THE OXFORD ENGLISH
DICTIONARY

SECOND EDITION

THE OXFORD ENGLISH DICTIONARY

First Edited by

JAMES A. H. MURRAY, HENRY BRADLEY, W. A. CRAIGIE
and C. T. ONIONS

COMBINED WITH

A SUPPLEMENT TO THE OXFORD ENGLISH DICTIONARY

Edited by

R. W. BURCHFIELD

AND RESET WITH CORRECTIONS, REVISIONS
AND ADDITIONAL VOCABULARY

THE OXFORD ENGLISH DICTIONARY

SECOND EDITION

Prepared by

J. A. SIMPSON *and* E. S. C. WEINER

VOLUME IX

Look–Mouke

CLARENDON PRESS · OXFORD

1989

Oxford University Press, Walton Street, Oxford OX2 6DP
Oxford New York Toronto
Delhi Bombay Calcutta Madras Karachi
Petaling Jaya Singapore Hong Kong Tokyo
Nairobi Dar es Salaam Cape Town
Melbourne Auckland
and associated companies in
Berlin Ibadan

Oxford is a trade mark of Oxford University Press

British Library Cataloguing in Publication Data
Oxford English dictionary.—2nd ed.
1. English language-Dictionaries
I. Simpson, J. A. (John Andrew), 1953-
II. Weiner, Edmund S. C., 1950-
423
ISBN 0-19-861221-4 (vol. IX)
ISBN 0-19-861186-2 (set)

Library of Congress Cataloging-in-Publication Data
The Oxford English dictionary.—2nd ed.
prepared by J. A. Simpson and E. S. C. Weiner
Bibliography: p.
ISBN 0-19-861221-4 (vol. IX)
ISBN 0-19-861186-2 (set)
1. English language—Dictionaries.   I. Simpson, J. A.
II. Weiner, E. S. C.   III. Oxford University Press.
PE1625.087 1989
423—dc19   88-5330

Data capture by ICC, Fort Washington, Pa.
Text-processing by Oxford University Press
Typesetting by Filmtype Services Ltd., Scarborough, N. Yorks.
Manufactured in the United States of America by
Rand McNally & Company, Taunton, Mass.

KEY TO THE PRONUNCIATION

THE pronunciations given are those in use in the educated speech of southern England (the so-called 'Received Standard'), and the keywords given are to be understood as pronounced in such speech.

I. *Consonants*

b, d, f, k, l, m, n, p, t, v, z *have their usual English values*

g as in *go* (gəʊ)
h ... *ho!* (həʊ)
r ... *run* (rʌn), *terrier* ('tɛrɪə(r))
(r) ... *her* (hɜː(r))
s ... *see* (siː), *success* (sək'sɛs)
w ... *wear* (wɛə(r))
hw... *when* (hwɛn)
j ... *yes* (jɛs)

θ as in *thin* (θɪn), *bath* (bɑːθ)
ð ... *then* (ðɛn), *bathe* (beɪð)
ʃ ... *shop* (ʃɒp), *dish* (dɪʃ)
tʃ ... *chop* (tʃɒp), *ditch* (dɪtʃ)
ʒ ... *vision* ('vɪʒən), *déjeuner* (deʒøne)
dʒ ... *judge* (dʒʌdʒ)
ŋ ... *singing* ('sɪŋɪŋ), *think* (θɪŋk)
ŋg ... *finger* ('fɪŋgə(r))

(FOREIGN AND NON-SOUTHERN)

ʎ as in It. *serraglio* (ser'raʎo)
ɲ ... Fr. *cognac* (kɔɲak)
x ... Ger. *ach* (ax), Sc. *loch* (lɒx), Sp. *frijoles* (fri'xoles)
ç ... Ger. *ich* (ɪç), Sc. *nicht* (nɪçt)
ɣ ... North Ger. *sagen* ('zaːɣən)
c ... Afrikaans *baardmannetjie* ('baːrtmanəci)
ɥ ... Fr. *cuisine* (kɥizin)

Symbols in parentheses are used to denote elements that may be omitted either by individual speakers or in particular phonetic contexts: e.g. *bottle* ('bɒt(ə)l), *Mercian* ('mɜːʃ(ɪ)ən), *suit* (s(j)uːt), *impromptu* (ɪm'prɒm(p)tjuː), *father* ('fɑːðə(r)).

II. *Vowels and Diphthongs*

SHORT

ɪ as in p*i*t (pɪt), -*ness*, (-nɪs)
ɛ ... p*e*t (pɛt), Fr. *sept* (sɛt)
æ ... p*a*t (pæt)
ʌ ... p*u*tt (pʌt)
ɒ ... p*o*t (pɒt)
ʊ ... p*u*t (pʊt)
ə ... *another* (ə'nʌðə(r))
(ə) ... *beaten* ('biːt(ə)n)
i ... Fr. *si* (si)
e ... Fr. *bébé* (bebe)
a ... Fr. *mari* (mari)
ɑ ... Fr. *bâtiment* (bɑtimɑ̃)
ɔ ... Fr. *homme* (ɔm)
o ... Fr. *eau* (o)
ø ... Fr. *peu* (pø)
œ ... Fr. *boeuf* (bœf) *coeur* (kœr)
u ... Fr. *douce* (dus)
ʏ ... Ger. *Müller* ('mʏlər)
y ... Fr. *du* (dy)

LONG

iː as in *bean* (biːn)
ɑː ... *barn* (bɑːn)
ɔː ... *born* (bɔːn)
uː ... *boon* (buːn)
ɜː ... *burn* (bɜːn)
eː ... Ger. *Schnee* (ʃneː)
ɛː ... Ger. *Fähre* ('fɛːrə)
aː ... Ger. *Tag* (taːk)
oː ... Ger. *Sohn* (zoːn)
øː ... Ger. *Goethe* ('gøːtə)
yː ... Ger. *grün* (gryːn)

NASAL

ɛ̃, æ̃ as in Fr. *fin* (fɛ̃, fæ̃)
ɑ̃ ... Fr. *franc* (frɑ̃)
ɔ̃ ... Fr. *bon* (bɔ̃)
œ̃ ... Fr. *un* (œ̃)

DIPHTHONGS, etc.

eɪ as in *bay* (beɪ)
aɪ ... *buy* (baɪ)
ɔɪ ... *boy* (bɔɪ)
əʊ ... *no* (nəʊ)
aʊ ... *now* (naʊ)
ɪə ... *peer* (pɪə(r))
ɛə ... *pair* (pɛə(r))
ʊə ... *tour* (tʊə(r))
ɔə ... *boar* (bɔə(r))

aɪə as in *fiery* ('faɪərɪ)
aʊə ... *sour* (saʊə(r))

The incidence of main stress is shown by a superior stress mark (') preceding the stressed syllable, and a secondary stress by an inferior stress mark (ˌ), e.g. *pronunciation* (prəˌnʌnsɪ'eɪʃ(ə)n).

For further explanation of the transcription used, see *General Explanations*, Volume I.

LIST OF ABBREVIATIONS, SIGNS, ETC.

Some abbreviations listed here in italics are also in certain cases printed in roman type, and vice versa.

a. (in Etym.)	adoption of, adopted from
a (as *a* 1850)	*ante*, 'before', 'not later than'
a.	adjective
abbrev.	abbreviation (of)
abl.	ablative
absol.	absolute, -ly
Abstr.	(in titles) *Abstract, -s*
acc.	accusative
Acct.	(in titles) *Account*
A.D.	*Anno Domini*
ad. (in Etym.)	adaptation of
Add.	Addenda
adj.	adjective
Adv.	(in titles) *Advance, -d, -s*
adv.	adverb
advb.	adverbial, -ly
Advt.	advertisement
Aeronaut.	(as label) in Aeronautics; (in titles) *Aeronautic, -al, -s*
AF., AFr.	Anglo-French
Afr.	Africa, -n
Agric.	(as label) in Agriculture; (in titles) *Agriculture, -al*
Alb.	Albanian
Amer.	American
Amer. Ind.	American Indian
Anat.	(as label) in Anatomy; (in titles) *Anatomy, -ical*
Anc.	(in titles) *Ancient*
Anglo-Ind.	Anglo-Indian
Anglo-Ir.	Anglo-Irish
Ann.	Annals
Anthrop., Anthropol.	(as label) in Anthropology; (in titles) *Anthropology, -ical*
Antiq.	(as label) in Antiquities; (in titles) *Antiquity*
aphet.	aphetic, aphetized
app.	apparently
Appl.	(in titles) *Applied*
Applic.	(in titles) *Application, -s*
appos.	appositive, -ly
Arab.	Arabic
Aram.	Aramaic
Arch.	in Architecture
arch.	archaic
Archæol.	in Archæology
Archit.	(as label) in Architecture; (in titles) *Architecture, -al*
Arm.	Armenian
assoc.	association
Astr.	in Astronomy
Astrol.	in Astrology
Astron.	(in titles) *Astronomy, -ical*
Astronaut.	(in titles) *Astronautic, -s*
attrib.	attributive, -ly
Austral.	Australian
Autobiogr.	(in titles) *Autobiography, -ical*
A.V.	Authorized Version
B.C.	Before Christ
B.C.	(in titles) British Columbia
bef.	before
Bibliogr.	(as label) in Bibliography; (in titles) *Bibliography, -ical*
Biochem.	(as label) in Biochemistry; (in titles) *Biochemistry, -ical*
Biol.	(as label) in Biology; (in titles) *Biology, -ical*
Bk.	Book
Bot.	(as label) in Botany; (in titles) *Botany, -ical*
Bp.	Bishop
Brit.	(in titles) *Britain, British*
Bulg.	Bulgarian
Bull.	(in titles) *Bulletin*
c (as *c* 1700)	*circa*, 'about'
c. (as 19th c.)	century
Cal.	(in titles) *Calendar*
Cambr.	(in titles) *Cambridge*
Canad.	Canadian
Cat.	Catalan
catachr.	catachrestically
Catal.	(in titles) *Catalogue*
Celt.	Celtic
Cent.	(in titles) *Century, Central*
Cent. Dict.	Century Dictionary
Cf., cf.	*confer*, 'compare'
Ch.	Church
Chem.	(as label) in Chemistry; (in titles) *Chemistry, -ical*
Chr.	(in titles) *Christian*
Chron.	(in titles) *Chronicle*
Chronol.	(in titles) *Chronology, -ical*
Cinemat., Cinematogr.	in Cinematography
Clin.	(in titles) *Clinical*
cl. L.	classical Latin
cogn. w.	cognate with
Col.	(in titles) *Colonel, Colony*
Coll.	(in titles) *Collection*
collect.	collective, -ly
colloq.	colloquial, -ly
comb.	combined, -ing
Comb.	Combinations
Comm.	in Commercial usage
Communic.	in Communications
comp.	compound, composition
Compan.	(in titles) *Companion*
compar.	comparative
compl.	complement
Compl.	(in titles) *Complete*
Conc.	(in titles) *Concise*
Conch.	in Conchology
concr.	concrete, -ly
Conf.	(in titles) *Conference*
Congr.	(in titles) *Congress*
conj.	conjunction
cons.	consonant
const.	construction, construed with
contr.	contrast (with)
Contrib.	(in titles) *Contribution*
Corr.	(in titles) *Correspondence*
corresp.	corresponding (to)
Cotgr.	R. Cotgrave, *Dictionarie of the French and English Tongues*
cpd.	compound
Crit.	(in titles) *Criticism, Critical*
Cryst.	in Crystallography
Cycl.	(in titles) *Cyclopædia, -ic*
Cytol.	(in titles) *Cytology, -ical*
Da.	Danish
D.A.	*Dictionary of Americanisms*
D.A.E.	*Dictionary of American English*
dat.	dative
D.C.	District of Columbia
Deb.	(in titles) *Debate, -s*
def.	definite, -ition
dem.	demonstrative
deriv.	derivative, -ation
derog.	derogatory
Descr.	(in titles) *Description, -tive*
Devel.	(in titles) *Development, -al*
Diagn.	(in titles) *Diagnosis, Diagnostic*
dial.	dialect, -al
Dict.	Dictionary; *spec.*, the *Oxford English Dictionary*
dim.	diminutive
Dis.	(in titles) *Disease*
Diss.	(in titles) *Dissertation*
D.O.S.T.	*Dictionary of the Older Scottish Tongue*
Du.	Dutch
E.	East
Eccl.	(as label) in Ecclesiastical usage; (in titles) *Ecclesiastical*
Ecol.	in Ecology
Econ.	(as label) in Economics; (in titles) *Economy, -ics*
ed.	edition
E.D.D.	*English Dialect Dictionary*
Edin.	(in titles) *Edinburgh*
Educ.	(as label) in Education; (in titles) *Education, -al*
EE.	Early English
e.g.	*exempli gratia*, 'for example'
Electr.	(as label) in Electricity; (in titles) *Electricity, -ical*
Electron.	(in titles) *Electronic, -s*
Elem.	(in titles) *Element, -ary*
ellipt.	elliptical, -ly
Embryol.	in Embryology
e.midl.	east midland (dialect)
Encycl.	(in titles) *Encyclopædia, -ic*
Eng.	England, English
Engin.	in Engineering
Ent.	in Entomology
Entomol.	(in titles) *Entomology, -logical*
erron.	erroneous, -ly
esp.	especially
Ess.	(in titles) *Essay, -s*
et al.	*et alii*, 'and others'
etc.	et cetera
Ethnol.	in Ethnology
etym.	etymology
euphem.	euphemistically
Exam.	(in titles) *Examination*
exc.	except
Exerc.	(in titles) *Exercise, -s*
Exper.	(in titles) *Experiment, -al*
Explor.	(in titles) *Exploration, -s*
f.	feminine
f. (in Etym.)	formed on
f. (in subordinate entries)	form of
F.	French
fem. (rarely f.)	feminine
fig.	figurative, -ly
Finn.	Finnish
fl.	*floruit*, 'flourished'
Found.	(in titles) *Foundation, -s*
Fr.	French
freq.	frequent, -ly
Fris.	Frisian
Fund.	(in titles) *Fundamental, -s*
Funk or *Funk's Stand. Dict.*	*Funk and Wagnalls Standard Dictionary*
G.	German
Gael.	Gaelic
Gaz.	(in titles) *Gazette*
gen.	genitive
gen.	general, -ly
Geogr.	(as label) in Geography; (in titles) *Geography, -ical*

Geol. (as label) in Geology;
(in titles) *Geology, -ical*
Geom. in Geometry
Geomorphol. in Geomorphology
Ger. German
Gloss. Glossary
Gmc. Germanic
Godef. F. Godefroy, *Dictionnaire de l'ancienne langue française*
Goth. Gothic
Govt. (in titles) *Government*
Gr. Greek
Gram. (as label) in Grammar;
(in titles) *Grammar, -tical*
Gt. Great

Heb. Hebrew
Her. in Heraldry
Herb. among herbalists
Hind. Hindustani
Hist. (as label) in History;
(in titles) *History, -ical*
hist. historical
Histol. (in titles) *Histology, -ical*
Hort. in Horticulture
Househ. (in titles) *Household*
Housek. (in titles) *Housekeeping*

Ibid. *Ibidem*, 'in the same book or passage'
Icel. Icelandic
Ichthyol. in Ichthyology
id. *idem*, 'the same'
i.e. *id est*, 'that is'
IE. Indo-European
Illustr. (in titles) *Illustration, -ted*
imit. imitative
Immunol. in Immunology
imp. imperative
impers. impersonal
impf. imperfect
ind. indicative
indef. indefinite
Industr. (in titles) *Industry, -ial*
inf. infinitive
infl. influenced
Inorg. (in titles) *Inorganic*
Ins. (in titles) *Insurance*
Inst. (in titles) *Institute, -tion*
int. interjection
intr. intransitive
Introd. (in titles) *Introduction*
Ir. Irish
irreg. irregular, -ly
It. Italian

J., (J.) (quoted from) Johnson's *Dictionary*
(Jam.) Jamieson, *Scottish Dict.*
Jap. Japanese
joc. jocular, -ly
Jrnl. (in titles) *Journal*
Jun. (in titles) *Junior*

Knowl. (in titles) *Knowledge*

l. line
L. Latin
lang. language
Lect. (in titles) *Lecture, -s*
Less. (in titles) *Lesson, -s*
Let., Lett. letter, letters
LG. Low German
lit. literal, -ly
Lit. Literary
Lith. Lithuanian
LXX Septuagint

m. masculine
Mag. (in titles) *Magazine*
Magn. (in titles) *Magnetic, -ism*
Mal. Malay, Malayan
Man. (in titles) *Manual*
Managem. (in titles) *Management*
Manch. (in titles) *Manchester*
Manuf. in Manufacture, -ing
Mar. (in titles) *Marine*

masc. (*rarely* m.) masculine
Math. (as label) in Mathematics;
(in titles) *Mathematics, -al*
MDu. Middle Dutch
ME. Middle English
Mech. (as label) in Mechanics;
(in titles) *Mechanics, -al*
Med. (as label) in Medicine;
(in titles) *Medicine, -ical*
med.L. medieval Latin
Mem. (in titles) *Memoir, -s*
Metaph. in Metaphysics
Meteorol. (as label) in Meteorology;
(in titles) *Meteorology, -ical*
MHG. Middle High German
midl. midland (dialect)
Mil. in military usage
Min. (as label) in Mineralogy;
(in titles) *Ministry*
Mineral. (in titles) *Mineralogy, -ical*
MLG. Middle Low German
Misc. (in titles) *Miscellany, -eous*
mod. modern
mod.L modern Latin
(Morris), (quoted from) E. E. Morris's *Austral English*
Mus. (as label) in Music;
(in titles) *Music, -al; Museum*
Myst. (in titles) *Mystery*
Mythol. in Mythology

N. North
n. neuter
N. Amer. North America, -n
N. & Q. *Notes and Queries*
Narr. (in titles) *Narrative*
Nat. (in titles) *Natural*
Nat. Hist. in Natural History
Naut. in nautical language
N.E. North East
N.E.D. *New English Dictionary*, original title of the *Oxford English Dictionary* (first edition)
Neurol. in Neurology
neut. (*rarely* n.) neuter
NF., NFr. Northern French
No. Number
nom. nominative
north. northern (dialect)
Norw. Norwegian
n.q. no quotations
N.T. New Testament
Nucl. Nuclear
Numism. in Numismatics
N.W. North West
N.Z. New Zealand

obj. object
obl. oblique
Obs., obs. obsolete
Obstetr. (in titles) *Obstetrics*
occas. occasionally
OE. Old English (= Anglo-Saxon)
OF., OFr. Old French
OFris. Old Frisian
OHG. Old High German
OIr. Old Irish
ON. Old Norse
ONF. Old Northern French
Ophthalm. in Ophthalmology
opp. opposed (to), the opposite (of)
Opt. in Optics
Org. (in titles) *Organic*
orig. origin, -al, -ally
Ornith. (as label) in Ornithology;
(in titles) *Ornithology, -ical*
OS. Old Saxon
OSl. Old (Church) Slavonic
O.T. Old Testament
Outl. (in titles) *Outline*
Oxf. (in titles) *Oxford*

p. page
Palæogr. in Palæography

Palæont. (as label) in Palæontology;
(in titles) *Palæontology, -ical*
pa. pple. passive participle, past participle
(Partridge), (quoted from) E. Partridge's *Dictionary of Slang and Unconventional English*
pass. passive, -ly
pa.t. past tense
Path. (as label) in Pathology;
(in titles) *Pathology, -ical*
perh. perhaps
Pers. Persian
pers. person, -al
Petrogr. in Petrography
Petrol. (as label) in Petrology;
(in titles) *Petrology, -ical*
(Pettman), (quoted from) C. Pettman's *Africanderisms*
pf. perfect
Pg. Portuguese
Pharm. in Pharmacology
Philol. (as label) in Philology;
(in titles) *Philology, -ical*
Philos. (as label) in Philosophy;
(in titles) *Philosophy, -ic*
phonet. phonetic, -ally
Photogr. (as label) in Photography;
(in titles) *Photography, -ical*
phr. phrase
Phys. physical; (*rarely*) in Physiology
Physiol. (as label) in Physiology;
(in titles) *Physiology, -ical*
Pict. (in titles) *Picture, Pictorial*
pl., plur. plural
poet. poetic, -al
Pol. Polish
Pol. (as label) in Politics;
(in titles) *Politics, -al*
Pol. Econ. in Political Economy
Polit. (in titles) *Politics, -al*
pop. popular, -ly
Porc. (in titles) *Porcelain*
poss. possessive
Pott. (in titles) *Pottery*
ppl. a., pple. adj. participial adjective
pple. participle
Pr. Provençal
pr. present
Pract. (in titles) *Practice, -al*
prec. preceding (word or article)
pred. predicative
pref. prefix
pref., Pref. preface
prep. preposition
pres. present
Princ. (in titles) *Principle, -s*
priv. privative
prob. probably
Probl. (in titles) *Problem*
Proc. (in titles) *Proceedings*
pron. pronoun
pronunc. pronunciation
prop. properly
Pros. in Prosody
Prov. Provençal
pr. pple. present participle
Psych. in Psychology
Psychol. (as label) in Psychology;
(in titles) *Psychology, -ical*
Publ. (in titles) *Publications*

Q. (in titles) *Quarterly*
quot(s). quotation(s)
q.v. *quod vide*, 'which see'

R. (in titles) *Royal*
Radiol. in Radiology
R.C.Ch. Roman Catholic Church
Rec. (in titles) *Record*
redupl. reduplicating
Ref. (in titles) *Reference*
refash. refashioned, -ing
refl. reflexive
Reg. (in titles) *Register*

reg.	regular	str.	strong	Trop.	(in titles) *Tropical*
rel.	related to	Struct.	(in titles) *Structure, -al*	Turk.	Turkish
Reminisc.	(in titles) *Reminiscence, -s*	Stud.	(in titles) *Studies*	*Typog., Typogr.*	in Typography
Rep.	(in titles) *Report, -s*	subj.	subject		
repr.	representative, representing	*subord. cl.*	subordinate clause	ult.	ultimately
Res.	(in titles) *Research*	subseq.	subsequent, -ly	*Univ.*	(in titles) *University*
Rev.	(in titles) *Review*	subst.	substantively	unkn.	unknown
rev.	revised	*suff.*	suffix	*U.S.*	United States
Rhet.	in Rhetoric	superl.	superlative	U.S.S.R.	Union of Soviet Socialist
Rom.	Roman, -ce, -ic	Suppl.	Supplement		Republics
Rum.	Rumanian	*Surg.*	(as label) in Surgery;	usu.	usually
Russ.	Russian		(in titles) *Surgery, Surgical*		
		s.v.	*sub voce,* 'under the word'	*v., vb.*	verb
S.	South	Sw.	Swedish	*var(r)., vars.*	variant(s) of
S.Afr.	South Africa, -n	s.w.	south-western (dialect)	*vbl. sb.*	verbal substantive
sb.	substantive	*Syd. Soc. Lex.*	Sydenham Society, *Lexicon*	*Vertebr.*	(in titles) *Vertebrate, -s*
sc.	*scilicet,* 'understand' or		*of Medicine & Allied*	*Vet.*	(as label) in Veterinary
	'supply'		*Sciences*		Science;
Sc., Scot.	Scottish	syll.	syllable		(in titles) *Veterinary*
Scand.	(in titles) *Scandinavia, -n*	Syr.	Syrian	*Vet. Sci.*	in Veterinary Science
Sch.	(in titles) *School*	*Syst.*	(in titles) *System, -atic*	viz.	*videlicet,* 'namely'
Sc. Nat. Dict.	*Scottish National Dictionary*			*Voy.*	(in titles) *Voyage, -s*
Scotl.	(in titles) *Scotland*	*Taxon.*	(in titles) *Taxonomy, -ical*	*v.str.*	strong verb
Sel.	(in titles) *Selection, -s*	techn.	technical, -ly	*vulg.*	vulgar
Ser.	Series	*Technol.*	(in titles) *Technology, -ical*	*v.w.*	weak verb
sing.	singular	*Telegr.*	in Telegraphy		
Sk.	(in titles) *Sketch*	*Teleph.*	in Telephony	W.	Welsh; West
Skr.	Sanskrit	(Th.),	(quoted from) Thornton's	wd.	word
Slav.	Slavonic		*American Glossary*	Webster	*Webster's (New*
S.N.D.	*Scottish National Dictionary*	*Theatr.*	in the Theatre, theatrical		*International) Dictionary*
Soc.	(in titles) *Society*	*Theol.*	(as label) in Theology;	*Westm.*	(in titles) *Westminster*
Sociol.	(as label) in Sociology;		(in titles) *Theology, -ical*	WGmc.	West Germanic
	(in titles) *Sociology, -ical*	*Theoret.*	(in titles) *Theoretical*	*Wks.*	(in titles) *Works*
Sp.	Spanish	Tokh.	Tokharian	w.midl.	west midland (dialect)
Sp.	(in titles) *Speech, -es*	tr., transl.	translated, translation	WS.	West Saxon
sp.	spelling	*Trans.*	(in titles) *Transactions*		
spec.	specifically	*trans.*	transitive	(Y.),	(quoted from) Yule &
Spec.	(in titles) *Specimen*	*transf.*	transferred sense		Burnell's *Hobson-Jobson*
St.	Saint	*Trav.*	(in titles) *Travel(s)*	*Yrs.*	(in titles) *Years*
Stand.	(in titles) *Standard*	*Treas.*	(in titles) *Treasury*		
Stanf.	(quoted from) *Stanford*	*Treat.*	(in titles) *Treatise*	*Zoogeogr.*	in Zoogeography
	Dictionary of Anglicised	*Treatm.*	(in titles) *Treatment*	*Zool.*	(as label) in Zoology;
	Words & Phrases	*Trig.*	in Trigonometry		(in titles) *Zoology, -ical*

Signs and Other Conventions

Before a word or sense

† = obsolete
‖ = not naturalized, alien
¶ = catachrestic and erroneous uses

In the listing of Forms

1 = before 1100
2 = 12th c. (1100 to 1200)
3 = 13th c. (1200 to 1300), etc.
5-7 = 15th to 17th century
20 = 20th century

In the etymologies

* indicates a word or form not actually found,
 but of which the existence is inferred
:— = normal development of

The printing of a word in SMALL CAPITALS indicates that further information will be found under the word so referred to.

.. indicates an omitted part of a quotation.

- (in a quotation) indicates a hyphen doubtfully present in the original; (in other text) indicates a hyphen inserted only for the sake of a line-break.

PROPRIETARY NAMES

THIS Dictionary includes some words which are or are asserted to be proprietary names or trade marks. Their inclusion does not imply that they have acquired for legal purposes a non-proprietary or general significance nor any other judgement concerning their legal status. In cases where the editorial staff have established in the records of the Patent Offices of the United Kingdom and of the United States that a word is registered as a proprietary name or trade mark this is indicated, but no judgement concerning the legal status of such words is made or implied thereby.

look (lʊk), *sb.* Forms: 2–6 loke, 3–5 lok, 4, 8–9 *Sc.* luke, (6 lowke), 6–7 looke, 8–9 *Sc.* leuk, 5– look. [f. LOOK *v.*]

1. a. The action or an act of looking; a glance of the eyes; a particular direction of the eyes or countenance in order to look at something. †Also *occas.*, sight, view (quot. 1390). Phr. †***to have*** (or ***get***) ***a look of***: to be looked at by. ***to have a look at*** (colloq.): to look at for the purpose of examining. † ***at a look***: (*a*) at first sight; (*b*) in the twinkling of an eye. ***if looks could kill*** (or ***slay***): used to denote an expression of hostility in a look.

c **1200** *Trin. Coll. Hom.* 215 ȝif þe hodede..ledeð hem [women] his life eȝen for to sechen hire loke. *c* **1375** *Sc. Leg. Saints* xvii. (*Martha*) 46 þe quhilk..As fyr gregois brynt at a luke. *c* **1386** CHAUCER *Man of Law's T.* 955 At the firste look he on hire sette. **1390** GOWER *Conf.* III. 179 In alle mennes lok A part up in his hond he tok. *a* **1400–50** *Alexander* 5256 Him þoȝt hire like at a loke his lady his modire. **1423** JAS. I *Kingis Q.* li, My luke vnto the hevin I threwe furthwith. **1508** DUNBAR *Gold. Targe* 232 Sudaynly, in the space of a luke, All was hyne went. **1591** SHAKS. *Two Gent.* II. iv. 108 Too meane a seruant To haue a looke of such a worthy a Mistresse. **1592** —— *Ven. & Ad.* 464 For lookes kill loue, and loue by lookes reuiueth. **1753** L. M. *Accomplished Woman* II. 125 Their every action is forced; their looks and smiles are all studied. **1798** CHARLOTTE SMITH *Yng. Philos.* III. 120 Medora watched her every look with distressing solicitude. **1807–8** W. IRVING *Salmag.* (1824) 346 Lovely virgins..darting imperial looks of conquest. **1813** SCOTT *Rokeby* I. xix, One dying look he upward cast. **1885** MABEL COLLINS *Prettiest Woman* ii, In the meantime I shall have a look at Warsaw. **1887** R. BUCHANAN (*title*) A look round literature. **1895** E. BOWEN ROWLANDS in *Law Times* XCIX. 464/2 It is at the first look hard to see why [etc.]. **1913** F. L. BARCLAY *Broken Halo* xxxvii. 372 If looks could slay, Margaret would not have left that room alive. **1922** F. HARRIS *My Life & Loves* I. ii. 37 When they let me up, I looked at Jones and if looks could kill, he'd have had short shrift. **1943** K. TENNANT *Ride on Stranger* iv. 31 Just then she saw me..and if looks could have killed!

b. With epithet denoting the feelings expressed by the look.

It is sometimes difficult to say whether particular instances should be referred to this sense or to 2.

1535 COVERD. *Ps.* xvii[i]. 27 Thou shalt..bringe downe the hye lokes of the proude. **1567** MAPLET *Gr. Forest* 76 b, She hath alwayes a cheerefull looke towardes him. **1576** FLEMING *Panopl. Epist.* 281 Hee casting vppon mee a sower visage, and a sterne looke. **1635** J. HAYWARD tr. *Biondi's Banish'd Virg.* 97 It being not likely that shee should ever get a good looke of her Father. **1686** tr. *Chardin's Coronat. Solyman* 111 There was not one living soul that vouchsaf'd him a kind look. **1703** ROWE *Fair Penit.* I. i. 109 With looks averse, and Eyes that froze me. *a* **1717** BLACKALL *Wks.* (1723) I. 158 True Religion does not consist..in singular Behaviour, in a down Look, in Sighing and Sobbing. **1810** SCOTT *Lady of L.* III. xii, Roderick, with impatient look. **1833** TENNYSON *Dream Fair W.* xxvi, With sick and scornful looks averse. **1883** R. W. DIXON *Mano* IV. iii. 147 And Sir Giroie failed nought of courtesy, And gave to us good looks and welcome great.

c. ***upon the look***: engaged in looking *for*.

1819 BYRON *Juan* II. clxxiv, At last her father's prows put out to sea, For certain merchantmen upon the look.

2. Appearance, aspect.

a. With reference to persons, often with mixture of sense 1: Appearance of the countenance (sometimes, of the whole person); visual or facial expression; personal aspect. † ***of a good look*** = of good appearance.

c **1385** CHAUCER *L.G.W.* 1605 *Hypsip.*, And of his lok as real as a leoun. *c* **1400** *Arth. & Merl.* 1582 (Lincoln's Inn MS.), þe whyte dragoun lay him by, Steorne of lok and grysly. **1508** DUNBAR *Tua mariit wemen* 267 Be of your luke like innocentis, thoght ȝe haif euill myndis. *a* **1548** HALL *Chron., Edw. IV* 237 b, This palenes of visage, and dedly loke doth prognosticate yᵉ time of my death. **1611** BIBLE *Ecclus.* xix. 29 A man may bee knowen by his looke. **1632** J. HAYWARD tr. *Biondi's Eromena* 68 Being the first time that a joyfull looke was seene in that Court, sithence the departure of the Princesse. **1697** DRYDEN *Virg. Georg.* III. 87 The Mother Cow must wear a low'ring Look. **1700** T. BROWN *Amusem. Ser. & Com.* 146, I see another Man of a very good Look come into the Circle, and no body takes the least Notice of him. **1724** RAMSAY *Vision* xi, With bauld forbidding luke. **1748** RICHARDSON *Clarissa* (1811) I. ii. 9 Indeed, gay and lively as he is, he has not the look of an impudent man. **1809** MALKIN *Gil Blas* VII. ii. (Rtldg.) 228 They had all the look of a deputation from a better world. **1860** READE *Cloister & H.* xxxviii. (1896) 109 Denys wore a look of humble apology. **1867** TROLLOPE *Chron. Barset* I. xxii. 190 The look of his face as he spoke was by no means pleasant.

b. *pl.* With the same meaning as sing. Sometimes = GOOD LOOKS. Also phr. ***to be in good looks***: to be looking well, to present a healthy appearance.

1564 HAWARD *Eutropius* II. 15 After they were dead keping stil theyr grim lokes. **1589** GREENE *Menaphon* (Arb.) 45 At last her eyes glaunced on the lookes of Melicertus. **1616** R. C. *Times' Whistle* III. 959 Most of our women are extreamly proud Of their faire lookes. **1697** DRYDEN *Virg. Georg.* IV. 371 Lean are their Looks, and shagged is their Hair. **1709** BERKELEY *Th. Vision* §9 We often see shame or fear in the looks of a man. **1724** *Lond. Gaz.* No. 6283/3 Abraham Shaw,..aged 38 Years,.. pale Looks. **1766** GOLDSM. *Vic. W.* xxix, When I survey these emaciated looks, and hear those groans. **1786** BURNS *Twa Dogs* 225 They..lee-lang nights, wi' crabbit leuks, Pore owre the devil's pictur'd beuks. **1798** JANE AUSTEN *Northang. Abb.* (1833) I. ii. 11 Catherine was in very good looks. **1815** —— *Emma* I. i, Everybody in their best looks. **1896** A. E. HOUSMAN *Shropsh. Lad* xxiii, And few that will carry their looks or their truth to the grave.

c. Of inanimate and immaterial things: Appearance, esp. as expressive of their quality or nature. Also in pl., esp. in ***from*** or ***by the looks*** (***of***).

1567 MAPLET *Gr. Forest* 10 b, A certaine vaine of the earth,..having the verie looke and face of Golde. **1710** T. FULLER *Pharm. Extemp.* 411 This colourless Syrup..gives no unpleasing colour, nor alters the look of the Medicine in the least. *a* **1716** BLACKALL *Wks.* (1723) I. 84 The beautiful Look of the forbidden Fruit. **1754** RICHARDSON *Grandison* II. iv. 40 If you fall I shall have the worst of it, from the looks of the matter. **1782** COWPER *Convers.* 862 Though such continual zigzags in a book, Such drunken reelings, have an awkward look. **1847** L. HUNT *Men, Women, & B.* II. xi. 269 What curious little circumstances conspired to give a look even of fabulous and novel-like interest to his adventures. **1875** JOWETT *Plato* (ed. 2) V. 27 Life is to wear, as at Athens, a joyous and festive look. **1877** W. H. RUSSELL *Pr. Wales' Tour* viii. 344 There are no minarets, mosques or Hindoo temples, to detract from the European look of the place. **1882** R. ABERCROMBY in *Nature* XXVI. 572 In common parlance, any particular 'look' of the sky is called a prognostic. **1883** R. CLELAND *Inchbracken* iv. 28 It micht be e'en a bairn by the looks o' the bun'le. **1923** 'B. M. BOWER' *Parowan Bonanza* v. 54 You're just ahead of a big storm, by the looks, Mr. Rayfield. **1975** J. SYMONS *Three Pipe Problem* ix. 65 Acting doesn't pay too well from the looks of it.

d. ***to have a look of***: to resemble vaguely, to remind the spectator of the appearance of (a person or thing).

1860 EMILY EDEN *Semi-attached Couple* II. 62 This picture which I think has a great look of you.

e. Colloq. phr. ***for the look of the thing***: for the sake of appearances.

1876 TROLLOPE *Prime Minister* IV. xiii. 217 'I shall go down and vote for them of course,' said Mr. O'Mahony, 'just for the look of the thing.' **1910** 'SAKI' *Reginald in Russia* 63 He often wished, for the look of the thing, that people would sometimes burn candles at his shrine. **1924** M. KENNEDY *Constant Nymph* xv. 212 Save for the look of the thing she had no particular wish for a reconciliation. **1940** L. H. MYERS *Pool of Vishnu* IV. v. 191 Why are they willing to die, and to send those whom they love to their death, for the sake of—what shall I call it?—the look of the thing?

f. *Fashion.* With defining word(s): an appearance or effect indicated by the preceding word(s). Occas. without defining word (quot. 1973).

1938 [see *little-girl* attrib. (LITTLE *a.* 14)]. **1939** *Vogue* 15 Apr. 2 (Advt.), Accent on That Fresh Young Look. **1940** *Mademoiselle* Mar. 56 Formold created for you that Tall Look of 1940. **1948** *Vogue* Mar. 41 The New Look has fined down... Length has crystallized into eleven inches from the ground for formal wear. **1966** *Listener* 3 Feb. 171/1 This year..the geometrical look is in. **1971** *Daily Mail* 3 Feb. 3 A specially-created hair-style to complete the hot-pants look. **1973** *Sunday Times* 28 Jan. 43/2 The clothes are created on them, and a whole look is painstakingly put together. **1974** *Country Life* 17 Jan. 107/1 The peasant look in knitwear.

3. *Comb.* With advs. forming combs. corresponding to various phrases under the vb., as ***look-back, -down, -forward, -on, -up***; **look-on net**, one of the nets pulled up as a test of the condition of the others.

1597 MIDDLETON *Wisdom of Solomon* xii. 15 Thou orderest every thing with look-on sight. **1813** L. HUNT in *Examiner* 11 Jan. 19/1 He..takes away confidence from their look-up to him. **1850** HAWTHORNE *Scarlet L., Custom House* (1886) 56 A dreary look-forward, this, for a man who [etc.]. **1853** JERDAN *Autobiog.* III. 7 The look-back is wearisome. **1862** H. MARRYAT *Year in Sweden* II. 401 The look-down on the works below..is awful. **1877** HOLDSWORTH *Sea Fisheries* 60 [Drift net fishing]. Whilst the nets are in the water, the warp is occasionally hauled in till the first net is reached; this is called the 'look-on' net. **1887** HALL CAINE *Deemster* I. x. 207 Dan..asked the skipper to try the 'look-on' net.

look (lʊk), *v.* Forms: 1 lócian, 2 lokien, (locan), (3 lokin, loky), 3–4 loc, lok(en, locken, 3–6 loke, (4 loki), 4–5 *north.* luk, 4–8 luke, (5 lokyn), 5–6 *Sc.* lowke, 5–7 looke, 6 *arch.* looken, *Sc.* louk, leuk, luck, luik, luick, lwik, 5– look. [OE. *lócian* = OS. *lôcon* (in a gloss), MDu. *loeken*:—OTeut. type **lôkôjan*; a form **lôgæ̂jan*, app. of identical meaning, appears in OHG. *luogên* (MHG. *luogen*, mod.G. dial. *lugen*) to see, look, spy.

Brugmann (*Grundriss* I. 384) suggests that the type **lôkô-* may represent OTeut. **lôkkô-*:—pre-Teut. **lāghná-* or *lōghná-*, from the root **lāgh-* or **lōgh-* (Teut. **lôg-*) represented by the Ger. vb.]

I. To direct one's sight.

1. *intr.* To give a certain direction to one's sight; to apply one's power of vision; to direct one's eyes upon some object or towards some portion of space. **a.** with phrase or adv. expressing the direction or the intended object of vision. (See also branches IV and V.)

The usual prep. introducing the object of vision is now *at*; the older ***to look on***, ***to look upon***, are in the literal sense either *arch.*, or include a mixture of the notion of mental watching or contemplation.

a **1000** *Boeth. Metr.* xxii. 20 Efne swa sweotole swa he on ða sunnan mæȝ..on locian. *c* **1000** *Ags. Gosp.* Mark vi. 41 He on heofon locode & hi bletsode. *c* **1200** *Vices & Virtues* (1888) 47 Ac me þincþ ðat tu lokest aweiward. *a* **1225** *St. Marher.* 2 Alle hire luueden þat hire on lokeden. **1362** LANGL. *P. Pl.* A. VIII. 123 'Lewede lorel!' quod he 'luite lokestou on þe Bible'. *c* **1380** WYCLIF *Serm.* Sel. Wks. I. 143 Lokynge in þe first myrour. *c* **1400** *Destr. Troy* 8658 Achilles ..Woundit hym [*sc.* Ector] wickedly, as he away loked. *c* **1450** *St. Cuthbert* (Surtees) 393 þe childe loked here and þare. *c* **1475** *Babees Bk.* 65 And yf they speke withe yow.. Withe stable Eye loke vpone theym Rihte. **1598** tr. *Aristotle's Pol.* 379 Wee forbid them also to looke on leud pictures, or dishonest fables. **1611** BIBLE *Acts* iii. 4 And Peter fastening his eyes vpon him, with Iohn, said, Looke on vs. [But *looke at* (fig.) in 2 Cor. iv. 18: see 3 a.] *a* **1626** BACON *New Atl.* (1900) 3 But the Servant tooke them not, nor would scarce looke upon them. **1634** SIR T. HERBERT *Trav.* 212 Her finnes so little that they are like the Dodoes wings, more to looke at, then for execution. **1688** BOYLE *Final Causes Nat. Things* ii. 61 The camelion may look directly forward with the right eye, and with the other at the same time, directly backwards. **1773** *Life N. Frowde* 32 Before she could well look upon me, I addressed her. **1797** MRS. RADCLIFFE *Italian* i, They walked quickly, looking neither to the right nor left. **1830** TENNYSON *Mariana* 15 She could not look on the sweet heaven, Either at morn or eventide. **1842** —— *Locksley Hall* 72 Such a one do I remember, whom to look at was to love. **1860** TYNDALL *Glac.* I. xi. 72 We went out to look at the firmament. **1872** GEO. ELIOT *Middlem.* I. 205 Every nerve and muscle in Rosamond was adjusted to the consciousness that she was being looked at. **1895** *Pall Mall Mag.* Nov. 393 Such a look as schoolboys exchange when the master is looking another way.

¶ Phrases. (***fair***, etc.) ***to look at***, † ***on***, † ***upon***: with respect to appearance; ***to look at him*** (***me***, ***it***, etc.): *colloq.* = judging from his (my, etc.) appearance; ***not to look at*** († ***on***, ***upon***); often emphatically for 'not to touch, taste, meddle with'; also, ***not to look at*** (someone): to find unattractive, to show no sexual interest in (someone); occas. in positive contexts; so ***cannot look at*** (colloq.) = 'has no chance against'; ***as quick*** (or ***soon***) ***as look at you*** (or ***him***, etc.): very rapidly and readily; 'at the drop of a hat'; ***not to know which way to look***: to be embarrassed.

a **1300** *Cursor M.* 23228 Fell dragons and tades bath þat ar apon to lok ful lath. *c* **1400** *Destr. Troy* 1554 Large on to loke, louely of shap. **1526** SKELTON *Magnyf.* 2208 What wylte thou skelpe me? thou dare not loke on a gnat. **1535** COVERDALE *Zech.* v. 6 Euen thus are they (yᵗ dwell vpon the whole earth) to loke vpon. **1611** BIBLE *Gen.* xii. 11, I know that thou art a faire woman to looke vpon. **1814** JANE AUSTEN *Mansf. Park* I. v. 101 She came up to me..and talked and laughed till I did not know which way to look. I felt that I must be the jest of the room. **1817** M. EDGEWORTH *Harrington* xi. 247 Nor did I know well which way to look, when his lordship..asked Miss Montenero if she could possibly imagine that any such vulgar prejudices existed. **1846** *Bentley's Misc.* XX. 433 No one would think me more than five or six-and-thirty, to look at me. **1859** TENNYSON *Enid* 1515 If he rise no more, I will not look at wine until I die. **1861** C. M. YONGE *Young Step-Mother* xxviii. 420 Albinia did not know which way to look when all was ascribed to Mr. Kendal's great kindness to him. **1888** 'R. BOLDREWOOD' *Robbery under Arms* II. iii. 46 He was awful shook on Mad; but she wouldn't look at him. **1894** SOMERVILLE & 'ROSS' *Real Charlotte* II. xx. 78 There was no other woman here that signified except Miss Dysart, and it didn't seem likely she'd look at him. **1895** *Daily News* 26 Aug. 7/1 When he [a bowler] went on for the second time the batsmen..'could not look at him'. **1922** JOYCE *Ulysses* 347 Give it to him too on the same place as quick as I'd look at him. **1926** I. MACKAY *Blencarrow* xi. 105 Supposing Kathrine wouldn't look at him in any case? **1937** M. SHARP *Nutmeg Tree* xx. 266 If I married you I'd never look at another man so long as I lived. **1941** H. NICOLSON *Diary* 8 July (1967) 177 He then stalks out of the room. We are left ashamed and wretched and do not know which way to look. **1946** E. O'NEILL *Iceman Cometh* (1947) III. 167 From what I've seen of 'em..they'd run over you as soon as look at you. **1955** J. I. M. STEWART *Guardians* III. ii. 214 The novelists.. constantly endow sensitive women with husbands whom, in fact, they would never *look at.* **1971** M. TORRIE *Bismarck Herrings* xi. 156 Threatened to report you to the council as soon as look at you, she did. **1973** W. M. DUNCAN *Big Timer* iv. 29 You have to watch it nowaways. Jump you as soon as look at you. **1974** P. DICKINSON *Poison Oracle* ii. 37 Will she even look at a male chimp? Doesn't she think she's human?

b. with the direction or object left indeterminate, or merely implied by the context. Sometimes said of the eye. †In early use also: To possess or receive the faculty of vision (= Gr. βλέπειν, ἀναβλέπειν). † ***to live and look***: to retain one's faculties.

971 *Blickl. Hom.* 173 And blinde men mid his bedum [Petrus] ȝehælde þæt hie locodan. *c* **1200** *Trin. Coll. Hom.* 181 Eien lokeð, and eare lusteð. *c* **1275** *Passion our Lord* 54 in *O.E. Misc.* 39 þe blynde he makede loki. *a* **1300** *Cursor M.* 1338 Cherubin, þat angel blyth, Bad him ga lok þe thrid syth. **1362** LANGL. *P. Pl.* A. IX. 49 But ȝif I may liuen and loken I schal go lerne betere. **1390** GOWER *Conf.* I. 54 For ofte..Betre is to winke than to loke. *c* **1470** HENRY *Wallace* VI. 468 The kingis palȝone..couth weyll luk and wynk, with the ta E. *c* **1550** R. BIESTON *Bayte Fortune* B ij, Looke therfore ere thou leape. **1667** MILTON *P.L.* x. 993 But if thou judge it hard and difficult, Conversing, looking, loving, to abstain From Loves due Rites. **1697** DRYDEN *Virg. Georg.* III. 334 He looks, and languishes, and leaves his Rest. **1709** BERKELEY *Th. Vision* §7 When we look only with one eye. **1875** E. WHITE *Life in Christ* IV. xxv. (1876) 422 The eye looks, but it is the mind that sees. **1896** *Law Times Rep.* LXXIII. 616/1 If he had looked he must have seen the light of the approaching train. **1901** 'IAN MACLAREN' *Yng. Barbarians* vii. 141 At the most critical moment he was afraid to look.

c. To direct one's eyes in a manner indicative of a certain feeling; to cast a look of a certain significance; to present a specified expression of countenance. With *adv.* or *phrase.*

Now only with the object or direction specified as in a; otherwise this sense now merges in 9.

c **1205** LAY. 2266 He stod bi-foren Locrine & laðelich him lokede on. **1297** R. GLOUC. (Rolls) 5348 Vre louerd mid is

eyen of milce on þe lokeþ þeruore. **1393** LANGL. *P. Pl.* C. II. 164 On ous he lokyde with loue. **1483** CAXTON *G. de la Tour* E viij b, He euer loked on her of a wantoun and fals regard. **1500–20** DUNBAR *Poems* lviii. 9 Bot, Lord! how petewuslie I luke, Quhen all the pelfe they pairt amang thame. *a* **1548** HALL *Chron., Rich. III*, 53 b, Least that it might be suspected that he was abasshed for feare of his enemyes, and for that cause looked so piteously. **1611** BIBLE *Gen.* xl. 7 Wherefore looke ye so sadly to day? **1642** R. CARPENTER *Experience* II. i. 133 The man look'd bloodily when he spoke it. **1842** TENNYSON *Talking Oak* 116, I look'd at him with joy. **1859** —— *Enid* 1279 He turn'd and look'd as keenly at her As careful robins eye the delver's toil.

d. *occas.* To give a look of surprise, to stare. Now *colloq.*

1610 B. JONSON *Alchemist* v. ii, Doctor 'tis true (you looke) for all your Figures. I sent for him, indeed. *Mod.* Yes, you may look!

e. quasi-*trans.* in such phrases as *to look* (a person or thing) *in the face*: see FACE *sb.* 2 b. *to look a gift horse in the mouth*: see HORSE *sb.* 21.

The object in sentences of this kind was prob. originally in the *dative*: cf. G. *einem ins gesicht sehen.*

c **1375** *Sc. Leg. Saints* xix. (*Cristofore*) 28 He sa mekil, sa hee and auchful vas, þat few du[r]ste luk hyme in þe face. *a* **1625** FLETCHER *Hum. Lieutenant* IV. i, I'll neuer look a horse i' th' mouth that's giuen. *a* **1716** SOUTH *Serm.* (1823) VI. 330 The soldier..converses with dangers, and looks death in the face. **1737** BRACKEN *Farriery Impr.* (1757) II. 184 Many who, altho' they have pretended knowledge in Horses, have been looked in the Mouth (as we say). *a* **1850** ROSSETTI *Dante & Cir.* I. (1874) 141 This lady..Look'd thee so deep within the eyes, Love sigh'd And was awakened there. **1880** G. MEREDITH *Trag. Com.* xiii. (1892) 194 She ..looks you straight at the eyes, perfectly unabashed. **1891** *Strand Mag.* II. 530/2 An eye that looks one through and through. **1892** R. KIPLING *Ball. East & West* 83 They have looked each other between the eyes, and there they found no fault. **1896** A. E. HOUSMAN *Shropsh. Lad* xlii, With.. friendly brows and laughter He looked me in the eyes.

f. with cogn. obj.

1592 SHAKS. *Rom. & Jul.* v. iii. 112 Eyes, looke your last. **1599** SHAKS. etc. *Pass. Pilgr.* 46 Such lookes as none could looke but beauties queen. **1643** TRAPP *Comm. Gen.* xlii. 29 *And they came to Jacob*, who had looked many a long look for them, no doubt. **1781** COWPER *Hope* 726 A transport glows in all he looks and speaks. **1850** TENNYSON *In Mem.* xlix, And look thy look, and go thy way. **1896** A. E. HOUSMAN *Shropsh. Lad* viii, Terence, look your last at me, For I come home no more.

g. *trans.* With complement or prep.: To bring by one's looks into a certain place or condition. Now *rare.* (Cf. *look down*, 33 e.)

1611 SHAKS. *Cymb.* v. v. 94 Thou hast look'd thy selfe into my grace. **1624** MASSINGER *Renegado* III. ii, Thrust out these fiery eies, that yesterday Would haue lookde thee dead. **1633** G. HERBERT *Temple, Glance* iii, Thou shalt look us out of pain. **1694** DRYDEN *Love Triumph.* IV. i, While you stay,.. every moment looks a part of me away. **1700** —— *Secular Masque* 51 Mars has looked the sky to red. **1766** GOLDSM. *Vic. W.* v, They had early learnt the lesson of looking presumption out of countenance. **1776** *Hist. Eur.* in *Ann. Reg.* 58/1 That armed force which was to have looked all America into submission. **1860** TROLLOPE *Castle Richmond* I. xii. 234, I really thought Mrs. Townsend would have looked him into the river when he came to her.

h. To express by a look or glance, or by one's countenance; to cast looks of (compassion, etc.) or looks which threaten (death, etc.). *to look daggers*: see DAGGER 3 b.

1727 THOMSON *Summer* 845 [1188] They..sigh'd, and look'd unutterable Things. **1742** YOUNG *Nt. Th.* iv. 635 With that soft eye..deign to look Compassion to the coldness of my breast. **1750** CHESTERF. *Lett.* (1774) III. 127 The same things differently expressed, looked, and delivered, cease to be the same things. **1818** BYRON *Juan* I. xv, Some women use their tongues— she *look'd* a lecture, Each eye a sermon, and her brow a homily. **1837** DICKENS *Pickw.* vi, The old lady..looked carving-knives at the.. delinquent. **1837** THACKERAY *Ravensw.* i, The Captain, looking several tremendous canings at him, walked into the back room. **1867** *Gd. Words* 335/2, I was obliged to be contented with looking my pleasure. **1947** A. MENEN *Prevalence of Witches* ii. 36 Suddenly his eyes looked mischief again. **1956** H. GOLD *Man who was not with It* (1965) vi. 53, I looked a question at her.

2. a. With indirect question expressed or contextually implied: To apply one's sight to ascertain (*who, what, how, whether*, etc.). Now only used when the question is regarded as capable of being answered at a single glance.

[*c* **1000** *Ags. Gosp.* Mark vi. 38 Ða cwæð he hu fela hlafa hæbbe ȝe gað & lociað.] *c* **1175** *Lamb. Hom.* 41 Heo tweien eoden..in to helle..for to lokien hu hit þer ferde. *c* **1200** *Trin. Coll. Hom.* 121 Ure drihten..beih of heuene to mannen and lokede gif here ani understoden oðer bisohten him. *c* **1250** *Gen. & Ex.* 2600 Ghe adde or hire dowter sent, To loken quider it sulde ben went. **1297** R. GLOUC. (Rolls) 315 Brut sende vp þere þre hondred men iarmed wel, to loke ȝwat lond þat were. *c* **1425** *Crafte Nombryng* (E.E.T.S.) 30 Multiply þat digit by anoþer diget,..and loke qwat comes þere-of. *a* **1584** MONTGOMERIE *Cherrie & Slae* 463 Luik quhair to licht before thou loup. **1588** A. KING tr. *Canisius' Catech.* in *Cath. Tractates* (1901) 205 Lowke quhat day of the age of the moone it is. **1590** SPENSER *F.Q.* I. iv. 19 Scarse could he once uphold his heavie hedd, To looken whether it were night or day. **1710** SWIFT *Jrnl. to Stella* 30 Nov., O, but one may look whether one goes crooked or no and so write on. **1819** CRABBE *T. of Hall* x, I loved my trees in order to dispose, I number'd peaches, look'd how stocks arose. **1848** J. H. NEWMAN *Loss & Gain* III. iii. 318 He glanced from one article to another, looking who were the University-preachers of the week, who had taken degrees [etc.]. *Mod.* I will look what time the train starts.

†**b.** Phr. *look else*: see whether it be not so. (See ELSE 4 c.) *Obs.*

1622 MASSINGER *Virg. Mart.* II. i, I kicke for all that like a horse, looke else.

c. *go look*: = 'find it out'; a contemptuous manner of refusing information. Now *dial.*

1595 LYLY *Woman in Moon* v. i. 86 (Bond), If you aske me why I sing, I say yee may go looke.

3. *fig.* **a.** 'To direct the intellectual eye' (J.); to turn or fix one's attention or regard. With advs. or phrases as in 1 a. (See also branches IV and V.) Now usually const. *at*; formerly *on* or *upon.*

a **1548** HALL *Chron., Hen. V*, 37 b, Let the kyngdome of the assiriens be your example, and if that suffise not, then loke on the Percians. **1560** DAUS tr. *Sleidane's Comm.* 37 b, Lokyng more narrowly upon domestical evils. **1562** WINȜET *Cert. Tractates* i. Wks. 1888 I. 12 Thay..luckis bakwart with the Israelitis to the potis of flesche in Egypt. **1570** *Satir. Poems Reform.* xii. 10 He man luke lawer, and enter in the Spreit, And than he sall persaif the cause fra hand. **1583** GOLDING *Calvin on Deut.* xxi. 124 Looke me vpon the Turkes: they haue some reuerence to their religion. **1602** SHAKS. *Ham.* IV. iv. 37 (1604 Qo.) He that made vs with such large discourse, Looking before and after. **1611** BIBLE *2 Cor.* iv. 18 While we looke not at the things which are seene, but at yᵉ things which are not seene. *a* **1625** BEAUM. & FL. *Bonduca* II. iv, Ods so infinite Discretion durst not look upon. *a* **1699** STILLINGFL. (J.), We are not only to look at the bare action, but at the reason of it. **1824** BENTHAM *Bk. Fallacies* Wks. 1843 II. 455 Instead of reforming others..let him look at home. **1845** M. PATTISON *Ess.* (1889) I. 2 Because ideas change, the whole mode and manner of looking at things varies with every age. **1861** DICKENS *Gt. Expect.* lv, What I look at, is the sacrifice of so much portable property. **1885** F. ANSTEY *Tinted Venus* 70 'That's the proper way to look at it', said he. **1885** SIR N. LINDLEY in *Law Rep.* 30 Ch. Div. 14 The case of *Stokes* v. *Trumper* is not really in point when we come to look at it closely. **1890** MRS. H. WOOD *House of Halliwell* I. vii. 175, I marry a medical student!..I look a little higher than that. *Ibid.* III. viii. 207 Your friends will look at position as well as gentle blood.

b. To take care, make sure, see (*that* or *how* something is done; also with omission of *that*). Now *arch.*

c **897** K. ÆLFRED *Gregory's Past.* lix. 451 Lociað nu ðæt ðios eowru leaf ne weorðe oðrum monnum to biswice. *a* **1300** *Cursor M.* 1966 Fixs and flesse, o bath i sai, Lok ai þe blod ȝee cast a wai. *a* **1300** *Ibid.* 16814 + 15 Pilat..bad þat þai suld loke þat he wore ded for-thy. *c* **1380** WYCLIF *Wks.* (1880) 38 Seynt petyr comaundiþ ȝif ony speke, loke he speke as goddis wordis. *c* **1440** *Anc. Cookery* in *Househ. Ord.* (1790) 434 Loke hit be stondynge. **1470–85** MALORY *Arthur* I. xvi. 60 Loke eueryche of yow kynges lete make suche ordinaunce. **1561** T. HOBY tr. *Castiglione's Courtyer* III. (1577) O viij, And you (my L. Margaret) looke yee beare it well awaye. **1604** SHAKS. *Oth.* IV. iii. 8 Dismisse your Attendant there: look't be done. **1621–31** LAUD *Serm.* (1847) 133 The State must look their proceedings be just, and the Church must look their devotions and actions be pious. **1646** J. HALL *Horæ Vac.* 22 We ought to looke how wee spend our houres here. **1690** E. GEE *Jesuit's Mem.* 89 Censor to look that no man lived idly. **1819** SHELLEY *Cyclops* 477 When I call, Look ye obey the masters of the craft. **1865** *Jrnl. R. Agric. Soc.* Ser. II. I. II. 242 We must look, therefore, that we have the ..wide chest, straight back, &c. **1871** R. ELLIS tr. *Catullus* lxiv. 231 Look that warily then deep-laid in steady remembrance These our words grow greenly.

c. To expect. Const. *to* with *inf.* †Formerly also with clause, usually introduced by *that.* †Also, to expect, await the time *when* something shall happen; to be curious to see *how, whether*, etc.; also *impers.* in *passive.*

c **1513** MORE *Rich. III* (ed. Lumby) 7 Whose life hee looked that euil dyete shoulde shorten. *Ibid.* 11 In these last wordes that euer I looke to speake with you. **1535** COVERDALE *Isa.* v. 4 When he loked yᵗ it shulde bringe him grapes, it brought forth thornes. **1568** GRAFTON *Chron.* II. 112 Lokyng every day when his Barons and their confederates would cruelly set upon him. *c* **1586** C'TESS PEMBROKE *Ps.* LXIX. viii, Some I lookt would me uphold. **1593** SHAKS. *Rich. II*, I. iii. 243. **1604** E. G[RIMSTONE] *D'Acosta's Hist. Indies* III. xi. 156 The wind being contrary and stormy, they looked all to perish. **1605** CAMDEN *Rem.* (1637) 271 Then it was looked how he should justifie that fact. **1611** HEYWOOD *Gold. Age* I. i. Wks. 1874 III. 10, I neuer heard she was committed to prison; yet t'is look't euery houre when she shall be deliuered. *a* **1626** BACON *New Atl.* (1900) 9 Wee..saluted him in a very lowly and submissive manner; As looking that from him, wee should receyve Sentence of Life, or Death. **1651** HOBBES *Leviath.* III. xlii. 271 By whom we look to be protected. **1657** AUSTEN *Fruit Trees* II. 64 God lookes every one should be fruit-full under all his dispensations. **1760–72** H. BROOKE *Fool of Qual.* (1809) IV. 141, I never look to have a mistress that I shall love half as well. **1830** SOUTHEY *Lett.* (1856) IV. 168, I too had been looking to hear from you. **1852** MRS. STOWE *Uncle Tom's C.* vii, I'm glad mas'r didn't go off this morning, as he looked to. **1893** *Field* 11 Mar. 362/3 The.. labourer..looks to go to work at a fixed hour. **1896** A. E. HOUSMAN *Shropsh. Lad* xxvi, Two lovers looking to be wed.

†**d.** with indirect question: To consider, ascertain (*who, when, whether*, etc.); to try (*if* something can be done, etc.). Also *simply*, to consider the matter, make inquiry; *esp.* in phr. *whoso will look*, etc. *Obs.*

1375 BARBOUR *Bruce* VIII. 419 The king can furth his vais ta,..for till luk gif he Micht recouer his cuntre. *c* **1375** *Sc. Leg. Saints* xl. (*Ninian*) 93 He vmthocht he wald luke Gyf he in sic corne cuth set huke. *c* **1380** WYCLIF *Serm.* Sel. Wks. I. 319 But diversite is greet here and þere, whoso wole loke. **1399** LANGL. *Rich. Redeles* III. 255 That ich leode lokide what longid to his age. *c* **1400** *Lanfranc's Cirurg.* 51 þou muste loke wheþer þat þe bodi be ful of wickide humouris, eiþer be clene. *c* **1450** *Merlin* 9 Than made he hir suster come on a saterday,..to loke yef he might gete hir in that manere. **1573** *Satir. Poems Reform.* xlii. 403 Schir, luk ȝe and se Gif that the teindis of this countrie May not do all that we have tauld. *c* **1585** R. BROWNE *Answ. Cartwright* 50 If he looke well, this proofe serueth against him. **1692** LOCKE *3rd Let. Toleration* ix. Wks. 1727 II. 394 Whether.. your pretending Gain to them,..be a greater Mockery, you were best look.

4. Idiomatic uses of the imperative.

a. Used to bespeak attention: = 'see', 'behold', 'lo'. In mod. colloq. use often *look you* (in representations of vulgar speech written *look'ee*) = 'mind this'; also *look here*, a brusque mode of address prefacing an order, expostulation, reprimand, etc. *looky here* U.S. regional variant of 'look here'; also *look-a-here.* Also, *look who's* (or *what's*) *here*: see who (or what) is here.

c **1000** ÆLFRIC *Gram.* xxxviii. (Z.) 231 *En* efne oððe loca nu, her hit is. *c* **1250** *Gen. & Ex.* 3331 Quod moyses, 'loc! her nu is bread'. *c* **1460** *Towneley Myst.* xxx. 141 Here is a bag full, lokys, of pride and of lust. **1513** DOUGLAS *Æneis* Exclamatioun 18 Lo, heir he failȝeis, se thar he leis, luik! **1575** GASCOIGNE *Glasse Govt.* IV. i, Poems 1870 II. 59, I would be glad to talke with Maister Gnomaticus..and looke where he commeth in haste. **1594** MARLOWE & NASHE *Dido* 372 *N.'s Wks.* (Grosart) VI. 22 Looke where she comes: Æneas, view her well. **1597** SHAKS. *2 Hen. IV*, II. ii. 116 (1600 Qo.) Looke you how he writes. **1611** —— *Wint. T.* III. iii. 116 Heauy matters, heauy matters: but looke thee heere boy. **1672** VILLIERS (Dk. Buckhm.) *Rehearsal* I. i. (Arb.) 33 For, look you, Sir, the grand design..is to keep the Auditors in suspence. **1709** STEELE *Tatler* No. 34 ¶ 4 Look ye, said I, I must not rashly give my Judgment. **1710** *Ibid.* No. 206 ¶ 2 Look'ee, Jack, I have heard thee sometimes talk like an Oracle. **1782** COWPER *Retirement* 283 Look where he comes. *a* **1814** *Woman's Will* IV. ii. in *New Brit. Theatre* IV. 111 Lookee there now! You can soon create a cause for quarrel, my Lady. **1843** LONGF. *Sp. Student* II. vi, Look, here he comes. **1861** DICKENS *Gt. Expect.* li, Now, look here, my man..I'll have no feelings here. **1865** —— *Mut. Fr.* II. xiv, 'Now, lookee here, my dear,' returned old Betty,—'asking your excuse for being so familiar'. **1872** [see *gum-game* (GUM *sb.*[2] 9)]. **1875** TENNYSON *Q. Mary* II. i, Look you, Master Wyatt, Tear up that woman's work there. **1876** 'MARK TWAIN' *Tom Sawyer* x. 94 And besides, look-a-here—maybe that whack done for *him*! **1925** E. O'NEILL *Desire under Elms* I. ii. 20 Looky here! Ye'd oughtn't t' said that, Eben. **1935** Z. N. HURSTON *Mules & Men* I. iv. 95 'Looka here, folkses,' Jim Presley exclaimed. 'Wese a half hour behind schedule.' **1943** 'C. DICKSON' *She died a Lady* v. 38 Looky here... Burn it all, all I was tryin' to do was see what she'd do flat out on an open road. **1945** A. KOBER *Parm Me* 75 'Well, look who's here!' exclaimed the host. **1949** N. MARSH *Swing, Brother, Swing* iii. 48 'Well, well, well,' he said. 'Look who's here.' **1969** *Listener* 1 May 614/1 Look, my Bill doesn't include any blanket condemnation of unofficial strikes. **1971** *Black Scholar* June 54/2 Looka-here, Dr. Hare, I don't have a picture at this time. **1973** *Black World* Apr. 62 Lookahere Sammy... I'm glad to see ya. **1973** G. SIMS *Hunters Point* xiii. 115 Look, we don't have to sit here. We could go down to the beach. **1974** *Daily Mail* 1 Oct. 8/5 *Look you!* Plaid Cymru protested to the BBC yesterday over the timing of its only party political broadcast.

†**b.** Prefixed to interrogative pronoun or adv., or relative conj., forming indefinite relatives = *whoever, whatever, however*, etc. Also, in later use, emphasizing the correspondence of relative and antecedent, as in *look as* = 'just as'. *Obs.*

The absence of examples between the 12th and the 16th c. is remarkable: the idiom was prob. preserved in some non-literary dialect.

c **1000** ÆLFRIC *Gen.* xvi. 6 Þrea hiȝ, loca hu þu wylle. —— *Josh.* ii. 19 And loca hwa ut gange, licge he ofslaȝen. *a* **1123** *O.E. Chron.* an. 1101 (Laud MS.) Loc hweðer þæra ȝebroðra oðerne oferbide, wære yrfeweard ealles Englalandes. **1535** COVERDALE *Ps.* i. 3 His leeues shal not fall off, and loke what soeuer he doth, it shal prospere. —— *Ecclus.* i. 13 The loue of God is honorable wiszdome: loke vnto whom it appeareth, they loue it. **1568** GRAFTON *Chron.* I. 94 And looke what he commaunded, that was done, though some did murmure. **1597** J. T. *Serm. Paules C.* 56 But looke as thou sinnest, so shalt thou haue the wages of sinne. *a* **1600** HOOKER *Eccl. Pol.* VII. vi. §9 He added farther, that look what duty the Roman Consuls did execute..the like charge had the Bishop. *c* **1600** SHAKS. *Sonn.* xxxvii. 13 Looke what is best, that best I wish in thee. **1611** BIBLE *1 Macc.* iv. 54 Looke at what time, and what day the heathen had prophaned it, euen in that was it dedicated with songs, and cittherns, and harpes, and cimbals. **1615** W. LAWSON *Country Housew. Gard.* (1626) 23 And looke how farre a tree spreads his boughs aboue, so far doth he put his roots vnder the earth. **1625** BURGES *Pers. Tithes* 31 And looke what the Lawes..enioyne, that thou must doe, or be a Rebell. **1675** BROOKS *Gold. Key* 321 Look, as God cannot but be just, so he cannot but be true. *Ibid.* 301, 302.

5. look sharp. Originally (with *sharp* as adv.) = 'to look sharply after something', 'to keep strict watch'. In later use (which is merely colloquial) the sense is commonly 'to bestir oneself briskly', 'to lose no time' (the vb. being app. taken in a sense belonging to branch III, and *sharp* regarded as a complementary adj.).

1711 STEELE *Spect.* No. 132 ¶ 1 The Captain..ordered his Man to look sharp, that none but one of the Ladies should have the Place he had taken fronting the Coachbox. **1713** R. BENTLEY *Remarks Late Disc. Free-th.* II. Wks. 1838 III. 472 It is time for us then to look sharp, to observe every period. **1732** BERKELEY *Alciphr.* vi. §1, I must, therefore, look sharp, and well consider every step I take. **1788** LD. AUCKLAND *Corr.* (1861) II. 69 At nine o'clock we began to look sharp for our house. **1803** in *Spirit Pub. Jrnls.* VII. 128 Mr. Robson will attend to the old peers..while Mr. Faulder will look sharp after the fortune-hunters. **1818** COBBETT *Pol. Reg.* XXXIII. 91, I see that the Ministers are very shy of dissolving the Parliament; and they shall look sharp if they act before I am ready for them. **1834** LANDOR *Exam. Shaks.* Wks. 1853 II. 285/2 But let her look sharp, or spectacles may be thrust upon her nose that shall make her eyes water. **1840**

DICKENS *Old C. Shop* xxxix, Kit..ordered..him to bring three dozen..oysters, and to look sharp about it! **1846** S. R. MAITLAND *Ess.* etc. 258 Would he not be startled if one told him that he would have to look sharp for five-and-twenty [martyrs]? **1874** *Punch* 8 Aug. 64 Glass of ale, young woman; and look sharp, please! **1890** FENN *Double Knot* I. viii. 191 You'd better look sharp,..they're all ready and waiting.

6. Transitive uses, chiefly synonymous with various intransitive uses with prepositions.

a. To look at, behold; to view, inspect, examine. Now *dial.* ***to look babies***: to gaze at the reflection of one's face in another's eyes.

13.. *Coer de L.* 3030 Rychard bad his men seche For some wys clerk and sertayn leche,..For to loke his uryn. **1382** WYCLIF *Num.* xxiv. 17, I shal inwardly loke hym [Vulg. *intuebor illum*] but not nyȝ. *c* **1400** *Destr. Troy* 7525 Leches full lyuely lokid his wound. **1471** J. PASTON in *P. Lett.* III. 7 That no body look my wryghtynges. **1509** BARCLAY *Shyp of Folys* (1570) 113 When he a while his glasse hath loken. **1523** FITZHERB. *Husb.* §40 Than let the shepeherde turne them, and loke them on euery syde. *a* **1578** LINDESAY (Pitscottie) *Chron. Scot.* (S.T.S.) II. 158 He mowit wpe to the hill heid of Tarbitt..to awew and luik the congregatioun. **1607** BEAUM. & FL. *Woman Hater* III. i, I cannot thinke, I shall become a coxcombe, To ha' my hare curl'd, by an idle finger,..Mine eyes lookt babies in. **1615** BRATHWAIT *Strappado* 80 Or when none that's iealous spies To looke babbies in his eyes. **1647** TRAPP *Comm. Ep. & Rev.* App. 669 Many Heathens have advised the angry man to look his face in a glasse, and to grow ashamed of his distemper. **1655** *New Haven Col. Rec.* (1858) II. 151 Robert Cranfeild..testifyed..that he went to looke oxen. **1721** RAMSAY *Morning Interview* 34 He frown'd, and look'd his watch. **1874** W. H. L. RANKEN *Domin. Australia* vi. 105 Plains are scoured and every piece of timber looked. **1882** J. WALKER *Jaunt to Auld Reekie* etc. 10 He looks his hand: behold the sooty meal The secret tells. **1897** CROCKETT *Lad's Love* xi. 115, I was engaged in 'looking the sheep'—that is, numbering them and seeing that none had strayed. **1957** J. BRAINE *Room at Top* xi. 107, I could see my face in her pupils... 'You're looking babies,' she said.

†**b.** To look into, examine; to consider, have regard to, regard. *Obs.*

c **1300** *Beket* 284 The King from Normandie com To Engelond to Look the stat of his Kynedom. **1340** HAMPOLE *Pr. Consc.* 205 He that right ordir of lyfyng wil luke Suld bygyn thus, als says the boke. *c* **1375** *Lay Folks Mass Bk.* (MS. B.) 271 When þou prayes, god lokes þi wille. *a* **1400** *Prymer* (1891) 45 For he lokede the mekenesse of his handmayde. **1430–40** LYDG. *Bochas* IX. xxxiii. (1558) 34 The matter who so list to loke. **1533** GAU *Richt Vay* 19 God lukis notht the wtuert richtfulnes quilk mony keipis. *c* **1560** A. SCOTT *Poems* (S.T.S.) xxxiv. 1 ȝe blindit luvaris, luke The rekless lyfe ȝe leid.

†**c.** To consult or refer to (an author, a book, or a place in it); to 'turn up'. In the imper. = VIDE. Also, to search for (a word etc.) in a book of reference. (Cf. *look up*, 45 g.) *Obs.*

a **1300** *Cursor M.* 9334 Þat yow tels sent Ieremi, If yee wald lok his propheci. *c* **1386** CHAUCER *Pard. T.* 250 Looketh the Bible, and ther ye may it leere. *a* **1420** HOCCLEVE *De Reg. Princ.* 3099 As þe boke can expresse: Whoso it lokith, fynde it shal no lesse. **1529** RASTELL *Pastyme, Hist. French* (1811) 69 Therfor loke Julius Cesar his commentaryes. **1596** HARINGTON *Metam. Ajax* 60 Looke it sirra there in the dictionarie. **1598** FLORIO, *Aria*, looke *Aere*. **1599** NASHE *Lenten Stuffe* 58 For his ensainting, looke the Almanack in the beginning of Aprill. **1611** COTGR., *Anonexie*, Looke *Anorexie*. **1611** BIBLE *1 Macc.* xii. 7 *marg.*, Areus: looke Ioseph. Ant. lib. 13. cap. 8. **1640** FULLER *Joseph's Coat* etc. 125 *marg.* Look Lord Bacon in his life. **1656** H. PHILLIPS *Purch. Patt.* (1676) 157 Take the compass of the tree..look this compass in the Table. **1813** J. ADAMS *Wks.* (1856) X. 49, I found that if I looked a word to-day, in less than a week I had to look it again.

d. To seek, search for; = *look for* (15 b). Also, to be on the look-out for, seek or search out. *rare* (now *dial.*).

c **1394** *P. P. Crede* 593 Now mot a frere..loken hem lesynges þat likeþ þe puple. *c* **1470** HENRYSON *Mor. Fab.* I. (*Cock & Jasp*) v, I had leuer ga scrapit heir with my naillis ..and luik my lyfis fude. **1595** MUNDAY *John a Kent* (Shaks. Soc.) 22 Moorton shall looke him now an other bryde. **1600** SHAKS. *A. Y. L.* II. v. 30 He hath bin all this day to looke you. **1622** MABBE tr. *Aleman's Guzman d'Alf.* II. 152 You neuer left any Crownes nor Royals with me: Goe looke your Crownes and Royals else-where. **1650** T. VAUGHAN *Anima Magica* To Rdr., He knew it was bootles to look fatal Events in the Planets. **1664** PEPYS *Diary* 3 Sept., In the morning she chid her mayds for not looking the fleas a-days. **1668** DRYDEN *All for Love* IV. i, Octavia, I was looking you, my love. **1683** TRYON *Way to Health* xix. (1697) 417 Or else the poor Lass after the Wedding-Cloathes are made, must go look her an Husband. **1716** B. CHURCH *Hist. Philip's War* (1865) I. 162 He went with his new Souldier to look his Father. **1752** JOHNSON *Rambler* No. 138 ⁋11 At her leisure hours she looks goose eggs. **1782** MISS BURNEY *Cecilia* VII. v, I'll go look him [a dog], however, for we went at such a rate that I never missed him. **1821** CLARE *Vill. Minstr.* I. 88 Pinders, that such chances look, Drive his rambling cows to pound. **1879** *Boy's Own Paper* 18 Jan. 14/3 [The monkeys] both set to work and 'look fleas' in the hare's fur. **1961** F. G. CASSIDY *Jamaica Talk* vii. 148 A very common usage makes *look* into a transitive verb meaning look for, gather: 'Arthur and I joined a group of boys to *look wood*.'

†**e.** To take care of, keep, guard, watch over, preserve in safety; to observe (a day). Also *refl.* To guard oneself, beware; to abstain (*from*). Also *absol.* or *intr.*: To watch. *Obs.*

c **1175** *Lamb. Hom.* 45 We aȝen þene sunne dei swiþeliche wel to wurþien and on alle clenesse to locan. *c* **1250** *Gen. & Ex.* 3193 He dede binden & faire loken Alle ðe bones ðe he ðor token. *Ibid.* 3511 Loke ðe wel ðat ðu ne stele. *a* **1300** *K. Horn* 800 Rymenhild þu kep and loke. *a* **1300** *Cursor M.* 8297 'Godd þe loke', he said, 'sir king'. *c* **1330** R. BRUNNE *Chron.* (1810) 129 Þat othe sald he wele loke. **1340** *Ayenb.* 42 þet hi ham loki uram þise zenne. *Ibid.* 235 Þe prestes þet lokeden chastete ine þe temple weren todeld uram þe oþren þet hi ne loren hire chastete. *c* **1460** *Towneley Myst.* xiii. 219 God looke you all thre!

†**f.** To provide, appoint, ordain, decree, decide. *Obs.*

c **1175** *Lamb. Hom.* 73 Þer fore hit wes iloked bi godes wissunge ine halie chirche þet mon scule childre fulhten. *a* **1225** *Leg. Kath.* 1206 As his ahne goddlec lahede hit ant lokede. **1297** R. GLOUC. (Rolls) 1230 Þe kyng he sende word aȝen, þat he adde is franchise In is owe court, vorto loke domes & assise. *c* **1305** *St. Kenelm* 301 in *E.E.P.* (1862) 55 Þe bischop hadde iloked þat hit scholde þider beo ibore. *c* **1330** R. BRUNNE *Chron.* (1810) 36 Þe right lawes did he loke for fals men & fikelle. *a* **1400–50** *Alexander* 3404 (Ashm. MS.) Syn it lokid [*Dublin MS.* lukkyd] has þe largenes of þe lord of heuen. *c* **1460** *Launfal* 783, I am a redy for to tho All that the court wyll loke.

†**g.** To expect, look forward to, look for. *Obs.*

1560 DAUS tr. *Sleidane's Comm.* 311 What ende at the length doe you loke of this obstinacy and vnloyaultie. *a* **1572** KNOX *Hist. Ref.* Wks. 1846 I. 4 We crave of all the gentill Readaris, not to look of us such ane History. *c* **1586** C'TESS PEMBROKE *Ps.* CXIX. K. i, What I look't from thee..I now enjoy. **1595** DANIEL *Civ. Wars* II. viii, His fortune gives him more than he could looke. **1611** SHAKS. *Wint. T.* IV. iv. 369 The gifts she lookes from me, are packt and lockt Vp in my heart.

II. To have an outlook, face a certain way.

7. a. *intr.* To have or afford a certain outlook; to face, front, or be turned *towards*, *into*, *on to*, etc.

1555 COVERDALE *Jer.* i. 13, I do se a seethinge pot, looking from out of the north hitherwarde. *a* **1586** SIDNEY *Arcadia* III. (1633) 304 Each of these chambers had a little window to looke into the hall. **1596** DALRYMPLE tr. *Leslie's Hist. Scot.* IX. 193 That parte of the Castel that luikis to Tued. **1611** BIBLE *Num.* xxi. 20 Pisgah, which looketh toward Ieshimon. **1668** DRYDEN *All for love* II. i, Unbar the Gate that looks to Cæsar's Camp. **1732** BERKELEY *Alciphr.* iii. §1 A summer parlour which looks into the garden. **1866** M. ARNOLD *Thyrsis* ii, The signal-elm that looks on Ilsley Downs. **1886** BEAT. M. BUTT *Lesterre Durant* I. v. 61 The windows looking north. **1893** *Strand Mag.* VI. 268/2 The dining-room looks on to the Melbury Road.

b. Of parts of the body, or the like: To face or turn (in a particular direction).

1656 RIDGLEY *Pract. Physic* 243 The Knee and Foot look inwards. **1692** SIR W. HOPE *Fencing-Master* (ed. 2) 17 The points of your Fingers must not look upwards, but pointing towards your Adversary. **1776–96** WITHERING *Brit. Plants* (ed. 3) I. 388 Bearing the flowers underneath, the florets looking downwards. **1863** HUXLEY *Man's Place Nat.* i. 23 Their nostrils have a narrow partition, and look downwards.

8. a. To show a tendency; to tend, point (in a particular direction).

1647 *Power of Kings* iv. 84 The context looketh wholly that way. **1674** N. FAIRFAX *Bulk & Selv.* 188 The Argument drawn from Gods unbounded power and goodness, as looking towards the behoof of the Creature will ever fall short upon this score. **1692** R. L'ESTRANGE *Josephus' Antiq.* II. ix. (1733) 44 The Barbarity of this bloody Decree look'd several ways. **1703** MAUNDRELL *Journ. Jerus.* (1732) 42 Its sense seems to look that way. *c* **1800** K. WHITE *Lett.* (1837) 320 He thinks it looks towards epilepsy. **1869** GOULBURN *Purs. Holiness* x. 93 In this direction look the words of our Lord to St. Thomas. **1881** P. GREG *Ivy* III. vi. 122 All the facts look the other way.

†**b.** To tend *to*, promise *to*. *Obs. rare.*

1607 SHAKS. *Cor.* III. iii. 29 He speakes What's in his heart, and that is there which lookes With vs to breake his necke.

III. To have a certain appearance. [App. in part developed from 1 c; but cf. the similar use in passive sense of other verbs of perception, like *smell*, *taste*, *feel*.]

9. a. *intr.* To have the appearance of being; to seem to the sight. (This sense when used of persons often retains some mixture of the notion of 1 c.) Const. a predicative sb. or adj., or a predicative adv. (as *well*, *ill* = 'in good, bad health').

For the fig. phr. *to look black*, *blue*, *foolish*, *small*, etc., see the adjs.

c **1400** *Destr. Troy* 8742 Ymages..Lokend full lyuely as any light angels. **1500–20** DUNBAR *Poems* liii. 37 God waith gif that scho loukit sour! **1526** *Pilgr. Perf.* (W. de W. 1531) 266 Resolueth all the grosenesse of the oyle, and maketh it to loke clere. **1658** WOOD *Life* 5 Apr., He look'd elderly and was cynical and hirsute in his behavior. **1697** DRYDEN *Æneid* XI. 99 All pale he lies, and looks a lovely Flow'r. **1712** HEARNE *Collect.* (O.H.S.) III. 486 'Twould have look'd vain, and ostentatious. **1715** POPE *Iliad* III. 208 She moves a Goddess, and she looks a Queen! **1761** MRS. F. SHERIDAN *Sidney Biddulph* I. 18 He is grown fat, and looks quite robust. **1788** COWPER *Pity for poor Africans*, You speak very fine, and you look very grave. **1802** MAR. EDGEWORTH *Moral T.*, *Forester* (1806) I. 65 Henry looked in great anxiety. **1857** RUSKIN *Pol. Econ. Art* i. 1, I see that some of my hearers look surprised at the expression. **1871** M. ARNOLD *Friendship's Garland* v. 36 'You made me look rather a fool, Arminius', I began. **1886** BEAT. M. BUTT *Lesterre Durant* I. xix. 304 London was certainly not looking its best. **1888** SARAH TYTLER *Blackhall Ghosts* II. xvii. 65 Kitty did not look the lady she was not. **1897** *Windsor Mag.* Jan. 274/1 No. 1.. looked such a much larger house than it was..No. 2..was such a much larger house than it looked.

b. with adv. of manner (†or advb. phrase): To have a certain look or appearance.

This use is often indiscriminately condemned, but is justly censurable only where *look* is virtually equivalent to *seem*, so that it requires a predicative complement and not a qualification of manner. (So, e.g., in quot. 1645.) Owing, however, to the prejudice excited by the inaccurate use, *look* now rarely occurs with advs. of manner other than *well*, *ill*, *badly*. In some early instances the apparent adv. may possibly be an adj. in ME.

a **1300** *XV Signa* 56 in *E.E.P.* (1862) 9 Hi sul..lok as bestis þat cun no witte. **1377** LANGL. *P. Pl.* B. v. 189 So hungriliche [1362 A. v. 108 hungri] and holwe sire Heruy hym loked. **1542** BOORDE *Dyetary* xxxix. (1870) 300 For that wyll cause a man to loke agedly. **1546** J. HEYWOOD *Prov.* 50 Though your pasture looke barreinly and dull. *c* **1586** C'TESS PEMBROKE *Ps.* CV. viii, Watry Nilus lookes with bloudy face. **1610** SHAKS. *Temp.* III. i. 32 You looke wearily. *Ibid.* IV. i. 146 You doe looke (my son) in a mou'd sort. **1611** —— *Wint. T.* III. iii. 3 The skies looke grimly. **1645** T. HILL *Olive Branch* (1648) 40 This would make you look more amiably and smell more sweetly. **1683** TRYON *Way to Health* xix. (1697) 413 How base a thing it is, and how unnaturally it looks, that men should value Money more than the Law of God. **1712** J. JAMES tr. *Le Blond's Gardening* 21 Points and Corners advancing..look very ill upon the Ground. **1719** DE FOE *Crusoe* II. i. (1840) 7 The world looked awkwardly round me. *Ibid.* II. xv. 314 To see who looked with most guilt in their faces. **1781** COWPER *Retirement* 567 Nature indeed looks prettily in rhyme. **1802** MRS. J. WEST *Infidel Father* II. 188 Do I also look meanly in her eyes? **1826** COBBETT *Rur. Rides* (1885) II. 57 Fields of Swedish turnips, all looking extremely well. **1849** MACAULAY *Hist. Eng.* ix. II. 497 On the whole, however, things as yet looked not unfavourably for James. **1855** *Ibid.* xx. IV. 471 It tasked all the art of Kneller to make her look tolerably on canvass. **1891** SIR A. WILLS in *Law Times* XCI. 233/2 Things had, by that time, begun to look badly for all concerned.

c. Const. *inf.* To seem to the view. *lit.* and *fig.*

1775 BURKE *Sp. Conc. Amer.* Sel. Wks. I. 192 It looks to me to be narrow and pedantic, to apply the ordinary ideas of criminal justice to this great public contest. **1793** W. ROBERTS *Looker-On* No. 84 (1794) III. 345 To make a display..looks to be, with the major part, the real object which assembles them. **1890** CLARK RUSSELL *Ocean Trag.* I. vi. 123 A little hat that looked to be made of beaver. **1893** *Graphic* 25 Mar. 298/1 The Queen looked to be in good health.

d. ***to look as if*** (or †*as*) ——: to have an appearance suggesting the belief that ——. Often with indefinite subject, ***it looks*** (or ***things look***) ***as if*** ——.

1500–20 DUNBAR *Poems* liii. 9 He leuket as he culd lern tham a. **1611** B. JONSON *Catiline* IV. v, Looke they, as they were built to shake the world? *a* **1700** DRYDEN *Flower & Leaf* 57, I took the way, Which through a path, but scarcely printed, lay;..And looked as lightly pressed by fairy feet. **1700** T. BROWN *Amusem. Ser. & Com.* 91 It looks as if Physicians learnt their Gibberish for no other purpose, than to embroil what they do not understand. **1790** BURKE *Fr. Rev.* (1898) 11 It looks to me as if I were in a great crisis. **1809** MALKIN *Gil Blas* V. i. ⁋27 Pedro was dumb-founded, and looked as if he could not help it. **1867** FREEMAN *Norm. Conq.* (1876) I. App. 774 This looks as if Harold were now quartered in Denmark. **1892** *St. Nicholas Mag.* XIV. 538/1 It looked as if there was going to be a free fight. **1898** FLOR. MONTGOMERY *Tony* 9 She looked as if she were thoroughly bored.

e. quasi-*trans.* To have an appearance befitting or according with (one's character, condition, assumed part, etc.). ***to look one's age***: to have the appearance of being as old as one is. ***to look oneself***: to appear to be in one's usual health.

1828 *Examiner* 756/1 She looked the character extremely well. **1842** L. HUNT *Men, Women & B.* (1876) 373 Though people do not always seem what they are, it is seldom they do not look what they can do. **1852** DICKENS *Bleak Ho.* xxxiv, But what's the matter, George?..you don't look yourself. **1879** MISS YONGE *Cameos* Ser. IV. xvii. 187 She looked her full forty-three years. **1883** *Manch. Exam.* 29 Oct. 5/3 Miss Anderson looked the part to perfection. **1891** L. MERRICK *Violet Moses* II. xii. 134 He assuredly did not look his age.

10. look like. a. To have the appearance of being. (See LIKE A. 1 b ⁋.) Also, (*it*) ***looks like***: it seems likely (*colloq.*, chiefly *U.S.*).

c **1440** *York Myst.* xxx. 273 He lokis like a lambe. **1581** STUDLEY *Hippolytus* 67 Lyke lusty young Perithous he looketh in the face. **1628** EARLE *Microcosm.*, *High Spirited Man* (Arb.) 91 One that lookes like a proud man but is not. **1662** STILLINGFL. *Orig. Sacr.* II. v. §3 There is some thing looks very like this in the proceedings of the people of Israel against the Prophet Jeremiah. **1699** T. BAKER *Refl. Learning* 58 This Plan, as laid down by him, looks liker an Universal Art than a distinct Logic. **1711** ADDISON *Spect.* No. 50 ⁋8 The Women look like Angels. *a* **1715** BURNET *Own Time* (1724) I. 606 He had a humour in his leg, which looked like the beginning of the gout. **1773** GOLDSM. *Stoops to Conq.* II. (*end*), My dear 'squire, this looks like a lad of spirit. **1861** M. PATTISON *Ess.* (1889) I. 40 The payment in kind, and not in money, looks like a customary acknowledgement from an old established guild. **1884** W. C. SMITH *Kildrostan* 43 She ..looked like a monument planted there. **1910** W. M. RAINE *Bucky O'Connor* 55 Your cook, Anderson, kid-napped the child, looks like to me. **1929** J. BUCHAN *Courts of Morning* 13, I admitted that it looked like it, and said that if Blenkiron had been captured by bandits..his captors had done the worst day's work of their lives. **1936** M. MITCHELL *Gone with Wind* I. i. 11 Don't it look to you like she would of asked us to stay for supper? **1970** N. MARSH *When in Rome* v. 127 'Wouldn't it be a fly?'..you were The Man?' 'Do I look like it?' **1972** G. BROMLEY *In Absence of Body* viii. 101 'And now I suppose you've got to find a replacement?' 'Looks like it.' **1973** *Guardian* 31 Jan. 4/7 Looks like your child's birthday is news again this year.

b. with gerund, vbl. sb., or *occas.* sb.: To give promise of, show a likelihood of.

1593 SHAKS. *Lucr.* 585 Thou look'st not like deceipt; do not deceiue me. **1747** *Gentl. Mag.* XVII. 383 Parties may be abolish'd, but the late dissolution of the parliament don't look much like it. **1883** J. W. SHERER *At Home & in India* 158 Later on, indeed, after supper, he grew worse—looked like biting—and..tore the bouquet in pieces. **1888** H. F. LESTER *Hartas Maturin* II. ii. 34 It looks like rain. **1973** A.

Broinowski *Take One Ambassador* ii. 21, I look like being in and out of the office a lot in the next few days.

IV. Specialized uses with prepositions.

11. look about ——. (Cf. 25.)

a. To turn one's eyes to, or make searches in various parts of (a room, etc.); to go about observing in (a country, town, etc.).

1375 Barbour *Bruce* iii. 579 Men mycht se mony frely fute About the costis thar lukand. **1530** Palsgr. 614/1, I loke aboute the contraye, *je pourjecte le pais*. *a* **1548** Hall *Chron., Rich. III* 28 [He] leapte out of his bed and loked about the chambre. **1604** Shaks. *Oth.* ii. iii. 255 Iago, looke with care about the Towne.

b. With pron. (used *refl.*), *to look about one*: to turn one's eyes or attention to surrounding objects; to consider, or take account of, one's position and circumstances; to be watchful or apprehensive.

c **1400** Maundev. (Roxb.) xix. 87 Sum of þam..er lukand douneward to þe erthe, and will noȝt luke aboute þam. **1484** Caxton *Fables of Æsop* v. v, Whanne the catte was vpon a tree he loked aboute hym and sawe how the dogges [etc.]. **1562** Cooper *Answ. Priv. Masse* Pref. Rdr., A man maye thinke they had good cause to startle at the matter, and somewhat to loke aboute them, leste they seemed altogether carelesse. **1596** Shaks. *Tam. Shr.* i. ii. 141 Master, master, looke about you: Who goes there? ha. **1666–72** Harvey *Morb. Angl.* vii. 18 If upon these Signs, you find a wasting of your flesh, then look about you. **1712** Arbuthnot *John Bull* i. xii, John began to think it high time to look about him. **1744** Ozell tr. *Brantome's Sp. Rhodomontades* 104 [They] had found the Enemy upon them, before they could look about 'em. **1849** Macaulay *Hist. Eng.* ii. I. 173 At length he returned; and, without having a single week to look about him,..he was at once set to rule the state. **1891** *Strand Mag.* II. 482/1 He looked about him anxiously.

12. look after ——.

a. To follow with the eye; to look in the direction of (a person departing); *fig.* to think regretfully of (something past). †Also, to observe the course of (a person).

971 *Blickl. Hom.* 121 þa hie þa in þone heofon locodan æfter him, & hie Drihten ȝesawon upastiȝendne. **1535** Coverdale *Exod.* xxxiii. 8 All the people rose vp,..and loked after Moses, tyll he was gone in to the Tabernacle. **1580** Sidney *Ps.* xxxvii. vii, Thou shalt see The wicked by his own pride banisht; Looke after him, he shall be vanisht. **1593** Shaks. *2 Hen. VI*, iii. i. 219. **1858** Bushnell *Serm. New Life* xi. (1869) 153 His soul still looking covertly after the goods she has lost.

†b. To search for. *Obs.*

c **1330** *Spec. Gy Warw.* 786 Tweye manere shame men fint in boke, Who-so wole þerafter loke. *a* **1425** *Cursor M.* 11086 (Trin.) þenne loked aftir sir Zakary tables & poyntel tyte. *c* **1449** Pecock *Repr.* 77 Such that his suer treuthe is not lokid aftir neither souȝt aftir. **1611** Shaks. *Cymb.* iii. v. 55 That man of hers, Pisanio,..I haue not seene these two dayes. Go, looke after. **1711** Addison *Spect.* No. 120 ¶1 He has caught me twice or thrice looking after a Bird's Nest. **1727** Boyer *Eng.-Fr. Dict.*, To look after (to seek) a thing, *chercher quelque chose*.

†c. To anticipate with desire or fear; to look forward to. *Obs.*

1377 Langl. *P. Pl.* B. xii. 181 þere þe lewed lith stille and loketh after lente. **1393** *Ibid.* C. iv. 249 þe lest lad þat longeþ to hym..Lokeþ after lordshep oþer oþere large mede. **1413** *Pilgr. Sowle* (Caxton 1483) iv. xxx. 78 They were lokyng after their help til they were deceyued. **1477** *Paston Lett.* III. 194 He lokyth afftr that ye sholde come see hym. **1533** Gau *Richt Vay* 37 Ve lwik efter ane blissit hop and the glorious cuming of the greit God. *a* **1555** Ridley *Confer. w. Latimer* (1556) E7, Hetheriunto ye se..how I haue in wordes onely made..a florishe before the fight, which I shortly loke after. **1611** Bible *Luke* xxi. 26.

d. To seek for, demand (qualities).

1604 Shaks. *Oth.* ii. i. 251 The knaue..hath all those requisites in him, that folly and greene mindes looke after. **1692** Locke *Educ.* §94 Wks. 1714 III. 41 There is yet another Reason, why Politeness of Manners, and Knowledge of the World, should principally be look'd after in a Tutour. **1822** Coleridge *Lett., Convers.*, etc. II. 98 Those marks which too frequently are overlooked,..but which ought to be looked for and looked after, by every woman who has ever reflected on the words 'my future Husband'.

e. To busy oneself about, concern oneself with; to give consideration to, consider.

1650 Cromwell *Let.* 17 July in *Carlyle*, O how good it is to close with Christ betimes: there is nothing else worth looking after. **1662** Stillingfl. *Orig. Sacr.* ii. vii. §3 God himself did dispense with the strict ceremoniall precepts of the Law, where men did look after the main and substantiall parts of the worship God required from them. **1695** Woodward *Nat. Hist. Earth* iii. ii. 162 My Subject does not necessarily oblige me to look after this Water, or to point forth the place whereinto 'tis now retreated. **1701** W. Wotton *Hist. Rome, Alex.* i. 430 He could not look after his Sons' Education. **1849** Macaulay *Hist. Eng.* ix. II. 536 Under pretence of looking after the election, Clarendon set out for the West.

f. To attend to; to take care of; to 'see to' the safety or well-being of.

1375 Barbour *Bruce* iv. 616 Eftir the fyre he lukit fast. **1598** Shaks. *Merry W.* ii. ii. 146 Saist thou so (old Iacke)..Ile make more of thy olde body then I haue done: will they yet looke after thee? **1601** —— *Twel. N.* i. v. 144 He's in the third degree of drinke: hee's drown'd: go looke after him. **1737** Bracken *Farriery Impr.* (1756) I. 341 The many Boys I have had to look after my Horses. **1777** Sheridan *Sch. for Scand.* ii. i, I shall just call in to look after my own character. **1847** Marryat *Childr. N. Forest* iv, You must look after the pony and the pigs. **1885** F. Anstey *Tinted Venus* 30 The person who 'looked after him' did not sleep on the premises. **1891** *Law Times* XCI. 32/2 In theory, no doubt, the investor should look after his own interests.

g. To keep watch upon. ? *rare.*

1603 Shaks. *Meas. for M.* i. ii. 148 Is Lechery so look'd after? **1672** C. Manners in *12th Rep. Hist. MSS. Comm.* App. v. 25 Our Navy puts out again to sea..and wee shall then looke after the Holland Indian fleete. **1821** *Examiner* 742/1 The police look after all breaches of the peace.

†13. look against ——. To look at (something dazzling). *Obs.*

a **1225** *Leg. Kath.* 1597 Swuch leome & liht leitede þrinne, þæt ne mahten ha nawt lokin þer aȝeines. **1598** Shaks. *Merry W.* ii. ii. 254 Shee is too bright to be look'd against.

look at ——. See senses 1 and 3.

14. look behind ——. With pron. used refl. (For literal uses see 1 a and behind *prep.*) *not* or *never to look behind one*: colloq., to have an uninterrupted career of advancement or prosperity.

1852 Serj. Bellasis in E. Bellasis *Mem.* (1893) 150 He did not look behind him, but got better and better.

look beside ——. See beside *prep.* 4 a.

15. look for ——.

a. To expect, to hope for, anticipate, be on the watch for.

c **1513** Q. Kath. in Ellis *Orig. Lett.* Ser. iii. I. 153 The Scotts being soo besy..and I lokyng for my departing every houre. **1526** Tindale *2 Pet.* iii. 13 Neverthelesse we loke for a neve heven and a newe erth accordynge to his promes. **1548** Udall, etc. *Erasm. Par. John* 74 a, If thou be that very Messias whome we look for, tell it vs openly without all colour. **1568** Grafton *Chron.* II. 21 Into England, where he was sooner arryved than he was looked for. **1611** Bible *Matt.* xi. 3 Art thou hee that should come? Or doe wee looke for another? **1684** *Contempl. State Man* i. vii. (1699) 77 Death steals..upon us, when we least look for it. **1756** C. Lucas *Ess. Waters* I. 121 We may look for the residuum..to be in general very compound. **1828** *Examiner* 403/1 We must not look for figs from brambles. **1853** Mrs. Carlyle *Lett.* II. 229, I must write..to tell them they may look for me any day. **1868** Bain *Ment. & Mor. Sci.* 161 Looking for favour, we may encounter contumely. **1887** E. F. Byrrne *Heir without Heritage* I. iii. 56, I look for you to join us. *ellipt.* *a* **1548** Hall *Chron., Hen. V* 47 Informed by his espialles that the daie of battaill was nerer then he loked for. **1596** Dalrymple tr. *Leslie's Hist. Scot.* vi. 332 Henrie tariet langre thair than ony man luiket for.

b. To seek, to search for.

1586 Whitney *Choice of Emblems* To Rdr. (1866), A pearle shall not bee looked for in a poore mans purce. **1598** Shaks. *Merry W.* iii. i. 3 Which way haue you look'd for Master Caius. **1861** Dasent *Burnt Njal* I. 31 He had best look for a wife. **1871** R. H. Hutton *Ess.* (1877) I. 39 It..studies to find the higher unity..by looking for a uniting power. **1875** Jowett *Plato* (ed. 2) III. 52 People who sweep the house to look for a thing. **1892** *Black & White* 26 Nov. 609/2 Caroline went to look for her a few hours afterwards.

c. *Sc.* To look at, to observe.

1785 Burns *Halloween* x, Nell's heart was dancin' at the view, She whisper'd Rob to leuk for't.

16. look into ——.

¶a. After L. *respicere in* of the Vulgate: To have respect to. *Obs.*

a **1400** *Prymer* (1891) 56 (Ps. ci[i.]) He lokede in to [Vulg. *respexit in*] the preiere of meeke men.

b. To direct one's sight to the interior of. (See 1 a and into *prep.*) Also, to consult (a book) in a cursory manner.

1535 Coverdale *Ezek.* xxi. 21 To axe Councell at the Idols, and to loke in to the lyuer. *a* **1674** Clarendon *Surv. Leviath.* (1676) 336 Not only that the Scriptures are the Mount,..but that they may not be look'd into. **1709** Steele *Tatler* No. 47 ¶5, I so far observed his Counsel, that I looked into Shakespear. **1732** Berkeley *Alciphr.* v. §17 To be convinced of this truth, you need only look into Thucydides. **1832** Tennyson *Mariana in South* 75 An image seem'd..To look into her eyes and say, [etc.]. **1841** Lane *Arab. Nts.* I. 99 The fisherman, looking into the lake saw in it fish of different colours. **1849** Macaulay *Hist. Eng.* i. I. 27 With such feelings, both parties looked into the chronicles of the middle ages. Both readily found what they sought.

c. To examine (a matter) minutely; to investigate (a question).

a **1586** Sidney *Arcadia* i. (1590) 37 Those imperfections..you by the daily mending of your mind haue of late bin able to looke into them, which before you could not discerne. **1598** Shaks. *Merry W.* iii. i. 245 Well, I wil looke further into 't. **1604** E. G[rimstone] *D'Acosta's Hist. Indies* ii. iii. 86 Let vs now looke into the temperature of Panama and all that coast. **1689** *Tryal Bps.* 126 The only thing that is to be lookt into. **1859** Tennyson *Enid* 1771 Thither came The King's own leech to look into his hurt. **1879** Huxley *Hume* vi. 117 It is needful to look narrowly into the propositions here laid down. **1890** A. Gissing *Village Hampden* III. i. 15 Read your newspapers; look into the rights of things.

d. To enter (a house, etc.) for a few moments in passing. Cf. *look in* (37 b).

1849 Macaulay *Hist. Eng.* viii. II. 296 It is said..that His Majesty deigned to look into the tennis court.

†17. look of ——. Confusedly used for *look on.*

1530 Tindale *Deut.* vi. 4–7 *marg.*, It is heresy with vs for a laye man to loke of gods worde or to reade it. **1570** T. Wilson tr. *Demosthenes' Olynthiacs* Ep. to Sir W. Cecil, Often he woulde englyshe his matters out of the Latine or Greeke vpon the sodeyne, by looking of the booke onely. *c* **1592** Marlowe *Jew of Malta* iv. iv, *Curt.* And where didst meet him? *Pil*... Within 40 foot of the Gallowes, conning his neck-verse I take it, looking of a Fryars Execution.

18. look on ——. (See also senses 1 and 3.)

a. To pay regard to; to hold in esteem; to respect; = *look upon*, 24 a. Now *dial.*

a **1548** Hall *Chron., Hen. VI* 175 [He] shewed to them his letters Patentes, but neither he nor his writyng, was once regarded or looked on. **1593** Shaks. *3 Hen. VI*, v. vii. 22, I am not look'd on in the world. **1689** Luttrell *Brief Rel.* (1857) I. 616 Father Petre is now at Rome, but is not much lookt on there. **1859** Geo. Eliot *A. Bede* li, He'd be a fine husband for anybody,..so looked-on an' so cliver as he is.

b. To regard or consider *as*; = *look upon*, 24 c.

1629 Earle *Microcosm., Good old Man* (Arb.) 89 All men looke on him as a common father. **1662** Stillingfl. *Orig. Sacr.* i. ii. §9 Mercuriall books,..which none of the wiser Heathens did ever look on as any other then Fables. *a* **1715** Burnet *Own Time* (1724) I. 606 So they looked on him as a dead man. **1818** Cruise *Digest* (ed. 2) III. 240 It was to be looked on as an evidence, that [etc.]. **1851** *Jrnl. R. Agric. Soc.* XII. i. 190, I should look on them as omens of bad success. **1892** *Monthly Packet* Mar. 316 Every one..looked on victory as certain.

c. To regard with a specified feeling; = *look upon*, 24 b.

1846 Keble *Serm.* xiii. (1848) 325 As, in medicine, wise men look coldly on remedies which profess to be quite perfect and infallible. **1878** R. H. Hutton *Scott* ix. 93 A publisher..looks on authors' MSS...with distrust. **1881** Gardiner & Mullinger *Study Eng. Hist.* i. iii. 40 Edwin and Morcar..looked on him with family jealousy.

d. *to look on* (or *to*) *the bright* (or *worst*, etc.) *side*: to regard or consider something with optimism (or dismay, etc.). Cf. side *sb.*[1] 10.

a **1784** Johnson in E. Fuller *Thesaurus Quots.* (1941) 667/1 The habit of looking on the best side of every event is worth more than a thousand pounds a year. **1833** W. F. Hook *Let.* 9 Dec. in W. R. W. Stephens *Life & Lett. W.F. Hook* (1878) I. iv. 258, I am a bit of an optimist, I always look to the bright side of things. **1839** [see bright *a.* 1 e]. **1848** J. Ruskin *Let.* 17 Mar. in M. Lutyens *Ruskins & Grays* (1972) xi. 98 My disposition is to look to the worst side of things and..I feared you were entirely ruined. **1852** Mrs. Stowe *Uncle Tom's Cabin* II. xxiv. 82 Well, of course, if you can look on the bright side, pray do. **1914** R. Frost *North of Boston* 69 But I don't count on it as much as Len. He looks on the bright side of everything. **1942** 'P. Wentworth' *Pursuit of Parcel* xi. 51 Well, ducks, I shouldn't take on. Look on the bright side.

19. look over ——. (See also simple senses and over *prep.*) **a.** To peruse or inspect cursorily; †to examine, pass in review.

1590 Shaks. *Mids. N.* iv. ii. 38 Euery man looke ore his part: for..our play is preferred. **1675** South *Serm.* (1823) I. 301 Look over the whole creation, and you shall see, that [etc.]. **1684** Creech tr. *Juvenal* xiii. 164 Look o'er the present and the former time. **1780** Charlotte Burney in *Mad. D'Arblay's Early Diary* (1889) II. 288 My father and him next went to looking over the prints. **1820** W. Irving *Sketch Bk.* (1859) 3 When..I look over the hints and memorandums I have taken down. **1848** *Jrnl. R. Agric. Soc.* IX. ii. 369 The plantation would be looked over every year, and the weakest trees..taken out. **1855** Ld. Houghton in T. W. Reid *Life* (1891) I. xi. 527 Mrs. Gaskell asked me to come and look over Miss Brontë's papers.

b. To ignore, leave out of consideration. Now only, to overlook, pardon (a fault).

1666 Bunyan *Grace Ab.* ¶50 Though I endeavoured at the first to look over the business of Faith. **1887** *Murray's Mag.* II. 425 He forgave her, and looked over her conduct. **1890** A. Gissing *Village Hampden* II. xii. 263 Let us just warn the man, and look over it this time.

c. *Sc.* To look after, take care of.

1790 Burns *Kind Sir, I've read* 21 Royal George, the Lord leuk o'er him.

20. look through ——. (Cf. 43.)

a. To direct one's sight through (an aperture, a transparent body, or something having interstices); also *fig.* †*to look through one's fingers at*: to pretend not to see; to connive at. †*to look through a hempen window*: to be hanged.

1508 Dunbar *Tua mariit wemen* 15 Throw pykis of the plet thorne I presandlie luiket, Gif ony persoun wald approche. **1549** Latimer *5th Serm. bef. Edw. VI* (Arb.) 152 Thei loke thorow ther fyngers and wil not se it. **1580** Lyly *Euphues* (Arb.) 289 Since your eyes are so sharpe, that you cannot onely looke through a milstone, but cleane through the minde. **1592** Shaks. *Jul. C.* i. ii. 202 He lookes Quite through the Deeds of men. **1601** —— *All's Well* ii. iii. 226 So my good window of Lettice fare thee well, thy casement I neede not open, for I look through thee. *c* **1610** Sir J. Melvil *Mem.* (1683) 1 For revenge Henry VIII looked through his fingers at the preachers of the Reformed Religion. **1627** J. Taylor (Water P.) *Armado* Wks. (1630) i. 77/2 Making their wills at Wapping or looking thorow a hempen window at St. Thomas Waterings. **1628** Earle *Microcosm., Meere Formall Man* (Arb.) 30 When you haue seene his outside, you haue lookt through him. **1709** Steele *Tatler* No. 44 ¶5 The World is grown too wise, and can look through these thin Devices. **1830** Tennyson *Lilian* 10 She, looking thro' and thro' me, Thoroughly to undo me, Smiling, never speaks. **1870** Bryant *Iliad* I. iv. 123 Why look through The spaces that divide the warlike ranks?

†b. To be visible through. *Obs.*

1596 Shaks. *Tam. Shr.*, Induct. ii. 12 Such shooes as my toes look through the ouer-leather. **1602** —— *Ham.* iv. vii. 152 That our drift looke through our bad performance, 'Twere better not assaid.

c. To direct one's view over the whole of; to peruse cursorily from end to end; to glance through (a book).

1565 Golding *Ovid's Met.* ii. (1567) 16 Looke through the worlde so round..aske what thou lykest best. **1633** Ford *'Tis Pity* i. i, Looke through the world, And thou shalt see a thousand faces shine More glorious, then this Idoll thou ador'st. **1732** Pope *Ess. Man* i. 32 But of this frame the bearings, and the ties,..Gradations just, has thy pervading soul Look'd thro'? **1858** Macaulay in Trevelyan *Life* (1876) II. xiv. 452, I looked through ——'s two volumes.

21. look to ——. (See also 1, 3, 6, and to *prep.*)

a. To direct a look or glance to. In early use chiefly *Sc.*, equivalent to the mod. *look at* (see 3 a).

1375 BARBOUR *Bruce* IV. 321 Than lukit he awfully thame to. *c* **1375** *Sc. Leg. Saints* xviii. (*Egipciane*) 336 þane stud þe monk..to þe erde lukand. *c* **1450** HOLLAND *Howlat* 900 He lukit to his lykame that lemyt so licht. **1508** DUNBAR *Tua mariit wemen* 120, I dar nought luk to my luf for that lene gib. **1602** SHAKS. *Ham.* I. iv. 77 (1604 Qo.), The very place puts toyes of desperation..into euery brain That lookes so many fadoms to the sea And heares it rore beneath. **1611** BIBLE *1 Sam.* xvi. 12 He was..of a beautifull countenance, and goodly to looke to. **1860** TYNDALL *Glac.* I. xviii. 123 We looked to the sky at intervals.

b. To direct one's attention to; to select for consideration. In Biblical use, *occas.* to regard with favour.

c **897** K. ÆLFRED *Gregory's Past.* xli. 300 To hwæm locige ic buton to ðæm eaðmodum? **1340** *Ayenb.* 89 Hy ssolden loki to hare zoþe uorbysne Ihesu crist. *c* **1400** *Cursor M.* 28877 (Cott. Galba) Crist lukes noght to þe almus dede,..bot efter gude will of þe gifer. *a* **1569** KINGESMYLL *Confl. Satan* (1578) 5 Loke to thy former wayes what they have bene. **1580** SIDNEY *Ps.* XVIII. vii, I walk'd his [God's] waies,..Still to his judgmentes look't. **1604** E. G[RIMSTONE] *D'Acosta's Hist. Indies* III. iii. 126 Speaking..of the qualitie of the windes, we must..looke to the coastes or partes of the world from whence they proceede. **1611** BIBLE *Isa.* lxvi. 2 To this man will I looke, even to him that is poore and of a contrite spirit. **1844** MILL *Ess.* 87 If we look only to the effects which are intended. **1847** *Jrnl. R. Agric. Soc.* VIII. I. 12 Graziers look more to quality than quantity of wool. **1891** *Law Times* XCII. 18/2 We incline to think that there will be an appeal, ..looking to the terms of sect. 49 of the Judicature Act.

c. To attend to, take care of; †to tend, nurse (a sick person).

a **1300** *St. Gregory* 1088 in *Archiv Stud. neu. Spr.* LVII. 70 An holy man..þat dygne were þer to done [*sc.* to be made pope] and cristendome to loke to. *c* **1320** *Cast. Love* 1659 And ȝe comforted me in prison eke, And loked to me whan I was seke. *a* **1548** HALL *Chron., Hen. VI* 152 b, After the death of this prelate,..the affayres in Fraunce, were neither well loked to, nor [etc.]. **1549** LATIMER *Serm. Ploughers* (Arb.) 24 Ye that be prelates loke well to your office. **1590** SHAKS. *Com. Err.* v. i. 412 Come go with vs, wee'l looke to that anon. **1611** BIBLE *Jer.* xxxix. 12 Take him, and looke well to him, and doe him no harme. **1840** THACKERAY *Paris Sk.-bk., Beatrice Merger*, Mother would never let me leave her, because I looked to my little brothers. **1855** MACAULAY *Hist. Eng.* xvi. III. 635 He ordered his own surgeon to look to the hurts of the captive. **1864** *Jrnl. R. Agric. Soc.* XXV. I. 88 The cider should be looked to every morning. **1865** DICKENS *Mut. Fr.* II. vii, The yard gate-lock should be looked to, if you please; it don't catch.

d. In the *imperative* or in injunctive contexts: To direct one's solicitude to (something) as endangered or needing improvement.

1593 SHAKS. *Rich. II*, v. iii. 39 My Liege beware, looke to thy selfe. **1602** *2nd Pt. Return fr. Parnass.* IV. ii. 1880 Fellow looke to your braines; you are mad. **1630** HALES *Gold. Rem.* I. (1673) 281 The Refuter must be sure to look to the strength of his reasons. **1797** MRS. RADCLIFFE *Italian* vii, 'Look to your steps', said a voice. **1813** SHELLEY *Q. Mab* IV. 237 Look to thyself, priest, conqueror, or prince! **1869** T. HUGHES *Alfred Gt.* iii. 35 It behoved even the Holy Father to look to his fighting gear. **1889** *Repent. P. Wentworth* II. v. 118 Then look to your own ways and manners, sir!

e. *to look to it*: to be careful, beware. Often with *clause*, to take care, see *that*.

1590 SHAKS. *Mids. N.* III. i. 34 There is not a more fearful wild-fowl than your lion living; and we ought to look to 't. **1600** —— *A.Y.L.* III. i. 4 Looke to it, Finde out thy brother wheresoere he is. **1672** VILLIERS (Dk. Buckhm.) *Rehearsal* I. i. (Arb.) 45 *Thun.* Let the Critiques look to 't. *Light.* Let the Ladies look to 't. **1703** MAUNDRELL *Journ. Jerus.* (1732) 30 And they have reason to look well to it. **1842** TENNYSON *Dora* 26 In my time a father's word was law, And so shall it be now for me. Look to it. **1892** *Gd. Words* May 292/1 She would look to it that they had a roof over their heads.

f. To keep watch upon.

c **1400** *Destr. Troy* 6257 Lokis well to þe listes, þat no lede passe! *a* **1548** HALL *Chron., Hen. V* 58 b, His kepers looked more narrowly to hym then thei did before. **1577–87** HOLINSHED *Chron.* (1807–8) II. 235 He committed him to the keeping of certeine gentlemen, which without much courtesie looked streightlie inough to him for starting awaie. **1593** *Nottingham Rec.* IV. 238 That all the alhousess of the back syd of the towne may be loukte tow. **1634** SIR T. HERBERT *Trav.* 83 For two yeares hee [a prisoner] was strictly lookt too. **1752** J. LOUTHIAN *Form of Process* (ed. 2) 209 And then desires the Keeper to take A. B. the Prisoner from the Bar, and look to him, for he stands convicted of High Treason. **1802** MAR. EDGEWORTH *Moral T.* (1816) I. xix. 167 Constable, look to your prisoner. **1819** SHELLEY *Cenci* IV. iv. 54 Sound the alarm; Look to the gates that none escape!

g. To direct one's expectations to; to rely on (a person, etc.) *for* something.

1611 BIBLE *Ecclus.* xxxiv. 15 Blessed is the soule of him that feareth the Lord: to whom doeth he looke? **1806** WINDHAM *Speech* 22 Dec., 'Man and steel, the soldier and his sword', are the only productions of a country that can be looked to with confidence for its protection and security. **1822** *Examiner* 227/2 To them then are the holders..to look for payment? **1885** *Law Times Rep.* LIII. 226/2 The consignee is the person to whom a carrier looks for the price of the carriage of goods. **1892** *Blackw. Mag.* CLI. 220/2, I look to you to help us.

h. To look forward to (see 36); to expect, count upon.

1782 COWPER *Table Talk* 495 A terrible sagacity informs The poet's heart, he looks to distant storms, He hears the thunder ere the tempest lowers. **1804** WELLESLEY in Owen *Desp.* 274 The French have never ceased to look to the re-establishment of their power. **1824** *Examiner* 108/1 Baron Gifford..looks to the Seals, when Lord Eldon retires. **1845** STOCQUELER *Handbk. Brit. India* (1854) 31 Clerkships in the public offices is the line of employment which the body of them look to.

i. To show affinity to. *rare.*

1835 KIRBY *Hab. & Inst. Anim.* II. xxiv. 514 The bear seems to look towards the sloth; and the feline race, in their whiskers and feet, look to the hares and rats.

22. a. look toward(s ——. (See simple senses and TOWARD, TOWARDS *prep.*)

a **1240** *Lofsong* in *Cott. Hom.* 211 Leoue louerd iesu crist loke toward me ase ich ligge lowe. *a* **1310** in Wright *Lyric P.* 69 Ihesu,..With thine suete eȝen loke towart me. **1821** SHELLEY *Epipsych.* 516, I have fitted up some chambers there Looking towards the golden Eastern air.

b. *to look towards a person*: in vulgar speech, to drink his health (? *obs.* exc. *jocular*). Also, *to look at* (a person).

1848 THACKERAY *Van. Fair* liii, The ladies drank to his 'ealth, and Mr. Moss, in the most polite manner 'looked towards him'. **1853** 'C. BEDE' *Verdant Green* II. iii, The Pet ..drank their healths with the prefatory remark 'I looks to-wards you gents!' **1880** STEVENSON & HENLEY *Deacon Brodie* I. 24 Deacon, I looks towards you. **1890** B. L. FARJEON *Mystery of M. Felix* I. iii. 26 Mrs. Middlemore,..you're a lady after my own heart... Here's looking towards you. **1910** A. NOYES *Coll. Poems* I. 241, I looks to-wards you, Prester John, you've done us very proud! **1930** J. DOS PASSOS *42nd Parallel* I. 119 'Pard, have that on me.'.. 'Thanks, here's lookin at you.'

c. = *look to*, 21 i (where see quot. 1835).

1879 A. W. TOURGEE *Fool's Errand* xliv. 330 There could be nothing looking towards marriage between us. **1903** A. T. HADLEY *Relations between Freedom & Responsibility* 15 A series of negotiations rather than discussions, looking toward compromise rather than toward mutual enlightenment. **1904** T. N. PAGE in *McClure's Mag.* 621 The South regarded jealously any teaching of the Negroes which looked toward equality. **1932** T. J. GRAYSON *Leaders & Periods Amer. Finance* xiii. 278 The thing to do was to take no precipitate action looking toward resumption.

23. look unto ——. *arch.* = *look to*, in various senses: see 21 a–f.

a **1300** *Cursor M.* 14333 Iesus he loked vnto þe lift. **1526** TINDALE *Heb.* xii. 2 Lokynge vnto Iesus, the auctor and fynnyssher of oure fayth. **1545** RAYMOND *Byrth Mankynde* Y v, In a fayre garden..if it be not regarded and loken vnto, the weedes..wyll [etc.]. ? *a* **1550** *Freiris Berwik* 99 in *Dunbar's Poems* (1893) 288 The gudwyf lukit vnto the Freiris tway. **1591** SPENSER *M. Hubberd* 292 For ere that unto armes I me betooke, Unto my fathers sheepe I usde to looke. **1593** SHAKS. *2 Hen. VI*, I. i. 208 Then lets make haste away, And looke vnto the maine. **1598** tr. *Aristotle's Politiques* 379 And it should especially be looked vnto children, that they neither heare nor see such things. **1611** BIBLE *Isa.* xlv. 22 Looke vnto mee, and be ye saued. **1642** C. VERNON *Consid. Exch.* 88 Abuses..will grow like ill weeds.. unless they be looked unto and weeded out.

24. look upon ——. (See also senses 1 and 3.)

†**a.** To pay regard to; *esp.* to regard favourably, hold in esteem; = *look on*, 18 a. *Obs.*

c **1515** in Ellis *Orig. Lett.* Ser. III. I. 181 Yf yt had nott ben lokyd upon betymes, I suppose yt wold not have ben abull to have contynuyd a Monastery ffower yeres. **1533** CROMWELL *Let.* 9 July in Merriman *Life & Lett.* (1902) I. 357 For lacke..whereof ye haue forfaited to the kinges highnes the Somme of one thousande markes which..ye ought substauncially e to loke uppon for the king is no person to be deluded..with all. **1533** GAU *Richt Vay* 101 God hes lukit apone ye powerte of his madine or scruand. **1611** BIBLE *2 Macc.* vii. 6 The Lord God looketh vpon vs.

b. With *adv.* or *adj. complement*: To regard with a certain expression of countenance, or with a certain feeling; = *look on*, 18 c.

1619 MIDDLETON *Inner Temple Masque* 23 The nearest kin I have looks shy upon me. **1629** MAXWELL tr. *Herodian* (1635) 61 The Romane Citizens being thus surrounded with direfull mis-haps..begaune to look sowre upon Commodus. **1633** MASSINGER *Guardian* IV. ii, I look with sore eyes upon her good fortune, and wish it were mine own. **1711** ADDISON *Spect.* No. 37 ¶5, I look upon her with a mixture of Admiration and Pity. **1740** tr. *De Mouhy's Fort. Country-Maid* (1741) I. 273, I fancied he look'd something sweet upon me. **1847** MARRYAT *Childr. N. Forest* xxv, Edward was ..satisfied that he was not quite looked upon with indifference by Patience Heatherstone. **1864** TENNYSON *Enoch Arden* 56 And all men look'd upon him favourably.

c. To regard *as*, †to consider *to be* so-and-so (cf. 18 b). †Also, *to look upon it*: to be of opinion *that*.

1662 STILLINGFL. *Orig. Sacr.* III. ii. §9 Both Pythagoras and Plato looked upon *constitutionem sylvæ* to bee *opus providentiæ*. **1665** BOYLE *Occas. Refl.* IV. Advt., A Change of Circumstances, has occasion'd the Publication of these Papers,..in such a way as will make most Readers look upon them as containing a story purely Romantick. **1674** BREVINT *Saul at Endor* 237 It is lookt upon, as one of those very strange things, which if she doth, it is seldome. **1711** ADDISON *Spect.* No. 31 ¶2 This Objection was looked upon as frivolous. *Ibid.* No. 191 ¶7 This Morning..I set up an Equipage which I look upon to be the gayest in the Town. **1756** C. LUCAS *Ess. Waters* I. 151 The antients looked upon water as the..first principle of all created things. **1793** SMEATON *Edystone L.* §300, I now looked upon it that we might think ourselves secure. **1822** *Examiner* 203/1 You are looked upon as a kind lord.

V. With adverbs.

25. look about. *intr.* See simple senses and ABOUT *adv.*; *fig.* to be on the watch, on the look-out. Also const. *for* (†*after*): to be in search of. (Cf. *to look about one*, 11 b.)

a **1300** *K. Horn* 1087 He lokede aboute, Myd is collede snoute. **1375** BARBOUR *Bruce* XIX. 669 The fox..Lukit about sum hoill to se. *c* **1420** LYDG. *Assembly of Gods* 347 She loked euer about as though she had be mad. *a* **1425** *Cursor M.* 11744 (Trin.) As þei to gider talkyng were þei loked aboute fer & nere. *c* **1489** CAXTON *Sonnes of Aymon* xx. 445 And whan rowlande was come out of the cave, he loked about for to know where they were. **1530** PALSGR. 613/2, I loke aboute, as one dothe that taketh the vewe of a place or contray. **1566** ADLINGTON *Apuleius* VII. xiii. (1893) 152 The shepheards looking about for a Cow that they had lost. **1592** SHAKS. *Rom. & Jul.* III. v. 40 The day is broke, be wary, looke about. **1610** —— *Temp.* I. ii. 410. **1611** BIBLE *Tobit* xi. 5 Now Anna sate looking about towards the way for her sonne. **1704** NORRIS *Ideal World* II. x. 395 Like the man who..looks about after the candle which he has all the while on his own head. **1724** DE FOE *Mem. Cavalier* (1840) 155 It was time to look about. **1750** *Student* I. 323 The fidler..soon after enter'd..and then every man look'd about for his partner. *Mod.* The last time I saw him he was looking about for something to do.

26. look abroad. *intr.* See simple senses and ABROAD *adv.*

c **1450** [see ABROAD *adv.* 4]. **1664** WALLER *From a Child* 4 Before our Violets dare look abroad. **1784** COWPER *Task* v. 738 He looks abroad into the varied field Of nature. **1834** L. RITCHIE *Wand. by Seine* 192 The young men do not look abroad for a wife.

†**27. look again, againward.** *intr.* To look back. Also *fig.* *Obs.*

a **1225** *Leg. Kath.* 2351 Heo as me ledde hire, lokede aȝeinward, for ludinge þæt ha herde. *c* **1320** [see AGAINWARD *adv.* 1]. *c* **1380** WYCLIF *Wks.* (1880) 41 No man sendynge his hond to þe plowȝ and lokenge a-ȝen is able to þe kyngdom of god. *c* **1400** [see AGAIN *adv.* 1 a].

†**28. look aloft.** *intr.* To aspire, be ambitious. *Obs.*

1533 FRITH *Agst. Rastell* (1829) 236 If the remnants of sin fortune at any time to look aloft and begin to reign, then he sendeth some cross of adversity or sickness to help to suppress them. **1567** [see ALOFT 11]. **1568** GRAFTON *Chron.* I. 162 By this mariage, Egeldred began to looke a loft, and thought much of himselfe.

†**29. look alow.** *intr.* To humble oneself.

1582 BENTLEY *Mon. Matrones* II. 33 There is no sainct so perfect..but looking a-lowe, shall find himselfe vnworthy, and so stop his mouth.

30. a. look around. *intr.* To look in several directions; *fig.* to take a comprehensive view of things.

1754 A. MURPHY *Gray's Inn Jrnl.* No. 93 He looked around, and saw a reverend Form advance towards him. **1791** MRS. RADCLIFFE *Rom. Forest* (1820) I. 185 Louis looked around in search of La Motte. **1847** MRS. A. KERR *Hist. Servia* 239 When the Servians now looked around, they congratulated themselves on having made a successful campaign. **1880** NEWMAN SMYTH *Old Faiths in New Light* ii. (1882) 32 We look around sceptical of our own impressions.

b. = *look round* (sense 42 c). Also, to search about *for*.

1883 'MARK TWAIN' *Life on Mississippi* xliii. 437 I'll look around a little, and if I can't do better I'll come back and take it. **1927** H. CRANE *Let.* 14 Mar. (1965) 290 I'm looking around for some sort of 'avocation'. **1974** 'M. INNES' *Appleby's Other Story* x. 81 Upper servants are frequently left in residence as caretakers... If it happens at Elvedon, it will give you time to look around.

31. look aside. *intr.* To turn aside one's eyes; to look obliquely.

1508 DUNBAR *Gold. Targe* 225 On syde scho lukit wyth ane fremyt fare. **1530** PALSGR. 613/2, I loke asyde by chaunce, or caste myn eye asyde. *Ibid.*, I loke asyde upon one by disdayne. **1855** BROWNING *Andrea del Sarto* 147 They pass and look aside.

look askance, askew, asquint: see the advs.

32. look back. *intr.*

a. To turn and look at something in the direction from which one is going or from which one's face is turned.

1538 ELYOT *Dict.*, *Respicio*, to loke backe, to haue regarde [etc.]. *a* **1586** SIDNEY *Arcadia* I. (1590) 2 At yonder rising of the ground she turned her selfe, looking backe toward her woonted abode. **1594** SHAKS. *Rich. III*, III. v. 19 Looke back, defend thee, here are Enemies. **1667** MILTON *P.L.* XII. 641 They looking back, all th' Eastern side beheld Of Paradise, so late thir happie seat. **1712–14** POPE *Rape of Lock* III. 138 Thrice she look'd back, and thrice the foe drew near. **1797** MRS. RADCLIFFE *Italian* xii, Often they looked back to the convent, expecting to see lights issue from the avenue.

b. To direct the mind to something that is past; to think on the past. Const. *into*, *on*, *upon*, *to*.

1599 SHAKS. *Hen. V*, I. ii. 102 Gracious Lord..Looke back into your mightie Ancestors. **1651** BAXTER *Saints' Rest* IV. 130 Is it not a very little time when thou lookest back on it? **1711** STEELE *Spect.* No. 100 ¶1 A Man advanced in Years that thinks fit to look back upon his former Life. **1849** MACAULAY *Hist. Eng.* vii. II. 200 He would have looked back with remorse on a literary life of near thirty years. **1889** MALLOCK *Enchanted Island* 221 Experiences like these are always fresh to look back upon. **1892** *Eng. Illustr. Mag.* IX. 331 One portion of my life is not pleasant to look back to.

†**c.** To look *to* a person *for* something. (? After L. *respicere*.) *Obs.*

1646 P. BULKELEY *Gospel Covt.* I. 52 The whole creation lookes backe unto him that made it for preservation in their being.

†**d.** *trans.* = *look back to*. *Obs.*

1606 SHAKS. *Ant. & Cl.* III. xi. 53 See How I conuey my shame, out of thine eyes, By looking backe what I haue left behinde Stroy'd in dishonor.

e. *colloq.* in negative contexts: To show signs of retrogression or (interrupted progress. (Cf. 14.)

1893 *Daily News* 5 Jan. 3/6 Since that day St. Simon has never, to use a slang phrase of the day, 'looked back.' **1928** *Observer* 17 June 27/4 Since they adopted the bold experiment..of changing the date of their regatta..Marlow Amateur Regatta has never looked back. **1936** 'N. BLAKE' *Thou Shell of Death* i. 17 His origin is shrouded in mystery. .. Turned up suddenly in the R.F.C. early in the war, and never looked back. **1949** *Radio Times* 15 July 17/1 Jules Verne..wrote *Five Weeks in a Balloon*, scored an immediate success, and never looked back. **1973** *Times* 23 Apr. 4/7 The play ran into the war, and she has never looked back.

33. look down.

a. *intr.* See simple senses and DOWN *adv.*

c **1200** [see 45 a]. *c* **1375** *Sc. Leg. Saints* xxvii. (*Vincencius*) 326 Keparis of þe presone, þat thru smal holis lokit done. *c* **1470** HENRY *Wallace* v. 146 Vpon Fawdoun as he was lukand doune. **1562** PILKINGTON *Expos. Abdyas* Pref. 3 Hee that sittes on hygh looked doune to the lowe dungeon of the pryson, and raised Joseph to be ruler. **1610** SHAKS. *Temp.* v. i. 201 Looke downe you gods And on this couple drop a blessed crowne. **1726** SWIFT *Gulliver* II. viii, I looked down upon the servants,..as if they had been pigmies, and I a giant. **1871** FREEMAN *Norm. Conq.* (1876) IV. xviii. 212 Thus is formed the promontory of Lincoln looking down upon the river to the South of it.

b. fig. *to look down on, upon*: to hold in contempt, to scorn; to consider oneself superior to.

1711 ADDISON *Spect.* No. 255 ¶9 A solid and substantial Greatness of Soul looks down with a generous Neglect on the Censures and Applauses of the Multitude. **1728** VENEER *Sincere Penitent* Ded., Looking down upon it with a generous contempt of all its vanities. **1889** JESSOPP *Coming of Friars* ii. 85 The monks looked down upon the parsons, and stole their endowments from them. **1893** *Chamb. Jrnl.* 29 July 476/1 They are..looked down upon and scorned.

†**c.** To have a downcast or mournful look.

1500–20 DUNBAR *Poems* lvi. 12 It is no glaid collatioun Quhair ane makis myrrie, ane vther lukis doun.

d. *Comm.* To tend downwards in price.

1806 *Ann. Reg.* 49 The bounties would begin soon, in the language of 'Change Alley, to 'be looking down'. **1825** HONE *Every-day Bk.* I. 173 Who, when the shares 'look down', try to sell.

e. *trans.* To quell or overcome by one's looks.

1812 *Niles' Reg.* III. 45/2 Volunteer companies..are rolling to the frontiers, in force sufficient to look down opposition. **1837** *Knickerbocker* IX. 361 We're a free trader ..and are forced to go well armed, to look down all resistance. **1838** J. F. COOPER *Homeward Bound* I. viii. 194 If the people cannot control and look down peculiarity..one might as well live in a despotism at once. **1840** DICKENS *Humphrey's Clock, Clock-case* 33, I never could look the boy down. **1847** MRS. GORE *Castles in Air* xxx. (1857) 285 Having no importunate witnesses present..to look me down while I was bragging.

34. look downward. *intr.* = *look down*, 33.

c **1400**, **1562** [see DOWNWARD A. 1 b]. **1667** MILTON *P.L.* III. 722 Look downward on the Globe whose hither side With light from hence, though but reflected, shines. **1823** *Examiner* 104/1 Consols were rather looking downward.

35. look forth. *intr.* To look out (of a window, etc., on to something). Now *arch.* and *poet.*

c **1420** LYDG. *Assembly of Gods* 1982 Then lokyd I forthe as Doctryne me badde. **1508** DUNBAR *Tua mariit wemen* 308, I salbe laith to lat him le, quhill I may luke furth. **1611** BIBLE *Song Sol.* ii. 9 He looketh forth..at the windowe. **1667** MILTON *P.L.* XII. 209 Through the Firey Pillar and the Cloud God looking forth will trouble all his Host. *c* **1775** T. LINDSEY *Song*, Look forth, look forth, my fairest! Thy faithful knight is nigh. **1781** COWPER *Friendship* 80 Jealousy looks forth distressed On good that seems approaching. **1813** SCOTT *Rokeby* I. i, The warder..from old Baliol's tower looks forth. **1828** LYTTON *Pelham* xvii, The chevalier looked wistfully forth.

36. look forward. *intr.* (See FORWARD B. 1 b.) Const. *to*, occas. *for*, †*on*.

1603 SHAKS. *Meas. for M.* IV. iii. 61 Looke forward on the iournie you shall go. **1737** POPE *Hor. Ep.* II. ii. 314 Pleas'd to look forward, pleas'd to look behind. *a* **1766** MRS. F. SHERIDAN *Nourjahad* (1767) 71 The loss of Mandana imbitters all my joys, and methinks I begin to look forward with disgust. **1844** H. H. WILSON *Brit. India* III. 48 They ..looked forward to the speedy expulsion of the intruders. **1861** THACKERAY *Adv. Philip* xxxii, The way in which we looked forward for letters from our bride and bridegroom. **1892** *Temple Bar* Nov. 379 We were looking forward to a merry time.

37. look in.

a. See simple senses and IN *adv.*

a **1300** *Cursor M.* 17288 + 188 (Cott.) Iohne..loked in & saȝe þe schetez, bot he dorst not gang in. **1483** *Cath. Angl.* 223/2 To Luke jn, *jnspicere*. **1500–20** DUNBAR *Poems* xlviii. 10 Me thocht Aurora..In at the window lukit by the day. **1535** COVERDALE *Song Sol.* ii. 9 He..loketh in at the wyndowe, & pepeth thorow the grate. **1591** SHAKS. *1 Hen. VI*, I. iv. 62 Here, through this Grate..Let vs looke in, the sight will much delight thee. **1830** TENNYSON *Mermaid* 26 That great sea-snake..Would..look in at the gate With his large calm eyes. **1839** LONGF. *Vill. Blacksm.* iv, And children coming home from school Look in at the open door.

b. To enter a room, etc. for the purpose of seeing something; hence, in mod. use, to make a call, to call (*upon* a person); to 'drop in' for a short stay or interview.

1604 SHAKS. *Oth.* v. ii. 257 Looke in vpon me then, and speake with me. **1610** —— *Temp.* v. i. 167 This Cell's my Court:..pray you looke in. **1799** in *Spirit Pub. Jrnls.* III. 121 To fashionably and carelessly look in at Tattersall's. **1837** DICKENS *Pickw.* ii, Will 10 o'clock be too late to look in for half an hour? **1884** G. GISSING *Unclassed* III. vi. i. 136 Could you manage to look in at the office tomorrow? **1890** CLARK RUSSELL *Ocean Trag.* III. xxvi. 4 I'll look in upon him after breakfast. **1892** *Temple Bar* Oct. 164 He would look in at the jeweller's at once and get her that bracelet. **1892** MRS. OLIPHANT *Marriage Elinor* II. xviii. 46 Some prodigious reception to which people 'looked in' for half an hour.

c. [After *listen in*, LISTEN *v.* 2 e.] *intr.* To watch a television programme. *colloq.*

1927 *Pictorial Weekly* 5 Mar. 100/1 We shall then 'look-in' by wireless and see events and scenes at a distance. **1928** *Daily Sketch* 7 Aug. 11/1 The public..can 'listen-in' or 'look-in' to the transmissions. **1950** *Ann. Reg. 1949* 418 At the end of October there were..206,000 [television] sets licensed and..as many as a million people regularly looking-in. **1959** J. BOLAND *Operation Red Carpet* v. 67, I often look-in when he's on.

†**38. look off.** To turn one's eyes away. *Obs.*

1710–11 SWIFT *Jrnl. to Stella* 4 Jan., No, no, look off, don't smile at me. **1738** —— *Pol. Conv.* 25 Why then, Mr. Neverout, do you see, if you don't much like it, you may look off of it. **1762–71** H. WALPOLE *Vertue's Anecd. Paint.* (1786) V. 113 Another small head of a man looking off.

39. look on. *intr.*

a. To direct one's looks towards an object in contemplation or observation; often, to be a mere spectator (and not a participator in the action). *to look on ahead*: to look forward into the future.

c **1000** ÆLFRIC *Deut.* xxviii. 32 Sin þine suna and þine dohtra ȝeseald oðrum folce, þær þu on locie [L. *videntibus oculis tuis*]. *c* **1315** SHOREHAM (E.E.T.S.) I. 1295 So schulle þe rederes now Hy rede and conne on lowke. **1456** SIR G. HAYE *Law Arms* (S.T.S.) 303 A tyrand of the proprieteis..that salbe gude and prouffitable for all men that on lukis. **1592** SHAKS. *Rom. & Jul.* I. iv. 38 Ile be a Candle-holder and looke on. **1628** EARLE *Microcosm., Bowle Alley* (Arb.) 61 He enioyes it that lookes on and bets not. **1744** OZELL tr. *Brantome's Sp. Rhodomontades* 21 Miscarrying in that Design too, he contented himself, for a while, to lye-bye and look on. **1823** J. F. COOPER *Pioneers* iii. (1869) 14/1 One who looked on a-head to the wants of posterity. **1875** JOWETT *Plato* (ed. 2) III. 63 Potters' boys are trained to the business by looking on at the wheel. **1879** M. PATTISON *Milton* x. 118 The world looks on and laughs.

b. colloq. *to look on* (*with*): to read from a book, etc., at the same time (with another person).

1893 *Cornh. Mag.* Jan. 64 They seem to have had a scarcity of music, necessitating a good deal of 'looking on'.

40. look out.

a. *intr.* (See simple senses and OUT.) To look from within a building or the like to the outside; also, to put one's head out of an aperture, e.g. a window.

1390 GOWER *Conf.* II. 352 That I be nyhte mai arise, At som wyndowe and loken oute. *c* **1450** HOLLAND *Howlat* 63 To luke out on day licht. *a* **1548** HALL *Chron., Hen. VIII* 91 b, A prison and a man lokyng out at a grate. **1567** HARMAN *Caveat* 38 [She] wente vnto her hall windowe.. and loking out therat, pointed with her fingar. **1607** SHAKS. *Timon* v. i. 131 Lord Timon, Timon, Looke out, and speake to Friends. *a* **1625** FLETCHER *False One* I. ii. (Song) Looke out, bright eyes, and blesse the ayre: Even in shadowes you are faire. **1635** J. HAYWARD tr. *Biondi's Banish'd Virg.* 13 Looking out at it [the doore] all afrighted. **1855** TENNYSON *Maud* I. ix. 3 The sun look'd out with a smile Betwixt the cloud and the moor.

transf. **1809** MALKIN *Gil Blas* VII. ii. (Rtldg.) 5 They.. looked out at the corners of their eyes.

†**b.** To appear, show itself. *Obs.*

1606 SHAKS. *Tr. & Cr.* IV. v. 56 Her wanton spirites looke out At euery ioynt, and motiue of her body. **1606** —— *Ant. & Cl.* v. i. 50 The businesse of this man lookes out of him. **1607** —— *Timon* III. ii. 80.

c. To be on the watch or look-out; to exercise vigilance, take care. (Cf. LOOK-OUT.)

1602 B. JONSON *Poetaster* II. i, These Courtiers runne in my minde still; I must looke out. **1655** C. CHAUNCY in Quincy *Hist. Harvard Univ.* (1840) I. 469 That..your petitioner..[may not be] enforced to look out to alter his condition. **1704** F. FULLER *Med. Gymn.* (1711) Pref., It is high time to look out, and set upon a resolute Course of Riding. **1740** tr. *De Mouhy's Fort. Country-Maid* (1741) I. 79 Let us look out sharp where we are, this is the Place we lost her in. **1769** FALCONER *Dict. Marine* (1780) s.v. *Look-out*, The mate of the watch..calls often from the quarter-deck, 'Look out afore there!' **1829** LANDOR *Imag. Conv., Miguel & his Mother* Wks. 1853 I. 560/1 Before that time I will look out sharply, and afterward you must. **1840** THACKERAY *Gt. Hoggarty Diamond* vi, 'Look out', said that envious McWhirter to me. **1886** BESANT *Childr. of Gibeon* II. ix, You'd better look out. Melenda's in a rage. **1892** *Black & White* 10 Sept. 301/2 We shall lose India if we don't look out.

d. To field, 'scout' (at cricket). ? *nonce-use.*

1837 DICKENS *Pickw.* vii, Several players were stationed, to 'look out', in different parts of the field.

e. *to look out for*: to watch or search for; to be on the look-out for; to await vigilantly.

1669 LADY CHAWORTH in *12th Rep. Hist. MSS. Comm.* App. v. 11 Some [are] so foolish now to cry the Duchess hath done itt, to looke out for love letters. **1712** STEELE *Spect.* No. 268 ¶3 Where shall we find the Man who looks out for one who places her chief Happiness in the Practice of Virtue? **1742** BERKELEY *Let. to Gervais* 2 Feb., Wks. 1871 IV. 284, I wrote..to Dean Browne to look out for a six-stringed bass viol of an old make and mellow tone. **1766** GOLDSM. *Vic. W.* xxvi, Prepare then this evening to look out for work against to-morrow. **1828** SCOTT *F.M. Perth* xxvi, Rely on my looking out for your safety. **1831** O'CONNELL *Speech Ho. Comm.* 27 June, [They] begin to look out for disturbances—or as the sailors say, to look out for squalls. **1892** *Chamb. Jrnl.* 4 June 361/2 I'll look out for something to do.

f. To have or afford an outlook (*on, over*, etc.).

1686 tr. *Chardin's Coronat. Solyman* 84 The great Portal of his Palace that looks out into the Royal square. **1820** W. IRVING *Sketch Bk., Roscoe* (1821) I. 23 The windows of the study, which looked out upon the soft scenery I have mentioned. **1859** MRS. CARLYLE *Lett.* III. 6 The back court that my windows look out on. **1866** W. COLLINS *Armadale* I. 162 The bedroom looked out over the great front door. **1874** RUSKIN *Hortus Inclusus* (1887) 3 His own little cell, looking out on the olive woods.

†**g.** To make any brief excursion. (Cf. *look in*, 37 b.) *Obs.*

1551 T. WILSON *Rule of Reason* (1580) 46 He looked not out of his house all that daie. **1699** DAMPIER *Voy.* II. I. 127 The Fish is presently sent to the Market in one of their Boats, the rest looking out again for more. **1793** SMEATON *Edystone L.* §296 It was not till the 12th instant that we were able to look out to sea further than to supply the seamen on board the buss with provisions.

h. *trans.* To find by looking; to choose out by looking.

1535 COVERDALE *Ezek.* xxi. 29 Thou hast loked the out vanities, & prophecied lyes. *c* **1590** MARLOWE *Faust.* viii. 7 She has sent me to look thee out; prithee, come away. **1607** SHAKS. *Timon* III. ii. 67 Ile looke you out a good turne, Seruilius. **1611** BIBLE *Gen.* xli. 33 Let Pharaoh looke out a man discreet and wise. **1658** *Plymouth Col. Rec.* (1855) III. 141 Liberty is graunted vnto Mr. Josias Winslow,..to look out a place to suply him with twenty fiue acres of land. **1768** E. CLEAVELAND in B. P. Smith *Hist. Dartmouth Coll.* (1878) 36 The Deputy Surveyor,..offered his assistance to look out the township and survey it. **1789** MRS. PIOZZI *Journ. France* II. 133, I am tired of looking out words to express their various merits. **1838** DICKENS *O. Twist* viii, You're a-staring at the pocket-handkerchiefs! eh, my dear!.. We've just looked 'em out, ready for the wash. *c* **1884** 'EDNA LYALL' *We Two* xix, She went..to the Bradshaw, and looked out the afternoon trains.

41. look over. a. *trans.* To cast one's eyes over; to scrutinize; to examine (papers, or the like).

c **1450** *St. Cuthbert* (Surtees) 11 Saynt cuthbert lyfe.. Who so lykes to luk it oure, He sall' fynde it part in foure. **1706** HEARNE *Collect.* 8 Mar. (O.H.S.) I. 201 Dr. Kennett.. look'd them [MSS.] all over. **1712** *Ibid.* III. 301 Gronovius hath publish'd some extracts out of Josephus with emendations... I must look them over. **1809** MALKIN *Gil Blas* XI. ii. (Rtldg.) 396 The minister..looked me over from head to foot. **1861** HUGHES *Tom Brown at Oxf.* ii. (1889) 14 Tom had time to look him well over, and see what sort of man had come to his rescue. **1892** *Temple Bar* Apr. 467, I have a number of papers to look over.

b. *colloq.* = *look on*, 39 b.

42. look round. *intr.*

a. To look about in every direction.

1526 TINDALE *Mark* iii. 5 He loked rounde aboute on them angrely. **1667** MILTON *P.L.* VI. 529 Others from the dawning Hills Lookd round, and Scouts each Coast light armed scoure. **1781** COWPER *Expost.* 27 Let the Muse look round From East to West, no sorrow can be found. **1791** MRS. RADCLIFFE *Rom. Forest* (1820) I. 100, I looked round in search of a human dwelling. **1863** GEO. ELIOT *Romola* xxix, Tito looked round with inward amusement at the various crowd. **1892** *Black & White* 19 Mar. 367/2, I had now time and daylight enough to look round.

b. *fig.* To search about *for*.

1849 MACAULAY *Hist. Eng.* vii. II. 161 In great perturbation men began to look round for help.

c. (See quot. 1914.)

c **1869** TAYLOR & DUBOURG in M. R. Booth *Eng. Plays of 19th Cent.* (1973) III. 250 I've begged and prayed to him for time—only to look round. **1914** *Conc. Oxf. Dict.* Add., *Look round*, (esp.) examine the possibilities &c. with a view to deciding on a course. **1950** J. CANNAN *Murder Included* i. 8 Hugo..is out of the army and looking round; there was some talk of him starting a dairy herd. **1974** 'R. TATE' *Birds of Bloodied Feather* iii. 74, I looked round for a job and found a modest occupation.

43. look through.

a. *trans.* To penetrate with a look or glance; to search. *lit.* and *fig.*

c **1450** HOLLAND *Howlat* 49, I sawe ane Howlat..Lukand the laike throwe. **1667** DRYDEN *Ind. Emperor* III. ii. (1668) 32 Fate sees thy Life lodg'd in a brittle Glass, And looks it through, but to it cannot pass. **1737** POPE *Hor. Ep.* I. i. 108 Who bids thee face with steady view Proud Fortune, and look shallow Greatness thro'. **1887** *Edin. Rev.* July 231 His eye glaring at a stranger with a gaze that seemed to look him through and through.

b. To examine or survey exhaustively.

1742–3 YOUNG *Nt. Th.* VI, Look nature through, 'tis revolution all. **1781** COWPER *Conversat.* 749 Look human nature through.

†**c.** *intr.* To become visible or obvious. *Obs.*

1597 SHAKS. *2 Hen. IV*, IV. iv. 120 Th' incessant care.. Hath wrought the Mure, that should confine it in, So thinne, that Life lookes through, and will breake out.

d. *to look right* (or *straight*) *through* (a person): to pretend not to see (someone), to ignore (someone) deliberately.

1959 B. KOPS *Hamlet of Stepney Green* I. 9 Like me? He never even sees me. He looks straight through me. **1963** P. WILLMOTT *Evolution of Community* ix. 98 It's awful when they look right through you, because they think you're not as good as them. **1973** G. MITCHELL *Murder of Busy Lizzie* ii. 26 Clothilde's straight-laced mamma boycotted Eliza.. and Clothilde..looked straight through the poor woman.

†**44. look under.** *intr.* To look down. *Obs.*

1700 DRYDEN *Pal. & Arc.* II. 340 Thus pondering, he looked under with his eyes.

45. look up.

a. See simple senses and UP *adv.*; to raise the eyes, turn the face upward.

c **1200** *Trin. Coll. Hom.* 173 Đanne..þo wreches..lokeð up and dun and al abuten. *c* **1220** *Bestiary* 187 Ne deme ðe noȝt wurdi ðat tu dure loken up to ðe heueneward. *a* **1300** *Cursor M.* 21393 Constantin..lok up..He sagh þar cristis cros ful bright. *c* **1386** CHAUCER *Sir Thopas* Prol. 8 Approche neer, and looke vp murily. **1535** COVERDALE *Ps.* xl. 12 My synnes haue taken soch holde vpon me, that I am not able to loke vp. **1608** SHAKS. *Per.* I. ii. 55 How dares [*sic*] the plants looke vp to heauen, From whence they haue their nourishment? **1637** MILTON *Lycidas* 125 The hungry Sheep look up, and are not fed. *a* **1800** COWPER *Jackdaw* 10 Look up—your brains begin to swim. **1855** TENNYSON *Brook* 204 And he look'd up. There stood a maiden near. **1892** *Longm. Mag.* Jan. 247 She looked up from her writing.

†**b.** Of a plant: To show itself above the ground.

1657 R. LIGON *Barbadoes* (1673) 97 If it be suffer'd to look up in a Garden, it will wind about all Herbs and Plants that have Stalks.

†**c.** To cheer up, take courage, be cheerful.

1597 SHAKS. *2 Hen. IV*, IV. iv. 113 My Soueraigne Lord, cheare vp your selfe, looke vp. **1602** —— *Ham.* III. iii. 50 Then Ile looke vp, My fault is past. **1611** —— *Wint. T.* v. i. 215.

d. *to look up to* (†*occas. at*): (*a*) to direct the look or face up towards; to raise the eyes towards, in adoration, supplication, etc.; (*b*) *fig.* to have a feeling of respect or veneration for.

a **1626** BACON *New Atl.* (1627) 7 Let vs looke vp to God, and euery man reforme his owne wayes. **1719** *Freethinker* No. 157 ¶6 These Three Ladies..look up to him, as their Patron and Defender. **1757** MRS. GRIFFITH *Lett. Henry & Frances* (1767) III. 100 The rest seem to look up at you, as of an higher Order of Intelligence. **1794** C. PIGOT *Female Jockey Club* 141 Are these the patriots, to whom England was to look up for Salvation? **1843** *Jrnl. R. Agric. Soc.* IV. I. 210 Sweden looks up to British agriculture as the model for imitation. **1855** MACAULAY *Hist. Eng.* xx. IV. 447 The Whig members still looked up to him as their leader. **1881** GARDINER & MULLINGER *Study Eng. Hist.* I. x. 178 In Pitt England had at last found the man to whom it could look up.

e. *slang.* To improve. Chiefly *Comm.*: cf. *look down*, 33 d.

1806 R. COCHRANE *Let.* 6 Jan. in J. Steele *Papers* (1924) I. 461 One cause why it has been so low at this market was the scarsity of salt; our river is now full enough for Boats to run, I think the Article will look up. **1822** *Examiner* 725/1 Foreign Securities are generally looking up. **1835** *Tait's Mag.* II. 211 The Radicals are, to use a mercantile phrase, looking up. **1884** G. ALLEN *Philistia* I. xi. 303 Trade is looking up. **1888** SARAH TYTLER *Blackhall Ghosts* III. xxix. 85, I don't believe that agriculture will look up in this country for many a day.

f. *Naut.* (See quot.)

1867 SMYTH *Sailor's Word-bk.*, *To look*, the bearing or direction, as, *she looks up*, is approaching her course.

g. To search for (something) in a dictionary or work of reference, among papers, or the like; to consult (books) in order to gain information.

1692 WOOD *Life* 24 July, They decided to look up it [Athenae Oxon.]—to see what I said of the Presbyterians. **1865** MILL *Exam. Hamilton* 458, I have only looked up the authorities nearest at hand. **1876** MISS YONGE *Womankind* vi. 44 She had better look the definitions up at the beginning of the books of Euclid. **1890** FENN *Double Knot* I. iii. 113, I have been looking up the Glens. Not a bad family, but a younger branch.

h. To call on, go to see (a person). *colloq.*

1852 DICKENS *Bleak Ho.* xlix, George will look us up..at half-after four. **1885** *Illustr. Lond. News* 21 Feb. 208/3 So do look me up..and you will be most welcome. **1892** *Harper's Mag.* LXXXIV. 246/2 You'd better look him up at his hotel.

i. To search for.

1468 *Paston Lett.* II. 329 The obligacion of the Bisshop of Norwychys oblygacion, I never sye it that I remembre; wherfor I wolde and prey my modre to loke it up. **1473** SIR J. PASTON in *P. Lett.* III. 37, I..praye yow to loke uppe my *Temple of Glasse*, and send it me by the berer herof. **1636** EARL MANCH. in *Buccleuch MSS.* (Hist. MSS. Comm.) I. 276 It will be best for every one to..look up the exemptions they have. **1669** *Plymouth Col. Rec.* (1856) V. 27 The Court haue ordered that..the said Winge be required to looke vp the said Indian, and bringe him..before some one of the majestrates. **1861** HUGHES *Tom Brown at Oxf.* iv. (1889) 30 He was..a sort of boating nurse, who looked-up and trained the young oars. **1894** WOLSELEY *Marlborough* I. 278 Hearing of some rebels in the neighbourhood of Taunton, he sent a small party of Oxford's regiment to look them up.

j. To direct vigilance to.

1855 MRS. MARCH *Heiress of Haughton* II. 52 Phillips is new to his place, remember;—you must look him up, if he is careless. **1862** MRS. H. WOOD *Channings* II. 235 A pretty time o' day this is to deliver the letters!.. You letter-men want looking up.

k. *to look* (a person) *up and down*: to scrutinize his appearance from head to foot.

1892 *Standard* 3 Oct. 4/7 They prefer to look his Viceroy up and down and all round before giving him a character. **1893** *Strand Mag.* VI. 125/2 People looked her up and down.

†**46. look upon.** = *look on*, 39 a. *Obs.*

1593 SHAKS. *3 Hen. VI*, II. iii. 27 Whiles the Foe doth.. looke vpon, as if the Tragedie were plaid in iest, by counterfetting Actors. **1606** —— *Tr. & Cr.* v. vi. 10 *Aia.* Ile fight with him alone, stand Diomed. *Dio.* He is my prize, I will not looke vpon. *Troy.* Come both you coging Greekes, haue at you both. **1611** —— *Wint. T.* v. iii. 100.

47. *Comb.* (used *attrib.* or as sbs.): **look-ahead**, an action of judging what can happen or is likely to happen in the (immediate) future; **look-and-say**, a method of teaching reading by identifying each word as a whole (as opposed to treating a word as a series of separate letters needing to be spelt); **look-around, -round** [cf. *to look (a)round*, senses 30, 42], an inspection, scrutiny, search; **look-like-a-goose** *sb.*, one who has a stupid look; **look-through** *Papermaking* (see quots.).

1963 I. FLORES *Logic Computer Arithmetic* iv. 78 Another solution is to examine the inputs to a number of stages and, somehow, simultaneously predict the carry outputs for this group of stages. This is called the carry lookahead. *Ibid.* v. 83 Let us examine an adder which performs the carry function with a lookahead on several levels. **1967** A. BATTERSBY *Network Analysis* (ed. 2) xii. 210 The effect of a 'look ahead' decision rule is shown. **1973** *Sci. Amer.* June 93/3 Since the number of legal moves available to a player at each turn averages about 30, a full look-ahead to a depth of four would require examination of about 30^4, or 810,000 moves. **1909** B. DUMVILLE *Sci. of Speech* xii. 167 The books on school method usually mention three methods of teaching to read—the Alphabetic, the Look-and-Say, and the Phonic. **1964** M. CRITCHLEY *Developmental Dyslexia* iv. 16 Many have blamed the analytic, look-and-say, 'flash' or global systems of teaching—whereby the child learns to identify each word as a whole. **1973** *Guardian* 7 Mar. 5/2 The use of highly speculative Gestalt psychology as the theoretical basis for 'look and say' methods. **1947** *Ann. Reg. 1946* 157 Field-Marshal Smuts found time to fly to Berlin for what he described as a 'private look around' with no special..objectives. **1967** M. MCLUHAN *Medium is Massage* 10 'The Medium is The Massage' is a look-around to see what's happening. **1624** BP. MOUNTAGU *Gagg* 300 He hath the figure of a man as Will Summer had, though he be indeed as very a Look-like-a-goose as he was. **1914** R. FROST *North of Boston* 65 We took one look round. **1932** J. BUCHAN *Gap in Curtain* ii. 97 He hoped, while in the country, to have a look round. **1937** E. J. LABARRE *Dict. Paper* 149/1 *Look-through*, a term applied to the appearance of paper when held to the light, thus disclosing the texture or formation. **1973** C. COHEN *Watermarks* (William Sommerville & Son Ltd.) 8/1 *Look-through*, the appearance of a sheet of paper when held up to the light: may be clear or mottled.

look, var. LOUK; obs. f. LOCK *sb.*[1]

look-a-here: see LOOK *v.* 4 a.

look-alike. *N. Amer.* [LOOK *v.* 9 + ALIKE *a.*] Something or someone that closely resembles another in appearance. Also *attrib.* or as *adj.*

1947 *Time* 1 Dec. 78 Lisle Maxwell Sanders..is often called 'Mr. Kieran' for his famed look-alike. **1949** J. ROEBURT *Tough Cop* xvi. 180 There were enough look-alikes in the flat photography of the period to puzzle me. **1961** M. BEADLE *These Ruins are Inhabited* (1963) ii. 31 Those look-a-likes, the two-shilling piece and the half-crown. **1969** L. GREENBAUM *Out of Shape* (1970) xxv. 175 Asher was flanked by his pregnant wife and a long-haired student. Except for the wife's stomach, the two women were look-alikes. **1972** *Islander* (Victoria, B.C.) 27 Feb. 10/3 This is the critical test, such misleading lookalikes as serpentine and its brother, bowenite, permitting no passage of light even through the finest sliver. **1974** *Publishers Weekly* 11 Feb. 62/3 He meets Gabrielle, Simone's look-alike sister, and falls in love all over again.

'look-down. *U.S.* [f. vbl. phr. *look down*: see LOOK *v.* 33.] A carangoid fish, the Horse-head or Moon-fish, *Selene vomer*.

1882 JORDAN & GILBERT *Fishes N. Amer.* (*Bull. U.S. Nat. Mus.* III) 439.

looke, obs. form of LOCK *sb.*[1]

looked (lʊkt), *ppl. a.*[1] [f. LOOK *v.* + -ED[1].] In senses of the vb., with advs., as *after*, *for*, *up*.

1548 ELYOT *Dict.*, *Expectatus*, desyred, taried, & looked for. **1565** COOPER *Thesaurus* s.v. *Expectatus*, The long loked day was come. **1606** etc. [see *long-looked-for*, LONG *adv.* 9 a]. **1823** COBBETT *Rur. Rides* (1885) I. 369 His anxiously looked-for event. **1885** H. O. FORBES *Nat. Wand. E. Archip.* 168 The Balai, always the best looked-after building in a village. **1895** *Westm. Gaz.* 7 Sept. 2/1 He..was one of the most looked-up-to gentlemen about. **1900** *Ibid.* 10 Aug. 2/3 A welcome beggar, a looked-for guest.

†**looked**, *ppl. a.*[2] *Obs.* [f. LOOK *sb.* + -ED[2].] Having an aspect of a certain kind: preceded by a defining adj.; see also ILL-LOOKED, WELL-LOOKED.

1593 SHAKS. *Rich. II*, II. iv. 11 Leane-look'd Prophets whisper fearefull change. **1666** PEPYS *Diary* 17 Aug., A strange fortune for so odd a looked mayde. **1694** MOTTEUX *Rabelais* IV. xxix. (1737) 121 This Meagre-look'd Shrovetide. **1716** B. CHURCH *Hist. Philip's War* (1865) I. 82 A great surly look'd fellow took up his Tomhog, or wooden Cutlash, to kill Mr. Church. **1725** DE FOE *Voy. round World* (1840) 267 He was as ugly a looked fellow as ever I saw.

lookee: see LOOK *v.* 4 a.

looker ('lʊkə(r)), *sb.* Also 4, 6 loker, 5 locar, 5–6 lokar, 6 *Sc.* luker, 7 lowker. [f. LOOK *v.* + -ER[1].]

1. a. One who looks, in senses of the vb. Const. with preps., as *at*, *on*, *to*, *upon*.

1556 J. HEYWOOD *Spider & Flie* xcii. 181 You are the myrrors; that all lookers look in. **1579** TWYNE *Phisicke agst. Fort.* I. lxxxv. 108 b, A diligent looker to the profite of the Common wealth. *c* **1580** SIDNEY *Ps.* XXII. v, The lookers now at me, poore wretch, be mocking. **1596** DALRYMPLE tr. *Leslie's Hist. Scot.* I. 17 Quhilke brig haveng 8 bowis, is ane gret delectatione to the lukeris vpon it. **1671** VILLIERS (Dk. Buckhm.) *Rehearsal* I. i. (Arb.) 27, I have ever observed that your grave lookers are the dullest of men. **1675** OTWAY *Alcibiades* III. i. Wks. 1728 I. 39 An anxious Looker on this Tragic Scene.

b. With advbs., as *looker about*, *in*, *out*, etc. *spec.* **looker-out**, in the book-trade, one who looks out wanted volumes from stock; **looker-upper** *colloq.*, one who looks something up.

1382 WYCLIF *Ecclus.* vii. 12 God forsothe the loker about is. *c* **1400** *Apol. Loll.* 2 If we wil, we mai calle bischoppis, locars up on. **1767** *Pol. Reg.* I. 363 The lookers-out have not been able to prevail on any man of consequence to accept [an office]. **1826** *New Monthly Mag.* XVII. 241, I have always casual lookers-in, and it is my cue..to keep..an open house. **1836** *Scottish Christian Herald* I. 286/2 Like the keepers of a puppet-show, to extort money from every looker-in. **1850** GROTE *Greece* II. lxiii. VIII. 140 The Peloponnesian fleet completely eluded the lookers-out of Thrasyllus. **1901** *Daily Chron.* 4 Dec. 9/2 (Advt.), Lookers-up (2 experienced); also several boys in beer factory. **1926** W. J. LOCKE *Old Bridge* II. viii. 134 The result..if sought, is there for the looker-round to behold. **1939** H. HODGE *Cab, Sir?* ii. 20 At the blind corners, where the separate sections are too far apart to keep in touch, there's a 'looker-out'. He waves up the cabs from one section to another. **1951** 'J. TEY' *Daughter of Time* vii. 91 'Marta..said you wanted something looked up.' 'And are you a looker-upper?' **1961** *Evening Standard* 14 July 19/4 Publisher has vacancy for warehouse-man to train as looker-out.

c. looker on, looker-on, one who looks on; a beholder, spectator, eye-witness. Often, one who merely looks on, without taking part. Cf. *onlooker*.

1539 TAVERNER *Erasm. Prov.* (1552) 22 Tearynge a sunder theyr visours..not without great laughynge of the lokers on. **1586** SPENSER *Sonn. to G. Harvey*, Sitting like a Looker-on Of this worldes Stage. *a* **1627** MIDDLETON & ROWLEY *Sp. Gipsy* v. iii. 84, I all this while Stand but a looker-on. **1711** BUDGELL *Spect.* No. 161 ¶2 To gain the Approbation of the Lookers-on. **1800** WINDHAM *Speeches Parl.* 18 Apr. (1812) I. 339 Accidents to the lookers-on do sometimes happen at bull-baiting. **1850** SMEDLEY *F. Fairlegh* (1894) 9 Every fool knows that lookers-on see most of the game. **1898** L. STEPHEN *Stud. Biog.* II. iv. 128 As an undergraduate he was a looker-on at..the Oxford Movement.

d. looker-in: a viewer of television. Also (now *rare*) *looker*.

The more usual word is *viewer*.

1927 *Pictorial Weekly* 5 Mar. 101 A speech which the 'looker-in' can actually see being delivered. **1928** *Daily Tel.* 30 Oct. 12/5 This afternoon 'lookers-in' will be given a chance of seeing the first still pictures to be publicly broadcast in this country. **1933** *Radio Times* 14 Apr. 72/2 *The First Television Revue*..should draw the majority of Britain's 'lookers' to their receivers. **1953** *Sunday Times* 25 Jan. 9/4 Producers should never allow themselves to be influenced by the knowledge that their audience contains many doggedly *literal* lookers. **1959** *Listener* 16 July 100/3 If the looker-in [of a televised church service] can only be a looker-on it would be better he did not watch.

2. a. One who looks after or has charge of anything (e.g. †children, cattle, land, a farm, woods, etc.); a guardian, keeper, shepherd, farm-bailiff, steward. Now only *local.*

1340 *Ayenb.* 220 þe children of riche men ssolle habbe guode lokeres and oneste. *a* **1400–50** *Alexander* 2591 þan mas he laddis ouire to lend & lokars of bestis. **1609** *MS. Acc. St. John's Hosp., Canterb.*, Payd to the lowker of Moserd Wood xij*d.* **1793** *Trans. Soc. Arts* IV. 49 Where my looker and family, with two or three labourers constantly resides. **1797** MRS. A. M. BENNETT *Beggar Girl* II. 103 Old Frazer.. had..filled the office of looker at Castle Gowrand—a phrase that implicates the combined duties of steward and bailiff. **1806–7** A. YOUNG *Agric. Essex* (1813) I. 62 *note*, Leaving their farms to the management of bailiffs, whom they call lookers.

b. With prefixed sb.: An official inspector of (what the sb. denotes). (Cf. LEAVE-LOOKER.) *local.*

1835 *1st Rep. Munic. Corporat. Comm.* App. III. 1627 [Morpeth] There is no election of fish and flesh lookers. *Ibid.* 1600 [Lancaster] Other officers of the Corporation are, Auditors,..Hedge-lookers. *Ibid.* 1484 [Clitheroe] Other officers are, Market Lookers,..Lookers of Hedges and Ditches. **1899** *Daily News* 23 Aug. 3/5 T. Thornton, cloth looker, Briercliffe.

3. A person, usu. a woman, of particularly pleasing appearance. *colloq.* (orig. *U.S.*).

1893 S. CRANE *Maggie* v. 41 The young men of the vicinity said, 'Dat Johnson goil is a puty good looker.' **1898** E. N. WESTCOTT *David Harum* 322, I was alwus a better goer than I was a looker. **1909** E. RICKERT *Beggar in Heart* 207 She isn't much of a looker—my missus has other points than looks. **1923** L. J. VANCE *Baroque* vii. 65 Just because daughter's a swell looker don't make father out an innocent. **1933** AUDEN *Witnesses* in *Listener* (Poetry Suppl.) 12 July p. ii, The days went by, he grew mature; He was a looker you may be sure. **1947** J. STEINBECK *Wayward Bus* vii. 80 She was a looker too—fine well-filled legs with rounded thighs. **1971** R. PARKES *Line of Fire* iv. 42 Bit of a looker... Otherwise..a ranking detective on a priority case, would hardly have bothered driving her home. **1973** *Washington Post* 5 Jan. 8/2 Sandra Archer, who plays the heroine from the Peace Corps..is such a looker that she can't help but make the Quest for Revolutionary Consciousness appear hopelessly glamorized.

looker ('lʊkə(r)), *v. dial.* [f. the sb.] *trans.* and *intr.* To tend and guard (farm animals).

1887 PARISH & SHAW *Dict. Kentish Dial.* 95 *Looker*, to perform the work of a looker. 'John? Oh! he's *lookering*.' **1961** *John o' London's* 5 Oct. 400/3 In East Sussex a shepherd is still called a 'looker' and his occupation 'lookering'. **1962** R. JEFFRIES *Exhibit No. 13* x. 97 Jones was 'lookering' his bullocks. The ministry man was due..and.. the bullocks had to be treated with all possible care and attention.

look-in, *sb.* [f. LOOK *sb.* + IN *adv.*]

1. A hasty glance; a peep. Hence, a short visit.

1847 L. HUNT *Men, Women & B.* I. xv. 293 The Induction to the 'Mirror of Magistrates' is a look in at the infernal regions. **1865** DICKENS *Mut. Fr.* IV. iii, He has given me another look-in, to make sure of..our stock-in-trade being correct.

2. *colloq.* An opportunity to take part in something, usually with a chance of success; a share of attention.

1870 *Bell's Life* 12 Feb. 3/6 If Fawcett imagines he has got a look in, Mullins will fight him for all the money he can get together. **1898** *Westm. Gaz.* 12 July 10/2 For the Beaufort Stakes Mr. L. de Rothschild should have a good look in. **1902** KIPLING *Traffics & Discov.* (1904) 27 We might even be able to give our Native Army a look in. **1905** *Official Guide Nat. Assoc. Professional Baseball Leagues* 58 With a team which never had a look-in for anything better than cellar championship..the club made money. **1911** G. B. SHAW *Getting Married* 244 We shall none of us have much of a look-in when Mrs. George comes. **1916** *Lit. Digest* 1 Jan. 7/2 Between Colonel Roosevelt and the diplomatic correspondence of this epoch the dictionary business is getting a look-in all right. **1916** 'TAFFRAIL' *Pincher Martin* xvii. 330 It's time we had a look in at something. **1936** *Times Lit. Suppl.* 17 Oct. 837/1 The faithful, unmarried lover who never gets a look-in. **1964** *Word Study* Apr. 1/1 Nor would a quack bonesetter get a look-in at a position in a modern

clinic. **1968** *Listener* 26 Sept. 390/1 An acknowledged modern artist gets a look-in at illustration 52.

looking ('lʊkɪŋ), *vbl. sb.* [f. LOOK *v.* + -ING¹.]

1. a. The action of the vb. LOOK; look, gaze.

c **1175** *Lamb. Hom.* 145 þer scal beon.. Lokinge wið-uten winkinge. *a* **1225** *Ancr. R.* 50 Vor nabbe ȝe nout þene nome ..of tollinde lokinges. **13..** *E.E. Allit. P.* A. 1048 þurȝ woȝe & wone my lokyng ȝede. *c* **1400** *Lanfranc's Cirurg.* 119 Crokidnes, or ellis lokynge asquynt of þe iȝen. *a* **1450** *Knt. de la Tour* (1868) 17 The eldest suster [was] for her highe and unferme loking forsaken. **1567** *Gude & Godlie Ball.* (S.T.S.) 74 The prydeful luking of my eine. *c* **1592** MARLOWE *Jew of Malta* III. i, Zoon's what a looking thou keep'st! *a* **1716** SOUTH *Serm.* (1823) IV. 318 Anger passes, in the gospel account, for murder; and looking and lusting, for adultery. **1821** BYRON *Heav. & Earth* iii. 92 After long looking o'er the ocean wide. **1861** J. EDMOND *Childr. Ch. at Home* ix. 138 Looking is seeing with attention.

Proverb. a **1624** BP. M. SMITH *Serm.* (1632) 154 By looking comes liking, you know the proverb.

b. With adverbs.

1526 *Pilgr. Perf.* (W. de W. 1531) 86 b, Whiche for ones lokynge backwarde was turned in to a salt stone. **1840** BROWNING *Sordello* III. 361 Which evidence you owed To some slight weariness, some looking-off Or start-away. **1870** J. H. NEWMAN *Gram. Assent* II. x. 412 A sensitive looking-out in all that happens..for tokens [etc.].

c. With prepositions, used *absol.*, or advs. ***looking after, on, to, unto***, care, attention; ***looking for***, expectation; ***looking over***, inspection. † ***to give (a person) the looking on***: to look on without interference or participation in his activity.

c **1513** MORE *Rich. III* (ed. Lumby) 33 The yonger, which besides his infancie that also nedeth good loking to, hath a while ben so sore diseased [etc.]. **1560** DAUS tr. *Sleidane's Comm.* 11 b, Or if the Frenche kinge warre upon Charles.., shall he geve them the lokyng on? [L. *num ociosus erit spectator?*] *Ibid.* 64 b, His advise and counsell, whiche unlesse they woulde folowe, he would gyve them the lokyng on. **1611** BIBLE *Heb.* x. 27 A certaine fearefull looking for of iudgement. **1660** H. MORE *Myst. Godl.* To Rdr. 21 To make the People believe..that Religion is worth the looking after. **1722** DE FOE *Plague* (1840) 44 If any person visited do fortune by negligent looking unto..to come..from a place infected. **1832** TENNYSON *Miller's Dau.* 241 That loss but made us love the more, With farther lookings on. **1890** 'ROLF BOLDREWOOD' *Col. Reformer* (1891) 328 My old horse ..wants a bit of looking after now. **1895** R. KIPLING in *Pall Mall G.* 29 July 2/1 Mowgli always attended a Looking-over.

d. looking-in *Television* = VIEWING *vbl. sb.* Also *attrib.*

1926 *Daily Herald* 31 Dec. 1/2 It is predicted that before many years have passed the family looking-in set will be as common in the home as is now the listening-in set. **1927** *Pictorial Weekly* 5 Mar. 101/2 'Looking-in' on Mr. Baird's apparatus is an interesting experience. **1951** *Ann. Reg. 1950* 414 From America came alarming reports of the craze for looking-in. **1957** R. HOGGART *Uses of Literacy* vi. 156 An undiscriminating looking-in, night after night, at T.V.

†**2.** Supervision, care, charge, custody. *Obs.*

a **1300** *K. Horn* 360 (Camb. MS.) Aylmar, þe gode kyng, Dude him on mi lokyng. **1340** *Ayenb.* 8 To ham þet habbeþ þe lokingge ous to teche. *Ibid.* 128 þe zeneȝere is ase þe ilke þet is ine prison..and ine greate lokinge.

†**3.** Decision, judgement. *Obs.*

1297 R. GLOUC. (Rolls) 7409 þat vpe þe popes lokinge of rome he ssolde it do. *c* **1330** R. BRUNNE *Chron.* (1810) 86 Philip..askid if þei wild stand to þer lokyng.

†**4.** Look, expression of countenance, appearance. *Obs.*

a **1300** *Cursor M.* 17288 + 108 His lokyng was als briȝt os is þe rede lempninge. **1388** WYCLIF *Dan.* ii. 31 The lokyng [Vulg. *intuitus*] therof was ferdful. *c* **1430** *Syr Gener.* (Roxb.) 4707 Wene ye that hir louely looking Pleaseth vs any maner thing As it dooth you. **1610** SHAKS. *Temp.* II. i. 309 Why how now hoa; awake, why are you drawn? Wherefore this ghastly looking?

5. *attrib.*

1519 HORMAN *Vulg.* 281 b, Order me a lokyng place in the play. **1552** HULOET, Lokynge place to se about, *theatrum*. **1670** DRYDEN *1st Pt. Conq. Granada* IV. ii. Wks. 1883 IV. 94 But yet my toil May be rewarded with a looking-while. **1843** MARRYAT *M. Violet* xi, A dog would..squat upon his looking-out place.

looking ('lʊkɪŋ), *ppl. a.* [f. LOOK *v.* + -ING².]

1. That looks or gazes. *rare.* † ***looking up***: having an upward aspect or direction; sloping.

1649 BLITHE *Eng. Improv. Impr.* (1653) 63 The other [spade] may be Six Inches wide, whose Tree must be made more compass and looking up, by far, than your usuall Spades are. **1722** RAMSAY *Three Bonnets* II. 12, I scarce can trow my looking een, Ye're grown sae braw.

2. Forming combinations. **a.** with a preceding adjective, substantive (now *rare*), or phrase. (See also GOOD-LOOKING, ILL-LOOKING.)

1590 SHAKS. *Com. Err.* v. i. 240 A needy, hollow-ey'd, sharpe-looking wretch. **1756** MRS. F. BROOKE *Old Maid* No. 25. 213 A well looking old woman..asked from the upper window, who he pleased to want? **1781** MAD. D'ARBLAY *Diary* Aug., I care not what looking horse I have; I never think of his appearance. **1782** MORITZ in *Brit. Tourist* (1809) IV. 33 Paddington, a very village-looking little town, at the west end of London. **1802** MAR. EDGEWORTH *Moral T.* (1816) I. xviii. 148 A hard, stout looking man. **1818** LADY MORGAN *Autobiog.* (1859) 249 The celebrity entered: a grave-looking elderly gentleman. **1825** *Greenhouse Comp.* II. 83 Phylica ericoides..a small heath-looking shrub from the Cape. **1834** *Tait's Mag.* I. 803/2 A book printed in a dull, muddy, everyday-looking type. **1840** CARLYLE *Heroes* (1858) 360 Most rude, chaotic, all these Speeches are; but most earnest-looking. **1881** W. H. MALLOCK *Romance 19th C.* II. 5 He was a small dissipated-looking man.

b. with adverbs of direction: Having a certain aspect or direction.

1884 BLACK *Jud. Shakes.* xx, There was a touch of it on the westward-looking gables of one or two cottages.

looking-forward. [f. LOOKING *vbl. sb.* + FORWARD *adv.*] The action of looking forward; an anticipation of future events.

1837 DICKENS *Let.* 3 Nov. (1965) I. 328 Anxious lookings-forward to the pleasure of your society. **1867** *People's Hymnal* 205/2 One the earnest looking forward, One the hope our God inspires. **1871** G. V. SMITH *Bible & Pop. Theol.* xxiv. 248 Any conscious looking forward by the writer to a greater and more genuine sacrifice to come. **1915** BEERBOHM *Lett. to R. Turner* (1964) 242 Well, dearest Reg, again all apologies..and all lookings-forward to later on. **1955** E. BOWEN *World of Love* xi. 221 Were there not those who said that everything *has* already happened, and that one's lookings-forward are really memories?

'looking-,glass. [f. LOOKING *vbl. sb.* + GLASS.]

1. a. A glass to look in, in order to see one's own face or figure; a mirror made of a plate of glass coated at the back with an amalgam of quicksilver; †applied *occas.* to a metal mirror (cf. GLASS *sb.*¹ 8 b).

1526 *Pilgr. Perf.* (W. de W. 1531) 1 b, Wherein dayly & hourly I myght loke, as in a myrour or lokyng-glass. **1605** SHAKS. *Lear* v. iii. 261. **1608** WILLET *Hexapla Exod.* 857 The brasen lauer was indeed made of the womens looking glasses. **1712** ADDISON *Spect.* No. 451 ⁋1 Seeing all her Wrinkles represented in a large Looking-glass. **1728** RAMSAY *Lass & Mirror* 3 The leal-hearted Looking-glass With truths addrest the lovely Lass. **1771** WESLEY *Jrnl.* 22 July, The sea was smooth as a looking-glass. **1831** BREWSTER *Optics* ii. 19 Let AB, fig. 16., be a plane mirror or looking-glass. **1876** A. LAING *Lindores Abbey* xxvi. 384 The looking glass was invariably covered up in the chamber where the dead lay.

b. *fig.* (In the 16th and 17th cents. frequently used in the titles of books.) Now *rare* (= 'mirror').

1556 *Aurelio & Isab.* L iij, The parson of a kinge is a thorrou persinge an sheninge lookinge glasse, in the whiche all the subgects sees them selfs. **1575** TYMME (*title*) A Looking Glasse for the Court. **1587** GOLDING *De Mornay* xvii. 269 The holy Scripture, is..a Looking glass to shew vs our spotes and blemishes. **1600** BRETON *Pasquils Mad-cappe* ii, Beautie is but a Babies looking glasse. **1656** TRAPP *Comm. Ps.* xxxv. 18 Great men are the Looking-glasses of the Country, according to which most men dress themselves. **1658** W. SANDERSON *Graphice* 5 The Eyes, the Looking-glasses of Nature. **1792** (*title*) The Looking-Glass for the Mind; or Intellectual Mirror. **1847** EMERSON *Poems* (1857) 74 Each to each a looking-glass, Reflects his figure that doth pass.

2. As the name of a material: Plate glass, or glass silvered for use as a mirror.

1682 N. O. *Boileau's Lutrin* I. 97 The Tester was all fac'd with Looking-Glass. **1764** DELAVAL in *Phil. Trans.* LIV. 233 Inclosed between small plates of thick looking-glass. **1799** G. SMITH *Laboratory* I. 178 How to Quicksilver the inside of Glass Globes, so as to make them look like Looking-glass. **1886** D. C. MURRAY *Cynic Fortune* viii, He took stock of his features in the little triangle of cracked looking-glass affixed to the wall.

3. In the plant-names **lady's looking-glass, Venus' looking-glass** (*Campanula Speculum*): see LADY, VENUS.

4. *slang.* A chamber-pot.

1622 BEAUM. & FL. *Beggar's Bush* II. iii, Ha! A Looking-glasse! **1638** BRATHWAIT *Barnabee's Jrnl.* II. (1818) 59 Mid-night waking, And a looking-glasse there taking, Chamber-pot was hol'd quite thorow. **1709** *Brit. Apollo* II. No. 43. 2/2 *Q.* Why is a Chamber-Pot call'd a Looking-Glass? *A.* Because many rarely see their Faces in any other.

5. *attrib.* and *Comb.*, as ***looking-glass calm, -fitter, -frame, -maker, -man, -plate, -tin***; ***looking-glass-panelled*** adj.; **looking-glass carp** (see quot.); **looking-glass image** *rare* = *mirror image*; **looking-glass tree**, *Heritiera littoralis*, the leaves of which are silvery on the under side; **looking-glass world** (or **land**), a vision of the world as it would be if seen, reversed, through a looking-glass; **looking-glass writing**, writing done backwards, so as to be legible by means of a mirror.

1840 COL. HAWKER *Diary* (1893) II. 194 A *looking-glass calm with bitter cold white frost. **1890** *Daily News* 8 Sept. 5/5 A '*looking-glass carp'..differs from the ordinary carp in having very few, and those very large, scales. *a* **1903** *Mod. Advt.*, Junior *Looking-glass Fitter wanted. **1688** PARKER & STALKER *Japaning* v. 25 *Looking-glass-frames. **1929** A. HUXLEY *Do what you Will* 44 The professional Don Juan destroys his spirit as fatally as does the professional ascetic, whose *looking-glass image he is. **1896** B. BERENSON *Italian Painters of Renaissance* (1930) II. ii. 63 He cannot persuade himself of the unreality of *Looking-Glass Land until he has touched the back of the mirror. **1909** CHESTERTON *Tremendous Trifles* 234 Always the Kingdom of Heaven is 'at hand', and Looking-glass Land is only through the looking-glass. **1911** —— *Innocence of Father Brown* viii. 225 An unspeakable certainty that there was something still unexplained... Could not be fully explained by his fancy about 'looking-glass land'. **1611** COTGR., *Miroaillier*, a *looking-glasse maker. **1723** *Lond. Gaz.* No. 6137/4 William Turing,..Looking-glass-maker. **1682** T. FLATMAN *Heraclitus Ridens* No. 67 (1713) II. 164 The *Looking-glass-man you almost promised to deal withal the last time we met. **1902** *Westm. Gaz.* 3 July 3/2 The cheapest bedroom furniture means a *looking-glass panelled wardrobe. **1703** T. N. *City & C. Purchaser* 152 These *Looking-glass-plates are ground smooth and flat, and Polished. **1703** T. S. *Art's Improv.* I. 55 Take a Plate of Polish'd Steel, which cover with that Orange, Tawny Mineral, call'd Mine de Plomb, Ground with Linseed-Oil and *Looking-glass Tin. **1866** *Treas. Bot.*, **Looking-glass tree*, Heritiera. **1871** 'L. CARROLL' *Through Looking-Glass* xii. 218 You've been along with me, Kitty—all through the *Looking-Glass world. **1963** *Daily Tel.* 15 Aug. 18/1 It is quite conceivable that there might exist a kind of looking-glass world, in which all matter is made up from anti-matter. **1967** 'A. GILBERT' *Visitor* xii. 203, I felt as if I were in a Looking-Glass world where everything goes the wrong way. **1902** *Westm. Gaz.* 29 Aug. 3/1 Notes..made with the left hand in '*looking-glass' writing.

lookit ('lʊkɪt), *int.* and *v. U.S. colloq.* [f. LOOK *v.* with arbitrary final element.]

a. *int.* Listen! **b.** *v. trans.* Only in imp.: look at (something or someone).

1917 *Dialect Notes* IV. 396 *Look-at*, used among school children for *look!*.. Cf. *look-it* in Mass., Mich. **1925** T. DREISER *Amer. Trag.* (1926) I. xiv. 103 Oh, isn't that just the classiest, darlingest little coat you ever saw! Oh, do look at those sleeves... Lookit the collar. And the lining! And those pockets! **1926** *S.P.E. Tract* XXIV. 124 *Lookit*, listen to me. **1927** M. OSTENSO *Mad Carews* (1929) iv. 49 But lookit! Lookit the nice stockin's Mrs. Bowers made for ye. **1938** D. BAKER *Young Man with Horn* IV. iv. 242 'Lookit the jig-men,' Olga said. 'I thought you'd give us the go-by.' **1966** M. BREWER *Man against Fear* i. 8 Lookit my hair—whiter it gets every day. **1968** [see JEEZ(E *int.*]. **1972** D. BLOODWORTH *Any Number can Play* xxiii. 231 Just get a load of that stuff, will you? It's not even killing the lousy jungle, lookit. It's bringing it alive!

'look out, look-out. *Pl.* look-outs, *rarely* looks out. [f. vbl. phr. *look out*: see LOOK *v.* 40.]

1. The action (*occas.* the faculty or the duty) of looking out. *lit.* and *fig.* Chiefly in phrases ***to keep*** (rarely ***to take***) ***a*** (***good***, etc.) ***look-out***; ***to be, place, put on*** or ***upon the look out***; const. *for*, *to*, and *to* with *inf.*; orig. *Naut.*

1748 *Anson's Voy.* III. vi. 346 We..kept a good look-out for the rocks of Vele Rete. *c* **1760** S. NILES in *3 Mass. Hist. Coll.* (1837) VI. 161 They were upon the constant look-out and had two forts not far distant from thence. **1766** BRICE in *Phil. Trans.* LVI. 67, I wished to put other people upon the look-out. **1768** GOLDSM. *Good-n. Man* II. Wks. (Globe) 622/2, I think if anything was to be foreseen, I have as sharp a look-out as another. **17..** WILKES *Corr.* (1805) III. 81 He ..keeps a very good look-out to futurity. **1815** *Sporting Mag.* XLVI. 4 The gamekeeper of Mr. Blundell was upon the look-out for poachers. **1849** W. IRVING *Crayon Misc.* 192 At one time, in crossing a hill, Beatte..took a look-out, like a mariner from the mast-head at sea. *c* **1860** H. STUART *Seaman's Catech.* 85 You are placed on the look out. **1864** BOWEN *Logic* i. 26 Anything new or peculiar..puts us upon the lookout to detect a possible absurdity. **1875** BEDFORD *Sailor's Pocket Bk.* iii. (ed. 2) 57 The very great majority of collisions happen through bad look-out and neglect to show lights. **1883** STEVENSON *Treas. Isl.* II. x, We were running down for it with a bright look-out day and night. **1887** *Pall Mall G.* 3 Aug. 2/2 In these ships the men go from look-out to wheel, from wheel to look-out. **1894** J. KNIGHT *D. Garrick* ii. 21 He had been on the look-out for such information.

2. In various concrete applications.

a. A station or building from which a look-out can be kept. orig. *Naut.*

1700 *S. Carolina Stat. at Large* (1837) II. 161 The Look-out formerly built on Sullivan's Island..is by a late storm overthrown to the ground. **1766** W. STORK *Acc. E. Florida* 33 To the back part of the house is joined a tower, called in America a look-out, from which there is an extensive prospect towards the sea. **1791** BENTHAM *Panopt.* I. 145 A Look-out or Exterior Inspection-Lodge. **1855** LONGF. *Hiaw.* xix. 5 Another vulture, watching From his high aerial look-out. **1861** J. EDKINS in *Chinese Scenes and People* (1883) 271 It is now used as a site for a high look-out by the rebels. **1893** F. ADAMS *New Egypt* 244 A battery of four guns, with a telegraph station and look-out attached. **1935** A. J. POLLOCK *Underworld Speaks* 73/1 *Look-out*, gambling house employee who observes the bets of players and the pay-off of dealers for regulatory purposes. **1961** *Canada Month* 6 Oct. 42/3 However, the forestry people want money to buy greater preparedness through more lookouts, men, planes and equipment.

b. A person employed to keep a look-out; a watchman, scout; a party of men so employed. Also, see quot. 1889.

1699 COWLEY *Voy.* (1729) 12 We took their look-outs who told us the news. **1720** DE FOE *Capt. Singleton* xiv. (1840) 240 We..kept a look-out upon the hill. **1840** R. H. DANA *Bef. Mast* xiv. 35 One man on deck as a look-out. **1872** *Routledge's Ev. Boy's Ann.*, Apr. 266/2 The 'Cambria' sailed ..with looks-out at her mast-heads. **1881** *Daily Tel.* 24 Feb., Those aboard are divided into three look-outs, giving each look-out four hours on deck and eight hours below. **1888** *Century Mag.* Feb. 498/2 These lookouts or forerunners having returned, the herds are set in motion as early in the spring as may be. **1889** FARMER *Americanisms*, *Look-out*, an attendant who, at the gaming-table, is supposed to see that matters are conducted fairly. **1893** *Harper's Mag.* May 939/2 By each dealer's side sits the 'lookout'..lazily looking on in the interests of such fair play as is consistent with professional gambling. **1955** J. S. GOWLAND *Smoke over Sikanaska* 16 The look-out had to be an expert woodsman, be able to read meteorological instruments, have an excellent degree of physical fitness and good eyesight.

c. A reconnoitring boat or vessel.

1761 *Descr. S. Carolina* 36 Eight Look-outs, which are also laid aside. **1841** J. T. HEWLETT *Parish Clerk* II. 203 Ere the channel was full enough for the look-outs to intercept her.

3. A more or less distant view; a prospect.

1779 H. SWINBURNE *Trav. Spain* xxiii. 184 This leads to a little tower..The look-out charming. **1842** MRS. F. TROLLOPE *Visit Italy* II. xi. 199 A walk through the Villa Reale..seemed..to promise advantageous look-outs

without end. 1883 *Eng. Illustr. Mag.* Nov. 68/2 The traveller feels weary and disgusted with the ugliness of the look-out.

b. In immaterial sense: A prospect or prospective condition, an outlook.

*c*1825 *Houlston Tracts* II. No. 47. 2 It was bad already with them, and a worse look out. 1840 Dickens *Old C. Shop* xix, 'He's going at the knees.' 'That's a bad look-out.' 1886 *Times* (weekly ed.) 6 Aug. 13/3 The look-out for the shooting-season is satisfactory. 1889 'Rolf Boldrewood' *Robbery under Arms* xxxv, It seemed a rather blue look-out.

4. †**a.** An object of desire (*obs.*). **b.** With possessive sb. or pron., ***that is ——'s look-out***: i.e. the matter concerns only his interest, which others are not bound to consider if he neglects it.

1795 Nelson in Nicolas *Disp.* (1845) I. 45 The loaves and fishes are all the look out. 1844 Dickens *Mart. Chuz.* xxvii, If he took it into his head that I was coming here for such or such a purpose, why, that's his look-out. 1858 R. S. Surtees *Ask Mamma* xix. 63 That however is more the Earl's look-out than ours. 1884 Sir F. North in *Law Times Rep.* LII. 51 The result would be that a less price would be got, but that is the vendor's look out.

5. *attrib.*, as *look-out-boat, -man, -ship*, etc.

1781 T. Jefferson *Corr.* Wks. 1859 I. 301 *Look-out boats have been ordered from the seaboard of the eastern shore. 1798 Capt. Moss in *Naval Chron.* (1799) I. 248 Our *look-out canoes have watched them. 1860 G. H. K. in *Vac. Tour.* 123 The deer..save the hinds a great deal of *look-out duty. 1806 A. Duncan *Nelson* 177 The Swedish squadron had been seen by the *look-out frigates. 1835 *Court Mag.* VI. 64/1 Over these ruins towered a tall *look-out house. 1830 Marryat *King's Own* xxx, The *look-out men at the mastheads. 1884 *Mil. Engineering* (ed. 3) I. II. 41 A '*look-out' place for noting the effect of the fire..should be constructed. 1834-47 J. S. Macaulay *Field Fortif.* (1851) 272 Where to place videttes, *look-out posts, or telegraphs. 1804 Capt. Dance in *Naval Chron.* XII. 138, I recalled the *look-out Ships. 1872 Baker *Nile Tribut.* xv. 264, I ordered some of my men every day to ascend this *look-out station. 1748 *Anson's Voy.* II. xii. 259 On..some small eminences there are several *look-out towers. 1897 R. Baden-Powell in *Daily News* 23 Apr. 6/2 Up on the roof of the hall is a *look-out turret.

look-over. [f. look *v.* 19.] An examination, a survey.

1909 R. A. Wason *Happy Hawkins* 183 Then I..took a stroll around to see that no one had been givin' us the look-over. 1916 'B. Cable' *Action Front* 216, I want you to go down quickly and have a look over at the new ground. 1952 *Irish Digest* Feb. 8/2, I have myself treated one farmer..who was sent to me for a general 'look over'. This disclosed a malunited fracture of the ulna.

'look-see. *slang.* Also looksee. [Pidgin-like formation from look *sb.* or *v.* + see *v.*]

1. A survey; a tour of inspection, a reconnaissance; an investigation. Also *rare* (quot. 1926), appearance, looks.

1883 *Boy's Own Paper* 22 Dec. 185/1, I 'spec she just come here to makee look see how de people get on. 1906 J. London *Let.* 25 Apr. (1966) 204 Would you care to have a look-see at it for publication in the magazine? 1908 *St. George's Rev.* I. 156 China..opium problem... It was my business to go out there and have what my John would call a 'look-see'. 1924 *Blackw. Mag.* Sept. 356/2, I sat up, and had a look-see. The ground sheet was crawling with scorpions. 1926 M. Leinster *Dew on Leaf* 82, I distrust the look-see of things. 1927 *Observer* 9 Oct. 22 We must be grateful to the B.B.C. for letting us have a 'looksee', as the Chinese say. 1928 *Sat. Even. Post* 4 Feb. 105/3 And I can take a look-see at what they're doing in aviation over there. 1939 J. Pascoe *Unclimbed N.Z.* v. 67 A hurried reconnaissance, or in Colonial argot, a 'look-see', disclosed that. 1942 C. Barrett *On Wallaby* iii. 52 We had a looksee at Merre Gudda, which, the blacks say, is a haunted cave. 1943 C. H. Ward-Jackson *Piece of Cake* 41 *A look-see*, a reconnaissance. Thus, 'Let's get some facts first; go down to the flights and take a look-see.' 1957 I. Cross *God Boy* (1958) xv. 123 I'll wander up and have a look-see. 1967 B. Copper *No Flowers for General* xi. 142 I'll have a looksee at the front. 1968 A. Diment *Bang Bang Birds* ii. 13, I took a long looksee through my..binoculars.

2. (See quot.) *rare.*

1925 Fraser & Gibbons *Soldier & Sailor Words* 147 *A look see*, a telescope, a periscope.

3. *attrib.*

1929 *Amer. Speech* V. 149 Several pidgin English terms are now accepted American slang:..'chow-chow' for food, and 'look-see man' for tourist or sightseer. 1971 M. Tak *Truck Talk* 101 *Look-see window*, a window in the rear of the sleeper that assists the driver in backing up by increasing his visibility. 1973 *Times* 17 May 27/2 As a result of his 'look-see' trip Lewis..came back home with around £100,000 worth of export orders. 1973 *Sci. Amer.* Oct. 114/1 'Look-see' diagrams that offer visual proof of complex algebraic formulas.

look-up ('lʊkʌp). [f. vbl. phr. *to look up* (see look *v.* 45).] **1.** A call, a visit. *rare.*

1855 D. G. Rossetti *Let.* 25 Nov. (1965) I. 278 Hughes..gave them a look up about it. 1888 'R. Boldrewood' *Robbery under Arms* I. xiv. 191 We foraged up Aileen's mare, and made it up to ride over to George Storefield's, and gave him a look-up.

2. The action of (or a facility for) looking something up in a dictionary, file, etc.; retrieval of information about items in an ordered collection. Freq. *attrib.*

1948 *Math. Tables & Other Aids to Computation* III. 157 Operations such as division, square root, table look-up, etc., where the required time cannot be predicted. 1958 A. D. Booth in *Aspects of Translation* 88 All that had been produced was a programme which would enable a computing machine to perform look-up operations which a human translator would perform with a dictionary. 1960 E. Delavenay *Introd. Machine Transl.* vi. 93 An appreciable amount of time will thus be saved in dictionary look-up. 1964 *Discovery* Oct. 55/1 The programme does this in several stages: (1) a dictionary look-up which provides information about parts of speech, [etc.]. 1967 Cox & Grose *Organiz. Bibliogr. Rec. by Computer* iv. 79 These citations are then found in the main file by a 'look-up' procedure. 1971 A. J. Aitken in R. A. Wisbey *Computer in Lit. & Ling. Res.* 14 In addition, TLF also has a computer 'look-up' which in effect lists certain predictable collocations of certain common function words so that the computer can subdivide its examples according to these collocations.

looky here: see look *v.* 4a.

[**lool.** Error for loob (sense 1), a vessel to receive the washings of metallic ores.

[1674 Ray *Collect. Words, Prepar. Tin* 121 The dross and earth..is carried all along the trough to a pit or vessel, into which the trough delivers it, called a loob.] 1753 Chambers *Cycl. Suppl.*, Lool (citing *Ray's English Words* p. 121). Hence in 1846 Buchanan *Technol. Dict.*, and some later Dicts.]

loom (luːm), *sb.*¹ Forms: 1 **ȝelóma**, 3 **leome**, 3-7 **lome**, 5-7 **loome**, 6 *Sc.* **lwme**, (**lowme, lumme**, *Sc.* **lwime**), 6-7 **lomb(e**, 6, 9 *Sc.* **lume**, 9 *Sc.* **leem**, *dial.* **leumm**, 7- **loom**. [ME. *lome*, aphetic repr. OE. *ȝelóma* wk. masc., utensil, implement, f. *ȝe-* y- *prefix*) + *lóma* as in *andlóman* (often *andluman, andlaman*) pl., apparatus, furniture.

The ulterior etymology is obscure: some have suggested connexion with OE. *ȝelóme* (= OHG. *kilômo*) often (see ylome); on this hypothesis the primary sense would be 'things in frequent use'. The simple **lóma* is cited in some dicts. as occurring in the Leiden glosses and the Corpus Glossary; but the Latin lemmata seem to show that the entries belong to different words.]

1. a. An implement or tool of any kind. *Obs.* exc. *Sc.* and *north. dial.*

*c*900 tr. *Bæda's Hist.* iv. xxviii. (Schipper) 521 þa bead se Godes mon þæt him mon issern geloman [*ferramenta*] mid hwæte þider brohte þæt land mid to teȝenne. *a*1225 *Ancr. R.* 124, I blesced beo þi muð..vor þu makest me leome þerof to timbren, & to echen me mine crune. 13.. *Gaw. & Gr. Knt.* 2309 He lyftes lyȝtly his lome, & let hit doun fayre, Wiþ þe barbe of þe bitte bi þe bare nek. *a*1310 in Wright *Lyric P.* xii. 41 So hit wes bistad, That nomon hem ne bad, huere lomes to fonde. *c*1375 *Sc. Leg. Saints* xvi. (*Magdalena*) 518 Þai had na lomys to wil, for to make a gannand grawe. 1393 Langl. *P. Pl.* C. vi. 45 The lomes þat ich laboure with and lyflode deserue Ys pater-noster and my prymer. *a*1400 *Sir Perc.* 2032 Fulle evylle myght any mene smale,..With siche a lome fighte. *c*1440 *Promp. Parv.* 312/1 Loome, or instrument (*S.* loombe), *utensile.* 1513 Douglas *Æneis* vi. iii. 53 Enee..With lume in hand fast wirkand like the laif. 1584 Hudson *Du Bartas' Judith* i. (1608) 15 The Craftsman now his lumes away hath laide. 1641 Best *Farm. Bks.* (Surtees) 49 An outligger carryeth but onely one loome to the field, and that is a rake. 1819 W. Tennant *Papistry Storm'd* (1827) 51 Your hands are toom O' chappin-stick and weirlike loom, To batter at the bawd o' Rome. 1894 Latto *Tam Bodkin* iv. 31 'They wad get the contents o' that lume i' their wames, though!' said Willie, pu'in' oot a muckle horse pistol.

†**b.** The penis. *Obs.*

*a*1400-50 *Alexander* 4750 And large was his odd lome þe lenthe of a ȝerde. 1508 Dunbar *Tua mariit wemen* 175 His lwme is vaxit larbar. 1568 *Satir. Poems Reform.* xlvii. 95.

†**c.** = heirloom. *Obs.*

1424 *E.E. Wills* (1882) 56, I wull he haue my grete maser..for þe terme of his life, and so from heir to heyr lome. *a*1814 *Sailors' Ret.* ii. iii. in *New Brit. Theatre* II. 340 With all the appurtenances, messuages, tenements, hereditaments, looms heir, rights of court, leet, and baron..thereto appertaining and belonging.

d. *dial.* Applied to persons, with adjs. of contemptuous meaning. (Cf. *tool.*)

*a*1650 *Sir Aldingar* 47 in Furnivall *Percy Folio* I. 168 'Goe with me', saide our comly king, 'This lazar for to see'. .. 'there is a lodly lome', says Harry King, 'for our dame Queene Elinor!' 1878 *Cumbld. Gloss., Leumm*, loom; a tool; a term of reproach. 'He's an ill leumm'.

2. a. An open vessel of any kind, as a bucket, tub, vat, etc. *Obs.* exc. *Sc.*

*a*1300 *E.E. Psalter* xxxii. 7 Samenand als in lome watres of se. 13.. *Childh. Jesus* 659 in *Archiv Stud. neu. Spr.* LXXIV. 336 Thies clathis sente he..ffor to litte thayme..Doo thayme in ȝone lomys three. *c*1420 *Pallad. on Husb.* xi. 447 In lomys smaller hent this must, and vse hit as wyn pestilent. 1509 *Market Harboro' Rec.* (1890) 233 Item a growt lome and a lome for grenys vjd. 1577 *Burgh Rec. Glasgow* (1832) 80 þe third falt brekin of pair lwmes, delyng of the brewing [etc.]. 1586 *MS. Inv., Hatfield Woodhouse, Yorks*, It. kyts, stands, lombes, boules, dyshes, chyrne, flackets. 1630 in *Descr. Thames* (1758) 66 No Fisherman..shall use..any Weel called a Lomb, or a Mill-Pot, or any other Engine. 1816 Scott *Antiq.* xxiii, 'Ay, and there's something to pit it in', said the mendicant, eyeing the ram's horn—'that loom's an auld acquaintance o' mine'. 1858 Ramsay *Remin.* Ser. i. (1860) 154 Having referred to the accident [of falling from his gig], Balnamoon quietly added, 'Indeed, I maun hae a lume that'll had in'.

†**b.** Vessel, boat. *Obs. rare.*

13.. *E.E. Allit. P.* B. 314 And þus of lenþe & of large þat lome [*sc.* the Ark] þou make. *Ibid.* 443.

3. a. A machine in which yarn or thread is woven into fabric by the crossing of threads called respectively the warp and weft. (In quots. 1535, 1566 app. used for: The beam of a loom.)

Often with prefixed word indicating (*a*) the kind of material produced, as †*linen, ribbon*, †*woollen*, etc. *loom*; (*b*) the method of operation, as *hand, power loom*; (*c*) some particular form of construction, as *circular, draw loom*; (*d*) the inventor or improver, as *Jacquard loom*: for which see those words.

1404 *Nottingham Rec.* 27 Aug. II. 22 Item, j lynyn lome, et j. warpyngstok et warpyngtree, et j. wheel, appretiata ad ijs. iiijd. *c*1440 *Promp. Parv.* 312/1 Loome of webbarys crafte (*K.P.* of webstare), *telarium.* 1444 *Rolls of Parlt.* V. 106/1 To serche all maner Worstedes, or to do serche, as well within the Lomes as oute of the Lomes. 1535 Coverdale *1 Sam.* xvii. 7 The shaft of his speare was like a weauers lome. 1566 *Eng. Ch. Furniture* (1866) 107 Johnne Craile who haith made a weavers lomb therof. 1632 Massinger & Field *Fatal Dowry* iv. i, His vestaments sit as if..art had wrought 'em on the same loome as nature fram'd his Lordship. 1675 C. Hatton in *H. Corr.* (1878) 120 Those weavers who had loomes without engines broke open ye houses of all those weavers who had loomes wth engines. 1717 Lady M. W. Montagu *Let. to Mr. Pope* 1 Apr., These wenches..pass the time at their looms under the shade of the trees. 1840 Thirlwall *Greece* VII. lv. 89 The looms of Ionia were kept in constant activity to supply purple robes for the Courtiers. 1843 Macaulay *Lays Anc. Rom., Horatius* lxx, And the goodwife's shuttle merrily Goes flashing through the loom. 1867 Smiles *Huguenots Eng.* vi. (1880) 96 The artizans set up their looms, and began to work at the manufacture of..cloth.

fig. 1603 Dekker *Wonderfull Yeare* A iv, Whatsoeuer they weaue in the motley-loome of their rustie pates. 1635-56 Cowley *Davideis* ii. 97 All like a comely Youth in Lifes' fresh Bloom; Rare Workmanship, and wrought by heav'nly Loom. 1645 Z. Boyd *Holy Songs* in *Zion's Flowers* (1855) App. 13/1 Sorrows are as threeds a crosse; in this our earthly loome. 1761 Gray *Fatal Sisters* ii, Glitt'ring lances are the loom, Where the dusky warp we strain, Weaving many a soldier's doom. 1787 *Minor* 54 The best wrought piece that ever issued from his intellectual loom. 1864 Longf. *Hawthorne* 7 The great elms o'erhead Dark shadows wove on their aërial looms.

†**b.** *transf.* Attributed to a spider or caterpillar; *occas.* used *poet.* for the web itself. *Obs.*

1590 Greene *Orl. Fur.* (1599) 58 Finest silke, Fetcht from the natiue loomes of labouring wormes. 1592 Nashe *P. Penilesse* (ed. 2) 8b, Spiders..that wont to set vp their loomes in euery windowe. 1606 Dekker *Sev. Sinnes* i. (Arb.) 15 O thou that on thy pillow (lyke a Spider in his loome) weauest mischeuous nets. 1647 H. More *Poems* 152 Like spider in her web, so do we sit Within this spirit, and if ought do shake This subtile loom we feel as it doth hit.

4. Put for: The art, business, or process of weaving.

1676 Worlidge *Cyder* (1691) 236 The dressing and preparing of hemp and flax from the stalk to the loom. 1697 Dryden *Æneid* vii. 1096 Unbred to Spinning, in the Loom unskill'd. 1784 Cowper *Task* i. 416 Who..Renounce the odours of the open field For the unscented fictions of the loom. 1829 Scott *Anne of G.* iii, Clothes..of much fines cloth, the manufacture of the German loom. 1846 McCulloch *Brit. Empire* (1854) II. 1 The intervention of merchants and dealers gives a continuous motion to the plough and the loom. 1859 Tennyson *Enid* 693 And one among his gentlewomen Display'd a splendid silk of foreign loom.

5. The shaft, i.e. the part between the blade and the handle of an oar; also, limited to the part of the oar between the rowlock and the hands in rowing; also, loosely, the handle.

1697 Dampier *Voy.* (1729) I. 54 Of the young Trees Privateers use to make Loom, or Handles for their Oars. 1769 Falconer *Dict. Marine* (1780) D d iv, That part of the oar..which is within-board, is termed the loom. 1829 Marryat *F. Mildmay* ii, The oar meeting no resistance, its loom or handle came back upon the bosom of..Sally. 1857 P. Colquhoun *Comp. Oarsman's Guide* 30 The oar or scull [consists] of handle, loom, shank, and blade. 1883 Clark Russell *Sailors' Lang., Loom*,..the part of an oar that is in a boat when the rest of it is out. 1893 F. M. Crawford *Childr. King* i. 5 Out go the sweeps,..and the men throw themselves forward over the long slender loom, as they stand.

6. *Electr.* **a.** Flexible tubing which is fitted over the ordinary insulation of an electric wire to provide additional protection.

1917 A. L. Cook *Interior Wiring* xiii. 235 For wires carrying more than 300 volts or for damp places, flexible conduit or armored cable must be used. The flexible tubing used is sometimes called 'circular loom'. 1939 H. P. Richter *Pract. Electr. Wiring* xi. 158 Where wires cross each other, slip loom over both wires.

b. A group of parallel insulated wires bound together into a bundle; (see also quot. 1949).

1949 *Gloss. Aeronaut. Terms* (*B.S.I.*) ii. 23 *Loom*, one or more cables pre-assembled for installation in an aircraft. 1962 *Which? Car Suppl.* Oct. 139/1 A wiring loom prevented the dipstick being removed or replaced easily. 1972 C. E. Jowett *Electronic Engin. Processes* iv. vi. 141 The forming of looms should preferably be by means of plastic ties, at an approximate pitch of 25 or 38 mm.

7. *attrib.* and *Comb.*: **a.** simple attrib., as ***loom-beam, -pattern, -post, -spoke, -room, -treadle, weight***; **b.** instrumental, as ***loom-made, -wrought*** adjs.; **c.** objective, as ***loom-maker, -worker***; **d.** locative, as ***loom-bred*** adj.; **e.** special comb., as †**loom-flitter**, a weaver; **loom-house**, a building or factory in which weaving is carried on; **loom-lace**, lace made in a loom; **loom-lord** *nonce-wd.*, the proprietor of weaving machinery; **loom-picture**, a picture woven in textile fabric; **loom-shed, -shop, -stance, -stead** = *loom-house*; **loom-state** *a.*, of woollen fabrics, in the state in which they came from the loom, untreated; †**loom-work**, weaving.

1606 Sylvester *Du Bartas* ii. iv. i. *David* 88 His Lance a *Loom-beam, or a Mast (as big) Which yet he shaketh as an Osier twig. 1812 W. Tennant *Anster F.* ii. xxxviii. 36 Dunfermline, too..Sends out her *loom-bred men. *a*1653 G. Daniel *Idyll* iv. 86 Children..can name Oligarchy, wth

more Ease Then a *Loome-flitter, can Church Hierarchies. **1819** *Western Rev.* I. 303 The other two young women slept in a *loom house adjoining. **1864** B. Brierley *Layrock of Langley-side* ix. 121 We'st be as quiet as a empty loomheawse. **1689** *Lond. Gaz.* No. 2493/4 A Wastcoat lac'd with broad Silver knotted *Loom-lace. **1870** Emerson *Soc. & Solit.* vi. 123 There has been a nightmare bred in England of indigestion and spleen among landlords and *loomlords. **1890** *Daily News* 13 Nov. 5/5 Finest *loom-made Spanish lace. **1851** in *Illustr. Lond. News* 5 Aug. (1854) 119 Occupations of the People, *loom-maker. **1835** Ure *Philos. Manuf.* 259 *Loom-pattern drawing. **1870** J. K. Hunter *Life Studies* xxii. 155 He had a wee box on the tap o' his loom .., and he had a slate that hung on his *loompost. **1845** *Knickerbocker* XXV. 448, I went out to look at the *loom-room. **1835** Ure *Philos. Manuf.* 351 A *loom-shed. *Ibid.* 263 The master of a *loom-shop. *c* **1817** Hogg *Tales & Sk.* V. 178 The destructive weaver seized a *loomspoke, and began a-beating me. **1876** S. R. Whitehead *Daft Davie* 6 The shop, containing generally several looms—a *loom-stance being often sublet by the householder—was on the other [side]. **1961** Blackshaw & Brightman *Dict. Dyeing* 101 **Loomstate*, woven fabrics in the condition in which they come from the loom. For practical purposes the term is synonymous with *Grey* (adjective). **1972** *Times* 9 May 20/6 Lists of cotton 'grey' (loomstate) goods. **1869** I. Burns *Life W. C. Burns* iv. (1870) 101 The weaving *loomsteads. **1831** Carlyle *Sart. Res.* (1858) 145 Religion .. weaving for herself new Vestures;—Teufelsdröckh himself being one of the *loom-treadles? **1881** *Archæologia* XLVI. 468 The *loom weights of chalk .. were used to weigh down the warp in the process of weaving. **1598** W. Phillips *Linschoten* (1864) 179 These clothes .. being verie costly wrought with *Loome-worke. *a* **1640** Day *Peregr. Schol.* (1881) 68 She taught Arachne her curiouse lomeworke. **1659** Torriano, *Telaruólo*, a weaver or *loom-worker of any kind of cloth. **1870** Morris *Earthly Par.* III. iv. 199 Its woven waters seemed to fall, Its trees, its beasts, its *loom-wrought folk, Now seemed indeed as though they woke.

loom (luːm), *sb.*[2] Also 7 lumb, 7–9 **lumme**, 9 **lumne**. [In Shetland repr. a. ON. *lóm-r*; in mod. literary use partly from Shetland dialect and partly a. mod.Sw. and Da. *lom.*] A name given in northern seas to species of the Guillemot and the Diver, esp. *Alca bruennichi* and *Colymbus septentrionalis* (Red-throated Diver). Cf. loon *sb.*[2]

[**1678** Ray *Willughby's Ornith.* 343 It is common among the Norwegians and Islanders, who in their own Country Language call it Lumme.] **1694** Narborough, etc. *Voy.* II. 80 The Lumb .. is quite black at the top, but underneath his belly even to the neck, he is snow-white. **1755** Amory *Mem.* (1769) I. 129 On the water, near the rocks, there were thousands of lummes and razor-bills. **1772–84** Cook *Voy.* (1790) V. 1761 The greater lumme, or diver, found in the northern parts of Europe. **1835** Sir J. Ross *Narr. 2nd Voy.* iv. 51 We saw a few looms and shear-waters. **1876** Davis *Polaris Exped.* xvi. 391 One lumne. **1886** A. W. Greely *Arctic Service* I. 49 On the face of these sea-ledges of Arveprins Island Bruennich's guillemots, or looms, gather in the breeding season .. by tens of thousands.

b. The flesh of these birds as an article of food.

1878 A. H. Markham *Gt. Frozen Sea* iii. 46 We revelled in 'loom soup', 'loom pie', 'roast loom' [etc.].

loom (luːm), *sb.*[3] [f. loom *v.*[2]]

1. A seaman's term for the indistinct and exaggerated appearance or outline of an object when it first comes into view, as the outline of land on the horizon, an object seen through the mist or darkness, etc.

1836 Marryat *Midsh. Easy* xxvi, We're very near the land, Captain Wilson; thick as it is, I think I can make out the loom of it. **1839** —— *Phant. Ship* xii, I did not see anything but the loom of her hull. **1862** H. Kingsley *Ravenshoe* li, A dark line, too faint for landsmen's eyes, far ahead, which changed into a loom of land. **1881** *Times* 30 May 6/4 Suddenly the loom of a rock was seen right ahead. **1889** Doyle *Micah Clarke* 244 Looking back there was nothing but a dim loom to show where we had left the great vessel.

fig. **1870** Lowell *Among my Bks.* Ser. i. (1873) 231 No mirage of tradition to give characters and events an imaginative loom.

2. *dial.* (See quot. and cf. loom *v.*[2] 1.)

1878 *Cumbld. Gloss.*, *Loom*, the slow and silent motion of the water of a deep pool.

loom (luːm), *a.* (or *sb. attrib.*) *Naut.* Also 6 **lum**, 7 **loome**, **loume**. [Perh. corruptly a. Da. *lugn*: see loun *a.*, *dial.*] Of a breeze or wind: Easy, gentle. *Obs.* exc. in **loom gale**, 'an easy gale of wind, in which a ship can carry her whole topsails atrip' (Smyth *Sailor's Word-bk.* 1867).

1587 J. Davis *Traverse Bk.* in *Hakluyt* (1810) III. 154 An island of ice was carried by the force of the current as faste as our barke could saile with lum wind, all sailes bearing. **1609** in Purchas *Pilgrims* (1625) IV. ix. v. 1733 By the feruent heat and loomes breezes, many of our men fell sicke of the Calenture. **1626** Capt. Smith *Accid. Yng. Sea-men* 17 A spoute, a loume gaile, an eddy wind. **1627** —— *Seaman's Gram.* x. 46 A faire Loome Gale is the best to saile in, because the Sea goeth not high, and we beare out all our sails. **1644** Digby *Nat. Bodies* xxviii. (1658) 304 We had run .. wth all the sails abroad we could make, and in a fair loom way. **1694** Motteux *Rabelais* v. x, We .. stood for the Offing with a fair loom Gale.

loom (luːm), *v.*[1] *rare.* [f. loom *sb.*[1]]

1. *trans.* To weave (a fabric).

1548 Hooper *Decl. Ten Command.* x. 161 He .. is as long in the morning to set his berd in an order, as a godlie crawftis man would be in loming of a peace of karsey. **1887** Moloney *Forestry W. Afr.* 145 The cloth loomed from the cotton thread of the country.

2. Weaving. *to loom the web*: to 'mount' the warp on the loom. Also *absol.*

1827 Taylor *Poems* 58 (E.D.D.) Thou's begun to loom thy wab, I'se thinking yer a wabster bred. **1851** L. D. B. Gordon in *Art Jrnl. Illust. Catal.* p. vii**/2 The 'lease' now being taken, and the cross bands or threads being introduced for the purpose of 'looming', or drawing in of the weaver's beam. **1883** A. Brown *Power-Loom* (ed. 4) 86 The process of looming the web.

Hence **'loomed** *ppl. a.*, woven.

1729 Savage *Wanderer* I. 277 He .. with loom'd Wool the native Robe supplies.

loom (luːm), *v.*[2] Also 7 **lome**, 7, 8 **loam**. [Skeat suggests that the original meaning may have been 'to come slowly (towards)', and compares EFris. *lômen*, Sw. dial. *loma* to move slowly, MHG. *luomen* to be weary, from *luomi* slack (related by ablaut to lame *a.*). Cf. also *loomy* (Sc. and north. dial.) misty, cloudy (E.D.D.).]

†**1.** Of a ship, also of the sea: To move slowly up and down. *Obs. rare.*

1605 Sir T. Smith *Voy. Russia* C 1 b, To behold one of the 3. gallant spectacles in the world, a Ship vnder sayle, loming (as they tearme it) indeede like a Lyon pawing with his forfeet. **1667** Colepresse in *Phil. Trans.* II. 481 Being in a Calm, that way which the Sea began to Loom or move, the next day the Wind was sure to blow from that point of the Compass towards which the Sea did Loom the day before. **1678** *Yng. Man's Call.* 93 This is to him as the due ballast to the ship, which makes the vessel indeed loome somewhat deeper, but keeps it from tossing too lightly upon the uncertain waters.

2. *intr.* To appear indistinctly; to come into view in an enlarged and indefinite form. Also with *up*. Often with adj. compl., as *to loom large*.

1591 Sylvester *Du Bartas* i. vii. 55 Here smokes a Castle, there a City fumes, And here a Ship upon the Ocean looms [orig. *Et là flote vne nef sur Neptune irrité*]. **1658** Phillips *s.v.*, A Ship Loomes a great or a small sail, a term used in Navigation, and signifieth as much as a Ship seems a great or a little Ship. **1769** Falconer *Dict. Marine* (1780) s.v. *Looming*, She looms large afore the wind. *Ibid.* ii, *Mirer*, to loom, or appear indistinctly. **1835** Sir J. Ross *Narr. 2nd Voy.* vi. 87 We saw the land looming. **1840** R. H. Dana *Bef. Mast* xxxvi. 136 A great ship loomed up out of the fog. **1846** Keble *Lyra Innoc.* (1873) 73 The hard stern outlines loom around Of hill by many a frost embrowned. **1853** Kane *Grinnell Exp.* xv. (1856) 110 Men are magnified to giants, and brigs 'loom up', as the sailors term it, into ships of the line. **1860** Tyndall *Glac.* i. xvi. 112 Still the summit loomed above us. **1865** Dickens *Mut. Fr.* i. xiv, A mist through which Mr. Inspector loomed vague and large. **1900** J. G. Frazer *Pausanias*, etc. 53 The haze through which the sun's disc looms red and lurid.

transf. (*jocular*).

1862 Mrs. H. Wood *Channings* v. 37 He understood it was quite a ladies' affair, and loomed in, dressed up to the nines.

b. *fig.* and of immaterial things.

1591 Sylvester *Ivry* 180 But, lo My Liege: O Courage! there he comes: What Ray of Honour round about him Looms? **1650** B. *Discolliminium* 6 Reasons .. which lowme so big in some mens eyes. **1809** W. Irving *Knickerb.* (1861) 69 Thus loom on my imagination those happier days of our city. **1827** Scott *Jrnl.* 7 July, Cash affairs loom well in the offing. **1850** Tennyson *In Mem.* xxiv, And is it that the haze of grief Makes former gladness loom so great? **1851** H. Mayo *Pop. Superstit.* 101 The facts which loom so large in the dawning light. **1875** Stubbs *Const. Hist.* III. xviii. 26 Political difficulties .. were looming at no great distance. **1878** Browning *La Saisiaz* 42 Shrunk to atom size, That which loomed immense to fancy low before my reason lies.

c. *causative.* To make to loom or appear unnaturally large. *rare.*

1817 *Chron.* in *Ann. Reg.* 473 It possesses the quality of looming, or magnifying objects, .. making the small billets of wood appear as formidable as trees.

loom, obs. form of lamb, loam.

loomb(e, obs. form of lamb, loom.

loomer ('luːmə(r)). [f. loom *v.*[1] 2 + -er[1].] (See quot. 1892.)

1881 *Daily News* 12 Sept. 3/6 The Loomers .. are still on strike. **1892** *Labour Commission* Gloss., *Loomers*, those who take the warp as it comes from the 'taper', and prepare it for the loom.

loomery ('luːmərɪ). [f. loom *sb.*[2] + -ery.] The place where looms or guillemots flock together for breeding.

1859 McClintock *Voy. Fox* 151 Our shooting parties have twice visited a loomery upon Cape Graham. **1882** L. Smith in *Standard* 22 Aug. 2/5 At Cape Stephen there was a large loomery, and at Cape Forbes there were a few looms.

looming ('luːmɪŋ), *vbl. sb.*[1] [f. loom *v.*[2] + -ing[1].] A coming indistinctly into view.

1627 Capt. Smith *Seaman's Gram.* xi. 53 The looming of a ship is her prospectiue, that is, as she doth shew great or little. **1634** *Relat. Ld. Baltimore's Plantat.* (1865) 7 At the first loaming of the ship vpon the river, wee found .. all the Countrey in Armes. **1684** *Bucaniers Amer.* (1698) ii. 84 This day we saw the looming of a very high land. **1790** Roy in *Phil. Trans.* LXXX. 266 Wherever the most faint looming of the land in a very clear day can be discerned. **1807** *Europ. Mag.* LII. 441/2 [Sailor *loq.*] 'Split me but I know the loaming of the land hereabouts.' **1829** *Nat. Philos. Optics* xviii. 56 (U.K.S.) The elevation of coasts, ships, and mountains above their usual level, when seen in the distant horizon, has been long known and described under the name of Looming. **1853** Kane *Grinnell Exp.* ix. (1856) 69 No evidences of refraction visible, except some slight loomings of the more distant bergs. **1861** C. J. Anderson *Okavango* vii. 87 A crashing and cracking .. announced the approach of elephants; in a few moments afterwards the looming of a dozen huge unwieldy figures in the distance told of their arrival.

fig. *a* **1839** Galt *Demon of Destiny* vii. (1840) 50 Tremendous loomings of eternal things.

looming ('luːmɪŋ), *vbl. sb.*[2] [f. loom *v.*[1] + -ing[1].] The action or process of 'mounting' the warp on the loom. In quot. *attrib.*

1851 L. D. B. Gordon in *Art Jrnl. Illust. Catal.* p. vii**/1 The warp was then taken from this [sizing-] machine to a machine for winding it on a roller-beam, after which it was taken to the looming-frame, and next to the loom.

looming ('luːmɪŋ), *ppl. a.* [f. loom *v.*[2] + -ing[2].] That looms, in the senses of the vb.

1855 M. Arnold *New Sirens* 182 In the midst of river-meadows Where the looming deer are laid. **1876** T. Hardy *Ethelberta* (1890) 217 As if divers social wants and looming penuriousness had never been within her experience. **1876** Ouida *Winter City* vi. 119 Her silvery marabouts glancing like hoar-frost in the shadows of the looming walls.

loon (lun), *sb.*[1] Chiefly *Sc.* and *north. dial.* Forms: 5 **lowen**, 5–6 **loone**, 6 **lound**, 6–9 **loun(e**, **lown(e**, 7– **loon**. [In 16th c. *lowen*, *lowne*, rhyming with *chenoun*, *downe*. Of obscure origin; the early forms do not favour the current hypothesis of connexion with early mod.Du. *loen* 'homo stupidus' (Plantijn and Kilian) which seems to be known only from dictionaries. The ON. *lúenn*, beaten, benumbed, weary, exhausted (pa. ppl. of *lýja* to beat, thrash) has been suggested as a possible etymon. The order of development of the senses is somewhat uncertain.]

1. A worthless person; a rogue, scamp (esp. in ***false loon***, ***to play the loon***); a sluggard, idler.

c **1450** *St. Cuthbert* (Surtees) 7957 þe clerkis þat were þare, leþir lowens [*rime* chenouns]. *c* **1470** Henryson *Fables* 2413 in *Anglia* IX. 475 Than lichtlie in the bukket lap the loun .. The tod come hailland vp, the wolf yeid doun. **1508** Kennedy *Flyting w. Dunbar* 485 Fra honest folk deuoide this lathly lown. **1514** Barclay *Eclog.* ii. (1570) B iij, That men shall call the malapart or dronke, Or an abbey lowne or limmer [*printed* limner] of a monke. **1548** Patten *Exped. Scot.* G. viii b, Cum here loundes, cum here tykes. **1571** *Satir. Poems Reform.* xxviii. 68 To loup on lassis, lait, and play the Lowne. **1590** Marlowe *Edw. II*, i. iv. 82 For shame, subscribe, and let the lowne depart. *a* **1600** Montgomerie *Misc. Poems* xxxiii. 36 Let not sik louns with teasings ȝou allure. **1604** Shaks. *Oth.* ii. iii. 95 He held them [breeches] all to deere, With that he cald the Tailor Lowne. **1605** —— *Macb.* v. iii. 11 The diuell damne thee blacke, thou cream-fac'd Loon. **1637** Rutherford *Lett.* (1862) I. 289 Looking on with their hands folded behind their back when louns are running with the spoil of Zion on their back. **1674–91** Ray *N.C. Words* 47 The Scots say, a fausse, i.e. false Loon. **1700** Dryden *Cock & Fox* 589 But the false loon who cou'd not work his will By open force employ'd his flatt'ring skill. **1762** Churchill *Prophecy Famine* Poems I. 114 When with a foreign loon she stole away. **1851** Longf. *Gold. Leg.* iv. *Refectory*, Out upon him, the lazy loon!

appositively. **16..** in Row *Hist. Kirk* (Wodrow Soc.) 392 Christ's minister may not preach Christ's trueth, if a loun minister neare by him have taught lies, except the Bishop give him leave so to doe.

b. Of a woman: A strumpet, concubine.

c **1560** A. Scott *Poems* (S.T.S.) iv. 87 The gayest grittest loun. *c* **1600** in Gordon Fraser *Wigtown* (1877) 392 Bad hir swithe [*printed* snyithe] pack hir furthe the harlot lowne. **1714** Ramsay *Elegy J. Cowper* vii, He ken'd the bawds and louns fou well. *a* **1800** in Scott *Minstr. Scot. Bord.* (1802) II. 68, I trow some may has plaid the lown. **1828** Scott *F.M. Perth* ii, Thou art too low to be their lawful love, and too high to be their unlawful loon.

2. A man of low birth or condition; in phrase ***lord and loon***. Now only *arch.*

1535 Stewart *Cron. Scot.* (1858) I. 45 Thus for ane loun than lichlyit is ane lord. **1548** Patten *Exped. Scot.* I viii b, The Lurdein was, in a maner, all one wyth the Lorde, and the Lounde wyth the Larde. **1608** Shaks. *Per.* iv. vi. 20 Wee should haue both Lorde and Lowne, if the peeuish baggadge would but giue way to customers. *a* **1650** *Capt. Carr* in Furnivall *Percy Folio* I. 81, 'I will not geve over my hous,' she saithe, 'Neither for lord nor lowne.' **1840** Barham *Ingol. Leg.*, 'Monstre' Balloon, The peer and the peasant, the lord and the loon.

3. A boor, lout, clown; an untaught, ill-bred person.

1619 *Bk. Demeanor* 12 in *Babees Bk.*, With manlike cheere, Not like a rustic lowne. **1784** *Unfortunate Sensibility* I. 133, I contrasted him with the ill-bred loons who had addressed my mother in my behalf. **1790** Burns *Ep. R. Graham* 11 [He] Came shaking hands wi' wabster lowns. **1798** Coleridge *Anc. Mar.* i. iii, Now get thee hence, thou grey-beard Loon. **1828** Scott *F.M. Perth* vii, Go to your Provost, you lorrel loons. **1872** Blackie *Lays Highl.* 49 A titled loon of high degree.

4. A fellow, man, 'chap'.

a **1550** *Christis Kirke Gr.* xii, The wyves .. fand lyfe in the loune. **1728** Starrat *To Ramsay* 15 in *R.'s Poems*, And learn'd the Latin lowns sic springs to play As gars the world gang dancing to their tune. **1901** *Scotsman* 28 Feb. 8/3 Wherever Moray loons may gather.

5. A boy, lad, youth.

c **1560** A. Scott *Poems* (S.T.S.) ii. 107 For thair wes nowdir lad not loun Mycht eit ane baikin loche For fowness. **1659–60** Pepys *Diary* 11 Jan., I .. went in to see Crowly who was now grown a very great loon and very tame. **1791** Boswell *Johnson* 17 Sept. an. 1773, The usual figure of a Sky-boy is a lown with bare legs and feet. **1821** Clare *Vill. Minstr.* II. 75 Urging each lown to leave his sports in fear. **1891** 'H. Haliburton' *Ochil Idylls* 127 As when ye roamed, a hardy loon, Upon the banks o' May. **1893** Crockett

Stickit Minister (1894) 202 The family, , consisted of three loons and a lassie.

loon (lu:n), *sb.*[2] [App. an alteration of LOOM *sb.*[2] q.v., perh. by assimilation to prec. sb.] A name for certain aquatic birds.

1. a. Any bird of the genus *Colymbus*, esp. the Great Northern Diver (*C. glacialis*), remarkable for its loud cry.

1634 W. WOOD *New Eng. Prosp.* (1865) 34 The Loone is an ill shap'd thing like a Cormorant. **1672** JOSSELYN *New Eng. Rarities* 12 The Loone is a Water Fowl, alike in shape to the Wobble. **1678** RAY *Willughby's Ornith.* 341 Greatest speckled-Diver, or Loon. **1759** B. STILLINGFL. tr. *Biberg's Econ. Nature* Misc. Tracts (1762) 90 The diver or loon.. lays also two eggs. **1766** PENNANT *Zool.* (1768) II. 414 On the Thames they [the grey speckled divers] are called Sprat loons, for they attend that fish during its continuance in the river. **1831** *A. Wilson & Bonaparte's Amer. Ornith.* III. 255 *Colymbus glacialis*.. Great Northern Diver, or Loon. **1839** MARRYAT *Diary Amer.* Ser. I. I. 187 Listening to the whistling of the solitary loon. **1860** *All Year Round* No. 75. 586 The loons hallooed and laughed at our approach. **1880** FITZGIBBON *Trip to Manitoba* ix. 101 The weird cry of the loon diving.

b. In phrases with *loon's* (see quots.). Also freq. ***as crazy as a loon*** (in reference to its actions in escaping from danger and its wild cry) and varr.; so, ***as drunk as a loon***; ***to hunt the loon*** (see quot. 1880).

1830 *Kentucky Intelligencer* (Flemingsburg) 29 May 4 Patton informed me that McLaughlin had just gone from Elizabethville, and was 'drunk as a loon'. **1834** C. A. DAVIS *Lett. J. Downing* 42, I saw thru' it in a minute, and made it all as strait as a loon's leg. **1834** S. SMITH *Sel. Lett. J. Downing* 110 He begun to sing out like a loon for us to come and take him. **1840** C. F. HOFFMAN *Greyslaer* I. i. xi. 129 After tramposing for twenty-four hours on a stretch, with not even a loon's nap at the end of it. **1845** C. M. KIRKLAND *Western Clearings* 83 Why, you're both as crazy as loons! **1865** 'MARK TWAIN' in Harte & 'Twain' *Sk. Sixties* (1926) 163 Our reserve.. came filing down the street as drunk as loons. **1880** *Harper's Mag.* Dec. 31 Miss Lois had been hunting the loon with a hand-net—a Northern way of phrasing the wearing of the willow. **1931** W. FAULKNER *Sanctuary* vi. 57 You're as crazy as a loon. **1934** J. T. FARRELL *Young Manhood* xxiv. 398 Jesus, I'm drunk as a loon. I'm drunk, Kelly. Drunk. **1951** *Publ. Amer. Dial. Soc.* xv. 66 Crazy as a loon.

c. *transf.* A crazy person; a simpleton.

Perhaps influenced by LOONY *a.* and *sb.*

1885 'C. E. CRADDOCK' *Prophet Gt. Smoky Mts.* xii. 230 But ye air a smart man ter that loon, fur.. he dunno he air a loon. **1918** C. SANDBURG *Cornhuskers* 99, I am a loon about the sea. **1945** *Coast to Coast 1944* 72 There we were, bottled up in camp because the loon in charge couldn't get the order signed for the trucks to leave.

2. a. The Great Crested Grebe (*Podiceps cristatus*). **b.** The Little Grebe or Dabchick (*P. fluviatilis* or *minor*).

1678 RAY *Willughby's Ornith.* 339 The greater Loon or Arsfoot. *Ibid.* 340 The Didapper, or Dipper, or Dobchick, or small Doucker, Loon, or Arsfoot. **1766** PENNANT *Zool.* (1768) II. 395, 398. **1828** FLEMING *Hist. Brit. Anim.* 131 *P[odiceps] cristatus*,.. Greater Loon. *Ibid.* 132 *P. minor*,.. Small Loon. **1880** *Times* 28 Sept. 4/4 Loon is a name for a small bird of the grebe tribe, and much better known as the dabchick.

3. An early type of guided missile developed by the U.S. Navy.

1947 *Newsweek* 17 Mar. 64/2 The Navy also displayed a 'bat bomb' and a 'loon', two hitherto secret radio-controlled missiles. **1951** COGGINS & PRATT *Rockets, Jets, Guided Missiles & Space Ships* iii. [28/1] Later the [U.S.] Navy built its own improved version of the V-1, called the 'Loon'. It can be launched from a submarine far at sea in a surprise attack against a harbor or convoy. **1952** *Jane's Fighting Ships 1952–53* 410/1 'Loon' missile is contained in a watertight steel hangar and takes off from a ramp fixed to the submarine's deck.

4. *attrib.*, as *loon-skin*.

1807 P. GASS *Jrnl.* 166 Some have robes made of muskrat skins.. and I saw some of loon-skins.

Hence **'looning** *nonce-wd.*, the cry of the loon.

1857 THOREAU *Maine W.* (1894) 307 This of the loon—I do not mean its laugh, but its looning,—is a long-drawn call, as it were, sometimes singularly human to my ear.

loon (lu:n), *sb.*[3] *dial.* (Cheshire). Also 7 **lound, loone**, 9 (? *erron.*) **loom.** [? Corruption of *lond* LAND *sb.*[1]] = LAND *sb.*[1] 7.

1611 *Will* (Cheshire) in *31st Rep. Comm. Inq. Charities* (1837) 361 Two butts of ground containing one lound. **1688** R. HOLME *Armoury* III. 136/2 Butt is half the quantity of a Loon. *Ibid.* 137/1 [see LAND *sb.*[1] 7]. **1844** PALIN in *Jrnl. R. Agric. Soc.* V. I. 62 A large portion of the flat clay-land has been formed, ages ago, into butts or loons, varying in width from 15 to 50 feet. **1855** MORTON *Cycl. Agric.* II. 724/2 *Looms*, (Chesh.), are wide lands, wider than *butts*.

loon (lu:n), *sb.*[4] *colloq.* [f. the vb.] *pl.* A style of close-fitting casual trousers widely flared from the knees to the ankles. Also (in *sing.*) *attrib.*, as ***loon pants, trousers***.

1971 *Melody Maker* 13 Nov. 50 (Advt.), New velvet and cord loon pants with 28" flare... New cotton drill loons and military trousers. **1972** *Guardian* 15 Aug. 17/3 As dead as tucked up loon pants. **1974** 'D. CRAIG' *Whose Little Girl are You?* v. 94 They had bloody long-hairs in the police now and kids in loon trousers. **1974** D. WINSOR *Death Convention* xii. 98, I wriggled into a pair of brown velvet loons, dropped a cream lace tunic over them.

loon (lu:n), *v.* [Etym. unknown.] *intr.* Esp. of young people: to spend one's leisure time in a pleasurable way, e.g. by dancing to popular music; to lie *about* or wander *about*. So **'looner**, one who loons; **'looning** *vbl. sb.* Cf. LOON *sb.*[4]

1966 *Melody Maker* 30 July 8/6 The younger members of the MM staff spend a lot of time doing something called 'looning'. To judge by their general condition the next morning I gather this is what used to be known as 'raving'. **1969** *It* 4–17 July 12/2 It's sort of music essentially to loon about to. **1969** *Daily Tel.* 14 July 11 (*heading*) Long enough to loon in. *Ibid.*, A fashion designer.. has just completed his first collection of clothes aimed purely for after work. He calls them 'looning' clothes. **1969** *Melody Maker* 13 Sept. 12/4 In the company of looners like Eric Burdon and Brian Auger, Zoot was the king looner. Zoot became a much beloved symbol of good fun and good time music. **1971** *It* 2–16 June 21/3 Children and the younger adults alike looning about in wonderful costumes.

loon(e, obs. form of LOAN.

†**'loonery.** *Obs.* In 6– **lounrie, -y**, 7 **lownry.** [f. LOON *sb.*[1] + -ERY.] The disposition and habits of a loon or rascal; lechery, villany.

1508 DUNBAR *Flyting w. Kennedie* 100 Thow art bot Gluncoch with thy giltin hippis, That for thy lounry mony a leisch hes fyld. **1567** *Satir. Poems Reform.* viii. 37 Euir þe mair þow wald be trowit, The les þi lounrie Is allowit. **1606** ROLLOCK *On 2 Thess.* 114 In thy lownry thou cannot haue an eye to God. **1686** G. STUART *Joco-ser. Disc.* 47 Upon trial found a rogue For all his lownry was discovered.

loong, obs. form of LUNG.

loongee, loonghie, var. forms of LUNGI.

†**loon-slatt**, *slang. Obs. rare*⁻⁰. [Perh. f. LOON *sb.*[1] + SLATT (*slang*) half-crown.] A name for the Scottish merk, the value of which in the 17th c. was 13½*d*, the proverbial amount of the hangman's fee. (Cf. quot. 1785 s.v. HANGMAN.)

a **1700** B. E. *Dict. Cant. Crew, Loon-slatt*, a Thirteen Pence half Penny.

loony ('lu:nɪ), *a.* and *sb. colloq.* Also **looney, luny.** [Shortened form of LUNATIC + -Y.]

A. *adj.* **1.** Lunatic, crazed, daft, dazed, demented, foolish, silly.

1872 B. HARTE *Heiress of Red Dog* (1879) 93 You're that looney sort of chap that lives over yonder, ain't ye? **1883** E. C. MANN *Psychol. Med.* 424 (Cent.) His fits were nocturnal, and he had frequent 'luny spells' as he called them. **1900** F. W. BULLEN *With Christ at Sea* xiii. 253, I sh'd a ben fair loony long ago.

2. *Pol.* Of (the members of) a political faction or tendency: unacceptably radical; extremist, fanatical. Esp. as *loony left* and derivs. Cf. HARD *a.* 12 d and *lunatic fringe* s.v. LUNATIC *sb.* 1 c.

1977 *Economist* 2 Apr. (Survey) 22/1 The views of the loony left are well known in the democratic world. **1983** *N.Y. Times* 29 July A4/6 A military analyst here attributed the change in policy to 'a loony, fringe group'. **1985** *N.Y. Times Mag.* 24 Feb. 28/5 'Red Dawn', described widely as of the loony-right and paranoid, was not a very good movie. **1985** *Economist* 16 Nov. 41/3 It could be a picture of complacency, corruption, cronyism, loony-leftism or all four. **1987** *City Limits* 19 Feb. 6 The press has branded Deirdre Wood a 'loony lefty'.

B. *sb.* **1.** A lunatic.

1884 *St. James's Gaz.* 29 Mar. 6/2 An excellent system whereby one loony was brought to bear upon another. **1897** KIPLING *Captains Courageous* 27 Dad sez loonies can't shake out a straight yarn.

2. loony bin [BIN *sb.* 7], a facetious term for a mental hospital; also *fig.* and *ellipt.*; **loony-doctor** *slang*, a doctor who treats mental illnesses, a psychiatrist.

1919 WODEHOUSE *My Man Jeeves* 195 If you're absolutely off your rocker, but don't find it convenient to be scooped into a luny-bin, you simply explain.. it was just your Artistic Temperament. **1921** —— *Indiscretions of Archie* xxv. 303 Nine out of ten of them had views on Art which would have admitted them to any looney-bin, and no questions asked. **1938** J. PHELAN *Lifer* xix. 201 Left him behind us there, we did, stone balmy. Finished in a loony. **1942** N. STREATFEILD *I ordered Table for Six* 216 Mrs. Framley must have thought him fit for a looney bin. **1959** *New Statesman* 28 Mar. 434/3 In short, I do not want men to live for ever in a sort of global loony-bin. **1962** J. SYMONDS *Bezill* 68 Yes, Aunt Marion. She's locked up, you know, in the looney bin. **1974** *Times* 9 Feb. 10/4 (*heading*) In the looney bin. **1925** WODEHOUSE *Carry on, Jeeves!* vi. 139 Old Sir Roderick, who's a loony-doctor and nothing but a loony-doctor, however much you may call him a nerve-specialist. **1936** BENTLEY & ALLEN *Trent's Own Case* iv. 39 'Once, I remember, he said that the worst of these loony-doctors——.' 'Did he say "loony-doctors"?' **1960** WODEHOUSE *Jeeves in Offing* ii. 18 She's browsing with Sir Roderick Glossop, the loony-doctor.

loop (lup), *sb.*[1] Forms: 5–6 **loupe**, 6 **loppe**, *Sc.* **lowpe**, 7 **lope, loupe**, 7– **loop.** [Of obscure etymology.

Prof. Skeat (*Concise Etym. Dict.*) suggests that the word may be a. ON. *hlǫup, hlaup* LEAP *sb.*, comparing the Sw. *löp-knut*, Da. *løb-knude, løb-øie*, running-knot. These compounds, however, seem to be merely modern Germanisms; the relevant sense of the verb, Sw. *löpa*, Da. *løbe*, being app. foreign to early Scandinavian, and due to the influence of the corresponding G. *laufen* (LG. *lōpen*). Further, the mod.Sc. form of ON. *hlǫup* would be regularly *loup*, pronounced (lʌup), whereas the word *loop* is in Sc. pronounced (lup); the spelling *lowpe* in G. Douglas is ambiguous, but prob. represents (lup); cf. *drowpe* = droop. The Irish and Gael. *lub*, formerly suggested by Prof. Skeat, presents at least a noteworthy resemblance of sound and meaning to the Eng. word.]

1. a. The doubling or return into itself of a portion of a string, cord, thong, or the like, so as to leave an aperture between the parts; the portion so doubled, commonly fastened at the ends. Often used as an ornament for dress (cf. *loop-lace*). † ***crochets and loops***: hooks and eyes. † ***to prick in the loop***: to play FAST AND LOOSE: cf. ***pricking in the garter*** (GARTER *sb.* 7).

c **1400** *Destr. Troy* 2806 Paris with pyne, & his pure brother,.. Lauset loupis fro the le; lachyn in Ancres. *c* **1450** *Bk. Curtasye* 446 in *Babees Bk.*, With crochettis and loupys sett on lyour. **1513** DOUGLAS *Æneis* v. v. 66 The todir part [of a snake cut in two] lamyt, clynschis and makis hir byde, In lowpis thrawin and lynkis of hir hyde. **1530** PALSGR. 241/1 Loupe to holde a button, *fermeau*. **1551** MATHEW *Bible, Exod.* xxvi. 4 Then shalt thou make loupes of Iacyncte coloure, alonge by the edge of yᵉ one curtayne. **1657–8** in Swayne *Churchw. Acc. Sarum* (1896) 332 A Crooke and Loope to put yᵉ Sword in, 2*s.* 6*d.* **1669** STURMY *Mariner's Mag.* v. xii. 49 There is a Brass Pin in the Center at C for to hang the Plummet and String, with the Lope upon. **1690** EVELYN *Ladies Dressing-R., Fops Dict.* 21 *Sultane*, a gown trimm'd with Buttons and Loops. **1718** LADY M. W. MONTAGU *Let. to C'tess Mar* 10 Mar., Those gold loops so common on birthday coats. **1762–71** H. WALPOLE *Vertue's Anecd. Paint.* (1786) V. 118 A woman.. in.. a cloak with loops hanging behind. **1771–2** *Ess. fr. Batchelor* (1773) II. 66 This is the identical Jack, who played prick in the loop with so many Lord Lieutenants, and cheated them all. **1782** COWPER *Gilpin* 103 The cloak did fly.. Till, loop and button failing both, At last it flew away. **1802** C. JAMES *Milit. Dict., Loop*, is.. used to signify an ornamental part of a regimental hat. **1815** ELPHINSTONE *Acc. Caubul* (1842) I. 351 There are rows of buttons and loops down the breast of the tunic. **1879** BUTCHER & LANG *Odyss.* 73 And fixed the oars in leathern loops all orderly. **1890** JULIA P. BALLARD *Moths & Butterflies* 120 A loop-and-link as if he had begun to make a chain. **1891** W. C. SYDNEY *Eng. 18th Cent.* II. 110 So late as 1799.. footmen wore their hair tied up behind in a thick loop called a hoop.

b. *spec.* in *Needlework* (see quots.).

1880 *Plain Hints Needlework* 93 To speak correctly, we believe it can be proved that we should speak of a *mesh* in netting, a *loop* in knitting. **1882** CAULFEILD & SAWARD *Dict. Needlework, Loop*, a term used instead of stitch in Crochet, Knitting, Netting, and Tatting. In Lace-making the word Loop is sometimes employed instead of Picot.

c. *Mining.* (See quot. 1891.)

1883 GRESLEY *Gloss. Coal Mining*, It [the D Link] is a loop in which one man is lowered and raised in an engine-pit. **1891** *Labour Commission* Gloss., *Loops*, slings attached to the end of the ropes which formerly drew the corves to the pit-mouth of a coal mine. **1897** *Westm. Gaz.* 13 May 7/1 There were about 200 men in the pit, who had to be brought out by another shaft in loops.

d. = LOOPFUL.

1901 *Brit. Med. Jrnl.* No. 2089 Epit. Med. Lit. 8 A loop of this second dilution is placed.. on each cover glass.

e. *U.S.* The looped portion of a lasso. **f.** = NOOSE *sb.* 1.

1907 S. E. WHITE *Arizona Nights* I. v. 93 Some few whirled the loop, but most cast it with a quick flip. **1933**, etc. [see HONDA]. **1944** *Living off Land* vii. 138 Knots.. nooses (or loops). **1970** G. R. STEWART *Amer. Place-Names* 264/1 *Loop* Texas: so called because the postmaster-to-be, at the time of suggesting a name, was playing with the loop of his lasso.

2. A ring or curved piece of metal, etc. employed in various ways, e.g. for the insertion of a bolt, ramrod, or rope, as a handle for lifting, etc.; *dial.* a door-hinge.

1674–91 RAY *N.C. Words* 44 A Loop; An Hinge of a Door. **1715** DESAGULIERS *Fires Impr.* 131 A Cover.. with a Loop to move it easily. **1735** DYCHE & PARDON *Dict., Loop*,.. in a Gun, tis a small Hole in the Barrel, to fasten it to the Stock or Carriage by. **1802** C. JAMES *Milit. Dict., Loop*, in a ship-carriage, made of iron,.. through which the ropes or tackle pass, whereby the guns are moved. **1824** P. HAWKER *Instr. Yng. Sportsm.* (ed. 3) 54 Parts of a Gun... *Loops*, eyes to barrel which receive the bolts that fasten it into the stock. **1847** *Infantry Man.* (1854) 33 Put it [the ramrod] into the loops. **1867** SMYTH *Sailor's Word-bk., Loops of a Gun-carriage*, the iron eye-bolts to which the tackles are hooked. **1875** KNIGHT *Dict. Mech., Loop*, a sleeve or collar, as that upon the middle of a neck-yoke. **1878** JEWITT *Ceramic Art* I. 15 It has on its central band four projecting handles or loops, which are pierced. Nine other looped examples, from Cornwall. **1881** GREENER *Gun* 239 The ribs are then soft-soldered on, and the loop fitted in.

3. Something having the shape of a loop, e.g. a line traced on paper, a part of a written character (as the upper part of the usual script *b*, *h*, *l*), a part of the apparent path of a planet, a bend of a river.

1668 WILKINS *Real Char.* IV. i. 388 Adverbs.. may be expressed by a Loop in the same place. **1814** SCOTT *Lines to Dk. Buccleuch* 13 Aug. in *Lockhart* xxxiii, For this mighty shoal of leviathans lay On our lee-beam a mile, in the loop of the bay. **1818** —— *Rob Roy* i, I wish.. you would write a more distinct current hand.. and open the loops of your l's. **1851** MAYNE REID *Scalp Hunt.* xviii. 127 Our path trended away from the river, crossing its numerous 'loops'. **1865** DICKENS *Mut. Fr.* III. x, He set out.. described a loop, turned, and went back again. **1880** C. & F. DARWIN *Movem. Pl.* 2 The apex often travels in a zig-zag line, or makes small subordinate loops or triangles. **1900** R. C. THOMPSON *Rep. Magicians Nineveh* II. p. lxxxix, Jupiter.. appears to have formed a 'loop' near Regulus. **1900** *Blackw. Mag.* July 58/1 James Bay, the Southern loop of Hudson's Bay.

4. *spec.* in scientific and technical applications.

a. *Anat.* A looped vessel or fibre. ***loop of Henle***, the looped part of a uriniferous tubule.

1846 TOYNBEE in *Medico-Chirurg. Trans.* XXIX. 309 Loops, convolutions, and dilatations, freely intercommunicating, characterize the tubuli of the surface.

1858 H. Gray *Anat.* 442 Occasionally the elementary [nerve-] fibres are disposed in terminal loops or plexuses. **1885** Landois & Stirling *Human Physiol.* II. 518 The spiral tubule.. passes into the descending portion of Henle's loop.

b. *Zool.* In brachiopods, the folding of the brachial appendages.

1851–6 Woodward *Mollusca* 211 In *Terebratula* and *Thecidium* it [the internal skeleton] takes the form of a loop, which supports the brachial membrane, but does not strictly follow the course of the arms. **1860** Reeve *Elem. Conchol.* II. 182 In *Terebratula dilatata*.. the loops are long. **1881** P. M. Duncan in *Academy* 19 Mar. 210 The comparative sizes are also given, and the internal skeleton or loop also.

c. *Math.* (See quot. 1877.)

1858 J. Booth in *Proc. Roy. Soc.* IX. 261 The difference between the lengths of the loop and the infinite branch is equal to an arc of the parabola together with a right line. **1877** W. K. Clifford in *Math. Papers* (1882) 243 A path going along any line from O to very near A, then round A in a very small circle, and then back to O along the same line, will be called a loop. **1891** Wolstenholme *Math. Probl.* 322 Also prove that the area of the loop is....

d. *Acoustics.* The portion of a vibrating string, column of air, etc., between two nodes.

1878 Ld. Rayleigh *Theory of Sound* §255 II. 46 Midway between each pair of consecutive nodes there is a loop, or place of no pressure variation. *Ibid.*, The loops are the places of maximum velocity, and the nodes those of maximum pressure variation. **1879** W. H. Stone *Sound* i. 9 The breaking-up of the string into a number of nodes with intervening loops or ventral segments.

e. *Railways* and *Telegraphy.* (i) A line of rails or a telegraph wire diverging from, and afterwards returning to, the main line or circuit. Hence in *Electr.*, any complete circuit or path for a current.

1863 Culley *Handbk. Telegr.* 122 Supposing the resistance of the loop to be 100 units. **1873** *Act 36 & 37 Vict.* c. 56 Sched. I. Note *a & b*, On single lines of Railway, each connection with a portion of double line at loops, terminal stations, or junctions to be stated. **1878** F. S. Williams *Midl. Railw.* 132 For some years the Midland.. used the loop via Worcester only for the local traffic. **1889** J. K. Jerome *Three Men in Boat* v, They.. thought the train was the Southampton express, or else the Windsor loop. **1909** Webster, *Loop*, a complete electric circuit. **1922** Glazebrook *Dict. Appl. Physics* II. 659/1 If a stout wire be temporarily used to connect the two banks of plates inside, the condenser may be measured as a loop at telephonic frequencies. **1967** *Electronics* 6 Mar. 132/1 The feedback loop is formed by connecting the amplifier's inverting input (pin 2) to potentiometer. **1970** J. Earl *Tuners & Amplifiers* iv. 95 Small mains currents can flow in the loops formed by the several earths, and these can induce hum into the system.

(ii) *Electr.* A point on an aerial at which the current or the voltage is a maximum.

1922 Glazebrook *Dict. Appl. Physics* II. 1034/1 A standing wave forms on the simple antenna just as in an organ-pipe with stopped end, there being a node of current at the upper end and a loop at the earthed connection. **1928** [see feeder 10 b]. **1968** *Radio Communication Handbk.* (ed. 4) xiii. 3/1 At positions of current loops, the current-to-voltage ratio is high and the wire will behave as a low impedance circuit.

f. In a 'centrifugal railway' or the like: That portion of the path which forms a circuit, along the upper portion of which the passenger travels head downwards. Also, a similar path described by an aeroplane. (Cf. loop *v.*[1] 6.) Phr. ***to knock for a loop*** [knock *v.* 6 e] and varr.

1900 *Scientif. American* 22 Sept. 186/1 [The car] plunges down the incline of 75 feet,.. whirls round the loop, and reaches the station after running up a heavy grade. **1913** *Aeroplane* 25 Sept. 350/2 M. Pégoud succeeded in looping the loop completely. **1923** *Cosmopolitan* Apr. 84/1 It took Hurricane Sherlock just two boisterous rounds to smite 12-Punch O'Bernstein 'for a loop', as Hurricane put it. **1936** J. G. Brandon *Pawnshop Murder* v. 46 Something had happened which had knocked even the imperturbable Wibley for the loop. **1968** J. Wainwright *Web of Silence* 126 Have you lost your marbles, Pervert?.. Have you gone for a complete loop? **1969** E. Ambler *Intercom Conspiracy* (1970) vi. 110, I was really confused. That memorandum threw me for a loop. **1971** *Country Life* 18 Feb. 374/2 It was over Tewkesbury that I pointed my nose at the Mill and did my first loop. **1973** D. Ramsay *Deadly Discretion* 153 That little charade of hers had knocked him for a loop.

g. *Skating.* A curve crossing itself, or any of several elaborations upon this.

1869 Vandervell & Witham *Syst. Figure-Skating* x. 187 The Large Loop. This being done entirely on one edge throughout, requires some medium degree of speed. **1901** *Encycl. Sport* IV. 370/1 Loops are of three kinds—the ordinary variety, the turn loop, and the bracket loop. **1935** *Encycl. Sports* 560/1 'Loop' is effected by over-balancing the body and recovering equilibrium by a quick turn of the foot. **1962** T. D. Richardson *Art of Figure Skating* vii. 60 Loops are not skated in the normal positions.. and what is more, they require an entirely different timing. **1973** *Times* 7 Feb. 15/8 Hoffmann was fourth in the rocker but skated the best loops.

h. A configuration in finger-prints.

1880 H. Faulds in *Nature* 28 Oct. 605/1 The right ring-finger.. has an oval whorl, but the corresponding left finger shows an open loop. **1894** 'Mark Twain' in *Century Mag.* June 235 The bewildering maze of whorls or curves or loops which constituted the 'pattern' of a 'record' stand out bold and black. **1938** G. W. Wilton *Fingerprints* xvi. 78 Galton had experimented only with thumbprints, grouping his lineations into three classes of arches, loops and whorls. **1970** P. Laurie *Scotland Yard* ix. 193 There are two basic finger-print patterns: loops, where the lines turn through two right angles, and triradii.

i. A slack length of film, flexible strip, or the like left between two mechanisms to allow for a difference between the supply and take-up motions, esp. (in cinematographic equipment) one between a sprocket that turns continuously and one that turns intermittently.

1912 F. A. Talbot *Moving Pict.* vii. 70 A slight loop is made at either end of the gate. **1939** Spencer & Waley *Cinema To-Day* ii. 25 A flickering motion of these loops absorbs the difference between the steady feed of the sprocket wheels and the intermittent feed of the claw. **1962** G. A. T. Burdett *Automatic Control Handbk.* ix. 54 When metal strip is being wound or reeled it is usual to form loops in the feed line to allow for flexibility and avoid undue tension.

j. = *loop aerial* (see 6).

1922 Glazebrook *Dict. Appl. Physics* II. 1058/1 Before the advent of high amplification, it was impracticable to use single loops of manageable dimensions. **1936** *Jrnl. R. Aeronaut. Soc.* XL. 175 To obtain a full direction finding service, it is usual to instal an external circular loop which can be rotated and orientated by the operator when taking a bearing. **1966** *McGraw-Hill Encycl. Sci. & Technol.* I. 445/2 Use of small loops concealed within the set is a standard practice for broadcast receivers in areas where signal strength is high.

k. A length of film or magnetic tape whose ends have been joined to form an endless strip, so that continuous repetition of the recording is made possible (e.g. in rehearsing the synchronization required for dubbing a foreign-language sound track).

1931 K. F. Morgan in L. Cowan *Recording Sound for Motion Pict.* x. 151 The machine is provided with a film elevator attachment for running a continuous loop of sound track. This attachment is particularly useful for the dubbing of continuous background sounds. **1951** R. Spottiswoode *Film & its Techniques* xii. 355 It is most important [in dubbing].. not to upset the recording order of an emotional scene which has had to be broken down into several loops. **1959** Halas & Manvell *Technique Film Animation* xix. 216 Each pencil-test is shot on negative and projected in loops so that it can be viewed over and over again. **1962** A. Nisbett *Technique Sound Studio* 258 A tape loop may be used (*a*) to provide a repeated sound structure or rhythm (in radiophonics), (*b*) for an 'atmosphere' track where this is regular in quality, (*c*) in tape delay techniques. **1968** *Punch* 31 Jan. 153 At the Rank Organisation's Pinewood Studios they tell how Sophia Loren dubbed sixty-four loops in an hour and a half, against an average of ten or twelve loops an hour.

l. A sequence of control operations or activities in which each depends on the result of the previous one; *esp.* (more fully *closed loop*), one in which there is feedback, the result of a later operation being made to affect one earlier in the sequence, usu. so as to maintain the output at a desired level.

1945 L. A. MacColl *Fund. Theory Servomechanisms* viii. 70 This procedure of adding feedback loops to internal parts of a servomechanism is employed frequently when it is necessary to take special steps to insure that the performances of those parts shall be accurate and reliable. **1948** Brown & Campbell *Princ. Servomechanisms* vii. 227 Figure.. shows internal loop within a main closed loop. **1954** M. H. Lajoy *Industr. Automatic Controls* i. 9 The automatic washing machine which operates on a time basis and is not dependent upon whether or not the clothes are clean is an open loop system. **1962** F. I. Ordway et al. *Basic Astronautics* ix. 366 There are two basic control systems: the open-loop system and the closed-loop system. The open-loop system is familiar to us all. Examples of this are.. a light switch, or the horn button on an automobile... In the closed-loop system a portion of the output is sensed and fed back to the input. The input is then altered to achieve a co-ordinated response at the output... A good example is the modern air conditioning system in which room air is fed back to the thermostat control. **1971** J. Z. Young *Introd. Study Man* vii. 107 Certain cells in the hypothalamus.. are very sensitive to slight rises in temperature above the normal (37°C). They then discharge nerve impulses that set in action the mechanisms that cool the body, such as sweating. This cools the blood and switches off the hypothalamus. In order to study such closed-loop feedback systems engineers use the device of 'opening' the loop. This has been done.. by putting heating electrodes in the hypothalamus and arranging that they keep it at a constant temperature a few tenths of a degree above normal in spite of the cooling blood.

m. *Computers.* A sequence of instructions which is executed repeatedly (usu. with an operand that changes in each cycle) until some previously specified criterion is satisfied.

1947 Goldstine & von Neumann in J. von Neumann *Coll. Works* (1963) V. 86 When a simple induction takes place, C travels during each step of the induction over a certain path, at the end of which it returns to its beginning. Hence this path may be visualized as a loop. We will call it an induction loop or a simple induction loop. **1954** *First Gloss. Programming Terminol.* (Assoc. Computing Machinery) 12 *Loop*, the repetition of a group of instructions in a routine. **1955** R. K. Richards *Arithmetic Operations in Digital Computers* xii. 359 Any one program may contain many loops which may interlock one another in a complex manner. **1964** C. Dent *Quantity Surveying by Computer* iii. 28 It will be seen that *s* in instruction 4 is reduced by unity at every cycle of the loop, by reason of instruction 7, and that eventually.. the conditional jump instruction will decide that the number stored by instruction 5 is negative. Control then proceeds with the next sequence according to instruction 9. **1969** P. B. Jordain *Condensed Computer Encycl.* 294 The terminating condition test is usually the last instruction of the loop, but it may be anywhere. **1970** O. Dopping *Computers & Data Processing* xiv. 215 Loops.. are basic to the economy of automatic data processing. It costs a few dollars to have an instruction written, but the computer executes it at a price which may be only a fraction of a cent below what the same operation would cost if it were executed by a human being. The only way of amortizing programming is to arrange for most instructions to be repeated a great number of times.

n. *Nuclear Engin.* A system of pipes passing through or associated with a reactor that forms a closed circuit (under operating conditions).

1957 *New Scientist* 23 May 33/1 The chemical behaviour of such systems has to be investigated in a reactor by passing a pipe containing a portion of the system under investigation through or close to the reactor core. Such a pipe, with the necessary measuring equipment, is called a test loop. **1958** H. Etherington *Nucl. Engin. Handbk.* v. 142 To satisfy the demand for testing operation under conditions of high temperature and pressure in those reactors using a primary water loop, high-pressure loops have been developed. Questions of fuel stability, heat transfer, water chemistry, radiation-accelerated corrosion, fission-product leakage, and fuel stability under desired operating conditions may be answered in high-pressure water loops. **1974** *Times* 21 Jan. 15/2 The CEGB's first two plants.. would be the 52nd and 53rd of their type—the Westinghouse four-loop design, in which a single reactor is linked to four steam-generating boilers. **1974** *Encycl. Brit. Macropædia* XII. 897/1 Pressurized water both cools the reactor and carries away the fission-produced heat through the primary system (or loop) to a heat exchanger... The pressurized water then circulates back through the reactor in a constant cycle. In the secondary loop (which is sealed off from the radioactive primary coolant water) the water boils and expands into steam.

o. A type of intra-uterine contraceptive device. Cf. Lippes loop.

1962 [see Lippes loop]. **1965** *Guardian* 28 May 6/3 The medical council has authorized the intra-uterine contraceptive device... The IUCD would nearly always prevent pregnancy... The 'loops'.. cost only a few pence. **1967** *Times* 9 Oct. 4/4 [Pakistan] Although the 1970 target of 500,000 vasectomies and five million loop insertions might seem low,.. the main object was to retard or halt the growing birth rate. **1971** *Petticoat* 17 July 6/4 There's one excellent method (the coil or loop) only suitable for someone who's already had a baby. **1974** *Guardian* 25 Mar. 10 Will the loop make your periods more painful? If you have comfortable periods before you have a loop fitted, you are unlikely to develop painful periods afterwards.

5. (See quots.) [Perh. a different word.]

1674–91 Ray *S. & E.C. Words* 105 A *Loop*; A Rail of Pales, or Bars join'd together like a Gate, to be removed in and out at pleasure. *a* **1825** Forby *Voc. E. Anglia*, *Loop*, the part of a pale-fence between one post and another.

6. *attrib.* and *Comb.*, as ***loop-handle***, ***-head***, ***-lock***, ***method***, ***-net***, ***road***, ***system***, ***way***; ***loop-maker***; ***loop-like***, ***-shaped*** adjs.; **loop aerial, antenna** *Radio*, an aerial consisting of one or more loops of wire; **loop-artery**, an artery that forms a loop alongside the main-duct; **loop-drag, -eye** (see quots.); **loop film**, a loop (sense 4 k) of cinematographic film; **loop-knot**, †(*a*) a reef-knot (*obs.*); (*b*) a single knot tied in a doubled cord, so as to leave a loop beyond the knot (1875 in Knight *Dict. Mech.*); **loop-lace**, (*a*) a kind of ornament consisting of a series of loops; (*b*) a kind of lace consisting of patterns worked on a ground of fine net; hence **loop-laced** *a.*; **loop-line**, (*a*) see 4 e; (*b*) a fishing-line used with the loop-rod (*q.v.*) to which it is attached by a loop; **loop pile** (see quot. 1963); **loop-rod**, a spliced fishing-rod with a strong loop of horse-hair at the top for the attachment of the line; **loop-stitch**, a kind of fancy stitch consisting of loops; also as *v. trans.*, to connect or attach by means of loop-stitches; so **loop-stitching**, such work; **loop system**, a method of connecting electrical supply points (as lamp roses) by taking the wires to each point from terminals at its switch and at the previous supply point, instead of making a separate joint elsewhere in the circuit; **loop-test** (see quot.); **loop-tube** = *looped tube* (see looped *ppl. a.*[1] 1); **loop-work**, work consisting of loops or looped stitches; also *attrib.*; **loop-worm** = looper 1; **loop yarn** (see quot. 1940).

1913 *Year-Bk. Wireless Telegr.* 314 For the directive aerial, the writer had been employing a closed circuit or *loop aerial, tuned with a condenser. **1966** J. P. Hawker *Outl. Radio & Television* xxii. 367 The main advantage of the loop aerial is the two sharp null positions as the loop is rotated, occurring when the plane of the loop is parallel to the wave front. **1968** M. Woodhouse *Rock Baby* xiii. 131, I packed the D.F. set, the loop aerial, and the little transceiver into my rucksack. **1906** J. A. Fleming *Princ. Electr. Wave Telegr.* iv. 280 (*caption*) Stationary potential oscillations set up on *loop antennæ. **1932** F. E. Terman *Radio Engin.* xvi. 588 All practical direction-finding systems make use of a loop antenna. **1968** A. L. Weeks *Antenna Engin.* ii. 56 Small loop antennas are frequently employed for low-frequency receiving applications. **1899** *Allbutt's Syst. Med.* VI. 239 The blood can enter at each end of the short *loop arteries. **1881** Raymond *Mining Gloss.*, **Loop-drag*, an eye at the end of a rod through which tow is passed for cleaning bore-holes. **1868** Joynson *Metals* 19 Vertical bars, to which they [horizontal bands] are attached by *loop-eyes or strong screw-bolts. **1940** *Chambers's Techn. Dict.* 510/2 **Loop film*, the same as band film or cycle film. **1957** *Oxf. Pocket Bk. Athletic Training* (ed. 2) 9 Get a loop film taken of your technique at normal and slow motion speeds. **1949** W. F. Albright *Archaeol. of Palestine* vi. 115 These craters were supplied with two tilted horizontal *loop-handles. **1969** E. H. Pinto *Treen* 387 Some 19th-century planes have 17th-century type 'loop' handles. **1876** J. S. Ingram *Centenn.*

Exposition ix. 318 These were the larger and most important part of the exhibit, while the rest was made up of..prop nuts, *loop heads, offsets and stay ends. **1795** Hutton *Math. Dict.* s.v. *Knot*, A **Loop knot* [explained as = *reef-knot*]. **1894** *Outing* (U.S.) XXIV. 351/2 We took a stout rope, made a strong loop-knot in it for each person. **1632** J. Hayward tr. *Biondi's Eromena* 52 The sleeves..were cut from the highest to the lowest part..and rejoind with small blacke *loope-lace. **1683** *Lond. Gaz.* No. 1797/4 A new-fashion'd Campaign Coat..gold Loop-Lace down the Seams. **1883** *Daily News* 22 Oct. 7/1 Common Valenciennes and loop laces. **1691** *Lond. Gaz.* No. 2686/4 One Flanders *Loop-laced Combing-cloath. **1896** *Pop. Sci. Monthly* Feb. 535 A tendency to draw a *looplike rudimentary contour soon emerges. **1859** G. A. Sala *Twice round Clock* 261 Then from the beginning of Italian opera in England, a grand trunk line extending to our days, I shunt off on to innumerable little branches and *loop-lines. **1869** *Bradshaw's Railway Manual* XXI. 115 A loop line from Peterborough, through Boston and Lincoln, rejoining the main line at Retford. **1885** D. Webster *Angler & Loop-Rod* iv. 71, I..constantly use the spliced rod and loop-line. **1908** *Daily Chron.* 16 May 1/5 The loop-line railway linking up all the railway termini. **1956** *Railway Mag.* Nov. 745/1 The up main and goods loop lines were destroyed or heavily damaged for about 70 yd. **1970** *Ibid.* Oct. 585/2 Passenger trains were diverted over the loop line via Lochwinnoch which is rarely used by other than freight services. **1888** G. M. Hopkins *Poems* (1918) 90 Then with *loop-locks Forward falling..his twiny boots Fast he opens. **1727** Boyer *Fr. Dict.*, *Loop-maker, *faiseur d'Agrémens*. **1901** L. W. Waterhouse *Conduit Wiring* 51 The wiring in this building has been carried out entirely on the '*loop' method, there being no joints in any of the wires or cables. **1869** *Game Laws Illinois* in *Fur, Fin & Feather* (1872) 175 That it shall be unlawful..to take or catch fish..by means of any seine, gill-net, tramel net, pike-net, or *loop-net. **1924** R. Beaumont *Carpets & Rugs* vii. 262 The *loop pile may wear flat or bare, but it remains part of the carpet structure. **1963** *Which?* Mar. 69/1 A loop pile carpet has closed loops while a cut pile has the top of the loop cut open. **1909** *Daily Mail* 5 Aug. 5/2 To construct *loop-roads for fast motor traffic round villages. **1960** *New Left Rev.* July–Aug. 23/1 Loop roads for buses would penetrate some distance into the pedestrian precinct. **1963** *Times* 7 Mar. 7/4 Whether the town is to have a loop road or..the High Street is to be widened. **1973** M. Yorke *Grave Matters* iv. ii. 76 He took the loop road that led away from the village. **1885** D. Webster (*title*) The Angler and the *Loop-Rod. *Ibid.*, Pref. p. viii, The art of fishing with what may be styled the loop-rod and line. **1870** Rolleston *Anim. Life* 134 We see a *loop-shaped gland. **1857** *Abridgm. Specif. Patents, Sewing* etc. 19 Then carrying through the latter a loop of the first thread, so as to form a double *loop-stitch. **1901** *Lady's Realm* X. 619 Fig. 22 is the way open loop-stitch is worked. .. When drawn through, the needle is put in a little way beyond the loop formed. **1932** D. C. Minter *Mod. Needlecraft* 189/1 In fig. 30 the patch edge..is *loop-stitched to the paper. **1951** *Good Housek. Home Encycl.* 213/2 The wrong side of the garment is neatened by *loopstitching the two raw edges together. **1969** *Jane's Freight Containers 1968–69* 544/1 One such hook and, at the other end, loop-stitching for permanent fixing to container sides. **1896** R. Robb *Electr. Wiring* v. 119 The object of confining this construction to the *loop system is to prevent joints being made in concealed places. **1925** G. A. Willoughby *House Wiring* ii. 73 The loop system of wiring does away with this possibility of fire, because the wires are looped from outlet to outlet and all joints are made within outlet boxes. **1867** Culley *Handbk. Telegr.* (ed. 2) 145 A *loop-test, when two similar wires are disconnected from earth at the distant end and joined together, is free from this source of error. **1876** Preece & Sivewright *Telegraphy* 276 The advantage of the loop test consists in its being independent, within certain limits, of the resistance of the fault. **1885** Landois & Stirling *Human Physiol.* II. 518 Here it [*sc.* the narrow loop of Henle] becomes wider..and enters a medullary ray, where it constitutes the ascending *loop-tube. **1929** *Times* 1 Nov. 18/3 Traffic proceeding towards London is being diverted at Hatton cross roads, *via* Cranford lane to the Bath road and London (A.A. *loop-way). *Ibid.*, A.A. loop-way signs. **1857** *Abridgm. Specif. Patents, Sewing* etc. 4 Apparatus for producing *loopwork ornaments on woven fabrics. **1888** *Art Jrnl.* 379 By leaving portions of the silk loopwork uncut a less raised pile is produced. **1880** *Libr. Univ. Knowl.* (N.Y.) III. 388 [Canker-worms] are often called..*loop worms or geometers. **1940** *Chambers's Techn. Dict.* 511/1 **Loop yarn*, a fancy yarn, with small loops; composed of three threads folded together, one of which is an effect thread and forms the loops, which are bound by another thread. **1957** Simpson & Weir *Weaver's Craft* (ed. 8) xvi. 214 *Curl or Loop Yarn* is made by turning a comparatively thick thread around a much finer ground thread so as to form a succession of curls or loops along the surface of the yarn. **1964** [see bouclé *a.*].

loop (luːp), *sb.*² Forms: 4–6 loup(e, 5–6 lowp(e, 6 loope, 5–7 lope, 7– loop. [Prob. connected with MDu. *lûpen* (mod.Du. *luipen*), to lie in wait, watch, peer; cf. MDu. *glûpen* (mod.Du. *gluipen*) of similar meaning, mod.Du. *gluip* narrow opening, crack of a door. An Anglo-Lat. *loupis* abl. pl., app. repr. this word, is cited by Du Cange from a document of 1394.]

1. An opening in a wall, to look through, or to allow the passage of a missile; a loop-hole.

13.. *Gaw. & Gr. Knt.* 792 Wyth mony luflych loupe, þat louked ful clene. **1393** Langl. *P. Pl.* C. xxi. 288 Eche chyne stoppe, þat no light leope yn at louer ne at loupe. *a* **1470** Gregory in *Hist. Coll. Lond. Cit.* (Camden) 213 They hadde..loupys with schyttyng wyndowys to schute owte at. **1494** Fabyan *Chron.* vii. 664 A place with a particioun atwene both prynces..made with a lowpe, that eyther myght se other. **1512** *MS. Acc. St. John's Hosp., Canterb.*, For makyng off a loope in þe dorter at þe susters syde vjd. *a* **1532** Ld. Berners *Huon* clxvi. 655 The sayd wacheman came to yᵉ wall syde, where as there was a strayte lope into Florence chaumbre. **1577–87** Holinshed *Chron.* III. 1215/1 One of them could not so soone looke out at a loope, but three or foure were readie to salute him. **1596** Lodge *Marg. Amer.* 63 A square and curious chamber, with fiue loopes to yeeld light. **1600** Fairfax *Tasso* xi. xxxii. 201 Some at the loopes durst scant out peepe. **1628** Coke *On Litt.* 5 a, *Tenellare* or *tanellare*, is to make holes or loopes in walls to shoote out against the Assailants. **1797** Mrs. Radcliffe *Italian* i. (1826) 12 Some remains of massy walls, still exhibited loops for archers. *c* **1822** Beddoes *Pygmalion* Poems 160 A blinded loop In Pluto's madhouse' green and wormy wall. **1846** *Guide Archit. Antiq. Neighbourhood Oxford* 164 On the first floor [Northleigh Ch. tower] the windows are plain Norman loops. **1864** Browning *Worst of It* xii, I spy the loop whence an arrow shoots.

b. *fig.* and in figurative contexts.

1863 Kinglake *Crimea* II. 118 Closing the loops by which a general might seek to escape from the obligation of having to make the venture. **1879** T. L. Cuyler *Heart-Culture* 102 The soul becomes luminous until the interior light and glow blaze out through every loop and crevice.

†**2.** An opening in the parapet of a fortification; an embrasure. *Obs.*

c **1477** Caxton *Jason* 14 b, They of Oliferne..ran unto the bateillement and lowpes of the walles. **1525** Ld. Berners *Froiss.* II. cccxxi. 499 At another lope of the wall on a ladder ..the lorde of Sercell..fought hande to hande with his enemyes. **1544** *Late Exped. Scot.* 6 in Dalyell *Fragm. Sc. Hist.* (1798), They repulsed the Scottyshe gonners from the loupes of the same [gate]. **1553** Brende *Q. Curtius* Cc viii, The walle..was very narowe in the toppe not divided with lopes..but enclosed with one whole and continuall battilment rounde about. **1575** Churchyard *Chippes* (1817) 148 Some beate the lowps, some ply the walles with shot. **1686** Plot *Staffordsh.* 381 A yew tree..cut on the top with loop and crest, like the battlements of a Tower.

fig. *a* **1533** Ld. Berners *Gold. Bk. M. Aurel.* (1546) Q vj b, Euery lightnes done in youth breketh down a loope of the defence of our lyfe.

3. *Comb.*, as ***loop-window***.

1573–80 Baret *Alv.* C 161 A loupe windowe or casement. **1848** Rickman *Styles Archit.* (ed. 5) 94 Some windows of this style are long and narrow,..Similar loop windows with square tops occur occasionally also in Norman work. **1892** A. Heales *Archit. Ch. Denmark* 68 A small round-headed loop-window.

†**loop**, *sb.*³ *Obs. rare*⁻¹. [Of obscure origin; perhaps a use of loop *sb.*¹ (cf. loop *v.*¹ 2); but cf. lop *sb.*¹] A wood-louse or hog-louse.

1612 *Enchir. Med.* ii. 58 Your Millepedes, which I take to be loopes or Hog-lice. **1615** Thomas *Lat. Dict.*, *Oniscus*, a lope, a worme which bendeth himselfe like to a bowe when he goeth. It is called of some *Millepeda*.

loop (luːp), *sb.*⁴ Also 5–6 loupe, 9 loup. [ad. F. *loupe*, which has all the senses. Cf. G. *luppe*.]

1. *Metallurgy.* A mass of iron in a pasty condition ready for the tilt-hammer or rolls; a bloom.

1674 Ray *Collect. Words, Iron Work* 127 The sow at first they roll into the fire, and melt off a piece of about three fourths of a hundredweight which so soon as it is broken off becomes a Loop. **1686** Plot *Staffordsh.* 163 The Metall in an hour thickens by degrees into a lump or mass, which they call a loop. **1731** in Bailey vol. II. **1794** H. Cort in *Repertory of Arts & Manuf.* (1795) III. 365 The method and process, invented, by me, is to continue the loops in the same furnace,..and to heat them to a white or welding heat. **1825** J. Nicholson *Operat. Mechanic* 768 The ore..loses its fusibility, and is collected into lumps called loops. **1881** Raymond *Mining Gloss.*, *Loup*, the pasty mass of iron produced in a bloomary or puddling furnace.

attrib. **18..** Whitman *To Working Men* 6 Iron works—the loup-lump at the bottom of the melt at last.

†**2.** A precious stone of imperfect brilliancy, *esp.* a sapphire. *Obs.*

c **1400** Maundev. (1839) xiv. 160 Of the Saphire Loupe, and of many other Stones. **14..** Lydg. *Commend. Our Lady* 92–3 Semely saphyre, depe loupe, and blewe ewage, Stable as the loupe, ewage of pite. **1545** *Test. Ebor.* VI. 228 A flower of golde diverslie enamylede, with a rubie, a saphire lupe and a perle. *a* **1548** Hall *Chron., Hen. VIII* 130 In the uppermost Rose, was a faire Saphier loupe perced.

3. A knot or bur, often of great size, occurring on walnut, maple, oak, and some other trees.

In some mod. Dicts.

4. 'A small magnifying-glass' (*Cent. Dict.*).

loop (luːp), *v.*¹ [f. loop *sb.*¹ App. of recent origin; not in Johnson or Todd. Cf. looped *ppl. a.*¹, which is recorded from the 16th c.]

1. *trans.* To form into a loop or loops; also with *round*.

1856 Kane *Arct. Expl.* I. xxx. 412 The other end is already looped, or as sailors would say, 'doubled in a bight'. **1872** Yeats *Techn. Hist. Comm.* 342 The eyes of the needles were formed by looping the metal round at the head. **1891** *Nature* 10 Sept., The larva..loops its body to and fro with a kind of lashing movement..in the water.

2. *intr.* To form a loop; *spec.* of certain larvæ.

1832 *Fraser's Mag.* VI. 384 The roots..twist themselves among the masonry, and the huge boughs come looping through the holes. **1854** Woodward *Mollusca* ii. 173 *Pedipes afra*..loops in walking, like truncatella. **1885** *Atlantic Monthly* LVII. 595 The currant worms went looping and devouring from twig to twig. **1898** E. Coues in *J. Fowler's Jrnl.* p. xxii, Fowler..went a roundabout way, looping far south to heads of the Whitewater and Verdigris rivers before he crossed the Neosho.

3. *trans.* To put or form loops upon; to provide (a garment) with loops.

1894 Blackmore *Perlycross* 24 The broad valley..looped with glittering water. **1900** *Blackw. Mag.* Sept. 336/1 Snow loops every ledge and curtains every slope.

4. To encircle or enclose *in* or *with* something formed into a loop.

1840 Lardner *Geom.* 248 Let a pencil be looped in the thread... Thus placed, let the pencil be moved in the loop of the thread. **1863–76** Curling *Dis. Rectum* (ed. 4) 102 Metallic wire..sufficient..to admit of the surgeon.. looping his finger with it.

5. a. Chiefly with *adv.* or *phrase*: To fasten (*back, up*) by forming into a loop, or by means of an attached loop; to join or connect by means of a loop or loops. Also *intr.* for *refl.*

1837 J. Kirkbride *Northern Angler* 3 Loop on the dropper-flies; the tail-fly should also be looped. **1840** Browning *Sordello* ii. 199 For him was..verse..A ceremony that..looped back the lingering veil Which hid the holy place. **1843** Carlyle *Past & Pr.* ii. viii, His frock-skirts looped over his elbow. **1844** Hood *Bridge of Sighs* 31 Loop up her tresses Escaped from the comb. **1853** *Mechanics' Mag.* LVIII. 375 Each needle carries a separate thread, which are looped into each other alternately. **1863** Alford in *Life* (1873) 366 Their narrow..streets, shady and lofty, looped together with frequent arches from side to side. **1873** Black *Pr. Thule* ii. 28 She had an abundance of dark hair looped up. **1880** N. Smyth *Old Faiths* v. (1882) 208 Every thread of life is inextricably looped with a thousand other threads. **1881** *Encycl. Brit.* XIII. 99/1 The basal processes loop with the horizontal fibres.

b. loop in. *trans.* (i) To connect into an electric circuit by the loop system.

1893 W. J. Hopkins *Telephone Lines & their Properties* xiii. 203 It was the custom..to 'loop in' the several telephones, that is, to place them in series. **1899** W. P. Maycock *Electr. Wiring* iii. 242 At A, three lamps *L* and switches *S* are 'looped in' to one fuse *F*. **1965** J. H. M. Sykes *Beginner's Guide Electr. Wiring* v. 113 Lighting circuits may be looped in, using three-plate ceiling roses, to avoid the necessity for joints.

(ii) To form (a wire) into a loop and insert it into a terminal.

1911 A. Bursill *Princ. & Pract. Electr. Wiring* vi. 37 The wires must never be cut where they are looped-in. **1952** W. E. Steward *Mod. Wiring Pract.* 140 Frequently, the description of this [*sc.* looping-in] system given in books on wiring methods tends to create a false impression in the mind of the reader. From these descriptions it would appear that one length of cable is bared at intervals and looped in at switch and lighting terminals. In practice, when wiring in conduit, the two lengths of wire forming the loop are threaded in separately and the junction is made at the switch, light, or other terminal. **1967** G. A. T. Burdett *Electr. Installations* 226 (*heading*) Looping-in the cable.

6. ***to loop the loop***, to perform the feat of circling in a vertical loop, orig. on a specially prepared track (see loop *sb.*¹ 4 f), later in an aeroplane. Also *transf.*, *fig.*, and as *sb.*

Orig. a fairground phrase.

1902 *Strand Mag.* June 708 (*heading*) Looping the loop on a bicycle. *Ibid.* 708/1 'Looping the loop' in America has become even more popular than shooting the chutes. *Ibid.* 708/2 At first he could not induce the ball to loop the loop. **1903** G. Bell *Let.* 8 July (1927) I. 166 We went on a switchback that looped the loop... Hugo..was distinctly conscious of being upside down..for the fraction of a second. **1903** *Outing* XLII. 552/1 He knows how to win the steeplechase..and has been 'thrown out' for standing up in the loop-the-loops. [**1908** A. Bazin in *L'Aérophile* 15 May, Pourquoi pas 'looping the loop' tout de suite?] **1911** A. P. Thurston *Elem. Aeronaut.* iii. 33 A glider..can be made to 'loop the loop', or follow any one of a number of curved paths. **1913** [see loop *sb.*¹ 4 f]. **1922** A. S. Eddington *Theory of Relativity* 3 The planets literally looped the loop in fantastic curves called epicycles. **1922** Wodehouse *Clicking of Cuthbert* ix. 209 A girl of such pronounced beauty that Ramsden Waters' heart looped the loop twice in rapid succession. **1935** [see falling *ppl. a.* 5 b]. **1940** O. Nash *Face is Familiar* (1954) 10 It's pleasant to loop the loop, To daringly seize The flying trapeze With a cry of Allez-oop! **1960** B. Keaton *Wonderful World of Slapstick* (1967) 73 The climax of the act came when he started doing loop the loops, riding upside down. **1961** [see aerobatics *sb. pl.*]. **1968** *Michelin Guide N.Y. City* 124 Coney Island..scenic railways, loop-the-loops and Ferris wheels compete with phantom trains, tunnels of love, sputniks.

7. *intr.* *Computers.* To execute a loop (loop *sb.*¹ 4 m).

1958 Gotlieb & Hume *High-Speed Data Processing* vi. 98 A common procedure is to use one sequence of instructions, cycling or looping through this sequence as often as required. **1969** P. B. Jordain *Condensed Computer Encycl.* 293 The ability to loop, and thus reuse instructions without duplicating them and wasting memory, is probably the single most important advantage gained by stored-program computers.

†**loop**, *v.*² [f. loop *sb.*⁴] *intr.* Of heated iron-ore: To form a loop (see loop *sb.*⁴).

1674 Ray *Collect. Words, Iron Work* 125 Care also must be taken that it be not too much burned, for then it will loop, i.e. melt and run together in a mass.

loop, *v.*³ [f. loop *sb.*² Cf. looped *ppl. a.*²] *trans.* To furnish with loop-holes.

1846 Z. Taylor *Let.* 9 Nov. in *N.Y. Morn. Express* (1847) 22 Jan. 2/3 The houses are of stone..all looped up for musketry.

‖**loop** (lɔʊp), *int.* *S. Afr.* [Afrikaans, f. Du. imp. of *lopen* to walk.] A word of command to an animal to move forward.

1811 W. J. Burchell *Jrnl.* 18 June in *Trav. S. Africa* (1822) I. viii. 169 Philip mounted his seat,..with an animated voice calling out to the oxen, *Loop!* **1927** W. Plomer *I Speak of Afr.* i. 40 'Loop!' he ordered in a loud voice. Shilling cracked his whip and shouted to the oxen. The voorlooper's head could just be seen through a forest of horns. **1937** F. B. Young *They seek a Country* ii. i. 162 'Ay, Blauwberg, would you?' (The long lash curled in the air like a salmon cast and stung the off-leader's muzzle.) '*Loop*, you devils, *loop*!'

looped (luːpt), *ppl. a.*¹ Also 6 *Sc.* lowpit, 7 louped. [f. LOOP *sb.*¹ and *v.*¹ + -ED.]

1. Coiled or wreathed in loops; †intertwined. '*looped tubes of Henle*, the narrower portion of the urinary tubule in the kidney' (*Syd. Soc. Lex.*).

1513 DOUGLAS *Æneis* II. iv. 9 Lo! twa greit lowpit ederis, with mony thraw, Fast throw the fluide towart the land can draw. **1850** NICHOL *Archit. Heav.* 83 Others [nebulæ] are in the meantime apart; but nevertheless of remarkable aspects: for instance Sir John Herschel's curious looped shape, the 30 Doradûs. **1860** REEVE *Elem. Conchol.* II. 182 A variously elaborated system of apophyses, or looped skeletons. **1877** GRAY *Anat.* (ed. 8) 704 The tubes taking the course above described form a kind of loop, and are known as the looped or recurrent tubes of Henle. **1878** [see LOOP *sb.*¹ 2].

†**2.** Having, or fastened with, a loop. Of a dart: Furnished with a thong or strap for throwing.

1589 RIDER *Bibl. Scholast.*, Looped, or latched with loopes, *amentatus*. **1609** HOLLAND *Amm. Marcell.* XXXI. vii. 413 They..assailed one another on both sides with louped darts and such like casting weapons.

3. Of lace: Wrought upon a ground of fine net (cf. *loop-lace* (b) in LOOP *sb.*¹ 6). ***looped pile*** (see quot. 1888). ***looped stitch, looped work*** = *loop-stitch, loop-work* (see LOOP *sb.*¹ 6).

1698 *Lond. Gaz.* No. 3356/4 Lost.., two Looped Lace Pinners. **1720** *Ibid.* No. 5868/9, 2 Pair of fine Mechlin looped Lace Mens Ruffles. **1740** C'TESS HARTFORD *Corr.* (1805) I. 226 There are..four fine laced Brussels heads—two looped and two grounded. **1851** *Illustr. Catal. Gt. Exhib.* 304 Circular looped fabric machine frame for the manufacture of woolen cloths and hosiery goods. **1857** *Abridgm. Specif. Patents, Sewing* etc. (1871) 8 Apparatus for producing ornamental tambour or looped work on lace or other fabrics. *Ibid.* 20 The well-known chain or looped stitch. **1888** J. PATON in *Encycl. Brit.* XXIV. 467/1 Looped pile is any fabric in which the woven loops remain uncut, as in Brussels and tapestry carpets, and terry velvets.

4. Held in a loop, held *up* by a loop.

1869 *Routledge's Ev. Boy's Ann.* 264 She wore the classical costume..a looped-up tunic. **1893** *Spectator* 23 Dec. 909/2 The plough-teams, with looped-up splinter bars banging against the trace-chains. **1898** *Speaker* 8 Oct. 437 In loops at the lower end of the ropes crouched some of the crew. At each stronger puff of wind the looped sailors would push off from the boat with their toes against the gunwale.

5. Intoxicated, drunk. *slang* (chiefly *U.S.*).

1934 in M. H. WESEEN *Dict. Amer. Slang* xviii. 279. **1951** 'M. SPILLANE' *Big Kill* ii. 46 The sap sounded half-looped. **1959** A. BAILEY *Making Progress* vi. 63 Slater..was almost looped on the Veuve Clicquot. **1962** J. POTTS *Evil Wish* ii. 28 Joe had gotten looped and called here. **1973** 'R. MACDONALD' *Sleeping Beauty* xxxviii. 221 The message.. didn't come through too clear. She talked as if she was slightly looped.

looped (luːpt), *ppl. a.*² [f. LOOP *sb.*² + -ED².] Having loop-holes.

1605 SHAKS. *Lear* III. iv. 31 (1st Qo. 1608) How shall.. Your loopt [Fo. 1623 lop'd] and windowed raggednes defend you From seasons such as these?

looper¹ ('luːpə(r)). [f. LOOP *v.*¹ + -ER¹.] One who or that which makes loops.

1. The larva of any geometrid moth. Also *attrib.*

1731 ALBIN *Birds* I. 2 A..number of green Caterpillars call'd Loopers. **1819** G. SAMOUELLE *Entomol. Compend.* 250 Caterpillars half loopers. **1840** J. & M. LOUDON tr. *Köllar's Treat. Insects* III. 212 The most ruinous insect for fruit-trees is assuredly the green looper-caterpillar. **1869** *Eng. Mech.* 24 Dec. 345/2 The extensive family known as the Geometers or Loopers..proceed by a regular series of strides, the middle of the body forming a loop. **1882** *Garden* 25 Feb. 132/2 The caterpillars of these [Swallow-tail] moths are called Loopers. **1932** E. STEP *Bees, Wasps, Ants* 184 A more striking..case is that of some 'looper' caterpillar,..from which a hundred *Microgaster* larvæ have broken out. **1964** V. B. WIGGLESWORTH *Life of Insects* x. 149 We have a whole series of insect larvae, of Noctuid moths, of 'looper' or Geometrid caterpillars, saw-fly larvae and others, all of which resemble pine needles.

2. a. A contrivance for making loops, e.g. in a sewing-machine. **b.** An implement for looping strips together in making rag-carpets.

1857 *Abridgm. Specif. Patents, Sewing* etc. (1871) 99 It [the diagonal needle] immediately becomes a simple looper to take the thread from the vertical needle. **1891** *19th Cent.* 941 In 1880 a machine called the 'looper' was invented. *Note.* The looper is the shuttle of a double-thread sewing-machine, which holds the under thread. **1895** *Chamb. Jrnl.* 21 Sept. 599/2 Making a chain-stitch by means of a revolving looper.

3. *Aeronaut.* One who loops the loop, or who has done so; a machine specially adapted for looping the loop.

1914 *Aeroplane* 15 Jan. 63/1 Two more names have been added to the roll of loopers. *Ibid.* 12 Mar. 284/2 Mr. Hucks ..first flew his two-seater, and later on the 'looper' at 700 feet, made one loop.

looper² ('luːpə(r)). *S. African.* Also loper. [a. Du. *looper*, lit. 'runner'.] *pl.* A kind of large buck-shot.

1886 P. GILLMORE *Hunter's Arcadia* iii. 18, I quickly substituted cartridges of lopers (buckshot) for the No. 3 that my chambers had previously contained. **1889** RIDER HAGGARD *Allan's Wife* 47 Now, boy, the gun, no, not the rifle, the shot-gun loaded with loopers. **1900** *Westm. Gaz.* 16 May 5/2 Mr. Green was only armed with a shot gun and cartridges loaded with loopers. **1932** C. FULLER *Louis Trigardt's Trek* x. 120 They espied a fully armed Native and scared him away with a charge of *lopers*.

loopful ('luːpfʊl). [f. LOOP *sb.*¹ + -FUL.] So much as is contained in a loop of (platinum) wire.

1896 *Pop. Sci. Monthly* Apr. 857 A pure culture..was prepared and a sterilized loopful deposited. **1901** *Brit. Med. Jrnl.* No. 2089/8 A loopful of this [fluid] is..mixed with ½ to 1 c. cm. of distilled water.

loop-hole, loophole ('luːphəʊl), *sb.*¹ [f. LOOP *sb.*² + HOLE *sb.*]

1. *Fortification.* A narrow vertical opening, usually widening inwards, cut in a wall or other defence, to allow of the passage of missiles.

1591 *Garrard's Art of Warre* 302 That not one of the towne do so much as appeare at their defences or loop holes. *a* **1625** FLETCHER *Nice Valour* II. i. 1st Song, Thou that makest a heart thy Tower, And thy loop-holes, Ladies eyes. **1697** DRYDEN *Æneid* IX. 711 Shoot through the Loopholes, and sharp Jav'lins throw. **1781** GIBBON *Decl. & F.* (1869) III. lxviii. 716 Incessant volleys were securely discharged from the loop-holes. **1805** SOUTHEY *Ballads & Metr. T.* Poet. Wks. VI. 59 Bishop Hatto..barr'd with care All the windows, doors, and loop-holes there. **1840** BROWNING *Sordello* II. 981 Ah, the slim castle!..gone to ruin—trails Of vine through every loop-hole. **1859** F. A. GRIFFITHS *Artil. Man.* (1862) 263 *Loop-holes* are oblong holes, from 15 to 18 inches long, 6 inches wide within, and 2 or 3 without. They are cut through timber, or masonry, for the service of small arms.

†**b.** *Naut.* A port-hole. Also (see quot. 1769).

1627 CAPT. SMITH *Seaman's Gram.* ii. 7 They fit Loop-holes in them for the close fights. **1632** J. HAYWARD tr. *Biondi's Eromena* 40 Her mast and loope-holes gracefully adorned with banners, and flags of cloth of gold. **1634-5** BRERETON *Trav.* (Chetham Soc.) 166 The Waves flashed into the Ship at the loop-holes at the stern. **1769** FALCONER *Dict. Marine* (1780), *Loop-holes*,..small apertures..in the bulk-heads and other parts of a merchant ship, through which the small arms are fired on an enemy who boards her. **1867** in SMYTH *Sailor's Word-bk.*

2. A similar opening to look through, or for the admission of light and air.

1591 PERCIVALL *Sp. Dict.*, *Miradero*, a watch tower, a loophole. **1606** HOLLAND *Sueton.*, *Nero* xii, His manner was to beholde them..through little loope-holes. **1667** MILTON *P.L.* IX. 1110 The Indian Herdsman..tends his pasturing Herds At Loopholes cut through thickest shade. **1719** DE FOE *Crusoe* II. iv. (1840) 92 Having a fair loophole..from a broken hole in the tree. **1789** BRAND *Hist. Newcastle* I. 175 This passage..has three or four loop holes on each side, all widening gradually inwards. **1828** P. CUNNINGHAM *N.S. Wales* (ed. 3) II. 291 Loop-holes and slides at top and bottom for the admission of air. **1848** ELIZA COOK *Curls & Couplets* xvi. 16 The callow raven tumbles, From the loop-hole of his hiding. **1901** *Q. Rev.* Apr. 505 Not two dozen were capable of duty beyond watching behind loopholes.

b. *fig.* (Cowper's phrase 'loopholes of retreat' has been used by many later writers.)

1784 COWPER *Task* IV. 88 'Tis pleasant through the loop-holes of retreat To peep at such a world. **1853** *Chr. Remembrancer* Jan. 59 The loop-holes through which we view the household manners of these times may be few and contracted. **1879** G. MEREDITH *Egoist* xiii. (1889) 117 Dim as the loophole was, Clara fixed her mind on it till it gathered light.

c. (See quot.)

1842-59 GWILT *Archit.* Gloss. s.v. *Loop*, A loophole is a term applied to the vertical series of doors in a warehouse, from which the goods, in craning, are delivered into the warehouse.

3. *fig.* An outlet or means of escape. Often applied to an ambiguity or omission in a statute, etc., which affords opportunity for evading its intention.

[Perh. after Du. *loopgat*, in which the first element is the stem of *loopen* to run.]

1663-4 MARVELL *Corr.* Wks. 1872-5 II. 143 It would be much below You and Me,..to have such loop-holes in Our souls, and to..squeeze Our selves through our own words. **1682** DRYDEN *Dk. of Guise* Dram. Wks. 1725 V. 327 Their Loop-Hole is ready, that the Cæsar here spoken of, was a private Man. *a* **1700** T. BROWN *Wks.* (1709) IV. v. 329 Some of the Doctor's Counsel has found out a Loop-hole for him in the Act. **1768** FOOTE *Devil on 2 Sticks* I. Wks. 1799 II. 253 A legal loop-hole..for a rogue now and then to creep through. **1807** JEFFERSON *Writ.* (1830) IV. 73 What loop-hole they will find in the case, when it comes to trial, we cannot foresee. **1855** MACAULAY *Hist. Eng.* xi. III. 80 The Test Act..left loopholes through which schismatics sometimes crept into civil employments. **1875** STUBBS *Const. Hist.* II. xvii. 518 Even the 'confirmatio cartarum' had left some loopholes which the king was far too astute to over-look. **1888** ANNIE S. SWAN *Doris Cheyne* iv. 70 Under the guise of motherly solicitude..she had left her without a loophole of escape.

4. *attrib.* and *Comb.*, as ***loop-hole door, frame***; ***loophole-lighted*** adj.

1855 *Act 18 & 19 Vict.* c. 122 §14 Loophole frames may be fixed within one inch and a half of the face of any external wall. **1866** *N. & Q.* 3rd Ser. IX. 447/2 A solidly constructed stone staircase that conducts to several dark and loophole-lighted chambers. **1891** *Daily News* 16 Nov. 7/1, I broke and cut a board from one of the loophole doors.

'loop-hole, *sb.*² *rare.* [f. LOOP *sb.*¹] The aperture of a loop.

1812-16 J. SMITH *Panorama Sci. & Art* I. 360 A thread.. having a loop-hole at its extremity. In this loop-hole fix a pin.

'loop-hole, *v.* [f. LOOP-HOLE *sb.*¹] *trans.* To cut loop-holes in the walls of; to provide with loop-holes.

1810 WELLINGTON in Gurw. *Desp.* (1838) VI. 504 The first [village] is loop-holed and there is an abbatis in its front. **1827** SOUTHEY *Hist. Penins. War* II. 184 He had been advised..to have the houses loop-holed. **1842** GEN. P. THOMPSON *Exerc.* III. 43 *note*, He [Napoleon]..lies all night in sight of the other army loop-holing its farm-houses. **1842** ALISON *Hist. Europe* (1849-50) X. lxvi. §83. 196 The houses adjoining the point expected to be breached were loopholed. **1883** STEVENSON *Treas. Isl.* IV. xvi, A stout log-house,..loopholed for musketry on every side.

Hence **'loopholed** *ppl. a.*, **'loopholing** *vbl. sb.*

1664 BUTLER *Hud.* II. i. 651 This uneasy loop-hol'd jail,.. Cannot but put y'on mind of wedlock. **1870** *Pall Mall G.* 24 Aug. 10 The..loopholing of such farmyards..as occupied places of tactical importance. **1885** *Gloucestersh. Chron.* 14 Feb. 2 From the loopholed walls the rifle puffs shot out continuously. **1900** *Blackw. Mag.* Aug. 244/1 Near the river was the village of Dubba with loopholed houses filled with armed men.

loop-in. [f. vbl. phr. *to loop in* (see LOOP *v.*¹ 5 b).] A connection between two lengths of wire made at a terminal in the loop system. Usu. *attrib.*, as ***loop-in system*** = *loop system* (s.v. LOOP *sb.*¹ 6).

1908 *Installation News* II. 86/2 In comparing the third method with the second, which is the usual method of loop-in wiring adopted, it will be found that there is a saving of wire in the new method. **1911** A. BURSILL *Princ. & Pract. Electr. Wiring* vi. 35 Fig. 18 shows four lamps connected in parallel on the loop-in system. **1960** E. L. DELMAR-MORGAN *Cruising Yacht Equipment & Navigation* xvii. 187 Even with the 'loop in' system one or at most two pairs of fuses will be sufficient. **1967** G. A. T. BURDETT *Electr. Installations* 224 To overcome the inherent dangers of using an ordinary three-plate ceiling rose as a looping-in point for the live feed an entirely new purpose-made loop-in ceiling rose has been introduced. *Ibid.* 226 More recent patterns..have a fourth terminal which is intended for the earth continuity conductor loop-in.

looping ('luːpɪŋ), *vbl. sb.*¹ [f. LOOP *v.*¹ + -ING¹.]

a. The action of LOOP *v.*¹, in various senses.

1480 *Wardr. Acc. Edw. IV* (1830) 140 Corde and liour for liring and lowping of the same arras. **1856** TODD & BOWMAN *Phys. Anat.* II. 81 Evidence of loopings..is wanting. In the cochlea of the bird, however, we have seen at one end a plexiform arrangement of nucleated fibres ending in loops. **1874** WOOD *Nat. Hist.* 704 Their mode of progression is popularly and appropriately termed 'looping', and the caterpillars are called 'loopers'. **1914** *Isis* (Oxf.) 28 Feb. 5/1 The 'looping' looked simplicity itself. A sudden plunge straight towards the earth..a sudden reversal and a perpendicular climb, which gradually brought the airman upside down and..a second downward plunge. **1929** E. WILSON *I thought of Daisy* III. 123 'I'm not out for any looping,' said Daisy... 'I think I'll go home and go to bed.' **1964** E. BACH *Introd. Transformational Gram.* iii. 46 Care must be taken to ensure that unwanted recursion (looping) does not occur.

attrib. **1857** *Abridgm. Specif. Patents, Sewing* etc. (1871) 27 Combining this needle with a looping apparatus.

b. *concr.* Material formed into loops; loops as a trimming.

1690 *Lond. Gaz.* No. 2531/4 A Red Pye Coat with black and white Looping.

c. looping in (cf. LOOP *v.*¹ 5 b), connection by the loop system.

1899 W. P. MAYCOCK *Electr. Wiring* iii. 243 The advantages of looping-in, as applied to the interconnection of switches and ceiling roses. **1902** F. C. RAPHAEL '*Electrician' Wireman's Pocket Bk.* 33 (*caption*) Simplex looping-in ceiling rose. **1930** —— *Electr. Wiring of Buildings* ii. 23 Looping in has become absolutely general, for not only does it save the danger of bad joints, but it is actually less expensive than to make joints. **1967** [see LOOP-IN].

looping ('luːpɪŋ), *vbl. sb.*² [f. LOOP *v.*² + -ING¹.] The running together of ore into a mass.

1753 in CHAMBERS *Cycl. Supp.* **1848** in CRAIG.

looping ('luːpɪŋ), *ppl. a.* [f. LOOP *v.*¹ + -ING².] That forms loops. ***looping-snail***, a snail of the genus *Truncatella.* ***looping caterpillar*** = LOOPER¹ 1.

1854 WOODWARD *Mollusca* II. 175 The end of the long muzzle is also frequently applied, as by the Looping-snails (*Truncatellæ*), and used to assist in climbing. **1869** BLACKMORE *Lorna D.* i, The vale is spread with looping waters. **1875** HUXLEY & MARTIN *Course Elem. Biol.* x. 95 The polypes..are capable of crawling about by a motion similar to that of the looping caterpillar.

loopist ('luːpɪst). *rare.* [f. LOOP *v.*¹ 6 + -IST.] = LOOPER¹ 3.

1914 *Aeroplane* 15 Jan. 63/1 One of the latest loopists is M. Galtier, who on January 7th looped the loop at Chateaufort.

looplet ('luːplɪt). [-LET.] A small loop.

1876 WHITNEY *Sights & Ins.* xxxi. 301 A little magic looplet opens in the very hills.

loopy ('luːpɪ), *a.* [f. LOOP *sb.*¹ + -Y.]

1. Full of loops; characterized by loops.

1856 DICKENS *Lett.* (1880) I. 425 Many a hand have I seen with many characteristics of beauty in it—some loopy, some dashy. **1885** W. F. CRAFTS *Sabb. for Man* (ed. 7) 109 Such loopy laws net no one. The big fish break them and the small ones creep through. **1890** H. M. STANLEY *Darkest Africa* II. xxviii. 236 It is a loopy,..crooked stream. **1902** *Westm. Gaz.* 19 June 3/2 A loopy sort of braid.

2. *Sc.* ? Crafty, deceitful.

1824 SCOTT *Redgauntlet* ch. xx, When I tauld him how this loopy lad, Alan Fairford, had served me, he said I might bring an action on the case.

3. *slang.* Crazy, 'cracked'.

1925 FRASER & GIBBONS *Soldier & Sailor Words* 147 *Loopy*, silly, daft. **1928** E. WAUGH *Decline & Fall* I. xiii. 145 He'll get off on a plea of insanity. Loopy, you know. **1942** 'M. INNES' *Daffodil Affair* II. 40 One does not want a loopy

colleague when embarked upon so distinctly rummy an investigation as the present. **1957** I. Cross *God Boy* (1958) vi. 44 Honestly, the pair of them were looking at me as though I was loopy. **1961** P. White *Riders in Chariot* iv. 88 'I will not waste my breath arguing with loopy Louie,' replied Mrs Jolley. **1970** *New Yorker* 15 Aug. 68/2 The wife ..is mad neither in the sense of loopy nor in the sense of furious. **1973** A. Hunter *Gently French* xiv. 125 He was loopy over her. If she said jump, he'd fall off a cliff.

loor (lʊə(r)). *dial.* Forms: α. 8 loore, lure, 9 loor, lore, lewer. β. 6 loue, 8 lough, 9 lo(o, low. [Origin and correct form uncertain.] Foot-rot.

1587 Mascall *Govt. Cattle, Oxen* (1596) 77 The loue is a disease which breedeth in the clawes of a beast. *a* **1722** Lisle *Husb.* (1757) 296 Farmer Elford of Upcern in Dorsetshire tells me, cows will be so sore between their claws that they cannot stand,..this he and others informed me, in that country was called the loore. **1787** Grose *Prov. Gloss., Lure*, a sore on the hoof of a cow, cured by cutting it cross-ways. West. **1799** C. Cooke in Beddoes *Contrib. Phys. & Med. Knowl.* 393 The lough, swellings of the udder, and cow-pox. **1840** *Jrnl. R. Agric. Soc.* I. iii. 320 Another form of this complaint [foot-rot], and known also by the names of foot-halt, lore, &c...generally proceeds from a strain or blow. **1848** *Ibid.* IX. ii. 445 Foul in the foot, or Low. **1882** Armatage *Cattle* 213 Foul in the Foot.—Paronychia Boum, Loo or Low. **1883** *Hampsh. Gloss., Lewer*, a disease in the feet of cattle. **1890** *Glouc. Gloss., Loor, Loo, Lo*, a sore on a cow's hoof.

loor, obs. Sc. f. *liefer* compar. of lief *a.*, dear.

1836 M. Mackintosh *Cottager's Dau.* 39 Far loor in a rape I'd see him hinging As 'mong heretics I'd hear him singing.

loor, obs. form of lower *v.*

loord, variant of lourd *Obs.*

loore, obs. form of lore, lure.

loorequet, variant of lorikeet.

loorie, var. loerie.

loos, loosable, obs. ff. lose, loss, losable.

loose (luːs), *sb.* Also 6 lose, lowse, 7 lewse, 8 louse. [f. loose *v.* and *a.*]

1. *Archery.* The act of discharging an arrow

1519 Horman *Vulg.* 283 b, Geue a smarte lose with thyn arowe and thy stryng. **1526** *Pilgr. Perf.* (W. de W. 1531) 160 b, In the loose of the stryng..the..arowe is caryed to the marke. **1545** Ascham *Toxoph.* ii. (Arb.) 146 An other I sawe whiche,..after the loose, lyfted vp his ryght legge. **1622** Drayton *Poly-olb.* xxvi. 338 The loose gaue such a twang, as might be heard a myle. **1636** B. Jonson *Discov.* (1641) 115 In throwing a Dart, or Iavelin, wee force back our armes, to make our loose the stronger. **1879** M. & W. H. Thompson *Archery* iii. 22 The loose being the delicate part of archery, a very small defect in the archer's gear will materially affect the smoothness of the loose.

fig. **1599** *Warn. Faire Wom.* ii. 394 The only mark whereat foul Murther shot, Just in the loose of envious eager death, ..Escap'd the arrow aim'd at his heart. **1599** B. Jonson *Ev. Man out of Hum.* iii. iii, Her braine's a quiuer of iests, and she do's dart them abroad with that sweete loose and iudiciall aime, that [etc.]. **1703** De Foe *True-born Eng.* Explan. Pref. 4 To allow me a Loose at the Crimes of the Guilty.

†**2.** The conclusion or close of a matter; upshot, issue, event. ***at*** (or ***in***) ***the*** (***very***) ***loose***: at the last moment. *Obs.*

1588 Shaks. *L.L.L.* v. ii. 752 The extreme parts of time, extremelie formes All causes to the purpose of his speed: And often at the verie loose decides That, which long processe could not arbitrate. **1589** Puttenham *Eng. Poesie* iii. xvi. (Arb.) 184 We vse to say marke the loose of a thing for marke the end of it. **1600** Holland *Livy* x. xxxv. 376 In the verie loose and retreat, rather than in the combat and medley, they found that many more were hurt and slain of their part. *Ibid.* xxii. ix. 437 The late battell..was more joious and fortunat in the loose and parting, than light and easie in the conflict and fighting. **1601** —— *Pliny* II. 403 A smacke it [a fountain] hath resembling the rust of yron, howbeit this tast is not perceiued but at the end and loose only. **1608** Bp. Hall *Epistles* i. iii, How all godless plots, in their loose, have at once deceived, shamed, punished their author. **1612** Bacon *Ess., Cunning* (Arb.) 442 You shall see them finde out pretty looses in the conclusion, but are no waies able to examine or debate matters. **1647** Sanderson *Serm.* II. 209 The unjust steward..resolveth..to shew his master a trick at the loose, that should make amends for all, and do his whole business.

†**3.** A state or condition of looseness, laxity, or unrestraint; hence, free indulgence; unrestrained action or feeling; abandonment. Chiefly in phr. ***at*** (***a*** or ***the***) ***loose***: in a state of laxity or freedom; unrestrained, unbridled, lax. ***to take a loose***: to give oneself up to indulgence. *Obs.* exc. as in b.

1593 'P. Foulface' *Bacchus Bountie* C, After these came young Cicero, who, for the large loose that he had in turning downe his liquor, was called Bicongius. *a* **1626** W. Sclater *2 Thess.* (1629) 86 Saint Paul stickes not to impute demencie to seduced Galathians... In his loose, imputes no lesse then ..madnesse or losse of wits vnto them. **1646** Sir T. Browne *Pseud. Ep.* v. v. 240 Although they act them-selves at distance, and seem to be at loose; yet doe they hold a continuity with their Maker. **1657** *Burton's Diary* (1828) II. 43, I would have you as careful in penning the clause as may be, but not wholly to leave these things at a loose. **1703** Rowe *Fair Penit.* i. i, Melts in his Arms, and with a loose she loves. **1703** C. Leslie in S. Parker *Eusebius' 10 Bks. Eccl. Hist.* p. xvi, From all this, that dreadful Loose has proceeded of Prophaneness,..which we now see before our Eyes. **1706** Mary Astell *Refl. Marriage* 13 The Man takes a loose; what shou'd hinder him? *a* **1734** North *Lives* (1826) III. 75 Such looses and escapes as almost all men there [in Turkey] are more or less guilty of. **1760–72** H. Brooke *Fool of Qual.* (1809) IV. 24 In the midst of all his enjoyments, of a loose to the gratification of every sensual desire.

b. ***to give a loose*** (occas. ***give loose***) ***to***: to allow (a person) unrestrained freedom or laxity; to give full vent to (feelings, etc.); to free from restraint. *occas.* To give (a horse) the rein.

1685 Dryden *Horace's Ode* i. xxix. 21 Come, give thy Soul a loose, and taste the pleasures of the poor. **1709** Steele *Tatler* No. 8 ¶6 They now give a Loose to their Moan. **1712** Addison *Spect.* No. 327 ¶11 The Poets have given a loose to their Imaginations in the Description of Angels. **1735** Somerville *Chase* iii. 84 Now give a Loose to the clean gen'rous Steed. **1752** Fielding *Amelia* iv. ix, Amelia's inclinations, when she gave a loose to them, were pretty eager for this diversion. **1770** Burke *Pres. Discont.* Sel. Wks. 1897 I. 72 They gave themselves..a full loose for all manner of dissipation. **1823** Scott *Quentin D.* xxviii, He..gave loose..to agitation, which, in public, he had found himself able to suppress so successfully. **1858** Thackeray *Virgin.* (1879) I. 391 The little boy..gave a loose to his innocent tongue, and asked many questions. **1876** Bancroft *Hist. U.S.* VI. xxxviii. 195 Were I to indulge my present feelings, and give loose to that freedom of expression which [etc.].

†**4.** The act of letting go or parting with something. Phrase, ***a cheerful loose***. *Obs.*

1615 S. Ward *Coal fr. Altar* 28 Without zeale the widowes mites are no better then the rest; It is the cheerefull loose [ed. 1627 lose], that doubleth the gift. **1667** J. Howard *All Mistaken* iii. (1672) 33 *Ping.* I must run with my Breeches in My hand, my Purge visits My Bumgut so intollerable often. *Doct.* Now Sir for a Cheerful Loose.

†**5.** The action of getting free, the fact of being set free, liberation, release. ***to make a loose from***: to get away from the company of. *Obs.*

1663 Dryden *Wild Gallant* i. ii, I must make a loose from her, there's no other way. **1672** —— *Marr. à la Mode* ii. i, I was just making a loose from Doralice, to pay my respects to you. *a* **1734** North *Lives* (1826) II. 177 After his first loose from the university, where the new philosophy was then but just entering.

†**6.** An impetuous course or rush. *Obs.*

1700 Prior *Carmen Sec.* 217 The fiery Pegasus..runs with an unbounded loose. **1735** Somerville *Chase* iii. 150 Hah! yet he flies, nor yields To black Despair. But one Loose more, and all His Wiles are vain. **1737** Bracken *Farriery Impr.* (1757) II. 148 It is running a Horse in Looses or in Pushes that makes the Sweat come out best.

7. *Comb.*: †**loose-giving**.

1567 Maplet *Gr. Forest* 52 b, Isidore saith that the best of it [myrrh] cummeth by resolution and loose-giving within it-selfe. [Isid. *Etym.* xvii. viii. 4 *Gutta ejus sponte manans pretiosior est.*]

loose (luːs), *a.* and *adv.* Forms: 3 (in definite form), 5–7 lousse, (also 8–9 *dial.*) lowse, (4 loss), 4–5 lause, loos, 4, 6 lose, 4–7 lous, 4–8 louse, 5 lawse, 5–6 lewse, loce, 6 *Sc.* lowis, lowsz, 7 lowsse, 5– loose. [ME. *lōs* (with close *ō*), in north. dial. *lous*, a. ON. *lǫus-s*, *laus-s* (Sw. *lös*, Da. *løs*), = OE. *léas* lease *a.*, q.v. for the ulterior etymology.] **A.** *adj.*

1. Unbound, unattached.

For *to break loose, cast loose, cut loose, let loose, shake loose, turn loose*, etc., see the verbs.

a. Of living beings or their limbs: Free from bonds, fetters, or physical restraint. Now used only in implied contrast with a previous, usual, or desirable state of confinement. *spec.* of horses etc.: allowed to run free in travelling or marching. Of money, cash, etc.: in relatively small denominations; in coins (as opp. to notes). So ***loose change*** (orig. *U.S.*), a quantity of coins kept or left in one's pocket, etc., for casual use.

a **1300** *Cursor M.* 13333 Quat man þat þou lesses o band, For lous [*Fairf.* lause, *Trin.* louse] he sal in heuen stand. **1303** R. Brunne *Handl. Synne* 10581 So fast þey neuer hym bonde, þat lose a noþer tyme þey hym fonde. *c* **1375** *Sc. Leg. Saints* xxix. (*Placidas*) 976 þe emperoure..commandit his men..to..bynd þame in a place..& lyons loss lat to þaim ga. *c* **1386** Chaucer *Reeve's T.* 218 This Millere..boond hire hors, it sholde nat goon loos. —— *Cook's Prol.* 28 For in thy shoppe is many a flye loos. *c* **1400** *Destr. Troy* 13190 He deliuert me lowse, & my lefe felow. **1526** Tindale *Matt.* xxvii. 17 Whether wyll ye that y geve losse vnto you [cf. Luther: *welchen soll ich euch los geben?*] barrabas or Iesus? **1590** Spenser *F.Q.* iii. x. 36 The gentle Lady, loose at randon lefte. **1598** Shaks. *Merry W.* i. i. 304 You are afraid if you see the Beare loose, are you not? **1608** *Burgh Rec. Glasgow* (1876) I. 285 That na maner of swyne be hadin lows within this bruche or burrow ruidis. **1672** Dryden *Conq. Granada* i. i, When fierce Bulls run loose upon the Place. **1794** Cowper *Faithf. Bird* 8 They sang as blithe as finches sing That flutter loose on golden wing. **1811** Jane Austen *Sense & Sens.* I. xvii. 217 My loose cash would..be employed in improving my collection of music and books. **1827** A. Sherwood *Gazetteer Georgia* 112 It would be a kind of generous charity, to leave with the tavern-keepers..some of the loose change. **1843** *Oregon Hist. Soc. Q.* (1901) II. 191 About fifty wagons, with those who had large droves of loose cattle, now left. **1845** J. C. Frémont *Rep. Exploring Expedition* 10 A few loose horses, and four oxen..completed the train. **1846** W. G. D. Stewart *Altowan* II. i. 41 The neighing of the loose troops, that ever and anon, broke forward to snatch the opportunity of browsing ere the crowd advanced. **1872** E. Eggleston *End of World* 173 Unless he means to part with all his loose change. **1882** Ouida *Maremma* I. 41 A fine long time he [a bandit] has been loose on these hills. **1885** *Outing* VII. 21/2 All drove pack and loose animals before them. **1895** A. Machen *Three Imposters* 81 He never returned, but his watch and chain, a purse containing three sovereigns in gold, and some loose silver, with a ring..were found three days later. **1900** *Speaker* 29 Dec. 340/2 Loose horses, blankets, bags and helmets littering the road. *a* **1903** *Mod.* He struggled until he got one hand loose. **1927** C. A. Siringo *Riata & Spurs* v. 54 That little burg saw the need of saloons and dance-halls to relieve the cowboy of his loose change. **1950** Wilkinson & Frisby *They're Open* ii. 19 *Capacious left-hand pocket*,.. in order that a large bulk of loose change may be carried. **1970** G. F. Newman *Sir, You Bastard* viii. 245 He got rid of the loose change in his pocket. **1973** *Woman's Own* 4 Aug. 36 (Advt.), The clip-to coin section is just the right size for all your loose change.

b. *transf.* and *fig.*, e.g. of something compared to a wild animal. Also of the tongue: Not 'tied', free to speak. † ***to have one's feet loose***: to be at liberty to travel (cf. *loose-footed* 10 d *fig.*).

1726 *Wodrow Corr.* (1843) III. 239 To recover this,.. were my feet loose, and my health served me, I would willingly make a London journey. **1781** Cowper *Conversat.* 354 We sometimes think we could such speech produce Much to the purpose, if our tongues were loose. **1817** Shelley *To W. Shelley* i. 7 The winds are loose, we must not stay. **1879** B. Taylor *Stud. Germ. Lit.* 115 Then swords are drawn, and murder is loose.

c. In immaterial sense: Freed from an engagement, obligation, etc.; at liberty. *Obs.* exc. *dial.*, e.g. in the sense 'free from apprenticeship, having completed a term of service' (E.D.D. s.v. *Lowse*).

1553 T. Wilson *Rhet.* (1580) 59 The seruitude of these twoo, where the one is so muche beholding and bounde to the other, that neither of them bothe would be lose though thei might. *a* **1600** Montgomerie *Misc. Poems* xxi. 27 Quhen I wes lous, at libertie I lap; I leugh vhen ladyis spak to me of love. **1608** Rowlands *Humors Looking Gl.* 14 My friend seeing what humours haunt a wife, If he were loose would lead a single life. **1880** *Antrim & Down Gloss., Loose*, unoccupied. 'I want to see the mistress when she's loose'.

†**d.** With *prep.*: Free *from* or *of*; released or disengaged *from*; unattached *to*. *Obs.*

c **1374** Chaucer *Boeth.* iv. pr. vi. 106 (Camb. MS.) In so moche is the thing moore fre and laus fro destinye as it.. holdeth hym nere to thilke centre of thinges. *c* **1400** *Destr. Troy* 10996 Philmen the fre kyng, þat he in fyst hade, He lete to þe large, lause of his hondes. **1456** Sir G. Haye *Law Arms* (S.T.S.) 249 [He] is lousse of his promess. **1526** *Pilgr. Perf.* (W. de W. 1531) 28 Hauyng thy herte lose from all worldly pleasure. *a* **1677** Barrow *Serm.* Wks. 1716 III. 179 To suppose that a Gentleman is loose from Business is a great mistake. **1695** Addison *Sir J. Somers* Misc. Wks. 1726 I. 5 If yet your thoughts are loose from State Affairs. **1713** Berkeley *Guardian* No. 3 ¶1 After getting loose of the laws which confine the passions of other men. **1761** Churchill *Rosciad* Poems 1763 I. 51 Loose to Fame, the muse more simply acts. **1784** Cowper *Task* v. 512 Her champions wear their hearts So loose to private duty, that [etc.]. **1821** Scott *Pirate* xxxvi, I wish we were loose from him [*sc.* the pirate captor].

†**e.** Loosely clad; ungirt; naked. *Obs.*

1423 Jas. I *Kingis Q.* xlix, Halflyng louse for haste. **1555** Eden *Decades* 56 They are excedynge swyfte of foote by reason of theyr loose goinge from theyr chyldes age. **1709** Prior *Pallas & Venus* 3 Venus, loose in all her naked Charms.

f. Of an inanimate thing: Not fastened or attached to that to which it belongs as a part or appendage, or with which it has previously been connected; detached. Phr. ***to come, get loose***.

a **1728** Woodward *Nat. Hist. Fossils* (1729) I. ii. 39 [A fossil] found loose on the Side of a pretty high Hill near Stokesley. **1833** J. Holland *Manuf. Metal* II. 276 These bolts may be..withdrawn, either by means of a loose key or a stationary handle on the outside of the door. **1856** Kane *Arct. Expl.* II. xxiii. 233, I remember once a sledge went so far under..that the boat floated loose. *Mod.* Some of the pages have come loose. It would be more convenient if the volume had a loose index.

g. Not joined to anything else. Of a chemical element: Free, uncombined.

1828 Hutton *Course Math.* II. 75 When a loose line is measured, it becomes absolutely necessary to measure some other line that will determine its position. **1873** Ralfe *Phys. Chem.* 178 Carbonic acid is present in the blood in two conditions; viz., loose and stable.

h. Having an end or ends hanging free. Also in fig. context. (See also loose end.)

1781 Cowper *Anti-Thelyphthora* 102 The marriage bond has lost its power to bind, And flutters loose, the sport of every wind. **1820** Shelley *Sensit. Plant* iii. 68 Like a murderer's stake, Where rags of loose flesh yet tremble on high. **1870** J. H. Newman *Gram. Assent* ii. viii. 277 As to Logic, its chain of conclusions hangs loose at both ends.

i. Not bound together; not forming a bundle or package; not tied up or secured.

1488 *Inv. R. Wardrobes* (1815) 4 Fund in the maist of the said cofferis lous & put in na thing bot liand within the said coffyr[is] 570 rois nobilis. **1596** Spenser *Prothalamion* 22 With goodly greenish locks, all loose untyde. **1597** Shaks. *Lover's Compl.* 29 Her haire nor loose nor ti'd in formall plat. **1634** Sir T. Herbert *Trav.* 159 Who compiled the Alcoran out of Mahomets loose paper. **1668** Dryden *Dram. Poesie* Ep. Ded., As I was lately reviewing my loose papers, amongst the rest I found this Essay. **1781** Cowper *Charity* 176 Loose fly his forelock and his ample mane. **1818** Shelley *Rosalind & Helen* 7 Thy loose hair in the light wind flying. **1840** Browning *Sordello* ii. 194 This calm corpse with the loose flowers in his hand. **1850** Hannay *Singleton Fontenoy* I. i. 97 Jingling the loose cash in their pockets. **1888** F. Hume *Mad. Midas* i. ii, Slivers had pushed all the scrip and loose papers away.

j. In immaterial sense: Unconnected; rambling; disconnected, detached, stray, random. ? Now *rare*.

1681 Dryden *Span. Friar* Ep. Ded. A 2 b, I..am as much asham'd to put a loose indigested Play upon the Publick.

1705 STANHOPE *Paraphr.* II. 256 These would check all our loose Wanderings. **1710** STEELE *Tatler* No. 215 ¶2 These are but loose Hints of the Disturbances in humane Society, of which there is yet no Remedy. **1739** HUME *Hum. Nature* I. iv. (1874) I. 319 Were ideas entirely loose and unconnected, chance alone wou'd join them. **1741** WATTS *Improv. Mind* I. xvii. Wks. 1753 V. 279 Vario will spend whole mornings in running over loose and unconnected pages. **1783** BURKE *Rep. Affairs India* Wks. XI. 307 He gives various loose conjectures concerning the motive to them. **1871** CARLYLE in *Mrs. Carlyle's Lett.* I. 247 Some real scholarship, a good deal of loose information.

k. Free for disposal; unattached, unappropriated, unoccupied. *Obs.* exc. in some jocular expressions. † ***loose shot***: marksmen not attached to a company. ***loose card*** (see quot. 1763[1]).

1479 *Bury Wills* (Camden) 51, I will that the seid priste be founde the residue of the seid vij yeers wt my loose godes. *Ibid.* 52 My executors pesably to ocupye my loose goodes. **1590** SIR J. SMYTH *Disc. Conc. Weapons* 17 Mosquettiers.. are not to be imployed as loose shot in skirmishes. **1613** SHAKS. *Hen. VIII*, v. iv. 59 A File of Boyes,..loose shot. **1633** T. STAFFORD *Pac. Hib.* II. xxi. (1810) 418 The Enemy thereupon put out some of their loose Shot from their battle, and entertayned the fight. **1759** HUME *Hist. Eng.* (1806) III. 798 Such as could render themselves agreeable to him in his loose hours. **1763** HOYLE *Whist* 82 Loose Card, Means a Card in a Hand that is of no Value, and consequently the properest to throw away. **1763** JOHNSON *Let. to G. Strahan* 16 Apr. in *Boswell*, I hope you read..at loose hours, other books. **1821** SHELLEY *Prometh. Unb.* IV. 154 In the void's loose field. **1839** I. TAYLOR *Ancient Chr.* I. iv. 465 A devout and wealthy layman resolves to spend a loose five and twenty thousand pounds on sacred architecture. **1900** *Daily News* 30 Mar. 3/3 With a handful of hastily levied farmers,..aided by the 'loose talent' of Europe.

l. *Gram.* Of certain syntactical elements: not essential to the meaning or construction, etc.

1932 E. KRUISINGA *Handbk. Present Day Eng.* (ed. 5) II. III. 235 The members of a loose group may be connected by other words or not... We distinguish *linked* groups and *unlinked* groups. **1933** O. JESPERSEN *Essent. Eng. Gram.* xxxiv. 357 A non-restrictive (or loose) clause,..may be left out without injury to the precise meaning of the word it is joined to, as in 'The Prince of Wales, who happened to be there, felt sorry for the prisoners.' **1961** R. B. LONG *Sentence & its Parts* iii. 68 They [*sc.* subordinate interrogatives] function also as loose adjuncts... We went with Larry, *who knew everyone.* **1972** HARTMANN & STORK *Dict. Lang. & Ling.* 135 *Loose apposition*, a word or phrase used in apposition and often separated by sustained juncture in speech or by commas in writing.

2. a. Not rigidly or securely attached or fixed in place; ready to move in or come apart from the body to which it is joined or on which it rests.

For *loose in the haft*, *in the hilt(s*, *to have a screw* or *a tile loose*, *a loose pin*, *slate*, see the sbs.

a **1225** *Ancr. R.* 228 Heo bið ikest sone adun, ase þe leste [*MS. T.* lowse, *MS. C.* lousse] ston is from þe tures coppe. *c* **1380** WYCLIF *Serm.* Sel. Wks. I. 70 þei wolen be louse in us as nailes in a tree. **1479** *Inv.* in *Paston Lett.* III. 273, j. candilstykke with a lous sokett. **1530** PALSGR. 700/2, I shake, as a tothe in ones heed that is lose. *a* **1548** HALL *Chron., Hen. VIII* 58 Spangels..set on Crymosyn satten lose and not fastened. **1568** GRAFTON *Chron.* I. 27 Moses..whose eyes were never dimme, nor his Teeth loose. **1613** SHAKS. *Hen. VIII*, IV. i. 75 Hats, Cloakes..flew vp, and had their Faces Bin loose, this day they had beene lost. **1669** STURMY *Mariner's Mag.* I. 19 We are within shot; let all our Guns be loose. **1724** DE FOE *Mem. Cavalier* (1840) 97 His bridge was only loose planks. **1784** COWPER *Task* I. 194 Rills..chiming as they fall Upon loose pebbles. **1839** URE *Dict. Arts* 1074 The said sheaves or pulleys are connected by a crown or centre wheel D, loose upon b, b. **1842** C. HODGE *Way of Life* III. ii. 78 Loose matter flies off from revolving bodies. **1860** TYNDALL *Glac.* II. xi. 292, I sent Simond to the top to remove the looser stones.

b. Of dye: Not fast, fugitive.

1844 G. DODD *Textile Manuf.* II. 72 A 'loose' colour.. easily washed out from those parts.

†c. Of the eyes: Not fixed, roving. *Obs.*

1603 DEKKER *Grissil* (Shaks. Soc.) 7 Their loose eyes tell That in their bosoms wantonness doth dwell. **1751** H. WALPOLE *Lett.* (1846) II. 381 Prince Edward is a very plain boy, with strange loose eyes.

d. Of a cough: Producing expectoration with little difficulty; not 'fast' or 'tight'.

1833 *Cycl. Pract. Med.* I. 316/2 Tightness across the chest, which yields as the cough becomes loose.

3. a. Of strings, reins, the skin, etc.: Not tightly drawn or stretched; slack, relaxed. ***with a loose rein*** (fig.): slackly, indulgently, without rigour.

c **1460** J. RUSSELL *Bk. Nurture* 907 His gurdelle..be it strayt or lewse. **1553** EDEN *Treat. Newe Ind.* (Arb.) 37 Neyther haue they theyr bellies wrimpeled or loose. **1565** COOPER *Thesaurus* s.v. *Laxus*, *Funes laxi*,..Cordes lewse or vnbounde. **1634** MILTON *Comus* 292 What time the labour'd Oxe In his loose traces from the furrow came. **1718** JACOB *Compl. Sportsman* 50 His [sc. a Greyhound's] Neck long,.. with a loose and hanging Weasan. **1775** BURKE *Sp. Conc. Amer.* Sel. Wks. 1897 I. 184 The Sultan..governs with a loose rein, that he may govern at all. **1799** M. UNDERWOOD *Dis. Children* (ed. 4) II. 61 Some such application as the following will soon brace the loose gums. **1819** SHELLEY *Cenci* IV. iii. 17 My knife Touched the loose wrinkled throat. **1908** *Animal Managem.* 17 The skin..when handled, should feel 'loose' and freely movable over the structures beneath.

b. Of clothes: Not clinging close to the figure; loosely-fitting.

1463 *Extracts Aberd. Reg.* (1844) I. 24 The saide Dauy sall cum bar fute, with his gowne louse. **1596** SHAKS. *1 Hen. IV*, III. iii. 4 My skinne hangs about me like an olde Ladies loose Gowne. **1606** HOLLAND *Sueton.* 147 Veiled all over in a loose mantle of fine Sendall. **1680** OTWAY *Orphan* II. iv, Thy garments flowing loose. **1727-46** THOMSON *Summer* 1291 Rob'd in loose array, she came to bathe Her fervent limbs. **1859** W. J. HOGE *Blind Bartimeus* vi. 115 Bartimeus..'cast away his garment', his loose upper robe. **1901** *Speaker* 17 Aug. 548/1 Men in loose flannel jackets sang old songs.

fig. **1605** SHAKS. *Macb.* v. ii. 21 Now do's he feele his Title Hang loose about him, like a Giants Robe Vpon a dwarfish Theefe.

c. Of the joints: Slack, relaxed from weakness. Also, of a person's 'build': Ungainly, looking unsuited for brisk movement.

1848 DICKENS *Dombey* ii, He was a strong, loose, round-shouldered, shuffling shaggy fellow, on whom his clothes sat negligently. **1893** STEVENSON *Catriona* 66 My eyes besides were still troubled, and my knees loose under me.

d. Of persons, etc.: relaxed or easy, calm; uninhibited. Esp. *predic.* (quasi-*adv.*) in phr. ***to hang*** (or ***stay***) ***loose***. *slang.* (orig. *U.S.*).

1968 R. COOVER *Universal Baseball Assoc.* viii. 242 'Hang loose,' he says, and pulling down his mask, trots back behind home plate. **1968–70** *Current Slang* (Univ. S. Dakota) III–IV. 40 *Down loose*, opposite of uptight.—College students, both sexes, Minnesota. **1970** S. BELLOW *Mr Sammler's Planet* iv. 161 Daddy had a bad thing about me, made me financially too independent. You know—pampered me and let me hang too loose. **1974** L. DEIGHTON *Spy Story* xviii. 195 This is the Captain. Stay loose, everybody. It's just their E.C.M. **1977** C. MCFADDEN *Serial* (1978) iv. 14/2 'And remember,' he told him, waving, 'stay loose'. **1977** *Zigzag* Mar. 12/3 The owners were like alcoholics, but they were nice people..loose. **1982** W. SAFIRE in *N.Y. Times Mag.* 28 Nov. 16 The sympathetic farewell is undiminished: *Hang in there* vies with *Hang tough* and *Hang loose*, and *Walk light* may cheer up the overweight.

4. Not close or compact in arrangement or structure. **a.** *gen.* Used e.g. of earth or soil: Having the particles free to move among themselves. Of a fabric or tissue or its texture: Having spaces between the threads.

c **1374** CHAUCER *Boeth.* II. metr. iv. 30 (Camb. MS.) The lavse [*ed.* 1532 lose] sandes refusen to beren the heuy wyhte. **1577** B. GOOGE *Heresbach's Husb.* (1586) 44 You must beware, that whyle the ground is loose and soft, you let not in the water. **1592** SHAKS. *Rom. & Jul.* v. iii. 6 So shall no foot vpon the Churchyard tread, Being loose, vnfirme with digging vp of Graues. **1603** OWEN *Pembrokeshire* (1891) 73 This Marle..is to be cast on baren lowse and drie land. **1626** BACON *Sylva* §34 The Ashes with Aire betweene, lie looser; and with Water, closer. **1726** LEONI *Alberti's Archit.* I. 40/1 A loose soft Mud. **1822–34** *Good's Study Med.* (ed. 4) IV. 50 A current of blood superfluous in quantity but loose and unelaborate in crasis. **1846** J. BAXTER *Libr. Pract. Agric.* (ed. 4) II. 38 It is a common custom to lay a quantity of loose earth of some kind over the yard.

b. Of array or order of men: Not dense or serried.

1630 *R. Johnson's Kingd. & Commw.* II. 218 In their marches in loose troopes, they are billeted in the next houses at the countries charges. **1667** MILTON *P.L.* II. 887 With Horse and Chariots rankt in loose array. **1697** DRYDEN *Virg. Georg.* II. 374 Extend thy loose Battalions largely wide. **1744** OZELL tr. *Brantome's Sp. Rhodomontades* 193 They began to break their Order, and retir'd in a very loose Manner. **1777** ROBERTSON *Hist. Amer.* v. Wks. 1813 II. 122 They repelled, with little danger, the loose assault of the Mexicans. **1818** SHELLEY *Rev. Islam* VI. vii, The loose array Of horsemen o'er the wide fields murdering sweep.

c. *Bot.* = LAX *a.* 3 b. Also (see quots. 1814–30 and 1839).

1776 J. LEE *Introd. Bot.* Explan. Terms 78 *Laxus*, loose, easily bent. **1776–96** WITHERING *Brit. Plants* (ed. 3) IV. 290 Gills loose. **1787** tr. *Linnæus' Fam. Plants* I. 63 The leaflets longer than the floret, loose, permanent. **1814–30** *Edinb. Encycl.* IV. 40/2 Leaves..Loose, (*solutum*) a cylindrical or subulate leaf, which is loosely attached to its stem. **1839** LINDLEY *Introd. Bot.* (ed. 3) 472 Loose (*laxus*); of a soft cellular texture, as the pith of most plants. *Ibid.* 492 Loose (*laxus*); when the parts are distant from each other, with an open light kind of arrangement; as the panicle among the other kinds of inflorescence.

d. Occurring in book-names of certain plants of a straggling habit (see quots.).

1837 MACGILLIVRAY *Withering's Brit. Plants* (ed. 4) 71 Loose Panick-grass. **1861** MISS PRATT *Flower. Pl.* VI. 38 Loose Pendulous Sedge.

e. Of handwriting: Not compact, straggling.

1711 HEARNE *Collect.* (O.H.S.) III. 105 [A transcript] wch is written in a pretty large and loose Hand. **1866** SKEAT *Melusine* (E.E.T.S.) Pref. (*init.*), It is written..in a clear but somewhat loose handwriting.

f. Applied to exercise or play in which those engaged are not close together or in which there is free movement of some kind. (See also quots. 1897 and cf. B. 2.)

1802 C. JAMES *Milit. Dict.*, s.v. *Loosen*, The lock step was introduced for the purpose of counteracting the mischievous effects of loose marching. **1833** *Regul. Instr. Cavalry* I. 146 The loose play, or independent practice, should first be attempted at a walk. **1897** *Encycl. Sport* I. 253/2 *Loose croquet*, the striking of the player's ball when both are set together, without putting one's foot upon it. *Ibid.* 144/2 (Broadsword), *Loose play*, a contest in which the combatants deliver strokes and effect parries, not in any regular sequence, but as they think each may be most effective. **1899** SHEARMAN in *Football* (Badm. Libr.) 195 The real feature of the loose game..was the additional importance it gave to the three-quarter back.

5. a. Wanting in retentiveness or power of restraint.

1390 GOWER *Conf.* I. 131 His lose tunge he mot restreigne. **1604** SHAKS. *Oth.* III. iii. 416 There are a kinde of men, So loose of Soule, that in their sleepes will mutter Their Affayres. **1613** —— *Hen. VIII*, II. i. 127 Where you are liberall of your loues and Councels, Be sure you be not loose. **1865** CARLYLE *Fredk. Gt.* VII. iv. (1872) II. 283 A rash young fool; carries a loose tongue.

b. Of the bowels: Relaxed. Also said of the person.

1508 KENNEDY *Flyting w. Dunbar* 484 A rottyn crok, louse of the dok. **1594** J. DICKENSON *Arisbas* (1878) 56 The brats of Usurers should be alwaies siche of the loose disease, neuer able to holde anything long. **1671** H. M. tr. *Erasm. Colloq.* 9, I have more need to stay it's looseness, for my belly is too loose. **1707** FLOYER *Physic. Pulse-Watch* xxi. (1710) 154 To keep the Body loose is very beneficial, but much Purging.. is very injurious. **1783** J. C. SMYTH in *Med. Commun.* I. 202 It..gave her two loose stools. **1879** J. M. DUNCAN *Dis. Wom.* xiv. (1889) 95 The patient tells you that her bowels are always either very constipated or very loose—implying by looseness rather frequency of motions than thinness or liquidity of the stools.

6. a. Of qualities, actions, statements, ideas, etc.: Not rigid, strict, correct, or careful; marked by inaccurate or careless thought or speech; hence, inexact, indefinite, indeterminate, vague.

1606 SHAKS. *Tr. & Cr.* III. iii. 41 Lay negligent and loose regard vpon him. **1622** BACON *Holy War* Misc. Wks. (1629) 114 It is but a loose Thing to speake of Possibilities, without the Particular Designes. **1649** MILTON *Eikon.* Pref., The loose and negligent curiosity of those who took upon them to adorn this Booke. **1651** HOBBES *Leviath.* III. xxxvi. 226 Prophets..at Delphi..of whose loose words a sense might be made to fit any event. **1711** STEELE *Spect.* No. 188 ¶1 It is an Argument of a loose and ungoverned Mind to be affected with the promiscuous Approbation of the Generality of Mankind. **1752** HUME *Pol. Disc.* x. 216 No attention ought ever to be given to such loose, exaggerated calculations. **1790** PALEY *Horæ Paul.* i. 3 We have only loose tradition and reports to go by. **1839** I. TAYLOR *Anc. Chr.* I. iii. 173 Not merely a loose resemblance but a close analogy. **1844** LINGARD *Anglo-Sax. Ch.* (1858) I. App. A. 317 The loose and indefinite word *interea*, or in the meanwhile. **1895** R. L. DOUGLAS in *Bookman* Oct. 23/1 His style is..free from that loose rhetoric which is so wearisome to the reader who loves history for its own sake.

b. Of literary productions, style, etc.

1638 BAKER tr. *Balzac's Lett.* (vol. III.) 31 This kind of writing is rather a loose poetry, than a regular Prose. **1687** MIEGE *Gt. Fr. Dict.* II, A loose Discourse, that does not hang together, *discours qui n'est pas bien lié.* **1709** FELTON *Classics* (1718) 173 That Loose and Libertine Way of Paraphrasing. **1754** GRAY *Poesy* 61 Loose numbers wildly sweet. **1872** MINTO *Eng. Prose Lit.* Introd. 6 A sentence so constructed as to be noticeably loose. **1884** CHURCH *Bacon* ix. 215 Nothing can be more loose than the structure of the essays.

c. Qualifying an agent-noun.

a **1568** ASCHAM *Scholem.* (Arb.) 116 Colde, lowse, and rough writers. **1847** L. HUNT *Men, Women & B.* II. i. 3 Lady Dorset was accounted a loose speaker. **1865** LIGHTFOOT *Galatians* (1874) 120 No stress can be laid on the casual statement of a writer so loose and so ignorant of Greek. **1875** WHITNEY *Life Lang.* ii. 29 We are loose thinkers and loose talkers. **1902** *Blackw. Mag.* May 590/2 Here too are traps for the loose rider.

†d. Of conditions, undertakings, or engagements: Lacking security, unsettled. *Obs.*

1603 *Contn. Adv. Don Sebastian* in *Harl. Misc.* (1810) V. 468, I hold it no policy to deliver it [a letter] her; considering it as a loose adventure, in such dangers, to trust a woman. **1645** RUTHERFORD *Tryal & Tri. Faith* (1845) 80 We make loose bargains in the behalf of our Souls. **1687** MIEGE *Gt. Fr. Dict.* II, To be in a loose (or unsettled) Condition, *n'avoir point d' Etablissement.*

e. *Cricket.* Of bowling: Wanting in accuracy of pitch. Of fielding, etc.: Careless, slack.

1859 *All Year Round* No. 13. 306 The loose balls we hit for fours and fives; the good ones we put away for singles. **1877** Box *Eng. Game Cricket* 454 *Loose*, this adjective is frequently applied to batting, bowling, and fielding too. **1884** *Lillywhite's Cricket Ann.* 103 P. M. Lucas punishes loose bowling severely.

f. *colloq.* Of an appointed time: Not strictly adhered to.

1892 SIR H. MAXWELL *Meridiana* 45 Breakfast is not on the table till a loose ten.

7. Of persons, their habits, writings, etc.: Free from moral restraint; lax in principle, conduct, or speech; chiefly in narrower sense, unchaste, wanton, dissolute, immoral.

c **1470** HENRYSON *Mor. Fab.* III. (*Cock & Fox*) xx, He was sa lous, and sa lecherous. *a* **1578** LINDESAY (Pitscottie) *Chron. Scot.* (S.T.S.) I. 197 He had ane lous man with him in his companie callit Makgregour quhilk he suspectit gif ony thing war in missing it wald be found of tymes throw his handis. **1588** GREENE *Perimedes* 43 By being lose in my loues,..to disparage mine honour. **1588** SHAKS. *L.L.L.* v. ii. 776. **1591** PERCIVALL *Sp. Dict.*, *Amancebado*,..a loose liuer. **1650** BAXTER *Saints' R.* I. vii. (1662) 104 Now every old companion and every loose-fellow is putting up the finger. **1660** PEPYS *Diary* 9 Oct., I find him to be a merry fellow and pretty good natured, and sings very loose songs. **1683** TRYON *Way to Health* xix. (1697) 428 The Spermatick Vessels, whence proceed wanton Desires, and loose Imaginations. **1700** DRYDEN *Pref. Fables* Wks. (Globe) 502, I am sensible..of the scandal I have given by my loose writings. **1722** DE FOE *Col. Jack* (1840) 170 He had led a loose life. *a* **1770** JORTIN *Serm.* (1771) IV. i. 5 The Pagans though loose enough in other points of duty. **1784** COWPER *Task* II. 378 Loose in morals, and in manners vain. **1849** MACAULAY *Hist. Eng.* vi. II. 118 He was a loose and profane man. **1879** F. W. FARRAR *St. Paul* (1883) 675 The leading hierarchs resembled the loosest of the Avignon cardinals.

8. Applied to a stable in which animals are kept 'loose' (sense 1 a) or without being fastened up. So also ***loose box*** (see BOX *sb.*[2] 12).

1813 *Sporting Mag.* XLII. 54 The reader will have noticed my frequent warm recommendations of the loose stable. **1833** LOUDON *Encycl. Cottage Archit.* §1091 The stables, loose-house (stable or place for a sick horse..&c.),.. to be neatly causewayed. **1839** GREENWOOD *Hints Horsemanship* (1861) 128 A horse should have a loose

standing if possible, if he must be tied in a stall it should be flat. **1849** THACKERAY *Pendennis* lxxv, Gentlemen hunting with the..hounds will find excellent Stabling and loose boxes for horses at the 'Clavering Arms'. **1871** M. COLLINS *Mrq. & Merch.* I. ii. 89 Loose boxes for no end of horses.

9. In certain specialized collocations: **loose back**, a method of binding the spine of a book to make it open more easily; **loose body** *Med.* = *joint mouse* (JOINT *sb.* 15); usu. *pl.*; **loose coupling** *Electr.* (see COUPLING *vbl. sb.* 6 f (i)); **loose cover**, a detachable cover for a chair, couch, or car seat; also *attrib.*; **loose fall** *Whaling* (see FALL *sb.*[3]); **loose-fill, loose fill**, a type of house insulation (see quot. 1964); also *attrib.*; **loose fish**, (*a*) *colloq.* a person of irregular habits; †(*b*) a common prostitute; (*c*) (see quot. 1864); (*d*) *Whaling* (see quot. 1883); †**loose hand** = LOOSE END, in phr. ***at the loose hand***; **loose head**, see HEAD *sb.*[1] 26 c; **loose-housing**, a method of housing cattle in winter in partly covered barns with access to a feeding area, in which the cows are not confined to a single stall; also *attrib.*; hence **loose-housed** *a.*; **loose ice** (see quot. 1835); **loose pulley**, 'a pulley running loosely on the shaft, and receiving the belt from the *fast pulley* when the shaft is to be disconnected from the motor' (Knight *Dict. Mech.*); also ***fast and loose pulley*** (see FAST *a.* 11); **loose scrummage, loose scrum**, in *Rugby Football*, a scrum formed by the players round the ball during play, and not ordered by the referee: opp. *set scrum(mage)*; hence, **loose scrummaging**; **loose smut**, a disease of cereals, esp. barley and wheat, caused by the fungus *Ustilago nuda*; **loose whale**, a whale which remains beside its harpooned mate; †**loose work**, a kind of embroidery in which certain parts (e.g. those representing leaves of trees) are left free to move.

1923 H. A. MADDOX *Dict. Stationery* 46 **Loose back*, also termed open or spring back. *Ibid.* 47 A loose back may be created by simply casing the book... The spring or loose back is actually bound into the book. **1956** *Bookman's Conc. Dict.* 277 *Spring Back*, an inner joint in a bookbinding which allows the book to open flat; known as Hollow or Loose Back. **1961** T. LANDAU *Encycl. Librarianship* (ed. 2) 268/2 *Open back*, a style of construction in which the cover is separated from the spine of the book by a special lining... Also called Hollow and Loose Back. **1886** H. MARSH *Dis. Joints* xv. 185 On examining his joint when the acute attack has gone off, the patient detects the *loose body, and learns that it shifts its position. *Ibid.* 183 (*caption*) Specimens of the loose bodies found in the knee joint in Mr. Smith's case. **1952** [see *joint mouse* s.v. JOINT *sb.* 15]. **1961** R. D. BAKER *Essent. Path.* xxi. 578 Portions of the damaged articular cartilage, or fragments of the thickened peripheral bone, break off and become loose bodies in the joint cavities. **1876** M. W. COOK *Tables & Chairs* i. 52 You may prefer to have your curtains, as well as the *loose covers, of chintz. *Ibid.* 56 Nothing now-a-days looks so nice and ladylike, or is so economical as well fitting loose covers. **1911** F. B. JACK *Woman's Bk.* 613/2 Loose covers are not much used nowadays, and, at the best, they soon get out of order and become shabby looking. **1929** *Radio Times* 8 Nov. 438/1 Odd Jobs about the House—II, A Few Hints on Loose Cover Cutting. **1936** R. LEHMANN *Weather in Streets* I. v. 104, I might keep her on for the sewing. She's very clever at loose covers. **1953** M. SHERIDAN *Furnisher's Encycl.* IX. iii. 414 A loose cover service may substantially increase the furnisher's business. **1959** *B.S.I. News* Nov. 20 Specifies.. maximum foreign matter content for loose cover cloths made from cotton. **1973** A. BROINOWSKI *Take One Ambassador* xii. 206 Comfortable upholstery, not bottomlessly soft, with well-cut linen loose covers. [**1949** *Building Digest* IX. 305 The flat roof has a loose vermiculite filling.] **1950** *Archit. Rev.* CVIII. 332/2 A 4 in. thickness of vermiculite *loosefill for instance has the same thermal insulation as 24 times that thickness of concrete. **1956** *Good Housek. Home Encycl.* (ed. 4) 170/2 'Loose fill' which is poured or packed..between the joists. **1964** J. S. SCOTT *Dict. Building* 198 *Loose-fill insulation*, insulating materials such as granulated cork, loose asbestos.. vermiculite. Loose fill is placed between rafters or studs to increase the insulating value of a dry air space. **1969** *Daily Tel.* 16 Sept. 15 Most house-holders can climb into their lofts and lay mineral wool or glass fibre over the joists, or loose-fill between them. **1809** MALKIN *Gil Blas* VII. vii, Girls in a servile condition of life, or those unfortunate *loose fish who are game for every sportsman. **1827** EGAN *Anecd. Turf* 72 A game known among the loose fish who frequent races ..by the name of 'the thimble-rig'. **1864** *Sat. Rev.* July 84/1 That peculiar variety of Parliamentary species known as 'an outsider' or 'a loose fish,' but described by itself under the more flattering title of 'an independent member'. **1883** CLARK RUSSELL *Sailors' Lang.*, *Loose-fish*, a whaling term signifying that the whale is fair game for anybody who can catch it. *a* **1734** NORTH *Lives* (1742) 77 He was weary of being at the *loose hand as to company. **1907** 'OLD INTERNATIONAL' *Rugby Guide* 62 It was discovered that on the flank of the row where the ball came into the scrum there was a head overhanging the side of the scrum. This head was given the appellation of '*loose head'. **1917** [see HEAD *sb.*[1] 26 c]. **1927** [see HOOKER[1] 6]. **1960** C. VENABLES *Instructions to Young Rugger Players* iii. 37 When the two scrummages are formed they pack down and, of course, the heads of the two front rows are interlocked. But, with three men in each row, this clearly means that one man in each row will have his head free. This is known as the 'loose head' and it is on that side that the scrum half will put the ball in, for the good reason that his own hooker will be nearer to the ball than the hooker on the other side. **1960** E. S. & W. J. HIGHAM *High Speed Rugby* xiv. 191 The *loose-head prop* puts the *inside* foot forward. *Ibid.* 195 We will refer to the hooker who has the loose head..as the 'loose head hooker'. **1960** *Farmer & Stockbreeder* 5 Jan. 53/1 Half [the herd] is *loose-housed and zero-grazed. *Ibid.* 12 Jan. 78/1 Three sides of the yard accommodating the 55 pedigree..Friesians loose-housed are filled by the covered lying shed. **1963** C. T. M. HERRIOTT tr. *Craplet's Dairy Cow* v. xvii. 374 Loose-housed animals are less nervous than those kept in byres. **1946** *Agric. Engineering* XXVII. 499/2 The *loose-housing barn and milking parlor seemed to offer a possible improvement. **1948** *Pop. Bull. Washington Agric. Exper. Station* No. 190 (*title*) The loose housing and feeding of dairy herds. *Ibid.* 2 Loose housing is becoming popular. **1963** C. T. M. HERRIOTT tr. *Craplet's Dairy Cow* v. xvii. 369 Loose housing provides a well-compacted, thoroughly decomposed manure. *Ibid.*, Cows to be kept under a loose housing system can become accustomed to communal living. **1774** C. J. PHIPPS *Voy. N. Pole* 38 At one in the afternoon, being still amongst the *loose ice. **1835** SIR J. ROSS *Narr. 2nd Voy.* Explan. Terms p. xv, *Loose ice*, a number of pieces of ice near each other, but through which the ship can make way. **1825** J. NICHOLSON *Operat. Mechanic* 382 A strap passing from a drum over a *fast and loose pulley. **1873** J. RICHARDS *Wood-working Factories*, 62 Loose pulleys will give trouble now and then, no matter how well they are fitted. **1874** G. H. WEST *Rugby Union Football Ann.* 66 A light and very useful forward, especially in a *loose scrummage. **1936** Loose scrummage [see *heel-back* (HEEL *sb.*[1] 26)]. **1952** *Rugby Union Football* ('Know the Game' Series) (ed. 2) 26 A 'loose' scrum..is formed by..players closing round the ball when it is on the ground. **1958** PELMEAR & MORPURGO *Rugby Football* VIII. 339 Loose scrummaging (now sometimes known as 'rucking') was becoming the half-back's delight. **1960** E. S. & W. J. HIGHAM *High Speed Rugby* xiv. 201 It is possible to build up a loose scrum in two ways. **1890** *2nd Ann. Rep. Kansas State Exper. Station 1889* 213 The *loose smuts are four closely allied species found on oats, wheat, and barley. **1909** *Bull. Bureau Plant Industry, U.S. Dept. Agric.* No. 152. 7 The loose smut..is easily distinguished from the covered smut by its earlier appearance, by its olive-green spore-mass.., and by the early shedding of the spores. **1924** *Jrnl. Agric. Res.* XXIX. 263/1 Formaldehyde and some of the organic mercury compounds have been found to control the loose-smut of barley in certain varieties. **1968** *Times* 16 Dec. 7/1 Loose smut in barley..has become a serious problem again because of the preponderance of susceptible varieties. **1903** F. T. BULLEN in *Strand Mag.* Nov. 539/1 All through the combat..the whale-fishers will be closely beset by the '*loose' whale. *a* **1548** HALL *Chron., Hen. VIII* 58 b, Velvet, covered all over with braunches of hony suckels of fyne flat gold of dammaske, of *lose worke, every lefe of the braunche moving. **1577–87** HOLINSHED *Chron.* III. 844/2 A curious lose worke of veluet imbrodered with gold.

10. *Comb.* **a.** In concord with sbs., forming adjectival combs., as ***loose-needle, loose-wrist.***

1866 *Athenæum* No. 1997. 178/3 Loose-wrist practice [in pianoforte-playing] is a most excellent thing. **1883** GRESLEY *Gloss. Coal Mining*, *Dialling*, the operation of making a survey with the dial. There are two ways of using the instrument, known as loose needle and fast needle dialling.

b. with pples., *loose* being used as a complement, as ***loose-broke, -hanging, -hung, -let, -lying*** adjs.

1807 J. BARLOW *Columb.* v. 203 His troops press forward like a *loose-broke flood. **1598** MARSTON *Sco. Villanie* II. vii. F 6, Her *loose-hanging gowne For her loose lying body. **1851** LONGF. *Gold. Leg.* III. *Street in Strasburg*, What news do you bring with your loose-hanging rein? **1625** K. LONG tr. *Barclay's Argenis* II. xx. 133 The *loose-hung banners. **1872** A. DE VERE *Leg. St. Patrick, St. P. & Armagh Cath.*, With tangled locks and loose-hung battle-axe Ran the wild kerne. **1870** SWINBURNE *Ess. & Stud.* (1875) 261 Effeminate in build, loose-hung, weak of eye and foot. **1601** *Mary Magd. Lament.* VI. xxvi. (*Fuller Worthies Miscell.* II.), My *loose-let soule. **1814** SOUTHEY *Roderick* Poet. Wks. 1838 IX. 53 Soon they scoop'd Amid *loose-lying sand a hasty grave.

c. parasynthetic adjs., as ***loose-barbed, -curled, -flowered, -girdled, -handed, -hipped, -jointed, -limbed, -lived, -locked, -panicled, -principled, -robed, -spiked, -wived.***

1901 *Blackw. Mag.* Dec. 742/2 Their spears with *loose barbed points. **1882** OUIDA *Maremma* I. 152 Her bronze-hued, *loose-curled head. **1837** MACGILLIVRAY *Withering's Brit. Pl.* (ed. 4) 346 *Loose-flowered Alpine Carex. **1894** GLADSTONE *Horace's Odes* 35 With thee, *loose-girdled Graces come. **1870** LOWELL *Among my Bks.* Ser. I. (1873) 223 To draw the line..between a wise generosity and a *loose-handed weakness of giving. **1648** HERRICK *Hesper.* (1869) I. 64 First Jollie's wife is lame; then next, *loose-hipt, Squint-ey'd, hook-nos'd. **1859** JEPHSON *Brittany* iii. 28 Big-headed, *loose-jointed..carriage-horses. **1823** COBBETT *Rur. Rides* (1885) I. 303 The cattle appear to be all of the Sussex breed..*loose-limbed. **1889** DOYLE *Micah Clarke* 236 A long loose-limbed seaman came up from the mouth of the cave. **1641** J. TRAPPE *Theol. Theol.* 250 *Loose-lived ministers. *a* **1661** HOLYDAY *Juvenal* 94 *Loose-lock'd Sabines, who a battle stay'd. **1825** *Greenhouse Comp.* II. 43 *Otidialaxa*, *loose-panicled Otidia. **1858** J. MARTINEAU *Stud. Chr.* 188 A *loose-principled and unholy being. **1777** ELIZ. RYVES *Poems* 60 Where *loose-rob'd Pleasure careless roves. **1837** MACGILLIVRAY *Withering's Brit. Pl.* (ed. 4) 346 *Loose-spiked Rock Carex. **1606** SHAKS. *Ant. & Cl.* I. ii. 75 It is a heart-breaking to see a handsome man *loose Wiu'd.

d. Special combs.: †**loose-bellied** *a.*, having the bowels relaxed; **loose-bodied** *a.*, (of a dress) loose-fitting; †*fig.* lewd, wanton; †**loose-breech**, a slovenly lout; †**loose-clacked** *a.*, loquacious, chattering; **loose-ended** *a.*, ended or finished off in a slack, untidy, or inconclusive way; also *fig.*; hence **loose-endedness**; **loose-footed** *a.*, having a loose foot (in quot., said of a sail); †*fig.* ready on one's feet, at liberty to travel; **loose-gowned** *a.*, wearing a loosely-fitting dress; †*fig.* wanton; †**loose-hangled** *a.* [f. *hangle* HINGLE], loose-jointed; †**loose-hilted** *a.*, 'loose in the hilts', incontinent, wanton; **loose-kirtle** (quasi-*arch.*), a wanton; **loose-knit** *a.*, connected in a tenuous or ill-defined way; not closely linked; †**loose-legged**, †**loose-tailed** *adjs.*, unchaste, incontinent; **loose-lipped** *a.*, (*a*) loose-tongued; uninhibited in speech; (*b*) having full lips; **loose-mouthed** *a.* = *loose-lipped* adj.; **loose-skinned** *a.*, having skin wrinkled or hanging in folds; **loose-tongued** *a.*, blabbing; †**loose-waistcoateer**, ? a woman.

1565 COOPER *Thesaurus*, *Aluus liquanda*, he must be made *loose bealyed. **1596** SHAKS. *Tam. Shr.* IV. iii. 136 If euer I said *loose-bodied gowne, sow me in the skirts of it. **1621** B. JONSON *Gipsies Metam.* (1640) 67 Christian shall get her a loose bodide-gowne. **1625** SHIRLEY *School of Compl.* II. i, Hee's giddy-headed, and loose-bodied. **1672** DRYDEN *1st Pt. Conq. Granada* Epil., And oft the lacquey, or the brawny clown, Gets what is hid in the loose-bodied gown. **1575** *Gamm. Gurton* III. iii, I faith, sir *loose-breche, had ye taried, ye shold haue found your match! **1661** K. W. *Conf. Charac.*, *Informer* (1860) 45 His dam was..some *loose clackt bitch or other. **1867** J. R. LOWELL in *Atlantic Monthly* Jan. 24 *Loose-ended souls, whose skills bring scanty gold. **1937** *Times Lit. Suppl.* 15 May 379/1 The weaving of three themes through the tenuous and loose-ended plot. **1944** *Horizon* IX. 286 My purpose is to indicate..how we loose-ended mortals are dealt with. **1905** *Proc. Roy. Soc.* LXXV. 378 There was no slackness or *loose-endedness about him either physically or intellectually. **1968** *Punch* 3 Jan. 4/2 The problem, which mightn't worry some people but had teased me for a fortnight by its sheer loose-endedness. **1717** *Wodrow Corr.* (1843) II. 315 Were I as *loose-footed as I have been, I could come to London to have the benefit of reading it. **1878** J. H. BEADLE *Western Wilds* ii. 38 Every loose-footed man wanted to go. *Ibid.* xxviii. 442 Loose-footed young men erect a cabin, barely habitable in good weather. **1895** *Outing* (U.S.) XXVI. 46/1 Tricing up the tack if the sail is loose-footed. **1927** G. BRADFORD *Gloss. Sea Terms* 104/2 *Loose-footed*, a fore and aft sail not laced to (or without) a boom. **1948** R. DE KERCHOVE *Internat. Maritime Dict.* 433/2 *Loose-footed*, an expression used for denoting a fore-and-aft sail in which the foot is not laced to the boom. *a* **1717** PARNELL *Donne's 3rd Sat.* 36 Or for some idol of thy fancy draw Some *loose-gown'd dame. **1611** COTGR. s.v. *Long*, *Longue eschine*..a tall, ill-fauoured, *loose-hangled boobie. *a* **1652** BROME *New Academy* II. i. Wks. 1873 II. 28 Your *loose-hilted Mystresses. **1855** KINGSLEY *Westw. Ho!* xxx, Here's a fellow..talks about failing, as if he were a Barbican *loose-kirtle trying to keep her apple-squire ashore! **1906** T. HARDY *Dynasts* II I. vii. 42 As he shatters the moves of the *loose-knit nations to curb his exploitful soul's ambitions. **1957** E. BOTT *Family & Social Network* iii. 94 Networks become loose-knit when people move from one place to another... If both husband and wife have moved considerably before marriage, each will bring an already loose-knit network to the marriage. **1963** *Times* 11 Mar. 3/5 The Welsh forwards performed doughty deeds individually, but were too loose-knit to hold their opponents, which was bad luck on D. C. T. Rowlands, whose most effective game thrives on a dominant pack. **1968** *Daily Tel. Mag.* 8 Nov. 27/4 The ARB team is loose-knit and embraces a cross-section of specialists. **1599** MARSTON *Sco. Villanie* II. vi. 199 Here's one must inuocate some *lose-leg'd Dame. **1919** J. MASEFIELD *Reynard* 33 *Loose-lipped with song and wine and revel. **1924** W. DE LA MARE *Ding Dong Bell* 70 Hook-nosed was I; loose-lipped. **1924** COMPTON MACKENZIE *Heavenly Ladder* xiii. 186 It was sad to see a young woman of thirty so loose-lipped and blowsy. **1928** *Daily Mail* 13 Aug. 5/1 Her mastery of what Sir William Watson has called the loose-lipped lingo of the streets. **1934** H. G. WELLS *Exper. Autobiogr.* II. ix. 679 If I were to put my reputation before my autobiographical rectitude, I think I should just let this little volume decay and char and disappear... Most of it is very loose-lipped indeed. **1934** W. B. YEATS *King of Great Clock Tower* 29 Had de Valera eaten Parnell's heart No loose-lipped demagogue had won the day. **1872** J. G. WHITTIER *Pennsylvania Pilgrim* in *Poet. Wks.* (1874) 447 We may trace How *loose-mouthed boor and fine ancestral grace Sat in close contrast. **1931** W. FAULKNER *Sanctuary* xxii. 203 You'll know I ain't loose-mouthed. **1938** *Times Lit. Suppl.* 18 June 415/4 Were all Roman aristocrats loose-mouthed and pot-bellied? **1950** D. GASCOYNE *Vagrant* 53 He is apt to get oddly pedantic about the proprieties while even more loose-mouthed than ever. **1906** *Westm. Gaz.* 14 June 4/2 This old man had a full, *loose-skinned face, with a comic mouth and forlorn eyes. **1909** *Ibid.* 5 Jun. 2/2 The sail heaved like a gigantic loose-skinned animal awakening. **1937** V. WOOLF *Years* 397 His swarthy wrinkled face.. always made her think of some loose-skinned, furry animal. **1941** BLUNDEN *Thomas Hardy* v. 110 Hands very white and soft and loose-skinned. **1598** J. DICKENSON *Greene in Conc.* (1878) 147 Her *loose-taild gossips which first intic't her to folly. **1689** CARLILE *Fortune Hunters* IV. 43 You have fixt her in the Rank of loose-tail'd Ladies. **1647** WARD *Simp. Cobler* 25, I shall..make bold..to borrow a little of their *loose tongued Liberty. **1883** *Daily News* 7 Nov. 5/4 The Marquis thought some of his Paris Attachés had been rather too loose-tongued. *a* **1658** CLEVELAND *Pet. Poem* 18 So that my Doublet pin'd, makes me appear Not like a Man but a *Loose-wastcoateer.

B. quasi-*sb.* and *sb.*

1. *absol.* in phrases. **a.** ***on*** (or †***upon***) ***the loose***: (*a*) (behaving) in an unrestrained or dissolute fashion; 'on the spree'; (*b*) of women: living by prostitution; (*c*) *gen.*, not tied down; not answerable to anyone.

1749 J. CLELAND *Mem. Woman Pleasure* II. 9 The giddy, wildness of young girls once got upon the loose. **1849** J. HANNAY *King Dobbs* v. 76 One evening, when they were at Gibraltar, on the look-out for amusement—in modern parlance, 'on the loose',—they went into a little wine-shop [etc.]. **1859** *Punch* 9 July 22/1 Our friend prone to vices you never may see, Though he goes on the Loose, or the Cut, or the Spree. **1859** HOTTEN *Dict. Slang* 70 *On the loose*, obtaining a living by prostitution, in reality, on the streets. The term is applied to females only. **1872** *Ibid.* 20 July 23/1 Having to appear at the police court in order to give evidence for one of your fast friends who has been out upon the loose.

1879 Roget's Thesaurus 330 Impure; unclean &c...; on the streets, on the pavé, on the loose. 1890 Barrère & Leland Dict. Slang II. Loose, on the,..getting a living by prostitution. 1914 G. B. Shaw Fanny's First Play III. 201 Do you mean to say that you went on the loose out of pure devilment? 1935 N. Ersine Underworld & Prison Slang 51 Ted is on the loose. 1949 Partridge Dict. Underworld 483/2 On the loose, obtaining a living by prostitution. 1951 E. Paul Springtime in Paris i. 12 Just then Raoul was spending all his free time with the peace posters and Katya stayed at home. When the roles were reversed, and Katya was on the loose, no one knew precisely what she was about. 1958 Times Lit. Suppl. 30 May 293/2 A group of young Americans.., some being genuinely on the loose or moving from job to job. 1970 V. Canning Great Affair xvii. 319 There was a little mistiming at Sokota so your friend King Alfy is on the loose.

b. *in the loose*: not made up into or prepared in a particular form.

1898 Westm. Gaz. 19 Nov. 8/1 Of this [collection of cigar ends] about 1½ cwt. was sold in the loose to a tobacco manufacturer at 1s. per lb.

2. *Rugby Football*. That part of the play in which the ball travels freely from player to player, as distinguished from the *scrummage*.

1892 Pall Mall G. 25 Jan. 1/2 They carried the 'scrums', and were quicker in the 'loose'. 1894–5 Rugby Union Football Handbk. 11 'Offside' is still penalised in the loose, but not Solon himself..could define where a scrummage ends and the loose begins. 1900 Westm. Gaz. 12 Dec. 7/2 In the loose both packs did well, but the Oxford men were the more brilliant. 1922 'Touch Flag' Mod. Rugby Tactics 49 Dangerous attacks frequently originate from chance openings in the loose. 1963 Rugby World Aug. 8/3 Wightman and Rogers impressed in the loose for England. 1974 Country Life 5 Dec. 1717/1 The All Blacks..were.. gaining their expected supremacy at the line-out and in the loose.

C. *adv.*

1. Loosely; with a loose hold. *to sit loose* (fig.): to be independent or indifferent; to hold loosely *to*, not to be enslaved *to*; *occas.* not to weigh heavily *upon*. †So *to hang loose* (*to*). *to hold loose*: to be indifferent.

1591 H. Smith Pride Nabuch. 27 How earnest hee was about his dreame and how loose he sat after in his pallace. 1647 Trapp Comm. Epist. & Rev. 83 The best counsell I can give you, is that you hang loose to all these outward comforts. 1680 P. Henry Diaries & Lett. (1882) 281 Theref. get loose, my soul, from these th. & sitt loose to them. 1683 Temple Mem. Wks. 1731 I. 480, I found within a Fortnight after I arriv'd, that he sat very loose with the King his Master. 1706 Atterbury Funeral Serm. Bennet 6 To sit as loose from those Pleasures, and be as moderate in the use of them, as they can. 1711 Addison Spect. No. 119 ¶2 The fashionable World is grown free and easy; our Manners sit more loose upon us. 1858 Carlyle Fredk. Gt. II. xiii. I. 175 A fluctuating series of governors holding loose, and not in earnest. 1880 Macm. Mag. No. 245. 397 To the rubrical theories he simply sat loose.

2. *to play fast and loose* (†*loose or fast*): see fast and loose b.

a1555 Lyndesay Tragedy 196 We mycht full weill haue leuit in peace and rest, Nyne or ten ȝeris, and than playit lowis or fast.

3. *Comb.*, as *loose-driving*, *-enrobed*, *-fitting*, *-floating*, *-flowing*, *-living*, *-thinking*, *-wadded*, *-woven*, *-writ* adjs.

1729 Savage Wanderer I. 165 Yon limeless Sands *loose-driving with the Wind. 1598 Shaks. Merry W. IV. vi. 41 *Loose en-roab'd With Ribonds-pendant flaring 'bout her head. 1881 H. James Portr. Lady xxv, Ralph had a kind of *loose-fitting urbanity that wrapped him about like an ill-made overcoat. 1727–46 Thomson Summer 1316 In folds *loose-floating fell the fainter lawn. 1777 Potter Æschylus, Seven agst. Thebes 159 Their *loose-flowing hair. 1873 Longf. Milton 6 Its loose-flowing garments. 1607 Tourneur Rev. Trag. I. ii. Wks. 1878 II. 18 With easie Doctors, those *loose-liuing men. 1862 R. H. Patterson Ess. Hist. & Art 108 In this *loose-thinking style. 1841 Thackeray Men & Coats Wks. 1900 XIII. 610 Your *loose-wadded German schlafrock..is the laziest, filthiest invention. 1627–47 Feltham Resolves I. ii. 4 That which puts the *loose-woven minde into a whirling tempest. 1901 Kath. Steuart By Allan Water x. 275 Their webs of loose-woven cloth. a1720 Sheffield (Dk. Buckhm.) Wks. (1753) I. 76 The *loose writ libels of this age.

loose (lu:s), *v.* Forms: 3 leowsin (? *for* lowsin), 4 lauce, laus, lowss, loyse, 4–5 (also 9 *dial.*) lause, lawse, 4–6 lous, lose, loiss, (also 7–9 *dial.*) louse, lowse, (5 losyn, louce), 5–6 louss, loss, (6 looce, looze, los, loase, lows, lowis, lewce), 6–7 leuse, 4– loose. *Pa. t.* 4 laused, etc.; also 5 laust, 6 loust, 7 loost. *Pa. pple.* 4 laused, etc.; *strong* (rare) 4 losine, 6 losen. [f. loose *a.* Cf. leese *v.*²]

1. a. *trans.* To let loose, set free; to release (a person, an animal, or their limbs) from bonds or physical restraint.

a1225 Juliana 38 Ichulle þe leowsin [Bodl. MS. lowse] ant leauen hwen me þuncheð. a1300 Cursor M. 14356 [Lazar] in winding clath..was wonden,..'Louses him nu', he said. c1400 Destr. Troy 7884 Deliuert were þo lordes, lawsit of prisone. c1470 Henry Wallace x. 727 Schyr, loss me off my band. 1470–85 Malory Arthur xi. xii. 589, I requyre the lose me of my boundes. 1497 Extracts Aberd. Reg. (1844) I. 60 And nocht to be lousit out of the goif quhile the saide hour, for nay request. 1530 Palsgr. 615/1 Lowse this prisoner from his yrones, he muste be removed from this gaylle. 1535 Coverdale Mark xi. 4 They..founde the foale tyed by yᵉ dore..and lowsed it. 1581 Act 23 Eliz. c. 10 §4 So as they..doe presentlye loose and let goe everye Feasaunte and Partridge so taken. 1611 Bible Isa. li. 14 The captiue exile hasteneth that he may be loosed. 1697 Dryden Virg. Past. vi. 38 Loose me, he cry'd, 'twas Impudence to find A sleeping God, 'tis Sacrilege to bind. 1821 Shelley Prometh. Unb. II. ii. 94 How he [the chained Titan] shall be loosed. 1840 Browning Sordello II. 211 Like Perseus when he loosed his naked love. 1865 Trollope Belton Est. xx. 232 Belton had gone into the stable, and had himself loosed the animal.

b. In immaterial sense: To set free, release, emancipate; †to absolve (a person). Const. *from* (†*of*).

1340 Hampole Pr. Consc. 2182, I yhern..be loused away Fra þis life. c1375 Sc. Leg. Saints xvi. (Magdalena) 985 Syndry seke men gettis þare hele, & are lousit of mekil payne. c1400 Destr. Troy 13250 At the last, fro þat lady, I lausyt myselfe. c1425 Cursor M. 18327 (Trin.) From deþ of helle to lousen vs. 1533 Gau Richt Vay 24 Quhil we be lowsit of this mortal body. 1559 Bk. Com. Prayer, Occas. Prayers, Let the pitifulnes of thy great mercy lose vs. 1570–6 Lambarde Peramb. Kent (1826) 149 Loosing them from al duty of allegiance to their Prince. 1611 Bible Luke xiii. 12 Woman, thou art loosed from thy infirmitie. 1637–50 Row Hist. Kirk (1842) 130 It was concluded,..that he shall be lowsed fra the said sentence. 1784 Cowper Task II. 39 They [sc. slaves] themselves once ferried o'er the wave That parts us, are emancipate and loosed. 1842 Tennyson Godiva 37 She sent a herald forth, And bad him cry,..that she would loose The people. 1902 A. M. Fairbairn Philos. Chr. Relig. III. ii. 542 God as interpreted through Him [Christ] was loosed from the qualities that bound Him to a peculiar people.

c. *esp.* with allusion to Matt. xvi. 19, xviii. 18. Also *absol.*

a1300 Cursor M. 18189 Quat art þou þat louses þaa þat formast sin sua band in wa? 1340 Hampole Pr. Consc. 3852 Alle þat þou lowses in erthe right Sal be loused in heven bright. c1375 Sc. Leg. Saints I. (Petrus) 17 To bind and louss quhowm-euer þou will Plane powar is gewin þe þare-till. c1400 Maundev. (Roxb.) iii. 9 To wham Godd gaffe full powere for to bynd and to louse. 1526 Pilgr. Perf. (W. de W. 1531) 225 b, What so euer thou loose in erth, it shall be losen in heuen. a1548 Hall Chron., Edw. IV 199 Havyng full aucthoritie to bynd and to lose, to contracte and conclude. 1567 Gude & Godlie Ball. (S.T.S.) 192 Saif Christ onlie that deit on tre He may baith louse and bind. 1892 E. P. Barlow Regni Evangelium i. 57 What they have bound no other hand must loose.

d. To free (the lips, tongue, etc.) from constraint.

a1375 Joseph Arim. 49 Louse þi lippes a-twynne & let þe gost worche. 1567 Gude & Godlie Ball. (S.T.S.) 127 My lippis Lord than louse thow sall. 1629 Sir W. Mure True Crvcifixe 2283 Now doe the wicked louse their tongues to lyes. 1822 Shelley Zucca x. 8 Sounds of softest song..Had loosed the heart of him who sat and wept. 1842 Tennyson Vision Sin 88 Let me screw thee up a peg: Let me loose thy tongue with wine. 1902 Expositor May 383 The wine loosed the tongues of the guests.

†e. To set free from disease. *Obs.*

a1637 B. Jonson Praises Country Life 58 Or the herb Sorrell, that loves Meadows still, Or Mallowes loosing bodyes ill.

2. a. To undo, untie, unfasten (fetters, a knot); to break (a seal); †*occas.* with *up*. † *to loose down* (Sc.): to unfasten and let down. Now *dial.* or *poet.*

a1300–1400 Cursor M. 12823 (Gött.), I es noght worthi to louse [Cott. lese] þe thwanges of his scho. c1375 Sc. Leg. Saints xix. (Cristofore) 510 þai..lousit þare beltis spedly. 1388 Wyclif Acts xvi. 26 Alle the doris weren openyd, and the boondis of alle weren lousid. a1400–50 Alexander 788* þus lowtes þis lede on low & lowsys hys chynez. 1530 Palsgr. 494/1 You have so confused this yerne that it can nat be losed asonder. Ibid. 615/2 Lowse the knotte of my garter. 1535 Coverdale Rev. v. 2 Who is worthy to open the boke, and to loose the seales therof? c1560 A. Scott Poems (S.T.S.) iv. 42 It settis not madynis als To latt men lowis thair laice. 1563 Mirr. Mag., Somerset xvi, When the chiefe lynke was lewced fro the chayne. 1591 Spenser Bellay's Visions ix, With side-long beard, and locks down hanging loast. 1725 Ramsay Gentle Sheph. IV. i, The witch..Lows'd down my breeks. 1742 Young Nt. Th. v. 30 Wit calls the graces the chaste zone to loose. 1822 Shelley Triumph Life 147 They..Throw back their heads and loose their streaming hair.

fig. 1535 Coverdale Mark vii. 35 His eares were opened, and the bonde of his tonge was lowsed. 1548 Udall, etc. Erasm. Par. Matt. xii. 71 Loused the knot of the question. c1620 A. Hume Brit. Tongue (1865) 9 The knot [is] harder to louse, for nether syde wantes sum reason. 1713 Addison Cato II. i. 20 Other Prospects Have loosed those Ties and bound him fast to Cæsar. 1859 Tennyson Vivien 192 Then our bond Had best be loosed for ever.

b. To unlock or unpack (a chest, etc.); to unpack (goods). Also with *forth*, *out*; *occas.* absol. Chiefly *Sc.*

Phr. (Sc.) † *to loose the box*: to open one's coffers, to pay up. † *to loose one's poke, pack*: to open one's budget, to 'out with it'.

13.. Gaw. & Gr. Knt. 2376 He kaȝt to þe knot & þe kest lawsez. 1545 Ascham Toxoph. (Arb.) 108 Lette vs returne agayne vnto our matter, and those thynges whyche you haue packed vp, in so shorte a roume, we wyll lowse them forthe. 1583 Leg. Bp. St. Androis 228 in Satir. Poems Reform. xlv, He pat him off with mowis and mockis, And had no will to louse the boxe. 1725 Ramsay Gentle Sheph. II. i, But loose your poke; be 't true or fause let's hear. 1785 Burns Jolly Beggars Recit. viii, The jovial thrang The poet did request, To lowse his pack, an' wale a sang. 1855 Robinson Whitby Gloss., To Lowse out, to untie, to unloose or unpack goods.

†c. To unjoin or unclasp (hands). *Obs.*

1548–9 (Mar.) Bk. Com. Prayer, Matrimony, Then shall they..looce theyr handes. 1566 Child-Marriages 69 Then the[y] losid hands. 1588 Shaks. Tit. A. II. iii. 243.

d. To detach, cast loose, let go: chiefly *Naut.* †Also with *forth*. † *to loose out* (a knife): to unsheathe it. †Also, to remove (an article of clothing) from the body.

1382 Wyclif Exod. iii. 5 Lowse thow thi shoyng fro thi feyt. c1400 Destr. Troy 2806 Paris..and his pure brother.. Lauset loupis fro the le; lachyn in Ancres [L. solutis itaque funibus, subductis anchoris]. c1400 Melayne 1067 The Sarazene..lawses out a knyfe full righte. c1470 Henry Wallace vii. 1160 Bownd on the trest in a creddill to sit, To lous the pyne quhen Wallace leit him witt. 1513 Douglas Æneis III. iv. 110 Do lows the rabandis, and lat doun the sail. 1530 Palsgr. 615/2 Lowse your shoe and gyve hym upon the heed withall. 1535 Coverdale Luke v. 5 Vpon thy worde I wil lowse forth the nett. a1578 Lindesay (Pitscottie) Chron. Scot. (S.T.S.) I. 324 The king..past to his chamber and loussit his claithis and maid him to his bede. 1632 Massinger City Madam I. ii, I will not loose a hat To a hairs breadth, move your Bever, I'le move mine. 1669 Sturmy Mariner's Mag. I. 16 Therefore up a hand and loose fore Top sail in the Top, that the Ships may see we will Sail. 1706 Phillips (ed. Kersey) s.v. Let-fall, If the Main-Yard, or Fore-Yard be struck down, so that the Sails may be loosed before the Yard be hoised, then the Mariners do not say, Let fall the Sail, but Loose the Sail. 1769 Falconer Dict. Marine (1780), To Loose, to unfurl or cast loose any sail, in order to be set, or dried, after rainy weather. 1821 Shelley Boat on Serchio 88 The chain is loosed, the sails are spread. 1863 Geo. Eliot Romola lxi, She loosed the boat from its moorings. 1867 Smyth Sailor's Word-Bk., To loose a rope, to cast it off, or let it go.

e. *Sc.* To detach the team from (a plough, etc.). Also *absol.*

c1480 Henryson Mor. Fab. 2253 in Anglia IX. 471 The oxin waxit mair reulie at the last, Syne efter thay lousit [etc.]. a1568 Wyfe of Auchtermuchty ii. in Bannatyne Poems (1873) 342 He lowsit the pluche at the landis end. Ibid. xiii. 345 She lowisit the plwch and syne come hame. 1791 J. Learmont Poems 56 Twa lads..War gaen at pleugh their forenoon yokin: At length baith tir'd wi' heat o' noon, They loos'd an' on the lee lay down. 1893 Crockett Stickit Minister 117 He was oot a' nicht, an' I havna seen him since he lowsed.

†f. To carve (a pheasant). *Obs.*

c1500 For to serve a Lord in Babees Bk. (1868) 395 To lose or unlase a fesaunt.

†g. *intr.* for *refl.* To come unfastened. *Obs.*

1760–72 H. Brooke Fool of Qual. (1809) IV. 84 The picture..suddenly looses from its ribband.

3. †a. *to loose the anchor*: to weigh anchor. Also, *to loose one's bark*. *Obs.*

c1450 St. Cuthbert (Surtees) 675 þe man went and loused þe ankir. 1555 Eden Decades (Arb.) 69 They lowsed theyr ankers and departed from Guadalupea. 1567 Turberv. Ovid's Epist. Q ij b, Auale and lose thy Barcke, take seas. 1596 Dalrymple tr. Leslie's Hist. Scot. x. 307 The frenche shipis beginis to lous thair anker, and stryk sail at Bristoo.

b. Hence *absol.* To weigh anchor. *occas.* with *up*.

1526 Tindale Acts xxvii. 2 We entred into a shippe of Adramicium, and lowsed from lond. 1587 Fleming Contn. Holinshed III. 975/1 The baron de la Gard..leused from Déepe with twelue gallies. 1594 Marlowe & Nashe Dido IV. iii, To stay my Fleete from loosing forth the Bay. 1635 Foxe & James Voy. N.W. (Hakluyt Soc.) I. 180 This noone he loost up for the shore. 1677 Lond. Gaz. No. 1245/3 This morning the light Ships that were at Anchor in this Bay, loosed, and are sailed to the Northwards. 1690 W. Walker Idiomat. Anglo-Lat. 277 Our ship loosed from the harbour. 1867 Smyth Sailor's Word-bk. Loosing for sea, weighing the anchor.

4. a. To shoot or let fly (an arrow); to let off (a gun).

c1400 Maundev. (Roxb.) xxiv. 112 Ga and louse ȝone arowes. 1473 Warkw. Chron. (Camden) 8 The Kynge.. losyde his gonnys of ordynaunce uppone them. 1530 Palsgr. 615/1, I lowse, as a gonner lowseth a pece of ordonaunce. 1582 N. Lichfield Castanheda's Discov. E. Ind. I. lvii. 120 As the Nayre loosed off his arrow. 1599 Shaks. Hen. V, I. ii. 207 As many Arrowes loosed seuerall wayes Come to one marke. 1638 Junius Paint. Ancients 324 Such archers..use..to loose their arrowes in a more comely manner. 1814 Cary Dante, Par. I. 122 That strong cord that never looses dart But at fair aim. 1818 Shelley Rev. Islam x. xxvi, Like a shaft loosed by the bowman's error. 1916 'Boyd Cable' Action Front 48 The artillery made a regular practice of loosing off a stated number of rounds per night. 1944 R.A.F. Jrnl. Aug. 286 Dropped our bomb-load..an' loosed off all our ammo.

transf. 1820 Shelley Vis. Sea 4 When lightning is loosed.

b. *absol.* or *intr.* To shoot, let fly. Also said of the gun. Now usu. with *off*. Also *loosing off*.

1387 Trevisa Higden (Rolls) VII. 77 þe childe losed and schette. 1530 Palsgr. 615/1, I thought full lytell he wolde have lowsed at me whan I sawe hym drawe his bowe. Ibid. 681/2 Se howe yonder gonne reculeth or ever she lowse. 1545 Ascham Toxoph. (Arb.) 161 Houlde and nocke trewlye, drawe and lowse equallye. a1548 Hall Chron., Hen. VIII 56 b, Al the .II. C. archers shot and losed at once. 1588 Shaks. Tit. A. IV. iii. 58 (He giues them the Arrowes.) Too it Boy, Marcus loose when I bid. 1603 B. Jonson Sejanus III. iii, Nor must he looke at what, or whom to strike, But loose at all. 1889 Rider Haggard Allan's Wife 80 Reserving their fire till the Zulus were packed like sheep in a kraal, they loosed into them with the roers. 1893 Field 25 Mar. 456/3, I threw up my gun mechanically, but had no intention of 'loosing' at the poor thing. 1900 Daily News 1 Oct. 7/3 Paget's artillerymen dashed forward, unlimbered, and loosed on the foe. 1906 Westm. Gaz. 9 Mar. 4/1 The man for whom the whole of shooting is comprised in the gunning—in the 'loosing off', as he will call it. 1926 Punch 28 July 86/2 The bowler would acquire the trick of looking at one [wicket] while really he was loosing off at the other. 1928 Blunden Undertones of War ii. 8 The howitzer loosing off occasionally outside punctuated these amenities. 1946 J. Irving Royal Navalese 110 To loose off, to open fire.

c. *trans.* (*transf.* and *fig.*) To give vent to, emit; to cause or allow to proceed from one.

1508 Kennedy Flyting w. Dunbar 28 Ramowd rebald, thow fall doun att the roist, My laureat lettres at the and I lowis. 1600 Shaks. A.Y.L. III. v. 103 Loose now and then A scattred smile, and that Ile liue vpon. 1601 —— All's Well II. iii. 172 Both my reuenge and hate Loosing vpon thee. 1687 Evelyn Diary 19 Apr., His..delicateness in extending and looseing a note with incomparable softnesse. 1847

TENNYSON *Princess* II. 407 And loose A flying charm of blushes o'er this cheek.

†**5.** To weaken the adhesion or attachment of; = LOOSEN *v.* 3; to make unstable or insecure in position. Also *intr.* for *pass.* Now only *arch.*

13.. *E.E Allit. P.* B. 957 þe rayn rueled doun .. Gorde to gomorra þat þe grounde laused. **1375** BARBOUR *Bruce* VI. 253 A gret stane .. That throu the gret anciente Was lowsyt, reddy for to fall. *c* **1420** *Chron. Vilod.* st. 1117 þen sye he how his fedris weron lewesode ychone. **1523** FITZHERB. *Husb.* §126 With the wyndynge of the edderynges thou dost leuse thy stakes and therfore they must nedes be .. hardened agayne. **1526** *Pilgr. Perf.* (W. de W. 1531) 254 The hole frame of the ioyntes of his body dissolued and losed. **1530** PALSGR. 615/1, I lowse a tree or herbe from the roote. *Ibid.*, Se howe the heate hath made these bordes to lowse asonder. *c* **1550** LLOYD *Treas. Health* (? 1550) H iij, A stroke or faul, wherby the ioyntes of the backe bone ar loused. **1611** BIBLE *Ecclus.* xxii, 16 As timbers girt and bound together in a building cannot be loosed with shaking. **1864** SWINBURNE *Atalanta* 1062 The firm land have they loosed and shaken.

6. a. To make loose or slack; to loosen, slacken, relax, make less tight; †*pass.* (of nerves) to be unstrung. † ***to loose a bridle to***: to indulge. Now *arch.* exc. in colloq. phr. ***to loose hold***: to let go.

c **1440** *Promp. Parv.* 314/1 Losyn, or slakyn, *laxo, relaxo.* **1530** PALSGR. 720/2, I lowse a thynge that was to strayte tyed. **1577** B. GOOGE *Heresbach's Husb.* (1586) 67 The olde Rosyars must haue the Earth loosed about them in Februarie, and the dead twigges cutte of. **1581** G. PETTIE tr. *Guazzo's Civ. Conv.* (1586) II. 117 Our lyfe is like to instruments of Musicke, which sometime wresting vp the strings, and sometime by loosing them, become more melodious. **1596** DALRYMPLE tr. *Leslie's Hist. Scot.* II. 152 Occasione frilie to louse a brydle to al thair appetites. *c* **1614** SIR W. MURE *Dido & Æneas* I. 220 A prince imposed To let or loose their rains, as he commands. **1697** DRYDEN *Virg. Georg.* IV. 586 The slipp'ry God will try to loose his hold. **1737** WHISTON *Josephus, Hist.* VI. viii. §4 Their nerves were so terribly loosed .. they could not flee away. **1865** LIGHTFOOT *Galatians* (1874) 118/2 Sin and law loose their hold at the same time. **1868** BROWNING *Ring & Bk.* V. 822 He bid them loose grasp. **1875** W. S. HAYWARD *Love agst. World* 18 'Loose your hold of the lady's bridle', cried Walter. **1901** METHUEN *Peace or War S. Africa* vii. 158 He will know when to loose and when to tighten the rein.

†**b.** *transf.* To relax or loosen (the bowels). Also *absol. Obs.*

c **1400** *Lanfranc's Cirurg.* 51 þou maist .. lose þe wombe if þat he be costif. **1528** PAYNEL *Salerne's Regim.* (1541) 77 The brothe of coole wortes .. leuseth the bealy. *Ibid.* 87 Blacke pepper throughe the heate and drynes therof, leuseth quickely. **1533** ELYOT *Cast. Helth* II. vii. (1541) 20 b, Soure grapes are colde, and do also lowse, but they are harde of dygestyon. **1612** WOODALL *Surg. Mate* Wks. (1653) 187 It is dangerous to loose the belly upon a former loosenesse. **1651** WITTIE *Primrose's Pop. Err.* I. 58 If their bellies be but abundantly loosed.

†**7. a.** [Cf. L. *solvere.*] To break up, dissolve, do away with. Chiefly *fig. Obs.*

1340 HAMPOLE *Pr. Consc.* 1792 þe dede .. louses alle thyng And of ilk mans lif mas endyng. **1387** TREVISA *Higden* (Rolls) VII. 149 Whos chirche dissolved and lowsed þoruȝ longe rotnes he reparailde. **1435** MISYN *Fire of Love* II. ix. 91 þat frenschyp þat is kyndely sal not be lausyd. **1526** *Pilgr. Perf.* (W. de W. 1531) 15 It dissolueth and loseth all vowes. **1530** PALSGR. 688/1, I resolve, I lose thynges, or melte them, or parte thynges asonder, *je resolue.* **1819** SHELLEY *Cenci* I. ii. 23 By assuming vows no Pope will loose.

†**b.** *intr.* To crumble away; to dissolve, melt.

c **1375** *Sc. Leg. Saints* xlv. (*Cristine*) 234 Til þe fals ydol don can fal, & in poudre lousyt al smal. **1481** CAXTON *Myrr.* II. xxvii. 120 The moisture .. is in thayer assembled and amassed .. And the sonne causeth it to lose and to falle on therthe.

†**8.** To break (faith); to violate (a peace). *Obs.*

13.. *Gaw. & Gr. Knt.* 1784 If ȝe .. folden fayth to þat fre, festned so harde, þat yow lausen ne lyst. **1456** SIR G. HAYE *Law Arms* (S.T.S.) 149 The man .. may nocht lous his faith. **1568** GRAFTON *Chron.* II. 309 By reason whereof the peace betwene them agreed might be losed or broken.

†**9.** To solve, explain. *Obs.*

1596 SPENSER *F.Q.* V. xi. 25 He had red her Riddle, which no wight Could ever loose but suffred deadly doole. **1660** R. COKE *Justice Vind., Arts & Sci.* 1 This doubt is after-wards loosed by Aristotle himself.

10. a. To redeem, release or obtain by payment; to pay for. *Sc.* Hence perh. Coverdale's use: †To buy (*obs.*).

1473 *Ld. Treas. Acc. Scotl.* (1877) I. 48 Item to Dauid Quhytehede and Thome of Stanly .. for Doctor Andres dispensacione lousyt be thaim in Bruges xvj*li.* **1500** *Ibid.* (1900) II. 98 Item, .. to Jacob lutar to lows his lute that lay in wed xxxij*s.* **1504-5** *Ibid.* (1901) III. 127 To Alexander Kers to lous the Kingis stope quhilk wes tane quhen he wes Abbot of Unreson vj*li* xiij*s.* iiij*d.* **1535** COVERDALE *Jer.* xxxii. 25 That I shall loose a pece of londe vnto my self. **1824** SCOTT *St. Ronan's* ii, As for the letters at the post-mistress's—they may bide in her shop-window—till Beltane, or I louse them. **1825-80** JAMIESON, To *Louse* .. , to pay for; as, 'Gie me siller to louse my coals at the hill'.

†**b.** *Sc.* To free (an estate) from incumbrance.

1494 *Acta Dom. Conc.* (1839) 361/2 Or the landis war lowsit, quhilkis are now lowsit.

11. *Sc. Law.* To withdraw (an arrestment).

1522 *Extracts Aberd. Reg.* (1844) I. 100 The arrest laid one the gudes aboune writin be Patrik Leslie... And the said Patrik offerit the said gudis, and the rest maid thar one to be loussit, incontinent thar findand souerty [etc.]. **1544** *Ibid.* I. 205 The said day, Thomas Menzeis, provest of Aberdene .. hes lowsit the arrestment made vpoun ane scheip, and certane tymmer being thairin, pertening to Robert Patersoune and vtheris. **1609** SKENE *Reg. Maj.* 75 b, The moueable gudes of the defender, sould be first attached, and arreisted, vntill he finde securitie be pledges, to compeir and answere to the complainer; and then the arreistment sould be lowsed. **1681** VISCT. STAIR *Instit. Law Scot.* III. i. (1693) 373 When he whose Goods or Sums are arrested, findeth Caution, and thereby louseth the Arrestment. *a* **1768** ERSKINE *Instit.* III. vi. §12 (1773) I. 509.

12. *pass.* and *intr.* To finish working; (of a school, factory, etc.) to close, disperse, 'break up'. Also in phr. ***loose-all***, the signal to stop work given in the pits. *dial.*

a **1813** WILSON *Maggie Weir* (E.D.D.), Ploughman chields lous'd frae their wark. **1829** HOGG *Sheph. Cal.* I. vi. 151 He wad hear it [a song] every day when the school looses. **1851** GREENWELL *Coal-trade Terms Northumb. & Durh.* 35 *Loose* ('Lowse')!—Finish working! **1893** SNOWDEN *Tales Yorksh. Wolds* 110 One Sunday afternoon just as the chapel had 'loosed'. **1911** D. H. LAWRENCE *White Peacock* vii. 485, I heard the far-off hooting of the 'loose-all' at the pits, telling me it was half-past eleven. **1913** —— *Sons & Lovers* ii. 30 Some men were there before four o'clock, when the whistle blew loose-all.

loose, obs. form or variant of LOSE, LOSS.

loosed (lu:st), *ppl. a.* [f. LOOSE *v.* + -ED[1].] In senses of the vb.

1580 SIDNEY *Ps.* XXII. viii, Whose loosed bones quite out of joynt be wried. **1661** LOVELL *Hist. Anim. & Min.* Introd. b, The eares are moveable ..; in horses, and labouring beasts, they shew their spirits, being micant in the fearfull, .. and loosed in the sick. **1887** G. MEREDITH *Ballads & P.* 150 He rose like the loosed fountain's utmost leap.

loose end.

1. An extremity of a string or the like left hanging loose; *fig.* of something left disconnected, undecided or unguarded. Chiefly *pl.*

1546 HEYWOOD *Prov.* (1867) 37 Some loose or od ende will come man. **1577** HARRISON *England* II. v. (1877) I. 110 The cleargie men .. are beloued generallie .. except peraduenture of some hungrie wombes, that couet to plucke & snatch at the loose ends of their best commodities; with whom it is .. a common guise, when a man is to be preferred to an ecclesiasticall liuing, what part thereof he will first forgo and part with to their vse. **1868** BAIN *Ment. & Mor. Sci.* 6 A completed connexion between the extremities of the body and the cells of the grey matter, or else between one cell and another of the central lump; there are no loose ends. **1897** *Boston* (Mass.) *Jrnl.* 1 Jan. 4/5 No loose ends of controversy along these lines will be left to be taken up by the new Administration.

2. Phr. ***at*** (***after, on***) ***a loose end***: not regularly occupied, having no settled employment; not knowing what to be at. Also (***to leave a matter***) ***at a loose end***: unsettled. *colloq.*, orig. *dial.* (cf. *loose hand*, LOOSE *a.* 9).

1851 MAYHEW *Lond. Labour* (1864) II. 55 One informant told me that the bird-catchers, .. when young, .. were those who 'liked to be after a loose end', first catching their birds, as a sort of sporting business, and then sometimes selling them in the streets. **1856** P. THOMPSON *Hist. Boston* 714 'He's on a loose end', without employment. **1860** GEO. ELIOT *Mill on Fl.* VI. iv. III. 54 When I've left off carrying my pack, and am at a loose end. **1864** *Fraser's Mag.* LXIX. 412/1 But to stop short of that is to leave the whole matter at a loose end. **1870** E. PEACOCK *Ralf Skirl.* III. 228 On the Saturday evening he, like Bob, was at the 'lowse end', but he had full employment. **1889** MALLOCK *In Enchanted Isl.* 262 Excepting myself he was the only stranger in Cyprus who was thus at a loose end, as it were, and not on some professional duty.

3. *Mining.* (See quots.)

1865 BOWER *Slate Quarries* 17 A 'loose end', as quarry-men call it, should always be selected for carrying on operations on the top rock. **1881** RAYMOND *Mining Gloss.*, *Loose-end*, a gangway in *long-wall* working, driven so that one side is solid ground while the other opens upon old workings. **1883** GRESLEY *Gloss. Coal Mining*, *Loose End*, the limit of a stall next to the goaf, or where the adjoining stall is in advance.

loose-leaf, *a.* Of a note-book, file, or the like: made to facilitate the insertion or removal of each leaf separately. Also as *sb.*

1902 *Accountant* 29 Nov. 1240/1 The difficulty he mentions is partly met by using a 'loose leaf' Ledger. **1907** *Daily Chron.* 6 Dec. 11/4 'Loose-Leaf' notebooks and diaries, .. in which pages can be taken out or added at will, have already won a well-deserved popularity. **1917** H. B. TWYFORD *Purchasing & Storing* 409 A copy of every printed form used should be posted on a loose-leaf sheet. **1930** 'J. J. CONNINGTON' *Two Tickets Puzzle* xv. 232 Dr. Selby-Onslow nodded again: crossed the room to his desk; and pulled from a drawer a large loose-leaf volume. **1937** I. O. EVANS *Cigarette Cards* 122 Sheets made up in this fashion could also be filed after the manner of the loose-leaves. **1955** W. GADDIS *Recognitions* II. vi. 559 In the window was a large loose-leaf book, whose lined pages were filled in a cramped round hand. **1967** *Listener* 21 Sept. 370/2 The large loose-leaf notebook in which he wrote rehearsal notes. **1971** *Ann. Rep. Curators Bodl. Libr. 1969-70* 49 Transferring of the old handlists to typescript sheets in looseleaf binders continued. **1975** *BSI News* May 6/3 The third revision of BS 2782 *Methods of test for plastics* is being issued in a loose-leaf form.

loosely ('lu:slɪ), *adv.* Forms: 4 loselyche, lousely, 4–5 loseliche, 5 losly, 5–6 losely, 6 lowslie, lowsel(e)y, lously, loocely, loos(e)lye, 7 loosly, 6– loosely. [f. LOOSE *a.* + -LY[2].] In a loose manner.

1. Not tightly, slackly; without tightness, closeness, rigidity, or cohesion. Also *fig.*

c **1400** *Lanfranc's Cirurg.* 82 Bynde it [a ligature] losely at þe mouþ of þe wounde. *Ibid.* 146 þe seuenþe is bounde loseliche to þe first spondile. *c* **1440** HYLTON *Scala Perf.* (W. de W. 1494) I. xii, The more þat this desyre is the faster is Iesu knytte to the soule: The lesse that this desyre is þe loslyer is he knytte. **1583** STUBBES *Anat. Abus.* II. (1882) 37 It is a worlde to see how lowsely they shall be sowed, .. euerie stitch an inch or two from another. **1597** A. M. tr. *Guillemeau's Fr. Chirurg.* 26 b/2 It fasteneth the gummes vnto the teethe, when as they hange looselye theron. **1667** MILTON *P.L.* VII. 425 Part loosly wing the Region, part more wise In common, rang'd in figure wedge thir way. **1811** LATHAM *Facts conc. Diabetes* 87 Matters capable of such fermentation .. have their sugar so weakly and loosely oxygenated as to be again readily evolved by the secretory action of the kidneys. **1842** BISCHOFF *Woollen Manuf.* II. 64 Articles of wool which were so loosely manufactured, that they could be easily converted again into wool. **1860** B. JOWETT in *Ess. & Rev.* 389 In modern times .. all languages sit loosely on thought. **1878** BROWNING *La Saisiaz* 81 Not so loosely thoughts were linked, Six weeks since.

2. Without care, strictness, or rigour; not strictly; carelessly, negligently, laxly. Said esp. of thought or its expression.

1377 LANGL. *P. Pl.* B. XII. 213 For he is in þe lowest of heuene .. And wel loselyche lolleth þere by þe lawe of holy-cherche. **1387** TREVISA *Higden* (Rolls) VII. 163 But Emme lousely i-kept [L. *laxius custodita*], wroot unto þe bisshoppis of Engelond. **1566** DRANT *Horace's Sat.* II. i. E vij b, Some thynke my satyres too to tarte to kepe no constant lawe, And some have thought it lously pende. **1638** R. BAKER tr. *Balzac's Lett.* (vol. III.) 6 Though you write nothing loosly, yet you write nothing with streyning. **1647** CLARENDON *Hist. Reb.* I. §106 The .. revenue had been very loosely managed. **1793** BEDDOES in *Observ. Nature Demonstr. Evid.* 133, I have already loosely observed, that their system supposes [etc.]. **1824** SCOTT *Fam. Lett.* 14 Nov. (1894) II. xx. 222 All men talk loosely in their ordinary conversation. **1838** PRESCOTT *Ferd. & Is.* (1846) I. Introd. 19 The laws were often loosely administered by incompetent judges. **1885** *Leeds Mercury* 31 Jan. 6/5 The ideas thus loosely expressed. **1899** *Allbutt's Syst. Med.* VII. 448 In this country the word 'stammering' is used loosely for all forms of speech defect.

3. Without moral strictness; immorally.

1548 UDALL, etc. *Erasm. Par. Matt.* xi. 20-24 Ye be not geuen to riot and excesse so openly and loosly. **1605** CAMDEN *Rem.*, *Wise Sp.* 188 In this age when a Bishop living loosely was charged that his conversation was not according to the Apostles lives, he [etc.]. **1699** DRYDEN in *Four C. Eng. Lett.* 140 Licence which Mrs. Behn allow'd herself, of writing loosely, and giving .. some scandall to the modesty of her sex. **1855** MACAULAY *Hist. Eng.* xvii. IV. 36 He was .. a far more dangerous enemy of the Church than .. if he had .. lived as loosely as Wilmot.

4. Without being confined or restrained. Now *rare.*

1590 SPENSER *F.Q.* I. xi. 51 Her golden locks for hast were loosely shed About her eares. *c* **1611** CHAPMAN *Iliad* XXI. 437 Ioues wife could put on no such raines, But spake thus loosly. **1633** P. FLETCHER *Poet. Misc.* 75 Or as the hairs which deck their wanton heads, Which loosely fly, and play with every winde. **1635-56** COWLEY *Davideis* III. 261 The wind admir'd, which her hair loosely bore, Why it grew stiff, and now would play no more. **1818** SHELLEY *Rev. Islam* X. xxv, Sheathed in resplendent arms, or loosely dight To luxury. **1892** TENNYSON *Akbar's Dream*, And what are forms? Fair garments, plain or rich, and fitting close Or flying looselier.

5. With free evacuation of the bowels.

1612 DEKKER *If it be not good* Wks. 1873 III. 288 Your guilded pills .. slip so smoothly doune Your Subiects throates, that all (vpon a sudden) Are loosely giuen. **1897** *Allbutt's Syst. Med.* III. 741 If the bowels are only opened once loosely he takes but one dose.

6. *Comb.* (with *ppl. adjs.*), as ***loosely-adherent***, ***-branched***, ***-fitting***, ***-knit***, ***-packed***, ***-woven***, etc. Cf. *loose-knit* adj. s.v. LOOSE *a.* 10 d.

1746 J. WARTON *Ode to Fancy* 9 O Nymph, with loosely-flowing hair. **1862** H. SPENCER *First Princ.* II. xix. §149 (1875) 403 Not unfrequently a piece of trap [rock] may be found reduced .. to a number of loosely-adherent coats, like those of an onion. **1887** MOLONEY *Forestry W. Afr.* 299 A loosely-branched tree. **1899** *Allbutt's Syst. Med.* VIII. 903 [Bacilli] occasionally in loosely packed bundles. **1935** HUXLEY & HADDON *We Europeans* i. 13 It [*sc.* group-sentiment] has spread beyond the family, the tribe, the loosely-knit federation of tribes to the yet more extensive aggregate, the nation. **1957** C. HUNT *Guide to Communist Jargon* xlvi. 153 It [*sc.* the Decree of the Central Committee] replaced the loosely-knit Union of Proletarian Writers by a single Union of Soviet Writers.

loosen ('lu:s(ə)n), *v.* Forms: 4 losne, lousen, loosne, 6 loozen, 7 losen, 9 *dial.* lowsen, 4, 7– loosen. [f. LOOSE *a.* + -EN[5]. ON. had *losna* intr., to become loose, from the wk. grade of the root.] To make loose or looser.

1. a. *trans.* To set free or release from bonds or physical restraint. *Obs.* exc. *poet.* (rare) and *dial.*

1382 WYCLIF *Ps.* cxlv. 7 The Lord losneth the gyuede. *Ibid.* ci. 21 That he shulde .. loosen the sones of the slayne. **1530** PALSGR. 766/2, I unbynde, I losen, *je deslie.* **1804** COUPER *Poetry* I. 88 The oussen, lousen'd frae the plough, Spread oure the grassy plain. **1887** BOWEN *Virg. Æneid* II. 153 Lifting his hands now loosened from chains.

b. *transf.* and *fig.* Now only in the phrase ***to loosen*** (a person's) ***tongue***, and in certain poetical or rhetorical uses (? after Shelley).

1645 MILTON *Tetrach.* Wks. 1851 IV. 192 And therfore doth in this Law, what best agrees with his goodnes, loosning a sacred thing to peace and charity, rather then binding it to hatred and contention. *Ibid.* 222 And this their limiting that which God loosen'd and their loosning the sinnes that he limited. **1695** DRYDEN *Dufresnoy's Art Painting* 185 This is an admirable Rule; a Painter ought to have it perpetually present in his Mind and Memory... It loosens his hands, and assists his understanding. **1821** SHELLEY *Prometh. Unb.* III. iii. 81 Thou breathe into the many-folded shell, Loosening its mighty music. **1850** TENNYSON *In Mem.* xlviii. 14 But [Sorrow] rather loosens from the lip Short swallow-flights of song. **1869** TROLLOPE

He knew xliv. (1878) 246 By degrees her tongue was loosened. **1893** E. H. BARKER *Wand. S. Waters* 222 The fragrance of the valley was loosened. **1895** ZANGWILL *Master* I. x. 110 The action seemed to loosen his tongue.

2. To undo, unfasten (bonds, a knot, or the like). Now usually: To render looser or less tight, to relax, slacken.

1382 WYCLIF *Isa.* xx. 2 Go, and loosne the sac fro thi leendis. **1611** BIBLE *Judith* ix. 2 Who loosened the girdle of a maide to defile her. **1686** tr. *Chardin's Trav. Persia* 384 The Grooms..walk the Horses, then they cloath them and loosen their Girts. **1806** SURR *Winter in Lond.* III. 54 The manacles were loosened from my hands. **1820** KEATS *St. Agnes* xxvi, She..Loosens her fragrant boddice. **1884** *Law Times* 3 May 1/2 A Government not accustomed to loosen their purse strings. **1899** *Allbutt's Syst. Med.* VII. 258 On loosening the ligatures the rabbit often gave a sudden jump forward. **1902** A. E. W. MASON *Four Feathers* xv. 141 That access of panic which had loosened his joints when first he saw the low brown walls of the town.

fig. **1871** R. ELLIS tr. *Catullus* lxiv. 367 Neptune's bonds of stone from Dardan city to loosen.

3. a. To weaken the adhesion or attachment of; to unfix, detach.

1667 MILTON *P.L.* VI. 643 From thir foundations loosning to and fro They pluckt the seated Hills. **1680** MOXON *Mech. Exerc.* 232 The manner of loosning all the other inward Spheres is as the Former. *Ibid.*, Loosen it out of the Wax. **1726** LEONI tr. *Alberti's Archit.* I. 72/2 The water..routs up the bottom, and..carries away every thing that it can loosen. **1855** MACAULAY *Hist. Eng.* xiii. III. 326 A wall which time and weather had so loosened that it shook in every storm. **1879** N. SMYTH *Old Faiths in New Light* ii. (1882) 45 The ivy creeping up the wall of the church does not loosen its ancient stones. **1882** OUIDA *Maremma* I. 28 Loosen the image from my hat.

†**b.** *fig.* To detach in affection, make a breach between. *Obs.*

1605 SHAKS. *Lear* v. i. 19 (1st Qo. 1608), I had rather loose the battaile, then that sister should loosen him and mee.

c. slang. ***to loosen*** (a person's) ***hide***: to flog.

1902 *Daily Chron.* 11 Apr. 9/2 He thought the only way to make them decent members of society was 'to loosen their hides'.

d. *intr.* for *refl.* or *pass.* To become loose.

1677 MOXON *Mech. Exerc.* 46 The square on the Spindle will be apt to loosen in the square of the Wheel. **1680** *Ibid.* 178 These Puppets stand the firmer, and are less subject to loosen. *Ibid.* 231 The Cube or Dy will loosen. **1726** SWIFT *Gulliver* IV. ix, They have a kind of Tree, which at Forty Years old loosens in the Root. **1899** J. HUTCHINSON *Archives Surg.* X. 157 A whitlow formed, and the nail loosened and was shed in fragments. **1901** W. M. RAMSAY in *Contemp. Rev.* Mar. 390 His old ideas had been slowly loosening and dissolving.

4. *trans.* To make less coherent; to separate the particles of.

1697 DRYDEN *Virg. Georg.* II. 488 With Iron Teeth of Rakes..to move The crusted Earth, and loosen it above. **1787** WINTER *Syst. Husb.* 62 Manures plowed in, loosen and divide the soil. **1846** J. BAXTER *Libr. Pract. Agric.* (ed. 4) II. 329 The workman then with his spade loosens..the texture of the..soil. **1860** TYNDALL *Glac.* I. xxvii. 202 He struck the snow with his baton to loosen it.

fig. *a* **1862** BUCKLE *Civiliz.* (1873) II. viii. 510 Society was loosened and seemed to be resolving itself into its elements.

5. a. To relax, relieve the costiveness of, cause a free evacuation of (the bowels).

1587 GOLDING *De Mornay* viii. 95 Esculapius..was esteemed as a God for teaching..to loozen the Belly. **1626** BACON *Sylva* §41 Feare looseneth the Belly. **1676** WISEMAN *Surg.* V. i. 352 Also use..lenient Purgatives, to loosen the body. **1761** W. LEWIS *Mat. Med.* (ed. 2) 181 To loosen the belly; to promote perspiration, urine, and the uterine purgations. **1822–34** *Good's Study Med.* (ed. 4) II. 617 The bowels [must] be loosened with some gentle aperient.

b. To render (a cough) 'looser'.

1833 *Cycl. Pract. Med.* I. 316/1 To loosen the cough..small doses of ipecacuanha or tartarized antimony are often most effectual. **1898** *Allbutt's Syst. Med.* V. 39 To mature, that is to loosen the [bronchial] catarrh.

6. To relax in point of severity or strictness.

1798 MALTHUS *Popul.* (1878) 10 The restraints to population are..loosened. **1858** BUCKLE *Civiliz.* (1873) II. viii. 568 Even the Inquisition was..made to loosen its hold over its victims. **1872** G. B. CHEEVER *Lect. Pilgr. Progr.* V. 152 The strictness of his imprisonment had been loosened. **1873** HOLLAND *A. Bonnic.* vii. 119 Mr. Bird seemed to take a special pleasure in our society, and while loosening his claim on us as pupils, to hold us as associates and friends more closely. **1899** T. S. BALDOCK *Cromwell* 291 The men neither straggled nor loosened their discipline.

7. *absol.* with *up*. **a.** To give money willingly, to talk freely, etc. *U.S. colloq.*

1908 K. MCGAFFEY *Sorrows of Show-Girl* xi. 125 Loosen-up... You've got to donate for a couple of tickets to the annual benefit. **1911** G. S. PORTER *Harvester* xx. 516 You're tight-mouthed... Loosen up! **1922** C. SANDBURG *Slabs of Sunburnt West* 6 Come across, kick in, loosen up. Where do you get that chatter? **1923** R. D. PAINE *Comrades of Rolling Ocean* xi. 187 Somebody will have to loosen up to pay for the damage to my nervous system. **1927** *Ladies' Home Jrnl.* 114 That is the first time he has ever loosened up. **1949** WODEHOUSE *Uncle Dynamite* i. 8 You will generally find women loosen up less lavishly than men.

b. In *Sport* or *Dancing*, to exercise the muscles before concentrated physical effort, to limber up. Also ***loosening-up*** vbl. sb. and ppl. adj.

1955 M. GILBERT *Sky High* xii. 165 The General came to a stop in the middle of his loosening-up exercises. **1956** R. ALSTON *Test Commentary* xvi. 139 Lindwall was given a couple of loosening-up overs. **1973** M. RUSSELL *Double Hit* viii. 55 Make it an hour. I'll be twenty minutes loosening up. .. I'm after the exercise.

loosened ('luːs(ə)nd), *ppl. a.* [f. LOOSEN *v.* + -ED[1].] In senses of the vb.; slackened, relaxed; rendered loose or easily detachable; also *dial.* liberated from service.

1680 DRYDEN *Ovid's Ep.* vii. 9 While you, with loosen'd Sails, and Vows, prepare To seek a Land, that flies the Searchers Care. **1697** —— *Virg. Georg.* III. 307 He scours along the Field, with loosen'd Reins. **1755** J. G. COOPER *Estimate of Life* III. 64 in Dodsley *Coll. Poems* III. 224 Despair, that hellish fiend, proceeds From loosen'd thoughts, and impious deeds. **1798** LANDOR *Gebir* II. 136 His chaplets mingled with her loosened hair. **1821** JOANNA BAILLIE *Metr. Leg., Lord John* xxix, But his loosen'd limbs shook fast. **1845** MRS. S. C. HALL *Whiteboy* xi. 91 Then will come the loosened soldier. **1855** BROWNING *Transcendentalism* 25 He..turned with loosened tongue to talk with him. **1860** TYNDALL *Glac.* I. xxv. 185 The loosened avalanches..upon the mountain heads.

loosener ('luːs(ə)nə(r)). [f. as prec. + -ER[1].]

1. One who loosens or makes loose.

1843 BROWNING *Blot in 'Scutcheon* II. Wks. 1896 I. 343/1 No loosener O' the lattice. **1852** R. A. COFFIN tr. *Liguori's Glories of Mary* (1868) 87 Loosener of my bonds..listen to my prayers.

2. Something which serves to loosen anything.

1630 BRATHWAIT *Eng. Gentlem.* (1641) 99 Immoderation is a loosener of the sinewes and a lessener of the strength. **1643** CARYL *Sacr. Covt.* 5 It is a loosner of affection. **1684** tr. *Bonet's Merc. Compit.* I. 9 It is not good to use looseners, as Apples, Prunes..frequently. **1784** JEFFERSON *Corr.* Wks. 1859 I. 334 The most powerful looseners of the bands of private friendship. **1871** R. ELLIS tr. *Catullus* ii. 13 The golden apple..Late-won loosener of the wary girdle.

looseness ('luːsnɪs). Forms: see LOOSE *a.* [f. LOOSE *a.* + -NESS.] The attribute of being loose.

1. Freedom from restraint, attachment, rigid connexion, tightness, or density. *lit.*, *transf.*, and *fig.*

c **1400** *Lanfranc's Cirurg.* 64 Þe enchesoun of cause coniuncte is compounned of þe mouþis of þe veynes and arteries,..or ellis to greet febilnes or to greet losenes. **1562** TURNER *Baths* 8 b, They are good for the lousnes and to muche sofftnes of the pappes. **1587** GOLDING *De Mornay* xiii. 223 After that maner therefore may we wade..betweene Loocenesse and Bondage by leauing their mouings free. **1607** MARKHAM *Caval.* II. (1617) 92 Hold vp his head, so as by no meanes he may..win it to such a loosnesse from the riders hand, that [etc.]. **1621** T. WILLIAMSON tr. *Goulart's Wise Vieill.* 34 Loosenesse of teeth. **1635–56** COWLEY *Davideis* III. 640 Not all that Saul could threaten or persuade, In this close Knot the smallest Looseness made. **1675** A. BROWNE *App. Art Limning* 20 The third thing Excellent in a Good Draught is Loosness, that is, that the Body be not made Stiff in any part. **1889** J. M. ROBERTSON *Christ & Krishna* xvii. 107 The looseness and flexibility of the materials of which the cumbrous mythology of the Hindu epic poems is composed.

2. Lack of strictness; laxity of principles or practice.

1585 FETHERSTONE tr. *Calvin on Acts* xviii. 17 This loosenesse must bee imputed not so much to the sluggishnes of the deputie as to the hatred of the Iewish religion. *a* **1639** W. WHATELEY *Prototypes* I. xix. (1640) 191 They know how to tie others hard and leave themselves loose, through the loosenesse of an evill conscience. *a* **1665** J. GOODWIN *Filled w. the Spirit* (1867) 465 Any looseness or lightness of spirit. **1723** WODROW *Corr.* (1843) III. 58 The Non-subscribing principle has a natural and necessary tendency to looseness and the opening a door for error. **1855** *N.Y. Express* Sept. (Bartlett), The perfect looseness, with which books not on the invoice were sold [at auction]. **1878** LECKY *Eng. in 18th C.* II. vii. 290 The greater looseness of their principles. **1891** *Daily News* 28 Oct. 2/3 It is confessed by members of the Stock Exchange that their methods of dealing sometimes encourage a certain amount of looseness.

b. Lack of exactness or accuracy.

1769 BURKE *Late St. Nat.* Wks. II. 70 The looseness and inaccuracy of the export entries. **1797** GODWIN *Enquirer* I. vi. 42 Misunderstandings..may be traced to..looseness of expression. **1849** RUSKIN *Sev. Lamps* p. vij, The looseness of the drawing..may perhaps diminish their credit. **1873** M. ARNOLD *Lit. & Dogma* (1876) 142 The incurable looseness with which the circumstances of what is called and thought a miracle are related. **1885** SIR A. WILLS in *Law Times Rep.* LII. 518/1 Throughout the Act there is not the smallest indication of looseness of phraseology.

3. Moral laxity; licentiousness or lewdness in conduct, speech, or thought.

1576 WOOLTON *Chr. Manual* H v b, Nature hath mingled pleasure with thinges necessarye... If pleasure come alone, it is lousnesse. **1581** J. BELL *Haddon's Answ. Osor.* 25 This chastitie may be seduced in processe of tyme to loosenesse. **1599** R. CROMPTON *Mansion Magnanimity* N iv b, The said noble Earle..knowing the loosenesse of soldiers..caused the Ladies..to be safely conveyed out of the Citie. **1693–4** WOOD *Life* 3 Mar., He told him that such a College in Oxford was a debauch'd college, that they were all given to loosness. **1709** FELTON *Classics* (1718) 26 The Looseness of his Thoughts, too immodest for chaste Ears to bear. **1868** MILMAN *St. Paul's* 302 Looseness too often sinking into obscenity. **1900** W. M. SINCLAIR *Unto You Young Men* x. 187 Scenes of luxury or looseness.

4. Laxity (of the bowels), esp. as a morbid symptom; diarrhœa; †an attack of diarrhœa.

1586 T. RANDOLPH in Ellis *Orig. Lett.* Ser. II. III. 121 He fell into a greate losenes of his bodye. **1600** SURFLET *Country Farme* I. xv. 97 For the loosenes of the belly, some make them meate of the husks of barlie steept in wine. **1663** BOYLE *Usef. Exp. Nat. Philos.* II. v. xi. 232 If rubarb be justly affirmed to be an excellent medicine in loosenesses. **1702** J. PURCELL *Cholick* (1714) 163 The Pains grew violent, and a great Looseness succeeded. **1737** BRACKEN *Farriery Impr.* (1749) I. 217 In Diarrhœa's or Loosenesses. **1755** *Gentl. Mag.* XXV. 28 His looseness encreased to a great excess, which brought on much weakness. **1760** GRAY *Let.* Poems (1775) 283 A violent looseness carried him off. **1897** *Allbutt's Syst. Med.* II. 242 A certain looseness of the bowels..is a common symptom of the disease [i.e. of whooping-cough]. **1898** P. MANSON *Trop. Diseases* xvii. 271 The preliminary looseness in such cases [of cholera] is called the 'premonitory diarrhœa'.

loosenger, variant of LOSENGER *Obs.*

loosening ('luːs(ə)nɪŋ), *vbl. sb.* [-ING[1].] The action of LOOSEN *v.* in various senses.

1597 A. M. tr. *Guillemeau's Fr. Chirurg.* 26 b/2 Without hurtinge of the gummes, and looseninge of the same. **1615** HIERON *Wks.* I. 654 Thus is death a loosening to the children of God. **1626** BACON *Sylva* §435 The Loosening of the Earth, which comforteth any Tree. **1860** TYNDALL *Glac.* II. xix. 333 Ice gives evidence of a loosening of its crystalline texture. **1876** MISS BRADDON *J. Haggard's Dau.* I. 35 A signal for the loosening of everyone else's tongue. **1883** R. W. DIXON *Mano* III. v. 126 Like the tightening and the loosening of a cord.

'**loosening**, *ppl. a.* [-ING[2].] That loosens, in various senses of the vb.

1665 HOOKE *Microgr.* 13 The strange loosening nature of a violent jarring motion. **1694** SALMON *Bate's Dispens.* (1699) 529/1 Laxative or Loosening Tartar. **1758** J. S. *Le Dran's Observ. Surg.* (1771) Dict. Cc ij, Laxative, or Loosening Medicines. **1801** SOUTHEY *Thalaba* IX. xlii, Thalaba Watches her snowy fingers..Unwind the loosening chain. **1886** C. SCOTT *Sheep-Farming* 15 They are fed upon roots..which exert a loosening effect on the teeth.

looser ('luːsə(r)). [f. LOOSE *v.* + -ER[1].] One who or something which looses.

1528 PAYNEL *Salerne's Regim.* (1541) 82 b, Mustarde sede is a great leuser, consumer, and clenser of fleumaticke humidities. **1591** PERCIVALL *Sp. Dict.*, *Soltador*, a looser, an expounder of drems or ridles. **1871** R. ELLIS tr. *Catullus* lxvii. 28 A sturdier arm, that franker quality somewhere, Looser of youth's fast-bound girdle. **1882** NARES *Seamanship* (ed. 6) 199 The sail loosers..keep fast the..booms.

loosestrife ('luːsstraɪf). Also 6 lose-, lous(e)strife, lostriffe. [f. LOOSE *v.* + STRIFE *sb.*; a mistransl. of late L. *lysimachia*, also *-machion*, a Gr. *λυσιμάχιον*, f. the personal name *Λυσίμαχος* Lysimachus, an application of the adj. *λυσίμαχος* 'loosing' (i.e. ending) strife, f. *λυσι-*, combining stem of *λύειν* to loose + *μάχη* strife.

The form **λυσιμαχία* (found only in Pliny's Latin transliteration) would be correct Gr. for 'the action of loosing strife'. The misinterpretation of the word is ancient; Pliny, though stating that the plant was discovered by one Lysimachus, also says that oxen that are made to eat it are rendered more willing to draw together. Ancient writers mention two kinds of *lysimachia*, the purple and the yellow, the descriptions of which agree with the two plants referred to in 1 below. Modern botanists have appropriated *Lysimachia* as a generic name to the 'yellow loosestrife'.]

1. The name for two common herbaceous plants resembling each other closely in growth (upright and tall) and habitat (margins of ditches and streams).

a. *Lysimachia vulgaris* (N.O. *Primulaceæ*), flowering in July, and bearing racemes of golden-yellow flowers; called *spec.* Golden or Yellow Loosestrife. Also a book-name for the genus.

1548 TURNER *Names of Herbes* (1881) 50 Some cal it *Lycimachiam luteam*..it may be called in englishe yealow Lousstryfe or herbe Wylowe. **1562** —— *Herbal* II. 44 It may be well called after the etimologi of the worde and also of yͤ vertue that it hath lous strife. **1578** LYTE *Dodoens* I. li. 75 The yellow Lysimachus or golden Louse stryfe. **1640** PARKINSON *Theatr. Bot.* 543 Common yellow Loosestrife or Willow herbe. **1861** MISS PRATT *Flower. Pl.* IV. 236 Great Yellow Loosestrife... Its large yellow panicle has leaves growing among the blossoms.

b. *Lythrum Salicaria* (N.O. *Lythraceæ*), blooming in summer months, with a beautiful showy spike of purplish-red flowers; called *spec.* Red, Purple, or Spiked Loosestrife. Also a book-name for the genus.

1548 TURNER *Names of Herbes* (1881) 50 *Lycimachia purpurea*..may be called in englishe red loosstryfe, or purple losestryfe. **1567** MAPLET *Gr. Forest* 51 Other will haue it called Lostriffe or Herbe Willow. It beareth a red flower. **1633** JOHNSON *Gerarde's Herbal* II. cxxix. 478 This lesser purple Loose-strife of Clusius. **1785** MARTYN *Rousseau's Bot.* xx. (1794) 278 Purple Loosestrife is a handsome plant. **1838** MARY HOWITT *Pheasant* i, The loose-strife's purple spear. **1866** M. ARNOLD *Thyrsis* xiii, When through the Wytham flats, Red loosestrife and blond meadow-sweet among,..We tracked the shy Thames shore. **1889** P. H. EMERSON *Eng. Idyls* 83 Their sea-boots crushed the purple loosestrife into the ground.

2. Applied (as a book-name) with qualifications to plants of other genera (see quots.).

1760 J. LEE *Introd. Bot.* App. 317 Podded Loose-strife, *Epilobium*. *Ibid.*, Yellow Virginian Loose-strife, *Gaura*. **1787** tr. *Linnæus' Fam. Plants* I. 254 *Gaura*, Virginian Loosestrife. **1866** *Treas. Bot.* 695/1 False Loosestrife, *Ludwigia*. Swamp-L., *Deocodon*. West Indian L., *Jussiæa suffruticosa*.

Looshai, var. LUSHAI *a.* and *sb.*

loosing ('luːsɪŋ), *vbl. sb.* [f. LOOSE *v.* + -ING[1].] The action of the vb. LOOSE.

†**1.** Letting go; setting free, release. *Obs.* or *arch.*

1415 SIR T. GREY in *43 Deputy Keeper's Rep.* 587 Ye mon shulde cum agayn on Tiseday to tel ye way of yair lawsyng. **1504** *Plumpton Corr.* (Camden) 186 The letter that come from William Elison, the which I had mynd in for loyssing of Edmund Ward, for I have gotten him forth by the wayes of William Ellyson. **1591** PERCIVALL *Sp. Dict., Soltura,* loosing, deliuering, *solutio, dimissio.*

†**2.** The making or rendering loose in a socket or the like; the untying (of a knot). *Obs.*

1482 *Monk of Evesham* (Arb.) 38 Some were also rasyd with fyry naylys vnto the bonys and to the lowsing of her ioyntys. **1576** FLEMING *Panopl. Epist.* 249 Rather then I wil tarrie the loosing of them [*sc.* knottes], I wil cutt them in sunder. **1599** *Life Sir T. More* in Wordsw. *Eccl. Biog.* (1853) II. 99 The old man's purse was made fast to his girdle, which the thief spying gave it the looseing.

3. A setting free, absolving, or discharging (from guilt, sentence, or obligation); remission of a sin or penance.

c **1357** *Lay Folks Catech.* (MS. T.) 345 At thair bother assent for to lyve samen Withouten ony lousyng to thair life lastes. **1526** *Pilgr. Perf.* (W. de W. 1531) 226 This power of byndyng & losynge of synne, is deriuyed from ye apostles to ye mynysters of Christes chirche. **1659** PEARSON *Creed* (1839) 505 What is the remission [of sins] itself, or the loosing of that obligation? **1686** J. SCOTT *Chr. Life* (1747) III. 462 The Pardon or Remission of Sins..consists in the loosing of sinful Men from that Obligation to eternal Punishment. **1871** SPROTT *Sc. Liturgies Jas. VI* (1901) Notes 151 This has always been regarded as a notable example of binding and loosing by the minister.

†**4.** The action of weighing anchor or setting free the moorings of a ship; getting under weigh.

1632 LITHGOW *Trav.* II. 54 Vpon the second day after our loosing from Clissa, we arriued at Ragusa.

†**5.** The action of letting-go the drawn string of a bow. *Obs.*

c **1400** *Laud Troy-bk.* 7797 [He] drow an Arwe vp to the vale; And as he was In his losyng, Diomedes..to him rode, Ar euere arwe fro him glode. **1545** ASCHAM *Toxoph.* (Arb.) 107 What handlyng is proper to the Instrumentes? Standynge, nockyng, drawyng, holdyng, lowsing, wherby commeth fayre shotynge. **1612** SELDEN in *Drayton's Poly-olb.* xvii. Notes 268 His death by an infortunate loosing at a deer out of one Walter Tirrel's hand.

6. A sum of money paid on the completion of a contract or obligation.

1889 W. MARCROFT *Ups & Downs* 10 On my coming to be 21 years of age there must be a loosing paid of one guinea.

7. *Sc. Law.* A release.

1495 *Rolls of Parlt.* VI. 481/2 If ther shall fortune a resonable consideracion or consideracions to be upon the making of the said Leasses, for lossyng of the same. **1564-[65]** *Reg. Privy Council Scot.* I. 317 Providing alwayis that the lowsing of the said arreistment..sall na wyise be hurtful. **1798** *Monthly Mag.* VI. 176 (Scots Law Phrases) A *Loosing of Arrestment*, a Writ to discharge such attachment, which issues of course on the debtor giving security for payment of the debt.

8. *Comb.*: **loosing-place** *Sc.* [cf. LOSSING], a place for unloading vessels (? *obs.*); **loosing-time**, the time of release from work (*dial.*).

1805 FORSYTH *Beauties Scotl.* III. 35 The bottom or tail.. of this bank..as a loosing place, experienced mariners prefer to any other harbour in the frith. **1824** SCOTT *St. Ronan's* xv, Looking at their watches..lest they should work for their master half an instant after loosing time.

'loosing, *ppl. a.* [f. LOOSE *v.* + -ING^2.] Relaxing; laxative.

1665 SIR J. LAUDER (Fountainh.) *Jrnl.* (S.H.S.) 43 In my experience I fand it very loosing, for before I was weill accoustened wt it, if I chanced to sup any tyme any quantity of the pottage, I was sure of 2 or 3 stools afternoon wt it.

loosing, obs. form of LOZENGE.

loosish ('lu:sɪʃ), *a.* [f. LOOSE *a.* + -ISH.] Somewhat loose.

1824-9 LANDOR *Imag. Conv.* Wks. 1846 I. 46 A loosish man and slippery in foul proclivities. **1853** G. J. CAYLEY *Las Alforjas* II. 202 Eruptive hills with loosish sandy slopes.

loosome, Sc. form of LOVESOME.

loot (lu:t), *sb.*^{1} Also 7 lute. [See LUTE *sb.*^{3}.] A name applied in the Cheshire and Staffordshire salt-works to the ladle used to remove the scum from the brine-pan.

1669 W. JACKSON in *Phil. Trans.* IV. 1065 This bloudy brine at the first boyling of the Pann, brings up a scumm, which they are careful to take off with a Skimmer, made with a woodden handle thrust through a long square of Wainscot-board, twice as bigg as a good square trencher: this they call a Loot. **1686** PLOT *Staffordsh.* 94. **1880** C. H. POOLE *Staffordsh. Gloss., Loot,* a brine ladle.

loot (lu:t), *sb.*^{2} [a. Hindī *lūt*, according to some scholars repr. Skr. *lōtra, lōptra* booty, spoil, f. the root *lup* = *rup* to break; others refer it to Skr. *lunt* to rob.] **1.** Goods (esp. articles of considerable value) taken from an enemy, a captured city, etc. in time of war; also, in wider sense, something taken by force or with violence; booty, plunder, spoil; now sometimes *transf.*, illicit gains, 'pillage' (e.g. by a public servant). Also, the action or process of looting.

[**1788** *Indian Vocab.* (Y.), *Loot*, plunder, pillage.] **1839** *Blackw. Mag.* XLV. 104 He always found the talismanic gathering-word *Loot* (plunder), a sufficient bond of union in any part of India. **1858-9** RUSSELL *Diary India* (1860) II. xvii. 340 Why, the race [of camp followers] is suckled on loot, fed on theft, swaddled in plunder, and weaned on robbery. **1860** HOOK *Lives Abps.* (1862) II. vii. 505 The horses in the archbishop's stables the murderers appropriated as their own fee,—or, as we should now say, as loot. **1876** *Blackw. Mag.* CXIX. 115/1 Public servants [in Turkey] have vied with one another in a system of universal loot.

2. *slang.* Money.

1943 HUNT & PRINGLE *Service Slang* 44 *Loot*, Scottish slang for money received on pay day. **1956** B. HOLIDAY *Lady sings Blues* (1973) ii. 16 There was nothing to do except for Mom to go back slaving away as somebody's maid. In Baltimore she couldn't make half the loot she could up North. **1959** *Encounter* Oct. 73/1 MacInnes's teen-agers.. are all economically self-supporting, in their own phrase, they've got the loot. **1968** J. SANGSTER *Touchfeather* xiii. 141 When you've got his sort of loot I don't suppose it matters. **1973** *Center City Office Weekly* (Philadelphia) 9 Oct. 3 Jefferson Medical College picks up $362,949 in loot for.. continuing research in hemophilia.

loot (lu:t), *sb.*^{3} *U.S. Mil. slang.* Shortened from Amer. pronunciation of LIEUTENANT 2.

1898 F. P. DUNNE *Mr. Dooley in Peace & War* 11 R-run over an' wake up th' loot at th' station. **1918** *Stars & Stripes* 27 Dec. 7 He's a loot-colonel now and a D.S.C. **1921** B. MATTHEWS in *S.P.E. Tract* v. 6 In the United States this officer is called the *lootenant*, which the privates of the American Expeditionary Force in France habitually shortened to '*loot*'. **1944** K. LEVIS in Murdoch & Drake-Brockman *Austral. Short Stories* (1951) 423 Some nitwit of a loot's in charge that don't know a bush track from Pitt Street. **1948** J. G. COZZENS *Guard of Honor* 331 Don't thank the loot!

loot (lu:t), *v.* [f. LOOT *sb.*^{2}] **a.** *trans.* To plunder, sack (a city, building). **b.** To carry off as loot or booty. **c.** *absol.*

a. 1845 W. H. SMITH in *Colburn's United Service Mag.* II. 10 He has attacked and looted several villages under our protection. **1861** GRESLEY *Sophron & N.* 135 The summer palace of the Emperor..has been..unceremoniously looted. **1889** JESSOPP *Coming of Friars* ii. 99 A gang of fellows..seems to have looted the manors of Dunton and Mileham.

b. 1847 LD. MALMESBURY in *Mem. Ex-minister* (1884) I. 192 Went to see Marshal Soult's pictures which he looted in Spain. **1858** K. YOUNG *Diary* (1902) App. D. 328 My Sirdar-bearer who..looted all my traps. **1860** DICKENS *Uncomm. Trav.* xiv, A place of temporary security for the plunder 'looted' by laundresses [*sc.* of Inns of Court chambers]. **1887** *Daily News* 18 July 5/4 The dervishes are reported to be looting cattle and grain.

c. 1842 [implied in LOOTING *vbl. sb.*]. **1859** *Times* 30 May 10/4 He who 'loots' is almost sure to make acquaintance with the 'haslinger'. **1878** R. TAYLER in *N. Amer. Rev.* CXXVI. 243 The gentle 'Tigers' [soldiers] were looting right merrily, diving in and out of wagons with the activity of rabbits in a warren.

Hence **'looted** *ppl. a.*

1897 *Daily News* 24 Mar. 7/6 All the looted cattle and women were recaptured.

loot, var. LOTE lotus, LOTH; obs. Sc. f. LOUT.

loot, Sc. pa. t. of LET *v.*^{1}

lootable ('lu:təb(ə)l), *a.* *rare*$^{-1}$. [f. LOOT *v.* + -ABLE.] That may be looted or taken as loot.

1885 *Ch. Times* 30 Jan. 75/3 The amount of lootable income would be a very different matter.

lootah: see LOTA(H.

loote, obs. form of LOT, LOTA(H.

looter ('lu:tə(r)). [f. LOOT *v.* + -ER^1.] One who loots.

1858-9 RUSSELL *Diary India* (1860) II. xvii. 340 Those insatiable 'looters'—men, women, and children, all are at it. **1872** *Daily News* 19 Aug., Those begging gentlemen who march at the tail of political parties like the looters behind armies.

looth(e, looþ, obs. forms of LOATH *a.*

‖**lootie** ('lu:tɪ). *Anglo-Ind.* Also 8 louchee, 9 lutee. [Hindī *lūṭī*, f. *lūṭ* LOOT *sb.*^{2}] In *pl.* A term applied, in India, to a body of native irregulars whose chief object in warfare was plunder. In wider sense, a band of marauders or robbers. Also rarely in *sing.*, one of such a band or gang. Hence **lootie-wallah** [Hindī *lūṭīwālā*: see WALLAH], a member of a gang of looties.

1757 ORME *Hist. Milit. Trans.* (1778) II. VII. 129 A body of their Louchees, or plunderers, who are armed with clubs ..attacked the houses of the natives. **1782** I. MUNRO *Narr. Mil. Operat. Coromandel Coast* (1789) 295 Even the rascally Lootywallahs, or Misorian hussars..now pressed upon our flanks and rear. **1791** *Gentl. Mag.* LXI. 77/1 These irregulars of the enemy [in the East Indies], distinguished by the name of Looties, continued their depredations. **1800** T. T. ROBARTS *Indian Gloss., Lootywalla*, see *Looties*. **1802** C. JAMES *Milit. Dict., Lootywallow*, Ind., a term of the same import as Looties. **1827** SCOTT *Surg. Dau.* xii, I will find the dagger of a Lootie which shall reach thee, wert thou sheltered under the folds of the Nawaub's garment. **1876** GRANT *Hist. India* I. iv. 279/1. **1884** W. L. WHIPPLE in *Bib. Soc. Rec.* Sept. 131 (Stanf.) A noted lutee, or rogue.

looting ('lu:tɪŋ), *vbl. sb.* [f. LOOT *v.* + -ING^1.] The action of the vb. LOOT. Also *attrib.*

1842 LD. ELLENBOROUGH *Let.* 17 May in *Indian Administr.* (1874) 194 The plunderers are beaten whenever they are caught, but there is a good deal of burning and 'looting' as they call it. **1859** M. THOMSON *Story Cawnpore* iii. 48 For downright looting commend me to the hirsute Sikh. **1862** L. OLIPHANT *Earl Elgin's Mission China* I. 135, I observed, in the suburb large looting parties, composed of Chinese blackguards, ransacking the houses.

†**loove, love.** *Obs. rare.* [repr. OE. *láf*: see LAVE *sb.*] Relict, widow.

1387 TREVISA *Higden* (Rolls) VIII. 75 Henry..ȝaf hym to wyf Constauns contas of Bretayne, þe loove [*v.r.* wydowe, L. *relictam*] of his sone Gaufred. *Ibid.* 173 Constans, Geffray his love [*v.r.* loove, L. *relicta*]. **1492** *Churchw. Acc. St. Dunstans, Canterb.* in *Kentish Gloss.* s.v. *Love*, Item payde for the buryng of Ellerygge's loue..iiij^s. **1514** *MS. Acc. St. John's Hosp., Canterb.*, Rec. off Pett's loove wyth owt west gaat ij*d*. **1557** *Will Jno Shoo*, Item I give to Counstables love xx^d to Steres love xx^d.

loover, obs. form of LOUVRE.

looves, -ys, obs. pl. of LOAF *sb.*^{1}

loovesum, obs. form of LOVESOME.

loo-warm, variant of LEW-WARM.

loowe, obs. form of LOW.

looz, variant of LOSE *sb. Obs.*, praise.

†**lop** (lɒp), *sb.*^{1} *Obs.* Forms: 1, 5 loppe, 7- lop. [OE. *loppe* wk. fem., of obscure origin. Cf. LOB *sb.*^{1}] A spider.

c **888** K. ÆLFRED *Boeth.* xvi. §2 ȝe furþum þeos lytle loppe hine [*sc.* man] hwilum deadne ȝedeþ. *c* **1000** ÆLFRIC *Gloss.* in Wr.-Wülcker 121/27 *Loppe*, fleonde næddre, *uel* attorcoppe. *c* **1391** CHAUCER *Astrol.* I. §3 Shapen in manere of a net or of a webbe of a loppe. *Ibid.* §19 From this senyth ..ther come a maner krokede strikes like to the clawes of a loppe. *c* **1400** *Ragman Roll* 72 in Hazlitt *E.P.P.* I. 72 Ye lade longe sydyde as a loppe.

lop (lɒp), *sb.*^{2} Now *dial.* [prob. a. ON. **hloppa* wk. fem. (Sw. *loppa*, Da. *loppe*), f. root of *hlǫupa* (*hlaupa*) to LEAP.] A flea.

c **1460** *Towneley Myst.* viii. 306 Grete loppys ouer all þis land thay fly [*sc.* the plague of 'flies']. **1480** CAXTON *Chron. Eng.* D vij b, After this Boor shall come a lambe that shall haue feet of leed an hede of bras an hert of a loppe. **1597** G. HARVEY *Trimming Nashe* Wks. (Grosart) III. 43 But see, what, art thou heere? *lupus in fabula*, a lop in a chaine? **1662** *Rump Songs* I. 192 Lay-interlining Clergy, a device That's nick-name to the stuff call'd Lops and Lice. **1674** RAY *N.C. Words* 31 Lops and Lice, used in the South, i.e. Fleas and Lice. **1755** in JOHNSON. **1787** GROSE *Provinc. Gloss., Lop*, a flea. N. **1863** ROBSON *Bards of Tyne* 237 The sheets lily-white, though aw says it mysel'; Maw darlin', nee lops there to touch us. **1877** in *N.W. Linc. Gloss.*

lop (lɒp), *sb.*^{3} Also 5-8 loppe, (7 lope), 6-7 lopp. [Commonly supposed to be f. LOP *v.*^{1}, but more probably the source of that word. Senses 2 and 3, however, are from the vb.

The etymology is obscure. An OE. **lopp* would represent a pre-Teut. type **lupno-* 'what is stripped off', f. root **lup-* (see LEAF *sb.*^{1}); but the word does not appear before the 15th c., and is not found in other Teut. dialects. Cf. Norw. dial. *loppa* v., to pluck, snatch, *lopa, lopna* (of bark) to be loosened by moisture.]

1. The smaller branches and twigs of trees, such as are not measured for timber; faggot-wood, loppings. Also, a branch lopped off. Phr. ***lop and top***, waste branches cut from timber trees, usually after the trees have been felled; also ***lop and crop***.

c **1420** *Pallad. on Husb.* VI. 45 And stones yf thee lacketh, this is boote: Sarment, or stre, or loope [L. *vel quibuscunque virgultis*] in hit be graued. **1464** *Rolls of Parlt.* V. 547/1 The Loppes and Croppes of Woode, falled withynne our fryth of Leycestre. **1532** *Dial. on Laws Eng.* II. lv. 153 b, What thynke they if a man sell the loppes of his woode, whether any tythe ought there to be payd? **1573** TUSSER *Husb.* xxxiii. (1878) 73 Let lop be shorne that hindreth corne. **1613** SHAKS. *Hen. VIII*, I. ii. 96 We take From euery tree, lop, barke, and part o' th' timber. **1651** G. W. tr. *Cowel's Inst.* 265 Where any one is killed, with the fall of an Arme or Lopp of a Tree..after warning given by the parties who are ..lopping. **1669** WORLIDGE *Syst. Agric.* (1681) 92 A certain gentleman..obtained a parcel of Elm-trees lops and tops. **1726** AYLIFFE *Parergon* [506], Lops of Trees above twenty years Growth pay no Tithes. **1774** T. WEST *Antiq. Furness* (1805) 228 Anye kind of underwoods, topps, loppes, croppes, or other woods. **1805** *Trans. Soc. Arts* XXIII. 135, I also considered the value of the tops and lop, or trimmings of the trees. **1819** W. FAUX *Mem. Days Amer.* (1823) 176 What [trees] are cut down, together with the lop, are rolled by levers into heaps and burnt. **1826** COBBETT *Rur. Rides* (1885) II. 238 What is the price of this load of timber?.. taking in lop, top and bark..ten pounds a load at least. **1842** BRANDE *Dict. Sci.* etc., s.v. *Lopping*, When timber trees are sold the purchaser bargains to take them either with or without the lop and crop. **1862** T. L. PEACOCK *Mem. Shelley* Wks. 1875 III. 448 The gardener had cut it [*sc.* a holly-tree] up into a bare pole, selling the lop for Christmas decorations. **1892** *Times* 24 Oct. 3/1 Cord wood is the smaller limbs of oak, the lop and top of the branches when the trees are felled. **1938** C. P. ACKERS *Pract. Brit. Forestry* vi. 194 Lop and top may be overcome either by burning or by stacking it in 'trenches'. **1972** *Country Life* 30 Mar. 789/3 'Lopp and Topp'—the side and top branches—were the college property and if from ash or oak fetched 8s. to 9s. 6d. a load.

fig. **1579** SPENSER *Sheph. Cal.* Feb. 57 Ah, foolish old man! .. Now thy selfe hast lost both lopp and topp, Als my budding braunch thou wouldest cropp. *a* **1641** BP. MOUNTAGU *Acts & Mon.* (1642) 94 Lop and top, hip and thigh, bough and branch, root and stemme, all and singular should be eradicated. *c* **1645** HOWELL *Lett.* I. v. xxvii, They three [*sc.* Italian, French, and Spanish] Are only lops cut from the Latian tree.

†**2.** A lopped tree or the lopped part of a tree. *Obs. rare.*

a **1640** SIR W. JONES *Rep.* (1675) 280 They must..not cut the Loppes flat, so that the water may stand on them, and rot

them. **1656** W. D. tr. *Comenius' Gate Lat. Unl.* §371. 105 Hee pruneth every year, that new branches may spring from the Lope, or pruned tree.

†**3.** The action or process of lopping a tree or its boughs. *Obs.*

1576 TURBERV. *Venerie* 198 What loads of haye, what grasse for bief, what store of wood for loppe. *a* **1600** HOOKER *Eccl. Pol.* VII. i. §2 It hath not seemed expedient to offer the edge of the axe unto all three boughs at once, but rather to .. strike at the weakest first, making show that the lop of that one shall draw the more abundance of sap to the other two.

4. *Comb.*: **lop-limbed** *a.*, having one or more limbs cut off; **lop-stick** (*Canadian*), a tree which has had its branches lopped and the name of the lopper cut in its trunk; also **lobstick**; **lop-wood**, branches, etc. lopped from a tree.

1809 MALKIN *Gil Blas* VII. xii, The *lop-limbed captain would have gone raving mad at it. **1821** N. GARRY *Diary* 19 Aug. (1900) 149 After Dinner we observed that two of our Men had lopped away the Boughs and all the Lower Branches of two Trees leaving a Top. This is called a *Lop-Stick. **1847** J. B. NEVINS *Two Voy. Hudson's Bay* iv. 90 Two gentlemen were travelling a short time since, and lobsticks were cut for them. **1873** G. M. GRANT *Ocean to Ocean* vii. 196 There is an old superstition that your health and length of days will correspond to your lobstick's. **1892** W. PIKE *North. Canada* 209 Often on the lonely waterways of the Northern country one sees a lop-stick showing far ahead on the bank, and reads a name celebrated in the annals of the Hudson's Bay Company or in the history of Arctic exploration. **1923** *Beaver* Aug. 421 To commemorate this great battle, three lobsticks were cut on each side of the river. **1949** *Argosy* Apr. 13 On the far side of the lake, if you must portage, use the 'lop-stick' mark. This is made by cutting all branches from one side of a tall tree which may be seen either from water or land. Its unnatural appearance attracts the eye; the side from which branches are cut indicates the direction of portage. **1964** *Islander* (Victoria, B.C.) 18 Oct. 1/12 There was a tradition among the Northern Indians that a lobstick honouring an individual would fall when its sponsor died. **1693** EVELYN *De la Quint. Compl. Gard.* 75 They afford both much *Lop-wood and Fruit. **1794** T. STONE *Agric. Surv. Linc.* (1800) 115 [Trees] which will consequently produce most bark, and top or lop-wood. **1888** *Academy* 4 Feb. 71/1 The curious customs of 'lop-wood' or privileges of cutting fuel from pollards at certain seasons of the year.

†**lop**, *sb.*[4] *Obs. rare.* [Related to LOP *v.*[2], expressing the notion of something hanging loose. Cf. LAP *sb.*[1], LOB *sb.*[2]] A lobe (of the liver).

1601 HOLLAND *Pliny* I. 342 The land Frogs of Toads kind, have one lop or lappet of the Liver, which Ants will not touch.

†**lop**, *sb.*[5] *Tanning. Obs.* [Of obscure origin; cf. LOB *sb.*[2] 5.] The infusion of bark and ooze used in tanning leather. (Cf. LOPPING *vbl. sb.*[3])

1773 *Encycl. Brit.* III. 886/2 The bark should be rounder beat, and more given to the lop, for large hides than small ones; and consequently larger leather should lie longer in the lop.

lop (lɒp), *sb.*[6] *Naut.* [Onomatopœic (connected with LOP *v.*[3]). Cf. LAP *sb.*[2], *v.*[1]] A state of the sea in which the waves are short and lumpy.

1829 COL. HAWKER *Diary* (1893) I. 360 There was too much 'lop'. **1838** *Ibid.* II. 153 The wigeon .. were always on a 'lop of the sea'. **1847** *Illustr. Lond. News* 10 July 18/2 There being a 'lop' on, the boat lurched to windward. **1899** F. T. BULLEN *Way Navy* 38 Quite a 'lop' of a sea gets up, but these battleships take no heed of it.

lop (lɒp), *sb.*[7] [Short for *lop-rabbit*: see LOP *v.*[2]] A variety of rabbit with long drooping ears. Also with word prefixed, as *full-*, *half-*, *oar-lop* (see quot. 1868), ***horn-lop***.

1868 DARWIN *Anim. & Pl.* I. iv. 107 When one parent, or even both, are oar-laps [*sic*], that is, have their ears sticking out at right angles, or when one parent or both are half-lops, that is, have only one ear dependent, there is nearly as good a chance of the progeny having both ears full-lop, as if both parents had been thus characterized. But I am informed, if both parents have upright ears, there is hardly a chance of a full-lop. **1877** C. RAYSON *Rabbits* xiii. 70 In rearing lops, little divergence need be made from the usual mode adopted. **1884** R. O. EDWARDS *Rabbits* vii. 54 It is very difficult to arrive at whether or not the drooping of the ears of the Lop is natural. *Ibid.* 55 Oar Lops, Half Lops, and Horn Lops, are not .. to be considered anything fancy.

lop, *sb.*[8] = *lop-grass* (see LOP *v.*[2] 4).

lop (lɒp), *v.*[1] Also 6 **loppe**. [prob. f. LOP *sb.*[3]]

1. *trans.* To cut off the branches, twigs, etc.: *rarely* the top or 'head', of (a tree); to cut away the superfluous growth of, to trim.

1519 HORMAN *Vulg.* 172 Vynes .. shuld be lopped or cut about the .xx. day of march. **1523** FITZHERB. *Husb.* §132 If yᵉ haue any trees to shrede, loppe, or croppe for the fyre wode. **1562** TURNER *Herbal* II. 75 If a Date tre be topped or lopped it will lyue no longer after. **1620** MARKHAM *Farew. Husb.* (1625) 160 In the moneth of December .. lop hedges and trees. **1667** MILTON *P.L.* IX. 210 What we by day Lop overgrown, or prune, or prop, or bind, One night or two with wanton growth derides, Tending to wilde. **1714** SCROGGS *Courts-leet* (ed. 3) 32 Whether any Copyholder .. Hath .. lopped or topped any Timber-Trees. **1750** JOHNSON *Rambler* No. 25 ¶4 A few strokes of an axe will lop a cedar. **1813** SIR H. DAVY *Agric. Chem.* (1814) 259 By lopping trees, more nourishment is supplied to the remaining parts.

b. *transf.* and *fig.*; *esp.* To cut off the head or limbs of (a person). †Also with *away*, *off*.

1602 *Narcissus* (1893) 696 My webb is spunne; Lachesis, loppe thy loome. **1603** DRAYTON *Odes* xvii. 47 When our grandsire great, Claiming the regal seat, By many a War-like feate, Lop'd the French lillies. **1682** OTWAY *Venice Preserved* II. i. Wks. 1727 II. 290 Lop their Nobles To the base Roots, whence most of 'em first sprung. **1683** [see LOPPING *vbl. sb.*]. **1725** POPE *Odyss.* XVIII. 99 A tyrant .. Who casts thy mangled ears and nose a prey To hungry dogs, and lops the man away. **1733** *Revolution Politicks* VII. 7 He would never be at Peace till he had lopped the Queen off shorter by the Head. **1742** YOUNG *Nt. Th.* I. 251 Some, .. In battle lopt away, with half their limbs, Beg bitter bread. **1869** BLACKMORE *Lorna D.* xxiv, A man in the malting business had tried to take up the brewer's work, and lop the King, and the Duke of York.

2. To cut off (the branches, twigs, etc.) from a tree; to shorten by cutting off the extremities. Also (now chiefly) with *away*, *off*.

1593 SHAKS. *Rich. II*, III. iv. 64 Superfluous branches We lop away, that bearing boughes may liue. **1611** BIBLE *Isa.* x. 33 The Lord of hostes shall lop the bough with terrour. **1651** N. BACON *Disc. Govt. Eng.* II. xiii. 118 He lopped off the tops as they sprang up. **1667** MILTON *P.L.* IV. 630 Branches overgrown, That .. require More hands then ours to lop thir wanton growth. **1748** *Anson's Voy.* III. x. 415 Their masts are made of trees, .. fashioned .. by barking them, and lopping off their branches. **1808** SCOTT *Marm.* VI. xi, As wood-knife lops the sapling spray. **1830** CUNNINGHAM *Brit. Paint.* I. 221 Lop carefully away all wild or over-flourishing branches. **1870** BRYANT *Iliad* II. xxi. 281 Lopping with an axe the boughs of a wild fig-tree. **1874** C. GEIKIE *Life in Woods* iii. 41 We had to lop off the branches.

b. *transf.* and *fig.*; *esp.* To cut off (a person's limbs or head). Also in gen. sense, to cut off, reduce by cutting. Also with advbs. as *away*, *down*, *off*.

c **1586** C'TESS PEMBROKE *Ps.* LXXVI. v, The Lord .. Who loppeth princes thoughts, prunes their affection. **1588** SHAKS. *Tit. A.* I. i. 143 Alarbus limbs are lopt, And intrals feede the sacrifising fire. **1591** —— *1 Hen. VI*, v. iii. 15 Ile lop a member off, and giue it you. **1608** HEYWOOD *Rape Lucrece* I. ii, With bright steele Lop downe these interponents, that withstand The passage to our throane. **1656** COWLEY *Pref. to Wks.* (1668) B iij b, Shakspear, Fletcher, Johnson, and many others; part of whose Poems I should take the boldness to prune and lop away. **1714** J. MACKY *Journ. Eng.* (1724) II. v. 77 The Keeper .. not to be absent .. on Pain of 20 Shillings to be lopped off from his Salary. **1725** POPE *Odyss.* XXII. 240 Thee first the sword shall slay, Then lop thy whole posterity away. **1732** —— *Ess. Man* II. 49 Expunge the whole, or lop th' excrescent parts Of all our Vices have created Arts. **1775** DE LOLME *Eng. Const.* I. vi. (1784) 67 In their endeavours to lop off the despotic power. **1809** CRABBE *Tales* 74 The worthy George must now a cripple be; His leg was lopp'd. **1846** LANDOR *Imag. Conv.*, *Southey & Landor* Wks. 1846 II. 67, I would lop off the whole from 'Spirits of purest light' v. 661, to 831. **1864** HAWTHORNE *Grimshawe* xx. (1891) 265 It will not lop off any part of your visit to me.

3. *absol.* or *intr.* Also *fig.*

1588 SHAKS. *Tit. A.* II. iv. 17 What sterne vngentle hands Hath lopt, and hew'd, and made thy body bare Of her two branches. **1622** R. HAWKINS *Voy. S. Sea* (1847) 189 One plowing, another harrowing, another sowing, and lopping. **1651** [see LOP *sb.*[2] 1]. **1856** MISS WINKWORTH *Life Tauler* ix. (1857) 249 They leave the roots of vice and evil dispositions alive in the heart, and hew and lop at poor nature, and thereby destroy this noble vineyard.

†**4.** *trans.* 'To cut partly off and bend down; as to lop the trees or saplings of a hedge'. *Obs.* (? or some error).

1828 in WEBSTER; and in later Dicts.

lop (lɒp), *v.*[2] [Perh. of onomatopœic origin; cf. LOB *v.*, which is closely akin in sense; also LAP *sb.*]

1. a. *intr.* To hang loosely or limply; to droop; to flop or sway limply *about*. Also ***to lop out***: to protrude in an ungraceful or lop-sided manner.

1578 LYTE *Dodoens* I. lxxxiii. 123 Nine or ten yellow floures .. hanging lopping downewardes. **1854** *Blackw. Mag.* LXXV. 524 Three exterior walls encompass it, and an eccentric work lops out at either side. **1874** T. HARDY *Far fr. Madding Crowd* II. xx. 230 These [sheep] filed in about nine o'clock, their vermiculated horns lopping gracefully on each side of their cheeks. **1882** *Century Mag.* XXIII. 652 The señora tried to brace up triumphantly, but could only lop about in her saddle. **1892** *Harper's Mag.* June 17/1 His under jaw lopped, and his brow contracted. **1892** *Temple Bar* Jan. 36 Her .. figure was rather disguised than set off by garments that fell lopping round her.

b. *trans.* To droop (the ears).

1828 WEBSTER s.v., A horse lops his ears. **1864** *Jrnl. R. Agric. Soc.* XXV. II. 556 The animals .. do not lop their ears, nor droop their heads.

2. a. *intr.* To move in a slouching manner; to 'hang about' idly. Also ***to lop about***.

1587 M. GROVE *Pelops & Hipp.* (1878) 122 To take the vewe this boyish clowne dyd nothing aye appall, .. But loppeth to the vpper end, his cap vpon his head. **1852** MRS. STOWE *Uncle Tom's C.* viii, She .. cried about it, she did, and lopped round, as if she'd lost every friend she had. **1881** BESANT & RICE *Chapl. of Fleet* I. x. (1883) 74 Some debauched, idle fellow who lies and lops about all day.

b. ***to lop down***, to sit down, to lie down. *U.S. colloq.*

1839 C. M. KIRKLAND *New Home* ii. 17 Jist come in, and take off your things, and lop down, if you're a mind to. **1861** MRS. STOWE *Pearl of Orr's Island* I. viii. 67 Ruby said she thought she'd just lop down a few minutes on the old sofa. **1892** F. P. HUMPHREY *New Eng. Cactus* 34 You'd best lop down on the lounge and get a nap.

3. With mixture of the sense of LOPE *v.*: To move with short irregular bounds.

1895 K. GRAHAME *Gold. Age* 102 The staidest of the rabbits was lopping demurely about the grass. **1902** CORNISH *Naturalist Thames* 91 Lopping easily along, a fox crosses through the teazles.

4. *Comb.*: *lop-brimmed* adj. **lop-eaves**, eaves which hang down at the sides; **lop-grass** (also simply lop) *dial.*, *Bromus mollis* (cf. *lob grass*, LOB *sb.*[2] 6); **lop-rabbit** (see LOP *sb.*[7]). Also LOP-EAR, LOP-EARED.

1901 S. E. WHITE *Westerners* xvi. 131 His broad hat—straight-brimmed in a *lop-brimmed camp—was pushed to one side. **1880** *Scribner's Mag.* Feb. 491 A most picturesque old dwelling, with low *lop-eaves. *c* **1832** *Glouc. Farm Rep.* 14 in *Husbandry* (L.U.K. 1840) III, All the seeds of grass, *lop-grass, and other seeds, which come up amongst the barley. **1883** in *Hampsh. Gloss.* **1886** BRITTEN & HOLLAND *Plant-n.*, Lob, or Lop Grass. *Bromus mollis* ... It is sometimes called simply Lop. **1884** R. O. EDWARDS *Rabbits* vii. 52 The *Lop Rabbit.

lop (lɒp), *v.*[3] [Cf. LOP *sb.*[6]] *intr.* Of water: To break in short lumpy waves. Cf. LOPPING *ppl. a.*[3]

1897 *Westm. Gaz.* 24 Aug. 7/2 The bow is being canvassed over to prevent, as much as possible, the water lopping in.

lop (lɒp), *v.*[4] *dial.* Also 6 loppe. [Cogn. w. ON. *hlǫup* (*hlaup*) coagulation, *hløypa* to curdle.] *intr.* To curdle. (Cf. LOPPER *v.* 1.)

1570 LEVINS *Manip.* 169/16 To Loppe as milk, *coagulare.* **1893** *Northumbld. Gloss.*, *Lop*, to curdle, applied to milk that curdles without the application of an acid.

lope (ləʊp), *sb.* [A dialectal var. of LOUP *sb.* a. ON. *hlǫup*: see LEAP *sb.*[1] Some of the uses may be from Du. *loop*, which is etymologically identical, and others are prob. from the Eng. vb.]

†**1.** = LEAP *sb.*[1] in various senses. *Obs.*

14.. *S. Eng. Leg.* (MS. Bodl. 779) in Herrig's *Archiv* LXXXII. 402/47 He ordeyned þat ech man þat prest wolde be scholde vndirfong þe ordres fro gre to gre; wit-oute lope & defaute. *a* **1420** HOCCLEVE *De Reg. Princ.* 3436 He at a lope was at hir, and hir kist. *c* **1440** CAPGRAVE *Life St. Kath.* II. 223 Tyme goth fast, it is full lyght of lope. **1483** *Cath. Angl.* 220/2 A Lope, *saltus.* **1596** DALRYMPLE tr. *Leslie's Hist. Scot.* I. 51 Quhairfor, ony Lope thocht wondirful, is .. commounlie called the Salmont lope. **1662** COTGRAVE *Wits Interpreter* (ed. 2) 323 He makes no more to run on a rope, Then a Puritan does of a Bishop or Pope. And comes down with a vengeance at one single lope. *a* **1734** NORTH *Exam.* III. viii. §47 (1740) 618, I cannot do the Author Justice .. without taking a large Lope, over the next Reign, into that which followed.

2. A long bounding stride. Now used chiefly of people.

1809 M. L. WEEMS *Life F. Marion* xii. 108 He dashed off at a charging lope. **1846** T. B. THORPE *Backwoods* 13 [The mustang pony] goes rollicking ahead, with the eternal lope .. a mixture of two or three gaits, as easy as the motions of a cradle. **1889** R. KIPLING *Fr. Sea to Sea* (1900) I. xx. 430 The Jap soldier .. doubles with the easy lope of the 'rickshaw coolie. **1894** CROCKETT *Lilac Sunbonnet* 310 At his usual swift wolf's lope he was out of sight .. speedily. **1910** C. E. MULFORD *Hopalong Cassidy* xxi. 135 As he rode at an easy lope he kept a constant lookout for signs of rustling. **1953** R. CHANDLER *Let.* 15 Mar. in *R. Chandler Speaking* (1966) 28 Walks with a forward-leaning lope, huh? **1961** L. VAN DER POST *Heart of Hunter* I. ii. 25 The others followed close on her heels with a strange stumbling lope. **1973** *Houston* (Texas) *Post* 14 Oct. (Spotlight Suppl.) 15/4 Somehow .. Hero Hazard reaches the Sphinx .. and evades the grisly Arab agents after a lope up and down the Great Pyramid.

3. *Comb.*: **lope-way** (see quots.)

1736 PEGGE *Kenticisms* (E.D.S.), *Lope-way*, a private footpath. **1791** *Gentl. Mag.* LXI. II. 928 A lope-way in Kent is now a short or quick way or bridle-way.

lope (ləʊp), *v.* Also 7–8 loap(e. [A dial. var. of LOUP *v.*, a. ON. *hlǫupa*: see LEAP *v.*]

1. *intr.* To leap, jump, spring. Also with *about*. *Obs.* exc. *dial.*

1483 *Cath. Angl.* 220/2 To Lope, *salire, saltare.* **1529** LYNDESAY *Complaynt* 251 And go, all, to the hie boirdall: Thare may we lope at lybertie, Withouttin ony grauitie. **1549** *Compl. Scot.* xvii. 151 Buciphal the grit horse of allexander .. syne tholit hym to lope on hym. **1581** N. WOODES *Conflict Conscience* III. iv. D iij b, In gude feth sir, this newis de gar me lope. **1623** MIDDLETON & ROWLEY *Sp. Gipsy* IV. i. (1653) G, He that loapes on the Ropes, shew me such an other wench. *a* **1734** NORTH *Lives* (1826) I. 62 Not by such large strides as he made in getting money, and loping into preferments. *a* **1734** —— *Exam.* I. ii. §82 (1740) 73 It is plain, his Malice lopes at a Venture. **1891** ATKINSON *Last of Giantkillers* 69 The Staff itself leaping—or rather loping—about with a startling activity.

†**b.** Of the pulse: To beat, throb. *Obs. rare.* Cf. Cornwall Dial. *lopping*, throbbing with pain.

a **1600** MONTGOMERIE *Misc. P.* xliv. 31, I quake for feir —my puncis lope—I shake betuix dispair and hope.

2. *intr.* To run, run away. Now only *slang* and *dial.* (see Eng. Dial. Dict.).

c **1572** GASCOIGNE *Fruites Warre* lii, Yet was he forst, alwayes from lawes to lope. *a* **1592** GREENE *Jas. IV* (1598) A iij b, This whinyard has gard many better men to lope then thou. **1632** I. L. *Womens Rights* 146 They may lope ouer ditch and dale. *a* **1700** B. E. *Dict. Cant. Crew*, *Let's buy a Brush*, or *Let's Lope*, let us scour off, and make what shift we can to secure our selves from being apprehended. **1785** GROSE *Dict. Vulgar Tongue*, *Loap*, to run away; he loaped down the dancers, he ran down stairs.

3. To run with a long, bounding stride. Also with *along*, *away*. (Said chiefly of animals.)

a **1825** FORBY *Voc. E. Anglia*, *Lope*, to take long strides; particularly with long legs. **1848** *Blackw. Mag.* LXIV. 27 The larger wolves .. lope hungrily around. **1863** H. KINGSLEY *A. Elliot* I. 78 He .. laid his leaf-like ears back, drooped his tail, .. and loped, or lurked in his Walk, which means, that he moved the two legs which were on the same side of him together. **1865** KINGSLEY *Herew.* xxiv, The hares and rabbits loped away, innumerable. **1891** *Field* 7 Mar.

331/1 The first fox..was seen loping over the uplands. **1893** *Spectator* 10 June 767 A regular Hindostanee carrier..will ..lope along over a hundred miles in twenty-four hours. **1897** G. BARTRAM *People of Clopton* viii. 233 Carter walked at a great pace, and we had to lope now and then to keep up with him. **1899** *Daily News* 6 Nov. 5/4 A Boer pony..hardly knows how to gallop or trot, but goes loping along in a leisurely, monotonous way.

b. *causative.* To make to run with a long, bounding stride.

1885 T. ROOSEVELT *Hunting Trips* viii. 261 For seven or eight miles we loped our jaded horses along at a brisk pace.

lop-ear (ˈlɒpˈɪə(r)), *sb.* (and *a.*) [LOP *v.*[2]]

1. *pl.* Ears that droop or hang down.

1692 *Lond. Gaz.* No. 2805/4 A plain strong bay Gelding, ..a Blase in his Face, Lop-ears. **1853** KINGSLEY *Hypatia* xxi. 258 The faithful Bran, whose lop-ears and heavy jaws, unique in that land of prick-ears and fox-noses, formed the absorbing subject of conversation.

2. A variety of rabbit with long drooping ears: see LOP *sb.*[7] Also *attrib.*

1877 C. RAYSON *Rabbits* xiii. 67 The Lop-ear. **1884** R. O. EDWARDS *Rabbits* vii. 52 The Lop-ear has often been termed the Prince of all rabbits. **1901** 'IAN MACLAREN' *Yng. Barbarians* iv. 92 'Did ye say rabbits?' 'Lop-ears', said Nestie... 'Lop-ear rabbits, and he feeds them himself.'

lop-eared (ˈlɒpˈɪəd), *a.* Also 7 lap-. [f. LOP *v.*[2] + -ED[2].]

1. Of an animal: Having ears which lop or hang loosely downwards.

1687 MIEGE *Gt. Fr. Dict.* II. s.v. *Lap*, Lap-eared, *qui a les Oreilles pendantes.* **1692** *Lond. Gaz.* No. 2801/4 An Iron grey Horse, lop Ear'd. **1724** *Ibid.* No. 6294/3 Stolen, ..a.. Gelding, ..a little Lop-Ear'd. **1859** JEPHSON *Brittany* v. 55 They [pigs] are long-legged, hump-backed, ..lop-eared. **1868** DARWIN *Anim. & Pl.* I. iv. 106 English lop-eared rabbits. **1871** L. STEPHEN *Playgr. Europe* x. 250 The queer lop-eared sheep.

†¶ **2.** [Confused with LOP *v.*[1]] = CROP-EARED 2.

1798 CHARLOTTE SMITH *Yng. Philos.* III. 26 The strait-laced lop-eared puritans of the United States.

†**ˈlopeholt.** *Obs. rare.* [App. formed after LOPESKONCE; the second part may be Du. *holte* hollow, hole.] A place of refuge.

1616 J. LANE *Cont. Sqr.'s T.* iv. 424 Yet so, as theire seavn mountes bee mand all waies, to serve for lopeholtes on contrarie sayes. *Ibid.* ix. 224 Algarsif, Horbell, Leifurcke, Gnartolite, retierd eake to theire lopeholt [1630 lopesconce], fortifite.

†**ˈlopeman.** *Obs. rare.* [a. Du. *loopman* (obs.), f. *loopen* to run + *man* MAN *sb.*] A runner.

a **1625** FLETCHER *Noble Gent.* III. iv, What a stile is this? Methinks it goes like a Duchy lope-man.

loper (ˈləʊpə(r)). [f. LOPE *v.* + -ER[1].]

†**1.** A leaper, dancer. *Obs.*

1483 *Cath. Angl.* 220/2 A Loper, *saltator, saltatrix.*

2. *Ropemaking.* A swivel upon which yarns are hooked at one end while being twisted into cordage. [Perh. another word, a. Du. *looper* runner.]

1794 *Rigging & Seamanship* 55 *Loper*, used to lay lines, has two iron swivel-hooks at each end, for the line to hang on. **1797** *Encycl. Brit.* XVI. 485/1 [*Rope-making*] This is put on one of the hooks of a swivel called the loper.

3. *Cabinet-making.* (See quots.)

1833 LOUDON *Encycl. Cottage Archit.* 302 In the second [bureau bookcase], the sloping flap falls down, and rests on two sliding pieces, technically called lopers. **1952** J. GLOAG *Short Dict. Furnit.* 323 Sliding rails which pull out from the carcase of a bureau to support the fall are called lopers. **1963** *Times* 20 Apr. 11/7 The bureau bookcase has continuously changed its outline, wood and fashionable finish according to the dictates of fashion, but apart from the invention, in this century, of the automatic opening loper, no basic improvement in it has been found possible between the reigns of Queen Anne and Queen Elizabeth II. **1971** *Canad. Antiques Collector* Mar. 10/1 The name 'pembroke' should be saved for a particular sort of small 4-legged dropleaf tables, usually with a drawer, the leaves supported on lopers (pull-out bars).

loper, var. LOOPER[2].

†**ˈlopeskonce.** *Obs.* [a. Du. *loopschans*, f. *loopen* to run + *schans* SCONCE.] An intrenchment.

1624 CAPT. SMITH *Virginia* IV. 158 Such another Lope Skonce would I haue had at Onawmanient. **1630** J. LANE *Cont. Sqr.'s T.* 149 *note*, Algars, Orbell, Leyfurcke, Gnartolite, retierd to their lopeskonces fortifyte.

†**ˈlope-staff.** *Obs.* Also 7 loape-. Pl. lope-staves. [f. LOPE *v.* + STAFF.] A pole used for leaping dykes, etc. in the Fens and Low Countries.

1603 DRAYTON *Bar. Wars* I. xliii, Such as in fens and marsh-lands us'd to trade, The doubtful fords and passages to try, With stilts and lope-staves that do aptliest wade. **1611** COTGR. s.v. *Bout, Baston a deux bouts*, a quarter-staffe; or, a Lope-staffe, wherewith Low-countrey men leape ditches. **1630** *R. Johnson's Kingd. & Commw.* I. 27 Tis usuall for the Bores of Holland, some with firelocks, and some with Loapestaves, to make out parties of foot to goe a-bootehaling. **1654** E. JOHNSON *Wond. workg. Provid.* 20 The Ditch..was so wide, that they could not leap over with a lope-staffe.

lopez-root (ˈləʊpɛz,ruːt). [= mod.L. *radix lopeziana*; orig. applied to the root of an East African species of the same genus, discovered by Juan *Lopez* Pinheiro (see Redi *Esper. Cose Nat.*, 1671).] The root of an East Indian plant, *Toddalia aculeata*, used as a remedy for diarrhœa.

1791 W. LEWIS *Mat. Med.* (ed. 4) II. Index Eng. Names, Lopez root. **1822** GOOD *Study Med.* I. 237 The lopez-root (*lopezia Mexicana*) [this is a mistake] which by Gaubius was preferred to the simarouba. **1856** MAYNE *Expos. Lex.*, *Lopez*, name given to the root of an unknown tree growing, it is said, at Goa.

†**lop-heavy,** *a. Obs.* [f. LOP *v.*[2] + HEAVY *a.* Cf. *top-heavy.*] Heavy with a weight which causes lopping, hanging down, or drooping.

1583 GOLDING *Calvin on Deut.* v. 29 We doe but creepe vppon the Earth, or rather be so loppeheauie [F. *si pesans*] that wee sinke still downeward. **1602** WARNER *Alb. Eng.* x. liv. (1612) 242 That Spanish-Iewish Atheist, and Lop-heauie-headed Leach, ..fowle Lopas, we impeach. *a* **1652** BROME *Queene's Exch.* II. ii. Wks. 1873 III. 478 It is indeed a divelish Lopheavy Bell. I would the Churchwarden that Should have mended it..were Hang'd in's Place. *a* **1722** LISLE *Husb.* (1757) 180 When they [*sc.* ears of wheat] are in shock, they spread and lay over, being lop-heavy.

lophine (ˈləʊfaɪn, ˈləʊfɪn). *Chem.* Also -in. [F. *lophine* (Laurent 1844), of unexplained formation: see -INE.] An organic base, a derivative of aldehyde, obtained by heating amarine.

1856 in MAYNE *Expos. Lex.* **1858** *Fownes' Chem.* (ed. 7) 611 Amarine (Benzoline). Strongly heated in a retort it decomposes with production of ammonia, ..and a new body *pyrobenzoline* or *lophine.* **1888** MORLEY & MUIR *Watts' Dict. Chem.* I. 474/2 Lophine $C_{21}H_{16}N_2$.

lophiodon (ləʊˈfaɪədɒn). *Palæont.* [f. Gr. λόφιον, dim. of λόφος crest + ὀδοντ-, ὀδούς tooth, after *mastodon*, etc.] A genus of fossil mammals of the Eocene period, the typical genus of the *Lophiodontidæ*; a fossil mammal of this genus.

1833 LYELL *Princ. Geol.* III. 221 Cuvier also mentions the remains of a species of lophiodon as occurring among the bones in the Upper Val d'Arno. **1836** BUCKLAND *Geol. & Min.* I. 82 The Lophiodon is..allied most nearly to the tapir and rhinoceros, and, in some respects, to the hippopotamus. **1864** OWEN *Power of God* 50 To match the eocene lophiodon we fetch the tapir from South America.

lophiodont (ˈləʊfɪəʊdɒnt), *a.* and *sb.* [See prec.]

A. *adj.* Pertaining to or resembling the lophiodon; belonging to the family *Lophiodontidæ.*

1864 in WEBSTER (citing DANA). **1873** FLOWER in *Proc. Roy. Instit.* (1875) VII. 100 Another offset from the ancient Lophiodont stock..constitutes the family *Tapiridæ.*

B. *sb.* An animal of the family *Lophiodontidæ.*

1873 FLOWER in *Proc. Roy. Instit.* (1875) VII. 99 These Lophiodonts possess a dental character which distinguishes them from all other *Perissodactyles.*

Hence **lophioˈdontine, lophioˈdontoid** *adjs.*, = LOPHIODONT *a.* **lophioˈdontous** *a.*, 'having hairy or bristly teeth' (*Syd. Soc. Lex.* 1889).

1887 E. D. COPE in *Amer. Nat.* XXI. 994 It is impossible to separate the Hyracotheriine sub-family as a family from the Lophiodontine. **1890** *Century Dict.*, *Lophiodontoid.*

lophioid (ˈləʊfɪɔɪd), *a.* and *sb. Ichthyol.* [f. mod.L. *Lophi-us* (app. f. Gr. λόφος or λοφιά mane, back-fin of fishes) + -OID.]

a. *adj.* Pertaining to the family *Lophiidæ*, of which the typical genus is *Lophius*, represented by the Angler or Fishing-frog. **b.** *sb.* A lophioid fish.

1854 OWEN in *Circ. Sci.* (*c* 1865) II. 56/1 Certain lophioid fishes..are enabled to hop after the..tide. **1859–62** SIR J. RICHARDSON etc. *Mus. Nat. Hist.* (1868) II. 134 The skeletons of the Lophioids are fibrous. **1883** *Rep. Copepoda coll. 1873–6* in *Challenger Rep.* VIII. 137 The curious Lophioid genus *Ceratias.*

lophiostomate (ləʊfɪˈɒstəmət), *a. Bot.* and *Zool.* [f. Gr. λόφιο-ν crest + στόμα mouth + -ATE[2].] Having a crested mouth or aperture.

1862 in COOKE *Man. Bot. Terms.* **1889** in *Syd. Soc. Lex.*

lopho- (ˈləʊfə, ləʊˈfɒ), before a vowel loph-, comb. f. of Gr. λόφος crest, in many scientific words, as **lophoˈcercal** *a.* [Gr. κέρκος tail] (see quot.). **lophoˈcercy**, the lophocercal stage of development of the fin-system of Ichthyopsida. **lophoderm** (ˈləʊfədɜːm) [Gr. δέρμα skin], a crested or spiny back. **lophodont** (ˈləʊfədɒnt) *a.* and *sb.* [Gr. ὀδοντ-, ὀδούς tooth], (*a*) *adj.*, characterized by having transverse or longitudinal ridges on the crowns of the molar teeth; (*b*) *sb.*, an animal with this kind of dentition. ‖**lophopoda** (-ˈɒpədə) [Gr. ποδ-, πούς foot], *sb. pl.*, the fresh-water Polyzoa, which have a horseshoe-shaped lophophore. **lophosteon** (-ˈɒstɪɒn) [Gr. ὀστέον bone], the median bone, including the keel, of the sternum of a carinate bird.

1885 J. A. RYDER in *Amer. Nat.* XIX. 92 *Lophocercy.—The second stage of development of the median fin-system of Ichthyopsida is what I have called **lophocercal*.. when it consists of continuous folds..or exceptionally of discontinuous folds..which do not include permanent rays. *Ibid.* 97 Lophocercal larva of the codfish. **1836** *Blackw. Mag.* XXXIX. 306 The thorny *lophoderm of a centronote or stickleback. **1854** BADHAM *Halieut.* 117 His [the perch's] prickly lophoderme is indeed a formidable affair. **1887** E. D. COPE *Orig. Fittest* vii. 246 The subordinate types of *Lophodonts. *Ibid.* 247 Four types of Lophodont dentition. **1880** PASCOE *Zool. Classif.* (ed. 2) 68 *Lophopoda. **1889** SEDGWICK tr. *Claus' Zool.* II. (ed. 2) 78 The Lophopoda are mainly distinguished by the bilateral arrangement of the numerous tentacles on the two-armed lophophore. **1884** COUES *Key N. Amer. Birds* 143 The median ossification, which includes the keel, is the *lophosteon.

lophobranch (ˈləʊfəbræŋk), *a.* and *sb. Ichthyol.* [ad. mod.L. *Lophobranchii*, f. Gr. λόφο-ς crest, tuft + βράγχια gills.] = LOPHOBRANCHIATE *a.* and *sb.*

1859–62 SIR J. RICHARDSON, etc. *Mus. Nat. Hist.* (1868) II. 157 The Lophobranchs have an osseous internal skeleton. **1890** *Century Dict.*, *Lophobranch* a. and sb.

lophobranchian (ləʊfəʊˈbræŋkɪən), *a. Ichthyol.* [f. as prec. + -AN.] = LOPHOBRANCHIATE *a.*

1835 KIRBY *Hab. & Inst. Anim.* II. xxi. 392 Lophobranchian Fishes. So called because their gills are not pectinated, but disposed in tufts.

lophobranchiate (ləʊfəʊˈbræŋkɪət), *a.* and *sb. Ichthyol.* [f. as prec. + -ATE.] **a.** *adj.* Belonging to or having the characteristics of the order *Lophobranchii*; having the gills disposed in tufts. **b.** *sb.* A lophobranchiate fish; *pl.*, the order *Lophobranchii* (see quot. 1842).

1834 McMURTRIE *Cuvier's Anim. Kingd.* II. 228 Lophobranchiate fishes..eminently distinguished by the gills, which..are divided into small round tufts. **1842** BRANDE *Dict. Sci.* etc., *Lophobranchiates*, an order of Osseous fishes, comprehending those in which the gills are in the form of small tufts, and disposed in pairs along the branchial arches; as in the pipe-fish and hippocamp. **1881** SEELEY in *Cassell's Nat. Hist.* V. 12 In..the Plectognathi and Lophobranchiates, the otolites are represented by calcareous dust.

So **lophoˈbranchous** *a.*

1856 J. E. GRAY *Kaup's Catal. Lophobranchiate Fish Brit. Mus.* Pref., Lophobranchous Fishes.

lophoite (ˈləʊfəʊaɪt). *Min.* [Named by A. Breithaupt, 1841 (*Lophoit*), f. Gr. λόφο-ς crest, cock's-comb + -ITE.] An obsolete synonym of prochlorite (A. H. Chester, 1896).

1882 DANA *Man. Min.* (ed. 4) 319.

lophophore (ˈləʊfəfɔə(r)). [f. Gr. λόφο-ς crest + -φόρ-ος bearing. (In sense 2, ad. mod.L. *Lophophorus.*)]

1. *Zool.* In Polyzoa, the oral disc at the free end of the polypide, bearing the tentacles.

1850 ALLMAN in *Brit. Assoc. Rept.* (1851) 307 The sort of disc or stage which surrounds the mouth and bears the tentacula, I have called *Lophophore.* **1855** *Eng. Cycl.*, *Nat. Hist.* III. 861/1. **1885** A. S. PENNINGTON *Brit. Zoophytes* 19.

2. A bird with crested crown and brilliant plumage, belonging to the genus *Lophophorus* of the family *Phasianidæ.* [Cf. F. *lophophore.*]

1883 *Fortn. Rev.* 1 Sept. 348 One of her dresses..made up principally of the feathers of the bright-plumaged lophophore. **1884** *Western Daily Press* 29 May 3/7 A butterfly, made of the feathers of the lophophore.

Hence **loˈphophoral** *a.*, of or pertaining to a lophophore (sense 1).

1890 in *Century Dict.*; and in other recent Dicts.

lophyropod (ˈlɒfɪrə,pɒd). *Zool.* [ad. mod.L. *Lophyropoda* neut. pl., f. pseudo-Gr. *λόφυρος 'hairy' (misreading of λόφουρος bushy-tailed) + ποδ-, πούς foot.] A crustacean of the group *Lophyropoda.*

1842 BRANDE *Dict. Sci.*, etc., *Lophyropods*, a section of Entomostracous Crustaceans, comprehending those species with cylindrical or conical ciliated or tufted feet. **1852** DANA *Crust.* II. 1308 The Cyclops section of Lophyropods.

loping (ˈləʊpɪŋ), *vbl. sb.* Also 6 *Sc.* lopene. [-ING[1].] The action of the verb LOPE.

1483 *Cath. Angl.* 220/2 A Lopynge, *saltacio, saltus.* **1549** *Compl. Scot.* vi. 66 It vas ane celest recreation to behald ther lycht lopene. **1886** *S.W. Linc. Gloss.* s.v., He's fond of loping.

loping (ˈləʊpɪŋ), *ppl. a.* Also lopeing. [f. LOPE *v.* + -ING[2].] Characterized by long, bounding strides; having a gait of this kind.

1707 *Lond. Gaz.* No. 4327/8 A brown bay Nag, ..of a loping Carriage. **1826** J. F. COOPER *Mohicans* (1829) I. ii. 26 Generally content to maintain a lopeing trot. **1841** — *Deerslayer* ii, A loping red-skin. **1865** KINGSLEY *Herew.* i, A man on foot coming up behind him at a slow, steady, loping, wolf-like trot. **1883** J. BURROUGHS *Fresh Fields* i, A loping hare started up before me.

lopister, obs. form of LOBSTER.

loplolly, variant of LOBLOLLY.

lopolith (ˈlɒpəʊlɪθ). *Geol.* [See quot. 1918 and -LITH.] A large intrusive mass similar to a laccolith but having the base centrally sunken.

1918 F. F. GROUT in *Amer. Jrnl. Sci.* CXCVI. 518 Professor John Barrell has suggested that as igneous forms they deserve a distinct name... The name proposed by the writer is 'lopolith' (from [Greek] λοπάς, a basin, a flat earthen dish, and λίθος, a stone). *Ibid.*, Pronunciation, lŏˈpolith. **1962** [see INTRUSIVE *sb.*]. **1972** M. P. BILLINGS *Struct. Geol.* (ed. 3) xvi. 343 In plan, lopoliths are arcuate or circular.

Hence **lopoˈlithic** *a.*

1959 *Econ. Geol.* LIV. 1208 Cooling of a lopolithic mass would proceed under the influence of two cooling gradients. **1968** R. W. FAIRBRIDGE *Encycl. Geomorphol.* 281/2 The second type [of intrusive dome mountain] is the complex laccolith (or lopolithic) intrusion with broad sill-type interfingering tongues of igneous material penetrating the surrounding sediments.

†'loppage. *Obs. rare*$^{-1}$. [f. LOP *v.*^{1} + -AGE.] The loppings from trees; lop.

1683 PETTUS *Fleta Min.* II. 14 Blink.. is also applyed to the .. brouse or loppage of Trees given to Deer. **1911** FLETCHER & KIPLING *School Hist. Eng.* ii. 32 Laws they made in the Witan, the laws of flaying and fine—Common, loppage and pannage, the theft and the track of kine.

loppard ('lɒpəd). [f. LOP *v.*^{1} + -ARD, after *pollard*.] 'A tree with the top lopped or cut off; a pollard' (Worcester 1846, *citing* Allen).

lopped (lɒpt), *ppl. a.* [f. LOP *v.*^{1} + -ED^{1}.] In senses of the verb. *Bot.* and *Zool.*: Truncate.

1570 LEVINS *Manip.* 49/27 Lopped, *tonsus.* **1611** SHAKS. *Cymb.* v. v. 454 The lofty Cedar, Royall Cymbeline, Personates thee: And thy lopt Branches point Thy two Sonnes forth. **1645** WALLER *Of the Queen* 26 By cutting hope, like a lopt limbe, away. **1721** RAMSAY *Marquis of Bowmont* 40 His lop'd-off locks. **1787** tr. *Linnæus' Fam. Plants* I. 3 Headlet flat, with the side declining to the nectary lop'd, perforated. *Ibid.*, Seeds very numerous, oblong, lop'd. **1791** COWPER *Odyss.* x. 533 So tumble his lopp'd head into the dust. **1812** BARCLAY, *Lopped*, in botany, appearing as if cut off with a pair of scissars; the leaves of the great bindweed are lopped at the base; the petals of the periwinkle are lopped at the end. **1847** HARDY in *Proc. Berw. Nat. Club* II. No. v. 234 Labial palpi filiform, or the last joint but slightly enlarged and lopped. **1867** TROLLOPE *Chron. Barset* II. lxxxii. 365 A hope that the lopped tree may yet become green again. **1872** GEO. ELIOT *Middlem.* lxxiii, She needed time to get used to her maimed consciousness, her poor lopped life. **1898** A. BALFOUR *To Arms* xxi. 241 He might have had the unenviable experience of a lopped-off head.

b. *Her.* (See quots.)

1828–40 BERRY *Encycl. Her.* I, *Lopped*, or *Snagged*, differs from couping, which does not show the thickness, whereas, this is cut off to sight. **1884** BURKE *Gen. Armory* p. xli, *Lopped*, or *snagged*, cut so as to show the thickness.

†loppel. *Obs.* [Cf. Du. *luifel.*] (See quot.)

1626 A. SPEED *Adam out of E.* iii. (1659) 28 He causeth to be built a little sleight shade or loppel with poles covered with straw or some sleight stuff on the top where he ties up his oxen.

lopper ('lɒpə(r)), *sb.*^{1} [f. LOP *v.*^{1} + -ER^{1}.] One who lops (a tree).

1538 ELYOT *Dict.*, *Frondator*, a brouser, a wodlopper [1545 wode lopper]. **1552** HULOET, Lopper, or shragger, *arborator, frondator.* **1572** —— (ed. Higgins), Hence lopper on the hautie hill, shall sing with voyce on highe. **1613** JACKSON *Creed* I. xxi. §1 A great oak.. spoiled of boughs by the lopper's axe. **1755** in JOHNSON. **1883** *Leisure Hour* 505/1 Beeches unscathed by topper and lopper.

lopper ('lɒpə(r)), *sb.*^{2} *Sc.* and *north. dial.* in form lapper. [f. LOPPER *v.*] A curdled or coagulated state or condition (of blood or milk). Also, partly-melted snow, 'slush'.

c **1817** HOGG *Tales & Sk.* V. 345 The country became waist-deep of lapper or half-melted snow. **1880** JAMIESON s.v. *Lapper*, The milk's into a lapper. **1895** CROCKETT *Men of Moss Hags* ii, The ground about was all a-lapper with blood.

lopper ('lɒpə(r)), *a. Obs.* exc. *Sc.* Also 4, 9 loper, 9 lapper. [? f. LOPPER *v.*] = LOPPERED.

1340 HAMPOLE *Pr. Consc.* 459 Whar he had na other fode Bot wlatsom glet, and loper blode. **1816** SCOTT *Antiq.* x, Lapper-milk. **1823** CRABB *Technol. Dict.*, *Lopper Milk* (Husband.), old milk turned to curds. *a* **1894** J. SHAW *Dumfr. Dial.* in Wallace *Country Schoolm.* (1894) 350 *Loper snow*, snow in a state of slush.

lopper ('lɒpə(r)), *v.* Now only *Sc.* and *north. dial.* Forms: 4 lopir, 5 leper, 9 lapper, lopper. [Perh. a derivative (with suffix -ER^{5}) of ON. *hlǫup* (*hlaup*) coagulation (of milk or blood). Cf. ON. *hløypa* trans. to curdle, Sw. *löpe*, Da. *løbe*, Norw. dial. *löper, löyper* rennet. Cf. LOP *v.*^{4}]

1. *intr.* Of milk: To curdle.

a **1300** [see LOPPERED]. *a* **1340** HAMPOLE *Psalter* cxviii. 70 As mylk in þe kynd is fayre and clere, bot in lopirynge it waxis soure. *c* **1400** MAUNDEV. (Roxb.) vii. 27 Take a drope of bawme.. and putte þerto gayte mylke; and, if þe balme be gude, alsone þe mylke sall leper. **1812** FORBES *Poems* 34 (E.D.D.) A muckle plate That ha'ds our milk to lapper. *a* **1825** FORBY *Voc. E. Anglia*, *Lopper*, to turn sour and coagulate by too long standing.

b. *trans.* To turn to curds; to curdle.

1882 G. MACDONALD *Castle Warlock* 13 Drinkin' soor milk—eneuch to lapper a' i' the inside o' 'im!

2. 'To dabble, to besmear, or to cover so as to clot' (Jam.).

1818 SCOTT *Rob Roy* xxx, Sic grewsome wishes, that men should be slaughtered like sheep—and that they may lapper their hands to the elbows in their heart's bluid.

loppered ('lɒpəd), *ppl. a. Obs.* exc. *Sc.* and *north. dial.* Forms: 3 lop(e)red, 4 lopird, 5 lopyr(r)de, 6 lopp(e)rit, 6–7 lopperd, 7–8 lappered, 8 lopered, 9 lapoured, lappert, loppert, lappered, loppered. [f. LOPPER *v.* + -ED^{1}.] Clotted, coagulated, curdled. Chiefly of milk and blood. Also *fig.*

a **1300** *E.E. Psalter* cxviii. 70 Lopred als milk es hert of þa. **1483** *Cath. Angl.* 220/2 Lopyrde (*A.* Lopyrryde). As mylke; *concretus.* Lopyrde mylke, *ivnctata.* **1513** DOUGLAS *Æneis* III. ix. 64 Thir wretchit mennis flesche, that is his fude, And drinkis worsum, and thair lopperit blude. **1597** LOWE *Chirurg.* (1634) 381 There remaineth lappered bloud. **1724** RAMSAY *Tea-t. Misc.* (1733) I. 91 And there will be lapper'd milk kebbucks. **1806** A. HUNTER *Culina* (ed. 3) 243 The preparation will become what, in this country, is called laboured. **1826** G. BEATTIE *John o' Arnha* 35 The.. stains Of lappert blood and human brains. *a* **1856** *Denham Tracts* (1895) II. 327 When cows.. give bloody or lappered or stringy milk.

loppestere, obs. form of LOBSTER.

loppet ('lɒpɪt), *v. dial.* [Onomatopœic extension of LOP *v.*^{2}] *intr.* To move or run with a heavy gait. Usually of an animal, as a hare or rabbit, *rarely* of a person. Hence **'loppeting** *vbl. sb.*

1864 C. BRYANT in Buckland *Log-bk.* (1875) 320 They [seals] travel by lifting themselves from the ground on their fore-legs, and hitching the body after them with kind of side-ways loppeting gallop. **1888** *Berksh. Gloss.*, *Loppettin'*, walking with an ungainly movement and heavy tread.

loppiness. *rare.* [f. LOPPY *a.*^{3}] The quality of being loppy or choppy.

1908 *Daily Chron.* 10 Aug. 1/4 He complained that the loppiness of the water had taken the strength out of him.

lopping ('lɒpɪŋ), *vbl. sb.*^{1} [f. LOP *v.*^{1} + -ING^{1}.]

1. The action of LOP *v.*^{1}

This was the cant term used by the Rye House conspirators for the killing of the King and the Duke of York: see *Tryals of Walcot, Hone, etc. for High-treason* (1683) 12.

c **1511** in Swayne *Churchw. Acc. Sarum* (1896) 63 For ffellynge of an Elme & for the loppynge therof byfore vjd. **1641** MILTON *Animadv.* Wks. 1851 III. 243 A punishment .. for the lopping, and stigmatizing of so many free borne Christians. *a* **1715** BURNET *Own Time* (1724) I. 543 Walcot .. liked the project of a rising, but declared he would not meddle in their lopping. **1793** JEFFERSON *Writ.* (1830) IV. 479 No lopping-off of territory could be made without a lopping-off of citizens. **1848** LYTTON *Harold* XII. i, The trees were dwarfed in height by repeated loppings.

2. (Chiefly *pl.*) Branches and shoots lopped from a tree. Also, material for lopping.

1589 J. RIDER *Bibl. Scholast.* 884 The loppings of trees, *concædes.* **1600** SURFLET *Country Farme* I. x. 49 He shall gather vp the loppings to make fewell of. **1665** MANLEY *Grotius' Low C. Warres* 956 Filling them with earth and small loppings of Trees. **1766** *Museum Rusticum* 80 It is also the best kind to plant.. by the sides of rills, etc. where they will produce larger lopping. **1818** SOUTHEY in *Q. Rev.* XIX. 49 The loppings and leaves of the elm.. dried in the sun, prove a great relief to cattle when fodder is dear.

3. *attrib.*

1659 HOWELL *Voc.* xv, A lopping hook, *vn falcinello.* **1787** *Minor* 160 The idea of foreign surgeons using their lopping knives. **1875** KNIGHT *Dict. Mech.*, *Lopping-shears*, a pair of heavy shears for trimming bushes, hedges, etc.

lopping ('lɒpɪŋ), *vbl. sb.*^{2} [f. LOP *v.*^{2} + -ING^{1}.] Of the ears: The condition of hanging loosely.

1868 DARWIN *Anim. & Pl.* I. iv. 116 Even the elongation and lopping of the ears have influenced in a small degree the form of the whole skull. *Ibid.* 118 In breeding lop-eared rabbits the length of the ears, and their consequent lopping and lying flat on the face, are the chief points of excellence.

†'lopping, *vbl. sb.*^{3} *Obs. rare.* [Cf. LOP *sb.*^{5}] The process of barking or tanning leather.

1773 *Encycl. Brit.* III. 886/2 Of Lopping, or what is more properly called Tanning. This part of the operation is designed to preserve the fibres from corruption.

lopping ('lɒpɪŋ), *ppl. a.*^{1} [f. LOP *v.*^{1} + -ING^{2}.] That lops or cuts away.

1722 SEWEL *Hist. Quakers* (1795) I. II. 112 By the lopping axe the sturdy oak Improves her shade.

lopping ('lɒpɪŋ), *ppl. a.*^{2} [f. LOP *v.*^{2} + -ING^{2}.]

1. Of the ears: That lop or hang down.

1685 *Lond. Gaz.* No. 2099/4 A gray Horse with a large Head and lopping Ears. **1770** G. WHITE *Selborne* xxviii. 79 The ears [of the moose] were vast and lopping. **1792** W. ROBERTS *Looker-on* No. 20 (1794) I. 279 The Land of Secrets, where dwell a people with long lopping ears and little gimlet eyes. **1868** DARWIN *Anim. & Pl.* I. iv. 119 The left zygomatic arch on the side of the lopping ear.

2. Of an angler's fly.

1885 W. H. RUSSELL in *Harper's Mag.* Apr. 769/1 With limber rod and far-reaching lopping fly.

lopping ('lɒpɪŋ), *ppl. a.*^{3} [f. LOP *v.*^{3} + -ING^{2}.] Of the sea: Rising and falling in short waves.

1887 *Spectator* 29 Oct. 1453 Lying-to in a lopping sea. **1889** W. S. GILBERT *Foggerty's Fairy*, etc. (1892) 305, I rose and fell in the sulky lopping sea.

loppy ('lɒpɪ), *a.*^{1} *Obs.* exc. *dial.* [f. LOP *sb.*^{2} + -Y.] Full of or infested with 'lops' or fleas.

1483 *Cath. Angl.* 220/2 Loppy, *pulicosus.* A Loppy place, *pulicetum.* **1876** *Whitby Gloss.* s.v. *Lopping*, *Loppy*, infested with fleas. **1886** *S.W. Linc. Gloss.*, *Loppy.*

loppy ('lɒpɪ), *a.*^{2} [f. LOP *v.*^{2} + -Y.] That hangs loosely; limp.

1855 S. BROOKS *Aspen Crt.* II. viii. 106 He would even put on the same smeared and loppy shirt-collar three mornings in succession. **1893** ELIZ. B. CUSTER *Tenting* 163 The droop of his [a dog's] head was rendered even more 'loppy' by the tongue, which dropped outside the sagging jaw.

loppy ('lɒpɪ), *a.*^{3} [f. LOP *v.*^{3} + -Y.] Of the sea: 'Lumpy', 'choppy'; cf. LOPPING *ppl. a.*^{3}

1883 *Pall Mall G.* 17 May 3/2 The Channel was somewhat loppy, as usual. **1891** J. H. PEARCE *Esther Pentreath* IV. ix, The sea was getting 'loppy' in the crowded little harbour.

loppy ('lɒpɪ), *sb. Austral. slang.* [Prob. from LOPPY *a.*^{1}] A handyman on rural stations.

1898 *Bulletin* (Sydney) 1 Oct. 14/3 A few more Western Queensland slang words... In a shearing shed: The boss is the 'finger', the shearers the 'brutes', the rouseabouts 'leathernecks', 'spoonbills', 'loppies' or 'Jacks'. **1933** *Ibid.* 8 Feb. 21 The loppies, who are meek and spry To shearers and the rest, Are perky chaps when I am by.

lopscourse, obs. form of LOBSCOUSE.

1792 G. GALLOWAY *Poems* 38 Now grog and lopscourse fill'd our stamacks.

lopseed ('lɒpsi:d). [? f. LOP *v.*^{2}] 'A North American herb, *Phryma Leptostachya*, with spikes of small purple flowers, which in fruit are bent back close against the axis' (*Cent. Dict.*).

1850 MRS. LINCOLN PHELPS *Lect. Bot.* App. 53 *Phryma*,.. lopseed. **1856** GRAY *Man. Bot. North. U.S.* (ed. 2) 299.

lop-sided, lopsided (ˌlɒp'saɪdɪd), *a.* Also 8–9 lapsided, 9 lobsided. [f. LOP *sb.*^{2} or *v.*^{2} + SIDE *sb.* + -ED^{2}.] That lops or appears to lop or lean on or towards one side; having one side lower or smaller than the other. Orig. *Naut.* (of a ship): Disproportionately heavy on one side; unevenly balanced.

1711 W. SUTHERLAND *Shipbuild. Assist.* 27 You will certainly have the Misfortune of a lapsided Ship. **1769** FALCONER *Dict. Marine* (1780), *Lap-sided*, the state of a ship, which is built in such a manner as to have one side heavier than the other. **1820** PRAED *Surly Hall* 221 He drew me once ..('twas lopsided, And squinted worse than ever I did). **1842** DICKENS *Amer. Notes* viii, An odd, lop-sided, one-eyed kind of wooden building. **1878** D. KEMP *Man. Yacht & Boat Sailing* 356 *Dict.*, *Lob Sided*, larger or heavier on one side than on the other. **1901** *Athenæum* 10 Aug. 198/1 The church.. was.. lop-sided, as one aisle.. was narrower than the other.

b. *fig.*

1850 KINGSLEY *Alt. Locke* x. (1876) 118 The sooner we get the balance [of classes] equal the better; for it's rather lop-sided just now no one can deny. **1868** GREEN *Lett.* II. (1901) 200 The.. article.. is very lop-sided and unfair. **1891** F. W. NEWMAN *Life J. H. Newman* 11 So lobsided morality, if propounded in a Mormon Bible or by a Hottentot Potentate, would be spurned as self-confuted.

Hence **lop'sidedly** *adv.*, **lop-'sidedness.**

1843 H. JAMES *Let.* 11 May in R. B. Perry *Tht. & Char. W. James* (1935) I. 46 Thought heaped up to topheaviness and inevitable lopsidedness. **1875** *Carpentry & Join.* 76 A degree of instability or lop-sidedness which should not exist. **1896** *Nat. Observer* 21 Mar. 561/1 A turban.. hanging lopsidedly over one ear. **1946** *Nature* 21 Dec. 890/2 He makes, incidentally, a powerful case for some attempt to redress the lopsidedness of scientific advance.

lopstar, -er(e, obs. forms of LOBSTER.

lop-stick: see LOP *sb.*^{3} 4.

†lop-web. *Obs. rare.* [f. LOP *sb.*^{1} + WEB.] A spider's web; a cobweb.

c **1391** CHAUCER *Astrol.* I. §21 The riet of thin Astrelabie with thy zodiak, shapen in maner of a net or of a lop-webbe. *c* **1412** HOCCLEVE *De Reg. Princ.* 2819 Riȝt as lop-webbys flyes smale & gnattes Taken, and suffre grete flyes go.

†lopyn. *Obs. rare.* [a. OF. *lop(p)in.*] A morsel or lump of food; a 'gobbet'.

c **1430** *Pilgr. Lyf Manhode* III. xl. (1869) 156 Alle goode lopyns [Fr. *loppins*] j plounge and drenche. *Ibid.* 157.

loquacious (ləʊ'kweɪʃəs), *a.* [f. L. *loquāci-*, *loquāx* (f. *loqu-ī* to speak) + -OUS.]

1. Given to much talking; talkative.

1667 MILTON *P.L.* x. 161 To whom sad Eve.. Confessing soon, yet not before her Judge Bold or loquacious, thus abasht repli'd. **1712** STEELE *Spect.* No. 296 ¶1 The chief Exercise of the Female loquacious Faculty. **1725** POPE *Odyss.* XIX. 110 Loquacious insolent! she cries, forbear. **1791** COWPER *Iliad* II. 253 Thersites only of loquacious tongue Ungovern'd. **1814** D'ISRAELI *Quarrels Auth.* (1867) 338 The new.. philosophy insisted that men should be less loquacious, but more laborious. **1849** MACAULAY *Hist. Eng.* iv. I. 460 He was not loquacious: but, when he was forced to speak in public, his natural eloquence moved the envy of practised rhetoricians. **1901** *Longm. Mag.* June 152 Abel, in an unusually loquacious mood, repeated his question.

2. *transf.* Of birds, water, or the like: Chattering, babbling. Chiefly *poet.*

1697 DRYDEN *Virg. Georg.* III. 654 He fills his Maw with Fish, or with loquacious Frogs. —— *Æneid* XII. 694 The black Swallow.. To furnish her loquacious Nest with Food. **1708** J. PHILIPS *Cyder* II. 445 Blind British bards, with volant touch Traverse loquacious strings. **1725** POPE *Odyss.* v. 86 The chough, the sea-mew, the loquacious crow. **1888** BARRIE *When a Man's Single* (1900) 66/2 For a moment the water was loquacious as.. punts shot past.

Hence **lo'quaciously** *adv.*, **lo'quaciousness.**

1727 BAILEY vol. II, *Loquaciousness*, talkativeness. **1766** FORDYCE *Serm. Yng. Wom.* (1767) I. vi. 220 She preserves the due mean between taciturnity and loquaciousness. **1807** G. CHALMERS *Caledonia* I. I. i. 18 The taciturnity of history, and the loquaciousness of archaiology. **1854** HAWTHORNE *Eng. Note-Bks.* (1879) I. 83 The rooks were talking together very loquaciously.

loquacity (ləʊˈkwæsɪtɪ). [ad. F. *loquacité*, ad. L. *loquācitās*, f. *loquāci-*, *loquāx* (see LOQUACIOUS).] The condition or quality of being loquacious; talkativeness. Also *pl.*, instances of this.

1603 HOLLAND *Plutarch's Mor.* 60 To reproove..the loquacity of Euripides. **1664** POWER *Exp. Philos.* III. 184 These are they that..glut the Press with their Canting Loquacities. **1664** H. MORE *Myst. Iniq.* 333 Alluding to the Loquacity of the Magpie. **1711** ADDISON *Spect.* No. 135 ⁋1 A Man who is sparing of his Words, and an Enemy to Loquacity. **1869** BUCKLE *Civiliz.* III. iv. 203 When a preacher was once in the pulpit, the only limit to his loquacity was his strength.
transf. *a* **1716** SOUTH *Serm.* (1823) V. 423 A loquacity of countenance, and a significance of gesture.

loquat (ˈləʊkwæt). Also lacott, loquet, loquette, loquot. [a. Chinese (Canton dial.) *luh kwat*, literally 'rush orange'.]

a. The fruit of *Eriobotrya japonica*, a native of China and Japan, introduced into southern Europe, India, and Australia. **b.** The tree itself. Also ***loquat tree***.

1820 *Trans. Hort. Soc. London* III. 229 You desire me [*sc.* Lord Bagot] to give you some information as to my mode of treating the Lo-quat. *Ibid.* 301 In 1813 ripe fruits of the Lo-quat were presented to the Horticultural Society by Lord Bagot. **1829** E. HOOLE *Narr. Mission S. India* ix. 75 The lacott, a Chinese fruit, not unlike a plum, was produced also in great plenty. **1833** C. STURT *South Australia* I. Introd. 58 The pear and the loquette grow side by side. **1837** J. D. LANG *New S. Wales* I. 435 A fruit-tree of Chinese origin, called loquet, has been long naturalized. **1854** STOCQUELER *Brit. India* 314 Apples, citrons, loquats. **1880** C. R. MARKHAM *Peruv. Bark* 341 Behind the house grew peach, apple, plum, and loquot trees. **1884** tr. *J. J. Rein's Japan* I. vii. 139 A Japanese fruit-tree, the Loquat (Eriobothrya japonica Lindl.), which the English have transplanted to their tropical and subtropical colonies. **1969** *Oxf. Bk. Food Plants* 104/2 Loquat..is also sometimes known as Japanese medlar... The yellow pear-shaped fruits are the size of crab apples and have a sweetish acid flavour.

†**loquel.** *Obs. rare*⁻¹. [ad. L. *loquēla*, f. *loquī* to speak. Cf. OF. *loquele*.] Speech.

1694 MOTTEUX *Rabelais* v. 252 Where Rules to polish Loquels are prescrib'd [Fr. *où la lime est pour les locutions*].

loquence (ˈləʊkwəns). *rare.* [ad. late L. *loquentia*: cf. LOQUENCY.] Speaking; talk.

1677 T. HARVEY tr. *Owen's Epigrams* 199 Thy Tongue is loose, thy Body close; Both ill: With Silence this, with Loquence that doth kill. **1886** R. F. BURTON tr. *Arabian Nights* VIII. 346 When the Princess Miriam beheld Nur al-Din and heard his loquence and verse and speech, she made certain that it was indeed her lord Nur al-Din.

loquency (ˈləʊkwənsɪ). *rare.* [ad. late L. *loquentia*, f. *loquent-* LOQUENT.] Talking, speech.

1623 COCKERAM, *Loquentie*, speaking. **1891** G. MEREDITH *One of our Conq.* I. iv. 51 [His] exuberance in loquency had been restrained by a slight oppression, known to guests.

loquent (ˈləʊkwənt), *a. rare.* [ad. L. *loquent-em*, pres. pple. of *loquī* to speak.] That speaks.

1593 R. HARVEY *Philad.* 101 He would be loquent as Mithridates, that could speake 22 languages. *a* **1619** FOTHERBY *Atheom.* II. xii. §1 (1622) 332 Of things loquent, and silent; of things moueable, and vnmoueable. **1654** H. L'ESTRANGE *Reign Chas. I* (1655) 135 So rare is it for a man very eloquent, not to be over loquent. **1885** G. MEREDITH *Diana of Crossways* xi. (1890) 99 Redworth would have yielded her the loquent lead.

Hence ˈ**loquently** *adv.*, in point of talking.

1891 G. MEREDITH *One of our Conq.* I. xii. 222 The loquently weaker of the pair.

loqueram, variant of LOCKERAM *Obs.*

loquet(te, loquot, variant forms of LOQUAT.

lor', lor (lɔː(r)). *int. vulgar.* A clipped form of LORD, used as an interjection and in certain exclamatory phrases. (Cf. LAW, LAWK(S.)

1835–6 DICKENS *Sk. Boz, Characters* iv, 'Lor! how nice!' said the youngest Miss Ivins. **1865** —— *Mut. Fr.* I. ix, 'Lor-a-mussy [= Lord have mercy]!' exclaimed Mrs. Boffin. **1870** MISS BRIDGMAN *Ro. Lynne* I. xiii. 213 Lor'! what a fuss.

lora: see LORE *sb.*³ 2 a.

†**lorain.** *Obs.* Forms: 4 lorein, lorom, 4–5 loreyn, lorem(e, 5 loran, loreine, lorayn(e. [a. OF. *lorain*:—late L. type **lōrānum*, f. L. *lōrum* thong. Cf. med.L. *loranum*, *lorenum* (Du Cange s.v. *loramentum*).] The straps (often spoken of as gilt, studded with metal, or jewelled) forming part of the harness or trappings of a horse.

c **1290** *Beket* 248 in *S. Eng. Leg.* I. 113 His loreins weren al of seluer. *a* **1300** *Cursor M.* 25464 Nu ask i noþer gra ne grene, Ne stede scrud, ne lorem [*Fairf.* lorom] scene. ?*a* **1400** *Morte Arth.* 2462 The lawnces with loraynes, and lemande scheldes. *a* **1400–50** *Alexander* 793* Than strenys he hys streropes..Lad hym by þe loran. *c* **1460** *Launfal* 888 Wyth sadell and brydell of Champayne, Har lorayns lyght gonne leme.

loral (ˈlɔərəl), *a.* (and *sb.*) *Zool.* [f. L. *lōr-um* thong or strap, LORE *sb.*³ + -AL¹.] Pertaining to the lore. Hence as *sb.* = *loral shield* or *plate* (see LORE *sb.*³ 2 c). Cf. LOREAL.

1874 COUES *Birds N.W.* 134 The fore..parts and sides of the head are buff,..there is no yellow loral stripe. **1889** SAUNDERS *Man. Brit. Birds* 92 A black loral patch descends diagonally from below the eye.

†**lorament.** *Obs. rare*⁻⁰. [ad. L. *lōrāmen-tum*, f. *lōrum* thong.] A thong or band of leather.

1623 in COCKERAM. **1658** in PHILLIPS.

Loran (ˈlɔə-, ˈlɒræn). orig. *U.S.* Also loran. [f. the initial letters of *lo*ng-*ra*nge *n*avigation.] A hyperbolic navigation system employing the difference in the times of arrival of pulsed radio signals from different stations. Freq. *attrib.*; also *ellipt.* for a Loran receiver.

[**1942** (*title*) Development of airborne receiver model LRN-1: report on project 191. (Radio Corporation of Amer. License Div. Lab. Rep. No. 207 (PB 32732), 9 Sept.).] **1943** (*title*) Development of Loran receiver trainer: report on project 191 (extension). (Radio Corporation of Amer. License Div. Lab. Rep. (PB 23321), 17 Mar.) **1945** *Tuscaloosa* (Alabama) *News* 18 Oct. 5 In the airplane, a loran receiver measures the difference in radio wave travel time in millionths of a second. **1945** [see HYPERBOLIC *a.* 2 b]. **1946** J. P. BAXTER *Scientists against Time* ix. 151 The beauty of Loran for wartime use was that the ship or plane which used it emitted no signal that might give away its position. **1960** M. SHARCOTT *Place of Many Winds* i. 6 We passed Spring Island, where there is a Department of Transport Loran station. **1966** *McGraw-Hill Encycl. Sci. & Technol.* VII. 585 The distance at which reliable loran fixes are generally obtained is about 800 nautical miles over water from the pair of transmitting stations during daytime and about 1500 miles at night. **1972** K. CAMPBELL *Thunder on Sunday* 11 'Get a Loran fix.'.. Peter Spence had his face glued into the rubber eye-piece of the Loran... He counted the jumping electric lines and the long number blips... He then transferred his eyes to the Loran map.

loran, variant of LORAIN.

lorandite (ˈlɔərəndaɪt). *Min.* [ad. Hung. *lorandit* (J. Krenner 1894, in *Matemat. és Természett. Értesitö* XII. 473), f. the name of *Loránd* Eötvös, 19th-century Hungarian physicist: see -ITE¹.] A sulphide of thallium and arsenic, $TlAsS_2$, found as scarlet monoclinic crystals.

1895 *Mineral. Mag.* XI. 32 Professor Krenner, of Budapest,..describes a mineral containing no less than 59·5 per cent. of thallium, to which he has given the name Lorandite. **1946** [see CROOKESITE]. **1957** *Contrib. Mineral. & Petrol.* XVI. 45 A new find of the thallium-arsenic-sulphosalt mineral lorandite in the Triassic dolomite of the famous Lengenbach quarry in Binnatal, Ct. Wallis (Switzerland) is described.

loranth (ˈlɔərænθ). *Bot. rare.* [ad. mod.L. *Lōranthus*, name of the typical genus of the order *Loranthaceæ*: f. L. *lōr-um* strap + Gr. ἄνθος flower.] Any plant of the N.O. *Loranthaceæ* (see next).

1846 LINDLEY *Veg. Kingd.* 789 *Loranthaceæ*—Loranths. ..It is customary to call the floral envelopes of the genera of Loranths by the name of sepals in Viscum.

loranthaceous (lɔərænˈθeɪʃəs), *a. Bot.* [f. mod.L. *Lōranthāceæ*, f. *Lōranthus*: see prec. and -ACEOUS.] Of or belonging to the N.O. *Loranthaceæ* (the mistletoe family).

1856 in MAYNE *Expos. Lex.*

loranthad (lɔˈrænθæd). *Bot. rare.* [f. *Loranth-us* (see prec.) + -AD.] = LORANTH.

1893 *Athenæum* 18 Nov. 701/1 Among the Amazonian plants found at Santa Cruz..may be mentioned..the loranthad *Oryctanthus ruficaulis*.

lorate (ˈlɔəreɪt), *a. Bot.* [f. L. *lōrum* strap + -ATE².] Strap shaped.

1836 LOUDON *Encycl. Plants* 243 *Pancratium littorale*... Leaves..lorate. **1880** GRAY *Struct. Bot.* 419/1.

lorayn(e, variant of LORAIN *Obs.*

lorcha (ˈlɔːtʃə), **lorch** (lɔːtʃ). [a. Pg. *lorcha* (occurring in Pinto 1540: see Yule and Burnell); of uncertain origin.] A fast sailing vessel built in China with the hull after a European model, but rigged in Chinese fashion, usually carrying guns.

1653 H. COGAN tr. *Pinto's Trav.* xv. (1663) 47 They entred our Lorch where most conveniently they could. **1857** COBDEN *Speeches* (1878) 370 A vessel called a lorcha—which is a name derived from the Portuguese settlement at Macao, and which merely means that it is built after the European model not that it is built in Europe. **1896** *Gen. Register of Shipping* 2 Sept., *Abbreviations*..*Lor.*, Lorcha.

lorche, -er, obs. forms of LURCH, -ER.

lorchipe, -uppe, obs. forms of LORDSHIP.

lord (lɔːd), *sb.* Forms: 1 **hláfweard, hláford, -erd, (hlábard, hláfard), 2 laford, -erde, hlouerd, leverd, lhoaverd, lourde, lowerd,** *Orm.* **laferrd, 2–4 laverd, (3 lavard, læverd), 3–4 lover(e)d, lovuerde, (4 lhord, lorld(e), 4–6 lorde (4 *gen. pl.* lordene), 4, 6–8 lard(e, 4– lord.** Also *Sc.* LAIRD. In exclamations **6 leard, 7–8 lawd, 8 laud, lurd;** also LUD. [OE. *hláford*, once *hláfweard* (Ps. civ. 17; Thorpe's 'to hálf-wearde' is a misprint: see note in Gr.-Wülck.), repr. a prehistoric form **hlaibward-*, f. **hlaib* (OE. *hláf*) bread, LOAF + **ward* (OE. *weard*) keeper (see WARD *sb.*). In its primary sense the word (which is absent from the other Teut. langs.) denotes the head of a household in his relation to the servants and dependents who 'eat his bread' (cf. OE. *hláf-æta*, lit. 'bread-eater', a servant); but it had already acquired a wider application before the literary period of OE. The development of sense has been largely influenced by the adoption of the word as the customary rendering of L. *dominus*. The late ON. *lávarðr* is adopted from ME.

With regard to the etymological sense, cf. mod.G. *brotherr*, lit. 'bread-lord', an employer of labour. In the mod. Scandinavian langs. 'meat-mother' (Sw. *matmoder*, Da. *madmoder*, Icel. *matmóðir*) is the designation applied by servants to their mistress.

For the phonology of the OE. word see Bülbring *Ae. Elementarbuch* §§367, 411, 562. In the 14th c. the word became monosyllabic through the dropping of the intervocalic *v* and the crasis of the vowels thus brought into contact.]

I. A master, ruler.

†**1.** A master of servants; the male head of a household. *Obs.*

c **950** *Lindisf. Gosp.* Matt. xxiv. 46 Eadiȝ ðe ðeȝn ðone miððy cymes hlaferd his on-fand sua doende. *c* **1000** *Ags. Gosp.* John xv. 15 Se ðeowa nat hwæt se hlafor[d] deð. *a* **1175** *Cott. Hom.* 241 Nan ne mai twan hlaforde..samod þowie. *c* **1250** *Gen. & Ex.* 1388 Ðis maiden wile ic..to min louerdes bofte bi-crauen. *a* **1300** *Cursor M.* 6691 If he [his thain] liue ouer a dai or tuin, þe lauerd sal vnderli na pain. *c* **1420** *Sir Amadace* (Camden) l, He wold gif hom toe so muche, or ellus more, As any lord wold euyr or qware. *c* **1450** HOLLAND *Howlat* 145 Bot thir lordis belyf [thai] the letteris has tane. **1611** BIBLE *Matt.* xxiv. 46.

2. a. One who has dominion over others as his subjects, or to whom service and obedience are due; a master, chief, prince, sovereign. Now only *rhetorical*. Also ***lord and master***. Also, a husband (now usu. *joc.*); cf. sense 4 below.

Beowulf (Z.) 3141 Alegdon ða to middes mærne þeoden..hlaford leofne. *c* **893** K. ÆLFRED *Oros.* I. i. §13 Ohthere sæde his hlaforde, Ælfrede cyninge, þæt [etc.]. *a* **1175** *Cott. Hom.* 221 Forte don him [*sc.* man] understonden, þat he [*sc.* God] his hlaford was. *c* **1250** *Gen. & Ex.* 275 Ðo ne miȝte he [Lucifer] non louerd ðhauen. *c* **1300** *Havelok* 607 Þis is ure eir þat shal ben louerd of denemark. *c* **1330** *Amis. & Amil.* 2030 The squier biheld the coupes tho, First his and his lordes also. **1340–70** *Alex. & Dind.* 174 A wel-langaged lud let þe king sone Aspien..ho were lord of hur land. *c* **1350** *Will. Palerne* 3405 Swiche a lorld of lederes ne liued nouȝt, þei held. *c* **1400** *Destr. Troy* 4054 Agamynon the gret was..Leder of þo lordis. **14..** *Voc.* in Wr.-Wülcker 629/22 *Ciliarcha*, a lord of thowsond knyȝtes. **1513** DOUGLAS *Æneis* x. v. 4 Eneas, the Troiane prynce and lard. **1530** PALSGR. 680/1 It is a pytuouse case..whan subjectes rebell agaynst their naturall lorde. **1555** EDEN *Decades* (Arb.) 52 Stoope Englande stoope, & learne to knowe thy lorde & master. **1604** E. G[RIMSTONE] *D'Acosta's Hist. Indies* III. xx. 185 The Citie of Cusco, (the ancient Court of the Lordes of those Realmes). **1628** DIGBY *Voy. Medit.* (Camden) 42 Ceremonies of dutie..they said were due to him being lord of the port. **1665** R. VERNEY *Let.* 5 June in M. M. Verney *Mem.* (1899) IV. iv. 122 Peg Gardner saw your Lord and Master with some gentlemen in Parke. **1667** MILTON *P.L.* XII. 70 Man over men He made not Lord. **1739–40** RICHARDSON *Pamela* (1740) II. 251 Your lord and master came in very moody. **1781** GIBBON *Decl. & F.* (1869) II. xlii. 575 The common people [in Mingrelia] are in a state of servitude to their lords. **1816** JANE AUSTEN *Emma* III. xvi. 300, I am waiting for my lord and master. **1841** JAMES *Brigand* iii, Who is lord here upon the side of the mountain but I? **1855** MACAULAY *Hist. Eng.* xiii. III. 321 A race which reverenced no lord, no king but himself. **1864** C. M. YONGE *Trial* I. vii. 126 She was not going to be one of the womankind sitting up in a row till their lords and masters should be pleased to want them! **1922** JOYCE *Ulysses* 639 The erring fair one begging forgiveness of her lord and master. **1961** [see DROIT¹ 1 b]. **1975** P. HARCOURT *Fair Exchange* II. 121 'You're a Counsellor, a senior official..what advice would you give?'..'I can't see our lords and masters asking me.'
transf. **1588** SHAKS. *L.L.L.* IV. i. 38 When they [wives] striue to be Lords ore their Lords. **1596** —— *Merch. V.* III. ii. 169 But now I [Portia] was the Lord Of this faire mansion, master of my seruants.

b. *fig.* One who or something which has the mastery or preeminence. ***lords of (the) creation***: mankind; now jocularly, men as opposed to women.

a **1300** *Cursor M.* 782 O wityng bath god and ill ȝee suld be lauerds at ȝour will. **1398** TREVISA *Barth. De. P.R.* VIII. xvi. (1495) 322 The sonne is the lorde of planetes. **1508** DUNBAR *Gold. Targe* 229 The Lord of Wyndis..God Eolus. **1591** SPENSER *Ruins Rome* xiv, As men in Summer fearles passe the foord Which is in Winter lord of all the plaine. **1592** SHAKS. *Rom. & Jul.* v. i. 3 My bosomes L. [*sic*] sits lightly in his throne. **1604** E. G[RIMSTONE] *D'Acosta's Hist. Indies* III. ii. 119 There are some windes which blow in certaine regions, and are, as it were, Lordes thereof. **1643** [ANGIER] *Lanc. Vall. Achor* 7 Fire is a cruell Lord. **1667** DRYDEN *Ess. Dram. Poesie* Dram. Wks. 1725 I. 19 He is the envy of one, who is Lord in the art of quibbling. **1697** —— *Virg. Georg.* III. 380 Love is Lord of all. **1744** HOBART in *Lett. C'tess Suffolk* (1824) II. 207, I..thought..they [women] might attain to a sagacity equal to that of the lords of the creation. **1774** GOLDSM. *Nat. Hist.* (1776) I. 400 The lowest animal finds more conveniencies in the wilds of nature, than he who boasts himself their lord. **1779** JEFFERSON *Corr.* Wks. 1859 I. 213 Are they so far lords of right and wrong as that [etc.]. **1797** MRS. A. M. BENNETT *Beggar Girl* II. x. 189 'Tis really a mighty silly thing for a lord of the creation..to take up his residence in a boarding house..where there are pretty women. **1830** J. G. STRUTT *Sylva Brit.* 10 The attribute of strength by which the lord of

the woods is more peculiarly distinguished. **1884** BROWNING *Ferishtah, Family* 27 A leech renowned World-wide, confessed the lord of surgery.

†**c.** *vocatively.* Sometimes = mod. *Sir!*

c **1050** *Byrhtferth's Handboc* in *Anglia* VIII. 322 Hyt ʒedafenað la wynsuma hlaford. *c* **1205** LAY. 14078 Þa queð Hengest to þan kinge, Lauerd hærcne tiðende. *c* **1300** *Havelok* 621 Lowerd, we sholen þe wel fede. *c* **1350** *Will. Palerne* 1439 Leue lord & ludes lesten to mi sawes! **15..** *Adam Bel* 467 in Hazl. *E.P.P.* II. 158 They sayed, lord we beseche the here, That ye wyll graunt vs grace.

d. An owner, possessor, proprietor (of land, houses, etc.). Now only *poet.* or *rhetorical.* (Cf. LANDLORD.)

a **1300** *Cursor M.* 601–602 Als oure lauerd has heuen in hand Sua suld man be lauerd of land. **1377** LANGL. *P. Pl.* B. VII. 156 Amonges lowere lordes þi londe shal be departed. *c* **1475** *Rauf Coilȝear* 128 To mak me Lord of my awin. **1480** *Waterf. Arch.* in *10th Rep. Hist. MSS. Comm.* App. v. 316 All suche lordes as have gutters betuxte thar houses. **1581** MULCASTER *Positions* xxxv. (1887) 125 Like two tenantes in one house belonging to seuerall lordes. *a* **1637** B. JONSON *Sad Sheph.* II. i, A mightie Lord of Swine! *Ibid.*, I am a Lord of other geere! **1674** RAY *Collect. Words, Making Salt* 142 Divers persons have interest in the Brine pit, so that it belongs not all to one Lord. **1697** DRYDEN *Virg. Georg.* IV. 189 Lord of few Acres, and those barren too. —— *Æneid* XII. 535 Turnus..Wrench'd from his feeble hold the shining Sword; And plung'd it in the Bosom of its Lord.

e. *Mining.* (See quot.)

1874 J. H. COLLINS *Metal Mining* Gloss., *Lord*, the owner of the land in which a mine is situated is called the 'lord'.

f. A 'magnate' in some particular trade. (Cf. *king.*) Often used with some transferred notion of sense 8.

1823, etc. [see COTTON LORD]. **1841** COBDEN in Morley *Life* (1902) 28 The cotton lords are not more popular than the landlords. **1900** *Westm. Gaz.* 17 Jan. 10/1 A suspicion that the 'coal-lords' are hoarding their supplies.

3. *spec.* A feudal superior; the proprietor of a fee, manor, etc. So *lord of the manor* (see MANOR); also, rhyming slang for 'tanner' (sixpence, now equal to 2½ pence); also (*ellipt.*) *lord.* ***lord mesne, paramount*** (see those words). †*lord in gross* (see quot. 1696, and cf. GROSS B. 2 e).

Lord of Ireland (*Dominus Hiberniæ*) was part of the official designation of the Kings of England from Henry II to Henry VII.

a **1000** *O.E. Chron.* an. 924, Hine ʒeces..to hlaforde Scotta cyning. **1258** *Charter Hen. III* in Tyrrell *Hist. Eng.* (1700) II. App. 25 Henry thurg Godes fultome King on Englene-loande Lhoauerd on Yrloand [etc.]. **1297** R. GLOUC. (Rolls) 3662 Cadour erl of cornwayle..To þe king is louerd wende. **1433** *Rolls of Parlt.* IV. 447/2 Savyng allwey to the Lorde of the Fee, eschates. **1435** *Ibid.* 487 Aswell the Lordes and ye Citezeins of Citees, as the Lordes and Burgeises. **1497** *Act 12 Hen. VII*, c. 12 Preamb., The Kyng of Scottis..ought..to..holde of you Sovereign Lorde his seid realme. **1530** PALSGR. 675/1 He was baylyffe of the towne, but the lorde hath put hym out. **1563** *Homilies* II. *Rogation Week* IV. (1859) 496 The Lords records..be perverted..to the disinheriting of the right owner. **1691** WOOD *Ath. Oxon.* II. 110 The antient Family of Des Ewes, Dynasts or Lords of the dition of Kessell. **1696** PHILLIPS (ed. 5), *Lord in Gross*, is he who is a Lord without a Mannor, as the King in respect of his Crown. **1778** PRYCE *Min. Cornub.* 324 Lord of the land or fee. **1818** CRUISE *Digest* (ed. 2) III. 427 The lord may seise the copyhold to his own use. **1839** KEIGHTLEY *Hist. Eng.* I. 77 The rights of the Lord of a town extended to the levying of tolls and customs. **1839** H. BRANDON *Poverty, Mendicity & Crime* 163/2 *Lord of the manor*, sixpence. **1882** *Sydney Slang Dict.* 5/2 *Lord of the Manor*, sixpence. **1901** *Speaker* 11 May 149/2 It might have weakened the feudal relation between lord and tenant. **1933** *Times Lit. Suppl.* 16 Nov. 782/1 Twenty years ago you might hear a sixpence described as a 'Lord' meaning 'Lord of the Manor'; that is, a tanner. **1972** *Lebende Sprachen* XVII. 8/3 *Lord of the Manor*, tanner (*old sixpence*).

4. A husband. Now only *poet.* and *humorous.* (Cf. LADY *sb.* 7.)

831 *Charter* in Sweet *O.E. Texts* 445 Ymbe ðet lond et cert ðe hire eðelmod hire hlabard salde. *a* **1225** *Ancr. R.* 52 Eue ..nom & et þerof & ȝef hire louerd. **1297** R. GLOUC. (Rolls) 8902 Damaisele..þi louerd ssal abbe an name Vor him & vor is eirs vair wiþoute blame. ?*a* **1400** *Morte Arth.* 3918 Scho [Gaynore] kayres to Karelyone, and kawghte hir a vaile,.. And alle for falsede, and frawde, and fere of hir louerde! **1596** SHAKS. *Tam. Shr.* v. ii. 131 Tell these head-strong women What dutie they doe owe their Lords and husbands. **1681** VISCOUNTESS CAMPDEN in *12th Rep. Hist. MSS. Comm.* App. v. 56 My Lady Skidmore and her lord was at Mr. Comsbys house upon a visette. **1860–6** PATMORE *Angel in Ho.* II. II. iv, Love-mild Honoria, trebly mild With added loves of lord and child. **1861** MISS YONGE *Yng. Stepmother* xxv. 371 She was come to take leave of home, for her lord was not to be dissuaded from going to London by the evening's train.

5. [Cf. 2 b.] *Astrol.* The planet that has a dominant influence over an event, period, region, etc.

1391 [see ASCENDANT]. **1585** LUPTON *Thous. Notable Th.* (1675) 93 When the Almuten or the Lord of the Ascendent is infortunate in his fall. **1653** R. SANDERS *Physiogn.* 152 The Sun, when he is Alfridary or Lord of a Cholerick, he causeth him to be of a brown colour. **1819** WILSON *Dict. Astrol.*, *Lord*, that planet is called the lord of a sign whose house it is... The lord of a house is that planet of which the sign or domal dignity is in the cusp of such house... The lord of the geniture is that planet which has most dignities in a figure... The lord of the hour is the planet supposed to govern the planetary hour at the moment of a nativity, or at the time of asking a horary question. The lord of the year is that planet which has most dignities, or is strongest in a revolutional figure... The lord of the geniture is..supposed to rule the disposition and propensities of the native.

6. a. the Lord (vocatively **Lord**): God. Also (*the*) ***Lord God***, and occas. ***my, thy, our*** (now *rarely*: see 7), ***his***, etc. ***Lord.*** Cf. DRIGHTIN.

In the O.T. *the Lord*, a translation of the Vulgate *Dominus*, LXX. ὁ κύριος, commonly represents the ineffable name *yhwh* (see JEHOVAH), for which ADONAI was substituted by the Jews in reading; in a few instances *Adonai* occurs in the Hebrew text.

c **1000** ÆLFRIC *Hom.* II. 562 Sy lof þam Hlaforde ðe leofað on ecnysse. *c* **1175** *Lamb. Hom.* 71 Lauerd god we biddeð þus. *c* **1200** *Vices & Virtues* (1888) 7 Ðat ic am swiðe forȝelt aȝeanes mine laferde god almihtin. *c* **1200** ORMIN 11391 Þe birrþ biforr þin Laferrd Godd Cneolenn meoclike & lutenn. *c* **1250** *Gen. & Ex.* 33 To thaunen ðis werdes biginninge, ðe, leuerd god, to wurðinge. *a* **1300–1400** *Cursor M.* 6163 (Gött.) To moyses þan vr lauerd teld, Quat wise þai suld þair pask held. **1362** LANGL. *P. Pl.* A. I. 131 For to loue þi louerd leuere þen þiseluen. **1382** WYCLIF *1 Kings* xviii. 36 Lord God of Abraham, and of Ysaac, and of Yrael. *a* **1400** *Pistill of Susan* 164 Bi þe lord and þe lawe þat we onne leeue. *c* **1420** LYDG. *Assembly of Gods* 2093 But the wey thedyrward to holde be we lothe, That oft sythe causeth the good Lorde to be wrothe. **1560** *Extracts Aberd. Reg.* (1844) I. 328 Be the lewing Lord, the eternal God..I do heir promise..that [etc.]. **1593** SHAKS. *Rich. II*, III. ii. 57 The breath of worldly men cannot depose The Deputie elected by the Lord. **1613** —— *Hen. VIII*, III. ii. 161 The Lord increase this businesse. **1728** P. WALKER *Life Peden* (1827) 45 At Bothwel-bridge.. the Lord's People fell and fled before the Enemy. **1827** C. SIMEON in *Life* (1847) 609 This is the Lord's work, and fit for a Sabbath-day. **1897** R. KIPLING *Recessional*, Lord God of Hosts, be with us yet.

b. Phrases. (*the*) ***Lord knows who, what, how,*** etc.: used flippantly to express emphatically one's own ignorance of a matter. ***Lord have mercy*** (***on us***): (*a*) in serious use, as a prayer (it used to be chalked on the door of a plague-stricken house); (*b*) in trivial use (vulgarly ***Lord-a-mercy*** and in other corrupt forms: cf. LAWKS), as an interjection expressing astonishment. Similarly (in trivial use only) ***Lord bless me.*** Also ***Lord*** (or ***lor'***) ***lumme*** (= lord love me).

†**Lord have mercy on me,** the 'iliac passion'.

1585 HIGINS *Junius' Nomenclator* 433 *Ileus*..the Illiake passion..which the homelier sort of Phisicians doe call, Lorde haue mercy vpon me. **1588** SHAKS. *L.L.L.* v. ii. 419 Write, *Lorde haue mercie on vs*, on those three. **1592** NASHE *Summers last Will* 1706 Wks. (Grosart) VI. 153, I am sick, I must dye: Lord haue mercy on vs! *c* **1634** R. WEST in *Randolph's Poems* (1668) B 5, The Titles of their Satyrs fright some, more Then *Lord have mercy* writ upon a door. **1692** R. L'ESTRANGE *Fables* ccxlvi. (1708) 262 'Tis not a bare *Lord have Mercy upon us*, that will help the Cart out of the Mire. **1713** SWIFT *Cadenus & Vanessa* Wks. 1755 III. II. 30 She was at lord knows what expence To form a nymph of wit and sense. **1722** —— *Stella's Birthday* ibid. 114 It cost me lord knows how much time To shape it into sense and rhyme. **1751** SMOLLETT *Per. Pickle* xxx, What became of him afterwards, Lord in heaven knows. **1784** H. WALPOLE *Let.* 8 June (1858) VIII. 480 Mr. Conway wonders why I do not talk of Voltaire's 'Memoirs'. Lord bless me! I saw it two months ago. **1808** ELEANOR SLEATH *Bristol Heiress* V. 159 There she died. Lord-a-mercy upon those that had a hand in such a business. **1830** GEN. P. THOMPSON *Exerc.* (1842) I. 253 Meetings to be called by the Lord Lieutenant,..and the Lord knows who. **1846** MRS. GORE *Sk. Eng. Char.* (1852) 33 People comprised under the comprehensive designation of 'the Lord knows who'. **1888** J. PAYN *Myst. Mirbridge* I. iii. 49 Lord a mercy, is that how she talks? **1902** E. NESBIT *Five Children & It* ii. 61 'Lor' lumme,' said Billy Peasemarsh, 'if there ain't another on 'em!' **1903** J. LONDON *People of Abyss* i. 8 Lord lumme, but it'll be the last I see af you if yer don't py me. *Ibid.* iv. 31 'Lor' lumme,' she laughed.

c. As interjection; a mere exclamation of surprise originating from the use in invocations. (Cf. LOR, LUD.)

Now only in profane or trivial use; in 14–16th c. often employed in dignified and even religious writing.

c **1384** WYCLIF *Sel. Wks.* III. 358 Lord! in tyme of Jesus Crist..were men not bounden to shryve hem þus. *c* **1400** *Lanfranc's Cirurg.* 298 O lord, whi is it so greet difference betwix a cirurgian & a phisician. *a* **1548** HALL *Chron.*, *Hen. VI* 161 Lorde how glad the poore people were of this Pardone. **1560–77** *Misogonus* III. iii. 69 (Brandl) O Leard, Leard, wone woude take him for a foole by his gowne and his capp. **1564–78** BULLEYN *Dial. agst. Pest.* (1888) 10 Lorde God, howe are you chaunged! **1590** SHAKS. *Com. Err.* III. i. 50 O Lord I must laugh. **1632** MASSINGER & FIELD *Fatal Dowry* IV. i, O Lard, hee has made me smell (for all the world) like [etc.]. **1687** CONGREVE *Old Bach.* II. iii, Lard, Cousin, you talk odly. **1721** AMHERST *Terræ Fil.* No. 44 (1754) 236 Lawd! lawd! Dick, what shall's zay to our Kate, for leaving her at whome? **1741** RICHARDSON *Pamela* (1824) I. 177 Laud, madam,..I wonder you so much disturb yourself. **1792** WOLCOT (P. Pindar) *Odes to Gt. Duke* vii. Wks. 1792 III. 10 Lord! what a buying, reading, what a racket! **1837** MARRYAT *P. Keene* xxii, Lord, what a state I shall be in till I know what has taken place.

7. a. As a title of Jesus Christ. Commonly ***our Lord*** (now often with capital O); also ***the Lord.***

a **1175** *Cott. Hom.* 243 Ure laford ihesu crist þe seið *Sine me nichil potestis facere.* *c* **1200** ORMIN Ded. 186 Forr an godnesse uss hafeþþ don þe Laferrd Crist onn erþe. *c* **1200** *Vices & Virtues* (1888) 7 Ac bidde we alle ure lauerd Crist. *a* **1225** *Leg. Kath.* 644 Lauerd, wune wið me. *a* **1300** *Cursor M.* 28088 To my lard ic am of-sene to crist ic haue vnbuxum bene. *a* **1300** *Crede* in Maskell *Mon. Rit.* II. 240 Ihesu Krist [h]is anelepi sone, hure laverd. *c* **1400** *Lay Folks Mass Bk.* App. iii. 125 Þou art a sooþfaste leche, lord. **1500–20** DUNBAR *Poems* xc. 3 Oure Lorde Jhesu..Fastit him self oure exampill to be. *a* **1548** HALL *Chron.*, *Hen. VI* 113 And it happened in the night of the Assencion of our lorde, that Pothon..issued outof Champeigne. **1579** E. K. *Spenser's Sheph. Cal.* Gen. Argt. §4 Our..eternall redeemer the L. Christ. **1653** W. BASSE in *Walton's Angler* iii. 81 For so our Lord was pleased, when He Fishers made Fishers of men. **1823** BENTHAM *Not Paul* 26 He informs the Lord what he had heard about Paul. **1882** TENNYSON *In Mem. W. G. Ward*, How loyal in the following of thy Lord!

b. (*in*) ***the year of our Lord*** (†***God***), †***of our Lord's incarnation***: = ANNO DOMINI.

1389 in *Eng. Gilds* (1870) 89 In ye ȝere of houre louerde a Thousande yre hundred sixti and seuene. **1463** *Bury Wills* (Camden) 19 The day and the yeer of oure lord of my departyng from this wourld. *a* **1548** HALL *Chron.*, *Edw. IV* 208 b, This was in the yere of our lordes blessed incarnacion .M.C.lxx. **1596** DALRYMPLE tr. *Leslie's Hist. Scot.* v. 268 *marg.*, King Achai dies the ȝeir..of our Lourd 819. **1604** E. G[RIMSTONE] *D'Acosta's Hist. Indies* III. xi. 154 In the yeere of our Lord God, one thousand five hundred seaventy nine. **1625** PURCHAS *Pilgrims* II. 1705 In the yeare of our Lord God 1567.

c. In certain syntactical combinations: **the Lord's Prayer** [= L. *oratio Dominica*], the prayer taught by Jesus to His disciples: see Matt. vi. 9–13. **the Lord's Supper** [= L. *cena Dominica*, Gr. τὸ κυριακὸν δεῖπνον 1 Cor. xi. 24], the Holy Communion. **the Lord's Table** [= Gr. τραπέζα κυρίου 1 Cor. x. 21: cf. *God's, the Lord's board* (see BOARD *sb.* 6)] = ALTAR 2 b; also the Holy Communion. Also LORD'S DAY.

1548–9 (Mar.) *Bk. Com. Prayer, Public Baptism*, The Crede, *the Lordes prayer, and the tenne commaundementes. **1646** J. HALL *Poems* I. 13 [She] makes one single farthing bear The Creed, Commandments and Lords-prayer. **1876** BANCROFT *Hist. U.S.* II. xxx. 248 She had never learned the Lord's prayer in English. **1382** WYCLIF *1 Cor.* xi. 20 Therfore ȝou comynge to gidere into oon, now it is not for to ete *the Lordis sopere. **1555** RIDLEY (*title*) A brief Declaracion Of the Lordes Supper. **1645** FULLER *Good Th. in Bad T.* (1646) 141 The Lords Supper, ordained by our Saviour to conjoyn our Affections, hath disjoyned our Judgements. **1755** CHAMBERLAYNE *Pres. St. Gr. Brit.* II. II. (ed. 17) 75 Some Time before the Lord's Supper is administred, the Congregation is to have Notice of it from the Pulpit. **1535** COVERDALE *1 Cor.* x. 21 Ye cannot be partetakers off *the lordes table, and off the table off deuyls. **1660** JER. TAYLOR *Worthy Commun.* i. §1. 22 It [the Holy Sacrament] is by the Spirit of God called..the Lord's Table. **1704** NELSON *Fest. & Fasts* II. iv. (1707) 494 Upon the Penalty of being excluded from the Lord's Table. **1852** HOOK *Ch. Dict.* (1871) 467 The Lord's Table is one of the names given to the altar in Christian churches.

II. As a designation of rank or official dignity.

In these applications it is not used vocatively, exc. in the form *my Lord* (see 15) and as a prefixed title (see 13).

8. a. In early use employed vaguely for any man of exalted position in a kingdom or commonwealth, and in a narrower sense applied to the feudal tenants holding directly of the king by military or other honourable service: see BARON 1. In modern use, equivalent to NOBLEMAN in its current sense: A peer (usually, a temporal peer) of the realm, or one who by courtesy (see 13) is entitled to the prefix Lord, or some higher title, as a part of his ordinary appellation.

13.. *Coer de L.* 2284 We are betrayd and y-nome! Horse and harness, lords, all and some! *c* **1350** *Will. Palerne* 4539 To fare out as fast with his fader to speke & with lordesse [= lordes] of þat lond. **1386** *Rolls of Parlt.* III. 225/1 To the moost noble and worthiest Lordes, moost ryghtful and wysest Conseille to owre lige Lorde the Kyng. *a* **1420** HOCCLEVE *De Reg. Princ.* 442 Men myghten lordis knowe By there arraye, from oþir folke. **1453** *Rolls of Parlt.* V. 266/2 If such persone bee of the estate of a Lord, as Duc, Marques, Erle, Viscount or Baron. **1480** CAXTON *Chron. Eng.* III. (1520) 26/1 It was denyed hym..by the instygacyon of a lord called Pompei. **1505** in *Mem. Hen. VII* (Rolls) 276 What attendance he hath abouts hym of lords and nobles of his reame. **1548** LATIMER *Ploughers* (Arb.) 25 For ever sence the Prelates were made Loordes and nobles the ploughe standeth. **1593** SHAKS. *Rich. II*, IV. i. 19 Princes, and Noble Lords: What answer shall I make to this base man? **1614** SELDEN *Titles Hon.* 59 Our English name Lord, whereby we and the Scots stile all such as are of the Greater Nobilitie i. Barons, as also Bishops. **1826** DISRAELI *Viv. Grey* III. iii, The Marquess played off the two Lords and Sir Berdmore against his former friend. **1876** BROWNING *Shop* v, He's social, takes his rest On Sundays, with a Lord for guest. **1900** *Daily Express* 21 July 5/7 The Englishman of to-day still dearly loves a lord.

b. Phrases. ***to live like a lord***: to fare luxuriously. ***to treat*** (a person) ***like a lord***: to entertain sumptuously, to treat with profound deference. ***drunk as a lord***: completely intoxicated; so †***to drink like a lord.*** Similarly, ***to swear like a lord.***

1531 ELYOT *Gov.* I. xxvi. (1880) I. 275 For they wyll say he that swereth depe, swereth like a lorde. **1623** MIDDLETON & ROWLEY *Sp. Gipsy* IV. i. (1653) F 4, Flowre bancks or Mosse be thy bourd, Water thy wine, *San.* And drinke like a Lord. **1651** EVELYN *Charact. Eng.* (1659) 48 The Gentlemen are most of them very intemperate, yet the Proverb goes, 'As drunk as a Lord'. **1681** T. FLATMAN *Heraclitus Ridens* No. 6 (1713) I. 36 They were as drunk as Lords with Bottle-Air. **1770** *Gentl. Mag.* XL. 560 As drunk as a Lord. **1809** MALKIN *Gil Blas* II. vii. ¶3 The landlord.. said,..we will treat you like a lord. **1861** THACKERAY *B. Lyndon* xviii. (1869) 254 She ran screaming through the galleries, and I, as tipsy as a lord, came staggering after. **1892** SIR W. HARCOURT *Speech* 20 Apr., We had changed that now, and the Chancellor of the Exchequer lived like a lord.

†**c.** *occas.* A baron as distinguished from one of higher rank. *Obs.* (Cf. 13.)

1526 *Pilgr. Perf.* (W. de W. 1531) 7 b, Farre excellyng ye state of lordes, erles, dukes or kynges.

d. ***lord-in-waiting, lord of the bedchamber***: the designation given to noblemen holding certain offices in attendance on the person of the sovereign.

1717 H. PELHAM in *Lett. C'tess Suffolk* (1824) I. 18 The King forbad the lord of the bedchamber inviting Lord Townshend..to dine with him at Newmarket. **1755** *Gentl. Mag.* XXV. 184 His majesty went to the house of peers, attended by..the ld of the bedchamber in waiting. **1860** W. G. CLARK in *Vac. Tour* 45 Furniture..the property, I suppose, of gold-sticks, and..lords-in-waiting. *a* **1865** GREVILLE *Mem.* II. (1885) II. 44 She had already given orders to the Lord-in-waiting to put all the Ministers down to whist. **1886** *Encycl. Brit.* XXI. 37/2 There are eight lords and eight grooms,..described as 'of the bedchamber' or 'in waiting', according as the reigning sovereign is a king or a queen.

9. a. pl. ***the Lords***: the peers, temporal and spiritual, as constituting the higher of the two bodies composing the legislature (of England, Scotland, and Ireland, when they existed as separate kingdoms; afterwards of the kingdom of Great Britain; and now of the United Kingdom). ***the Lords Temporal***: the lay peers. ***the Lords Spiritual***: the bishops who are peers of the realm, and (in England before the Reformation) the mitred abbots. ***the Lords' Act*** (see quot. 1800).

This branch of the legislature now consists of the English noblemen of baronial rank, the English bishops (with some exceptions), and elected representatives of the peers of Scotland and Ireland.

1451 *Paston Lett.* I. 204 To make requisicion..to the Lords espirituallx and temporelx in this present Parlement assembled. **1568** GRAFTON *Chron.* II. 349 The Lordes of the upper house, and the common house assembled together. **1655** FULLER *Ch. Hist.* x. vii. §1 The House of Commons presented to the Lords Spirituall and Temporall a Petition. **1675** MARVELL *Corr.* ccliv. Wks. 1872–5 II. 474 To desire the Lords concurrence herein. **1751** H. WALPOLE *Lett.* (1846) II. 388 In the Lords there were but 12 to 106, and the former the most inconsiderable men in that House. **1765** BLACKSTONE *Comm.* I. 50 The legislature of the kingdom is entrusted to three distinct powers,..first, the king; secondly, the lords spiritual and temporal. **1800** *Asiat. Ann. Reg., State Papers* 7/1 Rules for extending to insolvent debtors the relief intended by act 32 Geo. II. commonly called 'The Lords' Act'. **1812** MOORE *Intercepted Lett.* ii. 47 Quite upturning branch and root Lords, Commons, and Burdétt to boot. **1830** CROLY *Geo. IV* 218 An embassage from the lords and commons was sent with them from London. *a* **1865** GREVILLE *Mem.* II. (1885) II. 408 He got the House of Commons to sit on Saturday,..in order to send the Bill up to the Lords on Monday. **1879** MCCARTHY *Hist. Own Times* (1887) II. 257 The Lords..suspended the sitting until eleven at night. **1884** S. DOWELL *Tax. & Taxes Eng.* II. 303 The duke of Wellington leading in the Lords. **1897** OUIDA *Massarenes* iv, Don't suppose I shall ever live to get into the Lords.

b. ***House of Lords***, † ***Lords' House*** (see HOUSE *sb.* 4 d). Also (*slang.*), a lavatory.

1672 PETTY *Pol. Anat.* (1691) 35 [They] may..be call'd by Writ into the Lords House of England. **1818** CRUISE *Digest* (ed. 2) V. 332 This case having been heard in the House of Lords, the Judges were directed to give their opinions. **1845** POLSON *Eng. Law* in *Encycl. Metrop.* II. 811/1 The House of Lords is in the habit of referring certain bills to the opinion of the learned judges. **1961** in PARTRIDGE *Dict. Slang* Suppl. 1139/1. **1967** *Listener* 21 Dec. 802/2 In between you have the Business Man Jocular: 'I say, where's the geography, old son?' or 'When you need the House of Lords, it's through there.' **1969** J. ALEXANDER *Where have All Flowers Gone?* I. 46 Half way up the stairs there was a lavatory... 'The House of Lords,' said Jake.

†**c.** *transf.* in *Rom. Hist.* = Senators. *Obs.*

1618 BOLTON *Florus* (1636) 212 The Knights, and Gentlemen of Rome separated themselves from the Lords.

10. *Sc.* In various collocations (chiefly *Hist.*), as ***Lords of the Articles, of the Congregation, of Daily Council, of Justiciary, of Police, of Regality, of Session*** (see these sbs.).

11. Applied, with subjoined defining word or phrase, to the individual members (whether peers or not) of a Board appointed to perform the duties of some high office of state that has been put in commission, as in ***Lords Commissioners*** (in ordinary language simply ***Lords***) ***of the Admiralty, of the Treasury; Lords Commissioners of the Great Seal***. Also ***Lords Justices*** (***of Ireland***): the Commissioners to whom, in the early 18th c., the viceregal authority was entrusted. ***Civil Lord***: the one civilian member (besides the First Lord) of the Board of Admiralty, the others being ***Naval Lords***.

1642 C. VERNON *Consid. Exch.* 54 Lords Commissioners of the Treasury. **1711** SWIFT *Jrnl. to Stella* 16 May, Three books I got from the Lords of the Treasury for the college. **1724** —— *Drapier's Lett.* Wks. 1755 V. II. 38 As if it were a dispute between William Wood on the one part, and the lords justices, privy-council, and both houses of parliament on the other. **1739** LADY MURRAY *Mem. Baillies* (1822) 24 He was made one of the Lords of the Admiralty, and soon after one of the Lords of the Treasury. **1759** DILWORTH *Pope* 72 He was one of the lord-justices of Ireland. **1818** CRUISE *Digest* (ed. 2) VI. 151 The Lords Commissioners in Barnes v. Crowe appeared to have held, that [etc.]... Lord Commissioner Eyre stated the particular circumstances. **1834** MARRYAT *P. Simple* xxxix, A letter from your lordship to the First Lord—, only a few lines. **1879** MCCARTHY *Hist. Own Times* (1887) II. 409 Mr. Gathorne Hardy was made Secretary for War and Mr. Ward Hunt First Lord of the Admiralty. **1884** S. DOWELL *Tax. & Taxes Eng.* II. 116 George Grenville as a junior lord of the admiralty. **1893** MAXWELL *W. H. Smith* II. 182 He..became First Lord of the Treasury and leader of the House of Commons. **1898** *Hazell's Ann.* 447 The Works Department of the Admiralty is presided over by officers of the Royal Engineers, its supervision resting with the civil lord.

12. a. Forming part of various official titles, e.g. ***Lord*** (***High***) ***Admiral, Lord Chamberlain, Lord*** (***High***) ***Chancellor, Lord Chief Justice, Lord High Commissioner, Lord Deputy, Lord Marshal, Lord President, Lord Privy Seal, Lord Treasurer, Lord Warden***, etc., for which see the second member in each case. †**Lord** (**High**) **General**, a commander-in-chief (*obs.*). **Lord-rector**, an honorary title for the elected chief in certain Scotch Universities; hence ***Lord-rectorship***. Also LORD-LIEUTENANT, LORD MAYOR.

1598 BARRET *Theor. Warres* IV. i. 116 [The Colonel] ought to know how to performe the parts and office of a Lord high Generall. **1650** WHITELOCKE *Mem.* (1853) III. 207 (25 June) The lord general Fairfax. *Ibid.* 237 (7 July) The council of state ordered the narrative made by the lord general's [Cromwell's] messenger to be read in all churches. **1660** [see 15 a]. **1827** HALLAM *Const. Hist.* (1876) II. x. 287 The parliament having given him [Monk] a commission as lord-general of all the forces in the three kingdoms. **1864** BURTON *Scot Abr.* I. v. 249 Hence the catalogue of Lord Rectors soars far above respectability and appropriateness: it is brilliant. **1867** *Nation* (N.Y.) 3 Jan. 4/2 The candidates for the lord-rectorship of Aberdeen University this next year are Mr. Grote, historian, and Mr. Grant Duff.

b. In ceremonious use, prefixed to the titles of bishops, whether peers of parliament or not.

1639 (*title*) A Relation of the Conference between William Lawd..now Lord-Arch-Bishop of Canterbury: and Mr. Fisher the Jesuite. *a* **1673** W. BLAXTON in Bp. L. Coleman *Ch. Amer.* ii. 23, I came from England because I did not like the lord-bishops, but I cannot join with you, because I would not be under the lord-brethren. **1858** *Royal Charter University Lond.* §5 The Lord Bishop Maltby; the Lord Bishop of St. Davids.

†**c.** Formerly sometimes prefixed to a title of nobility. *Obs.*; but see 15 a (*c*).

1444 *Extracts Aberd. Reg.* (1844) I. 13 Quhat time it be plessand to the said Lord Erle [of Orkynnay].

d. ***Lord of the Flies***, a name for Beelzebub [tr. Heb. *ba'al-zĕbhūbh*: see BEELZEBUB]; also, used allusively of the book (1954) by William Golding (1911–) of the same name, in which a group of schoolboys marooned on an uninhabited tropical island revert to savagery and primitive ritual. (Use in quot. 1971 is *joc.*)

1931 A. HUXLEY *Cicadas* 37 But 'tis the shitten Lord of Flies Who with his loathsome business now fulfils On us their prayers. **1948** —— *Ape & Essence* (1949) 69 Such..is the inscrutable justice of the Lord of Flies. *Ibid.* 90 The Lord of Flies, who is also the Blowfly in every individual heart. **1965** *Listener* 24 June 933/1 The ship's figurehead.., removed from its place by the children, becomes a kind of Lord of the Flies. **1967** J. BLACKBURN *Flame & Wind* II. 72 Beelzebub—the Lord of the Flies—the Prince of the Hebrew devils. **1969** I. & P. OPIE *Children's Games* 13 Such accounts..have..influenced educational practice..leading us to believe that a *Lord of the Flies* mentality is inherent in the young. **1971** *Guardian* 9 Feb. 8/4 Instead of the orgasmic moment, we arrive at Mr Neville's playtime: the lord of the flies.

13. a. As a prefixed title, forming part of a person's customary appellation. Abbreviated Ld., formerly †L. (*pl.* LL.), Lo.

The rules now accepted for its use are as follows. In other than strictly ceremonial use it may be substituted for 'Marquis', 'Earl', or 'Viscount' (whether denoting the rank of a peer, or applied 'by courtesy' to the eldest son of a peer of higher rank); the word *of*, when it occurs in the more formal designation, being dropped. Thus 'Lord Hartington', 'Lord Derby', 'Lord Manvers', 'Lord Palmerston', may be used instead of 'The Marquis of Hartington', 'The Earl of Derby', 'Earl Manvers', 'Viscount Palmerston'. A baron (whether a peer, or a peer's eldest son known by the title of his father's barony) is always called by his title of peerage (either a surname or a territorial designation) preceded by 'Lord', as 'Lord Tennyson'; if the Christian name is mentioned for distinction, it comes first, as 'Alfred, Lord Tennyson'. The territorial titles given by courtesy to judges in Scotland are treated like those of barons, as 'Lord Monboddo'. The younger sons of dukes and marquises have the courtesy title of 'Lord' followed by the Christian name and surname, as 'Lord John Russell'. These rules were, for the most part, already formulated in the 16th c., but were for a long time seldom accurately observed except by experts in heraldry.

In early use the prefixed title had most commonly the form *my Lord* (see 15) or *the Lord*. The latter survives in certain formal uses, and in the superscription of letters.

1455 *Rolls of Parlt.* V. 332/2 William Bonvyle Knyght, Lord Bonevile, his servauntes and adheraunts. **15..** *Bk. of Precedence* in *Q. Eliz. Acad.* 27 All marquises Eldest sonnes are named no Earles, but lord of a place or barrony... And all his other bretheren Lordes, with the addition of there Christoned name. An Earles Eldest sonn is called a lord of a place or Baron[y], and all his other sonnes no lords. **1545** *Extracts Aberd. Reg.* (1844) I. 214 George Erle of Huntlie, Lord Gordoun and of Bangzenocht. **1568** GRAFTON *Chron.* II. 294 Also on the French part the Lorde John Cleremount fought under his awne Banner. **1591** SHAKS. *1 Hen. VI*, IV. vii. 61–64 Valiant Lord Talbot Earle of Shrewsbury: Created..Lord Talbot of Goodrig and Vrchinfield, Lord Strange of Blackmere, Lord Verdon of Alton [etc.]. **1593** —— *Rich. II*, II. ii. 53 The L. Northumberland. **1636** TRUSSELL *Contn. Daniel's Hist. Eng.* 93 Sir Iohn Oldcastle in right of his Wife called in courtesie Lord Cobham. **1781** (*title*) The Trial of the Right Honourable George Gordon, commonly called, Lord George Gordon. *a* **1865** GREVILLE *Mem.* II. (1885) II. 171, I dined with Lord and Lady Frederick FitzClarence and Lord Westmoreland. *Ibid.* III. 458 Whether Lord Derby or Lord any-body else is in office. **1879** MCCARTHY *Hist. Own Times* (1887) II. 405 Mr. Bruce was raised to the Peerage as Lord Aberdare.

b. ***the Lord Harry***: see HARRY 6.

c. Lord Derby, a large green and yellow-skinned variety of cooking apple, or the tree that produces it.

1876–85 HOGG & BULL *Herefordshire Pomona* II. plate 73 Lord Derby. The origin of this apple is unknown. It has probably been cultivated in the orchards for some years, without special notice. **1933** HALL & CRANE *Apple* II. 27 Some varieties, like Lord Derby, have a markedly upright habit. **1962** *Listener* 27 Sept. 495/1, I am thinking of cooking apples like..that good old-fashioned one, Lord Derby. **1966** C. R. THOMPSON *Pruning Apple Trees* II. 194 There are a few varieties from which large apples are wanted early in the season, such as early Victoria and Lord Derby.

14. Jocular uses. **a.** As a mock title of dignity given to the person appointed to preside on certain festive occasions. So ***Lord of Christmas*** (see CHRISTMAS 4), ***Lord of Misrule*** (see MISRULE), ***Summer Lord***, etc. (*obs.* exc. *Hist.*), ***Harvest Lord*** (see HARVEST *sb.* 7).

1556 *Chron. Gr. Friars* (Camden) 73 Item the iiijth day of January [1551–2] the lorde of Crystmas of the kynges howse came thorrow London..to the lorde mayer's to denner. **1571** GRINDAL *Injunc. at York* C iij, The Minister & churchwardens shall not suffer any Lordes of misrule or Sommer Lordes..to come vnreuerently into any Church [etc.]. **1628** in *Crt. & Times Chas. I* (1848) I. 311 On Saturday last, the Templars chose one Mr. Palmes..their lord of misrule. **1806** BLOOMFIELD *Wild Flowers* Poems (1845) 217 Many a Lord, Sam, I know that, Has begg'd as well as thee.

b. *slang.* A hunchback. (Cf. LORD-FISH.)

The origin of this use is obscure, but there is no reason for doubting the identity of the word. The *Dict. Canting Crew* has a parallel sense of *Lady*.

a **1700** B. E. *Dict. Cant. Crew, Lord*, a very crooked, deformed..Person. **1725** in *New Cant. Dict.* **1751** SMOLLETT *Per. Pic.* xxviii, His pupil..was..on account of his hump, distinguished by the title of My Lord. **1817** NEUMAN *Eng.-Sp. Dict.* (ed. 3), Lord..8 (Joc.) *Hombre jorobado*. **1826** LAMB *Elia* II. *Pop. Fallacies*, That a deformed person is a lord. **1887** BESANT *The World went* I. iii. 86 He was, in appearance, short and bent, with rounded shoulders, and with a hump (which made the boys call him My Lord).

c. ***Lord Muck***, a pompous self-opinionated man (see quot. 1966). *slang.*

1937 in PARTRIDGE *Dict. Slang* 539/1. **1955** J. THOMAS *No Banners* xxix. 287 Hey, Lord Muck! May we have the honour of introducing ourselves! **1966** 'L. LANE' *ABZ of Scouse* 63 *Lord Muck of Muck Hall*, a bombastic person; a swollen-headed man who likes to asserts his authority.

15. my Lord (usually pronounced (mɪˈlɔːd).

a. Prefixed to a name or title. (*a*) Formerly the ordinary prefix used in speaking to or of a nobleman, where we now commonly use simply 'Lord' (see 13); in early use the preposition *of* before territorial designations was commonly retained. (Now only *arch.*) (*b*) ***my Lord of*** (***London, Canterbury***, etc.): a respectful mode of referring to a bishop (*obs.* or *arch.*). (*c*) Prefixed to a title of rank or office; now only *vocatively*, as in ***my Lord Mayor, my Lord Duke, my Lord Marquis***.

c **1440** *York Myst.* xvii. 73 Mi lorde ser Herowde! *a* **1470** GREGORY in *Hist. Coll. Lond. Cit.* (Camden) 230 The mater was put to my Lorde of London. **1481–90** *Howard Househ. Bks.* (Roxb.) 321 The same day, my Lord rekened with his lokyer. **1530** PALSGR. 433/2, I am somoned by a sergent at armes to apere byfore my lorde chaunceller. **1533** T. CROMWELL *Let.* 25 July in *C.'s Life & Lett.* (1902) I. 385 My Lorde Abbot I recommende me vnto you [etc.]. *c* **1560** *Satir. Poems Reform.* xxviii. 57 Than my Lord Arrane from Albany ye Duke Obtenit the gift of Murray. **1561** *Stanford Churchw. Acc.* in *Antiquary* XVII. 168/1 At my lorde of Sarums commandment. **1583** STUBBES *Anat. Abus.* II. (1882) 104 May a bishop be called..by the name of 'my Lord bishop, my Lords grace'. **1584** *Leycesters Commonw.* (1641) 68 By your opinion my Lord of Leycester is the most learned of all his kindred. **1613** SPELMAN *De non Temer. Eccl.* (1646) 23 My Lord Coke also in the second part of his Reports, saith, that [etc.]. **1635** PAGITT *Christianogr.* (1640) I. 199 A petition to my Lords Grace of Canterbury. **1660** PEPYS *Diary* 3 Mar., My Lord General Fleetwood told my Lord that he feared the King of Sweden is dead. **1679** EVELYN *Mem.* 5 Nov., I was invited to dine at my Lord Tividale's. **1709** STEELE *Tatler* No. 17 ¶4 The Courage and Capacity of my Lord Galway. **1742** FIELDING *J. Andrews* Pref. ¶8, I apprehend, my Lord Shaftesbury's Opinion of mere Burlesque agrees with mine.

b. Used separately. (*a*) As the usual polite or respectful form of address to a nobleman under the rank of duke, and to a bishop; also (now only by persons greatly inferior in position) in speaking of them. (*b*) As the formal mode of address to a Lord Mayor, a Lord Provost, and to the Lord Advocate (Scotland). (*c*) In courts of law used in addressing a judge of the Supreme Court (or, formerly, a judge of any of the 'superior courts' now merged in this); in Scotland and Ireland in addressing a judge of any of the superior courts.

The hurried or affected pronunciation prevalent in the courts of law has often been derisively represented by the spelling *my Lud* or *m'lud* (see LUD).

1543 *Extracts Aberd. Reg.* (1844) I. 190 My lord, we recommend our hartlie and humil seruice vnto your lordschip. **1599** Shaks. *Much Ado* II. i. 294 [*Beatrice to Don Pedro*] So I would not he should do me, my Lord. **1601** Munday *Downf. Earl Huntingdon* II. ii. (1828) 34 *Robin.* What, Much and John! well met in this ill time. *Little John.* In this good time my lord. **1789** Wolcot (P. Pindar) *Subj. for Painters* 28 'Bravissimo! my Lor', replied Squalind. **1830** N. S. Wheaton *Jrnl.* 198, I could not help noticing the affected way in which they [H. of Lords clerks] pronounce the words *My Lord*.. as if they were written *My Lud.* **1870** Dickens *E. Drood* iv, He has been spoken to in the street as *My Lord*, under the impression that he was the Bishop. **1893** Sir A. Gordon *Earl Aberdeen* 191 The minister.. turned to the loft in which 'my Lord' was seated.

c. As nonce-vb., *to 'my lord'* (a person).

1831 Carlyle *Sart. Res.* III. vi, Who ever saw any Lord my-lorded in tattered blanket, fastened with wooden skewer? **1868** Yates *Rock Ahead* I. viii, His tenant.. would ..'My lord' him until the wine had done its work.

d. pl. ***my lords***: (*a*) the usual form of address to a number of noblemen or bishops, and in courts of law to two or more of the superior judges sitting together; (*b*) in the official correspondence of a department of state, used as a collective designation for the ministers composing it.

1500–20 Dunbar *Poems* lxxix. 1 My Lordis of Chacker, pleis ȝow to heir My coumpt. **1555** Ridley in Coverd. *Lett. Martyrs* (1564) 101 My Lordes, if in times past ye haue [etc.]. **1593** Shaks. *3 Hen. VI*, IV. vii. 16 My Lords, We were fore-warned of your comming. **1727** Pope etc. *Art of Sinking* 122 Separate divisions for the two houses of parliament, my lords the judges, &c. **1871** *Routledge's Ev. Boy's Ann.* Aug. 495 Speedily got himself into hot water with 'my lords' at Whitehall.

III. 16. *attrib.* or *appositive*, and in *Comb.*, as ***lord-lover***, ***-suitor***; ***lord-hating***, ***-loving***, ***-ridden*** adjs.; **lord and lady (duck)** *N. Amer.*, a pair of harlequin duck, *Histrionicus histrionicus*; **lord-breed** *nonce-wd.*, a breed or race of lords; **lord-farmer**, one who holds an episcopal manor by a rent paid to the bishop; † **lords' room**, app. a room or compartment on the stage of a theatre, reserved for privileged spectators.

1770 G. Cartwright *Jrnl.* 29 July (1792) I. 20, I shot four eider ducks, and seven *lords and ladies. **1835** E. Wix *Six Months Newfoundland Missionary's Jrnl.* (1836) 162, I had a fine view of a patch fox in my walk, saw several seals, and some of those very beautiful birds, called by the people of Newfoundland 'lords and ladies'. **1930** *Canad. Geogr. Jrnl.* I. 32/2 The Harlequin Duck.. is known to trappers and prospectors in the far west as 'Lord and Lady Duck'. **1959** W. L. McAtee *Folk-Names Canad. Birds* (ed. 2) 16 Harlequin Duck [is also called] lord and lady (Usually in the plural, 'lords and ladies'. In allusion to the handsome plumage.) **1862** Darwin in *Life & Lett.* (1887) II. 385 Ablest men are continually raised to the peerage, and get crossed with the older *Lord-breeds. **1718** R. Frampton in T. Evans *Life* (1876) 161 The *lord farmer there had been offering a small fine to renew with the two preceding Bishops who both refused. **1777** *Town & Country Mag.* June 335 Death. John Shadwell, Esq.; lord-farmer of Horfield manor, in Somersetshire. **1828** *Blackw. Mag.* XXIII. 384 The *lord-hating gang to which he.. appertains. **1855** Tennyson *Maud* I. XXII. v, O young *lord-lover, what sighs are those, For one that will never be thine? **1856** Emerson *Eng. Traits, Char.* Wks. (Bohn) II. 63 The conservative, money-loving, *lord-loving English are yet liberty-loving. **1849** R. Cobden in Morley *Life* (1902) xviii. 68/2 A servile aristocracy-loving, *lord-ridden people. **1599** B. Jonson *Ev. Man out of Hum.* II. i, Hee powres them out as familiarly, as if hee had tane Tabacco with them ouer the stage, in the *Lords roome. **1609** Dekker *Guls Horne-bk.* vi. 28 Let our Gallant.. presently aduance himselfe vp to the Throne of the Stage, I meane not into the Lords roome (which is now but the Stages Suburbes). **1868** Browning *Ring & Bk.* IV. 471 He likes to have *lord-suitors lounge.

lord (lɔːd), *v.* Also 3–4 **laverd**. [f. Lord *sb.*]

1. *intr.* †**a.** To exercise lordship, have dominion.

a **1300** *E.E. Psalter* cii[i]. 19 Laverd in heven graiþed sete his, And his rike til alle sal Laverd [Vulg. *dominabitur*] in blis. **1489** Caxton *Faytes of A.* I. i. 8 Metridates whiche lorded vpon xxiiij. contrees.

b. To play the lord; to behave in a lordly manner, assume airs of grandeur; to rule tyrannically, domineer. Now *rare* exc. const. *over*.

1377 Langl. *P. Pl.* B. x. 84 Þe more he.. lordeth in londes þe lasse good he deleth. **1548** Latimer *Ploughers* (Arb.) 24 For they [the Apostles] preached and lorded not. And nowe they lorde and preache not. **1579** Spenser *Sheph. Cal.* Dec. 70 The grieslie Tode-stoole groune there mought I se, And loathed Paddocks lording on the same. **1594** —— *Amoretti* x, She lordeth in licentious blisse Of her freewill. **1633** P. Fletcher *Elisa* II. vii, Her.. sister.. Alicia, in whose face Love proudly lorded. **1641** Milton *Ch. Govt.* vi. Wks. 1851 III. 124 The hatefull thirst of Lording in the Church.. first bestow'd a being upon Prelaty. **1671** —— *Samson* 265 They had by this.. lorded over them whom now they serve. **1685** Dryden tr. *Lucretius* III. 242 That haughty King, who lorded ore the Main,.. Him Death, a greater Monarch, overcame. **1777** Burke *Address King* Wks. 1842 II. 402 Much less are we desirous of lording over our brethren. **1833** Chalmers *Const. Man* (1835) I. iii. 156 Its unhappy patient is lorded over by a power of moral evil. **1871** B. Taylor *Faust* (1875) I. xiv. 151 Methinks, instead of in the forest lording, The noble Sir should [etc.]. **1881** Blackmore *Christowell* xxxi, I am not one to be lorded over by a man no better than myself.

c. So *to lord it*, chiefly with *over*.

1579 Spenser *Sheph. Cal.* July 176 They.. lord it as they list. **1593** Shaks. *2 Hen. VI*, IV. viii. 44, I see them Lording it in London streets. **1638** *Penit. Conf.* vii. (1657) 145 Lording it over the Consciences of the people. *a* **1704** T. Brown *Praise Drunkenness* Wks. 1730 I. 37 She [drunkenness] lords it over Poland, Sweden and Norway. *a* **1716** South *Serm.* (1823) V. 409 Though reason and judgment would veil to Christ, yet the man does not, because his affections lord it. **1775** Mad. D'Arblay *Let.* Nov. in *Early Diary*, He disdains submitting to the great or Lording it over the little. **1820** W. Irving *Sketch Bk.*, *Rip Van Winkle* ¶ 1 The Kaatskill mountains.. are seen.. swelling up to a noble height and lording it over the surrounding country. **1855** Tyndall in *Lett. Educ.* 192 We lord it over Matter, and in so doing have become better acquainted with the laws of Mind. **1900** *Q. Rev.* Oct. 337 This barbarian.. lorded it over many waters from the Canaries to Candia.

2. *trans.* To be or act as lord of; to control, manage, rule. *rare.*

c **1586** C'tess Pembroke *Ps.* LXXVIII. xxii, [Their] heritage he shared to the race.. of godly Israell, To lord their lands. *Ibid.* CVI. xv, [God] Left them to be.. Lorded by foes. **1691** J. Wilson *Belphegor* I. ii, Simple Merit Lords few Mens Horoscope. **1807** J. Barlow *Columb.* v. 660 Austria's titled hordes, with their own gore, Fat the fair fields they lorded long before. **1818** Keats *Endym.* II. 894 The look Of his white palace.. And all the revels he had lorded there.

3. †**a.** To make (a man) a lord or master. **b.** To confer the title of lord upon; to ennoble.

a **1340** Hampole *Psalter* xviii. 14 If þai ware noght lordid of me [Mistransl.: L. *si mei non fuerunt dominati*]. **1610** Shaks. *Temp.* I. ii. 97 He being thus Lorded, did beleeue He was indeed the Duke. **1643** Wither *Campo Musæ* 69 Ev'ry one of those That hath for any services, beene Lorded. **1720** *Humor. Lett. Lond. Jrnl.* (1721) 16 Thou shalt be told.. Who gets an Estate in the Alley, and is afterward Knighted or Lorded. **1787** *Minor* 307 Sir Cadwallader Pleadwell.. has been lately Lorded. **1889** Furnivall in *Pall Mall G.* 14 Dec. 1/3 It was with no little pleasure then that I found Lord Tennyson (before he was lorded) making me known.. to Mr. Robert Browning.

c. To address or speak of as 'Lord'.

1636 Rutherford *Lett.* lx. (1862) I. 161 My newly printed book against Arminians was one challenge: not lording the prelates was another. **1656** S. H. *Golden Law* 92 Is not Sarah commended for obeying, and lording her husband? **1660** *Charac. Italy* 56 Before they merit the degree of Knighthood, they must be Lorded.

lordan(e: see Lurdan.

lord-borough. One who has quasi-manorial rights in certain English boroughs: see quot.

1751 *Eng. Gazetteer* II. s.v. *Wolverhampton*, The dean is Ld.-borough of Wolverhampton, Codsall, Hatherton and Petshall.. and hath all manner of privileges bel. to the view of frank-pledge, felons goods, deodands, escheats [etc.].

lord-dom ('lɔːddəm). For forms see Lord *sb.* [OE. *hláford-dóm*, f. *hláford* Lord *sb.* + -dom.]

†**a.** The position of being lord, lordship (*obs.*). **b.** *nonce-use.* The state of things characterized by the existence of lords.

c **897** K. Ælfred *Gregory's Past.* xvii. 121 Se ðe on lareowes onlicnesse ða ðenenga ðæs ealdordomes ȝecierð to hlaforddome. *c* **1200** Ormin 11851 Te laþe gast Aȝȝ eggeþþ hise þeowess.. To ȝeornenn affterr laferrddom. *c* **1230** *Hali Meid.* 11 Is al to muchel lauerddom & meistrie þrinne þis cunde imerred tus. **1824** *New Monthly Mag.* X. 521 There is no country.. in which the system of lord-dom and servility is so manifestly supported as in England.

lorden: see Lurdan.

† **'lordfast**, *a.* *Obs.* *rare*⁻¹. In 5 -fest. [f. Lord *sb.* + Fast *a.*] Bound to a lord.

c **1460** *Towneley Myst.* xiii. 20 These men that ar lord fest thay cause the ploghe tary.

'lord-fish. [Cf. Lord *sb.* 14 b.] (See quot.)

1836 Yarrell *Brit. Fishes* II. 165 Some years since, I obtained from a fisherman at the mouth of the Thames a fresh-caught example of a species of *morrhua*, with the middle dorsal and the first anal fins short... Among the fishermen it was by some considered to be an accidental deformity, with injury of the spine, and their name for it was Lord-fish.

lordful ('lɔːdfʊl), *a.* *rare*⁻¹. [f. Lord *sb.* + -ful.] Having the bearing of a lord; lordly. Hence **'lordfully** *adv.*, in a lordly manner; nobly.

c **1450** *Mirour Saluacioun* 1178 This lordfulle child [*sc.* Jesus]. **1836** Gen. P. Thompson *Exerc.* (1842) IV. 185 They [the Lords] have said boldly and lordfully, 'Here we stand, the offspring of the by-gone time'.

† **'lordhead.** *Obs.* For forms see Lord *sb.* and -head. [f. Lord *sb.* + -head.] = Lordship.

c **1250** *Gen. & Ex.* 190 In ðe moste and in ðe leste he forles His louerd-hed quuanne he mis-ches. *a* **1300** *Cursor M.* 4837 We prai þi lauerd-hed þat þou wald vs help in nede. *c* **1325** *Metr. Hom.* (1862) 61 Of that tour nou spek I, For laverdhed and for maistri, That Nembrot havid first of man.

† **'lordify**, *v.* *Obs.* *rare*⁻¹. [f. Lord *sb.* + -(i)fy.] *trans.* To make a lord of.

1663 T. Porter *Witty Combat* III. i, I'le lordifie thee, John ..: thou shalt no more be plain John.. but my lord John.

lording ('lɔːdɪŋ), *sb.* Forms: 1 **hláfording** (Sweet), 2–3 **lover(e)ding**, 3 *Orm.* **laferrdinng**, 3–4 **laverding**, (**lhording**), 3– **lording**. [f. Lord *sb.* + -ing³.]

1. = Lord *sb.* 2. Frequent as a form of address, rarely *sing.* = Sir!, frequent in *pl.* = Sirs! Gentlemen! Also, ***my lording!*** *Obs.* exc. *arch.*

c **1200** *Trin. Coll. Hom.* 179 Þe riche þe ben louerdinges struien þe wrecche men, þe ben underlinges. *c* **1200** Ormin 918 Nu, laferrdinngess, loke we Whatt tiss maȝȝ us bitacnenn. *c* **1205** Lay. 27394 Lauerdinges, quæð Luces þa, Mahun eou beo liðe. *c* **1250** *Kent. Serm.* in *O.E. Misc.* 27 Lordinges and leuedis þis is si glorius miracle. *c* **1250** *Gen. & Ex.* 833 Neȝ ilc burȝe hadde ise louereding. *c* **1320** *Sir Tristr.* 402 Of a prince proude in play Listneþ, lordings dere. **1340** *Ayenb.* 67 Þis zenne is ine uele manneres ase ine sergons aye hire lhordinges. **1375** Barbour *Bruce* I. 445 Lordingis, quha likis for till her, The Romanys now begynnys her. **1382** Wyclif *Deut.* x. 17 The Lord oure God he is.. Lord of lordyngis. *a* **1400–50** *Alexander* 2573 Þe leche lokid ouire þe lynes 'my lording' he said, 'I am noȝt gilty of þis gile'. *c* **1450** Holland *Howlat* 628 Quhat fele armes.. Of lordingis and sere landis.. The said persewant bure. **1568** T. Howell *Newe Sonets* (1879) 149 Lo Lordynges, here by take a vewe. **1591** *Troub. Raigne K. Iohn* (1611) 29 Lordings forbeare, for time is comming fast, That deeds may trie what words can not determine. **1599** Shaks., etc. *Pass. Pilgr.* xv, It was a Lordings daughter, the fairest one of three. **1622** Fletcher *Beggars Bush* v. i, If't be worth His Lordships thanks anon, when 'tis done, Lording, Ile looke for't. **1865** Kingsley *Herew.* II. xxi. 363 Have a care for yourselves, lordings! The Wake is loose.

2. As diminutive of Lord: A little lord, a petty lord, usually in a contemptuous sense.

c **1577** Stanyhurst *Æneis*, etc. *Epit. Ld. Louth* (Arb.) 150 The Lord Baron of Louth.. was trayterously murthred by Mackmaughoun, an Irish Lording, about the year 1577. **1589** Puttenham *Eng. Poesie* III. xix. (Arb.) 229 Such termes are vsed to be giuen.. for a kind of contempt, as when we say Lording for Lord. **1611** Shaks. *Wint. T.* I. ii. 62 Ile question you Of my Lords Tricks, and yours, when you were Boyes: You were pretty Lordings then? **1651** N. Bacon *Disc. Govt. Eng.* II. vi. 59 Had future Ages pursued the flight as it was begun, these Lordings might have beaten the Air, without making any speedy way.

3. A sort of apple or pear. (Cf. Lordling 2.)

1664 Evelyn *Kal. Hort.*, *Aug.* (1679) 22 Pears.. Windsor ..Sugar-Pear, Lording Pear, &c. *Ibid.*, *Sept.* 24 Apples.. Summer Pearmain, Lording-apple. **1676** Worlidge *Cyder* (1691) 210 The Lording is a fair, green, and sharp apple.

lording ('lɔːdɪŋ), *vbl. sb.* [f. Lord *v.* + -ing¹.] The action of Lord *v.* in various senses.

1549 Coverdale, etc. *Erasm. Par. Pet.* 14 The office of a right bysshop is ferre of from lordinge. **1610** Guillim *Heraldry* III. xvii. (1611) 150 When they sit, they hold their heads steady and without motion: which stately action Spencer in his Shepheard's calender calleth the lording of Frogs. [See Lord *v.* 1 b, 1579.] **1648** Milton *Tenure Kings* (1650) 46 The censorious and supercilious lording over conscience. **1657** W. Morice *Coena quasi κοινὴ* xxi. 193 To exonerate themselves they transferre this Lording.. on the Bishop's. **1864** Burton *Scot Abr.* I. iii. 112 Possibly the fifteen days' lording it at Sluys may have broken in.. on his outfit. **1890** T. Hardy in *New Rev.* Jan. 20 The present lording of nonage over maturity.

attrib. **1611** Speed *Hist. Gt. Brit.* IX. ix. (1623) 607 As was the fashion of those Lording times. **1863** W. Lancaster *Præterita* 54 Zeus.. metes me out a little lording nook.

lording ('lɔːdɪŋ), *ppl. a.* [f. Lord *v.* + -ing².] That lords, in senses of the vb.

c **1400** tr. *Secreta Secret.*, *Gov. Lordsh.* 54 A man may.. by tokenynges perseyue whether wyt or no wyt be yn a kynge lordand. *c* **1629** Layton *Syons Plea* (ed. 2) 6 Where the Spirit recounteth by name all the sorts of Ministery,.. Eph. iv. 11 there is not one word of such a Lording Ministry. **1641** R. Brooke *Eng. Episc.* II. vii. 112 The.. Cruell Tyranny of some Lording Prelates. **1880** G. Meredith *Tragic Com.* (1881) 39 She tried to be revolted by his lording tone.

lordkin ('lɔːdkɪn). *nonce-wd.* [f. Lord *sb.* + -kin.] A little or young lord.

1855 Thackeray *Newcomes* II. 143 Princekin or lordkin from his earliest days has nurses, dependents [etc.].

lordless ('lɔːdlɪs), *a.* [OE. *hláfordléas*, f. *hláford* Lord *sb.* + *-léas* -less.] Without a lord; having no lord. Of a woman: Husbandless.

Beowulf (Z.) 2934 Oððæt hi oð-eodon earfoðlice in hrefnes holt hlaford-lease. *c* **1290** *Beket* 678 in *S. Eng. Leg.* I. 126 Ase men þat weren louerdlese—heo nusten ȝwat a-bide. **1297** R. Glouc. (Rolls) 2987 Þou ast ymad.. moni child wiþ oute fader, & moni wif louerd les. *c* **1440** Capgrave *Life St. Kath.* III. 489 Hoo is hir lord, or wheder is she lordles? **1643** T. Case *Serm.* in Kerr *Covenants & Covenanters* (1895) 249 Your diocese [shall be] bishopless and your sees lord-less. **1823** Joanna Baillie *Collect. Poems* 312 An armed band From Moorham's lordless hall. **1867** Freeman *Norm. Conq.* (1876) I. iii. 91 The lordless man became a kind of out-law. **1868–70** Morris *Earthly Par.* I. I. 137 And many a lordless, troubled land Fell scarce loth to his dreaded hand.

lordlet ('lɔːdlɪt). *jocular.* [f. Lord *sb.* + -let.] A little or young lord.

1884 *Chr. Commonw.* 13 Nov. 63/5 Suppose the private soldier had assaulted the ducal lordlet. **1901** *Contemp. Rev.* Jan. 102 Why should I be filled with envy on beholding some lordlet.. dash by me?

'Lord-lieu'tenant. Pl. lords-lieutenant(s, lord-lieutenants.

1. The title of various high officials holding deputed authority from the sovereign.

†**a.** In Scotland. *Obs.*

1453 *Extracts Aberd. Reg.* (1844) I. 403 He wald noght find caucion and sourete that the lord Lievtenand suld haue ferme and stable quhat the said Ranald did. **1547** *Reg. Privy Council Scot.* I. 81 As salbe thocht expedient be my Lord Lieutennent.

b. In Ireland: The Viceroy.

In 1640 the earl of Stafford who had till then borne the title of 'Lord Deputy', was promoted to the higher dignity of 'Lord Lieutenant'.

1614 Selden *Titles Hon.* 57 Some succeeding Princes.. had their.. Lord Lieutenants or Deputies (as at this day they are called) of Ireland,.. then whom, no Lieutenants in

Christendome..comes neerer Kinglike State. **1648** *Art. Peace* in *Milton's Wks.* (1847) 257/1 To such other place as his majesty's lord lieutenant..shall appoint. **1702** *Lond. Gaz.* No. 3841/3 Lawrence Earl of Rochester, Lord Lieutenant of Ireland. *a* **1865** GREVILLE *Mem.* II. (1885) II. 34 No appointment is known but that of Lord de Grey as Lord Lieutenant of Ireland.

c. In a county: The chief executive authority and head of the magistracy, usually a peer or other large land-owner, appointed by the Sovereign by patent. Under him and of his appointing are deputy-lieutenants. The position is now mainly ceremonial, though he retains some of his former powers (see quots.), including the recommendation of persons for appointment as justices of the peace.

Lord-lieutenants, when first introduced in the 16th c., were to take an active part in the defence of the realm, and down to 1871 they had extensive powers with regard to the militia, etc., which then reverted to the Crown.

1557-8 *Act 4 & 5 Phil. & Mary*, c. 3 §5 The Lorde Leiutenante or the Lorde Wardeine..duryng the tyme of any his or their Commission shall and maye heare order and determine the same Offences by his or their discretyons. **1642** *Declar. Lords & Comm., For Rais. Forces* 22 Dec. 7 That the Lord Lieutenants..do..appoint one experienced Souldier in every Regiment to be an Adjutor, to be resident in the sayd Counties to exercise the severall Companies of the sayd Regiments. **1710** CHAMBERLAYNE *Pres. St. Gt. Brit.* I. II. (ed. 23) 143 For furnishing Ammunition, and other Necessaries, the Lord Lieutenant..may levy every Year one fourth part..of each Man's Proportion in the Tax of 70,000*l.* a Month. **1839** *Penny Cycl.* XV. 216/1 From the reign of Philip and Mary the lords-lieutenants have had the charge, under the sovereign, of raising the militia in their respective counties. *a* **1865** GREVILLE *Mem.* II. (1885) III. 65 At Court yesterday to make Lord Grey Lord-Lieutenant of Northumberland. **1962** W. O. HART *Hart's Introd. Law Local Govt. & Admin.* ii. 64 With the disappearance of the militia the lord lieutenant has ceased to have a county force to command. His position has come to be largely one of great honour with no active duties to perform. **1963** *Times* 10 May 19/2 At the moment it was contemplated that there would be one lord lieutenant for the Greater London area, with a number of deputy lieutenants to assist him. **1963** K. B. SMELLIE *Hist. Local Govt.* iii. 42 The Lord Lieutenant and the Sheriff have mainly ceremonial duties. **1972** *Whitaker's Almanack 1973* 631 The duties of the Lord Lieutenant are to advise the Lord Chancellor as to the appointment of magistrates to the county bench... The Lord Lieutenant is usually a peer or baronet..and is often appointed *custos rotulorum* (keeper of the records).

†**2.** Applied to the second-in-command of an army, when a peer. *Obs.*

1544 *Late Exped. Scot.* 4 in Dalyell *Fragm. Sc. Hist.* (1798), Wherof my Lorde Admyral ledde the vantgard, and Therle of Hertford, beinge Lorde Lieutenaunt, the battayll. *Ibid.* 6 The Lord Lieutenaunt sent with diligence to the vanwarde, that they shulde merche towardes the towne.

Hence **'lord-lieu'tenancy**, the office of a lord-lieutenant.

1876 BANCROFT *Hist. U.S.* IV. xxx. 58 He had just obtained the lord-lieutenancy of Ireland for his brother. **1884** S. DOWELL *Tax. & Taxes Eng.* II. 103 Carteret, turned out of the lord-lieutenancy about the same time, was now in open opposition.

lordlike ('lɔːdlaɪk), *a.* and *adv.* [See -LIKE.]

A. *adj.* Resembling, befitting, or characteristic of a lord; lordly. Now *rare*.

c **1470** HENRY *Wallace* IX. 56 Ledys on luff burd, with a lordlik fer. **1500-20** DUNBAR *Poems* xviii. 11 Be I ane lord, and not lord lyk, Than [etc.]. **1546** *Supplic. Poore Commons* (E.E.T.S.) 89 They trust to optayne therby lordlyck liuinges out of the porsion of the poore. **1600** HOLLAND *Livy* XXV. xxii. 565 Anniball made this glorious and lordlike aunswere with a majestie. **1603** B. JONSON *Sejanus* v. viii, Officious Friendes..start before My great, proud Lord, to get a Lord-like nod! **1646** EARL MONM. tr. *Biondi's Civil Warres* IX. 208 His Lordlike looks..captivated the good-will of the standers by. **1839-40** I. TAYLOR *Anc. Chr.* (1842) II. viii. 400 He disclaims any lordlike authority in the Church.

Hence †**lordlikeness**.

c **1470** HENRY *Wallace* VII. 402 It can nocht be, but fredome, lordlyknes.

†**B.** *adv.* After the fashion of a lord, domineeringly. Also, as befits a lord; sumptuously. *Obs.*

1555 RIDLEY in Coverdale *Lett. Martyrs* (1564) 101 So many (I say) would at these my wordes Lordelike stampe and spurne and spit thereat. **1574** tr. *Marlorat's Apocalips* 10 Behaue not your selues lordlike ouer the Clergie [1 Pet. v. 3]. **1599** HAKLUYT *Voy.* II. II. 79 Manie great estates and gouernours there be, that during their office are lodged Lordlike. **1700** DRYDEN *Iliad* I. *Fables* 202 Lord-like at ease..the People to devour. **1727** BOYER *Fr. Dict.*, Lord-like, *en grand seigneur*.

lordlily ('lɔːdlɪlɪ), *adv. rare.* [f. LORDLY *a.* + -LY².] In a lordly fashion.

1611 COTGR., *Pontificalement*, pontiffically, lordlily. **1891** R. KIPLING *City Dreadf. Nt.* 46 Young men who smoke bad cigars and carry themselves lordlily.

lordliness ('lɔːdlɪnɪs). [f. LORDLY *a.* + -NESS.]

†**1.** The condition or state of a lord. *Obs.*

c **1380** WYCLIF *Wks.* (1880) 384 Clerkis & religious folke that louen unkyndely þes lordlynes willen glose here & say þat [etc.]. *c* **1400** tr. *Secreta Secret., Gov. Lordsh.* 42 Techinge falland to lordlynes of lordes. **1549** CHEKE *Hurt Sedit.* (1641) 10 By ambition yee seek Lordlinesse, much unfit for you. **1577-87** HOLINSHED *Chron.* I. 150/1 To ferret out concealed lands for the supporte of their owne priuat lordlines. **1606** SHAKS. *Ant. & Cl.* v. ii. 161 Doing the Honour of thy Lordlinesse To one so meeke. **1641** 'SMECTYMNUUS' *Answ.* xviii. (1653) 77 Men would be adding to Gods institution, what..Lordlinesse their phansie suggested unto them. **1669** WOODHEAD *St. Teresa* I. xxxiii. 236 The Lords, we are wont to meet within this world,..place all their Lordliness in some acted Authorities.

2. The disposition proper to a lord; dignity, grandeur. Frequent in bad sense: Arrogance, haughtiness, imperiousness.

1549 COVERDALE, etc. *Erasm. Par. Titus* 28 He must overcome more by..gentylnes, than by lordelynes. *a* **1585** CARTWRIGHT in R. Browne *Answ. Cartwright* 93 Pharisaicall pride and Lordlinesse in teaching. **1618** BOLTON *Florus* I. viii. (1636) 21 The intolerable Lordlinesse of Superbus did some good. **1670** G. H. *Hist. Cardinals* I. I. 14 From hence it is the Grandeur and Lordlyness of the Cardinals does spring. **1723** DK. WHARTON *True Briton* No. 42 II. 365 The Arbitrary Temper and Lordliness of Calvin. **1741** RICHARDSON *Pamela* (1824) I. 117 See the lordliness of a high condition! **1883** J. PARKER *Tyne Chylde* 200 There are instincts of lordliness in man which are to be accounted for. **1884** CHURCH *Bacon* ix. 225 The Latin in which [the *Novum Organum*] is written..has..the lordliness of a great piece of philosophical legislation.

lordling ('lɔːdlɪŋ). [f. LORD *sb.* + -LING.]

1. A little or puny lord: often in contemptuous sense. Occas. = LORDING *sb.* 1.

c **1275** LAY. 12664 Lusteþ louerdlinges. *c* **1380** *Sir Ferumb.* 1518 Lordlynges, wel ȝe wyteð alle, how [etc.]. *c* **1590** GREENE *Fr. Bacon* ix. 85 What say you Royall Lordlings to my Fryer? **1746** SMOLLETT *Reproof* 163 While the young lordling struts in native pride. **1782** ELIZ. BLOWER *Geo. Bateman* II. 47, I should sink myself to a level with the scoundrel lordling who employs you. **1820** COLERIDGE *Lett., Convers.* etc. I. 125 How long will..this hive of nations submit to the guidance of litterateurs and lordlings? **1824-9** LANDOR *Imag. Conv.* Wks. 1846 II. 229 The said conjurors..possess the faculty of making the precious metals out of..the skulls of young lordlings and gentlefolk. **1872** LONGF. *Wayside Inn* II. *Interlude bef. Student's T.* Listen, Lordlings, while I tell. **1887** M. MORRIS *Claverhouse* x. (1888) 170 One of these independent lordlings, Colin MacDonald of Keppoch.

†**2.** A kind of apple. *Obs.* (cf. LORDING *sb.* 3.)

1725 BRADLEY *Fam. Dict.* II. s.v. *October*, Apples now in prime..are the..Costard Lordling Parsley Apples.

lordly ('lɔːdlɪ), *a.* and *adv.* Forms: see LORD *sb.* and -LY. [OE. *hláfordlic*, f. LORD *sb.* + -LY.]

A. *adj.*

1. Of or pertaining to a lord or lords; consisting of lords; administered by lords. Now *rare*.

a **1000** in Napier *O.E. Glosses* (Anecd. Oxon.) 187/1 *Heroicus, id est nobile*, hlafordlic. *c* **1200** *Trin. Coll. Hom.* 23 Chireche..is cleped on boc kiriaca .i. dominicalis, þat is on englis louerdlich hus. *c* **1450** *Voc.* in Wr.-Wülcker 623/14 *Herilis*, lordlyche. **1530** PALSGR. 317/2 Lordlyke belongyng to a lorde. **1645** J. COTTON *Way Ch. New Eng.* 36 The Government of his [Christ's] Kingdome is not Lordly, but Stewardly and Ministeriall. **1653** J. HALL *Paradoxes* 4 Lordly or absolute Monarchy is the best and most natural Government. **1841** MIALL in *Nonconf.* I. 241 Pensioning off supernumerary members of lordly houses. **1862** R. VAUGHAN *Nonconformity* 392 The more learned of this class were ardent in their support of a lordly prelacy.

2. Of persons: Having the character, attributes, appearance, or demeanour of a lord. Of actions: Befitting a lord; honourable, noble.

? *a* **1400** *Morte Arth.* 138 Thow arte þe lordlyeste lede þat ever I one lukyde. *Ibid.* 396 Þe conquerour..Alowes þame gretly theire lordly a-vowes. *a* **1533** LD. BERNERS *Gold. Bk. M. Aurel.* (1546) G vij, Some will be so lordely and valyaunt in vertues. **1829** GEN. P. THOMPSON *Exerc.* (1842) I. 124 The..aggregate of good which arises to the lordlier part of the creation. **1840** CARLYLE *Heroes* (1858) 263 It is truly a lordly spectacle how this great soul takes in all kinds of men and objects, a Falstaff, an Othello, a Juliet, a Coriolanus. **1859** C. BARKER *Associat. Principle* i. 28 Falconry and the chase afforded to the abbot..the most lordly recreation of the time. **1886** SPURGEON *Treas. Dav.* Ps. cxxxvi. 3 He is more lordly than all emperors and kings condensed into one.

b. Haughty, imperious, lofty, disdainful.

1377 LANGL. *P. Pl.* B. III. 160 Lawe is so lordeliche and loth to make ende. **1530** PALSGR. 661/1 Are you waxen so lordely that you can nat plucke of your hosen your selfe? *a* **1548** HALL *Chron., Rich. III* 39 Whome he..had..compelled by lordely and streite commaundemente. **1588** J. UDALL *Demonstr. Discipl.* (Arb.) 45 A minister may not be Lordly ouer Gods people [1 Pet. v. 3]. **1600** HOLLAND *Livy* XLV. xxxv. 1225 He was an imperious and lordly commaunder. **1612** T. TAYLOR *Comm. Titus* iii. 2 (1619) 582 It suffereth not the Minister to be lordly in his doctrine or discipline. **1665** MANLEY *Grotius' Low C. Warres* 151 The Lordly domineering of the English, was not forgotten in France. **1681** DRYDEN *Abs. & Achit.* 454 And like a Lion..He..with a Lordly Rage, his Hunters tears. **1768-74** TUCKER *Lt. Nat.* (1834) I. 625 The lordly West-Indian tortures his poor Negroes. **1849** MACAULAY *Hist. Eng.* iii. I. 303 The Captain..treated the Master with lordly contempt. **1862** MRS. BROWNING *Ragged Schools* ix, Lordly English, think it o'er. **1880** L. STEPHEN *Pope* iv. 93 Swift, indeed, had..a lordly indifference to making money by his writings.

3. Of things: Suitable for a lord; hence, grand, magnificent, noble.

1535 COVERDALE *Judg.* v. 25 She..broughte forth butter in a lordly diszshe. **1570** B. GOOGE *Pop. Kingd.* I. 6 b, In placeing of his kinsemen hie, in loftie Lordely chayre. **1604** DRAYTON *Owl* 37 Under th' extensure of whose lordly arms, The small birds warbled their harmonious charms. **1810** SCOTT *Lady of L.* I. xiv, On this bold brow, a lordly tower. **1832** TENNYSON *Pal. Art* i, I built my soul a lordly pleasurehouse. **1890** H. G. DAKYNS *Xenophon* I. p. lxxxviii, Cyrus was flying at lordlier game than certain irrepressible hill tribes.

4. *absol.* (In early use quasi-*sb.*, a lordly person.)

c **1470** *Golagros & Gaw.* 1276 To that lordly on loft that lufly can lout. **1535** COVERDALE *Job* xxxiv. 19 He hath no respecte vnto the personnes of yᵉ lordly. **1849** JAMES *Woodman* iv, No meeting of the high, the rich, and the lordly. **1849** C. BRONTË *Shirley* xvi. 244 He still advocated the lordly, liberal, and effective.

5. *Comb.*

1860-6 PATMORE *Angel in Ho.* II. II. iii, I am so proud of Frederick, He's so high-bred and lordly-like With Mrs. Vaughan!

B. *adv.* After the manner of a lord; in a lordly manner (both in good and bad sense).

1393 LANGL. *P. Pl.* C. xx. 241 Lordliche for to lyuen, and likyngliche be clothed. **1398** TREVISA *Barth. De P.R.* XVII. clxxx. (1495) 722 By his socour..that..sauyth all lordly and myghtly. *c* **1420** *Anturs of Arth.* 489 (Douce MS.) And at þe listes one þe lande lordely done liȝte. *c* **1440** *Promp. Parv.* 312/2 Lordly, *dominanter*. **1589** GREENE *Menaphon* (Arb.) 61 To rebuke him for tyrannising so Lordlie ouer the boies. **1728** SAVAGE *Bastard* 45 Lordly neglectful of a worth unknown. **1812** COMBE *Picturesque* VII. (Chandos) 26 'If I' said he, 'remember right, I was most lordly drunk last night'. **1870** MORRIS *Earthly Par.* II. III. 279 In a land where few were poor, if none Were lordly rich. **1875** JOWETT *Plato* (ed. 2) III. 467 Love is his tyrant, and lives lordly in him. *Comb.* **1864** DASENT *Jest & Earnest* (1873) II. 263 Who is yon lordly-dressed man who is walking along the street?

Lord Mayor.

1. A title formerly limited to the mayors (see MAYOR) of London, York, and Dublin, but subsequently extended to the mayors of some other large towns, e.g. Liverpool, Birmingham, Sheffield, etc.

Lord Mayor's coal (see quot. 1842). *Lord Mayor's day*, Nov. 9, the day on which the Lord Mayor goes in procession with the Aldermen and other city dignitaries to and from Westminster, where he receives from the Lord Chancellor the assent of the Crown to his election. *Lord Mayor's man*: see *quota-man*, QUOTA 4. *Lord Mayor's show*, the procession on Lord Mayor's day.

c **1554** BALE *Decl. Bonner's Articles* i. 7 b, Here is as wise an order towardes, as maister Harry my Lord Mayres foole had bene of counsell therein. **1589** J. RIDER *Bibl. Scholast.* 885 The Lorde maior, or chiefe iustice, *præfectus prætorio*. **1605** MARSTON *Dutch Courtezan* III. i. D 4 b, All will scarce make me so high as one of the Gyants stilts that stalkes before my Lord Maiors pageant. **1638** BAKER tr. *Balzac's Lett.* (vol. II.) 38 Had it not been to see my Lord Mayors shew, I had not been seene in the citie. **1678** *Will of R. Saunders* (Somerset Ho.), A Lord Mayor's spoon. **1717** PRIOR *Alma* I. 377 If you dine with my lord mayor, Roast-beef and venison is your fare. **1761** *Ann. Reg.* 235 A proverb, that the lord mayor's day is generally a bad one. **1807** SIR R. WILSON *Jrnl.* 7 June in *Life* (1862) II. viii. 253, I..would not have exchanged meals with the Lord Mayor of London. **1842** BARHAM *Ingol. Leg.*, *Aunt Fanny*, Had the coal been a 'Lord Mayor's coal',—viz. a slate. **1859** H. KINGSLEY *G. Hamlyn* xxxii. (1860) 286 Burnside was in the habit of saying that he was like the Lord Mayor's fool—fond of everything that was good. *a* **1865** GREVILLE *Mem.* II. (1885) II. 51 The Queen must have known it was Lord Mayor's Day.

2. *slang.* 'A large crowbar' (Farmer).

1889 D. C. MURRAY *Danger. Catspaw* 24 There's..the crowbar, from a Lord Mayor down to a pocket jemmy.

Hence **Lord-'Mayoralty**, the position of Lord Mayor.

1882 *Society* 4 Nov. 16/1 Lord mayoralties and high shrievalties follow almost as a matter of course.

lordolatry (lɔː'dɒlətrɪ). *jocular.* [f. LORD *sb.* + -(O)LATRY.] Worship of lords.

1846 THACKERAY *Bk. Snobs* iii, The extent and prevalence of Lordolatry in this country. **1881** R. F. BURTON in *Academy* 1 Oct. 258/3 England, with her peculiar 'lordolatry', thinks it enough to send a peer when other nations send an explorer.

‖**lordosis** (lɔː'dəʊsɪs). *Path.* [mod.L., a. Gr. λόρδωσις, f. λορδός bent backward.] **a.** Anterior curvature of the spine, producing convexity in front (occurring as a physical deformity).

1704 HARRIS *Lex. Techn.*, *Lordosis*, by some Writers, is the Term for the bending of the Back-bone forwards in Children, &c. **1822-34** *Good's Study Med.* (ed. 4) IV. 249 *Lordosis*, imported procurvation of the head and shoulders or anterior crookedness. **1894** *Lancet* 3 Nov. 1030 Very extreme lordosis is present. **1899** *Allbutt's Syst. Med.* VII. 165 A lordosis was very evident.

b. A temporarily assumed posture, characteristic of some female mammals during mating, in which the back is arched downwards; the assumption of such a posture.

1941 *Endocrinology* XXIX. 411 Two males exhibited lordosis and hopping behavior typical of the sexually-receptive female [rat]. **1947** *Physiol. Rev.* XXVII. 243 Some female rats in heat display lordosis each time they are mounted by the male. **1965** *Science* 15 Jan. 306/3 Frequency of lordosis, ear-wiggling, and crouching (all indications of receptivity) were recorded. **1968** M. DIAMOND *Perspectives in Reproduction & Sexual Behavior* xx. 321 Normal males [*sc.* rats] rarely exhibit lordosis. **1971** *New Scientist* 13 May 370/3 The rats with no sense of smell were much more likely to show the typical lordosis (a posture where the belly is lowered and the rump stuck up in the air) that is normal in sexually receptive animals.

Hence **lordotic** (-'dɒtɪk) *a.* [see -OTIC], pertaining to or affected with lordosis.

1856 in MAYNE *Expos. Lex.* **1971** *New Scientist* 13 May 370/3 With these animals removal of both olfactory lobes increased the likelihood of going into a lordotic posture. **1972** *Science* 5 May 519/1 After a 9-hour delay, the typical lordotic reactions and sticky estrous discharge had generally disppeared.

Lord's (lɔːdz). Also **Lords**. The cricket ground at St. John's Wood, London, named after its founder Thomas *Lord* (1757–1832); now the headquarters of the Marylebone Cricket Club.

1799 *Times* 1 June 3/4 The colours..were presented..to the corps in Lord's cricket-ground. **1823** H. BENTLEY *Cricket Matches played by Mary-le-bone Club*, Lord's.—26th August, 1793. Eleven of England against Twenty-two of the County of Middlesex. **1863** A. J. MUNBY *Diary* 10 July in D. Hudson *Munby* (1972) 167 Miss Williams had asked me to go with her party to the Eton and Harrow cricket match at Lord's. **1910** *Blackw. Mag.* 90/1 The Australians had won the toss at Lords... Our visitors had already on a Lords wicket pretty thoroughly extended a M.C.C. eleven. **1930** E. WAUGH *Labels* 88 There was an interval, during which everyone..strolled about..as people do at Lord's between the innings. **1959** *Listener* 19 Feb. 344/1 He loyally goes through the motions, military and social (Bank Picquet, Tower Guard, débutantes' balls, Ascot, Lord's), that are required of him. **1972** K. WARD *Put Lock On!* ix. 99 When there's a Test on at Lords..radio stations cater to the thousands who sit up until dawn.

'lordsake, *int. Sc. colloq.* [Short for 'for the Lord's sake'.] An exclamation expressing surprise.

1861 RAMSAY *Remin.* Ser. II. 91, 'I am going to send the young laird abroad..to see the world';..'But lord sake, Laird, will no the world see him?' **1891** H. HALIBURTON *Ochil Idylls* 63 Lordsake, what's come owre the year?

lords and ladies. 'A very general name for *Arum maculatum* L., given in reference to the dark and light spadices, the dark being the lords, the light the ladies' (Britten & Holland *Plant-n.*).

1760 J. LEE *Introd. Bot.* App. 317 Lords and Ladies, *Arum.* **1821** CLARE *Vill. Minstr.* I. 99 Oft under trees we nestled in a ring, Culling out 'lords and ladies'. **1901** *Longm. Mag.* Apr. 533 She set boys to collect roots of lords and ladies.

Lord's day. [Properly, *The Lord's Day* = L. *dies Dominicus, -ca* (whence F. *dimanche*, Sp. *Domingo*, It. *Domenica*), Gr. ἡ κυριακὴ ἡμέρα Rev. i. 10.] A Christian appellation for Sunday.

In the 17–18th c. *Lord's day* (without the article) was somewhat widely used (not exclusively among Puritans) as an ordinary name for the day. This use seems to be partially retained by some Nonconformists (expressions like 'next Lord's day' appearing occasionally in announcements of services). Otherwise, *the Lord's day* is the only form now current, and it is commonly employed only when the intention is to refer expressly to the sacred character of the day.

c **1175** *Lamb. Hom.* 41 Sunedei is ihaten þes lauerdes dei. **1398** TREVISA *Barth. De P.R.* IX. xxi. (1495) 358 The fyrste day hyght the lordes day and Sonedaye. **1639** *Bury Wills* (Camden) 177 Vpon euery Lord's day, called Sonday, throughout euery yere of the said terme. **1660** PEPYS *Diary* 4 Mar., 4th. Lord's day. Before I went to church I [etc.]. **1677** *Act 29 Chas. II*, c. 7 §1 For the better observation and keeping holy the Lord's day commonly called Sunday. *c* **1710** C. FIENNES *Diary* (1888) 301 They come in Coaches and drive round, but it is only Lords day nights and some nights. **1759** B. FAWCETT *Pref. to Baxter's Saints' R.* (1836) 42 On Lord's days..a person..might overhear hundreds of families engaged in singing psalms. **1882** JEAN L. WATSON *Life R. S. Candlish* viii. 97 Multitudes were thus induced to travel on the Lord's day.

attrib. **1901** *Whitaker's Almanack* 285 (Societies and Institutions.) Lord's Day Observance Society.

lordship ('lɔːdʃɪp), *sb.* For forms see LORD *sb.* and -SHIP. Also 4 **lordchip**, 5 **lorchuppe**.

1. a. The dignity and functions of a lord; dominion, rule, sovereignty; ownership *of* or dominion †*on*, *over* (something specified); rarely *pl.*

c **897** K. ÆLFRED *Gregory's Past.* xxviii. 200 Đonne we agyltað wið ða hlafordas, ðonne agylte we wið ðone God þe hlafordscipe ȝescop. *c* **1330** R. BRUNNE *Chron.* (1810) 18 Tille Adelwolf gaf he..Lordschip ouer alle þe londes bituex Douer & Tuede. **1388** WYCLIF *Rom.* vi. 9 Deeth schal no more haue lordschip on hym. ? *a* **1400** *Morte Arth.* 646 Sir Mordrede..Salle be my leuetenante, with lordchipez ynewe. *c* **1400** MAUNDEV. (Roxb.) i. 4 Þis apple betakens þe lordschepe þat he had ouer all þe werld. *c* **1425** *Eng. Conq. Irel.* 136 The kynges of Englond owen wel to haue the lordshyp of Irland. **1450–1530** *Myrr. our Ladye* 74 The lordeshyp of all sinne may be so caste out of vs..that [etc.]. **1561** T. NORTON *Calvin's Inst.* IV. 59 Peter..exhorteth them so to fede the flocke, not as vsing a Lordship ouer the Clergie. **1585** FETHERSTONE tr. *Calvin on Acts* xiv. 19 They challenge to themselues no Lordship, they hunt after no gaine. **1611** BIBLE *Mark* x. 42 They which are accompted to rule ouer the Gentiles, exercise Lordship ouer them. **1625** MASSINGER *New Way* III. ii, Spite of his Lordship and his Collonelship,..I will make him render..a strict accompt. **1645** MILTON *Tetrach.* Wks. 1738 I. 218 Our first parent had Lordship over Sea, and Land, and Air. **1685** BAXTER *Paraphr. N.T.* Mark viii. 38 Will Preferment, Lordship, and Pomp,..recompense him? **1807** WORDSW. *White Doe* II. 55 But not for lordship or for land, My Father, do I clasp your knees. **1851** DIXON *W. Penn* xxi. (1872) 184 They claimed the lordship of the soil. **1876** BANCROFT *Hist. U.S.* IV. i. 313 Parliament had asserted an absolute lordship over the colonies in all cases whatsoever. **1900** *Edin. Rev.* July 57 The Templars acquired lordship over not less than 9,000 manors.

¶ Used to render L. *dominatio*, as the title of an order of angels.

c **1000** ÆLFRIC *Hom.* I. 342 Dominationes sind hlafordscypas ȝecwedene. *a* **1175** *Cott. Hom.* 219 He ȝescop tyen engle werod..Dominationes, hlafordscipe.

†**b.** *collect.* = lords. *Obs.*

1340–70 *Alisaunder* 335 Þe Lordship of Laceedemonie loþed hem þan.

2. a. The land belonging to a lord, the territory under his jurisdiction; a domain, estate, manor, seignory.

c **1380** WYCLIF *Wks.* (1880) 392 If eny siche lordeschips be ..Alienyd or take fro hem. **1399** *Rolls of Parlt.* III. 452/1 Castels, Maners, Lordeshipes, and other Possessions. **1422** tr. *Secreta Secret., Priv. Priv.* 135 Who-so covetyth a roialme or a lorchuppe to Purchase. **1513** BRADSHAW *St. Werburge* I. 183 The boundes and lorshyppes of the sayd Mercyens..were large and myghty. **1574** tr. *Littleton's Tenures* 17 b, In divers lordeshippes and mannoures there is suche custome. **1589** *Extracts Burgh Rec. Glasgow* (1876) I. 144 Walter, commendatour of Blantyre, lord fewar of the lordschipe and regalitie of Glasgw. **1607** NORDEN *Surv. Dial.* (1608) 211, I know a Lordship of my Landlords..it is much pestered with Broome. *a* **1710** BP. BULL *Serm.* xviii. Wks. 1827 I. 448 A good many years ago such a lordship was in such a family. **1765** T. HUTCHINSON *Hist. Mass.* I. iv. 103 This house was built with..four thousand acres for a manor or lordship. **1806** *Gazetteer Scotl.* (ed. 2) 423 That abbacy was erected into a temporal lordship in the family of Keith. **1849** MACAULAY *Hist. Eng.* vii. II. 261 The new envoy.. bore a title taken from the lordship of Zulestein. **1873** DIXON *Two Queens* I. I. i. 6 Owner of one of the widest lordships in the Kingdom. **1896** T. F. TOUT *Edw. I*, iii. 51 The Christian lordships in the Levant were reduced by this time to the slenderest proportions.

†**b.** A government, province, district. *Obs.*

c **1400** *Three Kings of Cologne* 55 Þer is an oþir londe þat is clepid Galilee, þe which is a greet lordschippe. *c* **1470** HENRY *Wallace* v. 1075 A squier than rewllyt that lordschip haill. **1535** COVERDALE *Josh.* xi. 2 The kynges that dwelt.. in the lordshippes of Dor by the see syde. **1578** T. N. tr. *Conq. W. India* 5 In the province of Anigua Iaqua and other lordships which were not as yet pacified.

†**3.** Lordliness, arbitrariness. *Obs.*

1634 CANNE *Necess. Separ.* (1849) 65 Without any other reason but mere lordship, the whole incorporation and I were dismissed to wait his pleasure.

†**4.** The protection given by a lord; patronage.

a **1420** HOCCLEVE *De Reg. Princ.* 1791 May no lordschepe, sone, þe auayle, ffor al þi long seruice & þi trauaile? **1470–85** MALORY *Arthur* VII. xxxv. 269 Said the kynge..ye shall haue my loue and my lordship in the vttermest wyse that may lye in my power.

5. a. The personality of a lord, esp. with possessive pronouns. ***your lordship***(*s*: a form of address to noblemen (except archbishops and dukes), and to judges. †Formerly abbreviated *Lop.*, *Lo*[p].

c **1489** CAXTON *Sonnes of Aymon* vi. 136 Thys worde I haue sayd afore your lordeshyppes for to [etc.]. **1540** MORYSINE *Vives' Introd. Wysd.* Pref. A iv, My poore harte myghte better haue served his lordeshyppe. **1550–3** *Decaye of Eng.* (1871) 8 Beseechynge your Hyghnes,..and honourable lordshyppes. **1593** SHAKS. *3 Hen. VI*, IV. viii. 34 Cousin of Exeter, what thinkes your Lordship? **1613** —— *Hen. VIII*, II. ii. 62 Health to your Lordships. **1681** PRIDEAUX *Lett.* (Camden) 98 Last Friday out goes about 20 of them to desire his Ldship to [etc.]. **1705** ADDISON *Italy* Ded., I here present your Lordship with the Remarks that I make in a Part of these my Travels. **1755** JOHNSON *Let. to Ld. Chesterfield* 7 Feb., Two papers, in which my Dictionary is recommended to the publick, were written by your Lordship. **1797** MRS. RADCLIFFE *Italian* iii. (1826) 20 If it is Signora Rosalba whom your lordship means. **1818** CRUISE *Digest* (ed. 2) III. 235 We must call that case to the consideration of your Lordships from your Journals. **1858** J. B. NORTON *Topics* 160 His Lordship in Council observes that [etc.]. **1884** *Illustr. Lond. News* 29 Nov. 527/3 Their Lordships then adjourned until next Monday.

b. *humorously.* (Not uncommon *colloq.* as a mock complimentary designation for ordinary persons.)

1892 LOWNDES *Camping Sketches* 43 After half an hour's walking we dropped down on his lordship [the donkey] browsing unconcernedly.

6. *Sc.* A percentage on sales of books; a royalty (on a mine or a book).

1859 J. BLACKWOOD *Let.* 18 Sept. in Geo. Eliot *Lett.* (1954) III. 160 Your warning voice about G.E.'s new novel keeps me uncertain. I incline to offer £3000, or £2000 with a lordship not to begin until so many are sold. **1861** STEPHENS & BURN *Bk. Farm-Buildings* 171 The contractor will have Kinpurney quarry, free of lordships, for all the stones necessary. **1886** J. BARROWMAN *Gloss. Scottish Mining Terms* 43 *Lordship*, rate per ton or other measure paid to the proprietor of minerals, royalty. **1887** DUKE OF ARGYLL in *19th Cent.* XXII. 612 The plan proposed of a fixed lordship or percentage of sales seems the only proposal which meets all the difficulties of the case. *Mod. Sc.* The publisher offered the author a lordship of 10 per cent. on the amount of sales.

7. *Comb.*: †**lordship-marcher**, ? a district under the government of a lord marcher.

1613 HAYWARD *Norm. Kings* 181 This being a Lordship marcher, hath enioyed royall liberties, since the time wherein it was first subdued. *a* **1648** LD. HERBERT *Hen. VIII* (1683) 435 Offenders..being not able..to..fly from one lordship Marcher to another.

lordship ('lɔːdʃɪp), *v.* [f. LORDSHIP *sb.*]

†**1.** *intr.* To exercise lordship; to be a lord or ruler. Const. *of*, *to*, *up*. *Obs.*

a **1325** *Prose Psalter* ix. 27 [x. 5] Þe ryȝtful shal lord-shipen of alle hys enemys. *Ibid.* xlviii. 15 [xlix. 14] Þe riȝtful shul lord-shippe vp hem in ioie. **1382** WYCLIF *Judg.* xiv. 4 Forsothe that tyme Philistien lordshipide to Yrael. *c* **1430** *Pilgr. Lyf Manhode* I. xxxiii. (1869) 21 Whan he hadde seruauntes he was lord and lordshipinge [Fr. *et seigneurissant*]. *c* **1430** LYDG. *Reas. & Sens.* (E.E.T.S.) 2445 He lordshyppeth, and hath cure Of euery maner creature.

2. *trans.* To exercise lordship over; to govern.

a **1325** *Prose Psalter* lxxxviii. 10 [lxxxix. 9] Þou lordshippest þe pouste of þe seo. *Ibid.* cv. 38 [cvi. 41] Hij þat hated hem lord-shipped hem.

3. To address as 'Your lordship'.

1740 tr. *De Mouhy's Fort. Country-Maid* (1741) II. 80 She Lordship'd every one who did her the Honour to address themselves to her. **1880** W. J. FITZ-PATRICK *Life Dr. Doyle* I. 91 Some of the priests..lordshipped him.

Hence †**'lordshipping**, the action of the vb., dominion, ownership. Also †**'lordshipper**, one who exercises lordship; a ruler.

c **1380** WYCLIF *Wks.* (1880) 385 Þis is þe mooste cyuylite or seculer lordeschipinge þat eny kynge or lorde haþ on his tenauntes. —— *Micah* v. 2 Of thee [Bethlem] shal gon out to me, whiche is lordshiper in Yrael. —— *2 Pet.* ii. 10 Hem that walken aftir flesch,..and despijsen lordscheping.

lordsmear ('lɔːdzmɪə(r)). *Mining.* [f. *lord's*, gen. of LORD *sb.* + MEAR.] The mear of land in mining ground belonging to the lord of the mine.

1747 HOOSON *Miner's Dict.* s.v. *Barmaster*, [The] Barmaster..looks after..Lordsmears, Pringaps [etc.].

†**'lordswike.** *Obs.* [OE. *hláfordswica*, f. *hláford* LORD *sb.* + *swica* deceiver.] A deceiver of his lord; a traitor.

c **1000** *Kalendar* in *Sax. Leechd.* III. 228 Ne þearf he him na ondrædan helle witan butan he beo hlafordswica. *c* **1205** LAY. 22138 Swa fule biwite þæt he weore lauerd-swike. **1297** R. GLOUC. (Rolls) 6399 Alle traitours & louerd suiken god late hom so spede. **1306** *Song on Simon Fraser* in *Pol. Songs* (Camd.) 220 For that he wes lordswyke, furst he wes to-drawe Upon a retheres hude. *c* **1325** *Chron. Eng.* 1033 in Ritson *Metr. Rom.* II. 313 For he wes loverdsuyke, Heo ladden him to Warewyke,..Ther his heved wes of smyte.

lordwood ('lɔːdwʊd). [a rendering of *Xylon Effendi*, the name current in Cyprus.] = *Liquidambar orientalis* (see LIQUIDAMBAR 2).

1866 in *Treas. Bot.*

lordy, *int.* orig. *U.S.* = LORD *sb.* 6 c. Also *lordy me* (= lord help me).

1853 *Southern Lit. Messenger* Oct. 602/2 On the sofa..you sank down and bounded up and said Lordy! **1857** *Knickerbocker* L. 236 O Lordy me Sir! I'm so dreadful afeard you're both on you Dorrites! **1897** R. M. STUART *In Simpkinsville* 155 Lordy, but it all takes my breath away. **1926** S. ANDERSON *Let.* 25 Apr. in R. L. White *S. Anderson/G. Stein* (1972) 52 It was a beautiful story, beautifully done. Lordy but that man can write. **1928** *Sat. Even. Post* 12 May 20/3 But seven hundred dollars and his pocket piece back again! Phew! Lordy! **1959** N. MAILER *Advts. for Myself* (1961) 198 Well, Lordy-me..I could introduce you to a good many of us. **1968** *Melody Maker* 30 Nov. 25/7, I have..seen many blues groups and have yet to hear one shouting 'Lordy, Lordy, yes'. **1973** *Bulletin* (Sydney) 25 Aug. 44/2 Oh lordy, that buffet car. **1973** E. TAYLOR *Serpent under It* (1974) xiv. 209 Lordy, ma—if you pamper me like this you'll unfit me for ordinary existence. **1974** N. FREELING *Dressing of Diamond* 88 A kidnapping... And lordy, it's the child of a magistrate.

lore (lɔə(r)), *sb.*[1] Forms: α. 1 **lár, laar**, 2 **lar**, 2–3 **lare**. Also *north.* and *Sc.* 4–5 **lar**, 5 **layre**, 6 **layr**, 4–5, 9 **lare**, 5– **lair**. See also LEAR. β. 4–6 **loore**, 5 **loor**, 7 **loare**, 3– **lore**. [OE. *lár* str. fem. = OS. *lêra* (MDu. *le(e)re*, Du. *leer*), OHG. *lêra* (MHG. *lêre*, G. *lehre*):—OTeut. **laizâ*, f. root *lais-*: cf. LEARN *v.*]

1. The act of teaching; the condition of being taught; instruction, tuition, education. In particularized use: A piece of teaching or instruction; a lesson. Now *arch.* and *dial.* Phr. †***to set to lore***: to place under instruction, send to school. ***at, to the lair*** (Sc.): at or to school.

971 *Blickl. Hom.* 47 Ne sceolan þ a lareowas aȝimeleasian þa lare. *a* **1225** *Leg. Kath.* 116 Hire feder hefde iset hire earliche to lare. *a* **1300** *Cursor M.* 12416 Yeitt þe folk soght eft as ar, To sett iesu to werld lar. *c* **1375** *Sc. Leg. Saints* xl. (*Ninian*) 25 Wele entendand til his lare he wes al tyme. *c* **1380** WYCLIF *Serm.* Sel. Wks. I. 392 What kyn þingis ben writun ben writun to oure lore. **1387** TREVISA *Higden* (Rolls) VI. 83 Oswy bytook his douȝter to þe lore of Hilda. *a* **1413** HOCCLEVE *Compl. Soule* 294 Wks. (1897) III. p. lx, Placebo mvst go before, As doth the Crosse in the litel childes lore. *c* **1440** *York Myst.* xi. 181 A! lorde of lyffe, lere me my layre. *c* **1470** HENRYSON *Mor. Fab.* iv. (*Fox's Confess.*) v, Weill worth my father, that send me to the lair. **1502** ARNOLDE *Chron.* (1811) 207 Who wil not for shame a short tyme suffir lore and lerne. **1526** SKELTON *Magnyf.* 1980 Take this caytyfe to thy lore. **1667** MILTON *P.L.* II. 815 She finish'd, and the suttle Fiend his lore Soon learnd. **1771** *Antiq. Sarisb.* 6 Therein you may find many an excellent Lore that unto your Wives you may teach. **1798** COLERIDGE *Nightingale* 41 We have learnt A different lore. **1855** ROBINSON *Whitby Gloss.*, *Lare* or *Lear*, learning, instruction. **1866** NEALE *Sequences & Hymns* 59 In the Cross we found our pulpit, In the Seven great Words, our lore.

2. That which is taught; (a person's) doctrine or teaching. Applied chiefly to religious doctrine, but used also with reference to moral principles (e.g. ***virtue's lore***). Now *poet.* or *arch.*

c **950** *Lindisf. Gosp.* John vii. 16 Min laar ne is min ah ðæs seðe sende mec. *c* **1175** *Lamb. Hom.* 13 Gif ȝe cherrat from me ower heortam and to-brecað mine lare. *c* **1275** *Moral Ode* 129 (Jesus Coll. MS.) Bilef sunne hwil þu myht, and do bi godes lore. *c* **1386** CHAUCER *Prol.* 527 But cristes loore, and hise Apostles twelue, He taughte, and first he folwed it hym selue. *c* **1420** LYDG. *Assembly of Gods* 2074 Walke ye the way of Vertu hys loore. **1483** CAXTON *G. de la Tour* Prol. A ij, They shal remembre somme good ensample or some good

lore. **1551** CROWLEY *Pleas. & Pain* 591 Directyng their wayes by Gooddis holy lore. **1567** *Gude & Godlie Ball.* (S.T.S.) 13 From unbeleue, and Lollardis lair. **1571** T. FORTESCUE *Forests* 98 He began first to honour the Christians, permitting them to live after their loore and order. **1590** SPENSER *F.Q.* I. i. 5 So pure and innocent.. She was in life and every vertuous lore. **1622** MASSINGER *Virg. Mart.* II. ii, So deepe a blow To the Religion here and Pagan lore As this. **1671** MILTON *P.R.* I. 483 Most men admire Vertue, who follow not her lore. **1805** SCOTT *Last Minstr.* I. viii, Can piety the discord heal..Can Christian lore, can patriot zeal, Can love of blessed charity? **1838** TRENCH *Honor Neale* 39 in *Sabbation*, etc. 23 Where the pure doctrine and the lore of Christ Was truly taught.

†**b.** *pl.* Doctrines, precepts, ordinances. *Obs.*

971 *Blickl. Hom.* 35 We sceolan..healdan..þa lara þara feower godspellera. *a* **1300** *Cursor M.* 21346 þir four [ewangelistes] for us ai prai to dright þat we mai folu þair lares right. *c* **1380** WYCLIF *Wks.* (1880) 303 Takynge hede to spiritis of errour & to loris of fendis. **1551** ROBINSON tr. *More's Utop.* II. (1895) 211 We haue taken vpon vs to shewe and declare theyr lores and ordenaunces. **1580** H. GIFFORD *Gilloflowers* (1875) 146 His lores (quoth will) are very sowre, His precepts are but colde.

†**c.** A form of doctrine, a creed, religion. *Obs.*

a **1225** *Leg. Kath.* 1011 Leaf þi lease wit..& liht to ure lare. *c* **1330** *Owayn Miles* (1837) 22 Of man and wimen that ther lay That crid allas and waileway For her wicked lore. **14..** *Sir Beues* 1187 (MS. C.), Y haue leuyd on false lore. **1560** DAUS tr. *Sleidane's Comm.* 190 If we should forsake this fayth, and fal vnto their lore. *c* **1550** *Exam. W. Thorpe* in Foxe *A. & M.* (1583) I. 533 To mayntayne theyr sect & lore agaynst the ordinaunce of holy Church.

†**d.** Rule of behaviour. *Obs.*

13.. *E.E. Allit. P.* A. 236 Enclynande lowe in wommon lore. *c* **1485** *Digby Myst.* (1882) II. 110 By my trowth than be ye changyd to a new lore. A seruand ye are and that a good.

3. Advice, counsel; instruction, command, order.

a **1300** *K. Horn* 472, I schal..do, lemman, þi lore [*v.r.* do after þi lore]. *c* **1320** *Sir Tristr.* 258 And bad al schuld be boun And to his lores liþe. *c* **1400** *Rom. Rose* 5153 For alle yede out an oon ere That in that other she dide lere; Fully on me she lost hir lore. **14..** *Sir Beues* 1386 (MS. M.), I wyll ffor-sake hym nevure the more For none oþure kynges lore. *c* **1530** H. RHODES *Bk. Nurture* 140 in *Babees Bk.*, Pare not thy nayles, fyle not the cloth; see thou obserue this lore. **1556** ABP. PARKER *Ps.* G iv, We will renounce that they pronounce, their loores as stately lordes. **1667** MILTON *P.L.* IX. 1128 Understanding rul'd not, and the Will Heard not her lore.

†**4.** Used vaguely, esp. in alliterative poetry, for: Something that is spoken; information; story; language. *Obs.*

c **1350** *Will. Palerne* 2070 Mi ladi for ani lore lengeþ in þis cite ȝut. *a* **1400-50** *Alexander* 523 If ȝow likis of þis lare to lesten any forthire. *Ibid.* 5652 Sum in latens lare sum langage of grece. *c* **1420** *Chron. Vilod.* st. 1013, Y nyl not þerof speke now to ȝow no more.

5. That which is learned; learning, scholarship, erudition. Now only *arch.* and *Sc.* (in the form *lair*, LEAR). Also, in recent use, applied (with a colouring derived from contexts like quot. 1766) to the body of traditional facts, anecdotes, or beliefs relating to some particular subject; chiefly with attributive sb., as ***animal, bird, fairy, plant lore.***

In the *Gentl. Mag.* for June, 1830, p. 503, a correspondent suggested that Eng. compounds of *lore* should be substituted for the names of sciences in *-ology*: e.g. *birdlore* for ornithology, *earthlore* for geology, *starlore* for astronomy, etc. The suggestion was never adopted, though some few words out of the long list of those proposed are occasionally used, not as names of sciences, but in the sense above explained. In German, several compounds of the equivalent *lehre* are in regular use as names of sciences or departments of study: e.g. *sprachlehre* (= speech-lore) grammar. Cf. FOLKLORE.

a **1225** *Ancr. R.* 134 Of dumbe bestes & of dumbe fueles leorneð wisdom & lore. *a* **1225** *Leg. Kath.* 939 þes is al þe lare þat ich nu leorni [L. *hic est philosophia mea*]. *c* **1350** *Will. Palerne* 2917 þat comli quen hade a prest a konyng man of lore. **1398** TREVISA *Barth. De P.R.* XVIII. xliv. (1495) 805 Elephauntes kepeth loore and dysciplyne of the sterres and in wexyng of the mone go to ryuers. *c* **1400** *Cursor M.* 29400 (Cott. Galba) A maister of lare may bete a clerk bot noght ouer sare. *c* **1460** *Towneley Myst.* IX. 40 My counsellars so wyse of lare. **1513** DOUGLAS *Æneis* XII. vii. 34 [He] Had lever haue knawin the sciens and the layr, The mycht and fors of strengthy herbys fyne. **1663** BUTLER *Hud.* I. ii. 223 Learn'd he was in Med'c'nal Lore. **1762** FALCONER *Shipwr.* III. 150 Unskill'd in Grecian or in Roman lore. **1766** GOLDSM. *Hermit* xiii, Skill'd in legendary lore. **1780-1808** J. MAYNE *Siller Gun* III. xxvi. (1836) 72 Nor is it only classic lair, Mere Greek and Latin, and nae mair. **1812** MOORE *Intercepted Lett.* viii. 35 Thou know'st the time, thou man of lore! It takes to chalk a ball-room floor. **1827** KEBLE *Chr. Y., 2nd Sund. Advent* iv. 8 For all the light of sacred lore. **1857** HUGHES *Tom Brown* II. iii. (1871) 256 Arthur was initiated into the lore of bird's eggs. **1901** *Expositor* Nov. 375 The Rabbis were the sole depositaries of sacred lore.

†**b.** A body of knowledge, a science. *Obs.*

c **1290** *S. Eng. Leg.* I. 438/235 Arsmetrike is alore þat of figurs al is. **1500-20** DUNBAR *Poems* lxv. 4 Off euerie study, lair, or discipline. **1551** RECORDE *Pathw. Knowl.* Pref., The Shippes on the sea with Saile and with Ore, were firste founde, and styll made, by Geometries lore.

6. *Comb.*: †**lore-child**, a scholar, apprentice; †**lore-father**, a master in learning; †**lore-master** = *lore-father*. Also LORESPELL.

a **1300** *Cursor M.* 27237 *Lare child wit-vten buxumnes. *c* **1200** ORMIN 16625 þatt tu..o Godess hallfe arrt sennd *Larfaderr her to manne. *a* **1340** HAMPOLE *Psalter* xlv. 7 Apostils and haly larefadirs. **1790** GROSE *Prov. Gloss.* (ed. 2) Suppl., *Larefather*, a schoolmaster or instructor. North. *c* **1425** *Cursor M.* 19679 (Trin.) His *lore maistir I shal be.

†**lore**, *sb.*² *Obs.* Also 3 **loar.** [OE. *lor*, ? neut. f. **lor-, lur-*, wk. grade of Teut. root **leus-*: see LEESE *v.*¹ Cf. LOSS *sb.*] Loss, destruction.

971 *Blickl. Hom.* 69 To hwon sceolde þeos smyrenes þus beon to lore ȝedon? *c* **1250** *Gen. & Ex.* 177 And him to pine, and loar her, God made wirme and wilde der. *c* **1330** *Spec. Gy Warw.* 187 Hij sholen haue euere among Lore of catel and seknesse. *c* **1430** *Syr Gener.* (Roxb.) 5457 That othre were grete shame and lore, I shal tel you wel wher-fore. **14..** *Stacyons of Rome* 642 in *Pol. Rel. & L. Poems* (1866) 137 The thyrde parte of alle þy lore.

lore (lɔə(r)), *sb.*³ [ad. L. *lōrum* strap, thong; in sense 2 cf. F. *lore.*]

†**1.** A strap, thong, rein. *Obs. rare.*

1621 G. SANDYS *Ovid's Met.* XIII. Notes (1632) 445 [tr. *Iliad* XVIII. 479–80] First forg'd a strong and ample shield..: round about he threw Three radiant rings (a siluer lore behind). **1636** R. GRIFFIN in *Ann. Dubrensia* (1877) 52 Stately coursers..champe their scorned Lores, Trample the groaning earth.

2. *Nat. Hist.* A strap-like appendage or surface in certain animals: **a.** in insects a horny appendage in the mouth of certain Hymenoptera, upon which the *mentum* or chin is carried (also in quasi-L. form lora); **b.** in birds, a space between the eye and the side of the superior mandible, sometimes naked; **c.** in snakes, a region between the eye and the nostril, sometimes covered by certain plates called *lorals.*

1826 KIRBY & SP. *Entomol.* III. 367 Lora (the *Lora*), a corneous angular machine observable in the mouth of some insects, upon the intermediate angle of which the Mentum sits. **1828** FLEMING *Hist. Brit. Anim.* 132 Horned Grebe.. Lores crimson. **1837-43** YARRELL *Brit. Birds* I. 97 The black hairs on the lore, or space between the base of the beak and the eye. **1890** COUES *Field & Gen. Ornithol.* II. 145 The next commonest [form of head-nakedness] is definite bareness of the lores, as in all herons and grebes.

lore, variant of LAURE *Obs.*, LOOR *dial.*

a **1400-50** *Alexander* 4972 Like oliues out of lebany, & lores so grene.

lore, str. pa. t. and pple. of LEESE *v.*¹

loreal (ˈlɔərɪəl), *a.* and *sb. Zool.* [? irreg. f. LORE *sb.*³ + -AL¹.] = LORAL.

1849 J. E. GRAY *Catal. Specim. Snakes Brit. Mus.* 35 The frontal shields two pairs, small; loreal shield none. **1858** GÜNTHER *Catal. Colubrine Snakes Brit. Mus.* 19 *Homalosoma*..one loreal, one anterior, two posterior oculars. **1878** MACALISTER *Morphol. Vertebr. Anim.* 137 *Dryadinæ*..loreal often absent.

lored (ˈlɔərd), *a. rare.* [f. LORE *sb.*¹ + -ED².] Learned; stored with knowledge.

a **1839** GALT *Demon of Destiny* III. (1840) 25 The lored elder, half evasive, then Replied.

lorein(e, variant of LORAIN *Obs.*

†**lorel**, *sb.* and *a. Obs.* Also 4–6 -elle, 4 7 -ell, 6–7 lorrel(l. [ME. *lorel*, f. *loren*, pa. pple. of LEESE *v.*, as LOSEL from the variant *losen.*]

A. *sb.* A worthless person, rogue, blackguard; = LOSEL. In 16th c. often opposed to *lord.*

1362 LANGL. *P. Pl.* A. VIII. 123 'Lewede lorel!' quod he, 'luite lokestou on the bible'. *c* **1374** CHAUCER *Boeth.* I. pr. iv. 13 (Camb. MS.), I se þat euery lorel shapith hym to fynde owt newe fraudes. *c* **1380** WYCLIF *Wks.* (1880) 191 Herefore ben many proude & lecherous lorelis founden & dowid wiþ temperal & worldly lordischipis. *c* **1440** *Gesta Rom.* x. 28 (Harl. MS.) If þou be so bold to telle of me, I shall breke þine hed; what lorell art thou! **1509** BARCLAY *Shyp of Folys* (1874) II. 320 To lorellys often the lorde moste lowt. **1522** MORE *De quat. Noviss.* Wks. 84/1 While the lorel playth the lord in a stage playe. *a* **1529** SKELTON *Agst. Garnesche* iii. 14, I am laureate, I am no lorelle. **1530** PALSGR. 659, I play the lorell or the loyterer. **1559** *Mirr. Mag., Dk. York* xx. 61 b, That cruell Clifford, lord, nay Lorell wilde. **1579** SPENSER *Sheph. Cal.* July 93 Thou speakes lyke a lewde lorrell. **1647** G. W. *Pluto's Progr. Gt. Brit.* 15 Thou talk'st like a Lorrell.

b. Cock Lorel. The name of the owner and captain of the boat containing jovial reprobates of all trades, in a humorous and sarcastic poem *Cocke Lorelles Bote* (printed by Wynkyn de Worde *c* 1515), partly imitating the *Shyp of Folys.* Afterwards used allusively with the force of 'rogue, reprobate'.

c **1515** *Cocke Lorell's B.* (1843) 4 Here is fyrst, Cocke Lorell the knyght. *c* **1545** *Doctour Double Ale* 390 in Hazl. *E.P.P.* (1866) III. 319. *a* **1577** GASCOIGNE *Fable of F. Geronimi* Wks. (1587) 206 A peece of Cocklorels Musicke.. such as I might be ashamed to publish in this company. **1577** FULKE *Confut. Purg.* 376 Then you shall not neede to rowe in Cockelaurels bote. **1581** J. BELL *Haddon's Answ. Osor.* 394 This clownish Cocklorrell therefore wandring abroad over hilles and dales. **1621** B. JONSON *Gipsies Metam.* Wks. 1640 II. 70 Cock-Lorrell would needs have the Devill his guest.

B. *adj.* Good-for-nothing; = LOSEL B.

1590 LODGE *Euphues' Gold. Leg.* (1592) E 2, Ah Lorrell lad, what makes thee Herry loue? **1614** J. DAVIES (Heref.) *Eclogue* 83 An Heydeguies, Pipt by Tom-piper, or a Lorrel-lad.

Hence †ˈ**lorelship**, rascality, lewdness.

c **1380** WYCLIF *Wks.* (1880) 156 þei wasten pore mennus liflode in hordom & glotonye & lernen lorelschipe.

Lorelei (ˈlɔərəlaɪ). Also 9 **Loreley.** [Name of a rock on the Rhine near Coblenz.] In German legend, a beautiful woman with long blonde hair who sat on the Lorelei rock and with her fine singing distracted boatmen, so that they drowned when their ships foundered on the rock. Also *transf.* Cf. SIREN *sb.* 2.

1878 *Chambers's Encycl.* VIII. 745/1 The Loreley of the Rhine is only a river-siren, though a more exquisite enchantress than ever Greek fancy conceived. **1910** 'O. HENRY' *Strictly Business* (1917) i. 10 Instead of being motoring bacchanalians and diamond-hungry *loreleis* they are businesslike folk. **1927** N. WAINWRIGHT tr. *Dekobra's Madonna of Sleeping Cars* ix. 125 My little Lorelei had unfastened her hair, which fell in a blonde cascade. **1965** 'A. GILBERT' *Passenger to Nowhere* iii. 42 Probably thought you were the original Lorelei. **1971** R. SALE *Man who raised Hell* III. vii. 249 She..evolved into the most devastating Lorelei of Mayfair, with an utterly intriguing contempt for the men she could so easily fetter.

loreless (ˈlɔəlɪs), *a. rare.* [f. LORE *sb.*¹ + -LESS.] Without learning or knowledge.

a **1300** *Five Evil Things* in *E.E.P.* (1862) 161 Bissop lorles, Kyng redeles. *a* **1327** in *Pol. Songs* (Camden) 254 For niht is liht, the lond is loreles. **1836** *Tait's Mag.* III. 447 The poetry of his loreless soul.

†**lorelly**, *adv. Obs.* [f. LOREL + -LY².] Like a 'lorel'.

c **1450** *Bk. Curtasye* 135 in *Babees Bk.*, Ne spit not lorely, for no kyn mede, Be-fore no mon of god for drede.

lorem, variant of LORAIN *Obs.*

loren, pa. pple. of LEESE *v.*¹

†**lorendriver.** *Obs. rare*⁻¹. [ad. Du. *lorrendraaier* smuggler.] A smuggler.

1649 in *Rec. Convent. Roy. Burghs* (1878) III. 348 Enterloperis, lorendryvers, staplebreakers.

Lorentz (ləˈrɛnts). *Physics.* The name of H. A. *Lorentz* (1853–1928), Dutch physicist, used *attrib.* to designate various concepts and phenomena described by him, as **Lorentz (-FitzGerald) contraction** = *FitzGerald contraction*; so ***Lorentz-contract*** vb. trans.; **Lorentz-covariant, -invariant** adjs., covariant, or invariant, under a Lorentz transformation; so ***Lorentz-covariance***; **Lorentz transformation** [named in Fr. by H. Poincaré 1905, in *Compt. Rend.* CXL. 1505], the set of equations which in the special theory of relativity relate the space and time co-ordinates of one frame of reference to those of another moving rectilinearly with respect to the first; **Lorentz triplet**, a group of three spectral lines produced by the splitting of a single line with the frequency of the middle one by a magnetic field (the Zeeman effect, first interpreted by Lorentz).

¶ See also LORENZ.

1908 *Sci. Abstr.* A. XI. 687 The equations for moving bodies, when subjected to a Lorentz transformation, are converted into the corresponding equations for the transformed quantities. **1916** *Monthly Notices R. Astron. Soc.* LXXVII. 155 The well-known Lorentz-contraction. **1920** [see COVARIANT B]. **1922** A. D. UDDEN tr. *Bohr's Theory of Spectra* II. iii. 47 It follows immediately from this result according to the principle of correspondence that each fine structure component must be expected to split up into a normal Zeeman effect (Lorentz triplet). **1923** C. D. BROAD *Sci. Thought* iv. 135 The Lorentz-Fitzgerald Contraction, if taken as a physical fact, affects all kinds of matter equally. **1955** R. PEIERLS *Laws of Nature* vi. 126 When one first hears of this 'Lorentz contraction' it sounds most artificial and unreasonable. **1955** W. HEISENBERG in W. Pauli *Niels Bohr* 21 Such an interpretation..would destroy..just the decisive symmetry property of the theory of relativity, namely the Lorentz invariance, and it must therefore be considered inappropriate. **1955** W. PAULI *Ibid.* 35 Lorentz-invariant quantized field theories. **1955** J. LINDHARD *Ibid.* 189 The reason for this is that the field acting on an electron is Lorentz contracted. **1964** E. A. POWER *Introd. Quantum Electrodynamics* iii. 23 The former is the more deep and can be made explicitly Lorentz covariant. **1965** P. CAWS *Philos. of Sci.* xxii. 167 Einstein found the Lorentz transformations at hand when he needed them. **1970** G. K. WOODGATE *Elem. Atomic Struct.* viii. 147 This so-called Lorentz triplet of one π and two σ lines is characteristic of the 'normal' Zeeman effect in electric dipole radiation. **1970** *Nature* 17 Oct. 272/3 Measuring scales..are assumed to be Lorentz-contracted by a factor $(1 - \omega^2 r^2/c^2)^{1/2}$.

Lorenz (ləˈrɛnts). *Physics.* Also (erron.) Lorentz. The name of L. V. *Lorenz* (1829–91), Danish physicist, used *attrib.* and in the possessive to designate the ratio $k/\sigma T$ (k = thermal conductivity, σ = electrical conductivity, T = temperature), which has approximately the same value for many metallic elements over a wide range of temperatures.

1922 GLAZEBROOK *Dict. Appl. Physics* I. 459/2 They found that for seven pure metals..the value of Lorenz's constant $K/\lambda T$ was nearly the same over the range 18° to 100°C. **1966** C. R. TOTTLE *Sci. Engin. Materials* v. 122 The electron influence on the thermal conductivity of metals is normally far greater than the lattice contribution. When this is the case, the Lorentz constant holds reasonably well. **1966** PHILLIPS & WILLIAMS *Inorg. Chem.* II. xix. 23 On the free-electron theory [of metals] it is predicted that there should be a direct relation between the thermal, k, and electrical, σ, conductivities... The Lorenz number, $k/\sigma T$, has the theoretical value of $2{\cdot}45 \times 10^{-8}$ watt ohm deg⁻².

lorer, obs. form of LAUREL.

lorer, riming alteration of LOREL.
c **1400** *Laud Troy Bk.* 6891 With tene smot he that lorer, That he brast helme and his viser.

† **'loresman.** *Obs.* [f. *lores*, genitive of LORE *sb.*[1] + MAN *sb.*] A teacher, instructor.
1377 LANGL. *P. Pl.* B. XII. 183 The lewed..as his loresman leres hym bileueth and troweth. **1390** GOWER *Conf.* II. 161 The loresman of the Schepherdes. *c* **1394** *P. Pl. Crede* 290 Loke houȝ þis loresmen lordes betrayen.

† **'lorespell.** *Obs.* Forms: 1 lárspell, 2–3 larspel, 3 larspell, (3 lorspel(l, lærspel, larspæl), 4 lorespelle. [f. LORE *sb.*[1] + SPELL *sb.*] A sermon, instructive discourse.
c **1000** ÆLFRIC *Saints' Lives* (1881) I. 58 Se bisceop..þam folce sæde..lar-spell. *c* **1175** *Lamb. Hom.* 63 Bred on grikisce is Larspel to us fuliwis. *c* **1200** *Trin. Coll. Hom.* 143 þa iherde hie seggen þat ure drihte on his lar-spelle sede þat alle men sholden deað polien. *c* **1205** LAY. 12654 þa bi-gon he lar-spæl & of gode spæc swide wel. **13..** *Minor Poems fr. Vernon MS.* xxxvii. 124 þreo þinges þer beþ..Seide me þe prest in his lore-spelle For whom I ouȝte loue Ihesu.

lorestinus, obs. form of LAURUSTINUS.
1664 S. BLAKE *Compl. Gard. Pract.* 81.

‖ **lorette** (lɒ'rɛt). *slang.* [Fr.] A courtesan of a class which at one time had its headquarters in the vicinity of the Church of Notre Dame de Lorette in Paris. Hence **lorettism** (lə'rɛtɪz(ə)m), the condition of life of the lorettes of Paris.
1862 *Sat. Rev.* 1 Feb. 122/2 No doubt Mr. Coleridge was quite right in saying that Lorettism culminated in Miss Rogers, alias Willoughby. **1865** *Pall Mall G.* 9 Sept. 9/2 The brilliant ball given by the aristocracy of the Parisian *lorettes*—for even lorettism has its aristocracy.

Lorettine (lə'rɛtaɪn, -iːn). [f. *Loretto*, name of a town in Italy + -INE.] A nun of any order of Our Lady of Loretto.
In recent Dicts.

† **lorey.** *Obs.* Also lory(e, lorray, lorre. [Of unknown origin; prob. AF. Cf. *lete lory* s.v. LETE.] A dish in ancient cookery.
14.. *Burlesque Poem* in *Relig. Ant.* I. 81 Ther was pestells in porres, and laduls in lorres. **14..** *Nom.* in Wr.-Wülcker 740/36 *Hoc lattum*, lorray. *c* **1430** *Two Cookery-bks.* 25 Lorey de Boolas. Take Bolas, and seþe hem a lytil [etc.].

loreyn, variant of LORAIN *Obs.*

‖ **lorgnette** (lɔː'njɛt, lɔrɲjɛt). [Fr., f. *lorgner* to squint: see -ETTE.] **a.** A pair of eye-glasses held in the hand, usually by a long metal, ivory, or tortoise-shell handle. **b.** An opera-glass.
[**1776** *Monthly Rev.* LIII. 536 Concerning Achromatic spying Glasses... We have thus translated the word *Lorgnettes*.] **1803** *Lett. Miss Riversdale* III. 320 Mr. Drummore moved on..with his lorgnette to his eye, scrutinising every dish. **1820** HOGG in *Blackw. Mag.* VI. 392 When eyes meet eyes, what need of Lorgnette? **1859** G. A. SALA *Twice round Clock* 253 Surveyed, through powerful-lensed lorgnettes. **1882** SERJT. BALLANTINE *Exper.* vii. 72 The court was crowded with ladies..furnished with lorgnettes. **1952** H. INNES *Campbell's Kingdom* 75 To my astonishment she quizzed me through a gold lorgnette as I entered the room. **1970** V. CANNING *Great Affair* vi. 104 My aunt..favoured Edwardian dress.., feathered hats, lorgnettes, [etc.].
attrib. **1873** BROWNING *Red Cott. Nt.-cap* 982 Lace gets more homage than from *lorgnette*-stare.
Hence **lor'gnetted** *a.*, furnished with lorgnettes.
1860 *All Year Round* No. 52. 34 Down the staircase came the..crinolined, lorgnetted, opera-cloaked..throng.

‖ **lorgnon** (lɔrɲɔ̃). [Fr.] **a.** A single or double eye-glass; a lorgnette. **b.** An opera-glass.
1846 MRS. BROWNING *Lett.* (1899) I. 422 On the glass of his own opera-lorgnon. **1848** THACKERAY *Van. Fair* xxix, The General..took up his Opera-glass—the double-barrelled lorgnon was not invented in those days. **1898** *Century Mag.* Jan. 333/2 Several times the lorgnons of the house had veered around.

lori, variant of LORIS.

loric ('lɒrɪk). *rare.* [ad. L. *lōrīca* (see next).] A corselet or cuirass.
1855 BROWNING *Protus* 4 Each with..loose-thonged vest, Loric and low-browed Gorgon on the breast.

‖ **lorica** (lə'raɪkə). [L. *lōrīca*, f. *lōrum* strap.]
1. *Rom. Antiq.* A cuirass or corslet of leather.
1706 PHILLIPS (ed. Kersey), *Lorica*, a Coat of Mail, a piece of Armour worn in old Times. **1797** *Encycl. Brit.* (ed. 3) X. 295 The Roman lorica was made like a shirt. **1840** FOSBROOKE *Encycl. Antiq.* 858 At the time of Trajan, the lorica was shortened, being cut straight round above the hips.
†**2.** The coping or protecting head of a wall.
1706 PHILLIPS (ed. Kersey), *Lorica*,..the Coping or Head of a Wall, made to cast off the Rain.
3. *Old Chem.* A kind of lute or paste with which vessels were coated before being subjected to heat.
1753 CHAMBERS *Cycl. Supp.*, *Lorica*, a name given..to a peculiar lute made for the coating over vessels, which are to bear a very vehement fire. **1855** in OGILVIE, Suppl.
4. *Zool.* The protective case or sheath of some infusorians and rotifers; also applied to the carapace of crustaceans.
1856–8 W. CLARK *Van der Hoeven's Zool.* I. 46 Animalcules enclosed in a membranous lorica or calcareous test. **1870** NICHOLSON *Man. Zool.* I. 301 *Lorica*, the protective case with which certain *Infusoria* are provided. **1896** HARTOG *Rotifers* (Camb. Nat. Hist.) 205 The cuticle..in the Loricata firm and of definite shape, constituting a *lorica*.
5. *Bot.* The integument or hard external casing of vegetable seeds.
1839 LINDLEY *Introd. Bot.* (ed. 3) 244 The *testa*, called also *lorica* by Mirbel.

loricarian (lɒrɪ'kɛərɪən), *a.* and *sb.* [f. mod.L. *Lōricāria* name of the typical genus (f. LORICA) + -AN.] Belonging to the *Loricariidæ*, a family of freshwater fishes of tropical America, which have the head and body cuirassed or loricated; *sb.* a fish of this family. Also **lori'carioid** *a.* and *sb.*
In mod. Dicts.

loricate ('lɒrɪkeɪt), *a.* and *sb.* *Zool.* [ad. L. *lōrīcāt-us*, f. LORICA: see -ATE[2].]
A. *adj.* Covered with 'armour' or adjoining plates or scales; having a lorica.
1826 KIRBY & SP. *Entomol.* IV. 347 Loricate (*Loricatum*). When the disk of the thigh appears covered with a double series of oblique scales like a coat of mail. **1843** OWEN *Lect. Invertebr. Anim.* I. 34 The loricate genera are *Noteus*, *Anuræa* [etc.]. **1870** ROLLESTON *Anim. Life* 33 In the loricate [reptiles] a neurocentral suture is permanent.
B. *sb. pl.* [repr. mod.L. *Loricati* or *Loricata*.] **a.** A small group of edentate mammals, including the pangolin and the armadillo. **b.** A group of reptiles comprising the alligators, crocodiles, and gavials. **c.** A group of infusorians protected by a test or shell.
1855 OGILVIE, Suppl., *Loricata*, *Loricates*, an order of reptiles... 2. A group of polygastric animalcules. **1877** DAWSON *Orig. World* xv. 338 Far in advance of any modern reptiles even of the order of Loricates.

loricate ('lɒrɪkeɪt), *v.* [f. L. *lōrīcāt-*, ppl. stem of *lōrīcāre*, f. LORICA.] *trans.* To enclose in or cover with a protective coating.
1623 COCKERAM, *Loricate*, to arme one with a coat of defence. **1691** RAY *Creation* II. (1692) 39 Therefore hath Nature loricated or plaistred over the sides of the fore-mentioned Hole with Ear-wax. **1753** CHAMBERS *Cycl. Supp.* s.v. *Lorication*, When vessels are exposed to a fire too strong for their structure..they crack and burst; for the preventing of which the operator has recourse to this method of coating or loricating his vessels. **1818** in TODD.

loricated ('lɒrɪkeɪtɪd), *a.* [Formed as LORICATE *a.* + -ED[1].] Protected by a covering of plates or scales, or of other matter; armed with a lorica; *Zool.* = LORICATE *a.*
1623 COCKERAM II. A Þij b, Armed with a coate of defence. *Loricated.* **1698** FRYER *Acc. E. India & P.* 7 The Bark of an Ash colour, loricated. **1795** SMITH in *Phil. Trans.* LXXXV. 268 The imbricated or loricated appearance of the scales which cover part of the sclerotic coat of the eye. **1834** PLANCHÉ *Brit. Costume* 17 Three loricated bands with three commanders wearing golden torques. **1871** HUXLEY *Anat. Vert. Anim.* i. 44 In the *Mammalia* the development of a dermal exoskeleton is exceptional, and occurs only in the loricated *Edentata*. **1875** BLAKE *Zool.* 52 The dermal bony armour of the Armadillos like that of loricated Saurians. **1884** *Q. Jrnl. Microsc. Sci.* July 336 Each of these groups is sub-divided into a loricated and an il-loricated family.

lorication (lɒrɪ'keɪʃən). [f. LORICATE *v.*: see -ATION.] **a.** The action of loricating (see quots.). **b.** *concr.* A defensive covering or casing.
a **1706** EVELYN *Sylva* (1776) 314 Cones..with pretty broad thick scales..and the entire lorication smoother couched than those of the Fir-kind. **1706** PHILLIPS (ed. Kersey), *Lorication*, a fencing with a Coat of Mail, a harnessing; in Masonry, the filling of Walls with Morter; in Chymistry, the covering of a Vessel call'd a Retort with Loam or Clay, before it is set over a naked fire. **1741** tr. *Cramer's Art Assaying Met.* 74 When the Vessels are exposed naked to the greatest Fire; it easily happens, that they burst... For the preventing of which, you must have Recourse to Lorication or Coating.

loricoid ('lɒrɪkɔɪd), *a.* [f. LORICA + -OID.] Pertaining to or resembling a lorica; loricated. Also applied to the fossil-footprints supposed to have been made by loricated animals.
In recent Dicts.

lorie, var. LORY.

lorification, erron. form of LORICATION.
1730–6 BAILEY (folio), *Lorification*, the covering a vessel, call'd a retort, with..clay, before it is set over a naked fire.

lorikeet (lɒrɪ'kiːt). Also 8 loriquet, loorequet, lorrykeet. [f. LORY + *-keet* in PARRAKEET.] A name for small brightly-coloured parrots of the Malay Archipelago, comprehending the genera *Charmosyna*, *Loriculus*, and *Coriphilus*.
1772–84 COOK *Voy.* (1790) I. 217 Loriquets, cockatoos, parrots. **1779** FORREST *Voy. N. Guinea* 66 He presented me with a Loorequet of beautiful plumage, mostly green and yellow. **1869** A. R. WALLACE *Malay Archip.* II. 42 The little lorikeet (*Charmosyna placentis*).

lorimer, loriner ('lɒrɪmə(r), 'lɒrɪnə(r)). Now *Hist.* Forms: *α.* 5 loryner, lorriner, 6– loriner; *β.* loyrymer, 5–6 lorymar, -er, 6 loremar, lorymere, lormener, (*Sc.*) loremair, lowriemeir, 3– lorimer. [a. OF. *loremier*, *lorenier* (F. *lormier*), f. *lorain* (see LORAIN). For the substitution of *m* for *n* cf. LATIMER.] A maker of bits and metal mountings for horses' bridles; also, a spurrier, and (generally) a maker of small iron ware and a worker in wrought-iron.
(The name persists only in the title of one of the London livery companies.)
[*c* **1225** GARLANDE in Wright *Voc.* 123 Lorimarii dicuntur a loris (seu loralibus) quæ faciunt.] *a* **1225** *Ancr. R.* 184 He is þi uile [*MS. T.* þat lorimers habben], & uileð awei al þi rust. **1415** in *York Myst.* Introd. 22 Sporiers..Lorymers. **14..** *Nom.* in Wr.-Wülcker 686/21 *Hic lorinarius*, a loryner. **1453** *Mem. Ripon* (Surtees) III. 161 Et de 6*d.* sol. loyrymer pro..emendale de les barres fenestrarum. **1469** *Mann. & Househ. Exp.* (Roxb.) 538 Item, my master paid to lorymer of London fore vj. brydille bittes..vij.*s.* ij.*d.* *a* **1500** *Voc.* in Wr.-Wülcker 593/33 *Lorimarius*, a sporyare, or a lormener. **1503** *Privy Purse Exp. Eliz. of York* (1830) 97 Item to Symond Warde..lorymere for v DD bittes at xiiijs. the DD, lxxs. **1536** LELAND *Itin.* IV. II. 186 b, Many Loriners that make Bittes. **1603** STOW *Surv. Lond.* 542 Lorimars, the warden and two persons. **1656** BLOUNT *Glossogr.*, *Lorimers*, is one of the Companies of London, that makes bits for horse bridles, spurs, and such like small iron work. **1833** J. HOLLAND *Manuf. Metal* II. 313 The manufacture of all the metallic parts of horse furniture was carried on..by artisans, incorporated under the denomination of loriners and spurriers. **1884** *Rep. Comm. Livery Comp. Lond.* III. 567 The Loriners of London appear first to have recorded their ordinances as a mystery in 1245. **1898** BESANT *Orange Girl* I. i, Alderman Paul Halliday, Citizen and Loriner.

lorimer: see LORYMER, obs. f. LARMIER.

lorin, pa. pple. of LEESE *v.*[1]

loriner, variant of LORIMER.

† **'loring**, *vbl. sb.*[1] *Obs.* [f. LORE *sb.*[1] + -ING[1].] Teaching, instruction.
1596 SPENSER *F.Q.* v. vii. 42 They..Her wisedome did admire, and hearkned to her loring.

loriot ('lɒrɪət). Also 7 loriote, lariot, lorion. [a. F. *loriot* (also *lorion* Cotgr.), a corruption (due to misapprehension of the prefixed article) of OF. *oriot*, altered form of *oriole* ORIOLE.] The Golden Oriole, *Oriolus galbula*.
1601 HOLLAND *Pliny* I. 287 The Witwall or Lariot..is all ouer yellow. *Ibid.* II. 628 A pale coloured bird called the Lariot. **1658** PHILLIPS, *Loriot*, A Bird called a Witwall, Woodpecker, or Greenfinch. **1676** COLES, *Lorion*, *-ot*, a Witwal, Yellow-peck, or Hickway. **1724** BAILEY, *Loriot*, a Bird, that being look'd upon, by one that has the Yellow Jaundice, cures the Person, and dies it self. **18..** R. H. STODDARD *Chinese Songs* Poems (1880) 231 The swallow and the loriot Are not so swift of wing.

loripede ('lɒrɪpiːd). *Conch.* Also -ped. [ad. L. *lōriped-*, *lōripēs*, lit. 'strap-footed', f. *lōrum* strap + *pēs* foot.
The L. word meant *fig.* a person of little endurance or resolve; so used (in pl. *loripedes*) by Jer. Taylor *Gold. Grove* Serm. Winter xiii. 165.]
A bivalve mollusc of the group *Conchifera*, now included in the genus *Lucina*; esp. *L. lactea*.
1837 *Partington's Brit. Cycl.*, *Nat. Hist.* III. 62 *Loripede*, a genus of molluscs. **1864** CRAIG Suppl., *Loriped*, a molluscan animal, having the foot prolonged into a kind of cylindrical cord.

loriquet, obs. form of LORIKEET.

loris ('lɔərɪs). Also *erron.* lori, lory. [a. F. *loris* (Buffon); said to be a. Du. †*loeris* booby, clown. Used as a mod.L. generic name (E. Geoffroy Saint-Hilaire 1796, in *Mag. Encycl.* I. 48).] **a.** A small arboreal primate of the genus so called, distinguished by grey or black fur, large eyes, and thin limbs, and found in Sri Lanka (Ceylon) and southern India; also called ***slender loris***. **b.** A larger primate of similar form but heavier build, belonging to the genus *Nycticebus* and found in south-east Asia; also called ***slow loris***.
1774 GOLDSM. *Nat. Hist.* II. 373 A little four-handed animal of the Island of Ceylon, which Mr. Buffon calls the *lori*. **1781** PENNANT *Hist. Quadrupeds* I. 213 Loris... Monkey with a produced dog-like visage. **1802** BINGLEY *Anim. Biog.* (1813) I. 101 This Loris is about the size of a small Cat. **1827** E. GRIFFITH tr. *Cuvier's Animal Kingdom* I. 229 The Loris, commonly, Lazy Monkeys. **1835** KIRBY *Hab. & Inst. Anim.* II. xxiv. 477 The lory, or sloth ape, so called from the excessive slowness of its movements. **1859** TENNENT *Ceylon* I. 133 The little loris, which..has acquired the name of the 'Ceylon Sloth'. **1861**, **1883** [see KUKANG]. **1891** FLOWER & LYDEKKER *Mammals* 692 The Gray Loris (*Nycticebus cinereus*). **1909** E. PROTHEROE *Handy Nat. Hist. Mammals* iii. 73 The Slender Loris is a small animal only eight or nine inches long. **1967** J. R. & P. H. NAPIER *Handbk. Living Primates* II. 206 The Slender Loris is not a particularly successful animal in captivity owing to delicacy and irascible temper. **1972** T. A. VAUGHAN *Mammalogy* vii. 119 Lorises occur in Africa south of the Sahara, in India, Ceylon, and South-east Asia.

lorisid (ˈlɔːrɪsɪd), *sb.* and *a.* [f. mod.L. family name *Lorisidæ*, f. generic name *Loris* (see above).]
A. *sb.* A member of the family Lorisidæ, which includes lorises, pottos, and, in certain classifications, galagos. **B.** *adj.* Of or pertaining to this family.
1969 *Nature* 22 Nov. 821/1 Lorisid primates. *Ibid.*, The only lorisids which live in open country today are some of the galagines of Africa. **1970** *Ibid.* 25 July 356/1 The talonids of tarsiids, plesiadapids and lorisids. **1972** *Ibid.* 24 Mar. 180/2 Unlike the condition of the symphysis in living tarsiers, lorisids or lemur..show distinct separation of the superior and inferior transverse tori.

lorisoid (ˈlɔːrɪsɔɪd), *sb.* and *a.* [f. mod.L. name of suborder *Lorisoidea*, f. generic name *Loris* (see above).] **A.** *sb.* A member of the suborder Lorisoidea, introduced by C. Tate Regan in 1930 and used in some recent classifications of primates. **B.** *adj.* Of or pertaining to this suborder.
1930 C. T. REGAN in *Ann. & Mag. Nat. Hist.* VI. 385 The continent formed by the union of Africa and South America ..was the original home of the Lemuroids and Lorisoids. *Ibid.* 387 In the Eocene there were in existence animals with many Lorisoid characters. **1953** W. C. O. HILL *Primates* I. 101 Their [*sc.* dwarf-lemurs'] general affinities are certainly more lemuroid than lorisoid. *Ibid.* 105 Lorisoids tend to possess more rounded heads, with shorter faces, than the average lemuroid. **1965** *Punch* 21 Apr. 580/1 Dr. Manley's studies on social behaviour and reproductive patterns in lorisoid primates have been extended to include the Angwantibo. **1970** *Nature* 25 July 355/2 Such diverse groups of primates as the omomyids, most lemuroids, lorisoids or the platyrrhines.

lork(e, obs. form of LURK.

lormery (ˈlɔːmərɪ). *Hist.* Also 5 **lormerie**, 6 **lormary**. [a. OF. *lormerie*, f. *lormier* LORIMER.] The small ironware produced by lorimers. Also, a place where such ironwork was made or sold.
[**1260** *Liber Custumarum* (Rolls) I. 78 Ces sount les purveaunces qe les forgeours de la lormerie de Londres ount purveu.] **1419** *Liber Albus* (Rolls) I. 231 Lormerie. **1583** *Rates Custom ho.* D ij, Lormary the c. contayning v. xx, xii.*l.* **1725** HEARNE *R. Brunne* Gloss. (1810) II. 613/2 In the Parish of North St. Michael's in Oxford..was an Alley, or Lane, call'd The Lormery, it being the Place where such sort of Iron works were sold for all Oxford. [**1899** *Cal. Let. Bk. A. Lond.* 32 The sum of £24 for saddles and lormery.]

lorn (lɔːn), *ppl. a.* [pa. pple. of LEESE *v.*[1]]
†**1.** Lost, perished, ruined; doomed to destruction. *Obs.*
For early instances of predicative use, see LEESE *v.*[1]
a **1300** *Cursor M.* 22080 Al þat birth þat þar es born be wick, and fals, and felun lorn. *a* **1400–50** *Alexander* 5 Sayntis, þat lete þer lifis be lorne for oure lordis sakc. **1513** DOUGLAS *Æneis* XII. vi. 9 O, stanch ȝour wraith for schame, or all is lorn! **1556** ABP. PARKER *Ps.* lxxxvii. Argt., Hierusalem most fortunate, To nurse both Iewe and gentile lorne. **1805** SCOTT *Last Minstr.* I. xxiii, If thou readest, thou art lorn! Better hadst thou ne'er been born!
2. Abandoned, left alone; bereft *of*; lonely, desolate, wretched; = FORLORN 4, 5.
c **1475** *Partenay* 3885 Raymound, out fro wit for wo almoste lorn. **1563** SACKVILLE *Mirr. Mag.* Induct. lxxvii, With gastly lookes as one in maner lorne. **1579** SPENSER *Sheph. Cal.* Jan. 62, I..am forlorne, (alas! why am I lorne?). **1607** *Schol. Disc. agst. Antichr.* I. i. 57 If any thing excuse Iehosophat or Hezechias for suffering the Idolatrous Temples..it was because they were lorne, forlorne. **1748** COLLINS *Ode Death Thomson* viii, Lorn Stream, whose sullen tide No sedge-crown'd Sisters now attend. ?**1793** COLERIDGE *Lines beautiful Spring* 18 The rustic..Whistling lorn ditties leans upon his crook. **1817** MOORE *Lalla R.* II. (1850) 66 That sky Hath nought beneath it half so lorn as I. **1820** KEATS *Hyperion* I. 118 Space starr'd, and lorn of light. *a* **1839** PRAED *Poems* (1864) II. 363 When lorn lovers sit and droop. **1876** T. HARDY *Ethelberta* (1890) 281 She might be despised by my lord's circle, and left lone and lorn.
Hence **ˈlornness**, forlornness.
1866 *Lond. Rev.* 28 Apr. 470/2 The very lornness of his condition won for him their tender consideration.

lorom, lorray, var. LORAIN, LOREY *Obs.*

Lorraine (lɒˈreɪn). The name of a province in NE. France used *attrib.* in *Lorraine cross* = *cross of Lorraine* (CROSS *sb.* 18). Also *cross Lorrain*(*e*).
1830 T. ROBSON *Brit. Herald* III. Gloss., *Cross patriarchal* or *double cross*, (French, *croix double*) composed of one piece in pale, and two transverse horizontal pieces... But French heralds form their cross patriarchal somewhat different, and often call it a *cross Lorrain*. **1894** GOUGH & PARKER *Gloss. Terms Heraldry* 173 It is often blazoned as a *cross Lorraine*. **1920** WEBSTER, Lorraine cross. **1970** *Guardian* 13 Nov. 1/1 Lorraine crosses, the symbol of the Gaullist Resistance.

Lorrainer (lɒˈreɪnə(r)). [f. LORRAINE + -ER[1].] A native or inhabitant of Lorraine. Also *attrib.* Cf. LOTHARINGIAN *sb.* and *a.*
1743 *Gentl. Mag.* Aug. 447/1 Of the Lorrainers..it is affirmed, that they are with Difficulty restrained from declaring in favour of their Sovereign. **1903** F. W. MAITLAND in *Cambr. Mod. Hist.* II. xvi. 574 The Lorrainers were not France. **1933** KIPLING *Souvenirs of France* ii. 58, I love that imperturbable Lorrainer [*sc.* Poincaré]. **1966** M. R. D. FOOT *SOE in France* vii. 163 He was one of three brothers, barons of Lorrainer origin, landed gentry of the Limousin.

lorre, variant of LAURE *Obs.*, laurel.
c **1420** *Anturs of Arth.* iii, Vnder a lorre þey lighte.

lorrei, lorrell(e, vars. LAURY, LOREL *Obs.*

lorrer, obs. form of LAUREL.

lorry (ˈlɒrɪ, ˈlʌrɪ), *sb.* Also 9 **lorrie, lurrie, larry, lurry**. [Of obscure etymology; cf. dial. *lurry* to pull, drag.]
1. a. A long flat wagon without sides running on four low wheels. Also, a truck or wagon used on railways or tramways.
1838 *Civil Engin. & Arch. Jrnl.* I. 115/1 There was a luggage lorry..between the engine and carriages for passengers. *Ibid.* 145/1 A luggage train was perceived..with three lurries attached to it. **1851** *Illustr. Catal. Gt. Exhib.* 256 Liverpool town float, lorrie and coal cart. **1855** MRS. GASKELL *North & S.* vii, Great loaded lurries blocked up the not over-wide thoroughfares. **1863** P. BARRY *Dockyard Econ.* 255 The plates are conveyed from the furnaces to the rolls on long iron trucks or lurries. The wheels of the lurrie run in grooves. **1879** JESSE FOTHERGILL *Probation* III. 179 Omnibuses, carts, and lorries were struggling in a 'lock' in the middle of the street. **1881** *Daily News* 6 Sept. 2/2 The time-honoured 'lorry,' or open cart, indigenous to Liverpool. **1882** OGILVIE, *Larry*, a coal truck on a railway;.. a lorry. **1900** *Engineering Mag.* XIX. 764/1 Greater interest ..now seems to center in the lorry, or automobile wagon for heavy duty.
b. A large motor vehicle for carrying goods, etc., by road. Also *attrib.*
1911 *Encycl. Brit.* XVIII. 927/2 (*caption*) Halley's van or lorry chassis. **1915** *Autocar Handbk.* (ed. 6) i. 11 Commercial motor vehicles, such as heavy motor lorries.. are not *specifically* dealt with. **1925** *Morris Owner's Manual* p. xiv (Advt.), Morris cars vans & lorries. **1930** *Amer. Speech* V. 274 American English has universally chosen *motor truck* and *truck* rather than *auto-truck* or the British *lorry*. **1955** *Times* 23 May 4/4 He spoke from a lorry on Waun Y Pound, a mountain top between Tredegar and Ebbw Vale. **1972** *Guinness Bk. Records* (ed. 19) 130/2 The world's largest lorry is the M-200 Lectra Haul built by Unit Rig and Equipment Co. of Fort Worth, Texas with a capacity of 200 tons.
2. *Mining.* A running bridge over a pit.
1883 GRESLEY *Gloss. Coal Mining*, *Lorry* (Yorkshire), a running bridge over a sinking pit top upon which the bowk is placed after it is brought up for emptying. *Ibid.*, *Lurry*,.. a movable platform on wheels, the top of which is made on a level with the bank or surface. It is run over the mouth of a pit-shaft for a bowk to be lowered down upon when reaching the pit top.
3. *Comb.*, as ***lorry driver, driving, load, -man, -wheel; lorry-borne*** adj.; **lorry-bus**, a lorry used as a vehicle for public transport; also **lorribus**; **lorry-hop** *v.*, to hitch-hike by lorry; so **lorry-hopping** *vbl. sb.*; **lorry-jump** *v.* = *lorry-hop* vb.; so **lorry-jumping** *vbl. sb.*; **lorry park**, an open space or lot reserved for the parking of lorries.
1937 B. H. L. HART *Europe in Arms* xxiv. 323 The inability of these temporarily *lorry-borne infantry to attack effectively after they had dismounted. **1943** *R.A.F. Jrnl.* Aug. 7 Our aircraft..have operated against..armoured formations and lorry-borne infantry. **1919** *Daily Mail* 12 June 4/4 In the welter of London's crowded streets we grasped at the relieving '*lorribus' (the converted Army lorry doing the duty as an emergency omnibus). **1963** *Economist* 23 Nov. 758/2 Ghana's ubiquitous lorry-buses, or mammywagons. **1926** *C.M.U.A. Jrnl.* Apr.–May 29 It sometimes happened that a *lorry driver, arriving at noon, was told to go away and return next morning, as railway trucks were being loaded. **1972** *Times* 30 Nov. 5/6 Lorry drivers will meet dockers' representatives to-morrow. **1937** D. L. SAYERS *Busman's Honeymoon* viii. 166 Odd jobs of *lorry-driving and taxi-work. **1975** J. WAINWRIGHT *Square Dance* 246 Shurrup, lad... Stick to lorry-driving, and learn. **1933** A. G. MACDONELL *England, their England* xvii. 286 He walked a bit from Alton, and then *lorry-hopped, in army fashion, as fas as..Alresford. **1947** *Penguin New Writing* XXI. 98 An ex-convict..who lorry-hops across England in order to escape the police. **1925** FRASER & GIBBONS *Soldier & Sailor Words* 147 **Lorry hopping* (or *jumping*), a familiar term at the Front for travelling by begging 'lifts' from passing transport vehicles. **1928** BLUNDEN *Undertones of War* 201 By luck or judgment in lorry-hopping..one reached Boulogne. **1931** *Times Lit. Suppl.* 12 Nov. 899/3 She 'hitch-hiked', the American equivalent for 'lorry-hopping'. **1947** L. HASTINGS *Dragons are Extra* v. 101 He ..*lorry-jumped his way back to his own battery. **1963** *Guardian* 6 Apr. 4/5 The moral dangers of young girls 'lorry jumping' or frequenting roadside cafés. **1928** C. T. BRUNNER *Probl. Motor Transport* vi. 101 The expense of railway transport,..could be reduced by packing the goods in containers..of a weight which would constitute a *lorry load. **1972** *Times* 30 Nov. 23/4 Mr John Peyton..has actively stimulated opposition to the present EEC proposals for standardizing lorry loads. **1888** *Pall Mall G.* 23 Jan. 10/2 A railway *lorryman. **1968** *Listener* 14 Mar. 335/1 Eight caravans..had been parked as a final gesture of despair in the middle of a Walsall Corporation *lorry park. **1971** *Daily Tel.* 13 Sept. 3/6 Recommendations..to replace traditional transport cafés with a network of guarded lorry parks. **1974** *Ibid.* 9 Mar. 2/5 The removal of guard dogs, closed circuit television and the £1 parking fee at a high security lorry park has led to a record number of lorries using it. **1880** *Daily News* 6 Oct. 6/4 A girl was blown under a *lorry wheel.

lorry (ˈlɒrɪ), *v.* [f. the sb.] *trans.* To transport or convey by means of a lorry or lorries. Hence **ˈlorried** *ppl. a.*
1920 *Blackw. Mag.* Jan. 125/1 They were 'lorried' to the Lys front. **1949** W. S. CHURCHILL *Second World War* II. II. xxiii. 416 Tanks..and artillery in front, and with lorried infantry in the centre. **1958** G. DONALDSON *Shetland Life under Earl Patrick* 61 Only since such calls [at individual ports] ceased have all goods for places on the Mainland been landed at Lerwick and then lorried to their destinations. **1975** *Daily Tel.* 9 Sept. 12/6 There will be in 1 British Corps, three lorried infantry battalions.

lorry, lorrykeet, vars. LAURY *Obs.*, LORIKEET.

lors (lɔːz), *int.* A vulgar corruption of LORD used as an exclamation. (Cf. *laws* s.v. LAW *int.*)
1860 GEO. ELIOT *Mill on Floss* II. 170 But, lors! I shouldn't know what to say to 'em. **1880** MRS. PARR *Adam & Eve* xiii. (1881) 65 'Lors' exclaimed Joan.

†**lorthew.** *Obs.* Forms: 2 **larþeow, -þeaw, -þeu, -þeau, -þaw**, 2–3 **larðew**, 3 **lorðeau, -ðeu, -ðew, -þeaw**. [repr. OE. **lárþéow* (f. *lár* teaching, LORE *sb.*[1] + *þéow* slave), presumed earlier form of *láréow* LAREW.] A teacher, preceptor, instructor.
c **1160** *Hatton Gosp.* John i. 38 Rabbi þæt ys ȝecweðen & ȝe-reaht larðeow [*c* 1000 lareow]. *c* **1175** *Lamb. Hom.* 117 He [þe biscop] godes budel is and to larþeawe iset þan leawede folke. *c* **1200** *Trin. Coll. Hom.* 7 þe lauerd sainte powel is heued lorðeau of alle holie chirechen. *a* **1250** *Prov. Ælfred* 105 in *O.E. Misc.* 108 þe mon þe on his youhþe yeorne leorneþ wit and wisdom..he may beon on elde wenliche lorþeu.

‖**lorum** (ˈlɔːrəm). *Nat. Hist.* Pl. lora (ˈlɔːrə). [L. *lōrum* = strap, thong.] = LORE *sb.*[3]
In mod. Dicts.

lory (ˈlɔːrɪ). Forms: 7 **lourey**, 8 **laurey, lowry**, 8–9 **loory, lury**, 9 **loeri, lorie, lowrie**, 8– **lory**. [a. Malay *lūrī*, dial. var. of *nūrī*, whence the synonym NORY. Cf. F. *lori* (Buffon).] A name applied to a number of parrot-like birds of brilliant plumage, chiefly bristle-tongued and belonging to the family *Loriinæ*, found in South-eastern Asia, the Asiatic Archipelago, and Australia. Cf. LOERIE.
1692 *Lond. Gaz.* No. 2811/4 An East-India Lourey, Paraquits, and several other outlandish Birds. **1704** tr. *Nieuhoff's Voy. E.-Indies* in *Churchill's Voy.* II. 357 The Lory Bird is a Bird as big as a Parrot, but of a much finer Colour. **1731** ALBIN *Nat. Hist. Birds* I. 13 The Laurey. **1751** G. EDWARDS *Nat. Hist. Birds* IV. 173 The Long-tailed Scarlet Lory... It differs principally from the three last foregoing Lories, in being smaller. *Ibid.* 174 The Lory-Parakeet. **1779** FORREST *Voy. N. Guinea* 112 From Saba and Sao are brought large red loories, also black ones. **1800** *Asiat. Ann. Reg.*, *Misc. Tracts* 208/2 The most remarkable birds to be seen in Amboyna are luries. **1810** SOUTHEY *Kehama* x. xix, 'Twas Camdeo riding on his lory, 'Twas the immortal Youth of Love. **1848** H. W. HAYGARTH *Recoll. Bush Life Austral.* xii. 139 The lorie, with his splendid livery of blue and green. **1850** CLUTTERBUCK *Port Phillip* iii. 40 The King Parrot is the most beautiful, and that called the Lowrie is, perhaps, the most docile. **1859** H. KINGSLEY *G. Hamlyn* xviii. (1894) 147 Flaming lories..fly whistling.. through the gloomy forest.

lory, loryel: see LORIS, LAUREL.

lorymer, obs. form of LARMIER.
a **1490** BOTONER *Itin.* (1778) 269 A resaunt lorymer. **1850** PARKER *Gloss. Archit.*, *Larmier, Lorymer*, the corona. **1877** F. G. LEE *Gloss. Liturg. Terms*, *Lorymer*.. 1. The eave of a house. 2. The slanting brow or coping of a wall, serving to throw off the rain. This term is not unfrequently found in churchwardens' accounts.

los, obs. f. LOSE, LOSS; and see LO *int.*[1]

losable, loseable (ˈluːzəb(ə)l), *a.* Also 7 **losable**. [f. LOSE *v.*[1] + -ABLE.] Capable of being lost.
1611 COTGR., *Perdable*, loosable; fit, or likelie, to be lost. **1647** TRAPP *Marrow Gd. Auth.* in *Comm. Ep.* 683 Grace in itself is losable. **1658** BAXTER *Saving Faith* vi. 49 There are many common gifts in man that are no more loseable then saving Grace. **1674** BOYLE *Tracts, Positive Nat. Cold* vii. 49, I heard him make inquiry,..Whether the frigorifick faculty of these Corpuscles be loosable or not? **1877** T. A. TROLLOPE *Life Pius IX*, II. III. v. 45 Those who might be supposed losable by it, are lost already.
Hence **ˈlosableness**.
1658 BAXTER *Saving Faith* vi. 49, I do not think..that the loosing of one, and not loosening, or not loosableness, of the other, will prove a specifick difference.

losane, losang(e, obs. forms of LOZENGE.

losanger, losaniour, variants of LOSENGER.

†**ˈlosard.** *Obs.* = LOSEL.
13.. *Coer de L.* 1864 Have ye no doutance Of all these English cowards, For they ne be but losards. *Ibid.* 1875 Now let come these French losards.

losce, loscion, obs. ff., LOSS, LOTION.

†**lose**, *sb.*[1] *Obs.* Forms: 3–5 (9 *arch.*) **los**, (4 **looz**), 4–5 **loes, loose**, 4–6 **loos, lose**, *Sc.* **loiss**, (5 **loce**, *Sc.* **loyse**, 6 *Sc.* **loze, loys**), 5–6 **loss(e**, *Sc.* **lois**. [a. OF. *los, loz, loos*:—L. *laudēs*, pl. of *laus* praise.] Praise; renown, fame. Also in neutral sense, (good or bad) reputation; *occas.* ill fame. ***out of lose***: to one's dispraise.
1297 R. GLOUC. (Rolls) 3917 þe kinges los so wyde sprong ynow..þat hor herte to him drou. *a* **1300** *Cursor M.* 8750 Of þis doom [of Solomon's] fer sprong þe loos. **1340** *Ayenb.* 26 Ypocrites þet..doþ manie penonces an guode principalliche uor þe los of þe wordle. **1387–8** T. USK *Test. Love* I. vi. (Skeat) l. 179 Yevynge me name of badde loos. **1390** GOWER *Conf.* I. 351 A Duc.. Which was a worthi kniht of los. *c* **1400** MAUNDEV. (1839) x. 89 In that time there weren 3 Heroudes, of gret Name and Loos for here crueltee. **14..** LYDG. *Flour of Curtesye* 234 Lest out of lose any word asterte In this

metre, to make it seme lame. *c* **1440** *Promp. Parv.* 313/2 Loos or bad name, *infamia*. **1456** SIR G. HAYE *Law Arms* (S.T.S.) 141 He did nocht his dedis of honour.. for hir sake, but for his awin los. *c* **1460** *Towneley Myst.* xxii. 202 Youre knyghtes of good lose. **1513** DOUGLAS *Æneis* XIII. iii. 51 O glory and renown of loys, in vayn. **1589** PUTTENHAM *Eng. Poesie* III. xix. (Arb.) 244 That thy loze, ne name may neuer dye. **1596** SPENSER *F.Q.* VI. xii. 12 Besides the losse of so much loos and fame. **1825** SCOTT *Talism.* vii, I am a belted knight, and come hither to acquire los and fame in this mortal life.

lose (lu:z), *sb.*[2] *slang.* [f. LOSE *v.*[1]] An instance of losing (a race). ***lose bet, game***, one in which the loser of the game wins the stakes.

1884 *Illustr. Lond. News* Nov. 410/3 The rate of pay recognised by the Jockey Club, which is five guineas for a 'win', and three guineas for a 'lose'. **1964** A. WYKES *Gambling* vi. 143 (*caption*) A 'lose' bet is that the shooter will throw a crap. **1971** *Jrnl. Gen. Psychol.* LXXXV. 268 High-risk bets are again more typical of the lose game.

lose (lu:z), *v.*[1] Forms: 1 losian, 2–3 losie(n, 5 *Sc.* loyse, 5–6 losse, *Sc.* lois(s, 5, *Sc.* 6- loss, 5–8 loose, 6 *Sc.* los, loce, (loase, 7 loze), 3- lose. *Pa. t.* 1 losode, -ade, 1–3 -ede, 4 *Sc.* losit, 4–6 loste, *Sc.* lossit, -yt, 6 *Sc.* loissit, loussit, (7 loosed, losed), 3- lost. *Pa. pple.* 1 (ȝe)losod, -ad, 3 ilosed, -et, 3–5 ilost, 4 losed, 4–5 i-, ylost(e, 4–6 loste, (*Sc.* losit, -yt, 5–6 loissit, lossit, -yt, 6 loist, loseit, 7 loissed), 3- lost. [OE. *losian*, f. *los* LOSS, used almost exclusively *intr.* (sense 1); sometimes with indirect obj. in dative, as *me losode hit* = I lost it. The transitive use, which occurs twice in ONorthumbrian and appears in general use early in 13th c., seems to have arisen partly from interchange of function between the indirect obj. and the subj. where these were not distinguishable by case-form (cf. LIKE *v.*, LOATHE *v.*), and partly from the perfect conjugated with *be* (OE. *hit is ȝelosod* = it is lost), which admits of being apprehended as passive. The later sense-development of the vb. has been influenced by the cognate LEESE *v.*, with which it became synonymous, and which it in the end superseded.

The regular mod. Eng. pronunciation repr. OE. *losian* would be (ləʊz); the standard Eng. pronunciation (lu:z) seems to be due to association with LOOSE *v.*, which in some contexts (e.g. *to loose hold*) closely approaches this vb. in meaning. Many dialects have the phoentic form normally descending from the OE. vb. The Sc. form *loss* is prob. evolved from the pa. t. and pa. pple. *lost*.]

†**1.** *intr.* To perish; also, to be lost or missing.

c **888** K. ÆLFRED *Boeth.* xxxi. §2 Swa swa seo beo sceal losian þon heo hwæt irringa stingð. *c* **897** —— *Gregory's Past.* xxx. 205 Ðætte nu foraldod is ðæt is forneah losad. *a* **1175** *Cott. Hom.* 245 Forþan þe ic imete mi sceap þe me losede. *c* **1175** *Lamb. Hom.* 117 Þenne losiað fele saulen. **13..** *E.E. Allit. P.* A. 907 Þer lyuez lyste may neuer lose.

†**2. a.** *trans.* To destroy, ruin, bring to destruction or perdition; to be the ruin of. *Obs.*

c **950** *Lindisf. Gosp.* Luke xvii. 27 And cuom þæt flod & losade *vel* spilde alle. **13..** *E.E. Allit. P.* B. 909 Alle þe londe with þise ledez we losen at-onez. *c* **1380** WYCLIF *Serm.* Sel. Wks. I. 49 Þe kyng.. sent his ostis and loste þese mansleeris. *c* **1440** *Jacob's Well* iii. 23 Þou schalt haue als manye peynes as þou hast loste soules! **1483** CAXTON *G. de la Tour* lxxxiv. G viij, The fyre sprang oute and loste his hand. **1538** BALE *God's Promises* II. (1744) 11 Lose hym not yet, Lorde, though he hath depely sworved. **1591** SYLVESTER *Du Bartas* I. iii. 845 Lest heat, wet, wind, should roste, or rot, or lose it. **1602** SHAKS. *Ham.* III. ii. 205 What to our selues in passion we propose, The passion ending, doth the purpose lose. **1628** tr. *Mathieu's Powerfull Favorite* 122 *marg.*, We ought not proudly to despise prodegies, this neglect lost Alexander.

b. To ruin in estimation. *rare.*

1605 SHAKS. *Lear* I. i. 236 Such a tongue, That I am glad I haue not, though not to haue it, Hath lost me in your liking. **1677** SEDLEY *Ant. & Cl.* v. i. Wks. (1766) 191 'Twas I that lost you in each Roman mind. **1882** J. C. MORISON *Macaulay* 44 His want of aspiration.. has lost him in the opinion of many readers.

c. *pass.* To be brought to destruction, ruin, or misery; to perish; to be killed; in a spiritual sense (of the soul), to be damned. Of a ship, its crew, passengers, or cargo: To perish at sea.

[*c* **897**: see 1.] *a* **1310** in Wright *Lyric P.* xxxvi. 99 Ichabbe be losed mony a day. *c* **1366** CHAUCER *A.B.C.* 152, I am wounded.. þat j am lost almost. *c* **1375** *Cursor M.* 6006 (Fairf.) Dede & loste was al þaire fe. *c* **1397** CHAUCER *Lack Stedf.* 7 Al is loste for lac of stedfastnesse. *c* **1470** HENRY *Wallace* v. 507, I trow nocht ȝeit at Wallace losyt be: Our clerkys sayis, he sall ger mony de. *a* **1533** LD. BERNERS *Huon* xxi. 63 Yf ye speke to hym ye are lost for euer. *a* **1533** —— *Gold. Bk. M. Aurel.* (1546) E vii b, To play at the tables and dice with suche as be lost and naught. **1604** E. G[RIMSTONE] *D'Acosta's Hist. Indies* v. i. 332 By this meanes God is dishonoured, and man lost in all parts by idolatry. **1610** SHAKS. *Temp.* I. i. 52 All lost, to prayers, to prayers, all lost. **1713** ADDISON *Cato* IV. i. 46 The Woman that Deliberates is lost. **1781** COWPER *Truth* 479 And is the soul indeed so lost! **1798** *Monthly Mag.* VI. 437 (Scotticisms) Poor man, he was *lost* in the river; drowned. **1817** SELWYN *Law Nisi Prius* (ed. 4) II. 921 The property insured was lost. **1861** J. A. ALEXANDER *Gosp. Jesus Christ* xiii. 182 You are not in danger of perdition, but are lost already. **1885** *Law Times Rep.* LIII. 60/2 The vessel.. sank in a short time, all hands being lost.

3. To incur the privation of (something that one possesses or has control of); to part with through negligence or misadventure; to be deprived of.

a. with obj. a material or immaterial possession, lands, goods, a right, quality, etc. †*occas.* with *away*, *up*, (? *U.S. rare*) *out*.

c **1205** LAY. 29159 Þus losede Bruttes al þas kine-londes. *c* **1330** R. BRUNNE *Chron.* (1810) 272 Þou losis þi dignite. **1427** *Waterf. Arch.* in *10th Rep. Hist. MSS. Comm.* App. v. 295 The accusere shal losse his fraunches for ever. *a* **1470** GREGORY in *Hist. Coll. Lond. Cit.* (Camden) 189 That same yere was the most pa[r]te of Normandy y-loste. **14..** *Childe of Bristowe* 402 in Hazl. *E.P.P.* I. 125 Thu has played atte dice,.. and lost up, sone, that thu had. *c* **1530** LD. BERNERS *Arth. Lyt. Bryt.* (1814) 6 He lost away and wasted.. his londes and goodes. **1632** LITHGOW *Trav.* II. 66 In all, the Christians loosed but eleuen Gallies. **1779** COWPER *Yearly Distress* 55 One talks.. of pigs that he has lost By maggots at the tail. **1869** H. BUSHNELL *New Life* viii. 110 The child brought up a thief gets an infinite power of cunning.. and loses out just as much in the power of true perception. **1878** S. WALPOLE *Hist. Eng.* II. 458 Sir Joseph Yorke told him that he would lose his place if he did not keep his temper.

b. with obj. a limb, a faculty, one's life, etc. ***to lose one's head***: see HEAD *sb.*[1] 56. ***to lose heart***: to become discouraged. ***to lose one's heart***: to fall in love. † ***to lose one's breath***: to die. ***to lose one's legs*** (slang): to get drunk. ***to lose one's nerve*** (NERVE *sb.* 10): to become scared, uneasy. ***to lose sleep over*** (or ***about, for***, etc., something): to worry about (something) (usu. in negative contexts).

c **1205** LAY. 25918 Hire lif heo losede sone. **13..** *E.E. Allit. P.* B. 586 If he has losed the lysten. **1432–50** tr. *Higden* (Rolls) VII. 315 Makynge a statute that whosoever toke a beste þer scholde lose oon eie. **1470–85** MALORY *Arthur* IV. ix. 130 Syr Arthur lost so moche blood that it was merueille he stode on his feet. **15..** in *Lett. Roy. & Illustr. Ladies* (1846) II. 4 She was like to have lost her mind. **1530** PALSGR. 429/2, I am spechelesse, as a sycke body is that hath lost the use of his speche. **1596** B. GRIFFIN *Fidessa* vi, Oh better were I loose ten thousand breaths, Than euer liue in such vnseene disgrace. **1597** BACON *Coulers Gd. & Evill* (Arb.) 152 As to a monoculos it is more to loose one eye, then to a man that hath two eyes. **1633** FORD *Broken H.* III. v, 'Tis long agone since first I lost my heart. **1671** MILTON *Samson* 914 Though sight be lost, Life yet hath many solaces. **1711** ADDISON *Spect.* No. 60 ¶4 In a little Time after he lost his Senses. **1744** OZELL tr. *Brantome's Sp. Rhodomontades* 186 As soon as They were dead, every one lost Heart, having lost their Chief Supports. **1749** LAVINGTON *Enthus. Methodists & Papists* II. vi. (1752) 46 A religious Nun, devoted to St. Xavier, famed for Skill in Music and a fine Voice, had her Voice lost by a Hoarsness for ten Years. **1770** *Gentl. Mag.* XL. 560 To express the Condition of an Honest Fellow and no Flincher under the Effects of Good Fellowship, he is said to.. [have] Lost his legs. **1804** G. ROSE *Diaries* (1860) II. 193 She.. rode to Southampton, where she lost some blood. **1842** TENNYSON *Edw. Gray* 3 And have you lost your heart? .. And are you married yet? **1852** MRS. STOWE *Uncle Tom's C.* xxvii. 253 She acquired an influence over the mind of the destitute child that she never lost. **1912** *Chambers's Jrnl.* Nov. 739/1 There's nothing here to lose one's nerve about. **1934** G. B. SHAW *Too True to be Good* III. 86 When I was wounded and lost my nerve for flying, I became an army chaplain. **1942** H. C. BAILEY *Dead Man's Shoes* iv. 19 'I'd like to know why you didn't tell me.' 'You told me not to lose any sleep over it.' **1944** 'N. SHUTE' *Pastoral* ii. 41 'I wasn't losing any sleep for them.'.. 'Those two have been at this for years.' **1959** [see CHANCER *sb.*]. **1959** N. MAILER *Advts. for Myself* (1961) 241 It's not the sort of thing I lose sleep over. **1967** J. PORTER *Dover & Unkindest Cut of All* x. 109 Dover hadn't lost any sleep over them... 'You can't win 'em all,' he used to say. **1971** *Guardian* 10 July 9/1 Stolid and conservative Midwesterners.. never lost much sleep over the Negroes' troubles. **1974** *Ibid.* 18 Mar. 6/5 Although increasing restrictions on immigration.. had been criticised .. it is doubtful whether the immigrants themselves have lost much sleep over them. **1975** *Times* 24 Feb. 14/7 You just have to get straight back on, or else you lose your nerve. The others are far more concerned with the loose horse than the girl lying face down in the dirt.

c. With obj. a person: To be deprived of (a relative, friend, servant, etc.) by death, by local separation, or by severance of the relationship. Also, in somewhat specific sense, of a commander, an army: To suffer loss of (men) by death, capture, wounds, etc. Of a medical man: To fail to preserve the life of (a patient). Also, to fail to give birth to (a live baby); to suffer a miscarriage of (a pregnancy), or the death of (a baby) soon after its birth (*colloq.*).

c **1205** LAY. 5704 Heo loseden monie þusend godere monnen. *c* **1386** CHAUCER *Knt.'s T.* 78 We losten alle oure housbondes at that toun. *c* **1460** *Towneley Myst.* v. 48 Why shuld I apon a day lovse both my sonnes? **1530** PALSGR. 749/2 The folysshe gyrle toke on for thought as if she had loste her father she coulde have done no more. **1722** DE FOE *Moll Flanders* (1840) 117 The apprehensions of losing such a friend. **1780** *Westm. Mag.* VIII. 249 The Resolution had the good luck to come up with the Prothée.. and took her without losing a man. **1842** BROWNING *Waring* I. iv, How much I loved him, I find out now I've lost him. **1847** TENNYSON *Princess* I. 256 When we came where lies the child We lost in other years. **1880** WHEELER *Short Hist. India* 604 The English had lost more than 2,400 officers and men. **1882** S. WELLS *Ovar. & Uterine Tumours* 185 He [McDowell] lost only the last of his first five cases of ovariotomy. **1883** HOWELLS *Woman's Reason* II. xx. 176 She had lost her father, who died very suddenly a few days after he sailed. **1895** GEORGE *Battles Eng. Hist.* 208 While Wellington lost about 1300 men, Massena lost considerably over three times that number. **1928** E. O'NEILL *Strange Interlude* IV. 148 He's unhappy now because he thinks he isn't able to give me a child. And I'm unhappy because I've lost my child. **1958** L. URIS *Exodus* (1959) II. x. 264 For five consecutive years she lost children through early miscarriages. **1975** G. BOURNE *Pregnancy* (1981) viii. 120 Pseudocyesis.. occurs in some women who have lost a pregnancy or a baby. **1986** J. B. HILTON *Moondrop to Murder* xvi. 142 She finally gave up hope of losing her baby. She had prayed that exertion, fatigue, suspense and terror would loosen that embryo from the walls of her womb.

d. To fail to maintain (a position, a state of mind or body), e.g. ***to lose patience, one's temper, to lose caste, hold, one's balance***, etc. ***to lose ground***: to fail to keep one's position; esp. *fig.* to decline in reputation, favour, health, etc.

[**1436**: see GROUND *sb.* 11.] **1470–85** MALORY *Arthur* IV. ix. 131 But alweyes he helde vp his shelde and lost no ground nor bated no chere. *a* **1586** SIDNEY *Arcadia* I. (1590) 27 At length, the left winge of the Arcadians began to loose ground. **1622** MABBE tr. *Aleman's Guzman d'Alf.* II. 53 How had they almost made me to lose my patience, and my judgement! **1640** tr. *Verdere's Rom. of Rom.* I. xvi. 68 They brake their staves bravely, without losing their saddles. **1667** MILTON *P.L.* VI. 838 They astonisht all resistance lost, All courage. **1712** W. ROGERS *Voy.* 291 A Current setting to Leeward, we rather lost than got ground. **1775** JOHNSON *Let. to Mrs. Thrale* 13 June, Boswell is a favourite but he has lost ground since I told them that he is married. **1782** PRIESTLEY *Corrupt. Chr.* I. IV. 379 Those suspicions were not likely to lose ground. **1844** DICKENS *Mart. Chuz.* xi, Chuffey boggled over his plate so long, that Mr. Jonas, losing patience, took it from him at last. **1877** SPURGEON *Serm.* XXIII. 320 He has lost caste and lost all ground of glorying.

e. *occas.* To cease to have, to get rid of (something undesirable, e.g. an ailment).

1667 MILTON *P.L.* II. 607 To loose In sweet forgetfulness all pain and woe. **1677** LADY CHAWORTH in *12th Rep. Hist. MSS. Comm.* App. v. 42 The Dutchesse hath had an ague in her lyeing inne but hath soone lost it. **1742** W. COLLINS *Hassan* 83 O! let me teach my heart to lose its fears. **1859** MRS. TREVELYAN *Let.* in Trevelyan *Life Macaulay* (1876) II. xv. 477 Never, as long as I live, can I lose the sense of misery that I ever left him after Christmas day. *a* **1903** *Mod.* I have not yet lost my rheumatism.

f. Of a thing: To be deprived of or part with (a portion of itself, a quality, or appurtenance). Also with *off*.

c **1330** R. BRUNNE *Chron.* (1810) 221 Þe day lost his coloure, & mirk was as þe nyght. *c* **1386** CHAUCER *Frankl. T.* 288 Til that the brighte sonne loste his hewe. **1598** SHAKS. *Merry W.* v. v. 239 This deceit looses the name of craft. **1629** MILTON *Hymn Nativity* 99 The Air such pleasure loth to lose, With thousand echo's still prolongs each heav'nly close. **1784** COWPER *Task* I. 648 And have thy joys Lost nothing by comparison with ours? **1874** *Rep. Vermont Board Agric.* II. 717, I think that tin buckets are preferable for catching sap to wooden ones, as they.. have no hoops to lose off. **1881** LE CONTE *Sight* 51 When.. the hypermetropic eye loses its power of adjustment. **1894** HALL CAINE *Manxman* IV. x. 233 Her household duties had lost their interest. **1906** *Dialect Notes* III. 145 A wheel lost off as they were driving to town.

†**g.** with cognate obj., ***to lose a loss***. Also, ***to lose*** (= incur) ***a fine***. *Obs.*

1498 *Old City Acc. Bk.* in *Archæol. Jrnl.* XLIII, Item for a fyne lost by John Stone.. xxd. **1525** LD. BERNERS *Froiss.* II. xxxvii. 109 The countrey of Bierne this hundred yere neuer loste suche a losse. *a* **1541** WYATT in *Tottel's Misc.* (Arb.) 87 Graunt them good Lord,.. To freate inward, for losyng such a losse. **1614** S. WARD *Let.* in *Ussher's Lett.* (1686) 33 We have lost.. a great loss by Mr. Casaubon's untimely decease.

†**h.** with *inf.*: To be deprived of the power or opportunity (of doing something). *Obs.*

1616 B. JONSON *Forest, Ep. Lady Aubigny* 4 What th' haue lost t' expect, they dare deride. **1671** MILTON *P.R.* I. 378 Though I have lost.. To be belov'd of God, I have not lost To love.

i. The *passive* is often used without any reference to a determinate person or thing as 'losing'; e.g. (of an art, etc.) to cease to be known or practised; (of a quality, etc.) to cease to be present. Cf. LOST *ppl. a.*

1667 MILTON *P.L.* XII. 429 This God-like act Annuls thy doom, the death thou shouldst have dy'd, In sin for ever lost from life. **1670** RAY *Prov.* 117 It's not lost that comes at last. All is not lost that is in danger. **1700** DRYDEN *Fables* Pref. (Globe) 505 The name of its author being wholly lost. **1722** QUINCY *Lex. Physico-Med.* (ed. 2) 264/1 In all Percussions the Stroke is proportional to the Force lost. **1779–81** JOHNSON *L.P., Cowley*, If what he thinks be true, that his numbers are unmusical only when they are ill-read, the art of reading them is at present lost. **1842** TENNYSON *Morte Arth.* 90 Surely a precious thing.. Should thus be lost for ever from the earth. **1870** M. ARNOLD *St. Paul & Protestantism* (1900) 69 From which [chapters] Paul's whole theology, if all his other writings were lost, might be reconstructed. **1897** *Allbutt's Syst. Med.* IV. 818 The quality of the voice may be unaltered or completely lost.

j. ***to lose a dinner*** (or ***a meal***): to vomit (what one has recently eaten).

Examples are *Austral.* and *U.S.*

1941 BAKER *Dict. Austral. Slang* 44 *Lose a meal*, to vomit up food. **1952** M. R. RINEHART *Swimming Pool* xxv. 227 I'm going to lose my dinner.

4. *absol.* or *intr.* **a.** To suffer loss; to cease to possess something; to be deprived of or part with some of his or its possessions, attributes, or qualities; to become deteriorated or incur disadvantage.

c **1230** *Hali Meid.* 41 Ha beon eauer feard for to losen [*elsewhere, and here in MS. Bodl.* leosen]. *c* **1470** HENRY *Wallace* IV. 336 Now want, now has; now loss, now can wyn. **1596** SHAKS. *Tam. Shr.* Induct. ii. 101 Thou shalt not loose by it. **1611** BIBLE *Eccl.* iii. 6 A time to get, and a time to lose. **1643** BURROUGHES *Exp. Hosea* iv. (1652) 75 There is nothing lost in being willing to lose for God. **1697** DRYDEN *Ded. Æneis* Ess. (ed. Ker) II. 229 Thus, by gaining abroad, he lost

at home. **1838** MACAULAY *Temple* Ess. (1887) 440 He never put himself prominently before the public eye, except at conjunctures when he was almost certain to gain and could not possibly lose. **1850** TENNYSON *In Mem.* xxvii, 'Tis better to have loved and lost Than never to have loved at all. **1895** GEORGE *Battles Eng. Hist.* 313 Fortunately the Sikhs had lost so severely that no evil consequences followed. **1898** *Folk-Lore* Sept. 198 The other was undertaken by a publisher, who lost on it. *Mod.* Both armies lost heavily.

b. Of an immaterial thing: To be deprived of its power or force. *rare.*

1794 MRS. PIOZZI *Synon.* II. 56 Our authors plunder French comedies in vain; the humour loses and evaporates. **1900** R. J. DRUMMOND *Relat. Apost. Teach.* i. 33 The words are only understood in their setting. They lose immensely when isolated.

c. Const. *in*, †*of*, with partitive sense.

1642 FULLER *Holy & Prof. St.* III. v. 163 Gold alwayes worn in the same purse with silver loses both of the colour and weight. **1753** A. MURPHY *Gray's Inn Jrnl.* No. 33 These Allurements soon began to lose of their Influence. **1791** BOSWELL *Johnson* (1831) I. 86 Hawkins told him it would lose of its beauty if it were so published. **1802** BEDDOES *Hygëia* v. 54 Every muscle, steeped in a heated medium, loses of its contractility. **1902** *Chambers's Jrnl.* July 441/2 A bird does not gather speed when sailing in the air, as a falling stone would, neither does it lose in pace. **1913** *Q. Rev.* Oct. 413 As a consequence the work loses in freshness and even in clearness. **1947** *Harrap's Stand. French & Eng. Dict.* II. 728/2 The incident did not lose in the telling... To lose in value, in interest.

d. orig. *U.S.* ***to lose out***: to be unsuccessful, to fail.

1858 H. BUSHNELL *Sermons for New Life* ix. 176 The child brought up a thief gets an infinite power of cunning..and loses out just as much in the power of true perception. **1909** 'O. HENRY' *Roads of Destiny* iv. 66, I know you've lost out some by not having me to typewrite 'em. **1913** E. D. BIGGERS *Seven Keys to Baldpate* xiii. 165 But it's over, and you've lost out. **1930** C. JOHNSON *Negro in Amer. Civilisation* (1931) xxvi. 396 Is it not true that the Negro female is losing out in personal service? So often newspapers are specifying white in their want ads. **1942** E. PAUL *Narrow St.* xvii. 133 Daladier made a bid for the premiership and lost out because Briand would not play ball with him. **1947** 'G. ORWELL' *Eng. People* 38 The American tendency is to burden every verb with a preposition that adds nothing to its meaning (*win out, lose out, face up to*, etc.). **1959** *Encounter* Sept. 16/1 It will probably lose out in the competition. **1963** S. DOUGLAS *Years of Combat* x. 251 Tracers might come whistling past one's ears, indicating all too clearly that the enemy..was on the attack. If that happened it meant that we had lost out in the preliminary tactical manoeuvrings. **1966** *Listener* 10 Mar. 337/2 It could be that both China and America are losing out to the Russians. **1971** *Guardian* 23 July 5/2 We are going to lose out unless the Government are prepared to do a tremendous public relations job for the tourist industry here. **1972** *Newsweek* 10 July 15/2 Rep. Bella Abzug..lost out in her bid for a second term in Congress. **1973** *Times* 30 June 13/6 The monstrous proliferation of redundant prepositions in the ever more popular usages 'check up on', 'lose out to', 'meet up with'.

e. Of a clock, watch, etc.: to become slow (SLOW *a.* 12); to indicate a time earlier than the correct time. Also *trans.*, to run slow by the amount of (a specified period).

1861, 1870, 1917 [see GAIN *v.*² 3 d]. **1955** *Oxf. Jun. Encycl.* VIII. 81/2 A pendulum clock with a steel rod loses $2\frac{1}{2}$ seconds per day for a rise of temperature of 10°F. **1972** *Which?* Aug. 244 At the same time each day the amount they had gained or lost was noted, and they were wound.

5. a. To become, permanently or temporarily, unable to find in one's own possession or custody; to cease to know the whereabouts of (a portable object, an animal, etc.) because it has strayed or gone unawares from one's possession, or has simply been mislaid.

c **950** *Lindisf. Gosp.* Luke xv. 4 ʒif forloraδ *vel* losaδ enne of δæm. **1382** WYCLIF *Luke* xv. 4 What man of ȝou that hath an hundrid scheep, and if he hath lost oon of hem [etc.]. *c* **1422** HOCCLEVE *Jonathas* 318 Y haue a fere..thow woldest it leese, As thow lostist my ryng. **1567** *Gude & Godlie Ball.* (S.T.S.) 37 My Sone was loste, and now is found. **1591** SHAKS. *Two Gent.* II. i. 23 Like a Schoole-boy that had lost his A.B.C. **1655** tr. *Com. Hist. Francion* VII. 12 We demanded if they had not taken up a hawk which we had lost. **1718** PRIOR *Dove* 8 Venus wept the sad disaster Of having lost her favourite dove. **1743** BULKELEY & CUMMINS *Voy. S. Seas* 110 She told me Mr. B——n had lost his Hat. **1847** TENNYSON *Princess* IV. 179 Since her horse was lost I left her mine. **1871** MORLEY *Voltaire* (1886) 5 Humanity had lost its title-deeds and he had recovered them.

b. To fail to keep in sight. Also, ***to lose sight of*** (lit. and fig.): see SIGHT. Also *occas.*, to cease to hear (*poet.*); †to fail to follow (a person) in argument (*obs.* or *arch.*).

1587 IANES in Hakluyt *Voy.* (1600) III. 111 The Master..was afrayd his men would shape some contrary course while he was asleepe, and so he should lose vs. *a* **1592** H. SMITH *Serm.* (1637) 349 This is our life while we enjoy it, we lose it like the Sunne which flies swifter than an arrow, and yet no man perceives that it moves. **1628** DIGBY *Voy. Medit.* (1868) 3 If wee should chance at any time to loose each other, vpon sight againe [etc.]. **1634** SIR T. HERBERT *Trav.* 11 Wee once more got sight of the Carracke, and lost her for euer, in two houres after. **1640** SHIRLEY *Constant Maid* IV. F 2 b, I cannot see i' th' darke with spectacles, And mine owne eyes ha' lost him o' the suddaine. **1725** *Wodrow Corr.* (1843) III. 173, I thought, upon infinity, he was running into Sir Isaac Newton's notion of infinite space being the divine sensorium,..but, indeed, many times I lost him. **1833** TENNYSON *Dream Fair Wom.* 245 Losing her carol I stood pensively.

c. To draw away from, be no longer near or among; to leave hopelessly behind in a race.

1704 POPE *Autumn* 60 Here where the mountains less'ning as they rise Lose the low vales, and steal into the skies. **1748** *Anson's Voy.* II. v. 180 We did not lose them [flying-fish] on the coast of Brazil, till we approached the southern tropic. **1886** SIR F. H. DOYLE *Remin.* 63 Where his great stride and iron legs would have enabled him, in the language of the turf, to lose his antagonist.

†**d.** To fail to retain in the mind or memory; to forget. Also said of the mind or memory. ***to lose it that***..: to forget that. *Obs.*

1530 PALSGR. 556/1, I forget, I have loste a thynge out of remembraunce. **1590** SHAKS. *Mids. N.* I. i. 114 Being ouer-full of selfe-affaires, My minde did lose it. **1592** —— *Ven. & Ad.* 408 The lesson is but plaine, And once made perfect, neuer lost againe. **1612** DEKKER *If it be not good* Wks. 1873 III. 299 My memorie had quite lost you. **1613** SHAKS., etc. *Hen. VIII*, II. i. 57 Heare what I say, and then goe home and lose me. **16..** MILTON *Ps.* lxxxiii. 16 That Israels name for ever may Be lost in memory. **1703** ROWE *Fair Penit.* v. i, Here let Remembrance lose our past Misfortunes. **1712** S. SEWALL *Diary* 11 Apr., Had quite lost it that the Meeting was at Mr. Stoddard's. [**1870** M. ARNOLD *St. Paul & Protestantism* (1900) 148 Who can ever lose out of his memory the roll and march of those magnificent words of prophecy?]

e. To cease to follow (the right track); also, to cease to find (traces of a person, etc.). Chiefly in ***to lose one's way*** (lit. and fig.). †Of a river: To diverge from (its channel).

1530 PALSGR. 771/1, I wander, as one dothe that hath loste his waye. **1582** N. LICHEFIELD tr. *Castanheda's Conq. E. Ind.* I. viii. 20 They had willingly lost their course. **1615** G. SANDYS *Trav.* II. 94 Nor is it a thing extraordinary for riuers to lose their channels. **1709** PRIOR *Chloe Hunting* 3 She lost her way, And thro' the Woods uncertain chanc'd to stray. **1849** MACAULAY *Hist. Eng.* iii. I. 373 Pepys and his wife, travelling in their own coach, lost their way between Newbury and Reading. **1893** *Fam. Herald* 132/1 After she had walked a little farther, she lost trail altogether.

†**f.** To allow to escape from one's power or influence. *Obs.*

a **1715** BURNET *Own Time* (1724) I. 378 Instead of prevailing on the Prince, he lost him so entirely, that all his endeavours afterwards could never beget any confidence in him.

g. To let slip one's knowledge of (a language).

1718 LADY M. W. MONTAGU *Let. to Lady Rich* 16 Mar., I am in great danger of losing my English.

6. a. To spend unprofitably or in vain; to waste, get no return or result for (one's labour or efforts); to let slip (opportunities) without using them to good purpose; to waste (time).

a **1340** HAMPOLE *Psalter* xxvi. 20 Suffre that thou suffirs for god and of god, for wa is þaim þat losis suffrynge. *c* **1374** CHAUCER *Troylus* II. 1700 (1749) Lest tyme I loste, I dar not with yow dele. *c* **1400** *Rom. Rose* 5153 Fully on me she lost hir lore. *c* **1450** *Merlin* 6 And so shold ye loose youre tyme. **1470–85** MALORY *Arthur* XVIII. xvi. 754 She is not the fyrst that hath loste her payn vpon yow. **1500–20** DUNBAR *Poems* lxvi. 13 The leill labour lost, and leill seruice. **1581** PETTIE *Guazzo's Civ. Conv.* I. (1586) 26 Now to loose no more time about this point, I saie vnto you, y^t [etc.]. **1590** SPENSER *F.Q.* I. iii. 24 But, when she saw her prayers nought prevaile Shee backe retourned with some labour lost. **1615** W. LAWSON *Country Housew. Gard.* (1626) 12 All your labour past and to come about an Orchard is lost vnlesse you fence well. **1632** SANDERSON *Twelve Serm.* 233 True zeale..will not loose the opportunity of doing what it ought, for waiting till others beginne. **1634** MILTON *Comus* 271 Ill is lost that praise That is addrest to unattending Ears. **1738** SWIFT *Pol. Conversat.* 127 Fall to, you know Half an Hour is soon lost at Dinner. **1770** FOOTE *Lame Lover* II. Wks. 1799 II. 80 The constables will be here in a trice, so you have not a moment to lose. **1819** CRABBE *T. of Hall* IX, How much she grieved to lose the given day In dissipation wild, in visitation gay. **1847** MARRYAT *Childr. N. Forest* v, There is no time to be lost. **1896** G. BOOTHBY *In Strange Comp.* II. vi. 55/1 A..fellow who never lost a chance of making himself objectionable.

b. ***to be lost on*** or ***upon***: to have no effect upon, to fail to influence.

1610 SHAKS. *Temp.* IV. i. 190 On whom my paines Humanely taken, all, all lost, quite lost. [**1692** BURNET *Past. Care* ix. 111 Niceties of Style are lost before a common Auditory.] **1697** DRYDEN *Æneid* XI. 1059 Thir Stratagems, and Tricks of little Hearts Are lost on me. **1833** HT. MARTINEAU *Brooke Farm* xi. 131 Your kindness is not lost upon me. **1844** DISRAELI *Coningsby* I. iii. I. 32 Nothing, however, was ever lost upon Lord Monmouth. No one had a more retentive memory, or a more observant mind. **1900** J. A. H. MURRAY *Evolution Eng. Lexicogr.* 6 The real humour of the situation..was..lost upon the House of Commons.

7. a. To fail to obtain (something one might have had): *occas.* const. *to.* Also, to fail to catch (a train, etc.). † ***to lose aim***: to miss one's mark.

1387 TREVISA *Higden* (Rolls) VI. 185 He schal lese [*MS.* γ luse] hevene þat wil hem take awey. **1390** GOWER *Conf.* I. 153 Adam for Pride loste his pris. *c* **1460** *Towneley Myst.* iii. 363 Wheder I lose or I wyn In fayth, thi felowship. *a* **1548** HALL *Chron., Hen. VI* 141 b, Meanyng not to lose so great a prey. **1603** SHAKS. *Meas. for M.* I. iv. 78 Our doubts are traitors And makes vs loose the good we oft might win, By fearing to attempt. **1606** —— *Ant. & Cl.* IV. xiv. 71 Shall I do that which all the Parthian Darts, (Though Enemy) lost ayme, and could not. **1611** BIBLE *Matt.* x. 42 Hee shall in no wise lose his reward. **1632** MASSINGER *Maid of Honour* v. i. (1632) K 2, *Cam...* If you forsweare your selfes wee shall not prosper. I'll rather lose my longing. **1650** BAXTER *Saint's R.* iv. (1656) 132 Where God loses his praise, man will certainly lose his comforts. **1711** SWIFT *Jrnl. to Stella* 12 May, Mr. Secretary..brought me to our town's end in his coach: so I lost my walk. **1775** HARRIS *Philos. Arrangem.* Wks. (1841) 339 The swift-footed Salius lost the prize to young Euryalus. **1830** J. JEKYLL *Corr.* (1894) 256 Rather than lose her legacy, she hung him on to the window bar. **1884** *Congregationalist* June 493, I once nearly lost a train on account of it. **1900** F. ANSTEY *Brass Bottle* ii. 22 'A guinea. For the last time. You'll lose it, sir', said the auctioneer to the little man.

b. To fail to apprehend by sight or hearing; not to 'catch' (words, points of a discourse).

1599 SHAKS. *Much Ado* III. i. 32 Then go we neare her that her eare loose nothing. **1604** E. G[RIMSTONE] tr. *D'Acosta's Hist. Indies* II. vii. 97 Being too farre off from any thing, wee loose the sight, and too neere likewise, we cannot see it. **1784** COWPER *Task* III. 599 Fearing each to lose Some note of Nature's music from his lips. *Mod.* I did not lose a word of his speech.

†**c.** To fail to attend; to 'miss'. *Obs.*

Also formerly at Cambridge University, ***to lose one's week***: not to be allowed to count towards the obligatory number of weeks of residence a week in which the required number of chapels had not been kept.

1711 SWIFT *Jrnl. to Stella* 4 Aug., I lost church to-day. **1847** TENNYSON *Princess* Prol. 161 They lost their weeks; they vext the souls of deans.

d. *Hunting.* To fail to catch (an animal).

1567 MAPLET *Gr. Forest* 68 b, I had rather (as they say lose the Hare) then to take such infinite paines as to hunt so farre for hir. **1883** LD. SALTOUN *Scraps* I. 104 The grey-hounds took up the chase, and either killed or lost her.

8. a. To be deprived of (something) in a contest or game; to forfeit (a stake); hence, to be defeated in (a game, battle, lawsuit); to fail to carry (a motion). Also in *Cricket*: To have (a wicket) taken by an opponent. Const. *to.*

a **1533** LD. BERNERS *Huon* liii. 180 She lost ye game wherof Huon was ioyfull. **1560** DAUS tr. *Sleidane's Comm.* 210 Foughte a battell in Piedmont, with the Frenchemen..and lost the felde. **1594** SHAKS. *Rich. III*, IV. iv. 538 While we reason here, A Royall battell might be wonne and lost. **1607** —— *Cor.* I. vii. 4 If we loose the Field, We cannot keepe the Towne. **1671** LADY M. BERTIE in *12th Rep. Hist. MSS. Comm.* App. v. 22 Wee play sometimes at trante a courante where my old ill lucke follows mee to loose my money. **1710** *Act 9 Anne*, c. 19 §2 Any Person or Persons..who shall at any Time or sitting by playing at Cards..lose to any One or more..Persons..the Sum..of Ten Pounds. **1799** H. K. WHITE *Let. to bro. Neville*, The Corporation versus Gee, which we..lost. **1836** DICKENS *Sk. Boz, Our Parish* iv, The motion was lost by a majority of two. **1843** *Blackw. Mag.* LIV. 171, I lost my wicket to the first ball. **1847** TENNYSON *Princess* VI. 9 When our side was vanquish'd and my cause For ever lost. **1872** *Punch* 27 Jan. 41/2 We never lost a game to a professional at billiards without hearing him assign his triumph chiefly to his flukes. **1885** *Manch. Exam.* 10 July 5/1 The Southerners had scored 78 without losing a wicket.

b. *absol.* To be defeated; also, to forfeit money by defeat in a game.

a **1548** HALL *Chron., Hen. VI* 116 Accordyng to the chaunce of war, the one part gat, and the other lost. **1593** SHAKS. *Lucr.* 730 A captiue victor that hath lost in gaine. **1605** —— *Lear* v. iii. 15 Who looses, and who wins; who's in, who's out. **1622** MABBE tr. *Aleman's Guzman d'Alf.* I. 21 Their game was Primera..; my mother, shee got the money, for my father was willing to lose to her. **1669** LADY CHAWORTH in *12th Rep. Hist. MSS. Comm.* App. v. 11, I heere your horse hath lost. **1738** SWIFT *Pol. Conversat.* 198 She lost at one Sitting to the Tune of a hundred Guineas. **1822** SHELLEY *Calderon's Magico Prodig.* i. 151 The battle's loss may profit those who lose. **1885** O. W. HOLMES, jr. in *Law Q. Rev.* Apr. 172 Tacitus says that the Germans would gamble their personal liberty and pay with their persons if they lost.

9. Causal senses. **a.** To cause the loss of: often const. *dative* of the person suffering loss.

1428 *Waterf. Arch.* in *10th Rep. Hist. MSS. Comm.* App. v. 295 Whatt ever man..bringe warre upon the citie whereby they bene prayed and losid thair goods. **1596** SHAKS. *1 Hen. IV*, III. i. 187 Pride, Haughtinesse [etc.],..The least of which, haunting a Nobleman, Loseth mens hearts. **1602** —— *Ham.* I. iii. 76. **1605** —— *Lear* I. i. 125. *a* **1611** BEAUM. & FL. *Philaster* IV. iv, I pray that this action loose not Philaster the hearts of the people. **1640–1** *Kirkcudbr. War-Comm. Min. Bk.* (1855) 76 If they [shoes] come not with expedition the want of thame will lose all our sogers. **1699** WOTTON *Let.* in Bentley *Phal.* Pref. 12, I did not think that a sufficient reason, why I should lose that Treatise to the World. **1763** HOYLE *Whist* 25 Do not overtrump him, which may probably lose you two or three Tricks. **1803** J. MARSHALL *Const. Opin.* (1839) 8 A loss of the commission would lose the office. **1871** FREEMAN *Hist. Ess.* Ser. I. vii. 195 The crimes of John lost him all the northern part of his French possessions.

b. To cause (a person) to 'lose his way'; to bewilder. Esp. in phr. ***you('ve) lost me*** = 'I failed to follow what you were saying'.

1648 *Eikon Bas.* xvi. 157 Nor are constant Formes of Prayers more likely to flat, and hinder the Spirit of prayer, ..then un-premeditated and confused variety to distract, and lose it. **1692** S. PATRICK *Answ. Touchstone* 15 He only endeavours to lose his Reader in a mist of Words. **1962** L. DEIGHTON *Ipcress File* vii. 42 'They have money..to investigate what they call "synthesised environment".' I said, 'You've lost me now—without trying.' **1967** H. VAN SILLER *Biltmore Call* 103 Frazer..looked up, frowning. 'You've lost me. What do you mean, exactly?' **1970** R. LEWIS *Wolf by Ears* i. 11 You will have to be a little more explicit in your statements. I'm a bit lost. *Ibid.* 17 'You've lost me.' 'Put simply, it's this way.' **1973** *Observatory* Oct. 162 You lost me at one stage.

†**c.** ? To cause to be forgotten. *Obs.*

1667 DRYDEN *Tempest* IV. iv, Have fifteen years so lost me to your knowledge, That you retain no memory of Prospero? **1724** *Wodrow Corr.* (1843) III. 130 It requires a much better memory than mine to resume such long work, and one harangue loses the former to me.

†**d.** To reject (a bill in parliament). *Obs.*

1663 PEPYS *Diary* 26 July, A Bill for the Lord's day, which it seems the Lords have lost, and so cannot be passed.

10. *refl.* (with corresponding *passive*).

a. To lose one's way, go astray. Also *fig.*

1535 COVERDALE *Ps.* cxviii[i]. 176, I go astraye as a shepe that is lost. **1581** LAMBARDE *Eiren.* IV. iv. (1602) 390 The

hearer would be many times lost, before I shoulde come to the end. **1581** PETTIE *Guazzo's Civ. Conv.* I. (1586) 14 But to what end goe I to loose my selfe in the intricate labirinth of the abuses & disorders of our time. **1593** SHAKS. *3 Hen. VI*, III. ii. 174 Like one lost in a Thornie Wood. **1604** E. G[RIMSTONE] tr. *D'Acosta's Hist. Indies* I. xxi. 69 They must of necessitie loose themselves, having no knowledge where they were. **1643** SIR T. BROWNE *Relig. Med.* I. §9, I love to lose my selfe in a mystery. **1667** MILTON *P.L.* II. 561 In wandring mazes lost. **1780** J. HARRIS *Philol. Enq.* Wks. (1841) 484 Arabian poetry is so immense a field, that he who enters it is in danger of being lost. **1859** TENNYSON *Elaine* 225 O'er these waste downs whereon I lost myself.

b. To lose one's (or its) identity; to become merged (*in* something else). *lit.* and *fig.*

1604 E. G[RIMSTONE] tr. *D'Acosta's Hist. Indies* II. vi. 93 Ten great rivers which loose themselves entring into that Lake. **1781** J. MOORE *View Soc. It.* (1790) I. xli. 445 The Via Sacra was a street leading to the Forum, and lost in it. **1796** JANE AUSTEN *Pride & Prej.* vii. (1813) 195 All surprise was shortly lost in other feelings. **1822** LAMB *Elia* Ser. II. *Detached Th. on Bks. & Read.*, I love to lose myself in other men's minds. **1871–4** HORT *The Way*, etc. ii. (1894) 62 By the Resurrection and Ascension His Apostleship had been visibly lost in His Sonship.

c. To become deeply absorbed or engrossed (*in* thought, etc.); to be bewildered, overwhelmed (*in* wonder); †to be distracted, lose one's wits (from emotion or excitement).

1604 E. G[RIMSTONE] *D'Acosta's Hist. Indies* V. v. 339 They were lost in their own imaginations and conceipts. **1605** SHAKS. *Macb.* II. ii. 71 Be not lost So poorely in your thoughts. **1606** —— *Ant. & Cl.* I. ii. 121 These strong Egyptian Fetters I must breake, Or loose my selfe in dotage. **1626** SHIRLEY *Maid's Rev.* IV. i. (1639) G 2b, I almost lose my selfe In joy to meete him. **1728** ADDISON *Hymn*, '*When all thy mercies*', Transported with the view, I'm lost In wonder, love, and praise. **1798** LANDOR *Gebir* I. 97, I neither feed the flock nor watch the fold; How can I, lost in love? **1809** W. IRVING *Knickerb.* III. i. (1820) 153 As I pace the darkened chamber and lose myself in melancholy musings. **1875** JOWETT *Plato* (ed. 2) I. 231 He seemed to be lost in the contemplation of something great. **1890** HALL CAINE *Bondman* III. vi, Her voice was low at first, but she soon lost herself, and then it rose above the other voices. **1899** *Allbutt's Syst. Med.* VIII. 239 For a time they become lost and dazed.

d. To become hidden from view, obscured (*in* clouds, etc.).

1697 DRYDEN *Æneid* VIII. 79 When the setting Stars are lost in Day. **1725** POPE *Odyss.* VII. 354 Woody mountains half in vapours lost. **1784** COWPER *Task* I. 194 Rills that.. lose themselves at length In matted grass. **1845** M. PATTISON *Ess.* (1889) I. 11 A vast ocean of tillage..losing itself in the vapour of the distant horizon. **1847** TENNYSON *Princess* I. 227 A pillar'd porch, the bases lost In laurel.

†**e.** Of water: To leak away. *Obs.*

1712 J. JAMES tr. *Le Blond's Gardening* 189 The Vials..are joined to the Pipes with Wax or Mastick, so that the Water rises into the Vials, without losing itself any where. *Ibid.* 194 Gravel, or Sand-Stone, upon which the Water will run without losing itself.

11. *Comb.*, with sense 'one who or something which loses...', as †*lose-all*, †*-office*; so †**lose-time** *a.*, time-wasting.

1603 FLORIO *Montaigne* I. xxv. (1632) 78 Jugling tricks, or other idle lose-time sports. **1623** PENKETHMAN *Handf. Hon.* IV. xlii, More loue to purchase, each good turne requite, Lest a Loose-office thou be termed right. **1650** W. BROUGH *Sacr. Princ.* (1659) 220 The third [heir] is commonly a lose-all.

†**lose**, *v.*² *Obs.* Also 4 loose, 5 lowse. [f. LOSE *sb.*¹, or perh. aphetic f. ALOSE *v.*] *trans.* To praise. Also *absol.*

1377 LANGL. *P. Pl.* B. XI. 411 Þow with rude speche Lakkedest, and losedest þinge þat longed nouȝt to be done. **1388** WYCLIF *1 Esdras* iv. 12 What maner wise passith not the kyng bifore oothere, that thus is loosid? *a* **1400–50** *Alexander* 1960 (Dublin MS.) Of all Lordes Lord lowsed þorow þe werld. *c* **1430** *Pilgr. Lyf Manhode* II. cii. (1869) 112, I am þilke þat of olde am cleped and losed [*v.r.* alosed] þe eldeste.

Hence †**losed** *ppl. a.*, praised, renowned. Also used as *sb.*, one praised.

c **1305** *Edmund Conf.* 245 in *E.E.P.* (1862) 77 So noble a losed þer nas non in al þe vniuersite. **1422** tr. *Secreta Secret., Priv. Priv.* 160 The force of good kynge Dauy..the loset of force and of vertue. *c* **1440** CAPGRAVE *Life St. Kath.* I. 7 A losyd lorde was he.

lose, obs. form of LOOSE, LOSS.

loseable: see LOSABLE.

losel ('ləʊzəl), *sb.* and *a. arch.* and *dial.* (See *E.D.D.*) Forms: 4–7 losell, 5–6 loselle, (6 losyll), 6–7 lozel(l, (6 lozile, lozzel, 7 lozzell), 6–7, 9 *Sc.* lossel, 7 lossell, 4– losel. [app. f. *losen*, pa. pple. of LEESE *v.* (cf. LOREL from the more usual *loren*, and BROTHEL similarly f. OE. *broðen*, pa. pple. of *bréoðan* to be ruined). The etymological sense is thus 'one who is lost', 'a son of perdition'.]

A. *sb.* A worthless person; a profligate, rake, scoundrel; in weaker sense, a ragamuffin, ne'er-do-well.

1362 LANGL. *P. Pl.* A. Prol. 74 Losels þat lecherie haunten. ? *a* **1400** *Morte Arth.* 252 We hafe as losels liffyde many longe daye. *c* **1400** *Destr. Troy* 12096 þe losell to þe lady launchid full swithe. *c* **1460** *Towneley Myst.* xvi. 154 Losels ye ar and thefys. **1561** T. NORTON *Calvin's Inst.* I. 42 Augustine, whome those losells do most hate. **1596** SPENSER *State Irel.* Wks. (Globe) 624/1 Many of them be such losells and scatterlings, as that they cannot easely by any sheriff,.. or other ordinarye officer be gotten. **1601** DENT *Pathw. Heaven* 170 There be many lazy lozels..which doe nothing all the day long, but walke in the streets, sit vpon the stalles, and frequent Tauerns and Ale-houses. **1609** C. BUTLER *Fem. Mon.* iii. (1623) G iv, The Drone..hath been alwaies reputed a greedy lozell. **1624** BP. MOUNTAGU *Gagg* 187 Yet it is possible and I could doo it, to puzzle such a Lozzell as yourself. **1650** TRAPP *Comm. Deut.* 123 The sword devoureth one, as well as another,..it spares neither lord nor losel, as they say. **1671** ANNAND *Myst. Pietatis* 94 How soon might the rude swaine, the country lossel, the clownish Boor,..find out a way, for nobilitating his family. **17..** *Heir of Linne* II. xx. in Ritson *Sc. Songs* (1794) II. 137 If we shold hang any losel heere, The first we wold begin with thee. **1832** CARLYLE in *Fraser's Mag.* V. 407 Do not recruiting sergeants drum through the streets..and..collect ragged losels enough? **1843** BROWNING *Blot 'Scutcheon* II. Wks. 1896 I. 343/2 Wretched women..tied By wild illicit ties to losels vile. **1897** 'L. KEITH' *Bonny Lady* viii. 78 The school-master knew it was no village losel hired by the hour.

B. *adj.* Good-for-nothing, worthless.

1601 MUNDAY *Downf. Earl Huntingdon* II. ii. (1828) 35 Yonder comes a lazy lozel Friar. **1633** P. FLETCHER *Pisc. Ecl.* II. xv, Why should you plain, that lozel swains refuse you? **1642** MILTON *Apol. Smect.* Wks. 1851 III. 296 Where didst thou learn to be..so pusillanimous, thou lozel Bachelour of Art. **1809** W. IRVING *Knickerb.* (1861) 57 He saw the losel porpoises, which had betrayed them into this peril, some broiling on the Gridiron, and others hissing on the Frying-pan! **1883** R. W. DIXON *Mano* II. i. 65 This bad daughter of a better sire With a vile losel dweller of the wild Was playing now.

†'**loseling**, *a. Obs. rare*⁻¹. [f. prec. + -ING².] Worthy of a losel, rascally.

1624 GEE *Foot out of Snare* vii. 64 A prettie drouzy,.. lozeling Argument this was against taking the Oath.

loselism ('ləʊzəlɪz(ə)m). *rare.* [f. LOSEL + -ISM.] The quality or state of a losel; losels collectively.

1831 CARLYLE *Let.* 21 Oct. in Froude *Life* (1882) II. 214 All the Loselism of London will be about the church next Sunday.

†'**loselled**, *ppl. a. Obs. rare*⁻¹. [f. LOSEL + -ED².] = LOSEL *a.*

1606 *Wily Beguiled* G, If I had been such a great long, large Lobcockt, loseld burden, as Master Churms is,..I should neuer haue got Pegge as long as I had liu'd.

†'**loselly**, *a. Obs. rare.* [f. LOSEL + -LY¹.] Like a losel, good-for-nothing, idle, lazy.

1611 COTGR., *Poltronesque*, lazie, lozellie, sluggish, idle. **1694** MOTTEUX *Rabelais* IV. lix, These lozelly Gulligutted Gastrolaters.

loselry ('ləʊzəlrɪ). *arch.* [f. LOSEL + -RY.] Performance characteristic of a losel; profligacy, debauchery, rascality.

1480 CAXTON *Chron. Eng.* cxcviii. 178 The false spencers, the whiche he mayntened thurgh loselrye ageynst his honour. **1522** SKELTON *Why nat to Courte?* 661 By sorsery Or suche other loselry. **1594** O. B. *Quest. Profit. Concern.* 13 To haue him Lord it out thus vnder my nose, and I to sweate and swinke, to maintaine his lozelrie. **1894** F. S. ELLIS *Reynard the Fox* 215 Surely my first thought was that she Had been judged for some loselry.

losen, obs. pa. pple. of LEESE *v.*¹, LOOSE *v.*

losen, variant of LOZEN *Sc.*

loseng(e, obs. form of LOZENGE.

†**losenge**, *v. Obs.* Also 5 losynge. [a. OF. *losenger* = Pr. *lauzengar*, Sp. *lisonjar*, Pg. *lisonjear*, It. *lusingare*; f. OF. *losenge*, *losange* sb. flattery = Pr. *lauzenga*, *lauzenja*, Sp., Pg. *lisonja*; app. adopted by the other Rom. langs. from Pr. *lauzenga* = OF. *loenge* (F. *louange*) praise:—med.L. *laudēmia*, a derivative (? on analogy of *vindēmia*) of L. *laud-em* praise: see LOSE *sb.*¹] *trans.* To flatter, compliment unduly. Const. *of.*

1422 tr. *Secreta Secret., Priv. Priv.* 129 Thay losyngid the kynge of Wayne-glory of the force of his hoste. **1480** CAXTON *Ovid's Met.* XIII. xvii, Thanne began Glaucus to call her and losenge her.

†**losengeous**, *a. Obs. rare*⁻¹. In 7 losungeous. [f. next with substitution of suffix: see -OUS.] Lying, flattering.

1632 LITHGOW *Trav.* III. 108 What a selfe Losungeous fellow hath this fustian companion proued.

†**losenger.** *Obs.* Forms: 4 loseniour (= *-jour*), -gour, losaniour (= *-jour*), lozengiour, -eour, 4–5 losengeour, -gere, -ynger(e, 4–6 losanger, (5 -ere, losengeoure, -joure, lousenger, lesingour, *Sc.* lossingere, 6 -geir, loosenger, losinger), 4–7 losenger. [a. OF. *losengeour*, *-ere*, agent-n. f. *losenger* LOSENGE *v.*]

1. A false flatterer, a lying rascal, a deceiver.

13.. *Seuyn Sag.* (W.) 674 Thou schalt ben an-honged, thou losenjour. **1303** R. BRUNNE *Handl. Synne* 3504 What sey men of þese loseniours, þat haue here wurdys feyre as flours? *c* **1385** CHAUCER *L.G.W.* Prol. 328 In youre court is manye a losenger. *a* **1400–50** *Alexander* 1923 Laches me þis losengere & ledis me him hedire. **1484** CAXTON *Ryall Bk.* C iij, But this synne [*sc.* of boasting] doubleth in them that folowe and flatre these vauntours and losengers. **1508** DUNBAR *Tua mariit wemen* 258 Gif yov nought list be forleit with losingeris vntrew. **1577–87** HOLINSHED *Chron., Hist. Scot.* 63/1 There to end their liues with shame, as a number of such other loosengers had often doone before them. **1616** BULLOKAR, *Losenger*, a flatterer, a Lyar.

¶**2.** *Sc.* A sluggard. [? Confused with *losel.*]

1513 DOUGLAS *Æneis* VIII. Prol. 178 Thus lysnit I, as lossingeir, sic lewidnes to luik. *Ibid.* XII. Prol. 281, I knew it was past four howris of day, And thocht I wald no langar ly In May Les Phebus suld me losanger attaynt.

†**losengery.** *Obs.* Forms: 4 (losingerie), lozengerie, 4–5 losengerie, -gerye, (4 -grie, -grye), 5 -gry, (-gri), (5 losangerye, losyng(e)rie). [a. OF. *losengerie*: see prec. and -ERY.] Flattery, deceit.

13.. *Seuyn Sag.* (W.) 1959 Gold and siluer to wille he wan Bi losengerie. **1303** R. BRUNNE *Handl. Synne* 3512 Kepe þe þan fro losengrye, For feyre spekyng man kan weyl lye. **1377** LANGL. *P. Pl.* B. VI. 145 In lecherye and in losengerye ȝe lyuen. **1422** tr. *Secreta Secret., Priv. Priv.* 157 Ouer-myche to Preyse is suspecte of losengry. **1484** CAXTON *Ryall Bk.* D j, Therof growen many sinnes,..That is to wete losangerye, flaterye [etc.].

loser ('lu:zə(r)). [f. LOSE *v.*¹ + -ER¹.]

†**1.** A destroyer. *Obs.*

a **1340** HAMPOLE *Psalter* Cant. 512, I sall be glad in god.. my saueoure, noght in þe warld my losere. **1388** in *Wyclif's Sel. Wks.* III. 459 þis court is..loser of al þe worlde. *c* **1611** CHAPMAN *Iliad* XVIII. 109 And when the loser of my friend his death in me shall find; Let death take all.

2. a. One who loses or suffers loss.

a **1548** HALL *Chron., Hen. VIII* 60 b, One daie thone parte lost, and the other gained, and likewise the losers regained. **1555** EDEN *Decades* 303, I may vppon iust occasion thynke my selfe a looser manye wayes. **1602** SHAKS. *Ham.* IV. v. 143 You will draw both Friend and Foe, Winner and Looser. **1608** *Burgh Rec. Glasgow* (1876) I. 283 That thay be nocht loseris of thair provisioun. *a* **1703** BURKITT *On N.T.* Mark x. 31 We may be losers for Christ, we shall never be losers by him. **1849** MACAULAY *Hist. Eng.* vii. II. 267 He always declared that he had been a loser by his mission.

Proverb. [**1533** MORE *Debell. Salem* Wks. 1018/2 Hit is an olde curtesye at the cardes perdy, to let the leser haue hys wordes.] **1562** J. HEYWOOD *Prov. & Epigr.* (1867) 146 Let the loosers haue their wordes. **1599** SANDYS *Europæ Spec.* (1632) 123 The wisest men have beene..pleased, that losers should have their words. **1634** SIR T. HERBERT *Trav.* 47 Giue loosers leaue to prate. *a* **1716** SOUTH *Serm.* (J.), Losers and malecontents, whose portion and inheritance is a freedom to speak.

b. A squanderer or waster (of time).

1650 JER. TAYLOR *Holy Living* i. §1. 8 If one of the Speakers be..trifling, he that hears, and he that answers.. are equal losers of their time. **1691** WOOD *Ath. Oxon.* I. 354 The author was no loser of his time.

c. A horse that loses in a race.

1902 J. BURNS in *Speaker* 11 Jan. 419/1 The workman works hard five days, but on the sixth is generally found at the 'Corner Pin' spotting winners and catching losers.

d. *a bad, poor* (or *good*) *loser*: a person who loses with bad (or good) grace.

1892 A. W. PINERO *Magistrate* I. 28 I hate a bad loser, don't you, Guv? **1917** *Dialect Notes* IV. 326 *Loser* n., differentiated as good loser and bad loser. Not local. 'Those college boys are good losers and do not complain at defeat, but the academy boys..are sure bad losers.' **1931** D. L. SAYERS *Five Red Herrings* xiii. 146 He was a bad loser. A slice off the tee..would put him off his game for the afternoon. **1947** 'G. ORWELL' *Eng. People* 14 The admiration for a 'good loser'. **1951** [see CLOBBER *v.*³]. **1973** A. MANN *Tiara* xvii. 164 The British were always talking about 'being a good loser'. **1973** *Radio Times* 20–27 Dec. 10/1, I like to win at things. But..I'm a good loser.

e. An unsuccessful or incompetent person, a failure.

1955 *Amer. Speech* XXX. 304 *Loser*,..someone.. hopeless. **1959** *Ibid.* XXXIV. 154 Those limited in ability or old-fashioned in dress or manners, [are] losers. *Ibid.*, The opposite of a B[ig] M[an] O[n] C[ampus] is a loser. **1972** *Melody Maker* 25 Nov. 53 (*heading*) Jiving K. Boots. The adventures of a loser musician. **1974** J. STUBBS *Painted Face* xiii. 180 Poor fellow... A born loser, every time.

3. *Billiards.* A losing hazard.

1873 BENNETT & 'CAVENDISH' *Billiards* 281 There may be a loser left off the white. **1902** J. ROBERTS jun. *Mod. Billiards* 88 The angle is not suitable for a following loser, so the play is again a loser off the cushion.

4. *U.S. slang.* A convicted criminal, a person who has served a sentence in prison. So ***two-time*** (or ***three-time***, etc.) ***loser***, a person who has been in prison twice (or three, etc., times).

1912 D. LOWRIE *My Life in Prison* xi. 127 T'day some four 'r five time loser'll drive up with a year. *Ibid.* xxvii. 337 He was a 'ten-time loser' the last time I saw him; *i.e.*, he had served nine previous terms at either San Quentin or Folsom. **1914** JACKSON & HELLYER *Vocab. Criminal Slang* 56 *Loser* noun, current amongst prison habitues. An ex-convict... Examples: 'Three-time losers cop life in some states.' **1926** *Clues* Nov. 161/2 *Loser*, one who has served a prison sentence. **1931** *Amer. Speech* VII. 117 *Two-time loser*, a prisoner who has been convicted twice. 'He's a two-time loser; got the book the second time.' **1939** E. S. GARDNER *D.A. draws Circle* (1940) xii. 213 He's a two-time loser. **1950** H. E. GOLDIN *Dict. Amer. Underworld Lingo* 129/1 *Loser*, anyone convicted of a felony. (A second felony conviction makes one a 'two-time loser'; a third conviction, a 'three-time loser', etc.) 'I'm a four-time loser on the next pinch (arrest).' **1973** *Houston* (Texas) *Chron. Texas Mag.* 14 Oct. 4/1 Bob, a three-time loser with a long line of busts and drug abuse..was sick of his life.

5. *Bridge.* **a.** A losing card.

1917 E. BERGHOLT *Royal Auction Bridge* (ed. 2) 56 The opponent will be able to make two tricks in that suit before Y has had a chance of discarding his two losers. **1921** F. IRWIN *Compl. Auction Player* ii. 48 You hold five losers. That is a two-bid, no more. **1964** *Contract Bridge* ('Know the Game' Series) (ed. 2) 29/1 You should not play any trumps but utilize them to ruff losers. **1964** *Official Encycl. Bridge* 334/1 At no trump, all cards below the ace and not in sequence with it are possible losers.

b. loser-on-loser (see quot. 1964).

[**1929** *Auction Bridge Mag.* Jan. 328/1 (*title*) Discarding a loser on a loser...discarding a losing card on a loser..may be the only play to secure the contract or game.] **1947** T. REESE *Reese on Play* xi. 162 Loser-on-loser play makes the hand against any defence... Some very complicated positions can arise after a loser-on-loser elimination. **1964** *Official Encycl. Bridge* 334/1 *Loser on loser*, the act of playing a card that must be lost on a losing trick in some other suit.

† **'losery.** *Obs.* [f. LOSE *v.*¹ + -ERY.] Losing; opportunity or chance of losing.

c **1400** *Beryn* 924 Al othir gamys that losery was in. *Ibid.* 1228 For in such losery he hath lost many a ffrank.

loseyite ('ləʊzɪaɪt). *Min.* [f. the name of Samuel *Losey* (*c* 1833–1906), U.S. mineral collector + -ITE¹.] A basic carbonate of zinc and manganese, $(Zn,Mn)_7(CO_3)_2(OH)_{10}$, found as bluish-white monoclinic crystals at Franklin, New Jersey, U.S.A.

1929 BAUER & BERMAN in *Amer. Mineralogist* XIV. 150 This mineral is named loseyite in honor of Mr. Samuel R. Losey, a native of Franklin and for many years, until his death, an ardent collector of the minerals occurring there. **1968** I. KOSTOV *Mineral.* II. xi. 542 Loseyite is also monoclinic (*A2/a*), found as bluish white radiating bundles of lath-like crystals.

loseyn, obs. form of LOZEN.

losh (lɒʃ), *sb.*¹ Also 7 losy. [a. Russ. *los'*.]

† **1.** An elk. *Obs.*

1591 [see OLEN]. **1599** HAKLUYT *Voy.* I. 463 An Elke or Loshe, the Red deere of the countrey. **1613** PURCHAS *Pilgrimage* IV. xvii. 431 They worship the Sunne, the Ollen, and the Losy and such like. *a* **1674** MILTON *Hist. Mosc.* ii. Wks. 1851 VIII. 482 People riding on Elks and Loshes.

2. *losh hide, leather*: the untanned hide of the elk, and later of the buffalo and ox, prepared with oil; a soft buff-coloured leather; wash-leather. (Cf. LASCH *sb.*)

1583 CARLILE in *Hakluyt's Voy.* (1600) III. 184 Losshe hides, rich Furres, and other such like. **1591** G. FLETCHER *Russe Commw.* (Hakl. Soc.) 10 Their losh or buffe hide is very faire and large. **1662** *Irish Stat.* (1765) II. 409 Losh hides, the piece £1. **1756** *Gentl. Mag.* XXVI. 61 Losh, or buff-leather, drest in oil. **1852** MORFIT *Tanning & Currying* (1853) 433 Oiled leather is commonly known as..wash-leather... It is also called losh leather. **1864** CRAIG, Suppl., *Losh-hide*, a hide not dressed in any way, but simply oiled.

losh (lɒʃ), *sb.*² [a. F. *loche* = LOACH.] A name in Canada and Alaska for the burbot.

1884 GOODE, etc. *Nat. Hist. Useful Aquatic Anim.* I. 236 In Alaska..it is known as 'Losh'; in Canada, as 'la Loche'. **1884** *Riverside Nat. Hist.* (1888) III. 273.

† **losh,** *v. Obs.* [? Onomatopœic.] *intr.* ? To fall with a splash; to go stumbling.

1629 GAULE *Holy Madn.* 170 Yet am I not so sheepish, to losh into the Ditch. **1847–78** HALLIWELL, *Losh*, to splash in water. *North.* **1859** WHITEHEAD *Leg.* (1896) 19 (E.D.D.) An laykes and loshes ower the steaynes.

losh (lɔʃ), *int. Sc.* A distortion of LORD, used in certain exclamations.

a **1779** D. GRAHAM *Leper the Taylor* (1785) 17 The losh preserve me, sirs. **1792** G. GALLOWAY *Poems* 40 Tax shoon! losh how the snobs will glunch. **1826** J. WILSON *Noct. Ambr.* Wks. 1855 I. 244 Losh me! that's beautiful language. **1901** *Blackw. Mag.* Mar. 363/1 'Losh! the body's cracked'.

losien, losin, obs. forms of LOZEN.

losine, obs. pa. pple. of LEESE *v.*

losing ('lu:zɪŋ), *vbl. sb.* [f. LOSE *v.*¹ + -ING¹.]

1. The action of LOSE *v.*¹ †**a.** Perdition, destruction; the being lost or destroyed (*obs.*). **b.** Used, chiefly *gerundially*, in various senses of the vb. † *to be on losing*: to be in process of being lost.

a. *c* **950** *Lindisf. Gosp.* Matt. vii. 13 Weȝ ðiu lædas to losing. **13..** *E.E. Allit. P.* B. 1031 He most ay lyue in þat loȝe in losyng euer-more. **1530** PALSGR. 241/1 Losyng, *perdition.* **1597** BEARD *Theatre God's Judgem.* (1631) 234 The citie beeing besieged, and in some danger of losing. *c* **1660** WRIOTHESLEY *Chron.* I. 136 An armye of Gelderland ..was in great daunger of loosinge.

b. *c* **1387** TREVISA *Higden* (Rolls) IV. 295 As a goldene fischhook, þe loosynge þerof may be i-quytte by non wynnynge of taking of fische. *c* **1470** HENRY *Wallace* II. 221 Compleyne his payne in dolour thus that duellis; In langour lyis, for losyng of thar luff. **1526** *Pilgr. Perf.* (W. de W. 1531) 241 How shorte they be in duryng: how feerfull in kepyng: how sorowful in losynge. **1639** FULLER *Holy War* (1647) 218 At his arrivall, the last stake of the Christians was on losing. **1668** PEPYS *Diary* 1 Jan., To see how differently one man took his losing from another. **1725** J. GLANVILL *Poems* 63 France shall meet with no Repair From Losings here, by healing Winnings there. **1847** TENNYSON *Princess* I. 140 Odes About this losing of the child. **1900** F. T. BULLEN *With Christ at Sea* iii. 53 We arrived..without..adventure except the losing of an anchor. **1901** *Q. Rev.* July 178 It was the scene of Charles Fox's chief losings at the faro table.

2. *attrib.* in **losing-money**, a payment allowed to the loser in certain competitions.

1880 *Daily Tel.* 7 Sept., There is a pound per win to each man.., and there is losing money at half rates every time your boat answers the starting gun.

'losing, *ppl. a.* [f. LOSE *v.*¹ + -ING².] That loses, or that results in loss. **losing game,** (*a*) a game played with ill-success; (*b*) a game in which the loser of the game wins the stakes. **losing hazard, loadum,** see the sbs.

1519 HORMAN *Vulg.* 280 b, A sengle ace is a losynge caste. **1596** SHAKS. *Merch. V.* IV. i. 62, I follow thus A loosing suite against him. **1601** —— *Jul. C.* V. v. 36, I shall have glory by this loosing day. **1668** LADY CHAWORTH in *12th Rep. Hist. MSS. Comm.* App. V. 10 [He] deserves a better fate than to be ever of the loosing side. **1708** POPE *Let. to H. Cromwell* 1 Nov., You are return'd by this time..to the old Diversions of a losing Game at Picquet with the Ladies, and half a Play ..at the Theatre. **1720** DE FOE *Capt. Singleton* xv. (1840) 265 This was a losing voyage. **1755** MAGENS *Insurances* I. 60 They came to a losing Market. **1763** HOYLE *Whist* 23 Do not trump it, but throw away a losing Card. **1893** F. ADAMS *New Egypt* 26, I think we're playing a losing game in Egypt.

Hence **'losingly** *adv.*, in a losing manner.

1864 in CRAIG, Suppl.

losing(e, obs. form of LOZENGE.

loss (lɒs, -ɔ:-) *sb.*¹ Forms: 1–3 los (only in dat. lose, in Lay. occas. written leose), 4–5 los, loos, (5 loose, 6 *Sc.* lois), 4–7 losse, (5 losce), 4– loss. [Prob. two distinct formations. The OE. *los* (? neut.), found only in the phr. *tó lose* (*weorðan*, *ȝedón*), corresponds to ON. *los* neut., 'breaking up of the ranks of an army' (Vigf.):—OTeut. **loso-m* (a parallel formation with OE. *lor* LORE *sb.*²:—OTeut. **lozo-m*), f. **lus-*, wk. grade of the root **leus-*, **laus-*: see LEESE *v.*, LEASE *a.*, LOOSE *a.* (The etymological sense may be rendered by 'dissolution'; cf. the ON. use.) As this word occurs in OE. and early ME. only in the dative (which if it had survived would have normally become *lōse* with voiced *s*), it cannot, unless the uninflected cases were preserved unrecorded, account for the mod. form. The word in its later use as a noun of action to *leese*, *lose* vbs., appears first in the middle of the 14th c., and may have been a back-formation from the pa. pple. *lost*; cf. LOST *sb.*, which is of contemporary date.]

1. Perdition, ruin, destruction; the condition or fact of being 'lost', destroyed, or ruined. Now only with mixture of other senses; cf. LOSE *v.*¹ 2 b.

c **897** K. ÆLFRED *Gregory's Past.* xxxvi. 249 Ðonne ȝe to lose weorðað. *c* **1205** LAY. 3903 Heore lif heom eode al to leose [*for* lose; *riming with* neose = nose]. *c* **1275** *Ibid.* 22844 And so hi solle go to lose. **1483** CAXTON *Cato* G j b, Whan they seken..the losse and the dethe of yonge chyldren. *a* **1548** HALL *Chron., Hen. VI* 115 Bothe her body and soule, wer gotten again out of eternall losse and perdicion. **1605** SHAKS. *Lear* III. vi. 102 His life With thine, and all that offer to defend him, Stand in assured losse. **1667** MILTON *P.L.* III. 308 Thou hast..quitted all to save A World from utter loss. **1743** BULKELEY & CUMMINS *Voy. S. Seas* 104 The Loss of the Ship, was the Loss of him. **1784** COWPER *Tiroc.* 166 Describe a Saviour's cross As God's expedient to retrieve his loss. **1839** MACAULAY *Ess., Gladstone on Ch. & State* (1880) 481 Is not the loss of one soul a greater evil than the extinction of many lives?

2. The fact of losing (something specified or contextually implied). See the senses of LOSE *v.*¹ Const. with *of* or objective genitive.

a. The being deprived of, or the failure to keep (a possession, appurtenance, right, quality, faculty, or the like).

1377 LANGL. *P. Pl.* B. xix. 287 Losse of worldely catel. **1398** TREVISA *Barth. De P.R.* VI. v. (1495) 193 Chyldren wepe more for the losse of an apple than for the losse of theyr heritage. **1562–3** *Act 5 Eliz.* c. 14 §12 Persons that shall so offende..shall have Imprisonement, losse of Eares, slytting and searing of Nose. **1620** T. GRANGER *Div. Logike* I. xxxvii. 109 The losse of power, and vertue in all liuing things..is the privation thereof. **1671** MILTON *Samson* 67 O loss of sight, of thee I most complain! **1774** GOLDSM. *Nat. Hist.* (1776) III. 180 William the Conqueror..punished such as were convicted of killing the wild boar in his forests, with the loss of their eyes. **1849** MACAULAY *Hist. Eng.* ii. I. 194 The Papists of Ireland attributed to him the loss of their lands. **1864** TREVELYAN *Compet. Wallah* (1866) 299 The words, 'loss of caste', convey to an English gentleman's mind no more terrible idea than that of marrying his laundress. **1896** J. H. CLARKE *Cold-Catching, Cold-Preventing*, etc. 66 Among the sequelae of a cold in the head..may be mentioned loss of taste and smell.

b. *loss of life*: the being put to death (as a punishment). Also, in generalized sense, the destruction or 'sacrifice' of human lives.

c **1386** CHAUCER *Knt.'s T.* 1685 Vp peyne of los of lyf. **1582** N. LICHEFIELD tr. *Castanheda's Conq. E. Ind.* I. viii. 20 Not willing they should..susteine crueltie, or losse of lyfe. **1595** SHAKS. *John* IV. iii. 106, I lou'd him, and will weepe My date of life out, for his sweete liues losse. **1611** BIBLE *Acts* xxvii. 22 There shall be no losse of any mans life among you. **1898** *Daily News* 12 Apr. 3/3 These men estimate the loss of life —that is, the ruthless waste and destruction of human life during the sixteen years that the Khalifa has ruled—at seventy-five per cent. of the entire population.

c. The being deprived by death, separation, or estrangement, of (a friend, relative, servant, or the like). Often *contextually*, the death (of a person regretted).

a **1450** MYRC 1279 For los of frendes or of any þynge. *c* **1645** HOWELL *Lett.* I. VI. xlv. 237 Ther be many sad hearts for the loss of my Lord Robert Digby. **1692** R. L'ESTRANGE *Fables* (1708) I. 543 The Case of a Lady that kept her Bed for the loss of a Favorite Puppy she had. **1710** STEELE *Tatler* No. 198 ⁋1 Affliction for the Loss of her Mother. **1798** *Monthly Mag.* VI. 309 [Died] John Case Browne, esq. whose loss will be severely felt..by the whole neighbourhood. **1805** J. QUINCY in *Life* 74 The loss of Mr. Griswold from the national legislature. **1831** BREWSTER *Newton* (1855) II. xxi. 269 Newton had to mourn the loss of his earliest and best friend.

d. The losing of or being defeated in (a battle, game, or contest). †Formerly also without specific mention of the object: The state of being a loser, defeat (*obs.*).

13.. *E.E. Allit. P.* C. 174, I lovne þat we lay lotes on ledes vchone, & who-so lympes þe losse, lay hym þer-oute. *a* **1548** HALL *Chron., Hen. VIII* 136 Of the takyng of the Kyng their Master, and of the losse of the feld. **1593** SHAKS. *3 Hen. VI*, IV. iv. 4 What losse of some pitcht battell Against Warwicke? **1611** —— *Cymb.* II. iii. 2 Your Lordship is the most patient man in losse, the most coldest that euer turn'd vp Ace. **1744** OZELL tr. *Brantome's Sp. Rhodomontades* 205 As a great many Captains have done after the Loss of a Battle. **1822** SHELLEY *Calderon's Magico Prodig.* i. 151 The battle's loss may profit those who lose.

e. Failure to take advantage or make good use (of time, etc.).

c **1385** CHAUCER *L.G.W.* 997 *Dido*, It nere but los of tyme. **1535** COVERDALE *Exod.* xxi. 19 He shal paye the losse of his tyme. **1593** SHAKS. *Lucr.* 1420 But for losse of Nestors golden words, Its seem'd they would debate with angrie swords. **1632** J. HAYWARD tr. *Biondi's Eromena* 29 She without losse of time, buried the Poyniard up to the hilts. **1709** ADDISON *Tatler* No. 131 ⁋10 To..take to some honest Livelihood without Loss of Time. **1814** SCOTT *Wav.* xxxi, Instant reimbursement for loss of time. **1860** TYNDALL *Glac.* I. xi. 75 This error caused us the loss of an hour.

f. Failure to gain or obtain. (Cf. LOSE *v.*¹ 7.)

a **1614** D. DYKE *Myst. Self-deceiving* (ed. 8) 41 A word that signifieth..losse of victory. *Mod.* I do not wish to risk the loss of my train.

† **3.** *occas.* Cause or occasion of ruin or deprivation. *Obs.*

c **1386** CHAUCER *Wife of Bath's Prol.* 720 Womman was the los of al mankynde. *a* **1548** HALL *Chron., Hen. VI* 130 The negligence of the kynges counsaill..was the losse of the whole dominion of Fraunce.

4. a. In particularized sense: An instance of losing. Also, a person, thing, or amount lost.

c **1369** CHAUCER *Dethe Blaunche* 1302 That was the losse.. that I had lorne. **1463–4** *Coldingham Priory Papers* (Surtees) 191 Our grete lossez in plee for Coldyngham. **1560** DAUS tr. *Sleidane's Comm.* 406 b, That those which had bene faithfull to him, and therfore had chaunced into extreme miserie, should first be recompensed their losse. **1599** SHAKS. *Much Ado* IV. ii. 87 A rich fellow enough, goe to, and a fellow that hath had losses. **1685** EVELYN *Mrs. Godolphin* 150 Thus ended this incomparable Lady: our never to be sufficiently lamented losse. **1718** *Freethinker* No. 1 ⁋6 It is not possible to trade to much Advantage without some Losses. **1883** R. W. DIXON *Mano* II. viii. 95 But soon 'twas heard (a loss of little woe) That he had stolen away the gallant quean. **1891** *Law Times* XC. 283/2 The company wrote off the loss as a bad debt.

b. *spec.* (*Path.*) A loss of blood by uterine hæmorrhage.

1901 *Brit. Med. Jrnl.* No. 2089. 86 The patient gave a history of having had a loss a few days previously.

c. *to cut one's loss*(*es*): to cease carrying on a losing transaction.

1912 *Q. Rev.* Jan. 287 It is now made the basis of the argument that England should 'cut her loss', and Ireland be sent adrift. **1926** T. E. LAWRENCE *Seven Pillars* (1935) VIII. xciv. 519 Feisal had..made one of his lightning decisions to cut the loss; a wise decision, though it hurt us sorely. **1927** *Daily Express* 13 July 8/2 The only reasonable thing is for Great Britain to..cut her losses, and bring the whole matter to an end. **1939** 'G. ORWELL' *Coming up for Air* II. vii. 123 The trouble over Joe aged Father a great deal. To lose Joe was merely to cut a loss, but it hurt him. **1944** A. BRYANT *Yrs. of Victory* ii. 39 Bonaparte..saw that he was beaten and, like the great man he was, cut his losses. **1969** *Listener* 28 Aug. 269/1 For this reason the CIA is cutting its losses, reducing its labyrinthine commitments.

5. a. Diminution of one's possessions or advantages; detriment or disadvantage involved in being deprived of something, or resulting from a change of conditions; an instance of this. (Opposed to *gain*.)

1377 LANGL. *P. Pl.* B. Prol. 195 Better is a litel losse than a longe sorwe. **1380** WYCLIF *Wks.* (1880) 212 Drede of worldly shame & loos. *c* **1400** *Destr. Troy* 1719 Of þe harmys þat we haue & þe hoge lose. *Ibid.* 9781 Me is leuer for to lyue with losse þat I haue. *a* **1548** HALL *Chron., Hen. VI* 141 b, Gain is not alwaies perdurable, nor losse alwaies continuall. **1603** SHAKS. *Meas. for M.* III. i. 181 No losse shall touch her by my company. **1611** BIBLE *Phil.* iii. 7 What things were gaine to me, those I counted losse for Christ. **1627** MILTON *Vacat. Exerc.* 9 Small loss it is that thence can come unto thee. **1686** tr. *Chardin's Trav. Persia* 8 No wonder if their Trade decrease, and turn to loss rather then profit. **1784** COWPER *Task* VI. 750 Nor can the wonders it records be sung To meaner music, and not suffer loss. **1841** TRENCH *Parables* xix. (1877) 341 Earthly losses are remedies for covetousness. **1848** NEWMAN (*title*) Loss and gain. **1866** MISS YONGE *Dove in Eagle's Nest* I. 76 No matter..'Tis only her loss [refusing to drink].

b. *to have a* (*great*) *loss in* (or *of*): to suffer severely by losing (usually, a person).

1680 AUBREY *Lives, E. Davenant* (1813) II. 300 He was not only a man of vast learning, but of great goodness and charity; the parish and all his friends will have a great losse in him. **1757** MRS. GRIFFITH *Lett. Henry & Frances* (1767) IV. 15 What a Loss shall I have of him! **1824** JEKYLL *Corr.* (1894) 144, I feel a sad loss of poor dear Mr. Stanley. **1836** MOORE *Mem.* (1856) VII. 164 As the time approaches for the departure of our dear little Nell, we begin to feel more and more the loss we shall have of her. **1881** TROLLOPE *Dr. Wortle's School* IV. xi, She had a certain charge..as to the school..; and very well she did her work. I shall have a great loss in her.

¶ **c.** *a* (*great*, etc.) *loss* (in this sense) is often idiomatically predicated of the person or thing lost, where in strictness the subject of the sentence should be the loss or deprivation of this. (The more correct expression, as in quot. 1605, is obsolete.) *dead loss*: see DEAD *a.* 30.

[**1605** BACON *Adv. Learn.* II. iii. §4 For apophthegms, it is a great loss of that book of Cæsar's.] *a* **1903** *Mod.* Our opponents are welcome to their new convert; he is no loss. **1940** W. FAULKNER *Hamlet* I. i. 16 Major De Spain's barn taken fire and was a total loss. **1943** *Scrutiny* XI. 288 If you apply serious standards, then P. G. [Wodehouse] is a total loss.

d. *one person's loss is another's gain*: a semi-proverbial expression. Also with non-personal subject and complement.

1914 G. B. SHAW *Misalliance* 41 It civilizes them. And it uncivilizes us. Their gain. Our loss. **1925** *New Yorker* 22 Aug. 9/1 When the fighting was over she remained... Our loss was their gain. **1949** B. A. BOTKIN *Treas. S. Folklore* II. i. 147 What is history's loss is folklore's gain. **1973** *Times* 22 Jan. 9/5 (*heading*) Newcastle's loss is Doncaster's gain.

6. *Mil.* The losing (by a commander or an army) of men by death, wounds, or capture; also (*sing.* and *pl.*) the number of men so lost.

a **1400–50** *Alexander* 3171 ȝit me is better.. in bataile be slayne, þan se þe lose of my ledis. *a* **1548** HALL *Chron., Hen. VI* 130 Trustyng.. shortly to be lorde of the citee and towne, without any greate losse or battaill. **1840** GRESLEY *Siege Lichf.* 45 The loss of each army.. was about equal. **1846** GROTE *Greece* (1869) II. II. viii. 446 They were repulsed with loss. **1899** SIR G. WHITE *Disp. to Buller* 16 Dec., The loss of 12,000 men here would be a heavy blow to England.

†**7.** Lack, default, want. *in the loss of question*: provided there is no dispute. *Obs.*

1603 SHAKS. *Meas. for M.* II. iv. 90 As I subscribe not that, nor any other, But in the loss of question. **1632** LITHGOW *Trav.* III. 85 The Villages for losse of ground are all built on the skirts of Rockes.

†**8.** *Tennis.* A lost chase (see CHASE *sb.*¹ 7).

1591 [see CHASE *sb.*¹ 7]. **1619** DRUMM. OF HAWTH. *Convers. B. Jonson* xvii. (1842) 30 A Lord playing at Tenis, and having asked those in the gallerie Whither a strock was Chase or Losse? A Brother of my Lord Northumberland's answered, it was Loss.

9. at a loss, †at loss. Of a hound: Having lost the track or scent; at fault. Hence of persons: At fault; utterly uncertain what to say or do (often with indirect questions introduced by *how*, *what*, etc.); unable *to* understand, imagine, discover, explain, etc. *at a loss for*: unable to discover or obtain (something needed).

1592 WARNER *Alb. Eng.* VII. xxxvi. (1612) 175 The Hound at losse doth ouer-giue. **1596** SHAKS. *Tam. Shr.* Induct. i. 23 He cried vpon it at the meerest losse, And twice to day pick'd out the dullest sent. **1663** SOUTH *Serm.* (1823) III. 424 The justness of his government left them at a loss for an occasion [*sc.* of rebellion]. **1668** HALE *Pref. to Rolle's Abridgm.* b j b, Many that are much conversant in subtilties of Logick.. are at a loss in it, and can make little of it. **1671** MILTON *P.R.* IV. 366 Satan now Quite at a loss, for all his darts were spent, Thus to our Saviour with stern brow reply'd. **1699** BENTLEY *Phal.* 332 His wonderfull Learning was at a loss. **1711** STEELE *Spect.* No. 53 ⁋8, I stood utterly at a loss how to behave my self. *Ibid.* No. 157 ⁋1, I am very much at a loss to express by any Word that occurs to me in our Language, that which is understood by *Indoles* in Latin. **1773** *Life N. Frowde* 23 If they were at a Loss for any thing, I cry'd out, can I find it, Sir? **1781** COWPER *Hope* 345 All speakers, yet all language at a loss. **1823** J. BADCOCK *Dom. Amusem.* 33 We are at a loss, however, for any direct knowledge of the means used by them. **1827** HALLAM *Const. Hist.* (1876) I. vi. 302 They were at a loss how to obtain his release. **1863** F. A. KEMBLE *Resid. Georgia* 17, I therefore am at a loss to understand what made her hail the erection of one [mill] at Charleston as likely to produce such.. happy results.

10. *attrib.* and *Comb.* **loss leader** *Comm.*, an article put on sale at a non-profit-making price in order to attract potential buyers of other articles; also *transf.*; hence **loss-leading** *vbl. sb.*; **loss-maker**, a business, etc., consistently working at a loss; **loss-making** *vbl. sb.*, the making of a loss (in business, etc.); also as *ppl. a.*, that makes a loss.

1922 HAYWARD & WHITE *Chain Stores* vii. 109 Many chains have a fixed policy of featuring each week a so-called '*loss leader'. That is, some well known article, the price of which is usually standard and known to the majority of purchasers, is put on sale at actual cost to the chain or even at a slight loss.. on the theory.. that people will be attracted to this bargain and buy other goods as well. Loss leaders are often termed 'weekly specials'. **1942** H. LEVY *Retail Trade Assoc.* xviii. 211 Prohibitions on 'loss leaders'. **1958** *Times* 15 Dec. 9/3 No doubt price cutting in individual lines often goes beyond the point where it is justified by reduction in direct cost: it is in point the loss-leader technique. People are attracted into a shop by some very low prices, and buy many other articles which give a handsome margin. **1969** *Daily Tel.* 7 Mar. 19 Sir Stanley Raymond, chairman of the Gaming Board, said yesterday he was convinced that Bingo was often used as a 'loss leader' to induce housewives into 'hard' gambling. In many cases Bingo provided only half of the takings in clubs. **1970** *Ibid.* 15 May 21/5 Some would like to see bank charges on personal accounts reduced or abolished, as a 'loss leader' to the existing personal customers. **1971** *New Scientist* 21 Jan. 102/1 The ranks of loss leaders and unrepeatable offers. **1964** *New Statesman* 28 Feb. 343/1 This concession was necessary to get any bill past his own back-benchers; and there are a few more.. concessions.. in particular a ban on *loss-leading. **1968** *Daily Tel.* 12 Nov. 17/8 Only a madman or a company making a genuine attempt at loss leading would reduce rates. **1971** *Guardian Weekly* 23 Jan. 22 What happens when two companies, both *lossmakers, merge into one? The answer, as often as not, is one big loss-maker. **1973** *Times* 24 Aug. 17/2 The company declined to give reasons for its withdrawals except to say that the bookstalls did not fit into its 'economic pattern' or plans for the future. It said the stalls were not lossmakers. **1971** *Sunday Times* 15 Aug. 41 He started by picking up a 40% stake in the *lossmaking Carson's chocolate business in March 1964. **1974** *Times* 7 Mar. 19/6 The company has been loss-making since 1971.

†**loss**, *sb.*² *Obs.* Also 5–6 losse, (5 lossem), 6 los, 7 loz. [a. MDu. *los* = OE. *lox*, OHG., MHG. *luhs* (mod.G. *luchs*); akin to Sw. *lo* of the same meaning. Caxton's *lossem* represents the unexplained variant *lossen* of the Du. original.] A lynx.

1481 CAXTON *Reynard* xxxviii. (Arb.) 105 The rulers and kepars of the felde was the lupaert and the losse. *Ibid.* xli. 111 The kepars of the felde, the lupaerd and the lossem. **1598** FLORIO, *Lince*, a beast like vnto a woolfe,.. called a los or linx. *Lince*,.. Also a losse, or a linx. **1624** T. HEYWOOD *Gunaikeion* VII. 329 The beast called a Loz or Lynx.

†**loss**, *v.* *Sc. Obs.* Also 5–6 los, 6–7 loiss. [a. Du. *lossen* (whence G. *löschen*, Da. *losse*, Sw. *lossa*), f. *los* adj., loose (:—OTeut. **lusso-*), cogn. w. *loos* (:—OTeut. **lauso-*: see LOOSE *a.*).] *trans.* To unload (a vessel), discharge (goods from a vessel). Also *absol.* of a ship: To unload.

1482 *Charters Edinb.* (1871) 168 Of ilk stane bait cumand and losand in the havin *id. Ibid.* 169 That na.. stapill gudis of strangearis remane.. langare in Leith eftir it be dischargit and losit than [etc.]. **1537** *Burgh Rec. Edinb.* (1871) II. 86 Jhone Sleith.. confessit that he loissit the pok of forest woll pertening to Mungo Tennend efter that the samyn wes schippit and stowit in his schip. **1565** *Reg. Privy Council Scot.* I. 332 Nane of thame sall brek bouk,.. quhill the tyme that thair gudis be housit, and the schip lost, and avysit with the conservatour how the marcat is. **1609** *Burgh Rec. Glasgow* (1876) I. 302 Be making of mercat thairof [*sc.* goods].. befoir they be lossit.

loss(e, var. Sc. f. LOSE *v.*¹; var. LOSE *sb.*¹ *Obs.*, praise; obs. f. LOOSE.

löss, variant of LOESS.

lossel, variant of LOSEL.

lossen, lossenge, obs. ff. LOZEN, LOZENGE.

lossenite (ˈlɒsənaɪt). *Min.* [Named by Milch in 1894, after Prof. C. A. *Lossen*: see -ITE.] Arsenate of iron and lead, occurring in small reddish-brown crystals.

1895 *Amer. Jrnl. Sci.* L. 76 Lossenite.

†ˈ**losset.** *Obs. dial.* Also 8 losad. [Ir. *losad* (OIr. *losat*) kneading-trough.] A wooden tray.

1645 BOATE *Irel. Nat. Hist.* xx. (1652) 155 Certain woodden trayes, amongst the English in Ireland peculiarly called Lossels [*sic*]. **1674–91** RAY *N.C. Words* 135 A *Losset*, a large flat wooden dish not much unlike a Voider. **1782** VALLANCY *Collect. De Rebus Hibern.* x. 82 This fine may be exchanged for losads, sieves, kneading troughs [etc.].

†ˈ**lossful**, *a.* *Obs.* [f. LOSS *sb.*¹ + -FUL.] Productive of loss; detrimental; unprofitable.

1611 SPEED *Hist. Gt. Brit.* IX. xii. §108. 694 Hee.. retired himselfe with losse-full hast into the bosome of France. **1623** in *Hartlib's Legacy* (1655) 287 As the rate of Money now goeth, no man can let his Timber stand.. but it will be very losse-full to him. **1675** BROOKS *Gold. Key* Wks. 1867 V. 421 It is a gainful loss to suffer for the truth; it is a lossful gain.. to provide for our present safety.. and ease.

†ˈ**lossing**, *vbl. sb.* *Sc. Obs.* [f. LOSS *v.* + -ING¹.] The action of unloading a vessel, or of discharging goods.

1531 *Extracts Aberd. Reg.* (1844) I. 142 Thair masteris of warke suld gar amend the prame of the brig,.. and lat hir and the prouestis greit keile to fraucht to the losing and laidnyng of schippis. *c* **1575** R. BANNATYNE *Jrnl.* (1806) 147 All horsmen and footmen went furth doun to Leyth to the lossing of the said bark, which incontinent was broght vp to the castell efter there lossing. **1597** *Sc. Acts Jas. VI* (1816) IV. 137/2 Þe conseruatour sall not.. admit onye cocquet,.. except the mercheandis,.. euerie ane of thame, befoir the loissing of onie of þair gudis, mak faith.. That he hes na forbiddin gudis [etc.].

lossingeir, -gere, Sc. variants of LOSENGER.

ˈ**lossless**, *a.* [f. LOSS *sb.*¹ + -LESS.] †**a.** Without loss. *Obs.*

1587 THYNNE *Contn. Hist. Scot.* 409 in *Holinshed*, They were.. suffered harmelesse of bodie, and losselesse of furniture to depart. **1642** MILTON *Apol. Smect.* Wks. 1851 III. 303 Miraculous and losselesse victories. **1669** in Picton *L'pool Munic. Rec.* (1883) I. 276 Saved harmles, lossles, & indemnifyed from any suit.

b. *Electr.* Characterized by or causing no dissipation of electrical or electromagnetic energy.

1952 *Proc. IRE* XL. 1651/1 If.. the system is lossless, then the transverse electromagnetic (TEM) mode can be propagated. **1962** CORSON & LORRAIN *Introd. Electromagn. Fields* xi. 357 Lossless dielectrics, good conductors, and low-pressure ionized gases. **1969** P. M. CHIRLIAN *Basic Network Theory* i. 46 Inductors and capacitors are called lossless elements.

lossom, -um, obs. forms of LOVESOME.

loss-proof (ˈlɒspruːf, -ɔː-), *a.* [f. LOSS *sb.*¹ + PROOF *a.* 1 b.] Guaranteed against loss, inflation, fluctuation in market value, etc.

1963 *New Yorker* 8 June 107 (Advt.), Travelers cheques.. Loss-proof and theft-proof. **1969** *Daily Tel.* 22 Nov. 14 (Advt.), The guaranteed loss-proof investment that *grows* despite Stock Market ups and downs.

lossy (ˈlɒsɪ, -ɔː-), *a.* *Electr.* [f. LOSS *sb.*¹ + -Y¹.] Characterized by or causing dissipation of electrical or electromagnetic energy.

1948 H. A. LEITER in Smullin & Montgomery *Microwave Duplexers* ix. 378 Lossy cables are used.. in order to isolate the oscillator from effects of mismatch in the unit under test. **1949** L. L. LANGTON *Radio-Frequency Heating Equipment* v. 76 A lossy capacitor. **1969** *Sci. Jrnl.* Dec. 44/3 At optical frequencies a metal transmission line structure would be very 'lossy' and only transparent dielectric materials such as glass can be considered. **1970** J. EARL *Tuners & Amplifiers* iv. 94 Most transformers are 'lossy' at the sub-bass end of the spectrum.

†**lost**, *sb.* *Obs.* Also loste. [app. f. *lost*, pa. pple. of LOSE *v.*] = LOSS *sb.*¹ *to go to lost*: to perish, go to ruin.

c **1374** CHAUCER *Boeth.* II. p. iv. 30 (Camb. MS.) Men do no more fors of the lost than of the hauyinge. **1387** TREVISA *Higden* (Rolls) IV. 213 For þey schulde defende hem þe manloker for drede of so greet lost [L. *metu tanti damni*]. **1390** GOWER *Conf.* I. 147 Which is of most cost And lest is worth and goth to lost? **1422** tr. *Secreta Secret., Priv. Priv.* 151 Of the lordshupp of Cursid men comyth many lostis and myschefis. *c* **1425** *Eng. Conq. Irel.* lx. 147 Al thynge vnder hys newe men yede to loste. **1473** *Waterf. Arch.* in *10th Rep. Hist. MSS. Comm.* App. v. 310 He shall.. make goode of all the losts that is done. **1505** *Galway Arch.* ibid. 391 All such costes, lostes and damages as he shuld sustayne. **1519** HORMAN *Vulg.* vii. 86 For in that delynge is great lost of tyme. **1671** *Woodbury Churchw. Acc.* (E.D.D.), Collected by vertue of a Briefe for a lost by ffire.

lost (lɒst, -ɔː-), *ppl. a.* [Pa. pple. of LOSE *v.*¹]

1. a. That has perished or been destroyed; ruined, esp. morally or spiritually; (of the soul) damned.

a **1533** LD. BERNERS *Gold. Bk. M. Aurel.* (1546) K vj, The greatteste signe of a loste man is to lease his time in naughty workes. **1590** SIR R. WILLIAMS *Disc. Warre* 58 Wee were lost men but for our owne wits and resolution. **1678** BUNYAN *Pilgr.* I. 15 As the sinner is awakened about his lost condition. *a* **1715** BURNET *Own Time* (1724) I. 548 He was reckoned a lost man. **1780** FALCONER *Dict. Marine, Lost*, the state of being foundered or cast away; expressed of a ship when she has either sunk at sea, or struck upon a rock. **1818** SHELLEY *Rosalind & Helen* 392 In my lost soul's abandoned night. **1895** [see BOOZE *sb.* 1 c]. **1923** D. H. LAWRENCE *Ladybird* 224 The lost-soul look of the men. **1937** *Discovery* May 150/2 It emits a weird screaming wail like a lost soul.

b. Having the mental powers impaired. *lost of wits*: imbecile (cf. dial. use of *lost* in this sense).

1821 SHELLEY *Ginevra* 12 Deafening the lost intelligence within. **1861** THACKERAY *Four Georges* i. 6 One thinks of a descendant of his two hundred years afterwards, blind, old, and lost of wits, singing Handel in Windsor Tower.

†**c.** *transf.* Desperate, hopeless. *Obs.*

1709 MRS. MANLEY *Secr. Mem.* (1736) II. 101 He loved me after a lost manner. **1720** —— *Power of Love* (1741) III. 214 She loves you in a lost manner, she is ready to die.

2. Of which some one has been deprived; not retained in possession; no longer to be found. Also, of a person or animal: Having gone astray, having lost his or its way. *to get lost*: see GET *v.* 33.

1526 TINDALE *Matt.* xv. 24, I am not sent but vnto the loost shepe of the housse of Israhel. **1560** BIBLE (Genev.) *Lev.* vi. 4 He shal then restore.. the lost thing which he founde. **1667** MILTON *P.L.* I. 55 The thought Both of lost happiness and lasting pain Torments him. **1756** C. LUCAS *Ess. Waters* Ded., The grateful votaries [desired] to teach others how to recover lossed health. **1809** *Laws of Cricket* (rev. ed.), If lost Ball is call'd, the Striker shall be allowed four, but if more than four are run before lost Ball is call'd, then the Striker to have all they have run. **1828** MOORE (*title*) Limbo of Lost Reputations. **1830** LYELL *Princ. Geol.* I. 4 The imperfect remains of lost species of animals and plants. **1845** BROWNING (*title*) The Lost Leader. **1849** *Chambers's Inform. People* II. 652/2 If a 'Lost ball' be called, the striker shall be allowed six runs. **1849** DICKENS *Dav. Copp.* xlvi, It occurred to me that she might be more disposed to feel a woman's interest in the lost girl. **1896** A. E. HOUSMAN *Shropshire Lad* xxxiii, To this lost heart be kind. **1967** *Laws of Cricket* ('Know the Game' Series) 15 If a ball in play cannot be found or recovered, any fieldsman may call 'Lost Ball', when 6 runs shall be added to the score.

Comb. *a* **1845** HOOD *Lost Heir* 24 Has ever a one seen anything about the streets like a crying lost-looking child?

¶ *to give* (*over* or *up*) *for lost*, also *to give lost*: see GIVE *v.* 31 b.

3. Of time, labour, space: Not used advantageously; spent in vain; †hence, vain, groundless. Of opportunities: Not turned to account, missed.

a **1500** *Chaucer's Dreme* 156 It were but paine and lost travaile. **1535** [see LABOUR *sb.* 1 b]. **1594** SHAKS. *Rich. III*, II. ii. 11 It were lost sorrow to waile one that's lost. **1604** —— *Oth.* v. ii. 269 Do you go backe dismaid? 'Tis a lost feare. **1622** MABBE tr. *Aleman's Guzman d'Alf.* II. 111 My friend.. repented himselfe of the lost time and charges, which he had spent in the sute. **1855** HOPKINS & RIMBAULT *Organ* xxxvii. 274 It can never be correctly said that 'unoccupied space' in an Organ, within reason, is 'lost room'. **1889** 'R. BOLDREWOOD' *Robbery under Arms* xv, He began.. to make up for lost time.

4. Of a battle, game: In which one has been defeated. Also *transf.* Of a person: That has lost the day; defeated (*poet.*).

1724 De Foe *Mem. Cavalier* (1840) 298, I saw it was a lost game. **1808** Scott *Marm.* vi. xxxii, In the lost battle, borne down by the flying. **1822** Shelley *Hellas* 294 So were the lost Greeks on the Danube's day.

5. *to be lost to*: **a.** To have passed from the possession of; to have been taken or wrested from.

1667 Milton *P.L.* ix. 479 Other joy To me is lost. **1744** Ozell tr. *Brantome's Sp. Rhodomontades* 63 This Battle being lost to us. **1796** Jane Austen *Pride & Prej.* xliii, My uncle and aunt would have been lost to me; I should not have been allowed to invite them. **1845** S. Austin *Ranke's Hist. Ref.* III. 363 The basis of power.. was thus of necessity lost to the Five Cantons. **1850** Tennyson *In Mem.* xliii. 9 So then were nothing lost to man. **1870** Morris *Earthly Par.* II. iii. 10 In the lore long dead, Lost to the hurrying world, right wise she was.

b. Of a person: To be so depraved as to be inaccessible (to some good influence); to have no sense of (right, shame, etc.). Also *rarely* in neutral sense, to be 'dead' to, to have lost all interest in.

1640 Shirley *St. Patrick* iv. F4 Thou lost thing to goodnesse. **1654** *State Case Commw.* 8 So lost and loose were that party of men to all former principles. **1682** T. Flatman *Heraclitus Ridens* No. 78 (1713) II. 228 Being lost to all Humanity. **1711** Steele *Spect.* No. 30 ⁋1 Who are not so very much lost to common Sense, but that they understand the Folly they are guilty of. **1769** Sir W. Jones *Pal. Fortune* Poems (1777) 31 Resign'd to heaven, and lost to all beside. **1819** Crabbe *T. of Hall* vi, A creature lost to reason. **1849** Macaulay *Hist. Eng.* vi. II. 92 Lost to all sense of religious duty. **1859** Tennyson *Vivien* 63 He lay as dead And lost to life and use and name and fame.

†**c.** To be forgotten by, unknown to (the world).

1626 Shirley *Brothers* ii. i. (1652) 19 Men whose expectations are like yours Come not with honour to court such as I am, (Lost to the World for want of portion) But with some untam'd heat of blood. **1636** —— *Duke's Mistress* iii. iii. (1638) F2 My Lord I know not with what words to thanke Your feeling of my sufferings. I will now Beleeve I am not lost to all the World.

6. In special collocations: **lost cause**, a cause (cause *sb.* 11) that has failed or that is unlikely to succeed; *spec.* the cause of the South in the American Civil War (1861–65); **lost day, level** (see quots.); **lost generation**, *spec.* that of the period of the 1914–18 war, a high proportion of whose men were killed in the trench warfare; also used more generally of any generation judged to have 'lost' its values, etc.; **lost motion**, imperfect transmission of motion between two parts of a machine which communicate one with the other, due to faulty construction or looseness of the parts; **lost property**, lost articles found but not claimed; so ***lost property department, office***, an office dealing with (the disposal of) lost property; **lost river** *U.S.*, a river which disappears into the ground and re-emerges elsewhere; **lost rock** *U.S.*, a travelled boulder; **lost stone** *U.S.* = *lost rock*; **lost Sunday** (see Sunday); **lost wax** = cire perdue; **lost weekend**, one spent in dissolute living; also *transf.*

1865 M. Arnold *Ess. Criticism* p. xix., Oxford... home of *lost causes, and forsaken beliefs, and unpopular names, and impossible loyalties! **1866** E. A. Pollard (*title*) The lost cause. **1901** 'Mark Twain' *Speeches* (1923) 231 You testify by honoring two of us, once soldiers of the Lost Cause. **1914** *Times Lit. Suppl.* 7 Aug. 378 Oxford has often been called 'the home of lost causes', or, as Mr. Cram puts it, 'of causes not lost but gone before'. **1933** C. Mackenzie (*title*) The lost cause. A Jacobite play. **1938** J. Betjeman *Oxf. Univ. Chest* v. 112 Wytham and Binsey are the less hackneyed of Oxford's lost causes on the edge of Oxford. **1940** C. F. Adams *And Sudden Death* xvii. 155 Why should I go round championing a lost cause? **1948** D. Wecter in J. G. Kerwin *Civil-Military Relationships in Amer. Life* 31 Their late adversaries, the United Confederate Veterans, licked their wounds and dwelt lovingly upon the Lost Cause. **1949** D. S. Freeman in B. A. Botkin *Treas. S. Folklore* p. viii, Perhaps every land that has the tradition of a Lost Cause builds its monuments in a certain sentimental determination and seeks through its memorials both to exemplify and to perpetuate its ideal. **1867** Smyth *Sailor's Word-bk.*, **Lost day*, the day which is lost in circumnavigating the globe to the westward, by making each day a little more than twenty-four hours long. **1926** E. Hemingway *Sun also Rises* (*title-page*), 'You are all a *lost generation.'—Gertrude Stein in conversation. **1930** R. Macaulay *Staying with Relations* iv. 57, I was nineteen when the affair [*sc.* the war] ended... I belong practically to the Lost Generation. **1939** C. Day Lewis *Child of Misfortune* ii. i. 146 'Ha,' Alec yelled. 'We're the Lost Generation.' **1951** E. Paul *Springtime in Paris* xi. 197 The era of the Lost Generation and the notorious expatriates. **1959** *Listener* 15 Oct. 616/2 Thomas Wolfe, F. Scott Fitzgerald, Sinclair Lewis, Ernest Hemingway, and Katherine Anne Porter—members of the so-called 'lost generation', strove and strayed on the left banks between the wars. **1969** [see hippie, hippy *sb.* and *a.*]. **1970** D. T. Turner in Z. N. Hurston *Mules & Men* 11 New York was an exciting place for young black intellectuals and artists during the mid-Twenties. Afro-American culture had been rediscovered... The 'Lost Generation' danced wildly to jazz rhythms. **1860** *Eng. & For. Mining Gloss.* (Cornwall Terms), **Lost levels*, levels which are not driven horizontally. **1877** Raymond *Statist. Mines & Mining* 421 The movement being continuous and rapid in one direction—so that there is no *loss motion [*sic*]. **1884** Knight *Dict. Mech.* Suppl., *Lost Motion*, looseness of fitting, incident to wear of parts. **1844** A. W. Kinglake *Eothen* xxii. 340 The Governor..saw the value which I set upon the *lost property. **1922** Joyce *Ulysses* 56 His lost property office secondhand waterproof. **1923** H. C. Bailey *Mr. Fortune's Practice* vi. 156 He was only calling on the lost property department to leave a lady's bag. **1941** V. Nabokov *Real Life S. Knight* (1945) x. 86 She fails to get the..job in the lost property office. **1959** *Manch. Guardian* 7 Aug. 12/2 A home-made double bass.. will be included in a lost property sale. **1971** 'A. Garve' *Late Bill Smith* ii. 49 Everyone with any kind of problem was bringing it to Sue. She was harbour-master, postmaster, nurse, lost property office. **1843** 'R. Carlton' *New Purchase* I. ix. 58 Out come the mole rivers that have burrowed all this time under the earth, and which, when so unexpectedly found are styled out there, —'*lost rivers'! And every district of a dozen miles square has a lost river. **1872** R. W. Raymond *Statistics of Mines* 197 The great 'lost river' which bursts out of the vertical side of the cañon of the Snake. **1831** J. M. Peck *Guide for Emigrants* ii. 136 Scattered over the surface of our prairies are large masses of rock, of granitic formation, roundish in form, usually called by the people **lost rocks*... These stones are denominated *boulders* in mineralogy. **1857** *Trans. Illinois Agric. Soc.* II. 347 Another curiosity is the boulders, or 'lost rocks', as they are frequently called, which are found on the surface of the earth in the middle and northern sections of Illinois. **1819** H. C. McMurtrie *Sk. Louisville* 29 (Th.), [Certain stones] in the Illinois and Missouri territories are denominated *lost-stones, from their being strangers to the soil where they are found. **1933** H. F. Lenz *Alfred David Lenz Syst. Lost Wax Casting* 9 The modeling wax for casting in the 'cire perdue' or '*lost wax' method has several requirements. **1947** J. C. Rich *Materials & Methods of Sculpture* vi. 146 The 'lost-wax' or *cire-perdue* process is the traditional method of casting in bronze... The ancient Egyptians employed the lost-wax method, casting over ash cores. **1972** *Times* 28 Sept. 18/6 The bronzes were made by the lost-wax process in which the mould is destroyed. **1944** C. Jackson (*title*) *Lost weekend. **1947** M. McCarthy in *Partisan Rev.* May–June 303 It was..comic that a man should have one name..for his wife..and another..for trips and 'lost' week ends. **1955** Koestler *Trail of Dinosaur* 56 He is the classic type who becomes addicted to the Communist drug, and never finds his way back from the lost weekend in Utopia. **1960** K. Amis *Take Girl like You* xix. 229, I quite expected to find you on the couch this morning, especially after your lost-weekend act. **1968** A. MacLeod *Dam* iii. 32 I'll have to go down to the pub and replenish the stock... And that will mean another bloody lost weekend. **1969** 'E. Lathen' *Come to Dust* iii. 34 He seems to feel that if Patterson emerges from some lost weekend, the press will seize on his connection with Neil Marsden. **1975** M. Kenyon *Mr Big* vii. 65 The *Express* used one paragraph headed Lost Weekend.

7. *absol.* **a.** (with *the*).

1849 Aytoun *Buried Flower* 72 All I loved is rising round me, All the lost returns again. **1871** R. Ellis tr. *Catullus* viii. 2 Lost is the lost, thou know'st it, and the past is past. *Ibid.* lxxvi. 18 A help to the lost.

b. *pl.* Advertisements of lost articles.

1761 *Ann. Reg.* 242 The number of losts..in the *Daily Advertiser* of next day.

lost(e, obs. f. lust; pa. pple. of loss *v.* *Obs.*

†**lostell.** *Obs.* In phr. *a lostell* = OF. *à l'ostel* (see hostel), 'to your quarters!', 'disperse!'

a **1548** Hall *Chron., Edw. IV* 197 b, The kyng..caused the Heraldes to cry, a lostell, and every man to departe. **1847** Halliwell, *Lostell*, the cry of the heralds to the combatants that they should return home.

loster, lostfalle, obs. ff. lustre, lustful.

†**losthope.** *Obs. rare*[−1]. [Cf. forlorn hope.] An abandoned person.

c **1540** tr. *Pol. Verg. Eng. Hist.* I. (Camden No. 36) 102 The Scottes..on all sides assemblinge the lostehopes and raskalls [L. *collectis undique perditis hominibus*].

†'**lostless**, *a.* *Obs.* [f. lost *sb.* + -less.] Free from loss.

1459 *Waterf. Arch.* in *10th Rep. Hist. MSS. Comm.* App. v. 300 That he save the citie lostlesse againste the King for all chelanges that he or his officers wil make.

lostling ('lɒstlɪŋ, -ɔː-). [f. lost *ppl. a.*, after *foundling*.] A person or thing lost.

1872 Raymond *Statist. Mines & Mining* 197 The great 'lost river' which bursts out of the vertical side of the cañon of the Snake—a torrent from the solid rock; a foundling rather than a lostling. **1898** C. Benham *Fourth Napoleon* 24 Evidently she spent her existence on the look-out for the lostling.

†'**lostly**, *adv.* *Obs.* [f. lost *ppl. a.* + -ly².] In a lost manner; hopelessly.

1660 tr. *Amyraldus' Treat. conc. Relig.* i. i. 3 Such eyes must be lostly obtenebrated, which do not perceive him therein.

lostness ('lɒstnɪs, -ɔː-). [f. lost *ppl. a.* + -ness.] The condition or state of being lost.

1728 P. Walker *Life Peden* (1827) 133 An enlightened believing Soul, that sees its Lostness, and Need of Christ. **1839** Bailey *Festus* (1852) 195 The desolation of the soul.. A sense of lostness that leaves death But little to reveal. **1891** *Punch* 23 May 246/1 My feeling of lostness is utter.

lostriffe, lostvol, obs. ff. loosestrife, lustful.

losungeous, variant of losengeous *a.* *Obs.*

‖**los von Rom** (loːs fɔn roːm). [Ger., = 'free from Rome'.] A slogan used by and applied to a movement which arose in Austria and Germany at the end of the 19th c., seeking to reduce the political influence of the Roman Catholic Church. Also used allusively of other policies of this kind.

1899 *Times* 8 Apr. 8/2 The really significant feature of the conversion of Herr Wolf, the Pan-Germanic member of the Reichsrath, and perhaps the most active promoter of the 'Los von Rom' agitation, is..his acceptance by the Evangelical community. **1920** W. T. Whitley in *Encycl. Relig. & Ethics* XI. 326/2 This Los von Rom movement seems..to have been anti-Slav, and reinforced Protestants quite as much, the tendency being to pave the way for these provinces to join the German Empire. **1923** G. M. Trevelyan *Manin & Venetian Revolution of 1848* ix. 165 Irritated by the Pope's Italian nationalism, the German Catholics might drift toward the position of *los von Rom.* **1957** *Oxf. Dict. Chr. Ch.* 822 *Los von Rom...* The Movement, which owed its name to the shout of a student at the Deutscher Volkstag at Vienna (1897), came to have its centre at Innsbruck. **1963** *Listener* 28 Feb. 360/1 None of the Five, not Dr Adenauer nor any other German, is likely to cry '*los von Rom*'.

losy, losyn, obs. forms of losh, lozen.

losynge, losyngye, obs. forms of lozenge.

losynger(e, variant of losenger.

lot (lɒt), *sb.* Forms: 1 **hlot, hlott, hlodd**, 2–8 **lott**, 4–6 **lote**, 4–7 **lotte**, (4 **loth**, 4–6 **loot**, 5 **loote**, **lootte**), 2– **lot**. [OE. *hlot* neut. (rendering L. *sors*, *portio*):—OTeut. type **hluto-m*, f. the wk. grade of the root **hleut-* (: *hlaut-*: *hlŭt-*) occurring in the str. vb. OE. *hléotan*, OS. *hliotan*, OHG. *liozan* (MHG. *liezen*), ON. *hlióta*, to cast lots, obtain by lot. The precise formal equivalent of the Eng. word is not found elsewhere exc. perh. in OFris. *hlot* (? neut.), MDu. *lot* neut. (also masc.), Du. *lot* neut.; but synonymous sbs. from the same root appear in all the Teut. langs. From the wk. grade are, besides those already mentioned, OHG. (*h*)*luz* masc., ON. *hlut-r*, *hlot-r* masc. (MSw. *luter*, *loter*, Sw. *lott*, Da. *lod*), *hlute* wk. masc.; from the form **hlaut-* are OE. *hlýt*, *hlét*, *hlíet* masc. (:—OTeut. **hlauti-z*), Goth. *hlaut-s* masc. (rendering κλῆρος), OS. *hlôt* masc., OHG. (*h*)*lôz* masc. and neut. (MHG. *lôz* masc. and neut., mod.G. *loos*, *los* neut.); cf. also ON. *hlaut* fem., blood of sacrifice. The Teut. word was adopted into the Rom. langs.: F. *lot* (whence *lotir* to divide, in OF. to cast lots), It. *lotto* game of chance, Sp., Pg. *lote* lot, Sp. *loto* 'lot' put up to auction. Probably some of the uses of the Eng. word are due to the influence of F. *lot*.

The primary meaning of the Teut. root **hleut-* is uncertain. Schrader has suggested that it may have been formed by secondary ablaut from the wk.-grade **hlut-* (repr. pre-Teut. *kld-*: see holt) in the sb. **hluto-m*, the primary sense of which would then be the piece of wood used in casting lots. But this conjecture is very doubtful, and not free from difficulties.]

1. a. An object (app. usually a piece of wood) used in a widely diffused ancient method of deciding disputes, dividing plunder or property, selecting persons for an office or duty, etc., by an appeal to chance or the divine agency supposed to be concerned in the results of chance. The 'lots', each bearing the special mark of one of the competitors, were placed in a receptacle (in Homeric Greece a helmet); according to Greek procedure the vessel was shaken, the winning lot being that which fell out first; in Scandinavia (see Vigf. s.v. *hlutr*) the winning lot was drawn out by an uninterested party. In Eng. (exc. in rare modern instances, chiefly translations from ancient langs.) the word in this sense occurs only in the phr. *to cast, draw* (†also *lay, put, send, throw, warp*) *lots* (or †*lot*); followed by *on* or *upon*, *over*, *between*, *for* (the object or objects concerned); also by inf. or indirect interrog. clause.

In genuine OE. idiom the vb. governing *hlot* was *weorpan* to throw (see warp *v.*); cf. G. *das loos werfen*, L. *sortes conicere*, Gr. κλῆρον βάλλειν. In ME. *werpe* was superseded by the synonymous *cast* and *throw*. The OE. use of *sendan* is a Latinism, after *mittere* of the Vulgate. The only forms of the phrase that survive are *to cast lots* (*arch.*) and *to draw lots* (cf. F. *tirer au sort*), which is interpreted as synonymous with *to draw cuts* (cut *sb.*¹ 1).

971 *Blickl. Hom.* 229 Hie sendon hlot him betweonum, hwider hyra ȝehwylc faran scolde to læranne. *c* **1000** *Ags. Gosp.* Matt. xxvii. 35 Hiȝ to-dældon hys reaf & wurpon hlot [L. *sortem mittentes*] þær-ofer. *c* **1205** Lay. 13858 Vmbe fiftene ȝer þat folc his isomned..& heore loten werpeð vppen þan þe hit faleð he scal uaren of londe. *c* **1275** *Passion our Lord* in *O.E. Misc.* 50 Ac hi casten heore lot hwes he scolde beo. *a* **1300** *E.E. Psalter* xxi. 18 And mi clepinge lote kaste þai on. *c* **1330** R. Brunne *Chron.* (1810) 124 Lotes did þei kast, for whom þei had þat wo. **1382** Wyclif *1 Sam.* xiv. 42 Sende ȝe lot bitwixe [**1535** Coverdale Cast the lot ouer, **1611** Cast lots betweene] me and Jonathas my sone. *c* **1385** Chaucer *L.G.W.* 1933 *Ariadne*, Euery thridde yere.. They caste lot, and as it fil a-boute On riche or pore, he muste his sone take [etc.]. *c* **1420** Lydg. *Assembly of Gods* 1569 Mathy and Barnabe, drawyng lottys, stood. *c* **1475** *Partenay* 3184 Thay haue caste ther loote certes you vppon. **1568** Grafton *Chron.* II. 455 The French men..had divided the prisoners

and spoyles among them, and had cast lottes for them. **c1611** CHAPMAN *Iliad* VII. 153 Each markt his lot, and cast it in, to Agamemnons caske. **1647** JER. TAYLOR *Lib. Proph.* xi. 171 The lot was throwne, and God made to be Judge. **1703** BURCHETT *Naval Trans.* III. xix. (1720) 391 That the Regiments should cast Lots which of them should go on shore first. **1725** POPE *Odyss.* XIV. 239 *note*, The sons cast lots for their patrimony. **1744** *Col. Rec. Pennsylv.* IV. 722 The several Nations had drawn Lots for the performance of the Ceremony. **1813** HOGG *Queen's Wake* 26 Their numbers given, the lots were cast, To fix the names of first and last. **1840** J. H. NEWMAN *Par. Serm.* (1842) V. xv. 296 Supposing we had to cast lots for some worldly benefit. *a***1851** JOANNA BAILLIE *Ethwald* III. iv. Wks. (1851) 150 *Ethw.* (giving a soldier a helmet filled with lots) Here, take the lots and deal them fairly round. **1875** JOWETT *Plato* (ed. 2) III. 341 Some ingenious kind of lots which the less worthy may draw. **1888** E. B. TYLOR in *Archæol. Rev.* Mar., Specimens of the sticks or other lots cut with patterns, which were used in the re-distribution of the communal plots of land.

b. In abstract sense: The casting or drawing of lots, or the use of any equivalent process, to obtain a decision. Chiefly in phr. ***by lot*** (occas. †***by lots***). Also *fig.*

1297 R. GLOUC. (Rolls) 2415 Þe stalworþest me ssal bi choys & bi lot al so Chese out. **1382** WYCLIF *Num.* xxxiii. 54 The which ȝe shal dyuyde to ȝou bi lot. **1390** GOWER *Conf.* III. 130 So as it falleth upon lot. **1568** GRAFTON *Chron.* I. 95 They were of the Countrie of Germany, and put out of their Countrie by a maner & sort of a Lot, which is sundrie times used in the sayde lande. *a***1591** H. SMITH *Serm.* (1637) 797 Mathias is chosen by lots, to the Apostleship. **1642** R. HARRIS *Serm.* 43 Let's put it to the Lot. **1649** MILTON *Eikon.* xv, But that controversy divine lot hath ended. **1651** HOBBES *Leviath.* II. xxx. 184 Good Counsell comes not by Lot, nor by Inheritance. **1802** PALEY *Nat. Theol.* xxvi. (1819) 457 The distribution of provision may be made by lot, as it is in a sailor's mess. **1875** JOWETT *Plato* (ed. 2) V. 125 The ancients knew that election by lot was the most democratic of all modes of appointment. **1884** tr. *Lotze's Logic* 400 The only remaining possibility is either the lot, or the decision of some external will.

c. The choice resulting from a casting of lots. In phr. ***the lot falls*** (†***limps***) ***on*** (a person or thing).

c1205 [see 1]. **13..** *E.E. Allit. P.* C. 194 And ay þe lote, vpon laste, lymped on Ionas. **1568** GRAFTON *Chron.* I. 29 Then he caused lots to be cast out, to know who should be king, and the lot fell upon the tribe of Beniamin. **1653** H. COGAN tr. *Pinto's Trav.* xxix. 115 Lots were cast five times ..and all those five times the lot fell still on a little Boy of seven years of age. **1855** PRESCOTT *Philip II*, II. vii. (1857) 284 The lot fell on Egmont to devise some suitable livery.

d. fig. ***the lot is cast***: the decisive step is taken. (Cf. DIE *sb.*)

1682 OTWAY *Venice Preserv.* IV. i, Now the lot's cast, and, fate, do what thou wilt. **1855** BROWNING *Statue & Bust* 55 Calmly he said that her lot was cast, That the door she had passed was shut on her Till the final catafalk repassed.

e. Phr. ***to cast*** (or ***throw***) ***in one's lot with***: to associate oneself with and share the fortunes of. (After Prov. i. 14 where the expression has its literal sense, with reference to partition of plunder.)

1382 WYCLIF *Prov.* i. 14 Lot ley with vs, o bagge of monee be of vs alle. **1535** COVERDALE *ibid.*, Cast in thy lott amonge us, we shal haue all one purse. **1678** BUNYAN *Pilgr.* I. 6, I intend to go along with this good man, and to cast in my lot with him. **1740** WESLEY *Wks.* (1872) I. 283 Seven or eight and forty likewise..desired to cast in their lot with us. **1834** GEN. P. THOMPSON *Exerc.* (1842) III. 39 She [England] must abide the chances with those with whom she hast cast in her lot. **1867** FREEMAN *Norm. Conq.* (1876) I. App. 708 We find East-Anglia heartily throwing in its lot with Wessex. **1870** [see THROW *v.*^{1} 41 e]. **1927** *Daily Express* 15 June 11/7 Mr. Patrick O'Maille..threw in his lot recently with Professor Magennis' party, Clainn Eireann.

†**f.** ***to put in lot***: ? to put (money) in a joint venture or speculation. *Obs.*

1594 BLUNDEVIL *Exerc.* I. xii. (1636) 34 Foure Merchants did put their money in lot in this manner.

†**g.** *sing.* and *pl.* Applied to games of chance. Also, to divinatory appeals to chance; hence *occas.* a sortilege, spell. *Obs.*

1577 NORTHBROOKE *Dicing* (1843) 139 Whosoeuer vseth this chaunce of lottes in ydle and trifling things taketh the name and prouidence of God in vaine. **1621** BURTON *Anat. Mel.* II. ii. IV. (1651) 275 Many too nicely take exceptions at Cardes, Tables and Dices, and such mixt lusorious lots. **1625** BACON *Ess., Envy* (Arb.) 515 There is no other Cure of Enuy, but the cure of Witchcraft: and that is, to remoue the Lot (as they call it) and to lay it vpon another. **1649** *Alcoran* 63 Consult not with Southsayers or Lots, it is a great sin. **1777** JOHNSON *L.P., Cowley*, I cannot but suspect Cowley of having consulted on this great occasion the Virgilian lots.

†**h.** *pl.* As the name of a particular game. *Obs.*

1579 TWYNE tr. *Petrarch's Physic agst. Fortune* I. xxvi. 35, I delight moreover to play at Lottes [L. *calculis*]. *Reason.* O chyldishe desyre..for olde doating men to stande gaping ouer a payre of tables, and a fewe rouling peeces of wood, by stealth robbing or falling in.

2. What falls to a person by lot.

a. That which is assigned by lot to a person as his share or portion in an inheritance, or in a distribution of property; a division or share of property made by lot. Phr. † ***to give in*** or ***to lot*** (or ***lots***) ***to***: to allot to. Also, ***to fall to*** (or †***in***) ***the lot of***.

*c***950** *Lindisf. Gosp.* Luke xv. 12 *Da mihi portionem substantiae*, sel me dæl *vel* hlodd fæes. **958** *Grant* in Birch *Cartul. Sax.* III. 230 On Fearnes felda ȝe byrað tweȝa manna hlot landes in to Sudwellan. *a***1300** *Cursor M.* 6964 In a land þat hight sichim, Was gin in loth to ioseph kin [*Fairf.* was giuen to loth Ioseph kin]. *a***1300** *Ibid.* 10385 To godd þe lambes he gaf to lottes. **1382** WYCLIF *Josh.* xv. 1 The lot [1388 part] of the sones of Juda, bi her kynredis, was this. **1398** TREVISA *Barth. De P.R.* XIV. xii. (1495) 473 Effraym had many pertyculer hylles and dennes, for all y lotte of the lygnage is moost in mountaynes & in wodes. *c***1400** MAUNDEV. (Roxb.) xiii. 58 Þat cuntree es called Galilea Gentium, and it fell in þe lote of Zabulon and of Neptalim. **1535** COVERDALE *Ps.* xv[i]. 6 The lott is fallen vnto me in a fayre grounde, yee I haue a goodly heretage. **1697** DRYDEN *Æneid* x. 739 Thy Barrs, and Ingots, and the Sums beside, Leave for thy Childrens Lot. **1737** BOLINGBROKE *Study & Use Hist.* vii. 188 The whole ten provinces were thrown into the lot of France. **1850** ROBERTSON *Serm.* Ser. III. vii. 92 When the revenues of a cathedral or a cure fell to the lot of a monastery. **1862** STANLEY *Jew. Ch.* (1877) I. xii. 225 One lot, and one only, they were to have; the rest they were to carve out for themselves.

b. Phr. † ***to have*** (or ***win***) ***lot with*** (a person) ***of*** or ***in*** (a thing), also † ***to have lot and dole*** (***cut, cavel***) ***with***: to have a share with. Now only ***to have no*** (***neither***) ***part nor lot in***, after Acts viii. 21.

*c***1150** *Burgh Lawis* liv. in *Anct. Laws & Cust. Burghs Scot.* (1868) 26 Et sciendum est quod stallangiator nullo tempore potest habere loth cut neque cavyl de aliquo mercimonio cum burgense nisi infra quando quilibet potest habere loth et cavyl. *c***1200** ORMIN 4030 Ȝiff þatt teȝȝ wolldenn habbenn lott Wiþþ himm inn eche blisse. *Ibid.* 9847 & winnenn lott wiþþ Abraham Off eche blisse inn heoffne. *c***1200** *Vices & Virtues* (1888) 111 Nis non mihte on godes temple ðat ne hafþ lott and dole mid ðessere eadiȝe mihte. *a***1240** *Ureison* in *Lamb. Hom.* 187 Hwa se euer wule habbe lot wiþ þe of þi blisse, he mot deale wiþ þe of þine pine on eorþe. *c***1449** PECOCK *Repr.* III. i. 277 The preestis and dekenes of the Oold Testament schulden not haue part and lott in the firste parting of the lond of Iewry. **1582** N. T. (Rhem.) *Acts* viii. 21 Thou hast no part, nor lot in this word. **1611** *Ibid.*, Thou hast neither part nor lot in this matter [Gr. οὐκ ἔστι σοι μερὶς οὐδὲ κλῆρος ἐν τῷ λόγῳ τούτῳ]. **1825** MACAULAY *Ess., Milton* (1851) I. 24 Having neither part nor lot in human infirmities. **1833** HT. MARTINEAU *Cinnamon & P.* vi. 102 Rayo and his countrymen had no part nor lot in the harvests of their native land.

†**c.** One's turn (to do something); originally, as determined by lot. *Obs.*

*c***1200** ORMIN 133 Att ænne time whanne hiss lott Wass cumenn upp to þeowwtenn, He toc hiss reclefatt onn hand, Annd ȝede innto þe temmple. *c***1385** CHAUCER *L.G.W.* 1887 *Ariadne*, Now cometh thy lot, now comestow on the rynge. *c***1386** —— *Friar's Prol.* 27 Lat hym seye to me What so hym list; whan it comth to my lot, By god, I shal hym quiten euery grot. **1611** BIBLE *Luke* i. 9. **1667** MILTON *P.L.* IV. 561 Gabriel, to thee thy cours by Lot hath giv'n Charge and strict watch that to this happie place No evil thing approach or enter in.

d. *fig.* That which is given to a person by fate or divine providence; esp. one's destiny, fortune, or 'portion' in this life; condition (good or bad) in life. Phr. ***the lot falls*** (***to*** a person), (***it***) ***falls to the lot of*** (a person), or ***it falls to*** (him) ***as his lot*** (to have or to do something). Also in colloq. phr. ***to be*** or ***to have had*** (one's) ***lot***.

*a***1300** *Cursor M.* 14108 Þe better lott has mari chosen. *Ibid.* 14555 Þat was sir Iudas scarioth Of alle him fell þe werst lot. **1549** COVERDALE, etc. *Erasm. Par. Eph.* 2 We wer chosen vnto the lotte and enheritaunce of immortalitie. **1576** FLEMING *Panopl. Epist.* 226 A minde satisfied with his appointed lotte. **1586** B. YOUNG *Guazzo's Civ. Conv.* IV. 179 Therefore let vs make triall, to whose Lot it shal befall to beare the swaie. **1611** BIBLE *Transl. Pref.* ¶2 If any man conceit, that this is the lot and portion of the meaner sort onely. —— *Isa.* xvii. 14 This is the portion of them that spoile vs, and the lot of them that robbe vs. **1667** MILTON *P.L.* IX. 952 However I with thee have fixt my Lot, Certain to undergoe like doom. **1671** —— *Samson* 1743 Bewailing His lot unfortunate in nuptial choice. **1684** BUNYAN *Pilgr.* II. 205 Shall it be my Lot to go that way again. **1711** STEELE *Spect.* No. 155 ¶1 That Part of the Fair Sex whose Lot in Life is to be of any Trade. **1764** GOLDSM. *Trav.* 178 He sees his little lot the lot of all. **1769–72** *Junius Lett.* Pref. 10 They ..confess that they are dissatisfied with the common lot of humanity. **1799** R. SICKLEMORE *Agnes & Leonora* II. 196 Agnes..enjoyed a greater portion of real bliss than in general falls to the lot of mortals. **1813** SCOTT *Rokeby* III. xxviii. *Song*, A weary lot is thine, fair maid. **1820** W. IRVING *Sketch Bk.* I. 7 It has been either my good or evil lot to have my roving passion gratified. **1884** W. C. SMITH *Kildrostan* 72 Some pet scheme or other, To remedy the lot of our poor folk. **1891** SIR R. WEBSTER in *Law Times* XC. 431/1 It falls to my lot to express in a few words [etc.]. **1960** *Observer* 24 Jan. 5/2 When the bogies sus you and take your trousers to the forensic lab you've had your lot. **1961** J. MACLAREN-ROSS *Doomsday Book* I. vii. 77 Any trouble, mush, and it's your lot. *Ibid.* II. v. 156 That's your lot, Marsh! This isn't one of your crime-plays, d'you hear. **1968** *Listener* 18 July 77/2 'Mummy, Tristram has just dropped your handbag into something rustic.' 'Right, that's your lot. Into the car, and we'll get back to civilisation.' **1973** *Times* 12 Dec. 2/7 Hate slogans scrawled on a blackboard. One read, 'Tina Wilson is going to be done over,' and another, 'Tina Wilson has had her lot tonight.'

†**3.** In the Ormulum: A part, portion, or division of anything; a number (of things or persons) forming part of a larger whole. *Obs.* (Cf. sense 8.)

*c***1200** ORMIN 10939 Þise cullfress þat sinndenn i þiss middellærd An lott off manne fode. *Ibid.* 15248 Þe maste lott tatt heȝhesst iss Iss þatt lærede genge þatt iss ȝuw sett abufenn ȝuw To ȝemenn & to lærenn..Þiss lott off all Crisstene follc Iss heȝhesst unnderr Criste. *Ibid.* 19017, 19150.

4. a. A tax, due, or custom. ***scot and lot*** (formerly also †***lot and scot***): see SCOT.

1530 PALSGR. 241/1 Lotte or shotte, *escot.* **1628** COKE *On Litt.* 283 That it was done by authority of the Commission of Sewers for Lotte or Taxe assessed by that Commission.

b. *Derbyshire Mines.* A payment of the thirteenth 'dish' of lead as royalty to the lord of the mine. (Cf. *lot-lead* in 10.)

1631, *a***1661** [see COPE *sb.*^{3} 3]. **1653** MANLOVE *Lead Mines* 76 The thirteenth dish of oar within their mine, To th' Lord for Lot, they pay at measuring time. **1747** HOOSON *Miner's Dict.* M j b, The chief Proprietor and Lord of the Mine; to whom Lot or Farm is paid by the Miner. **1851** *Act. 14 & 15 Vict.* c. 94 Sched. i. §9 The Duty called Lot is and shall be One Thirteenth Part of all Ore raised within the Jurisdiction of the Barmote Courts.

†**5.** A prize in a lottery. ***great lot, chief lot***, the highest prize. *Obs.* [After Rom. uses; cf. F. *le gros lot*] Also in the card-game (see LOTTERY).

† ***it is lots to blanks*** = 'it is a thousand to one'.

1567 *Lottery Chart* Aug., The number of Lots [in a Lottery] shall be Foure hundreth thousand, and no moe: and euery Lot shall be the summe of Tenne shillings sterling onely, and no more. **1607** SHAKS. *Cor.* v. ii. 10 It is Lots to Blankes, My name hath touch't your eares. **1634** WITHER *Emblems*, Direction at end, If it be the upper Figure, whose Index you moved, than, that Number where-upon it resteth, is the number of your Lot, or Blancke. **1698** *Wheel of Fortune* 2 Some more lucky Sot, Had march'd off with his Lot, And that was the Thousand pound Chance. **1709** STEELE *Tatler* No. 170 ¶6 You, who have both the furnishing and turning of that Wheel of Lots. **1710** *Ibid.* No. 203 ¶2 The Chief Lot he was confident would fall upon some Puppy. **1711** ADDISON *Spect.* No. 191 ¶1 Each of these..thinks he stands fairest for the great Lot. **1850** *Bohn's Handbk. Games* 327 (*Lottery*), One of them [dealers] deals a card to each player; all these cards are to remain turned, and are called the *lots*. **1876** 'CAPT. CRAWLEY' *Card Players' Man.* 235 (*Lottery*), One dealer gives to every player a card, face downwards, for the lots or prizes.

6. a. (Now chiefly *U.S.*) A plot or portion of land assigned by the state to a particular owner. Hence, any piece of land divided off or set apart for a particular purpose, e.g. for building or pasture. Phr. ***across*** or ***cross lots***: across the lots or fields as a short cut (*U.S. colloq.*). Also *attrib.*, as ***lot gate***. **b.** (? Influenced by sense 7.) One of the plots or portions in which a tract of land is divided when offered for sale. Also, land round a film studio where outside filming may be done.

1633 *Mass. Col. Rec.* (1853) I. 102 The westermost part of the Governors greate lot. **1641** *Connect. Col. Rec.* (1850) I. 505 To Jacob, my sonne, I giue my howse and lotts, meadow, homelotte and great lott and lottes whatsoeuer on this side the great Riuer. **1689** *Col. Rec. Pennsylv.* I. 317 If ye Province will build me a house in the City, vpon my Lott. **1776** G. SEMPLE *Building in Water* 154 E. and F. are twenty Lots for Docks,..p. and q. Thirty Lots for principal Merchants..to store their Imports and Exports. **1805** FORSYTH *Beauties Scotl.* II. 473 Each of these freemen possesses what is called a *lot* or *freedom*, containing about four acres of arable land. **1836** *Backwoods of Canada* 47 Every little dwelling..has its lot of land. *Ibid.* 89 The plains are sold off in park lots. **1840** MISS MITFORD in L'Estrange *Life* III. vii. 109 The lot, about an acre, is to be sold on the first of next month. *a***1852** F. M. WHITCHER *Widow Bedott Papers* (1883) xxii. 87 You see yer uncle and me went hum by the turnpike instid o' gwine cross lots. **1854** *Jrnl. Discourses* I. 83 [I dreamed that] I cut one of their throats from ear to ear, saying, 'Go to hell across lots.' **1858** J. R. LOWELL *Two Gunners* in *Poetical Works* II. 125 Joe looked roun' And see (acrost lots in a pond..) A goose. **1859** BARTLETT *Dict. Amer.* s.v., 'I left the road and went across lots, to shorten the distance', i.e. across the open fields or meadows. **1875** JOWETT *Plato* (ed. 2) III. 700 Each of the lots in the plain had an appointed chief..the size of the lot was a square of ten stadia each way. **1879** H. GEORGE *Progr. & Pov.* VII. i. (1881) 303 A house and the lot on which it stands are alike property. **1887** *Scribner's Mag.* Dec. 735/1 He'd have had to foot it by the path 'cross lots... He's sold his hoss. **1928** 'R. WEST' *Strange Necessity* 205 The worst of making war, as of acting for the 'movies', is the amount of waiting around on the lot. **1929** W. FAULKNER *Sartoris* IV. 281 Restless hounds waited for them at the lot gate. **1937** PARTRIDGE *Dict. Slang* 538/1 The most picturesque phrase of all is 'the lot', which is always used to describe the company's land surrounding the studio. It has been in use since the days when..hard-pressed pioneers rented vacant building lots. **1938** M. K. RAWLINGS *Yearling* xv. 153 As he clicked the lotgate, doves flew from the pines with a whistling of wings. **1948** 'N. SHUTE' *No Highway* vi. 151 Don't you ask me why, I'll tell you when I see you on the lot. **1966** *Listener* 15 Dec. 880/1 Many lots are devoted to the less arduous and expensive work of turning out films for television networks. **1969** in Halpert & Story *Christmas Mumming in Newfoundland* 174 Then commenced the chase, up lanes, 'across lots', down lanes.

7. a. An article, or set of articles, offered separately at a general sale; *esp.* each of the items at a sale by auction.

1704 *Lond. Gaz.* No. 4060/5 Lot 65. Cont. Brown Sugar. **1755** JOHNSON, *Lot* (4), a portion; a parcel of goods as being drawn by lot: as, what lot of silks had you at the sale? **1772–84** COOK *Voy.* (1790) V. 1571 In general, we paid for each lot or separate article as we received them. **1821** BYRON *Juan* III. xv, He had chain'd His prisoners, dividing them like chapters In number'd lots. **1859** *Chamb. Jrnl.* 23 Apr. 270/2 Lot after lot was disposed of..at what were considered good prices. **1901** *19th Cent.* 426 Lot 1 was brought up in a box.

b. *transf.* Applied with depreciatory epithet to a person; chiefly in ***a bad lot***.

1862 MRS. H. WOOD *Channings* xxxvii, [A schoolboy says:] Charley's not a bad lot, and he sha'n't be harmed. **1881** J. GRANT *Cameronians* I. i. 7 He had come home..with the current reputation, among his set, of being 'a bad lot'. **1894** MRS. H. WARD *Marcella* III. 345, I'm a bad lot, I know —well, an idle lot—I don't think I am a *bad* lot.

8. a. *gen.* A number of persons or things of the same kind, or associated in some way; a quantity

or collection (of things); a party, set, or 'crew' (of persons); also, a quantity (of anything). Now only *colloq.*, except with reference to articles of commerce, goods, live stock, and the like. Often with some degree of depreciation, either implied, or expressed by an epithet. (Cf. sense 3.)

c **1575** J. Hooker *Life Sir P. Carew* (1857) 49 The next day the people, like a lot of wasps, were up in sundry places. **1725** in G. Sheldon *Hist. Deerfield, Mass.* (1895) I. 449 Our men..discovered a partie of the Enemy that had killed a mare & a Lott of men. **1789** Bentham *Princ. Legisl.* xvi. §16 On the one hand a lot of punishment is a lot of pain; on the other hand the profit of an offence is a lot of pleasure. **1805** T. Holcroft *Bryan Perdue* I. 30 Put all the countries in the world in a bag, and the whole lot of them not worth little Ireland. **1854** Mrs. Carlyle *Lett.* (1883) II. 249 Mr. C—— being too busy with his book to waste a month at present, besides having a sacred horror of two several lots of children who were to be there. **1872** Raymond *Statist. Mines & Mining* 140 The Good Samaritan, on the dump of which a large lot of ore has accumulated. **1879** W. Benham *Mem. Cath. & Crau. Tait* 501 Their crew seem to have been a lazy lot. **1883** *Harper's Mag.* Jan. 206/2 The men who do this work are an interesting lot. **1884** E. R. Turner in *Law Times* 30 Aug. 310/1 The defendant saw the calves, one of which, the only wye calf in the lot, was poorly. **1884** *West. Morn. News* 30 Aug. 1/6 The above will be found to be an altering lot of Stock. **1897** Mary Kingsley *W. Africa* 348 He said the natives were an exceedingly bad lot.

b. ***the lot*** = the whole of a certain number or quantity. *colloq.*

1867 Mrs. H. Wood *Orville Coll.* I. xi. 252, I caught young Dick buying a quart [of gooseberries]. He's crunching the lot. **1877** *Fraser's Mag.* XVI. 381 'What is your fare?'..'A shilling for the lot'. **1886** Stevenson *Dr. Jekyll* i. (ed. 2) 8 There was something about the lot of us that meant mischief. **1936** W. R. Titterton *Chesterton* i. ii. 30 If I quoted much of that marvellous essay I should have to quote the lot. **1956** H. & M. Williams *Plays of Year* XV. 178 It was to be a big wedding—the full treatment—Royalty—the lot. **1958** *Listener* 3 July 10/2 They are said to cure everything from rheumatism to ringworm, colic to snake-bite..—the lot. **1961** [see croak *v.* 5]. **1970** *Times* 7 Jan. 7/5 The death of his father..triggers off a crisis for him too, producing a temporary breakdown, dismissal from his job, separation from his wife, the lot. **1974** 'P. B. Yuill' *Bornless Keeper* vii. 65 They've searched the island twice—helicopters, dogs, the lot.

9. *colloq.* A considerable number, quantity, or amount; a good deal, a great deal. Used in sing. (*a lot*) and plur.; also as quasi-adv. Often *absol.*, without explicit mention of the persons or things intended. Also with adj., as ***a good lot, a great lot, (this, that) little lot.***

1812 *Spirit Pub. Jrnls.* XVI. 191 Lots of our Senators have of late been subject to the awful visitation. **1816** 'Quiz' *Grand Master* ii. 47 Gallons of Arrack, lots of beer. **1835** Keble in Sir J. T. Coleridge *Mem.* (1869) 201 Till you have read a good lot of the Fathers. **1849** Clough *Poems*, etc. (1869) I. 158 You see lots of villas, six or seven at least, in ruins. **1853** Ld. Houghton in T. W. Reid *Life* (1891) I. xi. 491 General B... who is factotum of the Court, and who has lots of gossip. **1858** Mrs. Carlyle *Lett.* II. 368 Having had lots of time to unpack and dress. **1886** *Cornh. Mag.* July 41 There was plenty of cider—a lot too much, indeed. **1891** E. Peacock *N. Brendon* I. 69 Good bye, I've lots to do. **1894** H. Nisbet *Bush Girl's Rom.* 306 The colony could get lots more to take your post, if they hanged you. **1898** J. D. Brayshaw *Slum Silhouettes* 141 Yus, it's a nobby little turn-out, ain't it?.. Mine? Lor' luv a duck! No, that's Sal Hogan's little lot. **1901** *Blackw. Mag.* Aug. 223/1, I would give a lot to have had Raeburn paint her. **1901** A. Hope *Tristram of Blent* x. 113 But, mind you, Duplay's a very superior fellow. He knows the deuce of a lot. **1920** J. Mander *Story N.Z. River* v. 76, I just love you, lots. **1957** 'J. Wyndham' *Midwich Cuckoos* iii. 24 That there Miss Ogle ain't 'alf goin' to cop 'erself a basinful of 'Er Majesty's displeasure over this little lot. **1961** B. Crump *Hang on a Minute* 91 Have a bo-peep at this little lot, Jack, called Sam from the back of the truck. **1965** [see buster 2b]. **1968** *Listener* 1 Aug. 148/1 Mr Donoghue, like any good critic, doesn't mean us, he means you lot. **1975** P. G. Winslow *Death of Angel* 125 A group of lads she doesn't care about. .. Next stop Wormwood Scrubs, that little lot.

10. *Comb.*, as (sense 6) *lot-holder*; (sense 1) *lot-casting* ppl. adj.; **lot-jumper** *U.S.*, one who appropriates another's lot; †**lot-layer** *American*, one appointed to lay out land in lots; †**lot-lead** *Mining* (see quot. and cf. sense 4b); **lot-man**, †(*a*) a pressed seaman; †(*b*) an alleged synonym for *pirate*; (*c*) *Sc.* see quot. 1890; **lot-mead, -meadow**, a common meadow, the shares in which are apportioned by lot; **lot-money** (see quot. and sense 7); †**lot-monger**, one who practises sortilege; †**lot-pot**, an urn from which lots are shaken or drawn (cf. *lottery-pot* s.v. lottery 5); **lot-seller, -selling** (see quots.); †**lot-teller**, a fortune-teller.

1569 J. Sanford tr. *Agrippa's Van. Artes* 2b, A *lot-castinge Arithmetician. **1852** Grote *Greece* ii. lxxix. X. 407 Kleruchs or *lot-holders. **1869** *Overland Monthly* III. 63 Then there had been a *lot jumper's fight down at the end of the street. **1889** in J. B. Thoburn *Stand. Hist. Oklahoma* (1916) I. xx. 223 Gamblers, liquor dealers,..lot-jumpers. **1931** G. F. Willison *Here they dug Gold* 241 Counterfeiters, lot-jumpers, mine-jumpers,..and ruffians in general. **1677** *New Eng. Hist. & Gen. Reg.* (1873) XXVII. 48 It was agreed that..the *lot layers of both ends of the town..are apointed to consider tender cases. *c* **1480** *Mendip Laws* in Phelps *Hist. Somerset* vii. (1839) 6 So that he doth ..pay his *lott lead, which is the tenth pound which shall be blown on the hearth or hearths. **1758** J. Blake *Plan Mar. Syst.* 28 The number of volunteer seamen, together with the *lot-men.., may not be sufficient to man the navy. **1887** Smyth *Sailor's Word-bk.*, *Lotman*, an old term for pirate. **1890** *Scots Observer* 1 Feb. 296/1 The lotman was the thresher and he was to be found erewhile on every farm of the Lowlands. **1553** *Stanford Churchw. Acc.* in *Antiquary* XVII. 117/2 For grasse in the *loot mede yt belongythe to ye churche ijs. **1659–70** Aubrey *Topogr. Collect. Wilts* (1862) 198 Here [Wanborough] is a Lott-mead celebrated yearly with great ceremony. **1813** T. Davis *Agric. Wilts* App. 259 *Lot-Meads*, common meadows divided into acres or equal sized pieces; but the property to the hay of each piece being determined yearly by lot. **1675** W. Leonard *Reports* iv. 43 Where many have *Lot-Meadow to be divided every year by lot who shall have the Grass of such an Acre, and who of such an Acre, &c. **1878** G. B. L. Marriott tr. *E. de Laveleye's Prim. Property* 114 In many English villages meadows are still found divided into parts, which are annually assigned by lot among the co-partners. These are called lot meadows or lammas land. **1725** *Lond. Gaz.* No. 6363/2 The Buyer is to pay down in Part Five Guineas each Lott, and the Goods are to be taken away..on or before the 21st of May.., or the *Lott-Money forfeited. **1549** Chaloner *Erasm. on Folly* Rivb, That law was fyrste ordeined against *lottemongers, enchaunters, and sorcerers. **1603** Florio *Montaigne* i. xix. (1632) 31 Of all shak't is the *lot-pot [Hor. *Carm.* ii. iii. 26 *omnium versatur urna*]. **1619** Gataker *Lots* 4 The tickets or tokens that were cast into the Lot-pot. **1851** Mayhew *Lond. Labour* I. 447 The *Lot-sellers proper, are those who vend a variety of small articles, or 'a lot', all for 1*d*. *Ibid.*, The origin of '*lot-selling', or selling 'penny lots' instead of penny articles, was more curious. **1575** (*title*) A Dialogue of Witches, in foretime named *Lot-tellers, and now commonly called Sorcerers [tr. Danæus].

lot (lɒt), *v.* Also 5 lote, 6 lott(e, *Sc.* loitt. [f. lot *sb.* Cf. F. *lotir* to cast lots, assign by lot.]

I. *intr.*

1. To cast lots. Const. interrog. clause; also with *for*. *rare.*

1483 Caxton *Gold. Leg.* 65/1 Wherfore now stande euerich in his tribe and we shal lote who shal be our kyng. [**1600** Heywood *1st Pt. Edw. IV*, iii. i. Wks. 1874 I. 46 *King.* Well, let's cast lots whether thou shalt go with me [etc.]. *Hobs.* Lot me no lotting. I'll not go with thee.] **1642** R. Harris *Serm.* 43 Let's put it to the Lot. Lot upon your selves; and let each Parliament man say, Am I ready? *a* **1657** W. Bradford *Plymouth Plant.* (1856) 216 A cowe [was given] to 6. persons or shars, & 2. goats to ye same, which were first equalised for age & goodnes, and then lotted for. **1795** J. Sullivan *Hist. Maine* 188 The house lots were all lotted for, except such as were allowed to be pitched by the old proprietors.

2. *Sc.* To pay a 'lot' or assessment. Only in connexion with scot *v.*, q.v.

3. ***to lot upon***, to count or reckon upon; rest one's hopes on; depend or rely on; look for, hope for, expect. Now *U.S.*

[**1633** D. Rogers *Treat. Sacraments* i. 165 Doe ye know the way unto him by the Supper..? Doe ye lot upon it, that there (if any where)..the broken peace of your consciences ..is to be revived?] **1642** —— *Naaman* 565 Its a maxime: lot upon it, whether thou see it or not, it will be so. **1658** Gurnall *Chr. in Arm.* ii. ver. 16. xix. 656 The soul that was even now pining to death with despair, and lotting upon hell in his thought. **1662** *Ibid.* iii. ver. 18. ii. xix. §2. 642 As the Saints are covetous of prayers, so they lot upon it that you do pray for them. **1868** Mrs. Whitney *P. Strong* ii. (1869) 27, I can't help lotting on it all the time. **1894** M. E. Wilkins in *Brit. Weekly* 16 Aug. 258 All these six weeks..had Emma Jane lotted upon it.

II. *trans.*

4. To assign *to* one as his share or portion; to assign as one's lot or destiny. Also with *out*; and in indirect passive.

1524 Wolsey *Let. to Hen. VIII* in Strype *Eccl. Mem.* I. iv. 53 Your archers shall be lotted and appointed..to every part. **1562** Eden *Let. to Sir W. Cecil*, xxli thereof to be lotted to me for an earnest penye to begynne the booke. **1594** Carew *Huarte's Exam. Wits* xiii. (1596) 219 He who first deuised Chesse-play..lotted as many cheefe men to the one side as to the other. **1596** Drayton *Legends* iii. 286 So well had Fortune lotted out my hap. **1606** Warner *Alb. Eng.* xv. xcix. 391 Though she lack not of the age that Scriptures lot to man. **1611** Heywood *Gold. Age* ii. i. Wks. 1874 III. 29 She Must be her bed-companion, so tis lotted. **1648** Symmons *Vind. Chas. I* 291 They being by the Providence of God lotted under his government. **1823** Byron *Age of Bronze* vi, A live estate, existing but for thrall, Lotted by thousands, as a meet reward For the first courtier in the Czar's regard. **1832** *Fraser's Mag.* V. 684 Was more e'er lotted to the vulgar swarm? **1898** T. Hardy *Wessex Poems* 71 Fifty thousand sturdy souls..Who..were lotted their shares in a quarrel not theirs.

†**b.** To appoint or allot *to do* or *to be* (something): = allot *v.* 4. *Obs.*

1573 Twyne *Æneid* xii. (1584) Sviij, And I alonly lotted am King Turnus to assay. **1637** B. Jonson *Sad Sheph.* ii. i, Your brother Lorells prize! For so my largesse, Hath lotted her, to be your brothers Mistresse.

†**5.** To impose a tax, due, or impost upon. *Obs.*

1543–4 *Act 35 Hen. VIII*, c. 11 §4 Two Iustices of peace shall haue ful power..indifferently to lot and tax euery citie boroughe and towne within the shire.

6. To divide (land) into lots, esp. for assignment to private owners. Usually with *out*: To portion out and allot (*to* a person or persons).

c **1449** [see lotting *vbl. sb.*]. **1561** Norton & Sackv. *Gorboduc* i. ii. 151 As for diuiding of this realme in twaine, And lotting out the same in egall partes To either of my lordes your Graces sonnes. **1622** Peacham *Compl. Gentl.* ix. (1634) 73 Every man had his owne portion of ground lotted and laid out to him. **1634** *Rec. Muddy River & Brookline, Mass.* (1875) 9 That Hogg Island shall be lotted out unto the inhabitants and freemen of this town. **1647** *Mass. Col. Rec.* (1853) II. 195 Waymoth haveing a swamp, supposed to be above 100 acres, they are granted liberty to lot it out amongst themselues. **1736** in E. Hyde *Hist. Winchendon, Mass.* (1849) 75 The Committee to lot and lay out the first division. **1805** Forsyth *Beauties Scotl.* (1808) V. 202 A village is lotted out, and to each lot of building ground is appropriated a small croft. **1823** Byron *Juan* x. xxxv, Lotting others' properties Into some sixty thousand new knights' fees. **1836** A. A. Parker *Trip to the West* 167 A few years ago a town was lotted out in this place. **1879** Lubbock *Addr. Pol. & Educ.* ix. 156 A considerable part of the site was..lotted out in sites for cottages. **1891** E. Chase *Dartmouth Coll.* I. 611 The remainder of the grant..was lotted, and some of it rented on long leases about 1821.

7. To divide or group into lots for sale. Also with *out*.

1709 *Lond. Gaz.* No. 4595/4 They are lotted into small Parcels. **1821** Byron *Juan* iv. xci, Lady to lady, well as man to man, Were to be chain'd and lotted out per couple, For the slave-market of Constantinople. **1837** *Advt.* in Willis & Clark *Cambridge* (1886) III. 120 The Stone Wall..and the Coping..surmounted by Nine Balls..will be sold in one Lot; excepting the Balls, which will be lotted in Pairs. **1861** *Temple Bar* I. 145 The furniture was lotted out for the auctioneer's hammer. **1880** *Advt.* in *Echo* 23 Nov. 4/2 A Stock of about 300 dozen choice Wines, lotted to suit the Trade and Private Buyers. **1893** Vizetelly *Glances Back* II. xxvii. 110 The auctioneer's man who lotted the goods.

8. To cast lots for; to divide, apportion, or distribute by lot. Now *rare*.

1703 S. Sewall *Diary* 22 Mar., Mr. Banister and I Lotted our Fence on Cotton-Hill:..He chose to put it to Lot. **1723** *Ibid.* 2 Mar., The Children's Plate and Linen is divided into Six parts, and then Lotted. **1839** Bailey *Festus* xiii. (1848) 124 Men who have..bought up truth for the nations; parted it, As soldiers lotted once the garb of God.

9. To choose (pressed men) by lot for service. *Obs.* exc. *Hist.*

1758 J. Blake *Plan Mar. Syst.* 5 The other captain..is.. to send the officers under him on board merchant ships, in order to lot the men. **1893** J. H. Turner *Hist. Brighouse* 254 John Marsden who was lotted or pressed for a soldier in Wellington's time.

10. To portion *off* by lot.

1849 Grote *Greece* ii. xlvi. V. 496 The newly-created panels of salaried dikasts, lotted off in ten divisions from the aggregate Heliæa.

lot, var. late *sb.*[1] *Obs.*, look, sound.

lot, obs. form of lote, lotus.

‖**lota, lotah** ('ləʊtə). *Anglo-Ind.* Also lootah, loote, loto. [Hindi *lota.*] A spheroidal water-pot, usually made of polished brass.

1809 *Chron.* in *Ann. Reg.* 310/1 On returning the loote to one of the officiating Brahmins, he found a little left which he swallowed with great avidity. **1810** T. Williamson *E. India Vade M.* II. 284 A lootah, or brass water-vessel. *c* **1813** Mrs. Sherwood *Stories Ch. Catech.* x. 73 Taking the old man's brass lota, which was all the riches he had. **1858** J. B. Norton *Topics* 100 We shall still hear of men selling their lotahs to provide themselves with the necessaries of life. **1860** W. H. Russell *Diary India* I. 145 Each man carries his bamboo latee shod with iron, with a bundle at one end, and the unfailing lota..at the other. **1881** Monier Williams in *19th Cent.* No. 49. 509 A metal reservoir filled with water,.. and two or three Lotas.

lotarie, obs. form of lottery.

lotaustralin (ləʊ'taʊstrəlɪn). *Chem.* [f. mod.L. *Lot-us*, the generic name, + *austral-is*, the specific epithet (see Australian *sb.* and *a.*), of the lotus (lotus 5) from which it was first isolated: see -in[1].] A toxic crystalline compound, $C_{11}H_{19}NO_6$, which occurs in *Lotus australis* and in white clover (*Trifolium repens*).

1938 Finnemore & Cooper in *Jrnl. Soc. Chem. Industry* May 165/1 The cyanogenetic constituent is in the main composed of the glucoside of the cyanohydrin of methyl ethyl ketone. This is new and it is proposed to call it lotaustralin. **1964**, **1973** [see linamarin].

lote (ləʊt), *sb.*[1] *arch.* Also 6 lot. [Anglicized form of lotus.] = lotus in various senses.

1. The Nettle-tree: = lote-tree a.

c **1510** Barclay *Mirr. Gd. Manners* (1570) Fiij, In hye grounde or hilles reioyseth the Peretree, But the Lote and Planetree where waters often flowe. **1597** Gerarde *Herbal* iii. cxvii. 1308 Of the Lote or Nettle tree. The Lote whereof we write, is a tree as big as a Peare tree. **1665–76** Rea *Flora* (ed. 2) 221 The Lote or Nettle tree.

2. [After Homer's λωτός.] Some kind of clover, trefoil, or melilot: = lotus 3. ***bird's-foot lote*** = *Lotus corniculatus*.

1548 Turner *Names of Herbes* 49 Lotus syluestris... It maye be called in english wylde lote [*Melilotus officinalis*, Willd.]. **1615** Chapman *Odyss.* iv. 802 Where the broad fields beare Sweet Cypers grasse; where men-fed Lote doth flow. **1676** Hobbes *Iliad* (1677) 33 The horses..upon lote and cinquefoil feeding were. **1713** Petiver in *Phil. Trans.* XXVIII. 208 These Pods are lightly joynted like the Birds foot Lote.

3. The food of the Lotophagi (usually identified with the berry of *Zizyphus Lotus*: see lotus 1).

1638 Farley *Emblems* xxxi. E 8, Thus cralling for its food, my soule can fret And tasting Lote, his Country doth forget. **1726** Pope *Odyss.* xxiii. 335 How to the land of Lote unblessed he sails. **1830** Lindley *Nat. Syst. Bot.* 114 The fruit of Zizyphus..is often wholesome and pleasant to eat, as in the case of the Jujube and the Lote, the latter of which is now known to have given their name to the classical Lotophagi. **1855** Bailey *Mystic* 80 That heart-soothing herb, not less renowned Than lote, nepenthes, moly, or tolu.

4. The lotus-lily: see lotus 4.

1561 A. SCOTT *New Yeir Gift to Q. Mary* 218 Fragrant flour formois, Lantern to lufe, of ladeis lamp and lot. **1650–60** WHARTON *Disc. Soul World* Wks. (1683) 657 The Lote (which shutteth its Leaves before Sun Rise, but when he Ascendeth openeth them by degrees).

5. *attrib.* and *Comb.*, *as* **lote-berry**, **-eater**, **-leaf**; **lote-bush**, *Zizyphus Lotus.*

1611 COTGR., *Micocoules*, *Lote berries (be round, and hang by long staulkes like Cherries). **1846** LINDLEY *Veg. Kingd.* 582 The *Lote-bush, which gave its name to the Ancient Lotophagi, is to this day collected for food by the Arabs of Barbary. **1587** GOLDING tr. *Solinus Polyhistor* (1590) S iij, In the innermost part of the bigger *Syrt*.. inhabited the *Loteaters. **1638** MAYNE *Lucian* (1664) 355 Your example of the Lote-eaters, and instance of the Syrens, carry no resemblance to my case. **1865** SWINBURNE *Laus Veneris* 185 Softer than the Egyptian *lote-leaf.

†**lote**, *sb.*[2] The eel-pout (*Lota vulgaris*).

1611 COTGR., *Marmote*,..also, the riuer Lote; a little muddie fish, headed, skinned, and finned, like an Eele.

†**lote**, *v.*[1] *Obs.* Also 3 lotie(n, 4 lotye, ? 5 loyt. [? OE. *lotian, f. *lut-, ablaut-variant of *lūt- in the synonymous OE. *lútian* = OHG. *lûzên* (MHG. *lûzen*); the root is prob. identical with that in the str. vb. OE. *lútan* to bow down (see LOUT *v.*).] *intr.* To lurk, lie concealed.

c **1200** *Trin. Coll. Hom.* 217 On þesse fewe litele wored lotieð fele gode wored ȝif hie weren wel ioponed. *c* **1275** LAY. 21509 And dude ȝam alle cleane into þan sipes grunde, and hehte heom lotie [*c* **1205** lutie] wel, þat Cheldrich nere noht war. **1377** LANGL. *P. Pl.* B. XVII. 102 For outlawes in the wode and vnder banke lotyeth. *c* **1386** CHAUCER *Sec. Nun's T.* 186 He foond this hooly olde Vrban anon Among the Seintes buryeles lotynge. **1387** TREVISA *Higden* (Rolls) IV. 397 Latere a Latyn is lotye. **1398** —— *Barth. De P.R.* XVII. liii. (Tollem. MS.), Wormes loteþ under þe schadow þerof.

Hence †'**loting** *vbl. sb.* (in comb. *loting-place*).

13.. *K. Alis.* 6203 He say the ekeris wonynge, And the fysches lotynge. **1398** TREVISA *Barth. De P.R.* XIV. liii. (Tollem. MS.), A caue is proper lotynge and hidynge place of bestes, þat wonen in dennes and dowers.

†**lote**, *v.*[2] *Obs.* [a. ON. *láta* = LET *v.*[1]]

1. *trans.* To forsake, fail.

c **1250** *Gen. & Ex.* 3131 Ne sal ic ȝu noȝ[t] loten Of ðat ic haue ȝu bi-hoten.

2. *intr.* To take account *of.*

c **1400** *Laud Troy Bk.* 8598 Ther is no man that lengur lotes Off these gay golden cotes.

†**lote**, *v.*[3] *Obs.* [f. L. *lōt-*, ppl. stem of *lavāre*; or perh. back-formation from LOTION.] *trans.* To wash with a solution.

1547 BOORDE *Brev. Health* cclxxix. 93 Use the water of plantein with Tutty loted, and ever use colde thynges to the eyes.

lote, variant of LATE *sb.*[1] *Obs.*, look, sound.

lote, obs. form of LOTH *sb.*; variant of LOUT.

†'**loteby.** *Obs.* Forms: 4 lotebi, ludby, lut(t)by, 4–5 loteby, 5 lotby. [f. LOTE *v.*[1] + BY *adv.*] A lover, a paramour.

1303 R. BRUNNE *Handl. Synne* 1731 But þere þe wyfe haunteþ foly Undyr here husbande a ludby, Comunly she wyl neuere blynne. **13..** *Seuyn Sag.* (W.) 1443 Sche stal awai..And wente to here lotebi. *c* **1325** *Metr. Hom.* 82 When scho left Criste hir leve luttby, And toke hir to a synfull man. **1362** LANGL. *P. Pl.* A. III. 146 To holde lemmons and lotebyes al heor lyf-dayes. *c* **1425** *Seven Sag.* (P.) 2148 Anothyr lotby scho nam. **1426** AUDELAY *Poems* 5 He wold here selle that he had boȝt,..And takys to hym a loteby.

lotery, obs. form of LOTTERY.

lote-tree. *arch.* Also 7 loat-. [LOTE *sb.*[1]] **a.** The Nettle-tree, *Celtis australis.* **b.** The jujube-tree, *Zizyphus Lotus*, identified with the tree that bore the mythical lotus-fruit. **c.** The date-plum, *Diospyros Lotus* (*Treas. Bot.* 1866). **d.** Identified with the lotus-lily (LOTUS 4), erroneously supposed to be a tree.

1548 TURNER *Names of Herbes* 24 Celtis..it hath a leafe lyke a Nettel, therfore it may be called in englishe Nettel tree or Lote tree. **1601** HOLLAND *Pliny* I. 494 At Rome..there is yet to be seene a Lote tree standing before the said chappell. **1611** COTGR., *Micocoulier d' Afrique.* Th' African Lote, or Nettle, tree; of whose blacke wood excellent Flutes are made. **1626** BACON *Sylva* § 583 The Lasting of Plants is most in those that are Largest of Body; as Oakes, Elme, Ches-nut, the Loat-Tree, &c. **1678** CUDWORTH *Intell. Syst.* I. iv. § 18. 336 As the Egyptian Hieroglyphick for Material and Corporeal things, was Mud or floating Water, so they pictur'd God, *in Loto arbore sedentem super Lutum*, sitting upon the Lote-tree above the Watery Mud. **1741** *Compl. Fam.-Piece* II. iii. 374 Lote or Nettle-tree. **1825** *Greenhouse Comp.* II. 82 Z[*izyphus*] *Lotus*, a small tree from Barbary, supposed by some to be the Lote-tree of Pliny. **1855** PLANCHÉ *Fairy T. C'tess d' Aulnoy* (1858) 359 A part of the river-side, shaded by willows and lote-trees [Fr. *alisiers*]. **1884** J. PAYNE *1001 Nts.* VIII. 70 The lote-tree doth itself array In some fresh beauty every day. **1887** BROWNING *Parleyings, G. de Lairesse* v, Could I gaze intent On Dryope plucking the blossoms red..Whereat her lote-tree writhed and bled.

attrib. **1607** TOPSELL *Four-f. Beasts* 627 The Loote-tree-root [tr. L. *loti radix*]. **1833** TENNYSON *Œnone* Poems 56 The smoothswarded bower..with lotetree-fruit thicket. **1884** J. PAYNE *Tales fr. Arabic* II. 31 *note*, Lote-tree leaves dried and powdered..are strewn over the dead body.

‖**loth** (ləʊt), *sb.* Also 8 lote, 8–9 loot. [Ger.; a specific use of *loth* LEAD *sb.*[1] Also Du. *lood* (obs.).] A denomination of weight in use in Holland, Germany, Austria, and Switzerland. It varies locally in amount, but is always $\frac{1}{32}$ of the local pound, or half the local ounce.

1683 PETTUS *Fleta Min.* I. (1686) 29 The Mark in the Grain-weight, is parted into Loths and Grains. **1753** HANWAY *Trav.* (1762) I. II. xi. 51, 1 ounce is 2 loot. *Ibid.* VI. lxxxi. 371, 32 Lotes = 1 pound. **1799** W. TOOKE *View Russian Emp.* III. 530 They..heighten the colour afterwards with 3 lote of allum to every pound of berries. **1839** URE *Dict. Arts* 1124 The earthy deposit contains from $\frac{1}{4}$ to $\frac{3}{8}$ of a loth of silver per cwt. **1868** SEYD *Bullion* 146 For Silver, it [Carat] is the mark divided into 16 loths of 18 grains each.

loth, alternative form of LOATH *a.*

Lotharingian (ləʊθə'rɪndʒɪən), *sb.* and *a.* [f. *Lotharingia* (see below) + -AN.] **A.** *sb.* A native or inhabitant of the ancient duchy of Lotharingia in northern Europe, situated between the Rhine and the Scheldt from Frisia to the Alps. **B.** *adj.* Of or pertaining to Lotharingia or its inhabitants, or to modern Lorraine (see quot. 1969). Cf. LORRAINER.

1607 TOPSELL *Four-f. Beasts* 46 They [*sc.* beavers] are vsed by the Lotharingians and Sauoyens for meat allowed to be eaten on fish-daies. **1883** *Encycl. Brit.* XV. 5/1 By the treaty of Bonn (921) the Lotharingian duchy was ceded formally to France. *Ibid.*, The ever-restless spirit of the Lotharingians broke out into new commotions. **1909** J. H. B. MASTERMAN *Dawn Mediæval Europe* xxiii. 216 Louis the German and Charles both fell upon his [*sc.* Lothair's] Lotharingian lands like birds of prey. **1959** *Chambers's Encycl.* VIII. 694/1 In a struggle with the turbulent Lotharingian magnates, the young king was killed. **1964** *Times Rev. Industry* Jan. 73/3 The river Our..is situated within 100 miles of the Belgian coalfields, the Ruhr, the Lotharingian steel industry,..and the Luxembourg iron industry. **1969** *Listener* 6 Feb. 165/2 In this new economic Europe, which hinges on the Rhine and the Rhône—the Lotharingian axis, as it's sometimes called—Brittany tends to feel even more isolated.

Lothario (ləʊ'θɛərɪəʊ). Allusive use of the name of one of the characters in Rowe's *Fair Penitent*: often qualified by *gay.*

The name had previously been used for a somewhat similar character by Davenant in his *Cruel Brother* 1630.

A libertine, gay deceiver, rake.

[**1703** ROWE *Fair Penit.* V. i. H 3 Is this that Haughty, Gallant, Gay Lothario?] **1756** *World* No. 202 ⁋8 The gay Lothario dresses for the fight. **1812** MOORE *Intercepted Lett.* viii. 31 Both gay Lotharios. **1849** LYTTON *Caxtons* XVIII. vi. III. 278 No woman could have been more flattered and courted by Lotharios and lady-killers than Lady Castleton has been. **1887** W. S. GILBERT *Ruddigore* I, A devil of a fellow—a regular Lothario.

lothe, obs. form of LEWTH.

†**lothen**, *a. Obs.* [a. ON. *loðenn.*] Shaggy.

? *a* **1400** *Morte Arth.* 778 Lothene and lothely, lokkes and oþer. *Ibid.* 1097 Lyme and leskes fulle lothyne.

lotherwit(e, corrupt form of LAIRWITE.

1579 *Expos. Terms Law* 143 *Lotherwite*, that is, that you may take amendes of him which doth defile your bondwoman without your licence. **1686** PLOT *Staffordsh.* 279 The Lords enjoy another odd Custom, or privilege of Lotherwits or Lyerwits at this day.

loth(e)some, lothness: see LOATH-.

lotic ('ləʊtɪk), *a. Ecol.* [f. L. *lōtus* washing (Needham & Lloyd *Life of Inland Waters* (1916) vi. 315).] Of fresh-water organisms or habitats, situated in rapidly moving water. Cf. LENITIC *a.*

1916 NEEDHAM & LLOYD *Life Inland Waters* vi. 363 The animals of lotic societies are mainly small invertebrates. **1931** R. N. CHAPMAN *Animal Ecol.* xvii. 347 Along the shores of the Great Lakes there are lotic communities where the wave action is incessant, thus producing the fundamental conditions of a lotic environment and presenting an exception to the general statement that all lotic environments are streams. **1970** F. J. & W. B. VERNBERG *Animal & Environment* ii. 44 Fresh-water systems are generally divided into two groups based on the activity or rate of movement of the water: (1) standing quiet (lentic) waters..; and (2) flowing (lotic) waters.

lotiform ('ləʊtɪfɔːm), *a. Arch.* [As if ad. L. **lōtiformis*, f. *lōtus*: see LOTUS and -(I)FORM.] Shaped like the lotus-lily.

1897 *Edin. Rev.* Oct. 470 The cloistered court of lotiform pillars.

lotion ('ləʊʃən), *sb.* Also 5 loscion, 6 locion, lotyon. [ad. L. *lōtiōn-em* washing, f. *lavāre* (ppl. stem *laut-*, *lōt-*) to wash: see LAVE *v.*]

†**1.** *gen.* The action of washing (the body), ablution. Also, washing with a medicinal preparation (cf. 3). *Obs.*

1549 LATIMER *6th Serm. bef. Edw. VI*, U j b, Their doctrine was vnsauery, it was but of Lotiones [*misprinted* Loliones] of decimacions of anets seade, and Cummyn and suche gere. **1599** A. M. tr. *Gabelhouer's Bk. Physicke* 43/2 Everye weeke twice washe his head, and after the lotion of the same, strawe agayne of this poulder in the sores. **1615** G. SANDYS *Trav.* 64 Their customary lotions, and daily frequenting of the Bannias. **1659** H. L'ESTRANGE *Alliance Div. Off.* 152 It was..necessary that they should be washed and cleansed before they entered the sacred Font: This day was set apart for that lotion. **1707** FLOYER *Physic. Pulse-Watch* 206 The Lotion of the Head, Feet and Hands. **1797** *Encycl. Brit.* X. 297 *Lotion*, is, strictly speaking, such washing as concerns beautifying the skin.

b. *Eccl.* = LAVATORY 2 a. ? *Obs.*

1529 *Will of J. Robinson* (Somerset Ho.), Between the effectory and the first locion. **1552** in Money *Ch. Goods in Berks* (1879) 39 Two towelles one for the communyon thother for Drieng after lotyon. **1599** SANDYS *Europæ Spec.* (1632) 179 In the Priests Lotions at Masse.

†**2.** The 'washing' of metals, medicines, etc. in water to cleanse them from impurities, etc. *Obs.*

1612 WOODALL *Surg. Mate* Wks. (1653) 272 Lotion is a preparation of medicaments by water, or some other liquor to remove some evil and hurtful thing, and to procure some good and profitable quality in them. **1686** W. HARRIS tr. *Lemery's Course Chym.* I. ix. (ed. 3) 284 But let there be never so many lotions they can never wash away a certain inveloping or cover that is given to the Antimony by the fixt Saltpetre. **1756** C. LUCAS *Ess. Waters* I. 83 The Chemist.. uses [water] for..precipitation, lotion or ablution, crystallisation, distillation [etc.]. **1796** KIRWAN *Elem. Min.* (ed. 2) I. 137 Separated by lotion and coction.

3. *Pharm.* A liquid preparation used externally for healing wounds, relieving pain, beautifying the skin, etc.

c **1400** *Lanfranc's Cirurg.* 165 *marg.*, A loscion for wondis within the brest. **1599** A. M. tr. *Gabelhouer's Bk. Physicke* 308/2 [A recipe for] a precious vulneraryе water, or lotion, which on divers Persons hath bin tryed. **1606** WARNER *Alb. Eng.* XVI. ci. (1612) 400 And ye that haue the Aire parfum'd, bathe oft in Lotions sweete. **1758** JOHNSON *Idler* No. 40 ⁋5 The vender..sells a lotion that repels pimples. **1780** COWPER *Progr. Err.* 299 To hide the shocking features of her face Her form with dress and lotion they repair. **1807–26** S. COOPER *First Lines Surg.* (ed. 5) 338 A drachm of Bates's camphorated lotion in two ounces of water. **1883** J. HAWTHORNE *Dust* I. 24 Bathe the shoulder with a lotion.

4. *slang.* Alcoholic drink.

1876 HINDLEY *Adv. Cheap Jack* 82 The one who could take the most 'lotion' without being so [*sc.* drunk].

lotion ('ləʊʃən), *v. nonce-wd.* [f. LOTION *sb.*] *trans.* To treat with lotions.

1768 FOOTE *Devil on 2 Sticks* III. Wks. 1799 II. 275 Full power..to pill, bolus, lotion,..and poultice, all persons.

†'**lotium.** *Obs.* [L. *lōtium*, urine.] Stale urine used by barbers as a 'lye' for the hair. Also *attrib.*

1601 B. JONSON *Poetaster* III. i, [To an apothecary.] Thou stinkst of Lotium and the syringe. **1609** —— *Sil. Wom.* III. ii, *Mor.*..Let him [*sc.* 'that cursed barber'] be glad to eate his sponge, for bread. *Trv.* And drinke lotium to it. **1608** MIDDLETON *Trick to Catch Old One* IV. iv, To take away the scent of..my barber's lotium-water.

†**lotium**, vulgar form of LOTION.

a **1657** R. LOVEDAY *Lett.* (1659) 186 If you have a Recipe from Dr. B. of some soveraign lotium, it will be gratefully welcom.

†'**lotless**, *a. Obs. rare*[−1]. [? f. LOT *sb.* (sense 2 b).] App. = without harm or injury.

1470–85 MALORY *Arthur* X. iv. 419, I am sure and I doo bataille with you I shalle not escape with oute grete hurtes and as I suppose ye shalle not escape alle lotles.

†'**lotment.** *Obs.* exc. *dial.* (see *E.D.D.*). [f. LOT *v.* + -MENT.] An allotment of land.

1656 *First Cent. Hist. Springfield, Mass.* (1898) I. 253 To cleare and scoure the brooke soe far as their lott or lottments is in breadth in the same meddow. **1720** *Connect. Col. Rec.* (1872) VI. 208 This Assembly do enact and order, that the lotments in said town shall be taxed.

loto: see LOTA and LOTTO.

lotong (ləʊ'tɒŋ). Also lutung. [Malay.] A leaf monkey of the genus *Presbytis*, esp. *P. obscurus.*

1821 T. S. RAFFLES in *Trans. Linn. Soc.* XIII. 247 *Simia maura*? Linn. Lotong of the Malays. **1824** T. HORSFIELD *Zool. Res. Java* s.v. *Semnopithecus Maurus.* The name of the latter [monkey] is Lutung; but the Malays and Europeans apply this name to both species... In Sumatra the name of the 'Maure' is Lotong. **1839** T. J. NEWBOLD *Pol. & Statistical Acct. Straits of Malacca* I. vii. 432 Of the genus Semnopithecus are..the Lotong, or Semnopithecus Maurus, of F. Cuvier; the kra, etc. **1903** J. L. BONHOTE in *Fasciculi Malayenses: Zoology* I. 6 The lôtong is very generally distributed over those parts of the Peninsula that we visited. **1936** G. B. GARDNER *Keris & Other Malay Weapons* v. 95 They have a curved iron handle forged on, resembling the tail of a *lotong* monkey. **1965** C. SHUTTLEWORTH *Malayan Safari* 10 A *lotong* (leaf monkey) chattered its alarm call near by.

‖**Lotophagi** (ləʊ'tɒfədʒaɪ), *sb. pl.* Also 7 -ie. [L., a. Gr. Λωτοφάγοι, f. λωτό-ς LOTUS + φαγεῖν to eat.] The lotus-eaters; a people in Greek legend who lived on the fruit of the lotus, which was said to cause a dreamy forgetfulness in those who ate it.

1601 HOLLAND *Pliny* I. 397. **1615** CHAPMAN *Odyss.* IX. 139 The shore, Where dwell the blossome-fed Lotophagie. **1725** POPE *Odyss.* IX. 107 Lotos, the name; divine, nectareous juice! (Thence called Lotophagi.)

lotophagist (ləʊ'tɒfədʒɪst). *rare*[−1]. [See prec. and -IST.] A lotus-eater.

1839 *Blackw. Mag.* XLV. 289 Like most of our country-men who have become habituated to the..gentle ethics of that singular place, he is what he calls a lotophagist.

lotophagous (ləʊ'tɒfəgəs), *a. rare.* [See prec. and -OUS.] Lotus-eating, resembling the Lotophagi. Hence **lo'tophagously** *adv.*

1855 EMERSON in *Corr. w. Carlyle* II. 244, I have even fancied you did me a harm by the valued gift of Antony Wood; which and the like of which I take a lotophagous pleasure in eating. **1882** PIDGEON *Engineer's Holiday* I. 83 Thus lotophagously sailing, we landed one morning on a beautifully wooded point.

lotsa ('lɒtsə). Colloq. contraction of *lots of*.

1927 [see HOT *a.* 1 e]. **1945** A. KOBER *Parm Me* 18 Mmm, is good the cake... You must use lotsa ecks [*sc.* eggs] fa such a cake. **1967** 'P. CHAMBERS' *Bad die Young* x. 146 We got lotsa time. **1969** in Halpert & Story *Christmas Mumming in Newfoundland* 88 The social drinkers soon left, even though the host was protesting that there was 'lotsa time to stay'. **1971** *It* 9–23 Sept. 4/2 The Notting Hill Carnival was lotsa fun for seven days and nights.

lotta ('lɒtə). Also **lotter**. Colloq. contraction of *lot of*.

1906 E. NESBIT *Railway Children* viii. 175, I gets a lotter green paint and I paints her stem to stern. **1928** [see BULLSHIT 1]. **1944** C. HIMES *Black on Black* (1973) 198 Lotta hustlers up there. **1945** A. KOBER *Parm Me* 34, I hadda do a lotta talking to get her to come. **1965** 'D. SHANNON' *Death-Bringers* (1966) xiii. 164 A lotta people know my name who I don't know. **1969** *Coast to Coast 1967–68* 9 No, I'm a lotta things, but I ain't crazy. **1971** *Black World* Apr. 56 Lotta big talk, but when you get there nothin is happenin.

lottarie, obs. form of LOTTERY.

lotted ('lɒtɪd), *ppl. a.* [f. LOT *v.* + -ED[1].] In senses of the verb: Assigned by lot or as a lot, allotted, etc. Of a pressed seaman: Chosen by lot.

1568 T. HOWELL *Arb. Amitie* (1879) 46 Of bodies two, one corps is made, So linckt in lotted loue. **1568** —— *Newe Sonets* (1879) 137 The litle Byrde . . doth then . . greet oft his lotted feare. **1647** H. MORE *Song of Soul* II. ii. II. xiv, And so of life they'll want their 'lotted fee. **1758** J. BLAKE *Plan Mar. Syst.* 25 That the master of the merchant-ship, from which they were taken by lot, be obliged . . to make up such lotted seaman's accounts. **1823** BYRON *Age of Bronze* v, Thy lotted people and extinguish'd name.

b. With *adv.* (nonce-use) ***well-lotted***: fortunate in one's lot.

1709 PRIOR *Ladle* Moral, Some Sense, and more Estate, kind Heav'n To this well-lotted Peer has given.

lotter ('lɒtə(r)). [f. LOT *sb.* or *v.* + -ER[1].] ? One who rents an allotment of land.

1845 *Statist. Acc. Scot.* XV. 73 The tenants or lotters live on their respective farms or townships.

† **'lotterel.** *Obs.* [Cf. LODDER; also LOITER *v.*] A term of opprobrium: ? Scoundrel.

c **1440** *York Myst.* xxxii. 259 Latte we þat lotterell liffe ought long, It will be fonde, in faith, foly. *Ibid.* 382.

lottery ('lɒtərɪ). Forms: 6 **lottary(e, -erye, lottre,** 6–7 **lotarie, -ery, lotterie,** 7 **lottarie, lottire, lottrie, lottry,** 6– **lottery.** [ad. It. *lotteria* (whence F. *loterie*, 1658 in Hatz.-Darm.), f. *lotto*: see LOT *sb.*, LOTTO.]

1. An arrangement for the distribution of prizes by chance among persons purchasing tickets. Slips or lots, numbered in correspondence with the tickets, and representing either prizes or blanks, are drawn from a wheel. Usually intended as a means of raising money for the benefit of the promoters, of the State, or of some charitable institution. † ***lottery general***, a public or state lottery.

1567 *Lottery Chart* Aug., A very rich Lotterie generall, without any Blanckes, contayning a great number of good Prices, aswel of redy Money as of Plate, . . the same Lotterie is erected by Her Maiesties order, to the intent that suche commoditie as may chaunce to arise thereof, . . may be conuerted towards the reparation of the Hauens, and strength of the Realme. **1568** *Nottingham Rec.* IV. 132 The proclamasyon for the Lottre. **1587** STOW *Summarie Chron.* 434 A Lotery for meruailous rich and bewtifull armour, was begun to be drawen at London. **1588** FRAUNCE *Lawiers Log.* II. xvii. 116 Every rule were written in a severall schrole, every schrole being put into an earthen pitcher as they use in lottaries. **1626** DONNE *Serm.* iv. (1848) I. 62 He comes not to the Sacrament as to a Lottery where perchance he may draw Salvation. **1668** *Advt.* in *Lond. Gaz.* No. 261/4 Mr. Ogilby's Lottery of Books opens on Monday the 25th instant. **1710** STEELE *Tatler* No. 170 ⁋5 Tickets for the Lottery appointed by the Government. **1731** FIELDING *Lottery* ii. 28, I had no Fortune, but what I promis'd my self from the Lottery. **1769** *Junius Lett.* (1804) I. 7 If it must be paid by Parliament, let me advise the Chancellor of the Exchequer to think of some better expedient than a lottery. **1805** *Hansard's Parl. Deb.* VI. 358 Mr. Alderman Combe presented a petition from several persons, owners . . of houses, . . praying leave to dispose of the same by way of lottery. **1842** MISS MITFORD in L'Estrange *Life* III. ix. 153 My mother's fortune was large, my father's good, legacies from both sides, a twenty thousand prize in the lottery—all have vanished.

b. *transf.* and *fig.*

1596 SHAKS. *Merch. V.* I. ii. 32 The lotterie that hee hath deuised in these three chests of gold, siluer, and leade. **1596** DRAYTON *Leg.* II. 153 Thinke how thou liu'st here publikely in Court, . . Being a Lotterie whereat few doe winne. **1642** FULLER *Holy & Prof. St.* III. xxii. 212 Marriage shall prove no lottery to thee, when the hand of providence chuseth for thee, who, if drawing a blank, can turn it into a prize by sanctifying a bad wife unto thee. **1768** STERNE *Sent. Journ.* (1775) I. 14 (*Desobligeant*) Knowledge and improvements are to be got by sailing and posting for that purpose; but whether useful knowledge and real improvements, is all a lottery. **1771** SMOLLETT *Humph. Cl.* 10 July, If I have not been lucky in the lottery of life. **1866** GEO. ELIOT *F. Holt* (1868) 19 Such desires make life a hideous lottery, where every day may turn up a blank. **1901** *Scotsman* 28 Feb. 7/2 What a lottery it is, this being mentioned in dispatches.

† **2.** Decision by casting or drawing of lots, sortilege, appeal to the lot. Also: Chance, issue of events as determined by chance. *Obs.*

1570 LEVINS *Manip.* 105/5 A Lottery, *sortilicium.* **1584** R. SCOT *Discov. Witchcr.* XI. x. (1886) 159 The cousening art of sortilege or lotarie. **1601** SHAKS. *Jul. C.* II. i. 119 So let high-sighted-Tyranny range on, Till each man drop by Lottery. **1606** —— *Tr. & Cr.* II. i. 140 Who shall answer him? *Achil.* I know not, 'tis put to Lottry. **1613** BEAUM. & FL. *Honest Man's Fort.* IV. i, Fainting under Fortunes false Lottery. **1619** GATAKER *Lots* 6 Lotery is the deciding or determination of a doubt by some casuall euent. **1663** *Aron-bimnucha* 4 Such was the Lotery that discovered the Theft and Sacriledge committed at Jericho.

† **3.** Something which comes to a person by lot or fortune. *Obs.*

1606 SHAKS. *Ant. & Cl.* II. ii. 248 If Beauty, Wisedome, Modesty, can settle The heart of Anthony: Octauia is A blessed Lottery to him.

4. A round game at cards, in which prizes are obtained by the holders of certain cards.

1830 R. HARDIE *Hoyle made familiar* 84 Lottery. This is one of the most amusing of those games which are played merely for amusement. *Ibid.* 86 Each player . . stakes a certain number of counters . . which are placed in a box or pool as a fund for the lottery. **1876** 'CAPT. CRAWLEY' *Card Players' Man.* 233.

5. *attrib.* and *Comb.*, as ***lottery-book***, ***-mania***, ***-subscription***, ***ticket***; † **lottery-ball**, ? a ball used for drawing at a lottery; † **lottery-barber** (see quot.); † **lottery-broker**, one who acts as agent for the sale of lottery tickets; † **lottery-cavalier** (see quot.); † **lottery-fool**, ? a buffoon employed to attract custom to a lottery; † **lottery-lantern**, a lantern bearing transparencies advertising a lottery; **lottery-man** = *lottery-broker*; **lottery-office**, an office for the carrying on of lotteries; hence ***lottery-office-keeper***; † **lottery-pot** = *lot-pot* (see LOT *sb.* 10); † **lottery-puff**, **-squib**, an interested advertisement of a lottery; † **lottery-vagrant**, ? a vagrant making a pretence of selling lottery tickets; **lottery-wheel**, a piece of mechanism used in lotteries, consisting of a vertical wheel bearing on its axis a drum into which the numbered slips are placed and from which they are drawn after being shuffled by the revolution of the wheel.

1696 E. LHWYD in *Phil. Trans.* XXVII. 463, I have one given me, cut like a *Lottery-ball, and perforated. **1777** *Ann. Reg.* 207 *Lottery barbers, where a man for being shaved and paying three-pence may stand a chance of getting ten pound. **1783** BP. PERCY *Let. to S. Pegge* in Nichols *Illust. Lit. Hist.* (1858) VIII. 225 Could you procure access to the Commissioners' own *Lottery Books, and thence inform me of the fate of No. 24,380. **1794** C. PIGOTT *Female Jockey Club* Pref. 20 Contemplate the adventurous *lottery brokers, driving their hard bargains, with a . . peculating minister. **1682** DRYDEN *Epil. to 'Unhap. Favourite'* 5 Not *lottery cavaliers are half so poor. [*Note. 'Lottery cavaliers' are poor loyal officers, to whom the right of keeping lotteries was granted by patent in Charles II's reign.*] **1690** CROWNE *Eng. Friar* v. Dram. Wks. 1874 IV. 100 The honour of a dueller is but the honour of a *lottery-fool. **1774** FOOTE *Cozeners* I. Wks. 1799 II. 155 De *lottery-lanthorns hang up in de streets, vid large red letters, write on all sides. **1697** *Lond. Gaz.* No. 3333/4 Mr. Sherwood a *Lottery Man. **1775** *Misc.* in *Ann. Reg.* 190/1 My whole house had . . been infected with the *lottery mania,—(if I may be allowed the expression). **1772** *Town & Country Mag.* 130 Mr. Jesson, who keeps a *lottery-office under the piazzas, Covent Garden. **1827** *Gentl. Mag.* XCVII. II. 513 In truth we could name 'lottery-office-keepers' in real holy orders and pretended holy orders. **1629** H. BURTON *Babel no Bethel* 1 Scroles shufled together in a *lottery pott. **1806** SURR *Winter in Lond.* (1824) II. iii. 68 By taking out a couple of sudden deaths, a fire in Oxford-market, a *lottery puff, [etc.] . . we make room for the paragraph. **1817** *Parl. Debates* 732 Those misrepresentations and fabrications called lottery puffs. **1806** SURR *Winter in Lond.* (1824) III. v. 180 Curse me if the stupid dunce of an editor did not put it in the puffing corner, with two *lottery squibs and a wonderful cure of the gout by electricity. **1844** THACKERAY *May Gambols* Wks. 1900 XIII. 420 The *lottery-subscription lies in limbo. **1697–8** *Act 9 Will. III* c. 37 §2 The more orderly Payment of the *Lottery Tickets for the said Annuities. **1873** H. SPENCER *Stud. Sociol.* vii. 149 In the holder of a lottery ticket, hope generates a belief utterly at variance with probability as numerically estimated. **1799** *Naval Chron.* II. 318 An idle or suspicious character, or *lottery vagrant. **1819** SHELLEY *P. Bell 3rd* VI. xiii. 5 A world of words—false, true—and foul and fair—As in a *lottery-wheel are shook. **1827** HONE *Every-day Bk.* II. 1439 [An engraving of] The Lottery Wheel, 1826.

lotting ('lɒtɪŋ), *vbl. sb.* [f. LOT *v.* + -ING[1].] The action of the verb LOT.

c **1449** PECOCK *Repr.* III. i. 278 The firste departing, soorting, and lotting of the al hool land. **1579** FENTON *Guicciard.* XIV. (1599) 668 At last they fell to the custome of lotting of voyces in the Conclaue. **1770** A. HALL *Gospel Worship* (1829) II. xxii. 305 Directions concerning the lawful use of lotting must be suggested. **1825** J. NICHOLSON *Operat. Mechanic* 755 In the lotting of the ores, care should be taken to have small portions from different specimens.

attrib. **1514** *Will of J. Kirkby* (Somerset Ho.), My Lotting tables.

lottire, obs. form of LOTTERY.

lotto, loto ('lɒtəʊ, 'ləʊtəʊ). [a. It. *lotto*, F. *loto*: see LOT *sb.*]

1. A game played with cards divided into numbered and blank squares and numbered discs to be drawn on the principle of a lottery.

Each player has one or more cards before him; one of the discs is drawn from a bag, and its number called; a counter is placed on the square that has the same number, the player who first gets one row covered being the winner.

1778 WARNER *Let. to G. Selwyn* 28 Nov. in *G. Selwyn & his Contemp.* (1844) III. 353, I wonder how you could endure loto. **1819** *Banquet* 33 Or bid enlivening loto for a while, Or cogitative chess, the eve beguile. **1836** T. HOOK *G. Gurney* II. 121 Others diverted themselves at the more interesting game of loto. **1894** *Contemp. Rev.* Aug. 246 The children played draughts, bagatelle, lotto, or tiddlywinks. **1899** R. WHITEING *No. 5 John St.* 77 The toiling infants under age are found at the game of loto.

attrib. **1779** WARNER *Let. to G. Selwyn* 3 Jan. in *G. Selwyn & his Contemp.* (1844) III. 381 Lord Fitzwilliam . . received your loto-box.

‖ **2.** A lottery (of the Italian kind).

[**1787** P. MATY tr. *Riesbeck's Trav. Germ.* III. lxv. 248 The *lotto* of Genoa, which, though decorated with a smooth and splendid name, is in fact no more than a Pharaoh table.] **1827** HONE *Every-day Bk.* II. 1535 To the honour of the Hanoverian government, no *Lotto* was ever introduced into it, though many foreigners offered large sums for permission to cheat the people in this manner. **1884** *Sat. Rev.* 14 June 774/2 The love of gambling is a national characteristic; and . . Lotto—that is, the official weekly lottery—is the most dangerous of the forms it takes.

lottre, lottrie, lottry, obs. ff. LOTTERY.

'lot-tree. An alleged name for the Whitebeam Tree, *Pyrus Aria*.

1866 *Treas. Bot.*

† **'loture.** *Obs.* [a. L. *lōtūra* washing.] Washing: = LOTION *sb.* 2. Also *concr.*, the water in which any substance has been 'washed'.

1601 HOLLAND *Pliny* II. XXXIV. xviii. 519 Lead doth yeeld from it selfe a certaine substance by way of loture, which is of right great and manifold vse in physicke. **1657** TOMLINSON *Renou's Disp.* 100 Rusticks in Summer decoct the Loture of honey-combes.

lotus ('ləʊtəs). (Also **lotos** 7 *erron.* **lutes.**) Pl. **lotuses.** [a. L. *lōtus*, Gr. λωτός, the name of several dissimilar plants; it is not known whether the word in the various applications is etymologically identical; in sense 3 Herodotus speaks of it as Egyptian.]

1. The plant yielding the fruit which was the food of the LOTOPHAGI of Greek legend; represented by Homer (*Od.* IX. 90 ff.) as producing in those who ate it a state of dreamy forgetfulness, and loss of all desire to return home. Hence often *allusively*.

The Homeric lotus was identified by later Gr. writers with a North African shrub, the descriptions of which are thought by most naturalists to refer to the jujube-tree (*Zizyphus Lotus*), though other identifications have been proposed.

1540–41 ELYOT *Image Gov.* 39 Whan the Companions and seruantes of Ulisses had eaten abundantly of the herbe called Lotos. **1591** SPENSER *Virg. Gnat* 193 And them amongst the wicked Lotos grew, Wicked for holding guilefully away Vlysses men. *a* **1600** T. DELONEY *Thomas of Reading* (1632) G j b, Then would I be like those men (that eating of the tree Lutes) forget the Country where they were borne. **1628** LE GRYS tr. *Barclay's Argenis* 182 What Lotos in Africa doth hinder thy returne hither? **1725** POPE *Odyss.* IX. 106 Lotos, the name; divine, nectarious juice! **1773** JOHNSON *Journ. West. Isl.* Wks. X. 400 At Dunvegan I had tasted lotus and was in danger of forgetting that I was ever to depart. **1832** TENNYSON *Lotos-Eaters* 105 Eating the Lotos day by day. **1900** *Contemp. Rev.* July 57 If it had all been Yalta, I could have eaten of the lotus for many a day, but Sebastopol is grim and grey [etc.].

2. A tree mentioned by ancient writers, distinguished by its hard, black wood, of which statues, flutes, etc. were carved; prob. the nettle-tree, *Celtis australis*. Also, the date-plum, *Diospyros Lotus*.

1551 TURNER *Herbal* I. H vj b, Affryca . . bryngeth furth an excellent tree called lotus, . . the wood hath a black color and is myche desyred of men for to make pypes. **1669** WORLIDGE *Syst. Agric.* (1681) 99 The Larch and Lotus . . deserve to be propagated for their rarity, excellent Shade, and durable Timber. **1760** J. LEE *Introd. Bot.* App. 317 Lotus or Lote-tree, *Celtis*. *Ibid.*, Lotus, supposed, of Homer, *Diospyros*.

3. a. The water-lily of Egypt and Asia, *Nymphæa Lotus* (and other species), and *Nelumbium speciosum*. **b.** *Arch.* An ornament representing the Egyptian water-lily: cf. *lotus blossom*, etc. in 6.

1584 RICH tr. *Herodotus* II. 92 b, In time of the floude . . there arise in the water great plenty of lyllyes, which the people of Ægypt call Lotos. **1601** HOLLAND *Pliny* I. 397 The Ægyptian Lotus . . groweth in the marishes of Ægypt. **1785** WILKINS *Bhagvat* v. 45 The leaf of the lotus. **1859** TENNENT *Ceylon* I. I. iii. 123 The chief ornaments of these neglected sheets of water are the large red and white Lotus. **1877** LONGF. *Kéramos* 286 The grand Osiris holding in his hand the lotus. **1883** V. STUART *Egypt* 204 The blue and pink lotus of India. **1900** MAX MÜLLER in *19th Cent.* Nov. 732 After death the souls enter into the calyx of a lotus.

c. The plant treated symbolically in Hindu and Buddhist thought; also, in Yogic exercises,

a bodily position said to resemble the lotus blossom. Cf. *lotus gospel*, *pose*, etc. in 6.

1848 J. D. HOOKER *Himalayan Jrnls.* Nov. (1854) I. x. 229 Low stone dykes, into which were let rows of stone slabs, inscribed with the sacred 'Om Mani Padmi om'.—'Hail to him of the lotus and jewel.' **1887** E. ARNOLD (*title*) Lotus and jewel, containing 'In an Indian temple', 'A casket of gems'..with other poems. **1949** S. MUZUMDAR *Yogic Exercises* 103 There are insuperable impediments because of which many will fail to master the Lotus. **1973** R. RENDELL *Some lie & some Die* xviii. 183 Vedast..had taken up a Yoga position, a half-Lotus, on the floor.

4. Some kind of clover or trefoil (referred to by Homer as food for horses). †*wild lotus*, perh. *Melilotus officinalis*.

1562 TURNER *Herbal* II. 42 a, Lotus syluestris that is called wylde lotus, which som call yᵉ less trifoli, groweth in Libia. *c* **1611** CHAPMAN *Iliad* XIV. 294 With his leaves did dewy lotus store Th' Elysian mountain. **1682** WHELER *Journ. Greece* I. 3 Yellow Flowers..like those of wild Lotus. **1709** ADDISON *Tatler* No. 147 ¶4 While the Earth beneath them sprung up in Lotus's, Saffrons, Hyacinths [etc.]. **1820** SHELLEY *Hymn to Mercury* xvii. 6 When with rush-grass tall, Lotus and all sweet herbage, every one Had pastured been. **1842** TENNYSON *Œnone* 96 And at their feet the crocus brake like fire, Violet, amaracus and asphodel, Lotos and lilies.

5. Adopted by botanists as the name of a genus of leguminous plants; hence in popular language *spec.* the Bird's-foot Trefoil, *Lotus corniculatus*.

1753 CHAMBERS *Cycl. Supp.* s.v., The species of lotus, enumerated by Mr. Tournefort, are these. 1. The smooth hand cinquefoil lotus, called the smaller smooth horned lotus [and 22 others]. **1813** SIR H. DAVY *Agric. Chem.* (1814) 65 He was examining particularly a species of lotus. ? **1842** LANCE *Cottage Farmer* 9 Buckwheat, rye, tares, lucern, rape, white clover, trefoil, lotus; some one or other of these will grow readily in sandy land. **1865** GOSSE *Land & Sea* (1874) 7 The scarlet-tipped blossoms of the little bird's-foot lotus.

6. *attrib.* and *Comb.*, as ***lotus-blossom, -branch, -dust, -flower, -flute, -leaf*** (also *attrib.*), ***-lily, -pond, -seed***; (*Buddhism* and *Yoga*) ***lotus gospel, pose, position, posture, seat, throne***; ***lotus-like*** adj.; ***lotus-headed, -leafed, -leaved, -paven, -petalled*** adjs.; **lotus-berry**, *Byrsonima coriacea*; **lotus-bird** *Austral.* (see quot.); **lotus capital, -column** *Egyptian Arch.*, a capital or column ornamented with lotuses; **lotus-grass** = sense 4; **lotus-land**, the fabled land of the lotus-eaters; a land of ease and delight; **lotus-tree** = LOTE-TREE (*Treas. Bot.*).

1864 GRISEBACH *Flora W. Ind.* 785 *Lotus-berry. **1890** LUMHOLTZ *Cannibals* 22 The *Parra gallinacea*, which in Australia is called the *lotus-bird. It sits on the leaves that float on the water, particularly those of the water-lily. **1850** G. WILKINSON *Arch. Anc. Egypt* 7 The *lotus blossom, the papyrus head. **1834** *Baboo* I. xviii. 317 A piece of jewellery, representing a *lotus-branch. **1850** G. WILKINSON *Arch. Anc. Egypt* 47 The *lotus (or 'full blown lotus') capital. *Ibid.* 60 The full-blown *lotus column. **1832** TENNYSON *Lotos-Eaters* 149 Round and round the spicy downs the yellow *Lotos-dust is blown. **1856** R. A. VAUGHAN *Mystics* (1860) I. 228 The *lotus-flowers are not the Nile. **1833** TENNYSON *Poems* 101 Melody o' the Lybian *lotus-flute. **1911** E. A. GORDON (*title*) The *Lotus Gospel or Mahayana Buddhism and its symbolic teachings. **1820** SHELLEY *Œdipus* II. i. 63 In fresh dews Of *lotos-grass and blossoming asphodel. **1891** T. HARDY *Tess* (1900) 87/2 The smoke..rose from the chimney..like a *lotus-headed column. **1842** TENNYSON *Lotos-Eaters* 154 In the hollow *Lotos-land to live and lie reclined On the hills like Gods together. **1902** *Longm. Mag.* Jan. 214 He lived in 'lotos land'—the Garden Isle of England. **1813** COLERIDGE *Night-Sc.* 53 The God, who floats upon a *lotos leaf. **1865** J. H. INGRAHAM *Pillar of Fire* (1872) 262 Majestic columns, with lotus-leaf capitals. **1852** R. S. SURTEES *Sponge's Sp. Tour* (1893) 101 It cost a vast of money—fifty guineas! to say nothing of the *lotus-leafed pedestal it's on. **1837** *Penny Cycl.* IX. 318/1 (*Egyptian Architecture*) The bell-shaped and *lotus-leaved capitals. **1800** *Asiatic Ann. Reg., Misc. Tracts* 350/2 The dust of whose *lotos-like feet is holy. **1862** G. WILSON *Relig. Chem.* 21 *Lotus-lilies sucked up from the Nile and exhaled as vapour the snows that are lying on the tops of our hills. **1878** GOSSE *Rivers of Bible* 68 The sweet lotus-lilies that are set in porcelain vases. **1820** SHELLEY *Witch Atl.* lix, *Lotus-paven canals. **1881** W. G. PALGRAVE in *Macm. Mag.* XLV. 26 The same massive tree-like columns,..the same *lotus-petaled capitals. **1863** ALCOCK *Capital Tycoon* II. 165 He found temporary refuge in a *lotus-pond. **1966** 'A. HALL' *9th Directive* ii. 17 He sat with his legs crossed under him in the *Lotus pose. **1962** T. C. LETHBRIDGE *Witches* v. 57 There are so many ways in which the Indian gods agree with those of Western Europe, even to their sitting in the '*lotus' position. **1964** I. FLEMING *You only live Twice* i. 21 Since Bond had arrived in Japan he had assiduously practised sitting in the lotus position. **1968** *Guardian* 29 Feb. 8/4 Sitting in the lotus position..concentrating upon one's navel and repeating the mystic syllable, 'Om, Om'. **1884** RAM CHANDRA BOSE *Hindu Philos.* vi. 177 It is called Padmâsana (*lotus-posture), and is highly beneficial in overcoming all diseases. **1965** W. SWAAN *Jap. Lantern* xii. 136 Ideally, one should assume the cross-legged 'Lotus Posture' familiar from Buddha images. **1937** F. YEATS-BROWN *Yoga Explained* ii. 71 (*caption*) The pupil is shown in the *Lotus Seat, padmasana, but any comfortable position can be adopted. **1893** EARL DUNMORE *Pamirs* II. 233 The favourite dish of a Chinaman, namely, *lotus seed. **1911** E. B. HAVELL *Ideals Indian Art* iii. 32 The whole spirit of Indian thought is symbolised in the conception of the Buddha sitting on his *lotus-throne.

lotus-eater. Also lotos-. **a.** One of the LOTOPHAGI. **b.** *transf.* One who gives himself up to dreamy and luxurious ease.

1832 TENNYSON (*title*) The Lotos-eaters. **1838** THIRLWALL *Greece* II. xii. 95 The fable of the Lotus-eaters. **1847** W. E. FORSTER 27 Aug. in T. W. Reid *Life* (1888) I. vii. 209 He [Carlyle] is busy sleeping, and declares himself lazy as a lotos-eater. **1856** R. A. VAUGHAN *Mystics* (1860) I. 22 So those spiritual Lotos-eaters will only..hearken what the inner spirit sings, There is no joy but calm. **1893** *Times* 30 Dec. 9/3 A summer like that of 1893 may be all very well for the lotus-eater, but is a calamity to people who have to get their living out of English land.

Similarly **lotus-eating** *vbl. sb.* and *ppl. a.* Hence (as a back-formation) **lotus-eat** *v. intr.*

1861 WILSON & GEIKIE *Mem. E. Forbes* vi. 165 Day-dreaming and such Lotus-eating idleness as befits the intellectual Castle of Indolence. **1883** F. M. CRAWFORD *Mr. Isaacs* 5 The attractive waters of lotus-eating Saratoga. **1898** W. J. LOCKE *Idols* v. 64 'What have you been doing with yourself all this time?' she said... 'Oh, Lotus-eating, generally,' he replied. **1911** —— *Glory of Clementina Wing* xv. 211 The week had evidently passed pleasantly for Quixtus... He was lotus eating. **1972** J. POTTER *Going West* 60 Every dream fades. If he drank and lotus-ate, he would think. **1973** 'B. MATHER' *Snowline* xix. 231 Hippies..come here..from Bombay—lotus-eat for a month..and off they go.

lotye, variant of LOTE *v.*[1] *Obs.*, to lurk.

lotyon, obs. form of LOTION.

lou, Sc. form of LOW *sb.* and *v.*

loubber, loubee, -ie, obs. ff. LUBBER, LOOBY.

loubel(l, obs. variant of LOW-BELL.

louce, louch(e, obs. ff. LOOSE *v.*, LOCH[1] *Sc.*

‖**louche** (luʃ), *a.* [F. *louche* squinting, OF. *lousche*, orig. only fem.:—L. *lusca*, fem. of *luscus* one-eyed.] Oblique, not straightforward. Also, dubious, shifty, disreputable.

1819 LADY MORGAN *Autobiog.* (1859) 318 There is something *louche* about him, which does not accord with the *abandon* of careless, intimate intercourse. **1849** THACKERAY *Pendennis* lxix, There's something louche regarding him. **1873** G. H. LEWES *Diary* 16 Jan. in Geo. Eliot *Lett.* (1956) V. 368 The whole thing appeared *louche* and unpromising. **1905** G. B. SHAW *Lett. to G. Barker* (1956) 53 You could play Snobby. I want a slim, *louche*, servant-girl-bigamist, half-handsome sort of rascal. **1921** A. HUXLEY *Crome Yellow* xvii. 182 There had seemed to be something a little *louche* in the way she had suddenly found herself alone with Ivor. **1945** AUDEN *Sea & Mirror* ii. 46 A quick cold clasp now and then in some *louche* hovel. **1945** E. WAUGH *Brideshead Revisited* 236, I knew of a louche little bar quite near here. **1959** P. H. JOHNSON *Humbler Creation* xlviii. 328 As if he were an unfrocked priest due for reception into the world of the *louche* and the lost. **1970** *Times* Mar. (Saturday Suppl.) p. iv/6 There is plenty of marvellous delicate comedy and superbly *louche* menace. **1974** *Daily Tel.* (Colour Suppl.) 14 June 30/4 His louche greeting, 'Ladeez and Gentle*men*' was a byword among..BBC Light Programme listeners.

‖**loucherbem** (luʃebɛm). Also loucherbème. [f. Fr. *boucher* butcher.] The name given to a type of French slang formed by the transposing of certain letters and addition of others.

1937 J. ORR tr. *Iordan's Introd. Romance Lang.* iv. 360 The butchers of La Villette speak, or spoke, a slang called *loucherbem*, or *largongi*... The process..is a deliberate modification of an existing word. **1938** I. GOLDBERG *Wonder of Words* viii. 155 In French there is the *loucherbème* language, so called because its model of transformed words is *boucher*. **1939** L. H. GRAY *Foundations of Lang.* 31 Only in a few instances do they actually change the form of words, as in the relatively recent French *loucherbème*. **1942** PARTRIDGE *Usage & Abusage* (1947) 160/2 *Gibberish* is applied..to the Loucherbem of the Paris butchers (*loucherbem* for *boucher* is itself Loucherbem).

Loucheux (luʃø), *sb.* and *a.* [Canad. Fr., f. F. *louche* squint-eyed (see quot. 1828).]

A. *sb.* **a.** A North American Indian people inhabiting the Yukon and Mackenzie River areas. **b.** The language of this people. **B.** *adj.* Of, pertaining to, or designating this people or their language.

1828 J. FRANKLIN *Narr. Second Expedition Polar Sea* i. 23 The fact is, that Loucheux, or Squinter, was intended to convey the sense of the Indian name..Deguthée Dennee, which means, 'the people who avoid the arrows of their enemies, by keeping a look out on both sides'. *Ibid.*, The tribe of Indians whom Mackenzie calls the Quarrellers, but whom the traders throughout the fur country name the Loucheux. *Ibid.* 29 The Red River contributes its waters to the Mackenzie..and..is remarkable as being the boundary between the lands claimed by the Loucheux Indians and those of the Esquimaux. **1867** *Ann. Rep. Board of Regents Smithsonian Inst. 1866* 311 The physical characteristics of the Loucheux nation are..the same as those of the other aborigines of North America. *Ibid.*, The Loucheux language is a dialect of the Chepewyan. *Ibid.*, The Loucheux, though sunk in barbarism, are rather more intelligent than the other tribes. *Ibid.*, The Loucheux proper is spoken by the Indians of Peel's river. **1890** J. G. FRAZER *Golden Bough* II. iii. 127 The Loucheux and Hare-skin Indians..are forbidden by custom to eat the sinew of the legs of animals. **1921** E. SAPIR *Lang.* iv. 71 Such languages as Navaho,..Chipewyan, Loucheux. **1971** *Times* 22 Feb. (Canada Suppl.) p. v/1 In the north of the Yukon close by the Alaska border, a small band of Loucheux Indians have stood up to be counted: they do not want oil and gas exploration in their territory. *Ibid.*, The caribou move..through these flats, and the Loucheux take about 1,000 of them a year for food.

loud (laud), *a.* Forms: 1 hlúd, 3–4 lud(e, 4–7 loude, lowd(e, 4 loud. [Com. WGer.: OE. *hlúd* = OFris. (*h*)*lûd*, OS. *hlûd* (MDu. *lût*, *lûd*-, mod.Du. *luid*), OHG. *hlût* (MHG. *lût*, mod.G. *laut*):—OTeut. type **hlûdo*-:—pre-Teut. **klūtó*-, a passive pple. from the Aryan root **kleu*- to hear (Teut. **hleu*- in Goth. *hliuþ* listening attention; see LITHE *v.*[3]), whence Gr. κλύειν to hear, κλέος renown, L. *cluēre* to be famed, *cliens* (pres. pple., lit. 'hearer') dependent, client, OSl. *slava* glory, *slovo* word, Skr. *çru* to hear, *çravas* glory. Outside Teut. the ppl. adjs. have a different ablaut-grade and meaning; so Gr. κλυτός, L. (*in*)*clutus*, OIr. *cloth*, Skr. *çruta* renowned.

For the remoter cognates representing the extended form **kleus*- of the Aryan root, see LIST *sb.*[1]]

1. a. Of sounds or voices: Strongly audible; making a powerful impression on the sense of hearing. Hence, with agent-noun: That (speaks, sings, etc.) with a loud voice.

971 *Blickl. Hom.* 15 He þa cleopode hluddre stefne. *c* **1200** *Trin. Coll. Hom.* 89 þo þe after him comen remden lude stefne *Osanna filio dauid.* *a* **1225** *Ancr. R.* 210 Uorte makien noise—lud dream to scheauwen hore horel. *a* **1250** *Owl & Night.* 5 þat playd wes stif & starc & strong Sum hwile softe & lud among. **13..** *Sir Beues* 3129 (MS. A.) Iosian..spak to hire wiþ loude gret. **1398** TREVISA *Barth. De P.R.* VII. xxxii. (1495) 246 Thryste and sethinge and lowde brethynge. *c* **1450** HOLLAND *Howlat* 764 Claryonis lowde knellis. **1548–9** (Mar.) *Bk. Com. Prayer, Morn. Prayer*, The priest..shall begynne with a loude voyce the Lordes prayer. **1576** FLEMING *Panopl. Epist.* 280 Yᵉ man..fel into a lowd laughter. *a* **1645** A. STAFFORD *Apol. Fem. Glory* (1869) p. xcix, Priscian, a Bishop..said in somewhat too lowd a whisper [etc.]. **1697** DRYDEN *Virg. Georg.* IV. 666 Her fellow Nymphs the Mountains tear With loud Laments. **1732** BERKELEY *Alciphr.* IV. §7 Is the voice of man louder than that of thunder? **1816** SCOTT *Antiq.* vii, The mendicant and Lovel exerted their voices in a loud halloo. **1855** BAIN *Senses & Int.* II. ii. §6 (1864) 214 A loud speaker is exciting. **1875** JOWETT *Plato* (ed. 2) III. 651 A great body of sound is loud, and the opposite is low.

b. Of musical instruments, the sea, winds, etc.: Making a loud sound, sonorous. Chiefly *poet.*

c **897** K. ÆLFRED *Gregory's Past.* xxxvii. 266 Witodlice ðæt ar, ðonne hit mon slihð, hit bið hludre ðonne ænig oðer andweorc. **1390** GOWER *Conf.* I. 137 Thei speke and sounen in his Ere As thogh thei lowde wyndes were. **1604** E. GRIMSTONE *Hist. Siege Ostend* 143 The North-winde was somewhat loude. **1667** MILTON *P.L.* VI. 59 Nor with less dread the loud Ethereal Trumpet from on high gan blow. **1728** LD. LYTTELTON *Blenheim* 81 Silent a while, and smooth, The Current glides, till..down the Steep it falls, In loud Cascades. **1791** MRS. RADCLIFFE *Rom. Forest* vi, The storm was now loud. **18..** CAMPBELL *Lord Ullin's Daughter*, 'Twas vain: the loud waves lash'd the shore, Return or aid preventing. **1898** W. K. JOHNSON *Terra Tenebr.* 35 Let the loud seas thunder here.

c. Of a place, etc.: Full of noise, re-echoing. *rare.*

1595 SHAKS. *John* V. iv. 14 For if the French be Lords of this loud day He meanes [etc.]. *a* **1645** HEYWOOD *Fort by Land & Sea* III. i. Wks. 1874 VI. 396 All ways are loud, and hue and cry sent forth Through every hundred. **1871** SWINBURNE *Eve of Revolution* 123 Lands that are loud through all their length with chains. **1878** C. STANFORD *Symb. Christ* iv. 105 Streets and factories loud with life and black with the dust of toil.

2. *fig.* **a.** Clamorous, noisy; also, in more favourable sense, emphatic or vehement in expression.

1530 TINDALE *Wks.* (1573) 327/2 After the loudest maner he setteth out the cruelnes of the Emperor's souldiours. **1611** BIBLE *Prov.* vii. 11 She is loud and stubburne, her feet abide not in her house. **1647** MAY *Hist. Parl.* I. viii. 88 Many Subjects in Europe have played lowder parts upon the Theatre of the world. **1680** OTWAY *Orphan* III. iv. 865 Calls sawcy loud Suspicion, Public Zeal. **1711** ADDISON *Spect.* No. 128 ¶5 When we see a Fellow loud and talkative. **1734** BERKELEY *Analyst* §1 Several who make the loudest claim to those qualities. **1849** MACAULAY *Hist. Eng.* vi. II. 1 The Church was louder than ever in professions of attachment to him. **1879** MORLEY *Burke* viii. 148 The French were held up to the loudest admiration. **1884** TENNYSON *Freedom* x. Poems (1894) 576/2 Men loud against all forms of power. **1888** M. MORRIS *Claverhouse* viii. 147 Churchill's voice was loudest for battle.

absol. **1711** ADDISON *Spect.* No. 239 ¶11 Gold..silences the Loud and Clamorous.

†**b.** Of motives: Pressing, urgent. *Obs.*

1604 SHAKS. *Oth.* I. i. 151 For he's embark'd With such loud reason to the Cyprus Warres.

†**c.** Grandiloquent, pompously laudatory. *Obs.*

1651 JER. TAYLOR *Holy Dying* i. §2 (1686) 10 Many men ..labour onely for a pompous Epitaph, and a loud title upon their Marble.

†**d.** Manifest, palpable, flagrant. Chiefly of a lie. *Obs.*

1535 *Goodly Primer* To Rdr. (1834) 5, I omit the right loud lie before the Mass of *Recordare*. **1579** E. K. *Gloss. to Spenser's Sheph. Cal.* Apr. 120 Certain fine fablers, and loude lyers. **1590** NASHE *Pasquil's Apol.* I. C b, How durst you presume to make so lowde a lie? **1632** SANDERSON *Twelve Serm.* 64 But what doe I speak of these, but petty things in comparison of those her lowder impieties? **1645** MILTON *Tetrach.* Wks. (1847) 193/1 There is a loud exception against this law of God. **1650** BULWER *Anthropomet.* 12 Many have held opinion, that Pliny and Aulus Gellius were loud liars. **1678** RAY *Prov.* (ed. 2) 89 A great Lie..That's a loud one. *a* **1700** B. E. *Dict. Cant. Crew*, *Hummer*, a loud Lie.

3. *transf.* Of smell or flavour: Powerful, offensive. Now chiefly *U.S.*

1641 MILTON *Reform.* II. 20 Their..mouths cannot open without the strong breath and loud stench of avarice. **1842**

DICKENS *Amer. Notes* xiv, Pretty loud smell of varnish, sir? **1887** GOODE etc. *Fisheries U.S.* Sect. v. II. 473 The natives ..prefer to have the meat tainted rather than fresh, declaring that it is most tender and toothsome when decidedly 'loud'. **1899** J. PENNELL in *Fortn. Rev.* LXV. 122 The gas-lamp [for cycles] seems to make a very bright light. It is also said to make a very loud smell.

4. Of colours, patterns, dress, manners, etc.: Vulgarly obtrusive, flashy. Opposed to *quiet*.

1849 THACKERAY *Pendennis* xxxix, The shirts too 'loud' in pattern. **1878** BESANT & RICE *Celia's Arb.* xxxix. (1887) 287 The flashy rings upon his fingers;..the loud pattern of his trousers. **1883** *Century Mag.* XXVII. 106 Stained glass, indeed! loud, garish, thin, painty. **1884** *Stationery Trades Rev.* Sept. 215/2 Fine envelopes are not sold in such loud colours as they were a few years ago. **1889** 'J. S. WINTER' *Mrs. Bob* (1891) 118 The girls were dreadfully loud in their dress.

5. *absol.* †*in loud*, †*on loud*: ALOUD, with a loud voice. †*to the loudest*: at the top of one's voice.

c **1430** *Pistill of Susan* 161 (MS. Cott. Calig. A. II.) Then sayde þo loselles on lowde [*a* **1400** (Vern.) aloude] to þat lady. *c* **1450** *St. Cuthbert* (Surtees) 5835 Þe childe cryed on lowde, allase. **1611** SHAKS. *Wint. T.* II. ii. 39 I'le..undertake to bee Her Aduocate to th' lowd'st. **1682** *New Hampsh. Prov. Papers* (1867) I. 456 My father..desired him in loud to go out of his house to his lodgings.

6. *Comb.*, chiefly parasynthetic, as ***loud-flavoured***, ***-minded***, ***-mouthed***, ***-talking***, ***-tongued***, ***-voiced*** adjs.; also **loud-lashed** *a.*, lashed into loud uproar; **loud-mouth** *a.*, loud-mouthed, noisy; as *sb.*, a person given to loud and self-assertive talk; hence as vb., to talk in this manner, to bluster; **loud-mouthing** *vbl. sb.*

1866 HOWELLS *Venet. Life* vi. 84 A *loud-flavoured broth. **1818** HAZLITT *Eng. Poets* iii. (1870) 68 The sea..*loud-lashed by furious storms. **1845** CARLYLE *Cromwell* II. 234 A certain loud-tongued, *loud-minded Mr. Feak. **1668** E. HOWARD *Usurper* 63 Curse on these *loud-mouth Hounds! **1934** J. O'HARA *Appointment in Samarra* iv. 111 He was a loud-mouth and a good one-punch fighter. **1940** J. B. PRIESTLEY *Postscripts* 17 You will find that the laziest loud-mouth in the workshop has suddenly been given power. **1950** A. LOMAX *Mister Jelly Roll* (1952) v. 235 Morton, the old whorehouse pianist who seemed to be trying to loud-mouth his way back to big time. **1959** *Daily Mail* 31 Jan. 4/2 These 625 vain, devious loud-mouths..are our elected representatives. **1968** M. RICHLER *Cocksure* ix. 52 We are most decidedly not done for. My goodness, the last loudmouth to make that mistake was Hitler. **1628** FORD *Lover's Mel.* III. i, I haue a *loud-mouth'd Cannon of mine owne to batter her. **1867** TROLLOPE *Last Chron. Barset* I. xli. 353 How, from the abjectness of his own humility..he would rebuke the loud-mouthed triumph of the bishop's wife. **1901** *Expositor* July 21 They were heretics of the blatant sort, loud-mouthed and shallow-minded. **1924** G. B. SHAW *St. Joan* I. i. 7 The self-assertive, loud-mouthed, superficially energetic, fundamentally will-less Robert. **1966** *Listener* 27 Oct. 609/1 The Surrey amateur with an Oxford background and the loud-mouthed crowd from the foundries suddenly coalesced. **1971** C. BONINGTON *Annapurna South Face* vii. 85 He was well built, very self-confident yet not loudmouthed. **1950** W. L. JAMES in A. Dundes *Mother Wit* (1973) 431 Famous among those yet surviving names are 'corn field holler'..and '*loud mouthing'. **1973** *Daily Tel.* (Colour Suppl.) 26 Jan. 7/3 Money talks and there will be a lot of loud-mouthing before the future of the fourth channel is settled. **1848** MRS. GASKELL *Mary Barton* I. i. 3 Merry and somewhat *loud-talking girls. **1925** T. DREISER *Amer. Trag.* (1926) I. I. ix. 56 He was too smooth and loud-talking. **1622** MASSINGER *Virg. Mart.* I. i, *Lowd tong'd Fame The harbinger to prepare their entertainment. **1857** GEO. ELIOT *Scenes Cleric. Life, Janet's Repentance* (1878) II. 184 Loud-tongued abuse. **1850** MRS. BROWNING *Poems* I. 28 *Loud-voiced imagery.

loud (laʊd), *adv.* Forms: 1 hlúde, 2–4 lud(e, 3–4 loude, (4 lhoude, louthe), 4–7 lowd(e, (5 louȝde), 4– loud. [OE. *hlúde* = OS. *hlúdo* (Du. *luid*), OHG. *lûto*, *lûto* (MHG. *lûte*, G. *laut*):—OTeut. **hlûdô*, f. **hlûdo-* LOUD *a.*]

1. a. Loudly, with a loud noise or voice; aloud.

971 *Blickl. Hom.* 149 Hwæt is..þis folc þe her þus hlude singeþ? *c* **1175** *Lamb. Hom.* 43 Summe of þan monne..swa deor lude remeð. *a* **1225** *Ancr. R.* 290 Ȝif þe ne cumeð nout sone help, gred ludture mid hote heorte. *c* **1375** *Sc. Leg. Saints* vii. (*Jacobus Minor*) 208, & prayand fore þame Increly & lovd, þat al hard þis, can cry. *c* **1420** *Chron. Vilod.* 3793 þey..knokkede fast & louȝde at þe gate. *c* **1491** *Chast. Goddes Chyld.* 8 Some crye lowde wyth an hye woys. **1590** SPENSER *F.Q.* I. vi. 27 A Lyonesse.., That roaring all with rage did lowd requere Her children deare. **1632** MILTON *Penseroso* 126 Kercheft in a comely cloud While rocking winds are piping loud. **1671** —— *P.R.* XI. 339 While they loudest sing The vices of thir Deities, and thir own. **1771** GOLDSM. *Hist. Eng.* II. 211 The inhabitants clamoured so loud for a surrender. **1819** HAZLITT *Pol. Ess.* 148 He asserts a fact the louder, as he suspects it to be without proof. **1894** A. ROBERTSON *Nuggets* etc. 216, I shouted 'hurrah', and laughed loud and long.

†**b.** ***loud and still***: under all circumstances. [So MDu. *lude en stille.*] *Obs.*

1300–1400 *R. Gloucester's Chron.* (Rolls) App. xx. 352 Þat wolde libbe in ryot & habbe al hare wille In robberiȝe & prute boþe loude & stille. **1340** HAMPOLE *Pr. Consc.* 103 We suld pray, bathe loud and stille, For al cristen saules. *c* **1430** *Syr Gener.* (Roxb.) 8368, I must nedes doo his wil In al that I can loude or still. **1636** HEYWOOD *Loves Maistresse* II. i. Wks. 1874 V. 108 Let me hear some music, loud and still.

†**c.** With *to lie*: Openly, palpably. (Cf. LOUD *a.* 2 d.) *Obs.*

a **1400** *Pistill of Susan* 343 (Vernon MS.) Now þou liest loude, so helpe me vr lord. **1600** HOLLAND *Livy* XXXVIII. lv. 1019, I would rather thinke that the clerke..faulted with his pen in writing the copies, than the authour lied so lowd with his tongue.

d. ***out loud***, aloud, without restraint. Cf. OUT-LOUD.

1821 M. EDGEWORTH *Let.* 22 Nov. (1971) 277 Lord Andover in the presence of Lord and Lady Suffolk and speaking *out loud* said 'Miss Dutton..be so good to walk with me into the library.' **1844** [see OUT-LOUD]. **1881** TROLLOPE *Ayala's Angel* III. xlix. 67 He knew it would make me laugh out loud. **1924**, **1933** [see CRY *v.* 21 e]. **1939** G. B. SHAW *In Good King Charles's Golden Days* II. 104 Even a dissolute court, as they say mine is—I suppose they mean a court where bawdy stories are told out loud instead of whispered. **1941** [see CRY *v.* 21 e].

e. Phr. ***loud and clear***: (said, etc.) in a way that reduces or avoids confusion or misunderstanding; (esp. in radio or tele-communication) (heard or received) loudly and clearly; also *transf.*

1871 'L. CARROLL' *Through Looking-Glass* vi. 133, I said it very loud and clear; I went and shouted in his ear. **1940** H. G. WELLS *Babes in Darkling Wood* III. ii. 256 I'd have to play the Star Spangled Banner, loud and clear, one hundred per cent. **1958** 'CASTLE' & HAILEY *Flight into Danger* ix. 123 Hullo, Vancouver. 714 answering. Receiving you loud and clear. Over. **1959** *Listener* 19 Feb. 319/1 It seems desirable to say so loud and clear. **1962** L. DEIGHTON *Ipcress File* vii. 43 Dalby looked up. 'You are receiving me?' 'Loud and clear,' I said. **1962** A. SHEPARD in *Into Orbit* 104, I also contacted..the chase planes—and heard them loud and clear. **1963** J. N. HARRIS *Weird World Wes Beattie* (1964) iii. 25 The fact is I remember that black Dodge loud and clear. **1970** C. COLLINGWOOD *Defector* iv. 33, I read you loud and clear. Now, suppose something does go wrong, what do I do? **1972** D. LEES *Zodiac* 90 They don't seem able to make up their minds whether to warn me off or knock me off but I do get the message loud and clear and..I'm going.

2. Of smell: Strongly, offensively. (Cf. LOUD *a.* 3 and ALOUD *adv.* 2.)

1871 JOAQUIN MILLER *Songs Italy* (1878) 104 Carry.. some drug that smells loud.

3. *Comb.* with *pres.* and *pa. pples.* of verbs denoting or implying the production of sound, e.g. ***loud-acclaiming***, ***-bellowing***, ***-laughing***, ***-ringing***, ***-roaring***, ***-screaming***, ***-singing***, ***-squeaking***, ***-thundering***, ***-ticking***, etc.; ***loud-roared***, etc. Also **loud-spoken** *a.*, given to loud speaking.

1591 SYLVESTER *Du Bartas* I. ii. 733 The loud-roaring Thunder. *Ibid.* vi. 905 Loud-thundring Canons. *a* **1631** DONNE *Poems* (1650) 87 Some lowd squeaking Cryer Well pleas'd with one leane thred-bare groat for hire. *a* **1649** DRUMM. OF HAWTH. *Poems* Wks. (1711) 36 The christal-streaming Nid, loud-bellowing Clyde. **1667** G. C. *Pref. to H. More's Div. Dial.* (1713) 5 Those two loud-singing Nightingals of Arcadia. **1725** POPE *Odyss.* IV. 464 Loud-acclaiming Greeks the victor bless'd. **1768–74** TUCKER *Lt. Nat.* (1834) I. 596 Intemperate Jest, loud-laughing Mockery, and hood-winked Misrule. **1838** DICKENS *O. Twist* xii, A very large and loud-ticking gold watch. **1859** GEO. ELIOT *A. Bede* v, A broad-faced, broad-chested, loud-screaming rascal. **1882** STEVENSON *New Arab. Nts.* I. 138 Sir Thomas was..loud-spoken, boisterous and domineering.

loud(e, obs. form of LAUD *v.*

loude: see LUDE (= *lūde*) ME., noise.

louden ('laʊd(ə)n), *v.* [f. LOUD *a.* + -EN^{5}.]

1. *intr.* To become or grow loud or louder.

a **1848** R. W. HAMILTON in *Chr. Sabbath* (1852) xiii. 367 The birthday song of creation may well rise and louden into a new song. **1855** KINGSLEY *Westw. Ho!* (1861) 505 An angry growl from the westward heavens..rolled and loudened nearer and nearer.

2. *trans.* To make loud or louder. *rare*$^{-1}$.

1898 BODLEY *France* I. I. iv. 236 Internecine strife ought to be hushed instead of being loudened.

Hence '**loudening** *ppl. a.*, that grows louder.

1805 A. WILSON in *Poems & Lit. Prose* (1876) II. 173 Groaning we start! and at the loudening war, Ask our bewildered senses where we are. **1864** R. F. BURTON *Dahome* I. 183 A loudening hum of voices heralded a rush of warriors into the Uhon-nukon, or cleared space, with its central tree.

louderback ('laʊdəbæk). *Geol.* [Named after G. D. *Louderback* (1874–1957), American geologist.] A cap of old lava on a tilted fault-block.

1930 W. M. DAVIS in *Bull. Geol. Soc. Amer.* XLI. 299 It seems to me highly appropriate that the lava sheets, which were thus spread unconformably on the Powell surface of the worn-down King mountains, and which now cover the back slopes of the tilted Gilbert blocks, should be called Louderbacks, after their discoverer. **1965** W. D. THORNBURY *Regional Geomorphol. U.S.* xxiv. 473/2 Some of the range have lava caps, called by Davis (1930) louderbacks. **1968** R. W. FAIRBRIDGE *Encycl. Geomorphol.* 679/1 Since the original [lava] flow would normally have filled a valley, the louderback is usually also a form of inverted topography.

[**loudful**, *a.* Error for *loud full.*

[**1606** MARSTON *Sophonisba* I. ii. B 4 b, The Cornets and Organs playing loud full Musicke for the Act.] **1864** WEBSTER, *Loudful*, full of sound; noisy; ringing. (*Obs.*) 'Loudful music' *Marston.* Hence in some later Dicts.]

loud-hail, *v.* [Back-formation from next.] *trans.* and *intr.* To speak or call through a loud-hailer; to address (someone) through a loud-hailer; also *fig.* Also **loud-hailing** *ppl. a.* and *vbl. sb.*

1943 *Combined Operations, 1940–42* (Ministry of Information) xvii. 130 We 'closed' the 'Calpe', struggling with our loud-hailing equipment which remained resolutely silent. **1964** R. PETRIE *Murder by Precedent* i. 19 I'd just left again and gone to Despatch when they loud-hailed me. **1965** *Listener* 3 June 837/1 Ku Klux Klan men, assorted torchbearers,..and a loud-hailing director. **1969** C. CARFAX *Silence with Voices* xviii. 129 She went back into the cabin after Dr Ford loud-hailed her. **1969** J. ELLIOT *Duel* I. ii. 43 'The extraordinary thing is——' Harry loud-hailed so that people at the next table were forced to listen.

loud-'hailer. [f. LOUD *a.* 1 + HAILER.] A megaphone or other device for amplifying the voice, especially as used at sea. Also *transf.* and *attrib.*

1941 *Illustr. London News* 20 Sept. 366/3 Orders, signals and instructions..given over about one-eighth of a mile of water, orally, by the 'Loud Hailer' from Captain to Captain. **1943** *Combined Operations, 1940–42* (Ministry of Information) xvii. 131 'Maintain a smoke screen half a mile inshore and to the westward,' came over the loud hailer from the 'Calpe'. **1955** G. FREEMAN *Liberty Man* i. 2 Two metallic pipe-notes sounded through the loud-hailer system. **1956** J. MASTERS *Bugles & Tiger* xxii. 283, I heard a loud hailer calling my name. **1959** C. MACINNES *Absolute Beginners* 13 There was a loud-hailer echo up and down the flights. **1971** B. W. ALDISS *Soldier Erect* 241 They were allowed to use loud-hailers, even if the Japs would not trust them with rifles. **1971** *Daily Tel.* 16 Apr. 17/3 [He] alerted the Thames Coastguard..and then used a loudhailer to direct them to the highest point on the sandbank. **1973** C. BONINGTON *Next Horizon* xix. 264 John..ran out with the loud-hailer, shouting..the conventional form of greeting.

louding: see LUDING (= *lūding*) ME., noise.

loudish ('laʊdɪʃ), *a.* [f. LOUD *a.* + -ISH.] Somewhat loud.

1860 READE *Cloister & H.* II. 35 The voices had for some time been loudish round a table at the bottom of the hall. **1866** CARLYLE *Remin.* (1881) I. 290 Criticism..loudish universally and nowhere accurately just.

loudly ('laʊdlɪ), *adv.* [f. LOUD *a.* + -LY^{2}.] In a loud manner. **a.** In a loud tone or voice; †*fig.* with *to lie*, openly, palpably. **b.** Clamorously, noisily. **c.** With reference to dress: Flashily, showily.

a **1400–50** *Alexander* 1709 (Dublin) Hys litilayke & hys liknes he loudly [*Ashmole* laythly] dispysez. **1508** DUNBAR *Tua mariit wemen* 240 Loudly lauchand the laif allowit hir meikle. **1589** *Pasquil's Ret.* C iv b, He lyeth loudlie. **1590** SPENSER *F.Q.* I. i. 17 Therewith enrag'd she loudly gan to bray. **1602** SHAKS. *Ham.* v. ii. 410 The Souldiours Musicke, and the rites of Warre Speake lowdly for him. **1635** J. HAYWARD tr. *Biondi's Banish'd Virg.* 40 Yet blush'd he not to lye loudly, when it made any way for his ends. **1776** GIBBON *Decl. & F.* xiii. I. 375 Loudly complaining of the protection afforded by the Romans to rebels. **1845** S. AUSTIN *Ranke's Hist. Ref.* I. 83 The King of Bohemia.. insisted loudly on his rights. **1849** THACKERAY *Pendennis* xxx. Medical students, gallant, dashing, what is called 'loudly' dressed. **1875** JOWETT *Plato* (ed. 2) III. 260 Calling each man loudly by his name.

Comb. **1874** MICKLETHWAITE *Mod. Par. Churches* 294 A loudly-coloured pavement is very objectionable.

loudness ('laʊdnɪs). [OE. *hlúdnis*, f. *hlúd* LOUD + *-nis* -NESS.] **1.** The quality or condition of being loud; an instance of this. Also, the (great or small) extent to which a sound is heard as loud.

c **1050** *Byrhtferth's Handboc* in *Anglia* (1885) VIII. 332 Clamor on lyden on englisc ys hludnys. *c* **1440** *Promp. Parv.* 314/1 Lowdenesse, *altitudo.* **1530** PALSGR. 241/1 Loudnesse, *haultesse.* **1647** CRASHAW *Poems* 131 His prayers took their price and strength Not from the loudness nor the length. **1733** SWIFT *New Simile for Ladies* 21 When th' alarum-bell is rung Of Xanti's everlasting tongue, The husband dreads its loudness more Than lightning's flash or thunder's roar. **1860** TYNDALL *Glac.* I. ii. 16 These echos would diminish in loudness just as the images of the candle diminish in brightness. **1881** H. JAMES *Portr. Lady* xxv. in *Macm. Mag.* XLIII. 413 Naturally, he couldn't like her style, her loudness, her want of repose. **1881** BROADHOUSE *Mus. Acoustics* 394 They produce beats, or loudnesses separated by silences. **1937** *Ann. Reg. 1936* 65 It was suggested that an overall loudness of 90 phons at a lateral distance of 18 ft. should be the maximum permitted for a private car running on full throttle at 30 m.p.h. **1948** P. M. MORSE *Vibration & Sound* (ed. 2) vi. 226 Corresponding to the physical quantities intensity and frequency are the physiological (or, rather, psychophysiological) quantities loudness and pitch. *Ibid.* 227 The bottom curve, for zero loudness, is the threshold of hearing, below which a sound..is inaudible to the average person. **1959** *Chambers's Encycl.* XII. 728/1 It is important to distinguish between sound intensity—a physical quantity measurable in definite physical units; and loudness—the magnitude of the auditory sensation produced by that sound and therefore a subjective quantity depending upon personal judgements. **1961** G. A. BRIGGS *A to Z in Audio* 117 Although loudness depends primarily on actual intensity, it is also strongly affected by frequency. **1962** A. NISBETT *Technique Sound Studio* xi. 196 Equal loudness from the two voices will not generally be required.

2. *attrib.*, as ***loudness level***, ***scale***; **loudness control**, a device on an audio amplifier which corrects for the change in quality of reproduced sound at low volumes by boosting the bass (and often also the treble) relative to the middle frequencies, either combined with a volume control or as a separate on-off switch.

1961 G. A. Briggs *A to Z in Audio* 117 When the volume is turned down, music tends to sound thin and emaciated. The effect may be counteracted to some extent by bass and treble boost in the amplifier. A *loudness control is a device which automatically applies bass and treble boost as volume is reduced. **1970** J. Earl *Tuners & Amplifiers* i. 18 An idea which is popular in Europe and America (though not often liked in Great Britain) is the so-called loudness control. *Ibid.*, Some amplifiers are equipped only with a loudness control, while others feature the ordinary (non-compensated) volume control which can be changed to loudness control action by means of a switch. **1975** *Gramophone* May 2026 (Advt.), Separate loudness control. **1938** *Bell Lab. Rec.* XVI. 213/1 The intensity level of the 1000-cycle reference tone was defined as the *loudness level of this tone, and any other sound which is judged by listeners to be equally loud is said to have an equal value of loudness level. *Ibid.* 214/2 The unit to be used for intensity level measurements is the decibel, but the unit to be used for the equivalent loudness level measurements is the phon. **1934** *Discovery* Dec. 346/2 The number of phons and decibels coincides for the *loudness scale applying to the frequency 1,000 cycles per second, but for no other frequency.

loud-speaker (laʊdˈspiːkə(r)). Also loud speaker, loudspeaker. [f. LOUD *a.* + SPEAKER.]

1. Any instrument for converting variations in an applied electric current or voltage (of appropriate magnitude and frequency) into corresponding sound waves that are able to be heard at a distance from the instrument.

Loud-speaking (see next) was formerly the usual term employed to refer to such instruments. Quot. 1884 is an isolated early example of *loud-speaker*.

1884 *English Mechanic* 26 Sept. 95/3 Before troubling to make or buy a 'loud speaker', 'Pathologist' might try the following dodge... Fix an ordinary 'toy' telephone over one ear... Fasten the end of the string from the 'toy' to the centre of the diaphragm of the Bell..and, at the middle of the string, hang a small weight..to keep it taut... The voice is almost..as clear as when using the Bell direct. **1920** *Telegraph & Telephone Jrnl.* VI. 111/2 It was quite remarkable how far and how distinctly it was possible to hear the talk from the loud-speakers. **1923** *Daily Mail* 1 Mar. 9 For each concert there will be seating accommodation..for 1,000 people, and to these the concert will be delivered by powerful loud speakers. **1924** *Wireless Weekly* 8 Oct. 745/1 Loud speakers of all kinds are an outstanding feature of the show. **1930** J. Buchan *Castle Gay* xiii. 208 Their ears were greeted by the bray of a loud-speaker to which the wives by their house-doors were listening. **1931** B. Brown *Talking Pict.* v. 117 In some form or other the dynamic or moving coil loud speaker, well known in radio, is..always used for sound picture work. **1943** J. B. Priestley *Daylight on Saturday* v. 27 They were now putting canned music over the loud speakers. **1957** L. F. R. Williams *State of Israel* ix. 158 Regulations strictly forbid..loudspeakers in their [*sc.* the polling stations'] immediate vicinity. **1970** J. Earl *Tuners & Amplifiers* iii. 76 Headphones..can nowadays give a subjective impression of quality, spaciousness and stereo effect equally as good as the best loudspeakers.

2. *attrib.*, as ***loud-speaker enclosure, system, unit, van.***

1962 A. Nisbett *Technique Sound Studio* iv. 76 A manufacturer of *loudspeaker enclosures invited members of the public to judge and compare the quality of three different stereo speaker systems. **1971** *Daily Tel.* (Colour Suppl.) 22 Oct. 57 (Advt.), Twin sealed loudspeaker enclosures, each containing 2 speakers (bass and treble). **1958** *Times Lit. Suppl.* 10 Oct. 583/2 The installation of *loudspeaker systems in churches has rendered..manner even less important than matter in sermons than ever before. **1970** J. Earl *Tuners & Amplifiers* i. 25 A loudspeaker *system* is a box, usually called enclosure or cabinet, carrying a socket or couple of terminals at the rear with a grille at the front through which the sound comes. Such a loudspeaker system is scientifically designed in conjunction with the loudspeaker units inside. **1925–6** *T. Eaton & Co. Catal.* Fall & Winter 391 This *Loud Speaker Unit when attached to your gramophone tone arm, makes the horn act as a loud speaker. **1970** Loud-speaker unit [see *loud-speaker system* above]. **1945** H. Nicolson *Let.* 3 July (1967) 474 One of my workers said something mean on the *loud-speaker van. **1973** J. Drummond *Bang! Bang! You're Dead!* xlii. 144 A police loud-speaker van..pointed out that nothing could be gained by further resistance.

loud-speaking (ˈlaʊdˌspiːkɪŋ), *a.* Also without hyphen (as one word). [f. LOUD *adv.* + SPEAKING *ppl. a.*] Speaking loudly (in quot. 1855, *fig.*); *spec.* (the usual sense), capable of producing sound that can be heard at a distance; fitted with or employing a loud-speaker.

1855 Longf. *Hiaw.* xv. 117 The loud-speaking thunder helps me. **1879** *Telegraphic Jrnl.* VII. 112/2 The new telephone receiver of Mr. Edison is, undoubtedly, the greatest step..towards rendering the telephone a loud-speaking instrument. **1897** *Pearson's Mag.* July 51/1 This head-gear would hardly be necessary if a loud-speaking telephone were employed. **1921** *Sci. Amer.* Dec. 100/3 With a loud-speaking telephone on the living-room table and with a simple receiving set the members of the family can receive all the news..followed by a musical program. **1923** *Radio Times* 28 Sept. 14 A loud-speaking equipment that will enable all..to hear perfectly without headphones. **1951** *Catal. of Exhibits, South Bank Exhib., Festival of Britain* 82/2 Combined two-way loudspeaking intercommunication from bridge to selected points. **1960** *20th Cent.* Apr. 308 Loud-speaking cars toured hour by hour, giving names of known survivors.

loue, obs. variant of LOOR *dial.*

louffe, obs. form of LUFF.

†**lough**^{1}. *Obs.* Forms: 4 louh, 4–5 loȝe, 5 logh(e, loughe, 6 lowgh, 4– lough. See also LOW *sb.*^{3} [ME. *lough, loȝe*, perh. repr. ONorthumb. *luh* (?*lúh*), rendering L. *fretum* and *stagnum* in the Lindisfarne Gospels; the use for *fretum* suggests that it is a. Irish *loch* (see LOCH^1), though the vowel perh. agrees better with the British word represented by Welsh *llwch* (:—**luksu-*) lake, pool.]

1. A lake, pool. In ME. alliterative poetry sometimes used for: Water, sea.

c **1330** R. Brunne *Chron. Wace* (Rolls) 1423 Þe grete Lough of Rusticiadan. *Ibid.* 10197 In þat louh ar sexti iles. **13..** *E.E. Allit. P.* A. 119 Alle þe loȝe lemed of lyȝt. *c* **1400** Maundev. (Roxb.) xxi. 95 In þat ile also es a deed see; and it es in maner of a lowgh... Beside þat logh growez redez of a wonderfull lenth. *c* **1420** *Anturs of Arth.* 31 (Ireland MS.) He ladde þat lady so longe by that loghe sydus. *Ibid.* 83 Thare come a lowe one the loughe..In the lyknes of Lucyfere. **1538** Leland *Itin.* VII. 58 Divers Springes cummeth owt of Borodale, and so make a great Lowgh that we cawle a Poole; and ther yn be iii Isles. **1562** Turner *Herbal* II. 65 Nymphea..ii sorts..grow both in meres loughes lakes and in still or standyng waters. **1577** B. Googe *Heresbach's Husb.* (1586) 173 About Turwan in Fraunce..you shall finde in Loughes and Rayne Waters..great abundance of Fishe. *c* **1645** Howell *Lett.* (1650) IV. 110 Haerlam Mere, a huge inland lough. **1725** De Foe *Tour Gt. Brit.* II. I. 121 There is a little Lake or Lough of Water in the Middle of it [Litchfield]. [In ed. 7 (1769) II. 416 this passage is altered as follows: There is a kind of slow, sluggish Lough, or Water, which runs, or rather glides heavily through it, and so on for four or five Miles farther into the Trent.] **1829** Brockett *N. Country Words* (ed. 2) *Lough*, a lake.

b. *Sc.* (lux) = LOCH^1. ? *Obs.*

Cf. the Sc. form *louch* (14–16th c.) under LOCH^1; also the pl. *lowis* (16th c.): see LOW *sb.*^{3}

1785 Burns *Address Deil* vii, Wi' you, mysel, I gat a fright Ayont the lough [*rimes with* sough]. **1786** —— *Tam Samson's Elegy* iv, When to the loughs the Curlers flock.

2. *attrib.*: **lough-diver, -plover,** names for the female smew; **lough-leech** = *loch-leech* (see LOCH^1 2).

1678 Ray *Willughby's Ornith.* 338 The Female is described by Gesner under the title of *Mergus glacialis*, which Mr. Johnson Englisheth the **Lough-diver.* **1829** Col. Hawker *Diary* (1893) II. 11 A lough diver, or female smew. **1562** Turner *Herbal* II. 31 Horsleches or *lougheleches. **1578** Lyte *Dodoens* II. ccii. 305 Loughleaches.

lough^2 (lɒx). *Anglo-Irish.* Forms: 4 lowe, 6 logh, 6– lough. [The written form belongs to LOUGH^1, from which this need not have been separated but for the fact that, while the spelling *lough* survived in Ireland, the spoken word which it represented became obsolete, being superseded by the native Irish *loch* (lɒx): see LOCH^1.] A lake or arm of the sea; equivalent to the Scottish LOCH^1.

1387 Trevisa *Higden* (Rolls) I. 349 He wolde sende hir hym to þe Lowe Lacheryn. **1512** *Galway Arch.* in *10th Rep. Hist. MSS. Comm.* App. v. 395 The fishers of the logh bringe to the market thre dais in the wicke. **1567** in E. P. Shirley *Hist. Monaghan* 88 *note*, That fortification..is in 'sartin ffreshwater loghes' in his country. **1600** Fairfax *Tasso* I. xliv. 10 Whom Ireland sent from loughes and forrests hore. **1690** *Lond. Gaz.* No. 2540/2 Several Ships arrived that day in the Lough of Carrickfergus. **1708** *Brit. Apollo* No. 73. 2/1 There is a Lough in the North of Ireland, call'd Neugh. **1882** Mrs. Riddell *Pr. of Wales's Garden-Party* 230 On the other side of the lough..lay the green hills. **1900** *Blackw. Mag.* Oct. 580/1 Down in Mayo I had ridden out..to fish for white trout in a little lough that lies at the foot of Nephin.

†**lough**^{3}. *Obs.* = LOCH^2. Also *attrib.* in **lough-water** (see quot.).

1672 Flamsteed in Rigaud *Corr. Sci. Men* (1841) II. 153 Lough-water... 'Tis found in the midst of a firm stone in the lead mine. **1747** Hooson *Miner's Dict.* E iij, With this..we Chissel the Ore out of Loughs in Pipe Works.

†**lough,** *v. Obs.* [? repr. OE. *lóȝian* to place in order, f. *lóh* place.] *trans.* To stack (turf).

c **1630** Risdon *Surv. Devon* (1810) 11 Then drying and loughing those turfs into burrows, and so burning them.

lough, obs. pa. t. of LAUGH; obs. var. LOOR.

lough, louȝ, obs. forms of LOW *a.*

lougheen (ˈlɒxiːn). *Anglo-Irish.* [f. LOUGH^2 + dim. suffix *-een* (= Irish *-in* as in COLLEEN); cf. GIRLEEN.] A little lough.

1882 *Cornh. Mag.* Mar. 322 The countless multitude of loughs and lougheens.

lought, obs. variant of LOATH *a.*

16.. T. Heywood & Rowley *Fort. by Land & Sea* I. i. (1655) 3 Nor is he such a darling in mine eye, that I am lought to have him from my sight.

louh, louin, obs. forms of LOW, LOWN.

louie, var. LOOEY.

‖**louis** (ˈluːiː). *Hist.* Pl. louis. Also 7–8 in English form **lewis,** *pl.* lewis('s. [F. *louis*, appellative use of the Christian name borne by many French kings.] = LOUIS D'OR. Also †*silver lewis*: the French *écu* of the 17–18th c.

1689 *Lond. Gaz.* No. 2498/4 They took away..a quantity of Broad Pieces, Guinea's, Lewis's, Medals, &c. **1704** *Royal Proclam.* 18 June ibid. No. 4029/1 Ecu's of France, or Silver Lewis, Seventeen Peny-weight Twelve Grains, Four Shillings and Six Pence. **1794** Mrs. Radcliffe *Myst. Udolpho* v, He threw down all the money he had, except a very few louis. **1818** Byron *Juan* I. cviii, A good deal may be bought for fifty Louis. **1900** Ld. Rosebery *Napoleon* iii. 54 He sends with the challenge a gun and six louis which he had borrowed of his enemy.

louis, variant of LEWIS.

‖**louis d'or** (luːiː ˈdɔː(r)). *Hist.* Also in English or semi-English form 7 luidore, 8 lewi(s)dore, loui(s)dore. [F. *louis d'or*, lit. 'gold louis'; see prec.] A gold coin issued in the reign of Louis XIII and subsequently till the time of Louis XVI.

When first coined in 1640 its weight was 103·273 grains. In 1717 its legal value in England was fixed at 17*s.* In the Bourbon reigns following the Restoration the name was transferred to the 20 franc piece or Napoleon.

1689 *Lond. Gaz.* No. 2495/4 Lost..a Silk Purse,..therein two 5*l.* pieces of Gold, 13 or 14 Guinea's, and 3 Luidores. **1691** *Ibid.* No. 2643/4 The Ring is of Gold,..of the value of about 50 Lewis d'Or's. **1702** Farquhar *Inconstant* I. i. Wks. 1892 I. 335 He has ordered me to bespeak a dinner for us at Rousseau's at a louis-d'or a head. **1756** Nugent *Gr. Tour* III. 43 Spanish pistoles and French lewidores are current in this journey. **1832** Motley *Corr.* (1889) I. ii. 14 My room for the rest of this Semester..costs me three louis d'or and a half. **1883** Stevenson *Treas. Isl.* I. iv, The coins were of all countries and sizes—doubloons, and louis-d'ors, and guineas.

Louis heel. Also **Louis Quinze heel.** [f. the name of Louis XV (1715–74), King of France, in whose reign it became fashionable.] A type of heel used on a woman's shoe (see quot. 1968).

1872 *Young Englishwoman* Dec. 651/1 She knows that it is impossible to walk gracefully with the high-pointed heel, and never wears any but the demi-talon Louis Quinze. **1901** F. H. Burnett *Making of Marchioness* I. ii. 30 'She's got Louis Quinze heels,' returned his Lordship. **1906** *Daily Chron.* 23 Feb. 6/5 From the pretty shop-girl..to the daughter of the upper classes the Louis heel is regarded amongst women as a pedestal of superiority to be appropriated for personal adornment. **1968** J. Ironside *Fashion Alphabet* 136 It is of any height or shape... Its character is defined by the sole material which..is attached to the breast (front) of the heel by adhesive... *But* the term 'Louis' is generally applied to a high heel with curved waist, flared at the base.

Louisianian (luːiːz-, luːiːzɪˈænɪən, luːiːzɪˈɑːnɪən), *a.* and *sb.* [f. *Louisiana* (see below), named after Louis XIV of France.] **A.** *adj.* Of or pertaining to the State of Louisiana at the mouth of the Mississippi. **B.** *sb.* A native or inhabitant of Louisiana.

1775 J. Adair *Hist. Amer. Indians* 240 The illustration of this may..shew our southern colonies what they may still expect from the masterly abilities of the French Louisianians. **1835** J. H. Ingraham *South-West* I. ix. 101 Americans; that is to say, Anglo-Americans as distinguished from the Louisianian French. **1854** C. E. A. Gayarré *Hist. Louisiana* (*French Domination*) I. 13 Is not this the very poetry of landscape, of Louisianian landscape? **1945** *Chicago Daily News* 26 July 2/3 The slow but straight-talking Louisianian is extremely popular with his junior officers. **1949** B. A. Botkin *Treas. S. Folklore* IV. i. 552 Marylanders grow lyrical over Brunswick stew..and Louisianians, over the superiorities of the Cajun and Creole cuisine. **1967** Mrs. L. B. Johnson *White House Diary* 5 Dec. (1970) 597 This is a warm, loving, family-type house..crowded to the limit with..Louisianians.

louisine (luːɪˈziːn). [f. *Louis* or *Louise* a proper name + -INE^4.] (See quot. 1882.)

1882 Caulfeild & Saward *Dict. Needlework, Louisine*, a very thin plain silk material, suitable for children's wear, and for slight summer costumes. **1901** *Westm. Gaz.* 7 Mar. 3/2 Louisine, that new and fascinating silk, a sort of shimmering, larger-grained *peau de soie*.

Louis-Philippe (luːiːfɪˈliːp). The name of Louis-Philippe, King of France from 1830 to 1848; used *attrib.* or *ellipt.* to designate the style of architecture, furniture, and interior decoration characteristic of his reign.

1908 A. Bennett *Old Wives' Tale* iii. 307 He minutely examined his mouth in the glass of the Louis Philippe wardrobe. **1919** W. S. Maugham *Moon & Sixpence* xi. 46 It was a very small room, overcrowded with furniture of the style which the French know as Louis Philippe. **1951** N. Mitford *Blessing* II. iv. 183 To be able to tell at a glance whether an object was Louis XV or Louis Philippe, First or Third Empire. **1970** *Oxf. Compan. Art* 441/1 The slightly monotonous interiors..foreshadow the bourgeois interiors of Louis-Philippe. **1975** *Country Life* 6 Feb. (Suppl.) 31/2 Five piece gilt suite of the Louis Philippe period.

‖**Louis Quatorze** (luːiː kæˈtɔːz). Louis XIV, King of France, 1643–1715. Used adjectively to designate the styles in architecture, furniture, decorative art, etc., characteristic of his reign. So **Louis Quinze** (-kæ̃z), Louis XV, 1715–74. **Louis Seize** (-seɪz), Louis XVI, 1774–93. **Louis Treize** (-treɪz), Louis XIII, 1610–43. Hence rarely **Louis** as *adj.* to designate what was prevalent in two or more of the above-mentioned reigns.

1855 Ogilvie Suppl., Louis-Quatorze Ornament..Louis Quinze Ornament. **1876** Pollen *Anc. & Mod. Furniture* x.

103 The broken shell-shaped woodwork, popularly known as Louis quinze work, began to be adopted for the frames of large glasses. **1878** Eastlake *Househ. Taste* ii. (ed. 4) 55 Their notions of the beautiful are..derived from traditions of the Louis Quatorze period. **1882** Caulfeild & Saward *Dict. Needlewk.* 329 Louis Quinze Lace is formed of a braid known as Louis Treize. **1892** Litchfield *Hist. Furniture* 61 During the 'Louis Treize' period chairs became more comfortable. *Ibid.* 162 The familiar 'Louis Seize' riband surmounting the two oval Sèvres china plaques. **1901** *Contemp. Rev.* Sept. 381 Useful arts..are reduced to copies of the Louis styles.

†**louk**, *sb. Obs.* [f. LOUK *v.*] = LOCKCHESTER.

c **1400** *Payne MS.* (Dr. Frazer's), Contra pannum & maculam [oculorum] vermis claudens se cum tangitur .i. louk.

†**louk**, *v.*[1] *Obs.* Forms: *Inf.* 1 lúcan, 2-4 luke(n, 3 *Orm.* lukenn, 4 luk, louke(n, lowke, 6 lowk, 7 louk. *Pa. t.* 1 léac, *pl.* lucon, 3 læc, lec, loc, *pl.* loke(n, luken, 4 leke. *Weak forms*: 3-4 louked, luked, 4 loukid(e, 6 *Sc.* lowkyt. *Pa. pple.* 1 locen, 2-5 (i-, y-) i-loke(n, 3 *Orm.* lokenn, 3-4 luken, -in, 4-5 lokin, -on, -yn, (5 lukkin), *Weak forms*: 4 loukid, 5 lowked, *Sc.* lowkyt. [A Com. Teut. str. vb.: OE. *lúcan* = OFris. *lûka*, OS. (*ant-, bi-*)*lûkan* (MDu. *lûken*, Du. *luiken*), OHG. (*ant-, ar-, pi-*) *lûchan* (MHG. *lûchen*), ON. *lúka*, Goth. **lûkan* (in *galûkan* to close, *uslûkan* to open); f. Teut. root **leuk-*: *lauk-*: *lŭk-*, whence LOCK *sb.*[2] Outside Teut. no certain cognates have been found.

The str. pa. pple. survived the other parts of the vb., being regarded as belonging to LOCK *v.*[1]]

1. *trans.* To close, shut, fasten; *esp.* to fasten (a door or chamber) with lock and key, to lock; also, to close (the jaws, the eyes). Also *fig.*

a **1000** *Andreas* 1259 (Gr.) Hrim & forst..hæleða eðel lucon. *c* **1175** *Lamb. Hom.* 141 Þe ȝeten weren ilokene. *c* **1205** Lay. 15311 He ærde to Glochæstre & þe ȝates læc [*c* **1275** loc] ful feste. *c* **1220** *Bestiary* 513 Ðis cete ðanne hise chaueles lukeð. *c* **1250** *Gen. & Ex.* 3779 Ðis erðe is togidere luken, Als it ne were neuere or to-broken. *c* **1275** *Luue Ron* 147 in *O.E. Misc.* 97 He haueþ bi-tauht þe o tresur And bit þe luk þine bur. **1297** R. Glouc. (Rolls) 10189 Þe doren after hom wepinde [hii] loke vaste. *a* **1300** *Sarmun* xxxvi. in *E.E.P.* (1862) 5 Vn-do þin hert þat is iloke wiþ couetise and pryde. *a* **1300** *Cursor M.* 5224 Ioseph þi sun sal luke þin ei. **13..** *Seuyn Sag.* (W.) 929 He lek his eghen & gan to slape. *c* **1330** *Owayn Miles* (1837) 10 With lockе and keye the gate to louken. *a* **1340** Hampole *Psalter* cxlvii. 2 Þe ȝates of heuen eftire þe day of dome sall be loukid til. ? *a* **1400** *Morte Arth.* 3954 The gud kynge Lokes one his eye-liddis, þat lowkkide ware faire. *a* **1400** *Pol. Rel. & L. Poems* (E.E.T.S.) 257 Þe ȝates of Parais þoruth eue weren iloken. *c* **1422** Hoccleve *Jereslaus's Wife* 334 Left was the Erles Chambre dore vnstoken; To which he com and found it was nat loken. **1467** in *Eng. Gilds* (1870) 379 The same quayer to be put in a boxe called a Caskett, loken. **1513** Douglas *Æneis* ix. viii. 68 Nor I, thy moder, laid not thy corps on beyr, Nor wyth my handis lowkyt thyne eyn so cleyr. *a* **1600** Montgomerie *Misc. Poems* xv. 8 The dum solsequium..louks his leavis throu langour of the nicht. **1631** A. Craige *Pilgr. & Heremite* 8 Then who shall bee seene, To louk thy dead Eine?

2. *intr.* for *refl.* To close up, form one mass. Also with *together*. Of a lace: To have a fastening.

a **1000** *Phœnix* 225 (Gr.) Siþþan þa yslan eft onginnað æfter liȝþræce lucan togædre. *c* **1250** *Gen. & Ex.* 3276 God him bad helden up his hond to-ward ðis water, in a morgen quile ðe se luked. **13..** *E.E. Allit. P.* B. 441 Þenne lasned þe loȝ lowkande togeder. **13..** *Gaw. & Gr. Knt.* 217 A lace lapped aboute, þat louked at þe hede.

3. *trans.* To lock or shut up (const. *in, within*); to enclose, surround; also, to lock or shut *out*. *lit.* and *fig.* **to louk in clay** or **lead** = to bury.

c **1200** Ormin 1091 He wass himm sellf..lokenn þær wiþþinnenn. *c* **1205** Lay. 32202 His ban beoð iloken faste i guldene cheste. *c* **1250** *Gen. & Ex.* 362 Ðhu salt ben ut in sorȝe luken. *a* **1300** *Cursor M.* 6338 Sum-kin takening suld þar be Loken in þir wandes thre. *Ibid.* 9891 Þis castel es..wit walles loken four a stan. *Ibid.* 17411 Ioseph..Yee luked under lok and sele. *c* **1330** R. Brunne *Chron. Wace* (Rolls) 3258 For loue in armes ilk oþer þey loken. *c* **1330** *Amis & Amil.* 492 Hir pines were so harde and strong, She wald be loken in clay. **1377** Langl. *P. Pl.* B. xviii. 243 Lo! how the sonne gan louke Her liȝte in herself. *c* **1380** Wyclif *Sel. Wks.* III. 42 [God] loukide hem in þe myȝt of her enemyes. *c* **1386** Chaucer *Nun's Pr. T.* 55 Trewely she hath the herte in hoold Of Chaunteclеer loken in every lith. *c* **1400** *Rom. Rose* 3839 Thou shalt be bounde, And faste loken in a tour. *a* **1400-50** *Alexander* 5005 Þat oþir loken ouire with leues as it ware liȝt siluir. **1414** Brampton *Penit. Ps.* 18 Late noȝt myn enemyes makyn here game Of me, whan I am lokyn in leed. **1438** *Buke Alex. Great* 108 That hed him lukkin in luffis lace.

Hence †**louked** (*weak*) *ppl. a.* See also LOKEN, LUCKEN.

1513 Douglas *Æneis* xii. Prol. 101 The lowkyt buttonis on the gemmyt treis Ourspredand leyvis of naturis tapestreis.

louk, *v.*[2] *Obs.* exc. *dial.* Forms: 1 lúcan (*pres. ind.* 3 *sing.* lýcð), 3 luken, 5 lowke, 7-9 lowk, 9 look, luke, louk. *Pa. t.* 1 léac, 3 læc, leac, *pl.* 1 lucon, 3 luken. *Pa. pple.* 1 locen, 4 lokyn. [A Com. Teut. str. vb.: OE. *lúcan* = OFris. *lûka*, MDu. *lûken*, OHG. (*er-, ûz-*) *liuhhan* (MHG. *lûchen, liechen*, mod.G. dial. *liechen* to pull), Goth. (*us-*)*lûkan* to draw (a sword). Some regard the root (pre-Teut. **leug-*) as identical with that of Lith. *lúszti, láužyti* to break, Skr. *ruj* to shatter.]

1. *trans.* To pull up or out. Now only *dial.*, to pull up (weeds); to weed (corn).

a **1000** *Boeth. Metr.* xii. 28 (Sedgefield) Swa swa londes ceorl Of his æcere lycð yfel weod moniȝ. *c* **1205** Lay. 29072 Seiles heo up droȝen, ..luken rapes longe. *Ibid.* 29661 Up he læc þene staf, þat water þer after leop. *a* **1225** *Leg. Kath.* 2128, Ichulle leoten luken & teon þe tittes awei of þine bare breosten. *c* **1275** *XI Pains Hell* 136 in *O.E. Misc.* 151 Snakes heore eyen lukeþ. *a* **1400** *Octavian* 1274 Whan his swyrde was y-brokyn, A Sarasyns legge hath he lokyn, Therwyth he can hym were. **1483** *Cath. Angl.* 221/2 To Lowke (or weyde), *rvncare, sarculare*. **1674** Ray *N.C. Words* 31 To *Lowk*; i.e. to weed Corn, to look out weeds. **1825** Brockett *N.C. Words, Look, louk*, to weed, clear.

†**2.** *intr.* To burst *out*. *Obs.*

c **1205** Lay. 30274 Þa isah he of Brien his teres ut luken.

Hence '**louking** *vbl. sb.*, weeding. Also '**louker**, one who weeds.

14.. *Nom.* in Wr.-Wülcker 697/25 *Hic runcator*, lowker. **1491-2** *Durham Acc. Rolls* (Surtees) 159 Pro le lukkyng jus Spring apud Thonnokmyre. **1624** Best *Farm. Bks.* (Surtees) 156 July 20. Reckoned with Leonard Goodale, pd him for his mowing, and his wife lowkinge and haymakinge. 12*s*. **1641** *Ibid.* 142 Lookers have..3*d* a day.

†**louke**. *Obs.* App. a boon companion.

c **1386** Chaucer *Cook's T.* 51 Ther is no theef with-oute a lowke, That helpeth hym to wasten and to sowke Of that he brybe can or borwe may. [**1880** C. H. Poole *Gloss. Stafford* 15 *Lowk*, a sharp fellow.]

loukoum(i, varr. LOCOUM.

Loular, -ard, Louller: see LOLLARD, LOLLER[1].

loulou ('luːluː). [Fr., f. *loup* wolf.] A nickname for a Pomeranian dog.

1894 G. du Maurier *Trilby* II. vi. 208 The same old couples petting the same toutous and loulous! *Ibid.* (*footnote*), Loulou—a Pomeranian dog. **1916** E. V. Lucas *Vermilion Box* ccv. 237 One of our sights for visitors here is a dog. A real dog, not a toutou or a loulou, but a great collie kind of thing.

loun, obs. pa. ppl. of LIE *v.*[2]; var. of LOWN *Sc.*

lounder ('lundər), *sb. Sc.* [? Onomatopœic.] A heavy, swingeing blow.

1723 Ramsay *Monk & Miller's Wife* 263 Wha lent him on the neck a lounder That gart him o'er the threshold founder. **1816** Scott *Antiq.* xxi, I wad likeit weel just to hae..gien him a lounder wi' my pike-staff. **1862** W. Hunter *Biggar & Ho. of Fleming* xix. 231 [The] unwary cur..received such a lounder as sent him howling to his den.

lounder ('lundər), *v. Sc.* [f. LOUNDER *sb.*] *trans.* To beat, cudgel, thrash. Also, to hurl with violence *on* (something), in quot. *fig.*

1806 in Whitelaw *Bk. Sc. Ballads* (1875) 284/1 His back they loundert, mell for mell. **1816** Scott *Old Mort.* iv, If they come to lounder ilk ither, as they did last time, suldna I cry on you. **1893** Stevenson *Catriona* 330 Why is all this shame loundered on my head?

Hence, '**loundering** *vbl. sb.* '**loundering** *ppl. a.*, (of a blow) swingeing, severe.

1725 Ramsay *Gentle Sheph.* i. ii, To lend his loving wife a loundering lick. **1818** Scott *Hrt. Midl.* xviii, Her daughter had never seen Jock Porteous..since he had gien her a loundering wi' his cane. **1849** C. Bronte *Shirley* xxx. 437, I should rather relish a loundering whack.

†'**lounderer**. *Obs.* [a. Du. *lunderaar* (in Kilian *lunderer*), f. *lunderen* to idle.] A skulker.

c **1425** Wyntoun *Chron.* ii. viii. 740 Thai mycht..That lordschipe wyn in herytage, For to leve it fayntly, And lyve as lowndreris cayttevely. ? *c* **1530** *Test. W. Thorpe* in Foxe *A. & M.* (1583) I. 543/1 Lousengers and lounderers are wrongfully made and named Heremites.

†**loune**, *v. Obs.* [Echoic; cf. *looning* s.v. LOON *sb.*] *intr.* To utter the cry of the crane.

c **1325** *Gloss. W. de Bibbysw.* in Wright *Voc.* 152/3 Le bouf mugist (lowes), la grwe (crane) growle (lounet).

lounge (laundʒ), *sb.* [f. LOUNGE *v.*]

1. a. An act, spell, or course of lounging; a leisurely walk, a saunter, stroll; also, a lounging gait or manner of reclining.

1806 Surr *Winter in Lond.* II. 177 The gentlemen had arranged a morning lounge at Tattersall's. **1824** T. Hook *Say. & Doings* I. 18 The disembarrassed lounge on her own ottoman. **1833** M. Scott *Tom Cringle* xvi. (1859) 435, I am off to have a lounge with him. **1837** Lytton *Maltravers* ii. i. I. 166 What else have we to do with our mornings, we women?..Our life is a lounge from the cradle to the grave. **1860** Thackeray *Roundabt. P.* viii. Wks. 1869 XX. 85 'The Prince's lounge' was a peculiar manner of walking which the young bucks imitated. **1872** Black *Adv. Phaeton* xxx. 405 When we went out for a lounge after luncheon. **1889** D. C. Murray *Danger. Cats-paw* 18 Esden had slackened his pace to a mere lounge.

b. A pastime. Also *slang* (Eton and Cambridge), 'a treat, a chief meal' (Farmer).

1788 *Trifler* No. 21. 276 If..you have invented a new lounge, communicate it in your next. **1844** Disraeli *Coningsby* i. vi. I. 69, I don't care for dinner. Breakfast is my lounge.

2. a. A place for lounging; a gathering of loungers.

1775 Sheridan *Rivals* i. i, But pray, Mr. Fag, what kind of a place is this Bath?..*Fag*..'tis a good lounge. **1798** Jane Austen *Northang. Abb.* (1833) I. v. 20 Every search for him was unsuccessful, in morning lounges, or evening assemblies. **1798** *Monthly Mag.* VI. 171 If a man were asked to take a walk into the High-street in a morning—'He voted it a bad lounge.' **1800** Mrs. Hervey *Mourtray Fam.* IV. 135 Her house..was voted to be the most delightful lounge in London. *a* **1865** Greville *Mem.* ii. (1885) II. 170 This is a great lounge, attended by all the people of the town.

b. The drawing-room of a private house; the public sitting-room in a hotel or institution. Also *transf.*

1881 J. T. Slugg *Remin. Manch.* xxvi. 306 The lounge or drawing-room..was extremely elegant. **1908** *Daily Chron.* 13 Nov. 4/6 London hotels are extending their lounges. **1938** E. Bowen *Death of Heart* ii. i. 186 The sea..seemed an annexe of the livingroom... She learned later that Daphne called this the lounge. **1954** J. Betjeman *A Few Late Chrysanthemums* 94 It's ever so close in the lounge dear, But the vestibule's comfy for tea. **1965** M. Bradbury *Stepping Westward* iv. 181 Expressly for the purpose of hunting down Walker and bringing him to the English department faculty lounge, wherein the faculty were even now assembled. **1973** *Houston* (Texas) *Chron. Mag. People, Places, Pleasures* 14 Oct. 21/1, I am in a mobile lounge which is about to roll out from Dulles Airport to the supersonic Concorde. **1973** *Times* 8 Dec. 26/4 Burns Hotel... Licensed restaurant, bar lounge.

c. Ellipt. for *lounge-coat, -jacket, -suit.*

1893 J. Tomlin *Bond St. Syst. Cutting* 44 There are many different styles in which the Lounge is produced. **1905** *Daily Chron.* 16 Mar. 8/7 (Advt.), Good coat presser and baister for lounges and morning coats. **1928** *Tailor & Cutter* 29 Nov. 899/3 I'll take the lad; and..in six calendar months he will be able to make a lounge. **1968** A. A. Whife *First Course Gentlemen's Garment Cutting* (ed. 4) 69 The Reefer, Sports Jacket, Hacking Jacket..are designed on lines which originate in the basic structure of the Lounge.

3. A kind of sofa or easy chair on which one can lie at full length.

1830 J. F. Watson *Ann. Philadelphia* 183 Formerly they had couches of worsted damask..in lieu of what we now call sophas or lounges. **1845** *Knickerbocker* XXV. 446 The hard-bottomed chairs were the same, and the lounge, and the tall mahogany clock. **1852** Mrs. Stowe *Uncle Tom's C.* xxvi. 240 The graceful bamboo lounges were amply supplied with cushions. **1895** Mrs. B. M. Croker *Village Tales* (1896) 46 The patient was promoted into a cane lounge in the sitting-room. **1915** in B. A. Botkin *Treas. S. Folklore* (1949) iii. ii. 538 He stayed in the barn nights..and slept on an ol' lounge he carried out from the house. **1972** E. Staebler *Cape Breton Harbour* xvi. 142 There is always some one sitting on the rocker or on the wooden lounge built into the corner.

4. *attrib.* ('suitable for lounging'), as ***lounge-book, -chair, -coat, -hour, -jacket, -suit, -wear***; cf. LOUNGING *vbl. sb.* b; also (sense 2 b) ***lounge-diner*** (also ***lounge/diner***), ***-hall***; **lounge bar**, a bar in a public-house which is furnished with the amenities of a lounge; **lounge lizard** *slang* (orig. *U.S.*), a man who spends his time idling in fashionable society, esp. in search of a wealthy patroness.

1937 *Hotel & Catering Management* Sept. 23/1 Smoke-room or *lounge bars are obviously larger than cocktail bars, and provision has to be made for the serving of draught beers. **1971** 'H. Calvin' *Poison Chasers* vii. 83 Two of the security men..came into the public bar, and the rest of the customers..went into the lounge bar. **1800** Coleridge in *Sir H. Davy's Rem.* (1858) 82, I am compelled..to give a volume of letters from Germany, which will be a decent *lounge book, and not an atom more. **1902** *Westm. Gaz.* 25 Jan. 2/1 A sort of shudder sweeps over the limp forms in the *lounge-chairs. **1898** *Ibid.* 22 Sept. 8/2 Frock coats, and tail coats, and *lounge coats, and top coats. **1961** *Evening Standard* 3 July 23/4 (Advt.), Modern s/d house... Hall, *lounge/diner, kitchenette. **1966** Lounge-diner [see *garden gnome* s.v. GARDEN *sb.* 6]. **1974** *Country Life* 7 Mar. (Suppl.) 21/1 Excellent Family House..study/TV room, 31 ft. lounge/diner, breakfasting kitchen. **1910** *Bradshaw's Railway Guide* Apr. 1046 Lord Warden Hotel... Orchestra plays..in the beautiful *lounge hall every evening. **1933** D. C. Peel *Life's Enchanted Cup* xi. 126 This house..contained .. what house agents now call a lounge-hall. **1939** O. Lancaster *Homes Sweet Homes* 66 The luxury flat..is divided up..into a dining-room, drawing-room, lounge-hall, three bed, two bath, a kitchen and all the usual offices. **1810** *Sporting Mag.* XXXV. 311 A Boxing Match took place in Conduit-Street during the *lounge hours. **1887** E. B. Giles *Hist. Cutting in Eng.* i. 70 When repose is required [we use] the lounge jacket or dressing gown. **1899** R. Whiteing *No. 5 John St.* xxviii. 284 The billycock and the lounge jacket are, I think, my strong point. **1918** *Hatchet* 4 Apr. 39/1 (*caption*) Nautical *lounge lizards. **1921** *Daily Colonist* (Victoria, B.C.) 10 Apr. 4/4 The delicate, poetic cast of features, and the misplaced eyebrow adorning the nether lip of these lounge lizards, denizens of dansants and cabarets. **1926** *Punch* 17 Nov. 534/1 Formal recognition of those firmly attached appendages of Society, the lounge-lizards. **1973** *Times* 29 Dec. 7/7 The £50 a week contract which..lets her keep her lounge lizard husband, Queckett, in the manner to which he is accustomed, lacks conviction. **1901** *Westm. Gaz.* 25 Nov. 5/2 A navy blue serge *lounge suit. **1969** *Sears Catal.* Spring/Summer 3 Now—and all through the summer—Sears has the answer to just what you're looking for in *loungewear. **1974** *News-Palladium & Herald-Press* (Benton Harbor, Mich.) 8 May (Advt. Suppl.), See this utterly feminine loungewear in enchanting prints.

lounge (laundʒ), *v.* Also 7 loundge, 8 *Sc.* lunge; and in derivatives 7 lundge, 8 lownge. [Of obscure origin; perh. suggested by LUNGIS.]

1. *intr.* To move indolently, resting between-whiles, or leaning on something for support. Also with *about, away, in, out, up*. (In the early instances perh. rather: To skulk, to slouch.)

1508 Dunbar *Flyting w. Kennedie* 174 Ay loungand, lyk ane loikman on ane ledder. **1639** J. Clarke *Parœmiologia* 259 He loundge's as a dog that hath lost his tayle. **1755** Ramsay *To Jas. Clerk* 3 Works 1877 II. 307 Whase owsen

lunges o'er a plain Of wide extent. **1757** SMOLLETT *Reprisal* I. i, While I go down to the cabin..you may lounge about and endeavour to over-hear their conversation. **1838** LYTTON *Alice* 131 Vargrave lounged into the billiard-room. **1862** MRS. H. WOOD *Channings* xvii, Roland lounged in, not more presentable than the rest. **1863** FR. A. KEMBLE *Resid. in Georgia* 26 Filthy negroes, who lounge in and out. **1874** DEUTSCH *Rem.* 176 Egyptian officials, lounging about armed with weighty sticks. **1900** *Blackw. Mag.* Aug. 260/2 He would lounge up and say—'Now come really'.

2. To recline lazily, to loll.

1746 *Exmoor Scolding* (E.D.S.) 42 Eart lunging, eart squatting upon thy tether End. **1778** *Ibid.*, Gloss., *Lounging* or *Lundging*, leaning on any Thing, such as a Gate or a Stile, like a lazy Creature that hath nothing else to do. **1822–34** *Good's Study Med.* (ed. 4) III. 246 The complaint ..shows itself by..an unwonted desire to lounge and loll about. **1827** LYTTON *Pelham* I. xii. 39 You must not lounge on your chair. **1840** DICKENS *Old C. Shop* ii, The other stood lounging with his foot upon a chair. **1850** MAURICE *Mor. & Met. Philos.* (ed. 2) 162 Lounging upon their couches. **1859** C. C. BARKER *Associat. Princ.* iii. 63 'Squires..lounging on the rushes before the great hall fire.

3. To pass time indolently or without definite occupation; to idle.

1671 SKINNER *Etymol. Ling. Angl.*, *Lounge*, cunctari, movari, cessare, vide *Lungis*. **1755** JOHNSON, *Lounge*, to idle; to live lazily. **1784** J. BARRY in *Lect. Paint.* v. (Bohn 1848) 197 It would be at least some amusement..to lounge over what the other artists had done. **1856** LD. COCKBURN *Mem.* (1874) vii. 393 Scott..breakfasted and lounged from nine to eleven.

4. *trans.* To pass (time, etc.) *away* (rarely *out*) with lounging; also, †to lounge in (a place) (*obs.*).

1776 DK. RICHMOND in *Burke's Corr.* (1844) II. 113, I suppose you lounge away whole months whistling for want of thought. **1810** *Splendid Follies* I. 129, I never go to the play for any entertainment, except kicking up a row and lounging the lobbies. **1814** JANE AUSTEN *Mansf. Park* (1851) 67 They all returned to the house together, there to lounge away the time as they could with chit-chat. **1871** BURR *Ad Fidem* (ed. 2) iii. 39 The able-bodied and able-minded person who..lounges out his youth and lounges out his manhood. **1879** FROUDE *Cæsar* 104 He then returned to Rome to lounge away the remainder of his days in voluptuous magnificence.

lounge, variant of LUNGE; obs. form of LUNG.

lounger ('laʊndʒə(r)). [f. LOUNGE *v.* + -ER[1].]

a. One who lounges, an idler, a do-nothing.

1508 DUNBAR *Flyting w. Kennedie* 121 Lene larbar, loungeour, baith lowsy in lisk and lonȝe. **1513** DOUGLAS *Æneis* VIII. Prol. 122 Quhat bern be thou in bed..Lurkand like a longeour? **1711** STEELE *Spect.* No. 54 ⁋6, I shall enquire into such about this Town as have arrived at the Dignity of being Loungers by the Force of natural Parts. **1750** *Student* I. 21 Idle people called Lowngers, whose whole business it is to fly from the painful task of thinking. **1803** MAR. EDGEWORTH *Manufacturers* ii. (1832) 106 Our hero was ridiculed most unmercifully by all the Bond-street loungers. **1862** MERIVALE *Rom. Emp.* (1865) VI. xlviii. 66 The loungers of the baths and porticoes sallied forth from their cool retreats. **1878** *N. Amer. Rev.* CXXVI. 7 He went to Europe as a student, not as a lounger.

b. An article of furniture or of dress designed to be used for relaxation.

1964 G. SIMS *Terrible Door* xviii. 98 She wore..blue woollen stockings and highly polished, brown moccasin loungers. **1969** *Sears Catal.* Spring/Summer 3 Ankle length loungers with their own carefully constructed Bra sewn right in. **1969** A. LASKI *Dominant Fifth* v. 182, I am sitting in a lounger under an umbrella. **1971** *Daily Tel.* 11 May 13/5 The best 'loungers' are those which allow the legs to be raised slightly above the body.

lounging ('laʊndʒɪŋ), *vbl. sb.* [f. LOUNGE *v.* + -ING[1].] **a.** The action of LOUNGE *v.*

1793 LD. N. SPENCER in *Ld. Auckland's Corr.* (1862) III. 121 Two or three hour's lounging in a place called a club. **1823** BYRON *Juan* XI. lxvi, His afternoons he pass'd in visits, luncheons, Lounging, and boxing. **1901** *Edin. Rev.* Apr. 439 Seldom or never is the pulpit used..to denounce idleness, lounging or laziness.

b. *attrib.*, as ***lounging-book, -chair, -coat, -hall, -jacket, -place, robe, -room.***

1790 H. WALPOLE in *Walpoliana* clxxiv. 79 A catalogue *raisonnée* of such [novels] might be itself a good *lounging book. **1825** *Gentl. Mag.* XCV. I. 159 We assure our readers that the compilation is..an excellent lounging-book. **1841** R. P. WARD *De Clifford* III. viii. 123 See these superb sofas, carpets, tables, and *lounging-chairs. **1867** TROLLOPE *Chron. Barset* I. xxv. 217 [He] was sitting in a lounging-chair and smoking a cigar. **1971** *Daily Tel.* 11 May 13/5 Now, this year, Vogue have a lounging chair which lets you get your head down. **1920** B. E. STEVENSON *Gloved Hand* 11, I paused only to open my bag, change into a *lounging-coat, and brush off the dust of the journey. **1960** *Harper's Bazaar* Oct. 87 A chiffon lounging coat printed with cinnamon flowers. **1785** *Lounger* No. 8 ⁋2 If you will make Dun's rooms a *Lounging Hall instead of a Chapel. **1861** HUGHES *Tom Brown at Oxf.* xxxiii. (1889) 319 The owner of the mansion was seated at table in a *lounging jacket. **1837** HAWTHORNE *Twice Told T.* (1851) II. xii. 183 Peter had long absented himself from his former *lounging-places. **1908** *Sears Roebuck Catal.* 1117 (*heading*) Long kimonos or negligees and bath or *lounging robes. **1945** R. CHANDLER *Let.* 13 Oct. in *R. Chandler Speaking* (1966) 44 The great man appeared..clad in an expensive lounging robe. **1863** MRS. GASKELL *Dark Night's Work* iv. 42 He used the study for a smoking and *lounging-room principally. **1887** C. D. WARNER *Their Pilgrimage* (1888) i. 2 In the spacious office and general lounging-room, sea-coal fires glowed in the wide grates.

lounging ('laʊndʒɪŋ), *ppl. a.* [f. LOUNGE *v.* + -ING[2].] **a.** That lounges. **b.** Characterized by, occupied in, or adapted for lounging.

1674 N. FAIRFAX *Bulk & Selv.* 35 The foul stalking lundging body of that Og of Bashan. **1789** CHARLOTTE SMITH *Ethelinde* I. 108 There is not any of his..lounging, tonish friends of his half so well looking. **1807** KNOX & JEBB *Corr.* I. 326 There is..much of what is 'flat, stale, and unprofitable' in a lounging life. **1825** J. NEAL *Bro. Jonathan* I. 16 He..walked with a sort of lounging stoop. **1851** MAYNE REID *Scalp Hunt.* xxxviii. 289 The horses stand in lounging attitudes, asleep. **1857** HAWTHORNE *Eng. Note-Bks.* (1879) II. 210 The library is..lounging and luxurious.

loungingly ('laʊndʒɪŋlɪ), *adv.* [f. LOUNGING *ppl. a.* + -LY[2].] In a lounging attitude or manner.

1799 *Spirit Pub. Jrnls.* (1805) III. 126 Throw yourself loungingly into a chair at Owen's, cut up a pine [etc.]. **1855** *Chamb. Jrnl.* III. 49 He comes straight on, rather loungingly. **1882** *Macm. Mag.* XLVI. 326/2 Romeo can half sit loungingly against the fountain.

loungoute, var. LUNGOUTE *Sc. Obs.*, locust.

loungy ('laʊndʒɪ), *a.* [f. LOUNGE *sb.* + -Y[1].] Suggestive of lounges or lounging.

1911 CHESTERTON *Innocence of Father Brown* v. 124, I mean little, loungy men, who had just enough to live on and had nothing to do but lean about in bar-rooms and bet on horses.

lounie: see LUNYIE.

loup (laʊp), *sb.*[1] *Sc.* [a. ON. *hlǫup* = LEAP *sb.*[1]] = LEAP *sb.*[1] *lover's loup*: cf. LOVER[1] 4.

1375 BARBOUR *Bruce* VI. 638 Till thame that faucht vith his man A lowp richt lychtly maid he than. **1725** RAMSAY *Gentle Sheph.* I. i, Yonder's a craig, since ye have tint all hope, Gae till 't your ways, and take the lover's lowp. **1821** GALT *Ann. Parish* viii. 85 The horses gave a sudden loup, and couped the coach. **1900** *Speaker* 19 May 190/1 Two sheep dogs raced forward with long loups.

†**loup**, *sb.*[2] *Sc. Obs.* [a. ON. *lǫup-r* = LEAP *sb.*[2]] A weel or fishing basket; = LEAP *sb.*[2] 2.

1581 *Sc. Acts Jas. VI* (1814) III. 218/2 Halding of cruuis, lynis or loupis wᵗin fresche watteris.

‖**loup** (lu), *sb.*[3] [a. F. *loup*, lit. 'wolf':—L. *lupum*. Cf. LOO *sb.*[2]] A light mask or half-mask of silk or velvet worn by females.

1834 JAMES *J. Marston Hall* xxii, The black velvet mask, called a *loup*, which was then very generally used by women in the higher classes, under the pretext of defending their complexions. **1876** OUIDA *Winter City* x. 327 Their white teeth shone under the lace of their loups.

‖**loup** (lu), *sb.*[4] [Fr., lit. 'wolf'.] In full, ***loup de mer***. The sea-bass, *Dicentrarchus labrax*, found off the coasts of western Europe and in the Mediterranean.

1766 SMOLLETT *Trav.* I. xviii. 291 One of the best fish of this country, is called *Le Loup*, about two or three pounds in weight; white, firm, and well-flavoured. **1938** E. BOWEN *Death of Heart* I. iv. 76 Filing off wet third-class decks of lake steamers, choking over the bones of *loups de mer*. **1966** P. V. PRICE *France: Food & Wine Guide* 44 The *loup de mer*, so often found grilled over fennel sticks all over the south, is a sort of sea-perch or sea-bass. **1969** J. ELLIOT *Duel* I. v. 117 Keith..had lines out trolling for *rouget* and *loup de mer*. **1969** *New Yorker* 27 Sept. 120/2, I have seen more herbs thrown on the coals beneath, somewhat as fennel is blazed under a *loup*, the wolfish sea bass, at its last minutes on the grill.

loup (laʊp), *v. Sc.* Also 4–9 lowp(e, 6 loupe, (8 loop). [a. ON. *hlǫupa*: see LEAP *v.*] *intr.* and *trans.* = LEAP *v.* in various senses.

1375 BARBOUR *Bruce* XIII. 652 And it [wheel of fortune], that wondir lawch wer ere, Mon lowp on loft in the contrere. *c* **1375** *Sc. Leg. Saints* xxxvi. (*John Baptist*) 506 þe wikit wife gert hir dochtir ga..& spring & loupe befor þaim al. **1535** STEWART *Cron. Scot.* (1858) III. 413 Sum he gart loupe and droun into the deip. **1567** *Gude & Godlie Ball.* (S.T.S.) 222 Quhen that I heir hir name exprest, My hart for Ioy dois loup thairfor. *a* **1578** LINDESAY (Pitscottie) *Chron. Scot.* (S.T.S.) I. 197 The bischope quha was than loupand on hors. *a* **1584** MONTGOMERIE *Cherrie & Slae* 463 Luik quhair to licht before thou loup. **1693** *Scot. Presbyt. Eloq.* (1783) 138 That like new-spean'd Fillies they may loop over the Fold-dikes of Grace. **1788** BURNS *Ep. to H. Parker* 30 O, had I power like inclination, I'd..loup the ecliptic like a bar. **1826** J. WILSON *Noct. Ambr.* Wks. 1855 I. 175 The trouts are loupin in the water. **1871** C. GIBBON *Lack of Gold* vii, With ..your purse full you'll get dozens of them ready to loup at you. **1894** CROCKETT *Raiders* (ed. 3) 46 Gin I haena the strength o' airm to gar ye lowp mysel'.

b. *Comb.*: **loup-the-dike** *a.*, giddy, flighty.

1823 GALT *Entail* II. 276 She jealouses that your affections are set on a loup-the-dyke Jenny Cameron like Nell Frizel. **1824** SCOTT *Redgauntlet* ch. xxiii, I have my finger and my thumb on this loup-the-dyke loon.

loup, obs. form of LOOP.

‖**loup cervier** (lu sɛrvje). [F. *loup cervier*, ad. L. *lupus cervārius* (Pliny) the lynx (*lupus* wolf, *cervārius* that hunts stags, f. *cervus* stag).] The Canada lynx (*Lynx Canadensis*), a species of wild cat with a short tail.

1725 COATS *Dict. Heraldry*, *Loup-cervier* is a very large Sort of Wolf. **1744** A. DOBBS *Hudson's Bay* 41 The Loup Cervier, or Lynx, is of the Cat Kind.

loupe (luːp). [Fr.: cf. LOOP *sb.*[4]] A small magnifier used by a watchmaker or jeweller.

1909 in *Cent. Dict.* Suppl. **1940** C. MCCULLERS *Heart is Lonely Hunter* (1943) II. ii. 105 He noticed the distorted look of Kelly's right eye as it appeared through his watchmaker's loupe. **1949** H. C. WESTON *Sight, Light & Efficiency* iv. 122 Simple spectacle loupes are generally made to give a magnification of $2\frac{1}{4}$ or $2\frac{1}{2}$. **1962** R. WEBSTER *Gems* II. xxxiii. 598 It is now possible to discuss the various types of simple microscopes, such as the ordinary magnifiers with which jewellers are so familiar. These magnifiers, or loupes as they are sometimes called, must be considered with two points of view in mind. **1964** E. BRUTON *Finsbury Mob* viii. 111 On an old kitchen table were a pair of jeweller's scales, a loupe,.. various other bits of jewellers' paraphernalia, and a packet of detergent.

loupe, louped: obs. forms of LOOP, LOOPED.

†**loupegarth.** *Obs.* [Cf. MSw. *löpe gatulop* (Söderwall) to run the gantlope.] = GANTLOPE.

1637 R. MONRO *Exped.* I. 45 Other slight punishments.. as the Loupegarthe, when a Souldier is stripped naked above the waste, and is made to runne a furlong betwixt two hundred Souldiers,..where his Camerades whip him with small rods.

†'**louper.** *Obs.* Some kind of artificial fly.

1496 *Fysshynge w. Angle* (1883) 34 The blacke louper, the body of blacke wull & lappyd abowte wyth the herle of þe pecok tayle.

‖**loup-garou** (lugaru). Also 7 lou-garou. [F. *loup-garou*, f. *loup* wolf + *garou*, OF. *garoul*, a. OHG. **werawolf* WERWOLF.] = WERWOLF.

1579–80 NORTH *Plutarch, Alcib.* (1595) 218 Timon surnamed Misanthropus (as who would say Loup-garou [so Fr. in Amyot (1565) I. 136] or the manhater). **1648** C. WALKER *Hist. Independ.* I. 130 Dead mens Graves are not secure from these Lycanthropi, these Lou-garous. **1847** LONGF. *Ev.* I. iii. 13 He told them tales of the Loup-garou in the forest. **1939** H. M. MINER *St. Denis* vii. 136 The devil, in various forms, and *loup-garous* were abroad in the land and were a considerable problem. **1961** R. M. PATTERSON *Buffalo Head* ii. 69 Jerome, certain that the loup garou had come for him at last, backed closer to the fire.

louping ('laʊpɪŋ), *vbl. sb.* [f. LOUP *v.* + -ING[1].] The action of LOUP *v.*

c **1440** *Promp. Parv.* 316/1 Lowpynge or skyppynge, *saltus*. *a* **1584** MONTGOMERIE *Cherrie & Slae* 279 Ay houping, throu louping, To win to liberty. **1824** SCOTT *Redgauntlet* let. ix, Louping and laughing..would soon make the powder flee out of his wig.

b. *Comb.*: **louping ague**, 'a disease resembling St. Vitus's dance' (Jam.); **louping ill**, 'a disease of sheep, which causes them to spring up and down when moving forward' (Jam.); **louping-on stone**, a mounting-block.

1792 *Statist. Acc. Scot., Forfarsh.* II. 496 A singular kind of distemper, called the *louping ague, has sometimes made its appearance in this parish. **1816** SCOTT *Bl. Dwarf* x, The *louping-ill's been sairer amang his sheep than ony season before. **1902** *Dundee Advertiser* 31 May, Professor Hamilton ..has..discovered the bacilli of loupin'-ill in sheep. **1728** in A. Laing *Lindores Abbey* (1876) xxvi. 400 A petition given in by George Grant..To ye baillies and Councill..for ye liberty of building a *louping on ston at the south side of the house in Newburgh he possesses. **1814** SCOTT *Wav.* xxix, He had..by the assistance of a 'louping-on-stane',.. elevated his person to the back of..a broken-down blood-horse. **1902** C. G. HARPER *Holyhead Road* I. 263 Mile-stones..resembling 'louping on' stones or 'upping blocks'.

lour, lower (laʊə(r), 'laʊə(r)), *sb.*[1] For forms see the vb. [f. LOUR *v.*]

1. A gloomy or sullen look; a frown, scowl.

13.. *Seuyn Sag.* (W.) 1952 Whi makest thou swich scher and foul lour? **1530** PALSGR. 241/1 Loure an yvell loke. **1578** T. PROCTER *Gorg. Gallery* L iij, What are your sweet smiles, quite turnd into lowres? **1598** DRAYTON *Heroic. Ep.* Wks. (1748) 83 In one smile or lowre of thy sweet eye Consists my life. **1704** STEELE *Lying Lover* I. i. 2 Han't I a down bookish Lour? a wise Sadness. **1814** SCOTT *Wav.* xviii, A sudden, though transient lour of the eye, shewed a hasty, haughty, and vindictive temper.

2. Of the sky, weather, etc.: Gloominess, threatening appearance; an instance of this.

1596 B. GRIFFIN *Fidessa* (1876) 35, I am no leauing of al-withering age, I haue not suffred many winter lowres. **1686** GOAD *Celest. Bodies* II. iv. 214 [It] is apt to Heat, and some-times..to Dryth; but more frequently to Lowr, Bluster, Rain. **1808** SCOTT *Marm.* v. Introd., For thy dark cloud, with umber'd lower, That hung o'er cliff, and lake, and tower. **1816** J. WILSON *City of Plague* II. ii. 209 Alike unto that fearless flower..The sunlight's smile—the tempest's lower.

lour, lower (laʊə(r), 'laʊə(r)), *sb.*[2] *slang.* Also 6, 9 lowre, 9 loaver. Money.

1567 HARMAN *Caveat* 85 Hast thou any lowre in thy bonge? **1622** FLETCHER *Beggar's Bush* II. i, Except you do provide me hum enough, and Lour to bouze with! **1670** COTTON *Scoffer Scofft* (1675) 184 But e're this life I'le longer lead I'le stroll for Lower, or begg my bread. **1834** W. H. AINSWORTH *Rookwood* V. i. (1878) 341, I knows I owes you my life, and I thank you for it. Take back the lowre. **1851** MAYHEW *Lond. Labour* I. 424 They don't mind tipping the loaver (money). **1889** CLARKSON & RICHARDSON *Police* 321 Bad money (coin), *gammy lower*.

lour, lower (laʊə(r), 'laʊə(r)), *v.* Forms: 3–6 loure, 3–4 lure, 5–8 lowr(e, (6 loour, 7 lowere), 6– lour, lower. [ME. *loure-n*, perh. repr. an OE. **lúrian*; other Teut. langs. have forms app.

corresponding, but they have not been traced to any early date.

Cf. early mod.Du. *loeren* (Kilian) to frown, knit the brows; to look askance; to wink; to watch stealthily, to lie in wait (now only, to spy, lie in wait); late MHG. and MLG. *lûren* to lie in wait (mod.G. *lauern*), Sw. *lura*, Da. *lure* to lie in wait, also to doze, nap (Sw., Da. *lur* a nap), mod.Icel. *lúra* to doze, nap, *lúr* a nap.

The spelling *lower* (cf. *flower*) renders the word identical in its written form with LOWER, to bring or come down, and the two vbs. have often been confused: when said of clouds, *lower* ('laʊə(r)) to look threatening, has some affinity in sense with *lower* ('ləʊə(r)) to descend, and it is not always possible to discover which vb. was in the mind of a writer.]

1. *intr.* Of persons, their eyes, countenances, etc.: To frown, scowl; to look angry or sullen. † Also, to be depressed or mournful. Const. *at*, *on*, *upon*; rarely in indirect passive.

c **1290** *S. Eng. Leg.* I. 294/16 He..lourede with sori semblaunt: and þeos wordes out he caste. *a* **1300** *K. Horn* 286 Heo sende hire sonde Aþelbrus to honde, þat he come hire to, And also scholde horn do al in to bure, ffor heo gan to lure. *c* **1350** *Will. Palerne* 2119 þe liȝtere he let þer-of, ac lourand he seide [etc.]. *c* **1384** CHAUCER *H. Fame* I. 409 For had he lawghed, had he loured, He moste haue be devoured Yf Adriane ne had y-be. *c* **1412** HOCCLEVE *De Reg. Princ.* 703 Now I am mys-lokyd on & loured. *c* **1440** *Jacob's Well* 92 þou..lowryst, & chaungyst thi chere, & fleest companye. **1472** J. PASTON in *P. Lett.* III. 75 They that lowryd, nowe laughe upon me. **1568** TILNEY *Disc. Mariage* B viij, Can there be any greater disorder, than for the husbande to be merie abrode, and lowre at home? **1580** BABINGTON *Exp. Lord's Prayer* (1596) 75 Wee either loure or laugh to be tolde, we should come in. **1642** ROGERS *Naaman* 560 Love him.. lowre not upon him. **1671** MILTON *Samson* 1057 Nor from that right to part an hour, Smile she or lowre. *a* **1701** SEDLEY *Poems* Wks. 1722 I. 16 The Man's unkind, the cheated Woman low'rs. **1750** *Student* I. 323 A young man, who lower'd very much in his countenance, and stood in a melancholy posture. **1816** 'QUIZ' *Grand Master* I. 20 His tone of insolence and pow'r, Made all the passengers to low'r. **1862** J. GRANT *Capt. Guard* xx, His brows knit and his eyes loured. **1879** BUTCHER & LANG *Odyss.* 360 Then Odysseus of many counsels loured on them. **1883** A. FORBES in *19th Cent.* Oct. 722 The convict faces lowering over the bulwark of the barracoon.

b. quasi-*trans.* To express by frowning.

1746 WESLEY *Wks.* (1872) II. 21 The other part [of the crowd] remained a little way off, and loured defiance.

2. *transf.* and *fig.* Chiefly of the clouds, sky, a tempest, etc.: To look dark and threatening. Const. *on*, *over*, *upon*.

[*a* **1450**, etc.: see LOURING.] **1590** MARLOWE *Edw. II*, IV. vi. 63 O my starres! Why do you lowre vnkindly on a King? **1594** SHAKS. *Rich. III*, I. i. 3 The clouds that low'rd vpon our house. **1614** EARL STIRLING *Dooms-day* XII. vi. (1637) 261 No threat'ning cloud, all charg'd with hailstones lowres. **1667** MILTON *P.L.* IX. 1002 Skie lowr'd and..som sad drops Wept. **1713** ADDISON *Cato* I. i, The dawn is over-cast, the morning lours. **1768** BEATTIE *Minstr.* II. xxxii, When the dark shades of melancholy lower. **1835** I. TAYLOR *Spir. Despot.* ii. 70 Let commercial perplexity lour over a people as it may. **1842** BARHAM *Ingol. Leg.*, Ser. II. *Bloudie Jacke*, So sour Its ugly grey walls seem to lour. **1846** KEBLE *Lyra Innoc.* (1873) 74 Their day, in gloom or tempest born, Lowers on till noon and night. **1866** M. ARNOLD *Thyrsis* v, A shadow lour'd on the fields. **1887** BOWEN *Virg. Æneid* II. 397 Where night in her darkness lowers.

† **3.** Chiefly *Sc.* To crouch, lurk, skulk. *Obs.*

c **1450** *St. Cuthbert* (Surtees) 4528 Of paynyms lorells þat her by loures. *c* **1470** HENRYSON *Mor. Fab.* IX. iii. in *Anglia* IX. 463 And lowrand law, thow can gar hennis de. **1501** DOUGLAS *Pal. Hon.* I. lviii, On kneis I crap, and law for feir did lowre. **1513** —— *Æneis* VII. vii. 5 Alecto..prively begouth awach and loure About his spouse queyne Amatays boure. **1571** *Satir. Poems Reform.* xxix. 22 Quhen Dauid vnder þe sek did loure. **1622** MALYNES *Anc. Law-Merch.* 255 Philosophers..haue determined that the sperme, or seed of all things,..doth in a secret manner lowre within the two Elements of Water and Earth. **1647** H. MORE *Song of Soul* I. I. liii, Make their brisk sprights to lout and lowly lowr? **1824** W. TAYLOR in *Monthly Mag.* LVII. 509 The murderers of his nephew, whom he lour'd for.

† **lour, lowr**, *int. Obs.* [? contraction for *lo where*.] = Lo or look where! or simply Lo!

[*c* **1205** LAY. 21171 Lou [*c* **1275** lo] war her biforen us heðene hundes.] *a* **1225** *Ancr. R.* 152 Lour hit her: read gold & hwit seoluer inouh. *a* **1225** *Leg. Kath.* 2436 Lowr! her ich abide þe bite of sweordes egge.

lour, Sc. f. *liefer*, compar. of LIEF *a.*

† **lourd**, *a.* and *sb. Obs.* Also 4 lourde, 5 lowrde, lowryd(e, 6 lowrd, loord, lurde, 7 lowr'd. [a. F. *lourd* heavy.]

A. *adj.* Sluggish, dull, sottish, stupid.

1390 GOWER *Conf.* II. 149 To se so lusti on as sche Be coupled with so lourde a wiht. *c* **1425** WYNTOUN *Cron.* VIII. x. 1670 Made hym bot lowryd chere. **1564** MARTIALL *Treat. Cross* 119 b [Images] quicken the memory which in many is fickle, help ignoraunce, which in some is lurde. ? **1590** A. HUME *Poems* (S.T.S.) 19 The mortall, caduck, carnall corps (a lowrd and brukill mas). **1594** *Ibid.* 85. **1681** COLVIL *Whigs Supplic.* (1751) 101 The lowr'd mistakings of some men. [**1790** H. WALPOLE *Let. to Miss A. Berry* 29 Nov. (1846) VI. 381 The *lourd* want of grace in Guercino.]

B. *sb.* A sottish fellow, a lout.

1579 SPENSER *Sheph. Cal.* July 33 Syker, thous but a laesie loord, And rekes much of thy swinck. **1590** —— *F.Q.* III. vii. 12 A laesy loord, for nothing good to donne.

Hence † **lourdish**, † **lourdly**, **lourdy** *adjs.*, in the same sense.

1600 *Hosp. Incur. Fooles* 41 Of dottuls and shallow-pated Fooles..These Infortunate and Lourdish sort. **1674** RAY *S. & E.C. Words* 71 Lourdly, Sluggish. Suff. **1721** BAILEY, *Lourdy*, slothful, sluggish. *Suss.*

lourd (lurd). *Sc.* [Alteration of *lour*, var. of *lever* LIEFER, the structure of the phrase suggesting a pa. pple. as appropriate.] Only in *I had* or *wad lourd* = 'I had rather'.

? **17..** *Child Morice* in Child *Ballads* II. 275, I rather lourd it had been my sel Than eather him or thee. **1799** SCOTT *Sheph. Tale*, But I had lourd melle with fiends of hell Than with Clavers and his band. *a* **1802** *Jamie Telfer* xliii. in Child *Ballads* IV. 7, I wad lourd have had a winding-sheet And helped to put it ower his head. *a* **1802** *Broom of Cowdenknows* xviii. ibid. IV. 199 And ere he had taken the lamb he did I had lourd he had taen them a'.

lourdain(e, -an, -ayne, variants of LURDAN.

lourde, obs. form of LORD.

† **lourderie**. *Obs.* In 6 luerdrie. [a. F. *lourderie*, f. *lourd*: see LOURD.] Stupidity.

1555 BRAHAM *To Rdr.* in *Lydg.'s Chron. Troy*, The trifelinge tales and barrayne luerdries of Robyn Hode [etc.].

lourdin, variant of LURDAN *Obs.*

† **loure**. *Obs.* [a. F. *loure*, an old name for the musette or bagpipe, also a tune adapted to that instrument.] ? An air suited to the bagpipe.

1706 P. SIRIS *Art Dancing* 50 Quadruple-Time is made use of in slow Airs, and the Tunes called Loures. **1724** *Explic. For. Words Mus.* 42 *Loure*, is the name of a French Dance, or the Tune thereunto belonging, always in Triple Time, and the Movement, or Time, very Slow and Grave. **1811** in BUSBY *Dict. Mus.*

loure, lourey, obs. ff. LOWER *v.*, LORY.

lourie: see LOERIE.

louring, lowering ('laʊərɪŋ), *vbl. sb.* [f. LOUR, LOWER *v.* + -ING[1].] The action of LOUR *v.*, frowning, scowling, sullenness.

a **1250** *Owl & Night.* 423 Grucching and luring him both rade. *a* **1450** *Knt. de la Tour* (1868) 35 There was neuer pees betwene hem, but euer glomyng, louring, and chiding. **1549** COVERDALE, etc. *Erasm. Par. Rom.* 34 Lette it be done withoute sadnes and louryng. **1581** J. BELL *Haddon's Answ. Osor.* 486 b, Neither was Queene Elizabeth ever..afrayd of any her subjectes lowring or browbeating. **1665** BRATHWAIT *Comment Two Tales* 179 There was nothing there [at the bridal] but Pouting, Louring, and Cloudy Weather. **1820** W. IRVING *Sketch Bk.* I. 180 These lourings of gloomy reflection.

louring, lowering ('laʊərɪŋ), *ppl. a.* [f. LOUR, LOWER *v.* + -ING[2].]

1. Of persons (†occas. of animals), their looks, etc.: Frowning, scowling; angry-looking, gloomy, sullen.

13.. *K. Alis.* 525 Louryng semblaunt on hire he made. **1340** *Ayenb.* 256 The lourinde chiere [to-þrauþ] þe wordes of the missiggere. **1393** LANGL. *P. Pl.* C. VI. 163 He lokeþ al louryng and 'lordein' hym calleþ. **1443** JAS. I. *Kingis Q.* clxi, And quhilum In hir chiere thus a lyte Louring sche was. **1546** LANGLEY *Pol. Verg. De Invent.* VI. vii. 123 b, A lowring loke & a laughyng herte. *c* **1550** CHEKE *Matt.* vi. (1843) 37 When ye fast be not lowring lijk hypocrijts. **1607** TOPSELL *Four-f. Beasts* (1658) 48 They call him [a bull] fierce, valiant, and louring. **1641** MILTON *Animadv.* Wks. 1851 III. 186 To be angry, and..to cast a lowring smile. **1697** DRYDEN *Virg. Georg.* III. 87 The Mother Cow must wear a low'ring Look. **1712** BUDGELL *Spect.* No. 425 ¶5 In his Look a louring Roughness. **1741** BETTERTON *Eng. Stage* v. 66 A louring and dark Visage is the Index of Misery. **1819** L. HUNT *Indicator* No. 4 (1822) I. 25 With eyes a little shut and lowering. **1849** MACAULAY *Hist. Eng.* iii. I. 400 The young candidate..was strictly interrogated by a synod of louring Supralapsarians. **1862** J. GRANT *Capt. Guard* xiv, 'Fooll!' reiterated the Chancellor, with a louring brow and flashing eyes. **1888** F. HUME *Madame Midas* I. Prol., The other did not take the slightest notice of his friend's lowering looks.

2. *transf.* Of the clouds, sky, weather, etc.: Gloomy, dark, threatening. Sometimes *fig.* of attendant circumstances. Occas. influenced by association with LOWERING *ppl. a.*

a **1450** *Fysshynge w. Angle* (1883) 20 Ye schall angle as y seyde be for in darke lowryng wedur. **1530** PALSGR. 317/2 Lowring as the wether is, whan it is disposed to rayne, *sombreux*. *a* **1548** HALL *Chron. Hen. VI* 168 Iames Butler.. seyng fortunes loweryng chaunce..with a great numbre fled away. **1579** TWYNE (*title*) Physicke against Fortune..as well in tyme of the bryght shynyng sunne of prosperitie, as also of the foule lowryng stormes of aduersitie. **1593** SHAKS. *Rich. II*, I. iii. 187 Nor euer write, regreete or reconcile This lowring tempest of your home-bred hate. **1611** BIBLE *Matt.* xvi. 3 The skie is red and lowring. **1669** PEPYS *Diary* 1 May, And mighty earnest to go, though the day was very lowering. *a* **1720** SHEFFIELD (Dk. Buckhm.) *Wks.* (1753) II. 51 Our Climate is..perpetually cloudy, low'ring, and uncertain. **1746–7** HERVEY *Medit.* II. 36 Virtue gains Loveliness from a louring Providence. **1772–84** COOK *Voy.* (1790) V. 1697 A storm came on, preceeded by a lowering darkness. **1804** J. GRAHAME *Sabbath* 814 So light displays its loveliest effect In lowering skies. **1821–2** PRAED *Eve of Battle* Poems (1864) II. 3 A lowering sound of doubt and fear Breaks sudden on the startled ear. **1873** BLACK *Pr. Thule* i. 3 The black peaks were holding converse with the louring clouds. **1878** LECKY *Eng. in 18th C.* I. iii. 474 The calm or louring aspect of foreign affairs.

† **b.** Of liquor: Turbid. *Obs.*

1703 *Art & Myst. of Vintners* 35 Sack that is lumpish or lowring.

† **3.** Lurking, skulking. *Obs.*

? *a* **1400** *Morte Arth.* 1446 We lurkede undyr lee as lowrande wreches! **1575** GASCOIGNE *Pr. Pleas. Kenilw.* (1821) 8, I..Have led a low'ring life in restless pain. **1583** *Leg. Bp. St. Androis* 716 Nor it had bene ane hieland quow Lurcane and lowring, I wat not how.

Hence '**louringly**, '**loweringly** *adv.*, gloomily, sullenly, threateningly; '**loweringness**.

1530 PALSGR. 241/1 Lowringnesse of the wether, *sombrevseté*. **1576** GASCOIGNE *Philomene* (Arb.) 106 And now on hir, and then on him, Full lowringly did leare. **1680** AUBREY *Lives, Sir H. Blount* (1898) I. 110 They..looked louringly on him. **1834** M. SCOTT *Cruise Midge* xxiii. (1842) 477 The day broke very loweringly. **1872** *Daily News* 12 Aug., The clouds come loweringly down to meet the mist.

loury, lowery ('laʊərɪ), *a.* Also 7 lowry. [f. LOUR *sb.*[1] + -Y.] Of the sky, etc.: Dull, gloomy, threatening.

1648 J. BEAUMONT *Psyche* VII. xix, And in my wretched Beings lowry morn Dawn'd not eternal Night. *Ibid.* XVII. xxxii, But strait their Sunshine turn'd to lowry weather. **1686** GOAD *Celest. Bodies* I. xiii. 67, XXI 1 m. close, H. wd m. often lowry, some shedding o. **1735** DYCHE & PARDON *Dict.*, *Lowry*, hazy, dull dark Weather, when the Air looks thick..and Rain is threatened. **1864** D. G. MITCHELL *Sev. Stor.* 39 The day was lowery. **1888** BARRIE *Auld Licht Idylls* xi. (1902) 84/1 Loury grew the sky.

loury, obs. form of LOWRIE *Sc.*

lous, obs. or dial. form of LOOSE *v.*

louse (laʊs), *sb.* *Pl.* lice (laɪs). Forms: 1 lús, luus, 3 luse, 4 lous, 4–5 lowce, 4–7 lows(e, 6– louse. *Pl.* 1 lýs, 4–5 luys, 4–6 lys(e, (4 lyes(e, -yse, 5 lies(e, lise), 6 *Sc.* lyiss, 4–7 lyce, 6– lice. [A Com. Teut. fem. cons.-stem: OE. *lús* = MLG., MDu. *lûs* (Du. *luis*), OHG., MHG. *lûs* (mod.G. *laus*), ON. *lús* (Da., Sw. *lus*).]

1. a. A parasitic insect of the genus *Pediculus*, infesting the human hair and skin and causing great irritation by its presence. Applied also to the numerous other kinds of insects parasitic on mammals, birds, and plants, and to the degraded crustaceans which infest fishes: often with qualification, as ***bird-, fish-, plant-, sea-louse***.

c **725** *Corpus Gloss.* (Hessels) P. 310 *Pedacla*, luus. *c* **1000** *Hexam. Basil* xvii. (1849) 24 Hine byton lys. *c* **1000** ÆLFRIC *Hom.* II. 192 He afylde eal heora land mid..hundes lusum. *a* **1300** *Sarmun* v. in *E.E.P.* (1862) 1 Of þi schuldres and of þi side þou miȝte hunti luse and flee. **1340** HAMPOLE *Pr. Consc.* 651 þou forth bringes of þi-self here Nites, lyse, and other vermyn sere. **1377** LANGL. *P. Pl.* B. v. 196 A tauny tabarde of twelue wynter age..ful of lys crepynge. **1387** TREVISA *Higden* (Rolls) VI. 387 Arnulphus..[was] destroyed, and i-ȝete with luys riȝt to þe deth. **1460–70** *Bk. Quintessence* 19 Medicyn..for to distrie lies þat ben engendrid of corrupt humouris. **1597** BEARD *Theatre God's Judgem.* (1612) 389 In time it corrupted his flesh, and turned into lice. **1615** LATHAM *Falconry* (1633) Words explained, *Lice*, are a small kinde of white vermine, running amongst the feathers of the Hawke. **1673** *Phil. Trans.* VIII. 6038 In a Lowse I observe indeed..a short tapering nose with a hole in it. **1732** ARBUTHNOT *Rules of Diet* I. 247 It has always been believed that the immoderate use of them [*sc.* Figs] generates Lice. **1802** BINGLEY *Anim. Biog.* (1813) III. 345 When we examine the human Louse with the microscope, its external deformity strikes us with disgust. **1897** MARY KINGSLEY *W. Africa* 253 Sleep impossible—mosquitoes! lice!!

b. In phrases and proverbs (mostly *obs.*), chiefly as a type of something worthless or contemptible, as ***not worth a louse***, ***not to care (three skips of) a louse***. † ***to prick a louse***, to be a tailor.

1588 GREENE *Alcida* (1617) I 2, Lest thy..Logike prooue not worth a lowse. **1598** B. JONSON *Ev. Man in Hum.* I. iii. (end), Care 'll kill a cat, vp-tailes all, and a louse for the hang-man. **1633** —— *Tale Tub* II. i, I care not, I, Sir, not three skips of a Lowse for you. **1630** *Articles agst. Cosin in C.'s Corr.* etc. (Surtees) I. 198 Many yeares before John Cosin could tell how to prick a lowse in his fathers shopp at Norwich. **1678** OTWAY *Friendship in F.* 50 The very poets themselves that were wont to stand in awe of me, care not a louse for me now. **1699** SWIFT *Mrs. Harris's Petit.*, 'Tis not that I value the money three skips of a louse. **1749** CHESTERF. *Lett.* (1792) II. cxciii. 219, I..don't care a louse if I never see it again. **1785** BURNS *Addr. to Deil* xi, When the best wark-lume i' the house..Is instant made no worth a louse. **1836** MARRYAT *Midsh. Easy* xii, I say, Mr. Gossett, have you got the spirit of a louse?

2. *transf.* Applied in scorn to human beings.

1633 *Costlie Whore* I. ii. in Bullen *O. Pl.* IV, Come away, fellow louse, thou art ever eating. **1901** R. KIPLING *Kim* i. 25 Why hast thou allowed this louse Lutuf to live so long?

3. *attrib.* and *Comb.*, as *louse-mite*; **louse-berry (tree)**, *Euonymus europæus*; **louse-borne** *a.*, of diseases: transmitted by lice; **louse-burr**, *Xanthium strumarium*; **louse-disease**, PHTHIRIASIS; **louse-land** (*slang*), Scotland; † **louse-powder**, powder for destroying lice; † **louse-pricking**, tailoring, also *attrib.*; † **louse-seed**, ? fleabane; **louse-trap** *dial.* and *slang*, a comb.; **lousewort**, † (*a*) Stinking Hellebore, *Helleborus fœtidus*; (*b*) any plant of the genus *Pedicularis*, esp. *P. palustris* and *P. sylvatica*; (*c*) Yellow Rattle, *Rhinanthus Cristagalli*; (*d*) *Delphinium Staphisagria* (Britten & Holland).

1866 *Treas. Bot.*, *Louseberry-Tree, *Euonymus europæus*. **1919** W. BYAM et al. (*title*) Trench fever: a *louse-borne disease. **1942** *Times* 21 Sept. 5/3 Typhus, which is louse-borne,..was overcome by active measures of disinfestation. **1964** M. HYNES *Med. Bacteriol.* (ed. 8) xxi. 322 *Trep. recurrentis obermeieri* is typical of the louse-borne disease.

1970 *Control of Communicable Dis. in Man* (Amer. Public Health Assoc.) (ed. 11) 275 (*heading*) Typhus-fever, epidemic louse-borne. **1974** PASSMORE & ROBSON *Compan. Med. Stud.* III. xii. 75/1 Louse-borne relapsing fever is a disease of cold weather. **1578** LYTE *Dodoens* I. viii. 14 *Xanthium*, *Louse Burre, or the lesser Clote. **1879** J. R. REYNOLDS *Syst. Med.* V. 973 *Louse-disease..may last indefinitely if unchecked. *a* **1700** B. E. *Dict. Cant. Crew*, *Louse-land, Scotland. **1877** MURRAY *List Coll. Econ. Entomol.* 14 *Sarcoptidæ* (Itch and *Louse Mites). **1578** LYTE *Dodoens* III. xxxix. 372 This herbe is called..in base Almaigne *Luyscruyt*, and the seede made into powder *Luysepouder*, that is to say, *Lousepowder. **1710** *London's Medicinal Informer* 53 His Father's *Louse-pricking Trade, i.e. Tayloring. **1756** TOLDERVY *Hist. 2 Orphans* I. 164 It would be well for you, if you'd stay at home, and mind your louse-pricking. *c* **1265** *Voc. Plants* in Wr.-Wülcker 559/6 *Psillium*, *lusesed. *a* **1700** B. E. *Dict. Cant. Crew*, *A Scotch *Louse-trap*, a Comb. [See Eng. Dial. Dict.] **1578** LYTE *Dodoens* III. xxvi. 351 *Louswurt..Fuchsius counteth for a kinde of blacke hellebor. **1597** GERARDE *Herbal* II. ccccxxi. 913 Of red Rattle, or Lousewoort. **1756** J. HILL *Brit. Herbal* 120 Our farmers have an opinion that sheep feeding on them [Coxcombs] become subject to vermin, whence the English name lousewort. **1901** *Speaker* 21 Sept. 692/2 Yellow louseworts.

louse (laʊz), *v.* Also 5 lowsyn, 6 lowze, 6–7 louze, lowse. [f. LOUSE *sb.*]

1. a. *trans.* To clear of lice, remove lice from (a person, oneself, a garment).

c **1440** *Promp. Parv.* 316/2 Lowsyn, *pediculo.* **1514** BARCLAY *Cyt. & Uplondyshm.* (Percy Soc.) 11 Efte was she busy, them lowsynge and kemynge. **1596** SPENSER *State Irel.* Wks. (Globe) 631/2 Howe handsome it is to lye and sleepe, or to lowze themselves in the sunn-shine. **1596** LODGE *Wits Miserie* (1879) 112 Goe wretche as thou art and louse thyselfe. **1663** PEPYS *Diary* 6 June, To York House, where the Russia Embassador do lie: and there I saw his people go up and down louseing themselves. **1795** S. HEARNE *Journ. to N. Ocean* 325 He frequently set five or six of his strapping wives to work to louse their hairy deer-skin shifts. **1822** E. D. CLARKE *Trav. Russia* (1839) 52/1 [They] were lousing each other; and it surprised us that they did not discontinue their work..as we entered. **1824** *Edin. Rev.* XL. 482 Prince Potemkin..used to louse himself at dinner.

fig. **1596** NASHE *Saffron Walden* 15, I haue here tooke the paines to nit and louze ouer the Doctours booke.

b. *intr.* for *refl.*

1570 in Levins *Manip.* 225/2 [printed *Bouse*]. **1655** tr. *Com. Hist. Francion* 27 That little Beggers brat..was taken not long since lowsing under a hedge. **1673** R. HEAD *Canting Acad.* 27 We beg'd together, lay together and louz'd together. **1727** SOMERVILLE *Fable* xiv. III. 119 A tailor despicably poor, In every hole for shelter crept, On the same bulk, botch'd, lous'd, and slept.

2. *intr.* To be infested with lice. *Obs. rare*[−1].

1605 SHAKS. *Lear* III. ii. 29 The Codpiece that will house, before the head has any; The Head, and he shall Lowse.

3. a. With *up*. To infest with lice. orig. *U.S.*

1931 *San Francisco Examiner* 29 Jan. 34/4 Lousey, now fixed in Broadway actor jargon, is from small time troupers. .. The Maine tavern keeper who refused lodging to a repertoire company..explained: 'The last troupe loused up the beddin'.' **1931** *Gang World* Jan. 14 The precinct was fumigated yesterday, an' you ain't gonna louse it up again. **1955** R. P. HOBSON *Nothing too Good for Cowboy* i. 15, I got loused up in that cabin once. **1968** *Listener* 9 May 601/2, I was occasionally loused-up myself, and people, rather than pass me, used to go on the other side of the road.

b. *slang.* To spoil, to mess up. Const. *up*. Also **loused-up** *a.* orig. *U.S.*

1934 J. O'HARA *Appointment in Samarra* ii. 61 There's fifty bucks in it for you on account of lousing up your date. **1938** *Amer. Speech* XIII. 195 Louse up the show. **1948** *Sat. Even. Post* 25 Sept. 41 The hospital field is loused up enough. **1957** F. & R. LOCKRIDGE *Practise to Deceive* (1959) ii. 29 Of all the loused-up operations. **1958** E. DUNDY *Dud Avocado* II. i. 185 He said if I'm really serious about getting a part..the easiest way to louse it up would be to turn up with a hundred other people. **1959** *Tamarack Rev.* XII. 24 What a way to louse up this new magenta outfit... You'd think she'd spent her afternoon at a Yiddish tear-jerker. **1959** 'S. RANSOME' *I'll die for You* x. 119 Had a rough time getting her to come back... Damned if I'll let you louse me up now. **1967** [see next]. **1969** *N.Y. Rev. Bks.* 10 Jan. 38/2 It is safe to predict that President-elect Nixon will look for some outstanding public figure for this job, even though it may louse up the table of organization. **1972** *Human World* Nov. 48 If..he tries to sabotage his actions—he louses up a machine he is purporting to work, for example [etc.]. **1973** R. LUDLUM *Matlock Paper* i. 7 A loused-up army record. **1975** *New Yorker* 5 May 115/1 The picture is a cheerfully loused-up reworking of the legend of King Arthur's Grail hunt.

Hence '**lousing** *vbl. sb.*, also *attrib.*

a **1640** MASSINGER *Very Woman* III. ii. (1655) Dost thou think any State Would..trust thee with a secret above lousing? **1707** J. STEVENS tr. *Quevedo's Com. Wks.* (1709) 226 He went into the lousing Room, and turn'd a little Board that hung at the Door, on which was written, *One is lousing.*

louse, Sc. and north. form of LOOSE.

lousenger, loush, var. ff. LOSENGER, LUSH.

louser. [f. LOUSE *v.* + -ER.] **a.** One who louses. **b.** One who spoils things: used as a general term of abuse. Also **louser-up**.

1575 R. B. *Apius & Virginia* B 1, Yea but what am I, ..A Louse or a louser, a Leeke or a Larke. **1960** B. MOORE *Luck of Ginger Coffey* iv. 86 You louser... What the hell do you know about love? All you want is to get up some woman's skirts. **1966** A. PRIOR *Operators* viii. 110 He entered her, cursing all women... The sluts, bags, lousers, slags. **1967** C. COCKBURN *I, Claud* xxxv. 438 Hardly anyone can be packed off to some social equivalent of the Russian 'virgin lands' for lousing things up, because almost every louser-up can convincingly claim that he was not really responsible for the thing that happened. **1968** 'N. BLAKE' *Private Wound* vii. 108 If any of you lousers interfere I'll plug him in the belly.

lousily ('laʊzɪlɪ), *adv.* [f. LOUSY + -LY[2].] In a lousy manner; filthily, meanly, scurvily.

1611 L. BARRY *Ram Alley* v. i. H 2 b, For I had rather dye, then in a street liue poore and lowsily.

lousiness ('laʊzɪnɪs). [f. LOUSY + -NESS.] The condition of being lousy; *fig.* meanness, vileness. †Also a mock-title.

1530 in PALSGR. 241/1. **1547** BOORDE *Brev. Health* §273 In greke it is named *Phthiriasis*. In Englyshe it is named lousines. **1608** MIDDLETON *Trick to Catch Old One* I. iv, May it please your worshipful lousiness. **1664** EVELYN *Sylva* xxvii. (1679) 141 Trees (especially Fruit-bearers) are infested with the Measels..to this commonly succeeds lousiness. **1682** SHADWELL *Medal* 89 Who by reviling Patriots, think to be From louziness and hunger ever free. **1822** GOOD *Study Med.* IV. 645 Species I. Malis Pediculi. Lousiness. **1872** W. AITKEN *Sci. & Pract. Med.* (ed. 6) I. 200 Lousiness is a morbid state in which lice develop themselves to such an extent that a pruriginous eruption is produced.

lousious, obs. form of LUSCIOUS.

lou'sologist. *humorous nonce-wd.* One who has a scientific knowledge of lice.

1835 SYD. SMITH in Lady Holland *Mem.* (1855) II. 367 Mineralogists, astronomers, ornithologists, and lousologists.

louss(e, loust, obs. ff. LOOSE, LUST.

lousy ('laʊzɪ), *a.* Also 4–8 lowsy(e, (4 lousi, 5 lowse, -i), 6–7 lous-, lowsie, -ye, -zie, -zy, 8 lowsey. [f. LOUSE *sb.* + -Y.]

A. *adj.* **1. a.** Full of lice, infested by lice.

1377 LANGL. *P. Pl.* B. v. 195 With an hode on his hed a lousi hatte aboue. **1486** *Bk. St. Albans* B v, A medecyne for an hawke that is lowse. **1523** FITZHERB. *Husb.* §117 There be horses that wyll be lowsy, and it cometh of pouertie, colde and yll kepynge. *a* **1572** KNOX *Hist. Ref.* Wks. 1846 I. 74 Your cord and lowsie coit and sark. **1652** CULPEPPER *Eng. Physic.* (1809) 134 Some authors say, the eating of them [figs] makes people lousy. **1653** WALTON *Compl. Angler* 130 If I catch a Trout in one Meadow, he shall be white and faint, and very like to be lowsie. **1677** JOHNSON in *Ray's Corr.* (1848) 127 The sight of one of these [salmon] makes a fisher leap for joy, especially if his gills be lousy. **1697** *Phil. Trans.* XIX. 394, I call him the Lousie Beetle, because when taken, he is generally found to be infested with small Vermin, like Lice. **1707** MORTIMER *Husb.* 253 The Sweet-bryar and Gooseberry that are only lousie in dry times or in very hot and dry places. **1710** ADDISON *Tatler* No. 229 ¶1 A very ordinary Microscope shows us, that a Louse is itself a very lousy Creature. **1890** C. PATMORE *Let.* 23 May in B. Champneys *Mem.* (1900) II. 136 These are both large fish, but they are habitually what the fishermen call 'unclean' and 'lousy'; so they don't try to catch them. **1901** R. KIPLING *Kim* i. 26, I do not give to a lousy Tibetan.

†**b.** Characterized by the presence of lice. ***lousy disease, evil*** = PHTHIRIASIS. *Obs.*

1519 HORMAN *Vulg.* iii. 34 Antiochus, Sylla, and Herodde dyed in the lowsy euyll. **1538** ELYOT *Dict.*, *Pherecydes*,.. which dyed of the lousy sickenesse. **1579–80** NORTH *Plutarch, Sylla* (1595) 520 Acastus the sonne of Pelias died of the lowsie euill. **1774** GOLDSM. *Nat. Hist.* (1776) VII. 274 The Pthiriasis [*sic*], or lousy disease, though very little known at present, was frequent enough among the ancients. **1830** LINDLEY *Nat. Syst. Bot.* 138 The lousy diseases to which people are very subject in those countries.

c. lousy grass, †(*a*) Stinking Hellebore, *Helleborus fœtidus*; (*b*) *Spergula arvensis* (1875 in Britten & Holland).

1597 GERARDE *Herbal* II. ccclxi. 827 The thirde and fourth [kinds of Black Hellebore] are named in the Germane toong *Lowszkraut*, that is *Peduncularis*, or Lowsie grasse. **1611** COTGR. s.v. *Ellebore*.

d. 'Swarming' with; abundantly supplied with (money, people, etc.); full of. Const. *with. slang* (orig. *U.S.*).

1843 *Spirit of Times* 4 Mar. 7/3 He was lousy with money, and dared any man to face him. **1856** *Democratic State Jrnl.* (Sacramento, Calif.) 6 Oct. 2/3 The bed of the river is perfectly 'lousy' with gold. **1864** A. J. MUNBY *Diary* 15 July in D. Hudson *Munby* (1972) 199 Why Sir, these unfortunates are all over the place: the ground (he added with a gesture of disgust) is *lousy* with them. **1928** S. VINES *Humours Unreconciled* i. 13 The Totsuka Club was..in the words of Mr. Podler, 'just lousy with liars'. **1934** V. M. YEATES *Winged Victory* xix. 150 And if the Dover Patrol was costly in life, were not shipping magnates lousy with shekels? **1936** W. HOLTBY *South Riding* II. i. 89 Leckton told me last month they threw in sixteen and a half couple of hounds and couldn't see a dog. Lost in thistles and willow herb—but lousy with foxes. **1956** R. BRADDON *Nancy Wake* xiii. 153 The town was lousy with Germans, she noted.

2. *fig.* Dirty, filthy, obscene. Also as a general term of abuse: Mean, scurvy, sorry, vile, contemptible. Also, inferior, poor, bad; ill; in low health or spirits.

c **1386** CHAUCER *Friar's T.* 169 A lowsy Iogelour kan deceyue thee. **1532** MORE *Confut. Tindale* Wks. (1557) 463/2 He loueth her with suche a lewde lowsye loue, as the lewde lousy louer in lechery loueth himself. **1568** GRAFTON *Chron.* II. 613 His base birth and lowsy lynage. **1596** NASHE *Saffron Walden* 34 It is no vpright conclusion to say whatsoever is long laboured, is lowsie and not worth a straw. **1663** DRYDEN *Wild Gallant* I. i, And to discredit me before Strangers; for a lousie, paltry sum of Mony? **1708** *Brit. Apollo* No. 38. 2/1 Wicked Rhimes..sung to lowsey Tunes. **1768** STERNE *Sent. Journ.* (1775) I. 65 (*Remise Door*) You can never after..be any thing in it [the church], said Pride, but a lousy prebendary. **1786** *Trials, etc. J. Shepperd*, I might pick up the lousy guinea myself and be damned! **1822** D. O'CONNELL *Let.* 22 May in *Corr.* (1972) II. 391 Perhaps to save some lousy postage you wrote across the letter. They stop all such letters in France. **1849** A. GORDON *Diary* 12 July in W. E. Woodward *Way Our People Lived* (1944) viii. 268, I wish I could never hear the word *lousy* again. I am willing to bet that Tommy Plunkett uses it fifty times a day, but he is no worse than the others. It is 'lousy' this and 'lousy' that. The rain is lousy, the trail is lousy, the bacon is lousy, and Gus Thorpe, losing in the card game, has just said that he has had a lousy deal. **1893** STEVENSON *Catriona* 65 The lousiest, lowest, story to hand down to your namesakes in the future. **1922** JOYCE *Ulysses* 18 You come along with your lousy leer and your gloomy jesuit jibes. *a* **1930** D. H. LAWRENCE *Last Poems* (1932) 197 Oh great god of the machine What lousy archangels and angels you have to surround yourself with! **1932** N. MITFORD *Christmas Pudding* xiv. 220, I still think it's lousy of you not to have taken me last night. **1933** 'N. WEST' *Miss Lonelyhearts* (1949) 46, I felt swell before you came, and now I feel lousy. **1937** L. BROMFIELD *Rains Came* I. xxxix. 170 Life is so short and so lousy. **1950** 'S. RANSOME' *Deadly Miss Ashley* xv. 171 She felt too lousy to come to work. A foul cold, she said. **1959** J. BRAINE *Vodi* xi. 153 A dirty rotten little whore, who couldn't wait six months for her husband, not six lousy months before she went off with another man. **1959** R. GANT *World in Jug* 136 That sudden, nervous sweep which made him to my mind one of the lousiest drivers in Paris, city of lousy drivers. **1968** K. WEATHERLY *Roo Shooter* 23 You're not a bad bastard, Hunter,..in spite of your lousy cooking. *Ibid.* 74 'I got fifty-two last night,' he said... 'I only got a lousy twelve,' replied Hunter. **1973** P. MOYES *Curious Affair of Third Dog* xi. 148 A brisk, pretty, coloured nurse came in... 'Ah, you're awake... How do you feel?' 'Lousy,' said Henry.

B. As *adv.* 'Lousily', extremely. Chiefly *N. Amer.*

In quot. 1971 a mere intensive.

1932 *Amer. Speech* VII. 436 A man drunk is..'lousy drunk'. **1936** C. DAY LEWIS *Friendly Tree* xiv. 210 Well, not lousy-drunk. Just comfortable. **1971** D. HEFFRON *Nice Fire & Some Moonpennies* iv. 33 But she didn't lousy come to school that day! What a blow.

lout (laʊt), *sb.*[1] Also 6 loute, loughte, 6–7 lowt(e. [perh. of dialectal origin, connected with LOUT *v.*[1] (cf. ON. *lút-r* stooping) or LOUT *v.*[2]]

1. An awkward ill-mannered fellow; a bumpkin, clown.

a **1548** HALL *Chron., Hen. VI* 110 Callyng them, cowardes, dastardes, and loutes. **1565** GOLDING *Ovid's Met.* (1567) Pref. A iij b, The wyse, the foole: the countrie cloyne: the lerned and the lout. **1591** SHAKS. *Two Gent.* IV. iv. 71 'Tis no trusting to yond foolish Lowt. **1636** T. RANDALL in *Ann. Dubrensia* (1877) 18 Ill thrive the Lowt, that did their mirth gaine-say. **1660** R. COKE *Justice Vind., Arts & Sci.* 20 Will any man say, a great Lout new whipt, is probably like to make a good Schollar. *c* **1720** PRIOR *Old Gentry* 4 His son, and his son's son, Were all but ploughmen, clowns and louts. **1821** CLARE *Vill. Minstr.* I. 19 A more uncouthly lout was hardly seen. **1871** CARLYLE in *Mrs. C.'s Lett.* I. 317 Her particularly stupid huge lout of a son. **1901** *Longm. Mag.* Apr. 546 That lout has actually dared to make love to me.

†**2.** In occasional use: A servant. *Obs.*

1567 DRANT *Horace's Ep.* I. x. E j, Collected coyne is Lord or lowte to eche possessinge man. **1626** SPELMAN *Gloss.* s.v. *Leudes*, Anglis veteribus loute, pro seruiente et subdito.

3. *Rugby School slang.* A common fellow, 'cad'.

1857 HUGHES *Tom Brown* I. v, We never wear caps here. Only the louts wear caps. *Ibid.* I. viii, They would roar out instances of his..shirking some encounter with a lout of half his own size.

lout (laʊt), *sb.*[2] *dial.* [Cf. CLOUT *sb.*[1]] A blow.

c **1650** *Turke & Gowin* 142 in Furnivall *Percy Folio* I. 95 Thou shalt see a tenisse ball that neuer knight in Arthurs hall is able to giue it a lout. **1877** *N.W. Linc. Gloss.* s.v., I fetch'd him a lout upo' th' side o' th' heäd.

†**lout**, *sb.*[3] *Obs.* [f. LOUT *v.*[1]] An inclination, bend.

1596 DALRYMPLE tr. *Leslie's Hist. Scot.* I. 44 Thair the land bowing the selfe be litle and litle, with a certane laich lout and bend with her bosum.

†**lout**, *sb.*[4] *Obs. rare*[−1]. [f. LOUT *v.*[4]] A bellowing noise.

?*a* **1500** *Chester Pl.* vii. 172 Yender lad..The lowt [*v.r.* lowde (? = LUDE[1])] of this horne he shall heare.

lout (laʊt), *v.*[1] Pa. t. and pa. pple. louted. Now *arch.*, *poet.* and *dial.* Forms: 1 lútan, 3 luten, (lutien), *Orm.* lutenn, 4 lute (lote, louȝte, lutte), 5–7 loute, lowte, (5 loutte, lowth, lowtt), 6 lewt(e, 6, 9 *Sc.* loot, 4– lout. *pa. t.* α. *strong* 1 léat, *pl.* luton, 3–4 leat, *pl.* luten. β. *weak* 3 lotte, ? lute, lowtede, 3–5 lut(te, luted, 4–6 lowted, 4– louted. [Orig. a str. vb., OE. *lútan*, pa. t. *léat*, pl. *luton*, pa. pple. *loten*, corresponding to ON. *lúta*, pa. t. *lǫut*, pl. *lutu*, pa. pple. *lotenn* (Sw. *luta*, Da. *lude*), f. Teut. root **leut-*: *laut-*: *lŭt-*:—pre-Teut. **leud-*: *loud-*: *lŭd-*.

The primary sense of the root is prob. that represented in this vb.; it also appears in the senses 'to lurk' (see LOTE *v.*, LOUT *v.*[2], and cf. the cognates there mentioned), 'to deceive' (as in Goth. *liut-s* hypocrite, *lutōn* to deceive, OE. *lot* deceit, *lytegian* to defraud) and 'to be small' (see LITTLE *a.*). Outside Teut., probable cognates are Lith. *liū́deti* to mourn, *liū́dnas* sad, cast down, OSl. *luditi* to deceive, *ludŭ* foolish.]

1. *intr.* To bend, bow, make obeisance; also, to stoop. Occas. *refl.*; also with *down*.

c **825** *Vesp. Psalter* xciv. 6 Cumað weorðien we and forð luten we biforan god. *c* **1200** ORMIN 11392 Þe birrþ biforr þin Laferrd Godd Cneolenn meoclike & lutenn. *c* **1200** LAY. 1880 Ofte hes luten a-dun. *a* **1300** *Cursor M.* 5156 Hailsand forwit him þai lute. *Ibid.* 11614 þai þam luted vnder him. **13**

.. *E.E. Allit. P.* B. 798 Loȝe he loutez hem to Loth to þe grounde. **1375** BARBOUR *Bruce* v. 253 Thar-with-all he lowtit, and his leyf has tane. **1398** TREVISA *Barth. De P.R.* v. xii. (Tollem. MS.) Foure fotid bestis, þat hauen hedes loutynge doun to þe erþewarde. **c 1440** *Gesta Rom.* xxxvi. 144 (Add. MS.) The Steward .. lowted downe, and thanked the Emperour of his grete mercy. *c* **1450** *Merlin* 98 The archebisshop lowted to the swerde, and sawgh letteres of golde in the stiel. **1513** DOUGLAS *Æneis* x. ix. 84 The Troiane prynce down lowtis hym abone. **1590** SPENSER *F.Q.* I. i. 30 He faire the knight saluted, louting low. **1658** CLEVELAND *Rustick Rampant* Wks. (1678) 403 The limber Knights .. who .. can kiss the Hand and lowt with more Grace. *a* **1755** G. WEST *Abuse Trav.* (Imit. Spenser) xli. in Dodsley *Coll. Poems* (1755) II. 98 Tho' to that old mage they louted down. **1826** J. WILSON *Noct. Ambr.* Wks. 1855 I. 147 Dinna loot wi that lang back o yours. **1891** CONAN DOYLE *White Company* iii, I uncovered and louted as I passed.

b. Const. dative or *till, to, unto*: To bow or make obeisance to, reverence. †Also *trans.*

971 *Blickl. Hom.* 223 Sanctus Martinus .. leat forð to ðæm men ðe hine slean mynte. *c* **1200** ORMIN 8961 And till hemm baþe he lutte & bæh. *a* **1225** *St. Marher.* 12 Heo leat lahe to hire leoue lauerd. **1340** *Ayenb.* 239 Þer com on of þe princes, and leat to him. *c* **1375** *Sc. Leg. Saints* xxxiii. (*George*) 343 Þat scho suld god lofe & lowte. *c* **1380** WYCLIF *Wks.* (1880) 306 3if a frere be a mastir .. he shal be loutid & worshipid. *c* **1485** *Digby Myst.* (1882) III. 926 Why lowtt ȝe nat low to my lawdabyll presens? **1522** *World & Child* (Roxb.) Bj, To me men lewte full lowe. **1596** SPENSER *F.Q.* IV. iii. 5 Thrise lowted lowly to the noble Mayd. **1612** DRAYTON *Poly-olb.* v. 78 All lowting lowe to him, him humbly they observe. **1813** SCOTT *Rokeby* IV. viii, To Rokeby, next, he louted low, Then stood erect.

c. *fig.* To bow, stoop, submit (to).

c **1330** R. BRUNNE *Chron.* (1810) 282 Þe ildes aboute alle salle loute vnto þat lond. *c* **1350** *Will. Palerne* 2900 He ga[r]te þe grettest to hire prison louȝte. *c* **1500** *Elegy on Henry* 45 in *Percy's Reliv.*, To whome grete astates obeyde and lowttede. **1568** C. WATSON *Polyb.* 100 The Carthaginenses perceiving how they were not able at that present to cope with the Romans, louted for the time. **1801** MACNEILL *Poems* (1844) 118 'He ne'er can lout', I musing said, 'To ply the fleeching fawning trade'. **1819** KEATS *Otho* III. i. 17 Was't to this end I louted and became The menial of Mars?

2. *trans.* To bow (the head); to let (the countenance) fall. *rare.*

1297 R. GLOUC. (Rolls) 2479 Hengist vaire him þonkede & is heued lotte [*v.r.* lowtede] adoun. *a* **1300** *Cursor M.* 16350 Iesus thoght ful mikel scam, and luted dun his cher.

† **lout** (laʊt), *v.*² *Obs.* Forms: 1 lútian, 3 lutien, 4 lute(n, 5 loute, lowt. [OE. *lútian* weak vb. = OHG. *lûzên* (MHG. *lûzen*) f. Teut. root **leut-*: *laut-*: *lŭt-* (see LOUT *v.*¹); cf. OHG. *loscên* (:—*OTeut. stem **lut-skǣ-*) to lurk, LUSK.] *intr.* To lurk, lie hid, skulk, sneak. Used both in material and immaterial sense.

c **825** *Vesp. Hymns* xiii. 26 Ðu wunda lutiendra god ætstondes lece. *c* **1000** ÆLFRIC *Josh.* ii. 16 Farað eow nu .. to muntum and lutiað þær þry daȝas. *c* **1205** LAY. 21509 Duden heom alle clane into þan scipen grunde & hæhte heom þere lutie [*c* **1275** lotie] wel. *c* **1230** *Hali Meid.* 43 Ha [*sc.* prude] luteð iþe heorte. *a* **1250** *Owl & Night.* 373 Þe hare luteþ al day, Ac noþeles i-seo he may, 3if [etc.]. *c* **1250** *Long Life* 29 in *O.E. Misc.* 156 Ac deþ luteþ in his scho. **1390** GOWER *Conf.* I. 107 For love is of himself so derne, It luteth in a mannes herte. *c* **1470** HARDING *Chron.* cxx. ix, Thus semeth well in armes a knight to dye, And not in bed to lye, loure, and loute, Tyll death hym kyll with paynes cruelly. **1483** CAXTON *Gold. Leg.* 378/2 Valeryan .. fonde this holy man urbane lowtyng emonge the buryellys.

b. *simply.* To lie.

c **1460** J. RUSSELL *Bk. Nurture* 579 Þey [fish] must be tekyn of as þey in þe disshe lowt.

lout, *v.*³ Also 6–7 lowt(e. [? f. LOUT *sb.*¹]

1. *trans.* To treat with contumely, mock. (Cf. FLOUT *v.*) Also, *to lout* (a person) *out of* (something). *Obs.*

c **1530** REDFORD *Play Wit & Sci.* (1848) 41 So mokte, so lowted, so made a sot! *a* **1553** UDALL *Royster D.* III. iii. (Arb.) 44 He is louted and laughed to skorne, For the veriest dolte that euer was borne. **1581** J. BELL *Haddon's Answ. Osor.* 258 b, Here is no want of any thing nowe, but of some gyering Gnato, which may lowt this Thraso out of hys paynted coat. **1591** SHAKS. *1 Hen. VI*, IV. iii. 13, I am lowted by a Traitor Villaine, And cannot helpe the noble Cheualier. **1591** HARINGTON *Orl. Fur.* XII. xxii, She will finde some sleight and pretie shift, With her accustom'd coynes him to lout. *c* **1650** *Eger & Grine* 672 in Furnivall *Percy Folio* I. 375 Eger .. lay and heard her lowte him like a knave.

2. *intr.* To act as a lout; to loll about.

1807 W. IRVING *Salmag.* No. 3 (1811) I. 59 Those sprigs of the ton .. Who lounge, and who lout, and who booby about, No knowledge within, and no manners without.

† **lout,** *v.*⁴ *Obs.* Also 6 lowte. [? Echoic: cf. ROWT, LOW *vbs.*] *intr.* To low or bellow.

1530 PALSGR. 615/2, I lowte as a kowe or bull dothe. *a* **1700** B. E. *Dict. Cant. Crew*, To Lout, to Low like a Cow, or Bellow like a Bull. **1847** in HALLIWELL.

† **'loutardly,** *a. Obs. rare*⁻¹. [f. LOUT *sb.*¹ + -ARD + -LY¹.] ? Lubberly.

1658 tr. *Bergerac's Satyr. Char.* xiii. 53 That loutardly shepheard.

† **'louter.** *Obs. rare.* [f. LOUT *v.*¹ + -ER¹.] One who bows (to a person); a worshipper.

a **1340** HAMPOLE *Psalter* xxi. 29 Whare verray louters loutes þe fadere. *Ibid.* cxxxi. 7 Verray louters of God.

loutheris = *lochtris*, obs. pl. of LACHTER *Sc.*

c **1375** *Sc. Troy-bk.* (Horstm.) II. 2989 Loutheris frome his hed cane ryf. **1535** STEWART *Cron. Scot.* 2990 Loutheris of his faire ȝallow haire.

'louting, *vbl. sb. Obs.* exc. *arch.* [f. LOUT *v.*¹ + -ING¹.] The action of LOUT *v.*¹; bowing, cringing.

1340 HAMPOLE *Pr. Consc.* 7847 Þare es lowtyng and reverence. *c* **1410** LOVE *Bonavent. Mirr. Sacr. Christ's Body* (Gibbs MS.) lf. 124 Þe kyng with loutynge of hys heued .. dyde reuerence. **1549** COVERDALE, etc. *Erasm. Par. Eph.* Prol., Promotion obtained by .. hipocritical lowting. **1683** CHALKHILL *Thealma & Cl.* 81 Their low lootings lift them a step higher. **1819** KEATS *Let. to J. Taylor* 23 Aug., Is this worth louting or playing the hypocrite for?

'louting, *ppl. a.*¹ [f. LOUT *v.*¹ + -ING².] Bowing down, deferential.

1602 *2nd Pt. Return fr. Parnass.* III. iv. 1389 Iustly to esteeme my verses lowting pitch. **1603** FLORIO *Montaigne* I. xlii. (1632) 141 If he [a king] chance to be jealous or capricious, will our lowting-curtzies .. bring him in tune againe? **1886** STEVENSON *Kidnapped* xv. (1888) 138 Our lowland beggars .. had a louting, flattering way with them.

† **'louting,** *ppl. a.*² *Obs.* [f. LOUT *v.*² + -ING².] That louts or skulks. In quot. *absol.*

a **1325** *Names of Hare* in *Rel. Ant.* I. 133 He shal saien on oreisoun In the worshipe of the hare .. The louting, the westlokere.

louting ('laʊtɪŋ), *ppl. a.*³ [f. LOUT *sb.*¹ + -ING².] Acting like a lout, loafing.

1836 W. IRVING *Astoria* I. 11 A louting train of Indians, hanging about the establishment, eating and drinking at his expense. **1864** PALGRAVE *Norm. & Eng.* IV. 28 Ejecting the lazy, louting, secular canons.

loutish ('laʊtɪʃ), *a.* [f. LOUT *sb.*¹ + -ISH.] Characteristic of a lout, clumsy, clownish, lubberly.

a **1553** UDALL *Royster D.* III. i. (Arb.) 39 Rather than with such a loutishe dolte to marie. **1590** NASHE *Pasquil's Apol.* I. D b, What a lazie, lowtish kind of argument is this. **1616** R. C. *Times' Whistle* v. 1755 Helottes .. which wer their slaves, A sort of loutish abject-minded knaves. **1821** SCOTT *Kenilw.* xiii, His loutish savage-looking demeanour. **1900** F. T. BULLEN *With Christ at Sea* iii. 57 The big loutish boy who was my colleague.

Hence **'loutishly** *adv.*, **'loutishness.**

a **1553** UDALL *Royster D.* III. v. (Arb.) 55 He disgraced hym selfe, his loutishnesse is suche. **1580** HOLLYBAND *Treas. Fr. Tong, Lourdement*, loutishlye. **1871** MISS MULOCK *Fair France* 158 The .. small, wiry, active frame was merged into a larger-limbed, honest loutishness. **1888** MRS. H. WARD *R. Elsmere* 489 The Arabs outside made loutishly flattering remarks.

† **'loutlike,** *a. Obs. rare*⁻¹. [f. LOUT *sb.*¹ + -LIKE.] = prec.

1567 GOLDING *Ovid's Met.* XIV. (1593) 335 The shepherd .. with his lowtlike leapes Did counterfet their minion dance.

‖**loutrophoros** (luːtrəʊ'fɔərɒs). *Cl. Antiq.* [Gr. λουτρο-φόρος, f. λουτρόν water for a bath + -φορός bearing.] A tall two-handled vessel used for carrying water to the nuptial bath.

1896 C. H. SMITH in *Catal. Greek & Etruscan Vases Brit. Mus.* III. 366 Beside her is a box or table on three legs terminating in lions' paws, on which stand a pyxis and an oinochoè with tall handle and neck (loutrophoros?). **1931** *Times Lit. Suppl.* 16 July 563/2 A splendid loutrophoros by Polygnotus. **1935** RICHTER & MILNE *Shapes & Names Athenian Vases* 5 *Loutrophoros*, .. tall vase with high, funnel-shaped neck, slender body, and flaring mouth. Water was brought in it from the fountain Kallirrhoe for the nuptial bath, and it was placed on tombs of unmarried persons. **1967** R. S. FOLSOM *Handbk. Greek Pott.* 157 The loutrophoros usually was an amphora, but sometimes the form appears as a hydria with three handles.

louvre ('luvə(r)). Forms: 4 luver, 4–7 lover, (5 lewer, lovyre, lowere, luvere, 5–6 lovery, -ie, 6 lofer, lour, lovour), 6–9 loover, (7 loovar, loure, lower), 9 luffer, *dial.* luvver, 7–9 louvre, 7– louver. The form **louvre** is now usual in the U.K. and **louver** in the U.S. [a. OF. *lover, lovier*, perh. an alteration (with euphonic *v* as in *pouvoir* POWER) of **loer*:—med.L. **lōdārium* cogn. w. the synonymous med.L. *lodium* (quot. *c* 1425). The ultimate etymology is obscure; some have compared the mod.Icel. *hlóð* pl., hearth, chimney-place. The form *louvre* arises from confusion with F. *Louvre* (see next).]

1. A domed turret-like erection on the roof of the hall or other apartment in a mediæval building with lateral openings for the passage of smoke or the admission of light. (Cf. LANTERN 4.)

1367–8 *Durham Acc. Rolls* (Surtees) 386 In sclatario operanti super aulam .. pro luuers de novo factis. **1393** LANGL. *P. Pl.* C. XXI. 288 Cheke we and cheyne we and eche chyne stoppe, þat no light leope yn at louer ne at loupe. *c* **1425** *Voc.* in Wr.-Wülcker 667/32 *Hoc lodium*, lowere. *c* **1470** HENRYSON *Mor. Fab.* III. (*Cock & Fox*) xxvii, The cok ouer the feildis tuke his flicht, And in at the wedowis lewer couth he lycht. **1496** *Dives & Paup.* (W. de W.) I. xliv. 85/2 Whan smoke medled with fyre cometh out of an house .. by the louerys, men .. wyll saye that that house shall go on fyre. **1544–5** in Willis & Clark *Cambridge* (1886) II. 219 To a carpenter for makynge yᵉ lover in yᵉ hall vijˢ. **1575** T. CARTWRIGHT *2nd Replie agst. Whitgift* 621 To proue a bishop ouer the ministers off a diocese .. is to set the fondacion vpon the louer. **1596** SPENSER *F.Q.* VI. x. 42 Ne lightned was with window, nor with louer. **1599** HALL *Sat.* V. i. 119 Whose shrill saints-bell hangs on his louerie. **1599** MARSTON *Sco. Villanie* II. v. 197 He .. Hath drawn false lights from pitch-black loueries. **1601** MUNDAY *Death Earl Huntington* L 3, For all the issue both of vent and light, Came from a loouer at the towers toppe. **1650** W. BROUGH *Sacr. Princ.* (1659) 173 Fly to the windows of glory, mount to those louvers on high. **1756** C. LUCAS *Ess. Waters* III. 50 Every bath [has] a louvre or opening at top, to give a current to the air. **1849** FREEMAN *Archit.* 251 *note*, A cloister runs round the lowest stage, crowned with a sort of square louvre. **1865** KINGSLEY *Herew.* iv, The smoke went out through a louver in the roof.

†**2.** A similar erection serving as a dovecote. *Obs.*

?**1583** *MS. Bursary Acc. St. John's Coll. Oxon.*, Lofer. **1585** LUPTON *Thous. Notable Th.* (1675) 150 Hang a great glass in the top of the Lovour. **1605** SYLVESTER *Du Bartas* II. iii. I. *Vocation* 872 Pigeons .. Stooping at this and that, that to their Louver .. they hardly can recover. *a* **1661** FULLER *Worthies, Northamptonsh.* II. (1662) 279 Pigeons .. famished for want of food, as unable to fly .. out at the Lover.

3. A hole in a roof for the passage of smoke; a chimney. *Obs.* exc. *dial.* (see E.D.D.).

1375–6 *Abingdon Abb. Acc.* (1892) 30 In factura j louer pro cotagio juxta, vijd. **1519** HORMAN *Vulg.* 140 Moche of the showre felle into the louer [L. *impluvium*]: but moche more into the barton.

transf. **1609** HEYWOOD *Brit. Troy* VII. xii. 143 There is a steepe decliuy way lookes downe, Which to th' Infernall Kingdome Orpheus guides, Whose loouer, vapors breathes.

4. a. Chiefly *pl.* An arrangement of sloping boards, laths or slips of glass overlapping each other, so as to admit air, but exclude rain. Originally, such a contrivance as used to close the apertures of a 'louvre' (sense 1). Cf. *louvre-board* in 5. Also used for other purposes, e.g. to deflect air issuing from an opening or to prevent the direct passage of light through it. Used in *sing.* in same sense; also, an individual slat or strip of such an arrangement.

1555 EDEN *Decades W. Ind.* (Arb.) 376 The roofe of thynne boordes open in sundry places lyke vnto louers to lette in the ayer. **1833** J. C. LOUDON *Encycl. Cottage, Farm & Villa Archit.* 1128/2 *Louvre*, see *Luffer-boards.* **1854** RONALDS & RICHARDSON *Chem. Technol.* (ed. 2) I. 300 The .. louvres or shutters in the top are then opened, when the moist air is discharged, and a fresh supply admitted. **1858** SIMMONDS *Dict. Trade, Luffer*, a frame of laths to admit air or light; the wooden window in a church steeple. **1869** E. A. PARKES *Pract. Hygiene* (ed. 3) 131 Glass louvres, which can be more or less closed. **1872** ELLACOMBE *Bells of Ch.* iv. in *Ch. Bells Devon* etc. 249 The louvres of the windows should be so constructed as to let out the sound of the bells. **1884** WALMISLEY *Iron Roofs* 14 Both roofs are crowned with lanterns fitted with side louvres for ventilation. **1920** W. NEUBECKER *Pract. Sheet Metal Duct Construction* xiv. 155 (*caption*) Formation of movable louvre. *Ibid.*, When movable louvres are used they are pivoted on rods. **1923** *Man. Seamanship* (Admiralty) II. 282 An ideal system of ventilation for a small compartment. A small adjustable flap and louvre .. is fitted in the supply trunk. **1933** MOYER & FITTZ *Air Conditioning* ix. 236 The two-point thermostat *A* is located near the fresh-air intake louver. **1957** *Economist* 23 Nov. 710/1 Heat is distributed not only in conventional radiators but through louvres in the skirting board. **1966** D. F. GALOUYE *Lost Perception* xvi. 169 He had managed to .. check on the intake louvre... The simple removal of four screws would unfasten the grating and provide access to the ventilation duct. **1968** *Autocar* 25 Jan. 30/2 The wheels splashed through puddles .. and steam blew back from the bonnet louvres. **1972** *Sci. Amer.* June 127/3 The temperature probes can be housed in a box that has louvers large enough to ensure the free circulation of air.

†**b.** *transf.*

1542 UDALL *Erasm. Apoph.* 214 b, He putte abrode the louvres of the tente [L. *tentorii vela*] with a ruttocke that he had in his hande.

5. *attrib.* and *Comb.*, as *louvre door, -hole, -light, screen, slat, slate, -tower*; *louvre-roofed* adj.; †**louvre-bands** = *louvre-strings*; **louvre (luffer) boards** (see 4); so *louvre-boarding*; **louvre damper**, a louvre the inclination of whose slats may be varied to regulate the flow of air through them; †**louvre-strings**, strings to open or close the louvres (see 4); **louvre-ways, -wise** *adv.* (see quot.).

1469–70 in *Fabric Rolls York Minster* (Surtees 1859) 73 Diversis cordulis emptis pro les *loverbandes, 12*d.* **1448–9** *Abingdon Abb. Acc.* (1892) 124 In ij *louerboordes emptis pro tenemento Henrici Baret. **1856** F. E. PAGET *Owlet Owlst.* 9 Even the luffer-boards protected by netting. **1895** *Edin. Rev.* Apr. 355 Fitted with 'luffer-boards' that could be opened and shut like Venetian blinds. **1851** *Ord. & Regul. R. Engineers* xix. 101 The Storekeeper .. will determine .. the nature of the Guard, whether of Wire or *Louvre Boarding. **1920** W. NEUBECKER *Pract. Sheet Metal Duct Construction* xv. 160 (*caption*) *Louvre dampers for large size ducts. **1953** N. W. KAY *Mod. Building Encycl.* 410/1 *Louvre door. **1967** *Boston Sunday Herald* 26 Mar. III. 5/7 (Advt.), Set up louver door. **1622** MABBE tr. *Aleman's Guzman d'Alf.* I. 16 If the Doue-house hold vp, .. we shall lacke no Pigeons, as long as there is a *Louer-hole for the poore fooles to get in at. **1659** SHIRLEY *Honoria & Mammon* III. iv. 48 Bid him .. cap the Chimney, least my Lady fly Out at the Lover-hole. **1618** FIELD *Amends for Ladies* I. (1639) B 4, If your Lady-ship be talking in the same roome with any Gentle-man, I can read on a booke, .. looke up at the *loover light, heare and be deafe. **1688** R. HOLME *Armoury* III. 400/1 A cornered tower or chamber, between 2 square turrets, all *loover roofed. **1948** C. ISHERWOOD in *Penguin New Writing* XXXIV. 127 Movable *louvre-screens take the place of port-holes. **1969** *Sears Catal.* Spring/Summer 910 Louver

slats fitted into 1½-in. thick frame. **1842** *Ecclesiologist* I. 10 Four-centered belfry windows..filled up to the top with *louvre slates. **1356-7** *Durham Acc. Rolls* (Surtees) 558 Et in ij fadom de *louerstringes empt. pro novo Solario. **1833** *Penny Cycl.* XIV. 116/2 Handsome *Louvre tower. *c* **1850** *Rudim. Navig.* (Weale) 130 **Louver-wise* or **louver-ways.* To place battens on boards at a certain angle, so as to admit air but not wet.

Hence **louvred** *ppl. a.*, (*a*) Arranged like louvres. (*b*) Provided with a louvre or louvres.

1846 YOUNG *Naut. Dict.*, *Loovered-boards* or *Loovered-battens*, boards or battens framed like Venetian blinds, used for admitting air into a vessel's ports. *c* **1850** *Rudim. Navig.* (Weale) 130 The louvered or battened parts of ships' wells are fixed in this manner. **1881** *Daily News* 12 Dec. 2/2 Glass roofing..surmounted by..'louvred openings', which secure ventilation while they serve to keep out the hot glare of a summer's day. **1891** T. HARDY *Tess* (1900) 80/1 The louvred belfry. **1898** F. W. MACEY *Specifications in Detail* 264 Louvred doors are generally required for ventilation in various places. **1934** H. M. VERNON *Princ. Heating & Ventilation* ix. 170 A fresh-air shaft may be necessary, with a louvered opening above the level of the building. **1950** *Engineering* 7 Apr. 376/2 The long-distance transport of fruit and vegetables is being investigated..with special reference to the performance of a new type of louvred van. **1969** *Daily Tel.* 14 Jan. 15/4 Wardrobes..are better with louvred doors. **1972** *Gloss. Electrotechnical, Power Terms* (*B.S.I.*) IV. iii. 21 *Louvered ceiling*, luminaire system comprising a large installation of louvres above which are mounted the lamps.

‖**Louvre** (luːvr), *sb.*² *Obs.* [Fr.; named after the *Louvre*, the palace of the French kings at Paris.] Some kind of dance.

1729 S. JENYNS *Art Dancing* II. Whether her Steps the Minuet's Mazes trace Or the slow Louvre's more majestic Pace. **1760-72** H. BROOKE *Fool of Qual.* (1809) III. 135 The Louvre..was a dance of the newest fashion.

lovability, loveability (lʌvəˈbɪlɪtɪ). [f. LOVABLE *a.*¹ + -ITY.] Lovableness.

1834 *New Monthly Mag.* XLI. 310 He is quite *passé* as to loveability. **1886** G. ALLEN *Maimie's Sake* xviii, It is a tribute to your personal lovability.

lovable, loveable (ˈlʌvəb(ə)l), *a.*¹ Forms: 4-5 lufabyll(e, 5 luffable, luffeabille, 5, 9 loveable, 9 lovable. [f. LOVE *v.*¹ + -ABLE.] Deserving of being loved; amiable; attractive, pleasing.

c **1340** HAMPOLE *Prose Tr.* (1866) 2 Ihesu, desederabill es thi name, lufabyll and comfortabyll. *c* **1400** *Destr. Troy* 3097 Ne no lede to hir lykyng halfe so luff-able. **1483** *Cath. Angl.* 222/2 Lufabylle (*MS. A.* Luffeabille); *amabilis.* **1570** LEVINS *Manip.* 3/2 Loueable, *amabilis.* **1611** COTGR., *Aimable*,..loueable. **1814** MAR. EDGEWORTH *Patronage* v, 'She is..very loveable—that is the exact word'. 'I fear it is not English', said Miss Hauton. **1823** SCOTT *Fam. Lett.* (1894) II. xix. 171 Teviotdale is a very loveable district. **1870** H. SMART *Race for Wife* ii, He had married..a sweet, lovable girl. **1874** GREEN *Short Hist.* viii. §10. 585 The wide sympathy with all that is human which is so loveable in Chaucer and Shakspere. **1898** L. STEPHEN *Stud. Biogr.* II. i. 1 The man..who could display such reverent and loyal affection was certainly lovable.

†**b.** Friendly. *Obs. rare*⁻¹.

1691 LUTTRELL *Brief Rel.* (1857) II. 280 That the loveable cantons shal be guarantees of the treaty.

†**lovable,** *a.*² *Obs.* Forms: 4, 6 lovabil(l, 5 lovabile, 6 -byll, 4-7 lovable, 5-6 loveable. [f. LOVE *v.*² + -ABLE.

Not distinguishable with certainty from the adopted form of the synonymous but unconnected F. *louable* LOWABLE. The examples with *u* or *v* are all placed here, though it is possible that in some of them the letter is a vowel.]

Praiseworthy, laudable.

a **1340** HAMPOLE *Psalter* Cant. 505 Wha is thi like..aghful and louabil and doand wondirs. **1388** WYCLIF *Bible* IV. 439 (*Ep. Laodiceans*) And whiche been hool, and sooth, and chast, and rightwijs, and louable, do ȝe. *c* **1400** *Destr. Troy* 7062 Hit is lelly not louable in no lede oute, Of no wise mon to wale. *c* **1400** tr. *Secreta Secret.*, *Gov. Lordsh.* 53 It ys growyng of vertuz & rote of alle goodes loueables & worschipfull. **1496** *Extracts Aberd. Reg.* (1844) I. 59 For vphaldin of the auld louable consuetud..and plesour of this burgh. **1501** *Ibid.* 70 Conforming to the alde louabile rite. **1513** DOUGLAS *Æneis* x. v. 169 The worthy actis of ȝour eldaris bygane, Thar lovabyll fame, and ȝour awyn renowne. **1579** in *Home MSS.* (Hist. MSS. Comm., 1902) 50 Lett it rest..quhill the lovable custum be verifiit be the maist skilfull Borderers of baith the realmes. **1609** in *E. Burt's Lett. N. Scotl.* (1818) II. 242 The louable Acts of Parliament of this realme.

ˈlovableness, ˈloveableness. [f. LOVABLE *a.*¹ + -NESS.] The quality of being lovable.

1842 C. WHITEHEAD *R. Savage* (1845) II. ix. 290 Beauty she had..a loveableness (to coin a word) of mien upon the stage almost irresistible. **1876** MISS BRADDON *J. Haggard's Dau.* III. 9 The soft lovableness of her disposition. **1894** *Pop. Sci. Monthly* XLIV. 559 His thoughtfulness and wisdom and lovableness.

lovably, loveably (ˈlʌvəblɪ), *adv.*¹ [f. LOVABLE *a.*¹ + -LY².] In a lovable manner.

1825 *New Monthly Mag.* XVI. 237 How loveably vivid seems the victim to look at us! **1863** GEO. ELIOT *Romola* xvii, Her radiant beauty, made so lovably mortal by her soft hazel eyes.

†**lovably,** *adv.*² *Obs.* [f. LOVABLE *a.*² + -LY².] In a laudable manner.

1456 SIR G. HAYES *Law Arms* (S.T.S.) 217 Thai that had ever wele and lovably governyt.

lovage¹ (ˈlʌvɪdʒ). Forms: 4-7 lov(e)ach(e, 6-7 leuish, liuish, 8 loveage, 5- lovage. [ME. *loveache*, an etymologizing alteration (as if *love-ache* 'love-parsley': see ACHE *sb.*²) of OF. *levesche, luvesche* (mod.F. *livèche*, earlier *levesse*, whence Du. *lavas*):—late L. *levisticum*, whence It. *levistico, libistico*, various Slavonic and Lithuanian forms, and (with etymologizing perversion) OE. *lufestice*, OHG. *lubestecco, lubistechal* (MHG. *lübisteche, lubstickel*, mod.G. *liebstöckel*). The late L. *levisticum* is believed to be a corruption of L. *ligusticum* (app. denoting the same plant), neut. of *ligusticus* LIGURIAN; this was adopted by Linnæus as the name of the British genus, while he gave the name *Levisticum* to the south European genus.]

a. The umbelliferous herb *Levisticum officinale*, a native of southern Europe, grown in old gardens, and used as a domestic remedy. **b.** A later book-name for the British umbelliferous genus *Ligusticum*, esp. *L. scoticum*. **c.** Formerly also applied to *Smyrnium Olusatrum* (black lovage), to *Laserpitium Siler* (bastard or Lombardy lovage), and to *Œnanthe crocata* (water lovage).

a **1387** *Sinon. Barthol.* (Anecd. Oxon.) 11 *Apium levisticum*, loveache. *a* **1400** *Pistill of Susan* 109 (Vernon MS.) þe lilye, þe louache [*Ingilby* louage; *Cotton* louge], launsyng wiþ leue. *c* **1420** *Liber Cocorum* (1862) 18 Take a handfulle of herb lovache. **1548** TURNER *Names of Herbes* 48 *Ligusticum*..I haue sene it in Italy, but no where els. It maye be called in englishe Lumbardy Louage. *Ibid.* 75 *Smyrnium*..maye be called in englishe blacke Louage. **1563** HYLL *Art Garden.* (1593) 62 Lumbardie Louage. **1573** TUSSER *Husb.* xlv. (1878) 97 Necessarie herbes to growe in the garden for Physick... Louage for the stone. **1597** GERARDE *Herbal* II. ccccvi. 892 *Siler montanum officinarum.* Bastard Louage. **1601** HOLLAND *Pliny* II. 30 As for Loueach or Liuish, it..loueth alone to grow of it self among the mountains of Liguria. **1633** JOHNSON *Gerarde's Herbal* (1636) 1060 The roots of this plant..are dayly by the ignorant women in Cheape-side sold..by the name of Water Louage. **1751** SMOLLETT *Per. Pic.* (1779) II. xliv. 72 A sauce composed of pepper, lovage, coriander, &c. **1806** A. HUNTER *Culina* (ed. 3) 147 Lovage and chives, half a handful.

d. *attrib.*, as *lovage root, -seed.*

c **1450** *ME. Med. Bk.* (Heinrich) 125 Loueache seed. **1502** ARNOLDE *Chron.* (1811) 171 Drynke noo stronge ale and vse louach see[d] and letews. **1876** tr. *von Ziemssen's Cycl. Med.* VI. 169 The vegetable diuretics, such as lovage root.

†**lovage**². *Obs.* Also louage, lowage. [perh. f. LOVE *v.*² + -AGE; perh. miswritten for *louāge* = *louange*, LOENGE.] Praise, honour.

1489 *Burgh Rec. Edinb.* (1869) I. 58 Thair petitioun was consonant to ressoun and to the lovage of God. **1500** *Ibid.* 80 Desyrand for the lovage of God..that [etc.]. **1522** *State P. Hen. VIII*, VI. 102 He shall..attayne moche lowage amonges all goode Cristen people. **1523** BERNERS *Froissart* I. i. 1, I..wyll treat and recorde an hystory of great louage and prayse.

lovally: see LOVERLY *a.*²

lovalto, obs. variant of LAVOLTA.

lovaˈnenty, *int. Sc.* An exclamation of surprise.

1824 MACTAGGART *Gallovid. Encycl.*, *Loveanendie!* an exclamation, 'O! strange'. **18..** in RAMSAY *Remin.* (1861) Ser. II. 10, I debar all those who use such minced oaths as..losh! gosh! and lovanenty! [*ed.* 18 lovanendie]. **1894** CROCKETT *Raiders* 191 Lovenenty me! but she'll hae gi'en ye anither kind o' a kiss than an auld wife like me.

Lovat (ˈlʌvət). The name of a place in Inverness-shire, used *attrib.* and *ellipt.* to denote a muted green colour, a tweed (suit), or another garment or material of this colour.

1907 *Daily Chron.* 21 Nov. 7/4 The famous 'Lovat' shades of tweed are very popular among lady motorists. **1911** *Daily Colonist* (Victoria, B.C.) 5 Apr. 2/5 (Advt.), Sweater Coats —New consignment, white, navy, lovat and camel hair, for ladies and gentlemen. **1914** C. MACKENZIE *Sinister St.* II. III. xi. 719 This world of light-green Lovat tweeds, of fashionable rusticity. **1922** J. BUCHAN *Hunting-tower* i. 16 A most disreputable tweed suit..had once been what..is called a Lovat mixture, but was now a nondescript sub-fusc. **1930** H. NICOLSON *Diary* 22 Feb. (1966) 42 The Prime Minister appears in Lovat plus-fours. **1937** D. L. SAYERS *Busman's Honeymoon* iv. 87 Will you wear the Lovats or the grey suit? **1940** *Illustr. London News* CXCVII. 640 (Advt.), Overcoats... A wide choice of brown, fawns, greys or lovat. **1953** J. TRENCH *Docken Dead* vi. 81 He wore a shapeless suit of Lovat tweed. **1969** J. WOOD *Three Blind Mice* i. 9 He wore ..lovat-green socks.

love (lʌv), *sb.*¹ Forms: 1 lufu, (lufo), 2-4 luve, 3 lou, 4, 6 loove, 5 louf, loof, 4-5 lof, lofe, 5 luf, lufue, (*Sc.* 4-6 luf(e, luff, 5, 8 luffe, 6 luif(e, 6, 8 luve, 6 luwe, luyf, luiff, lwiff, loif), 3- love. [OE. *lufu* str. fem. (also declined weak) = OHG. *luba*:—Teut. type **lubâ*, not found elsewhere, though Goth. has (*brôþru-*)*lubô* wk. fem., love, and *lubains* (stem *-aini-*) str. fem., hope; f. the weak-grade of the Teut. root **leub-*: *laub-*: *lub-*:—OAryan **leubh-*: *loubh-*: *lubh-*. Other derivatives of the wk.-grade are OS. *lubig* loving, and the Com. Teut. **lubo-m*, **lobo-m* LOF and its derivative **lobôjan* LOVE *v.*²; also OHG. *gilob* precious. Cognates belonging to the other grades of the root (1) from the *eu* grade, Com. Teut. **liubo-* LIEF *a.*, and its derivatives OHG. *liobôn* (MHG., mod.G. *lieben*), Du. *lieven* (obs., superseded by *liefhebben* lit. 'to have dear'), OE. *léofian*, MDu. *lieven*, OHG. **liubên* (MHG. *lieben*) to be dear or agreeable, OHG. *liuben* (MHG. *lieben*) to endear, to show kindness; MDu., Du. *liefde* fem., love; OHG. *liubî* wk. fem., *liuba* str. fem. (MHG. *liebe*), MDu. *lieve* fem., love; (2) from the *au* grade, the Teut. types **laubâ*, **galaubon-*, **galaubjan*, etc. (see LEAVE *sb.*¹, BELIEF, BELIEVE *v.*).

Outside Teut. the Aryan root is represented by L. *lubet* (*libet*) it is pleasing, *lubīdo* (*libīdo*) desire, OSl. *ljubŭ* dear, *ljuby* love, *ljubiti* to love, Skr. *lubh* to desire, *lōbha* masc. desire.]

1. a. That disposition or state of feeling with regard to a person which (arising from recognition of attractive qualities, from instincts of natural relationship, or from sympathy) manifests itself in solicitude for the welfare of the object, and usually also in delight in his or her presence and desire for his or her approval; warm affection, attachment. Const. *of, for, to, towards.*

c **825** *Vesp. Psalter* cviii. 5 Settun wið me yfel fore godum & laeððu fore lufan minre. *c* **1000** *Ags. Gosp.* John xv. 13 Næfð nan man maran lufe þonne ðeos ys þæt hwa sylle his lif for his freondum. *c* **1250** *Gen. & Ex.* 8 And to alle cristenei men beren pais and luue bi-twen. *a* **1300** *Cursor M.* 20300 Vre leuedi wep, saint iohan alsua, Treu luue was omang þam tua. **1387** TREVISA *Higden* (Rolls) I. 155 Wommen moste be ouercome with fairenesse and loue, and nouȝt wiþ sternesse and drede. *c* **1400** MAUNDEV. (Roxb.) Pref. 2 What lufe he had til his sugets. **1470-85** MALORY *Arthur* I. viii. 44 He wende that al the kynges & knyghtes had come for grete loue and to haue done hym worship at his feste. **1535** COVERDALE *2 Sam.* i. 26 Thy loue hath bene more speciall vnto me, then the loue of wemen. **1588** SHAKS. *L.L.L.* v. ii. 415 My loue to thee is sound sans cracke or flaw. **1597** MORLEY *Introd. Mus.* Pref., Adiuring me by the loue of my contrie. **1611** BIBLE *Dan.* i. 9 God had brought Daniel into fauour and tender loue with the Prince of the Eunuches. **1765** COWPER in Southey *Life & Wks.* (1835) I. 155 My heart was full of love to all the congregation. **1818** CRUISE *Digest* (ed. 2) II. 346 The natural love which Thomas Kirby bore to his brother. **1836** W. IRVING *Astoria* I. 279 His dominant spirit, and his love for the white men, were evinced in his latest breath. **1871** MORLEY *Voltaire* (1886) 2 They should prove their love of him whom they had not seen, by love of their brothers whom they had seen.

b. Viewed as an abstract quality or principle. (Sometimes *personified.*)

c **1050** *Voc.* in Wr.-Wülcker 343/32 *Affectu*, for hylde and lufe. *a* **1300** *Cursor M.* 99 O reuth o loue and charite, Was neuer hir mak. **1377** LANGL. *P. Pl.* B. I. 146 For trewthe telleþ þat loue is triacle of heuene. **1422** tr. *Secreta Secret.*, *Priv. Priv.* 135 Humylite Engendryth lowe that destrueth envy and hatredyn. **1557** SEAGER *Sch. Vertue* 815 in *Babees Bk.*, Loue doth moue the mynde to mercie. *a* **1628** PRESTON *Breastpl. Love* (1631) 8 Love and hatred are..the great Lords and Masters, that divide the rest of the affections between them. **1811** COLERIDGE *7 Lect.* (1856) 70 Love is a desire of the whole being to be united to some thing, or some being, felt necessary to its completeness.

c. In particularized use: An instance of affection. †Also, an act of kindness.

c **1000** *Prayers of Exeter Bk.* iv. 115 Wæs a cearu symle lufena to leane. *c* **1200** *Moral Ode* 314 in *Trin. Coll. Hom.*, þe þe þos two loues halt and wile hes wel healde. **1595** SHAKS. *John* IV. i. 49 What good loue may I performe for you? **1632** LITHGOW *Trav.* v. 189, I met with an English ship..whose loues I cannot easily forget. *a* **1853** ROBERTSON *Lect.* i. (1858) 25 The same feelings and anxieties and loves.

†**d.** In OE. (contrasted with *laȝu* law): Amicable settlement, as opposed to litigation. Hence, in later use, *occas.* rendering L. *fœdus* treaty, covenant. Also, ***under love and law***; a phrase used to denote the position of being a member of a frankpledge. *Obs.*

a **1000** *Laws of Æthelred* III. c. 13 §1 (Schmid) And þar þeȝen aȝe tweȝen costas lufe oþþe laȝe and he þonne lufe ȝeceose. **1432-50** tr. *Higden* (Rolls) I. 99 Oreb..the mownte of fere and of luffe [L. *mons terroris et fœderis*]. *Ibid.* 347, IV. 123. *a* **1500** in Arnolde *Chron.* (1811) 90 Yf ther bee ony persone wythin the warde that is not vnder francpledge that is to saye under loue and lawe.

e. *(give) my love to..*, or *love to..*: a formula of request that the person addressed will convey the expression of the speaker's or writer's affection to a third person. Also ***to send one's love***; ***love from...***

1630 WINTHROP in *New Eng.* (1825) I. 378 Commend me to all our friends. My love and blessing to your brother and sisters [etc.]. **1765** COWPER *Let. to J. Hill* 14 Aug., My love to all your family. **1785** LADY NEWDIGATE *Let.* May in A. E. Newdigate-Newdegate *Cheverels* (1898) iv. 67 Love from all here Adieu. **1793** —— *Let. to W. Hayley* 24 Feb., With Mary's kind love. **1837** DICKENS *Pickw.* ix, Love to Tuppy! **1854** W. COLLINS *Hide & Seek* II. iv. (1861) 183, 'I will write and comfort your mother this very afternoon ——' 'Give her my love', interposed Zack. **1913** W. OWEN *Let.* 19 Oct. (1967) 202 Love, Hopes, and Kisses from your own Wilfred. **1921** A. HUXLEY *Let.* 21 Nov. (1969) 205, I will telephone or write about both these dates. Love from Aldous. **1949** D. SMITH *I capture Castle* xi. 188 Dear Cassandra, it was nice of you to write... Love from Neil.

2. In religious use, applied in an eminent sense to the paternal benevolence and affection of God towards His children, to the affectionate devotion due to God from His creatures, and to the affection of one created being to another so far as

it is prompted by the sense of their common relationship to God. (Cf. CHARITY 1.)

Theologians distinguish the ***love of complacency***, which implies approval of qualities in the object, and the ***love of benevolence***, which is bestowed irrespective of the character of the object.

c **975** *Rushw. Gosp.* John v. 42 Ah ic cuðe iowih þætte lufo ȝodes ne habbas ȝe in iow. *c* **1200** *Trin. Coll. Hom.* 141 Ure drihten forgiaf hire hire sinnen for two þinge, an is muchel leðe to hire sunne oðer muchel luue to him. *a* **1310** in Wright *Lyric P.* 70 Jhesu, suete love the dude gredyn. **1526** TINDALE *1 John* v. 3 This is the love of god, that we kepe his commaundementes. **1611** BIBLE *1 John* iv. 16 God is loue, and hee that dwelleth in loue, dwelleth in God. **1650** E. LEIGH *Annot. New Test.* 220 There is a two fold love in God. 1. *Amor benevolentiæ*, a love of well willing..2. *Amor complacentiæ*, a love of complacency. **1794** COLERIDGE *Relig. Musings* 192 Lord of unsleeping Love, From everlasting Thou! **1876** MOZLEY *Univ. Serm.* ii. 29 Love in the Gospel sense is that general virtue which covers the motives.

3. Strong predilection, liking or fondness *for*, or devotion *to* (something). Const. *of, for, to* (arch.), †*unto*. †***to give, bear love to***: to be devoted or addicted to.

c **900** tr. *Bæda's Hist.* IV. xxvii. (Schipper) 514 Swa mycel lufu to godcundre lare. *c* **1250** *Gen. & Ex.* 4067 And for luue of ðis hore-plaȝe Manie for-leten godes laȝe. **1422** tr. *Secreta Secret., Priv. Priv.* 218 Philosophie is no more but loue of witte and cvnnynge. *a* **1548** HALL *Chron., Edw. IV* 237 b, Blynde avarice and love of money. **1611** BIBLE *Transl. Pref.* 2 For the loue that he bare vnto peace. **1726** POPE *Postscript to Odyssey* V. 305 Let our love to Antiquity be ever so great. **1773** MRS. CHAPONE *Improv. Mind* (1774) II. 32 The love of truth, and a real desire of improvement. *c* **1810** COLERIDGE in *Lit. Rem.* (1838) III. 303 Those vicious habits in which there is no love to sin. **1877** GLADSTONE *Glean.* I. 148 The love of freedom itself is hardly stronger in England than the love of aristocracy. **1887** FOWLER *Princ. Mor.* II. i. 11 Among these primary desires should be specified the love of ease and the love of occupation. **1888** C. PATMORE in B. Champneys *Mem.* (1900) II. iv. 43 When I was about fifteen my love for poetry began to get the better of my love for science.

4. a. That feeling of attachment which is based upon difference of sex; the affection which subsists between lover and sweetheart and is the normal basis of marriage. ***for love*** (†***in love***): by reason of love (often placed in opposition to pecuniary considerations); also in weakened sense; ***love at first sight***: the action or state of falling in love with someone whom one has never previously seen; ***love's young dream***: the relationship of young lovers; the object of someone's love, a man regarded as the perfect lover.

c **1000** ÆLFRIC *Gen.* xxix. 20 Iacob him hirsumode þa seofan ȝear for Rachele and hit þuhte him feawa daȝa for þære lufe, þe he to hire hæfde. *c* **1230** *Hali Meid.* 47 For to drahen his luue toward hire. *c* **1374** CHAUCER *Troylus* I. 508 Now art þow yn þe snare That whilom Iapedest at loues peyne. *Ibid.* II. 667 This was a sodeyn love, how mighte it be That she so lightly lovede Troilus Right for the firste sighte; ye, pardee? *a* **1400–50** *Alexander* 226 Þe lede lawid in hire lofe as leme dose of gledis. **1500–20** DUNBAR *Poems* xlvi. 4, I hard a merle with mirry notis sing A sang of lufe. **1540** HYRDE tr. *Vives' Instr. Chr. Wom.* (1592) N ij, They that mary for love, shall lead their life in sorrow. *a* **1593** MARLOWE *Hero & Leander* (1598) I. 175 Where both deliberat, the loue is slight, Who euer lov'd, that lov'd not at first sight? **1667** MILTON *P.L.* IV. 750 Haile wedded Love, mysterious Law, true source Of human offspring. **1776** JOHNSON in Boswell 28 Mar., It is commonly a weak man who marries for love. **1822** HAZLITT *Table-Talk* II. xvi. 354, I do not think that what is called *Love at first sight* is so great an absurdity as it is sometimes imagined to be. *a* **1834** MOORE *Irish Mel., Love's Yng. Dream* i, But there's nothing half so sweet in life As love's young dream. **1839** [see BEAT *v.*[1] 10]. *a* **1849** POE *Annabel Lee* 9 We loved with a love that was more than love—I and my Annabel Lee. **1868** W. COLLINS *Moonstone* I. vii. 91 You have heard of beautiful young ladies falling in love at first sight, and have thought it natural enough. **1898** J. K. JEROME *Second Thoughts* 155 The stout lady, now regarded as a would-be blighter of love's young dream, was hustled into the back seat. **1903** KIPLING *Traffics & Discov.* (1904) 132 'Do you want a tow to Brixham?'.. 'What for?'.. 'For love; for nothing.' **1920** GALSWORTHY *Skin Game* I. 33, I don't mean any tosh about love's young dream; but I do like being friends. **1937** D. L. SAYERS *Busman's Honeymoon* xv. 307 There now!.. If there ain't love's young dream a-comin' up the path. **1952** *Scrutiny* XVIII. 273 We know that what we have here is no drama of romantic love-at-first-sight. **1961** C. MCCULLERS *Clock without Hands* iv. 89 In early youth, love at first sight, that epitome of passion, turns you into a zombie. **1966** L. SOUTHWORTH *Felon in Disguise* viii. 121 It calls for a sweetheart act, a proper 'Love's Young Dream' routine. **1975** D. BAGLEY *Snow Tiger* xvi. 138 Don't you believe in love at first sight?

b. As a motive in imaginative literature.

1779–81 JOHNSON *L.P., Addison* The greatest weakness of the play is in the scenes of love.. Yet the love is so intimately mingled with the whole action, that [etc.]. **1859** MACAULAY *Biogr., W. Pitt* (2nd par.), This piece.. is in some respects highly curious. There is no love. The whole plot is political.

c. An instance of being in love. Also *collect. pl.*, amatory relations, love-affairs.

1589 PUTTENHAM *Eng. Poesie* III. xxiii. (Arb.) 276 Nothing is so vnpleasant to a man, as to be encountred in his chiefe affection, and specially in his loues. **1590** SPENSER *F.Q.* I. ii. 3 Like a young Squire, in loves and lusty-hed His wanton daies that ever loosely led. **1604** SHAKS. *Oth.* v. ii. 41 *Oth.* Thinke on thy sinnes. *Des.* They are Loues I beare to you. **1697** DRYDEN *Virg. Georg.* IV. 490 All the Rapes of Gods, and ev'ry Love, From ancient Chaos down to youthful Jove. **1738** SWIFT *Pol. Conversat.* 103, I suppose, the Colonel was cross'd in his first Love. **1844** DISRAELI *Coningsby* VIII. ii, The sweet pathos of their mutual loves. **1849** JAMES *Woodman* ii, The loves of Mars and Venus.

d. ***babe of love***: = LOVE-CHILD.

1728–42 POPE *Dunc.* II. 158 Two babes of love close clinging to her waist. **1807** CRABBE *Par. Reg.* I. (1810) 70 Recorded next a Babe of love I trace! Of many loves, the Mother's fresh disgrace.

5. a. (With capital.) The personification of sexual affection; usu. masculine, and more or less identified with the Eros, Amor, or Cupid of classic mythology; formerly sometimes feminine, and capable of being identified with Venus. (See also 8 a.)

13.. in Wright *Lyric P.* xvi. 53 To love y putte pleyntes mo. *c* **1374** CHAUCER *Troylus* I. 353 For loue bygan his fetheres so to lyme. **1435** MISYN *Fire of Love* II. xii. 102 Weil it is sayd in play 'luf gos before & ledis þe dawns'. **1566** PAINTER *Pal. Pleas.* I. 79 b, Notwithstanding dame Love is so favourable unto mee. **1588** SHAKS. *L.L.L.* IV. iii. 380 Fore runne faire Loue, strewing her way with flowers. **1667** MILTON *P.L.* IV. 763 Here Love his golden shafts imploies, here lights His constant Lamp, and waves his purple wings. **1805** SCOTT *Last Minstr.* III. ii, In peace, Love tunes the shepherd's reed; In war, he mounts the warrior's steed. **1868** FITZ-GERALD tr. *Omar* cviii. (1899) 103 Ah Love! could you and I with Fate conspire.

b. with *pl.* A Cupid; one of the multitude of nameless gods of love imagined by mythologists; a figure or representation of the god of love.

1594 SPENSER *Amoretti* xvi, Legions of loves with little wings did fly. **1663** COWLEY *Acme & Septimius*, All around The little Loves, that waited by, Bow'd, and bless'd the Augury. **1731** SWIFT *Strephon & Chloe* Wks. 1755 IV. I. 150 The smiling Cyprian goddess brings Her infant loves with purple wings. ? **1793** COLERIDGE *Autumn. Evening* 49–50 A thousand Loves around her forehead fly; A thousand Loves sit melting in her eye. *a* **1839** PRAED *Poems* (1864) II. 63 Where'er her step in beauty moves, Around her fly a thousand loves.

6. The animal instinct between the sexes, and its gratification.

c **1375** *Sc. Leg. Saints* xxxvii. (*Vincencius*) 13 Fals erroure, & lufe vnclene, & warldis dout als. **1387** TREVISA *Higden* (Rolls) V. 185 A ȝongelynge.. þat hadde obleged hym self to the devel for þe love of a wenche. *c* **1560** A. SCOTT *Poems* (S.T.S.) vi. 27 A leddy als, for luf, to tak Ane propir page, hir tyme to pass. **1567** *Satir. Poems Reform.* iv. 28 Hir licherous luife, quhilk kindlit ouer hait. **1611** BIBLE *Prov.* vii. 18 Come, let vs take our fill of loue vntill the morning. **1697** DRYDEN *Virg. Georg.* III. 102 Six Seasons use; but then release the Cow, Unfit for Love, and for the lab'ring Plough.

7. Phrases (chiefly with prepositions).

a. ***for the love of***: for the sake of, on account of. †Also ***for my*** (***our***, etc.) ***love*** = for my (our, etc.) sake. ***for the love of Mike***: for goodness' sake! (a colloq. exclamation of exasperation or surprise, with no notion of the literal sense; prob. f. MIKE *sb.*[4]).

Now only where some notion of the literal sense is implied (chiefly in adjurations); in early use often merely idiomatic, = L. *causa, gratia*. In OE. the sb. was often *plural*.

c **888** K. ÆLFRED *Boeth.* xxii. §2 Ic wille [þe oðewan] forlustlice for þinum lufum [L. *tui causa libenter*]. **971** *Blickl. Hom.* 23 Eal þis he þrowode for ure lufan. *c* **1200** *Vices & Virtues* (1888) 7 Alle ðe ðis iseiȝð.. i bidde and warni, for ðe luue of gode.. þat ȝie hatien.. ðes awerȝhede senne. *a* **1300** *Cursor M.* 14683 Forþ in dedes gode... We wil noght stan þe, parfai! But.. for þe luue o þi missau. *c* **1375** *Sc. Leg. Saints* xxix. (*Placidas*) 163 Sa hyme, for þe luf of me, þat in my nam he baptis þe. **1470–85** MALORY *Arthur* XIII. xvi, We shalle destroye alle the knyghtes of kyng Arthurs.. for the loue of syr Galahad. *a* **1548** HALL *Chron., Hen. V.* 62 Required the Englishe lordes for the love of God that the truce might continue. **1587** IANES in Hakluyt *Voy.* (1600) III. 112 The Sauages came to the Island.. and tore the two vpper strakes, and carried them away onely for the loue of the yron in the boords. **1588** SHAKS. *L.L.L.* v. ii. 850 Impose some seruice on me for thy loue. **1601** —— *Twel. N.* II. iii. 92 For the loue o God, peace. **1710** SWIFT *Jrnl. to Stella* 8 Dec., I begged Mr. Harley, for the love of God, to take some care about it. **1859** TENNYSON *Vivien* 410 A Table Round, That was to be, for love of God and man And noble deeds, the flower of all the world. **1922** JOYCE *Ulysses* 763 O move over your big carcass out of that for the love of Mike listen to him. **1925** T. DREISER *Amer. Trag.* (1926) I. I. ix. 57 For de love o' Mike, will you listen to dat, now. **1934** J. BROPHY *Waterfront* i. 14 For the love of mike.. shut those blasted windows. **1935** W. D. HUBBARD *Thousandth Frog* i. 7 Dick could not repress an exclamation of astonishment. 'For the love of Mike. Look at them.' **1941** *Penguin New Writing* VIII. 91 Well, for the luvva Mike! **1942** *R.A.F. Jrnl.* 3 Oct. 11 Tired? Well for the love of mike! What about me? **1957** A. MACNAB *Bulls of Iberia* xv. 181 For the love of Mike, let's hope he's brave.

†**b.** ***for*** or ***of all*** (***the***) ***loves, upon all loves, of all love***: a phrase of strong adjuration or entreaty. Similarly, ***for love's sake***. *Obs.*

c **1400** *Sowdone Bab.* 1587 Sir, for alle loues, Lete me thy prisoneres seen. *a* **1425** *Cursor M.* 20380 (Trin.) Whi wepestou what is þe For alle loues [*earlier texts*, for felaured, for felauschip,] telle now me. **1565** COOPER *Thesaurus*, Amabo.. Of felowshippe: of all loues: I pray the: as euer thou wilte doe me good turne. **1590** SHAKS. *Mids. N.* II. ii. 153 Speake of all loues; I sound almost with feare. **1618** USSHER *Lett.* (1686) 64, I do intreat you of all Love, to look over the first Edition. **1620** MIDDLETON *Chaste Maid* III. i. 31 O sweet Father, for Loues sake pittie me. **1624** BP. MOUNTAGU *Immed. Addr.* 185 She.. intreateth him that was worshipped vpon the Altar, of all loves, mercies, and works of wonder, to restore her vnto her health. *c* **1646** in *2nd Rep. Hist. MSS. Comm.* 87/1 [*tol.*] which I desire you of all love to pay upon sight of this my letter. **1655** J. S. *Phillis of Scyros* III. iv. 63 For loves sake, doe not press me to relate So long a story now. **1829** WHEWELL in *Life* (1881) 133 Beg her of all love to establish herself in a more collegiate part of Cambridge.

c. ***for love or money***: at any price, by any means. (Used in negative contexts.)

[**971** *Blickl. Hom.* 43 Ne for feo, ne for nanes mannes lufon. **13..** *Coer de L.* 1476 Neythyr for love, neyther for eye. **1377** LANGL. *P. Pl.* B. I. 101 And neuer leue hem for loue ne for lacchyng of syluer.] **1590** C. S. *Right Relig.* 18 Then should not men eyther for loue or money haue pardons. **1609** DEKKER *Guls Horne-bk.* vi. 30 If you can (either for loue or money) prouide your selfe a lodging by the water side. **1712** SWIFT *Jrnl. to Stella* 7 Aug., No more ghosts now for love or money. **1837** SIR F. PALGRAVE *Merch. & Friar* i. (1844) 18 Any person who, for love or money, might be induced to take the letter in his charge. **1869** MARCH *Gram. Anglo-Saxon* Pref. iv, He let me.. use.. Anglo-Saxon texts not elsewhere to be had for love or money.

d. ***in love*** (***with***): enamoured (of), imbued with love (for); *transf.* very fond (of) or much addicted (to).

[Cf. F. '*Estre en amour*, said of birds that bill, tread, or breed' (Cotgr.).]

1508 DUNBAR *Tua mariit wemen* 191 He is for ladyis in luf a right lusty schadow. **1577** B. GOOGE *Heresbach's Husb.* (1586) 5 He would talke.. of the stories of the Scripture, so sweetely.. as I was wonderfully in loue with him. **1581** PETTIE *Guazzo's Civ. Conv.* III. (1586) 140 A woman cannot possibly doe any thing y^t may make her husband more in love with her, then to play the good huswife. **1591** SHAKS. *Two Gent.* II. i. 87, I was in loue with my bed. **1664** BUTLER *Hud.* II. i. 267 Quoth she, Y' have almost made m' in Love With that which did my pity move. **1690** LOCKE *Hum. Und.* IV. xvii. §24 He that believes, without having any reason for believing, may be in love with his own fancies. **1727** GAY *Begg. Op.* I. x. (1729) 14 What, is the fool in love in earnest then? **1828** MACAULAY *Ess., Hallam's Const. Hist.*, Its conduct, we are told, made the excellent Falkland in love with the very name of Parliament. **1881** L. B. WALFORD *Dick Netherby* xvii. 213 He was not himself in love. **1896** A. E. HOUSMAN *Shropsh. Lad* xviii, Oh, when I was in love with you, Then I was clean and brave.

e. ***out of love*** (***with***): the opposite of *in love* (*with*); disgusted (with).

1581 PETTIE tr. *Guazzo's Civ. Conv.* I. (1586) 10 Hee seemeth either too farre in loue with himselfe, or to farre out of loue with others. **1591** SHAKS. *Two Gent.* IV. iv. 210, I should haue scratch'd out your vnseeing eyes, To make my Master out of loue with thee. **1603** —— *Meas. for M.* III. i. 174, I am so out of loue with life. **1722** DE FOE *Relig. Courtsh.* I. i. (1840) 4 What's the matter, that you are so out of love with the world all on a sudden? **1754** RICHARDSON *Grandison* III. xi. 83 Lord W.'s animosity to my father made him out of love with his name.

f. ***to fall*** (†***be taken*** or ***caught***) ***in love***: to become enamoured; *transf.* to become very fond of, dote upon. Const. *with.* †Also, ***to fall, be brought into love's dance***.

Cf. F. *tomber en amour* (15th c. in Littré).

1423 JAS. I *Kingis Q.* xlv, So ferre I-fallyng Into lufis dance. **1530–1866** [see FALL *v.* 38 b]. *c* **1530** *Hickscorner* (Manly) 204 Than in-to loves daunce we were brought. **1568** GRAFTON *Chron.* I. 37 Locryne fell in great phancy and love with a faire Damosell. **1579** LYLY *Euphues* (Arb.) 345 Of which water who so drinketh, shall bee caught in Love. **1596** SPENSER *F.Q.* IV. vi. *heading*, He sees her face; doth fall in love, And soone from her depart. **1606** W. W[OODCOCKE] *Hist. Ivstine* XLIII. 134 With the pleasantnesse of which, they were so taken in loue, that [etc.]. **1887** RIDER HAGGARD *Jess* iv, John Niel was no chicken, nor very likely to fall in love with the first pretty face he met.

g. ***to make love***: to pay amorous attention; now more usually, to copulate. [After F. *faire l'amour* or It. *far l'amore*.] Const. *to.*

1580 LYLY *Euphues* (Arb.) 290 A Phrase now there is which belongeth to your Shoppe boorde, that is, to make loue. **1590** SHAKS. *Mids. N.* I. i. 107 Demetrius.. Made loue to Nedars daughter. **1602** —— *Ham.* v. ii. 57 Why, man, they did make loue to this imployment. **1605** —— *Macb.* III. i. 124 Thence it is That I to your assistance doe make loue. **1605** —— *Lear* v. iii. 88 If you will marry, make your loues to me. **1663** COWLEY *Hymn to Light* ii, Thou golden Shower of a true Jove! Who does in thee descend, and Heav'n to Earth make love! **1712** ADDISON *Spect.* No. 517 ¶2 The Widow Lady whom he had made love to. **1768** STERNE *Sent. Journ.* (1775) I. 31 (*Remise Door*) You have been making love to me all this while. *a* **1845** HOOD *Poems* (1846) I. 213 Oh there's nothing in life like making love. **1860** *Sat. Rev.* IX. 306 How often.. do we make love to the charms of cousins and avuncular expectations. **1950** M. PEAKE *Gormenghast* xxix. 173 One of the Carvers made love to her and she had a baby. **1966** AUDEN *About House* 15 Stocktaking, horseplay, worship, making love. **1967** B. WRIGHT tr. *Queneau's Between Blue & Blue* xiv. 151 When you make love on a bunk,.. the man has to bump his head. **1971** *Daily Tel.* 15 Jan. 17/1 Couples who make love frequently are more likely to have sons than those who do so less often.

†**h.** ***in the love of***: beloved by. *Obs. rare.*

1631 WEEVER *Anc. Funeral Mon.* 417 He also departed this world, in the loue of all good men.

8. In various proverbs and proverbial phrases.

a. Proverbs.

c **1470** HENRYSON *Mor. Fab.* III. xvii. in *Anglia* IX. 357 The prouerbe sayis 'als gude luif cummis as gais'. **1474** CAXTON *Chesse* III. iii, Herof men say a comyn proverbe in englond, that loue lasteth as longe as the money endurith. **1596** SHAKS. *Merch. V.* II. vi. 36 Loue is blinde. **1611** COTGR. s.v. *Amour*, Loue, and the Cough cannot be hidden. *a* **1618** RALEIGH *Rem.* (1664) 35 Love needs no teaching.

b. ***labour of love***: work undertaken either from fondness for the work itself, or from desire to benefit persons whom one loves.

[An allusion to 1 Thess. i. 3, 'Your worke of faith and labour of loue', and Heb. vi. 10.]

1673 *Lady's Call.* II. iii. §12 Women.. founded Hospitals, and yet with a labor of love, as the Apostle styles it, Heb. vi. 10, disdain'd not somtimes to serve in them. **1853** KINGSLEY

Hypatia ix, The humble stock phrases in which they talked of their labours of love. **1878** BLACK *Goldsmith* xiv. 131 During this labour of love [the composition of the *Deserted Village*].

c. *love in a cottage*: a euphemistic expression for marriage with insufficient means.

1812 MAR. EDGEWORTH *Absentee* iv, Lady Clonbrony had not..the slightest notion how anybody..could prefer, to a good house..and a proper establishment, what is called love in a cottage. [**1820** KEATS *Lamia* II. i, Love in a hut, with water and a crust, Is—Love, forgive us!—cinders, ashes, dust.] **1894** H. GARDENER *Unoff. Patriot* 239 Here's more love in a cottage business for you.

d. *there's no love lost between them*: an ambiguous phrase, which has been employed with two contrary implications. †(*a*) Their affection is mutual. *Obs.*

c **1640** R. DAVENPORT *Surv. Sci.* Wks. (Bullen 1890) 327 Oh my sweete! Sure there is no loue lost when you two meete. **16..** *Children in Wood* ii. in Percy *Reliq.* (1765) III. 172 No love between these two was lost, Each was to other kinde. **1696** M. HENRY *Life P. Henry* (1699) 8 Dr. Busby.. took a particular Kindness to him,..and there was no Love lost betwixt them. **1706** MOTTEUX *Quix.* II. xxxiii. (1749) III. 266, I love him well, and there's no love lost between us. **1749** SMOLLETT *Gil Bl.* (1797) III. 233, I have a friendship for you..And I can assure thee, child (said I), there is no love lost [Fr. *que tu n'aimes pas un ingrat*]. **1773** GOLDSM. *Stoops to Conq.* IV, As for murmurs, mother, we grumble a little now and then, to be sure. But there's no love lost between us. **1823** LAMB *Elia* Ser. II. *New Year's Coming of Age*, There was no love lost for that matter. **1824** N. DRAKE *Noontide Leisure* II. 54 Give me your hand..and let me tell you..there is no love lost between us.

(*b*) Now always: They have no love for each other.

?**1622** J. TAYLOR (Water-P.) *Trav. Twelve-pence* Wks. (1630) I. 71 They loue me not, which makes 'em quickly spend me. But there's no great loue lost 'twixt them and mee, We keepe asunder and so best agree. **1748** RICHARDSON *Clarissa* (1768) III. 134 He must needs say, there was no love lost between some of my family and him; but he had not deserved of them what they had of him. **1858** THACKERAY *Virgin.* xvii. I. 134 There was not a great deal of love lost between Will and his half-sister. **1866** HOWELLS *Venet. Life* 121 Americans do not like these people and I believe there is no love lost on the other side. **1889** T. A. TROLLOPE *What I remember* III. 91 Between Italian and French radicals there is really no love lost.

9. a. A beloved person: *esp.* a sweetheart; chiefly applied to a female person, but sometimes to a male. (Often used as a term of endearing address.)

a **1225** *Leg. Kath.* 1531 He is mi lif & mi luue. *c* **1369** CHAUCER *Bk. Duchesse* 91 And wher my lord, my love, be deed? **1377** LANGL. *P. Pl.* B. IV. 49 Rose Regineldes loue [*text A* lemmon]. *c* **1386** CHAUCER *Prol.* 672 Ful loude he song 'Com hider, love, to me'. **14..** *Sir Beues* 2019 (MS. M.) Beuys, loue dere, Ryde nat fro me in no manere! **1470–85** MALORY *Arthur* VII. xxxv. 269 He is my fyrst loue and he shal be the laste. *a* **1592** MARLOWE *Pass. Sheph. to his Love*, Liue with me and be my Loue. **1596** SHAKS. *Merch. V.* IV. i. 277 Whether Bassanio had not once a Loue. **1600** *Dr. Dodypoll* III. v. in Bullen *Old Plays* III. 135 Why, love? doubt you that? *Ibid.* 136 Thou art growne passing strange, my love. *c* **1606** WITHER *Love Sonn.* iii. in *Descr. Love* (1638) C 4 In Summer-time to Medley My love and I would goe. **1767** SIR W. JONES *Seven Fountains* Poems (1777) 37 Told to their smiling loves their amorous tales. **1818** SCOTT *'Old Song'* in *Br. Lamm.* xxix, It is best to be off wi' the old love, Before you be on wi' the new. *a* **1834** MOORE *Yng. May Moon* 1 The young May moon is beaming, love. **1860** C. PATMORE *Faithful for ever* III. ii. 180 And there's another thing, my Love, I wish you'd show you don't approve. **1895** A. W. PINERO *Second Mrs. Tanqueray* III. 104 Paula love, I fancied you and Aubrey were a little more friendly. **1900** BARRIE *Tommy & Grizel* xxv. 303 There are poor dogs of men..who open their letters from their loves, knowing exactly what will be in them. **1966** *New Yorker* 29 Jan. 22/3 'Sit over here, love,' he said as another actress entered. **1967** *Listener* 5 Oct. 429/3 Lovely, loves, I loved it. And Alison here was hysterical, weren't you, Alison? **1975** J. SYMONS *Three Pipe Problem* iii. 25 But Sher. love, it was only a read-through. You don't expect me to *act*.

b. *transf.* of animals.

1697 DRYDEN *Æneid* VIII. 288 One Heifar who had heard her Love complain, Roar'd from the Cave. **1792** WOLCOT (P. Pindar) *Wks.* III. 259 Her feather'd Partner..Now for his loves pursues his airy way, And now with food returns.

†**c.** In reference to illicit relations: A paramour; said of both men and women. *Obs.*

c **1400** MAUNDEV. (1839) xiv. 154 And whan thai wil have ony companye of man..than thei have Loves, that usen hem. **1462** *Paston Lett.* II. 98 He bydeth but a tyme that he myght gete a summe of money to geders..and to gone ther with a love of his sojornyng as yette in Hokehold. **1588** M. KYFFIN tr. *Terence's Andria* I. iii. C iv b, Whether she be wife to Pamphilus, or but his loue, I knowe not. **1598** SHAKS. *Merry W.* III. v. 79 To serch his house for his wiues Loue. **1613** PURCHAS *Pilgrimage* (1614) 768 They haue one wife, many loues.

d. *gen.* The object of love; the beloved (of..).

1734 POPE *Ess. Man* IV. 190 The lover and the love of human-kind. **1754** CHATHAM *Lett. Nephew* iv. 28 Make yourself the love and admiration of the world. **1818** BYRON *Ch. Har.* IV. clxx, In the dust The fair-hair'd Daughter of the Isles is laid, The love of millions!

e. A charming or delightful person or thing; a 'duck'. *colloq.*

1814 JANE AUSTEN *Lett.* (1884) II. 241 The garden is quite a love. **1831** LADY GRANVILLE *Let.* 28 Feb., A pretty, tiny daughter, whom my girls think a love. **1841** S. WARREN *Ten Thous. a-year* II. 75 He's a love of a man, pa, isn't he? **1844** L. HUNT *Blue-Stocking Revels* i. 26 Poems 103 Such doves of Petitions, and loves of sweet Pray'rs. **1864** W. H. AINSWORTH *John Law* Prol. vi. (1881) 35 Nankin has the tiniest teacups you ever beheld—perfect loves! **1889** 'ROLF BOLDREWOOD' *Robbery under Arms* xxiv, What a love of a chain!

f. *love in disguise*: (see quots.).

1877 E. S. DALLAS *Kettner's Bk. of Table* 282 *Love in disguise* is a calf's heart stuffed, then surrounded with forcemeat, next rolled in vermicelli, lastly deposited in a baking dish..and sent to the oven. **1958** W. BICKEL tr. *Hering's Dict. Cookery* 451 *Love in disguise*, calf's heart, soaked in water, larded, boiled until tender, dried, coated with veal forcemeat, rolled in crushed raw noodles, roasted in butter in oven and basted frequently.

10. a. *for love*: without stakes, for nothing; applied to the practice of playing a competitive game for the pleasure of playing.

1678 BUTLER *Hud.* III. i. 1007 For these at Beste and L'Ombre [you] wooe, And play for love and money too. **1813** *Sporting Mag.* XLI. 296 A match of..single-stick, was played..for what is technically termed *Love and a Belly-full.* **1821** LAMB *Elia* Ser. I. *New Year's Eve*, I play over again for love, as the gamesters phrase it, games for which I once paid so dear. **1844** DICKENS *Mart. Chuz.* xxxii, Mrs. Todgers..proposed that..they should play for 'love'.

b. In various competitive games of skill, e.g. whist, football, tennis, racquets: No score, nothing; meaning that the party said 'to be *love*' has scored no points in the game then in progress. *love all*: no score on either side.

1742 HOYLE *Whist* i. 13 If your Adversary is 6 or 7 Love, and you are to lead. **1780** *Gentl. Mag.* L. 322/2 We are not told how, or by what means Six love comes to mean Six to nothing. **1797** *Encycl. Brit.* (ed. 3) XVIII. 380/2 As the games are won, so they are marked and called; as one game love, two games to one, &c. **1885** *Pall Mall G.* 2 Mar. 10/2 In the Rugby game Northampton beat Coventry by a try to love. **1898** *Encycl. Sport* II. 242/1 The marker's..duty is to call the game..from the start at 'love all'.. 'Love', in the game of rackets, as in other games, signifies nothing.

c. Applied *attrib.* to a game or set of games in which there is nothing scored on one side.

1833 T. HOOK *Parson's Dau.* (1847) 57 Can't make a hazard..and has lost two love games. **1878** J. MARSHALL *Ann. Tennis* 158 *Love-set*, a set in which one player wins six consecutive games; or, in case of an advantage-set, seven consecutive games. **1884** *Pall Mall G.* 25 Apr. 3/2 In the two first days' play the whole of the heats were love victories.

†**11.** A game of chance in which one player holds up a certain number of fingers, and the other, without seeing, guesses their number. = MORA. *Obs.*

1585 HIGGINS *Junius' Nomenclator* 297/2 *Micare digitis*,.. a play vsed in Italy,..it is called there..the play of loue. **1611** COTGR., *Mourre*, the play of loue. **1653** URQUHART *Rabelais* I. xxii. 94 There he played..At love [orig. *a la mourre*]. **1725** BAILEY *Erasm. Colloq.* (1733) 205 The Countrymens Play of holding up our Fingers (*dimicatione digitorum, i.e.* the Play of Love).

12. A variant of the game of EUCHRE.

1886 *Euchre* 41 Slam, Love, or Skunk.

†**13.** 'A kind of thin silk stuff' (J.), formerly used when in mourning; a border of this. Orig. *love-hood*. *Obs.* (Cf. *love-ribbon* in 16 below.)

1663 BOYLE *Exper. Colours* III. ix. (1664) 198 Such a kind of Transparency, as that of a Sive, a piece of Cyprus, or a Love-Hood. **1747** MRS. DELANY *Let. to Mrs. Dewes* in *Life & Corr.* 478, I shall make no more dark things; after three months black silk is worn with love hood. **1751** *Lond. Daily Advertiser* 21 Dec. (*N. & Q.* 1st Ser. X. 206) A black velvet cloak with a love coarsely run round it. **1825–9** MRS. SHERWOOD *Lady of Manor* II. x. 63 He was dressed in white, having a sash of black love.

14. a. An old name for Traveller's Joy or Virgin's Bower, *Clematis Vitalba*; also *love-bind* (see 16 b). **b.** (See quot. 1874.)

1640 PARKINSON *Theat. Bot.* 384 In English of most country people where it groweth [called] Honestie; and the Gentlewomen call it Love, but Gerard coyned that name of the Travelours joy. **1657** S. PURCHAS *Pol. Flying-Ins.* I. xv. 95 Bees gather of these flowers following..In July..Love. **1874** *Treas. Bot.* Suppl., *Love*, a name used in Tasmania for *Comesperma volubile*.

15. Obvious combinations. **a.** simple attributive, as *love-adept, -adventure, -allegory, -ballad, -bed, -bite, -bond, -charm, -dance, -desire, -discourse, -ditty, -dream, -drug, -duel, -duet, -elegy, -eye, -fit, -flight, -game, -gift, -glance, -god, intrigue, -laughing, -light, -look, -lore, -lyric, -madness, -magic, -marriage, -melancholy, -mourning, -note, -ode, -passion, -plot, -poem, -poet, -poetry, †-prate, -quarrel, -rime, -secret, -service, -shaft, -sonnet, -speech, †-spring, -talk, -talking, -tear, -theme, -thought, -toy, -trick, -verse, -word*, etc.

1821 SHELLEY *Prometh. Unb.* I. i. 738 Dreaming like a *love-adept. **1711** SHAFTESB. *Charac.* (1737) I. 271 In relation to common amours and *love-adventures. **1933** R. TUVE *Seasons & Months* iv. 189 All this is to be found in the *love-allegory of the *Golden Targe.* **1565** COOPER *Thesaurus* s.v. *Amor, Componere amores*..To make *loue balades. **1594** SHAKS. *Rich. III*, III. vii. 72 He is not lulling on a lewd *Loue-Bed. **1934** DYLAN THOMAS *18 Poems* 19 Invisible, your clocking tides Break on the lovebeds of the weeds. *a* **1963** S. PLATH *Crossing Water* (1971) 33 Musky as a lovebed the morning after. **1749** J. CLELAND *Mem. Woman Pleasure* II. 63 Then the turtle-billing kisses, and the poignant painless *love-bites. **1903** H. ELLIS *Stud. Psychol. Sex* III. 71 We may find references to love-bites in the literature of ancient as well as of modern times... In the Indian *Kama Sutra* of Vatsyayana a chapter is devoted to this subject. **1972** *Daily Tel.* 29 Jan. 3/1 Once I saw her sitting in class with a love bite on her neck. **1951** L. MACNEICE tr. *Goethe's Faust* II. v. 295 Rapture which yearns ever, *Love-bond which burns ever. **1889** *Cent. Dict.*, *Love-charm. **1935** *Amer. Speech* X. 119/2 Certain generic epithets..have become so conventionalized that they too tell their tales... Love thief, love nest, love lure, love charm, love potion. **1948** B. G. M. SUNDKLER *Bantu Prophets S. Afr.* vi. 222 Various Native 'Chemist' shops sell..love-charms. **1911** J. A. THOMSON *Biol. Seasons* II. 233 The long larval period of two or three years in the water, and the short aerial *love-dance lasting for an evening or two. **1934** *Discovery* Nov. 309/1 For a few weeks they [*sc.* the termites] revive their ancestral free-living life in a mad love-dance. **1628** FORD *Lover's Mel.* IV. iii, The Incense of my *loue-desires are flam'd Vpon an Altar of more constant proofe. **1591** SHAKS. *Two Gent.* II. iv. 126, I know you ioy not in a *Loue-discourse. *a* **1711** KEN *Christophil* Poet. Wks. 1721 I. 476, I..Who for Two thousand Years, or rather more, Have sung the like *Love-ditties o're and o're. **1808** SCOTT *Marm.* I. vii, And frame love-ditties passing rare. *a* **1400** *Minor Poems fr. Vernon MS.* 449/20 þou make in me þi *loue-dreem. **1959** *Chambers's Dict.* Suppl., **Love-drug*, dagga. **1969** *Rolling Stone* 17 May 3/4 The new 'love drug', MDA (3,4-methylenedioxy-phenyl-iso-propylamine). **1880** 'MARK TWAIN' *Tramp Abroad* 58 This was not a *love duel, but a 'satisfaction' affair. **1932** R. CAMPBELL *Taurine Provence* ii. 44 The great 'Lou Pouvenco'..bore a small fortune between his horns, until he was killed in a love-duel by a younger rival. **1946** *Essays & Stud.* XXXI. 105 Anyone who takes the trouble to get the score of Verdi's *Otello*, and compare the *love-duet at the end of the first act, in particular Otello's solo passages, with the last but two and last but one paragraphs of the *Anna Livia* episode, will discover some very interesting similarities in phrasing. **1975** *Times* 12 Feb. 23/6 The dance of Discord and War..has to be reconciled by the love duet. **1616–61** HOLYDAY *Persius* 295 Weak *Love-elegies, such as Rome's nobles speak. *c* **1400** *Destr. Troy* 3128 Lokyng on lenght with a *loue ee. **1582** STANYHURST *Æneis* IV. (Arb.) 112 Or fro this hoat *looue fits I shal bee shortlye retrayted. **1679** J. GOODMAN *Penitent Pardoned* II. i. (1713) 150 Taken with an agony of mind, or a kind of love-fit. **1821** BYRON *Sardan.* III. i. 401 Again the love-fit's on him. **1908** E. J. BANFIELD *Confessions of Beachcomber* I. vii. 232 The *love flight of the green and gold butterfly. **1936** *Brit. Birds* XXIX. 307 The love-flights of many species depend on a subtle change in the character of the wing-beat, most marked perhaps in the waders. **1925** F. HARRIS *My Life & Loves* I. 182, I waited a little while and then began the *love game. **1973** B. FREEMANTLE *Goodbye to Old Friend* iv. 54 He wondered if Anne were playing some odd kind of love game. **1645** RUTHERFORD *Tryal & Tri. Faith* (1845) 379 Christ is God's highest *love-gift. **1876** BROWNING *Cenciaja* 279 The simpleton must ostentatiously Display a ring, the Cardinal's love-gift. **1821** KEATS *Lamia* I. 102 The *love-glances of unlovely eyes. *c* **1600** SHAKS. *Sonn.* cliv, The little *Loue-God lying once asleepe. **1887** BOWEN *Virg. Æneid* I. 662 She addresses the Love-god plumed for the flight. **1684** OTWAY *Atheist* II. i. Wks. 1728 I. 34 Your *Love-Intreagues are not so closely manag'd, but that [etc.]. **13..** *Gaw. & Gr. Knt.* 1777 With *luf-laȝyng [= laughing] a lyt. **1833** COLERIDGE *Song, 'She is not Fair'* 10, I cease not to behold The *love-light in her eye. **1839** BAILEY *Festus* (1852) 513 Her bright heart With lovelight glowed. **1637** S. RUTHERFORD *Let.* 10 June (1891) clxxv. 331 Any little communion with Him [*sc.* Christ], one of His *love-looks, should be my begun heaven. **1904** *Windsor Mag.* June 305/2 Do you think I don't know a love-look when I see it? **1754** H. WALPOLE *Lett.* (1846) III. 64 That living academy of *love-lore, my Lady Vane. **1856** *National Rev.* III. 372 The *love-lyric..is probably the most intense expression of primitive passion. **1962** L. DURRELL *Spirit of Place* (1969) 19 He had just published a sequence of love-lyrics called *Kingcup.* **1974** P. DICKINSON *Poison Oracle* ii. 44 You get a basic story, but inside it you get dramatic sections and love lyrics. **1884** *Harper's Mag.* Dec. 134/1 *Love-madness is nothing new. **1949** M. MEAD *Male & Female* iii. 56 How the..human sacrifice or *love-magic fitted into the whole. **1850** THACKERAY *Pendennis* II. xxi. 209 Look at your *love-marriages... The love-match people are the most notorious of all for quarrelling afterwards. **1973** *Archivum Linguisticum* IV. 93 A love-marriage (as opposed to an arranged marriage). **1621** BURTON *Anat. Mel.* III, *Love Melancholy. *a* **1290** *S. Eustace* 111 in Horstm. *Altengl. Leg.* (1881) 213 Ssore i-bounden..wiþ *loue mourninge Of Crist þat alle þinge shop. **1840** MRS. NORTON *Dream* etc. 205 The borrowed *love-notes of thy echoing lyre. **1689** PRIOR *Ep. Fleetwood Shephard* 50 Pigs might squeak *love-odes, dogs bark satire. **1583** T. WATSON *Poems* To Rdr. (Arb.) 27 In respect of my trauaile in penning these *loue-passions. **1670** DRYDEN *2nd Pt. Conq. Granada* I. ii, I'll your *love-plot quickly countermine. **1847** TENNYSON *Princess* IV. 102 And this A mere *love-poem. **1923** J. M. MURRY *Pencillings* 224 *Love poets are seldom the singers of happiness in love. **1965** *New Statesman* 16 July 87/2 Donne..has a title to be our greatest love poet. **1865** *Reader* 20 May 561/2 Claim passionate tenderness as especially feminine, and the inquiry is made whether all the best *love-poetry in existence..has not been written by men. **1872** GEO. ELIOT *Middlem.* III. v. xlvii. 75 Verifying in his own experience that higher love-poetry which had charmed his fancy. **1971** *Guardian* 14 July 11/2 The best of his [*sc.* Attlee's] poems are political ballads... The others (not so good) run even to love poetry. **1600** SHAKS. *A.Y.L.* IV. i. 206 You haue simply misus'd our sexe in your *loue-prate. **1671** MILTON *Samson* 1008 *Love-quarrels oft in pleasing concord end. **1588** SHAKS. *L.L.L.* III. i. 183 Don Cupid, Regent of *Loue-rimes. **1754** RICHARDSON *Grandison* I. xxxvii. 265 And has he, can he have, *so many* *Love-secrets, and yet..not let them transpire to such a sister? **1923** R. GRAVES *Feather Bed* 25 This meek ex-novice rifled Of her love-secrets? **1561** T. HOBY tr. *Castiglione's Courtyer* III. (1577) N v b, With what sober mode they shewe fauor to who so is in their *loue seruice. **1590** SHAKS. *Mids. N.* II. i. 159 Cupid..loos'd his *loue-shaft smartly from his bow. **1870** D. G. ROSSETTI *Let.* 26 Feb. (1965) II. 804 The *love-sonnets are the preponderant portion. **1958** BLUNDEN *War Poets* ii. 15 In the pre-war poems of Brooke something like a premonition can be seen recurring. A love-sonnet dated 1909 powerfully includes it. *a* **1225** *Ancr. R.* 204 Mid tollinde wordes, oðer mid *luue speche. *a* **1310** in Wright *Lyric P.* 70 Jhesu..Thy *love sprenges tacheth me. **1590** SHAKS. *Com. Err.* III. ii. 3 Shall Antipholus Euen in the spring of Loue, thy Loue-springs rot? **1599** —— *Hen. V*, v. ii. 101 Tearmes, Such as will..pleade his *Loue-suit to her gentle heart. **1862** G. MEREDITH *Mod. Love* xxxiii. 65 My wife, read this! Strange *love talk, is it not? **1968** 'N. BLAKE' *Private Wound* v. 69

She used none of the experienced woman's verbal tricks to arouse me, none of the shameless, titillating, love-talk. **13..** *Gaw. & Gr. Knt.* 927, I hope þat may hym here Schal lerne of *luf-talkyng. *a* **1310** in Wright *Lyric P.* 70 Of *love teres he weop a flod. **1938** R. Graves *Coll. Poems* p. xxi, With the *love-theme went the old fear-theme, sharpened rather than blunted by the experiences of peace. **1957** Manvell & Huntley *Techniques Film Music* i. 21 Examples of original music by Griffith and Briel included a prominent love-theme (for the Little Colonel and Elsie Stoneman). **1601** Shaks. *Twel. N.* I. i. 41 *Loue-thoughts lye rich, when canopy'd with bowres. *a* **1586** Sidney *Arcadia* III. (1598) 390 These are your *loue-toyes, which still are spent In lawlesse games. **1647** Trapp *Comm. Col.* iv. 16 Other good books must be read..yet not idle pamphlets, and love-toies. **1590** T. Watson *Eglogue Death Sir F. Walsingham* 266 Let them suppose sweete Musicke out of vse, and wanton *louetricks to be foolish toies. **1611** Cotgr., *Amourettes*, loue-trickes. **1826** Syd. Smith *Wks.* (1859) II. 90/2 All the various love-tricks of attempting to appear indifferent. *a* **1708** Walsh in Dryden *Misc.* (1727) IV. 335 Petrarch.. being by much the most famous of all the Moderns who have written *Love-Verses. *a* **1240** *Ureisun* in *Cott. Hom.* 201 Hwi ne con ich wowen þe wið swete *luue wordes. *a* **1651** Calderwood *Hist. Kirk* (1843) II. 352 Manie love words she useth to Bothwell in this letter. **1883** *Longm. Mag.* Aug. 368 Why did her love-words echo in his ear?

b. objective and objective genitive, as ***love-breathing***, ***-darting***, ***-devouring***, ***-inspiring***, ***-lacking***, etc.; ***love-†frayner*** (= asker), ***-monger***, etc.

1730–46 Thomson *Autumn* 593 In rapture warbled from *love-breathing lips. **1605** Sylvester *Du Bartas* II. iii. IV. *Captains* 849 Her sweet, *love-darting Eyn. **1634** Milton *Comus* 753 Love-darting eyes. **1592** Shaks. *Rom. & Jul.* II. vi. 7 Then *Loue-deuouring death do what he dare. *a* **1400** *Relig. Pieces fr. Thornton MS.* (1867) 59 Þat he ne do no trispase agayne þe rewle..of þis relegion, and of þase *lufe frayners. **1797** Mrs. M. Robinson *Walsingham* I. 277 The *love-inspiring dames of luxurious Italy. **1532** More *Confut. Tindale* Wks. 403/1 His false *loue-lacking charitie. **1592** Shaks. *Ven. & Ad.* cxxv, Loue-lacking vestals, and selfe-louing Nuns. **1588** —— *L.L.L.* II. i. 253 Thou art an old *Loue-monger. **1882** *Spectator* 9 Dec. 1579 His [Sterne's] *lovemongering was altogether contemptible. **1592** Shaks. *Rom. & Jul.* III. ii. 5 Spred thy close Curtaine *Loue-performing night. **1742** Pope *Dunc.* IV. 306 *Love-whisp'ring woods, and lute-resounding waves.

c. adverbial (chiefly instrumental) and parasynthetic, as ***love-born***, ***-crossed***, ***-deep***, ***-dittied***, ***-enthralled***, ***-fond***, ***-illumined***, ***-inspired***, ***-instructed***, ***-laboured***, ***-laden***, ***-learned***, ***-lighted***, ***-lit***, ***-mad***, ***-open***, ***-pensive***, ***-proof***, ***-quick***, ***†-shaked***, ***-smitten***, ***-spent***, ***-starved***, ***-stricken***, ***-touched***, ***wounded*** adjs.

1725 Pope *Odyss.* x. 398 *Love-born confidence. **1834** Lytton *Pompeii* III. ii, Thy Master was *love-crossed. **1885–94** R. Bridges *Eros & Psyche* Oct. iv, Many an old love-crost And doleful ditty would she gently sing. **1832** Tennyson *Eleanore* 76 The languors of thy *love-deep eyes. **1725** Pope *Odyss.* I. 532 *Love-dittied airs, and dance, conclude the day. **1665** Brathwait *Comment Two Tales* 23 We are now to..descend to our *love-enthralled Absolon. **1823** Roscoe *Sismondi's Lit. Eur.* (1846) II. xxxvi. 458 The melancholy soul of a *love-fond poet. **1781** E. Darwin *Bot. Gard.* I. (1791) 19 Guard from cold dews her *love-illumin'd form. **1768** Wolcot (P. Pindar) *Elegy Fleas Teneriffe* ix, The *love-inspir'd Fandango warms no more. *a* **1586** Sidney *Arcadia* I. (1598) 90 Then did he slacke his *loue-enstructed pace. **1667** Milton *P.L.* v. 41 The night-warbling Bird, that now awake Tunes sweetest his *love-labor'd song. **1820** Shelley *Skylark* ix, Soothing her *love-laden Soul in secret hour With music sweet as love. **1595** Spenser *Epithal.* 88 The birds *love-learned song. **1785** T. Dwight *Conquest of Canäan* (1788) III. 78 For earth too bright were these *love-lighted fires! **1904** *Daily Chron.* 9 Feb. 5/2 Peering through the pale miracle of spring at his violets,..his blear eyes love-lighted. **1855** J. R. Lowell *Indoors Out* in *Uncoll. Poems* (1950) 107 No glimmering beacon's *love-lit rays Will homeward guide the wand'rer's feet. **1948** Blunden *Shakespeare to Hardy* (1964) 208 Here she is in her father's garden, flowering, love-lit, awaiting the slow old Nurse. **1839** Hallam *Hist. Lit.* IV. IV. vi. §5. 259 *Love-mad and yet talking in gallant conceits. *a* **1586** Sidney *Arcadia* I. (1598) 91 His *loue-open eye..that eu'n did marke her troden grasse. **1717** Fenton *Poems* 101 Wand'ring *Love-pensive near his Amber Stream. **1810** *Splendid Follies* III. 121 The widow..placed herself opposite this *love-proof hero. **1595** Daniel *Civ. Wars* II. lxxv, [She] her *love-quicke eyes, which ready be, Fastens on one. **1600** Shaks. *A.Y.L.* III. ii. 385, I am he that is so *Loue-shak'd, I pray you tel me your remedie. **1848** Thackeray *Van. Fair* lvii, This *love-smitten and middle-aged gentleman. **1648** Herrick *Hesper.*, *To Willow-tree* (1869) 112 The *love-spent youth, and love-sick maid. **1909** *Westm. Gaz.* 24 July 2/1 *Love-starved young Keats hath cast his gift of clay. **1955** *New Yorker* 25 June 59/1 The heroine is a love-starved American secretary. **1805** Surr *Winter in Lond.* (1806) II. x. 247 Bless me, the youth is *love-stricken! **1872** A. de Vere *Leg. St. Patrick*, *Arraignm. St. P.* 7 Like birds that cannot stay their songs *Love-touched in Spring. **1591** Shaks. *Two Gent.* I. ii. 113 *Loue wounded Protheus.

16. a. Special combs.: **love-affair**, in early use *pl.* the experiences connected with being in love; now *sing.* (in somewhat disparaging use) an amatory episode in a person's life, an amour; also *fig.*; **†love amour**, sexual love as distinguished from friendship; **†love-badge**, ? a badge indicating profession of amorous allegiance; **love beads**, a necklace of coloured beads worn as a symbol of universal love; **love-begotten** *a.*, illegitimate; **†love-bend**, the 'fetters' of love; **love-blink** *Sc.*, a look of love; **love-book**, (*a*) the book of 'the Song of Solomon'; (*b*) a book treating of love; **†love-boy**, a catamite; **†love-brat** = LOVE-CHILD; **†love-broker**, one who acts as an agent between lovers; so **love-broking**; **love-call**, a call or note used as a means of amorous communication between the sexes; **†love-cause** = *love-affair*; **love comic**, a comic (sense B. 2) in which the principal ingredient of the stories is love; **love-cup**, †(*a*) a philtre; (*b*) a loving-cup; **love-curl**, a lovelock, esp. on the forehead; **love-dart**, an organ found in certain snails (see quot.), the *spiculum amoris*; **†love-deed**, an action proceeding from love; **†love-dose**, **-draught**, a philtre; **†love-dread**, the fear that proceeds from love, 'filial' fear; **†love-drunk**, intoxication with love; **†love-eie** (= *awe*) = *love-dread*; **love-favour** (see FAVOUR *sb.* 7); **†love-feat**, an act of courtship; **love-hate**, (orig. a psychoanalytic) term used to describe ambivalent feelings of love and hate existing towards the same object; freq. *attrib.*; so as *vb.*; also *love-hatred*; **†love-hood** (see sense 13); **love-interest**, a theme or episode in a story, film, etc., of which the main element is the affection of lovers; **love-juice**, †(*a*) a juice which dropped upon the eyes has the effect of a philtre; (*b*) an aphrodisiac; (*c*) a sexual secretion; **†love-lace**, the snare of love; **†love-lad**, a lover; **†love-lake** = *love-sport*; **†love-lass**, a sweetheart; **†love-late**, amorous looks or demeanour; **†love-libel**, a love-letter or message; **love-life**, relations between the sexes as they affect a particular person; **†love-liking**, sexual affection; **†love-line** *nonce-wd.*, a love-letter; **love-match**, a marriage of which the motive is love, not worldly advantage or convenience; **love-money**, coins broken in two and divided between lovers or friends as a token of remembrance; **love-nest**, a secluded retreat for (esp. illicit) lovers; **†love-nettled** *a.*, deeply in love; **love-object**, the object on which love is centred; **†love-paper** *nonce-wd.*, a love-letter; **love-pass** = *love-passage*; **love-passage**, an incident of amatory experience; **love-pat**, a smart tap given out of love (cf. *love-tick*); **love-pennant**, ? a pennant with which a departing ship is decorated; **love-philtre**, often redundantly = PHILTRE; **love-play**, wooing, caressing, spec. *foreplay*; also *fig.*; **love-potion**, a philtre = LOVE-DRINK; **†love-powder**, (*a*) a powder administered as a philtre; (*b*) *nonce-use*, the explosive stuff of love; **love-ribbon**, a narrow gauze ribbon with satin stripes (cf. sense 13); **†love-ron**, **-rune**, a tale or song of love; **love-scene**, a scene, esp. in a story or play, consisting of an interview between lovers; **love-seal**, a seal with a device appropriate to amatory correspondence; **love-seat**, a special form of arm-chair (also, of sofa) designed for two occupants; **†love-soken** (see quot.); **love-spoon**, a wooden spoon, sometimes with a double bowl, carved for presentation to one's intended wife; **love-sport**, amorous play or dalliance; **love-story**, a story in which the main theme is the affection existing between lovers; **love-tale** = prec.; **love-tap**, a tap or gentle blow to indicate love; **†love-thing**, ? a pledge of love; **†love-tick** = *love-tap*; **†love-tiding**, a message of love; **love-tight** *a.*, so as to be proof against love; **†love-tooth**, an inclination for love; **love-up** [cf. LOVE *v.*[1] 1 d] *slang*, an act of caressing, hugging, etc.; **†love-wine**, wine served out to a company in a loving-cup.

1591 Shaks. *Two Gent.* III. i. 254, I'le..confer at large Of all that may concerne thy *Loue-affaires. **1862** *National Rev.* XIV. 220 They have suggested that some irregular love-affair was unprosperous. **1867** Trollope *Chron. Barset* I. xxv. 217, I think you are aware that you have got a love-affair on hand. **1969** *Times* 25 Mar. 9/4 The crazy world of Erogenous Zones [*sc.* a play] is the result of 25-year-old Mike Stott's love affair with American strip cartoons. **1974** *Times* 4 Dec. 17 This century's love-affair with the motor-car. *c* **1350** *Ipomadon* (Kölbing) 127 Nowghte she covthe of *love amowre. **1656** Sir J. Mennis & J. Smith *Musarum Deliciæ* 35 Another ask't me..Whether I wore a *Love-bagge on my shoulder? **1968** *Daily Colonist* (Victoria, B.C.) 20 June 1/5 *Love beads draped on him by Pierre Trudeau, adorn former Prime Minister Pearson at Toronto political rally. **1969** R. Lowell *Notebk. 1967–68* (1970) 217 Our love-beads Rattling together to show that we were young. **1973** 'B. Mather' *Snowline* xiii. 155 Weirdo fringed shirts, headbands, love beads..as unsavoury a bunch of love children as I have ever seen. **1771** Smollett *Humph. Cl.* 24 May, That he had been a *love-begotten babe, brought up in the workhouse. **1784** *Registers of River, Kent (MS.)*, Mary, daughter of Ann Allen—Love begotten, [baptized]. *c* **1250** *Hymn to Virgin* 35 in *Trin. Coll. Hom.* App. 256 Ic êm in þine *loue bende. **13..** *Guy Warw.* (A.) 324 Leuer him wer walk & wende, & dye in trewe loue bende. **1508** Dunbar *Tua mariit wemen* 228, I cast on him a crabbit E..And lettis it is a *luf-blenk. **1636** Rutherford *Lett.* (1862) I. 155 My Bridegroom's love-blinks fatten my weary soul. *a* **1225** *Ancr. R.* 102 Ase mi leofmon þet seið to me, iðe *luue boc, 'osculetur me osculo oris sui'. **1587** F. Clement *Petie Schole* 36 Bookeloue I say, but I meane not louebookes, which..be the enemies of vertue. **1591** Shaks. *Two Gent.* I. i. 19 For I will be thy beadesman, Valentine. *Val.* And on a loue-booke pray for my successe? **1936** C. S. Lewis *Allegory of Love* iv. 172 Hence those strange comings and goings in every medieval love-book. *a* **1656** Ussher *Ann.* VI. (1658) 131 Pausanias, being discovered by Argilius, his *love-boy. ? **16..** *Old Chap-bk.* (N.), Four *love brats will be laid to thee. **1601** Shaks. *Twel. N.* III. ii. 39 There is no *loue-Broker in the world, can more preuaile in mans commendation with woman, then report of valour. **1808** E. S. Barrett *Miss-led General* 165 What money Mr. Greentimber disbursed on account of the great man's *love-broking affairs. **1824** Miss Mitford *Village* Ser. I. 198 In less than two minutes Harriet heard the *love-call sounded at Sally's gate. **1887** *Athenæum* 31 Dec. 901/3 He [Mr. Rowbotham] disagrees with Darwin in finding the origin of all instrumental music in the love-call. **1600** Shaks. *A.Y.L.* IV. i. 97 In all this time there was not anie man died in his owne person (*videlicet*) in a *loue cause. **1951** M. McLuhan *Mech. Bride* (1967) 151/2 It recently shifted a large section of its enterprises from murder to *love comics. **1970** G. Greer *Female Eunuch* 214 The market is contested by..love comics and fotoromance. **1561** Daus tr. *Bullinger on Apoc.* (1573) 128 Poysoning *louecuppes, and inchauntments, were in the tyme of S. John most frequented throughout the Romayne Empyre. **1849** Rock *Ch. of Fathers* IV. xi. 86 The love-cup was sent about. **1850** H. Melville *White Jacket* II. xxxvii. 240 Many sailors, with naturally tendril locks, prided themselves upon what they call *love curls. **1926** T. E. Lawrence *Seven Pillars* (1935) lxxxvi. 479 In command was young Metaab, stripped to his skimp riding-drawers for hard work, with his black love-curls awry. **1877** F. P. Pascoe *Zool. Classif.* 122 A curious organ is a pyriform muscular sac, containing one or two slender conical styles, which can be thrust out through the aperture of the sac; they are found in certain snails, and with them they pierce each other's skin. They are known as '*love-darts'. **13..** *Minor Poems fr. Vernon MS.* liv. 62 And þis I made for Monkynde, Mi *loue-dedes to haue in mynde. **1709** J. Johnson *Clergym. Vade M.* II. 69 Pharmacy probably signifies here..the compounding of philtrums or *love-doses. **1647** R. Stapylton *Juvenal* 85 Their *love-draughts, charmes, and druggs. **1841** Borrow *Zincali* I. II. i. 228 The women..dealing in love draughts and diablerie. **1906** *Westm. Gaz.* 27 Aug. 3/1 The love-draught which Tristram and Iseult drink together. *c* **1380** Wyclif *Serm.* Sel. Wks. II. 316 *Love-drede is in men wiþouten siche servile drede. *c* **1440** *Jacob's Well* xxxviii. 243 For þe loue-dreed þat sche hadde to god. **1390** Gower *Conf.* III. 11 *Lovedrunke is the meschief Above alle othre the most chief. *a* **1225** *Ancr. R.* 428 Liðe wordes..þerof kumeð þinge best—þet is *luue-eie. **1597** Bp. Hall *Sat.* I. ii. B 3 b, Deck't with *love-fauors. **1588** Shaks. *L.L.L.* v. ii. 123 And euery one his *Loue-feat will aduance Vnto his seuerall Mistresse. **1925** J. Riviere et al. tr. *Freud's Coll. Papers* IV. 79 So the second antithesis, *love-hate, reproduces the polarity pleasure-pain, which is bound up with the former. **1937** H. Nicolson *Diary* 16 June (1966) 302 Goering..has the love-hate complex of the average German bourgeois for England. **1950** E. J. Simmons *Dostoevsky* xix. 315 Versilov's..love-hate relations with Katerina which conclude with his mad attempt to murder her. **1967** A. Wilson *No Laughing Matter* II. 216 *She* love-hates him enough to be unable to leave him. **1972** Ld. Robens *Ten Year Stint* ii. 15 My personal relationship with the men and their leaders was schizophrenic—a sort of love-hate relationship. **1951** H. Hatfield *Thomas Mann* iii. 36 The protagonists in *Two Friends*, a novella of the *love-hatred between a responsible burgher and a ne'er-do-well, afford a certain parallel to Thomas and Christian Buddenbrook. **1961** *Times* 18 Mar. 11/4 The love-hatred of Isolde for Tristan. **1892** H. James *Notebks.* (1947) 129 There must be a '*love-interest'—which is one and the same with the other parts of the situation. **1938** R. G. Collingwood *Princ. Art* v. 84 The cinema, where it is said to be a principle accepted by almost every manager that no film can succeed without a love-interest. **1961** C. S. Lewis *Exper. in Crit.* iv. 38 The story of excitement or mystery usually has a 'love interest' tacked on to it. **1973** *Time Out* 2–8 Mar. 59/3 'Love-interest' rears its inept head just as the medical satire should show its teeth. **1590** Shaks. *Mids. N.* III. ii. 89 Thou hast mistaken quite And laid the *loue iuyce on some true loues sight. **1896** Farmer & Henley *Slang* IV. 241/1 Love-juice. **1965** J. Gaskell *Fabulous Heroine* 59 The sheets smelt of linen instead of love-juice. **1968** L. Berg *Risinghill* 122 'What is "love-juice"?' 'The liquid produced in the vagina of a woman when she is sexually excited.' **1972** 'R. Crawford' *Whip Hand* I. ix. 54 She was drugged by love-juices and on the brink of sleep. **1972** *Pussycat* XXXIII. LIX. 7/2, I could feel his lovejuice so hot, trickling down into the start of my stomach. *c* **1330** *Arth. & Merl.* 2251 (Kölbing) He was nomen wiþ *loue las. **1586** W. Webbe *Eng. Poetrie* (Arb.) 84 The Cornation that among the *loue laddes wontes to be worne much. *c* **1320** *Sir Tristr.* 2020 Her *loue laike þou bi hald For þe loue of me. **1610** Niccols *Eng. Eliza* Induct. *Mirr. Mag.* 776 So soone as Tython's *love-lasse gan display Her opall colours in her Easterne throne. *a* **1225** *Ancr. R.* 90 His eie euer bihalt te ȝif þu makest..eni *luue lates touward unðeauwes. **1602** Dekker *Satiromastix* Wks. 1873 I. 215 *Sir Vau...* I desire you to..read this Paper. *Miniver.* Ile receive no *Love libels perdy, but by word a mouth. **1919** M. K. Bradby *Psycho-Anal.* v. 59 The character and development of the infantile love for father and mother will have an influence on the whole *love-life of later years. **1934** 'R. West' *Mod. Rake's Progress* 74 Ecclesiastics..called out to sanctify the love-life of our puny little George. **1959** A. Christie *Cat among Pigeons* viii. 89 Even Games Mistresses may have their love lives. **1972** T. Ardies *This Suitcase* xiii. 140 He's the guy who's trying to break up my love life. *c* **1386** Chaucer *Sir Thopas* 2040 Of romances that been royales, Of popes and of cardinales, And eek of *love-lykinge. **1601** Shaks. *All's Well* II. i. 81 To giue great Charlemaine a pen in's hand And write to her a *loue-line. **1749** Fielding *Tom Jones* XIII. viii, This was a *love-match, as they call it, on both sides; this is, a match between two beggars. **1869** Trollope *He Knew* etc. xxv. (1878) 138 It was little enough she got by marrying him... But it was a love-match. **1856** W. H. Smyth *Rom. Fam. Coins* 281 The custom of breaking *love-money, as a pledge of fidelity. **1919** U. Sinclair *Brass Check* xi. 65 So before long we began to notice dark hints in the newspapers; such esoteric phrases as 'Sinclair's *love-nest'. **1970** G. Greer *Female*

Eunuch 154 Nobody knew of his love-nest. **1972** 'H. Howard' *Nice Day for Funeral* ix. 124 Pamela and Frankie were sharing a love-nest at Lakeland Towers. **1586** D. Rowland *Lazarillo* II. (1672) X viii, I was so *love-nettled, that if they had asked me the Phenix.. I would have given it them. **1923** J. T. MacCurdy *Probl. Dynamic Psychol.* xvi. 191 The 'sentiment of love'.. consists in identification with the *love object. **1925** J. Riviere et al. tr. *Freud's Coll. Papers* IV. 45 In the choice of their love-object they have taken as their model not the mother but their own selves. **1960** C. Day Lewis *Buried Day* vii. 137 When it became apparent that.. as a love-object, I myself was unsatisfactory, she started on dogs. **1967** M. E. Romm in C. W. Wahl *Sexual Probl.* 221 Fetishism is.. the utilization in sex of a substitute for the love object. **1973** S. Fisher *Female Orgasm* xv. 437 Orgasm difficulties were observed to be linked to concern about the instability or potential loss of love objects. *c* **1613** Middleton *No Wit like a Woman's* I. ii, Peruse this *love-paper as you go. [*Giving letter.*] **1872** Hardy *Under Greenwood Tree* I. I. viii. 113 Good luck attended Dick's *love-passes during the meal. He sat next Fancy. **1845** C. M. Kirkland *Western Clearings* 106 No one .. had ever been able to ascertain whether there had actually been any '*love-passages' between them or not. **1865** Tylor *Early Hist. Man.* iii. 43 Love-passages of the gods and heroes. **1876** C. D. Warner *Wint. Nile* i. 24 Garibaldi received one of his wounds, a sort of *love-pat of fame. **1889** Doyle *Micah Clarke* 377 You are like the same ship when the battle and the storm have.. torn the *love-pennants from her peak. **1834** Lytton *Pompeii* ii. 20 The very air seems to have taken a *love-philtre, so handsome does every face without a beard seem in my eyes. **1911** *Love-play [see courting *vbl. sb.* 3]. **1944** T. Rattigan *While Sun Shines* II. 226 You're both very much mistaken if either of you imagines that you're going to have twopence-worth of verbal loveplay with my fiancée on my telephone. **1963** A. Heron *Towards Quaker View of Sex* 55 Adult heterosexuality presents fewer problems where early love play is tolerated than where it is suppressed. **1964** L. Nkosi *Rhythm of Violence* 46 Lili: Jo, I don't want to play. Jojozi: [tries to kiss her.] Not even love-play? **1647** R. Stapylton *Juvenal* 85 *margin*, Philters or *love-potions. **1623** Webster *Duchess of Malfi* v. ii, Confesse to me Which of my women 'twas you hyr'd to put *Loue-powder into my drinke? **1678** Butler *Hud.* III. i. 661 When he's with Love-powder laden, And Prim'd, and Cock'd by Miss, or Madam. **1742** J. Yarrow *Love at First Sight* 14 There are Things call'd Charms, Bribes, and Love-Powder. *c* **1805** Mrs. Sherwood in *Life* xix. (1847) 329, I made her and Annie new caps, which I trimmed with rosettes of black *love-ribbon. **1882** Caulfeild & Saward *Dict. Needlewk.*, *Love-ribbon*,.. was employed to tie on Crape Hat-bands when worn at funerals, and is now occasionally worn by ladies in their caps. *a* **1225** *Leg. Kath.* 109 Nalde ha.. nane *luue runes leornin ne lustnen. *c* **1275** *A Luue Ron 2* in *O.E. Misc.* 93 A Mayde cristes me bit yorne þat ich hire wurche a luue ron. **1639** Massinger *Unnat. Combat* III. iii. 181, I will bring you Where you.. may see The *love-scene acted. **1818** *Theatrical Inquisitor* XIII. 183 Love-scenes.. which both French and English writers.. regard as absolutely essential to their drama. **1850** Hannay *Singleton Fontenoy* I. iii. I. 35 Circe resumed a love-scene between Adèle and the tender *forçat*. **1932** R. Campbell *Taurine Provence* 37 Read his [*sc.* Shaw's] miserable love-letters (published) and his 'love-scene' between Caesar and Cleopatra. **1975** *Country Life* 6 Feb. 326/2 Intimate, tender love-scenes. **1877** W. Jones *Finger-ring* 21 The impress being two human heads.. the prototype of the numerous '*love seals' of a later period. **1904** *Love-seat [see *double chair* (double *a.* A. 6)]. **1915** F. W. Burgess *Antique Furnit.* 205 Such settees which closely resemble an adaptation of two single chairs, are commonly called 'love-seats'. **1970** *Canad. Antiques Collector* Dec. 21/1 A Victorian love seat Mr. Daniel saw being hauled away in a garbage truck. **1973** 'D. Halliday' *Dolly & Starry Bird* x. 151 Johnson.. kissed her, and then.. found a love seat and dropped there beside her. **1523** Fitzherb. *Surv.* 9 b, But and he [the tenant] bye his corne in the market or other places, he is than at lybertie to grynde where he may be best serued, that maner of gryndyng is called *loue Socone, and the lordes tenauntes be called bonde socon. **1918** W. R. Butterfield in *Connoisseur* Aug. 191/1 At first,.. *love-spoons did not differ greatly from the wooden spoons in ordinary use in the household. **1968** J. Arnold *Shell Bk. Country Crafts* 193 The Welsh carvers.. produced a great deal of fine work, amongst which were the celebrated love-spoons. **1972** *Country Life* 20 Jan. 160/2 These [*sc.* stay busks] were rather in the manner of Welsh love-spoons and were made by young men for their intended marriage partners. **1605** Chapman *All Fools* I. i, Where I am cloyde, And being bound to *loue sports, care not for them. **1623** Massinger *Bondman* I. iii, They cannot.. Vsher vs to our Litters, tell *loue Stories. **1890** Barrie *My Lady Nicotine* xxiii. (1901) 70/1 The tragedy.. is led up to by a pathetic love-story. **1633** Shirley *Bird in Cage* v. I 2 b, Forgetting all their legends, and *Loue tales Of Venus, Cupid, and the scapes of Ioue. **1667** Milton *P.L.* I. 452 The Love-tale Infected Sions daughters with like heat. **1802** Ritson *Anc. Engl. Metr. Rom.* I. p. vii, The love-tales of Longus, Heliodorus, and Xenophon of Ephesus. **1889** 'Mark Twain' *Yankee at Crt. K. Arthur* xxxiii. 383 When I make up my mind to hit a man, I don't plan out a *love-tap. *c* **1205** Lay. 169 For he heo heuede swiþe ilofed, & *luf-ping hire biheite. **1493** *Dives & Paup.* x. viii. I iij b, Yᵗ mischeif is noo curse but a *louetyk of god. **1627** Bp. Hall *Passion Serm.* Wks. 429 These were but loue-ticks to what His soule endured. **1635** Quarles *Embl.* III. vi. 146 Her frownes.. may chance to show An angry love-trick [*read* -tick] on his arme, or so. *a* **1250** *Owl & Night.* 1035 Ich mai do þar gode note, And bringe hom *lovetiþinge, Vor ich of chirche songe singe. **1875** McLaren *Serm.* Ser. II. iv. 71, I can shut it out, sealing my heart *love-tight against it. **1580** Lyly *Euphues* (Arb.) 350, I am nowe olde, yet haue I in my head a *loue tooth. **1953** 'Caddie' *Sydney Barmaid* xxv. 136 Come on, wot about a little bit of a *luv-up? **1968** M. Allwright *Roundabout* ix. 65 He looked so beaten by the world that I wanted to gather him in my arms on the spot and give him a good love-up. **1641** Best *Farm. Bks.* (Surtees) 117 They perhaps have *love wine ready to give to the company when they light.

b. In names of plants and animals: **love-and-idle(s**, dial. var. of *love-in-idleness* (E.D.D.); **love-bind**, the plant Traveller's Joy (Halliwell); **love-bush**, the Jamaican name for dodder *sb.* 1; **love-entangle, -entangled** = *love-in-a-mist* (*a*); **love-grass**, a grass of the genus *Eragrostis*: **love-in-a-mist**, (*a*) the Fennel-flower, *Nigella damascena*; (*b*) a West Indian species, *Passiflora fœtida* (cf. G. *liebe im nebel*); **love-in-a-puzzle**, *Nigella damascena*; **love-in-idleness** (also †**love-in-idle**), the Heartsease, *Viola tricolor*; **love-parrakeet, -parrot** = love-bird; **love-shell** (see quot.); **love-tree**, the Judas-tree, *Cercis Siliquastrum* (*Treas. Bot.* 1866); also ***tree of love***; **love-vine**, 'any species of *Cuscuta*, dodder' (Webster, Suppl.).

1630 J. Taylor (Water-P.) *Wks.* II. 134/2 Amongst all Pot-herbes growing on the ground, Time is the least respected, I haue found.. When passions are let loose without a bridle, Then precious Time is turnd to *Loue and Idle. **1814** J. Lunan *Hortus Jamaicensis* I. 266 Cuscuta Americana... The negroes of Liguanea mountains call it *love-bush. **1954** *Farmer's Guide* (Jamaica Agric. Soc.) 582 The common Love-bushes of Jamaica comprise about four species of *Cuscuta*. **1962** S. Wynter *Hills of Hebron* ii. 35 Pale yellow tendrils of the 'lovebush' wrapping themselves around the prickly arms of the cactus. **1847** Halliwell, **Love-entangle*, the nigella. *Cornw.* **1841** S. C. Hall *Ireland* I. 128 Sometimes they are overgrown by weed called '*love-entangled', and the golden stone-crop. **1702** Petiver in *Phil. Trans.* XXIII. 1257 What is peculiar in this *Love-grass is its having just under each spike, its stalk clammy. **1760** J. Lee *Introd. Bot.* App. 318 *Love in a Mist, *Passiflora*. **1834** Mary Howitt in *Tait's Mag.* I. 445/2 I'd a noble root of love-in-a-mist. **1824** H. Phillips *Flora Hist.* II. 151 *Love in a puzzle, Love in a mist,.. *Nigella Damascena*. **1664** S. Blake *Compl. Gardeners Pract.* 50 *Lowe in idle, or two faces under a hood, is a Flower that is much like Violets. **1578** Lyte *Dodoens* II. ii. 149 This floure is called.. in English, Pances, *Loue in idlenes, and Hartes ease. **1590** Shaks. *Mids. N.* II. i. 168 The bolt of Cupid.. fell vpon a little westerne flower; Before, milke-white; now purple with loues wound, And maidens call it, Loue in idlenesse. **1864** T. L. Phipson *Utilization Minute Life* vii. 155 Other species of Cypræa known.. by the English as '*Love-shells', are used as ornaments, etc. [**Love-tree*: cf. **1760** J. Lee *Introd. Bot.* App. 317 Tree of Love, *Cercis*.] **1885** Lady Brassey *The Trades* 325 The long tendrils of the *love-vine rolled up into coils, which he assured us would live and grow for years, if hung on a nail indoors.

love, *sb.*² [Of obscure origin.] One of a set of transverse beams supporting the spits in a smoke-house for the curing of herring.

1865 [see spit *sb.*¹ 4 d]. **1895** A. Patterson *Man & Nature on Broads* 44 A savoury bloater, fresh down from the 'loves', is engrossing our own attentions. **1962** Granville *Dict. Sailors' Slang* 73/2 *Loves*, wooden splines in a herring curing loft on which the fish are suspended to dry.

love (lʌv), *v.*¹ Forms: 1–2 lufian, 2–3 luvie(n, 3 lovin, *Orm.* lufenn, lufie, lofvie, 3–4 luven, loven, lovie, luvie, -ye, 4 *Sc.* lowe, luff, 4–5 lofe, luffe, 4–6 luve, luf(e, 5 loufe, lovyn, *Sc.* low, 6 loove, (lub(be), *Sc.* luif, lwf, luyf, lwiff, (lude = *luf it*), 8–9 *Sc.* lo'e, 3– love. *Pa. t.* 1 lufode, 2–3 luvede, 3 lufede, lovede, 4 lovied, lofde, louved, lufud, -ed, luv(e)d, lufd, lovyd, *north.* luffet, lofit, 4–5 lovet, lowyt, 4–6 *Sc.* lovit, luf(f)it, -yt, 5 luf(f)ed, lofed, -id, -yd, loffyd, 6 *Sc.* luifed, luif(f)et, lwffit, lowitt, lude, lwd, luid, 4– loved. *Pa. pple.* 1 ȝe-lufod, 2–3 iloved, y-, iluved, ileoved, 4–5 yloved, 4- (as in pa. t.). [OE. *lufian*, f. *lufu* love *sb.*¹]

1. a. *trans.* With personal obj. or one capable of personification: To bear love to; to entertain a great affection or regard for; to hold dear.

c **825** *Vesp. Psalter* xvii. 1 Ic lufiu ðe dryhten meȝen min. **1154** *O.E. Chron.* an. 1137 (Laud MS.) Hi luueden God & gode men. *c* **1250** *Gen. & Ex.* 2042 An litel stund, quhile he was ðer, So gan him luuen ðe prisuner. *a* **1300** *Cursor M.* 2328 Þis abram.. Ful wel was luued wit god of heuen. **1375** Barbour *Bruce* I. 360 All men lufyt him for his bounte. *a* **1420** Hoccleve *De Reg. Princ.* 1260 God in holy writ seith ..'Whom so I loue, hym wole I chastyse'. *c* **1470** Henry *Wallace* x. 725, I sall, quhill I may leiff, Low yow fer mar than ony othir knycht. *a* **1548** Hall *Chron.*, *Edw. IV* 234 b, I love hym as my brother, and take hym as my frende. *a* **1600** Montgomerie *Misc. Poems* x. 45 Love nane bot vhare thou art lude. **1647** Clarendon *Hist. Reb.* vi. §406 He.. loved his country with too unskilful a tenderness. **1653** Walton *Angler* vii. 153 Tie the frogs leg above the upper joint to the armed wire, and in so doing use him as though you loved him. **1769** Goldsm. *Hist. Rome* (1786) I. 432 Caesar.. was loved almost to adoration by his army. **1856** Froude *Hist. Eng.* (1858) I. ii. 128 A man who loved England well, but who loved Rome better. **1885** *Ch. Times* 13 Nov. 883 Our nation is not much loved across the Atlantic.

b. *spec.* with reference to love between the sexes. ***to love paramours***: see paramour.

c **1000** Ælfric *Gen.* xxiv. 67 Isaac.. underfeng hiȝ to wife and lufode hiȝ [etc.]. **1297** R. Glouc. (Rolls) 9549 In som þing The quene louede as me wende more him þan þe king. **1375** Barbour *Bruce* x. 554, I.. lufit ane vench her in the toune. **1470–85** Malory *Arthur* VII. xxxv. 269, I loue her aboue all ladyes lyuynge. **1567** *Satir. Poems Reform.* iv. 15 Lancit with luif she luid me by all wycht. **1604** Shaks. *Oth.* IV. i. 111, I neuer knew woman loue man so. **1667** Milton *P.L.* IX. 832 So dear I love him, that with him all deaths I could endure. **1711** Ramsay *Elegy on Maggy Johnstoun* iii, To bonny lasses black or brown, As we loo'd best. **1794** Burns *Red, Red Rose* ii, And I will luve thee still, my dear, Till a' the seas gang dry. **1859** Tennyson *Elaine* 674–5 If I love not him, I know there is none other I can love.

†**c.** Occasional uses, with cogn. obj. with complement, etc. *Obs.*

1470–85 Malory *Arthur* IX. viii. 364 The good loue that I haue loued you. **1672** Dryden *Marr. à la Mode* I. i. Wks. 1883 IV. 261 We loved, and we loved, as long as we could, 'Till our love was loved out in us both. **1678** —— *All for Love* II. Wks. 1883 V. 369 We have loved each other Into our mutual ruin.

d. With *up*. To caress, fondle; to engage in love-play with. *colloq.* (orig. *U.S.*).

1921 J. Dos Passos *Three Soldiers* II. iii. 83 You said you were goin' back and love up that goddam girl. **1928** *Dialect Notes* VI. 62 If a hillman [in the Ozarks] does admit that he loved a woman he means only that he caressed and embraced her—and he usually says that he *loved her up*. **1932** K. S. Prichard *Kiss on Lips* 167 Why don't you give her a hug.. love her up a bit? **1957** J. Braine *Room at Top* xix. 166 If you love me up, I'll be as warm as toast. **1968** M. Allwright *Roundabout* ix. 59, I never meant any harm; it was just as if he was a puppy I was loving up.

2. a. Proverbs.

1546 J. Heywood *Prov.* (1867) 76 Loue me, loue me dog. *a* **1548** Hall *Chron.* (1809) 444 The olde Proverbe loue me little and love me longe. **1553** T. Wilson *Rhet.* (1580) 192 A man maie loue his house well, and yet not ride vpon the ridge. *a* **1633** G. Herbert *Jacula Prudentum* 141 Love your neighbour, yet pull not downe your hedge.

b. In certain vulgar ejaculations: (***Lord***) ***love you*** (or ***your heart***), etc.

c **1810** W. Hickey *Mem.* (1913) II. i. 10 Lord love your honour, to be sure I will. **1821** Scott *Pirate* I. i. 15 But, Heaven love you, Mr Mertoun, think what you are purposing. **1833** T. Hook *Parson's Dau.* (1847) 231 Love your heart, sir, a path's never straight. **1841** Lytton *Nt. & Morn.* II. ix. II. 15 Quiet! Lord love you! never heard a noisier little urchin! **1843** Dickens *Christmas Carol* iii. 85 They said it was a shame to quarrel upon Christmas Day. And so it was! God love it, so it was. **1894** R. Bridges *Feast of Bacchus* II. 579 Lord love you, I'm not surprised at any one wanting to marry you. **1898** J. D. Brayshaw *Slum Silhouettes* I Mister Bloomfiel'? Lor' lummy! there ain't no misters 'ere. *Ibid.* 141 Mine? Lor' luv a duck! No, that's Sal Hogan's little lot. **1916** 'Taffrail' *Pincher Martin* xii. 218 'Lord love us!.. d'you mean to say'—Words failed him. **1922** Joyce *Ulysses* 176 Lord love a duck, he said, look at what I'm standing drinks to! **1934** T. S. Eliot *Rock* ii. 65 What's that? Lor-love-a-duck, it's the missus! **1938** 'J. Bell' *Port of London Murders* xv. 247 ''Lor love us!' I says to meself. 'Something's up.' **1954** W. Sansom (*title*) Lord love us. **1955** M. Allingham *Beckoning Lady* iv. 55 Orf come 'is 'at, and lord luva duck!

c. ***to love one's love with an A, with a B***, etc.: a formula used in games of forfeits.

[**1620** *Swetnam Arraigned* (Grosart) 24 A husband.. so complete As if he had been pickt out of the Christ-Crosse row... Ile begin with A.. comparing his good parts as thus: for A, hee is Amiable, Bountefull, Courteous.. now for Z he's Zealous.] **1672** Marvell *Reh. Transp.* I. Wks. 1776 II. 61 One would think that.. you should have learnt when J.O. came into play, to love your love with an J, because he is judicious, though you hate your love with an J, because he is jealous: and then to love your love with an O, because he is oraculous, though you hate your love with an O, because he is obscure. **1678** Butler *Hud.* III. i. 1006 For these you play at purposes, And love your love's with A's and B's. **1865** Dickens *Mut. Fr.* II. i, I'll give you a clue to my trade, in a game of forfeits. I love my love with a B because she's Beautiful; I hate my love with a B because she's Brazen; I took her to the sign of the Blue Boar, and I treated her with Bonnets; her name's Bouncer, and she lives in Bedlam.

d. ***he loves me, he loves me not***, etc.: a formula used in divining-games. Also *transf.*

[**1909** A. E. Gillington *Old Hampshire Singing Games* facing p. 1 Then they say 'David Bailey' (Boy's name), Do you love me? Yes, No, etc. till the skipping girl stops. The two trilling the rope say—'Alma Bailey' (Girl's name), Do you love him? Yes, No, etc.] **1946** A. Uttley *Country Things* v. 64 He loves me. He don't. He'll have me. He won't. He would if he could, But he can't. **1959** I. & P. Opie *Lore & Lang. Schoolch.* xv. 339 Much energy and calculation is devoted to skipping through the alphabet... the following sequence being that used by an 11-year-old Portsmouth girl: Does he love me? Yes, no, yes, no... Will he marry me? Yes, no, yes, no. **1971** *Guardian* 10 July 11/2 Eric Lubbock's private game of 'he loves me, he loves me not' with press and politicians is coming to a blessed end.

e. Phrases. ***an*** (or ***as***) ***you*** (or ***thou***, etc.) ***love me***, if (or since) you love me: used as an imprecation; ***to love and leave you***: a formula of departure; ***love them and leave them***, etc.: seduce and abandon women.

1818 Carlyle *Early Lett.* (1886) 148 Send a letter quickly, an thou love me. **1823** J. F. Cooper *Pioneers* I. i. 28 Natty—you need say nothing of the shot, nor of where I am going—remember, Natty, as you love me. **1885** R. Holland *Gloss. County of Chester* 212 *Love you and leave you*, a common saying when any visitor is going to take his departure. 'Well a' mun *love ye, and leave ye*.' **1917** 'S. Rohmer' *Si-Fan Mysteries* xxxv. 264 But in waiting for one who is stealthily entering a room, don't, as you love me, take it for granted that he will enter *upright*. **1930** *Amer. Speech* Dec. 92 Love'em and leave'em. **1938** W. G. Hardy *Turn back River* 33 Love 'em and leave 'em; that was the idea. **1946** K. Tennant *Lost Haven* (1947) xvi. 259, I wouldn't try to keep me if I was you... Love me and let me leave. **1960** K. Amis *Take Girl like You* ii. 36 I'm afraid I shall have to love you and leave you. **1967** J. Morgan *Involved* 11 'Dewi, I have to love you and leave you,' Frankie said. 'I'm supposed to be on duty.' **1975** H. McCutcheon *Instrument of Vengeance* vii. 123 'I have many interests.' 'But no girls? .. You just love them and leave them, no?'

3. *absol.* and *intr.* **a.** To entertain a strong affection; *spec.* to have a passionate attachment to a person of the opposite sex; to be in love.

c **1250** *Hymn Virgin* 45 in *Trin. Coll. Hom.* App. 256 Nis non maiden.. þat swo derne louiȝe kunne. *a* **1300** *Cursor M.* 4510 Qua leli luues for-gettes lat. ? *a* **1366** Chaucer *Rom. Rose* 85 Harde is the heart that loueth nought In Mey. *a* **1550** *Christis Kirke Gr.* iv, He wald haif lufit, scho wald not lat him. **1604** Shaks. *Oth.* v. ii. 344 One that lou'd not

wisely, but too well. **1650** BAXTER *Saints' R.* III. x. §6 No man else can tell me whether I Believe and Love, if I cannot tell my self. **1710** LADY M. W. MONTAGU *Let. to W. Montagu* 25 Apr., I can esteem, I can be a friend, but I do not know whether I can love. **1850** TENNYSON *In Mem.* xxvii, 'Tis better to have loved and lost, Than never to have loved at all.

†**b.** in reciprocal sense; in ME. *to love together* (or *samen*). *Obs.*

1340 HAMPOLE *Pr. Consc.* 1849 Þe body and þe saul with þe lyfe Lufes mare samen þan man and hys wyfe. **1387** TREVISA *Higden* (Rolls) III. 373 It is spedful þat frendes love wel. **1470–85** MALORY *Arthur* XVIII. i. 725 They loued to gyder more hotter than they did to fore hand. **1568** GRAFTON *Chron.* I. 173 They loved after, as two brethren, during their naturall lyves. **1593** SHAKS. *2 Hen. VI*, IV. vii. 139 Let them kisse one another: For they lou'd well When they were aliue. **1601** —— *Jul. C.* IV. iii. 131 Loue, and be Friends. **1790** COWPER *Let. to Newton* 15 Oct., The day of separation between those who have loved long and well is an awful day. **1791** BURNS '*Ae fond kiss*' ii, Had we never lov'd sae kindly. *a* **1849** [see LOVE *sb.*[1] 4].

c. *to love with*: to bear or make love to; to be in love with. *Obs.* or *arch.*

1665 BRATHWAIT *Comment Two Tales* 96 That they may have Husbands Meek, to live with, Young, to love with, and Fresh, to lie with. **1883** R. W. DIXON *Mano* I. iii. 7 He was so gentle and so fair a knight, Who loved with Blanche.

4. *trans.* With a thing as obj.:

a. To be strongly attached to, to be unwilling to part with or allow to perish (life, honour, etc.).

c **950** *Lindisf. Gosp.* John xii. 25 Seðe lufað sauel his spildeð hia. *c* **1175** *Lamb. Hom.* 15 Þu aȝest luuan heore saule for cristes luue. **13..** *Gaw. & Gr. Knt.* 2368 Bot for ȝe lufed your lyf, þe lasse I yow blame. *c* **1412** HOCCLEVE *De Reg. Princ.* 462 Lordes, if ye your estat and honour Louen, fleemyth this vicius errour! **1432–50** tr. *Higden* (Rolls) VII. 25 The erle..preide her as sche luffed hir lyfe that [etc.]. **1530** PALSGR. 735/1 No man styrre and he love his lyfe. **1649** LOVELACE *Lucasta, Going to Wars* iii, I could not love thee (Deare) so much, Lov'd I not Honour more. **1661** MARVELL *Corr.* Wks. 1872–5 II. 71 As you loue your own affairs,..be pleased..to let me know your minds in these points.

b. To have a strong liking for; to be fond of; to be devoted or addicted to. In the U.S. a frequent vulgarism for *like*.

c **1200** *Trin. Coll. Hom.* 99 It warð on eches muð wat mete se he mest luuede. **1297** R. GLOUC. (Rolls) 7698 Game of houndes he louede. *c* **1386** CHAUCER *Cook's T.* 12 He loved bet the Taverne than the shoppe. *c* **1400** tr. *Secreta Secret., Gov. Lordsh.* 113 Þis man ys lycherous, deceyuant, and loufand lecherye. **1432–50** tr. *Higden* (Rolls) IV. 393 This Nero luffede gretely instrumentes musicalle. **1611** BIBLE *Prov.* xx. 13 Loue not sleepe, lest thou come to pouertie. **1622** FLETCHER *Beggars Bush* IV. v, I love a fat goose, as I love allegiance. **1690** LOCKE *Hum. Und.* II. xx. §4 When a Man declares..that he loves Grapes, it is no more, but that the taste of Grapes delights him. **1738** SWIFT *Pol. Conversat.* 10 Colonel, Don't you love Bread and Butter with your Tea? **1796** MRS. GLASSE *Cookery* iii. 19 Some love a pig brought whole to table. **1801** GOUV. MORRIS in Sparks *Life & Writ.* (1832) III. 146, I respect the English nation highly, but I do not love their manners. **1817** SCOTT *Search after Happiness* xviii, She loved a book, and knew a thing or two. **1849** MACAULAY *Hist. Eng.* iv. I. 447 The new king, who loved the details of naval business. **1859** BARTLETT *Dict. Amer.*, To Love, for to *like*. 'Do you love pumpkin pie?'

c. To take pleasure in the existence of (a virtue, a practice, a state of things) in oneself, in others, or in the world generally.

a **1225** *Leg. Kath.* 431 Ȝef ha nalde leauen þet ha ȝet lefde, & hare lahe luuien. *c* **1250** *Old Kent. Serm.* in *O.E. Misc.* 28 We mowe..luuie þo ilek [*read* ilke] þinkes þat he luued. *a* **1300** *Cursor M.* 20114 Ne luued scho notþer fight ne strijf. **1387** TREVISA *Higden* (Rolls) VIII. 25 He..loved wel pees and quyet. **1422** tr. *Secreta Secret., Priv. Priv.* 122 Euer lowynge ryght and verite. **1567** *Gude & Godlie Ball.* (S.T.S.) 122 Thow luiffis treuth, gude Lord. **1653** WALTON *Angler* xiii. 246 All that hate contentions, and love quietnesse, and vertue, and Angling. **1775** BURKE *Corr.* (1844) II. 26, I love firm government. **1902** *Edin. Rev.* July 84 Universal humanity loves sharp practice.

5. Of plants or animals: To have a tendency to thrive in (a certain kind of situation). Cf. L. *amare, diligere*.

1601 HOLLAND *Pliny* I. 462 The Pitch-tree loveth the mountains and cold grounds. **1706** LONDON & WISE *Retir'd Gard'ner* I. xi. 157 Fig-trees..love loose, hot ground. **1760** BROWN *Compl. Farmer* II. 85 All sorts of pease love limed or marled land. **1774** GOLDSM. *Nat. Hist.* (1776) IV. 22 Rabbits are found to love a warm climate, and to be incapable of bearing the cold of the north. **1796** C. MARSHALL *Garden.* xix. (1813) 331 Willow herb..loves moisture. **1866** B. TAYLOR *Proposal* Poems 257 The violet loves a sunny bank.

6. a. Const. *inf.* To have great pleasure in doing something. †Also *rarely* of things (= L. *amare*, Gr. φιλεῖν) to be accustomed (*obs.*).

c **1350** *Will. Palerne* 162 Ȝe þat louen & lyken to listen a-ni more. **14..** *Sir Beues* (MS. M.) 82 He lovith not with me to rage. **1581** PETTIE *Guazzo's Civ. Conv.* III. (1586) 126 Those women that loue not to curle vp their haire roistinglie, but vse to kembe it downe smoothlie. **1601** HOLLAND *Pliny* I. 462 The Larch tree..loveth to grow in the same places. **1614** RALEIGH *Hist. World* v. iii. §15. 436 Young men..loue to seeme wiser then their fathers. **1626** BACON *Sylva* §703 Salmons and Smelts loue to get into Riuers, though it be against the Streame. **1704** F. FULLER *Med. Gymn.* (1711) 103 They don't love to be told the Truth, tho' it is ever so necessary. **1728–46** THOMSON *Spring* 402 Down to the river, in whose ample wave Their little naiads love to sport at large. **1859** BARTLETT *Dict. Amer.* s.v., 'I'd love to have that bonnet'. **1875** JOWETT *Plato* (ed. 2) I. 246, I love to hear you wise men talk.

†**b.** with acc. and inf. or obj.-clause: To desire or like (something to be done). *Obs.*

c **1380** WYCLIF *Wks.* (1880) 440 He louyde hem not to be worldly riche. **1682** T. FLATMAN *Heraclitus Ridens* No. 74 (1713) II. 205 Our Whigs don't love Justice should be executed without 'em.

7. To embrace affectionately. (A childish use.)

1877 HABBERTON *Helen's Babies* 31, 'I was only a-lovin' you, cos you was good, and brought us candy'. **1889** *Harper's Mag.* July 271/2 Putting his arms round her neck, [he] 'loved' her with his cheek against hers. **1893** OLIVE SCHREINER *Story Afr. Farm* II. i. 132 Some pale-green, hairy-leaved bushes..meet over our head; and we sit among them, and kiss them, and they love us back.

8. *Comb.*: **love-and-tear-it** *dial.* [corruption of *Lavatera*], the tree mallow, *Lavatera arborea*; †**love-man,** cleavers, *Galium Aparine*; †**love-pot** *a.*, drunken.

1598 FLORIO, *Philantropo*, the herbe goose-grasse or loue man. **1611** *Ibid.*, *Berghinellare*, to gad abrode a gossoping as a pratling loue-pot woman. **1611** COTGR., *Riéble*, Cleauer,.. Loue-man, Goose-grasse. **1880** ADELAIDE SARTORIS *Past Hours* II. 55 'Love-and-tear-it!'—the name..down in our part of the world for..the mallow.

†**love,** *v.*[2] *Obs.* Forms: 1 lofian, 3 *Orm.* lofenn, 4 louve, 4–5 loove, lof(e, *Sc.* loyf, 4–6 love, *Sc.* low(e, 5 lowf, 5–6 *Sc.* loif(e, 6 loave, *Sc.* lowff, loff. [OE. *lofian* = OS. *lobon* (Du. *loven*), OHG. *lobôn, lobên* (MHG., mod.G. *loben*), ON. *lofa* (Sw. *lofva*, Da. *love*):—OTeut. *lobôjan, -ǣjan*, f. **lobo-* praise: see LOF.]

1. *trans.* To praise, extol.

a **1000** *Cædmon's Gen.* 508 Ic ȝehyrde hine þine dæd & word lofian on his leohte. *c* **1200** ORMIN 3484 Menn shollden cnawenn himm & lofenn himm & wurrþenn. *a* **1300** *Cursor M.* 18487 Loues nu vr lauerd dright. **14..** *How Good Wife taught Dau.* 140 (in *Barbour's Bruce*, etc. 529) Loyf all leid, and no man lak. **1456** SIR G. HAYE *Law Arms* (S.T.S.) 27 He was lufit, and lovit, and honourit throuout all the warld. *c* **1470** HENRY *Wallace* XI. 1460, I yow besek,..Quha will nocht low, lak nocht my eloquence. **1513** DOUGLAS *Æneis* I. Prol. 427 Virgill did diligence.. Eneas for to loife and magnify. **1535** COVERDALE *Ps.* cvi. 32 They wolde exalte him in the congregacion of the people, & loaue him in the seate of the elders. *a* **1586** MONTGOMERIE *Misc. Poems* I. 1 Luiffaris, leif of to loif so hie ȝour ladyes.
with cogn. obj. a **1300** *E.E. Psalter* cv. 12 Þai..looued his lofe [Vulg. *laudaverunt laudem ejus*]. **1340** HAMPOLE *Pr. Consc.* 321 Þai..loved his lovyng als þai couth say.

b. *absol.* To give praise; also, to flatter.

c **1000** *Ags. Ps.* (Th.) lxx. 21 Mine weleras ȝefeoð, wynnum lofiað. *c* **1470** HENRYSON *Fables* III. xxx. in *Anglia* IX. 360 To loif and le that settis thair haill delite. *c* **1475** *Rauf Coilȝear* 87 For first to lofe, and syne to lak, Peter! it is schame. **1549** *Compl. Scot.* xv. 130 To loue vitht out flattery. **1596** DALRYMPLE tr. *Leslie's Hist. Scot.* II. x. 474 Gif tha Loue, praise ouermekle, or commend.

2. To appraise, estimate or state the price or value of.

c **1200** *Trin. Coll. Hom.* 213 Þe sullere loueð his þing dere. .. Ðe beȝer bet litel þar fore. *c* **1440** *Promp. Parv.* 314/2 Lovon, and bedyn as chapmen, *licitor*. *c* **1460** *Towneley Myst.* xx. 239 Now, Judas, sen he shalbe sold How lowfys thou hym? **1530** PALSGR. 614/2, I love, as a chapman loveth his ware that he wyll sell... Come of, howe moche love you it at?

love, variant of LOF, LOOVE; obs. f. LOOF, LUFF.

loveable, etc.: see LOVABLE, etc.

loveache, loveage, obs. ff. LOVAGE[1].

'love-apple. Also **apple of love.** [tr. F. *pomme d'amour*, G. *liebesapfel*. (A 16th c. example in Lacurne refers to the use of the fruit as a philtre; but possibly this notion may have been suggested by the name.)] The fruit of the TOMATO, *Lycopersicum esculentum*. †Formerly also applied to the BRINJAL, *Solanum esculentum*.

1578 LYTE *Dodoens* III. lxxxv. 438 There be two kindes of Amorus or Raging Love apples. **1597** GERARDE *Herbal* II. lv. §5. 275 The apple of Loue is called in Latine..*Poma Amoris*. **1604** E. G[RIMSTONE] *D'Acosta's Hist. Indies* IV. xxxi. 294 There is at the Indies any good thing that Spaine brings foorth..as..*Becengenes*, or apples of love,..vetches, and finally whatsoever groweth heere of any profite. **1707–12** MORTIMER *Husb.* (1721) II. 211 Apples of Love. **1785** MARTYN *Rousseau's Bot.* xvi. (1795) 201 Tomatos or Love-Apple..is also admitted to the table and eaten with impunity. **1825** *Greenhouse Comp.* I. 235 Baron Tschoudi.. informs us that he has grafted the love-apple on the potatoe.
allusively. **1812** H. & J. SMITH *Rej. Addr.*, *Living Lustres*, I mean the love-apples that bloom in the eyes.

'love-bird. 1. A diminutive bird of the parrot tribe, esp. the West African Lovebird, *Agapornis pullarius*, remarkable for the affection it shows for its mate. The name is also given to the other species of the genus *Agapornis*; to several American species of *Psittacula*; and to certain small Australian Parrakeets, esp. *Euphema undulata*.

1595 LYLY *Woman in Moon* V. i. 105 Ile giue thee..Loue birdes whose feathers shalbe beaten gold. **1841** *Penny Cycl.* XIX. 92/2 The latter [*Agapornis*], a ready example of which occurs in the Lovebirds,..was separated from *Psittacula*. **1860–1** THACKERAY *Lovel* iv. (1869) 214 Unless they are two behind a carriage perch they pine away, I suppose,..as one love-bird does without his mate. **1886** MISS BRADDON *Fatal Three* I. ii, A pair of Virginian love-birds were twittering in their gilded cage. **1897** BLACKMORE *Dariel* xviii. 179 A pair of what are called 'lovebirds', of whom, if one hops the final twig, the other pines into the darkness and dies.

2. A lover.

1911 *Maclean's Mag.* Nov. 39/2 Seems as if I'd lighted on a pretty nest of love-birds. **1949** A. HYND *We are Public Enemies* iv. 121 Ma barged in on the love birds. **1974** J. MITCHELL *Death & Bright Water* xx. 242 'Lovebirds, lovebirds,' Randy Blythe said. Callan sat up, one arm still round Helena.

'love-child. A child born out of wedlock.

1805 EUGENIA DI ACTON *Nuns of Desert* II. 10 Miss Blenheim being, what in that country is denominated, a love-child. **1820** SHELLEY *Hymn to Mercury* xxxviii. 6 And where the ambrosial nymph..Bore the Saturnian's love-child, Mercury. **1889** G. D. LESLIE *Lett. to Marco* xxi. (1893) 140 Many of the little children..called themselves 'love children'. 'Please, sir, she's a love child.' **1894** FROUDE *Erasmus* i. 2 Legend says that Erasmus was what is called a love-child.

¶ *allusively.*

1884 SYMONDS *Shaks. Predecess.* xv. 618 No sane critic will maintain that the 'Jew of Malta' was a love-child of its maker's genius.

†**'lovecop, 'lufcop.** *Obs.* [? a. ON. **lofkaup*, f. *lof* licence, leave + *kaup* purchase.] Some kind of local market-duty.

1278 in Jeake *Charters Cinque Ports* (1728) 11 Et quod habeant Infangtheff. Et quod sint Wrecfree & Wittfree, Lastagefree, & Lovecopefree. **1299** in Harrod *Deeds & Rec. King's Lynn* (1874) 93 Lufcop. **1374** *Ibid.* 83 Lovecop [*mentioned with* tronage *and* measurage]. **1857** *Times* 27 May 11/4 [Law Cases.] A decree had been agreed upon..the effect of which would be to declare his Royal Highness.. entitled..to a moiety of the custom or duty of 'lofcop', that is, to one moiety of the duties levied specifically upon corn, grain, or seeds exported by water from the port..of Lynn.

loved ('lʌvd, 'lʌvɪd), *a.* Also 3–4 **lovid,** *Sc.* 4–5 **lowit, luffit,** 5 **lufyd, lwfyt,** 5–6 **lowyt, luifit,** 6 **luvit,** 6–7 **lovit,** (9 *arch.* **lovite**). [f. LOVE *v.*[1] + -ED[1].]

1. a. In senses of the vb.; in attributive use now chiefly *poet.*, exc. with prefixed adv. as *dearly-loved, much-loved*; ordinarily superseded by BELOVED.

a **1300** *Cursor M.* 10416 Þis leuedi was o mikel prise, Loued and lered, bath war and wise. *c* **1375** *Sc. Leg. Saints* xxxvi. (*John Baptist*) 322 Þis is my luffit sone & dere. *c* **1470** HENRY *Wallace* VIII. 1639 O lowit leid, with worschip wys and wicht. **1513** DOUGLAS *Æneis* II. xii[i]. 46 Thy weping.. Quhilk thou makis for thi luifit Crewsay. **1590** SPENSER *F.Q.* III. ii. 46 To compas thy desire, and find that loved knight. **1621** G. SANDYS *Ovid's Met.* VI. (1632) 209 In loued lakes they striue. **1706** ROWE *Ulysses* v. Wks. 1747 I. 407 I'll fly, as I have sworn For thy lov'd sake, far from the Sight of Man. **1750** GRAY *Elegy* (1st draught) 92 Thy once loved haunt, this long deserted shade. **1866** M. ARNOLD *Thyrsis* xii, Many a dingle on the loved hill-side.

b. *absol.* or *sb.* A person beloved.

1435 MISYN *Fire of Love* II. viii. 87 Þer spekys þe lufyd to þe hart of þe lufar. **1596** SPENSER *F.Q.* IV. v. 29 Britomart.. Upon her first adventure forth did ride, To seeke her lov'd. **1831** CARLYLE *Sart. Res.* II. v, By what Pre-established Harmony of occurrences did the Lover and the Loved meet one another in so wide a world? **1898** G. MEREDITH *Odes Fr. Hist.* 51 This loved and scourged of angels.

c. *loved one.* (i) A beloved, a lover; *pl.*, one's family or relations. (ii) A dead relation (spouse, etc.). Freq. with capital initials.

1862 M. B. CHESNUT *Diary* 9 June (1949) xiv. 240 How many, many of your friends and loved ones this scrap of paper may tell you have gone to their death. **1879** GEO. ELIOT *Let.* 20 Feb. (1956) VII. 104, I want, if I can, to write a '*characteristik*' of my loved one—no memoir, but a brief sketch. **1906** CHESTERTON *Charles Dickens* viii. 187 To ask for the loved one, and then not to dare to cross the threshold. **1926** A. HUXLEY *Jesting Pilate* IV. 272 Lay the Loved Ones to rest in—Graveyard, the Cemetery Unusual. **1938** D. CASTLE *Do Your Own Time* iii. 35, I sat idly drawing designs on my writing-paper while nineteen heartsick men began writing to their loved ones. **1948** E. WAUGH (*title*) The loved one. **1968** *Guardian* 17 Aug. 8/1 Montpellier has just acquired..Europe's first funeral parlour on the American model..the Loved Ones make their final appearances in rooms done up in sky blue, water green, pink, or beige. **1971** *Progress* (Cape Town) May 8/3 In many cases these people would have to travel more than two or three hundred miles to be with their loved ones. **1973** *Advocate-News* (Barbados) 22 Jan. 12/1 (Advt.), For a smaller charge, we do not only intimate about the Birth, Baptism, Confirmation, Marriage and Death of your loved ones in our Classified Columns we also give a lasting record of the event for posterity.

2. *Sc.* In royal and feudal documents, prefixed to personal names or designations; equivalent to the 'trusty and well-beloved' of English charters. †Often with plural ending.

1460 *Charters* etc. *Peebles* (1872) 135 Our lwfyt burges Ihon Smayll. **1461** *Ibid.* 140 Our luffit burges and nychtbur Andro Mylner. **1543** *Extracts Aberd. Reg.* (1844) I. 189 Thair lowyt seruitour, Maister Edward Menzes. **1545** *Ibid.* 217 To our louittis cousingis, bailzeis, counsale, and communitie of Abirdene. **1637** *Sc. Prayer Bk. Proclam.*, Charles..to our Lovits Messengers. **1868** *Act 31 & 32 Vict.* c. 101 Sched. (QQ), ['Form to be used under this Act'.] It is humbly shown to us by our lovite *A.B.*, complaner, against *C.D.* [etc.].

loved, obs. form of LOAFED.

1597 GERARDE *Herbal* II. xxxvi. §5. 246 There is another sort of Cabbage or loued Colewoort.

†**'loveday.** *Obs.* Forms: see LOVE *sb.*^{1} and DAY. [tr. med.L. *dies amoris* (Du Cange).]

1. A day appointed for a meeting with a view to the amicable settlement of a dispute; hence, an agreement entered into at such a meeting.

c **1290** *S. Eng. Leg.* I. 445/510 Ofte huy nomen louedai: ake þet contek euere i-laste. **1387-8** T. USK *Test. Love* I. ii. (Skeat) I. 95 Moste of all, maked I not a louedaie, bitwene God and mankind? **1390** GOWER *Conf.* I. 39 Helle is full of such descord That ther may be no loveday. *c* **1420** LYDG. *Assembly of Gods* 692 Fyghters, brawlers, brekers of lofedayes. **1493** *Festivall* (W. de W. 1515) 79 There was made a fynyte loveday betwene the kyng & Thomas [à Becket]. **1519** HORMAN *Vulg.* vii. 66 b, He is more redy to make a fraye than a loue daye. **1588** SHAKS. *Tit. A.* I. i. 491 This day shall be a Loue-day Tamora. **1655** FULLER *Waltham Abb.* 9 The Townsmen..desired a Love-day.

attrib. **1502** ARNOLDE *Chron.* (1811) 95 Also ye shal be no loueday maker.

2. *nonce-use.* A day devoted to love-making.

1590 GREENE *Mourn. Garm.* (1616) D 3 b, Oft haue I heard my liefe Coridon report on a loue-day, When bonny maides doe meete with the Swaines in the vally by Tempe.

'love-drink. A drink to excite love; a philtre.

c **1320** *Sir Tristr.* 1710 Sche tok þat loue drink. **13..** *Minor Poems fr. Vernon MS.* liv. 167 A loue-drynke I asked of þe. *c* **1386** CHAUCER *Wife's Prol.* 754 That for he sholde alwey vp-on hire thynke, She yaf him swich a manere loue drynke, That he was deed, er it were by the morwe.

†**love-drury.** *Obs.* [f. LOVE *sb.*^{1} + DRU(E)RY. Cf. *love-amour*, LOVE *sb.*^{1} 16.] **a.** Love, love-making, courtship: = DRUERY 1. **b.** A love-token or keepsake: = DRUERY 2.

a. *c* **1300** *Havelok* 195 Til þat she were tuelf winter hold, And of speche were bold; And þat she couþe of courteysye, Gon, and speken of luue-drurye. *c* **1386** CHAUCER *Sir Thopas* 184 Of bataille and of chiualry And of ladyes loue drury Anon I wol yow telle.

b. **13..** *K. Alis.* 7610, Y wol sende hire love-drewry. **1513** DOUGLAS *Æneis* v. x. 48 A Sidoun steid..quham Dido..gaif hym in luif drowry [L. *pignus amoris*]. **1550** LYNDESAY *Sqr. Meldrum* 1003 And he gaif hir ane lufe drowrie, Ane Ring set with ane riche Rubie.

lovee (ˌlʌ'viː). *nonce-wd.* [f. LOVE *sb.*^{1} + -EE^1.] A recipient of love.

1754 RICHARDSON *Grandison* (1781) VI. xi. 44 The Lover and Lovee make generally the happiest couple. **18..** LADY C. LINDSAY in *Academy* 20 Jan. (1894) 49/2 Papa, mama, lover, and lovee,..played their parts to perfection.

lovee, variant of LOVEY.

'love-feast.

1. *Eccl. Antiq.* Used as a rendering of Gr. ἀγάπη, Eccl. Latin AGAPE. Among the early Christians, a meal partaken of, in token of brotherly love, by the members of the church; app. originally in connexion with the eucharistic celebration.

1580 HOLLYBAND *Treas. Fr. Tong, Agape*, a loue, banquet [? *read* loue banquet], or feaste that was vsed in the Primitiue Church. **1610** T. GODWIN *Moses & Aaron* I. 20 Their Love-feasts,..now antiquated thorowout Christendome. **1737** WATERLAND *Eucharist* 29 In the Apostolical Times, the Love-Feast and the Eucharist, tho' distinct, went together. **1881** N.T. (R.V.) *2 Pet.* ii. 13 Revelling in their love-feasts while they feast with you. **1902** *Expositor* Aug. 126 In 2 Peter the feasts are Christian love-feasts.

2. Among Methodists, and some other modern sects, a religious service held at intervals in imitation of the Agape of the early church.

Its special features are the partaking of a simple meal (usually only of bread and water), and the relation of religious experiences by various members of the congregation.

1738 WESLEY *Wks.* (1872) I. 93 That on the Sunday seven-night following be a general love-feast. **1761** —— *Jrnl.* 19 July, The very design of a Love-feast is a free and familiar conversation. **1807-8** W. IRVING *Salmag.* (1824) 144 She..was frequent in her attendance at love-feasts. **1870** [see EBENEZER 1]. **1882** *19th Cent.* Nov. 740 They who turn aside to attend a Ranters' Love-feast..must be wrong in the head. **1909** F. CALHOUN *Miss Minerva* 96 She was always on hand at the Love Feast and the Missionary Rally. **1922** G. EDWARDS *From Crow-scaring to Westminster* iii. 35 One form of [Primitive Methodist] service was called a 'love-feast' at which small pieces of bread were taken round with water.

3. Transferred to other gatherings.

1876 *Solano Republican* (Suisun, Calif.) 24 Aug. 2/1 A regular old-fashioned Democratic love-feast was engaged in by the many-scarred war-horses of the party. **1893** *Nation* (N.Y.) 19 Jan. 44/1 On the evening of inauguration day the Populists held a 'love-feast'. **1943** K. TENNANT *Ride on Stranger* iii. 28 Aunt Edith beamed over the love-feast. **1948** *Minneapolis Star* 17 Sept. 1/3 Senator Joseph H. Ball and Gov. Luther Youngdahl had a sort of love feast at the capitol Thursday. **1973** 'S. HARVESTER' *Corner of Playground* I. v. 47 Several of their customs had Egyptian overtones, including a 'love-feast'..close to the Pharaonic *agapes*.

Hence **love-feaster**, one who participates in a love-feast.

1749-51 LAVINGTON *Enthus. Meth. & Papists* (1820) 298 She was the mother of the Agapetae, or love-feasters.

loveful ('lʌvfʊl), *a.* [f. LOVE *sb.*^{1} + -FUL.]

†**1.** Regardable with love; lovable. *Obs.*

1382 WYCLIF *Eccl.* xv. 13 The Lord hateth al cursing of errour, and it shal not ben looueful [Vulg. *amabile*] to men dredende hym. **1596** R. L[INCHE] *Diella* etc. F 7 b, His loue-ful face is now her soules sole essence.

2. Abounding in love. Now *rare.*

a **1225** *Ancr. R.* 222 So lufful & so reouðful is hire heorte. **1598** SYLVESTER *Du Bartas* II. ii. III. *Colonies* 505 The everlasting Voyce Which now again re-blest the love-full choyce Of sacred Wedlock's secret binding band. **1645** R. SYMONDS *Diary Civ. War* (Camden) 275 Do not persuade a loveful maid there's any heaven but he. **1854** H. STRICKLAND *Trav. Th. & Fancies* 87 Cheerful, hopeful, loveful feelings, instead of the old religions of fear.

love-in ('lʌvɪn). [-IN^3.] A gathering for the purpose of establishing and enjoying love relationships.

1967 *Times* 28 Mar. 4/7 The 'love-in' in Elysian Park, Los Angeles, was equally odd but caused no more than a traffic jam. **1967** *Observer* (Colour Suppl.) 3 Dec. 12/1 The imitation 'Love-in' at the Alexandra Palace..attracted 'horrible yobs'. **1971** M. BUTTERWORTH *Flowers for Dead Witch* ix. 127 We had a few love-ins up on the cliffs... We'd go for moonlight swims, and then dry off with a little horseplay.

lovekin ('lʌvkɪn). Also **lovekins.** [f. LOVE *sb.* + -KIN.] A lover.

1922 JOYCE *Ulysses* 418 Reels off a credit. Lovey lovekin. **1925** T. DREISER *Amer. Trag.* II. II. xliii. 36 He'll be with me most of the time—the lovekins will.

'love-knot. A knot or bow of ribbon tied in a peculiar way, supposed to be a love token. Also, a representation of such a knot. Cf. *true love knot.*

c **1386** CHAUCER *Prol.* 197 He hadde of gold ywroght a ful curious pyn: A loue knotte in the gretter ende ther was. **1598** MARSTON *Pygmal.* III. 149 His windows strow'd with Sonnets, and the glasse Drawne full of love-knots. **1842** TENNYSON *Talking Oak* 65 Leg and arm with love-knots gay. **1877** W. JONES *Finger-ring* 371 The circular box on the top..contains a sort of love-knot.

b. *fig.* and *allusive.*

1393 LANGL. *P. Pl.* C. XVIII. 127 Lyf, and loue, and leaute in o by-leyue and lawe, A loue-knotte of leaute and of leel by-leyue. *a* **1586** SIDNEY *Arcadia* III. (1590) 263 b, If it were a bondage, it was a bondage onely knitte in loue-knots. *c* **1600** F. DAVISON *Ps.* cxxxii. in Farr *S.P. Eliz.* (1845) II. 328 Where this love-knot remaines vnbroken, God heapes of blisse doth send.

Lovelace ('lʌvleɪs). The name of Robert *Lovelace*, a character in Richardson's *Clarissa Harlowe* (1747-8), used allusively for 'a seducer'.

[**1751** RICHARDSON *Clarissa* (ed. 3) VIII. 294 Ladies.. should rather prefer the honest heart of a Hickman..than the volatile mischievous one of a Lovelace. **1812** SHELLEY *Let.* 11 Jun. (1964) I. 305, I regard charges of resembling Lovelace with contemptuous indifference.] **1850** THACKERAY *Pendennis* II. ix. 92 If Arthur had been the most determined *roué* and artful Lovelace who ever set about deceiving a young girl, he could hardly have adopted better means. **1944** S. PUTNAM tr. *E. da Cunha's Rebellion in Backlands* II. iv. 127 A scandal in which a certain local bigwig, a police sergeant, was *magna pars*, the Lovelace of the episode.

'love-lay. Chiefly *poet.* A love-song.

a **1400-50** *Alexander* 6 And sum has langing of lufe lays to herken. **1600** FAIRFAX *Tasso* XVI. xiii, A woondrous bird.. That in plaine speech sung louelaies loud and shrill. **1830** TENNYSON *Dualisms* Poems 145 Two bees..Hum a lovelay to the westwind at noontide. **1856** R. A. VAUGHAN *Mystics* (1860) I. 258 These love-lays he interspersed with riddles and rhyming proverbs.

loveless ('lʌvlɪs), *a.* [f. LOVE *sb.*^{1} + -LESS.]

1. Having no love; **a.** not feeling love; **b.** not loved.

? **1311** *Pol. Songs* (1839) 255 For frend is fo, the lond is loveles. **1362** LANGL. *P. Pl.* A. v. 98 Thus I liue loueles lyk a luther dogge. **1390** GOWER *Conf.* I. 259 Envie, which is loveles, And Pride, which is lawles. *Ibid.* III. 362 Sche which deide gulteles For love, and yit was loveles. **1509** BARCLAY *Shyp of Folys* (1570) 72 A lorde or state whom many men doth drede With loueles feare. **1599** SHAKS. etc. *Pass. Pilgr.* xv, Long was the combat doubtfull, that loue with loue did fight To leave the master louelesse, or kill the gallant knight. **1612** SHELTON *Quix.* I. i. (1620) 7 The Knight Errant that is louelesse, resembles a tree that wants leaues and fruit. **1735** POPE *Ep. Lady* 125 From loveless youth to unrespected age No Passion gratify'd except her Rage. **1825** COLERIDGE *Aids Refl.* (1848) I. 149 The anxiety to be admired is a loveless passion. **1877** DOWDEN *Shaks. Prim.* vi. §8. 79 An absolute cynic, loveless and alone. *Ibid.* 80 The loveless solitude, haunted by terrible visions of his victims. **1901** H. BLACK *Culture & Restr.* xii. 372 A loveless saint thus becomes a contradiction in terms.

†**2.** Unlovely. *Obs.*

1601 HOLLAND *Pliny* II. 432 These [Tortoises] are ilfavored to see to, and yet as louelesse as they be, they are not without some medicinable vertues.

Hence **'lovelessly** *adv.*, **'lovelessness.**

1616 J. LANE *Cont. Sqr.'s T.* x. 189 Was never love more lovelesselie requitted. **1823** BYRON *Stanzas to a Hindoo Air*, How the long night flags lovelessly and slowly. **1852** ROBERTSON *Serm.* Ser. II. 167 Men of withered affections excuse their lovelessness by talking largely of the affection due to God. **1891** F. PAGET *Spirit Discipl.* (ed. 2) 214 The mysterious terror of everlasting lovelessness is seizing on his heart.

'love-letter. A letter written by a lover to the beloved, and expressing amatory sentiments.

[*a* **1240** *Wohunge* in Cott. *Hom.* 283 A swete ihesu þu oppnes me þin herte for to cnawe witerliche and in to reden trewe luue lettres.] **1598** SHAKS. *Merry W.* II. i. 1 What! haue I scap'd loue-letters in the holly-day-time of my beauty, and am I now a subiect for them? **1622** MABBE tr. *Aleman's Guzman d'Alf.* II. 260 A loue-letter brought her by her maid. **1718** LADY M. W. MONTAGU *Let. to Lady Rich* 16 Mar., I have got for you, as you desire, a Turkish love-letter. **1824** MISS MITFORD *Village* Ser. I. 21 Our village beauty had fairly reached her twentieth year..without the slightest suspicion of her having ever written a love-letter. **1901** *Blackw. Mag.* Oct. 496/1 The young people interchange love-letters.

love-lies-(a)-bleeding. The garden-plant *Amaranthus caudatus*, having a long drooping purplish-red spike of bloom.

Also applied *dial.* to some other plants (see E.D.D. and *W. Som. Gloss.*).

[*c* **1610** BEAUM. & FL. (*title*) Philaster, or Love lies a Bleeding.] **1664** S. BLAKE *Compl. Gardeners Pract.* 57 Princes-feathers. Otherwise called, My Love lieth a bleeding. **1665** REA *Flora* II. ix. 185 This [*Amaranthus*] is.. called by some Country women, Love lies a bleeding. **1760** J. LEE *Introd. Bot.* App. 318. **1809** CAMPBELL *O'Connor's Child* xvi, And cherish, for my warrior's sake—'The flower of love lies bleeding'. **1842** WORDSW. *Love lies bleeding* 1 You call it 'Love lies bleeding',—so you may, Though the red Flower, not prostrate, only droops.

lovelify ('lʌvlɪfaɪ), *v. rare.* [f. LOVEL(Y *a.* + -IFY.] *trans.* To render lovely. So **'lovelified** *ppl. a.*, **'lovelifying** *vbl. sb.*

1897 G. B. SHAW *Our Theatres in Nineties* (1932) III. 73 Life, death, love and mankind are no longer themselves: they are glorified, sublimified, lovelified. **1935** *Punch* 17 July 65/1, I have heard of a 'Hairdresser and Beautician' who offers to 'lovelyfy' the ladies of Manchester; and, from New York of a Youthifying Beauty Cream. And here is a pretty piece from *The Windsor Magazine*:—'A hand cream..has a lovelifying effect on hands roughened from gardening.'

lovelihead ('lʌvlɪhɛd). *rare.* [f. LOVELY *a.* + -HEAD.] Loveliness. In quot. 1633 *concr.*

1633 B. JONSON *Underwoods* xciii. *Epithalamium* xxi, Those Sweet and Sacred fires Of Love betweene you and your Lovely-head. **1881** ROSSETTI *Ball. & Sonn.* xcvi. 258 As thy love's death-bound features..alway keep..Than all new life a livelier lovelihead.

'lovelike, *a. rare.* [f. LOVE *sb.*^{1} + -LIKE.] Of a nature appropriate to love. †Also = LOVELY.

1621 LADY M. WROTH *Urania* 296 Her haire was..of a dainty, and loue-like browne. **1839** BAILEY *Festus* (1852) 447 Musing, as wont, With love-like sadness, upon sacred things.

Hence †**love-likely** *adv.*, lovelily.

1621 LADY M. WROTH *Urania* 81 Shee lookt sadly, and wept so loue-likely, as all pittied her.

lovelily ('lʌvlɪlɪ), *adv.* Also 4 **luflyly, luuelili, luflely,** 5 **louelyly,** 6 *Sc.* **luuilelie.** [f. LOVELY *a.* + -LY^2.] In a lovely manner; †**a.** in a loving or friendly manner (*obs.*); **b.** in a way to stimulate love; beautifully.

a **1300** *Cursor M.* 25582 Suete iesu!..al luuelili þou vs lere þe to luue wit sothfast rede. **1375** BARBOUR *Bruce* XVII. 315 Thair capitane Tretit thame sa luflely. ? *a* **1400** *Morte Arth.* 2292 Bot sir Arthure..Laughte hym vpe fulle louelyly with lordlyche knyghttez. **1596** DALRYMPLE tr. *Leslie's Hist. Scot.* x. 459 Efter be the burgesses of Edinburgh verie luuilelie, and honorablie was receiuet. **1671** H. M. tr. *Erasm. Colloq.* 245 Moreover, how lovelily do the Graces cling to one another. **1763** CHURCHILL *Duellist* II. Poems 1769 II. 69 Courage, a Youth of royal race, Lovlily stern, possess'd a place. **1813** BYRON *Br. Abydos* I. iii, So lovelily the morning shone. **1897** *Academy* 27 Mar. 357/2 The 'bowery loneliness' of 'Paradise Lost' is less lovelily beautiful.

loveliness ('lʌvlɪnɪs). [f. LOVELY *a.* + -NESS.] The quality of being lovely; exquisite beauty; †lovableness.

a **1340** HAMPOLE *Psalter* cxlviii. 13 Til whaim na thynge may be like in fayrhed & luflynes & in kyndnes. **1535** COVERDALE *Song Sol.* vi. 4 Thou art pleasaunt (o my loue) euen as louelynesse itself. *c* **1600** SHAKS. *Sonn.* iv, Unthrifty loveliness, why dost thou spend Upon thyself thy beauty's legacy? **1628** COKE *On Litt.* 395 a, For a farewell to our jurisprudent, I wish unto him..the lovelinesse of temperance, the stability of fortitude [etc.]. **1657** BAXTER *Agst. Quakers* 2 A Catholick Love to all Christians.. proportionable to their several degrees of loveliness. **1741** RICHARDSON *Pamela* I. Introd. 20 It adorn'd her with such unpresum'd Increase of Loveliness. **1816** BYRON *Ch. Har.* III. xxiv, Cheeks..which but an hour ago Blush'd at the praise of their own loveliness. **1818** KEATS *Endym.* I. 2 A thing of beauty is a joy for ever: Its loveliness increases. **1884** PAE *Eustace* 8 It was a face of surpassing loveliness.

b. *pl.* Lovely qualities, traits of loveliness. *rare.*

1790 G. WALKER *Serm.* II. xxi. 131 Let us adopt..into the rule of our lives, all the lovelinesses, which compose the character of the disciple of Christ.

loveling ('lʌvlɪŋ). *rare.* [f. LOVE *sb.*^{1} or *v.*^{1} + -LING.] ? A lovely creature; ? an object of love, a 'darling'.

1606 SYLVESTER *Du Bartas* II. iv. II. *Magnif.* 692 These frolick lovelings fraighted Nests do make The balmy Trees o'r-laden Boughs to crack. **1853** MISS E. S. SHEPPARD *Ch. Auchester* II. 111 'And Herr Hummel', my loveling went on, pursing his lips, 'said' [etc.]. **1882** J. PAYNE *1001 Nts.* I. 155 Upon the imperial necks she walks, a loveling bright.

lovelock ('lʌvlɒk). [f. LOVE *sb.*^{1} + LOCK *sb.*^{1}] A curl of a particular form worn by courtiers in the time of Elizabeth and James I; later, any curl or tress of hair of a peculiar or striking character.

1592 LYLY *Midas* III. ii. 43 Wil you haue..your loue-locke wreathed with a silken twist, or shaggie to fal on your shoulders? **1628** PRYNNE (*title*) The Vnlovelinesse of Love-lockes. **1840** MARRYAT *Poor Jack* i, Lovelocks, as the sailors term the curls which they wear on their temples. **1894** A. GRIFFITHS *Secrets Prison Ho.* II. IV. ii. 63 Bandoline, which

she used in making love-locks to adorn her fore-head and her temples.

transf. **1886** MAXWELL GRAY *Silence Dean Maitland* I. i. 12 Each [cart-] horse wore his mane in love-locks.

'love-longing. The longing felt by those who are in love.

a **1300** *Cursor M.* 24629 þar lai i in mi luue langing. *a* **1310** in Wright *Lyric P.* 61 A suete love-longynge myn herte thourh out stong. *c* **1386** CHAUCER *Miller's T.* 493 To Alison now wol I tellen al My loue-longing. **1522** *World & Child* (Roxb.) A iij b, And in loue longynge my harte is sore sette. **1593** DRAYTON *Sheph. Garl.* viii. (Roxb.) 117 This lad would neuer from her thought: she in loue-longing fell. **1882** CHILD *Ballads* I. 23/1 An elf-knight, by blowing his horn, inspires Lady Isabel with love-longing.

'love-lorn, *a.* Forsaken by one's love; forlorn or pining from love.

1634 MILTON *Comus* 234 Where the love-lorn Nightingale Nightly to thee her sad Song mourneth well. **1746** COLLINS *Ode to Simplicity* 16 By her [*sc.* the nightingale] whose lovelorn woe [etc.]. **1768** SIR W. JONES *Solima* Poems (1777) 5 O'er Azib's banks while love-lorn damsels rove. ? **1795** COLERIDGE *To Nightingale* 1 Sister of love-lorn poets, Philomel! **1810** SCOTT *Lady of L.* VI. i, The love-lorn wretch starts from tormenting dream. **1902** *Longm. Mag.* Aug. 334 Some love-lorn thrush serenaded his mate.

Hence **'lovelornness,** lovelorn condition.

1863 GEO. ELIOT *Romola* lxi, It was the story of that fair Gostanza who in her love-lornness desired to live no longer. **1888** R. A. KING *Leal Lass* I. xi. 210 His love-lornness, his sense of self-importance.

lovely ('lʌvlɪ), *a.* Forms: see LOVE *sb.*[1] and -LY[1]. [OE. *luflic*, f. *lufu* LOVE *sb.*[1] + *-lic* -LY[1].]

†**1. a.** Loving, kind, affectionate. *Obs.*

c **1000** *Sax. Leechd.* III. 190 Mona se twelfta on eallum weorcum nytlic ys..cild acenned god luflic. *c* **1200** *Trin. Coll. Hom.* 5 For þanne beð no man siker ar he ihere þat lufliche word of ure louerd ihesu cristes swete muðe Cumeð ȝe ibletsede. *a* **1225** *Ancr. R.* 428 Swuch ouh wummone lore to beon—luuelich & liðe. *a* **1300** *K. Horn* 484 Seie ich him biseche Wiþ loueliche speche þat he adun falle Bifore þe king. *a* **1300** *Cursor M.* 13260 He sermund wit his loueli spek, And heild mani þat war seke. *c* **1374** CHAUCER *Anel. & Arc.* 142 For sheo to him so lovely was and trewe. *c* **1400** *Laud Troy Bk.* 565 And welcomed hem with louely chere. **1533-9** T. ST. AUBYN in *Lisle Papers* XIII. 96 (MS.) With much hearty and lovely recommendations. **1602** *Narcissus* (1893) 129 Wee are..the kings owne lovely subiects.

†**b.** Amorous. *Obs.*

1470-85 MALORY *Arthur* VII. xxi. 246 And they had goodely langage & louely countenaunce to gyder. **1556** *Aurelio & Isab.* (1608) A ij, Whatsoever man that was unto the lovely passions disposed, soudenly..burned for her. **1587** M. GROVE *Pelops & Hipp.* (1878) 74 The letter of a friend of a wounded Louer,..to disswade him from this louelie follie. **1592** LYLY *Midas* III. iii, Amerula, another tale or none, this is too louely. *Sua.* Nay let me heare anie woman tell a tale of x lines long without it tend to love, and I will [etc.]. **1599** SHAKS. etc. *Pass. Pilgr.* iv, Sweet Cytherea ..Did court the Lad with many a louely looke.

†**c.** Friendly, amicable. *Obs.* (? *Sc.*)

1409 in *Exch. Rolls Scotl.* IV. ccx, [Thai] sal nocht tak that caus furth bot in lufely manere as the lach will. *a* **1649** DRUMM. OF HAWTH. *Hist. Scot.* (1655) 12 After lovely advice at the Council-Table..he was freely dismist.

2. Lovable; worthy of love; suited to attract love. *Obs.* exc. with etymological allusion.

c **1000** *Ags. Ps.* (Spelman) lxxxiii. 1 Hu luflice [Vulg. *quam dilecta*] ȝeteld ðin. **1375** BARBOUR *Bruce* I. 389 Quhen he wes blyth, he was lufly. *c* **1450** tr. *De Imitatione* III. lv. 131 Louely fader, it is worþy þat þis houre þi seruaunt suffre somwhat for þe. **1513** BRADSHAW *St. Werburge* I. 1443 But, moost louely father I pray you hertfully Take no dysplesure. *a* **1586** SIDNEY *Arcadia* I. (1590) 66 Being beloued in all companies for his louely qualities. **1638** JUNIUS *Paint. Ancients* 192, I am almost loth to say it, (sayth Quintilian) because it may be mistaken that shamefastnesse is a vice, but a lovely one. **1748** G. WHITE *Serm.* (MS.), Though God be ..more lovely than Man, yet 'tis more natural and easy..for us in our present state to love men than God. **1812** LANDOR *Ct. Julian* I. iii, What we love Is loveliest in departure! **1846** RUSKIN *Mod. Paint.* II. III. II. v. §12 If his mind be..sweetly toned, what he loves will be lovely.

3. Lovable or attractive on account of beauty; beautiful. Now with emotional sense, as a strong expression of admiring or delighted feeling: Exquisitely beautiful.

a. with reference to beauty of person.

a **1300** *Cursor M.* 16635 Þai spitted on his luueli face. **13..** *Gaw. & Gr. Knt.* 52 Þe louelokkest ladies þat euer lif haden. **1340** HAMPOLE *Pr. Consc.* 690 Be he never swa stalworth and wyght, And comly of shap, lufly and fayre. *c* **1420** *Anturs of Arth.* 162 My lyre als the lely, lufely to syghte. **1590** MARLOWE *2nd Pt. Tamburl.* I. iii, This lovely boy, the youngest of the three. *Ibid.*, Well, lovely boys, ye shall be emperors both. **1596** SHAKS. *Tam. Shr.* Induct. i. 67 Til the teares..Like enuious flouds ore-run her louely face. **1720** MRS. MANLEY *Power of Love* (1741) I. 22 The Brother was not only more lovely than the Sister, but handsome beyond all Things. **1722** B. STAR tr. *Mlle. de St. Phale* vii. 220, I never saw two lovelier Gentlemen in my Life, nor so beautiful a Virgin. **1751-2** FIELDING *Covent Gard. Jrnl.* No. 37 Wks. 1784 X. 72 The ladies..covered their lovely necks. **1801** COLERIDGE *Christabel* II. 507 He bids thee come without delay..And take thy lovely daughter home. **1898** FLOR. MONTGOMERY *Tony* 14 What a lovely face!

absol. or *sb.* Now usu. a woman or girl of glamorous loveliness, esp. one who takes part in an entertainment or 'show'. Also *transf.*

c **1420** *Anturs of Arth.* 397 Withe a launce one loft þat louely cone lede; A freke one a fresone him folowed, in fay. *c* **1470** *Golagros & Gaw.* 1003 Thai luschit and laid on, thai luflyis of lyre. **1652** BENLOWES *Theoph.* To my Fancy, Should one Love knot all lovelies tie. **1753** HOGARTH *Anal. Beauty* xi. 81 Tho' the lovely seems likewise to have been as much the sculptor's aim. **1786** COWPER *Let. to Unwin* 3 July, Wks. 1836 V. 342 Our love is with all your lovelies, both great and small. **1859** E. FITZGERALD tr. *Omar* xxi. (1899) 76 The loveliest and best That Time and Fate of all their Vintage prest. **1933** [see FRIPPET]. **1938** AUDEN & ISHERWOOD *On Frontier* III. ii. 108 It [*sc.* the working class] prefers our larger and livelier organs of enlightenment, which can afford snappier sports news,..and bigger photographs of bathing lovelies. **1940** H. G. WELLS *Babes in Darkling Wood* II. i. 143 Not for many years have I had that hungry craving for everything, give and receive, from another human being. I can't imagine the man. What a marvel, what a lovely he'd have to be! **1957** J. BRAINE *Room at Top* xvi. 150, I was taking Susan not as Susan, but as a Grade A. lovely, as the daughter of a factory-owner. **1966** T. PYNCHON *Crying of Lot 49* iii. 63 One of the girls, a long-waisted, brown-haired lovely in a black knit leotard. **1967** *Stage* 2 Mar. 7/1 The six lovelies comprising Marie de Vere's Ballet Montparnasse. **1974** *Times* 22 Jan. 11 Gone are the remorseless parade of whey-faced classic lovelies, each indistinguishable from the other.

b. said of inanimate things.

13.. *E.E. Allit. P.* A. 692 As quo says lo ȝon louely yle, Þou may hit wynne if þou be wyȝte. *c* **1400** *Laud Troy Bk.* 4193 Day is dawed and is day, It was a louely morn. *c* **1400** *Destr. Troy* 1541 Was neuer sython vnder son Cite so large, ..Non so luffly on to loke in any lond oute. *c* **1403** *Cuckow & Night.* 72 They coude that servyce al by rote; Ther was many a lovely straunge note. *c* **1560** A. SCOTT *Poems* (S.T.S.) xix. 33 Nane may..in to þat lufly bour Mak residens. **1634** SIR T. HERBERT *Trav.* 79 See how mischiefe appeares in a louely and vndistempered Scene. *Ibid.* 214 Corall, white and louely. **1708** BURNET *Lett.* (ed. 3) 193 Crusted with inlayings of lovely Marble, in a great Variety. **1866** M. ARNOLD *Thyrsis* iii, And that sweet city with her dreaming spires..Lovely all times she lies, lovely tonight. **1884** Q. VICTORIA *More Leaves* 123 We came upon Loch Ard, and a lovelier picture could not be seen.

c. with reference to moral or spiritual beauty. (See also sense 2.)

1805 SOUTHEY *Lett.* (1856) I. 315 The life and death of that man were equally lovely. *a* **1851** MRS. SHERWOOD *Poor Burruff* 15, I hope that all the little boys who read this, may learn thereby how lovely it is to be kind to dumb creatures. **1861** J. EDMOND *Childr. Ch. at Home* iii. 50 Make us like the lovely child Jesus.

4. Used as a term expressive of enthusiastic laudation: Delightful, highly excellent. *colloq.*

1614 MARKHAM *Cheap. Husb.* (1623) 121 [The Swine] though he is counted good in no place but the dish onely, yet there he is so louely and so wholesome, that all other faults may be borne with. **1653** WALTON *Angler* iii. 73 Come lets to supper. Come my friend Coridon, this Trout looks lovely. **1681** CHETHAM *Angler's Vade-m.* iv. §21 (1689) 53 Tis a lovely Bait for Winter, and Spring. **1860** C. PATMORE *Faithful for ever* III. i. 171 Dear Fred wrote, Directly, such a lovely note. **1872** GEO. ELIOT in Cross *Life* III. 164 Mr. Lewes had 'a lovely time' at Weybridge.

†**'lovely,** *adv.* *Obs.* Forms: see LOVE *sb.*[1] and -LY[2]. [OE. *luflíce*, f. *lufu* LOVE *sb.*[1] + *-líce* -LY[2].]

1. Lovingly, affectionately.

c **897** K. ÆLFRED *Gregory's Past.* Pref. 3 Ælfred kyning hateð gretan Wærferð biscep his wordum luflice & freondlice. *c* **1175** *Lamb. Hom.* 17 Bide hine luueliche þet he þe do riht. *c* **1205** LAY. 7892 He..þus spec wið his folke & lueliche spilede. *c* **1220** *Bestiary* 381 in *O.E. Misc.* 12 Ðus is ure louerdes laȝe luuelike to fillen. *c* **1350** *Will. Palerne* 975 William was gretliche glad & loueliche hir þonked. *a* **1400** *Pistill of Susan* 237 Loueliche heo louted, and lacched her leue At kynred and cosyn þat heo hed euere iknawen. **1503** HAWES *Examp. Virt.* xii. 23 Dame Clennes loked vpon me louely. **1596** SPENSER *F.Q.* IV. iii. 49 Instead of strokes, each other kissed glad, And lovely haulst, from feare of treason free.

b. Willingly, with joy.

c **900** tr. *Bæda's Hist.* IV. xi. (Schipper) 406 þæt he luflice swa dyde. *c* **1175** *Lamb. Hom.* 133 Euric mon þe lusteð lueliche godes wordes and ladeð his lif rihtliche þer efter he scal habben eche lif. *a* **1300** *Cursor M.* 9106 Al he tok in goddis nam, And thold luueli al þat scam.

2. Lovably, beautifully.

a **1400-50** *Alexander* 426 A lyons heuyd was on-loft louely coruyn. *c* **1430** *Freemasonry* 706 Al the whyle thou spekest with hym, Fayre and lovelyche bere up thy chyn. **1596** SHAKS. *1 Hen. IV*, III. i. 125 Where, being but young, I framed to the Harpe Many an English Dittie, louely well. **1604** —— *Oth.* IV. ii. 64 Oh thou weed: Who art so louely faire, and smell'st so sweete. **1708** J. PHILIPS *Cyder* II. 344 The defecated liquor..Spouts into subject vessels, lovely clear. **1811** W. R. SPENCER *Poems* 191 Lovelier beams the noon-day splendour.

love-making ('lʌv,meɪkɪŋ). Amorous proposals or intercourse, courtship.

c **1450** *Merlin* 87 Vlfyn is som-what a-quytte of the synne that he hadde in the love makinge. **1829** LYTTON *Devereux* II. ii, I looked round that mart of millinery and love-making, which was celebrated in the reign of Charles II. **1831** CARLYLE *Sart. Res.* (1858) 114 The whole Borough, with all its love-makings and scandal-mongeries.

fig. **1625** BACON *Ess., Truth* (Arb.) 500 The Inquirie of Truth, which is the Loue-making, or Wooing of it.

attrib. **1830** MOORE *Mem.* (1854) VI. 135 My sweet Bess and I recollected the time when we used, in our love-making days, to stroll for hours there together.

So **'love-maker, 'love-making** *a.*

1747 SARAH FIELDING *Fam. Lett.* 81 The Conversation of Fools and general Love-makers. **1868** BROWNING *Ring & Bk.* VI. 1532, I..bear no more love-making devils: hence!

love-mate ('lʌvmeɪt). Also 6 **loves-mate.** [f. LOVE *sb.*[1] + MATE *sb.*] The person with whom one is mated in love; a lover or sweetheart.

1582 STANYHURST *Æneis* IV. (Arb.) 108 At my tears showring dyd he sigh?..dyd he yeeld ons mercye toe loouemate? **1591** GREENE *Farew. to Follie* 2nd Ded. (1617) A 3 b, Sweet Companions, and Loue-mates of Learning. **1602** WARNER *Alb. Eng.* vi. 20 For her her mother Ceres and her Loves-mate did complaine. **1817** BYRON *Lament Tasso* v, A Princess was no love-mate for a bard. **1902** *Edin. Rev.* Oct. 319 The willing, or it may be unwilling, love-mate of Paris.

†**'loveness.** *Obs. rare*[−1]. [irreg. f. LOVE *sb.*[1] + -NESS.] Love.

a **1240** *Wohunge* in *Cott. Hom.* 285 Tac hit to þe nu leve lif wið treowe luuenesse.

lover[1] ('lʌvə(r)). Forms: *α.* 3, 5 luffer(e, 4-6 lufer, 4 lufere, lovere, luver, 5 loufer, lovare; *Sc.* 4-5 lufare, 4-6 luffar, 4 lyffar, 5 lufar, 6, 8 luver, 6 luvar, luvear, luwair, luif(f)ar, 7 luiver. *β.* 4 (8, 9 *dial.*) lovier, 4 loviere, lovyere, 4, 5, 8 lovyer, 8 loveyer, 4- lover. [f. LOVE *v.*[1] + -ER[1].] One who loves.

1. a. One who is possessed by sentiments of affection or regard towards another; a friend or well-wisher. Now *rare.*

a **1340** HAMPOLE *Psalter* i. 1 His verray lufers folous him fleand honur. *c* **1400** *Destr. Troy* 5277 He was a frynde to my fader, & a fyn louer. **1432-50** tr. *Higden* (Rolls) VIII. 231 The luffers of seynte Edmund were displeasede with hym gretely þerfore. *c* **1485** *Digby Myst.* (1882) III. 800 He ys þi lover, lord, suerly. **1524** *Sir R. Sutton's Will* in Churton *Life* App. 543 Make a new feoffment to ten persones of my lovers and frends. **1535** COVERDALE *1 Sam.* Contents xviii, Ionathas and Dauid are sworne louers. **1598** B. JONSON *Ev. Man in Hum.* Ded., To.. Mr. Cambden..your true lover, Ben. Jonson. **1601** SHAKS. *Jul. C.* III. ii. 49, I slewe my best Louer for the good of Rome. **1625** BACON *Ess., Friendship* (Arb.) 171 Men so Wise,..and so Extreme Louers of Themselues, as all these were. **1661** MORGAN *Sph. Gentry* IV. iii. 44 The loving Company of the order of the garter hath received you their Brother Lover and fellow. **1760-72** H. BROOKE *Fool of Qual.* (1809) III. 15 A stranger, but a very warm lover of yours. **1796** WOLFE TONE *Autobiog.* (1828) 147, I made my bow, and followed my new lover to his hotel. **1898** W. K. JOHNSON *Terra Tenebr.* 34 The earth was foe to him, Let the sea be lover.

b. In the spiritual sense.

c **1300** *Cursor M.* 20870 Petre was..luuer o lauerd, alsua niter. *c* **1375** *Sc. Leg. Saints* xviii. (*Egipciane*) 1085 God ..þat gyfis mare to his luferis þan þai cane ask. **1577** *St. Aug. Manual* (Longman) 108 God their lover will not take it [love] away from his lovers against their wils. **1740** C. WESLEY *Hymn*, Jesu, Lover of my Soul. **1748** G. WHITE *Serm.* (MS.), Every true Lover of God. **1866** J. H. NEWMAN *Gerontius* §1 Lover of souls! great God! I look to Thee.

2. a. One who is in love with, or who is enamoured of a person of the opposite sex.

a **1225** *Ancr. R.* 256 Leouere me beoð hire wunden þen uikiinde [*MS. C.* lufferes] cosses. *c* **1374** CHAUCER *Troylus* IV. 295 (323) O ye loueres þat heyhe vpon the whiel Ben set of Fortune. *c* **1375** *Sc. Leg. Saints* xxi. (*Clement*) 455 And hyre enbrasit with al his macht, as lyffaris þat had bene intwyne. *c* **1386** CHAUCER *Prol.* 80 A louyere, and a lusty Bacheler. **1423** JAS. I *Kingis Q.* clxxix, Awak! awake! I bring, lufar, I bring The newis glad. **1500-20** DUNBAR *Poems* xlviii. 60 The birdis did with oppin vocis cry, O, luvaris fo, away thow dully nycht. **1525** LD. BERNERS *Froiss.* II. xxx. 85 Loyes Rambalte had at Bride a fayre woman to his louer, whome he loued parfitely. **1557** NORTH *Gueuara's Diall Pr.* Gen. Prol. ¶ 7/1 He [Nero] counted seuerally al the haires that his louer Pompeia had on her head. **1601** B. JONSON *Poetaster* II. i, If I freely may discouer, What woulde please mee in my Louer: I woulde haue her faire, and wittie [etc.]. **1606** SHAKS. *Ant. & Cl.* V. ii. 298 The stroke of death is as a Louers pinch, Which hurts, and is desir'd. **1768** *Woman of Honor* III. 52 You will find few,..such desperately true lovyers. **1821** BYRON *Juan* III. iii, In her first passion, woman loves her lover. *a* **1825** FORBY *Voc. E. Anglia, Lovier*, a lover. A vulgarism, but no corruption. Not peculiar to us. **1847** EMERSON *Repr. Men, Plato* Wks. (Bohn) I. 290 If he had lover, wife, or children, we hear nothing of them. **1885** BURTON *Arab. Nts.* (1887) III. 101 She..said ..'I am a lover separated from her beloved'.

b. One who loves illicitly; a gallant, paramour.

1611 BIBLE *Jer.* iii. 1 Thou hast played the harlot with many louers. **1716** LADY M. W. MONTAGU *Let. to Lady Rich* 20 Sept., A woman looks not for a lover as soon as she is married. **1841** LANE *Arab. Nts.* I. 89 She answered, Thy wife has a lover.

c. A pimp. *U.S. slang.*

1904 'No. 1500' *Life in Sing Sing* 250/1 *Lover*, a man who receives support from a prostitute. **1963** R. I. MCDAVID *Mencken's Amer. Lang.* 727 A pimp is a..McGimp, fish and shrimp, lover, Latin lover and many others.

d. As a form of address (to a lover, or casually). *colloq.* (orig. and chiefly *U.S.*).

1911 G. S. PORTER *Harvester* x. 194 'Hello, lover!' cried Doctor Carey... 'Are you married yet?' **1920** F. SCOTT FITZGERALD *This Side of Paradise* II. i. 209 *Rosalind*: Lover! Lover! I can't do with you, and I can't imagine life without you. **1959** N. MAILER *Advts. for Myself* (1961) 389 Maybe I wouldn't hear all the jazz you hear, lover, but I could develop her talent. **1963** D. HEYES *12th of Never* (1964) v. 31 'You got it, lover,' the waitress said. **1966** L. DEIGHTON *Billion-Dollar Brain* iv. 41 It's nothing like that, lover. I'm not going to get myself hurt. **1972** J. BURMEISTER *Running Scared* iv. 72 She swung her legs off the bed. 'How about some coffee, lover?'

3. One who has an affection, predilection, fancy, or liking for (a thing, action or idea).

1340 *Ayenb.* 270 O men ne byeþ naȝt..louieres of þe wordle. *Ibid.*, Yet eft þe wordle þyestre, uor þe louyeres of þe wordle byeþ þyestre. **1388** WYCLIF *1 Pet.* iii. 13 And who is it that schal anoye ȝou if, ȝe ben sueris and louyeris of goodnesse. *c* **1420** LYDG. *Assembly of Gods* 902 Fysshers of sowles, and lovers of clennes. **1568** GRAFTON *Chron.* I. 8 Tuball..was a great lover of Musick. **1647** CLARENDON *Hist. Reb.* I. §122 He was a great lover of his country. **1655** WALTON *Angler* xxi. (1661) 255 *Pisc.* And upon all that are lovers of Vertue, and all that love to be quiet and go a fishing. **1748** HUME *Ess., Parties Gt. Brit.* 97 Lovers of Liberty, but greater Lovers of Monarchy. **1828** SCOTT *F.M. Perth*

Introd., Freed from the odious presence of this lover of cleanliness. **1901** *Longm. Mag.* Oct. 543 The book will be eagerly read by all lovers of Selborne.

4. *Comb.*, as **lover-loving** adj. Also **lover boy, man** *slang* (orig. *U.S.*), a lover, an attractive man, a woman-chaser; also used as a form of address; †**lovers' lair** *Sc.*, the bed of love; **lover's knot** = LOVE-KNOT; **lovers' lane**, a road or any other secluded place to which lovers resort; **lover's leap** (see LEAP *sb.*[1] 2); often applied to a precipice in connexion with some legend about the suicide of a lover by leaping down; also (*allusive nonce-use*), a matrimonial venture; **lover's (lovers') quarrel**, a dispute between lovers; also *transf.*

15.. *Littill Interlud* 76 in *Dunbar's Poems* (1893) 316 Lassis..Wald ga to luvaris lair. *c* **1560** A. SCOTT *Poems* (S.T.S.) vi. 25 So luvaris lair no leid suld lak. **1592** LYLY *Gallathea* IV. ii. 22 (Bond) First you must vndoe all these Louers knots, because you tyed them. **1677** (*title*) The lovers quarrel: or, Cupids triumph. **1809** MALKIN *Gil Blas* X. xii. (1866) 383, I answered by expressing my surprise at her honouring me with the offer of her hand... To this she replied, that having a considerable fortune, it would give her pleasure to share it in her life-time with a man of honour.. then, rejoined I, you have made up your mind to take a lover's leap. **1812** BYRON *Ch. Har.* I. lxxxi, While on the gay dance shone Night's lover-loving Queen. **1823** C. LAMB *Let.* 9 Jan. (1935) II. 364 Henceforth I retract all my fond complaints of mercantile employment; look upon them as lovers' quarrels. **1831** CARLYLE *Sart. Res.* II. vi, The river of his History..here dashes itself over that terrific Lover's Leap; and, as a mad-foaming cataract, flies wholly into tumultuous clouds of spray! **1842** LYTTON *Zanoni* I. II. ii. 137 The mysterious warning of Zanoni then suddenly occurred to him; he had forgotten it in the interest of his lover's quarrel with Viola. **1851** RUSKIN *Stones Ven.* (1874) I. viii. 98 Tying the shafts together in their centre, in a lover's knot. **1881** *Golden Gate Gaz.* (San Francisco) 26 Oct. 2/2 Sunday afternoon as a young lady and gentleman were promenading through 'Lovers' Lane' they were attacked by a ferocious dog. **1918** BARRIE *What Every Woman Knows* IV. 134 There is a romantically damp little arbour at the end of what the villagers call the Lovers' Lane. **1941** *Time* 25 Aug. 41/1 In England, a young pair who had had a lovers' quarrel took 50 years to cool off, finally got the knot tied. **1942** R. FROST *Witness Tree* 52, I had a lover's quarrel with the world. **1947** *News of World* 26 Jan. 3/6 Her..body..was found in a 'lovers' lane' on an empty building site. **1952** S. ELLIN *Key to Nicholas Street* I. i. 14 Here was lover boy walking around with milady's key. **1958** M. PROCTER *Man in Ambush* xvi. 196 Lover boy's been talking to you. Take no notice. **1959** C. WILLIAMS *Man in Motion* iii. 26 He's a Lover Boy, one of those big, flashy, conceited types that has to..give all the girls a break. **1961** H. S. TURNER *Something Extraordinary* ii. 28 Clive..has never been able to stop her calling him 'loverboy' in tones of scorn. **1966** J. PEARL *Crucifixion P. McCabe* (1967) ix. 136 How would I know that I'd find Donna Lord parked in a lovers' lane at Briarwood Lake? **1968** L. DEIGHTON *Only when I Larf* xvii. 226 'There's no hurry, loverman,' she said. **1972** F. WARNER *Lying Figures* II. 9 Out on the prowl tonight, lover-boy? **1972** J. BROWN *Chancer* xv. 208 Our arty friend, lover man, he was running a photography business. **1974** *Daily Tel.* (Colour Suppl.) 18 Jan. 34/4 Elisabeth Foster's body was found on January 3, 1972, under a hedge by a 'lovers' lane' near the picturesque village of Wrea Green.

†**lover**[2]. *Obs.* [f. LOVE *v.*[2] + -ER[1].] One who praises, an eulogist.

a **1340** HAMPOLE *Psalter* ix. 24 þat thynge has man delite to doe in þe whilk þai hafe sum louere & nan with takere. *Ibid.* xxi. 33 To be his lufere and louere.

lover, loverd(e, obs. ff. LOUVER, LORD.

†ˈ**lovered**, *sb. Obs.* Forms: 1 lufræden, 3 luuered, 4 lufreden(e, louered, lufredyn, 4–5 louerede, 5 louerede, loueraden(e, *Sc.* 4 luferand, 5 lufrant, 5–6 luferent, 6 luifrent. [OE. *lufræden*, f. *luf-u* LOVE *sb.*[1] + OE. *rǽden* condition: see -RED.] The condition or state of relations in which one person loves another; the emotion or feeling of love; warm affection, good will, kindness; *Sc.* lust.

c **1000** *Lamb. Ps.* cviii. 5 (Bosw.-T.) Hiȝ ȝesetton hatunge for lufrædenne minre. *a* **1300** *Cursor M.* 9812 A bird wald thinc, His grett luuered, his mikel suinc þat wald sua first vr liknes haf. *c* **1325** *Metr. Hom.* 30 He..Com to mak him glad and blithe, And his lufredene til him to kithe. *c* **1340** HAMPOLE *Prose Tr.* xxiv. 3 Thai doe wickidly to get thaim the fauour and lufredyn of this warld. *c* **1375** *Sc. Leg. Saints* xxiv. (*Alexis*) 160 Quhene he can luk one It, sic luferand he tuk, þat he þare dwelt in body & thocht. *a* **1425** *Cursor M.* 13255 (Trin.) Of his sarmoun spek many man And of þe louerede þat he wan. **1456** SIR G. HAYE *Law Arms* (S.T.S.) 254 A conquest bairn..is callit in the lawis adopcioun; that is to say..a conquest barne be favour and luferent. *Ibid.* 263 A man has despyte at hys wyf, for haterent of hir, or luferent of ane othir. **14..** *How Good Wife taught Dau.* 90 (in *Barbour's Bruce* etc. 528) For nakit lying lufrent will gendir. **1543** *Aberd. Reg.* (Jam.), The said gudis war frelie geivin.. to his said dothir for dothirlie kindness and luferent. **1560** ROLLAND *Crt. Venus* I. 656 Our life wplift throw feruour and luifrentis.

Hence †**lovereden** *a.*, beloved; †**loveredenly** *adv.*, in a loving manner.

c **1425** *Orolog. Sapient.* i. in *Anglia* X. 331/40 þat I am in alle tymes..so loueradenlye bisye abowte þe as þei..I ȝaf entente onelye to þe. *Ibid.* 375/41 O þis gracyous and loveraden worde.

lovered (ˈlʌvəd), *ppl. a.* [f. LOVER[1] + -ED[1].] Provided with, or having a lover.

1597 SHAKS. *Lover's Compl.* 320 Who, young and simple, would not be so louer'd? **1879** H. MERIVALE in *Theatre* Nov. 213 The veriest..minx, who would never have been fathered by that fine old Duke, or lovered by the manful Orlando.

loverhood (ˈlʌvəhʊd). [f. LOVER[1] + -HOOD.] The state or condition of being a lover.

1891 HANNAH LYNCH *G. Meredith* 154 The fluted tenor of romance twangs the guitar of loverhood musically.

lovering (ˈlʌvərɪŋ), *vbl. sb.* [f. LOVER[1] + -ING[1].] Courting, fondling. Also *attrib.*

1884 in R. LAWSON *Upton-on-Severn Words* 22. **1907** *Daily Chron.* 27 Nov. 3/3 Where the schoolboy demands gore in his books, she asks for 'lovering', as she calls it. *Ibid.*, Let him only think of the possibilities of that new 'mixed' school, where the headmaster kept a 'lovering table', at which dined the spoony couples. **1919** GALSWORTHY *Saint's Progress* I. ii. 20 Between these two young people no actual word of love had yet been spoken. Their lovering had advanced by glance and touch alone. **1922** C. ORR *Kate Curlew* xi. 178 She's nae objections to a bit of lovering behind her sister's coats. **1926** R. MACAULAY *Crewe Train* II. ix. 169 People like the lovering couple usually stayed out.. for long hours on end.

loverless (ˈlʌvəlɪs), *a.* [f. LOVER[1] + -LESS.] Having no lover, deprived of a lover.

1824 MISS MITFORD *Village* Ser. I. 64 She paid her faithless suitor the compliment of remaining loverless for three weary months. **1853** C. BRONTE *Villette* xiii, Loverless and inexpectant of love. **1892** *Temple Bar* Apr. 525 Until quite lately she was loverless.

loverlike (ˈlʌvəlaɪk), *a.* and *adv.* [f. LOVER[1] + -LIKE.] Like a lover; of a character or in a manner befitting a lover.

1552 HULOET, Louerlyke or lyke a louer, *amatorie*. **1641** MILTON *Reform.* II. Wks. 1851 III. 65 There is no act.. wherein passes more loverlike contestation betweene Christ and the Soule. **1748** RICHARDSON *Clarissa* (1811) I. 164 A mere loverlike correspondence which my heart condemns. **1808** ELEANOR SLEATH *Bristol Heiress* I. 183, I delight to delineate, with a lover-like minuteness, the various.. perfections..of Miss Percival. **1894** H. NISBET *Bush Girl's Rom.* 155 Lover-like he fixed on one star and connected it with the maiden.

loverly (ˈlʌvəlɪ), *a.*[1] and *adv.* [f. LOVER[1] + -LY.] **A.** *adj.* Like a lover. **B.** *adv.* In the manner of a lover.

1875 J. PAYN *Halves* xxii. II. 182, I only hushed her lips in loverly fashion. **1886** G. MACDONALD *What's Mine's Mine* xli. III. 101 Said the chief abruptly, 'I want only herself!' A very loverly way of speaking. **1887** STEVENSON *Misadv. J. Nicholson* ii. 4 The highest point of loverly exaltation. **1890** *Temple Bar* Nov. 441 He murmured loverly something about 'the light..of her jacinth hair'.

Comb. **1885** STEVENSON *Pr. Otto* iii. 30 They made a loverly-looking couple.

Hence ˈ**loverliness**.

1879 G. MEREDITH *Egoist* I. 154 He fluted away in loverliness, forgetful of Crossjay.

loverly, *a.*[2] Also **lovally**. Repr. a Cockney pronunc. of LOVELY *a.*

1907 [see JELLIED *a.* 3]. **1937** in PARTRIDGE *Dict. Slang* 497/2. **1956** LERNER & LOEWE *My Fair Lady* (1958) I. i. 13 All I want is a room somewhere, Far away from the cold night air;..Oh, wouldn't it be loverly? **1968** J. WAINWRIGHT *Web of Silence* 28 He 'ad the ackers—believe me—wiv a car like that... A loverly job, it was.

lovership (ˈlʌvəʃɪp). [f. LOVER[1] + -SHIP.] The state or condition of being a lover. Also used as a form of address to a lover.

1837 F. TROLLOPE *Vicar of Wrexhill* III. xiv. 325 Your lovership must excuse me if I declare that it is my intention to accompany the young lady myself. **1876** G. DAWSON *Authentic Gosp.* v. 77 The divine things in man are of God —I mean fatherhood, motherhood, lovership, patriotism.

†ˈ**lovertine**, *a. Obs. nonce-wd.* [f. LOVER[1], after *libertine*.] Addicted to love-making.

1603 DEKKER, etc. *Pat. Grissill* Wks. (Grosart) V. 231 These Gentlemen louertine, and my selfe a hater of loue.

loverwise (ˈlʌvəwaɪz), *adv.* [f. LOVER[1] + -WISE.] In the manner of a lover.

1872 HOWELLS *Wedd. Journ.* (1892) 155 They sat down here loverwise. **1884** RIDER HAGGARD *Dawn* II. i. 3 They journeyed loverwise, with their arms around each other.

lovery, obs. form of LIVERY, LOUVER.

loves, obs. pl. of LOAF *sb.*[1]

lovescape (ˈlʌvskeɪp). *rare.* [f. LOVE *sb.* after LANDSCAPE.] A view or prospect of love.

1876 G. M. HOPKINS *Wreck of Deutschland* xxiii, in *Poems* (1967) 59 With the gnarls of the nail in thee, niche of the lance, his Lovescape crucified. **1969** *Punch* 19 Feb. 286/1 It is finely elegiac and the townscapes and lovescapes are vivid.

ˈ**loveship**. *Obs. rare*[−1]. [f. LOVE *sb.*[1] + -SHIP.] The action of making love; courtship.

a **1500** *Piers of Fullham* 320 in Hazl. *E.P.P.* II. 13 Loueship goith ay to warke [*read* wrake], When that presence is put a bake.

lovesick (ˈlʌvsɪk), *a.* [f. LOVE *sb.*[1] + SICK *a.*] Languishing for or with love.

1530 PALSGR. 317/2 Lovesycke enamowered, *enamourée*. **1588** SHAKS. *Tit. A.* v. iii. 82 When..he did discourse To loue-sicke Didoes sad attending eare. **1606** —— *Ant. & Cl.* II. ii. 198 Purple the Sailes: and so purfumed that The Windes were Loue-sicke with them. **1697** DRYDEN *Virg. Past.* IX. 54 Where Nightingales their Love-sick Ditty sing. **1739** A. NICOL *Nature without Art* 67 Cure me of this love-sick fever. **1894** MRS. OLIPHANT *Hist. Sk. Q. Anne* i. 14 Her great general sighed like a lovesick boy whenever he was absent from her.

Hence **lovesickness**, lovesick condition.

1707 FLOYER *Physic. Pulse-Watch* 10 He, by mentioning the Name of Pylas to a sick Woman, found some alteration in her Pulse, by which he discover'd her Love-Sickness. **1874** SPURGEON *Treas. Dav.* Ps. lxxxiv. 2 He had a holy lovesickness upon him.

lovesome (ˈlʌvsəm), *a.* Now *arch.* or *dial.* Forms: 1–6 **lufsum**, 3 **luffsumm**, 3–5 **lussum**, 3 **luvesum**, 4 **luffsum**, **lufsom**, **lufsome**, **lussom**, **lossum**, **lossom**, **loovesum**, 4–5 **lofsom**, **lufsom**, **lovesum**, 4–6 **lovesom**, 6 **loveseme**, **lusum**, ?**luxom(e**, **lufesum**, **lufesome**, *Sc.* **luifsum**, 5– **lovesome**. [OE. *lufsum*, f. *luf-u* LOVE *sb.*[1]: see -SOME. (The contracted forms *lussom*, *lossom*, *-um*, seem to occur only in sense 2.)]

1. Worthy of love; having qualities that inspire love; lovable.

a **1000** *Crist* 913 (Gr.) Lufsum and liþe leofum monnum to sceawianne þone scynan wlite. *c* **1200** ORMIN 3583 Daviþess name..itt uss tacneþþ stang wiþþ hannd, & luffsumm onn to lokenn. *a* **1225** *Juliana* 13 Ihesu crist..þat ich on leue & luuie as leoflukest & lufsumest lauerd. *c* **1325** *Deo Gratias* 29 in *E.E.P.* (1862) 125 A louesum buirde he lihte with-Inne þe worþiest þat euer was. **1430** *Hymns Virg.* 29 Hise louesum lijf þat alle men siȝe[n], Ful myldeli he out gan lete. **1570** *Satir. Poems Reform.* xv. 33 Thow luifsum Lark & gay Goldspink,..Lat be ȝour heuinly noitis. **1676** ETHEREDGE *Man of Mode* III. iii, Wild, witty, lovesome, beautiful and young. **1899** SWINBURNE *Rosamund* III. 60, I know not Aught lovesome save the sweet brief death of sleep.

2. Lovable on account of beauty; lovely, beautiful.

a **1225** *St. Marher.* 3 Ant wel hire schal iwurthen for hire lussum leor. *a* **1240** *Wohunge* in *Cott. Hom.* 269 þu art lufsum on leor, þu art al schene. *a* **1300** *Cursor M.* 604 A luuesum land at lenger in. *a* **1310** in Wright *Lyric P.* 26 Hire rode is ase rose that red is on rys, With lilye-white leres lossum he is. *Ibid.* 51 A burde of blod ant of bon Never ȝete y nuste non lussomore in londe. *c* **1320** *Sir Tristr.* 2816 Ysonde haue þere he wald Luffsum vnder line. *c* **1374** CHAUCER *Troylus* v. 465 O lufsom lady bryght, How haue ye faren syn þat ye were þere? *c* **1420** *Anturs of Arth.* 344 (Douce MS.) A lady, lufsom of lote, ledand a kniȝte. *c* **1450** *St. Cuthbert* (Surtees) 1215 He saw..Com fra heuen a lufsom lyght. **15..** in *Dunbar's Poems* (1893) 326 Fair lufsum lady, gentill and discret. **1820** SCOTT *Monast.* xiv, The handsomest, the very lovesomest young man I ever saw with sight. **1842** TENNYSON *Beggar Maid* 12 One praised her ancles, one her eyes, One her dark hair and lovesome mien. **1868** MORRIS *Earthly Par.* II. 323 He heard a sudden lovesome song begun.

absol. **13..** *Gaw. & Gr. Knt.* 1814 'Nay..' Quod þat lufsum vnder lyne. **13..** *E.E. Allit. P.* A. 398 þen sayde þat lufsoum of lyth & lere [etc.].

3. Loving, friendly.

c **1200** ORMIN 1547 Aȝȝ to follȝhenn soþ meocleȝȝc Wiþþ luffsumm æddmodnesse. **1566** DRANT *Horace's Sat.* I. ii. Bb, But they, the sillye fonded fooles,..Do feaste him, for his louesom loue. **1868** BROWNING *Ring & Bk.* VIII. 20 Won't we hold Our little yearly lovesome frolic feast. **1901** H. C. WELCH *Anselm* iii. 48 This increasing influence was due to the happy lovesome temper which plays through his letters.

4. Amorous.

1720 MRS. MANLEY *Power of Love* (1741) 150 Caton, who being naturally Lovesome, put herself in his way at every opportunity, so that he could not help saying soft things to her. **1844** KINGLAKE *Eothen* vii. (1878) 92 Shrubs that twined their arms together in lovesome tangles. **1883** *Longm. Mag.* Sept. 533 While lovesome and moansome thereon spake and falter'd the dove to the dove.

Hence †**lovesomehead** = LOVESOMENESS.

a **1300–1400** *Cursor M.* 5792 (Gött.), I sal þaim bring fra þat thralhede, And into a land of lufsum-hede.

†ˈ**lovesomely**, *adv. Obs.* [f. LOVESOME *a.* + -LY[2]. (OE. had *lufsumlic* adj.)] Lovingly, affectionately.

c **1200** ORMIN 1663 Nohht ne maȝȝ ben don Allmahhtiȝ Godd tocweme, But iff itt be wiþþ witt & skill & luffsummlike forþedd. *a* **1225** *Juliana* 12 [He] seide hire lufsumliche þat [etc.]. *a* **1300** *Cursor M.* 7989 þan com til him an angel clere,..And lufsumli to david spak. **1375** BARBOUR *Bruce* XVII. 315 Thair capitane Tretit thame sa lusumly. *c* **1475** *Rauf Coilȝear* 558 His leif at the Coilȝear He tuke lufesumly.

lovesomeness (ˈlʌvsəmnɪs). [f. LOVESOME *a.* + -NESS.] The quality of being lovesome.

a **1000** *Voc.* in Wr.-Wülcker 218/34 *Delectatio*, lustbærnes, *vel* lufsumnes. **1550** BALE *Image Both Ch.* viii. H vij b, They mixed yᵉ truth in falshede, they poysoned the waters, they toke awaye the louesomnesse of them. *a* **1568** *Bannatyne Poems* (Hunter. Club) 657 Weill lasit with luifsumnes. **1869** MISS MULOCK *Woman's Kingd.* II. 19 [She] was not beautiful..but there was a lovesomeness about her.

love-song (ˈlʌvsɒŋ). A song of love, an amorous song.

a **1310** in Wright *Lyric P.* 74 Iesu, thi love is suete ant strong..Tech me, Ihesu, thi love song, With suete teres ever among. **1591** SHAKS. *Two Gent.* II. i. 20 First, you haue learn'd..to rellish a Loue-song. **1653** WALTON *Angler* i. 29 Solomon..wrote that..holy amorous love-song, the Canticles. **1833** TENNYSON *Miller's D.* 65 A love-song I had somewhere read. **1883** H. DRUMMOND *Nat. Law in Spir. W.* (ed. 2) 154 The bird..listens to the love-song of its mate.

love-token ('lʌv,təʊk(ə)n). Something given as a sign or token of love.

Beowulf (Z) 1863 Sceal hring naca ofer hea þu bringan lac & luf tacen. **1590** SHAKS. *Mids. N.* I. i. 27 Thou hast giuen her rimes, And interchang'd loue-tokens with my childe. **1626** BP. HALL *Contempl., O.T.* xx. viii, What Church in the world can show such deare love-tokens from the Almighty as this? **16..** *Child Maurice* xxii. in Child *Ballads* II. 265/2 For thou hast sent her loue-tokens, More now then two or three. **1836** J. H. NEWMAN in *Lyra Apost.* (1849) 26 Yes! let the fragrant scars abide Love-tokens in thy stead. **1877** W. JONES *Finger-ring* 343 He sent two diamond rings, as love-tokens to Mary, Queen of Scots.

loveward(s ('lʌvwəd(z)), *adv. rare.* [f. LOVE *sb.* + -WARD or -WARDS.] Towards love.

1927 JOYCE *Watching Needleboats at San Sabba* in *Pomes Penyeach*, I heard their young hearts crying Loveward above the glancing oar. **1971** G. M. BROWN *Fishermen with Ploughs* 76 The children of the valley Drifted lovewards.

†**lovewende**, *a. Obs.* [OE. *lufwęnde*, f. *lufu* LOVE *sb.*^{1} + *-węnde* f. *węndan* to turn. Cf. *hálwende* wholesome, *hwílwende* transitory.] Beloved; loving; lovely.

a **1000** *Gloss.* in Wr.-Wülcker 222/21 *Dilectaque rura*, and þa lufwende eardas. *c* **1000** *Sax. Leech.* III. 186 Cild acenned..soðfæst, lufwende. *a* **1225** *Juliana* 65 Ich..luuie þe to leofmon luuewende lauerd.

loveword, variant of LOFWORD *Obs.*

'**love-worth**, *sb. rare.* [f. LOVE *sb.*^{1} + WORTH *sb.*] Worthiness of love.

c **1611** CHAPMAN *Iliad* To Rdr. 85 Homer..should be belov'd, Who euerie sort of loue-worth did containe.

†**love-worth**, *a. Obs.* [f. LOVE *sb.*^{1} + WORTH *a.*] = next.

a **1225** *Ancr. R.* 112 Ower deorewurðe spus, þe luuewurðe Louerd. *a* **1225** *Juliana* 53 þi luuewurðe leofmon. *a* **1240** *Ureisun* in *Lamb. Hom.* 187 Alre þinge leofluccst and luue wurðest.

loveworthy ('lʌvwɜːðɪ), *a.* [f. LOVE *sb.*^{1} + WORTHY *a.*] Worthy to be loved.

a **1240** *Wohunge* in *Cott. Hom.* 269 Inwið þe ane arn alle þe þinges igedered þat euer muhen maken ani mon luuewurði to oðer. **1621** LADY M. WROTH *Urania* 289 Neræna, the most loue-worthy of her sex. **1633** W. STRUTHER *True Happiness* 31 If these small goods be love-worthy, with what a love should we adhere to the fountain-good. **1867** THIRLWALL *Lett.* (1881) I. 278 It may happen..that..the child makes the painful discovery that the person whom it most tenderly loves is not loveworthy. **1880** SWINBURNE *Stud. Shaks.* 227 A living god-garland of the noblest earth-born brothers and love-worthiest heaven-born sister.

Hence **loveworthiness**.

1867 THIRLWALL *Lett.* (1881) I. 278 The perception of His loveworthiness must tend to swallow up our sense of benefits received from him. **1899** F. P. COBBE in *Daily News* 27 May 7/1 The nobility and loveworthiness of human nature.

lovey ('lʌvɪ). Also lovy, lovee, lovie. [f. LOVE *sb.*^{1} + -Y.] A term of affectionate address: = 'Dear love', 'darling'.

1731 FIELDING *Lett. Writers* I. v, You don't look pretty in it, lovey, indeed you don't. **1764** FOOTE *Mayor of G.* I. Wks. 1799 I. 169, I go, lovy: good-day to my father-in-law. **1770** —— *Lame Lover* I. ibid. II. 67 Why, really, lovee, 'tis a large sum of money. **1801** MACNEILL *Poems* (1844) 19 Sullen moods, and scolding frays, When lovie's absent for some days. **1884** *Punch* 20 Dec. 294 And what would Dovey do if Lovey were to die?

lovey-dovey ('lʌvɪ'dʌvɪ), *sb.* and *a.* [f. LOVEY + DOVIE, DOVEY.] **A.** *sb.* = LOVEY; also, brotherly love.

1819 [see DOVIE, DOVEY]. **1904** *Daily Chron.* 26 Mar. 6/5 We will..love one another as much as we can, lovey dovey. **1946** H. L. MENCKEN in *Life* 5 Aug. 46/2 And bring in a reign of peace, prosperity and lovey-dovey.

B. *adj.* Fondly affectionate; namby-pamby.

1886 *Harper's Mag.* Dec. 134/1, I would wear gray, which mamma prefers, but which I think looks lovey-dovey. **1900** H. LAWSON *On Track* 65 Just as lovey-dovey talk is important to her and nonsense to you. **1967** 'D. SHANNON' *Chance to Kill* (1968) vii. 91 You want to act all broad-minded and lovey-dovey with the dinges, O.K., but I got a right to feel how I like too. **1969** *Sunday Times* (Colour Suppl.) 19/3 There had been a fight. 'There was none of the usual lovey-dovey stuff between them.' **1973** 'H. CARMICHAEL' *Too Late for Tears* viii. 99 This woman hadn't been all lovey-dovey with her husband... They'd been squabbling for months.

So '**lovey-'doveyness** [-NESS], a state of maudlin sentimentality.

1923 D. H. LAWRENCE *Stud. Classic Amer. Lit.* x. 210 He [*sc.* Melville] wanted the lovey-doveyness of perfect mutual understanding. **1968** *Punch* 29 May 788/3 The fond pleasures, dear upsets and general lovey-doveyness of family life.

loveyer, lovier, obs. forms of LOVER *sb.*^{1}

'**loving**, *vbl. sb.*^{1} Now *rare.* [f. LOVE *v.*^{1} + -ING^1.] The action of the vb. LOVE^1.

c **1375** *Sc. Leg. Saints* iii. (*St. Andrew*) 766 Fore, criste,.. I ȝarne our althinge, to be and dwel in þi lovynge. *c* **1385** CHAUCER *L.G.W.* Prol. 544 For she taughte al the craft of fyn louinge. *c* **1400** *Cursor M.* 27746 (Cott. Galba) Wreth.. of gude lufing it brekes þe band. **1538** ELYOT *Dict.* Addit., *Amatio*, a louynge. **1600** SHAKS. *A.Y.L.* II. vii. 181 Most frendship is fayning; most Louing, meere folly. **1633** P. FLETCHER *Poet. Misc.* 79 What fool commends a stone for never moving?.. Cease then, fond men, to blaze your constant loving. **1855** BROWNING *One Word More* v, Dante ..Hated wickedness that hinders loving. **1885–94** R. BRIDGES *Eros & Psyche* May xxii, This was the lover she had lack'd, and she, Loving his loving, was his willing bride.

†'**loving**, *vbl. sb.*^{2} *Obs.* [f. LOVE *v.*^{2} + -ING^1.] Praise, laudation; *pl.*, praises, songs of praise.

a **1300** *Cursor M.* 13245 Iesus þat well wist..Quarfor sant ion was don o lijf; To þe Iues..In his louing he made sermon. *a* **1300** *E.E. Psalter* ix. 15 þat I schewe forth to sprede þine loueynges euerilkone. **1375** BARBOUR *Bruce* VI. 283 Now demys, quhethir mair lovyng Suld Tedeus haf, or the king! *c* **1400** tr. *Secreta Secret., Gov. Lordsh.* 51 He þat gyues his good to hem þat hauys no myster, he purchases no louynge þerof. **1476** *Burgh Rec. Edinb.* (1869) I. 33 For the honour and loving of Gode Almichty. **1477** EARL RIVERS (Caxton) *Dictes* I To gyue therfore synguler louynges & thankes. **1533** GAU *Richt Vay* (1888) 13 Thay that desiris lowine or vane gloir. **1539** *Test. Ebor.* (Surtees) VI. 83, I.. beinge of holl and perfite mynde..lovinge be to God. **1590** A. HUME *Hymns* ii. 32 The maiestie of God was praisd with louings loud on hight. **1596** DALRYMPLE tr. *Leslie's Hist. Scot.* II. x. 343 He did the legacie and office..with sik lofeng and comment. **1721** BAILEY, *Lovingis*, praises, Scotch.

loving ('lʌvɪŋ), *ppl. a.* [f. LOVE *v.*^{1} + -ING^2.]

1. a. That loves; affectionate.

In 16th c. 'your loving friend' was an ordinary form of subscription for letters. 'Our loving subjects' has at various times been a usual phrase in royal proclamations.

c **1000** ÆLFRIC *Gram.* vi. (Z.) 10 *Hic amans uir*, þes lufienda wer;..*hoc amans mancipium*, þes lufienda þeowa man. *a* **1240** *Ureisun* in *Cott. Hom.* 185 Ler to loue þe..þe louende louerd. **1320** *Cast. Love* 290 And foure dowghtryne hede this kyng, And to uche he wes lovyng. **1375** BARBOUR *Bruce* IV. 7 Thaim that till hym luffand wer, Or kyn, or freynd. *c* **1460** *Towneley Myst.* iv. 102 Now, who would not be glad that had A child so lufand as thou art? *c* **1491** *Chast. Goddes Chyld.* 44 It is yeuen us and sende us fro our louyng fader. **1513** MORE in Grafton *Chron.* (1568) II. 781 A lovyng man and passyng well beloved. **1529** —— *Let.* Wks. 1419/2 At Woodestok..by the hand of Your louing husbande Thomas More knight. **1568** GRAFTON *Chron.* I. 82 They were loving and kinde to him, and he to them. **1741** RICHARDSON *Pamela* II. 330 They are the honestest, the loveingest, and the most conscientious Couple breatheing. **1809** MALKIN *Gil Blas* v. i. ¶11 They got to be as loving as turtles. **1835** MACAULAY *Hist. Eng.* xvi. III. 723 He brought that force only for the defence of his person and for the protection of his loving subjects. **1866** J. H. NEWMAN *Gerontius* §1 O loving friends, your prayers! *Ibid.*, Help, loving Lord! Thou my sole Refuge, Thou.

†**b.** *absol.* A lover; one who loves. *Obs.*

a **1300** *Cursor M.* 14313 Lauerd, o selcut þat es slei, þi lufand þus, qui let þou dei? *c* **1340** HAMPOLE *Prose Tr.* (1866) 3 Fyllys þe luffande of gastely joye. *c* **1375** *Cursor M.* 14597 (Fairf.) Haue I na tome þidder to fare for na wele louande haue I þare.

c. *transf.* Tending to be closely attached, clinging, adhesive. *dial.*

1641 BEST *Farm. Bks.* (Surtees) 148 By this meanes the strawe is made lovinger, and is allsoe kept from growinge on the howacs. [Common in mod. dialects: see Eng. Dial. Dict.]

2. Of words, actions, etc.: Manifesting love; proceeding from love. Hence *occas.* of persons with respect to their demeanour or conduct (const. *to*).

c **1450** MYRC 1697 Louynge serues and godely speche, Agayn enuye ys helpe and leche. **1509** HAWES *Past. Pleas.* xxvii. (Percy Soc.) 119 Her lovynge countenaunce so hyghe dyd appere, That it me ravyshed. **1634** SIR T. HERBERT *Trav.* 39 They continue that louing custome [widow burning] deuoutly to this day. **18..** TENNYSON *Early Spring* i, Once more the Heavenly Power..domes the red-plow'd hills With loving blue. **1862** LYTTON *Str. Story* II. 177 Faber's loving account of little Amy. **1868** BROWNING *Ring & Bk.* III. 1303 His fingers pushed their loving way Through curl on curl. **1894** J. T. FOWLER *Adamnan* Introd. 54 He was held in most loving remembrance.

3. Preceded by a *sb.*, in various *comb.*, as ***fun-, home-, money-, pleasure-loving***.

1726 SWIFT *Gulliver, Lament. Glumdal.* 33 That Money-loving Boy To some Lord's Daughter sold the living Toy. **1838** ELIZA COOK *Old Dobbin* xi, We fun-loving urchins would group by his side. **1871** S. B. JAMES *Duty & Doctrine* 192 A pushing, eager, pleasure-loving, money-loving age! **1902** *Westm. Gaz.* 3 June 1/2 The Boer is, above all things, a home-loving man.

4. *Comb.*, as ***loving-heartedness***; ***loving-hearted, -kind, -kindly*** adjs.

1903 HARDY *Dynasts* I. I. vi. 33 In its early, loving-kindly days Of gracious purpose. **1909** *Westm. Gaz.* 27 Feb. 4/3 The loving-hearted but hot-tempered musician who was head of the Conservatoire at Naples. **1909** R. BROOKE *Coll. Poems* (1918) 99 Quiet and strange, and loving-kind, you sleep. **1926** *Contemp. Rev.* Feb. 226 It may have been the *sirocco*, which never makes for loving-heartedness. **1960** *Clergy Rev.* Jan. 14 More's way, detached, peaceful and loving-kind, must have set him dreaming.

loving cup. [LOVING *ppl. a.* 2.] A large drinking vessel, usually of silver, having two or more handles, by which it is readily passed from hand to hand amongst friends or guests assembled together, each of whom successively drinks from its contents, generally at the close of a banquet.

1808 [In Minute-bk. of Committee for the Lord Mayor's banquet 9 Nov. (Dr. R. R. Sharpe).] **1812** J. BRADY *Clavis Calend.* (1815) II. 351 The Lord Mayor drinks to you in the Loving Cup, and bids you all heartily welcome. **1827** HONE *Every-day Bk.* II. 312 The loving cup..is..passed to the guest on his left hand. **1868** BREWER *Dict. Phrase & Fable* (ed. 3) 527 In drinking the loving cup, two adjacent persons always stand up together.

loving-kindness ('lʌvɪŋ'kaɪndnɪs). [f. LOVING *ppl. a.* + KINDNESS. Originally two words; the combination was introduced by Coverdale.] Affectionate tenderness and consideration; kindness arising from a deep personal love, as the active love of God for his creatures.

1535 COVERDALE *Ps.* xxv. 6 Call to remembraunce, O Lorde, thy tender mercyes & thy louinge kyndnesses, which haue bene euer of olde. *Ibid.* lxxxix. 33 Neuerthelesse, my louynge kyndnesse wil I not vtterly take from him. **1554–9** *Songs & Ball.* (1860) 3 What great lovyng kyndnes did God show in thys cace? *a* **1729** J. ROGERS *19 Serm.* (1735) 349 The amiable Attributes of Goodness and Loving-kindness. **1807–8** W. IRVING *Salmag.* (1824) 144 A lady of unbounded loving-kindness. **1871** MORLEY *Voltaire* (1886) 2 The infinite mercy and loving-kindness of a supreme creator.

Hence (back-formation) **loving-kindly** *adv.*

1840 LOWELL *Love*, A love..that seeth faults, Not with flaw-seeking eyes..But loving-kindly ever looks them down.

†**loving-knot.** *Obs.* = LOVE-KNOT.

c **1588** *1st Pt. Jeronimo* (1605) C iij b, Heere seale the letter with a louing knot.

†'**lovingly**, *a. Obs. rare*$^{-1}$. [f. LOVING *ppl. a.* + -LY^1.] Of loving disposition.

1567 *Gude & Godlie Ball.* (S.T.S.) 222, I knaw nane sic as scho is one, Sa trew, sa kynde, sa luiffandlie.

lovingly ('lʌvɪŋlɪ), *adv.* [f. LOVING *ppl. a.* + -LY^2.] In a loving manner.

1398 TREVISA *Barth. De P.R.* VI. xiii. (1495) 197 Louyngly the man auyseth his wyfe yf she doo amys. **1435** MISYN *Fire of Love* I. vii. 15 To prays god parfytely,..louandly to syng in hym. **1535** COVERDALE *Jer.* xxxi. 20 Gladly and louyngly will I haue mercy vpon him, saieth the Lorde. **1611** BIBLE *1 Sam.* xx. (chapter-summary), Ionathan louingly taketh his leaue of Dauid. **1641** T. HAYNE *Luther* 136 He was very lovingly affectioned towards his children. **1709** STEELE *Tatler* No. 118 ¶4 We live very lovingly together. **1883** R. W. DIXON *Mano* IV. iii. 147 And ever on him leaned she lovingly.

lovingness ('lʌvɪŋnɪs). [f. LOVING *ppl. a.* + -NESS.] The quality or habit of being loving.

1574 tr. *Marlorat's Apocalips* 25 Be thou a patterne to the faithfull, in word, in conuersation, in louingnesse,..and in chastitie. *a* **1586** SIDNEY *Arcadia* II. (1590) 115 b, Caryìng thus in one person the only two bands of good will, loue-lines & louingnes. **1621** LADY M. WROTH *Urania* 348 Such were her allurements, her sweetnesses, louingnesses [etc.]. **1799** W. TAYLOR in Robberds *Mem.* I. 297 There is a lovingness of heart about Parr..which would endear him even without his Greek. *a* **1859** L. HUNT *Bk. Sonnet* (1867) I. 66 The very lovingness of his nature. **1865** J. GROTE *Moral Ideas* viii. (1876) 108 That φιλία or lovingness which creates, so to speak, a kindred and brotherhood.

b. Used as a mock title of honour.

a **1636** LYNDE *Case for Spectacles* (1638) 91 Instead of the Emperours name, he assumes the Popes person, saying, Your lovingnesse wrote to me.

lovis, -ys, obs. pl. of LOAF *sb.*^{1}

lovy, variant of LOVEY.

lovyer(e, obs. form of LOVER *sb.*^{1}

low (ləʊ), *sb.*^{1} Also 3–5, 9 lowe, 6 looe, 7 loe. Cf. LAW *sb.*^{3} [OE. *hláw*, *hlǽw* masc., = OS. *hlêo* (dat. *hlêwe*) grave-mound, OHG. *hlêo* (MHG. *lê*) grave-mound, hill, Goth. *hlaiw* neut., grave (whence *hlaiwasnôs* pl., graves):—OTeut. **hlaiwoz-, -iz-* neut.:—pre-Teut. **kloiwos-, -es-*, f. root **klei-* to slope: see LEAN *v.* and cf. L. *clīvus* hill.]

1. = LAW *sb.*^{3} I. *arch.*

Beowulf (Z.) 1120 Wand to wolcnum wælfyra mæst hlynode for hlawe. *c* **1200** ORMIN 9205 And illc an lawe and illc an hill Shall nibþredd beon and laȝhedd. *c* **1300** *Havelok* 1699 þo stod hauelok als a lowe Aboven [þo] þat þer-inne wore. *a* **1400–50** *Alexander* 1090 May þou oght, lede, yonder low lift on þi shulder. *c* **1500** *Cov. Corp. Chr. Plays, Shearmen & Taylors* 218 Harke! I here owre brothur on the looe; This ys hys woise. *a* **1650** *Sir Lionell* 70 in Furnivall *Percy Folio* I. 78 The Gyant lyes vnder yond low. *a* **1765** *R. Hood & Guy of Gisborne* xlvi. in Child *Ballads* III. 93/2 That beheard the sheriffe of Nottingham, As he leaned vnder a lowe. **1847** MARY HOWITT *Ballads* 66 And some they brought the brown lint-seed, and flung it down from the Low. **1901** *Speaker* 20 Apr. 77/1 The coarse meadows swell up into rounded or pointed 'lows'.

2. A burial-mound; a tumulus. ? *Obs.*

a **1000** *Boeth. Metr.* x. 43 Hwa wat nu þæs wisan Welandes ban, on hwelcum hi hlæwa hrusan þeccen. **1686** PLOT *Staffordsh.* 402 A barrow or Low, such as were usually cast up over the bodies of eminent Captains. **1778** *Eng. Gazetteer* (ed. 2) s.v. *Wiggington*, Near this place are certain Lows, which are reckoned among the Roman Tumuli.

low, lowe (lou), *sb.*^{2} Chiefly *Sc.* and *north.* Also 3 loȝhe, 4 lou, (lawhe, lo), 5 logh, (lawe). [a. ON. *loge* wk. masc. (Da. *lue*) = OFris. *loga*:—OTeut. type **logon-* (*lugon-*), pre-Teut. *lukón-*, cogn. w. MHG., mod.G. *lohe* fem.:—OTeut. type **lohâ* (*luhâ*):—pre-Teut. **lúkā*, f. **luk-* wk. grade of the Aryan root **leuk-*: see LEYE, and LIGHT *sb.*]

1. Flame; a flame, a blaze.

a **1225** *Ancr. R.* 356 Cherubines sweorde..of lai [*MS. T.* lohe]. *c* **1250** *Gen. & Ex.* 643 Al-so heȝe ðe lowe sal gon, So ðe flod flet de dunes on. *a* **1300** *Cursor M.* 5739 Him thoght brennand he sagh a tre Als it wit lou war al vm-laid. **1340** HAMPOLE *Pr. Consc.* 9430 Lowe and reke with stormes melled. *c* **1470** HENRY *Wallace* VIII. 1054 The rude low rais

LOW 62 LOW

full heych adown that hauld. **1533** BELLENDEN *Livy* I. xvi. (S.T.S.) 88 His hede apperit (as It war blesand) in ane rede low. **1631** A. CRAIGE *Pilgr. & Hermit* 8 The Coale that mee burnes to the bone, will I blow, Though Liver, Lungs, and Lights, fly vp in a low. **1785** BURNS *Vision* I. 39 By my ingle-lowe I saw..A tight, outlandish Hizzie. **1816** SCOTT *Bl. Dwarf* iii, The low of the candle, if the wind wad let it bide steady. **1849** C. BRONTE *Shirley* iv, A verse blazing wi' a blue brimstone low. **1892** R. KIPLING *Barrack-r. Ball.* etc. 126 For every time I raised the lowe That scared the dusty plain, ..I'll light the land with twain. **1901** *Trans. Stirling Nat. Hist. Soc.* 51 The Dead Candle... A blue lowe, moving along slowly about three feet from the ground.

b. Phrases. (*to be, set*) *in, on a low*, in a flame, on fire; ***to put the low to***, to set fire to; ***to take a low***, to catch fire.

c **1200** ORMIN 16185 All alls itt wære all oferr hemm O loȝhe. *c* **1330** R. BRUNNE *Chron. Wace* (Rolls) 14692 Þe fir, þe tonder, þe brymston hot, Kyndled on lowe, & vp hit smot. *c* **1422** HOCCLEVE *Learn to die* 703 Whan þat a greet toun set is on a lowe. *a* **1584** MONTGOMERIE *Cherrie & Slae* 745 Will flatterit him,..An set him in an low. **1722** RAMSAY *Three Bonnets* II. 103 Soon my beard will tak' a low. **1815** SCOTT *Guy M.* x, She [a vessel] was..in a light low. **1826** J. WILSON *Noct. Ambr.* Wks. 1855 I. 130 A..boy fell off his chair a' in a low, for the discharge had set him on fire. **1865** G. MACDONALD *A. Forbes* viii. 25 Ye wad hae the hoose in a low aboot oor lugs.

2. *spec.* **a.** A light used by salmon-poachers.

1814 J. HODGSON in J. Raine *Mem.* (1857) I. 146 For making lows or fish-lights for fishing in the night. **1856** *Denham Tracts* (1892) I. 315 This used to be done with a low and a leister.

b. A light or piece of candle used by miners.

1816 in I. H. H. HOLMES *Coal Mines Durham*, etc. 245. **1865** *Trapper's Petit.* in *Our Coal & Coal-fields* 155 'Tis very dark and that small low You gave me soon will burn away.

†**low**, *sb.*[3] *Obs.* [var. of LOUGH[1].] A lake, loch, river, water.

1387 [see LOUGH[2]]. **1513** DOUGLAS *Æneis* XII. Prol. 153 Swannys swouchis throw owt the rysp and redis Our al thir lowys. **1539** in *Rec. Peebles* (1872) 57 Woddis, lowis, fischingis [etc.]. [**1563** *Ibid.* 72 Louchis.]

†**low**, *sb.*[4] *Sc. Obs.* [aphetic f. *allow sb. f. ALLOW *v.*] Allowance, permission.

1535 STEWART *Cron. Scot.* (1858) III. 464 [He] passit hame awa, But lowe or leif that tyme of ony wicht.

low (ləʊ), *sb.*[5] [f. LOW *v.*[4]] The action of lowing; the ordinary sound uttered by an ox or cow.

1549 *Compl. Scot.* vi. 39 The nolt maid noyis vitht mony loud lou. **1599** SHAKS. *Much Ado* v. iv. 48 Bull Ioue, sir, had an amiable low. **1726–46** THOMSON *Winter* 85 The cattle from the untasted fields return, And ask with meaning low their wonted stalls. **1821** CLARE *Vill. Minstr.* I. 111 On list'ning ears so sweet Fall the mellow low and bleat. **1861** HUGHES *Tom Brown at Oxf.* xxxvii. (1889) 360 A comfortable low came at intervals from the cattle, revelling in the abundant herbage.

low, *sb.*[6] See LOOR (= foot-rot in cattle).

low (ləʊ), *a.* and *sb.* Forms: 2–3 **lah** (*inflected* **laȝe**), 3 **lahȝh, laih**, 3–4 **laȝh**, 4 **lagh(e**, 3 **lohe, louh**, 3–4 **loȝ(e**, 4 **loghe**, 4–5 **louȝ(e**, (4 **lowh, loewȝ**), 5 **lough, lowȝe**, 3–7 **lowe**, (5 **loe**, 7 **lo**), 4– **low**. Also *Sc.* and *north.* 4–6 **lawe**, 4, 7 **lau(e**, 4–5 **lauch(t, lawch**, 5 **lawgh**, 6 **lewche**, 6–9 **leuch(e**, 8–9 **leugh**; see also LAIGH. [Early ME. *lāh* (*lāȝ-*), a. ON. *lág-r* (Sw. *låg*, Da. *lav*) = OFris. *lêge, lêch*, MDu. *lage, laech, lege, leech* (Du. *laag*), MHG. *læge* flat (early and dial. mod.G. *läg*), OE. with different meaning **lǣge* in *lǣghrycg* (see LEA *a.*):—OTeut. **lǣgio-* from the root of LIE *v.*[1]]

A. *adj.* (Usually the opposite of *high*.)

I. Literal senses.

1. a. Of small upward extent or growth; not tall; little, short. (Now rarely of persons, though still commonly said of stature.)

c **1150** *Grave* 17 in Thorpe *Analecta* (1834) 142 Þin hus..bið unheh and lah,..ðe hele-waȝes beoð laȝe, sid-waȝes unheȝe. *c* **1200** ORMIN 15232 Þær wass an bennkinnge lah. **1375** BARBOUR *Bruce* XVII. 380 The vallis of the toune than wer Sa law, that [etc.]. *c* **1420** *Pallad. on Husb.* III. 304 Make hem [*sc.* trees] lough in cleuis that decline. **1530** PALSGR. 452/2, I..make a thynge so lowe that it be levell with the grounde. **1558** *Galway Arch.* in *10th Rep. Hist. MSS. Comm.* App. v. 388 The said John..ys bound to make..ther but a loe gardinge, not plantinge anny great tres. **1593** SHAKS. *Lucr.* 663 Low-shrubs wither at the Cedars roote. **1607** TOPSELL *Four-f. Beasts* (1658) 474 It is a little low hearb. **1610** SHAKS. *Temp.* IV. i. 250 We shall..be turn'd..to apes With foreheads villanous low. **1638** JUNIUS *Paint. Ancients* 245 Low men love to stand on tiptoes. **1660** F. BROOKE tr. *Le Blanc's Trav.* 80 Their cowes are low, and their horns grow only skin deep. **1724** R. WODROW *Life J. Wodrow* (1828) 55 My mother was of a stature rather low than tall. **1771** SIR J. REYNOLDS *Disc.* iv. (1876) 348 Agesilaus was low, lame and of a mean appearance. **1827** DISRAELI *Viv. Grey* VII. viii. V. 95 Her full voluptuous growth gave you..the impression that she was somewhat low in stature. **1849** MACAULAY *Hist. Eng.* iv. I. 483 His forehead low as that of a baboon. **1855** BROWNING *How it Strikes a Contemporary* 102 Who..stood about the neat low truckle bed. **1860** TROLLOPE *Framley P.* II. ix. 183, I do remember the young lady,..a dark girl, very low, and without much figure. **1874** PARKER *Goth. Archit.* I. iii. 56 Early Norman buildings were generally low.

b. Rising but little from a surface. ***low relief*** (*a*) = BAS-RELIEF 1; (*b*) = BAS-RELIEF 2.

1711 SHAFTESB. *Charac.* (1737) III. 380 The low-relieves, and ornaments of columns and edifices. **1901** *19th Cent.* July 100 The modelling in low-relief of a life-sized bull in painted terra cotta.

c. Of a woman's dress: Cut so as to leave the neck exposed.

1857 TROLLOPE *Barchester T.* xxxvi. (1858) 299 I'm sorry you've come in such low dresses, as we are all going out of doors. **1899** RIDER HAGGARD *Swallow* iii, A lovely lady in a low dress.

2. a. Situated not far above the ground or some other downward limit; not elevated in position. †Formerly prefixed to names of countries or districts, denoting the part near the sea-shore (now only in the comparative LOWER), as ***Low Germany, Low Egypt*** (*obs.*). Also LOW-COUNTRY. (Cf. *Low* DUTCH, *Low* GERMAN.)

13.. *E.E. Allit. P.* B. 1761 Þe myst dryues þorȝ þe lyst of the lyfte, bi the loȝ medoes. **1382** WYCLIF *Isa.* xxxiv. 9 Turned shuln ben his stremes in to pich, and his loewȝ erthe in to brunston. *c* **1400** MAUNDEV. (Roxb.) Pref. 3 Egipte þe hie and þe lawe. *c* **1400** *Destr. Troy* 6952 He led hom forth lyuely by a law vale. *c* **1470** HENRY *Wallace* x. 622 The lauch way till Enrawyn thai ryd. **1509** HAWES *Past. Pleas.* xxxv. (Percy Soc.) 183 We were glad when ye had forsaken The lowe vale. *a* **1548** HALL *Chron.*, *Hen. VIII* 259 b, She was laden with much ordinaunce, and the portes left open, whiche were very lowe. **1577–87** HOLINSHED *Chron.* I. 75/1 All alongst the sea coasts of low Germanie. *a* **1578** LINDESAY (Pitscottie) *Chron. Scot.* (S.T.S.) II. 38 [They] draw thaim selffis to ane leuche place out of the Inglischemenis sight. **1626** BACON *Sylva* §832 The Raine-Bow consisteth of a Glomeration of Small Drops, which cannot possibly fall, but from the Aire, that is very Low. **1653** R. SANDERS *Physiogn.* 221 The second Cardinal house is the fourth, called the low heaven. **1707** CHAMBERLAYNE *St. Gt. Brit.* III. iii. 274 His [an Earl's] Coronet hath the Pearls raised upon Points, and Leaves low between. **1744** BERKELEY *Siris* §25 Trees growing in low and shady places do not yield so good tar. **1796** COLERIDGE *Destiny of Nations* 19 In this low world Placed with our backs to bright reality. **1846** MCCULLOCH *Acc. Brit. Empire* (1854) I. 47 Orfordness, a low beach running out into the sea.

b. Of a heavenly body: Near the horizon.

1676 WALTON & COTTON *Angler* II. ii. (1875) 228 The sun grows low. **1801** CAMPBELL *Hohenlinden* 1 On Linden, when the sun was low, All bloodless lay the untrodden snow. **1811** A. SCOTT *Poems* 8 (Jam.) The moon, leugh i' the wast, shone bright. **1859** TENNYSON *Enid* 598 The third day..Made a low splendour in the world. **1889** 'ROLF BOLDREWOOD' *Robbery under Arms* xvi, There was a low moon.

c. Lying dead, or dead and buried. Now only ***predicative***. †Formerly also *absol.*

c **1315** SHOREHAM *Poems* (E.E.T.S.) v. 329 Þat body þat he tok of hys oȝen, Hou mytte hyt ligge amang þe loȝen. **1808** BYRON (*title*) And wilt thou weep when I am low? **1826** SCOTT in *Croker Papers* 19 Mar., My head may be low—I hope it will—before the time comes. **1852** TENNYSON *Death of Wellington* 18 The last great Englishman is low.

†**d.** Of the ear: 'Bowed down'. *Obs.*

c **1400** *Destr. Troy* 2650 Let your lordship lystyn with a loue ere.

e. Of an obeisance: Profound, deep.

a **1548** HALL *Chron.*, *Edw. IV* 234 He toke of hys cappe, and made a low and solempne obeysance. **1596** SHAKS. *Tam. Shr.* Induct. i. 53 With a lowe submissiue reuerence Say [etc.]. **1602** *2nd Pt. Return fr. Parnass.* II. vi. 947 He presently doffes his cap most solemnly, makes a low-leg to his ladiship. **1632** J. HAYWARD tr. *Biondi's Eromena* 157 Rising up to make him a low congey, she proceeded. **1667** MILTON *P.L.* IX. 835. **1887** W. P. FRITH *Autobiog.* I. xix. 237 'I am very much obliged to you', making a low bow.

f. *Phonetics.* Of a vowel sound: Produced with the tongue or some part of it in a low position. Also *Comb.*, as ***low-back, -central, -front, -mid, -rising***, used chiefly attributively or quasi-adj.

1876 [see HIGH *a.* 4 b]. **1924** H. E. PALMER *Gram. Spoken Eng.* I. 13 Low-Rising. Nucleus-tone. **1934** J. J. HOGAN *Outl. Eng. Philol.* 14, æ: low-front. **1934** WEBSTER, Low-back, low-central. **1944** T. H. WETMORE in *Studies in Speech & Drama in Honor of A. M. Drummond* 244 (*title*) The dialectal significance of the non-phonemic low-back vowel variants before R. **1951** Z. S. HARRIS *Methods Struct. Ling.* vi. 57 Low-rising intonation. **1962** *Amer. Speech* XXXVII. 165 The low-central free vowel /ɑ/. **1964** Low-front [see HIGH *a.* 4 b]. **1965** *Language* XLI. 346 A low-back /ɔ/. *Ibid.*, In disyllabic words, Ngbaka shows only four sequences: high-mid, mid-high, mid-low, and low-mid. **1970** *Publ. Amer. Dial. Soc.* 1968 L. 13 Sometimes..it occurs as a retracted low-front or as a low-central monophthong.

g. *Path.*

1898 P. MANSON *Trop. Diseases* xix. 317 Occasionally it [*sc.* epidemic gangrenous rectitis] may begin higher up—in the colon. In this case it is called the ' high' form; in the other, the 'low' or rectal form.

h. Phr. ***low to paper***: of type, of less than normal height.

[**1683–4** J. MOXON *Mech. Exerc. Printing* (1962) 346 Low against Paper.] **1888** *Encycl. Brit.* XXIII. 698/2 Types lower than the ordinary dimension are said to be *low to paper*, and if surrounded by higher types will not give a perfect impression. **1922** D. B. UPDIKE *Printing Types* I. ii. 34 The standard height-to-paper is 0·918 inch. Types exceeding or falling short of this measurement are termed respectively 'high-to-paper' and 'low-to-paper'.

†**3.** Situated under the level of the earth's surface, far down in the ground; deep. *Obs.* in positive; cf. LOWER, LOWEST.

a **1340** HAMPOLE *Psalter* xvii. 30 He mekis þaim in til þe lawe pitt of hell. *c* **1440** *Promp. Parv.* 314/1 Low, or lowe, *profundus*. *c* **1470** HENRY *Wallace* II. 157 And ek thar to he was in presoune law. **1533** GAU *Richt Vay* (1888) 49 He first passit dwne to ye law portis of the zeird. **1718** G. JACOB *Compl. Sportsman* 53 The good Dogs produc'd in a deep Low-Country, will always excel the good Dogs upon the Plains.

4. Of a liquid: Less in vertical measurement than the average, or than is usual; shallow. Hence of a river, a spring, etc.: Containing or yielding less water than usual. See also LOW TIDE, LOW WATER. (For *low ebb* lit. and fig., see EBB *sb.*)

c **1440** *Promp. Parv.* 314/2 Lowe, or ny the drestis, *bassus*. **1568** GRAFTON *Chron.* II. 269 The river..when the flood is gone, it is so low, yt it may be passed without all daunger. **1621** T. WILLIAMSON tr. *Goulart's Wise Vieillard* 98 He..compares old age to Wine that is lowe and almost nothing but lees. **1695** WOODWARD *Nat. Hist. Earth* IV. (1723) 234 The Springs and Rivers are very low. **1855** MACAULAY *Hist. Eng.* xii. III. 236 The ships were in extreme peril: for the river was low.

II. Transferred and figurative senses.

5. Of humble rank, station, position, or estimation.

Not now (in the positive) said of persons exc. in contemptuous use (see 7 c); but cf. LOWER *a.*

c **1200** *Trin. Coll. Hom.* 35 Ne was þe engel isend ne to none heȝe..men..ac to loȝe and edeliche men. *c* **1205** LAY. 686 Nis þar nan swa laih þæt [etc.]. **1303** R. BRUNNE *Handl. Synne* (E.E.T.S.) 6560 Ȝyf a cursed man hadde cumpany with one or ouþer, logh or hy. **1310** in Wright *Lyric P.* 73 Pore ant loȝe thou were for ous. **1390** GOWER *Conf.* II. 119 He hath set al his corage..Upon a Maide of low astat. *a* **1420** HOCCLEVE *De Reg. Princ.* 2805 Al such mayntenance..Sustened is naght by persones lowe. *c* **1470** HENRY *Wallace* IV. 184 King Eduuardis man he was..Off rycht law byrth. **1500–20** DUNBAR *Poems* xx. 18 Hie vertew may stand in law estait. **1531** LATIMER *Let. to Baynton* in Foxe *A. & M.* (1563) 1324/1 We lowe subiectes are bounde to obey powers and their ordinaunces. **1687** SETTLE *Refl. Dryden* 49 The lowest Boy in Westminster would have told him that [to be Borne] was a passive verb. **1718** *Freethinker* No. 7 ¶8, I shall subjoin a Matrimonial Story in Low-Life. **1770** *Gentl. Mag.* XL. 426 That the low people never taste flesh is a proof of their extreme poverty. **1810** BENTHAM *Packing* (1821) 140 One law for gentlemen, another for low people. **1844** THIRLWALL *Greece* VIII. lxvi. 441 Andriscus, a young man of low birth,..had been..acknowledged as king. **1874** DEUTSCH *Rem.* 327 Men low in the social scale.

absol. *a* **1200** *Moral Ode* 162 Þer sculen eueningges bon þe riche and þe laȝe. *c* **1275** LAY. 22928 For þar sal þe heȝe be efne to þan lowe. *a* **1586** SIDNEY *Arcadia* I. (1590) 17 All the people of this countrie from high to lowe, is giuen to these sportes of the witte. **1852** MRS. STOWE *Uncle Tom's C.* xviii, Look at the high and the low, all the world over, and it's the same story. **1890** *Spectator* 22 Nov., Having..the benefit of vast experience of the low.

6. a. Of inferior quality, character, or style; wanting in elevation, commonplace, mean.

a **1225** *Ancr. R.* 140 Þet so unimete louh þinc..schal drawen into sunne so unimete heih þinc. *c* **1450** tr. *De Imitatione* III. lvi. 133 (*ch.-heading*) That man must ȝeue him to lowe workes [L. *humilibus operibus*] whan hye workes failen. **1598** FLORIO Ep. Ded. 1 My poore studies may in so lowe a cottage entertaine so high..dignities. **1665** G. HAVERS *P. della Valle's Trav. E. India* 91 Which low School of Reading and Writing, the said Fathers keep for more convenience of Children. **1725** POPE *Postscr. to Odyssey* (1840) 389 There is a real beauty in an easy, pure, perspicuous description even of a low action. **1743** FIELDING *J. Wild* II. vii, They passed an hour in a scene of tenderness, too low and contemptible to be recounted. **1753** *Adventurer* No. 39 The low drudgery of collating copies,..or accumulating compilations. **1855** MACAULAY *Hist. Eng.* xx. IV. 467 Much parliamentary ability of a low kind. **1856** KINGSLEY *Plays & Puritans* 31 To discriminate between high art and low art, they must have seen both. **1899** *Allbutt's Syst. Med.* VIII. 173 In patients of low type of intelligence.

b. Of literary style, words, expressions, hence of a writer: The opposite of sublime; undignified.

1672 DRYDEN *Def. Epil.* Ess. (ed. Ker) I. 172 Never did any author precipitate himself from such height of thought to so low expressions, as he often does. **1709** POPE *Ess. Crit.* 347 And ten low words oft creep in one dull line. **1725** —— *Postscr. to Odyssey* (1840) 389 But whenever the poet is obliged by the nature of his subject to descend to the lower manner of writing, an elevated style would be affected. **1765** in *Priv. Lett. Ld. Malmesbury* I. 130 Superior to Runkenius ..whose language is rather low. **1779–81** JOHNSON *L.P.*, *Prior*, Prior is never low, nor very often sublime.

c. Of races of mankind: Inferior in degree of civilization, little advanced. Of animals or plants, their type, etc.: Not highly organized.

1859 J. R. GREENE *Protozoa* Introd. xviii, The lowest form of animal life with which we are acquainted. **1865** TYLOR *Early Hist. Man.* iv. 79 Languages spoken by very low races. **1881** TYNDALL *Ess. Floating Matter Air* 125 Germs of bacteria and other low organisms.

7. As a term of reprobation or disgust.

a. In a moral sense: Abject, base, mean.

1559 *Mirr. Mag.*, *Mowbray's Banishment* xvii, Through flattery loe, I dyd hys yll vpholde. **1666** PEPYS *Diary* 8 Sept., Much..discourse..of the low spirits of some rich men in the City, in sparing any encouragement to the poor people that wrought for the saving their houses. **1790** H. WALPOLE in *Walpoliana* clxiv. 75 Low-cunning, self-interest, and other mean motives. **1799** J. ROBERTSON *Agric. Perth* 401 Flattery or fawning or other low arts. **1895** A. F. WARR in *Law Times* XCIX. 507/1 Whenever a dramatist wished to introduce intrigue, chicanery, or other dirty work, his *dramatis personæ* included a low attorney.

b. Degraded, dissolute.

1599 in *10th Rep. Hist. MSS. Comm.* App. IV. 431 [Paid] to John Wosley for his horse and dragge to be used for the whippinge of low woomene, 4*d.*

c. Wanting in decent breeding; coarse, vulgar; not socially 'respectable'.

1759 DILWORTH *Pope* 18 Notwithstanding Mr. Wycherley's low behaviour to Mr. Pope. **1780** MAD. D'ARBLAY *Diary* May, She has evidently kept low company.

1838 DICKENS *Nich. Nick.* xii, Tilda's friends are low people. 1849 MACAULAY *Hist. Eng.* iv. I. 483 A considerable number of low fanatics..regarded him as a public benefactor. 1861 R. G. WILBERFORCE *Life S. Wilberforce* (1882) III. i. 27 They [Irish priests] are generally low fellows—McHale is a very coarse low fellow himself. 1872 *Punch* 6 Jan. 5/1 What is there in common between a respectable shopkeeper who pays rates and a low person who wheels a barrow? 1912 *Chambers's Jrnl.* Aug. 533/1 He may feel that he is the superior in every way of some of the 'low whites' with whom he comes into daily contact.

8. a. Wanting in bodily strength or vigour; poorly nourished, weak.

1398 TREVISA *Barth. De P.R.* IV. iii. (1495) 83 Dryenesse makyth the body lene and lowe. 1486 *Bk. St. Albans* c j, Sum put hawkys in mew at high estate, and sum when thay be right low. 1530 PALSGR. 317/2 Lowe of complexyon, *fieble*. 1607 TOPSELL *Four-f. Beasts* (1658) 155 They keep them low and down by subtraction of their meat. 1684 *Lond. Gaz.* No. 1912/4 A Plain Black Gelding,..low of flesh. 1697 DRYDEN *Virg. Georg.* III. 321 Before his Training, keep him poor and low. *a*1715 BURNET *Own Time* (1724) I. 585 He was so low, that it was not probable he could live many weeks. 1783 H. WATSON in *Med. Commun.* I. 165 She..grew low from loss of appetite. 1802 MRS. E. PARSONS *Myst. Visit* II. 62 So low and ill, that she gladly accepted a small cup of usquebaugh. 1887 *Poor Nellie* (1888) 162 When I had my severe crisis off Vera Cruz, I was frightfully low at the time. 1899 *Allbutt's Syst. Med.* VIII. 575 If..the patient is in low condition, an improvement in the diet may be of service.

b. Emotionally depressed; dejected, dispirited, dull, esp. in phr. ***low spirits***.

1744 BERKELEY *Siris* §101 Lives which seem hardly worth living for bad appetite, low spirits, restless nights. 1779 BURKE *Corr.* (1844) II. 302, I am low and dejected at times, in a way not to be described. 1822–34 *Good's Study Med.* (ed. 4) III. 49 An undue secretion of melancholia..was supposed..to produce a low or gloomy temperament. 1860 EMILY EDEN *Semi-attached Couple* II. 121 Lady Eskdale was low, and sent off a groom with a bulletin. 1894 HALL CAINE *Manxman* III. xii. 170 She's wake and low and nervous, so no kissing.

c. Of diet, feeding: Affording little nourishment or stimulation; poor.

*a*1715 BURNET *Own Time* (1897) I. I. 386 These were both ..men of great sobriety, and lived on a constant low diet. 1752 BERKELEY *Th. on Tar-water* Wks. III. 503 Such low diet as sour milk and potatoes. 1863 FR. A. KEMBLE *Resid. in Georgia* 111, The general low diet of the slaves. 1886 C. SCOTT *Sheep-Farming* 55 Low Feeding of Sheep. 1897 *Allbutt's Syst. Med.* III. 367 The patient should be put on a low diet. 1899 *Ibid.* VIII. 214 The percentage of children ..who presented low nutrition.

9. a. Little above the minimum, not high, in amount or degree of intensity. (Often with implied reference to position in a graduated scale.)

1390 GOWER *Conf.* I. 34 Right now the hyhe wyndes blowe, And anon after thei ben lowe. 1715 CHEYNE *Philos. Princ. Relig.* I. (ed. 2) 321 We see an Image of this slow and low kind of Life in Swallows, Insects, Vipers [etc.]. 1736 BUTLER *Anal.* Introd., Such low presumption, often repeated, will amount even to moral certainty. 1742 *Lond. & Country Brew.* I. (ed. 4) 72 The Grinding also must be considered, according to the high or low Drying of the Malt. 1789 W. BUCHAN *Dom. Med.* (1790) 239 The fever is kept low, and the eruption greatly lessened. 1823 J. BADCOCK *Dom. Amusem.* 154 When the flour is too fine, the colour will be low. 1822–34 *Good's Study Med.* (ed. 4) I. 688 Low or slow Nervous Fever. *Ibid.* III. 48 *note*, Hence, also, the terms high madness and low madness. 1831 BREWSTER *Optics* ix. 83 Muriatic acid has too low a refractive and dispersive power to fit it for [etc.]. 1840 *E. Turner's Chem.* (ed. 7) II. 447 Heating the mixture to low redness. 1860 TYNDALL *Glac.* I. xxii. 151 Friends who visited me always complained of the low temperature of my room. 1875 FORTNUM *Majolica* xii. 132 Grotesques..in low olive tint on a blue ground.

b. of price, rate, numbers, amounts, etc.

1601 SHAKS. *Twel. N.* I. i. 13 Nought enters there, Of what validity and pitch so ere, But falles into abatement and low price Euen in a minute. 1602 *2nd Pt. Return fr. Parnass.* IV. iii. 1794 If we can intertaine these schollers at a low rate. 1683 *Apol. Prot. France* ii. 23 Merchants subsist by their Credit: if their credit be low, they must fall. 1691 LOCKE *Lower. Interest* Wks. 1727 II. 72 It [the Exchange] is Low, when he pays less than the Par. 1693 J. DRYDEN, jun., in *Dryden's Juvenal* xiv. (1697) 355 So of old Was Blood, and Life, at a low-Market sold. 1831 J. DAVIES *Manual Mat. Med.* 227 The low price of lime. 1885 *Manch. Exam.* 12 Nov. 5/2 Chinese workmen..work for low wages.

c. *Geog.* Of latitude: Denoted by a low number; at a short distance from the equator.

1748 [see LOWER 1]. 1867 SMYTH *Sailor's Word-bk.*, *Low Latitudes*, those regions far removed from the poles of the earth towards the equator, 10° south or north of it.

d. Of things: Having a low value, price, or degree of some quality. (Chiefly with the specific reference expressed or contextually indicated.) †Of gold: Not reaching a high standard of fineness. Of a card: Of small numerical value.

1727 A. HAMILTON *New Acc. E. Ind.* I. i. 8 Sena abounds in Elephants Teeth and low Gold, of 18 or 19 carects Fineness. 1740 *Wimble's List of Snuffs* in F. W. Fairholt *Tobacco* (1876) 268–9 English Rappee..Best Dunkerque Rappee..Rappee Bergamot..Low Rappee. 1798 *Monthly Mag.* VI. 236 Horses still continue low [*sc.* in price]. 1835 URE *Philos. Manuf.* 140 Hence, by the plan of mixture, much low English wools are consumed in our cloth manufacture, that would otherwise find no market at all. 1885 PROCTOR *Whist* ii. 33 In general a low card is to be played second hand. 1900 G. NEWMAN *Bacteria* (ed. 2) 116 'Low' yeasts..sink in the fermenting fluid, act slowly, and only at the low temperature of 4° or 5° C.

e. Of condition: Not flourishing or advanced.

1596 SHAKS. *Merch. V.* III. ii. 319 My Creditors grow cruell, my estate is very low. 1686 tr. *Chardin's Trav. Persia* 68 During the weak and low Condition of the Eastern Emperors. 1844 T. WRIGHT *Anecd. Lit.* 23 Of course we ought to make great allowances for the low state of this branch of philology in Tyrwhitt's time.

10. a. Of or in reference to musical sounds: Produced or characterized by relatively slow vibrations; grave.

1422 tr. *Secreta Secret., Priv. Priv.* 231 Tho..haue the voice atte the begynnynge of the worde grete and lowe. 1530 PALSGR. 845/1 With a low voyse, *a basse voyx*. 1597 MORLEY *Introd. Mus.* 166 Songs which are made..in the low key. *a*1600 MONTGOMERIE *Misc. Poems* iii. 14 Sing sho tua notis, the one is out of tone, As B acre lau and B moll far abone. 1878 in *Grove's Dict. Mus.* I. 27/1 These [words] are 'high' and 'low', the former denoting greater, the latter less, rapidity of vibration.

b. Of the voice, a sound: Not loud.

*c*1440 *Promp. Parv.* 314/2 Lowe, or softe yn voyce, ..*submissus*. 1605 SHAKS. *Lear* V. iii. 273 Her voice was euer soft, Gentle, and low, an excellent thing in woman. 1724 R. WODROW *Life J. Wodrow* (1828) 98 His voice was but low and none of the strongest. 1839 MARRYAT *Phant. Ship* xxxviii, A low tap at the door was heard. 1852 IDA PFEIFFER *Journ. Iceland* 172 The explosions are always preceded by a low rumbling. 1863 WOOLNER *My beautiful Lady* 15 Her warbling voice, though ever low and mild. 1887 BOWEN *Virg. Æneid* III. 320 Bending her face to the ground, in a whisper low she replies.

11. Humble in disposition, lowly, meek. Now *rare*.

1377 LANGL. *P. Pl.* B. xx. 36 Nede is next hym..as low as a lombe for lakkyng of that hym nedeth. 1390 GOWER *Conf.* I. 118 Thou most..with low herte humblesce suie. *c*1403 *Cuckow & Night.* 3 The god of love..can make of lowe hertes hye, And of hye lowe. 1426 in *Surtees Misc.* (1888) 5 þe law submission of þe said John Lyllyng. 1533 GAU *Richt Vay* (1888) 30 God hes al tyme hwyd the richt visdome.. and schawis it to thayme that ar simpil and law. *a*1578 LINDESAY (Pitscottie) *Chron. Scot.* (S.T.S.) II. 38 In the meane tyme held thame selffis lewche and quyit. 1836 MRS. BROWNING *Poet's Vow* II. viii, I thought..The teachings of the heaven and earth Did keep us soft and low.

12. a. (With allusion to sense 4.) Of one's pockets, stock of money or any commodity: Nearly empty or exhausted. Hence of persons, ***to be low in pocket***, etc.

1700 S. L. tr. *Fryke's Voy. E. Ind.* 94, I thought it high time..to recruit my Pockets, which were now very low. 1821 SCOTT *Pirate* xxxiv, We have junketed till provisions are low with us. *Ibid.* xxxi, My own [money] was waxing low. 1894 HALL CAINE *Manxman* 40 And you talk of being low in your pocket.

b. ***low on***: deficient in, short of. *colloq.*

1966 *Listener* 23 June 926/2 Low on credibility however was *They Were So Few*. 1969 *Ibid.* 22 May 732/2 Her difficulty is that she is incapable of fulfilling herself, partly because she seems to be low on energy. 1974 J. WAINWRIGHT *Evidence I shall Give* xxxv. 200 He brewed instant coffee. He was low on sugar.

13. Of an opinion, estimate: Attributing small value or poor quality; depreciatory, disparaging.

*a*1903 *Mod.* I have a very low opinion of his abilities.

14. Of a date: Relatively recent. Chiefly in *compar.* and *superl.*

*a*1903 *Mod.* The date assigned by this critic to Ecclesiastes seems to be too low.

15. Said of religious doctrine, as the opposite of *high* in various applications (see HIGH *a.* 15); often *colloq.* = Low CHURCH.

1854 S. WILBERFORCE *Let.* in *Life* (1881) II. vi. 234 The Church of England will seem to be committed to Low doctrine, which she does not teach, as to this sacrament. 1881 TROLLOPE *Dr. Wortle's School* I. i, Among them [Low Church prelates] there was none more low, more pious, more sincere.

III. In complemental use with verbs both *trans.* and *intr.* where the complement frequently indicates the result of the action.

16. ***to bring low***: to bring into a low condition, with respect to health, strength, wealth or outward circumstances; also, to bring to the ground. Cf. *low-brought* in 23 below.

1387 TREVISA *Higden* (Rolls) V. 277 His son Occe..was byseged at York, and [i]-brouȝte lowe [L. *humiliato*]. 1530 PALSGR. 468/1 For all his great bely, this syckenesse hath brought hym lowe ynoughe. 1535 COVERDALE *1 Sam.* ii. 7 The Lorde..bryngeth lowe and exalteth. 1611 BIBLE *Job* xl. 12 Looke on euery one that is proud, and bring him low. 1655 STANLEY *Hist. Philos.* I. (1701) 16/1 His Father.. brought his Estate so low, as to want even necessaries. 1756–7 tr. *Keysler's Trav.* (1760) I. 360 The nobles of Savoy have long since been brought low. 1819 SHELLEY *Julian & Maddalo* 601 Perhaps remorse had brought her low.

absol. 1871 B. TAYLOR *Faust* (1875) II. II. iii 129 At one quick blow Shoot, and bring low!

17. ***to lay low***: **a.** To lay flat; to bring to the ground, to overthrow in fight, to stretch lifeless. **b.** To lay in the ground, to bury. **c.** in immaterial sense or *fig.*: To abase, humble.

a. *c*1386 CHAUCER *Manciple's T.* 118 She shal be cleped his wenche, or his lemman. And..Men leyn that oon as lowe as lith þat oother. *c*1470 *Golagros & Gaw.* 726 Schir Edmond loissit has his life, and laid is full law. 1470–85 MALORY *Arthur* XX. xxii, For I wene thys day to laye the as lowe as thou laydest me. 1667 MILTON *P.L.* I. 137 The dire event..Hath..all this mighty Host In horrible destruction laid thus low. 1740 LADY M. W. MONTAGU *Let. to Lady Pomfret* 25 Nov., I bought a chaise at Rome..; and had the pleasure of being laid low in it the very second day after I set out. 1791 BURNS *Lament for Earl Glencairn* ix, O! had I met the mortal shaft Which laid my benefactor low! 1815 W. H. IRELAND *Scribbleomania* 111 Whenever morality hitches the toe, Delinquent with crab-stick shou'd straight be laid low.

b. 1340 HAMPOLE *Pr. Consc.* 862 When it es in erth layd lawe, Wormes þan sal it al to-gnaw. 1595 SHAKS. *John* II. i. 164, I would that I were low laid in my graue. 1795 *Jemima* II. 187 Little did his now laid low Lordship think his days were so closely numbered. 1896 A. E. HOUSMAN *Shropsh. Lad* xxiv, Use me ere they lay me low Where a man's no use at all.

c. *a*1225 *Juliana* 62 Ant þeo þet heieð ham her leist ham swiðe lahe. *a*1425 *Cursor M.* 1649 (Trin.), I shal hem laye ful lawe þat sett so litil of myn awe. *c*1586 C'TESS PEMBROKE *Ps.* LX. vi, [God] shall lay our haters low. 1611 BIBLE *Isa.* xiii. 11, I..will lay low the hautinesse of the terrible.

18. ***to lie low***: **a.** *literally.* To lie in a low position or on a low level, deep down; also, to crouch. **b.** To lie on or in the ground, lie prostrate or dead; *fig.* to be humbled, abased. Of an erection: To be overthrown or broken down, to lie in fragments. **c.** *Mod. slang.* To keep quiet, remain in hiding; to bide one's time.

a. *c*1250 *Death* 166 in *O.E. Misc.* 178 þu schald nu in eorþe liggen ful lohe [*Jes. Coll. MS.* lowe]. 1560 ROLLAND *Crt. Venus* I. 56 Behind the Bus (Lord) bot I liggit law. 1567 *Gude & Godlie Ball.* (S.T.S.) 76 To ly rycht law in till ane Crib. 1590 SPENSER *F.Q.* II. i. 40 Beside a bubling fountaine low she lay. 1653 H. MORE *Antid. Ath.* II. iii. (1712) 49 Whether it might not have laid so low in the Earth as never to have been reached. 1674 JOSSELYN *Voy. New Eng.* 171 It lyeth low, by reason whereof it is much indammaged by flouds.

b. *a*1300 *Cursor M.* 1649, I sal do þam lij ful lau þat letes sua lightly on min au. 1307 *Elegy Edw. I* ii, Of wham that song is that y synge, Of Edward kyng that lith so lowe. *Ibid.* iv, Aȝeyn the hethene for te fyhte, To wynne the croiz that lowe lys. *c*1375 *Sc. Leg. Saints* xiv. (*Lucas*) 80 þe angel his trumpe sal blav, & gcr þame ryse þat lyis law. 1387–8 T. USK *Test. Love* II. ii. (Skeat) l. 58 His auter is broke, and lowe lyth. 1393 LANGL. *P. Pl.* C. xx. 10 That Lucifers lordshup ligge sholde ful lowe. *c*1400 *Cato's Morals* 171 in *Cursor M.* App. iv, Loke þou lere sum craft, quen þi hap turnis baft, and logh þou lise. 1513 DOUGLAS *Æneis* X. x. 18 Lo now he liggis law, for al his feris. 1535 STEWART *Cron. Scot.* (1858) I. 297 The castell als thai gart it lig full law. 1599 SHAKS. *Much Ado* V. i. 52 If he could but rite himselfe with quarrelling, Some of vs would lie low. *a*1822 SHELLEY *Marg. Nicholson Fragment* 12 Monarch thou For whose support this fainting frame lies low. 1871 R. ELLIS tr. *Catullus* lxviii. 22 All our house lies low mournfully buried in you. 1879 J. D. LONG *Æneid* II. 730 Priam by the sword Lies low.

c. 1880 J. C. HARRIS *Uncle Remus* ii. (1881) 20 De Tar-Baby, she sot dar, she did, en Brer Fox, he lay low. 1892 *Pall Mall G.* 11 Mar. 3/1 Mr. N——..has not really been dead at all, but only 'lying low' in Canada. 1894 MARG. VERNEY *Mem. Verney Fam.* III. 475 Royalists who had lain low were showing signs of life. 1901 *Scotsman* 2 Mar. 9/4 To that end the opposition lay low.

19. With certain other verbs, the meaning of which includes the notion 'to make' or 'to become'; ***to burn low*** (see BURN *v.* 2 c); †***to go low***, (*a*) to become worsted; (*b*) to become exhausted; ***to run low*** (see RUN).

*c*1330 R. BRUNNE *Chron.* (1810) 23 þe Kyng herd þat telle, þat his side ȝede lowe. 1377 LANGL. *P. Pl.* B. XI. 61 Pouerte pursued me and put me lowe. 1555 BRADFORTH in Strype *Eccl. Mem.* III. App. xlv. 131 Other men in England whose stoutnes must be plucked lowe. 1583 STOCKER *Civ. Warres Lowe C.* III. 117 b, Their victuals went very low. 1768–74 TUCKER *Lt. Nat.* (1834) I. 621 Should I chance on some distant journey to be reduced low in pocket.

IV. In Combination.

20. In concord with sbs. forming combinations used attributively or quasi-adj., as ***low-altitude***, ***-angle***, ***-blast***, ***-budget***, ***-calorie***, ***-carbon***, ***-caste***, ***-class***, ***-consumption***, ***-contrast***, ***-cost***, ***-density***, ***-drag***, ***-energy***, ***-fat***, ***-field***, ***-flash***, ***-flux***, ***-ground***, ***-heel***, ***-impedance***, ***-income***, ***-intensity***, ***-neck***, ***-noise***, ***-power***, ***-pressure***, ***-price***, ***-rank***, ***-rental***, ***-risk***, ***-status***, ***-sulphur***, ***-temperature***, ***-tension***, ***-tread***, ***-type***, ***-value***, ***-velocity***, ***-voltage***, ***-wage***, ***-warp***, ***-wattage***, ***-wing***.

1925 R. W. G. KINGSTON in E. F. Norton *Fight for Everest 1924* 286 *Low-altitude deserts. 1966 *Electronics* 3 Oct. 181 Dornier System GmbH last year made a successful low-altitude recovery with a paraglider that unfolds its wings for descent. 1971 C. BONINGTON *Annapurna South Face* iii. 34 He [*sc.* Kelvin Kent] had also organized our low-altitude porters, whose job it was to carry all the gear up to Base Camp. 1907 *Yesterday's Shopping* (1969) p. xliii/4 *Low angle planes. 1956 *Nature* 17 Mar. 500/1 Low-angle X-ray patterns from two durains of different rank. 1966 *Electronics* 14 Nov. 48 An antenna lacking the low-angle coverage.. would not be able to communicate with the satellite unless the plane flew farther south. 1875 KNIGHT *Dict. Mech.*, *Low-blast Furnace*, a metallurgic furnace in which the air of the blast is delivered at moderate pressure. 1958 R. SILL in *Film Daily Yearbk. Motion Pict.* 985/1, 20th Century Fox.. proclaimed that it has budgeted $65,000,000 for the production of 65 features this year, including 25 from.. Regal Films, which specialize in *low-budget films. 1961 B. PAULU *Brit. Broadcasting in Transition* vii. 129 Audiences seem to show no more enthusiasm for high-cost television than low-budget radio music. 1973 E. BULLINS *Theme is Blackness* 129 Short, low-budget films that could be distributed nationally. 1969 *Lancet* 8 Dec. 1190/2 On *low-calorie high-fat diets, fat and thin subjects developed the same levels of ketones in the blood. 1970 *Sunday Times* 26 Apr. 28/2 Jars of low-calorie instant soup. 1900 *Engineering Mag.* XIX. 751/2 Copper and *low-carbon ingot steel. 1894 *Pop. Sci. Monthly* XLIV. 500 The *low-caste Hindus. 1898 *Daily News* 11 Nov. 5/1 All such *low-class methods. 1960 *Farmer & Stockbreeder* 8 Mar. 61/1 The north-east, a *low-consumption area. 1975 *Times* 11 Mar. (Italian Industry Suppl.) p. v/1 Petrol has never been cheap in Italy, so low

consumption motors were developed there. 1966 D. G. Brandon *Mod. Techniques Metallogr.* i. 14 The curves for a 'soft', *low-contrast, fast emulsion and a 'hard', high-contrast, slow emulsion are shown. 1934 H. L. Ickes *Diary* 10 Mar. (1953) I. 152 Obviously it wasn't a model of *low-cost housing for people on the very lowest rung of the economic order. 1960 *Times* 21 Nov. (Canada Suppl.) p. xiii/7 Efficient and low-cost producers. 1969 *New Statesman* 11 Apr. 506/1 There is no cheaper way of running a radio station than sitting a low-cost young man in a studio to talk about his breakfast and his fan mail. 1960 *New Left Rev.* May–June 70/2 *Low density, two-storey three-bedroom housing. 1962 F. I. Ordway et al. *Basic Astronautics* iii. 58 Since it [*sc.* the Moon] is a low-density world, there is little likelihood of extensive concentrations of metallic iron and nickel. 1964 *Ann. N.Y. Acad. Sci.* CXV. 569 The resulting digital data, when stored on low-density (200 characters per inch) digital tape, would fill 84 digital tapes. 1962 F. I. Ordway et al. *Basic Astronautics* xi. 428 An aerodynamic shroud.. provides a *low-drag housing for the entire vehicle. 1971 *Flying* Apr. 2/1 A low-drag high-speed wing. 1942 J. D. Stranathan *'Particles' of Mod. Physics* xiii. 535 The mean free path may be longer, and the mean life correspondingly longer, for high energy mesotrons than it is for *low energy mesotrons. 1960 *Farmer & Stockbreeder* 8 Mar. 149/2 A low-energy ration contained 750 cal per lb. 1960 *Times* 20 Sept. (Pure Food Suppl.) p. iii, None of the *low-fat girls had better skins than at the start of the experiment. 1972 J. Ball *Five Pieces Jade* xii. 150 He poured some cornflakes into a bowl, covered them with.. low-fat milk. 1962 Corson & Lorrain *Introd. Electromagn. Fields* iii. 91 All that varies from one *O'* to another is the fact that sometimes the point lies in a high-field region, within a molecule, for example, and other times it lies in a *low-field region. 1894 *Westm. Gaz.* 25 July 2/3 *Low-flash oils, imported chiefly from America. 1956 *Nature* 4 Feb. 205/2 The rent of experimental facilities in [the nuclear reactor] DIDO may vary from £100 a day down to £10 a day for those in less-attractive *low-flux positions. 1897 *Westm. Gaz.* 1 Sept. 1/3 The high and *low ground game fauna of the country. 1712 Steele *Spect.* No. 526 ¶6 Such as appear discreet by a *low-heel shoe. 1962 Simpson & Richards *Physical Princ. Junction Transistors* ii. 26 The device thus passes most of the emitter current from a *low-impedance generator to a high-impedance load. 1952 M. Laski *Village* xvi. 219 Roy Wilson may start in a *low-income group, but if he can make a success, well, he's worth more than people who can't. 1971 *Guardian* 7 July 24/4 Up to 60,000 children in low income families have lost their right to free school meals. 1953 N. Tinbergen *Herring Gull's World* xiii. 109 *Low-intensity copulations can be seen early in the season. 1964 P. Delattre in D. Abercrombie et al. *Daniel Jones* 51 Very low-intensity vowel. 1971 D. E. Westlake *I gave at the Office* (1972) 14 Marijuana was legal in the United States until 1935, and it was just a sort of low-intensity fact in American culture. 1901 *Lady's Realm* X. 646/2 With the coat and skirt the *low-neck blouse is wofully out of place. 1961 *Times* 5 Apr. 6/4 Special 'maser' *low-noise amplifiers will be used in the reception of the very weak signals from the satellites. 1878 Abney *Photogr.* (1881) 306 The student is recommended to commence with a comparatively *low-power objective. 1833 N. Arnott *Physics* (ed. 5) II. i. 97 The high-pressure or condensed steam.. expands.. until it becomes *low-pressure steam. 1873 B. Stewart *Conserv. Energy* iv. 108 Let us take, for example, the low-pressure engine. 1897 *Allbutt's Syst. Med.* IV. 564 Those exceptional cases of Bright's disease, in which a low-pressure pulse is found. 1851 in O. Hudson *Martin Tupper* (1949) x. 121 Shepherd's mammoth *low price clothing emporium, Chesnut street above Third. 1944 A. G. Hatcher in *Mod. Lang. Notes* LIX. 516, I have seen ..*low-price shoes*. 1968 D. E. Allen *Brit. Tastes* viii. 204 Low-price catering. 1956 *Nature* 17 Mar. 501/1 The decreased intensity of the diffuse scattering [of X-rays] at very low angles for the *low-rank coals. 1965 *Times Lit. Suppl.* 25 Nov. 1057/3 Artistic low-rental areas. 1951 S. A. Stouffer in Parsons & Shils *Toward Gen. Theory Action* iv. v. 492 *Low-risk and high-risk situations. 1956 J. Klein *Study of Groups* vii. 102 One thus obtains four types of sub-groups: high-status mobile, and non-mobile; *low-status mobile, and non-mobile. 1974 J. Burnett *Useful Toil* i. 31 Farm labouring gradually sank during the course of the [nineteenth] century into a low-status occupation. 1965 G. J. Williams *Econ. Geol. N.Z.* xviii. 322/1 The coal is a *low-sulphur lignite of lower grade than the lignites of Benhar and Mataura. 1909 *Installation News* III. 133/2 The *low-temperature system of healing by means of convectors. 1957 R. Hoggart *Auden* iii. 32 He seems to be aiming not at a widely-acceptable demotic speech but at a low-temperature verse of intelligent observation and comment. 1898 *Ibid.* V. 983 Not infrequently.. the *low-tension pulse presents marked fluctuation of the base line. 1948 *Penguin New Writing* XXXV. 93 Poetry of a kind which is at present particularly in need of rescue from oblivion: what may be called low-tension poetry. 1957 *Railway Mag.* Mar. 159/2 A cubicle containing the majority of the low-tension control equipment is housed in a van compartment in the motor coach. 1885 Howells *Silas Lapham* (1891) I. 71 An easy *low-tread staircase. 1897 W. C. Hazlitt *Ourselves* 122 It is natural that this *low-type Realism should be ruled by circumstances. 1962 A. Battersby *Guide to Stock Control* viii. 76 At the other end of the scale, spare parts should be in the *low-value, long-residence class. 1956 *Nature* 21 Jan. 120/2 In areas where deep weathering or drift presents difficult *low-velocity-layer correction problems, the reflexion times down to a known shallow marker-bed will give the necessary corrections for the deeper horizons. 1975 N. Luard *Robespierre Serial* vi. 45 A low-velocity hand-gun. 1922 Glazebrook *Dict. Appl. Physics* II. 748/1 On *low-voltage alternating-current systems these [switches] consist of movable blades bridging two contacts. 1971 L. Payne *Even my Foot's Asleep* i. 7 The soft glow of a low-voltage lamp. 1920 *Act 10 Geo. V* c. 10 §1, Part of the contributions payable in respect of *low-wage earners. 1971 *Times* 19 Mar. 6 There had been a suggestion that steel might be imported from low-wage producers like Japan. 1899 Mackail *Life Morris* II. 46 The *low-warp loom he dismissed, as useless for his purpose. 1962 A. Wise *Death's Head* xi. 131 A few *low-wattage wall lights. 1971 W. Hanley *Blue Dreams* xix. 314 Erotic light.. suffused the rooms, cast by the low-wattage red light bulbs. [1923 *Flight* XV. 122/2 The choice of *low wing position has doubtless been made mainly on account of a desire to keep the wing in one piece.] 1942 *R.A.F. Jrnl.* 16 May 15 This is a conventional two-seater low-wing monoplane. 1950 *Gloss. Aeronaut. Terms (B.S.I.)* I. 30 *Low-wing monoplane*, a monoplane in which the main planes are located at or near the bottom of the fuselage.

21. Parasynthetic derivatives in -ED[2], unlimited in number, as *low-arched, -backed, -bodied, -boughed, -bowed, -ceiled, -ceilinged, -conceited, -conditioned, -crowned, -eaved, -filleted, -flighted, -fortuned, -heeled, -levelled, -masted, -minded* (hence *low-mindedness*), *-panelled, -powered, -priced, -purposed, -quartered, -rented, -rimmed, -roofed, -sided, -sized, -statured, -studded, -thoughted, -toned, -tongued, †-vanitied, -vaulted, -voiced, -waisted, -wheeled, -withered, -witted*; **low-blooded**, of low blood, race, or descent; **low-necked**, (of a dress) cut low in the neck or bosom.

1821 Joanna Baillie *Metr. Leg., Lady G. Baillie* i. 7 By *low-arched door. 1681 *Lond. Gaz.* No. 1656/4 A Sorrel Mare, about 13 hands high,.. a little *low Back'd. 1827 Lady Morgan *O'Briens & O'Flahertys* IV. 60 A low-backed car is the common vehicle used for the purposes of husbandry. 1839 *Times* 19 Mar., It failed, as *low-blooded knavery always does. 1892 E. Reeves *Homeward Bound* 28 The passing of weak, low-blooded paupers by careless selectors. 1882 Stevenson *New Arab. Nts., Prov. & Guitar* ii, Léon looked at her, in her *low-bodied maroon dress. 1824 Miss Mitford *Village* Ser. i. 54 The peacock.. dropping it [his tail] gracefully from some *low-boughed tree. 1898 R. Kipling in *Morning Post* 5 Nov. 5/3 The *low-bowed battleships slugged their bluff noses into the surge. 1904 W. de la Mare *Henry Brocken* 106 The room in which we sat was *low-ceiled and cheerful. 1864 Hawthorne *S. Felton* (1883) 266 The *low-ceilinged eastern room where he studied. 1648 Bp. Hall *Select Th.* §10 Humble and *low-conceited of rich endowments. 1632 Massinger *Maid of Hon.* v. ii, Of.. an abject temper,.. poore and *low condition'd. 1600 Rowlands *Lett. Humours Blood* v. 72 A little *low cround Hatte he alwayes weares. 1856 Lever *Martins of Cro' M.* 141 His.. low-crowned oil-skin hat, and leather gaiters. 1905 *Westm. Gaz.* 20 May 5/3 *Low-eaved houses, cobbled streets, and quiet squares. 1687 *Lond. Gaz.* No. 2271/4 Stolen or strayed.., a Chesnut Gelding.., *low-Fillited. 1592 Nashe *Strange Newes* F 3, The Portugals and Frenchmens feare will lend your Honors richer ornaments, than his *low-flighted affection (fortunes summer folower) can frame them. 1627–47 Feltham *Resolves* 430 The *low-fortuned ploughman. 1687 *Lond. Gaz.* No. 2295/4 A Roan Gelding.., about 14 hands, all his paces, *low-heel'd before. 1810 Scott *Lady of L.* iii. xxvii, The *low-levell'd sunbeams. 1696 Phillips (ed. 5), **Low-masted*, a Ship is said to be low-masted, or under-masted, when her Mast is too small, or too short. 1730–46 Thomson *Autumn* 188 Giddy fashion and *low-minded pride. 1829 Southey *Sir T. More* (1831) II. 48 Not so much from the *low-mindedness of individuals, as from the circumstances wherein they are placed. 1901 *Westm. Gaz.* 30 July 6/3 A *low-necked wedding gown. 1902 *Blackw. Mag.* May 653/2 Entering under a *low-panelled door, we found ourselves in a long and wide bar. 1903 *Daily Chron.* 3 Aug. 3/7 A motor-car, however *low-powered or slow it may be. 1953 R. Lehmann *Echoing Grove* 211 Put a frame round the amorphous semi-transparent mass of low-powered energy that seemed himself. 1972 'G. North' *Sgt. Cluff rings True* xv. 114 The glow from a low-powered bulb in a standard lamp. 1722 De Foe *Col. Jack* (1840) 171 He.. falling into some *low-prized rogueries afterwards,.. was.. transported. 1842 Bischoff *Woollen Manuf.* II. 199 The German cloths are not so well manufactured as ours, particularly the low-priced cloth. 1895 *Montgomery Ward Catal.* 5/1 This is one of the best made low priced suitings that we ever received. 1923 *Radio Times* 28 Sept. 22/2 Headphones specially low priced at 24/- per pair. 1729 Savage *Wanderer* v. 298 The *low-purpos'd, loud, polemic Fray. 1860 Reade *Cloister & H.* III. 59 They [shoes] were *low-quartered and square-toed. 1802 *Trans. Soc. Arts* XX. 348 To live in *low-rented houses. 1598 Sylvester *Du Bartas* ii. i. iv. *Handie-Crafts* 90 The *low-rooft broken wals (In stead of Arras) hang with Spiders' cauls. 1671 Milton *P.R.* iv. 272 Philosophy.. From Heaven descended to the low-roofed house Of Socrates. 1874 J. W. Long *Amer. Wild-Fowl Shooting* 78 A small, *low-sided boat.. might be.. dangerous on large waters. 1882 Nodal & Milner *Gloss. Lancs. Dial.* 186 **Low-sized*, little, short of stature. 1907 Joyce *Let.* 1 Mar. (1966) II. 218 They were low-sized and quince-coloured. 1938 S. Beckett *Murphy* 97 A low-sized corpulent middle-aged woman. 1635 R. Johnson *Hist. Tom a Lincoln* (1828) 100 A very *low-statured dwarf. 1854 B. P. Shillaber *Life & Sayings Mrs. Partington* 16 A tall man could not stand erect in the *low-studded room. 1884 Low-studded [see studded *ppl. a.* 6]. 1934 E. Wharton *Backward Glance* x. 251 It was a tiny garden patch, and a few steps brought us to the door of a low-studded cottage in a gap of the hanging woods. 1634 Milton *Comus* 6 With *low-thoughted care Confin'd. 1847 Tennyson *Princess* vii. 208 So she *low-toned; while with shut eyes I lay Listening; then look'd. 1871 G. Meredith *H. Richmond* li, Your dear mother had a low-toned nervous system. 1909 R. Fry *Let.* 15 Jan. (1972) I. 310 The *Fur Jacket*.. is.. exceedingly low-toned. 1941 *B.B.C. Gloss. Broadcasting Terms* 18 *Low-toned*, manifesting a form of frequency distortion in which the lower audio-frequencies are accentuated. 1969 *Word* XXV. 155 Possessive prefixes are usually low-toned. 1606 Shaks. *Ant. & Cl.* iii. iii. 15 Didst heare her speake? Is she shrill tongu'd or *low? 1830 Tennyson *Adeline* 51 Doth the low-tongued Orient Wander from the side of the morn. 1748 Richardson *Clarissa* (1811) IV. 86 Your foolish, your *low-vanity'd Lovelace. 1869 J. R. Lowell *Foot-Path* in *Under Willows* 225 Those angel stairways in my brain, That climb from these *low-vaulted days To spacious sunshines far from pain. 1606 Shaks. *Ant. & Cl.* iii. iii. 16 Madam, I heard her speake, she is *low voic'd. 1895 A. W. Pinero *Second Mrs. Tanqueray* ii. 63 She is a low-voiced, grave girl. 1953 'N. Blake' *Dreadful Hollow* 148 He stared up at her, and caught Charles's low-voiced words. 1923 A. Huxley *Antic Hay* ix. 124 *Low-waisted summer frocks. 1966 *Guardian* 27 July 6/4 A long, lean, low-waisted jumper top. 1974 *Country Life* 24 Oct. 1242/3 The long, low-waisted black jersey evening dress. 1842 Tennyson *Talking Oak* 110 Sitting straight Within the *low-wheel'd chaise. 1884 *St. Stephen's Rev.* 28 June 14/2 Saddles.. suited to the *low-withered Arab horses.

22. In combination with pres. and pa. pples., forming ppl. adjs., corresponding to the vbl. phrases in senses 16–19, as *low-burning, -laid, -lying, -made.*

1904 E. Rickert *Reaper* 8 His mother sat by the *low-burning peat. 1974 E. Hardwick *Seduction & Betrayal* 131 Miss Kilman.. is hanging on.. to a low-burning encounter with religion. 1611 Shaks. *Cymb.* v. iv. 103 Be content, Your *low-laide Sonne, our Godhead will vplift. 1811 Shelley *Tear* iv. 7 Sure man.. May weep in mute grief o'er thy low-laid shrine. 1856 Lever *Martins of Cro' M.* 611 A mild, soft day, with *low-lying clouds. 1567 Golding *Ovid's Met.* viii. (1593) 202 And ducking downe their heads, within the *low-made wicket came.

23. Special combinations and collocations: **low-alloy** *a. Metallurgy*, containing a small proportion of alloying elements; **low bailiff** (see quot.); **low boat** *U.S. Sport*, that which secures the smallest quantity of fish or game (*Cent. Dict.*); †**low-brought** *ppl. a.*, reduced to distress, weakness, or subjection (see sense 16); **low-bush** *N. Amer.*, used *attrib.* to designate low-growing plants or their fruit, esp. **low-bush blackberry**, one of several species of *Rubus*; **low-bush blueberry**, a variety of *Vaccinium angustifolium*; **low-bush cranberry**, in Canada, *Viburnum edule*; **low celebration** *Eccl.* (see quot.); †**low-cheered** *a.*, mild-faced, having a meek look; **low comedian**, an actor of low comedy; **low comedy**, (*a*) comedy in which the subject and treatment border upon farce; (*b*) *Theat. slang* = *low comedian*; also *attrib.*; †**low-day**, any day that is not a Sunday or feast-day; **low definition**: see definition 5 c; **Low Dutch** *a.* and *sb.* (see Dutch A. 1, B. 1 and 3); hence ***Low-Dutchman*** (cf. Dutch 3 b); †**Low Easterday** = Low Sunday; **low embroidery, fermentation** (see quots.); **low-fidelity** *a.*, characterized by an absence of 'high fidelity' (see high fidelity); **low gear**: see gear *sb.* 7 b; **Low German** *a.* and *sb.* (cf. German A. 1 b, B. 1 b, 2 b); **low grade** *Philol.* [grade *sb.* 9 a], a reduced form, generally represented by [ə], in an ablaut series; **low grinding** = *low-milling*; **low-key** *Photogr.* (see quot. 1959); also *attrib.* and *fig.*, esp. muted, restrained, of modest ambition; so **low-keyed** *a.* (in *fig.* senses); **Low Latin** *a.* and *sb.* [= F. *bas-latin*], late Latin or mediæval Latin; hence **Low-Latinist**, a scholar in Low Latin; **low-loader**, a lorry with a low deck (usu. without sides) to facilitate loading of heavy loads, esp. other vehicles; **low-loss** *a. Electr.*, characterized by or causing little dissipation of electric or electromagnetic energy; **low maple** *U.S.*, the mountain maple, *Acer spicatum*; **low mass** (see mass); **low-milling** (see milling *vbl. sb.*); **low-molecular** *a. Chem.*, having a low molecular weight; **low-neck**, a low-necked dress; †**low-pad** *cant* = footpad; †**low-parted** *a.*, of no great parts or abilities; †**Low parties** *pl.*, the Netherlands; **low-pass** *a.*, denoting a filter that attenuates components with a frequency greater than some cut-off frequency and passes components of lower frequency; **low profile**, (*a*) *attrib.* of a motor-vehicle tyre, having a relatively great width in proportion to its height; (*b*) (of or pertaining to) a low-keyed and unobtrusive policy, restrained or inconspicuous behaviour, etc.; **low quarters** [quarter *sb.* 20 c] *pl. U.S.* (see quots. 1916, 1971); also **low-quarter** *attrib.*; **low-residue** *a.*, (of a meal or diet) designed to give rise to relatively little fæces and urine; **low-rise** *a.*, of a building: low, of one storey or few storeys; also *transf.*; as *sb.*, a low building; **low-rope** = *slack-rope*; **low-sail** (*Naut.*) = *easy sail* (cf. easy *a.* 5); **low tea** *U.S.*, a plain tea; †**low Toby** (see quot.); **Low Week**, the week following Easter week; †**low-wood** = copsewood 2; **low-worm** (see quot.); **low-yield** *a.*, producing little, giving a low return; *spec.* applied to a nuclear weapon having a relatively low explosive force.

1931 *Iron Age* CXXVIII. 1142/1 The *low alloy steels were described [by H. J. French] as those containing usually no more than 6 or 7 per cent of the alloying metal. 1956 W. D. Hargreaves in D. L. Linton *Sheffield* 287 Rotherham produces about a million tons per year of carbon and low alloy steel. 1972 *Jrnl. Austral. Inst. Metals* XVII. 175/1 Where additional durability is required, a widely employed technique is to use a low-alloy 'marine grade' of steel. 1835 *1st Munic. Corp. Comm. Rep.* App. iii. 1601 [Lancaster.]The Bailiff of the Commons, sometimes called the *Low Bailiff, is elected at an annual meeting of the free burgesses from among the commons. 1459 *Paston Lett.* No. 331 I. 444 He.. is ryte *lowe browt, and sore weykid and

feblyd. **1545** *Primer Hen. VIII* DD iv, Beholde, how I am lowe brought from the cruel pursuers. **1596** Spenser *State Irel.* (Globe ed.) 614/2 How comes it then to pass, that having once beene soe lowe brought, and throughly subjected, they afterwardes lifted themselves soe strongly agayne? **1833** C. P. Traill *Let.* 18 Apr. in *Backwoods of Canada* (1836) 144 The *low-bush cranberries are brought in great quantities by the Indians to the towns and villages. **1857** A. Gray *First Less. Bot. & Vegetable Physiol.* 122 *R[ubus] trivialis*, Michx. (Low Bush-Blackberry). **1891** J. M. Coulter *Bot. W. Texas* I. 104 Low bush blackberry. A southern blackberry, apparently common in eastern, southern, and western Texas. **1958** *Edmonton* (Alberta) *Jrnl.* 26 July 39/6 For the most part, housewives pick high and low bush blueberries..and in the fall, low bush cranberries. **1962** M. W. Murie *Two in Far North* i. i. 15 And sometimes had time to pick a handful of bright red low-bush cranberries. **1969** E. H. Pinto *Treen* 91 The harvesting of lowbush blueberries..begins in Maine in late July and August. **1867** Walker *Ritual Reason Why* 79 *Low celebration is the administration of the Holy Communion without the adjuncts of assistant ministers and choir. **1377** Langl. *P. Pl.* B. xix. 258 Grace gaue Piers a teme, foure gret oxen: þat on was Luke, a large beste and a *lowe-chered. **1749** W. R. Chetwood *Hist. Stage* 82 *note*, A well-esteem'd *low Comedian. **1890** Barrie *My Lady Nicotine* xiii. (1901) 43/1 This is the low comedian Kempe. **1608** Day *Humour out of breath* i. B 4 b, Attendance sirra, your *low Commedie, Craues but few Actors, weele breake company. **1671** Dryden *Evening's Love* Pref. *Ess.* (ed. Ker) I. 135 Low comedy especially requires, on the writer's part, much of conversation with the vulgar, and much of ill nature in the observation of their follies. *c* **1750** T. Aston *Suppl. to Cibber* 12 There being no Rivals in his dry, heavy, downright Way in Low Comedy. **1849** *Theatrical Mirror* 17 Sept. 19 Whether in consequence of the non-arrival of the second low-comedy man, I would undertake his part in the last piece. **1885** J. K. Jerome *On the Stage* 39 Our low comedy, who knew the whole piece by heart. **1886** in J. R. Ware *Passing Eng.* (1909) 171/2 The success of *Indiana* mainly depends upon the extravagant humours of the chief low-comedy merchant. **1906** E. Dyson *Fact'ry' Ands* xviii. 239 Feathers had some reputation as a yarn spinner. His low-comedy style was popular. **1961** *John o' London's* 6 July 8/2 She lacks the low-comedy sense which Kingsley Amis shows in his poetry. *c* **1613** T. Campion *To Henry, Ld. Clifford* Wks. (1889) 64 The vulgar *low-days undistinguished, Are left for labour, games, and sportful sights. **1592** Nashe *P. Penilesse* 23 b, The Germaines and *lowe Dutch..should bee continually kept moyst with the foggie aire and stinking mistes that arise out of their fennie soyle. **1764** Harmer *Observ.* Pref. 8 Egmont's and Heyman's Travels..translated from the Low Dutch. **1576** Newton *Lemnie's Complex.* (1633) 63 The Netherlanders, and *low Dutchmen bordering upon the Sea. **1603** Owen *Pembrokeshire* (1892) 271 The second..on Ester Monday..the third on *Lowe Esterday. **1882** Caulfeild & Saward *Dict. Needlewk.*, **Low Embroidery*. This term includes all the needlework formed with Satin or other fancy stitches upon solid foundations, whether worked upon both sides alike, or slightly raised (not padded) by run lines from the foundation. **1881** Tyndall *Floating Matter Air* 257 This beer is prepared by what is called the process of *low fermentation; the name being given partly because the yeast ..falls to the bottom of the cask; but partly also because it is produced at a low temperature. **1947** *Amer. Speech* XXII. 132 The relatively *low-fidelity aluminum disks might not always record it clearly enough to interfere with established habits of transcription. **1962** Simpson & Richards *Physical Princ. Junction Transistors* xviii. 451 For low-fidelity communication links using portable equipment a narrow-band FM system..may be used. **1963** T. Pynchon *V* v. 113 Each anchor man had a walkie-talkie, tied in on a common network to Zeitsuss's office and a low-fidelity 15-inch speaker mounted on the ceiling. **1845** S. Austin *Ranke's Hist. Ref.* I. 287 The champion of the modern views,—a *low German, Erasmus of Rotterdam. **1887** [see German A. 1 b]. **1901** *Jrnl. Gmc. Philol.* III. 265 Skr. *i*: Gr. α<ə, as *low grade of a long vowel. **1907** *Mod. Philol.* V. 269 OE. *þwīnan*, pre-Germ. *tụino-* may represent the low grade of a base *tāu-ịo-* from *tā-ụo-* from *tā-*. **1884** *Bath Herald* 27 Dec. 6/4 [Flour Mill.] The system in vogue up to a dozen years ago was *low grinding. **1895** *Leeds Mercury* Suppl. 5 Jan. (E.D.D.), Sarah wor in a varry *low key. **1907** *Westm. Gaz.* 19 Jan. 14/2 There is not the slightest reason why we should not exploit this low-key type of picture. **1953** K. Reisz *Technique Film Editing* i. 65 The elegant low-key lighting (which is utterly unrealistic). **1959** W. S. Sharps *Dict. Cinematogr.* 108/1 *Low-key*, the term applied when a majority of the tones in the subject or image lie at the dark end of the grey scale. **1965** *Listener* 2 Dec. 934/3 Pleasant, low-key entertainment. **1972** *Guardian* 11 July 12/2 With the UDA building its barricades, how long can the 'low key' phase last. **1960** R. Davies *Voice from Attic* 19 Nothing could be farther from my intention, and I know that many readers are happiest with a *low-keyed and antitheatrical approach to their pleasure. **1969** *Daily Tel.* 11 Feb. 16/1 A fairly low-keyed inquiry. **1973** *Publishers Weekly* 30 May 40/3 A girl spending the winter recovering from a long illness, and her pet hamster are the elements in this low-keyed fantasy. **1872** Yeats *Growth Comm.* 159 The Hanseatic league derives its name from the *Low Latin 'hansa'. **1927** *Times* (Weekly ed.) 3 Nov. 495/4 Two open coaches mounted on six-cylindered *low-loader commercial chassis. **1960** *Guardian* 23 Nov. 11/4 Efforts were still being made to tow the low loader out of the hedge. **1973** J. Leasor *Host of Extras* i. 23, I may have to carry them [*sc.* old cars] round the country on a low loader to show them to someone who can't come to London. **1928** *Times* 23 Mar. 20/1 The effect of connecting up a valve amplifier with a highly efficient tuned circuit employing a coil of the *low-loss type. **1946** *Nature* 9 Nov. 671/1 The oxides in powder form were mixed in various proportions with a low-loss, non-magnetic binder, paraffin wax. **1962** Corson & Lorrain *Introd. Electromagn. Fields* xii. 418 This type of wave guide is found in almost all types of electronic equipment for use both at low and at high frequencies. The medium of propagation is a low-loss dielectric. **1813** H. Muhlenberg *Catal. Plant.* 95 Mountain maple or *low maple. **1832** D. J. Browne *Sylva Amer.* 102 It is sometimes called Low Maple, from the dwarfish stature of the tree. **1897** G. B. Sudworth *Nomencl. Arborescent Flora U.S.* 282 *Acer spicatum*. Mountain Maple... Low Maple (Tenn.). **1946** *Nature* 28 Dec. 925/1 Crystallization phenomena in rubbers show certain similarities to, but also striking differences from, crystallization in ordinary *low-molecular systems. **1866** Howells *Venet. Life* xx. 329 Ladies planted in formal rows of *low-necks and white dresses. **1909** *Englishwoman* Apr. 319 Magazines with 'types of beauty'—in tights, ballet dancers' skirts or low-necks. **1922** Low-neck [see *bathing-suit* (bathing *vbl. sb.* 2)]. **1673** R. Head *Canting Acad.* 65 The Ruffler is metamorphosed into a *Low-Pad. **1662** Gurnall *Chr. in Arm.* verse 18. ix. §2. 577 The heart [may be] sound and sincere, where the head is *low-parted. **1502–9** Henry VII in J. Gairdner *Lett. Rich. III & Hen. VII* 449 He [would shew] unto us mervelous conclusions touching the rule and [governance] of these *Lowe parties. **1929** J. H. Morecroft *Elem. Radio Communication* vii. 250 A simple calculation, say, of the *low-pass type, will show the reason for the particular performance of filters. **1950** *Engineering* 17 Feb. 186/3 The model..consists essentially of a headpiece made up of successive layers of flexible material, felt and iron arranged so as to constitute a low-pass acoustic filter. Such a filter does not cause appreciable attenuation of the low and voice frequencies, but cuts out those frequencies which give rise to harmful shrillness. **1964** *Language* XL. 203 'Content-free speech' has also come to refer to doctored recorded corpora of speech which have been run through low-pass filters, so that features conveying affective qualities are retained while linguistic intelligibility is suppressed. **1967** *Guardian* 25 Sept. 3/8 A production Aston Martin..with..*low profile tyres. **1970** *Ibid.* 24 Aug. 3/2 The Nixon doctrine of 'low profile' involvement, in other words a maximum of aid and a minimum of US troops. **1971** *Publishers' Weekly* 6 Dec. 19/2 Los Angeles.. more than lives up to its reputation as a low-profile, seemingly endless sprawl with no center. **1972** *Times* 2 Aug. 14/5 Whittaker Hunt has been adopting an altogether lower profile. **1973** *Listener* 4 Jan. 7/3, I admire the brisk creativeness of American English. 'Low profile' is a perfectly vivid phrase for 'conciliatory demeanour'. **1880** 'Mark Twain' *Tramp Abroad* 275 He wore very *low-quarter patent-leather shoes. **1916** *Dialect Notes* IV. 269 *Low-quarters*, Oxford shoes. 'He wears *low quarters* all the year round.' [New Orleans; Also N. Car.] **1971** *Current Slang* (Univ. S. Dakota) VI. 7 *Low quarters*, army dress shoes. **1962** A. Shepard in *Into Orbit* 98, I had a *low residue breakfast of orange juice, a filet mignon wrapped in bacon, and some scrambled eggs. **1971** *New Scientist* 11 Mar. 551/2 Waste can be minimised by the careful planning of low-residue diets..but it will always present a problem [in space flight]. **1957** *Fortune* Sept. 213/2 What kind of people..prefer 'high-rise' apartment buildings, what kind of people prefer two-to-five-storey '*low-rise' houses? **1967** *London* (Ontario) *Free Press* 23 June 38/4 Hip Briefs for today's low-rise trousers. **1971** *Rand Daily Mail* (Home Owner) 27 Mar. 7/4 High rise for young couples or old folk, low-rise for couples with older children. **1972** *Sat. Rev.* (U.S.) 17 June 47/2 The finished units..were stacked 3-high..to form low-rise garden units. **1697** Dryden *Ded. to Æneis* in *Ess.* (1900) II. 201 This is like Merry Andrew on the *low rope. **1805** in Nicolas *Disp. Nelson* (1846) VII. 134 *note*, Saw the Enemy to leeward under *low-sail on the larboard tack. **1883** Howells *Woman's Reason* II. xviii. 133 The world..sent her invitations to little luncheons and *low teas. **1825** Knapp & Baldw. *Newgate Cal.* III. 438/1 A *low Toby, meaning it was a footpad robbery. **1884** *Catholic Dict.* 604 From Holy Saturday till Saturday in *Low Week. **1684** *Scanderbeg Rediv.* v. 115 In the midst of the Copse or *Low-wood. **1704** *Dict. Rust.*, **Low-worm* is a Disease in Horses, hardly known from the Anthony-Fire or the Shingles..'tis a Worm that is bread on the back of a Horse..or runs along the Neck to the Brain. **1957** *Wall St. Jrnl.* 25 Jan. 1/3 Only *low-yield nuclear tests will be conducted at the Frenchman's Flat Proving Ground... The announcement added high-yield devices (hydrogen bombs) are never tested in Nevada. **1959** *Times* 20 Oct. 19/3 Substantial two-way business in industrial shares partly reflected switching out of low-yield shares into higher yielding second rankers. **1972** *Sat. Rev.* (U.S.) 6 May 31/2 Localized Soviet attacks would be countered..by the Pentomic army equipped with a variety of sophisticated, low-yield nuclear weapons.

B. Quasi-*sb.* and *sb.*

I. The neuter *adj.* used *absol.*

1. What is low, a low place, position, or area.

c **1175** *Lamb. Hom.* 79 Adam ure forme feder þet alihte from hehe in to lahe. *a* **1340** Hampole *Psalter* lviii. 10 þou takis me vp fra my laghe in til þi heghe. *c* **1375** Barbour *Bruce* vi. 518 Schir Ameryis rout he saw, That held the playn ay & the law. **1484** Caxton *Fables of Auian* xxvi, To thende he falleth not from hyhe to lowe. **1597** Hooker *Eccl. Pol.* v. xxxviii. 1 Musical harmony..being but of high and low in sounds a due proportionable disposition. **1875** Browning *Aristoph. Apol.* 5120, I..Face Low and Wrong and Weak and all the rest.

†**2.** With preps. *at, in, on low*: down low, on the ground, below, on earth = alow 1. *Obs.*

a **1300** *Cursor M.* 11260 On hei be ioi, and pes on lagh. **13..** *S. Erkenwolde* 147 in Horstm. *Altengl. Leg.* (1881) 269 Such a lyche here is, Has layne lokene here one loghe, how longe is vnknawene. **1340** *Ayenb.* 119 þanne ine ous beginneþ þise graces..ine loȝ and sseweþ an heȝ. *a* **1400–50** *Alexander* 3261 Now in leuell, nowe on-loft, nowe in law vnder. *c* **1460** *Towneley Myst.* xiv. 570 And truly, syrs, looke that ye trow That othere lord is none at-lowe.

II. As *sb.*

3. (with *a* and *pl.*) **a.** A piece of low-lying land. *spec.* in E. Anglia, a hollow or valley between dunes; a pool left by the tide in such a hollow.

1790 *Trans. Soc. Arts* VIII. 92 This Low, as it is called, traversing the best part of our saltings. **1855** *Trans. Philol. Soc.* 33 [Norfolk words.] *Low*, a loch left by the tide on the shore. **1878** *Pop. Sci. Monthly* July 310 These high and low areas, or 'highs' and 'lows' as they are technically known, travel. **1878** Miller & Skertchly *Fenland* ix. 291 The Tides..having a larger and deeper channel run with greater velocity into Lynn Deeps, and set westward through the lows in the sands into Boston Deeps, the Tide being about 20 minutes later there than in Lynn Deeps. **1929** *Jrnl. Ecol.* XVII. 138 Very characteristic of the Blakeney dunes are the 'lows'—narrow valleys between the dune-ridges, corresponding to the 'slacks' of the west-coast dunes. The lows differ from slacks in not being permanently moist..and in being liable to flooding by unusually high tides. **1964** V. J. Chapman *Coastal Vegetation* vi. 156 After flooding by the tide, water may remain in the low for some time. **1970** G. E. Evans *Where Beards wag All* xxi. 240 These men lived in these huts which they'd placed down there in the Low.

b. An area of low barometric pressure. Also, an area of low gravitational field strength.

1966 *McGraw-Hill Encycl. Sci. & Technol.* 166/2 Gravity maps display highs and lows. **1972** *Nature* 3 Mar. 24/1 The main feature of the present map..is the large gravity 'low' in the Moray Firth.

c. A low point or minimum in price, temperature, numbers, or the like. Cf. *all-time* adj. (all E. 13).

1911 *N.Y. Times* 20 Sept., Calumet and Hecla opened 17 points off at 373, which is 47 points above the established low of 1897. **1929** *Observer* 17 Nov. 3/4 The sharp rally.. called the weighted average of eight leading industrial stocks up to 149·0 from the new low of 133·0. **1933** A. R. Longworth *Crowded Hours* viii. 133 In 1906 the finances of the Longworths, though they were on the way, had not reached their present 'low'. **1934** Wodehouse *Thank You, Jeeves* xiv. 203 But the heart was still sinking. And when I hear him snort emotionally in the darkness it touched a new low. **1953** —— *Performing Flea* 193 The population of Dormitory 309 fluctuated between a high of 68 and a low of 57. **1955** *Ann. Reg. 1954* 82 The death rate fell to a new low of 8·7 per thousand. **1964** *Financial Times* 3 Mar. 2/6 A new low for many years was reached in stocks of refined tin in London Metal Exchange official warehouses last week. **1968** *Globe & Mail* (Toronto) 17 Feb. 1/6 The predicted high for Elliot Lake today is 5 below; the low tonight 20 below. **1971** *Sci. Amer.* Sept. 107/2 The interior temperature of the house sometimes reached 80 degrees, and the nightly lows were seldom below 70. **1973** *Jrnl. Genetic Psychol.* CXXII. 186 Scores could range from a high of 64..to a low of 1.

4. In *All-fours*: The deuce of trumps, or the lowest trump dealt. (Earlier books have 'highest, lowest', etc.)

1818 Todd s.v. *All-fours*, The all-four are high, low, Jack, and the game. **1830** [see game *sb.* 8 f]. **1897** in Webster.

5. = *low gear* (see gear *sb.* 7 b).

1934 in Webster. **1968** C. Nicole *Self Lovers* ii. 30 He descended the hill from his house in low, partly to minimise the potholes..and partly to enjoy the view. **1970** T. Hillerman *Blessing Way* xiii. 119 Put it in low and angle to the left. **1973** 'A. Hall' *Tango Briefing* viii. 96, I dragged the manual into low to kill the rest of the speed.

low (ləʊ), *adv.* Forms: 3 lah(e, 3–5 laȝ(e, loȝ(e, 3–6 lowe, (4 louwe), 4–5 lau, 4–6 *Sc.* and *north.* law(e, 4– low. Also laigh. [ME. *laȝe, lahe, loȝe*, f. the adj.]

1. a. In a low position; on or under the ground; little above the ground or some base. *to carry low* (see carry 32, 32 c). † *to dance low*: to dance lifting the feet but little from the ground.

Cf. low *a.* 18; the adv. and the complementary adj. are often difficult to distinguish.

a **1225** *Ancr. R.* 130 Fleoð heie, & holdeð þauh þet heaued euer lowe. *c* **1230** *Hali Meid.* 5 þeos..wuneð lahe on eorðe. *c* **1250** *Lutel Soth Serm.* 37 in *O.E. Misc.* 188 Loȝe heo holdet hore galun. *c* **1290** *S. Eng. Leg.* 50/131 Him þouȝte it was wel vuele i-do þat he lai so lowe þere, þat he nere i-bured in herre stude. **1340** Hampole *Pr. Consc.* 3062 When þe ryche man, þat in helle sat lawe, Lazar in Abraham bosom sawe. **1423** Jas. I. *Kingis Q.* ciii, Law in the gardyn, ryght tofore myn eye. **1535** Stewart *Cron. Scot.* (1858) II. 288 Tha..Passit ouir Esk richt lauch ouir Sulwa sand. *a* **1548** Hall *Chron., Edw. IV* 233 b, The towne standeth lowe, and the Ryver passeth thorough. **1753** Chambers *Cycl. Supp.* s.v. *Liberty*, Care must be taken not to make the liberty too high, lest it ..make the horse carry low. **1782** *Ann. Reg.* ii. 12 *note*, Persons of all ranks here [in Naples] dance very low. *a* **1800** Cowper *Needless Alarm* 25 The spotted pack, With tails high mounted, ears hung low.

b. *fig.* Humbly; in a low condition or rank; on poor diet; at a low rate. † *to breed* (a person) *low*: to educate in an inferior way (cf. low-bred). *to play low*: to play for stakes of small amount.

c **1374** Chaucer *Anel. & Arc.* 95 For in her sight to her he bare him lowe. *a* **1400–50** *Alexander* 1012 Lord, with ȝoure leue we lawe ȝow be-sechis. **1530** Palsgr. 449/2, I beare lowe, I behave my selfe humbly, *je me humilie*. **1593** Shaks. *3 Hen. VI*, iv. vi. 20 That I may conquer Fortunes spight, By liuing low, where Fortune cannot hurt me [etc.]. **1673** *Ess. Educ. Gentlewom.* 3 The Barbarous custom to breed Women low, is grown general amongst us. **1758** Chesterf. *Let. to Son* 5 Sept. (1892) III. 1234 Live cool for a time, and rather low. **1832** Ld. Houghton in T. W. Reid *Life* I. 122 The doctor here tells me that I..must live very low while I remain in Rome. **1900** *Longm. Mag.* Dec. 98 You value yourself too low.

2. a. To a low point, position, or posture; also, along a low course, in a low direction.

a **1225** *St. Marher.* 14 þe engles..þe seoð ham lihten swa lah of so swiðe heh. *c* **1275** *Passion Our Lord* 8 in *O.E. Misc.* 37 He þet is and euer wes in heuene myd his fadere Ful lowe he alyhte. **13..** *E.E. Allit. P.* B. 798 Loȝe he loutez hem to Loth to þe grounde. *a* **1400–50** *Alexander* 2289 'Mi louely lorde', quod þe lede & law him declines. **1530** Palsgr. 739/2 Stryke lowe, stryke, *lachez jusques a terre*. **1590** Shaks. *Comm. Err.* iii. ii. 143 Oh sir, I did not looke so low. **1602** Dekker *Satiro-mastix* Epilogus M 2 b, You my little Swaggerers that fight lowe: my tough hearts of Oake that stand too't so valliantly. **1611** Bible *Deut.* xxviii. 43 Thou shalt come downe very low. **1667** Milton *P.L.* ii. 81 With what compulsion and laborious flight We sunk thus low? **1726** Shelvocke *Voy. round World* 383 We ought..to.. bream as low as we could to destroy the worm. **1842** Macaulay *Lake Regillus*, So answered those strange horsemen, And each couched low his spear. **1850–6** O. W. Holmes *Disappointed Statesm.* 60 Party fights are won by aiming low. **1871** 'M. Legrand' *Cambr. Freshm.* 129 The Captain was 'a fellow who smokes his cigars very low'.

b. *fig.* and in figurative contexts. ***clean and low*** (see CLEAN *adv.* 6).

1526 *Pilgr. Perf.* (W. de W. 1531) 15 b, Anone they depresse hym as lowe in mysery & wretchednes. **1638** BAKER tr. *Balzac's Lett.* (vol. II.) 21 When I see the sonne of the great Cecile let downe his spirits so low as to mine. **1781** COWPER *Expostul.* 547 Verse cannot stoop so low as thy desert. **1805** *Morn. Chron.* in *Spirit Pub. Jrnls.* (1806) IX. 284 He never descended so low as to steal pint pots and door-scrapers. **1871** FREEMAN *Norm. Conq.* (1876) IV. xviii. 208 Had the royal power ever fallen as low in England as it fell in Germany and Italy.

3. With reference to the voice, the wind, etc.: In a low tone, gently, softly. Also of singing, etc.: At a low pitch, on low notes. (Cf. LOW *a.* 10.)

c **1300** *Havelok* 2079 Speke y loude, or spek y lowe, þou shalt ful wel heren me. ? *a* **1366** CHAUCER *Rom. Rose* 717 Summe highe and summe eek lowe songe. **1390** GOWER *Conf.* I. 77 Thogh thei [wyndes] beginne lowe, At ende thei be noght menable. **1601** SHAKS. *Twel. N.* II. iii. 42 O stay and heare, your true loues coming, That can sing both high and low. **1662–3** PEPYS *Diary* 1 Mar., He read his sermon . . so brokenly and low, that nobody could hear at any distance. **1713** ADDISON *Cato* V. iv. 59 Lucia, speak low, he is retired to rest. **1776** *Trial of Nundocomar* 76/2 You say, the writer read the bond low: was it so low that you could not hear what was said? **1818** SHELLEY *Rosalind & Helen* 244 Low muttering o'er his loathed name. **1853** KINGSLEY *Hypatia* xxiv, Now, Wulf, speak low. **1856** MRS. MARSH *Evelyn Marston* I. i. 9 The wind howls low and mournfully around the chimneys. *Mod.* I can't sing so low as that.

4. With reference to time: Far down, or to a point far down; late.

1658 SIR T. BROWNE *Hydriot.* Introd. (1736) 2 As low as the Reign of Julian we find, that [etc.]. **1710** HEARNE *Collect.* (O.H.S.) III. 45 The IId. vol. of his Church History of Britain . . is to come as low as King Charles IId. **1732** in *Wesley's Jrnl.* (1830) I. 390 Easter fell low that year. **1734** SWIFT *Reasons agst. Bill Tithe Flax & Hemp* Wks. 1745 VIII. 101 The Clergy had the sole right of taxing themselves . . as low as the restoration. **1774** WARTON *Hist. Eng. Poetry* (1840) II. 108 This alliterative measure . . remained in use so low as the sixteenth century. **1845** STEPHEN *Comm. Laws Eng.* (1874) I. 64 These reached as low as the time of Pope Alexander the third.

5. *Comb.* **a.** Forming with ppl. adjs. used attrib. numerous quasi-compounds, usually hyphened; as ***low-bellowing, -bended, -bowed, -built, -cut, -flying, -growing, -hung, -paid*** (also *absol.*), ***-ranking, -rated, -slung, -trained*** (also as pa. pple.), ***-yielding***, etc. Also † **low-cast**, (of a valley) deep; **low-ebbed**, *lit.* of waves, having ebbed to a low point; †*fig.* of persons, 'at a low ebb', impoverished; **low-flung** *a. U.S. colloq.*, of low character or standing.

1727–46 THOMSON *Summer* 505 A hollow moan . . *low-bellowing round the hills. **1597** BP. HALL *Sat.* II. iii. 27 The crowching Client, with *low-bended knee . . Tels on his tale. **1633** FORD *Broken H.* III. v, With *low-bent thoughts Accusing such presumption. **1726–46** THOMSON *Winter* 77 The low-bent clouds Pour flood on flood. **1872** A. DE VERE *Leg. St. Patrick, Arraignm. St. P.*, Ceasing, he stood *Low-bowed, with hands upon his bosom crossed. **1592** NASHE *Summers Last Will* (1600) I j b, This *lowe built house, will bring vs to our ends. **1691** *Lond. Gaz.* No. 2625/4 Also a low-built Watch with a String, the Box Gilt. **1697** CREECH tr. *Manilius* IV. 33 But hotter Climates narrower Frames obtain, And low-built Bodies are the growth of Spain. **1843** JAMES *Forest Days* (1847) 60 It was, in fact, a large, though low-built house. **1613–16** W. BROWNE *Brit. Past.* II. v, A *low-cast valley. **1613** R. ZOUCHE *Dove* B, The *low-coucht Seas. **1757** DYER *Fleece* IV. 591 Proud Buenos Aires, low-couched Paraguay. **1667** MILTON *P.L.* IX. 180 Like a black mist *low creeping. **1818** KEATS *Endym.* I. 257 Low-creeping strawberries. **1601** SHAKS. *Jul. C.* III. i. 43 *Low-crooked-curtsies, and base Spaniell fawning. **1897** *Sears, Roebuck Catal.* 203/3 Men's *low cut canvas pumps. **1932** 'E. M. DELAFIELD' *Thank Heaven Fasting* II. 44 Lady Marlowe, superb . . in her low-cut green satin, with an emerald tiara. **1962** P. GREGORY *Like Tigress at Bay* iv. 40 Steve was forced to admit to himself that she presented a beautiful picture, sitting there in the spotlight in her low-cut, strapless gown. **1593** SHAKS. *Lucr.* 1705 May my pure mind with the fowle act dispence, My *low declined honor to aduance? **1625** MILTON *Death Fair Infant* 32 Hid from the world in a *low delved tomb. **1728–46** THOMSON *Spring* 720 Her pinions . . *low-drooping, scarce Can bear the mourner to the poplar shade. **1735** SOMERVILLE *Chase* I. 251 Strait Hams . . And his *low-dropping Chest confess his Speed. **1601** ? MARSTON *Pasquil & Kath.* II. 119 Why, this same boy's . . A *low-eb'd gallant. **1820** KEATS *Hyperion* II. 136 When the waves Low-ebb'd still hid it up in shallow gloom. **1830** TENNYSON *Poems* 99 Keen knowledges of *low-embowèd eld. **1633** FORD *Love's Sacr.* V. iii, Let thy smooth, *Low-fawning parasites renowne thy Act. **1830** TENNYSON *Mermaid* 32, I would fling on each side my *low-flowing locks. **1843** *Missouri Reporter* (St. Louis) 11 Apr. (Th.), Here we have a beautiful specimen of the dishonesty and *low-flung slang of the clique. **1844** *Knickerbocker* XXIII. 506 Who wants a parcel of low-flung 'outside barbarians' to go in cahoot with us? **1853** J. G. BALDWIN *Flush Times Alabama* 24 He . . denounced Jefferson as a low-flung demagogue. **1861** *Oregon Argus* 28 Dec. (Th.), It would be impossible to attempt a controversy with such low-flung dogs. **1963** *Times Lit. Suppl.* 8 Feb. 95/2 The *low-flying beginning of this book is much better than its high-flying philosophic end. **1864** TENNYSON *Aylmer's F.* 612 A breathless burthen of *low-folded heavens. **1883** *Harper's Mag.* Oct. 726/2 He is *low-going, and a wide-goer behind. **1877** RAYMOND *Statist. Mines & Mining* 326 Masses of *low-growing plants. **1906** *Westm. Gaz.* 26 May 11/3 The topmost bough of some low-growing tree or shrub. **1958** W. J. STOKOE *Caterpillars Brit. Moths* (new ed.) I. 299 Greater plantain (*Plantago major*) and other low-growing plants. **1876** GEO. ELIOT *Dan. Der.* II. xxx. 246 The *low-hanging clouds. **1700** DRYDEN *Pal. & Arc.* III. 863 Like a *low-hung cloud. **1902** *Q. Rev.* Oct. 484 The low-hung narrow-windowed mansion in Butcher Row. **1916** D. H. LAWRENCE *Amores* 104 The low-hung lamps stretched down the road . . as I hastened to meet The low-hung light of her eyes. **1924** E. SITWELL *Sleeping Beauty* xvi. 54 It seemed a low-hung country of the blind. **1377** LANGL. *P. Pl.* B. XII. 265 To *lowe-lybbyng men the larke is resembled. **1964** W. L. GOODMAN *Hist. Woodworking Tools* 138 Comparatively *low-paid labourers. **1974** *Times* 5 Dec. 4/4 The TUC had . . recognized the low-paid as a special case. **1672** DRYDEN *Maiden Queen* V. i, You teach me to repent my *low-placed love. **1727** DE FOE *Syst. Magic* I. ii. (1840) 43 The *low-prized learning of the magicians answered very well. **1958** W. J. H. SPROTT *Human Groups* ix. 152 The less popular members of the consistently *low-ranking teams did not change their allegiance. **1599** SHAKS. *Hen. V*, IV. Prol. 19 The . . ouer-lustie French Doe the *low-rated English play at dice. **1895** THOMSON & THOMAS *Electr. Tab. & Mem.* 15 A *low-reading voltmeter. **1826** MILMAN *A. Boleyn* 162 Ha! thou *low-rolling doubling drum—I hear thee! **1634** MILTON *Comus* 315 Ere morrow wake, or the *low roosted lark From her thatch't pallat rowse. *a* **1613** OVERBURY *Charact., Taylor* Wks. (1856) 78 He . . raiseth the *low set roofe of his crosse-legged fortune. **1931** *Morning Post* 21 Aug. 11/7 His *low-slung car simply hurtled down the straight and was lost to view. **1965** G. MCINNES *Road to Gundagai* ii. 31 A very full, low-slung muskmelon moon. **1973** 'R. MACLEOD' *Nest of Vultures* ii. 30 Sleek Ferraris, opulent Rolls-Royces and an occasional low-slung Lamborghini. **1854** MRS. GASKELL *North & S.* x, Some trivial, *low-spoken remark. **1615** G. SANDYS *Trav.* 99 Slow Nile with *low-sunke streames shall keepe his braies. **1691** NORRIS *Pract. Disc.* 13 This low-sunk, wretched and deplorable Degeneracy of Soul. **1742** YOUNG *Nt. Th.* III. 507 Slender tributes *low-tax'd Nature pays For mighty gain. **1820** SHELLEY *Vision Sea* 12 The *low-trailing rack of the tempest. **1869** *Rep. Comm. Agric. 1868* (U.S. Dept. Agric.) 249 *Low-trained hedges may be necessary where land is limited in area, and high in price. *Ibid.*, Evergreens or shrubs may be formed, trimmed, and low-trained a long time without pleaching. **1946** *Nature* 23 Nov. 762/2 The replacement of existing virus-infected, *low-yielding clonal stocks of raspberries is a pressing necessity. **1968** *Economist* 2 Mar. 61/2 Town and City has always been a favourite low-yielding property share.

b. With agent-nouns or nouns of action, as ***low-flyer, -flying*** (so ***low-fly*** vb.), ***-living, -loading***, †***-lying***, †***-riding***.

1881 O. WILDE *Poems* 69 Young Mercury *Low-flying to the dusky ford of Dis. **1949** *Happy Landings* July 8/1 One pilot, low flying over the Continent, had his aircraft blown-up. **1958** G. DUTTON in B. James *Austral. Short Stories* (1963) 288 He low-flies through the unforeseeable complications of tree and rock. **1708** MRS. CENTLIVRE *Busie Body* I. i. 14 For then we are all thought to be . . High-Flyers, or *Low-Flyers, or Levellers. **1942** *Tee Emm* (Air Ministry) II. 78 The pilot who is recklessly daring . . in properly authorised *low-flying practices. **1945** *Ibid.* V. 33 There is . . a fascination about low-flying. **1896** *Allbutt's Syst. Med.* I. 386 The claims made for their several methods by those who have enjoined high-living, *low-living, 'vegetarianism'. **1940** *Chambers's Techn. Dict.* 512/2 **Low-loading amplifier*, a more recent name for a loaded push-pull amplifier. **1962** *Times* 8 May 16/5 The luggage boot, with its flat, low-loading floor. **1691** T. H[ALE] *Acc. New Invent.* p. lxii, The *low-lying of the Head-springs of . . this River. **1599** JAS. I *Βασιλ. Δῶρον* III. 121 Use . . *lowe-ryding for handling of your sworde.

c. In comb. with another adv., as ***low-deep***.

1595 DANIEL *Civ. Wars* I. xcvii, Pry Into the lowe-deepe-buried sinnes long past. *a* **1649** DRUMM. OF HAWTH. *Poems* Wks. (1711) 25 He . . will not deny you grace, But low-deep bury faults, so ye repent.

low (ləʊ), *v.*[1] *Obs.* exc. *dial.* Forms: 3 *Orm.* **laȝhenn, 3–6 lowen, 4 loȝen, -ȝy, 4–6 *Sc.* and *north.* law(e(n, (5 lou, louȝe, lowyn), 5– low.** *pa. pple.* **3 i-lahet, 4 y-loȝed, lawene.** [f. LOW *a.*]

1. *trans.* To make or bring low (chiefly in immaterial sense); to abase, humble, lower.

c **1200** ORMIN 13965 Whi wollde Godess Sune Crist . . himm sellfenn laȝhenn. *Ibid.* 18257 Forrþi þeȝȝ wolldenn niþþrenn Crist & laȝhenn himm þe mare. *c* **1230** *Hali Meid.* 28 Ha neren nawt ihurt, þah ha weren ilahet. *c* **1315** SHOREHAM *Poems* IV. 154 Þench þou nart bote esche, And so þou loȝe þe. **1375** BARBOUR *Bruce* XIII. 658 Quhen the Kyng Eduardis mycht Wes lawit, Kyng Robert lap on hicht. **1382** WYCLIF *Phil.* ii. 7 He lowyde him silf, takynge the foorme of a seruant. *a* **1400–50** *Alexander* 3293 Þat he þat lawene has a lede may lyft, if him thinke. **1422** tr. *Secreta Secret., Priv. Priv.* 245 The sonne louyth hym fro oure regioun. *c* **1449** PECOCK *Repr.* III. iv. 302 He schulde louȝe him silf in inward feeling of herte. *c* **1470** HENRYSON *Mor. Fab.* v. (*Parl. Beasts*) xxi, The grit cameill . . I can him law als litill als ane mous. **1496** *Dives & Paup.* (W. de W.) I. xv. 47/2 The prayer of hym that loweth hym in his prayer thyrleth the clowdes. **1523** FITZHERB. *Surv.* xi. (1539) 26 High no man for no hate, and lowe no man for noo loue. **1533** GAU *Richt Vay* (1888) 91 He lawit hime selff and twik apone hime ye schaip of man. *a* **1555** LYNDESAY *Tragedy* 140 Who dois exault hymself God sall hym law. **1567** *Gude & Godlie Ball.* (S.T.S.) 190 The Ignorant peple sa lawit bene and febill, That thay wat nocht quhome to wyte. **1661** GLANVILL *Van. Dogm.* 101 [God] in his Word, is pleas'd to low himself to our capacities. **1790** A. SHIRREFS *Poems* 219 The merry fowks that were the ben, By this time 'gan to low their strain.

b. *intr.* for *refl.*

13.. *K. Alis.* 5746 The sonne loweth and west helt. **1390** GOWER *Conf.* III. 295 Now it [Fortune] hiheth, now it loweth. *c* **1430** *Hymns Virg.* 120 Euery hylle Shalle lowe, valeys For to Fylle. **1501** DOUGLAS *Pal. Hon.* I. 55 Now thow promittis, . . now lowis, now defyis.

2. a. *trans.* To diminish, lessen; to lessen the value of (a coin); to depreciate. **b.** *refl.* To depreciate (oneself); to run down. **c.** *intr.* for *refl.* Of a fault: To be extenuated.

1340 *Ayenb.* 28 Þet guode los to abatye and hyre guodes to loȝy. *Ibid.* 49 Þis zenne an-heȝeþ and loȝeþ be þe stat of þe persones þet hit doþ. *c* **1375** *Sc. Leg. Saints* l. (*Katerine*) 167 Catone forbad his sowne . . To law hyme-self or lof gretely. **1494** FABYAN *Chron.* VII. 493 He areryd & lowyd ye coynes & moneys of his lande. **1793** T. SCOTT *Three Auld Men, Poems* 338 To lawe their price they will be sorry, Ae single doit.

3. *trans.* To lower, to hold or put in a lower position; to lower the level of (ground).

c **1450** *Merlin* 397 Than he lowed his spere. **1463** *Bury Wills* (Camden) 39 To lowe ye grownd that the dore may be of a resonnable heyghte. **1654** A. GRAY *Serm. on Death* (1755) 151 The other graces must low the sail to faith.

low (ləʊ), *v.*[2] *Obs.* exc. *dial.* Also **5 lowyn, law, 9 lowe.** [a. ON. *loga*, f. *loge* LOW *sb.*[2] Cf. MHG. *lohen.*] *intr.* To flame, blaze, glow; *fig.* to glow, be 'on fire' with passion, etc. Also with *up*.

13.. *Gaw. & Gr. Knt.* 236 Grener . . þen grene aumayl on golde lowande bryȝter. *a* **1400–50** *Alexander* 226 Þe lede lawid in hire lofe as leme dose of gledis. *a* **1440** *Sir Degrev.* 1436 Arcangelus of rede golde . . Lowynge ful lyȝth. *c* **1440** *Promp. Parv.* 315/1 Lowyn, or flamyn as fyyr, *flammo.* **1697** W. CLELAND *Poems* 34 When stocks that are half rotten lowes, They burn best. **1724** RAMSAY *Tea-t. Misc.* (1733) I. 25 Dryest wood will eithest low. *a* **1758** —— *Mill* i, A' lowing with love, my fancy did rove. *a* **1810** TANNAHILL *When John & me were married Poems* (1846) 116 And love will lowe in cottage low, As weel's in lofty ha'. **1827** J. WILSON *Noct. Ambr.* Wks. 1855 I. 278 *North.* Look at your right hand . . . *Shepherd.* Its a' lowin. **1870** E. PEACOCK *Ralf Skirl.* I. 197 Each individual brick shone and 'lowed' with the intense heat. **1893** STEVENSON *Catriona* 362 It lowed up in my mind that this was the girl's father. **1894** CROCKETT *Raiders* (ed. 3) 66 Transferring the flame when it lowed up to the bowl of his . . pipe.

†**low**, *v.*[3] *Obs.* Forms: 4 **lu, loouwe, 4–5 lowe, 6–7 low, 7– 'low.** [Partly a. OF. *louer, loer* (mod. F. *louer*):—L. *laudāre*; partly aphetic f. ALLOW *v.* Some of the forms coincide with northern spellings of LOVE *v.*[2], which has some of the senses of this *vb.*, and may sometimes have been confused with it.

For the mod. vulgarism *'low* for *allow*, see ALLOW *v.*]

1. *trans.* = ALLOW *v.* in various senses.

13.. *Cursor M.* 20034 (Edin.) Þu mi wille me al wil lu [*other texts* alou]. **1382** WYCLIF *Wisd.* iii. 6 As brent sacrifise of ost he loouwede them [Vulg. *accepit eos*]. *c* **1400** *Rom. Rose* 4532 A foolis word is nought to trowe, Ne worth an appel for to lowe. *c* **1440** *Gesta Rom.* liv. 187 (Harl. MS.) The knyȝt hadde noon Excusacion, ne wolde not lowe himselfe. **1587** TURBERV. *Trag. T.* (1837) 139 He lowde him scope, without suspect of ill. **1609** DANIEL *Civ. Wars* VIII. lxvi, Least they [her looks] should 'low More then her heart might meane. **1881** J. C. HARRIS *Nights with Uncle Remus* (1884) xvi. 81 Brer Fox 'low dat he know dat ar place same ez he do he own tater-patch. **1911** G. S. PORTER *Harvester* xvi. 367 She 'lowed to make him a big man. **1938** [see JES, JES']. **1948** G. V. GALWEY *Lift & Drop* iv. 65 Wind's backed four points . . . We've got to 'low for it.

2. *intr.* To bid a price. (Cf. LOVE *v.*[2])

1607 NORDEN *Surv. Dial.* I. 9 *note*, Tenants striuing in lowing and bidding, inhanceth fines and rents.

low (ləʊ), *v.*[4] Forms: 1 **hlówan, 3 lhouen, 4 lo(o)wen, louwen, 5 lawe, loe, lowyn, 6 lo(o)we, 7 lough, lowgh, 4– low.** [A Com. Teut. reduplicating str. vb. (preserved as such only in OE.; elsewhere conjugated weak); OE. *hlówan*, pa. t. *hléow* = ODu. (OLFrankish) *hluoien* (MDu. *loeyen*, Du. *loeien*), OHG. *hluojen* (MHG. *lüejen*), ? ON. *hlóa* (once, with sense 'to roar'); f. Teut. root **hlô-*:—W. Aryan **klā-*; cf. L. *clāmāre* to shout, Gr. *κικλήσκειν* to call.]

1. *intr.* Of cattle: To utter their characteristic sound (in recent use apprehended as denoting a more subdued sound than *bellow*); to moo.

c **1000** ÆLFRIC *Gram.* xxii. (Z.) 129 *Bos mugit*, oxa hlewð. *c* **1240** *Anc. Songs* (Ritson) 4 Awe bleteþ after lomb lhouþ after calue cu. **13..** *Poem times Edw. II* 183 in *Pol. Songs* (Camden) 332 Hit nis noht al for the calf that kow louweth. **1382** WYCLIF *Job* vi. 5 Whethir . . an oxe shul loowen, whan befor the fulle cracche he shal stonde? *a* **1400–50** *Alexander* 4744 Vmquile he noys . . as a nox quen he lawes. **1432–50** tr. *Higden* (Rolls) III. 27 Oon of the calfes of golde that Iheroboam made loede scharpely in the natiuite of Heliseus. **1560** BIBLE (Genev.) *Job* vi. 5 Doeth the wilde asse braye when he hathe grasse? or loweth the oxe when he hathe foddre? **1611** BIBLE *Ibid.* **1647** WARD *Simp. Cobler* 84 Should I heare . . a Cat lowgh like an Oxe, . . it would scare mee. **1770** GOLDSM. *Des. Vill.* 118 The sober herd that lowed to meet their young. **1805** WORDSW. *Prelude* 208 The heifer lows, uneasy at the voice Of a new master. **1820** SHELLEY *Hymn to Mercury* xix. 7 Hermes dragged forth two heifers, lowing loud. **1897** tr. *Nansen's Farthest North* II. ix. 452 We . . could hear them [walruses] . . lowing like cows.

2. *transf.* To make a loud noise, to bellow, howl. Of a cavern: To reverberate with a noise.

a **1000** *Elene* 54 (Gr.) Hleowon hornboran, hreopan friccan. **1382** WYCLIF *Jer.* li. 52 In al his lond loowen shal the woundid. **1513** DOUGLAS *Æneis* III. x. 36 How cavernis or furnys of Ethna round Rummist and lowit. *a* **1661** HOLYDAY *Juvenal* 22 No she-priest here lows in a horn.

3. *trans.* To utter in a voice like that of cattle; to bellow *forth*.

a **1547** SURREY *Æneid* II. 281 Like to the sound the roring bull fourth loowes. **1633** J. FISHER *Fuimus Troes* IV. i. G j b, Which Caucasus may as a Catch repeate, And Taurus lough the same. **1644** SIR E. DERING *Prop. Sacr.* ciii, Others do lough forth the tenour. **1871** G. MEREDITH *H. Richmond* xxxviii, 'Oh I thank you!' I heard the garlanded victim lowing. **1876** 'ANNIE THOMAS' *Blotted out* iii. 27, I shudder under the conviction that she is going to low reproof at me, and so she does.

low, obs. pa. t. of LAUGH *v.*

†**'lowable**, *a. Obs.* [ad. F. *louable*:—L. *laudābilis* LAUDABLE. (Perhaps partly confused with LOVABLE².)] Permissible, desirable, commendable.

1393 LANGL. *P. Pl.* C. VI. 103 Ich rede þe..rape þe to bygynne þe lyf þat ys lowable and leel to þe soule. **1483** CAXTON *Gold. Leg.* 249/2 Thyrdly for the lowable dystrybucion of the tresours that he gaf alle to poure men wysely. **1538** J. BUTLAR *Let. to Cranmer* in *C.'s Misc. Writ.* (Parker Soc.) II. 373, I have declared to the prior that his third Article is not lowable. **1545** RAYNOLD *Byrth Mankynde* Prol. Bvj, Honest and helthsum decoration & clendlynes, alwaies most lowable and commendable in a woman. **1639** CHAS. I *Declar. Tumults Sc.* 63 According to the lowable lawes and constitutions received in this Realm.

†**lowage**. *Obs. rare.* In 6 lowaige. [? ad. F. *louage* hiring.] Some kind of charge on shipping.

1531 *Charterparty* in R. G. Marsden *Sel. Pl. Crt. Adm.* (1894) 37 All stowage lowaige wyndage pety lodmanage and averages acustomyd shalbe taken.

lowan ('ləʊən). *Austral.* [Aboriginal name.] = *mallee bird, fowl, hen* (MALLEE).

1861 H. W. WHEELWRIGHT *Bush Wanderings* iv. 63 The lowan is a plain dull-coloured bird, brownish black, a little larger than the common fowl. **1888** 'R. BOLDREWOOD' *Robbery under Arms* II. ii. 23 The lowan (Mallee hen, they're mostly called) and tallagatta (brush turkey) were thick enough in some of the scrubby corners. **1939** *Nature* 12 Aug. 272/2 It [*sc.* Wyperfeld (Mallee) National Park, Victoria] is probably..the last home of that wonderful bird—the mound builder called the lowan, which incubates its eggs in the vegetative centre of mounds which it builds. **1963** [see *incubator-bird* (INCUBATOR 5)].

lowan, variant of LOWN.

lowance ('laʊəns). Now *dial.* [aphetic f. ALLOWANCE.] A limited portion of food or drink or its equivalent in money given in addition to wages.

c **1565** R. BAKER in Hakluyt *Voy.* (1589) 141 Our lowance waxt so small..it waxed lesse and lesse. **1612** ROWLANDS *Knaue of Harts* 36 You drinke too deepe, Your lowance you exceed. **1846** M. A. RICHARDSON *Borderer's Table-bk.* VI. 199 (E.D.D.) Besides their lowance. **1881** CUSSANS *Hist. Hertfordsh.* III. *Cashio* 320 *Beaver*, lunch; in the harvest field, when supplied by the master, sometimes called 'lowance.

†**'lowbell, low-bell**, *sb. Obs.* Also 6 lowe-bell, 6–7 low-bel, 7 logh-bell, loobel, loubel(l. [? f. LOW *a.* + BELL.

On the assumption that sense 2 is the original, the word has generally been referred to LOW *sb.*²; cf. Phillips (ed. Kersey 1706), '*Luff* or *Lough*, a Light or Flame, to Fowl with a Low-bell'. But it is difficult to see how sense 1 can be a transferred application of sense 2, while the reverse development would be quite normal.]

1. A small bell, *esp.* a cow-bell or sheep-bell; *jocularly*, a bell generally.

1578 G. BEST in *Hakluyt's Voy.* (1600) III. 59 The captaine..knowing wel how they greatly delighted in our toyes, and specially in belles, he rang a pretty lowbell, making signes that he would giue him the same that would come and fetch it. [*Afterwards*: he rang a louder bell.] **1598** FLORIO, *Sampogna*,..a bell hanged about sheepe or goates, a lowe-bell. *a* **1625** FLETCHER *Woman's Prize* I. iii, Peace gentle low-bell. *a* **1634** RANDOLPH *Muse's Looking-gl.* III. i, I'le get a high crown'd hat with five Low-bels. **1661** MORGAN *Sph. Gentry* IV. iii. 33 Two cowes..with collers and lowbells. **1664** COTTON *Scarron.* 66 In a pretty wooden steeple A Low-Bell hung to call the people.

2. A bell used in fowling at night.

The process of fowling with 'low-bell and hand-net' is elaborately described in *Dict. Rusticum et Urbanicum* (1704). The birds are to be stupefied with terror by the noise of the bell and the sudden glare from lights contained in a tin-lined box serving as a dark lantern; when they are thus rendered motionless, the net is to be thrown over them.

1581 *Act 23 Eliz.* c. 10 §6 Others, which..take any Partridges or Feasaunts by night vnder any Tramel, Lowbell, Roadenete or other Engyn. **1589** RIDER *Bibl. Schol.*, A Lowebell to catch birdes with all in the night, *campinula*. **1607** HIERON *Defence* I. 210 But belike M. H. thought, that the word *accursed*, would sound both lowder and fowler, and so amaze men (as a loobel doth Larks) till he threw his nett upon them. **1661** BOYLE *Style of Script.* 27 Some he catches..with frights (as Black-birds with..a Low-Bell). **1707** CHAMBERLAYNE *St. Gt. Brit.* III. vii. 313 The Nobility and Gentry have their..Guns for Birding, Lowbells [etc.]. **1709** W. KING *Art Love* I. 47 The fowler's low-bell robs the lark of sleep. **1792** OSBALDISTONE *Brit. Sportsm.* 445 The sound of the low-bell causes the birds to lie close, and not to stir when the net is over them. **1821** *Sporting Mag.* IX. 11 Hays, nets, low-bells, hare-pipes.

fig. **1653** MILTON *Hirelings* (1659) 132 Now commonly he who desires to be a minister, looks not at the work, but at the wages; and by that lure or loubel may be toald from parish to parish all the town over.

'lowbell, *v.* Now only *dial.* [f. prec.]

†**1.** *trans.* **a.** To capture (birds) by the use of a low-bell. **b.** *transf.* To scare or bewilder as the lowbeller does birds. *Obs.*

1581 LAMBARDE *Eiren.* IV. iv. (1588) 444 If any person whatsoever, have taken..any Phesants or Partriches..by lowbelling or tramelling. **1642** *Broken Title Episcop. Inher.* §2 A muster of a few Exoticke obsolete Saxon termes to Low-bell his Ignorant Examiner. **1651** R. CHILD in *Hartlib's Legacy* (1655) 91 Larks..may be taken in snares, or by day-nets, Low-belling, &c. **1660** H. MORE *Myst. Godl.* To Rdr 23 Weak Christians..are so low-belled by this terror as to be taken up and captivated by the Church of Rome. *Ibid.* 24 [They] do not low-bell men into their own errour by either uncharitable censurings or bloody persecutions.

2. *dial.* To greet with 'rough music' (i.e. beating of pots and kettles, blowing of horns, etc.) as an expression of popular disapprobation.

Current in Northants, Warwickshire, and Worcestershire: see E.D.D.

Hence **'lowbeller**, †(*a*) one who uses a lowbell in fowling (*obs.*); (*b*) *dial.* one who joins in 'low-belling' an unpopular person.

1581 *Act 23 Eliz.* c. 10 §6 This acte shal not..extende to Lowbellers, Tramellers or others, which shall vnwillingly happen to take any Partridges. **1706** PHILLIPS (ed. Kersey), *Low-beller*, one that goes a Fowling with a Light and a Bell.

lowbie, obs. form of LOOBY.

'low-born, *a.* [f. LOW *adv.* + BORN *ppl. a.*]

1. Born in a low station.

c **1205** LAY. 22041 Ne beo he noht swa loh iboren, ful wel he beoð iborȝen. **1611** SHAKS. *Wint. T.* IV. iv. 156 This is the prettiest Low-borne Lasse, that euer Ran on the greene-sord. [**1732** POPE *Ep. Bathurst* 138 Corruption..Shall deluge all; and Av'rice, creeping on, Spread like a low-born mist, and blot the Sun.] **1849** MACAULAY *Hist. Eng.* x. II. 657 The fact that the low born young barrister was appointed to so honorable and important a post.

2. As *sb.* A low-born person. *nonce-use.*

1879 E. ARNOLD *Lt. Asia* VII. 202 Wrapped in a clout, shorn, sandalled, craving food Of low-borns.

low-boy.

†**1.** One who supports the 'low' party in matters of church polity, etc., in opposition to the 'high-flyers' or 'high-boys'; a Whig and Low-churchman.

1715 MRS. CENTLIVRE *Gotham Election* 70 No Fire and Faggot; no Wooden Shoes; no Trade-Sellers; a Low Bow, a Low Bow [*sic*]. *Ibid.* 72 That rascally, cheating, canting Low Boy.

2. orig. *U.S.* A low chest of drawers.

1899 *House Beautiful* (Chicago) Aug. 140 Antique mahogany chair and low-boy. **1929** *Burlington Mag.* LIV. 313 The 'Lowboy'..is the pendant piece to the 'Highboy' and also has no counterpart in England. **1970** *Canad. Antiques Collector* May 11/2 Rare William and Mary lowboy of excellent proportions in burr-walnut and inlays of herringbone. **1973** *Country Life* 29 Mar. (Suppl.) 38/2 Queen Anne walnut two drawer lowboy..Height 2 ft. 3 ins. **1975** *Times* 6 Feb. 9/1 Hand made, hand finished traditional lowboy, in walnut.

low-bred, *a.* [f. LOW *adv.* + BRED *ppl. a.*; cf. †*to breed low* (LOW *adv.* 1 b).] Brought up in a low, inferior, vulgar fashion; characterized by low breeding, conduct, or manners.

1757 GARRICK *Lilliput* I. ii. 39 Let low-bred Minds be curb'd by Laws and Rules. **1775** SHERIDAN *Duenna* I. ii, I don't mention your lowbred, vulgar, sound sleep. **1847** J. WILSON *Chr. North* (1857) I. 138 Like other low-bred creatures, they are covered with vermin. **1848** KINGSLEY *Saints' Trag.* III. iii. 169 She'll wed some pink-faced boy—The more low-bred and penniless, the likelier.

lowbrow, low-brow ('ləʊbraʊ), *sb.* and *a. colloq.* (orig. *U.S.*). [f. LOW *a.* 1, in contrast with HIGHBROW, HIGH-BROW *sb.* and *a.*] **A.** *sb.* One who is not, or does not claim to be, highly intellectual or æsthetically refined.

1906 S. FORD *Shorty McCabe* iii. 64 The spaghetti works was in full blast, with a lot of husky low-brows goin' in and out. **1907** *Collier's* 30 Mar. 23/2 The overwhelming majority of Low Brows, who never read 'Peer Gynt'. **1914** 'HIGH JINKS, JR.' *Choice Slang* 15 *Low brow*, an uneducated person usually prone to exhibit his deficiencies. **1915** E. WALLACE *Melody of Death* ii. 20 If you only knew how the low-brows are pitying you..you would not be posing for a picture of 'The Ruined Gambler'. **1926** *Glasgow Herald* 13 Mar. 4 The highbrows will be overwhelmed..: the lowbrows will be unmoved. **1927, 1929** [see *broad-brow, broadbrow* (BROAD *a.* D. 2)]. **1935** *Discovery* Sept. 281/1 If we can persuade the lowbrows and free-livers of the present day that there is something heroic, even sporting, in the cultivation of the higher regions of the mind, we shall have won more than half the battle. **1947** [see CLASSICAL *a.* 6 c]. **1953** [see *Aunt Edna* (AUNT 6)]. **1974** *Times* 30 Nov. 8/2 They considered themselves lowbrows and..preferred a rattling good yarn to all that highbrow twaddle.

B. *adj.* Of, pertaining to, or characteristic of a lowbrow; not highly, or not pretentiously, intellectual; unrefined, unæsthetic. Also quasi-*advb.*

1913 H. A. FRANCK *Zone Policeman 88* i. 28 With all its excellences it would be unjust to complain that the Zone 'Y.M.' is a trifle 'low-brow' in its taste. **1914** S. LEWIS *Our Mr. Wrenn* v. 61 You ain't neither too highbrow or too lowbrow. **1923** *Spectator* 22 Sept. 391/2 Often the sole reason why he [*sc.* the man of genius] does not write 'low-brow' is because he cannot. **1928** *Collier's* 10 Nov. 30/1 The doctor who is sufficiently adventurous, or lowbrow, to visit a soda-fountain occasionally. **1934** S. R. NELSON *All about Jazz* i. 24 From the many attempts of our leaders to substitute..'symphonic syncopation', 'modern rhythm', and the like, it is obvious that the much-maligned and obvious 'low-brow' caste of the word has rendered it necessary for us to designate our music with something that is emphatically not—jazz! **1963** [see HIGHBROW, HIGH-BROW B. *adj.*]. **1974** *Country Life* 9 May 1126/2 Another enormous price was the £22,000 paid..for a mid-18th-century print of an actor by Toyonobu;..but, as all the subjects of such prints..seem to me to represent deplorably ham actors, I remain wholly unimpressed. Now I come to think of it, what a low-brow criticism.

absol. **1927** *Daily Express* 7 May 9/6 Our aim will be..to steer a course between the 'highbrow' and the 'low-brow' in music.

So **'lowbrowism**, the condition of being lowbrow; lack of interest in intellectual or æsthetic matters.

1931 A. HUXLEY *Music at Night* 222 The snobbery of culture..has now to wrestle with an organized and active low-browism. **1946** *Amer. Speech* XXI. 121 The Australian dislike of elegance and affectation leads to a general 'low-browism' of expression and a careless enunciation. **1957** R. HOGGART *Uses of Literacy* x. 255 At a time when it is so easy to be led into arrogant low-browism, some retain an idealistic love for 'things of the mind'. **1971** *Listener* 2 Dec. 763/3, I am not at all arguing for a populist lowbrowism.

low-browed, *a.* [f. LOW *a.* + BROW *sb.*¹ + -ED².]

1. Of persons: Having a low brow (see BROW *sb.*¹ 3 and 5). Also *absol.*

1855 J. E. COOKE *Ellie* 71 The man, who was a coarse, low-browed fellow. **1868** BROWNING *Ring & Bk.* VI. 669 A low-browed verger sidled up. **1899** CROCKETT *Kit Kennedy* 305 Dick always had with him now a low-browed, smartly-dressed man. **1905** *McClure's Mag.* May 20/1 Exactly the type of low-browed ruffian and professional thug that they were hiring over there. **1936** G. B. SHAW *Shaw on Theatre* (1958) 251 The simplicity of the lowbrowed.

fig. **1863** I. WILLIAMS *Baptistery* I. viii. (1874) 91 When low-brow'd cares our mighty yearnings balk.

2. *transf.* Of rocks: Beetling. Of a building, doorway, etc.: Having a low entrance; hence, dark, gloomy. The prevailing sense, app. due to Milton's use of the word.

1632 MILTON *L'Allegro* 8 There under..low-brow'd Rocks,..In dark Cimmerian desert ever dwell. **1717** POPE *Eloisa* 244 Low-browed rocks hang nodding o'er the deep. **1810** SCOTT *Lady of L.* VI. xii, They halted by a low-brow'd porch. **1824** MISS MITFORD *Village* Ser. I. 263 The picturesque, low-browed, irregular cottage. **1889** D. C. MURRAY *Danger. Catspaw* 20 He paused before a sombre low-browed little shop.

lowbye, lowce, obs. forms of LOOBY, LOUSE.

Low Church, *a.* and *sb.* [app. deduced from *Low Churchman* (see next) and used attrib. as in *Low Church party*, and then substantively.]

A. *adj.* or *attrib. phrase.* Of, belonging to, or characteristic of Low Churchmen (see next), their principles or practice.

1710 in *Select. fr. Harl. Misc.* (1793) 566 That occasioned the queen to change the low-church ministry. **1711** SWIFT *Examiner* No. 43 ⁋4 To exalt the king's supremacy beyond all precedent, was low-church, Whiggish, and Moderate. **1714** —— *Pres. St. Affairs* Wks. 1755 II. I. 218 Secure in the affections, the principles and the professions of the low-church party. **1867** TROLLOPE *Chron. Barset* II. lxvii. 250 One lady connected with low-church clergymen..was named as a probable successor.

B. *sb.* [orig. short for *Low Church party*, *Low Church principles*.] The party or the principles of Low Churchmen (see next).

1702 *Charac. Church-Man* 15 Having the Imputation of Fanaticism and Low-Church fixt upon them. **1715** MRS. CENTLIVRE *Gotham Election* Wks. 1760 III. 171 *Friendly* [dressed like a Frenchman]..If dese plaguey Low-Church get de Day,—dey vill make it Treason for any one to send der Children to France, Begar. **1751** EARL ORRERY *Remarks Swift* (1752) 24 The chief ministers of that Queen [Anne], whether distinguished under the titles of Whigs or Tories, of High Church or of Low Church. **1841** SHAFTESB. in *Life* ix. (1887) 185 The Low Church, as they are called, will believe and will preach too, that Popery is encouraged and promoted. **1888** C. A. LANE *Notes Eng. Ch. Hist.* II. VI. XXVII. §1. 213 High Church and Low Church agreed in denouncing the heretical bishop [Hoadley].

Hence **Low-'Churchism**, Low-Church principles, doctrine, or practice.

1864 F. OAKELEY *Hist. Notes* 60 The various gradations of Dissent and Low-Churchism.

Low Churchman. [Cf. HIGH CHURCHMAN.] A member of the Church of England holding opinions which give a low place to the authority and claims of the episcopate and priesthood, to the inherent grace of the sacraments, and to matters of ecclesiastical organization, and thus differ relatively little from the opinions held by Protestant Nonconformists.

The term, invented as an antithesis to *High Churchman*, was in the early part of the 18th c. used as equivalent to LATITUDINARIAN. Afterwards it fell into disuse, but was revived in the 19th c., when the designation *High Churchman* had obtained a new currency as applied to those who inclined to the theology and ritual of pre-Reformation times. In this later use, *Low Churchman* has for the most part been viewed as equivalent to EVANGELICAL, and has rarely been applied to members of the Broad Church School.

1702 *Charac. Church-Man* 18 He is for shewing the Low Church Men in their own proper Colours. **1703** DE FOE *Short. Way Peace* Misc. 463 We have had it Printed, with an Assurance I have wondred at, That the moderate Members of the Church of England, call'd Low Church Men, are worse than the Dissenters. **1708** *Phenix* II. Pref. 13 It shows the first rise of that party which were afterwards called Latitudinarians, and are at this day our 'Low-Churchmen'. **1710** H. BEDFORD *Vind. Ch. Eng.* 132 He..is known to be so wretched a low Churchman, as to dispute all the Articles of the Christian Faith. *a* **1715** BURNET *Own Time* (1734) II. 347 All [of the clergy] that treated the Dissenters with temper and moderation..were called Low Churchmen. **1845** BP. WILBERFORCE in A. R. Ashwell *Life* (1879) I. 314 Taking as your prominent subject..Baptismal Regeneration, and its side against Low Churchmen.

Hence **Low-'Churchmanism** = *Low-Churchism.*

1829 [see HIGH-CHURCHMANISM].

low-country.

1. A region or district whose level is lower than that of the surrounding country.

1530 PALSGR. 241/1 Lowe countree, *plat pais.* **1797** *Last Advice of C. Pettigrew to Sons* (MS.) (D.A.E.), You may think it best to sell your possessions in this low country, and to move westwardly. **1823** E. JAMES *Acct. Expedition Rocky Mts.* I. 38 Here commences the low country, which extends west to the Mississippi. **1828** W. CARR *Dial. Craven* (ed. 2) I. 302 *Low-country*, East Riding of Yorkshire, being, in general flat, particularly when contrasted with this mountainous district. **1874** 'H. CHURTON' *Toinette* x. 114 He came from somewhere down in the low country. **1963** R. I. MCDAVID *Mencken's Amer. Lang.* vi. 299 Low Country, especially in the South, denotes the Coastal Plain of South Carolina and Georgia, as distinguished from the Piedmont or Up Country. **1974** *State* (Columbia, S. Carolina) 15 Feb. 17-A/8 Sen. Strom Thurmond, R-S.C., said Thursday arrangements have been made for an additional 1.4 million gallons of gasoline for the South Carolina Low-country.

attrib. **1837** J. R. MCCULLOCH *Statist. Acc. Brit. Empire* II. 54 The webs manufactured in North Wales are.. strong, or high country, cloth, and small, or low country, ditto. **1886** STEVENSON *Kidnapped* 172 You Low-country bodies have no clear idea of what's right and wrong. **1899** *West. Gaz.* 14 Apr. 3/2 On a low-country shooting, which has no house attached to it, a bag of mixed game generally costs at least five shillings a head.

2. a. *pl.* **Low Countries**, the district now forming the kingdoms of Holland and Belgium, and the grand-duchy of Luxembourg.

[*a* **1548** HALL *Chron., Hen. VII* 32 b, To all the cytyes of the Gaule Belgique or lowe countrey.] *a* **1548** *Ibid., Hen. VIII* 136 The lowe countreis, of Brabant, Flaunders, and Zealande. **1592** NASHE *P. Penilesse* 21 b, It would not conuert clubs and clowted shoone from the flesh pots of Egipt, to the Prouant of the Lowe countreyes. **1656–9** B. HARRIS *Parival's Iron Age* 43 The war was.. hot in the Low-Countries. **1858** LONGF. *M. Standish*, etc. Pref., The career of poor but daring spirits in the age of Elizabeth was often sought in the Low Countries. **1887** M. MORRIS *Claverhouse* v. (1888) 80 He had served his apprenticeship to the trade of war in the Low Countries.

b. *attrib.*, quasi-*adj.* Belonging to the Low Countries. In 17th c. often of soldiers: Having served in the Low Countries.

1625 BACON *Ess., Seditions* (Arb.) 407 The Low-Countrey-Men, who haue the best Mines, aboue ground, in the World. **1678** BUTLER *Hud.* III. i. 1440 But I have sent him for a Token To your Low-Countrey Hogen Mogen. **1889** CORBETT *Monk* ii. 15 The plain Low Country officer. **1889** DOYLE *Micah Clarke* 34 Baggy low-country knee-breeches.

3. *S. Afr.* = LOWVELD. Cf. BUSHVELD b.

1879 [see BUSHVELD]. **1929** D. REITZ *Commando* xiv. 126 Our road ran through the Sabi low country teeming with big game of all descriptions. **1930** *Official Year Bk. S. Afr.* No. 11. 18 The Low Country stretches from the Limpopo valley behind the escarpment past the eastern end of Zoutpansberg southwards to meet the South-Eastern region below the escarpment east of Carolina. **1947** J. STEVENSON-HAMILTON *Wild Life S. Afr.* xxiii. 189, I have weighed a good number of low-country leopards immediately after death.

lowd(e, obs. form of LOUD.

lowder ('ludər). *Sc.* and *north.* Also looder. [a. ON. *lúðr* (Norw. *luder, lur*).] **a.** The stand or foundation on which a mill rests. **b.** (Short for *lowder-tree*, which is also in use.) A wooden lever or handspoke used for lifting the millstones; any long, stout rough stick (Eng. Dial. Dict.).

a **1585** MONTGOMERIE *Flyting w. Polwart* 98, I promise thee heere to thy chafts ill cheir, Except thou goe leir to licke at the lowder. *a* **1706** in J. Watson *Collect. Scot. Poems* I. 44 He.. Ran to the Mill and fetcht the Lowder, Wherewith he hit her on the Shou'der. **1881** *Contemp. Rev.* Aug. 190 The cure for this was to throw a fire-brand down the 'lighting-hole' in the 'looder'. **1899** J. SPENCE *Shetland Folk-Lore* 172 In a corner of the looder stood a toyeg.. containing as much corn as would be a hurd o' burstin. **1910** *Old-Lore Misc.* III. i. 9 The table or bin on which the quern stands is called lúðr in Edda and looder in Orkney.

low down, *a.* and *adv.* [f. LOW *a.* and *adv.* + DOWN *adv.*] **a.** Used as a more emphatic synonym for the adj. in predicative use, and for the adv. (Written as two words.) **b.** In attributive use; chiefly *U.S.*, degraded, abject. (Written with hyphen.)

In quot. 1850 in b used in the geographical sense, and in quot. 1908 in a physical sense.

a. 1548 ELYOT *Dict., Demissus*, humble, lowe downe. **1689** LOCKE *Civ. Govt.* II. v. §38 (1694) 194 In that part of the World which was first inhabited,.. even as low down as Abrahams time, they wandred with their Flocks and their Herds.. freely up and down. *a* **1860** J. A. ALEXANDER *Gosp. Jesus Chr.* xv. (1861) 201 They put the date of Messiah's advent too low down. **1870** KINGSLEY in *Gd. Words* 205/2 To see Sirius,.. not, as in our dog-days, low down on the horizon, but riding high in heaven. **1890** L. C. D'OYLE *Notches* 20 They had played it rather low down on the preacher. **1935** [see GROWL *v.*[3] 3]. **1959** 'F. NEWTON' *Jazz Scene* 291 The widespread practice of equating joy with height.. and grief with depth... Thus the quality most desired in the old blues is that it should be *low-down* or *dragging*.

b. 1850 *Congress. Globe* 25 Apr. 821/1 The 'low-down' Virginia Democracy had to yield to the western mountain Democracy. **1865** *Nation* (N.Y.) I. 586 His manners and conversation, showed him to be a good-deal above that class commonly called 'low-down, triflin' people', or poor white trash. **1869** *Overland Monthly* III. 130 There are the delusive 'kettlings', among the 'low-down' people. **1881** CABLE *Mad. Delphine*, etc. 104 It was so much better than he could have expected from his 'low-down' relative. **1882** *Daily Tel.* 24 June, Lucas effected a beautiful low-down catch. **1888** EGGLESTON *Graysons* xviii. 197 Her archaic speech was perhaps a shade better than the 'low-down' language of Broad Run. **1897** MARY KINGSLEY *W. Africa* 158 There is another low-down pigeon domesticated at Talagouga. **1901** *Scribner's Mag.* XXIX. 484/1 Every low-down Neapolitan ice-creamer in the town. **1908** *Sears, Roebuck Catal.* 604/2 The closet.. is a syphon jet bowl with a low down tank and seat. **1915** F. M. HUEFFER *Good Soldier* III. i. 140 Low-down Bowery tough. **1916** 'TAFFRAIL' *Pincher Martin* xii. 214 They considered that Pincher had played them a low-down trick in ignoring their charms and in going elsewhere for an object for his affections. **1928** *Variety* 15 Aug. 49/4 There were as many as 35 or 40 dark-skinned musicians on the stand, kidding around and giving their conception of low-down tunes. **1968** *Blues Unlimited* Sept. 10 John Lee Hooker comes here a lot, an' he plays some really lowdown things.

Hence **low-downer** *U.S.*, a 'poor white' of the southern States.

1871 DE VERE *Americanisms* (1872) 45 [Given as the designation current in North Carolina]. **1883** STEVENSON *Silverado Sq.* 131 They are at least known by a generic by-word, as Poor Whites or Low-downers.

'low-down, *sb. slang* (orig. *U.S.*). [f. the adj. or adv.] The fundamental, though not generally known, facts *on* (about) a person, situation, etc.; the 'inside story'.

1915 *San Francisco Call & Post* 2 Dec. 12 (*caption*) Aw, give us the low down on them, Bill. **1920** *Collier's* 15 May 57/2 He calls me back, and in about twenty minutes I have got the low down on Monsieur Kane Halliday. **1924** WODEHOUSE *Leave it to Psmith* ix. 184 Listen, Ed, while I slip you the low-down. **1930** *Punch* 5 Feb. 144/1 Our own book, Percival and I have decided, is to be called the Low-down on Taxi-drivers. **1930** ADE *Let.* 19 Dec. (1973) 149 You certainly shattered some of my early idols, although I think I had figured out the low-down on most of them before I read your book. **1935** AUDEN & ISHERWOOD *Dog beneath Skin* I. ii. 34 The Old Man sent for me before I left. Wants me to get the low-down on the Dripping merger. **1939** *War Illustr.* 18 Nov. p. ii/3, I have often smiled in recollecting this bit of 'low down' on the exile of Doorn—possibly for the first time here divulged. **1946** R. CAMPBELL *Talking Bronco* 13 To have the low-down from their cross-Fates, Predicting tons of human phosphates Imported here in flesh and bone. **1957** N. MICKLEM *Box & Puppets* v. 102, I was occasionally able to do him some slight service in return by giving him 'the low-down' on theologians about whom he was required to compose orations. **1959** G. JENKINS *Twist of Sand* iv. 73 I'll give the low-down, charts, position, damage and all the rest of it. **1973** M. MACKINTOSH *King & Two Queens* x. 147 One of his minions will.. give me the official low-down on Fisher. Possible police record, etc.

lowe, obs. f. LOW *a.*, LOUGH[2]; obs. pa. t. of LAUGH *v.*; obs. pa. t. and pa. pple. of LIE *v.*[2]

löweite ('lœːvəaɪt). *Min.* [Named, 1846, by Haidinger after A. *Löwe* of Vienna.] Sulphate of magnesium and sodium occurring in yellowish crystalline masses.

1850 DANA *Min.* 678 Löweite is a saline mineral from Ischl. **1885** *Erni's Min.* 278.

†'lower, *sb. Obs.* Forms: 4–5 lower(e, 6 looer. [ad. OF. *louier* reward.] Reward, guerdon, recompense.

c **1330** *Arth. & Merl.* 372 (Kölbing) þurch ous þou art in þi power: 3if ous now our lower! *a* **1400–50** *Alexander* 5368 Ser, if þou lessen my life na lowere þou wynnes. *c* **1450** *Merlin* 59 A knyght axed his body when he was deed vpon the seide crosse, and it was graunted hym of Pilate in lower of his servyse. *a* **1550** *Image Ipocr.* I. in *Skelton's Wks.* (1843) II. 415 Thoughe Christ be the doer, They force not of his looer, They sett therby no stoore.

lower ('ləʊə(r)), *a.* (*sb.*) and *adv.* Forms: 3 **laȝghere, lah(e)re, lahȝhre**, 4 **lagher, law(i)er, logher**, 5 **lougher, louȝer, lowyr**, *Sc.* **lavar, -war**, 4, 7 *Sc.* **lauer**, 4– **lower**. [f. LOW *a.* + -ER[3].]

A. *adj.* The comparative of LOW *a.*

1. As an ordinary comparative (capable of being followed by *than*): see the senses of LOW *a.*

c **1200** ORMIN 2664 þohh wass ȝho miccle lahre, þann ure laffdiȝ Marȝe wass. *Ibid.* 3746 Lasse þann hiss enngell, & lahȝhre inoh. *c* **1230** *Hali Meid.* 36 Hwa-se, of engel, lihteð to iwurðen lahre, þen a beast.. loki hu ha spede! *a* **1300** *Cursor M.* 9467 Sua hei na-thing was euer wroght, þat.. ne moght Fall dun in to lagher [*Gött.* lauer] state. **1375** BARBOUR *Bruce* I. 58 Thai said, successioun of Kyngrik Was nocht to lawer feys lik. **1435** MISYN *Fire of Love* II. i. 69 Qwen tha ar far lawar. **1450–80** tr. *Secreta Secret.* 39 Of whiche lougher men in degre mowe lerne gret.. doctryne. *c* **1460** FORTESCUE *Abs. & Lim. Mon.* xv. (1885) 145 What lower man was þer sytinge in þat counsell, þat [etc.]. *c* **1560** A. SCOTT *Poems* (S.T.S.) xxvi. 40 They wald with nobill men be nemmit, Syne laittandly to lawar leinde. **1667** MILTON *P.L.* IV. 76 And in the lowest deep a lower deep Still threatning to devour me opens wide. **1671** —— *Samson* 1246 Stalking with less unconsci'nable strides, And lower looks. **1740** LD. BALTIMORE in *Gentl. Mag.* X. 586 The Estimate of the Navy.. is lower.. than that which was laid before us the last Session. **1774** T. HUTCHINSON *Diary* 7 Oct., The people of Norfolk are generally of a lower size, and very few tall. **1839** YEOWELL *Anct. Brit. Ch.* vii. (1847) 73 It seems difficult to place their origin at a lower period than the apostolic age. **1849** MACAULAY *Hist. Eng.* iii. I. 294 A small body of grenadier dragoons, who came from a lower class and received lower pay. **1862** TROLLOPE *Orley F.* I. xxxii. 254 Hush-sh-sh. For heaven's sake, Mr. Mason, do be a little lower. **1868** JOYNSON *Metals* 115 The solder, of course, has a much lower fusion point than the metals to be joined. **1873** PRINCESS ALICE in *Mem.* 26 July (1884) 308, I feel lower and sadder than ever. **1895** ZANGWILL *Master* II. ii. 139 Try and keep that lower in tone.

absol. **1869** J. MARTINEAU *Ess.* II. 186 Can the lower create the higher? **1885** TENNYSON *Locksley H. 60 Yrs. after* 124 So the Higher wields the Lower, while the Lower is the Higher.

2. a. Used in contradistinction to UPPER or HIGHER, as the specific designation of an object, a class or group of objects, a part or parts of some whole (with reference either to local situation or to rank, dignity, or place in classification); occas. in partitive concord (= 'the lower part of'), esp. in geographical names.

1590 SIR J. SMYTH *Disc. Weapons* Proëme 16 All higher and lower Officers of Armies under the Generall. **1606** SHAKS. *Ant. & Cl.* III. vi. 10 Lower Syria. **1611** BIBLE *Gen.* vi. 16 With lower, second, and third stories shalt thou make it. **1631** MASSINGER *Beleeve as you list* II. ii, This is the bodye of Antiochus, Kinge of the lower Asia. **1667** MILTON *P.L.* v. 410 Both contain Within them every lower facultie Of sense. **1702** J. PURCELL *Cholick* (1714) 3 The outward Muscles and Skins of the Lower-Belly. **1730** A. GORDON *Maffei's Amphith.* 131 In the lower Ages the Legend on Medals did not often allude to a particular Fact. **1758** J. S. *Le Dran's Observ. Surg.* (1771) 42 The Corner of the Lower-Lip. **1783** BURKE *East India Bill* Wks. IV. 72 The lower sort in the camp it seems could not be restrained. **1831** R. KNOX *Cloquet's Anat.* 101 The Lower Wall or the Floor of the Orbit is nearly plain. **1840** MACAULAY *Ess., Von Ranke* (1843) III. 220 Merchants from the Lower Danube. **1852** H. MARTINEAU *Let.* 7 Apr. in R. K. Webb *H. Martineau* (1960) x. 301 Thinking men & women of the *lower middle*, & working classes. **1861** MILL *Repr. Govt.* iii. 67 A benefit of the same kind.. is produced on Englishmen of the lower middle class by their liability to be placed on juries and to serve parish offices. **1869** BOUTELL *Arms & Arm.* x. 193 The sleeves of the hauberk sometimes were cut short about the middle of the lower arm. **1873** DAWSON *Earth & Man* iii. 36 The Huronian or Lower Cambrian. *Ibid.* iv. 56 The Lower Silurian is the Upper Cambrian of Sedgwick. **1873** HELPS *Anim. & Mast.* i. (1875) 5 The treatment of the lower animals by man. **1881** LADY MONKSWELL *Diary* 26 Apr. in E. C. F. Collier *Victorian Diarist* (1944) 52 Presently an old lady, rather 'lower middle class', with grey hair & no cap, appeared and welcomed us. **1883** *Harper's Mag.* Aug. 448/2 Strong lower-sail winds. **1889** POLLOCK, etc. *Fencing* ii. (Badm. Libr.) 43 There are four lines in fencing; two upper and two lower. **1898** F. T. BULLEN *Cruise Cachalot* iii. (1900) 23 An immense fourfold tackle from the main lowermast-head. **1930** *Archit. Rec.* Feb. 113/1 The wages of the lower income groups will indeed have to be raised. **1937** *Daily Tel.* 15 Oct. 22/5 'American Dream' has many of the hall-marks of a lower-middlebrow best-seller. **1951** M. MCLUHAN *Mech. Bride* (1967) 35/2 Kindly human thoughts such as keep ordinary men in the lower-income brackets. **1968** D. LAWTON *Social Class, Lang. & Educ.* ii. 7 The lower working class consists of groups traditionally outside the educational system. *Ibid.* v. 78 The typical lower working-class environment. **1971** R. ROBERTS *Classic Slum* vii. 105 Before 1914.. lower-working-class men did not generally shave themselves, but patronised a barber twice a week. **1972** A. DAVIDSON tr. *Moravia's Two of Us* I. 10, I was struck by his language, half courtly, half bureaucratic and, in any case, lower middle-class. **1973** *Guardian* 19 Apr. 4/4 Mario Biaggi, probably the most popular candidate for Mayor of New York among the city's lower income white population.

b. Phrase. † *to have the lower hand*: to have lost the superiority; to be second best off.

1693 *Mem. Count Teckely* III. 72 When they have once the lower-hand,.. they no longer distinguish what they do.

3. quasi-*sb.* **a.** One lower; an inferior.

c **1200** ORMIN 10739 Whase laȝheþþ himm Bineþenn his lahȝhre. **1340** *Ayenb.* 175 þe zinne is gratter.. ine ane prelat þanne ine ane loȝer. *c* **1400** *Apol. Loll.* 104 þei are vnfeiþful to þer souereyns, vneuyn to þer lowar. *c* **1450** tr. *De Imitatione* III. xxi. 89 Wheþir he suffre of his prelate or of his piere, or of his lower. **1921** *Chambers's Jrnl.* 30 July 545/1 Appreciation of beauty.. is that which most distinguishes the humans from their lowers. **1967** *Listener* 21 Dec. 802/1 If a man spoke rather loudly.. keeping his vowels open, then he was an Upper. If he attempted this and just failed, then he was a Middle. If.. his voice carried the flavour of the area in which he was born, then he was a Lower.

† b. The lower part or parts *of* (something). *Obs.*

a **1340** HAMPOLE *Psalter* lxii. 9 Into þe lavgher of þe earth.

c. A lower plate of artifical teeth.

1878 C. HUNTER *Mech. Dentistry* i. 7 For edentulous uppers or lowers plaster is employed. **1939** A. THIRKELL *Before Lunch* vi. 162 'And how are the new lowers?'.. Mrs. Pucken smiled broadly with a slightly seasick motion of her lower teeth. **1963** J. OSBORNE *Dental Mech.* (ed. 5) ix. 170 In function there is a tendency for upper dentures to be moved forwards and lowers backwards.

4. Special collocations: **lower-boy**, a boy in the *lower school* (see below); **lower-case** *Printing* (see CASE *sb.*[2] 9); also *attrib.*; **lower chamber** = *lower-house*; **lower classes**, those below the middle rank in society; **lower criticism**, verbal or textual criticism (cf. *higher criticism*, s.v. CRITICISM 2 b); **lower critic**, one who is occupied with lower criticism; **lower deck**, the deck immediately over the hold, orig. only of a ship with two decks; also *attrib.*; **Lower Empire** [= F. *bas empire*], the later Roman Empire (formerly, in numismatic use, from the reign of Gallienus; now usually, from the reign of Constantine, or some still later epoch); **lower fourth, fifth**, etc., the lower division of the fourth, fifth, etc. form in a public school; also *attrib.*; **lower house**, the inferior branch of a legislature consisting of two houses; also of the

convocation of the Church of England; **lower** †**order** or **orders** = *lower classes*; **lower school**, in public schools, usually the forms below the fifth; also *attrib.*; (*the* or *this*) **lower world**, earth as opposed to heaven or the heavenly bodies.

1844 DISRAELI *Coningsby* I. I. viii. 92 The *lower boy or fag,..asked his master whether he had further need of him. **1857** G. A. LAWRENCE *Guy Livingstone* i. 1 A mob of two hundred lower-boys. **1683** MOXON *Mech. Exerc., Printing* xiv. ¶1 The Stem, and other Fat Stroaks of *Lower-Case Roman. **1797** *Encycl. Brit.* (ed. 3) VII. 383/2 The letters of the lower case. **1890** MORRIS in Mackail *Life* (1899) II. 251 The type is getting on: I have all the lower-case letters (26). **1885** LOWE *Bismarck* I. 293 The *Lower Chamber would not yield an inch to the Crown and the Upper House. **1772** (the *lower classes of the people), **1806** (the lower class) [see CLASS *sb.* 2]. **1849** THIRLWALL *Rem.* III. 346 Efforts..to elevate the intellectual condition of the lower classes. **1897** RENDEL HARRIS in *Contemp. Rev.* Sept. 342 Resch is not merely a '*lower critic' busied with readings of the existing Gospels. *Ibid.*, The *Lower Criticism of the New Testament. **1709** *Lond. Gaz.* No. 4521/2 We fired, with the utmost Vigour,..part of our *Lower-deck Guns. **1758** J. BLAKE *Plan Mar. Syst.* 2 The ports of the said lower-deck to be grated on the inside. **1790** BEATSON *Nav. & Mil. Mem.* 246 The lower-deck ports were then opened. **1900** *Westm. Gaz.* 12 Apr. 4/3 Lieutenant..is the highest step to which a lower-deck rating can attain. **1797** *Encycl. Brit.* (ed. 3) VI. 573/2 (*Empire*) The *lower empire comprehends near 1200 years, reckoning [from 260] down to the destruction of Constantinople in 1453. **1857** HUGHES *Tom Brown* I. viii, The driving of this *lower-fourth must have been grievous work. *Ibid.*, He and the other lower-fourth boys. **1579** FULKE *Heskins' Parl.* 50 He..placeth him in the *lower house. **1760–72** H. BROOKE *Fool of Qual.* (1809) IV. 49 Exultation was heard through all the lower house. **1852** BP. WILBERFORCE *Let.* in R. G. Wilberforce *Life* (1881) II. iv. 140 Suppose that..the Lower House [of Convocation] elected another [Prolocutor]. **1862** *Acts Massach.* 254 Lower House. **1869** ROGERS *Hist. Gleanings* Ser. I. 23 Ultimately, however, the Lower House [Commons] conceded the demands of the Upper. **1712** (the *lower Order of Britons), **1749** [see ORDER *sb.* 2]. **1796** G. M. WOODWARD *Eccent. Excurs.* 14 The adjoining skittle-ground is filled with people of the lower order (according to fashionable denomination). **1822** COBBETT *Weekly Reg.* 27 Apr. 196, I will make your Aristocratic insolence bend before the superior mind of the 'Lower Orders'. **1857** T. HUGHES *Tom Brown* I. v, There's nothing like candour for a *lower-school boy. **1593** SHAKS. *Rich. II*, III. ii. 38 The Globe that lights the *lower World. *a* **1599** SPENSER *Mutability* vi. 14 Mean-while the lower World..was darkned quite. **1675** SOUTH *Serm.* (1823) I. 301 All the light and influence that the heavens bestow upon this lower world.

5. *Comb.* **a.** Forming comparatives to the combinations of LOW *a.* (see LOW *a.* IV).

1622 H. SYDENHAM *Serm. Sol. Occ.* II. (1637) 25 Apprehensions lower-roofed. **1851** KINGSLEY *Yeast* xiii. 242 Smaller, clumsier, lower-brained, and weaker-jawed than their elders.

b. With duplication of *lower*: belonging in the lower reaches of a 'lower' class or grade.

1955 T. H. PEAR *Eng. Social Differences* iii. 89 There are few serious impersonations of the lower-lower class. **1970** 'D. CRAIG' *Young Men may Die* ix. 68 We languish at an almost unbelievable and entirely unspeakable lower-lower-middle Costa Blanca resort.

B. *adv.* **a.** The comparative of LOW *adv.*, q.v. ***lower down***: the comparative of LOW DOWN.

a **1548** HALL *Chron., Edw. IV* 209 The kynges shyp..descended lower, before a towne in Holland. **1570** *Satir. Poems Reform.* xiii. 10 Quha that wald the mater vnderstand, He man luke lawer. **1588** SHAKS. *L.L.L.* IV. i. 120 She her selfe is hit lower. *a* **1600** MONTGOMERIE *Misc. Poems* xlviii. 143 Come no lauer. *a* **1635** NAUNTON *Fragm. Reg.* (Arb.) 20 No Prince living..descended lower in presenting her person to the publique view. **1641** J. JACKSON *True Evang. T.* II. 122 Let us continue on the story down lower still. **1648** FAIRFAX, etc. *Remonstrance* 17 Then he fell to play lower. **1715** LEONI *Palladio's Archit.* (1742) I. 80 How it was performed, we shall teach lower in this Book. **1731** P. SHAW *Three Ess. Artif. Philos.* 62 A viscous clammy..Mixture, scarce at all disposed to ferment, before 'tis let down lower with Water. **1771** *Junius Lett.* liv. 288 The lower they are degraded..the more submissively they must depend upon his favour. **1782** COWPER *Truth* 170 Your portion is with them,—nay, never frown, But, if you please, some fathoms lower down. **1838–9** HALLAM *Lit. Europe* II. i. §48 We find not a few editions..:—Cicero de Officiis..1553; Virgil, 1570;..Horace and Juvenal, 1574. It is needless to proceed lower, when they become more frequent. **1878** HUXLEY *Physiogr.* 64 Still farther north [the snow line] reaches yet lower.

b. *Comb.*

1960 F. C. STERN *Chalk Garden* vii. 74 *P[aeonia] obovata alba*..is a lower-growing plant with rather smaller flowers. **1972** *Guardian* 24 Nov. 10/1 Lower-paid hospital workers are resorting to a series of unofficial strikes. **1972** *Times* 24 Nov. 2/7 Incomes standstill blow to lower-paid clergymen. **1975** *Times* 3 Jan. 2/3 Teachers should be looking after their lower-paid colleagues. **1975** *Times* 11 Jan. 7/6 Show a minimum by bidding Two Hearts or a near minimum by bidding Two Diamonds (a lower ranking suit).

lower ('ləʊə(r)), *v.* Also 7 loor, lour, lowre. [f. LOWER *a.*]

1. a. *trans.* To cause or allow to descend, to let down gradually (e.g. a boat, a drawbridge, a thing or person suspended from above); to haul down (a sail, a flag). Also with *away* (Naut.), *down*.

1659 D. PELL *Impr. Sea* 611 Being almost at my desired Port, I will strike and lower down my Fore-top-sail. **1669** STURMY *Mariner's Mag.* I. 17 Loure the Yard, and furl the Sail. **1695** WOODWARD *Nat. Hist. Earth* IV. 198 The Water..sustains these Particles..till..its motion begins to remit,..when by degrees it lowers them. **1762–9** FALCONER *Shipwr.* II. 384 Now down the mast the yard they lower away. **1795** SOUTHEY *Joan of Arc* VII. 548 The foe advance to meet us..look! they lower The bridge! **1821** SCOTT *Pirate* xxxvi, The sloop immediately lowered a boat. **1874** GREEN *Short Hist.* viii. §9. 562 A summons from Blake to lower the Dutch flag was met by the Dutch admiral..with a broadside. **1894** WEYMAN *My Lady Rotha* xiv. 151 My lady..waved adieu to him, and he lowered his great plumed hat to his stirrup. **1895** *Manch. Guard.* 14 Oct. 5/6 The workmen have to be lowered by ropes down the face of the cliff.

b. *absol.* (*Naut.*)

1769 FALCONER *Dict. Marine* (1780), *Lower handsomely!* and *lower cheerly!* are opposed to each other, the former being the order to lower gradually, and the latter to lower expeditiously. **1842** BARHAM *Ingol. Leg.* Ser. II. *Smuggler's Leap*, Now lower away, come lower away! We must be far ere the dawn of the day. **1898** F. T. BULLEN *Cruise Cachalot* iii. (1900) 21 We lowered and left the ship.

c. *trans.* To make lower, diminish the height of.

1858 LARDNER *Hand-bk. Nat. Phil., Hydrostatics* etc. 33 The water escapes..until the level of C has been lowered to that of B. **1870** F. R. WILSON *Ch. Lindisf.* 103 The bell-cot..had been lowered to the porch.

d. *Wood-engraving.* To remove by cutting or scraping, or to depress (the surface of a block).

1839 CHATTO *Wood Engraving* ix. (1861) 586 The part which appears white in A [should be] lowered out. **1849** *Chambers's Inform.* II. 723/1 If lowered, the designs will require to be re-sketched on the wood.

e. To drink (beer or other liquor); to empty (a bottle or glass of liquor) by drinking. *colloq.*

1895 *Punch* 27 July 39/1 If you'd just seen me lower the beer. **1899** C. ROOK *Hooligan Nights* iv. 63 Out comes a bloke wiv a razzo like 'arf a boiled beetroot... Looked as if you wouldn't like to pay for the 'arf of what 'e could lower. **1920** 'SAPPER' *Bull-Dog Drummond* ii. 64 During the time that he took to drink a mild nightcap, Mr. Benton succeeded in lowering three extremely strong glasses of spirit. **1933** A. G. MACDONELL *England, their England* vii. 113 The gallant Major..had already lowered a quart and a half of mild-and-bitter. **1962** 'L. GREX' *Terror wears Smile* ix. 143 He could lower a whole bottle of three-star brandy without batting an eye. **1974** P. LOVESEY *Invitation to Dynamite Party* v. 56 He's more accustomed to lowering pints than lifting weights.

f. ***to lower the boom***: to inflict a physical defeat *on* (someone), to treat someone severely, to put a stop to an activity. *N. Amer. slang.*

1950 *Western Folklore* Apr. 118 *Lower the boom.* In a fight, to knock out your adversary with one punch. 'I sure lowered the boom on him. He had to take down his pants to blow his nose.' **1951** *New Yorker* 30 June 21/1 Just as they were about to pawn my studs.., my patience evaporated and I lowered the boom on them. **1963** J. N. HARRIS *Weird World Wes Beattie* (1964) xv. 186 Wes had been borrowing from everybody and his brother, and the boys had lowered the boom on him. **1973** *Times* 14 July 5 Senator Inouye asked if President Nixon's actions, after being told all by Mr Dean, could be considered as 'lowering the boom'—the phrase used by the former Attorney General, Mr John Mitchell, in his testimony this week.

2. a. *intr.* To descend, sink (also *fig.*); † to cower, crouch (*obs.*). Often with *down.* Also *Naut.* of a yard: To admit of being let down.

1606 SHAKS. *Ant. & Cl.* I. ii. 129 The present pleasure, By reuolution lowring, does become The opposite of it selfe. **1680** HICKERINGILL *Meroz* Wks. 1716 I. 240 For the Crown to Veil and Lower to the Stool of Repentance, Oh abominable and Vile! **1720** T. GORDON *Humourist* I. 92 The brute Part of the Creation are affected by the Turns of Weather; the Deer, we say, runs to Covert, the Bird lowers. **1727** *Philip Quarll* (1816) 38 The main yard could not lower. **1799** J. ROBERTSON *Agric. Perth* 323 When snow is falling..the shepherds drive their flocks..round the top of a hill in a circle, to keep them from lowring and being smothered. **1806** H. SIDDONS *Maid, Wife, & Widow* I. 146, I immediately lowered down and hid myself among some shrubs. **1852** DICKENS *Bleak Ho.* i, Smoke lowering down from chimney-pots.

b. To slope downwards.

1813 SOUTHEY *Nelson* II. 104 To the north of Helsinburg the shores are steep and rocky; they lower to the south. **1875** LYELL *Princ. Geol.* I. II. xxv. 638 The top of the escarpment where it lowers towards Ottajano.

†**c.** *trans.* To descend (a hill). *Obs.*

1780 A. YOUNG *Tour Irel.* I. 133 Lowering the hill the scenery is yet more agreeable.

3. a. *trans.* To diminish in amount, price, proportion, etc. **b.** *intr.* To become lower in price.

a. 1690 CHILD *Disc. Trade* Pref. (A) 7 b, Some People..may..not know it is for their Advantage to lower their Interest. **1729** SWIFT *Intelligencer* No. 19 ¶5 The Value of Guineas was lowered in England from 21*s.* 6*d.* to only 21*s.* **1765** BLACKSTONE *Comm.* I. 172 The value of money is very considerably lowered since the bishop wrote. **1823** BYRON *Age of Bronze* xiv, Did the tyrant..lower wheat? **1833** HT. MARTINEAU *Manch. Strike* i. 3, I suppose your wages are lowered. **1886** EARL SPENCER *Speech at Leeds* 3 May, They lowered the rents.

b. 1697 *First Cent. Hist. Springfield* (1899) II. 347 Soe soon as that grain vizt Indian Corne lowers of the abovesaid price..then [etc.]. **1823** *Examiner* 448/2 Meat will lower in price. **1891** *Daily News* 13 June 5/5 Poultry is gradually lowering in price.

4. a. To make lower in quality or degree; to lessen the intensity or elevation of.

1780 MAD. D'ARBLAY *Diary* 6 Dec., My illness..alone never yet lowered my spirits as they are now lowered. **1818** JAS. MILL *Brit. India* II. v. vii. 623 The Mahratta government..might have been induced to lower its tone. **1834** LISTER *Anne Grey* xxvi. II. 115 Lowering his voice so that she alone could hear. **1860** TYNDALL *Glac.* I. vi. 46 The light of both is lowered in the same proportion. **1887** RUSKIN *Præterita* II. 193 In washing, the Chiaroscuro is lowered from the high lights..to the middle tones. **1899** *Allbutt's Syst. Med.* VII. 629 Another time-honoured fashion of lowering intracranial tension is by purgatives.

†**b.** To reduce the strength or quality of (a liquid, the air); to dilute *with* (water, etc.). *Obs.*

1731 P. SHAW *Three Ess. Artif. Philos.* 145 This Art of purifying Arracs with Milk, were tolerable, if they did not, at the same time, lower them with Water also. **1753** CHAMBERS *Cycl. Supp.*, Lowering a sample [of spirits] to the proof strength. **1771** SMOLLETT *Humph. Cl.* 8 June, Milk..lowered with hot water. **1793** BEDDOES *Lett. Darwin* 39 It would be more advantageous to lower the atmospheric air with hydrogene than with azotic air. **1809** MALKIN *Gil Blas* II. i. ¶5 [She made] him take a good draught of wine, a little lowered at proper intervals. **1844** DICKENS *Mart. Chuz.* ix, Wot do you go a lowerin' the table-beer for then?

c. *Mus.* To depress in pitch, to flatten.

1889 E. PROUT *Harmony* (ed. 10) xvii. §448 If we take the second inversion of a chord of the seventh..and lower the bass note a chromatic semitone, we shall obtain a new combination.

d. *intr.* To become lower in intensity.

1818 SCOTT *Hrt. Midl.* vii, The lurid light, which had filled the apartment, lowered and died away.

e. *Phonetics.* To replace (a sound) with an allophone or phoneme of lower tongue position (Webster).

1888 H. SWEET *Hist. Eng. Sounds* 21 In diphthongs of the (ij)-type there is a tendency to make the cleaving more distinct to the ear by divergence, the first element being lowered and retracted. **1927** E. V. GORDON *Introd. Old Norse* IV. ii. 255 Neither *i* nor *u* was lowered if *i* or *j* stood in the next syllable. **1959** A. CAMPBELL *Old Eng. Gram.* 122, *ǣ* had been unrounded to *ē*, and *ȳ* unrounded and lowered to *ē*.

5. a. *trans.* To bring down in rank, station, or estimation; to degrade, dishonour. Const. *to.*

1771 *Junius Lett.* liv. 282 His letter has lowered him in my opinion. **1774** J. BRYANT *Mythol.* II. 65 The history of Persius had been greatly misapplied and lowered, by being inserted among the fables of Greece. **1827** LYTTON *Pelham* iv, In marriage a man lowers a woman to his own rank. **1849** MACAULAY *Hist. Eng.* vi. II. 75 What had passed must have had the effect of raising his own Church in his esteem, and of lowering the Church of England. **1859** TENNYSON *Enid* 347 Turn, Fortune, turn thy wheel and lower the proud. **1882** JEAN WATSON *Life A. Thomson* iii. 44 Lowering his character as a minister of the Gospel.

b. *intr.* for *refl.*

1842 TENNYSON *Locksley Hall* 45 Thou shalt lower to his level day by day.

6. *trans.* To bring down to a lower position on a graduated scale.

1860 TYNDALL *Glac.* II. xxi. 344 To lower the melting point of the Montanvert ice. **1871** B. STEWART *Heat* §98 It is possible to lower the freezing point by various means.

lower: see LOUR *v.*; obs. form of LOUVER.

lowerable ('ləʊərəb(ə)l), *a.* [f. LOWER *v.* + -ABLE.] Capable of being lowered.

1889 H. M. DOUGHTY *Friesland Meres* 230 Top-masts lowerable under bridges.

lowerd, lowere, obs. ff. of LORD, LOUVER.

lowered ('ləʊəd), *ppl. a.* [f. LOWER *v.* + -ED[1].] In various senses of the vb. In *Her.*, of an ordinary: = ABASED 2.

1707 E. SMITH *Phædrus & Hipp.* III. 31 The suppliant Nations..with lower'd Sails Confess the Ocean's Queen. **1826** SCOTT *Jrnl.* 8 June, The affectionate care that used to be ready, with lowered voice and stealthy pace, to smooth the pillow. **1828–40** BERRY *Encycl. Herald.* I, *Lowered.* **1839** CHATTO *Wood Engraving* ix. (1861) 614 When lowered blocks are printed at a common press, it is necessary that [etc.]. **1847** *Gloss. Heraldry*, *Lowered*: see *Abased.* **1860** GEO. ELIOT *Mill on Floss* III. 167 A great tear fell from under her lowered eyelids. **1869** E. A. PARKES *Pract. Hygiene* (ed. 3) 63 A general lowered state of health among the population. **1877** SWEET *Handbk. Phonetics* 12 The intermediate heights are distinguished as 'lowered' and 'raised', thus the 'lowered high-front' has a position below the 'high-front'.

lowerer ('ləʊərə(r)). [f. LOWER *v.* + -ER[1].] One who or something which lowers.

1890 SWEET *Primer Phonetics* 15 Intermediate positions between the nine cardinal ones are marked by diacritics: ⊥ 'raiser', ⊤ 'lowerer'..⊣ ⊤ 'backward lowerer'.

lowering ('ləʊərɪŋ), *vbl. sb.* [f. LOWER *v.* + -ING[1].] The action of LOWER *v.* in various senses.

1669 STURMY *Mariner's Mag.* I. 16 Such indifferent things as..hoising, looring, and the like. **1671** F. PHILLIPS *Reg. Necess.* 15 A striking or louring of Sail by the Ships of other Nations. **1753** CHAMBERS *Cycl. Supp.*, *Lowering*,..the debasing of the strength of any spirituous liquor by mixing water with it. **1868** LOCKYER *Guillemin's Heavens* (ed. 3) 193 The lowering of the temperature in February and May. **1890** 'ROLF BOLDREWOOD' *Col. Reformer* (1891) 171 A continuous course of baiting, lowering and hauling up. **1899** *Allbutt's Syst. Med.* VIII. 556 A previous lowering of vitality may usher it [psoriasis] in.

lowering ('ləʊərɪŋ), *ppl. a.* [f. LOWER *v.* + -ING[2].] That lowers, in senses of the vb.

1895 *Daily News* 3 June 7/2 The felt branches continue dull, at lowering prices. **1899** GRIFFITH-JONES *Ascent thro. Christ* I. iii. 120 There are lowering influences in the environment.

lowering: see LOURING.

†**'lowermore,** *a. Obs.* [f. LOWER *a.* + MORE *adv.*, after next.] = LOWER *a.*

1668 CULPEPPER & COLE *Barthol. Anat.* I. xxviii. 69 The lowermore round ligament of the Womb. *Ibid.* II. iv. 93.

lowermost ('ləʊəməʊst), *a.* [f. LOWER *a.* + -MOST.] = LOWEST *a.* (Cf. HIGHERMOST.)
1561 T. HOBY tr. *Castiglione's Courtyer* IV. (1577) X iv a, The Sunne..in winter season draweth to the lowermost signe. **1669** STURMY *Mariner's Mag.* v. xii. 71 As you may see by the Figure out of the lowermost Gun of the Castle. **1759** *Ann. Reg.* 74 The lowermost mast would likewise have gone, had not the weather proved fine. **1899** *Allbutt's Syst. Med.* VII. 295 The lowermost extremity of the ascending frontal convolution.

lowery: see LOURY.

lowest ('ləʊɪst), *a.* (*sb.*) and *adv.* Forms: 3 *Orm.* laȝhesst, 4 lauest, louwest, 5 lagh-, lau-, law-, lowist, -yst, 5–6 lawest, *Sc.* -ast, 6 *Sc.* leuchest, 3- lowest. [f. LOW *a.* + -EST.]
A. *adj.* **1. a.** The superlative of LOW *a.* in its various senses.
c **1200** ORMIN 15276 Þiss follc iss laȝhesst. **1297** R. GLOUC. (Rolls) 2437 Þe mone lowest is. *a* **1300–1400** *Cursor M.* 357 (Gött.) Þe lauest [*Cott.* neþermast] Þan es water and erde. **1362** LANGL. *P. Pl.* A. I. 115 Lucifer louwest liȝth of hem alle. **1435** MISYN *Fire of Love* I. iv. 8 Slyke soþly ar moste haly, & ȝit of men ar haldyn laghyst. *a* **1548** HALL *Chron., Hen. V.* 33 b, The lowest sorte of the vile and rusticall people. *a* **1578** LINDESAY (Pitscottie) *Chron. Scot.* (S.T.S.) II. 89, I sall mak..the hiest stone the leuchest. **1602** SHAKS. *Ham.* III. ii. 383 You would sound mee from my lowest Note to the top of my Compasse. **1681** FLAVEL *Right Man's Refuge* 179 When things have been brought to the lowest ebb. **1780** COWPER *Table T.* 419 Perjury..Sells oaths by tale and at the lowest price. **1860** TYNDALL *Glac.* II. iii. 247 The lowest atmospheric strata. **1862** *Building News* 23 May 1/2 The Board do not bind themselves to accept the lowest or any Tender. **1900** J. G. FRAZER *Pausanias*, etc. 46 The lowest fetish-worshippers of Western Africa.
b. In partitive concord: The lowest part of. *poet.*
1596 SPENSER *F.Q.* V. v. 2 But, when she list, it raught Downe to her lowest heele. **1611** BIBLE *Ps.* lxxxvi. 13. **1667** MILTON *P.L.* II. 882 That the lowest bottom shook Of Erebus.
2. *Comb.* Forming superlatives to the combinations of LOW *a.*
a **1640** EARL STIRLING *Anacrisis* in *Wks. of Drumm. of Hawth.* (1711) 160 In a more abject manner than the lowest minded man could have descended to conceive.
B. *absol.* or as *sb.* **1.** The lowest part, position or pitch. *Obs.* exc. with *at.*
a **1225** *St. Marher.* 14 Þe engles..Þe seoð ham lihten swa lah of so swiðe heh, from Þe heste in heouene to Þe laheste in helle. **1388** WYCLIF *Matt.* xxvii. 51 And lo! the veil of the temple was to-rent in twey parties, fro the hiest to the lowest. *c* **1450** tr. *De Imitatione* II. x. 53 Put Þe euer atte lowist, and Þe hyest shal be ȝoven to Þe; for Þe hiest may not stonde wiÞoute Þe lowist. **1640** tr. *Verdere's Rom. of Rom.* III. xxxvii. 156 When a man thinks them at the lowest of the wheele, hee shall be sure to find them on the top. **1659** HAMMOND *On Ps.* cvii. 39–41 Paraphr. 546 Just when they are brought to the lowest. **1860** MILL *Repr. Govt.* (1865) 140/1 Men who had been brought up to their duties, and had fulfilled them for many years, at lowest without disgrace. **1897** C. HEADLAM *Sel. Brit. Satirists* 64 When taste was almost at its lowest in England.
2. He who or that which is lowest.
1785 COWPER *Task* IV. 588 The rich, and they that have an arm to check The licence of the lowest in degree. **1830** R. HARDIE *Hoyle made Familiar* 62 [*Cassino.*] When three persons play..the two lowest subtract their points from the highest. **1843** PUSEY *Serm. Holy Euch.* 15 Lowest is joined on with highest, earth with heaven..man with God.
C. *adv.* The superlative of LOW *adv.* in its various senses; also in *Comb.*
1390 GOWER *Conf.* I. 65 Whanne he berth lowest the Seil, Thanne is he swiftest to beguile The womman. **1759** HUME *Hist. Eng.* (1834) III. xxiii. 231 The period in which the people of Christendom were the lowest sunk in ignorance. **1834** *Tait's Mag.* I. 725/1 In 1799 the salary of our lowest-paid Judges was £1000. **1926** *Daily Chron.* 13 May 1/7 Any such agreement should..not adversely affect in any way the wages of the lowest-paid men. **1974** *Guardian* 24 Jan. 4/3 His scheme would help the lowest paid. **1975** *Times* 8 Mar. 7/7 East..invited a switch to the lowest-ranking suit.

Lowestoft ('ləʊstɒft). The name of a town in Suffolk, used *attrib.* or *ellipt.* to denote a soft-paste porcelain made from 1757.
1790 E. GILLINGWATER *Hist. Acct. Lowestoft* ix. 423 It was agreed upon to open a subscription..in order to raise a sum sufficient for building a man of war..on which occasion the town of Lowestoft subscribed as follows:—Mr Walker, for the proprietors of the Lowestoft porcelain manufactory £10 10s. 0d. **1875** L. TROUBRIDGE *Life amongst Troubridges* (1966) 106 Two pretty old Lowestoft bowls. *Ibid.* 9 June 120 In the windows was a most beautiful tea-set of old blue Lowestoft. **1912** C. MACKENZIE *Carnival* xviii. 181 'But what a terrible teapot.'..'It's old Lowestoft.' **1968** R. H. R. SMITHIES *Shoplifter* (1969) 8 A small irregular pair of Georgian silver candlesticks flanked a bowl of armorial Lowestoft..the gold tracery glittering against the ultramarine glaze and the creamy porcelain. **1974** *Country Life* 6 June 1517/2 Rare Lowestoft coffee pot..circa 1776.

loweth, lowey, var. ff. LOWTH *Obs.*, LOWY.

lowffe, obs. form of LUFF.

†**'lowffing,** *vbl. sb. Obs. rare*$^{-1}$. [Cf. 'Luff or Lough, a Light or Flame, to Fowl with a Low-Bell' (Phillips, ed. Kersey, 1706).] ? = LOWBELLING.
1581 *Act 23 Eliz.* c. 10 § 1 No maner of..persons..shal..take, kill, or destroye any Fesauntes or Parteridges, with any maner of Nettes, Snares, Ginnes, Enginnes, Rowsting, Lowffing or other deuices whatsoeuer, in the night time.

low 'frequency. [f. LOW *a.* + FREQUENCY 4.]
1. a. A frequency (see FREQUENCY 4 b) having a relatively small number of cycles in a second; applied esp. to an electric current or voltage, an electromagnetic wave, or a sound wave. Abbrev. *L.F.*, esp. in radio and telecommunications, where it also refers specifically to electromagnetic waves of 30–300 kilohertz.
1900 M. A. OUDIN *Stand. Polyphase Apparatus* xiv. 242 Transmissions of power are accomplished at a comparatively low frequency. **1928** *Daily Mail* 25 July 18/1 The best Gramophone and Wireless Sets at present in use fail to reproduce the low-frequency of bass notes in anything like proper proportion. **1933** *B.B.C. Year-Bk.* 384 Actually the microphone responds from very low frequencies up to about 8000 cycles per second. **1934** [see HIGH FREQUENCY 1 a]. **1943** C. L. BOLTZ *Basic Radio* vii. 121 In considering an imaginary capacitance, that of a tumbler switch,..we judged its capacitance in thousandths of a $\mu\mu$F. At low frequencies the reactance of such a switch is in perhaps millions of megohms. **1960** H. CARTER *Dict. Electronics* 169 *Low frequency.* (1) A relative term used to distinguish waves or oscillations of a particular frequency or band of frequencies from those of higher frequencies. (2) More specifically applied to radio waves of frequencies between 30 and 300 kc/s, corresponding to the long wave range. (3) The term is also loosely applied to the audio-frequency signals in a radio receiver to distinguish them from the 'high frequency', i.e. the radio- and intermediate-frequency signals. **1962** A. NISBETT *Technique Sound Studio* iv. 78 The second harmonic [of the mains frequency] is generally the most serious component [of hum] except in certain types of hi-fi loudspeaker cabinet which provide a high output at low frequencies.
b. A low rate of occurrence, in space or time.
1935 [see HIGH FREQUENCY 1 b].
2. *attrib.* (usu. with hyphen).
a. In sense 1 a.
1900 *Engineering* 28 Sept. 412/3 Low frequency induction telegraphy experiments..were not considered in this report. **1920** H. M. DOWSETT *Wireless Telegr.* v. 118 Low-frequency amplification is the process applied to the signal current after its form has been altered by rectification so that it can affect a telephone. **1923** *Radio Times* 28 Sept. 36 Its volume is limited only by the amount of low frequency amplification employed in the receiving set. **1926** J. S. HUXLEY *Ess. Pop. Sci.* xvii. 191 The special sense-organs for perceiving low-frequency vibrations in water which, like a herring or any other fish, it [*sc.* the tadpole] carries on a 'lateral line' along its flank. **1934** *B.B.C. Year-Bk.* 385 The output from the microphone is taken to a two-stage low-frequency amplifier. **1941** *Electronic Engin.* XIV. 404 Low frequency response is expressed in the form of a curve showing variation in power output at different frequencies. **1964** W. JASSEM in D. Abercrombie et al. *Daniel Jones* 344 The level of this low-frequency noise in the spectrum is 20–25 db below the peak at the higher frequencies. **1973** BOYD & PARKES *Dark Number* viii. 83 Some stimuli are so reverberant they just hum on as a low-frequency signal programmed into your unconscious.
b. In sense 1 b: occurring rarely, involving relatively few instances.
1957 *Publ. Amer. Dial. Soc.* XXVIII. 78 Low-frequency verbs like *asseverate, reiterate, aver*, etc.,..would rarely be initials without *that*, or parenthetically. **1963** ERVIN & MILLER in J. A. Fishman *Readings Sociol. of Lang.* (1968) 79 The evidence..reveals a high degree of similarity in the existence of such sequences of high-frequency and low-frequency items. **1971** *Brit. Med. Bull.* XXVII. 19/1 Much of the risk to people from tribes where the frequency [of cancer of the penis] is high is lost when they move to low-frequency areas.

lowgh, var. LOUGH^1, *Obs.*; obs. f. LOW *v.*^{4}

lowgit, obs. form of LUGGED *ppl. a.*^{2}

low-grade, *a.* [LOW *a.* 20.] **a.** Of low or inferior quality.
1878 [see HIGH-GRADE *a.*]. **1879** H. GEORGE *Progr. & Pov.* III. vi. (1881) 191 It is not low wages which will cause the working of low-grade ore. **1899** *Jrnl. R. Agric. Soc.* Mar. 133 Maize flour of a low-grade quality has taken the place of low-grade wheaten flour in the manufacture of boots. **1926** J. S. HUXLEY *Ess. Pop. Sci.* iv. 39 If the good types are now crossed together, a stock will be produced..not containing harmful recessive factors and therefore not continually producing a certain proportion of low-grade individuals. **1940** J. H. JAGGER *English in Future* i. 12 Low-grade mental vocabularies consist of the auxiliary words common to all of us. *a* **1963** L. MACNEICE *Astrol.* (1964) ii. 46 The Moon is especially responsible for rather low-grade persons. **1964** *Ann. Reg. 1963* 389 Going on from this, scientists found strains of bacteria which throve on the normally poisonous metal copper, and began research into the possibility of pumping solutions of such bacteria into cracks in rocks above low-grade copper ore. **1974** E. MCGIRR *Murderous Journey* 39 A cheap low-grade snooper.
b. Not high in amount or degree of intensity. Cf. LOW *a.* 9.
1940 A. HUXLEY *Let.* 24 Apr. (1969) 452 There seems to be some kind of long-standing low-grade infection at work. **1950** A. L. ROWSE *England of Elizabeth* p. viii, The accumulation of capital then—as against its erosion in a low-grade consumption now. **1961** *Lancet* 19 Aug. 402/2 Because of continuing low-grade colonic obstruction,..the left colon was excised.

lowh, obs. pa. t. of LAUGH.

low-headed, *a.* [LOW *a.* 21.] **a.** Of trees: having a low crown of foliage.
1861 *Trans. Illinois Agric. Soc.* IV. 328 Plant dwarf, or dwarfed, low-headed cherries, only. **1869** *Rep. Comm. Agric. 1868* (U.S. Dept. Agric.) 201 The silk tree (*Albizzia julibrissin*) is a low-headed, spreading tree, possessed of the most graceful foliage.
b. *transf.* Favouring low-headed trees.
1865 *Trans. Illinois Agric. Soc.* V. 205 We have never..been identified with the ultra low headed orchardists.
c. Of animals: carrying their heads low.
1932 W. FAULKNER *Light in August* xiv. 311 The low-headed and eager dogs..began to bay.

lowie: see LOWY.

löwigite ('lœːvɪgaɪt). *Min.* [Named, 1861, by Mitscherlich after K. J. *Löwig*, who first analysed it.] Hydrous sulphate of aluminium and potassium, found in yellowish nodules (A. H. Chester).
1862 *Amer. Jrnl. Sci.* XXXIV. 215 Löwigite..the variety of alunite analysed by Löwig. **1892** DANA *Min.* 976.

†**lowing,** *vbl. sb.*^{1} *Obs.* [f. LOW *v.*^{1} + -ING^1.] The action of LOW *v.*^{1}; descent; obeisance; humiliation, etc.
c **1394** *P. Pl. Crede* 508 He loueth in markettes ben met WiÞ..lowynge of lewed men. **1398** TREVISA *Barth. De P.R.* IX. viii. (1495) y vj, Wynter bygynnyth whan the sonne is in ..Capricornus, and is ende of discencyon and the lowynge of the sonne in yᵉ myddaye. *c* **1440** HYLTON *Scala Perf.* (W. de W. 1494) II. xxvi, The nether clowde is downe puttyng and a lowenge of his euencristen.

†**lowing,** *vbl. sb.*^{2} *Obs.* [f. LOW *v.*^{2} + -ING^1.] The action of LOW *v.*^{2}; flaming.
c **1440** *Promp. Parv.* 315/2 Lowynge, or lemynge of fyyr, *flammacio.*

†**lowing,** *vbl. sb.*^{3} *Obs.* [f. LOW *v.*^{3} + -ING^1.] The action of LOW *v.*^{3}; *concr.* an allowance.
1533 *Burgh Rec. Edin.* (1871) II. 64 And has na lowing to vphald the samyn..bot oure ouklie penny gaderyt amangis the brether of the said craft. **1607** [see LOW *v.*^{3} 2].

lowing ('ləʊɪŋ), *vbl. sb.*^{4} [f. LOW *v.*^{4} + -ING^1.] The action of LOW *v.*^{4}; the mooing of cattle; also *transf.*
a **1225** *Leg. Kath.* 144 Lowinge of Þæt ahte, ludinge of Þe men. *c* **1440** *Promp. Parv.* 315/2 Lowynge, or cryynge of nette, *mugitus.* **1579** A. M[UNDAY] *Captiv. J. Fox* in Hakluyt *Voy.* (1589) 153 Amongst the Turkes was one..who..fell off from the toppe of the prison wall, and made such a lowing that the inhabitants..came and dawed him. **1610** SHAKS. *Temp.* IV. i. 179 Calfe-like, they my lowing follow'd. **1794** WORDSW. *Guilt & Sorrow* lviii, Melancholy lowings intervene Of scattered herds. **1848** DICKENS *Dombey* v, Here Miss Nipper made a horrible lowing. **1876** A. LAING *Lindores Abb.* etc. xxiv. 309 The blowing of his horn, and the lowing of his charge.

lowing ('ləʊɪŋ), *ppl. a.*^{1} Now *dial.* [f. LOW *v.*^{2} + -ING^2.] Burning, flaming, flashing.
13.. *Gaw. & Gr. Knt.* 679 A lowande leder of ledez in londe hym wel semez. **1721** RAMSAY *Horace to Virgil* iii, Prometheus..staw A lowan coal frae heav'n's high ha'. **1785** BURNS *Holy Fair* xxii, A vast, unbottom'd, boundless pit, Fill'd fou o' lowin brunstane. **1852** A. ROBB *Poems & Songs* 123 Dearest, return The lowin' love I hae for you.

lowing ('ləʊɪŋ), *ppl. a.*^{2} [f. LOW *v.*^{4} + -ING^2.] That lows, as cattle do.
1382 WYCLIF *Wisd.* xvii. 18 The stronge vois of loowende bestes. **1616** B. JONSON *Forest, To Sir R. Wroth* 16 'Mongst loughing heards. **1750** GRAY *Elegy* 2 The lowing Herd winds slowly o'er the Lea. **1882** *W. Worc. Gloss.*, (*Proverbs*) A lowing cow soon forgets her calf.

lowing, variant of LOYN *Obs.*

lowins, var. LOW WINES.

lowis, obs. f. LOOSE.

lowish ('ləʊɪʃ), *a.* [f. LOW *a.* + -ISH.] Somewhat low. Also in *comb.*
1689 *Lond. Gaz.* No. 2476/4 Taken..from two Gentlemen,..a grey gelding.., lowish back'd [etc.]. **1741** RICHARDSON *Pamela* I. 81 Money runs a little lowish, after what I have laid out. **1886** MRS. RANDOLPH *Mostly Fools* I. iii. 64 The boy found his level..—a lowish one.

lowk(e, variant of LOUK *v.*^{1} *Obs.* and *v.*^{2}

lowland ('ləʊlənd), *sb.* and *a.* Also 6–9 **lawland,** 8 **lawlin,** 9 **laighland, lawlant.** Also LALLAN. [f. LOW *a.* + LAND.] **A.** *sb.*
1. Low or level land; land which is on a lower level than the adjoining districts. Usually *pl.*
sing. **1841** THOREAU *Jrnl.* 8 Feb. in *Writings* (1906) VII. 207 Upland and lowland, forest and field have been ransacked. **1843** *Knickerbocker* XXII. 5 Everywhere, in lowland and highland,..nothing is more evident than the..degradation of the negro. **1855** KINGSLEY *Heroes, Theseus* II. 205 The lowland grew blue beneath his feet. **1885** BIBLE (R.V.) *Jer.* xxxiii. 13 In the cities of the lowland.
pl. **1693** DRYDEN *Ovid's Met.* I. Poems 1743 II. 176 No Nat'ral Cause she found from Brooks, or Bogs, Or marshy Lowlands, to produce the Fogs. **1725** DE FOE *Voy. round World* (1840) 266 So high above the valley that it looked like the lowlands in England do below Box Hill in Surrey. **1870** YEATS *Nat. Hist. Comm.* 106 The central lowlands must be the coldest part of North America.
fig. **1864** LOWELL *Fireside Trav.* 118 The lowlands and levels of ordinary palaver.
2. *spec.* **a.** (Now always *pl.*) The less mountainous region of Scotland, situated south and east of the Highlands.
1631 in *Thanes of Cawdor* (Spalding Club) 273 The necessitie of his advis doeth ofttymes invite him to the

lowlandis. *a* 1687 PETTY *Pol. Arith.* iv. (1691) 69 Whether England and the Low-Lands of Scotland, can maintain a fifth part more People than they now do..the said Territories of England, and the Low-Land of Scotland, contain about Thirty Six Millions of Acres. *c* 1730 BURT *Lett. N. Scotl.* (1818) I. 37 The Kirk..distinguishes the Lowlands from the Highlands by the language generally spoken by the inhabitants. 1822 GALT *Provost* xiii. 98 Mr. Keg..had come in from the Laighlands..to live among us. 1938 DUKE OF MONTROSE in R. Bain *Clans & Tartans* 11 The Tartan as a dress properly belongs to the Highlands, and not to the Lowlands. 1961 C. R. MACKINNON *Highlands in Hist.* 95 Montrose had mustered his army at Blair Atholl, and decided to open his campaign in the Lowlands in order to encourage the king's supporters in the south.

b. *pl.* The Low Countries.

c 1685 in *Roxburghe Ballads* (Ballad Soc.) (1887) VI. II. 421 And it is called the Sweet Trinity, And was taken by the false Gallaly, sailing in the Low-lands. 1923 G. B. HARRISON *Shakespeare's Fellows* iii. 100 Between his service in the Lowlands and the success of *Every Man in his Humour*, 1598, he had tried acting. 1961 T. HENROT *Belgium* 28 Some fifteen Spanish grandees were named successively governors of the Spanish Low Lands.

3. *lowlands*: the Lowland (Scottish) dialect. (Cf. *Lallans* s.v. LALLAN.) *Sc.*

1832–53 BALLANTINE *Whistle-Binkie* (Scot. Songs) Ser. III. 27 My young cousin Peggy cam doun frae Dunkeld, Wi' nae word o'lawlants ava, man. *a* 1878 H. AINSLIE *Land of Burns* (1892) 335 Has gude braid lawlan's left the land?

B. *attrib.* or *adj.*

1. Of, pertaining to, or inhabiting low land or a level district; occas. pertaining to the 'nether regions'.

1567 *Reg. Privy Council Scot.* I. 555 To eschew sic contemptuus oppressioun in a peciabill cuntre and lawland. 1691 DRYDEN *K. Arthur* I. 7 His Errand was, to draw the Low-land damps..from the foggy Fens. 1711 SHAFTESB. *Charac.* (1737) III. 52 Israel was constrain'd to go down to Egypt, and sue for maintenance to these..low-land states. 1721 RAMSAY *Answer to Burchet* 8 He..Doups down to visit ilka lawland ghaist. 1823 in Hone *Every-day Bk.* II. 926 Our lowland vapours..deranged her constitution. 1863 WOOLNER *My Beautiful Lady* 138 Well coerced by Lowland William's [i.e. William III's] craft. 1865 WHITTIER *Revisited* 41 Bring down, O lowland river, The joy of the hills to the waiting sea. 1868 W. W. HUNTER *Compar. Dict. Lang. India* 2 The English have studied and understand the lowland population as no conquerors ever studied or understood a subject race.

2. Of, belonging to, or characteristic of the Lowlands of Scotland.

1508 DUNBAR *Flyting w. Kennedie* 56 Ane lawland ers wald mak a bettir noyis. 1610 HOLLAND *Camden's Brit.* I. 155 The Scots are divided into Hechtlandmen and Lawlandmen. 1752 FAWKES *Descr. May* Pref., The Lowland Scotch language, and the English, at that time, were nearly the same. 1785 BURNS *Jolly Beggars* Air iv, A Highland lad my love was born, The Lawlan' laws he held in scorn. 1896 N. MUNRO *Lost Pibroch* (1902) 88 In her house on the Lowland road Jean Rob starved. 1898 CROCKETT *Standard Bearer* i. 6 Lambs which had just been brought from a neighbouring lowland farm.

lowlander ('ləʊləndə(r)). [f. LOWLAND + -ER^{1}.] An inhabitant of the low-lying or level portion of a country or district.

1835 THIRLWALL *Greece* I. iv. 105 The hostility of the Lowlanders, the Lapiths, whom they certainly never subdued. 1865 KINGSLEY *Herew.* I. 4 The lowlander, on the other hand, has his own strength.

b. *spec.* An inhabitant of the Lowlands of Scotland.

1692 *Lond. Gaz.* No. 2732/3 The Clan Gregor, and many others, both Highlanders and Lowlanders,..are now come in. *c* 1775 JOHNSON in Hawkins *Life* (1787) 490 Of the..state of the whole Earse nation, the Lowlanders are, at least, as ignorant as ourselves. 1900 *Blackw. Mag.* Oct. 468/1 The little lowlander strutted as he played the evening melody.

Lowler, variant of LOLLER^{1} *Obs.*

low-level, *a.* [LOW *a.* I and II.] **1.** Situated near or below ground level; *fig.* not advanced in skill, culture, etc.; low-ranking, unobtrusive, restrained.

1881 W. D. HAY *300 Years Hence* vii. 149 The Sahara Desert, or rather the low-level parts of it. 1908 *Chambers's Jrnl.* Sept. 647/1 The conformation of the barrier which it pierces compelled an abnormally long low-level tunnel. 1910 *Jrnl. R. Inst. Brit. Archit.* Apr. 472 The scheme [of Leonardo da Vinci] comprises a system of low-level streets for commercial purposes, and an upper residential stratum. 1914 W. OWEN *Let.* 2 Feb. (1967) 232 Once fixed in a low-level Rut one is ever-after straightened there;—straightened intellectually and socially as surely as financially. 1923 OGDEN & RICHARDS *Meaning of Meaning* vii. 255 A useful low-level shorthand. 1930 *Times Educ. Suppl.* 11 Jan. p. i/2 We saw low-level sea ice. 1941 *Flight* 9 Jan. 23/1 During such low-level attacks it was easy to see what damage had been done, and there is a vivid report from an aircraft which roared over a main railway station at just below 100 feet. 1955 *Bull. Atomic Sci.* Jan. 5/1 Finally, the long-range genetic danger of exposure of mankind as a whole to low-level, but widespread and persistent radioactivity—the most ominous but least well understood of all dangers of the new age—is only beginning to be dimly perceived. 1955 T. H. PEAR *Eng. Social Differences* xi. 264 An atmosphere of low-level excitement. 1964 E. BACH *Introd. Transformational Gram.* iv. 59 Thus a 'high-level' rule is a rule that is placed earlier in an ordered list than a 'low-level' rule. 1972 *Village Voice* (N.Y.) 1 June 53/2 Lee is obsessed with a woman who has let him down; Harry, who would rather sleep than hear the horny details, tells him, 'Obsession is low-level awareness.'

2. *Computing.* Of a language: reflecting the structure of a particular kind of computer; *spec.* in which each instruction corresponds to a single instruction in machine language. Cf. *high-level* s.v. HIGH *a.* 22 a.

1961 *Communications Assoc. Computing Machinery* IV. 492/1 (*heading*) Low level language subroutines for use within Fortran. 1980 C. S. FRENCH *Computer Sci.* xxv. 189 Each computer manufacturer normally devises a low level language which corresponds closely to the particular machine language used by that manufacturer. 1985 *Personal Computer World* Feb. 162/1 It also frequently needs sections to be written in low-level language due to its restricted areas of application.

'low-life, *a.* and *sb.* [LOW *a.* 20.] **A.** *adj.* Coarse, disreputable, vulgar.

1794 WOLCOT (P. Pindar) *Ode to For. Soldiers* Wks. 1812 III. 248 Saint Crispin..The low-life Cobler's Tutelary Saint. 1861 M. B. CHESNUT *Diary* 8 Dec. (1949) 171 Mr. Shuford he goes for low life things, hurting people's feelings. 1885 F. ANSTEY *Tinted Venus* 95 The peculiar stave by which a modern low-life Blondel endeavours to attract notice. 1910 G. B. SHAW *Brieux: a Preface* 16 Servants, solicitors, and other low life personages. 1931 W. FAULKNER *Sanctuary* xxvi. 265 A durn low-life Jew. 1939 *Time* 18 Dec. 21/1 There can be nothing very awful about even such ostentatiously 'low-life' dives as the Nut Club in Greek Street. 1959 P. BULL *I know Face* xi. 198 Soho low-life stories. 1964 *English Studies* XLV. 368 Could minor low-life characters speak at once so feelingly and with our own voice, to their mistress, at a tragic climax? 1972 *Listener* 10 Aug. 184/3 Low-life action and local vernacular.

B. *sb.* Pl. usu. *low-lifes*. A coarse, vulgar, or no-good person. (Esp. in Jewish use.)

1911 M. GLASS *Potash & Perlmutter* i. 8 'If you think Pincus Vesell done me up good, Noblestone,' Potash said, 'you are mistaken. I got better judgment as to let a low-life like him get into me.' 1932 L. GOLDING *Magnolia St.* II. xiv. 467 *Nu*, and what do you expect from such a low life? 1933 *Omaha* (Nebraska) *World-Herald* 25 Oct., Police Commissioner Bolan in opening a school of correct English for policemen yesterday, remarked that such study would 'refine the tastes' of the men, but his noble prospect left most of the city's lowlifes cold. 1955 J. POTTS *Death of Stray Cat* (1966) xxii. 209 Why, that low-life! Stealing my stuff. 1959 H. PINTER *Birthday Party* (1960) III. 50 Keep an eye open for low-lives, for schnorrers and for layabouts. 1964 *Amer. Folk Music Occasional* I. 7 It would be an error to conclude that such songs are found only among the low-life. 1971 *Black World* Apr. 38/2 Our responsible leaders sniffed their disdain of the low-lifes and begged aristocrats for white-collar jobs.

lowlihead ('ləʊlɪhɛd). *arch.* [f. LOWLY *a.* + -HEAD.] Humility, lowliness.

c 1403 CLANVOWE *Cuckow & Night.* 156 Lowliheed, and trewe companye. 1426 LYDG. *De Guil. Pilgr.* 7995 Meknesse & lavlyhede. 1830 TENNYSON *Isabel* i, The stately flower.. Of perfect wifehood and pure lowlihead. *c* 1850 ROSSETTI *Dante & Circ.* I. (1874) 90 The lamp of her meek lowlihead. 1889 BROWNING *Pope & Net* vii, The thing was gone—That guarantee of lowlihead.

'lowlihood. $rare^{-0}$. [+ -HOOD.] = prec.

1818 in TODD (but his quot. has *lowlyhede*). Hence in mod. Dicts.

lowlily ('ləʊlɪlɪ), *adv.* [f. LOWLY *a.* + -LY^{2}.] In a lowly fashion or manner.

c 1340 HAMPOLE *Prose Tr.* (1866) 11 þat þay..serve þame mekely and gladly and lawlyly. 1587 GOLDING *De Mornay* xxx. 481 He shall..enter into the Citie very poorely and lowlily. 1844 MRS. BROWNING *Drama Exile* Poems 1850 I. 79 Live and love—Doing both nobly, because lowlily. 1881 SHAIRP *Asp. Poetry* iv. 116 Only by thinking lowlily of himself, and highly of those better than himself.

lowliness ('ləʊlɪnɪs). [f. LOWLY *a.* + -NESS.] The quality or condition of being lowly.

1. Meekness, humility; an instance of this.

a 1413 HEN. PR. WALES *Ep. to Hen. IV* (Nat. MSS. I. 37), Alle the lowlinesse that any subget kan thenkke or devise. *c* 1440 *Partonope* 224 Lat fayle no curtasy And lowlynesse bothe to smalle and grete. 1509 HAWES *Past. Pleas.* iv. (Percy Soc.) 20 Than were endued Her crystall eyes full of lowlenes. 1535 COVERDALE *Prov.* xvi. 1 Lowlynes goeth before honoure. 1601 SHAKS. *Jul. C.* II. i. 22 'Tis a common proofe, That Lowlynesse is young Ambitions Ladder. 1764 J. WOOLMAN *Jrnl.* (1840) 127 By so travelling..I might set an example of lowliness before the eyes of their masters. 1855 TENNYSON *Maud* I. xii. v, O Maud were sure of Heaven If lowliness could save her. 1864 PUSEY *Lect. Daniel* (1876) 285 Greatness in lowliness.

2. Low state or condition; abjectness, poverty.

1596 SPENSER *State Irel.* (Globe ed.) 614/2 They say that they continued in that lowlyness, untill the time that the division betweene the two howses of Lancaster and Yorke arose. 1891 T. K. CHEYNE *Origin Psalter* vii. 353 Sympathy ..made the Messiah like unto common men in their lowliness.

†'lowling. *Obs.* $rare^{-1}$. [f. LOW *a.* + -LING.] A low-bred fellow.

1581 MULCASTER *Positions* xxxviii. (1887) 178 Yet some petie lowlinges, do sometimes seeke to resemble.

low-lived ('ləʊˌlaɪvd), *a.* Also 8–9 **-lifed**. [f. LOW *a.* + *live-*, LIFE + -ED^{2}.] Of persons: Living a low life; vulgar, mean. Hence of actions, expressions, etc.

1760 C. JOHNSTON *Chrysal* (1822) I. 155 She could not think of letting any common low-lived fellow come near her. *Ibid.* III. 177 How can you take delight in such a low-lived trick? 1766 GOLDSM. *Vic. W.* xi, Your Ladyship should except..your own things in the Lady's Magazine. I hope you'll say there's nothing low-lived there? 1781 J. RIPLEY *Sel. Orig. Let.* 77 The low-lifed fellow who wrote this letter. 1836–48 B. D. WALSH *Aristoph.* 46 *note*, Aristophanes is.. unmerciful upon low-lived, vulgar people. 1882 FR. A. KEMBLE *Later Life* I. 82 An ignoble, low-lived expression occasionally startled..one, on a countenance noble and intellectual.

lowly ('ləʊlɪ), *a.* Somewhat *arch.* Forms: 4 **lou(e)lich, louli,** 4–7 *north.* **lawly, -lie,** (7 **laulie**), 6 **lowely, lowlie,** 4– **lowly.** [f. LOW *a.* + -LY^{1}.]

1. Humble in feeling or demeanour; not proud or ambitious.

c 1374 CHAUCER *Anel. & Arc.* 142 She to him so louly was and trewe. 1377 LANGL. *P. Pl.* B. XIV. 227 For loulich he loketh and loueliche is his speche. 1426 LYDG. *De Guil. Pilgr.* 21034 Yiff thow do to myn Image, Lowly worshepe and homage. *a* 1450 in *Shillingford Lett.* (Camden) 132 Y.. byseke yow yn the lowlokyst wyse that [etc.]. *c* 1470 HENRY *Wallace* VIII. 1664 Wallace on kne, with lawly obeysance. 1535 COVERDALE *Micah* vi. 8 To be lowly, and to walke with thy God. 1601 SHAKS. *Twel. N.* III. i. 110 'Twas neuer merry world, Since lowly feigning was call'd complement. 1659 HAMMOND *On Ps.* cl. 3 Annot. 719 Without the lowlyest posture of the body. 1709 STEELE *Tatler* No. 18 ⁋3 The Pope has written to the French King on the Subject of a Peace, and his Majesty has answered in the lowliest Terms. 1781 COWPER *Truth* 93 God accounts him proud; High in demand, though lowly in pretence.

absol. 1535 COVERDALE *Prov.* iii. 34 He shal geue grace vnto the lowly. 1611 BIBLE *ibid.*

2. a. Humble in condition or quality. Usually with some notion of sense 1: Modest, unpretending.

1634 MILTON *Comus* 323 Courtesie..is sooner found in lowly sheds..then in tapstry Halls. 1784 COWPER *Task* IV. 141 All the comforts that the lowly roof Of undisturbed retirement..knows. 1791 J. LEARMONT *Poems* 278, I'd sit fu' happy i' my lowly ben. 1802 WORDSW. *Sonn.*, '*Milton! thou should'st be living*', Thy heart The lowliest duties on herself did lay. 1859 DARWIN *Orig. Spec.* iv. (1873) 98 The continued existence of lowly organisms offers no difficulty. 1860 TYNDALL *Glac.* I. iii. 23, I put up at a very lowly inn. 1871 G. V. SMITH *Bible & Pop. Theol.* xi. 116 They remembered the origin of Jesus and saw his lowly condition. 1871 FREEMAN *Norm. Conq.* (1876) IV. xviii. 143 The sons of Harold who were within the walls of Exeter came of a lowlier and doubtful stock.

absol. 1725 POPE *Odyss.* VIII. 600 Say..what the name you bore..(For from the natal hour distinctive names, One common right, the great and lowly claims). 1852 MRS. STOWE (*title*), Uncle Tom's Cabin; or, Life among the Lowly.

b. Of plants or animals, comparatively undeveloped.

1876 *City-Road Mag.* Jan. 44/2 There can be very little doubt that lowly forms can exist..at temperatures not much below 150° Fahr. 1886 A. GEIKIE *Class-Bk. Geol.* xv. 293 The progress of life from its earliest appearance in lowly forms of plant or animal has been continuous. 1912 *Q. Rev.* Apr. 528 The most conspicuous physical features in Europe ..had no existence when these lowly organisms lived and died. 1927 PEAKE & FLEURE *Apes & Men* 13 Birds first appear in the Jurassic system, while traces of lowly mammals have been found from the Trias onwards.

3. a. Low in situation or growth, usually with allusion to sense 1. (Cf. HUMBLE *a.*)

1593 SHAKS. *Rich. II*, II. iv. 21 Thy Sunne sets weeping in the lowly West. 1697 DRYDEN *Virg. Past.* IV. 2 Lowly Shrubs and Trees that shade the Plain, Delight not all. 1715 POPE *Iliad* II. 638 Those who dwell..where Boagrius floats the lowly Lands. 1728–46 THOMSON *Spring* 449 Where purple violets lurk With all the lowly children of the shade. *a* 1729 CONGREVE *Mourn. Muse Alexis* Wks. 1730 III. 208 As lofty Pines o'ertop the lowly Reed, So did her graceful Height all Nymphs exceed. 1852 WHITTIER *Question of Life* 123 In lowliest depths of bosky dells The hermit Contemplation dwells. 1853 KANE *Grinnell Exp.* xxvii. (1856) 225 And the sun, albeit from a lowly altitude, shone out in full brightness.

b. ? *nonce-use.* ? Lying low.

1591 SHAKS. *1 Hen. VI*, III. iii. 47 As lookes the Mother on her lowly Babe, When Death doth close his tender dying Eyes.

¶ **4.** *occas.* Low in character, mean.

1741 RICHARDSON *Pamela* (1824) I. 124 This proud letter of the lowly Lady Davers..*Lowly*, I say, because she could stoop to such vain pride. 1843 JAMES *Forest Days* (1847) 289 His name was never stained with any lowly act.

5. *Comb.*, as ***lowly-built, -lovely, -minded*** (hence ***lowly-mindedness***) adjs.

a 1822 SHELLEY *Tear* iv. 3 Over thy *lowly-built sepulchre bending. 1864 TENNYSON *Aylmer's F.* 168 She—so *lowly-lovely and so loving. 1540 COVERDALE *Fruitf. Less.* i. (1593) K 3 b, Christ..teacheth vs to bee *lowly minded and humble. 1859 GEN. P. THOMPSON *Audi Alt.* II. lxxxvii. 57 The stamp of *lowly-mindedness.

lowly ('ləʊlɪ), *adv.* Forms: 4 **loȝly, louheliche, lowelyche, laweliche,** 4–5 **louli, -y,** 4–6 **lowely,** 5 **loughly, louely,** 5–6 **lawly,** 6 *Sc.* **lau-, lawle, -lie,** 6–7 **lowlie,** 9 *Sc.* **laighly, leuchly,** 4– **lowly.** [f. LOW *a.* + -LY^{2}.]

1. In a lowly manner (= LOWLILY); humbly, reverently; modestly. In *to bow lowly* with mixture of sense 2.

13.. *E.E. Allit. P.* B. 614 Lenge a lyttel with þy lede I loȝly biseche. *c* 1385 CHAUCER *L.G.W.* 2062 *Ariadne*, But I yow serve as louly In that place. 1393 LANGL. *P. Pl.* C. x. 141 Lewede eremytes, That loken ful louheliche to lacchen mennes almesse. 14.. *Why I can't be a Nun* 161 in *E.E.P.* (1862) 142, I, as lowly as I can, Wolle do yow servyse nyȝt and day. 1513 DOUGLAS *Æneis* I. ii. 24 To quham as than lawle thus Juno said [etc.]. 1529 FRITH *Antithesis* Wks. (1573) 98/1 Christ full lowly and meekely washed his disciples feete. 1588 A. KING tr. *Canisius' Catech.* 79 We maist humblie, and laulie prosterne our selfs. 1629 MILTON *Nativity Ode* 25 O run, prevent them with thy humble ode,

And lay it lowly at his blessed feet. **1667** —— *P.L.* v. 144 Lowly they bow'd adorning, and began Thir Orisons. **1802** WORDSW. *Farewell* 28 A gentle Maid, whose heart is lowly bred. **1844** DISRAELI *Coningsby* III. ii, As he bowed lowly before the Duchess.

2. In a low manner or degree.

a. In a low position or posture; along the ground. In examples from 18th c. there is mixture of sense 1.

13.. *Guy Warw.* (A.) 1384 So wele his strok he sett That his heued fram þe bodi flei, He ȝede him laweliche neye. **1590** SPENSER *F.Q.* II. i. 24 A pleasant dale that lowly lay Betwixt two hills. **1784** COWPER *Task* III. 663 Some clothe the soil that feeds them, far diffused And lowly creeping. **1785** —— *Poplar Field* 14, I must ere long lie as lowly as they [felled trees]. **1795** BURNS *Song*, '*Their groves o' sweet myrtles*', Where the blue-bell and gowan lurk lowly unseen. **1811** A. SCOTT *Poems* 144 (Jam.) Auld Reekie stands sweet on the east sloping dale, An' leuchly lurks Leith, where the trading ships sail.

b. In a low voice. Now only *poet.*

c **1440** *Promp. Parv.* 314/2 Lowely, or softe yn voyce, *submisse*. **1810** SHELLEY *Zastrozzi* iv. Pr. Wks. 1888 I. 17 He sometimes spoke lowly to himself. **1839** BAILEY *Festus* (1852) 127 A maiden sat in her lonely bower Sadly and lowly singing. **1863** WOOLNER *My Beautiful Lady* 95 What are thou whispering lowly to thy babe, O wan girl-mother?

†**c.** In an inferior manner, meanly. *Obs.*

1601 SHAKS. *All's Well* II. ii. 3, I will show my selfe highly fed, and lowly taught.

d. With a low opinion. *rare.*

1742 RICHARDSON *Pamela* III. 63 They always think highly of the beloved Object, and lowly of themselves. **1852** H. NEWLAND *Lect. Tractarianism* II. 68 'Why', said he [South], 'the High Church are those who think highly of the Church, and lowly of themselves; the Low Church are those who think highly of themselves, and lowly of the Church'.

e. In a low degree. *rare.*

1870 ROLLESTON *Anim. Life* 30 The walls of the lung are but very lowly vascular.

3. *Comb.*, as *lowly-born*, *-breathed*, *-cultivated*, *-organized*.

1613 SHAKS. *Hen. VIII*, II. iii. 19 Tis better to be *lowly borne.. Then [etc.]. **1872** F. W. ROBERTSON *Hist. Ess.* 234 We may long look in vain for the name of a lowly born man amongst the Roman magistracy. **1827** KEBLE *Chr. Y.*, 1st Sund. after Christm. ii, A sick man's *lowly-breathed sigh. **1856** KANE *Arct. Expl.* II. xxi. 212 That apathetic fatalism which belongs to all *lowly-cultivated races. **1859** DARWIN *Orig. Spec.* iv. (1873) 99 *Lowly organised forms appear to have been preserved to the present day.

†**'lowly**, *v. Obs.* Also 6 *Sc.* lawly. [f. LOWLY *a.*] *trans.* To humble; *refl.* to condescend.

1535 STEWART *Chron. Scot.* (1858) I. 512 Louyng to God Almycht, Hes lawleit him so far to schaw the rycht Of this tirrane quhilk wes oure prince and king. **1577–87** HOLINSHED *Chron.* III. 1218/2 Were not the charge I present.. I should lowlie my person to meet you six English miles. **1583** GOLDING *Calvin on Deut.* xxi. 125 Wee see howe God lowlieth himselfe and stoopeth to our rudenesse.

low man, 'lowman. [f. LOW *a.* + MAN. Cf. also HIGHMAN.] In *pl.* Dice loaded so as to turn up low numbers. (Cf. LOW-RUNNER.)

1592 KYD *Sol. & Pers.* II. i. 223 Heere are tall men and little men... Hie men and low men, thou wouldst say. **1596** LODGE *Wits Miserie* (1879) 47. **1608** DEKKER *Belman Lond.* E 3. *a* **1612** HARINGTON *Epigr.* I. lxxix. (1618) D 3 b, Then play thou for a pound or for a pin, High men are low men, still are foysted in. **1622**, *a* **1643** [see HIGHMAN].

lowme, obs. form of LOOM *sb.*[1]

lowmost ('ləʊməʊst), *a.* and *adv.* Now *dial.* [f. LOW *a.* or *adv.* + -MOST.] = LOWEST *a.* and *adv.*

1548 UDALL, etc. *Erasm. Par. Mark* xiii. 87 From the hyghest pole of heauen to the lowmoste. **1578** LYTE *Dodoens* II. lxvi. 233 The leaues.. that grow lowmoste are somewhat larger. **1820** *Blackw. Mag.* VII. 260 The lowmost at the royal board, but foremost still in war. **1865** E. WAUGH *Besom Ben* ii. 23 Every time his head came lowmost he looked at his master with imploring eyes.

lowmpe, obs. form of LAMB.

lown (laʊn), *a.*, *sb.*, and *adv. Sc.* and *north. dial.* Forms: 5–7 lowne, 6 louin, loun, 7–8 lownd, 8 lowen, 9 lowan, lound, 6– lown. [a. ON. **lugn* (*u* stem; Icel. *lygn* adj., *logn* neut. sb., MSw. *lughn*, Sw. *lugn*, Da. *luun* adj. and sb.). The derived LOWN *v.* occurs earlier.] **A.** *adj.*

1. a. Of the weather, water, a locality: Calm, quiet, still, unruffled.

c **1450** HOLLAND *Howlat* 18 The land lowne was and le, with lyking and luf. *c* **1470** HENRYSON *Mor. Fab.* VII. (*Lion & Mouse*) xxxviii, The fair forest with leuis lowne and lie. **1513** DOUGLAS *Æneis* III. viii. 60 Within the havin goith loune. **1536** BELLENDEN *Cron. Scot.* (1821) I. Proheme to Cosmogr. 11 In weddir louin and maist tempestius haill, But ony dreid, I beir ane equall saill. **1583** *Leg. Bp. St. Androis* 156 Then sett he to, with saill and ayre, To seik some lowner harbore thayre. **1584** HUDSON *Du Bartas' Judith* I. (1608) 19 The variant winde is still and lowne. **1683** G. MERITON *Yorks. Dialogue* 346 How comes thy Clathes seay flurr'd, Barne, this Lownd day? **1826** J. WILSON *Noct. Ambr.* Wks. 1855 I. 118 Ye may hear him, on a lown day, at every farm house in the village. **1894** CROCKETT *Raiders* 221 The wind came.. in lown-warm puffs.

b. Of persons, their actions, circumstances, demeanour, talk, etc.: Calm, gentle, quiet, silent, soft, still.

1714 RAMSAY *Elegy John Cowper* ix, To keep a' things hush and lown. **1768** ROSS *Helenore* (1789) 92 My lad, my counsel's ye be lown. **1816** SCOTT *Antiq.* xxiv, Sir Richard .. had a fair offspring o' his ain, and a' was lound and quiet till his head was laid in the ground. **1823** J. WILSON *Trials Marg. Lyndsay* xxxiii. 270 But do you think your brother will like Nether-Place? It will be oure lown for him. **1827** —— *Noct. Ambr.* Wks. 1855 I. 277 You'll keep a lowner sugh or you get halfway from Dalnacarnoch.

2. Sheltered; cozy, snug.

1728 RAMSAY *Ram & Buck* 6 And drave them frae the lowner bield, To crop contented frozen fare. **1867** N. MACLEOD *Starling* i, Turnips and stubble are no' to be compared wi'.. the win'y taps o' the hills, or the lown glens.

B. *sb.* [= Icel. *logn*.] Quiet, calm, stillness, tranquillity; also, shelter.

1787 GROSE *Prov. Gloss.*, *Lun*, or *Lewe*, under cover, or shelter. Under the lun or lewe of a hedge. W. **1830** GALT *Lawrie T.* VI. ii. (1849) 257 To hear the far-off Kirk-bell ringing shrilly in the lown of a Sunday morning. **1880** WATT *Poet. Sketches* 60 (E.D.D.) Oor bit hoosie that stood i' the lown o' the shaw.

C. *adv.* Quietly, softly.

1535 STEWART *Cron. Scot.* 24125 Befoir the wynd thai saillit lone and still. **1816** SCOTT *Old Mort.* xlii, For God's sake, speak lound and low.

lown (laʊn), *v. Sc.* and *north. dial.* Also 5 llown, 9 lownd. [f. LOWN *a.*]

1. a. *intr.* To become calm, to calm; also with *down*. †**b.** *trans.* To make calm, to lull. *Obs.*

c **1400** *Sc. Trojan War* (Horstm.) II. 1012 The see-tempestes llownyt not. **1513** DOUGLAS *Æneis* VII. ii. 5 Eftir the wyndis lownit war at will. *Ibid.* x. ii. 113 The wyndis eik thar blastis lownit sone. **1737** RAMSAY *Sc. Prov.* (1797) 24 Blaw the wind ne'er so fast it will lown at the last. **1894** R. W. REID *Poems* 59 The win' was lownin' doon.

2. To shelter.

1375 BARBOUR *Bruce* xv. 276 And a myle was betuix the seis, And that wes lownyt all with treis. **1802** COLERIDGE *Lett.* 26 Aug. (1895) 400, I was sheltered (in the phrase of the country, *lownded*) in a sort of natural porch on the summit of Sca Fell.

Hence **lowned** (*lownit*) *ppl. a.*, calmed, still.

1513 DOUGLAS *Æneis* v. iv. 107 Scherand the lownit air, [scho] Doun from the hycht discendis soft and fair.

lown(e, variant of LOON *sb.*[1]

lowndrer, var. LOUNDERER *Obs.*, skulker.

lowness ('ləʊnɪs). [f. LOW *a.* + -NESS.]

1. The quality or condition of being LOW.

a. In physical applications: Smallness of elevation from the ground or of prominence from a surface; situation at a low level; †shortness of stature.

1398 TREVISA *Barth. De P.R.* VII. xxxi. (1495) 245 Amonge the tokens of Tysyk ben.. lowenesse of the roundenesse of eyen. *c* **1440** *Promp. Parv.* 314/2 Lownesse, or depnesse, *profunditas*. Lownesse, ny the grounde, *bassitas*. **1442** *Rolls of Parlt.* V. 44/1 By cause of the lowenes and straitenes of the said Brigge. **1606** SHAKS. *Ant. & Cl.* II. vii. 22. **1626** BACON *Sylva* §32 The Lownesse of the Bough .. maketh the Fruit greater, and to ripen better. *a* **1637** B. JONSON *Underwoods* (1640) 181 Can I discerne how shadowes are decreast, Or growne; by height or lownesse of the Sunne? **1638** F. JUNIUS *Paint. Ancients* 256 Augustus.. was of a low stature,.. but.. his lownesse was hid by the fitnesse and equalitie of his members. **1781** *Hist. Eur.* in *Ann. Reg.* 7/2 Their own lowness.. preserved them.. from the fire of the batteries. **1836** MACGILLIVRAY tr. *Humboldt's Trav.* xxi. 298 The island of Tortuga remarkable for its lowness and want of vegetation.

b. Low or depressed condition with regard to station, rank, fortune, or estimation; †degradation, abasement.

a **1225** *Ancr. R.* 278 Edmodnesse is.. luue of lute hereword & of louhnesse. **1340** HAMPOLE *Pr. Consc.* 8500 Þus salle þai haf gret powere, And heghnes, for þair awen gret lawnes here. **1393** LANGL. *P. Pl.* C. XVII. 18 That al here lyf leden in lowenesse and in pouerte. **1548** UDALL, etc. *Erasm. Par. Matt.* xvi. 20–23 But no man can truely glory in him, but he whiche is not offended with hys humilitie and lownes. **1598** DALLINGTON *Meth. Trav.* G iij b, He raysed the afflicted lownesse of the desolate King. *c* **1655** A. SIDNEY in *19th Cent.* (1884) Jan. 63 The lownesse and meannesse of my fortune and person forbids me to hope. **1779–81** JOHNSON *L.P.*, *Prior*, The lowness of his original. **1886** *Book-lore* Feb. 58 After disposing of the charge of lowness of birth.

†**c.** Humility, lowliness, meekness. *Obs.*

c **1330** R. BRUNNE *Chron. Wace* (Rolls) 8765 And ȝit wyþ gret lownesse of hert, þat pruyde turne hit nought ouerthwert. **1393** LANGL. *P. Pl.* C. XVI. 133 Loue and leaute and louhnesse of herte. *c* **1430** LYDG. *Reas. & Sens.* 1501 She the proude kan enclyne To lownesse and humilyte. *c* **1440** *Promp. Parv.* 314/2 Lownesse, or mekenesse, *humilitas*. Lownesse, and goodnesse in speche, *affabilitas*.

d. Low degree of any quality; low pitch (of a note); smallness of amount, price, temperature, etc.

1597 MORLEY *Introd. Mus.* 3 A Cliefe is a character.. shewing the heigth and lownes of euery note standing on the same Verse. **1690** CHILD *Disc. Trade* (ed. 4) 31 The lowness of interest of money in Holland.. proceeds only from their abundance of coin. **1708** J. C. *Compl. Collier* (1845) 18 They have not the Benefit of the lowness of Price as at the Pits. **1797–8** WELLINGTON in Owen *Desp.* 779 Measures having lowness of freight and freedom of trade in view may be adopted upon two principles. **1860** TYNDALL *Glac.* II. xx. 336 This lowness of temperature.

†**e.** Want of elevation in literary style; an instance of this. *Obs.*

1673 DRYDEN *Marr. à la Mode* Ded., If there be any thing in this Play wherein I have rais'd my self beyond the ordinary Lowness of my Comedies. **1725** POPE *Postscr. to Odyssey* (1726) V. 299 The more he was forc'd upon figures and metaphors to avoid that lowness. *Ibid.* 306 He, who ventur'd.. to imitate Homer's Lownesses in the Narrative. **1728** DR. HERRING in J. Duncombe *Lett.* (1773) I. 287 The inaccuracies of style, the lownesses of expression,.. in this translation.

f. Want of elevation in character; meanness, baseness.

1662 STILLINGFL. *Orig. Sacr.* I. ii. §8 Who could but imagine a strange lowness of spirit in those who could fall down and worship the basest.. of creatures? **1884** LADY VERNEY in *Contemp. Rev.* Oct. 554 Wickedness and lowness are necessary to show forth the good and the high.

g. Mental or nervous depression. Now only explicitly *lowness of spirits*.

1739 WESLEY *Jrnl.* 12 July (1830) I. 210, I went to a gentleman who is much troubled with what they call lowness of spirits. **1782** J. C. SMYTH in *Med. Comm.* I. 72 *note* 2 She had.. a small quick pulse, with great lowness. *c* **1815** JANE AUSTEN *Persuas.* (1833) I. xi. 300 She had to struggle against a great tendency to lowness. **1822** GOOD *Study Med.* II. 437 Great languor, lowness and oppression at the præcordia. **1843** BETHUNE *Sc. Peasant.* 45 He felt occasionally that lowness of spirits from which, when their prospects are clouded,.. few are wholly exempted.

2. As a mock title of dignity.

1771 P. PARSONS *Newmarket* I. 1 Such a salutation would affront their Highnesses and Lownesses. **1790** H. WALPOLE *Let. to Miss Berrys* 8 Nov., His turbulent Lowness of Brabant. **1860** RUSSELL *Diary India* II. 235 There sat his Highness the Rajah, and here stood his lowness the correspondent.

†**3.** *concr.* The low part of a country. *Obs.*

c **1400** MAUNDEV. (1839) v. 46 In Egipt there ben 2 parties; the Heghte, that is toward Ethiope; and the Lowenesse, that is towardes Arabye.

lownin, obs. form of LOANING *sb.*

lownly ('laʊnlɪ), *adv. Sc.* [f. LOWN *a.* + -LY[2].] In a 'lown' manner. **a.** Calmly, quietly; in a low tone. **b.** In shelter, under fostering care.

1788 PICKEN *Poems* 56 His todlan wee anes.. Nurs't lownly up aneath his care. **18..** R. CHAMBERS *Wheesht!* Speak loundly about it; and don't say I told you. **1890** J. SERVICE *Thir Notandums* viii. 53 Lownly my faither leuch to himsel'.

lowp(e, obs. f. LOOP *sb.*[1], *sb.*[2]; var. LOUP *v.*

low-pitched, *ppl. a.* [In sense 1 f. LOW *adv.* + PITCHED *pa. pple.* of PITCH *v.*; in sense 2 f. LOW *a.* + PITCH *sb.* + -ED[2].]

1. Pitched in a low key or tone, *lit.* and *fig.*; but little elevated; of low quality.

1622 DRAYTON *Poly-olb.* xxv. 358 The Muse, which seem'd too slacke in these two low-pitcht layes. **1641** MILTON *Animadv.* xiii. Wks. (1847) 70/1 Poor and low-pitched desires. **1873** M. ARNOLD *Lit. & Dogma* v. 145 It is .. eminently natural; but it is above common, low-pitched nature. **1898** *Allbutt's Syst. Med.* V. 277 The continuous low-pitched rumbling sound produced by the contraction of the muscles.

2. Of a roof: Having but a slight angular elevation. Hence of a room: Having a low ceiling.

1833 LOUDON *Encycl. Archit.* Gloss. Index, Low-pitched roof. **1843** JAMES *Forest Days* ii, One of the tables in the low-pitched parlour. **1884** *Century Mag.* XXVII. 827 A one-story and garret house, with a low-pitched roof.

lowre, obs. f. LOUR, LOUVRE, LOWER *v.*

lowrell, obs. form of LAUREL *sb.*[1]

lowrie ('laʊrɪ). *Sc.* Also 6 lawrie, loury, 6–8 lowry. [Short for LAURENCE[1].]

1. The fox; used as a quasi-proper name.

1500–20 DUNBAR *Poems* xxxii. 16 The tod.. wes ane lusty reid haird lowry. **1728** RAMSAY *Fox & Rat* 27 The Monarch pleas'd with Lowry, wha durst gloom? **1835** *Laird of Logan* (1841) 163 A' my customers hae been worrying at me like as many jowlers in the neck o' poor tod lowrie. **1885** 'S. MUCKLEBACKIT' *Rhymes* 91 As sheep when lowrie tod they see, Man, wife, and wean, in panic flee!

2. A crafty person; a 'fox'; a hypocrite.

1567 *Gude & Godlie Ball.* (S.T.S.) 209 Had not that blissit bairne bene borne,.. Lowreis, zour lyues had been forlorne. **1571** *Satir. Poems Reform.* xxix. 21 3itt I beleieff ols mony myndis thochte, ha, loury, ha, ha! **1583** *Leg. Bp. St. Androis* 55 Men heiring tell how Lowrie landit, The congregatione him commandit To serve a kirk and keip a cure.

lowrie, var. LAURY *Obs.*; Australian var. LORY.

lowrier, obs. form of LAUREL *sb.*[1]

†**low-runner.** *Obs.* A false die loaded so as to run on the low numbers. (Cf. LOWMAN.)

1670 [see HIGH-RUNNER].

lowry ('lɔːrɪ). *U.S. Railways.* [? Cf. LORRY *sb.*] An open box-car (Knight *Dict. Mech.* 1875).

lowry: see LOURY *a.*, LOWRIE.

lows(e, obs. or dial. form of LOOSE *v.*, LOUSE.

lowse, obs. f. LUCE a pike; var. LOSE *v.*[2] *Obs.*

lowsey, -ie, obs. forms of LOUSY.

†**'lowship.** *Obs.* In 3 louhschipe. [f. LOW *a.* + -SHIP.] Lowness; humility.

a **1225** *Ancr. R.* 358 Scheome & louhschipe þet heo her uor Godes luue mildeliche þolieð.

low side window. A small window lower than the other windows, found in some old churches. Cf. *leper window* (LEPER *sb.*[2] A. b), LYCHNOSCOPE.

1847 *Archæol. Jrnl.* IV. 314 No part of our ancient churches has so completely baffled the enquiries of antiquaries [etc.] as the low side windows which so frequently occur near the west end of the chancel, usually on the south side, but sometimes on the north, and sometimes on both sides; occasionally also near the east end of the nave, and in other situations. **1848** *Ecclesiologist* VIII. 375 Where neither low side window nor bell-cot existed. **1852** ROCK *Ch. Our Fathers* III. I. Contents p. v, The low side or ankret's window. **1894** *Murray's Handbk. Oxfordsh.* 103 On the S. is a low side window, blocked.

low-'spirited, *a.* [f. LOW *a.* + SPIRIT *sb.* + -ED[2].] Having low spirits. †**a.** Mean in spirit; abject, base, cowardly, paltry (*obs.*). **b.** Wanting in animation or sprightliness; dejected, dispirited.

a. 1588 SHAKS. *L.L.L.* I. i. 250 That low spirited Swaine, that base Minow of thy myrth. **1655** E. TERRY *Voy. E. Ind.* 79 People..so low-spirited..that they dare not fight. **1760-72** H. BROOKE *Fool of Qual.* (1809) III. 67 Low-spirited scoundrels, who rob the widow and the fatherless. **1795** LD. AUCKLAND *Corr.* (1862) III. 283 This country is very low-spirited as to continental politics.

b. 1753 N. TORRIANO *Gangr. Sore Throat* 120 She was very low-spirited and hysterical. **1778** MISS BURNEY *Evelina* xxiii. (1791) I. 134 When we returned home, we were all low-spirited. **1833** J. H. NEWMAN *Lett.* (1891) I. 432, I was low-spirited about the state of things and thought nothing could be done. **1869** CLARIDGE *Cold Water Cure* 55 Where the patient is low spirited or unwell.

Hence **low-'spiritedness**, the condition of being low-spirited; †(*a*) Cowardice, meanness (*obs.*). (*b*) Dejection, depression, faint-heartedness.

1652 J. WRIGHT tr. *Camus' Nat. Paradox* VII. 145 Our low-spiritedness stretched out the neck to this blow. **1711** SHAFTESB. *Charac.* (1737) I. 230 Nor shou'd I..charge 'em with meanness and insufficiency on the account of this low-spiritedness which they discover. **1741-70** MRS. CARTER *Lett.* (1808) 351 The low spiritedness..of which you complain, assures me you cannot be well. **1812** W. TAYLOR in *Monthly Mag.* XXXIV. 410 The reverse of low-spiritedness is gaiety.

lowss, obs. Sc. form of LOOSE.

Low Sunday. [Cf. quot. 1866.] The Sunday next after Easter Sunday.

1431 in *Eng. Gilds* (1870) 275 Ye sonday next aftyr low-sonday. **1511** *Nottingham Rec.* III. 329 In ye weke next after Lowe Sondey. *a* **1633** AUSTIN *Medit.* (1635) 168 Low-Sunday. *Inferius Pascha.* The Lower Easter-Sunday. **1710** HEARNE *Collect.* 16 Apr. (O.H.S.) II. 373 This Day being Low-Sunday. **1866** *Annot. Bk. Com. Pr.* 107 The popular name of Low Sunday has probably arisen from the contrast between the joys of Easter and the first return to ordinary Sunday services.

lowt(e, obs. form of LOUT *sb.* and *v.*

†**lowth.** *Obs.* [f. LOW *a.* + -TH[1].] Lowness.

1526 TINDALE *Rom.* viii. 39 Nether heyth, nether lowth [A.V. and R.V. depth], nether eny other creature. **1535** COVERDALE *Rom.* viii. 39 Nether heyth ner loweth. [**1691** RAY *Collect. Words* Postscr. 171 That which lies under the Hills, especially down by Humber and Ouse side,..is called by the Country-people the Lowths, i.e. The low Country in contradistinction to the Wauds.]

low tide: see TIDE.

lowveld ('ləʊfɛlt, -vɛlt). *S. Afr.* Also hyphenated and with capital initial(s). [ad. Afrikaans *Laeveld* low country.] The low-lying region of the eastern Transvaal and of Swaziland; also applied to corresponding regions of adjoining territories. Freq. *attrib.*

1878 A. AYLWARD *Transvaal of Today* iii. 44 Bushveld and Lowveld are convertible terms. **1905** *Transvaal Agric. Jrnl.* Oct. 141 (*title*) Notes on the native flora and crops of the Lowveld of the Eastern Transvaal. **1929** J. STEVENSON-HAMILTON *Low-Veld* 1 The Transvaal Province of the Union of South Africa is divided into three zones of altitude known respectively as High, Middle, and Low Veld... It is not unusual to hear an altitude of three thousand feet referred to as 'Low-Veld'... The Low-Veld of the Transvaal lies approximately between the twenty-second and the twenty-sixth parallels of south latitude. **1931** *Discovery* Aug. 259/2 At Barberton [Transvaal], where problems connected with the improvement of cottons for low-veld areas are dealt with. **1949** *Cape Argus Mag.* 5 Nov. 9/5 The lowveld hills around Umgungundhlovu. **1959** *Cape Times* 4 Feb. 1/1 Mr. Ray Stockil yesterday announced his intention to retire as Leader of the Opposition in the Southern Rhodesia Parliament and to devote his attention to the economic development of the lowveld of the country. **1968** C. BURKE *Elephant across Border* v. 189 A shallow ravine, covered in those lowveld succulents which are able to grow out of small patches of moss and cracks in the rock.

low water. The state of the tide when the surface of the water is lowest; the time when the tide is at the lowest ebb. (Cf. HIGH WATER.) †Also, in a river, a time when the stream is shallow.

1530 PALSGR. 241/1 Lowe water, *leave basse.* *a* **1548** HALL *Chron., Edw. IV* 209 As nere as their great shyppes could come at the lowe water. **1582** in Turner *Select. Rec. Oxford* 426 At everye hyghe and ragynge water youre slueses.. should be drawne upp... And at everye lowe water your.. sluses should be..shutte. **1670** SPEED in Bedloe *Popish Plot* 21 He bid him observe the Tide, and be sure to do it within an hour of low water. **1762** BORLASE in *Phil. Trans.* LII. 420 At Kinsale,..near dead low-water, the tide rose suddenly on the strand. **1853** SIR H. DOUGLAS *Milit. Bridges* (ed. 3) 50 A certain number of pontoons would..be left aground at every low water. **1882** E. P. EDWARDS in *Gd. Words* Apr. 248 Rocky peaks showing only above low-water.

fig. **1877** *Gd. Words* XVIII. 18/2 In summer..everything is at dead low-water.

b. *attrib.* †Of a soldier = FRESHWATER 2 b.

1643 [ANGIER] *Lanc. Vall. Achor* 7 Fire is a cruell Lord, and dreadfull object to fresh and low-water souldiers.

c. *fig.* Chiefly in phr. ***in low water***: 'hard up', impoverished.

1785 GROSE *Dict. Vulg. Tongue, Low tide* or *Low water*, when there is no money in a man's pocket. **1885** *Chamb. Jrnl.* 21 Feb. 125/2 Law-breakers..who, having been 'put away', and done their time, found themselves in low water upon their return to the outer world. **1886** MISS BRADDON *Mohawks* I. iv. 94 His lordship was in low water financially.

low-'water-mark. The line or level reached by the tide at low-water; a mark set up to indicate this. (Cf. HIGH-WATER-MARK.)

1526 in Dillon *Customs of Pale* (1892) 87 Anie wrak rivinge or drivinge in the sea without the Lowe water marke. **1629** H. C. *Drayning Fennes* C ij, When the out-fals shall bee opened to Low water marke. **1776** G. SEMPLE *Building in Water* 2, 2 Inches above the Low-water Mark... 8 Inches above Low-water Mark. **1783** PAGE in *Phil. Trans.* LXXIV. 16 It continued in vast quantity almost to the spring tide low-water-mark. **1880** GEIKIE *Phys. Geog.* iii. §17. 154 The lower limit of the beach or low-water mark.

b. *fig.* The lowest point reached in number, quality, quantity, intensity, etc.

1651 N. BACON *Disc. Govt. Eng.* II. xxxvii. (1739) 167 The state of Learning and Holiness was now at the low-water mark. **1745** H. WALPOLE *Lett.* (1846) II. 9 My ink is at low water-mark for all my acquaintance. **1838** DICKENS *O. Twist* viii, I'm at low-water-mark myself—only one bob and a magpie. **1890** *Spectator* 29 Mar., Destroying the truths of which most social conventions are the low-water mark.

†**low-wines.** *Obs.* Also 7 *sing.* low wine, 8 *Sc.* lowins. *pl.* The first spirit that comes off in the process of distillation. (Cf. FAINTS.)

1641 FRENCH *Distill.* i. (1651) 26 There will come forth a weak Spirit, which is called low Wine. **1657** R. LIGON *Barbadoes* (1673) 93 The first Spirit that comes off, is a small Liquor, which we call low-wines. **1701** *Lond. Gaz.* No. 2717/1 An Act for Granting to His Majesty several Duties upon Low-Wines or Spirits of the first Extraction. **1790** A. WILSON *Poems* 91 Whauks o' gude ait-far'le cowins, Synt down wi' whey, or whisky lowins. **1820** *Broderip & Bingham's Rep.* I. 436 *Terry* v. *Huntington*, when the commissioners determined low wines to be strong waters.

lowy. *Obs.* exc. *Hist.* [a. OF. *louee, lieuee*:—late L. *leucāta*, f. *leuca* (F. *lieue*) LEAGUE *sb.*[1]] A liberty extending for about a league outside a town.

1570-6 LAMBARDE *Peramb. Kent* 329 Round about the Towne of Tunbridge, lyeth a territorie, or compasse of ground, commonly called, the Lowy, but written in the auncient Recordes and Histories Leucata [*printed* peucata] or Leuga, and being (in deede) a French League of ground. **1598** HAKLUYT *Voy.* I. 18 The Port of Hastings ought to finde three ships. The lowie of Peuensey, one. **1780** *Descr. Tunbridge-Wells* 39 Great Bounds..was so called, because it was the extreme boundary of the lowy or liberty of Tunbridge. **1809** BAWDWEN *Domesday Bk.* 257 In Ripon the Archbishop has the Lowy of St. Wilfrid. **1880** R. C. JENKINS *Canterbury* 170 Gilbert de Clare did homage for the Castle and lowy of Tonbridge.

lox (lɒks, ɛl əʊ ɛks), *sb.*[1] Also **LOX.** [orig. f. *l*iquid *ox*ygen *explosive*; later interpreted as repr. *l*iquid *ox*ygen.] **a.** An explosive device which uses liquid oxygen as an oxidant (see quot. 1946).

1923 *Chem. Abstr.* XVII. 2646 Wood pulp as an ingredient renders LOXs less sensitive to detonation. **1933** *Mining & Metall.* XIV. 368/1 This research was to be centered upon the absorbent material used in the manufacture of LOX cartridges. **1946** G. J. YOUNG *Elem. Mining* (ed. 4) v. 127 Lox consists of a canvas cartridge filled with granular carbonaceous material, moistened, which when soaked in liquid oxygen, removed from the soaking box, and placed in the drill hole can be detonated and is an effective blasting agent. **1966** S. FORDHAM *High Explosives & Propellants* v. 63 A type of explosive..which achieved popularity for a time and is still used in some countries, is the liquid oxygen explosive or LOX.

b. Liquid oxygen, esp. when used as a rocket propellant.

The 1923 example may have been intended in sense a. **1923** *Chem. Abstr.* XVII. 2646 The ballistic pendulum was found suitable for tests of LOX explosives. **1940** *News* (San Francisco) 3 Oct. 19/4 That liquid is called liquid oxygen, or 'L-O-X', as the mining men say. **1949** *Time* 6 June, The Viking burns alcohol and 'lox' in a single combustion chamber. **1959** *Adv. Space Sci. & Technol.* I. 193 Existing LOX systems probably will not function properly under weightlessness. **1962** *Flight Internat.* LXXXI. 168/2 The Buccaneer is the first Naval aircraft to use lox.

Hence as *v. trans.*, to fuel with liquid oxygen; **'loxing** *vbl. sb.*

1961 A. B. SHEPARD in *Astronauts* Suppl. 4 The Red-stone was loxed. **1962** J. GLENN in *Into Orbit* 187 One of the loxing valves stuck and the technicians had to shift a smaller valve to complete the loading process. **1970** R. TURNILL *Lang. of Space* 72 Loading the lox into the launch vehicle's fuel tanks from a ground supply is referred to as loxing.

lox (lɒks), *sb.*[2] Pl. lox, loxes. [f. Yiddish *laks*, f. G. *lachs* salmon.] A kind of smoked salmon.

1941 S. LONGSTREET *Last Man around World* xii. 135 Listen, you lox-eater—until last year you thought herring was the only thing they took from the sea. **1950** F. ALLEN *Let.* Oct. in G. Marx *Groucho Lett.* (1967) 73 At the stage delicatessen..the lox is running good and the cream cheese is spreading easily. **1961** B. MALAMUD *New Life* (1962) 121 I'll bet lox to bagels that Gerald will get more for the department. **1969** A. GLYN *Dragon Variation* ix. 293 He.. folded himself on to a stool at the counter, and ordered coffee and a bagel with lox. **1972** *Times* 21 July 12/8 Where in Paris,..can one enjoy a breakfast of beigles, lox (Yiddish for salmon) and cream cheese? **1973** *Daily Colonist* (Victoria, B.C.) 16 Sept. 35/5 The bagel..often is eaten with smoked salmon or lox from Nova Scotia.

lox, ? obs. pl. of LOCK *sb.*[1] (see sense 2 *note*).

1668 *Clevelands Old Gill* ii. in *J.C. Revived* (ed. 4) 32 Her Breath smells like Lox.

Loxa ('lɒksə). [The name (now spelt *Loja*) of a province in Ecuador, South America.] *attrib.* in ***Loxa bark***: the pale Peruvian bark obtained from the cinchona-tree (*C. condaminea*).

1825 *Amer. Jrnl. Sci.* IX. 364 Loxa, or Crown Bark. **1837** *Penny Cycl.* VII. 172 (*Cinchona*), Loxa or crown bark, called also true Loxa bark, is obtained either exclusively from the C. Condaminea or from it and C. scrobiculata. *Ibid.*, The false Loxa bark, confessedly a very bad bark. **1885** A. B. GARROD *Ess. Mat. Med.* (ed 11) 292 Pale or Loxa barks.

‖**loxarthrus** (lɒk'sɑːθrəs). *Surg.* [mod.L., f. Gr. λοξ-ός oblique + ἄρθρον joint. Cf. F. *loxarthre.*] (See quot.)

1822-34 *Good's Study Med.* (ed. 4) III. 237 Loxarthrus in surgery, an obliquity of a joint of any kind, without spasm or luxation.

‖**loxia**[1] ('lɒksɪə). [mod.L., f. Gr. λοξ-ός oblique. (So called by Gesner, from the oblique crossing of the mandibles.)] A genus of birds of which the Crossbill is the type.

1706 PHILLIPS (ed. Kersey), *Loxias*, the Cross-beak or Shell-apple; a Bird that is common in several Parts of Germany, and sometimes found in England. **1753** CHAMBERS *Cycl. Supp., Loxia.* **1834** PRINGLE *Afr. Sk.* 25 Whose slender sprays above the flood Suspend the loxia's callow brood In cradle-nests.

‖**loxia**[2] ('lɒksɪə). *Path.* [mod.L., f. Gr. λοξ-ός: see prec.] A deformity of the neck in which it is drawn to one side; wry-neck.

1844 in HOBLYN *Dict. Med.*

Loxian ('lɒksɪən), *sb.*[1] *rare*[−1]. [f. L. *Loxi-as*, Gr. Λοξίας surname of Apollo + -AN.] Apollo.

1840 BROWNING *Sordello* I. 601 The Loxian's [*note* Apollo (the bowman)] choicest gifts of gold.

loxian ('lɒksɪən), *a.* and *sb.*[2] [f. LOXIA + -AN.] **A.** *adj.* Of or belonging to the genus *Loxia.* **B.** A bird of this genus.

In recent Dicts.

loxic ('lɒksɪk), *a. Med.* [ad. mod.L. *loxicus*, f. Gr. λοξ-ός oblique: see -IC.] Distorted in position or direction; awry.

1856 in MAYNE *Expos. Lex.* **1890** in J. S. BILLINGS *Nat. Med. Dict.*

loxoclase ('lɒksəʊkleɪs). *Min.* [mod. (Breithaupt, 1846) f. Gr. λοξό-ς oblique + κλάσις fracture.] A variety of orthoclase, containing sodium.

1846 *Amer. Jrnl. Sci.* II. 414 Loxoclase is near feldspar in its characters. **1852** C. U. SHEPARD *Min.* (ed. 3) 187 Loxoclase..occurs in regular crystals. **1893** CHAPMAN *Blowpipe Pract.* 259 Loxoclase is also a variety but resembles Oligoclase in composition.

loxocosm ('lɒksəkɒz(ə)m). [f. Gr. λοξό-ς oblique + κόσμ-ος world. Cf. F. *loxocosme.*] 'An instrument to illustrate the effect of the obliquity of the earth's axis in different seasons upon the length of the day' (*Cent. Dict.* 1890).

Loxodon ('lɒksədɒn). *Zool.* [ad. mod.L. *Loxodonta* pl. (Cuvier), f. Gr. λοξ-ός oblique + ὀδοντ-, ὀδούς tooth.] 'A sub-genus of elephants, so called from the rhomb-shaped discs of the worn molars' (Ogilvie, 1882).

1857 FALCONER in *Q. Jrnl. Geol. Soc.* XIII. 315 For this subgeneric group [of Elephants] the name of Loxodon, first indicated by Frederick Cuvier, has been adopted. *Ibid.* 321 Two of the Loxodons,..have a ridge-formula which is identical or nearly so with that of *Stegodon insignis.* **1863** LYELL *Antiq. Man* xxii. 438 A remarkable dwarf species.. has been discovered belonging, like the existing *E. Africanus*, to the group Loxodon.

So **'loxodont. a.** *adj.* Having teeth like those of an elephant belonging to the group *Loxodon.* **b.** *sb.* An elephant with this dentition.

In recent Dicts.

loxodrome ('lɒksədrəʊm). [f. Gr. λοξό-ς oblique + δρόμ-ος course.] = *loxodromic line.*

1880 *Libr. Univ. Knowl.* (N.Y.) X. 436 The loxodrome, or loxodromic line. **1888** GREENHILL *Integral Calculus* 31 A loxodrome on the sphere, cutting the meridians at a constant angle.

loxodromic (lɒksəʊˈdrɒmɪk), *a.* and *sb.* [Formed as prec. + -IC. Cf. F. *loxodromique.*]

A. *adj.* Pertaining to oblique sailing, or sailing by the rhumb. ***loxodromic chart, projection***, another name for Mercator's projection. ***loxodromic curve, line, spiral***, a rhumb-line. ***loxodromic tables***, traverse tables.

1702 J. RALPHSON *Math. Dict., Loxodromick Line.* **1727–41** CHAMBERS *Cycl.* s.v. *Table, Loxodromick Tables.* **1834** *Nat. Philos., Navigation* II. iv. §51. 19 (U.K.S.) The oblique rhumb line is called also the Loxodromic curve. **1839** *Penny Cycl.* XIV. 183/1 *Loxodromic spiral*, the curve on which a ship sails when her course is always on one point of the compass. It is called in English works Rhumb Line. **1855** MAURY *Phys. Geog. Sea* (1859) §123 These..counter-currents are also made to move in a sort of spiral or loxodromic curve.

B. *sb.* = *loxodromic line, table.* **b. loxodromics**: the art of oblique sailing.

a **1679** SIR J. MOORE *Syst. Math.* (1681) II. 120 Loxodromiques or Traverse-Tables of Miles, with the Difference of Longitudes and Latitudes. **1704** J. HARRIS *Lex. Techn., Loxodromiques*, is the Art or Way of oblique sailing by the Rumb... Hence the Tables of Rhumbs, or the Traverse Table of Miles,..is by Sir J. Moore, and others, called by this Name of Loxodromiques. **1762** DUNN in *Phil. Trans.* LIII. 66 If rightly correspondent with the loxodromiques or rhumbs. **1860** MAURY *Phys. Geog. Sea* iv. §235 It is diverted from the great circle path and forced to take up its line of march, either in spirals about a point on the surface of the earth, or in loxodromics about its axis. **1867** SMYTH *Sailor's Word-bk., Loxodromic*, the line of a ship's way when sailing oblique to the meridian.

loxodromical (lɒksəʊˈdrɒmɪkəl), *a.* [Formed as prec. + -AL[1].] = LOXODROMIC *a.*

1704 J. HARRIS *Lex. Techn.* s.v. *Loxodromiques*, Loxodromical Tables. **1706** PHILLIPS (ed. Kersey), *Loxodromical* or *Loxodromick*, (in Navigat.) belonging to the Method of oblique Sailing.

Hence **loxoˈdromically** *adv.*

1867 SMYTH *Sailor's Word-bk., Mercator's sailing.* Performed loxodromically by means of Mercator's charts.

loxodromism (lɒkˈsɒdrəmɪz(ə)m). [Formed as prec. + -ISM. Cf. F. *loxodromisme.*] The tracing of or moving in a loxodromic line or curve.

1853 TH. ROSS *Humboldt's Trav.* III. xxxii. 374 Occupied ..by the parallelism, or rather the loxodromism of the strata,.. I was struck with [etc.]. **1855** OGILVIE, Suppl., *Loxodromism*, the tracing of a loxodromic curve or line.

loxodromy (lɒkˈsɒdrəmɪ). [Formed as prec. + -Y. Cf. F. *loxodromie.*] A loxodromic line or course; also = *loxodromics.*

a **1656** USSHER *Ann.* (1658) 98 Anaximander..first observed the Loxodromie, or biassing motions of the stars, in the Zodiac. **1706** PHILLIPS (ed. Kersey), *Loxodromy*, such a Course in Sailing. **1712** DESAGULIERS tr. *Ozanam's Geog.* 114 A Ship which..sails along any Oblique Rumb.. describes upon the Terraqueous Globe a Spiral Line, which we have call'd a Loxodromick Line, Loxodromy, or Oblique Course. **1855** OGILVIE, Suppl., *Loxodromy*, a loxodromic curve or spiral; loxodromics.

loxolophodont (lɒksəʊˈləʊfədɒnt), *a.* and *sb.* [f. Gr. λοξό-ς oblique + *lophodont*: see LOPHO-.]

A. *adj.* Belonging to the genus *Loxolophodon* of fossil mammals, having obliquely crested molar teeth. **B.** *sb.* An individual of this genus.

1887 E. D. COPE *Orig. Fittest* vii. 259 The Loxolophodonts. *Ibid.* 263 The..Loxolophodont types of molar structure.

loxotic (lɒkˈsɒtɪk), *a. Med.* [ad. mod.L. *loxōticus* (Mayne *Expos. Lex.* 1856), f. Gr. λοξό-ς oblique: see -OTIC.] = LOXIC.

1889 *Syd. Soc. Lex.* **1890** J. S. BILLINGS *Nat. Med. Dict.*

loxotomy (lɒkˈsɒtəmɪ). [ad. mod.L. *loxotomia*, f. Gr. λοξό-ς oblique + τομία cutting.] A method of amputation characterized by cutting obliquely through the limb.

1856 in MAYNE *Expos. Lex.* In some recent Dicts.

†**loy**[1]. *Obs. rare.* Also 6 loye. [a. OF. *loie, loy*, or aphetic for ALLOY.] Alloy.

1598 FLORIO, *Caráto*, the touch or refining, or loye of gold. *Ibid., Coppella*, a refiner's woord, called the test or loye of siluer or gold. **1622** MABBE tr. *Aleman's Guzman d' Alf.* I. 127 We see euery thing want some-what in the finenesse of it's Loy and true touch.

loy[2] (lɔɪ). *Anglo-Irish.* [a. Irish *laighe.*] A kind of spade used in Ireland (see quots.).

1763 *Museum Rusticum* I. lxxxiii. 358 The iron part of the loy, or Irish spade, is not quite half so broad at the edge as the English garden spade. **1780** A. YOUNG *Tour Irel.* I. 286 All the tillage is by the irish loy. **1892** JANE BARLOW *Irish Idylls* 181 There be the loys and graips lying around.

loyal (ˈlɔɪəl), *a.* and *sb.* Also 6–7 loyall, 7 loial(l. [a. F. *loyal*, OF. *loial, leial*, semi-popular ad. L. *lēgāl-em* (see LEGAL *a.*), f. *lēg-*, *lēx* law. Cf. LEAL *a.*]

A. *adj.* **1.** True to obligations of duty, love, etc.; faithful to plighted troth.

1604 SHAKS. *Oth.* IV. ii. 35 Your wife my Lord: your true and loyall wife. **1611** —— *Cymb.* III. ii. 47 So he wishes you all happinesse, that remaines loyall to his Vow, and your encreasing in Loue. **1651** HOBBES *Leviath.* III. xxxv. 217 Abraham..the Father of the Faithfull; that is, of those that are loyall. **1676** DRYDEN *Aurengz.* I. i. 186 Darah from Loyal Aurenge-Zebe is fled. **1697** —— *Æneid* VI. 607 [There] Chast Laodamia, with Evadne, moves: Unhappy both, but loyal in their Loves. **1859** TENNYSON *Elaine* 558 Nor often loyal to his word. **1871** R. ELLIS tr. *Catullus* lxiv. 182 Nay, but a loyal lover, a hand pledg'd surely, shall ease me. **1871–74** J. THOMSON *City Dreadf. Nt.* v. iv, A home of peace by loyal friendships cheered.

2. Faithful in allegiance to the sovereign or constituted government. Also, in recent use, enthusiastically devoted or reverential to the person and family of the sovereign.

Originally a contextual application of sense 1. As in the case of other words of similar or opposite meaning (as *leal, feal; traitor, treason*) the specific feudal use has in English become a distinct sense, and the one most prominent in use.

1531 ELYOT *Gov.* Proheme, I..do nowe dedicate it vnto your hyghnesse [the King]..verely trustynge that your moste excellent wysedome wyll therein esteme my loyall harte and diligent endeauour. **1593** SHAKS. *Rich. II*, I. i. 181 A Iewell in a ten times barr'd vp Chest, Is a bold spirit, in a loyall brest. **1595** —— *John* II. i. 271 He that proues the King To him will we proue loyall. **1611** BIBLE *2 Macc.* xi. 19 If then you wil keepe your selues loyall to the state [LXX. ἐὰν μὲν οὖν συντηρήσητε τὴν εἰς τὰ πράγματα εὔνοιαν]. **1620** J. WILKINSON *Coroners & Sherifes* 3 That all coroners.. should be chosen..of the most convenientest and most loialst people that may be found in the said counties. *a* **1677** BARROW *Serm.* Wks. 1686 III. 48 He must reign over us, if not as over loyal Subjects to our comfort, yet as over stubborn Rebels to our confusion. **1702** DENNIS *Monument* xxxvi. 76 His loyal'st Subjects too divided were. **1784** COWPER *Task* VI. 661 The simple clerk, but loyal,..did rear right merrily, two staves, Sung to the praise and glory of King George. **1849** MACAULAY *Hist. Eng.* vii. II. 209 The king pressed them, as they were loyal gentlemen, to gratify him. **1887** TENNYSON *Jubilee Q. Victoria* iv, And in each let a multitude Loyal, each, to the heart of it,..Hail the fair Ceremonial Of this year of her Jubilee. **1897** SIR W. LAURIER *Speech* in *Daily News* 5 July 4/3 We [*sc.* French Canadians] are loyal because we are free.

3. Of things, actions, etc.: Characterized by or exhibiting loyalty; ***loyal toast***, a toast proposed and drunk (in the U.K. and British Commonwealth) to the monarch or (elsewhere) to some other important personage.

1598 SHAKS. *Merry W.* v. v. 68 Each faire Instalment, Coate, and seu'rall Crest, With loyall Blazon, euermore be blest. **1600** HOLLAND *Livy* XLV. 1209 They had received great helpe at his hands in the Punick warre by his valiant and loiall service. **1601** SHAKS. *Twel. N.* I. v. 289 *Ol.* Why, what would you? *Vio...* Write loyall Cantons of contemned loue. **1799** *Times* 1 June 3/4 Many Loyal Toasts were given, and the day spent with great conviviality. **1802** WORDSW. *Sonn.*, '*Is it a reed that's shaken*', A seemly reverence may be paid to power; But that's a loyal virtue, never sown In haste. **1835** DICKENS *Sk. Boz*; *Public Dinners*, The other 'loyal and patriotic' toasts having been drunk with all due enthusiasm. **1858** [see HIGHLAND *a.* 2a]. **1872** BLACKIE *Lays Highl.* 67 For strong men who knew to do and dare I drop the loyal tear. **1970** M. KELLY *Spinifex* xi. 166 'Gentlemen—' Matsuda barked.. 'The Loyal Toast!' **1972** *Guardian* 9 May 15/4 It was the most miserable meal I have ever presided over, and I had not the heart to propose the Loyal Toast at the end. **1974** *Ibid.* 25 Jan. 10/4 The time was come for toasts and speeches. After the Loyal Toast, Blackadder clipped his cigar.

†**4.** = LEGAL in certain senses. **a.** Of a child: Legitimate. **b.** Of money: Genuine, legally current. Of goods: Of the legal standard of quality. *Obs.*

1605 SHAKS. *Lear* II. i. 86 Loyall and naturall Boy. **1660** WATERHOUSE *Arms & Arm.* 34 Cognizance is taken..of what House Gentlemen are, from what branch of that House, whether loyall or spurious. **1690** CHILD *Disc. Trade* (ed. 4) 159 Our Laws that oblige our people to the making of strong, substantial (and, as we call it, loyal) cloth of a certain length.

5. *Manege.* (See quot.; cf. F. *cheval loyal, bouche loyale.*) ? *Obs.*

1727 BAILEY vol. II. s.v., A Horse is said to be loyal, who freely bends all his Force in obeying and performing any manage he is put to; and does not..resist, altho' he is ill treated. Loyal Mouth [of a Horse]..of the Nature of such Mouths, as are usually called Mouths with a full rest upon the Hand.

6. *Comb.*, as ***loyal-hearted*** adj.

1599 *Warn. Faire Wom.* I. 468 To his wife, in all this city, none More kind, more loyal-hearted. **1850** TENNYSON *In Mem.* cx, On thee the loyal-hearted hung.

B. *sb. pl.* †**a.** Those who are bound by allegiance; liege subjects (*obs.*). **b.** In recent use: Loyal subjects, as opposed to disaffected persons.

c **1540** tr. *Pol. Verg. Eng. Hist.* (Camden No. 36) I. 177 After the forthe yeare of his [Ethelbertus'] reigne he was semblabie murthered of his owne loyals. **1602** CAREW *Cornwall* 97 Being destitute of horses and treasure, he [Earl Richard] prayed therein ayde of his loyals. **1885** *Fortn. Rev.* Oct. 604 From the Diamond Fields alone a large contingent of loyals can always be reckoned upon. **1887** RIDER HAGGARD *Jess* xxvii, Whoever says that the English have given up the country..and deserted its subjects and the loyals and the natives, is a liar.

loyalism (ˈlɔɪəlɪz(ə)m). [f. LOYAL *a.* + -ISM.] The principles or actions of a loyalist; adherence to the sovereign or government; loyalty.

1837 LOCKHART *Scott* lxiii. (1842) 556 This feature of Irish loyalism was new to the untravelled Scotch of the party. **1887** *Chamb. Jrnl.* IV. 12 Why, then, should I, a student, foresee, beneath this wealth of loyalism, a rising power that would crush and kill both the lauders and the lauded.

loyalist (ˈlɔɪəlɪst), *sb.* (and *a.*) [f. LOYAL *a.* + -IST.] **a.** One who is loyal; one who adheres to his sovereign or to constituted authority, *esp.* in times of revolt; one who supports the existing form of government; *spec.* (freq. with capital initial) an Irish advocate or supporter of parliamentary union between Great Britain and Northern Ireland (or, before partition, the whole of Ireland).

United Empire Loyalist (Amer. Hist.): see quot. 1897. For the quot. from *Howell's Vocal Forest* (1640) given by Johnson to illustrate this word, see LOYOLIST.

[**1647** *The Royall, and the Royallist's Plea* (*running title*) The Royall and the Loyallists Plea.] **1685** J. KETTLEWELL (*title*) The Religious Loyalist: or, a Good Christian Taught. How to be a Faithful Servant both to God and the King. **1712** E. COOKE *Voy. S. Sea* 294 The wounded were above 400 of the Loyalists. **1721** *Wood's Ath. Oxon.* (ed. 2) II. 98/2 It was then the hap and fortune of one Dr. Tho. Bayly a great Loyallist, to meet with this Nobleman. **1781** S. PETERS *Hist. Connect.* 357 Colonel Street Hall, of Wallingford, a loyalist, was appointed General. **1812** *Gen. Hist.* in *Ann. Reg.* 205 The provinces of Spanish America were still the theatre of a sanguinary civil war between the two parties of independents and loyalists. **1852** THACKERAY *Esmond* I. (1876) 2 This resolute old loyalist..was with the King whilst his house was thus being battered down. **1885** *Times* 11 Nov. 7/2 A meeting of the Loyalists of the county Wexford..was held to-day..in order to declare a firm adherence to the legislative union between Ireland and Great Britain. **1886** LADY MONKSWELL *Jrnl.* 1 Feb. in *Victorian Diarist* (1944) I. 125 If he [*sc.* Mr. Gladstone] proposes Home Rule I almost think the loyalists will fight. **1893** *Times* 11 May 9/2 The Loyalists in Ireland repudiated with one voice the Legislative Council proposed in the [Home Rule] Bill. **1893** *Times* 11 May 9/3 Mr. Rentoul asserted that the Loyalists in Ireland repudiated with one voice the Legislative Council proposed in the Bill. **1897** J. G. BOURINOT *Canada* xxi. 291 This event was the coming to the provinces of many thousand people, known as United Empire Loyalists, who during the progress of the war..left their old homes in the thirteen colonies. *Ibid.* 297 Those loyalists..who joined the cause of Great Britain before the Treaty of Peace in 1783, were allowed the distinction of having after their name the letters U.E. to preserve the memory of their fidelity to a United Empire. **1934** *Hansard Lords* 25 July 1073, I am glad to understand that the Irish loyalists are not suffering from any injustice or persecution by reason of their political faith. **1975** *Irish Times* 10 May 11/1 It is politic, of course, for the Loyalists to cut sober figures these days. **1986** *Daily Tel.* 14 May 1/7 Several Loyalists were arrested in Northern Ireland yesterday in connection with rioting during an illegal parade.

b. *attrib.* or as *adj.*

1885 *Times* 19 Oct. 12/4 (*heading*) The loyalist union in Ireland. **1934** *Times* 7 May 11/6 The immediate object for which the Irish Loyalist Imperial Federation has been formed is to assert the constitutional rights and privileges of all loyal South Irish-born subjects of the King. **1970** [see MARITIME *sb.* 1 b]. **1986** *Sunday Tel.* 11 May 3/1 A territory the 'loyalist' extremists were designating 'Catholic-free'.

†**loyality.** *Obs.* [f. LOYAL *a.* + -ITY.] Loyalty.

1646 EARL MONM. tr. *Biondi's Civil Warres* VIII. 152 Richard being now King found like loyality in his subjects, as whilest He was a subject, he used to the King his Nephew.

loyalize (ˈlɔɪəlaɪz), *v.* [f. LOYAL *a.* + -IZE.] *trans.* To make loyal; to restore to faithful allegiance; also, to attach to the loyalist party.

1825 SYD. SMITH *Sp.* Wks. 1859 II. 206/1 My remedy for these evils is, to enter into an alliance with the Irish people —to conciliate the clergy,..to loyalise the laity. **1867** *Pall Mall G.* 7 Aug. 1 To pacify, loyalize, and content at once those who have land and those who desire it.

Hence **ˈloyalized** *ppl. a.*

1851 C. R. EDMONDS *Milton* xvi. 224 The treacherous faction of loyalized presbyterians.

†**loyallement**, *adv.* *Obs. rare*[−1]. [a. F. *loyalement.*] In a loyal manner, faithfully.

1548 HOOPER *Ten Commandm.* x. 159 It sufficithe vs, loyallement, and with good faythe to hyre this commaundement.

loyally (ˈlɔɪəlɪ), *adv.* [f. LOYAL *a.* + -LY[2].] In a loyal manner, with loyalty; faithfully.

1572 HULOET (ed. Higgins), Loyally or faythfully, *fideliter.* **1600** E. BLOUNT tr. *Conestaggio* 270 Such as faithfully without promises..had loially serued them. **1725** POPE *Odyss.* XI. 449 Wealthy Kings are loyally obey'd. **1853** J. H. NEWMAN *Hist. Sk.* (1876) I. [II.] I. iv. 181 Its [China's] power of persevering so loyally in its old institutions through so many ages. **1891** E. PEACOCK *N. Brendon* I. 185 He was loyally anxious to serve his employer.

loyalness (ˈlɔɪəlnɪs). [f. LOYAL *a.* + -NESS.] The state or condition of being loyal; loyalty.

1592 STOW *Ann.* (an. 1566) 1125 The Queenes maiestie.. was of all the students..so honorably and ioyfully receiued, as..their loialnes towardes the Queenes maiestie..did require. **1642** ROGERS *Naaman* 380 Loyalnesse and love. **1727** BAILEY vol. II, *Loyalness*, loyalty.

loyalty (ˈlɔɪəltɪ). Also 5 loyaltee, -aulte, 6–7 loyal-, loialtie, 7 loialty, loyaltye. [a. OF. *loialté* (mod. *loyauté*), f. *loyal* LOYAL *a.*: see -TY.]

1. Faithful adherence to one's promise, oath, word of honour, etc.; †conjugal faithfulness, fidelity. †Also in phrase ***by my loyalty***.

c **1400** *Rom. Rose* 6783 This noble dide such labour To susteyne euer the loyaltee, That he to moche agilte me. *c* **1477** CAXTON *Jason* 21 By my loyaulte saide there Corsus sire alle that I haue sayd procedeth not from ony fere..that I haue of all your enemyes. *c* **1532** DU WES *Introd. Fr.* in Palsgr. 927 In my loyaltie, *en ma loyaulté.* **1591** SHAKS. *Two Gent.* IV. ii. 7 When I protest true loyalty to her, She twits me with my falsehood to my friend. **1612** CHAPMAN *Widdowes Teares* II. Dram. Wks. 1873 III. 23 If you be sure

of your wiues loialtie for terme of life. **1697** DRYDEN *Virg. Past.* VIII. 130 These Garments once were his; and left to me The Pledges of his promis'd Loyalty. **1770** GOLDSM. *Des. Vill.* 406 And piety with wishes placed above, And steady loyalty, and faithful love. **1856** EMERSON *Eng. Traits, Ability* Wks. (Bohn) II. 36 In the courts, the independence of the judges and the loyalty of the suitors are equally excellent. **1871** R. S. CANDLISH in *Life* xiv. (1882) 149 Thy right hand hath not lost its cunning, nor thy heart its loving loyalty to the gentle craft.

2. a. Faithful adherence to the sovereign or lawful government; *spec.* of government employees. Also, in recent use, enthusiastic reverence for the person and family of the sovereign.

1531 ELYOT *Gov.* III. vi, For the subiecte or seruaunt to his soueravne or maister it is proprely named fidelitie, and in a frenche terme loyaltie. **1568** GRAFTON *Chron.* I. 176 In this battaile Canutus proved the Loyaltie and manly prowesse of the Englishe men. **1605** SHAKS. *Macb.* I. iv. 22 The seruice, and the loyaltie I owe, In doing it, payes it selfe. **1630** J. LEVETT *Ord. Bees* (1634) 69 They offer unto him all their services and loyalties. *a* **1677** BARROW *Serm.* Wks. 1686 III. xli. 471 Whoever of those rebels willingly should come in.. and promise future loyalty, or obedience to his laws.. should..obtain rewards from him. **1784** COWPER *Task* v. 331 We too are friends to loyalty. We love The king who loves the law. **1807-8** SYD. SMITH *Plymley's Lett.* Wks. 1859 II. 176/1 Loyalty within the bounds of reason..is one of the greatest instruments of English happiness. **1874** GREEN *Short Hist.* vii. §6. 399 Under the rule of Elizabeth loyalty became more and more a passion among Englishmen. **1955** *Bull. Atomic Sci.* Apr. 132 Commissioner Murray, concurring in the result, found Dr. Oppenheimer a risk on grounds of loyalty which he newly defined as obedience to security regulations. **1956** M. GRODZINS *Loyal & Disloyal* v. 230 Loyalty-security programs threaten to cripple the entire foreign service. *Ibid.* 231 Governments must guard themselves against harm and destruction, and there can therefore be no criticism of the objectives of loyalty investigations for government employees and scientists who work on government projects. **1964** GOULD & KOLB *Dict. Social Sci.* 397 In the United States since the end of World War II, loyalty has been an important issue in politics... Under President Truman..there was an elaborate procedure for determining the 'loyalty' of servants of the U.S. government.

b. *attrib.* in † *loyalty loan*; **loyalty oath** *U.S.*, an oath, usually mandatory, required of a prospective public employee or other person in which he swears to abstain from subversive activities.

1800 *Asiatic Ann. Reg., Proc. Parl.* 23/2 The.. advantageous disposal of the loyalty loan. **1952** M. McCARTHY in *Reporter* (N.Y.) 8 July 32/2 In order to.. work for the Columbia Broadcasting System you have to sign a loyalty oath which is presented with your contract. **1969** L. GREENBAUM *Out of Shape* xxii. 162 The older man had his contract terminated under a clause dealing with loyalty oaths. Apparently he was a card-carrier and hadn't said so. **1971** M. McCARTHY *Birds of America* 250 Berkeley is horrible... You have to swear a loyalty oath... It's natural that the students would finally rebel. **1973** *Black Panther* 12 May 6/1 After signing a loyalty oath to the school, students are required to present two identification cards, one issued since November 16th, before gaining entrance to the campus.

† 3. Lawfulness, legality (of marriage). *Obs. rare*$^{-1}$.

1660 R. COKE *Power & Subj.* 193 In all the reign of H. 3. ..if any issue were joyned upon loyalty of marriage, general bastardy, or such like, the King did ever write to the Bishop of the diocese..to certifie the loyalty of the marriage.

loyeter, obs. form of LOITER.

† loyn. *Obs. rare.* Also 5 **loigne, loyne,** 8 **lowing.** See also LUNE. [a. OF. *loigne* (also *longe*):—med.L. *longia, longea,* f. *long-us* LONG *a.*] A length (of cord); a leash for a hawk. Also *fig.*

c **1400** *Rom. Rose* 3882 The loigne [F. *longe*] it is so longe Of Bialacoil, hertis to lure. *Ibid.* 7050 He shal have of a corde a loigne [F. *longe*], With whiche men shal him binde and lede. *c* **1430** *Pilgr. Lyf Manhode* III. xxiii. (1869) 148 Yif me a loyne [F. *longe*], if thou wolt, and peyre gessis. **1575** TURBERV. *Faulconrie* 129 Let hir be loose from all hir furniture, that is without either loyne or cryaunce. **1702** J. K. *Dict.*, The Lowings or thongs of an hawk.

loyn, obs. form of LINE *v.*^{1}

† Loyolan, *a. Obs. rare*$^{-1}$. In 7 **Leiolan.** [f. *Loyola* (see LOYOLITE) + -AN.] Pertaining to Loyloa or the Jesuits.

1613 PURCHAS *Pilgrimage* (1614) 171 Thus dis Abraham ..; this must the Iesuite do when an Ignatian Superiour commands, or else he is no Holocaust for the Leiolan Altar.

Loyolism ('lɔɪəlɪz(ə)m). [Formed as next + -ISM.] The doctrine or principles of Loyola or the Jesuits.

1800 W. TAYLOR in *Monthly Mag.* VIII. 599 Intelligence, artfully tinctured with the essential oil of Loyolism.

† 'Loyolist. *Obs.* (Often in Howell.) [Formed as next + -IST. Cf. F. *Loyoliste.*] = LOYOLITE.

1640 HOWELL *Dodona's Gr.* 80 The Societies of the Loyolists. *Ibid.* 102 By the Instigation of the Loyolists.

Loyolite ('lɔɪəlaɪt). Also 7 **Loiolite.** [ad. mod.L. *Loyolīta*, f. the name of Ignatius *Loyola*, the founder of the Society of Jesus: see -ITE.] A Jesuit.

a **1670** HACKET *Abp. Williams* I. (1693) 172 Dr. Laud.. galled Fisher with great Acuteness. Which the false Loiolite traduced..in his Reports. **1679** OLDHAM *Sat. Jesuits* III. (1685) 36 And when in time these Contradiction meet; Then hope to find 'em in a Loyolite. **1818** RANKEN *Hist. France* V. ii. §4. 356 The members have been called sometimes, from his name, Inighists and Loyalites [*sic*], but they are more generally known by the name of Jesuits. **1875** M. PATTISON *Casaubon* v. 304 We shall all soon be mere slaves of the loyolites.

† loys. *Obs. rare.* Some kind of stone.

1295 *Visitat. S. Paul's* (Du Cange), Unum superaltare de Loys. **1486** *Bk. St. Albans, Her.* A iij, The..v. stone is calde a Loys..a sanquine stone or synamer hit is calde in armys.

loyse, obs. f. LOOSE *v.*; var. LOOSE *Obs.*, praise.

loysyn, obs. form of LOZEN.

loyte, -er, obs. ff. LITE *sb.*^{4}, LIGHTER *sb.*^{1}

loytre, loytron, obs. forms of LOITER.

loz, loze, var. ff. LOSS^{2} *Obs.*, LOSE *sb. Obs.*

lozel(l, variant of LOSEL.

lozen ('lɒzən). Chiefly *Sc.* Forms: 4-5 **los(e)yn, lozeyn, loysyn,** 6 **losan(e, losin,** 7 **losien, lossen,** 9 **losen,** 8-9 **lozen.** [? a. OF. *loseigne (once *loseingne*), var. of *losange* LOZENGE *sb.*]

† 1. *Cookery.* ? A thin cake of pastry. *Obs.*

? *c* **1390** *Form of Cury* (1780) 21 Take obleys oþer wafrous [wafrons] in stede of lozeyns and cowche in dysshes. *Ibid.* 46, 61, 62. *c* **1420** *Liber Cocorum* (1862) 40 Lay þer in þy loseyns abofe þe chese with wynne..þose loysyns er harde to make in fay.

† 2. A lozenge-shaped figure. *Obs.*

1542 *Inv. R. Wardr.* (1815) 60 Item ane uther dyamont ground oure with losanis ennamelit with the freir knott. **1593** *Sc. Acts Jas. VI* (1816) IV. 48/2 On the vther syde ane losane with ane thrissill on euery nuke.

3. A (lozenge-shaped) pane of glass.

1665 SIR J. L. FOUNTAINHALL *Jrnl.* (1900) 114 One of his servantes brook a lossen. *a* **1813** A. WILSON *2nd Ep. to J. Dobie* Poet. Wks. (1846) 51 While rains are blatt'ring frae the south, And down the lozens seeping. **1824** SCOTT *Redgauntlet* let. i, And who taught me to pin a losen, head a bicker, and hold the bannets? Alan once more. **1865** C. S. GRAHAME *Mystifications* 16 Lord Gillies was reminded of the time when he was an ill prettie laddie, and of breaking the lozens of one of her windows. **1896** N. MUNRO *Lost Pibroch* (1902) 40 The window-lozens winked with the light of big peat-fires within.

b. *transf.* A glass of a pair of spectacles.

1834 M. SCOTT *Cruise Midge* xi. (1842) 200 Auld Durie Squake..caught such a bash on the nose that baith the lozens were dang out of his barnacles.

4. *attrib.* and *Comb.* **a.** *attrib.* or *adj.* ? Embroidery with lozenge patterns.

1500-20 DUNBAR *Poems* xiv. 19 Sic losin sarkis, so mony glengoir markis Within this land was nevir hard nor sene. **1507** *Ld. Treas. Acc. Scotl.* (1901) III. 253 Ane gret losin doublat for the king. **1546** *Extracts Aberd. Reg.* (1844) I. 239 Tua losin sarkis.

b. *Comb.*, as † *lozen-wise* adv.

1625 in Rymer *Fœdera* XVIII. 236 Dyamonds cutt lozen wise.

Hence **'lozened** *a.* = LOZENGED. Also **'lozenless** *a. rare.*

1770 BP. FORBES *Jrnl.* (1886) 306 A circular Window, lozened by Arches of polished Stone meeting in the Centre. **1898** N. MUNRO *John Splendid* xiv, The place lay tenantless and melancholy,..the windows lozenless.

lozenge ('lɒzɪndʒ), *sb.* Forms: 4-7 **loseng(e,** 5-6 **losang(e, losing(e,** 5 **losyngye, (losynge, lesyng, lozingge),** 5-7 **lozeng,** 6-7 **lossenge, loosing,** 6-8 **lozange,** (8 **lozinge**), 7- **lozenge.** [a. OF. *losenge, losange* (mod.F. *losange*) = Sp. *losanje*, Catal. *llosange*, It. *lozanga*; perh. a derivative of the word which appears as Prov. *lausa*, Sp. *losa*, Catal. *llosa*, Pg. *lousa*, slab, tombstone, ? OF. *lauze* roofing slate.

It has been suggested that Prov. *lausa*:—late L. **lapidea* (f. *lapid-*, *lapis* stone) has been adopted into the other Rom. langs.; the presumed derivative *losenge* first occurs in Fr. (13th c.).]

1. A plane rectilineal figure, having four equal sides and two acute and two obtuse angles; a rhomb, 'diamond'. In *Heraldry*, such a figure used as a bearing, less elongated than the FUSIL, and placed with its longer axis vertical. † ***in lozenge*** = LOZENGY. ***grand lozenge***, † ***lozenge in point***: a lozenge the angles of which touch the sides of the shield. ***lozenges in cross***: four or more lozenges disposed so as to form a cross.

Guillim's definition (quot. 1610) would require that the acute angles should be of 60°; but the rule is not strictly followed by heraldic draughtsmen.

[*a* **1327** in Parker *Gloss. Her.* s.v., Sire Gerard de Braybrok, de argent a vij lozenges de goules.] ? *a* **1366** CHAUCER *Rom. Rose* 893 A [robe] with losenges [F. *losenges*] and scochouns,..wrought ful wel. *c* **1384** —— *H. Fame* III. 227 Somme crouned were as kinges, With crounes wroght ful of losenges. **1452** in Willis & Clark *Cambridge* (1886) I. 282 The Bemes shalbe. xij. inche imbowed with lozinggys. **1486** *Bk. St. Albans, Her.* F iv b, Off losyngys how and what maner of wyse they be made. **1519** HORMAN *Vulg.* 242 Paper or lyn clothe straked a crosse with losynges make fenestrals in stede of glasen wyndowes. **1577-87** HOLINSHED *Chron.* III. 802/2 The walles..coloured white & greene losengis, and in euerie losing either a rose or a pomegranat. **1610** GUILLIM *Heraldry* IV. xix. (1660) 354 A Losenge differeth from a Fusill in that the space between its two collaterall or middle Angles equals the length of any of the four Geometricall lines whereof it is composed. **1658** SIR T. BROWNE *Gard. Cyrus* iii. 54 Their mutual intersections make three Lozenges at the bottom of every Cell. **1688** R. HOLME *Armoury* I. 95/1 He beareth Or, a Losenge in point, (or extending to all sides of the Escochion) Gules. *a* **1695** WOOD *Oxford* (O.H.S.) III. 129 Over his head are his armes engraven... Over hers in lozenge, parted per fess, a lozenge counterchanged [etc.]. **1718** LADY M. W. MONTAGU *Let. to C'tess Mar* 10 Mar., Her shift [was] fastened at the bottom with a great diamond, shaped like a lozenge. **1818-20** E. THOMPSON *Cullen's Nosolog. Method.* (ed. 3) 323 Scales have at first the figure and extent of the cuticular lozenges. **1855** BROWNING *Cleon* 84 See, in the chequered pavement opposite, Suppose the artist made..a lozenge, then a trapezoid. **1870** F. R. WILSON *Ch. Lindisf.* 73 The font is panelled in lozenges.

b. A lozenge-shaped shield upon which the arms of a spinster or widow are emblazoned.

[**1696** PHILLIPS (ed. 5), *Lozenge*... This figure is particularly us'd in Heraldry, for the Bearings of Women not under Covert Baron.] *a* **1797** H. WALPOLE *Mem. Geo. III*, III. vii. 199 The royal arms in a widow's lozenge were pictured over the bed. **1835** MARRYAT *Olla Podr.* xxi, Nine out of ten have the widow's lozenge. **1868** CUSSANS *Her.* (1893) 42 *note*, The custom of emblazoning the arms of ladies upon lozenges did not generally obtain in England until the sixteenth century.

c. *Math.* = RHOMBUS. Now only in ***spherical lozenge***: see quot.

1551 RECORDE *Pathw. Knowl.* I. Defin., The thyrd kind is called losenges or diamondes whose sides bee all equall, but it hath neuer a square corner. **1889** CASEY *Spherical Trigon.* 18 If the four sides of a spherical quadrilateral be equal, the diagonals are perpendicular to each other, and they bisect its angles. Such a figure is called a spherical lozenge.

d. One of the lozenge-shaped facets of a precious stone when cut (see quots.).

1750 JEFFRIES *Treat. Diamonds & Pearls* (1751) *Explan. Techn. Terms*, Lozenges are common to Brilliants and Roses. In Brilliants they are formed by the meeting of the skill and star facets on the bezil: In Roses, by the meeting of the facets In the horizontal ribs of the crown. **1883** A. H. CHURCH *Precious Stones* 20 The old brilliant-cut..requires ..58 facets thus arranged:..4 Quoins or lozenges [etc.].

e. *Arch.* Short for *lozenge moulding*.

1841 BLOXAM *Goth. Archit.* 69 What were the mouldings principally used in the decoration of Norman churches?.. The cable moulding. The double cone... The lozenge [etc.]. **1850** PARKER *Gloss. Archit.* II. 47 Mouldings and Ornaments... Star... Lozenge... Enriched Lozenge.

† 2. *Cookery.* **a.** A lozenge-shaped cake. **b.** A lozenge-shaped ornament used to garnish a dish.

c **1430** *Two Cookery-bks.* 44 Lesynges de chare... And þan kytte þe cakys þorw with an knyf in maner of lesyngys. *c* **1440** *Douce MS.* 55 lf. 38 b, Cutt hem in the maner of losenges and make feyre batur..& close the sydes of the losynges ther with. **1494** FABYAN *Chron.* VII. 599 Viand royall plantyd losynges of golde.

3. A small cake or tablet, originally diamond-shaped, of medicated or flavoured sugar, etc. to be held and dissolved in the mouth. The name is also used, *e.g.* in ***meat lozenge***, for a tablet of a substance (indicated by the prefixed word) in a concentrated form.

1530 PALSGR. 241/1 Losange of spyce, *losange.* **1547** BOORDE *Brev. Health* II. xvii. 8 Dregges and losanges made to breake wynde. **1591** *Treas. Hid. Secrets* lvii. C 7, Lay on it your gold leafe,..cut your Losings [1627 Loosings] Diamond fashion, and so keep them. **1607** TOPSELL *Four-f. Beasts* (1658) 583 The Liver of a Wolf being made in the form of a dry Electuary and given as a Lozeng. *c* **1623** LODGE *Poor Man's Talent* (1881) 26 It shall not bee amiss to take a loosing of *Diaphisopi* or *Diaireas Salomonis.* **1629** MASSINGER *Picture* IV. ii, Eate presently These lozenges, of forty crownes an ounce. **1721** N. HODGES *Hist. Acc. Plague Lond.* 221, I..kept in my mouth some Lozenges all the while I was examining them. **1795** BURKE *Regic. Peace* iv. Wks. IX. 56 Boxes of epigrammatick lozenges. *a* **1845** HOOD *To J. Hume* v, Talk till hoarse; Have lozenges—mind Dawson's—in your pocket. **1898** *Cycling* 27 Meat lozenges are far preferable.

4. One of the lozenge-shaped panes of glass in a casement.

1656 BLOUNT *Glossogr.*, *Lozenge*,..also a quarry of a glass window. **1882** in OGILVIE, and in other recent Dicts.

5. *Manege.* (See quot.)

1897 *Encycl. Sport* I. 341/2 *Lozenge*, the slang term for a circular piece of leather with a hole in the centre to fit round the mouthpiece of the bit.

6. *attrib.* or *adj.* **a.** Lozenge-shaped, lozenge-like.

1658 SIR T. BROWNE *Gard. Cyrus* iii. 47 The..Lozenge seeds of the noble flower of the Sunne. **1688** R. HOLME *Armoury* II. 93/1 A Lozenge leaf, or double pointed leaf, or pointed at both ends. *c* **1790** IMISON *Sch. Art* II. 44 Gravers are of two sorts, square and lozenge. **1862** RICKMAN *Goth. Archit.* 382 The lozenge interval is formed by some of the ribs of the fan running though it.

b. Of or composed of lozenges; ornamented with lozenges. Of strokes: Crossed so as to form lozenge-shaped interstices.

1658 SIR T. BROWNE (*title*) The Garden of Cyrus or the Quincuncial Lozenge, or Net-work Plantations of the Ancients..Considered. **1688** R. HOLME *Armoury* I. 33/2 The Bends..wrought upon with Fusil or Lozenge work, which consisteth of two colours. **1797** *Encycl. Brit.* (ed. 3) VI. 671/2 The cross strokes ought to be very lozenge. **1812-16** J. SMITH *Panorama Sci. & Art* I. 156 The pier.. became, in its plan, lozenge, and formed the decorated pier. **1823** RUTTER *Fonthill* 36 Their openings are filled with bronze lozenge lattice. **1868** BROWNING *Ring & Bk.* I. 481, I..stepped out on the narrow terrace..And paced its lozenge-brickwork. **1870** F. R. WILSON *Ch. Lindisf.* 68 The arches..rich with billet and lozenge ornament. **18..** *Archit.*

Publ. Soc. Dict., *Lozenge Molding* or *Lozenge Fret*, an ornament used in Norman Architecture presenting the appearance of diagonal ribs inclosing diamond-shaped panels.

7. *Comb.* **a.** General comb.: simple attrib., as ***lozenge-machine***; ***lozenge-like*** adj.; parasynthetic, as ***lozenge-figured***, ***-shaped*** adjs.

1658 SIR T. BROWNE *Gard. Cyrus* iii. 47 Wherein [*sc.* the Sunflower] in *Lozenge figured boxes nature shuts up the seeds. **1551** RECORDE *Pathw. Knowl.* I. Defin., Ther corners are like the corners of a losing, and therfore ar they named *losengelike. **1859** R. F. BURTON *Centr. Afr.* in *Jrnl. Geog. Soc.* XXIX. 315 The depth of the temporal fossæ,.. producing, with the peaked and weakly retreating chin..a lozenge-like aspect. **1875** KNIGHT *Dict. Mech.*, **Lozenge-machine*, a machine for rolling out and cutting lozenges. **1833** HT. MARTINEAU *Three Ages* ii. 72 The summer flowers in the *lozenge-shaped parterres. **1860** READE *Cloister & H.* (1861) I. 70 The panes were very small and lozenge-shaped.

b. Special comb.: **lozenge-base**, the material used as a 'base' in the manufacture of lozenges; **lozenge-coach** (*nonce-use*), a coach with the owner's coat of arms emblazoned on a lozenge (see 1 b), a dowager's or widow's coach; **lozenge lion**, a Scotch gold coin called a 'lion', of the reign of Jas. I. (1406–37), having on the obverse the arms of Scotland in a lozenge shield.

1898 *Rev. Brit. Pharm.* 16 Trochiscus Sulphuris... It is not made with one of the *lozenge-bases. **1746** H. WALPOLE *Let. to Mann* 21 Aug., I am retired hither like an old summer dowager; only that I have no toad-eater to take the air with me in the back part of my *lozenge-coach. **1890** SERVICE *Notandums* ix. 67 There were..Gold Pennies and Mailles, *Lozenge Lions [etc.].

lozenged ('lɒzɪndʒd), *a.* [f. LOZENGE + -ED^2, after F. *losangé* (OF. *losengié*) LOZENGY.] Ornamented with lozenges of alternate colours; divided into lozenges or lozenge-shaped spaces.

1523 LD. BERNERS *Froiss.* I. ccccxix. 734 Some had cotes ..losenged with whyte and blacke. **1611** COTGR., *Lozengé*, lozenged. **1820** D. TURNER *Tour Normandy* II. 186 The archivolts are encircled by two rows of lozenged squares. **1822** *Gentl. Mag.* XCII. I. 30 The floor is lozenged of black and white. **1847** C. BRONTË *J. Eyre* xxviii, There shot out the friendly gleam again, from the lozenged panes of a very small latticed window. **1872** BROWNING *Fifine* xxx. 17 What outside was noon, Pales, through thy lozenged blue, to meek benefic moon.

lozengeour, variant of LOSENGER *Obs.*

lozenger ('lɒzɪndʒə(r)). Also 6 **losinger.** [f. LOZENGE + -ER.]

†**1.** = LOZENGE *sb.* 1. *Obs.*

1527 *Test. Ebor.* (Surtees) V. 244 Unum le diamond vocatum a losinger.

2. = LOZENGE *sb.* 3. *U.S.* and *north. dial.*

1860 O. W. HOLMES *Elsie V.* (1887) 59 Boxes containing 'lozengers', as they were commonly called. **1887** T. E. BROWN *Doctor* 6 Somethin just to be haulin out For the kids —a lozenger or the lek.

lozengerie, variant of LOSENGERY *Obs.*

†**lozengeways**, *adv. Obs.* Also **lazange-.** [f. LOZENGE *sb.* + -WAYS.] = LOZENGEWISE.

1610 GUILLIM *Heraldry* I. v. (1611) 3 A Cross pierced Losenge-ways, that is, after the form of a Losenge, with the points or acute Angles, streight upward and downward. Some say pierce Losengee. *Ibid.* II. vii. 70 Piercing..is threefold. That is to say Round, Losengwaise, Quadrate. **1668** LEYBOURN *Platform Purch.* 116 They are..laid Lazange wayes, one of white, another of black, laid angle to angle.

lozengewise ('lɒzɪndʒwaɪz), *adv.* [f. LOZENGE + -WISE.] So as to form a lozenge or lozenge pattern; *spec.* in *Her.* = LOZENGY *a.* 1.

1530 PALSGR. 844/2 Dyamant wyse, loserige [*sic*] wyse, trewlove wyse. **1577** B. GOOGE *Heresbach's Husb.* (1586) 71 My trees stand..losingwise or diamonde wise. **1610** GUILLIM *Heraldry* I. x. 116 He beareth Argent, nine Losenges Losengewise (or in Losenge) Gules. **1696** *Lond. Gaz.* No. 3217/4 The Arms of Andrew, being a Cross, set Lozengewise. **1725** BRADLEY *Fam. Dict.* s.v. *Plover*, Leap-Nets, whose Meshes are Lozengewise. **1864** BOUTELL *Her. Hist. & Pop.* ix. (ed. 3) 43 It is common for the upper of two cushions to be set lozengewise upon the lower.

lozengiour, variant of LOSENGER *Obs.*

lozengy ('lɒzɪndʒɪ), *a.* Forms: 6–7 **lozengie**, 7 **losengy**, **lozengee**, 8 **lozengé**, 9 **lozengée**, 7– **lozengy**. [a. OF. *losangié* (13th c.), f. *losange* LOZENGE.]

1. *Her.* Of a field: Covered with lozenges of alternate tinctures; divided into lozenges. †Also of a bearing: Shaped like a lozenge.

1562 LEIGH *Armorie* 157 He beareth Losengye, Argent, and Sable. **1572** BOSSEWELL *Armorie* II. 38 b, One fermaulx lozengie, Gules. **1610** [see LOZENGEWAYS.] **1727** BAILEY vol. II, *Lozengé*, *Lozangy*..is a Shield or an Ordinary of all Lozenges. **1864** BOUTELL *Her. Hist. & Pop.* (ed. 3) 35 A Field Lozengy..is divided into Lozenge-shaped figures. *Ibid.* 361 Lozengée erm. and sa.

b. **lozengy barry**, divided into lozenges, which are divided again horizontally. **lozengy-bendy** (see quot. 1838). †**lozengy in point** (see quot. 1688). †**semi-lozengy** (see quot. 1612).

1612 PEACHAM *Gentl. Exerc.* III. 160 If ther be aboue the number as I said of fiue and twentie or sixe and twentie, you must say Semi-lozengie. **1688** R. HOLME *Armoury* I. 105/2 He beareth Gules, two Piles Barwise Agent... This is by others Blazoned, a pale Losengie in point, or extending to the sides..of the Escochion. **1838** *Penny Cycl.* XII. 142/1 [A shield Fusily] if parted per pale and per bend, would be either Lozengy-bendy, or Fusily-bendy, according to the width of the space between the lines.

2. *transf.* **a.** Resembling a lozenge, lozenge-like. **b.** Composed of or divided into lozenges.

1602 CAREW *Cornwall* 99 b, In the mouth of the harbour, lyeth S. Nicholas Iland, in fashion, losengy. **1686** PLOT *Staffordsh.* 125 The Choir..is paved Lozengy, black and white. **1845** M. A. LOWER *Rep. to Brit. Archæol. Assoc.* Nov., A lozengy or network pattern.

lozeyn, lozzel(l, obs. ff. LOZEN, LOSEL.

Lozi ('ləʊzɪ). [Native name.] **A.** *sb.* **a.** A Bantu people inhabiting Zambia. **b.** Their language. **B.** *adj.* Of or pertaining to the Lozi.

1948 M. GUTHRIE *Classification Bantu Lang.* 53 Nominals are used as sentences. For example,..in Lozi..*ze kilitipa* 'these are the knives'. **1949** M. GLUCKMAN in M. Fortes *Social Struct.* 146 The Lozi.. call them *Mawiko*, 'the people of the West'. *Ibid.*, I worked through Lozi, a lingua franca which most Wiko men..speak and understand. *Ibid.* 151 The hostility of the Wiko..to their Lozi and Kwongwa neighbours. **1953** D. T. COLE in D. Hymes *Lang. in Culture & Society* (1964) VIII. 549/1 These [languages] include.. Lozi of Barotseland in Northern Rhodesia. **1959** G. D. MITCHELL *Sociol.* 82 We shall be concerned with the Lozi system, which since British influence has undergone some modifications. **1967** *Economist* 11 Nov. 617/1 The.. conference..saw Barotseland's Lozi leaders lose much of their status in the party... Barotseland's development is lagging behind..because of..Lozi cultural indifference... Mr Kaunda could galvanise the Lozis into political co-operation. **1972** *Times* 18 Sept. 12/4 President Kaunda of Zambia has had to face..a Lozi challenge.

L. S. D.^{1}, **£. s. d.** (ˌɛlɛs'diː), abbreviation for 'pounds, shillings, and pence' (see the letters L, S, D); hence often used = 'money'. Hence **L. S. Deism** (*humorous*), worship of money.

1853 HOOD *Dead Robbery* i, But p'rhaps, of all the felonies de se,..Two-thirds have been through want of *L. s. d.!* **1880** MRS. LYNN LINTON *Rebel of Family* ii, For his own part he preferred £. S. D. **1892** *Cornh. Mag.* Aug. 170 L. S. Deism ..the modern worship.

LSD^2 (ˌɛlɛs'diː). Also (*rare*) **L.S.D.** [f. G. *lysergsäure-diäthylamid*, lysergic acid diethylamide.] Lysergic acid diethylamide (see LYSERGIC *a.*). Freq. with the number 25 appended.

[**1947** W. A. STOLL in *Schweizer Arch. für Neurol. und Psychiatrie* LX. 279 Dieser Stoff ist das Lysergsäure-diäthylamid (LSD).] **1950** *Diseases Nervous Syst.* XI. 243/1 We believe that L.S.D. 25 is a drug which induces a controllable toxic state within the nervous system, that re-activates anxiety and fear with apparently just enough euphoria to permit recall of the provoking experiences. *Ibid.* 243 Supplies of L.S.D. 25 for this study were made available by the manufacturer, Sandoz Pharmaceuticals, New York City. **1955** *Sci. News Let.* 26 Feb. 135/1 LSD has been used by psychiatrists recently to bring on a mental disease state in healthy persons in the hope of learning more about how to treat or prevent real mental sickness. **1958** A. HUXLEY *Let.* 11 Jan. (1969) 843 A session with an RC psychiatrist, who had reluctantly submitted to taking LSD25. **1962** *Observer* 15 July 1/5 The American Medical Association has given a warning that use of the drug known as LSD-25, or lysergic acid, can lead to suicide, and that LSD-25 has joined the ranks of black-market drugs like marijuana and heroin. **1964** *Daily Tel.* 28 Mar. 9/3 The tablets are believed to be a solid form of LSD, lysergic acid diethylamide. They can be obtained in certain clubs and public houses in London and other big cities. **1964** D. F. DOWNING in M. Gordon *Psychopharmacol. Agents* I. xiii. 569 The effective oral dose in man amounts to 0·02–0·05 mg and (+)-LSD-25 is therefore 10^4 times as active as mescaline in causing a psychotomimetic effect and the most powerful psychotomimetic substance known. **1965** *New Scientist* 22 Apr. 225/1 Bizarre though the symptomatology may seem, the intensive research which has taken place in the 23 years since LSD 25 was discovered has failed to reveal any seriously deleterious effect which the drug may have on brain chemistry or biophysics. **1966** *Daily Tel.* 31 Mar. 25 New York County Medical Society has called for severe penalties against the illicit manufacture, distribution and sale of the hallucination-producing drug known as LSD. It has described the drug as 'far more dangerous than heroin'. **1968** A. HOFMANN in A. Burger *Drugs affecting Cent. Nervous Syst.* II. v. 205 In the case of a very intensive reaction to LSD, the normal feeling of the identity with the own self is weakened (depersonalization). The test person at the same time appears to himself as a stranger watching him and judging his actions coolly and critically. *Ibid.*, LSD produces a state of hypersuggestibility, which is characterized by an enormous sensitiveness to the influence of sensory and cognitive stimuli and which is of decisive importance for the use of LSD as an adjuvant in psychotherapy. **1973** E. BULLINS *Theme is Blackness* 162 Not many of us smoked as much pot as before. And L.S.D. almost disappeared from our circle.

Ltd., abbrev. of LIMITED *ppl. a.* (sense 2 b).

1900 *Times* 19 Oct. 12/1 (Advt.), Employees of Bovril Ltd. ..are not eligible to compete. **1922** JOYCE *Ulysses* 152, I am hastening to purchase the only reliable ink-eraser *Kansell*, sold by Hely's Ltd, 85 Dame Street. **1967** *Times Rev. Industry* Feb. 37 (Advt.), Dictation systems Dictaphone Company Ltd. **1974** *Spectator* 22 June 774/3 Chater & Scott Ltd... Specialists in motoring books.

lu, obs. form of LOO.

luau ('luːaʊ). [ad. Hawaiian *lu'au.*] **a.** A party or feast with Hawaiian food and usually accompanied by Hawaiian entertainment; also *attrib.* **b.** A cooked dish of young taro leaves served with coconut cream and octopus or chicken.

1843 L. SMITH *Diary* 3 Aug. in M. D. Frear *Lowell & Abigail* (1934) 168 The table..was..loaded with an immense quantity of food—pigs, turkies,..taro, luau, etc., etc. **1853** *Putnam's Mag.* II. 19/1 It was on a Saturday afternoon in the year 1852, that a merry party of us started forth to attend a *luau* or native feast, given by a chief who lived some miles from Honolulu. **1905** *Hartford* (Connecticut) *Courant* 24 Apr. 8/5 A *luau* is a square meal with roast pig and poi in it. **1951** H. WOUK *'Caine' Mutiny* 62 Willie and Keefer..full of hog meat and whisky which they had consumed at a hilarious luau. **1957** *New Yorker* 19 Jan. 14 Choose from a range of restaurants..from quaint Japanese tea house to lively Hawaiian luau. **1960** *Ibid.* 26 Mar. 152 (Advt.), Luau dinners and after theater suppers. **1964** *Asia Mag.* 16 Aug. 20/1 In the old days, the luau was an expression of thanksgiving to the gods. Today, it is a feast for sight and palate. *Ibid.*, Guests sit cross-legged around the low luau table and eat with their fingers. **1966** *New Yorker* 22 Oct. 20 (Advt.), Charge everything from a surfboard to a luau on your American Express Credit Card.

lubard, obs. form of LEOPARD.

lubba ('lʌbə). Also 8 **lobba**. A name used in Shetland and Orkney for coarse grass or sedge (see quots.). Also *attrib.*

c **1794** T. JOHNSTON in Shirreff *Agric. Surv. Shetld.* (1814) App. 46 On the berry heather and lobba pastures they [sheep] are at their prime from five to seven years old. **1795** G. LOW in *Statist. Acc. Scot.* XIV. 316 [The hills] are covered with heath, and what we call lubba, a sort of grass which feeds our cattle in the summer time; it generally consists of different species of carices, plain bent, and other moor grasses. **1822** S. HIBBERT *Descr. Shetl. Isl.* III. 435 Lubba comprises those common productions of the hills which are found where heath is absent.

lubbard ('lʌbəd). *Obs.* exc. *Sc.* and *north. dial.* Also 7 **lubberd**, 8 **lubber'd**, 9 **lobbart**, **lubbart**, **-ert**. [Altered form of LUBBER: see -ARD.] = LUBBER *sb.*

1586 in Neal *Hist. Purit.* (1754) I. 321 That all cathedral churches may be put down... They are the dens of idle loitering lubbards. **1612** tr. *Benvenuto's Passenger* I. i. 3 Thou slouenly lubberd, and toyish fellow, what idle toyes goest thou fantasticating. **1712** STEELE *Spect.* No. 466 ¶1 In all the Dances he invents..he keeps close to the Characters he represents. He gives to Clowns and Lubbards clumsy Graces. **1724** RAMSAY *Health* 306 Sciatic, jaundice, dropsy, or the stone, Alternate makes the lazy lubbard groan. **1823** SCOTT *Peveril* xxxv, I need only instance..the celebrated downfall of Goliah, and of another lubbard. **1867** SMYTH *Sailor's Word-bk.*, *Lubber*, or *Lubbart*, an awkward unseamanlike fellow. **1899** H. PEASE *Tales Northumbria* 173 Thoo great clumsy lubbert, see what thoo's done!

b. *attrib.*, *appositive* or quasi-*adj.*: Lubberly.

1679 EARL ROCHESTER in *Roxb. Ball.* (1883) IV. 567 So have I seen at Smithfield's wondrous Fair,..A lubbard Elephant divert the Town. **1710** *Medley* No. 2/3 His lubber'd Genius from its Byass crost, In heaps of false Arithmetick is lost. **1711** *Ibid.* No. 39/1 The other..was such a Lubbard Trickster, so aukward at Mischief. **1784** COWPER *Task* III. 400 Conscious how much the hand Of lubbard Labour needs his watchful eye. **1817** J. F. PENNIE *Roy. Minstr.* v. 5 Ocean..stretches its lubbard arms Along the shores low growling.

lubbe, obs. form of LOVE *v.*

lubber ('lʌbə(r)), *sb.* Forms: 4 **lobre**, **lobur**, 6 **lober**, **loubber**, **lubbo(u)r**, **lub(b)ur**, **luber**, **lubbarre**, 6–7 **lubbar**, 6– **lubber**. [The form may possibly belong to an adoption of OF. *lobeor* swindler, parasite, agent-n. f. *lober* to deceive, sponge upon, mock; but if so the sense has been altered by association with LOB *sb.*^{2} (cf. the Du. and Norw. cognates mentioned under that word).]

1. a. A big, clumsy, stupid fellow; esp. one who lives in idleness; a lout. Also in phr. † ***to play the lubber***. In early quots. frequently applied to a monk (cf. ABBEY-LUBBER). *Obs.* exc. *arch.* or *dial.*

1362 LANGL. *P. Pl.* A. Prol. 52 Grete lobres [MS. H. (*c* 1400) loburs] and longe þat loþ weore to swynke Cloþeden hem in Copes. **1515** BARCLAY *Egloges* III. (1570) Cij b/2 Some be forgetfull,..Some craftles fooles, some proude and negligent, If thou chaunge some better for to haue, Thou voydest a lubber and hast agayne a knaue. **1530** [see LUBBER *v.*] *c* **1530** LD. BERNERS *Arth. Lyt. Bryt.* liv. (1814) 198 Two greate lubbers brought after hym the heed of the monster, in a great basket. *a* **1533** FRITH *Disput. Purgat.* A viij, That we shuld no lenger..be dyspoyled and robbed of a syght of sturdie lubbarres. *a* **1568** ASCHAM *Scholem.* II. (Arb.) 88 They went to the Grammer schole, little children: they came from thence great lubbers: alwayes learning, and litle profiting. **1590** NASHE *1st Pt. Pasquils Apol.* Wks. (Grosart) I. 241 Will he neuer leaue to play the lubber? what a lazie lowtish kind of argument is this. **1605** SHAKS. *Lear* I. iv. 101 If you will measure your lubbers length againe, tarry. **1671** J. WEBSTER *Metallogr.* i. 18 Idle Lubbers that dare not adventure from the air of their Countries. **1750** GRAY *Long Story* (end), And so God save our noble King, And guard us from long-winded Lubbers. **1812** *Sporting Mag.* XL. 159 The sparks which flew from the pipe of a lubber who was blowing smoke and fire about at the door of the Angel. **1871** B. TAYLOR *Faust* (1875) I. xix. 172 Now is the lubber tame! **1888** *Berksh. Gloss.*, *Lubber*, or *Lubber-yead*, one very stupid indeed.

transf. c **1826** HOOD in A. A. Watts *Life A. Watts* (1884) II. 25 It..is but a hulking lubber of a paper.

b. *esp.* A sailor's term for: A clumsy seaman; an unseamanlike fellow. (Cf. LAND-LUBBER.)

1579 GOSSON *Sch. Abuse* 33 b, To lye wallowing like Lubbers in the Ship of the common wealth, crying Lord, Lord, when wee see the vessel toyle. **1748** SMOLLETT *Rod. Rand.* xxiv, He swore woundily at the lieutenant, and called him..swab and lubber. **1769** FALCONER *Dict. Marine* (1780) Cc ij, Afraid..of being stigmatized with the opprobrious epithet of *lubber*. **1824** SCOTT *Redgauntlet* ch. iii, The cowardly lubbers have all made sail. **1890** BESANT *Armorel of Lyonesse* I. 39 Two lubbers! They ought not to be trusted with a boat.

†**c.** An inferior servant, drudge, scullion. *Obs.*

1538 ELYOT *Dict.*, *Mediastinus*, a drudge or lubber, which doth in the howse all maner of vyle seruice, as swepe or clense the house, carie wodde to the kytchen, and other like drudgery. **1706** PHILLIPS (ed. Kersey), *Lubber*, a mean Servant, that does all base Services in a House; a Drudge.

2. a. *attrib.* and *appositive* passing into *adj.* (In ***lubber lips*** perh. a different word; cf. *blubber-lip*.)

c **1530** *Hickscorner* 421 (Manly), Thou lubber Imagynacyon. **1599** PORTER *Angry Wom. Abington* G, Sow vp your lubber lips. **1673** DRYDEN *Amboyna* Epil. 14 Venetians do not more uncouthly ride, Than did their Lubber-State Mankind bestride. **1730-46** THOMSON *Autumn* 562 Astride The lubber Power in filthy triumph sits. **1832** SIR S. FERGUSON *Forging Anchor* 57 The kraken's back,..a lubber anchorage for sudden shallow'd miles. **1874** TENNYSON *Vivien* 117 Then narrow court and lubber King, farewell! **1875** BROWNING *Inn Album* i. 7 Lubber prose o'ersprawls, And straddling stops the path from left to right. **1891** HALL CAINE *Scapegoat* xxvii, His thick lubber lips working visibly.

b. Special comb.: **lubber-grasshopper**, a name for two large-bodied clumsy insects of the U.S.; (*a*) *Brachystola magna*, of the western plains; (*b*) *Romalea microptera*, of the Gulf States; **lubber-head**, a stupid person, a blockhead; hence ***lubber-headed*** adj. (E.D.D.); **lubber-lift** *v.* (see quot. 1905); **lubber's line, mark, point** *Naut.*, a vertical line inside a compass-case, indicating the direction of the ship's head; †**lubber-wort**, the (imaginary) herb that produces laziness; also, a lubber. Also LUBBER FIEND, LUBBERLAND, LUBBER'S HOLE.

1877 *Field & Forest* II. 160 The '*Lubber' grasshopper [is the] large grasshopper *Romalia microptera*. **1885** *Riverside Nat. Hist.* (1888) II. 194 The 'Lubber Grasshopper', or the Clumsy Locust, of the plains, *Brachystola magna*,..is..confined to the central portion of North America. **1962** METCALF & FLINT *Destructive & Useful Insects* (ed. 4) xii. 577 Large and small, lubberly grasshoppers often invade cotton from near-by waste lands and defoliate the plants... Lubber grasshoppers, differential grasshoppers. **1847** HALLIWELL, **Lubber-head*, a stupid fellow. **1849** *Sidonia Sorc.* II. 286 If..the thoughtless lubberhead, had not let the ring fall. **1797** *Spirit of Farmer's Museum* (1801) 85 Our Democrats begin to muster, Rolling around an anxious eye, Some '*lubber lifting' power to spy. **1905** *Terms Forestry & Logging* (U.S. Dept. Agric. Bureau Forestry) 42 *Lubber lift*, to raise the end of a log by means of a pry, and through the use of weight instead of strength. **1858** *Merc. Marine Mag.* V. 34 The *lubber's line of a compass. **1884** KNIGHT *Dict. Mech.* Suppl., *Lubber's Mark (*Nautical*). **1840** RAPER *Pract. Navig.* §142. 42 Care is taken to place the box so that **lubber's point* in the bowl, and the centre of the card, are in a line fore and aft, or parallel to the keel. But as lubber's point deviates a little from its proper position when the ship is heeled over, seamen do not implicitly depend upon it, as indeed the name implies. **1881** CLARK RUSSELL *Sailor's Sweeth.* III. iv. 156, I..set the two compasses down with the lubber's points exactly parallel. **1547** BOORDE *Brev. Health* cli. (1557) 55 b, Whyles they do take theyr medecine [for the 'fever lurden'] put no *Lubber-worte into theyr potage. **1575** LANEHAM *Let.* (1871) 23 A loouely loober woorts, freklfaced, red headed, cleen trust in his doobletʼ.

lubber (ˈlʌbə(r)), *v.* [f. LUBBER *sb.*] *intr.* To behave as a lubber; to loaf about; to navigate a boat like a lubber. †Also ***to lubber it.*** Now chiefly in *pres. pple.* and in **ˈlubbering** *ppl. a.*

1530 PALSGR. 615/2, I lubber, I playe the lubber, *je loricarde*. You lubber as well as any knave in this towne. **1611** COTGR., *Loricarder*, to luske, lowt, or lubber it; to loyter about like a masterlesse man. **1837** WHEELWRIGHT tr. *Aristophanes, Birds* III. iv, By the brown owls I will no longer spare thee, Whom I behold thus slow and lubbering. **18..** MRS. H. E. P. SPOFFORD *Pilot's Wife*, He began to grumble about being ashamed to be seen lubbering round so. **1885** *Century Mag.* XXX. 742/1 As the..wind grew.., we soon found ourselves lubbering over the beautiful lake.

lubberd, lubber'd, obs. forms of LUBBARD.

lubber fiend. [Cf. LUBBER *sb.* 1 c.] A beneficent goblin supposed to perform some of the laborious work of a household during the night; a 'Lob-lie-by-the-fire'. Also *transf.*

1632 MILTON *L' Allegro* 110 Tells how the drudging Goblin swet, To ern his Cream-bowle duly set,..Then lies him down the Lubber Fend, And stretch'd out all the Chimney's length, Basks at the fire his hairy strength. **1831** *Edin. Rev.* LIV. 175 The lubber-fiend has nothing of the sly humour of Robin Goodfellow about him. **1889** MORRIS in Mackail *Life* (1899) II. 222 Except that the parson is a lubber-fiend, and that the people are as poor as may be, nothing need be better.

Lubberland (ˈlʌbəlænd). An imaginary land of plenty without labour; a land of laziness.

1598 FLORIO, *Cocagna*, as we say Lubberland. **1614** B. JONSON *Bart. Fair* III. ii, Good mother, how shall we finde a pigge, if we doe not looke about for't? will it run off o' the spit, into our mouths thinke you? as in Lubberland? and cry, *we, we?* **1633** SHIRLEY *Gamester* III. (1637) F 2 b, And so I commend mee to all your friends in Lubber-Land. **1681** W. ROBERTSON *Phraseol. Gen.* (1693) 621 Weak-witted; a wittal; a fool; born in Lubberland. **1827** SCOTT *Napoleon* IV. 206 A Grand Elector, who was to be the very model of a king of Lubberland. **1856** R. A. VAUGHAN *Mystics* (1860) I. 238 Pining after your Lubberland, as usual,—your Millennium of mere ease and plentiful supply. **1893** MCCARTHY *Red Diamonds* I. 160 Luxuriously enjoying his monarchy of the lubberland of bed.

lubberlike (ˈlʌbəlaɪk), *a.* and *adv.* [f. LUBBER *sb.* + -LIKE.] **A.** *adj.* Of, pertaining to or characteristic of a lubber. **B.** *adv.* After the manner of a lubber.

1572 HULOET (ed. Higgins), Lubberlike, vnhandsome or lowtishe, *secors*. **1575** GASCOIGNE *Posies*, *Flowers* 117 Though you thinke it lubberlike to leese Yet shoulde you lende that one halfe of your cote. **1588** FRAUNCE *Lawiers Log.* Ded., Sheepes skinnes cast over their lubberlike shoulders. **1636** T. RANDALL in *Ann. Dubrensia* (1877) 17 How lubber-like they loll upon the Plaines! **1851** H. MELVILLE *Whale* xiii, The jeering glances of the passengers, a lubber-like assembly.

lubberliness (ˈlʌbəlɪnɪs). [f. LUBBERLY + -NESS.] The attribute of being lubberly.

1598 FLORIO, *Zottichezza*, clownishnes,..lubbarlines. **1707** T. BROWN *Lett. from Dead* II. (ed. 2) 67 A lazy Hulk, whose stupendious Magnitude is full big enough to load an Elephant with Lubberliness. **1882** SPURGEON in *Homilet. Rev.* Mar. 342 There is a lumpishness and lubberliness innate in the elements of some men's constitution.

lubberly (ˈlʌbəlɪ), *a.* and *adv.* [f. LUBBER *sb.* + -LY.] **A.** *adj.*

1. Of the nature of a lubber; coarse of figure and dull of intellect, loutish; clumsy; lazy; stupid; sometimes *transf.* of animals and inanimate things. Also of things: Appropriate to or characteristic of a lubber.

1573 TUSSER *Husb.* ix. (1878) 17 To raise betimes the lubberly, Both Snorting Hob and Margery. **1598** SHAKS. *Merry W.* v. v. 195, I came yonder at Eaton to marry Mistris Anne Page, and she's a great lubberly boy. **1618** BOLTON *Florus* (1636) 171 They..according to their lubberly wits, assayd to stop it first with their bodies. **1671** CLARENDON *Dial.* Tracts (1727) 323 Those lubberly fellows, who come from great schools after they are nineteen or twenty years of age. **1728** VANBR. & CIBBER *Prov. Husb.* I. Wks. (1730) 230, I wonder..you will encourage that lad to swill his guts thus with such beastly, lubberly liquor. **1759** WESLEY *Wks.* (1872) II. 477 All but four or five lubberly men seemed almost persuaded to be Christians. **1838** DICKENS *O. Twist* x, 'I did that, sir', said a great lubberly fellow, stepping forward. **1847** J. WILSON *Chr. North* (1857) I. 139 Great lubberly Leicesters or Southdowns [sheep]. **1859** MISS CARY *Country Life* (1876) 188 A lubberly, yellow-haired boy of twelve years old kicks open the door. **1862** J. GRANT *Capt. Guard* xxii, Great lubberly barges were dragged to and fro by horses of equally lubberly aspect. **1864** BURTON *Scot Abr.* I. iv. 184 James..in his lubberly schoolboy-like complaints about his mother, showed that he knew about them.

2. In nautical use: Resembling, pertaining to, or characteristic of a lubber; unseamanlike. Of a vessel: Managed in an unseamanlike manner.

[**1695** CONGREVE *Love for L.* II. 29 D'ee think shee'll ever endure a great lubberly Tarpawlin?] **1795-7** SOUTHEY *Minor Poems* Poet. Wks. II. 81 You lubberly landsmen don't know when you're well! **1831** TRELAWNEY *Adv. Younger Son* I. 44 You don't take me for that lubberly school-mastering parson on board, do you? **1849** GROTE *Greece* II. xlvii. VI. 87 His seamen had full leisure to contemplate what they would despise as lubberly handling of the ships. **1884** *Manch. Exam.* 27 Dec. 5/1 There never was a clearer case of lubberly navigation. **1887** BESANT *The World went* vi. 49 One [ship]..is obedient to her helm, the other shall be lubberly and difficult to steer.

B. *adv.* In a lubberly manner; like a lubber; unskilfully, clumsily.

1594 NASHE *Unfort. Trav.* 6 Ouer my necke he throwes himselfe verie lubberly. **1693** DRYDEN *Orig. & Progr. Satire* Ess. (ed. Ker) II. 56 A company of clowns on a holiday, dancing lubberly. **1823** *Examiner* 320/1 A large frigate,.. lubberly handled. **1884** *Manch. Exam.* 8 May 5/2 It is difficult to imagine that..either vessel can have been so lubberly managed as to run into the other.

lubber's hole. *Naut.* Also 8 **lubber-hole**. A hole in the ship's top, close to the mast, affording an easier way of ascent or descent than by climbing the futtock shrouds.

1772-84 COOK *Voy.* (1790) VI. 1194 He becomes as much an object of ridicule, as a sailor who descends through lubber's hole. **1792** WOLCOT (P. Pindar) *Peter's Prophecy* Wks. 1792 III. 75 And yet, Sir Joseph, fame reports you stole To Fortune's topmast through the lubber-hole. **1833** MARRYAT *P. Simple* vii, He proposed that I should go through lubber's hole. **1882** NARES *Seamanship* (ed. 6) 233 Pass a hawser..through the lubber's hole.

lubbert, variant of LUBBARD.

lubbor, -our, -ur, obs. forms of LUBBER.

lubbord, obs. form of LARBOARD.

lube (l(j)u:b, lu:b), *sb.* and *v.* Chiefly *N. Amer.* and *Austral.* Colloquial shortening of LUBRICANT *sb.*, LUBRICATION, LUBRICATE *v.* (cf. HYDROLUBE). Freq. *attrib.*, as ***lube bay, job, oil.***

1934 *Industr. & Engin. Chem.* Feb. 194/2 Refineries where lube oil is not manufactured. **1947** *Lubrication Engin.* Sept. 26 (*heading*) Lube spots. **1951** *Chem. & Engin. News* 24 Dec. 5456/1 (*heading*) Synthetic lube oil announced by Defense Department. **1956** *Ibid.* 3 Sept. 4247/2 (*heading*) Better lubes needed. **1957** CASAMASSA & BENT *Jet Aircraft Power Syst.* (ed. 2) xiv. 195/1 On the rear face are mounted the main lube and scavenge pump [etc.]. **1961** B. MALAMUD *New Life* (1962) 259 He had once lubed Levin's car. **1962** *Engineering* 31 Aug. 285/2 A reinforced plastic coating can be laid on without putting the tank out of commission if the products are crude or lube oils. **1964** *N.Z. Listener* 11 Dec. 5/1 A new office girl passed the lube-bay... Windy was so upset he got grease all over everything. **1965** J. M. CAIN *Magician's Wife* (1966) xv. 115 I'm just about due, I think, for the works—wash, lube job, tyre checks, gas—the usual. **1973** R. HAYES *Hungarian Game* liii. 323 The grease nipples were dry; the car needed a lube. **1973** *Tucson* (Arizona) *Daily Citizen* 22 Aug. 60/1 (Advt.), Clean and lube backing plates.

Lubecker (ˈl(j)u:bɛkə(r)). [f. *Lubeck* (see LUBISH) + -ER[1].] A Lubeck merchant vessel.

1627 in *Crt. & Times Chas. I* (1848) I. 196 They would set out..to intercept the Lubeckers and Hamburghers coming forth of the Sound. **1711** *Lond. Gaz.* No. 4850/1 A Lubecker sailing towards Sweden.

Lubeck(e)s: see LUBISH.

†ˈ**lubency.** *Obs. rare.* Also 7 lubentie. [f. L. *lubent-*, *libent-em* willing: see -ENCY.] Willingness or pleasure (in regard to action or activity).

1623 COCKERAM, *Lubentie*, mirth, pleasantnesse. *a* **1640** JACKSON *Creed* x. xxvi. §2 Their Natural Freedom as it is opposed to that which we call Spontaneum or Lubency in Vegetables only, or meer sensitive Creatures. **1669** *Addr. Young Gentry Eng.* 8 The idle person..stands ready to let out himself Post, on the easy rates of the next stirring device and lubency.

luber, obs. form of LUBBER.

lubfish, var. LOBFISH.

ˈ**Lubish**, *a.* *Comm. Obs.* exc. *Hist.* Also 6 Lub(b)is, Lubyes, Lup, Lupis, 7 Lupish, Lups, Lubeck(e)s, 9 Lubesh, Lubs. [a. G. *lübisch*, Du. *lubeksch*, f. *Lübeck*, Lubeck.] Of or belonging to *Lubeck*, a town of northern Germany, formerly a member of the Hanseatic League.

1. In ***mark Lubish, schilling Lubish***, denominations belonging to a money of account formerly in extensive mercantile use in North Germany.

15.. *Aberdeen Reg.* (Jam.), xij Lubbis sh, xx merkis Lubis. **1563** *Ibid.* XXV. (Jam.), Aucht daleris & tuelf Lup schilling... To pay x sh. for ilk mark lupis. *c* **1575** *Balfour's Practicks* (1754) 88 One thousand lubyes stok fish is ane last. **1622** MALYNES *Anc. Law-Merch.* 177 The Mariners are to haue two shillings lups for euery Last for doing of it. *Ibid.* 415 The said Doller was valued at two markes Lubish, euery marke being sixteene shillings Lubish. **1823** CRABB *Technol. Dict.*, *Lubs* or *Lubesh*, a term applied to the money of Lubeck and Hamburgh, as sterling is to English money. **1858** HOMANS *Cycl. Comm.* 1324/2 The mark Lubs, or Lubec mark, used at Hamburgh, is a money of account, equal to 29½ cents.

†**b.** *transf.* Genuine, authorized. Cf. *sterling*.

1632 LITHGOW *Trav.* VI. 271 Although they be bastards & wooden blocks, yet are they better clad, then their lupish legitimate ones.

†**2.** ***Lubecks beer***: a strong beer brewed at Lubeck.

[**1594** NASHE *Unfort. Trav.* E 1 b, Thy horses..shall kneed vp to the knees..in spruce beere and lubeck licour.] **1608** HEYWOOD *Rape of Lucrece* sig. E 4 Were it in Lubeckes or double double beere their owne naturall liquor i'de pledge it. **1639** GLAPTHORNE *Albertus Wallenstein* III. iii. F 3 b, I thinke you'r drunk With Lubecks beere or Brunswicks Mum.

‖**lubra** (ˈl(j)u:brə). [Native Australian.] **a.** An aboriginal woman of Australia.

1847 CAPT. C. STURT *Narr. Exped. Central Austral.* (1849) I. 127 He [an aboriginal] placed his lubra and infant child in it [a canoe]. **1864** SIMCOX *Outward Bound* 87 Many lubras so black, with their load on their back. **1881** MRS. C. PRAED *Policy & P.* I. 67 We white women are no better off than the lubras.

b. More generally: a woman. *Austral. slang.*

1966 W. S. RAMSON *Austral. Eng.* 129 *Gin* and *lubra* are used of Aboriginal women and occasionally, though only in slang and never as a compliment, of women in general.

lubrefaction, variant of LUBRIFACTION.

lubric (ˈl(j)u:brɪk), *a.* [a. F. *lubrique* or ad. L. *lūbric-us*, f. Aryan root **sleub-*: see SLIP *v.*]

1. Smooth and slippery. Now *rare.*

1490 CAXTON *Eneydos* vii. 32 Fortune..sette..vnder the feet of the righte chaste quene, thyng slypper and lubrik, for to make hir to ouerthrowe. **1609** HUME *Admonit. Poems* (S.T.S.) 171 Behold at how narrow a rift that awld lubrik serpent hathe slydin in. **1646** CRASHAW *Musicks Duell* 64 in *Steps to Temple* 105 Sobs, whose thundring volleyes float And roule themselves over her lubricke throat In panting murmurs. **1681** COTTON *Wond. Peak* (ed. 4) 61 The Roof does sloping rise In a steep, craggy, and a lubrick Shore. **1813** HOGG *Queen's Wake* 290 The glossy sea was heaving bright..While far on her lubric bosom were seen The magic dyes of purple and green. **1852** *Fraser's Mag.* XLVI. 84 They..turn up successively a dirty white belly or brown lubric back. **1867** J. B. ROSE tr. *Virgil's Æneid* 120 A lubric serpent.

†**2.** *fig.* Slippery, shifty; unsteady, unsettled; prone to danger or error. *Obs.*

1631 R. H. *Arraignm. Whole Creature* xiv. §1. 230 For life it selfe, alas how uncertaine Lubrick and fraile is it. **1646** J. HALL *Horæ Vac.* 109 Lubrick is the estate of Favorites. **1660** J. LLOYD *Prim. Episc.* 44 These adorations of the Cross &c.

..were very lubrick, so that it was a difficult matter to stand upright in them, and not to fall to superstition or idolatry.

3. Lascivious; wanton.

1490 CAXTON *Eneydos* ix. 36 Ne to make foul the holy purpose of thy castymonye by thuntrue note of lubryke & slypper luxurye. **1535** STEWART *Cron. Scot.* I. 103 This king he wox rycht vile..Lubrik and louss, with licherous appetyte. **1592** R. D. *Hypnerotomachia* 44 My venerious Lubric and incessing spurre of desire. *a* **1637** DEKKER *Witch Edmonton* III. Wks. 1873 IV. 388 If I finde Any loose lubrick scapes in him. **1686** DRYDEN *Elegy Miss A. Killigrew* 63 This lubrique and adult'rate age. **1909** J. JUSSERAND *Lit. Hist. Eng. People* III. 436 Here we have a Bellario, all virtue and sweetness..opposed to a series of lubric and ferocious monsters.

'lubrical, *a.* ? *Obs.* [Formed as prec. + -AL[1].] = prec. in various senses; also, voluble.

1601 B. JONSON *Poetaster* v. i, What, shall thy Lubricall and glibbery Muse Liue, as she were defunct, like Punque in Stewes! **1656** BLOUNT *Glossogr.*, *Lubrical*, *Lubricious*, slippery, deceitful, incertain; stirring, wanton, lascivious. **1657** TOMLINSON *Renou's Disp.* 164* A smooth, continuall, equall and lubricall juice. **1867** LONGF. *Dante's Par.* XXIII. 57 All the tongues That Polyhymnia and her sisters made Most lubrical with their delicious milk.

lubrican, obs. form of LEPRECHAUN.

lubricant ('l(j)uːbrɪkənt), *a.* and *sb.* [f. L. *lūbricant-em*, pr. pple. of *lūbricāre* to LUBRICATE, f. *lūbric-us* LUBRIC.] **A.** *adj.* Lubricating.

1822-34 *Good's Study Med.* (ed. 4) II. 214 This matter, instead of being mild and lubricant as in health, is now not only viscid, but acrimonious and corrosive.

B. *sb.* A material, usually an oil, used to lubricate machinery. Hence *transf.* **a.** A fluid which makes motion or action smooth or removes friction. **b.** (*jocular*) Any oily or greasy substance.

1828 WEBSTER, *Lubricant n.*, that which lubricates. **1856** KANE *Arct. Explor.* I. xv. 171 Grating it [potato] down nicely..and adding the utmost oil as a lubricant, it is as much as I can do to persuade the mess to shut their eyes and bolt it. *a* **1882** SIR R. CHRISTISON *Life* (1885) I. 395 Paraffin-oil..had been found the best of all anti-friction lubricants. **1890** *Spectator* 2 Aug., Etiquette is a mere lubricant of the order of society. **1897** *Allbutt's Syst. Med.* III. 309 Most external secretions are concerned in digestion either as lubricants, such as saliva, or as digestants, such as saliva, gastric and pancreatic juice.

lubricate ('l(j)uːbrɪkət), *a.* *rare*$^{-1}$. [ad. L. *lūbricāt-us*, pa. pple. of *lūbricāre*: see next and -ATE[2].] Slippery; smooth and oily.

1848 LYTTON *Harold* IV. vii, A fat priest with a lubricate and shining nose. **1882** OGILVIE, *Lubricate*, slippery. (Rare.)

lubricate ('l(j)uːbrɪkeɪt), *v.* [f. L. *lūbricāt-*, ppl. stem of *lūbricāre*, f. *lūbric-us* LUBRIC.]

1. a. *trans.* To make slippery or smooth; to render smooth the motion or action of (something) by applying a fluid or unguent.

1623 COCKERAM, *Lubricate*, to make slipper. **1732** ARBUTHNOT *Rules of Diet* 425 Relaxing and lubricating the passages and quieting the Spasms by Opiates. **1806** *Med. Jrnl.* XV. 574 A fluid which serves to lubricate the canal for the passage of the fæces. **1835-6** TODD *Cycl. Anat.* I. 307/1 There are two glands which secrete a fluid to lubricate the ball of the eye. **1862** TYNDALL *Mountaineer.* vi. 43 The liquid appeared to lubricate every atom of my body. **1866** TATE *Brit. Mollusks* iv. 68 All molluscous animals secrete a mucous fluid to lubricate the skin.

b. To apply oil or some other substance to (a machine) in order to minimize the friction and make it run easily.

1742 YOUNG *Nt. Th.* IX. 2186 Man's..balmy bath, That supples, lubricates, and keeps in play, The various movements of this nice machine. **1789** E. DARWIN *Bot Gard.* I. (1791) Notes 21 He used oil or grease to..lubricate the cylinder. **1863** TYNDALL *Heat* i. §9 (1870) 8 We are careful to lubricate the axles of our railway carriages.

c. *gen.* To oil or grease.

1791 COWPER *Odyss.* XVII. 105 Wash'd and lubricated with fresh oils. **1866** LIVINGSTONE *Last Jrnls.* (1873) I. xii. 315 Dark brown fat which they use to 'lubricate' their hair.

d. *Photogr.* To cover (a print) with a glazing agent as a preliminary to burnishing.

1892 WOODBURY *Encycl. Photogr.* s.v. *Burnisher*, The face of the mounted print is lubricated with soap.

2. *transf.* and *fig.* **a.** In general use.

1784 COWPER *Task* IV. 65 Here rills of oily eloquence in soft Meanders lubricate the course they take. **1833** COLERIDGE *Table-t.* 6 July, Fine music..has a sensible effect in..animating and as it were, lubricating my inventive faculty. **1856** EMERSON *Eng. Traits* xvii. Wks. (Bohn) II. 130 There seemed a pool of honey about his heart, which lubricated all his speech and action with fine jets of mead.

b. *slang.* To ply with drink; also *intr.* to drink (Farmer *Slang* 1896).

1900 *Daily Express* 26 June 7/3 His late employers..had ..dismissed him for..'lubricating the police'.

c. To grease the palm of; to bribe.

1928 *Daily Express* 12 July 1/1 He made specific charges. One was that taxicab proprietors have to 'lubricate' Scotland-yard before their taxicabs are passed for licensing.

3. *absol.* or *intr.* To act as a lubricant.

1726 LEONI tr. *Alberti's Archit.* II. 11/1 Between the Axis and the Circle in which it turns, there shou'd be some-what to lubricate. **1739** S. SHARP *Operat. Surg.* 77 The Patient is ..relieved by..the Mucilaginous, the Saponaceous, &c. [remedies], some of which lubricate, and others both lubricate and stimulate.

lubricated ('l(j)uːbrɪkeɪtɪd), *ppl. a.* [f. prec. + -ED[1].] Made slippery or smooth; oiled, oily.

1781 COWPER *Retirement* 57 The shapely limb and lubricated joint. **1836** BRODERIP in *Penny Cycl.* V. 24/1 His [a boa constrictor's] stretched jaws and lubricated mouth and throat. **1864** in Wilberforce *Life Bp. Wilberforce* (1882) III. v. 141 He [Lord Westbury] said the 'judgement is simply a series of well lubricated terms'.

'lubricating, *vbl. sb.* [f. LUBRICATE *v.* + -ING[1].] The action of LUBRICATE *v.*; lubrication.

1775 ASH, Suppl., *Lubricating*, the act of making smooth and slippery. **1875** KNIGHT *Dict. Mech.* 1361/2 For lubricating and for electrotyping, the mineral [graphite] should be used in impalpable condition.

'lubricating, *ppl. a.* [f. LUBRICATE *v.* + -ING[2].] That lubricates; adapted for lubrication.

1691 RAY *Creation* II. (1704) 327 Both the Ingredients are of a lubricating Nature. **1768** LYSONS in *Phil. Trans.* LIX. 12 Using bleeding, with anodyne and lubricating medicines. **1858** GREENER *Gunnery* 423 The patent lubricating bullet, with the lubricating composition, effectually lubricates the inner surface of the chamber as far as the bullet enters. **1867** *Amer. Jrnl. Sci.* XCIII. 348 The lubricating oils are of very low specific gravity. **1878** BROWNING *Poets Croisic* cxvi, A sweetmeat teazed beneath Palate by lubricating tongue. **1974** *Sci. Amer.* May 97/1 As lubricating oil circulates through a machine it picks up myriads of wear particles.

lubrication (l(j)uːbrɪ'keɪʃən). [f. LUBRICATE *v.*: see -ATION.] The action of lubricating or the condition of being lubricated. Also *attrib.*

1802 PALEY *Nat. Theol.* viii. (1804) 132 The healing lubrication of the mucilage. **1870** YEATS *Nat. Hist. Comm.* 206 Rape oil is more suitable than any other oil for the lubrication of machinery. **1906** *Westm. Gaz.* 23 July 8/2 Motor-'buses, fitted with the new automatic lubrication appliance. **1907** *Ibid.* 13 Nov. 9/1 The lubrication system.. can be regulated to suit all engine speeds. **1951** M. MCLUHAN *Mech. Bride* (1967) 124 He brings you our 78 years of lubrication experience. **1975** *D. Bristow's Catal. Miscellany* 1/75 14 (*Operation manual*). The Singer Car.. with lubrication chart loosely inserted.

lubricational (l(j)uːbrɪ'keɪʃənəl), *a.* [f. LUBRICATION + -AL.] Of, pertaining to, or for lubrication.

1909 *Westm. Gaz.* 18 Nov. 4/2 An automatic lubricational oil pump is fitted at the end of the cam-shaft.

lubricative ('l(j)uːbrɪkətɪv), *a.* [f. LUBRICATE *v.* + -IVE.] Having the property of lubricating.

a **1881** S. LANIER *Eng. Novel* xi. (1883) 267 In some oily and lubricative way.

lubricator ('l(j)uːbrɪkeɪtə(r)). [f. LUBRICATE *v.* + -OR.]

1. One who lubricates. In quot. *fig.*

1883 EARL GRANVILLE in *Standard* 3 May 3/3 In the House of Commons you have some good oilers. I can conceive no better lubricators than..Mr. Cotes, and Mr. Duff.

2. A lubricating substance; a lubricant. *Photogr.* An agent for glazing prints before burnishing.

1756 BURKE *Subl. & B.* IV. xxi, Water..is found, when not cold, to be a great resolver of spasms, and lubricator of the fibres. **1874** ABNEY *Instr. Photogr.* xxxi. (1888) 255 For burnishing, the print must be quite dry, and a dry lubricator used, Castile soap answering for that purpose.

b. *transf.* and *fig.*

1869 *Spectator* 3 July 780 If Lord Carnarvon will leave out one or two features in his proposal..we see no serious objection to its acceptance as a lubricator for the Bill. **1890** 'ROLF BOLDREWOOD' *Miner's Right* (1899) 81/1 Gold, the universal lubricator.

3. An oil-cup or other contrivance for lubricating a machine or instrument.

183. E. J. WOOLSEY in Ure *Dict. Arts* (1839) 782 When you wish to see the quantity of oil remaining in the lubricator. **1871** C. H. OWEN *Mod. Artillery* 133 The solid residue (from the powder) left within the bore after firing, would..foul the bore if allowed to remain in it; but this residue is got rid of by the lubricator. The lubricator consists of three parts. **1887** D. A. LOWE *Machine Draw.* (1892) 32 The journal is lubricated by a needle lubricator.

4. *U.S. slang.* = GREASER 2.

1872 C. KING *Mountain. Sierra Nev.* xiv. 285 'String him up!' 'Burn the doggoned lubricator!

lubricious (l(j)uː'brɪʃəs), *a.* [f. L. *lūbric-us* LUBRIC + -IOUS.] = LUBRICOUS, in various senses.

1583 STUBBES *Anat. Abus.* I. (1879) 71 *margin*, Womens lubricious minds neuer content with any thinge when it is well. **1656** BLOUNT *Glossogr.* [see LUBRICAL]. **1698** R. FERGUSON *View Eccles.* 93 How Lubricious a Friend and Changeable a Partizan he will be to any Soveraign. **1706** PHILLIPS (ed. Kersey), *Lubricious*, slippery, uncertain, unconclusive, as A lubricious Hope, a lubricious Argument. **1884** C. READE in *Contemp. Rev.* May 711 He deserted pure for lubricious morality.

Hence †**lu'briciousness** *rare*$^{-0}$.

1731 in BAILEY vol. II.

†**lu'bricitate**, *v.* *Obs.* *rare*$^{-0}$. [? f. L. *lūbric-us* LUBRIC, after *facilitate*.] (See quot.)

1706 PHILLIPS (ed. Kersey), *Lubricitate* (in *Physick* and *Philos.*), to make slippery. **1721** in BAILEY. **1755** in JOHNSON.

lubricity (l(j)uː'brɪsɪtɪ). [ad. F. *lubricité* or L. *lūbricitās*, f. *lūbricus* LUBRIC.]

1. Slipperiness, smoothness; oiliness. Also in *pl.*

1601 HOLLAND *Pliny* II. 477 The same liquor is easie to diuide into drops, and as apt again by the lubricitie thereof, to run into an humor. **1633** T. CAREW *Coel. Brit.* (1634) 5 Hebe, through the lubricity of the pavement tumbling over the Halfe-pace. **1668** H. MORE *Div. Dial* I. ii. 179 The manifold Incompossibilities and Lubricities of Matter, that ..would [not] be fit for any thing, if its shapes..were not.. infinitely varied. **1784** COWPER *Task* v. 165 The same lubricity was found in all, And all was moist to the warm touch. **1822-34** *Good's Study Med.* (ed. 4) I. 383 The shrillness or roughness of the voice depends on the internal diameter of the glottis, its elasticity, motility, and lubricity. **1831** SYD. SMITH *Sp.* Wks. 1859 II. 219/1 Hands, accustomed to the scented lubricity of soap. **1878** EMERSON *Misc., Fort. Repub.* Wks. (Bohn) III. 391 In creeping out of one snake-skin into another of equal..lubricity.

†**b.** *spec.* in *Pathology*. *Obs.*

1547 BOORDE *Brev. Health* iii. 8 Abhorsion..maye come by ventositie and lubricite of humours in the matryx. *c* **1550** LLOYD *Treas. Health* (1585) Dij, For yᵉ lubricitie of yᵉ bowelles when the meate cometh furth vndigestyd. **1710** T. FULLER *Pharm. Extemp.* 225 It..roborates the Bowels, corects their Lubricity. **1755** JOHNSON *Let. to Miss Boothby* 31 Dec., A very probable remedy for indigestion and lubricity of the bowels.

2. *fig.* **a.** 'Slipperiness', shiftiness; unsteadiness, instability; elusiveness. Also with *pl.*

1613 R. CAWDREY *Table Alph.* (ed. 3), *Lubricitie*, lightnesse, slipery, inconstant. *c* **1645** HOWELL *Lett.* I. III. xxi, The lubricity of mundan greatnesse. **1664** H. MORE *Myst. Iniq.* 213 How necessary it is that the holy Prophecies should..be made of uncertain Interpretation by undeterminable lubricities. **1792** W. ROBERTS *Looker-On* No. 30 (1794) I. 428 This lubricity of manner, and alienation of thought in his neighbour. **1842** MIALL in *Nonconf.* II. 505 The speech, in their judgment, exhibits more of the lubricity of the clever tactician than of the serious designs of the minister. **1874** MOTLEY *Barneveld* (1879) II. xi. 47 The one ally on whom they had a right to depend..was slipping out of their grasp with distracting lubricity.

†**b.** Volubility, glibness. *Obs.*

1603 HOLLAND *Plutarch's Mor.* 202 The bulwarke of reason should..be set against it [the tongue], which..may stay.. that overflowing and inconstant lubricitie which it hath. **1657** HAWKE *Killing is M.* Pref. 1 Defamation proceeding from the lubricity of the tongue.

c. Mobility, suppleness. *rare.*

1809 MALKIN *Gil Blas* II. ii. ¶2 You would not have been a martyr to the gout, and your limbs would have performed their functions with lubricity.

3. Lasciviousness, lewdness, wantonness. Also with *pl.* an instance of this.

1491 CAXTON *Vitas Patr.* (W. de W. 1495) I. ii. 108 a/1 The poore doughter was two yere liuynge in lubrycyte and lecherye. **1593** MUNDAY *Def. Contraries* 83 Mens vaine pleasures and idle lubricities. **1611** *Coryat's Crudities* Panegyr. Verses, The ladyes of Lubricity that live in the Bordello. **1693** DRYDEN *Disc. Satire* Ess. (ed. Ker) II. 53 From the lechery of those Fauns [he] thinks he has sufficiently proved that satire is derived from them: as if wantonness and lubricity were essential to that sort of poem. **1777** G. FORSTER *Voy. round World* I. 457 This lubricity was ..very far from being general, and we had reason to believe that not a single married woman was guilty of infidelity. **1870** ROCK *Text. Fabr.* Introd. vii. 140 Mischief and lubricity are..shadowed forth in the likeness of the monkey. **1883** M. ARNOLD in *Pall Mall G.* 13 Nov. 2/1 What man is there that knoweth not that the city of the French is a worshipper of the great goddess Lubricity? **1902** *Onlooker's Note-Bk.* ii. 12 Women gaze unmoved on the most risky plays and freely canvass the lubricities of life.

lubricous ('l(j)uːbrɪkəs), *a.* Also 6 *Sc.* lubricus. [f. L. *lūbric-us* LUBRIC + -OUS.]

1. Slippery, smooth; slimy; oily.

1659 H. MORE *Immort. Soul* II. vi. 177 It is not such a lubricous Substance as the Animal Spirits, nor so disunited. **1695** WOODWARD *Nat. Hist. Earth* III. i. (1723) 145 The Parts of it being very voluble and lubricous,..it easily insinuates it self into..the Tubes. **1794** G. ADAMS *Nat. & Exp. Philos.* III. xxxiii. 344 Consider the fluid in a vessel.. to consist of a vast number of small, equal, lubricous, spherical globules. **1835** KIRBY *Hab. & Inst. Anim.* II. xvii. 119 Without falling..from their lubricous or seemingly perilous station. **1835-6** TODD *Cycl. Anat.* I. 543/2 The skin of the Cephalopods is thin and lubricous. **1861** H. MACMILLAN *Footn. Nature* 163 [*Ulva bulbosa*] with its excessively soft and lubricous masses, appearing as if in a state of fermentation.

2. *fig.* **a.** 'Slippery', shifty; unstable; elusive.

1646 *Speech without Doors defended without Reason* 7 He.. leaves the safety of Embassadors in a most lubricous posture. **1655-87** H. MORE *App. Antid.* (1712) 203 This proof or reason is the most lubricous and unmanageable of any that I have made use of. **1722** WOLLASTON *Relig. Nat.* v. 125 All observations of this kind must be very lubricous and uncertain. **1822** T. TAYLOR *Apuleius* 230 She..transferred, with a lubricous mobility [L. *mobilitate lubrica*], her nefarious love to a far more pernicious hatred.

†**b.** Voluble, glib. *Obs. rare.*

1715 M. DAVIES *Athen. Brit.* I. Pref. 49 Such a lubricous Faculty of spouting out so many Prodigal Expressions.

†**c.** Insinuating. *Obs. rare.*

1792 W. ROBERTS *Looker-on* No. 51 (1797) III. 20 A certain magical grace of manner, a lubricous insinuating softness slides into every action and gesture.

3. Lascivious, wanton. *rare.*

1535 STEWART *Cron. Scot.* II. 533 Rycht lubricus with sic lust and delyte, As brutell best takis his appetyte. **1898** *Q. Rev.* Jan. 193 The lubricous fancies of a half-demented day-dreamer [Rousseau].

lubri'faction. ? *Obs.* Also lubre-. [irreg. f. L. *lūbric-us* LUBRIC + -FACTION. Cf. next and

LUBRIFY.] The making slippery or smooth; lubrication. Also *Path.* (Cf. LUBRICITY 1 b.)

1542 BOORDE *Dyetary* xii. (1870) 265 Euery thynge that is vnctyous is noysome to the stomacke, for as moche as it maketh lubryfactyon. **1547** —— *Brev. Health* xviii. 13 This infyrmitie [vomiting] doth come..of lubryfaction of the intestines. **1626** BACON *Sylva* §41 Lubrefaction, and Relaxation. As we see in Medicines Emollient; Such as are Milke, Honey..and others.

lubrification (l(j)uːbrɪfɪˈkeɪʃən). ? *Obs.* [f. LUBRIFY: see -FICATION. So in Fr.] = prec.

1691 RAY *Creation* II. (1704) 327 A..Liquor prepared for the..Lubrification of their [*sc.* bones'] Heads or Ends.

lubrify (ˈl(j)uːbrɪfaɪ), *v.* Now *rare.* [ad. F. *lubrifi-er* (16th c.), irreg. f. L. *lūbric-us* LUBRIC: see -FY.] *trans.* To make slippery or smooth; to lubricate. Hence **ˈlubrifying** *ppl. a.*

1611 COTGR., *Lubrifier*, to lubrifie, or make slipperie. **1628** VENNER *Baths of Bath* (1637) 341 Some lubrifying, clensing extract. **1638** A. READ *Chirurg.* xxvii. 201 Into these nutritive clysters no oyle must enter, because it will too much lubrifie the guts. **1718** BLAIR in *Phil. Trans.* XXX. 888 A certain quantity of Moisture, fit to lubrifie the Muscles of the Ossicles. **1866** *Eng. Mechanic* 7 Sept. 515 This water lubrifies the piston, and dispenses with necessity for grease.

lubritorium (l(j)uːbrɪˈtɔərɪəm). Chiefly *U.S.* Also **ˈlubritory.** [f. LUBRI(CATE *v.* + *-torium* as in *auditorium, sanatorium.*] A greasing bay in a service station; a service station.

1930 *Amer. Speech* V. 329 In New Philadelphia, Ohio, there is a 'lubritorium' which I presume is intended to assist automobiles to a proper degree of lubricity. In Ann Arbor, Michigan, there is a 'Lubritory' which serves the same purpose. **1942** BERREY & VAN DEN BARK *Amer. Thes. Slang* §544 *Lubritory*, a gas station. **1954** *Encounter* June 13/1 The effort to 'professionalise' work has become the major means of giving one's job a badge of honorific quality... So the garage becomes the 'lubritorium'. **1963** *Punch* 24 Apr. 579/3 The sign outside a Glasgow service station: Lubritorium. **1969** M. PEI *Words in Sheep's Clothing* (1970) xxi. 209 'Lubritorium' is so much more learned a word than 'service station'. **1969** *West Australian* 5 July 71/5 (Advt.), Lubritorium and driveway attendant..required.

Lubs, var. f. LUBISH.

lubur, obs. f. LUBBER.

Lucan (ˈl(j)uːkən), *a.* Also **Lukan.** [f. L. *Lūcas* Luke + -AN.] Pertaining to the evangelist St. Luke.

1876 J. DARE tr. *Zeller's Acts Apostles* II. 303 The expression ὀπτάνεσθαι, ver. 3, and the description of the angel, ver. 10, are also specifically Lukan. **1890** W. H. SIMCOX *Lang. N.T.* 76 ἡ ἐπαγγελία τοῦ πνεύματος is a Lucan phrase, υἱοθεσία a Pauline. **1895** W. M. RAMSAY in *Expositor* Feb. 129 He accepts the Lucan authorship. **1896** *Ibid.* Feb. 146 Westcott and Hort with their great knowledge of Lukan style consider it to involve a corruption.

Lucanian (luːˈkeɪnɪən), *sb.* and *a.* [f. *Lucania*, name of a district of southern Italy, also called Basilicata.] **A.** *sb.* A member of the Lucani, a branch of the Sabelline race, inhabiting Lucania. **B.** *adj.* Of, pertaining to, or belonging to Lucania; *spec.* ***Lucanian ox, cow*** (see quots.).

1709 [see APULIAN *a.* and *sb.*]. [**1797** *Encycl. Brit.* X. 314 *Lucæ boves* denoted elephants; first seen in Pyrrhus's wars in Lucania, whence the appellation (Pliny).] **1863** W. K. KELLY *Curiosities Indo-European Trad. & Folk-Lore* i. 5 The Romans gave the name of Lucanian *ox* to the elephant. **1878** J. R. KING tr. *Cicero's Philippic Orations* XIII. v. 230 He ..took possession of his estates in the Lucanian territory. **1879** LEWIS & SHORT *Latin Dict.* 1079/1 *Luca bos*, Lucanian cow, for elephant (because the Romans first saw this animal in Lucania, in the army of Pyrrhus). **1907** A. E. ZIMMERN tr. *Ferrero's Greatness & Decline Rome* I. iv. 85 The Samnites and Lucanians, who were still under arms, sent ambassadors. *Ibid.* v. 89 Only the Samnites and the Lucanians, as being still in revolt, were to be excepted. **1949** *Oxf. Classical Dict.* 313/1 The Romans first encountered elephants ('Lucanian oxen') in Pyrrhus' army, but seldom used them in battle. *Ibid.* 514/2 Lucanian communities had an official known as *meddix.* **1957** *Encycl. Brit.* XIV. 456 The Social War, in which the Lucanians took part with the Samnites. **1960** *Times* 29 June 15/7 Slogans on the walls of a Lucanian town: 'We are Italians too.'

lucanid (luːˈkeɪnɪd), *a.* and *sb.* [f. mod.L. family name *Lucanidæ*, f. generic name *Lucanus* (J. A. Scopoli *Entomologia Carniolica* (1763) 1), f. L. *Lūcānus* Lucanian, f. *Lucania* (see prec.).]

A. *adj.* Of or pertaining to a stag-beetle of the family Lucanidæ. **B.** *sb.* A member of this family.

1925 A. D. IMMS *Gen. Textbk. Entomol.* 512 Lucanid larvae inhabit the rotting wood of trees or their roots. **1932** J. S. HUXLEY *Probl. Relative Growth* vii. 208 A peculiarly interesting example..is provided by the Lucanid beetle *Cyclommatus tarandus*, with markedly heterogonic male mandibles. **1959** E. F. LINSSEN *Beetles Brit. Is.* II. 115 While not having the extraordinarily developed mandibles of male Lucanids, there is in the present family [*sc.* Scarabæidæ] a great complexity of 'outgrowth-horns'.

lucar, obs. form of LUCRE.

lucarne (l(j)uːˈkɑːn). Forms: α. 6 lucane, -ayne, 8 lucerne, 9 lucarne. (See also LUTHERN.) β. *corruptly* 6–7 (?) leucomb, lucombe (*Arch. Publ. Soc. Dict.*), 7 lucome, luke-home, 9 *dial.* lucam, lewcome. (See also E.D.D.) [a. OF. *lucane*, mod.F. *lucarne*, of obscure origin; cf. OF. *lucquet* of similar meaning.

Some scholars have suggested OHG. *lukkâ* opening (mod.G. *lücke* cavity, gap) as the source. Diez' proposal to connect the word with L. *lucerna* (see LUCERNE[1]) is untenable.]

An opening made in a roof to let in the light; a skylight, a dormer or garret window. (Now only as Fr.) Also ***lucarne window.***

In quot. 1792 the word appears to be misused.

a **1548** HALL *Chron. Hen. VIII* 97 Great towers embattailed and vauted with lopes Lucanes like Masonry. **1554** *Acc. Rolls Durham Castle* 3 Nov. (Parker *Gloss. Archit.*), For ij dayes & dim. in mendyng of the gret Lucayne, in the gallere and lying of fyletts. **1565** JEWELL *Def. Apol.* (1611) 523 Hanged by the necke, out of a great Lucane window into the street. **1631** CORNWALLIS *Ess.* II. xlvii. 296 Many entries, landing places, and Lucomes. **1657** REEVE *God's Plea* 124 A dozen casements above, and two wide luke-homes below. **1792** BURNS *Let. to W. Nicol* 20 Feb., I look up to thee, as doth a toad through the iron-barred lucerne of a pestiferous dungeon, to the cloudless glory of a summer sun! **1823** E. MOOR *Suffolk Words* 212 *Lewcome*, a window projecting in the roof, generally a 'Lewcome window', but the word is applied to the gable end of a house. *a* **1825** FORBY *Voc. E. Anglia*, *Lucam.* **1859** JEPHSON *Brittany* xi. 187 The lucarne windows from which she saw the reek of the burning camp. **1873** BROWNING *Red Cott. Nt.-cap* I. 611 That grey roof, with the range of lucarnes.

Lucas (ˈl(j)uːkəs, ‖lyka). *Math.* The name of F. Édouard A. *Lucas* (1842–91), French mathematician, used *attrib.* to designate (*a*) the sequence of integers 1, 3, 4, 7, . . . , formed in the same way as the Fibonacci numbers; (*b*) the sequences generated by the recurrence relation $u_{n+2} = Pu_{n+1} - Qu_n$ when $u_0 = 0$, $u_1 = 1$ (the Fibonacci numbers being a particular case corresponding to $P = 1$, $Q = -1$) and when $u_0 = 2$, $u_1 = P$, which are respectively defined by $u_n = (a^n - b^n)/(a - b)$ and $u_n = a^n + b^n (n = 0, 1, 2, ..)$, where *a* and *b* are the roots of $x^2 - Px + Q = 0$.

[**1919** L. E. DICKSON *Hist. Theory Numbers* I. xvii. 393 (*heading*) Recurring series; Lucas' u_n, v_n.] **1953** *Scripta Math.* XIX. 278 (*heading*) Linear expressions for the powers of Fibonacci and Lucas numbers. *Ibid.*, The *i*th term of the Lucas sequence 1, 3, 4, 7... **1954** *Duke Math. Jrnl.* XXI. 608 If any term of (*W*) vanishes, (*W*) is essentially the well-known Lucas sequence $L_n = (\alpha^n - \beta^n)/(\alpha - \beta)$. **1961** *Pacific Jrnl. Math* XI. 385 It would be interesting to make a numerical study of several recurrences..to endeavor to find out whether the two Lucas sequences 0, 1, *P*, ... and 2, *P*, $P^2 - 2Q$, ... and their translates are essentially the only ones for which a global characterization of the divisors is possible. **1966** OGILVY & ANDERSON *Excursions in Number Theory* 164 The Lucas numbers satisfy the same recursion relation as the Fibonacci numbers, but have starting values $L_1 = 1$, $L_2 = 3$. **1972** P. RIBENBOIM *Algebraic Numbers* i. 8 Prove: (a) Two consecutive Lucas numbers are relatively prime. (b) $b_n^2 - b_{n-1}b_{n+1} = (-1)^n.5$ for every $n \geqq 1$.

lucasite (ˈl(j)uːkəsaɪt). *Min.* [Named, 1886, after H. S. *Lucas*: see -ITE.] A micaceous mineral, occurring at Corundum Hill, N. Carolina.

1886 T. M. CHATARD in *Amer. Jrnl. Sci.* 3rd Ser. XXXII. 735.

lucayne, obs. form of LUCARNE.

Lucca (ˈluːkə). [The name of a city and province in northern Italy.] ***Lucca lamb***, a variety of processed lambskin, used mainly to make headwear; ***Lucca oil***, a superior quality of olive oil.

1725 J. STEUART *Letter-Bk.* (1915) 238 A Chist of finest Cucca [*sic*] oil. **1734** C. MORTIMER in W. Ellis *Mod. Husbandman* (1750) VII. II. 84 His Wife rubbed in..the Sallad-oil (which I had bought by the Name of Lucca-oil). [**1861** S. SMITH in Mrs. Beeton *Bk. Househ. Managem.* 244 Four times the spoon with oil of Lucca crown, And twice with vinegar.] *c* **1938** *Fortnum & Mason Price List* 52 (*caption*) Superfine Lucca oil. **1956** J. G. LINKS *Bk. Fur* ii. 52 Persian lamb..and all the odd varieties of processed lamb (beaver, Tuscan,..Lucca and..others). **1962** —— *How to look at Furs* (rev. ed.) 108 The merino can be sheared less or more than it is in the case of beaver lamb. If it is sheared less, the result is often called by such names as Lucca lamb or Tuscan lamb (Italian lambs are often treated in this way). **1966** J. S. COX *Illustr. Dict. Hairdressing* 92 *Lucca oil*, olive oil. **1970** *Kay & Co. (Worcester) Catal. 1970–71* Autumn/Winter 287/1 Lucca Lamb Fur Hat. Get the feel of luxury with this fashionable..hat made in real Lucca lamb.

Hence **ˈLuccan** *a.* and *sb.*

1911 H. GERARD tr. *Maurel's Little Cities of Italy* I. I. vi. 63 Mirrors planted by the Luccan army on the towers of Asciano. *Ibid.*, The Luccans added a charming porch of elegant proportions. *Ibid.* 69 Matteo must have wandered often about the Luccan country. **1936** *Times Lit. Suppl.* 29 Aug. 690/2 He..finds the Pisan school Byzantine and the Luccan Roman. **1961** C. C. BAYLEY *War & Society in Renaissance Florence* i. 7 Florence emerged..with only a secondary prize, the former Luccan dependency of Pistoia. **1968** E. HYAMS *Mischief Makers* iv. 51 Olives yielding an oil of almost Luccan quality.

luce[1] (l(j)uːs). Also 5 lus(e, luyss, luy3s, lewse, 6 leuse. [a. OF. *lus, luis*, repr. late L. *lūcius*.] The pike (*Esox lucius*), *esp.* when full grown.

[**1338** *Durham Acc. Rolls* (Surtees) 35 In j Luc' pro Suppriore, iij d.] *c* **1386** CHAUCER *Prol.* 350 Many a breem and many a luce in stewe. **14..** *Nom.* in Wr.-Wülcker 704/34 *Hic lucius*, a lewse. **14..** *Two Cookery-bks.* 113 Nym luyss or tenge, or other manere fish. **1577** B. GOOGE *Heresbach's Husb.* (1586) 173 The best Pikes and Luces, were thought to be in the Riuer of Tyber. **1653** WALTON *Angler* vii. 142 The Luce, or Pikrell, or Pike breeds by Spawning. **1740** R. BROOKES *Art of Angling* I. xxxi. 68 The Pike, Luce or Pickerel..with us in England is a very common Fish. **1836** YARRELL *Brit. Fishes* I. 383 The Pike. Pickerell. Jack. Luce. **1892** *Pall Mall G.* 21 July 31/1 Two mighty eels, three fatted tench, and a couple of luce were at once secured.

b. *Her.* as a charge.

1587 FLEMING *Contn. Holinshed* III. 370/1 A fesse indented sable charged with four leuses heads eirant rased or. **1598** SHAKS. *Merry W.* I. i. 16 All his Ancestors..may giue the dozen white Luces in their Cote.

2. ***luce of the sea, sea-luce***: the hake, *Merlucius vulgaris.*

1598 STOW *Surv.* 71 [In a Fishmongers' pageant] Sixe and fortie armed Knightes riding on horses, made like luces of the sea. **1655** MOUFET & BENNET *Health's Improv.* (1746) 246 Luces, properly called Pikes of the Sea, are so rare in Spain that they are never seen. **1880–4** F. DAY *Fishes Gt. Brit.* I. 301 The hake..has also been termed..sea-luce, or sea-pike.

†**luce**[2]. *Obs.* = *flower-de-luce*, FLEUR-DE-LIS.

c **1645** HOWELL *Lett.* (1650) II. 128 (*The Vote*) Her [*sc.* Henrietta Maria's] fruit, sprung from the rose and luce.

†**luce**[3]. *Obs.* [App. a. G. *luchs*: see LOSS[2].] A lynx.

1564 in *Catal. Harl. MSS.* (1808) II. 360 Abstract of an Agreement made..for the annuall painting of that Cities four Giants, one Unicorne, one Dromedary, one Luce, one Camell, one Asse, one Dragon.

lucence (ˈl(j)uːsəns). *rare.* Also 5 lucens(e. [f. LUCENT: see -ENCE.] = next.

c **1485** *Digby Myst.* III. 715 O lux vera, gravnt vs 3ower lucense. *Ibid.* 770 Lucens. **1888** A. S. WILSON *Lyric Hopeless Love* cxix. 340 Love which opes the Soul to see Is lucence from divinity.

lucency (ˈl(j)uːsənsɪ). [f. LUCENT: see -ENCY.] Luminosity, brilliance. *lit.* and *fig.*

1656 S. HOLLAND *Zara* (1719) 146 Only a certain Star appeared in the East part of the Horizon, which afforded a glimmering Lucency. **1672** S. S. *Dorastus & Fawnia* 7 With winged haste (by Luna's lucency) He passes through the city postern gate. **1837** CARLYLE *Fr. Rev.* III. I. vi, These are the Septemberers (*Septembriseurs*); a name of some note and lucency,—but lucency of the Nether-fire sort. **1892** *Athenæum* 2 Jan. 29/2 His manner..is not unlike that of D. Teniers the elder, but it possesses much greater warmth and lucency.

lucent (ˈl(j)uːsənt), *a.* Also 5 *erron.* **lucyant.** [ad. L. *lūcent-em*, pres. pple. of *lūcēre* to shine.]

1. Shining, bright, luminous.

a **1500** in *Q. Eliz. Acad.* (1869) p. xix, Afferik, Sumtyme namyt the land lucyant in the partis of Orient. **1535** STEWART *Cron. Scot.* I. 203 Thair steill helmes, and bureall basnetis bryoht, Lik lucent lantrynis ... ane aureat lycht. **1597** A. M. tr. *Guillemeau's Fr. Chirurg.* 25 Cause the patient to sit in a verye lucent and lightsome place. **1616** B. JONSON *Epigr.* I. lxxvi. 8, I meant the dog-star should not brighter rise Nor lend like influence from his lucent seat. **1667** MILTON *P.L.* III. 589 The Sun's lucent Orbe. **1800** *Phil. Trans.* XC. 172 Two drams of soda phosphorata and two ounces of water, mixed with herring-light, formed a very lucent fluid. **1853** RUSKIN *Stones Ven.* II. vi. §8. 156 Ledges of porphyry sloping under lucent sand. **1894** D. C. MURRAY *Making of Novelist* 48 The roofs and spires..were outlined against a lucent belt of sky.

b. *transf.* and *fig.*

1639 G. DANIEL *Ecclus.* i. 30 How much resplendent She! How lucent in all flesh! **1831** CARLYLE *Sart. Res.* I. ii. (1872) 6 The Volume on Clothes, read and again read, was in several points becoming lucid and lucent. **1858** —— *Fredk. Gt.* x. vii. II. 664 Algarotti..a man beautifully lucent in society.

2. Translucent; lucid, clear.

1820 KEATS *Eve St. Agnes* xxx, Lucent syrops, tinct with cinnamon. **1865** MERIVALE *Rom. Emp.* VIII. lxiv. 126 Remains have been detected, at the bottom of the lucent Nemi, of a wooden ship or raft.

Hence **ˈlucently** *adv.*

1826 *Examiner* 323/2 His sea-waves flow lucently.

†**luceret.** *Obs.* Also 7 luseret. [Obscurely related to LUCERN[1], LUSARD.] = LUCERN[1].

1632 T. MORTON *New Eng. Canaan* II. v. (1838) 53 The Luseran, or Luseret, is a beast like a Catt. **1674** JOSSELYN *Voy. New Eng.* 85 The Wild-cat, Lusern or luceret, or Ounce as some call it.

lucern[1] (l(j)uːˈsɜːn). *Obs.* exc. *Hist.* Forms: 6 **luzarne, lyserne, 6–7 lusern, luzern(e, 7 leuz-, lewzerne, lewxern, lucirne, luseran, 7– lucern(e.** [Prob. a. early mod.G. *lüchsern* adj., pertaining to the lynx, f. *luchs* lynx (see LOSS[2]); the word was app. introduced as a name for the fur of the lynx; for a similar instance of an adjective becoming a sb., cf. MARTEN.

The spelling *lewxerne* (quot. 1662), if not a misprint, is conclusive evidence in favour of this derivation. Etymologists have usually supposed the word to be an alteration of the OF. *loucerve, leuserve*, female lynx, a fem. of unexplained from corresponding to the masc. *loup-cervier* repr. L. *lupus cervārius* (Pliny) lynx, lit. 'stag-hunting wolf' (*lupus* wolf, *cervārius* adj. f. *cervus* stag). But this hypothesis does not account for the form of the Eng. word, nor can it be satisfactorily referred to the OF. *loup cervin* (as if L. **lupus cervinus* = *lupus cervarius*) of which Godef. gives one example. Possibly there may have been in OF. a confusion between *loup-cervier* and an adopted Teut. synonym.]

1. The lynx. **b.** The skin or fur of the lynx, formerly held in high esteem.

1532–3 *Act 24 Hen. VIII*, c. 13 §1 Ne also weare..any Furres of Blake Jenettes or Luserns. **1536** *Wardr. Acc. Hen. VIII* in *Archæologia* IX. 249 With twelve lusarne skynnes. **1549** in *Egerton Papers* (Camden) 11 That no man under the degree of an Erle, weare..any..sabel, luzarnes, or black genetes. **1578** PARKHURST *Let.* in *Hakluyt's Voy.* (1600) III. 133 There are many other kinds of beasts, as Luzarnes and other mighty beastes like to Camels in greatnesse. **1585** *Sir W. Dixie's Pageant* in Nichols *Progr. Q. Eliz.* I. 446 A straunger, straungly mounted, as you see, Seated upon a lusty Luzern's back. **1591** G. FLETCHER *Russ. Commw.* 10 Their beasts of strange kinds are the Losh, the Ollen,..the Lyserne, the Beauer, the Sable [etc.]. *c* **1611** CHAPMAN *Iliad* XI. 417 As when a den of bloodie Lucerns [*orig.* θῶες] cling About a goodly palmed Hart. **1617** MIDDLETON *Love & Antiq.* Wks. (Dyce) V. 288 The Triumphant Chariot of Love..drawn with two luzerns. **1622** FLETCHER *Beggars Bush* III. iii, The Polcat, Marterne and the rich skind Lucerne. **1628** DEKKER *Brit. Hon.* Wks. 1873 IV. 105 Two Luzernes, The Supporters of the Skinners Armes. **1662** *Stat. Irel.* (1765) II. 406 Lewxerns skins the piece £2 10s. 0d. **1698** A. BRAND *Emb. Muscovy to China* 59 Hereabouts are abundance of Lucerns and Sables, which are in great esteem among the Chineses. **1727** BAILEY vol. II, *Lucern*, a wild beast in Russia.

¶ **2.** Used by Chapman for: A kind of hunting dog. (Cf. quot. *c* 1611 in 1.)

1607 CHAPMAN *Bussy d'Ambois* III. Dram. Wks. 1873 II. 43 Let me haue My lucerns too (or dogges inur'd to hunt Beasts of most rapine).

†**lucern**². *Obs.* [App. an erron. extension of LUCE¹, after prec.] The full-grown pike; = LUCE¹.

1615 MARKHAM *Pleas. Princes* iv. (1635) 23 The Luce or Lucerne, which indeed is but the over-growne Pyke.

lucernal (l(j)uːˈsɜːnəl), *a.* [f. L. *lucerna* lamp + -AL¹.] Pertaining to a lamp: only in ***lucernal microscope***, a microscope in which the object is illuminated by a lamp or other artificial light.

1787 G. ADAMS *Ess. Microscope* 22 About the year 1774, I invented the improved lucernal microscope. **1839** G. BIRD *Nat. Philos.* 386 The magic-lantern being nothing more than a lucernal microscope of low magnifying power.

lucernarian (l(j)uːsəˈnɛərɪən), *a.* and *sb. Zool.* [f. mod.L. *Lucernaria* (see below), f. *lucerna* lamp.] **A.** *adj.* Belonging to the genus *Lucernaria* typical of the family *Lucernariidæ* of hydrozoa. **B.** *sb.* A hydrozoan of this genus or family.

1854 A. ADAMS, etc. *Man. Nat. Hist.* 355 Lucernarians.

So **luˈcernarid, lucerˈnaridan**, *a.*, pertaining to the *Lucernarida*, a sub-class of hydrozoa; *sb.* a member of the *Lucernarida*. **luˈcernaroid**, the reproductive zooid of any of the *Lucernarida*.

1861 J. R. GREENE *Man. Anim. Kingd.*, *Cœlent.* 123 A fixed and sexless 'Lucernaroid'. *Ibid.*, The developmental cycle of each Lucernarid. **1870** NICHOLSON *Zool.* I. 90 The *Hydra-tuba* thus constitutes the fixed 'Lucernaroid', or the 'trophosome' of one of the *Rhizostomidæ*.

lucerne¹ (l(j)uːˈsɜːn). ? *Obs.* exc. *Antiq.* [ad. L. *lucerna*, f. *luc-* ablaut-variant of *lūc-*, *lūx* light.] A lamp, lantern.

a **1500** *Envoy to Alison* 23 (Skeat's *Chaucer* VII. 360) Lucerne a-night, with hevenly influence Illumined. **1500–20** DUNBAR *Poems* lxxxv. 3 Lucerne in derne, for to discerne Be glory and grace devyne. **1883** C. C. PERKINS *Ital. Sculpture* III. iv. 375 A multitude of wreaths, tablets, masks, festoons, lucernes, genii holding lyres [etc.].

lucerne², **lucern** (l(j)uːˈsɜːn). Also 7 **luceran**, 8–9 **lusern(e**, 9 **luzern**. [a. F. *luzerne* (16th c.), in Cotgr. also *luserne*, ad. mod.Pr. *luzerno* of unascertained etym. Cf. F. *lauserne, lauserte*, 'Shrub Trefoile, Milke Trefoile, Citisus Bush' (Cotgr.). In Eng. agricultural books of 17th and 18th c. the word constantly occurs as *la lucerne*, with the Fr. article prefixed.] The leguminous plant *Medicago sativa*, resembling clover, cultivated for fodder; purple medick.

native or ***paddy lucerne*** = Queensland hemp, *Sida rhombifolia* (Morris *Austral Eng.*).

1626 A. SPEED *Adam out of E.* v. (1659) 38 Clovergrass..is a grass very hardy, not much inferior to Luceran. **1649** BLITHE *Eng. Improv. Impr.* (1653) 186 Chap. xxvii Speaks of the usage of St. Foyne and La-lucern. **1669** WORLIDGE *Syst. Agric.* (1681) 31 It is not so good as La Lucerne..only this will grow on drier and poorer Land than Lucern. **1733** TULL *Horse-hoeing Husb.* xv. (Dubl.) 200 La Luserne is that famous *Herba Medica* so much Extoll'd by the Ancients. *Ibid.* 201 Luserne in Grass is much sweeter than St. Foin. **1762** *Gentl. Mag.* 262 One acre of Lucerne can maintain three or four horses. **1817–18** COBBETT *Resid. U.S.* (1822) 5 Warm and fine. Grass pushes on. Saw some Lucerne in a warm spot, 8 inches high. **1844** STEPHENS *Bk. Farm* II. 552 *Lucern.*—This kind of forage plant has never been successfully cultivated in Scotland, nor has it taken much hold in England. **1846** J. BAXTER *Libr. Pract. Agric.* (ed. 4) II. 25 Lucern is much superior to clover for soiling milch cows. **1873** BROWNING *Red Cott. Nt.-cap* I. 25 All its growth unsheaved Of emerald luzern bursting into blue. **1883** V. STUART *Egypt* 136 After the cotton is gathered we immediately sow lucerne.

b. *attrib.*, as ***lucerne field, grass, paddock, seed.***

1724 *Act 11 Geo. I*, c. 7 (Bk. Rates), Seed, vocat Lucerne Seed the C. wt. 0. 10. 0. **1733** TULL *Horse-hoeing Husb.* xv. 201 Tho' one Luserne Root be much more taper than another. *Ibid.* 211 Luserne Plants. **1760** J. LEE *Introd. Bot.* App. 318 Lucern Grass, *Medicago.* **1890** 'ROLF BOLDREWOOD' *Col. Reformer* (1891) 125 An old working bullock in a lucerne field. *Ibid.* 218 A lucerne paddock.

†**lucet**¹. *Obs.* In 6 lucette, 7 lucit. [a. OF. *lucet*, f. *lus* LUCE¹.] A pike; = LUCE¹.

c **1550** *Battle of Otterburn* xlvi. in Child *Ballads* III. 297 The lucettes and the cressawntes both; The Skottes favght them agayne. **1658** R. FRANCK *North. Mem.* (1821) p. xxix, The artist [i.e. fisherman] (if expert) may summons up lucit, and the generous race of salmon.

lucet² (ˈl(j)uːsɪt). ? *Obs.* (See quot. 1858.)

a **1650** in Furnivall *Percy Folio* (1868) II. 402 Shee that liues by nille and tape, & with her bagge & lucett beggs. **1858** SIMMONDS *Dict. Trade*, *Lucet*, a lady's lace loom, made of bone, ivory or wood.

luche, obs. form of LUTCH *v.*, *dial.*

Lucian (ˈluːʃ(ɪ)ən). The name (repr. Gr. Λουκιανός, L. *Lūciānus*) of a celebrated writer of Greek dialogues (*c* 160 A.D.); *allusively*, a witty scoffer. Hence †**Lucian** *v. intr.* in ***to Lucian it***, to imitate the style of Lucian, to play the scoffer; **Lucianesque**, in a Lucianic style; **Luciˈanic** *a.*¹, †**Luciˈanical** *a.*, pertaining to or characteristic of Lucian and his style; marked by a scoffing wit; **Luciˈanically** *adv.*; **Lucianism**, admiration and emulation of Lucian.

1561 DAUS tr. *Bullinger on Apoc.* (1573) 230 b, Their most light, and wanton Lucianicall wittes. **1592** G. HARVEY *Four Lett.* 8 My betters neede not take it grieuously, to be taunted ..in that booke, where Saint Peter, & Christ himselfe are Lucianically & scoffingly alleadged. *a* **1641** BP. MOUNTAGU *Acts & Mon.* (1642) 53 Erasmus scoffingly, as his manner was, in a Lucianicall style. **1655** FULLER *Ch. Hist.* VI. i. §34 Erasmus in his Dialogues..though..he doth Lucian it too much, yet truth may be discovered under the varnish of his scoffing wit. **1750** HODGES *Chr. Plan* (1755) Pref. 7 Ridiculed by men of light heads and bad hearts, the Lucians and facetious drolls of their respective ages. **1820** SHELLEY in Lady Shelley *Mem.* (1859) 136, I had written a Lucianic essay to prove the same thing. **1888** DOBSON *Goldsmith* 70 A little in the Lucianic spirit of Fielding's 'Journey from this World to the Next'. **1922** P. S. ALLEN *Erasmus* 6 The outcome of his thoughts..was a Lucianic composition, *Moriae Encomium.* **1925** A. M. HARMON tr. *Lucian* IV. 111 The source and character of the reply contribute a truly Lucianic fillip of surprise. **1937** C. R. THOMPSON (*title*) Lucian and Lucianism in the English Renaissance: an introductory study. **1962** R. P. ADAMS *Better Part of Valor* IV. 48 Erasmus couples Lucianic irony with his own special form of wit. **1969** G. HOLMES *Florentine Enlightenment 1400–50* iv. 112 *Momus* is the most substantial of his Lucianesque creations.

†**Lucianist**¹. *Obs.* [f. *Lucian* (see prec.) + -IST.] **a.** A disciple of Lucian (see prec.).

1585 FETHERSTONE tr. *Calvin on Acts* viii. 13. 189 The Epicures & Lucianists doe professe that they believe, where as notwithstanding they laugh inwardly. **1592** G. HARVEY *Four Lett.* 29 A contemner of God, and man: a desperate Lucianist: an abhominable Aretinist.

b. A student, admirer, or emulator of Lucian.

1940 C. R. THOMPSON *Translations of Lucian* i. 1 Erasmus ..was the paramount Lucianist of the Renaissance. **1941** H. H. HUDSON tr. *Erasmus's Praise of Folly* p. xix, Enough has been said, though more is available, to prove him a Lucianist. *Ibid.* p. xx, Rabelais..was both a Lucianist and an Erasmian. **1946** L. F. DEAN tr. *Erasmus's Praise of Folly* 17 By 1506 he had become a thorough Lucianist.

Lucianist² (ˈluːʃ(ɪ)ənɪst). *Eccl. Hist.* Also **Lucanist.** [ad. late L. *Lūciānista*, f. *Lūciān-us*: see -IST.] The name of two sorts of heretics: **a.** A follower of Lucianus the Marcionite (of the 2nd century). **b.** A kind of Arian; = COLLUCIANIST.

1727–41 CHAMBERS *Cycl.*, *Lucianists*, or *Lucanists*, a religious sect, so called from Lucianus, or Lucanus,..a disciple of Marcion... There was another sect of Lucianists, who appeared some time after the Arians. **1805** H. ADAMS *View Relig.* I. 187/2 *Lucianists*, so called from Lucianus, a disciple of Marcion. **1824** C. BUCK *Theol. Dict.* (ed. 2) 313/2 *Lucianists*,..a sect so called from Lucianus,..a heretic of the second century, being a disciple of Marcion, whose errors he followed. *Ibid.*, There was another sect of Lucianists, who appeared some time after the Arians. They taught, that the Father had been a Father always,..even before he begot the Son, as having in him the power and faculty of generation. **1874** J. H. BLUNT *Dict. Sects* 262 *Lucianists*, a section of the Marcionites, followers of Lucian. .. The particular tenet by which the Lucianists were distinguished from the Marcionites..was that, in the resurrection from the dead, neither the actual body nor the actual soul..would arise. **1882** H. M. GWATKIN *Stud. Arianism* ii. 31 Disciples of Lucian—Eusebius.., Menophantus.., and Leontius... These are all the Lucianists whom we can trace. *Ibid.* iii. 73 Eusebius himself was the ablest of all the Lucianists. **1903** J. F. BETHUNE-BAKER *Introd. Early Hist. Christian Doctrine* xii. 163 The Lucianists thought that logic could settle everything. **1958** J. N. D. KELLY *Early Christian Doctrines* III. ix. 230 He and Eusebius.., he implied, were 'fellow-Lucianists', and Eusebius is elsewhere described as a disciple of Lucian. **1960** A. BULL tr. *Ricciotti's Age of Martyrs* v. ii. 265 The Origenists and the Lucianists were interested to see whether or not the unity of God..could be reconciled with their particular school.

Hence **Luciˈanic** *a.*²

1882 H. M. GWATKIN *Stud. Arianism* iii. 72 We find him using the Lucianic creed. **1903** J. F. BETHUNE-BAKER *Introd. Early Hist. Christian Doctrine* xii. 174 The Lucianic origin of the Creed has, however, been called in question in recent times. *Ibid.* 175 The Fourth Creed assigned to this Council, which might be Lucianic. **1962** *Catholic Dict. Theol.* I. 139 They could never hope to pass off the rambling and old-fashioned Lucianic creed as one that would now rally all theologians of the West.

lucible (ˈl(j)uːsɪb(ə)l), *a. rare.* [ad. L. *lūcibil-is*, f. *lūcēre* to shine: see -BLE, -IBLE.] Bright, lucent.

1623 COCKERAM, *Lucible*, that which is light of its selfe. **1656** BLOUNT *Glossogr.* **1893** STORRS *Sp.* in *Independent* (N.Y.) 19 Oct., In letters of lightning, lucible and not frightful.

lucid (ˈl(j)uːsɪd), *a.* [ad. L. *lūcid-us*, f. *lūcēre* to shine. Cf. F. *lucide.*]

1. Bright, shining, luminous, resplendent. Now *poet.* and *techn. Ent.* and *Bot.* = Smooth and shining. *Astr.* Of a star: Visible to the naked eye.

1591 SPENSER *M. Hubberd* 1259 With his azure wings he cleav'd The liquid clowdes, and lucid firmament. **1654** VILVAIN *Theol. Treat.* ii. 45 The Air is not a lucid body like the Sun. **1667** MILTON *P.L.* XI. 240 Over his lucid Armes A Militarie Vest of purple flowd. **1693** BENTLEY *Boyle Lect.* viii. 5 There are great multitudes of lucid Starrs even beyond the reach of the best Telescopes. **1772–84** COOK *Voy.* (1790) V. 1743 Supposed to be an animal which contributes to that lucid appearance often observed at sea in the night. **1797** *Encycl. Brit.* (ed. 3) III. 443/2 [*Botany.*] A Surface is..Lucid, as if it were illuminated. **1800** HULME in *Phil. Trans.* XC. 180 Another lucid dead glow-worm was put into warm water, at 114°. **1833** TENNYSON *Poems* 60 Her lucid neck Shone ivorylike. **1845** WESTWOOD *Brit. Moths* II. 221 *Aphelosetia lucidella* (the lucid). **1847** W. E. STEELE *Field Bot.* Gloss. 16 *Lucid*, with a bright and shining surface. **1870–74** J. THOMSON *City Dreadf. Nt.* I. i, The lucid morning's fragrant breath. **1893** SIR R. BALL *Story Sun* 333 Beta Lyræ..is among the coolest of the lucid stars.

fig. *a* **1652** J. SMITH *Sel. Disc.* iv. 112 The intellectual world, being..made all lucid, intellectual, and shining with the sunbeams of eternal truth. **1742** BARNARD *Char. Lady E. Hastings* 39 To bring them into the lucid Path of Vertue and Religion.

2. Translucent, pellucid, clear.

1620 VENNER *Via Recta* Introd. 4 The lucide and cleare substance of it [*sc.* air]. **1647** H. MORE *Poems* 5 Thus they stood by that good lucid spring Of living bliss. **1725** POPE *Odyss.* VI. 102 The lucid wave a spacious bason fills. **1791** COWPER *Odyss.* III. 1 The sun, emerging from the lucid waves. **1832** LYTTON *Eugene A.* I. x, How singularly pure and lucid the atmosphere becomes. **1882** F. W. H. MYERS *Renewal of Youth* 314 Let many a heat distil Her lucid essence from the insurgent ill.

3. lucid interval. Also in early use in med.L. form (pl.) ***lucida intervalla.*** **a.** A period of temporary sanity occurring between attacks of lunacy. (So F. *intervalle lucide.*) †Formerly also, in wider use, an interval of apparent health between the attacks or periods of a disease.

[The Latin phrase 'non est compos mentis, sed gaudet lucidis intervallis' is common in English legal documents from the 13th to the 15th c.; so also in the med.L. commentators on Justinian's *Institutes.* For the etymological notion presumably underlying the expression, cf. c.]

1603 SIR C. HEYDON *Jud. Astrol.* xxi. 425 Sometimes shee [the moon] graunteth to them [lunatics] *Lucida interualla.* **1625** B. JONSON *Staple of N.* v. i, They are almost mad! But I forgiue their *Lucida Interualla.* *c* **1645** HOWELL *Lett.* (1650) II. 42, I had a shrewd disease hung lately upon me. .. After som gentle slumbers, and unusuall dreames..I had a lucid intervall. *a* **1655** VINES *Lord's Supper* (1677) 213 A mad man may have lucid intervals. **1659** STANLEY *Hist. Philos.* XIII. (1701) 624/2 As for that Pain which is lasting, it is not only gentle, but hath many lucid intervals. **1686** J. DUNTON *Lett. fr. New-Eng.* (1867) 23, I had between whiles those lucid intervals [in sea-sickness]. **1769** BLACKSTONE *Comm.* IV. 25 If a lunatic hath lucid intervals of understanding, he shall answer for what he does in those intervals. **1839** I. RAY *Med. Jurispr. Insanity* xiv. 298 It was decided by the court, Sir Willian Wynne, that she had a lucid interval, while making the will. *a* **1859** MACAULAY *Hist. Eng.* xxv. V. 294 James lingered three days longer. He was occasionally sensible during a few minutes, and, during one of these lucid intervals [etc.].

b. *transf.* and *fig.* A period of rest or calm in the midst of tumult or confusion; an interval during which there is a reversion to a normal, reasonable, or desirable condition.

1581 W. ALLEN *Apol. Eng. Seminaries* iii. 22 Which [Arianisme] though it troubled the world some hundred yeres together, yet it..had *lucida interualla*, gaue seasons of calme and rest to holy Bishops. **1622** BACON *Hen. VII* Wks. 1861 VI. 32 Which [dissensions] although they had had.. lucid intervals and happy pauses; yet did they ever hang over the kingdom. **1650** FULLER *Pisgah* IV. ii. 34 The devil heaped afflictions upon him, allowing him [Job] no lucid intervalls. **1682** DRYDEN *MacFl.* 22 Some beams of wit on other souls may fall, Strike through and make a lucid interval. **1751** SMOLLETT *Per. Pic.* xxii, Neither was his whole time devoted to the riotous extravagancy of youth. He enjoyed many lucid intervals. **1822** R. G. WALLACE *15 Yrs. in India* 194 It is quite impossible to transact business with a chief, except in that lucid interval between..one debauch, and..another. **1900** *19th Cent.* Sept. 386 Italy is just passing through one of these lucid intervals.

¶ **c.** In the etymological sense: An interval of sunshine in a storm.

1655 TUCKNEY *Good Day well Impr.* 8 Some short *lucida intervalla*, as the sun in a rainy day, looking out now and then a little. **1749** CAPT. STANDIGE in *Naval Chron.* III. 207 It being then day-light, and a lucid interval between showers of snow.

4. Marked by clearness of reasoning, expression, or arrangement; easily intelligible.

1786 COURTENAY *Lit. & Mor. Charac. Johnson* 24 And lucid vigour mark'd the general style. **1803** *Med. Jrnl.* X.

182 Arranged in that lucid order which is so necessary to assist the student. **1838** DICKENS *Nich. Nick.* xxiv, Mrs. Curdle sat listening to this lucid explanation. **1871** MORLEY *Voltaire* (1886) 7 His expression was incomparably lucid. **1876** C. M. DAVIES *Unorth. Lond.* 103 The sermon was long but lucid.

5. Of persons: Clear in intellect; rational, sane.

1843 CARLYLE *Past & Pr.* II. i, Any lucid, simple-hearted soul like him. **1859** G. MEREDITH *R. Feverel* xxx, Two apparently lucid people. **1887** *Times* 11 Aug. 5/2, I believe you are insane on that one point. On everything else you are lucid and bright.

6. With agent-noun: That performs the action implied in a lucid manner.

1879 MCCARTHY *Own Times* II. xxix. 372 There never was a more lucid and candid reasoner.

‖**lucida** (ˈl(j)uːsɪdə). *Astr.* [L. (sc. *stella* star) fem. sing. of *lūcidus* LUCID.] (See quot. 1877.)

1727–51 CHAMBERS *Cycl.* s.v. *Corona Borealis*, Names and situations of the stars... Lucida of the *corona*... That following the lucida to the south. **1877** G. F. CHAMBERS *Descript. Astron.* (ed. 3) 917 *Lucida*, a word occasionally used in sidereal astronomy to indicate the brightest star of the constellation, or group, &c. mentioned.

†**lucidary.** *Obs.* [f. L. *lūcid-us* LUCID + -ARY[1].] App. a name 1687–90 for a newly invented light or lighting apparatus.

1687 *MS. Reg. Middle Temple* 10 June, Some proposals had been made him by the Undertaker for setting up his lucidarys in the several Courts and Avenues of the House. **1690** *Lond. Gaz.* No. 2596/4 The Proprietors of the Lucidaries, or new Lights.

†**lucident,** *a. Obs. rare*$^{-1}$. [f. L. *lūcid-us* LUCID + -ENT.] Bright, lucent. Hence †**lucidently** *adv.*

14.. *Nine Ladies Worthy* 22 O pulchrior sole in beauty full lucident. *c* **1480** *St. Ursula* (Roxb.) Aj, Cryste with thy Comforte Illumyn me lucydently.

lucidity (l(j)uːˈsɪdɪtɪ). [ad. L. *lūciditās*, f. *lūcid-us* LUCID: see -ITY. Cf. F. *lucidité*.] The quality or condition of being lucid; brightness, luminosity; now chiefly *fig.* intellectual clearness; transparency of thought or expression.

1656 BLOUNT *Glossogr.*, *Lucidity*, brightness. **1664** H. MORE *Myst. Iniq.* 497 Touching the Lucidity of Christ's Body after his Ascension. *a* **1688** CUDWORTH *Immut. Mor.* (1731) 259 There is indeed a Brightness or Lucidity in the Sun. **1794** G. ADAMS *Nat. & Exp. Philos.* IV. xlix. 346 Light frequently does not sensibly act otherwise than as the cause of lucidity, or of luminous phenomena. **1851** NICHOL *Archit. Heav.* 253 His precision of language and peculiar lucidity of exposition. **1855** M. ARNOLD *Resignation* 298 Fate gave, what chance shall not control, His sad lucidity of soul. **1874** MAUDSLEY *Respons. in Ment. Dis.* vii. 229 Through their long intervals of lucidity. **1875** H. JAMES *R. Hudson* vi. 200 He looked at him with eyes of such radiant lucidity. **1884** F. TEMPLE *Relat. Relig. & Sci.* i. (1885) 10 The question..put by Hume..was handled by him with singular lucidity.

lucidly (ˈl(j)uːsɪdlɪ), *adv.* [f. LUCID + -LY[2].] In a lucid manner; with lucidity; brightly, clearly.

c **1705** BERKELEY *Commonpl. Bk.* in Fraser *Life* (1871) 459 All ye carefully and lucidly to be set forth. **1820** MISS MITFORD in L'Estrange *Life* (1870) II. v. 97 With such eyes! so purely, so lucidly blue! **1844** THIRLWALL *Greece* VIII. lxv. 349 The consul..expounded the phrase very lucidly. **1885** *Manch. Exam.* 25 Feb. 3/3 The chapters..are..admirably arranged and lucidly written.

lucidness (ˈl(j)uːsɪdnɪs). [f. LUCID + -NESS.] Lucidity.

1648 W. MOUNTAGUE *Devout Ess.* I. xxi. §1. 385 The smoothness and lucidness of Glass. **1680** BOYLE *Aerial Noctiluca* 38 The Constant Noctiluca..in which the lucidness was constant, though the Vial that contain'd it, was kept stopt. **1694** [see LUCIFEROUS 1]. **1727** BAILEY vol. II, *Lucidness*, brightness. **1800** HULME in *Phil. Trans.* XC. 172 The fluid acquired a great degree of lucidness. **1836** JAS. GRANT *Random Recoll. Ho. Lords* ix. 189 The lucidness of his arrangement, the appropriateness of his arguments, and the transparency of his style.

lucifee, lucivee (ˈluːsɪfiː, -viː). *Canada* and *local U.S.* [Corruption of LOUP-CERVIER.] The Canadian lynx.

1823 COBBETT *Rur. Rides* (1885) I. 371 When in New Brunswick I saw the great wild grey cat, which is there called a Lucifee. **1902** WEBSTER Suppl., *Lucivee*.

Lucifer (ˈl(j)uːsɪfə(r)). [L. *lūcifer* adj., light-bringing; used as proper name of the morning star; f. *lūc(i)-*, *lūx* light + *-fer* bearing. Cf. the equivalent Gr. φωσφόρος, after which it was prob. formed.]

I. As proper name, and allusively.

1. The morning star; the planet Venus when she appears in the sky before sunrise. Now only *poet.*

c **1050** *Byrhtferth's Handboc* in *Anglia* (1885) VIII. 320 Þær æfter on þam circule lucifer up arist. *c* **1374** CHAUCER *Boeth.* III. metr. i. 50 (Camb. MS.) After þat lucifere the day sterre hath chasyd awey the dirke nyht. **1388** WYCLIF *Job* xxxviii. 32 Whether thou bryngist forth Lucifer, that is dai sterre, in his tyme. **1629** MILTON *Nativity* 74 The Stars.. will not take their flight, For all the morning light, Or Lucifer that often warn'd them thence. **1744** AKENSIDE *Pleas. Imag.* (1779) I. 148 Lucifer displays His beaming forehead through the gates of morn. **1887** BOWEN *Virg. Æneid* II. 801 Now on the mountains of Ida was rising Lucifer bright.

†**b.** *fig.* (Cf. DAY-STAR.) *Obs.*

a **1585** CARTWRIGHT in R. Browne *Answ. to C.* 87 Vntill such time as the day starre spring & Lucifer do rise in our hearts. **1599** *Broughton's Let.* viii. 26 You Cynosura and Lucifer of nations, the stupor and admiration of the world.

2. The rebel archangel whose fall from heaven was supposed to be referred to in Isa. xiv. 12; Satan, the Devil. Now *rare* in serious use; current chiefly in the phrase ***as proud as Lucifer***.

The Scripture passage (Vulg. 'Quomodo cecidisti de cælo, Lucifer, qui mane oriebaris?' A.V. 'How art thou fallen from heauen, O Lucifer, sonne of the morning?') is part of a 'parable against the king of Babylon' (Isa. xiv. 4); but the mention of a fall from heaven led Christian interpreters to suppose that 'king of Babylon' was to be interpreted spiritually, as a designation of the chief of 'the angels who kept not their first estate'. Hence the general patristic view that *Lucifer* was the name of Satan before his fall. The Latin word was adopted in all the Eng. versions down to 1611; the Revised version has *daystar*.

a **1000** *Christ & Satan* 367 (Gr.) Wæs þæt encgelcyn ær ʒenemned, Lucifer haten, leohtberende. *a* **1300** *Cursor M.* 442 And for þat he was fair and bright, lucifer to nam he hight. *c* **1380** WYCLIF *Wks.* (1880) 30 þese nouelries maad of ydiotis & synful wrecchis of lucifers pride. *c* **1450** *Mirour Saluacioun* 4377 With feendes and lucifere..in helle. **1567** *Gude & Godlie Ball.* (S.T.S.) 175 Proude Lucifer, the greit maister of hell. **1613** SHAKS. *Hen. VIII*, III. ii. 371 And when he falles, he falles like Lucifer, Neuer to hope againe. **1625** PURCHAS *Pilgrims* I. IV. 571 His Pride is such, as may teach Lucifer. **1667** MILTON *P.L.* VII. 131. **1771** FLETCHER *Checks* Wks. 1795 II. 352 A fall into pride may drive me nearer Lucifer. **1814** SCOTT *Wav.* lvii, A second Lucifer of ambition and wrath. **1839** BAILEY *Festus* (1852) 55 Men say—as proud as Lucifer—Pray who would not be proud with such a train?

Comb. **1553** BECON *Reliques of Rome* (1563) 1 His.. Lucifer-like pride. **1581** J. BELL *Haddon's Answ. Osor.* 219 With such an incredible inordinate desire of luciferlike superioritie.

¶ Misused for: A devil.

1887 RUSKIN *Præterita* II. 72 The temper of eight little Lucifers in a swept lodging.

†**b.** *allusively.* One who commits the sin of Lucifer, i.e. who seeks to dethrone God; *occas.* applied to one who presumptuously rebels against an earthly sovereign. *Obs.*

1549 CHEKE *Hurt Sedit.* (1641) 12 That presumption of challenging Gods seat, doth shew you to have been Lucifers. **1579** FULKE *Heskins's Parl.* 305 What Lucifer is that, that wil oppose him selfe against the flatt commaundement of the holie ghost. **1602** WARNER *Alb. Eng.* IX. l. 229 Yea, too blasphemous, they incroch vpon the Deitie, Though of these Lucifers haue been that perish through a Flie. *a* **1618** RALEIGH in Gutch *Coll. Cur.* I. 89 Although they be perpetual Lucifers, they must always be Angels, and live in plenty.

II. As a common noun. (Usu. with lower-case initial.)

3. Orig. **lucifer match.** A friction match made usually of a splint of wood tipped with an inflammable substance ignitable on a roughened or otherwise prepared surface.

1831 *John Bull* 28 Nov. XI. 379/1 [Jones *v.* Watts, speech of plaintiff's counsel.] Mr. Jones had, some time ago, invented a match to produce an instantaneous light..and he had given his ingenious invention the name of 'Promethean'... Subsequently the plaintiff invented another description of match, which he designated with the frightful name of 'Lucifer'... For the 'Lucifers' he had not ..secured his right as the patentee... The defendant made an exact imitation of the 'Lucifer Match.' **1836** BRANDE *Man. Chem.* (ed. 4) 543 Matches tipped with some of these inflammable mixtures, and called *Lucifers*, are now in common use, and are inflamed either by friction or by the contact of sulphuric acid. *Ibid.* 1274 Gen. Index, Lucifer matches. **1837** *Ann. Reg.* 80 Several other lucifer matches were lying about, one of them having the appearance of having been drawn through the sandpaper. **1849** MRS. CARLYLE *Lett.* II. 42 When we had put a lucifer to some sticks in the grate. **1876** 'CAPT. CRAWLEY' *Card Players' Man.* 120 Cribbage..is played with a full pack of fifty-two cards,..and two pegs (that may be of ivory, or lucifer matches, with the phosphorus ends cut off). **1884** E. YATES *Recoll.* I. ii. 45 The lucifer, or Congreve match as it was called,..was ignited by friction on sandpaper, and had a very unpleasant smell.

Comb. **1858** SIMMONDS *Dict. Trade*, *Lucifer-box*. **1862** H. MARRYAT *Year in Sweden* II. 400 Mr. Lundström..showed me over his lucifer-manufactory.

Hence †**'Lucifering** *a. nonce-wd.*, acting the part of Lucifer.

1602 WARNER *Alb. Eng.* IX. l. 229 Of which Conuerting, Christo-fers yee [Popes] thenceforth shalbe said: If not, apply and perish in your Luciferring Traid.

luciferase (l(j)uːˈsɪfəreɪz, -s). *Biol.* [ad. F. *luciférase* (R. Dubois 1887, in *Compt. Rend.* CV. 691): see LUCIFERIN and -ASE.] Any enzyme which catalyses a reaction by which a specific luciferin produces light.

It was formerly believed that a single enzyme, luciferase, was common to all organisms which produce light.

1888 *Jrnl. R. Microsc. Soc.* 26 From the luminous parts of the animal the author [*sc.* R. Dubois] has succeeded in extracting two substances, the contact of which in the water, determines the appearance of the light. One of them was obtained in the crystalline state... It is soluble in water, and hardly soluble in alcohol; it may be called luciferine. The other body is an active albuminoid of the class of soluble ferments, and may be called luciferase. **1920** *Nature* 26 Aug. 843/1 The production of light by animals is due to the burning or oxidation of a substance called luciferin in the presence of an enzyme or catalyst called luciferase. **1952** [see LUCIFERIN]. **1971** *Country Life* 9 Sept. 605/1 The luciferin, or light-producing material, in a glow-worm's body is oxidised and broken down, with the aid of an enzyme called luciferase, to release light energy with practically no wastage.

Luciferian (l(j)uːsɪˈfɪərɪən), *a.*[1] and *sb.*[1] ? *Obs.* Also 6 **Luceferian, Lucifrian,** 7 **Luciferan.** [f. LUCIFER + -IAN.] **A.** *adj.* Of or pertaining to Lucifer; Satanic, devilish. Often with reference to pride: 'As proud as Lucifer'.

1570 *Homilies* II. *Wilful Rebell.* III. (1574) 576 A luceferian pride and presumption. **1598** MARSTON *Pygmal.* II. 146 From haughty Spayne, what brought'st thou els beside, But lofty lookes, and their Lucifrian pride? **1613** DEKKER *Strange Horse-Race* Wks. (Grosart) III. 350 For now he saw the Dilaceration of his owne Luciferan Kingdome. **1673** *Lady's Call.* I. v. §10 What a Luciferian fall will they have from their honors. **1691** WOOD *Ath. Oxon.* II. 312 He fell on the Bishops generally, calling them Luciferian Lord Bishops. **1704** NORRIS *Ideal World* II. x. 396 We have so much of the Luciferian ambition, as to aspire to be like to the most high. **1773** J. ROSS *Fratricide* I. 782 (MS.) Darting a ghastly Luciferian look After their footsteps.

†**B.** *sb.* A Luciferian or Satanic person. *Obs.*

1647 TRAPP *Comm. Matt.* xix. 17 None but a proud Luciferian would have said, as Vega, the Popish perfectionary did [etc.].

Luci'ferian, *a.*[2] and *sb.*[2] Also 6, 8 **Luciferan.** [f. L. proper name *Lūcifer* (see below) + -IAN.]

A. *adj.* Of or pertaining to the sect founded by Lucifer, bishop of Cagliari in the fourth century, who separated from the Church because it was too lenient (as he thought) towards Arians who repented of their heresy.

1607 TOPSELL *Four-f. Beasts* (1658) 106 You, saith he, (speaking to the Luciferian hereticks) run away from the vain shaking of feathers, like the fearfull Harts. **1638** CHILLINGW. *Relig. Prot.* I. ii. §36 While you thus inveigh against Luther, and charge him with Luciferian heresies. **1865** LIGHTFOOT *Comm. Galat.* (1874) 228 Hilary the Roman deacon..attached himself to the Luciferian schism.

B. *sb.* An adherent of this sect.

c **1555** *Life Bp. Fisher* in *F.'s Wks.* (E.E.T.S.) II. 135 Saint Jerom against Helvidius, Jovinianus, Vigilantius, and the luciferans. **1585** FETHERSTONE tr. *Calvin on Acts* xix. 7. 458 No man thinks that the grace of the Spirit is annexed to such a ceremonie, as doeth Jerome against the Luciferians. **1681** BAXTER *Answ. Dodwell* ii. 16 Novatians, Luciferians, Donatists..had all Orders in Episcopal Communion. **1797** W. JOHNSTON tr. *Beckmann's Invent.* III. 406 In the altercation between a Luciferan and an Orthodox, he relates that an adherent of the schismatic Lucifer disputed. **1882–3** SCHAFF *Encycl. Relig. Knowl.* II. 1358 As the Luciferians considered themselves the true and pure church, they utterly repudiated the name of a sect.

luciferin (l(j)uːˈsɪfərɪn). *Biol.* Formerly also -ine. [ad. F. *luciférine* (R. Dubois 1887, in *Compt. Rend.* CV. 691), f. L. *lūcifer* light-bearing: see -IN[1].] Any substance which is present naturally in an organism (such as the glow-worm) and which when oxidized in the presence of a specific enzyme (a luciferase) is capable of producing light.

It was formerly believed that one single substance, luciferin, was common to all organisms which produce light.

1888, 1920 [see LUCIFERASE]. **1952** E. N. HARVEY *Bioluminescence* p. xi, Luciferin and luciferase are general names used for these compounds manufactured by luminous animals, but it is probable that the luciferin or luciferase from a species in one group may be quite different chemically from that in another. **1954** HARVEY & TSUJI in *Jrnl. Cell. & Compar. Physiol.* XLIV. 71 Luciferin may properly be defined as the oxidizable substance supplying molecules capable of absorbing enough excess energy to emit in the visible region. **1966** JOHNSON & HANEDA *Bioluminescence in Progress* 10 Bacterial luciferin has become a matter of definition... $FMNH_2$ may be considered the 'luciferin' of this system. **1971** [see LUCIFERASE].

†**Luciferine,** *a. Obs.* [f. LUCIFER + -INE[2].] = LUCIFERIAN *a.*[1]

c **1546** JOYE in Gardiner *Decl. Art. Joye* (1546) 14, I passe ouer his [Gardiner's] luciferin pryde,..vicious lyuyng, &c. **1588** PARKE tr. *Mendoza's Hist. China* 376 Nobunanga..was slaine by a captaine of his, and punished by God by this meanes for his luciferine pride.

†**Luciferous,** *a.*[1] *Obs.* [f. LUCIFER + -OUS.] = LUCIFERIAN *a.*[1]

c **1554** BALE *Declar. Bonner's Art.* i. [8], Els wold ye couple your sorcerous masmongers with Gods maiestye in one honour which we wil not take at your luciferus perswasyons. **1593** NASHE *Christ's T.* (1613) 54 God forbid I should be so Luciferous passionatiue-ambitious. **1623** COCKERAM, *Luciferous*, haughtie, proud.

luciferous (l(j)uːˈsɪfərəs), *a.*[2] [f. L. *lūcifer* light-bearing (see LUCIFER) + -OUS.]

1. That brings, conveys, or emits light. Now *rare* in serious use.

1656 BLOUNT *Glossogr.*, *Luciferous*, that brings or causeth light. **1686** PLOT *Staffordsh.* 116 The clammy moisture of Oysters that shines in the dark of a violet colour, comes from luciferous wormes that have their holes in the shells. **1694** SALMON *Bate's Dispens.* I. 351/1 The lucidness of the Luciferous matter. **1805** tr. *St. Vincent's Voy. Afr. Seas* 42 These luciferous animals [F. *animaux lucifères*] almost all belong to the class of transparent..worms. **1821** *Blackw. Mag.* X. 560 Combustible and luciferous matter. **1856** GRINDON *Life* xxxii. 283 The nearer we stand to the luciferous orb [*sc.* the sun]. **1859** THACKERAY *Virgin.* xxv, Let us..bless Mr. Price and other Luciferous benefactors of

mankind, for banishing the abominable mutton of our youth.

2. *fig.* Affording illumination or insight; luminous, illuminating. In 17th c. common in ***luciferous experiment***, after Bacon's *lucifera experimenta* (*Nov. Org.* I. §70, 99, *et al.*).

1648 PETTY *Adv. to Hartlib* 20 How to make the most of experiments,..all being equally Luciferous, although not equally Lucriferous. **1660** BOYLE *New Exp. Phys. Mech.* xv. 104 So Luciferous an Experiment. **1676** GLANVILL *Ess.* iii. 28 A rare and luciferous Theory. **1811** *Edin. Rev.* XIX. 229 These..are the only luciferous experiments, of which geology can yet boast.

Hence **lu'ciferously** *adv.*, **lu'ciferousness.**

1665 *Phil. Trans.* I. 48 The Luciferousness of such Experiments. **1682** SIR T. BROWNE *Chr. Mor.* III. §3 Embrace not the opacous and blind side of opinions, but that which looks most Luciferously or influentially unto Goodness.

lucific (l(j)uː'sɪfɪk), *a.* [ad. late L. *lūcific-us*, f. *lūc(i)-*, *lūx* light: see -FIC.] Light-producing.

1701 GREW *Cosm. Sacra* II. ii. §14. 38 When they [the rays] are made to Converge,..though their Lucifick motion be continu'd, yet..that equal motion, which is the Colorifick, is interrupted. **1800** HULME in *Phil. Trans.* XC. 173 The degree of illumination in these liquids must depend upon the quantity of lucific matter applied. **1825** COLERIDGE *Aids Refl.* (1848) I. 168 The dry light..the lucific vision,..meaning thereby..reason in contradistinction from the understanding. **1876** J. ELLIS *Caesar in Egypt* 53 Lucific orbs.

luciform ('l(j)uːsɪfɔːm), *a.* Now *rare.* [ad. L. **lūciform-is* (repr. Gr. αὐγοειδής), f. *lūc(i)-*, *lūx* light: see -FORM.] Having the character of light, luminous: applied *spec.* to the 'vehicle' of the soul (αὐγοειδὲς ὄχημα) imagined by the Neo-Platonists; *occas.* to the spiritual body of the Resurrection.

1668 H. MORE *Div. Dial.* Schol. (1713) 560 It may well be questioned, whether the Pythagoreans held a distinct Notion of this kind of luciform Body. **1678** CUDWORTH *Intell. Syst.* I. v. 788 These Ancients say, that there is another Heavenly Body, always conjoyned with the Soul and Eternal, which they call Luciform and Star-like. **1710** R. WARD *Life H. More* 39 What the Platonists call the Luciform Vehicle of the Soul. **1862** ELLICOTT *On 1 Thess.* iv. 17 The glorified and luciform body will be caught up in the..clouds. [**1881** SHORTHOUSE *J. Inglesant* I. xvii. 313 To keep in order this luciform vehicle of the soul, as the Platonists call it.]

Lucifrian: see LUCIFERIAN *a.*[1]

lucifugous (l(j)uː'sɪfjʊgəs), *a. Nat. Hist.* [f. L. *lūcifug-us*, f. *lūc(i)-*, *lūx* light + *fug-ĕre* to fly: see -OUS.] Shunning the light.

1654 GAYTON *Pleas. Notes* IV. vi.-vii. 211 Such designes as these were Lucifugous, and would not endure the face of Heaven. **1655** STANLEY *Hist. Philos.* I. (1701) 14/1 These ill Dæmons..Aquatile, and Subterraneous, and Lucifugous. **1737** OZELL *Rabelais* II. 121 *note*, Lucifugous Nycticoraces. **1835-6** TODD *Cycl. Anat.* I. 599/2 The habits of which [animals] are more completely lucifugous and retired than any others. **1865** OAKELEY *Hist. Notes* 36 Owls and bats and other such shy and lucifugous creatures.

So **lu'cifugal** *a.*, in the same sense.

1889 in *Syd. Soc. Lex.*

lucigen ('l(j)uːsɪdʒɛn). [f. L. *lūc(i)-*, *lūx* light + -GEN.] An illuminant produced by burning a spray of oil mixed with air.

1887 *Pall Mall G.* 16 Sept. 12 Lucigen, as the new illuminant is called, is the invention of Mr. Hannay, of Glasgow, and is already extensively used in large engineering works, and for lighting large open spaces. **1892** *Ibid.* 26 Jan. 5/2 It is proposed to make experiments at the Woolwich Ferry with the lucigen light.

†**lu'cigenous**, *a. Obs.*$^{-0}$ [f. L. *lūc(i)-*, *lūx* light + -GENOUS.] (See quot.)

1727 BAILEY vol. II, *Lucigenous*, born or begotten in the Day Time.

lucimeter (l(j)uː'sɪmɪtə(r)). [Hybrid f. L. *lūc(i)-*, *lūx* light + -METER.]

1. An instrument for measuring the intensity of light; a photometer.

1825 HAMILTON *Hand-bk. Terms*, *Lucimeter*, in Optics, an apparatus for measuring the intensity of light proceeding from different bodies. **1875** in KNIGHT *Dict. Mech.*

2. 'A sunshine recorder designed to measure the combined effect of the duration and intensity of sunshine in promoting evaporation' (*Cent. Dict.*).

‖**Lucina** (l(j)uː'saɪnə). Also 6 (*anglicized*) Lucyne. [L. fem. of adj. *lūcīnus*, f. *lūc-*, *lūx* light: see -INE[1].] In Roman mythology, the goddess who presided over childbirth, sometimes identified with Juno or with Diana; hence, a midwife.

c **1386** CHAUCER *Knt.'s T.* 1227 But for hir child so longe was vnborn Ful pitously Lucyna gan she calle. **1608** SHAKS. *Per.* III. i. 10 Lucina, oh! Diuinest patrionesse, and my wife gentle To those that cry by night. **1631** MILTON *Epit. March. Winch.* 26 And now with second hope she goes, And calls Lucina to her throws. **1658** SIR T. BROWNE *Hydriot.* v. 27 Death must be the Lucina of life. **1701** C. WOLLEY *Jrnl. New York* (1860) 27 Neither..the nice attendance of Nursekeepers, nor the art of a dextrous Lucina. **1759** STERNE *Shandy* II. xi, A daughter of Lucina is put..over thy head.

b. By identification with Diana, put for: The moon. *poet.*

1500-20 DUNBAR *Poems* xxxv. 1 Lucina schynnyng in silence of the nicht. **1508** —— *Gold. Targe* 2 Quhen gone to bed war Vesper and Lucyne. **1503** HAWES *Examp. Virt.* ix. 2 For Lucyna eke dyd her shrowde. **1594** GREENE & LODGE *Looking-glass* (1598) F 2 b, An hoast of blacke and sable cloudes Gan to eclips Lucinas siluer face.

lucioid ('l(j)uːsɪɔɪd). *Ichth.* [f. L. *luci-us* pike + -OID.] **A.** *sb.* A fish of the family *Esocidæ*; a pike. **B.** *adj.* Belonging to this family (*Cent. Dict.*).

1836 YARRELL *Brit. Fishes* (ed. 3) I. 343 This expert ichthyologist has restricted the *Esocidæ* (Lucioids), or family of Pikes, to the single genus *Esox*. **1859-62** SIR J. RICHARDSON, etc. *Mus. Nat. Hist.* (1868) II. 153 Lucioids (*Esocidæ*).

lucirne, obs. form of LUCERN.

lucit, variant of LUCET[1] *Obs.*

Lucite ('l(j)uːsaɪt). Also lucite. [f. L. *luc(i)-*, *lux* light + -ITE[1].] A proprietary name for a solid, transparent plastic that is a methyl methacrylate resin; perspex.

1937 *Official Gaz.* (U.S. Patent Office) 6 July 9/1 E. I DuPont de Nemours and Company. Lucite. For thermoplastic synthetic resin material, known as methyl methacrylate, in the form of sheets, rods, and tubes, and in powdered or granular form. **1939** *Reader's Digest* Feb. 81/1 Light flows through rods made of Lucite, a du Pont plastic, as water flows through a pipe. **1953** J. Y. COUSTEAU *Silent World* 89 Through the lucite windows [of the *Bathyscaphe*] the pilots could look into a landscape lighted by exterior floodlamps. **1973** R. HAYES *Hungarian Game* xv. 98 The system had two Lucite indicators, one red the other green.

lucius, obs. form of LUSCIOUS.

lucivee: see LUCIFEE.

luck (lʌk), *sb.* Also 5-6 luk(e, 6-7 lucke. [a. LG. (Du., OFris.) *luk*, a shortened form of *geluk* (MDu. *gelucke* = MHG. *gelücke*, mod.G. *glück*). Parallel adoptions of the LG. word are Icel. *lukka* (14th c.), MSw. *lukka*, *lykka* (mod.Sw. *lycka*), Da. *lykke*. Probably it came into English as a gambling term; the LG. dialects were a frequent source of such terms in 15-16 centuries.

The ultimate etymology of MHG. *gelücke* (:—OHG. **gilucchi*:—OTeut. type **galukkjo-m*) is obscure. So far as meaning is concerned nothing could be more plausible than Paul's view (*Beitr.* VII. 133 *note*) that the word is connected with G. *gelingen* (OHG. *gilingan*) to succeed, turn out well or ill, as G. *druck* pressure with *dringen* to press, *schluck* gulp with *schlingen* to swallow, *ruck* wrench with *ringen* to wrench. But morphologically this assumption seems quite inadmissible, and most scholars deny the existence of etymological affinity in any of these instances. Formally, the word might be cognate with LOUK *v.*[1] or *v.*[2], or with G. *locken* to entice (OHG. *lockôn*) and the synonymous OHG. *lucchen*; but no probable hypothesis seems to have been formed to connect the meaning of the sb. with that of any of these vbs.]

1. a. Fortune good or ill; the fortuitous happening of events favourable or unfavourable to the interests of a person; a person's condition with regard to the favourable or unfavourable character of some fortuitous event, or of the majority of the fortuitous events in which he has an interest. Often with adj., as ***bad, hard, evil luck***, GOOD-LUCK, ILL-LUCK. Also, the imagined tendency of chance (esp. in matters of gambling) to produce events continuously favourable or continuously unfavourable; the friendly or hostile disposition ascribed to chance at a particular time.

1481, *a* **1529** [see GOOD LUCK]. **1530** PALSGR. 241/1 Lucke, happe, *hevr.* *a* **1547** SURREY in *Tottel's Misc.* (Arb.) 220 And if to light on you my luck so good shall be, I shall be glad to fede on that that would haue fed on me. **1563** B. GOOGE *Eglogs* vii. (Arb.) 61 Let vs here what lucke you haue had in loue. **1576** FLEMING *Panopl. Epist.* 39 It was his hard lucke & curssed chaunce,..to finde [etc.]. **1590** SHAKS. *Com. Err.* III. ii. 93, I haue but leane lucke in the match. **1602** *2nd Pt. Return fr. Parnass.* II. v. 823 It hath beene my luck alwayes to beat the bush, while another kild the Hare. **1653** WALTON *Angler* ii. 60 Wel Scholer, you must indure worse luck sometime, or you will never make a good Angler. **1738** SWIFT *Pol. Conversat.* 18 Yes; Tom sings well; but his Luck's naught. **1791** MRS. RADCLIFFE *Rom. Forest* xv, I hope we shall have better luck next time. **1856** WHYTE MELVILLE *Kate Cov.* xvii, The Arch-croupier below, they say, arranges these matters for beginners; but the luck turns at last. **1882** OUIDA *Maremma* I. ii. 41 'He has got his deserts', and Jaconda.. 'Luck always changes'. **1883** HOWELLS *Woman's Reason* II. xx. 178 He bade him..get fire to light the beacon. Giffen refused. 'No, sir; better not have any of my luck about it'.

†**b.** A piece of (good or bad) luck. *Obs.*

1530 PALSGR. 580/2, I have a shreude chaunce or a shreude tourne, or I have an yvell lucke, *il me meschiet.* **1603** DRAYTON *Bar. Wars* IV. xxxiv, Those evill Lucks, in numbers many are, That to thy footsteps do themselves apply.

c. In generalized sense: Chance regarded as a cause or bestower of success and failure. Sometimes *personified.*

1534-5 MORE *Dauy the Dycer* Wks. 1433 Long was I, lady Lucke, your seruing man. **1576** FLEMING *Panopl. Epist.* 83 One refuge yet remaineth, that is patiently to suffer what so euer lucke allotteth. **1630** DAVENANT *Cruel Bro.* I. i. B 2, Report is then become a Bawde to Luck; Whom Fortune doth enrich, Fame doth flatter. **1899** MAJ. A. GRIFFITHS in *Fortn. Rev.* LXV. 307 Luck, in the great game of war, is undoubtedly lord of all. **1902** A. E. W. MASON *Four Feathers* iii. 23, I told you luck might look my way. Well, she has. I go out to Egypt on General Graham's Staff.

d. Predicatively, ***it is good*** or ***bad luck*** = 'it is a good or bad omen' (to do so-and-so).

a **1903** *Mod.* You should never put boots on the table: it's bad luck.

2. a. Good fortune; success, prosperity or advantage coming by chance rather than as the consequence of merit or effort. Phr. ***to have the luck*** = to be so fortunate as (*to* be or do something). †***to have no luck to***: to be unfortunate in.

14.. *Pol. Rel. & L. Poems* (1866) 38 Wher-for lucke and good hansselle my hert y sende you. ? *a* **1480** *Promp. Parv.* (Winchester MS.) 316/2 Luk, *lucrum.* [*So Camb. MS. and ed. Pynson*; *Harl. MS. reads* (*prob. correctly*) Lukre or wynnynge, *lucrum.*] **1535** STEWART *Cron. Scot.* II. 46 That neidfull war thai wantit thair nothing, At thair lyking, with greit larges and luke [*rime* instruct]. **1583** HOLLYBAND *Campo di Fior* 145 No man can have luck alwayes at playe. **1590** SHAKS. *Mids. N.* v. i. 439 If we haue vnearned lucke, Now to scape the Serpents tongue. *a* **1656** HALES *Gold. Rem.* (1688) 348 Only plutarch, whatever the matter is has no luck to the latin, and therefore I would advise you either to read him in French or in English. **1661** BOYLE *Style of Script.* (1675) 36 A hint, which..I have since had the luck to improve sufficiently. **1784** COWPER *Tiroc.* 329 How he was flogged, or had the luck to escape. **1835** W. IRVING *Tour Prairies* 164 One of the rangers, however, had little luck to boast of, his horse having taken fright..thrown his rider, and escaped. **1856** KANE *Arct. Expl.* I. xxviii. 374, I have been off with a party..on a hunt inland. We had no great luck. **1866** GEO. ELIOT *F. Holt* (1868) 20 Like most energetic natures, he had a strong faith in his luck. **1874** GREEN *Short Hist.* vii. §1. 350 Catherine Parr, had the luck to outlive the King. **1883** STEVENSON *Silverado Sq.*, *With Children of Israel* 1, The luck had failed, the mines had petered out. **1891** N. GOULD *Double Event* 8 At cards, Captain Drayton seemed to have the 'devil's own luck'.

†**b.** (*one's*) ***luck of***: (one's) good fortune in obtaining. *Obs.*

1762-71 H. WALPOLE *Vertue's Anecd. Paint.* (1786) I. 104 A man, whose luck of fame was derived from all the circumstances which he himself reckoned unfortunate.

c. A piece of luck or good-fortune. ? *Sc.*

1856 MRS. CARLYLE *Lett.* II. 289 It was a luck for me yesterday..that I had these live things to look after.

¶**d.** *occas.* In appellations of objects on which the prosperity of a family, etc., is supposed to depend.

This use originates with 'The Luck of Eden Hall', which is an oriental glass goblet (of the 15th c. or earlier) in the possession of the Musgraves of Eden, Cumberland, so called from a superstition embodied in the words, 'If this glass will break or fall, Farewell the luck of Eden-hall'.

a **1800** *Ballad* in Lysons *Britannia* IV. Cumb. (1816) p. ccix, God prosper long from being broke The Luck of Edenhall. **1842** LONGF. (*title*) The Luck of Edenhall [transl. from Uhland]. **1870** B. HARTE (*title*) The Luck of Roaring Camp. **1901** E. F. BENSON *Luck of Vails* 16 When the Luck of the Vails is lost, Fear not fire nor rain nor frost.

3. a. Phrases. ***as*** (***good, ill***) ***luck would have it***: by (good, ill) fortune; ***bad luck to*** (a person or thing)!: a vulgar form of imprecation, expressive of ill-will, disgust, or disappointment; ***best of Arab*** (or ***Welsh***) ***luck***: cf. BRITISH *a.* 6; ***better luck another*** (or ***next***) ***time***: an expression of encouragement to endure a disappointment; ***devil's own luck***: uncannily good luck; ***down on*** (occas. ***in***) ***one's luck***: in ill-luck, in misfortune (*slang*); ***for luck***: in order to bring good luck (expressing the purpose of some superstitious action); ***in luck***: fortunate, enjoying good luck; ***good luck to*** (a person or thing): see GOOD LUCK; ***just my*** (or ***his, our***, etc.) ***luck***: typical of my (his, our) bad luck, or occas., of my good luck; (***one's***) ***luck is in***, or ***is/runs out***: luck is on one's side, or, one has come to the end of one's run of luck; ***luck of the draw***: an expression of resignation to chance; ***no such*** (***good***) ***luck***: the thing is beyond the power even of good fortune, unfortunately not; ***out of luck***: having bad luck, in misfortune; ***push*** (or ***crowd, ride***) ***one's luck***: to expect or count on an even better run of good fortune than one has had already; cf. *to push one's fortune* (PUSH *v.* 11 b); †***to strike*** (a person) ***luck***: see STRIKE *v.*; ***to try one's luck***: see TRY *v.*; †***upon luck's head***: on chance (*obs. Sc.*); ***worse luck*** = unfortunately, 'more's the pity' (*colloq.*); ***you can never know your luck***: you cannot be sure that luck won't change for the better, you may be lucky. For ***run, stroke of luck***, see the sbs.

1598 SHAKS. *Merry W.* III. v. 83 As good lucke would haue it..they conuey'd me into a bucke basket. **1637** RUTHERFORD *Lett.* I. xli. (1675) 87, I would believe in the Dark upon Luck's head, and take my hazard of Christ's goodwill. **1680** A. RADCLIFFE in Rochester *Poems* 147 As luck wou'd have it in came Will. **1687** J. PHILIPS tr. *M. de Cervantes's Don Quixote* I. I. ii. 9 As ill luck would have it, it happen'd to be upon a Friday Night. **1789** WOLCOT (P. Pindar) *Sir J. Banks & Emp. of Mor.* 17 Quite out of breath, and out of luck. **1849** THACKERAY *Pendennis* lxi, The Chevalier was..to use his own picturesque expression ..'down on his luck'. **1854** E. TWISLETON *Let.* 29 June (1928) 213 They..asked us to a dinner a fortnight off, when

as ill-luck would have it, we were engaged. **1855** F. W. FABER *Growth in Holiness* xvi. 297 When we fall we must rise again, and go on our way, wishing ourselves, after a Christian fashion, better luck another time. **1857** HUGHES *Tom Brown* I. viii, By Jove, Flashey, your young friend's in luck. **1857** C. M. YONGE *Dynevor Terr.* II. xii. 176 'When you break down anywhere, send me a telegraph.' 'No such good luck,' sighed Clara. **1858** TROLLOPE *Doctor Thorne* II. iv. 74 No harm had been done, and he might have better luck next time. **1861** MISS YONGE *Yng. Stepm.* xvii. 234 He.. should see enough of him when Mr. Hope came, worse luck. **1862** W. COLLINS *No Name* I. I. xi. 150 All *he* ever said was better luck next time. **1867** F. FRANCIS *Angling* vi. (1880) 233 Like a dissipated house-fly out of luck. *c* **1874** D. BOUCICAULT in M. R. Booth *Eng. Plays of 19th Cent.* (1969) II. 190 Well, as the divil's luck would have it, there was only .. a tailor's thimble, an' they couldn't get it full. **1876** C. M. DAVIES *Unorth. Lond.* 185 A clever rogue momentarily down on his luck. **1882** R. BURTON in *Athenæum* No. 2880. 11/3 The miner down in his luck. **1883** STEVENSON *Treas. Isl.* III. xv, There are some of Flint's hands aboard; worse luck for the rest of us. **1884** JESSOPP in *19th Cent.* Mar. 402 Labour is scarce and he is down in his luck. **1891** E. DOWSON *Let.* 30 June (1967) 205, I came here.. & found as luck would have it a Rosière going on. **1892** R. L. STEVENSON *Let.* 29 May (1911) IV. 54 No such luck; the ship delayed, and at last, about three, I had to send them home again. **1894** G. S. LAYARD *Tennyson & Pre-Raphaelite Illustr.* iv. 45 Oriana ties her kerchief round the wings of her lover's helmet, whilst he strings his bow for luck against her foot. **1898** J. D. BRAYSHAW *Slum Silhouettes* 29 Well, yer never know yer luck; an' his was 'ard enuff, Gawd knows. **1900** *Blackw. Mag.* July 99/1, I was in luck when I tumbled amongst them. **1901** ADE *Forty Mod. Fables* 156 Adams had a Run of Luck and he crowded it. **1902** A. E. W. MASON *Four Feathers* xxiii. 227, I, worse luck, was not one of them. **1903** G. B. SHAW *Man & Superman* I. 21 'She'll marry you.' .. 'No such luck, Jack!' **1907** —— *John Bull's Other Island* IV. 82 He has the divil's own luck, that Englishman, annyway. **1909** GALSWORTHY *Strife* I. 195 Just our luck, the men finding a fanatical firebrand like Roberts for leader. *a* **1911** D. G. PHILLIPS *Susan Lenox* (1917) II. xxi. 494 Don't be a fool. Let's push our luck, now that things are coming our way. **1916** A. BENNETT *These Twain* III. xx. 488 You never know your luck. If she'd been free I might have been fool enough to get married. **1923** *Brewer's Dict. Phr. & Fable* (new ed.) 689/1 *He has.. the devil's own luck*, he is extraordinarily lucky; everything he touches turns to gold. **1926** J. BUCHAN *Dancing Floor* I. ii. 53 Something about the features.. struck me as familiar. As luck would have it, it turned out to be Vernon. **1927** E. O'NEILL *Marco Millions* I. iii. 45 Better luck next time. He'll learn! **1928** —— *Strange Interlude* VIII. 274 The damned radio has to pick out this time to go dead!.. Just my luck! *a* **1930** D. H. LAWRENCE *Phoenix II* (1968) 146 Gilbert at her side took step after step, and thought to himself his luck was out as regards women. **1938** R. D. FINLAYSON *Brown Man's Burden* 60 Just my luck to be caught in a thunderstorm. **1938** G. GREENE *Brighton Rock* III. i. 99 'You ever come across this Kolley Kibber?' she asked. 'No such luck,' the barman said. **1956** J. POTTS *Diehard* vii. 116 He paused. Was he pushing his luck too far? **1959** 'J. WELCOME' *Stop at Nothing* i. 11 He had never won the Derby and.. had.. announced that he would not die until he did. As he must by now be touching eighty.., this was pushing his luck pretty hard. **1963** A. SMITH *Throw out Two Hands* vii. 79 If our luck was in we might hit Madagascar, but there is quite enough luck needed in ballooning without attempting to stretch it, and to hope for a landfall on a solitary island. **1966** 'S. HARVESTER' *Treacherous Road* xix. 183 And the best of Arab luck to you, mate. **1966** M. R. D. FOOT *SOE in France* x. 341 *Cinema-phono* had never been a lucky circuit, and its luck now ran out altogether. **1967** *Listener* 23 Nov. 667/2 As luck, or history, if you like, would have it, the Russian Revolution coincided with the spread.. of wireless telegraphy. **1967** 'J. ASHFORD' *Forget what you Saw* iii. 14 You never know your luck—one of these days we might actually set sail. **1967** M. CHILDS *Taint of Innocence* (1968) iii. 177 'It's so unfair.' 'Well, the luck of the draw.' **1969** 'A. GARVE' *Boomerang* iii. 132 'Anything else?' 'I don't think so—Except to wish you the best of Welsh luck!' **1970** N. MARSH *When in Rome* v. 127 Don't tell me you *are* the Lord Chamberlain... It would have been just my luck. **1972** M. BABSON *Murder on Show* v. 58 My luck was in and I caught a taxi. **1973** 'H. HOWARD' *Highway to Murder* iii. 37 Some say first impressions are best. Mine have been wrong as often as they've been right, so I guess it's the luck of the draw. **1974** I. MURDOCH *Sacred & Profane Love Machine* 75 If I.. was never heard of again. Thank you very much! No such luck! **1975** J. SYMONS *Three Pipe Problem* xv. 131 You ain't going to find no killer... I reckon this is some amateur riding his luck.

†**b.** ***luck in a bag.*** A name for some (? swindling) contrivance resembling a LUCKY-BAG, in which the prizes were few. Hence, a rare piece of good luck, an unlikely or unexpected stroke of luck.

1649 LIGHTFOOT *Battle w. Wasps Nest* Wks. 1825 I. 405 It was luck in a bag then, that he that is so direct in all his gospel from end to end, as never to change one story out of its proper time and place, should do it here to serve Mr. Heming's turn so pat. **1701** *Walk to Smith-field* in G. Daniel *Merrie Eng.* xx. (1874) 273 The spectators were shuffled together like little boxes in a sharper's Luck-in-a-bag. **1711** SWIFT *Jrnl. to Stella* 8 Sept., You have luck indeed; and luck in a bag. What a devil is that eight shilling tea-kettle? copper, or tin japanned? It is like your Irish politeness, raffling for tea-kettles.

†**4.** A sign of future (good or ill) luck; an omen.

[**1548** ELYOT *Dict.*, *Omen*, the lucke of some thynge to come, gathered of some woorde or saiyng before spoken.] **1570** LEVINS *Manip.* 184/2 Lucke, *fortuna, omen.* *c* **1600** A. HOME in *Bellenden's Livy* v. (1822) 479 The quhilk voice being herd abroad,.. the senate did think the samin to be the luck and presage of sum thing to come.

5. *attrib.* and *Comb.*: **luck-money** = next; **luck-penny**, a piece of money given or kept 'for luck'; a certain sum which local custom prescribes to be returned by the seller to the buyer, esp. in the sale of live-stock; †**luck-sign**, an augury; †**luck-stroken** *a.*, ? having received the luck-penny.

1877 *N. & Q.* 5th Ser. VII. 488 In all agricultural dealings connected with cattle or corn it is customary when receiving payments to return a small sum to the customer, which is termed '*luck money'. **1898** *Daily News* 17 Aug. 2/7 The butchers assert that luck money was customarily granted in Lincoln until the auction system was started. **1788** BURNS *Let. to Mrs. Dunlop* 2 Aug., I am, indeed, seriously angry with you at the quantum of your *luckpenny. **1823** SCOTT *Fam. Lett.* 8 Jan. (1894) II. xix. 162 Builders.. have drain'd my purse, otherwise the luck penny should have been better worth your acceptance. **1824** MISS MITFORD *Village* Ser. I. 262 All the savings of a month, the hoarded halfpence, the new farthings, the very luck-penny, go off *in fumo* on that night. **1890** *Times* 25 Feb. 10/1 The defendant bought a hunter for £100 from the plaintiff and received back £5 'luck penny'. **1587** GOLDING *De Mornay* xxxiii. 621 He tooke a *Lucksigne at the sight of a Lyonnesse [Fr. *Il prend augure d'vne Lyonne*]. **1597** BP. HALL *Sat.* II. v. 17 Go take possession of the church-porch-doore, And ring thy bels; *luck stroken in thy fist, The parsonage is thine or ere thou wist.

luck, *v.* [? a. Du. *lukken*, f. *luk* LUCK *sb.* (But possibly an Eng. formation, though in our quots. appearing earlier than the vb.)]

1. a. *intr.* To chance, happen. Usu. with defining adv.: To turn out *well*, *ill*, etc., to have (good or bad) luck. Also *impers.* (with or without *it*). *Obs.* exc. *dial.*

14.. *Billa posita super hostium majoris* in Hartshorne *Metr. T.* 225 See wich a scrowe is set on thie gate Warning the of harde Happes For and it lukke thou shalt have swappes. **1481** CAXTON *Reynard* (Arb.) 35 Whan it so lucked that we toke an oxe or a cowe. *a* **1547** SURREY *Æneid* II. 494 Our first labor thus lucked well with us. **1596** DALRYMPLE tr. *Leslie's Hist. Scot.* IX. 218 With thame of Cathnes lucket sa il, that [etc.]. **1601** OGLE *Vere's Parlie at Ostend* in *Sir F. Vere's Comm.* 144 The first (and that is the worst) did lucke well, judging the fact by the event. **1681** FLATMAN *Heracl. Ridens* No. 14 (1713) I. 92 They that Addressed were the only Freeborn English, and they that did not Address, were to be Slaves to them, if they had luck't right. **1810** COCK *Strains* II. 65 (E.D.D.) Lat me tell ye, thro' the week Your wark wad luck the better.

b. To be lucky, prosper, succeed. *Obs.* exc. *dial.*

a **1584** MONTGOMERIE *Cherrie & Slae* 643 Thocht thay now, I say now, To hazard hes na hart; ȝit luck we, and pluck we The fruit, they would haue part. **1877** GORDON FRASER *Wigtown* 212 Ill-gotten gear can never luck.

c. With *upon*: To hit upon by chance; to chance to find or meet with.

1670 EACHARD *Cont. Clergy* 35 Whereas there be so many thousand words in the world, and that he should luck upon the right one. *a* **1683** OLDHAM *Art Poetry, Some New Pieces* (1684) 30 When such a lewd, incorrigible sot Lucks by meer chance upon some happy thought. **1712** OLDISWORTH *Odes of Horace* II. 27/1 The most Renowned Thomas Gale.. has luckt upon another Interpretation. **1946** MEZZROW & WOLFE *Really Blues* 376 Luck up on: get by luck, come into possession of unexpectedly. **1962** E. LACY *Freeloaders* i. 9 This is the best writing pad I've ever lucked up on. **1971** *Black World* Apr. 56 All of em hopin to luck up on a few grand by hittin on me. **1973** *Black Panther* 29 Sept. 2/3 Riggs happened to luck up on a good hustle by attacking women's rights in tennis.

d. With *inf.*: To chance, to have the good luck (*to* do something). *Obs.* exc. *dial.*

1724 RAMSAY *Lochaber No More* iii, If I should luck to come gloriously hame. **1787** W. TAYLOR *Scots Poems* 103 Gin I shou'd luck to get a plummy sowd.

e. *to luck out* (*U.S.*), to achieve success or advantage by good luck in a difficult, testing, or dangerous situation.

1954 *Amer. Speech* XXIX. 303 He lucked out on the final examination... I just 'lucked out' on that shot... He really 'lucked out'. He didn't get any Saturday classes. **1967** *Boston Sunday Herald* 7 May VI. 8/4 If you luck out, good. If not, you've still got your original bookings. **1971** J. BALL *First Team* (1972) xxi. 317 Since we pretty much had to choose one from one.. it looks as if we lucked out. **1972** J. WAMBAUGH *Blue Knight* (1973) ii. 22, I started making inquiries.. and damned if I didn't luck out and get steered into a good job.

f. *to luck into*, to acquire by good fortune.

1959 *Time* (Atlantic ed.) 6 July 15/1 Loveless.. lucked into booming revenues from old taxes as.. Iowa expanded. **1966** S. MORROW *Moonlighters* (1967) ix. 98 He lucked into a prime location there. **1970** J. POTTS *Affair of Heart* viii. 63 The rent was fantastically low; she had lucked into it a couple of years ago through an artist friend.

†**2.** *trans.* To bring good luck to. *Obs.*

1530 PALSGR. 615/2, I lucke one, I make hym luckye or happye, *je heure.* He is a happy person, for he lucketh every place he commeth in.

luck, dial. form of LOCK *sb.*[1] (sense 2).

luckely, obs. form of LUCKILY.

ˈ**lucken**, *pa. pple.* and *ppl. a. Sc.* and *north. dial.* [str. pa. pple. of LOUK *v.*[1] See also LOKEN.] Closed, locked, shut up, close-joined; said e.g. of the hand or fist (*lit.* and *fig.*); also *spec.* of web-feet.

c **1470** HENRYSON *Mor. Fab.* XIII. (*Frog & Mouse*) vi, 'With my twa feit', quod scho, 'lukkin and braid, In steid of airis, I row the streme full still'. **1632** LITHGOW *Trav.* x. 469 Mine armes being broake, my hands lucken and sticking fast to the palmes of both hands, by reason of the shrunke sinewes. **1721** RAMSAY *Genty Tibby* ii, Fresh as the lucken flowers in May. **1790** FISHER *Poems* 104 Lucken hands, she ne'er had nane To man or beast.

b. *Comb.*: **lucken-browed** *a.*, having the eyebrows close together; **lucken-footed** *a.*, web-footed.

1683 G. MERITON *Yorksh. Dial.* 73 Thou lucken-brow'd Trull. **1710** SIBBALD *Hist. Fife* (1803) 109 This [Turtur maritimus insulae Bass] is palmipes, that's luckenfooted.

c. lucken booths, booths which can be closed or locked up; hence, the place or quarter where such booths are permanently erected in a town.

1456 in *Charters etc. Peebles* (1872) 113 Land awest half the Cors and on the North Rau som tym was callet the Lwkyn Bothys. **1625** *Ibid.* 413 In ane hows at the bak of the Lwikinbuithis. *a* **1835** J. M. WILSON *Tales Borders* (1839) V. 10/2 The buildings of the jail and Luckenbooths hid that part of the street. **1896** CROCKETT *Grey Man* ii. 13 Buying of trittle-trattles at the lucky-booths.

lucken, *v.*[1] *Sc.* ? *Obs.* [? f. LUCKEN *pa. pple.*] *trans.* To lock, fasten together; to gather up (cloth) in folds; to knit (the brows).

c **1560** A. SCOTT *Poems*, '*Quha is perfyte*' 35 Baith our hartis ar ane, luknyt in luvis chene. *a* **1670** SPALDING *Troub. Chas. I* (1851) II. 388 Haddoche prepairit him self noblie for death, and causit mak ane syd Holland cloth sark, luknit at the heid for his winding scheit. **1806** JAMIESON *Pop. Ball.* II. 173 While anger lucken'd his dark brows.

†**lucken**, *v.*[2] *Obs. rare.* [f. LUCK *sb.* or *v.* + -EN[3].] *intr.* To happen, chance; = LUCK *v.* 1.

1674 N. FAIRFAX *Bulk & Selv.* 56 Which shall be likewise set down in somewhat a mingled way, as they may lucken most readily to come into mind.

luckenes, obs. form of LUCKINESS.

lucken golland, lucken gowan. *dial.* Also 6–7 locker goulons, lockron gowlons, (8–9 -ans). [f. LUCKEN *ppl. a.* + GOLLAND, GOWAN.] A north. dial. name for the Globe-flower, *Trollius Europæus*. (By Turner app. erron. applied to the Marsh Marigold, *Caltha palustris*.)

1548 TURNER *Names of Herbes* (1881) 26 Chameleuce.. is called in Northumberlande a Lucken gollande. **1597** GERARDE *Herbal* II. ccclí. 809 Locker Goulons, or globe Crow-foote. *Ibid.* 810 The globe flower is called.. Lockron gowlons. **1640** PARKINSON *Theat. Bot.* 333, 1740. **1724** RAMSAY *Yng. Laird & Katy*, We'll pou the daisies on the green, The lucken gowans frae the bog. **1760** J. LEE *Introd. Bot.* App. 317 Locker Gowlans, *Trollius.* **1821** HOGG *When the kye comes hame* iv. Poet. Wks. 1840 V. 73 When.. the bonny lucken gowan Has fauldit up her ee.

luckily (ˈlʌkɪlɪ), *adv.* Also 6 luckely, luckilie, luckyly. [f. LUCKY *a.* + -LY[2].

The form *luckely*, frequent in 16th c., may belong to LUCKLY *adv.*; cf., however, *luckenes* = LUCKINESS.]

1. In a lucky manner; with good luck, successfully, prosperously, happily. Now *rare.*

1530 PALSGR. 836/2 Happely, luckely, *par eur, par bon eur.* **1548** UDALL, etc. *Erasm. Par. Matt.* xiii. 1–9 Other sum fel vpon a good and a frutful grounde, and springing vp luckeli, brought furth fruit. *a* **1553** —— *Royster D.* I. v. (Arb.) 31 My dere spouse.. whom.. God luckily sende home to both our heartes ease. **1561** DAUS tr. *Bullinger on Apoc.* lxxviii. 546 The Romanistes.. make their boaste, that.. no Kinges.. haue yet luckely assayled Rome. **1585** J. B. tr. *Viret's Sch. Beastes* B, The esterne winde. Which brought you hither luckely. **1647** CLARENDON *Hist. Reb.* I. §104 He.. carried himself so luckily in Parliament, that he did his Master much service. **1668** DRYDEN *Dram. Poesy* Ess. (1900) I. 80 All the images of Nature were still present to him, and he drew them, not laboriously, but luckily. **1748** *Anson's Voy.* II. iii. 141 Several fine runs of.. fresh water,.. some of them so luckily situated, that the casks may be filled.. with an hose. **1766** GOLDSM. *Vic. W.* iii, 'This,' cried he, 'happens still more luckily than I hoped for'.

2. Now chiefly used as a qualification of the sentence as a whole, indicating that the fact or circumstance stated is a lucky one.

1717 LADY M. W. MONTAGU *Let. to Miss Sar. Chiswell* 1 Apr., Luckily for me, I was so well deceived that I knew nothing of the matter. **1762** KAMES *Elem. Crit.* viii. (1774) I. 288 Luckily.. our speculations are supported by facts. **1815** W. H. IRELAND *Scribbleomania* 236 *note*, The poor blind man.. told his tale; which, luckily for him, was believed. **1871** L. STEPHEN *Playgr. Europe* x. (1894) 236 Climbing a long snow-slope which was luckily in fair order.

luckiness (ˈlʌkɪnɪs). Also 6 luckenes, luckynesse. [f. LUCKY *a.* + -NESS.] The quality or condition of being lucky; fortunateness.

1561 DAUS tr. *Bullinger on Apoc.* xxiv. 149 The eyes signifie a foresighte, watchefulnes, subtilties, and luckenes in doynge of thinges. **1571** GOLDING *Calvin on Ps.* x. 6 Hee speaketh of the luckye state of the ungodly.. and complayneth of this their luckynesse. **1662** PETTY *Taxes* 53 A lottery therefore is properly a tax upon unfortunate selfconceited fools; men that have a good opinion of their own luckiness. **1690** LOCKE *Hum. Und.* IV. xvii. §24, I know not whether the luckiness of the accident will excuse the irregularity of his proceeding. **1832** tr. *Tour Germ. Prince* II. ix. 148, I have often been tempted to think that luckiness and unluckiness are a sort of subjective properties which we bring with us into the world.

luckite (ˈlʌkaɪt). *Min.* [Named (in Fr.) by A. Carnot 1879 from the 'Lucky Boy' silver-mine in Utah: see -ITE.] A variety of melanterite.

1885 in *Cassell's Encycl. Dict.*

luckless ('lʌklɪs), *a.* (In 6 *superl.* **lucklest.**) [f. LUCK *sb.* + -LESS.]

1. Having no 'luck' or good fortune; attended with ill-luck; unlucky, hapless, ill-starred, unfortunate. (Of persons and things.)

1563 SACKVILLE *Induct. Mirr. Mag.* xvii, The drery destinie And luckeles lot for to bemone of those, Whom Fortune [etc.]. *a* **1586** SIDNEY *Arcadia* III. (1598) 389 Mine is the lucklest lot, That euer fell to honest woman yet. **1590** SPENSER *F.Q.* I. vi. 19 Glad of such lucke, the luckelesse lucky mayd. **1593** SHAKS. *3 Hen. VI*, II. vi. 18, I, and ten thousand in this lucklesse Realme. **1697** DRYDEN *Virg. Past.* VIII. 81 Let the whelming Tide, The lifeless Limbs of luckless Damon hide. **1782** COWPER *Gilpin* 201 Ah, luckless speech, and bootless boast! **1874** GREEN *Short Hist.* v. §1. 213 [Chaucer] was luckless enough to be made prisoner. **1876** L. STEPHEN *Eng. Th. 18th C.* I. 102 It was a luckless performance so far as his temporal interests were concerned.

†**2.** Presaging or foreboding evil, ominous of ill.

1633 P. FLETCHER *Purple Isl.* XII. xxxiv, On his dangling crest A lucklesse Raven spred her blackest wings. **1637** B. JONSON *Sad Sheph.* II. ii, The shreikes of lucklesse Owles Wee heare! and croaking Night-Crowes in the aire.

Hence '**lucklessly** *adv.*, '**lucklessness**.

1830 H. ANGELO *Remin.* I. 452 When lucklessly engaging to subdue a fine Arabian..he was thrown, and..was killed on the spot. **1868** BROWNING *Ring & Bk.* v. 44 Show men the lucklessness, the improvidence Of the easy-natured Count. **1876** GREEN *Stray Stud.* 368 Michelet has with singular lucklessness selected Angers as the type of a feudal city.

† '**luckly**, *a.* and *adv. Obs.* [f. LUCK *sb.* + -LY.]

A. *adj.* Lucky, fortunate, successful.

a **1568** ASCHAM *Scholem.* I. (Arb.) 62 Experience of all facions in yougthe, beinge, in profe, alwaise daungerous, in isshue, seldom lucklie. **1589** WARNER *Alb. Eng.* VI. xxxi. (1612) 156 So lesser sute hath luclier speede. **1612** T. ADAMS *Gallants Burd.* 15 The peaceable dayes of the Wicked, and their luckly proceedinges in this world.

B. *adv.*

[**1530**, **1548**, **1561**, etc.: see LUCKILY I.] **1582** STANYHURST *Æneis* I. (Arb.) 30 Doubtlesse thee gods al greatlye doe tender Thy state, neere Tyrian citty so lucklye to iumble.

luckwarm, obs. form of LUKEWARM.

lucky ('lʌkɪ), *sb.*[1] *Sc.* Also **luckie**. [? f. LUCKY *a.* 6.] A familiar name for an elderly woman; *spec.* a grandmother. (Used as a form of address, and prefixed as a title to the proper name.) Also applied, jocularly or affectionately, to a woman of any age; a wife, mistress, etc. **b.** *spec.* The mistress of an ale-house, a landlady.

1717 RAMSAY *Elegy on Lucky Wood* 30 Poor facers now may chew pea-hools, Since Lucky's dead. **1725** —— *Gentle Sheph.* II. iii. (*init.*), How does auld honest lucky of the glen? **1770** BP. FORBES *Jrnl.* (1886) 324 We dined at Lucky Mac Fun's. *a* **1794** *Lass of Ecclefechan* ii. in *Burns' Wks.*, O haud your tongue now, Luckie Laing. —— *Lady Onlie* i. *ibid.*, Lady Onlie, honest Lucky, Brews guid ale at shore o' Bucky. **1816** SCOTT *Antiq.* iv, I said to Luckie Gemmels, 'Never think you, Luckie', said I. **1827** WATT *Poems* 56 (E.D.D.) Gin the kye o' milk be dryin', Some luckie's been her cantrips tryin'. **1857** STEWART *Character* 145 (E.D.D.) The gawcy change-house luckies lauch and mulct the drunken fule. **1893** STEVENSON *Catriona* 134 Alan..must..carry on to the new luckie with the old story.

lucky ('lʌkɪ), *sb.*[2] *slang.* In phr. ***to cut*** or ***make one's lucky***: to get away, escape, decamp.

1834 M. M. G. DOWLING *Othello Travestie* I. ii. 7 He's in such a rage—you'd better cut your lucky. **1837** DICKENS *Pickw.* x, Wot's the use o' runnin' arter a man as has made his lucky, and got to t'other end of the Borough by this time. **1859** LEVER *Davenport Dunn* xiv. 119 Simpson, of the Bays, has cut his lucky this morning.

Lucky ('lʌkɪ), *sb.*[3] [ellipt. f. *Lucky Strike*, a U.S. brand of cigarettes.] A Lucky Strike cigarette.

1934 A. HUXLEY *Beyond Mexique Bay* 153 If Luckies are to sell here, they will have to be put under the patronage of Saint Joseph. **1949** O. NASH *Versus* 139 As a Lucky Striker, Whenever I offer smart folk a Lucky [etc.]. **1953** A. BARON *Human Kind* 184 He fumbled for a packet of Luckies and offered Casey a fresh cigarette. **1963** 'D. RUTHERFORD' *Creeping Flesh* i. 63 I smoked six Luckies. *Ibid.* 80 A packet of Luckies, please. **1969** N. FREELING *Tsing-Boum* xxii. 160 Those French ones—no thanks. I only smoke Luckies, really.

lucky ('lʌkɪ), *a.* Also 6 **luckye, lukie, lukky**, 6–7 **luckie**. [f. LUCK *sb.* + -Y[1].]

1. Of persons: Having, or attended by, good luck. In early use often, Fortunate, successful, prosperous. Now with narrower meaning: Favoured by chance; successful through causes other than one's own action or merit.

1502 ARNOLDE *Chron.* (1811) 159 God Almyghty yeue you parte of his saluacion and make you lukky. **1530** TINDALE *Gen.* xxxix. 2 And the Lorde was with Ioseph, and he was a luckie felowe. **1552** LATIMER *Serm. Lincolnsh.* i. (1562) 68 And therefore there is a common sayinge The more wicked, the more lucky. **1624** GATAKER *Transubst.* 120 He never is luckie in the framing of his consequences. **1625** BACON *Ess., Negotiating* (Arb.) 89 Vse also such, as haue beene Luckie and Preuailed before in Things wherein you haue Emploied them. **1641** J. JACKSON *True Evang. T.* II. 96 It is part of the description of a lucky, and prosperous man, that his Cow calveth. **1827** SCOTT *Two Drovers* ii, Wakefield was lucky enough to find a chap for a part of his drove. **1849** MACAULAY *Hist. Eng.* ii. I. 183 A dexterous and lucky player. **1865** KINGSLEY *Herew.* xiii, He must be a luckier man than you are.

†**b.** Of a person: Having the knack of success; 'handy' (Davies). *Obs.*

1703 MRS. CENTLIVRE *Love's Contriv.* I. Wks. 1761 II. 19 You used to be a lucky Rogue upon a Pinch.

c. Of actions or experiences: Attended by good luck.

1548 UDALL, etc. *Erasm. Par.* Pref. 10 Whose fortunate and luckye spede in all hys woorthye entrepryses. **1548** LADY ELIZ. HOWARD *Let. to Q. Dowager Parr*, Praying the Almighty God to send you a most lucky deliverance [in childbirth]. **1560** DAUS tr. *Sleidane's Comm.* 184 b, Geuing thankes to his god, for that lucky successe. **1697** DRYDEN *Æneid* IX. 454 Ev'n then he dreamt of Drink and lucky Play. **1736** BUTLER *Anal.* I. iii. (1849) I. 62 There are instances of reason and real prudence preventing men's undertaking what, it hath appeared afterwards, they might have succeeded in by a lucky rashness. **1807** CRABBE *Par. Reg.* III. 699 And what's good judgement but a lucky guess? **1864** TENNYSON *En. Ard.* 537 Less lucky her home-voyage.

d. Of a literary composition: Having an unstudied or unsought felicity.

1700 T. BROWN tr. *Fresny's Amusem. Ser. & Com.* 6 There is more Wit in disguising a Thought of Mr. Lock's, than in a lucky Translation of a Passage from Horace. **1779–81** JOHNSON *L.P.*, *Cowley*, He has no elegance either lucky or elaborate. *Ibid.*, *Waller*, Genius now and then produces a lucky trifle. We still read the Dove of Anacreon, and Sparrow of Catullus.

e. ***lucky him*** (or ***you***, etc.): phrases expressing envy at another's good fortune.

1857 C. M. YONGE *Dynevor Terr.* II. xi. 171 She's..the finest figure in the whole county; lucky him who gets her. *Ibid.* xii. 176 Lucky you to have work at home, and to stay with it. **1893** W. ELWIN *Let.* 4 May in E. Lutyens *Blessed Girl* (1953) x. 190 Lucky you to be mothered by Betty. **1965** A. ROUDYBUSH *Season for Death* (1966) xxviii. 165 'I'm going to the flicks.' 'Lucky you. God bless!' **1972** R. HILL *Fairly Dangerous Thing* I. iv. 36 ' I'm busy every night but tonight.' 'Lucky you,' said Joe.

2. Of events or circumstances: Of the nature of good luck; occurring by chance and producing happy results.

a **1547** SURREY *Praise of meane & constant estate* in *Tottel's Misc.* (Arb.) 28 When lucky gale of winde All thy puft sailes shall fil. **1653** WALTON *Angler* xi. 207 Well met, Gentlemen, this is luckie that we meet so just together at this very door. **1726** SWIFT *Gulliver* I. v, By the luckiest chance in the world, I had not discharged myself of any part of it. **1752** JOHNSON *Rambler* No. 192 ¶2 His heir..sometimes by a wealthy marriage, sometimes by lucky legacies, discharged part of the encumbrances. **1796** JANE AUSTEN *Pride & Prej.* x. (1813) 213 This was a lucky recollection—it saved her from something like regret.

3. With superstitious reference: Presaging or likely to promote good luck; well-omened. Often applied to objects carried as charms, as in ***lucky penny, sixpence*** (usually one bent or perforated; sometimes an old or foreign coin), ***lucky stone*** (often, one with a natural hole through it: see E.D.D.).

lucky day, etc. may be used also in sense I c.

1549 COVERDALE, etc. *Erasm. Par. 1 Cor.* 44 With all good and luckye woordes, blessed..bee God. **1555** BRADFORD *Let.* in Foxe *A. & M.* (1583) II. 1632/1 Looke not vppon these dayes..as dismall dayes..but rather as lucky dayes. **1601** SHAKS. *All's Well* I. iii. 252 That his good receipt Shall for my legacie be sanctified By the luckiest stars in heauen. **1614** B. JONSON *Barth. Fair* II. ii, They say, a Foole's hansel is lucky. **1637** MILTON *Lycidas* 20 So may som gentle Muse With lucky words favour my destin'd Urn. **1718** *Freethinker* No. 62. 46 Sneezing..might be interpreted Lucky, or Unlucky, according to the Occasions. **1727** POPE *Th. Var. Subjects* in *Swift's Wks.* (1755) II. I. 231 Augustus meeting an ass with a lucky name foretold himself good fortune. **1792** W. ROBERTS *Looker-on* No. 22 (1797) I. 332 It has often happened..that a dream, by presenting to the imagination a lucky number, has induced a poor man to commit himself in the lottery. **1819** CRABBE *T. of Hall* xix, She praised her lucky stars, that in her place She never found neglect, nor felt disgrace. **1852** DICKENS *Bleak Ho.* xxxii, Mr. Guppy nods, and gives him a 'lucky touch'. **1855** Q. VICTORIA *Life Highlands* 10 Sept. (1868) 105 The new house seems to be lucky, indeed; for, from the first moment of our arrival, we have had good news. **1905** A. BURVENICH *Eng. Idioms* 219 To be born under a lucky star. **1911** C. E. W. BEAN '*Dreadnought' of Darling* xxxv. 317 The Australian should probably thank Providence and his lucky star. **1920** W. J. LOCKE *House of Baltazar* xv. 187 It doesn't seem to be one of the House of Baltazar's lucky days. **1959** J. BRAINE *Vodi* xxv. 261 Thank your lucky stars to be well out of it. **1973** A. BEHREND *Samarai Affair* xii. 115 Richardson wondered if this was going to be his lucky day.

4. Occurring by chance; depending on chance; casual, fortuitous. *rare.*

1691 RAY *Creation* I. (1692) 23 It were beyond the Possibility of the Wit of Man to perswade him that this was done by the temerarious dashes of an unguided Pen..or by the lucky Projection of so many Letters at all adventures. **1701** ROWE *Ambit. Step-Moth.* I. i, My Royal Mistress Artemisa's Fate, And all her Son young Artaban's high hopes Hang on this lucky Crisis. **1836** EMERSON *Nat., Lang.* Wks. (Bohn) II. 150 There is nothing lucky or capricious in these analogies..they are constant, and pervade nature.

5. *dial.* Used to indicate an amount not less, and usually greater, than what is actually stated; full, good. (For this and other dialect uses of the word, consult the *Eng. Dial. Dict.*)

1649 *Last Sp. Visct. Kenmure* in *Sel. Biog.* (Wodrow Soc. 1845) I. 384 God..plucked them from their deceiving hopes, before they got half a bellyful, yea, or a lucky mouthful of the world. **1823** GALT *R. Gilhaize* II. xxxii. 315 The sun has been set a lucky hour. **1828** J. RUDDIMAN *Tales Sc. Par.* (1889) 125, I aye had my doubts..o' cats in general, for the lucky half o' them are but handmaidens to witches.

6. *Sc.* Used as a term or address of endearment, esp. to a woman. [Cf. Icel. *heill* good luck, 'in mod. usage as a term of endearment' (Vigfusson).] Hence **lucky-dad, -daddy**, a grandfather; **lucky-minny (-minnie)**, a grandmother. (Cf. LUCKY *sb.*[1])

a **1555** LYNDESAY in *Bannatyne Poems* (Hunter. Club) 465 [Cotter addressing his wife] Ye gaif me leif, fair lucky dame. **1721** KELLY *Scot. Prov.* 164 Ha'd your Feet, luckie daddie, old Folk are not feery. **1742** FORBES *Ajax Sp.* etc. *Jrnl.* (1755) 30 Lucky-minny. *a* **1758** RAMSAY *Fox turned Preacher* 36 'Tis cruel, and a cruelty By which we are expos'd (O sad!) To eat perhaps our lucky dad. **1818** SCOTT *Hrt. Midl.* xlvii, The bits o' bairns, puir things, are wearying to see their luckie-dad. **1867** SMYTH *Sailor's Word-bk.*, *Lucky minie's lines*, the long stems of the sea-plant *Chorda filum*. **1868** G. MACDONALD *R. Falconer* xxiii. (1870) 150 That auld luckie-minnie o' his.

7. *Comb.*, as ***lucky-starred*** adj.; **lucky dip**: see DIP *sb.* 1 h; **lucky dog**, someone considered by others to be lucky; **lucky-proach** *Sc.* = FATHER-LASHER.

1841 S. BAMFORD *Passages in Life of Radical* (ed. 2) I. xxix. 175 They were a set of 'lucky dogs'... They escaped. **1844** DICKENS *Mart. Chuz.* xii, He has come into his property... He's a lucky dog. **1922** JOYCE *Ulysses* 634 You were a lucky dog if they didn't set the terrier at you directly you got back. **1836** YARRELL *Brit. Fishes* I. 63 Father-Lasher, Long-Spined Cottus. Lucky Proach. *Scotland.* **1876** PATMORE *The Rosy Bosom'd Hours* 3 He lock'd us in, ah, lucky-starr'd.

'**lucky-bag.** [f. LUCKY *a.* Cf. *luck in a bag*, LUCK *sb.* 3 b.]

1. A bag, at fairs and bazaars, in which, on payment of a small sum, one dips one's hand and draws an article of greater or less value. Often *fig.*

1825 R. T. in Hone *Every-day Bk.* II. 1309 Here is Rebecca Swain with her..lucky-bag. **1887** W. E. NORRIS *Major & Minor* xxxiv, Who knows what is in the lucky-bag. **1891** *Confectioners' Union* IV. 530/1 (Advt.), Farthing Goods... Pick-me-up Lucky Bags. **1902** *Blackw. Mag.* Feb. 290/2 A regular lucky-bag of fighting men. **1927** W. E. COLLINSON *Contemp. Eng.* 20 The term lucky bag is still used to denote a bag stuffed full of miscellaneous objects. **1931** A. UTTLEY *Country Child* iii. 37 There the paper bag lay, 'Monster Lucky Bag', with some others..on the counter, asking her to open it. **1968** 'E. PETERS' *Grass Widow's Tale* vii. 90 This trifle, hardly too big to have fallen out of a child's lucky-bag. **1973** *Dalesman* May 144/1, I well remember..the lucky bags which cost a ha'penny. These bags were pink, yellow or green and contained some sweets and a little novelty or toy.

2. *U.S.* 'A receptacle on a man-of-war for all clothes and other articles of private property carelessly left by their owners' (*Cent. Dict.*).

1832 E. C. WINES *Two Yrs. in Navy* (1833) I. 55 All property that falls in his [*sc.* the master-at-arms'] way for which he cannot find an owner, is thrown into the 'lucky bag'. **1840** *Southern Lit. Messenger* VI. 233/2 Every man-of-war, you know, has her lucky bag, containing a little of every thing, and something belonging to everybody. **1884** S. B. LUCE *Seamanship* 310 (Cent.) Have the master-at-arms with you in this inspection, to gather up all articles of private property and put them in the lucky bag.

lucombe, lucome, obs. forms of LUCARNE.

† '**lucrate**, *v. Obs.*[—0] [f. L. *lucrāt-*, ppl. stem of *lucrāri* to gain, f. *lucrum* gain.] *trans.* To gain, win.

1623 in COCKERAM.

† **lu'cration.** *Obs.* [ad. late L. *lucrātiōn-em*, n. of action f. *lucrāri* to gain.] The action of gaining, an instance of this.

1658 PHILLIPS, *Lucration*, a gaining or winning. **1775** in ASH. **1812** SOUTHEY *Ess.* (1832) I. 112 The gain which can be extracted from him, the quantum of lucration of which he can be made the instrument.

lucrative ('l(j)uːkrətɪv), *a.* Also 5 **lucratijf, -tyf(e**, 6 **-tyve**. [ad. L. *lucrātīv-us*, f. *lucrāri* to gain.]

1. Yielding gain or profit; gainful, profitable. ***lucrative office***: an office to which compensation is attached.

14.. *Wyclif's Bible* (1850) IV. 684[b], Addit. Prol. Luke, Manye clerkis lernen lucratijf sciencis, to gete richessis. *c* **1412** HOCCLEVE *De Reg. Princ.* 659 An office also hadde I lucratyf. **1526** *Pilgr. Perf.* (W. de W. 1531) 237 b, To abstayne from..bodyly labours, & specyally from them that be lucratyue. **1625** BACON *Ess., Usury* (Arb.) 544 The Trade of Merchandize, being the most Lucratiue, may beare Vsury at a good Rate. **1725** BROOME *Notes Pope's Odyss.* XIV. 259 III. 350 The more lucrative..method of life by Agriculture. *a* **1763** SHENSTONE *Ess.* Wks. 1765 II. 146 Necessity may be the Mother of lucrative invention. **1777** ROBERTSON *Hist. Amer.* (1778) I. I. 29 At length, the Soldans of Egypt established a lucrative trade in that port. **1808** SCOTT *Prose Wks.* IV. Biographies II. (1870) 37 A lucrative contract warded off the blow for a time. **1849** MACAULAY *Hist. Eng.* iii. I. 388 It became clear that the speculation would be lucrative. **1874** GREEN *Short Hist.* vii. §5. 387 A more lucrative traffic had already begun with the coast of Guinea.

b. *Scots Law.* Chiefly in ***lucrative succession*** (after L. *lucrativa acquisitio*, Ulpian *Dig.* xliv. §4): the acceptance by an heir apparent, in the lifetime of his ancestor, of a free gift of any part of the estate to which he would have succeeded.

To prevent this being done to the defrauding of creditors, the law provides that the 'lucrative successor' becomes liable for all the debts of the grantor contracted before the time of the grant.

1681 VISCT. STAIR *Instit.* III. vii. (1693) 489 Lucrative Successors, how this passive Title is extended, and how Limited by our Practise..Lucrative Dispositions of any part of the Heretage infer this passive Title. **1848** WHARTON *Law Lex., Lucrative Succession.*

†**2.** Of persons, their actions and sentiments: Bent upon or directed towards making of gain; avaricious, covetous. *Obs.*

1549 LATIMER *7th Serm. bef. Edw. VI* (Arb.) 53 He requyres no such diligence as the most part of our lucratiue lawyers do vse. **1603** DANIEL *Epist. to Sir T. Egerton* xxiii, To binde the hands of Iustice vp so hard, That lest she falling to prooue Lucratiue Might basely reach them out to take reward. **1630** DONNE *Serm.* xiii. 131 Let not thy prayer be Lucrative nor Vindicative. **1744** HARRIS *Three Treat.* Wks. (1841) 52 May we not venture..to pass the same sentence on the lucrative life, as we have already on the political. **1750** BEAWES *Lex Mercat.* (1752) 258 Attributed..not to any lucrative view of unnecessarily swelling my book. **1792** W. ROBERTS *Looker-on* No. 32 (1794) I. 458 To enter upon..a cure..on which perhaps I should not wish to reside long, would show more of the lucrative mind than the pastoral care. **1797** S. JAMES *Narr. Voy.* 58 To show what a man will do to compass his lucrative desires.

Hence **'lucratively** *adv.*, **'lucrativeness.**

1726 LEONI tr. *Alberti's Archit.* I. 37 The Censors, in farming out..Estates, always began with the Lake Lucrinus, because of the Lucrativeness of its Name. **1848** WEBSTER, *Lucratively*, profitably. **1871** *Echo* 4 Apr. 1/2 The device..ingeniously and lucratively extricates authorities from a serious difficulty. **1899** SIR G. DOUGLAS *Hogg* v. 96 His pen being abundantly and lucratively occupied.

†**'lucratory,** *a. Obs.* [f. L. *lucrāt-* (see LUCRATE *v.*) + -ORY².] Relating to the getting of gain.

1646 GAULE *Cases Consc.* 6 Witch-seekers..whose lucratory skil and experience is not much improved above the outward senses.

lucre ('l(j)uːkə(r)), *sb.* Forms: 5 lukir, lukre, 6 lucar, lucur, (?) lycur, 6–7 luker, 7 lukar, 4– lucre. [ad. (either directly, or through F. *lucre*) L. *lucrum*, f. WAryan root **lŭ-, leu-, lou-*, whence Gr. ἀπο-λαύειν to enjoy, Goth. *launs*, OHG. *lôn*, mod.G. *lohn* wages, reward.]

1. Gain, profit, pecuniary advantage. Now only with unfavourable implication: Gain viewed as a low motive for action; 'pelf'. ***filthy lucre***: (see FILTHY 4 b); so †***foul lucre.*** †Also *pl.*

c **1380** WYCLIF *Wks.* (1880) 172 þ ei traueilen faste aboute here owene worldly honour and lucre. **1388** —— *Ezek.* xxii. 27 In suynge lucris gredili. *c* **1412** HOCCLEVE *De Reg. Princ.* 1544 þus bothe oure þanke & lucre gon a-weye. **1477** *Rolls of Parlt.* VI. 187/2 They shuld have for lucre, favorable Enquestes of comers to the said Feyres. **1503–4** *Act 19 Hen. VII*, c. 19 Preamble, For their owne spede and lucre they suffer their ledder to passe untruly coryed. *a* **1533** LD. BERNERS *Gold. Bk. M. Aurel.* (1546) U v, Theyr owne handes open for theyr owne propre lucres. **1540** TAVERNER *Flores Aliquot Sentent.* A vj b, Preferre dammage afore fowle lucre. **1576** FLEMING *Panopl. Epist.* 283 They sel the fruits of their lands with lucre. **1605** BACON *Adv. Learn.* I. v. §11. 26 Men haue entered into a desire of Learning and Knowledge..for lukar and profession. **1611** BIBLE *1 Sam.* viii. 3 His sonnes..turned aside after lucre, and tooke bribes. **1669** GALE *Crt. Gentiles* I. I. ix. 49 The Phenicians, for lucres sake, sailed throughout the world. **1697** DRYDEN *Virg. Georg.* II. 717 From his lov'd Home no Lucre him can draw. **1734** BERKELEY *Let. to T. Prior* 2 Mar., Wks. 1871 IV. 215 A greater greediness for lucre than I hope I shall ever have. **1768** BEATTIE *Minstr.* I. lx, At lucre or renown let others aim. **1804** WELLINGTON in Gurw. *Desp.* III. 23 Putting lucre out of the question, I am of opinion that we shall gain more influence. **1834** LYTTON *Pompeii* II. ii, In the earlier times of Rome the priesthood was a profession, not of lucre but of honour. **1862** LD. BROUGHAM *Brit. Const.* App. iii. 457 He wrote for lucre the party's speech which he was to deliver in his own person.

personified. **1606** *Wily Beguiled* 30 Thus Lucre, set in golden Chaire of state, When learning's bid Stand by, and keepes a loofe.

†**2.** Const. *of.* **a.** Gain or profit derived from (something) (*obs.*). **b.** Acquisition of (something profitable) (*obs.* exc. *arch.*).

The phr. ***lucre of gain***, frequent in 17th c., is echoed as an archaism by some writers of the 19th c.

c **1386** CHAUCER *Prioress' T.* 39 Foule vsure and lucre of vileynye. **1390** GOWER *Conf.* III. 380 Uppon the lucre of merchandie, Compassement and tricherie Of singuler profit to wynne. *c* **1430** LYDG. *Reas. & Sens.* (E.E.T.S.) 1335 For now vnneth[e] ther ys noone That loueth but for lucre of gode. **1576** FLEMING *Panopl. Epist.* 267 Such as..sell their skill and labour for lucre of monie. **1632** B. JONSON *Magn. Lady* v. vi, Love to my Child, and lucre of the portion Provok'd me. *a* **1667** COWLEY *Agric.* in *Verses & Ess.* (1687) 99 The Utility [of Agriculture] (I mean plainly the Lucre of it) is not so great now in our Nation as arises from Merchandise. **1697** *C'tess D'Aunoy's Trav.* (1706) 198 These Men of War ought not to carry any Merchants Goods, but the Lucre of Gain tempts them. **1704** N. N. tr. *Boccalini's Advts. fr. Parnass.* I. 73 To write a Barbarous Recipe, purely for the Lucre of a Guinea. **1720** DE FOE *Capt. Singleton* (1840) xviii. 309 A Malabar, for the lucre of a knife, conducted them to a Dutch town. **1758** JOHNSON *Idler* No. 67 ⁋5 It is..love, and not lucre of gain. **1805** SOUTHEY *Lett.* (1856) I. 314, I am going to make a book for the lucre of gain. *a* **1849** H. COLERIDGE *Ess.* (1851) I. 85 Sometimes, too, the prolific are led, by the lucre of gain, to deck the childless with parental honours. Adopted books are as common as adopted children.

Hence †**'lucre** *v.*, to make gain. †**'lucring** *vbl. sb.* and *ppl. a.*

1570 LEVINS *Manip.* 78/26 To Luker, *lucrari. Ibid.* 182/35 To Lucre, *lucrari.* **1573** A. ANDERSON *Expos. Hymn Benedict* 75 b, Such popish Masse priestes..frame themselues to euery chaunge, thereby to satisfy their lucring lust. **1615** BRATHWAIT *Strappado* (1878) 105 Such lucring Mammonists the heauens displease.

lucrefie, variant of LUCRIFY *v. Obs.*

Lucretian (l(j)uː'kriːʃ(ɪ)ən), *a.* (*sb.*) [f. *Lucrēti-us*, the name of a Latin poet and Epicurean philosopher + -AN.] Pertaining to, characteristic of, or resembling Lucretius or his philosophy.

1712 BLACKMORE *Creation* 113 Say, did you e'er reflect, Lucretian tribe? **1768–74** TUCKER *Lt. Nat.* (1834) II. 652 The Lucretian comfort is none to me. **1900** *Speaker* 1 Sept. 602 The Lucretian philosophy. **1902** *Q. Rev.* Oct. 500 (*Giordano Bruno in England*), Part of his Lucretian poem, 'De Immenso', must have been written here.

b. quasi-*sb.* (The adj. used *absol.*) A follower of Lucretius, an adherent of his philosophy.

1881 S. WAINWRIGHT *Sci. Sophisms* i. (1883) 31 It is the ideal Lucretian himself who is the speaker.

†**lucri'faction.** *Obs. rare*⁻¹. [as if ad. L. **lucrifactiōn-em*, n. of action f. *lucrifacĕre*, f. *lucrum* gain, LUCRE + *facĕre* to make.] The action or practice of making or getting gain.

1606 BIRNIE *Kirk-Buriall* (1833) F 2 b, The Iewes do comprise all titular rights vnder one of three: acquisition, like Abrahams..heredation like Isaacs..lucrifaction, like Iacobs, whose wealth was the winning of his owne hand-hammers.

†**lu'criferous,** *a. Obs.* [f. L. *lucr-um* + -(I)FEROUS.] Bringing gain; lucrative, profitable.

1648 PETTY *Adv. Hartlib* 23 Schollers..would quickly help themselves by opening treasures with the Key of Luciferous Inventions. **1669** NEWTON in Rigaud *Corr. Sci. Men* (1841) II. 294 Being the most luciferous, and many times lucriferous experiments too in philosophy. **1707** SLOANE *Jamaica* I. 53 Those from Angola run away from their masters,..which is no lucriferous experiment, for on hard usage they kill themselves.

Hence †**lu'criferousness,** the quality of being lucriferous or profitable.

1663 BOYLE *Usef. Exp. Nat. Philos.* I. ii. 45 If we impartially consider the Lucriferousness..of the properties of Things, and their Medical Virtues, we shall find, That [etc.].

†**lu'crific,** *a. Obs. rare*⁻⁰. [ad. L. *lucrific-us*, f. *lucrum* gain: see -FIC.] Producing gain.

1727 in BAILEY vol. II. **1755** in JOHNSON.

†**lu'crificable,** *a. Obs.* [ad. L. *lucrificā-bilis*: see next and -ABLE.] = prec.

1623 in COCKERAM.

†**lu'crificate,** *v. Obs. rare*⁻⁰. [f. L. *lucrificāt-*, ppl. stem of *lucrificāre*, f. *lucrific-us* LUCRIFIC.]

1656 BLOUNT *Glossogr., Lucrificate*,..to gain, or get, to make after gain.

†**'lucrify,** *v. Obs.* Also 6 lucrefie, lucrifie. [ad. L. *lucrificāre*: see prec. and -IFY.] **a.** *trans.* To gain, win. **b.** To make gain of or by; to turn to account.

1563–87 FOXE *A. & M.* (1596) 323/1 By the which the Deuill is ouercome, and plenty of soules be lucrified and wonne to Christ. **1564–78** BULLEYN *Dial. agst. Pest.* (1888) 140 God hath geuen you a talent full godlie, you doe lucrefie the same and hide it not. *a* **1598** ROLLOCK *Comm. 2 Thess.* iii. (1606) 144 Peter..sayes, They lucrifie soules vnto Christs, by their lyves without any speach [1 *Pet.* iii. 1].

Lucrine ('l(j)uːkraɪn), *a.* [ad. L. *Lūcrīn-us.*] The designation of a lake near Baiæ in Campania, and of the oysters (highly esteemed by the Romans) which were procured from it.

a **1637** B. JONSON *Praises Country Life* 49 Not Lucrine Oysters I could then more prize. **1835** *Penny Cycl.* III. 168/1 The Lucrine Lake was filled up by an eruption.

lucriouse, erroneous form of LUCROUS *Obs.*

†**lu'cripetous,** *a. Obs.* [f. L. *lucripet-a* (f. *lucr-um* gain + *pet-ĕre* to seek) + -OUS.] Eager for gain.

1675 PLUME *Life Bp. Hacket* (1865) 122 When he was made a Bishop no man was less lucripetous, he desired to hold nothing *in commendam.*

†**'lucrous,** *a. Obs.* Also 6 lukerous, *erron.* lucrious. [ad. L. *lucriōsus*, f. *lucrum* LUCRE: see -OUS.] Pertaining to lucre; gainful. Also, avaricious, covetous.

15.. *Kalender of Sheph.* (? 1528) L viij b, O ye marchauntes..Of lukerous wynnynge ye haue greate pleasure. **1551** BECKE *Bible, Ded. to Edw. VI*, Your graces Chancelers, Iudges, Iustices & such as intermedle wyth the lucrous lawe. **1570** LEVINS *Manip.* 226/2 Lucriouse, *lucriosus.* **1755** J. G. COOPER *Tomb Shaks.* 143 Free from the muck-worm miser's lucrous rage. **1796** *Mod. Gulliver's Trav.* 138 Vilpi Tico enables even the most avaricious to gratify their lucrous appetites.

†**luc'tation.** *Obs.* [ad. L. *luctātiōn-em*, n. of action f. *luctāri* to struggle.] Struggling, wrestling; an instance of this.

1651 HOWELL *Venice* 207 She [Venice] having clos'd in actuall luc[t]ation with that great Eastern Giant. **1660** tr. *Amyraldus' Treat. conc. Relig.* I. vii. 121 The luctation and combate of reason against the corporeal appetites. **1698** FRYER *Acc. E. India & P.* 255 At Noonday we overcame an high mountain after a troublesome Luctation.

b. *transf.* Agitation due to chemical reaction. Also, a struggling for breath.

1678 GREW *Luctation* 6 Sometimes the Luctation begins presently upon mixture. **1693** J. CLAYTON *Acc. Virginia* in *Misc. Cur.* (1708) III. 351 The Swelling and Luctation at his Breast, was as if he would burst. **1693** MOULEN in *Phil. Trans.* XVII. 625, I pour'd good Spirit of Salt on a parcel of this Sand, but could observe no Luctation thereby produc'd.

†**luc'tiferous,** *a. Obs. rare*⁻¹. [f. L. *luctifer* (f. *luct-us* sorrow + *-i-fer* bearing) + -OUS.] Bringing sorrow, mournful, gloomy.

1656 in BLOUNT *Glossogr.* **1775** in ASH. **1824** MISS FERRIER *Inher.* liii, An equipage and attendants of—of—of the most luctiferous description.

Hence **luc'tiferousness.**

1731 in BAILEY vol. II.

†**luc'tific,** *a. Obs.* [ad. L. *luctificus*, f. *luct-us* grief: see -FIC.] Causing sorrow or mourning.

1727 in BAILEY vol. II. **1775** in ASH.

†**luctificable,** *a. Obs.* [ad. L. *luctificābilis*, f. **luctificāre*, f. *luctificus* LUCTIFIC.] That is sorrowful (Bailey 1721).

†**luctisonant,** *a. Obs. rare*⁻⁰. [f. L. *luctison-us* (see next + -ANT: cf. SONANT *a.*] Mournful-sounding.

1656 in BLOUNT *Glossogr.*

†**luctisonous,** *a. Obs. rare*⁻⁰. [f. L. *luctison-us* (f. *luct-us* grief + *son-* root of *sonus* sound) + -OUS.] = prec.

1721 in BAILEY.

†**'luctual,** *a. Obs.* [f. L. *luctu-s* mourning + -AL¹.] Mournful, sorrowful.

1613–18 DANIEL *Coll. Hist. Eng.* (1626) 17 [He] found meanes to maintaine publique manners, without that luctuall remedy of bloud. **1646** BUCK *Rich. III*, II. 41 The turbulent and luctuall times, which were towards the end..of his..Raigne. **1655** H. VAUGHAN *Silex Scint.* II. *Rainbow* (1858) 173 Thy light as luctual and stained with woes I'll judge.

†**'luctuate,** *v. Obs. rare*⁻¹. [f. as prec. + -ATE³.] *trans.* To render mournful or gloomy.

1772 NUGENT tr. *Hist. Fr. Gerund* II. 320 Sumptuous tombs..irradiated with lights and luctuated with baize.

†**'luctuous,** *a. Obs. rare*⁻⁰. [ad. L. *luctuōsus*, f. *luctu-s* mourning: see -OUS.] Mournful.

1721 BAILEY, *Luctuous*, sorrowful, full of sorrow.

lucubrate ('l(j)uːkjuːbreɪt), *v.* [f. L. *lūcubrāt-*, ppl. stem of *lūcubrāre*, f. *lūc-*, *lūx* light.]

1. *intr.* Literally, To work by artificial light. In mod. use, to produce 'lucubrations', discourse learnedly in writing.

1623 in COCKERAM. **1755** in JOHNSON. **1804** *Europ. Mag.* XLV. 18, I have often lucubrated for your Magazine. **1817** BYRON *Beppo* xlvii, I like to speak and lucubrate my fill. **1824** ARNOLD in *Life* (ed. 5) 75, I could lucubrate largely *de omni scibili*, but paper happily runs short. **1832** *Fraser's Mag.* V. 755 In spite of this neglect Gioja and others have within the last four years flourished and lucubrated in Italy. **1900** *Speaker* 29 Dec. 347/1 This is not Mr. Alfred Austin lucubrating in the columns of the *Times.*

2. *trans.* To produce (literary compositions) by laborious study.

(In recent Dicts.)

Hence †**'lucubrated** *ppl. a.*, (*a*) consumed in lucubration; (*b*) studied or done by artificial light (Bailey vol. II, 1727).

1645 QUARLES *Sol. Recant.* I. 8 We..Spare neither sweat nor lucubrated Oyle.

lucubration (l(j)uːkjuː'breɪʃən). [ad. L. *lūcubrātiōn-em*, n. of action f. *lūcubrāre* to LUCUBRATE.]

1. The action or occupation of lucubrating; nocturnal study or meditation; study in general; an instance of this.

1595 BELL *Surv. Popery* Ep. Ded., Who haue spared no labour, no watchinges, no lucubrations, to atchieue exact knowledge in the holie scriptures. **1649** EVELYN *Liberty & Servitude* iv. Misc. Writ. (1805) 25 The very lamp of earth wherewithall he used to illuminate his lucubrations, was sold for three thousand drachmas. *a* **1658** CLEVELAND *Wks.* (1687) 63 Life is, since he is gone, But a Nocturnal Lucubration. **1709** STEELE *Tatler* No. 140 ⁋1 That state of Mind which is proper for Lucubration. **1776** GIBBON *Decl. & F.* iii. I. 79 The virtue of Marcus Aurelius Antoninus was ..the well-earned harvest of..many a midnight lucubration. **1817** COLERIDGE *Lay Serm.* 403 If Plato himself were to return and renew his sublime lucubrations. **1847** tr. *Feuchtersleben's Psychical Med.* 296 Immoderate lucubration with overstrained mental exertion. **1875** CUSIN tr. *F. Godet's Luke* II. 40 The light which the Rabbins had not found, or had lost, in their theological lucubrations.

2. quasi-*concr.* Usually *pl.* The product of nocturnal study and meditation; hence, a literary work showing signs of careful elaboration. Now somewhat derisive or playful, suggesting the notion of something pedantic or over-elaborate.

1611 CORYAT *Crudities* 432 His learned lucubrations and most solid workes of Diuinity. **1622** WOTTON in *Reliq.* (1672) 248 Which unfinished lucubration (for so I may justly call it, having been for the most part born in the

night). **1693** N. MATHER *Pref. to Owen's Holy Spirit* 4 There are some other Lucubrations of his on Subjects nearly allied unto these. **1709** STEELE & SWIFT *Tatler* No. 70 ⁋2 Having read your Lucubrations of the 10th Instant. **1745** FIELDING *True Patriot* Wks. 1775 IX. 285 The encouragement with which those lucubrations are read, may seem..more difficult to be accounted for. **1791** BOSWELL *Johnson* 20 Mar. an. 1750, Unconnected fragments of his lucubrations were purposely jumbled together. *c* **1800** K. WHITE *Rem.* (1837) 385 A future number of my lucubrations. **1828** J. BALLANTYNE *Exam. Hum. Mind* 26, I have divided my Lucubrations into Four Parts. **1862** CARLYLE *Fredk. Gt.* VIII. v. (1872) III. 36 We search in vain through tons of dusty lucubration. **1876** A. LAING *Lindores Abb.* xiii. 127 [She] endeavoured to turn his pious lucubrations into French Verse.

†**lucubratist.** *Obs.* [f. L. *lūcubrāt-* (see LUCUBRATE *v.*) + -IST.] = LUCUBRATOR.
1759 *Misc.* in *Ann. Reg.* 429/1 It would be more consonant to the epithet our modern lucubratists assume.

lucubrator (ˈl(j)uːkjuːbreɪtə(r)). [agent-n. f. *lūcubrāre* to LUCUBRATE.] **a.** A nocturnal student. **b.** One who produces lucubrations.
1775 S. J. PRATT *Liberal Opin.* cxxiii. (1783) IV. 137, I remained in his lucubratory, which, in point of exterior, surpassed everything but the lucubrator. **1828** MRQ. NORMANBY *Engl. in France* II. 240 The most idle and unprofessional of lucubrators. **1833** LYTTON *Eng. & Engl.* IV. ii. II. 55 This quality..is entirely new in an essayist. I know of no other lucubrator who possesses it.

†**lucubratory**, *a.* and *sb.* *Obs.* [ad. L. *lūcubrātōrius*, f. *lūcubrāre*.] **A.** *adj.* Pertaining to lucubration; meditative. **B.** *sb.* (*jocular.*) A 'thinking-shop', a place of midnight study.
1656 BLOUNT *Glossogr.*, *Lucubratory*, of or belonging to studying or working by candle-light. **1711** POPE *Let.* 21 Dec. (1735) I. 122 You must have a sober dish of coffee and a solitary candle at your side to write an Epistle lucubratory to your friend. **1775** [see LUCUBRATOR].

lucule (ˈl(j)uːkjuːl). *Astr.* Also in Lat. form *pl.* luculæ, *incorrectly* luculi. [a. F. *lucule*, ad. mod.L. *lūcula*, dim. of *lūx* light.] (See quot. 1869.)
1864 WEBSTER, *Lucule*, a luminous spot on the sun. **1867–77** G. F. CHAMBERS *Astron.* I. i. 32 The term luculi has been applied to the constituent specks [on the Sun's surface]. **1869** PHIPSON tr. *Guillemin's Sun* (1870) 216 Hence those lines of light and shade, luminous and obscure ridges [on the Sun's disc], which have been called luculæ.

†ˈ**luculence.** *Obs. rare*⁻⁰. [ad. L. *lūculentia*, f. *lūculentus* LUCULENT.] **a.** Trimness, fineness, beauty (1727 in Bailey vol. II). **b.** Clearness, certainty (1775 in Ash).

†ˈ**luculency.** *Obs.* [as prec.] Brightness, beauty.
1656 in BLOUNT *Glossogr.* **1696** in PHILLIPS.

luculent (ˈl(j)uːkjʊlənt), *a.* [ad. L. *lūculentus*, f. *lūc-*, *lūx* light.]

1. Full of light; bright, clear, shining. Now *rare.*
c **1420** *Pallad. on Husb.* x. 191 Trie out the grape vnhurt, neither to ripe Neither to sowre, as gemmys luculent. **1645** EVELYN *Mem.* (1857) I. 188 It emitted a luculent flame as bright and large as a small wax candle. **1657** TOMLINSON *Renou's Disp.* 631 Vipers..must be cocted on a luculent, but not a violent fire. **1726–46** THOMSON *Winter* 710 Luculent along The purer rivers flow. **1892** C. E. NORTON *Dante's Par.* XXII. 143 The most luculent of those pearls.

2. †**a.** Of oratory, compositions in general: Brilliant, admirable; hence of a writer or orator (*obs.*). **b.** Of evidence, arguments: Clear, convincing. Of explanations: Lucid, luminous.
a **1548** HALL *Chron., Hen. VII* (1809) 450 The kyng.. gaue good eare to his luculent & eloquent oracion. **1597** HOOKER *Eccl. Pol.* v. xl. §2 The most luculent testimonies that Christian Religion hath. **1603** *Eng. Mourn. Garm.* in *Harl. Misc.* (Malh.) II. 486 She was still confident in her Saviour,..as appeared by many luculent examples. **1606** DEKKER *Newes fr. Hell* Wks. (Grosart) II. 103 Luculent Poet, Elegant Orator. **1641** J. JACKSON *True Evang. T.* Title, Three Sermons..upon that luculent Prophecie of Peace, and Union, *Esay* chap. II. v. 6. 7. and 8. **1675** SIR E. SHERBURNE *Manilius* Pref. 10 Having illustrated so Obscure a Subject in such Luculent Verse. **1693** J. H. in *Dryden's Juvenal* x. Notes 19 Mr. John Dryden Junior's method therein is more Luculent than the Dauphin's famous Tutors. **1702** C. MATHER *Magn. Chr.* III. III. (1852) 532 A most luculent and practical exposition. *a* **1734** NORTH *Lives* (1826) II. 217 The redundance..may be indulged as a worthy remembrance of a most luculent example. **1824** *Blackw. Mag.* XVI. 6, I now desire Mr. James Ballantyne.. to set up in brevier the following luculent observations. **1851** 'NIMROD' *The Road* 61 A luculent chapter on the astonishing convenience of our public conveyances. **1858** CARLYLE *Fredk. Gt.* VIII. v. II. 356 These glimpses of the Crown-Prince..are not very luculent to the reader. **1885–6** F. D. ALLEN in *Papers Amer. School at Athens* (1888) IV. 39 A luculent case is in n. 58.

3. Of persons: Brilliant; illustrious. *Obs.*
1599 B. JONSON *Ev. Man out of Hum.* II. iii, Most debonaire, and Luculent Ladie. *c* **1600** *Timon* II. iv. (1842) 31 By what faulte or fate of mine (luculent not lutulent Serjeants) shall I say it is come to passe. *c* **1620** J. TAYLOR (Water-P.) *Wks.* (1630) III. 117/2 Saint George comes: and seeing so bright and luculent a Goddesse..demanded entertainement.

luculently (ˈl(j)uːkjʊləntlɪ), *adv.* [f. LUCULENT + -LY².] In a luculent manner; clearly.
1613 in R. CAWDREY *Table Alph.* (ed. 3). **1641** J. JACKSON *True Evang. T.* III. 177 So luculently foretold by this our Prophet Esaias. *a* **1734** NORTH *Exam.* I. ii. §131 (1740) 102 A Declaration..which most luculently solves all. **1864** MAX MÜLLER *Sci. Lang.* (1880) II. xi. 570 Nowhere has the transition of physical mythology into epic poetry..been so luculently shown as here. **1862** MERIVALE *Rom. Emp.* (1865) VI. xlix. 120 It deserved to be explained more luculently.

luculia (luːˈkuːlɪə). [mod.L. (R. Sweet *Brit. Flower Garden* (1826) II. 145), f. *luculi swa* native name of *L. gratissima* in India.] A large deciduous shrub of the genus so called, belonging to the family Rubiaceæ, native to northern India and China, and bearing corymbs of fragrant pink flowers.
1826 R. SWEET *Brit. Flower Garden* II. 145 (*heading*) Delightfully fragrant Luculia. **1885** W. J. MAY *Greenhouse Managem.* (ed. 2) vi. 236 The best place for Luculias is in the beds or borders of a conservatory where they have plenty of room to grow. **1962** *Amat. Gardening* 21 Oct. (Suppl.) 32/3 The luculias need plenty of room and are best planted out in a well drained, peaty soil in the greenhouse.

Lucullan (l(j)uːˈkʌlən), *a.* [L. *Lucullanus*, *Lucullianus*.] = LUCULLIAN, -EAN *a.*
1857 BOSTOCK & RILEY tr. *Pliny's Nat. Hist.* VI. XXXVI. ii. 307 The largest of these columns, pillars of Lucullan marble ..were erected in the atrium of Scaurus. *Ibid.* viii. 325 L. Lucullus was consul; the same person who gave its name, it is very evident, to the Lucullan marble. **1909** G. G. RAMSAY tr. *Tacitus' Annals* II. XI. xxxii. 41 Messalina took herself off to the Lucullan Gardens. **1913** *Chambers's Jrnl.* 11 Jan. 87/1 Two thousand pounds for a really Lucullan feast as planned ..by one who plans them constantly. **1935** *Times Lit. Suppl.* 11 Apr. 245/2 This is definitely a Lucullan book, of use only to the hostess with a chef and a large staff. **1935** J. M. COBBAN *Senate & Provinces* iv. 116 Clodius and his fellows were acting at the direct instigation of the 'anti-Lucullan' party at Rome. *Ibid.* 123 Pompey..whom we have seen to be the prime force behind the anti-Lucullan movement. **1966** *Punch* 4 May 669/3 He gives us a Lucullan feast of stories, but my favourite is the tale of Mrs. Keppel.

Lucullian, -ean (l(j)uːˈkʌlɪən, ˌl(j)uːkəˈliːən), *a.* [Two forms: (1) ad. *Lucullīānus*, f. *Lucull-us* (see -IAN); (2) f. L. *Lucullē-us* + -AN.] Pertaining to or characteristic of L. Licinius Lucullus, a Roman famous for his wealth and the profuse luxury of his banquets. † ***Lucullean marble*** (tr. L. *marmor Lucullеum*): some kind of black marble; by mineralogists of the 18th c. identified with the mineral now called lucullite or anthracoxenite.
1601 HOLLAND *Pliny* II. 572 Consull L. Lucullus..gaue the name to Lucullean marble..he brought it first to Rome, and had a speciall fancy thereto, notwithstanding it were black. **1842** W. SMITH *Dict. Gr. & Rom. Antiq.* s.v. *House, Roman* 494 Columns of black marble, called Lucullean, thirty-eight feet high. **1892** K. GOULD tr. *Conversat. Döllinger* i. 8 The display, the Lucullian feast, and the introduction of the bride are merely intended to present forcibly to one's mind what the priest is called on to renounce. **1897** *Daily News* 21 Oct. 7/7 To draw company to the house to entertain her he gave Lucullian banquets.

Luˈcullic, *a.* = LUCULLAN *a.*
1904 J. MCCABE tr. *Haeckel's Wonders of Life* xi. 98 The careful choice and preparation of savoury food..was just as important..as it is to-day in royal banquets or the Lucullic dinners of millionaires.

lucullite (l(j)uːˈkʌlaɪt). *Min.* [f. *Lucull-us* (see LUCULLIAN, -EAN *a.*) + -ITE. Named by J. F. John, 1814, after the former designation 'marmor *Lucullеum*'.] = ANTHRACOXENITE (A. H. Chester 1896).
1819 BRANDE *Man. Chem.* 517 The black variety [of limestone] known under the name of Lucullite. **1821** R. JAMESON *Mineral.* 49 Lucullite..is divided into three kinds, viz. Compact, Prismatic, and Foliated.

‖**Lucuma** (l(j)uːkjʊmə). Also 8 lucoma, 9 lucama. [Peruvian.] A genus of American trees (N.O. *Sapotaceæ*) bearing sweet fruit.
1745 P. THOMAS *Jrnl. Anson's Voy.* 91 The natural Fruit of Peru are Guavas, Lucomas, Holos and Wallnuts. **1748** *Earthquake Peru* iii. 210 The Lucumas..are there very plentiful. **1848** in WEBSTER (citing Gardner); **1866** in *Treas. Bot.*; and in mod. Dicts.

‖**lucumo** (ˈl(j)uːkjuːməʊ). Also in anglicized form **lucumon.** [L. *lucumo*, *lucumon-*, an Etruscan title.] One of the Etruscan nobles, who united in themselves the character and functions of priest and prince.
1837 LANDOR *Pentam.* iii. Wks. 1853 II. 331/1 The lucumons of Etruria. **1842** MACAULAY *Horatius* xxiii, Now might the burghers know, By port and vest..Each warlike Lucumo. **1847** TENNYSON *Princess* II. 113 She..spoke of those That lay at wine with Lar and Lucumo.

lucumony (ˈl(j)uːkjuːmənɪ). *Rom. Hist.* Also 9 *erron.* **lucomony.** [ad. F. *lucumonie*, f. L. *lucumo*: see prec.] A name given by modern writers to each of the twelve states of the Etruscan federation.
1763 SWINTON in *Phil. Trans.* LIV. 104 Fæsulæ..with its district..formed of the twelve lucumonies, or free states. **1882** OUIDA *Maremma* I. 36 Etruscan lucomonies had had their fortresses and their tombs away yonder.

lucur, obs. form of LUCRE.

‖**lucus a non lucendo** (ˈluːkʌs ɑː nɒn luːˈkɛndəʊ, ˈl(j)uːkʌs eɪ nɒn l(j)uːˈsɛndəʊ). [L. phr., 'a grove, (so-called) from the absence of *lux* (light)', discussed by Quintilian in *De inst. oratoria* i. 6. 34.] A paradoxical or otherwise absurd derivation; something of which the essence or qualities are the opposite of what its name suggests. Also **lucus a non.**
1711 ADDISON *Spectator* 8 May, He composed an..Epic Poem..consisting of four and twenty Books, having entirely banished the Letter *A* from his first Book, which was called *Alpha* (as *Lucus a non lucendo*) because there was not an *Alpha* in it. *c* **1728** SWIFT in W. King *Dreamer* 88 And make his ignorance discerned, To get the name of council learned; (As *lucus* comes *à non lucendo*). **1749** FIELDING *Tom Jones* III. VIII. iv. 172 This Sun, into which Jones was now conducted, was truly named as *Lucus a non lucendo*; for it was an Apartment into which the Sun had scarce ever looked. **1823** BYRON *Don Juan* VI. lv. 240 Thus..has been shown 'Lucus a *non* Lucendo', *not* what *was*, But what *was not*; a sort of style that's grown Extremely common in this age. *Ibid.* XI. xxi. 54 Through Groves, so called as being void of trees, (Like *lucus* from *no* light;). **1845** R. FORD *Hand-bk. Trav. Spain* II. 941 *St. Jean de Luz*..is not a 'city of light', but of 'mud', and a Lutetia or lucus a non lucendo. **1848** J. R. LOWELL *Fable for Critics* 69 'Illustrations'..are said to illustrate, because, as I view it, Like *lucus a non*, they precisely don't do it. **1904** W. F. H. KING *Classical & Foreign Quotations* 186 To the *Lucus a non lucendo* principle, as it is called, are referred all such paradoxical derivations and descriptions which involve a contradiction in the mere stating of them. **1924** A. HUXLEY *Little Mexican* 13 Their philology was the picturesque *lucus a non lucendo*, bloody from by-our-Lady type. **1958** R. LIDDELL *Morea* III. 219 Was its name Hydraea (watery), a *lucus a non lucendo*—it is singularly waterless today.

lucy (ˈluːsɪ). *Her.* [ad. L. *lūcius.*] = LUCE¹.
1610 GUILLIM *Heraldry* IV. viii. (1660) 299 Azure, three Dolphins..between two paire of Lucyes Saltier. **1780** in EDMONDSON *Heraldry* II. **1864** BOUTELL *Her. Hist. & Pop.* xv. (ed. 3) 181 Gu., three lucies haurient in fesse arg.

†**lud**¹. *Sc. Obs.* [Cf. Norw. *ludden* thick, broad; and see LUDDOCK.] In *pl.*, the buttocks.
a **1568** *Bannatyne MS.* (Hunter. Club) 764 On thair luddis Thay get grit skuddis In nakit bed.

lud² (lʌd). Minced form of LORD *sb.* †**a.** As an exclamation or in trivial phrases, = LORD *sb.* 6 b, c (*obs.*). **b.** In comic representations of the affected or hurried pronunciation used by lawyers addressing a judge in court, and by clerks in the House of Lords: see LORD *sb.* 15 b.
1725 VANBRUGH *Prov. Wife* IV. iii. [2nd vers.], That Fellow wou'd have ravish'd me. *2nd Watch.* Ravish! Ravish! O lud! O lud! O lud! Ravish her! **1767** G. S. CAREY *Hills of Hybla* 33 To make me soldier 'gainst my will, and go the lud knows where. **1773** GOLDSM. *Stoops to Conq.* II. Wks. (Globe) 657/2 O lud! he has almost cracked my head. **1777** SHERIDAN *Sch. Scand.* III. i, Lud! Sir Peter, I hope you haven't been quarrelling with Maria? **1818** SCOTT *Rob Roy* v, 'Read whom, ma'am?—I do not even remember the author's name'. 'O lud! on what a strand are you wrecked!' replied the young lady. **1821** CLARE *Vill. Minstr.* I. 36 But soldiers, they're the boys to make a rout,..Lud, clowns are almost mad where'er they come. **1830** [see LORD *sb.* 15 b]. **1898** BESANT *Orange Girl* II. xii, 'My Lud', said Mr. Caterham, 'my case is completed'.

lud, var. LEDE *Obs.*; obs. f. LIDE, LOUD.

ludby, variant of LOTEBY *Obs.*

†**ludden.** *Obs.* [Variant of LEDEN.] A refrain; the burden (of a song or complaint).
1607 *Schol. Disc. agst. Antichr.* I. ii. 61 The first sort of them singe the old ludden. **1654** WHITLOCK *Zootomia* 121 The Patient wanteth but Pen and Ink, and he will prescribe his Physick, which at last must be some Cordiall or strengthning (the Ludden of Them all).

Luddism (ˈlʌdɪz(ə)m). [f. *Lud* or *Ludd* (see next) + -ISM.] **a.** The practices of the Luddites.
1812 *Chron.* in *Ann. Reg.* 115 Several persons have been apprehended [at Huddersfield] on various charges of Luddism. **1817** *Ann. Reg.* 79 That atrocious system of combination, outrage, and hired assassination, which has prevailed in some of the midland counties, under the name of Luddism. **1893** *Athenæum* 5 Aug. 189/1 Her family on both sides had lived in the thick of Luddism.

b. Also **luddism.** More generally, intense dislike of or opposition to technological innovation.
1967 *Sunday Times* 16 Apr. 24 Systems men are just as susceptible to Luddism as anyone else. **1986** *Times* 22 Apr. 13/2 The NUJ's warning to the luddism of the print unions.

Luddite (ˈlʌdaɪt), *sb.* (*a.*) [f. the proper name *Lud* or *Ludd* + -ITE.
According to Pellew's *Life of Lord Sidmouth* (1847) III. 80, Ned Lud was a person of weak intellect who lived in a Leicestershire village about 1779, and who in a fit of insane rage rushed into a 'stockinger's' house, and destroyed two frames so completely that the saying 'Lud must have been here' came to be used throughout the hosiery districts when a stocking-frame had undergone extraordinary damage. The story lacks confirmation. It appears that in 1811–13 the nickname 'Captain Ludd' or 'King Lud' was commonly given to the ringleaders of the Luddites.]

A member of an organized band of English mechanics and their friends, who (1811–16) set themselves to destroy manufacturing

machinery in the midlands and north of England.
1811 *Hist. Eur.* in *Ann. Reg.* 93/2 The rioters assumed the name of Luddites and acted under the authority of an imaginary Captain Ludd. **1812** *Examiner* 4 May 277/1 The Luddites at Nottingham..have relinquished their system of frame-breaking. The person known by the name of King Ludd is taken..His name is Walker; he was a collier. **1816** BYRON *To Moore* 24 Dec., Are you not near the Luddites? And down with all kings but King Ludd? **1888** F. PEEL *Risings of Luddites* 32 The names they assumed were 'Ludds', 'Ludders', and 'Luddites'. **1897** S. & B. WEBB *Industrial Democracy* (1902) 220 *note*, We need only remind the reader..of such angry insurrections as those of the Luddites in 1811.

b. *transf.* One who opposes the introduction of new technology, esp. into a place of work.
1970 *New Scientist* 10 Sept. 549 They [*sc.* errors] can be prevented by improved systems and organization. But first it is necessary to overcome the professional and official luddites. **1986** *Economist* 10 May 13/1 By suggesting..that the modern world has lost control of its technology, both [accidents] help to strengthen the hands of Luddites who would halt technology and therefore a lot of economic growth.

2. *attrib.* or *adj.* Pertaining to the Luddites.
1812 *Gentl. Mag.* LXXXII. I. 285/1 The Luddite system. **1814** *Ibid.* LXXXIV. II. 387/2 The Luddite ring-leader..dropped dead. **1874** GREEN *Short Hist.* x. §4. 806 The Luddite, or machine-breaking, riots. **1957** *Ann. Reg.* *1956* 23 A Labour spokesman..assured the Minister that organized workers were by no means wedded to a 'Luddite' philosophy. **1965** *Times* 29 Dec. 5 Port capacity can be greatly increased by quick installation of modern equipment—if the Indian Government is really determined to override the Luddite resistance of wharf labour. **1976** *Survey* Summer–Autumn 212 The Luddite view..is particularly tempting when it comes to military technology. **1986** *N.Y. Times* 5 May A10/3 There seemed to be no real desire to turn back, no sweeping Luddite reaction to all technology.

Hence **ˈLudditism** = LUDDISM.
1830 *Fraser's Mag.* II. 426 A bill..for the suppression of Ludditism in Nottinghamshire. **1971** *Guardian Weekly* 19 June 20 In an uprising against ignorance and psychopathology Ludditism has no place. **1983** *Times Lit. Suppl.* 18 Mar. 256/4 The blame for world catastrophe is to be placed..on the blind forces of unscientific nature, which might include items like messianic Ludditism. **1986** *Financial Times* 11 Feb. 38/3 More efficient farmers should not be penalised by institutionalised Ludditism.

†**ˈluddock.** *Obs.* [? f. LUD¹ + -OCK. (But it is possible that the *lud* may be really a shortened form.)] The loin, or the buttock.
c **1420** *Liber Cocorum* (1862) 43 Take befe and sklice hit fayre and thynne, Of þo luddock with owte or ellis with in. *c* **1460** *Towneley Myst.* xxx. 314 His luddokkys thai lowke like walk-mylne cloggys. *c* **1490** *Promp. Parv.* 296/1 Leend, lym of a beeste (*MS. K.*, *Pynson* or luddok), *lumbus*.

†**lude¹.** *Obs.* Also 3 loude. [ME. *lūde*. repr. OE. *hlȳd* str. fem. (:—**hlūdjâ*), cogn. w. *hlúd* LOUD *a.* (The form *loude* in the second text of Layamon is prob. due to a misinterpretation of the spelling *lude* in the first text.)] Noise, clamour.
c **1205** LAY. 2591 þa hunten wenden æfter mid muchelen heora lude [*c* **1275** loude]. *a* **1275** *Prov. Ælfred* 687 in *O.E. Misc.* 138 He wole maken fule luden, He wole grennen, cocken and chiden. [But this may belong to LEDEN.]

†**lude².** *Obs.* [ad. L. *lūd-us* play.] A game.
1694 MOTTEUX *Rabelais* v. (1737) 230 Ludes omniform are there invented.

lude, var. LEDE *Obs.*; obs. f. LIDE, LOUD.

lude, obs. Sc. pa. t. of LOVE *v.*¹

†**ˈludent.** *Obs. nonce-wd.* [ad. L. *lūdent-em*, pres. pple. of *lūdĕre* to play.] A player.
1573 G. HARVEY *Letter-bk.* (Camden) 133, I helpe to make a ludent, And nare a student.

luderick (ˈluːdərɪk, ˈlʌdrɪk). *Austral.* Also ludrick. [Aboriginal name.] A perciform herbivorous food fish, *Girella tricuspidata*, which has a dark-coloured back and silvery belly; also called blackfish, black bream or perch.
1898 E. E. MORRIS *Austral Eng.* 275/2 Luderick, or Ludrick, an aboriginal Gippsland name for a local variety of the fish *Girella simplex*. **1951** T. C. ROUGHLEY *Fish & Fisheries Austral.* 92 In 1947, when a conference of fisheries officials from all Australian States was held to discuss the question of the diversity of the names of fish in the various States, it was decided to adopt the Victorian name of 'luderick' for this fish throughout Australia... The luderick is an estuarine fish found in all Australian States, but it occurs in its greatest numbers in New South Wales, southern Queensland, and Victoria. **1969** *Man* (Austral.) Mar. 12/2 Over the seasons you get a variety of fish you'd be scratching to find anywhere else—drummer, luderick, [etc.].

†**Ludgate.** *Obs.* The name (from its situation near the City gate so called) of an ancient debtors' prison in London; phr. †*to take Ludgate* (see quot. 1585). Hence †**Ludgatian** (**-thian, -tion**), a debtor, bankrupt.
1585 HIGGINS *Nomenclator* 324 *Argentariam dissoluere*..To play the bankerupt: to take Ludgate. **1600** B. JONSON *Ev. Man out of Hum.* I. i, Alwaies beware you commerce not with Bankroutes, or poore needie Ludgathians. **1606** DEKKER *Sev. Sins* I. (Arb.) 11 The Master, the Keepers, and all the Prisoners of Ludgate. *Ibid.* 12 It was a bird pickt out of purpose (amongst the Ludgathians) that had the basest and lowest voice, and was able in a Terme time, for a throat, to giue any prisoner great ods for ye box at the grate. **1607** [E. SHARPHAM] *Cupid's Whirligig* III. i. E 3, I am none of these Ludgations that beg for fourscore and ten poore men: my suite is only for my selfe. *a* **1700** B. E. *Dict. Cant. Crew*, *Lud's-bulwark*, Ludgate Prison.

ludge, -eing, etc., obs. Sc. ff. LODGE, LODGING.

Ludian (ˈl(j)uːdɪən). Also **Lūd, Lude, Ludic, L'üdikš, Lüdish.** [f. Olonetsian *liūdi* (? ad. Russ. *ljudi*, people) + -AN, -IAN.] A language of the Finnish group of the Finno-Ugrian family of languages, used by a small number of speakers in the region of Olonets, now in the north-west part of the Russian Soviet Federative Socialist Republic.
1921 M. STENBÄCK in T. Homén *East Carelia & Kola Lapmark* II. ii. 122 Among the Onega Wepsians... Those who speak Wepsian are said to speak *l'üdikš*. **1933** L. BLOOMFIELD *Lang.* 68 The other languages of the Baltic branch [of the Finnish-Lapponic languages], *Carelian, Olonetsian, Ludian, Vepsian, Livonian, Ingrian*, and *Votian*, are far smaller, and some of them are near extinction. **1939** L. H. GRAY *Foundations of Lang.* 369 The languages of the Uralic family are as follows: (1) *Finnish* group: Finnish proper.., Karelian.., Olonetzian, Ingrian, Lüdish, Vepsian, [etc.]. **1954** PEI & GAYNOR *Dict. Ling.* 127 *Ludian*, a dialect (also called *Lüdish*) of the Finnish group of the Finno-Ugric (or Uralic) sub-family of the Ural-Altaic family of languages. **1955** B. COLLINDER *Fenno-Ugric Vocab.* p. ix, Lude.., spoken in the region west of lake Onega, is a kind of intermediary between Olonets and Veps. **1959** *Chambers's Encycl.* XIV. 200/2 Lüd, spoken to the north and west of Petrozavodsk. **1967** D. S. PARLETT *Short Dict. Lang.* 81 *Ludian* 10 th[ousand] speakers in region of Olonets (north east of Leningrad on shore of Lake Ladoga) of a series of patois, basically northern Vepsian but with influences of Carelian, and forming a transition between the two. Impregnated with Finnish and Russian. **1974** *Encycl. Brit. Micropædia* V. 709/3 Ludic, a minor group of dialects spoken to the south of Karelian, is considered to be a blend of Karelian and Veps.

†**ˈludible,** *a. Obs.*—⁰ [ad. med.L. *lūdibilis*, f. L. *lūdĕre* to play.] Playful.
1656 BLOUNT *Glossogr.*, *Ludible*,..apt to play, sportive.

ludibrious (l(j)uːˈdɪbrɪəs), *a.* [ad. late L. *lūdibriōs-us*, f. *lūdibrium* sport, jest, f. *lūdĕre* to play.]
†**1.** Apt to be a subject of jest or mockery. *Obs.*
1563–87 FOXE *A. & M.* (1596) 85/1 The youth in skuls flocke and run togither, and craue that they may haue Agnes their ludibrious preie. **1597** BEARD *Theatre God's Judgem.* (1612) 41 Baiazet the Turke, to what a miserable and ludibrious end came hee. **1650** SIR W. MURE *Cry of Blood* 266 Ludibrious Clay Dare craule on borrowed legges, and Heaven defy. **1675** BROOKS *Gold. Key* Wks. 1867 V. 493 Ludibrious acts, and mere follies!
2. Full of scorn; inclined to scoff; scornful, mocking. Also *transf.* Now *rare.*
1641 J. SHUTE *Sarah & Hagar* (1649) 62 Samson more patiently endureth the boring out of his eyes, than the ludibrious scoffs of the Philistines. **1780** J. HOWIE in Shields *Faithf. Contend.* Pref. 21 This lukewarm and ludibrious generation. **1807** J. BARLOW *Columb.* IX. 647 He..Leaves to ludibrious winds the priceless page.

†**ˈludibry.** *Obs.* [ad. L. *lūdibrium*: see prec.] Derision, contempt; *concr.* an object of derision.
1637 BASTWICK *Litany* II. 5 Brought vpon euery stage, and into the pulpit, as fittest for ludibry by the Players, Preists, and Prelats. **1722** WODROW *Hist. Ch. Scotl.* (1833) III. 225 This step of Mr. Cargill's hath been matter of much reproach and ludibry to the enemies of the Church of Scotland. **1723** MᶜWARD *Contend. for Faith* 346 (Jam.) By Popish artifice,..the most renowned court in the world is made the ludibrie and laughing-stock of the earth.

†**ˈludibund,** *a. Obs. rare.* [ad. L. *lūdibund-us*, f. *lūdĕre* to play.] Playful. Hence †**ˈludibundness.**
1664 H. MORE *Myst. Iniq.* 316 That ludibundness in Nature in her Gamaieu's and such like sportful and ludicrous productions. **1668** —— *Div. Dial.* III. xvi. (1713) 214 Though the Phancy of Cuphophron may seem more than ordinary ludibund and lightsomely sportful. **1727** BAILEY vol. II, *Ludibund*, full of play.

ludic (ˈl(j)uːdɪk), *a.* [ad. F. *ludique*, f. L. *ludĕre* to play.] Of or pertaining to undirected and spontaneously playful behaviour.
1940 HINSIE & SHATZKY *Psychiatric Dict.* 323/2 This excess-energy must be expended (without purpose) in some way, most usually in play-activity, called *ludic activity*. **1969** P. L. BERGER *Rumor of Angels* iii. 76 Ludic, or playful, elements can be found in just about any sector of human culture. **1971** D. G. BOYLE *Lang. & Thinking in Human Devel.* vi. 65 Ludic play and symbolism are among the defining characteristics of humanity. **1972** *Times Lit. Suppl.* 3 Mar. 234/5 Poetry is sacred..for the same reasons that eroticism is sacred: it is ludic, that is to say useless. **1973** M. AMIS *Rachel Papers* 207 My existence, too, was a prismatic web of mendacity—but for me it was..far more ludic, literary, answering an intellectual rather than an emotional need.

†**ˈludicral,** *a. Obs. rare*—⁰. [f. L. *lūdicr-us* LUDICROUS + -AL¹.] Ludicrous.
1656 BLOUNT *Glossogr.*, *Ludicral*, pertaining to play or mirth, mocking, light, childish. *Greg.* **1727** BOYER *Dict. Roy.*, *Ludicral*, or *Ludicrous*.

†**ˈludicrism.** *Obs.* [f. L. *lūdicr-us* LUDICROUS + -ISM.] Burlesque.
1830 R. BROWN *Mem. Curl. Mab.* in *Blackw. Mag.* (1831) XXX. 979/2 [This lay of the laureate was forthwith] duly turned into ludicrism by a burlesque song.

ludicro- (ˈl(j)uːdɪkrəʊ), used as combining form of L. *lūdicrus* LUDICROUS, in the sense 'ludicrous and..', as ***ludicro-pathetic, -serious, -splenetic.***
1751 J. BROWN *Shaftesb. Charac.* 242 The ambiguous expression, and the ludicro-serious of the gentle essayist, perfectly secure him from the rough handling of the logical disputer. **1813** COLERIDGE *Lett.* (1895) II. 607 A ludicro-splenetic copy of verses. **1828** *Westm. Rev.* IX. 432 The ludicro-pathetic effect resulting from..levity and feeling in the character of the lower Irish.

ludicrosity (l(j)uːdɪˈkrɒsɪtɪ). *rare.* [f. LUDICROUS: see -OSITY.] Ludicrousness.
a **1856** H. MILLER *Cruise Betsey* (1858) 399 Unintentional ludicrosities. **1856** J. BROWN *Let.* in *Life Cairns* xv. (1895) 422 There is a sort of sublime ludicrosity about it.

ludicrous (ˈl(j)uːdɪkrəs), *a.* [f. L. *lūdicr-us* (app. evolved from the neut. sb. *lūdicrum* sportive performance, stage-play, f. *lūdĕre* to play) + -OUS.]
†**1.** Pertaining to play or sport; sportive; intended in jest, jocular, derisive. *Obs.*
1619 GATAKER *Lots* iii. 34 Easty onely maketh foure sorts; diuine..; diabolicall..; politicall..; ludicrous, for sport and pastime. **1653** ASHWELL *Fides Apost.* 25 Both in ludicrous toyes, as in Childrens sports, and in weightier matters. **1664** H. MORE *Myst. Iniq.* xiii. 44 But he rewarding my blind devotion with a ludicrous blessing and loud laughter, I presently found my errour. **1668–83** OWEN *Expos. Heb.* (1790) IV. 281 It is not a ludicrous contest that we are called to, but it is for our lives and souls. **1709** J. JOHNSON *Clergym. Vade M.* II. 174 [tr. *Canons of Carthage* lxvi] If any one desire to forsake any Ludicrous Exercise [*i.e.* any theatrical or gladiatorial employment], and become a Christian. **1779–81** JOHNSON *L.P.*, *Pope*, The 'Rape of the Lock'..is universally allowed to be the most attractive of all ludicrous compositions.
†**2.** Given to jesting; trifling, frivolous; also, in favourable sense, witty, humorous. *Obs.*
1687 H. MORE *Contn. Remark. Stor.* (1689) 428 But to entangle things thus is an usual feat of these ludicrous Spirits. **1711** ADDISON *Spect.* No. 191 ¶1 Some ludicrous Schoolmen have put the Case, that if an Ass were placed between two Bundles of Hay [etc.]. **1736** BUTLER *Anal.* II. vi, Men may indulge a ludicrous turn so far as to lose all sense of conduct and prudence in worldly affairs. **1778** BP. LOWTH *Transl. Isa.* (ed. 12) Notes 332 A heathen author, in the ludicrous way, has..given idolatry one of the severest strokes it ever received. **1792** COWPER *Let. to T. Park* 27 Apr., The man is as formidable for his ludicrous talent, as he has made himself contemptible by his use of it. **1827** *Burton's Anat. Mel.* (ed. 13) Advt. 7 The ludicrous Sterne has interwoven many parts of it [Burton's 'Anatomy'] into his own popular performance.
3. Suited to occasion derisive laughter; ridiculous, laughably absurd. (The only current sense.)
1782 MISS BURNEY *Cecilia* II. iii, The ludicrous mixture of groups, kept her attention unwearied. **1813** SHELLEY *Q. Mab* VI. 64 How ludicrous the priest's dogmatic roar! **1834** MACAULAY *Pitt* Ess. (1887) 321 The Duke was in a state of ludicrous distress. **1875** JOWETT *Plato* (ed. 2) IV. 380 Plato delights to exhibit them [Sophists] in a ludicrous point of view. **1898** F. T. BULLEN *Cruise Cachalot* xxiii. (1900) 298 This subdivision was often carried to ludicrous lengths. **1901** N. MUNRO in *Blackw. Mag.* May 659/2 Count Victor stood before him a ludicrous figure.
4. *absol.* (in senses 2 and 3).
1798 FERRIAR *Illustr. Sterne* i. 7 The ludicrous, by its nature, tends to exaggeration. **1858** O. W. HOLMES *Aut. Breakf.-t.* iv. 36 The ludicrous has its place in the universe. **1884** YATES *Recoll.* I. 67 A bright charming fellow,..with a real appreciation of the ludicrous.

ludicrously (ˈl(j)uːdɪkrəslɪ), *adv.* [f. LUDICROUS + -LY².] In a ludicrous manner; †sportively, jestingly, humorously (*obs.*); ridiculously, absurdly.
a **1678** MARVELL in *Life* Wks. 1776 III. 462 You do not mean to treat me ludicrously by these munificent offers. **1742** H. WALPOLE *Lett. H. Mann* (1834) I. xli. 166 It was of a piece with her saying 'that Swift would have written better if he had never written ludicrously'. **1758** BLACKSTONE *Comm.* (1765) I. Introd. i. 14 They will give me leave, however, to suggest, and that not ludicrously, that it might frequently be of use [etc.]. **1779–81** JOHNSON *L.P.*, *Pope*, Circumstances were sometimes added, which..produced what Perrault ludicrously called 'comparisons with a long tail'. **1844** EMERSON *Lect.*, *New Eng. Ref.* Wks. (Bohn) I. 262 As soon as he leaves the University, as it is ludicrously styled, he shuts those books for the last time. **1899** E. GRIFFITH-JONES *Ascent thro. Christ* i. 3 This calculation was ludicrously inadequate.

ludicrousness (ˈl(j)uːdɪkrəsnɪs). [f. LUDICROUS + -NESS.] The state or quality of being ludicrous.
1664 H. MORE *Antid. Idolatry* i. Theol. Wks. (1708) 773 The Ludicrousness and Fugitiveness of our wanton Reason might otherwise find out many Starting-holes [etc.]. **1785** BOSWELL *Tour Hebrides* 160 The ludicrousness, absurdity, and extraordinary contrast between what the fellow fancied, and the reality, was truly comick. *a* **1800** J. WARTON *Dryden's Ilias, D.'s Poet. Wks.* (1811) IV. 530 Homer sometimes introduced his gods and goddesses in scenes of ludicrousness. **1865** RUSKIN *Crown Wild Olive* iii. (1866) 162 There is a ghastly ludicrousness in this.

†**ludificable,** *a. Obs. rare*—⁰. [ad. L. *lūdificābil-is*, f. *lūdificāre* (see LUDIFY *v.*).] (See quot.)
1623 COCKERAM II, Deceiuing, *Ludificable*. **1721** BAILEY, *Ludificable*,..that maketh Sport and Pastime.

†**ludificate**, *v.* *Obs.* *rare*⁻⁰. [f. L. *lūdificāt-*, ppl. stem of *lūdificāre*: see LUDIFY *v.*] (See quots.)

1623 COCKERAM, *Ludificate*, to deceiue, to beguile. **1775** ASH, *Ludificate*,..to mock, to deceive, to frustrate.

ludification (l(j)uːdɪfɪˈkeɪʃən). Now *rare*. [ad. L. *lūdificātiōn-em*, f. *lūdificāre*: see LUDIFY *v.*] A deception or mocking.

1623 COCKERAM, *Ludification*, a beguiling. **1635** HEYWOOD *Hierarch.* IX. Comm. 612 More gentle and of less Malice were those ludifications and deceptions of Zedechias the Jew. **1674** JOSSELYN *Voy. New Eng.* 181 All [are] like Æthiopians white in the Teeth, only full of ludification and injurious dealing. *a* **1683** SIDNEY *Disc. Govt.* iii. §18 (1704) 308 Such ludifications of the most sacred things. **1838** G. S. FABER *Inquiry* 198 In order to see whether this ludification be not properly of demons and not of men.

†**ludificatory**, *a.* *Obs.* *rare*⁻¹. [ad. L. *lūdificātōri-us* deceptive: see -ORY².] Deceptive.

a **1677** BARROW *Serm.* (1686) III. 450 In the Sacraments.. there is nothing empty (or vain), nothing ludificatory.

†ˈ**ludify**, *v.* *Obs.* *rare*⁻¹. [ad. L. *lūdificāre* to delude, f. *lūd-us* sport: see -FY.] *trans.* To deceive.

1447 BOKENHAM *Seyntys, Eliz.* (Roxb.) 244 Why art thou so..cautelous me for to ludyfye? *Ibid.* 276 And þat no successyoun shuld her ludyfye Of werdly prosperyte. **1623** COCKERAM, *Ludifie*, to deceiue.

†ˈ**luding**. *Obs.* Also 3 loudinge. [ME. *lūdinge*, n. of action (see -ING¹) f. **lūden*:—OE. *hlýdan* to resound (:—**hlūdjan*) related to *hlúd* LOUD *a.* For the form *louding* in the second text of Layamon cf. LUDE¹.] Noise.

c **1205** LAY. 10715 Þa iherde þe king mucle ludinge. *Ibid.* 24873 And þa luding alæid [*c* **1275** And þe loudinge alay].

ludlamite (ˈlʌdləmaɪt). *Min.* [Named, 1877, after H. *Ludlam*, by Field.] A green crystalline hydrous phosphate of iron.

1877 *Mineral. Mag.* I. 138 Ludlamite..is a new hydrated basic ferric phosphate. **1892** *Dana's Min.* 841.

Ludlovian (lʌdˈləʊvɪən), *a.* *Geol.* [f. *Ludlovia*, med.L. name of Ludlow, town in Salop (Shropshire) in the vicinity of which are exposures of this series: see -IAN.] Of, pertaining to, or designating the latest of the three divisions of the Silurian, preceding the Downtonian (or the second latest, if the Silurian is taken to include the Downtonian). Also *absol.*

1855 J. PHILLIPS *Man. Geol.* vi. 104 This stage contains no less than seventy-eight species—the genera being mostly Wenlockian and Ludlovian. **1946** L. D. STAMP *Britain's Struct.* xii. 109 Though various divisions of the Silurian have been proposed the old three-fold one into: (3) Ludlow Series or Ludlovian; (2) Wenlock Series or Wenlockian; (1) Llandovery Series or Valentian; has stood the test of time and is most convenient. **1969** BENNISON & WRIGHT *Geol. Hist. Brit. Isles* vi. 121 There is..an almost perfect transition in the Welsh Borders from the Ludlovian into the Dittonian reflecting a gradually changing environment from marine to non-marine. *Ibid.* 120 *Monograptus scanicus* suggests a low Ludlovian age for these deltaic deposits.

ludo (ˈl(j)uːdəʊ). [a. L. *lūdo* I play.] A game, played with dice and counters on a special board.

1898 *Westm. Gaz.* 4 Jan. 2/1 Cards, tiddley-winks, and ludo are played, but gambling is strictly forbidden. **1955** L. P. HARTLEY *Perfect Woman* xxxvi. 324 The four ludo-players identified her. **1973** *Times* 4 Oct. 2/5 Pedestrians feel like pawns on a vast spongy chess and ludo board. **1975** R. PLAYER *Let's talk of Graves* iv. 108 Our dear Miss Grigg produced a new Ludo set and..a few crackers.

Ludolph (ˈluːdɒlf). [The name of *Ludolph* van Ceulen (1540–1610), who was born at Hildesheim (Germany), taught mathematics in the Netherlands, and calculated π to 35 decimal places.] ***Ludolph's number***; the number π (see PI *sb.*).

[**1887** *Encycl. Brit.* XXII. 434/2 In Germany the 'Ludolphische Zahl' is still a common name for the ratio.] **1894** F. CAJORI *Hist. Math.* 154 The value of π is therefore often named 'Ludolph's number'. **1959** *Webster's Biogr. Dict.* s.v. *Ceulen, Ludolph van*... Known for computations of the value of π (Ludolphian, or Ludolph's number).

Hence **Luˈdolphian** *a.*

1886 G. S. CARR *Synopsis Pure & Appl. Math.* I. II. 901/1 (Index), Ludolphian number. **1905** *Westm. Gaz.* 14 Oct. 3/1 The history of the search for this ratio, the Ludolphian number..is practically the early history of mathematics itself. **1953** H. EVES *Introd. Hist. Math.* iv. 92 Ludolph van Ceulen of Germany computed π to 35 decimal places by the classical method, using polygons having 2^{62} sides. He spent a large part of his life on this task and his achievement was considered so extraordinary that the number was engraved on his tombstone, and to this day is frequently referred to in Germany as 'the Ludolphian number'.

‖ˈ**ludus**. *Med. Obs.* [Mod.L. (Paracelsus), app. an application of L. *lūdus* play (perh. taken in the sense 'freak of nature').] A name applied to certain septarian nodules formerly regarded as specific in cases of calcareous concretionary disease.

a **1728** WOODWARD *Nat. Hist. Fossils* (1729) I. 83 He [Dr. Grew] supposes the Waxen-Vein to be the same with the Ludus of Paracelsus and Van Helmont. *Ibid.* 84 Sir I. Newton gave me a Piece of this kind of Body brought over from Germany by the younger Helmont, as the true Ludus of his Father; which does not differ..from those commonly found in England.

ludwigite (ˈluːdvɪgaɪt). *Min.* [Named by Tschermak, 1874, after Prof. E. *Ludwig*: see -ITE.] A black fibrous borate of magnesium and iron.

1875 DANA *Min.* App. II. 35 Ludwigite occurs altered to limonite. **1887** *Mineral. Mag.* VII. 43 A. Renard..examines the optical properties of Ludwigite.

Ludwig's angina (ˈlʊdvɪgz ænˈdʒaɪnə). *Path.* [tr. mod.L. *angina Ludovici*, f. the name of W. F. von *Ludwig* (1790–1865), German surgeon, who described it in 1836.] Severe inflammation of the tissues of the floor of the mouth (usu. caused by streptococci).

[**1875** *Brit. Med. Jrnl.* 25 Dec. 778/2 (*heading*) A note on Angina Ludovici. **1885** *Lancet* 26 Sept. 571/2 (*heading*) Two cases of angina Ludovici.] *Ibid.*, Ludwig's angina is a name applied to the condition known as submaxillary cellulitis. **1939** *Bull. Hist. Med.* VII. 1124 Ludwig's Angina is a comparatively rare disease despite the fact that the disease picture is fairly well known to all students of medicine. **1971** D. F. MITCHELL et al. *Oral Diagn.* (ed. 2) xiv. 344 In this case, all of the spaces of the floor of the mouth (submandibular, sublingual, submental) are involved and the condition is called Ludwig's angina.

Ludwigsburg (ˈluːdvɪgzbɜg). The name of a town in Württemberg used *attrib.* or *absol.* to designate a variety of hard-paste porcelain made there from 1758 to 1824, characterized by its suitability for figure-modelling.

1863 W. CHAFFERS *Marks Pott. & Porc.* 185 Ludwigsburg, or Louisburg, called also Kronenburg porcelain. **1960** R. G. HAGGAR *Conc. Encycl. Cont. Pott. & Porc.* 188/1 (*caption*) Ludwigsburg porcelain miniature group. *Ibid.* 189/1 Ludwigsburg porcelain Chinese groups. *Ibid.* 273/1 Ludwigsburg models were reproduced at Amberg..during the nineteenth century.

lue, lew (l(j)uː), *v.* *Tin* and *Silver mining. trans.* To sift with a sieve.

1674 RAY *Collect. Words, Smelting Silver* [Cardiganshire] 116 That which is thus Buddled they lue with a thick hair sieve close wrought in a tub of water. *Ibid., Prepar. Tin* [Cornwall] 122 The fine [tin] is lewed in a fine sierce. **1799** MAR. EDGEWORTH *Lame Jervas* viii, I had new models made of the sieves for lueing.

lue, lued, obs. ff. LEW, LIEU, LOO, LEDE.

luef, luer, obs. forms of LIEF, LURE.

‖**lues** (ˈl(j)uːiːz). *Med.* [L. *luēs* plague.] A plague or pestilence; a spreading disease, *esp.* syphilis (*Lues venerea*); also, a contagious disease amongst cattle.

1634 SIR T. HERBERT *Trav.* 86 [The bath] is preualent too against the *lues venerea*. **1721** BAILEY, *Lues*, a Pestilence or Plague; also a Murrain in Cattle. **1803** *Med. Jrnl.* IX. 573 The reason why blennorrhagy so seldom produces lues, is [etc.]. **1880** BARWELL *Aneurism* 96 Many syphilitic persons have atheromatous arteries; but..a great number who have suffered from the *lues* have also had acute rheumatism.

Hence **luetic** (l(j)uːˈɛtɪk) *a.* [badly formed, after *herpetic*, etc.], of or belonging to lues.

1899 *Allbutt's Syst. Med.* VII. 688 In contradistinction to atheroma, luetic endarteritis is limited to single arteries.

‖**lues Boswelliana** (ˈl(j)uːiːz bɒzwɛlɪˈeɪnə, -ˈɑːnə). [f. LUES: cf. BOSWELLIAN *a.*, -IANA.] A disease of admiration; a biographer's tendency to magnify his subject.

1834 MACAULAY in *Edin. Rev.* Jan. 508 Biographers, translators, editors,—all, in short, who employ themselves in illustrating the lives or the writings of others, are peculiarly exposed to the *Lues Boswellianæ*, or disease of admiration. **1928** [see FUROR 4]. **1931** *Times Lit. Suppl.* 8 Oct. 765/3 Though he decidedly comes to praise Caesar, not to bury him, he avoids any excessive *lues Boswelliana*.

lueshite (ˈl(j)uːəʃaɪt). *Min.* [a. F. *lueshite* (A. Safiannikoff 1959, in *Bull. d. Séances, Acad. r. d. Sci. d'Outre-Mer* V. 1255), f. *Lueshe*, name of a locality north of Goma in eastern Zaïre where it was discovered: see -ITE¹.] A black orthorhombic niobate of sodium, $NaNbO_3$.

1961 *Mineral. Mag.* XXXII. 966 Lueshite. **1968** I. KOSTOV *Mineral.* I. 250 The chief minerals [of the perovskite group] are perovskite ($CaTiO_3$), lueshite ($NaNbO_3$), and loparite ($NaCeTi_2O_6$).

lueve, obs. form of LIEF.

lue-warm, variant of LEW-WARM *a.*

luf, obs. form of LIEF, LOVE.

lufand, lufare, obs. ff. LOVING, LOVER.

lufe, obs. form of LOOF, LOVE, LUFF.

lufesome, -sum, obs. forms of LOVESOME.

luff (lʌf), *sb.*¹ *Naut.* Forms: 3 lof, (*pl.* lofes, 3–5 loves), 4–5 lofe, 5, 8 loff, 5 louffe, lowffe, 7 loufe; 6–7 loofe, looff(e, *Sc.* luif(e, 3–9 loof; 6 luf(fe, 6–7 lufe, 5– luff. [Early ME. *lof*, *loof*, app. a. OF. *lof* (Wace, 12th c.), later *louf*, used in sense 1 below. Senses 2–4 are common to various mod. langs.: F. *lof*, Sp., Pg. *ló*, Du. *loef* (whence LG. *loff*, G. *luv*, Da. *luv*, Sw. *luf*). The manner of their development is obscure, and it is uncertain whether they originated in Fr., Eng., or (? most prob.) Du. Sense 5 is peculiar to Eng., and it is not easy to connect it with any of the other senses.

Certain other meanings which the word has had in Du. and Fr. need to be accounted for before any hypothesis as to the primitive meaning and sense-development can be regarded as satisfactory. In early mod.Du. *loef, loeve* is explained as 'thole-pin' (*scalmus*, Kilian). In the 17th c. the F. *lof* or *loo* is stated to mean 'the distance from the mast to the place on the side to which the sheet is fastened when the vessel is close-hauled'. (See the quot. from Nicot in Godef., s.v.) In the existing uncertainty as to the primary meaning, the ultimate etymology remains obscure; the current view that it represents a Teut. word cogn. with ON. *lófe* palm, LOOF *sb.*¹, depends on the doubtful assumption that the 'lof' of sense 1 was a steering paddle.]

†**1.** ? Some implement or contrivance for altering the course of a ship. Phrases, ***to turn, wend the luff*** (= Anglo-Latin *obliquare dracenam*), to change one's course; also *fig.* *Obs.*

Commonly supposed to have been either a rudder or a paddle to assist in steering. Comparison with the various senses which the word has had in Eng. and other langs. (see above) suggests that it may have been some kind of machine for operating on the sails.

c **1205** LAY. 7859 Heo scuuen ut heore lof & læiden to þon londe. *Ibid.* 20949 Heo wenden heore lofes [*c* **1275** loues] & liðen toward londe. *Ibid.* 30922 Heo rihten heore loues and up droȝen seiles. *a* **1225** *Ancr. R.* 104 Hu swetelich þi spus spekeð, & cleopeð þe to him so lueueliche, & ter after hu he went þene lof, & spekeð swuð grimliche, ȝif þu wendest vt. *a* **1259** MATTHEW PARIS *Chron. Maj.* (Rolls) III. 29 Perrexerunt igitur audacter, obliquando tamen dracenam, id est loof, acsi vellent adire Calesiam. **13..** *Coer de L.* 71 And her loof and her wyndas Off asure forsothe it was. *c* **1330** R. BRUNNE *Chron. Wace* (Rolls) 12088 Somme aforced þe wyndas, Somme þe loof [*Petyt MS.* lofe], somme þe bytas [*orig.* 11491 Li un s'esforcent al vindas, Li autre al lof et al betas]. **13..** *E.E. Allit. P.* C. 106 Þay layden in on ladde-borde & the lofe wynnes [? *read* wyndes]. ? *a* **1400** *Morte Arth.* 744 Tytt saillez to þe toppe, and turnez the lufe. **1485** *Naval Acc. Hen. VII* (1896) 38 Chenes for the Loves ..j.

†**2.** The weather-gauge, or part of a ship toward the wind. *Obs.*

? *a* **1400** *Morte Arth.* 750 Launchez lede apone lufe, lacchene ther depe. *a* **1500** *Piers of Fullham* 263 in Hazl. *E.P.P.* II. 11 What worde for to sey he ys yn dowt: eyther, war the looff, or fall, or bye. **1609** *T. Ravenscroft's Pammelia* No. 55 D4b, Looke to the looffe wel, beware the lee still. **1622** R. HAWKINS *Voy. S. Sea* xlix. 118 The Vice Admirall a mile right to le-wards of vs; the Reare Admirall in a manner right a head, some Culvering shott; and one vpon our loofe, within shott also.

3. In various phrases. †***on luff***, †***at a luff***, †***at luff and lie***, ***luff a luff***: hugging the wind closely, close to the wind. †***a luff***: see ALOOF *adv.* 1, 2. †***to go by luff*** (***by love***), ***to keep one's luff***: to keep close to the wind; to keep away to the windward, keep one's distance (from another vessel, etc.). ***to spring one's luff***: to bring the ship's head closer to the wind; *transf.* (in jocular use) to show agility in climbing. (Also said of the ship, ***to keep her luff***, ***spring her luff***, ***spring a loof***.)

c **1400** *Laud Troy Bk.* 3610 The wynd was good to ther byhoue, Thei sailed on brod and gon by-loue, Til thei come to Troye land. **1535** STEWART *Cron. Scot.* (1858) I. 124 Sum bade on luffe, and other sum hald by. *a* **1568** *Satir. Poems Reform.* xlvi. 6 Se that hir hatchis be handlit richt, Wᵗ steirburd, baburd, luf and lie. *Ibid.* 11 Bot at ane lufe scho lyis behind. **1583** *Leg. Bp. St. Androis* Pref. 104 He lattis his scheip tak in at luife and lie. **1591** RALEIGH *Last Fight Rev.* (Arb.) 19 Diuerse of the formost, who as the Marriners terme it, sprang their luffe. *c* **1595** CAPT. WYATT *R. Dudley's Voy. W. Ind.* (Hakl. Soc.) 57 She verie stoutlie keepinge her loofe bare with us. **1628** DIGBY *Voy. Medit.* (1868) 21 He sprung his loofe and went as neere the wind as he could. **1682** HICKERINGILL *Black Non-Conf.* Concl., Wks. 1716 II. 157 Then, Charity (Hussy!) stand off, keep your 'loof and your distance. **1697** *Lond. Gaz.* No. 3318/3 The Hospital-Ship prudently springing her Loof quickly came near us. **1754** EELES in *Phil. Trans.* XLIX. 143 If they sail upon a wind from the center of the shower toward the extremity, they may safely venture to keep their luff. **1762** FALCONER *Shipwr.* II. 51 The mizen draws; she springs aloof once more. **1805** ADM. STIRLING in *Naval Chron.* XV. 80 We sprung our luff. **1849** *Florist* 305 And so we quietly kept our luff. **1870** *Routledge's Ev. Boy's Ann.* 251, I just want to know who 'spring their luffs' most nimble up the rigging. **1887** E. J. MATHER *Nor'ard of Dogger* (1888) 172 He stated that they had passed the Leman Light, and was steering southerly, luff a luff (close haul to the wind).

4. 'The weather part of a fore-and-aft sail, in other words, the side next the mast or stay to which it is attached' (Young *Naut. Dict.* 1846).

1513 DOUGLAS *Æneis* v. xiv. 7 Now the lie scheit, and now the luf, thai slak. **1549** *Compl. Scot.* vi. 40 Hail doune the steir burde lufe harde a burde. *c* **1860** H. STUART *Seaman's Catech.* 48 Name the parts of a fore-and-aft sail. Head, luff, leech, and foot. **1883** *Harper's Mag.* Aug. 449/2 A mainsail which is..short on the luff or on the part which is made fast to the mast. **1893** MAX PEMBERTON *Iron Pirate* 39 The mainsail presently showed a great rent near the luff.

5. The fullest and broadest part of a ship's bow, where the sides begin to curve in towards the stem. †***luff for luff***: (of two vessels) close alongside.

1624 CAPT. SMITH *Virginia* IV. 128 They brauely boorded vs loofe for loofe. **1627** —— *Seaman's Gram.* ii. 9 The Bow is broadest part of the Ship before, compassing the Stem to the Loufe, which reacheth so farre as the Bulkhead of the Fore-castle extendeth. **1694** MOTTEUX *Rabelais* v. xviii, With Cables fasten'd to the Bits abaft the Manger in the Ship's Loof. **1711** W. SUTHERLAND *Shipbuild. Assist.* 47 Raise what you can regularly in the Bulge and Loof. *c* **1850** *Rudim. Navig.* (Weale) 130 *Luff* or *loof*, the fullest or roundest part of the bow. **1875** BEDFORD *Sailor's Pocket Bk.* vi. (ed. 2) 214 The two bowmen to gather down on the luff.

6. = *luff-tackle* (see 7). ***luff upon luff***, a luff-tackle attached to the fall of another, to increase the purchase.

1840 R. H. DANA *Bef. Mast* xxix. 99 Two more luff tackles [were] hooked on, with dogs,..and thus by luff upon luff, the power was multiplied. *c* **1860** H. STUART *Seaman's Catech.* 8 A long luff for a fore and aft tackle should be used for steadying the boat. **1882** NARES *Seamanship* (ed. 6) 58 The double block of the luff is hooked to the lanyard.

7. *attrib.* and *Comb.*: † **luff board**, ? = sense 2; † **luff hook** (see quot. 1627); † **luff-law, -lew, -low** [second element obscure], ? = sense 5; **luff-piece** (see quot.); **luff-rope**, ? the rope of a luff-tackle; **luff-tackle**, a purchase composed of a double and a single block, used for various purposes.

c **1470** HENRY *Wallace* IX. 56 Ledys on *luff burd, with a lordlik fer: Lansys laid out, to [luik] thar passage sound. **1485** *Naval Acc. Hen. VII* (1896) 73 *Lofe hokes. **1495** *Ibid.* 158 Loff hokes. **1532** *Inv. Gt. Barke* 6 Oct. (Jal), Item, a snatche polly; a Luffhooke. **1627** CAPT. SMITH *Seaman's Gram.* v. 24 The Loofe hooke is a tackle with two hookes, one to hitch into a chingle of the maine, or fore saile,..and the other to strap spliced to the chestres to bouse or pull downe the saile to succour the tackes in a stiffe gale of wind. **1495** *Naval Acc. Hen. VII* (1896) 192 Devettes stondyng at the *louffelawes oon asterborde an other a latheborde. *Ibid.* 203 Lowffelewes. *Ibid.* 215 Loff-lowes. **1815** *Falconer's Marine Dict.* (ed. Burney), *Loof*, the after part of a ship's bow;..hence, the guns which lie here are called *loof-pieces. **1895** *Times* 29 Jan. 11/2 Before the wheel could turn G. [a workman] had to be let down in his basket from the axle in order to take off a *luff rope. **1698** T. SAVERY *Navig. Impr.* Plate, A pice of Iron, to which a *luff Takle may bee Fixed, to lift those [paddles] that are to Heavey for mens Strength. **1731** BAILEY vol. II, *Loof Tackle.* **1775** FALCK *Day's Diving Vessel* 51 Belay all safe with stout salvages and loff-tackles. **1793** SMEATON *Edystone L.* §253 That buoy.. was confined to the side of the Weston by a small luff-tackle which laid hold of it. *c* **1860** H. STUART *Seaman's Catech.* 61 They are..transported to their places by luff tackles. **1884** *Mil. Engineering* I. II. 66 The luff tackle used for loading and unloading the magazine.

luff (lʌf), *sb.*^{2} *colloq.* = LIEUTENANT.

1836 E. HOWARD *R. Reefer* xxxiii, The Hon. Mr. B., our junior luff. **1898** *Westm. Gaz.* 17 Oct. 2/3 The future 'Luffs' —in other words, the naval cadets at Dartmouth—are to be reduced in point of numbers.

luff (lʌf), *v.* orig. *Naut.* Forms: 4 love, 6-8 loff, louffe, 7 looft, loute, luffe, *Sc.* luif, 6-8 loof(e, 6- luff. [f. LUFF *sb.*^{1}; cf. Du. *loeven*, F. *lofer*.]

1. *intr.* To bring the head of a ship nearer to the wind; to steer or sail nearer the wind; to sail in a specified direction with the head kept close to the wind. Also with advs., †*by*, *in*, *off*, *to*, *up*, etc. ***luff round*** or *alee*: see quot. 1769.

1390 GOWER *Conf.* II. 369 So nyh the weder thei wol love. **1557** W. TOWRSON in Hakluyt *Voy.* (1589) 119 He loffed too and was able to lie as neere as he did before. **1578** BEST *Frobisher's 2nd Voy.* in Hakluyt (1600) III. 64 Hauing mountaines of fleeting yce on euery side, we went roomer for one, and loofed for another. **1579-80** NORTH *Plutarch, Antonius* (1595) 999 He was driuen also to loofe off to haue more roome. **1591** RALEIGH *Last Fight Rev.* (Arb.) 19 The ships that wer vnder his lee luffing vp, also laid him aboarde. *a* **1600** MONTGOMERIE *Misc. Poems* xlviii. 143 Come no lauer, bot luif a lytill we. **1600** *Hakluyt's Voy.* III. 589 The vice-admirall of the Spaniards..loofed by and gaue the Concord the two first great shot. **1687** B. RANDOLPH *Archipelago* 61 The ship..luffing too near the great island. **1697** DAMPIER *Voy.* (1729) I. 550 We lufft in for the Downs. **1697** DRYDEN *Æneid* v. 23 Contract your swelling sails and luff to Wind. **1706** PHILLIPS (ed. Kersey) s.v., To *Loof into a Harbour*, is to sail into it close by the Wind. **1748** *Anson's Voy.* II. i. 112 By means of the head-way we had got, we loofed close in. **1769** FALCONER *Dict. Marine* (1780), *Luff*, the order..to put the helm towards the lee-side of the ship [etc.]... Hence, luff round, or luff alee; the excess of this movement by which it is intended to throw the ship's head up in the wind, in order to tack her, &c. **1806** A. DUNCAN *Nelson* 110 He had the satisfaction to luff under his stern. **1833** MARRYAT *P. Simple* xv, 'Luff now, all you can, quarter-master', cried the captain. **1840** R. H. DANA *Bef. Mast* xxxvi. 136 She luffed at the same moment, and we just passed one another. *a* **1895** LD. CLARENCE PAGET *Autobiog.* i. (1896) 8 The unfortunate vessel was in a sinking state,.. she luffed up and grounded on the rocks.

2. *trans.* To bring the head of (a vessel) nearer to the wind. Also with *up*. Also ***luff the helm*** (the call or order to the steersman).

1606 SHAKS. *Ant. & Cl.* III. x. 18 She once being looft, The Noble ruine of her Magicke, Anthony, Claps on his Sea-wing, and..flyes after her. **1694** MOTTEUX *Rabelais* IV. xxii. (1737) 95 Loff, loff, cry'd the Quarter-master..keep her full, loff the Helm. Loff: it is, answer'd the Steer-man. **1800** WEEMS *Washington* xi. (1810) 137 Washington..with a hard-a-lee, luffed up his ship at once to the gale. **1831** TRELAWNEY *Adv. Younger Son* cv, We carefully luffed her up to the wind.

3. a. In yacht-racing: To get the windward side of (an opponent). Also with *away*.

1894 *Times* 23 July 11/2 Vigilant at once began to luff Britannia. **1898** *Daily News* 23 Sept. 3/2 In four or five lengths she was alongside and to windward. She failed, however, to luff her antagonist away.

b. To obstruct (an opponent's yacht which is attempting to pass to windward on the same course) by sailing one's own yacht closer to the wind.

1912 HECKSTALL-SMITH & DU BOULAY *Compl. Yachtsman* xiii. 299, I make it a fixed rule to luff every vessel that attempts to pass me to windward. **1960** E. SCHIÖTTZ *Pract. Yacht Racing* ix. 89 If a yacht clear astern sails between two yachts ahead she has no right to luff the windward one. **1965** *Sailing* ('Know the Game' Series) (ed. 2) 34/1 A yacht may luff a yacht clear astern or a windward yacht, until helmsman of windward yacht comes abreast of the mainmast of the leeward yacht.

†**4.** ? To attach (the anchor) to the ship's luff.

1627 CAPT. SMITH *Seaman's Gram.* ix. 38 Loofe fast your Anchor with your shank-painter.

5. *trans.* To alter the inclination of (the jib of a crane or derrick); to raise or lower in a vertical plane. Also with adverbs, as ***luff in***, to raise (the jib), so moving the hook nearer to the operator; similarly ***luff out***.

1913 H. WILDA *Cranes & Hoists* ii. 128 The lifting and lowering of the load is effected by means of multiple pulley blocks, the horizontal movement of the load by luffing the jib. **1922** H. H. BROUGHTON *Electr. Handling of Materials* III. ii. 32 The load follows a horizontal path when luffing-in the jib. **1932** S. J. KOSHKIN *Mod. Materials Handling* v. 78 A derrick boom can be changed in inclination, or luffed, to give one of the components of motion to the load. *Ibid.* 80 The boom is luffed-in or out as little as possible. **1963** R. HAMMOND *Mobile & Movable Cranes* vi. 180 This arrangement reduces the power required to luff in the jib.

Hence **'luffing** *vbl. sb.*; so ***luffing-in, -out***; **luffing crane**, a crane whose jib can be luffed in operation; **luffing-match**, a struggle for 'weather berth' (between racing yachts).

1775 ASH, Suppl., *Loofing*, the act of bringing to the wind. **1886** CAULFIELD *Seamanship Notes* 2 Luffing..would be correct. **1893** *Westm. Gaz.* 9 Aug. 4/1 Plenty of luffing matches took place. **1896** *Daily News* 2 July 4/4 Satanita soon made an attempt for Britannia's weather, but Carter put his boat sharply up and a determined luffing match ensued. **1913** *Engineering* 9 May 632/1 Most of these luffing-cranes are now fitted with some sort of compensating gear to keep the load approximately level while the luffing operation is being carried out. *Ibid.*, Greater acceleration in luffing is also obtained. **1922** H. H. BROUGHTON *Electr. Handling of Materials* III. ii. 41 The design is exceedingly simple, the level path being obtained by the automatic paying-out or taking-in of the load rope during the operations of luffing in and luffing out respectively. **1963** R. HAMMOND *Mobile & Movable Cranes* vi. 181 The luffing motion control equipment consists of a negative-phase sequence panel, with contactors to give plain rotor-controlled 'luffing-in' and 'luffing-out' by the unbalancing of the stator voltages of the motor through an inbuilt transformer. **1967** *Courier-Mail* (Brisbane) 8 July 1/9 The cries of wharf laborer Derek Beuttel, 54, were not heard by fellow workmen because of the noise of three large luffing cranes.

luff, obs. form of LOOF *sb.*^{1} *Sc.*, LOVE.

luffer, obs. f. LIVER *sb.*^{1}; var. LOUVER.

luffeword, variant of LOFWORD *Obs.*, praise.

luffsum(m, obs. form of LOVESOME.

lufftenande, obs. form of LIEUTENANT.

lufful, obs. form of LOVEFUL.

lufly (*lufliche*, etc.), obs. form of LOVELY.

lufray(e, lufre, obs. Sc. forms of LIVERY *sb.*

lufsom(e, -s(o)um, obs. forms of LOVESOME.

luft(e, obs. form of LEFT and LIFT *sb.*^{1}

luftenand, obs. form of LIEUTENANT.

‖**luftmensch, luftmensh** ('lʊftmɛnʃ). Pl. luftmenschen. [Yiddish, f. G. *luft* air + *mensch* person.] An impractical visionary.

1907 I. ZANGWILL *Ghetto Comedies* 240 The word 'Luftmensch' flew into Barstein's mind. Nehemiah was not an earth-man... He was an air-man, floating on facile wings. **1960** *Commentary* June 530/1 The revolutionary student, the nihilist-anarchists, the *Luftmenschen.* **1966** *New Society* 12 May 11/2 Americans, children of the soil, have become traders in air, advertising men, *luftmenschen.* **1968** L. ROSTEN *Joys of Yiddish* 212 The prototype of the luftmensh was one Leone da Modena,..who listed his skills and cited no fewer than twenty-six professions... Why would so accomplished a man be classified as a *luftmensh*? Because out of all twenty-six professions.., he barely made a living. **1969** *Sat. Rev.* (U.S.) 26 Apr. 44/2 Menachem-Mendl, *luftmensch* extraordinary, a veritable Don Quixote of Eastern European commerce.

‖**Luftwaffe** ('lʊftvafə). [Ger., 'air-weapon'; cf. LIFT *sb.*^{1}] The German air force before, and until the end of, the 1939-45 war. Also *attrib.*

1935 *Times* 23 May 15/1 The armed forces are henceforth known collectively as the Wehrmacht (Defence Force) and consist of the Army (*Heer*), Navy (*Kriegsmarine*), and the Air Arm (*Luftwaffe*). **1939** *War Illustr.* 21 Oct. 169 The German Luftwaffe—literally 'air weapon'—has been built up by Field-Marshal Goering and General Milch into a formidable force both in size and quality. **1941** *Ann. Reg.* *1940* 66 The repulse..broke down the legend of the invincibility of the German *Luftwaffe.* **1941** H. G. WELLS *You can't be too Careful* v. ii. 244 The Luftwaffe he [*sc.* Goering] had launched. **1942** *Electronic Engin.* XV. 240 Generally the receiving valves are..similar to those used in German Luftwaffe sets. **1946** *R.A.F. Jrnl.* May 174 One Group alone has disposed of thousands of tons of Luftwaffe equipment. **1957** *Encycl. Brit.* I. 453/1 As soon as the arms limitation of the Versailles treaty had been repudiated, Germany embarked upon the creation of a great Luftwaffe.

lug (lʌg), *sb.*^{1} Now *dial.* Also 3-6 lugge, 8-9 lugg. [Of obscure etymology: there is no clear affinity of sense with LUG *v.* or LOG *sb.*^{1}]

1. A long stick or pole; the branch or limb of a tree. (See also LOG *sb.*^{1} 1 d.)

a **1250** *Owl & Night.* 1609 An evereuch man is widh me wrodh, An me mid stone and lugge threteth. **1447** *Yatton Churchw. Acc.* (Somerset Rec. Soc.) 88 It. to Iohn Styvor makyng of to baner luggus..iiij^d. **1567** TURBERV. *Epit.* etc. 26 b, And from the bodies [of pines and oaks] the boughes and loftie lugges they beare. **1609** C. BUTLER *Fem. Mon.* v. (1623) M, These sides are fitly made of inch-board, or of a cleaft Lug of Withie or other wood. **1795** BILLINGSLEY *Agric. Surv. Somerset* (1797) 88 Covering the same with strong lugs or poles. **1853** *Jrnl. R. Agric. Soc.* XIV. II. 441 In Herefordshire the ordinary mode of gathering the fruit is by sending men to beat the trees with long slender poles or rods,..these poles are provincially termed 'polting lugs'.

2. A measure **a.** of length: a pole or perch, varying according to local custom; usually of 16½ feet, sometimes of 15, 18, 20, or 21 feet (? = *great lug* in quot. 1623).

1562-3 *Act 5 Eliz.* c. 4 §11 What Wages every Woorckman..shall take..for ditching..by the Rodd, Perche, Lugg, Yard [etc.]. **1590** SPENSER *F.Q.* II. x. 11 For the large leape which Debon did compell Coulin to make, being eight lugs of grownd. **1610** W. FOLKINGHAM *Art of Survey* II. iv. 52 Sixteen Foote ½ make a Pearch, Pole, or Lug. **1623** BOYLE in *Lismore Papers* (1886) II. 73, I paid..eight pounds ster: for every great Lugg of the playn worck of the town wall. **1681** GLANVILL *Sadducismus* II. (ed. 2) 176 [He] followed the Apparition about ten Lugs (that is Poles) farther into the Copse. **1771** *Antiq. Sarisb.* 91 This [channel] was brought down..about 20 lug below the Bridge. **1811** T. DAVIS *Agric. Wilts.* App. 268 A Lug..is of three lengths in this county: 15, 18, and 16½ feet. **1858** SIMMONDS *Dict. Trade, Lug*..in Gloucestershire, a land-measure of six yards.

b. of surface: a square pole or perch; † ***acre by lug*** = *lug-acre* (see 3).

1602 *Burford Reg.* (Hist. MSS. Comm.) *Varr. Collect.* I. 164 Mowinge of barley for every acre by lugge not above v^d. **1727** BRADLEY *Fam. Dict.*, *Acre*, a Measure of Land, consisting of..an hundred and sixty square Lug or Perch of Land. **1772** *Ann. Reg.* 115 He had inclosed with a hedge about four lug of the land. **1794** J. CLARK *View Agric. Herefordsh.* 31 One standard is left to each forty-nine square yards, here called a lugg. **1845** *Morn. Chron.* 22 Nov. 5/2, I have seen a sack [of potatoes] a lug on some land,—that is 160 sacks per acre. **1885** *Berksh. Vicar* in *Standard* 17 Aug. 2/2 Allotments of twenty luggs each (i.e. one-eighth of an acre).

3. *attrib.* and *Comb.*: † **lug-acre**, an acre based on that value of the pole or perch to which the name *lug* was locally applied; † **lug-fall**, the length of a lug; a pole or perch; **lug-pole** *U.S.* (= sense 1).

1635 *Burford Reg.* (Hist. MSS. Comm.) *Varr. Collect.* I. 169 Wages... For reaping and binding of wheate..for every *lugg aker not above ij^s. vj^d. **1863** J. SCOTT *Com. Bench Repts.* XII. 91 [Somerset Law Case.] The right..to enter.. upon a part or strip, to wit, a *lug fall [*margin*, A perch] of the said close. **1773** *Mass. Gaz.* 4 Feb. (Suppl.) 1/2 A Defect in the Chimney, by Reason of the Wooden *Lug-pole burning out. **1848** D. DRAKE *Pioneer Life Kentucky* (1870) v. 107 The tea kettle swung from a wooden 'lug pole'.

lug (lʌg), *sb.*^{2} Chiefly *Sc.* and *north.* Also (6 *Sc.* louge), 6-7 lugg(e. [Of obscure etymology.

As a synonym of *ear*, it first appears early in the 16th c., and in colloquial Sc. use has entirely superseded the older word. Presumably this application is a transferred use of a word that existed earlier with some other meaning. It is possible that the sense 'ear-flap of a cap', which is the earliest represented in our quots., may really be prior to the sense 'ear'; for similar transferences of words from parts of clothing to the parts of the body covered, cf. *breech*, *crown*, *sole*. If so, the word may perh. be of Scandinavian origin, with a general sense of 'something that can be pulled or laid hold of', specialized differently in Sw. *lugg* forelock, with which cf. Eng. dial. (Sheffield, North Derb., etc.) 'to pull (somebody's) lugs', meaning not as in Scotland, the ears, but the hair. (See LUG *v.*)]

1. One of the flaps or lappets of a cap or bonnet, covering the ears.

1495 *Ld. Treas. Acc. Scotl.* (1877) I. 225 Item, fra Henry Cant, ij cappis wyth luggis; price xxxvj*s.* **1549** *Compl. Scot.* vi. 43 Euyrie scheiphird hed ane horne spune in the lug of there bonet. **1737** RAMSAY *Sc. Prov.* (1797) 35 He has a bee in his bannet lug. **1822** GOLDIE *Poems* 115 (E.D.D.) Cock yer bonnet hie, An' frae its lug let tartans flee.

2. a. = EAR *sb.*^{1} 1 and 3. Now *colloq.* or *joc.*

By the 19th cent. it had become the only word in use in Sc. *ear* having become *obs.* exc. in combination (though it is now standard). Eng. writers of 16-17th c. use *lug* as a slang or jocular synonym (see quots. 1592 and 1625, and cf. b).

1507 *Extracts Aberd. Reg.* (1844) I. 437 That na craftis-men by hidis bot as the law requires, that is to say, the louge and the horne elik lang. **1515** *Edin. Counc. Rec.* in A. Laing *Lindores Abbey* xxii. (1876) 297 To be scurgeit to the gallows and thair his lug takkit to the beame. **1549** *Compl. Scot.* vi. 64 Kyng midas gat tua asse luggis on his hede be cause of his aureeis. **1581** *Satir. Poems Reform.* xliv. 109 Sathan in ȝour knauish luggis bleu. **1592** GREENE *Conny-catching* Wks. (Grosart) XI. 62 Then the gentle-woman let loose his eares, and let slip his head, and away went he home with his bloody lugges. **1625** B. JONSON *Staple News* v. i, A fine round head when those two lugs are off To trundle through a pillory. **1659** SHIRLEY *Content. Ajax & Ulysses* i, If you have a mind to lose one of your lugs,..Talk on. **1721** RAMSAY *Lucky Spence* xiii, I..Roun'd in his lug, that there was a Poor

country Kate. **1786** BURNS *Scotch Drink* 4 Let other Poets.. grate our lug. **1824** SCOTT *Redgauntlet* let. xii, Dinna blaw in folk's lugs that gate. **1893** STEVENSON *Catriona* 52, I heard the balls whistle in our lugs. **1908** *Old-Lore Misc.* I. VII. 270 Lang an last, da laird grippit him be da lug. **1916** 'TAFFRAIL' *Pincher Martin* ii. 28 Give 'im a clip under the lug! **1922** *Banffshire Jrnl.* 26 Sept. 6 An' hame-brewn sets th' lugs a crackin'. **1922** JOYCE *Ulysses* 192 Has the wrong sow by the lug. *Ibid.* 261 Cowley's red lugs and Adam's apple in the door of the sheriff's office. **1939** —— *Finnegans Wake* 500 The snare drum! Lay yer lug till the groun.

†**b.** In other than Sc. use, sometimes taken in specialized meanings: (*a*) the lobe of the ear; (*b*) a large ugly ear. *Obs.*

1602 *2nd Pt. Return fr. Parnass.* v. iv. 2232 Like a great swine by his long leane eard lugges. **1611** COTGR., *Le mol de l'oreille*, the lug or list of th' eare. **1650** BULWER *Anthropomet.* viii. (1653) 158 The prominency of our Eares serve also for a defence [etc.]..all which commodities our mickle-wise Mothers defraud us of by their nice dislike of Lugs, and as they call them in reproach, Prickeares. **1706** PHILLIPS (ed. Kersey), *Lug*, the tip of the Ear. **1764** O'HARA *Midas* 60 Dare you think your clumsey lugs [*printed* lungs] so proper to decide, as The delicate ears of Justice Midas?

c. In phrases similar to those s.v. EAR *sb.*[1] Also, fig. ***to get one's lug in one's loof***, to be severely taken to task; ***by the lug and the horn***, by main force; ***to hang by the lug of***, to keep a firm hold of.

a **1652** BROME *Mad Couple* III. i. Wks. 1873 I. 47 You.. were found by my servants at Luggs with your brace of Corps bearers. *a* **1693** M. BRUCE *Good News in Evil T.* (1708) 54 Since the Cause is put in his Hand, ye have ay good Reason to hing by the Lug of it. **1744** ADAM SMITH in *Life W. Cullen* (1832) I. 481, I shall get my lug in my lufe, as we say, for what I have written. **1770** BP. FORBES *Jrnls.* (1886) 300 The poor Brutes..cock'd their Lugs when they came in sight of Maryburgh. **1828** MOIR *Mansie Wauch* xx. 291 We carried them by the lug and the horn before a justice of peace. **1883** THOMSON *Leddy May* 109 (E.D.D.) Up in debt owre the lugs, he is happy for a'.

3. An object resembling the external ear.

a. The handle of a pitcher, etc. Also *techn.* in various uses, denoting an appendage by which an object may be lifted or suspended; cf. EAR *sb.*[1] 8, 8 b, 13.

1624 *Invent.* in *Archæologia* XLVIII. 151 One copper pan with 2 lugges. *a* **1693** *Urquhart's Rabelais* III. xlv, Instructors of Children shake the heads of their Disciples, as one would do a Pot in holding it by the Lugs. **1794** W. FELTON *Carriages* (1801) II. Suppl. 51 Sewing on one old lug or flap..o. o. 6. **1819** SCOTT *Leg. Montrose* iv, The lady's auld posset dish, that wants the cover and one o' the lugs. **1862** *Macm. Mag.* Oct. 510 That, when they 'pree' or examine a corner or lug of their nets, they may find it glitter with the silvery sheen of the fish. **1867** SMYTH *Sailor's Word-bk.*, *Lugs*, the ears of a bomb-shell, to which the hooks are applied in lifting it. **1871** OWEN *Mod. Artill.* 98 There are three natures of mortar shells..the two higher natures have either lugs or lewis holes. **1881** WHITEHEAD *Hops* 69 A lug or ear is left on each side of the mouth of the pocket. **1895** *Month* Sept. 53 Its [the haddock's] head had been cut off, and it hung by the lug, or ear.

b. = EAR *sb.*[1] 9.

1833 HOLLAND *Manuf. Metal* II. 215 In the centre of this fulcrum are two projecting lugs, one on each side. **1855** HOPKINS *Organ* ii. 16 The fork-shaped piece of wood that projects from the hanging end of the feeder [in the blowing-action], called the lug. **1875** *Carpentry & Join.* 33 A neat iron tank, with lugs to allow of its being screwed to a bench. **1881** GREENER *Gun* 262 The lugs of the barrels..should be oiled occasionally. **1882** NARES *Seamanship* (ed. 6) 39 Top-gallant yards are..fitted with an iron band and lug round the centre of the yard. **1897** *Encycl. Sport* I. 271/2 The [bicycle] Frame is made of steel tubes, inserted at their points of junction into hollow stampings or castings of metal, known as 'lugs'.

c. The side-wall (of a fire-place or other recess); a (chimney) corner.

1784 BURNS *Ep. to Davie* i, Frosty winds blaw..Ben to the chimla lug. **1843** J. BALLANTINE *Gaberlunzie's Wallet* xii. 276 He likit the lug o' the kitchen fire best.

d. ***to put*** (or ***pile***) ***on lugs***, to put on airs. *U.S. slang.*

1889 K. MUNROE *Golden Days* xvii. 188 If you notice me ..piling on any lugs..you just bump me down hard. **1896** ADE *Artie* vi. 54 The family did n't put on no such lugs in them days. **1903** A. BENNETT *Leonora* iv. 106 American women..put on too much lugs, at any rate for an Englishman. **1905** *Springfield* (Mass.) *Weekly Republ.* 15 Sept. 12 Dr. Hall puts on no 'lugs', and is not above sitting on a cracker barrel in a country grocery for a chat with old acquaintances. **1920** S. LEWIS *Main St.* 326 Oh, the lugs he puts on—belted coat, and piqué collar.

e. A demand for borrowed or exacted money. Esp. in phr. ***to put the lug on***, to extort, to put pressure on. *U.S. slang.*

1929 D. RUNYON in *Hearst's Internat.* Aug. 73/2 Why do you not put the lug on him? **1935** A. J. POLLOCK *Underworld Speaks* 84/2 *Out on the lug*, engaged in begging racket. *Ibid.* 93/1 *Put the lug on*, to borrow; to beat up a racketeer with blackjack or brass knuckles for muscling in on forbidden territory. **1936** *Kansas City* (Missouri) *Star* 15 Oct. 6/1 Indiana uses the 'Lug'. **1938** *Kansas City* (Missouri) *Times* 14 Feb. 1/6 The Democratic organization's lug on all city and county employees—for its campaign fund..has been started. **1940** *Topeka* (Kansas) *State Jrnl.* 26 Mar. 1/8 Shakedowns in Topeka are known to have ranged from $20 to $50 monthly, depending on the amount of illegal business done by the individuals on whom the lug was put. **1973** M. TRUMAN *Harry S. Truman* vii. 129 My father also knew, from his inside contacts with Missouri Democrats, that the governor..was 'putting the lug' (to use Missouri terminology) on state employees to contribute to his campaign fund.

4. *Tobacco trade* (see quots.).

1835 J. MARTIN *New Gazetteer Virginia* 175 An eminent tobacco manufacturer of Richmond has offered the inhabitants of this district to take all of their tobacco, (lugs included) at $10 a hundred. **1851** *Southern Planter* (Richmond, Virginia) June 192/1 We quote lugs $5 25 to $7. **1888** PATON & DITTMAR in *Encycl. Brit.* XXIII. 424/2 The leaves [of tobacco] are..sorted into qualities, such as 'lugs', or lower leaves, 'firsts' and 'seconds'. **1896** P. A. BRUCE *Econ. Hist. Virginia* I. 442 The lowest grade was known as lugs as early as 1686.

5. Chiefly *N. Amer. slang.* Used contemptuously of a person: a lout, a sponger.

1931 *Broadway Brevities* 19 Oct. 2/1 Is his only sin the fact that he was born a lug? **1935** A. J. POLLOCK *Underworld Speaks* 73/2 *Lug*, an incapable person who frequently borrows small sums of money. **1936** R. CHANDLER *Black Mask* June 24/1 The girl snapped at me: 'Is this lug your partner?' **1952** *Landfall* VI. 265 Now there's your sermon! .. No, no, no. These lugs would never understand. **1953** K. TENNANT *Joyful Condemned* xxix. 284 The big fellows slip through my fingers, leaving some tough lug to take the rap. **1968** B. TURNER *Sex Trap* xi. 98 'The other lug's at June's,' Louis said. **1973** *Hansard* (Canada) 20 Mar. 2388/1, I will stand down when Mr. Speaker tells me to, not when you lugs tell me to. **1973** 'B. MATHER' *Snowline* x. 116 Any other names you can come up with?.. You don't owe these lugs anything.

6. *attrib.* and *Comb.*, as (sense 1) ***lug-cap***; (sense 2) ***lug-drum***, ***-trumpet***; (sense 3) ***lug-end***, ***-knee***; **lug-bab** *Sc.*, an ear-drop (cf. BOB *sb.*[1] 3); **lug-bolt**, a cylindrical bolt, to which is welded a flat iron bar (*Cent. Dict.*); **lug-chair**, an easy-chair with side-pieces for the head; **lug-haul** *v.*, to pull by the ears; **lughole** *dial.* and *colloq.*, ear-hole; **lug-knot**, a knot of ribbons worn at the ear; **lug-mark**, *sb.* and *v.* = EAR-MARK; **lug sole** *N. Amer.* (see quot. 1961).

1725 *Cock-laird* in *Orpheus Caledonius*, Craig-claiths, and *lug-babs, And rings twa or three. **1898** *Westm. Gaz.* 4 Mar. 3/1 The black skull cap of silk or cotton, the common *lug-cap [etc.]. **1901** N. MUNRO in *Blackw. Mag.* Mar. 347/1 Humped in his *lug-chair, he would forget his duty. **1865** YOUNG *Pict.* 169 (E.D.D.) The whistlin' and the skirlin'..Rings through ane's *lug-drum like a bullet. **1894** BOTTONE *Electr. Instr. Making* (ed. 6) App. 228 These plates must be perforated all over..to within about $\frac{3}{8}$ in. of the top, or *lug-end. **1829** HOGG *Sheph. Cal.* I. vii. 201 Speak plain out, else I'll have thee *lug-hauled, thou dwarf! **1895** J. S. FLETCHER *Wonderful Wapentake* 72 I'll come..and pelt thi *lughoil for tha. **1898** B. KIRKBY *Lakeland Words* 96 Stuff thi lug-whols wi' woo. **1966** F. SHAW et al. *Lern Yerself Scouse* 20 *Is lugole*, his ear. **1973** *Times* 25 Aug. 10/8 A session with *Hello, Cheeky* is like being exposed to some noisy, rude and unstoppable urchin who wins you round or at least averts a skull-shattering clout about the lughole simply because he will go on regardless. **1874** THEARLE *Naval Archit.* 39 Plate XVI. and fig. 7, show the kind known as *lug knees, the lugs being forged to the knee. **17..** *Muirland Willie* xii. in Ramsay *Tea-t. Misc.* (1788) I. 9 Our bride's maidens were na few, Wi' tap-knots, *lug-knots, a' in blew. **1685** M. SHIELDS *Faithf. Contend.* (1780) 181 Imprisoning,..*lugg-marking, banishing, and killing. **1802** C. FINDLATER *Agric. Surv. Peebles* 191 They [lambs] receive ..marks cut into the ear with a knife, designed lug mark. **1892** *Newcastle Daily Jrnl.* 28 Mar. 5/6 A Northumberland farmer..in identifying a heifer in dispute, stated that he lug-marked it. **1893** CROCKETT *Stickit Minister* etc. 68 Every sentence has got the 'Gallowa' lug-mark' plain on it. **1961** WEBSTER, **Lug sole*, a thick rubber sole that has deep indentations in a pattern designed to provide good footing and is used on sport and work shoes. **1970** *Toronto Daily Star* 24 Sept. 16/2 (Advt.), Heavy duty lug sole. **1830** J. WILSON *Noct. Ambr.* (1864) III. 54 Gin he uses a *lug-trumpet.

†**lug**, *sb.*[3] *Obs.* [Cf. LUG *v.* (sense 3) and *sb.*[7]; also LG. *lug*, Du. *log*, slow, heavy, and LOG *sb.*[1]] Something heavy and clumsy; in quot. applied to a massive bow.

1545 ASCHAM *Toxoph.* I. (Arb.) 28 The other [bowe] is a lugge slowe of cast, folowing the string, more sure for to last, then pleasaunt for to vse. **1565** COOPER *Thesaurus*, *Vastus arcus*, a lugge, or mighty bigge bowe.

lug (lʌg), *sb.*[4] Also 7 **lugg**, 7, 9 **log**. [Cf. prec.; also LURG.] A large marine worm (*Arenicola marina*) which burrows in the sands of our coasts and is much used for bait. Also *Comb.*, as **lug-worm**; **lug-fork** (see quot. 1883).

1602 CAREW *Cornwall* 34 b, The Lugg is a worme resembling the Tag-worme or Angle-touch, and lying in the ose somewhat deepe, from whence the women digge them vp, and sell them to the Fishermen. **1793** *Statist. Acc. Scot.* V. 277 All the above [fish]..are taken with lines baited with mussels and lug. **1802** BINGLEY *Anim. Biog.* (1813) III. 409 Lug-worms are marine animals. **1859** ATKINSON *Walks & Talks* (1892) 315 A sufficient supply of 'log', or the worms found in the sea-sand. **1883** *Fisheries Exhib. Catal.* 13 Lug Fork..used..for digging large Lugworms.

†**lug**, *sb.*[5] *Obs.* [Of obscure origin.
The mod. Cornwall dialect has '*Lugg*, the undergrowth of weed in a field of corn', but the identity of the word is doubtful.]

= FLAG *sb.*[1] 1.

1538 TURNER *Libellus*, Lug, *acorum.* **1859** W. K. CLAY *Waterbeach* 21 Lugs (flags)..made a coarse kind of hay for foddering their cattle in the winter.

lug (lʌg), *sb.*[6] Short for LUG-SAIL. Also *Comb.*, as ***lug-rigged*** adj.; **lug-boat** (see quot. 1867).

1830 MARRYAT *King's Own* xiii, Up with the lugs. **1859** *All Year Round* No. 33. 148 My eye lights..on certain lug-rigged boats bobbing along the waves. These are fishing-boats. **1860** NARES *Seamanship* 100 Sling a dipping lug $\frac{1}{3}$ from the foremost yard arm; standing lug $\frac{1}{4}$. **1867** SMYTH *Sailor's Word-bk.*, *Lug-boat*, the fine Deal boats which brave the severest weather; they are rigged as luggers, and dip the yards in tacking. **1884** H. COLLINGWOOD *Under Meteor Flag* 9 She was jogging easily along under her fore and mizzen lugs and a small jib.

lug (lʌg), *sb.*[7] [f. LUG *v.*] The action of lugging; a rough pull; **b.** *concr.* (*U.S.*) see quot. 1828.

a **1616** BEAUM. & FL. *Nice Valour* III. ii, All but a lugg byth'eare. **1687** MIEGE *Fr. Dict.*, To give one a lug, *tirer l'Oreille à quêcun tout d' un coup.* **1708** *Brit. Apollo* No. 34. 3/2 I'll soundly lug his ears.. The Lug might more be fear'd by you. **1828** WEBSTER, *Lug*,..something heavy to be drawn or carried. (Vulgar.) **1897** WEBSTER, *Lug*, the act of lugging; as, a hard lug; that which is lugged; as, the pack is a heavy lug. (*Colloq.*)

lug (lʌg), *v.* Also 4 **logge**, 4–8 **lugg(e**. [Prob. of Scandinavian origin; cf. Sw. *lugga* to pull a person's hair, f. *lugg* forelock, also nap of cloth.
Normally an ON. **lugg* might be cogn. w. a vb. **loggva*:—OTeut. **lauwan*, represented only by MDu. *lauwen*, *gelauwen* to snatch at, seize.]

1. *trans.* To pull, give a pull to, to pull *by* (the ear, hair, etc.); to tease, worry, bait (a bear, bull, etc.). *Obs.* exc. *dial.*

In South Yorkshire and the adjacent counties the most common use is in the sense 'to pull the hair of (a person)'.

1390 GOWER *Conf.* III. 149 Be the chyn and be the cheke Sche luggeth him riht as hir liste. **1399** LANGL. *Rich. Redeles* II. 173 This lorell that ladde this loby awey..was ffelliche ylauȝte and luggid fful ylle. **1533** J. HEYWOOD *Pardoner & Friar* (1830) B iij, Leue thy railynge..Or by Iys Ish lug the by the swete eares. **1621–23** MIDDLETON & ROWLEY *Changeling* II. i. 81 Like a common Garden-bull, I do but take breath to be lugg'd again. **1647** TRAPP *Comm. Matt.* x. 6 These also [*sc.* swine] when lugged..will hie to their home. **1678** R. L'ESTRANGE *Seneca's Mor.* (1702) 242 He was Lugg'd and Tumbled by the Rabble. **1682** OTWAY *Venice Pres.* III. i. Wks. 1727 II. 298 I'll have my Footmen lug you, you Cur. **1693** DRYDEN *Persius Sat.* i. 277 To see a Strumpet tear A Cynick's Beard, and lug him by the Hair. *c* **1720** POPE *Let. to Earl Burlington* Wks. 1737 VI. 20 Mr. Lintott lugg'd the reins, stopt short, and broke out, 'Well Sir, how far have you gone?' **1775** *Francis Lett.* (1901) I. 231 Some with Pincers pulling out their own Beards, and Lugging their Ears. **1805** W. TAYLOR in *Ann. Rev.* III. 64 The dog..still fawns on the master who is lugging his ears. **1833** MARRYAT *P. Simple* xxviii, So saying, he lugged me by the ear, upon which I knocked him down for his trouble.

2. *intr.* To pull, tug. Of a horse: To press heavily *on* (the bit or reins).

a **1375** *Lay Folks Mass Bk.* App. iv. 350 Wiþ his teth anon He logged þat al in synder gon lasch. *a* **1550** *Christis Kirke Gr.* vii, Lord, than how they luggit! **1598** *Hakluyt's Voy.* (1599) I. 601 This huge and monstrous galliasse, wherein were contained three hundred slaues to lug at the oares. **1876** BROWNING *Pacchiarotto* xxi, A whip awaits shirkers and shufflers Who slacken their pace, sick of lugging At what don't advance for their tugging. **1894** CROCKER *Educ. Horse* 57 A colt thoroughly bitted with this bridle will never lug on the reins. *Ibid.* 133 A horse that lugs on the bit.

†**b.** To take a pull *at* (liquor, the breast). Also *trans.* To pull at (the breast). *Obs.*

1577 HARRISON *England* II. xviii. (1877) I. 295 How our maltbugs lug at this liquor. *a* **1591** H. SMITH *Serm.* (1622) 467 When we have lugged the brest almost drie. **1615** CROOKE *Body of Man* 969 That he might cease to be trouble-some to his mother, and not lie alwaies lugging at her brests. **1617** J. MOORE *Twofold Cord Consolat.* ii. 43 The brests of the world, (which we alwayes would be lugging).

c. To move *about*, *along*, heavily and slowly; to drag. *rare* now only *techn.*

In South Yorkshire, etc. a comb is said to 'lug' when it meets with resistance in passing through the hair.

13.. *E.E. Allit. P.* B. 443 As þat lyftande lome [*sc.* the Ark] luged aboute. **1690** DRYDEN *Don Sebastian* IV. i, My flagging Soul flyes under her own pitch, Like Fowl in air too damp, and lugs along, As if she were a body in a body. **1841** SAVAGE *Dict. Printing* 446 When balls stick together in distributing they are said to lug. **1888** JACOBI *Printers' Vocab.* 78 When rollers are tacky or stick together they are said to lug.

3. *trans.* To pull along with violent effort; to drag, tug (something heavy). Also with *advs.* (cf. 5). † ***to lug forth***, absol. (nonce-use) = *to lug out* (5 b).

c **1400** *Destr. Troy* 11029 þe Mirmydons,..Lepyn to þere lord, lugget hym away. *Ibid.* 12323 The lady þat the lede lugget of þe toure. **1565** COOPER *Thesaurus* s.v. *Cœnum*, *Ineluctabile cœnum*, out of whiche one can not lugge his legges. **1577** HANMER *Anc. Eccl. Hist.* (1619) 114 They lugged me foorth and carried me away. **1682** DRYDEN *Epil. to King & Queen* 31 Think on your souls; but by your lugging forth, It seems you know how little they are worth. **1684** EARL ROSCOMMON *Ess. Transl. Verse* (1709) 180 There Sweat, there Strain, there lug the laborious Oar. **1719** DE FOE *Crusoe* I. xiii, I lugged this Money home to my Cave, and laid it up. **1728** MORGAN *Algiers* II. iv. 291 The Turkish Admiral..caused his Janizaries..to lug along all the heavy Artillery, in Slings, on their Shoulders. **1782** CHARL. A. BURNEY *Jrnl.* 15 Jan. in *Mad. D'Arblay's Early Diary*, Mr. Seward came up..lugging a chair into the middle of the room for me. **1835** W. IRVING *Tour Prairies* 332 She lugged from the fire a huge iron pot. **1898** A. BALFOUR *To Arms* viii. 90, I was lugged headlong up a steep stair.

b. *colloq.* with a hyperbolical suggestion of ponderousness in the object.

1652 CULPEPPER *Eng. Physic.* 260 It is..more convenient ..than to lug a Galli-pot along with him. **1717** POPE *Let. to Lady M. W. Montagu* Oct. in *M. W. M.'s Lett.* (1887) I. 306 Allow me..to lug an old *busto* behind you, and I shall be proud beyond expression. **1747** H. WALPOLE *Lett. H. Mann* (1834) II. 196 The Countess used to lug a half-length picture..behind her postchaise. **1871** L. STEPHEN *Playgr. Eur.* i. (1894) 8 Boswell..succeeded in lugging him [Johnson] into the wilds of the Highlands. **1874** HELPS *Soc.*

Press. vii. 91 And how can you expect that a man who is being lugged forward [etc.]. **1896** NEWNHAM-DAVIS *Three Men* etc. 14 His wife lugged it [a marble god] down here with her yesterday.

4. *fig.* To introduce in a forced manner, or irrelevantly; = DRAG *v.* 2.

1721 AMHERST *Terræ Fil.* (1754) App. 320 There is scarcely an enormity in the university, which you have not luggd-in. **1774** MAD. D'ARBLAY *Let. to Mr. Crisp* Apr. in *Early Diary*, In Raphael's School of Athens..I like his picture of the..Dwarf, which for fun and spite he lugg'd by head and shoulders into that fine composition. **1901** *Scotsman* 1 Mar. 5/3 Counsel for the other side had lugged in every thing he could to prejudice the case.

5. lug out. a. *trans.* See prec. senses and *out*.

c **1400** *Destr. Troy* 6663 Weghis of his aune Luggit hym out to þe laund. **1722** DE FOE *Col. Jack* (1840) 12 The major lugged out the goods. **1840** THACKERAY *Catherine* vi, Mr. Brock lugged out five guineas. **1840** —— *Paris Sk.-bk.* (1869) 178 The little fellow was obliged to lug out his sword. **1889** J. K. JEROME *Three Men in Boat* 23 You land and lug out the tent.

fig. **1755** *Barnaby Bright's New Jrnl.* 3, I thought of.. lugging out my florid style, which I keep by me for Holidays. **1891** *Speaker* 2 May 532/2 The *Quarterly* reviewer also lugs out again that 'very ancient and fish-like' fallacy which distinguishes between duties and rights.

b. *absol.* or *intr.* To draw one's sword; to pull out money or a purse. Now only *arch.* †Also *fig.*, To launch out in talk.

1684 DRYDEN *Prol. to 'Disappointment'* 62 They caterwaul,..Call sons of whores, and strike, but ne'er lug out. **1700** *Step to the Bath* (ed. 2) 4 They call'd for a Bill, which was presently brought; out I lugg'd, and was going to Discharge, but [etc.]. **1748** SMOLLETT *Rod. Rand.* (1760) I. iv. 17 My poor uncle..was obliged to lug out in his own defence. **1787** *Minor* IV. v. 214, I lugged out in the most feeling manner on my sad situation. **1826** SCOTT *Woodst.* xxv, Put up both of you, or I shall lug out as thirdsman. **1854** W. COLLINS *Hide & Seek* I. ix. 287 If the patrons of art don't lug out handsomely to get..that picture ——. **1889** DOYLE *Micah Clark* 75, I..might have had more, had that young fool not lugged out at me.

†**6.** *intr.* ? To draw swords (= *lug out*, 5 b); or ? to tussle. *Obs.*

1605 *1st Pt. Ieronimo* III. ii. 121 Lug with him, boy; honors in bloud best swim.

lug, obs. Sc. form of LODGE *sb.*

lugage, obs. form of LUGGAGE.

lug-aleaf. *Cornish dial.* ? *Obs.* = BRILL *sb.*[1]

1686 RAY *Willoughby's Hist. Pisc.* IV. iii. 95 *Rhombus non aculeatus squamosus*... Lug-aleaf *Cornubiensibus.* *a* **1705** —— *Syn. Pisc.* (1713) 31 The Pearl *Londinensibus, Cornubiensibus* Lug-aleaf. **1740** R. BROOKES *Art Angling* 116 Of the Pearl or Lug-Aleaf.

Luganda (l(j)uːˈgændə). A language of the Bantu group, spoken in Uganda.

1889 R. P. ASHE *Two Kings of Uganda* p. ix, Buganda is the country itself, '*Muganda*' a native of the country, '*Baganda*' the plural of '*Muganda*', and '*Luganda*' is the language. **1902** *Encycl. Brit.* XXXIII. 541/2 The languages spoken in the Uganda Protectorate belong to the following stocks:—... *Bantu* (Lu-Ganda, [etc.]). **1933** L. BLOOMFIELD *Lang.* iv. 67 The languages of the Bantu family,..are very numerous,..; among the better known are *Luganda*, [etc.]. **1955** *Times* 6 July 8/3 Similar statements have been prevalent in Luganda newspapers and in the resolutions of some district councils outside Buganda. **1966** B. KIMENYE *Kalasanda Revisited* 15 His Luganda was spoken with a sharp accent. **1971** *Guardian* 22 Apr. 10/3 He was brought up at Bombo in Buganda and speaks excellent Luganda.

Lugbara (lʊgˈbɑːrə), *sb.* and *a.* Also **Logbara, Lugbware, Lugwari. A.** *sb.* **a.** A people inhabiting the border area of Uganda and Zaïre; a member of this people. **b.** The Sudanic language of this people. **B.** *adj.* Of or pertaining to this people.

1925 R. E. MCCONNELL in *Jrnl. R. Anthrop. Inst.* LV. 439 The Lugwari Tribe of the West Nile District of Uganda does not seem to have been described, so I venture to record some notes. *Ibid.* 442 Though not aggressive, The Lugwari are a fearless and warlike people in defence. *Ibid.* 448 The Lugwari women very usually wear large clumsy iron rings around their ankles. **1932** C. G. & B. Z. SELIGMAN *Pagan Tribes Nilotic Sudan* viii. 282 Rain-stones..said to be of Bari origin..taken from the Lugbware some years previously. **1933–5** A. N. TUCKER in *Bull. Sch. Oriental Stud.* VII. 868 The Lugbara (also called 'Lugwari') live in the North-East Congo..and extend into the West Nile District of Uganda. **1935** THOMAS & SCOTT *Uganda* v. 86 Languages of the Moru-Madi group [are spoken] by the Lugbara..and Lendu..of the West Nile. **1953** TROWELL & WACHSMANN *Tribal Crafts Uganda* i. 57 The Madi and Lugbara smoke their tobacco in a water-cooled pipe with a small clay bowl. **1959** *Chambers's Encycl.* XIII. 257/1 Sudanic languages... Sudan-Nile (Lugbara, Logo, Lendu, Baka in Belgian Congo and the Sudan). **1960** J. P. CRAZZOLARA (*title*) A study of the Logbara, Ma'di, language, grammar and vocabulary. **1971** *Sunday Nation* (Nairobi) 11 Apr. 14/2 On January 25, 1971, a modestly educated Lugbara voice haltingly read out to the nation eighteen reasons why the army had taken over power. **1974** *Guardian* 26 Mar. 1 Amin's recent policy of cracking down on Lugbara officers. *Ibid.*, Ondoga was a Lugbara from the western Nile.

lugdor(re, variant of LOCKDOR *Obs.*, woodlouse.

14.. *Voc.* in *Promp. Parv.* 311 *note*, Multipes, lugdorre.

luge (luːʒ), *sb.* [Swiss dialect.] A sledge, of Swiss origin, of the bob-sleigh type. Also *attrib.*

1905 *Sci. Amer.* Suppl. 15 Apr. 24488/1 The 'luge' is a small sled peculiar to the Grisons. **1907** *Ladies' Field* 19 Jan. 278 On the ascent the luge flies straight up into the air. **1919** *Daily Mail* 10 Dec., (*caption*) A pair of winter holiday-makers in Switzerland enjoying a run on a Canadian luge. **1968** *Globe & Mail* (Toronto) 13 Jan. 41/4 Canada's luge team..will be announced Monday. The Canadian luge championships are scheduled Sunday.

Hence **luge** *v. intr.*, to toboggan on a luge. Also **ˈlugeing, ˈluging** *vbl. sb.*, **ˈluger**.

1907 *Ladies' Field* 19 Jan. 278 The gentle art of Luging... Les Avants is the most obvious place from which to luge... Caux is the only other [place] where lugers assemble in force. **1909** *Westm. Gaz.* 26 Jan. 5/2 Les Avants..has one of the finest natural luging courses in Europe. **1924** *Yorksh. Post* 28 Jan. 10/7 There is good curling, bob sleighing, and lugeing. **1927** *Daily Express* 28 Dec. 3/1 Youths..'luged' in a reckless, haphazard style.

luge, obs. Sc. form of LODGE *sb.* and *v.*

luge(i)ng, obs. form of LODGING *vbl. sb.*

lugent (ˈl(j)uːdʒənt), *a.* *rare*$^{-0}$. [ad. L. *lūgent-em*, pr. pple. f. *lūgēre* to mourn.] **a.** Weeping. **b.** (See quot. 1889.)

1656 in BLOUNT *Glossogr.* **1889** *Syd. Soc. Lex.*, *Lugent*, weeping. Applied to plants with drooping branches.

Luger (ˈluːgə(r)). Also (erron.) **Lueger, Lüger.** The name of G. *Luger*, German firearms expert, used *attrib.* or *absol.* to designate a German type of automatic pistol. Cf. PARABELLUM.

1904 W. B. WALLACE *Text Bk. Small Arms* 178 The Borchardt Leuger or 'Parabellum' automatic pistol belongs to Class I. **1912** H. M. RIDEOUT *William Jones* 139 For arms he carried only a Luger pistol. **1933** 'P. CAIN' *Fast One* 229 Faber lifted the flap of the right side pocket, slipped a black Luger out onto the seat beside him. **1934** D. TEILHET *Talking Sparrow Murders* ii. 34 A short Lüger thudded to the floor. **1947** *Landfall* I. 264 He held a Lueger pistol. **1957** 'D. RUTHERFORD' *Long Echo* viii. 159 He picked up the Luger and began to extract the magazine. **1961** *Sunday Express* 12 Mar. 17/8 Two middle-aged men..shoot at one another, one with a Luger and the other with a ·38. **1970** R. A. STEINDLER *Firearms Dict.* 171/2 s.v. *Pistole Parabellum*. The name of Georg Luger has been linked to the gun to such an extent that the gun is often simply called the 'Luger'. **1975** P. SOMERVILLE-LARGE *Couch of Earth* iii. 39, I would have expected..a Luger or a Walther.

luggage (ˈlʌgɪdʒ). Also 7 loggage, luggadge, -edge, lugage. [f. LUG *v.* + -AGE.]

1. a. †In early use: What has to be lugged about; inconveniently heavy baggage (*obs.*). Also, the baggage of an army. Now, in Great Britain, the ordinary word for: The baggage belonging to a traveller or passenger, esp. by a public conveyance.

1596 NASHE *Saffron Walden* F 1 b, I hearing the fellow so forlorne and out of comfort with his luggage, gaue him his *Charons Naulum* or ferry three half pence, & so dismist him to go to the place from whence he came. **1596** SHAKS. *1 Hen. IV*, v. iv. 160 Come bring your luggage Nobly on your backe. **1609** ARMIN *Two Maids More-clacke* A 2 [*Stage-direct.*] Enter two watermen with luggedge. **1615** BEDWELL *Moham. Imp.* II. §90 The pilgrimes do stay, and dispose of their..luggage where they meane to rest themselues. **1631** in *Crt. & Times Chas. I* (1848) II. 127 The residue..taken prisoners, with all their..luggage. **1665** GLANVILL *Def. Vain Dogm.* p. xii, If the Luggage be prized equally with the Jewels, none will be cast out, till all be lost and shipwrack't. **1726** SWIFT *Gulliver* II. ii, We had no other Company but a Boy of the House, who rode after us with the Luggage. **1827** R. NESBIT in *Mem.* (1858) ii. 47, I got all my heavy luggage on board. **1851** GALLENGA *Italy* 489 Heavy losses of cannon, ammunition, and luggage. **1902** *Blackw. Mag.* Oct. 464/1 The ladder-cart is loaded with luggage.

b. *fig.* and in figurative contexts.

1612 DONNE *Progr. of Soul, Harbinger* 9 No soule—whiles with the luggage of this clay It clogged is—can follow thee halfe way. **1687** DRYDEN *Hind & P.* III. 1033 A lively faith will bear aloft the mind And leave the luggage of good works behind. **1776** G. CAMPBELL *Philos. Rhet.* (1801) II. 356 The luggage of particles such as pronouns, prepositions and auxiliary verbs clogs the expression. **1820** LAMB *Elia* Ser. I. *Two Races Men*, Getting rid of the cumbersome luggage of riches. **1876** GEO. ELIOT *Dan. Der.* lxii. IV. 224 The continued visit of that familiar sorrow which had lately come back, bringing abundant luggage.

†**c.** Goods in general. *Obs.* *rare*$^{-1}$.

1624 CAPT. SMITH *Virginia* 54 Powhatan..presented him with twentie Turkies... Now..he presented Captaine Smith with the like luggage.

2. †**a.** With *a*. An encumbrance (*obs.*). **b.** *pl.* *nonce-use* = IMPEDIMENTA.

1614 RALEIGH *Hist. World* III. (1634) 52 Those uncountable multitudes..are..rather a luggage than an aide. **1629** SHIRLEY *Wedding* v. ii, My mis-fortune made mee thinke..My very soule a luggage. **1693** LISTER in *Phil. Trans.* XVII. 643 Why should the Shell it self be brought, an useless Luggage so far. **1864** CARLYLE *Fredk. Gt.* IV. 8 His whole army with its luggages.

†**3.** The quality or condition of having to be lugged; heavy weight. *Obs.*

1667 *Observ. Burning Lond.* in *Select. Harl. Misc.* (1793) 445 Four commodities, which, for their luggage and cumbersomeness, could not be rescued from the jaws of that unmerciful element, that is, wine, tobacco, spices, and books.

4. *attrib.* and *Comb.*, as ***luggage-boat, -boot, -carrier, -grid, -label, -porter, -rack, -rest, -ticket, train, -van***; **luggage locker**, a locker (sense 5) at a railway station, air terminal, etc., for use by passengers.

1720 DE FOE *Capt. Singleton* xii. (1840) 206 He sent him.., in a great *luggage-boat, a cow. **1837** CARLYLE *Fr. Rev.* III. IV. ii, A leathern Diligence, with its post-bags and *luggage-boots [etc.]. **1972** *Country Life* 7 Dec. 1592/3 The luggage boot is..fairly well filled by the spare wheel. **1760–72** H. BROOKE *Fool of Qual.* (1809) III. 64 The burden of the *luggage-carriers was..lightened. **1907** *Westm. Gaz.* 12 Feb. 4/2 A telescopic *luggage-grid capable of taking heavy trunks. **1928** Luggage grid [see GRID 9]. **1969** *Guardian* 21 Aug. 9/6 The dreary rows of *luggage lockers. **1971** M. KELLY *25th Hour* i. 9, I drove to the main station ..and..I put my case in a luggage locker. **1901** *Daily Chron.* 2 Oct. 9/3 Joseph Durisch, *luggage porter at the Walsingham House Hotel. **1905** *Daily Chron.* 18 May 4/5 Holding on..to the *luggage-rack in the narrow..boxes which serve for [train] compartments. **1928** *Chambers's Jrnl.* Jan. 21/2 Just below the luggage-rack is an indicator by which the passenger may control the amount of steam entering the radiator. **1973** C. WILLIAMS *Man on Leash* (1974) i. 5 The room was cool... He dropped the bag on a luggage rack. **1941** 'N. BLAKE' *Case of Abominable Snowman* viii. 83 That *luggage-rest..at the end of the bed. **1898** H. S. MERRIMAN *Roden's Corner* xxiii. 231 Give your *luggage ticket to the hotel porter. **1846** R. FORD *Gatherings from Spain* v. 49 A handful of opponents..may..burn the engines.., particularly smashing the *luggage train. **1853** *Mechanics' Mag.* LVIII. 394 To indicate..the class of the train that had last passed, whether ordinary, express, or luggage. **1899** O. WILDE *Importance of being Earnest* III. 127 Apprised, sir, of my daughter's sudden flight.., I followed her at once by a luggage train. **1876** GEO. ELIOT *Dan. Der.* xxxv. III. 23 Like the sprite of ill-luck you..see grinning at you from the top of your *luggage-van.

Hence **ˈluggaged** *ppl. a.*, loaded with luggage; †**ˈluggaging** *vbl. sb.*, carrying luggage.

1691 J. WILSON *Belphegor* III. i, My Back's almost broke with Luggaging. *a* **1847** ELIZA COOK *Rhymes by Roadside* i, We're losing fast the luggaged roof, The whistling guard and ringing hoof.

luggageless (ˈlʌgɪdʒlɪs), *a.* [f. LUGGAGE + -LESS.] Without luggage.

1855 *Chamb. Jrnl.* III. 177, I was taking a short, harmless, luggageless journey. **1887** *Bicycling News* 27 Aug. 327/1 He arrived at the Royal Oak luggageless.

luggar (ˈlʌgə(r)). Also **lugger, luggur.** [Hindī *laggar.*] = JUGGER (properly, the female bird).

1893 NEWTON *Dict. Birds* 522 Luggar, the *Falco juggur* of ornithology.

†**ˈluggard.** *Obs.* [f. LUG *v.* + -ARD.] One who moves heavily; a sluggard. (Cf. LAGGARD.)

a **1529** SKELTON *Dyties Solacyous* 26 Behold, thou lyeste, luggard, alone! **1847** in HALLIWELL.

lugge, obs. form of LUG.

lugged (lʌgd), *ppl. a.*[1] [f. LUG *v.* + -ED[1].] Pulled by the ears. Of a bear: Baited.

1596 SHAKS. *1 Hen. IV*, I. ii. 84, I am as Melancholly as a Gyb-Cat, or a lugg'd Beare. **1598** BP. HALL *Sat.* IV. i. 72 His ears hang laving, like a new-lug'd swine. **1605** SHAKS. *Lear* IV. ii. 42 (1st Qo. 1608), A gracious aged man, Whose reuerence euen the head-lugd beare would lick. **1654** GAYTON *Pleas. Notes* II. v. 52 You know how pitifully a lugg'd sow looks. **1851** MRS. MARSH *Ravenscliffe* II. i. 10 He was..as surly as a lugged bear.

lugged, *ppl. a.*[2] *Obs.* exc. *dial.* Also 5 lwgyt, 6 lugde, lowgit, 6, 9 lug'd, luggit, 8 lugget. [f. LUG *sb.*[2] + -ED[2].] Having 'lugs' or ears.

1489 *Ld. Treas. Acc. Scotl.* (1877) I. 146 Item, the xxij da of Fabruar, for a lwgyt cap and a bonat to the king, price xxxjs. **1535** *Aberd. Reg.* XV. 674 (Jam.), vj lowgit dischis of pewtyr. **1594–5** *Inventory* in *Archæologia* XLVIII. 132 Item ij copper lugde pannes ijs. vjd. **1598** MARSTON *Sco. Villanie* III. x. H 7 b, The long fooles coate, the huge slop, the lugg'd boot From mimick Piso, all doe claime their roote. **1718** RAMSAY *Christ's Kirk Gr.* III. xxi, Hutchon with a three-lugged cap. *a* **1779** D. GRAHAM *Writings* (1883) II. 142 Ye see the hens turns ay red lugget or they begin to lay. **1786** BURNS *Scotch Drink* x, O rare! to see thee fizz an' freath I' th' lugget caup! **1834** H. MILLER *Scenes & Leg.* xix. (1857) 281 Send one of your companions for your lugged water-stoup.

luggee (lʌˈgiː). *nonce-wd.* [f. LUG *v.* + -EE.] One who is lugged or pulled.

1830 GREVILLE *Mem. Geo. IV* (1875) I. ix. 350 The luggee holds by this tackle, and the guide goes before him.

luggen, obs. form of LIE *v.*[1]

luggenis, obs. Sc. pl. of LODGING *vbl. sb.*

lugger (ˈlʌgə(r)), *sb.*[1] [f. LUG *v.* + -ER[1].] One who lugs; spec. an oarsman who depends on mere strength. Also in ***beef, ship lugger***.

1611 COTGR., *Tireur*, a drawer, puller,..lugger, tugger. **1881** *Daily News* 14 Feb. 5/5 His Australian competitor, though by no means such a mere 'lugger' as his country-man Trickett, trusts much less to..mechanical finish. **1904** *Sun* (N.Y.) 5 Aug. 1 It was reported that beef luggers in all the cold storage plants were to be called out. *Ibid.* 11 Aug. 3 The men who are called ship luggers, and who load meat aboard the steamships.

lugger (ˈlʌgə(r)), *sb.*[2] [perh. f. *lug* in LUGSAIL; but cf. Du. *logger*, perh. f. MDu. *loggen, luggen* to fish with a drag-net.] **a.** (See quot. 1867.)

1757 *Gentl. Mag.* Jan. 45/2 On the 25th inst. a French lugger drove a vessel ashore at Hastings. **1795** *Hull Advertiser* 25 July 2/4. **1809** J. ADAMS *Wks.* (1854) IX. 317 In a general impressment..it cost the nation, in cutters, luggers, press-gangs,..a hundred pounds for every man they obtained. **1817** W. IRVING in *Life & Lett.* (1864) I. 385 He..is as slow getting under way, as a Dutch lugger. **1837** MARRYAT *Dog-fiend* xxx, The lugger pulled eighteen oars, was clinker built, and very swift. **1867** SMYTH *Sailor's Word-bk.*, *Lugger*, a small vessel with..four-cornered cut sails, set fore and aft, and [*sic*] may have two or three masts.

1884 PAE *Eustace* 217, I am captain of the lugger you see yonder.

b. *attrib.* (*appositive*) and *Comb.*

1801 NELSON in A. Duncan *Life* (1806) 194 Flats (lugger-rigged). **1819** J. H. VAUX *Mem.* I. 70 A beautiful French lugger privateer, of fourteen guns.

†'lugger, *v. Obs.* [f. LUG *v.* + -ER^{5}.] *trans.* **a.** To drag or carry about. **b.** To tease.

1654 FLECKNOE *Ten Years Trav.* 78 Apes which had young, with 2 or 3 claspt about their neck,..which they went thus luggering, till [etc.]. **1679** CROWNE *Ambit. Statesman* III. 32 When e're I see Authority Lugger a heavy fool upon her sholders Before me. **1782** ELIZ. BLOWER *Geo. Bateman* II. 174 The child don't like to lugger folks.

luggerheaded, obs. form of LOGGERHEADED.

luggie ('lʌgɪ). *Sc.* [f. LUG *sb.*^{2} + -IE.] A small wooden vessel with a 'lug' or handle.

1725 RAMSAY *Gentle Sheph.* III. ii, Beech luggies mingle, On skelfs forgainst the door. **1785** BURNS *Halloween* xxxii, In order on the clean hearth-stane, The luggies three are ranged. **1876** C. GIBBON *R. Gray* xxxvii, Two strapping lassies..preparing the luggies..for the evening's milk. **1901** R. ANDERSON *Hist. Kilsyth* iv. 30 There were 'luggies' in the morning filled with porridge.

lugging ('lʌgɪŋ), *vbl. sb.* [f. LUG *v.* + -ING^{1}.] The action of the vb. LUG.

?*a* **1500** *Chester Pl.* vii. 212 On this loyne thou may have good lugging. **1523** SKELTON *Garl. Laurel* 1309 With myghty luggyng..He pluckid the bull By the hornid scull. **1614** MARKHAM *Cheap. Husb.* v. xiii. (1668) 105 The lugging of Swine with Dogs.

lugging ('lʌgɪŋ), *ppl. a.* [f. LUG *v.* + -ING^{2}.] That moves slowly and heavily. (Cf. LUG *v.* 2 c.)

1816 W. TAYLOR in *Monthly Mag.* XLI. 527 The lugging baggage-waggons oxen drag.

luggis, obs. Sc. pl. of LODGE *sb.*

†'luggish, *a. Obs.* [? f. LUG *v.* + -ISH.] ? Miserly.

1684-5 WOOD *Life* 1 Jan., Verie rich, having been alwaies of a covetuous and luggish disposition.

lugin, obs. form of LODGING *vbl. sb.*

†'luginar. *Sc. Obs.* [f. *lugin* LODGING *vbl. sb.* + -AR, -ER^{1}.] One who lets lodgings.

1503 *Sc. Acts Jas. IV* (1814) II. 243/1 All prowest & balȝeis..avis wt þar luginaris & hostillaris w'in þar bondis anent þe lugin.

luging, obs. form of LODGING *vbl. sb.*

lugis, obs. pl. of LODGE *sb.*

lugit, obs. Sc. pa. t. and pa. pple. of LODGE *v.*

†lug-loaf. *a.* (? or *sb.*) *Obs.* [f. LUG *v.*]

1606 *Wily Beguiled* (1623) E4b, Shee had little reason to take a Cullian lug-loafe, milke sop slaue When she may haue a Lawyer.

Lugol ('lu:gɒl). [The name of Jean *Lugol* (1786–1851), French physician.] ***Lugol's iodine, solution,*** a solution of 5% iodine and 10% potassium iodide in water, which is used for the internal administration of iodine and as a biological stain.

1880 P. SQUIRE *Compan. Brit. Pharmacopœia* (ed. 12) 177 (*heading*) Lugol's solution. **1917** *Jrnl. Pharmacol.* IX. 363 The increase in resistance to Lugol's solution did not go beyond three times. **1948** L. MARTIN *Clin. Endocrinol.* iv. 83 If thyroidectomy be chosen for a case of thyrotoxic heart failure, it is best to secure the maximum improvement possible with strict rest in bed, digitalis, and the mercurial diuretics before giving Lugol's iodine. **1961** *Lancet* 23 Sept. 688/1, 30 minims Lugol's iodine were administered intravenously during the night. **1972** *Acta Path. & Microbiol. Scand.* A. LXXX. 185 The substance displays some properties similar to those of classic amyloid, such as ..responsiveness to methyl-violet, iodine green and Lugol's solution.

lugre, obs. form of LIGURE.

'lug-sail. [Formation uncertain: perh. f. LUG *v.* or LUG *sb.*^{2}] A four-cornered sail, bent upon a yard which is slung at about one-third or one-fourth of its length from one end, and so hangs obliquely. Also *attrib.*

1677 *Lond. Gaz.* No. 1194/4 She is open in the Midships, and sails with a Lugsail, and one Topsail. **1769** FALCONER *Dict. Marine* (1789), *Voile de Fortune*, the square or lug sail of a galley or tartane. **1799** *Naval Chron.* I. 214 A lug-sail boat from Calais. **1892** STEVENSON *Across the Plains* 212 The boats with their reefed lugsails scudding for the harbour mouth.

†lugubre, *a. Obs.* [a. F. *lugubre*, ad. L. *lūgubris*, f. *lūgēre* to mourn.] Lugubrious.

1727 LADY M. W. MONTAGU *Let. to C'tess Mar* July, You see my philosophy is not so lugubre as yours. **1835** J. ROMILLY *Diary* 26 Feb. (1967) 69 In a fly..to drink tea with Mrs Clarkson..the affair most lugubre.

lugubriosity (l(j)u:gju:brɪ'ɒsɪtɪ). *rare.* [f. L. *lūgubri-s* + -OSITY.] Mournfulness.

1840 *Tait's Mag.* VII. 259 Our Church music is.. characterized by a long-drawn funereal lugubriosity. **1846** WORCESTER cites *Q. Rev.*

lugubrious (l(j)u:'gju:brɪəs), *a.* [f. as prec. + -OUS.] Characterized by, expressing or causing mourning; doleful, mournful, sorrowful.

1601 DENT *Pathw. Heaven* (1831) 305 The sea shall roar and make a noise in most doleful and lugubrious manner. **1639** HAMMOND *Pastors Motto* Wks. 1684 IV. 546 To act no passionate, lugubrious, tragical part. **1792** MARY WOLLSTONECR. *Rights Wom.* vi. 267 The severe graces of Virtue must have a lugubrious appearance to them. **1847** LEWES *Hist. Philos.* (1867) II. 567 A grotesque and lugubrious farce was played on the day of his quitting the establishment. **1877** BLACK *Green Past.* xxi. (1878) 173 The enforced silence of the room was rather a painful and lugubrious business. **1900** *Q. Rev.* July 113 The lugubrious fresco in the Campo Santo at Pisa.

Hence **lu'gubriously** *adv.*, **lu'gubriousness.**

1848 WEBSTER, *Lugubriously.* **1860** GEN. P. THOMPSON *Audi Alt.* III. cxv. 49 It points lugubriously to the fact, that the ways of dishonour are not always ways of pleasantness. **1879** R. H. ELLIOT *Written on Foreheads* I. 16 They did not cultivate lugubriousness in general. **1900** H. W. SMYTH *Greek Melic Poets* 389 Some of his [Bacchylides'] lugubriousness is no doubt mere literary veneer.

†lu'gubrous, *a. Obs.* [f. L. *lūgubr-is* + -OUS.] = LUGUBRIOUS.

1632 J. HAYWARD tr. *Biondi's Eromena* 54 Windowes shut up with cloath curtaines, to make the ceremonies seeme more lugubrous. **1664** EVELYN tr. *Freart's Archit.* Ep. Ded. 14, I onely had the affliction to be present at the lugubrous Object. **1708** OZELL tr. *Boileau's Lutrin* iv. (1730) 177 Now the lugubrous Instrument resounds, And every Ear with hideous Clangor wounds. [In some mod. Dicts.]

Lugwari, var. LUGBARA *sb.* and *a.*

lug-worm: see LUG *sb.*^{4}

Luian, var. LUVIAN *sb.* and *a.*

luidore, obs. form of LOUIS D'OR.

luif(e, luif(f, obs. forms of LOOF *sb.*^{1}, LUFF.

luif(f)ar, obs. form of LOVER^{1}.

luifsum, obs. Sc. form of LOVESOME.

Luing (lɪŋ). [Name of an island in the Hebrides.] The name giv..ı to cattle evolved from a crossing of the beef shorthorn and Highland breeds. (See quots. 1970.)

1970 *Times* 8 July 2/4 The Luing (pronounced Ling) bred from the Highland and the Beef Shorthorn, confined itself to the new commercial cattle section... Some purists have queried whether it is..a breed within the strict meaning of the term. **1970** *Radio Times* 24–30 Oct. 51/1 The three Cadzow brothers..had to create the first new beef cattle breed for nearly two centuries—Luing cattle. To accomplish their task they turned the Hebridean island of Luing into a huge experimental ranch. **1971** *Country Life* 6 May (Suppl.) 32b, 87 arable acres support the hill flock and herd of pedigree Luing. **1972** *Field* 7 Dec. 1352 (*caption*) A new breed of beef cattle, the Luing. The breed was evolved by the Cadzow brothers..on the island of that name in the Inner Hebrides... The Luing is based on beef Shorthorn *x* Highland.

Luiseño (lu:i:'seɪnjəʊ). Also **San Luiseño.** [Sp., f. *San Luis Rey*, a mission established in S. California in 1798.] The name, orig. San Luiseño, given to a Shoshone Indian people; a member of this people or the language spoken by them. Also *attrib.* or as *adj.*

1858 *Daily Even. Bulletin* (San Francisco) 5 Nov., The true native Americans of the wild forests—such as the Yumas,..San Luiseños,..predominate. **1875** H. H. BANCROFT *Native Races Pacific States* I. iv. 460 The villages of the San Luiseños are in a section of country adjacent to the Cahuillas. **1884** H. H. JACKSON *Ramona* 244 In the Luiseno tongue that is Majel. **1965** R. F. SPENCER et al. *Native Americans* vi. 263/1 The Luiseño myth of their origins revealed a surprising loftiness of concept. *Ibid.* 264/2 These events have combined to substantially eliminate the Luiseño as an ethnic and cultural group. **1965** *Canad. Jrnl. Ling.* Spring 139 The Luiseno sub-branch of languages in South-western California.

luite, variant of LITE *sb.*^{4}, little.

†lu'ition. *Obs. rare*$^{-0}$. [ad. L. *luitiōn-em*, n. of action f. *luĕre* to pay.] Payment of a ransom.

1656 BLOUNT *Glossogr.*, *Luition*, a paying a ransome.

luiver, obs. form of LOVER^{1}.

lujula. *Obs.* [a. It. *lugliola*, f. *Luglio* JULY.] An old name of Wood Sorrel, *Oxalis Acetosella.*

1651 BIGGS *New Disp.* ⁋166 So also vegetables may assume a vitriolate energy, as Lujula, Limons, succory. **1657** W. COLES *Adam in Eden* cxxiii. 179 It [Wood-Sorrel] is called by the Apothecaries in their Shops, Alleluja and Lujula..the other [name] came corruptly from Juliola, as they of Calabria in Naples do call it. **1687** CLAYTON in *Phil. Trans.* XLI. 152 The Sorrel-tree bears a Leaf something like a Laurel, in Taste much resembling Lujula.

luk, obs. f. LOOK *v.*, LUCK; var. LOUK *v.*^{1} *Obs.*

Lukan, var. LUCAN *a.*

Lukanism ('l(j)u:kənɪz(ə)m). [f. *Lukan* LUCAN *a.* + -ISM.] A form of expression characteristic of St. Luke.

1919 S. C. CARPENTER *Christianity acc. Luke* 69 There are in the passage certain Lukanisms of style.

Lukanize ('l(j)u:kənaɪz), *v.* [f. as prec. + -IZE.] *trans.* To invest with a Lucan character.

1919 S. C. CARPENTER *Christianity acc. Luke* 81 It would no doubt be possible to assert that he determined at all costs ..to Paulinize and Lukanize the Master.

lukar, obs. form of LUCRE.

luke (l(j)u:k), *sb. slang.* Nothing.

1821 in *Life Haggart* 172 *Gloss.* **1864** in *Slang Dict.*

†Luke, Lukes, *proper name. Obs.* Also 5 luks. The anglicized name of the town of Lucca in Italy; used *attrib.*

[**1393** LANGL. *P. Pl.* C. v. 194 Lumbardes of lukes. *Ibid.* IX. 109 By þe rode of lukes.] **1483** *Wardr. Acc.* in Grose *Antiq. Repert.* (1807) I. 49, ij canopies, oon with luks gold garnyssht with frenge of venys gold. **1640** *Rates* in *Noorthouck's Lond.* (1773) 839/1 Silk, wrought satins, of Bolonia, lukes, jean [etc.]. **1682** WHELER *Journ. Greece* I. 35 Cephalonia is fruitful in Oyl, and excellent Wines, especially red Muscatels (which we call Luke Sherry). **1684** G. MERITON *Praise Yorks. Ale* (1685) 2 Briskets, Luke Olives, Anchoves, Caveare, Neats Tongues [etc]. **1700** PETIVER *Musei Petiver.* 66 Its about the bigness of a Lucca (Luke) Olive.

luke (l(j)u:k), *a. Obs.* exc. *dial.* Forms: 4 lheuc, 4–5 lewk(e, 5 leuk(e, (luk, 6 *Sc.* luik), 3–6, 9 luke. [The ME. forms *lheuc*, *leuk*, and the modern pronunciation, appear to point to a derivation from OE. *hléow* LEW *a.*, perh. through the medium of a vb. **hliewcian*: see LUKE *v.*

Notwithstanding the resemblance in form and meaning, it seems impossible to connect the word etymologically with mod.Du. *leuk* (pronounced løk) lukewarm, LG. *lūk*, *luke*, *lök*, tepid, weak, slack. See LUKEWARM.]

1. = LUKEWARM 1.

c **1205** LAY. 27557 And opened wes his breoste. þa blod com forð luke. **13..** HAMPOLE *Pr. Consc.* 7481 (MS. Harl.) Als a lewke bath nouther hate ne calde. **1387** TREVISA *Higden* (Rolls) VII. 149 In reward of which flamme oure fire is but lewk. *c* **1420** *Pallad. on Husb.* IV. 61 Yf luk water hem biwepe They wole be grete. **1491** CAXTON *Vitas Patr.* II. (W. de W. 1495) 228b/2 He dranke luke water. **1837** DICKENS *Pickw.* xxxiii, Let me have nine penn'orth o' brandy and water luke.

2. = LUKEWARM 2.

1340 *Ayenb.* 31 He is fyeble and lheuc to alle guodes to done. **1388** WYCLIF *Rev.* iii. 16 Thou art lew [*v.r.* lewk] and nether cold, nether hoot. *c* **1449** PECOCK *Repr.* II. viii. 184 Thouȝ in ech chapel..may be ymagis of God and of Marie and of Seintis forto make bi hem sengil and leuke remembrauncis. *c* **1450** tr. *De Imitatione* I. xxv. 37 The negligent religiose & þe leuke haþ tribulacion.

3. *Comb.*, as ***luke-hearted*** adj.; **luke-hot** *a.* = LUKEWARM.

1398 TREVISA *Barth. De P.R.* XVII. iii. (1495) 605 Oyle of almondes clensyth and purgyth matere of eeres yf it be luke hote [*Bodl. E. Mus. MS.* wlache hote] droppyd therin. *c* **1450** *ME. Med. Bk.* (Heinrich) 217 Mak alle þus lewk hot to geder. **1508** DUNBAR *Tua mariit wemen* 498, I am so loik [*MS. M.* luik] hertit.

Hence **†'lukely** *adv.*, **†'lukeness.**

1340 *Ayenb.* 31 Huanne þe man loueþ lite and lheucliche oure lhord, þet he ssolde louye bernindeliche. *c* **1440** *Promp. Parv.* 302/1 Lewkenesse, *tepor.* **1597** J. KING *On Jonas* (1618) 406 His lukenesse and neutrality of dealing in his seruice did so much offend him.

†luke, *v. Obs. rare.* In 5 lewk(e. [? repr. OE. **hliewcian*, f. **hléow* LEW *a.*; for the formation cf. *ieldcian* to delay, f. *eald* old, and *ȝearcian* to prepare, f. *ȝearo* ready.

The existence of such a vb. in OE. must app. be assumed in order to account for the formation of LUKE *a.*; but the recorded vb. may be a new formation on the adj.]

trans. To make lukewarm.

a **1400** *Stockh. Med. MS.* in *Anglia* XVIII. 314 Modir wort..ȝif it be lewkyd with oyle of roset [cures fevers].

luke, obs. or Sc. form of LOOK; obs. f. LUCK.

luke-home: see LUCARNE.

luken, var. LOUK *v.*^{1} *Obs.*; obs. f. LOUK *v.*^{2}

luker, obs. form of LOOKER *sb.*, LUCRE.

†lukes, *a. Obs.* Also 6 lewkes, lukys. [ad. Du. *Luiksch*, f. *Luik* Liège, a town and province of Belgium.] Made at Liège; said *esp.* of velvet.

[**1472** in Rogers *Agric. & Prices* III. 351/1 Lukys [iron].] **1536** *Wardr. Acc. Hen. VIII* in *Archæologia* IX. 248 A coote of blacke lukys veluette. **1545** *Lanc. Wills* II. 63 A jaket of fyne lukes velvet. **1547** BOORDE *Introd. Knowl.* xii. (1870) 155 The lond of Lewke is a pleasaunt countre. The cheefe towne is the cytie of Lewke; there is Lewkes veluet made, & cloth of Arys.

Lukes: see LUKE *proper name*, Lucca.

†'Lukesmas. *Sc. Obs.* Forms: 5 luxmess, 6 lukismes, 7 loukismes, lucsmes, lukemasse, ? lukesmasse. [= *Luke's* MASS.] The festival of St. Luke, kept on 18 Oct. (Formerly a customary date for payment of accounts.)

1470 *Burgh Rec. Prestwick* (Maitland Club) 15 To be in bande fra beltane till luxmess. **1590** *Burgh Rec. Glasgow* (1876) I. 153 To be payit in maner following,..tuentie pundis at Lukismes. **1671** *Corshill Baron-court Bk.* in *Ayr & Wigton Archæol. Coll.* IV. 95 Since loukismes last.

† **'luket.** *Obs.* Also 6 lukette. [a. OF. *luquet.*] A casement.

1564 BULLEYN *Dial. agst. Pest.* 21 b, Drawe the Curtaines, open the lukette [**1572–8** luket] of the windowe. **1599** NASHE *Lenten Stuffe* 44 Hope..made her at breake of day..to vnloope her luket or casement, to looke whence the blasts came.

† **lukeward.** *Obs.* The name of a variety of cherry.

16.. *MS. Ashm.* 1461 lf. 19 The Luke ward Chery ripe June the 10. **1664** EVELYN *Kal. Hort., June* (1679) 18 Cherries..Luke-ward, early Flanders [etc.]. **1707** MORTIMER *Husb.* (1721) II. 297 The..Lukeward, one of the best of Cherries.

lukewarm ('l(j)uːkwɔːm), *a.* and *sb.* Forms: 4–7 lukewarme, 5 lewk(e)-warm(e, (lowk warm), 5–6 leuk(e)-warm(e, (7 luk warme, 8 luckwarm), 6– lukewarm. [f. LUKE *a.* + WARM *a.* Cf. LEW-WARM and LG. *lukwarm* (also *slukwarm*).]

A. *adj.*

1. Moderately warm, tepid.

1398 TREVISA *Barth. De P.R.* XVII. xciii. (1495) 661 The broth of clete..comfortyth the teeth: yf it be luke warme hote [*Bodl. E. Mus. MS.* lewke hote] holde in the mouth. *c* **1400** tr. *Secreta Secret., Gov. Lordsh.* lxiii. 82 þe firste be cold, þe seconde leuk-warme, þe þrydde hoot. *c* **1450** *ME. Med. Bk.* (Heinrich) 213 Stampe hyt wyþ vynegre lewk warm. **1546** PHAER *Bk. Childr.* (1553) T ij, Lette the chylde drynke of it twise or thrise a day luke warme. **1590** SPENSER *F.Q.* I. ix. 36 All wallowd in his own yet luke-warme blood. **1658** A. FOX *Wurtz' Surg.* II. ix. 80 Apply the Collyrium luke-warm. **1762** WOOD in *Phil. Trans.* LII. 416 The water ..close to the flame is only luckwarm. **1840** DICKENS *Old C. Shop* xix, Sickening smells from many dinners came in a heavy lukewarm breath upon the sense.

2. Of persons, their actions, attributes, etc.: Having little warmth or depth of feeling, lacking zeal, enthusiasm or ardour, indifferent.

c **1522** MORE *De quat. noviss.* Wks. 83/1 Like as god said in thapocalips vnto the church of Loadice. Thou arte neyther hote nor cold but luke warme, I would thou were colde y^t thou mighteste waxe warme. **1593** G. HARVEY *Pierce's Super.* 108 Some that called him the lukewarme Doctor, and likened him to milke from the Cowe. **1623** tr. *Favine's Theat. Hon.* v. i. 55 The strength of youth and Manhood is now become but luke-warme. **1691** WOOD *Ath. Oxon.* I. 154 Whittyngham..was but a luke-warm conformist at best. **1718** BP. HUTCHINSON *Witchcraft* 86 That shewed the Zeal of their Time above our lukewarm Temper. **1771** *Junius Lett.* lix. 303 The lukewarm advocate avails himself of any pretence to relapse into..indifference. **1804** J. GRAHAME *Sabbath* 86 No lukewarm accents from my lips should flow. **1883** FROUDE *Short Stud.* IV. I. ix. 96 The clergy were lukewarm in his interests.

So † **lukewarmed** *a.* = prec. sense 1.

1545 RAYNOLD *Byrth Mankynde* 71 The beryes of iuniper ..dronke with luke warmed wine, wyl [etc.].

B. *sb.* A lukewarm person; one who is by no means enthusiastic.

1693 W. FREKE *Sel. Ess.* xxxi. 188 Let such Cowards and Lukewarms do what they will, —I shall always Condemn Vice and Sin. **1835** C. BRONTË in Mrs. Gaskell *Life* viii. (1858) 107 But the Opposition is divided, Red-hots, and Luke-warms. **1890** *Pall Mall G.* 25 June 1/2 One enthusiast is worth a dozen 'lukewarms'.

'lukewarm, *v.* *Obs. rare*⁻¹. [f. LUKEWARM *a.*] *trans.* To make lukewarm.

1592 G. HARVEY *Pierce's Super.* (1593) 185 Can..the tempest calme, or loue quench, or Zeale luke-warme, or valour manicle, or excellencie mew-vpp, or perfection geld, or supererogation combe-cutt itselfe?

'lukewarmish, *a. nonce-word.* [-ISH.] Rather lukewarm.

1827 SCOTT *Jrnl.* 25 Apr., Good blank verse and stately sentiment, but something lukewarmish.

† **'lukewarmling.** *Obs.* [f. LUKEWARM *a.* + -LING¹.] A lukewarm person. Also *attrib.*

1626 W. FENNER *Hidden Manna* (1652) 31 Art thou a swearer, a lyar, or a luke-warmling? *a* **1640** —— *Sacrif. Faithfull* (1648) 15 The lukewarmling deadhearted and vaine-thoughted professor. *Ibid.* 167.

'lukewarmly, *adv.* In a lukewarm manner.

1611 COTGR., *Tiedement*, luke-warmely. **1675** TRAHERNE *Chr. Ethics* 169 To be beloved lukewarmly is to be embraced with polluted and filthy armes. **1880** *Mem. Sir J. Paget* v. 295 We and some more are 'on the whole' and 'rather luke-warmly' in favour of their admission.

lukewarmness ('l(j)uːkwɔːmnɪs). [+ -NESS.] The quality or condition of being lukewarm.

1561 DAUS tr. *Bullinger on Apoc.* (1573) 58 b, He expoundeth more fully the sinne of the Laodicians, and what is the cause of their lukewarmenesse. **1665** BOYLE *New Exp. & Observ. Cold* 37 The many degrees of Coldness.. betwixt Lukewarmness and the Freezing degree of Cold. **1720** WELTON *Suffer. Son of God* I. xii. 310 Their Luke-warmness and Indifferency towards God. **1875** MANNING *Mission H. Ghost* i. 28 The lukewarmness with which we allow His Graces and Mercies to pass by us.

lukewarmth ('l(j)uːkwɔːmθ). Now *rare.* [f. LUKEWARM + -TH¹.] = LUKEWARMNESS.

1598 FLORIO, *Tepidezza*, luke warmth. **1620** GRANGER *Div. Logike* I. xxxv. 104 As lukewarmth partaketh of heate, and cold. **1716** ADDISON *Freeholder* No. 8 ¶9 The.. perfidiousness of certain faithless men, and..the lukewarmth and indifference of others. **1842** J. AITON *Domestic Econ.* (1857) 333 Seventy degrees is but just warm, a gentle luke-warmth. **1895** J. DAVIDSON *Earl Lavender* 49 Being well-known for the luke-warmth of my allegiance to the Guild.

lukie, lukky, obs. forms of LUCKY.

‖ **lukiko** (luː'kiːkəʊ). Also lukiiko. [Luganda, = audience-hall, council, levee.] A levee; the council or parliament of the Buganda people of Uganda.

1889 R. P. ASHE *Two Kings of Uganda* vi. 53 He, like us, has come to 'kika', that is to present himself at Mutesa's grand 'lukiko', or levee. **1902** *Encycl. Brit.* XXXII. 539/1 The native parliament or 'Lukiko' was reorganized and its powers were defined. [**1904** G. R. BLACKLEDGE *Luganda-Eng. Vocab.* 51/1 *Lukiko*, audience room, council, levee.] **1955** *Ann. Reg. 1954* 122 It was suggested..that..the Lukiko should be given the opportunity to decide whether to recall the exiled Kabaka or to elect a new Kabaka, as a constitutional monarch. **1955** *Times* 3 Jan. 7/3 The compromise was not made public until after the Great Lukiko had debated the Namirembe reforms. **1969** *Times* 15 Sept. (Uganda Suppl.) p. ii/3 The Buganda Lukiko (Parliament) is not the only regional body to have suffered an eclipse. **1971** *Sunday Nation* (Nairobi) 11 Apr. 11/4 The Lukiiko..demanded that Obote's government should quit the soil of Buganda.

lukir, lukre, obs. forms of LUCRE.

Lukismes, variant of LUKESMAS *Sc. Obs.*

lulav ('l(j)uːlɑːv). Also lulab, lulov. [Heb. *lūlābh* branch.] (See quot. 1959.)

1892 I. ZANGWILL *Childr. Ghetto* I. 265 He bore to synagogue the tallest *Lulav* of palm-branches. **1893** *Ibid.* (ed. 3) 409 *Lulov*, palm-branch dressed with myrtle and willow, and used at the Feast of Tabernacles. **1959** D. D. RUNES *Conc. Dict. Judaism* 157/1 *Lulav*, palm frond, one of four species waved at Sukkoth services (others are citron, myrtle, willow). These plants are interpreted as representing various types of man. **1972** C. RAPHAEL *Feast of Hist.* iii. 72/1 An oil lamp..bearing symbols familiar in Jewish art, including..a *lulav* for Sukkot. **1973** *Jewish Chron.* 10 Aug. 18/5 Succot is a festival of thanksgiving for the harvest... What is the lulav for? *Ibid.*, The lulav represents the palm-tree and its dates are delicious. **1973** *Synagogue Light* Sept. 50/1 The required length of the stock of a Lulab, besides its upper leaves, should measure four hand-breadths.

† **lulibub.** *Obs.* ? Earlier form of LOLLIPOP.

c **1710** CELIA FIENNES *Diary* (1888) 17 Severall little Cake-houses where you have fruits lulibubs and sumes Liquours.

lull (lʌl), *sb.*¹ [f. LULL *v.*]

1. Something which lulls; *spec.* a lulling sound, etc.

1719 YOUNG *Revenge* v. ii, Yonder lull Of falling waters tempted me to rest. **1820** KEATS *Isabella* v, Sweet Isabella's untouch'd cheek..Fell thin as a young mother's, who doth seek By every lull to cool her infant's pain.

† **b.** Soothing drink, 'nepenthe'. *Obs.*

1659 *Lond. Chanticleers* ix. 20 Mine Host Welcom has a Cup of blessed Lull.

2. A lulled or stupefied condition.

1822–56 DE QUINCEY *Confessions* (1862) 238, I fleeted back into the same opium lull. **1902** *Blackw. Mag.* Apr. 553/1, I sat listening in a kind of lull of terror and disgust.

3. A brief period of intermission or quiescence in a storm. Also *fig.*

1815 EARL DUDLEY *Let.* 15 Apr. (1840) 93 What..so many wiser people mistook for a calm, turns out to be only a lull. **1851** GALLENGA *Italy* ii. 90 The lull that occurred in Lombardy..was sheer dread and horror of French interference. **1860** MOTLEY *Netherl.* (1868) I. iii. 69 There was a lull on the surface of affairs. **1901** *Edin. Rev.* Jan. 196 There seemed for a time a lull in the storm.

lull (lʌl), *sb.*² *Whaling.* [a. Du. *lul* tube.] A tube to convey blubber into the hold. Also *lull-bag.*

1836 *Uncle Philip's Convers. Whale Fishery* 99 From the speck-trough, [the pieces of blubber]..pass through the lull, into tubs fixed in the hold. **1867** SMYTH *Sailor's Word-bk., Lull-bag*, a wide canvas hose in whalers for conducting blubber into the casks, as it is 'made off'.

lull (lʌl), *v.*¹ [Imitative of the repetition of (lʌ lʌ) or similar sounds, appropriate to the purpose of singing a child to sleep. Cf. Sw. *lulla*, Da. *lulle*, to hum a lullaby, to lull, early mod.Du. *lullen* 'numeros canere' (Kilian), mod.Du. *lullen* to prattle; cf. MDu. *lollen* to mutter (see LOLLARD).

A similar onomatopœia occurs in L. *lallāre*, of equivalent meaning.]

1. *trans.* To soothe with sounds or caresses; to induce to sleep or to pleasing quiescence.

13.. *Leg. Rood* (1871) 133 Feet and fayre hondes þat nou ben croised I custe hem ofte, I lulled hem I leid hem softe. *c* **1386** CHAUCER *Clerk's T.* 495 And gan the childe to kisse And lulled it and after gan it blisse. —— *Merch. T.* 579 He lulleth hire he kisseth hire ful ofte. *c* **1400** *Destr. Troy* 647 We will seasse till, now sone, the sun be at rest,..And yche lede, as hym list, lullit on slepe. *a* **1500** *Songs & Carols 15th C.* (Percy Soc.) 9 In a manjour of an as Jhesu lay and lullyd was. **1530** PALSGR. 615/2 She can lulle a childe as hansomly aslepe as it were a woman of thurty yere old. **1587** TURBERV. *Trag. T.* (1837) 12 Minerva luld him on her lappe, and let him many a kisse. **1607** SHAKS. *Cor.* III. i. 114 The Virgin voyce That Babies lull a-sleepe. **1666** BUNYAN *Grace Ab.* §110 Continual rocking will lull a crying child. **1710** STEELE *Tatler* No. 161 ¶1 The Musick of the Birds..lull'd me asleep before I was aware of it. **1715–20** POPE *Iliad* XIV. 191 And lull the Lord of Thunders in her arms. *c* **1718** PRIOR *Young Gentl. in Love* 4 Take me, my Celia, to thy breast, And lull my wearied soul to rest. **1800** WORDSW. *Hart-leap Well* ii. 150 Asleep he sank, Lulled by the fountain in the summer-tide. **1825** D. WELSH *Life T. Brown* i. 3 His mother used to lull him asleep with *The flowers of the forest*, a tune, to which [etc.]. **1871** B. TAYLOR *Faust* (1875) I. xii. 141 Lulled in my lap with many a song, It smiled, and tumbled, and grew strong.

2. *fig.* and in fig. context. †Also with *up.*

1575 LANEHAM *Let.* (1871) 35, I was lulld in such liking.. that mooch a doo..had I, to fynde me whear I waz. **1576** FLEMING *Panopl. Epist.* 199 As though you were in likelyhoode to possesse peace, and to be lulled in the lap of safetie. **1582** BRETON *Flourish upon Fancy* (Grosart) 60/2 So (luld in this my deepe distresse) some comfort lend to me. *a* **1586** SIDNEY *Arcadia* II. (1590) 108 b, The young Musidorus..was yet for some yeares after..lulled vp in as much good luck [etc.]. **1615** W. MARTYN *Twenty Kings Eng.* 178 The said Petition was thereby lulled fast asleepe. **1775** SHERIDAN *Rivals* v. i, You may lull your keen regret to slumbering. **1810** SCOTT *Lady of L.* I. xxxiii, Not Ellen's spell had lulled to rest The fever of his troubled breast.

b. *esp.* To quiet (suspicion) by deception; to delude into a sense of security.

1601 HOLLAND *Pliny* II. 153 To drinke wine upon an emptie stomacke fasting..dulleth the vigor and quicknesse of the spirit: fitter indeed to bring and lull men asleepe in the bed of securitie. **1636** E. DACRES tr. *Machiavel's Disc. Livy* II. 255 Who,..partly beguil'd by some devises hee shall make use of to lull them a sleepe, are easily kept from stirring. **1734** tr. *Rollin's Anc. Hist.* (1827) II. II. 68 Antiochus imposed upon and lulled asleep by his flatterers. **1833** MARRYAT *P. Simple* lxii, A superior is equally bound to prefer a charge, or to give notice that that charge will be preferred,..instead of lulling the offender into security. **1859** JEPHSON *Brittany* xvi. 254 By a feigned devotion to the interests of his new master, [he] succeeded in lulling all his suspicions. **1900** W. WATT *Aberdeensh.* iv. 85 They were soon lulled into a sense of security.

† **3.** *intr.* To be lapped in soothing slumbers.

Possibly these quots. may belong to LOLL *v.*¹ 4. On the other hand, it is possible that some of the quots. there given should have been placed here.

a **1450** *Cov. Myst.* (Shaks. Soc.) 182 My lytylle childe lyth alle lame, That lullyd on my pappys! **1576** FLEMING *Panopl. Epist.* 291 Some there be that lie lulling on the softe pillow of slouth. **1594, 1635, 1778** [see LOLL *v.*¹ 4].

4. *trans.* To bring to a state of comparative quiescence (winds, sea, etc.).

1680 DRYDEN *Ovid's Epist.* vii. 52 Stay but a little, 'till the Tempest cease, And the loud Winds are lull'd into a Peace. **1819** BYRON *Juan* II. clxviii, Lull'd like the depth of ocean when at rest. *a* **1854** H. REED *Lect. Eng. Hist.* ix. 283 The tempest, that was only lulled, comes back again.

5. *intr.* Of the sea or wind: To become lulled, or gradually diminished in force or power.

1808 PIKE *Sources Mississ.* (1810) 10 The wind lulling, we encamped on the point of an island. **1835** MOTLEY *Corr.* (1889) I. iii. 57 The wind lulling a little, we became encouraged. **1836** MARRYAT *Midsh. Easy* xxvi, The wind lulled, the rain came down in a deluge. **1853** KANE *Grinnell Exp.* xxiv. (1856) 193 This [nipping], too, continued through the day, sometimes lulling for a while into comparative repose. **1869** PARKMAN *Disc. Gt. West* xii. (1875) 144 When at length the tempest lulled, they re-embarked.

b. *fig.* To become quiescent or inactive.

1850 H. BUSHNELL *God in Christ* 287 The instinct of system lulls in its activity, as spiritual life quickens in the soul. **1862** NEALE *Hymns East. Ch.* 16 Lulling at the death of Constantine, the persecution again broke out in the latter years of his successor Leo.

† **lull,** *v.*² *Obs.* Also 6 loll. *trans.* To pull about (by the ears).

1530 PALSGR. 614/1, I lolle one aboute the eares. *Je luy tire les oreilles.* I shall lolle you aboute the eares tyll I make your eares cracke. **1568** *Hist. Jacob & Esau* II. ii. C ij, Oh that I had his eare betwene my teeth now, I should shake him euen as a dog that lulleth a sow.

lull, obs. form of LOLL *v.*¹

† **'lulla,** *int.* *Obs.* Also lullay, lully. [Onomatopœic: see LULL *v.*¹] = LULLABY.

? *c* **1450** in *Cov. Myst.* (Shaks. Soc.) Notes 414 Lully, lulla, thow littell tine child; By, by, lully, lullay, thow littell tyne child. *c* **1450** *Ibid.* 137 'Fayr chylde, lullay', sone must she syng. *c* **1460** *Towneley Myst.* xiii. 442, 445 Sing lullay thou shall, for I must grone, And cry outt by the wall on mary and Iohn,..Sing lullay on fast When thou heris at the last. *c* **1485** *Digby Myst.* (1882) IV. 719, I sange lullay to bringe you on slepe. *a* **1500** *Songs & Carols* (Percy Soc.) 12 And ever among A mayden song Lullay, by by, lullay. [*Other verses simply* by by, lullay.] *Ibid.* 19 Lullay, my chyld, and slepe. **1590** [see next]. *c* **1600** *Mother's Lullaby* in Ritson *Anc. Songs* (1792) 198 My little sweete derlinge, my comforte and ioye Singe Lullyby Lully... Singe Lully Lully Lully, Sweete baby, Lully Lully, sweete baby, Lully Lully. *a* **1764** [see next, sense 1].

lullaby ('lʌləbaɪ), *int.* and *sb.* Forms: 6 lulley by, 6–7 lullabie, 7 lull-a-ba, lullyby, 8 lullabye. [f. prec. + *-by*, as in *by-by*, BYE-BYE¹: cf. HUSHABY, ROCKABY.]

1. *int.* A soothing refrain, used to please or pacify infants. Also *gen.*, any soothing refrain. (Sometimes preceded by *lulla.*)

c **1560** RICHARDES *Misogonus* IV. I. 76 (Brandl) When my maistrisse lay in and we Sange lulley by baby and bore ye. **1588** GREENE *Pandosto* (1843) 27 The good wife learned to sing lullaby at home with her yong babe. **1588** SHAKS. *Tit. A.* II. iii. 29 Whiles Hounds and Hornes, and sweet Melodious Birds Be vnto vs as in a Nurses Song Of Lullabie, to bring her Babe asleepe. **1590** —— *Mids. N.* II. ii. 14–19 Sing in your sweet Lullaby, Lulla, lulla, lullaby, lulla, lulla, lullaby, Neuer harme, nor spell, nor charme, Come our louely Lady nye, So good night with Lullaby. **1651** N. BACON *Disc. Govt. Eng.* II. xl. (1739) 174 King James conquering all enmity, spake Peace abroad, and sang Lullaby at home. **1739** A. NICOL *Poems* 14 Where once, of late the Nurse's Lull-a-ba Made all the Place delightful to the Eyes Now all's dispersed. *a* **1764** LLOYD *Ode to Obliv.* Poet. Wks. 1774 I. 128 And, hollow blasts, which never

cease to sigh, Hum to each care-struck mind their lulla-lulla-by! **1807–8** W. IRVING *Salmag.* (1824) 217 She with 'lulla-by-baby' beguiles it [a child] to rest. *a* **1845** HOOD *Serenade* i, Lullaby, oh, lullaby! The brat will never shut an eye.

†**b.** Used for 'farewell', 'good-night'. *Obs.*

1599 *Pass. Pilgr.* xv, Then lullaby the learned man hath got the lady gay, For now my song is ended. **1601** SHAKS. *Twel. N.* v. i. 48 Marry sir, lullaby to your bountie till I come agen.

2. *sb.* A song sung to children to soothe them to rest. Also, any song which soothes to rest.

1588 GREENE *Pandosto* (1607) 12 Alas sweet vnfortunate babe..shalt thou haue the whistling windes for thy Lullaby. **1779** BURNEY in *Phil. Trans.* LX. 206 In Italy the ninne nonne, or lullabies, are fragments of elegant melodies. **1842** LYTTON *Zanoni* 24 You thought you heard the lullaby which a fairy might sing to some fretful changeling. **1900** *Contemp. Rev.* Aug. 247 The feeling of quietness evoked by an evening landscape or by a lullaby.

b. *transf.* and *fig.*

1611 RICH *Honesty Age* (Percy Soc.) 10 Hee that would please the time must learne to sing lullaby to Folly, and there is no musicke so delightfull as the smoothing vp of sinne. **1622** T. SCOTT *Belg. Pismire* 11 Rockt asleepe in desperate securitie, with a lullabie of peace and safety, hee derides all happie admonition. **1679** *Vind. Sir T. Player* 2/2 The rest of his Sheet consists of Wheadle and Lullabies. **1796** BURKE *Regic. Peace* i. Wks. VIII. 196 Would not this warm language of high indignation have more of sound reason in it..than all the lullabies of flatterers? **1819** S. ROGERS *Human Life* 2 The bees have hummed their noon-tide lullaby.

3. *attrib.* and *Comb.*, as ***lullaby-song***, ***-sound***, ***-speech***, ***-strain***; **lullaby-cheat** *Cant*, a baby.

1671 R. HEAD *Eng. Rogue* I. iv. (1680) 35 His Doxie.. carried at her back a Lullaby-cheat. **1687** MIEGE *Fr. Dict.* II, Lullaby, a Lullaby-Song. **1795** MASON *Ch. Mus.* i. 63 That these lullaby strains should be exclusively adhered to. **1822–34** *Good's Study Med.* (ed. 4) I. 437 The Greeks, from the letter λ (*lambda*), denominated this *lambdacismus*; the Romans with more severity, *lallatio*, or lullaby-speech. *a* **1849** POE *Annie* Poems (1859) 118 Water that flows With a lullaby sound. *a* **1849** H. COLERIDGE *Ess.* (1851) II. 158 Still-life lullaby poetry.

ˈlullaby, *v.* [f. prec.] *trans.* To soothe with a lullaby; to sing to sleep. Also *transf.* and *fig.*

1592 G. HARVEY *Pierce's Super.* (1593) 194 No man could ..lullaby the circumspectest Argus more sweetly. **1596** COPLEY *Fig for Fortune* 59 Sweet Sound that all mens sences lullabieth. **1607** WALKINGTON *Opt. Glass* 19 It..lullabees the senses, yea, intoxicates the..soule, with a pleasing poyson. **1647** HOWELL *Twelve Treat.* (1661) 268 In Holland ..he was..pourtrayed lying in his cradle lullaby'd and rock'd asleep by the Spaniard. **1818** HAZLITT *Pol. Ess.* (1819) 340 When we see a poor creature like Ferdinand VII ..lullabied to rest with the dreams of superstition [etc.]. **1890** JEAN MIDDLEMASS *Two False Moves* III. xiv. 210 Ruth ..kissed and lullabyed her to sleep. **1893** A. AUSTIN *Conv. Winckelmann*, etc. (1897) 157 Then I..lullaby my pain with plaintive song.

b. *absol.* or *intr.*

1603 FLORIO *Montaigne* I. xix. (1632) 31 No song of birds, no musikes sound Can lullabie to sleepe profound. **1866** CARLYLE *Remin.* I. 101 Waves..beautifully humming and lullabying on that fine long sandy beach.

lullay, variant of LULLA *int. Obs.*

lulled (lʌld), *ppl. a.* [f. LULL *v.*^{1} + -ED^1.] Quieted; reduced to calmness.

1787 *Generous Attachment* IV. 44 Give me again, ye shades,..your lulled repose! **1852** MUNDY *Our Antipodes* (1857) 185 Amid thunderings and lightnings..but with lulled airs,..we doubled the North Cape. **1862** TRENCH *Justin Martyr* Poems 11 And the lulled Ocean seemed to say, 'With me is quiet, come away'.

†**ˈluller.** *Obs.* [f. LULL *v.*^{1} + -ER^1.] One who lulls; ? a woman who chants spells, a witch.

14.. *Voc.* in Wr.-Wülcker 575/14 *Contravaria*, a luller. *Ibid.* 582/7 *Facuminaria*, a lullere. **1611** COTGR., *Mignardeur*, a luller, dandler, cherisher.

Lullian (ˈlʌlɪən), *a.* [f. proper name *Lulli-us* + -IAN.] Of or belonging to the mystical philosophy of Lullius (Raymund Lull 1234–1315).

1653 R. SANDERS (*title*) Physiognomie and Chiromancie.. the subject of dreams, divinative, steganographical and Lullian Sciences, etc. **1669** *Phil. Trans.* IV. 1093 To show the Defects and Difficulties in the famous Lullian Art. **1933** *Times Lit. Suppl.* 29 June 433/2 No records remain to us of the early Centenaries, but their nature can be safely deduced from that of the Lullian cult, which was practised for hundreds of years both in Majorca and on the mainland. **1946** E. A. PEERS *Fool of Love* vii. 108 He rifled the Lullian library of the College of Sapiencia. *Ibid.* 109 With Pasqual began a new orientation of Lullian studies.

Hence †**Lullianist** = LULLIST.

1610 B. JONSON *Alch.* II. i, *Sub.*.. Who are you? *Ana.* A faithful Brother... *Sub.* What's that? A Lullianist? a Ripley? *Filius Artis*? Can you sublime and dulcifie?

lulliloo (ˈlʌlɪluː), *v. rare.* [Imitative.] *intr.* To utter the cries by which certain African peoples express delight.

1857 LIVINGSTONE *Trav.* i. 25 The women clapping their hands..and lullilooing for joy. **1886** BURTON *Arab. Nts.* (Abr. ed.) I. 191 Then the singing-girls beat their tabrets and lulliloo'd with joy. [**1889** H. M. STANLEY in *Daily News* 26 Nov. 5/8 The female followers..set up a shrill lululus on seeing their own lake again.]

lulling (ˈlʌlɪŋ), *vbl. sb.* [f. LULL *v.*^{1} + -ING^1.] The action of LULL *v.*^{1}

c **1394** *P. Pl. Crede* 77 And at þe lulling of oure Ladye þe wymmen to lyken. *c* **1440** *Promp. Parv.* 317/1 Lullynge of yonge chylder.., *neniacio*. **1575** R. B. *Apius & Virginia* B 1 b, What culling: what lulling: what stur haue wee here? **1633** G. HERBERT *Temple, Pearl* iii, I know the wayes of pleasure, the sweet strains, the lullings and relishes of it. **1865** *Cornh. Mag.* Sept. 269 The mother..began to soothe it..interspersing her lulling with thanks to Molly.

†**b.** *concr.* A soothing song. *Obs.*

1398 TREVISA *Barth. De P.R.* VI. v. (Tollem. MS.), þey [nurses] use to singe lullynges and oþer cradel songis to plese þe wittis of þe childe.

lulling (ˈlʌlɪŋ), *ppl. a.* [f. LULL *v.*^{1} + -ING^2.] That lulls.

c **1440** *Promp. Parv.* 317/1 Lullynge songe, *nenia*. **1672** *Chaucer's Ghoast* 26 He sang him such a lulling Song, that he the Giant brought asleep. **1711** ADDISON *Spect.* No. 29 ¶8 An English Composer should not follow the Italian Recitative too servilely..He may copy out of it all the lulling Softness. **1748** LADY M. W. MONTAGU *Fashion* 76 in Dodsley *Coll. Poems* III. 277 Let Italy give mimick canvass fire, Carve rock to life, or tune the lulling lyre. **1821** SHELLEY *Prometh. Unb.* I. i. 225 My wings are folded o'er mine ears: ..Yet..through their lulling plumes arise, A Shape, a throng of sounds. **1847** DISRAELI *Tancred* III. iv, Its lulling influence is proverbial.

lullingly (ˈlʌlɪŋlɪ), *adv.* [f. prec. + -LY^2.] In a lulling manner; with lulling effect.

1834 *Fraser's Mag.* X. 646 That pensive vacancy which.. rural scenes so lullingly diffuse over the mind. **1890** *Temple Bar* Aug. 458 The soothing voice..lullingly reading him to sleep.

Lullist (ˈlʌlɪst). [f. proper name *Lull* (see LULLIAN) + -IST.] A follower of Raymund Lull.

1569 J. SANFORD tr. *Agrippa's Van. Artes* 2 b, A prating Lullist. **1596** PLAT *Jewell-ho.* III. 89 These yong gallants were right ioyful of this good successe, desiring nothing more then to become Lullistes. **1711** KING tr. *Naude's Ref. Politics* iv. 138 Let some Alchymist,..Lullist, or Cabalist begin to shew their tricks. **1839** *Penny Cycl.* XIV. 195/1 The 'Ars Magna Lulli, or the Lullian Art', which found a few admirers who styled themselves Lullists [etc.].

Hence **ˈLullism**, the philosophy or beliefs of Lull or his followers.

1929 E. A. PEERS *Ramon Lull* xviii. 377 Ample evidence exists, supplied alike by the friends of Lullism and its enemies, as to the veneration with which its author was regarded. **1933** *Times Lit. Suppl.* 29 June 433/3 That Lullism could survive so long,..is an astonishing testimony to the hold which the Doctor Illuminate had upon his fellow-countrymen. **1946** E. A. PEERS *Fool of Love* vii. 109 At this very time Lullism was taking a fresh impetus both in Spain and abroad. **1954** T. MAYNARD *Long Road of Father Serra* (1956) ii. 27 Students from all over Spain were attracted to this main center of Lullism.

†**ˈlully.** ? *dial. Obs.*$^{-0}$ [? compressed form of OE. *lundlaȝa* kidney.] The kidney (of a cow).

1688 R. HOLME *Armoury* II. 171/2 Intrals [of a Bull, etc.] ..The Kidneys or Lullies.

lully, variant of LULLA *int. Obs.*

lulte, luly-whit, obs. ff. LILT, LILY-WHITE.

lulu (ˈluːluː). *slang* (orig. *U.S.*). [Of obscure origin.] A remarkable or wonderful person or thing; freq. used ironically; also *attrib.*

1886 *Lantern* (New Orleans) 10 Nov. 6/3 Farrell's two baser was a lu-lu. **1896** ADE *Artie* ix. 76 Mebbe you think I ain't got a lulu of a head on me this morning. **1904** 'O. HENRY' *Cabbages & Kings* xvii. 301, I smelt a million violets. She was a lulu. I told her I came in a private yacht. **1922** H. TITUS *Timber* iii. 38 *She's* a lulu though! **1940** R. STOUT *Over my Dead Body* xiii. 176 You certainly picked a lulu for an adopted daddy. **1946** J. IRVING *Royal Navalese* 111 *Lulu*, a lady of infinite allure but questionable character. **1963** *Economist* 9 Nov. 578/1 Its own rationale..of why it suddenly became obligatory for [oil] companies to consult governments before changing prices..might be described as a lulu performance. **1968** *Jazz Monthly* Oct. 19/2 A muddle unparalleled in the history of jazz record issues—and there have been some Lulus—seems to have taken place. **1969** *Islander* (Victoria, B.C.) 13 July 6/1 His first job was, to use modern parlance, a lulu—census taker for the Island's west coast. **1971** *Black Scholar* Sept. 43/2 Joyce, honey, when you goof, its a lulu. **1972** D. SALE *Love Bite* iv. 50, I do hope you're not scared of earth tremors... This one was a real lulu. **1974** *Evening News* (Edinburgh) 23 Nov. 8/4 There are some parts of a new book on spying that aren't fit to be printed... This one is a lulu. As long as two years ago, legal proceedings were initiated.

‖**luluai** (ˈluːluːaɪ). *New Guinea.* [Native name.] A man appointed by the administration to be responsible for the maintenance of order in a village; a village headman.

1924 J. AINSWORTH *Rep. Administrative Arrangements Natives New Guinea* 17/1 in *Austral. Parl. Papers 1923–4* IV. 1819 A luluai or kukurai is the political head of the particular section of which he is either the hereditary or appointed headman. **1930** M. MEAD *Growing up in New Guinea* 372 *Luluai*, headman of village. **1937** *Official Handbk. New Guinea* IV. 302 For the purpose of local government, the Administration has appointed two native representatives in each village. The senior of these is called a '*luluai*' and the junior, his assistant, a '*tul-tul*'. The work of the *luluai* is that of a village headman. **1957** M. WEST *Kundu* v. 63 There is a luluai in every village appointed by the Kiap in Goroka. **1965** *Sunday Mail* (Brisbane) 10 Oct. 2 In the next village the headman, the 'luluai', had a wife who was dying of kuru. **1970** L. P. MAIR *Austral. in New Guinea* (ed. 2) v. 72 The native authorities were known..as luluais..and tultuls... The luluais are responsible for good order and control in the villages.

Lulworth (ˈlʌlwəθ). The name of Lulworth Cove, Dorset, used *attrib.* in **Lulworth skipper** to designate a butterfly, *Thymelicus acteon*, of the family Hesperiidæ (cf. SKIPPER *sb.*^{1} 2 c), first found there in 1833 by J. C. Dale.

1833 J. CURTIS *Brit. Entomol.* X. 442 (*heading*) The Lulworth Skipper. **1894** W. FURNEAUX *Butterflies & Moths* 199 The Lulworth Skipper..is a very local species. **1945** E. B. FORD *Butterflies* vii. 149 In England the Lulworth Skipper only flies within a mile or two of the sea. **1973** T. G. HOWARTH *South's Brit. Butterflies* 27 The Lulworth Skipper... The coloration of this butterfly is somewhat dingy.

lum (lʌm). *north. dial.* and *Sc.* Also 6 **lumbe**, 7 **lume**, 8 **lumb**. [Of obscure etymology; possibly an application of OF. *lum* light (:—L. *lūmen*); cf. the uses of F. *lumière* in the sense of 'aperture, passage'. The resemblance in form and sense to Welsh *llumon* chimney is noteworthy.]

†**1.** ? An opening in a roof; a skylight. *Obs.*

1507–8 *Durham Acc. Rolls* (Surtees) 659, ij ropez ad le lumbe pro lumine in pandoxatorio.

2. A chimney; also a chimney-top.

1697 [see 3]. **1701** BRAND *Orkney*, etc. (1703) 145 They carefully fix their Eyes upon the Lums or Chimney Heads of this House. **1742** FORBES *Ajax Sp.* etc. *Jrnl.* (1755) 30 Gin I had been gain out at the lum o' a house. *a* **1774** FERGUSSON *Hallowfair* Poems (1845) 13 Upon the tap of ilka lum The Sun began to keek. **1785** BURNS *Halloween* viii, He bleez'd owre her, an' she owre him,..Till fuff! he started up the lum. **1862** G. MACDONALD *Dav. Elginbrod* I. 33 By the side of the wide chimney, or more properly *lum*, hung an iron lamp. **1883** GRESLEY *Gloss. Coal-mining*, *Lum*, a chimney placed on the top of an upcast shaft to carry off the smoke, &c., and to increase the ventilating current.

3. *Comb.*: **lum-hat**, a chimney-pot hat; **lum-head**, the upper part of a chimney, whence the smoke escapes; **lum-sweeper**, a chimney-sweeper.

1888 BARRIE *When a Man's Single* (1900) 86/2 It's Rob Angus come home in a *lum hat. **1768** ROSS *Helenore* (1789) 55 The sun begins to leam, And clouds of reek frae *lumb-heads to appear. **1818** SCOTT *Hrt. Midl.* xxvii, The..blue reek that came out of the lum-head. **1697** *Parish Reg.* in Brand *Hist. Newcastle* (1789) I. 619 James Brown *lume sweeper.

lum: see LOOM *a.*, LUMB^2.

lumachella (l(j)uːməˈkɛlə). *Min.* Also 8 **lumachelli**, 9 **lumachel**, **lumachelle**, **lumachello**. [a. It. *lumachella* little snail, f. *lumaca* snail. Cf. F. *lumachelle*.] A dark-coloured compact limestone containing shells which frequently emit fire-like reflections; fire-marble.

1784 KIRWAN *Min.* 30 Marbles..which abound in petrifactions are called lumachellis. **1791** *Ibid.* (ed. 2) I. 116 The marble called Lumachelli, found at Bleyberg in Carinthia. **1804** *Phil. Trans.* XCIV. 386 The shells forming the lumachella of Bleyberg, which still possess the lustre and iridescence of their original nacre. **1850** DANA *Min.* 208 Fire marble or lumachelle is a dark brown shell marble. **1869** tr. *Hugo's By King's Command* I. 12 The brown corridor in Astracan lumachel. **1894** *Geol. Mag.* Oct. 463 The shelly limestone below the clay is in part an Oyster lumachelle.

†**ˈlumany.** *Obs. rare*$^{-1}$. [? Blunder for LUNARY.] Some plant or substance used in alchemy.

1592 LYLY *Galathea* II. iii, Then our Mettles, Saltpeeter, Vitrioll, Sal tartar, Sal perperat..Egrimony, Lumany, Brimstone..and what not, to make I know not what.

†**lumb**^{1}. *Obs.* [ad. L. *lumb-us*.] The loin.

1541 R. COPLAND *Guydon's Quest. Chirurg.* I iij b, The kydnees..are situate vpon the lumbes [*printed* tumbes]. **1599** A. M. tr. *Gabelhouer's Bk. Physicke* 135/1 Let the dampe therof ascende into the Arsgutte, & soe into his Lumbes.

lumb^2. Also 8–9 lum.

1. *Mining.* †**a.** A well for the collection of water in a mine. *Obs.*

1747 HOOSON *Miner's Dict.* M iij, When Shafts are sunk down and troubled with Water, we Sink two or three Yards deeper than the Design of the Shaft, on purpose to hold Water one Night at least,..and this we call a Lumb.

b. (See quot. 1883.)

1747 HOOSON *Miner's Dict.* s.v. *Break-off*, An Alteration in a Vein, made by a jumbled Place, or Lumb of Softness. **1883** GRESLEY *Gloss. Coal-mining*, *Lum* [in Derbyshire], a basin or natural swamp in a coal seam, often running several hundred yards in length.

2. 'A deep pool in the bed of a river' (E.D.D.).

1790 GROSE *Prov. Gloss.*, *Lum*, a deep pool.

lumb, obs. f. LOOM *sb.*^{2}; var. LUM *dial.*

lumbaginous (lʌmˈbeɪdʒɪnəs), *a.* [f. L. *lumbāgin-*, LUMBAGO + -OUS.] Pertaining to, resembling, or afflicted with lumbago.

1620 VENNER *Via Recta* (1650) 311 Some soft woollen cloth..which will preserve from lumbaginous pains. **1834** JEFFREY in Ld. Cockburn *Life* (1852) II. let. cxxii. 266 God bless us, I am dyspeptic and lumbaginous and cannot sleep. **1875** SWINBURNE *Ess. Chapman* 21 A ponderous and lumbaginous licence of movement.

lumbago (lʌmˈbeɪgəʊ), *sb. Med.* [a. L. *lumbāgo*, f. *lumb-us* loin.] A rheumatic affection in the lumbar region of the body. Also *attrib.*

1693 in *Blancard's Phys. Dict.* (ed. 2). **1707** FLOYER *Physic. Pulse-Watch* 398 As in a Lumbago, with pain in the Back. **1771** JOHNSON *Let. to Mrs. Thrale* 7 July, The old rheumatism is come again into my face and mouth, but nothing yet to the lumbago. **1804** WELLINGTON in Gurw. *Desp.* (1837) II. 706, I am much annoyed by the lumbago, a disorder to which I believe, all persons in camp are liable. **1899** *Allbutt's Syst. Med.* VI. 750 'Muscular rheumatism' (of the lumbago type).

lumˈbago, *v.* [f. LUMBAGO *sb.*] *trans.* To afflict with lumbago.

1796 'A. PASQUIN' *New Brighton Guide* (ed. 6) 26 He's lumbago'd [by the north or east wind] the rest of his days. **1880** *Gentl. Mag.* Oct. 504 Roasting his knees and nose, while his back is lumbagoed by exposure to the..cold air.

†**ˈlumbal**, *a.* and *sb. Anat. Obs.* [ad. mod.L. *lumbāl-is*, f. L. *lumbus* loin.]

A. *adj.* = LUMBAR *a.*

1696 COWPER in *Phil. Trans.* XIX. 302 The Lumbal pain encreast on the left side. **1713** CHESELDEN *Anat.* II. ii. (1726) 123 The first lumbal Vertebra. **1803** *Med. Jrnl.* IX. 152 The sciatic, lumbal, and intercostal nerves.

B. *sb.* = LUMBAR *sb.*[1]

1708 J. KEILL *Anim. Secret.* 50 The Spermatic Arteries.. dilate as big, if not bigger than one of the Lumbals. **1722** QUINCY *Lex. Physico-Med.* (ed. 2) 32 Six lumbals, each 434·2.

lumbar (ˈlʌmbə(r)), *a.* and *sb.*[1] *Anat.* [ad. mod.L. *lumbār-is*, f. L. *lumbus* loin.]

A. *adj.* **a.** Of, belonging to, or situated in the loin.

1656 BLOUNT *Glossogr.* s.v. *Vein*, *Lumbar vein*, the vein of the loins, etc. **1741** MONRO *Anat. Nerves* (ed. 3) 67 The five lumbar Nerves on each Side communicate with the Intercostal. **1756** DOUGLAS tr. *Winslow's Struct. Hum. Body* (ed. 4) II. 24 The Lumbar Arteries go out posteriorly from the inferior descending Aorta. **1800** *Med. Jrnl.* III. 232 Invest the whole of the abdominal and lumbar regions with a large..plaster. **1870** ROLLESTON *Anim. Life* 3 The diaphragm and the lumbar muscles. **1882** *Quain's Dict. Med.* 854/2 The skin of the lumbar region is remarkable for its..thickness.

b. Of, pertaining to, or performed on or within the spinal cord in the lumbar region.

1895 *Brit. Med. Jrnl.* Suppl. 27 Apr. 65/2 Fürbringer.. recalls how Quincke, in 1891, at Wiesbaden, made known his method of lumbar puncture in cases of meningitis of various kinds. **1947** *Physiol. Rev.* XXVII. 253 The bitch exhibits normal estrous and mating despite complete lumbar section. **1963** *Lancet* 12 Jan. 116/1 In three infants the fundus oculi was examined, and in two a lumbar puncture was done.

B. *sb.* [From the elliptical use of the adj.] An artery, nerve, vein or vertebra situated in the loin.

1858 H. GRAY *Anat.* 518 The first [lumbar nerve] appears between the first and second lumbar vertebræ, and the last between the last lumbar and the base of the sacrum. **1866** HUXLEY *Preh. Rem. Caithn.* 148 The processes [of the vertebræ] are coarser and stronger, and the lower oblique processes of the last lumbar are unusually far apart. **1881** MIVART *Cat* 281 The last dorsal nerve sends back a branch which unites with the first lumbar.

†**lumbar**, *sb.*[2] *Obs.* [app. = LOMBARD.] A kind of ship.

13.. *K. Alis.* 6063 In schipes cayvars, In dromondes, and in lumbars [*MS. Laud* in shippes lumbars].

lumbar, obs. form of LOMBARD, LUMBER.

†**lumbard.** *Obs.* Also 6 *Sc.* lumbart. [app. = LOMBARD.] A particular kind of sleeve.

1542 *Inv. R. Wardr.* (1815) 99 Item, the body and lumbartis of ane jornay of velvott of the collour of selche skin. *a* **1650** CALDERWOOD *Hist. Kirk* (1845) VII. 55 The bishops were ordeaned [in 1610] to have their gownes with lumbard sleaves.

lumbard(e, obs. f. LOMBARD, LUMBER(-PIE).

lumbardar, variant of LAMBARDAR.

†**lumbary**, *a. Anat. Obs.* [f. L. *lumb-us* loin + -ARY.] = LUMBAR *a.*

1672 *Phil. Trans.* VII. 5009 The two Lumbary veins. **1681** tr. *Willis' Rem. Med. Wks.* Vocab., *Lumbary*, belonging to the loins.

lumber (ˈlʌmbə(r)), *sb.*[1] Also 6 lumbor, 7 lumbar. [Prob. f. LUMBER *v.*[1], which occurs much earlier. But as a LUMBER-HOUSE or pawnbroker's shop was in fact a storehouse for such odds and ends of property as are denominated 'lumber', the word was prob. at one time more or less associated with LUMBER *sb.*[2]]

1. a. Disused articles of furniture and the like, which take up room inconveniently, or are removed to be out of the way; useless odds and ends.

1552 HULOET, Baggage, lumbor, or trumperye, *scruta.* **1587** *Wills & Inv. N.C.* (Surtees) II. 300 The tobs, kyrnes, stands, dishes, formes, chaires, stoles, and other lumbar. **1596** *Unton Invent.* (1841) 2 In the Warthrope..ij paire of olde virginalls, and other lumber there. **1622** MABBE tr. *Aleman's Guzman d' Alf.* I. 3 A deale of lumber and luggage. **1716** LADY M. W. MONTAGU ? *Let. to Pope* 10 Oct. in *Lett.* (1887) I. 130 A catalogue of the rest of the lumber. **1817** L. HUNT *Let. to C. C. Clarke* in *Gentl. Mag.* May (1876) 601 All the chaos of packed trunks, lumber,..&c. **1884** *Globe* 6 Oct. 2/1 Three pictures..stowed away for nearly fifty years as lumber.

b. *fig.* Useless or cumbrous material.

1649 MILTON *Eikon.* xvii. Wks. 1851 III. 466 When Ministers came to have Lands, Houses, Farmes, Coaches, Horses, and the like Lumber. **1709** POPE *Ess. Crit.* 613 The bookful blockhead..With loads of learned lumber in his head. **1768** GOLDSM. *Good-n. Man* II. i, I'm to be a mere article of family lumber. **1858** DARWIN in *Life & Lett.* II. 127, I should be mere living lumber.

2. Superfluous fat, esp. in horses.

1806–7 J. BERESFORD *Miseries Hum. Life* (1826) i. Introd., With all my fleshy lumber about me. **1885** *Sat. Rev.* 6 June 749/2 Plenty of muscle and no lumber. **1891** H. S. CONSTABLE *Horses, Sport & War* 15 Good thorough-bred horses have also lost what goes by the name of 'lumber'—such as lumps of flesh and fat..on the top of the neck. *Ibid.* 18 Sir Tatton seldom praised a horse without adding 'there is no lumber about him'.

3. *N. Amer.* Timber sawn into rough planks or otherwise roughly prepared for the market.

1662 *Suffolk* (Mass.) *Deeds* 26 Aug., Freighted in Boston, ..with Beames, for houses, boards..and other Lumber. **1755** *Gentl. Mag.* XXV. 16 The principle articles of their [Rhode Islanders] trade are horses, lumber, and cheese. **1862** TROLLOPE *N. Amer.* I. 107 Timber in Canada is called lumber. **1900** *Contemp. Rev.* July 60 The millwright operated the mill giving the supply of bread and lumber. **1928** *Chambers's Jrnl.* Feb. 119/1 Behind the lumber grand-stand, which..resembled every natural wooden grand-stand in the world, stretched a grass meadow. *Ibid.* 120/1 We found Miss J. and Miss N. in a home where the lumber had mellowed—featuring an entrancing tint. **1941** *Sun* (Baltimore) 15 Oct. 5/5 They take nuts and bolts out of packing cases, pick up broken and abandoned field telephone wire along the roadsides, whittle scrap lumber with penknives and produce workable Morse sending keys. **1945** J. J. MATHEWS *Talking to Moon* 66, I had lumber left over from the building of the chicken and pheasant houses. **1965** *Globe & Mail* (Toronto) 5 Jan. B5 A company that will manufacture prefabricated homes in the United Kingdom with Canadian lumber.

4. *attrib.* and *Comb.*, as (sense 1) ***lumber-cellar, -garret, -house*** (cf. LUMBER-HOUSE), ***-office, -place, -raft; lumber-headed*** adj.; (sense 3) ***lumber-boat, -business, -field, -king, -merchant, -products, -raft, -steamer, -wharf; lumber-laden, -preparing*** adjs.; **lumber-act**, ?an act of parliament regulating the lumber-trade; **lumber baron** *U.S.*, a leading or wealthy timber merchant; **lumber-camp**, a camp in which lumbermen dwell; **lumber-carrier**, (*a*) a vessel employed in the lumber-trade; (*b*) a vehicle for carrying lumber; **lumber-cart**, ? = *jockey-cart* (JOCKEY *sb.* 9); **lumber-jack, lumberjack**, a lumberman; **lumber jacket** orig. *N. Amer.*, a warm jacket of the type worn by lumbermen; **lumber-line**, a railway constructed primarily for carrying lumber; **lumber-mill**, a sawmill for cutting up lumber; **lumber-money**, a tax levied upon lumber; **lumber-port**, (*a*) a port-hole in the bow or stern of a ship for loading or unloading timber; (*b*) a seaport from which lumber is shipped; **lumber-raft**, a raft made of logs, boards, or the like; **lumber-scaler**, one who measures up timber; **lumber-shover**, a labourer in a lumber-yard (*slang*); **lumber town** *U.S.*, a town chiefly engaged in the timber trade; **lumber-trade**, the trade in rough timber; †**lumber-troop**, a convivial society of London citizens (dissolved in 1859), with a quasi-military organization, its president being styled the 'colonel'; also *allusively*; hence **lumber-trooper**; **lumber-wood**, a wood where lumber is cut; **lumber-wagon** *N. Amer.*, a springless wagon of a type used for hauling lumber or for general transport (see also quot. 1962); **lumber-yard** *N. Amer.*, a *timber-yard*. Also LUMBERMAN, LUMBER-ROOM.

1721 *New Hampsh. Prov. Papers* (1869) III. 834 A message to the house..for repealing the *lumber Act. **1888** *N.Y. Life* 18 Feb. 27/2 One of the..*lumber 'Barons' of Michigan. **1948** *Time* 29 Nov. 24/1 In many ways he seemed a throwback to the lumber barons, the cattle kings and the mining magnates who had ruled the West before him. **1902** *Westm. Gaz.* 28 Aug. 2/1 Flat, ugly, *lumber-boats. **1792** J. BELKNAP *Hist. New-Hampshire* III. 211 Husbandry..is much preferable to the *lumber business. **1896** *Vermont Agric. Rep.* XV. 79 Gov. Woodbury has spent years as superintendent of the Burlington branch of J. R. Booth's gigantic lumber business. **1882** HOWELLS *Mod. Instance* II. 139 Down there in the *lumber camp. **1700** *New Hampsh. Prov. Papers* (1869) III. 104 Coasting vessels and *lumber carriers. **1928** *Collier's* 29 Dec. 5/4 On the left were rows of twenty-foot lumber piles, trams laid between them, and electric lumber carriers rolling on the trams. **1830** CUNNINGHAM *Brit. Paint.* II. 228 He was stopt at Whetstone turnpike by a *lumber or jockey cart. **1832** *Chambers's Edin. Jrnl.* 24 Mar. 59/2 Stone bottles.. collected from all the *lumber-cellars in the country. **1910** *Daily Chron.* 18 Jan. 3/4 A cramped and pokey lumber-cellar. **1881** *Chicago Times* 4 June, Pineries, *lumber-fields [etc.]. **1838** J. W. CROKER in *C. Papers* (1884) 1 Nov., I should look with more expectation to the *lumber garrets than to the muniment room. **1818** T. G. FESSENDEN *Ladies' Monitor* 38, I would not wish your pedant *lumber-headed. **1891** ATKINSON *Last of Giant Killers* 100 The usually lumber-headed old giants. **1720** in A. McF. Davis *Tracts Currency Mass. Bay* (1902) 385 Hemp, Flax, Turpentine.. to be stored up in the *Lumber-house. **1728** POPE *Dunc.* III. 193 A Lumber-house of books in ev'ry head. **1899** H. B. CUSHMAN *Hist. Indians* 162 A lumberhouse and granary, each 18 × 20 ft. **1831** in E. C. Guillet *Valley of Trent* (1957) VI. 236 My misfortunes have been brought upon me chiefly by an incorrigible..race of mortals called *lumberjacks*, whom, however, I would name the Cossacks of Upper Canada. **1896** *New York Weekly Witness* 30 Dec. 13/1 To lose the lumber-jack vote meant to lose the election. **1902** S. E. WHITE *Blazed Trail* 41 Typical native-born American lumber-jacks powerful in frame. **1972** *Daily Colonist* (Victoria, B.C.) 2 Feb. 16/5 She later became a lumberjack and spent three months in the woods. **1939** *These are our Lives* (Federal Writers Project, N. Carolina) 107 He was dressed in riding breeches and leather *lumber-jacket. **1943** *R.A.F. Jrnl.* Aug. 16 They wore lumber jackets. **1952** S. KAUFFMANN *Philanderer* (1953) vii. 107 He went into the middle of the group and squatted next to Jake (he still remembered the smell of the woollen lumber-jacket). **1956** T. H. RADDALL *Wings of Night* 70, I pulled on my old lumber jacket and went out to do the firewood chore. **1968** J. IRONSIDE *Fashion Alphabet* 37 In its modern meaning, the lumber-jacket is very similar to an anorak. It is a short, straight jacket, reaching to the hips, with a centre-front fastening (usually zipped) and buckled at the sides to make it fit snugly. **1975** P. SOMERVILLE-LARGE *Couch of Earth* ix. 148 A black and red lumber-jacket, the sort American hunters wear. **1889** W. H. WITHROW *Our Own Country: Canada* 372 One of the great *lumber-kings of the country. **1941** *Yankee* Dec. 19/3 They were..Anderton's lumber kings; so nobody minded their smelling strongly of horses, even in the Methodist basement. **1879** *Lumberman's Gaz.* 19 Nov., The '*lumber lines' are now getting their new cars ready. **1789** *Boston Directory* 181 Dillaway, Samuel, *lumber-merchant. **1825** J. NEAL *Bro. Jonathan* I. 23 The preacher..had been..a lumber-merchant. **1830** *Deb. Congress U.S.* 11 Mar. 606/2 You will not find..such constant, unceasing labor as in our *lumber mills. **1901** *19th Cent.* Oct. 550 Lumber mills, saw mills, grist mills. **1715** *New Hampsh. Prov. Papers* (1868) II. 682 An account of the *lumber mony and excise mony. **1687** T. BROWN *Saints in Uproar* Wks. 1730 I. 82 Carry that..halbard to my *lumber-office. **1744** W. COLE in Willis & Clark *Cambridge* (1886) I. 296 Laid up in a *Lumber Place. **1838** *Yale Lit. Mag.* III. 76 The pirates had knocked out the *lumber port, with the intention of sinking her [*sc.* a ship]. **1883** *Wheelman* I. 333 Calais [in Maine], the great lumber port of this part of the country. **1837** W. JENKINS *Ohio Gazetteer* 62 The Hockhocking river..furnishes..a downward navigation for flat boats and *lumber rafts. **1898** *Engineering Mag.* XVI. 96 Lumber-rafts can easily be built. **1961** B. FERGUSSON *Watery Maze* v. 111 Irrawaddy lumber-rafts. **1896** *New York Weekly Witness* 30 Dec. 13/1 A famous *lumber-scaler. **1880** *Harper's Mag.* Aug. 354/1 A cheerful little *lumber town lying high among the hills. **1904** S. E. WHITE *Blazed Trail Stories* I. 3 The sawdust streets..of the lumber town were filled with people. **1972** R. NEELY *Sexton Women* (1974) ii. 12 She had been..brought up in a lumber town.. near the Oregon border. **1689** in *Mass. Hist. Soc. Coll.* (1834) 3rd Ser. I. 98 They are supplied..with the *lumber trade. **1732** COL. DUNBAR *Let.* 25 Aug. in *Calendar State Papers* (*Colonial Ser.*) (1939) 201 The undertaker for the masting has and does carry on a greater lumber trade than any man in N. Engld. **1884** S. E. DAWSON *Handbk. Canada* 129 Quebec [city] is..the centre of the lumber-trade. **1963** *Canada Month* Nov. 22/1 The lumber trade furnished employment for thousands of lumber jacks, river drivers, and sailors. **1745** *E. Ward's Compl. Acc. Clubs* title-p., A Compleat and Humorous Account of all the Remarkable Clubs and Societies in the Cities of London and Westminster, From the R—l-S—y down to the *Lumber-Troop, &c. **1805** M. A. SHEE *Rhymes on Art* (1806) 76 Dolts, ..Pass muster in the lumber troop of Taste. *c* **1742** in Hone *Every-day Bk.* II. 525 All other institutions, whether.. Hiccubites, *Lumber-Troopers, or Free-Masons. **1831** S. STODDARD *Diary* 30 Nov. in *Mich. Hist. Mag.* (1927) XI. 472 Breakfast swallowed we stepped into our next rig, which was a *lumber wagon drawn by two very good horses. **1887** C. D. WARNER *Their Pilgrimage* (1888) xiii. 288 At this season one meets them [*sc.* the hop-pickers] on all the roads driving from farm to farm in lumber wagons. **1902** E. BANKS *Autobiogr. Newspaper Girl* I Gathered about the little village station in hard-seated lumber-wagons. **1961** *Edmonton* (Alberta) *Jrnl.* 24 July 11/7 They forded the North Saskatchewan River in a lumber wagon. **1962** *Amer. Speech* XXXVII. 270 *Lumber wagon*, an old, broken-down automobile, particularly one that rides rough. **1858** SIMMONDS *Dict. Trade*, *Lumber-wharf, a timber-yard. **1891** *N.Y. Sun* in *Boston* (Mass.) *Jrnl.* Nov., A man that works in the *lumber-woods. **1786** *Maryland Jrnl.* 4 Apr. (Th.), *Lumber-yard, at the head of Baltimore Bason. **1851** C. CIST *Sk. Cincinnati in 1851* 207 Connected with the machinery is a lumber yard. **1961** W. E. GREENING *Ottawa* 108 The district close to the lumberyards was full of waterfront dives. **1973** C. WILLIAMS *Man on Leash* (1974) iv. 52 Lew was..running a lumberyard and building supply here.

†**ˈlumber**, *sb.*[2] [variant of LOMBARD *sb.*[1]]

1. †**a.** A pawnbroking establishment; = LOMBARD *sb.*[1] 3. *Obs.*

1617 MINSHEU *Voc. Hisp. Lat.*, *Mónte de piedád*, a lumber or bancke to lend money for a yeare, for those that need, without interest. **1749** LADY MURRAY *Lives G. Baillie & Lady Grisell B.* (1822) 53 They put up the little plate they had..in the Lumber, which is pawning it.

b. Phrases. ***to put to lumber***: to put in pawn or pledge. ***to be in lumber*** (slang): to be imprisoned; also, to be in trouble.

1671 SKINNER *Etymol. Ling. Angl.* s.v., To put one's Clothes to Lumbar, *pignori dare.* **1812** J. H. VAUX *Flash Dict.* s.v., A man..sent to gaol is said to be lumbered, to be in lumber, or to be in Lombard-Street. **1963** J. PRESCOT *Case for Hearing* viii. 125 My poor old dad was in and out of lumber all his life. **1965** A. PRIOR *Interrogators* xi. 202 We're out on a limb hoping for a confession, and if we don't get it we're in dead lumber. **1967** 'M. CARROLL' *Begotten Murder* iv. 104 It rather looks to me as if someone is trying to get Susan in lumber. **1972** L. HENDERSON *Cage until Tame* vi. 43

I've got to keep at it. Break my bloody leg or something stupid like that and I'm in lumber.

†**2.** Money due with respect to articles pawned. *Obs.*

a **1680** BUTLER *On Critics* 94 And, by an action falsely laid of Trover, The lumber for their proper goods recover.

3. *slang.* A house or room; *spec.* one where stolen property is hidden; a house used by criminals.

1753 J. POULTER *Discoveries* (ed. 2) 33 They pike up the Prancers, that is, go up Stairs, and fisk the Lumbers, that is, search the Rooms. *a* **1790** H. T. POTTER *New Dict. Cant & Flash* (1795) 40 *Lumber*, a house convenient for the reception of swindlers, sharpers, and cheats. **1800** G. PARKER *Life's Painter* xiv. 117 Have you any body in the lumber behind the bar? *Ibid.* xv. 140 *Lumber*, a room. **1846** *Swell's Night Guide* 34 The polka is greatly in favour with the femmes of this lumber. *Ibid.* 74 His long room, or 'slanging lumber', is the scene of many a choice spree and downey movement. **1923** S. T. FELSTEAD *Underworld of London* iii. 108 The proprietor of the 'lumber', where stolen property is stored pending a suitable buyer, also wants his whack. **1938** F. D. SHARPE *Sharpe of Flying Squad* xiv. 151 Her husband was taken into custody at a 'lumber' (hide-out for stolen property) in Walthamstow. **1950** R. FABIAN *Fabian of Yard* xxxiv. 206 *Lumber*, address used by a prostitute for her profession only.

'lumber, *sb.*[3] [f. next.] A rumbling noise.

1750 SMITH in *Phil. Trans.* XLVI. 729 One other Person ..heard the Noise [of an earthquake], but judged it to be an odd Lumber above Stairs.

lumber ('lʌmbə(r)), *v.*[1] [Possibly two or more words may have coalesced. ME. *lomere* may have been a frequentative formation on *lome* LAME *a.* With sense 2 cf. Sw. dial. *lomra* to roar (Rietz). The word, however, may be partly of direct imitative formation in Eng.]

1. *intr.* To move in a clumsy or blundering manner; in later use only, to move heavily on account of unwieldiness of bulk and mass. Now always with defining adv. or advb. phr.

13.. *E.E. Allit. P.* B. 1094 Summe lepre, summe lome, and lomerande blynde. **1530** PALSGR. 586/1, I hoble, or halte, or lomber, as a horse dothe, *je cloche.* **1697** DRYDEN *Virg. Georg.* III. 229 Let 'em not..lumber o'er the Meads: or cross the Wood. **1728** POPE *Dunc.* III. 294 Thy giddy dullness still shall lumber on. **1771** FOOTE *Maid of B.* III. Wks. 1799 II. 229 Hush! I hear him lumbering in! **1830** SCOTT *Demonol.* iii. 100 The massive idol leapt lumbering from the carriage. **1852** HAWTHORNE *Blithedale Rom.* I. viii. 138 We..were pretty well agreed as to the inexpediency of lumbering along with the old system any further. **1899** CROCKETT *Kit Kennedy* xxii. 153 'Ouch..!' barked Royal lumbering outwards like a great pot-walloping elephant through the shallows. **1902** *Blackw. Mag.* Mar. 400/1 They lumbered to attention as I entered.

2. To rumble, make a rumbling noise. ? *Obs.* exc. *U.S.*

a **1529** SKELTON *Agst. Comely Coystrowne* 29 He lumbryth on a lewde lewte, Roty bully joyse, Rumbyll downe, tumbyll downe, hey go, now, now. **1530** PALSGR. 615/2, I lumber, I make a noyse above one's head... You lumbred so over my heed I coulde nat slepe. [**1584** CLEM. ROBINSON *Handf. Ples. Delites* (Arb.) 47 A proper new Dity..To the tune of Lumber me.] *c* **1611** CHAPMAN *Iliad* XVII. 643 A boisterous gust of wind Lumbering amongst it. [**1621–1782**: see LUMBERING *vbl. sb.*[1]]**1855** J. E. COOKE *Ellie* 207 Keeping the footman lumberin at the knockers on both sides o' the street. **1890** *Dialect Notes* I. 65 'Listen how he lumbers', said of a deep-mouthed dog's barking when he has treed a 'coon or 'possum. **1904** T. WATSON *Bethany* (1920) 165 And he himself did not always know what he had on his mind until he pushed back his specs, and began to 'lumber' [= hold forth].

†**3.** *trans.* ? To utter with a rumbling noise. *Obs.*

a **1529** SKELTON *Col. Clout* 95 They lumber forth the lawe, ..Expoundyng out theyr clauses.

lumber ('lʌmbə(r)), *v.*[2] [f. LUMBER *sb.*[1]]

1. a. *trans.* Orig., to cover, fill up, or obstruct with lumber; to burden uselessly, encumber. Now usu., to leave (someone) *with* something unwanted or unpleasant; to get (someone) into trouble or difficulties; freq. *pass.* Said both of personal agents, and of the things which form the encumbrance. Sometimes with *over*, *up*.

1642 O. SEDGWICKE *Eng. Preserv.* 5 An indigested Thicket, lumbred all over with weedes. **1741** RICHARDSON *Pamela* II. 81, I hope it [*sc.* a chapel] will never be lumber'd again. **1798** MILLER in Nicolas *Nelson's Disp.* (1846) VII. p. clviii, We..sent our prisoners and their baggage which lumbered our guns, on board the Goliath. **1824** W. IRVING *T. Trav.* I. 328 Empty bottles lumbered the bottom of every closet. **1825** LOCKHART *Let.* in Smiles *Mem. J. Murray* (1891) II. xxvii. 229, I..should be sorry to have them [*sc.* packages] lumbering your warehouses. **1840** R. H. DANA *Bef. Mast* xxix. 98 The decks were lumbered up with everything. **1845** FORD *Handbk. Spain* I. 49 There is no worse mistake than lumbering oneself with things that are never wanted. **1861** TULLOCH *Eng. Purit.* ii. 247 The mere details of controversy..lumber his style. **1866** HOWELLS *Venet. Life* 148, I could not, in any honesty, lumber my pages with descriptions. **1867** TROLLOPE *Chron. Barset* I. xxxvii. 319 One side and two angles of the court are always lumbered with crates, hampers, [etc.]. **1901** *Edin. Rev.* Oct. 261 The ships of war were lumbered up with the soldiers. **1924** E. WALLACE *Room 13* i. 9 'If they lumbered you with the crime, it was because you was a mug,' said Lal complacently. 'That's what mugs are for—to be lumbered.' **1951** A. BARON *Rosie Hogarth* III. iv. 180, I suppose you're afraid... Of getting lumbered, eh? **1958** T. HALL in P. Gammond *Decca Bk. Jazz* xix. 233 Poor old Don Rendell.. got really lumbered. He left his clarinet with Gee's with the proviso that it would be forfeited if the trousers and windcheaters weren't returned by the following Monday. Needless to say, they weren't. **1961** SIMPSON & GALTON *Four Hancock Scripts* 35/2 Every time I travel on a train I get lumbered with a carriageful of the most miserable-looking bunch of face-aches you've ever seen in your life. **1964** G. DAVIS *Friday before Bank Holiday* i. 11, I want to realise on the cottage..but I'm lumbered unless I can find another home for Fiddler. **1968** J. LOCK *Lady Policeman* xii. 113, I tell him I'm lumbered for court in the morning.

b. *intr.* To lie as lumber.

1850 D. MACMILLAN in *Life* (1882) ii. 11 A queer mass of rubbish to lie lumbering in any one's brain.

2. To heap or place together as lumber, without order or method; to deposit as lumber.

1678 T. RYMER *Trag. Last Age* 41 In Rollo we meet with so much stuff lumberd together. **1733** MALLET *Verbal Crit.* 16 With all their refuse lumber'd in his head. **1805** M. A. SHEE *Rhymes on Art* 369 How that [*sc.* picture], long.. lumber'd in some filthy broker's stall, Lay, lost to fame.

3. a. *intr.* To perform the labour or carry on the business of cutting forest timber and preparing it for the market. occas. *trans.* (*N. Amer.*)

1809 KENDALL *Trav.* III. lxviii. 73 The verb to lumber has also the..sense, to procure or even to manufacture lumber. **1870** *Maine Rep.* LVI. 566 The plaintiff lumbered on his township called Holeb. **1891** R. A. ALGER in *Voice* (*N.Y.*) 15 Oct., I..commenced lumbering in a small way. *Ibid.*, We then lumbered a million and a quarter feet a year. **1893** *Scribner's Mag.* June 711/1 They bought and lumbered timber on their own account.

b. *trans.* To go over (ground) cutting the timber on it.

[**1831** *Trans. Lit. & Hist. Soc. Quebec* II. 269 His intention..was to clear land and lumber some.] **1851** J. F. W. JOHNSTON *Notes N. Amer.* I. 52 We clean up two or three acres every year of the lumbered land (land from which the timber has been cut). **1871** R. L. DASHWOOD *Chiploquorgan* v. 60 This part of the country has never been 'lumbered', being too difficult of access. **1900** *U.S. Dept. Agric. Yearbk.* 365 The cut-over lands..which..have been lumbered heavily, not only for timber but also for fuel. **1971** *Lebende Sprachen* XVI. 9/2 This valley was lumbered in 1955. We lumbered more than a million acres last year.

'lumber, *v.*[3] *slang.* [f. LUMBER *sb.*[2]] *trans.* To deposit (property) in pawn; hence (orig. in *passive*), to put away privily, to imprison, arrest.

1812 J. H. VAUX *Flash Dict.* s.v., To lumber any property, is to deposit it at a pawnbroker's..; to retire to any..private place, for a short time is called lumbering yourself. A man ..sent to gaol is said to be lumbered. **1840** *Fraser's Mag.* XXII. 578 Revelling in the reminiscences of the number of times they have been lumbered. **1882** *Sydney Slang Dict.* 6/1 *Lumber*, to take or carry away to the lock-up. **1931** *Police Jrnl.* Oct. 501 Did the detective (busy) arrest (lumber) Jack? **1953** K. TENNANT *Joyful Condemned* ii. 17 Don't you worry about the police. If there's a warrant out for you..they'll lumber you sooner or later. **1961** B. CRUMP *Hang on a Minute* 136 We were sneaking into the church to bunk down last night when the johns lumbered us. **1970** M. KENYON *100,000 Welcomes* iv. 30 We're pros—twice in twelve years I've been lumbered... Only twice in twelve years screwing.

lumberdar, var. LAMBARDAR.

†**lumberdyne.** *Obs. rare*[−1]. [? Connected with *Lombardy*; cf. *pleasance* from *Placentia*, Piacenza.] A kind of black lawn.

a **1548** HALL *Chron., Hen. VIII* (1809) 514 Their faces, neckes, armes & handes, couered with fyne pleasaunce blacke: Some call it Lumberdynes, which is merueylous thine, so that the same ladies semed to be nygrost or blacke Mores.

lumbered ('lʌmbəd), *a.* [f. LUMBER *v.*[2] + -ED[1].] Filled or encumbered with lumber. Sometimes with *up*.

1745 P. THOMAS *Jrnl. Anson's Voy.* 288 She was so lumbered that she could not fight all of them. **1803** W. RAMSAY in *Naval Chron.* IX. 269 Many ships going in a lumbered state from Gravesend. **1898** F. T. BULLEN *Cruise Cachalot* 109 Soon the lumbered-up decks began to resume their normal appearance. **1900** *Longm. Mag.* Oct. 547 [He] hunted a dusty creel from out of a lumbered corner.

lumberer ('lʌmbərə(r)), *sb.*[1] *N. Amer.* [f. LUMBER *v.*[2] + -ER[1].] One engaged in the lumber or timber trade.

1809 KENDALL *Trav.* III. 33 To this mill, the surrounding lumberers or fellers of timber bring their logs. **1861** WOODS *Pr. of Wales in Canada* 152 The lumberers, who in Ottawa welcomed the Prince in their procession of canoes. **1884** LD. BLACKBURN in *Law Rep.* 9 App. Cases 410 The legislature confined the enactment to the seasons during which lumberers ordinarily ply their trade.

'lumberer, *sb.*[2] *Obs.* exc. *slang.* [f. LUMBER *v.*[3] + -ER[1].] A pawnbroker.

1802 W. TAYLOR in *Robberds' Mem.* I. 419 The Jew lumberers exhibit..candlesticks purchased of the church-robbers. **1807** —— in *Ann. Rev.* V. 296 We believe the term broker, for a furniture broker, is gradually disused, and that the term lumberer is introducing itself. **1896** FARMER *Slang, Lumberer*..2. (American thieves').—A pawnbroker.

'lumberer, *sb.*[3] [f. LUMBER *v.*[1] + -ER[1].]

1. One who goes clumsily or blunderingly.

1593 NASHE *Christ's T.* (1613) 128 So many cow-baby-bawlers and heauy-gated lumberers into the ministry are stumbled.

2. *slang.* †**a.** ? A tramp, vagrant (*obs.*). **b.** 'A swindling tipster' (Barrère & Leland).

1764 *Low Life* (ed. 3) 99 Lumberers taking a Survey of the Streets and Markets, and preparing to mount Bulks instead of Beds. **1897** HALL CAINE *Christian* IV. iv. 376 The pick-pocket, the card-sharper, the 'lumberer',..and the faker of every description laid his snares on this holy spot [Epsom Downs]. **1901** *Sketch* 18 Dec. 351/1 It is a pity means could not be devised to rid the Turf of the 'lumberers'.

†**lumber-house.** *Obs.* = LUMBER *sb.*[2] 1.

1677 YARRANTON *Eng. Improv.* 7 A lumber-house, whereby all poor people may have Moneys lent upon Goods at very easie Interest. **1720** *Lond. Gaz.* No. 5859/9 Subscriptions for erecting Lumber-Houses, Loan-Offices, &c. **1723** *Ibid.* No. 6164/1 Lumber-Houses or Banks for lending Money on Pledges.

lumbering ('lʌmbərɪŋ), *vbl. sb.*[1] [f. LUMBER *v.*[1] + -ING[1].] The action of LUMBER *v.*[1]

1621 LADY M. WROTH *Urania* 486 Wee heard a noise.. continuing with increase of lumbring. **1782** COWPER *Gilpin* 232 The lumbering of the wheels. **1816** SCOTT *Old Mort.* xviii, The lumbering of the old guns backwards and forwards shook the battlements.

lumbering ('lʌmbərɪŋ), *vbl. sb.*[2] [f. LUMBER *v.*[2] + -ING[1].]

1. The action of filling with lumber.

1775 in ASH, Suppl.

2. The trade or business of a lumberer; dealing or working in timber.

1792 J. BELKNAP *Hist. New-Hampsh.* III. 213 Towns adjoining the river, in which lumbering was formerly the chief employment. **1898** G. F. R. HENDERSON *Stonewall Jackson* I. i. 10 Young men had to serve a practical apprenticeship to lumbering and agriculture.

b. *attrib.*, as ***lumbering-camp***, ***season***.

1857 THOREAU *Maine W.* (1894) 143 Here were the ruins of an old lumbering-camp. **1873** *Wisconsin Rep.* XXXI. 424 The coming lumbering season.

lumbering ('lʌmbərɪŋ), *ppl. a.* [f. LUMBER *v.*[1] and [2] + -ING[2].]

Ponderous in movement, inconveniently bulky. *lit.* and *fig.*

1593 NASHE *Four Lett. conf.* G 3 Master Stannyhurst.. trod a foule lumbring boystrous wallowing measures [*sic*] in his translation of Virgil. **1594** —— *Terrors Nt.* Wks. (Grosart) III. 275 And yet me thinkes it comes off too goutie and lumbring. **1606** J. RAYNOLDS *Dolarney's Prim.* (1880) 118 There might be heard, the hideous lumbring swasher. **1736** *New Hampsh. Prov. Papers* (1870) IV. 713 We had only time..to save our lumbering stuff, such as tables and chairs. **1792** WOLCOT (P. Pindar) *Ode to the Pope* ii. Wks. III. 256 Upon the sportsman's breaking back, A lumb'ring eighteen pounder. **1811** SCOTT *Fam. Lett.* (1894) I. vii. 229, I agree with you respecting the lumbering weight of the stanza. **1855** MRS. GATTY *Parables fr. Nat.* Ser. I. (1869) 3 A caterpillar, who was strolling along a cabbage leaf in his odd lumbering way. **1885** *Sat. Rev.* 6 June 758/1 How lumbering all their rapier play Beside your finished carte and tierce. **1900** *Longm. Mag.* Oct. 574 It was a great heavy lumbering travelling coach.

†**b.** Rumbling. *Obs.*

1678 BUNYAN *Pilgr.* I. 159 A lumbring noise as of fire. **1684** *Ibid.* II. 27.

Hence **'lumberingly** *adv.*, **'lumberingness**.

1850 *Bentl. Misc.* Jan. 12 'Come—be alive!' and Meg moved lumberingly out. **1860** *Rutledge* 112, I..ran up stairs followed lumberingly by the housekeeper. **1869** *Echo* 13 Feb., The intolerable lumberingness of its action [*sc.* of the House of Commons]. **1885** D. C. MURRAY *Rainbow Gold* III. VI. iii. 214 A drunken sailor who howled a song and danced lumberingly. **1900** N. MUNRO in *Blackw. Mag.* Oct. 451/1 The beast..fell lumberingly on its side.

lumberly ('lʌmbəlɪ), *a.* [f. LUMBER *v.*[1] + -LY[1].] Clumsy, cumbrous.

1805 COLERIDGE *Lett.* (1895) II. 488 The latter word shall have become an incurable synonym, a lumberly duplicate. **1855** ROBINSON *Whitby Gloss.*, *Lummerly* or *Lumberly*, awkward, cumbrous. **1880** J. A. H. MURRAY *Address to Philol. Soc.* 30 England is stirring, in a slow, lumberly, and timorous fashion.

lumberman ('lʌmbəmən). *N. Amer.* [f. LUMBER *sb.*[1] + MAN.] One whose work is among lumber or rough timber, *esp.* one who fells and dresses timber in the forest.

a **1817** T. DWIGHT *Trav. New Eng.*, etc. II. (1821) 166 The lumbermen were without employment. **1870** EMERSON *Soc. & Solit.* Wks. (Bohn) III. 1 He envied every drover and lumberman in the tavern. **1893** *Scribner's Mag.* June 711/1 The veteran lumberman and politician, Hon. Philetus Sawyer, is a conspicuous example.

†**lumber-pie.** *Obs.* Also **lumbar-pie.** [See LOMBARD *a.* 2.] A savoury pie made of meat or fish and eggs.

1656 MARNETTÈ *Perf. Cook* II. 1 To make a Lumbar Pye. Take three pound of Mutton [etc.]. **1663** in Jupp *Acc. Carpenters' Comp.* (1848) 206 It is..ordered..that the provision be as followeth; vizt. Roast Turkey, Lumberpie, Capon, Custurd, and codling tart. **1688** R. HOLME *Armoury* III. 83/1 Lumber pie, made of Flesh or Fish minced and made in Balls..with Eggs..and so Baked in a Pye with Butter. **1694** MOTTEUX *Rabelais* (1737) IV. lix. 243 Lumber-Pyes, with hot Sauce. **17..** E. SMITH *Compl. House wife* (1750) 150 To make a Lumber pye. Take a pound and a half of veal, &c. **1849** W. H. AINSWORTH *Lanc. Witches* III. ix, There were lumbar pies, marrow pies, quince pies [etc.].

lumber-room. [f. LUMBER *sb.*[1]] A room for the reception of lumber or disused chattels.

1741 RICHARDSON *Pamela* (1824) I. 132 My own little chapel, which has not been used for any thing but a lumber-room. **1812** H. & J. SMITH *Rej. Addr.*, *Baby's Debut*, The chaise..Stood in the lumber room. **1884** J. HATTON *H.*

Irving's Impress. Amer. (ed. 2) I. 4 The apartments were lumber-rooms until lately.

b. *fig.*

1748 CHESTERF. *Lett.* clx. (1792) II. 72 Many great readers ..make lumber-rooms of their heads. **1827** HARE *Guesses* Ser. II. (1873) 446 The memory ought to be a store-room. Many turn theirs rather into a lumber-room. **1879** J. A. H. MURRAY *Address to Philol. Soc.* 33 They are included by Lepsius in his provisional lumber-room of 'Isolated Languages'.

lumbersome ('lʌmbəsəm), *a.* [f. LUMBER *v.*[1] + -SOME.] Cumbrous, unwieldy.

1834 M. SCOTT in *Blackw. Mag.* XXXV. 314 Sprawl.. invariably wore with his back to him, and so lumbersome and slowly, that the Commodore usually had wheeled..long before Mr. Sprawl came round. **1837** C. LOFFT *Self-formation* I. 142, I was like a young greyhound, sprawling, uncouth, and lumbersome. **1873** BROWNING *Red Cott. Nt.-cap* II. Wks. 1898 II. 396/2 The large and lumbersome and ..dignified And gentry-fashioned old-style haunts of sleep.

lumbert(te, obs. form of LOMBARD.

‖**lumbiplex** ('lʌmbɪplɛks). *Anat.* [f. L. *lumbus* loin + PLEX-US.] The lumbar plexus of nerves. Hence **lumbi'plexal** *a.*, pertaining to the lumbiplex.

1890 *Cent. Dict.* refers to COUES.

lumbo- ('lʌmbəʊ), used as combining form of L. *lumbus* loin, as **lumbo-abdominal** *a.*, pertaining to the loins and the abdomen (cf. ABDOMINAL); so ***lumbo-aortic***, ***-costal***, ***-inguinal***, etc. (see *Syd. Soc. Lex.* 1889), ***-sacral***, ***-vertebral*** adjs.; ‖**lumbodynia** [mod.L.; hybrid f. Gr. ὀδύνη pain] = LUMBAGO.

1899 *Allbutt's Syst. Med.* VI. 660 Neuralgia of the lumbar plexus, or *lumbo-abdominal neuralgia. **1866** A. FLINT *Princ. Med.* (1880) 805 The affection is commonly known as lumbago. Valleix designated it **lumbodynia*. **1840** E. WILSON *Anat. Vade M.* (1842) 107 The *lumbo-iliac ligament is triangular in form. **1856** *Quain's Anat.* (ed. 6) II. 632 *note*, Schmidt describes them as separate nerves, naming the genital branch, external spermatic, and the crural branch, *lumbo-inguinal. **1840** E. WILSON *Anat. Vade M.* (1842) 14 The *lumbo-sacral nerve. **1878** T. BRYANT *Pract. Surg.* I. 258 The lumbo-sacral portion of the column is more frequently affected than any other. **1899** *Allbutt's Syst. Med.* VI. 217 The *lumbo-vertebral anastomotic trunk of Braune.

lumbor, obs. form of LUMBER *sb.*[1]

†**lumbric.** *Obs.* Also 5 **lumbryke.** [ad. L. *lumbrīcus*: see LUMBRICUS.] A worm.

c **1440** *Promp. Parv.* 316/2 Lumbryke, *lumbricus*. **1828–32** WEBSTER, *Lumbric*, a worm. *Med. Repos.*

lumbrical (lʌm'braɪkəl), *a.* and *sb.* *Nat. Hist.* [ad. mod.L. *lumbrīcāl-is*: see LUMBRICUS and -AL[1].]

A. *adj.* Pertaining to or resembling a lumbricus or worm; *Anat.* applied to certain fusiform muscles in the hand and the foot which assist in flexing the digits.

1694 *Phil. Trans.* XVIII. 230 The Lumbrical Muscles (which lye in the Palm of the Hand). **1722** QUINCY *Lex. Physico-Med.* (ed. 2) 2 The Tendon of one of the lumbrical Muscles. **1775** ASH, *Lumbrical*.., belonging to the earth-worm. **1802** BINGLEY *Anim. Biog.* (1813) III. 394 The Lumbrical and Vermicular Ascaris. **1847–9** TODD *Cycl. Anat.* IV. 757/2 The fourth digital nerve..gives a filament to the second lumbrical muscle. **1866** *Treas. Bot.*, *Lumbrical*, worm-shaped; a term applied to the worm-like lobes of the frond of certain seaweeds.

B. *sb.* Often in L. form **lumbricalis**, pl. **-es** (lʌmbrɪ'keɪlɪs, -i:z). A lumbrical muscle.

1706 PHILLIPS (ed. Kersey), *Lumbricales*, Muscles of the Finger, so nam'd from their Figure. **1800** *Phil. Trans.* XC. 12 The fingers are bent to a certain degree by the long muscles that lie upon the fore-arm, to the tendons of which a set of smaller muscles are attached, called lumbricales. **1872** HUMPHRY *Myology* 188 There is in each limb only one lumbricalis. **1887** *Brit. Med. Jrnl.* 2 Apr. 733/1 The lumbricals of the hand and foot. **1899** *Allbutt's Syst. Med.* VI. 660 The two radial lumbricals are not paralysed.

lumbriciform (lʌm'braɪsɪfɔ:m), *a.* [ad. mod.L. type **lumbrīciformis*: see LUMBRICUS and -FORM.] Resembling a lumbricus; vermiform.

1828–32 in WEBSTER. **1874** COUES *Birds N.W.* 269 The tongue..resembles that of the Woodpeckers, in its length and lumbriciform slenderness.

lumbricine ('lʌmbrɪsaɪn), *a.* *Zool.* [ad. mod.L. *lumbrīcīna*: see LUMBRICUS and -INE.] Pertaining to the group *Lumbricina* of annelids; lumbriciform.

1890 in *Century Dict.*

So **lumbri'cinan**, a worm of this group.

1835 KIRBY *Hab. & Inst. Anim.* I. xii. 334 The third [order] he [Savigny] names Lumbricinans.

lumbricoid ('lʌmbraɪkɔɪd), *a.* and *sb.* *Zool.* [ad. mod.L. *lumbrīcoīd-ēs*: see LUMBRICUS and -OID.]

A. *adj.* Resembling the lumbricus or round-worm, *Ascaris lumbricoides*. **B.** *sb.* The round-worm.

1849–52 TODD *Cycl. Anat.* IV. 853/2 The presence of lumbricoid ascarides in the intestine. **1882** *Quain's Dict. Med.* 855/2 All the larger round-worms infesting man and animals are apt to be called *lumbricoids*. **1892** *Lancet* 20 Jan. 284/2 The possible relations between micro-organisms and these lumbricoids being thus established.

lumbricous (lʌm'braɪkəs), *a.* *Path.*, etc. [f. LUMBRIC-US + -OUS. Cf. late L. *lumbrīcōsus*.]

a. Infested with lumbrici. **b.** = LUMBRICIFORM.

1856 MAYNE *Expos. Lex.*, s.v. *Lumbricodes*. **1900** JACKSON *Gloss. Bot. Terms*.

lumbriculus (lʌm'brɪkjʊlʌs). [mod.L. (A. E. Grube 1844, in *Archiv für Naturgeschichte* X. 207), f. mod.L. *Lumbricus* (cf. LUMBRICUS) the name of a genus of earthworms + *-ulus*.] An aquatic, oligochæte worm of the genus so called, resembling an earthworm.

1901 [see DIVISION 1 f]. **1927** HALDANE & HUXLEY *Animal Biol.* ix. 172 The same (multiplication) would have been true if instead of a Planarian you had cut up the little polyp Hydra, and almost the same with the smaller Annelid worms such as Lumbriculus. **1963** R. P. DALES *Annelids* viii. 154 *Lumbriculus* has been found capable of regenerating the head twenty-one times in succession.

‖**lumbricus** (lʌm'braɪkəs). *Zool.* Pl. **lumbrici** (lʌm'braɪsaɪ). [L. *lumbrīcus*.] **a.** The earth-worm, *L. terrestris*. **b.** The round-worm which infests the intestines, *Ascaris lumbricoides* (frequently referred to *Lumbricus*).

c **1400** *Lanfranc's Cirurg.* 150 Leie aboue lumbricus of þe erþe, þat beth erþe-wormes staumpid & boilid wiþ oile of rosis. **1802–12** BENTHAM *Ration. Judic. Evid.* (1827) V. 202 In a relaxed constitution of the body politic, acquitted and unprosecuted malefactors..are no less congenial..than the tænia, the lumbricus, and the ascaris are to the natural body. **1808** *Med. Jrnl.* XIX. 307 Since taking the electuary, [he] has voided another lumbricus. **1841–71** T. R. JONES *Anim. Kingd.* (ed. 4) 248 In the Lumbrici,..every ring..is found to support a series of sharp retractile spines.

attrib. **1822–34** *Good's Study Med.* (ed. 4) I. 82 The contents of the stomach, together with a lumbricus worm.. were effused in the chest.

lumbrous ('lʌmbrəs), *a.* *rare.* [f. LUMBER *sb.*[1] + -OUS.] Heavy and unwieldy; lumbering.

1836 J. HILDRETH *Dragoon Campaigns Rocky Mts.* I. iii. 26 Our lumbrous vessel heavily groped her way through the waters. **1847–8** H. MILLER *First Impr.* xi. (1857) 170 The lumbrous dignity of Shenstone's elegiacs. **1887** HALL CAINE *Deemster* ii. (1888), A lumbrous, jolting sound of heavy wheels.

lume, Sc. var. LOOM *sb.*[1]; obs. f. LEAM *v.*[1]

‖**lumen** ('l(j)u:mɛn). Pl. **lumina** ('l(j)u:mɪnə). [L. = light; an opening.]

1. An opening, passage, or canal. **a.** *Anat.* and *Zool.* **b.** *Bot.* **c.** *Surg.* The passage of any tube in an instrument.

a. 1873 T. H. GREEN *Introd. Pathol.* (ed. 2) 81 The vessel thus calcified, loses its..contractility; its lumen is diminished. **1888** BEDDARD in *Encycl. Brit.* XXIV. 680/2 A longitudinal fold on the dorsal side which projects into the lumen of the intestine. **1893** SHIPLEY *Zool. Invertebr.* 214 In the lumen of the siphon is a small valve.

b. 1887 GARNSEY & BALFOUR tr. *De Bary's Fungi* 321 The hyphæ..usually have their walls thickened till the lumina disappear. **1900** JACKSON *Gloss. Bot. Terms*, *Lumen*, the space which is bounded by the walls of an organ, as the central cavity of a cell.

c. 1889 *Lancet* 9 Nov. 949/1 Tracheotomy was resorted to, the larger lumen of the tube affording a freer vent. **1894** *Ibid.* 3 Nov. 1033 The lumen of the catheter.

2. [First adopted, in Fr., by A. Blondel 1894, in *La Lumière électrique* 7 July 10.] A unit of luminous flux (now incorporated into the International System of Units), equal to the flux emitted by a point source of intensity one candela (formerly, one candle) into a solid angle of one steradian.

The total flux emitted by a source of one candela is 4π (= about 12·57) lumens.

1898 *Astrophysical Jrnl.* VII. 300 Luminous current is defined as the rate at which luminous energy is emitted by a point-source through a solid angle of one steradian. Unit: The luminous current of one candle, i.e., of one Hefner lamp. Name: 'Lumen'. Proposed by L. Weber. **1937** *Times* 13 Apr. p. iv/2 Electric discharge lighting..has been recently installed to give an even and intense illumination of 1,120,000 lumens so that any flaw or defect in the panels being produced may be detected at once. **1953** AMOS & BIRKINSHAW *Television Engin.* I. vii. 125 The efficiency of electric lamps is usually expressed in lumens per watt... For gas-filled lamps the efficiency increases steadily with the rating and is approximately 10 lumens per watt for 25 W lamps, 13 lumens per watt for 100 W lamps and 17·5 lumens per watt for 1 kW lamps. Thus a 100 W lamp radiates a total of 1,300 lumens and is equivalent to a source of $1{,}300/4\pi$, i.e., approximately 100 candle-power. **1974** *Which?* Mar. 88/3 The long-life bulbs gave a light output of about 600 lumens after one hour of life.

3. Special Comb.: **lumen-hour**, the quantity of light corresponding to a flux of one lumen radiated for one hour; similarly **lumen-second**.

1925 *Trans. Illuminating Engin. Soc.* (U.S.) XX. 630 The Lumen-hour is the unit of quantity of light. It is equal to a flux of one lumen continued for one hour. **1975** *Times* 21 Mar. 20/3 The public wanted a certain package of candlepower (expressed in lumens); the industry assured certain fixed wattages, and then aimed at the minimum cost per lumen-hour for those wattages. **1930** tr. *L. P. Clerc's Photogr.* ii. 7/2 The unit of exposure is the lumen-second or candle-metre-second. **1958** *Newnes Compl. Amat. Photogr.* x. 110 The light output of a flash-bulb is measured in lumen seconds.

lumen, obs. pl. of LIMB *sb.*[1]

‖**lumen siccum** ('l(j)u:mɛn 'sɛkʌm). [L., = dry light.] The dry light of rational knowledge or thought.

1605 BACON *Adv. Learn.* II. f.48 But this same *Lumen siccum*, doth parch and offend most mens watry and soft natures. **1819** COLERIDGE *Philos. Lect.* (1949) xiii. 374 Must there not be some power, call it with Lord Bacon the '*lumen siccum*'; or 'the pure light', with Lord Herbert;..that stands in human nature but in some participation of the eternal and the universal by which man is enabled to question, nay to contradict, the irresistible impressions of his own senses, nay, the necessary deductions of his own understanding? **1946** *Mind* LV. 285 Taylor's intellect was no *lumen siccum*, but was always strongly personal in its approach and attitude.

†**lumer.** *Obs.* *rare*$^{-1}$. [? a. OF. *lumiere*, F. *lumière* light.] Light, illumination.

c **1468** in *Archæol.* (1846) XXXI. 334 To encrese the lumer of the said hall, one every side vii other candelstickes, one eche iiii lyghtis.

lumeter ('l(j)u:mi:tə(r)). [f. L. *lūm-en* light + -METER.] = LUXMETER.

1911 *Trans. Optical Soc.* XII. 104 Messrs. R. & J. Beck, Ltd., the makers of the 'Lumeter' instrument. **1923** L. C. MARTIN *Colour* 178 The lumeter reads in foot-candles, that is to say the brightness which a perfectly reflecting and diffusing surface would have if illuminated by so many foot-candles. **1947** *Brit. Jrnl. Psychol.* XXXVIII. 89 The apparatus was calibrated for intensity of illumination (as this would appear to the subject's eye) by placing a lumeter in the position of the tube T.

lumichrome ('l(j)u:mɪkrəʊm). *Chem.* [ad. G. *lumichrom* (P. Karrer et al. 1934, in *Helv. Chim. Acta* XVII. 1010), f. L. *lūmi(n-*, *lūmen* light + Gr. χρῶμ-α colour.] 6,7-Dimethylalloxazine, $C_{12}H_{10}N_4O_2$, a crystalline compound that is formed by ultra-violet irradiation of riboflavin in acidic solution and shows a sky-blue fluorescence.

1935 *Chem. Abstr.* XXIX. 798 Straw-yellow crystals of lumichrome..are obtained by irradiating solns. of lactoflavin with sunlight. **1949** *Proc. Soc. Exper. Biol. & Med.* LXX. 585/2 The presence of lumichrome crystals in the media containing riboflavin after growth of the tubercule bacillus indicated that the loss of the vitamin was due to conversion to lumichrome. **1962** S. UDENFRIEND *Fluorescence Assay in Biol. & Med.* xiv. 460 Fresh milk and cream emit greenish-yellow fluorescence which is due mainly to riboflavin. When exposed to daylight for appreciable periods of time or irradiated in any other way, the fluorescence turns from yellow to blue. The latter is characteristic of lumichrome. **1972** *Plant Physiol.* XLIX. 991/2 The present report establishes the formation of lumichrome, presumably from either free or bound riboflavin, by the action of light on etiolated shoots of corn and oats and on yeast cells.

Lumière (l(j)u:mi:ɛə(r)). *Photogr.* The name of the brothers Auguste (1862–1954) and Louis (1864–1948) *Lumière*, French photographers, used *attrib.* to denote a process of colour photography invented by them involving a colour screen consisting of a glass plate coated with a mixture of starch grains dyed in the primary colours which was placed in front of the panchromatic emulsion on exposure and for viewing; also applied to plates used in this process. Cf. AUTOCHROME *a.* and *sb.*

1907 *Westm. Gaz.* 24 Aug. 14/2 In some respects the new Lumière process is old. *Ibid.* 20 Sept. 4/3 Even in the case of the Lumière plate a keen eye can detect the red and blue grains upon the lighter portions. **1920** *Chambers's Jrnl.* Apr. 238/2 Twelve volumes, illustrated by 1260 plates of his [*sc.* Burbank's] most beautiful creations, reproduced in colour from original *lumière* plates. **1955** G. R. SHARP tr. *Lorelle's Colour Bk. Photogr.* 199 In the Lumière process a transparent film base carries a mosaic pattern of microscopic coloured filters which is coated with a fine grain panchromatic emulsion. **1966** LACOUR & LATHROP *Photo Technol.* xv. 194/2 To produce the Lumiere Autochrome plate, starch grains were pulverized and one third dyed blue, one third dyed green and the remaining grains dyed red. The colored grains were remixed and spread in a very thin layer on a glass plate.

lumiflavin (l(j)u:mɪ'fleɪvɪn). *Chem.* [f. L. *lūmi(n-*, *lūmen* light + FLAVIN 2.] 6,7,9-Trimethylisoalloxazine, $C_{13}H_{12}N_4O_2$, a crystalline compound that is formed by ultra-violet irradiation of riboflavin in alkaline solution and shows a yellow-green fluorescence.

1934 *Chem. Abstr.* XXVIII. 2036, 1000 l. whey yields 170 mg. pure lumiflavin. **1946** *Jrnl. Biol. Chem.* CLXII. 96 Lumiflavin can either inhibit or stimulate the use of riboflavin or FAD by *Lactobacillus casei*, depending upon the relative amounts of lumiflavin present. **1956** *Jrnl. Biochem.* (Tokyo) XLIII. 643 To estimate the fluorescence of flavin separately from similar fluorescent substances in living body, the procedure of converting flavins to lumiflavin is of excellent one [*sic*]. **1962** S. UDENFRIEND *Fluorescence Assay in Biol. & Med.* vii. 243 Riboflavin can also be converted to the more highly fluorescent derivative, lumiflavin, by photodecomposition in alkaline solution, the formation of lumiflavin involving cleavage between the ribitol and flavin ring.

†**luminair.** *Sc. Obs.* Also 5 lumynar, -air. [a. F. *luminaire*, ad. med.L. *lūmināria*: see LUMINARY *sb.*] = LUMINARY *sb.*

1456 SIR G. HAYE *Law Arms* (S.T.S.) 210 God..maid twa lumynaris..that are callit the grete lumynar and the small lumynar. *c* **1477** CAXTON *Jason* 84 Whan..all the lumynaire brende about the body of Appollo. **1560** ROLLAND *Crt. Venus* II. 125 Of all palice it was the luminair. **1588** A. KING tr. *Canisius' Catech.* 81 All outuard apparell and ornaments of this vnbloody sacrifice as haly vestments, vessell, luminairs and vther cæremonies.

luminaire ('l(j)uːmɪnɛə(r)). orig. *U.S.* [Fr.; see LUMINARY *sb.*] An electric light and its fittings; such a lighting unit. Cf. LUMINAIR.

1921 *Trans. Illuminating Engin. Soc.* (U.S.) XVII. 249 The matter of a generic term for 'lighting unit' was considered by the Committee... The suggested term 'luminaire' was deemed to be the most acceptable... It is not a coined word but is a term already in use in the French language. **1925** M. LUCKIESH in Cady & Dates *Illuminating Engin.* ix. 363 In school lighting..luminaires should not be spaced farther apart than a distance of 1·5 times their elevation above the desk-tops. **1933** *Trans. Illuminating Engin. Soc.* (U.S.) XXVIII. 274 A luminaire is a complete lighting unit consisting of a light source, together with its direct appurtenances, such as globe, reflector, refractor, housing and such support as is integral with the housing. **1940** *Chambers's Techn. Dict.* 513/2 *Luminaire*,..a term sometimes used in America to denote an electric-light fitting. **1960** *How TV Works* iv. 24 The ceiling of a large studio such as Studio 6 in Manchester..may be fitted out with up to a hundred different lights, or 'luminaires' as they are more often called. **1971** *Daily Tel.* 21 Aug. 10 The British Standards Institution's committee responsible for electric light fittings has announced that in the interests of international standardisation it recommends the use of the word 'luminaire' instead of 'lighting fittings' in future. **1971** *Bahamian Rev.* Nov. 32/2 The 'Night Guard' luminaire is turned on automatically at dusk and switched off automatically at dawn, providing night-long security and safety. **1972** HENDERSON & MARSDEN *Lamps & Lighting* xix. 341 Luminaires can be divided into two categories: those which are essentially decorative and those which are essentially functional. Decorative luminaires are usually in the form of an assembly of decorative components around a light source, ranging from a simple pendant to the large..prestige chandelier. **1973** *Times* 1 Feb. 22/8 It is preposterous for BSI to force *luminaires* upon us.

luminal ('l(j)uːmɪnəl), *a.* [f. L. *lūmin-*, LUMEN + -AL[1].] Of or belonging to a lumen.

1897 *Amer. Naturalist* Jan. 67 The luminal walls of these intestinal cells are strong and thick.

Luminal ('l(j)uːmɪnæl), *sb. Pharm.* Also luminal. [prob. f. L. *lūmin-*, *lūmen* light (as a rendering of PHEN-) + -AL[2].] A proprietary name of phenobarbitone.

1912 *Trade Marks Jrnl.* 20 Mar. 402 Luminal... A medicine for human use as a sedative and hypnotic. The Bayer Company, Limited,..Manchester; manufacturers. **1928** *Daily Express* 7 Dec. 12 Gave him five grains of luminal. He'll sleep for a few hours and wake up penitent. **1937** *Times* 6 Sept. 7/5 For the defence, it was suggested that the shock of the collision, together with the use of luminal (a narcotic), would account for the symptoms. **1951** 'E. CRISPIN' *Long Divorce* iv. 37 As a doctor, she had remedies to hand—barbitone, nembutal, luminal. **1960** W. G. LENNOX *Epilepsy* II. xxvi. 860 Luminal (Winthrop-Stearns) is phenobarbital that costs more.

'**luminance.** [f. next: see -ANCE.]

1. Luminousness.

1880 OUIDA *Moths* III. xi. 282 Her eyes have a serious sweet luminance. **1884** E. A. B. HODGETTS tr. *Remin. Gen. Skobeleff* 322 The bright luminance of our freedom shall shine forth to be seen by the whole world. **1893** MARIE CORELLI *Barabbas* iii. (1894) 15 The flickering luminance thus given only making the native darkness of the place more palpable.

2. *Physics.* The amount of luminous flux emitted by unit area of a source into unit solid angle (the objective analogue of subjective brightness).

1950 JENKINS & WHITE *Fund. Optics* (ed. 2) vii. 104 To distinguish it from the visual sensation of brightness, it is usually termed the luminance in the technical literature, but ..we shall use the commoner name brightness, with the understanding that..the photometric quantity..is meant. **1952** *Electronics* Nov. 208/2 Luminance is a purely photometric quantity. Use of this name permits brightness to be used entirely with reference to the sensory response. **1957** V. J. KEHOE *Technique Film & Television Make-Up* viii. 95 As to..the reception of a color telecast on a monochromatic receiver, only the luminance portion will be supplied to the single electron gun in the monochrome tube to produce a black-and-white version of the signal. **1968** *Sci. Amer.* Nov. 8/2 Consider two areas that have the same luminance but one of which is seen against a dark background while the other is seen against a light background. The former will appear to be brighter. **1970** *Jrnl. Gen. Psychol.* LXXXII. 111 Midway between these red apertures a yellow spot, three minutes of arc in diameter and 3·1 ftL in luminance, provided the fixation. **1972** *Sci. Amer.* June 101/1 Measurements of a photograph of the vase ..showed that the luminance of the moon was 15 foot-lamberts and the space one moon diameter below was 20 foot-lamberts. The contour effect is so strong that the apparent brightness of the two areas is just the reverse of the objective luminance.

luminant ('l(j)uːmɪnənt), *a.* and *sb.* [ad. L. *lūminant-em*, pres. pple. of *lūmināre* to LUMINATE.]

A. *adj.* Illuminating, luminous.

1891 MISS DOWIE *Girl in Karp.* xviii. 237 There would be three more hours of light..before the luminant star-freaked dark. **1893** *Black & White* 22 July 100/2 His discussion is luminant only in flashes.

B. *sb.* An illuminant.

18.. *Elect. Rev.* XXIV. 334 (Cent.) Public institutions and factories are very much in favour of the new luminant. **1884** *Daily News* 3 Sept. 3/5 The different luminants—gas, oil, and electricity—which are being experimented with.

lumi'narious, *a. rare.* [f. LUMINARY + -OUS.] Luminous.

1773 J. ROSS *Fratricide* II. 853 (MS.) See! the clouds descend With luminareous glory. **1823** *Spirit Publ. Jrnls.* (1825) I. 271 Falling flat before the luminarious orb.

luminarism ('l(j)uːmɪnərɪz(ə)m). [-ISM, after LUMINARIST.] The art or doctrine of the luminarists.

1903 *Edin. Rev.* Oct. 373 We shall probably hear less of Turner as the pioneer of impressionism, luminarism, and pre-Raphaelitism. **1953** *New Republic* 6 July 18 In our own art the progression from linear to formal, formal to coloristic, and finally to the complete luminarism of the 1870s has been a slow process.

luminarist ('l(j)uːmɪnərɪst). [ad. F. *luminariste* (Littré *Suppl.*), f. L. *lūmin-*, *lūmen* light.] A painter who treats light effectively, or whose 'colour' is luminous.

1888 *Academy* 21 Jan. 48/2 The finest works of that great and subtle luminarist Adrian van Ostade. *a* **1900** R. A. M. STEVENSON *Introd. Armstrong's Sir H. Raeburn* (1901) 18 Oil-paint is the least abstract or conventional of the mediums. It is the medium of the luminarist and the man who would render an account of the full aspect of nature.

luminary ('l(j)uːmɪnərɪ), *sb.* [ad. F. *luminaire* masc. (early OF. *luminarie*), ad. med.L. *lūminārium*, *lūmināre*, f. *lūmin-*, *lūmen* light: cf. -ARY.]

1. A natural light-giving body, *esp.* a celestial body; pre-eminently applied to the sun or the moon. †*the luminaries* often = the sun and moon.

1489 CAXTON *Faytes of A.* IV. xvii. 279 The golde representeth the sonne whiche is a right noble lumynarye. **1559** W. CUNNINGHAM *Cosmogr. Glasse* 11 Imagining the luminaries to haue their course vnder all the other Planetes. **1615** TOMKIS *Albumazar* v. i. K 2 b, Search your Natiuitie: see if the Fortunates And Luminaries be in a good Aspect. **1665** BOYLE *Occas. Refl.* Pref. (1848) 24 For though the stars cannot, the Luminaries can, cloathe the..vapours of the air, with the colour of Gold and of Roses. **1667** —— in *Phil. Trans.* II. 606 Both of them [rotten Wood and burning Coal] are Luminaries, that is, give Light. **1667** MILTON *P.L.* III. 576 Where the great Luminarie Alooff the vulgar Constellations thick,..Dispenses Light from farr. **1774** GOLDSM. *Nat. Hist.* (1776) I. 8 All other planets that depend upon our great luminary for their support. **1820** SCOTT *Abbot* i, The level surface of the lake..was gilded with the beams of the setting luminary. **1881** ROUTLEDGE *Science* i. 15 Pythagoras conceived the planets to revolve around the central luminary.

b. *transf. nonce-use.* (As if 'astrological signs'.)

a **1639** WOTTON *Life Dk. Buckhm.* in *Reliq.* (1651) 77 Who, I know not upon what Luminaries he spyed in his face, disswaded him from Marriage.

2. An artificial light; †in Caxton *collect. sing.* (cf. F. *luminaire*); †in 17th c. *pl.*, illuminations betokening rejoicing (so med.L. *luminaria*).

1483 CAXTON *G. de la Tour* cxxxvi. 193 She..gaf these torches, and alle suche other lumynary as it neded therto. *c* **1510** BARCLAY *Mirr. Gd. Manners* (1570) G ij, None closeth in a corner a kindled luminary. **1605** B. JONSON *Masque Blackness* Wks. 1616 I. 897 The dressing of her head antique; & crown'd with a Luminarie, or Sphere of light. *c* **1645** HOWELL *Lett.* (1650) I. 135 There were luminaries of joy lately here for the victory that Don Gonzalez de Cordova got over Count Mansfelt in the Netherlands. **1692** LUTTRELL *Brief Rel.* (1857) II. 598 There were extraordinary luminaries in all the windows in the publick streets. **1706** COTES tr. *Dupin's Eccl. Hist. 16th C.* II. IV. xviii. 266 The Church..has introduced Ceremonies, such as mystical Benedictions, Luminaries [etc.]. **1892** STEVENSON *Across the Plains* 213 [They] began to garnish their windows with our particular brand of luminary.

3. *fig.* A source of intellectual, moral, or spiritual light (now only of persons, formerly also *occas.* of things); a person of 'light and leading'.

a **1450** *Cov. Myst.* (Shaks. Soc.) 288 [To Herod] O thou luminarye of pure lightnes! *a* **1529** SKELTON *Prayer to Father of Heaven*, O radiant Luminary of lyght intermynable, Celestial Father. **1557** PAYNEL *Barclay's Jugurth* 89 The glorious dedes..of forefathers be like an example or luminary vnto their of spring or progeny. **1643** SIR T. BROWNE *Relig. Med.* I. §12 In this mass of nature there is a set of things which to wiser..Reasons serve as Lumenaries in the Abyss of knowledge. **1692** BENTLEY *8 Serm.* (1724) 108 A late happy Discovery by two great Luminaries of this Island. **1773** JOHNSON in *Boswell* 19 Oct., We were now treading that illustrious island, which was once the luminary of the Caledonian regions. **1797** GODWIN *Enquirer* II. ix. 324 Mr. Fox..the greatest luminary of the present house of commons. **1854** H. ROGERS *Ess.* II. i. 2 Like the other great luminaries of philosophy and science, Locke has shone on with tolerably uniform lustre. **1860** TROLLOPE *Framley P.* i, Here is one of the luminaries of your diocese.

'**luminary,** *a. rare.* [f. L. *lūmin-*, *lūmen* light + -ARY.] Pertaining to light.

1794 G. ADAMS *Nat. & Exp. Philos.* II. xxi. 416 Without the influence of light, vegetables would..be deprived of their beautiful shades by the interception of the luminary fluid. **1889** *Anthony's Photogr. Bull.* II. 399 While the so-called cirri or land clouds have an average height of 13 kilometres, the luminary night clouds float at a height of 75 kilometres.

†'**luminate,** *a. Obs.* [ad. L. *lūmināt-us*, pa. pple. of *lūmināre* (see next).] Lighted.

1560 ROLLAND *Crt. Venus* II. 925 Thair luminat lampis of gret valour.

luminate ('l(j)uːmɪneɪt), *v. Obs.* or *arch.* [f. L. *lūmināt-*, ppl. stem of *lūmināre*, f. *lūmin-*, *lūmen* light.] *trans.* To light up, ILLUMINATE.

1623 COCKERAM, *Luminate*, to giue light. **1693** W. DE BRITAINE *Hum. Prud.* v. (ed. 6) 36 Whether the Stars be but Earth luminated, as Thales maintained, or [etc.]. **1799** SIR H. DAVY in Beddoes *Contrib. Phys. & Med. Knowl.* (1799) 87 The atmosphere [above 45 miles high] is amazingly rare, being composed of phosoxygen highly luminated. **1813** T. BUSBY *Lucretius* I. I. 634 Would proper principles in Nature lie, To furnish earth and luminate the sky?

Hence '**luminated,** '**luminating** *ppl. adjs.*

1652 BENLOWES *Theoph.* VII. xix. 97 The Stars..That stud the luminated sphear. **1746** WATSON in *Phil. Trans.* XLIV. 87 The luminating Power which is gained by Calcination. **1882** G. MACDONALD *Castle Warlock* i. xx. 320 He had been inwardly beholding a large breadth of gently luminated spiritual sky.

lumination (l(j)uːmɪ'neɪʃən). *rare.* [ad. L. **lūminātiōn-em*, n. of action f. *lūmināre*: see prec.] A shedding or emission of light. †Also *concr.* an illumination (cf. LUMINARY *sb.* 2).

1654 tr. *Scudery's Curia Pol.* D j b, The glory of terrestrial Soveraignty..transcendeth..inferiour lights and luminations. **1709** *Proclamation* in K. Steuart *By Allan Water* iii. (1901) 104 The haill inhabitants to put out and mak luminations in the windows of their houses. **1794** J. HUTTON *Philos. Light* etc. 291 Most powerful for exciting heat, proportionally to its lumination. **1858** MOTLEY *Dutch Rep.* Hist. Introd. VII. 39 The liberty of the Netherlands, notwithstanding several brilliant but brief luminations,.. seemed to remain in almost perpetual eclipse.

‖**luminator** ('l(j)uːmɪneɪtə(r)). *Hist.* [med.L. *lūminātor* (f. *lūmināre*: see LUMINATE *v.*); the word occurs as the designation of an official who kept the accounts of expenditure for the lighting and 'fabric' of a church. Cf. OF. *luminier* of the same meaning (in Auvergne, a churchwarden). See Du Cange s.vv. *Luminator*, *Luminaria.*] In St. Andrews University, a student (one in each class) who was privileged to attend the professor's lectures without payment, and to receive certain dues from the other students, in return for services rendered by him.

The former Librarian of the University, Mr. J. Maitland Anderson, informed us that the first student whom he found described in the records as 'luminator' entered the University in 1697; it is, however, probable that the title goes back to mediæval times. It is supposed that the 'luminator' originally provided lights and fires to the classes; but there is no contemporary evidence of this. Between 1800 and 1827 his duties seem to have been those of a clerk (cf. quot. *a* 1808). The office was abolished about 1830.

It is commonly stated that the University seal contains a representation of a 'luminator' holding a candle while a professor is lecturing. But whether the object is a candle or something else (? a mace), and whether the figure holding it is meant for the 'luminator', seems to be quite uncertain.

Called *illuminator* in Lyon's *St. Andrews* (1838) 171.

a **1808** *Bye-laws United College* (MS.), *clause added by Prof. Adamson*, The Luminator of each class to give in to the Hebdomadar each Monday a list of absents [from church] on the preceding Sunday. **1827** *Evidence Univ. Commission* (1837) III. 292 Each class has a Luminator, who originally furnished lights and fires to the classes for a certain remuneration from the students... He is still privileged to attend the class of which he is Luminator, without payment of a fee to the Professor; and..he continues to receive..2*s.* 6*d.* from each Secondar of the class, and 1*s.* 6*d.* from each Ternar, except [etc.].

lumine ('l(j)uːmɪn), *v.* Now *rare* or *Obs.* [a. OF. *lumine-r*, med.L. *lūmināre*, f. L. *lūmin-*, *lūmen* light. Cf. LIMN *v.*, ILLUMINE *v.*] *trans.* To light up, illumine. †In early use, to illuminate (manuscripts or books); see LIMN *v.* Hence '**lumined** *ppl. a.*, '**lumining** *vbl. sb.*

1387 TREVISA *Higden* (Rolls) VII. 295 Þis bisshop hymself schonede not to write and lumine and bynde bookes. **1483** *Cath. Angl.* 223/2 To Lumine, *illuminare*. **1512** in *Ld. Treas. Acc. Scotl.* IV. 379 In part pament of lummyng [? *read* lumining] of the Kingis grete portuus x Franch crounis. **1577–87** HOLINSHED *Chron.* III. 857/1 The outward part of the place lumined the eies of the beholders, by reason of the sumptuous worke. **1596** SPENSER *Heavenly Love* 280 Blinding the eyes, and lumining the spright. **1729** SAVAGE *Wanderer* III. 139 From lumin'd windows glancing on the eye, Around, athwart, the striking shadows fly. **1823** J. F. COOPER *Pioneers* xli, A smile of joy lumined his wrinkled features.

†**luminer(e.** *Obs.* Also -our. See also LIMNER. [f. LUMINE *v.* + -ER[2].] = ILLUMINATOR 5.

1330–31 *Durham Acc. Rolls* (Surtees) 517 Radulpho Luminour pro libr. de Merington illuminand. xijd. **1491** in *York Myst.* Introd. 39 Tixt-wryters, luminers [etc.].

luminesce (l(j)uːmɪ'nɛs), *v.* [Back-formation from LUMINESCENT.] *intr.* To become luminescent.

1896 S. P. THOMPSON in *Jrnl. Oxf. Univ. Junior Scientific Club* II. No. 40. 67 Substances such as glass lose the power of luminescing when raised to temperatures such that they become conductors of electricity. **1898** SIR W. CROOKES

Addr. Brit. Assoc. 22 Fluor-spar, which by prolonged heating has lost its power of luminescing when re-heated.

luminescence (l(j)uːmɪˈnɛsəns). [f. next: see -ENCE.] Luminescent condition or quality.

1889 [tr. *E. Weidemann* in] *Philos. Mag.* Ser. v. xxviii. 151, I have ventured to employ the term luminescence for all those phenomena of light which are more intense than corresponds to the actual temperature. **1896** *Q. Rev.* Apr. 497 Electrical luminescence. **1899** D. SHARP *Insects* II. (Camb. Nat. Hist.) 259 It is remarkable that there should be three successive seats of luminescence in the life of the same individual.

luminescent (ˈl(j)uːmɪˈnɛsənt), *a.* [f. L. *lūmin-, lūmen* light + -ESCENT.] **a.** Emitting light, or having the property of emitting light, otherwise than as a result of incandescence. **b.** Pertaining to luminescence.

1889 [tr. *E. Weidemann* in] *Philos. Mag.* Ser. v. XXVIII. 155 Luminescent light is in a high degree dependent in colour and intensity upon the mode of production. **1896** S. P. THOMPSON in *Jrnl. Oxf. Univ. Junior Scientific Club* II. No. 40. 64 The colour emitted by the luminescent body.

luminiferous (l(j)uːmɪˈnɪfərəs), *a.* [Formed as prec. + -(I)FEROUS.] Producing or transmitting light *esp.* in ***luminiferous ether*** (see ETHER 5).

1801 YOUNG in *Phil. Trans.* XCII. 22 The actual velocity of the particles of the luminiferous ether. **1842** PARNELL *Chem. Anal.* (1845) 270 The principal luminiferous constituents of coal-gas are [etc.]. **1863** TYNDALL *Heat* xi. 293 The luminiferous ether fills stellar space. **1866** J. MARTINEAU *Ess.* I. 137 The luminiferous, the calorific, and the chemical rays. **1878** BELL tr. *Gegenbaur's Comp. Anat.* 394 The paired luminiferous organ of these animals.

luminism (ˈl(j)uːmɪnɪz(ə)m). [f. L. *lūmin-, lūmen* light + -ISM.] = LUMINARISM.

1905 *Sat. Rev.* 11 Feb. 174 And now, stated in general terms, what is the principle of Monet's luminism? **1920** *Glasgow Herald* 27 Aug. 4 The world of art has given us Futurist, Cubist, Vorticist, luminism and others. **1927** F. J. MATHER *Hist. Mod. Painting* 365 The theoretical Cubists merely turned upon the prevailing Expressionism the criticism which Cézanne had applied to Luminism. **1970** R. LOWELL *Notebk.* 245 One misses Emerson drowned in luminism.

luminist (ˈl(j)uːmɪnɪst). *rare.* [f. L. *lūmin-, lūmen* light + -IST.] = LUMINARIST.

1901 *Edin. Rev.* Oct. 492 The Barbizon school, the realists, the luminists, the impressionists [etc.].

luminize (ˈl(j)uːmɪnaɪz), *v.* [f. L. *lūmin-, lūmen* light + -IZE.] *trans.* To make luminous; to apply a luminous substance to.

1958 *Oxford Mail* 9 July 1 Home radiation hazard in luminizing clocks. **1959** *Times* 30 Apr. 6/5 A Swiss firm was using strontium to luminize their watches. **1967** *Health Physics* XIII. 613/2 Where large numbers of the same type of dial are to be luminised, the paint is often applied by machine.

Hence **ˈluminized** *ppl. a.*, **ˈluminizing** *vbl. sb.*; **ˈluminizer**, one who luminizes objects.

1958 *Times* 20 June 11/7 Luminizing belongs to the daunting group of hazards associated with radiation. **1958** *Ann. Rep. Chief Inspector of Factories on Industr. Health 1957* 36 in *Parl. Papers 1958–9* (Cmnd. 558) XIII. 183 The case of a female luminiser, aged 42, is of special interest. **1959** *New Scientist* 19 Nov. 980/2 The clock industry has its own luminizing regulations. **1967** *Health Physics* XIII. 613/1 It was possible to make body radio-activity measurements on almost all the personnel employed on luminising in these workshops. *Ibid.* 613/2 Radium luminous compound is usually obtained by the luminiser in the form of a powder. *Ibid.* 614/1 In some cases the rest periods are spent on work with luminised articles.

luminol (ˈl(j)uːmɪnɒl). *Chem.* [f. L. *lūmin-, lūmen* light + -OL.] A pale yellow crystalline bicyclic hydrazide, $C_8H_7N_3O_2$, which gives a blue luminescence when oxidized in alkaline solution and is used in the determination of oxidizing agents and metal ions.

1934 E. H. HUNTRESS et al. in *Jrnl. Amer. Chem. Soc.* LVI. 241/1 It is the purpose of the present note to offer an improved method for the synthesis of this material [*sc.* 3-aminophthalhydrazide], which in the interest of simplicity we have long referred to as 'Luminol'. **1965** *Analytical Biochem.* XII. 309 This assay [for hematin iron] is based on the luminescence of alkaline luminol in the presence of hematin iron and hydrogen peroxide. **1970** R. P. WAYNE *Photochem.* iv. 120 The oxidation of luminol..in alkaline solution by ferricyanide..is one of the best-known chemiluminescent reactions. **1974** *Nature* 25 Jan. 193/2 Using a ^{60}Co-γ-source, irradiated saccharides give a bright blue light (≈4,460 Å) when they are dissolved in luminol solution.

luminologist (l(j)uːmɪˈnɒlədʒɪst). [f. L. *lūmin-, lūmen* light + -OLOGIST.]

1. One who studies the luminescent phenomena in living organisms.

1888 *Nature* 1 Mar. 411/1 Luminologists such as Giglioli, Dubois, and others.

¶ **2.** One versed in the study of illuminations of manuscripts. *rare*$^{-0}$.

1890 in *Century Dict.* (with quot. of sense 1).

luminophore (ˈl(j)uːmɪnəfɔə(r)). Also -phor. [f. L. *lūmin-, lūmen* light + -O + -PHORE.]

a. A luminescent substance.

1907 *Jrnl. Chem. Soc.* XCII. II. 419 The addition of sodium or potassium sulphate to the mixture intensified both this green phosphorescence and that due to the luminophore added. **1930** *Chem. Abstr.* XXIV. 785 (*heading*) Contribution to the preparation of luminophores. **1950** H. W. LEVERENZ *Introd. Luminescence of Solids* v. 147 Luminescent materials in general (luminophors)..have the additional property of being able to convert part of the absorbed primary energy into emitted luminescence radiations whose spectral characteristics are determined almost entirely by the luminophor. *Ibid.*, The generic term *luminophor* is subclassified into fluorophors..and phosphors. **1968** *Proc. Internat. Conf. Luminescence, Budapest 1966* I. 1290 Precipitates of uniform size..are demanded especially by the luminophore industry.

b. A group of atoms in a molecule which is considered to be responsible for its luminescence.

1910 *Encycl. Brit.* X. 72/1 H. Kauffmann..suggested that the property [of fluorescence] is due to the presence of at least two groups. The first group, named the 'luminophore', is such that when excited by suitable aetherial vibrations [it] emits radiant energy; the other..acts with the luminophore in some way or other to cause the fluorescence. **1949** P. PRINGSHEIM *Fluorescence & Phosphorescence* v. 392 The strong absorption of visible light which is characteristic of dyes was ascribed to the presence of certain unsaturated groups, such as the azo group $-N{=}N-$, the ethylene group $-HC{=}CH-$, and the carbonyl group $>C{=}O$, which were called chromophors. These chromophors were at first supposed also to be the carriers of fluorescence as 'luminophors'.

luminosity (l(j)uːmɪˈnɒsɪtɪ). [f. LUMINOUS: see -ITY, -OSITY.]

1. a. The quality or condition of being luminous.

1634 BP. HALL *Contempl., N.T.* IV. vii, As it is in the sun ..the luminosity of it being no whit impaired by that perpetual emission of lightsome beams. **1851–9** OWEN in *Man. Sci. Enq.* 369 The phenomena of oceanic luminosity. **1865** E. C. CLAYTON *Cruel Fortune* II. 148 To impart additional luminosity to your ideas. **1871** DARWIN *Desc. Man* I. x. 345 The purpose of the luminosity in the female glowworm is..not understood. **1895** ZANGWILL *Master* II. i. 120 Luminosity of colour, richness of handling, grip of composition.

b. The effectiveness of light of any particular wavelength in producing the sensation of brightness when perceived.

[**1888** *Amer. Jrnl. Sci.* CXXXVI. 359 While..the luminosity of any spectral ray increases proportionately to the heat in this ray, and indeed is but another manifestation of the same energy..there is..a failure to recognize how totally different optical effects may be produced..according to the wave-length.] **1898** *Astrophysical Jrnl.* VII. 303 That particular property of any color which determines its value as an illuminant is called its 'luminosity'. **1936** *Proc. R. Soc.* A. CLV. 664 The relative luminosity (visibility) in the red region has been measured..as far as 770 mμ. In this paper an account is given of measurements up to 900 mμ. At this wavelength the relative luminosity is one-sixty millionth of that at 556 mμ. **1950** F. H. ADLER *Physiol. Eye* xx. 645 The luminosity of any one wave length is usually compared to that of 550 mμ. **1966** C. W. WILMAN *Seeing & Perceiving* xiv. 116 Curve *Ph* in Fig. 78 represents the relative luminosity (brightness) of various parts of the spectrum.

c. *Astr.* The intrinsic brightness of a heavenly body (as distinct from its apparent brightness, diminished by distance); the rate of emission of electromagnetic radiation (visible or invisible) within any part of the spectrum.

1906 *Astrophysical Jrnl.* XXIII. 248 Prevailing opinion.. admits the presence in the heavens of at least a few stars of extraordinary intrinsic brilliancy...stars having a luminosity exceeding that of the Sun by ten-thousand fold or more. **1924** H. DINGLE *Mod. Astrophysics* vi. 74 By brightness we mean—at present, at any rate—the apparent brightness of a star, which will be determined by the star's distance from us as well as by its intrinsic luminosity. **1930** R. H. BAKER *Astron.* ix. 369 The apparent magnitude of a star relates to its brightness as we observe it, depending on its real brightness, or luminosity, and on its distance. **1974** *Nature* 1 Mar. 34/2 We have..assumed a thermal spectrum, with an electron temperature of 2×10^6 K, in deriving an upper limit to the X-ray luminosity of the source. *Ibid.*, A 3σ upper limit was obtained to the source luminosity of 4·0 (±1·0) × 10^{32} erg s^{-1} for the energy range 0·5 to 1·5 keV.

2. Something luminous; a luminous point or area.

1853 KANE *Grinnell Exp.* xxvii. (1856) 223, I thought I saw a luminosity overhead. **1873** BROWNING *Red Cott. Nt.-cap* 232 Then his face grew one luminosity. **1895** ZANGWILL *Master* II. ii. 142 The strange warm luminosities Matt professed to see on London tiles.

3. Special Comb.: **luminosity curve**, a graph showing how emitted energy, or perceived brightness, varies with wavelength; **luminosity function** *Astr.*, a function giving the number or proportion of heavenly bodies with an absolute magnitude equal to, or greater than, any chosen value.

1886 ABNEY & FESTING in *Phil. Trans. R. Soc.* CLXXVII. 425 By successive alterations in the distance of the comparison-light other pairs of points in the spectrum are determined until the limits of the visible spectrum are reached. The curves of intensities of different parts of the spectrum plotted from these observations will be found to be fairly smooth. This curve we call the 'luminosity curve'. *Ibid.* 452 We..determined the luminosity-curve of a candle. **1900** *Astrophysical Jrnl.* XI. 220 (*heading*) Determining the luminosity curve of the solar spectrum. **1937** *Nature* 6 Mar. 409/2 The maximum of this luminosity curve was at 510 mμ. This was a mean value for forty-eight young observers. **1941** J. D. COBINE *Gaseous Conductors* xiii. 514 The luminosity curve for an incandescent lamp is shifted slightly toward the long wave lengths compared with sunlight. **1951** *Proc. IRE* XXXIX. 1143/2 The luminosity curve expresses the relation..between the luminance and the radiance of spectrum colors. *Ibid.* 1144/1 Based on the new definition of the lumen, and on the new International Temperature Scale, the peak value of the luminosity curve corresponds to 680 lumens per watt. **1924** *Astrophysical Jrnl.* LIX. 13 The comparison..is easily made with the aid of what may be called the apparent luminosity function..which expresses the frequencies of absolute magnitudes among the stars brighter than m_0. **1958** *Ibid.* Suppl. III. 211 Distances of galaxies are correlated with their apparent magnitude; however the uncertainty of the luminosity function of galaxies complicates and weakens the statistical treatment.

luminous (ˈl(j)uːmɪnəs), *a.* Also 5 luminos(e, lumynouse. [ad. L. *lūminōs-us*, f. *lūmin-, lūmen* light. Cf. F. *lumineux*.]

1. a. Full of light; emitting or casting light; shining, bright. *occas.* jocular = shiny.

1432–50 tr. *Higden* (Rolls) I. 113 The frute of olives is vnctuous, luminose, and delicious. **1471** RIPLEY *Comp. Alch.* Pref. in Ashm. *Theatr. Chem. Brit.* (1652) 121 Whose Luminos Bemes obtundyth our speculation. **1630** *Tinker of Turvey* 55 His eyes were luminous, Chrystalline and beauteous. **1792** MAR. RIDDELL *Voy. Madeira* 20 The phaenomenon of the luminous sea, well known to naturalists. **1835** W. IRVING *Tour Prairies* 147 As the night thickened the huge fires became more and more luminous. **1839** URE *Dict. Arts* 1191 In circumpolarization it [sugar] bends the luminous rays to the right. **1863** TYNDALL *Heat* i. §11 (1870) 11 Here are two quartz-pebbles: I have only to rub them together to make them luminous. **1877** W. H. BALMAIN *Brit. Pat. 4152* 7 Nov., My invention relates to a method of rendering paints, varnishes, whitewashings, and temperings luminous, and consists in the introduction into ordinary paints, varnishes, or washes of a phosphorescent substance, by which means the object to which the paint, or varnish, or wash is applied is made visible in the dark and more or less capable of imparting light to other objects. **1900** *Blackw. Mag.* July 58/2 The maples and birches..shone with a strange luminous beauty. **1926** R. W. LAWSON tr. *Hevesey & Paneth's Man. Radioactivity* xxv. 194 These radioactive 'luminous substances' differ from the phosphorescent substances formerly used, in that they do not require previous illumination. **1929** *Jrnl. Amer. Med. Assoc.* 9 Feb. 466/1 (*heading*) Occupational poisoning in manufacture of luminous watch dials. **1953** KIRK & OTHMER *Encycl. Chem. Technol.* X. 658 Of increasing commercial importance are the luminous pigments which produce fluorescent and phosphorescent effects of value in interior decoration, for direction signs and safety devices, television picture tubes, special military applications, and the like. **1958** *New Statesman* 28 June 846/3 The sins of the hitch-hiking undergraduates were drainpipes, luminous socks, and frying sausages in their bedrooms. **1969** R. F. LANG tr. *Henglein's Chem. Technol.* 546 Radium salts are used..for manufacturing luminous paint mixed with ZnS and CaS. **1975** K. BARCLAY tr. *Orum's Whipping-Boy* xi. 82 My alarm clock has a luminous dial.

b. Of a room: Well lighted.

1610 G. FLETCHER *Christ's Tri.* II. xxx, Their sunny Tents and houses luminous. **1624** WOTTON *Elem. Archit.* I. 55 Our Master..seems to haue beene an extreame Louer of Luminous Roomes. **1775** JOHNSON *Tour West. Isl. Scot.* 10 The library..is elegant and luminous. **1791** BOSWELL *Johnson* 21 Sept. an. 1777, The church of Ashbourne, which is one of the largest and most luminous that I have seen in any town of the same size.

c. Applied to animals or plants which emit light.

1845 DARWIN *Voy. Nat.* ii. (1879) 30 The rings in one instance retained their luminous property nearly twenty-four hours after the death of the insect. **1851–6** WOODWARD *Mollusca* 30 Some of the cuttle-fishes are slightly luminous. **1900** *Nature* 12 July 264/2 Dr. J. D. F. Gilchrist exhibited ..four fishes showing luminous organs.

d. ***luminous efficiency***, (of radiant energy) the ratio of the luminous flux to the total flux; (of a light source) the ratio of the luminous flux to the total flux emitted by, or power supplied to, the source.

1902 *Encycl. Brit.* XXVIII. 89/1 The luminous efficiency of any source of light, that is to say, the percentage of rays emitted which affect the eye as light compared with the total radiation, is dependent upon its temperature. In an ordinary oil lamp the luminous rays do not form much more than 3 per cent of the total radiation. **1927** H. N. RUSSELL et al. *Astron.* II. xvi. 529 The luminous efficiency of sunlight is obtained by dividing the luminous flux by the total radiant flux..and comes out 100 lumens, or about 8 candles per watt. **1961** CARNT & TOWNSEND *Colour Television* iii. 55 Objects moving across the screen may..leave a yellow trail ..as the red and green phosphors continue to glow after the blue phosphor has ceased... The luminous efficiency of these phosphors is low, only a few per cent of the electrical energy being converted into radiant energy... Ten or so lumens per watt can be obtained at 20 kV.

2. *transf.* and *fig.*; said esp. of writers, expressions, literary treatment, etc.

*c*1450 *Mirour Saluacioun* 1261 This virgine fulle of splendour and thorgh out lumynouse. **1618** BOLTON *Florus* To Rdr. (1636) A 7 Whose writings are altogether as luminous, as acuminous. **1787** SHERIDAN in *Sheridaniana* 98 If you..read the luminous page of Gibbon. **1799** *Med. Jrnl.* I. 397 The solid and luminous theory of Lavoisier and La Place. **1809** KNOX & JEBB *Corr.* I. 559 When I say that Watts was not luminous, I mean strictly to distinguish that word from *lucid*; for this I think he was. **1855** MACAULAY *Hist. Eng.* xxv. IV. 447 His State papers..are models of terse, luminous, and dignified eloquence. **1881** G. ALLEN *Vignettes fr. Nat.* xxii. 222 Mr. Wallace's luminous researches on the geographical distribution of animals.

ˈluminously, *adv.* [f. LUMINOUS + -LY^2.] In a luminous manner; with luminosity.

1816 T. L. PEACOCK *Headlong Hall* ix, So luminously expounding the nature of Owen Thomas' mistake. **1884** *Harper's Mag.* Aug. 362 Where swim medusæ luminously.

1888 H. R. Reynolds *Expos. St. John* xxi, Vers. 14–18 are.. eminently and luminously Johannine.

ˈluminousness. [f. as prec. + -NESS.] Luminous quality or condition; luminosity.

1667 Boyle in *Phil. Trans.* II. 591 Whether stinking Fish, that shines, be of the same nature as to Luminousness with Rotten Wood, that shines too. **1773** Johnson *Let. to Mrs. Thrale* 25 Aug., A library that for luminousness and elegance may vie at least with the new edifice at Streatham. **1873** J. H. Newman *Hist. Sk.* III. ii. v. 284 Expounding a sacred dogma with a luminousness which is almost an inspiration.

lumirhodopsin (ˌl(j)uːmɪrəʊˈdɒpsɪn). *Biochem.* Also **lumi-rhodopsin.** [f. L. *lūmi(n-, lūmen* light + RHODOPSIN.] An orange intermediate that is formed when rhodopsin is bleached by light and changes spontaneously to metarhodopsin.

1950 G. Wald et al. in *Science* 17 Feb. 180/1 On exposing the solution to light at these low temperatures, the maximum shifts about 5 mμ toward the blue, rising about 5% in height in cattle rhodopsin, falling about this amount in frog rhodopsin, still with little change in shape. This is the light reaction. We shall call its product lumirhodopsin. **1975** *Nature* 3 Jan. 56/2 Lozier and Stoeckenius have observed [in *Halobacterium halobium*] four spectrally distinct intermediates analogous to the rhodopsin, prelumirhodopsin, lumirhodopsin and metarhodopsin of invertebrates.

lumisterol (l(j)uːˈmɪstərɒl). *Biochem.* [ad. G. *lumisterin* (A. Luttringhaus 1931, in *Chemikerzeitung* 12 Dec. 956/2), f. L. *lūmi(n-, lūmen* light + *-sterin* after CHOLESTERIN, ERGOSTERIN, with altered ending (see -STEROL).] A steroid alcohol, $C_{28}H_{44}O$, which is a stereo-isomer of ergosterol and occurs as an intermediate when this is converted to vitamin D_2 by ultra-violet irradiation and warming.

1932 *Nature* 20 Feb. 277/1 In lumisterol the crystals are fine needles with *b* as needle axis. **1949** W. H. Eddy *Vitaminology* iii. 46 Lumisterol can be converted into calciferol and may form with it an addition compound consisting of one part lumisterol and one part calciferol... This addition compound.. was called vitamin D_1. **1967** W. R. Butt *Hormone Chem.* xi. 235 It has been established that acetate is the primary carbon source of cholesterol, there being probably about thirty separate reactions involved in the pathway through squalene and lumisterol to cholesterol. **1970** R. A. Morton *Fat-Soluble Vitamins* 187 The compound originally called vitamin D_1 was later found to be a mixture of ergocalciferol (D_2) and lumisterol, a photodecomposition product of D_2.

lumme, obs. form of LOOM *sb.*[2]

lumme (ˈlʌmɪ), *int.* Also **lummy.** A corruption of *(Lord) love me.*

1898 J. D. Brayshaw *Slum Silhouettes* 146 Wot! Pay for me death? Oh, lummy! not me. **1921** H. Williamson *Beautiful Yrs.* xviii. 205 He's an awful liar, you know, but can't he half climb a tree! Lumme, much better'n I can! **1934** P. Allingham *Cheapjack* xxii. 297 You've forgotten all about sister Alice! Lumme, you must get 'er something. **1935** D. L. Sayers *Gaudy Night* xvii. 370 'Lor' lumme!' I says, 'there's old Winderpane gawn.' **1942** *R.A.F. Jrnl.* 3 Oct. 33 Two years ago.. they set London on fire... Lumme, that was a night. **1963** *Times* 4 Mar. 5/2 A pitch which has evoked from Trueman the classic comment: 'Lumme! A green dusty.'

lummox (ˈlʌməks). *dial.* and *U.S.* Also **lommocks, lommox, lummicks, lummux,** etc. [Of obscure formation. Goes with the dial. verb *lummock* to move heavily or clumsily.] A large, heavy, or clumsy person; an ungainly or stupid lout.

a **1825** R. Forby *Vocab. E. Anglia* (1830) II. 201 Look o' yin great lummox, lazing and lolloping about. **1854** A. E. Baker *Gloss. Northamptonshire Words* I. 402 A great fat lommocks. **1854** 'Dow Jr.' *Patent Sermons* IV. 149 (Th.), Man in his original state is little more than a big lummux of a baby. **1857** J. G. Holland *Bay Path* 381 (Th.), I hope you'll leave somebody else to home besides this lazy lummox. **1893** W. K. Post *Harvard Stories* 186 Well, don't you be such a lazy lummox. **1919** H. L. Wilson *Ma Pettengill* iii. 92 Oswald is a big fair-haired lummox that sings tenor in the Presbyterian choir. **1924** F. Hurst (*title*) Lummox. **1934** [see GORMLESS *a.*]. **1952** J. Steinbeck *East of Eden* xvii. 172 Those great lummoxes would chew a little thing like you to the bone. **1953** K. Tennant *Joyful Condemned* vi. 54 There's that settee... This big lummox.. can sleep on that. **1957** J. Braine *Room at Top* iv. 45 The big lummox standing possessively beside her. **1971** T. Kilroy *Big Chapel* vi. 123 And that other lummox backing him up good-oh!.. A fine pair of cross-fire merchants the two of them! **1973** A. Garner *Red Shift* 55 You big lummox,.. He's talking about the Irish.

lummy (ˈlʌmɪ), *a. slang.* First-rate.

1838 Dickens *O. Twist* xliii, Jack Dawkins—lummy Jack—the Dodger—the Artful Dodger. **1864** *Slang Dict.*, *Lummy*, jolly, first-rate. **1883** *Punch* 28 July 38/1 London's gettin' more lummy each day; there's sech oshuns to see and enjoy!

lump (lʌmp), *sb.*[1] Also 4–6 lomp(e, lumpe, (5 lumppe). [ME. *lump*; not found in the early Teut. dialects; cf. early mod.Du. *lompe* (now *lomp*) rag; Du. *lomp*, LG. *lump* adj., coarse, heavy, rude; Ger. (from Du. or LG.) *lumpen* rag, *lump* ragamuffin; Sw. *lump* (Da. 16th c.) rag is from Ger. A sense nearer to that of the Eng. word occurs in Da. (16th c.) *lump(e* lump, Norw. and Sw. dial. *lump* block, stump, log, *lumpe* a sort of cake.

The ulterior etymology is quite uncertain. Usually the word has been regarded as cogn. w. LAP *sb.*[1] It might perh. be connected with OE. *(ge)limpan*, pa. pple. *(ge)lumpen*, to happen, the original notion being that of such a quantity as chance determines—such a portion as may offer itself, and not any measured or intentionally shaped piece.]

1. a. A compact mass of no particular shape; a shapeless piece or mass; often with implication of excessive size, protuberant outline, or clumsiness. Also *ellipt.*, = *lump of sugar.*

a **1300** *Cursor M.* 2869 (Cott.) Men findes lumpes [*Gött.* lompis] on þe sand O þer [*read with Gött.* Of ter] nan finer in þat land. *c* **1375** *Sc. Leg. Saints* xliii. (*Cecile*) 461 [He] gert men with lumpis of led dyng hyme til he ves ded. *c* **1400** Maundev. (Roxb.) xii. 50 Men may find.. grete lumppes þaroff, ȝa as grete as a hors, casten vp on þe land. **1426** Lydg. *De Guil. Pilgr.* 17834, I put vp many a lompe off bred In-to my sak. **1508** Kennedie *Flyting w. Dunbar* 462 Thow spewit, and kest out mony a lathly lomp. **1581** Pettie tr. *Guazzo's Civ. Conv.* ii. (1586) 59 Wee must frame all the bodie in such sorte, that it seeme neither to bee of one whole immoueable lumpe, neyther yet to be altogether loosely disioynted. **1601** Shaks. *All's Well* iii. vi. 30 When your Lordship sees.. to what mettle this counterfeyt lump of ours [Theobald 1726 *suggests* oare] will be melted. **1656** Cowley *Pindar. Odes, Nemæan Ode* v, Nature herself, whilst in the Womb he was, Sow'd Strength and Beauty through the forming Mass, They mov'd the vital Lump in every part. **1728** Pope *Dunc.* i. 102 So Watchful Bruin forms, with plastic care, Each growing lump, and brings it to a Bear. **1728** E. Smith *Compleat Housewife* (ed. 2) 213 When 'tis fine draw it into dry Bottles, and put a Lump of Sugar into every Bottle. **1738** Swift *Pol. Conversat.* 95 She gives the Child a lump of Sugar. **1860** Tyndall *Glac.* ii. xxv. 365 A tin vessel filled with lumps of lead and iron as a weight. **1899** H. James *Awkward Age* iii. xi. 101 Sugar?—isn't that the way to say it? Three lumps? **1901** *Speaker* 5 Jan. 375/2 American methods of handling do not readily lend themselves to the preservation of the coal in large lumps. *a* **1916** 'Saki' *Toys of Peace* (1919) 24 Little friendly questions about weak or strong tea, how much, if any, sugar, milk, cream, and so forth. 'Is it one lump? I forgot.' **1922** H. S. Walpole *Cathedral* i. v. 85 No, I'm afraid I don't—thank you, Mrs. Sampson. One lump, please.

b. ***a lump in one's throat***: (*a*) a swelling in the throat; (*b*) a feeling of tightness or pressure in the throat due to emotion. *popular.*

1803 *Med. Jrnl.* IX. 552 She feeling a lump, to use her own expression, in her throat, which obstructed her swallowing. **1863** Mrs. H. Wood *Vern. Pride* lvi. (1888) 361 A lump was rising in Lionel's throat. *a* **1878** P'cess Alice in *Biog. Sk.* (1884) 34 A lump always comes into my throat when I think of it.

c. ***lump of clay***: applied disparagingly to the human body, or to a person stigmatized as 'soulless'.

a **1400** *Cursor M.* 27647 (Galba) þou man þat in erth I say and wers þan a lump of clay. **1567** *Satir. Poems Reform.* iii. 7 Ane King at euin, with Sceptur, Sword, and Crown, At morne bot ane deformit lumpe of clay. **1591** Shaks. *1 Hen. VI*, ii. v. 13 Yet are these Feet, whose strengthlesse stay is numme, Vnable to support this Lumpe of Clay. *c* **1680** Beveridge *Serm.* (1729) I. 338 Being freed from these lumps of clay,.. we shall be made like to the glorious angels. **1763** Churchill *Gotham* iii. 175 One of the herd, a lump of common clay, Inform'd with life, to die and pass away. [**1855** Tennyson *Maud* i. xvi. i, This lump of earth has left his estate The lighter by the loss of his weight.]

d. *transf.* and *fig.*

1576 Fleming *Panopl. Epist.* 282 The man who is a lumpe or masse of foolishnesse, is the onely occasion of this motion. **1594** Shaks. *Rich. III*, i. ii. 57 Blush, blush, thou lumpe of fowle Deformitie. **1624** Middleton *Game at Chess* iv. iv. 81 Is it that lump of rank ingratitude. **1821** Lamb *Elia* Ser. i. *Old & New Schoolm.*, Some neglected lump of nobility or gentry. **1876** Mozley *Univ. Serm.* ii. 26 We come across some obstinate lump of evil that will not give way.

e. A great quantity; a 'lot', 'heap'. Also *pl.* 'lots', 'heaps'. *slang.* or *dial.*

1523 Skelton *Garl. Laurel* 733, I am not ladyn of liddyrnes with lumpis. **1549** Coverdale, etc. *Erasm. Par. James* 25 He that is pressed with sondry lumpes of sorowes. **1713** Warder *True Amazons* (ed. 2) 32 Now we are sure of a good lump of Honey. **1728** P. Walker *Life Peden* (1827) 118 Nothing will convince this Generation but Judgments, and a surprising Lump of them upon the West of Scotland. **1841** L. Hunt *Seer* (1864) 11 The merrier and happier they are in general, the greater the lumps of pain they can bear. **1869** Blackmore *Lorna D.* xv, Colonel Harding owed him a lump of money. **1880** *Antrim & Down Gloss.*, *Lump*.. (2) A quantity. 'A lump of people'. **1896** Farmer *Slang* s.v., 'I like that a lump'.

f. = *lump work* (LUMP *sb.*[1] 9). Of persons: those who contract to do work 'in the lump', i.e. for a lump sum.

[*a* **1852** H. Mayhew *London Labour* (1861) II. 330/1 The first man who agrees to the job takes it in the lump, and he again lets it to others in the piece.] **1902** *Eng. Dial. Dict.* III. 691/1 You can do it either by the day or lump. **1969** *Daily Mail* 3 Sept. 2/1 He then spelt out exactly how the thousands of 'labour only' sub-contractors—'The Lump' in building trade slang—deprive the Treasury of more than £3 million a year. **1970** *Daily Tel.* 27 May 11/1 In the building industry, the outgoing government argues, this employment of a quarter of a million men—known as 'the Lump' because it accepts a lump sum for its work and attends to its own tax and social insurance problems—has resulted in widespread tax and National Insurance evasion. **1972** *Times* 21 Nov. 21/2 They attribute much of the confusion in the building 'jungle', as they often call it, to the operations of the 'lump', the growing number of labour-only sub-contractors and 'self-employed'. **1973** *Guardian* 22 Feb. 9/5 A Bill which would prohibit 'lump' labour in the building and construction industry was given a formal first reading in the Commons... There had been a definite increase in the lump in the past 10 years. **1974** *Shelter News* Easter 3/2 Some companies already party to the agreement admit a limited use of lump labour and argue very convincingly that they have little choice if they are to meet completion dates.

g. *U.S. slang.* A parcel of food given to a tramp or vagrant. Cf. Eng. dial. *lump*, a luncheon (see *E.D.D.*).

1912 D. Lowrie *My Life in Prison* ix. 105, I noticed he had a lump (lunch) with him. **1914** Jackson & Hellyer *Vocab. Criminal Slang* 56 *Lump*, current chiefly amongst yeggs, hobos, and the indigent. A donation of victuals intended for consumption outside the house. **1926** J. Black *You can't Win* vi. 67 She'll give you a sit-down for yourself, chances are, but bring back a 'lump' for us. **1931** 'D. Stiff' *Milk & Honey Route* xiv. 161 It may be that he has the boy along only to wash his clothes or to bum his lumps. **1967** K. Allsop *Hard Travellin'* xviii. 214, I met a husky burly taking of his rest And he flagged me with a big lump and a can.

h. *pl.* Hard knocks, scolding.

1935 *Jrnl. Abnormal Psychol.* XXX. 363 *Lumps, get the*, to [be] beaten up. **1949** [see FOOT *sb.* 29]. **1970** J. H. Gray *Boy from Winnipeg* 32 My father would sit and take his verbal lumps, saying nothing. **1971** B. Malamud *Tenants* 130 Now I take my lumps, he thought. Maybe for not satisfying Mary.

2. a. Applied *spec.* (chiefly *fig.* in Biblical use) to the mass of clay taken up by a potter or sculptor for one operation, and to the mass of dough intended for one baking.

1526 Tindale *Rom.* ix. 21 Hath nott the potter power over the claye, even off the same lompe to make one vessell vnto honoure, and a nother vnto dishonoure? —— *1 Cor.* v. 6 Knowe ye not that a lytell leven sowereth the whole lompe of dowe? [**1611** leaueneth the whole lumpe.] *a* **1633** G. Herbert *Church, Holy Comm.*, Before that sin turned flesh to stone And all our lump to leaven. **1643** Shaks. *Hen. VIII*, ii. ii. 45 All mens honours Lie like one lumpe before him, to be fashion'd Into what pitch he please. **1847** A. M. Gilliam *Trav. Mexico* 272 The meddlesome Puritan,.. attempting to leaven the whole lump, will, I am afraid, often make the cake all dough. **1875** Jowett *Plato* (ed. 2) IV. 504 We have taken up a lump of fable, and have used more than we needed. **1884** H. W. S. *Secret Happy Life* i. 14 The lump of clay would never grow into a beautiful vessel.

†**b.** Hence, *allusively*, the whole mass or quantity of anything. Also, the 'mass', 'bulk', great majority. *Obs.*

1576 Fleming *Panopl. Epist.* 87 Now by this little crop, iudge you of the whole lumpe. **1659** Fuller *App. Inj. Innoc.* ii. 14 Who.. calleth the whole Lump of English Papists, the Catholick Party. **1674** Hickman *Hist. Quinquart.* (ed. 2) 81 God had not such a love for the whole lump of mankind, as to [etc.]. **1709** Steele *Tatler* No. 137 ⁋2 The Lump of these [Swearers] may, I think, be very aptly divided into the common Distinction of High and Low. **1711** —— *Spect.* No. 4 ⁋7 The thoughtless Creatures who make up the Lump of that Sex.

†**3.** An aggregate of units; a congeries, heap, clump, cluster; *occas.* a group (of persons). *Obs.*

1375 Barbour *Bruce* xv. 229 About him slayne lay his menȝe All in a lump, on athyr hand. *c* **1380** Wyclif *Wks.* (1880) 447 Lordis of þis world þat mayntenen lumpis of þes ordris and þer housis and possessiouns. ? *a* **1400** *Morte Arth.* 2230 Thus he layes one þe lumppe, and lordlye þeme served. **1611** Bible *1 Sam.* xxv. 18 An hundred clusters [*marg.* Or, lumps] of raisins, and two hundred cakes of figges. —— *2 Kings* xx. 7 Take a lumpe of figs. **1632** Lithgow *Trav.* x. 469 Vermin, which lay crawling in lumps.. about my body: yea, hanging in clusters about my beard. *Ibid.* x. 500 Lumpes of Wals, and heapes of stones. **1781** Archer in *Naval Chron.* XI. 283 They [ships] drew up into a lump.

4. a. A protuberance, swelling, or excrescence, *esp.* one caused by disease or injury in an animal body.

c **1475** *Pict. Voc.* in Wr.-Wülcker 784/16 *Hec ffalaa*, a lumpe of a walle. **1513** Douglas *Æneis* iv. ix. 87 The lump betuix the new born folis ene. **1631** *Googe's Heresbach's Husb.* (ed. Markham) 237 The Camell with two lumpes upon the backe. **1738** [see 5 f]. **1804** *Med. Jrnl.* XII. 320 Hard lumps appeared on the spots which had been covered by the pustules. **1899** *Allbutt's Syst. Med.* VIII. 894 The growths [of Xanthoma] occur either as thin flat plates.. or as nodules or lumps. *Mod.* I knocked my head and got a lump on my forehead.

b. *Naut.* (Cf. LUMPY *a.* 1 b.)

1849 N. Kingsley *Diary* (1914) 53 The farther north we get the more our anxiety is increased, as those big lumps are not quite eradicated from our minds yet. **1857** C. Gribble in *Merc. Marine Mag.* (1858) V. 3 Ship.. shipping heavy lumps of water on deck. **1865** *Athenæum* 23 Sept. 414/1 He ..chuckles over lumps of the sea. **1872** Talmage *Serm.* 107 There was what sailors call 'a big lump of a sea'.

5. Phrases with preps., belonging to the preceding senses. †**a.** ***at a lump***: in one mass; in a single piece or quantity. **b.** ***by the lump*** (rarely ***by lump***): = *in the lump*. †**c.** ***by lumps***: by instalments, piecemeal. †**d.** ***in a lump***: the whole together; all at once. **e.** ***in the lump*** (occas. †***in lump***): taking things as a whole without regard to detail; in the mass; in gross; wholesale. **f.** ***all of a lump***: altogether, in a heap; also, swollen so as to appear one lump.

a. **1596** Bp. W. Barlow *Three Serm.* 113 There are men.. to set out all at a lump in one day, not forethinking of an ensuing want. **1658–9** *Burton's Diary* (1828) IV. 47, I shall not be against the Judges, or the officers sitting there, but not to give all things away at a lump. **1686** tr. *Chardin's Trav. Persia* 337, I propounded to him to take all at a Lump, and never to make two Bargains. **1697** tr. *C'tess D'Annoy's Trav.* (1706) 220 This prodigious quantity of Silver, which comes all at a lump, is spread over all the World.

b. **1522** *MS. Acc. St. John's Hosp. Canterb.*, Paied for a certen of bryk by the lumpe of my lord of Seynt Gregorys xijd. **1699** Bentley *Phal.* 383, I must now consider half a

Dozen of Mr. B's Pages by the Lump. **1737** Bracken *Farriery Impr.* (1757) II. 277, I would not by the Lump decry any Body of People. **1760–72** tr. *Juan & Ulloa's Voy.* (ed. 3) I. 283 Other species of provisions are sold by the lump, without weight or measure. **1784** R. Bage *Barham Downs* 257, 'I accept of your conditions by the lump', replies the Professor. **1864** *Slang Dict.*, *Lump-work*, work contracted for, or taken by the lump. **1867** Smyth *Sailor's Word-bk.* s.v., *By the lump*, a sudden fall out of the slings or out of the top; altogether.

c. 1576 Gascoigne *Philomene* xviii, Common peoples love by lumpes, And fancie comes by fits.

d. 1640 Lenthall in Rushw. *Hist. Coll.* (1721) IV. 18 Were we not all in a lump by them intended to be offered up to Moloch? **1666** Temple *Let. to Ld. Arlington* Wks. 1731 II. 13 Whatever his Majesty's resolves to do, ought to be sudden, and in a Lump. **1709** Steele *Tatler* No. 106 ¶2, I .. asked him, Whether he would .. sell his Goods by Retail, or designed they should all go in a Lump? **1812** *Examiner* 24 Aug. 542/1 If we .. condemn, to use a vulgar expression, in a lump, we exasperate those whom we would wish to amend. **1825** Bentham *Ration. Reward* 154 When reward, instead of being bestowed in a lump, follows each successive portion of labour. **1923** H. G. Wells *Men like Gods* I. viii. 143 We shall all be .. judged in a lump. **1934** G. B. Shaw *Too True to be Good* Pref. 9 The unqualified assertion that the rich, in a lump, are miserable.

e. 1624 Bp. Mountagu *Immed. Addr.* 133 All they .. haue met with and obserued in lumpe. **1637** R. Humphrey tr. *St. Ambrose* II. 41 He chose rather to sell the corne .. then to give it away in the lumpe. **1676** Towerson *Decalogue* 22 How far they were from erring .. I come now to shew, and that both in the lump and the retail. **1727** Pope, etc. *Art Sinking* 86 A great genius takes things in the lump, without stopping at minute considerations. **1791** *Gentl. Mag.* 20/1 The Whitfieldians railed at rector, curate, doctrine, service, &c. &c. all in the lump. **1848** Mrs. Carlyle *Lett.* II. 28 Poor human creatures .. I am heartily sorry for them, severally, and in the lump. **1901** 'A. Hope' *Tristram of Blent* x. 117 'You seem to dislike the daughter too ..' 'Oh, I take the family in the lump'.

f. *c***1681** Hickeringill *Trimmer* vi. Wks. 1716 I. 385 Answer them by lump, for they are all of a lump. **1708** Nelson in *Phil. Trans.* XXVI. 141 The violence of the Thunder and Lightning .. melted a Watch and the Chain all of a Lump. **1738** Swift *Pol. Conversat.* 100 She must be hurt for certain .. her head is all of a Lump. **1873** *Routledge's Yng. Gentl. Mag.* Mar. 197 Oil-skin jacket and trousers, .. and high boots, into which he dropped all of a lump.

6. Applied to persons. **a.** As a term of opprobrium: A heavy, dull person. (Cf. 1 c.)

1597 *Pilgr. Parnass.* I. 80 All foggie sleepers and all idle lumps. **1714** Mandeville *Fab. Bees* II. (1733) 159 What awkward Lumps have I known, which the Dancing-master has put limbs to! **1735** Dyche & Pardon *Dict.*, *Lump*, .. a heavy, dull, unapprehensive Person. *c***1800** K. White *Athanatos* 39 Poems (1830) 124 A sluggish senseless lump to lie. **1888** A. Wardrop *Poems & Sk.* 202 The muckle diled lump didna like to spoil the nicht's performance.

b. A big sturdy creature. ? *dial.*

1630 *R. Johnson's Kingd. & Commw.* IV. 509 He being a corpulent man presumed to follow his pleasures .. At last, this lumpe was extinguished. **1842** S. Lover *Handy Andy* viii. 76 They were comely lumps of girls. **1879** Miss Jackson *Shropsh. Word-bk.*, *Lump*, a good-sized child .. 'How big are your children?' 'Oh, they bin lumps'. **1887** Hall Caine *Deemster* xx, When we were lumps of lads.

7. Technical senses.

a. A bloom or loop of malleable iron.

[**1686**, etc.: see loop *sb.*[4] 1.] **1875** in Knight *Dict. Mech.*

b. A kind of paving brick or tile (see quot. 1881).

1787 W. Marshall *Norfolk* (1795) II. 383 *Lumps*, barn-floor bricks. **1833** Loudon *Encycl. Cottage*, etc. *Archit.* §599 The Welsh or Stourbridge lumps at the sides should form with those of the back an angle of forty-five degrees or upwards. **1881** Young *Every Man his own Mechanic* §1224 'Lumps' which are thicker than tiles range in size from 12 in. to 36 in.

c. A barge or lighter used in dockyards.

1796 *Lond. Chron.* 2 June 528 A lump from the dockyard has this moment conveyed three new cables on an end to the Hind. **1858** Simmonds *Dict. Trade*, *Lumps*, .. dock-yard barges. **1867** in Smyth *Sailor's Word-bk.*

d. In firearms: (*a*) The nipple-seat on a gun-barrel; (*b*) 'In a break-joint breech-loader, an iron block on the barrel which descends into a recess in the action' (*Cent. Dict.*).

1844 *Regul. & Ord. Army* 106 A new lump for swivel, brazed and fitted on carbine. **1875** 'Stonehenge' *Brit. Sports* I. I. ii. §1. 27 The accident which sometimes occurs when from defective brazing the barrels and the lump part company. **1881** Greener *Gun* 198 A steel lump placed underneath the barrels, which engages in the face of the breech-action when the gun is closed.

e. Calico woven in long lengths.

1897 *Textile Stocks & Ex. Gaz.* 25 Oct., 150 lumps 9/8 Shirtings.

f. *Mining*, *S. Staffordsh.* (See quot.)

1883 Gresley *Gloss. Coal-mining*, *Lumps*, coal of largest size by one.

8. *slang.* The workhouse (see also quot. 1933).

1874 Hotten *Slang Dict.* 219 *Lump*, the workhouse; also called the Pan. **1898** J. D. Brayshaw *Slum Silhouettes* 146 If Sal can't bury me, the 'Lump''ll have to. **1933** 'G. Orwell' *Down & Out* xxxii. 236 These .. are some of the cant words now used in London. .. The lump—the casual ward. **1972** G. F. Newman *You Nice Bastard* 347 *In the lump*, in the workhouse.

9. *attrib.* and *Comb.*: ***lump-lac***, ***-tobacco***; **lump-account**, an account in which items are 'lumped' together without particulars or details; **lump-coal** (see quot. 1881); †**lump cotton**, some species of cotton plant, prob. *Gossypium barbadense*; **lump gold**, gold in nuggets; †**lump-love**, ? cupboard-love; **lump stone** (see quot.); **lump sugar**, loaf sugar broken into lumps or cut into cubes; **lump-sugary** *a.*, suggestive of lump-sugar; **lump sum**, a sum which covers or includes a number of items; **lump work**, work which is contracted for 'in the lump'.

*a***1700** B. E. *Dict. Cant. Crew*, *Dutch Reckoning*, .. a verbal or *Lump-account without particulars. **1877** Raymond *Statist. Mines & Mining* 288 The combustion is far more perfect than can be brought about with *lump-coal. **1881** —— *Mining Gloss.* s.v. *Coal*, *Lump* [coal] includes the largest lumps as they come from the mine. **1640** Parkinson *Theat. Bot.* 1552 *Gossipium*, The Cotton tree or plant .. 2 *Gossipium frutescens annum* [sic]. The bush of *lumpe Cotton. **1657** W. Coles *Adam in Eden* clxxiv, The bush of lump cotton .. riseth out of the ground with an upright stemme. **1898** *Daily News* 28 Jan. 5/7 Where it crosses the creeks, *lump gold is plentiful. **1815** Kirby & Spence *Introd. Entomol.* I. x. 317 In this country .. it is distinguished by the names .. *Lump-lac when melted and made into cakes. **1873** *Beeton's Dict. Commerce* s.v. *Lac*, Lump lac is the deposit [of lac] formed into cakes. **1909** *Chambers's Jrnl.* Sept. 585/2 The body has a dry, lump-sugary appearance. **17..** *Old Song* (N.), Now he ate, and he drank, and he kiss'd, and he toy'd, And all the delights of *lump-love he enjoy'd. **1829** *Glover's Hist. Derby* I. 91 There are lamellar gritstone of this class, capable of sustaining great heat; these are formed into round plates, called pye, pot, or *lump stones, and are used in the iron forges. **1657** R. Ligon *Barbadoes* (1673) 95 Making it into whites, which is that we call *Lump-Sugar in England. **1731** P. Shaw *Three Ess. Artif. Philos.* 31 The Art of refining Sugar into the different kinds of Clay'd, Lump, Loaf, &c. **1854** Dickens *Hard T.* II. vi. 184 The bread was new and crusty, the butter fresh, and the sugar lump. **1867** Smyth *Sailor's Word-bk.*, **Lump sum*, a full payment of arrears, and not by periodical instalments of money. **1883** T. Hardy in *Longm. Mag.* July 266 He .. receives a lump sum of 2*l.* or 3*l.* for harvest work. **1900** J. T. Fowler in *Durham Acc. Rolls* (Surtees) 729 The rents of each place are entered in a lump sum. **1851** C. Cist *Sk. Cincinnati in 1851* 244 Charles Bodmann .. manufactures *lump tobacco. **1851** Mayhew *Lond. Labour* (1864) II. 373/2 The natural tendency is for piecework to pass into *lump-work. *Ibid.* 374/2 'Lump' work, 'piece' work, work by 'the job', are all portions of the contract system. The principle is the same. **1892** *Star* 17 Mar. 3/3 There are three systems of payment—day work, piece work, and lump work; and lump work is the curse of the lot.

lump (lʌmp), *sb.*[2] Also 6–7 lumpe, 7 lompe. [Found also as MLG. *lumpen* (Diefenbach), MDu. *lompe*, G. *lump*, *lumpfisch*, F. *lompe*; hence mod.L. (specific name) *lumpus*, It., Sp. *lumpo*. By foreign etymologists it has commonly been supposed to be of Eng. origin, a use of lump *sb.*[1], with reference to the bulky figure of the fish; but the Du. and LG. forms are known from earlier examples than the Eng. Cf. Du. *lomp* heavy.]

1. A spiny-finned fish of a leaden-blue colour and uncouth appearance, *Cyclopterus lumpus*, characterized by a suctorial disk on its belly with which it adheres to objects with great force (whence its name of *lump sucker*); the sea-owl.

The arctic species is *C. spinosus*.

1545 Elyot *Dict.*, *Faber*, a fyshe of the Spanyshe sea .. is lyke to that fyshe, whyche is called a lump. **1591** Lyly *Endimion* III. iii, For fish these; crab, lumpe, and powting. **1601** Holland *Pliny* II. 428 The Lompe, Paddle or sea-Owle, a fish called in Latin orbis. **1655** Moufet & Bennet *Health's Improv.* (1746) 247 Lumps are of two sorts, the one as round almost as a Bowl, the other resembling the Fillets of a Calf. *a***1672** [see cock-paddle]. **1828** Fleming *Hist. Brit. Anim.* 190. **1844** *Knickerbocker* XXIV. 471 We discussed the merits of dun-fish, .. lump, halibut, .. and trout. **1867** [see bagaty, baggety]. **1969** A. Wheeler *Fishes Brit. Isles & N.-W. Europe* 345 (*heading*) Lumpsucker (Sea Hen, Hen-fish, Lump).

2. *Comb.*: **lump-fish, lump sucker**, = 1.

1620 Venner *Via Recta* iv. 76 Lompe-fish. The Lumpe or Lompe, is a fish so named from his shape and likenesse, and is in taste agreeable to the name. **1743** Parsons in *Phil. Trans.* XLII. 385 The *Phoca* .. is rather like a Lump-fish, and almost triangular. **1835** Kirby *Hab. & Inst. Anim.* II. xvii. 121 Under the name of lump-fishes I include all those whose ventral fins unite to form a disk or sucker by which they are enabled to adhere to the rocks. **1885** C. F. Holder *Marvels Anim. Life* 21 The lump-fish is .. accredited with being a nest builder. **1969** H. Horwood *Newfoundland* 223 A lumpfish that I weighed on a pier-head in Conception Bay a few years ago went over thirty pounds. **1972** *Country Life* 30 Nov. 1541/3 You can afford to entertain with the real thing [*sc.* Sevruga caviar] and not pass off Danish Lumpfish roe (dyed black) as a substitute. **1974** *Observer* (Colour Suppl.) 15 Dec. 76/2 The lumpfish, known also as the cock- or hen-paddle on account of the thick crest shaping its back, is a creature of character. *Ibid.*, There is lumpfish caviare, which comes dyed black, and pearly, in small glass pots from Iceland and Denmark. **1766** Pennant *Zool.* (1776) III. 117 Lump sucker. **1836** Yarrell *Brit. Fishes* (1859) II. 343 The Lump Sucker is remarkable for its very grotesque form. **1883** *Fisheries Exhib. Catal.* (ed. 4) 105 A Lump Sucker, caught at S. Leonards. **1959** A. Hardy *Fish & Fisheries* x. 193 Another surprise in this first haul was a lumpsucker *Cyclopterus lumpus* which I had previously decided to leave out of the book, thinking it to be an entirely coastal species. .. Its body is covered with little protuberances giving it a somewhat toad-like appearance; but it is bright with a pink hue on its lower parts. **1974** *Observer* (Colour Suppl.) 15 Dec. 76/2 They [*sc.* the female lumpfish] swim off leaving the males in charge, who cling to the rock by means of a suction disc between the pelvic fins—hence yet another name, lumpsucker.

lump (lʌmp), *v.*[1] Now *dial.* In 6 lompe. [Cf. the synonymous *lamp* (see E.D.D.) and Du. *lompen.*] *trans.* To beat, thresh; to beat or thresh *out*. Also *absol.*, to thresh.

1546 J. Heywood *Prov.* (1867) 47 But what neede we lumpe out loue at ones lashyng. **1550** Coverdale *Spir. Perle* vi. (1588) 75 As the .. laundresse washeth, beateth, lompeth, and clappeth the foule vnclenly and defiled clothes. **1821** Clare *Vill. Minstr.* I. 65 Delving the ditch .. Or lumping corn out in a dusty barn. *Ibid.* II. 31 The thresher once lumping, we heard him no more. **1847** Halliwell, *Lump*. (1) To beat severely. *Var. dial.*

lump (lʌmp), *v.*[2] [Of symbolic sound; cf. *dump*, *glump*, *grump*, *hump*, *mump*.]

1. *intr.* To look sulky or disagreeable. (In early quots. always in collocation with *lour*.)

1577 Stanyhurst *Descr. Irel.* in Holinshed *Chron.* (1807–8) VI. 5 They stand lumping and lowring .. for that they imagine that their evill lucke proceedeth of him. **1581** Rich *Farewell* Dd iv b, She beganne to froune, lumpe, and lowre at her housebande. **1593** *Tell-Troth's N. Y. Gift* 19 At home they will lumpe and lower. **1594** Lodge *Wounds Civ. W.* IV. i. F 2, How fare these Lords that lumping pouting proud Imagine how to quell me with their lookes? **1847** Halliwell, *Lump* .. (3) To be or look sulky. *Devon.*

2. *trans.* In antithesis with *like*: To be displeased at (something that must be endured). *colloq.*

1833 Neal *Down Easters* I. vii. 104 Let 'em lump it if they don't like it. **1835–40** Haliburton *Clockm.* Pref. (1862) 6 A man that would be guilty of such an action is no gentleman, that's flat, and if you don't like it you may lump it. **1878** Mrs. Stowe *Poganuc P.* xi. 94, I'll buy clothes as I see fit, and if anybody don't like it, why they may lump it, that's all. **1893** Grant Allen in *R. Blathwayt's Interviews* Pref. 11 Whether we like him or lump him, he [the Interviewer] is master of the situation.

lump (lʌmp), *v.*[3] [f. lump *sb.*[1]

Cf. lumping *ppl. a.* 2, which occurs much earlier than the verb.]

1. *trans.* **a.** To melt down into a lump. **b.** To form or raise into lumps. **c.** To cover with lumps.

1797 Mrs. M. Robinson *Walsingham* (1805) IV. xc. 256 Topas nicked the family plate, and has lumped it by this time, with my pink diamond into the bargain. **1852** *Meanderings of Mem.* I. 12, I the mattress spread, And equal lay whatever lumps the bed. **1879** G. Meredith *Egoist* xxiii, An old cuirass .. lumped with a strange adhesive concrete. **1893** Earl Dunmore *Pamirs* II. 293 Ploughed fields, one of which was 'lumped up' for melon planting, each lump a mound about two feet high.

2. To put altogether in one 'lump', mass, sum, or group, without discrimination or regard for particulars or details; to take, consider, or deal with 'in the lump'. **a.** *simply.* spec. in *Taxonomy*: To classify (plants and animals) without using minute variations as a basis for the establishment of a large number of different species or genera. Cf. lumper *sb.* 3.

1624 Bp. Mountagu *Immed. Addr.* 84 They agree not long with and amongst themselues, .. let them be lumped or consorted as they would haue it, as they please. **1721** C. King *Brit. Merch.* I. 223 They are as much out in their Estimation .. as they are in their other goods, which they lump at above 480000*l.* whereas they amount only to 168884*l.* **1781** Mad. D'Arblay *Diary* Mar., I have been .. provokingly interrupted in writing this, that I must now finish it by lumping matters at once. **1840** Marryat *Poor Jack* xiii, They always lump the petty officers and common seamen. **1852** H. C. Watson *Cybele Britannica* III. 8 Early training under the late Professor Graham, and geographical convenience, are very likely to have given to me .. a predisposition to 'lump' species. **1884** Browning *Ferishtah*, *Camel-Driver*, Man lumps his kind i' the mass. God singles thence Unit by unit. **1893** Lydekker *Horns & Hoofs* 75 Dr. Gray (who certainly did not err on the side of 'lumping' species). **1945** A. Young *Prospect of Flowers* xx. 151 Our Village Schoolmistress carries lumping to an extreme degree. **1962** Mackworth-Praed & Grant *Birds S. Third Afr.* I. p. xi, It will be noted that we have not followed the modern trend of 'lumping' species and that we keep specific rank in this work for more birds than is usual nowadays. **1973** *Nature* 30 Mar. 353/1 The general absence of subgenera and species groups [in Chiarelli's classification of primates], combined with some tendency to 'lump' has meant the virtual disappearance of certain significant distinctions.

b. *to lump together* (occas. *up*).

1692 Sir T. P. Blount *Ess.* 103 Take the World in Gross, and lump it together. **1726** Ayliffe *Parergon* 82 A compensation of Expences ought to be made, that is to say in English, the Expences ought to be lump'd together and divided. **1856** Maxwell in *Life* viii. (1882) 239 A tendency in the human mind to lump up all causes, and give them an aggregate name. **1895** F. Harrison in *19th Cent.* Aug. 314 All systems of unorthodox philosophy are lumped together by him as mere forms of contemporary superstition.

c. *to lump* (*together*) *in* or *into*, occas. ***under***.

1703 De Foe *Freeholder's Plea agst. Stockjobbing Elections* Misc. 182 Our Liberties and Armies, and Fleets, and Parliaments, and Nation, are not Lump'd into Bargains. **1839** J. Sterling *Ess.*, etc. (1848) I. 326 Mr. Carlyle lumps under the same condemnation all introspection of a man's being. **1883** Sir J. Bacon in *Law Rep.* 27 Ch. Div. 511 The premium and the principal are lumped in one sum. **1902** Bond *Lyly's Wks.* II. 249 The .. earlier work which I have lumped together under the wide title of Moralities.

d. *to lump* (something) *into* or (*in*) *with* (something else): see 2.

1796 Bentham *Prot. agst. Law Taxes* (1816) 56 It comes lumped to him in the general mass of law charges: a heap of items, among which no vulgar eye can ever hope to discriminate. **1831** T. L. Peacock *Crotchet C.* viii. Farmer Seedling lumps it in with his tithes... Lumps it in, sir! Lump in a charitable donation! **1857** Hughes *Tom Brown* I.

viii, 'I won't', said Tom, . . lumping them all in his mind with his sworn enemy. **1874** WHYTE MELVILLE *Uncle John* II. xviii. 193 The General lumped him in with a body of dancing men . . he was pleased to call the Light Brigade.

3. †**a.** To pay in a lump sum. *Obs. rare.*

1755 *Mem. Capt. P. Drake* I. xv. 147 The Turnkey proposed to us, to lump (as he called it) the coming down Money.

b. To lay the whole of (a particular sum of money) *on* a single object.

1864 *Derby Day* iii. 32 He lumped it all upon an outsider, and backed him to win the Chester Cup. **1872** BESANT & RICE *Ready Money Mort.* v, If I only had a dollar in the world . . I'd lump it all on my system.

4. *intr.* To collect *together* into a lump; to be formed or raised into lumps.

1720 ROBIE in *Phil. Trans.* XXXI. 122 [To] cause the Ashes to lump or clodder together. **1852** MORFIT *Tanning & Currying* (1853) 397 Leather thus made . . does not lump under the hammer. **1856** SYMONDS in H. F. Brown *Biog.* (1895) I. 82, I have a new cover and cushion made for my chair. It is much fatter and more comfortable than the old one, which used to lump up all in a heap.

5. To move heavily, 'stump' *along*; to drop *down* like a lump.

1861 F. W. ROBINSON *No-Church* Prol. (1863) 4 The old woman gave a snort like a sea-horse, lumped down in her bed, and drew her counterpane over her head. *Ibid.* viii. 61 He scrambled up with an oath, lumped down again in a sitting posture, and stared before him stupidly. **1879** G. MEREDITH *Egoist* I. Prel. 4 They lump along like the old loblegs of Dobbin the horse.

6. (Influenced by LUMPER *sb.* 1.) To act as a lumper, to load or unload cargoes. Hence, (*colloq.*) to carry or shift (something heavy) *about*.

1890 BARRÈRE & LELAND *Dict. Slang* II. 33/2 (Thieves), to *lump* the lighter, to be transported. In this case to *lump* signifies to load. **1905** *Westm. Gaz.* 10 Oct. 10/1 He . . soon had the squad of irregulars at hard work 'lumping' as heartily as any gang of dock labourers. **1911** 'KIWI' *On Swag* 14 For a month or so [I] was lumping on the wharf at the Spit. **1925** A. B. ARMITAGE *Cadet to Commodore* vi. 43, I earned sixteen shillings a week by 'lumping' in the docks. **1946** K. TENNANT *Lost Haven* (1947) xiii. 201 'I promised her a salmon.' He felt a fool lumping the great thing about.

lumpectomy (lʌmˈpɛktəmɪ). *Surg.* [f. LUMP *sb.*¹ + -ECTOMY.] Removal of a lump from a woman's breast in a case of suspected or diagnosed cancer, the remainder of the breast being left intact; an operation to perform this.

1972 *Daily Colonist* (Victoria, B.C.) 10 Feb. 28/4 Still another development in surgery is the lumpectomy, in which only the cancerous lump, plus some surrounding tissue, is removed. **1977** *Time* 28 Mar. 58/2 If the breast tumour is still small—no more than 4 cm. (1½ in.) in diameter —doctors first excise the growth in a relatively simple surgical procedure called a lumpectomy. **1985** *Times* 25 Feb. 13/5 Women who had been treated for breast cancer faced the risk of a local recurrence . . . This risk is believed to be greater among women who opt for lumpectomy and radiotherapy. **1985** *Amer. Jrnl. Psychiatry* CXLII. 34 (*heading*) Psychological outcome of lumpectomy versus mastectomy in the treatment of breast cancer.

lumped (lʌmpt), *ppl. a.* [f. LUMP *sb.*¹ and *v.* + -ED.] **1.** Made, shaped, or raised into a lump.

c **1425** *St. Christina* x. in *Anglia* VIII. 123/29 In þe maner of an vrchyn þe lumped body ȝode to þe owne shappe. **1882** J. WALKER *Jaunt to Auld Reekie* etc. 20 He limps awa and hauds his lumpit noddle. **1898** G. MEREDITH *Odes Fr. Hist.* 21 Like lumped grass Nid-nod to ground beneath the cuffing storm.

2. *Electr.* (Containing impedances or circuit elements) localized at a particular point or points, rather than distributed uniformly throughout part of a circuit.

1912 A. E. KENNELLY *Applic. Hyperbolic Functions to Electr. Engin. Probl.* iii. 35 This semi-angle cannot be correct, because it is based on a lumped leakance instead of a distributed leakance as assumed. **1948** E. G. BOWEN *Text-bk. Radar* xiii. 439 The units are connected by a low impedance coaxial cable which . . is equivalent to a lumped capacity at video frequencies. **1967** *Electronics* 6 Mar. 163/1 Factors that combine to make analysis of crosstalk difficult are: . . The distributed, rather than lumped, nature of the inductances and capacitances of the circuits involved. **1973** B. KINARIWALA et al. *Linear Circuits & Computation* i. 4 We will confine ourselves to the discussion of lumped circuits —that is, circuits composed entirely of lumped elements.

lumpenproletariat (ˌlʌmpənprəʊlɪˈtɛərɪət). [a. G. *lumpenproletariat* (K. Marx 1850, in *Die Klassenkämpfe in Frankreich* and 1852, in *Der achtzehnte Brumaire des Louis Bonaparte*), f. *lumpen*, rag (*lump* ragamuffin: see LUMP *sb.*¹) + *proletariat* (see PROLETARIATE, -AT).] A term applied, orig. by Karl Marx, to the lowest and most degraded section of the proletariat; the 'down and outs' who make no contribution to the workers' cause. So **ˈlumpenproleˈtarian** *a.* and *sb.* Also **ˈlumpen** *a.*, boorish, stupid, unenlightened, used derisively to describe persons, attitudes, etc., supposed to be characteristic of the lumpenproletariat; also *ellipt.* or as *sb.*

1924 H. KUHN tr. *Marx's Class Struggles France* I. 38 The financial aristocracy, in its methods of acquisition as well as in its enjoyments, is nothing but the reborn *Lumpenproletariat*, the rabble on the heights of bourgeois society. **1936** R. GESSNER *Some of my Best Friends are Jews* xxii. 306 No bandits dared attack her desperate inhabitants, the rough and dangerous Jews who had become lumpenproletarians under the Czar. **1937** F. BORKENAU *Spanish Cockpit* i. 15 A not unimportant number of these 'lumpenproletarian' elements have joined the anarchist movement. **1940** 'G. ORWELL' *Inside Whale* 132 The lumpen-proletarian fringe . . composed partly of genuine artists and partly of genuine scoundrels. **1942** *New Statesman* 17 Oct. 255/1 He [*sc.* Hitler] mixed with the *Lumpen-proletariat*, the nomadic outcasts in the no-man's-land of society. **1944** KOESTLER in *Horizon* Mar. 167 Thus the intelligentsia . . becomes the Lumpen-Bourgeoisie in the age of its decay. **1948** J. STEINBECK *Russ. Jrnl.* (1949) ix. 220 This journal will not be satisfactory either to the ecclesiastical Left, nor the lumpen Right. **1949** A. WILSON *Wrong Set* 57 Like called to like. The Colonel's lady and Lily O'Grady were both 'lumpen' under the skin. **1958** *Time* 28 June 35/3 At his cinematic best a shaggy lumpen-proletarian helplessly meshed in the woof of modern life . . Charlie Chaplin. **1963** D. MACDONALD *Against Amer. Grain* i. 58 The spoofs of Dada have now become the serious offerings of what one might call the lumpen-avant-garde. **1969** R. BLACKBURN in Cockburn & Blackburn *Student Power* 186 Regis Debray has suggested that the lumpen-bourgeoisie of Latin America substitute police vigilance for an authentic class consciousness. **1970** *New Yorker* 18 July 22/2 Cope, a well-known proponent of lumpen aesthetics, had met the challenge with cool authority. **1971** 'P. KAVANAGH' *Triumph of Evil* (1972) ii. 19 The rightist reaction of the white *lumpenproletariat* is easily imagined. Their instinctive response is racist and anti-intellectual. **1972** *Times Lit. Suppl.* 6 Oct. 1202/4 The *lumpenbourgeoisie*, behind a variety of leaders, is sick of dissent—student demonstrations, anti-apartheid, pornography, drug-taking, immigration, strikes, and crime. **1972** *Times* 14 Nov. 14/8 The underlying antipathy . . towards the *lumpen* masses. **1973** *Ann. N.Y. Acad. Sci.* CCXI. 128 Fortunately for a lumpen linguist like me, my job doesn't require exercise of the vernier virtuosity that one sees in Linguistic Atlas maps and synopses. **1974** *Black Panther* 27 Apr. 13/2 The outlaw and the lumpen will make the revolution. The people, the workers, will adopt it. **1974** *Listener* 2 May 598/2 These institutions are likely to be manipulated only by a comparatively favoured group in society . . leaving a real *lumpen* element at the bottom.

lumper (ˈlʌmpə(r)), *sb.* [f. LUMP *v.* + -ER¹.]

1. a. A labourer employed in loading and unloading cargoes, esp. timber. **b.** *Sc.* (See quot.)

1785 GROSE *Dict. Vulg. Tongue*, *Lumpers*, persons who contract to unload ships. **1796** COLQUHOUN *Police Metrop.* (ed. 3) 54 The prevailing practice of discharging and delivering the cargoes of ships by a class of aquatic labourers, known by the name of Lumpers and Scuffle-hunters. **1825** JAMIESON, *Lumper*, one who furnishes ballast for ships, Greenock; apparently from its being put on board in the lump. **1840** MARRYAT *Poor Jack* xviii, They go on board as lumpers to clear the ships. **1892** *Daily News* 5 Dec. 5/5 He was a rigger and lumper.

2. *slang.* **a.** A kind of river-thief (cf. 1). **b.** (See quot. 1851.) **c.** A militia-man. **d.** A small contractor, sweater.

a. *a* **1781** G. PARKER *View Soc.* II. 78 They then commence Lumpers, which is skulking about ships, lighters, &c. . . stealing old iron . . or whatever comes to hand.

b. 1851 MAYHEW *Lond. Labour* (1864) I. 413 He understood by a 'Duffer', a man who sold goods under false pretences, making out that they were smuggled . .; whereas a 'Lumper' would sell linens [etc.] . . which . . were made to appear new when they were old, or sold when they were flimsy.

c. *c* **1869** BLACKMORE *Lorna D.* xxxviii, He was going to bring the lumpers upon us, only he was afeared, last winter.

d. 1851 MAYHEW *Lond. Labour* (1864) II. 374 The first man who agrees to the job takes it in the lump, and he again lets it to others in the piece. . . The men to whom it is sublet only find labour, while the 'lumper', or first contractor, agrees for both labour and materials. **1892** *Labour Commission* Gloss., *Lumpers*, contractors, middlemen, sweaters. **1902** *Westm. Gaz.* 29 Mar. 9/1 In working in America for what are called 'front lumpers'.

3. *Taxonomy.* A taxonomist who is unwilling to use minute variations as a basis for the establishment of a large number of different species or genera.

1857 DARWIN in *Life & Lett.* (1887) II. 105 It is good to have hair-splitters and lumpers. **1894** *Cornh. Mag.* Mar. 295 Modern biologists are divided into the two camps of the splitters and the lumpers. The first are in favour of making a species out of every petty . . variety; the second are all for lumping unimportant minor forms into a single species. **1945** A. YOUNG *Prospect of Flowers* xx. 151 Botanists are divided into two classes, 'splitters' and 'lumpers', 'splitters' being those who split plants into a large number of species and sub-species, while 'lumpers', impatient of minute distinctions, are inclined to lump them together. **1967** A. W. JONES *Introd. Parasitol.* xxix. 419 The more conservative taxonomists, called irreverently 'lumpers', defended established categories from attack by the radical 'splitters'. **1972** *Sci. Amer.* Nov. 60/2 One can use the work of many different taxonomists, without regard to whether they are 'lumpers' or 'splitters' in their method of classification, as long as the work is self-consistent.

4. *Ireland.* A coarse variety of potato.

1840 *Tait's Mag.* VII. 278 [In Ireland] though their condition haply should not be much bettered, under any change, it is impossible that it can be worse, while lumpers will grow. **1841** LEVER *C. O'Malley* xxviii, You son of a lumper potato. **1843** —— *J. Hinton* xxvii, A miserable mud hovel, surrounded by, maybe half an acre of lumpers.

ˈlumper, *v. Obs.* exc. *dial.* [Cf. LAMPER, LOMPER *Obs.* Also LUMP *v.*³ 5.]

1. *intr.* To move clumsily; to stumble or blunder along. Also *fig.*

1581 J. BELL *Haddon's Answ. Osor.* 91 [They] have alwayes hetherto in the interpretation of that Epistle, gropyngly lyke nightowles lumpred in darknesse. *Ibid.* 311 As men you may lumper and trippe. **1787** GROSE *Prov. Gloss.*, *Lumper*, to stumble. A lumpering horse. W[est]. **1898** T. HARDY *Wessex Poems* 206 Over piggeries, and mixens . . They lumpered straight into the night.

†**2.** In pa. pple. ? Spread out. *Obs.*

c **1650** in Furnivall *Percy Folio* I. 114 Her lyppes lay lumpryd' on her chyn.

†**ˈlumperdee ˈclumperdee**, *adv.* ? *nonce-wd.* Used to express clumsy movement.

a **1553** UDALL *Royster D.* II. iii. (Arb.) 36 Ye shall see hir glide and . . Not lumperdee clumperdee like our spaniell Rig.

†**ˈlumpering**, *ppl. a. Obs.* [f. LUMPER *v.* + -ING.] Stumbling; ? causing to stumble.

1519 HORMAN *Vulg.* 247 b, All our iourney was by lumperynge grounde, and . . bryry placis. **1787** [see LUMPER *v.* 1].

lumpers (ˈlʌmpəz), *sb. pl. slang.* [f. *lump sum*: cf. -ER⁶.] A lump sum paid as compensation for loss of employment.

1960 *Economist* 23 July 352/2 They all give the impression that they remain happiest when a colonial official takes his 'lumpers' (lump sum compensation) and retires for good. **1963** *Punch* 17 July 77/2 The civil servants . . deprived . . of their career, have the consolation of their 'lumpers'— . . up to £10,000. **1965** *New Society* 11 Nov. 11/2 The settler saw the official receive the 'golden handshake' or 'lumpers'.

ˈlumpet. [f. LUMP *sb.* + -ET¹.] A small lump.

1812 COLERIDGE *Omniana* Lit. Rem. 1836 I. 366 The curd lumpets of various sizes.

lumpily (ˈlʌmpɪlɪ), *adv.* [f. LUMPY + -LY².] In a lumpy fashion; in lumps.

1878 ABNEY *Photogr.* (1881) 55 Note if the collodion flows freely, viscously, or lumpily. **1900** *Blackw. Mag.* Apr. 516/1 A white beard with amber streaks hung lumpily down to his waist.

lumpiness (ˈlʌmpɪnɪs). [f. LUMPY + -NESS.] Lumpy quality or condition. Also *concr.*

1805 R. W. DICKSON *Pract. Agric.* I. 27 To reduce and break down the lumpiness, and bring the land into a fine state. **1874** VAN BUREN *Dis. Genit. Org.* 7 A lumpiness may be left behind at the point of injury. **1886** J. K. JEROME *Idle Thoughts* 19 They [*sc.* a child's new shoes] lack symmetry and curve, and possess an indescribable appearance of lumpiness.

lumping (ˈlʌmpɪŋ), *vbl. sb.* [f. LUMP *v.*³ + -ING¹.]

1. The action of LUMP *vb.*³ in various senses.

1607 MARKHAM *Caval.* VII. (1617) 14 It is very good to save the blood . . and whilst he bleedes, to stirre it about for lumping. **1757** *Monitor* No. 96 II. 424 The lumping of characters together, and giving them in such general terms, as convey no distinct and clear idea. **1851** *Fraser's Mag.* Aug. 144 With . . a dryness and lumping in my throat. **1903** *Speaker* 14 Mar. 576/2 The Committee could object to the 'lumping' of votes.

2. The occupation or business of a 'lumper'.

1851 MAYHEW *Lond. Labour* (1861) III. 289 In order to become acquainted with the system of lumping.

ˈlumping, *ppl. a.* [f. LUMP *sb.*¹ or *v.*³ + ING².]

†**1.** Forming itself into lumps; coagulating.

1751 LAVINGTON *Enthus. Meth. & Papists* III. (1754) 94 The Blood begins to boil, and the Heat rarefies and disperses the lumping Mass.

†**2.** Weighing heavy. *Obs.*

13.. *Minor Poems fr. Vernon MS.* 620/303 Heore hertes were colde as lumpyng led.

b. Hence *colloq.*: Great, big. (Cf. *thumping*, *bouncing*, etc.) Formerly often in phr. (now *dial.*) ***lumping pennyworth*** = 'plenty for one's money'. Also ***lumping weight***, good or full weight.

1705 HICKERINGILL *Priest-cr.* II. viii. 73 But Money is Money . . and therefore a lumping peny-worth Priestcraft will afford you, as aforesaid. **1712** ARBUTHNOT *John Bull* IV. vi, Wilt thou purchase it, Nic.? thou shalt have a lumping Pennyworth. **1753** *Scots Mag.* 330/1 We are not to wonder at the lumping compliments. **1768** G. WHITE *Selborne* xiii, A full grown mus medius domesticus weighs . . one ounce lumping weight. **1825** BENTHAM *Offic. Apt. Maximized, Observ. Peel's Sp.* (1830) 16 One lumping assertion there is, upon which the whole strength of his argument rests. **1861** T. A. TROLLOPE *La Beata* II. xiv. 103 A family group with three or four lumping brats around her. **1881** CLARK RUSSELL *Ocean Free-Lance* II. 30 She should be a lumping boat, to judge by the size of her mainsail.

c. Of movement: Heavy, clumsy, attended by heavy shocks. Also of the noise produced by such movement.

1884 READE *Gd. Stories* 254 There was a lumping noise and a great clatter.

3. Characterized by putting things together indiscriminately or without regard for detail.

1802–12 BENTHAM *Ration. Judic. Evid.* (1827) I. 435 By lumping charges together, and (after a lumping mass of proof) pronouncing a lumping judgment on the whole mass, —a precedent has been set. **1896** *Engineering Mag.* XVI. 48 The factory manager accustomed to 'lumping' methods of cost-keeping.

Hence **ˈlumpingly** *adv.*, heavily and clumsily.

1847 *Blackw. Mag.* LXI. 741 The canvass flapped against the mast, as the old girl rolled lumpingly in the swell.

lumpish ('lʌmpɪʃ), *a.* Also 6 **lompish.** [f. LUMP *sb.*[1] (in some uses with mixture of the sense of LUMP *v.*[2]) + -ISH.]

1. Of material objects: Of cumbersome weight or bulk; not apt to be moved easily; heavy and unwieldy. ? *Obs.*

1545 ASCHAM *Toxoph.* II. (Arb.) 125 It is better to haue a shafte..somewhat to lyght than ouer lumpysshe. **1683** TRYON *Way to Health* 105 It [boiling] makes it [food] lumpish, close, heavy, dull, and gross on the Pallate. **1727** BRADLEY *Fam. Dict.* s.v. *Earth*, The Earth is called claiey or stiff Earth, when it..is lumpish, dull, heavy and cold.

2. Heavy and clumsy in appearance, shape, or movement.

c **1555** HARPSFIELD *Divorce Hen. VIII* (Camden) 226 Then should we have soon espied the lumpish and foul hands of our juggler. **1573** L. LLOYD *Pilgr. Princes* 19 From a rude & lumpish Chaos, the worlde waxed beautifull. **1671** BLAGRAVE *Astrol. Physic* 127 A man of..swarthy complection, and of a lumpish countenance. **1777** G. FORSTER *Voy. round World* II. 539 The amphibious and lumpish animals which dwelt on Southern Georgia. **1820** SCOTT *Monast.* xxix, Swelling lumpish hills. **1863** A. M. BELL *Princ. Speech* 179 A tongue which formerly lay lumpish and inert in the mouth. **1882** *Q. Rev.* Oct. 375 Seated statues, square and lumpish, like those brought from Branchidæ to the British Museum. **1894** MRS. H. WARD *Marcella* III. 122 A governess, a schoolgirl, or a lumpish boy.

3. Stupidly dull, heavy, or lethargic in action, thought, or feeling; sluggishly inactive; slow-minded, unapprehensive.

1528 PAYNEL *Salerne's Regim.* B iv b, A lumpishe spirite causeth a sluggishe body. **1598** R. BERNARD tr. *Terence, Heautont.* v. i. Q vj, To be called a blockpate, a dulhead, an asse, a lumpish sot. **1620** VENNER *Via Recta* vii. 141 The often and much vse of Lettuce..hindreth procreation,.. and maketh the body lumpish. **1702** POPE *Jan. & May* 420 The lumpish husband snoar'd away the night. **1777** BURKE *Let. to Fox* Wks. IX. 150 An heavy, lumpish acquiescence in Government. **1782** COWPER *To Lady Austen, on a Flood at Olney*, I then should have no need of wit, For lumpish Hollander unfit! **1868** DORAN *Saints & Sin.* II. 309 He was as nervous about dreams as the most lumpish of dairymaids. **1893** *Nation* (N.Y.) 12 Jan. 19/1 We do not believe this attitude of lumpish obstruction can be persisted in if the Democratic Senators do their duty.

†**b.** Insensible *to*. *Obs.*

1585 PARSONS *Chr. Exerc.* I. iv. 29 So dead we are, and lumpish to all goodnesse.

†**4.** Low-spirited, dejected, melancholy. *Obs.*

1534 MORE *Comf. agst. Trib.* II. Wks. 1196/1 He marketh well..mennes complexions..by whiche they be light hearted or lumpish. **1590** SPENSER *F.Q.* III. xii. 18 He looking lompish and full sullein sad. **1591** SHAKS. *Two Gent.* III. ii. 62 She is lumpish, heauy, mellancholly. **1602** ROWLANDS *Tis Merrie when Gossips meete* 9 The lumpish leaden melancholy thought. **1621** S. WARD *Life Faith* vii. 46 His faith cannot bee but lumpish and melancholly. **1647** TRAPP *Comm. Phil.* i. 14 Neither ever since that time have I felt any lumpish heavinesse. **1712** STEELE *Spect.* No. 518 ¶9 A contracted brow, a lumpish down-cast look. **1741** RICHARDSON *Pamela* II. 35 My Heart was so lumpish!

5. Of sound: Dull and heavy.

1742 FIELDING *J. Andrews* III. ix, He fell prostrated on the floor with a lumpish noise. *a* **1764** LLOYD *Ode to Genius* Poet. Wks. 1774 II. 174 Lifeless and lumpish as the bagpipes drowzy drone. **1806–7** J. BERESFORD *Miseries Hum. Life* (1826) xvi. 90 The dead, lumpish, tubby tones of the fourth and fifth strings of the guittar.

†**6.** In lumps, lumpy. *Obs.* (exc. as *nonce-use*).

1735 DYCHE & PARDON *Dict.*, *Lumpish*, in Clods or congealed Parcels. **1776** *Bedlam, a Poem* 8 When gloomy the black Bile prevails, And lumpish Phlegm the thicken'd Mass congeals. **1850** MAXWELL *Let.* in *Life* v. (1882) 145 Metallic bismuth..either powder or lumpish.

†**b.** Of liquor: Full of lumps, ropy. *Obs.*

1703 *Art & Myst. Vintners* 35 Sack that is lumpish or lowring.

7. *Comb.*

1632 DEKKER *Pref. Verse* in *Brome's North. Lasse*, Thy Daughter..Is chaste and witty to the time; Not lumpish-cold, as is her Clime. *a* **1645** HEYWOOD *Fort. by Land & Sea* I. i. Wks. 1874 VI. 366 Ther's no mirth in me, nor was I wont to be so lumpish sad. **1863** MRS. GASKELL *Dark Night's Work* xii. 223 They've quite a different style of hand [in horsemanship], and sit all lumpish-like.

lumpishly ('lʌmpɪʃlɪ), *adv.* [f. prec. + -LY[2].] In a lumpish manner; heavily and clumsily; †dejectedly; stupidly; sluggishly (*obs.*).

c **1430** *Stans Puer ad Mensam* 16 in *Babees Bk.*, Lumpischli caste not þin heed a-doun. **1583** GOLDING *Calvin on Deut.* lxxxviii. 543 Let vs looke that wee knowe Gods trueth aforehand..for without that wee shall goe lumpishly to worke. *a* **1652** BROME *Eng. Moor* I. iii. Wks. 1873 II. 12 'Tis your sullenness; Would you have brided it so lumpishly With your spruce younker? **1860** HAWTHORNE *Marb. Faun* II. vi. 81 She sought..to relieve his heart of the burden that lay lumpishly upon it. **1862** *Macm. Mag.* Sept. 424 The dark outline of the summit peaked or lumpishly rounded. **1890** CLARK RUSSELL *Ocean Trag.* II. xxi. 180 Bodies of vapour coming together over our mastheads, and compacting there lumpishly amid the stagnant air.

lumpishness ('lʌmpɪʃnɪs). [f. as prec. + -NESS.] The condition or quality of being lumpish; cumbrous heaviness; heavy and clumsy aspect; †sluggishness, drowsy inactivity, heaviness of heart (*obs.*); *rarely*, lumpiness.

1574 NEWTON *Health Mag.* 17 An ill diet bringeth heavinesse and drowsie lumpishnesse to the bodie. **1582** BENTLEY *Mon. Matrones* II. 174 Take from me ydlenesse and sloth, and heauie lumpishnesse. **1638** A. READ *Chirurg.* xvi. 117 A purgative medicament is to bee ministred..if the party have the headache or lumpishnesse. **1658** tr. *Porta's Nat. Magic* v. ii. 163 When the Lead hath lost its own earthy lumpishness, which is expelled by often melting. **1727** BAILEY vol. II, *Lumpishness*, a being in lumps; also dulness, heaviness. **1847** L. HUNT *Men, Women, & B.* I. iv. 65 His apparently indolent yet active lumpishness. **1848** RICKMAN *Archit.* App. 42 The chapels and aisle surrounding these apses, tends very much..to give that lumpishness mentioned above. **1880** G. MEREDITH *Tragic Com.* iv. 49 No dead stuff, no longer any afflicting lumpishness. His brain was vivifying light.

lumpkin ('lʌm(p)kɪn). *dial.* [f. LUMP *sb.*[1] + -KIN.] A clumsy, blundering person.

[**1773** GOLDSM. *Stoops to Conq.*, Dram. Pers., Tony Lumpkin.] **1901** 'ZACK' *Tales Dunstable Weir* 198 The lumpkin had reached the gate o' Morse's Yard. **1901** *Speaker* 12 Jan. 399/2 There's a silly old-fashioned lot of Lumpkins in our part.

lumpless ('lʌmplɪs), *a.* [f. LUMP *sb.*[1] + -LESS.] Having no lumps.

1908 *Daily Chron.* 3 Mar. 8/1 As soon as the ingredients are fairly worked into a lumpless, creamy whole, stop beating.

lump sucker: see LUMP *sb.*[2]

lumpy ('lʌmpɪ), *a.* [f. LUMP *sb.*[1] + -Y[1].]

1. a. Full of lumps.

1707 MORTIMER *Husb.* 286 This is one of the best Spades I have met with to dig hard lumpy Clays. **1809–16** COLERIDGE *Table-t.* (1884) 414 A lumpy soup full of knots of curds. **1845** G. E. DAY tr. *Simon's Anim. Chem.* I. 293 The blood remained perfectly fluid and slightly lumpy. **1885** *Times* 30 July 9/6 The soaked rice when subjected to steam-heat is liable to form a lumpy porridge instead of a mess in which the grains remain separate.

b. Applied to rough water when the surface is cut up by the wind into small waves. Also of broken weather.

1857 C. GRIBBLE in *Merc. Marine Mag.* (1858) V. 3 Hard gales..with a heavy lumpy sea. **1867** *Morn. Star* 19 Sept. 3 At this part of the river the water was extremely 'lumpy', the high wind meeting the ebb tide. **1875** 'STONEHENGE' *Brit. Sports* II. VIII. iv. §3. 664 They are capable of living through a great deal of lumpy lake or river. **1894** *Times* 6 Mar. 7/2 The head wind and lumpy water in this reach making the work very hard. **1928** *Sat. Even. Post* 10 Mar. 8/1 'Had good weather?' 'Lumpy weather all the way.'

c. ***lumpy jaw***: actinomycosis affecting the jaw, common in cattle.

1891–2 E. SALMON in *U.S. Rep. Bureau Anim. Indust.* (*title*), The Treatment of Lumpy Jaw. **1895** *Times* 4 Mar. 3/3 Should an animal be suffering from 'lumpy jaw' (actinomycosis),..the inspector condemns it.

2. Having an outline or shape characterized by lumps or roundish protuberances which impart a heavy and clumsy appearance.

1708 OZELL tr. *Boileau's Lutrin* 36 Leaning on one Arm his lumpy Head. **1794** U. PRICE *Ess. Picturesque* I. 262 [That] dead flatness of outline..which his own close lumpy plantations of trees always exhibit. **1828** SCOTT *Jrnl.* 3 Apr., I have not forgiven them for..building two lumpy things like mad-houses. **1865** GEIKIE *Scen. & Geol. Scot.* viii. 222 Schistose rocks..form large lumpy hills, with long smooth slopes. **1890** 'ROLF BOLDREWOOD' *Col. Reformer* (1891) 107 Young ones [horses] generally have a roundish, lumpy shoulder. **1899** *Allbutt's Syst. Med.* VI. 577 The disorder differs from other forms of obesity in its partial and lumpy distribution. **1926** A. BENNETT *Lord Raingo* I. xxxviii. 216 The fair but lumpy young woman silently left the room. **1928** E. O'NEILL *Strange Interlude* I. 14 Pretty vicious face under caked powder and rouge..lumpy body. **1934** *Times Lit. Suppl.* 8 Mar. 162/2 In the early nineties I was looking at Rubens's 'Rape of the Sabines' in the National Gallery, when a British workman beside me remarked, 'Lumpy lot to lift, eh?' **1959** I. & P. OPIE *Lore & Lang. of Schoolch.* ix. 168 The unfortunate fat boy..is known as..lumpy. **1973** *Observer* 5 Aug. 18/7 Lumpier and mousier, the girl grooms socialised affectionately with their ponies.

3. *slang.* Intoxicated, drunk.

1810 *Splendid Follies* III. 165 Doctor Lying..got cherry-merry, and came home as lumpy..as an ass. **1845** *Punch* VIII. 200 For 'boosey' we might substitute 'lumpy' to suit modern parlance. **1864** in *Slang Dict.*

‖**luna** ('l(j)uːnə). Also 7 anglicized **lune.** [L. *lūna* moon.] (In senses 1 and 2 written with capital L as proper name.)

1. The moon (personified).

a **1529** SKELTON *Bowge of Courte* 3 Whan Luna, full of mutabylyte, As emperes the dyademe hath worne Of our pole artyke. **1588** SHAKS. *L.L.L.* IV. ii. 39 *Dul.* What is dictima? *Nath.* A title to Phebe, to Luna, to the Moone. **1592** KYD *Sp. Trag.* II. iv. 19 And Luna hides her selfe to pleasure vs. **1836** M. MACKINTOSH *Cottager's Dau.* 319 Luna shone bright in the blue arch above.

2. †**a.** *Alch.* Silver (*obs.*). **b.** *Her.* The name used for argent, in the blazon of sovereign princes.

c **1386** CHAUCER *Can. Yeom. Prol. & T.* 273 Sol gold is, and Luna silver we threpe. **1594** PLAT *Jewell-ho.* III. 89 To melt one part of Luna with 3 parts of Venus. **1599** T. M[OUFET] *Silkwormes* 45 When Ioue they turne to Sol or Luna fine. **1606** J. DAVIES (Heref.) *Select Second Husband* (Grosart) 7/1 Though Beauty then seem Sol, at least as rich, It will be found but Lune, on Tryalls touch. **1641** FRENCH *Distill.* vi. (1651) 196 Take..of our lune, not of the vulgar, graines two. **1652** ASHMOLE *Theatr. Chem.* 198 Luna ys a pure white Body of clene Mercury & Sulphur white ingendered. **1709** HEARNE *Collect.* 6 Nov. (O.H.S.) II. 301 A Cross Patée Luna. **1758** [see JUPITER 2 b]. **1828–40** BERRY *Encycl. Her.*

c. **luna cornea** = HORN SILVER, chloride of silver fused. Also ***lunæ*** (incorrectly ***luna***) ***cornua***.

1706 PHILLIPS (ed. Kersey), *Luna Cornea* or *Lunæ Cornua*, a tough, tasteless Mass, almost like Horn, made by pouring Spirit of Salt..on Crystals of Silver. **1796** KIRWAN *Elem. Min.* (ed. 2) II. 33 One hundred parts of..salt, 235 parts of Luna cornua well dried. **1890** ABNEY *Photogr.* (ed. 6), Silver chloride, known to them [alchemists] as Luna cornua.

3. More fully ***luna-moth***: A large moth of North America, *Actias luna*, having crescent-shaped spots on the wings.

1884 *Riverside Nat. Hist.* (1888) II. 458 The luna moth, *Actias luna*, is unrivalled for loveliness and beauty. **1869** *Amer. Naturalist* II. 679/2 Luna moth. **1876** *Field & Forest* II. 72 Mr. Rodgers..gives the history of the Luna moth. **1948** *Natural Hist.* Dec. 451/1 The Hercules moth is a close relative of the well-known Luna moth. **1972** SWAN & PAPP *Common Insects N. Amer.* 267 Luna Moth: *Actias luna*... Wings are delicate green, shading to pale gray, with transparent eyespots... Larva..resembles the Polyphemus larva except that Luna has yellow lateral stripe and no oblique stripes on the side. **1974** A. DILLARD *Pilgrim at Tinker Creek* x. 159 Luna moths are those fragile ghost moths, fairy moths, whose five-inch wings are swallow-tailed, a pastel green bordered in silken lavender.

lunabase ('l(j)uːnəbeɪs). *Astr.* [f. L. *lūna* moon + BASE *sb.*[1] (as the sb. corresponding to the adj. *basic*, in the petrographic sense).] The lunar maria or lowlands (the dark-coloured regions as seen from the earth).

Orig. proposed for the rock composing them (see quot. 1944).

1944 J. E. SPURR *Geol. applied to Selenology* II. iv. 20 The differently colored formations which largely make up the marking of the lunar 'map' have, in the Imbrian study (volume I), been interpreted as probably corresponding to two main types of terrestrial rock: the light-gray 'uplands' as siliceous, the dark mare as basic or basaltic... In future descriptions the light-colored rocks may be called lunarite. The dark-gray mare..may be called imbase... In the mare formations south of the Mare Imbrium, a later, darker phase of presumably basic rock..may safely, and briefly, be called novabase (later lunar basaltic rock). And the inclusive term for both would be lunabase (lunar basaltic rock). **1966** *Earth Sci. Rev.* I. 231 Spurr (1944) gave the name 'lunarite' to the more highly reflective parts [of the moon's surface], and the name 'lunabase' to the darker parts. Large areas of lunarite are referred to as 'continents', and specific areas of lunabase are called 'maria'. **1967** *New Scientist* 2 Feb. 263/2 The mountains [on the moon] end with steep terminal slopes of 20° or so, which cannot be due to erosion as a result of melting by subsequent lavas from the mare region (the dark lunabase).

lunacy ('l(j)uːnəsɪ). [f. LUNATIC: see -ACY 3.]

1. The condition of being a lunatic; intermittent insanity such as was formerly supposed to be brought about by the changes of the moon; now applied *gen.* to any form of insanity (idiocy usually excepted). In legal use, such mental unsoundness as interferes with civil rights or transactions. †Also, a fit or attack of such insanity.

commission of lunacy, a commission, issuing from a court, authorizing an inquiry as to the soundness of a person's mind. ***commissioner in lunacy***, (*a*) the title given by the statute of 1842 to two officers then first appointed; in 1845 changed to *master in lunacy* (see below); (*b*) in subsequent use, a member of a board appointed by the Lord Chancellor to inspect asylums and grant licences to private persons who undertake the charge of lunatics. ***master in lunacy***, a legal officer whose duty it is to investigate the mental condition of persons alleged to be insane and to make orders dealing with the persons and estates of lunatics.

1541 *Act 33 Hen. VIII*, c. 20 §1 Suche persons..were.. than not mad nor lunatike, but sithen that time fallen to madnes or lunacy. **1602** SHAKS. *Ham.* III. i. 4 Grating so harshly all his dayes of quiet With turbulent and dangerous Lunacy. *Ibid.* III. iii. 7 The termes of our estate, may not endure Hazard so dangerous as doth hourely grow Out of his Lunacies. **1611** COTGR., *Lunatique*, Lunaticke, in a Lunacie. **1635** SWAN *Spec. M.* vii. §3 (1643) 334 This disease of lunacie, is a disease whose distemper followeth the course of the moon. **1764** BURN *Poor Laws* 55 Persons, who by lunacy or otherwise are furiously mad. **1818** CRUISE *Digest* (ed. 2) V. 307 Taking advantage of John Lord Brereton's being then under a commission of lunacy. **1874** BUCKNILL & TUKE *Psych. Med.* (ed. 3) 14 If the Lord Chancellor..employ a person not a Commissioner in Lunacy to inspect..the state of any asylum, hospital, gaol, house, or place wherein any lunatic is confined. **1880** *Libr. Univ. Knowl.* (N.Y.) IX. 198 Declared a lunatic..by the certificate of a master in lunacy. **1899** *Allbutt's Syst. Med.* VIII. 453 The tendency..of all lunacy is to set at naught first and most frequently the optional and then the obligatory rules of conduct.

b. *transf.* and *fig.* Mad folly. Often in much weakened sense.

1588 GREENE *Alcida* (1617) E, One while accusing loue as a lunacie, and then againe [etc.]. **1616** R. C. *Times' Whistle* IV. 1549 The hellish and mad lunacy Of them that doe commit apostacie For gold. **1733** CHEYNE *Eng. Malady* Pref. (1734) 3 To put a Stop to so universal a Lunacy and Madness. **1817** COLERIDGE *Lay Serm.* 425 The wicked lunacies of the gaming-table. **1884** *Manch. Exam.* 25 June 5/2 All talk of this kind is mere lunacy, involving, moreover, a more than lunatic disregard of facts.

c. *attrib.*

1881 *Encycl. Brit.* XIII. 112/1 The commencement of legislation such as that known in England as the Lunacy Acts. **1887** *Brit. Med. Jrnl.* 12 Feb. 338/2 Under the present lunacy law. **1897** *Daily News* 17 Feb. 5/1 Finding that he could not fill up the necessary lunacy forms.

†**2.** = Moon-blindness. (Cf. LUNATIC 2 b.)

1600 SURFLET *Country Farm* I. xxx. 200 The horse-mules are more tractable and more easie to guide and learne then the mare-mules be. Both of them are subiect to lunacie.

lu'nambulism. *rare.* [f. L. *lūna* moon, after *somnambulism.*] A kind of somnambulism supposed to be due to the moon's influence.

1846 TRENCH *Mirac.* v. (1862) 157 *note,* There are cases of lunambulism, in which, no doubt, it [the moon] has influence: but they are few and exceptional.

lunanaut: see LUNARNAUT.

Luna Park. The name of an amusement centre on Coney Island, Brooklyn, New York; also *transf.*, any such entertainment park. Also as *v. intr.*

1911 H. HAWTHORNE *New York* viii. 53 Luna Park and Dreamland are large sections of Coney.. within whose gates are real fairylands of plaster palaces. **1921** A. HUXLEY *Crome Yellow* ii. 8 The lights of Luna Park. **1930** J. COLLIER *His Monkey Wife* iii. 33 The Fun Fairs and Luna Parks of the carnal capitals of Europe. **1936** F. CLUNE *Roaming round Darling* xxiv. 244 Over a by-wash, then, Luna-parking down a big dipper, belly half-way up the other side. **1956** M. DUGGAN *Immanuel's Land* 90 Up at Tibidabo in the empty luna-park an aluminium aeroplane turns slowly at the end of a long pole. **1957** A. HEPBURN *Compl. Guide N.Y. City* (new ed.) 109 Biggest and best of the amusement centers are Steeplechase, Luna Park, Dreamland. **1967** G. GREENE *May we borrow your Husband?* 10 As squalid as a closed fun-fair with Lunar [*sic*] Park boarded up.

lunar ('l(j)uːnə(r)), *a.* and *sb.* [ad. L. *lūnār-is*, f. *lūna* moon: see -AR.] **A.** *adj.*

1. a. Of or belonging to the moon; situated in the moon; formerly often, influenced by or dependent upon the moon, or supposed to be so.

lunar race: a legendary race of Indian kings (*Candrávança*) supposed to have been descended from the moon.

1626 BACON *Sylva* §493 They haue denominated some Herbs Solar and some Lunar. **1661** LOVELL *Hist. Anim. & Min.* Introd., The Lunar [animals] are the cat, beaver, dog, goat, hart, otter. **1762** HOOLE *Tasso's Jerus. Delivered* VIII. 232 There full the lunar beam resplendent play'd. **1774** GOLDSM. *Nat. Hist.* (1776) I. 255 There are solar tides, and lunar tides. **1800** tr. *Lagrange's Chem.* I. 352 The alchemists gave the name of Solar Metals to those which are coloured; and that of Lunar to those which are white. **1841** ELPHINSTONE *Hist. Ind.* I. 259 The lunar race has but forty-eight names in the same period, in which the solar has ninety-five. **1854** W. K. KELLY *Arago's Astron.* (ed. 5) 73 The existence of lunar volcanoes is in no wise demonstrated. **1878** ABNEY *Photogr.* (1881) 303 Lunar photography. **1958** *Observer* 17 Aug. 1/6 It was new moon on Friday, and the 'lunar probe' must be launched in the next two or three days or postponed for a month. **1971** *Sci. Amer.* Oct. 49/3 Type *D* material consisted of miscellaneous fines smaller than a centimeter in diameter, material sometimes called lunar soil. **1972** *Science* 2 June 1014/3 It is appropriate to define the base of the 'lunar crust' at the discontinuity at 65 km.

b. Specialized collocations.

lunar cycle = *Metonic cycle* (see CYCLE *sb.* 2). **lunar day**, the interval of time between two successive crossings of the meridian by the moon. **lunar dial** (see quot.). **lunar distance**, in *Naut. Astr.*, the distance of the moon from the sun, a planet, or a fixed star, which is used in calculating longitude at sea. **lunar equation**, the intercalation of a lunar month after three lunar years; also, the correction of the epact in the Gregorian calendar necessitated by the error of the lunar cycle. **lunar horoscope** (see quot.). **lunar hour**, the 24th part of a lunar day. **lunar mansion** (see MANSION). **lunar method**, in *Naut. Astr.*, the method of determining longitude at sea by means of lunar distances. **lunar month**, the interval from one new moon to the next, about $29\frac{1}{2}$ days; in popular language often used for a period of 28 days (four weeks). **lunar nodes**, the point at which the orbit of the moon cuts the ecliptic. **lunar observation**, in *Naut. Astr.*, an observation of lunar distances in finding the longitude at sea. **lunar orbit**, (*a*) the orbit of the moon around the earth; (*b*) an orbit around the moon. **lunar rainbow**, one formed by the moon's rays. **lunar star**, a star whose geocentric distance from the moon is given in the Nautical Almanac for certain hours, so that the longitude may be found from them. **lunar tables**, (1) tables of the moon's motion from which its true place at any time may be found; (2) logarithmic tables for correcting the apparent distance of the moon from a star, on account of refraction and parallax. **lunar theory**, the deduction of the moon's motion from the law of gravitation. **lunar window**, a launch window for a mission to the moon. **lunar year**, a period consisting of twelve lunar months (about $354\frac{1}{3}$ days).

1704 HARRIS *Lex. Techn.* s.v. *Cycle of the Moon*, Enneadecaterides is, with some, the Name of this *Lunar Cycle. **1686** GOAD *Celest. Bodies* I. xii. 58 As there is a Lunar Month consisting of 28 or 29 Days, so there is a *Lunar Day. **1862** BACHE *Discuss. Magn. & Meteorol. Observ.* III. 8 The curves.. show two east and two west deflections in a lunar day. **1727–41** CHAMBERS *Cycl.* s.v. *Dial, Moon-Dial*, or **Lunar Dial*, is that which shews the hour of the night by means of the light, or shadow, of the moon, projected thereon from an index. **1830** HERSCHEL *Stud. Nat. Phil.* 27 A page of '*lunar distances' from the Nautical Almanack. **1712** DESAGULIERS tr. *Ozanam's Geog.* 66 The Addition of 30 Days to the third Lunar Year, is call'd the *Lunar Equation. **1727–41** CHAMBERS *Cycl.* s.v. *Horoscope*, **Lunar Horoscope* is the point which the moon issues out of, when the sun is in the ascending point of the east. This is also called the *part of fortune.* **1862** BACHE *Discuss. Magn. & Meteorol. Observ.* III. 1 Each observation was marked with its corresponding *lunar hour. **1860** WORCESTER, **Lunar method.* **1594** BLUNDEVIL *Exerc.* III. I. xlv. (1636) 358 The *Lunar month is that space of time which the Moone spendeth while she departing from the Sunne, returneth to him againe. **1727–41** CHAMBERS *Cycl.*, *Lunar periodical Months*, consist of twenty seven days, seven hours, and a few minutes. *Lunar synodical Months* consist of twenty nine days, twelve hours, and three quarters of an hour. **1766** BLACKSTONE *Comm.* II. 141 A month in law is a lunar month, or twenty eight days, unless otherwise expressed. **1883** P. SCHAFF *Hist. Church* I. II. xvi. 133 The month Nisan was the first of the twelve lunar months of the Jewish year. **1715** tr. *Gregory's Astron.* I. 37 If the abovementioned meeting of the Sun, and *Lunar Node, happens on the very Day of the New Moon. **1840** R. H. DANA *Bef. Mast* xxxi. 112 The Captain got a *lunar observation as well as his meridian altitude. **1728** *Chambers's Cycl.* II. 578/1 The transverse Diameter of the *Lunar Orbit. **1834** MRS. SOMERVILLE *Connex. Phys. Sci.* ii. 10 The reaction of that matter on the moon is the cause of a corresponding nutation in the lunar orbit. **1968** *Guardian* 28 Dec. 9/1 The Lunar Landing Module.. will shuttle two astronauts from lunar orbit, down to the moon's surface. **1969** *Daily Mail* 14 Jan. 1/2 For us, lunar orbit was the busiest time of the flight. **1969** *New Scientist* 17 July 114/2 They are inserted into an elliptical lunar orbit varying between 60 and 170 nautical miles above the Moon's surface. **1711** THORESBY in *Phil. Trans.* XXVII. 320 An Account of a *Lunar Rain-bow seen in Darbyshire. **1840** R. H. DANA *Bef. Mast* xxiii. 74 He knew every *lunar star in both hemispheres. **1864** WEBSTER, **Lunar Tables.* **1834** MRS. SOMERVILLE *Connex. Phys. Sci.* vi. 34 In the *lunar theory the sun is the great disturbing cause. **1883** *Encycl. Brit.* XVI. 800/1 The modern lunar theory commenced with Newton. **1969** *Guardian* 15 Jan. 18/2 A *lunar window exists for Russia at the moment. **1970** N. ARMSTRONG et al. *First on Moon* ii. 33 The time of launch.. had been chosen with great care. The date and the hour had been fixed to take full advantage of the so-called 'lunar window'. **1594** BLUNDEVIL *Exerc.* III. I. xliv. (1636) 357 Of *lunar yeeres there be two kinds, whereof the one is ordinary,.. and the other extraordinary or excessive,.. the ordinarie or common yeere, is the space of twelve Moones or changes. *Ibid.*, The extraordinarie Lunar yeere.. is the space of thirteene Moones or changes containing 384 daies. **1835** THIRLWALL *Greece* I. 221 The Greeks had begun to compensate for the defect of the lunar year, by the occasional addition of an intercalary month.

c. Employed in or relating to travel to or from the moon or on its surface; ***lunar* (*excursion*) *module***, a module designed to take an astronaut from an orbiting spacecraft to the moon's surface and back (abbrev. *LM, LEM* (L 7)).

1962 *Daily Tel.* 17 July 17/6 If anything should go wrong with the lunar space-craft and the astronauts found themselves unable to take off, from the moon, unmanned supply vehicles would be sent. **1962** *New Scientist* 19 July 123 At a hundred miles or so from the lunar surface retro-rockets will slow the craft into a lunar orbit. It will then be split in two, to form a mother craft and a lunar excursion module. **1965** *Punch* 20 Jan. 84/1 The great Apollo 'lunar project' by which the Americans, bless them, still hope to land a man, alive, on the Moon in 1970. **1966** *Electronics* 3 Oct. 134 The Lunar Excursion Module of the Apollo program has to descend safely as well as take off and rendezvous with the command module for the long trip home. **1967** *Technology Week* 20 Feb. 16 (*caption*) Full-size mockup of Apollo Telescope Mount.. is based on Apollo Lunar Module and is being used for placement of instruments. **1969** *Daily Mail* 14 Jan. 5/2 We were to test the lunar module, the vehicle which will land on the Moon, in a high Earth orbit. **1970** N. ARMSTRONG et al. *First on Moon* i. 20 By 1962.. the future programs were well designed and the lunar mission was going to become a reality. **1971** *New Scientist* 3 June 574/1 Special wire mesh wheels have been built for America's Lunar Roving Vehicle which.. is to drive around the lunar surface during the Apollo 15 mission in July. **1972** *Daily Tel.* 24 Apr. 1/4 They climbed into the lunar rover to drive 3·3 miles to North Ray Crater. **1975** S. JOHNSON *Urbane Guerilla* v. 181 Neil Armstrong at last stepped down from the lunar module *Eagle* on to lunar soil.

2. Transferred and figurative uses.

a. Monthly, menstrual. *rare.*

1683 TRYON *Way to Health* 630 In the time of Pregnancy, or her Lunar visits. **1822** GOOD *Study Med.* IV. 64 The cessation of her lunar discharge.

b. Having the character of the moon as opposed to that of the sun; not warmly bright; pale, pallid.

1742 YOUNG *Nt. Th.* III. 56 A theme so like thee, a quite lunar theme, Soft, modest, melancholy, female, fair. **1864** *Spectator* 425 Which we might call lunar poetry,—poetry without brilliancy, passion, or warmth, but yet containing glimpses of a pale but true beauty. **1902** SWINBURNE in *Q. Rev.* July 26 Even the lustre of Partridge [in *Tom Jones*] is pallid and lunar beside the noontide glory of Micawber.

c. ***lunar politics***: used allusively for 'matters of no practical concern'.

1868 HUXLEY *Lay Serm.* vii. (1870) 159 Hume's strong and subtle intellect takes up a great many problems about which we are naturally curious, and shows us that they are essentially questions of lunar politics, in their essence incapable of being answered.

3. Crescent-shaped, LUNATE. ***lunar bone*** (= medical L. *os lunare*): = B 3. Also, marked with crescent-shaped spots, as ***lunar underwing***.

1635 J. HAYWARD tr. *Biondi's Banish'd Virg.* 179 The Dwellings spreading.. from one point of the Heaven to the other in a lunar forme. **1693** DRYDEN *Iphis & Ianthe* Poet. Wks. (Aldine ed.) IV. 186 The lunar horns, that bind The brows of Isis. **1703** POPE *Thebais* 864 Who grasps the struggling heifer's lunar horns. **1759** W. WILKIE *Epigon.* II. (1769) 22 Each with a faulchion armed and lunar shield. **1843** WESTWOOD *Brit. Moths* I. 133 *Orthosia lunosa* (the lunar under wing). **1845** *Ibid.* II. 10 *Geometra lunaria* (the lunar thorn). **1863** REEVE *Land & Freshw. Mollusks* 50 Aperture broadly obliquely lunar. **1887** E. D. COPE *Orig. Fittest* vii. 264 The separation of the scaphoid and lunar bones.

4. Of or containing silver (see LUNA 2 a). **lunar caustic**, nitrate of silver fused.

1800 *Asiat. Ann. Reg., Misc. Tr.* 331/2 The little success attending the use of the lunar caustic in these experiments. **1822** GOOD *Study Med.* I. 313 The lunar pill of Boerhaave, formed from a preparation of silver, which may be regarded as a mild lunar caustic. **1826** OTTLEY *Dict. Chem., Silver, Nitrate of*; formerly called Lunar Nitre, Lunar Crystals, or Crystals of Silver, and when fused Lunar Caustic. **1899** *Allbutt's Syst. Med.* VI. 789 The cornea of both eyes was touched with a point of lunar caustic.

5. In Arabic grammar: The epithet of the class of consonants before which the *l* of the article is not assimilated; so called because including *q*, the initial of *qamar* moon. Opposed to *solar*.

1776 J. RICHARDSON *Arab. Gram.* iii. 8 The dentals and linguals are called *solar* letters, the rest *lunar*.

6. *Comb.*: **lunar-diurnal** *a.*, pertaining to the lunar day; **lunar-magnetic** *a.*, pertaining to magnetism as affected by the moon's position.

1856 SABINE in *Phil. Trans.* CXLVI. 499 The Lunar-diurnal Variations of the Inclination.. at that Station. **1862** BACHE *Discuss. Magn. & Meteorol. Observ.* III. 11 The lunar-magnetic interval for the Philadelphia station.

B. *sb.*

†**1.** A moon-like body, satellite. *Obs.*

1651 R. CHILD in *Hartlib's Legacy* (1655) 161 Mars, Jupiter, Saturn, have their Lunars or small Stars moving about them.

2. a. A lunar distance; a lunar observation.

1830 HERSCHEL *Stud. Nat. Phil.* 28 We steered towards Rio de Janeiro for some days after taking the lunars above described. **1875** BEDFORD *Sailor's Pocket Bk.* v. (ed. 2) 194 In taking Lunars, stars lying at about equal distances, east and west of the moon, should be chosen.

b. *colloq.* A look.

1906 GALSWORTHY *Man of Property* i. 21 Now and then he would level his umbrella and take a 'lunar', as he expressed it, of the varying heights. **1938** N. MARSH *Artists in Crime* v. 65 Let us take what used to be called a 'lunar' at the case. **1950** 'J. GUTHRIE' *Is this what I Wanted?* iii. 71 Charles took a lunar.

3. A bone of the wrist, shaped like a half-moon. Also in Latin form **lunare** (l(j)uː'nɛəriː).

1854 R. OWEN in *Circ. Sci.* (*c* 1865) II. 88/1 The carpal bones, answering to the scaphoid and lunar in the human wrist, are.. confluent. **1872** MIVART *Elem. Anat.* 169 The scaphoid coalesces with the lunare in the Carnivora.

lunaria: see LUNARY *sb.*[1]

lunarian (l(j)uː'nɛəriən), *a.* and *sb.* [f. L. *lūnāris* LUNAR + -IAN.]

A. *adj.* Inhabiting the moon.

1868 LOCKYER *Guillemin's Heavens* (ed. 3) 165 The lunarian observer situated on the invisible hemisphere.

B. *sb.*

1. A dweller in the moon.

1708 *Brit. Apollo* No. 13. 2/2 Be those Lunarians false or true. **1794** G. ADAMS *Nat. & Exp. Philos.* IV. xxxvii. 23 When it is what we call New Moon, we will appear as a Full Moon to the Lunarians. *a* **1849** POE *Mellonta Tauta* Wks. 1865 IV. 299 Creatures so diminutive as the lunarians. **1880** P. GREG *Acr. Zodiac* I. ii. 41 During an eclipse, the Lunarian would see round the Earth a halo created by [etc.].

2. One who observes or describes the moon; one who used the lunar method in finding longitude.

1817 E. WARD (*title*) The Lunarian, or Seaman's Guide; being a practical Introduction to the Method of ascertaining the Longitude at Sea. **1881** PROCTOR *Poetry Astron.* vi. 233 Nor does Schröter or any of the older lunarians indicate a crater at this part of the moon's surface. **1901** *Blackw. Mag.* Oct. 476/2 The expert lunarians—the men who found their longitude from observation of the moon—are gone.

lunarist ('l(j)uːnərɪst). *rare.* [f. LUNAR + -IST.] One who holds the 'lunar' theory of the causation of weather-changes.

1863 R. FITZROY *Weather Bk.* 213 In such grand disturbances as these [storms], the Lunarist and the Astro-meteorologist should endeavour to trace influences of moon and planets. **1864** *Intell. Observ.* No. 32. 105 The Lunarists and the Astro-meteorologists.

lunarite ('l(j)uːnəraɪt). *Astr.* [f. L. *lūna* moon + -ITE[1].] The lunar uplands (the light-coloured regions as seen from the earth).

Orig. proposed for the rock composing them (see quot. 1944).

1944, 1966 [see LUNABASE]. **1967** *New Scientist* 2 Feb. 263/3 In a few places the lunarite [lava] flows seem to dip under the lunabase of the surrounding plain, indicating that the lunarite and lunabase flows may at an early time have been contemporaneous.

‖**lunarium** (l(j)uː'nɛəriəm). [mod.L., f. L. *lūnāris* LUNAR.] An instrument representing the phases and motions of the moon. Cf. LUNARY *sb.*[2]

1786 JEFFERSON *Writ.* (1859) I. 507 What is become of the Lunarium for the King? **1794** G. ADAMS *Nat. & Exp. Philos.* IV. xliii. App. 171.

lunarnaut ('l(j)uːnənɔːt). Also **lunanaut.** [f. LUNAR *a.* + *-naut*, after *aeronaut, astronaut.*] One who travels or has travelled to the moon.

1965 *Guardian* 30 Aug. 12/1 The moon men (or lunarnauts, as they will doubtless come to be called) must be able to park their spacecraft. **1966** *Electronics Weekly* 27 July 29/2 (*heading*) Lunanauts will land with a reassuring 'bump'. **1969** *Scottish Daily Mail* 13 Jan. 2/6 Lunarnaut Frank Borman warned today that space flights are 'chancy'. **1971** *Daily Tel.* 30 Jan. 3/3 The Command and Service Module orbit the Moon while the lunarnauts carry out experiments and walk on its surface.

lunarscape ('l(j)uːnəskeɪp). [f. LUNAR *a.* + SCAPE *sb.*[3]] A picture or view of the moon's surface; the lunar landscape.

1965 *Newsweek* 25 Jan. 89 No one knows in detail what the lunarscape is like. **1966** *Punch* 27 Apr. 636/1 Superb blending of the Op and the Pop, comprising pointillist lunarscape in Coke bottle-tops. **1967** *Time* 25 Aug. 38

Lights flashed everywhere, bounding off the Day-Glo lunarscapes along the wall. **1970** *Guardian Weekly* 15 Aug. 12 The moon began to show out over the North Sea... Through my powerful binoculars I was able to study its face. The lunarscape looked like some great contoured globe. **1971** *New Scientist* 22 Apr. 224/1 These [paintings] include some dramatic lunarscapes.

lunary (ˈl(j)uːnərɪ), *sb.*^{1} ? *Obs.* Also 6–9 in Latin form **lunaria**. [ad. med.L. *lūnāria*, f. L. *lūna* moon.] **a.** The garden plant called HONESTY, *Lunaria biennis*. **b.** The fern called MOONWORT, *Botrychium Lunaria*.

Parkinson (1640 *Theat. Bot.* 508) says that 'there are so many herbes called by the name of *Lunaria* that it would make any man wonder how so many should be called'. The magical powers referred to in quots. 1642 and 1679 seem to have been ascribed to the fern.

c **1386** CHAUCER *Can. Yeom. Prol. & T.* 247 And herbes koude I telle eek many oon As Egrimoyne, Valerian, and lunarie. **1477** NORTON *Ord. Alch.* iii. in Ashm. (1652) 39 Vervaine, Lunara [*sic*], and Martagon. **1548** TURNER *Names of Herbes* (1881) 85 Lunaria is of two kyndes, the one is called in latine Lunaria maior... It maye be called in englishe great Lunari. Some cal it Shabub. The other kinde is called in latin Lunaria minor, which may be called in englishe litle Lunary or Maye Grapes. **1597** GERARDE *Herbal* II. lxxxv. 328 The small Lunarie springeth foorth of the ground with one leafe like Adders toong. **1627** DRAYTON *Agincourt*, etc. 127 Then sprinkles she the iuice of Rue.. With nine drops of the midnight dewe, From Lunarie distilling. **1642** FULLER *Holy & Prof. St.* IV. v. 261 They say of the herb Lunaria ceremoniously gathered at some set times, that laid upon any lock, it makes it flie open. **1679** *Hist. Jetzer* Pref. 2 The Fathers of that Society have the true Lunaria, which will open the strictest, strongest Locks or Fetters wherewith Conscience can be restrained. **1767** J. ABERCROMBIE *Ev. Man Own Gard.* (1803) 703/2 Lunaria, moon-wort or honesty. **1881** *Sat. Rev.* No. 1325. 374 The genus *botrychium*, the moon-fern or lunary, to the magical powers of which several of the Elizabethan poets bear testimony.

attrib. **1591** LYLY *Endym.* IV. i, You knowe that on the Lunary bancke sleepeth Endimion.

lunary (ˈl(j)uːnərɪ), *a.* and *sb.*^{2} Now *rare*. [ad. F. *lunaire*, L. *lūnāris*: see LUNAR and -ARY.]

A. *adj.*

1. Of or pertaining to the moon; = LUNAR *a.* 1. Also, inhabiting the moon.

1561 EDEN *Art of Navig.* II. vi. 30 These tymes [of conjunctions and oppositions] may be knowen..by the Ephimerides or Almanackes, or other tables, or Lunary instrumentes. **1610** HEALEY *St. Aug. Citie of God* 550 The yeare as it is now, consumate in twelve lunary revolutions Eastward. **1638** WILKINS *New World* I. (1684) 9 A Lunary Eclipse. *c* **1645** HOWELL *Lett.* (1692) II. 530 The Moon is peopled with Selenites or Lunary Men. **1651** J. F[REAKE] *Agrippa's Occ. Philos.* 48 There be here certain things which are Solary, and certain which are Lunary. **1690** LEYBOURN *Curs. Math.* 447 We are not to imagine..that the Lunary Seas, Lakes,..&c. are of the same Water with our Seas. **1727** BAILEY vol. II, *Lunary*, belonging to the moon. *a* **1849** POE *Ulalume* Wks. 1874 I. p. lxx, The limbo of lunary souls.

b. In *lunary month, year* (see LUNAR 1 b).

1602 FULBECKE *Pandectes* 4 Their [the Athenians'] twelue monethes did not exceed that number of daies which doth consist of the twelue lunarie monethes. [**1642** FULLER *Holy & Prof. St.* I. x. 25 Some erroneously compute the long lives of the Patriarks before the flood not by solary, but lunary years, making a moneth a yeare.] **1646** SIR T. BROWNE *Pseud. Ep.* IV. xii. 220 The Greeks observed the Lunary yeare, that is, twelve revolutions of the Moone 354. dayes. **1712** DESAGULIERS tr. *Ozanam's Geog.* 66 The Lunary Month, usually call'd Lunation.

2. *transf.* and *fig.* **a.** Monthly, menstrual.

1822–34 *Good's Study Med.* (ed. 4) III. 394 The ordinary return where anything like a regular period is established, is menstrual or lunary.

b. Lunatic.

c **1617** MIDDLETON *Witch* IV. i. 7 There is some difference betwixt my jovial condition and the lunary state of madness.

3. Crescent-shaped, LUNATE; = LUNAR.

1623 tr. *Favine's Theat. Hon.* III. iv. 359 His..Battalions should be ordered..in a Lunarie forme, and of a Crescent. **1668** CULPEPPER & COLE *Barthol. Anat.* I. xvii. 47 With their broad end they look towards the Cara, and with their sharp and lunary part they respect the Kidneys.

†**4.** ? Silvery. *Obs. rare*$^{-1}$.

1615 TOMKIS *Albumazar* II. iii, Hang'd round from toppe to bottome With pure white lunary Tapstry, or needle-worke; But if 'twere cloath of siluer, 'twere much better.

†**B.** *sb.*^{2} *Obs.*

1. A kind of apparatus for solving astronomical problems; = VOLVELLE.

14.. in Dyce *Skelton* (1843) II. 336 Now folowith here the volvelle, that sum men clepen a lunarie.

2. ? One born under the influence of the moon.

1605 TIMME *Quersit.* I. xi. 47 Starres which have their most colde and moyst spirites, as the Saturnalls and Lunaries.

3. A crescent or half-moon.

1610 W. FOLKINGHAM *Art of Survey* II. vi. 58 Parallelograms, Squares, Circles, Oualls, Lunaries.

lunate (ˈl(j)uːnət), *a.* Chiefly *Nat. Hist.* [ad. L. *lūnātus*, f. *lūna* moon: see -ATE^2.] Crescent-shaped, crescentiform.

1777 S. ROBSON *Brit. Flora* 11 Lunate, subrotund. **1806** GALPINE *Brit. Bot.* 329 Stipulæ lunate, toothed. **1828** STARK *Elem. Nat. Hist.* II. 174 Eyes linear, almost lunate. **1848** DALYELL *Rare Anim. Scotl.* II. 88 The lunate hydræ of Scotland falling within the sphere of my observation, are of three distinct genera. **1870** BENTLEY *Man. Bot.* 161 When a leaf is reniform but with the lobes at the base of the lamina pointed, it is lunate or crescent-shaped.

lunate (ˈl(j)uːneɪt), *sb. Archæol.* [f. the adj.] A small prehistoric stone (usu. flint) artifact which was probably used as an arrow-head and has an elongated half-moon shape with the straight edge unworked and the curved edge sharpened by chipping.

1932 *Jrnl. R. Anthrop. Inst.* LXII. 261 A fair proportion of lunates and other microliths showed a peculiar retouch... The back of the implement is not blunted in the ordinary way, but is trimmed obliquely from both surfaces, the result being to make it sharp instead of blunt. **1949** W. F. ALBRIGHT *Archaeol. of Palestine* iii. 59 The Natufian was a thorough-going microlithic culture, consisting largely of flint blades and points, most typical of which is the so-called lunate, a crescent or arc-shaped blade, probably used to tip reed arrows. **1960** K. M. KENYON *Archaeol. in Holy Land* ii. 36 Most characteristic of all are the lunates, very fine little flakes with a straight edge and a crescent-shaped back.

lunated (ˈl(j)uːneɪtɪd), *a.* Chiefly *Nat. Hist.* Now *rare*. [f. LUNATE *a.* + -ED^1.] = LUNATE *a.*

1673 E. BROWNE *Trav.* 82 A sort of Cross, which our Heralds do not dream of, which is a Cross Lunated after this manner. **1706** *Phil. Trans.* XXV. 2216 The *Jugulum* or lunated part of the Breast-bone. **1830** S. COOPER *Dict. Pract. Surg.* (ed. 6) 819 The operator..made a lunated incision. **1857** BIRCH *Anc. Pottery* (1858) I. 411 The Amazons have the pelta, or lunated shield. **1859** TODD *Cycl. Anat.* V. 156/2 The sacro-iliac facet..is lunated in shape.

ˈ**lunately**, *adv. rare*. [f. LUNATE *a.*] In a crescent form.

1872 H. C. WOOD *Contrib. Hist. Fresh-Water Algæ N. Amer.* 109 Cells..more or less lunately curved.

lunatic (ˈl(j)uːnətɪk), *a.* [ad. late L. *lūnātic-us*, f. L. *lūna* moon: see -ATIC. Cf. F. *lunatique*, Sp., It. *lunatico*.] **A.** *adj.*

1. Originally, affected with the kind of insanity that was supposed to have recurring periods dependent on the changes of the moon. In mod. use, synonymous with INSANE; current in popular and legal language, but not now employed technically by physicians.

c **1290** *S. Eng. Leg.* I. 369/99 He hadde ane douȝter þat was lunatyke. **1393** LANGL. *P. Pl.* C. x. 107 Þe whiche aren lunatik lollers and leperes a-boute, And mad as þe mone sitt. **1398** TREVISA *Barth. De P.R.* XVI. xcv. (1495) 587 The precyous stone Topazius..helpith ayenst the passyon Lunatyk. **1430–40** LYDG. *Bochas* VII. ii. (1554) 165 b, He was ..euery moneth once Lunaticke. **1564** in Strype *Eccl. Mem.* III. App. lviii. 197 All this trouble..was when you were lunatike and not your owne man. **1592** KYD *Sp. Trag.* III. viii. 5 (*Stage Direction*), She runnes lunaticke. **1600** *Hosp. Incur. Fooles* 77 If the moone be euill placed, either it maketh men extatical, lunatick, or subiect to the kings euill. **1604** S. GRAHAME *Pass. Sparke* E 4 b, The greatest Foole is wise if he be rich, And wisedome flowes from his Lunatique brayne. **1640** YORKE *Union Hon.* 110 This Alice fell lunaticke, and was divorced from the said Gilbert. **1759** ROBERTSON *Hist. Scot.* VII. Wks. 1813 I. 548 The presumptive heir to the throne was lunatic. **1885** *Sat. Rev.* 18 July 80/1 One of the most distinctive marks of the lunatic mind is that it reasons sanely from insane premises. **1889** *Spectator* 21 Dec., The House of Castile, which, after fighting and reigning for nearly eight hundred years, terminated in a lunatic girl.

b. Of things: indicating lunacy; crazy.

1605 SHAKS. *Lear* II. iii. 13 Bedlam beggers, who with roaring voices..Sometime with Lunaticke bans, sometime with Praiers, Inforce their charitie. **1614** B. JONSON *Barth. Fair* I. i, A notable hypocriticall vermine it is..of a most lunatique conscience, and splene. **1861** BUSHNELL *Char. Jesus* 48 There have been great enthusiasts in the world, and they have shown their infirmity by lunatic airs, appropriate to their extravagance.

c. *fig.* Madly foolish, frantic, idiotic, 'mad'.

1571 GOLDING *Calvin on Ps.* iv. 5 If lunatik rashnesse have caryed any into sinne. **1590** MARLOWE *Edw. II*, v. i. 113 Greefe makes me lunaticke. **1604** DEKKER *Honest Wh.* Wks. 1873 II. 71, I am sicke Of that disease, all Love is lunatike. **1612** DRAYTON *Poly-olb.* To Rdr. A, Nothing [is] esteem'd in this lunatique age but what is kept in cabinets. **1859** BRIGHT *Sp. India* 1 Aug. (1876) 47 No policy can be more lunatic than the policy of annexation. **1884** GEO. ELIOT *Ess.* (ed. 2) 14 The seventh [Satire]..contains nothing in particular except lunatic flattery of George I.

†**2. a.** Influenced by the moon. *Obs.*

c **1430** LYDG. *Reas. & Sens.* 6177 Ther [*sc.* women's] hertys chaunge never.. Ther sect ys no thing lunatyke. **1583** GREENE *Mamillia* Wks. (Grosart) II. 180 By natiuitie they be lunaticke, not taking this worde as the English men do, for starke mad, but as borne under the influence of Luna, and therefore as firme..as melting waxe. **1593** NASHE *Christ's T.* 14, I that was borne to suppresse & treade down sinne vnder foote, in the night time, (when that sinne-inhabited element is wont to be most lunaticke) walke on the crests of the surges as on the dry land.

b. *Farriery*. Affected with moonblindness; moon-blind, moon-eyed. *Obs.*

1577 B. GOOGE *Heresbach's Husb.* (1586) 124 Yᵉ broken wineded, the lunatike, and the mangines, called the Farcine. **1580** BLUNDEVIL *Curing Horses Dis.* 16 Of lunatike eies. **1607** MARKHAM *Caval.* VII. (1617) 22 Lunatike eyes, or Moone eyes. **1737** BRACKEN *Farriery Impr.* (1756) I. 136 In Lunatick or Moon-blind Horses.

B. *sb.* A lunatic person; a person of unsound mind; a madman.

1377 LANGL. *P. Pl.* B. Prol. 123 Thanne loked vp a lunatik, a lene thing with-alle. *c* **1380** WYCLIF *Serm.* Sel. Wks. II. 23 Lunatikes ben sich men þat han cours of þer siikenesse bi movyng of þe moone. **1590** SHAKS. *Mids. N.* v. i. 8 The Lunaticke, the Louer, and the Poet, Are of imagination all compact. **1628** COKE *On Litt.* I. 247 a, A Lunatique that hath sometime his vnderstanding and sometime not. **1735** MOTTE in *Swift's Lett.* (1768) IV. 107 An Hospital for Lunaticks and Idiots. **1742** *Act 15 Geo. II*, c. 30 Whereas Persons who have the Misfortune to become Lunaticks, may..be liable to be surprised into unsuitable Marriages. **1757** SMOLLETT *Reprisal* I. viii, An English lunatic at full moon, is a very sober animal when compared to a Frenchman in a passion. **1818** CRUISE *Digest* (ed. 2) I. 315 An infant, a person of nonsane memory, an idiot, a lunatic,..may also be grantees of a copyhold. **1828** SIR A. HALLIDAY *Pres. St. Lunatics* 30 In Perthshire, the idiots are two hundred and eight, the lunatics only one hundred and fifty-nine. **1881** *Encycl. Brit.* XIII. 113/1 Insane persons (although not lunatics so found by inquisition) may be placed under personal restraint. **1887** *Brit. Med. Jrnl.* 9 Apr. 808/2 A desperate encounter recently took place..between a lunatic who had escaped from Hatton Asylum and two keepers who were sent in pursuit.

b. *fig.* A madly foolish person.

1602 *2nd Pt. Return fr. Parnass.* II. iii. 665 She may be thy Luna, and thou her Lunaticke. *a* **1631** DONNE *Poems* (1650) 4 Vaine lunatique, against these scapes I could Dispute, and conquer, if I would. **1884** *Chr. World* 4 Sept. 667/1 Any man telling the farmers of Ireland not to pay their rents would be a lunatic.

c. *attrib.*: **lunatic asylum** (also **lunatic hospital**, † **house**), a hospital established for the reception and treatment of lunatics; **lunatic fringe**, a minority group of adherents to a political or other movement or set of beliefs; also *attrib.*; **lunatic soup** *Austral.* and *N.Z. slang*, alcoholic drink.

1762 WESLEY *Jrnl.* 21 Dec. (1827) III. 120, I doubt this is not the case of any other lunatic hospital. **1822–34** *Good's Study Med.* (ed. 4) III. 63 The proportion of patients returned as having been received into lunatic houses. **1828** SIR A. HALLIDAY (*title*) A General View of the Present State of Lunatics, and Lunatic Asylums, in Great Britain and Ireland. *Ibid.* 31 Dumfries has a small lunatic establishment, attached to the County Infirmary. **1885** *Times* 4 Aug. 9/4 A page from the lunatic entry book had been surreptitiously removed. **1887** *Brit. Med. Jrnl.* 2 Apr. 736/1 That the registered lunatic hospitals should not be subjected to special restrictions and disabilities. **1913** T. ROOSEVELT *Hist. as Lit.* 305 There is apt to be a lunatic fringe among the votaries of any forward movement. **1933** *Bulletin* (Sydney) 6 Sept. 42/1 Lunatic soup, as the few fellows about who knew him as Darkie called the brandy he drank. **1936** *Economist* 4 Jan. 3/1 Dr. Townsend has now left all his rivals behind in competition for the votes of the lunatic fringe. **1941** BAKER *Dict. Austral. Slang* 45 *Lunatic soup*, cheap red wine. **1945** 'G. ORWELL' *England your England* (1953) 56 The lunatic fringe even contrived to be simultaneously pro-Russian and pro-Nazi. **1951** E. PAUL *Springtime in Paris* iii. 59 Most of the paintings are imitations of other paintings, either conscious or unconscious, ranging from primitives and false primitives to the latest lunatic fringe. **1953** *Manch. Guardian Weekly* 21 May 15/4 Five [letters]..refer to his 'plug-ugly tactics', the 'lunatic fringe' brand of anti-communism. **1958** *Times* 9 Sept. 9/3 The lunatic fringe of society, to which only too many irresponsible hoaxers here and in America belong, finds the telephone its best friend. **1968** *Guardian* 12 Dec. 9/1 Lunatic-fringe Utopians call for something entirely new. **1969** *Observer* 23 Nov. 25/3 Views like these, as anyone who has listened to a few conversations on the verandahs of suburban Kingston will recognise, aren't lunatic fringe. **1970** *Ibid.* 11 Oct. 32/3 Both sides..have what you might call lunatic fringes; on the middle-aged right there are those who would lynch anyone with long hair, on the young left.. there are those who refuse to state their case rationally. **1973** D. RAMSAY *Deadly Discretion* 175 Antique shops were magnets for the lunatic fringe.

lunatical (l(j)uːˈnætɪkəl), *a. rare*. [f. LUNATIC + -AL^1.] = LUNATIC *a.*

1599 *Broughton's Let.* viii. 28 The Lunaticall conceits.. are thine owne. **1600** O. E. *Repl. Libel* I. ii. 43 Let this lunaticall or extaticall frier..forbeare to bragge. **1866** HOWELLS *Venet. Life* 100, He was of a most lunatical deportment. **1892** *Nat. Observer* 17 Dec. 101/2 The lunatical ignorance of politicians.

Hence **luˈnatically** *adv.*

1873 W. CORY *Lett. & Jrnls.* (1897) 311 The muezzin sang the prayers dismally, deathfully, lunatically.

†**lunaticness.** *Obs. rare.* The condition of being lunatic.

1662 J. CHANDLER *Van Helmont's Oriat.* 145 The immortall minde..doth not vary through Lunatickness or Franticknesse at a certain time of the Moon. **1727** BAILEY vol. II, *Lunatickness*.

lunation (l(j)uːˈneɪʃən). [ad. med.L. *lūnātiōn-em* (whence F. *lunaison*, It. *lunazione*, Sp. *lunacion*, Pg. *lunação*), f. *lūna* moon: see -ATION.]

1. The time from one new moon to the next, constituting a lunar month (= $29\frac{1}{2}$ days).

1398 TREVISA *Barth. De P.R.* IX. ix. (1495) 354 A monthe of the mone is also taken for a full lunacyon whyche duryth fro chaunge to chaunge. *c* **1400** MAUNDEV. (1839) xxx. 301 And there is not the Mone seyn in alle the Lunacioun. **1653** SHAKERLEY *Tabulæ Britan.* [117] A Table of the mean Lunations. **1664** POWER *Exp. Philos.* Pref. 4 Lunations of the inferiour Planets. **1690** LEYBOURN *Curs. Math.* 466 The Arabians..having respect to the Moon form their Year of 12 Synodical Lunations. **1712** STEELE *Spect.* No. 545 ¶ 13 The 8th day of the third lunation, and the 4th year of our reign. **1812** WOODHOUSE *Astron.* xxx. 295 From the inequality of the Moon's motion, this synodic period, or lunation, is not always of the same length. **1893** SIR R. BALL *Story of Sun* 132 Nineteen years is almost exactly equal to two hundred and thirty five lunations.

2. The time of full moon.

c **1549** in Froude *Hist. Eng.* (1881) IV. 405 They..intend at this or next lunation to conjure for treasure hid between Newbury and Reading. **1686** GOAD *Celest. Bodies* I. vi. 19 The Exuberance of the Tides at or neer the Æquinoctial Lunations. **1953** A. C. CLARKE *Prelude to Space* xxii. 115 If ..there's a last-minute hold-up, launching will be delayed

.., at the most, thirty-six hours. After that we'll have to wait for the next lunation—that is, for four weeks... We're anxious to land in daylight.

3. A menstruation. *rare.*

1822-34 *Good's Study Med.* (ed. 4) IV. 46 A tendency to keep up that periodical habit of depletion, which will probably prove advantageous against the ensuing lunations.

lunch (lʌnʃ), *sb.*[1] *Obs.* exc. *dial.* Also 5 **lonche.** [App. onomatopœic. Cf. DUNCH *sb.*] The sound made by the fall of a soft heavy body.

c **1440** *Promp. Parv.* 135/1 Dunche, or lonche (*H.P.* lunche), *sonitus, strepitus.* **1890** *Linc. N. & Q.* July 68 She heard a lunch, bud she thoht it was th' childer plaayin'.

lunch (lʌnʃ), *sb.*[2] [Perh. evolved from LUMP *sb.*[1], on the analogy of the apparent relation between *hump* and *hunch, bump* and *bunch.* Cf. 'Lounge, a large lump, as of bread or cheese' (Brockett *N. Country Words*, ed. 2, 1829).

It is curious that the word first appears as a rendering of the (at that time) like-sounding Sp. *lonja* slice of ham. LUNCHEON, commonly believed to be a derivative of *lunch*, occurs in our quots. 11 years earlier, with its present spelling. In sense 2 *lunch* was an abbreviation of *luncheon*, first appearing about 1829, when it was regarded either as a vulgarism or as a fashionable affectation.]

†**1.** A piece, a thick piece; a hunch or hunk. *Obs.*

1591 PERCIVALL *Sp. Dict., Lonja de tocino*, a lunch of bacon, *frustum, lardi.* **1600** SURFLET *Country Farm* VII. xxv. 850 He shall take breade and cut it into little lunches [Fr. *loppins*] into a pan with cheese. **1622** MABBE tr. *Aleman's Guzman d' Alf.* II. 280 Our Master was well content.. that we should roste a good lunch of porke. **1707** J. STEVENS tr. *Quevedo's Com. Wks.* (1709) 236, I clapp'd a good Lunch of Bread into my Pocket. **1785** BURNS *Holy Fair* xxiii, An' cheese an' bread.. Was dealt about in lunches.

2. a. A synonym of LUNCHEON *sb.* 2. (Now the usual word exc. in specially formal use, though formerly objected to as vulgar.) Also, a light meal at any time of the day.

1829 [H. BEST] *Pers. & Lit. Mem.* 307 The word *lunch* is adopted in that 'glass of fashion', Almacks, and *luncheon* is avoided as unsuitable to the polished society there exhibited. **1839-41** S. WARREN *Ten Thous. a-year* viii. I. 256 He happened to mention it at lunch. **1842** A. COMBE *Physiol. Digestion* (ed. 4) 266 We do not experience the same dislike to exertion after a light forenoon lunch. **1859** J. CUMMING *Ruth* v. 87 Parched corn was her only lunch in the midst of a day of ardour and of sunshine. **1865** TROLLOPE *Belton Est.* xxvi. 308 Lunch was on the table at half-past one. **1880** MRS. FORRESTER *Roy & V.* I. 20 Come to lunch to-morrow at one. **1901** R. D. EVANS *Sailor's Log* vi. 59 Every night during the mid watch a beautiful lunch was served to the officer of the deck. **1936** *S.P.E. Tract* XLV. 183 In several.. instances a word has been liberated in America from the restrictions that limit its application in England; for example ..*lunch.* **1950** E. A. MCCOURT *Home is Stranger* (1951) viii. 124 At midnight the womenfolk hurried out to the hall to prepare lunch. **1951** *Good Housek. Home Encycl.* 540 *Lunch*, the midday meal.. may cover anything from the sandwich lunch taken by some office and factory workers to the fairly elaborate formal meal given when guests are entertained at a public function or private party. **1960** S. PLATH *Colossus* (1967) 20, I open my lunch on a hill of black cypress. **1963** L. DIACK *Labrador Nurse* I. vii. 37 After a 'lunch' (i.e. a snack), all hands.. would set to work. **1965** J. S. GUNN *Terminol. Shearing Industry* I. 36 *Lunch*, a light snack which was taken at the mid-morning or mid-afternoon break... Lunch was food taken at any time away from main meals, even in the evening. **1968** *New Society* 22 Aug. 265/2 Though the U still have lunch (not dinner) in the middle of the day and U-dogs still have their dinner then, U-children have changed; they no longer have mid-day dinner, in the nursery, but have lunch with their mothers.

b. *out to lunch*: insane; stupid, unaware; socially unacceptable. *N. Amer. slang.*

1955 *Sci. Digest* Aug. 33/1 'Out to lunch' refers to someone who, in other years, just wasn't 'there'—and he is told immediately to 'Get with it!' **1959** *She* May 21/2 *Out to lunch* has nothing to do with social life but implies one is not in the groove. **1966** *Toronto Daily Star* 16 June 74/2 A girl who would be attracted to Bud's mean streak and bad temper must be a little out to lunch. **1974** *Melody Maker* 13 July 13/5, I think he's out to lunch. He's blown out—completely.

3. *attrib.* and *Comb.*, as *lunch-basket, -bell, -biscuit, -box, -break, -cake, -can, -counter, -date, -hour, -house, -money, -pail, -party, -room, -stand, -table, -tin, -wagon*; **lunch-dinner**, a meal that might be called either lunch or dinner, a mid-day dinner.

1901 *19th Cent.* Oct. 630, I.. snatched a hasty breakfast from my lunch basket. **1875** MRS. STOWE *We & Neighbors* v. 67 The ringing of the lunch bell interrupted the conversation. **1892** G. R. LOWNDES *Camping Sk.* 52 Trout, lunch biscuits, and cake, formed a reasonable lunch. **1864** *Rep. Comm. Patents 1862* (U.S.) I. 158 *Improved Lunch Box.* .. This invention consists of an arrangement of dishes, cups, etc., arranged within a case for the use of travellers. **1921** *Daily Colonist* (Victoria, B.C.) 23 Oct. 6/1 (Advt.), Folding lunch boxes. **1970** G. GREER *Female Eunuch* 233 Her house is ideally a base which her tired-warrior hunter can withdraw to.. while he.. is prepared by laundry and toilet and lunch-box for another sortie. **1960** *News Chron.* 14 June 6/6 Half of today's secretaries are married women and rely on the lunch break to do.. their shopping. **1971** C. STORR *Thursday* xii. 133 She timed herself to reach the [building] site just before the lunch break. **1886** M. L. DODS *Handbk. Pract. Cookery* (new ed.) 219 Lunch Cake,.. Bake in a moderate oven for one hour and a quarter. **1901** *Daily Colonist* (Victoria, B.C.) 27 Oct. 7/2 Our buns, scones and lunch cakes are the acme of perfection. **1951** *Good Housek. Home Encycl.* 540/2 *Lunch cake*, a fairly plain, substantial fruit cake. **1897** R. M. STUART *In Simpkinsville* 14 They'd give him biscuits out o' their lunch-cans. **1869** *Demorest's Young Amer.* Oct. 460 (*caption*) Eating at a small lunch counter or eating-saloon. **1904** G. S. FULLERTON *Syst. Metaphysics* xv. 242 To obtain a sandwich from the woman at the lunch-counter. **1934** *Archit. Rev.* LXXVI. 159/1 (*caption*) Lunch counter with recessed stainless steel front. **1960** *New Statesman* 26 Mar. 435/2 Possibly President Eisenhower will be a shade or two happier when a coloured Georgian and a white Georgian, seated on adjacent stools, have pie and coffee at a Woolworth lunch-counter in Atlanta —and possibly he may not. **1970** *Times* 23 Mar. 13/3 A nostalgic echo of those days when it seemed that all we had to do to achieve integration was to sit down at enough lunch counters together. **1933** *Radio Times* 14 Apr. 95 A tragic lunch date. **1968** *Listener* 25 July 103/3 A message came regretting he could not keep our lunch date, because he must be sure to cast his vote. **1878** SIR P. WALLIS in Brighton *Life* (1892) 201, I hope the good squire will take a lunch-dinner with me. **1908** KIPLING *Lett. of Travel* (1920) 129 Canadian Clubs.. assemble their members during the mid-day lunch-hour. **1909** H. G. WELLS *Ann Veronica* xiv. 302 She waited in the laboratory at the lunch-hour. **1929** *Radio Times* 8 Nov. 426/1, 1.15-2.0. A lunch hour concert. **1959** J. O'DONOVAN *Visited* xviii. 116 Edith sat by the phone all the lunch-hour. **1846** *Knickerbocker* XXVIII. 558 The following parody was found inscribed on the newspaper-board of a 'lunch-house' in Saint Louis, Missouri. **1902** G. H. LORIMER *Lett. Merchant* viii. 108 One of those fellows.. goes around and makes the boys give up their lunch money to buy flowers. **1955** M. GILBERT *Sky High* x. 144 Sixpence a week and their lunch money. That's all they get. **1891** M. E. WILKINS *New Eng. Nun* 44 Matilda came in her voluminous alpaca, with her tin lunch-pail on her arm. **1926** E. HEMINGWAY *Torrents of Spring* x. 71 He set down his lunch-pail. **1964** M. GALLANT in R. Weaver *Canad. Short Stories* 2nd Ser. (1968) 77 There was an unbridgeable gap.. between the girl whose father went off to work with a lunch pail and the daughter of a man who ate.. in the company cafeteria. **1884** F. M. CRAWFORD *Amer. Politician* I. iii. 43 At a lunch party.. they sat and talked about pictures. **1936** H. NICOLSON *Let.* 19 Feb. (1966) 244, I gave a lunch-party. **1961** NEW ENG. BIBLE *Luke* xiv. 12 When you give a lunch or dinner party. **1830** *N.Y. Mercantile Advertiser* 16 Aug. 4/6 His Breakfast, Lunch and Dining rooms are capacious and comfortable. **1919** Lunch room [see HOLE *sb.* 7b]. **1958** *New Statesman* 1 Feb. 143/1 By the end of the novel, Flem ..having by trickery acquired a half-interest in a Jefferson lunch-room has taken himself off to the county seat. **1887** C. B. GEORGE *40 Yrs. on Rail* v. 79 Superintendent Johnson.. noticed this lunch-stand, with its modest, yet appetizing display. **1890** 'ROLF BOLDREWOOD' *Col. Reformer* (1891) 277 The well-appointed lunch-table. **1950** *N.Z. Jrnl. Agric.* Aug. 191/1 Lunch tins which can be painted attractive colours are easily washed, inexpensive, and light and convenient to carry. **1894** *Life* 4 Oct. 215/1 'That, my dear,' responded Adalbert, 'is a lunch wagon.' **1959** N. MAILER *Advts. for Myself* (1961) 69 Inside, out of the rain, the lunch wagon was hot and sticky.

lunch (lʌnʃ), *v.* [f. LUNCH *sb.*[2]]

1. *intr.* To take lunch.

1823 D'ISRAELI *Cur. Lit.* Ser. II. I. 402 She is now old enough, she said, to have lived to hear the vulgarisms of her youth adopted in drawing-room circles. To lunch, now so familiar from the fairest lips, in her youth was only known in the servants hall. **1884** GRANT ALLEN *Philistia* II. 101 Miss Merivale lunched with the family. **1887** J. ASHBY-STERRY *Lazy Minstrel* (1892) 190 Here can we lunch to the music of trees. **1897** LD. TENNYSON *Mem. Tennyson* II. 222 On one occasion Ruskin lunched with us.

2. *trans.* To provide lunch for. *colloq.*

1892 *Temple Bar* Dec. 578 [She] does her duty.. warmly by her country friends—lunching, tea-ing, and dining them. **1893** *Westm. Gaz.* 15 June 2/1 Permission was given to lunch the pilgrims on board the *Victory.*

luncheon ('lʌnʃən). Also 7 **lunchen, lunchion, lunching,** 7-8 **lunchin,** 8 **lunshin.** [Related in some way to LUNCH *sb.*[2]

The ordinary view, that the spelling *lunching* represents the etymological form, appears somewhat unlikely. In our quots. the earliest form is *luncheon*, and this appears in our quots. earlier than *lunch*; and there is no evidence of a derivative verb in the 16-17th c. It is possible that *luncheon* might have been extended from *lunch* on the analogy of the relation between *punch, puncheon, trunch, truncheon.*]

†**1.** = LUNCH *sb.*[2] 1. *Obs.*

1580 HOLLYBAND *Treas. Fr. Tong, Lopin*, a lumpe, a goblet, a luncheon. **1617** MORYSON *Itin.* III. II. iv. 97 Eating a great lumpe of bread and butter with a lunchen of cheese. **1660** *Chas. II's Escape fr. Worcester* in *Harl. Misc.* (1809) IV. 444 The Colonel plucked out of his pocket a good luncheon of bread and cheese. **1703** THORESBY *Let. to Ray* (E.D.S.) s.v., A huge lunshin of bread, i.e. a large piece. **1760-72** H. BROOKE *Fool of Qual.* (1809) III. 62 A large luncheon of brown bread.. struck my eyes. **1824** SCOTT *Redgauntlet* let. x, Little Benjie.. was cramming a huge luncheon of pie-crust into his mouth.

fig. **1685** H. MORE *Paralip. Prophet.* xii. 98 No little scraps of bounty.. but large Lunchions of Munificence.

2. a. Originally, a slight repast taken between two of the ordinary meal-times, *esp.* between breakfast and mid-day dinner. The word retains this original application with those who use *dinner* as the name of the mid-day meal; with those who 'dine' in the evening, *luncheon* denotes a meal (understood to be less substantial and less ceremonious than *dinner*) taken usually in the early afternoon. Now somewhat *formal*: cf. LUNCH *sb.*[2] 2.

a **1652** BROME *Mad Couple* v. i. Wks. 1873 I. 92 Noonings, and intermealiary Lunchings. **1655** tr. *Com. Hist. Francion* III. 71 For our Breakfast and after-noons Lunchions [Fr. *à gouster*]. **1706** E. WARD *Writings* (ed. 3) II. 125 Then others more Hungry, their Stomachs to please, Sit down to their Luncheons of House-hold and Cheese. **1809** MALKIN *Gil Blas* III. ii. ¶3 As soon as we had released our kitchen-wench, I gave orders for a good luncheon. **1823** BYRON *Juan* XI. lxv, His afternoons he pass'd in visits, luncheons, Lounging and boxing. **1827** CARLYLE *Germ. Rom.* II. 318 The mother looked for the little ones, and brought them their evening luncheon. **1855** MRS. GASKELL *North & S.* i, They did not scruple to make a call at each other's houses before Luncheon. **1881** LADY HERBERT *Edith* 2 Have you had some luncheon? **1891** E. PEACOCK *N. Brendon* II. 2 Thornton stayed for luncheon.

b. *U.S.* Applied to a late supper.

1903 *Boston Even. Transcript* 3 Oct. 5 At this table, from 9 o'clock until midnight, a bountiful standing luncheon was served continuously.

3. *attrib.*, as *luncheon bar, -basket, bell, -hour, tent, -time*; **luncheon-car**, on a railway train, a restaurant-car where luncheons are provided; also *attrib.*; †**luncheon-dinner** = *lunch-dinner* (LUNCH *sb.*[2] 3); **luncheon meat**, a type of pre-cooked meat containing preservatives; **luncheon voucher**, a money voucher given to employees which is exchangeable for meals at certain restaurants.

1891 H. HERMAN *His Angel* 125 The cellar.. was occupied by a liquor and luncheon bar. **1859** QUEEN VICTORIA *Jrnl.* 7 Oct. in D. Duff *Victoria in Highlands* (1968) 159 Our pony carried the luncheon baskets. **1903** *Railway timetable*, Luncheon-baskets.. may be obtained at the principal stations. **1958** J. CANNAN *And be a Villain* I. 15 Ah, the Victorian railways!.. the luncheon baskets you wired ahead for. **1884** W. S. GILBERT *Princess Ida* 11, Merrily ring the luncheon bell. **1903** A. BENNETT *Leonora* vii. 203 The express, with its two engines, its gilded luncheon-cars, and its post-office van. *Ibid.* 204 Catching the luncheon-car attendant by the sleeve. **1909** *Westm. Gaz.* 8 Sept. 2/1 A new luncheon-car express, starting from King's Cross at 1.5 p.m. **1970** *Country Life* 31 Dec. 1293/1 On the next stage north there was a luncheon car, and at The Mound he ate his lunch. **1819** M. EDGEWORTH *Let.* 4 Mar. (1971) 178 After luncheon-dinner I finished at Oxford. **1882** W. D. HAY *Brighter Britain!* I. ii. 25 There are three common meals —breakfast, luncheon-dinner, and dinner-supper. **1888** J. PAYN *Myst. Mirbridge* I. ix. 146 From that very Pavilion he had slipped away during the luncheon-hour. **1945** 'R. CROMPTON' *William & Brains Trust* ix. 166 Although it meant opening her last remaining tin of Luncheon Meat. **1953** J. HUNT *Ascent Everest* IV. xii. 155 Over our bacon and, possibly, eggs, or fried luncheon meat. **1957** E. CRAIG *Collins Family Cookery* 814 Dice luncheon meat and use as a filling for bread. **1960** A. E. BENDER *Dict. Nutrition* 76/2 *Luncheon Meat*.. must have a meat content not less than 80%. **1899** E. PEACOCK in *Month* Feb. 208 To witness the servants of the Duke pitch the luncheon-tent. **1823** J. BADCOCK *Dom. Amusem.* 158 Allowing.. not a moment for meals, nor the well known luncheon-time. **1955** *Evening Standard* 28 Oct. 15/3 (*heading*) Doorman/timekeeper for staff and goods entrance... Pension scheme, welfare fund, luncheon vouchers, etc. **1966** A. LA BERN *Goodbye Piccadilly* v. 48 Their wallets contained more luncheon vouchers than treasury notes. **1973** *Times* 24 Jan. (Security Conf. Printing Suppl.) p. i/3 The notes in our wallets, stamps for letters.. luncheon vouchers.. are a few of the little pieces of paper so essential to modern life.

Hence **'luncheon** *v. intr.*, to take luncheon, to lunch; **'luncheonless** *a.*, without luncheon.

1883 LD. SALTOUN *Scraps* I. 190, I.. went luncheonless myself. **1885** *Fortn. in Waggonette* 94 A few minutes more saw an imposing party luncheoning on the grassy roadside. **1889** *Archæol. Æliana* XIII. 309 The Duke of Northumberland.. luncheoned at the 'Three Half Moons'.

luncheo'nette. orig. *U.S.* [LUNCHEON 2 + -ETTE.] A small restaurant or snack bar serving light lunches.

1924 *Public Opinion* 11 July 31/2 Luncheonettes supply icecream soda and a ham sandwich. **1930** J. O. DAHL (*title*) Soda fountain and luncheonette management. **1939** C. MORLEY *Kitty Foyle* viii. 74 Sparta's, a Greek candy and luncheonette a block farther up Main. **1959** *New Statesman* 24 Oct. 534/3 They sleep late, meet on the corners, drift in and out of the poolrooms and the luncheonettes. **1969** *New Yorker* 20 Sept. 38/2 A luncheonette, where a couple of young men in shirt sleeves sat hunched over the counter eating.. noodle soup. **1972** *Daily Tel.* 10 Apr. 9/8 France is to have 100 quick-lunch restaurants *à l'Anglaise*... These luncheonettes will all be along France's main highways. **1974** D. RAMSAY *No Cause to Kill* I. 44 She didn't care for luncheonette food.

luncher ('lʌnʃə(r)). [f. LUNCH *v.* + -ER[1].] One who lunches or takes lunch.

1840 *New Monthly Mag.* LX. 60 We therefore put it to the conscience of the ladies who indulge in hot luncheons (if a regular luncher can have a conscience). **1895** J. DAVIDSON *Earl Lavender* 248 The sound of the pipes.. reached the thirty lunchers in their barn.

lunching, *vbl. sb.* [f. LUNCH *v.*] The action of taking lunch. Also *attrib.*

1920 R. L. ALSAKER *Maintaining Health* 271 Lunching before going to bed is a bad habit. **1968** *Economist* 18 May 74/2 One can see bloated central staffs, outside directors who are appositely called 'lunching directors' and cannot control their management colleagues in any way.

'lunchless, *a.* [f. LUNCH *sb.*[2] + -LESS.] Having had no lunch; without lunch.

1904 KIPLING *Traffics & Discov.* 339, I found myself stranded, lunchless, on the sea-front. **1920** GALSWORTHY *In Chancery* III. i. 244 Sitting lunchless in the hall of his hotel. **1958** E. NEWBY *Short Walk in Hindu Kush* ii. 17 In my lunchless state I envied them.

'lunch-time. [f. LUNCH *sb.*[2] + TIME *sb.*] The time at which lunch is eaten. Also *attrib.*

1859 GEO. ELIOT *Let.* 10 Oct. (1954) III. 180 He can't take us wrongly any day either at 1 o'clock, (lunch-time) or at half past 5 (dinner). **1866** G. M. HOPKINS *Lett. to R. Bridges* (1955) 5 He.. left me at lunch-time. **1890** 'ROLF

BOLDREWOOD' *Col. Reformer* (1891) 276 It was on the right side of lunch-time. **1909** H. G. WELLS *Ann Veronica* xiv. 290 Capes came into the laboratory at lunch-time. **1929** *Radio Times* 8 Nov. 389/2 The lunch-time programme arranged by Mr. Christopher Stone. **1957** MANVELL & HUNTLEY *Technique Film Music* 235 Kisenga, an African musician..is seen playing this work in a reconstruction of the war-time National Gallery lunch-time concerts. **1963** *Times* 22 May 9/5 We'll be at the coast by lunchtime and the children can't wait for a swim and neither can I. **1968** J. BINGHAM *I love, I Kill* xv. 222 Have me thrown out, boyo. If you hurry up, it'll make the lunchtime editions. **1971** D. CRYSTAL *Ling.* i. 11 There is at least one teachers' common-room..where problems of etymology..provide the normal, lunch-time gossip.

†**lund.** *Obs.* Also 5 lunde. [a. ON. *lund.*] Disposition, nature; manners.

c **1200** ORMIN 7038 Gode menness clene lund. *Ibid.* 9785 All fulle off attriз lund. *c* **1450** *St. Cuthbert* (Surtees) 1460 In haly speche he lyked his lunde.

‖**'lunda.** Also 8 lunder. [repr. Icel. *lundi*, Norw. *lunde*, Sw. *lunn.*] A Scandinavian name for: The puffin.

1743 *Phil. Trans.* XLII. 612 Greenland produces.. Cormorants, Lunders, Parrots [etc.]. **1802** G. MONTAGU *Ornith. Dict.* (1833) 310 *Lunda*, a name for the Puffin. **1893** NEWTON *Dict. Birds, Lunda.*

lunder, lundge: see LOUNDER *v.*, LOUNGE *v.*

†**lundress.** *Obs.* [a. F. *Londreis* adj., f. *Londres* London.] (See quot. 1695.)

1695 W. LOWNDES *Amendm. Silver Coin* 17 A Sterling.. was once called a Lundress, because it was to be Coined only at London. **1706** in PHILLIPS; and in later Dicts.

‖**lundum** ('lʊndʌm). [Pg.] A primitive Portuguese song and dance, from which the *fado* probably developed.

1936 R. GALLOP *Portugal* xi. 252 The *lundum*..shared the affections of the Lisbon populace from the last quarter of the eighteenth to the middle of the nineteenth century. The *lundum* came to Portugal from Brazil... It reached Brazil from the west coast of Africa. **1957** R. CAMPBELL *Portugal* ix. 191 It was this crossing of the primitive sensual ferocity and black, wailing misery of the negro *lundum*..that gave us the *fado.* **1957** [see *belly-dancing* s.v. BELLY *sb.* 17]. **1969** S. BRADFORD *Portugal & Madeira* 27 With them [*sc.* Angolan slaves] went memories of their native dances, one of them being the lundum, a dance of Congolese origin.

Lundyfoot ('lʌndɪfʊt). [Named after Lundy Foot, a Dublin tobacconist, whose address is given as 8 Essex Bridge in Wilson's *Dublin Directory* 1776.] A kind of snuff.

1811 *Ora & Juliet* IV. 187 The sportive zephyrs carried the high-dried Lundyfoot into the eyes of the whole party. **1822** *Blackw. Mag.* XI. 370* He took so much of Lundy-Foot, That he used to snort and snuffle. **1866** *Daily Tel.* 11 Jan. 5/1 A pinch of Lundyfoot or brown Rappee.

lune[1] (l(j)uːn). *Hawking.* Also 5 lewne; and see LOYN. [var. of LOYN.] A leash for a hawk.

1470–85 MALORY *Arthur* VI. xvi, Thenne was he ware of a Faucon..and longe lunys aboute her feete. **1486** *Bk. St. Albans* B v b, The lewnes shulde be fastened to theym, with a payre of tyrettis. **1580** H. GIFFORD *Gilloflowers* (1875) 90 In fancie's lune I fast was cought. **1593** GREENE *Mamillia* I. E 3, The closer shee couered the sparke, the more it kindled: yea, in seeking to vnlose the Lunes, the more shee was intangled. **1611** COTGR., *Longe*,..a hawkes lune or leash. **1895** QUILLER-COUCH *Wandering Heath* 230 A gerfalcon lying with long lunes tangled about his feet.

lune[2] (l(j)uːn). *arch.* [ad. med.L. *lūna* lit. 'moon', hence 'fit of lunacy' (cf. LUNATIC), whence F. *lune*, MHG. *lûne* (G. *laune* whim, humour).] *pl.* Fits of frenzy or lunacy; mad freaks or tantrums. (Cf. LINE *sb.*[2] 29.)

1611 SHAKS. *Wint. T.* II. ii. 30 These dangerous, vnsafe Lunes i' th' King,—beshrew them. **1778** JOHNSON *Let. to Mrs. Thrale* 14 Nov., My master is in his old lunes and so am I. **1799** LAMB *John Woodvil* III, Let him alone. I have seen him in these lunes before. **1867** J. H. STIRLING in *Fortn. Rev.* Oct. 381 This is the central weak point, the special lunes of the De Quincey nature. **1883** SYMONDS *Renaiss. It., Ital. Lit.* II. II. x. 97 Their tales for the most part are the lunes of wanton love.

lune[3] (l(j)uːn). [a. F. *lune*:—L. *lūna* moon.]

1. *Geom.* The figure formed on a sphere or on a plane by two arcs of circles that enclose a space.

1704 HARRIS *Lex. Techn.*, *Lunes* or *Lunulæ.* **1839** in *Penny Cycl.* XIV. 199. **1854** MOSELEY *Astron.* xxxiv. (ed. 4) 119 Her [the moon's] crescent..now presents the appearance of a lune. **1891** CAYLEY in *Coll. Papers* (1897) XIII. 205 The two lunes *ACB* and *ABD* of figure 6.

2. Anything in the shape of a crescent or half-moon.

1706–9 WATTS *Lyric Poems* II. *Vict. Poles over Osman* 149 Faithful Janizaries..Fall'n in just Ranks or Wedges, Lunes or Squares. **1805** W. HERSCHEL in *Phil. Trans.* XCV. 36 This made them [the globules] gradually assume the shape of half moons..The dark part of these little lunes..did not appear sensibly less than the enlightened part.

lune, anglicized f. LUNA.

lünebergite (lʏnə'bɜːgaɪt). *Min.* [Named by C. Nöllner, 1870, from *Lüneberg*, Hanover, its locality: see -ITE.] A boro-phosphate of magnesium, found in fibrous masses.

1872 DANA *Min.* App. 10. **1893** *Chapman's Blowpipe Pract.* 179.

lunecye, obs. form of LUNACY.

lunel[1] (l(j)uː'nɛl). [f. *Lunel* (Hérault) a town in France.] A sweet muscat wine. Also *lunel-wine.*

1770 *Ann. Reg.* II. 158 He..made me drink bumper after bumper of his lunel wine. **1821** *Rouge et Noir* 85 A bumper of the true lunel. **1841** THACKERAY *Mem. Gormandising* Wks. 1900 XIII. 589 What could literary men mean by ordering lunel?

‖**lunel**[2] ('l(j)uːnɛl). *Her.* [Fr., a. Sp. *lunel*, f. *luna* moon.] A figure formed by four crescents appointé resembling a rose with four leaves.

1828–40 in BERRY *Encycl. Her.* I.

lunestice, obs. form of LUNISTICE.

‖**lunetta.** [It.] = LUNETTE 4 b.

1898 *Daily News* 10 Feb. 6/3 Under the lunetta is the Descent from the Cross, the Madonna kneeling.

lunette (l(j)uː'nɛt). Also 7–8 in anglicized form lunet(t. [a. F. *lunette*, dim. of *lune* moon.]

†**1.** A little moon, a satellite. *Obs.*

1645 BP. HALL *Peace-Maker* x. 81 Our predecessors.. could never have believed, that there were such Lunets about some of the Planets as our late Perspectives have described.

†**2.** The figure of a crescent moon. Also *attrib.*

1774 J. BRYANT *Mythol.* II. p. iv, Juno Samia Selenitis, standing in a lunette, and crowned with a lunette. **1787** M. CUTLER in *Life, Jrnls. & Corr.* (1888) I. 278 In this rock a flight of steps is cut, in a winding or kind of lunette form, from the road to the top of the hill.

3. *Farriery.* A horse-shoe consisting of the front semicircular portion only. Also *lunette-shoe.*

1580 BLUNDEVIL *Curing Horses Dis.* clii. 65 Pull off his shooes and shooe him with halfe Moone shooes called Lunette. **1688** R. HOLME *Armoury* III. 324/2 A Lunet shooe ..is used for Horses that have weak Heels. *c* **1720** W. GIBSON *Farrier's Guide* II. (1738) 256 The cure is..to shoe him with Lunets, or Half-Moon shoes. **1753** in CHAMBERS *Cycl. Supp.* **1816** *Sporting Mag.* XLVII. 27 A shoe in the form of the old lunette, or La Fosse's shoe. **1875** in KNIGHT *Dict. Mech.*

4. *Arch.* **a.** An arched aperture in a concave ceiling for the admission of light.

1613–39 I. JONES in Leoni *Palladio's Archit.* (1742) I. 39 The manner of Arches are..a Rotonda G, a Lunette P, and a Conca N and K. **1823** P. NICHOLSON *Pract. Build.* 114 Lunettes are used in large rooms or halls, and are made either in waggon-headed ceilings, or through large coves, surrounding a plane ceiling. **1842–59** GWILT *Archit.* (ed. 4) Gloss., *Lunette*, a cylindric, cylindroidic, or spherical aperture in a ceiling.

b. A crescentiform or semicircular space in a ceiling, dome, etc., decorated with paintings or sculptures; a piece of decoration filling such a space.

1722 RICHARDSON *Statues Italy* 117 The pictures are painted in a sort of Lunettes, form'd by a Semicircle within a Tall Arch ending in a Point, and [etc.]. **1853** RUSKIN *Stones Ven.* III. ii. 74 The painting which filled the lunette behind it [a sarcophagus]. **1857** MRS. JAMESON *Leg. of Madonna* Introd. (ed. 2) 60 It is comprised in five lunettes round the ceiling. **1873** OUIDA *Pascarel* I. 36 Above at a vast height there was a lunette with frescoes of the labours of Hercules. **1886** WILLIS & CLARK *Cambridge* III. 210 The lunette over the entrance-door [of the Fitzwilliam Museum].

5. *Fortif.* A work larger than a redan, consisting of two faces, and two flanks (Voyle *Mil. Dict.*).

1704 HARRIS *Lex. Techn.*, *Lunettes* in Fortification, are Envelopes, Countergardes, or Mounts of Earth cast up before the Curtain. **1706** PHILLIPS (ed. Kersey), *Lunette*.. In Fortification, a small Work generally rais'd before the Courtin in Ditches full of Water: It consists of two Faces making a Re-entring Angle, and serves to dispute the Passage of the Ditch. **1711** *Lond. Gaz.* No. 4883/2 His Grace..has given Orders for making several Lunettes in the Front of our Camp. **1759** B. MARTIN *Nat. Hist. Eng.* II. 200 An embattled Wall, with Lunets hanging over the River. **1778** *Eng. Gazetteer* (ed. 2) s.v. *Sandown Castle, Kent*, N. of Deal,..consists of four lunets of very thick arched work of stone... In the middle is a great round tower. **1834–47** J. S. MACAULAY *Field Fortif.* (1851) 11 The lunette, like the redan, is frequently open at the gorge. **1859** F. A. GRIFFITHS *Artil. Man.* (1862) 263 A Lunette has two faces, similar to the redan, and also two flanks.

6. A blinker for a horse.

1652 BP. HALL *Invis. World* III. §12 Make earthly things, not as lunets to shut up our sight, but spectacles to transmit it to spiritual objects. **1753** CHAMBERS *Cycl. Suppl.*, *Lunette* is also the name of two small pieces of felt made round and hollow, to clap upon the eyes of a vicious horse. **1875** in KNIGHT *Dict. Mech.*

7. †**a.** *pl.* Spectacles. *Obs.*

1681 COLVIL *Whigs Supplic.* (1751) 53 Then answered the whole croud, Bidding him read it out aloud. Seeking his Lunets [etc.]. **1693** EVELYN *De la Quint. Compl. Gard., Refl. Agric.* 49 One day Lunetts and Microscopes may possibly be Invented, whereby these Pores may plainly be seen and distinguished. **1796** *Mod. Gulliver's Trav.* 75 Fearful of more mistakes, for want of my useful lunettes, I made my bow of depart.

b. Given as the name for a special kind of concavo-convex lens for spectacles.

1855 in OGILVIE Suppl. **1875** in KNIGHT *Dict. Mech.*

8. A watch-glass of flattened shape. Also *lunette (watch-) glass.*

1832 G. R. PORTER *Porcelain & Gl.* ix. 233 Lunette glasses. **1849** DANA *Geol.* ix. (1850) 466 The curvature of a lunette watch-glass. **1884** F. J. BRITTEN *Watch & Clockm.* 156 *Lunette*, the usual form of rounded watch glass.

9. In the guillotine, the circular hole which receives the neck of the victim.

1859 F. E. PAGET *Curate of Cumberw.* 238 When the victim's head is fixed in the lunette. **1900** *Westm. Gaz.* 20 Oct. 6/2 His head had to be thrust into the lunette by two warders.

10. *Glass-making.* = LINNET-HOLE.

1839 URE *Dict. Arts* 587 The founding or melting furnace is a square brick building,..at each angle of this square a small oven or arch is constructed..vaulted within, and communicating with the melting furnace by square flues called lunettes.

11. *Antiq.* A crescent-shaped ornament.

1865 *Athenæum* 22 July 119/1 A pair of golden gorgettes or lunettes.

12. A forked iron plate into which the stock of a field-gun carriage is inserted.

1875 in Knight *Dict. Mech.*

13. (See quot.)

1884 R. F. BURTON *Bk. Sword* 124 This hilt-plate has dwindled in the French fencing-foil to a lunette, a double oval of bars shaped like a pair of spectacles.

14. *Eccl.* A circular crystal case, fitting into an aperture in the monstrance, in which the Host is placed for exposition.

1890 in *Century Dict.* **1893** in *Catholic Dict.*

15. *Physical Geogr.* A broad shallow mound of wind-blown material built up along the leeward side of a lake basin, esp. in arid parts of Australia, and typically having a crescent shape with the concave edge of the crescent along the lake shore.

1940 E. S. HILLS in *Austral. Geographer* III. VII. 15 (*title*) The lunette, a new land form of aeolian origin. *Ibid.* 15/1 Along the eastern shores of almost every lake and swamp in the plains of northern Victoria there occurs a crescentic ridge of silty clay or clay 'loam'... It is..proposed to designate them by a new term—*lunette.* **1942** C. A. COTTON *Geomorphology* (ed. 3) xx. 275 Dust captured from the air during gales that produce dust storms is brought down by spray whipped up from lakes, so that crescentic mounds of loamy material of this origin grow up immediately to leeward of the lakes. Being rarely more than 20 or 30 feet high these broad mounds are not conspicuous unless they rise from very level plains, as is the case in south-eastern Australia, where there are many examples of such landscape forms, there termed lunettes. **1957** G. E. HUTCHINSON *Treat. Limnol.* I. i. 127 The most important type of wind action in forming lake basins..is deflation or wind erosion. The clearest evidence of this process is provided by those cases in which the deflated material is piled up as a curved mound of sand or *lunette*..along the lee shore of the depression.

lung (lʌŋ). Forms: 1 **lungen**, 3–6 **lunge**, 3–4 **longen(e**, 4–6 **long(e**, 4–5 **lounge**, 5 **longon**, **lungen**, (5 **longhe**, **lunche**, 6 **longue**, **loong**), 6– **lung.** [OE. *lungen* str. fem. = OFris. *lungen*, MLG. *lunge*, MDu. *longe* (Du. *long*), OHG. *lungun* (MHG., mod.G. *lunge*); ON. with change of declension *lunga* wk. neut.; f. Teut. root **lung-*:—OAryan **lngh-* in Skr. *laghu-*, Gr. ἐλαφρός light: see LIGHT *a.*[1] (The lungs were so called because of their lightness: cf. LIGHTS.)]

1. a. Each of the two respiratory organs in man and most vertebrate animals, placed within the cavity of the thorax on either side of the heart and communicating with the trachea or windpipe.

c **1000** ÆLFRIC *Gloss.* in Wr.-Wülcker 160/34 *Pulmo*, lungen. *c* **1000** *Sax. Leechd.* II. 92 Mið þy sceal mon lacnian þone man þe biþ lungenne wund. *c* **1250** *Death* 172 in *O.E. Misc.* 178 Nu schal for-rotien þi liure and þi lunge. *c* **1275** LAY. 6499 þe longene and þe liure folle to þan grunde. **13..** *K. Alis.* 4719 Men to heom throewe drit and donge, With foule ayren, with rotheres lunge. *a* **1340** HAMPOLE *Psalter* l. 8 It purges þe longes of inflacioun. **1390** GOWER *Conf.* III. 100 The lunge yifth him weie of speche. **1393** LANGL. *P. Pl.* C. IX. 189 Lame men he lechede with longen of bestes. *c* **1420** *Pallad. on Husb.* I. 49 The longis hool and wynded with the best. *c* **1440** *Gesta Rom.* i. 3 (Harl. MS.) The archer ..hath y-schotte him selfe in þe lungen. *c* **1470** HENRY *Wallace* II. 409 Leuir and lounggis men mycht all redy se. **1481** CAXTON *Reynard* (Arb.) 91 The wulf..gaf to me but half the longes. **1513** DOUGLAS *Æneis* x. vii. 63 That all the blayd, vp to the hylt and hand Amyd his flaffand longis hyd hes he. **1535** COVERDALE *I Kings* xxii. 34 A certayne man.. shott the kynge of Israel betwene the lunge and ye longes. **1551** T. WILSON *Logike* (1569) 48 b, Oft fetchyng of winde, declares a sicknesse of the lungus. **1577** B. GOOGE *Heresbach's Husb.* (1586) 133 The sicknes of the Loongs is perceiued if the Dewlap be harde closed together very farre vppe. **1610** SHAKS. *Temp.* II. i. 174 Gentlemen,..of such sensible and nimble Lungs that they always vse to laugh at nothing. **1612** BACON *Ess., Studies* (Arb.) 13 Shooting [is good] for the Lungs and Breast. **1774** GOLDSM. *Nat. Hist.* (1776) II. 294 In those which breathe through the lungs, some have the heart composed of two ventricles, and some have it of one. **1831** R. KNOX *Cloquet's Anat.* 622 The Lungs ..are two spongy, cellular, expansible organs. **1872** MIVART *Elem. Anat.* xii. (1873) 462 The lungs are attached by their roots to the two branches of the windpipe.

b. *transf.* and *fig.*, esp. as in phrase *lungs of London* (etc.), applied to open spaces within or adjacent to a city.

1651 CLEVELAND *Poems* 10 Could not the Winds.. With their whole card of Lungs redeem thy breath? 1808 WINDHAM *Sp. agst. Encroachm. Hyde Park* 30 June, It was a saying of Lord Chatham, that the parks were the lungs of London. 1852 MUNDY *Our Antipodes* (1857) 4 Beyond this fence the outer domain.. acts as one of the lungs of Sydney. 1874 T. HARDY *Far fr. Mad. Crowd* II. i. 3 That Bathsheba was a firm and positive girl.. had been the very lung of his hope. 1876 —— *Ethelberta* (1890) 346 At length something from the lungs of the gale alighted like a feather upon the pane. 1900 *Q. Rev.* July 51 We can with perfect safety use these old burial grounds as lungs for the overcrowded city.

2. Applied to analogous organs in other animals.

1889 *Syd. Soc. Lex.* s.v., In Mollusca the Pulmonata, represented by the snail and slug, have a simple type of lung... In Amphibia.. the lung is a simple or double sac with a smooth lining near the termination of the trachea.

†**3.** *pl.* One who blows the fire; a chemist's assistant. *Obs.*

1610 B. JONSON *Alch.* II. i, That's his fire-drake, His lungs, his Zephyrus, he that puffes his coales. 1663 COWLEY *Adv. Exper. Philos. College* in *Verses & Ess.* (1669) 43 That the Company received into it be as follows... Two Lungs, or Chemical Servants. That the annual allowance.. be as follows... To each of the Lungs twelve pounds.

4. (See quot.) *dial.* (? *Obs.*)

1741 *Compl. Fam.-Piece* III. 504 Swine.. are subject to a Distemper which is called the *Thirst*, or *Lungs*.

5. lungs of (the) oak, oak lungs (see OAK *sb.* 8), *Sticta pulmonacea*; = LUNGWORT 5.

1856 W. L. LINDSAY *Brit. Lichens* 183 *Sticta Pulmonaria*... Its specific name, as well as its familiar designation, 'Lungs of Oak', or 'Tree Lungwort' are due to its efficacy, real or supposed, in pulmonary affections. 1863 J. R. WISE *New Forest* xvi. 176 One of the commonest remedies for consumption in the Forest is the 'lungs of oak'. 1866 *Treas. Bot.*, Lungs-of-the-oak.

6. *attrib.* and *Comb.* **a.** simple attributive, as ***lung-attack***, †***-blood***, ***cancer***, ***-cell***, ***-consolidation***, ***-disease***, ***function***, ***-parenchyma***, ***-substance***, ***-tissue***, ***-trouble***, ***-tubercle***, ***-vessel***. **b.** objective, as ***lung-bearing***, ***-bursting*** adjs. **c.** instrumental, as ***lung-breather***; ***lung-breathing***, adj.

1865 MRS. WHITNEY *Gayworthys* I. 206 A *lung attack.. when the three score and ten years are passed, can hardly leave a man exactly where it found him. 1888 G. ALLEN in *Gd. Words* 229 The *lung-bearing and air-breathing terrestrial animal. 1666 HARVEY *Morb. Angl.* xiv. 165 *Lung-blood generally appears somewhat lighter than a natural red, because it is conceived to be rendred more aereous by the Lungs. 1880 *St. James's Budget* 17 Sept. 12/1 The earliest *lung-breathers were amphibians. 1907 *Westm. Gaz.* 1 June 16/3 The complete proof of this evolution of the *lung-breathing four-footed creatures of the earth from purely aquatic forms has been lost. 1949 *Oxf. Jun. Encycl.* II. 359/2 If the larval form [of the Axolotl] is kept.. it will gradually turn into the mature, lung-breathing salamander. 1971 S. CAVELL *World Viewed* vii. 41 Baudelaire's.. *lung-bursting inflation of Delacroix. 1973 C. BONINGTON *Next Horizon* xxi. 286 The last length of rope.. was the most strenuous of all, taking two hours of lung-bursting effort to reach the top. 1926 *Jrnl. Amer. Med. Assoc.* 17 July 147/1 A diagnosis of endothelioma has been made frequently in primary *lung cancers. 1953 *Newsweek* 25 May 60 Dr. Alton Ochsner.. believes that lung cancer.. 'is unquestionably due to the carcinogenic effect of cigarette smoking'. 1975 'G. BLACK' *Big Wind* ii. 39 When she was still a deb.. lung cancer was still diagnosed as galloping consumption. 1853 MARKHAM *Skoda's Auscult.* 287 The *lung-cells and finer bronchial tubes are compressed by the distended blood-vessels. 1898 *Allbutt's Syst. Med.* V. 768 In like manner, the former auscultatory signs of *lung-consolidation vanish. 1897 *Ibid.* IV. 302 Passive congestion is a frequent cause of albuminuria, more especially in heart and *lung diseases. 1966 *Lancet* 24 Dec. 1386/1 Systematic *lung-function studies were not carried out in these patients. 1853 MARKHAM *Skoda's Auscult.* 44 Effusion of blood into the *lung-parenchyma. *Ibid.* 46 We scarcely ever find any considerable amount of *lung-substance deprived of air by pressure. *Ibid.* 269 Signs of Pneumonia, when the *Lung-tissue is permeable to air. 1899 *Allbutt's Syst. Med.* VIII. 356 Some secondary *lung trouble with which there is not nervous power to contend. *Ibid.* 309 Some decided signs of *lung tubercle are discovered early in the disease. 1898 *Ibid.* V. 403 The absence of clotting from blood within the *lung vessels.

7. Special combs.: **lung book**, a lamellate respiratory organ found in spiders, scorpions, and certain other arachnids; cf. *book-lung* (BOOK *sb.* 19); †**lung-cracked** *a.*, of breath, issuing from exhausted lungs; **lung-fever**, pneumonia; **lung-fish**, a fish having lungs as well as gills, a dipnoan; **lung-flower**, Gerarde's transl. of the Ger. name of the Marsh Gentian, *Gentiana Pneumonanthe*; **lung fluke**, a parasitic trematode flatworm of the genus *Paragonimus*; also *attrib.*; †**lung(s)-growing**, a disease in cattle, in which the lungs adhere to the side; †**lung-grown** *a.*, said of an animal affected with 'lung-growing'; also *sb.* = *lung-growing*; **lung-gymnastics**, 'the exercise of the respiratory powers in a regular and orderly manner for the prevention or cure of disease' (*Syd. Soc. Lex.*); **lung-juice**, serum from diseased lungs; **lung lichen** = LUNGWORT 5 (J. Smith *Dict. Pop. Names Plants* 1882); **lung-note**, the sound produced by tapping the chest of a healthy subject; †**lung-pipe** *sing.*, the trachea or windpipe, *pl.* the bronchial tubes; **lung-plague** (in cattle), pleuro-pneumonia; **lung-power**, power of voice; **lung-sick** *a.* and *sb.*, (*a*) *adj.* sick of a pulmonary complaint; (*b*) *sb.* a disease of the lungs, pleuro-pneumonia; so **lung-sickness**; **lung snail**, a snail of the order Pulmonata (see PULMONATE *sb.*); †**lung-woe**, disease of the lungs; **lung-worm**, a parasite infesting the lungs of cattle (see quot.).

[1861 J. BLACKWALL *Hist. Spiders Great Brit.* I. 4 The internal organs of respiration in connection with the anterior pair of stigmata present the appearance of membraneous sacs formed by lamellæ applied to one another like the leaves of a book.] 1881 E. R. LANKESTER in *Q. Jrnl. Microsc. Sci.* XXI. 541 The lamellæ of the Scorpion's *lung-book. 1932 BORRADAILE & POTTS *Invertebrata* xv. 447 The spiders, at least, have passed through a primitive lung-book stage from which they have not all emerged. In fact they show all the stages of replacement of lung books by tracheae. 1971 *Nature* 12 Feb. 455/1 The species [sc. *Micrathena gracilis*, a spider] possesses a well-developed stridulatory organ with a file on the cover of the lung book (the respiratory organ). 1636 W. DENNY in *Ann. Dubrensia* (1877) 12 The Racer.. might.. outward shoote His *lung-crackt-breath. 1852 H. W. PIERSON *Amer. Missionary Mem.* 229 His illness (*lung-fever) was sudden and unexpected. 1883 C. F. HOLDER in *Harper's Mag.* Dec. 107/2 The curious *lung-fish (*Protopterus*) builds a burrow. 1968 A. S. ROMER *Procession of Life* viii. 165 The dipnoans owe their popular name of lungfishes to the fact that, except for two ray-finned fishes.. they are the only living fishes to possess these air-breathing structures. 1597 GERARDE *Herbal* II. ciii. 355 *Viola Autumnalis*, or Autumne Violet.. the same that Valerius Cordus.. saith is named in the German toong *Lungen blumen*, or *Lung flower. 1900 STILES & HASSAL in *16th Ann. Rep. Bureau Animal Industry, U.S. Dept. Agric.* 560 (*title*) The *lung fluke (*Paragonimus westermanni*) in swine and its relation to parasitic hemoptysis in man. 1931 *Jrnl. Amer. Vet. Med. Assoc.* LXXVIII. 229 (*title*) Lung flukes of the genus Paragonimus in American mink. 1937 *Discovery* Feb. 34/2 The lung-fluke disease, or paragonim[i]asis, of which they [*sc.* mitten crabs] are a carrier in China, does not really threaten Europe as yet. 1970 *Black's Vet. Dict.* (ed. 9) 516/1 Lung flukes attack cats, dogs, pigs, and man in the Far East and the United States. 1704 *Dict. Rust.*, *Lungs-growing. 1730–6 BAILEY (fol.), *Lung's Growing*. 1775 ASH, *Lunggrowing*, .. a disease in cattle. 1614 MARKHAM *Cheap Husb.* (1623) 96 Of the diseases in the Lungs, especially the Lung-growne. *Ibid.*, A beast, which is *lung-growne, or hath his lungs growne to his side. 1898 *Allbutt's Syst. Med.* V. 46 *Lung gymnastics. 1885 KLEIN *Micro-Organisms* 89 Blood, pericardial exudation, and *lung juice from the fatal Nottingham case inoculated into ten animals.. produced fatal results in six. 1876 *Trans. Clinical Soc.* IX. 189 There was.. an entire want of *lung-note over the manubrium of the sternum. 1562 TURNER *Herbal* II. 35 Rosemary.. openeth the *lung pipes. 1657 REEVE *God's Plea* 88 Shall we be carried no further to Heaven, then.. a lungpipe-pant can blow us? 1884 *Encycl. Brit.* XVII. 60/1 Pleuro-Pneumonia or *Lung-Plague. 1900 J. KIRKWOOD *United Presbyt. in Ayrsh.* iv. 34 He could exercise his *lung power also in preaching. ?1520 tr. *Dial. Creat. Moral.* xxvii. I, He.. was made both *lungsyk and Reumatyke that he myght not occupye his accostomyd synnes. 1552 HULOET, Longe sycke, *pneumonicus* [sic]. 1899 *Strand Mag.* Mar. 270/1 For 'lung-sick' had reduced the.. team of sixteen to.. five [bullocks]. 1726 BAILEY, *Lung Sickness. 1730–6 —— (fol.), *Lung's Sickness*. 1899 WERNER *Capt. of Locusts* 100 [He] had just had heavy losses.. from the lung-sickness. 1909 *Westm. Gaz.* 26 June 15/2 The land and most of the freshwater snails belong to the *lung snails, the gills being reduced to a mere vestige. c1420 *Pallad. on Husb.* I. 50 The *longe [*v.r.* longis] woo cometh oft of yvel eire. 1882 *Cassell's Nat. Hist.* VI. 253 The *Lung Worm [*Strongylus micrurus*] is often fatal to calves.

lung(a: see LUNGI.

lungang, lungar: see LONGAN, LANGUR.

Lung-ch'üan (lʊŋtʃuːˈɑːn). The name of a district in the province of Chekiang, China, used to designate a type of Chinese celadon ware produced mainly during the Sung dynasty (A.D. 960–1279).

1904 E. DILLON *Porcelain* v. 63 Lung-chuan ware was made during Sung times. 1936 *Burlington Mag.* Jan. 9/1 The lovely green celadons of Lung-ch'üan... Soon it may be possible to identify the celadons made at the different factories of the Lung-ch'üan district. 1960 H. HAYWARD *Antique Coll.* 62/1 Typical [of Celadon wares] are.. the much-exported Lung-chüan celadons of the Sung and Ming dynasties. 1971 L. A. BOGER *Dict. World Pott. & Porc.* 56/1 The characteristic Sung Lung-ch'üan celadon has a body that approaches a white porcelain in character, but its main glory rests in the radiant, light bluish-green glaze.

lunge, longe (lʌndʒ), *sb.*[1] [a. F. *longe* halter, lunge, var. of OF. *loigne* (whence LOYN, LUNE[1]):—popular L. **longea*, f. L. *long-us* LONG *a.*]

†**1.** *gen.* A thong, cord. *Obs.*

1607 TOPSELL *Four-f. Beasts* 94 Their [Camels] feet (although fleshy) are so tyed together with little lunges that they neuer weare.

2. A long rope used in training horses, being fastened at one end to the horse's head and held at the other by the trainer, who causes the horse to canter round in a circle.

1720 W. GIBSON *Diet Horses* vii. (1726) 105 He recommends those who stand together in an open Stable,.. to be secured with two Bindings, and for that Purpose, the Ropes or Longes ought to be so long, that they may easily lie down. 1778 EARL PEMBROKE *Mil. Equitat.* 37 In the beginning a longe is useful.. to help both the rider and the horse. 1845 LADY STANHOPE *Mem.* I. vi. 201 And round this [green plat] the grooms, with longes, were made to run them [two mares] until they were well warmed.

3. a. The use of the lunge in training horses. **b.** A circular exercising-ground in which the lunge is used; 'the training ground for the instruction of a young horse' (Voyle *Mil. Dict.* 1872–6).

1833 *Regul. Instr. Cavalry* I. 40 One Manege will thus contain two good circles or longes. *Ibid.* 78 The horse has rested.. after the longe. 1839 GREENWOOD *Hints Horsemanship* 87 A horse.. should never be compelled to canter in the longe, though he may be permitted to do it of himself. 1886 'STONEHENGE' *Rur. Sports* (ed. 16) 469/2 The colt should be kept going round the lunge, until [etc.].

4. *attrib.*

1839 GREENWOOD *Hints Horsemanship* 88 Such powerful instruments as the longe-cord and whip. *Ibid.* 90 With the longe-whip in skilful hands. 1868 H. C. R. JOHNSON *Long Vac. Argent. Alps* xxix. 153 One of the girths of my saddle, the longe surcingle, and three or four large silk handkerchiefs.. gave me, as I thought, length enough.

lunge (lʌndʒ), *sb.*[2] Also 8–9 longe, 9 lounge. [Aphetic var. of ALLONGE, ELONGE.]

1. a. A thrust with a sword (spec. in *Fencing*) or other weapon.

1748 SMOLLETT *Rod. Rand.* xii. (1804) 62 My adversary.. made a great many half longes, skipping backward at every push. 1780 T. DAVIES *Mem. Garrick* (1781) I. iii. 23 With the first lunge he killed his adversary. 1809 ROLAND *Fencing* 5 The distance between the two feet will be found to be.. about two-thirds of the distance of the longe. 1823 SCOTT *Peveril* xxxii, A successful.. lounge, by which Peveril ran his gigantic antagonist through the body. 1835 LYTTON *Rienzi* I. iv, He made a desperate lunge at Adrian. 1880 SIR S. LAKEMAN *Kaffir-Land* 74 A lunge from an assegai through his thigh. 1885 *Sat. Rev.* 6 June 758/1 If.. parried lunges found their match In neat retorts.

b. (See quot.)

1817 WILBRAHAM *Glos. Chesh.* (1818) s.v. *Lungeous*, A lunge is common for a violent kick of a horse, though Dr. Ash has omitted it.

2. A sudden forward movement; a plunge, rush.

1845 J. J. HOOPER *Taking Census* in *Some Adventures Simon Suggs* 155 That was a most unfortunate lunge I made into that hole in the river. 1873 G. C. DAVIES *Mount. & Mere* xvii. 149 A heavy lunge that told of a big fish. 1882 J. WALKER *Sc. Poems* 127 With a lumbering lunge The freighted vessel left the quay. 1900 *Longm. Mag.* Aug. 455 The impatient farmer made a sudden lunge at them.

lunge (lʌndʒ), *sb.*[3] *N. Amer.* Also longe, 'longe, 'lunge. [? Short for MASKALONGE.] Either of two large North American freshwater fishes, *Salvelinus namaycush*, a char or lake trout found in northern lakes, or *Esox masquinongy*, a pike found in the Great Lakes.

1851 *Vermont Laws* 49 Such person or persons shall forfeit and pay.. the sum of one dollar for each trout or lunge so taken. 1857 *Porter's Spirit of Times* 11 Apr. 86/3 The lower end of the lake.. is supplied with the large catfish,.. Oswego, black, longe, great-bass, pike-perch, perch, &c. 1882 JORDAN & GILBERT *Fishes N. Amer.* 317 (*Bull. U.S. Nat. Mus.* III), Mackinaw Trout; Great Lake Trout; Longe (Vermont). 1884 G. B. GOODE etc. *Nat. Hist. Aquatic Anim.* 488 The Lake Trout has other appellatives, such as 'Lunge' in Canada.. 'Black Lunge', 'Silver Lunge', 'Racer Lunge', 'Black Salmon'. 1887 *Lit. World* (U.S.) 23 July 227/2 To troll for 'lunge' in the deep waters of Lake Memphremagog. 1894 *Outing* (U.S.) XXIV. 368/2 'It's a 'lunge,'.. 'He'll weigh at least fifteen pounds.' *Ibid.* 453/2, I led him alongside, where—as a played-out 'longe always will—he remained motionless.. for a few seconds. 1902 *Jrnl. Amer. Folk-lore* Oct. 246 *Longe* or *lunge*, a common abbreviation of *muskelunge* (*maskalonge*) among English-speaking people in the region about the Great Lakes. 1953 *Canad. Geogr. Jrnl.* XLVII. 17/1 Recently, thanks to government hatcheries, 'lunge has been added to the menu.

lunge (lʌndʒ), *v.*[1] Also 9 longe, lounge, [f. LUNGE *sb.*[2]]

1. *intr.* **a.** *Fencing.* To make a thrust with a foil or rapier. **b.** *Boxing.* To deliver a straightforward blow. Const. *at*.

1809 ROLAND *Fencing* 23 When longing in the position of tierce. 1814 *Sporting Mag.* XLIII. 55 Lunging with the right he hit short. 1836 SMART, *Longe*, to make a pass with a rapier. 1861 THACKERAY *Four Georges* ii. (1862) 84 Lunging with his rapier like a fencing master. 1900 N. MUNRO in *Blackw. Mag.* Oct. 456/1 Count Victor.. lunged and skewered him through the thick of the active arm.

c. quasi-*trans.* with cognate obj. To deliver (a kick, a thrust); also with *out*.

1735 *Gentl. Mag.* May 252 If Savage lunge'd a thrust, And brought the youth a victim to the dust. 1847 THACKERAY *Christm. Bks.* (1872) 33 The Mulligan.. lunged out a kick.

2. *trans.* To drive or thrust with or as with a lunge. Also *refl.* said of a heavy body (= 3).

1841 J. MILLS *Old Eng. Gentl.* xxvii. II. 206 M'Donald plunged the rowels deep into his flanks, and lunging him with all his power, hurled the excited creature to the ground. 1865 DICKENS *Mut. Fr.* I. i, What he had in tow, lunged itself at him sometimes in an awful manner when the boat was checked. 1875 BUCKLAND *Log-bk.* 140 The scorpion instantly lunged his sting into him.

3. *intr.* To move with a lunge; to make a sudden forward movement; to rush. Also with *up*.

1821 CLARE *Vill. Minstr.* II. 102 [Fish] at the worm no nibbles more repeat, But lunge from night in sheltering flag-retreat. 1827 HONE *Every-day Bk.* II. 330 He [an elephant] lounged furiously at the bars. 1831 DE QUINCEY in *Blackw. Mag.* XXIX. 63 [He] made for a fauteuil standing opposite to the fire. Into this he lunged. 1859 G. MEREDITH *R. Feverel* xxvii, Ripton lunged for the claret jug. 1880 MRS. WHITNEY *Odd or Even?* viii, Farmer Heybrook's old brown mare came lungeing up the steep hill. 1900 *Longm. Mag.*

Nov. 67 The jolting and swaying of the cart, as it lunged over the ruts, helped us.

Hence ˈ**lunging** *ppl. a.*

1857 HUGHES *Tom Brown* II. iii, Parrying the Slogger's lunging hits.

lunge, longe (lʌndʒ), *v.*² Also 9 lounge. [f. LUNGE *sb.*¹]

1. *trans.* To put (a horse) through his paces by the use of the lunge; to make a horse (*occas.* his rider) go round the lunge (see LUNGE *sb.*¹ 3 b).

1806 CUMBERLAND *Mem.* I. 263 You might as safely have backed Bucephalus, before Alexander had lunged him. **1815** *Sporting Mag.* XLVI. 116 At three [years old] put on the bits and lunge him. **1833** *Regul. Instr. Cavalry* I. 72 The horse may be longed to the right. **1845** *Jrnl. R. Agric. Soc.* V. II. 529 Being lounged in a circle with great care. **1848** THACKERAY *Van. Fair* xlvi, As the coachman was lunging Georgy round the lawn on the grey pony. **1862** H. MARRYAT *Year in Sweden* II. 406 Armed horsemen are seen lunging their chargers round and round after the manner of a modern circus. **1875** 'STONEHENGE' *Brit. Sports* II. I. viii. §5. 454 The colt.. may now be taken out and well lunged. **1889** HAYES *Illustr. Horse Breaking* ii. 64 The generality of men, when they lunge a colt or filly, will circle the young one more to the left than to the right.

2. *intr.* Of the horse: To go round the lunge in a specified direction.

1833 *Regul. Instr. Cavalry* II. 75 The rein on the hand to which the horse is longing.

lunged (lʌŋd), *ppl. a.* [f. LUNG + -ED².] Furnished with lungs, or something resembling lungs; as applied to human beings usually with prefixed adj., as ***small-, weak-lunged.***

1693 DRYDEN *Juvenal* x. (1697) 249 The Smith prepares his Hammer for the Stroke, While the Lung'd Bellows hissing Fire provoke. **1818** in TODD. **1860** in WORCESTER; and in later Dicts.

lungeous (ˈlʌndʒəs), *a. dial.* [f. LUNGE *sb.*² or *v.*¹ + -OUS.] †**a.** Of a fall: Heavy (*obs.*). **b.** Of persons: Rough-mannered, violent (in play).

1681 COTTON *Wond. Peak* (1741) 339 A lungeous Fall indeed, the Master said. **1787** GROSE *Prov. Gloss., Lungeous*, spiteful, mischievous. Derb. & Leic. **1817** WILBRAHAM *Gloss. Cheshire* (1818), *Lungeous*, ill tempered, disposed to do some bodily harm by a blow or otherwise. **1866** GEO. ELIOT *F. Holt* xxviii, A big lungeous fellow, who would speak disrespectfully of anybody. **1883** *B'ham Daily Mail* 3 Apr. 2/3 The rules of Rugby football allow.. a cruel latitude to lungeous players.

lunger¹ (ˈlʌŋə(r)). *colloq.* [f. LUNG + -ER¹.] One who is diseased or wounded in the lungs.

1893 KATE SANBORN *Truthf. Wom. in S. Calif.* 14 The rainy season is hard for 'lungers' and nervous invalids. **1896** *Westm. Gaz.* 14 Apr. 1/3 There were of course a good many English 'lungers' in the village. **1900** R. KIPLING in *Daily Mail* 25 Apr. 4/4 He was a badly-shotten 'lunger'.

lunger² (ˈlʌndʒə(r)). [f. LUNGE *v.*¹ + -ER¹.] One who lunges.

1842 LYTTON *Zanoni* II. i, A swifter lunger never crossed a sword. **1887** *Daily News* 26 July 5/2 The lunger is run through by the man who parries thus.

†**lungeteyn**, *a.* Also 5 LONTAIGNE. [ad. OF. *loingtain* (F. *lointain*):—popular L. **longitānum*, f. *longus* LONG.] Distant, remote.

c **1330** R. BRUNNE *Chron. Wace* (Rolls) 4190 *note*, [He] tok his leue at [þe] Romayns To wyne londes lungeteyns.

lungful (ˈlʌŋfʊl). [f. LUNG + -FUL.] So much as will fill the lungs; *spec.* a quantity of inhaled cigarette-smoke.

1860 PIESSE *Lab. Chem. Wonders* 109 A lungful of real fresh air. **1894** *Outing* (U.S.) XXIV. 70/1 Bracing lungfulls of morning air. **1942** *R.A.F. Jrnl.* 3 Oct. 33 The little man accepted a cigarette.., drawing down a lungful of smoke. **1964** 'E. LATHEN' *Accounting for Murder* (1965) xiv. 128 He sucked a healing lungful of smoke. **1973** A. HUNTER *Gently French* ii. 20 He pulled in a contemptuous lungful. **1973** P. MALLOCH *Kickback* xxix. 154 Hold your breath all the time. You don't want to get a lungful.

‖**lung-gom-pa** (ˈluŋgompa). Also **lung-pa.** [Tibetan.] A Tibetan monk who has the mystical power of walking many miles at great speed without stopping.

1931 A. DAVID-NEEL *With Mystics & Magicians in Tibet* vi. 200, I met the first *lung-gom-pa* in the Chang thang of Northern Tibet. *Ibid.*, The feat expected from the *lung-gom-pa* is one of wonderful endurance rather than of momentary extreme fleetness... True *lung-gom-pas* must be very rare. **1937** *Times Lit. Suppl.* 7 Aug. 579/1 He claims to have seen *lung-gom-pas* on two occasions. These are hermits who are said to have gained the power of travelling a hundred miles a day on their own feet. **1952** E. MOSSBACHER tr. *Maraini's Secret Tibet* iii. 51 *Lung-pa*,.. the 'wind-men' —monks who, after years of extreme asceticism and strenuous preparation, succeed in freeing themselves almost completely from the weight of the human frame and are therefore able to travel hundreds of miles in a single day. **1954** W. NOYCE *South Col* iii. 39 On the boat we read two books about Buddhism. I read of 'tumo'.. and 'lung-gompa', the art of going into a trance and travelling many miles at incredible speeds.

‖**lungi** (ˈlʊŋgiː). Also 7 lung, lunga, longee, longi, 7–9 lungee, lungie, lungy, 9 loongee, loonghie, lunggi, 20 longyi, lungyi. [Urdū (Persian) *lungī*, f. *lung* of the same meaning. Cf. LANGOOTY.] A loin cloth. Also, the material of which this is made.

1634 SIR T. HERBERT *Trav.* 197 A lung or cover to conceale their privy members. **1662** J. DAVIES tr. *Mandelslo's Trav.* I. (1669) 49 Some Cotton-cloaths.. of those kinds which are commonly called Dosternals,.. Longis, Allegiens, &c. **1698** FRYER *Acc. E. India & P.* 53 The Peer as well as Peasant, wrapping only a Lunga about his Middle. *Ibid.* 101 The Men and Women came down together to wash, having Lungies about their wastes only. **1727** A. HAMILTON *New Acc. E. Ind.* I. xxiv. 294 His Dress was only a Silk Lungie or Scarf made fast by a Girdle of Gold Plate, about his Middle. **1779** FORREST *Voy. N. Guinea* 229 Cloth.. made in the form of a Bengal lungy, or Buggess cloth. *c* **1809–10** F. BUCHANAN *Puraniya* III. 101 The Lunggi.. is wrapped simply two or three times round the waist, and hangs down to the knee. **1835** BURNES *Trav. Bokhara* (ed. 2) I. 52 He wore a very handsome loongee round his waist. **1882** CAULFEILD & SAWARD *Dict. Needlework, Loonghie*, a mixed fabric composed of richly coloured silk and cotton. **1901** *Daily News* 9 Jan. 3/5 Indian soldiers.. wearing lungis of beautifully woven silk. **1906** W. DEL MAR *Romantic East* i. 8 The lungyi.. whenever the wearer can afford it, is of thin silk and is simply a square of about five feet.. put on like a petticoat and folded in over the right hip. **1908** H. JONES *Let.* 2 May in H. J. W. Hetherington *Life & Lett. Sir H. Jones* (1924) II. 203 The boxers, all naked except for their ornamental silk *longyis* tied up hard between their legs and around their middle. **1934** [see ARAKANESE *a.* and *sb.*]. **1947** 'N. SHUTE' *Chequer Board* 105 A green *longyi* wrapped around her waist and falling to her feet. **1948** *Amer. Speech* XXIII. 228/2 *Longyi, lungyi*, Burmese skirtlike attire which falls to the ankles. The national dress, worn by both sexes. **1957** R. MASON *World of Suzie Wong* II. ii. 17 A Burmese woman.. with her bright red *longyi* taut over her thighs. **1959** *Times* 19 Mar. 14/6 The Burmese in their gaily coloured *lungyis*. **1959** *Ibid.* 10 Dec. 11/2 Burma, where men wear the *longyi*. **1971** *Nat. Geographic* Mar. 304/2 He wears the Burmese national costume, a wrap-around skirt called a *longyi*, derived from India, and a short formal jacket with three pockets and cloth buttons, derived from China.

lungie, variant of LONGIE.

lunging (ˈlʌndʒɪŋ), *vbl. sb.*¹ [f. LUNGE *v.*¹ + -ING¹.] The action of LUNGE *v.*¹

1847 MRS. GORE *Cast. in Air* xxiv. (1857) 217 One of the many merry mountebanks who are lost without the presence of a *plastron* against whom they may exercise their lunging.

lunging (ˈlʌndʒɪŋ), *vbl. sb.*² [f. LUNGE *v.*² + -ING¹.] The action of LUNGE *v.*²

1833 *Regul. Instr. Cavalry* I. 71 It is of little importance upon which hand the Longing is begun. **1875** S. SIDNEY *Bk. Horse* (1886) 558 Longeing properly employed teaches a horse obedience. **1892** W. H. HUTCHISON *Hints on Colt-breaking* 49, I.. without any lunging or preparation, put the saddle and bridle on him [etc.].

attrib. **1833** *Regul. Instr. Cavalry* I. 70 The horse being brought to the riding-house, or longing-ground, a.. snaffle bridle is to be placed in his mouth. **1862** H. KINGSLEY *Ravenshoe* I. iii. 27 The centre of this quad.. is occupied by a tan lunging ring.

†ˈ**lungis.** *Obs.* Also 6 longis, lundgis, 7 lunges, -eis. *pl.* 6 lungis. [a. OF. *longis*:—L. *Longinus* apocryphal name of the centurion who pierced our Lord with a spear, by popular etymology associated with L. *longus* long.] **a.** A long, slim, awkward fellow; a lout. **b.** One who is long in doing anything; a laggard, a lingerer.

c **1560** RICHARDES *Misogonus* II. ii, Let sungir [? *read* lungis, *Collier's conjecture*] lurke and drudges worke, We doe defie their slaverye. **1572** HULOET (ed. Higgins), Longis or a long slymme, *lungurio*. **1579** LYLY *Euphues* (Arb.) 115 If talle, [they term him] a lungis, if short, a dwarfe. **1592** NASHE *Summer's Last Will* (1600) E 4, No, that there is not, goodman Lundgis. **1611** BEAUM. & FL. *Knt. Burn. Pestle* II. iii, The foule great Lungeis laid vnmercifully on thee. **1706** PHILLIPS (ed. Kersey), *Lungis*, a slim Slow-back; a drowsy or dreaming Fellow.

lungless (ˈlʌŋlɪs), *a.* [f. LUNG + -LESS.] Devoid of lungs, without lungs.

1606 SYLVESTER *Du Bartas* II. iv. I. *Tropheis* 760 A Body heart-lesse, lung-lesse, tongue-lesse too, Where Satan lurks, not to give life thereto. **1861** WILSON & GEIKIE *Mem. E. Forbes* v. 145 The lungless sea slugs.. on which he laboured so much. **1901** *Daily Chron.* 6 July 5/1 Much has been written of these lungless salamanders.

lungoor, lungooty, vars. LANGUR, LANGOOTY.

†**lungoute.** *Obs.* Forms: 2–3 languste, 5 *Sc.* l(o)unguste. [ad. F. *langouste*, semi-popular repr. L. *locusta*.] A locust.

c **1200** *Trin. Coll. Hom.* 127 Wilde huni and languste his mete. **1456** SIR G. HAYE *Law Arms* (S.T.S.) 29 Thare come of that reik a maner of bestis callit Lungoutis. *Ibid.* 30 Loungoutis.

†ˈ**lungsought.** *Obs.* Forms: 6 long(e)saugh, -sought, *Sc.* lunsaucht, 6–7 long-sought. [f. LUNG + ON. **sóht* disease.] Lung-disease.

1523 FITZHERB. *Husb.* §59 An nother maner of sycknesse amonge bestes.. called longe soughte,.. ye shal perceyue it by his hoystynge. **1562** TURNER *Herbal* II. 170 The sede [of nettels].. is good for the long sought or inflammation of the lunges. **1579** LANGHAM *Gard. Health* (1633) 425 The seed of Romane Nettles.. is good for.. the old plurisie or Long-sought. **1598** *Trials for Witchcraft* in *Spalding Club Misc.* I. 120 Thow.. haillis the guidis, and preservis thame fra the lunsaucht and all vther diseasis.

lungung, obs. form of LONGAN.

lungwort (ˈlʌŋwɜːt). For forms see LUNG and WORT. [OE. *lungenwyrt*, f. *lungen* LUNG + *wyrt* WORT.] The English name of various plants.

†**1.** *Hieracium murorum*, also called ***French, golden lungwort.*** *Obs.*

c **1000** *Sax. Leechd.* II. 92 Nim.. lungenwyrt seo biþ ȝeolu ufeweard. **1597** [see FRENCH *a.* 5]. **1670** [see GOLDEN *a.* 10 b]. **1796** [see FRENCH *a.* 5].

†**2.** Black Hellebore. *Helleborus niger. Obs.*

c **1265** *Voc. Plants* in Wr.-Wülcker 557/27 *Eleborum*, ellebre, lungwurt. *a* **1400–50** *Stockh. Med. MS.* 184 Long-wourt or pelethre of Spanye (*Eleborus*). *c* **1450** *Voc.* in Wr.-Wülcker 580/2 *Eleborus niger*, longwort. **1611** COTGR., *Obre*, Bastard blacke Hellebore, Lungwort, Christs-wort.

3. The boraginaceous plant *Pulmonaria officinalis* (Common Lungwort), having leaves with white spots, fancied to resemble the spots in a diseased lung.

1538 ELYOT *Dict.*, *Pulmonaria*, an herbe callyd Lung-worte. **1577** B. GOOGE *Heresbach's Husb.* (1586) 134 Take a handfull of beasts Loongwoort, a handfull of other Loongwoort that serueth for the pot. **1688** R. HOLME *Armoury* II. 85/2 Lungwort, a kind of Moss, with broad tough leaves,.. spotted on the upper side. **1787** tr. *Linnæus' Fam. Plants* I. 100 *Pulmonaria* (Lung-wort). **1861** MISS PRATT *Flower. Pl.* IV. 31. **1882** G. ALLEN *Colours Flowers* ii. 49 The lung-wort (*Pulmonaria officinalis*) is also dark blue.

b. With qualification applied to plants of the allied American genus *Mertensia*.

1856 DELAMER *Fl. Gard.* (1861) 88 *Mertensia Sibirica*, the Siberian Lungwort, removed by modern botanists from the genus *Pulmonaria*,.. is also sometimes styled Forget-me-not. **1866** *Treas. Bot.*, Lungwort, smooth. *Mertensia*.

†**4.** The Great Mullein, *Verbascum Thapsus*; called also ***bullock's, clown's, cow's lungwort*** (see these sbs.). *Obs.*

1538 TURNER *Libellus*, Longwort, *Verbascum*. **1578** LYTE *Dodoens* I. lxxxi. 120 Mulleyn is called in.. English also.. Longworte. **1601** HOLLAND *Pliny* II. 246 Mvllen or Lung-wort with the yellow golden floure. **1607** TOPSELL *Four-f. Beasts* (1658) 477 If it come from the sickness of the Lungs, then the herb called Lungwort or Creswort, is the most present remedy in the World. **1706** PHILLIPS (ed. Kersey), *Candelaria*, the Herb Wooll-blade, Torchherb, Long-Wort, or Mullein.

5. A species of lichen (*Sticta pulmonacea* or *pulmonaria*), otherwise known as Lungs of Oak (see LUNG 5) and Tree Lungwort (see TREE).

1578 LYTE *Dodoens* III. lxxi. 412 The seconde kinde [of Moss] groweth also about trees, the whiche is called Lung-wurt. **1579** LANGHAM *Gard. Health* (1633) 374 Lvngwort of the Oke.. is good for the inflammations & ulcers of the lungs. **1756** WATSON in *Phil. Trans.* XLIX. 857 *Lichen pulmonarius arboreus sive Pulmonaria arborea*,.. Lung-wort, Oak Lungs. **1785** MARTYN *Rousseau's Bot.* xxxii. (1794) 498 Lungwort or Tree Lichen, which hangs from old Oaks, and beeches in woods, has very large jagged leaves, smooth and ending obtusely. **1861** H. MACMILLAN *Footnotes fr. Page Nat.* 106 The lung-wort (*Sticta pulmonaria*).. grows.. on trees and rocks in sub-alpine woods.

†**6.** Angelica, *Archangelica officinalis. Obs.*

[The form *lungwort* does not occur in this sense, and the ambiguous spelling *longwort* perh. indicates a distinct word, f. LONG *a.* But angelica was in fact used in ailments of the lungs.]

1552 ELYOT *Dict.* s.v. *Angelica*, Of this herbe be two kindes, one of the gardeyne.. an other wilde, named linge worte or longe wurt. **1565** COOPER *Thesaurus, Angelica*, an hearbe whereof be two kindes, one of the garden called angelica or imperial, the other wilde: named lingwourt or longewourt. **1706** PHILLIPS (ed. Kersey), *Long-wort* or Angelica, an Herb. **1731** BAILEY vol. II, *Long-wort*.

†**7.** Toothwort, *Lathræa Squamaria.* (Also ***clown's lungwort.***) *Obs.*

1597 GERARDE *Herbal* III. clxiii. 1387 Of great Toothwoorth, or Clownes Lungwoort. 1 *Dentaria maior Mathioli*. Great toothwoort, or Lungwoort. 2 *Dentaria minor*. Little Lungwoort. *Ibid.* 1388 Our countrey women do call it [*Dentaria*] Lungwoort, and do vse it against the cough and all other imperfections of the lungs.

lungy (ˈlʌŋɪ), *a.* [f. LUNG + -Y.] **a.** Affected with lung-disease.

1888 G. ALLEN *Devil's Die* I. xvii. 276 The mild Hindoos, lungy to a man, preferred.. a native doctor. **1899** *Pall Mall Mag.* Apr. 474, I got to know from a doctor at home that I was lungy.

b. Coming from the lungs.

1909 *Westm. Gaz.* 21 Apr. 2/1 As the armed companies turned this corner of the narrow road a lungey Oriental cheer.. saluted each. **1935** 'R. CROMPTON' *William—the Detective* ix. 211 Sounds lungy to me.

lungy, lung-yen: see LONGIE, LONGAN.

lungyi, var. LUNGI.

lunicurrent (ˌl(j)uːnɪˈkʌrənt), *a. rare*⁻⁰. [f. L. *lūna* moon + CURRENT *sb.*] Depending in current on the phases of the moon.

1864 in WEBSTER (citing BACHE). Hence in mod. Dicts.

†**luˈnific**, *a.* and *sb. Obs.* [f. LUNA (sense 2) + -(I)FIC.] **a.** *adj.* Producing silver. **b.** *sb. Alch.* A substance capable of transmuting other substances into silver.

1678 R. R[USSELL] *Geber* III. II. II. xvi. 207 To.. convert it [*sc.* argent vive].. into true Solifick and Lunifick. *a* **1693** *Urquhart's Rabelais* III. li. 414 The Lunifick Trees of Seres.

luniform (ˌl(j)uːnɪfɔːm), *a.* [f. L. *lūna* moon: see -FORM. Cf. F. *luniforme*.] Shaped like the moon; *spec* in *Nat. Hist.* (see quot.).

1826 KIRBY & SP. *Entomol.* IV. 268 Luniform, whose longitudinal section is lunate.

lunik (ˈl(j)uːnɪk). *Astronautics.* Also **Lunik**. [f. L. *lūn-a* moon + -NIK, after *sputnik*, or ad. Russ. *lúnnik* (similarly f. Russ. *luná* moon).] Any of a series of Russian spacecraft sent to or close by the moon.

1959 *Daily Tel.* 5 Jan. 16/6 The Russians had a word for the moon rocket soon enough: Lunik. Unlike Sputnik the word was not official. *Ibid.*, The only vocal demonstrations ..were from the generation still young enough to qualify for ..trips..aboard Luniks. **1959** H. NICOLSON *Let.* 14 Sept. (1968) 370, I hate the lunik for having bumped into the radiant moon. **1961** *Ann. Reg. 1960* 388 The Russians attempted no further 'lunik' shots. **1964** *Yearbk. Astron. 1965* 70 The Russians se[n]t up their Moon probe Lunik III, which represented the greatest triumph in space research up to that moment. [**1966** *Ann. dell' Istituto Univ. Orient., Sezione Slava* IX. 213 From the evidence presented above the fact seems to emerge that, even if *lunnik* was coined in Moscow on the morning of 3 January 1959, it was simultaneously fabricated in the West.] **1967** *Punch* 28 June 937/1 The Luniks were soon joined by American Surveyors and Lunar Orbiters and by the end of 1966, by no stretch of poetic imagination could the moon be described as companionless.

† **ˈlunish**, *a. Obs. rare*⁻¹. [? f. LUNE² + -ISH.] ? Productive of 'lunes'; maddening.

1657 F. COCKIN *Divine Blossomes* 34 Than Living Waters, he had rather sip His lunish Cups of Soul-confounding Drink.

lunisolar (ˌl(j)uːnɪˈsəʊlə(r)), *a. Astr.* [f. L. *lūna* moon + SOLAR. Cf. F. *lunisolaire*.] Pertaining to the mutual relations of the sun and moon, or resulting from their combined action. ***lunisolar period***: a cycle of 532 years, that number being the product of 19 and 28, the numbers of years in the cycles of the moon and sun respectively. ***lunisolar year***: a year whose divisions are regulated by the revolutions of the moon, while its average total length is made to agree with the revolution of the sun. ***lunisolar precession***: see PRECESSION.

1691 T. H[ALE] *Acc. New Invent.* p. xxxvii, A New Luni-Solar Year. *a* **1727** NEWTON *Chronol. Amended* (1728) 15 Hitherto the Lunisolar year had been in use. **1735** DYCHE & PARDON *Dict.*, *Luni-solar period.* **1751** *Phil. Trans.* XLVII. 319 The other luni-solar tables constructed from the numbers and measures of the illustrious Newton. **1792** H. CAVENDISH *ibid.* LXXXII. 385 In those parts of India in which this almanac is used, the civil year is lunisolar. **1795–8** T. MAURICE *Hindostan* (1820) I. I. ii. 81 The luni-solar year ..was..found to fall short of the true equinoctial year by five days and a quarter. **1879** J. W. BODDAM-WHETHAM *Roraima* xxv. 285 Luni-solar attraction. **1885** *Where Chinese Drive* 129 The Chinese year is lunisolar.

† **ˈlunist.** *Astrol. Obs.* [f. L. *lūna* moon + -IST.] One born under the influence of the moon.

1569 J. SANFORD tr. *Agrippa's Van. Artes* 50 b, She pronounceth..another a Venerean, Mercurialist, or Lunist. **1598** R. HAYDOCKE tr. *Lomazzo* II. 16 Nor an vndaunted Martiallist be like terrified..as a timerous Lunist.

lunistice (ˈl(j)uːnɪstɪs). *Astr.* Also 7 **lunestice**. [as if ad. mod.L. **lūnistitium*, f. *lūna* moon + *-stitium* a stopping, after *solstitium*.] The point at which the moon has the greatest northing or southing in her monthly course; the time at which she reaches this point.

1650 CHARLETON *Paradoxes* 43 The Sea conformes to either Lunestice. **1860** in WORCESTER, and in later Dicts.

luniˈtidal, *a.* [f. L. *lūna* moon + TIDAL.] Pertaining to the movements of the tide dependent on the moon. ***lunitidal interval*** (see quot.).

1851–9 WHEWELL in *Man. Sci. Enq.* 70 We add to them the other columns containing the moon's transit and the lunitidal interval calculated therefrom. **1889** SIR R. BALL *Time & Tide* 30 We speak of the interval between the transit of the moon and the time of high water as the luni-tidal interval.

lunk (lʌŋk). *colloq.* (orig. *U.S.*). [Abbrev. of LUNKHEAD.] A slow-witted, unintelligent person.

1867 *Harper's Weekly* 25 May 330/2 They're tigers, you thick-headed lunk. **1907** J. MASEFIELD *Tarpaulin Muster* iv. 70 He's dead all right... He might ha' known..going alone among them Indians... None but a red-headed runt'd have been such a lunk as to try it. **1931** F. HURST *Back St.* II. xxvi. 231 What a lunk he continued to be! **1955** W. GADDIS *Recognitions* I. vii. 229 Most artists have a great lunk of a man they trail around with them, they never know what to do with him, he gets drunk, he gets into trouble. **1975** *New Yorker* 24 Mar. 93/3 He looks incredulous, as if he couldn't figure out how he got turned into such a lunk.

lunkah (ˈlʌŋkə). [Orig. attrib. use of Hindi *laŋka*, the local term for the 'islands' of the Godavery Delta in which the tobacco is grown (Yule *Hobson-Jobson* 1886).] A kind of strong cheroot.

1889 DOYLE *Sign of Four* i. 5 Some murder has been done by a man who was smoking an Indian lunkah.

lunker (ˈlʌŋkə(r)). *N. Amer. colloq.* [Origin unknown.] An animal, esp. a fish, which is an exceptionally large example of its species; a 'whopper'. Also *attrib.*

1912 *Dialect Notes* III. 582 Isn't that calf a lunker. **1920** *Outing* July–Aug. 197, I said that I caught trout in a tin pan, and here's the proof. This old lunker of a rainbow gave me a bath. **1947** *Sports Afield* Dec. 21/1 A bronzed lunker came out of the shadowy depths and smashed the pigskin. **1968** *Globe & Mail* (Toronto) 3 Feb. 33/5 The area has been dubbed lunker country and anglers find it's more than just a slogan. **1972** *Angling Times* 6 Apr. 14/3, I shall be going out..in search of these lunker bass.

lunkhead (ˈlʌŋkhɛd). *colloq.* (orig. *U.S.*). A blockhead. Hence **lunkˈheaded** *a.*, thickheaded, stupid.

1884 'MARK TWAIN' *Huck. Finn* xxii. 225 So the duke said these Arkansaw lunkheads couldn't come up to Shakespeare. **1889** A. W. TOURGEE in *Chicago Advance* 19 Dec., You dear old lunkhead, I congratulate you! **1901** J. A. RIIS *Making an American* 315 A miserable little lunkhead quite beyond hope. **1885** J. HILL *Corsairs* 19 Prospecters tearfully eloquent to the horny-handed (and lunkheaded). **1908** *Daily Chron.* 23 July 3/2 Now do you see, you lunkhead? **1934** WODEHOUSE *Right Ho, Jeeves* v. 52 A lunkhead capable of mucking things up as Gussie had done. **1951** E. PAUL *Springtime in Paris* ix. 165 They are not all lunkheads or mountebanks. **1966** *Punch* 7 Dec. 868/1 The poor lunkhead's concerns soon get lost under all the modelling and backlighting.

lunn (lʌn). *rare.* Short for SALLY LUNN.

1874 CHR. ROSSETTI *Sp. Likenesses* 53 Tea and coffee, and potato-rolls, and lunns.

lunnite (ˈlʌnaɪt). *Min.* [named (*Lunnit*) in 1839 by J. J. Bernhardi after F. *Lunn*, who had analyzed it: see -ITE.] An obsolete synonym of pseudomalachite (A. H. Chester).

lunokhod (ˈl(j)uːnəkɒd, -xɒd). *Astronautics.* Also (as the proper name of individual vehicles) with capital initial. [a. Russ. *lunokhód*, f. *luná* moon + *-khod*, suffix denoting something that travels (f. *khodít'* to go).] A type of Russian self-propelled, radio-controlled vehicle for transmitting information about the moon as it travels over its surface.

1970 *Guardian* 18 Nov. 1/2 Russia is likely to try to bring its moon crawler Lunokod-1 back to earth. **1973** *Nature* 30 Nov. 241/2 The thickness of the regolith decreased as the lunokhod approached the rille and the lip consisted of a rock 'border' with boulders of at least 1 to 2 m. *Ibid.*, Magnetometer experiments, a new feature of Lunokhod-2.

lunshin, obs. form of LUNCHEON.

lunt (lʌnt), *sb. Sc.* Also 6 **luntt**. [a. Du. *lont* a match. Cf. LINSTOCK.]

1. A slow match; also, a torch. ***to set lunt to***: to set fire to.

1550 *Acts Privy Council* (1891) III. 89 One cᵗʰ weight of fyne corne powder, demi cᵗʰ of matches or luntes. **1571** R. BANNATYNE *Jrnl. Trans. in Scot.* (1806) 132 Some men that was going vpon the croftis with lunttis. **1582–8** *Hist. James VI* (1804) 126 Ane of thame..hade a loose lunt, quhilk negligently fell out of his hand amang the great quantity of poulder. **1706** in PHILLIPS (ed. Kersey). **1755** JOHNSON, *Lunt*, the matchcord with which guns are fired. **1816** SCOTT *Bl. Dwarf* ix, 'If ye step a foot nearer it wi' that lunt, it's be the dearest step ye ever made in your days'... 'We'll sune see that', said Hobbie, advancing fearlessly with the torch. **1828–40** TYTLER *Hist. Scot.* (1864) III. 237 They..laid a train, which was connected with a 'lunt', or slow match. **1887** MᶜNEILL *Blawearie* 57 The 'lunt' was used by the miner..for the purpose of kindling his lamp when he arrived at the stairhead. **1894** CROCKETT *Lilac Sunbonnet* xvi. 141 An' whiles they tied them to a bit stick an' set lunt to them.

2. Smoke, smoke with flame, esp. the smoke from a pipe. Also, hot vapour.

1785 BURNS *Halloween* xiii, She fuff't her pipe wi' sic a lunt. *Ibid.* xxviii, Till butter'd so'ns wi' fragrant lunt Set a' their gabs a-steerin. **1865** J. SHAW in R. Wallace *Country Schoolm.* (1899) 123 After she had discussed her 'lunt' she would crouch with her chin on her palms.

lunt, *a.* [Cf. Da. †*lunte* lazy (Kalkar).] †**a.** Of a horse: Spiritless, tame (*obs.*). **b.** *dial.* (See quot. *a* 1825.)

1639 T. DE GRAY *Compl. Horsem.* 303 He will become lunt, and utterly to have lost his mettle. *a* **1825** FORBY *Voc. E. Anglia*, *Lunt*, short; crusty; surly in speech or in manners.

lunt (lʌnt), *v.* [f. LUNT *sb.*]

a. *intr.* To smoke, emit smoke. **b.** quasi-*trans.* To smoke (a pipe). **c.** *intr.* Of smoke: To rise in wreaths, to curl. **d.** *trans.* To kindle, light *up*.

1830 D. VEDDER in Whitelaw *Bk. Sc. Song* (1875) 185/2 The carle..was luntin' his cutty before the fire. **1836** M. MACKINTOSH *Cottager's Dau.* 71 The curling reek was luntin' up the lum. **1861** R. QUIN *Heather Lintie* (1866) 172 Dumfries, to me thy very name Lunts up a soul-endearing flame. **1894** CROCKETT *Raiders* (ed. 3) 92 He sat ever by the chimney corner and lunted away on his cutty pipe.

ˈlunting, *ppl. a.* [f. prec. + -ING².] Smoking, blazing, glowing. Of the eyes: Flashing.

1786 BURNS *Twa Dogs* 133 The luntin pipe, an' sneeshin mill, Are handed round wi' right guid will. **1791** J. LEARMONT *Poems* 117 The fierce blaze o' simmer's luntin' heat Wad ruin a'. **1834** *Tait's Mag.* I. 428/2 They must kindle a lunting fire. **1893** STEVENSON *Catriona* 166 Peden wi' his lang chafts an' luntin' een. **1895** CROCKETT *Men of Moss Hags* 234 Nae beard like bristles, nae luntin' stinkin' pipes.

‖**lunula** (ˈl(j)uːnjʊlə). [L. *lūnula*, dim. of *lūna* moon.]

1. a. *Geom.* = LUNE³ 1, LUNULE 2. †**b.** (See quot. 1712). *Obs.*

1571 DIGGES *Pantom.* II. xiv. O j, Yᵉ last figure called a Lunula. **1579** —— *Stratiot.* 104 All others as the Lunula.. and Hexagonall Battailes. **1700** WALLIS in. *Phil. Trans.* XXI. 411 The Squaring a certain Lunula by Hippocrates Chius long since, hath been known..for many Ages. **1712** DESAGULIERS tr. *Ozanam's Mech.* 123 We call Lunula a Plain terminated by the Circumferences of Two Circles, which touch one another on the inside [etc.]. **1881** ROUTLEDGE *Science* ii. 37 The areas of the lunulae AFBD, BGCE.

†**2.** A satellite. *rare*⁻¹. *Obs.* (Cf. F. *lunule*.)

1676 GLANVILL *Ess.* iii. 18 The Ansulæ Saturni, the Asseclæ of Jupiter..By these Lunulæ 'tis thought that Jupiters distance from the Earth may be determined.

3. a. *Nat. Hist.* A crescent-shaped mark = LUNULE 1. **b.** The white crescent-shaped mark at the base of the finger-nails.

1828 QUAIN *Elem. Anat.* 699 At the posterior, or attached extremity [of the nail], a small portion will be observed differing in colour from the rest, and usually called lunula, from its form. **1874** COUES *Birds N.W.* 703 The frontal lunula reaches but little beyond the eyes, instead of nearly half an inch behind them. **1891** *Brit. Med. Jrnl.* 12 Sept. 624/2 A patient..who had a lunula on each thumbnail only. **1897** *Allbutt's Syst. Med.* II. 361 A white band and a furrow at the lunula of the nails.

4. a. *Conch.* = LUNULE 3. **b.** *Anat.* (See quot.)

1835–6 TODD *Cycl. Anat.* I. 711/2 The lunula does not occur in every genus of bivalve shell. **1856** *Quain's Anat.* (ed. 6) III. 240 [In the heart] two narrow lunated portions, one on each side of the nodule and adjoining the free margin of the valve. These parts..are named *lunulæ*. **1875** T. HAYDEN *Dis. Heart* 24 This is the lunula.

5. *Archæol.* A gold, crescent-shaped, neck ornament found in archaeological sites of the Early Bronze Age.

1719 J. HARRIS *Hist. Kent* I. II. 249/1 Many also of the *Lunulae* were found here. **1773** *Archæologia* II. 37 The small circular plates at the extremities of the Lunula. **1867** *Archæol. Jrnl.* XXIV. 197 In another remarkable discovery of golden relics.., namely the two *lunulæ* found at Padstow .., the precious deposit was likewise accompanied by an object of bronze. **1911** *Encycl. Brit.* II. 353/1 The flat, crescent-shaped, diadem-like objects called 'lunulae', which are..characteristic of Ireland. **1939** G. CLARK *Archaeol. & Society* v. 133 If the distribution of crescentic jet necklaces and the gold 'lunula' ornaments are together plotted on the map they will be found to coincide closely with the distribution of food vessels.

lunular (ˈl(j)uːnjʊlə(r)), *a.* and *sb. Geom.* Also 6 (as sb.; ? mod.L.) **lunulare**. [f. LUNULA + -AR.]

A. *adj.* Pertaining to a lune or lunule; in the form of a lunule, crescent-shaped.

1727–51 CHAMBERS *Cycl.* s.v. *Angle*, Lunular Angle..is that formed by the intersection of two curve lines; the one concave, and the other convex. **1740** ANDERSON in Rigaud *Corr. Sci. Men* (1841) I. 363 There is no need of the proportion of the arches..in order to measure the lunular segment. **1788** T. TAYLOR *Proclus* I. 168 Two circumferences, either making angles, as in the lunular figure, or [etc.]. **1797** *Encycl. Brit.* (ed. 3) III. 442/2 (*Botany*) The figure of Similitudes is..Lunular, crescent-shaped, subrotund.

†**B.** *sb.* A crescent-shaped figure. *Obs.*

1570 DEE *Math. Pref.* a iij b, A perfect Square,..Lunular, Ryng, Serpentine [etc.]. **1579** DIGGES *Stratiot.* 104 Causing them..to change from Triangle to Square, from Circulare to Lunulare. **1674** JEAKE *Arith.* (1696) 12 The Lunular Decrescent is the sign of the Quotient of any Division. **1789** T. TAYLOR *Proclus* II. 44 In lunulars and systroides.

lunulate (ˈl(j)uːnjʊleɪt), *a. Nat. Hist.* [a. mod.L. *lūnulāt-us*: see LUNULA and -ATE².]

= LUNULATED.

1760 J. LEE *Introd. Bot.* III. v. (1765) 178 Lunulate, Moon-shaped; when they are round, and hollowed at the Base, and the Lower Part has Angles. **1816** KIRBY & SP. *Entomol.* (1818) II. 407 Another cavity of a lunulate shape. **1847** HARDY in *Proc. Berw. Nat. Club* II. 253 The fifth [segment] with a deep lunulate impression. **1848** J. GOULD *Birds Austral.* IV. 57 A lunulate mark of white on either side of the neck. **1852** DANA *Crust.* I. 200 Crest entire, lunulate, sublateral. **1866** in GRAY *1st Less. Bot.* Gloss.

So **lunuˈlation**, a lunular or lunulate spot.

1888 P. L. SCLATER *Catal. Birds Brit. Mus.* XIV. 318 Well-marked black lunulations on the breast [etc.].

lunulated (ˈl(j)uːnjʊleɪtɪd), *a.* [f. as prec. + -ED.]

†**1.** Crescent-shaped. (Cf. LUNULAR *a.*) *Obs.*

1705 PETIVER in *Phil. Trans.* XXV. 1956 It's externally piped towards the Mouth, and above these lunulated. **1753** CHAMBERS *Cycl. Supp.* s.v. *Leaf*, *Lunulated* leaf, one in form of a crescent. **1772** FORSTER in *Phil. Trans.* LX. 412 The throat..blackish,..but mixed with white lunulated spots. **1797** *Encycl. Brit.* (ed. 3) III. 436/2 The antheræ are lunulated, or shaped like a crescent.

2. Marked with lunulæ or crescent-shaped spots.

a **1798** TENNANT *Journ. fr. Lond. to I. of Wight* (1801) II. 73, I saw here the lunulated Gilt-head and ancient Wrasse. **1836** YARRELL *Brit. Fishes* (1859) II. 149 Lunulated Gilt-head. **1848** J. GOULD *Birds Austral.* IV. 72 *Melithreptus lunulatus*, Lunulated Honey-eater. **1888** P. L. SCLATER *Catal. Birds Brit. Mus.* XIV. 317 Whole body below lunulated with black.

lunule (ˈl(j)uːnjʊl). [a. F. *lunule*, ad. L. *lūnula*, dim. of *lūna* moon.]

1. *Nat. Hist.* A crescent-shaped mark, spot, etc.

1828 STARK *Elem. Nat. Hist.* I. 138 Whitish lunules on the tail-feathers. **1845** WESTWOOD *Brit. Moths* II. 14 With two rather slightly marked strigæ (between which is a white lunule).

2. *Geom.* = LUNE[3] 1. (Cf. LUNULA 1 a.)

1737 in BAILEY vol. II. **1817** COLEBROOKE *Algebra*, etc. 96 A lunule or meniscus. **1872** DE MORGAN *Budget of Paradoxes* 45 This [Porta's *Elementa Curvilineorum*] is a ridiculous attempt, which defies description, except that it is all about lunules.

3. *Conch.* The crescent-shaped depression in front of the umbo. (Cf. LUNULE 4 a.)

1842 SOWERBY *Conch. Man.* (ed. 2) 179. **1851–6** WOODWARD *Mollusca* 298 *Cyprina*,.. umbones oblique; no lunule. **1863** J. G. JEFFREYS *Brit. Conchol.* II. 233 Lunule deep and heart-shaped. **1866** TATE *Brit. Mollusks* ii. 11.

Hence **ˈlunuled** *a.*, crescent-shaped.

1863 REEVE *Land & Freshwater Mollusks* 236 Shell large, oval-globose, slightly lunuled.

lunulet (ˈl(j)uːnjʊlɪt). *Nat. Hist.* [f. LUNULA + -ET[1].] A small crescent-shaped mark.

1826 KIRBY & SP. *Entomol.* IV. 286. **1838** WESTWOOD *Entomologist's Text Bk.* 278.

lunulite (ˈl(j)uːnjʊlaɪt). *Geol.* [ad. mod.L. *lūnulītēs* (J. Parkinson 1822): see LUNULA and -ITE.] A small fossil coral, more or less circular in shape.

1845 LYELL *Trav. N. Amer.* I. 137 The corals.. agree all generically with those of the Miocene beds of Europe, and some specifically, as a lunulite, the same as one from the Suffolk crag. **1864** in WEBSTER; and in later Dicts.

luny: see LOONY.

†**ˈlunyie.** *Sc.* ? *Obs.* Also 6 lonȝe, lounie, 7 leungyie, 9 lunzie, lungie. Var. of LOIN *sb.*

1508 DUNBAR *Flyting w. Kennedie* 121 Lene larbar, loungeour, baith lowsy in lisk and lonȝe. *a* **1520** —— *Poems* xxvi. 75 Belliall, with a brydill renyie, Evir lascht thame on the lunyie. **1575** R. B. *Apius & Virginia* iiij b, Your fatlings are feding well Sir, the Gods be praised, A goodly lounie of beef on them is all redy raised. **1686** G. STUART *Joco-Ser. Disc.* 13, I saw your Naig, else I'm a Whelp I took his Leungyie sike a Skelp. **1818** SCOTT *Br. Lamm.* xxii, Broad in his shouthers and narrow around the lungies. **1819** W. TENNANT *Papistry Storm'd* (1827) 14 He gave his lunzie sic a lounder As did the sillie man dumfounder.

Luo (ˈluːəʊ), *sb.* and *a.* Also Luoh, Lwo.

A. *sb.* **a.** The name of an East African people in Kenya and the upper Nile valley; a member of this people. **b.** The Nilotic language of this people. **B.** *adj.* Of or pertaining to the Luo or their language.

[**1905** C. ELIOT *E. Afr. Protectorate* viii. 148 Whereas the villages in the north are surrounded with mud walls, those of the Ja-luo are protected by a thick-set hedge of euphorbias and aloes.] **1911** *Encycl. Brit.* XV. 565/1 *Jur*, the Dinka name for a tribe of negroes of the upper Nile valley, whose real name is Luoh, or Lwo. **1942** *E. African Ann. 1941–2* 17/1 The Luo are a Nilotic negro tribe of agriculturalists living in the hot fertile country east of Lake Victoria. **1957** W. M. HAILEY *Afr. Survey* (rev. ed.) iii. 98 There are language committees concerned with the Kikuyu and Luo languages and an increasing volume of vernacular literature is being produced. **1964** C. WILLOCK *Enormous Zoo* v. 85 A mixed horde of Kikuyu, Luo and one Turkana appeared armed with pangas. **1968** *New Scientist* 12 Dec. 599/3 The Luo, the second largest tribe in Kenya after the Kikuyu. **1968** Y. R. CHAO *Lang. & Symbolic Syst.* 99 Dinka and Luo .. have almost 1 million speakers each. **1969** *Listener* 24 July 100/1 Mboya was the only Luo leader of stature still in the party hierarchy. **1970** *Guardian* 6 June 9/6 Josphat shouted something in Luo which I did not hear. **1970** *Language* XLVI. 402 Some of the so-called prefixing forms of Luo are almost isomorphic semantically with their suffixal counterparts in Tarascan.

luodic (l(j)uːˈɒdɪk), *a.* *Path. rare.* [f. LU-ES, after *spasmodic*, etc.] Having the characteristics of *lues* or syphilis.

1822 GOOD *Study Med.* IV. 80 Women who upon inspection had no marks.. of luodic blenorrhœa, or clap.

lupaerd, obs. form of LEOPARD.

‖**lupanar** (l(j)uːˈpeɪnɑː(r)). [L. *lupānar*.] A brothel.

1864 *Daily Tel.* 8 Aug., To see.. every lupanar that has been a plague-spot here. **1886** R. BUCHANAN in *Pall Mall G.* 20 Sept., It is a very phenomenal city whose existence can only be determined by its lupanars and its sewers.

lupard(e, lupart, obs. forms of LEOPARD.

lupe, variant of LOOP *sb.*[4]

‖**Lupercal** (ˈl(j)uːpəkæl), *sb.* *Rom. Antiq.* [L. *lupercāl*, subst. form of *lupercāle*, neut. of *lupercālis* pertaining to Lupercus, a Roman deity commonly identified with the Greek Pan.]

1. A grotto on the Palatine sacred to Lupercus.

1513 DOUGLAS *Æneis* VIII. vi. 72 He schew him eik,.. the cove, was call Full mony ȝeris in thair leid Lupercall,.. To Pan the god of Licie consecrait.

2. A festival held annually in February in honour of Lupercus. Also *pl.* **Lupercalia**.

1600 HOLLAND *Livy* I. v. 5 Even in those daies.. was the feastivall pastime Lupercal, used in mount Palatine. **1601** SHAKS. *Jul. C.* III. ii. 100 You all did see, that on the Lupercall, I thrice presented him a Kingly Crowne. **1740** J. DUPRÉ *Conform. Anc. & Mod. Cerem.* 101 The Pagans could say the same of their Saturnals, Bacchanals and Lupercals. **1901** *Edin. Rev.* Jan. 202 The Lupercalia was a Caesarian revival. *Ibid.* Oct. 328 His brother-conspirators of the proceedings at the Lupercal.

†**b.** *transf.* An orgy. *Obs.*

1591 SYLVESTER *Du Bartas* I. vii. 416 To turn God's Feasts to filthy Lupercals.

†**Luˈpercal,** *a.* *Obs. rare.* [ad. L. *lupercālis*: see prec.] Pertaining to the Lupercal or Lupercalia.

1607 TOPSELL *Four-f. Beasts* (1658) 112 The Romans and Grecians had also a custom to sacrifice a dog in their Lycæan and Lupercal Feasts. **1656** BLOUNT *Glossogr.* s.v., Lupercalia, or lupercal Sacrifices.

Lupercalian (l(j)uːpəˈkeɪlɪən), *a.* [f. L. *lupercālia* (see LUPERCAL *sb.* 2) + -AN.] Pertaining to the Lupercalia.

1884 in *Cassell's Encycl. Dict.*

lupiform (ˈl(j)uːpɪfɔːm), *a.* *Path.* [f. LUPUS + -(I)FORM.] Of the form of or resembling lupus.

1889 in *Syd. Soc. Lex.* **1890** in J. S. BILLINGS *Nat. Med. Dict.* II. 89.

‖**lupinaster** (l(j)uːpɪˈnæstə(r)). *Bot.* [mod.L. *lupinaster*, f. *lupin-us*: see LUPINE *sb.* and -ASTER.] The bastard lupine (*Trifolium Lupinaster*) of Siberia, an umbellate clover (N.O. *Leguminosæ*).

1753 in CHAMBERS *Cycl. Supp.* (as generic name). **1823** in CRABB; and in later Dicts.

lupine, lupin (ˈl(j)uːpɪn), *sb.* Also 5 lupyne. [ad. L. *lupīn-us*, *lupīn-um*.]

1. Any plant of the genus *Lupinus* (N.O. *Leguminosæ*); in the early quots. chiefly *L. albus*, cultivated in the warmer districts of Europe for the seed and for fodder. The species now common in flower-gardens are of American origin. The flowers, blue, rosy-purple, white and sometimes yellow, grow in clusters of long tapering spikes.

bastard lupine = LUPINASTER (*Treas. Bot.*). **small lupine**, *Psoralea Lupinella* (ibid.).

c **1420** *Pallad. on Husb.* I. 237 Lupyne and ficches slayn, and on their roote Vpdried, are as dongyng, londis boote. **1562** TURNER *Herbal* II. 43 The leues of lupines turne with yᵉ son. **1578** LYTE *Dodoens* IV. xxiii. 480 There be two sortes of Lupines, the white or garden Lupine, and the wild Lupine. **1697** DRYDEN *Virg. Georg.* I. 111 Where.. Stalks of Lupines grew (a stubborn Wood): Th' ensuing Season, in return, may bear The bearded product of the Golden Year. **1707–12** MORTIMER *Husb.* (1721) II. 150 Lupines are an excellent Pulse, and require little care. **1877** A. B. EDWARDS *Up Nile* xi. 290 Rows of blossoming lupins, purple and white. **1882** *Garden* 11 Feb. 91/2 Poor sandy soil suits Lupines well.

2. *pl.* The seed of this plant.

1398 TREVISA *Barth. De P.R.* XVII. xcv. (1495) 662 Some legumina ben bytter of themself as Lupines. *c* **1400** *Lanfranc's Cirurg.* 88 Þese medicyns ben sumwhat more driere: yrios,.. lupines, þe rotynes eiþer þe drie poudre of trees. *c* **1550** LLOYD *Treas. Health* (1585) B v, The Branne of Lupines or penny beane layd on the hearye place [etc.]. **1601** HOLLAND *Pliny* II. 143 There is not a thing more.. light of digestion than white Lupines, if they be eaten dry. **1699** BENTLEY *Phal.* xix. 530 As the Actors in Comedies paid all their Debts upon the Stage with Lupins, so a Sophist pays all his with Words. **1770** LANGHORNE *Plutarch* (1879) II. 950/2 He is said to have lived on lupines. **1898** F. M. CRAWFORD *Ave Roma Immort.* I. 9 The old men.. sunned themselves in the market-place, shelling and chewing lupins to pass the time, as the Romans have always done.

3. *attrib.*

1601 HOLLAND *Pliny* (1635) I. Table, Lupine meat medicinable. **1841** BROWNING *Pippa Passes* ii. Wks. 1896 I. 210 Hellward bound.. With food for both worlds.. Lupine-seed and Hecate's supper.

lupine (ˈl(j)uːpaɪn), *a.* [ad. L. *lupīn-us*, f. *lupus* wolf.] Having the nature of qualities of a wolf.

1660 GAUDEN *Serm. at Funeral of Brownrig* 236 That which in their Physiognomy is.. lupine or leoline (for so we read some men had lionly looks). **1851** KINGSLEY *Yeast* xiv, To send back the fugitive lamb into the jaws of the well-meaning, but still lupine wolf. **1883** EMMA PHIPSON *Anim. Lore Shaks. Time* 36 Ravages imagined to be committed by them [men and women] in their lupine shape. **1885** *Harper's Mag.* Mar. 648/1 The lupine foster-mother of Romulus and Remus.

lupinin (ˈl(j)uːpɪnɪn). *Chem.* Also -ine. [ad. F. *lupinine*, f. L. *lupīn-us*, LUPINE *sb.*: see -IN.] A bitter glucoside obtained from the seeds of *Lupinus albus*.

1839 URE *Dict. Arts*, etc., *Lupinine*. **1865** WATTS *Dict. Chem.*, *Lupinin*, a bitter non-nitrogenous substance obtained from lupine-seeds.

lupinite (ˈl(j)uːpɪnaɪt). *Chem.* [f. LUPINE + -ITE.] = prec.

1839 in *Penny Cycl.* XIV. 202/2.

lupinosis (l(j)uːpɪˈnəʊsɪs). [f. LUPINE, LUPIN *sb.* + -OSIS.] Poisoning of animals, esp. sheep, after ingestion of lupines, either that caused by the presence of lupine alkaloids in the lupines, or (and now usu. spec.) that caused by toxins produced by a fungus of the genus *Phomopsis* growing on lupines.

1899 E. V. WILCOX in *Bull. Montana Agric. Exper. Stat.* No. 22. 39 The symptoms have become so well known and are so constant and uniform that the disease caused by the lupine poisoning has been called lupinosis. **1905** MOUSSU & DOLLAR *Dis. Cattle, Sheep, Goats & Swine* II. vii. 242 The symptoms of lupine poisoning are so well known in Europe that chronic lupine poisoning has been given the name lupinosis. **1928** W. C. MILLER *Black's Vet. Dict.* 571/2 In Europe, by far the greater number of cases [of poisoning by lupines] are of a chronic type, which results in the production of a train of symptoms to which the name 'lupinosis' has been given. **1943** *N.Z. Jrnl. Agric.* LXVII. 83/3 There was considerable swelling about the head, and the skin came off the ears and the nose and also along the top of the head. These symptoms are identical with those described as occasionally occurring in cases of lupinosis. **1961** *Jrnl. Austral. Inst. Agric. Sci.* XXVII. 62/1 In 1880, 14,138 of a total number of 240,000 sheep in one district in Pomerania died of lupinosis. **1966** *Brit. Vet. Jrnl.* CXXII. 508 Lupinosis of sheep was shown to be due to the grazing of dead standing lupin roughage which had been exposed to rain after drying off in the spring. **1967** *Adv. Veterinary Sci.* XI. 86 Two distinct forms of injury are recognized in animals ingesting one or more of the several parts of lupines. The first of these is due to the pharmacologic activity of the bitter principle (a variable mixture of alkaloids) and has become variably known as lupine poisoning, alkaloidal poisoning, American lupinosis, or lupine madness. The second is an icteric disease caused by a hepatotoxin which was designated.. as 'ictrogen'... The disease was called 'lupinosis', or sometimes more specifically, 'European lupinosis'. **1972** *Mycologia* LXIV. 316 Typical signs of lupinosis were produced experimentally in Merino ewes fed either naturally infected lupines or pure cultures of the fungus [sc. *Phomopsis leptostromiformis*] on autoclaved white lupine seeds.

lupoid (ˈl(j)uːpɔɪd), *a.* *Med.* [f. LUPUS + -OID.] Of the nature of or resembling LUPUS.

1834 J. HOUGHTON in *Cycl. Pract. Med.* III. 173 An erysipelas, attacking the skin beside the lupoid patch. **1878** T. BRYANT *Pract. Surg.* I. 345 Ulceration of a lupoid character.

lupous (ˈl(j)uːpəs), *a.*[1] [f. L. *lup-us* wolf + -OUS.]

1. Resembling a wolf; wolfish, lupine.

1840 in MAUNDER *Sci. & Lit. Treas.*; and in later Dicts.

2. *Med.* Pertaining to or resembling LUPUS.

1883 PEPPER *Elem. Surg. Pathol.* 30 Lupous ulcers (vide Lupus). **1897** W. ANDERSON *Surg. Treat. Lupus* 12 His section has passed well below the lupous cell-growth.

Lups: see LUBISH *Obs.*

†**ˈlupulated,** *a.* *Obs.*[−0] [f. mod.L. *lupul-us* hop + -ATE + -ED[1].] Supplied with or containing hops.

1727 BAILEY vol. II, *Lupulated*, hopped.

lupulin (ˈl(j)uːpjʊlɪn). Also -ine. [f. mod.L. *lupul-us* hop + -IN.]

1. Small shining grains of a yellowish colour found under the scales of the calyx of the hop, first described by Dr. Ives of New York (*a* 1822).

1826 HENRY *Elem. Chem.* II. 332 *Lupulin*. This name has been given by Dr. Ives.. to an impalpable yellow powder, in which he believes the virtue of the hop to reside. **1870** *Eng. Mech.* 18 Mar. 651/3 A resinous waxy substance called 'lupuline'.

2. The bitter aromatic principle contained in the hop; also called *lupulite*.

1839 URE *Dict. Arts*, etc. 92 Lupuline is neither acid nor alkaline. **1893** LELAND *Mem.* II. 221, I.. substituted lupulin in the form of hops—that is to say, pale ale or 'bitter'.

3. *attrib.*

1829 TOGNO & DURAND tr. *Edwards & Vavasseur's Man. Mat. Med.* 144 Lupulin powder F.M. (Lupulin 1 part, sugar 2 parts)... Lupulin ointment [etc.]. **1839** URE *Dict. Arts* 101 In tearing them [hops] asunder, some of the lupuline powder is apt to be lost.

Hence **lupuˈlinic** *a.*, relating to LUPULIN; **lupuˈlinous** *a.* *Bot.* = LUPULINE *a.*

1845 COOLEY *Cycl. Pract. Receipts* (ed. 2) 571 Lupuline.. may be obtained by treating the aqueous extract of the yellow powder or lupulinic grains of the strobiles, along with a little lime [etc.]. **1866** *Treas. Bot.*, *Lupulinous*, resembling a head of hops. **1876** HARLEY *Mat. Med.* (ed. 6) 430 The lupulinic or hop glands. **1881** WHITEHEAD *Hops* 59 Hops are .. collections of imbricated scales, under which are yellowish, aromatic, lupulinic glands.

lupuline (ˈl(j)uːpjʊlaɪn), *a.* [ad. mod.L. *lupulīn-us*, f. *lupul-us* hop.] Resembling a bunch of hops.

1880 GRAY *Struct. Bot.* 419.

lupulite (ˈl(j)uːpjʊlaɪt). *Chem.* [f. mod.L. *lupulus* + -ITE.] = LUPULIN 2.

1839 in *Penny Cycl.* XIV. 202/2. **1842** BRANDE *Dict. Sci.* etc., *Lupulin*, the active principle of the hop; it is more properly called *lupulite*.

lupulone (ˈl(j)uːp(j)ʊləʊn). *Chem.* Also -on (-ɒn). [ad. G. *lupulon* (W. Wöllmer 1916, in *Ber. d. Deut. Chem. Ges.* XLIX. 781), f. mod.L. *lupulus*, used either as the specific epithet of the hop, *Humulus lupulus*, or †as a name for the genus *Humulus* (cf. L. *lupus* hop): see -ONE.] A bitter, crystalline, cyclic ketone, $C_{26}H_{38}O_4$, that

is an important constituent of hops and has strong antibiotic activity.

1919 *Chem. Abstr.* XIII. 495 The so-called α- and β-bitter acids..are more appropriately termed 'humulone' and 'lupulone'. **1937**, etc. [see HUMULONE]. **1967** *Chem. Rev.* LXVII. 26/1 While lupulone crystallizes from the soft resin of continental European hops, British and American hops yield cohumulone.

‖**lupus** ('l(j)uːpəs). [L. = wolf.]

†**1.** A wolf. *Obs.*

1583 *Leg. Bp. St. Androis* 6 God forwairns you..To ken the lupus in a lamb skyn lappit.

2. The wolf, a southern constellation situated to the south of Scorpio, and joined to Centaur.

1706 PHILLIPS (ed. Kersey), *Lupus*,..a Southern Constellation. **1839** *Penny Cycl.* XIV. 203/1 *Lupus* (the Wolf), one of the old constellations.

3. The pike or luce.

1706 PHILLIPS (ed. Kersey), *Lupus*,..the Pike, or Sturgeon, a Fish. **1854** BADHAM *Halieut.* 42 Sluggish mugils and the voracious lupus should be selected as easy to rear.

4. a. An ulcerous disease of the skin, sometimes erosive, sometimes hypertrophous.

[*c* **1400** *Lanfranc's Cirurg.* 208 Summen clepen it cancrum, & summen lupum.] **1590** BARROUGH *Meth. Physick* 331 Lupus is a malignant vlcer quickly consuming the neather parts; and it is very hungry like vnto a woolfe. **1693** *Blancard's Phys. Dict.* (ed. 2), *Lupus*, a sort of Canker in the Thighs and Legs. **1818–20** E. THOMPSON *Cullen's Nosol. Method.* (ed. 3) 333 Lupus: *Noli Me Tangere*. **1876** *Trans. Clinical Soc.* IX. 165 The comparatively rare..sebaceous Lupus or Bat's-wing disease. **1897** W. ANDERSON *Surg. Treat. Lupus* 1 Lupus is still as defiant as in the dark ages.

attrib. **1897** *Allbutt's Syst. Med.* IV. 685 The lupus patients treated by tuberculin. **1900** J. HUTCHINSON in *Archives Surg.* XI. 52 The lupus scar. *Ibid.* 53 The form of cancer..is very like lupus cancer. *Ibid.* 218 Lupus patches.

b. Used in various mod.L. (or sometimes Englished) collocations to designate various forms and manifestations of *lupus vulgaris* or to designate various other skin diseases: **lupus erythematosus** [tr. F. *lupus érythémateux* (Casenave 1850, in *Gaz. des Hôpitaux* 27 July 354/3): see ERYTHEMATOUS *a.*], a disease which is now considered to be manifested in two related forms, that of chronic discoid *lupus erythematosus*, which usu. involves only the skin and causes scaly red patches to form esp. on the face, and that of systemic *lupus erythematosus*, which produces a similar skin condition but involves the connective tissues generally and is attended by widespread symptoms of illness, esp. fever, malaise, and arthralgia; **lupus vulgaris**, a tuberculous disease of the skin, characterized by the formation of brownish nodules; = LUPUS 4.

1852 *Med. Times & Gaz.* XXVI. 141 (*heading*) Treatment of lupus exedens. **1857** *Lancet* 1 Aug. 116/2 (*heading*) Horrible deformity from lupus vorax. **1860** *Boston Med. & Surg. Jrnl.* LXII. 462 In lupus vulgaris it [*sc.* a liquid remedy] is seldom used, but in lupus erythematosus it may be considered a true specific. **1878** *Lancet* 13 July 35/1 (*heading*) Clincial lecture on disseminated follicular lupus. **1883** *Med. Chron.* (Baltimore) I. 271 (*heading*) Notes of a case of erythematous lupus complicated by the tubercular syphiloderm. **1947** *Sci. News* IV. 106 Tuberculosis can attack not only the lungs but also most other parts of the body—bones and joints, kidneys, glands, brain, and skin. In the last mentioned the disease is known under the Latin name of Lupus vulgaris. **1966** WRIGHT & SYMMERS *Systemic Path.* II. xxxix. 1547 In systemic lupus erythematosus the skin manifestations are merely part of a much more widespread disorder. **1974** PASSMORE & ROBSON *Compan. Med. Stud.* III. xxxi. 47/2 Lupus vulgaris most commonly begins in childhood.

lupyne, obs. form of LUPINE.

‖**lur**[1] (lʊə(r)). Also lure (l(j)ʊə(r)). Pl. lurer, lures, lurs. [Da., Norw., and Sw.] A Bronze Age musical instrument of the horn family found in Scandinavia.

1876 STAINER & BARRETT *Dict. Mus. Terms* 275/2 *Lures*, ancient Scandinavian trumpets. **1879** GROVE *Dict. Mus.* I. 56/2 There is a Swedish instrument of this kind called *Lure*. **1955** *Times* 24 May 5/5 The *lur* is still occasionally used in Denmark. **1961** C. W. MONK in A. Baines *Mus. Instruments* xi. 277 Some examples of the Danish Bronze Age *lurs*, cast in the shape of a mammoth tusk, have mouthpieces astonishingly like modern melodic brass instruments. **1968** G. JONES *Hist. Vikings* I. i. 18 The long, slender, gracefully curved lurs or trumpets. **1970** BRAY & TRUMP *Dict. Archaeol.* 136/1 Lurer come from the peatbogs of Denmark and are almost invariably found in pairs.

Lur[2] (lʊə(r)). A member of an aboriginal people inhabiting Luristan in western Iran. Chiefly in *pl.*

1845 *Encycl. Metrop.* XXIII. 272/2 The Lurs are divided into the Pish-kúh..and Pusht kúh. **1909** *Daily Chron.* 18 Feb. 5/1 Colonel Bell formed a favourable opinion of the Lurs as a whole. **1965** B. SWEET-ESCOTT *Baker St. Irreg.* iii. 89 Most of the Persian troops had not been paid for several weeks, and..when the surrender had taken place.., they had promptly sold their rifles to the neighbouring Lurs and Kurds.

lura ('lʊərə). *Anat.* [mod.L. use of L. *lūra* mouth of a bag or wine-skin.] 'The contracted foramen of the infundibulum of the brain.' Hence '**lural** *a.*, pertaining to the lura (*Cent. Dict.*).

1885 WILDER in *N. Y. Med. Jrnl.* 23 Mar. 328 (*Cent.*) The removal of the hypophysis leaves the orifice which I have called lura.

†**lurcate**, *v. Obs.*—⁰ [f. L. *lurcāt-*, ppl. stem of *lurcāre*, *-ārī*.] *intr.* To eat ravenously. Hence **lur'cation**.

1623 COCKERAM, *Lurcate*. **1644** *Vindex Anglicus* 6 (in list of 'ink-horn' terms). **1661** BLOUNT *Glossogr.* (ed. 2), *Lurcation*,..a greedy eating or gluttonizing.

lurch (lɜːtʃ), *sb.*[1] Also 6–7 **lurche, lurtch**. [a. F. *lourche* (erroneously written *l'ourche*) a game resembling backgammon, played in the 16th c.; also used as adj. in the phr. *demeurer lourche*, app. primarily to incur a 'lurch' (see 2 below) in this game, hence *fig.* to be discomfited or disappointed.

Obviously related in some way to this Fr. word are early and dial. mod.G. *lortsch, lurtsch, lorz, lurz*, the name of a game, also as adj. in *lurz werden*, a phrase in various games, expressing the failure to achieve some object aimed at; MHG. *lorz, lurz* (also *lerz*), mod.Ger. dial. *lurz, lurtsch* left (hand), wrong, whence MDu. *loorts, loyrtz, luers* left; MHG. *lürzen* (= OE. *belyrtan* BELIRT *v.*) to deceive, whence MDu. *lordsen*. The most plausible supposition with regard to the relation between these words is that the MHG. *lurz* left, wrong, or its derivative *lurtsch* (cf. *linksch* from *link*), was adopted into Fr. as a gaming term (*lourche* adj.), and that *lourche* sb. as the name of a game was developed from the adj. As a name for the game, the Ger. word is probably a readoption from Fr.]

†**1.** A game, no longer known, supposed to have resembled backgammon. *Obs.*

1611 COTGR., *Lourche*, the game called Lurche. **1653** URQUHART *Rabelais* I. xxii. 94 There he played..At the lurch. **1656** EARL MONM. tr. *Boccalini's Advts. fr. Parnass.* I. xli. (1674) 57 He might account business his pastime..instead of Picquet or Lurch. *a* **1693** *Urquhart's Rabelais* III. xii. 98 My Mind was only running upon the lurch and tricktrack.

2. Used in various games to denote a certain concluding state of the score, in which one player is enormously ahead of the other; often, a 'maiden set' or love-game, i.e. a game or set of games in which the loser scores nothing; at cribbage, a game in which the winner scores 61 before the loser has scored 31; in whist, a treble. *to save the lurch*: in whist, to prevent one's adversary from scoring a treble. Now *rare* (? or *Obs.*).

1598 FLORIO, *Marcio*, a lurch or maiden set at any game. **1606** DEKKER *Sev. Sins* IV. (Arb.) 32 What by Betting, Lurches, Rubbers and such tricks, they neuer tooke care for a good daies worke afterwards. **1608** —— *Belman Lond.* F 3, Whose Inne is a Bowling Alley, whose bookes are bowles, and whose law cases are lurches and rubbers. **1653** URQUHART *Rabelais* II. xii, By two of my table-men in the corner-point I have gained the lurch. **1674** *Gouldman's Lat. Dict.* (ed. 3) 1, A lurch, *duplex palma, facilis victoria*. **1742** HOYLE *Whist* i. 13 A Probability either of saving your Lurch, or winning the Game. **1745** *Gentl. Mag.* 606 A King!—we're up—I vow I fear'd a lurch. **1784** H. WALPOLE *Let.* 14 Aug. (1858) VIII. 495 Lady Blandford has cried her eyes out on losing a lurch. **1860** *Bohn's Handbk. Games* III. 83 The game [long whist] consists of ten points; when no points are marked by the losing partners, it is treble, and reckons three points;..This is called a lurch. **1876** 'CAPT. CRAWLEY' *Card Players' Man.* 18 *Lurch* (at Long Whist), not saving the double. *Ibid.* 128 [*Cribbage*] A lurch—scoring the whole sixty-one before your adversary has scored thirty-one—is equivalent to a double game. **1897** *Encycl. Sport* I. 129/2 (Bowls) *Lurch game*, a game in which one side has scored five before the other has scored one.

3. †**a.** A discomfiture. *Obs.*

1584 LODGE *Alarum* C ij b, If heereafter thou fall into the lyke lurch,..so then I will accompt of thee as a reprobate. *c* **1600** *Peele's Jests* (*c* 1620) 20 The Tapster hauing many of these lurches, fell to decay. **1608** ARMIN *Nest Ninn.* D b, Often such forwarde deedes, meete with backward lurches. **1679** *Heart & Right Soveraign* 119 The Italian out-wits the Jew in his part, and the lurch befalls the English side.

†**b.** *to give* (a person) *the lurch*: to discomfit, get the better of. *Obs.*

1598 E. GUILPIN *Skial.* (1878) 25 Gellia intic'd her good-man to the Citty, And often threatneth to giue him the lurch. ? *c* **1600** *Bride's Buriall* 38 in *Roxb. Ball.* (1871) I. 248 Faire Hellens face gaue Grecian Dames the lurch. **1626** BRETON *Pasquil's Mad-cap* (Grosart) 6/2 How ere his wit may giue the foole the lurch, He is not fit to gouerne in the Church.

†**c.** *to have* (*take*) *on* (*in, at*) *the lurch*: to have or take (a person) at a disadvantage. *Obs.*

1591 GREENE *Disc. Coosnage* (1592) 7 There was fourtie to one on my side, and ile haue you on the lurch anon. **1601** WEEVER *Mirr. Mart.* B viij b, Shee..Sels lyes for nothing, nothing for too much; Faith for three farthings, t'haue thee in the lurch. **1615** T. ADAMS *Black Devil* 74 Thus the great Parasite of the soule that heretofore..flatterd this wretch with the paucity of his Sinnes, now takes him in the lurch, and over-reckons him. **1649** G. DANIEL *Trinarch., Hen. IV*, clx, The Sage Span of a Circle tooke the Starres at Lurch, To Conspire Storme. **1692** D'URFEY *Pills* (1719) V. 3 He took me in the lurch.

†**d.** *in a person's lurch*: in his power. *Obs.*

1607 R. C[AREW] tr. *Estienne's World of Wonders* 195 Hauing him in his lurch and at his lure. **1641** J. SHUTE *Sarah & Hagar* (1649) 93 They lose their authority when they come within the lurch of their servants. **1643** T. GOODWIN *Trial Christian's Growth* 127 David, when he had Saul in his lurch, might as easily have cut off his head.

e. *to leave in the lurch*: to leave in adverse circumstances without assistance; to leave in a position of unexpected difficulty.

Cf. the somewhat earlier phr. *to leave in the lash* (see LASH *sb.*[1] 4).

1596 NASHE *Saffron Walden* 119 Whom..he also procured to be equally bound with him for his new cousens apparence to the law, which he neuer did, but left both of them in the lurtch for him. **1600** HOLLAND *Livy* 222 The Volscians seeing themselves abandoned and left in the lurch by them,..quit the campe and field. **1663** BUTLER *Hud.* I. iii. 764 And though th' art of a diff'rent Church, I will not leave thee in the lurch. **1711** ADDISON *Spect.* No. 119 ¶6 If the Country Gentlemen get into it they will certainly be left in the lurch. *a* **1716** SOUTH *Serm.* (1842) I. 345 In transubstantiation, where accidents are left in the lurch by their proper subject. **1873** E. FITZGERALD *Lett.* (1889) I. 357 My Eyes have been leaving me in the lurch again. **1879** BROWNING *Martin Relph* 66 He has left his sweetheart here in the lurch.

†**4.** A cheat, swindle. *Obs.*

(In our quots. the earliest recorded use.)

1533 J. HEYWOOD *Pardoner & Friar* (1830) B iv, No more of this wranglyng in my chyrch, I shrewe your hartys bothe for this lurche. *a* **1550** *Image Hypocr.* I. in *Skelton's Wks.* (1843) II. 432/2 They blered hym with a lurche. **1604** T. M. *Black Bk.* E iv, I giue and bequeath to thee..All such Lurches, Gripes, and Squeezes, as may bee wrung out by the fist of extortion. **1611** BADLEY in *Coryat's Crudities, Panegyr. Verses*, Briefly, for triall of a religious lurch Thou nimbd'st an image out of Brixias Church. ? **1616** CHAPMAN *Hymn to Hermes* 63 I'le have a scape, as well as he a serch, And over take him with a greater lurch.

lurch (lɜːtʃ), *sb.*[2] [f. LURCH *v.*[1]]

†**1.** An opportunity of 'lurching' or outstripping others in eating. (Cf. LURCH *v.*[1] 2.) *Obs.*

1568 NORTH *Gueuara's Diall Pr.* IV. vii. 125 b, And if perhaps a courtier come late, and the table be all ready full, and the lurch out, yet he will not be ashamed to eat his meat neuertheles. For albee it hee can not bee placed at his ease yet..rather than fayle he will syt of half a buttock.

2. *to lie at* (*on, upon the*) *lurch*: to lie concealed; to be in a lurking place; to lie in wait. *lit.* and *fig.*

1578 O. ROYDON in *T. Proctor's Gorg. Gallery, Pref. Verses*, The drowsie Drones doo neuer take such toyle, But lye at lurch, like men of Momus minde. **1589** R. ROBINSON *Gold. Mirr.* (Chetham Soc.) 25 Fained Friendship now layes on lurtch, his faithful friend to spil. **1621** BURTON *Anat. Mel.* Democr. to Rdr. (1651) 29 Another Epicurean company, lying at lurch as so many vultures, watching for a prey of Church goods. **16..** *Paradox* xvii. in *Third Collect. Poems* (1689) 25 Or H——, that lyes upon the Lurch, Who left the Charters, shall restore the Church. **1762** GOLDSM. *Nash* Wks. (Globe) 548/2 He chiefly laboured to be thought a sayer of good things; and by frequent attempts was now and then successful, for he ever lay upon the lurch. **1860** J. P. KENNEDY *W. Wirt* I. v. 68 The enemy of human happiness, always lying at lurch to make prey of the young.

lurch (lɜːtʃ), *sb.*[3] [Of obscure origin.

The word app. occurs as the second element of *lee-larches* in the first quot. below, for which later nautical and other dicts. substitute *lee-lurches*. If *lee-larches* in Falconer be not a misprint for *-lurches*, it may represent an altered pronunciation of the older *lee-latch*, in the word of command 'have a care of the lee-latch', i.e. 'look that the ship does not go to leeward of her course' (*Milit. & Sea Dict.* 1711). It seems possible that *lurch* originated in the compound *lee-lurch*, an alteration (by association with LURCH *sb.*[1] 3) of *lee-larch* for *lee-latch*, which prob. contains LATCH *sb.*[2], LETCH *sb.*[2] inclination (for the sense development cf. the etymological note on LIST *sb.*[5]).]

1. (Orig. *Naut.*) A sudden leaning over to one side, as of a ship, a person staggering, etc. Also, a gait characterized by such movements. Phr. *to give a lurch*.

[**1769** FALCONER *Dict. Marine*, *Lee-larches*, the sudden and violent rolls which a ship often takes to leeward in a high sea.] **1819** BYRON *Juan* II. xix, Here the ship gave a lurch, and he grew sea-sick. **1843** BETHUNE *Sc. Fireside Stor.* 35 The heavy *lurch*, told too plainly what he had been about. **1848** J. GRANT *Adv. Aide-de-C.* I. iv. 47 As the carriage swayed from side to side, I expected at every lurch, that the whole party would be upset. **1863** BARING-GOULD *Iceland* 266 They got the vessel afloat, and with a lurch, she ran out to sea. **1876** BESANT & RICE *Gold. Butterfly* i, There was the slightest possible lurch in their walk. **1901** *Speaker* 6 Apr. 10/2 We were soon clattering over cobbled streets with an ample lurch at intervals.

2. *U.S.* A propensity, penchant, leaning.

1854 MAR. CUMMINS *Lamplighter* xv. 92 She has a nateral lurch for it [learning], and it comes easy to her. **1878** A. PHELPS in E. S. Phelps *Memoir* (1891) 219, I think I got from Professor Stuart and Albert Barnes, both of whom were penurious letter-writers, a lurch adverse to such work.

lurch (lɜːtʃ), *v.*[1] [app. a variant of LURK *v.* The relation between the two forms is obscure; it is not analogous to that between *birch* and *birk*, *church* and *kirk*, *beseech* and *seek*, etc., where the OE. form has umlaut. The development of sense somewhat resembles that of FORESTALL *v.*, but has perh. been influenced by LURCH *sb.*[1] or *v.*[2]]

†**1.** *intr.* To remain in or about a place furtively or secretly, esp. with evil design. (Cf. FORESTALL *v.* 1.) Also, ? to avoid company, ? to sulk. *Obs.*

c **1420** *Chron. Vilod.* 1377 Þen come þe sexsten to serche þe chirche,..& sey hem in an hyron þere so lorche. **1570** LEVINS *Manip.* 190/33 To Lurche, *latitare*. **1575** R. B. *Apius & Virginia* E j b, Then gallope to see where her father doth

lurche. **1598** SHAKS. *Merry W.* II. ii. 26, I my selfe..hiding mine honor in my necessity, am faine to shuffle, to hedge, and to lurch. **1589** PUTTENHAM *Eng. Poesie* III. xix. (Arb.) 220 For when he is merry, she lurcheth and she loures, When he is sad she singes, or laughes it out by houres. **1630** J. TAYLOR (Water P.) *Wks.* II. 117/1 There's a crue of Thieues that prie and lurch, And steale and take the liuings of the Church. **1632** BROME *Novella* II. ii, I'le turne you off ..To lurch i' th' night betwixt eleaven and two To rob and drown for prey. *a* **1677** BARROW *Serm.* xxviii. Wks. 1687 I. 376 Not at least to be a Fox or a Wolf; either cunningly lurching, or violently ravening for prey. **1692** R. L'ESTRANGE *Fables* xii. 12 While the One was upon Wing, the Other stood Lurching upon the Ground, and flew away with the Fish. **1727** SOMERVILLE *Dainty new Ballad* 14 For Love, that little urchin About this widow lurching, Had slily fix'd his dart. **1749** FIELDING *Tom Jones* VI. x, The son of a whore came lurching about the house. **1790** POTTER *Dict. Cant* (1795), *Lurch*, to lay by, to sneak, to hang on.

b. Of greyhounds: (See quot. 1897).

1824 BYRON *Juan* XVI. lxxx, Whose hounds ne'er err'd, nor greyhounds deign'd to lurch. **1856** 'STONEHENGE' *Brit. Sports* I. III. ii. §3 (ed. 2) 155 [Greyhounds.] Remember that too much knowledge or cleverness soon leads to lurching. **1897** *Encycl. Sport* I. 210/1 *Lurching*, of the greyhound; running cunning, and leaving the most part of the work to its opponent.

2. *trans.* To get the start of (a person) so as to prevent him from obtaining a fair share of food, profit, etc. In later use, to defraud, cheat, rob. *Obs.* exc. *arch.*

1530 PALSGR. 616/1, I lurtche, as one dothe his felowes at meate with eatynge to hastyly, *je briffe.* Syt nat at his messe, for he wyll lurtche you than. **1568** ABP. PARKER *Corr.* (Parker Soc.) 337, I pray your honour be a mean that Jugge only may have the preferment of this edition; for if any other should lurch him to steal from him these copies, he were a great loser. **1573** TUSSER *Husb.* xxiii. (1878) 61 Yoong colts with thy wennels together go serue, least lurched by others they happen to sterue. **1592** GREENE *Def. Conny Catch.* (1859) 18 Was not this an old Cony catcher..that could lurtch a poore Conny of so many thousands at one time? **1604** MIDDLETON *Father Hubburd's Tales* Wks. (Bullen) VIII. 94 Where like villanous cheating bowlers, they lurched me of two of my best limbs. **1607** SHAKS. *Cor.* II. ii. 105 And in the brunt of seuenteene Battailes since, He lurcht all Swords of the Garland. **1609** B. JONSON *Sil. Wom.* v. iv, You haue lurch'd your friends of the better halfe of the garland. **1810** SCOTT *Lady of L.* VI. v, And 'tis right of his office poor laymen to lurch, Who infringe the domains of our good Mother Church.

†**3.** To be beforehand in securing (something); to consume (food) hastily so that others cannot have their share; to engross, monopolize (commodities); in later use, to get hold of by stealth, pilfer, filch, steal. (Cf. FORESTALL *v.* 2.) *Obs.*

c **1550** *Disc. Common Weal Eng.* (1893) 32 Ye lurched some of the coyne as sone as euer ye perceived the price of that to be enhaunced. **1568** V. SKINNER *Montanus' Inquisition* 39 b, Some of ye meat which he had lurched from the prisoners. **1587** TURBERV. *Trag. T.* (1837) 23 Her christall eyes had lurcht his yielding heart. **1599** *Broughton's Let.* viii. 28 Bel his priests priuily lurched the viands, which were supposed to be deuoured by the Idoll. **1613** F. ROBARTS *Revel. Gosp.* Title-p., The sacred offering broyles: the eagle spies, A gob she lurch'd, and to her young she flies. **1622** S. WARD *Christ All in All* (1627) 31 Oh how difficult is this for vs, not to lurch some part of the praise. **1625** BACON *Ess., Building* (Arb.) 548 Too farre off from great Cities, which may hinder Businesse; Or too neare them, which Lurcheth all Prouisions, and maketh euery Thing deare. **1630** *R. Johnson's Kingd. & Commw.* To Rdr. A ij, How much hath that..Plagiarie..closely lurcht out of this Author? **1642** VICARS *God in Mount* (1644) 39 Clergy-trash, who lay lurking in the Bee-hives of the Church, and lurching away the sweet honey from the laborious Bees. **1660** MILTON *Free Commw.* Wks. 1738 I. 595 If we can keep us from the fond Conceit..put lately into many Mens heads by some one or other suttly driving on under that notion his own ambitious ends to lurch a Crown.

†**b.** *absol. Obs.*

1593 NASHE *Christ's T.* (1613) 66 The Sonne could scarce refraine from biting out his Fathers throate-boule, when he saw him swallow downe a bit that he died for. The Mother lurcht from them both. **1620** MIDDLETON *Chaste Maid* III. ii, See how they lurch at the lower end. **1640** BP. HALL *Chr. Moder.* I. xi. 104 Wherein had he been a thiefe, if he had not ..meant to lurch out of the common Treasury?

4. To catch (rabbits) by means of lurchers.

1727 MATHER *Yng. Man's Companion* 12 He lurches Conies. [Given as an example of the word.] **1798** [see LURCHING *vbl. sb.*^{1} 2].

5. *Comb.*: †**lurch-church** (see quot.); †**lurch-line**, 'the line of a fowling-net, by which it was pulled over to enclose the birds' (Nares); †**lurch-man** (*nonce-wd.*), a pilferer.

1578 *Mirr. Mag., Harold* xii, Let hym go beate the bushe, I and my men to the lurche line will steale, And pluck the Net. **1603** BRETON *Mad World* (Grosart) 12/2 These may rather be called lurch-men then Church-men, who as they are not troubled with much learning, so they have no more honesty, then they may well away withall. *c* **1700** DE LA PRYME *Hist. Holy Trin. Ch. Hull* 321 (MS.), When a man that's in orders go's voluntarily and preaches in a Church to which he was never..instituted..our law gives him no title to the tithes but calls him a Lurch Church.

lurch (lɜːtʃ), *v.*^{2} [f. LURCH *sb.*^{1}]

1. *trans.* To beat, in various games of skill, sometimes by a specified number or proportion of points. (See LURCH *sb.*^{1} 2.)

c **1350** [implied in LURCHING *vbl. sb.*^{2}]. **1678** BUTLER *Hud.* III. ii. 1062 Your old foe, the hangman, Was like to lurch you at Back-gammon. *a* **1700** B. E. *Dict. Cant. Crew, Lurched*, beaten at any Game. **1760** FOOTE *Minor* I. Wks. 1799 I. 241 Lurch me at four, but I was mark'd to the top of your trick, by the baron, my dear. **1763** HOYLE *Piquet* 150 It is about two to one that the Eldest-hand does not lurch the Younger-hand. **1785** GROSE *Dict. Vulgar Tongue* s.v. *Lurch*, Those who lose a game of whist without scoring five are said to be lurched. **1830** R. HARDIE *Hoyle made Familiar* 61 [Cassino.] Lurched, is when your adversary has won the game, before you have gained six points.

b. *fig.* To defeat. ? *Obs.*

a **1716** SOUTH *Serm.* (1744) XI. 289 He will be lurched in that that admits of no after-game or reparation. **1829** *Examiner* 354/2 Chancery Reform was lurched the week before last.

2. To leave in the lurch, disappoint, deceive. ? *Obs.*

a **1651** C. LOVE in Spurgeon *Treas. Dav.* Ps. lxii. 10 How many have riches served as Absalom's mule served her master, whom she lurched, and left..hanging. **1692** SOUTH *Serm.* (1697) I. 29 Putting such an emptiness in them, as should so quickly fail and lurch the expectation. **1727** BAILEY vol. II, *Lurching*, leaving a Person under some embarrassment. **1791** WOLCOT (P. Pindar) *Apol. for Kings* Moral, Wks. 1816 II. 246 This little anecdote doth plainly show That ignorance, a king too often lurches. **1809** E. S. BARRETT *Setting Sun* II. 109 The Hon. Charles James Fox, ..having been lurched by lord North, turned his face to Whiggism. **1810** *Sporting Mag.* XXXVI. 68 They are foiled by fortune, who hath lurched generals in her time.

lurch (lɜːtʃ), *v.*^{3} (Orig. *Naut.*) [f. LURCH *sb.*^{3}]

1. *intr.* Of a ship, etc.: To make a lurch; to lean suddenly over to one side; to move with lurches.

1833 MARRYAT *P. Simple* xv, We heeled over so much when we lurched, that the guns were wholly supported by the breechings and tackles. **1845** R. COBBOLD *Marg. Catchpole* xx. II. 50 The boat lurched through the breakers like a log. **1866** NEALE *Sequences & Hymns* 37 Tempests of temptations Made our vessel lurch and dip. **1902** *Speaker* 9 Sept. 601/1 It lurches up and down like a ship at sea.

fig. **1858** CARLYLE *Fredk. Gt.* v. ii. (1872) II. 76 The Kaiser's Imperial Ostend East-India Company..made Europe lurch from side to side in a terrific manner.

2. To move suddenly, unsteadily, and without purpose in any direction, as, e.g. a person staggering.

1851 THACKERAY *Humourists* v. (1858) 241 Where the tipsy trainband-man is lurching against the post. **1851** D. G. MITCHELL *Fresh Gleanings* 16 My London beaver..lurched over and fell among them. **1870** E. PEACOCK *Ralf Skirl.* I. 263 The dogs lurched violently forward. **1879** HOWELLS *L. Aroostook* ii. 12 These men lurched in their gait with an uncouth heaviness.

lurcher^1 ('lɜːtʃə(r)). Also 6 **lorcher**, 8 **lircher**. [f. LURCH *v.*^{1} + -ER^1. In early Dicts. often used to render L. *lurco* glutton, with which it has no etymological connexion.]

†**1.** One who 'lurches' (see LURCH *v.*^{1} 2) or forestalls others of their fair share of food; hence, a glutton. *Obs.*

[*c* **1440**: see LURKER^1 3.] **1530** PALSGR. 241/1 Lurcher an exceeding eater, *galiffre. Ibid.* 500/2 Se howe he crammeth in his meate lyke a lurcher. **1591** LYLY *Endimion* II. ii, Is not loue a lurcher, that taketh mens stomacks away that they cannot eate, their Spleen that they cannot laugh [etc.]. **1608** MIDDLETON *Mad World* v. i. Wks. (Dyce) II. 407 Take heed of a lurcher, he cuts deep, he will eat up all from you. **1616** BOYS *Wks.* (1629) 821 The Mass-priests are gross lurchers at the Lord's Table.

2. One who pilfers or filches in a mean fashion; a petty thief, swindler, rogue.

1528 ROY *Rede me* (Arb.) 98 Ye but thorowe falce lorchers And vnthryfty abbey lobbers To povre folcke lytell they a forde. **1601** HOLLAND *Pliny* I. 459 No seale will serue to make sure either such lurchers themselues for filching, or keep the very locks and keies safe. **1705** PENN in *Pa. Hist. Soc. Mem.* X. 20 To be treated as a lurcher of the people.. is more..than any poor mortal could bear. **1714** GAY *Trivia* III. 64 Swift from his Prey the scudding Lurcher flies. **1831** TRELAWNEY *Adv. Younger Son* I. 72 This Caledonian lurcher..had three or four dozen of shirts, with every one a different mark. **1891** *Morn. Advert.* 3 Apr. (Farmer), It was quite time that the honest and respectable drivers sat down on the lurchers once and for all.

3. One who loiters or lies hidden in a suspicious manner; a spy.

1706 PHILLIPS (ed. Kersey), *Lurcher*, one that lies upon the Lurch or upon the Catch. **1760–72** H. BROOKE *Fool of Qual.* (1792) I. 199 Some..with outward bravade,..went searching along the walls and behind the posts for some lurcher. **1774** FOOTE *Cozeners* II. Wks. 1799 II. 172, I thought that I had detected love, that sly lurcher, lurking under the mask. **1814** SCOTT *Ld. of Isles* v. xxii, Our Lord may choose the rack should teach To this young lurcher use of speech. **1894** *Daily News* 7 June 2/7 The prisoner..said prosecutor was a lurcher, and was only sent out as a decoy.

4. A cross-bred dog, properly between the sheepdog or collie and the greyhound; largely used by poachers for catching hares and rabbits.

1668 WILKINS *Real Char.* II. v. 161 Greater Beasts; Greyhounds. Lesser Beasts; Lurchers. **1674** N. FAIRFAX *Bulk & Selv.* To Rdr., Why should the ears of all..be dinn'd..as if the whole world besides were all Weasils and Poulcats, vermine and Lurchers? **1675** *Lond. Gaz.* No. 1053/4 Lost.., a Pied Dog..somewhat shap't like a Lurcher. **1688** R. HOLME *Armoury* II. 185/1 The Tumbler, or Lurcher is..in shape like the Grey-hound. **1741** *Compl. Fam.-Piece* II. i. 304 The Lircher is a kind of Dog much like a Mungril Greyhound. **1819** SCOTT *Ivanhoe* i, A ragged wolfish-looking dog, a sort of lurcher, half mastiff, half greyhound. **1894** *Field* 9 June 813/2 The usual lurcher is between the greyhound and collie; they cross well, and the speed of one is combined with the sagacity of the other.

b. *slang.* A bumbailiff.

1785 GROSE *Dict. Vulg. Tongue* s.v., A lurcher of the law, a bum-bailiff, or his setter. **1839** W. H. AINSWORTH *Jack Sheppard* ii, 'But, where are the lurchers?' 'Who?' asked Wood. 'The traps!' replied a bystander.

'lurcher^2. *rare.* [f. LURCH *v.*^{3} + -ER^1.] One who lurches from side to side.

1878 BESANT & RICE *Celia's Arb.* I. ii. 164 The most lop-sided and lurcher-like of rustics was bound to become perpendicular.

'lurching, *vbl. sb.*^{1} [f. LURCH *v.*^{1} + -ING^1.] The action of LURCH *v.*^{1}

1. †**a.** The forestalling of others of their food (*obs.*). **b.** Pilfering, stealing.

1573 TUSSER *Husb.* lxxxviii. (1878) 178 No lurching, no snatching, no striuing at all, lest one go without and another haue all. **1611** COTGR., *Fortraction*, a lurching, purloyning; withdrawing. **1616** BOYS *Wks.* (1629) 844 Is not..the denying of the cup a notorious lurching at the Lord's Table?

2. The capturing of rabbits by means of lurchers.

1798 *Sporting Mag.* XII. 99 There are many ways of killing rabbits, of which lurching is in most common use.

3. *Comb.*: †**lurching-place**, a lurking place.

a **1656** USSHER *Ann.* VI. (1658) 573 There were so many lurching places, by reason of which, they could easily escape when assaulted.

'lurching, *vbl. sb.*^{2} [f. LURCH *v.*^{2} + -ING^1.] The gaining of a 'lurch' at play, *esp.* whist, piquet, etc.

c **1350** *MS. Reg.* 13 A. xviii. fol. 158 Lurchyng [given as one of two modes of winning at the 'long game' at tables, the other being 'lympoldyng']. **1763** HOYLE *Piquet* 125 The lurching of your Adversary..is so material that [etc.]. **1767** *Connoisseur* No. 60 (ed. 5) II. 192 A school for Whist would [teach] lurching,..finessing,..and getting the odd trick.

'lurching, *vbl. sb.*^{3} [f. LURCH *v.*^{3} + -ING^1.] The action of LURCH *v.*^{3}

1852 PFEIFFER *Journ. Iceland* 53 The lurching and pitching of the ship had covered it with traces of everything which had been on the table. **1880** EM. MARSHALL *Troub. Times* III. 244, I had a sudden wrench by the lurching of my horse.

'lurching, *ppl. a.*^{1} [f. LURCH *v.*^{1} + -ING^2.]

†**1.** Given to or characterized by forestalling others at meals, gluttonous. Also, pilfering. *Obs.*

1577 STANYHURST *Descr. Irel.* Ep. Ded. in *Holinshed*, Loath also in lurching wise to forstall anie man his travell, I was contented to leave them thumping in the forge, and quietlie repair to my usuall studies. **1619** DENISON *Heavenly Banq.* 127 This condemnes that lurching sacrifice, wherein oft times the Priest giues none to others, but retains al to himself. **1620** VENNER *Via Recta* viii. 167 All strange and confused sauces..abandon, as..acceptable onely to lurching and deuouring Belly-gods. **1655** tr. *Com. Hist. Francion* x. 23 Ah these are close lurching Companions. These are the Nimmers who would rob me of all my moveables.

2. Of a dog (see LURCH *v.*^{1} 1, 1 b, 4; the sense in the quots. is uncertain).

1613 *Uncasing of Machivil's Instr.* 25 A lurching Dog will range about the fields. **1824** SCOTT *Redgauntlet* let. x, My friend Benjie's lurching attendant..began to cock his tail. **1871** *Daily News* 5 Jan., A lurching cur who gnawed something under a waggon.

3. Lurking, 'sneaking'.

1661 K. W. *Conf. Charac., A Baily* (1860) 41 The wals should discover his lerching knavery. **1865** S. EVANS *Bro. Fabian* 5 A lurching, lean-lipped, lollardizing loon.

'lurching, *ppl. a.*^{2} [f. LURCH *v.*^{2} + -ING^2.] In senses of LURCH *v.*^{2} **a.** That wins a 'lurch' at a game. **b.** Given to deceiving, perfidious.

1604 T. M. *Black Bk.* in *Middleton's Wks.* (Bullen) VIII. 30 In came I with a lurching cast [of the dice], and made them all swear round again. **1728** VANBR. & CIBBER *Prov. Husb.* I. i. 17 A married Woman may..throw a familiar Levant upon some sharp lurching Man of Quality.

'lurching, *ppl. a.*^{3} [f. LURCH *v.*^{3} + -ING^2.] That lurches or leans suddenly over.

1884 'HUGH CONWAY' *Called Back* 12 A staggering, uncertain, lurching kind of step. **1892** G. LASCELLES *Falconry* (Badm. Libr.) 225 Whilst the falcons are fine-tempered generous birds,..the hawks are shifting, lurching fliers. **1895** *Daily News* 18 Dec. 5/4 The lurching movement and recoil of the ship prevented him. **1901** *Blackw. Mag.* June 751/2 The Devons tramp after over the lurching pontoon.

Hence **'lurchingly** *adv.*

1837 CARLYLE *Fr. Rev.* II. IV. v, It lumbers along, lurchingly with stress, at a snail's pace. **1851** H. MELVILLE *Whale* xxx. 142 Ahab lurchingly paced the planks.

lurck(e, obs. form of LURK.

lurdan ('lɜːdən), *sb.* and *a. Obs.* exc. *arch.* Also α. 4 **lourdeine**, 4–5 **lordein**, 4–6 **lordeyn(e**, **lurdayne**, **-eyn(e**, 4–6, 9 **lurdane**, 4, 7 **lordan**, 4, 7, 9 **lourdan**, 4–8 **lurden**, 5 **lorden**, 5–6 **lurdayn**, **lordayne**, 5–8 **lordane**, 6 **lurdon**, **lordenne**, **lourdaine**, **-yne**, 6–7 **lurdein(e**, **lourdan(e**, **-en**, 7 **lurdain(e**, **lur-daine**, **lourdin**, **lordant**, 9 *Sc.* **lordoun**. β. 6 **Lorde Dane**, **-Dene**, **lor-Dane**, 7 **Lord-Dane**, **Lur-Dane**. [a. OF. *lourdin*, f. *lourd* heavy: see LOURD.

The pseudo-etymology in quot. 1529 has affected the spelling of the word in many later examples.]

A. *sb.* A general term of opprobrium, reproach, or abuse, implying either dullness and

incapacity, or idleness and rascality; a sluggard, vagabond, 'loafer'. (Cf. FEVER-LURDEN.)

a **1300** *Cursor M.* 13660 'Herd yee þis lurdan,' coth þai, 'Hu he wald lere vs nu vr lai.' *c* **1330** R. BRUNNE *Chron.* (1810) 9 Sibriht þat schrew as a lordan [AF. *lers*] gan lusk, A suynhird smote he to dede vnder a thorn busk. **1375** BARBOUR *Bruce* IV. 108 For thar within wes a tratour, A fals lurdane, ane losengeour. *c* **1440** *Gesta Rom.* xxxvi. 145 (Harl. MS.) Sum of hem beþe thevis & some lurdaynes. **1529** RASTELL *Pastyme* (1811) 131 These Danys before were so proud, y[t] they kept the husbondmen lyke vyleyns;..the husbondmen called them Lorde Dane, which word now we use in obprobrye, callynge hym y[t] we rebuke Lurdayn. **1603** H. CROSSE *Vertues Commw.* (1878) 126 Some lur-daines that haue wealth left by their ancestors, holde it a poynt of wisedome to rest theyr idle limmes and spare their bodies. **1641** MILTON *Reform.* II. Wks. 1851 III. 44 Lourdan, quoth the Philosopher, thy folly is as great as thy filth. **1723** RAMSAY *Fair Assembly* xviii, These lurdanes came just in my light. **1820** SCOTT *Abbot* iv, I found the careless lurdane feeding him with unwashed flesh, and she an eyass. **1865** KINGSLEY *Herew.* v, Next to them by chance sat a great lourdan of a Dane.

Comb. **1607** R. C[AREW] tr. *Estienne's World of Wonders* 14 Lurden-like loutishnesse.

b. *rarely* applied to a woman.

1513 DOUGLAS *Æneis* VI. viii. 82 That strang lurdane [Helen]..quham weill ȝe ken.

¶ **c.** With allusion to the supposed etymology: see quot. 1529 above.

1589 *Mar Martine* 5 To make new upstart Jacks Lor-Danes, with coine to cram their chests. ? **1690** *Consid. Raising Money* 27 This [taxation] is a way to bring a Lord-Dane into every one of our Families.

B. *adj.* Worthless, ill-bred, lazy.

c **1375** *Sc. Leg. Saints* xxxvi. (*Baptista*) 632 ȝet he, þat of sic uertu wes, wes gefine til a lurdan las. **1582** MUNDAY *Eng. Rom. Life* iv. 29 Whereby the lazie lurden Friers that keepe the Church gettes more ritches. **1791** J. LEARMONT *Poems* 32 Lurdane Sloth O'ercoups them a' mang savage swarms O' Hun and Goth. **1819** W. TENNANT *Papistry Storm'd* (1827) 122 If I'se na soon exhibit sticket..This braggin' lordoun loun. **1859** TENNYSON *Ettarre* 436 In one [pavilion].. droned her lurdane knights.

Hence † **'lurdanry**, rascality.

1513 DOUGLAS *Æneis* VIII. Prol. 9 Leis, lurdanry, and lust ar our laid stern.

lurde, variant of LOURD *a.*

† **lurdge**, *v. Obs. rare*[−1]. [Cf. *lurgy* (dial.), lazy (E.D.D.).] *trans.* To indulge in laziness.

c **1580** JEFFERIE *Bugbears* IV. iv. in *Archiv Stud. neu. Spr.* (1897), It booteth not to lie, and lurdge my wery boanes.

† **lure**, *sb.*[1] *Obs.* Forms: 1 lyre, 2–4 lere, 3 leore, 3–4 lire, 3–5 lure(*ü*), (4 luere, lur). [OE. *lyre* masc.:—OTeut. type **luzi-z*, f. root **lus-* (:*leus-* :*laus-*) to lose: see LEESE *v.*] Loss, either the action or process of losing, or what is lost; destruction, perdition. Also *to bring to lure, to lie in lure.*

c **1000** ÆLFRIC *Colloq.* in Wr.-Wülcker 96 Mid lyre ealra þinga minra. *c* **1150** *Voc.* ibid. 540/31 *Iactura*, lure. *a* **1175** *Cott. Hom.* 221 þa wolde god ȝefyllan and ȝeinnian þone lere þe forloren was, of þan hefenlice werode. *c* **1200** ORMIN 5667 Whatt mann se itt iss þatt wepeþþ her Forr lire off eorþlike ahhte. *a* **1250** *Owl & Night.* 1151 Thu singst aȝen eiȝte lure. **1297** R. GLOUC. (Rolls) 10813 Him þoȝte it was a gret lere [*C.* lure] to al is kinedom. *a* **1327** in *Rel. Ant.* I. 263 On blac hors ryden other seon, That wol luere ant tuene buen. **13..** *Gaw. & Gr. Knt.* 355, I am þe wakkest, I wot, and of wyt feblest, & lest lur of my lyf, quo laytes þe soþe. *c* **1400** *Destr. Troy* 2241 Ouer lukes all lures to the last ende, What wull falle. *Ibid.* 8691 Alasse, the losse and the lure of oure lefe prinse!

lure (l(j)ʊə(r)), *sb.*[2] Also 5–6 leure, 6–7 lewre, 7 luer, lewer. [a. OF. *leurre, loerre, loire* = Pr. *loire*, cogn. w. It. *logoro* bait; prob. of Teut. origin; cf. MHG. *luoder*, mod.G. *luder* bait.]

1. An apparatus used by falconers, to recall their hawks, constructed of a bunch of feathers, to which is attached a long cord or thong, and from the interstices of which, during its training, the hawk is fed. *hawk of the lure*: see HAWK *sb.*[1] 1.

c **1440** *Promp. Parv.* 317/2 Lure for hawkys, *lurale.* **1530** PALSGR. 239/1 Leure for a hauke, *levrre.* **1575** TURBERV. *Faulconrie* 146 Fasten a pullet unto your leure and goe apart. **1592** SHAKS. *Ven. & Ad.* 1027 As Faulcons to the lure, away she flies. **1615** LATHAM *Falconry* (1633) Words of Art expl., Lver is that whereto Faulconers call their young Hawkes by casting it vp in the aire, being made of feathers and leather in such wise that in the motion it looks not vnlike a fowle. **1660** *Act 12 Chas. II*, c. 4 Rates Inwards..Lewers for Hawkes the peece js. iiiid. *a* **1682** SIR T. BROWNE *Tracts* 116 Though they [old Falconers] used Hoods, we have no clear description of them, and little account of their Lures. *c* **1704** PRIOR *Henry & Emma* 110 When Emma hawks: With her of tarsels and of lures he talks. **1814** CARY *Dante, Inf.* XVII. 123 As falcon, that hath long been on the wing, But lure nor bird hath seen. **1834** *Spectator* 1 Nov. 1036 The Duke of St. Albans has manned eight hawks, and their training with leash and crease and lure is now in actual progress. **1881** *Macm. Mag.* XLV. 39 First the hawk..is 'called off' to a piece of food held in the hand; next to a 'lure'.

b. The act or function of training the hawk to come to the lure. *rare.*

1615 LATHAM (*title*) Falconry; or the Faulcons Lure, and Cure.

c. Phrases. *to alight on the lure, to bring, call, come, stoop to* (*the* or *one's*) *lure*, etc. Often *fig.* †Also *at one's lure* (fig.): at one's command, under one's control; so † *to gain to one's lure.*

c **1386** CHAUCER *Friar's T.* 42 This false theef,..Hadde alway bawdes redy to his hond, As any hauk to lure in Engelond. —— *Manciple's Prol.* 72 Another day he wole peraueuture Reclayme thee, and brynge thee to lure. **1390** GOWER *Conf.* II. 11 Bot yit hire liketh noght alyhte Upon no lure which I caste. **1430–40** LYDG. *Bochas* V. xxxiv. (1554) 141 b, After this.. Came Jugurtha y[t] manly man to lure. **1509** HAWES *Past. Pleas.* xxxiv. (Percy Soc.) 171 She promised..To love you best..Though that Disdayne brought her to her lure. **1582** T. WATSON *Centurie of Love* xlvii, In time the Bull is brought to weare the yoake, In time all haggred Haukes will stoope the Lures. **1587** GOLDING *De Mornay* xi. 151 As much as thou canst, thou makest all things stoope to thy lure. **1599** T. M[OUFET] *Silkwormes* 52, I leaue to tell how she doth poison cure,..What canckars hard and wolfes be at her lure. **1611** MARKHAM *Country Content.* I. v. (1668) 30 After your Hawks are manned, you shall bring them to the Lure by easie degrees. **1643** SIR T. BROWNE *Relig. Med.* I. §10, I teach my haggard and unreclaimed Reason to stoope unto the lure of Faith. **1653** HOLCROFT *Procopius* I. 30 This mayd Antonina, by much soothing..at last gained to her lure. **1664** BUTLER *Hud.* II. iii. 614 The Rosycrucian way's more sure To bring the Devil to the Lure. **1670** G. H. *Hist. Cardinals* II. III. 186 He brought the Venetian to his Luer. **1688** [see LURE *v.* 2]. **1742** SOMERVILLE *Field Sports* 14 A docile Slave, Tam'd to the Lure, and careful to attend Her Master's Voice. **1819** SHELLEY *Peter Bell* VII. ii, A friend of ours—a poet: fewer Have fluttered tamer to the lure Than he. **1865** SWINBURNE *Poems & Ball., Gard. Proserpine* 76 Time stoops to no man's lure.

2. *Her.* A conventional representation of a hawk's lure, consisting of two birds' wings with the points directed downwards, and joined above by a ring attached to a cord. *in lure*: see quot. 1828–40.

1572 BOSSEWELL *Armorie* II. 132 b, The fielde is de Azure, two winges iointly en Lewre de argent. **1610** GUILLIM *Heraldry* VI. i. (1660) 384 Three pair of Wings joyned in lewer. **1828–40** BERRY *Encycl. Her.* I, *Lure*,..Wings conjoined with their tips turned downwards..are said to be in Lure. **1868** CUSSANS *Her.* (1883) 117. **1883** *N. & Q.* 23 June 484/2 Northern California..Argent, on a bend gules, cotised sable, three pairs of wings conjoined in lure of the field [etc.].

3. (orig. *fig.*) Something which allures, entices, or tempts.

c **1385** CHAUCER *L.G.W.* 1371 *Hypsip.*, Thou madest thyn recleyimyng and thyn luris To ladyes. *c* **1412** HOCCLEVE *De Reg. Princ.* 4140 He þat dispendith out of mesure Shal tast a-none pouertes bitternesse; ffoole largesse is ther-to a verray lure. **1528** LYNDESAY *Dreme* 278 Off Lychorye thay wer the verray luris. **1635** R. BOLTON *Comf. Affl. Consc.* 276 To hold out..as a prize and Lure, the freenesse of Gods immeasurable mercy. **1671** MILTON *P.R.* II. 194 How many have with a smile made small account Of beauty and her lures. **1747** SMOLLETT *Regicide* I. i. (1777) 6 Remained unshaken by the enchanting lure Which vain ambition spread before his eye. **1815** SHELLEY *Alastor* 294 Silent death exposed, Faithless perhaps as sleep, a shadowy lure. *a* **1832** MACKINTOSH *Rev.* 1688, Wks. 1846 II. 89 Whether the succession was actually held out to her as a lure or not, at least there was an intention..to prefer her to the Princess of Orange. **1902** *Contemp. Rev.* Sept. 359 He is mighty hard on those who dare to tempt fortune and follow its lure.

4. A means of alluring animals to be captured; in *Angling* a more general term than *bait*, which strictly denotes only something that fishes can eat.

a **1700** B. E. *Dict. Cant. Crew, Lure*,..a Bait. **1859** MARK LEMON *Christm. Hamper* (1860) 86 The barber..whose bow-windowed shop..is full of lures for fish. **1867** F. FRANCIS *Angling* v. (1880) 158 His line, guiltless of a lure, is extended on the surface of the water. **1878** STEVENSON *Inland Voy.* 44 The kind of fish for which they set their lures. **1900** *Blackw. Mag.* Sept. 340/2 The aim of the angler should be to present them with something..different.. from the lures with which they may have become familiar.

¶ **b.** Erroneously used for: A trap or snare (*fig.*).

1463 G. ASHBY *Prisoner's Refl.* 269 Poems (E.E.T.S.) 9 Was ther euyr lord so gret and so sure,..That may not fall in the snare and in the lure Of trouble. **1719** D'URFEY *Pills* (1872) IV. 269 And treacherously thou hast betrayed, Unto thy Lure a gentle Heart. **1870** DISRAELI *Lothair* xlii, The Colonel fell into the lure only through his carelessness. **1872** BROWNING *Fifine* iii, At wink of eve be sure They love to steal a march, nor lightly risk the lure.

5. The cry of a falconer recalling his hawk: *fig.* any alluring cry.

1653 MILTON *Hirelings* (1659) 132 By that lure or loubel may be toald from parish to parish all the town over. **1811** W. R. SPENCER *Poems* 199 Oh! where's thy guiding lure, —a mother's voice.

6. *attrib.*, as *lure-bait, -bird, -fish, -owl.*

1777 HOOLE *Comenius' Vis. World* (ed. 12) 68 He allureth birds, by the chirping of lure-birds. **1869** BROWNING *Ring & Bk.* VII. 678 You are a coquette, A lure-owl posturing to attract birds. **1876** G. B. GOODE *Anim. Resources U.S.* 41 Lure-fish used in taking Mackinaw trout. **1883** *Fisheries Exhib. Catal.* 195 Case of lure-baits and ornamented hooks from Alaska.

lure, *sb.*[3] *Obs.* exc. *Sc.* (Caithness, Aberdeensh.: see E.D.D.) [? Anomalous var. YURE *a.*, ON. *júgr.*] The udder of the cow and other animals.

c **1500** LACY *Wyl Bucke's Test.* (Copland) a iij, For the thrid course of the bucke. The potage Mogets and Nowmbleis stued,..bake dowcetts and tendreus, and the liuer rostid, and if it be a Doo take the lure.

lure (l(j)ʊə(r)), *sb.*[4] *techn.* Also looer, lewer. [Shortened from VELURE.] A pad of silk or velvet used by hatters for smoothing.

1858 SIMMONDS *Dict. Trade, Lewer*,..a hatter's name for a smoothing pad of silk, properly vellour from the French. **1875** KNIGHT *Dict. Mech., Looer, Lure.*

lure (l(j)ʊə(r)), *sb.*[5] Also loor. [ad. Da. and Norse *lur*, ON. *lúðr*. Cf. Shetland *looder-horn.*] A long curved trumpet, used for calling cattle.

1840 HT. MARTINEAU *Feats on Fiord* ix. (1841) 217 She.. took in her hand her lure, with which to call home the cattle ..and stole away. **1877** BURROUGHS *Birds & Poets* (1884) 162 At evening the cows are summoned home with a long horn, called the loor.

lure (l(j)ʊə(r)), *v.* Also 6 leur, 6–7 lewre, 7 lewer. [f. LURE *sb.*[2]; cf. F. *leurrer* (OF. *loirrer*).]

1. *trans.* To recall (a hawk) by casting the lure; to call (a hawk) to the lure.

c **1386** CHAUCER *Wife's Prol.* 415 With empty hand men may none haukes lure. **1562** J. HEYWOOD *Prov. & Epigr.* (1867) 215 Lewre falcones when ye list. **1601** SIR W. CORNWALLIS *Ess.* II. xxxv. (1631) 88 A Faulkoner would not have lured it. **1611** MARKHAM *Country Content.* I. v. (1668) 30 Short winged Hawks are said to be called, not lured. **1828** SIR J. S. SEBRIGHT *Hawking* 17 The falconer..should always *halloo* when he is luring.

2. *intr.* To call to a hawk while casting the lure.

1530 PALSGR. 616/1, I lure, as a falconer dothe for his haulke. **1575** TURBERV. *Faulconrie* 147 Take the lewre..and cast it about your heade crying and leuring aloud. **1688** R. HOLME *Armoury* II. 239/2 Lure, or Lewer, or Lewre, is to call the Hawk to Lure.

† **b.** To call loudly. *Obs.*

1601 HOLLAND *Pliny* I. 239 This boy lured for him & called Simo. **1607** TOPSELL *Four-f. Beasts* (1658) 543 He standeth lewring and making a terrible noise to affright the Swine. **1626** BACON *Sylva* §250 If you stand between a House, and a Hill, and lure towards the Hill. **1626** *Jests Scogin* (Hazl.) 65 At last Scogin did lewer and whoop to him [his horse].

† **c.** To call *at* contemptuously. *Obs.*

1693 J. H. in *Dryden's Juvenal* x. 5 He's mocked and lur'd at by the giddy Crowd.

† **3.** *trans.* To train (a hawk) to come to the lure.

1486 *Bk. St. Albans* D iv, Theys be hawkes of the towre: and ben both Ilurid to be calde and reclaymed. **1530** PALSGR. 616/1 Lure your haulke betyme I wolde advyse you. **1575** TURBERV. *Faulconrie* 129 When you woulde lure him, giue him unto some other man to holde and call him with a lure well garnished with meate.

4. To allure, entice, tempt.

1393 LANGL. *P. Pl.* C. VIII. 44 Ich am nat lured with loue, bote ouht lygge vnder þombe. *c* **1412** HOCCLEVE *De Reg. Princ.* 3069 Only þe richesse þer-to hem lurith. **1447** BOKENHAM *Seyntys* (Roxb.) 14 Hyr bewte sosore dede lure Hys herte. *a* **1547** SURREY in *Tottel's Misc.* (Arb.) 219 But that your will is such to lure me to the trade As other some full many yeres to trace by craft ye made. **1667** MILTON *P.L.* II. 664 In secret, riding through the Air she comes, Lur'd with the smell of infant blood. **1688** CROWNE *Darius* II. Dram. Wks. 1874 III. 406 Nay, Sir, but for a while, till he has lur'd Gods, and revolting nations to your aid. *a* **1763** SHENSTONE *Elegies* xxvi 27 Expense, and art, and toil, united strove; To lure a breast that felt the purest flame. **1825** J. NEAL *Bro. Jonathan* III. 407 His dog had gone off it appeared; having been lured away. *a* **1839** PRAED *Poems* (1864) I. 119 But go and lure the midnight cloud, Or chain the mist of morning. **1855** MACAULAY *Hist. Eng.* xx. IV. 511 He had been lured into a snare by treachery. **1900** W. WATT *Aberdeen & Banff* x. 250 By a feint..Montrose lured away a large portion of the defending force.

b. To entice to come *down* by a call.

1774 GOLDSM. *Nat. Hist.* (1776) VI. 134 The ducks flying in the air are often lured down..by the loud voice of the mallard.

† **5.** *intr.* To set a trap *for* (another). *fig. Obs.*

a **1591** H. SMITH *Serm.* (1614) 423 Yet Paul lured for Agrippa. Now he sues to the people. When he had caught the king, he spred his net for the people.

lure, obs. Sc. f. *liefer*, compar. of LIEF *a.*, dear.

1728 RAMSAY *Tit for Tat* 31 I'd lure be strung Up by the neck.

lure, str. pa. t. LEESE *v.*[1]; var. LOOR *dial.*

lured (l(j)ʊəd), *ppl. a.* [f. LURE *v.* + -ED[1].]

1. Of a hawk: Trained to come to the lure.

a **1576** *Common Conditions* 409 (Brandl) 613 The leured hauke, whose rowlyng eyes are fixed on Partredge fast. **1599** PORTER *Angry Wom. Abingt.* (Percy Soc.) 71 Like a well lur'de hawke she knowes her call.

2. Entrapped.

1720 GAY *Dione* II. ii. Poems II. 453 Bid the lur'd lark, whom tangling nets surprise, On soaring pinion rove the spacious skies.

lureful ('l(j)ʊəfʊl), *a. rare.* [f. LURE *sb.*[2] + -FUL.] Alluring. Hence **'lurefully** *adv.*

1887 G. MEREDITH *Ballads & P.* 39 Lureful is she, bent for folly. **1891** —— *One of our Conq.* II. xi. 267 His wreck, ..winked lurefully when abandoned. *Ibid.* III. v. 88 Her voice was lurefully encouraging.

lurement ('l(j)ʊəmənt). *rare.* [f. LURE *v.*[1] + -MENT.] Allurement.

1592 WYRLEY *Armorie* 155 No luerments wrought my constant mind to faile. **1825** HOGG in *Blackw. Mag.* XVII. 716 For vengeance I did it,..Without that, futurity lurements had none. **1898** H. CALDERWOOD *Hume* viii. 145 She, feeling the lurements of a gay court, was drawn into intrigue.

lurer[1] ('l(j)ʊərə(r)). [f. LURE *v.* + -ER[1].] One who or that which lures.
In mod. Dicts.

lurer[2] ('l(j)ʊərə(r)). [f. LURE *sb.*[4] + -ER[1].] One who smoothes felt hats with a 'lure'.
1881 *Instr. Census Clerks* (1885) 75 Hatter, hat-manufactures.. Felt Hat Making:.. Lurer.

'luresome, *a.* [f. LURE *v.* + -SOME.] Alluring.
1889 *Harper's Mag.* Jan. 179/2 Beneath a woman's tongue .. The subtlety its luresome lodging hath.

Lurex ('l(j)ʊərɛks). Also **lurex**. The proprietary name of a type of yarn which incorporates a metallic thread; also, fabric made from this yarn.
1945 *Official Gaz.* (U.S. Patent Office) 16 Oct. 360/1 The Dobeckmun Company, Cleveland Ohio... Lurex. For yarn and thread comprised either in whole or in part of laminated film having a metallic appearance, including gimp comprised of a filament of yarn spirally overwrapped with coated or laminated foil which has been slit to a narrow width, said overwrapping imparting a metallic appearance. **1958** *Spectator* 12 Dec. 853/1 The party from the Camberwell Jazz Club, dressed in Italian-cut jackets shot with lurex, were not enthusiastic. **1965** *Guardian* 31 Mar. 15/2 Far away in the Outer Hebrides, the crofter weavers have found pleasure as well as profit in weaving 'Lurex' threads into tweeds of an altogether new lightness and beauty. **1967** *Spectator* 4 Aug. 139/3 The curtain rises on Donald Pleasance, in lurex dressing-gown,.. kneeling before a marble urn and listening to Verdi. **1973** *Guardian* 18 June 15/2 Plain snakeskin Lurex blousons.

lurg (lɜːg). *local.* [? Cf. LUG *sb.*[4]] A British marine worm used for bait; the white-rag worm.
1880 *Antrim & Down Gloss.*, *Lurgan, Lurg, Lurk*, a whitish, very active sea-worm used for bait. **1882** *Cassell's Nat. Hist.* VI. 232 The White-rag Worm, or Lurg [*Nephthys cæca*], is common on the British shores, and varies from six to ten inches in length.

†**lurgg**. *Sc. Obs.* [repr. Gael. *cù luirg* (*cù* dog, *luirg* gen. of *lorg* track).] ***lurgg dog***: a bloodhound.
?**1605** in *Reg. Priv. Council Scot.* VII. 744 That in every parish there may be some lurgg dogges kept, one or moe,.. for following of pettie stouthes.

Lurgi ('lʊəgɪ, 'lɜːgɪ). The name of the *Lurgi* Gesellschaft für Wärmetechnik m.b.H., of Frankfurt, W. Germany, used *attrib.* to denote a method of gasification suitable for low-grade coal such as lignite by reaction with steam and oxygen at high pressure; so ***Lurgi gas, plant***.
1934 ROBERTS & JENKNER *Internat. Coal Carbonization* xi. 249 In the Lurgi process the heat transference occurs directly by means of hot gaseous products of combustion, which pass through the coal. **1950** D. A. TOWNEND in D. H. Bangham *Progress Coal Sci.* xxvi. 436 Lurgi gas from brown coal has the following composition. **1950** WARING & FOSTER in Foster & Lund *Econ. of Fuel Gas from Coal* v. 81 Table 17 gives.. the average analyses of the gas from the Lurgi plant at Bohlen. *Ibid.* 83 The economic advantage of the Lurgi process is that gasification of a cheaper, low-rank fuel is possible and that a comparatively high-Btu gas is delivered under pressure without the expense of carburetion with oil. **1973** *Nature* 7 Dec. 326/2 The well established Lurgi process is used to gasify the coal almost completely and a gas of low calorific value.. is produced. *Ibid.*, The Lurgi process converts almost all the coal into gas, unlike the system used to manufacture town gas which produces coke and tar as well. **1974** *Sci. Amer.* Mar. 20/2 In some places Lurgi plants made a gas that was distributed as city gas.

lurgy ('lɜːgɪ). Also **lurgi**. Usu. in phr. ***the dreaded lurgy***. A fictitious, highly infectious disease invented (?) and made a byword by the Radio Goons (GOON 4).
For the possibility that the word is not invented, cf. *fever-lurgy*, dial. var. of FEVER-LURDEN, and *E.D.D.* s.v. *lurgies*, *lurgy* adj. & sb.
1954 *Radio Times* 9 Nov. 20/3 The Goon Show... Poor Arnold Fringe is suddenly stricken with the Dreaded Lurgi. .. Within a few days Lurgi has claimed nine thousand victims. **1969** I. & P. OPIE *Children's Games* ii. 75 (*heading*) The dreaded lurgy. **1971** *It* 15–29 July 5/3 The youth of Australia have been saved once more from the dreaded lurgy, marijuana. **1974** H. MACINNES *Climb to Lost World* ix. 149, I was beginning to feel weak and knew that I had caught the dreaded swamp lurgy.

lurid ('l(j)ʊərɪd), *a.* [ad. L. *lūrid-us* pale yellow, wan, ghastly.]
1. Pale and dismal in colour; wan and sallow; ghastly of hue. Said e.g. of the sickly pallor of the skin in disease, or of the aspect of things when the sky is overcast.
1656 BLOUNT *Glossogr.*, *Lurid*, pale, wan, black, and blew. **1658** PHILLIPS, *Lurid*, pale, wan, of a sallow colour. **1669** COKAINE *Elegy Eliz. Repington* Poems 76 A lurid paleness sits upon the skin That did enclose the beauteous body in. **1746** COLLINS *Ode to Fear* 20 Whilst Vengeance, in the lurid air, Lifts her red arm, expos'd and bare. **1822–34** *Good's Study Med.* (ed. 4) IV. 82 Applied to the disease like our own term green-sickness, from the pale, lurid, and greenish cast of the skin. *Ibid.* 496 Lurid papulous scall. **1874** SYMONDS *Sk. Italy & Greece* (1898) I. i. 13 A leaden glare.. makes the snow and ice more lurid.
2. Shining with a red glow or glare amid darkness (said, e.g., of lightning-flashes across dark clouds, or flame mingled with smoke).
1727 THOMSON *Britannia* 79 Fierce o'er their beauty blaz'd the lurid flame. **1805** WORDSW. *Waggoner* I. 167 Save that above a single height Is to be seen a lurid light, Above Helm-crag—a streak half dead, A burning of portentous red. **1818** SCOTT *Hrt. Midl.* vii, The lurid light, which had filled the apartment, lowered and died away. **1836** W. IRVING *Astoria* I. 263 At night also the lurid reflection of immense fires hung in the sky. **1877** BLACK *Green Past.* xxvii. (1878) 220 A thick and thundery haze that gave a red and lurid tinge to the coast we were leaving. **1878** STEWART & TAIT *Unseen Univ.* ii. §84. 93 A gleam of lurid light seemed for a moment to illuminate the thick darkness.
b. Said *hyperbolically* of the eyes, countenance, etc.
1746 T. SEWARD *Conformity betw. Popery & Paganism* 55 The prating Grandame.. His Lips.. with lustral Juices arms From lurid Eyes and fascinating Charms [= *urentes oculos inhibere perita*, Persius II. v. 35]. **1826** DISRAELI *Viv. Grey* III. vi, The lurid glare of the anaconda's eye. **1852** MRS. STOWE *Uncle Tom's C.* xxxviii. 335 A softness gathered over the lurid fires of her eye. **1860** HAWTHORNE *Marble Faun* xix. (1879) I. 191 The glow of rage was still lurid on Donatello's face.
3. *fig.* (from either of the preceding senses), with connotation of 'terrible', 'ominous', 'ghastly', 'sensational'. Often in phr. ***to cast*** or ***throw a lurid light on*** (a subject).
1850 KINGSLEY *Alt. Locke* iv, Woe unto that man on whom that idea, true or false, rises lurid. **1865** DICKENS *Mut. Fr.* III. iv, Lurid indications of the better marriages she might have made, shone athwart the awful gloom of her composure. **1866** R. W. DALE *Disc. Spec. Occ.* viii. 273 The lurid, stormy eloquence of Edmund Burke. **1879** FARRAR *St. Paul* (1883) 127 He adds one fact more which casts a lurid light on the annals of the persecution. **1899** F. T. BULLEN *Log Sea-waif* 182 Peter's voice prattled on, its lurid language in the strangest contrast to the gentleness of his speech.
4. In scientific use: Of a dingy brown or yellowish-brown colour. †Applied *spec.* to plants of the order *Luridæ* of Linnæus (see quots. 1822–34).
1767 W. HARTE *Christ's Par. Sower* 41 Lurid hemlock ting'd with pois'nous stains. **1822–34** *Good's Study Med.* (ed. 4) II. 587 The lurid and umbellate narcotics. *Ibid.* IV. 92 Cataplasms of Hemlock, or the other umbellate or lurid plants in common use. **1826** KIRBY & SP. *Entomol.* IV. 281 *Lurid*, yellow with some mixture of brown. Dirty yellow. **1839** LINDLEY *Introd. Bot.* (ed. 3) 478 *Lurid*; dirty brown, a little clouded. **1856** HENSLOW *Dict. Bot. Terms*, *Lurid*, of a dingy brown, grey with orange. **1871** DARWIN *Desc. Man* II. xii. 25 In many species the body presents strongly contrasted, though lurid tints. **1871** W. A. LEIGHTON *Lichen-flora* 400 Ardellæ depressed, lurid, dark-purplish.
Hence **'luridly** *adv.*, **'luridness**.
1731 BAILEY vol. II, *Luridness*, black and blueness, paleness, &c. **1795–7** SOUTHEY *Min. Poems* Poet. Wks. II. 210 Yon cloud that rolls luridly over the hill Is red with their weapons of fire. **1845** HIRST *Poems* 13 Luridly Coursed the swift lightning through the sky. **1864** *Spectator* 20 Aug. 957/1 The writer has deliberately.. softened a hundred tints which would have increased the luridness of his picture.

lurido-. Used in *Bot.* as quasi-Latin combining form of *lūridus* LURID.
1871 W. A. LEIGHTON *Lichen-flora* 51 Lurido cinerascent. *Ibid.* 252 Lurido-fuscescent. *Ibid.* 288 Lurido-whitish.

luring ('l(j)ʊərɪŋ), *vbl. sb.*[1] [f. LURE *v.* + -ING[1].] The action of LURE *v.* in various senses.
1547 BOORDE *Brev. Health* cccv. 100 It may come by lewrynge, halowynge, or great cryeng. **1557** *Tottel's Misc.* (Arb.) 269 My luryng is not good, it liketh not thine eare. **1596** WILLOBIE *Avisa* (1880) 137 Trusse vp your lures, your luring is in vaine. **1603** BRETON *Dial. Pith & Pleas.* (Grosart) 7/1 Tyring of legges, and tearing of throates, with luring, and hollowing. **1634** HEYWOOD *Lanc. Witches* I. Wks. 1874 IV. 173 Tush let him passe, He is not worth our luring, a meere Coxcombe.

'luring, *vbl. sb.*[2] *techn.* [f. LURE *sb.*[4] + -ING[1].] The action of smoothing a hat with a lure.
1902 *Brit. Med. Jrnl.* No. 2146. 378 Finishing consists of 'shaving' with fine sand-paper and 'luring'... The 'luring' is done with a suitable pad.

'luring, *ppl. a.* [f. LURE *v.* + -ING[1].] That lures (in senses of the verb); enticing, attractive.
1570 *Satir. Poems Reform.* xxii. 24 Ane luiring bait fond fischis to wirk tene. **1575** TURBERV. *Faulconrie* 148 You must put hir on a payre of gret lewring bels. **1583** *Leg. Bp. St. Androis* 8 Ane lewrand lawrie licherous. **1592** WYRLEY *Armorie, Ld. Chandos* 30 Yet near vncaught the luring fruit doth stay. **1842** MANNING *Serm.* vii. (1848) I. 101 Some high and luring offer. **1863** I. WILLIAMS *Baptistery* I. xiv. (1874) 176 The world with luring glances, Leads them on. **1869** BROWNING *Ring & Bk.* x. 724 Fowlers.. eschew vile practice, nor find sport In torch-light treachery or the luring owl.

luringly ('l(j)ʊərɪŋlɪ), *adv.* [f. LURING *ppl. a.* + -LY[2].] In a luring or enticing manner.
1897 J. L. ALLEN *Choir Invisible* xvi, This second image.. drawing always nearer, summoning him more luringly. **1961** R. CRAFT *Diary* 31 Oct. in Stravinsky & Craft *Themes & Episodes* (1966) II. 203 He talks luringly of the Favors of a houri.

luripup, variant of LIRIPOOP.

Luristan (lʊərɪ'stɑːn). The name of a district in western Iran used *attrib.* to designate the engraved bronze articles and castings, of the twelfth century B.C., found in the region.
[**1935** L. BINYON *Spirit of Man in Asian Art* iv. 105 Persian art, as we see it in the bronzes of animals recently discovered in Luristan, propagated its motives of design among the outlying, unsettled, still nomad tribes.] **1961** *Times* 6 June 22/7 (Advt.), A pair of unique Luristan bronze cheekpieces from a bit. **1970** *Oxf. Compan. Art* 830/1 Scientific excavations.. have been held to show (though it is still unproven) that the Luristan bronzes are the handwork of the Medes, an Indo-European people who.. began to infiltrate into Persia at about this period. **1971** *Ashmolean Mus. Rep. of Visitors 1970* 16 *Purchased*: seventeen 'Luristan' and 'Amlash' bronzes, Iran, late 2nd to early 1st millennium B.C.

lurk (lɜːk), *sb.*[1] [f. LURK *v.*]
1. The action of prowling about. In phrase ***on the lurk***. Cf. LURCH *sb.*[2] 2.
1829 *Life & Death J. Wilson* (Farmer), Like Reynard sneaking on the lurk.
2. *slang.* **a.** A method of fraud.
c **1842** *Exposure of Impositions practised by Vagrants* 5 Persons who go on this lurk, generally represent themselves as Captains or Masters of merchant ships which have been wrecked, and they have, of course, lost all their property. **1851** MAYHEW *Lond. Labour* I. 363 The 'dead lurk'.. is the expressive slang phrase for the act of entering dwelling-houses during divine service. *Ibid.* (1861) II. 51 Thus initiated, Chelsea George could 'go upon any lurk'. **1864** *Slang Dict.*, *Lurk*, a sham, swindle, or representation of feigned distress. **1875** BRINE in Ribton-Turner *Vagrants & Vagrancy* (1887) 642 The 'bereavement lurk' is a lucrative one—(i.e.) the pretended loss of a wife [etc.].
b. Chiefly *Austral.* and *N.Z. slang*. A scheme, 'dodge', plan of action, ruse (not necessarily implying fraud). (See also quot. 1941.)
1916 C. J. DENNIS *Songs Sentimental Bloke* 125 *Lurk*, a plan of action. **1918** [see JERRY *v.*]. *c* **1926** [see FREEZE *sb.*[1] I (i)]. **1938** *Observer* 13 Nov. 11/3 *Dart*, a scheme or racket; *lurk*, ditto. **1941** BAKER *Dict. Austral. Slang* 45 *Lurk*, a 'dodge', scheme, racket. 2. A hanger-on, an eavesdropper or sneak. **1953** A. UPFIELD *Murder must Wait* xvii. 149 Thanks a lot for the antidote... It is one hell of a good lurk. **1961** *N.Z. Listener* 17 Mar. 3/1 The Navy.. is just a good lurk for those who want to delve deep into the public purse. *Ibid.* 15 Sept. 29/2, I suspect Barry Crump found he was on a good advertising lurk when he was interviewed for *Book Shop*. **1966** B. COOPER *Drown him Deep* xx. 165 She was a very rich girl indeed, and Hilary, with considerable influence over her, might well be on to a very good 'lurk'. **1967** C. DRUMMOND *Death at Furlong Post* xv. 182 If the hounds were out, the lurk was to get ahead of them and go to earth.
c. *Austral.* and *N.Z. slang*. A job.
1916 C. J. DENNIS *Songs Sentimental Bloke* 20, I found 'er lurk Wus pastin' labels in a pickle joint. *Ibid.* 125 *Lurk*, a regular occupation. **1958** R. STOW *To Islands* 126 'What's your lurk, mate?' 'Me? Stockman on a mission.' **1965** *Telegraph* (Brisbane) 2 June, O'Grady's current lurk is holidaying as an unpaid deck hand on the South Molle cruise ship Crest while he absorbs sunlight and material for a new book.
3. *dial.* A loafer. (E.D.D.) Cf. LURK *v.* 1 b.
4. *slang.* A hiding-place; a 'hang-out'.
1906 E. DYSON *Fact'ry 'Ands* viii. 97, I come out frim me lurk, 'n' went over ther ground. **1924** *Chambers's Jrnl.* 20 Sept. 683/2 Why did the old beggar come to this secret lurk in the East End and disguise himself? **1972** *N.Z. News* 26 Jan. 4/1 The first bar I saw was the Cockney's Pride—a completely new lurk for me. **1974** J. GARDNER *Return of Moriarty* 32, I met her in a servant's lurk.

†**lurk**, *sb.*[2] *Obs.* Some plant; ? = LURKYDISH.
1530 PALSGR. 241/2 Lurke an herbe.

lurk (lɜːk), *v.* Now *literary*. Forms: 4 lurkke, lork(e, 4–7 lurke, 6 lourke, 6–7 lurck, 7 lurcke. [app. f. *lūr-* LOUR *v.* with frequentative suffix as in *tal-k*. Cf. LG. *lurken* to shuffle along, Norw. *lurka* to sneak away, Sw. dial. *lurka* to be slow in one's work (Sw. *lurk* bumpkin).]
1. a. *intr.* To hide oneself; to lie in ambush; to remain furtively or unobserved about one spot. (Now only with indication of place.) Also, †to live in concealment or retirement.
c **1300** *Havelok* 68 Hwan he felede hise foos, He made hem lurken, and crepen in wros. ? *a* **1366** CHAUCER *Rom. Rose* 465 There lurked and there coured she, Fer pover thing, wher-so it be, Is shamfast, and despysed ay. *c* **1375** *Sc. Leg. Saints* xliii. (*Cecile*) 89 Valaryane.. fand þe bischope sanct urbane lurkand ymong pure men mekly. **1390** GOWER *Conf.* II. 355 And thus lurkende upon his stelthe In his await so longe he lai [etc.]. *c* **1400** *Destr. Troy* 1167 Silen to the Citie softly and faire; Lurkyt vnder lefe-sals loget with vines. *c* **1470** *Golagros & Gaw.* 1080 Sal neuer freik on fold, fremmyt nor freynde, Gar me lurk for ane luke, lawit nor lerd. **1547** BOORDE *Introd. Knowl.* xxiv. (1870) 181 To lyue in rest and peace in my cytye I do lourke. **1596** DALRYMPLE tr. *Leslie's Hist. Scot.* I. 20 Fisches lurking amang the stanes. **1605** CAMDEN *Rem.*, *Rythmes* 25 When Philip de Valoys the French King lurked in Cambray. **1650** FULLER *Pisgah* IV. i. 9 They shew also in this city the house or rather hole wherein Ananias.. dwelt or lurked, being a Cellar under ground. **1709** STEELE *Tatler* No. 33 ⁋7 Could you then steal out of Town, and lurk like a Robber about my House. **1761** HUME *Hist. Eng.* (1806) V. lxix. 185 Shaftesbury.. had left his house and secretly lurked in the city. **1772–84** COOK *Voy.* (1790) VI. 1962 The natives were seen lurking about the beach. **1826** COBBETT *Rur. Rides* (1885) II. 193 When quarters are good, you are apt to lurk in them; but really it was so wet, that we could not get away. **1863** MISS BRADDON *Eleanor's Vict.* III. ii. 22 There was a man lurking somewhere under the shadow of the evergreens. **1887** BOWEN *Virg. Eclog.* III. 93 Run, for a cold snake lurks in the grasses yonder unseen!
†**b.** To shirk work; to idle. *Obs.*
1551 CROWLEY *Pleas. & Pain* 287 You toke from them theyr heritage Leaueyng them nought wheron to worcke: Which lacke dyd make them learne to lurke. **1573** TUSSER *Husb.* (1878) 175 When Dinner is ended, set seruants to wurke, and follow such fellowes as loueth to lurke. *a* **1792** *Song, Poor Thresher* ii. in *Johnson's Museum* IV. 384 He never was known for to idle or lurk.

2. *trans.* and *fig.* Of things: To escape observation, to be concealed or latent.

c **1374** CHAUCER *Troylus* IV. 277 (305) O soule lurkinge in þis wo, vnneste, Fle forth out of myn herte and lat it breste. **1576** FLEMING *Panopl. Epist.* 18 Then ought you to denie that any vnfaithfulnes, fraude, or deceitfulnesse lieth lurking in our friendship. **1602** MARSTON *Antonio's Rev.* II. iii. Wks. 1856 I. 98 Griefe..lurkes in secret angles of the heart. **1661** BOYLE *Style of Script.* (1671) 206 Laziness and pride..both which lurk under the pretext of multiplicity of important avocations. **1697** DRYDEN *Virg. Past.* III. 58 Grapes in clusters lurk, Beneath the Carving of the curious Work. **1712** ADDISON *Spect.* No. 399 ⁋3 Those Vices that lurk in the secret Corners of the Soul. **1795** BURNS *Song, 'Their groves o' sweet myrtles'*, Where the blue-bell and gowan lurk lowly unseen. **1812** BYRON *Ch. Har.* II. lxxxii, But midst the throng in merry masquerade, Lurk there no hearts that throb with secret pain? **1883** R. W. DIXON *Mano* III. iii. 121 A dismal deed..The fame of which lurks in obscurity.

3. To move about in a secret and furtive manner; to 'steal' *along*, *away*, *out*. Now *rare*.

c **1350** *Will. Palerne* 25 þat litel child listely lorked out of his caue. *Ibid.* 2213 Lorkinde þurth londes bi niȝt so lumbardie þei passed. **1393** LANGL. *P. Pl.* C. III. 226 Lyghtliche lyere lep a-way þennes, Lorkynge þorw lanes. *c* **1400** *Destr. Troy* 12666 þe buernes..dang hym to deth in þe derk hole..& lurkit to þaire tentis. *Ibid.* 13106. **1572** *Satir. Poems Reform.* xxxiii. 297 First, thair come in, lurkand vpon ȝour gait, Pryde and Inuy. **1848** THACKERAY *Van. Fair* lxi, That second-floor arch in a London house,..commanding the main thoroughfare by which..cook lurks down before daylight to scour her pots and pans in the kitchen;..up which John lurks to bed. **1851** D. JERROLD *St. Giles* xiv. 142 That young nobleman has been seen lurking about here very much of late.

†**4.** To peer furtively or slyly. *Obs.*

c **1440** *York Myst.* xxix. 107 He lokis lurkand like an nape. **1513** DOUGLAS *Æneis* xiii. Prol. 78 Me thocht I lurkit vp vnder my hude To spy this auld.

5. [Perh. connected with LURCH *v.*²] In pa. pple.: beaten, lost (in a game of chance) (see also quot. 1929). *slang.*

1917 M. T. HAINSSELIN *Grand Fleet Days* xx. 172 'What-Ho!'..said the Admiral, 'not a bad idea at all! Let's have a garden...' '——' said the Watch-keepers, in the sheltered seclusion of the wardroom, knowing full well that they would be lurked for the digging. **1929** F. C. BOWEN *Sea Slang* 87 *Lurked, to be*, to be ordered to do some unpleasant job without a chance of avoiding it. **1938** C. MORGAN *Flashing Stream* III. 222 Four straight aces. Good enough? You're lurked, Sandford. **1946** J. IRVING *Royal Navalese* 111 The man who 'cuts' for drinks and loses is 'lurked for the round'.

lurk, north. dial. variant of LIRK.

lurker¹ ('lɜːkə(r)). [f. LURK *v.* + -ER¹.]

1. One who lurks or lies concealed: freq. employed as a term of abuse in early quots. *lit.* and *fig.*

a **1325** *Names of Hare* in *Rel. Ant.* I. 133 The wilde der, the lepere, The shorte der, the lerkere. **1399** LANGL. *Rich. Redeles* III. 57 But as sone as þey [the young birds]..steppe kunne, þan cometh and crieth her owen kynde dame, and they ffolwith þe vois,..and leueth þe lurker þat hem er ladde. *a* **1400–50** *Alexander* 3543 þou litill thefe, þou losangere, þou lurkare in cities. *c* **1470** HENRYSON *Fables* v. *Parl. Beasts* xl, 'For goddis lufe, my lord, gif me the law Of this lurker'; with that lowrence let draw. **1519** HORMAN *Vulg.* viii. 89 b, He is a starter a syde or a lurkar [L. *emansor*]. **1620** BP. HALL *Hon. Mar. Clergy* I. xxiv. 129 If this lawlesse Lurker had euer had any taste of the Ciuill or Canon Law, hee might haue beene able to construe that Maxime. **1641** MILTON *Ch. Govt.* I. vi. Wks. 1851 III. 121 It was well knowne what a bold lurker schisme was even in the houshold of Christ. **1702** C. MATHER *Magn. Chr.* VII. App. (1852) 631 Two men at Exeter were killed by some of the same dangerous lurkers. **1821** SCOTT *Kenilw.* xix, In hopes to find that the lurker had disappeared. **1870** MORRIS *Earthly Par.* II. III. 498 Then did the lurkers from the gully bound.

2. A begging impostor; a petty thief.

c **1842** *Exposure of Impositions practised by Vagrants* 4 Lurkers are persons who go about with briefs, containing false statements of losses by fire, shipwrecks, accidents, &c. **1851** MAYHEW *Lond. Labour* I. 219 Armed with these [sham official documents], the patterer becomes a 'lurker',—that is, an impostor. *Ibid.* 363 A lurker being strictly one who loiters about for some dishonest purpose. **1925** H. LEVERAGE in *Flynn's* IV. 869/2 *Lurker*, a swindler. **1973** G. BUTLER *Coffin for Pandora* i. 27, I knew the lingo. A macer was a cheat or a sharper and a lurker was a man with a story of hard luck to tell.

¶**3.** App. misused for LURCHER.

c **1440** *Promp. Parv.* 317/2 Lurcare.., *lurco.*

lurker² ('lɜːkə(r)). (See quots. 1825, 1880.)

1825 *Encycl. Lond.* XX. 435/1 [In pilchard fishing] the third boat is called the lurker, and carries three or four men. **1880** *W. Cornwall Gloss.*, *Lurker*, a boat in which the master seiner sits to give instructions. **1902** *Longm. Mag.* Aug. 349 The lurkers were lifted over mud and shingle, the crews sprang, tumbled, or were pushed on board.

lurking ('lɜːkɪŋ), *vbl. sb.* [f. LURK *v.*]

1. The action of LURK *v.*; a hiding or lying concealed.

1563 *Homilies* II. *Idleness* (1859) 518 If we give ourselves to idleness and sloth, to lurking and loitering. **1587** FLEMING *Contn. Holinshed* III. 1360/1 She hath caused some of these ..sowers of rebellion, to be discouered for all their secret lurkings. **1677** TEMPLE *Ess. Gout* Wks. 1731 I. 137 The Approaches or Lurkings of the Gout..may indispose Men to Thought and to Care. **1713** ADDISON *Guardian* No. 71 ⁋5 By the wanderings, roarings, and lurkings of his lions, he knew the way to every man breathing. **1824** W. IRVING *T. Trav.* II. 98 Who knew every suspicious character, and..all his lurkings. **1855** MACAULAY *Hist. Eng.* xvii. IV. 31 After about three years of wandering and lurking he..made his peace with the government.

2. *Thieves' slang.* Stealing, fraudulent begging.

1851 MAYHEW *Lond. Labour* I. 250 After a career of incessant 'lurking' and deceit. *Ibid.* 363 Many modes of thieving as well as begging are termed 'lurking'.

3. *attrib.*, as ***lurking-corner***, ***-den***, ***-hole***, ***-place***.

1545 ASCHAM *Toxoph.* I. (Arb.) 53 When the nyghte and *lurking corners, giueth lesse occasion to vnthriftinesse, than lyght daye. **1573** L. LLOYD *Marrow of Hist.* (1653) 252 The *lurking dens and secret snares of Cupid. **1567** MAPLET *Gr. Forest* 6 The most bolde and aduenterous men, are said, to seeke out the *lurking holes of the Dragon. **1678** LOCKE *Let. to Grenville* 6 Dec. in Fox Bourne *Life* (1876) I. vii. 394 No garrisons unreduced, no lurking-holes unsearched. **1772** *Ann. Reg.* 32/2 He was found hid in a chimney, covered with soot; a lurking-hole suited to its inhabitant. **1571** GOLDING *Calvin on Ps.* xvii. 12 He nameth their Dennes or privy *lurking-places. **1611** BIBLE *Ps.* x. 8. He sitteth in the lurking places of the villages. **1751** SMOLLETT *Per. Pic.* (1779) III. viii. 238, I was..discovered ..and hunted out of my lurking place. **1869** BROWNING *Ring & Bk.* x. 729 He..hies to the old lurking-place.

'lurking, *ppl. a.* [f. LURK *v.* + -ING².] That lurks; concealed, latent. Also, †skulking, lazy.

c **1400** *Destr. Troy* 1001 But a Sourdyng with sourgrem sanke in his hert, And a lourekand lust to Lamydon the kyng. **1570** *Satir. Poems Reform.* xiii. 176 Sa sall we se and heir Quhat lurkand lubers will tak thir Lymmers parts. **1667** MILTON *P.L.* IX. 1175, I..foretold The danger, and the lurking Enemie That lay in wait. **1676** GREW *Anat. Plants* IV. ii. (1682) 174 Keeping the Plants warm, and thereby enticing the young lurking Flowers to come abroad. **1705** STANHOPE *Paraphr.* I. 76 He will disclose many lurking motives. **1743** *Lond. & Country Brew.* II. (ed. 2) 107 It does ..draw forth that lurking, keen, sour Quality that the Wood has imbibed. **1772–84** COOK *Voy.* (1790) IV. 1274 We discovered a lurking rock, in the middle of one of the beds of weeds. **1807–8** WORDSWORTH *White Doe* vii. 1711 Why tell of mossy rock, or tree, By lurking Dernbrook's pathless side? **1871** FREEMAN *Norm. Conq.* (1876) IV. xvii. 91 And William..may have felt some lurking sympathy for those who had drawn on themselves the censures of the Church.

b. *slang.* Following the occupation of a 'lurker' or begging impostor.

1851 MAYHEW *Lond. Labour* (1864) I. 263 Among the more famous of the lurking patterers.

Hence **'lurkingly** *adv.*

1549 COVERDALE, etc. *Erasm. Par. Jude* 21 That kynde of men shall lurkingly crepe among the flocke of Christyanes. *a* **1693** *Urquhart's Rabelais* III. xviii. 149 Lurkingly, and in covert. **1929** R. B. C. GRAHAM *Thirty Tales & Sk.* 178 They eyed the women just as a starving dog looks at a butcher's shop, sideways and lurkingly.

'lurkingness. [f. LURKING *ppl. a.* + -NESS.] The quality of lurking.

1912 GALSWORTHY *Inn of Tranquility* 51 The mist.. seemed to have in its sheer silence a sort of muttered menace, a shuddery lurkingness.

'lurkman. *Austral. slang.* [f. LURK *sb.*¹ + MAN *sb.*¹] (See quot.)

1945 BAKER *Austral. Lang.* vii. 138 We are..originators of the following terms for various sharpers, tricksters and others who live by their wits: *spieler..lurk man*..and *amsterdam.*

lurky ('lʌrkɪ), *a. rare.* [f. LURK *v.* + -Y.] Inclined to be concealed.

1892 STEVENSON *Vailima Lett.* xxiii. (1895) 227 Compare these little lurky fevers with the fine healthy prostrating colds of the dear old dead days.

†**'lurkydish.** *dial.* (*Cheshire.*) The herb Pennyroyal, *Mentha Pulegium.*

1611 COTGR., *Pulege*, Pennie Royall..Lurkydish. **1820** WILBRAHAM *Gloss. Cheshire*, *Lurkey-dish.*

lurne, obs. form of LEARN.

lurrier ('lʌrɪə(r)). [f. LURRY *v.* + -ER¹.] An operative in textile-printing (see quot. 1897).

1897 C. F. S. ROTHWELL *Printing Textile Fabrics* 34 The lurrier brings the colour required from the colour shop, the pieces and back-greys from the stock room, and also does any odd jobs required by the printer. **1921** *Dict. Occup. Terms* (1927) §399 *Lurrier, lurryman*, colour carrier.

lurry ('lʌrɪ), *sb.*¹ *Obs.* exc. *dial.* Forms: 6 lerrie, 7 lirrie, -y, lurrie, 7–8 lurrey, 7, 9 *dial.* lerry, 9 *dial.* larry, lorry, 7– lurry. [Shortened from LIRIPOOP: cf. quots. *c* 1580, 1589.]

1. Something said by rote; a lesson, set speech, 'patter'; *fig.* a cant formula. *Obs.* exc. *dial.*

c **1580** JEFFERIE *Bugbears* v. vii. 28 in *Archiv Stud. neu. Spr.* (1897) 50 But I sent the knaves packinge I taught then [*sic*] thier lerrie & thier poop to for thier knacking. **1589** R. HARVEY *Pl. Perc.* (1590) 16 Why haue you not taught some of those Puppes their lerrie? **1602** MIDDLETON *Blurt* III. iii. F, Wee'll hencefoorth neuer goe to a cunning woman, since men can teach vs our lerrie. **1625** HEYLIN *Microcosmus* I. (ed. 2) 197 Hauing learned her lirrie of that Frier-monger, she composed an order of Religious Virgins. **1641** MILTON *Reform.* 3 Then was the Priest set to con his motions, and his Postures, his Liturgies, and his Lurries. **1651** BIGGS *New Disp.* ⁋60 Hear and learn the Galenicall Lurrey. **1669** BP. HOPKINS *Serm.* 1 Pet. ii. 12 (1685) 63 They had not learnt that lirry, that the saints are the only Lords of the world. **1719** D'URFEY *Pills* V. 220 He..begins his Lurrey. **1744–50** W. ELLIS *Mod. Husbandm.* VI. xvii. 101 Almost every shepherd..will..very likely plead: Such a Man tried a Thing, and it did no Good; [etc.] This is the common Lirry. **1887** *Kentish Gloss.*, *Lerry*, the 'part' which has to be learnt by a mummer who goes round championing. *Lorry*, *Lurry*, jingling rhyme; spoken by mummers and others.

2. A confusion of voices; babel, hubbub, outcry. *Obs.* exc. *dial.* (Cf. LARRY *sb.*¹)

c **1649** BP. GUTHRY *Mem.* (1702) 126 Notwithstanding the Lurry which had been express'd upon the first hearing of it, yet when the Convention of Estates assembled..not so much as one Man in all the City was heard to speak against it. **1690** *Andros Tracts* II. 57 The Lerry, Dinn, and Vociferations, which these Addressers make here. **1710–11** SWIFT *Jrnl. to Stella* 4 Mar., When this parliament lurry is over, I will endeavour to steal away. **1724** —— *Drapier's Lett.* vi. Wks. 1761 III. 111 Finding the whole town in a lurry, with bells, bonfires, and illuminations. **1776** J. ADAMS *Wks.* 1854 IX. 421 The election..was carried on, amidst all this lurry, with the utmost decency and order.

3. A confused assemblage (of persons) or mass (of things). *Obs.* exc. *dial.*

1607 R. C[AREW] tr. *Estienne's World of Wonders* 135 And is the lurry of lawyers quite worn out? *Ibid.* 187 Such a lurry and rable of poore farthing Friers. **1664** H. MORE *Myst. Iniq.* 464 In lieu whereof Antichrist brings in an heap and lurry of Superstitious Opinions, Rites and Ordinances. **18..** T. C. PETER *MS. Coll. Cornish Wds.* (E.D.D.), Thare ware sum lurry o' peepul theeare.

†**4.** Looseness (of the bowels). [Cf. *lurry* adj., 'of cows suffering from looseness' (*Wiltsh. Gloss.*).]

1689 T. PLUNKET *Char. Gd. Commander* 13 Such a lerry did possess his breech.

†**'lurry**, *sb.*² *slang. Obs.* [Cf. LOUR *sb.*²] (See quots.)

1673 R. HEAD *Canting Acad.* 11 But if the Cully naps us, And the Lurries from us take. *Explan. note*, Lurries, Mony, Watch, Ring, or any other moveable. *Ibid.* 191 The fifth is a Glasier, who when he creeps in: To pinch all the Lurry, he thinks it no sin. **1676** COLES, *Lurries*, c[*ant*], all manner of cloaths. *a* **1700** in B. E. *Dict. Cant. Crew.*

lurry ('lʌrɪ), *v. Obs.* exc. *dial.*

1. *trans.* To carry or drag along (a heavy body, a person, child); to 'lug'. Also, to drive by worrying. Now *dial.* (see E.D.D.).

1664 COTTON *Scarron.* 33 Seven lordly tups he wounded Mortal..These to his hungry mates he lurries. (Pray what's his due that Mutton worries?) **1879** *Cumbld. Gloss.* Suppl. s.v., Tak t' dog and lurry them sheep away.

2. *absol.* or *intr.* To push about, struggle.

1804 *Anderson's Cumberld. Ball.* 91 They fit, lugg'd, and lurry'd, aw owre blood and batter. *Ibid.* (1807) 142 The youngermak lurried ahint them.

lurry, lurtch, lury, lus: see LORRY *sb.*, LURCH, LORY, LUCE¹.

†**'lusard.** Also 6 lusart, luzard, luserde, 7 luswart. See also LUCERET. [Related to LUCERN; the formation is obscure.] The lynx; chiefly *pl.* the fur of the lynx.

1530 in Whitaker *Hist. Craven* (1812) 305 Item, a pair of white lusarts, 2l. **1535** *Wardr. Acc. Hen. VIII* in *Archæologia* (1789) IX. 245 A shamewe of blacke printed satten..furred with luzardis. **1550** in Strype *Eccl. Mem.* II. xxxiii. 538 Sables and lusards. **1572** in Whitaker *Hist. Craven* (1812) 324 A black velvett jackett..faced with luserdes. **1612** CAPT. SMITH *Proc. Virginia* 33 Some Otters, Beavers, Martins, Luswarts, and sables we found.

lusarde, obs. form of LIZARD.

Lusatian (l(j)uː'seɪʃ(ɪ)ən), *sb.* and *a.* [f. med.L. *Lusatia* + -AN.] **A.** *sb.* A native or inhabitant of Lusatia, name of a former region of eastern Germany between the Elbe and the Oder; = WEND *sb.* 1. **b.** The West Slavic language spoken in Lusatia. **B.** *adj.* Of or pertaining to Lusatia or its inhabitants.

1555 R. EDEN tr. *Martyr's Decades of Newe Worlde* 290 The Slauon tounge..vsed of..the Bohemians, Lusacians, Silesians, Morauians, [etc.]. **1862** R. G. LATHAM *Elem. Compar. Philol.* 766 Lusatian language. **1877** A. H. KEANE tr. *Hovelacque's Sci. of Lang.* 275 The Sorbian, or Sorabian, called also Wendic, or Lusatian comprises two distinct varieties, High and Low Sorbian. *Ibid.* 276 About the middle of the sixteenth century the Lusatian territory was twice as extensive as at present. **1921** *19th Cent.* May 894 We need only except Lessing, who was a Lusatian. **1933** L. BLOOMFIELD *Lang.* iv. 60 One of these, *Lusatian* (*Wendish, Sorbian*), survives as a speech-island of some 30,000 persons in Upper Saxony. **1949** *Archivum Linguisticum* I. I. 89 In view of the scarcity of Lusatian literature it is to be regretted that no selections have been supplied. **1972** W. B. LOCKWOOD *Panorama Indo-European Lang.* 158 Slavonic in Lusatia—it may be termed Sorbian or Lusatian as well as (Lusatian) Wendish—falls into two divergent dialect groups.

†**luschbald.** *Sc. Obs. rare.* ? A sluggard.

1508 KENNEDIE *Flyting w. Dunbar* 501 Lunatike, lymare, luschbald, louse thy hose.

luschburue, variant of LUSHBURG.

‖**'luscio.** *Obs.* [Sp. *lucio.*] A luce or pike.

1680 SHADWELL *Wom. Captain* I. 5 The Luscio, Eel, [etc.].

luscious ('lʌʃəs), *a.* Forms: 5 lucius, 6 lousious, looshiouse, 6–7 lussious, (6 -youse, 7 loushous), 6–8 lushious, (7 -yous), 6– luscious. [Of obscure origin.

The form *lucius*, occurring in a MS. which elsewhere has *licius* in the same sense (see LICIOUS) suggests (as Prof. Skeat has remarked) that the word may be an aphetic form of

DELICIOUS, with altered vowel. But phonetically this is unsatisfactory, and no better suggestion has been made.]

1. Of food, perfumes, etc.: Sweet and highly pleasant to the taste or smell.

c **1420** *Anturs of Arth.* 458 (Irel. MS.) With lucius drinkes, and metis of the best. **1566** DRANT *Horace's Sat.* II. iv. H, The stronge may eate good looshiouse meate. **1590** SHAKS. *Mids. N.* II. i. 251, I know a banke.. Quite ouer-cannoped with luscious woodbine. **1604** —— *Oth.* I. iii. 344 The Food that to him now is as lushious as Locusts, shalbe to him shortly, as bitter as Coloquintida. **1630** DRAYTON *Muses Elizium* (1892) 29 The lushyous smell of euery flower. **1655** FULLER *Waltham Abb.* 5 The grass.. is so sweet and lushious to Cattle, that they diet them. *a* **1700** DRYDEN *Daphnis & Chloris* Poems 1743 II. 40 Blown Roses hold their Sweetness to the last, And Raisins keep their luscious native taste. **1733** CHEYNE *Eng. Malady* II. v. §5 (1734) 159 The Means us'd commonly in making it [food] more luscious and palatable. **1758** JOHNSON *Idler* No. 96 ⁋4 The most luscious fruits had been allowed to ripen and decay. **1840** BROWNING *Sordello* 634 Like the great palmer-worm that.. Eats the life out of every luscious plant. **1869** BROWNING *Ring & Bk.* IX. 401 The luscious Lenten creature [*sc.* the eel]. **1870** H. MACMILLAN *Bible Teach.* ix. 187 Its luscious clusters of golden or purple fruit.

quasi-adv. **1588** T. HARIOT *Rep. Virginia* B 2 b, There are two kinds of grapes..: the one is small and sowre..: the other farre greater & of himselfe lushious sweet.

fig. **1665** BOYLE *Occas. Refl.* v. iii. (1848) 305 The luscious sweets of sin. *a* **1716** SOUTH *Serm.* (1823) IV. 309 May there not be.. something more glistering than a crown? and more luscious than revenge? **1848** KINGSLEY *Saint's Trag.* III. ii. 250 Sinking down In luscious rest again.

†**b.** *transf.* of a young person. *Obs.*

1742 FIELDING *J. Andrews* I. vii, He.. really is.. a strong, healthy, luscious boy enough.

2. In bad sense: Sweet to excess, cloying, sickly.

1530 PALSGR. 313/1 Fresshe or lussyouse as meate that is nat well seasoned, or that hath an unplesante swetenesse in it, *fade*. **1616** SURFL. & MARKH. *Country Farm* 239 The smell of them [*sc.* other Lillies] is lussious, grosse, and vnwholesome. **1706** PHILLIPS (ed. Kersey), *Lushious*, over-sweet, cloying. **1816** SCOTT *Old Mort.* Conclus., The last cup.. is by no means improved by the luscious lump of half-dissolved sugar usually found at the bottom of it. **1830** M. DONOVAN *Dom. Econ.* I. 275 Without the addition of water.. the resulting wine will be luscious and heavy. **1877** 'RITA' *Vivienne* III. vi, And the luscious dreary odours of.. fading flowers and trodden fruits, were heavy in the air.

3. Of immaterial things, esp. of language or literary style: Sweet and highly pleasing to the eye, ear, or mind. Chiefly in unfavourable use, implying a kind of 'sweetness' not strictly in accordance with good taste.

1651 FULLER *Abel Rediv., Berengarius* (1867) I. 4 He often.. adulced his discourse with all luscious expressions unto him. **1653** A. WILSON *Jas. I*, Pref. 8 Lushious words, that give no good rellish to the sense. **1708** BURNET *Lett.* (ed. 3) 304 All those luscious Panegyricks of Mercenary Pens. **1738** BIRCH *App. Life Milton* I. 78 A luscious Style stuffed with gawdy Metaphors and Fancy. **1822** HAZLITT *Table-t.* Ser. II. iii. (1869) 66 A stream of luscious panegyrics. **1840** KINGSLEY *Lett.* (1878) I. 50, I have shed strange tears at the sight of the most luscious and sunny prospects. **1902** *Longm. Mag.* Mar. 479 The *Lotus Eaters*.. is what may be called a luscious expansion of four or five lines of the Odyssey.

b. Of colouring, design, etc.

1849 RUSKIN *Sev. Lamps* ii. §15. 42 The groups of children,.. luscious in colour and faint in light. *Ibid.* iv. §13. 105 This extraordinary piece of luscious ugliness [a festoon].

†**4.** Of tales, conversation, writing, etc.: Gratifying to lascivious tastes, voluptuous, wanton. Rarely of a person: Lascivious. *Obs.*

a **1613** OVERBURY *A Wife* (1638) 63 She leaves the neat youth, telling his lushious tales. *a* **1694** TILLOTSON *Serm.* (1744) XI. ccviii. 4717 Those luscious doctrines of the Antinomians. **1702** POPE *Jan. & May* 379 Cantharides,.. Whose use old Bards describe in luscious rhymes. **1748** RICHARDSON *Clarissa* (1768) VII. xliv. 123 Calista [in 'The Fair Penitent'] is a desiring luscious wench. **1766** FORDYCE *Serm. Yng. Wom.* (1767) I. iv. 149 Their descriptions are often loose and luscious in a high degree. **1815** W. H. IRELAND *Scribbleomania* 143 Descriptions so luscious—such pictures of passion That prudes, ta'en with furor, to ruin might dash on.

5. *absol.* (with *the*).

1708 *Brit. Apollo* No. 78. 3/1 There's a Great deal of Wit, But the Devil a Bit Of the lushious, can I find In't. **1790** A. WILSON *Ep. to Mr. T—— B——* Poet. Wks. (1846) 87 A poet, Whose mem'ry will live while the luscious can charm.

lusciously (ˈlʌʃəslɪ), *adv.* [f. LUSCIOUS *a.* + -LY².] In a luscious manner.

1566 DRANT *Horace's Sat.* VIII. I vij, Some people.. Wyll.. make their cookes looshiously, theyr delicates to dresse. **1660** G. FLEMING *Stemma Sacrum* Ep. Ded. 6 The spices of Arabia are said to be lushiously redolent to those that are distant from it some hundreds of miles. **1710** PALMER *Proverbs* Pref. 14 An uncautious wanton writer can possibly give the vice he has too lusciously describ'd. **1779–81** JOHNSON *L.P., Milton* Wks. II. 147 The Latin pieces are lusciously elegant. **1897** MRS. LYNN LINTON *Geo. Eliot* in *Women Novelists* 64 Those lusciously suggestive epithets. *Ibid.* 68 Hetty Sorrel with her soft caressing lusciously-loving outside, and her heart 'as hard as a cherry-stone'.

lusciousness (ˈlʌʃəsnɪs). [f. LUSCIOUS *a.* + -NESS.] The quality of being luscious.

1594 PLAT *Jewell-ho.* III. 16 By allaying of the exceeding lusciousness of the mault with his bitterness. **1667** *Decay Chr. Piety* viii. ⁋15 To embitter those sensualities whose lusciousness serves to intoxicate us. **1742** FIELDING *J. Andrews* II. xii, If prudes are offended at the lusciousness of this picture they may take their eyes off from it. **1839** HALLAM *Hist. Lit.* IV. iv. vi. §42. 282 A versification sweet even to lusciousness. **1879** R. K. DOUGLAS *Confucianism* iv. 93 If a man has sumptuous viands laid before him and does not eat them, he does not know their lusciousness.

†**lu'scition.** *Obs. rare*⁻⁰. [ad. L. *luscitiōn-em* dimness of sight, f. *luscus* one-eyed.] (See quot.)

1656 BLOUNT *Glossogr.*, *Luscition*, dimness, pore-blindness of the eyes. **1676–1717** in COLES.

luse, luser(a)n, luserde, luseret: see LOUSE, LUCE¹, LUCERN¹, LUSARD, LUCERET.

†**lush,** *sb.*¹ *Obs.* [f. LUSH *v.*¹] A stroke, blow.

? *a* **1400** *Morte Arth.* 3848 With the lussche of the launce he lyghte one hys schuldyrs. *c* **1440** *York Myst.* xxviii. 271 Here with a lusshe, lordayne, I schalle þe allowe. **1887** *Jamieson's Dict.* Suppl., *Lush*, a stroke, blow, cut, as with a wand or cane.

lush (lʌʃ), *sb.*² *slang.* [Of obscure origin: perh. suggested by LUSH *a.*]

1. a. Liquor, drink.

1790 POTTER *Dict. Cant.* (1795), *Lush*, drink. **1796** *Grose's Dict. Vulg. Tongue*, *Lush*, strong beer. **1812** J. H. VAUX *Flash Dict.*, *Lush*, beer or liquor of any kind. **1829** LYTTON *Disowned* 5 I'll find the lush. **1840** COL. HAWKER *Diary* (1893) II. 189 Cheering the workmen with good words and 'lush'. **1872** MRS. LYNN LINTON *J. Davidson* viii. 160 'It's no use, governor' he said.. in his drunken way; 'work and no lush too hard for me, governor!

b. A drinking bout.

1841 COL. HAWKER *Diary* (1893) II. 214 We ended the day with a lush at Véry's. **1896** A. D. COLERIDGE *Eton in Forties* 363 On very special occasions.. there would be a 'lush', when every mess brewed its punch, or egg-flip.

c. A habitual drunkard, one addicted to drink.

1890 J. A. RIIS *How Other Half Lives* (1891) xix. 221 The first long step in crime taken by the half-grown boy.. is usually to rob a 'lush', i.e., a drunken man who has strayed his way. **1899** ADE *Doc Horne* i. 1 'My uncle didn't think so,' remarked the lush. *Ibid.* iv. 39 The drinking man, often mentioned as the lush. **1945** J. STEINBECK *Cannery Row* xxix. 124, I don't like to leave the place without a man. Some lush might get smart and the kids couldn't handle him. **1958** J. & W. HAWKINS *Death Watch* (1959) 135 She took a drink now and then, but she wasn't a lush. **1958** *Spectator* 14 Feb. 210/1 Some high-class Hollywood bitches and lushes. **1972** D. DELMAN *Sudden Death* (1973) iii. 94 He's a drunk, ain't he?.. He's a lush. And a lush is a lousy security risk.

2. *Comb.*: **lush-crib, -ken,** = *lushing-ken* (see LUSHING *vbl. sb.*); **lush-head, -hound,** a drunkard; **lush-roller, -worker,** one who steals from drunks.

1790 POTTER *Dict. Cant.* (1795), *Lush ken*, an alehouse. **1812** J. H. VAUX *Flash Dict.*, *Lush-crib* or *Lush-ken*, a public-house, or gin-shop. **1823** *Blackw. Mag.* XIII. 457 On leaving the lush-crib, we can figure them giving fippence to the drawer. **1925** H. LEVERAGE in *Flynn's* IV. 869/2 *Lush-roller*, one who robs drunken men. **1930** Lush-worker [see GLOM *v.*]. **1935** G. INGRAM *'Stir' Train* ii. 31 He's a 'lush-hound' and I knew he must be a coward. **1945** L. SHELLY *Jive Talk Dict.* 29/1 *Lush head*, chronic drinker. **1946** MEZZROW & WOLFE *Really Blues* (1957) Dedication, To all the junkies and lushheads in two bit scratchpads. **1948** MENCKEN *Amer. Lang.* Suppl. II. 682 A *creep-joint* or *panel-house* is one in which patrons are robbed, a *roller* or *mush-worker* is a girl who robs them, and a *lush-worker* is one who specializes in drunks. **1957** *Amer. Speech* XXXII. 278 *Zoot suit* meaning flashy clothes, and *lushhead* or *lush* for drunkard are no longer considered good jazz lingo, though they are or were in common nonjazz usage.

lush (lʌʃ), *a.*¹ Also 5 lusch, 6 lushe. [? Onomatopœic alteration of LASH *a.* 3.]

1. Lax, flaccid; soft, tender. *Obs.* exc. *dial.*

c **1440** *Promp. Parv.* 317/2 Lusch, or slak, *laxus*. **1567** GOLDING *Ovid's Met.* xv. 189 b, Then greene, and voyd of strength, and lush, and foggye, is the blade. **1580** BLUNDEVIL *Curing Horses* v. 4 b, The flesh of his lips and of all his bodie is lush and feeble. **1587** GOLDING tr. *Solinus* vii. G, Shrubbes, which so soone as they be in the deepes of the water, are lushe and almost like a grystle to touch. **1815** *Monthly Mag.* XXXIX. 125 (Essex Dialect), *Lush*, Loose. **1847** HALLIWELL s.v., Ground easily turned over is said to be *lush*. **1898** B. KIRKBY *Lakeland Wds.* (E.D.D.), That beef's varra lush and tender.

2. a. Of plants, esp. of grass: Succulent, and luxuriant in growth.

The literary currency of this sense (which seems still to exist in s.w. dialects) is due to the recollection of the instance in Shaks. (quot. 1610). A conjecture of Theobald's, adopted by Johnson and many later editors, substituted '*lush* woodbine' (*metri gr.*) for '*luscious* woodbine' in *Mids. N.* II. i. 251. The conjecture is now discredited, but the passage as emended has had many echoes in 19th c. literature.

1610 SHAKS. *Temp.* II. i. 52 How lush and lusty the grasse lookes? **1817** KEATS '*I stood tiptoe*' 31 And let a lush laburnum oversweep them. **1818** —— *Endym.* I. 941 Overhead, Hung a lush screen of drooping weeds. **1820** SHELLEY *Question* III. 1 In the warm hedge grew lush eglantine. **1832** TENNYSON *Dream Fair Wom.* xviii, And at the root thro' lush green grasses burn'd The red anemone. **1862** W. W. STORY *Roba di R.* i. (1864) 1 The broken arches of a Roman bridge, nearly buried in the lush growth of weeds, shrubs, and flowers. **1867** *Spectator* 6 Apr. 384 The lush tropical forests of South America. **1872** BLACK *Adv. Phaeton* xiii, Lush meadows, with the cattle standing deep in the grass. **1876** BROWNING *Pacchiarotto* Prol. ii, And lush and lithe do the creepers clothe Yon wall I watch, with a wealth of green. **1884** *Sat. Rev.* 19 July 80 Bound together by the lush growth of the bramble.

b. Of a season: Characterized by luxuriance of vegetation.

1818 KEATS *Endym.* I. 46 And, as the year Grows lush in juicy stalks, I'll smoothly steer My little boat [etc.]. **1891** T. HARDY *Tess* II. 109 The supernumerary milkers of the lush green season had been dismissed.

c. Luxuriantly covered *with*.

1863 LYTTON *Caxtoniana* xxii, The farmers.. allow their hedges to.. spread four yards thick, all lush with convolvulus and honeysuckle.

d. *transf.* and *fig.* Also, luxurious; of a woman: sexually attractive.

1851 MRS. BROWNING *Casa Guidi Wind.* I. 1088 Mow this green lush falseness to the roots. **1891** T. HARDY *Tess* II. 55 The æsthetic, sensuous, pagan pleasure in natural life and lush womanhood. **1939** *Punch* 8 Nov. 517/1 Business-men from neutral countries should be met with red-carpeted gangways and military bands, and passed in lush motor-cars from one feast to the next. **1942** [see BINT *sb.*²]. **1958** *Economist* 8 Nov. 497/2 The egg board's lush new London headquarters.

¶**3.** Shakspere's use has by some writers been misapprehended as referring to colour.

1744 *Shaks. Wks.* (ed. Hanmer) VI. Gloss., *Lush* [*Temp.* II. i. 52], of a dark deep full Colour, opposite to pale and faint. **1860** T. MARTIN *Horace* 60 The lush rose lingers late.

4. *Comb.*

1818 KEATS *Endym.* II. 52 Listening still, Hour after hour, to each lush-leaved rill. **1870** MORRIS *Earthly Par.* IV. 52 The lush-cold blue-bells.

Hence **'lushly** *adv.*, **'lushness.**

c **1440** *Promp. Parv.* 317/2 Luschly, *laxe* (K.P. *rare*). **1883** MISS BROUGHTON *Belinda* III. IV. iv. 231 The long lythrums growing lushly beside them. **1900** *Contemp. Rev.* Apr. 552 In the lushness of early summer. **1902** *Nation* (N.Y.) 9 Jan. 39/2 The customary lushness of rhetoric that is rather French than English.

lush (lʌʃ), *a.*² *slang.* (See quot.)

1812 J. H. VAUX *Flash Dict.*, *Lush*, or *Lushy*, drunk.

lush, *v.*¹ *Obs.* exc. *dial.* Forms: 4 **lusshe, luysche, lusse, lusche,** (*pa. t.* **loste, luste**), 5 **lusche, loushe, lusk,** 9 **losh,** 6– **lush.** [? Echoic variant of LASH *v.*]

1. *intr.* To rush, dash; to come *down* with a rush.

c **1330** *Arth. & Merl.* 8117 (Kölbing) Hou our wiȝtlinges so hende On þe heþen wiþ swordes losten. *c* **1330** R. BRUNNE *Chron. Wace* (Rolls) 2977 Mast & sayl, doun hit lusched [*v.r.* lussed], Cordes, kables, casteles, tofrusched. *a* **1350** *S. Anastasia* 114 in Horstm. *Altengl. Leg.* (1881) 26 Þe Emperours men.. Lusshed opon him. ? *a* **1400** *Morte Arth.* 1459 With lufly launcez one lofte they luyschene to-gedyres. *Ibid.* 2226 He laughte owtte a lange swerde, and luyschede one ffaste. *c* **1430** LYDG. *Min. Poems* (Percy Soc.) 114 He thought he harde the devylle loushe, He start into a bryer boushe. *c* **1470** *Golagros & Gaw.* 1003 Thai luschit and laid on, thai luflyis of lyre. **1566** DRANT *Horace* A iij, The bancke hath burst, that down they lush, and so be drente at laste. **18..** WHITEHEAD *Leg.* 19 (Cumberld. Gl.) For seun she grows a lusty beck An layks an loshes ower the steaynes.

2. *trans.* To strike.

c **1330** *Arth. & Merl.* 6875 (Kölbing) Þer was.. mani of his hors ylust. *Ibid.* 7750 Our cristen.. out of þe sadel mani lust. *Ibid.* 9797 Anoþer to þe chine he luȝste. *c* **1400** *Destr. Troy* 6730 He hurlet forth vnhyndly, harmyt full mony, Of þe ledis, þat hym led, luskit to ground. *c* **1440** *York Myst.* xxxi. 10 þus schall I.. lusshe all youre lymmys with lasschis. *Ibid.* xlvi. 37 Þei lusshed hym, þei lasshed hym. **14..** *MS. Soc. Antiq.* 101 lf. 72 (Halliw.) These lions been lushed and lased on sondir. **1890** *Glouc. Gloss.*, *Lush*, to beat down wasps with a bough.

†**3.** To bring *out* with a rush. In quot. *fig. Obs.*

c **1449** PECOCK *Repr.* I. xx. 129 Thei kunnen bi herte the textis of Holi Scripture and kunnen lussche hem out thikke at feest, and at ale drinking.

lush (lʌʃ), *v.*² *slang.* [f. LUSH *sb.*²]

1. *trans.* To ply with 'lush' or drink; to liquor.

1821 *Life D. Haggart* 18 We had lushed the coachman so neatly, that Barney was obliged to drive. **1838** COL. HAWKER *Diary* (1893) II. 142 To lush the Keyhavenites with four gallons of swill. **1888** E. J. GOODMAN *Too Curious* xxii, To lush me and feed me so as to get on my blind side.

2. a. *intr.* To drink, indulge in drink. Also *to lush it.*

1811 *Lex. Balatronicum*, *Lush*, to drink. **1825** C. M. WESTMACOTT *Eng. Spy* II. 252 Smoke, take snuff, lush. **1835** COL. HAWKER *Diary* (1893) II. 90 The captain and his mate having.. 'lushed it' ashore all night. **1851–61** MAYHEW *Lond. Labour* (1864) I. 187/2, I was out of work two or three weeks, and I certainly lushed too much.

b. *trans.* To drink.

1838 DICKENS *O. Twist* xxxix, Some of the richest sort you ever lushed.

3. With *up*. **a.** *intr.* To get drunk. **b.** *trans.* To ply with drink, to make (a person) drunk. **c.** *trans.* To provide with a luxurious standard of living.

1926 MAINES & GRANT *Wise-Crack Dict.* 10/2 *Lush up*, to get drunk. **1927** K. NICHOLSON *Barker* 150 *Get lushed up*, become intoxicated. **1927** *Punch* 25 May 573/1 He at once enclosed a bit of tennis-lawn for them [*sc.* rabbits] as a *manège*.. and altogether lushed them up to the good things of this world. **1933** WODEHOUSE *Mulliner Nights* ii. 48 If I lush this cat up satisfactorily, shall I not be in a position later on to make a swift touch? **1952** W. R. BURNETT *Vanity Row* (1953) xv. 107 Mr. Hobart got so lushed up... He was spilling drinks down the front of his shirt. **1959** R. GANT *World in Jug* 39 By that time Andy Mendoza had got himself lushed up and started careening around the set playing a slow drag. **1960** *News Chron.* 9 Apr. 3 (*caption*) You are lushed up on the good life and are convinced that we never had it so mechanised and marvellous. **1961** WODEHOUSE *Ice in Bedroom* i. 8, I see you're lushing up the dumb chums.

Lushai (ˈluːʃaɪ), *a.* and *sb.* Also Lhooshai, etc. [Native name.] **A.** *adj.* Of or pertaining to a mountainous region in India between Burma and Bangladesh, its inhabitants, or the language spoken by them. **B.** *sb.* **a.** A native or inhabitant

of this region. **b.** The Tibeto-Burman language spoken there.

1862 C. U. AITCHISON *Coll. Treaties India* I. 77 On the southern frontier of Cachar lies the territory of the Lhooshai Kookees... Timber merchants are..in the habit of employing Lhooshais in felling the trees in their forests. **1868** *Ann. Indian Administration* XII. 86 Mr. N. T. Davey remarks on the difficulties..likely to result in an attempt to explore..the hilly tract lying between Cachar and Chittagong. These hills are inhabited by the Looshais. **1873** E. BALFOUR *Cycl. India* III. 499/1 In the beginning of 1871, the Looshai made a prolonged raid on the North-East Provinces of British India, but were driven back. **1874** T. H. LEWIN *Progressive Colloq. Exercises in Lushai Dial.* 3 The Lushai dialect is in fact the *lingua frânca* of the country. The clan-name Lushai probably means 'the decapitators', being derived from 'lú' a head and 'shá' or 'shát' to cut. **1876** W. W. HUNTER *Statistical Acct. Bengal* VI. 59 The Lusháis or Kukis are a powerful and independent people, split up into different clans. **1887** C. A. SOPPITT *Short Acct. Kuki-Lushai Tribes* i. 2 The Lushai people have only been known to us within comparatively recent years. *Ibid.* 4 In Hill Tipperah there are three tribes, named Paitu, Omroi, Korêng, all nearly connected with the Lushais. *Ibid.* 79 (*heading*) Comparison of the dialects of the Kuki Lushai tribes and of the language known as Lushai. **1890** KIPLING *Barrack-Room Ballads* (1892) 17 We've chivied the Naga an' Looshai, we've give the Afreedeeman fits. **1910** *Encycl. Brit.* I. 773/1 The inner line formerly maintained along the Lushai border has since 1895 been allowed to fall into desuetude, but Lushais visiting Cachar are required to take out passes from the superintendent of the Lushai hills. **1915** *Encycl. Relig. & Ethics* VIII. 198/1 The Lushais are a superstitious people, and believe firmly in witchcraft. **1959** P. C. CHOUDHURY *Hist. People of Assam* iv. 95 The Central Chin group..includes the Lushâis and other allied peoples. **1972** *Language* XLVIII. 476 The most useful Kukish language for comparative purposes has hitherto been Lushai. **1972** W. B. LOCKWOOD *Panorama Indo-European Lang.* 227 To the south of these places [*sc.* Manipur and Tripura], in the southern tip of Assam, the local language is Lushai with 250,000 speakers. **1974** *Encycl. Brit. Micropædia* VI. 396/3 Lushai villages traditionally were situated on the crests of hills or spurs and..were fortified by stockades. *Ibid.*, The Kuki clans have been largely absorbed by the Lushai, adopting the Lushai customs and language.

† **'lushburg.** *Obs.* Forms: 4 lusshebourne, -borwe, -borue, -borgh, -burgh, lusseburgh, lusschebruys, lusshbourue, 4–5 lussheburghe, 5 -burne, luschburue, -bowrn, 7 *Hist.* lushbrough, -borow, -burgh, (lushoborow), 8 *Hist.* lushborough, -burg. [Anglicized name of Luxemburg.] A base coin made in imitation of the sterling or silver penny and imported from Luxemburg in the reign of Edward III. Also ***Lussheborue sterling.***

1346 *Rolls of Parl.* II. 160/2 Item, pur ce que plusours Marchantz..emportent la bone Moneie d'esterlyng hors de ceste terre, & de jour en autre reportent diverses fauxes Monoies appellez Lusshebournes [etc.]. **1351** *Ibid.* 239/1 Si homme apporte fause Monoie en cest Roialme..sicome la Monoie appelle Lusseburgh [etc.]. **1377** LANGL. *P. Pl.* B. xv. 342 As in lussheborwes is a lyther alay and ȝet loketh he lyke a sterlynge. *c* **1386** CHAUCER *Monk's T.* 74 God woot no lussheburgh payen ye. **1393** LANGL. *P. Pl.* C. xviii. 72 Men may lykne letterid men to a lussheborgh, oþer werse. *Ibid.* 82 Thus are þe lithere lykned to lussheborue sterlinges. *c* **1440** *Promp. Parv.* 317/2 Luschburue (*S.* lushburue, *papirus*). *a* **1500** *Piers of Fullham* 42 in Hazl. *E.P.P.* II. 11 No luschbowrns but money of fyne asaye. **1607** COWELL *Interpr.*, *Lushoborow*, is a base coine vsed in the daies of King Ed. the 3. coined beyond Seas to the likenes of English money. **1716** M. DAVIES *Athen. Brit.* III. 78 'Twas made High Treason in K. Edw. 3 Days, to bring in or receive the Counterfeit Money, call'd Lushburg.

'lusher. [f. LUSH *v.*^{2} 2.] One who is excessively self-indulgent, especially one who drinks excessively.

1895 G. MEREDITH *Amazing Marriage* II. xxxi. 80 The suspicion cast on the dreary lusher was the wife's wild shot at her husband. **1914** *Dialect Notes* IV. 110 Once all the politicians, nearly, were lushers. **1928** M. C. SHARPE *Chicago May* 288/1 *Lusher*, lone drinker.

lushing ('lʌʃɪŋ), *vbl. sb.* [f. LUSH *v.*^{2} + -ING^1.] The action of the vb. LUSH^2. Also *pl.*, abundance.

1829 SCOTT *Jrnl.* 18 Mar., Cigars in loads, whisky in lushings. [*So in Lockhart*; *ed.* 1890 *has* lashings; *reading of MS. perh. doubtful.*] **1890** H. NISBET *Bail Up!* i, You can have both grub and liquor here in lushings.

b. *Comb.*: **lushing-ken**, a drinking bar, low public house; **lushing-man**, a drunkard.

1859 MATSELL *Vocab.* (Farmer), With all the prigs and lushing-men, A hundred stretches hence. **1883** L. WINGFIELD *A. Rowe* I. v. 120 Unable..to steer clear of lushing-kens, or avoid the seductions of the gaming-table.

Lushington ('lʌʃɪŋtən). *slang.* [Punning use of the surname *Lushington*, with allusion to LUSH *sb.*^{2}

The 'City of Lushington' was the name of a convivial society (consisting chiefly of actors) which met at the Harp Tavern, Russell Street, until about 1895. It had a 'Lord Mayor' and four 'aldermen', presiding over 'wards' called Juniper, Poverty, Lunacy, and Suicide. On the admission of a new member, the 'Lord Mayor' (of late years at least) harangued him on the evils of excess in drink. The 'City' claimed to have existed for 150 years; if this claim be well-founded, the existence of LUSH *sb.*^{2} will be authenticated for a date considerably earlier than that of our first quot. Our information is from 'Sir' B. Davies, the last 'Lord Mayor of Lushington'.]

† **1.** In various jocular phrases referring to drink. (See quots.) *Obs.*

1823 'JON BEE' *Dict. Turf* s.v. *Lush*, 'Lushington' or 'dealing with Lushington', taking too much drink. **1823** EGAN *Grose's Dict. Vulgar Tongue*, s.v. *Lush*, Speaking of a person who is drunk they say, *Alderman Lushington is concerned*, or, he has been *voting for the Alderman.* **1826** *The Fancy* I. 31 He is reported not to take sufficient care of himself: Lushington is evidently his master.

2. A drunkard.

[**1840** *Comic Almanack* 39 A blessed School of Physic—half-and-half! The Lushington of each young Doctor's Commons; Medical Students—sons of gin and chaff—Going to pot.] **1851** MAYHEW *Lond. Labour* I. 64 If they have any..a little stale, at the end of a week, they sell it at the public-houses to the 'Lushingtons'. **1890** 'ROLF BOLDREWOOD' *Col. Reformer* xiii. 134 The best eddicated chaps are the worst lushingtons when they give way at all.

† **'lushish,** *a. Obs. rare*$^{-1}$. [? f. LUSH *a.* + -ISH.] ? Somewhat 'lush' or soft.

1661 LOVELL *Hist. Anim. & Min.* 190 The greater Sea Crabs..are strong and lushish, of hard digestion.

lushy ('lʌʃɪ), *a.*^{1} (and *sb.*) *slang.* Also lushey. [f. LUSH *sb.*^{2} + -Y^1.] Intoxicated, drunk. Also (*U.S.*) as *sb.*, a drunkard.

1811 *Lex. Balatronicum*, *Lushy*, drunk. The rolling kiddeys had a spree, and got blood lushey. **1821** *Life D. Haggart* 15 They were both pretty lushy and quarrelling. **1883** L. WINGFIELD *A. Rowe* I. v. 127 'Steady there!' bawled the Hebrew. 'Damn him! always lushy'. **1944** *New Yorker* 8 July 28/2 All our horn blowers were lushies. **1945** L. SHELLY *Jive Talk Dict.* 13/2 *Lushie*, a drunkard. **1946** MEZZROW & WOLFE *Really Blues* (1957) 94 The lushies didn't even play good music.

lushy ('lʌʃɪ), *a.*^{2} [f. LUSH *a.*^{1} + -Y^1.] = LUSH *a.*^{1}

1821 CLARE *Vill. Minstr.* I. 98 When April first..Its [*sc.* the Arum's] ear-like spindling flowers their cases burst, Beting'd with yellowish white or lushy hue. *Ibid.* II. 178 Flower of lushy red. **1882** J. WALKER *Jaunt to Auld Reekie*, etc. 16 Here milken curds and jugs o' lushy cream.

Lusian ('l(j)uːsɪən), *a.* and *sb.* [f. mod.L. *Lūsi-us* (= L. *Lūsitānus*) + -AN.] = LUSITANIAN I.

1776 W. J. MICKLE tr. *Camoens' Lusiad* 154 Heavens! shall the Lusian nobles tamely yield? **1812** BYRON *Ch. Har.* I. xiv, And soon on board the Lusian pilots leap. *Ibid.* xvi, Albion ..to the Lusians did her aid afford.

† **'lusion.** *Obs. rare*$^{-0}$. [ad. L. *lūsiōn-em*, n. of action f. *lūdere* to play.] (See quot.)

1656 BLOUNT *Glossogr.*, *Lusion*, a playing, game or pastime. **1721** in BAILEY.

† **Lusitan,** *a. Obs. rare.* [ad. L. *Lūsitān-us.*] = LUSITANIAN *a.* I.

1577–87 HOLINSHED *Hist. Scot.* 293/1 All which was doone in the sight of the rest of the Lusitan ships.

Lusitanian (ˌl(j)uːsɪ'teɪnɪən), *a.* and *sb.* [f. L. *Lūsitānia* (see below) + -AN.]

A. *adj.* **1.** Of or belonging to Lusitania; hence (chiefly *poet.*), of or pertaining to Portugal.

1720 SWIFT *Progr. Beauty* 48 Venus..Gave Women all their hearts could wish When first she taught them where to find White Lead and Lusitanian Dish. **1842** TENNYSON *Will Waterproof* i, Go fetch a pint of port:..such whose father-grape grew fat On Lusitanian summers. **1902** *Edin. Rev.* July 88 Later geographers..confounded Odusseia in the Sierra Nevada with the Lusitanian Olysippo.

2. *Biol.* Of plants or animals, having their origin in south-western Europe, esp. Portugal.

1907 R. F. SCHARFF *European Animals* v. 88 Almost all the members of that South-western, or Lusitanian, element in our fauna have a discontinuous range, which is a sure indication of great antiquity. **1927** PEAKE & FLEURE *Hunters & Artists* 38 It is a remarkable fact that the west of the Spanish peninsula and the south-west corner of Ireland share several peculiar plants and animals, such as the winter strawberry, the London pride, the great spotted slug, and a peculiar lacustrine shellfish. This so-called 'Lusitanian' association may be supposed to have lived on the Atlantic coast-lands of the Ice Age. **1935** *Discovery* Nov. 318/1, I look upon it [*sc.* the field cricket] as clearly a member of that group which Scharff has called Lusitanian. **1970** *Watsonia* VIII. 93 Several of the main phytogeographical elements in the British flora, including the Lusitanian, are represented in this section.

B. *sb.* An inhabitant of Lusitania, an ancient province of Hispania, almost identical with modern Portugal; hence, a Portuguese.

1607 TOPSELL *Four-f. Beasts* (1658) 97 A certain Lusitanian, whom he took in an Island of Portugal. **1634** SIR T. HERBERT *Trav.* 46 Some English Merchants ships (then too much abused, by the bragging Lusitanian..) helped them. **1709** J. CLARKE tr. *Grotius' Chr. Relig.* II. xviii. (1711) 128 *note*, See..Freita concerning the Empire of the Lusitanians in Asia. **1886** SHELDON tr. *Flaubert's Salammbô* 7 A Lusitanian, of gigantic height.

lusive ('l(j)uːsɪv), *a. rare*$^{-1}$. [f. L. *lūs-*, ppl. stem of *lūdere* to play + -IVE.] Playful.

1871 M. COLLINS *Inn of Strange Meetings* 184 A little tablet for love's lusive rhyme.

† **lusk,** *sb. Obs.* [f. LUSK *v.*] An idle or lazy fellow; a sluggard.

c **1420** LYDG. *Assembly of Gods* 714 Vnthryftys, & vnlustes came also to that game, With luskes, & loselles that myght nat thryue for shame. **1470–85** MALORY *Arthur* VII. v, What arte thou but a luske and a torner of broches and a ladyl wessher. *c* **1515** *Cocke Lorell's B.* 11 Luskes, slouens, and kechen knaues. **1600** HOLLAND *Livy* XXI. xliv. 418 Well may they bee cowards, and play the idle luskes. **1647** TRAPP *Comm. Rev.* ii. 26 That keepeth himself unspotted of the world, that foul lusk that lieth in that wicked one. **1694** MOTTEUX *Rabelais* V. 236 Idle Lusks.

Comb. **1611** COTGR., *Estourdi*, sottish, blockish..luske-like.

lusk (lʌsk), *a.* [f. prec. sb.] Lazy, sluggish.

1775 ASH, *Lusk*, lazy, worthless, idle. **1890** *Lippincott's Mag.* Jan. 99 The lapses of lusk water heard apart.

† **lusk,** *v. Obs.* [Of obscure origin.

The sense agrees with that of OHG. *loscên* (:—OTeut. **lut-skæ̂-* L. root **lut-*: see LOITER *v.*), which would correspond to an OE. **loscian.* For the phonology cf. DUSK *a.*]

intr. To lie hid; to lie idly or at ease, to indulge laziness; to skulk.

c **1330** R. BRUNNE *Chron.* (1810) 9 Sibriht þat schrew as a lordan gan lusk, A suynhird smote he to dede vnder a thorn busk. **1532** MORE *Confut. Tindale* 131 Frere Luther and Cate calate hys nonne lye luskynge togyther in lechery. **1533** —— *2nd Pt. Confut. Tindale* Wks. 526/1 He nothing seeketh, but corners to crepe in, where he may luske and lurke in the darke. **1591** SYLVESTER *Du Bartas* I. vii. 115 Not that I mean to fain an idle God That lusks in Heav'n and never looks abroad. **1621** T. WILLIAMSON tr. *Goulart's Wise Vieillard* 98 He lies lusking at home. **1662** J. COTGRAVE *Wits Interpr.* (ed. 2) 311 Nay now you puff, lusk, and draw up your chin.

† **luskard.** *Obs. rare*$^{-1}$. [Of obscure formation; app. coined to render (obs.) F. *foirard.*] A kind of grape which causes looseness of the bowels.

1653 URQUHART *Rabelais* I. xxv. 115 The muscadine, the verjuice grape and the luskard for those that are costive.

† **luskin.** *Obs. rare*$^{-1}$. [Perh. subst. use of LUSKING *ppl. a.*] = LUSK *sb.*

1593 B. BARNES *Parthenophil* in Arb. *Garner* V. 457 The lead-heeled lazy luskins louping, Fling out, in their new motley breeches! [**1824** MACTAGGART *Gallovid. Encycl.* 325 A luscan was lodged once in a farm-house,..and thought proper to walk off in the morning with the bed-clothes.]

† **'lusking,** *vbl. sb. Obs.* [f. LUSK *v.* + -ING^1.] Idling, skulking.

1579 TWYNE *Phisicke agst. Fort.* I. xxi. 27 Wouldest thou say rest, or lusking, or sleepe?

† **'lusking,** *ppl. a. Obs.* Also 5 luskand. [f. LUSK *v.* + -ING^2.] Slothful, lazy.

c **1460** *Towneley Myst.* xx. 750 Nay, luskand losell, lawes of the land Shall fayll bot we haue oure will. **1600** LANE *Tom Tel-troth* (1876) 128 Thither thus lusking lubber softly creeped.

† **'luskish,** *a. Obs.* [f. LUSK *sb.* + -ISH.] Slothful, lazy, sluggish.

15.. *Hye Way to Spyttil Hous* 117 in Hazl. *E.P.P.* IV. 28 Boyes, gyrles and luskysh strong knaues. **1533** MORE *2nd Pt. Confut. Tindale* Wks. 589/1 Thei haue in their traunce and theire sleepe played out all their luskishe lustes. **1548** UDALL, etc. *Erasm. Par. Mark* vi. 7–9 Suche a mynistre as is quicke and spedie, and not a luskysh loyterer or sluggerde. **1643** BURROUGHES *Exp. Hosea* v. (1652) 91 Away now with our..luskish desires, let us up and be doing. **1790** J. WILLIAMS *Shrove Tuesday* in *A Cabinet*, etc. (1794) 28 Luskish or fleet, lugubrious or glad. **1819** H. BUSK *Tea* 115 When luskish seasons their retreat delay And March enamour'd steals a kiss from May.

Hence **'luskishly** *adv.*, **'luskishness.**

1530 PALSGR. 839/1 Luskysshely, *en lourdault.* **1538** ELYOT *Dict.*, *Socordia*..Luskisshenesse. **1540** MORYSINE tr. *Vives' Introd. Wysd.* C ij, Those thinges..be occasions of great vices, as of insolent arrogancy, of luskyshenes [etc.]. **1596** SPENSER *F.Q.* VI. i. 35 But, when he saw his foe before in vew, He shooke off luskishnesse. **1637** GILLESPIE *Eng. Pop. Cerem.* Ep. A iv, Is it time for us luskishly to sit still, and to be silent? **1642** ROGERS *Naaman* 131 Formality in Religion, ease, sloath..and luskishnesse of spirit.

lusky ('lʌskɪ), *a.* [f. LUSK *sb.* + -Y.] Lazy, sluggish. (In quot. 1604 *transf.*)

1604 DRAYTON *Owl* 111 Rowse thee thou sluggish Bird.. and leaue thy Luskye nest. **1873** W. S. MAYO *Never Again* xxxii. 417 That I..would..Learn Hope to scorn and duty deprecate; And idly float on lush and lusky flow Of sense. **1886** *S.W. Linc. Gloss.*, *Lusky*, lazy, idle. 'Gret lusky things, they're too idle to work'.

Luso- ('luːsəʊ). [f. *Lusitania* = Portugal.] In *Comb.*: of Portugal, Portuguese.

1951 SMITH & MARCHANT *Brazil* v. 146 The Brazilian Negroes are blending physically and culturally with the national types, mostly Luso-Brazilian ethnically. **1957** R. CAMPBELL *Portugal* 20 The Luso-Spanish sieges of Numantia. **1958** *Archivum Linguisticum* X. I. 30 The Luso-Hispanic frontier. **1964** *New Statesman* 3 Apr. 514/1 Portugal's assertion of complete Luso-African unity. **1969** J. MANDER *Static Society* ii. 79, I have stressed the unity that Latin America possesses in virtue of its Luso-Hispanic inheritance. **1973** *Black World* Sept. 19/1 [Jorge de Lima] taught Luso-Brazilian literature at the Federal and National Universities.

† **lu'sorious,** *a. Obs.* [f. L. *lūsōri-us* belonging to a player (f. *lūsor* player) + -OUS.] Used in sport or as a pastime.

1613 T. GODWIN *Rom. Antiq.* (1625) 100 He did not beate the ayre, and flourish with those lusorious, and preparatory weapons, but he did truly fight. **1619** GATAKER *Lots* vi. 117 Lusorious Lots; and such as be vsed in game, sport or pastime, for recreation and delight. **1668** G. C. in H. More *Div. Dial.* Publ. to Rdr. a 4, The ill Tendency of such loose and lusorious Oratorie. **1697** POTTER *Antiq. Greece* II. xvi. (1715) 332 Of Lots there were four sorts, viz. Political, Military, Lusorious, and Divinatory.

lusory ('l(j)uːsərɪ), *a.* [ad. L. *lūsōri-us* (see prec.).] Used as a pastime; of the nature of play

or sport. Of composition: Written in a playful style.

1653 GATAKER *Vind. Annot. Jer.* 173 A lusorie Lot is lawful. *a* **1694** TILLOTSON *Serm.* (1743) XII. 5457 Which signifies just nothing, but is lusory and trifling. **1711** SHAFTESB. *Charac.* (1737) III. Misc. II. iii. 119 God, as a kind Tutor, was pleas'd to..bear with his Anger, and in a lusory manner, expose his childish Frowardness. **1779** JOHNSON *L.P., E. Smith* Wks. II. 456 Mr. Philips's ode.. after the manner of Horace's lusory or amatorian odes is.. a master-piece. **1791–1823** D'ISRAELI *Cur. Lit.* (1866) 361 There is a refined species of comic poetry,—lusory yet elegant.

lussh(e)borgh, -bourne, etc.: see LUSHBURG.

lussom, -um, obs. forms of LOVESOME.

lust (lʌst), *sb.* Also 3 *Orm.* lusst, 4 lost(e, 4–7 luste. [Common Teut.: OE. *lust* masc. corresponds to OFris. *lust* masc., OS. *lust* fem. (MDu., Du. *lust* masc.), OHG. *lust* fem. (MHG. *lust* masc. and fem., mod.G. *lust* fem.), Goth. *lustu-s* masc.:—O.Teut. **lustu-z*, prob. repr. a pre-Teut. **l̥s-tu-s*, f. the zero-grade of the root **las-* to long for, occurring in Gr. λιλαί-εσθαι (:—**li-lasy-*), Skr. *laṣ* (:—**la-ls*, a reduplicated form); the suffix *-tu-* forms nouns of action from verbal roots.

Cf. ON. *loste* wk. masc. (MSw. *luste, loste*), Da. *lyst*, mod.Icel. *lyst* (see LIST *sb.*), which are cognate and synonymous, but differ in declension. The mod.Sw. *lust* has been assimilated in form to the Ger. word.]

†**1.** Pleasure, delight. Const. *in, to, unto.* (Sometimes coupled with *liking*.) *Obs.*

c **888** K. ÆLFRED *Boeth.* xxiv. §3 þa sæde he [Epicurus] þ se lust wære þ hehste good. *c* **1275** *Luue Ron* 93 in *O.E. Misc.* 96 He [Jesus] is feyr and bryht on heowe..Of lufsum lost of truste treowe. **1340** *Ayenb.* 92 Of zuyche blisse and of zuyche loste no liknesse..ne may by yuounde..ine lostes of þe wordle. *c* **1380** WYCLIF *Serm.* Sel. Wks. I. 2 Sone, have mynde how þou haddist lust in this lyfe, and Lazar peyne. **1470–85** MALORY *Arthur* XI. x. 587 Allas my swete sones.. for your sakes I shalle lese my lykynge and lust. *a* **1529** SKELTON *E. Rummyng* 222 Whan we kys and play, In lust and in lykyng. *c* **1580** SIDNEY *Ps.* XXII. v, Let God save hym in whom was all his lust. **1593** SHAKS. *Lucr.* 1384 Gazing vppon the Greekes with little lust. **1607** —— *Timon* IV. iii. 492.

†**b.** *pl.* Pleasures. *Obs.*

c **1000** *Ags. Gosp.* Luke viii. 14 þa ðe..of carum..& of lustum þiss lifes synt for-þrysmede. **1340** *Ayenb.* 72 þer hy habbeþ..hire solas, hire blisse, and hire confort, and alle hire lostes. *c* **1369** CHAUCER *Dethe Blaunche* 581 My lyf, my lustes be me lothe. **1382** WYCLIF *2 Tim.* iii. 4 Loueris of lustis [Vulg. *voluptatum amatores*] more than of God. *c* **1400** *Destr. Troy* 3317 All your ledys..[shal] lyue in þis lond with lustes at ease. *c* **1420** *Anturs of Arth.* 213 This es it to luffe paramoures, and lustis [*v.r.* listes] and litys.

c. quasi-*concr.* A source of pleasure or delight; †an attraction, charm (*obs.*). *poet.*

1390 GOWER *Conf.* I. 46 O Venus,..Thou lif, thou lust, thou mannes hele. *Ibid.* II. 46 In kertles and in Copes riche Thei weren clothed..With alle lustés that eche knew Thei were enbrouded overal. **1423** JAS. I *Kingis Q.* lxv, Our lyf, oure lust, oure gouernoure, oure quene. **1549–62** STERNHOLD & H. *Ps.* lxii. 7 God is my glory and my health, my soules desire and lust.

†**d.** Liking, friendly inclination *to* a person. *Obs.*

c **1430** *Freemasonry* 506 For they were werkemen of the beste, The emperour hade to them gret luste. **1535** COVERDALE *Num.* xiv. 8 Yf the Lorde haue lust vnto vs [1611 If the Lord delight in vs].

†**2.** Desire, appetite, relish or inclination for something. Const. *of; to* (with sb. or inf.). Sometimes joined with *leisure* (cf. LIST *sb.*[4] 2). *Obs.*

Now merged in the stronger use 5 (influenced by 4).

a **900** tr. *Bæda's Hist.* v. xiii. [xii.] (1890) 436 Mid ungesweencedlice luste heofonlicra gode. *c* **1000** ÆLFRIC *Hom.* I. 86 Him wæs metes micel lust. *a* **1225** *Ancr. R.* 118 þeo hwule þæt te lust is hot toward eni sunne. **1340** *Ayenb.* 253 þe oþer stape is þet me zette mesure ine þe loste and mid þe likinge of þe wille. *c* **1400** MAUNDEV. (1839) xxviii. 285, I hadde no lust to go to tho parties. **1470–85** MALORY *Arthur* VI. i, The weder was hote about noone, and syre launcelot had grete lust to slepe. **15..** *Frere & Boye* 56 in Ritson *Anc. Pop. Poet.* 37 Hys dyner forth he drough: Whan he sawe it was but bad, Ful lytell lust therete he had. **1528** TINDALE *Obed. Chr. Man* To Rdr. 4 b, Yf we thurst, his [God's] trueth shall fulfill oure luste. **1530** PALSGR. 580/2, I have nothing so good luste to my worke as I had yesterdaye. **1570** FOXE *Serm. 2 Cor.* v, Ep. Ded. A iiij, Men wholy geuen ouer to worldly studyes haue litle leysure, and lesse lust, either to heare Sermons or to read bookes. **1611** BEAUM. & FL. *Knt. Burn Pestle* I. iii, If you would consider your state, you would haue little lust to sing, I wisse. **1627** W. SCLATER *Exp. 2 Thess.* (1629) 276, I have neither lust nor leasure to enter the question.

†**b.** with indefinite article. *Obs.*

1426 LYDG. *De Guil. Pilgr.* 23360, I had a lust..for to holden my passage. **1528** PAYNEL *Salerne's Regim.* (1535) 11 b, No man ought to eate but after he hath a luste. **1530** PALSGR. 616/1, I have a luste to gyve you a blowe on the cheke. **1549–62** STERNHOLD & H. *Ps.* lxxi. (1566) 167 From my youth I had a lust Stil to depend on thee. **1641** J. JACKSON *True Evang. T.* II. 161 Such as did seeke the Glory of Martyrs..out of a lust of dying.

†**c.** (One's) desire or wish; (one's) good pleasure. Phr. *at* (*after*) *one's lust. Obs.*

c **950** *Lindisf. Gosp.* John i. 13 Ðaðe ne of blodum ne of uillo *vel* of lust lichomæs ne from uillo *vel* lust [weres] ah Gode ȝecened sint. *a* **1300** *Cursor M.* 2899 Sua ferr your lust yee foln noght, þat yee for-gete him þat yow wroght. *c* **1386** CHAUCER *Knt.'s T.* 1620 Weepe now na more, I wol thy lust fulfille. *c* **1400** *Destr. Troy* 8852 All the pepull to þyne put and dethe at oure lust? *c* **1450** *Merlin* 268 Whan he was all to brosed and hym diffouled at her lust saf thei haue hym not slain. **1535** COVERDALE *Ps.* xci. 11 Myne eye also shal se his lust of myne enemies. **1576** FLEMING *Panopl. Epist.* 18 If by the law of your lust, you account me a craftie..felow. **1579** LYLY *Euphues* (Arb.) 59 Wil thy Father..giue thee libertie to lyue after thine owne lust? **1606** SHAKS. *Tr. & Cr.* IV. iv. 134 When I am hence, Ile answer to my lust. **1677** SEDLEY *Ant. & Cl.* I. 5 The Valiant cannot board, nor Coward fly, But at the lust of the unconstant Sky.

†**d.** = LONGING *vbl. sb.*[1] 2. *Obs.*

1530 PALSGR. 241/2 Luste as women with chylde have.

3. *spec.* in Biblical and Theological use: Sensuous appetite or desire, considered as sinful or leading to sin. Often *pl.* esp. in ***the lusts of the flesh, fleshly lusts.***

a **1000** *Juliana* 409 Him sylfum selle þynceð leahtras to fremman ofer lof godes lices lustas. *c* **1200** *Trin. Coll. Hom.* 29 Ðre þing beð þat mankin heuieð. On is þe selue lust, oðer is iuel lehtres. Ðe pridde flesliche lustes. *c* **1230** *Hali Meid.* 3 Pricunges of fleschliche fulðen to licomliche lustes. *a* **1400** *Cursor M.* 28749 (Cott. Galba) Fasting and gude bisines gers a man fle lustes of fless. **1526** TINDALE *1 John* ii. 16 All that is in the worlde (as the lust of the fleshe, the lust of the eyes, and the pryde of goddes). **1604** SHAKS. *Oth.* I. iii. 335 We haue Reason to coole our raging Motions, our carnall Strings, or vnbitted Lusts. **1641** WILKINS *Math. Magick* I. i. (1648) 2 Which set a man at liberty from his lusts and passions. **1857** MAURICE *Ep. St. John* viii. 130 These sensual pleasures, these gods of our creation, these lusts which we are feeding. **1900** J. WATSON in *Expositor* Sept. 193 This world with its pride and its riches and its lust and its glitter must pass away.

4. Sexual appetite or desire. Chiefly and now exclusively implying intense moral reprobation: Libidinous desire, degrading animal passion. (The chief current use.)

c **1000** *Sax. Leechd.* I. 358 Weres wylla to ȝefremmanne nime bares geallan & smyre mid þone teors & þa hærþan þonne hafað he mycelne lust. *a* **1100** *Voc.* in Wr.-Wülcker 524/34 *Ueneris*, lustes. *a* **1300** *Cursor M.* 26254 Man þat menges him wit best for his flexs lust to ful-fill. *c* **1315** SHOREHAM *Poems* I. 1981 Ne stren may nou encressy Wyþ-oute flesches loste. *c* **1400** MAUNDEV. (1839) iv. 27 The grete lust that he had to hire. *c* **1412** HOCCLEVE *De Reg. Princ.* 1563 Thou deemest luste and love convertible. **1592** SHAKS. *Ven. & Ad.* 800 Loue comforteth, like sun-shine after raine, But lusts effect is tempest after sunne. **1607** TOPSELL *Four-f. Beasts* (1658) 82 Cats,..in the time of their lust (commonly called 'catwralling'),..are wilde and fierce, especially the males. *a* **1635** NAUNTON *Fragm. Reg.* (Arb.) 15 He never spared man in his anger, nor woman in his lust. **1667** MILTON *P.L.* IX. 1015 In Lust they burne; Till Adam thus 'gan Eve to dalliance move. **1697** DRYDEN *Virg. Georg.* II. 637 Wine urg'd to lawless Lust the Centaurs Train. *a* **1704** T. BROWN *Sat. agst. Wom.* Wks. 1730 I. 56 We need not rake the brothel and the stews, To see what various scenes of lust they use. **1756** BURKE *Subl. & B.* I. x, The passion which belongs to generation, merely as such, is lust only. **1855** TENNYSON *Maud* II. I. ii, The feeble vassals of wine and anger and lust.

5. In mod. rhetorical use (with some transferred notion of sense 4): Lawless and passionate desire *of* or *for* some object. In poetry sometimes without implied reprobation: Overmastering desire (esp. of battle).

1678–9 DRYDEN & LEE *Œdipus* IV. i, He, who brings him forth, shall have reward Beyond ambition's lust. **1699** CIBBER *Xerxes* 11, The neighing Steeds too foam and champ,..and show a noble Lust of War. **1760** STERNE *Serm.* xi. Wks. 1815 III. 118 The insatiate lust of being witty. **1786** W. THOMSON *Watson's Philip III* (1839) 238 The monarch was governed by a lust of power. *a* **1797** H. WALPOLE *Mem. Geo. III* (1845) II. xii. 274 It appeared that he felt nothing really but the lust of applause. **1818** JAS. MILL *Brit. India* II. v. viii. 660 The very lust of pleasing the men on whose favour..their prosperity..depends. **1857** RUSKIN *Pol. Econ. Art* 12 A mean lust of accumulation. **1865** KINGSLEY *Herew.* vii, He felt the lust of battle tingling in his veins. **1868** MISS YONGE *Cameos* I. xxxiv. 293 From the time Edward I gave way to the lust of conquest, his history is one of painful deterioration.

†**6.** Vigour, lustiness; fertility (of soil). *Obs.*

1398 TREVISA *Barth. De P.R.* III. viii. (1495) 54 To restore the luste bothe in plantes and in beestes. **1521** FISHER *Serm. agst. Luther* Wks. (1876) 323 No lust of grenenes nor of lyfe appereth. *c* **1540** J. HEYWOOD *Four P.P.* (Copland) D j b, I left her in good helthe and luste. *a* **1591** R. GREENHAM *Serm.* i. (1599) 96 It putteth life and lust into vs,..to doe all those good workes which may glorifie God. **1605** BACON *Adv. Learn.* II. iv. §5. 19 Being as a plant that cometh of the lust of the earth without a formal seed. *c* **1616** S. WARD *Coal from Altar* (1627) 9 As courage to the souldier, mettle to the horse, lust to the ground. **1626** BACON *Sylva* §442 The increasing the Lust of the Earth or of the Plant. **1648** *Hunting of Fox* 5 The Vine..springs not up..out of the lust and fatnesse of the earth. **1682** *Weekly Mem. Ingen.* 44 The Salt and Lime together contribute some warmth, as well as lust and heat, to the Seed, and help the defect of other manure.

7. *attrib.* and *Comb.* **a.** simple attrib., as ***lust-bed, -fiend, -itch, -pandar, -storm***; **b.** objective, instrumental, etc., as ***lust-baiting, -belepered, -blind, -born, †-breathed, -burned, -burning, -cankered, -dieted, -engendered, -fired, -greedy, -grown, -stained, -stung, -tempting, -wearied*** adjs.; **c.** special comb., as †**lust-garden** [after G. *lust-garten*, Du. *lustgaard*], a pleasure-garden; †**lust-wort**, Gerarde's transl. of the Du. name of the Round-leaved Sundew, *Drosera rotundifolia*.

1599 MARSTON *Sco. Villanie* I. iii. 181 Taynting our Townes and hopefull Academes With your *lust-bating most abhorred meanes. *c* **1200** *Trin. Coll. Hom.* 77 þe heuenliche leche seinte poul..rere us of ure fule *lust bedde. **1633** FORD *'Tis Pity* IV. iii, I'le drag Thy *lust be-leapred body through the dust. **1600** ROWLANDS *Letting Humours Blood* xv. 21 This *lustblind Louer's vaine. **1887** BROWNING *F. Furini* iii, *Lust-born His Eve low bending took the privilege Of life. **1593** SHAKS. *Lucr.* 3 *Lust-breathed Tarqvin leaues the Roman host. **1613** HEYWOOD *Silver Age* III. Wks. 1874 III. 143 The *lust-burn'd and wine-heated monsters. **1591** SYLVESTER *Du Bartas* I. vi. 1108 Oft two Creatures of a divers kinde,..Confounding their *lust-burning seeds together, Beget an Elf, not like in all to either. **1608** MACHIN *Dumb Knt.* III. i. F 3 b, The putrefied sores Of these *lust-cankered great ones. **1605** SHAKS. *Lear* IV. i. 70 The superfluous, and *Lust-dieted man, That slaues your ordinance. **1633** FORD *Love's Sacr.* IV. ii, To hew your *lust ingendred flesh to shreds. **1609** MARKHAM *Famous Whore* (1868) 19 To breede in them this *lust-feind iealousie. **1599** MARSTON *Sco. Villanie* I. iii. 175 Like a swaggerer, *lust fiered. **1616** W. BROWNE *Brit. Past.* II. iii. 79 Walla..Was by a lust-fir'd Satyre 'mong our bowres Well-neere surpriz'd. **1873** E. BRENNAN *Witch of Nemi* 155 Purge my *lust-fretted soul of its remorse. **1589** *Troubl. Trav. Tyme* 10 The Paradise, or *Lust-garden of the Lord. **1598** SYLVESTER *Du Bartas* II. i. III. *Furies* 786 Like *Lust-greedy Goates. *a* **1586** SIDNEY *Arcadia* III. (1590) 302 A..*lust-growne rage. **1599** MARSTON *Sco. Villanie* I. iv. 189 Marry Alcides thirteenth act must lend A glorious period, and his *lust-itch end. *Ibid.* I. ii. 175 Ioues *lust-Pandar, Maias iuggling sonne. **1604** SHAKS. *Oth.* V. i. 36 Thy Bed *lust-stain'd, shall with Lusts blood bee spotted. **1605** SYLVESTER *Du Bartas* II. iii. IV. *Captains* 1125 Hurried with passion's windes Whither their *Lust-storms do transport their minds. **1597** BP. HALL *Sat.* I. ix. 22 Some *lust-stung letcher. **1601** MUNDAY *Death Earl Huntington* I. iii. (1828) 35 She is remov'd from his *lust-tempting eye. **1606** SHAKS. *Ant. & Cl.* II. i. 38 The neere *Lust-wearied Anthony. **1597** GERARDE *Herbal* III. clv. 1366 It is called.. in low Dutch *Loopichecruit*, which in English signifieth *Lust woort, bicause..cattell, if they do but onely taste of it, are prouoked to lust. **1760** J. LEE *Introd. Bot.* App. 318 Lust-wort, *Drosera*.

lust (lʌst), *v. literary* and *arch.* Also 4 loste, 4–7 luste. [f. LUST *sb.*; cf. ON. *losta*, and LIST *v.*[1]]

†**1.** *trans.* To please, delight (also *absol.*); *pass.* and *refl.* to be pleased or delighted. *Obs.*

c **1230** *Hali Meid.* 34 Hare muchele vnþeaw, þet bereð ham ase beastes to al þet ham lusteð. *a* **1300** *E.E. Psalter* lxxvi. 3 And i am lusted [Vulg. *delectatus sum*]. **1340** *Ayenb.* 246 þer he him uetteþ, þer he him losteþ, þer he him resteþ. *c* **1430** *Pilgr. Lyf Manhode* III. vii. (1869) 139 This is interieccioun sorweful wer inne is no thing that lusteth.

†**b.** *intr.* To delight *in* (something). *Obs.*

c **1400** *Destr. Troy* 3869 Noght ferfull, ne furse,..Louet he no lede þat lustide in wrange.

†**2.** *impers.* ***me lusteth***: I have a desire. *Obs.*

1390 GOWER *Conf.* II. 213 Him lusteth of no ladi chiere. *a* **1553** [see LIST *v.*[1] I b]. **1555** W. WATREMAN *Fardle Facions* I. v. 55 As thoughe me lusteth ware lawe.

†**3.** *intr.* To desire, choose, wish. **a.** Const. *inf.*

In the first quotation the verb may be impersonal: cf. LIST *v.*[1] 1, quot. *a* 1300.

a **1425** *Cursor M.* 22601 (Trin.) No creature shal luste [*Cott., etc.* list] play, Seint petur shal be doumbe þat day. **1459** *Somerset Medieval Wills* (1901) 192 Such time as God lustith to calle you owte of this present life. **1526** *Pilgr. Perf.* (W. de W. 1531) 24 Who so lusteth to rede this lytell treatyse. **1562–3** *Jack Jugler* (Grosart 1873) 43 You may saye ..That you lusted not this night any supper make. **1563** *Homilies* II. *Holy Ghost* II. (1859) 463 He that lust to see examples, let him search their lives. **1586** A. DAY *Eng. Secretary* I. (1625) 45 Insomuch as he that never lusted to helpe others, was not now able to helpe himselfe.

†**b.** With ellipsis of *inf.* (Chiefly in clauses introduced by relatives, *when, where*, etc.) *Obs.*

1526 TINDALE *Matt.* xvii. 12 They..have done vnto him whatsoever they lusted. **1536** in Strype *Cranmer* II. (1694) 36 A man is at his choiss to choose him what proctor he lust best. **1590** SPENSER *F.Q.* II. vii. 11 Do not I kings create,.. And, whom I lust, do heape with glory and renowne? **1605** CAMDEN *Rem.* (1637) 403 Here is Elderton lying in dust, Or lying Elderton, chuse which you lust. **1618** M. BARET *Horsemanship* I. 70 In letting him doe what hee lust, hee will become so stubborne and idle [etc.].

†**c.** *refl.* in the same sense. *Obs.*

a **1568** ASCHAM *Scholem.* I. (Arb.) 50 To giue them licence to liue as they lust them selues. **1583** STUBBES *Anat. Abus.* I. (1879) 34 To flaunt it out in what apparell he lusteth himself. **1599** HAKLUYT *Voy.* II. I. 271 They rate the goods without reason as they lust themselves.

†**d.** *trans.* To desire. *Obs.* (Cf. LIST *v.*[1] 3.)

1648 SANDERSON *Serm.* (1653) 4 The Spirit and the flesh are contraries, and they lust contrary things.

4. *intr.* To have a strong, excessive, or inordinate desire. Const. *for, after*, †*unto*; occas. with *inf.* or noun-clause. *arch.*

1530 TINDALE *Deut.* xiv. 26 Goo..and bestowe that moneye on what soeuer thy soule lusteth after. **1530** PALSGR. 616/1, I luste or longe for a thyng, as a woman with chylde doth. **1563** *Homilies* II. *Rogation Wk.* II. (1859) 492 If we be an hungred, we lust for bread. **1611** BIBLE *Gal.* v. 17. *a* **1701** SEDLEY *Tyrant of Crete* II. iv, So barbarous a place which dares do Any thing it lusts unto without regard Of laws or hospitality. **1761** STERNE *Tr. Shandy* IV. xxii, I have lusted earnestly, and endeavoured carefully..that these little books..might stand instead of many bigger books. **1882** *Pop. Sci. Monthly* June 211 All those who lusted after the gains and possessions of the Jews. **1898** *Pall Mall Mag.* June 221 The..Spaniards lusting for their destruction. **1898** G. W. STEEVENS *With Kitchener* 150 Charging with the cold bayonet, as they lusted to.

b. *spec.* of sexual desire.

1526 TINDALE *Matt.* v. 28 Whosoever eyeth a wyfe, lustynge affter her, hathe committed advoutrie with her alredy in his hert. **1596** SPENSER *F.Q.* IV. ix. 21 But Paridell of loue did make no threasure, But lusted after all that him did moue. **1605** SHAKS. *Lear* IV. vi. 166 Thou hotly lusts to

vse her in that kind, for which thou whip'st her. **1634** SIR T. HERBERT *Trav.* 200 Societie with that sex, is much lusted after by all inflamed Asiatiques. **1727** SWIFT *Circumcision E. Curll* Wks. 1755 III. I. 163 Instead of lusting after the real wives and daughters of our rich citizens, they covet nothing but their money and estates. **1838** LYTTON *Leila* I. vi, Yet dost thou lust after the daughter of our despised race.

lust: see LIST.

lustar, lustely, obs. ff. LUSTRE, LUSTILY.

luster ('lʌstə(r)). Now *rare*. [f. LUST *v.* + -ER[1].] One who lusts.

1591 LYLY *Endym.* III. iv, *Eum*... But did neuer any Louers come hether? *Ger.* Lusters, but not Louers. **1622** T. STOUGHTON *Chr. Sacrif.* xi. 156 Doth not the Apostle forbid the Corinthians..to be lusters after euill? **1705** STANHOPE *Paraphr.* III. 323 God gave the Lusters Flesh according to their Desire. **1847** C. BRONTE *J. Eyre* (1890) 371 A luster after power.

luster, obs. and U.S. form of LUSTRE.

lustful ('lʌstfʊl), *a.* Also 4 lostvol, 6–7 lustfull. [OE. *lustfull*: see LUST *sb.* and -FUL. Cf. ON. *lostafullr*.]

1. Having a strong or excessive desire (for something); eagerly or inordinately desirous *of* or *to do* (something). *Obs.* or *arch.*

c **893** K. ÆLFRED *Oros.* III. ii. §1 Gif his hwa sie lustfull mare to witanne, sece him þonne self þæt. **1598** GRENEWEY *Tacitus' Ann.* v. i. (1622) 117 Augustus rauished with her beauty..tooke her from her husband, shewing himselfe so lustfull of her, that [etc.]. **1660** F. BROOKE tr. *Le Blanc's Trav.* 277 They have so lustful a greedinesse to Mansflesh, that [etc.]. **1901** *Daily Chron.* 29 June 3/1 Lustful of inflicting and witnessing pain.

†**2.** Delightful, pleasurable. *Obs.*

1340 *Ayenb.* 80 Me can todele þri manere guodes, guod worþssiplich, guod lostuol, and guod uremuol. *Ibid.* 91, 92. **1394** *P. Pl. Crede* 605 Whereto beggen þise men..But for a lustfull lijf in lustes to dwellen?

3. Vigorous, lusty. *arch.*

1561 NORTON & SACKV. *Gorboduc* III. i. (1847) 127 This want of lustfull health. **1579** SPENSER *Sheph. Cal.* Jan. 37 My lustfull leafe is drye and sere. **1621** QUARLES *Esther* (1638) 95 In depth of silence there was heard the loud And lustfull language of Darius Horse. **1858** BUSHNELL *Serm. New Life* ii. (1869) 19 The first men are shewn as living out a thousand years of lustful energy. **1882** J. H. BROWN *Rambler's Cal.* 16 Neck to neck, The lustful darlings [greyhounds] race the ridgy earth.

4. Full of, imbued with, or characterized by, lust or unlawful desires; pertaining to, marked by, or manifesting sensual desire; libidinous.

1579 E. K. *Gloss. to Spenser's Sheph. Cal.* Mar. 97 By wounding in the hele, is ment lustfull loue. **1596** SHAKS. *Tam. Shr.* Ind. ii. 40 Wee'l haue thee to a Couch, Softer and sweeter then the lustfull bed On purpose trim'd vp for Semiramis. **1653** WALTON *Angler* i. 22 There are also lustful and chaste fishes, of which I shall also give you examples. **1667** MILTON *P.L.* XI. 619 Bred..to the taste Of lustful appetence. **1727** DE FOE *Syst. Magic* I. iv. (1840) 111 Injecting lustful or loose and wandering thoughts into her chaste Mind. **1815** W. H. IRELAND *Scribbleomania* 143 Libidinous themes will awake foul desires, And, banishing decency, light lustful fires. **1902** FAIRBAIRN *Philos. Chr. Relig.* I. iv. 167 The miseries that follow a lustful will.

†**5.** Provocative of lust. *Obs.*

1610 FLETCHER *Faithf. Shepherdess* II. ii. (1629) C4b, Therefore foule standergrasse, from me and mine I banish thee, with lustfull Turpentine. *a* **1667** COWLEY *Verses & Ess., Agric., Hor. Epod.* ii. (1687) 108 Not all the lustful Shell-fish of the Sea, Dress'd by the wanton Hand of Luxury [etc.].

'lustfully, *adv.* [f. prec. + -LY[2].] In a lustful manner; †with pleasure or delight; voluptuously (*obs.*); libidinously.

971 *Blickl. Hom.* 37 Se mildheorta Drihten..onfehþ swiþe lustfullice eallum þæm godum þe ænig man ȝedeþ. **1340** *Ayenb.* 51 Ine vif maneres me zeneȝeþ be mete and be drinke, Oþer uor þet þet me eth and dryngþ to-uore time, oþer to lostuolliche, oþer out of mesure, oþer [etc.]. **1388** WYCLIF *Lam.* iv. 5 Thei that eten lustfuli, perischeden in weies. **1610** HOLLAND *Camden's Brit.* I. 197 That King plied getting children so lustfully, as that hee was father of thirteen Bastards. **1665** MANLEY *Grotius' Low C. Warres* 331 The men that remained in the Town were slain, so also were some women after they had been lustfully abused. **1727** BAILEY vol. II, *Lustfully*, lecherously.

'lustfulness. [f. as prec. + -NESS.] Lustful condition or character; †delight, pleasurableness (*obs.*); libidinousness.

a **900** tr. *Bæda's Hist.* I. xvi. [xxvii.] (1890) 86 Seo lustfulnes bið þurh lichoman. *c* **1175** *Lamb. Hom.* 21 For þa licome lustfulnesse..we ne maȝen..halden crist bibode. **1611** COTGR., *Miesuresse*, incontinencie..lustfulnesse. **1654** GATAKER *Disc. Apol.* 56 The heat of lustfulness abates by degrees, and waxeth old with old age. **1893** in Barrows *Parl. Relig.* II. 896 The avoidance of cruelty, lying, lustfulness [etc.].

lust-house. [ad. Du. *lusthuis*, G. *lusthaus*, f. *lust* pleasure (= LUST *sb.* 1).] Used *occas.* to render the Du. and Ger. equivalents (which occur more frequently in their foreign form) in the senses: (*a*) A country-house, villa; (*b*) A tavern with a beer-garden.

1590 WOTTON in *Reliq.* (1685) 592 Concerning the Model of the Emperours Lust-house your honour may trust me with it. **1591** *Ibid.* 602 To get the plots of both the Lust-houses, the foundation is laid. **1818** *Blackw. Mag.* III. 530 Pass where you will, by lust-huis or by shop, You'll always find some Grizzy at her mop. **1834** BECKFORD *Italy* I. 36 [Amsterdam to Utrecht] Each lusthuys we passed contained some comfortable party dozing over their pipes. **1889** DOYLE *Micah Clarke* xxiii. 232 You may have a lust-haus of your own in a year or two, with a trimmed lawn [etc.]. *Ibid.*, Donner! There are other things beside lust-houses and flower-beds.

†**'lustick**, *a.* and *adv.* *Obs.* Also -ique. [a. Du. *lustig*; cf. F. (from Du. or Ger.) *loustic*, regimental buffoon.] **a.** *adj.* Merry, jolly; chiefly with reference to drinking. **b.** *adv.* Merrily, jovially.

1601 SHAKS. *All's Well* II. iii. 47 *Par*... Heere comes the King. *Ol. Laf.* Lustique [*Globe ed.* lustig], as the Dutchman saies. **1607** DEKKER *Sir T. Wyatt* Wks. 1873 III. 103 If my olde Maister be hanged, why so; If not, why rustické and lusticke. **1618** D. BELCHIER *Hans Beer-pot* G 2b, So now I am well, can walke a mile or two, As lustique as a Boore. *a* **1638** MEDE *Wks.* (1672) 163 Your Wine-mirth is but the smothering sometimes..of a deeper grief; like the lustick fit in some Countries of such as are going to execution. **1641** BROME *Joviall Crew* I. Wks. 1873 III. 366 As lustick and frolique as Lords in their Bowers. **1691** J. WILSON *Belphegor* II. iv, To eat well, drink lustick, care for nothing, and have my Flatterers as other Men.

lustihead ('lʌstɪhɛd). *arch.* [f. LUSTY + -HEAD.] = LUSTINESS in its various senses: pleasure, delight; vigour; lustfulness, libidinousness.

c **1369** CHAUCER *Dethe Blaunche* 27 Defaute of slepe and heuynesse Hath slayne my spyrite of quicknesse, That I haue loste al lustyheed. **1513** DOUGLAS *Æneis* XIII. v. 63 Quhayr is now thy schynand lustyhed, Thy fresch figour, thy vissage quhyte and reid? **1579** SPENSER *Sheph. Cal.* May 42 They..Passen their time..In lustihede and wanton meryment. **1621** AINSWORTH *Annot. Ps.* xc. 10 (1639) 137 *Their pride*, or prowesse, that is, the excellencie, or lusty-head of those yeeres, the bravest of them is but miserie. **1748** THOMSON *Cast. Indol.* II. vii, A knight..Of actiue mind and vigourous lustyhed. **1870** MORRIS *Earthly Par.* I. I. 62 And so all being said A little there we gathered lustihead.

lustihood ('lʌstɪhʊd). *arch.* [f. LUSTY + -HOOD.] Lustiness, vigour of body, robustness; *occas.* †lustfulness.

1599 SHAKS. *Much Ado* v. i. 76 His Maie of youth, and bloome of lustihood. **1606** —— *Tr. & Cr.* II. ii. 50. **1794** MATHIAS *Purs. Lit.* (1798) 6 In these latter days, they [Frenchmen] have been *neighing* after the constitutions of their neighbours in their lawless lustihood. **1806** H. SIDDONS *Maid, Wife, & Widow* III. 71, I had no money, but I had health in all its lustihood. **1822** W. IRVING *Braceb. Hall* (1823) I. 122 The oak, in the pride and lustihood [*ed.* 1845 lustiness] of its growth. **1826** SCOTT *Woodst.* xxix, Showing my lustihood at foot-ball. **1873** BROWNING *Red Cott. Nt.-cap* 1252 Youth, strength and lustihood can sleep on turf.

lustily ('lʌstɪlɪ), *adv.* Also 5–6 lustely(e, lustyly. [f. LUSTY + -LY[2].

It is difficult to say whether the form *lustely(e* in the 15–16th c. belongs to this word or to LUSTLY *adv.*]

†**1.** With pleasure or delight; pleasantly, pleasurably; delightfully. Also, gladly, willingly. (Cf. LUSTLY *adv.* 1.) *Obs.*

a **1225** *Juliana* 75 Lustnið lustiliche hali writes lare. ? *a* **1366** CHAUCER *Rom. Rose* 1319 A, lord! they lived lustily! [F. *cum menoient bonne vie!*] *c* **1386** —— *Knt.'s T.* 671 Whan þat Arcite hadde romed al his fille, And songen al the roundel lustily In-to a studie he fil sodeynly. *c* **1430** LYDG. *Reas. & Sens.* 275 Of Plyades and sterres sevene, That so lustely do shyne. *c* **1440** *Promp. Parv.* 318/1 Lustyly, or lystyly, *delectabiliter*. **1500–20** DUNBAR *Poems* x. 45 Now spring vp flouris fra the rute..Lay out ȝour levis lustely. **1526** SKELTON *Magnyf.* 1583 These wordes in myne eyre they be so lustely spoken, That [etc.]. *a* **1533** LD. BERNERS *Gold. Bk. M. Aurel.* xxi. Kiv, These fyve thynges..were lustely and willyngly graunted by the Senate.

2. With vigour or energy; vigorously, energetically; with a will, heartily, cheerfully. Now said only of physical activity.

c **1400** MAUNDEV. (1839) xxii. 238 Thei make Knyghtes to jousten in Armes fulle lustyly. *a* **1479** CAXTON *Bk. Curtesye* xliv, It is to a godly chyld wel syttynge..To harpe or lute or lustely to synge. **1535** COVERDALE *Ps.* xxxii. 3 Synge him a new songe, yee synge lustely unto him & with a good corage. **1599** SHAKS. *Hen. V*, IV. i. 201, I determine to fight lustily for him. **1632** BROME *North. Lasse* I. i. Wks. 1873 III. 2 *Tri.* What, married! *Luc.* Lustily promis'd Sir. Absolutely contracted. **1634** SIR T. HERBERT *Trav.* 156 They bowze it lustily, with varietie of meates and pleasure. **1685** WOOD *Life* 21 June, It began to raine lustily for a quarter of an hour. **1719** DE FOE *Crusoe* I. xix. (1840) 349 He..cried out to us..lustily. **1738** SWIFT *Pol. Conversat.* 35 If she ben't marry'd, at least she's lustily promis'd. **1829** SCOTT *Anne of G.* xxx, He saw him feed lustily as well as carve featly. **1877** A. B. EDWARDS *Up Nile* xxi. 641 Every inch of arable ground is turned to account. All that grows, grows lustily. **1898** G. S. TYACK *Bk. abt. Bells* x. 170 The bells pealing forth right lustily from the steeple of the parish church.

†**3.** Lustfully, carnally. *Obs.*

c **1410** LOVE *Bonavent. Mirr.* xxxiv. (Gibbs MS.) lf. 64 That a man þat seeþ a woman lustyly..is accounted a lechoure. **1520** *Caxton's Chron. Eng.* IV. 28 b/2 On a certayn nyght whan he wold lustely knowe his wyfe she dremed that she shold bere a chylde of myschefe. **1589** *Pappe w. Hatchet* B ij b, I think it [lecherie]..no harme if the tearmes be not abusde: for you must say, vertuously done, not lustily done.

lustiness ('lʌstɪnɪs). Also 5–6 lustines, -ynes(se. [f. LUSTY + -NESS.]

†**1.** Pleasantness, pleasure, delight. Also, beauty of attire (cf. LUSTY *a.* 2b). *Obs.*

c **1374** CHAUCER *Troylus* III. 128 (177) Beth glad and draweth yow to lustynesse. **1413** *Pilgr. Sowle* (Caxton) I. xx. (1859) 28 Thou myght..euer abyde in ioye and lustynesse. **1500–20** DUNBAR *Poems* lxiv. 2 Delytsum lyllie of everie lustynes. *a* **1547** SURREY in *Tottel's Misc.* (Arb.) 3 The sonne hath twise brought furth his tender grene, And clad the earth in liuely lustinesse. ? *a* **1550** in *Dunbar's Poems* 327 Dewoyd langour, and leif in lustines.

2. Vigour, robustness; †energy, activity.

c **1325** *Song of Mercy* 160 in *E.E.P.* (1862) 123 And lustines his leue hap take. We loue so sloupe and harlotrie. ? *a* **1366** CHAUCER *Rom. Rose* 1282 And after daunced.. Youthe, fulfild of lustinesse. **1413** *Pilgr. Sowle* (Caxton 1483) IV i. 58 That other [tree] drye withoute ony maner lustynesse or verdure. **1509** HAWES *Past. Pleas.* xl. (Percy Soc.) 203 My youth was past, and all my lustynes. **1607** MARKHAM *Caval.* I. (1617) 33 For a Horse..of youth, strength and lustinesse, eight Mares are a full number. **1740** DYER *Ruins of Rome* 476 For now the frame no more is girt with strength Masculine, nor in lustiness of heart Laughs at the winter storm. **1863** KINGLAKE *Crimea* II. ix. (1877) 102 He had too much lustiness of mind..to be capable of living on terms of close intelligence with the..statesmen of Berlin.

†**3.** Lustfulness; carnal nature or character.

c **1400** *Rom. Rose* 5118 Whan thou hast..spent thy youthe in ydilnesse, In waste, and woful lustinesse. *c* **1555** HARPSFIELD *Divorce Hen. VIII* (Camden) 247 Lest the vice of concupiscence and lustiness..should..break forth. **1580** FRAMPTON *Dial. Yron & Steele* 160 The powders of it [steele] are..good for the *Gonorea passio*, and for the lustinesse of man. **1619** FOTHERBY *Atheom.* I. x. §5 (1622) 111 When the heate of that lust and lustinesse is past, and they be come againe vnto their cold blood.

lusting ('lʌstɪŋ), *vbl. sb.* [f. LUST *v.* + -ING[1].] The action of the verb LUST in its various senses.

a **1300** *Seven Sins* viii. in *E.E.P.* (1862) 18 þat me giue lif and gode ending and to ȝou ȝiue gode lusting in þis silue place. **1580** SIDNEY *Ps.* XXXVII. iii, Delight in God, and he shall breede The fullnesse of thy own hartes lusting. **1677** GILPIN *Demonol.* (1867) 73 Paul's persecution, though a real gratification of his envious lustings, by his blinded understanding was judged duty. **1760** LAW *Spirit of Prayer* I. 54 By the flesh, and its lustings, are meant..the natural man, as he is by the fall. **1895** KIPLING *Seven Seas* (1896) 82 The lying, and the lusting, and the drink. **1909** *Westm. Gaz.* 18 Aug. 2/3 Thou art grim with the lusting of gain.

'lusting, *ppl. a.* [f. LUST *v.* + -ING[2].] That lusts; having lustful desires.

1559 T. BRICE *Compend. Reg.*, *Wishes Wise* ii, When shall the minde bee moued right To leaue hys lustyng life? **1591** GREENE *Maidens Dream* in *Shaks. Soc. Papers* (1845) II. 138 The lusting humor of the eyes..Could not allure his mind to think of vice. **1844** W. H. MILL *Serm. Tempt. Christ* iv. 91 The hopes of good which the lusting eye conceived in them while distant. **1875** JOWETT *Plato* (ed. 2) III. 118 The tyrannical man..is just a drinking, lusting, furious sort of animal.

lustless ('lʌstlɪs), *a.* Now *rare* or *Obs.* [f. LUST *sb.* + LESS.]

†**1.** Without vigour or energy: = LISTLESS. *Obs.*

c **1325** *Old Age* xi. in *E.E.P.* (1862) 150 þe tunge..lostles lowteþ in uch a liþ. **1398** TREVISA *Barth. De P.R.* IV. ix. (Tollem. MS.), A verry flewmatike man is in the body lustles [L. *deses*], heuy and slow. *c* **1412** HOCCLEVE *De Reg. Princ.* 3881 Whan þat þe paunche is ful, A fume clymbith vp in-to þe heed, And makiþ a man al lustles and al dul. **1549** COVERDALE, etc. *Erasm. Par. 2 Tim.* 24 Preache the worde of the ghospel stronglye, nether beyng frayed with aduersitie nor lustles in prosperitie. **1590** SPENSER *F.Q.* I. iv. 20 For in his lustlesse limbs..A shaking fever raignd continually. **1611** COTGR., *Detalenté*,..vnwilling, lustlesse, vndisposed, out of the humor. **1612** DRAYTON *Poly-olb.* XIII. 56 The Throstell, with shrill Sharps; as purposely he song T'awake the lustlesse Sunne.

†**2.** Joyless; without pleasure or delight. *Obs.*

1508 DUNBAR *Tua mariit wemen* 441 ȝone lustlese led so lelely scho luffit hir husband. *a* **1585** SIDNEY *Arcadia*, etc. (1622) 493 A lustless song.

3. Without lust or sexual appetite.

1586 MARLOWE *1st Pt. Tamburl.* III. (1590) C 7, He shall be made a chast and lustlesse Eunuke. **1610** HEALEY *St. Aug. Citie of God* XXII. xxiv. (1620) 848 The time shall come when we shall doe nothing but enioy our (lustlesse) beauties. **1611** COTGR., *Priapisme*, a lustlesse extention, or swelling of the yard.

Hence †**'lustlessness.**

1556 OLDE *Antichrist* 5 To dryue all lustlesnesse and sluggish drowsynes out of our myndes. **1611** COTGR., *Chasteté*, chastitie, continencie, lustlesnesse.

'lustly, *a.* [f. LUST *sb.* + -LY[1].]

1. Pleasant, pleasure-giving. *Obs.* or *arch.*

c **1200** *Trin. Coll. Hom.* 39 þe gode word of holi boc beð þe saules lustliche bileue. *c* **1380** WYCLIF *Wks.* (1880) 411 Poul vndirstondiþ bi fode, mete and drynk þat ben couenable to do betere þe seruyss of god; and not lustly deyntees of prestis. **1591** SYLVESTER *Du Bartas* I. iv. 673 The mealie Mountains (late unseen) Change their white garments into lustly green. **1894** F. S. ELLIS *Reynard Fox* 261, I ne'er have set My eyes on anything so rare, So lustly, costly, or so fair.

†**2.** Lustful; carnal. *Obs.*

c **1200** *Trin. Coll. Hom.* 79 Shune lustliche wil. **1618** FLETCHER *Chances* III. iv, There can be no hell To his that hangs upon his hopes; especially In way of lustly pleasures.

†**'lustly**, *adv.* *Obs.* [OE. *lustlíce*: see LUST *sb.* and -LY[2].]

1. With pleasure or delight; gladly, willingly.

971 *Blickl. Hom.* 47 þæt hi Sunnandaȝum & mæssedaȝum Godes cyrican ȝeorne secan, & þær þa godcundan lare lustlice ȝehyran. *c* **1000** ÆLFRIC *Gram.* xliv. (Z.) 264 *Libenter*, lustlice. *c* **1275** *Prov. Alfred* 212 in *O.E. Misc.* 115 þus quad Alfred: Lustlike lustne [*v.r.* lustnie]. [*c* **1430**, **1500–20**, *a* **1533** see LUSTILY *adv.* 1.]

2. Voluptuously; lustfully.

c **1440** *Promp. Parv.* 318/1 Lustly (*K.* lustili), *voluptuose*. *c* **1440** HYLTON *Scala Perf.* (W. de W. 1494) I. lxxii, Yf he

falle..eyther by excesse of tomoche etyng or to often or to gredely or to lustly & delicatly or tosone in untyme. [**1520**: see LUSTILY *adv.* 3.] **1598** GRENEWEY *Tacitus' Ann.* II. x. (1622) 48 Tiberius thought it better, that the yong man lustlie giuen, by the wanton laciuiousnesse of the citie, should bee better fashioned in the campe.

3. Lustily, vigorously.

[*a* **1479**: see LUSTILY *adv.* 2.] **1529** MORE *Dyaloge* I. Wks. 136/2 Forth he lymped on three legges so lustly, y[t] his maysters horse w[t] four fete, could scant ouertake him. *a* **1533** FRITH *Another Bk. agst. Rastell* C ix b, Rastell.. plaieth me the bal lustlye ouer the corde. [**1535**: see LUSTILY *adv.* 2.] **1546** BP. GARDINER *Declar. Art. Joye* 31 The unlerned arrogant reader wyl here waxe angry..and..go lustly forth to proue me a foole.

lustra, pl. of LUSTRUM.

†**lustrable**, *a. Obs.*$^{-0}$ [ad. L. **lūstrābil-is*, f. *lustrāre* to LUSTRATE.] 'That may be purged or purified' (Bailey 1727 vol. II).

lustral (ˈlʌstrəl), *a.* and *sb.* [ad. L. *lūstrāl-is*, f. *lūstr-um* LUSTRUM.] **A.** *adj.*

1. Pertaining to the Roman LUSTRUM or purificatory sacrifice; hence, pertaining to, of the nature of, or used in rites of purification; purificatory.

1533 BELLENDEN *Livy* III. vii. (S.T.S.) 270 þe capitoll was purgit be þe Sacrifice lustrale. **1677** GILPIN *Demonol.* (1867) 194 He [Julian] caused their meats and drinks to be sprinkled or mixed with the lustral water. **1776** GIBBON *Decl. & F.* I. *Notes* xv. p. lxviii, The assistants were sprinkled with lustral water. **1783** T. WILSON *Archæol. Dict.*, *Lustral day*, or *dies lustricus* amongst the Romans, was the day on which lustrations were performed for a child, and the name given. **1851** LAYARD *Pop. Acc. Discov. Nineveh* x. 251 Copper lustral spoons. **1853** MERIVALE *Rom. Rep.* iv. (1867) 133 The assassin..coolly washed his hands in the lustral waters of a neighbouring temple. **1862** RAWLINSON *Anc. Mon.* I. vi. 480 A lustral Ewer. **1874** H. R. REYNOLDS *John Bapt.* v. §2. 278 The Hindu worship has always consisted largely in lustral rites.

2. Occurring every five years; quinquennial.

1781 GIBBON *Decl. & F.* xviii. II. 71 As this general tax upon industry was collected every fourth year, it was stiled the Lustral Contribution. **1880** MUIRHEAD *Ulpian* i. §8 The lustral census in Rome.

†**B.** *sb.* A lustrum or period of five years. *Obs.*

a **1656** USSHER *Ann.* (1658) 807 When to this time five lustrals I had seen.

†**lustran.** *Obs. rare.* [f. LUSTR-UM + -AN (? or L. *an-nus* year).] The first year of a lustrum.

a **1656** USSHER *Ann.* vi. (1658) 766 The first [census] was made in the lustran, that is, in the year that they reckoned for the beginning of the space of five years.

†**ˈlustrant**, *a.*[1] *Obs. rare.* [ad. L. *lūstrant-em*, pres. pple. of *lūstrāre* to illuminate: see LUSTRE *sb.*[1]] Lustrous; *fig.* illustrious.

1549 *Compl. Scot.* vi. 38 His lustrant beymis var eleuat iiii. degres abufe oure oblique orisʒone. **1616** J. LANE *Cont. Sqr.'s T.* v. 479 Bold spirites, and lustrant heroes.

ˈlustrant, *a.*[2] *rare.* [ad. L. *lūstrant-em*, pres. pple. of *lūstrāre*: see next.] = LUSTRATING *ppl. a.*

1895 ELWORTHY *Evil Eye* 422 The application of the lustrant spittle with the middle or *infamis digitus*.

lustrate (ˈlʌstreɪt), *v.*[1] [f. L. *lūstrāt-*, ppl. stem of *lūstrāre*, to purify by lustral rites, to go round, review, survey, f. *lūstrum*: see LUSTRUM.]

1. *trans.* To purify by a propitiatory offering; to cleanse by (or as if by) lustration; *gen.* to purify.

1653 [see LUSTRATING below]. **1655** STANLEY *Hist. Philos.* I. (1701) 18/1 There was also a great Plague; the Oracle advis'd them to lustrate the City. *Ibid.* 57/1 He [Epimenides] is reported to be the first that lustrated Houses and Fields, which he performed by Verse. **1718** ROWE tr. *Lucan* III. 601 Barb'rous Priests some dreadful Pow'r adore, And lustrate ev'ry Tree with human Gore. **1746** T. SEWARD *Conform. betw. Popery & Paganism* 55 This Custom of Nurses lustrating the Children by Spittle. **1818** J. C. HOBHOUSE *Hist. Illustr.* (ed. 2) 319 The city was solemnly lustrated by holy water and missions,..to purge away the contagion of the French. **1891** tr. *De La Saussaye's Man. Sci. Relig.* xix. 160 The sacrificial animals were led round the object which was to be lustrated.

†**2. a.** *intr.* To pass or go *through* (a place). **b.** *trans.* To pass through or traverse. *Obs.*

1632 VICARS *Æn.* VIII. 303 Thrice through Aventines mount he doth lustrate. **1657–83** EVELYN *Hist. Relig.* (1850) I. 83 His soul lustrates and pervades through all things. **1721** BAILEY, *Gangweek*, the Time when the bounds of the Parishes are lustrated by the Parish-Officers, Rogation-Week.

†**3.** *trans.* To view, survey. *Obs.*

1623 COCKERAM, *Lustrate*, to view. *a* **1648** LD. HERBERT *Hen. VIII* (1683) Ep. Ded., The parts thereof, as fast as I could finish them, were lustrated by Your gracious Eye.

Hence **ˈlustrating** *vbl. sb.* and *ppl. a.*

1653 MANTON *Exp. James* iii. 17 Being in an idol temple, the lustrating water fell upon them. **1653** HAMMOND *Par. & Annot. N.T.*, *1 Cor.* iv. 13 Wks. 1659 III. 520 Περικαθαρματα [filth] signifies those things that are used in the lustrating of a city among the Gentiles. **1728** EARBERY tr. *Burnet's St. Dead* II. 52 Lustrating or purging Fires. **1846** *New Timon* (ed. 3) 178 The penitent offering the lustrating tide.

†**ˈlustrate**, *v.*[2] *Obs.* [f. LUSTRE *sb.*[1] + -ATE.] *trans.* To impart lustre to; = LUSTRE *v.*

1688 *Abridgm. Spec. Patents, Weaving* (1861) 1 Invencion of making, dressing, and lustrateing silke, called black plain, alamodes, ranforcees, and lutestringes. **1689** *Lond. Gaz.* No. 2454/4 Peter Du Clou who Dresseth and Lustrateth Silks, Stuffs, &c. **1697–8** *Act 9 Will. III*, c. 43 §13.

lustration (lʌˈstreɪʃən). [ad. L. *lūstrātiōnem*, n. of action f. *lūstrāre* LUSTRATE *v.*[1]]

1. The action of lustrating; the performance of an expiatory sacrifice or a purificatory rite (e.g. by washing with water); the purification by religious rites (*of* a person or place *from* something).

1614 RALEIGH *Hist. World* II. v. vi. §3. 621 A Muster, and ceremonious lustration of the Armie, was wont to be made at certeine times with great solemnitie. **1635** A. STAFFORD *Fem. Glory* (1869) 118 The Lustration of houses was yearely usuall with the Romans, in the Moneth of February. **1699** BENTLEY *Phal.* 380 The Lustrations of Cities and Countries from Plagues, Earthquakes, Prodigies. **1715** POPE *Iliad* I. 411 The host to expiate, next the king prepares, With pure lustrations, and with solemn prayers. **1768–74** TUCKER *Lt. Nat.* (1834) II. 414 Signatures of the cross, and lustrations by holy water. **1862** MERIVALE *Rom. Emp.* (1865) VI. l. 183 Enjoining the lustration of the city by solemn sacrifices. **1875** LIGHTFOOT *Comm. Col.* 171 There were other points of ceremonial observance, in which the Essenes superadded to the law. Of these the most remarkable was their practice of constant lustrations. **1883** *Encycl. Brit.* XV. 70/1 In Rome ..there was a lustration of the fleet before it sailed, and of the army before it marched.

b. *gen.* Washing. Chiefly *jocular*.

1825–9 MRS. SHERWOOD *Lady of Manor* III. xix. 82 The little girl..now too evidently bore the symptoms of long neglect, and Mrs. Cicely's plans of lustration were, therefore, the more needful. **1829** J. L. KNAPP *Jrnl. Naturalist* 310 Birds are unceasingly attentive to neatness and lustration of their plumage. **1887** LOWELL *Old. Eng. Dram.* (1892) 78 The other never paid his washer-woman for the lustration of the legendary single shirt without which [etc.].

2. *fig.* Purification, *esp.* spiritual or moral.

1655 [GLAPTHORNE] *Lady Mother* v. i. in Bullen *O. Pl.* II. 185 You may live To make a faire lustration for your faults And die a happie Convert. **1684** tr. *Bonet's Merc. Compit.* VI. 179 The..excrementitious matter is separated by this inward lustration from the bloud. **1777** EARL CHATHAM *Sp. on Addr.* 18 Nov., Let them [the prelates] perform a lustration; let them purify..this country, from this sin. **1882** FARRAR *Early Chr.* I. 140 St. Peter's mind is full of the Deluge as a type of the world's lustration. **1887** LOWELL *Democr.* 166 The lustration of the two vulgar Laises by the pure imagination of Don Quixote.

3. The action of going round a place, viewing, or surveying it; the review (of an army).

1614 [see 1]. **1623** COCKERAM, *Lustration*, a viewing, compassing. **1656** BLOUNT *Glossogr.*, *Lustration*, compassing, viewing or going about on every side. **1752** YOUNG *Brothers* I. i. (1777) 7 'Tis their great day, supreme of all their year, The fam'd lustration of their martial powers. **1849** JEFFREY in Cockburn *Life Jeffrey* (1852) I. 405, I have made a last lustration of all my walks and haunts, and taken a long farewell of garden, and terrace, and flowers.

†**4.** A perambulation, inspection, census. *Obs.*

1646 SIR T. BROWNE *Pseud. Ep.* VII. xi. 360 How deepely hereby God was defrauded in the time of David,..will easily appeare by the summes of former lustrations.

5. = LUSTRE *sb.*[2] *rare*$^{-1}$.

1853 F. W. NEWMAN *Odes of Horace* II. iv, One whose age runs fast to finish Its eighth lustration.

lustrative (ˈlʌstrətɪv), *a.* [Formed as LUSTRATE *v.* + -IVE.] Pertaining to lustration, expiatory purification, or (*jocularly*) washing.

1875 *Contemp. Rev.* XXV. 256 The Saxon..expends his lustrative energies upon his street and stairway, but never thinks of washing his own shirt. **1883** *Encycl. Brit.* XV. 70/1 Puppets suspended and swinging in the air (*oscilla*) formed one way of using the lustrative power of the air. **1889** *Edin. Rev.* No. 345. 67 The numerous and minute lustrative prescriptions..always included Gentile pollution.

lustratory (ˈlʌstrətərɪ), *a. rare.* [f. as prec. + -ORY.] Lustral, expiatory.

1727–41 CHAMBERS *Cycl.* s.v. *Lustration*, Lustrations, and lustratory sacrifices, were not only performed for men, but also for temples [etc.]. *a* **1883** E. FITZGERALD *Sp. Paullus Æmilius* in *Blackw. Mag.* (1889) Nov. 632 To Delphi; where to the presiding God A lustratory Sacrifice I made.

lustre (ˈlʌstə(r)), *sb.*[1] Also 6 *Sc.* lustir, 6– (now *U.S.*) luster. [a. F. *lustre* masc., = Sp., Pg. *lustre*, It. *lustro*, Rumanian *lustru*; a Com. Rom. vbl. sb. f. L. *lūstrāre* to illumine, prob. repr. an earlier **lūc-strāre* f. *lūc-*, *lūx* light.]

1. a. The quality or condition of shining by reflected light; sheen, refulgence; gloss.

Often with adj., as *metallic*, *pearly*, *silky*, *waxy lustre*.

c **1522** MORE *Dequat. noviss.* Wks. 73/2 He that by good vse and experyence, hathe in his eye the ryghte marke and very trewe lustre of the Dyamonte. **1529** —— *Dyaloge* I. ibid. 159/2 The iewell,..the bryght lustre where of bleryd eyes might not endure to beholde. **1601** SHAKS. *Jul. C.* I. ii. 124 That same Eye, whose bend doth awe the World, Did loose his Lustre. **1670** in *12th Rep. Hist. MSS. Comm.* App. v. 15 Theire ordnary designes [in tapestry]..with a whiles use will soone loose their luster. **1727–41** CHAMBERS *Cycl.* s.v., Curriers give a lustre, or gloss to their leather, several ways, according to the colour to be illustrated. **1738** GRAY *Tasso* 65 All stones of lustre shoot their vivid ray. **1830** D'ISRAELI *Chas. I*, III. vii. 135 The dark and dazzling lustre of her eyes frequently shone in tears. **1845** G. E. DAY tr. *Simon's Anim. Chem.* I. 77 Minute scales of caprate of baryta, of a fatty lustre. **1845** DARWIN *Voy. Nat.* i. (1879) 8 A coating of a hard glossy substance with a pearly lustre. **1871** W. H. G. KINGSTON *Banks Amazon* (1876) 111 The wool appeared very long, soft, fine, and of a silky lustre. **1878** HUXLEY *Physiogr.* 75 Cut a piece of lead or of zinc, and observe the lustre of its fresh surface.

b. *rarely* in pl. Appearances of lustre.

1614 TOMKIS *Albumazar* II. iii. (1615) D 4, By the whitenesse and bright sparkling lustres We allure th' Intelligences to descend. *a* **1625** BEAUM. & FL. *Custom Country* v. v, She being set in yeares next, none of those lusters Appearing in her eye, that warme the fancy. **1841–4** EMERSON *Ess.*, *Love* Wks. (Bohn) I. 76 Like opaline doves'-neck lustres, hovering and evanescent.

c. *concr. pl.* Applied to the eyes.

1810 F. DUDLEY *Amoroso* I. 118 (Fitzedw. Hall).

d. A material or composition used to impart a lustre to manufactured articles.

1727–41 CHAMBERS *Cycl.* s.v., For very black furs, they sometimes prepare a lustre of galls, copperas, Roman alum, ..and other ingredients. **1875** [see LUSTRING *vbl. sb.* b].

e. In ceramics, the surface sheen produced by glazing; the material used for glazing. Also *ellipt.*, = *lustre ware* below. Hence ***lustre-glazed***, ***-painted*** adjs.

1829 S. SHAW *Hist. Staffordshire Pott.* x. 227 The Lustre of our day is a good red clay body, with a fine brown glaze; upon which is laid, for Gold Lustre, a very thin coating of a chemical mixture containing a small quantity of Gold in solution. **1892** J. R. & F. KIDSON *Hist. Notices Leeds Old Pott.* 87 The Agate ware made at the Leeds Pottery was contemporary with the earliest makes of their Silver Lustre. **1897** *Sears, Roebuck Catal.* 681/2 Luster band, open Meakin's English-ware... The decorations are of a heavy luster band and a flower sprig in luster which resembles gold very closely. **1939** *Burlington Mag.* May 227/2 A lustre-glazed tile made at Valencia in the late fifteenth century. **1961** *Antiquaries Jrnl.* XLI. 9 A lustre-painted bowl of Malaga ware in the Staatliche Museen, East Berlin. **1969** G. LEWIS *Collector's Hist. Eng. Pott.* xvi. 157 The newly introduced technique of electro-plating made the silver lustre less popular and production ceased. **1973** *Country Life* 11 Nov. 1049/1 Morris's philosophy extended as much to..rush-bottomed chairs as to gold lustre.

2. a. Luminosity, brilliancy, bright light; luminous splendour.

1549 *Compl. Scot.* vi. 53 The spere & hauyn of Venus..is ane grit sterne of ane meruelous lustir. **1596** SPENSER *F.Q.* v. xi. 58 With bils and glayves making a dreadfull luster. **1632** J. HAYWARD tr. *Biondi's Eromena* 40 Her three lanthornes..afforded the greater lustre, because of the chrystal, cut diamond-wise. **1646** SIR T. BROWNE *Pseud. Ep.* I. v. 19 God expects no lustre from the minor stars. **1694** ADDISON *Ovid's Met.* Misc. Wks. 1726 I. 195 And now the scorching Sun was mounted high, In all its lustre. **1782** WOLCOT (P. Pindar) *Lyric Odes to R. Acad.* v, Thus stars, when pinch'd by frost, cast keener lustre. **1799** VINCE *Elem. Astron.* XXI. (1810) 229 Obstructing the lustre of the sun's beams. **1840** DICKENS *Barn. Rudge* xlvii, The sun was shining with uncommon lustre. **1893** SIR R. BALL *Story of Sun* 218 The lustre of the most remote part of the corona.. was about one eight-hundreth part of the brightness of the Moon.

b. *concr.* A shining body or form.

1742 YOUNG *Nt. Th.* v. 307 As glaring day Of these unnumber'd lustres robs our sight. **1814** CARY *Dante, Par.* v. 126, [I] turn'd Toward the lustre, that with greeting kind Erewhile had hail'd me.

3. *transf.* Radiant beauty or splendour (of the countenance, of natural objects, etc.).

1602 MARSTON *Antonio's Rev.* I. ii. Wks. 1856 I. 78 Till the soile of griefe Were cleared your cheeke, and new burnisht lustre Cloath'd your presence. **1727** GAY *Begg. Op.* I. vii, Virgins are like the fair flower in its lustre. **1728–46** THOMSON *Autumn* 1320 When Autumn's yellow lustre gilds the world. **1844** DISRAELI *Coningsby* I. i, His countenance, radiant with health and the lustre of innocence. **1887** BOWEN *Virg. Æneid* I. 591 Manhood's glorious lustre and noble joy in his eyes.

4. *fig.* in various applications, *esp.* Brilliance or splendour of renown; glory. Often in phrases, *to add lustre to*, *to shed* or *throw lustre on*, etc. Also, splendid beauty (of language, sentiments, etc.).

c **1555** HARPSFIELD *Divorce Hen. VIII* (Camden) 69 The third chapter..casteth forth a very jolly glistering lustre of many goodly illations of such things as..make little against us. **1580** SIDNEY *Ps.* XXXVII. iv, Like the light, he shall display Thy justice in most shining lustre. **1614** RALEIGH *Hist. World* III. (1634) 112 These actions, together with his honourable behaviour, which added much to their lustre, were more glorious than profitable. **1629** MAXWELL tr. *Herodian* (1635) 185 Hee affected popular Lustre by frequent exhibiting most Stately Shewes. **1634** W. TIRWHYT tr. *Balzac's Lett.* 85 The..chastity of Stile, which lendeth a luster to your elaborate writings. **1641** J. JACKSON *True Evang. T.* III. 202, I hold mine own Religion so good, as it needs not fetch lustre from the disgrace of another. **1713** ADDISON *Cato* I. i, How does the lustre of our father's actions, Through the dark cloud of ills that cover him, Break out. *a* **1715** BURNET *Own Time* (1724) I. 304 The Duke of Richmond was sent to give a lustre to that negociation. **1741** MIDDLETON *Cicero* I. i. 1 His birth..was attended by prodigies, foretelling the future eminence and luster of his character. **1756–82** J. WARTON *Ess. Pope* (ed. 4) I. iv. 239 The pomp and lustre of his language. **1760–72** H. BROOKE *Fool of Qual.* (1809) III. 3 She was..charmed by the lustre of his sentiments. **1769** ROBERTSON *Chas. V*, II. Wks. 1813 V. 295 It threw great lustre on his administration. **1776** GIBBON *Decl. & F.* xi. I. 295 The virtues of Claudius..place him in that short list of emperors who added lustre to the Roman purple. **1874** H. R. REYNOLDS *John Bapt.* IV. iv. 253 Mythical lustre illumined all the historic facts of Abraham's life. **1880** DISRAELI *Endym.* I. xix. 166 As she dilated on the past, she seemed to share its lustre and its triumphs. **1882** PEBODY *Eng. Journalism* xx. 152 Its future is a future which ..is likely to add fresh lustre to the Newspaper Press.

†**b.** Something that adds lustre; a glory. *Obs.*

a **1625** BEAUM. & FL. *Wit without M.* III. i, To thinke well of our selues, if we deserue it, is a luster in us. **1637–50** ROW *Hist. Kirk* (Wodrow Soc.) 436 Which virtues were most eminent in this singular servant of God, as a luster to his great learning. *a* **1647** HABINGTON *Surv. Worc.* in *Proc.*

Worc. Hist. Soc. III. 359 The degree of knighthood, which is not onely a luster to a family, but giueth a precedence. **1647** FULLER *Holy War* v. xxx, 286 The Persian or the Tartarian or some other obscure Prince..shall have the lustre from God to maul this great Empire.

†**c.** External splendour, magnificence. *Obs.*

1658 SIR T. BROWNE *Hydriot.* iv. (1736) 46 Solemnizing Nativities and Deaths with equal Lustre. *a* **1674** CLARENDON *Hist. Reb.* XI. §169 They inveighed vehemently against lord bishops, their pride and lustre.

5. a. †A glass ball placed among artificial lights to increase the brightness of the illumination (*obs.*); also, one of the prismatic glass pendants often attached in circles to a chandelier or hung round the edge of an ornamental vase. **b.** A chandelier [the usual sense in Fr.].

1682 WHELER *Journ. Greece* II. 187 Hung with many great Circles of Lamps..intermixed with Lustres or Balls of Glass. **1716** LADY M. W. MONTAGU *Let. to C'tess Mar* 8 Sept., The whole is made gay by pictures..and in almost every room large lustres of rock crystal. **1754** in Picton *L'pool Munic. Rec.* (1886) II. 160 A glass lustre or chandelier. **1812** MOORE *Intercepted Lett.* viii. 45 Many a maid, with busy feet That sparkle in the Lustre's ray. **1836–7** DICKENS *Sk. Boz, Scenes* xxi, The remains of a lustre, without any drops. **1842** FRANCIS *Dict. Arts, Lustre*, a bright brass chandelier, suspended from a ceiling, as we see in churches, theatres, &c. **1851** *Illustr. Catal. Gt. Exhib.* 1133 A bronze lustre for sixty candles. **1865** M. ARNOLD *Ess. Crit.* vii. (1875) 277 Lustres of coloured crystal.

6. a. A thin light dress material having a cotton (formerly also silk or linen) warp and woollen weft and a highly lustrous surface.

1831 G. R. PORTER *Silk Manuf.* 299 Poplins and lustres are..composed partly of silk and partly of worsted. **1877** BURROUGHS *Taxation* 555 Linen lustres..are dutiable. **1881** *Daily News* 26 Aug. 5/1 We do not believe there lives a woman whose partriotism would induce her to wear an English lustre if she is able to buy a French cashmere.

b. A kind of wool having a lustrous surface.

1894 *Times* 22 Jan. 13/4 The best lustres and demi-lustres are sure to be more in request than any other kinds.

7. *attrib.* and *Comb.*, as ***lustre bowl, china, jug, mug, process, tea-pot, trade, tile***; in sense 'having a lustrous or glossy surface', as ***lustre fabric, fleece, goods, wool***; objective gen., as ***lustre-maker***; **lustre mottling**, 'the peculiar mottling seen in pœcilitic rocks' (Webster *Suppl.* 1902); **lustre ware**, cheap pottery with surface ornamentation in bright metallic colours.; *spec.* pottery which is given a metallic lustre by the application of a metal oxide to its surface; also *transf.*

1908 *Sears, Roebuck Catal.* 359/4 Iridescent *luster bowl made of the most select Bavarian china. **1952** M. LASKI *Village* viii. 136 The furniture..consisted of..a painted pine corner cupboard with..some genuine old *lustre china inside. **1886** SCOTT *Sheep-Farming* 192 If *lustre fabrics are out of fashion the demand for home-grown wool diminishes. **1891** *Times* 15 Oct. 5/9 *Lustre and demi-lustre fleeces. **1884** *Pall Mall G.* 13 Sept. 4/2 France has again begun to give out orders for *lustre goods. **1908** J. M. SYNGE *Lett. to Molly* (1971) 276 Look round in Galway for *lustre jugs or Irish curios. **1881** *Daily News* 26 Aug. 5/1 The silk manufacturers of Lyons are..worse off while the taste for finely-wrought wool lasts than the Yorkshire *lustre makers. **1971** 'E. FERRARS' *Stranger & Afraid* i. 16 A good deal of clutter, in the way of Staffordshire teapots, *lustre mugs, Bohemian glass and photographs. **1900** *19th Cent.* Sept. 447 The *lustre process was known in Siena at a very early date. **1935** N. MITCHISON *We have been Warned* I. 107 Miss Waterhouse would now be giving..strong tea to her weaving class, pouring steadily from a beautiful *lustre teapot. **1943** D. WELCH *Maiden Voy.* vi. 46, I was only talking about the lustre teapot... It's shiny stuff—like metal, only china. **1933** *Burlington Mag.* Nov. 224/1 These spiral scrolls and leaves are familiar..in the thirteenth century *lustre tiles. **1895** *Daily News* 31 Dec. 2/7 In the twofold weft and *lustre trade there is an abundance of work. **1825** J. NICHOLSON *Operat. Mechanic* 476 *Lustre ware consists of an inferior quality of the materials worked into the usual forms, and having the hue of gold, platina, or copper, &c. fixed on the glaze. **1875** E. METEYARD *Wedgwood Handbk.* 312 After the commencement of the present century lustre-wares were generally made throughout the Potteries. **1938** *Times Lit. Suppl.* 17 Sept. 595/4 The household of the meek Jewish tailor and the home of the jolly publican are shining pieces of cockney lustre-ware. **1961** *Antiquaries Jrnl.* XLI. 1 A large cover of Hispano-Moresque lustreware, imported from Malaga. **1971** *Canad. Antiques Collector* Jan. 17/1 English lustre ware affords a fascinating variety of colour, charm and decoration for the collector. **1879** *Cassell's Techn. Educ.* IV. 238/1 The wool..has a glistening appearance, which has earned for it the name '*lustre wool'.

lustre ('lʌstə(r)), *sb.*² Also 6 *Sc.* lustir, 6– (now *U.S.*) luster. [Anglicized form of LUSTRUM.] A period of five years.

1387 TREVISA *Higden* (Rolls) VIII. 29 Thritty yere of vj. lustres. **1513** DOUGLAS *Æneis* I. v. 94 Eftir mony lustris and ȝeiris ourslidin is. **1685** BOYLE *Free Enq.* p. xiii, The following Discourse was written..some Lustres ago. **1715** GARTH *Claremont* 221 The fourth bright Lustre had but just begun To shade his blushing cheeks with doubtful down. **1855** THACKERAY *Newcomes* II. 9 So it will be the turn of you young folks, come eight more lustres, and your heads will be bald like mine. **1899** O. SEAMAN *In Cap & Bells* (1900) 27 After a lustre of celibacy She married with a publican.

† **'lustre,** *sb.*³ *Obs.* [ad. L. *lustrum.*] A cave.

1615 CHAPMAN *Odyss.* XVII. 159 But, turning to his luster, Calues and Dam, He shewes abhorr'd death, in his angers flame. **1658** PHILLIPS, *Lustre*,..a Den of wilde beasts.

† **'lustre,** *v.*¹ *Obs. rare.* [ad. L. *lūstrāre* to LUSTRATE.]

1. *trans.* To purify; = LUSTRATE *v.*¹ 1.

1645 RUTHERFORD *Tryal & Tri. Faith* (1845) 285 That all his actions moral be watered and lustered with faith.

2. To view, survey; = LUSTRATE *v.*¹ 3.

1541 PAYNEL *Catiline* xiv. 20 b, They trusted, that Jupiter, lustring and beholdynge all thynges, wolde discouer the counsailes..of those vngratious hopelostes. **1635** D. DICKSON *Pract. Wks.* (1845) I. 10 If a Pagan's life be well lustred.

lustre ('lʌstə(r)), *v.*² Also 7–9 **luster**. [ad. L. *lūstrāre*: see LUSTRE *sb.*¹]

†**1.** *trans.* **a.** To render illustrious. **b.** To throw light upon, illustrate. **c.** To render specious or attractive. *Obs.*

1591 SYLVESTER *Du Bartas* I. iv. 728 As a Husband's Nobl'ness doth lustre A mean-born Wife; so [etc.]. **1627** W. SCLATER *Exp. 2 Thess.* (1629) Ep. Ded. A iij, Worthies, loe to you at last; Saint Pauls Antichrist in such lineaments as that Apelles his pencell, or coale rather was pleased to shadow him in. Lustred I say not, vnuailed onely, and made more barefaced. **1637** GILLESPIE *Eng. Pop. Cerem.* II. iv. 20 The Policy then which is most simple and single, and least lustered with the pompe & bravery of Ceremonies [etc.]. **1644** BP. MAXWELL *Prerog. Chr. Kings* i. 17 Our Puritans have from hence learned to colour and lustre their ugly Treasons..with the cloake of Religion.

2. *intr.* To be or become lustrous. Now *rare.*

1582 STANYHURST *Æneis* II. (Arb.) 62 Eeune lyk as her deitee to the Saincts dooth luster in heunblisse. **1637** HEYWOOD *Royal Ship* 27 Her five bright Lanthorns luster round the seas, Shining like five of the seven Hyades. **1729** SAVAGE *Wanderer* III. 326 What bloom, what brightness lusters o'er her cheeks! **1902** *Westm. Gaz.* 6 Dec. 2/1 Their feathers lustered in the moonlight as they passed.

3. *trans.* To put a lustre upon (cloth, pottery, etc.).

1883 *Fisheries Exhib. Catal.* 201 Isinglass..used..in lustreing silk ribbons.

lustred ('lʌstəd), *a.* [f. LUSTRE *sb.*¹ or *v.*² + -ED.] Having a lustre; *spec.* in *Ceramics*, having a thin glaze or a metallic lustre.

1858 SIMMONDS *Dict. Trade, Lustred Seal*, a furrier's name for a dyed and prepared skin of the fur seal. **1868** MORRIS *Earthly Par.* I. I. 394 The lustred kingfisher. **1893** *Athenæum* 17 June 774/1 A small room in the Louvre has been appropriated to a collection of Persian lustred pottery.

‖**lustrée.** *Obs. rare.* [F. (*étoffe*) *lustrée.*] A lustred silk fabric.

1645 EVELYN *Diary* (1879) I. 244 Courtezans..cover their ..faces with a vaile of a certaine glittering taffeta or lustrée.

lustreful ('lʌstəfʊl), *a.* [f. LUSTRE *sb.*¹ + -FUL.] Lustrous.

1843 BAMFORD *Homely Rhymes* (1864) 76 And raven had never spread plume on the air Whose lustreful darkness with his might compare. **1885** G. MEREDITH *Diana* II. xiii. 333 Her eyes were proudly lustreful.

lustreless ('lʌstəlɪs), *a.* [f. LUSTRE *sb.*¹ + -LESS.] Without lustre: said freq. of the eyes.

1810 F. DUDLEY *Amoroso* II. 109 (Fitzedw. Hall). *a* **1814** *Spaniards* v. i. in *New Brit. Theatre* III. 246 Her eyes..Now lustreless are cast upon the ground, Or stare around her with a vacant gaze. **1851** RUSKIN *Stones Ven.* I. App. 393 No perfect or refined form can be expressed except in opaque and lustreless matter. **1898** P. MANSON *Trop. Diseases* xvi. 254 The skin..becomes dry, lustreless, and scurfy.

† **'lustrement.** *Obs. rare*⁻¹. [f. LUSTRE *sb.*¹ + -MENT.] Lustrous appearance.

a **1641** BP. MOUNTAGU *Acts & Mon.* (1642) 51 Notwithstanding all specious shewes, and lustrement, they retained the state and condition of sins.

† **'lustrical,** *a. Rom. Antiq. Obs.* [f. L. *lūstric-us*, f. LUSTRUM: see -ICAL.] Pertaining to purification. Only in ***lustrical day*** (L. *dies lustricus*): see quots.

1623 COCKERAM, *Lustricall day*, ones christning day. **1741** MIDDLETON *Cicero* I. i. 6 This name was..imposed..on the ninth day, called the lustrical, or day of purification.

† **lu'strific,** *a. Obs.* [ad. L. *lūstrific-us*: see LUSTRUM and -FIC.] Purificatory. †So **lu'strifical** *a.*

1656 BLOUNT *Glossogr., Lustrifical.* **1727** BAILEY vol. II, *Lustrifick*, purging. **1732** *Hist. Litteraria* III. 393 Sprinkling themselves with lustrifical Water.

† **lustrifi'cation.** *Obs.* [f. LUSTRE *sb.* + -(I)FICATION.] A making lustrous.

1631 *Celestina* I. 16 Shee made..oyntments for to make the face smooth, lustrifications, clarifications [etc.].

lustrify ('lʌstrɪfaɪ), *v. rare.* [f. LUSTRE *sb.* + -(I)FY.] *trans.* To make lustrous.

1886 *All Year Round* 28 Aug. 79 Ointments for various purposes of lustrifying and beautifying the complexion.

lustrine ('lʌstriːn). [a. F. *lustrine*, f. *lustre* LUSTRE *sb.*¹, after It. *lustrino.*] A glossy silk fabric.

1851 *Illustr. Catal. Gt. Exhib.* 1229 Specimens of figured silks: Lustrine, taffeta, English velvet. **1883** *Advt. 'great silk sale'* in *Daily News* 10 Oct. 7/4 Black and white Lustrines, from 13*d.* per yard.

lustring ('lʌstrɪŋ), *sb. Obs.* exc. *arch.* (See also LUTESTRING².) [Alteration of F. *lustrine* (see prec.), It. *lustrino*, as if f. LUSTRE *sb.*¹ + -ING¹ or -ING³.] A glossy silk fabric. Also *attrib.*

1697 *Lond. Gaz.* No. 3262/4 The Royal Lustring Company of England do give notice, that..their Ware-house..shall be opened every day to sell their Allamodes, Renforces, and Lustrings. **1732** LEDIARD *Sethos* II. VII. 75 All sorts of stuffs..of Italian lustrings. **1751** ELIZA HEYWOOD *Betsy Thoughtless* I. 68 A pink coloured French lustring. **1789** *Bath Jrnl.* 3 Aug. (Fashions), A stomacher of white lustring. **1822** LAMB *Elia* Ser. I. *Distant Correspondents*, As vapid as a damaged lustring. **1886** BYNNER *A. Surriage* xxix. 334 She must have new gowns of lustring and taffeta.

lustring ('lʌstərɪŋ), *vbl. sb. techn.* Also *U.S.* lustering. [f. LUSTRE *v.*² + -ING¹.] The action of LUSTRE *v.*²; the manner in which something is lustred. In *Metallurgy* = BRIGHTENING *vbl. sb.* 2.

1875 KNIGHT *Dict. Mech., Lustering (Metallurgy)*, the brightening of metal in the crucible at the moment of reaching its point of purity. **1892** *Athenæum* 6 Aug. 200/2 The style, colours, lustring, and other characteristics of the beautiful ceramic ware of Persia.

b. *concr.* = LUSTRE *sb.*¹ 1 d.

1875 KNIGHT *Dict. Mech., Lustering*, a polish; as black-luster for stoves, etc.

'lustring, *ppl. a.* [-ING².] Exhibiting a lustre; lustrous, shining.

1582 STANYHURST *Æneis* I. (Arb.) 29 O gay Godesse lustringe. **1708** *Brit. Apollo* No. 108. 2/2 Your Rayes so extensive, And Lust'ring Streamers so all-comprehensive. **1849** *Tait's Mag.* XVI. 245 O'er the image of the lustring moon Gloomily a sable speck is spreading.

† **'lustrious,** *a. Obs. rare.* [f. LUSTRE *sb.*¹, after *illustrious.*] Splendid, lustrous.

1651 FULLER *Abel Rediv.* 7 Most worthily may..Old Berengarius fairly shine Within this Skie of lustrious Starres, Who 'gainst Romes errors fought Truths wars. **1760–72** H. BROOKE *Fool of Qual.* (1809) III. 132 You will see folk there of much more lustrious attire.

lustrous ('lʌstrəs), *a.* [f. LUSTRE *sb.*¹ + -OUS. Cf. OF. *lustreux.*] Having lustre, sheen, or gloss.

1601 SHAKS. *All's Well* II. i. 41 My sword and yours are kinne, good sparkes and lustrous. **1742** COLLINS *Oriental Eclog.* i, But dark within, they drink no lustrous light. **1820** KEATS *Ode to Nightingale* 29 Where beauty cannot keep her lustrous eyes. **1842** TENNYSON *Locksley Hall* 162 Slides the bird o'er lustrous woodland. **1870** DICKENS *E. Drood* ii, Thick, lustrous, well-arranged black hair and whiskers. **1872** YEATS *Techn. Hist. Comm.* 135 The Romans manufactured a red lustrous ware on the banks of the Rhine.

b. *fig.* (Cf. LUSTRE *sb.*¹ 4.)

1605 BACON *Adv. Learn.* II. xx. §1 A certaine..lustrous masse of matter chosen to giue glory..to the eloquence of discourses. **1626** —— *Sylva* §956 The more Lustrous the Imagination is, it filleth and fixeth the better. **1822** LAMB *Elia* Ser. I. *Decay Beggars*, The Blind Beggar..whose story doggrel rhymes..cannot so degrade or attenuate, but that some sparks of a lustrous spirit will shine through the disguisements. **1898** G. MEREDITH *Odes Fr. Hist.* 40 She saw the Lustrous, her great lord, appear.

Hence **'lustrously** *adv.*, **'lustrousness.**

1839 BAILEY *Festus* (1848) 17/2 Like stars..They shall.. be lost All meanly in its moonlike lustrousness. **1849** E. B. EASTWICK *Dry Leaves* 56 The clemency and moderation, which shine so lustrously in the English crown. **1884** *Harper's Mag.* June 79/1 The steel..becomes lustrously white. **1892** HENLEY *Song Sword*, etc. *Lond. Voluntaries* ii. 26 With this enchanted lustrousness.

‖**lustrum** ('lʌstrəm). Pl. **lustra, lustrums,** *erron.* **lustras.** [L. *lūstrum*; usu. believed to be f. root of *luĕre* to wash (cogn. w. *lavāre* LAVE *v.*).]

1. *Rom. Antiq.* A purificatory sacrifice made by the censors for the people once in five years, after the census had been taken. Hence, the census itself.

1598 GRENEWEY *Tacitus' Ann.* XI. viii. (1622) 150 He [Claudius]..appointed a view to be taken of the city which is called Lustrum, and the number of the citizens to be inrolled. [**1780** *Ann. Reg., Chron.* 224/2 We hear from Rome that they had a lustrum (or a numbering of the people) there on the 24th of June, when it appeared there were in that city 155,184 inhabitants.]

2. A period of five years.

In Latin sometimes used for a period of *four* years.

1590 L. LLOYD *Consent of Time* To Rdr. a 3, Can any true accompt of time be made..by the censure of *Lustrum*, which the Grecians call *Penteterides.* **1601** HOLLAND *Pliny* I. 24 The Lustrum or computation of the fiue yeares beginneth at the leap yere, when the Dogstar doth arise. **1666** J. SMITH *Old Age* 264 Prolonging them..to so many years or Lustras. **1680** T. FLATMAN *Heraclitus Ridens* No. 71 (1713) II. 189 Till two short Lustra o're your Sacred Head shall flow. **1742** YOUNG *Nt. Th.* II. 173 We push time from us, and we wish him back; Lavish of lustrums, and yet fond of life. *a* **1849** POE *Morella*, Thus passed away two lustra of her life. **1901** M. T. F. MCCARTHY *Five Yrs. Irel.* xxiv. 343 There were, during the lustrum under review, 1077 men in Ireland who had been called to the Bar.

3. *U.S.* In college use.

1850 W. R. WILLIAMS *Relig. Progr.* ii. (1854) 36 It is the book not of an academic lustrum only, nor of a lifetime, but of generations. **1860** C. DURFEE *Hist. Williams Coll.* 290 A proposition was then submitted to the Alumni..that the classes in lustrums, or divisions of fours, engage to contribute two hundred and fifty dollars each.

† **'lustry,** *a. Obs. rare*⁻¹. [f. LUSTRE *sb.*¹ + -Y.] Lustrous.

1610 W. FOLKINGHAM *Art of Survey* I. iii. 5 The vyolet Hyacinth,..Lustrie Diamonde, shining Topaz.

† **'lustsome**, *a. Obs. rare.* [OE. **lustsum* (implied in *lustsumlic* pleasant) = OHG. (MHG., Ger.) *lustsam*, Goth. *lustusams*; see LUST *sb.* and -SOME.] ? Covetous, ? wilful.

a **1300–1400** *Cursor M.* 1641 (Gött.) All lustsum, all wicked-hede Has fild þis world on lenth and brede. *a* **1400** *Wyclif's Bible* Pref. Ep. vii. (1850) I. 72/1, I am not so lustsum and dul, that I shulde bihote thes thingis me to know.

lusty ('lʌstɪ), *a.* Also 3–5 lusti, 6 losty, 6–7 lustie. [f. LUST *sb.* + -Y. Cf. MHG. *lustic* (mod.G. *lustig*), ON. *lostig-r*.]

†**1.** Of persons and their attributes: Joyful, merry, jocund; cheerful, lively. *Obs.*

a **1225** *Leg. Kath.* 1693 Alle pleiende somet, alle lahinde somet, eauer iliche lusti. *c* **1386** CHAUCER *Knt.'s T.* 655 And from his courser, with a lusty herte, In to a groue ful hastily he sterte. **14..** *Epiphany* in *Tundale's Vis.* (1843) 109 With lusty hart and glad chere and myld of face. **1549** COVERDALE, etc. *Erasm. Par. Rom.* Prol., The lawe requireth a fre, a willinge, a lusty and a louynge hearte. **1552** ASCHAM *Germany* 16 The one so lusty with good luck that he had no lust to leave, and the other so chafed with losing that he still would venture. **1583** STUBBES *Anat. Abus.* II. (1882) 41 The gentlemen.. keepe sumptuous houses, lusty ports, and great hospitalitie. **1621** FLETCHER *Isl. Princess* II. vii, My most noble Princes, no discontents, but all be lustie, He that frownes this day is an open enemie.

b. Of singing, music, festivities: Merry, cheerful. Now *arch.* and *dial.*

1430–40 LYDG. *Bochas* Prol. (1554) 35 Their.. lustie freshe singing. *c* **1440** —— *Nightingale Poems* 3/37 Sche,.. all the someres nyght Ne seseth not with mony a lusty note. **1519** *Interl. Four Elem.* (Percy Soc.) 50 Let us some lusty balet syng. **1535** COVERDALE *Amos* vi. 7 The lusty chere [1611 banquet] of the wylfull shall come to an ende. **1596** SIR J. DAVIES *Orchestra* lxviii, With loftie turnes and capriols in the ayre, Which with the lustie tunes accordeth fayre. **1622** FLETCHER *Beggars Bush* IV. v, Well met sir, you are for this lusty wedding? **1818** SCOTT *Hrt. Midl.* iv, The lusty banqueting with sweetmeats and comfits. **1864** SKEAT tr. *Uhland's Poems* 262 Hark! a lusty horn is sounded. **1896** CROCKETT *Grey Man* xxvii. 183 Never once did we speak of wars and stratagems.. but all of friendship, of lusty daffing, and of leasome love.

†**2.** Pleasing, pleasant. *Obs.*

†**a.** Pleasing in appearance; beautiful. *Obs.*

a **1240** *Wohunge* in *Cott. Hom.* 269 þi leor is swa unimete lufsum and lusti on to loken. **1390** GOWER *Conf.* I. 35 Now be the lusti somer floures, Now be the stormy wynter shoures. **1412–20** LYDG. *Chron. Troy* I. vi, The medowes.. Tapited bene with diuers floures newe, Of sundry motlees lusty for to sene. **1513** DOUGLAS *Æneis* XI. ix. 86 Lavynia.. That doun for schame did cast hyr lusty eyn [L. *decoros*]. **1530** TINDALE *Gen.* iii. 6 The woman sawe that it was a good tree to eate of and lustie unto the eyes. **1562** TURNER *Baths* 9 a, Hillockes whych are pleasant and lusty to loke unto. *a* **1600** MONTGOMERIE *Misc. Poems* xvii. 63 Quhen throu hir garments, heir and thair, Appeirit hir lustie limis square.

†**b.** Of dress: Handsome, gay. Of persons: Gaily dressed. *Obs.*

c **1412** HOCCLEVE *De Reg. Princ.* 486 Who now moost may bere on his bak at ones Of cloth and furrour, hath a fressh renoun; He is 'a lusty man' clept for þe nones. **1508** DUNBAR *Gold. Targe* 58 Ane hundreth ladyes, lustie in to wedis, Als fresch as flouris that in May vp spredis. **1530** PALSGR. 318/1 Lusty or fresshe in apparayle, *frisque*. **1555** BRADFORD in Strype *Eccl. Mem.* III. App. xlv. 134 Ye shall prove their lustie lyveryes to be bought with exceeding great excesse. **1584** PEELE *Arraignm. Paris* I. i, Her lustie mantle wauing in the winde. **1603** DRAYTON *Odes* x. 7 Long since the Summer layd Her lustie Brav'rie downe. **1610** FLETCHER *Faithf. Shepherdess* I. i, Euery shepheards boy Puts on his lusty greene.

†**c.** Of seasons, places, etc.: Pleasant, delightful. *Obs.*

? *a* **1366** CHAUCER *Rom. Rose* 736 And with him, in that lusty place, So fair folk and so fresh hadde he. *c* **1386** —— *Sqr.'s T.* 44 Ful lusty was the weder and benigne. *c* **1430** LYDG. *Reas. & Sens.* (E.E.T.S.) 4807 In that fressh[e] lusty place Hem to disporte and solace. **1525** LD. BERNERS *Froiss.* II. lxxix. [lxxv.] 236 It was in the ioly lusty moneth of Aprell. *c* **1590** MARLOWE *Faust.* i. 149 That I may coniure in some lustie groue. **1610** FLETCHER *Faithf. Shepherdess* I. i, Since the lusty spring began.

†**d.** Pleasant to the taste. *Obs.*

c **1430** LYDG. *Compl. Bl. Knt.* 29 Till firy Tytan.. Had dried up the lusty lycour nywe, Upon the herbes in the grene mede. *a* **1450** MYRC 1436 Also ȝef þou synned hast In mete or drynke by lusty tast.

†**e.** Of language, eloquence, etc.: Pleasing, agreeable. *Obs.*

1399 *Pol. Poems* (Rolls) I. 372 That it be lore lawefulle, and lusty to here. *c* **1449** PECOCK *Repr.* II. xviii. 255 Into this eende.. thei vsiden certein colouris of rethorik, that with hem her spechis schulde be the more lusti. **1513** BRADSHAW *St. Werburge* I. 980 All the audyence Reioysed to here her lusty eloquence. *a* **1529** SKELTON *Replyc.* etc. Wks. 1843 I. 207 Yong scolers.. when they haue delectably lycked a lytell of the lycorous electuary of lusty lerning.

†**3.** Full of desire, desirous. Const. *to*, *for*. *Obs.*

c **1400** *Destr. Troy* 10598 Sum lordes to lenge lusty þai were. **1493** *Festivall* (W. de W. 1515) 96 Than George bad yᵉ kynge.. be lusty to goddes servyce. **1552** LATIMER *Serm. Lincoln.* vii. (1562) 124 b, These thynges are written for our sake, to make vs lustie to folowe oure vocation. **1657** S. PURCHAS *Pol. Flying-Ins.* 97 Lusty for labour.

†**4.** Full of lust or sexual desire; lustful. *Obs.*

c **1386** CHAUCER *Manciple's Prol.* 41 Fy stynkyng swyn fy, foule moot thee falle,.. A taketh heede sires, of this lusty man. **1483** *Cath. Angl.* 224/2 Lusty,.. *libidinosus*. **1523** FITZHERB. *Husb.* §68 It is better to kepe the horse frome the mares,.. for.. he shall be more lusty, and the moo horse coltes shall he gete. **1562** *Child Marriages* etc. 75 He went.. when he was lustie, to his wief, and vsid her companye in bed. **1610** FLETCHER *Faithf. Shepherdess* IV. ii, Prouoking thoughts that stirr vpp lusty fiers. **1611** COTGR., *Rechauffer vn chien*, to make him lustie, or desirous of the bitch. **1697** DRYDEN *Virg. Georg.* III. 104 While their Youth is fill'd with kindly Fire, Submit thy Females to the lusty Sire.

5. Full of healthy vigour.

a. Of persons and animals: Healthy, strong, vigorous. Also of a period of life: Characterized by vigour. Now somewhat *arch.* in literary use; common in dialects. †In early use often: Valiant, courageous, active (*obs.*).

c **1374** CHAUCER *Anel. & Arc.* 85 This.. knyght.. Was yong and there with all a lusty knyght. *c* **1386** —— Prol. 80 With hym ther was his sone a yong Squier A louyere, and a lusty Bacheler. **1486** *Bk. St. Albans* b vj b, That hawke was neuer so lusty nor so Joly before. **1521** in Ellis *Orig. Lett.* Ser. III. I. 281, I mett his Holynes, and my thought I never sawe hym mor losty. **1535** COVERDALE *Prov.* xvii. 22 A mery herte maketh a lusty age, but a sorowfull minde dryeth vp yᵉ bones. **1577** B. GOOGE *Heresbach's Husb.* (1586) 128 For milcking, or for feeding, it is best alwaies to choose such as are young, of lusty age. **1593** SHAKS. *Rich. II*, I. iii. 66. **1612** T. TAYLOR *Comm. Titus* i. 15 All idle, lustie, and wandring beggars, who ought not to eate. *a* **1648** DIGBY *Closet Open.* (1669) 27 Cause a lusty Servant (his Arms well washed) to mix the honey and water together. **1702** POPE *Jan. & May* 135 Old as I am, my lusty limbs appear Like winter greens, that flourish all the year. **1791** COWPER *Iliad* I. 175 A bark with lusty rowers well supplied. **1824** BYRON *Deformed Transf.* I. i, Though my brothers are So beautiful and lusty. **1876** BLACK *Madcap V.* vii. 65 But what pathos was there possible to those stalwart young fellows with their lusty throats, their tobacco, and beer and wine? **1884** *West Sussex Gaz.* 25 Sept., [To be sold] 10 prime lusty heifers.

transf. **1548** UDALL, etc. *Erasm. Par. Matt.* iv. 31 Make lusty the mynde of a Christian souldier. *a* **1677** BARROW *Serm.* Wks. 1716 II. 14 Truth is the natural food of our soul.. doth render it lusty, plump and active. **1871** BLACKIE *Four Phases* I. 33 *note*, They were.. the natural guides of the lusty young democracy. **1880** NEWMAN SMYTH *Old Faiths in New Lt.* i. (1882) 19 Much even of our most positive and lusty science is still only in its infancy.

†**b.** Phrases. ***Lusty Laurence*** (cf. LAURENCE): 'a good wencher' (Nares). ***Lusty Juventus***: the title of a morality play produced *c* 1550; often used allusively in 16th c. *Obs.*

1582 STANYHURST *Æneis* II. (Arb.) 64 You lustye iuuentus In yeers and carcasse prime. **1594** in Arber *Stationers' Reg.* (1875) II. 309 A ballad intituled Lustye Lawrence. **1594** BARNFIELD *Helens Rape* Poems (Arb.) 40 Old lad, and bold lad, such a Boy, such a lustie *Iuuentus*. **1598** MARSTON *Metam. Pigmal.* etc. *Sat.* iv. F 1 b, When strong backt Hercules.. Rob'd fifty wenches of virginity. Farre more then lusty Laurence. **1613** BEAUM. & FL. *Captain* IV. iii, Lusty Laurence, See what a Gentlewoman you have saluted. *a* **1625** FLETCHER *Woman's Prize* I. iii, Well, lusty Laurence, were but my night now, Old as I am, I would make you clap on Spurs, But I would reach you. **1636** DEKKER *Wonder of Kingd.* v. i. Wks. 1873 IV. 279 Hee'll proue a lustie Larrence.

c. With reference to vegetable growth. *arch.*

1600 SURFLET *Country Farm* III. viii. 434 In the spring and March when the trees are in flowers, and beginne to grow lustie. **1660** SHARROCK *Vegetables* 128 Thus you will have lusty slips. **1671** GREW *Anat. Plants* I. (1682) 8 The Plume,.. growing so lusty, as to mount up without them [the lobes]. **1820** KEATS *Isabella* ix, Great happiness Grew, like a lusty flower in June's caress.

†**d.** Of soil: Fertile, prolific. *Obs.*

1601 BP. W. BARLOW *Defence* 6 Pregnant natures, are like lustie groundes, these manured by industry, prooue soundly fertile.

†**6.** Insolent, arrogant, self-confident. *Obs.*

a **1568** ASCHAM *Scholem.* I. (Arb.) 54 To thinke well of him selfe, to be lustie in contemning of others. **1573** G. HARVEY *Letter-bk.* (Camden) 5 Purposing.. to show a lusti contempt of so silli a frend. **1588** J. HARVEY *Disc. Probl.* 46 The great emperor of Turkes.. is lately become,.. somewhat cranker and lustier, than his accustomed maner was. **1600** HOLLAND *Livy* VI. xxxvi. 242 The Coloners onely of Velitre, upon so long rest and quietnesse began to be lustie and wax wanton [L. *gestientes otio*]. *a* **1674** CLARENDON *Hist. Reb.* x. §102 When they found it fit to make any lusty Declaration against the Parliament,.. they allways inserted somewhat that might look like candour and tenderness towards the King's Party.

†**7.** Of inanimate agencies (e.g. a fire, wine, poison, a disease): Strong, powerful. *Obs.*

1576 FLEMING *Panopl. Epist.* 228 The husbandmen sat warming their shanckes by a lustie fire that filled the chimney. **1596** DRAYTON *Leg.* iii. 21 Many a low Ebbe, many a lustie Tide. **1622** FLETCHER *Beggars Bush* IV. iv, Strong lusty London beer. *a* **1647** *Prol. to Beaum. & Fl.'s Custom Country*, They.. dranke lusty wine, The nectar of the Muses. *a* **1649** DRUMM. OF HAWTH. *Conv. betw. B.J. & W.D.* Wks. (1711) 224 It was strong and lusty poison. **1683** TRYON *Way to Health* xvi. (1697) 380 The close Rooms, lusty Fires, drawn Curtains, and other torturing Circumstances. **1692** LOCKE *Educ.* §29 Distempers.. which, by too forward applications, might have been made lusty diseases.

†**b.** Of a ship: Sailing well. *Obs.*

1660 F. BROOKE tr. *Le Blanc's Trav.* 335 In an houre we cast more over-board then was laded in a day; and.. immediately we perceiv'd the Vessell to be more lusty. **1667** *Lond. Gaz.* No. 155/4 The *Paradox*.. had a sharp dispute with a lusty privateer, who got from him. **1669** STURMY *Mariner's Mag.* I. 19 The Chase is a lusty brave Ship.

8. Of actions (esp. those involving physical effort, as a blow, a shout): Vigourous. Of a meal, etc.: 'Hearty', abundant.

1672 *Chaucer's Ghoast* 14 He.. beheld the lusty Love which each of them to other made. *a* **1682** SIR T. BROWNE *Tracts* 122 A word drawn from the lusty shout of soldiers. **1710** STEELE *Tatler* No. 266 ⁋2 He drunk a lusty Draught. **1779** JOHNSON *Let. to Mrs. Thrale* 25 Oct., I hope Mr. Thrale once a day makes a lusty dinner. **1797** BURKE *Regic. Peace* iii. Wks. VIII. 271 The Turk.. gave him two or three lusty kicks on the seat of honour. **1840** THACKERAY *King of Yvetot*, And every day it came to pass That four lusty meals made he. **1872** BAKER *Nile Tribut.* xi. 177 She gave her a maternal welcome.. bestowing lusty blows on her back. **1894** HALL CAINE *Manxman* III. xiv. 175 There was some lusty disputation.

†**9.** Massive, substantial, large. *Obs.*

1640 *Lanc. Lovers* in Brand *Pop. Antiq.* (1849) II. 37 We will haue a lustie Cheese-cake at our sheepe-wash. **1645** EVELYN *Mem.* (1857) I. 196 The Arsenal has sufficient to arm 70,000 men,.. with divers lusty pieces of ordnance. **1647** LILLY *Chr. Astrol.* lxxvi. 432 Provided alwayes, it be not to hinder themselves from enjoying a lusty Benefice. **1670** EACHARD *Cont. Clergy* 127 If ten or twenty of the lustiest noble-mens estates of England were cleaverly sliced among the indigent. **1691** SHADWELL *Scourers* I. i, A bottle of Spirit of Canary and a lusty glass. **1842** S. LOVER *Handy Andy* xv. 133 Four boys and a little girl sat at a side table where.. a lusty loaf was laid under contribution.

¶**b.** ? Important, striking. ? *nonce-use.*

1788 H. WALPOLE *Let. Earl Strafford* 17 June (1846) VI. 292 To have Constantinople taken, merely as a lusty event.

10. Of persons: Massively built. Hence, corpulent, stout, fat.

1772–84 COOK *Voy.* (1790) IV. 1341 He was lusty and well made, though not tall. **1785** G. A. BELLAMY *Apology* IV. 5 That lady, playing the character of Arpasia.. being very lusty, the scene men found great difficulty to lift the chair into which she had thrown herself. **1792** CHARLOTTE SMITH *Desmond* II. 209 Quite a grand looking man, though not lusty, but rather thinnish. **1818** SCOTT *Hrt. Midl.* ii, Being a robust and lusty man, he.. found it impossible to get through between the bars. **1839** FR. A. KEMBLE *Resid. in Georgia* (1863) 180, I came upon a gang of lusty women, as the phrase is here for women in the family-way. **1886** ELWORTHY *W. Somerset Word-bk.*, *Lusty*.. 2. Obese; fat.

11. *Comb.* (parasynthetic), as ***lusty-handed***, †***-hued***, ***-limbed***, ***-lunged*** adjs.

1730–46 THOMSON *Autumn* 639 The.. heaps Of apples, which the *lusty-handed year,.. o'er the blushing orchard shakes. *c* **1400** *Rom. Rose* 3014 So *lusty hewed of colour. **1897** PULLEN-BURRY *Blotted Out* 17 Red-nosed *lusty-limbed swains. **1895** CLIVE HOLLAND *Jap. Wife* (ed. 11) 87 Instruments.. blown by other equally *lusty-lunged boys.

Hence † **'lusty** *sb.* (*Naut.*) = HEARTY *sb.*²

1805 *Spirit Pub. Jrnls.* (1806) IX. 375 Now then, my lusties, for a lug at the bowlines.

† **lusty gallant.** *Obs.*

1. The name of a dance; also of a dance-tune.

1569 ELDERTON in *Collect. B.L. Ball. & Broadsides* (1867) 14 A proper new Ballad in praise of my Ladie Marques, whose Death is bewailed to the Tune of New lusty gallant. **1577** BRETON *Wks. Yng. Wit* (Chappell *Mus. Old T.* I. 91), The youth must needs go dance, First galliards—then larousse, and heidegy—Old Lusty Gallant—All flowers of the broom. **1578** PROCTOR *Gorg. Gallery* D b, A propper Dittie. To the tune of lusty Gallant. **1594** NASHE *Terrors Nt.* Wks. (Grosart) III. 271 After all they danst Lustie gallant, & a drunken Danish Laualto or two.

2. A fanciful name for some tint of light red.

1587 HARRISON *Descr. Eng.* II. vii. 172 in *Holinshed*, I might here name a sort of hewes deuised for the nonce, wherewith to please phantasticall heads, as a gooseturd greene.. popingaie blue, lustie gallant. **1589** RIDER *Bibl. Schol.* 1709 Lusty gallant colour or light red, *spadiceus*. **1601** HOLLAND *Pliny* II. 110 The French vse therewith [the hyacinth] to die their light reds or lustie-gallant.

lusum, obs. form of LOVESOME.

‖**lusus naturæ** ('l(j)uːsəs nə'tjʊəriː). Also 9 simply lusus. [L. *lūsus nātūræ* a playing or sport of Naure.] A supposed sportive action of Nature to which the origin of marked variations from the normal type (of an animal, plant, etc.) was formerly ascribed. Chiefly *concr.*, a natural production deviating markedly from the normal type, or having the appearance of being a result of sportive design; a 'freak of nature'.

a **1661** FULLER *Worthies, Glouc.* (1662) I. 351 Others more probably account them [fossils] to be *Lusus Naturæ*. **1726** SWIFT *Gulliver* II. iii, They.. concluded unanimously, that I was only *relplum scalcath*, which is interpreted literally *lusus naturæ*. **1767** GOOCH *Treat. Wounds* I. 180 Doctor Hunter.. exhibits many arms.. shewing this *Lusus Naturæ*. **1816** BRACKENRIDGE *Jrnl. Voy. Missouri* 46 The wild turkey is invariably black: although, it is possible, that by some *lusus naturæ*, there may be white. **1833** SIR C. BELL *Hand* (1834) 35 The animals of the Antediluvian world were not monsters; there was no lusus or extravagance. **1845** FORD *Handbk. Spain* I. 334 A *lusus naturæ* called *el Torcal*, an assemblage of stones which look like a deserted town. **1850** MRS. BROWNING *Lost Bower* xlviii, I have found a bower today A green lusus—fashioned half in Chance, and half in Nature's play. **1880** GRAY *Struct. Bot.* 419/1 *Lusus*, a 'sport' or variation from a seed or bud. **1885** *Manch. Exam.* 18 Feb. 3/2 It is a veritable curiosity—a sort of fossilised *lusus naturæ*.

luswart, lut, var. forms of LUSARD, LITE.

† **'lutament.** *Obs.*⁻⁰ [ad. L. *lutāmentum*.] 'A wall or bridge made with morter' (Cockeram 1623).

lutanist, lutenist ('l(j)uːtənɪst). Also 7 lutonist, 7–8, (9 *arch.*) lutinist. [ad. med.L. *lūtānista*, f. *lūtāna* lute.] A lute-player.

1600 J. DOWLAND *2nd Bk. Songs* title-p., Batchelor of Musick, and Lutenist to the King of Denmark. *a* **1634** RANDOLPH *Muses Looking-gl.* IV. v. (1638) 84 The Lutanist takes Flats and Sharpes, And out of those so dissonant notes, does strike A ravishing Harmony. **1759** JOHNSON *Rasselas* ii,

I likewise can call the lutanist and the singer. **1789** BURNEY *Hist. Mus.* III. ii. 243 The celebrated Striggio a lutenist and voluminous composer. **1881** SHORTHOUSE *J. Inglesant* II. 52 An accomplished lutinist and singer. **1892** C. E. NORTON *Dante's Par.* xx. 135 As a good lutanist makes the vibration of the string accompany a good singer. **1898** S. LEE *Life Shaks.* xv, Lyrics..set to music by Robert Johnson, a lutenist in high repute.

'lutany. [? Formed after prec.] ? Lute-music.
1897 F. THOMPSON *New Poems* 41 [Minstrels] without end Reel your shrill lutany.

lutar, obs. form of LUTER.

†lu'tarious, *a. Obs. rare*⁻¹. [f. L. *lutāri-us* (f. *lut-um* mud) + -OUS.] Inhabiting mud.
1681 GREW *Musæum* I. iii. 38 A scaly tortoise shell..of the Lutarious kind.

†'lutary, *a. Obs. rare*⁻¹. [ad. L. *lutārius*: see prec.] = prec.
1661 LOVELL *Hist. Anim. & Min.* Introd., Lutarie torteise.

lutarynnauncer: see LUTHERANANCER.

†lu'tation. *Obs.* [n. of action, f. L. *lutāre* LUTE *v.*²] **a.** The process of luting. **b.** The material used in the process.
1611 FLORIO, *A lutatione*, a luting or lutation. **1612** WOODALL *Surg. Mate* Wks. (1653) 265 Then to Lutation have a care, therein be no abuse. *Ibid.* 272 Lutation..is a medicine thin or thick..which stoppeth most exactly the orificium of the vessel. **1657** in *Phys. Dict.*

lutby, variant of LOTEBY *Obs.*, paramour.

lutch, *v. Obs.* exc. *dial.* (*Yorks.*) Also 4 **luche**. *trans.* To lift.
13.. *E.E. Allit. P.* C. 230 In-to þat lodlych loȝe þay luche hym sone. **1888** *Sheffield Gloss.*, Lutch.

lute (l(j)uːt), *sb.*¹ Also 4 **loyt**, 5–6 **lutte**, **lewte**. [a. F. *lut* (Cotgrave; now written *luth*) whence It. *liuto*, Du. *luit*, Da. *lut*, MHG. *lûte* (G. *laute*); another form of the word appears in Pr. *laut*, Sp. *laud*, Pg. *alaude*; a. Arab. *al-ʿūd*, where *al-* is the definite article.]

1. A stringed musical instrument, much in vogue from the 14th to the 17th centuries, the strings of which are struck with the fingers of the right hand and stopped on the frets with those of the left.
1361–2 *Durham Acc. Rolls* 127 In uno viro ludenti in uno loyt. *c* **1386** CHAUCER *Manciple's T.* 268 For sorwe of which he brak his minstralcye, Bothe harpe, and lute, and giterne, and sautrye. *c* **1410** *Sir Cleges* 101 He hard a sovne.. Of harpis, luttis, and getarnys. **1481–90** *Howard Househ. Bks.* (Roxb.) 218 Item, to the menstrellis for the mendynge of a lewte ij.*s.* iiij.*d.* *a* **1529** SKELTON *Agst. Comely Coystrowne* 29 He lumbryth on a lewde lewte. **1535** COVERDALE *Ps.* xxxiii. 2 Synge psalmes vnto him with the lute and instrument of ten strynges. **1599** SHAKS. *Much Ado* II. i. 98 God defend the Lute should be like the case. **1663** COWLEY *Verses & Ess., Garden* iv. (1669) 117 When Orpheus strook th' inspired Lute, The trees danc'd round. **1717** LADY M. W. MONTAGU *Let. to C'tess Mar* 18 Apr., Four of them began to play some soft airs on instruments between a lute and a guitar. **1789** BURNEY *Hist. Mus.* (ed. 2) III. i. 143 The Lute of which hardly the sound or shape is known at present, was during the last two centuries the favorite chamber instrument of every nation of Europe. **1879** STAINER *Music of Bible* 22 A guitar and lute only vary with regard to the shape or length of the body and neck.
transf. **1820** KEATS *Isabella* xxxv, The forest tomb Had.. taken the soft lute From his lorn voice.

b. The name of a stop in some forms of the harpsichord (see quot. 1885).
1879 A. J. HIPKINS in *Grove's Dict. Mus.* I. 691/1 The so-called 'lute'-stop. **1885** *Encycl. Brit.* XIX. 70/2 To the three shifting registers of jacks of the octave and first and second unisons were added the 'lute', the charm of which was due to the favouring of high harmonics by plucking the strings close to the bridge, and the 'harp', a surding or muting effect [etc.].

2. *attrib.* and *Comb.*, as ***lute-case***, ***-lesson***, ***-maker***, ***-master***, ***-player***, ***-playing***, ***-tune***; ***lute-resounding***, ***-voiced*** adjs.; ***lute-fashion*** adv.; **lute-backed** *a.*, having a back shaped like a lute; **lute-fingered** *a.*, having fingers adapted to the lute; **lute-pin**, one of the pegs or screws for tuning the strings of the lute; **† lute shoulders** (cf. *lute-backed*), round shoulders; **lute-way** *adv.*, in the way in which the lute is played (cf. *lyra-way*). Also LUTE-STRING.
1601 HOLLAND *Pliny* I. 354 Those who are *Lute backed, thicke shouldered, and bending forward,..bee long liued. **1582** STANYHURST *Æneis*, etc. (Arb.) 141 This slut..with a head lyke a *lutecase. **1599** SHAKS. *Hen. V*, III. ii. 45 Bardolph stole a Lute-case; bore it twelue Leagues, and sold it for three halfepence. *a* **1734** NORTH *Life Ld. Keeper North* (1742) 12 His..Lyra Viol (which he used to touch, *Lute-fashion, upon his knees). **1873** BROWNING *Red Cott. Nt.-cap* I. Wks. 1898 II. 374/2 [Fiddles] sawn bow-hand-wise, Or touched lute-fashion and forefinger-plucked. **1820** KEATS *Lamia* I. 73 The soft, *lute-finger'd Muses. **1610** DOWLAND (*title*), Varietie of *Lvte-lessons. **1573** BARET *Alv.* L 672 A *lutemaker, *testudinarius.* **1610** DOWLAND *Var. Lute-lessons* D 2, Hans Gerle, Lutenist, Citizen and Lute-Maker of Nurenburge. **1665–6** PEPYS *Diary* 12 Feb., Then comes Mr. Cæsar, my boy's *lute-master. **1703** *Lond. Gaz.* No. 3921/4 Mr. Dupre, Lute-Master, has set up a School at the White-Periwig in King-street. **1596** NASHE *Saffron-Walden* F 4, Otherwise he looks like a case of tooth-pikes, or a *Lute pin put in a sute of apparell. **1612** ROWLANDS *Knaue of Harts* 10 My Breeches like a pair of Lute-pins be, Scarse Buttocke-roome, as euery man may see. **1587** GOLDING *De Mornay* vii. 91 He doth fondlie incorporate the spirit of the *Lute-plaier in the Lute. *Ibid.* xiv. 221 He cannot put his *Lute-playing in exercise. **1742** POPE *Dunciad* IV. 306 Love-whisp'ring woods, and *lute-resounding waves. **1500–20** *Lut schulderis [see LUTTERED]. *c* **1500** *Proverbs* in Grose *Antiq. Repert.* (1809) IV. 406 He that is a perfyte musicion Perceyvithe the *Lute tewnes and the goode proporcion. **1818** KEATS *Endym.* iv. 774 Thy *lute-voiced brother will I sing ere long. **1607** BREWER *Lingua* I. ix, Auditus, shall we here thee play, the Lyero-way, or the *Lute-way, shall we? **1611** J. MAYNARD (*title*), XII Wonders of the World... With some Lessons to play Lyra-wayes alone, or..with another Violl set Lute-way.

lute (l(j)uːt), *sb.*² See also LUTUM. [ad. OF. *lut* (F. *lut*) or med.L. (use of L. *lutum* mud).]

1. Tenacious clay or cement composed of various ingredients, and used to stop an orifice, to render air-tight a joint between two pipes, to coat a retort, etc., and to protect a graft. Also with *a* and *pl.* a particular kind of this substance. † ***lute of wisdom*** [= med.L. *lutum sapientæ*], a composition for hermetical sealing, variously described by alchemists. ***fat lute*** (see quot. 1836–41).
c **1400** *Lanfranc's Cirurg.* 195 þe mouþ of þis pott schal be ioyned to þe mouþ of þe pott þat is in þe erþe with good lute, þat þere mowe noon eir out þerof. **1460–70** *Bk. Quintessence* 4 ȝe schulen opene þe hoole of þe vessel in þe heed þat was selid with þe seel of lute of wijsdom, maad of þe sotillest flour, and of white of eyren, and of moist papere, ymeyngid so þat no þing respire out. **1599** A. M. tr. *Gabelhouer's Bk. Physicke* 57/1 Put it in a glass, agglutinate the same, with a lute made for that purpose. **1605** TIMME *Quersit.* III. 193 The ordinary lutes wherewith to stop vessels of glasse against faint vapours are these. **1660** SHARROCK *Vegetables* 68 Lute is made with horse-dung and stiff clay well mix'd together. **1662** R. MATHEW *Unl. Alch.* §89. 151 Take a good Retort of Glass, and put on it a good coat of strong Lute made of Blood, Lome, Hair, and sharp Sand. **1766** CAVENDISH in *Phil. Trans.* LVI. 153 A glass tube fitted into its mouth, and secured with lute. **1816** J. SMITH *Panorama Sci. & Art* II. 789 Lutes are compositions which are employed to defend glass and other vessels from the action of fire [etc.]. **1836–41** BRANDE *Chem.* (ed. 5) 1037 Fat lute, composed of pipe-clay and drying oil, well beaten to a stiff mass. **1868** JOYNSON *Metal.* 114 Make the box tight with a lute of sand and clay, in equal parts.

†2. In sense of L. *lutum*: Mud. Also *attrib.*
1694 MOTTEUX *Rabelais* (1737) V. 231 Lute, Unds, and Sands did long our March oppose. **1756** C. LUCAS *Ess. Waters* I. 143 Roundish granules of a pale lute colour.

3. 'A packing-ring of india-rubber placed between the lid and the lip of a jar, to prevent the access of air to the contents' (Knight *Dict. Mech.*).

lute (l(j)uːt), *sb.*³ *U.S. Brickmaking.* [a. Du. *loet* (whence also LOOT *sb.*¹).] (See quot. 1889.)
1875 in KNIGHT *Dict. Mech.* **1889** C. T. DAVIS *Manuf. Bricks* etc. (ed. 2) 142 There is a tool used for scraping off and levelling the moulding floor... It consists of a piece of light pine board,..set upright, with a long light handle in the centre. At the bottom is tacked a thin piece of steel, generally an old wood-saw blade, with the teeth turned upward... The tool is called a 'lute'.

†lute, *sb.*⁴ *Obs.* Short. f. LUTE-STRING².
1676 *Lond. Gaz.* No. 1099/4 Sarcenets, Alamodes, and Lutes.

lute (l(j)uːt), *v.*¹ Now *rare.* [f. LUTE *sb.*¹] **a.** *intr.* To play on the lute. **b.** quasi-*trans.* with cognate obj. or quoted words: To express by means of the lute. **c.** *intr.* To sound like a lute.
a. *a* **1479** CAXTON *Bk. Curtesye* xliv, To harpe and lute, or lustely to syng. **1509** HAWES *Past. Pleas.* xvi. (Percy Soc.) 64, I may not lute, or yet daunce or synge! **1549–62** STERNHOLD & H. *Ps.* lxxi. 23 Therefore thy faythfulnesse to prayse, I will both Lute and sing. *c* **1580** JEFFERIE *Bugbears* I. iii. 83 in *Archiv Stud. neu. Spr.* (1897) XCVIII. 313 He lutethe, he harpethe, and singethe all the day.
b. **1377** LANGL. *P. Pl.* B. XVIII. 423 Thanne luted Loue in a loude note, *Ecce quam bonum et quam iocundum, etc.* **1847** TENNYSON *Princess* IV. 111 Knaves are men, That lute and flute fantastic tenderness.
c. **1821** KEATS *Lamia* I. 167 Her new voice luting soft Cried, 'Lycius'.

lute (l(j)uːt), *v.*² [ad. L. *lutāre* (F. *luter*, 16th c.) f. *lut-um*: see LUTE *sb.*² Cf. ENLUTE.]

1. *trans.* To coat with lute, esp. to cover (a crucible, etc.) with lute as a protection against fire; to close or stop with or as with lute (an orifice or joint); to stop with lute the cracks or joints of (a vessel). Also with *about*, *up*.
1398 TREVISA *Barth De P.R.* XIX. xxxi. (1495) 878 Ocra brente Rede in newe crockes wel stoppyd and lutyd wyth newe claye. **1562** BULLEYN *Dial. Soarnes & Chir.* 25 b, Then ye shall lute the gappe, or mouthe of the vaines..with this medicen. **1594** PLAT *Jewell-ho.* II. 4 Before they distill, luting the Limbeck. **1599** A. M. tr. *Gabelhouer's Bk. Physicke* 67/1 Put this..in a nue pot, and lute the same verye close. **1601** HOLLAND *Pliny* I. 520 The better way is to lute it well, and close with clay. **1624** CAPT. SMITH *Virginia* II. 33 Their small boats, made of the barkes of trees, sowed with barke and well luted with gumme. **1639** T. DE GRAY *Compl. Horsem.* 349 Make a cake of clay and therewith lute up the pot. **1661** LOVELL *Hist. Anim. & Min.* 135 They make their nests of a longish hemispherical figure, of little twigs, and then lute them. **1662** HOBBES *Consid.* (1680) 52, I admire them when I see them lute an Alembick handsomely. **1688** R. HOLME *Armoury* III. 86/1 To Lute about the Oven stock with Clay..to keep the heat in. **1756** C. LUCAS *Ess. Waters* I. 59 Having luted the junctures..let the fire be gradually administered. **1763–6** W. LEWIS *Comm. Phil.-Techn.* 7 There is no occasion for the hoop being luted. **1854** H. MILLER *Sch. & Schm.* vii. 65 Producing gas by means of a tobacco pipe luted with clay. **1858** HOGG *Life Shelley* II. 424 Luting his retorts with pipe clay. **1893** *Chamb. Jrnl.* 29 July 479/1 These he places in an earthen vessel, which he lutes with moist earth.
fig. **1627** DONNE *Serm.* xliv. 440 Except the Lord open them [thy lips], it were better they were luted with the clay of the grave. **1650** R. STAPYLTON *Strada's Low C. Warres* x. 6 [They] had their eares..luted against the sound of Peace.

2. To fasten or fix with or as with lute; also with *about*, *down*, *in*, *on*, *together*, *up*; occas. with complement. Const. †*against*, *into*, *to*, *unto*. Said also of the luting material.
1489 CAXTON *Faytes of A.* II. xiv. 118 And luted theym wyth dong and stones ayenst the walles. **1563** T. GALE *Antidot.* II. 88 Put them..in to a still of glasse, and put his heade on it, & lute them well together. **1641** FRENCH *Distill.* i. (1651) 40 Lute it well thereunto. **1666** BOYLE *Orig. Formes & Qual.* 422 Then pour out the Mixture into a tall Glass Cucurbite, to which lute on a Head and a Receiver. **1668** R. L'ESTRANGE *Vis. Quev.* (1708) 48 A large Glass-Bottle, wherein was Luted up..a famous Necromancer. **1727** BRADLEY *Fam. Dict.* s.v. *Distillation of Oil*, Cover the Vessel, and adapt its Helm to it; lute 'em very well together with the Whites of Eggs and Flower. **1796** KIRWAN *Elem. Min.* (ed. 2) II. 87 Place the mixture in a Crucible..to which a cover should be luted. **1819** SOUTHEY in *Q. Rev.* XXI. 387 M. de Thury..opened the masonry of these wells, and luted into the opening the upper half of a broken bottle. **1879** *Cassell's Techn. Educ.* IV. 212/2 After charging them with the crude ore, the lids were luted down. **1881** TAIT in *Nature* XXV. 126 In the neck of the steel cylinder..there was luted a vertical glass tube.
transf. and *fig.* **1650** CHARLETON *Paradoxes* 103 Paracelsus was fast luted in his grave..about the year of Christs Incarnation 1541. **1856** KANE *Arct. Expl.* I. xi. 118 It was a wooden structure firmly luted to its frozen base.

lute: see LITE, LOOT, LOUT.

luteal ('l(j)uːtɪəl), *a.* [f. L. *lūte-us* yellow (in mod.L. *corpus luteum*: see CORPUS 2) + -AL¹.] Of or pertaining to the *corpus luteum*.
1927 *Amer. Jrnl. Anat.* XL. 211 The inhibitory effect of luteal tissue upon follicular development does not explain why certain animals have an anoestrum. **1932** E. ALLEN *Sex & Internal Secretions* xvi. 794 The lutenizing [*sic*] factor will not cause the luteal change in the ovary of an immature animal. *Ibid.* 795 During the luteal phase the so-called 'B' factor is utilized. **1939** S. R. M. REYNOLDS *Physiol. Uterus* iii. 69 The action of the luteal hormone. **1966** *Ann. Rev. Physiol.* XXVIII. 60 Prolactin may stimulate luteal function in the ferret. **1969** K. W. MCKERNS *Gonads* iii. 72 (*heading*) Factors affecting luteal activity in intact rabbits.

lutecium, var. LUTETIUM.

luted ('l(j)uːtɪd), *ppl. a.* [f. LUTE *v.*² + -ED¹.] Daubed or stopped with lute.
1601 HOLLAND *Pliny* Explan. Words Art, *Luted*, close stopped with clay, dough, or such like. **1725** BRADLEY *Fam. Dict.* s.v. *Nitre*, Put the Luted retort upon a furnace of close Reverberation. **1825** J. NICHOLSON *Operat. Mechanic* 757 Expose the luted crucible to a strong forge fire.

luteic (l(j)uː'tiːɪk), *a. Chem.* [f. L. *lūte-us* yellow + -IC.] ***luteic acid***: see quot.
1892 MORLEY & MUIR *Watts' Dict. Chem.*, *Luteic acid* $C_{26}H_{20}O_{12}$(?)..A yellow colouring matter prepared from the flowers of *Euphorbia Cyparissias*.

lutein ('l(j)uːtɪɪn). *Chem.* Also 9 **-ine**. [f. L. *lūte-um* yolk of egg (neut. of *lūteus* yellow) + -IN.] A substance of a deep yellow colour found in the yolk of eggs and the ovaries of animals.
1869 THUDICHUM in *Proc. Roy. Soc.* XVII. 253 Various parts of animals and plants contain a yellow crystallizable substance..to which..I assign the name 'luteine'. **1900** *Allbutt's Syst. Med.* V. 624 This [absorption band] is indicative of the presence of lutein, to which the colour of the serum is said to be due.

luteinization (ˌl(j)uːtiːnaɪ'zeɪʃən). *Physiol.* [f. LUTEIN + -IZATION.] The formation of lutein in the cells that remain of the Graafian follicle after expulsion of the ovum, during which process the follicle is converted into the *corpus luteum*; the formation of a *corpus luteum*.
1929 *Anatomical Rec.* XLIII. 239 (*heading*) The origin of the corpus luteum in the rat as indicated by studies upon the luteinization of the cystic follicles. **1931** *Amer. Jrnl. Physiol.* XCVII. 292 It [*sc.* the luteinizing hormone] does, however, cause luteinization of the follicles which are produced by the gonad stimulator. **1967** G. S. RICHARDSON *Ovarian Physiol.* ii. 22 Increased follicular growth without luteinization or corpus-luteum formation. **1968** PASSMORE & ROBSON *Compan. Med. Stud.* I. xxxvii. 18/2 Following ovulation and subsequent luteinization of the follicle, oestrogen synthesis is supplemented by the production of progestagens.

Hence **'luteinize** *v. trans.*, to cause (a tissue associated with the *corpus luteum*) to form lutein; **'luteinized** *ppl. a.*; **'luteinizing** *ppl. a.* and *vbl. sb.*; ***luteinizing hormone***, a glyco-protein hormone secreted by the adenohypophysis which in the female helps to induce ovulation and brings about the formation of the *corpus luteum*, and in the male promotes the secretion of androgen by acting on the Leydig cells of the testis (abbrev. LH (L 7)).

1929 *Anatomical Rec.* XLIII. 242 The cells of either the granulosa or the theca have become luteinized. **1931** *Amer. Jrnl. Physiol.* XCVII. 291 (*heading*) The gonad stimulating and the luteinizing hormones of the anterior lobe of the hypophesis [*sic*]. *Ibid.* 294 This preparation..does luteinize the follicles produced by the gonad stimulating fraction. *Ibid.*, The water soluble preparation contains primarily the gonad stimulating hormone with little or none of the luteinizing substance. *Ibid.* 295 Stimulation to luteinizing activity. **1935** *Endocrinology* XIX. 45 The ovary of the infantile rat can be luteinized to a much higher degree than was found in the above experiments with urine. **1966** *Ann. Rev. Physiol.* XXVIII. 61 Heavily luteinized ovaries. **1969** K. W. McKerns *Gonads* x. 279 Some 95 percent of the ovarian tissue consisted of luteinized cells. **1970** *Sci. Jrnl.* June 47/1 Three gonadotrophic hormones are produced by the anterior section of the pituitary gland: the mammotrophic hormone, prolactin, the follicle stimulating hormone (FSH) and the luteinizing hormone (LH). **1970** *Nature* 26 Sept. 1344/2 In the cyclic female albino rat, a release of pituitary luteinizing hormone (LH) occurs on the afternoon of proestrus.

lutenand, -a(u)nt, obs. forms of LIEUTENANT.

†**lutener.** *Obs. rare*⁻¹. [f. LUTE *sb.*¹, after LUTANIST.] A lute-player.
1626 Rous *Diary* (Camden) 8 The queenes lutener, a Frenchman, layd in the Tower.

lutenist: see LUTANIST.

luteo- (ˈl(j)uːtɪəʊ), used as the combining form of L. *lūteus* LUTEOUS in various scientific terms.

a. To signify the presence of a yellow colour with some other. ˌ**luteo-coˈbaltic** *a. Chem.*, containing a compound of cobalt with a yellow colour. ˌ**luteo-ˈfulvous** *a. Bot.*, of a tawny yellow colour. ˌ**luteo-fuˈscescent** *a. Bot.*, of a somewhat dusky yellow colour. ˌ**luteo-ˈfuscous** *a. Bot.*, between fuscous and yellow (Cassell). ˌ**luteo-ˈgallic (acid)** *Chem.*, the yellow colouring matter of gall-nuts. ˌ**luteo-hæmaˈtoidin** *Phys.*, a yellow modification of hæmatoidin. ˌ**luteo-ruˈfescent** *a. Bot.*, of a reddish yellow colour. ˌ**luteo-viˈrescent** *a. Bot.*, of a greenish yellow colour.
1889 *Syd. Soc. Lex.*, *Luteo-cobaltic salts. **1871** W. A. Leighton *Lichen-flora* 205 Apothecia *luteo-fulvous. *Ibid.* 246 Spores 1, *luteo-fuscescent, narrow-oblong [etc.]. **1861** Hulme tr. *Moquin-Tandon* II. III. v. 152 Gallic, ellagic, and *luteogallic acids. **1880** J. W. Legg *Bile* 39 The lutein of Thudichum appears to resemble the *luteo-hæmatoidin.. of Piccolo and Lieben. **1871** W. A. Leighton *Lichen-flora* 341 Apothecia *luteo-rufescent or reddish-flesh-coloured. *Ibid.* 267 *Lecidea melanochroza*, Leight. *luteo-virescent.

b. Also before a vowel **lute-**. Used as the combining form of *corpus luteum* (CORPUS 2), as in **luteˈolysis** *Physiol.* [LYSIS 3], degeneration of the *corpus luteum*, such as occurs when the discharged ovum is not fertilized, so **luteoˈlytic** *a.* [-LYTIC], bringing about or sufficient to bring about luteolysis. **luteˈoma** *Path.* [-OMA], an ovarian tumour consisting of cells resembling those of the corpus luteum.
1961 J. W. Everett in W. C. Young *Sex & Internal Secretions* (ed. 3) I. viii. 537/1 By luteolysis we shall refer to corpus luteum regression in any of its manifestations. **1965** *Endocrinology* LXXVI. 1218/1 The luteolysis induced by estrogen. **1971** *Nature* 23 Apr. 526/1 We have measured the output of prostaglandin from the uterus in one condition which is associated with premature luteolysis, uterine distension. **1974** *Ibid.* 10 May 176/2 In many species luteolysis is dependent upon the presence of the uterus and an intact utero-ovarian vasculature. **1961** *Recent Progress Hormone Res.* XVII. 122 This experiment..argues against the possibility that the luteolytic effect of progesterone is due to a direct action on the corpus luteum. **1965** *Endocrinology* LXXVI. 1214/1 Particular attention was focused on establishing the luteolytic dose of estradiol cyclopentylpropionate. **1971** *Nature* 23 Apr. 526/1 Prostaglandin $F_{2\alpha}$..has a luteolytic action in various species including the guinea-pig. **1931** R. J. E. Scott *Gould's Med. Dict.* (ed. 3) 749/1 *Luteoma*, a tumor developing from the corpus luteum. **1947** *Radiology* XLIX. 280/1 Figure 10 shows a mixed luteoma and tubular adenoma. **1966** R. W. Evans *Histol. Appearances Tumours* (ed. 2) xxviii. 666 There exists a rare though well-recognized ovarian tumour which, because of its debatable nature and genesis, has been variously and confusingly called: adrenocorticoid tumour or hypernephroma of ovary, virilizing lipoid-cell tumour, luteoma, androgenic hilus-cell tumour and masculinovoblastoma.

luteolein (l(j)uːtɪˈəʊliːɪn). *Chem.* [ad. F. *lutéoléine*.] Chevreul's term for a substance which accompanies, and is a product of the normal oxidation of luteolin (*Syd. Soc. Lex.* 1889).
1864 in Webster. **1882** in Ogilvie.

luteolin (ˈl(j)uːtɪəlɪn). *Chem.* Also -ine. [ad. F. *lutéolin*, f. mod.L. (*reseda*) *lūteol-a* weld.] The yellow colouring matter of weld (*Reseda luteola*).
1844 in Hoblyn *Dict. Med.* **1869** Thudichum in *Proc. Roy. Soc.* XVII. 255 Luteoline, from weld.

luteolous (l(j)uːˈtiːələs), *a. Nat. Hist.* [f. L. *lūteol-us* (dim. of *lūteus* LUTEOUS) + -OUS.] Somewhat luteous, yellowish.
1856 in Mayne *Expos. Lex.* **1874** H. C. Wood *Fresh-w. Algæ N. Amer.* 99 The microgonidia indefinite in number, much the smaller, pale or dirty green or luteolous.

†ˈ**luteon.** *Obs. rare*⁻¹. [? Misprint for *lutern* LUTHERN; but Moxon has both words.] (See quot.)
1679 Moxon *Mech. Exerc.* 147 Single light Windows or Luteons.

luteotrophic (ˌl(j)uːtɪəʊˈtrəʊfɪk), **-tropic** (-ˈtrəʊpɪk, -ˈtrɒpɪk), *a. Physiol.* [f. LUTEO- b + -TROPHIC, -TROPIC.] Maintaining or capable of maintaining the *corpus luteum* in being during pregnancy and thus counteracting luteolysis; ***luteotrop(h)ic hormone***, such a hormone which in rats and mice is produced by the adenohypophysis and which is probably identical with the hormone prolactin of other animals, including man (though attempts to demonstrate that prolactin is luteotrophic in these other animals have failed) (abbrev. LTH (L 7)).
1941 E. B. Astwood in *Endocrinology* XXVIII. 310 In speaking of a substance which will maintain the functioning of formed corpora lutea it has been found convenient to use the term 'luteotrophic' substance or 'luteotrophin'. **1955** *Jrnl. Endocrinol.* XIII. 19 Cutuly (1941) found that luteotrophic hormone stimulates corpora lutea of hypophysectomized rats sufficiently to allow implantation. **1961** *Recent Progress Hormone Res.* XVII. 120 The luteinizing hormone..may be luteotropic in animals other than rats and mice. **1964** H. H. Cole *Gonadotropins* i. 1 We know nothing of other possible pituitary luteotropic hormones. **1964** *Endocrinology* LXXV. 625/1 Such extracts have been shown to be luteotrophic in hypophysectomized rabbits. **1968** Passmore & Robson *Compan. Med. Stud.* I. xxxvii. 16/2 The factors which control the maintenance and regression of the corpus luteum are not understood, but during pregnancy a placental gonadotrophin exerts a powerful luteotrophic effect.

Hence ˌ**luteoˈtrophin, -ˈtropin**, any substance exerting a luteotrophic effect; *spec.* = *luteotrop(h)ic hormone*.
1941 [see LUTEOTROPHIC *a.*]. **1945** *Index-Catal. Library Surg.-General's Office, U.S. Army* 4th Ser. IX. 1323/1 Luteotropin: see Pituitary hormone. **1961** *Recent Progress Hormone Res.* XVII. 120 LH may have the dual role of causing ovulation and of acting as a luteotropin. **1961** W. C. Young *Sex & Internal Secretions* (ed. 3) I. viii. 530/2 The term luteotrophin was proposed by Astwood (1941) to refer to a substance that maintains function of corpora lutea, in distinction to substances that cause them to form. It is now conceded that the substance described in that paper was probably the lactogenic hormone... Although lactogen seems to be the hypophyseal luteotrophin in rats, such is not necessarily true for all species... Nevertheless, the expression luteotrophin in the generic sense continues to be desirable. **1965** *Endocrinology* LXXVI. 1218/1 It therefore appears..that a hypophysial luteotropin is only necessary for a short period after ovulation.

luteous (ˈl(j)uːtɪəs), *a.*¹ *Nat. Hist.* [f. L. *lūte-us* (f. *lūtum* yellow weed) + -OUS.] Of a deep orange yellow colour. Hence †ˈ**luteously** *adv.*
1657 Tomlinson *Renou's Disp.* I. v. i. 345 [Mandrake] bears Apples..luteously [*printed* lutrously] pallescent. *Ibid.* I. v. ii. 345 Flowers..out of whose middle erupts a luteous and specious tuft. **1661** Lovell *Hist. Anim. & Min.* Introd., Woodpecker..green luteous. **1731** Medley *Kolben's Cape G. Hope* II. 290 A fine luteous substance which is taken and dried for the painters, who use it in the place of yellow oker. **1848** Gould *Birds Austral.* IV. 78 Luteous Honey-eater.
Comb. **1819** Samouelle *Entomol. Compend.* 159 Olive-black above, luteous red beneath. **1877** Coues & Allen *N. Amer. Rod.* 28 In the prairie skins, the color is very bright; a rich fawn or luteous-brown.

†ˈ**luteous,** *a.*² *Obs.* [f. L. *lute-us* (f. *lutum* mud) + -OUS.] Of or pertaining to mud.
1656 in Blount *Glossogr.* **1715** tr. *Pancirollus' Rerum Mem.* II. i. 273 That [Sarsaparilla] is naught..which hath a dirty, luteous kind of Colour within. **1731** Medley *Kolben's Cape G. Hope* II. 284 These waters keep but a little while fresh; the luteous and saline particles, which are the life of 'em, falling quickly to the bottom of the vessel.

luter (ˈl(j)uːtə(r)). *Obs.* exc. *Hist.* Forms: 5–6 lutar, 6 leutare, lewter, 6– luter. [f. LUTE *v.*¹ + -ER¹.] A lute-player.
1474 *Ld. Treas. Acc. Scot.* (1877) I. 59 Item to the lutare, j elne ½ quarter of grene for his gowne. **1497** *Ibid.* 376 Giffin to ane lutar..ixs. **1502** *Privy Purse Exp. Eliz. of York* (1830) 29 Item..to Giles lewter for stringes for the Quene of Scottes lewte..xs. **1532** Hervet *Xenophon's Househ.* (1768) 65 To exercyse the hande, as harpers and luters do, that it may folowe the mind. **1654** Vilvain *Epit. Ess.* v. 73 Twixt Nightingal and Luter a strife extended. **1660** Haward *Crown Rev.* 25 Two Luters: Fee a piece..40 0 0. **1893** *Nat. Observer* 11 Mar. 415/1 The wooers and luters of Watteau's fans are phantasms.

lutescent (l(j)uːˈtɛsənt), *a. Nat. Hist.* [f. L. *lūteus* yellow + -ESCENT.] Inclining to yellow.
1819 Samouelle *Entomol. Compend.* 182 Hinder margin of the thorax red lutescent. **1887** W. Phillips *Brit. Discomycetes* 167 *Helotium Humuli.* Cup..becoming slightly concave, lutescent, firm.

b. in combining form **luteˈscenti-**.
1871 W. A. Leighton *Lichen-flora* 261 *Lecidea ochrococca*, Nyl. lutescenti-ochraceous, granulose, effuse [etc.]. *Ibid.* 297 Epithecium..slightly lutescenti-fuscescent ..or dusky.

ˈ**lute-string**¹. [f. LUTE *sb.*¹ + STRING *sb.*]

1. A string of (or adapted for) a lute.
1530 Palsgr. 241/2 Lutestryng, *cordeav, cordon de lus.* **1578** Lyte *Dodoens* I. ci. 143 Long threedes (like to very fine and small lutestrings). **1599** Shaks. *Much Ado* III. ii. 61 His iesting spirit, which is now crept into a lute-string, and now gouern'd by stops. **1630** Davenant *Cruel Bro.* v. i, Thy wrist vaynes are cut, Heere In this Bason bleed: till drynesse made them curle Like Lute-strings in the fire. **1731** Arbuthnot *Nat. Aliments* (1735) 157 A Lute-string will bear a hundred Weight without Rupture. **1820** Keats *Isabella* ii, Her lute-string gave an echo of his name. **1855** Browning *Fra Lippo* 52 There came..A sweep of lute-strings, laughs, and whifts of song.
attrib. **1683** Moxon *Mech. Exerc., Printing* xv. ¶9 Fine Lute-string Wyer..is.. fastned by twisting about half an Inch of the end of the Lute-string to the rest of the Lute-string.

2. A noctuid moth having lines resembling the strings of a lute on its wings.
1819 G. Samouelle *Entomol. Compend.* 402 The lesser Lutestring..The Poplar Lutestring. *Ibid.* Index, Lute-string moths. **1843** Westwood *Brit. Moths* I. 202.

lutestring² (ˈl(j)uːtstrɪŋ). [App. an alteration of LUSTRING (which, however, appears later in our quots.), assimilated to prec.] A kind of glossy silk fabric; a dress or a ribbon of this material.
1661 Pepys *Diary* 18 Feb., We went to a mercer's..and there she bought a suit of Lutestring for herself. **1686** *Lond. Gaz.* No. 2126/4 To be sold..a parcel of very good black narrow Lute-Strings, and Alamode-Silks. **1704** Pope *Lett.* (1736) V. 124 Think of flouncing the petticoat so very deep, that it looks like an entire coat of lute-string! **1767** *Woman of Fashion* I. 78 She was dressed in a flowing Negligee of white Lutestring. **1799** G. Smith *Laboratory* II. 46 To draw a pattern for a silver brocade lutestring. **1856** Mrs. Browning *Aur. Leigh* vi. 715 As if you had..held your trailing lutestring up yourself. **1887** *Macm. Mag.* LV. 108 A suit of white lutestring trimmed with large bunches of acorns.

†**b.** ***to speak in lutestring***: (meaning uncertain).
The phrase 'which I met with in the course of my reading' is several times derisively quoted by Junius as used by the Duke of Grafton. Cf. quot. *a* 1797 in c.
1771 *Junius Lett.* xlviii. 250, I was led to trouble you with these observations by a passage, which, to speak in lutestring, I met with this morning in the course of my reading.

c. *attrib.*
1759 *Compl. Lett.-writer* (ed. 6) 222 Dressed in a white lutestring gown and petticoat. **1768** C'tess Cowper *Let. to Mrs. Delany* in *Mrs. D.'s Life & Corr.* Ser. II. I. 186 Lord Spencer had a pale blue lutestring domino. *a* **1797** H. Walpole *Mem. Geo. III.* (1845) I. xiv. 210 He [Chas. Townshend] had said of the last arrangement before Fox was set at the head, that it was a pretty lutestring administration which would do very well for summer wear.

Lutetian (l(j)uːˈtiːʃ(ɪ)ən), *a.* [f. L. *Lutēti-a* an ancient city on the site of modern Paris + -AN.] Of or belonging to Lutetia or Paris; Parisian.
1740 Somerville *Hobbinol* II. 235 That Strength..Which ..by your great Forefathers taught, [might] have fix'd The British Standard on Lutetian Tow'rs.

lutetium (l(j)uːˈtiːʃɪəm, -sɪəm). *Chem.* Also lutecium. [ad. F. *lutécium* (G. Urbain 1907, in *Compt. Rend.* CXLV. 761), f. F. *Lutèce*, L. *Lutēt-ia* (see LUTETIAN *a.*): see -IUM.] A rare metallic element that is the heaviest member of the lanthanide series and forms colourless salts in which it is trivalent. Atomic number 71; symbol Lu.
1907 *Jrnl. Chem. Soc.* XCII. II. 956 (*heading*) A new element: lutecium, resulting from the decomposition of Marignac's ytterbium. **1929** *Encycl. Brit.* XIV. 490/2 Lutecium occurs along with ytterbium, erbium, etc., in the minerals gadolinite, euxenite, xenotime, etc. It is separated from the other members of the group by the fractional crystallization of the bromates, lutecium bromate being the most soluble passes into the mother-liquor. **1939** *Physical Rev.* LVI. 21 The half-life of the natural radioactivity of lutecium..is..$7{\cdot}3 \pm 2 \times 10^{10}$ years for Lu^{176}, which probably is the active isotope. **1952** *Chem. & Engin. News* 7 July 2843/2 The table of international atomic weights, as published by the 'Comptes Rendus' of the New York meeting of the Union for 1951..shows changes in the weights of seven elements... Lutetium replaces lutecium, to agree with the original Latin spelling Lutetia..instead of the French Lutèce. **1973** J. J. Lagowski *Mod. Inorg. Chem.* xvi. 604 Lutetium, the first element which follows the lanthanides, starts the last *d*-series, but it forms a M^{3+} cation with a filled 4*f* orbital. Thus, lutetium on the basis of its atomic and ionic radii also appears to be a member of the lanthanide series.

†**lutewiht.** *Obs. rare.*⁻¹ [f. ME. *lut* (see LITE *sb.*⁴) little + *wiht* thing.] A little.
a **1225** *Ancr. R.* 72 Auh hwon ȝe nede moten speken a lutewiht, leseð up ower muðes flodȝeten.

‖**luth** (lyt). [Fr.: ? transferred use of *luth* LUTE *sb.*¹] The Leather Turtle (see LEATHER *sb.* 6).
1883 *Fisheries Exhib. Catal.* (ed. 4) 176 The large Sun-fish ..the Luth..the group of Péron's Seals. **1884** [see *leather turtle* s.v. LEATHER 6]. **1901** Gadow *Amphibia & Reptiles* 333 *Sphargis* s. *Dermatochelys coriacea*, the Leathery Turtle or Luth..the largest of all recent Chelonians.

luther, obs. form of LITHER.

Lutheran (ˈl(j)uːθərən), *a.* and *sb.* Also 6 lutherane. [f. proper name *Luther* + -AN.]

A. *adj.* Pertaining to the German reformer Martin Luther (1483–1546), his opinions and followers.
In the 16th c. the designation was used by Roman Catholic writers as coextensive with PROTESTANT; applied, e.g., to the reformed Church of England. Now chiefly

applied to doctrinal views held by Luther in opposition to other reformers, e.g. his doctrine as to the nature of Christ's presence in the Eucharist (see CONSUBSTANTIATION), and as the appellation of those churches, principally in Germany and Scandinavia, which accept the Augsburg Confession as their official doctrinal symbol.

1530 CROMWELL in Merriman *Life & Lett.* (1902) I. 333 They wyll not discent from the lutheran sekt. **1650** STAPYLTON *Strada's Low-C. Warres* III. 53 Disliking his marrying into a Lutheran family. **1660** JER. TAYLOR *Duct. Dubit.* II. ii. rule vi. §10 The Lutheran churches..have..as little reason for their division. **1841** T. A. TROLLOPE *Summer W. France* I. viii. 128 Marechal de Saxe..lived and died in the Lutheran religion. **1875** BRYCE *Holy Rom. Emp.* xviii. (ed. 5) 336 In North Germany princes as well as people were mostly Lutheran.

B. *sb.* A follower of Luther; an adherent of his doctrines; a member of the Lutheran church.

1521 ABP. WARHAM in Ellis *Orig. Lett.* Ser. III. I. 240 The heryng wherof shuld be right..plesant to the open Lutheranes beyond the See. **1613** SHAKS. *Hen. VIII*, III. ii. 99 I know her for A spleeny Lutheran. **1700** S. L. tr. *Fryke's Voy. E. Ind.* 321 We had several Lutherans..these fell a Singing some Spiritual Hymns in the Temple. **1865** J. GILL *Banished Count* xxi. 219 There were large numbers of Lutherans at this time in Pennsylvania. **1900** R. J. DRUMMOND *Apostol. Teach. & Christ's* viii. 335 This is..the contention of Ritualists, be they Lutherans or Anglicans.

Hence **Lutheranancer** *nonce-wd.* = LUTHERAN *sb.*; **Luthe'ranic** *a.* (*rare*) = LUTHERAN *a.*

a **1562** G. CAVENDISH *Wolsey* (1893) 273 Depresse this newe pernicious sekt of the lutarynnauncers. **1848** W. H. MILL *Five Serm.* 132 *note*, Where..the palmary Lutheranic dogma is implied. *Ibid.* 139 *note*, Perhaps this is the Lutheranic interpretation of the words.

lutheran: see LUTHERN.

Lutheranism ('l(j)uːθərənɪz(ə)m). [f. LUTHERAN + -ISM.] The body of doctrine taught by Luther and his followers; the holding of Lutheran opinions.

1560 DAUS tr. *Sleidane's Comm.* 118 In this meane tyme beginneth anewe persecution in Fraunce, againste them that were anye thynge suspected of Lutheranisme. **1641** 'SMECTYMNUUS' *Answ.* §18 (1653) 71 The Papists upbraid the Protestants with their Lutheranisme. **1756–7** tr. *Keysler's Trav.* (1760) IV. 441 Pieces relating to the history of Lutheranism. **1847** LEWES *Hist. Philos.* (1867) II. 100 This centre of Lutheranism [Würtemberg]. **1876** TENNYSON *Q. Mary* III. iv, You yourself have been supposed Tainted with Lutheranism.

Lutheranize ('l(j)uːθərənaɪz), *v.* [f. LUTHERAN + -IZE.] **a.** *trans.* To render Lutheran; to convert to Lutheran doctrines and belief. **b.** *intr.* To become Lutheran; to incline to Lutheran doctrines. Hence '**Lutheranizer**.

1845 MANNING in Purcell *Life* (1896) I. xv. 311 Is it not strange that the Lutherans and Lutheranizers..hold a development? **1857** PUSEY *Real Presence* i. (1869) 95 A few leading Zwinglian preachers Lutheranised for a while. **1879** BARING-GOULD *Germany* II. 175 Ditmarschen..In 1532 it was Lutheranised.

luthere, obs. form of LITHER.

†**Lu'therian**, *a.* and *sb. Obs.* Also 6 lutheryan, (lauterian). [f. *Luther* + -IAN. Cf. F. *luthérien.*] = LUTHERAN *a.* and *sb.*

1526 *Pilgr. Perf.* (W. de W. 1531) 224 b, Agaynst the first parte of this artycle these lutheryans..hath maligned and erred. **1581** NICOL BURNE *Disput.* in *Cath. Tract.* (S.T.S.) 147 The Lauterianis, Zuinglianis, Calvinistis, and Anabaptistis. **1589** L. WRIGHT *Hunting Antichrist* 10 They were all called Waldenses till the time of Luther, when they began to be called Lutherians and Protestants.

Hence †**Lu'therianism** = LUTHERANISM.

1796 MORSE *Amer. Geog.* II. 54 Lutherianism was..finally established in 1593, by the synod of Upsal.

Lutherism ('l(j)uːθərɪz(ə)m). [f. as prec. + -ISM.] **a.** = LUTHERANISM. **b.** Something characteristic of Luther, or done or said in imitation of Luther.

a **1695** WOOD *Hist. & Antiq. Univ. Oxf.* (Gutch 1796) II. 29 Lutherism increased daily in the University. **1863** W. C. DOWDING *Life & Corr. G. Calixtus* vii. 51 Calixtus, who had hitherto been conversant with Lutherism, found here the headquarters of the German 'Reformed'. **1882–3** SCHAFF *Encycl. Relig. Knowl.* I. 72 The movement which led the population of Anhalt from Lutherism to Calvinism.

Lutherist ('l(j)uːθərɪst). [f. *Luther* + -IST.]

a. A student of Luther; one deeply read in his life-history and works. **b.** = LUTHERAN *sb.*

1883 *American* VII. 121 Only Dr. Th. Kolde contests with Dr. Köstlin the distinction of being the first of living Lutherists. **1884** *Ibid.* 330 The latest studies of the Lutherists of Germany.

luthern ('l(j)uːθən). Forms: 7 lutheran, -en, 8 luthron, 7– luthern. [? A corruption of LUCARNE. Cf. F. LUTEON.] A dormer-window. Also ***luthern-light, -window.***

1669 in Willis & Clark *Cambridge* (1886) II. 557 With hansome Lutheran windowes in the roofe. **1679** MOXON *Mech. Exerc.* 169 Luthern, See Dormer. **1690** LEYBOURN *Curs. Math.* 901 In measuring of Roofing, seldom any deductions are made for..the Vacancies for Lutheren Lights, and Sky-Lights. **1723–24** CHAMBERS tr. *S. le Clerc's Archit.* I. 109 We call Lutherns, those Windows rais'd over the Corniche of a Building, and in the Roof of the House. **1751** HALFPENNY *New Designs Farm Houses* 7, 2 Luthron Windows with Cheeks at 9/s. each. **1793** SMEATON *Edystone L.* Introd. 5 The inside of the dome..receives light from eight luthern windows regularly disposed. **1823** NICHOLSON *Pract. Builder* 587 Luthern. **1886** E. L. BYNNER *A. Surriage* xv. 167 The gambrel roof and luthern window.

Lutherolatry (l(j)uːθər'ɒlətrɪ). [See -LATRY.] The 'worship' of Luther. Hence **Luther'olatrist**, a 'worshipper' or idolizer of Luther.

1859 *Lit. Churchman* 16 June 217/1 Lutherolatry. **1883** *Ch. Times* XXI. 857 Our Lutherolatrists think [etc.].

luthier ('l(j)uːtɪə(r)). [a. F. *luthier*, f. *luth* LUTE.] A lute-maker.

1879 HIPKINS in *Grove's Dict. Mus.* I. 687 To leave this instrument as complete as the Cremona School of luthiers left the violin. **1932** *Times Lit. Suppl.* 4 Feb. 68/2 That [knowledge] which comes from the long practice of the craft of the *luthier*. **1951** H. M. ROBINSON *Cardinal* II. 183 With two luthiers in the house, a violin ought to get finished once in a while. **1974** *Daily Colonist* (Victoria, B.C.) 1 Sept. 16/8 Dunn learned to make the 16th-century instruments while sharing a shop with Canadian luthier Ray Nurse and now makes about 20 a year.

luthre, luthur, variant of LITHER *a.*

lutidine ('l(j)uːtɪdɪn). *Chem.* **a.** An alkaloid obtained from bone-oil and coal-tar products. **b.** A related alkaloid ('β-lutidine') obtained by distilling cinchonine with potassium hydrate.

1851 T. ANDERSON in *Trans. Royal Soc. Edin.* XX. 254 A base..which possesses precisely the constitution of toluidine, and to which I give the name of lutidine. **1864** *Proc. Royal Soc.* XIII. 305 The cinchonine base, which the author [Greville Williams] distinguishes by the name of β lutidine. **1881** *Athenæum* 21 May 691/3 'On the Physiological Action of β Lutidine'.

luting ('l(j)uːtɪŋ), *vbl. sb.*[1] [f. LUTE *v.*[1] + -ING[1].] The action of playing on the lute.

a **1440** *Sir Degrev.* 38 Off lewtyng,..He bare the pryes aey. **1484** MARG. PASTON in *P. Lett.* III. 314 Ther wer non dysgysyngs, ner harpyng, ner lutyng, ner syngyn, ner non lowde dysports. **1589** NASHE *Anat. of Absurditie* Epist. *Wks.* (Grosart) I. 8 Citterning and Luting. **1880** WATSON *Angelo* in *Prince's Quest*, etc. (1892) 120 My wife, sir, hath a pretty gift Of singing and of luting.

luting ('l(j)uːtɪŋ), *vbl. sb.*[2] [f. LUTE *v.*[2] + -ING[1].] The action of stopping joints or cracks with lute.

1608 BP. HALL *Char. Virtues & V., Presumptuous* Wks. (1627) 195 He is a confident alchymist... His glasse breakes; yet hee, vpon better luting, laies wagers of the successe. **1676** WORLIDGE *Cyder* (1691) 52 The head of the stock..covered to defend it from wet by good luteing of it. **1816** KIRBY & SP. *Entomol.* (1828) II. 500 Transfer the bees to a new hive which shall require a new luting.

attrib. **1789** J. KEIR *Dict. Chem.* 97/1 The whole luting apparatus is to be bound with a string.

b. *concr.* The material used for this purpose.

1527 ANDREW *Brunswyke's Distyll. Waters* A iij, A lutynge for a glasse that ryveth upon the fyre. **1662** MERRETT tr. *Neri's Art of Glass* xxxviii, Bath the joynts and lutings with warm water. **1777** PRIESTLEY *On Air* III. Introd. 4 As a luting I have found it most convenient. **1800** tr. *Lagrange's Chem.* I. 30 A luting is employed, called Fat Luting. **1861** GESNER *Coal, Petrol.* etc. (1865) 173 A good fine clay,..is the cheapest luting for retort lids. **1893** LLOYD & HADCOCK *Artillery* 219 The door or cover is made watertight with a mixture of beeswax and tallow, termed 'luting'.

luting ('l(j)uːtɪŋ), *ppl. a.*[1] [LUTE *v.*[1] 2.] That lutes, or sounds like a lute.

1887 G. MEREDITH *Ballads & P.* 131 This lady of the luting tongue.

'**luting**, *ppl. a.*[2] In senses of LUTE *v.*[2]

1853 KANE *Grinnell Exp.* xxx. (1856) 261 Your chin has a trick of freezing to your upper jaw by the luting aid of your beard.

lutinist, obs. form of LUTANIST.

lutist ('l(j)uːtɪst). [f. LUTE *sb.*[1] + -IST.] **a.** A lute-player. (Cf. LUTENIST.) **b.** A maker of lutes.

1627 HAKEWILL *Apol.* (1630) 254 Imitation of Claudian in expressing a controversie betweene a lutist and a nightingale. **1814** MRS J. WEST *Alicia de Lacy* II. 47 The lady retained..a taborer, a lutist, and a player on the rebeck. **1863** LONGF. *Wayside Inn* I. Prel. 280 The instrument on which he played..A marvel of the lutist's art.

lutite ('lʌtaɪt). *Geol.* Formerly also **-yte**. [f. L. *lut-um* mud + -ITE[1] 2 b.] = PELITE. So **lu'taceous** *a.* [-ACEOUS] = PELITIC *a.*

1904 A. W. GRABAU in *Amer. Geologist* XXXIII. 242 The third texture [*sc.* that of 'rock flour or impalpable powder'], finally, may be designated by the term *lutaceous*, (from *lutum*, mud), and for consolidated rocks of this type the term *lutyte* may be used, irrespective of chemical composition. Pelyte has been used particularly for argillaceous rocks of the group. **1941** F. H. LAHEE *Field Geol.* (ed. 4) 785 These terms [*sc.* psephite, psammite, pelite] are derived from the Greek. The equivalent terms, derived from the Latin and preferred by some geologists, are rudite.., arenite.., and lutite. **1959** W. W. MOORHOUSE *Study of Rocks in Thin Section* xviii. 334 The clastic sediments are classified according to size as rudytes (rudaceous), which are conglomerates, arenytes (arenaceous) which are sands, and lutytes (lutaceous), which are shales and muds. **1970** *Nature* 14 Mar. 1068/2 A sediment core..reveals the top 20 cm to be a greyish-brown fossiliferous lutite.

Lutomer ('l(j)uːtəʊmə(r)). Also **Ljutomer**. The Slovene name for the region of Slovenia in which wine is produced; used *attrib.* for the wine produced there.

Before the creation of Yugoslavia in 1918 both the region (then part of Austria) and the wine were known by their German name *Luttenberg*.

[**1851** C. REDDING *Wines* (ed. 3) xi. 288 The Luttenberg wines of Lower Styria are among the first.] **1954** 'BON VIVEUR' *A.B.C. of Wine Drinking* 74 *Lutomer Riesling*, sweetish—definitely—fairly sturdy and with a slight bouquet. **1965** *Sun* 23 Jan. 6/6 The favourite white, Lutomer Riesling, that great party standby. **1970** L. W. MARRISON *Wines for Everyone* ix. 122 One has the feeling that in those restaurants where carafe wines are available, the white is more likely to be lutomer riesling than graves or mâcon. **1971** J. JEFFS *Wines of Europe* 499 In a tasting of 1958 wines in 1964, the best was undoubtedly a lutomer traminer which..was very well balanced.

lutonist, obs. form of LUTANIST.

lutose ('l(j)uːtəʊs), *a.* [ad. L. *lutōs-us*, f. *lutum* clay.] Covered with mud; miry; *spec.* in *Ent.* (see quot. 1826). Hence †**lu'tosity**, muddiness.

1650 ASHMOLE *Chym. Collect.* 8 Which Tinctures..are separable from accidentall drosse, and earthly lutosity. **1826** KIRBY & SP. *Entomol.* IV. 275 Lutose, covered with a powdery substance resembling mud or dirt, which easily rubs off.

‖**lutrin** (lytrɛ̃). [Fr.] = LECTERN.

1837 CARLYLE *Fr. Rev.* III. v. iv. 314 Sacristies, lutrins, altar-rails are pulled down. **1856** *Ecclesiologist* XVII. 89 The *lutrin*, or great lettern, and other fittings.

lutrine ('l(j)uːtraɪn), *a.* [ad. mod.L. *lutrīnus*, f. L. *lutra* otter: see -INE[1].] Pertaining to the *Lutrinæ* or otter family.

1883 *Daily Tel.* 4 July 5/2 The lutrine tribes are greatly on the increase..upon some of the best trout-streams.

luttby, var. LOTEBY *Obs.*, paramour.

lutte, var. LITE, little; obs. f. LUTE *sb.*[1]

† '**lutter**, *a. Obs.* [OE. *hlútor, hluttor* = OS. *hlutter*, OHG. *hlúter, hlutter* (mod.G. *lauter*), Goth. *hlútrs*.] Pure.

971 *Blickl. Hom.* 209 On þa norð healfe þæs weofodes swiþe wynsum ond hluttor wæta utflowende. *c* **1200** ORMIN 5706 þe sexte seollþess ædiȝleȝȝc Iss clene & lutterr herrte.

† '**luttered**, *a. Obs.* Also 6 *Sc.* **luttaird**. ? Bowed, crooked.

? *a* **1400** *Morte Arth.* 779 Alle with lutterde legges, lokerde unfaire. **1500–20** DUNBAR *Poems* lx. 57 With lut schulderis, and luttaird back.

lutulence ('l(j)uːtjʊləns). *rare.* [f. next: see -ENCE.] Muddiness; mud, dirt.

1727 in BAILEY vol. II. *a* **1834** in Sir H. Taylor *Artevelde* Wks. 1864 I. 305 The after-stream with earth-sprung taints, And gathering lutulence, [is] made foul.

lutulent ('l(j)uːtjʊlənt), *a.* ? *Obs.* exc. *literary.* [ad. L. *lutulent-us*, f. *lutum* mud.] Muddy, turbid.

c **1600** *Timon* II. iv. (1842) 31 By what faulte or fate of mine (luculent, not lutulent Sergeants) shall I say [etc.]. **1614** T. ADAMS *Devil's Banquet* 17 The lutulent, spumy, maculatorie waters of Sinne. **1661** LOVELL *Hist. Anim. & Min.* Introd., The spleen, drawing thick lutulent and melancholick blood. **1755** in JOHNSON. [Hence in mod. Dicts.] **1922** JOYCE *Ulysses* 377 Exterior splendour may be the surface of a downwardtending lutulent reality.

† '**lutum.** *Obs.* [a. L. *lutum*.] = LUTE *sb.*[2]

1718 J. CHAMBERLAYNE *Relig. Philos.* (1730) II. xviii. §7 They [Chymists] try whether their Lutums (that is the matter which they apply to the Joints of their Vessels) are as close as they should be.

lutz (lʊts). [prob. f. name of Gustave *Lussi* (1898–), Swiss figure skater, who invented it.] A jump in ice-skating in which the skater takes off from the outside back edge of one skate and lands, after a complete rotation in the air, on the outside back edge of the opposite skate.

1938 D. CUMMINGS *Figure Skating* xv. 83 Similar to the flip jump is the *Lutz*; but it is more difficult. **1940** M. Y. VINSON *Advanced Figure Skating* vi. 175 A really fine lutz..is the ambition of every jumper. **1959** *Times* 12 Mar. 4/4 The title therefore was not awarded, in spite of Jones's splendid free skating programme, which included a fine..lutz. **1964** *Times* 3 Feb. 3/5 There was a momentary unsteadiness in landing the double lutz, but all her other jumps were splendidly executed. **1976** *Times* 19 Jan. 9/6 The rather perilous landing of a double lutz.

luv (lʌv, lʊv). Spelling used to represent an affectionate, dialectal, or colloquial, etc., occurrence of the word *love*: esp. freq. as a term of address.

1898 J. D. BRAYSHAW *Slum Silhouettes* 35 They say as luv is blind. **1909** R. BROOKE *Let.* 21 Aug. (1968) 174 Boxer's in Luv. **1957** J. BRAINE *Room at Top* vi. 52 T'lad's cum to enjoy hisen, 'aven't you, luv? **1966** 'L. LANE' *ABZ of Scouse* 63 *Luv*, ironical term of affection applied to the opposite sex. Often used by waitresses as in *what'll yer 'ave luv?* **1968** A. CLARKE *Darkened Room* x. 126 The nurses called me 'Luv' or 'Dear'. **1972** G. BELL *Villains Galore* xiii. 205 Watch that money, luv! It's not safe there.

luve, obs. f. LOVE.

luven, var. LEVE *v.*[2] *Obs.*

luver, luveray, obs. ff. LOUVER, LIVERY.

†**luvestiche.** *Obs.* [OE. *lufestice*, ad. late L. *levisticum*: see LOVAGE.] = LOVAGE.

c **1000** *Sax. Leechd.* I. 374 ȝenim..lufestice [etc.]..& ȝepuna ða wyrte to somne. *c* **1265** *Voc. Plants* in Wr.-Wülcker 555/11 *Leuisticum*, i. luuesche, i. luuestiche.

luvesum, obs. form of LOVESOME.

Luvian (ˈluːvɪən), *sb.* and *a.* Also **Luwian, Luian.** [f. G. *Luvisch, Luvier* from *Luvia*, name given to part of Asia Minor: see E. Forrer in *Mitteilungen Deut. Orient-Gesellschaft* (1921) LXI. 20–39: see -IAN.] **A.** *sb.* **a.** A member of an Anatolian people contemporary with the Hittites, known from cuneiform inscriptions. **b.** The language of the Luvians. **B.** *adj.* Of or pertaining to the Luvians or their language.

[**1923** H. R. HALL in Buckler & Calder *Anatolian Studies* 168 Although until we have the cuneiform texts before us it is quite impossible to control the work of Forrer..yet, whatever we may think at present of his elaborate analysis of the eight languages which he thinks the Hittites or their subjects spoke,..'Ur-Luvisch', 'Luvisch',..and so on, yet the rough historical results..can no doubt be accepted without demur.] **1924** *Cambr. Anc. Hist.* II. xi. 253 More [tablets], however, are couched in some six native allied dialects, according to the latest decipherers.., who agree in regarding the dialects as Indo-European... To the six dialects they give the names Kanesian, Luvian, [etc.]. **1933** C. D. BUCK *Compar. Gram. Greek & Latin* 15 Closely related to the cuneiform Hittite are the hieroglyphic Hittite and Luwian. **1934** WEBSTER, *Luian*,..an ancient language of the Hittite empire. **1939** L. H. GRAY *Foundations of Lang.* xi. 324 There are also Hittite inscriptions in pictographic or hieroglyphic characters... Their language may be akin to that seen in the thus far scanty fragments of *Luian* or *Luvian*, closely related to Hittite. **1952** O. R. GURNEY *Hittites* i. 18 Other Indo-European dialects (Luwian, Palaic, Lycian, and 'Hieroglyphic Hittite') established themselves in other parts of Anatolia. **1961** L. R. PALMER *Mycenaeans & Minoans* 26 The possibility..that the predecessors of the Greeks were Luvians from western Asia Minor should please both philologists and archaeologists. **1963** —— *Interpretation Mycenaean Greek Texts* 339 The word [*sc. a-ja-me-na*] may be a Luvian loan-word (*a-ja* 'do, make') in the sense 'wrought'. This possibility is strengthened by the fact that *kuwana-* occurs in Luvian and is held to be the source of Greek κύανος. **1966** J. PUHVEL in Birnbaum & Puhvel *Anc. Indo-European Dial.* 238 This linguistic division of the substrata is indirectly discernible in the divergent Hattic, Kaneshite, and Luwian pantheons within the hospitality of the state cults of the Hittite empire... 'Hieroglyphic Hittite' is in reality a dialectal form of Luwian ('East' or 'Late' Luwian). **1973** K. A. KITCHEN in D. J. Wiseman *Peoples of Old Testament Times* 67 Goliath (*Golyat*) is claimed as a dissimilated form of a Walwatta.., from a Luvian base *walwi/a*.

luvien, obs. form of LIVE, LOVE *vbs.*

Luwian, var. LUVIAN *sb.* and *a.*

†**lux**, *v. Obs.* [ad. F. *luxer*, ad. L. *luxāre*: see LUXATE *v.*] = LUXATE *v.* Hence **ˈluxing** *vbl. sb.*

1708 J. PHILIPS *Cyder* II. 488 The fall Luxt his neck-joint. **1725** POPE *Odyss.* XI. 80 Staggering I reel'd, and as I reel'd I fell, Lux'd the neck-joint. **1775** ASH, Suppl., *Luxing*, the act of putting out of joint.

lux (lʌks), *sb. Physics.* Pl. lux. [L., = 'light'.] A unit of illumination (now incorporated into the International System of Units) equal to the illumination of a surface all of which is one metre from a uniform point source of light of unit intensity (now one candela), i.e. (as now defined) one lumen per square metre.

1889 *Engineering* 13 Sept. 313/1 Mr. Preece was not.. fortunate with his unit of surface illumination, the 'lux' being the illumination produced by a lamp of one Carcel power at a distance of one metre, which is practically the same illumination as that afforded by an English standard candle at a distance of 1 ft... It is probable, sooner or later, that such a unit will be adopted. **1897** *Jrnl. Inst. Electr. Engin.* XXVI. 638 It was proposed by the Committee of the International Congress of Geneva that M. A. Blondel should present a report, with..a complete system of defining the dimensions and units of photometry... This report was submitted for examination of a commission.. and was accepted... Lux = Lumen/Square metre. **1911** A. P. TROTTER *Illumination* ii. 17 Sir William Preece..adopted the Carcel-metre, and he showed that it was equal to a standard candle of 1·058 foot. At the Paris Electrical Congress of 1889 he adopted the name 'lux' for this... The unit of illumination produced by a bougie-décimale at a metre has been called a bougie-metre, and the name 'lux' was revived at the Geneva Congress of 1896 and was applied to this unit... This lux is, roughly, one-twelfth of a foot-candle, or about one-fourteenth of Preece's lux. The illumination produced by a Hefner at a metre has also been called a 'lux', and it seems probable that the International candle at a metre may be called an International lux. **1927** *Forestry* I. 87 Experiments carried out..in a light intensity of 48,000 lux. *Ibid.*, The lux is a light intensity produced by a light of one candle-power at a distance of one metre. Forty-eight thousand lux is roughly equivalent to full sunlight at noon in midsummer in Germany. **1953** AMOS & BIRKINSHAW *Television Engin.* I. 279, 1 lux = 1 lumen per square metre = 0·0929 foot-candle. **1970** *Nature* 26 Dec. 1349/2 On many days during the growth of these plants light intensities reached 80,000 lux.

lux, obs. variant of LUXE.

†**ˈluxate**, *ppl. a. Obs.* [ad. L. *luxāt-us*, f. *luxāre*: see next.] = LUXATED.

1597 J. KING *On Jonas* (1618) 399 He..lieth not within our Land (sauing in a few disordered and luxate members). **1661** LOVELL *Hist. Anim. & Min.* 110 Applied with the ashes of a Womans haire it cureth luxate joynts.

luxate (ˈlʌkseɪt), *v.* [f. L. *luxāt-*, ppl. stem of *luxāre*, f. *luxus* dislocated, a. Gr. λοξός.] *trans.* To dislocate, put out of joint. Also *fig.*

1623 in COCKERAM. **1644** BARWICK *Querela Cantabr.* Pref., Thus the Knipperdolings of the age..luxated all the joints of Christianity in this kingdom. **1681** GLANVILL *Sadducismus* I. (1726) 57 Descartes by his jocular metaphysical Meditations has so luxated and distorted the rational Faculties of some, otherwise, sober..Persons. **1684** tr. *Bonet's Merc. Compit.* x. 368 The Spine luxated inwards cannot be restored. **1760** *Phil. Trans.* LI. 679 My father was sent for to a man who had luxated his thigh bone. **1835–6** TODD *Cycl. Anat.* I. 157/1 The foot..had been luxated. **1846** BRITTAN tr. *Malgaigne's Man. Oper. Surg.* 237 Depress the metacarpus to luxate the bones.

Hence **ˈluxated** *ppl. a.*, **ˈluxating** *vbl. sb.*

1634 T. JOHNSON *Parey's Chirurg.* Pref. (1678) 3 Who without Chirurgery can hope to cure Broken or Luxated parts? **1712** tr. *Pomet's Hist. Drugs* I. 195 Dragon's Blood.. strengthens luxated Joynts. **1775** ASH, Suppl., *Luxating*, the act of putting out of joint. **1899** *Allbutt's Syst. Med.* VI. 549 The projection of the luxated portion into the abdomen.

luxation (lʌkˈseɪʃən). *Surg.* [ad. L. *luxātiōn-em*, n. of action f. *luxāre*: see LUXATE *v.*] The action of dislocating or putting out of joint; the condition of being dislocated; dislocation; an instance of this.

1552 UDALL tr. *Geminie's Anat.* Pref., Luxacions and wrenches. **1580** T. NORTON *Let. to Ld. Burghley*, In a luxacion or unknittyng of their owne lymes. **1615** CROOKE *Body of Man* 1002 If at any time the luxation of the Talus doe happen, it is rather to the inner processe then to the vtter. **1676** WISEMAN *Surg.* VII. ii. 480 When..two Bones, which being naturally united make up a Joint, are separated from each other, we call it a Luxation. **1748** SMOLLETT *Rod. Rand.* xxvii. (1804) 180 As pretty a luxation of the *os humeri* as one would desire to see. **1830** R. KNOX *Béclard's Anat.* 115 New synovial membranes are sometimes formed, as is observed in false joints, after unreduced luxations. **1884** M. MACKENZIE *Dis. Throat & Nose* II. 430 The existence of luxation of the nasal bones was established.

b. *fig.*

a **1631** DONNE *Serm.* lxxxvi. Wks. (ed. Alford) IV. 85 There are other Luxations, other Dislocations of Jesus when we displace him for any worldly respect. **1658** W. BURTON *Itin. Anton.* 232, I could produce many such luxations of whole verses..out of Virgil. **1812** *Q. Rev.* VIII. 227 Discussions on the position of an accent, the luxation of a dochmiac, or the hallucination of some sinful copyist.

luxe. Also 7 lux. [a. F. *luxe*, ad. L. *luxus*.]

1. Luxury. Also *attrib.* or quasi-*adj.*

1558 in Froude *Hist. Eng.* VI. 399 *note*, While they..in luxe and lewdness, did sail in a sure port. *a* **1618** SYLVESTER *Spectacles* xviii, Ambition, Luxe, and Avarice. **1636** E. DACRES tr. *Machiavel's Disc. Livy* I. ii. 12 To exceed others in luxe and wantonnesse. **1661** EVELYN *Tyrannus* (ed. 2) 14 There will need no Sumptuary lawes to represse..the Lux which Men so much condemn in our Apparrel. **1718** PRIOR *Pleasure* 14 The power of wealth I tried, And all the various luxe of costly pride. **1746** SHENSTONE *Elegies* xxi. 39 Above or Persian luxe or Attic art, The rude majestic monument arose. **1908** *Westm. Gaz.* 28 July 11/3 We possess..a special department for hiring out luxe carriages. *Ibid.*, One of our Charron luxe cars fills all the essentials of a gentleman's private car. **1932** R. FRY *Let.* 26 Apr. (1972) II. 667 Epidauros..was all on a grand scale and tremendous *luxe* in the architecture. **1959** *N.Y. Times* 8 Nov. I. 98 (Advt.), The incomparable beauty and luxe of silk. **1961** *Ibid.* 26 Nov. I. 91 (Advt.), The great revival of the luxe little mesh evening bag. **1967** L. DEIGHTON *London Dossier* 124 Jermyn Street ..is a thoroughfare resonant with *luxe*. **1968** L. DURRELL *Tunc* iii. 94 For tonight the Pera hotel..will enable you to rest. There is every luxe. **1974** *New Yorker* 3 June 98/2 He looks round his palace of a house with sniffly and quite unfair resentment, considering its comfort and luxe.

‖**2.** The French *luxe* (lyks) occurs as an alien word with the sense: Luxuriousness, sumptuous elegance; esp. in ***édition de luxe, train de luxe.***

1819 *Edinb. Rev.* XXXII. 377 The paper used for printing, except in what are emphatically called *les éditions de luxe*, is very inferior to ours. **1885** *Athenæum* 25 July 111/2 The volume may fairly claim to be, in a modest way, an *édition de luxe*. **1886** *Westm. Rev.* Apr. 591 Paper and type are the very acme of refinement and *luxe*. **1888** *Pall Mall G.* 4 Aug. 2/2 These were not *luxe* or 'limited' trains with extra fancy fares. **1890** *Bradshaw's Cont. Rlwy. Guide* Jan. 49 'Train de Luxe', consisting of Sleeping Cars and Lits-Salons, number of places limited.

Luxembourgeois (ˈlʌksəmbuːʒwɑː), *a.* Of or pertaining to Luxemb(o)urg or to its inhabitants. Also as *sb. pl.*, the natives or inhabitants of Luxemb(o)urg.

1905 T. H. PASSMORE *In Further Ardenne* v. 121 If its effects upon conduct be any test of a religious system, Luxembourgeois Catholicism comes out brightly, for in the matter of honesty and chastity the people are resplendent. **1951** T. EDWARDS *Belgium & Luxembourg* vii. 80 A playground for both Luxembourgeois and Belgians. **1971** *Guardian* 8 June 11/4 Though the Luxembourgeois run the hotel, all have English as a working language. **1973** *Sunday Times* 21 Jan. 24/6 Many Luxembourgeois aristocrats have long ago departed.

Luxembourger (ˈlʌksəmbɜːgə(r)). A native or inhabitant of Luxemb(o)urg.

1913 G. RENWICK *Luxembourg* i. 38 During the two previous reigns German influence was supreme at Court... But..that is so no more, and to be a Luxembourger is not now a drawback. **1942** *R.A.F. Jrnl.* 16 May (recto rear cover), Luxembourgers paid tribute to fallen R.A.F. pilots and were punished for their gesture. **1951** W. J. TAYLOR-WHITEHEAD *Luxembourg* I. ii. 24 The Luxembourgers work hard, and they work long (though sometimes irregular) hours. **1956** B. MILES *Attic in Luxembourg* i. 3 Redouté, the rose-painter, was a Luxembourger. **1972** R. MAYNE *Europeans* vi. 164 Some European officials..smiled at Luxembourgers' accents in French or German. **1973** *Guardian* 23 Mar. 15/7 The Luxembourgers have been saying that they will sign, only if the bank has its headquarters in their capital.

Luxemburgisch (lʌksəmˈbɜːrgɪʃ). Also **Luxembourgish.** [f. *Luxemb(o)urg* + -ISH[1].] = LETZEBURGESCH.

1957 *B.B.C. Handbook* 251, 1940... 30 Nov. Luxembourgish broadcasts (as part of Belgian Service) began. **1961** R. E. KELLER *German Dial.* 10 These two dialects—or languages—are the daily medium of *all classes* of 300,000 people in the case of Luxemburgisch and of over three million people in the case of *Schwyzertütsch*. **1965** [see LETZEBURGESCH].

luxmeter (ˈlʌksmiːtə(r)). Also **luxometer.** [f. LUX *sb.* (+ -O) + METER *sb.*[3]] An instrument for measuring the luminance (brightness) or illuminance (illumination) of a surface.

1910 H. M. HOBART *Dict. Electr. Engin.* II. 319/2 *Luxmeter, photometric.* This is a photometer of the 'cat's-eye type'. **1912** W. C. CLINTON tr. *Bloch's Sci. of Illumination* v. 101 A further development..in the direction of greater portability and lightness has been made in the luxometer. **1915** GASTER & DOW *Mod. Illuminants* vii. 261 Another small instrument of the surface-brightness type, the 'Luxometer', has recently been introduced. **1932** *Proc. Internat. Illumination Congr., 1931* I. 215 Two types of luxmeter have been studied: the luxmeter with a scale of illuminations, and the luxmeter with a single comparison illumination, controllable either by the distance of the lamp or by the interposition of a photometric wedge. **1967** E. CHAMBERS *Photolitho-Offset* vii. 85 Meters can be purchased for measuring the number of Lux (luxmeters) or [*printed* of] foot-candela (foot-candela meters).

luxsorius, obs. form of LUXURIOUS.

luxullianite (lʌkˈsʌlɪənaɪt). *Min.* [f. *Luxullian* its locality in Cornwall + -ITE.] (See quots.)

1878 LAWRENCE tr. *Cotta's Rocks Class.* 199 The name Luxullianite has been proposed..for a porphyroidal granite, in which the mica is replaced by tourmaline. **1879** RUTLEY *Study Rocks* xii. 210 Luxullianite is composed of schorl, flesh-coloured orthoclase, and quartz.

†**ˈluxur.** *Obs. rare.* [? Back-formation from LUXURIOUS.] A lecher.

1604 T. M. *Blacke Booke* D 3 How many Villainies were in Spaine: how many Luxurs in Italie. **1604** T. M. *Father Hubburds Tales* E 2 b, The torment to a luxur due, Who neuer thinkes his harlot true. **1607** TOURNEUR *Rev. Trag.* I. i. Wks. 1878 II. 6 A parcht and juicelesse luxur.

†**luxure.** *Obs.* [a. F. *luxure* (13th c. in Littré), ad. L. *luxuria*: see LUXURY.] = LUXURY 1.

c **1374** CHAUCER *Boeth.* III. pr. vii. 62 (Camb. MS.) Who-so-euere wole remembryn hym of hyse luxures, he shal wel vndyrstonde þat [etc.]. **1390** GOWER *Conf.* III. 245 The Philosophre..conseileth to a king, That he the surfet of luxure Schal tempre.

luxuriance (lʌkˈsjʊərɪəns, lʌgˈʒʊərɪəns). [f. LUXURIANT: see -ANCE.] The condition of being luxuriant; superabundant growth or development; exuberance; an instance of this. Also quasi-*concr.*

1728–46 THOMSON *Spring* 92 The whole leafy forest stands displayed, In full luxuriance. **1770** LANGHORNE *Plutarch* (1879) I. 87/2 Each had the luxuriances of the citizens to prune. **1777** BURKE *Let. to Sheriffs Bristol* Wks. III. 203 The faults which grow out of the luxuriance of freedom. **1820** KEATS *Hyperion* I. 237 This calm luxuriance of blissful light. **1825** LYTTON *Zicci* ii, The luxuriance of his fancy was unabated. **1845** FORD *Handbk. Spain* 92 Vegetation..bursts forth in gigantic luxuriance and life. **1850** GOSSE *Rivers of Bible* (1878) 196 The cattle are driven ..from considerable distances to feed on its luxuriance. **1880** HAUGHTON *Phys. Geog.* vi. 312 The whole Equatorial zone is characterized by the extreme luxuriance of the vegetation.

luxuriancy (lʌkˈsjʊərɪənsɪ, lʌgˈʒʊərɪənsɪ). Now *rare.* [f. as prec.: see -ANCY.] = prec.

1648 W. MOUNTAGUE *Devout Ess.* I. xii. 143 The ranknes and luxuriancy of our tempers..ought rather to be the subject of our extirpation. **1672** DRYDEN *Defence* Wks. 1883 IV. 230 His malice keeps a poet within those bounds, which the luxuriancy of his fancy would tempt him to overleap. **1712** ADDISON *Spect.* No. 414 ¶5 A Tree in all its Luxuriancy and Diffusion of Boughs and Branches. **1737** *Common Sense* I. 25, I therefore prohibit all *Concetti*, and Luxuriancies of Fancy. **1748** *Anson's Voy.* I. x. 102 Such a luxuriancy of funguous flesh, as yielded to no remedy. **1804–6** SYD. SMITH *Mor. Philos.* (1850) 183 You do not expect wildness in walls, and luxuriancy in buttresses. **1818** C. M. J. CLAIRMONT *Jrnl.* in Dowden *Shelley* (1886) II. v. 203 The scenery to Bologna was flat, but of incredible luxuriancy.

luxuriant (lʌkˈsjʊərɪənt, lʌgˈʒʊərɪənt), *a.* Also 6 *erron.* **luxurient.** [ad. L. *luxuriant-em*, pres. pple. of *luxuriāre* to grow rank, f. *luxuria* LUXURY.]

1. Producing abundantly, prolific. Now *rare.*

c **1540** tr. *Pol. Verg. Eng. Hist.* (Camden) I. 19 The grownde is luxurient and frutefull. **1712** POPE *Vertumnus* 10 The growth of the luxuriant year. **1748** *Anson's Voy.* I. v. 44 The soil of the Island is truly luxuriant. **1756–7** tr. *Keysler's Trav.* (1760) III. 142 The country still retains a luxuriant fertility. **1794** S. WILLIAMS *Vermont* 131 The soil was.. fertile and luxuriant. **1877** M. M. GRANT *Sun-Maid* ii, It was luxuriant as the valleys of Devon.

†*transf.* **1650** BULWER *Anthropomet.* Pref., Here the luxuriant Chin quite down is mown.

2. Of plants, etc.: Growing profusely, exuberant, rank. †Of flesh: Growing to excess (*obs.*).

1661 LOVELL *Hist. Anim. & Min.* 230 If stamped and applied they compresse luxuriant flesh. *a* **1667** COWLEY *Death Mrs. K. Philips* iv., Wit's like a Luxuriant Vine. **1697** DRYDEN *Virg. Georg.* I. 166 [The Ploughman] Sends in his feeding Flocks betimes t' invade The rising bulk of the luxuriant Blade. **1749** FIELDING *Tom Jones* IV. ii, Her hair.. was so luxuriant, that it reached her middle. **1791** COWPER *Iliad* XVII. 64 The luxuriant olive by a swain Rear'd in some solitude. **1835** MISS MITFORD in L'Estrange *Life* III. iii. 35 The dark nasturtium is a fine colour, and very luxuriant. **1846** J. BAXTER *Libr. Pract. Agric.* (ed. 4) II. 365 The tops of white turnips are long and luxuriant at the commencement of the season. **1883** *19th Cent.* May 763 Strong and luxuriant hair is accompanied by regular and durable teeth.

b. *spec.* in *Bot.* (see quots. 1760, 1852).

1760 J. LEE *Introd. Bot.* I. xx. (1765) 53 A flower is said to be luxuriant, when some of the Parts of Fructification are augmented in Number, and others thereby excluded. **1776–96** WITHERING *Brit. Plants* (ed. 3) I. 251 When of a luxuriant growth, the numbers often increase, especially the number of the pistils. **1852** HENSLOW *Dict. Bot. Terms, Luxuriant*... Generally applied where a superabundance of nutriment causes the organs of nutrition to be more developed than those of fructification.

3. In immaterial applications. **a.** Of invention, genius, fancy, etc.: Exuberantly productive. Of speech, action, etc.: Abundant, profuse, excessive. Of ornamentation: Excessively rich or florid.

1625 BACON *Ess. Youth & Age* (Arb.) 263 A fluent and Luxuriant Speech.. becomes Youth well, but not Age. **1641** 'SMECTYMNUUS' *Vind. Answ.* iii. 53 If hee will give lesse scope to his luxuriant pen, speak more cautiously. **1675** TRAHERNE *Chr. Ethics* 443 Mistake not these things for arbitrary flourishes of luxuriant fancy. **1689** SWIFT *Ode to Temple* Wks. 1755 IV. I. 244 How is the muse luxuriant grown. **1765** BLACKSTONE *Comm.* I. 87 Restraining it [the common law] where it was too lax and luxuriant. **1780** A. YOUNG *Tour Irel.* II. xvii. 75 The irish jig, which they can dance with a most luxuriant expression. **1799** *Med. Jrnl.* I. 43 Brown was a luxuriant genius. **1848** MRS. JAMESON *Sacr. & Leg. Art* (1850) 91 The vivid colour, the luxuriant architecture remind us of Paul Veronese. **1855** BAIN *Senses & Int.* III. i. §55 (1864) 425 A luxuriant imagination implies the facility of retaining scenes of every description. **1882–3** SCHAFF *Encycl. Relig. Knowl.* II. 1200 Rules were given with respect to the luxuriant ornamentation of the churches.

†**b.** Excessively prosperous. *Obs.*

1654 tr. *Scudery's Curia Pol.* 76 Luxuriant and wanton times cause Princes like iron to rust for want of use. **1712** STEELE *Spect.* No. 330 ¶3 By many Losses.. reduced from a very luxuriant Trade and Credit to very narrow Circumstances. **1766** GOLDSM. *Vic. W.* xxix, The luxuriant great ones of the world shall no more tread us to the earth.

†**c.** Of a disease: Abundantly prevalent. *Obs.*

1656 J. SMITH *Pract. Physick* 24 Arthritis that is vagrant is Scorbutical... The parts affected are the Nerves; because it is very luxuriant in the back and the loins.

¶**4.** Misused for: LUXURIOUS.

1671 *Phil. Trans.* VI. 2129 Being the most delicious and luxuriant Cider.. that ever I knew. **1824** MISS FERRIER *Inher.* lix, Uncle A... had been left.. in a luxuriant apartment. **1885** C. GIBBON *Hard Knot* I. v. 69 It was a splendid apartment,.. luxuriant to a degree.

Hence **lu'xuriantly** *adv.*, †**lu'xuriantness.**

1725 C. PITT *Vida's Art Poet.* III. (1726) 66 In wide array luxuriantly he pours A crowd of words, and opens all his stores. **1775** ASH, *Luxuriantness.* **1786** BURNS *Ep. to a Young Friend* vi, The sacred lowe o' weel-plac'd love, Luxuriantly indulge it. **1840** BROWNING *Sordello* I. 637 Round each new discovery wreathed Luxuriantly the fancies infantine. **1863** LYELL *Antiq. Man* 16 Nowhere.. does this tree flourish more luxuriantly than in Denmark.

luxuriate (lʌkˈsjʊərɪeɪt, lʌgˈʒʊərɪeɪt), *v.* [f. L. *luxuriāt-*, ppl. stem of *luxuriāre*: see LUXURIANT.]

1. *intr.* Of a plant: To grow rank. Now *rare.* Also *fig.* †Of a writer: To write at exuberant length; to exceed one's limits. *Obs.*

1621 BURTON *Anat. Mel.* Democr. to Rdr. 10, I could haue more willingly luxuriated, and better satisfied my selfe and others. *Ibid.* III. II. I. 545 The mind is apt to lust, and hote or cold, As corne luxuriates in a better molde. **1658** J. ROBINSON *Eudoxa* IX. 48 Scorbutical Plants.. luxuriate, where the Scurvie is predominant. **1731** in BAILEY vol. II. **1832** G. DOWNES *Lett. Cont. Countries* I. 269 The vineyards hereabout are partly lopped, partly left to luxuriate. **1868** LIGHTFOOT *Comm. Philipp.* (1873) 259 Syria was a soil where such a plant would thrive and luxuriate.

†**b.** *fig.* To grow or develop exuberantly *into* (error, folly, etc.). *Obs.*

1651 N. BACON *Disc. Govt. Eng.* II. xvii. (1739) 90 The Clergy.. suffered the minds of young Scholars to luxuriate into Errours of Divinity. **1757** JOHNSON *Rambler* No. 172 ¶1 The powers of the mind.. more frequently luxuriate into follies, than blossom into goodness. **1808** ELEANOR SLEATH *Bristol Heiress* V. 121 The seeds of faults.. wanted but the soil in which.. to luxuriate into vices.

2. To indulge in luxury; to feast, revel, enjoy oneself. Now only with const. *in, on.*

1621 BURTON *Anat. Mel.* Democr. to Rdr. 56 Let them tyrannize, Epicurize, oppresse, luxuriate, and consume themselues. **1648** JOS. BEAUMONT *Psyche* XIX. xliv, 'Tis Worth enough, if a young Gallant can Look big, Luxuriate, and Write Gentleman. **1832** MRS. F. TROLLOPE *Dom. Manners Amer.* i. (1839) 2 A huge crocodile luxuriating in the slime. **1841** E. FITZGERALD *Lett.* (1889) I. 71, I had a long letter from Morton the other day—he is still luxuriating at Venice. **1866** MRS. STOWE *Lit. Foxes* 25 The Christmas-dinner, that solid feast of fat things on which we also luxuriated. **1878** BOSW. SMITH *Carthage* 278 The troops.. must have luxuriated in the easeful quarters which Hannibal's sword had opened for them.

b. In immaterial sense: To take great delight, revel *in* (something).

c **1650** tr. *Hales' Dissert. de Pace* in *Phenix* (1708) II. 357 Do they not luxuriate in this Wish? **1678** CUDWORTH *Intell. Syst.* I. iv. 550 They also did luxuriate in their other Many Creature-gods. **1830** HERSCHEL *Stud. Nat. Phil.* 71 The mind.. luxuriates in its newly found powers. **1880** N. SMYTH *Old Faiths in new Light* iv. (1882) 124 The Oriental mind.. luxuriates in dreams.

Hence **luxuri'ation**, the action or process of luxuriating; exuberant efflorescence.

1839 DE QUINCEY *Recoll. Lakes* Wks. 1862 II. 207 This book never could be very popular, from the.. luxuriation of its descriptions. **1854** —— *Autobiog. Sk.* Wks. II. 60 The same genial climate there was, the same luxuriation of nature in her early prime.

†**luxuriety.** *nonce-wd.* [f. LUXURIOUS, on the supposed analogy of *variety*, etc.] Luxuriance.

a **1768** STERNE *Serm.* xl. Wks. 1815 IV. 64 One may observe a kind of luxuriety in the description.

†**luxuriose**, *a. Obs. rare*$^{-0}$. = next.

1727 in BAILEY vol. II.

luxurious (lʌkˈsjʊərɪəs, lʌgˈʒʊərɪəs), *a.* Also 4 luxsorius, 5 luxurius, 7 luxurous. [ad. OF. *luxurius* (mod.F. *luxurieux*), ad. L. *luxuriōsus*, f. *luxuri-a*: see LUXURY and -OUS.]

†**1.** Lascivious, lecherous, unchaste. *Obs.*

c **1330** *Arth. & Merl.* 652 (Kölbing) Þe deuelen, þat houen abouen ous, Euer be luxsorius. *a* **1450** *Knt. de la Tour* (1868) 50 Havinge luxurious lokes, countenaunces and signes in her chirche atte the masse. **1456** SIR G. HAYE *Law Arms* (S.T.S.) 76 Ane [is] luxurius, ane othir chaste. **1599** MINSHEU *Span. Dial.* 53/2 Great hee-goats, which is a most luxurious beast. **1607** TOPSELL *Four-f. Beasts* (1658) 428 The beast beginneth to be luxurious, and prone to the rage of venery. **1630** *R. Johnson's Kingd. & Commw.* III. 430 They are exceeding luxurious, by reason whereof the Countrey swarmeth with Whores. **1697** DRYDEN *Virg. Past.* IV. 52 The luxurious Father of the Fold.

†**2.** Outrageous, extravagant, excessive; also, passionately desirous *after* something. *Obs.*

c **1374** CHAUCER *Boeth.* I. pr. iv. 13 (Camb. MS.) Euery luxurious tormentour [L. *flagitiosum quemque*] dar doon all felonye unpunysshed. *a* **1613** OVERBURY *Charact., Wise Man* Wks. (1856) 60 He.. is not luxurious after acquaintance. **1627** HAKEWILL *Apol.* IV. viii. §10. 384 As they were luxurious in the price, so were they likewise in the worke itself. **1665** NEEDHAM *Med. Medicinæ* 266 When this Sulphureous part is exalted, and becomes luxurious in the Bloud.

3. a. Of persons, their habits, etc.: Given to luxury, or self-indulgence, voluptuous.

1606 WARNER *Alb. Eng.* XIV. lxxxvii. 358 Luxurious, idle, Bacchanists. **1691** HARTCLIFFE *Virtues* 311 Corinth, the Metropolis of Achaia, was.. excessively proud and luxurious. **1722** DE FOE *Plague* (1840) 21 The monarchy being restored.. all people were gay and luxurious. **1774** GOLDSM. *Nat. Hist.* (1776) II. 71 The inhabitants lead a.. soft, luxurious life. **1836** J. H. NEWMAN in *Lyra Apost.* (1849) 85 He.. lets his feelings run, In soft luxurious flow. **1875** GLADSTONE *Glean.* (1879) I. 32 A wealthy country, with a large leisured class, in a luxurious age.

b. Of things: Of or pertaining to luxury; characterized by or making a display of luxury.

1650 BULWER *Anthropomet.* 99 The two most precious Pearls which Cleopatra dissolv'd and drunk as a luxurious expression of Love to Mark Antonie. **1667** MILTON *P.L.* XI. 784 Those whom last thou sawst In triumph and luxurious wealth. **1713** STEELE *Guardian* No. 18 ¶4 Conveyed to that luxurious Paradise. **1860** EMERSON *Cond. Life, Wealth* Wks. (Bohn) II. 348 A sumptuous ship has.. made it [the Atlantic] a luxurious hotel. *a* **1873** LYTTON *Pausanias* 30 An imitation of the luxurious galleys of the Barbarian. **1879** FARRAR *St. Paul* (1883) 491 The rich brought their luxurious provisions.

¶**4.** = LUXURIANT 2. Now *rare.*

1644 H. VAUGHAN *Serm.* 26 That is but a luxurious branch shot forth through the strength and heat of devotion. **1653** *Cloria & Narcissus* I. 59 Arrable grounds, every one intermixt with luxurious Vines. **1662** EVELYN *Chalcogr.* (1769) 16, I can only name them briefly, the field would be too luxurious to discourse upon them severally. **1801** CHARLOTTE SMITH *Lett. Solit. Wand.* I. 5 This luxurious grass spangled with wild flowers. **1826** SOUTHEY in *Q. Rev.* XXXIV. 103 Their villages are situated in the midst of the most luxurious groves. **1854** CARDL. WISEMAN *Fabiola* (1855) 349 She wiped them with her luxurious hair.

†**b.** Of unhealthy flesh: Granulating exuberantly, 'proud'. *Obs.*

1676 WISEMAN *Surg.* 378 If in the incarning the Wound the Flesh grow luxurious, touch it with a Vitriol-stone.

lu'xuriously, *adv.* [f. prec. + -LY^2.] In a luxurious manner. †**a.** Lasciviously, lustfully (*obs.*). **b.** In the enjoyment of luxury and pleasure; plentifully, sumptuously, voluptuously.

a. *c* **1540** tr. *Pol. Verg. Eng. Hist.* (Camden) I. 260 Emonge the captives was the wife of Sigifredus,.. whome the kinges sonn Edmundus hadd long since luxuriuslie deflowred. **1606** SHAKS. *Ant. & Cl.* III. xiii. 120 Besides what hotter houres.. you haue Luxuriously pickt out.

b. **1605** DANIEL *Ulysses & Syren* 15 To spend the time luxuriously Becomes not men of worth. **1693** DRYDEN *Juvenal* iii, Mice and rats.. with heroic verse luxuriously were fed. **1796** J. MOSER *Hermit of Caucasus* I. 65 The plain abounding in fruits, luxuriously supplied. **1883** FROUDE *Short Stud.* IV. I. xi. 141 Giraldus Cambrensis.. found the monks dining more luxuriously than the King. **1900** *Edin. Rev.* July 223 A great heiress living luxuriously in London.

lu'xuriousness. [f. as prec. + -NESS.] The quality or state of being luxurious; †lasciviousness (*obs.*); indulgence in luxury or pleasure, voluptuousness; also profuseness, prodigality.

1542 BOORDE *Dyetary* xxi. (1870) 285 Cucumbers restrayneth veneryousnes, or lassyuyousnes, or luxuryousnes. **1598** BARCKLEY *Felic. Man* (1631) 317 Ungodlinesse troubleth the Church, Injustice the commonwealth, Luxuriousnesse private families. **1651** N. BACON *Disc. Govt. Eng.* II. i. (1739) 4 Retaining a tincture of.. the luxuriousness of his great Grandfather Edward the Second. **1847** PUSEY tr. *Horst's Paradise* I. iii. (1871) I. 35 From all luxuriousness and uncleanness Deliver us. **1872** *Spectator* 7 Sept. 1142 The almost Asiatic luxuriousness with which it is illustrated. **1889** BRYDALL *Art in Scotl.* xiv. 311 A luxuriousness of effective light and shade.

'luxurist. *Obs.* or *arch. rare.* [f. LUXURY + -IST.] One addicted to luxury.

1689–90 TEMPLE *Ess. Poetry* Wks. 1731 I. 248 There are no where more abandoned Libertines, more refined Luxurists. **1830** JAMES *Darnley* xix. 83/1 In his history.. may be traced the yet unsated luxurist, and the incipient tyrant.

†**lu'xurity.** *Obs. rare.* [Irregularly f. LUXURIOUS + -TY.] **a.** Lasciviousness, lustfulness. **b.** = LUXURIANCE.

1563–87 FOXE *A. & M.* (1596) 225/2 Greedie couetousnesse, and filthie luxuritie. **1595** L. PIOT *Orator* 375 That proceedeth of nothing but idlenesse and gluttonie which provoketh luxuritie. **1630** T. WESTCOTE *Devon.* (1845) 391 Its fruitful glebe and luxurity thereof.

luxurius, luxurous, obs. ff. LUXURIOUS.

luxury (ˈlʌksjʊərɪ, ˈlʌkʃərɪ, ˈlʌgʒərɪ). Also 4–7 luxurie. [a. OF. *luxurie*, ad. L. *luxuria*, f. *luxu-s* abundance, sumptuous enjoyment. Cf. F. *luxure* (whence LUXURE), Sp. *lujúria*, It. *lussuria.*

In Lat. and in the Rom. langs. the word connotes vicious indulgence, the neutral senses of the Eng. 'luxury' being expressed by L. *luxus*, F. *luxe*, Sp. *lujo*, It. *lusso.*]

†**1.** Lasciviousness, lust; *pl.* lusts. *Obs.*

1340 *Ayenb.* 157 Þe dyeuel.. assayleþ.. þane sanguinien mid ioliuete and mid luxurie. *c* **1386** CHAUCER *Man of Law's T.* 827 O foule lust of luxurie. *c* **1450** *Knt. de la Tour* (1868) 58 Leude touchinge and handelyng.. makithe.. folke falle into orible synne of luxurie. **1577** tr. *Bullinger's Decades* (1592) 234 Therewithal he doth inclusiuely vnderstand all kindes of lust and luxurie. **1602** MARSTON *Antonio's Rev.* II. iii. Wks. 1856 I. 96 Mellida is light, And stained with adulterous luxury. **1661** LOVELL *Hist. Anim. & Min.* 89 The ashes of the claws with that of the skinne, being applied helpe luxury in man or woman. **1728** MORGAN *Algiers* I. v. 163 To say nothing of the Luxury and Debaucheries which reigned in the Camps, which he describes as the filthiest of Brothels. **1812** CRABBE *Tales, Squire & Priest* (1814) II. 91 Grov'lling in the sty.. of shameless luxury.

†**2.** = LUXURIANCE. *Obs.*

c **1611** CHAPMAN *Iliad* XXI. 262 Where now weake waters luxurie Must make my death blush. **1692** RAY *Disc.* ii. (1732) 108 Wonderful Fertility and Luxury of the Soil. **1695** WOODWARD *Nat. Hist. Earth* v. (1723) 262 The Luxury and Superabundance of the Productions of the Earth.

3. The habitual use of, or indulgence in what is choice or costly, whether food, dress, furniture, or appliances of any kind.

1633 P. FLETCHER *Elisa* I. xxv, I never knew or want or luxurie.. or base-bred flatterie. **1667** MILTON *P.L.* XI. 711 All now was turn'd to jollitie and game, To luxurie and riot, feast and dance. **1718** LADY M. W. MONTAGU *Let. to C'tess Mar* 10 Mar. II. xliv. 19 The piece of luxury that grieved my eyes was the table-cloth and napkins. **1755** YOUNG *Centaur* ii. Wks. 1757 IV. 134 On the soft beds of luxury most kingdoms have expired. **1791–1823** D'ISRAELI *Cur. Lit.* (1858) III. 400 Luxury is the cure of that unavoidable evil in society—great inequality of fortune! *a* **1832** BENTHAM *Man. Pol. Econ.* Wks. 1843 III. 37 Luxury is.. an inseparable accompaniment to opulence. **1866** GEO. ELIOT *F. Holt* (1868) 17, I suppose you have been used to great luxury. **1891** CHEYNE *Orig. Psalter* IV. ii. 167 The increase of luxury produced a similar current of song in ancient Palestine.

4. *transf.* Refined and intense enjoyment.

1715 GARTH *Claremont* in *Dryden's Miscell. Poems* VI. (1727) 255 Hard was their Lodging, homely was their Food; For all their Luxury was doing Good. **1749** FIELDING *Tom Jones* VII. v, She indulged herself.. in all the luxury of tender grief. **1764** GOLDSM. *Trav.* 22 And learn the luxury of doing good. **1805** FOSTER *Ess.* I. i. 1 Those who do not seek.. the luxury of pensiveness. **1810** D. STEWART *Philos. Ess.* II. Ess. i. vi. 299 Hence, to a botanist, the luxury of a garden. **1869** EADIE *Galat.* 45 The enlightenment of the apostle was not for his own individual luxury.

5. a. quasi-*concr.* Means of luxurious enjoyment; sumptuous and exquisite food or surroundings.

1704 ADDISON *Italy* (1705) 475 He has cut the Side of the Rock into a Flat for a Garden, and.. has made such a Spot of Ground of it as furnishes out a kind of Luxury for a Hermite. **1759** JOHNSON *Rasselas* ii, He often sat before tables covered with luxury. **1851** *Illustr. Catal. Gt. Exhib.* 200 Preserved fruits.. representing those articles of luxury removed by their character and costliness out of the ordinary category of human food.

b. In particularized sense: Something which conduces to enjoyment or comfort in addition to what are accounted the necessaries of life. Hence, in recent use, something which is desirable but not indispensable.

1780 BENTHAM *Princ. Legisl.* xviii. §17 *note*, Necessaries come always before luxuries. **1833** HT. MARTINEAU *Briery Creek* iv. 75 He buys a new luxury which will yield no good beyond his own selfish pleasure. **1849** MACAULAY *Hist. Eng.* iii. I. 267 A coach and six was a fashionable luxury. **1874** MICKLETHWAITE *Mod. Par. Churches* 99 A reredos is a luxury. **1878** JEVONS *Prim. Pol. Econ.* 21 That which is spent in early life upon mere luxuries and frivolities. **1902** *Fortn. Rev.* June 1006 The most expensive of luxuries in London is to keep clean.

6. *abstr.* Luxuriousness; abundance of appliances for comfort.

1849 MACAULAY *Hist. Eng.* ii. I. 267 The brilliancy of the shops and the luxury of the private dwellings far surpasses anything that England could then show. **1863** W. G. BLAIKIE *Better Days Work. People* i. (1864) 8 Such luxury as shall tempt them to forget that they are but strangers and pilgrims here.

7. *attrib.*, as ***luxury coach, cruise, duty, edition, flat, liner, shop, tax, trade.*** *Comb.*, as ***luxury-loving*** adj.

1936 O. LANCASTER *Progress at Pelvis Bay* 61 As many as fifty or sixty..luxury coaches leave daily from the square. **1941** N. COWARD *Australia Visited* 1. 5 Society ladies returning home exhausted after a lightning luxury cruise. **1971** E. CANDY *Words for Murder Perhaps* iv. 50 The drug pusher, the criminal classes. You don't get that sort of person in good hotels or on luxury cruises. **1904** *Hansard Commons* 19 Apr. 564 An article of luxury which might very fairly pay a luxury duty. **1930** T. E. LAWRENCE *Lett.* (1938) 709 We must do our best to get the whole of the luxury edition placed before the date of publication. **1937** *Night & Day* 9 Dec. 12 Luxury flat. A story by K. K. Busvine. **1939** O. LANCASTER *Homes Sweet Homes* 66 The luxury flat..is divided up with fiendish ingenuity into a dining-room, drawing-room, lounge-hall, three bed, two bath, a kitchen and all the usual offices. **1958** *New Statesman* 5 Apr. 439/2 A luxury-flat developer..instructed his architects to do neo-Georgian. **1934** G. B. SHAW *Too True to be Good* Pref. 11 The rich tourists in the palace hotels and luxury liners. **1947** L. MACNEICE *Dark Tower* 50, I followed you—but not on a luxury liner. Mine was a cargo boat. **1959** N. MARSH *Singing in Shrouds* iii. 38 A luxury liner and organised fun would be more his cup-of-tea. **1899** 'MARK TWAIN' in *Forum* Mar. 32 We are..the most luxury-loving people on the earth. **1927** H. WADDELL *Wandering Scholars* i. 25 It was an apple-orchard in blossom to his luxury-loving, exquisite and peaceful soul. **1962** H. R. LOYN *Anglo-Saxon Eng.* ii. 69 The gold coinage, papyrus, fine stuffs and spices point to the existence of a luxury-loving aristocracy. **1935** N. MITCHISON *We have been Warned* iv. 349 Turning..to Mayfair, they began to pass the discreet and rather impressive luxury shops. **1973** S. JACKMAN *Guns covered with Flowers* vi. 74 The luxury shops and the department stores. **1904** *Hansard Commons* 19 Apr. 564 The luxury tax at that time was 6*d.* **1974** R. JEFFRIES *Mistakenly in Mallorca* xiii. 122 The large cars on national or tourist plates whose owners were not forced to pay the luxury taxes that all Spaniards had to. **1905** *Westm. Gaz.* 9 Jan. 3/1 Their action deprives of employment persons who were..employed in luxury trades. **1966** G. GREENE *Comedians* I. iii. 84, I can see great possibilities of improvement. My mother was not catering for the luxury-trade.

‖**luxus** ('lʌksəs). *Phys.* [L. *luxus* excess.] A normal excess of proteid material supposed to exist in the blood. Only *attrib.* (see quots.).

1873 RALFE *Phys. Chem.* 78 The excess of the nitrogenous food taken into the system, but not employed, being at once oxidized and converted into urea: this view of its formation is known as the 'luxus consumption theory'. **1898** *Allbutt's Syst. Med.* V. 911 Persistent high pressure due to luxus-consumption.

luys, obs. pl. LOUSE.

†**luyte.** *Obs.* [a. OF. *luite* fem., f. *luiter*:—L. *luctāre* to wrestle.] Wrestling, grappling.

c **1477** CAXTON *Jaxon* 15 The luyte or wrastling of your wordes is not strong ynouh for to bete doun & ouercome the constaunce of my continence.

luytel, obs. form of LITTLE.

luzardis, variant of LUSARDS *pl. Obs.*

luzarne, luzern(e, obs. forms of LUCERN[1].

luzonite ('l(j)uːzənaɪt). *Min.* [f. *Luzon* its locality.] A sulph-arsenide of copper, similar to enargite (A. H. Chester 1896).

1883 *Encycl. Brit.* XVI. 396.

luzzel, variant of LAZULE *Obs.*

lwime, lwme, obs. forms of LOOM *sb.*[1]

LXX. The Roman numeral symbol for Seventy; hence used as an abbreviation for SEPTUAGINT.

1662 STILLINGFL. *Orig. Sacr.* III. iv. §9 The learned dissertation of the late learned Bishop of Chester upon the LXX. **1883** *Cath. Dict.* (1897) 617/2 The LXX entirely misses the sense; the Vulgate has 'loquens pro eo'.

attrib. **1900** MARGOLIOUTH in *Expositor* Jan. 33 The LXX. translator of the Song of Solomon.

ly, variant of LI[1].

1858 SIMMONDS *Dict. Trade*, *Ly*, a Chinese land-measure.

ly, abbrev. LANGLEY.

1959 S. L. HESS *Introd. Theoret. Meteorol.* ix. 131 The rate of receipt of solar energy is nearly constant at the equator where it varies between 790 and 895 ly day⁻¹. **1963** G. L. PICKARD *Descriptive Physical Oceanogr.* v. 51 One langley (ly) is one gram calorie per square centimetre.

ly, obs. f. LIE, LYE; var. LEYE *Obs.*, flame.

-ly, *suffix*[1]. (Forms: 1 -líc, -lic, 2-5 -lich, 4-5 -liche, 3-5 *north.* -lik(e, (3 *Orm.* -lic, -liȝ, -like), 3-6 -li, 4- -ly), appended to sbs. and adjs. to form adjs., represents the OE. *-līc*, corresponding to OFris., OS. *-lîk* (Du. *-lijk*), OHG. *-lîh* (MHG. *-lîch*, mod.G. *-lich*), ON. *-lig-r*, *-leg-r* (Sw., Da. *-lig*), Goth. *-leik-s*:—OTeut. *-lîko-*. The phonology of the OE. form, as also of the mod.G. and the ON. forms, is somewhat abnormal, the frequency in use of the suffix having caused loss of the original secondary stress, with consequent shortening of the vowel, and in ON. also voicing of the guttural. A further irregularity appears in the phonetic development in ME. The normal representation of OE. *-lic* was *-lik* in northern dialects and *-lich* in southern dialects. These forms are found as late as the 15th century; but the form *-li*, *-ly*, which (though parallel with the reduction of OE. *ic* to *I*, and of ME. *everich* to *every*) seems to be chiefly due to the influence of the Scandinavian *-lig-*, occurs in northern and midland dialects as early as the 13th c., and before the end of the 15th c. had become universal. In the *Ormulum* (*c* 1200) *-lic* (rarely *-like*) is used before a vowel and at the end of a line, and *-liȝ* before a cons.; the inflected form *-like* (disyllabic) seems often to be used, for metrical reasons, where grammar would require the uninflected form. In the comparative and superlative (OE. *-licra*, *-e*, *-licost*) the ME. form had regularly *-k* according to phonetic law in all dialects (in the south the usual 13-14th c. form was *-lukere*, *-lokere*); but where the positive had the form *-li* new comparatives and superlatives in *-lier*, *liest* were regularly formed from it.

The original Teut. adjs. in *-lîko-* were compounds of the sb. *lîkom appearance, form, body (see LICH). Thus **mannlîko-* ('manly') means etymologically 'having the appearance or form of a man'; *gôðolîko-* ('goodly') 'having a good appearance or form', or 'having the appearance or form of what is good'. The primitive force of the suffix may therefore be rendered by 'having the appearance or form indicated by the first element of the word'; but while in the historical Teut. langs. it has remained capable of expressing this meaning, it has in all of them acquired a much wider application.

When appended to sbs., the most general senses of the suffix in all Teut. langs. are 'having the qualities appropriate to', 'characteristic of', 'befitting'. In English of all periods it has been a prolific formative; the adjs. formed with it are most frequently eulogistic, as in *kingly*, *knightly*, *masterly*, *princely*, *queenly*, *scholarly*, *soldierly* (cf. *manly*, *womanly* with *mannish*, *womanish*); among the examples with dyslogistic sense are *beastly*, *beggarly*, *cowardly*, *dastardly*, *rascally*, *ruffianly*, *scoundrelly*. In OE., as in other Teut. langs., the suffix had often the sense 'of or pertaining to'; but the adjs. have, so far as this meaning is concerned, been to a great extent superseded by synonyms of Latin or Romanic etymology. Thus *manly* formerly admitted of the senses now expressed by *human* and *masculine*; for one of the older senses of *timely* we must now say *temporal*. Another use of the suffix, common to English with other Teut. langs., is to form adjs. denoting periodic recurrence, as *daily*, *hourly*, *monthly*, *nightly*, *weekly*, *yearly*.

When *-ly* is appended to an adj., the resulting derivative adj. often connotes a quality related to or resembling that expressed by its primary; cf., e.g., OE. *léof* 'dear' with *léoflic* 'lovely' (or, as it might be rendered, 'such as becomes dear'). The diminutive sense found in mod.G. *gelblich* yellowish, *süsslich* sweetish, though a very easy development from the original sense of the suffix, does not seem ever to have existed in English. Even in OE. *-lic* had app. ceased to be used in new formations from adjs.; the new adjs. f. adj. + *-ly* that have arisen in ME. or in mod.E. seem to be from the advs.

-ly, *suffix*[2]. (Forms: 1-2 -líce, 2-5 -liche, 4-5 -lich, 3-5 *north.* -like, (3 *Orm.* -like, -liȝ), 3-6 -li, 4- -ly), forming adverbs, represents OE. *-líce*, corresponding (functionally if not morphologically) to OFris. *-lîke*, OS. *-lîko* (M.Du. *-lîke*, Du. *-lijk*, MLG. *-lîke*, mod.LG. *-lik*), OHG. *-lîchô* (MHG. *-liche*, mod.G. *-lich*), ON. *-liga*, *-lega* (MSw. *-lika*, *-leka*, in mod.Sw. superseded by *-ligt*, *-ligen*; Da. *-lig*), Goth. *-leikô*, derived from *-lîko-* (see -LY[1]) with an adverb-forming suffix, OTeut. *-ô*, according to some repr. the ending of the abl. fem. (pre-Teut. *-ād*) or neut. (pre-Teut. *-ōd*); according to others that of the instrumental neut. (pre-Teut. *-ōm*).

The form-history of the suffix in Eng. is similar to that of -LY[1]: in ME. the OE. *-líce* was normally represented by *-līche* (southern), *-līke* (northern), the compar. being *-līker*, *-luker*, *-loker* (superl. *-est*).

The form *-li*, *-ly*, which was current in East Midland English in the 14th c., and became general in the 15th c., is probably due to the influence of the ON. *-liga*. In the strongly Scandinavianized dialect of the *Ormulum* (*c* 1200) *-liȝ* and *-like* are used indifferently, according to the requirements of the metre. Where the positive ended in *-li*, *-ly*, the comparative and superlative ended in *-lier*, *-liest*. In the 15-17th c. forms like *falslyer*, *traitorouslyer* (Malory), *softlier*, *justlier*, *widelier* (Long *Barclay's Argenis* 1625), *easilier*, *-est* (R. Baxter *Saving Faith* 1658) were common, but in later use the advs. in *-ly* are compared with *more*, *most*, the inflexional forms being only employed in poetry or for rhetorical effect.

In OTeut. an adv. with this suffix must have implied the existence of an adj. with the suffix corresponding to -LY[1]. In OE., however, there are several instances (e.g. *bealdlíce* boldly, *swétlíce* sweetly) in which an adv. in *-líce* has been formed directly from a simple adj. without the intervention of an adj. in *-lic*. In ME. the number of these direct formations was greatly increased, and when the final *-e*, which was the original OE. adverb-making suffix, ceased to be pronounced, it became usual to append *-ly* to an adj. as the regular mode of forming an adv. of manner. It was, down to the 17th c., somewhat frequently attached, with this function, even to adjs. in *-ly*, as *earlily*, *godlily*, *kindlily*, *livelily*, *lovelily*, *statelily*; but these formations are now generally avoided as awkward, while on the other hand it is felt to be ungraceful to use words like *godly*, *goodly*, *lovely*, *mannerly*, *timely*, as advs.; the difficulty is usually evaded by recourse to some periphrastic form of expression. In examples belonging to the 16th and 17th c. it is sometimes difficult to determine whether a writer intended the adv. *goodly* to mean 'in a good manner' or 'in a goodly manner', and there are other instances of similar ambiguity. In the words denoting periodical recurrence, as *daily*, *hourly*, the adj. and the adv. are now identical in form. A solitary example of an adv. f. sb. + *-ly*[2] with no related adj. is *partly*. From the early part of the 16th c. the suffix has been added to ordinal numerals to form advs. denoting serial position, as *firstly*, *secondly*, *thirdly*, etc. (cf. F. *premièrement*, etc.).

When *-ly* is attached to a disyllabic or polysyllabic adj. in *-le*, the word is contracted, as in *ably*, *doubly*, *singly*, *simply*; contractions of this kind occur already in the 14th c., but examples of the uncontracted forms (e.g. *doublely*) are found as late as the 17th c. *Whole* + *-ly* becomes *wholly*, but in all other similar instances the written *e* is retained before the suffix, e.g. in *palely*, *vilely*, *puerilely*. Adjs. ending graphically with *ll* lose one *l* before *-ly*, as in *fully* (in southern Eng. commonly pronounced with a single *l*, but in Scotland often with double or long *l*), *dully* ('dʌllɪ), *coolly* ('kuːllɪ). Adjs. of more than one syll. ending in *y* change *y* to *i* before *-ly*, as in *merrily*; in formations from monosyllabic adjs. the usage varies, e.g. *dryly*, *drily*; *gayly*, *gaily* (cf. *daily*, which is the only current form); *slyly*, *slily* (but always *shyly*); *greyly*, *grayly* has always *y*. Another orthographical point is the dropping of the *e* in the two words *duly*, *truly*. It is unusual to append *-ly* to an adj. in *-ic*; the ending of the adv. is nearly always -ICALLY, even when the only current form of the adj. ends in *-ic*.

‖**Lyæus** (laɪ'iːəs). [L., a. Gr. Λυαῖος.] A surname of Bacchus; hence used for: Wine.

1602 MARSTON *Antonio's Rev.* v. iv. Wks. 1856 I. 137 Let Lyeus flote In burnisht gobblets. **1851** THACKERAY *Eng. Hum.* ii. (1858) 92 When his honest hand was shaking..in the morning after libations to purple Lyaeus over-night.

lyam ('laɪəm), **lyme** (laɪm). *Obs.* exc. *Hist.* and *dial.* Forms: 4-6 lyame, 5 lyeme, ? 5, 7 lym, 6

lyalme, lyemme, 6–7 lyome, lime, 6–9 leam, liam, 7 leame, leon, 7, 9 lyme, 5- lyam. [a. OF. *liem* (mod.F. *lien*) = Pr. *liam-s*, Cat. *lligam*, Pg. *ligame*, It. *legame*:—L. *ligāmen*, f. *ligāre* to tie, bind. Cf. LIEN.]

1. A leash for hounds.

c **1400** *Parlt. Thre Ages* (text A) 38 My lyame than full lightly lete I doun falle. *Ibid.* 61, I hyede to my hounde and hent hym vp sone And louset my lyame and let hym vmbycaste. **1481–90** *Howard Househ. Bks.* (Roxb.) 287 My Lord paied to Mason for lyemes for his howndes..xxd. **1501** DOUGLAS *Pal. Hon.* I. 297 Of goldin cord wer lyamis, and the stringis Festinnit coniunct in massie goldin ringis. **1528** *MS. List of Jewelry* (P.R.O.), ij doggs collers of scoolewerk with lyalmes sylk and gold. **1541** *Knaresboro' Wills* (Surtees) I. 81 *note*, One copie of houndes and ther lyomes. **1570** CAIUS *De Canibus Brit.* 11 b, Nam Lyemme nostra lingua Lorum significat. ?*c* **1600** *Distracted Emp.* v. iv. in Bullen *O. Pl.* III. 255 Enter Eudon & Busse, leading in twoe lymes Byrtha & a Spaniell. **1611** COTGR., *Traict*,.. a lime, or line wherin a Bloud-hound is led. **1612** WEBSTER *White Devil* B iij, Let her not go to Church, but like a hounde In Leon at your heeles. **1686** BLOME *Gentl. Recr.* II. 82 A Hound will draw better when he is held short, than if he were let at the length of the Liam. **1829** SCOTT *Wav.* 2nd App. to Gen. Pref. iv, A large blood-hound tied in a leam or band. **1876** *Whitby Gloss.*, *Leam*, a leash or thong. **1897** MADDEN *Diary W. Silence* 23 The huntsman then held him [the bloodhound] short, pulling in the liam. **1898** *Pall Mall Mag.* Oct. 164 The second illustration shows the huntsmen with their hounds on the lyam seeking for deer.

b. *Her.* The representation of a lyam or leash.

1572 BOSSEWELL *Armorie* II. 43 A Lyon Couchante, & three Lyams in chefe d'argent. **1634** [see LYAM-HOUND c].

c. *Comb.*: **lyam-dog** = LYAM-HOUND.

1805 SCOTT *Last Minstr.* VI. vii, Stout Conrade, cold.. Was by a woodman's lyme-dog found.

2. Short for LYAM-HOUND.

1486 *Bk. St. Albans* F vj b, A Sute of a lyam. **1605** SHAKS. *Lear* III. vi. 72 Mastiffe, Grey-hound, Mongrill, Grim, Hound or Spaniell, Brache, or Lym [*1st Fo.* Hym].

lyam-hound, lyme-hound. *Obs.* exc. *Hist.* Forms: 6 lyam-, 6–7 lime-, 7 leame-, lim-, *erron.* lyne-, line-, liam- (also 9 *arch.*), 7, 9 lyme-. [f. LYAM + HOUND.] A bloodhound.

1527 *St. Papers Hen. VIII*, IV. 464 A cowple of lyam houndes. **1596** SPENSER *F.Q.* v. ii. 25 But Talus, that could like a lime-hound winde her,.. At length found out whereas she hidden lay. **1611** COTGR., s.v. *Mut*, *Chiens mut*,.. lyne-hounds, tearmed otherwise, *Limiers de mut.* **1616** SURFL. & MARKH. *Country Farm* VII. xxii. 673 This crie of hounds.. is in no sort allowed to the liam hound, so long as he draweth in the string. **1624** T. SCOT *Vox Populi* II. 17, I had my Leame-hounds ready in euery corner to draw after them dry-foote, and fetch the Authors *Coram nobis.* **1631** BRATHWAIT *Whimzies, Forrester* 35 He can do miracles with his line-hound, who by his good education ha's more sophistry than his master. **1657** R. LIGON *Barbadoes* (1673) 98 There is nothing in that Countrey so usefull as Liam Hounds, to find out these Thieves. **1674** J. WRIGHT tr. *Seneca's Thyestes* 45 So when the Vmbrian Lime-hound through the field Hunts on a Trayl; and in a Leash is held. **1801** *Sporting Mag.* XVIII. 100 One that leads a lime-hound for the chace. **1821** SCOTT *Kenilw.* iv, He has the stanch lyme-hound to track the wounded buck over hill and dale, but he hath also the fleet gaze-hound to kill him at view. **1852** KINGSLEY *Andromeda* 446 Him Até follows avenging; Slowly she tracks him and sure, as a lyme-hound. **1897** MADDEN *Diary W. Silence* 22 The huntsman brought with him his liam-hound, a pure-bred blood-hound used for finding and harbouring the deer.

b. *fig.* Applied to persons.

a **1611** BEAUM. & FL. *Philaster* IV. i, Oh, hee's a pernitious limhound, turne him vpon the pursue of any Lady. **1656** S. HOLLAND *Zara* (1719) 30 Or a second Helen proud of the Lime-hound Paris.

c. As a heraldic cognizance.

1634 HARRINGTON *Orl. Fur.* XLI. xxx. 344 His cosin had a Lyme-hound argent bright, His Lyme laid on his back.

†**lyance.** *Obs.* Also 4 leiance. [a. OF. *liance*, f. *li-er* to bind.]

1. Allegiance.

1390 GOWER *Conf.* III. 381 To him belongith the leiance Of Clerk, of knyght, of man of lawe.

2. A group of persons related to or allied with another; = ALLIANCE 4.

c **1380** *Sir Ferumb.* 1409 A knyȝt þar was of fraunce.. hwych was icomen of gret lyaunce. *Ibid.* 4098 þou ne dost noȝt ase þe wys If þow y-lyuest sir Alorys, oþer any of his lyaunce. *c* **1400** *Laud Troy Bk.* 1932 For we haue frendes gret plente, That ben alied to ȝow and me, That schal ben to us in mayntenaunce With alle her men and lyaunce. *c* **1400** *Destr. Troy* 1747 With a liaunce full large of other lege kyngis, þat we to helpe vs may haue. **1530** PALSGR. 239/1 Lyaunce kynred, *aliance*.

3. A kinsman or ally; = ALLIANCE 5.

14.. *Nom.* in Wr.-Wülcker 691/14 *Hec affinis*, a lyans. **1502** *Plumpton Corr.* (Camden) 164 Cousin, I.. pray you to be good master to Nycholas Lee, my lyanse [*printed* lyaufe].

lyantery, obs. form of LIENTERY.

†**lyar.** *Sc. Obs.* Also lyare, liare. [? f. LIE *v.*[1] + -ER[1].] ? A coverlet.

1497 *Ld. Treas. Acc. Scotl.* (1877) I. 369 Item, for xvj elne of damas, to be the Kingis lyare... Item, for xvj elne of bukram, to lyne the Kingis liare. **1530** *Inv. R. Wardr.* (1815) 48 Item, ane lyare of crammesy velvett, with twa cuschingis of crammesy velvett, bordourit with tressis of gold. **1542** *Ibid.* 96 Item ane lyar of purpour velvott.

lyar, var. LYRE[3], the shearwater.

lyard, lyart, *a.* and *sb. Obs.* exc. *dial.* Also 4–5 lyarde, 4–5, 8 liard, 5–6 lyerd. [a. OF. *liart*, of obscure origin; perh. f. *lie*, LEE *sb.*[2]]

A. *adj.* A designation of colour. **a.** Of a horse: Spotted with white or silver grey. **b.** Of hair: Grey, silvery grey approaching white. **c.** Applied by Burns to the colour of withered leaves.

In north Eng. dialects 'a white lyared horse means a grey one, or one dappled with white and black; and a red lyared one is dappled with bay or red and white' (E.D.D.).

[**1300** *Liber Quotid. Garderobæ* (1787) 78 Pro uno equo nigro liardo empto de eodem [etc.] 10 0 0. *Ibid.*, Pro uno equo griseo liardo empto de eodem ad opus Regis [etc.] 7 6 8. *c* **1386** CHAUCER *Friar's T.* 265 This carter þakked his hors..'Hayt now' quod he,..'þat was wel twight, myn owne lyard boy'. ? *a* **1400** *Morte Arth.* 2542 Laggene with longe speres one lyarde stedes. *c* **1420** *Pallad. on Husb.* IV. 826 Colouris now to knowe attendith ye:..The liard & the white, and broun is sure. **1438** *Bk. Alexander Gt.* (Bannatyne) 115 Yon ald man..With lyart berd and hare gresone. **1500–20** DUNBAR *Poems* lxi. 70 Tak in this gray horss, Auld Dunbar, Quhilk in my aucht with schervice trew In lyart changeit is in hew. **1590** *Wills & Inv. N.C.* (Surtees 1860) 247 To Oswin Fenwick a graie nagge. To William Fenwick the lyerd nagge. **1607** MARKHAM *Caval.* I. (1617) 22 The best colour for a stallyon, is browne bay dapled, dapple gray, bright bay, or white lyard. **1721** RAMSAY *Prospect Plenty* xvii, Nereus rising frae his wat'ry bed, The pearly drops hap down his lyart head. *c* **1750** MISS ELLIOT *Song, The Flowers of the Forest* iii, The bandsters are lyart and runkled and grey. **1785** BURNS *Holy Fair* 15 Twa had manteeles o' dolefu' black, But ane wi' lyart lining. **1785** —— *Jolly Beggars* 1 When lyart leaves bestrow the yird. **1804** J. GRAHAME *Sabbath* (1808) 14 The lyart veteran. **1895** CROCKETT *Men of Moss Hags* 156 His hair, lyart and long, fell upon his shoulders.

B. *sb.* As the proper name of a 'lyard' horse.

13.. *Pol. Songs* (Camden) 71 Thou shalt ride sporeles o thy lyard Al the ryhte way to Dovere ward. **1377** LANGL. *P. Pl.* B. XVII. 64 He lyȝte adown of lyard and ladde hym in his hande. *c* **1470** GREGORY *Hist. Coll. Lond. Cit.* (Camden) 238 As for beddyng, Lyard my hors had more ese thenn had sum good yeman. **1486–1504** in Denton *Eng. 15th Cent.* (1888) 319, I sall gyff yow to yowr plesure lyerd my horse.

lyard, lyas, obs. forms of LIARD *sb.*[1], LIAS.

lybard, lybbard(e, obs. forms of LEOPARD.

lybben, lybbet, obs. ff. LIVE *v.*, LIBBET[1].

lyberary, obs. form of LIBRARY.

lybet, Lybic: see LIBBET, LIBYC.

lybre: see LIBRE.

lycæm: see LYCEUM.

lycænid (laɪˈsiːnɪd), *sb.* and *a.* [f. mod.L. family name *Lycænidæ*, f. the generic name *Lycæna* (J. C. Fabricius 1807, in *Mag. für Insektenkunde* VI. 85), f. Gr. λύκαινα she-wolf.] **A.** *sb.* A butterfly of the family Lycænidæ, which includes the blues and the hairstreaks. **B.** *adj.* Of or pertaining to this family.

1892 W. L. DISTANT *Naturalist in Transvaal* 68, I have often mistaken it for a large Lycænid. **1913** *Oxf. Univ. Gaz.* 4 June 950/1 A beautiful series of 84 Lycaenid butterflies from the Nicobar Islands. **1972** L. E. CHADWICK tr. *Linsenmaier's Insects of World* 197/1 (*caption*) The hairstreaks, a large group of the lycaenids, spend most of the time in bushes and trees. **1974** *Nature* 1 Mar. 16/3 Eliot's paper is designed to evoke thought and curiosity about his lycaenid butterflies.

lycam, variant of LICHAM *Obs.*

lycanthrope (ˈlaɪkænθrəʊp, laɪˈkænθrəʊp). Also 7 lycanthrop. [ad. mod.L. *lycanthrōp-us*, ad. Gr. λυκάνθρωπ-ος lit. wolf-man, f. λύκο-ς wolf + ἄνθρωπος man.]

1. One who is afflicted with LYCANTHROPY, q.v.

1621 MOLLE *Camerar. Liv. Libr.* IV. xiii. 276 The organs of the fantasie of such foolish Lycanthrops. **1679** G. R. tr. *Boaystuau's Theat. World* III. 246 They will become Lycanthropes, and go naked like the Wolves.

2. By mod. writers used as a synonym of WEREWOLF; one of those persons who (according to mediæval superstition) assumed the form of wolves.

1831 A. HERBERT in Sir F. Madden *Will. & Werwolf* (1832) 16 Parthenophagy..is an enormity of the lycanthropes, and not of wolves. **1882** *St. James's Gaz.* 17 Feb. 7 These legends of the lycanthrope—the loupgarou—perhaps especially induce us to vilify the wolf.

fig. **1855** WHITTIER *Arisen at Last* 16 Hereaway, The fell lycanthrope finds no prey.

lycanthropic (laɪkænˈθrɒpɪk), *a.* [f. mod.L. *lycanthrōp-us* (see prec.) + -IC.] Of or belonging to lycanthropy; suffering from lycanthropy.

1829 LANDOR *Imag. Conv., Marvel & Bp. Parker* Wks. (1853) II. 108/2 He never drove men into holy madness with incessant howlings, like the lycanthropic saints of the north. **1887** H. S. OLCOTT tr. *D'Assier's Posth. Human.* 80 There is some reason to apprehend that this may be a lycanthropic manifestation of the human phantom.

lycanthropist (laɪˈkænθrəpɪst). [Formed as prec. + -IST.] = LYCANTHROPE.

1727 BAILEY vol. II, *Lycanthropist.* **1831** A. HERBERT in Sir F. Madden *Will. & Werwolf* (1832) 36 A wolf who.. prowls..in quest of human flesh, for which he alone, like the lycanthropist, has any taste remaining. **1882** *Pall Mall G.* 18 Apr. 4 Petrus Borel the lycanthropist.

ly'canthropous, *a.* [Formed as prec. + -OUS.] Pertaining to lycanthropy.

In recent Dicts.

‖**lycanthropus.** *Obs. Pl.* lycanthropi. Mod.L. form of LYCANTHROPE.

1584 R. SCOT *Discov. Witchcr.* v. i. (1886) 72 Another being Lycanthropus in the forme of a woolfe, had his woolves feet cut off. *a* **1627** MIDDLETON *Changeling* III. iii, The swift lycanthropi, that walk the round, We'll tear their wolvish skins, and save the sheep. **1657** TRAPP *Comm. Job* v. 22. 58 Such Lycanthropi, or beasts in the shape of men, Paul fought with at Ephesus.

lycanthropy (laɪˈkænθrəpɪ). Also in mod.L. form **lycanthropia.** [ad. Gr. λυκανθρωπία, f. λυκάνθρωπος: see LYCANTHROPE.]

1. A kind of insanity described by ancient writers, in which the patient imagined himself to be a wolf, and had the instincts and propensities of a wolf. Now occasionally applied as a name of those forms of insanity in which the patient imagines himself a beast, and exhibits depraved appetites, alteration of voice, etc., in accordance with this delusion.

1584 R. SCOT *Discov. Witchcr.* v. i. (1886) 73 Lycanthropia is a disease and not a transformation. **1594** T. B. *La Primaud. Fr. Acad.* II. 166 That malady, which is.. named by the Græcians..lycanthropie. **1621** BURTON *Anat. Mel.* I. i. I. iv, Lycanthropia,..or Wolf-madness, when men run howling about graves and fields in the night, and will not be persuaded but that they are wolves or some such beasts. *a* **1656** BP. HALL *St. Paul's Combat* i. Wks. 1808 V. 321 It is contrary to the delusions of lycanthropy. There, he, that is a man, thinks himself a beast; here, he, that is a beast, thinks himself a man. **1672** MARVELL *Reh. Transp.* I. 68 His Madness hath formed itself into a perfect Lycanthropy. He doth so verily believe himself to be a Wolf, that his speech is all turned into howling, yelling, and barking. *a* **1779** WARBURTON *Serm. on Matt.* iv. 24 Wks. 1788 V. 429 The madness called Lycanthropy. **1818** LADY MORGAN *Fl. Macarthy* (1819) III. ii. 75, I am not well, surely, Sir,..and thinks betimes that it's the lycanthropia I have got, which Maister Camden saith was common to the ancient Irish. **1891** DRIVER *Introd. Lit. O.T.* (1892) 469 Nebuchadnezzar's seven years' insanity (lycanthropy) with his edict respecting it. **1891** SYDNEY *Eng. 18th C.* I. 27 Young boys and girls were bred..in crime, even to the pitch of moral lycanthropy.

2. The kind of witchcraft which was supposed to consist in the assumption by human beings of the form and nature of wolves.

1830 SCOTT *Demonol.* vii. 210 Persons accused of the crime of lycanthropy. **1865** LECKY *Ration.* I. I. 82 Lycanthropy or the transformation of witches into wolves.

lycaon (lɪˈkeɪɒn). [mod.L. (S. Brookes in E. Griffith et al. tr. *Cuvier's Animal Kingdom* (1827) V. 151), f. Gr. λυκάων, L. *lycāon* a wolf-like animal.] A wild dog of the monotypic genus so called, found in Africa south of the Sahara; the African hunting dog.

1827 E. GRIFFITH et al. tr. *Cuvier's Animal Kingdom* V. 151 (*heading*) Burchel's Lycaon. **1915** ROOSEVELT & HELLER *Life-Hist. Afr. Game Animals* I. viii. 265 The skull of *Lycaon* is easily recognizable from that of a wolf or a jackal. **1945** C. L. B. HUBBARD *Observer's Bk. Dogs* 187 *Lycaon* is the most peculiar and interesting of all dog-like carnivores native to Africa. **1958** *Listener* 16 Jan. 102/2 The four-legged animal which deals out more destruction than almost any other is the lycaon, or wild dog.

Lycaonian (lɪkeɪˈəʊnɪən), *a.* and *sb.* Also Lykaonian. [f. L. *Lycaonia*, Gr. Λυκαονία Lycaonia + -AN.] **A.** *adj.* Of or pertaining to ancient Lycaonia in southern Asia Minor, its inhabitants, or the language spoken by them. **B.** *sb.* **a.** The language of Lycaonia. **b.** A native or inhabitant of Lycaonia.

1582 BIBLE (Reims) *Acts* xiv. 10 And the multitudes when they had seen what Paul had done, lifted vp their voice in the lycaonian tongue. **1890** W. M. RAMSAY *Hist. Geogr. Asia Minor* 392 When, in 361–2, it was found advisable to divide further the large province of Isauria, all the Lykaonian cities were taken from it and from Pisidia. **1893** —— *Church in Roman Empire* ii. 57 Greek then, and not Latin or Lykaonian, would be the common language of these two classes of the population. **1911** [see ICONIAN *a.* and *sb.*]. **1926** *Public Opinion* 25 June 582/1 The two gods to whom the Lycaonians..were accustomed to pray. **1957** *Encycl. Brit.* XIV. 511/2 The Lycaonians were to a great extent independent of the Persian empire... The mention of the Lycaonian language in the Acts of the Apostles..shows that the native language was spoken by the common people at Lystra as late as A.D. 50.

lyce, obs. form of LIST *sb.*[3]

1485 CAXTON *Chas. Gt.* 40 Thys fyerabras..came vnto the lyces of Kynge Charles..as he shold fyght al armed.

lyce, obs. f. *lice*, pl. of LOUSE; obs. f. LACE *v.*

lyceal (laɪˈsiːəl), *a.* [f. LYCÉE + -AL.] Of or pertaining to the French Lycées or similar establishments.

1904 G. S. HALL *Adolescence* I. 345 Marro tabulated the conduct of 3,012 boys in gymnasial and lyceal classes in Italy from eleven to eighteen years of age.

‖**lycée** (lise). [F. *Lycée*, ad. L. *Lycēum* (see LYCEUM).] The name given in France to a secondary school maintained by the State, in contradistinction to a *collège* or secondary school maintained by a municipality.

1865 *Q. Rev.* CXVII. 40 There are seventy-four *lycées* in France. **1900** *Speaker* 19 May 190/2 The population of the lycées and colleges has remained stationary.

‖**lycéen** (liseɛ̃). [Fr.: see LYCÉE.] A pupil at a *lycée* in France.

1883 H. JAMES *Little Tour in France* (1885) xiii. 90 Little pale-faced *lycéens*..who are about to be restored to those big educative barracks. **1909** *Daily Chron.* 23 Sept. 4/4 One is naturally led to inquire what steps are taken to ensure the discipline of the Lycéens out of school. **1971** G. STEINER *In Bluebeard's Castle* iv. 85 The Victorian public-school boy, the *Gymnasiast* or *lycéen*. **1974** *Guardian* 26 Mar. 4/4 A background of marching lycéens and charging police, not to speak of protesting school masters.

lycence, -ens, obs. forms of LICENCE, LICENSE.

lyceum (laɪˈsiːəm). Also 6–9 *erron.* lycæum. [a. L. *Lycēum*, ad. Gr. *Λύκειον*, neut. of *Λύκειος* epithet of Apollo, to whose temple the Lyceum was adjacent. Cf. F. *lycée*, Sp., It. *liceo*.]

1. (With capital initial.) The proper name of a garden with covered walks at Athens, in which Aristotle taught his philosophy. Hence, the Aristotelian philosophy and its adherents.

1579–80 NORTH *Plutarch, Sylla* (1595) 504 He feld down all the wood of the parke Lycæum. **1638** BAKER tr. *Balzac's Lett.* (vol. II.) 79 He makes use of them [riches] after the manner of the Academy, and of the Lyceum, which never thought them impediments to happinesse. **1671** MILTON *P.R.* IV. 253 Within the walls then view The schools of ancient sages..Lyceum there, and painted Stoa next. **1744** AKENSIDE *Pleas. Imag.* I. 591 Guide my way Through fair Lycéum's walk, the green retreats Of Academus [etc.]. **1838** THIRLWALL *Greece* II. ii. 63 The Lyceum, a garden at a short distance from Athens, sacred to the Lycian Apollo. **1901** LAWSON *Remin. Dollar Acad.* 29 He might have been taken for a resuscitated Grecian philosopher hastening to meet his pupils at the Lyceum.

b. *transf.*

1727–46 THOMSON *Summer* 1393 To Nature's vast Lyceum, forth they walk. **1809** *Ann. Reg.* 238 It seemed as if all the animal creation had been assembled in Covent Garden, as in a capacious lyceum.

2. Used allusively as the proper name of certain places of study or instruction. **a.** In Italy and Switzerland, the Latin title of certain universities or colleges (It. *Liceo*, F. *Lycée*). **b.** = F. *Lycée*, the name of an institution (afterwards called *Athénée*) founded at Paris in 1786, at which lectures on literature and science were delivered by eminent professors. **c.** In England, adopted as the title of many literary institutions established in the early part of the 19th c., and of the buildings erected for them, usually including lecture-rooms and class-rooms and a library.

1786 *Gentl. Mag.* LVI. I. 262/1 A literary establishment has lately been opened at Paris under the title of the Lyceum, where lectures are read by the following professors... The Lyceum is to open every day, morning and evening, and each professor is to read two hours in each week. **1832** G. DOWNES *Lett. Cont. Countries* I. xi. 159 (Zurich) Close by is the Lyceum, or Carolinian College. *Ibid.* xxix. 472 (Ferrara) We first went to visit the Lyceum, or University.

3. = LYCÉE.

1827 SCOTT *Napoleon* VI. 97 It was the policy of Bonaparte to diminish..the secondary or ecclesiastical schools, in order that the public education might be conducted at the public seminaries, called Lyceums or Academies. **1861** M. ARNOLD *Pop. Educ. France* Introd. 39 The French aristocracy could procure for its children..a better training than that which is now given in the lyceums.

4. *U.S.* (Cf. 2 b, c.) An institution in which popular lectures are delivered on literary and scientific subjects.

1820 *Amer. Jrnl. Sci.* II. 366 Abstract of the proceedings of the Lyceum of Natural History, New-York. **1837** HT. MARTINEAU *Soc. Amer.* III. 163 Colleges to receive the élite of the schools; and lyceums, and other such institutions, for the subsequent instruction of working men. **1850** W. R. WILLIAMS *Relig. Prog.* iv. (1854) 77 Men have expected..the Lyceum and the Lecture to close the dram-shop. **1893** LELAND *Mem.* I. 270 Let the aspirant begin by reading papers..before such societies or lyceums as will listen to him.

b. *attrib.*, as ***lyceum assembly***, ***bureau***, ***hall***, ***lecture***, ***lecturer***, ***lecturing***, ***system***.

1858 O. W. HOLMES *Aut. Breakf.-t.* vi. 55 Two lyceum assemblies, of five hundred each, are so nearly alike, that [etc.]. **1924** I. S. COBB *Kansas* ii. 20 Fate, personated by the booking agency of a lyceum bureau, decreed that I should jump out of the Teutonic comforts of St. Louis. **1831** *Mass. Private & Special Statutes* 4 Mar., They are hereby made a corporation, by the name of Lyceum Hall,..for the purpose of affording means..for the prosecution of literary and scientific studies [etc.]. **1837** H. MARTINEAU *Society in America* I. I. iii. 61, I attended another Lyceum lecture in Massachusetts. **1922** L. MUMFORD in H. E. Stearns *Civilization in U.S.* 6 The Lyceum lecture..was taken as a soporific rather than a stimulant. **1844** *Knickerbocker* XXIV. 294 The remark of a lyceum lecturer upon matrimony. **1881** *Harper's Mag.* Mar. 628/2 During the days of his lyceum lecturing, no man was more popular [than Dr. Chapin] upon the platform. **1843** 'R. CARLTON' *New Purchase* I. 174 The common school system, the lyceum system. **1863** W. PHILLIPS *Speeches* xi. 242 Appreciating the lyceum system as I do..I feel [etc.].

5. Used as the title of a book.

1809 BELFOUR (*title*) Lycæum of Ancient Literature; or Biographical..Account of Greek and Roman Classics.

6. (With capital initial.) The name of a theatre near the Strand in London, used *attrib.* to denote a performance characteristic of those given at this theatre, esp. of the melodramatic type associated with Henry Irving; also *transf.*

1898 G. B. SHAW *Let.* 29 Jan. in C. St. John *Ellen Terry & Bernard Shaw* (1931) 294 Henry [Irving]..is as much behind the times now as Pinwell's and Fred Walker's and Mason's pictures are (I always call them the Lyceum school). **1898** —— *Plays Pleasant & Unpleasant* p. xix, Popular entertainments like Gounod's opera or the Lyceum version, in which poetry and philosophy are replaced by romance. **1901** —— *Three Plays for Puritans* p. xi, I found that the whole business of stage sensuousness, whether as Lyceum Shakespear, musical farce, or sham Ibsen, finally disgusted me. **1936** 'N. BLAKE' *Thou Shell of Death* xiii. 229 Tones that would have done credit to a Lyceum melodrama. **1964** 'A. GILBERT' *Knock knock, who's There?* i. 21 This wasn't a cosy pub..it was all set for a Lyceum melodrama.

lych, var. LICH, LIGHT.

lych(e, obs. f. LIKE.

lyche, obs. form of LEECH *sb.*³, LIEGE *a.* and *sb.*

lychee, lych-gate, var. LITCHI, LICH-GATE.

‖**lychnapsia** (lɪkˈnæpsɪə). *Gr. Church.* [a. Gr. *λυχναψία* lighting of lamps.] A series of seven prayers for protection during the night, forming part of the lychnic.

1850 NEALE *East Ch.* Introd. I. 896 While this Psalm is being said, the Priest..saith the lychnapsia.

lychnic (ˈlɪknɪk). *Gr. Church.* [ad. eccl. Gr. *λυχνικόν* time of lamplighting, f. *λύχνος* lamp.] An office which accompanies the lighting of lamps, being the introductory part of vespers.

1850 NEALE *East. Ch.* Introd. I. 897 *note*, The Order of Philotheus directs the Priest..to begin the lychnics at the verse 'In wisdom hast Thou made them all'.

‖**lychnidea.** *Obs.* Also lichnidea. [mod.L., f. L. *lychnid-*, LYCHNIS.] 'An old garden name for the genus *Phlox*' (Britten & Holland).

1733 MILLER *Gard. Dict.* (ed. 2) s.v. *Lychnis*, Virginian Lychnidea..Carolina Lychnidea. **1741** *Compl. Fam.-Piece* II. iii. 379 In Beds made of light rich Earth,..plant your Cuttings of Lichnidea's. **1785** MARTYN *Rousseau's Bot.* xvi. (1794) 210 Such are all the species of Lychnidea: which you will know by their salver-shaped Corolla, with a bent tube.

†**lychˈnidiate**, *a.* *Ent. Obs.* [Hybrid f. Gr. *λυχνίδι-ον* (dim. of *λυχνίον* lamp-stand, f. *λύχνος* lamp) + -ATE².] Giving out light.

1826 KIRBY & SP. *Entomol.* IV. 307 *Lychnidiate*, when the Vertex, Frons and Postnasus are porrected so as to form a kind of rostrum which gives light in the night.

‖**lychnis** (ˈlɪknɪs). *Pl.* lychnides (ˈlɪknɪdiːz). [L., a. Gr. *λυχνίς* some red flower, f. *λύχνος* lamp.]

1. *Bot.* A genus of caryophyllaceous plants, including the Campion and Ragged Robin.

1601 HOLLAND *Pliny* II. 110 As touching Lychnis, that flaming hearbe surnamed Flammea [etc.]. **1664** EVELYN *Kal. Hort. May* (1679) 17 Flowers in Prime, or yet lasting..yellow Lillies, Lychnis, Jacea, Bellis, double, white and red. **1707–12** MORTIMER *Husb.* (1721) II. 229 Lychnis or Calcedon are single and double. **1824** H. PHILLIPS *Flora Hist.* II. 183 The Scarlet Lychnis is a perennial plant. **1884** JEFFERIES in *Chamb. Jrnl.* 1 Mar. 131/1 The pink lychnis or ragged robin grows among the grasses.

2. With defining word, applied by gardeners to various plants of other genera: see quots.

1760 J. LEE *Introd. Bot.* App. 318 Lychnis, Bastard, *Pholx.* Lychnis, Wild, *Agrostema.* **1787** tr. *Linnæus' Fam. Plants* I. 116 *Phlox*.... False Lychnis.

†ˈ**lychnobite.** *Obs.*⁻⁰ [f. Gr. *λυχνόβιος* (in Seneca), f. *λύχνο-ς* lamp + *βίος* life; after *cœnobite*.] One who turns night into day; a 'fast-liver'.

1727 BAILEY vol. II, *Lychnobite*, a Night Walker.

lychnoscope (ˈlɪknəskəʊp). *Arch.* [f. Gr. *λύχνο-ς* lamp + *-σκόπος* -SCOPE.] A name given to the LOW SIDE WINDOW on the supposition that its purpose was to allow lepers to see the altar lights.

1843 *Ecclesiologist* II. 71 A paper on the windows called 'Lychnoscopes', in the fourth edition of the [Cambridge Camden] Society's 'Hints on the Practical Study of Ecclesiastical Antiquities'. **1846** —— V. 165 Lychnoscopes are nothing else than the symbolical representation of the Wound in the Saviour's Side. **1848** B. WEBB *Continental Ecclesiol.* 57 The dwarf-wall is pierced by a broad fenestrella with a trefoliated head opening through into the aisle. This in England would be called a 'lychnoscope'. **1866** PARKER *Gloss. Terms Goth. Archit.*

Hence **lychnoˈscopic** *a.*

1849 *Ecclesiologist* IX. 314 Behind it is a small chamber with a kind of 'lychnoscopic' window. **1852** *Ibid.* XIII. 216.

lycht, obs. Sc. form of LIGHT.

Lycian (ˈlɪsɪən), *sb.* and *a.* [f. L. *Lycia*, Gr. *Λυκία* Lycia + -AN.] **A.** *sb.* **a.** A native or inhabitant of ancient Lycia in south-west Asia Minor. **b.** The language and script used in Lycia. **B.** *adj.* Of or pertaining to ancient Lycia, its inhabitants, or the language and script used by them.

1598 CHAPMAN tr. *Homer's Seaven Bookes of Iliades* 45 Sarpedon had the Lycians charge. **1607** TOPSELL *Four-f. Beasts* 115 These beasts are..plentifull..in Lycia:..the Lycian Roes doe neuer goe ouer the Syrian Mountaines. **1718** POPE tr. *Homer's Iliad* XVI. 570 Two sounding Darts the Lycian Leader threw. **1839** C. FELLOWS *Jrnl. Excursion Asia Minor* viii. 229 On the side of the tomb..under two lines of the peculiar characters of this town, (perhaps Lycian,) is a group of figures. **1841** —— *Acct. Discoveries Lycia* vii. 168 The tedious, but..useful occupation, of copying the Lycian inscription. **1845** [see BILINGUAL *a.* 2]. **1883** *Encycl. Brit.* XV. 92/2 It [*sc.* Lycia] was..inhabited from a very early period by a distinct people, known to the Greeks as Lycians. *Ibid.* 94/1 A few of these inscriptions are fortunately bilingual, in Greek and Lycian. **1913** H. R. HALL *Anc. Hist. Near East* vi. 270 There is a reference to Lycian pirates in another letter. **1933** [see CARIAN *sb.* and *a.*]. **1941** [see ILIAN *a.* (*sb.*)]. **1948** D. DIRINGER *Alphabet* 464 The Lycian alphabet..is certainly of Greek origin. **1951** J. B. BURY *Hist. Greece* (ed. 3) viii. 337 Cimon..constrained the Lycian communities to enrol themselves in the confederacy of Delos. **1972** R. MEIGGS *Athenian Empire* xvii. 307 The Lycians also had ceased to bring their tribute. *Ibid.*, The Carian and Lycian coasts were being used by pirates. **1973** *Times* 1 Oct. 17/6 Lycian is an Indo-European language and belongs to the Luwian sub-group of Anatolian. *Ibid.*, It would be important to know in which of the two Lycian dialects the inscription is written.

lycid (ˈlɪsɪd), *a.* and *sb.* [f. mod.L. family name *Lycidæ*, f. generic name *Lycus* (J. C. Fabricius *Mantissa Insectorum* (1787) I. 163), f. Gr. proper name *Λύκος*, L. *Lycus*: see -ID³.] **A.** *adj.* Of or pertaining to a beetle of the family Lycidæ. **B.** *sb.* A beetle of this family.

1932 J. S. HUXLEY *Probl. Relative Growth* vii. 237 See..Mjöberg's discussion (1925) on the larviform females of certain Lycid beetles. **1934** WEBSTER, *Lycid n.* and *adj.* **1962** *New Scientist* 6 Dec. 577/1 The cerambycid beetle *Elytroleptus ignitus* is a mimic of the lycid beetles *Lycus loripes* and *L. simulans*.... They are typical cases of Batesian mimicry, the cerambycids being palatable to predators but gaining protection by looking like the distasteful lycids. **1972** L. E. CHADWICK tr. *Linsenmaier's Insects of World* 165/1 There are a great many mimetic forms that resemble protected beetles (such as the already-mentioned lycids).

lycine (ˈlɪsaɪn). *Chem.* [f. LYCIUM: see -INE⁵.] A base found in Box-thorn.

1865 WATTS *Dict. Chem.*

†**lyciske.** *Her. Obs.* Also 7 lyciscus, 8 lycisca. [ad. med.L. *lyciscus* masc., *-ca* fem., f. Gr. *λύκος* wolf.] A fabulous beast supposed to be a hybrid between a wolf and a dog.

1572 BOSSEWELL *Armorie* II. 56 Two Lyciskes Passant. Lyciskes are called (as Plinie saithe) dogges, gendered of wolfes. **1610** GUILLIM *Heraldry* III. xxv. 179 Castorides, Dogges ingendred by a Fox and a Beuer; Lyciscus of a Wolfe and a Mastiffe. **1706** PHILLIPS (ed. Kersey), *Lycisca*, a Dog ingender'd of a Wolf and a Bitch.

†**lycium.** *Obs.* [late L., a. Gr. *λύκιον*, orig. neut. sing. of *Λύκιος* Lycian.] **a.** The shrub Box-thorn (*Lycium barbarum*). **b.** The fruit, and **c.** the extracted juice of the Box-thorn.

1597 GERARDE *Herbal* III. xxv. 1151 There is drawne out of the leaues and branches of Boxe Thorne..a iuice, which is named Lycium.... In English..it is also named Lycium of the iuice which is boiled out of it. **1657** *Physical Dict.*, *Lycium*, a decoction made of the juyce or decoction of the bramble root. **1661** LOVELL *Hist. Anim. & Min.* 36 Some adulterate the Indian Lycium with the gall hereof [*sc.* a Heifer]. **1753** CHAMBERS *Cycl. Supp.*, *Lycium*,..the name of a fruit called by the French *baye d' Avignon*, the Avignon berry. **1839** *Penny Cycl.* XIV. 210.

lycke, lycken, obs. ff. LICK *v.*, LIKEN *v.*

lyckore, obs. comparative form of LIKE.

lycoctonine (laɪˈkɒktənaɪn). *Chem.* [f. mod.L. *Lycocton-um* wolf's-bane (a. Gr. *λυκοκτόνον* lit. wolf-killer) + -INE.] An alkaloid extract of the Wolf's-bane.

1878 tr. *H. von Ziemssen's Cycl. Med.* XVII. 744 *Aconitum lycoctonum*..is the only species [of aconitum] that contains no aconitine, but another alkaloid, lycoctonine.

lycodont (ˈlaɪkədɒnt). *Ichthyol.* [ad. mod.L. *Lycodont-*, *-odon*, ad. Gr. *λυκοδόντ-ες* pl. (Galen), f. *λύκο-ς* wolf + *ὀδοντ-*, *ὀδούς* tooth.] A snake of the family *Lycodontidæ*, having caniniform teeth.

1887 *Encycl. Brit.* XXII. 190/2 In some [snakes] all the teeth are nearly of the same size; others possess in front of the jaws (Lycodonts) or behind in the maxillaries (Diacrasterians) a tooth..larger than the rest.

Hence **lycoˈdontine** *a.*, pertaining to the *Lycodontidæ* (Cent. Dict.).

lycomarasmin (ˌlaɪkəʊməˈræsmɪn). *Chem.* Also †lyco-marasmine. [ad. G. *lyco-marasmin* (Plattner & Clauson-Kaas 1945, in *Experientia* I. 196), f. mod.L. *lyco-persici* varietal or specific

epithet (taken as gen. of *lycopersicon*: see LYCOPERSICIN) + Gr. μαρασμ-ός withering + -IN[1].] A phytotoxic dipeptide, $C_9H_{15}N_3O_7$, which contains glycine and aspartic acid residues and was isolated from *Fusarium bulbigenum* var. *lycopersici*, the fungus which causes tomato wilt.

1945 *Experientia* I. 196 On hydrolysis lyco-marasmine yields glycine, aspartic and (probably) pyruvic acid and ammonia. **1956** *Ann. Rev. Microbiol.* X. 361 Lycomarasmin, therefore, causes iron deficiency in the stem and iron excess in the leaves. **1972** S. A. J. TARR *Princ. Plant Path.* xiii. 236 Lycomarasmin is a dipeptide which brings about wilting and yellowing of tomato cuttings, and its phytotoxicity is increased in the presence of iron.

†**lyco'panther.** *Obs.* [a. Gr. λυκοπάνθηρ, f. λύκο-ς wolf + πάνθηρ panther.] A fabulous hybrid between a wolf and a panther.

1607 TOPSELL *Four-f. Beasts* (1658) 448 The Lycopanthers are ingendred between wolves and panthers. *Ibid.* 581.

lycopene ('laɪkəʊpiːn). *Chem.* [f. LYCOP(IN + -ENE.] A polyunsaturated hydrocarbon, $C_{40}H_{56}$, which is a red carotenoid pigment present in tomatoes and many berries and fruits.

1935 *Jrnl. Biol. Chem.* CXII. 424 In an investigation of the plastid pigments of marsh dodder, . . α- and β-carotenes, γ-carotene, lycopene, and rubixanthin have been isolated. **1950** *Genetics* XXXV. 209 Tomatoes which contain principally *beta*-carotene differ from those which contain mostly lycopene by a single incompletely dominant gene. **1972** GOODWIN & MERCER *Introd. Plant Biochem.* xi. 279 The conversion of phytoene into coloured carotenoids involves a stepwise desaturation to neurosporene and lycopene which are then converted into the cyclic carotenoids.

‖**lycoperdon** (laɪkə'pɜːdən). *Bot.* [mod.L., irreg. f. Gr. λύκο-ς wolf + πέρδεσθαι to break wind: a rendering of the Eng. name *wolf's fist* (FIST *sb.*[2]).] The fungus Puff-ball, *Lycoperdon Bovista*.

1756 *Gentl. Mag.* XXVI. 430 The lycoperdon, or puff-ball. **1830** LINDLEY *Nat. Syst. Bot.* 335 Gasteromyci . . comprehending . . Lycoperdons and the like.

b. *attrib.*: **lycoperdon nut** (see quot.).

1886 *Treas. Bot.*, *Lycoperdon nuts*, the name under which the herbalists sell our common species of *Elaphomyces*.

Hence **lyco'perdoid** *a.*, resembling fungi of the genus *Lycoperdon*.

1871 W. A. LEIGHTON *Lichen-flora* 243 Verrucæ large, globular, . . lycoperdoid, eventually lacerato-dehiscent.

lycopersicin (ˌlaɪkəʊ'pɜːsɪkɪn). *Chem.* [f. mod.L. *lycopersic-on*, the name of the genus to which the tomato belongs, f. Gr. λύκο-ς wolf + περσικ-ός peach (f. Περσίς: see PERSIAN *a.* and *sb.*): see -IN[1].] **a.** = LYCOPENE.

1913 B. M. DUGGAR in *Washington Univ. Stud.* I. 23 Since the pigment derived from the tomato has now been demonstrated to be distinct from carotin . ., and since it was first described in the tomato, it seems well to suggest that, in view of the inappropriateness of the earlier terms, lycopersicin should be adopted instead.

b. = TOMATIN.

1945 G. W. IRVING et al. in *Science* 6 July 9/1 We have obtained from the expressed juice of Pan American tomato plants . . a preparation which . . possesses marked fungistatic activity toward Fol. This antibiotic agent, which will be designated 'lycopersicin', occurs throughout the mature plant. **1946** *Jrnl. Bacteriol.* LII. 601 In a recent publication . . this substance was referred to as 'lycopersicin'. Inasmuch as it has since been learned that the term 'lycopersicin' was once used . . as a synonym for 'lycopene', the red pigment of the tomato, the designation of the antibiotic agent has been changed to 'tomatin' to avoid possible confusion.

†**lycophosed**, *a.* *Obs.*[−1] [f. Gr. λυκόφως twilight, app. misapprehended to mean keen sight (f. λύκο-ς wolf + φῶς light) + -ED[2].] Keen-sighted. Also **lycophosy** in the same sense.

1600 TOURNEUR *Transf. Metam.* vi, Looke on my sight, you lycophosed eies, And tell me whether it be blear'd or no. *Ibid.* xlvii, His eies that 'fore were cleare lycophosie, Now cannot see but in a minery.

lycopin ('laɪkəʊpɪn). *Chem.* [f. mod.L. *lycopersicon* (see LYCOPERSICIN) + -IN[1].] = LYCOPENE.

1903 C. A. SCHUNCK in *Proc. R. Soc.* LXXII. 174 Believing that this substance has not been isolated before, or if it has, has been mistaken for carotin, I venture to apply to it the name *Lycopin*. **1965** BELL & COOMBE tr. *Strasburger's Textbk. Bot.* 43 Over seventy different carotinoids are known. Of these we need refer here only to the carotin of the carrot . ., to the lycopin of the tomato and other red fruits, and to the yellow violaxanthin.

lycopod ('laɪkəpɒd). *Bot.* [Anglicized form of LYCOPODIUM.] A club-moss, a plant of the N.O. *Lycopodiaceæ*, esp. of the genus *Lycopodium*.

1861 H. MACMILLAN *Footnotes fr. Page Nat.* 58 Lycopods may be said to present the highest type of cryptogamic vegetation. **1873** DYER in *Q. Jrnl. Microscop. Sci.* XIII. 152 The relationship of a Lycopod to a flowering plant.

Hence **ly'copodal** *a.*, pertaining to the lycopods; *sb.*, a plant belonging to the 'Lycopodal alliance'.

1835 LINDLEY *Introd. Bot.* (1848) II. 98 The Lycopodal Alliance. **1854** A. ADAMS, etc. *Man. Nat. Hist.* 525 Lycopodals.

lycopode ('laɪkəpəʊd). [a. F. *lycopode*, ad. mod.L. LYCOPODIUM.] = LYCOPODIUM 2.

1866 *Treas. Bot.*, *Lycopode*, vegetable brimstone.

lycopodiaceous (ˌlaɪkəpɒdɪ'eɪʃəs), *a.* *Bot.* [f. mod.L. *Lycopodiācе-æ* + -OUS.] Pertaining to the N.O. *Lycopodiaceæ*, of which LYCOPODIUM is the typical genus.

1852 TH. ROSS *Humboldt's Trav.* I. xiii. 428 Lycopodiaceous plants and mosses. **1892** *Natural Sci.* Mar. 57 A gigantic aquatic Lycopodiaceous plant.

lycopodite (laɪ'kɒpədaɪt). *Geol.* A fossil lycopodium.

1839 *Penny Cycl.* XIV. 212/1.

lycopodium (laɪkə'pəʊdɪəm). [mod.L., f. Gr. λύκο-ς wolf + ποδ-, πούς foot, from the claw-like shape of the root.]

‖**1.** *Bot.* A plant of the cryptogamous genus *Lycopodium*: a club-moss. In early use, *L. clavatum*.

1706 PHILLIPS (ed. Kersey), *Lycopodium*, Wolfs-claw, an Herb. **1756** [see CLUB-MOSS]. **1851** RICHARDSON *Geol.* vii. (1855) 174 The gigantic lycopodium-like, and cactoid plants of the coal measures . . all disappear. **1873** DYER in *Q. Jrnl. Microscop. Sci.* XIII. 155 The thickened prosenchymatous cells which are found in recent Lycopodiums.

2. The fine powder formed by the ripe spores of species of *Lycopodium*, known as 'vegetable brimstone' from its inflammability. Also *l. dust*, *powder*.

It is used in surgery as an absorbent; also in theatres for the production of stage lightning.

1836 J. M. GULLY *Magendie's Formul.* (ed. 2) 173 Starch or lycopodium powder washed with alcohol, appears to preserve the auriferous salts the best. **1856** TODD & BOWMAN *Phys. Anat.* II. 89 The vibrations of the paper are easily demonstrated by the movements of particles of fine sand, or lycopodium powder strewed upon it. **1876** DUHRING *Dis. Skin* 235 Asborbent dusting powders, consisting of lycopodium dust, will be found most useful.

lycor, obs. form of LIQUOR.

lycoras, -ess(e, -ice, etc., obs. ff. LIQUORICE.

lycorous(e, -oruse, variants of LICKEROUS.

lycotropal (laɪ'kɒtrəpəl), *a.* *Bot.* [f. Gr. λύκο-ς 'anything in the form of a hook' (L. & Sc.) + -τροπ-ος turning + -AL[1].] The term applied to an orthotropous ovule, curved downward in the form of a horse-shoe (*Treas. Bot.* 1866).

lycotropous (laɪ'kɒtrəpəs), *a.* *Bot.* [f. as prec. + -OUS.] = prec.

1878 HOBLYN *Dict. Med. Terms.*

lycour(e, -esse, obs. ff. LIQUOR, LIQUORICE.

lycoures, -ourous, -ours, var. LICKEROUS.

Lycra ('laɪkrə). Also **lycra**. A proprietary name of an elastic polyurethane fibre and fabric used esp. for underwear and swimming costumes.

1958 *Official Gazette* (U.S. Patent Office) 18 Nov. TM 87/1 E. I. du Pont de Nemours and Company... Lycra. For synthetic fibers and filaments for generalized use in the industrial arts. First use Feb. 3, 1958. **1959** *Trade Marks Jrnl.* 8 Apr. 380/2 Lycra... Raw or partly prepared natural or synthetic fibres; and untwisted and unspun filaments; . . E. I. Du Pont De Nemours and Company. **1961** *Harper's Bazaar* Sept. 103 Lycra, the ultimate in lightweight power. **1963** *Guardian* 8 Nov. 12/4 Proofed . . lycra jersey ski pants. **1968** *Vogue* 15 Apr. 23/2 This . . pantie-corselette . . of softest lycra power net. **1972** *Country Life* 18 May 1275/3 Beachwear in newest Lycra material, light but giving corselette support.

lyctus ('lɪktəs). [mod.L. (J. C. Fabricius *Entomologia Systematica* (1792) I. II. 502), f. Gr. Λύκτος, L. *Lyctus* name of a city in Crete.] A wood-boring beetle of the genus so called; a powder-post beetle. Also *attrib.* Hence **'lyctid** *sb.*, a beetle of the family Lyctidæ; as *adj.*, of or pertaining to this family.

1917 *U.S. Dept. Agric. Farmers' Bull.* No. 788 (*title*) Powder-post damage by *Lyctus* beetles to seasoned hardwood. **1926** E. O. ESSIG *Insects Western N. Amer.* 438 The European lyctus . . can be separated by the single row of large round shallow punctures on the elytra. **1936** *Discovery* Feb. 42/1 The Powder-Post or Lyctus beetles are menacing timber-yard pests. **1958** *Times Rev. Industry* May 18/3 Death watch beetles and furniture beetles . . are joined by . . the lyctus beetle. **1959** E. F. LINSSEN *Beetles Brit. Is.* II. 63 The dust made by Anobiid larvae is granular, that of the Lyctid grubs is a fine powder. **1963** N. E. HICKIN *Insect Factor in Wood Decay* v. 134 Lyctid beetles are small.

lycur, obs. form of LUCRE.

lycure, -esse, -yce, obs. ff. LIQUOR, LIQUORICE.

Lycurgan (laɪ'kɜːgən), *sb.* and *a.* Also **Lycurgean, Lycurgian.** [f. L. *Lycurgus*, Gr. Λυκοῦργος traditional lawgiver and founder of the Spartan constitution, dated in antiquity variously to the ninth and eighth centuries B.C.]

A. *sb. rare.* An adherent of Lycurgus or his methods. **B.** *adj.* Of, pertaining to, or characteristic of Lycurgus, or the constitutional innovations attributed to him; harsh, severe.

1584 W. ALLEN *True Defence Eng. Catholiques* vii. 149 By the meanes of such Lycurgians as this, we haue in England new lawes against al claime of iurisdiction spiritual or temporal, that can be made by anie person whosoeuer, borne out of the Realme. **1846** G. GROTE *Hist. Greece* II. II. vi. 454, I incline to adopt the opinion of Thucydides as to the time at which the Lycurgean constitution was introduced at Sparta. **1934** [see DIE-HARDISM]. **1956** A. TOYNBEE *Historian's Approach to Relig.* 242 The Lycurgean régime at Sparta was exceptional. **1962** *Listener* 30 Aug. 323/2 The Lycurgan training for public service enriched Greek 'paedeia'. **1970** *Oxf. Classical Dict.* (ed. 2) 1007/2 Proposals to revive the strictness of the Lycurgan training . . were obstructed by the ephors.

lydder, -ir, -yr, variants of LITHER *a.*

lydderne, -eryn, variants of LIDDERON *Obs.*

lyddite ('lɪdaɪt), *sb.* [f. name of *Lydd* in Kent (where this explosive was first tested in England).] A high explosive, chiefly composed of picric acid, and believed closely to resemble MELINITE; used in the manufacture of explosive shells in England.

1888 *I. of Wight County Press* 3 Nov. 3/4 Armstrong and Co... bought the patent from . . M. Turpin, who is now personally assisting in the manufacture of Lyddite, the English name for Melinite. **1898** *Westm. Gaz.* 26 Aug. 7/1 The new Lyddite shell. **1901** *Scotsman* 14 Mar. 7/3 The power of Lyddite has been described by experts . . as most destructive in a rocky country.

lyddite, *v. rare.* [f. the sb.] *trans.* To destroy, wreck, etc., by the explosion of lyddite.

1906 F. CAMPBELL *Dearlove* 78 She was pleased they had not dynamited or lyddited him.

lyder, -ir, -yr, variants of LITHER *a.*

Lydford law: see LAW *sb.*[1] 8 c.

Lydford, now a small village on the confines of Dartmoor, was formerly the chief town of the stannaries.

1399 LANGL. *Rich. Redeles* III. 145 Now, be þe lawe of lydfford . . þilke lewde ladde ouȝte euyll to thryue. *a* **1645** W. BROWNE *Wks.* (1772) III. 157, I oft have heard of Lydford law, How, in the morn they hang and draw, And sit in judgement after. **1656** BLOUNT *Glossogr.*, *Lydford Law*, is to hang men first, and indite them afterwards.

†**lydge**, *v.* *Obs.* [Back-formation f. *lydger*, LEDGER.] *intr.* To be a ledger ambassador.

a **1618** RALEIGH *Maxims St.* (1656) 31 [To] have some of his own Lydging abroad about their Princes Court, under colour of Embassage, or some other pretence.

lydgear, -er, obs. forms of LEDGER.

Lydian ('lɪdɪən), *a.* and *sb.* [f. L. *Lȳdi-us*, Gr. Λύδι-ος + -AN.]

A. *adj.*

1. Pertaining to the Lydians, a people of Asia Minor, or to their country, Lydia. Sometimes with allusion to the wealth of Crœsus king of Lydia.

1584 LYLY *Sapho & Phao* v. i, This shaft is headed with Lidian steel. *c* **1620** T. ROBINSON *Mary Magd.* 12 To whome the Lydian wealth . . is brought in lauish measure. **1626** MASSINGER *Rom. Actor* I. iii, We show no arts of Lidian Pandarisme. **1844** O. COCKAYNE in *Proc. Philol. Soc.* (1854) I. 275 The Lydian Hercules. **1901** *Edin. Rev.* July 29 The earlier Lydian civilization was Asiatic rather than European.

2. *spec.* in *Music.* **a.** The designation of one of the modes in ancient Greek music, characterized as soft and effeminate. **b.** The third of the authentic ecclesiastical modes, having F for its 'final', and C for its 'dominant'.

1579 E. K. *Gloss. to Spenser's Sheph. Cal.* Oct. 27 The Lydian and Ionique harmony. **1593** G. HARVEY *Pierce's Super.* 50 He regarded not the dainety Lydian, Ionian, or Æolian Melody. **1632** MILTON *L'Allegro* 136 Lap me in soft Lydian aires, Married to immortal verse. **1636** C. BUTLER *Princ. Mus.* I. i. 1 Ðe Lydian Mood' is a grav', ful, solemn Musik in Discant, for ðe most' part', of slow tim'. **1697** DRYDEN *Alexander's Feast* 97 Softly sweet, in Lydian measures, Soon he soothed his soul to pleasures. **1807** ROBINSON *Archæol. Græca* v. xxiii. 534 In music . . there were four principal νόμοι or modes: the Phrygian, the Lydian, the Doric, and the Ionic . . The Phrygian mode was religious, the Lydian plaintive. **1867** MACFARREN *Harmony* i. 13 The Lydian is the third mode of Ambrose's selection. *fig.* **1664** BUTLER *Hud.* II. i. 850 As skilful coopers hoop their tubs With Lydian and with Phrygian dubs.

3. Lydian-stone. *Min.* A black variety of jasper (basanite) used by jewellers as a touchstone for testing gold.

1720 STRYPE *Stow's Surv.* II. VI. i. 11/1 Within the Rails before the High Altar, is a curious in-laid Floor . . where . . there are set these several Sorts of Stones, the Jasper, . . Lydian, . . and Serpentine. **1746–74** HILL *Theophr. Stones* 25 Others serve for the Trial of Metals, as that called the Heraclian or Lydian Stone. **1836** MACGILLIVRAY tr. *Humboldt's Trav.* ii. 133 It did not exhibit the little veins of quartz so common in Lydian stone. **1879** RUTLEY *Study Rocks* xiv. 293 Lydian-stone (basanite, touch-stone, kiesel-schiefer) is . . an altered sandy slate.

B. *sb.* An inhabitant of Lydia. Also, the language of the Lydians.

1545 ASCHAM *Toxoph.* I. (Arb.) 40 Yet after by the meane of one Pactyas a verye headie manne amonges the Lydians they rebelled agaynste Cyrus agayne. **1696** PHILLIPS s.v. *Lydia*, It falling to Tyrrhenus his lot, he went out with a great multitude of Lydians. **1735** BOLINGBROKE *Study &*

Use Hist. iii. (1752) I. 76 Herodotus..proposed to publish all he could learn of the antiquities of the Ionians, Lydians, ..Medes, and Persians. **1886** SHELDON tr. *Flaubert's Salammbô* 3 Some Lydians feasted arrayed in the robes..of women.

lydite ('lɪdaɪt). *Min.* Also 9 lydit. [f. LYD(IAN *a.* and *sb.* + -ITE[1].] = *Lydian stone* (s.v. LYDIAN *a.* 3).

1816 R. JAMESON *Syst. Mineral.* (ed. 2) I. 192 Lydit. **1861** H. W. BRISTOW *Gloss. Mineral.* 223/2 Lydian Stone.. Lydite. **1907** *Q. Jrnl. Geol. Soc.* LXIII. 31 It is by no means a pure sand; there are no 'lydite' or other pebbles. **1948** *Proc. Prehist. Soc.* XIV. 129 Brown and purple quartzite cobbles, pieces of vein quartz and of lydite. **1968** *Mineral. Abstr.* XIX. 333/1 Six chemical analyses of phyllites and clay slates are listed; these are in zeolitic and greenschist facies and contain grapholite-bearing lydites.

lydron, -un, variants of LIDDERON *Obs.*

lydyate, obs. form of LIDGATE.

lye (laɪ), *sb.*[1] Forms: 1 léaȝ, (lǽȝ), léah, léȝ, 3 leihe, 4 leȝe, liȝe, (5 legh, leyȝe, leygh(e, lyhe), 5–9 lee, lie, ley, (5–6 leye, le, 7 ly), 5– lye. [OE. *léaȝ* (later *léah*, genit. *léaȝe*) str. fem., corresponds to MDu. *loghe* (Du. *loog*), OHG. *louga* (MHG., mod.G. *lauge*), lye, ON. *laug* bath:—OTeut. **laugâ*; prob. f. the root **lau-* to wash (see LATHER) + suffix *-gâ*:—OAryan *-qā*.]

1. a. Alkalized water, primarily that made by the lixiviation of vegetable ashes, but also applied (esp. with prefixed word as in *soap-lye*, *soda-lye*) to any strong alkaline solution, esp. one used for the purpose of washing. †Also ***water of lye.***

a **700** *Epinal Gloss.* 591 Lexiua, leaȝ [*Corpus* and *Erf.* læȝ]. *c* **1000** *Sax. Leechd.* I. 364 Scinseocum men wyrc drenc of hwites hundes þoste on bitere leȝe wundorlice hyt hæleð. *Ibid.* II. 338 Wyrc him leaȝe of ellen ahsan. *c* **1400** *Lanfranc's Cirurg.* 93 If þat þou waische hem boþe [a cankre & a foul vlcus] wiþ liȝe. *Ibid.*, þe vlcus is clensid wiþ þilke liȝe [*v.r.* leyȝe]. *c* **1420** *Pallad. on Husb.* II. 377 Wete hit [a tree] at the fulle Thrie euery mone a yer in lie allone. *c* **1430** *Two Cookery-bks.* 32 Take a gode quantyte of fyne leye, & put it on a potte..& whan þe ley is seþin hot, caste þe Pesyn þer-to. *c* **1440** *Jacob's Well* 195 Watyr of legh þat is made wyth asschys & watyr,..for asschys & hote watyr makyn good leyghe. **1502** *Ord. Crysten Men* (W. de W. 1506) I. ii. 10 But man shall be baptysed in necessyte with le. **1669** WORLIDGE *Syst. Agric.* (1681) 60 The Lee or Lixivium wherewith the Women usually scour their Clothes. **1704** N. N. tr. *Boccalini's Advts. fr. Parnass.* III. 287 Henry the Fourth, thought it an Honour to wash his Head..though some malicious People say, He did it not with Soap, but with hot scalding Lye. **1807** T. THOMSON *Chem.* (ed. 3) II. 544 Muriate of potash. This salt..is prepared from the waste leys of the soap-makers. **1898** F. T. BULLEN *Cruise Cachalot* iv. (1900) 32 The officers..were content with ley, which was furnished in plenty by the ashes from the galley fire.

b. In wider sense: Any detergent material used in washing; a cleansing substance. Also *fig.*

c **1200** *Vices & Virtues* 95 Nis ðar non swo god leiȝe se teares. **12..** *Prayer to our Lady* 19 in *O.E. Misc.* 193 Mi brune her is hwit bicume ich not for hwucche leihe. *c* **1330** *Spec. Gy Warw.* 828 þe hote teres of mannes eiȝe Makeþ clannere þan any liȝe. **1340** *Ayenb.* 145 þet is þet we byeþ alle y-wasse of onelepi leȝe, þet wes mid Iesu cristes preciouse blod. **1426** LYDG. *De Guil. Pilgr.* 21855 Wyth wych water, dame Penaunce Maketh a lye..To wasshen a-way al ordure. **1601** HOLLAND *Pliny* II. 324 The vrin of a yong Asse fole is supposed to thicken the haire: but there would be mixed some Spiknard with this washing lie, to rectifie the strong sent of the said vrine. **1648** HERRICK *Hesper.* (1869) 190 Feacie, some say, doth wash her clothes i' th' lie That sharply trickles from her either eye.

†**c.** A cosmetic for the hair. (Cf. LYE-POT.) *Obs.*

15.. WITHALS *Dict.* (1568) 51 a/2 Lie to wasshe the head with, *lixiuium.* **1561** T. HOBY tr. *Castiglione's Courtyer* II. (1577) L iij b, I reprehended a ladie of loue for occupying a certain kinde of lye y[t] shined much.

†**d.** Applied to urine used as a detergent; more fully CHAMBER-LYE. *Obs.*

14.. *Voc.* in Wr.-Wülcker 593/23 *Locium*, lye, or pysse.

2. Water impregnated with salts by decoction or lixiviation. Now *rare.*

1634 PEACHAM *Gentl. Exerc.* I. xxiii. 77 The Lie of Rue, (that is the water wherein you have sod your Rue or herb-grace). **1644** NYE *Gunnery* (1670) 14 Pour upon the said flower so much of the strained water, which I call lee or lime water, as will dissolve the flower. **1646** SIR T. BROWNE *Pseud. Ep.* VI. xii. 337 Colcothar or vitriol burnt..will make good Inke, and so will the Lixivium or Lye made thereof with warme water. **1811** *Self Instructor* 562 A ley made with tartar and gum-water. **1860** MAURY *Phys. Geog. Sea* i. §43 They [waters] find their way into the sea, and so make the lye of the earth brine for the ocean. *Ibid.* x. §461 The brine of the ocean is the ley of the earth.

3. The limpid acrid fluid which runs from a blister or the like; the 'water' which collects in the body in dropsy. Now only *dial.*

1615 CROOKE *Body of Man* 92 His Nauell suddenly opened whence issued so great quantity of the dropsy Lie, that his body fell to the wonted scantling. **1886** *S.W. Linc. Gloss.*, *Lee* (so pronounced),..the watery matter which issues from a wound or sore: as 'It's more like lee than matter'.

4. *attrib.* and *Comb.* (sense 1), as ***lye-ashes, -brush, -cask, hominy, -kettle, -leach, -trough, -tub, -vessel, -wash.*** Also LYE-POT.

1601 HOLLAND *Pliny* II. 599 Hereupon comes *Lixivus cinis*, i. Lie ashes, which being drunk is medicinable. **1605** TIMME *Quersit.* II. iii. 115 Lye-wash..is made of ashes and water. **1683** MOXON *Mech. Exerc., Printing* xi. ¶21 The Lye Brush is made of Hogs Bristles fastned into a Board with Brass-Wyer. *Ibid.*, A Lye-Kettle..commonly holds about three Gallons. *Ibid.*, The Lye-Trough..is a Square Trough made of Inch-Boards. **1743** *Lond. & Country Brewer* II. (ed. 2) 109 A Lye-tub, though generally neglected as the worst.. for a Cooler, has really proved the sweetest and safest of any. **1763** *Museum Rusticum* I. 53 The straw in the bottom of your lye-vessel. **1821** W. B. DEWEES *Lett. from Early Settler Texas* (1852) 20 Our subsistence was principally upon..a kind of lye hominy seasoned with hickory nut kernels. **1824** J. JOHNSON *Typogr.* II. 489 As soon as a form is wrought-off, the press-man to carry it to the lye-trough, and there completely rub it over with lye. **1843** 'R. CARLTON' *New Purchase* I. ix. 63 A lie-cask, or rather, an inverted pyramidical box to contain ashes. **1847** J. O. HALLIWELL *Dict. Archaic & Provincial Words* Lie-leach. **1854** M. J. HOLMES *Tempest & Sunshine* xv. 202 Now be keerful and not run afoul of the plaguey lye leech! **1882** J. SOUTHWARD *Pract. Printing* (1884) 406 Lye is applied to the forme with a lye brush. **1919** J. P. DUNN *Indiana* II. 1170 A woman situated like Mrs. McCoy, in her Indian boarding school, with no food but lye hominy in the house..'degraded her soul' by cooking lye hominy. **1948** E. N. DICK *Dixie Frontier* 290 Lye hominy was made by soaking the whole grains of corn in lye water to remove the hulls.

lye, *sb.*[2] [var. LIE *sb.*[2]] = LIE *sb.*[2] 4.

1855 OGILVIE *Imp. Dict.* Suppl., *Lye*, a term employed, in *railway lang.*, to denote the sidings or short offsets from the main line, into which trucks may be run for the purpose of loading or unloading. **1901** *Daily Record* (Glasgow) 31 Aug. 3 A boy..was accidentally killed at the lye of South Renfrew Station on Thursday night.

†**lye,** *v.*[1] *Cookery. Obs.* [a. F. *lier* to thicken (a sauce, etc.), lit. 'to bind':—L. *ligāre.*]

1. *trans.* To mix; to thicken (soups, sauces, etc.). Cf. *alye*, ALLY *v.* 5.

?*c* **1390** *Forme of Cury* (1780) 17 Make a lyre of raw ayrene and do þerto Safrone and powdour douce, and lye it up with gode broth. *c* **1420** *Liber Cocorum* (1862) 12 Loke þou lye hit with amydone. *c* **1430** *Two Cookery-bks.* 13 Take Vele..and hakke it to gobettys..and lye it with Flowre of Rys. *Ibid.* 19.

2. To bind or tie. In quot. *fig.*

1621 *Bury Wills* (Camden) 167 He shall neede noe bonde to lye him to it.

lye, *v.*[2] Also ley. [f. LYE *sb.*[1]] *trans.* To treat with lye.

1805 *Ann. Reg.* 875 Ley the thread once. **1823** E. JAMES *Acct. Expedition Rocky Mts.* I. 195 They sometimes prepare this hard corn for eating by the process of leying it, or boiling it in a ley of wood ashes for..an hour or two. **1888** *Sci. Amer.* 8 Dec. 356/2 The air is to be..excluded from the surface of fruits left standing after having been either lyed or washed.

lye: see LEE *sb.*, LEYE, LIE.

lyeas, str. pa. t. of LEESE *v.*[1]

lyeave, obs. form of LEAF.

lyed (laɪd), *ppl. a. U.S.* Also leyed, lied. [f. LYE *v.*[2] + -ED[1].] Treated with lye; steeped or washed in an alkaline fluid. ***lyed corn,*** maize or other grain steeped in weak lye to remove the husk.

1814 BRACKENRIDGE *Jrnl.* in *Views Louisiania* 202 Their food consists of lied corn homony for breakfast. **1823** E. JAMES *Acct. Expedition Rocky Mts.* I. 114 Another very acceptable dish was called leyed corn. **1825** W. BIGGS *Narr. Captivity among Kickapoo Indians* (1922) 35 Sandy hill cranes boiled in leyed corn. **1860** EMERSON *Cond. Life, Wealth* 70 Pride can go without domestics;..can eat potato, purslain, beans, lyed corn.

lyef(e, obs. f. LIEF.

lyefull, var. LEEFUL.

lyege, lyeg(e)aunce, obs. ff. LIEGE, LIGEANCE.

lyegge, lyeȝe, obs. forms of LIE *v.*[1], *v.*[2]

ly(e)ȝere, lyek(e, obs. ff. LIAR, LIKE.

lyen, obs. form of LIE *v.*[1], LIEN *sb.*[1], LION.

lyencephalous (laɪɪn'sɛfələs), *a. Zool.* [f. mod.L. *Lyencephal-a* (Owen) + -OUS.

According to Owen himself (*Classif. Mammalia*, 1859), his term *Lyencephala* is f. Gr. λύ-ειν to loose + ἐγκέφαλος brain (see ENCEPHALON), and signifies 'the comparatively loose or disconnected state of the cerebral hemispheres'.]

Of or belonging to the *Lyencephala*, in Owen's classification the lowest group of Mammals, including the Monotremes and the Marsupials.

1859 OWEN *Classif. Mammalia* 27 The Lyencephalous Mammalia. **1864** in WEBSTER. And in later Dicts.

lyepart(e, obs. form of LEOPARD.

†'**lye-pot.** *Obs.* [Cf. LYE *sb.*[1] 1 c.] An ornamental vessel to hold lye for use as a hair-wash.

1486 *Will of Lytton* (Somerset Ho.), A lye pott of siluer and gilt, a holy water stopp. **1599** NASHE *Lenten Stuffe* 45 Semiramis ranne out with her lie-pot in her hand, and her black dangling tresses about her shoulders. **1607** MIDDLETON *Five Gallants* I. i. 12 Lent..upon her gilt casting-bottle and her silver lie-pot, fifty-five shillings.

lyer(e, var. LEAR[2] *Obs.*; obs. f. LYRE[3], LIAR.

lyerne, -i, -y, obs. forms of LEARN.

lyeroway: see LYRA 5.

lyery ('laɪərɪ), *a.* Now *dial.* Also **lyary.** [Var. of LIRY *a.*] Of cattle: Having a superabundance of lean flesh.

[**1483**: see LIRY, s.v. LIRE *sb.*[1]] **1803** A. HUNTER *Georg. Ess.* IV. 351 Lyery, or black-fleshed. **1807** CULLEY in W. C. L. Martin *Ox* 51/1 Cattle, well known to the breeders adjoining the river Tees by the appellation of 'lyery', or 'double-lyered'; that is, black-fleshed. *a* **1843** SOUTHEY *Commpl. Bk.* IV. 400 Those [Lincolnshire oxen] that never fatten are called lyery. *c* **1847** W. C. L. MARTIN *Ox* 41/2 The cattle in general were large,..slow to fatten..and often black, or foul-fleshed, or as it is called in Yorkshire 'lyery'. **1855** STEPHENS *Bk. Farm* (ed. 2) II. 142/1 When the flesh [of an ox] becomes heavy on the thighs, making a sort of double thigh, the thigh is called *lyary*.

lyes, obs. form of LEASH; obs. pl. LOUSE.

lyese, lyesinge, vars. LEESE *v.*[1], LEASING.

lyf, obs. form of LEAF, LIFE.

lyfar, obs. Sc. comp. of LIEF, dear.

lyfe, obs. form of LIFE; Sc. form of LIEF.

lyff(e, lyffere, obs. forms of LIFE, LIVER.

†**lyfkie.** *Obs.* Also 6 leefekye. [a. Du. *lijfken* 'corpusculum, subucula, exomis' (Kilian), dim. of *lijf* body; cf. G. *leibchen.*] A bodice.

1579 LYLY *Euphues* (Arb.) 116 Their spots, their lawnes, their leefekyes, their ruffes, their rings: Shew them rather Cardinalls curtisans, then modest Matrons. **1609** T. COCKS *Diary* (1901) 73 W'th iij li before delivered her for my wives gowne and lyfkie.

lyfnoð, variant of LIVENATH *Obs.*

lyft(e, obs. form of LEFT, LIFT.

lyfve, lyfy, obs. forms of LIVE *v.*, LIFEY.

lyg, lygaunce, obs. ff. LIE *v.*[1], LIGEANCE.

lyger, see LEDGER.

lyg(g)e, obs. form of LIE *v.*[1], LIEGE.

lygham, see LICHAM.

lyghe, lyȝe, obs. ff. LIE; var. LEYE *Obs.*

lygher, lyȝer(e, obs. forms of LIAR.

lyght, obs. form of LIGHT; variant of LITE.

lyghteling, lyȝtmose, obs. form of LIGHTNING *sb.*, LITMUS.

lyhe, lyht(e, obs. forms of LYE, LIGHT *v.*[1]

lyicht, lyif, lyik, obs. ff. LIGHT, LIFE, LIKE.

lying ('laɪɪŋ), *vbl. sb.*[1] Forms: see LIE *v.*[1] [f. LIE *v.*[1] + -ING[1].]

1. a. The action of LIE *v.*[1] in various senses; resting, reclining, remaining in deposit, †being sick, etc.

a **1225** *Ancr. R.* 8 Fleschs forgon oþer visch, & alle oþer swuche þinges, of weriunge, of liggunge, of vres, of beoden. *a* **1300** *Cursor M.* 6686 þe smiter sal quite his lechyng, And þe scath of his liging. *c* **1380** WYCLIF *Serm.* Sel. Wks. I. 141 For boþe Cristis liynge in þe sepulcre and his dwellinge here in erþe was litil tyme. *a* **1400** *Cursor M.* 29091 (Cott. Galba) þe first [discipline es]..sighing, wepeing, and ill liging. **1526** *Pilgr. Perf.* (W. de W. 1531) 137 Soft lyenge, soft weryng, or moche fedyng of delycate meates. **1602** SHAKS. *All's Well* I. i. 167 'Tis a commodity will lose the glosse with lying; The longer kept, the lesse worth. **1634** *Lease by R. Kenward to W. Deane* verso (MS.), I..would never have bought it but for the convenient lying of it to my other ground. **1683** MOXON *Mech. Exerc., Printing* vii, Sugar-Chest..Stuff being commonly well-season'd, by the long lying of the Sugar in it. **1726** LEONI tr. *Alberti's Archit.* I. 34/1 Liquify'd by long lying in the Water. **1899** *Allbutt's Syst. Med.* VI. 574 This situation [of a bed sore] is determined..by the lying of the paralytic on that side.

†**b.** *spec.* The state of being buried; *concr.* place of sepulture. *Obs.*

1480 CAXTON *Chron. Eng.* ccxxx. 244 Kyng Edward chese his sepulture and his lyggyng at Westmynster. *a* **1676** GUNTON *Hist. Ch. Peterburgh* (1686) 77 The Heralds.. appointed..the place for the body to be Interred, which was devised over against the lying of Queen Katherine.

c. with adv. or advb. phr. (see LIE *v.*[1] IV). Also LYING-IN.

1382 WYCLIF *Rom.* ix. 10 Rebecca, of o liggynge by hauynge tweye sones of Ysaac, our fadir. **1387** TREVISA *Higden* (Rolls) VI. 93 Bote wiþ som manere rouschelynge þat he made in ligynge adoun his felowe awook. **1483** CAXTON *Gold. Leg.* 333/2 He hadde Subtyltee for teschewe the lyggynge in a wayte of his enemyes. **1530** PALSGR. 239/2 Lying in wayte, *aguaytance. Ibid.* 423, I am upon my lieng downe, as a woman that is nere her tyme. **1601** HOLLAND *Pliny* I. 87 From thence to the lying out of the mountaine Pyrenæus, Aquitania. **1611** BIBLE *Ps.* cxxxix. 3 Thou compassest my path, and my lying downe. **1611** —— *Acts* xx. 19 Many teares, and temptations, which befell me by the lying in wait [TINDALE layinges awayte] of the Iewes. **1623** MASSINGER *Bondman* II. i, There's a sport too Nam'd lying Perdieu..Which you must learne to play at. **1647** FULLER *Good Th. in Worse T.* (1841) 81 This lying along is an improper posture for piety. **1711** W. SUTHERLAND *Shipbuild. Assist.* 115 B. is the Fore-top-sail braced back, which is done..to stop her way, term'd Lying-by. **1711**

Lond. Gaz. No. 4910/2 The Admiral thought it proper..to make the Signal for lying by. **1792** CHARLOTTE SMITH *Desmond* II. 121 You have accused me of lying by in Company.

attrib. *c* **1834** N. P. WILLIS in G. Paston *Little Mem. 19th C.* (1902) 176 His [Disraeli's] eye..has the most mocking lying-in-wait expression conceivable. **1899** *Allbutt's Syst. Med.* VII. 460 If a change from the lying-down to the sitting-up position is rapidly made.

2. *concr.* With qualification (as *dry*, *soft*, *warm*, etc., *lying*): Accommodation for repose.

1853 DE QUINCEY *Autobiog. Sk.* Wks. I. 295 It was a subject of gratitude..to dwell upon the soft lying which was to be found in that..morass. **1868** NETTLESHIP *Browning* vii. 262 A poet from his birth, nursed in Nature's softest lying. **1886** *Weekly Times* 6 Aug. 13/3 There is no finer feeding or warmer lying in Scotland. **1898** *Westm. Gaz.* 20 May 10/2 Dry lying—a dry bed at night—is..essential to the welfare of deer.

3. *attrib.*, as **lying-ground**, **-place**; †**lying-house** (see quot. 1593); **lying-in-state**, (of the corpse of a public figure) being on display for public tribute before burial; **lying-press** (*Printing*) = *laying-press* (see LAYING *vbl. sb.* 3).

1895 CORNISH *Wild Eng.* 122 The paddock is a favourite *lying ground for hares. **1423-4** *Durham Acc. Rolls* (Surtees) 271 Pro ligatur pro hostio vocato trapdoure supra *lyng house, iiijd.; et pro seris et clavibus pro lyng house, xxd. **1593** *Rites & Mon. Ch. Durh.* (Surtees) 75 A strong prysonne call the Lynghouse [*MS. Cos.*, Lyinge house]. **1923** W. DE LA MARE *Riddle* 241 Positive constellations of candles as if for a Prince's..*lying-in-state. **1947** M. FIELD *Boys' & Girls' Film Bk.* 67 When he died thousands of people went to his lying-in-state. **1972** *Whitaker's Almanack 1973* 565/2 The Duke of Windsor's lying-in-state took place in St. George's Chapel, Windsor. **1382** WYCLIF *Prov.* vii. 17, I ha sprengd my *ligging place with myrre, and aloes. **1580** HOLLYBAND *Treas. Fr. Tong, Desbauger vn sanglier*, to raise a wilde Bore from his lying place. **1876** *Encycl. Brit.* IV. 43/1 By screwing the volume up in the *lying-press.

lying ('laɪɪŋ), *vbl. sb.*² Forms: see LIE *v.*² [f. LIE *v.*² + -ING¹.] The action of LIE *v.*²; the telling of lies. †In 16–17th c. sometimes in *plural.*

a **1300** *E.E. Psalter* v. 7 (MS. Egerton) þou leses alle þat speke liyhinge. **1340** *Ayenb.* 143 Him hit þingþ þet hit is al wynd and metinge and lyeȝynge. **1426** LYDG. *De Guil. Pilgr.* 13302 My condicioun ys to lye;..With lyyng I shal deceyue the. **1577** NORTHBROOKE *Dicing* (1843) 68 If for ydle wordes, what for hurtfull words? what for lyings? **1604** E. G[RIMSTONE] *D'Acosta's Hist. Indies* v. xxviii. 412 The Divell..did steale all that he could from the trueth, to imploy it in his lyings and deceits. **1656** E. REYNER *Rules Govt. Tongue* 16 Lying is an ungodly, devilish and damnable practice. **1827** MRS. A. OPIE (*title*) Illustrations of Lying in All its Branches. **1863** MRS. RIDDELL *World in Ch.* III. 41 Lying is the employment of the lower orders, and the recreation of the higher.

personified. **1606** DEKKER *Sev. Sins* II. (Arb.) 21 Lying is Father to Falshood, and Grandsire to Periury.

¶**b.** Alleged name for a 'company' of pardoners.

1486 *Bk. St. Albans* F vij, A Lyeng of perdeneris.

lying ('laɪɪŋ), *ppl. a.*¹ [f. LIE *v.*¹ + -ING².]

1. That lies, or rests in a recumbent, extended, stationary or inert position; also, †*absol.* (OE.) dead.

c **1000** *Leg. St. Swithun* etc. (Earle 1861) 110 þæt mægn þæs licgendan. **1382** WYCLIF *Jer.* xxxiii. 12 A dwelling place of shepperdus, of liggende flockus. **1422** tr. *Secreta Secret., Priv. Priv.* 224 The angry man Is wonyt to be of..a semely chyne and accordynge to the visage, and liggyne here. *a* **1450** *Fysshynge w. Angle* (1883) 16 The lying ground lyne with ovte floyte. **1842** TENNYSON *Vision Sin* 11 Sitting, lying languid shapes. **1862** *Remarks on Golf* 14 The Short-spoon ..is used for playing either good-lying or bad-lying balls. **1880** W. CARNEGIE *Pract. Trap.* 16 That most annoying eventuality, a 'lying' ferret.

b. *Sc.* Of money, goods, etc.: Put by.

1722 RAMSAY *Three Bonnets* I. 129 Your claiths, your lands, and lying pelf. **1799** J. ROBERTSON *Agric. Perth* 386 We are not informed, what lying stock they have, what donations they have received [etc.].

2. Special collocations: **lying-dog**, a setter; **lying-panel**, †(*a*) a panel which occupies the lowest place in a series; (*b*) a panel whose longest dimension, or one whose grain, lies horizontally; †**lying-stone**, the nether millstone; **lying-storm** (*Sc.*), a snow-storm when the snow lies; **lying-wall** *Mining* = FOOT-WALL (Raymond *Mining Gloss.*).

1818 SCOTT *Hrt. Midl.* xii, As if a penalty was inflicted by statute for any man who suld hunt or hawk, or use *lying-dogs. **1678** MOXON *Mech. Exerc.* I. 106 The *Lying Pannel, above the Base. **1823** P. NICHOLSON *Pract. Build.* 226 *Lying Panel*, a Panel with the fibres of the wood disposed horizontally. **1842-59** GWILT *Archit.* Gloss., *Lying panels*, those wherein the fibres of the wood, or the grain of it, lie in an horizontal direction. **1674** N. FAIRFAX *Bulk & Selv.* 151 As certain a cause as is that, by which the runner in a Mill does not sink through the *Lyingstone. **1787** BEATTIE *Scoticisms* 79 We use the word *storm* to signify a storm of snow, or snowy weather. We even speak of a *lying storm. **1844** H. STEPHENS *Bk. Farm* I. 298 Should the flakes be spicular and fall very thick and fast, then a heavy fall, or a 'lying storm'..may be expected.

lying ('laɪɪŋ), *ppl. a.*² Forms: see LIE *v.*² [f. LIE *v.*² + -ING².]

1. Of a person, his lips, etc.: That tells lies.

1535 COVERDALE *Ps.* cxix. 2 Deliuer my soule (o Lorde) from lyenge lippes. **1593** SHAKS. *2 Hen. VI*, II. i. 126 Then, Saunder, sit there, the lying'st Knaue in Christendome. **1610** B. JONSON *Alch.* IV. iv, Do not beleeue him, Sir. He is the lying'st Swabber! **1611** BIBLE *Prov.* x. 18 Hee that hideth hatred with lying lippes..is a foole. *a* **1758** RAMSAY *Eagle & Robin* 44 With a wickit lieand tung. **1886** W. J. TUCKER *E. Europe* 158 A canting, lying, hypocritical set.

2. Of impersonal things: Untruthful, mendacious; hence, deceitful, false.

a **1225** *Juliana* 2 Ant of þis lihinde lif leade us..into þe eche of heouene. *a* **1340** HAMPOLE *Psalter* i. 4 His worde sall noght..dissayuabile ne leghynge. **1535** COVERDALE *Jer.* vii. 4 Trust not in false lyenge wordes. **1611** BIBLE *Ps.* xxxi. 6, I haue hated them that regard lying vanities. **1718** PRIOR *Solomon* II. 673 And slavish bards our mutual loves rehearse In lying strains. **1855** MACAULAY *Hist. Eng.* xix. IV. 322 It was much easier..to put forth a lying prospectus.

'lying-'in. [LYING *vbl. sb.*¹ I c. See LIE *v.*¹ 23.]

a. The being in childbed; accouchement.

c **1440** *Promp. Parv.* 305/2 Lyynge yn, of childe bedde, *decubie.* **1580** HOLLYBAND *Treas. Fr. Tong, Gesine*, a lying in. **1698** FROGER *Voy.* 126 The women have good Lying's-in and the children are lusty. **1768-74** TUCKER *Lt. Nat.* (1834) I. 93 Those cushions your gossips stick with pins in hearts, lozenges, and various forms, against a lying-in. **1842** L. HUNT *Men, Women & B.* (1847) I. 342 The Queen talked to me [Madame de Sévigné] as long about my illness as if it had been a lying-in.

b. *attrib.*, as *lying-in-asylum*, *-chamber*, etc.

1770 HEWSON in *Phil. Trans.* LX. 412 The British Lying-in-Hospital. **1799** *Med. Jrnl.* II. 190 A lying-in ward has been lately established. **1823** J. CONSTABLE *Let.* 24 Aug. in *Corr.* (1964) II. 282 Miss Cookson is on a visit with another lying in sister. **1838** DICKENS *O. Twist* xxxvii, 'The lying-in room, I suppose?' said Mr. Bumble. **1861** D. G. ROSSETTI *Let.* 20 Apr. (1965) II. 396 Dr. Babington, head of the Lying-in Hospital. **1887** *Brit. Med. Jrnl.* 21 May 1101/1 Such sanitation..might be of service in lying-in institutions. **1895** *Daily News* 9 Dec. 3/7 A system of registration of all..lying-in houses. **1899** *Allbutt's Syst. Med.* VII. 797 Statistics of lying-in hospitals show that [etc.]. **1912** *Q. Rev.* July 60 A slight increase in the ratio of lying-in claims to the number of members... A lying-in benefit of 30*s.* **1964** D. OWEN *Eng. Philanthropy* I. ii. 50 The years 1749–65 saw the founding of..the British Lying-In (1749), the City of London Lying-In (1750),..these in addition to the Lying-In Charity,..established in 1757. **1975** *Country Life* 2 Jan. 50/3 Villages which had a mutual aid or 'lying-in society'.

So **lying-in** *ppl. a.*, that is in childbed.

1710-11 SWIFT *Jrnl. to Stella* 23 Mar., I..saw his lady sitting in the bed, in the forms of a lying-in woman. **1824** MISS MITFORD *Village* Ser. I. 174 The sick, the delicate,.. the lying-in. **1889** J. M. DUNCAN *Lect. Dis. Women* xxii. (ed. 4) 189 In lying-in or recently delivered women.

lyingly ('laɪɪŋlɪ), *adv.* [f. LYING *ppl. a.*² + -LY².] In a lying manner, mendaciously.

1382 WYCLIF *Jer.* vii. 8 To steln, to slen, to don auoutrie, to swern liendely, to offre to Baalym. —— *Ezek.* xiii. 22 For that the ȝe maden leeiȝyngli the herte of the iust man to mourne, whom Y made not sorewful. **1541** R. COPLAND *Guydon's Quest. Chirurg.* G iv, Of whiche .xij. rybbes there be .vij. very, and .v. false or lyengly. **1682** *Disc, Addresses or Presentm. to King* 20 Their Popes (who go lyingly under the Name of Christ's Vicars). **1804** ANNE SEWARD *Lett.* (1811) VI. 146 It reached his ear, that she had lyingly called him 'the thing of sound without sense'. **1895** *Times* 19 Jan. 11/6 He lyingly reported that he had sunk two of the French men-of-war.

†**lying-weight.** *Obs.* [LYING *ppl. a.*¹] **a.** A free weight placed in a scale, as distinguished from the hanging weight attached to a spring balance or a steelyard. **b.** = AVOIRDUPOIS.

1454 *Rolls of Parlt.* V. 275/1 [That no person buy wool by the fleece] nor weyed by the awncell, but only by the lying weight, after XIIII li to the stoon. **1502** ARNOLDE *Chron.* (1811) 191 Ther beth iij maner weyghtȝ that is to wele troy weyght, auncell weyghtis, and lyggynge weyght. *Ibid.*, The Lygginge weyght..therby is boughte and solde alle maner of Marchaundise..as is vsed to be solde be weyght, and of this weyght xvi vuncis made a pound and C. and xij li. is an C. **1545** *Rates Custom-ho.* d v b, Lyinge wayghte. Thys Lyinge and Haburdy peyse is all one.

lyk, obs. Sc. form of LIKE.

lykam(e, lykance, vars. LICHAM, LIKANCE.

lykanthropy, variant of LYCANTHROPY.

lyke: see LICH, LICHE, LICK *v.*, LIKE *v.*

lykeleod, -hood, obs. forms of LIKELIHOOD.

lyken, lykeny, obs. forms of LIKE *v.*¹, LIKEN *v.*

lykeres, obs. form of LIQUORICE.

lyker(o)us, -owse, etc., var. LICKEROUS *Obs.*

'lyke-wake, 'lykewake ('laɪkweɪk). Also 4, 9 **liche-wake**, 6, 9 **lyk(e)wa(i)ke**, 6–7 **like-, lyke-walk**, 8–9 **lake-wake**, 9 **lychwake**. Cf. LATE-WAKE. [f. *lyke*, LICH + WAKE *sb.*] The watch kept at night over a dead body.

c **1386** CHAUCER *Knt.'s T.* 2100 Ne how that lych wake was yholde Al thilke nyght,..kepe I nat to seye. **1513** DOUGLAS *Æneis* x. ix. 31 Quham that he etlis for to send from thens, To Pallas likewalkis. **1558** *Richmond Wills* (Surtees 1853) 127 Ther shall be no yong folkes at my lyke-waike. **1623** in Pitcairn *Crim. Trials* III. 549 At quhose lyke-walk..the ox foirsaid was slane and eittin. *a* **1775** *Fair Mary of Wallington* xix. in Child *Ballads* II. 311/2 Your daughter..bids you come to her sickening, or her merry lake-wake. **1832** CARLYLE *Misc.* (1857) III. 114 At all lykewakes, the doings and endurances of the Departed are the theme. **1878** W. C. SMITH *Hilda* (1879) 192, I heard them..moan their rugged lyke-wakes in the ancient Runic rhymes.

attrib. **1805** SCOTT *Last Minstr.* IV. xxvi, Our slogan is their lyke-wake dirge. **1837** SIR F. PALGRAVE *Merch. & Friar* (1844) 99 The lyke-wake train was seen advancing towards them.

lykey, lykke, -yn, obs. ff. LICK *v.*, LIKE *v.*

lykkerwys, lykky: see LICKEROUS, LIKE *v.*¹

lykne(n, -yn, obs. forms of LIKEN.

lykor, lykorise, obs. ff. LIQUOR, LIQUORICE.

lyky(e)n, obs. forms of LIKE *v.*¹

lykyrrhize, obs. form of LIQUORICE.

lylac, lyle, -ie, obs. forms of LILAC, LILY.

Lyle gun (laɪl gʌn). [Named from its inventor D. A. *Lyle* (d. 1937) of the U.S. Ordnance Dept.] A cannon, invented in 1877, designed to project a rope from the shore to a stranded ship to facilitate salvaging and rescue operations.

1880 *Ann. Rep. U.S. Life-Saving Service* 109 The keeper ..then proceeded to charge the Lyle gun. **1899** *Ibid.* 471 The sample submitted is designed for use with the 2½-inch Lyle gun. **1911** *Encycl. Brit.* XV. 606/2 The keeper fires a line over the wreck with the Lyle gun, a small bronze cannon ..having an extreme range of about 700 yards. **1927** G. BRADFORD *Gloss. Sea Terms* 106/2 *Lyle gun*, a life-saving gun designed to shoot a projectile with a line attached. This line ..establishes a connection with a stranded ship by which an endless line and tail block is hauled off and afterwards a hawser. **1944** H. NORBY *Questions & Answers* vi. 128 No part of Lyle gun equipment is to be used for any other purpose.

Lylian ('lɪlɪən), *a.* Also **Lylyan**. [f. the name of John *Lyly* (*c* 1554–1606), English dramatist and novelist.] Of, pertaining to, or having the characteristics of John Lyly or his works.

1923 E. K. CHAMBERS *Eliz. Stage* III. 36 The plays of the Lylyan school..illustrate very precisely, on the side of staging, that blend of the classical and the romantic tempers which is characteristic of the later Renaissance. **1928** E. A. GERRARD *Eliz. Drama* II. i. 145 The scene between Lucilla and the Enchanter is purely Lylian. **1959** *Times* 1 Sept. 11/2 It was Lyly who opened the door for Shakespeare, and when he was forced to abandon the Lylian view he abandoned comedy. **1962** G. K. HUNTER *John Lyly* iv. 164 The approach to Alexander is underlined for us in a typically Lylian way. *Ibid.* iv. 218 With typical Lylian balance the action returns to the point from which it started.

lylle, variant of LILL, LILLE *vbs. Obs.*

lyll(i)e, -y(e, obs. forms of LILY.

lym, lymail(le, obs. ff. LEAM *sb.*¹, LIMAIL.

Lyman ('laɪmən). *Physics.* The name of Theodore *Lyman* (1874–1954), U.S. physicist, used *attrib.* to designate a series of lines (individually designated alpha, beta, etc.) discovered by him in the ultraviolet part of the spectrum of atomic hydrogen, with wave numbers represented by the formula $R(1 - 1/m^2)$ (where R is the Rydberg constant and $m = 2, 3, \ldots$), the first line of which has a wavelength of 121·6 nanometres.

1922 *Encycl. Brit.* XXXII. 559/2 The formulæ for the hydrogen series are as follows:—Lyman series: $\nu = N/1^2 - N/m^2$ ($m = 2, 3, \ldots$). Balmer series: $\nu = N/2^2 - N/m^2$ ($m = 3, 4, \ldots$). Paschen series: $\nu = N/3^2 - N/m^2$ ($m = 4, 5, \ldots$). **1929** J. K. ROBERTSON *Introd. Physical Optics* xviii. 359 Lines of the Lyman series arise from electron drops from outer orbits to the innermost or normal orbit, for which $k = 1$. **1959** *Sunday Times* 5 Apr. 8/3 The sun itself has been photographed in the extreme ultra-violet (the Lyman-alpha) region of the spectrum. **1967** W. R. HINDMARSH *Atomic Spectra* ii. 13 Ritz..proposed his well-known combination principle in 1908; he recognized that the wave-numbers of the lines could always be represented as a difference between two terms... It was with the use of this principle that the Paschen, Lyman, Brackett and Pfund series in the spectrum of hydrogen were predicted..before they were known experimentally. **1968** G. M. B. DOBSON *Exploring Atmosphere* (ed. 2) viii. 158 Another possiblity is that the very strong radiation which is given out by hydrogen in the sun, at a wavelength of 1216 Ångstrom units (known as the Lyman alpha line) produces the *D* region [of the ionosphere].

lymasson, obs. form of LIMAÇON.

lymb(e, lym(e, obs. forms of LIMB *sb.*¹ and ².

lyme: see LYAM.

'lyme-grass. [? f. LIME *sb.*¹ with reference to the binding quality of the plant; the spelling is app. suggested by the mod.L. generic name.] The name for grasses of the genus *Elymus*, esp. *E. arenarius*, a grass which is planted on sand, that its roots may help to keep the sand in its place.

1776 WITHERING *Bot. Arrangement Veg.* I. 64 Lymegrass. Elymus. **1787** tr. *Linnæus' Fam. Plants* I. 52. **1854** S. THOMSON *Wild Fl.* III. (ed. 4) 299 The lyme grass (*Elymus*), by binding the sands..with its roots, assists in the resistance to the encroachments of the sea.

b. *attrib.* in the name of a moth.

1869 NEWMAN *Brit. Moths* 275 The Lyme Grass (*Tapinostola Elymi*).

lymer, lymet(t, obs. ff. LIMER, LIMIT.

lymfad, lyming, obs. ff. LYMPHAD, LIMING.

lymiter, lymme, obs. ff. LIMITER, LIMB *sb.*[1]

lymnite: see LIMNITE.

lymon, obs. f. LEMON.

lymph (lɪmf). Also 7–8 in L. form **lympha**. [ad. L. *lympha*, altered spelling (due to pseudo-etym. association with Gr. νύμφη NYMPH *sb.*) of **limpa* (whence *limpidus* LIMPID), **lumpa*; according to some scholars repr. a prehistoric **dumpa* cognate with the Oscan *Diumpais* 'Nymphis'.]

1. a. Pure water; water in general; a stream. Only *poet.* and *rhetorical*.

a **1630** *Roxb. Ball.* (1871) I. 176 Here rurall gods and tripping Nymphs Did bath their corps in the pure lymphs And christal streams. **1791** E. DARWIN *Bot. Gard.* I. 117 The Naiad-Nymph, Who hides her fine form in the passing Lymph. **1843** BORROW *Bible in Spain* xlix. (1872) 279 In the middle of the court was a fountain well supplied with the crystal lymph. **1860** LD. LYTTON *Lucile* II. v. §6. 17 Then.. the lymph Was the dwelling divine of a white-footed nymph. **1885** R. BRIDGES *Eros & Psyche* Dec. xxix, Its [*sc.* a fountain's] biting lymph may not be touch'd of man Or god, unless the Fates have so ordain'd.

fig. **1879** G. MEREDITH *Egoist* xvi. I. 302 It would be the pity of common sympathy, pure lymph of pity, as nearly disembodied as can be.

b. *transf.* (nonce-uses).

1784 COWPER *Task* III. 391 Sipping calm the fragrant lymph [*sc.* tea] Which neatly she prepares. **1878** W. T. THORNTON *Word for Word fr. Horace* 136 Not on wings.. shall I through aether's lymph be borne.

†**2.** *Bot.* A colourless fluid in plants; the sap.

1672–3 GREW *Anat. Plants* II. iii. (1682) 68 The Root of Dandelion being cut in November, seems to bleed both a Milk and a Lympha. **1784** COWPER *Task* VI. 136 That moved The pure and subtle lymph Through th' imperceptible meand'ring veins Of leaf and flow'r. **1807** J. E. SMITH *Phys. Bot.* 67 The sap, or lymph, of most plants.. appears to the sight and taste little else than water. **1830** LINDLEY *Nat. Syst. Bot.* 270 The juice of the fruit and the lymph of the stem of Musa are slightly astringent. [**1900** JACKSON *Gloss. Bot. Terms, Lymph*,.. Grew's term for sap.]

3. *Phys.* A colourless alkaline fluid, derived from various tissues and organs of the body, resembling blood but containing no red corpuscles.

1725 N. ROBINSON *Th. Physick* 59 The Pancreatic Juice, Lympha, and Bile are all fitted for their several Offices of Separation, Attenuation, and Dilution. **1793** J. HUNTER *Treat. Blood* etc. (1794) 28 The coagulating lymph of the blood being common, probably to all animals, while the red particles are not. **1805** W. SAUNDERS *Min. Waters* 446 The waters of Barege.. dissolve.. soap and animal lymph. **1830** R. KNOX *Béclard's Anat.* 120 To coagulate like the coagulable lymph of the blood. **1898** *Allbutt's Syst. Med.* V. 666 There is a continual outpouring of some of the contents of the capillaries into the tissues, which output, under the name of lymph, is roughly speaking *liquor sanguinis* deprived of much of its albumin.

4. a. The exudation from an inflamed tissue, from a sore, etc. **b.** In recent use often *spec.* for *vaccine lymph* (see VACCINE), the matter which is taken from the vesicles characteristic of cow-pox in a cow or calf or in a vaccinated human being, in order to be used in the operation of vaccination. Hence, in wider sense, any morbid matter taken from a person or animal suffering from a disease, in order to be employed in some prophylactic operation analogous to vaccination.

1800 *Med. Jrnl.* IV. 61 Several.. tumours.. discharged an acrid lymph. **1801** RING *Cow-pox* I. 295 Medical men in general.. think it [variolous matter] most active when it is a mere lymph, and inert as it becomes more opaque. **1810** JENNER in Baron *Life* (1838) II. 368, I send out a great deal of vaccine lymph on ivory points. **1866** J. HUTCHINSON in *J. R. Reynolds' Syst. Med.* I. 307 The rapid absorption of syphilitic lymph under mercurial influence. **1868** SEATON *Handbk. Vaccination* 109 Lymph should in every instance (where practicable) be inserted direct from arm to arm. **1873** ROBERTS *Handbk. Med.* 53 Fibrinous Exudation, Lymph, Coagulable Lymph, Inflammatory exudation. An exudation escapes from the vessels in some forms of inflammation, which is coagulable, containing much fibrine, and to this the above names have been applied. *Ibid.* 194 The lymph does not deteriorate or lose its protective power after passing through any number of individuals. **1893** *Dunglison's Med. Dict., Koch's lymph*.

5. *attrib.* and *Comb.* **a.** simple attributive, as ***lymph-cell**, **-channel**, **-corpuscle**, **-follicle**, **-gland**, **-globule**, **-path**, **-sinus**, **-space**, **-stoma*** (pl. *stomata*), ***-stream**, **-vessel***; **b.** objective, as ***lymph-absorption**, **-secretion**; **lymph-connective**, **-forming*** adjs.; **lymph-canalicular** *a.*, of or pertaining to lymph-channels; **lymph-cataract** (see quot.); **lymph-heart**, one of a number of contractile muscular sacs which pump the lymph forward; **lymph node**, any of several small rounded gland-like structures of the lymphatic system, which are disposed along the course of the lymph vessels and which are responsible for removing foreign bodies from the lymph stream and for producing lymphocytes and antibodies; a lymph gland.

1899 *Allbutt's Syst. Med.* VI. 213 The hypothesis of lymph-formation and *lymph-absorption. **1874** *Q. Jrnl. Microscop. Sci.* XIV. 278 The *lymph-canalicular system of Recklinghausen. **1844** HOBLYN *Dict. Med. Terms*, **Lymph-cataract*, the most frequent form of spurious cataract; so named by Beer. **1873** T. H. GREEN *Introd. Pathol.* (ed. 2) 208 Small spheroidal elements resembling *lymph-cells. **1867** *Quain's Anat.* (ed. 7) III. p. clxxxviii, The Lymph-sinus, or the *lymph-channel. **1899** *Allbutt's Syst. Med.* VI. 507 The *lymph-connective elements (spider-cells).. crowd upon the sheaths of the blood-vessels. **1872** PEASLEE *Ovar. Tumours* 14 The *lymph-corpuscle, becomes a diagnostic element of the peritoneal fluid. **1873** T. H. GREEN *Introd. Pathol.* (ed. 2) 264 The *lymph-follicles become enlarged from the multiplication of their elements. **1897** *Allbutt's Syst. Med.* IV. 13 Increase of uric acid.. may be an evidence of changes in *lymph-forming structures. **1856–8** W. CLARK *Van der Hoeven's Zool.* I. 15 *Lymph-glands are found only in higher animals. **1822–34** *Good's Study Med.* (ed. 4) I. 552 Globules void of colour, found floating in the serum, and which Sir Everard Home has called *lymph-globules. **1875** HUXLEY & MARTIN *Elem. Biol.* 172 The Frog possesses two pairs of *lymph-hearts. **1892** *Proc. N.Y. Path. Soc. 1891* 65 (*heading*) Large-celled indurative hyperplasia of the *lymph nodes. **1925** *Jrnl. Amer. Med. Assoc.* 28 Feb. 669/2 The cervical, axillary, epitrochlear and inguinal lymph nodes were moderately enlarged. **1955** *Sci. News Let.* 18 June 393/2 Antibodies, he found, are formed in lymph nodes, better known to the layman as glands. **1961** H. A. SKINNER *Origin Med. Terms* (ed. 2) 259/2 All of the early writers seem to have adhered to the term [lymph] gland.. and the term has been continued, although there is no indication of any gland function. This was a matter of vigorous debate at the anatomical congress at Basle [in 1895].. and Toldt especially advocated use of the term 'lymph node'. On the last ballot his suggestion was voted down by a large majority. In the Nomina Anatomica adopted at Paris in **1955** the term node was approved. **1972** J. W. SHIELDS *Tropic Function Lymphoid Elem.* xi. 71 The lymph nodes are characteristically oriented to receive substrate more or less directly from the peripheral tissues. **1878** HOBLYN *Dict. Med. Terms* (ed. 10), **Lymph-scrotum*, a peculiar disease of the scrotum, characterized by the formation of vesicles in the skin of the scrotum containing albuminous fluid, charged with corpuscles like those of the blood. **1899** *Allbutt's Syst. Med.* VII. 243 The whole question of *lymph secretion is at present in too unsettled a state to be discussed with much profit. **1867** *Lymph-sinus [see *lymph-channel*]. **1874** *Q. Jrnl. Microscop. Sci.* XIV. 91 The *lymph spaces existing between the tendinous fibres of fasciæ. **1875** E. R. LANKESTER *ibid.* XV. 260 Each fold contains between its lamellæ a lymph-space (part of the cœlom). **1899** *Allbutt's Syst. Med.* VII. 542 A pleural effusion closes the *lymph-stomata of the pleura. **1873** GREEN *Introd. Path.* 109 The transmission by the *lymph-stream of substances.. derived from the malignant growth. **1874** *Q. Jrnl. Microscop. Sci.* XIV. 91 The *lymph vessels on the opposite side.

lymphad ('lɪmfæd). Also 7 **lum-, lime-, lymfad.** [corruption of Gael. *longfhada*: see LANGFAD.] A one-masted galley propelled by oars. Now only *Hist.*; and *Her.* borne as a charge in the arms of some Scottish families.

1536 [see LANGFAD]. **1608** in *Burt's Lett. N. Scotl.* (1818) II. App. 238 Destroyit the haill gallayis, lumfaddis. **1641** *Sc. Acts. Chas. I.* (1814) V. 442/1 The nomber of boittis, or Lymfadis within the pairtis of this kingdome lying opposite to Irland. **1814** SCOTT *Diary* 12 Aug., He [Earl of Orkney] bears the royal arms.. quarterly, with a lymphad or galley, the ancient arms of the county. **1818** —— *Rob Roy* xxix, Our loch ne'er saw the Campbell lymphads. **1864** BOUTELL *Her. Hist. & Pop.* ix. 46 The Lymphad is borne by the Duke of Argyll and the Marquis of Abercorn. **1888** *Sat. Rev.* 25 Feb. 221 The MacDonalds can hardly go over in lymphads to Ulster and butcher another Shane O'Neil.

‖**lymphadenitis** (lɪmfædɪ'naɪtɪs). *Path.* [mod.L., f. LYMPH + Gr. ἀδήν gland + -ITIS.] Inflammation of the lymphatic glands.

1879 J. R. REYNOLDS *Syst. Med.* V. 134 **1897** *Allbutt's Syst. Med.* IV. 554 The.. condition of the spleen seen in cases of bacterial infection may be described as a splenitis and in some degree comparable to lymphadenitis.

lymphadenoid (lɪm'fædɪnɔɪd), *a.* [f. as prec. + -OID.] Resembling the tissue of a lymphatic gland.

1877 ROBERTS *Handbk. Med.* (ed. 3) I. 270 Lymphadenoid tissues are specially prone to tubercle. **1898** *Allbutt's Syst. Med.* V. 3 The root-particles lie in.. the lymphadenoid bodies of the lung.

‖**lymphadenoma** (,lɪmfædɪ'nəʊmə). [mod.L., f. L. *lympha* LYMPH + Gr. ἀδήν gland + *-oma*, after *carcinoma*, etc.] An abnormal development, or a tumour consisting of lymphoid tissue (*Syd. Soc. Lex.*). Hence **lymphade'nomatous** *a.*

1873 T. H. GREEN *Introd. Pathol.* (ed. 2) 145 Closely allied to the simple lymphomata are the growths now known as lymphadenoma. *Ibid.* 147 A lymphadenomatous tumour of the mediastinum.

lymphadenopathy (,lɪmfædɪ'nɒpəθɪ). *Med.* [f. LYMPH + ADENOPATHY.] Disease of the lymph nodes.

1920 *Bull. Johns Hopkins Hosp.* XXXI. 413/2 An acute infection associated with lymphadenopathy and lymphocytosis. **1973** *Nature* 27 July 206/2 The pertinent findings on physical examination were marked gingival hypertrophy, lymphadenopathy, petechiae of the lower extremities, and hepatomegaly.

†**'lymphæduct.** *Obs.* Also 7 **lymphiduct**, 7–8 **lympheduct**, 9 **lymphoduct**. [ad. mod.L. *lymphæductus*, f. *lymphæ* gen. of *lympha* LYMPH + *ductus* leading; formed after *aquæductus* AQUEDUCT.] = LYMPHATIC B.

1664 POWER *Exp. Philos.* III. 191 We had yet never known.. the Blood's Circulation, the Lymphiducts, and other admirable Curiosities in this fabrick of our Selves. **1691** RAY *Creation* II. (1692) 30 Certain Water-pipes or Lymphæ-ducts inserted in the Bulb of the Eye. **1694** W. WOTTON *Anc. & Mod. Learn.* (1697) 219 The Lympheducts.. were not fully traced till Steno and Briggs described them. **1725** BRADLEY *Fam. Dict.* s.v. *Skin*, Nervous Fibres.. full of Glandules and Lympheducts. **1768** CHESELDEN *Anat.* 209 Lymphæducts are small pellucid cylindrical tubes, which arise invisible from the extremities of the arteries.

b. In plants: A sap-vessel.

1672–3 GREW *Anat. Plants* II. iii. (1682) 68 Whether all Roots have Lymphæducts, is doubtful. **1675** *Phil. Trans.* X. 487 In some of which he finds Sap vessels to be only lymphæducts.

‖**lymphæmia** (lɪm'fiːmɪə). *Path.* [mod.L., f. L. *lympha* LYMPH + Gr. αἷμα blood.] (See quot.)

1889 *Syd. Soc. Lex. Lymphæmia*, a synonym of Leucocythæmia. **1898** *Allbutt's Syst. Med.* V. 635 [Virchow] drew a distinction between a lymphatic form of the disease in which there is an admixture in the blood of leucocytes from the enlarged lymphatic glands—'lymphæmia'—and a splenic form.

lymphagogue ('lɪmfəgɒg). *Med.* [f. LYMPH + Gr. ἀγωγός leading.] Something adapted to produce or increase the flow of lymph.

1892 STARLING *Elem. Hum. Physiol.* 73 The flow of lymph.. is also increased by the injection of certain substances into the blood. These substances have been termed lymphagogues by Heidenhain.

‖**lymphangiectasis** (,lɪmfændʒɪ'ɛktəsɪs). *Path.* [mod.L., f. as LYMPHANGIOMA + ECTASIS.] Dilatation of the lymphatics.

1882 *Quain's Dict. Med.*, *Lymphangiectasis*,.. lymphatic varix, or varicose dilatation of lymphatic vessels. **1899** *Allbutt's Syst. Med.* VI. 443 The dilatation of the lymphatics, or lymphangiectasis, may be very diffuse.

Hence **,lymphangiec'tatic** *a.*

(In recent Dicts.)

lymphangiography (,lɪmfændʒɪ'ɒgrəfɪ). *Med.* [f. LYMPH + ANGIOGRAPHY.] A technique or procedure for demonstrating and examining the lymph vessels *in vivo* by injecting a contrast medium into them and examining them with X-rays; an examination by this technique.

1941 DORLAND & MILLER *Med. Dict.* (ed. 19) 830/1 *Lymphangiography*, the roentgenologic visualization of lymphatic vessels following the injection of contrast medium. **1952** *Clin. Sci.* XI. 13 (*heading*) Lymphangiography in man. **1961** *Radiology* LXXVI. 179/1 Lymphangiography, the radiographic demonstration of the lymphatic system by intralymphatic injection of contrast material, has opened a new field of investigation. **1973** J. F. MEANEY et al. *Complications & Legal Implications Radiologic Special Procedures* ix. 92 Lymphangiography is usually considered a relatively simple procedure. *Ibid.*, Many outpatients having lymphangiographies do not have their temperatures recorded.

Hence **lym'phangiogram**, a radiograph taken by this technique; **,lymphangi'ographer**, one who carries out or employs lymphangiography; **lym,phangio'graphic** *a.*; **lym,phangio'graphically** *adv.*

1955 *Brit. Med. Jrnl.* 16 Apr. 941/1 (*caption*) Normal lymphangiogram: 6 ml. of 70% diodone was injected and the films were exposed one minute later. **1964** *Clin. Radiol.* XV. 346/1 We have encountered only one serious reaction during our series of fifty-five lymphangiograms. **1967** A. RÜTTIMANN *Progress Lymphology* 127 (*heading*) Lymphangiographic evaluation of lymphoma. **1968** *Proc. Conf. Lymph & Lymphatic Syst.* vii. 154 Kinmonth and associates reported the largest series of patients studied lymphangiographically. **1973** J. F. MEANEY et al. *Complications & Legal Implications Radiologic Special Procedures* ix. 99 Every lymphangiographer should be aware of the potential danger.

‖**lymphangioma** (lɪmfændʒɪ'əʊmə). *Path.* Pl. **-omata** (-'əʊmətə). [mod.L., f. as next + *-oma*, after *carcinoma*, etc.] A morbid growth in the lymphatics. Hence **lymphangi'omatous** *a.*

1876 DUHRING *Dis. Skin* 70 Blood vessels and lymphatics are also the seat of new growths, as seen in angioma and lymphangioma of the skin. **1899** *Allbutt's Syst. Med.* VI. 456 Some mesenteric cysts.. may be due to dilatation of lymphatic vessels and to lymphangiomatous growth.

‖**lymphangitis** (lɪmfæn'dʒaɪtɪs). *Path.* Also **-angeitis, -angiitis**. [mod.L., f. *lympha* LYMPH + Gr. ἀγγεῖον vessel + -ITIS. Cf. F. *lymphangite*.] Inflammation of the walls of the lymphatic vessels.

1842 DUNGLISON *Dict. Med. Sci.* (ed. 3) 425/2 Lymphangeitis. **1861** BUMSTEAD *Ven. Dis.* (1879) 128 Gonorrhœal lymphangitis may either be seated in the principal trunks or in the reticular network of these vessels. **1889** *Syd. Soc. Lex.* Lymphangiitis. **1898** P. MANSON *Trop. Diseases* xxxi. 470 Lymphangitis is a common occurrence in all forms of filarial disease. **1960** R. A. RUNNELLS et al. *Princ. Vet. Path.* xxii. 691/1 Epizootic lymphangitis is a chronic suppurative infection of horses, mules, and donkeys caused by the fungus *Zymonema farciminosum*. **1966** WRIGHT & SYMMERS *Systemic Path.* I. xxvi. 803/2 Elephantiasis of the penis and scrotum... Repeated attacks of lymphangiitis and the presence of a sufficient number of worms may, in the

course of time, block so many lymph channels that chronic oedema develops.

†'**lymphate**, *pa. pple. Obs. rare*⁻¹. [ad. L. *lymphāt-us*, pa. pple. of *lymphāre*, f. *lympha* water.] Diluted with water.

1610 BARROUGH *Meth. Physick* xxxi. (1639) 51 If his body be weake, let him drink wine well lymphate, or small Ale.

†'**lymphate**, *v. Obs. rare*⁻⁰. In 7 **lymphat**. [f. L. *lymphāt-*, ppl. stem of *lymphāre*: cf. LYMPHATIC.] *trans.* To drive mad.

1623 in COCKERAM.

Hence †**lymphated** *ppl. a.*, frenzied.

1727 in BAILEY vol. II. **1755** in JOHNSON. **1817** J. F. PENNIE *Roy. Minstrel* VI. 525 But a more furious storm rag'd in the breast Of the lymphated Saul.

lymphatic (lɪm'fætɪk), *a.* and *sb.* Also 7-8 **lymphatick**, (8 **limphatic**). [ad. L. *lymphātic-us* mad, frenzied, f. *lympha* LYMPH. In mod. scientific Latin the word has been used in the sense 'pertaining to lymph' (the ending having been prob. misapprehended to be identical with that of *spermatic*, etc.); so F. *lymphatique*, It. *linfatico*.

The classical Lat. word is difficult to account for; perh. it may be due to the association of *lympha* with *νύμφη* (see LYMPH); cf. Gr. *νυμφιᾶν* to be frenzy-stricken.]

A. *adj.*

†**I. 1.** Frenzied, mad. *Obs.*

1656 BLOUNT *Glossogr.* **1711** SHAFTESB. *Charac.* (1737) I. 51 Poets are fanaticks too. And thus Horace either is, or feigns himself lymphatick, and shews what an effect the vision of the nymphs and Bacchus had on him. **1727** BAILEY vol. II, *Lymphatick Persons.* **1822** S. BURDER *Orient. Lit.* I. 120 The frog, like the tortoise and crocodile, was an emblem ..of lymphatic prophecy.

II. In senses connected with LYMPH.

2. a. *Phys.* and *Anat.* Pertaining to lymph; concerned in the secretion or conveyance of lymph, as in ***lymphatic gland, vessel***; ***lymphatic system***, the lymphatic vessels and glands collectively; ***lymphatic heart*** = *lymph-heart*. Also, of the nature of lymph as in ***lymphatic fluid, humour*** (? obs.).

1649 EVELYN *Mem.* (1857) I. 257 Came to visit me Dr. Ioyliffe, discoverer of the lymphatic vessels, and an excellent anatomist. **1663** BOYLE *Usef. Exp. Nat. Philos.* II. v. x. 224 The late anatomical discoveries of the motion of the chyle and limphatick liquor..hath yet made men cure diseases much better than before. **1732** ARBUTHNOT *Rules of Diet* 428 In the serous part of the Blood affecting the lymphatick Arteries. **1747** tr. *Astruc's Fevers* 351 A lymphatic or lacteal humour and the blood circulate from the mother into the placenta and fœtus. **1804** ABERNETHY *Surg. Obs.* 34 Perhaps originating in lymphatic glands. **1830** R. KNOX *Béclard's Anat.* 213 The Lymphatic System comprehends, 1st, the vessels which carry the lymph and chyle into the veins, and 2dly, Enlargements which occur in their course, and which are called conglobate glands, or lymphatic ganglia. **1870** ROLLESTON *Anim. Life* Introd. 59 Upon their junction with the veins of this latter region, contractile sacs, the so-called 'lymphatic hearts', are developed. **1899** *Allbutt's Syst. Med.* VI. 457 Growth of this kind should..be called..lymphatic gland sarcoma.

†**b.** *Bot.* Containing or conveying sap. *Obs.*

1672-3 GREW *Anat. Plants* II. iii. (1682) 69 Whence it should seem that Lymphatick Rays and Milky Rings are in that Root [Dandelion] so far mixed together. **1836** LOUDON *Encycl. Plants* Gloss., *Lymphatic*, of or belonging to lymph or sap.

3. Of persons and their temperaments: Having the characteristics (flabby muscles, pale skin, sluggishness of vital and mental action) formerly supposed to result from an excess of lymph in the system.

1834 J. FORBES *Laennec's Dis. Chest* (ed. 4) 319 In..persons of a lymphatic habit, the skin becomes white. **1858** HAWTHORNE *Fr. & It. Note-Bks.* II. 31 A widow..of an easy, lymphatic, cheerful temperament. **1859** G. MEREDITH *R. Feverel* xxxv, With lymphatic approbation. **1872** HUXLEY *Physiol.* iii. 72 Persons of flabby, or what is called lymphatic constitution. **1885** *Truth* 28 May 850/2 Her flesh being.. lymphatic, and her outlines wanting in firmness.

B. *sb.*

†**1.** A lunatic, a madman. (See A. 1.) *Obs.*

1708 SHAFTESB. *Charac.* (1711) I. 50 All Nations have their Lymphaticks of some kind or another. *a* **1763** SHENSTONE *Elegies* xvi. 34 From Bethlem's walls the poor lymphatic stray'd.

2. Chiefly *pl.* Vessels similar to veins, whose special function is the conveyance of lymph. †Also applied to the sap-vessels in plants. *Obs.*

1667 *Phil. Trans.* II. 509 The trunk of the Lymphaticks. **1707** FLOYER *Physic. Pulse-Watch* 145 The Tumour.. breaks the Limphatics which abound near the Liver. **1768** HEWSON in *Phil. Trans.* LVIII. 219 Into this lymphatic some small branches from the kidneys seem to enter. **1826** GOOD *Bk. Nat.* (1834) I. 164 Like the perfect plant, it possesses lymphatics and air-vessels. **1881** MIVART *Cat* 349 The small lymphatics originate by the junction of nucleated cells.

†**lym'phatical**, *a.* and *sb. Obs.* [f. prec. + -AL¹.] **A.** *adj.* **a.** Of persons: Frenzied. **b.** Of or pertaining to frenzy; visionary. **B.** *sb.* A frenzied person (Cockeram 1623).

1603 HARSNET *Pop. Impost.* Pref., The Lymphaticall Priests of Baal. **1678** R. L'ESTRANGE *Seneca's Mor.* (1702) 106 For Captivity, Wounds and Chains, he only looks upon as false, and lymphatical Terrours. **1718** BP. HUTCHINSON *Witchcraft* Ded. 11 Witches, Conjurers, and Fairies, and all that Lymphatical Chimæra.

†**lym'phation**. *Obs.* [ad. L. *lymphātiōn-em*, n. of action f. *lymphāre* (see LYMPHATE *v.*).] The action of driving mad.

1623 in COCKERAM. **1712** OLDISWORTH *Odes Horace* x. 26/1 By *το metu* in the foregoing verse he understands Madness, Enthusiasm, Lymphation.

lymphatism ('lɪmfətɪz(ə)m). *Path.* [f. LYMPHAT-IC + -ISM.] (See quot.)

1878 HOBLYN *Dict. Med. Terms* (ed. 10) *Lymphatism*, a term recently associated with scrofula, from the idea that scrofula is the highest expression of the lymphatic temperament.

lymphault, obs. form of LIMPHALT.

'**lymphic**, *a. Obs. rare*⁻⁰. [f. LYMPH + -IC.] = LYMPHATIC *a.*

1681 tr. *Willis' Rem. Med. Wks.* Vocab.

†'**lymphid**, *a.* [f. L. *lympha* LYMPH, perh. after *limpid*.] = LYMPHOID.

1647-7 J. MOLINS *Anat. Obs.* (1896) 23 All parts being repleat with the Lymphid matter.

‖**lymphitis** (lɪm'faɪtɪs). *Path.* [f. LYMPH + -ITIS. Cf. F. *lymphite*.] = LYMPHANGITIS.

1861 BUMSTEAD *Ven. Dis.* (1879) 416 Simple lymphitis may be due to any of the causes already mentioned as producing a simple bubo.

lympho- ('lɪmfəʊ), comb. form of LYMPH 3, used in numerous biological and medical terms, as '**lymphoblast** *Biol.* [-BLAST], any cell which is a precursor of a small lymphocyte; so **lympho'blastic** *a.*; ˌ**lymphobla'stoma** *Path.* [-OMA], malignant proliferation of lymphoblasts; **lympho'genic** [-GENIC], **lym'phogenous** [-GENOUS], (*a*) producing lymph or lymphocytes; (*b*) arising in, produced by, or disseminated via the lymphatic system; '**lymphokine** *Immunol.* [f. Gr. *κινεῖν* to move], any of various soluble substances released by lymphocytes following activation by contact with an antigen which are thought to be involved in cell-mediated immunity but to lack the antigen-specificity of antibodies; **lympho'penia** [-PENIA], reduction in the number of lymphocytes in the blood; **lymphopoiesis** (-pɔɪ'iːsɪs) [-POIESIS], the formation of lymphocytes; so **lymphopoi'etic** *a.*

1909 *Cent. Dict.* Suppl., Lymphoblast. **1935** *Jrnl. Amer. Med. Assoc.* 7 Sept. 765/2 Lymphoblasts approach the structure of myeloblasts. **1962** *Lancet* 27 Jan. 206/2 In the early stages of the production pathway, the lymphocytes are large and possess an intensely basophilic cytoplasm; these are the cells which have often been called lymphoblasts. **1905** *Ibid.* 12 Aug. 465/2 Dr. Jones concluded,..secondly, that apparently a lymphoblastic marrow was usually accompanied by an increased production of erythroblasts, but that, on the other hand, a leucoblastic marrow was not associated with increased erythroblastic production. **1961** *Ibid.* 5 Aug. 291/2 In 2 cases biopsy of a lymph-gland was undertaken and reported as lymphoblastic lymphoma. **1920** *Jrnl. Urol.* IV. 137 (*title*) Lympho-blastoma (lymphosarcoma) of the prostate. **1926** *Jrnl. Amer. Med. Assoc.* 17 Apr. 1185/1 Lymphoblastoma, a name considered by some as synonymous with malignant lymphoma..may include lymphatic leukemia (lymphocytic and lymphoblastic), aleukemic lymphatic leukemia (pseudoleukemia, aleukemic lymphadenosis), lymphocytoma, Hodgkin's disease (lymphogranuloma), lymphadenoma, lymphomatosis, lymphosarcoma, round cell sarcoma, leukosarcoma and lymphadenosarcoma. **1970** S. D. KOBERNICK tr. *Masson's Human Tumors* II. x. 353 The structure is very simple: a chaotic mixture of small cells with round nuclei, larger in lymphoblastomas than in lymphocytomas. **1901** Lymphogenic [see LYMPHOMATOSIS]. **1968** *Proc. Conf. Lymph & Lymphatic Syst.* viii. 173 Experimental animals with lymphogenic encephalopathy have decreased response to pain. **1889** *Syd. Soc. Lex.*, *Lymphogenous*, producing lymph. **1909** *Practitioner* Nov. 656 The unilateral distribution of renal tuberculosis..is explained by lymphogenous infection. **1935** N. P. SHERWOOD *Immunol.* iii. 59. The four avenues [of spread of infectious agents] commonly mentioned are surface spread, dissemination by way of the lymphatics (lymphogenous), blood stream (hematogenous) and direct extension to adjacent tissues. **1968** *Proc. Conf. Lymph. & Lymphatic Syst.* viii. 169 (*heading*) Lymphogenous encephalopathy. **1969** D. C. DUMONDE et al. in *Nature* 4 38/1 In the guinea-pig these four phenomena are mediated by cell-free soluble factors, which are generated during interaction of sensitized lymphocytes with specific antigen, but which are expressed without reference to immunological specificity. The generic term 'lymphokine' is suggested to describe this group of biological activities. **1973** *Ibid.* 2 Mar. 22/2 When T cells are activated by antigen, they proliferate..but they..do not become antibody-secreting cells. They do, however, secrete a variety of non-antigen-specific factors ('lymphokines') such as migration inhibition factors (MIF), chemotactic factors, cytotoxic factors and mitogenic factors, at least some of which presumably play a role in cell-mediated immune responses, for which T cells are primarily responsible. **1974** *Sci. Amer.* Apr. 36/2 Transplantation antigens and other foreign material..stimulate the production and release of 'sensitized' lymphocytes, or effector cells... In addition to killing graft cells directly the sensitized lymphocytes secrete a variety of chemical agents called lymphokines, some of which act directly on the foreign cells and some of which attract other leukocytes..which digest damaged cells and cell fragments. **1909** *Cent. Dict.* Suppl., Lymphopenia. **1921** *Lancet* 10 Dec. 1205/2 The blood content passes from exhibiting a lymphopænia to a lymphocytosis. **1964** L. MARTIN *Clin. Endocrinol.* (ed. 4) i. 35 A leucocytosis of 10–15,000 per c.mm. is usual with a polymorph excess, lymphopenia and eosinopenia. **1918** STEDMAN *Med. Dict.* (ed. 5) 569/1 *Lymphopoiesis*,..the formation of lymphocytes. **1968** PASSMORE & ROBSON *Compan. Med. Stud.* I. xxvii. 2/2 In the lymphoreticular organs the reticulum cells..also differentiate into stem cells which divide and mature to form lymphocytes in the process known as lymphopoiesis. **1915** J. E. R. MCDONAGH *Biol. & Treatm. Venereal Dis.* xv. 144 (*heading*) Syphilis of the lympho- and haemopoetic [*sic*] system. **1966** M. W. ELVES *Lymphocytes* iii. 71 The lymphopoietic role of the thymus.

lymphocyte ('lɪmfəsaɪt). *Phys.* [f. *lympho-* comb. f. LYMPH + -CYTE.] A kind of small leucocyte which has a single round nucleus and little or no granulation in the cytoplasm, constitutes about a quarter of the total leucocytes in the blood stream, is found in large numbers in the lymph nodes and other lymphoid tissue, and is a major agent in most immunological processes. ***large lymphocytes***, which constitute a small proportion of the total number of lymphocytes, are larger than and apparently the precursors of the ***small lymphocytes***, which constitute the bulk of them.

1890 *Jrnl. Morphol.* IV. 108 It is quite generally agreed that the origin of the white corpuscles of the blood is to be found in the lymph leucocytes, or lymphocytes, to borrow a convenient term... The lymphocytes are characterized by a vesicular nucleus, usually with a nucleolus and a scanty reticulum, and by a very small protoplasmic envelope. **1891** *Rep. Lab. R. Coll. Physicians Edin.* III. 118 If this view of the nature of leucocytes is accepted, we at once realise the futility of the attempts..to establish distinctions between the leucocytes found in different situations,—the white blood corpuscles, the wandering cells in the tissues, the lymphocytes of the lymph, lymph-glands and spleen, the thymus-cells, the marrow-cells, &c. **1896** *Allbutt's Syst. Med.* I. 730 He recommends subcutaneous injections of pilocarpine, in order to raise artificially the number and ratio of the lymphocytes. **1905** A. STENGEL tr. *Ehrlich's Dis. Blood* 71 At the introduction to this chapter it was pointed out that a retrograde movement in hematology is in progress which attempts to establish the derivation of all the white blood-cells from the lymphocytes. **1913** GULLAND & GOODALL *Blood* II. vii. 58 Large lymphocytes have the same general characters as the small lymphocytes. **1962** *Lancet* 26 May 1098/2 The blood-picture was:..eosinophils 2%, lymphocytes 11%, monocytes 1%, [etc.]. **1968** PASSMORE & ROBSON *Compan. Med. Stud.* I. xxvii. 4/2 Lymphocytes, or more properly small lymphocytes, to distinguish them from their immediate precursors, the medium and large lymphocytes, are formed in the cortex of lymph nodes by the maturation and division of lymphoblasts and lymphoid stem cells. **1970** *Courier-Mail* (Brisbane) 28 Jan. 30 Unfortunately this desensitisation technique seems to affect only a proportion of the recipient's lymphocytes: the remainder attack the transplant.

attrib. **1902** *Brit. Med. Jrnl.* 5 Apr. 832 *note*, There was.. a high lymphocyte percentage.

Hence ˌ**lympho'cytic** *a.*, of or pertaining to, or characterized by the presence of, lymphocytes; ˌ**lymphocy'toma** (pl. **-'tomas, -'tomata**) *Path.* [-OMA], malignant proliferation of lymphocytes; any condition characterized by this; a tumour composed of lymphocytes; ˌ**lymphocy'tomatous** *a.*

1896 *Allbutt's Syst. Med.* I. 730 The number of 'neutrophile' cells falls rapidly, while the uninuclear or lymphocytic elements increase. **1908** OSLER & MCCRAE *Syst. Med.* IV. 827 The hyperplastic and neoplasm-like conditions of the lymph nodes depending upon an overgrowth of cells of the type of lymphocytes..are here brought into one general class, the lymphocytomata. This includes all the lymphocytomatous tumors classed variously as lymphoma, lymphadenoma, lymphosarcoma, pseudoleukæmia, adenia, lymphadenomatosis, lymphomatosis, etc. **1920** J. E. R. MCDONAGH *Venereal Dis.* iv. 55 (*heading*) Syphilitic lymphocytomata. **1949** *Year Bk. Radiol.* 406 The medical profession has believed that no attempt at treatment of lymphoid tumors (lymphosarcoma, lymphocytoma, Hodgkin's disease and macrofollicular lymphoma) will be successful.

‖**lymphocytosis** (ˌlɪmfəʊsaɪ'təʊsɪs). *Phys.* [f. LYMPHOCYTE + -OSIS.] A morbid increase in the number of lymphocytes.

1896 *Allbutt's Syst. Med.* I. 730 In the lymphocytosis he sees a prognostic sign of great value. **1900** *Allchin's Man. Med.* II. 291 The lymphocytes are generally increased to the greatest extent (lymphocytosis).

lymphœdema (lɪmfɪ'diːmə). *Path.* Also **lymphedema**. [f. LYMPH + ŒDEMA.] Œdema resulting from obstruction of lymph vessels or lymph nodes.

1889 *Syd. Soc. Lex.*, Lymphœdema. **1961** *Lancet* 19 Aug. 408/1 The XO female was noted to have peripheral lymphœdema and neck-webbing at birth. **1968** *Proc. Conf. Lymph & Lymphatic Syst.* vii. 153 In 1892, Milroy reported congenital, bilateral lymphedema of the legs in twenty-five of ninety-two members of one family.

Hence **lymphœ'dematous** *a.*

1934 *Arch. Internal Med.* LIV. 614 Lymphedematous swelling..is present at birth. **1962** D. I. ABRAMSON *Blood Vessels & Lymphatics* xxiv. 733 The protein content of tissue fluid from the lymphedematous area was similar to that of the serum.

lymphogranuloma (ˌlɪmfəʊgrænjʊ'ləʊmə). *Path.* [f. LYMPHO- + GRANULOMA.] Used, usu.

with mod.L. or Eng. adjs., to designate any of three diseases (see quot. 1958), esp. ***lymphogranuloma venereum*** (or ***lymphogranuloma inguinale***), a venereal disease, esp. of the tropics, caused by micro-organisms of the group Chlamydiæ, and manifested esp. as inflammation, followed by suppuration and breakdown, of the lymph nodes and lymph vessels, particularly in the inguinal region.

1924 J. SCHAUMANN in *Brit. Jrnl. Dermatol.* XXXVI. 515 When in November 1914, I described the disease I proposed designating by the anatomico-clinical name of benign lymphogranuloma, I had already detected the essential characteristics, which justified its classification amongst lymphadenic affections. **1932** DEWOLF & VAN CLEVE in *Jrnl. Amer. Med. Assoc.* 24 Sept. 1065/1 They [*sc.* Durand, Nicolas, and Favre] chose the name 'subacute inguinal lymphogranulomatosis' for the disease, a rather unfortunate designation because of the confusion to which it may lead. We have chosen the shorter designation, 'lymphogranuloma inguinale', as this name is becoming more widely used by European writers. **1958** R. W. RAVEN *Cancer* II. xxiv. 473 Few medical terms can have such different meanings in different countries as lymphogranuloma. When used without qualification, in English-speaking countries, 'lymphogranuloma' usually refers to 'lymphogranuloma inguinale' (Nicolas-Favré disease); in most European countries it implies Hodgkin's disease ('lymphogranuloma malignum') but in Scandinavia it refers to sarcoidosis ('lymphogranuloma benignum'). **1960** J. MARSHALL *Dis. Skin* xxv. 630 (*heading*) Hodgkin's disease (malignant lymphogranuloma of Paltauf-Sternberg). **1967** A. C. ALLEN *Skin* (ed. 2) xi. 423/1 At different stages in the evolution of the information on the disease, stress was placed on the involvement of one organ over others, as indicated by the application of the terms 'uveo-parotid fever', 'osteitis tuberculosa multiplex cystica', 'lupus pernio', and 'benign lymphogranuloma'. **1974** PASSMORE & ROBSON *Compan. Med. Stud.* III. xiii. 13/2 Lymphogranuloma venereum. Alternative names for this disease are lymphogranuloma inguinale and tropical bubo. It is caused by *Chlamydia* or *Bedsonia*.

lymphogranulomatosis (ˌlɪmfəʊgrænjʊləʊməˈtəʊsɪs). *Path.* [f. *lymphogranulomat-*, taken as stem of prec. + -OSIS.] Used, usu. with mod.L. or Eng. adjs., to designate any of three diseases, viz. ***lymphogranulomatosis benigna***, sarcoidosis; ***lymphogranulomatosis inguinalis*** [tr. F. *lymphogranulomatose inguinale* (Durand et al. 1913, in *Bull. et Mém. Soc. méd. d. Hôp. de Paris* XXXV. 274)], lymphogranuloma venereum; ***lymphogranulomatosis maligna***, Hodgkin's disease.

1911 DORLAND *Med. Dict.* (ed. 6) 470/1 *Lymphogranulomatosis*..Hodgkin's disease. **1915** J. E. R. MCDONAGH *Biol. & Treatm. Venereal Dis.* xlvi. 550 This case..would probably have been called lymphogranulomatosis on the Continent, and lymphadenoma or Hodgkin's disease affecting the skin in this country. **1926** *Arch. Dermatol. & Syphilol.* XIV. 36 In January, 1913, Nicolas, Durand and Favré published a report concerning a series of cases of lymphatic enlargement of the groins which they named 'lymphogranulomatosis inguinalis'. **1932** [see LYMPHOGRANULOMA]. **1935** *Brit. Jrnl. Dermatol.* XLVII. 225 The symptomatic triad of benign lymphogranulomatosis. *Ibid.*, I attributed the diabetes to the presence of lymphogranulomatosis benigna in this organ. *Ibid.* 227 The polynuclear leucocytosis in malign lymphogranulomatosis (Hodgkin's disease). **1971** BRUNSON & GALL *Concepts of Dis.* xxv. 925/1 In the United States and Great Britain, Hodgkin's disease is regarded generally as a malignant neoplasm; in Germany it is considered to be a peculiar inflammatory process and is designated by the term *lymphogranulomatosis*. **1973** R. B. SCOTT *Price's Textbk. Pract. Med.* (ed. 11) ix. 874 Sarcoidosis. *Synonyms.* Lymphogranulomatosis benigna [etc.].

lymphography (lɪmˈfɒgrəfɪ). [f. *lympho-* comb. form of LYMPH + -GRAPHY.] **1.** A description of the lymphatic vessels, their origin and uses.

1828 in WEBSTER; and in later Dicts.

2. A technique similar to lymphangiography but including demonstration and examination of lymph nodes.

1935 DORLAND & MILLER *Med. Dict.* (ed. 17) 776/1 *Lymphography*, roentgen visualization of the lymph vessels and nodes after the injection of a contrast medium. **1969** *Brit. Med. Jrnl.* 6 Dec. 579/1 Lymphovenous shunts have been detected in patients by lymphography with Ultrafluid Lipiodol. **1973** J. F. MEANEY et al. *Complications & Legal Implications Radiologic Special Procedures* ix. 96 Fraimow et al. demonstrated the physiologic effects of lymphography on the lungs.

lymphoid (ˈlɪmfɔɪd), *a. Phys.* [f. LYMPH + -OID.] Resembling lymph, lymph corpuscles, or the tissue of lymphatic glands; occas. = LYMPHATIC.

1867 *Quain's Anat.* (ed. 7) III. p. cxcix, This structure which prevails in the mucous membrane of the stomach, and intestines..is sometimes named lymphoid tissue from its resemblance to the interior tissue of the lymphatic glands. **1874** *Q. Jrnl. Microscop. Sci.* XIV. 279 Spherical or lymphoid cells, of which all intermediate sizes exist,..are seen in the lymph canalicular system. **1879** REYNOLDS *Syst. Med.* V. 217 The tissue known..as 'adenoid' consists of lymphoid corpuscles embedded in the meshes of a 'retiform' stroma.

Also **lymˈphoidal** *a.*

(In recent Dicts.)

‖**lymphoma** (lɪmˈfəʊmə). *Path.* Pl. **lymphomata.** [f. LYMPH, after *carcinoma*, etc.] A tumour having the structure of a lymphatic gland.

1873 T. H. GREEN *Introd. Pathol.* (ed. 2) 142 The Lymphomata are new formations consisting of lymphatic.. tissue. **1897** *Allbutt's Syst. Med.* IV. 590 Sharp, who distinguishes between lymphosarcoma and lymphadenoma, considers that each starts from a lymphoma.

Hence **lymˈphomatous** *a.*, of the nature of or resembling a lymphoma.

1876 *Trans. Clinical Soc.* IX. 87 An examination of the growth microscopically did not show..that it was lymphomatous. **1892** W. OSLER *Princ. Med.* 27 The lymphomatous nephritis..produces as a rule no symptoms.

lymphomatosis (lɪmfəʊməˈtəʊsɪs). *Path.* [f. *lymphomat-* (taken as stem of mod.L. LYMPHOMA) + -OSIS.] Any of various diffuse neoplastic or hyperplastic disorders originating in lymphoid tissue.

1900 DORLAND *Med. Dict.* 368/2 *Lymphomatosis*, general lymphatic engorgement. **1901** *Encycl. Medica* VII. 196 Among them [*sc.* synonyms of lymphadenoma] are adenia, lymphadenia, lymphogenic diathesis, lymphadenosis, lymphoma, lymphomatosis, pseudo-leukemia, lymphosarcoma, and the non-committal Hodgkin's disease. **1933** *Jrnl. Exper. Med.* LVIII. 254 Lymphomatosis (lymphoid leukosis) of chickens is identical with the similar disease of mammals. **1947** *Radiology* XLIX. 354/1 Terminal changes were mainly of two types: generalized atrophy (premature aging) and mediastinal lymphomatosis. **1961** *Brit. Vet. Jrnl.* CXVII. 323 Much confusion has resulted from the use of the term 'visceral lymphomatosis', which some workers understand to be a genuine lymphoid leucosis, whilst others use it to designate the visceral lesions associated with fowl paralysis. **1965** *New Scientist* 17 June 800/2 The three main leukaemias of poultry—lymphomatosis, erythroblastosis and myeloblastosis. **1970** JUBB & KENNEDY *Path. Domestic Animals* (ed. 2) I. iv. 386/1 All primary tumours of the lymphoreticular tissues are malignant... These tumours occur in all domestic animals. .. Very many names have been applied to them depending on the pattern of growth, the presence or absence of 'leucaemic' changes in the circulating blood, and the judgement of the observer on what was the chief cell involved. In the following discussion we shall include them all in the designation lymphomatosis.

‖**lymphorrhagia** (lɪmfəʊˈreɪdʒɪə). [f. *lympho-* comb. form of LYMPH + Gr. -ραγία a bursting.] A discharge of lymph produced by the bursting of a lymphatic vessel.

1876 tr. *Wagner's Gen. Pathol.* (ed. 6) 224 Lymphorrhagia is a term used to express the flow of lymph out of its natural channels. **1897** *Allbutt's Syst. Med.* II. 1078 The debilitating effects of the recurring attacks of lymphorrhagia.

Hence ˌ**lymphoˈrrhagic** *a.*, of or pertaining to lymphorrhagia.

1882 *Quain's Dict. Med.* s.v. *Lymphorrhagia*, A lymphorrhagic diathesis.

‖ˌ**lymphosarˈcoma.** *Path.* [f. as prec. + SARCOMA.] A sarcoma containing lymphoid cells, so as to resemble a lymphatic gland.

1874 JONES & SIEV. *Pathol. Anat.* (ed. 2) 155 When the proportion of cells is very large, Virchow has applied the name lymphosarcoma. **1898** J. HUTCHINSON in *Arch. Surg.* IX. 325 A case in which the adenitis of syphilis..passed on into lympho-sarcoma.

Hence ˌ**lympho-sarˈcomatous** *a.*

1880 M. MACKENZIE *Dis. Throat & Nose* I. 84 Cases..of the..lympho-sarcomatous character.

lymphotomy (lɪmˈfɒtəmɪ). [f. as prec. + Gr. -(ο)τομία cutting.] Dissection of the lymphatics.

1856 in MAYNE *Expos. Lex.*

lymphous (ˈlɪmfəs), *a. Phys.* [f. LYMPH + -OUS.] †**a.** Of vegetable fluids: Watery (*obs.*). **b.** Of animal fluids: Containing, of the nature of, or resembling lymph.

1672-3 GREW *Anat. Plants* II. iii. (1682) 67 The Milky Saps..agree, in being more Oyly than any of the Lymphous Saps. **1876** W. ROBERTS *Urin. & Renal Dis.* II. iv. (ed. 3) 323 The coagulum in lymphous urine resembles calf's foot or currant jelly. **1897** *Allbutt's Syst. Med.* II. 1078 The lymphous fluid soiling the patient's clothes.

lymphy (ˈlɪmfɪ), *a. Phys.* [f. LYMPH + -Y.] Of the nature of or resembling lymph.

1848 in WEBSTER. **1855** RAMSBOTHAM *Obstetr. Med.* 49 They are entirely destitute of the rich, interstitial, lymphy deposit. **1897** *Allbutt's Syst. Med.* II. 424 In the first or croupo-fibrinous variety [of dysentery] the lymphy or fibrinous deposit is of varying thickness and consistency.

†**lympold,** *v. Obs.* [? f. ***lympold*, var. of LIMPHALT *a.*] *trans.* To defeat (an opponent) at tables by one of the two methods recognized by the laws of the game. Hence **lympolding.**

a **1400** [see LURCHING *vbl. sb.*[2]].

lymtake: see *limb-take*, LIMB *sb.*[1] 5.

lymyter, -tour(e, obs. forms of LIMITER.

lyn, obs. form of LIE *v.*[1], LINE, LINN.

lyn, obs. pa. pple. LIE *v.*[1]

lynage, lynce, obs. ff. LINEAGE, LYNX.

lyncean (lɪnˈsiːən), *a.* Also 7 **lincean,** 7-9 **lyncæan,** 9 **lynxean.** [f. L. *lyncē-us* (a. Gr. λύγκειος, f. λύγξ LYNX) + -AN.

Some of the writers who have used the word have perh. intended a reference to *Lynceus*, the name of one of the Argonauts, celebrated for his sharp sight; cf. 'a more piercing Linceus sight' (Nashe *Lenten Stuffe* (1599) 67).]

Of the eyes, sight, etc.: Resembling that of a lynx, keen; also of persons: lynx-like; sharp-sighted.

1622 BP. HALL *Serm.* V. 129 Justice cannot be too lyncean to the being of things. *a* **1678** MARVELL *Def. John Howe* Wks. 1875 IV. 181, I wonder how in this lyncean perspicacity It oversaw a more remarkable errour of Mr. Howe's. **1793** W. ROBERTS *Looker-on* No. 85 (1794) III. 364 It was not long ere the..lyncean vigilance of the Baron detected the exchange of letters. **1816** KIRBY & SP. *Entomol.* II. 219 Hunted for by the lyncean eye of an entomologist. **1819** TURTON *Conchol. Dict.* p. xviii, This laborious and lyncean naturalist. [In mod. Dicts.]

†ˈ**lynceous,** *a. Obs.* Also 6 **lincious,** 7 **lyncius.** [formed as prec. + -OUS.] = LYNCEAN.

1592 R. D. *Hypnerotomachia* 82 b, Yet with a lincious eye, I never left to examine..the extreame beautie of the excellent Nymph. **1656** BLOUNT *Glossogr.*, *Lynceous.*

lyncet, variant of LINESEAT *Obs.*

lynch (lɪnʃ), *v.* Orig. *U.S.* [f. *Lynch*: see LYNCH LAW.] *trans.* To condemn and punish by lynch law. In early use, implying chiefly the infliction of punishment such as whipping, tarring and feathering, or the like; now only, to inflict sentence of death by lynch law.

1836 *Niles' Reg.* 1 Oct. 69/1 Some personal friend of Mr. Bronx..proceeded to the mansion of judge Bermudez, with a view to Lynch him. **1839** MARRYAT *Diary Amer.* Ser. I. III. 240 It may appear strange that people should be lynched for the mere vice of gambling. **1856** EMERSON *Eng. Traits* (1857) 154 The prison was burst open by the mob, and George [of Cappadocia] was lynched, as he deserved. **1884** SIR L. H. GRIFFIN *Gt. Repub.* 151 It is..unreasonable to insist on the guilt of an unfortunate who has been lynched after an acquittal in open court.

transf. **1839** LONGF. in *Life* (1891) I. 329, I have Lynched all the trees,—that is, tarred them.

¶ App. misused for: To render infamous.

1835 DISRAELI 9 May in *Corr. w. Sister* (1886) 37 If all the O'Connells were to challenge me, I could not think of meeting them now. I consider and everyone else that they are lynched.

lynch, variant of LINCH *sb.*[2]

lyncher (ˈlɪnʃə(r)). [f. LYNCH *v.* + -ER[1].] One who lynches; one who punishes or helps to punish by lynch law, esp. one who puts (an offender) to death by summary process.

1839 *Niles' Reg.* 15 June 256/2 Lynchers punished. **1847** *Harbinger* 7 Aug. 136/1 The company of lynchers once formed, they proceed to the execution of summary justice. **1881** *Times* 21 Feb. 5/6 The mob of lynchers numbered 200.

lynchet (ˈlɪnʃɪt). Forms: 7- **lynchet(t,** 9 **linchard,** 8-9 **linchet.** [f. LINCH *sb.*[2]; perh. by confusion with *lanchet*, LANDSHARD.]

1. A strip of green land between two pieces of ploughed land.

1674 RAY *S. & E.C. Words* 71 *A Lynchett*, a green balk to divide lands. *a* **1722** LISLE *Husb.* (1752) 67 There happened in this ground to be a linchet ploughed up in the winter. **1863** BARNES *Dorset Gloss.*, *Linchet* or *Linch*, *Lynchet* or *Lynch*,..the strip of green ground between two ploughed ledges. **1893** *Wiltshire Gloss.*, *Linch, Linchet,..Linchard*, &c.

2. A slope or terrace along the face of a chalk down. (Cf. LINCH *sb.*[2]). Also *attrib.*

1797 [see LINCH *sb.*[2]]. **1844** *Jrnl. R. Agric. Soc.* V. I. 169 The parings from road-sides, old banks, and linchets, ant-hills, &c., are burnt. **1888** T. HARDY *Wessex Tales* (1889) 26 The 'lynchets', or flint slopes, which belted the escarpment at intervals of a dozen yards. **1898** —— *Wessex Poems* 135 That Highway the Icen, Which trails its pale riband down Wessex O'er lynchet and lea. **1917** J. MASEFIELD *Old Front Line* 42 The line of the lynchet-top merges into the slope behind it.

b. *Archæol.* A cultivation terrace. Also *attrib.*

1796 *Gentl. Mag.* LXVI. 822/1 On the declivities of the elevated and chalky tracts of Wiltshire, Dorsetshire, and other counties, there very frequently occurs a beautiful assemblage of *terraces*, mostly horizontal, and rising in a continued series like the steps of Egyptian pyramids... These, which are commonly arable,..are popularly called *lynchets*... They are generally regarded in the neighbourhood as the offspring of human exertion in remote ages, to facilitate and extend the dominion of the plough. **1869** D. MACKINTOSH *Scenery Eng. & Wales* IV. ii. 89 Many terraces are still cultivated but..there is..a general desire to plough down the 'lynchets' (as they are locally called), and ..formerly their number was much greater than at present. **1908** A. H. ALLCROFT *Earthwork of Eng.* ii. 40 All but the very summits of the highest Downs were early ploughed, and the lynchets must in many cases be of mediæval, if not of Saxon date. **1953** R. J. C. ATKINSON *Field Archaeol.* (ed. 2) 19 When lynchets (cultivation terraces) are photographed facing a setting sun, the sloping faces of the terraces..will reflect more light than the surrounding ground. **1954** M. BERESFORD *Lost Villages* ix. 297 On the valley sides are lynchet-like terraces which look as if they mark where the ploughs moved. **1968** J. ARNOLD *Shell Bk. Country Crafts* 13 Celtic farmers increased the areas of their arable land by excavating some of the hillsides and making terraces or lynchets.

Hence ˈ**lynchetted** *ppl. a.*, of land: cultivated in this way.

1928 *Antiquity* June 171 To the south and west of the lynchetted area lies what is known as 'The Druid's Circle'. **1933** *Ibid.* VII. 494 The..rarity in Cumbria of the lynchetted form of settlement. **1954** S. PIGGOTT *Neolithic Cultures* ii. 33 Certain types of settlement, characterized by huts within irregular lynchetted areas, may be Neolithic in date.

lynching (ˈlɪnʃɪŋ), *vbl. sb.* [f. LYNCH *v.* + -ING¹.] The action of LYNCH *v.*; an instance of this.

1836 D. CROCKETT *Exploits & Adventures Texas* vii. 103 This is what we call Lynching in Natchez. **1837** *Southern Lit. Messenger* III. 648 The outrages of the borderers, the frontier law of 'regulation' or 'lynching', which is common to new countries all over the world, are ascribed to slavery. **1839** *Niles' Reg.* 14 Dec. 256/1 Horrible lynching. **1901** *N. Amer. Rev.* Feb. 281 Lynchings in the South are mainly caused by the peculiar nature of the crimes for which lynching is a penalty.

attrib. **1879** SIR G. CAMPBELL *White & Black* 171 Several lynching cases of atrocity occured before I had been many weeks in the States. **1884** SIR L. H. GRIFFIN *Gt. Repub.* 148 He was taken to the scene of the crime by a lynching party. **1900** *Congress Rec.* 31 Jan. 1369/1 They have sometimes had 'lynching bees',..they have sometimes lynched men for murder, for arson, for rape. **1903** C. T. BRADY *Bishop* ix. 172, I don't join no more lynchin'-bees. **1943** *Christian Cent.* 1 Dec. 1/2 Evidently there is a widespread and growing fear lest the United Nations..let loose in Europe what might turn out to be little less than a gigantic lynching bee.

lynch law. Orig. *U.S.* Also **Lynch law**; in early use **Lynch's (Linch's) law.** The practice of inflicting summary punishment upon an offender, by a self-constituted court armed with no legal authority; it is now limited to the summary execution of one charged with some flagrant offence.

'The origin of the expression has not been determined. It is often asserted to have arisen from the proceedings of Charles Lynch, a justice of the peace in Virginia, who in 1782 was indemnified by an act of the Virginia Assembly for having illegally fined and imprisoned certain Tories in 1780. But Mr. Albert Matthews informs us that no evidence has been adduced to show that Charles Lynch was ever concerned in acts such as those which from 1817 onward were designated as "Lynch's law". It is possible that the perpetrators of these acts may have claimed that in the infliction of punishments not sanctioned by the laws of the country they were following the example of Lynch, which had been justified by the act of indemnity; or there may have been some other man of this name who was a ring-leader in such proceedings. Some have conjectured that the term is derived from the name of Lynche's Creek, in South Carolina, which is known to have been in 1768 a meeting-place of the "Regulators", a band of men whose professed object was to supply the want of regular administration of criminal justice in the Carolinas, and who committed many acts of violence on those suspected of "Toryism".' (N.E.D.)

The particulars supplied by Ellicott, together with other evidence, clearly establish the fact that the originator of Lynch law was Captain William Lynch (1742–1820) of Pittsylvania in Virginia. According to Ellicott, 'this self-created judicial tribunal was first organised in the state of Virginia about the year 1776'; an article in the *Southern Lit. Messenger* (1836) II. 389 gives the date definitely as 1780.

1811 A. ELLICOTT in C. V. Mathews *A. Ellicott* (1908) 220 Captain Lynch just mentioned was the author of the Lynch laws so well known and so frequently carried into effect some years ago in the southern States in violation of every principle of justice and jurisprudence. **1817** S. ROANE in W. Wirt *Life P. Henry* (1818) 372 In the year 1792, there were many suits on the south side of the James river, for inflicting Lynch's law. **1819** W. FAUX *Diary* 29 Nov. in *Memor. Days in Amer.* (1823) 304 The people [of Princeton, Indiana].. deputed four persons to inform him, that unless he quitted the town and state immediately, he should receive Lynch's law, that is, a whipping in the woods. **1828** J. HALL *Lett. fr. West* 291 No commentator has taken any notice of Linch's Law, which was once the *lex loci* of the frontiers. **1835** W. IRVING *Tour Prairies* 41 'Lynch's law', as it is technically termed, in which the plaintiff is apt to be witness, jury, judge, and executioner. **1839** STONEHOUSE *Axholme* 112 The burning Reading's house was..a terrible example of what the Americans term lynch law. **1879** FARRAR *St. Paul* I. 570 They seized the opportunity of executing a little Lynch law. **1888** BRYCE *Amer. Commw.* III. 309 Lynch law, however shocking it may seem to Europeans, is far removed from arbitrary violence. **1902** J. LONDON *Daughter of Snows* 284 It's lynch law, you know, and their minds are made up. They're bound to get me. **1963** *Times* 18 Apr. 9/1 It smacks more of lynch law than the reasoned kind of wisdom one hopes for in our elected officials. **1974** *Times* 28 Nov. 8/7 Mr Jeremy Thorpe..urged..that the hijackers of the British Airways VC10 should not be handed over to the 'lynch law' of the Palestine Liberation Organization.

So **lynch-court** *nonce-wd.*, a self-constituted tribunal for exercising lynch law; **Judge Lynch**, the imaginary authority from whom the sentences of lynch law are jocularly said to proceed; **lynch mob**, a mob intent on lynching.

1838 H. MARTINEAU *Retrospect of Western Travel* II. 87 A distant Lynch mob was outraging..a free and innocent citizen. **1840** W. G. SIMMS *Border Beagles* 248 The murmurs began to close with the ominous inquiry after that venerable border magistrate, Judge Lynch. **1849** LYELL *2nd Visit to U.S.* II. 32 My companions..said..'If you were a settler there [in Florida], and had no other law to defend you, you would be glad of the protection of Judge Lynch'. **1890** CORBETT *Drake* v. 73 Few prisoners fared so well at Westminster..as did Thomas Doughty at that first Lynch-court amidst the desolation of Patagonia. **1972** B. GARFIELD *Line of Succession* (1974) III. 255 If he pulls through alive you'll just have to hold off a lynch mob.

Lynch-like, *a.* [f. *Lynch*: see LYNCH LAW.] Characteristic or suggestive of Judge Lynch.

1837 R. M. BIRD *Nick of Woods* I. 221 Since Stackpole, having endured the penalty for stealing him, considered himself as having a legal, Lynch-like right to the animal, which no one could dispute.

lynch-man. [Cf. LYNCH LAW.] One of the early administrators of lynch law.

1811 A. ELLICOTT in C. V. Mathews *A. Ellicott* (1908) 221 The Lynch-men associated for the purpose of punishing crimes in a summary way without the tedious and technical forms of our courts of justice. *Ibid.* 222, I should not have asserted it as a fact had it not been related to me by Mr. Lynch..together with several other Lynch-men as they are called.

lyncine (ˈlɪnsaɪn), *a.* [f. L. *lync-*, LYNX + -INE¹.] Of or pertaining to the genus *Lynx*.

1863 WOOD *Nat. Hist.* (1874) 41 The Lyncine group.

†**lyncury.** *Obs.* In 7 lyncurie. [ad. L. *lyncūrium* or *lyncūrius*: see LIGURE.] = LIGURE.

1638 FEATLY *Strict. Lyndom.* I. 184 By the Jesuits rule no Physician..should make use of..Lyncurie, because it issueth out of the body of a spotted beast, called Lynx. **1650** TRAPP *Comm. Num.* 51 The precious stone Lyncurie may issue out of the body of the Lynx, an unclean and spotted beast.

lyne, obs. f. LEAN, LINE, pa. pple. of LIE *v.*¹

lynee, lynesey: see LIGNEE, LINSEY.

lyng(e, obs. pres. pple. LIE *v.*¹; obs. f. LINE.

Lyngby (ˈlɪŋbɪ). Also **Lingby.** [See quot. 1964.] Used *attrib.* or *ellipt.* to designate a mesolithic culture of the Baltic area or its artefacts (see quots.).

1925 V. G. CHILDE *Dawn European Civilization* i. 11 The ..Lingby culture..belongs to the end of the ice-age or the very beginning of the Ancylus period. **1936** J. G. D. CLARK *Mesolithic Settlement of N. Europe* ii. 70 The tanged flake from Christiansund..is often spoken of as 'a Lyngby point'. *Ibid.* iii. 79 Our knowledge of the Lyngby culture apart from the reindeer antler objects is slight. **1951** A. COATES *Prelude to History* x. 253 To the east several cultures, the Ahrensburg..in north Germany, Lyngby in Jutland and Swiderian in north Poland, derive from the East Gravettian of the upper palaeolithic. **1964** W. L. GOODMAN *Hist. Woodworking Tools* 12 Their earliest tools, made of reindeer antler, with the stump of the brow tine sharpened to a cutting edge, are known as 'Lyngby axes', from the site at Norre-Lyngby, in Denmark, where they were first found.

lyngorm: see LINGWORM.

lyniament, obs. form of LINEAMENT.

lynk(e, lynkome, obs. ff. LINK, LINCOLN¹.

lynkwhytte, obs. form of LINTWHITE.

lynn(e, obs. form of LINN, LINE.

lynn, var. of LINN².

lynnin, -ing, -yn(e, obs. forms of LINEN.

lynolf, lynset: see LINGEL *sb.*¹, LINESEAT.

lynton, lyntquhit: see LINTERN, LINTWHITE.

lynwever, -ar: see LINE *sb.*¹ 5.

lynx (lɪŋks). Forms: 4–5 lenx, 4–7 linx, 6–8 lynce, 6–7 lince, 4– lynx. [a. L. *lynx, lync-em* (Sp., Pg., It. *lince*), a. Gr. λύγξ (genit. λυγκός), cogn. w. Lith. *luszi-s*, OHG. *luhs* (mod.G. *luchs*), OE. *lox*, Du. *los*, Sw. *lo*. Prob. related to Gr. λεύσσειν to see, the animal being named from its quickness of sight.]

1. An animal of any of several species of the genus *Felis* forming the sub-genus *Lynx*, having a tuft at the tip of the ear, usually a short tail, and the fur more or less spotted. The lynx of the ancients is the CARACAL.

With qualifying words, as ***banded lynx*** *L. fasciata*, ***bay lynx*** *L. rufa*, ***booted lynx*** *L. caligata*, ***Canada lynx*** = LOUP CERVIER.

1340, *c* **1375** [see b]. *a* **1400–50** *Alexander* 3573 Lebards, lesards & lenxis. **1555** EDEN *Decades* 231 They keepe in theyr pallacces the beste cauled Linx, being fayrer then a lyon. *c* **1611** CHAPMAN *Iliad* XIII. 96 The torne-vp fare Of Lynces, Wolues, and Leopards; as neuer borne to warre. **1697** DRYDEN *Virg. Georg.* III. 415, I pass the Wars that spotted Linx's make With their fierce Rivals, for the Female's sake. **1781** PENNANT *Quadrupeds* I. Pl. XXXII, Bay Lynx. Persian Lynx. *Ibid.* I. 281 Caspian Lynx. **1790** BEWICK *Hist. Quadrupeds* (1824) 236 A variety is found in the inner parts of the province of New York, which is called the *Bay Lynx*,..its general colour is a bright bay, obscurely marked with dusky spots. **1829** J. RICHARDSON *Fauna Boreali-Amer.* I. 101 *Felis Canadensis* Canada Lynx. *Ibid.* I. 104 *Felis fasciata* Banded Lynx. **1839** *Penny Cycl.* XIV. 219/2 *The Booted Lynx*,..sole and posterior part of the foot ..deep black. **1855** LONGF. *Hiaw.* XV. 95 A pouch of healing, Skin of beaver, lynx, or otter, filled with magic roots. **1855** BROWNING *An Epistle* 29 A black lynx snarled and pricked a tufted ear.

b. With allusion to its keenness of sight.

1340 HAMPOLE *Pr. Consc.* 576 A best þat men Lynx calles, Þat may se thurgh thik stane walles. *c* **1375** *Sc. Leg. Saints* xxxi. (*Eugenia*) 509 Wes neuir lenx þat schuttis fyre, mare fulfillit of breth & yre. **1423** JAS. I *Kingis Q.* clv, The percyng lynx; the lufar vnicorne. *a* **1548** HALL *Chron.*, *Hen. V*, 38 b, Vigilantly to forsee with Lincis iyes. **1598** BARCKLEY *Felic. Man* (1631) 670 In earthly things we have Lynces eyes; but in spirituell things we are blind as beetles. **1685** *Gracian's Courtier's Orac.* 189 It concerns them much to be ..sharp-sighted Linxes, that they may dive in truth, and discern falshood. **1818** KEATS *Endym.* I. 123 And now, as deep into the wood as we Might mark a lynx's eye, there glimmered light. **1865** CARLYLE *Fredk. Gt.* XVII. v. (1872) VII. 50 Half of the Prussian Force, lie, vigilant as lynxes, blockading here.

2. The fur of the lynx.

1839 *Penny Cycl.* XIV. 221/2 The European and northern Asiatic Lynxes and the Canadian Lynx produce the great supply of furs known by the furriers under the name of lynx. **1899** *Westm. Gaz.* 21 Sept. 3/2 Lynx one sees about in many of the furriers'.

3. One of the northern constellations.

[**1727–51** CHAMBERS *Cycl.* s.v. *Constellation.*] **1798** *Encycl. Brit.* (ed. 3) II. 548/1. **1868** LOCKYER *Guillemin's Heavens* (ed. 3) 321 The Giraffe and the Lynx, all the stars in which constellations are at most of the fourth magnitude.

4. *attrib.* and *Comb.*: **lynx-eye**, in quots. *fig.*, an eye as keen as that of a lynx; so **lynx-eyed** *a.*, (of persons) having eyes like those of a lynx; keen-sighted; **lynx-like** *a.*, resembling a lynx; (of the eye, etc.) resembling that of a lynx; keen; (of actions, qualities, etc.) keen-sighted; **lynx-sharp** *a.*, sharp as that of a lynx.

1828 CARLYLE *Misc.* (1857) I. 199 His *lynx-eye discerns the true relations of the world and human life. **1880** C. R. MARKHAM *Peruv. Bark* xvi. 166 Martinez,..to great experience in woodcraft, added a lynx eye for a Calisaya plant. **1597** J. KING *On Jonas* (1618) 129 How blind in our selues, how censorious and *lince-eied against our brethren. **1809–10** COLERIDGE *Friend* (1865) 133 The cautious balancing of comparative advantages,..the lynx-eyed watching for opportunities. **1883** *19th Cent.* May 874 The lynx-eyed agent of some loan society. **1591** SYLVESTER *Du Bartas* I. vii. 194 Hee [God] sees all secrets, and his *Lynx-like ey..doth every Thought descry. **1839** *Penny Cycl.* XIV. 218/1 The figures..have small tufts on the tips of their ears, and are otherwise inclined to be lynx-like. **1868** MILMAN *St. Paul's* xvi. 380 Lynx-like sagacity. **1812** W. TENNANT *Anster F.* II. xlix, The Muse's *lynx-sharp eye.

lynx, obs. pl. of LINK *sb.*

lynyall, linye, obs. ff. LINEAL, LINE.

lynyolf, obs. variant of LINGEL *sb.*¹

lyochrome (ˈlaɪəkrəʊm). *Biochem.* [ad. G. *lyochrom* (Ellinger & Koschara 1933, in *Ber. d. Deut. Chem. Ges.* LXVI. B. 317), f. Gr. λύ-ειν to loosen + -O + Gr. χρῶμ-α colour.] = FLAVIN 2.

1933 *Chem. Abstr.* XXVII. 2167 The name lyochrome is proposed for pigments of this class. **1938** [see INTRAVITAL *a.*]. **1964** WAGNER & FOLKERS *Vitamins & Coenzymes* iv. 48 The term 'lyochrome' was rejected, and the designation 'flavin' was adopted for these growth-promoting water-soluble pigments. **1974** *Encycl. Brit. Macropædia* IV. 922/2 (*heading*) Flavins (lyochromes).

lyomerous (laɪˈɒmərəs), *a. Ichth.* [f. mod.L. *Lyomerus* (f. Gr. λύειν to loosen + μέρος part, joint) + -OUS.] Of or pertaining to the *Lyomeri* or loose-jointed fishes.

1885 *Riverside Nat. Hist.* (1888) III. 110 Both of the types of lyomerous fishes have very peculiar pedunculated appendages in the place of the lateral line.

Lyon, shortened form, with an early spelling retained, of *Lyon King of Arms* (see KING-OF-ARMS), the title of the chief herald in Scotland; so named from the lion on the royal shield. Also *Lyon Herald* (see HERALD *sb.* 1 e), *Lyon King*.

[**1377** in *Exch. Rolls Scotl.* (1880) II. 553 Et in solucione facta magistro Nicholao cementario, de mandato regis, Leoni heraldo [etc.].] **1381** in *Cal. Docum. Scotl.* (1888) IV. 67 [Warrant for licence for 40 days to] Leon Heraud [of the K. of Scots]. **1502** *Ibid.* 336 Lion the haroulde. *a* **1548** HALL *Chron., Edw. IV* 245 The forsayd Lyon desired an abstinence of warre to be taken. **1592** *Sc. Acts Jas. VI* (1816) III. 555/1 Þe said lyoun and his brether herauldis. **1596** [see HERALD *sb.* 1 e]. **1633** DELL in *Coronation Jas. I* (1685) 19 The Earls..put on their Crowns, and the Lyon his. **1755** *Chamberlayne's St. Gt. Brit.* II. III. x. 147 Lion, and his Brethren the Heralds, have Power to visit the Arms of Noblemen and Gentlemen. **1808** SCOTT *Marm.* IV. ix, Strict was the Lion-King's command. **1900** A. LANG in *Longm. Mag.* Aug. 383 The office of Lyon has ever been highly respectable.

attrib. **1847** *Gloss. Terms Her.* 82 The Lyon Office, Edinburgh, and the Office of Arms, Dublin, have cognizance of the heraldry of Scotland and Ireland respectively.

lyon, -asse, -cell: see LION, -ESS, LIONCEL.

lyond, obs. pres. pple. of LIE *v.*¹

Lyonist (ˈlaɪənɪst). *Hist.* Also 7 Lionist. [ad. F. *Léoniste*, according to Bossuet (quoted in Littré) named from a certain Leo (*c* 300).] *pl.* Another name for the Waldenses.

1644 FEATLY *Roma Ruens* 34 The sect of the Waldenses or Lionists is more pernicious to the church of Rome then all other sects. **1727–41** CHAMBERS *Cycl.* s.v. *Vaudois*, The Vaudois..were also called Lyonists and Sabatez or Insabatez, or Ensabatez.

Lyonnais (liːəˈneɪ, ‖ljɔnɛ), *sb.* and *a.* Also **Lyon(n)ese** (liːəˈniːz); (fem.) **Lionnoise, Lyonnaise, Lyonoise.** [Fr.] **A.** *sb.* A native or

inhabitant of the city of Lyons (Fr. *Lyon*), or the former province of Lyonnais, in eastern France; these people collectively; also, the French dialect of this area.

1653 [see ANGEVIN *a.* and *sb.*]. **1768** STERNE *Sentimental Journey* II. 201 The maid was a Lyonoise of twenty, and as brisk and lively a French girl as ever moved. **1777** P. THICKNESSE *Year's Journey* II. xlii. 78 Two harangues made by the Emperor Claudius in the senate, in favour of the Lyonoise. **1867** C. M. YONGE *Pupils of St. John* xv. 249 To Irenæus and his Lyonnese such falsehood was the next thing to apostasy. **1868** J. S. NORTHCOTE *Celebrated Sanctuaries of Madonna* iv. 134 The devotion of the Lyonnese..clung rather to the crypt and the image of St. Pothinus. *Ibid.* 142 Suchet was a Lyonnese by birth. *Ibid.* 146 Nor must we..fail to notice the last ornament presented to the sanctuary by the piety of the Lyonnese. **1955** J. THOMAS *No Banners* xvii. 156 Fernande continued in her archaic *Lyonnais*: 'Joe's been arrested, too.' **1960** L. DURRELL *Spirit of Place* (1969) 327 No traveller will repeat these words to a Lyonnais without provoking the passionate cry: 'Unjust!' **1966** *Observer* 30 Oct. 5/2, I saw between 15,000 and 20,000 *Lyonnais* in the square. *Ibid.*, The *Lyonnaises* peered into an English bathroom in the Ideal Home Exhibition House. **1972** *Guardian* 11 Mar. 15/1 The nineteenth century writer, Edouard Aynard, described the Lyonnese as 'a northern race astray in the south'.

B. *adj.* Of, pertaining to, or characteristic of Lyons or its inhabitants; *spec.* designating either of two styles of book-binding associated with Lyons.

1801 C. WILMOT *Let.* 13 Dec. in *Irish Peer* (1920) 17, I have issued forth betimes, under the conduct of a Lyonese Laquais de Place. **1867** C. M. YONGE *Pupils of St. John* xiv. 224 The whole..day..was spent by this Lyonnese multitude in baiting these..men. **1893** S. T. PRIDEAUX *Hist. Sk. Bookbinding* i. 46 The Lyonnese binders..used very fine stamps. **1894** H. P. HORNE *Binding of Bks.* ii. 77 The use of azured tools..became a characteristic of Lyonese bindings. **1928** E. P. GOLDSCHMIDT *Gothic & Renaissance Bookbindings* I. 317 These bindings are generally referred to as being in the 'Lyonnese' style. It is quite possible that a good many may come from Lyons, but I have never found any proof for this. **1960** E. A. LOWE *Eng. Uncial* 3 The collection of Concilia in the sixth-century Paris MS. Lat. 12097 written mostly in half-uncial has many pages in almost contemporary uncial. Experts consider the collection Lyonese. **1960** L. DURRELL *Spirit of Place* (1969) 328 The first steam-powered boat was Lyonnais in conception and design. De Jouffroy of Lyons built it. **1966** M. R. D. FOOT *SOE in France* viii. 215 He made firm friends with two Lyonnais business men. **1972** R. COBB *Reactions to French Revolution* ii. 51 The 29 Mai..would *never* be forgotten,..another example no doubt of Lyonnais particularism.

b. *Cookery.* Designating food, esp. sliced potatoes, cooked or served with onions, or with an onion sauce. Freq. placed after the sb., and as *à la Lyonnaise.*

1846 C. E. FRANCATELLI *Mod. Cook* 8 Lyonnaise Sause. Peel..onions... Slice them... Fry them... put them into a small stewpan, with..brown sauce. [**1846** A. SOYER *Gastronomic Regenerator* 470 (*heading*) Pommes de Terre à la Lyonnaise.] **1866** H. ST. CLAIR *Dainty Dishes* 130 Potatoes à la Lyonnaise..are very good to eat with cutlets. **1877** E. S. DALLAS *Kettner's Bk. of Table* 359 *Lyonnese Potatoes* (Pommes-de-terre à la Lyonnaise).—These are cooked potatoes combined with cooked onions. **1939** A. SIMON *Conc. Encycl. Gastron.* I. 34 *Lyonnaise*, Sauce. A white wine and onion sauce. **1960** E. DAVID *French Provincial Cooking* 228 What is to be served after these sausage dishes?.. No dish requiring potatoes after the Lyonnais one. **1974** *Times* 2 May 8/1 Lyonnaise potatoes... Fried potatoes made with blanched raw potatoes... Sauté potatoes with onion.

Lyons ('laɪənz, liɔ̃). Also **Lyon.** [F. *Lyon* Lyons, a city in France.] Used *attrib.* to designate various products associated with the city (see quots.); also *absol.*

1765 STERNE *Tr. Shandy* VII. xxxi. 162, I could..sometimes not so much as see even a Lyons-waistcoat, but this remembrance..would present itself. **1778** F. BURNEY *Evelina* I. xvi. 100 We found her..very busy in wiping her negligee..as she said it was a new Lyon's silk. *Ibid.* III. xxi. 234 'Twill be a most excellent opportunity to shew off her best Lyons' silk. **1851** MAYHEW & BINNY *1851* xvi. 160 The jewels and the tapestry, and the Lyons silks, are not now the sole objects of attraction. **1855** DICKENS *Dorrit* (1857) I. i. 6, I can cut my bread..like Lyons sausage. **1869** 'MARK TWAIN' *Innoc. Abr.* (1870) xxx. 244 Lyons velvets rank higher in America than those of Genoa. **1872** *Young Englishwoman* Dec. 646/1 Lyons grosgrains and moire silks. **1874** W. CROOKES *Pract. Handbk. Dyeing & Calico-Printing* II. iii. 195 (*heading*) Aniline blues... *Lyons blue* (Girard and De Laire). **1895** *Brit. Warehouseman* Feb. 13/2 A triple-pleated blouse of purple Lyons velvet was worn. **1902** S. J. WEYMAN *In Kings' Byways* I. 161 The hiding-places..had been..contrived to hold runlets of Nantz and bales of Lyons. **1908** A. BENNETT *Old Wives' Tale* III. vi. 385 She bought..coffee, Lyons sausage, dried prunes. **1914** F. W. ATACK tr. *Wahl's Manuf. Org. Dyestuffs* III. xvi. 171 The monophenyl- and monotolyl-derivatives [of Pararosaniline] occur in the dyestuffs known as Phenyl violet,..Lyons blue, etc. **1924** A. T. DE MOUILPIED *Quest for Colour* iv. 20 Summary of the more important discoveries in the history of synthetic organic dyestuffs... 1860 Bleu de Lyon—a spirit soluble blue derived from Magenta. [Discoverer] Girard and De Laire. **1952** 'P. WENTWORTH' *Brading Collection* xi. 66 Great ladies..had bought changeable silks there, and fine Lyons velvet. **1959** D. OGRIZEK *France Observed* 211 The contribution local artists have made toward enhancing the prestige of Lyons silk has always been recognised. **1960** E. DAVID *French Provincial Cooking* 225 Randall & Aubin..sell a coarsely-cut garlic-flavoured sausage which is not unlike the Lyon sausage. **1971** *Colour Index* (Soc. Dyers & Colourists) (ed. 3) V. 5573 Commercial name..Lyon Blue ..C.I. Solvent Blue 3.

lyonsew(e, variant of LIONCEAU.

lyophile ('laɪəfaɪl), *a.* [ad. G. *lyophil* (Freundlich & Neumann 1908, in *Zeitschr. f. Chem. und Ind. d. Kolloide* III. 81/2), f. Gr. λύ-ειν to loosen; see -PHIL, -PHILE.] **1.** *Physical Chem.* = LYOPHILIC *a.*

1915 W. W. TAYLOR *Chem. Colloids* i. 7 The term *lyophile* has been applied to those systems in which there is a marked affinity between the phases and *lyophobe* to the others. **1927** H. S. VAN KLOOSTER tr. *Kruyt's Colloids* i. 10 Emulsoids, or lyophile colloids,..form disperse systems in which the properties of the dispersing phase are considerably modified by the disperse colloid. **1941** R. J. HARTMAN *Colloid Chem.* xviii. 358 The terms lyophobe ('hatred' toward external phase) and lyophile (' love' toward external phase) were suggested by Freundlich.

2. *Biol.* and *Med.* Also **lyophil** (-fɪl). Of, pertaining to, or employing lyophilization; lyophilized.

1934 S. MUDD et al. in *Jrnl. Immunol.* XXVI. 341 (*heading*) The preparation, properties and applications of lyophile serum proteins and complement. **1949** *Jrnl. Bacteriol.* LVII. 575 The lyophil process has been shown to be a successful method for the preservation of yeast cultures in a viable state. **1958** *Angiology* IX. 189/2 The condenser system of the lyophile apparatus should be cleaned and dried before re-use. **1961** *Phytopathology* LI. 259/1 (*heading*) Observations on lyophil preservation and storage of Pythium species.

lyophilic (laɪə'fɪlɪk), *a. Physical Chem.* [f. LYOPHIL(E *a.* + -IC.] Of a dispersed colloidal phase: having an affinity for the dispersion medium; not readily precipitated out by small quantities of electrolyte. Also applied to sols containing such a phase, which generally have a lower surface tension and a higher viscosity than the dispersion medium and which give gels on evaporation or cooling.

1911 [see LYOPHOBIC *a.*]. **1938** H. L. HIND *Brewing* I. vi. 111 The complex carbohydrates and proteins belong to the class of lyophilic colloids, which is much the more important class in brewing. **1940** GLASSTONE *Text-bk. Physical Chem.* xiv. 1210 Substances which most readily form lyophilic sols are those of high molecular weight; each particle, therefore, consists of a small number of molecules and in some instances possibly of only one large molecule. **1959** [see LYOPHOBIC *a.*]. **1969** G. D. PARFITT *Dispersion of Powders in Liquids* iii. 81 Solutions of macromolecules and association colloids are of the lyophilic type and form spontaneously when the components are brought into contact.

lyophilization (laɪˌɒfɪlaɪ'zeɪʃən). *Biol.* and *Med.* [f. LYOPHIL(E *a.* + -IZATION.] = FREEZE-DRYING *vbl. sb.*

1938 *Jrnl. Allergy* X. 3 The chief advantage of lyophilization lies in the means it offers to preserve antibodies and other labile serum components..over extended periods of time. **1949** E. P. ABRAHAM et al. in H. W. Florey et al. *Antibiotics* II. xv. 638 Solvent transfer and lyophilization still form the basis of all commercial penicillin production, processes. **1958** W. C. FRAZIER *Food Microbiol.* xvi. 214 Milk and other liquid dairy products may be dried by lyophilization. **1967** *Oceanogr. & Marine Biol.* V. 164 Lyophilization is probably the gentlest way to dry a tissue and is essential if delicate materials are to be preserved.

lyophilize (laɪ'ɒfɪlaɪz), *v.* [f. LYOPHIL(E *a.* + -IZE.] *trans.* To subject to lyophilization; to freeze-dry.

1938 *Jrnl. Allergy* X. 3 In each instance a negative Kahn reaction was obtained on the 'immune' serum before it was lyophilized. **1949** A. G. SANDERS in H. W. Florey et al. *Antibiotics* II. xvi. 684 Spores from these fungi can be lyophilized, that is, dried from the frozen state, without impairing their vitality. **1973** LANDHUIS & IDE in J. A. Capella et al. *Corneal Preservation* xii. 141 Tissue lyophilized without pretreatment in glycerin became hard, took longer to rehydrate, and healed more slowly.

Hence **ly'ophilized** *ppl. a.*; also **ly'ophilizate** [after *filtrate*, *precipitate*, etc.], a substance or material which has been lyophilized; **ly'ophilizer**, an apparatus for carrying out lyophilization.

1938 *Jrnl. Allergy* X. 9 Patients to be treated with lyophilized immune serum were selected. **1963** *Problemy Gematol. i Pereliv. Krovi* VIII. VI. 62 Both homogenates and lyophilizates may be used as a source of erythroplastin in experimental research and clinical laboratory tests for hemostasis. **1967** *Oceanogr. & Marine Biol.* V. 163 In a lyophilizer the water is sublimed away during a drying period lasting several hours but the tissue is at zero degrees as long as ice is present. **1971** *Times* (Suppl.) 27 July p. iii/6 Problems concerning skin replacement in burns have been tackled..where the preparation of lyophilized (freeze dried) and deep frozen skin has been successful. **1972** *Nature* 14 Apr. 347/1 The lyophilizate was then redissolved to give a final concentration of 5 × SSC. **1972** IZAK & LEWIS *Mod. Concepts in Hematol.* 76 Lyophilization was performed in a Virtis batch lyophilizer.

lyophobe ('laɪəfəʊb), *a. Physical Chem.* [ad. G. *lyophob* (Freundlich & Neumann 1908, in *Zeitschr. f. Chem. und Ind. d. Kolloide* III. 81/2), f. Gr. λύ-ειν to loosen: see -PHOBE.] = LYOPHOBIC *a.*

1915 [see LYOPHILE *a.* 1]. **1927** H. S. VAN KLOOSTER tr. *Kruyt's Colloids* i. 10 The suspensoids, or lyophobe colloids ..are systems in which most of their physical properties differ only slightly from their dispersion media. **1941** [see LYOPHILE *a.* 1].

lyophobic (laɪə'fəʊbɪk), *a. Physical Chem.* [f. LYOPHOB(E *a.* + -IC.] Of a dispersed colloidal phase: not having an affinity for the dispersion medium; readily precipitated out by small quantities of electrolyte. Also applied to sols containing such a phase, which generally have a similar surface tension and viscosity to those of the dispersion medium, and which on evaporation or cooling give solids which cannot readily be reconverted into sols.

1911 H. FREUNDLICH in *Chem. News* 22 Sept. 140/1 Colloidal solutions stand between these two extremes. One class, distinguished from coarse suspensions only by the ultramicroscopic dimensions of their particles, are termed 'Suspension-colloids' or 'Lyophobic Sols'. These include colloidal metals, sulphides, and many hydroxides. 'Emulsion-colloids', or 'Lyophilic sols', which include albumin, gelatin, starch, &c., approach more nearly to the true solutions. **1959** K. J. MUSELS *Introd. Colloid Chem.* viii. 181 If we consider a paraffinic solvent,..the alcohol group is now lyophobic and the hydrocarbons are lyophilic. **1968** *Physics Bull.* Nov. 377/1 The stability of lyophobic colloids, like a quartz suspension or gold sol, is due to the competition between electrostatic forces of repulsion..and the van der Waals attraction.

lyotrope ('laɪətrəʊp), *a. Physical Chem.* [ad. G. *lyotrop* (H. Freundlich *Kapillarchemie* (1909) 54), f. Gr. λύ-ειν to loosen + τροπή turn, turning.] = LYOTROPIC *a.* 1.

1915 W. W. TAYLOR *Chem. Colloids* i. 8 Among the reactions in which this lyotrope influence has been recognised are the following: the catalysis of esters, the inversion of cane sugar, the setting of gelatine, and the heat-coagulation of albumin. **1965** *Biol. Abstr.* XLVI. 480/2 Hofmeister's lyotrope salts modify the molecular structure of erythrocyte stroma protein.

lyotropic (laɪə'trɒpɪk, -'trəʊpɪk), *a. Physical Chem.* [f. LYOTROP(E *a.* + -IC: see -TROPIC.]

1. Associated with the change of internal pressure of a solution from that of the solvent which is caused by the solute. ***lyotropic series***, a series in which ions are arranged in order of their lytropic effects, esp. their ability to cause precipitation of a lyophilic sol.

1924 W. A. PATRICK in H. S. Taylor *Treat Physical Chem.* II. xx. 1285 Those properties of solutions or liquids that are in causal relation to the forces of molecular attraction are termed lyotropic. We thus have two great groups of properties of solutions, the colligative, and the lyotropic. **1925** G. BARGER tr. *Freundlich's Elem. Colloid Chem.* 27 The characteristic series of cations and anions so obtained..are called the lyotropic series. **1926** H. S. HATFIELD tr. *Freundlich's Colloid & Capillary Chem.* 49 We can therefore distinghish from the group of properties which are comprehended in the van't Hoff theory a second independent group, which are due to the change of the internal pressure by the solute. These properties will be described as lyotropic; the influence of the solute upon the surface tension, the compressibility, the solubility of difficultly soluble substances, and others will be called lyotropic influences. **1937** *Chem. Rev.* XX. 170 The numbers obtained in the case of salting-out experiments with lyophilic colloids play an important part in other lyotropic phenomena. *Ibid.* 179 Since the heat of hydration of ions depends on the electric field which surrounds them, the lyotropic effects are beyond doubt caused by the different electric field strengths of the ions. **1956** *Bacteriol. Rev.* XX. 51/2 Attempts have been made to correlate the toxicity of various salts to the lyotropic..series. **1970** *Biochemistry* IX. 2802/1 We have adopted an approach to the elucidation of lyotropic mechanism in which the effects of related perturbants on a standard collagen-buffer system have been compared.

2. Of a mesophase: having its phase transitions readily effected by a change of concentration. Also applied to the mesomorphism exhibited by such a mesophase.

1933 *Trans. Faraday Soc.* XXIX. 1008 (*heading*) Lyotropic mesomorphism. **1966** *Molecular Crystals* II. 55 Lyotropic systems are also thermotropic and it is the co-operative action of the temperature and of the solvent which enables them to pass successively from the solid crystalline state to the liquid crystalline state and to the isotropic liquid or dissolved state. **1969** *Analytical Chem.* Nov. 26A/3 Liquid crystals are divided into two major groups. One of these is identified as thermotropic, indicating that the class is prepared by heating... Lyotropic liquid crystals constitute the second major group and are prepared by mixing two or more components. In two-component systems involving water the second component is generally an amphiphile. Lyotropic systems can be large in number and varied in composition. **1974** P. G. DE GENNES *Physics Liquid Crystals* i. 5 For all the systems listed in this section, the transitions are induced most easily by changing the concentration of rods rather than the temperature; for this reason they are commonly called lyotropic. *Ibid.* 6 Depending on which..conditions hold, amphiphilic compounds may be lyotropic or thermotropic.

lyotropy (laɪ'ɒtrəpɪ). *Physical Chem.* [f. LYOTROP(E *a.* + -Y[3].] The change of internal pressure brought about in a solution by the solvent or solvents; the mechanism by which this is brought about.

1927 H. S. VAN KLOOSTER tr. *Kruyt's Colloids* xvii. 237 Lyotropy, therefore, is probably not a hydration pure and simple, but one that orients the dipoles of water. **1937** *Chem. Rev.* XX. 169 (*heading*) Quantitative lyotropy.

lyoun(e, -own, obs. forms of LION.

lyour(e, -owre, variants of LEAR[2] *Obs.*

lyparde, obs. form of LEOPARD.

lype (laɪp). *Sc.* Also **lipe**. [See LIPE *sb.*[1]] Part of the roof of a mine rendered dangerous by faults in the rock.
1835 *Trans. Highland Soc.* X. plate ix (*caption*) Lipes or 'glazed backs'. Dislocations or 'hitches'. **1883** W. S. GRESLEY *Gloss. Terms Coal Mining* 163 *Lypes*,.. irregularities in the *roof* indicating danger from *falls*. **1912** G. CUNNINGHAM *Verse* 70 'Boot up steps and doon steps, and veezes and lypes. **1920** A. H. FAY *Gloss. Mining & Mineral Industry* 411/1 *Lype* (Scot.), an irregularity in the mine roof... A projecting rock in a mine roof that may fall at any time. Usually in the plural, and sometimes spelled Lipe. **1952** B. HOLMAN *Behind Diamond Panes* 82 All the care in roof support did not prevent a 'fall' because of a 'greasy lipe'.

lypemania (lɪpɪˈmeɪnɪə). *Path.* [mod. (irreg.) f. Gr. λύπη grief + μανία MANIA. Cf. F. *lypémanie*.] A form of insanity characterized by extreme mournfulness.
[**1856** in MAYNE *Expos. Lex.* as a Lat. word.] **1874** MAUDSLEY *Respons. in Ment. Dis.* iii. 72 The chronic form of the disease.. which Esquirol proposed to distinguish as lypemania. **1896** *Allbutt's Syst. Med.* I. 828 In some cases, especially in women, the delirium [of typhoid fever] has more the character of lipemania.

lypnin, obs. form of LIPPEN.

lypothimy, -thymia: see LIPOTHYMY.

lyppart, obs. form of LEOPARD.

lyppe, obs. form of LIP, LIPE *sb.*[1]

lyppin, -yn, obs. forms of LIPPEN.

lyqueresse, -yce, obs. forms of LIQUORICE.

lyquet, -quid, lyquor, obs. ff. LIQUID, LIQUOR.

‖**lyra** (ˈlaɪərə). [L. *lyra*, a. Gr. λύρα.]
†**1.** A lyre. (Occas. in It. form *lira*.) See also 5.
a **1586** SIDNEY *Arcadia* II. (1598) 232 Til she had (taking a Lyra Basilius helde for her) song these Phaleuciakes. **1599** B. JONSON *Cynthia's Rev.* IV. iii, Vpon which I composde this ode, and set it to my most affected instrument, the lyra. **1606** BRYSKETT *Civ. Life* 147 Which verses.. were vsed to be sung at the tables of great men and Princes, to the sound of the Lyra. **1611** COTGR., *Lyre*, a Lyra, or Harpe. *c* **1714** POPE, etc. *Mem. M. Scriblerus* I. vi, I have here a small Lyra of my own, fram'd, strung, and tun'd after the ancient manner. **1724** *Explic. For. Words Mus.* 42 *Lira*, or *Lyra*, or *Lyre*.
2. *Astr.* (With capital L.) An ancient northern constellation: = HARP *sb.*[1] 3.
1658 in PHILLIPS. **1810** J. BRINKLEY in *Phil. Trans. C.* 204 My observations on α Lyræ.. now amount to 47. **1901** J. F. HEWITT *Mythmaking Age* I. i. 8 When Vega in the Constellation of the Vulture of Lyra became Pole Star.
†**3.** *Zool.* (With capital L.) **a.** A former genus of fishes including the Piper (*Trigla lyra*). **b.** A former genus, including the Harp-shell (*Harpa*).
1706 PHILLIPS (ed. Kersey), *Lyra*,.. Also the Rochet, a Sea-fish, call'd in Cornwall the red Gournard. **1753** CHAMBERS *Cycl. Supp.* s.v., There are three species of the lyra, or harp shell. 1. The common lyra. **1854** BADHAM *Halieut.* 48 The Lyra or gurnard [was offered] to Apollo.
4. *Anat.* 'The triangular portion of the under surface of the corpus callosum lying between the diverging posterior crura of the fornix, and marked with transverse, longitudinal, and oblique lines' (*Syd. Soc. Lex.*).
1756 DOUGLAS tr. *Winslow's Struct. Hum. Body* (ed. 4) II. 245 The interior Surface of the triangular Cieling, which lies between these arches, is full of transverse, prominent, medullary Lines; for which reason the Ancients called it Psalloides and Lyra, comparing it to a stringed Instrument, something like what is now called a Dulcimer. **1840** G. ELLIS *Anat.* 39 An appearance, called the *lyra*, or *corpus psalloides*. **1881** MIVART *Cat* 265.
†**5.** *attrib.* (sense 1), as ***lyra lesson***; **lyra** (also 7 *lero*) **viol**, a bass-viol, tuned and played according to the lute notation or 'tablature'; **lyra-way** (also 7 *lyero-*, *leero-way*), **-wise** (*Cent. Dict.*), according to the method of notation used for instruments of the lute-kind (see TABLATURE).
1661 PEPYS *Diary* 10 Apr., A base viall, on which he that played played well some *lyra lessons. **1666** *Ibid.* 16 Oct., Hearing my brother play a little upon the *lyra viall. **1669** PLAYFORD *Musicks Recreat.* Pref. 1 The Lero or Lyra-Viol. **1674** —— *Skill Mus.* II. 91 The Viol (usually called) de Gambo or Consort Viol, because the Musick thereon is play'd from the Rules of the Gam-vt, and not as the Lyra-Viol, which is by Letters or Tableture. *a* **1734** NORTH *Life Ld. Keeper North* (1742) 14 His Practice of Musick upon his Base, or Lyra Viol (which he used to touch, Lute-fashion, upon his Knees). **1607** *Lingua* I. ix. C ij, Auditus, shall we here thee play, the *Lyeroway, or the Lute-way? **1611** [see LUTE *sb.*[1] 2]. **1658** PHILLIPS, *Lyrick* verses,.. songs composed to the Lyre, or Harp, whence we say vulgarly, playing Leero-way on the Viol, which is corruptly used for Lyra-way, *i.e.* Harp-way. **1674** PLAYFORD *Skill Mus.* II. 101 A Bass-Viol to play Lyra-way, that is by Tableture.

Lyraid (ˈlaɪəreɪd), **Lyrid** (ˈlaɪərɪd). *Astr.* [f. LYR-A + -ID[2].] One of a group of meteors observed in some years about April 20th, apparently radiating from the constellation Lyra.
1883 *Encycl. Brit.* XVI. 111/2 Lyraids. **1885** *Athenæum* 16 May 634/1 The Lyrids.
b. *attrib.*
1899 *Edin. Rev.* Oct. 319 Biela's is not the only comet with meteoric appurtenances; there are Leonid, Perseid and Lyrid comets as well.

lyrate (ˈlaɪəreɪt), *a.* *Nat. Hist.* [ad. mod.L. *lyrāt-us*, f. *lyra* LYRE: see -ATE[2].] Shaped like a lyre. In *Bot.*, of a leaf: Pinnatifid, with the upper lobes much larger than the lower.
1760 J. LEE *Introd. Bot.* III. v. (1765) 179 *Lyrate*, *Lyre-shaped*. **1785** MARTYN *Rousseau's Bot.* xxiii. (1794) 323 Winter Cress with lyrate leaves, the outmost lobe roundish. **1852** DANA *Crust.* I. 86 Carapax lyrate. **1856–8** W. CLARK *Van der Hoeven's Zool.* II. 652 *Gazella*.. Horns lyrate. **1870** HOOKER *Stud. Flora* 30 Upper leaves toothed or lyrate. **1880** HUXLEY *Crayfish* v. 234 A characteristic lyrate mark upon the cephalic region of the carapace. **1893** SELOUS *Trav. S. E. Africa* 450 The elegant lyrate horns of the males.
b. Used in *comb.* with sense 'lyrate and ——', in ***lyrate-pinnate***, ***-pinnatifid*** adjs. Also in quasi-L. form **lyrato-** (laɪəˈreɪtəʊ).
1775 JENKINSON *Brit. Plants* Gloss., *Lyrato-hastated*, is shaped partly like a harp or lyre, and partly like a spear. **1806** GALPINE *Brit. Bot.* 96 Stipulæ lyrato-pinnatifid. **1845** LINDLEY *Sch. Bot.* v. (1858) 60 Radical leaves lyrate-pinnate. **1847** W. E. STEELE *Field Bot.* 105 Leaves glabrous, or hairy, the radical ones lyrate-pinnatifid.

lyrated (ˈlaɪəreɪtɪd), *a.* *Nat. Hist.* [Formed as LYRATE + -ED[1].] = LYRATE.
1753 CHAMBERS *Cycl. Supp.* s.v. *Leaf*, Lyrated Leaf, *folium lyratum*. **1834** *Penny Cycl.* II. 68/2 Sometimes they [*sc.* the horns of the antelope] are what is commonly called lyrated, or bend first backwards and then point forwards. **1871** DARWIN *Desc. Man* II. xvii. 254 The elegant lyrated horns of certain antelopes.

lyrately (ˈlaɪəreɪtlɪ), *adv.* *Nat. Hist.* [f. prec. + -LY[2].] In a lyrate form. (Cf. LYRATE b.)
1775 JENKINSON *Brit. Plants* Gloss., *Lyrately-pinnate*. **1880** GRAY *Struct. Bot.* III. iv. 101 Lyrately Pinnate denotes a leaf in which the terminal leaflet is largest and the lower small.

lyre[1] (laɪə(r)). Also 3 **lire**. [a. F. *lyre*, OF. *lire* (12th c. in Littré), ad. L. *lyra*, a. Gr. λύρα.]
1. A stringed instrument of the harp kind, used by the Greeks for accompanying song and recitation.
The word is used to translate the Gr. κιθάρα (in Homer κίθαρις) and φόρμιγξ, as well as λύρα; also sometimes used interchangeably with HARP. ***Æolian lyre***, the Æolian harp: see ÆOLIAN 2.
c **1205** LAY. 7003 Of harpe & of salterium, of fiðele & of corium, of timpe & of lire. **1598** FLORIO, *Lira*, an instrument of musicke called a lyre [1611 Lyra] or a harp. **1635–56** COWLEY *Davideis* I. 26 The tuneful Strings of David's Lyre. **1647** CRASHAW *Music's Duel* Poems 89 A holy quire Founded to th' name of great Apollo's lyre. **1697** DRYDEN *Alexander's Feast* 123 Now strike the golden lyre again. **1725** POPE *Odyss.* I. 197 To Phemius was consign'd the chorded lyre. *a* **1774** GOLDSM. *Surv. Exp. Philos.* (1776) II. 190 The Eolian lyre is easily made, being nothing more than a long narrow box of thin deal [etc.]. **1876** HUMPHREYS *Coin-Coll. Man.* v. 45 He [Arion] generally holds in one hand the lyre and in the other the plectrum.
b. *fig.* chiefly as the symbol of lyric poetry.
1683 DRYDEN *To Mem. Mr. Oldham* 5 One common note on either lyre did strike, And knaves and fools we both abhorred alike. **1754** GRAY *Progr. Poesy* I. i, Awake, Æolian lyre, awake. **1782** COWPER *Charity* 106 The painter's pencil, and the poet's lyre. **1819** SHELLEY *Ode West Wind*, Make me thy lyre even as the forest is. **1838** THIRLWALL *Greece* II. xii. 123 If we had been permitted to compare the happiest productions of the Æolian, the Dorian, and the Ionian lyre. **1850** TENNYSON *In Mem.* xcvi, One indeed I knew In many a subtle question versed, Who touch'd a jarring lyre at first, But ever strove to make it true.
2. *Astr.* = LYRA 2.
1868 LOCKYER *Guillemin's Heavens* (ed. 3) 348 Vega, the brightest star in the constellation of the Lyre.
3. *Anat.* = LYRA 4.
1900 DEAVER *Surg. Anat.* II. 522 The fibres of the under surface of the fornix behind are so arranged as to give rise to the designation *the lyre*.
4. 'A grade of isinglass; a trade name' (*Cent. Dict.* 1890).
[**1856** *Encycl. Brit.* (ed. 8) XII. 628/2 art. *Isinglass*, For *long* and *short staple*, it is twisted between three pegs, into the shape of a horse-shoe, harp, or lyre.]
5. *attrib.* and *Comb.*, as ***lyre-affecting*** adj.; **lyre-bat**, a species of bat, *Megaderma lyra*; **lyre-bird**, an Australian bird, *Menura superba* or *M. novæhollandiæ*, resembling a pheasant with a beautiful lyre-shaped tail; **lyre-fish**, the Harp-fish or Piper, *Trigla lyra*; **lyre-flower**, *Dielytra spectabilis* (Cassell); **lyre-man** *U.S.*, a cicada or harvest-fly; **lyre-pheasant** = *lyre-bird*; **lyre-shaped** *a.* = LYRATE; **lyre-tail** = *lyre-bird*; **lyre-turtle** *U.S.*, the leather back or trunk-turtle, *Dermochelys coriaceus*; †**lyre-viol** = *lyra-viol* (see LYRA 5).
1611 COTGR., *Aime-lyre*,.. Harpe-louing, *Lyre-affecting. **1834** G. BENNETT *Wand. New S. Wales* I. 277 The 'Native or Wood-pheasant', or '*Lyre bird' of the colonists. **1872** A. DOMETT *Ranolf* I. iii. 7 Curved like the lyre-bird's tail half spread. **1884** *Longm. Mag.* Mar. 530 The gurnards, one of which is known as the *lyre-fish. **1778** *Encycl. Brit.* (ed. 2) II. 1297/1 (*Botany*). *Lyratum*, *lyre-shaped; i.e. divided transversely into oblong horizontal segments, of which the lower ones are lesser and more distant from each other than the upper ones. **1901** *Q. Rev.* July 232 Spiral, lyre-shaped horns. **1660** PEPYS *Diary* 17 Nov., Then to my *lyre-viall, and to bed.

†**lyre**[2]. *Obs.* The name (med.L. *Lyra*) of a town in Brabant, now Lire or Liere, occurring in the designations of certain kinds of cloth, as ***black of lyre*** (*black a-lyre*, *black of lure*), ***green of lyre*** (*grene alyr*, *grene lyre*).
[**1390–1** *Earl Derby's Exped.* (Camden) 89 Pro xxiij[bus] uirgis panni nigri de Lyra. *Ibid.* 90 Pro j vlna et di. de blodeo de Lyra.] **1421** in *E.E. Wills* (1882) 97 *note*, Blac of lyre. **1434** *Ibid.* 97 An hode of black of lure, an a hod of blewe. **1439** *Ibid.* 118 My gowne of grene Alyre cloth of golde. **1490** *Ibid.* 97 *note*, Togam viridis coloris anglice grene lyre medley.
attrib. **1479** in *Eng. Gilds* (1870) 415 [The mayor of Bristol] in.. his skarlat cloke, furred, with his blak a lyre hode, or tepet of blak felwet.

lyre[3]. *Orkney* and *Shetland*. Also **lyer, lyrie, layer, lyar**. [a. Da. *lire*.] The bird Manx Shearwater, *Puffinus anglorum*.
1654 *Blaeu's Atlas Scot.*, *Orkney*, The Stour, where buildet that excellent foul, called the Lyer. **1701** J. BRAND *Descr. Orkney* (1703) 22 The Lyre is a rare and delicious Sea fowl. **1777** PENNANT *Zool.* (1812) II. 207. **1889** SAUNDERS *Man. Brit. Birds* 719 Lyrie.

lyre, variant of LEAR[2] *Obs.*, LIRE *sb.*[1] *Obs.*

lyric (ˈlɪrɪk), *a.* and *sb.* Also 6 **lirick**, 6–7 **lirique**, 7 **lyrike**, 7–8 **lyrick**. [a. F. *lyrique*, or ad. L. *lyric-us*, a. Gr. λυρικός, f. λύρα LYRE[1].]
A. *adj.*
1. Of or pertaining to the lyre; adapted to the lyre, meant to be sung; pertaining to or characteristic of song. Now used as the name for short poems (whether or not intended to be sung), usually divided into stanzas or strophes, and directly expressing the poet's own thoughts and sentiments. Hence, applied to the poet who composes such poems. ***lyric drama***, ***lyric stage***, the opera.
1589 PUTTENHAM *Eng. Poesie* I. xi. 20 They were called Lirique Poets. **1664** DRYDEN *Rival Ladies* Ep. Ded., This sweetness of Mr. Waller's lyric poesy was afterwards followed in the epic by Sir John Denham. **1671** MILTON *P.R.* IV. 257 Æolian charms and Dorian Lyric Odes. *a* **1727** NEWTON *Chronol. Amended* i. (1728) 59 Terpander was a Lyric Poet. **1778** JOHNSON *L.P.*, *Dryden*, Quatrains of lines alternately consisting of eight and six syllables make the most soft and pleasing of our lyric measures. **1825** W. AYRTON *Let.* 5 Apr. in J. Ebers *Seven Yrs. King's Theatre* (1828) 255 Signor Tramezzani,.. one of the finest singers and actors that ever graced the lyric stage, took the character of Guglielmo. **1838** THIRLWALL *Greece* II. xii. 125 The tyrants likewise cherished the lyric Muse. **1842** *Ainsworth's Mag.* I. 183 Still we hail with undiminished delight the lyric drama. **1849** TICKNOR *Sp. Lit.* III. 8 Herrera is too lyric.. to write good elegies. **1873** RUSKIN *Fors Clav.* III. xxxiv. 6 Lyric poetry is the expression by the poet of his own feelings. **1877** G. B. SHAW *How to become Mus. Critic* (1960) 22 The most exciting situation in lyric drama—the duet in the fourth act of Les Huguenots. *Ibid.* 28 It requires a faculty for light comedy, which is almost unknown on the lyric stage. **1880** VERNON LEE *Stud. Italy* II. iii. 38 Poetry which is lyric in spirit as well as in metre. **1938** *Oxf. Compan. Mus.* 526/2 *Lyric Drama*, another name for opera, covering all kinds. The term is applied not so much to any particular work as to the whole class—i.e. opera as distinct from the spoken play. **1957** *Oxf. Compan. Theatre* 589/1 Beethoven's .. solitary contribution to the lyric stage, 'Fidelio' (1805). **1958** A. JACOBS *New Dict. Mus.* 218 *Lyric drama*, occasional synonym for opera (especially in French, as *drame lyrique*); hence also *the lyric stage*, i.e. the operatic stage.
2. Of persons: Given to song; singing-. *poet.*
1814 SOUTHEY *Roderick* XXI. Poet. Wks. IX. 203 A richer, stronger strain Than that with which the lyric lark salutes The new-born day. **1820** KEATS *Cap & Bells* iv, While little harps were touch'd by many a lyric fay. **1871** BROWNING *Balaust.* 186 Here she stands, Balaustion! Strangers, greet the lyric girl!
B. *sb.*
1. *absol.* (with *the*): That which is lyrical; lyric style, verse, etc.
1586 W. WEBBE *Eng. Poetrie* (Arb.) 86 The most vsuall kindes [of verse] are foure, the Heroic, Elegiac, Iambick, and Lyric... Sometime the Lyric ryseth aloft, sometime the comicall. **1821** BRYON *Juan* III. lxxxv, His muse made increment of anything, From the high lyric down to the low rational.
†**2.** A lyric poet. *Obs.*
1594 R. ASHLEY tr. *Loys le Roy* 69 There hath bin a great companie of Tragicks, Comicks, Elegiacks, Lyricks [etc.]. **1630** BRATHWAIT *Eng. Gentlem.* (1641) 107 Horace, the most delicate of all the Roman Lyricks. **1699** BENTLEY *Phal.* 40 Simonides would speak thus of one of his Contemporary Lyrics. **1710** STEELE *Tatler* No. 214 ⁋3 That ancient Lyric, M. D'Urfey. **1839** tr. *Lamartine's Trav. East* 82/1 He is the first of sentimental poets!—the king of lyrics!
3. A lyric poem. Also *pl.*, verses in lyric metre.
1581 SIDNEY *Apol. Poetrie* (Arb.) 62 In the Earle of Surries Liricks, many things.. worthy of a noble minde. **1714** GAY *Sheph. Week*, *Wednesday* 16 At Wakes.. Where D—y's Lyricks swell in every Voice. **1758** JOHNSON *Idler* No. 2 ⁋6 The cook warbles her lyricks in the kitchen. *a* **1849** H. COLERIDGE *Ess.* (1851) II. 29 An Eton boy follows Virgil in longs, Tibullus in longs and shorts, and Horace in lyrics. **1879** *Fortn. Rev.* No. 155. 692 Wordsworth's fame will rest upon his lyrics, if we extend the term to include his odes, sonnets, and some narrative poems in stanzas.

4. The words of a popular song; freq. *pl.* Also *attrib.*, as *lyric-writer*.

1876 STAINER & BARRETT *Dict. Mus. Terms* 276/2 *Lyric*, poetry or blank verse intended to be set to music and sung. **1927** *Melody Maker* Aug. 759/3 On July 8 Edgar Leslie, the prolific and most successful lyric writer in America, arrived in London. **1933** *Punch* 16 Aug. 180/3 The gramophone plunged fervently into that lyric called 'I've Got a Date with an Angel'. **1934** C. LAMBERT *Music Ho!* IV. 272 The lowbrow poet—the type of writer who in the nineteenth century produced 'Champagne Charlie' and now produces revue lyrics. **1938** *Oxf. Compan. Mus.* 526/2 Another well-known poet constantly advertises himself in the British musical press as 'Lyric Author...2,000 songs...not one failure to give great pleasure'. **1946** E. O'NEILL *Iceman Cometh* (1947) II. 132 They all join in a jeering chorus, rapping with knuckles or glasses on the table at the indicated spot in the lyric. **1958** *Times* 2 Aug. 7/4 Teenagers in Minneapolis, believing that the words of some 'pop' songs can encourage juvenile crime, have..'opened a nation-wide "better lyrics" contest'. **1967** *Listener* 3 Aug. 130/1 Having introduced a new sound in the music, they saw that they had next to change the type of lyric. **1968** *Ibid.* 7 Nov. 610/1 According to Mick Farren, lyric-writer of the Deviants: 'Pop music is..the last free medium.' **1972** *Jazz & Blues* Sept. 12/1 The banality of the lyrics. **1973** *Listener* 19 Apr. 522/1 The bo' weevil fugues..in blues lyrics.

†**lyric**, *v.* *Obs. rare.* [f. prec.] *trans.* To sing (*over*) in a lyrical manner.

a **1704** T. BROWN *Lett. fr. Dead to Living* II. (1707) 163 Parson Punch..Lyricks over his part in an Anthem very handsomly. **1711** E. WARD *Quix.* I. 383 The Songster Lyrick'd o'er with all His Skill the following Madrigal.

lyrical (ˈlɪrɪkəl), *a.* [f. LYRIC *a.* + -AL[1].]

1. = LYRIC *a.* Also, having the qualities or characteristics of lyric poetry.

1581 SIDNEY *Apol. Poetrie* (Arb.) 67 Other sorts of Poetry almost haue we none, but that Lyricall kind of Songs and Sonnets. **1623** COCKERAM III, *Alceus*, a famous liricall Poet. **1685** DRYDEN *Pref. 2nd Misc.* Ess. (ed. Ker) I. 267 Somewhat of a finer turn and more lyrical verse, is yet wanting. **1697** —— *Ded. Æneis* ibid. II. 230 Mr. Cowley had found out that no kind of staff is proper for a heroic poem, as being all too lyrical. **1795** MASON *Ch. Mus.* iii. 195 Compleat Psalms..of sufficient brevity..should have the preference, because they form a Lyrical whole. **1798** *(title)* Lyrical Ballads. **1838** THIRLWALL *Greece* II. xii. 123 The loss we have suffered in the masterpieces of Greek lyrical poetry. **1853** MAURICE *Proph. & Kings* xix. 326 The lyrical freedom and richness of Isaiah's [style].

2. Resembling what is found in lyric poetry.

1817 COLERIDGE *Satyrane's Lett.* i. 194 Passing with a very lyrical transition to the subject of general politics. **1898** G. PARKER *Battle of the Strong* viii. 55 The Chevalier..tapped his lips with his fingers in a little lyrical emotion.

Hence **ˈlyrically** *adv.*, **ˈlyricalness**.

1803 W. TAYLOR in Robberds *Mem.* I. 443 A great deal is told by implication, and too lyrically. **1894** *Temple Bar* CI. 601 Lyricalness is the special mark of De Banville. **1900** *Q. Rev.* Oct. 434 He had handled, in a lyrically dramatic form, that legend of the Bride of Corinth.

†**lyrichord**. *Obs.* [f. LYRE[1], after HARPSICHORD.] A kind of harpsichord (see quot. 1883).

1741 in *Spec. Patents Music* (1871) 3 A new invention for ..meliorating..harpsichords; and lyrichords which are harpsichords, strung with catgut; and spinnets. **1768** S. BENTLEY *River Dove* 5 Soft touch'd is the Lyrichord String. **1883** A. J. HIPKINS in *Grove's Dict. Mus.* III. 639/1 The Lyrichord being a harpsichord strung with wire and catgut, made on the sostinente principle, and actuated by moving wheels instead of the usual quills, so that the bow of the violin and the organ were imitated.

lyricism (ˈlɪrɪsɪz(ə)m). [f. LYRIC + -ISM.] Lyric character or style; the pursuit or eulogy of the same; (with *pl.*), a lyrical expression or characteristic. *Occas.* (after F. *lyrisme*), affectation of high-flown sentiment or poetic enthusiasm.

1760 GRAY *Let. to Mason* 20 Aug., Lest people should not understand the humour of the thing (which indeed to do they must have our lyricisms at their finger ends). **1833** *New Monthly Mag.* XXXIX. 87 She got up a night or two of patriotic lyricism. **1834** COLERIDGE *Table-t.* 15 Mar., In Beaumont and Fletcher it [blank verse] is constantly slipping into lyricisms. **1870** *Daily News* 8 Sept. 4 The danger of what we may perhaps call Lyricism. We sincerely trust that the new Government will enter upon its duties in the most prosaic spirit possible. **1881** A. AUSTIN in *Macm. Mag.* XLIII. 403 Sheer lyricism just now is over much the mode.

lyricist (ˈlɪrɪsɪst). [f. LYRIC + -IST.] **a.** One who is skilled in or devoted to lyric composition.

1881 A. AUSTIN in *Macm. Mag.* XLIII. 402 The Lyricists pure and simple—and certainly, as far as verse is concerned, De Musset never became anything else.

b. A writer of lyrics (LYRIC *sb.* 4).

1909 *Pall Mall Gaz.* 12 Apr. 4/3 No doubt it could be paralleled in the works of our own music-hall 'lyricists'. **1932** *Amer. Speech* VII. 243 Scores of ways of saying 'I Love You' have been invented by the lyricists of popular songs. **1963** *Movie* Apr. 11/3 Music by Joseph Kosma. Lyricist: Jacques Prevert. English lyrics by Johnny Mercer, sung by Nat King Cole. **1971** *Daily Tel.* 11 Oct. 15 'Jesus Christ, Superstar', a 'folk opera' depicting the last seven days of Christ,..is making a fortune for its composer and lyricist.

lyricize (ˈlɪrɪsaɪz), *v. rare.* [f. LYRIC + -IZE.] *intr.* To sing lyrics.

1832 *Blackw. Mag.* XXXI. 326/1 That one should be so young and wise, And so adroitly lyricize.

lyrico- (ˈlɪrɪkəʊ), combining form of Gr. λυρικός LYRIC, as in *lyrico-dramatic*, *-epic* adjs.

1873 KINGSBURY in *Speaker's Comm.* IV. 665 The Song of Songs might be called a lyrico-dramatic poem. **1897** DOWDEN *Hist. Fr. Lit.* i. 4 *Cantilènes*, short lyrico-epic poems.

Lyrid: see LYRAID.

lyrie, variant of LYRE[3].

lyriform (ˈlaɪərɪfɔːm), *a.* [See -FORM. Cf. F. *lyriforme* (in Littré).] Lyre-shaped.

1856 in MAYNE *Expos. Lex.* **1893** NEWTON *Dict. Birds* 527 In the male of *M[enura] alberti* the tail is..not lyriform.

lyring, variant of *learing*: see LEAR[2].

lyrism (ˈlaɪərɪz(ə)m, ˈlɪrɪz(ə)m). [a. F. *lyrisme*, or ad. Gr. λυρισμός playing on the lyre, f. λύρα LYRE.] = LYRICISM. Also (*nonce-use*), lyrical performances, singing of songs.

1859 GEO. ELIOT *A. Bede* liii, The lyrism, which had at first only manifested itself by David's *sotto voce* performance of 'My love's a rose without a thorn', had gradually assumed a rather deafening and complex character. **1870** *Athenæum* 7 May 609 The extraordinary outburst of lyrism, which was witnessed thirty years ago in France. **1886** SYMONDS *Renaiss. Italy, Cath. React.* (1898) VII. viii. 97 Tasso developed the lyrism of the octave stanza. **1896** *Tablet* 18 July 86/2 Such flights of delirious lyrism as the following.

lyrist (ˈlɪrɪst). [ad. L. *lyrist-a*, ad. Gr. λυριστής, f. λύρα LYRE.]

1. A player on the lyre; one who sings and accompanies himself on the lyre.

1656 BLOUNT *Glossogr.*, *Lyrist*, a Harper, or one that sings to the Harp. **1725** POPE *Odyss.* XXIII. 133 While the sweet lyrist airs of rapture sings. **1763** J. BROWN *Poetry & Mus.* 163 In the early Times, the Offices of Poet and Lyrist were united in the same Person. **1811** BUSBY *Dict. Mus.* Introd. vi, David, it appears, was the best lyrist of his time. **1862** MERIVALE *Rom. Emp.* (1865) VII. lv. 3 The long loose robe was the garb also of the lyrist.

2. A lyric poet.

1813 EUSTACE *Class. Tour* (1821) II. vii. 240 The hills, the woods..which so often inspired the Roman Lyrist. **1821** SHELLEY *Adonais* xxx, From her wilds Ierne sent The sweetest lyrist of her saddest wrong. **1856** MASSON *Ess.* i. 9 Burns is a lyrist, pouring out his own feelings in song.

lys: see LIS[1], LISS, LISSE *v.*, LOUSE.

lysans, -aunce, -ence, -ense, obs. ff. LICENCE.

lysate (ˈlaɪzeɪt). *Biol.* [f. LYS(IS + *-ate*, after *filtrate*, *precipitate*.] A solution or preparation containing the products of lysis of cells, esp. bacterial cells.

1922 *Brit. Med. Jrnl.* 19 Aug. 298/2 The other point is the question of the effect of dispersion of the lysate—that is, the bacterial bodies in the emulsion used. **1954** *Sci. News* XXXIII. 91 This process of bacterial destruction is called 'lysis'; the resulting liquid is a 'lysate', and may contain over a hundred thousand million bacteriophage particles per cubic centimetre. **1973** *Nature* 12 Jan. 96/1 These antibodies gave strong reactions with ultrasonic lysates of both normal and CML leucocytes.

lysatinine (laɪˈsætɪnaɪn). *Chem.* [f. Gr. λύσις loosening, solution + the ending of CREATININE.] An organic base forming a crystalline double salt with silver nitrate, obtained by decomposition of various proteids.

1897 *Allbutt's Syst. Med.* IV. 7 Secondary products..of basic nature like lysine, lysatinine and ammonia.

lysch, obs. form of LIEGE *a.* and *sb.*

lyse (laɪz), *v. Biol.* [Back-formation from LYSIS 3: cf. *analysis*/*analyse*, *catalysis*/*catalyse*, etc.]

1. *trans.* To bring about lysis of (a cell, etc.).

1927 *Brit. Jrnl. Exper. Path.* VIII. 121 It [*sc.* an active phage] lysed certain laboratory strains of coliform bacilli. **1947** *New Biol.* II. 75 Fleming made the observation that the small bacterial colonies close to the mould colony were being 'lysed' (dissolved). **1967** *New Scientist* 13 July 97/1 It will burst open or lyse the offending bacteria. **1970** *Nature* 16 May 594/1 They lysed algal cells by treatment with penicillin.

2. *intr.* To undergo lysis (sense 3).

1933 *Jrnl. Infectious Dis.* LII. 272 The tendency of placental blood to lyse was found to be overcome by this use of hypertonic salt solution. **1971** *Nature* 22 Jan. 272/2 Many bacteria lyse when growth of the cultures ceases. *Ibid.* 26 Nov. 231/2 When leaves of these two species were slowly dried.., chloroplast lamellae and mitochondrial cristae often disintegrated or lysed while tonoplasts..usually remained intact.

So **lysed**, **ˈlysing** *ppl. adjs.*

1922 *Brit. Med. Jrnl.* 19 Aug. 290/1 The filtrate contains the bacteriophagic principle as active as the lysed non-filtered culture. **1924** *Jrnl. Bacteriol.* IX. 401 It is established that, though non-lysing, they carry *some* lytic agent. **1929** *Jrnl. Path. & Bacteriol.* XXXII. 41 The type of resistant colony is related to these characteristics of the lysing phage. **1934** *Biol. Rev.* IX. 338 Phage particles just liberated from a lysing bacterium are more active. **1949** H. W. FLOREY et al. *Antibiotics* I. i. 36 The lysates were known as Sentocym preparations, with a prefix to indicate the type of lysed organism which they contained.

lyse, obs. f. *lees* pl. of LEE *sb.*[2]; obs. pl. LOUSE.

lyse, obs. 3rd sing. ind. pres. LIE *v.*[1]

Lysenkoism (laɪˈsɛŋkəʊɪz(ə)m). [f. the name *Lysenko* (see below) + -ISM.] Belief in or advocacy of the views of the Russian agronomist T. D. Lysenko (1898–1976), who opposed modern genetics and advocated neo-Lamarckian views and who for a time achieved great influence in Soviet Russia. Cf. MICHURINISM.

1948 *Discovery* Nov. 325/1 The opponents of Lysenkoism did not remain silent. **1962** *New Scientist* 11 Jan. 101/2 It would mean that if genes can be offset by a non-hereditary factor, that very factor could in effect become hereditary... This, surely, would be Lysenkoism, or an aspect of it. **1969** I. M. LERNER tr. *Medvedev's Rise & Fall T. D. Lysenko* vi. 136 The period of absolute domination of Lysenkoism in Soviet biology and agronomy was relatively short-lived. **1974** *Nature* 11 Oct. 558/1 A convinced anti-Lysenkoist, whose career suffered considerably during the years of Lysenkoism, Astaurov became a focus for the anti-Lysenkoist reaction.

Hence **Lyˈsenkoist**, one who believes in or advocates the views of Lysenko; also as *adj.*

1949 *Jrnl. Heredity* XL. 197/1 The Lysenkoist offensive is a two-pronged attack. **1950** *New Biol.* VIII. 6 The argument between Lysenkoists and geneticists is in the tradition of those great controversies which periodically ruffle, sometimes convulse, the progress of a science. **1969** *Nature* 13 Sept. 1182/1 He describes the total failure of.. attempts to breed cows with high butter-fat by hybridization with Jerseys by Lysenkoist principles. **1973** *New Yorker* 24 Sept. 119/1 In 1971..Lysenkoists were still accusing classical geneticists of failure to achieve practical results.

lysergic (laɪˈsɜːdʒɪk), *a. Chem.* [f. *lys* (in HYDROLYSIS) + ERG(OT *sb.* + -IC.]

lysergic acid: **a.** A crystalline tetracyclic compound, $C_{16}H_{16}N_2O_2$, containing the indole nucleus and occurring in two enantiomorphic forms, the dextrorotatory one being produced by the hydrolysis of ergot alkaloids.

1934 JACOBS & CRAIG in *Jrnl. Biol. Chem.* CIV. 547 A new substance was obtained..which possessed both acid and basic properties and which we have named lysergic acid. **1961** *New Scientist* 2 Nov. 278 The alkaloids of ergot are all derivatives of lysergic acid, an indole compound. **1964** D. F. DOWNING in M. Gordon *Psychopharmacol. Agents* I. xiii. 572 Lysergic acid derivatives with biological activity are.. known to occur both in fungi and higher plants. The most active hallucinogenic substance (LSD-25) has, however, been obtained only by synthesis from (+)-lysergic acid. **1969** T. A. BAN *Psychopharmacol.* xviii. 347/1 Lysergic acid diethylamide, or, as commonly referred to, LSD_{25}, is a synthetic product prepared from lysergic acid.

b. Used *ellipt.* for *lysergic acid diethylamide*, or (less commonly) any derivative of the acid.

1952 *Jrnl. Mental Sci.* XCVIII. 314 High doses of glucose raising the blood sugar above 200 mgm. inhibit the action of lysergic acid (LSD. 25). **1954** *Brit. Jrnl. Psychol.* XLV. 2/4 The visions produced by such drugs as mescaline and lysergic acid. **1955** *Sci. Amer.* June 39/1 The creation of experimental psychoses with lysergic acid thus opens the way to studying treatments and the nature of mental illness. **1957** J. S. HUXLEY *Relig. without Revelation* vii. 168 Mescalin and lysergic acid induce remarkable intensifications and modifications of consciousness, including often a sense of transcendence of self. **1958** *Sunday Times* 1 June 7/5 Lysergic acid should be tried for its extraordinary property of resurrecting childhood. **1962** [see LSD[2]]. **1964** *New Statesman* 28 Feb. 347/3 (Advt.), Author seeks objective confirmation of subjective mystical experience under Lysergic Acid (LSD 25). **1969** T. A. BAN *Psychopharmacol.* xviii. 348/1 Other lysergic acids. Besides LSD_{25} there are at least eight other lysergic acid derivatives with psychotomimetic properties. **1972** *Daily Tel.* (Colour Suppl.) 11 Aug. 12/3 The acids, like the barbiturates and amphetamines, are synthetically produced, and the best known is lysergic acid, LSD.

Hence **lysergic acid diethylamide** (daɪˈɛθɪl-, daɪəˈθaɪləmaɪd), the diethylamide of lysergic acid (in which the group $-N(C_2H_5)_2$ replaces the hydroxyl group of the acid), an extremely powerful synthetic hallucinogen which can produce profound changes in perception (esp. vision) and mood, with psychotic symptoms resembling those of schizophrenia, and which has been given orally in psychotherapy, usu. as the water-soluble tartrate, a colourless odourless powder; also called LSD[2], LYSERGIDE.

1944 *Chem. Abstr.* XXXVIII. 1502 With $NHEt_2$ condensation gave *d*-lysergic acid diethylamide. **1950** *Diseases Nervous Syst.* XI. 241/1 Occasionally, it was observed that patients were able to verbalize the repressed components of their conflicts during a toxic delirium. This led us to consider various drugs that might induce a transitory delirious state. It was during this search that the Sandoz Company called to our attention and made available d-lysergic acid diethylamide (L.S.D. 25). **1955** *Sci. News Let.* 2 July 4/1 LSD, short for lysergic acid diethylamide, is a chemical that produces hallucinations and delusions in healthy persons like those in mental sickness. **1965** *New Scientist* 22 Apr. 224/3 Lysergic acid diethylamide (LSD 25) and mescaline are..often called 'psychotomimetic', because some of the symptoms which they produce create certain resemblances to schizophrenic illness. **1967** *Economist* 7 Oct. 20/1 The coming thing is lysergic acid diethylamide (LSD). **1969** [see sense a above]. **1971** *Nature* 29 Jan. 347/1 Small doses (~ 100 μg) of lysergic acid diethylamide (LSD) taken orally cause hallucinations and distortions of visual perception in man. *Ibid.* 16 July 191/1 Lysergic acid diethylamide (LSD-25) is believed to cause chromosome abnormalities.

lysergide (laɪˈsɜːdʒaɪd). *Pharm.* [f. LYSERG(IC *a.* + AM)IDE.] = *lysergic acid diethylamide.*
1965 *Jrnl. Amer. Med. Assoc.* 11 Jan. 93/1 Lysergic acid diethylamide..is the most potent of the hallucinogenic drugs, and is also referred to as LSD-25, lysergide, and delysid. **1968** M. SHEPHERD et al. *Clin. Psychopharmacol.* viii. 188 Lysergide has been administered to patients suffering from many types of mental illness. *Ibid.* 190 The dangers of lysergide therapy have been repeatedly stressed.

lyserne, obs. form of LUCERN[1], the Lynx.

lysigenetic (ˌlaɪsɪdʒɪˈnɛtɪk), *a.* [f. Gr. λύσι-ς + -GENETIC.] = LYSIGENOUS.
1884 BOWER & SCOTT *De Bary's Phaner.* 409 The middle layer is soon destroyed to form lysigenetic air-passages. **1887** GARNSEY tr. *De Bary's Fungi* 496.

lysigenic (laɪsɪˈdʒɛnɪk), *a.* [See -IC.] = next.
1885 GOODALE *Physiol. Bot.* (1892) 99 *note*, The first mode of development of intercellular spaces has been termed schizogenic, the latter lysigenic.

lysigenous (laɪˈsɪdʒɪnəs), *a. Bot.* [f. Gr. λύσι-ς loosening + -γεν-ής born + -OUS.] Of intercellular spaces: Produced by the breaking down of adjoining cells.
1881 VINES *Prantl's Elem. Textbk. Bot.* (ed. 2) 60 Cavities ..which have been formed..by the absorption of a mass of tissue (lysigenous). **1883** *Athenæum* 29 Dec. 870/2 The lysigenous origin of the reservoirs of ethereal oil in these plants [Hypericaceæ].

‖**lysimachia** (ˌlaɪsɪˈmeɪkɪə). Also 6 **lysimachion**, **-ium**, **lysimachus**, 7 **lisimachia**, **lecimachus**, *pl.* 6 **lysimachies** (? -iaes), 8 **lysimachias**. [L. *lysimachia*, a. Gr. *λυσιμαχία, λυσιμάχιον, f. Λυσίμαχος Lysimachus (see LOOSESTRIFE).] = LOOSESTRIFE 1.
1578 LYTE *Dodoens* I. li. 72 Especially foure, vnder whiche all the Lysimachies shalbe comprysed. *Ibid.* 73 *Lysimachion verum*. Yellow Lysimachion or Louse stryffe. *Ibid.* 74 In English Lysimachia, Willow herbe and Louse strife. *Ibid.* 75 The yellow Lysimachus or golden Louse stryfe. **1592** R. D. *Hypnerotomachia* 36 The flowring Lysimachia or willow hearbe. **1610** FLETCHER *Faithf. Shepherdess* II. ii, Yellow Lecimachus, to giue sweete rest To the faint Shepheard. **1657** S. PURCHAS *Pol. Flying-Ins.* I. xv. 94 Bees gather of these flowers following... In June..Lisimachia. **1753** CHAMBERS *Cycl. Supp.* s.v. *Lysimachia*, 6. The lesser yellow willow herb with leaves spotted with black. 7. The two-leaved yellow lysimachia with spiked flowers. **1864** in WEBSTER; and in some later Dicts.

lysimeter (laɪˈsɪmɪtə(r)). [f. Gr. λύσι-ς loosening + -METER.] (See quots.)
1879 L. STOCKBRIDGE *Investig. Rainfall* (Boston, U.S.) 3 The word 'lysimeter' means simply an instrument for measuring the natural percolation of rain falling upon the soil. **1889** *Syd. Soc. Lex.*, *Lysimeter*, an instrument for measuring the quantity of matter dissolved in a liquid.

lysin (ˈlaɪsɪn). *Biol.* Also †-ine. [ad. G. *lysine* (W. Kruse 1893, in *Beiträge zur path. Anat. und zur allgemeinen Path.* XII. 339), f. *lysis* LYSIS: see -IN[1].] Any substance (as a bacteriolysin or hæmolysin) which is able to lyse cells; *spec.* an antibody with this ability.
1900 A. C. JONES tr. *Fischer's Struct. & Functions Bacteria* xvii. 168 To formulate a theory of immunity that shall not be lost in clouds of hypothesis is at present impossible. The alexines, antitoxines, lysines, and antilysines, that the wordy research of the last few years has given us, are at present quite unknown. **1902** *Brit. Med. Jrnl.* 5 Apr. 845 Some immune serums appear to exercise an agglutination of the red cells immediately before the lysin action. *Ibid.* 12 Apr. 920 [The first-mentioned poisons] as well as..the lysin of cholera belong to the lysin group. **1922** *Brit. Jrnl. Exper. Path.* III. 259 Gengou..has described a bacteriolytic substance which he has found in extracts of leucocytes. He found, however, that the lysin was absorbed by saturation with the microbe. **1954** A. WHITE et al. *Princ. Biochem.* xxiv. 658 If the cells are lysed, the antibodies are lysins. **1966** *McGraw-Hill Encycl. Sci. & Technol.* VII. 637/2 Lysins vary in the range of host species whose cells they will attack and in their requirements for accessory factors for lysis; the immune lysins are strictest in their requirements.

lysine (ˈlaɪsiːn). *Chem.* Also †-in. [ad. G. *lysin* (E. Fischer 1891, in *Arch. f. Anat. u. Physiol., physiol. Abtheil.* 269), prob. f. *lysatinin* LYSATININE: see -INE[5].] An amino-acid, $COOH{\cdot}CH(NH_2){\cdot}(CH_2)_3{\cdot}CH_2NH_2$, which is probably a constituent of all proteins.
1892 *Jrnl. Chem. Soc.* LXII. 1500 Not lysine, but lysine carbonate..was obtained. **1897** [see LYSATININE]. **1919** Lysin [see HISTIDINE]. **1946** *Nature* 7 Sept. 349/2 Destruction of lysine by heat has been observed in milk, casein and oat protein. **1964** *Economist* 4 July 70/3 Lysine, a chemical that has great potentialities as a protein-forming additive for animal feedstuffs. **1965** LEE & KNOWLES *Animal Hormones* ii. 33 The structural formula of vasopressin is the same in all mammals except in the pig and the hippopotamus, where the amino acid arginine is replaced by lysine. **1973** *Daily Colonist* (Victoria, B.C.) 29 Sept. 28/1 Lysine is one of the amino acids that is an essential component of protein in human nutrition.

‖**lysis** (ˈlaɪsɪs). [L. *lysis*, Gr. λύσις a loosening.]
1. *Arch.* 'A plinth or step above the cornice of the podium of ancient temples, which surrounded or embraced the stylobate' (Gwilt *Archit.* 1842).
1847 LEITCH tr. *C.O. Müller's Anc. Art* §280. 270 The lysis above the corona of a short pillar, of which there is mention made twice, was probably a small echinus.
2. *Path.* 'An insensible or gradual solution or termination of a disease or disorder without apparent phenomena' (*Syd. Soc. Lex.* 1889). Opposed to CRISIS 1.
1822–34 *Good's Study Med.* (ed. 4) I. 590 If it [the matter of the disease] be carried off at different times, it is a lysis, or resolution. **1877** ROBERTS *Handbk. Med.* (ed. 3) I. 115 In short a combination of crisis and lysis is observed.
attrib. **1897** *Trans. Amer. Pediatric Soc.* IX. 146 The lysis cases showed physical signs..later than the crisis cases.
3. *Biol.* [perh. derived from the suffix *-lysis* in *bacteriolysis*, *hæmolysis* (see LYSIS 2).] The disintegration or dissolution of cells or cell organelles; *esp.* the dissolution of bacterial cells brought about by bacteriophage.
1902 *Jrnl. Exper. Med.* 17 Mar. 4 That complete agglutination has no effect upon subsequent solution (lysis) of the corpuscles will be shown when treating of the latter phenomenon. **1922** *Brit. Med. Jrnl.* 19 Aug. 296/2 The Twort phenomenon and the d'Herelle phenomenon are identical. They are two different aspects of..the transmissible lysis of bacteria. **1922** *Brit. Jrnl. Exper. Path.* III. 258 The lysis takes place with dead as well as with living bacteria. **1937** *Jrnl. Immunol.* XXXII. 1 (*heading*) A natural hemolysin from the rat producing nuclear lysis of chicken erythrocytes. **1940** *Jrnl. Gen. Physiol.* XXIII. 643 (*title*) The growth of bacteriophage and lysis of the host. **1970** *Nature* 11 July 138/1 Certain antibiotics can cause physical disintegration or 'lysis' of cells when added to growing cultures of sensitive bacteria.

-lysis (lɪsɪs). A word-forming element [f. Gr. λύσις a loosening, parting] in many technical terms, primarily denoting decomposition, disintegration, dissolution.
1. In words in which the first element indicates the agent; e.g. (in *Chem.*) ELECTROLYSIS (*c* 1840), HYDROGENOLYSIS; (in *Biol.*) BACTERIOLYSIS (sense 1), BIOLYSIS.
2. In words in which the first element indicates the substance or object affected; e.g. (in *Chem.* and *Biochem.*) FRUCTOLYSIS, GLYCOLYSIS (1892); (in *Biol.*) BACTERIOLYSIS (sense 2), HÆMOLYSIS (cf. LYSIS 3). **b.** In a few terms in *Surg.* *-lysis* denotes surgical detachment of a part indicated by the first element, as *cardiolysis*.
3. In words in which the first element indicates some other characteristic; e.g. (in *Biol.*) AUTOLYSIS, HETEROLYSIS (sense 1); (in *Chem.*) HETEROLYSIS (sense 2), HOMOLYSIS. (CATALYSIS (1836) was adopted directly from Gr. κατάλυσις dissolution.)

lyso- (ˈlaɪsəʊ), a comb. form of LYSIS (sense 3), used to form various biological and biochemical terms, as **lyso'lecithin** *Biochem.*, any compound obtained from a lecithin by the hydrolytic removal of one of the two fatty acid groups.
1923 LEVENE & ROLF in *Jrnl. Biol. Chem.* LV. 743 Thus the product was a mixture of several substances, which we propose to name lysolecithin and lysocephalin. Inasmuch as lecithins differ in the nature of their saturated fatty acids, it is probable that there exist several lysolecithins. **1972** *Sci. Amer.* Jan. 88/3 Lecithin, like the bile salts, is synthesized by the liver, and after it is secreted into the small intestine an enzyme secreted by the pancreas converts lecithin to lysolecithin. This substance breaks up cells by removing the lipids from their membranes.

lysogenesis (laɪsəʊˈdʒɛnɪsɪs). *Bacteriology.* [f. LYSO- + -GENESIS.] Orig., the production of lysis or a lysin; in mod. use = LYSOGENY.
1901 *Lancet* 19 Oct. 1031/1 Agglutination..is not concerned in lysogenesis, which is a function of the action of immune body to addiment alone. **1902** *Encycl. Brit.* XXVI. 68/1 It has been completely established that in this phenomenon of lysogenesis [*sc.* dissolution of bacterial cells] there are two substances concerned, one specially developed or developed in excess, and the other present in normal serum. **1932** *Jrnl. Path. & Bacteriol.* XXXV. 855 The use of *B. sanguinarium* as an indicator of lysogenesis arose out of previous work..on the characteristics of a lysogenic enteritidis strain. *Ibid.* 862 The phenomenon of lysogenesis. **1951** *Jrnl. Bacteriol.* LXII. 293 (*heading*) Studies on lysogenesis. I. The mode of phage liberation by lysogenic *Escherichia coli.* *Ibid.*, The stable association of a bacteriophage with a bacterial strain, known as lysogenesis, has received scarce attention. **1968** A. L. SMITH *Microbiol. & Path.* (ed. 9) xvi. 278/1 This kind of phage is referred to as a prophage, and this condition of mutual tolerance is termed lysogeny or lysogenesis.

lysogenic (laɪsəʊˈdʒɛnɪk), *a. Biol.* [f. LYSO- + -GENIC.] Pertaining to, or capable of producing or undergoing, lysis (sense 3); *spec.* applied to a bacterium which, without being attacked by a phage, can lyse and liberate phage, an effect which is due to the ability of such a bacterium to carry, through an indefinite number of generations, a phage which is integrated with the bacterial genome and normally replicates synchronously with it but which may, under a suitable stimulus, become detached from the bacterial genome, replicate rapidly, and lyse the bacterial cell.
1899 [see *immune body* s.v. IMMUNE *a.* (*sb.*) 3 b]. **1902** *Encycl. Brit.* XXVI. 68/1 The first of these is the lysogenic action, which consists in the production of a change in the corresponding bacterium whereby it becomes granular, swells up, and ultimately may undergo dissolution. *Ibid.*, Lysogenic action is not confined to the case of bacteria, but obtains also with other organised structures. **1911** STEDMAN *Med. Dict.* 499/1 *Lysogenic*, relating to the formation of lysins. **1929** *Austral. Jrnl. Exper. Biol. & Med. Sci.* VI. 277 (*heading*) Observations on a permanently lysogenic strain of *B. enteritidis gaertner*. **1929** J. H. DIBLE *Recent Adv. Bacteriol.* iv. 73 Of greater interest are certain strains which, whilst themselves resistant, have incorporated with them the lytic principle, which remains present through future subcultures. These are the 'lysogenic' strains of Bordet. **1930** F. M. BURNET in *Syst. Bacteriol.* (Med. Res. Council) VII. xxxix. 494 There are some bacterial strains that it is impossible to deprive of lysogenic power. **1934** *Biol. Rev.* IX. 346 The ability of certain bacterial strains, so-called lysogenic bacteria, to liberate phage during their growth. **1953** [see INDUCTION 9 d]. **1953** *Cold Spring Harbor Symp. Quant. Biol.* XVIII. 71/1 It is possible that the phage population is heterogeneous, containing lytic, lysogenic, etc. phages. **1965** *New Scientist* 21 Oct. 167/2 Strains of bacteria carrying prophage DNA are described as 'lysogenic'. **1970** PASSMORE & ROBSON *Compan. Med. Stud.* II. xviii. 101/2 The prophage is normally inhibited from replication in the lysogenic state by the presence of virus-specified repressor substance that controls the operon for the structural gene. **1971** LECHEVALIER & PRAMER *Microbes* xli. 430/1 Such phages (e.g., coliphage λ) are called lysogenic viruses.
Hence **lysoge'nicity**, **ly'sogeny**, the state or property of a bacterium of being lysogenic; the phenomenon of lysis of a lysogenic bacterium with the subsequent release of phage.
1932 *Jrnl. Path. & Bacteriol.* XXXV. 857 Double lysogenicity, *i.e.* the production of two distinct phage types by a single strain, is relatively common. *Ibid.* 857 In certain important bacterial groups lysogenicity is a normal characteristic. **1934** *Biol. Rev.* IX. 347 It was found that another group of Salmonellas..did show the existence of a common type of lysogenicity. **1954** *Genetics* XXXIX. 429 (*heading*) Segregation of lambda lysogenicity during bacterial recombination in *Escherichia coli* K12. **1956** *Nature* 14 Jan. 92/1 The occurrence of lysogeny in *SU*298 was demonstrated. **1962** *Lancet* 19 May 1054/2 Little is known about the mechanism of induction of tumours by viruses, and..it seems clear that nothing directly akin to bacteriophage lysogeny occurs. **1970** PASSMORE & ROBSON *Compan. Med. Stud.* II. xviii. 101/2 When a bacteriophage infects a sensitive bacterium, it can either replicate and lyse the host cell..or it may be incorporated in the host genome in a state of lysogeny.

lysogenization (laɪˌsɒdʒənaɪˈzeɪʃən). *Bacteriology.* [f. LYSOGEN(IC *a.* + -IZATION.] The process by which a bacterium acquires a phage which becomes stably integrated into its genome; the establishment of the lysogenic state.
1953 *Cold Spring Harbor Symp. Quant. Biol.* XVIII. 71 (*heading*) Studies on lysogenization in *Escherichia coli.* **1970** *Nature* 17 Jan. 226/1 The parallels between the lysogenization of bacteria by bacteriophage and the transformation of cells in tissue culture by DNA tumour viruses are too compelling to ignore.
Hence **ly'sogenize** *v. trans.*, (of a bacteriophage) to become stably integrated into the genome of (a bacterium); also *absol.*; **ly'sogenized** *ppl. a.*; **ly'sogenizing** *vbl. sb.*
1953 *Cold Spring Harbor Symp. Quant. Biol.* XVIII. 71/1 There do occur, however, *lambda* mutants that lysogenize poorly or not at all. *Ibid.*, Different strains of artificially lysogenized bacteria. **1957** *Virology* III. 42 (*heading*) Mutations in a temperate bacteriophage affecting its ability to lysogenize *E. coli.* **1961** *Jrnl. Molecular Biol.* III. 399 (*heading*) A mutation affecting the DNA content of bacteriophage lambda and its lysogenizing abilities. **1971** *Nature* 5 Nov. 12/1 The Paris group..set about isolating mutants of this phage which by lysogenizing CRT46 cells can cause the cells to replicate at 42° C.

lysol (ˈlaɪsɒl). [f. Gr. λύσ-ις a loosening + -OL 3.] A solution of coal-tar oil in soap.
1891 *Brit. Med. Jrnl.* 12 Sept. 598/1 Lysol differs from creoline..by its most perfect solubility in..water. **1898** P. MANSON *Trop. Diseases* viii. 163 [Of plague disinfectants] the best..are..lysol..and carbolic acid.

lysosome (ˈlaɪsəsəʊm). *Biol.* [f. LYSO- + -SOME[4].] A cytoplasmic cell organelle widely found in animal tissues which contains hydrolytic enzymes enclosed in a membrane.
1955 C. DE DUVE *et al.* in *Biochem. Jrnl.* LX. 615/2 For practical purposes, it is proposed to refer to these granules as lysosomes, thus calling attention to their richness in hydrolytic enzymes. **1970** *Sci. Jrnl.* Aug. 15/4 The invader is met by the lysosome, engulfed and destroyed by the enzymes.
Hence **lyso'somal** *a.*
1957 *Symp. Soc. Exper. Biol.* X. 59 All the lysosomal enzymes..were recovered to a large extent in the parenchymal cells. **1965** *Listener* 18 Mar. 404/1 Amoebae or other protozoa take particles into food vacuoles, release lysosomal enzymes into the vacuoles and so digest the particles.

lysozyme (ˈlaɪsəzaɪm). *Biochem.* [f. LYSO- + EN)ZYME.] Any of various similar enzymes of relatively low molecular weight which are widely found in animal and plant tissues and secretions and which are capable of hydrolysing a particular mucopolysaccharide found in the

cell walls of certain Gram-positive bacteria and hence of lysing such bacteria.

1922 A. FLEMING in *Proc. R. Soc.* B. XCIII. 306 In this communication I wish to draw attention to a substance present in the tissues and secretions of the body, which is capable of rapidly dissolving certain bacteria. As this substance has properties akin to those of ferments I have called it a 'Lysozyme', and shall refer to it by this name throughout the communication. **1934** J. H. PARSONS *Dis. Eye* (ed. 7) x. 144 The tears are not a good culture medium, and though they contain traces of lysozyme, they cannot be regarded as actively bactericidal. **1949** H. W. FLOREY et al. *Antibiotics* I. p. v, No consideration has been given to antibacterial substances of animal origin, such as lysozyme. **1962** FLORKIN & MASON *Compar. Biochem.* III. viii. 413 *Ficus* lysozyme is different from the egg white enzyme. **1965** PEACOCKE & DRYSDALE *Molecular Basis Heredity* xii. 144 Similar studies have been initiated on the genetically controlled structure of the lysozyme produced in bacteria infected by normal and mutant T4 bacteriophage.

‖ **lyssa** ('lɪsə). *Path.* Pl. lyssæ. [mod.L., a. Gr. λύσσα rage, rabies. Cf. LYTTA.]

1. Rabies or hydrophobia.

1706 PHILLIPS (ed. Kersey), *Lyssa* or *Lytta*, madness, properly of a dog. **1753** in CHAMBERS *Cycl. Supp.* **1822–34** *Good's Study Med.* (ed. 4) II. 141 Inflammation of the lungs is .. occasionally found as a symptom or sequel in .. lyssa, or canine madness. *Ibid.* III. 294 Ammonia was formerly employed in cases of lyssa. **1864** in WEBSTER; and in later Dicts.

2. *pl.* Used to signify the pustules supposed to be developed under the tongue in hydrophobia.

1864 in WEBSTER. **1889** in *Syd. Soc. Lex.*

Hence **'lyssic** a. *Path.*, pertaining to rabies. **1856** in MAYNE *Expos. Lex.* **1902** in WEBSTER Suppl.

lyssacine ('lɪsəsaɪn), *sb.* and *a.* *Zool.* Also **lyssakine.** [ad. mod.L. *Lyssacina* (Zittel, 1878).

App. an irregular formation intended to refer to the loose or detached growth of the spicules in these sponges (Gr. λύ-ειν to loosen, ἀκίs spicule).]

a. *sb.* A hexactinellid sponge of the division *Lyssacina.* **b.** *adj.* Of or pertaining to this division.

1882 *Cassell's Nat. Hist.* VI. 330 It is a Lyssakine with spicules .. crossing one another. *Ibid.*, A Lyssakine sponge. **1894** *Geol. Mag.* Oct. 467 The Hexactinellids [found] all belong to the Lyssakine division.

‖ **lyssophobia** (lɪsəʊ'fəʊbɪə). *Path.* [f. Gr. λυσσο-LYSSA + Gr. -φοβία, after *hydrophobia*.] A morbid dread of hydrophobia, the symptoms of which sometimes simulate those of the actual disease.

1889 in *Syd. Soc. Lex.* **1902** in WEBSTER Suppl.

ly'st, lyst, obs. 2nd sing. ind. pres. LIE *v.*[1]

lyst(e, obs. form of LEST, LIST *v.*

lystare, -er, obs. forms of LISTER

lyster, obs. form of LEISTER.

1611 *N. Riding Rec. Soc.* I. 209 For taking four Salmon .. with a Lyster.

lystny, lystyn, obs. forms of LISTEN.

lysure, variant of LISER *Obs.*

lysz, obs. Sc. 3rd sing. ind. pres. of LIE *v.*[1]

lyt, obs. f. LIT; variant of LITE *a.* and *sb.*[4]

lytarge, lytaster, obs. ff. LITHARGE, LITSTER.

lytche, obs. form of LICH.

lyte, obs. f. LEET *sb.*[2] *Sc.*, LIGHT *sb.*, LITE.

lyten, -ynge, obs. ff. LIGHTEN *v.*[2], LIGHTNING *sb.*

lyter, obs. form of LIGHTER *sb.*[1], LITTER.

lyteradg, -age, obs. forms of LIGHTERAGE.

lyterian (laɪ'tɪərɪən), *a.* *Path.* [f. Gr. λυτήρι-ος releasing, f. λύειν to loosen + -AN.] Terminating a disease: indicating the end of a disease.

1864 in WEBSTER; and in later Dicts.

lytester, obs. form of LITSTER.

lyth, lyth-: see LITH, LITH-.

† **lyth-coop.** *Obs.* Also **8** *dial.* lief-coup, **9** *dial.* litcop. [Perh. adopted (with change of sense)

from Du. *lijfkoop*, in MDu. also *litcoop, liefcoop,* a luck-penny on the conclusion of a bargain. The Du. forms are prob. affected by popular etymology; cf. G. *leitkauf* of the same meaning, believed to be f. *leit* (= Goth. *leipus*) ale + *kauf* purchase.] An auction of household goods.

1681 HICKERINGILL *Char. Sham Plotter* Wks. 1716 I. 213 He changes his Oaths, as Chapmen come, or (as at a Lyth-Coop) for—*who bids more?* **1736** LEWIS *Hist. Thanet* (ed. 2) 37 *Lief-coup, lieue-chepe,* a Sale or Market of Goods in the Place where they stand. [The form *lieue-chepe* appears to be merely Lewis's way of indicating what he supposes to be the etymology of *lief-coup.*] **1887** *Kent. Gloss., Lief-coup. Ibid., Litcop,* same as *Lief-coup.*

lythe (laɪð). *Sc.* Also **8** lyth, **9** lithe, lyd. A name in Scotland and Ireland for the pollack.

1769 *De Foe's Tour Gt. Brit.* IV. 19 Lyths, Spirlings, Soles .. are also caught on the Scottish coasts in great plenty. **1805** FORSYTH *Beauties Scotl.* II. 380 Sea-fish are to be found in the harbour... Scad, called here lyth or lyd. **1836** YARRELL *Brit. Fishes* II. 173 This fish [the pollack] is called Lythe in Scotland .. doubtless from its nimbleness and pliancy which the word signifies. *Ibid.*, In Ireland, the Pollack may be traced as occurring .. under the names of Pollack, Laith, and Lythe. **1844** W. H. MAXWELL *Sports & Adv. Scotl.* i. (1855) 28 A scull of lithes and pollocks. **1873** BLACK *Pr. Thule* ii. 28 A heavy string of lythe in her right hand.

lythe, obs. f. LIGHT, 3rd sing. ind. pres. LIE *v.*[1]

lythonthriptick, obs. form of LITHONTRIPTIC.

‖ **Lythrum** ('lɪθrəm). [mod.L. (Linnæus), ad. Gr. λύθρον gore, in allusion to the colour of the flowers.] A genus of plants (N.O. *Lythraceæ*), including among others the Purple Loosestrife (*Lythrum Salicaria*): see LOOSESTRIFE 1 b.

1862 DARWIN in *Life & Lett.* III. 301 You might have Lythrum in North America. **1879** *Athenæum* 5 Apr. 442/1 The numerous publications of the same author [Darwin] upon Primroses, Lythrums, and other plants.

lythurgyry, obs. form of LITHARGE.

lythylman, see LITTLE MAN.

lytic ('lɪtɪk), *a.* [ad. Gr. λυτικ-ός able to loose.]

1. *Med.* Of, pertaining to, or causing a lysis (sense 2).

1889 *Syd. Soc. Lex., Lytic,* of, or belonging to, a loosing or dissolving. **1907** *Practitioner* Apr. 500 It boots little whether that increase in heat [during fever] is due to an excessive production, as the 'genetic' protagonists proclaim, or an inadequate dissipation, as their 'lytic' opponents contend. **1962** *Lancet* 26 May 1123/2 Ice placed inside the oxygen tent and cold sponging are remarkably efficient in lowering the temperature of these infants to 86–88°F (31°C)... In our experience 'lytic' agents are not required.

2. *Bacteriology.* Pertaining to or causing lysis (sense 3); *lytic cycle,* the sequence of events that takes place from the infection of a bacterium by a virulent phage to lysis of the bacterium and the release of progeny phage.

1902 *Jrnl. Exper. Med.* 17 Mar. 281 Only when the lytic serum is very fresh will solution be effected. **1922** *Brit. Jrnl. Exper. Path.* III. 259 The lytic substance, lysozyme, is very stable. **1925** C. H. BROWNING *Bacteriol.* ix. 214 He concluded that the agent causing this solution or lytic action was a living virus. **1946** *Nature* 23 Nov. 745/1 The lytic effect of certain myxobacteria upon the true bacteria (eubacteria) has been known for some years. **1963** *Biol. Abstr.* XLI. 1198/2 Studies on control of enzyme induction and initiation of lytic cycle in a lysogenic bacterium. **1968** R. RIEGER *Gloss. Genetics & Cytogenetics* 34 The introduction by infection of the genetic material of virulent phages into a susceptible host results invariably in the death and dissolution of the cell with the release of (100–10000) new phages ('lytic cycle'). **1972** *Nature* 24 Mar. 144/3 It is much more likely that the tails kill sensitive cells either by injecting lytic enzymes or by acting at the cell surface.

-lytic ('lɪtɪk), ending of adjs. corresponding to sbs. that end in -LYSIS (some of the earliest examples of which, ANALYTIC, CATALYTIC, correspond to Gr. originals in -λυτικός: cf. LYTIC *a.*).

lytically ('lɪtɪkəlɪ), *adv. Bacteriology.* [f. LYTIC *a.*: see -LY[2].] (By infection) with a lytic phage.

1967 *Jrnl. Virol.* I. 917/2 The enzyme .. in lytically infected cells is dependent on virus genome for its development. **1969** A. M. CAMPBELL *Episomes* i. 5 Such specialized transduction is not observed with lytically grown phage. **1972** *Jrnl. Molecular Biol.* LXX. 68 The sequences

of SV40 RNA which appear only late in lytically infected cells.

lytier, see LITTER.

lytmos, lytnynge: see LITMUS, LIGHTNING *sb.*

lytoridge, lytour, obs. ff. LITHARGE, LITTER.

lytre, variant of LITRE[1] *Obs.*

lytt, obs. f. LEET *sb.*[2] and *v.* *Sc.*, LIGHT, LIT.

‖ **lytta** ('lɪtə). *Phys.* [mod.L., a. Gr. λύττα, Attic form of λύσσα LYSSA.] A vermiform structure in the tongue of various carnivora.

In the dog it is vulgarly called 'the worm', and supposed to be a parasite causing liability to rabies.

1601 HOLLAND *Pliny* II. 363 There is a certaine little worme in dogs tongues, called by a Greeke name Lytta, which if it be taken out when they are young whelpes, they will never after prove mad. **1706** PHILLIPS (ed. Kersey), *Lyssa* or *Lytta,* Madness, properly of a Dog; also a Worm under a Dog's Tongue, which makes him mad, if it be not taken out; the greedy Worm. **1889** in *Syd. Soc. Lex.*

lyttar, lytter(e, -ier, obs. ff. of LITTER *sb.*

lytte, obs. form of LIT *v.*, LITE *sb.*[4]

lyttit, obs. pa. pple. of LIT *v.*, to dye.

lyttmos(se, obs. form of LITMUS.

lytton(e, -yn, obs. forms of LITTEN.

lyttre, -ur, -yer, obs. forms of LITTER.

lyturgy, obs. form of LITHARGE.

lytyn, obs. forms of LIT *v.*, LITE *v.*[1]

lyun, obs. f. LION; obs. 3rd pl. ind. pres. LIE *v.*[1]

lyv-: see LIFE-, LIVE-.

lyve, obs. form of LIEF, LIFE, LIVE *v.*

lyveret, obs. form of LEVERET.

lyves, lyvez, obs. sing. gen. and pl. of LIFE.

lyvyatan, -on, obs. forms of LEVIATHAN.

lyw-: see LIV-.

lywn, obs. f. LION.

lyxoflavin (lɪksəʊ'fleɪvɪn). *Biochem.* Also -flavine. [f. LYXO(SE + FLAVIN 2.] A yellow crystalline flavin, $C_{17}H_{20}N_4O_6$, which is a lyxose derivative and occurs in heart tissue.

1949 *Arch. Biochem.* XXII. 64 We have succeeded in isolating L-lyxoflavine from the human heart muscle. This compound was obtained in the form of monoclinic crystals. **1953** *Proc. Soc. Exper. Biol. & Med.* LXXXII. 590/2 Relatively large amounts of lyxoflavin are required for such growth stimulation, and since available evidence indicates that the compound does not occur naturally, it cannot be considered a vitamin. **1963** J. P. LAMBOOY in Florkin & Stotz *Comprehensive Biochem.* XI. ii. 31 Lyxoflavin stimulates a small increase in the growth rate of rats, chicks, and pigs when adequate amounts of riboflavin are present in the diet.

lyxose ('lɪksəʊz, -s). *Chem.* [a. G. *lyxose* (Fischer & Bromberg 1896, in *Ber. d. Deut. Chem. Ges.* XXIX. 581), f. *xylose* XYLOSE by reversal of the first syllable.] A crystalline pentose sugar, $C_5H_{10}O_5$, which differs from xylose in the configuration of the carbon atom adjacent to the aldehyde group, is rare in nature, and is obtain synthetically by degradation of the calcium salt of galactonic acid.

1896 *Jrnl. Chem. Soc.* LXX. I. 348 The lactone can be reduced with 2½ per cent. sodium amalgam at 0° to the sugar, lyxose. **1961** *Tetrahedron* XV. 80 This is the first time that L-lyxose .. has been found in a natural product [*sc.* curamycin].

lyyf, lyyf-, obs. forms of LIFE, LIFE-.

lyyn, obs. and Sc. forms of LIE *v.*[1] and [2].

M

M (ɛm), the thirteenth letter of the modern and twelfth of the ancient Roman alphabet, represents historically the Greek *mū* and the Semitic *mēm*. The Phœnician form of the letter is 𐤌, whence the early Gr. and L. ᛘ, ᛗ, M. Its phonetic value has varied little; in Eng. it has always expressed what was doubtless its original sound, that of the bilabial nasal consonant, which is normally voiced, though when it is followed by an unvoiced consonant it has an unvoiced ending. Like the other nasals, *m* is capable of being used as a sonant or vowel, denoted by ((ə)m) in the phonetic notation here employed; but in Eng. this occurs only after (ð) and (z) at the end of words (of Gr. etymology), as *rhythm*, *spasm*, *schism*, and the suffix *-ism*; in these words many speakers substitute (-əm). The letter is never silent, exc. initially before *n* in Gr. derivatives, as *mnemonic*.

I. 1. a. The letter and its sound.

c **1000** ÆLFRIC *Gram.* iii. (Z.) 6 *Semivocales* syndon seofan: f, l, m, n, r, s, x. **1530** PALSGR. Introd. 17 These thre letters M, N or E fynall..be the very and onely causes why these thre vowelles A, E, O, be formed in the brest and sounded by the nose. *a* **1637** B. JONSON *Eng. Gram.* iv, M..is pronounc'd with a kind of humming inward, the lips clos'd. Open, and full in the beginning: obscure in the end: and meanly in the midd'st. **1710** STEELE & ADDISON *Tatler* No. 260 ¶5 Which would..pronounce the Letters M or N and in short, do all the Functions of a Genuine and Natural Nose. **1727-41** CHAMBERS *Cycl.* s.v., Quintilian observes, that the M sometimes ends Latin words, but never Greek. **1854** BUSHNAN in *Circ. Sci.* (*c* 1865) I. 288/1 The mouth is closed by the lips while *m* is pronounced. **1900** *Pilot* 3 Mar. 28 The middle stage of the evolution of the eagle, namely, its transformation from the Gothic M to the fleur-de-lis.

b. M roof: see quot. 1825.

1797 *Encycl. Brit.* (ed. 3) II. 246/2 Fig. 2. Exhibits an *M* roof. **1825** J. NICHOLSON *Operat. Mechanic* 573 In roofs of rectangular buildings..a valley is introduced, which makes the vertical section in the form of the letter M, or rather an inverted W; hence it has obtained the name of an M roof. **1842-59** GWILT *Encycl. Archit.* Gloss.

2. *Printing.* = EM. *Comb.* **m-thick**: see quot.

1683 MOXON *Mech. Exerc., Printing* xiii. §1 Some [types] are m thick; by m thick is meant m Quadrat thick, which is just so thick as the Body is high. **1863** *Daily News* 10 Aug., Compositors are allowed 60 cents per thousand m's (not reckoning by n's as in England). **1892** *Academy* 3 Sept. 199/3 (advt.), 49,000 American ems (equal to 98,000 English ens) were set in eight hours.

II. Symbolical uses.

3. Used like the other letters of the alphabet to denote serial order; applied e.g. to the thirteenth (or more usually the twelfth, either I or J being often omitted) group or section in classification, the twelfth sheet of a book or quire of a MS., etc.

1850 FORSHALL & MADDEN *Wyclif's Bible* Pref. 29 The MS. M (Queen's Coll. 23). **1899** *Blackw. Mag.* Sept. 354/1, I to M are the most original passages of the hymn. **1900** *Dundee Advert.* 21 Mar. 5, M Battery Royal Horse Artillery.

4. The Roman numeral symbol for: A thousand.

(In the 15–16th c. it could be substituted for the numeral word in any context; it is now rare exc. in dates.)

1412-20 LYDG. *Chron. Troy* I. ix, There came..seuen M knightes. **1535** COVERDALE *Judg.* xii. 6 There fell of Ephraim two & fortye M. **1553** *Short Catech.* 62 b, We be feble, weake, subiect to a thousand periles, a M. temptations. **1603** OWEN *Pembrokeshire* (1892) 139 The M of oysters at the waterside is vsuallie sold for x[d] or xij[d].

5. Further symbolic uses in science.

a. In *Physics M* is used to designate the series of X-ray emission lines of longer wavelength than the *L*-series obtained by exciting the atoms of any particular element (cf. L 7 a); these arise from electron transitions to the atomic orbit of third-lowest energy, with principal quantum number 3, which is thus termed the ***M-shell***, and electrons in this shell ***M-electrons***. **M-capture**, the capture by an atomic nucleus of one of the *M*-electrons.

1911 C. G. BARKLA in *Phil. Mag.* XXII. 408 From the similarity of the behaviour of all the elements we must then admit..the possibility of further series M, N, &c. **1923** H. L. BROSE tr. *Sommerfeld's Atomic Struct. & Spectral Lines* iii. 145 Electronic transitions that end in the M-shell, furnish differences of energy that correspond to emissions of lines of the M-series. **1924** *Phil. Mag.* XLVIII. 722 Krypton..has 2 K, 8 L, 18 M, and 8 N electrons. **1924** R. W. G. WYCKOFF *Struct. Crystals* ii. 72 The M-lines have been observed from the elements from dysprosium..to uranium. **1934** H. E. WHITE *Introd. Atomic Spectra* xvi. 306 Like the *K* and *L* series lines, the *M* series lines follow nearly straight lines on a Moseley diagram. **1968** *Physical Rev.* CLXVI. 944/2 The predicted exchange-overlap correction ..is even larger for *M* capture than for *L* capture. **1970** E. P. BERTIN *Princ. & Pract. X-Ray Spectrometric Analysis* i. 27 An electron that has enough energy to expel a *K* electron obviously can also expel any *L* or *M* electron.

b. In *Physics m* and *M* denote magnetic quantum numbers, corresponding to the component of an angular momentum (often indicated by a subscript) in some physically distinguished direction (usu. that of a magnetic field). [Introduced by A. Landé 1921, in *Zeitschr. f. Physik* V. 233.]

m is usually used for a single particle, and *M* for an assemblage of particles.

1923 *Jrnl. Optical Soc. Amer.* VII. 415 The numbers at the left show the magnetic quantum number *m* characterizing each level. **1926** *Proc. R. Soc.* A. CXII. 80 It is necessary also..to take into consideration the effect of the orientation of orbits with respect to an imaginary magnetic field, and such orientation involves a fourth quantum number *m*, which in turn is itself composite and is equal to the vector sum of two subsidiary quantum numbers m_a and m_s. **1962** H. D. BUSH *Atomic & Nucl. Physics* ii. 38 It is necessary to characterize electrons in atoms by four quantum numbers *n*, *l*, m_l, m_s. **1967** W. R. HINDMARSH *Atomic Spectra* I. vi. 72 We can also perform a simple calculation for the case where the Zeeman splitting is large compared with the hyperfine structure but still small compared with the fine structure. In this case the quantum numbers M_J and M_I (which defines the *z*-component of the nuclear spin) are well defined, but not *J* and *I*.

III. 6. Abbreviations. (Abbreviations given here with the full stop are frequently used without it.)

a. M. = various proper names, as Mark, Margaret, etc.; **M.** † = Majesty; used in ancient criminal procedure (see quots. 1487, 1727–41); **M.** = member, as in ***M.B.E.***, Member(ship) of the Order of the British Empire, ***M.C.***, Member of Congress, ***M.I.A.E.***, Member of the Institute of Automobile Engineers, ***M.I.C.E.***, Member of the Institution of Civil Engineers, ***M.I.E.E.***, Member of the Institution of Electrical Engineers, ***M.I.M.E.***, Member of the Institute of Mechanical Engineers, Member of the Institute of Mining Engineers, ***M.I. Mech. E.***, Member of the Institution of Mechanical Engineers, ***M.I. Struct. E.***, Member of the Institution of Structural Engineers, ***M.J.I.***, Member of the Institute of Journalists, ***M.L.A.***, Member of the Legislative Assembly, ***M.L.C.***, Member of the Legislative Council, ***M.P.***, (see as main entry), ***M.P.P.***, (in Canada) Member of Provincial Parliament, ***M.R.C.P.***, Member of the Royal College of Physicians, ***M.R.C.S.***, Member of the Royal College of Surgeons, ***M.V.O.***, Member of the Royal Victorian Order; **M.** *Mus.* = metronome; **M.** = middling: of paper, showing slight imperfections; **M.** *Math.* = modulus; **M.** = morphine; **M.** or **m.** in astronomical tables, etc. = meridian or meridional; also (after the numeral *twelve*) = L. *meridies* noon (cf. A.M., P.M.); **M.** or **m.** = million (£300 m. = three hundred million pounds); **m.** = mass, in *Mech.*; **m.** = metre; **m.** = minute; **m.** in log-books = mist; **m.** = molar, in dental formulæ; **m.** *Mus.* = It. *mano* or F. *main* (as *mano destra*, *main droite*, right hand), *mezzo* (as ***mf*** = *mezzoforte*), in organ music, *manual*; ***m-*** (Chem.) = META-[1] 6 b; **M.A.**, mental age; **M.A.D.**, **MAD**, magnetic anomaly (or airborne) detector (or detection); **M. and D.**, medicine and duty, marked on a serviceman's sick report when he is feigning illness; **M. and V.**, meat and vegetable(s); **M.A.P.**, Ministry of Aircraft Production; **M.A.S.H.** (*U.S.*), Mobile Army Surgical Hospital; **M.A.T.S.** (*U.S.*), Military Air Transport Service; **M.C.**, Military Cross (established 1915); **M.C.C.**, Marylebone Cricket Club, the governing body of English cricket; the official title of touring teams generally deemed to represent England; **Mcf**, **mcf**, etc., a thousand cubic feet; so **MMcf(d)**, etc., a million cubic feet (per day); **MCP**, male chauvinist pig; **M.C.P.A.**, 2-methyl-4-*c*hloro*p*henoxy*a*cetic-acid (salts and esters of which are used in sprays as herbicides); **M.C.R.**, middle common room (in the University of Oxford); **M.C.U.** (*Photogr.*), medium close-up; **M.D.**, Managing Director; **m.d.**, mental, or mentally, deficient or defective; **M.D.**, Musical Director; **M-day**, mobilization day; **m.e.** (*Bibliogr.*), marbled edges; **M.E.**, medical examiner; **M.E.**, Middle English (see ENGLISH *sb.* 1 b); **MEP**, Member of the European Parliament; cf. *Euro-MP* s.v. EURO- 2 b; **mF** (also ***mf***, etc.), microfarad; **M.F.**, **m.f.**, motherfucker; **M.F.**, machine-finish(ed), (MACHINE 9 c); **M.F.N.**, most favoured nation; **M.F.V.**, **m.f.v.**, motor fleet vessel; motor fishing vessel; **M.G.**, machine-glazed (MACHINE 10); **M.G.**, machine-gun; **M.G.** (*Building*), make good; **M.G.B.** [Russ. *Ministérstvo Gosudárstvennoĭ Bezopásnosti*], Ministry of State Security; **M.G.C.**, machine-gun company; **m.g.d.**, million gallons per day; **M.G.M.**, Metro-Goldwyn-Mayer (a film company); freq. *attrib.*, esp. to denote a roaring lion used as a symbol by this company; **MHD**, magnetohydrodynamic(s); **M.H.W.**, mean high water; **M.I.**, Military Intelligence (followed by numerals which indicate departments); **M.I.5**, **M.I.6**, sections of Military Intelligence which (until 1964) dealt with matters of state security; cf. *D.I.*; **M.I.**, Mounted Infantry; **MIA**, missing in action; **MICR**, magnetic ink character recognition; **mip**, mean indicated pressure; **MIRV**, multiple independently targeted re-entry vehicle (a type of missile); hence as *vb. trans.*, to equip with multiple independently targetable warheads; so ***MIRVed*** ppl. adj., ***MIRVing*** vbl. sb.; **M.I.T.**, Massachusetts Institute of Technology; **M.K.S.**, **m.k.s.**, metre-kilogramme-second; **M.L.**, motor launch; **M.L.D.**, **MLD**, minimum lethal dose; **M.L.F.**, multilateral force; **MLR**, minimum lending rate (see MINIMUM *a.* b); **M.L.W.**, mean low water; **M.M.**, Military Medal (established 1916); **m.m.f.**, **M.M.F.**, magnetomotive force; **M.M.P.I.**, Minnesota Multiphasic Personality Inventory; **M.O.**, mass-observation; **M.O.**, medical officer; **m.o.**, modus operandi; **M.O.**, **m.o.** (*Chem.*), molecular orbital; **M.O.**, money order; **M. of I.**, **M.O.I.**, Ministry of Information; **M.O.H.**, Medical Officer of Health; **M.O.L.**, manned orbiting (or orbital) laboratory; **MOR** (orig. *U.S.*) = MIDDLE-OF-THE-ROAD 2; **M.O.S.** (*U.S. Mil.*), Military Occupational Specialty; **MOS(T)**, metal-oxide-semiconductor (transistor); **M.O.T.**, **MoT**, Ministry of Transport; also *ellipt.*, a Ministry of Transport test to establish the roadworthiness of a motor vehicle; also *attrib.*; **m.p.**, **M.P.**, melting point; **M.P.**, military police(man); **m.p.g.**, miles per gallon; **m.p.h.**, miles per hour; so as *v. intr.* (nonce), to travel; **M.Q.** (*Photogr.*), metol-hydroquinone; **M.R.A.**, Moral Rearmament, BUCHMANISM; **M.R.B.M.**, medium range ballistic missile; **mRNA** (†**MRNA**), messenger RNA; **M.R.P.** [Fr. *Mouvement Républicain Populaire*], Popular Republican Movement, the Christian Democratic Party of France under the Fourth Republic; **M.S.** (*Photogr.*), medium shot; **M.S.**, minesweeper; **M.S.**, morphine (sulphate); **MS**, multiple sclerosis; **MSG**, monosodium glutamate; **MSH**, melanocyte-stimulating hormone; **M.S.I.** [It. *Movimento Sociale Italiano*], Italian Social Movement, the Fascist Party of Italy under the Republic; **M.T.**, machine translation; **M.T.**, motor transport; **M.T.B.**, motor torpedo boat; **M.T.C.**, Mechanized Transport Corps; **M.T.I.**, **m.t.i.**, moving-target indication (a radar system that gives prominence to moving objects); **M.V.D.** [Russ. *Ministérstvo Vnútrennikh Del*], Ministry of Internal Affairs, replacing the N.K.V.D.; **MX** (*U.S. Mil.*) [f. *m*issile, e*x*perimental], an experimental intercontinental ballistic missile with multiple warheads, designed to be easily movable from one location to another; also ***MX missile***; **M.Y.O.B.**, mind your own business. Also M AND B, M.B., M.D., M.S.[1], Ms[2], MUSA[2].

1869 D. G. ROSSETTI in Mackail *W. Morris* (1899) I. 204 The *Ms [= Morrises] at Ems. **1487** *Act 4 Hen. VII*, c. 13 Every suche persone so convicted for murdre, to be marked with a *M. upon the brawne of the lefte thumbe. **1581** J. HAMILTON in *Cath. Tract.* (S.T.S.) 75/3 His thankfull spreit tovart your M. **1727-41** CHAMBERS *Cycl.*, *M*, in law, the brand or stigma of a person convicted of manslaughter, and admitted to the benefit of clergy. **1599** A. M. tr. *Gabelhouer's Bk. Physick* 360 Take vnpeeled Barlye *M iiij. **1727-41** CHAMBERS *Cycl.*, **M*, in astronomical tables,..is used for *Meridional* or southern, sometimes for *Meridies* or mid-day.

1840 R. H. Dana *Bef. Mast* xxxiv. 129 At twelve M., it bore N.W.½N. **1889** G. M'Gowan tr. *Bernthsen's Text-bk. Org. Chem.* xvii. 329 The xylene of coal tar consists of a mixture of the three isomers, **m*-xylene being present to the extent of 70 to 85 p.c. **1929** L. A. Coles *Introd. Mod. Org. Chem.* xxvii. 327 *m*-Dinitrobenzene is always prepared by the nitration of benzene in two stages. **1968** R. O. C. Norman *Princ. Org. Synthesis* xi. 368 The t-butyl group is removed by reaction with more of the starting *m*-dialkylbenzene. **1971** *Nomencl. Org. Chem.* (I.U.P.A.C.) (ed. 3) A. 18 The position of substituents is indicated by numbers except that *o-* (*ortho*), *m-* (*meta*) and *p-* (*para*) may be used in place of 1,2-, 1,3-, and 1,4-, respectively, when only two substituents are present. **1894** *Amer. Dict. Printing & Bookmaking* 354/1 **M paper*, paper which is not up to the highest standard of the manufacturer. **1937** E. J. Labarre *Dict. Paper* 170/1 M paper is that which is not up to the first sorting, but in which the imperfections are trivial. **1948** *Words into Type* 545 M's or M paper. Paper not up to the standard quality. **1934** Webster, **M*,.. mega- (million). **1955** *Times* 3 May 10/3 (*heading*) $1M. declined. *Ibid.* 9 May 8/2 $28m. for aid to Spain. *a* **1912** W. T. Rogers *Dict. Abbrev.* (1913), **M.*, morphin. **1914** Jackson & Hellyer *Vocab. Criminal Slang* 60 *M*, or *Morph*, used by morphine fiends. Sulphate of morphia. **1922** M (= morphine) [see C C III. 3]]. **1935** A. J. Pollock *Underworld Speaks* 74/1 *M.*, morphine (a white alkaloid derived from opium). **1953** W. Burroughs *Junkie* xii. 125 When I have an H or M shooting habit I am non-sociable. **1940** R. S. Woodworth *Psychol.* (ed. 12) iv. 111 Of the two measures, *MA and IQ, which is the better index of intelligence? **1960** J. B. Carroll in Saporta & Bastian *Psycholinguistics* (1961) 340/1 There has been much interest in the relation between language maturity and measures of intellectual functioning such as MA or IQ. **1952** *Coronet* May 78/1 Scientists..thought, a compasslike magnetic device could be made to respond to even as small a body of metal as a submarine... U.S. Navy engineers tried dangling the tiny magnetic element on the end of a hundred-foot cable, through which electrical impulses traveled to a recording instrument in the plane. It worked, and *MAD (magnetic air-borne detector) was soon helping our Navy send U-boats to the bottom. **1967** *Sunday Mail Mag.* (Brisbane) 22 Jan. 6/3 The long metal shape of a sub shows up distinctly as MAD passes over the hull. **1968** A. Hine *Magnetic Compasses & Magnetometers* xi. 308 The purpose of M.A.D. is to find small irregularities in the general pattern of the Earth's magnetic field, which are associated with ferro-magnetic deposits of rock and oil-bearing strata. **1917** A. G. Empey *Over Top* 299 **M. and D.*, what the doctor marks on the 'sicker' or sick report when he thinks Tommy is faking sickness. **1919** W. H. Downing *Digger Dial.* 33 *M. & D.*, medicine and duty. A familiar sick-parade slogan. **1935** G. Blake *Shipbuilders* 256 If that wound's not healed by to-morrow it's M. and D. for you. **1925** Fraser & Gibbons *Soldier & Sailor Words* 148 **M and V*, a familiar expression for the tinned meat and vegetable ration. **1944** *R.A.F. Jrnl.* Aug. 260 We are given..a hot tin of M. & V. (Meat and Vegetable: you pour it into your mess tin and eat it with a spoon). **1944** A. Jacob *Traveller's War* 273 The spearhead of the Eighth Army will eat a Christmas dinner of tinned meat and vegetable stew (the famous 'M. and V.'), biscuits and tinned fruit and tea. **1972** A. Neave *Flames of Calais* iii. 34 By nightfall my troop was cooking M & V beneath the plane trees of the market place. **1942** Partridge *Dict. Abbrev.* 60/1 *M.A.P. **1946** *Happy Landings* (Air Ministry) July 1/2 Returning to England as Controller of Research and Development at M.A.P. **1953** *Economist* 14 Nov. 505/2 The Ministry of Aircraft Production. The problems that will confront the Atomic Energy Corporation have a family likeness..to those of MAP. **1950** *Army Information Digest* Dec. 51 Critical cases are flown by..helicopter direct to Mobile Army Surgical Hospitals (*MASH). **1970** *Monthly Film Bull.* (Brit. Film Inst.) July 140/2 *M-A-S-H*, U.S.A., 1969 Director: Robert Altman... Hawkeye Pierce, Duke Forrest and Trapper John McIntyre arrive to join the 4077th Mobile Army Surgical Hospital in Korea, and are kept busy operating on wounded men sent back from the front lines. **1955** R. J. Schwartz *Compl. Dict. Abbrev.* 109/1 *MATS. **1958** *Times* 24 July 9/7 M.A.T.S...has to have up-to-date aircraft capable of carrying freight as well as troops. **1917** *Illustr. London News* 30 June 759/1 The five classes of the Order [of the British Empire] are:..4. Officers (O.B.E.), 5. Members (*M.B.E.). **1936** *Discovery* Sept. 292/1 Major A. B. Klein, M.B.E. **1955** *Times* 8 July 15/2 Mr. Stace has recently been honoured with the M.B.E. and we are all extremely gratified that such an honour should have been conferred on another stalwart of the industry. **1972** *Times* 6 Dec. 32/3 In proud and ever loving memory..of Capt. John Henry Brunt, V.C., M.C...and his beloved father, T. H. Brunt, M.B.E. **1832** *Boston Even. Transcript* 29 June 2/2 Two bundles were lately received at the Opeloasas post office, franked 'H. A. Bullard, *M.C.' which contained two Marseilles vests for children in that parish. **1904** *N.Y. Even. Post* 23 Sept. 5 John Wesley Gaines, M.C., made a careful study some years ago of the evils of a President's eligibility to reëlection. *a* **1917** M.C. [see *D.S.O.* (D III. 3)]. **1969** S. Mays *Fall out Officers* viii. 51 He's only got one eye and a lump shot aff his knee; both shot aff when he got his M.C. **1862** *Lillywhite's Cricket Scores* I. 128 Neither the *M.C.C. books or 'Bentley' gave the name of the ninth batsman on the M.C.C. side. **1972** *Times* 6 Dec. 11/1 MCC's outcricket tightened up after an alarming start. **1960** V. B. Guthrie *Petroleum Products Handbk.* iii. 43 **Mcf*, 1,000 cu ft. *Ibid.* xvii. 18 *MCF*, abbreviation for thousand cubic feet. **1975** *Economist* 30 Aug. 8/3 Someone has interpreted mcf as million cubic feet whereas according to American practice this means 1,000 cubic feet. **1971** *Publishers' Weekly* 1 Nov. 22 *MCPs, you should know by now, are Male Chauvinist Pigs, an epithet that has grown so common it is now abbreviated. **1946** G. Blackman in *Jrnl. Ministry of Agric.* LIII. 17 These names ..are unlikely to be remembered, so that the abbreviations *MCPA and DCPA can perhaps serve better. *Ibid.*, White charlock, corn buttercup and shepherd's needle are best destroyed with MCPA. **1958** *New Biol.* XXVI. 45 The selective growth regulating herbicides such as M.C.P.A... and 2,4-D..are the most commonly used herbicides on pastures and the buttercup species differ in their sensitivity to these. **1971** *Arable Farmer* Feb. 12/2 MCPA, discovered during the war and still widely used alone or in mixture for cereals. **1966** *Rep. Comm. Inquiry Univ. Oxf.* II. 483 For those who enjoy the college atmosphere and who belong to a college which has a *MCR *and* which is usefully situated in relation to their living accommodation or place of work, this can largely supply their need. **1959** W. S. Sharps *Dict. Cinematogr.* 110/2 **M.C.U.*, abbreviation for Medium Close-up. **1955** R. J. Schwartz *Compl. Dict. Abbrev.* 110/2 **MD*..; Managing Director. **1963** *Times* 14 May p. i/4 (Advt.), Do give this a little thought and perhaps you might have a word with the Managing Directors of some of the subsidiary companies... Have you talked to the M.D.s about it? **1942** Partridge *Dict. Abbrev.* 61/1 **M.D.*, ..mentally deficient. **1968** 'L. Black' *Outbreak* xiv. 137, I just don't see..how the m.d. ward got infected. **1971** *Oz* May 5/1 He is classified in Orange County..as MDSO (mentally defective sexual offender). **1927** *Melody Maker* Apr. 397/1 It would be useless for any *M.D. to call a rehearsal and run through music *before* seeing the 'subject' he has to accompany. **1967** *Stage* 2 Mar. 3/2 Ernest Woodhouse the MD of Creswell Colliery Band. **1937** *Reader's Digest* Aug. 97 *M-day in America. **1970** N. Armstrong et al. *First on Moon* i. 18 That was M day, and a good one to remember. *a* **1912** W. T. Rogers *Dict. Abbrev.* (1913) 123/1 **m.e.* (book), marbled edges. **1952** J. Carter *ABC for Bk.-Collectors* 12 *M.e.*, marbled edges. **1961** Webster, **ME*,..medical examiner. **1968** H. Waugh *30 Manhattan East* (1969) 120 I'll give your boss the M.E.'s verdict as soon as I get it. **1874** H. Sweet in *Trans. Philol. Soc. 1873–4* 526 The word *greet* [in the eighteenth century] = *M.E. *greet* (O.E. *grēat*) is an example of exceptional retention of the older *ee*. **1927** *Englische Studien* 10 Nov. 74 The investigations which have been published hitherto with a view of classifying the ME. dialects by the aid of place-name material. **1972** M. L. Samuels *Ling. Evol.* v. 85 The plural *-ep* had been replaced by *-en* in the Midlands, and early ME texts from East Anglia show this feature as their only distinction of number. **1976** *Times* 11 Feb. 14/1 There is no doubt that the British Government can devise a means of electing *MEPs. **1984** *Which?* June 265/3 MEPs are paid the same as national MPs in their respective countries. **1914** E. A. Dawe *Paper* 157/2 (*index*) Machine finish (*M.F.). **1965** S. C. Gilmour *Paper* (ed. 2) xix. 218 M.F. papers are much used for printing formes of type with line blocks. **1892** C. T. & W. H. Jones *Telegr. Connections* 15/2 On one end of the condenser will usually be found a stamp like this: 2·5 *M.F. The microfarad (for which M.F. stands) is the one-millionth part of a farad. **1911** L. W. Bishop *Wireless Operators' Pocket-Bk.* v. 62 The highest capacity of a variable condenser should not be over ·004 mf. **1940** *Chambers's Techn. Dict.* 544/2 *mF.*, *μF.*, abbrev. for micro-farad. **1958** *Times Rev. Industry* May 32/1 Single phase 26V current in conjunction with a 1·5 mf tuning capacitor. **1969** C. M. Rodgers *Songs of Blackbird* 38 None of us can relax until the last *m.f.'s Been done in. **1971** B. Malamud *Tenants* 165 The blacks have to murder you white MF's for cripplin our lives. **1973** S. Henderson *Understanding New Black Poetry* 44, I am not speaking merely of words like 'nigger' and 'the big M.F.', as Ron Welburn calls it. **1942** Partridge *Dict. Abbrev.* 62/1 **M.F.N.*, most favoured nation. **1961** *Times* 16 May 15/7 Consequently, the M.F.N. concept is not helpful. **1948** *Hansard Commons* 8 Mar. 971/1, I hope I shall be able to satisfy the hon. Gentleman with the figures for..the number of fishery protection vessels. We have now..eight ships plus two *M.F.V.s. **1949** P. F. Anson *Scots Fisherfolk* 84 The fleet has also been increased by the addition of a large number of Admiralty-built, diesel-motor vessels (M.F.V.s), originally used by the Navy, but since allocated to fishermen. **1973** A. MacVicar *Painted Doll Affair* xiii. 148 They're at sea in that m.f.v. **1974** 'M. Hebden' *Pride of Dolphins* II. ix. 188 They were moving up astern of a big grey-painted vessel..an ex-naval M.F.V. **1914** E. A. Dawe *Paper* iv. 25 The paper passing round this heated cylinder is dried, and glazed on one side, hence the term *M.G., or machine-glazed paper. **1937** E. J. Labarre *Dict. Paper* 170/2 Characteristic of machine glazed papers (abbr. M.G.) is that they are only glazed on one (the under) side, the other being in the (rough) condition in which it comes from the wet end of the machine. **1965** S. C. Gilmour *Paper* (ed. 2) xix. 236 Litho posters are generally printed on M.G. paper. **1915** D. O. Barnett *Let.* 8 July 207 I'm going to be *M.-G. officer. **1969** S. Mays *Fall out Officers* xx. 154 Sergeant Yardley of M.G. Squadron. **1940** *Chambers's Techn. Dict.* 544/2 **M.G.* (Build.), abbrev. for make good. **1950** Webster Add., *M.G.B. **1974** T. P. Whitney tr. *Solzhenitsyn's Gulag Archipelago* I. i. iv. 145 The MGB wasn't interested in the truth and had no intention of letting anyone out of its grip once he was arrested. **1917** W. Owen *Let.* 12 Feb. (1967) 433 We have a Canadian,..various *M.G.C.'s, a S.W.B. **1963** F. D. Fawcett *Cycl. Initials & Abbrev.* 97/2 *MGC*, Machine Gun Corps, disbanded 1922. **1955** *Times* 7 July 1/5 (Advt.), The extent of the supply works to be supervised and maintained include the following... Ultimate maximum output of finished water 21·5 *m.g.d. **1935** Ade *Let.* 27 June (1973) 186 The sad facts in regard to *The County Chairman* are that *M.G.M. bought the talking rights and recently sold them to Fox. **1952** S. Kauffmann *Philanderer* (1953) iv. 68 What we want is some kind of gimmick or slogan or handle for the public to tie on to with this thing... Like 'Ask the man who owns one'. Or the M.G.M. lion. A trade-mark. **1974** W. Garner *Big enough Wreath* xvi. 250 He'd allowed his *id* an MGM roar. **1974** P. M. Hubbard *Thirsty Evil* i. 14 Jimmy was my agent... We had not reached the point yet where he had to haggle with M.G.M. over the film-rights. **1960** *Aeroplane* XCIX. 837/2 The latter included ion-drive, solar propulsion, plasmajet propulsion, photon-drive, and *MHD (Magneto-hydrodynamic) propulsion. **1965** *New Scientist* 3 June 652/2 By passing the exhaust gases from the MHD generator into a conventional steam-raising plant, an overall thermal efficiency of 55 per cent might be achieved. **1974** *Nature* 1 Mar. 89/3 In the post-war years Ferraro did much to encourage research in MHD. [**1920** *Tide Tables* (Admiralty, Hydrographic Dept.) I. p. xxi (*heading*) M.H.W.S...M.H.W.N.] **1923** N. Davey *Stud. Tidal Power* iv. 63 Taking the *M.H.W. and M.L.W. areas of the estuary at Salcombe..the half-tide outflow system will utilise a mean average of 49% of the maximum volume of water above M.L.W.S. level. **1964** V. J. Chapman *Coastal Vegetation* ii. 19 It is possible to regard the littoral as extending from mean high water (M.H.W.) to mean low water (M.L.W.); alternatively, it can be defined as reaching from extreme high water mark (E.H.W.M.) to extreme low water mark (E.L.W.M.). Most of the early ecological work is based upon one of these two definitions. **1939** D. Wheatley *Sixty Days to Live* vi. 58 'It's a matter which may affect the welfare of the whole nation. I really mean that'. 'Well, if you put it that way. Is this *M.I.5, or something?' **1940** H. Innes *Trojan Horse* ii. 32 The search of a representative of M.I.5. **1963** V. Gielgud *Goggle-Box Affair* xiii. 126 He ultimately opted for Polish nationality, promising apparently to do occasional jobs for M.I.6 on the side. **1964** M.I.5 [see D.I. (D III. 3)]. **1965** B. Sweet-Escott *Baker St. Irreg.* iii. 85 M.I.9..had the job of helping allied prisoners of war to escape. **1901** Kipling *Five Nations* (1903) 164 (*title*) *M.I. **1929** J. Buchan *Courts of Morning* II. i. 177 They've first-rate cavalry, but indifferent M.I. **1946** *Newsweek* 6 May 36/2 From D Day until May 6, 1945 ..more than 10 per cent of the total casualties were listed as *MIA. **1970** *Sunday Mail* (Brisbane) 8 Feb. 5/1 Diana O'Grady has groped through 34 months as the wife of an MIA (missing in action). *a* **1912** W. T. Rogers *Dict. Abbrev.* (1913) 125/1 **M.I.A.E.*, Member of the Institute of Automobile Engineers. **1935** *Discovery* Sept. 276 H. Warren, M.I.E.E., M.I.A.E. **1885** *List of Subscribers, Classified* (United Telephone Co.) (ed. 6) 89 *Engineers* (Civil)... Lowe J. E., *M.I.C.E., M.I.M.E. (of Bolling & Lowe). **1966** *MICR [see magnetic *a.* 1]. **1970** O. Dopping *Computers & Data Processing* iii. 62 MICR readers do not utilize the information contained in the vertical distribution of ink. They analyze only the horizontal distribution. *a* **1912** W. T. Rogers *Dict. Abbrev.* (1913) 125/2 **M.I.E.E.*, Member of the Institute of Electrical Engineers. **1937** *Discovery* Apr. p. xxviii/1 Professor John Hollingworth, M.A., D.Sc., F.C.G.I., M.I.E.E. *Ibid.*, Professor Dempster Smith, M.B.E., M.Sc.Tech., *M.I.M.E. **1909** *Cent. Dict.* Suppl., *M.I.Mech.E. **1961** Webster, *mip. **1962** *Engineering* 23 Nov. 662/2 A series of marine engines of various sizes, all having the high mip pressure of 10·4 kg per sq. cm. **1967** *Technology Week* 20 Feb. 12/3 A program to demonstrate the feasibility of a solid propellant Post Boost Control System (PBCS) to deliver Multiple Independent Re-entry Vehicle (*MIRV) payloads is expected to be funded shortly. **1968** *N.Y. Times* 3 Nov. iv. 7 MIRVing the Polaris system allows a dozen warheads to be fitted to a single Poseidon missile. **1970** *Time* 20 Apr. 22 Each MIRVed rocket is capable of carrying a number of warheads. **1974** L. Deighton *Spy Story* xii. 119 Can they retarget the MIRVs before launching? **1974** *Times* 5 Mar. 7/3 The multiple independently targeting technology for warheads (Mirvs) is the most striking Soviet advance adduced in the report. **1974** *Nature* 6 Dec. 431/1 Proposals for SALT-2 now include multiple warheads in the list of constraints,..presumably because it is considered economically desirable not to go the whole way on MIRVing. **1975** *Sci. Amer.* Jan. 48/1 The tentative agreement represents an incremental advance for arms control..in that for the first time it includes strategic bombers and limits at least the number of missiles that can be MIRVed. **1937** *Discovery* Mar. p. xx/1 W. B. McKay, M.Sc.Tech., *M.I.Struct.E. **1950** J. D. MacDonald *Brass Cupcake* (1955) xii. 124 Very distinguished Boston type. Taught mathematics at *M.I.T. **1954** D. Riesman *Individualism Reconsidered* v. 303 The M.I.T. students who brought us together dreamed up the whole idea, then found the means to implement it. **1968** Chomsky & Halle *Sound Pattern Eng.* p. x, The general point of view that underlies this descriptive study is one that several of us have been developing for more than fifteen years, at M.I.T. and elsewhere, at first independently, but increasingly as a joint effort. **1909** *Cent. Dict.* Suppl., *MJI. **1935** *Engineering* 26 July 95/1 This new system has been designated the Giorgi-*M.K.S. system, and in it the practical electrical units are essential constitutional elements in one-to-one relation, with the result that the numerical conversion factors need no longer be..memorised. **1963** Jerrard & McNeill *Dict. Sci. Units* 15 The Giorgi or M.K.S. system attracted little attention until about 1935 but after this interest in them [*sic*] increased and in 1948 the 9th International Conference on Weights and Measures adopted the M.K.S. definition as their definition of the ampere. **1968** M. S. Livingston *Particle Physics* xii. 208 In the rationalized mks system of electromagnetic units, charge becomes a fourth fundamental quantity. **1942** Partridge *Dict. Abbrev.* 63/1 **M.L.*,..motor launch. **1945** 'N. Shute' *Most Secret* i. 4 The *Raumboot* is rather like our own M.L., isn't it? **1897** *Medicine Hat* (Alberta) *News* 8 Apr. 4/2 Another of our *M.L.A.'s is to join his confreres in the new Western Eldorado, the marvellously rich Kootenay. **1933** *Bulletin* (Sydney) 6 Sept. 12/3 The combination of the guillotine and the division system is being developed to a stage when the main duty of an M.L.A. will be to sit on a bench and be counted like a sheep. **1970** *Globe & Mail* (Toronto) 26 Sept. 8/2 Indeed the new talk about Fraser power has been met with instant avowals of undying opposition from some of the Government's own MLAs in the Fraser Valley. **1971** *Sunday Australian* 8 Aug. 7/2 He is an old family friend and 'retainer' of Norman Smith, Labor MLA for the Mt Isa area from 1940 to 1960. **1849** *Niagara* (Ontario) *Chron.* 25 Oct. 3/2 J. Leslie, *M.L.C. **1930** L. G. D. Acland *Early Canterbury Runs* ii. 29 He..was a member of the old Provincial Council and an early M.L.C. **1971** *Hindustan Times Weekly* (New Delhi) 4 Apr. 3/4 Two MLAs and one MLC of Uttar Pradesh..joined the Congress (N) today. **1901** *M.L.D. [see addiment]. **1928** L. E. H. Whitby *Med. Bacteriol.* xx. 198 One M.L.D. is that amount of toxin which, on subcutaneous inoculation, will with certainty cause the death of a 250 gm. guinea-pig within four days. **1961** N. G. Pandalai *Textbk. Bacteriol.* (ed. 2) xii. 245 While the M.L.D. of atropine for an adult person is 130 mg., of strychnine 30–40 mg., and of cobra venom 4·4 mg., the M.L.D. of the crude tetanus toxin is only 0·2 mg. or even less. **1973** White & Tinbury *Essent. Immunol. & Microbiol.* II. vii. 120 The ultimate measured effect of toxin is the MLD. **1963** *Times* 10 June 10/5 Thus the first and perhaps most important objection to the multilateral force (*M.L.F.) has been largely removed. **1972** *Times* 23 Dec. 1/2 The Bank of England's minimum lending rate (*MLR)..rose by 1 per cent yesterday to 9 per cent. **1981** *Daily Tel.* 20 Aug. 17/2 As from today, MLR will cease to be posted except in very unusual circumstances. **1904** *Amer. Jrnl. Sci.* XVII. 335 The datum plane used..is mean low water—*M.L.W.—at the Battery as used by the Department of Docks and Ferries. **1923, 1964** M.L.W. [see *M.H.W.* above]. **1933** *M.M. [see Minnie[2], minnie]. **1971** D. Niven *Moon's a Balloon* v. 63, I caught a glimpse of the medal ribbons of the D.C.M. and M.M. on his chest. **1973** G. G. Spalding in P. Hepple *Outlook for Natural Gas* iv. 55 (*heading*) Estimated well deliverability (*MMCFD). **1974** *Petroleum Rev.* XXVIII. 792/2 The field came on

production in September 1971 and is currently producing 560 MMcfd. **1975** *North Sea Background Notes* (Brit. Petroleum Co.) 19 Under this agreement, BP undertook to deliver at least 50 million cubic feet of gas a day for a period of 15 years. Later revisions to the contract have resulted in a present commitment of 168 mmcfd as the basic contract rate. **1893** R. M. Walmsley *Wormell's Electr. in Service of Man* II. 392 The number of lines..which a magnetomotive force (*M.M.F.) can set up depends not only on its own magnitude but on the reluctance..of the path provided. **1962** *Newnes Conc. Encycl. Electr. Engin.* 467/1 The m.m.f. per metre length of path is *H*.., the value of *H* determining the magnetic flux density $B = \mu H$ at the point, where μ..is the absolute permeability of the medium. **1946**, etc. *MMPI [see Minnesota]. **1948** *Psychol. Bull.* XLV. 402 This would seem to indicate that..the MMPI scales do not actually differ from each other as they are supposed to. **1970** *Jrnl. Gen. Psychol.* LXXXIII. 70 Noting the discrepancy between behavior and test data (in this instance, the MMPI), Peterson..also concluded that the manifestations of psychosis in the MMPI..were instances of inaccurate diagnosis. **1939** Madge & Harrisson *Britain, by Mass-Observation* i. 10 Through *M-O you can already listen-in to the movements of popular habit and opinion. **1971** *Guardian Weekly* 10 Apr. 18/1 The MO reports now held by Sussex University have been cleverly worked over. **1916** F. M. Ford *Let.* 19 Dec. (1965) 80 The *M.O. who has just sounded my poor old lungs again says I am to be sent to Nice. **1924** *Army Q.* Oct. 138 Stop a minute—give this chit to the M.O. **1944** *Living off Land* v. 97 Day's travel from the nearest M.O. **1974** S. Gulliver *Vulcan Bulletins* 23 You have to get your ideas sorted out not to spend your time in the MO's queue asking for tranquillisers. **1955** R. J. Schwartz *Compl. Dict. Abbrev.* 114/3 **MO*,..method of operation (*modus operandi*). **1956** 'E. McBain' *Cop Hater* (1958) vii. 66 It was possible that the two deaths were unrelated..but not very probable. The m.o. was remarkably similar. **1974** R. Edwards *Dixon of Dock Green* 108 His m.o. was to pull two or three jobs in a line and then fade from the scene. **1937** *Trans. Faraday Soc.* XXXIII. 1481 The **m.o.* solution depends essentially upon the solution of a one-electron problem. **1947** *Q. Rev.* I. 151 The energy of a M.O. is lowest..when the component atomic orbitals overlap one another as much as possible. **1968** R. O. C. Norman *Princ. Org. Synthesis* ii. 35 In the lower-energy MO, termed the *σ1s* bonding orbital.., there is an accumulation of charge in the region between the nuclei. **1909** J. Joyce *Let.* 4 Sept. (1966) II. 246, I received your *M.O. for £3.5.0. **1940** H. Nicolson *Diary* 3 Aug. (1967) 104, I am feeling very depressed by the attacks upon the Ministry of Information... Since the *M. of I. should be an offensive instrument, its value to our war-effort will be diminished by this constant sniping from the rear. **1942** E. Waugh *Put out more Flags* 169, I will say for the Ministry of Information they were uncommon civil. Not at all like they are here. At the M. of I. they were never too busy to see one. **1909** *Cent. Dict.* Suppl., *MOH. **1911** G. B. Shaw *Doctor's Dilemma* Pref. p. lxxii, When one of the first-rate posts becomes vacant, all the leading M.O.H.s compete for it. **1961** *Lancet* 19 Aug. 440/1 She worked as assistant M.O.H. and inspector of midwives in Manchester. **1939** *War Illustr.* 18 Nov. p. iii/2 *M.O.I., Ministry of Information. **1957** J. Braine *Room at Top* x. 100 A MOI poster. **1963** *Aviation Week & Space Technol.* 16 Dec. 30 As described by Defense Secretary McNamara, the system, called *MOL for manned orbiting laboratory, will consist largely of hardware already under development. **1965** *Sci. News Let.* 2 Jan. 6/2 The most immediate USAF manned space project is the Manned Orbital Laboratory (MOL), scheduled for some time between 1967 and 1969. In the MOL two men will spend 30 days in orbit around the earth, studying both outer space and each other's reactions to it. **1969** *Times* 13 June 7/6 The cancelled Manned Orbiting Laboratory (M.O.L.) of the U.S. Air Force. **1970** *Billboard* 31 Jan. 35/1 *MOR stations have been forced into their present role by the recording artists in the easy listening field. **1975** [see middle-of-the-road 2]. **1982** *Face* May 31/4 With more determination they might have invented electro-country, but this is more like MOR pop. **1955** R. J. Schwartz *Compl. Dict. Abbrev.* 115/2 **MOS*,..Military Occupational Specialty. **1969** I. Kemp *Brit. G.I. in Vietnam* iii. 43 'What's your M.O.S.?' he barked. 'Operations and Intelligence Assistant, First Sergeant.' **1964** R. D. Lohman in *Semiconductor Products* May 31 The metal-oxide-semiconductor (*MOS) transistor is a new semiconductor device which combines many advantages of vacuum tubes and bipolar transistors. *Ibid.*, A typical n-channel MOS. **1967** Millman & Halkias *Electronic Devices & Circuits* xiv. 384 There are two types of field-effect transistors, the junction field-effect transistor (abbreviated JFET, or simply FET) and the insulated-gate field-effect transistor (IGFET), more commonly called the metal-oxide-semiconductor (MOS) transistor (MOST or MOSFET). **1971** *New Scientist* 8 July 77/2 With the very high-precision masking now used in MOS techniques the space between metallised paths can be 0·0003 in or less. **1973** *Sci. Amer.* Aug. 54/2 Today virtually all desk calculators and all pocket calculators are designed around MOS circuits. **1955** R. J. Schwartz *Compl. Dict. Abbrev.* 115/2 **MOT*,..Ministry of Transport. **1968** *Listener* 13 June 787/3 The annual MoT test could incorporate a check on noise, and any vehicle which had become noisier..than its original design limits would fail the test. **1971** *Exchange & Mart* 15 July 67 (Advt.), Spot cash!! For any make of Car or Van in any condition e.g. Failed M.O.T. and Damaged Vehicles. **1972** A. Aird *Automotive Nightmare* ii. 41 The inclusion of other items, and in particular corrosion, in the MOT test would also significantly increase the repair demand. **1973** J. Morris *Age of Arthur* 178 The roads are shown as classified by the Ministry of Transport (MoT). **1885** *Phil. Mag.* XX. 513, 2 [exceptions] are due to the *m.p. of carbon tetrabromide, CBr_4, being too high. **1947** *Sci. News* IV. 153 A polisher using a powder of oxamide (M.P. 417° C.)..did not produce any effect on speculum metal (M.P. 745° C.) or copper (M.P. 1,083° C.). **1917** A. G. Empey *Over Top* 300 *M.P., Military Police. Soldiers with whom it is unsafe to argue. **1967** *Coast to Coast 1965–66* 22 A bloody M.P. I suppose, that's what you were. **1972** D. E. Westlake *Cops & Robbers* (1973) vi. 91 What I really wanted was to drive a tank, but I wound up an M.P. **1931** *Daily Express* 28 Apr. 2/1 Petrol consumption..averages 20–26 *m.p.g. **1955** *Times* 30 Aug. 11/5 The petrol consumption is claimed to be at the rate of 100 m.p.g. on long journeys and 90 m.p.g. in town. **1973** *Country Life* 20 Sept. 802/3 The engine..is very thirsty for its size, giving me 14 mpg overall and nearer 12 mpg in town driving. **1909** *Cent. Dict.* Suppl., *m.p.h. **1935** *Discovery* Oct. 293/2 Speed was increased by only two m.p.h. **1942** *R.A.F. Jrnl.* 16 May 9 The qualities of this type of aircraft are judged..by its m.p.h., manoeuvrability and ascending speed. **1960** Wodehouse *Jeeves in Offing* xix. 185, I deposited Upjohn at the 'Bull and Bush' and started m-p-h-ing homeward. **1975** *Guardian* 20 Jan. 7/3 The car with.. a top speed of 107 mph, is aimed initially at the American market. **1826** *Colonial Advocate* (Toronto) 9 Feb. 2/4 John J. Lafferty, Esq. *M.P.P. was called to the chair. **1970** *Toronto Daily Star* 24 Sept. 35/1 Lewis, MPP for Scarborough West. *a* **1912** W. T. Rogers *Dict. Abbrev.* (1913) 129/1 **M.Q.*, Metol-Quinol (Developer). **1940** *Chambers's Techn. Dict.* 561/1 *M.Q.*, an abbrev. for metol-quinol or metol-hydroquinone developers. **1939** *Nation* (N.Y.) 5 Aug. 135/1 *M.R.A. and Hollywood were made for each other. **1949** *New Statesman* 15 Oct. 422/1 The success of M.R.A...is so brilliant that one cannot understand why the world is still in such a mess. **1969** *Listener* 3 July 19/3 Less than 1 per cent of our members are associated with MRA. **1960** *Acronyms Dict.* (Gale Research Co.) 126 *MRBM... Medium Range Ballistic Missile. **1961** *Ann. Reg. 1960* 167 Opposition to giving M.R.B.M.s to NATO was partly emotional. **1848** Thackeray *Pendennis* (1849) I. ii. 10 A professional friend, *M.R.C.S. **1936** *Discovery* June 182 Winifred de Kok, M.R.C.S., L.R.C.P. **1961** *M-RNA [see *messenger RNA* (messenger 7)]. **1965** *Jrnl. Molecular Biol.* XI. 187 A very small proportion of rapidly labeled RNA can be identified as M-RNA in the cell cytoplasm. **1965** *Ibid.* XIV. 257 [They] have presented evidence for the attachment of ribosomal particles to mRNA while the RNA is still attached to its DNA template. **1970** Ambrose & Easty *Cell Biol.* iv. 129 When the code has been transcribed from DNA on to mRNA, the latter leaves the nucleus, passing through the nuclear membrane into the cytoplasm. **1946** *Ann. Reg. 1945* 172 The Socialist Party (S.F.I.O.) and Christian Democrats (*M.R.P.) were in favour of *Yes.* **1958** *Spectator* 30 May 676/3 Feelings within the MRP were stiffening as in the Socialist Party. **1953** K. Reisz *Technique Film Editing* iv. 87 **M.S.* Father, daughter and doctor. **1923** *Man. Seamanship* (Admiralty) II. 177 The executive officer of a minesweeping vessel should first ascertain the allowed establishment of *M/S stores. **1953** W. Burroughs *Junkie* (1972) v. 52, I was getting sick and wondered if I would get home to the *M.S. I had stashed in my apartment. **1969** R. R. Lingeman *Drugs from A to Z* 176 When used by addicts, morphine is most commonly in the form of a salt, e.g., morphine sulfate (the origin of M.S., a slang term for morphine), which is soluble in water and hence injectable. **1955** *Sci. News Let.* 14 May 311/3 The search for twins with *MS, or multiple sclerosis, has yielded 33 identical sets so far, but the National Multiple Sclerosis Society would like to locate about 350 more, fraternal as well as identical. **1959** *Observer* 29 Mar. 8/4 Best results are obtained by dissolving *M.S.G. in the cooking liquor and adding towards the end of cooking. **1969** *New Scientist* 6 Mar. 505/2 Every packet soup, fish-finger and chicken croquette contains a dose of MSG to..'wake up all the flavour *nature* put in your food'. **1953** *MSH [see *melanocyte-stimulating hormone*]. **1958** MSH [see melatonin]. **1965** Lee & Knowles *Animal Hormones* x. 128 As in amphibians, the elasmobranch skin colour is controlled by the level of MSH. **1955** M. Grindrod *Rebuilding of Italy* viii. 79 The *MSI had..by 1952..built up some sort of status for itself. **1959** *Engineering* 6 Feb. 184/2 *MT is discussed in two general chapters, on dictionary searching, the 'stem-ending' method of analysis, identification of idioms and a possible method for resolving multi-meanings. **1966** Y. Bar-Hillel in *Automatic Transl. of Lang.* (NATO Summer School, Venice 1962) 20 On the other hand, the number of research groups which have taken up MT as their major field of activity is still on the increase. **1917** 'Contact' *Airman's Outings* 167 The Squadron Commander meets us... 'Seen anything?' he asks. 'Fourteen trains and some *M.T.,' I reply. **1946** *R.A.F. Jrnl.* May 174 There are W.A.A.F. clubs,.. W.A.A.F. on M.T. **1947** L. Hastings *Dragons are Extra* i. 25 He collected second-hand cars... Tinkering them up, and practising the same sort of cannibalism that long after became an M.T. necessity in modern war. **1938** *Jane's Fighting Ships* 140 A number of the *M.T.B.'s of the Thornycroft type are still in existence. **1944** *R.A.F. Jrnl.* Aug. 265 Cargo vessels, with M.T.B.'s weaving among them, leaving long white wakes. **1955** 'N. Shute' *Requiem for a Wren* 128 Left Gosport in an M.T.B. **1942** Partridge *Dict. Abbrev.* 65/2 *MTC. **1944** M.T.C. [see Croix de Guerre]. **1956** *Electronic Engin.* XXVIII. 15 A further important feature of this equipment is the *m.t.i. (moving target indicator) system, which is more effective in removing unwanted clutter and permanent echoes, and more stable in operation than any other previous type. **1966** *McGraw-Hill Encycl. Sci. & Technol.* VIII. 620/1 MTI is almost a necessity when moving targets are being sought over a region from which the ground clutter echoes are very strong. **1949** Koestler *Promise & Fulfilment* 262 At the bottom of their hearts they know quite well what the *M.V.D. has in store for them. **1959** *Listener* 4 June 996/3 One falls into the hands of the M.V.D. **1902** *Encycl. Brit.* XXXI. 339/2 The Royal Victorian Order..consists of..knights commanders (K.C.V.O.), commanders (C.V.O.), and members of the fourth and fifth classes (*M.V.O.), the distinction between these last divisions lying in the badge and in the precedence enjoyed by the members. **1973** *Aviation Week* 10 Sept. 15/3 The *MX still is in its formative stage, providing a low profile in budget requests. **1979** *N.Y. Rev. Bks.* 22 Mar. 38/2 Most ominous is the plan to develop the huge mobile ICBM, the MX, that would be equipped with as many as ten nuclear warheads. **1984** *Science* 22 June 1373/1 The impact of the MX on arms control efforts. **1985** *Ann. Reg. 1984* 383 Growing domestic pressure in the US..was reflected in a narrow Senate vote on the future of the MX missile. **1915** *Dialect Notes* IV. 246 *N.o.y.b.*, none of your business. Also **m.y.o.b.*, mind your own business. **1951** P. Branch *Lion in Cellar* xvi. 184 'Who are you?'..'M.Y.O.B.' **1972** J. Wilson *Hide & Seek* i. 8 'I had to go and collect something,' Alice mumbled. 'What?' 'M.Y.O.B.' 'Don't be cheeky.' **1974** L. Meynell *Fairly Innocent Little Man* xi. 140 'M.Y.O.B.,' Hooky said, 'if you know what that means.' 'At school we say it means Mess Your Own Breeches.'

b. Abbreviation for master: †(*a*) generally, and as a conventional title of address or mention = the later mister, Mr. Phr. ***to have*** (or ***carry***) ***an M under one's girdle***: to use a respectful prefix (Mr., Mrs.) when addressing or mentioning a person. (*b*) Used for *master* or the L. *magister* in academical degrees, as ***M.A.*** or ***A.M.*** (*magister artium*), Master of Arts; ***M.B.A.***, Master of Business Administration; ***M.Ch.*** (*magister chirurgiæ*), Master of Surgery; ***M.Litt.*** (*magister litterarum*), Master of Letters; ***M.S.*** (*U.S.*), ***M.Sc.***, Master of Science. ***M.Ed.***, Master of Education. (*c*) Also in ***M.A.A.***, Master-at-Arms; ***M.C.***, Master of the ceremonies; also as *v. trans.* and *intr.*; ***M.F.H.***, Master of fox-hounds; ***M.R.***, Master of the Rolls.

a **1540** Barnes *Wks.* (1573) 349/1 Our M. Christ teaching al creatures to pray. **1549** *Latimer's 2nd Serm. bef. Edw. VI* To Rdr. (Arb.) 52 The deuourer of townes and countryes as M. Latimer tearmeth them rightly. *a* **1553** Udall *Royster D.* iii. iii. (Arb.) 48 If faire fine mistresse Custance sawe you now Ralph Royster Doister were hir owne I warrant you. *R. Royster.* Neare an M by your girdle? **1553** Eden *Treat. Newe Ind.* (Arb.) 39 Where..the M. Pilate of this name lost his shippe. **1579** E. K. *Spenser's Sheph. Cal.* Epistle, Postscr., Now I trust, M. Harvey, that [etc.]. **1596** Spenser *Prothalamion* (heading), The two worthie Gentlemen M. Henry Gilford, and M. William Peter, Esquyers. **1605** B. Jonson, etc. *Eastw. Hoe!* iv, *Quick.* Must Golding sit upon us? *Con.* You might carry an M under your girdle, to Mr. Deputy's worship. **1712** *Great Britons Honycombe* (MS.) (N.), What, plaine Budwaies! have you nere an M. under your girdle. **1738** Swift *Pol. Conversat.* i. 28 You might have an M under your Girdle, Miss. **1816** Scott *Old Mort.* xxix, Ye might hae had an M under your belt for Mistress Wilson of Milnwood. **1730–6** Bailey (folio), M, is an abbreviation of *Magister*, as *M.A.* or *A.M. Magister Artium*, i.e. *Master of Arts.* **1811** Byron *Hints fr. Horace* 240 He.. retires M.A.; Master of arts! **1916** 'Taffrail' *Pincher Martin* vii. 117 'Petty Officer William Weatherley,' the M.A.A. went on, 'requests hextension o' leaf till two p.m. on Monday.' **1934** Webster *M.B.A.*, Master in, *or* of, Business Administration. **1965** *New Statesman* 26 Nov. 828/3 Even those few firms that give lip service to the idea of business schools are unwilling to regard a good MBA degree as representing more than one or two years of 'relevant experience'. **1790** E. Sheridan *Jrnl.* 5 Jan. (1960) 192 It was Tyson's Benefit, and as he is my acquaintance, independent of being M:C:, it was but decent that at least one of us should appear there. **1812** *Dramatic Censor 1811* 470 They are no more..co-equal with what they were, than the M.C. of a watering-place is on a par with the late Earl of Chesterfield in mind and manners. **1937** A. Upfield *Mr. Jelly's Business* viii. 74 Almost seventy people waiting for the M.C. to announce the first dance. **1843** Surtees *Handley Cross* I. v. 92 The loose riding M.C. sitting like 'the Drunken Hussar' at the circus. **1938** *New Yorker* 22 Oct. 23/3, I m.c'd and they had a couple of kids from the local dancing school doing tap. **1950** Webster Add., *m.c.*, *MC*, or *M.C.*..v.i. & t. **1954** E. Warner *Trial by Sasswood* (1955) x. 185 He was to m.c. an assemblage in the market compound. **1968** *Listener* 5 Sept. 307/1 With his mutton-chop whiskers John Peel appropriately looks like an MC at an Edwardian music hall. **1934** Webster, *M.Ed.*, Master of Education. **1937** *Discovery* June p. xlviii/1 G. P. McHugh M.Sc., Ph.D. (Lond), M.Ed. (Dunelm). **1843** Surtees *Handley Cross* II. vii. 147 First public day as an M.F.H. **1869** 'Bradwood' *O.V.H.* I. iii. 33 He was not the man to violate modesty by proposing himself to a nearly strange Hunt as a new M.F.H. **1909** *Cent. Dict.* Suppl., M.Lit. **1955** R. J. Schwartz *Compl. Dict. Abbrev.* 113/3 *M Litt*, Master of Letters. **1895** *Funk's Stand. Dict.*, M.R. **1964** *Mod. Law Rev.* XXVIII. iii. 274 Lord Denning M.R. said that Silverthorne was liable. **1909** *Cent. Dict.* Suppl., M.S. **1955** *Sci. Amer.* Sept. 36/3 He was born in Miami, Fla., and has a B.S. and an M.S. in physics from the University of Florida. **1909** *Cent. Dict.* Suppl., M.Sc. **1936** *Discovery* May 156 Julius Grant, Ph.D., M.Sc., F.I.C.

‖**c.** = monsieur (q.v.) as prefixed title.

d. *m* = milli-, as in **mA**, milliampere(s); **mg**, **mgm**, milligram(s); **ml**, millilitre(s); **mm**, millimetre; **mrad**, millirad(s).

1896 T. E. Herbert *Electr. in Applic. to Telegr.* iii. 27 1/1000 ampere or 1 m.a. **1927** *Wireless World* 16 Nov. 670/1 The..three valves..draw a high-tension current totalling 2 or 3 mA. **1970** *Which?* June 183/2 Even at maximum volume most transistor radios will not use more than 100 mA. **1894** J. Walker tr. *Ostwald's Man. Physico-Chem. Measurements* iii. 39 The correction is 0·00014, i.e. 0·14 mg. per gram. **1951** *Good Housek. Home Encycl.* 339/2 Its vitamin C content is low—1 mg. per oz. **1968** *Listener* 28 Nov. 703/1 The good effects of last year's Road Safety Act, making it an offence to drive with a level of alcohol in the blood of more than 80 milligrammes per 100 millimetres [*sic*], may be wearing off. This may well be because 80mg/100ml is such a high level. **1909** *Cent. Dict.* Suppl., *mgm.*, an abbreviation of *milligram.* **1939** *Nature* 11 Mar. 442/1 It is..possible to carry out exact estimations of carbon..using 2–3 mgm. of material. **1892** G. Collar *Notes on Metric System* 7, 10 millilitres (ml.) make 1 centilitre (cl.). **1968** ml [see *mg* above]. **1878** *Jrnl. R. Microsc. Soc.* I. 355 A quarter of a century ago..Harting proposed..micro-millimetre... Thus we had *m.* for the metre, *mm.* for the millimetre, and *mmm.* for the micromillimetre. **1897** *Sears, Roebuck Catal.* 583/1 Pin Fire Pistol Cartridges... In sizes 7 M-M is 32 caliber, 9 M-M is 38 caliber, 12 M-M is 44 caliber. **1971** *Guardian* 16 Dec. 1/2 The police did not identify the weapon but said that the ammunition was 9 mm. **1961** *New Scientist* 11 May 297/1 The average exposure in the course of radiological procedures was only of the order of 20 mrad annually, which is far less than the 100 mrad from natural background sources to which we are subjected. **1970** mrad [see dose *sb.* 1 b].

e. *M* = mega- b, as in **MeV** (also **Mev**, etc.), million electron volt(s); **MHz**, megahertz; **MW**, megawatt(s).

1934 *Physical Rev.* XLVI. 1109/2 The spectrum.. indicates gamma-ray lines of roughly 2, 4, 5·5 and 7 m.e.v.

Ibid., (*heading*) Energy in MEV. **1955** *Bull. Atomic Sci.* May 171/3 U-238 does not undergo fission with neutrons below 1·1 Mev. **1964** HEISENBERG in *Cambr. Rev.* 24 Oct. 48/1 A mass difference up to 400 MeV. **1951** *Physica* XVII. 213 Measurements have been carried out on paramagnetic resonance absorption in iron ammonium alum at a frequency of about 9200 MHz. **1970** *E. Afr. Standard* (Nairobi) 2 Jan. 11/7 (Advt.), B.B.C. listeners can also hear programmes in English for East Africa between 7.30 and 8.45 p.m. on 15·42 MHz. **1956** *Proc. CERN Symposium* I. 22/2 Production of the flutter fields by pole-face windings.. would require ~ a few MW of power per pole face. **1962** *Newnes Conc. Encycl. Electr. Engin.* 324/1 Fuel-fired steam power stations.. are now built for outputs up to 1,000 MW or more.

f. Designating a motorway. Also *fig.* and *Comb.*

1959 *Times* 10 Nov. 6/5 Two people were injured in an accident on the London-Birmingham motorway, the M.1, yesterday. **1963** *Listener* 10 Jan. 100/2 Some of the by-ways of sound radio—by-ways to me but no doubt a positive M1 to thousands of others—can be rewarding. **1964** *Daily Tel.* 3 Mar. 21/1 (*heading*) M-drivers 'can stop if drowsy'. **1966** 'A. YORK' *Eliminator* iv. 72, I would have thought you'd have wanted to try her on the M. **1973** *Guardian* 26 May 8/5 Bartholomew's new Motorway Atlas.. is a useful tool for those who go up and down the Ms all the time.

7. *Econ.* ***M***, used in measures of money supply, as ***M0***, the sum of notes and coin in circulation; ***M1***, Mo plus the amount held by residents of a country in current accounts; ***M2***, M1 plus the equivalent sum in deposit accounts; ***M3***, M2 plus all other kinds of deposit held by residents in the national banking sector.

1948 P. SAMUELSON *Economics* xiii. 291 If the total amount of all.. kinds of money is *M* and the price level is *P*, then according to the simplified quantity theory $M = kP$ or $P = \frac{1}{k}M$ where *k* is a factor of proportionality which remains constant if 'other things are equal'. **1963** FRIEDMAN & MEISELMAN *Relative Stability Monetary Velocity in U.S., 1897–1958* 242 Three.. definitions of money were considered. These were: M_1: Currency in public circulation + Adjusted demand deposits, $M_2 = M_1$ + Time deposits in commercial banks, $M_3 = M_2$ + Mutual savings bank deposits + Postal savings accounts + Savings and loan association shares. **1967** *Federal Res. Bank of St. Louis Rev.* Oct. 8/2 M equals the public's holding of currency, demand deposits, and time deposits. **1968** *Business Week* 26 Oct. 117/3 There are two basic definitions of the quantity of money in use: M_1—demand deposits plus currency in circulation... M_2—this includes not only demand deposits and currency, but also time deposits in the commercial banks. **1973** LD. ROBBINS *Against Inflation* (1979) xiii. 66 Since the end of June 1970.. M_3—the most commonly accepted measure of the credit base—had increased to last September by something of the order of magnitude of 40 per cent. **1985** *Times* 13 Sept. 16/3 US M1 money supply rose $1.4 billion in the week to September 2. **1986** *Economist* 11–17 Jan. 19/2 MO, the chancellor's favourite measure of the money supply, has grown by only $2\frac{1}{4}\%$ during the past 12 months.

m'. = MY *poss. adj.*

1712 [see MY *poss. adj.* 1 β]. **1837** J. F. COOPER *England* II. xii. 51, I take it, the polite way of pronouncing this word is by a sort of elision—as m'horse, m'dog, m'gun. *Ibid.*, I think more noble peers, however, said '*me* lurds', than 'm' lurds'. **1852** DICKENS *Bleak Ho.* (1853) i. 4 'Mr. Tangle,' says the Lord High Chancellor... 'Mlud,' says Mr. Tangle. **1907** R. BROOKE *Let.* 12 Aug. (1968) 99 M'uncle is changing his house or face or wife or something. **1908** [see HOUSE *sb.*[1] 4 c]. **1914** [see ÆSTHETE]. **1942** G. GREENE *Brit. Dramatists* 33 Lady Teazle 'm'ludding' and flirting a fan. **1945** E. WAUGH *Brideshead Revisited* I. ii. 47 A series of harrowing interviews with m'tutor. **1967** *Guardian* 31 July 5/1, I remember him playing the part of a prosecuting counsel.. full of patronising 'M'luds'. **1968** A. DIMENT *Gt. Spy Race* vii. 103 Why, chappie in m'tutors, doing four years in the Scrubs. **1970** O. NORTON *Dead on Prediction* v. 84 Not evidence, m'dear. Is it? **1972** J. PORTER *Meddler & her Murder* iii. 39 Allow me to carry the tray for you, Eve, m'dear.

'm. Var. MA'AM.

m-, a clipped form of ME sometimes found in Middle English before vowels.

c **1393** CHAUCER *Scogan* 36, I mexcuse. **1426** LYDG. *De Guil. Pilgr.* 9802 Out off my shyp make maryue.

-m, in I'M = I am: see BE *v.*, A. I. 1.

ma (mɑː). **a.** A childish and colloquial shortening of MAMMA. Now often ridiculed as *vulgar*. Also a familiar shortening of (or substitute for) MRS. Also applied *colloq.* to a middle-aged or elderly woman, esp. one in authority.

[**1823** MOOR *Suffolk Words* s.v. *Pa*, It is sometimes rather comic to hear a great chuckle-headed lout—*paa*-ing his father—or *maa*-ing his mother.] **1829** *Censor* 225 These exhibitions, though affording wonderous delight to affectionate *Pas* and *Mas*, are productive of the most injurious results to their children. **1829** LYTTON *Disowned* 20 How could he admire that odious cap of Ma's. **1836** T. HOOK *G. Gurney* I. 196 Gussy, as her ma' called her. **1885** F. ANSTEY *Tinted Venus* 119, I've got to dine with aunt and meet Matilda and her ma. **1932** J. CARY *Aissa Saved* xxxvii. 196 You come now, ma; she very sick. **1943** K. TENNANT *Ride on Stranger* iii. 27 'What-ho, Ma,' came a howl from the kitchen. 'Coming.' Beryl appeared wiping her hands. **1951** J. COMMON *Kiddar's Luck* xi. 161 My father called them the Ma gang, because they had a habit of always alluding to each other as Ma This and Ma That. *Ibid.*, It was becoming fairly regular to see Ma McGrewin, or Ma Smailes, or Ma Forbes sitting boldly by the fireside. **1966** WODEHOUSE *Plum Pie* v. 124 'Did Ma Purkiss make a speech?' 'Yes, Mrs. Purkiss spoke.' **1974** M. BABSON *Stalking Lamb* xvi. 120 'Here, Ma,' Aaron said, 'I've brought company.'

b. *Austral.* (With capital initial.) Popular name for New South Wales. So ***Ma State***.

1934 *Bulletin* (Sydney) 24 Jan. 25/1 The Cabbage Gardeners will have to be licked outright if Ma is to have a hope. **1945** BAKER *Austral. Lang.* 187 *New South Wales*, New South, the Ma State or Ma. **1949** *Geogr. Mag.* Feb. 373 *New South* and *The Ma State*, New South Wales (oldest state in the Commonwealth).

ma. (meɪ), *a.* Colloq. abbrev., in some schools, of *major* = the elder of two namesakes.

1791 [see MI. *a.*]. **1932** WODEHOUSE *Louder & Funnier* 12 Faber *ma* was so annoyed by his snorts and chuckles that he hit him over the head with a *croisson* or small French roll. **1963** *Times* 5 June 14/3 There was gentler satire from McGavin ma. with John Betjeman's 'Village Inn'.

ma., obs. abbreviation of MAJESTY, MASTER.

1579 E. K. *Spenser's Sheph. Cal.* Epistle, Myne owne good friend Ma. Harvey. **1605** BACON *Adv. Learn.* 11. To King 1 Since wee have so bright and benigne a starre, as your Ma: to conduct and prosper us.

ma: see MAKE *v.*, MAY *v.*, ME, MO, MY.

maa (mɑː), *v.* [Echoic, in imitation of the sound made by a sheep or goat. Cf. MAE *v.*] *intr.* To bleat. Hence as *sb.* and **'maaing** *vbl. sb.*

1827 DARLEY *Sylvia* II. i. 34 It will make me *ma-a* like a he-goat on a rock-top when he misses the beard of his charmer. **1886** J. STEWART *Twa Elders* 147 The boys would maa and bleat. **1922** JOYCE *Ulysses* 162 All are washed in the blood of the lamb, bawling maaaaaa. **1928** *Blackw. Mag.* Mar. 324/1 Poor old goat!.. His caperings were fantastic, his *maaings* continuous. **1940** N. MARSH *Surfeit of Lampreys* (1941) xvii. 268 'M-a-a-ah,' said Rattisbon with a formidable and sheep-like cry.

maa, obs. f. MAKE *v.*; var. MO *Obs.*, more.

maac, maad: see MAKE *v.*

maakins, variant of MACKIN(G)S.

†**maal.** *Obs. rare*⁻¹. Wyclif's transl. of L. *mālum* apple, taken by him to mean fir-tree, by confusion with *mālus* mast (see quot.).

1382 WYCLIF *Joel* i. 12 Poumgarnet, and palme tree, and maal tree, or fir, of whom mastis ben maad.

maale, obs. form of MAIL.

maalesh, var. MALEESH *int.*

maam (mɑːm). A South American bird, the TINAMOU.

1825 WATERTON *Wand. S. Amer.* 23 The forest contains an abundance of.. maams, maroudis and waracabas. *Ibid.* 32 The maam sends forth its plaintive note.

ma'am (mɑːm, mæm; usually unstressed məm, (ə)m). Also 7 **mam**. In representations of vulgar speech written **mem, mim, mum, 'm** Cf. MARM. A colloquial shortening of MADAM.

1. Used *vocatively*, as the usual oral equivalent of MADAM.

Now only used parenthetically or at the end of a sentence. Formerly the ordinary respectful form of address to a woman (originally only to a married woman) of equal or superior rank or station (unless entitled to be called 'my lady'). The present tendency is to confine it to the speech of servants or other persons of markedly inferior position. (Used at Court, instead of *madam*, in addressing the Queen or a royal princess.)

1668 DRYDEN *Evening's Love* III. i. (1671) 33 Madam me no Madam, but learn to retrench your words; and say Mam; as yes Mam, and no Mam, as other Ladies Women do. Madam! 'tis a year in pronouncing. **1765** FOOTE *Commissary* I. Wks. 1799 II. 8 Indeed, Ma'am, you'll kill yourself. **1838** DICKENS *O. Twist* xvii, Mrs. Mann, ma'am, good morning. *c* **1850** LYTTON *Lionel Hastings* ii. in *Life* (1883) I. II. xi. 180 'Well, Marm—' Mr. Cotton preserved that broad pronunciation of the ellipsis *Ma'am*, from *Madame*, which was formerly considered high bred, and is still the Court mode. **1854** DICKENS *Hard T.* I. xvi, 'Mrs. Sparsit ma'am', said Mr. Bounderby. 'I am going to astonish you'. **1885** F. ANSTEY *Tinted Venus* 142 'Now, marm', he said, in a voice which trembled with repressed rage. **1900** *Speaker* 23 June 324/2 In Thackeray's time every man among equals of a certain refinement was Sir, and every woman Ma'am.

β. **1700** CONGREVE *Way of World* II. v, *Minc.* O Mem, your Laship staid to peruse a Pecquet of Letters. **1840** DICKENS *Barn. Rudge* xix, 'Here's master, mim', said Miggs. 'Oh, what a happiness it is when man and wife come round again!' **1854** B. P. SHILLABER *Life & Sayings Mrs. Partington* 47 'This is grand weather, mem, for poor people' said Mr. Tigh, the rich neighbor of Mrs. Partington. **1867** *Good-wife at Home* i. 5 Eh! Dear be here, mem, is this you, In sic a byous day? **1876** E. B. RAMSAY *Reminisc. Scottish Life & Character* (ed. 21) iv. 78 Then I canna engadge wi' ye, mem; for 'deed I wadna gie the crack i' the kirkyard for a' the sermon. **1877** G. MACDONALD *Marquis of Lossie* III. ix. 161 But, mem,.. I canna lee. **1887** *Gordonhaven* xi. 104 'What have you been doing?' 'Nothing, mem'.

γ. **1847** A. BRONTË *Agnes Grey* xi. 177 For you know mum he's now't at all to live on, but what he gets fra' th' rector. **1866** TROLLOPE *Belton Estate* (ed. 3) III. vi. 159 The gentleman.. was blown up with all the ceremony of which Mrs. Bunce was capable. 'Here he be, mum.' **1885** F. ANSTEY *Tinted Venus* 116 'Dear me, mum, you don't say so!' exclaimed Leander. **1973** S. COHEN *Diane Game* (1974) vi. 62 It's me, mum... Are you having dinner in?

δ. **1864** J. S. LE FANU *Uncle Silas* I. iv. 37 He bowed gravely, with a: 'Yes, 'm—shall, 'm.' **1933** E. A. ROBERTSON *Ordinary Families* vii. 140 Her submissive 'Yes 'm' and 'No, miss'. **1945** in B. A. Botkin *Treas. S. Folklore* (1949) II. iv. 352 Mr. Linktum come down. Yes'm, Mr. Abe Linktum and his partner, Horace Greeley, comed down.

2. Prefixed to a surname. *Obs.* exc. *U.S. vulgar*. (See MADAM.)

1837, etc. [see MARM 2].

†**3.** A person addressed as 'ma'am', a married woman. *Obs.*

1765 *Meretriciad* (ed. 6) 43 Or when Mam walks, he, twenty steps behind. **1779** SHERIDAN *Critic* I. i, Then to be continually alarmed with misses and ma'ams piping hysteric changes on Juliets, and Dorindas.

4. *attrib.*: **ma'am-school** *U.S.*, a dame-school.

1857 S. G. GOODRICH *Recoll. Lifetime* iv. I. 39, I found a girl.. keeping a ma'am-school for about twenty scholars.

Hence **ma'am** *v. trans.*, to address as 'ma'am'.

1813 *Sketches Charac.* (ed. 2) I. 121 You should not 'sir' and 'ma'am' people as you do, unless you wish to keep them at a distance. **1887** G. R. SIMS *Mary Jane's Mem.* 6 Don't ma'am me—I'm a miss. **1889** H. JOHNSTON *Chron. Glenbuckie* v. 58 'Indeed, mem'... 'Ye needna' "mem" me .. I'm a common body like yoursel'.

ma'amselle. Corresponds to F. *mam'selle*, familiar abbreviation of MADEMOISELLE.

c **1794** *Search aft. Perfect.* I. i. in *New Brit. Theatre* (1814) III. 37 The first four out of the eleven were ma'amselles.

maand, variant of MAUND (basket).

maane, obs. form of MANE.

maar (mɑː(r)). *Geol.* Pl. ‖**maare, maars.** [G. dial., 'crater-lake'.] **a.** (Usu. with capital initial.) One of the craters or crater-lakes of the Eifel district in Germany. **b.** Any volcanic crater which does not lie in a cone and was formed by a single explosive event (and is usu. occupied by a lake).

1826 *Edin. Jrnl. Sci.* V. 152 The craters of this country [*sc.* Prussia] have nearly, without exception, become bodies of water, or *Maare*, as they are called by the natives. *Ibid.* 154 To the S.E. of Steffler, lies a small *maar*, or crater-lake. *Ibid.* 156 The water in the three lakes appears to stand at the same level... One only, the Schalkenonchrener maar, has any visible outlet. **1882** A. GEIKIE *Text-bk. Geol.* 560 Occasionally, as in some of the Maare of the Eifel, these non-volcanic fragments constitute most of the débris. **1895** *Bull. Philos. Soc. Washington* XII. 251 The maars are of still rarer occurrence, and represent the antithetic phase of volcanism. **1933** R. A. DALY *Igneous Rocks & Depths of Earth* viii. 161 Maars are relatively flat-floored craters of explosion at vents that are either coneless or else provided with inconspicuous cones. *Ibid.*, Reck has recently published.. fine illustrations of maars in Abyssinia. **1968** R. W. FAIRBRIDGE *Encycl. Geomorphol.* 681/1 Maare sometimes resemble calderas. **1971** *Nature* 30 July 330/2 The lake occupies the crater of a maar—a volcanic eruption crater lying below the general level of the surrounding country and surrounded by a low tuff ring.

maarmor, erron. form of MAORMOR.

maas (mɑːs). *S. Afr.* Also **amaaz, amas, amasi.** [f. Zulu (*pref.*) *ama-* + *si* milk.] Thickened sour milk.

1833 S. KAY *Trav. Caffraria* I. v. 121 Their general diet extremely simple. This ordinarily consists of milk, which.. they invariably use in a sour curdled state. It is called *amaaz*, and rendered thus thick and acidulous by being kept in leathern sacks or bottles. **1857** *Cape Monthly Mag.* I. 289 The men are not allowed to drink any amasi or thick sour milk from a kraal of which they may think of courting a girl. **1882** W. R. LUDLOW *Zululand & Cetewayo* vii. 73 Maas, which is the chief food of the Zulus, where there are large herds of cattle, is most delicious and nourishing food. **1946** J. HERTSLET *Bantu Folk Tales* v. 61 A wether had been killed and a large piece of its meat was put with the maas and beer. **1952** S. CLOETE *Curve & Tusk* (1953) iii. 33 He ate.. maas, the sour thickened milk of the indigenous people. **1953** R. CAMPBELL *Mamba's Precipice* ii. 24 They solidified the milk in calabashes and called it *Maas*. **1967** O. WALKER *Hippo Poacher* 18 He provided them with *amasi* or sour milk.

maas, maat, obs. forms of MACE, MATE.

maasbanker ('mas,baŋkər, mɔs'bɔŋkər). Also **maasbancker, maasbank, marsbanker, masbanker, massbanker.** [Afrikaans, f. Du. *marsbanker* MOSSBUNKER.] The South African name for the scad or horse mackerel, *Trachurus trachurus*.

1727 J. G. SCHEUCHZER tr. *Kæmpfer's Hist. Japan* I. I. xi. 136 *Adsi* is the *Maasbancker* of the Dutch. **1843** J. C. CHASE *Cape Good Hope* II. 169 Maasbank.. June.. Like Mackerel, but stronger, not always wholesome. **1853** L. PAPPE *Synopsis Edible Fishes Cape Good Hope* 25 *Caranx Trachurus* Lacep. (Maasbanker; Bastard Mackerel.).. Caught in winter at both ends of the Colony. Its flesh is well flavoured and wholesome. **1902** *Trans. S. Afr. Philos. Soc.* XI. 215 The Maasbanker.. is identical with the Maasbanker (*Caranx trachurus*) of Holland, and indeed is to be found almost everywhere within the temperate and tropical zones of both hemispheres. **1930** C. L. BIDEN *Sea-Angling Fishes of Cape* vii. 146 The English horse-mackerel is the masbanker of the Cape (*Trachurus trachurus*). **1947** *Cape Times* 2 May 9 Maasbankers continue to be plentiful. **1953** *Ibid.* 20 May 4/4 The Government has limited the number and capacity of plants which may be used for the manufacture of fish meal and fish oil from pilchards and massbankers. **1959** G. JENKINS *Twist of Sand* ii. 43 We'd had a fair haul of pilchard, stockfish and maasbanker. **1970** *Cape Times* (S.A. Fishing Rev.) 28 Oct. 2/2 The purse seine boats.. hunt the shoals of pilchard, mackerel, maasbanker and anchovy along the West Coast. **1972** L. G. GREEN *When Journey's Over* (1973) xii. 148 Nelson saw snoek and *marsbankers* in boxes and barrels or hanging up to dry.

Maastrichtian, var. MAESTRICHTIAN *a.*

‖**maat** (maːt). *S. Afr.* [Afrikaans = MATE *sb.*[2] 1.] A companion, partner, friend.

1812 W. BURCHELL *Trav. S. Afr.* 24 July (1822) II. 466 Another chieftain who was his *maat* (partner, or agent). *Ibid.* 555 Thus a Hottentot.. when he visits Litakun.. goes directly to the house of his correspondent, whom he calls his *maat* (a Dutch word identical with 'mate'). **1827** G. THOMPSON *Trav. S. Afr.* (ed. 2) I. xii. 238 Many of the Bechuanas selected *maats* or comrades.. from among their allies. **1932** C. FULLER *Louis Trigardt's Trek* x. 124 We drank it as my *maats* had just come to my wagon.

†**mab**, *sb. Obs.* [Cf. MAB *v.* and *map*, 17th c. form of MOP *sb.*; also *Mab*, short for *Mabel.*]

1. A slattern; a woman of loose character.

1557–8 *Jacob & Esau* v. vi. (1568) Gj, Come out thou mother Mab, out olde rotten witche. **1691** RAY *N.C. Words* 47 To *Mab*; to dress carelesly: *Mabs* are Slatterns. *a* **1700** B. E. *Dict. Cant. Crew*, *Mab*, a Slattern. *Mab'd up*, Drest carelesly, like a Slattern. **1725** *New Cant. Dict.*, *Mob*, or *Mab*, a Wench or Harlot.

2. A mop.

1623 WHITBOURNE *Newfoundland* 75 Thrummes for Pitch mabs, 000*li.* 01*s.* 6*d.*

†**mab**, *v. Obs.*$^{-0}$ [Belongs to MAB *sb.* Cf. MABBLE, MOB *vbs.*] *intr.* To dress untidily.

1691, *a* **1700** [see MAB *sb.*]. **1829** BROCKETT *N.C. Words*, *Mab*, v. to dress carelessly. Hence, *Mab-cap*, generally called *mob-cap*, a cap which ties under the chin—worn by elderly women.

†**mabble**, *v. Obs.* Also **mable**. [Cf. MOBLE *v.*] *trans.* To wrap or muffle up (the head).

1615 G. SANDYS *Trav.* 69 Their heads and faces so mabled in fine linnen, that no more is to be seene of them then their eyes. *Ibid.* 148 The elder mabble their heads in linnen.

mabela (mæ'biːla). *S. Afr.* Also **mabbele**. [ad. Zulu *i(li)bele*, pl. *amabele.*] Indian millet, *Sorghum vulgare*, or the meal or porridge made from it. Also *attrib.*

1824 W. J. BURCHELL *Trav. S. Afr.* II. xviii. 586 The plant resembles... Maize or Indian corn... The Bichuanas call it *mábbĕlĕ*.. and are fond of chewing the stalk. **1939** A. W. WELLS *S. Afr.: Planned Tour* xx. 228 (*caption*) Natives in a valley of mealies and mabela corn near the Caledon River. **1946** *Cape Argus Mag.* 14 Dec. 4/5 He.. set before him on a stool a bowl of mabela, a flat scone toasted on the coals and a calabash bowl of milk.

Mac[1] (mæk). Also MACK. [Irish and Gaelic *mac*:—OCeltic **makko-s*, cogn. w. Welsh *mab*: —OWelsh *map*:—OCeltic **makwo-s*.] The Gaelic word for 'son', occurring as a prefix in many Scottish and Irish names of Celtic origin, and thus equivalent to the Eng. suffix *-son*. Hence: A person whose name contains the prefix *Mac*; also a familiar form of address used to any stranger.

The prefix is written also *Mc*, *M^c*, *M'*; e.g. *Macdonald*, *MacDonald*, *McDonald*, *McDonald*, *M'Donald.*

1656 in BLOUNT *Glossogr.* **1689** [FAREWELL] *Irish Hudibras* 108 The Champions of the Irish Cause, A numerous Train of Mac's and O's. **1730** FIELDING *Tom Thumb* I. iii, Ireland her O's, her Mac's let Scotland boast. **1764** WILKES *Corr.* (1805) III. 126 The list of the company (of the Macs and Sawneys not in the French service) would divert you. **1828** SCOTT *F.M. Perth* vi, If the son of some great Mac or O was to become an artizan. **1830** N. S. WHEATON *Jrnl.* 472 A feather or two stuck in his bonnet denotes his allianc in the 50th degree with some Highland Mac. **1887** [see O *sb.*[2]]. **1898** *Tit-Bits* 21 May 148/1 In the house of Commons the 'Macs' are numerically strong enough to form a considerable party of their own. **1937** PARTRIDGE *Dict. Slang* 503/1. **1962** L. DEIGHTON *Ipcress File* xxv. 158 'Make on the feet, mack,' he said. **1963** *Landfall* XVII. 14 You'd only to hear my father ..to know where he stood, solid for intolerance, mac, but solid. **1965** *Sc. Nat. Dict.* VI. 169/2 *Mac*,.. in colloq. use applied in Eng. to anyone known or thought to be a Scotsman, in Scot. common as a fam. form of address to any stranger. **1968** *New Yorker* 16 Mar. 42 For the last time, Mac—we don't have any mead. **1973** J. WAINWRIGHT *Pride of Pigs* 128 The bouncer.. tapped him on the shoulder and said: 'Hey, mac.'

mac[2] (mæk). *colloq.* Short for MACADAM.

1851 MAYHEW *Lond. Labour* II. 197 The Scavengers call mud all that is swept from the granite or wood pavements, in contradistinction to mac which is scraped and swept on the macadamized roads. **1886** *Pall Mall G.* 2 Oct. 2/2 The thousands of yards of old mac that were taken off the roads for use elsewhere.

mac, var. MACK *sb.*[5]

mac: see MACK, MAKE *v.*

macabaa, -bao, variants of MACCOBOY.

macaberesque (mə,kɑːbə'rɛsk), *a.* [f. MACABRE + -ESQUE.] = MACABRE 2.

1876 *Encycl. Brit.* V. 104/1 A curious reaction is visible in the work of Peter Breughel (1510–1570) towards the grotesque *diablerie* and macaberesque morality of mediæval art.

‖**macabre** (mə'kɑːbr), *a.* (*sb.*) Also 5 **machabree**, 7 **machabray**, 9 **macaber**. [The form now usual represents F. *macabre*, an error for OF. *macabré*, whence the earlier Eng. forms.

The OF. word occurs first in Jean le Fèvre's *Respit de la Mort* (1376), where the author, if he be correctly interpreted by M. Gaston Paris (*Romania* XXIV. 131), claims to have written a work called *la danse Macabré*. The etymology of the word is obscure; so far as its form is concerned it might be a popular corruption of OF. *Macabé* = Maccabæus (an example of 'Judas Macabré' has been found), and in the 15th c. the 'Dance of Death' was called *chorea Machabæorum* in Latin (Du Cange cites a Besançon document of 1453), and *Makkabeusdans* in Du. M. Gaston Paris, however, thinks *Macabré* may have been the name of the artist who painted the picture which suggested the first poem on the subject.]

A. *adj.* **1.** ***danse macabre***, also in anglicized forms † ***dance of machabree, -bray*** (obs.), ***dance macaber***: the Dance of Death (see DANCE *sb.* 6 c).

14.. LYDG. (*title*) The daunce of Machabree wherin is liuely expressed and shewed the state of manne, and howe he is called at vncertayne tymes by death, and when he thinketh least theron. *Ibid.* Prol. iii, I toke on me to translaten all, Out of the Frenche Machabrees daunce. **1598** STOW *Surv.* 264 About this Cloyster was artificially & richly painted the dance of Machabray, or dance of death, commonly called the dance of Pauls. **1833** J. DALLAWAY *Disc. Archit. Eng.* 137 The Dance of Macabre (Holbein's Dance of Death) was painted on the walls of the cloisters. **1851** LONGF. *Gold. Leg., Nativ.* v. 12 *Elsie.* What are these paintings on the walls around us? *Henry.* The Dance Macaber! *Elsie.* What? *Henry.* The Dance of Death. **1870** C. M. YONGE *Caged Lion* ix. 166 It is the Danse Macabre... It was invented as a warning to those of sinful life. **1938** *Oxf. Compan. Mus.* 251/1 *Danse macabre.* The idea of Death as a dancer, or as a fiddling inciter to the dance, is very ancient. **1955** *Times* 19 May 3/7 This *danse macabre* could only have been written by a poet. **1966** *Listener* 17 Nov. 746/3 An *Allegretto* in G minor —a waltz-like *danse macabre*—which quotes the opening of the first cello concerto. **1974** H. WAUGH *Parrish for Defence* (1975) i. 5 The hours before dawn belonged to the souls of the dead... The restless whirling of their frenzies would be the *Danse Macabre.*

2. Characterized by the gruesomeness of the *danse macabre* (see 1): applied chiefly to literary or artistic productions.

1889 *Athenæum* 14 Sept. 347/2 One Dance of Death circles uninterruptedly from end to end... The book is macabre, but unaffectedly macabre. **1892** *Speaker* 29 Oct. 528/1 It was the material representation.. of the ghastly, the grim, and the macabre which Webster intended. **1902** *Spectator* 12 Apr. 557 Her habits are bizarre, even macabre.

B. *As sb.* A macabre happening.

c **1920** T. E. LAWRENCE *Lett.* (1938) facing p. 233 It's just struck me that there's all the elements of a macabre in the passage which R. G. censored. **1948** F. R. LEAVIS *Great Tradition* i. 19 The unfortunate *macabre* of the cab-journey.

Hence **ma'cabrely** *adv.*

1961 A. WILSON *Old Men at Zoo* ii. 107 The black suit she wore, against which her white face.. stared out so macabrely. **1964** *Economist* 24 Oct. 365/2 This is where [it] ..might become most macabrely relevant. **1968** D. FRANCIS *Forfeit* xiii. 163 What he said.. was macabrely at variance with the way he said it.

macac, variant of MACAQUE.

macaco[1] (mə'keɪkəʊ). Also 7–8 **macaquo**, (*erron.* **-guo**), 9 **macauco**, *vulgar* **maccacco**, **murkarker**. [a. Pg. *macaco* monkey, ape (whence *macaquear* to ape); cited (in the form *macaquo*) by Marcgrave *Hist. Nat. Brazil* (1648) 227 as the name used in Congo for this species of monkey.]

1. Originally, a South African monkey incidentally described by Marcgrave in his *Natural History of Brazil*, and after him by various writers on zoology. Subsequently applied to any monkey of the genus MACACUS (either in its earlier or later extension); = MACAQUE.

[**1693** RAY *Syn. Anim. Quad.* etc. 155 Cercopithecus angolensis major, Congensibus Macaquo Marcgr.] **1774** GOLDSM. *Nat. Hist.* IV. 233 Of the monkies of the ancient continent, the first, he [Buffon] describes, is the Macaguo; somewhat resembling a baboon in size. **1854** BUSHNAN in *Circ. Sci.* (*c* 1865) I. 290/2 In the mandril, pavian, and macacos, membranous sacs are observed. **1874** *Slang Dict.*, *Murkarker*, a monkey, vulgar Cockney pronunciation of Macauco... Jacko Macauco, or Maccacco, as he was mostly called, was the name of a famous fighting monkey, who used nearly fifty years ago to display his prowess at the Westminster Pit.

2. *Comb.*: **macaco-wood**, *Tococa guianensis*, a Brazilian shrub (Cassell); **macaco-worm**, the larva of a South American insect, *Dermatobia noxialis*, which infests the skin of animals.

1876 *Beneden's Anim. Parasites* viii. 175 A gadfly found at Cayenne is distinguished by the name of the Macaco Worm; it.. usually attacks the skin of oxen and dogs.

macaco[2] (mə'keɪkəʊ). Also 8 **mocock**, **mococo**, 8–9 **maucauco**, 9 **macauco**. [a. F. (Buffon) *mococo*; ulterior origin obscure. Cf. MAKI.] A name applied to certain lemurs, *esp.* to the genus *Lemur*.

1751 G. EDWARDS *Nat. Hist. Birds*, etc. IV. 197 The Maucauco.. is about the Bigness of a middling sized Cat. **1774** GOLDSM. *Nat. Hist.* IV. 239 The last of the monkey kind are the Makis... The first of this kind is the Mococo; a beautiful animal about the size of a common cat, but.. of a longer make. **1797** *Encycl. Brit.* (ed. 3) IX. 785 Lemur, the Maucauco.. 1. The tardigradus, or tail-less maucauco. **1797** S. JAMES *Narr. Voy.* 141 The tail of the mocock, is the most beautiful that can be imagined. **1834** *Nat. Philos., Phys. Geog.* 54/2 (U.K.S.) The flying macauco or lemur. **1839** *Penny Cycl.* XIII. 419/1 The Makis, or Macaucos, properly so called, *Lemur*. **1840** BLYTH tr. *Cuvier's Anim. Kingd.* (1849) 64 The Murine Macauco (*Lemur murinus*). **1884** *Riverside Nat. Hist.* (1888) I. 228 The Mongoose Lemur, or Woolly Macaco [*Lemur mongoz*].

‖**Macacus** (mə'keɪkəs). Pl. **macaci** (mə'keɪsaɪ). [mod.L., ad. F. *macaque*: see MACAQUE.] A genus of Old World catarrhine monkeys of the family *Cercopithecidæ*; originally including a great number of African and Asiatic species, but now restricted to species resembling the bonnet macaque or toque; a monkey of this genus.

1871 DARWIN *Desc. Man* I. i. 23 In.. baboons and some species of macacus the upper portions of the ear is slightly pointed. **1875** *Encycl. Brit.* II. 152/1 The *Macaci* present us with the most northern forms of apes. **1893** *Daily News* 8 June 5/3 A small monkey, a macacus, has been placed in his cell to keep him [an ourang-outang] company.

macadam (mə'kædəm). (Formerly with capital M; also Mac-Adam, McAdam.)

1. The name of John Loudon McAdam (1756–1836) used *attrib.* to designate the kind of roadway which he invented and the material used in making it: see MACADAMIZE.

Now apprehended as an attributive use of 2.

1824 MISS MITFORD *Village* Ser. I. 277 We shall see no more of him [our surveyor]; for the Mac-Adam ways are warranted not to wear out. **1878** *N. Amer. Rev.* CXXVI. 91 Closet warriors, in cozy studies, with smooth McAdam roadways before their doors. **1881** *Macm. Mag.* XLIV. 342 All piles of spare macadam material were carefully removed.

2. The material of which a macadamized road is made.

1826 J. WILSON *Noct. Ambr.* Wks. 1855 I. 178 What a.. rattle o' wheels!.. intolerable aneuch ower the macadam, but Lord hae mercy on us, when you're on the causeway! **1831** MOORE *Summer Fête* 121 Where never gleam of gas must dare 'Gainst ancient Darkness to revolt, Nor smooth Macadam hope to spare The dowagers one single jolt. **1856** FONBLANQUE in *Life & Labours* (1874) 520 He may gravely serve out Macadam for rations, and supply biscuit for making roads. **1862** *Athenæum* 30 Aug. 268 The drab-coloured mud of the macadam. **1892** *Times* 20 Apr. 7/4 It is broken up into macadam, and forms a splendid material for making roads.

fig. **1871** R. H. HUTTON *Ess.* II. 126 He sprinkles a little macadam of stony fact along the fair upland path of his imagination. **1892** *Academy* 29 Oct. 382/3 It is an unfinished macadam of inverted commas and references.

3. *nonce-use* as *adj.* Level as macadam.

a **1845** HOOD *St. to Tom Woodgate* v, Does that hard, honest hand now.. tug the oar, a gondolier On smooth Macadam seas?

macadamia (mækə'deɪmɪə). [mod.L. (F. von Mueller 1858, in *Trans. Phil. Inst. Victoria* II. 72), f. the name of John *Macadam* (1827–65), Scottish-born chemist, who was secretary of the Philosophical Institute of Victoria at that time.] An evergreen tree of the Australian genus so called, of the family Proteaceæ, esp. *Macadamia ternifolia*, the Queensland nut, which bears white-fleshed nuts in hard shells. Also *attrib.*

1904 J. H. MAIDEN *Forest Flora New South Wales* I. 217 Mr. Betche and I described a *Macadamia*.. from Camden Haven, N.S.W. **1929** M. D. FREAR *Our Familiar Island Trees* 64 Perhaps the best of these [recent introductions to Hawaii] is the Macadamia Nut, sometimes called the Queensland Nut from its native habitat. **1949** S. A. CLARK *All the Best in Hawaii* xx. 207 Macadamia nuts call for special pause and explanation, for mainlanders seem rarely to have heard of them... A man named E. W. Jordan brought some of these nuts from Tasmania to Honolulu about the year 1890. *Ibid.* 208 Some smooth-leaf varieties of macadamia produce smaller and less sweet nuts. As a delicacy.. macadamia nuts, salted and bottled, have hardly three decades of history... Several Honolulu concerns ship bottled macadamias anywhere. **1955** W. GADDIS *Recognitions* II. i. 295 She returned to her desk.. took a macadamia nut from the jar. **1963** *Economist* 14 Dec. 1198/3 Oils are available.. from.. macadamia nuts. **1969** *Coast to Coast 1967–68* 4 He could hear the familiar morning sounds through that hush,.. the sow's demanding squeals, the butcher-birds and magpies in the macadamia-trees. **1970** *Daily Colonist* (Victoria, B.C.) 23 Dec. 4/1 Economies [made by United Air Lines] have ranged from cancelling routes.. and ceasing to serve macadamia nuts—a Hawaiian delicacy—with drinks.

macadamite (mə'kædəmaɪt), *sb.* and *a.* Now *rare* or *Obs.* [f. MACADAM + -ITE.]

A. *sb.* One who practises or advocates McAdam's system of road-making.

1821 *Monthly Mag.* LII. 104 Some incidental remarks of mine in a paper I sent you in May last, have caused the Mackadamites to throw some of their spare dirt about. **1839** MURCHISON *Silur. Syst.* I. xxxix. 535 In certain districts.. they [boulders] are fast disappearing through the labours of the Macadamites.

B. *adj.* Pertaining to McAdam's system of road-making.

1824 MISS MITFORD *Village* Ser. I. 276 The Mac-Adamite enormity of the stony road. **1846** THACKERAY *Cornhill to Cairo* vii. Wks. 1900 V. 650 Roads were being repaired in the Macadamite manner.

macadamization (mə,kædəmaɪ'zeɪʃən). (Formerly with capital M.) [f. next + -ATION.] The process, practice, or system of making macadamized roads; rarely *concr.* a macadamized road. Also, the converting of stone into road-metal.

1824 *Lond. Mag.* X. 350 Major-Taylorization against Mac-adamization any day! **1824** *Newcastle Mag.* III. 27 The only road in our neighbourhood on which something like Macadamization has been attempted. **1825** *Blackw. Mag.* XVII. 87 A long street under the process of

Macadamization. **1826** Miss Mitford *Village* Ser. II. 2 That..turnpike-road..is now so perfect and so beautiful a specimen of Macadamization, that [etc.]. **1861** Musgrave *By-roads* 75 Mac-adamization. **1869** 'Bradwood' *O.V.H.* (1870) 184 Miss Warren..was cantering down the turf border that fringed the mac-adamisation. **1871** L. Stephen *Playgr. Eur.* v. (1894) 121 The glacier..crushed into smaller fragments, producing..a kind of incipient macadamisation. *fig.* **1847** *Tait's Mag.* XIV. 746 So very strange a macadamization of parties has taken place.

macadamize (mə'kædəmaɪz), *v.* Also **McAdamise, -ize.** [f. MACADAM + -IZE.]

1. *trans.* To make or repair (a road) according to J. L. McAdam's system, which consists in laying down successive layers of stone broken into pieces of nearly uniform size, each layer being allowed to consolidate under the pressure of ordinary wheel traffic before the next is laid upon it.

See McAdam's pamphlet, *Remarks on the Present System of Road-Making* (ed. 5, 1822). He did not approve of the placing of any kind of foundation under the layers of stone, of the use of sand or gravel as 'binding' material, or of the smoothing of the surface by heavy rollers; though the name of 'macadamizing' is now often given to methods in which some or all of these practices are admitted.

1826 *Lion Hunting* 78 The road..was what we now deemed a great luxury,—M'Adamized, instead of paved. **1828** Southey *To A. Cunningham* 23 A street not yet Macadamized. **1863** A. C. Ramsay *Phys. Geog.* (1878) 613 Basalts..are ill adapted for macadamising roads. **1871** L. Stephen *Playgr. Eur.* (1894) 135 A heap of granite stones prepared for macadamising a road.

absol. **1871** M. Collins *Mrq. & Merch.* I. vi. 188 There is no hard stone nearer than Mount Sorel, so they macadamize with something almost as soft as loaf sugar.

b. *fig.* To render level or even; to level, raze.

1826 J. Sherman in *Mem.* (1863) 219 Grace indeed macadamises the road, makes the stones smaller. **1827** Jelf *Let. to Pusey* in Liddon, etc. *Life P.* (1893) I. 117 Your mind is certainly macadamized; mine resembles the road between this [Berlin] and Strelitz. **1829** Marryat *F. Mildmay* iii, The enemy's centre should have been *macadamised* by our seven three-deckers. **1842** Orderson *Creol.* iv. 38 Our..Bishop has..macadamized the way for his successor. **1868** Peard *Water-Farm.* ii. 14 Each successful labour of to-day will macadamise the road for to-morrow.

2. To convert into road-metal.

1841 J. T. Hewlett *Parish Clerk* II. 154 Coarse, thick slates, that would certainly have been macadamized in these days as excellent materials for road-making.

b. *transf.* and *fig.* To break up (something hard or figured as being hard) *into* pieces. ? *Obs.*

1825 Good *Study Med.* (ed. 2) V. 539 By grinding, or as we should now perhaps call it macadamizing the stone into granules. **1825** *New Monthly Mag.* XV. 296 In Macadamizing a few broad, simple, and impressive sounds into passages of numberless rapid notes, there is no time left for giving the emphasis required. **1852** Smedley *L. Arundel* xxxvi. 270 Richard Frere..devoted himself to that indurated specimen of the original granite formation,..and by trying to mac-adamise her into small-talk [etc.]. **1855** —— *H. Coverdale* i. 2 Fathers have flinty hearts, and even the amenities of the nineteenth century have failed to macadamise them.

macadamized (mə'kædəmaɪzd), *ppl. a.* [f. MACADAMIZE + -ED[1].]

1. Of a road (see MACADAMIZE 1).

1827 *Blackw. Mag.* XXI. 791 We were not seen stumbling even upon a Macadamized road. **1837** *Civil Eng. & Arch. Jrnl.* I. 1/2 Filled in with broken stones, such as are used for M'Adamized roads. **1861** Musgrave *By-roads* 282, I found even a Mac-adamized road, which crosses the plain, miry enough, in heavy rain. **1889** G. Findlay *Eng. Railway* 49 A well-constructed macadamized road.

fig. **1827** Lytton *Falkland* 45 Neither in person nor in character was he much beneath or above the ordinary standard of men. He was one of Nature's Macadamized achievements. His great fault was his equality. **1863** Cowden Clarke *Shaks. Char.* xi. 291 The hard and macadamised road of dry duty and daily labour.

2. Broken up into road-metal. Also (*nonce-use*), strewn with broken stones.

1849 Capt. C. Sturt *Exped. Centr. Austral.* I. 238 We then proceeded..down the creek, keeping close upon its banks to avoid the macadamized plains on either side. **1888** *Times* (weekly ed.) 23 Nov. 3/3 Some loose macadamised stones lying about.

ma'cadamizer. [f. MACADAMIZE + -ER[1].]

1. One who makes macadamized roads.

1824 *Newcastle Mag.* III. 26 [The paviours] have..nothing to do but to transform themselves into Macadamizers. **1864** *Reader* 11 June 747/3 Our London macadamizers go about their work in a very unscientific way. **1881** *Instr. Census Clerks* (1885) 87 Paviour...Macadamiser.

2. One who rides on a macadamized road; *esp.* one who keeps to the roads when hunting.

1832 G. Downes *Lett. Cont. Countries* I. 11 Our little Gallic Macadamizer asked one of the Hibernians present [etc.]. **1838** Surtees *Jorrocks's Jaunts* 55 A private road and a line of gates through fields now greet the eyes of our M'Adamisers. **1869** 'Bradwood' *O.V.H.* I. xii. 219 'Here come all the roadsters!' growled the latter, as the hounds..crossed a bye-road—along which in the rear clattered some fifty macadamisers.

maca'damizing, *vbl. sb.* [-ING[1].] The action of the verb MACADAMIZE; macadamization.

1851-61 Mayhew *Lond. Labour* II. 181 The macadamizing of the latter thoroughfare. **1876** Page *Adv. Text-Bk. Geol.* vii. 136 Their extensive use in causewaying and macadamising.

ma'cadamizing, *ppl. a.* [-ING[2].] **a.** That macadamizes. **b.** (Cf. MACADAMIZER 2.)

1826 Bentham in *Westm. Rev.* VI. 457 It performs the function of a Mac-adamizing hammer, in breaking down the aggregate mass. **1860** O. W. Holmes *Prof. Breakf.-t.* i, This is the great Macadamizing place, always cracking up something. **1869** 'Bradwood' *O.V.H.* I. 224 Jack Marshall, in the safe pursuit of pleasure, as far as compatible with macadamising action, had suddenly espied..the Maule carriage.

macaleb, obs. form of MAHALEB.

macalive, variant of MACKALLOW *Obs.*

Macamethe, obs. form of MAHOMET.

‖**macana** (mə'kɑːnə). *South American.* [Said by Humboldt to be Haytian.] An ironwood club.

1622 R. Hawkins *Voy. S. Sea* §27 (1847) 98 Their armes for the warre, which is a sword of heavie blacke wood... They [the Indians of Brazil] call it macana, and it is carved and wrought with inlayd works very curiously, but his edges are blunt. *Ibid.* §41. 147 Their [the islanders of Mocha, Chile] weapons are bowes and arrowes and macanas. **1822** Sara Coleridge tr. *Dobrizhoffer's Hist. Abipones* [Paraguay] II. 360 The wooden club, *macana*. **1861** W. Bollaert tr. *P. Simon's Exped. Aguirre* (Hakl. Soc.) xix. 79 Darts and macanas (a sort of club). [The reference is to Peru.]

†**ma'cao.** *Obs.* Also **makao.** [f. the name of *Macao*, a Portuguese settlement on the coast of China, noted for gambling. In Fr. *macao.* Cf. MACCO.] A gambling game at cards, 'a kind of vingt-et-un' (Littré).

1778 Earl Malmesbury *Diaries & Corr.* I. 179 Macao, (a game much in vogue here at present). **1783** H. Walpole *Lett.* (1858) VIII. 388 When she wants to play at macao. **1794** C. Pigot *Female Jockey Club* 109 We have beheld her ready to burst with rage, when the consequences have been against her at Macao. **1827** *Sporting Mag.* XX. 58 A diplomatic character and member of a fashionable Club at Brussels, has been accused of cheating at Macao. **1883** *Times* 11 July 7 He consorted much with..needy players at..roulette, makao, and similar games of hazard.

macao, obs. form of MACAW.

macaque (mə'kɑːk). Also 8 **mocawk,** 9 **macac.** [a. F. *macaque*, ad. Pg. *macaco*: see MACACO[1].]

†**1.** Some Brazilian species of monkey. *Obs. rare*—1.

1698 Froger *Voy.* 115 We observed two sorts of Monkeys there [*viz.* Brazil], which they distinguished by the Names of Sagovins and Macaques [Fr. orig. *Macaqs*]... The Macaques are..of a brown Colour.

2. A monkey of the genus MACACUS.

1757 J. H. Grose *E. Indies* 41 The natives call it a Mocawk, and when taken young it soon grows very tame. **1840** Blyth tr. *Cuvier's Anim. Kingd.* (1849) 58 The Macaques (*Macacus*, Desm.). *Ibid.* 59 The Bonneted Macaque (*M. Sinicus*). *Ibid.*, The Pig-tailed Macaque... The Black Macaque. **1875** *Encycl. Brit.* II. 152/1 The Thibet Macaque (*Macacus thibetanus*). **1878** Browning *La Saisiaz* 590 What though monkeys and macaques Gibber 'Byron'? **1885** E. Balfour *Cycl. India* (ed. 3) II. 753/2 Macacus cynomolgus, common macac.

macare, obs. form of MAKER.

macarism ('mækərɪz(ə)m). *rare.* Also **makarism.** [ad. Gr. μακαρισμ-ός, f. μακαρίζειν: see next and -ISM.] **a.** (See quot. 1818-60; and cf. next vb.) **b.** = BEATITUDE 2.

1818-60 Whately *Commpl. Bk.* (1864) 25 *note*, The words 'felicitate' and 'congratulate' are used only in application to events, which are one branch only of 'macarism'. *Ibid.* 28 To admiration, contempt seems to be the direct contrary; censure to commendation; pity to macarism. *a* **1860** J. A. Alexander *Gosp. Matth.* (1861) 110 A series of *beatitudes* or macarisms [Footnote, μακαρισμός], so called from the word with which they severally open. **1882** A. B. Bruce *Parab. Teach. Christ* 380 The makarisms and woes with which Luke's version of the Sermon on the Mount begins. **1889** —— *Kingd. God* Introd. 10 Luke's..form of the 'macarisms'.

macarize ('mækəraɪz), *v. rare.* Also **macarise, makarize.** [f. Gr. μακαρίζειν, f. μάκαρ happy: see -IZE.] *trans.* To account or call happy or blessed (cf. quot. 1816-60).

1816-60 Whately *Commpl. Bk.* (1865) 9 A man is admired for what he is, macarized for what he has, praised for what he does. *Ibid.* (1864) 25 If a man possess a genius, or a person that is admirable, he is himself admired; but not if he has an admirable horse or house; the sentiment we feel towards him is of a different nature, and we have no English word to express it; so much are we at a loss as to resort to the word 'envy'. I should like to introduce the word 'macarise'. **1840** Arnold *Let.* in Stanley *Life & Corr.* (1844) II. ix. 227 Therefore I 'macarize' you the more, for having both an inherited home, and in a county and part of the county per se delightful. *a* **1871** Grote *Eth. Fragm.* v. (1876) 177 No man praises happiness, as he praises justice, but macarises (blesses) it as something more divine and better.

macaron, variant of MACAROON.

macaroni (mækə'rəʊnɪ). Pl. **-ies.** Also 6-9 **maccaroni,** 8 **mac(c)arone, makarony,** 9 **mackerony.** [a. It. *maccaroni* (Florio 1598), earlier form of *maccheroni* (Florio 1611) pl. of *maccherone*; the ulterior etymology is obscure.

Some scholars have suggested connexion with Gr. μακαρία, explained by Hesychius to mean a sort of barley-broth. Diez regarded the word as a derivative of It. *maccare* to bruise, crush.]

1. A kind of wheaten paste, of Italian origin, formed into long tubes and dried for use as food.

The same 'Italian paste' is prepared also in the form of VERMICELLI, q.v.

1599 B. Jonson *Cynthia's Rev.* II. i, He doth learne..to eat ænchouies, maccaroni, bouoli, fagioli, and cauiare. **1750** Chesterf. *Lett.* (1792) II. 345 You would do very well to take one or two such sort of people home with you to dinner every day; it would be only a little *minestra* and *macaroni* the more. **1769** Mrs. Raffald *Eng. Housekpr.* (1778) 285 To dress Macaroni with Parmesan Cheese. **1813** Sir H. Davy *Agric. Chem.* (1814) 142 The wheat of the south of Europe, in consequence of the larger quantity of gluten it contains, is peculiarly fitted for making macaroni. **1825** Lytton *Zicci* 45 Merton had heard much of the excellence of the macaroni at Portici. **1893** *Spectator* 10 June 768 A Sicilian sawyer fed on macaroni and melons.

2. *Hist.* An exquisite of a class which arose in England about 1760 and consisted of young men who had travelled and affected the tastes and fashions prevalent in continental society. **b.** *dial.* A fop, dandy.

[This use seems to be from the name of the Macaroni Club, a designation prob. adopted to indicate the preference of the members for foreign cookery, macaroni being at that time little eaten in England. There appears to be no connexion with the transferred use of It. *maccherone* in the senses 'blockhead, fool, mountebank', referred to in 1711 by Addison *Spect.* No. 47 ¶ 5.]

[**1764** H. Walpole *Let. Earl Hertford* 6 Feb. (1857) IV. 178 The Maccaroni Club (which is composed of all the travelled young men who wear long curls and spying-glasses).] **1764** —— *Let. Earl Hertford* 27 May *Ibid.* 238 Lady Falkener's daughter is to be married to a young rich Mr. Crewe, a Macarone, and of our Loo. **1770** *Oxford Mag.* June 228/2 There is indeed a kind of animal, neither male nor female, a thing of the neuter gender, lately started up amongst us. It is called a Macaroni. It talks without meaning, it smiles without pleasantry, it eats without appetite, it rides without exercise, it wenches without passion. **1773** Boswell *Johnson* 21 Aug., You are a delicate Londoner; you are a maccaroni; you can't ride. **1773** [C. Hitchcock] *Macaroni* I. 5, I wanted you to be a man of spirit; your ambition was to appear a first-rate Macaroni; you are returned fully qualified, and determined, I see, to shew the world what a contemptible creature an Englishman dwindles into, when he adopts the follies and vices of other nations. **1783** Mme. D'Arblay *Diary* 9 Dec., It is the custom, you know, among the Macaronies, to wear two watches. **1820** Lamb *Elia* Ser. I. South-Sea House, He wore his hair..in the fashion which I remember to have seen in caricatures of what were termed, in my young days, Maccaronies. **1854** A. E. Baker *N'hampton Words* II, *Macaroni*, a fop. Equivalent to the modern *dandy*; now nearly, if not quite, obsolete. **1859** Thackeray *Virgin.* (1879) I. 357 If he brags a little to-night..and talks about London and Lord March, and White's, and Almack's, with the air of a macaroni. **1881** *Athenæum* 5 Nov. 603/2 The weak chin,..resolute brow, and good forehead, portray Sheridan to the life, as he appeared, a macaroni and brilliant lounger in Carlton House. **1891** *Sheffield Gloss.*, *Mackerony*, an over-dressed, or gaudily-dressed person.

transf. **1778** [W. Marshall] *Minutes Agric.* 3 Feb. 1775 Harnessed the old oxen in all their new finery..; the Pantheon never saw two more ridiculous Macaronies.

3. A species of crested penguin, *Eudyptes chrysolophus.* In full ***macaroni penguin.***

[App. so called because its crest was thought to resemble the coiffure of the 'macaronies'. The *Pall Mall Gazette Extra* of 24 July 1884, p. 29/2 gives from a print of 1777 two figures of head-dresses then in use, one of which is called 'the macaroni'. Cf. also quot. 1820 in 2.]

1838 Poe *A. G. Pym* Wks. 1864 IV. 123 The maccaroni, the jackass and the rookery penguin. **1860** C. C. Abbott in *Ibis* 338 This bird is called in the Falkland Islands the Maccaroni Penguin... It has an orange-coloured crest. **1885** *Encycl. Brit.* XVIII. 492/1 *Eudyptes*, containing the crested Penguins, known to sailors as..'Macaronis'.

4. A medley (such as a macaronic poem).

1884 Rogers *Six Cent. Work & Wages* (1886) 166 Political songs in Latin or in a maccaroni of Latin and English.

5. In the West Indies, a coin of the value of a quarter of a dollar. ? *Obs.*

1834 M. G. Lewis *Jrnl. W. Ind.* 403 Each grown person received a present of half a dollar, and every child a maccaroni. **1838** W. Jameson in A. Robb *Gosp. Africans* (1861) iv. 88 The masters began to offer a *macaroni*, or 1s. sterling, a day.

†**6.** The name of a gambling-room at Newmarket. (Cf. MACCO.) *Obs.*

1771 P. Parsons *Newmarket* I. 186 The Maccaroni is no other than a pretty large and whimsically painted room.

7. (See quot.)

1876 R. L. Wallace *Canary Bk.* xiv. 165 Lizards [*sc.* canaries] are known among Scotchmen as 'macaronies'.

8. Short for *macaroni tool.*

1867 G. A. Rogers *Wood Carving* 12 Now take the macaroni and cut away the wood on either side of the vein. ..The maccaroni..is shaped to cut at both angles.

9. An Italian. *slang.*

1845 [see FROG[1] 3 b]. **1901** 'L. Malet' *Hist. R. Calmady* v. x. 461 You don't suppose I mean to stand here till the second anniversary of the Day of Judgment, watching your blithering chicken-shanked macaronies suck rotten oranges, do you? **1942** E. Paul *Narrow St.* xxix. 266 'Cut the throats of the macaronis,' Madame Absalom said. She disliked Italians slightly more than the rest of the human race. **1946** D. Hamson *We fell among Greeks* viii. 91 They dropped us practically on to the Italian garrison at Karpenisi... Doug was playing hidey-ho with a couple of macaronis, taking potshots round bushes at each other.

10. Nonsense, meaningless talk. *slang* (chiefly *Austral.*).

1924 LAWRENCE & SKINNER *Boy in Bush* iii. 46 Yes. Jam, macaroni, cockadoodle. We're plain people out here-aways, not mantle ornaments. **1941** BAKER *Dict. Austral. Slang* 45 *Macaroni*, nonsense, foolishness. **1945** —— *Austral. Lang.* vi. 128 *Macaroni*..and *borak* cover the same meaning of misleading chatter. **1965** J. VON STERNBERG *Fun in Chinese Laundry* (1966) iv. 67 What is flashed from the projector overhead will be the same old macaroni.

11. *attrib.*, as (sense 1) ***macaroni dealer, pudding, soup, -stall, wheat***; (sense 2) ***macaroni cane, dress, intelligencer, marquis, philosopher, shrug, train***; **macaroni cheese**, a savoury of which the principal ingredients are macaroni and cheese; † **macaroni fiddle**, ? some kind of small violin; † **macaroni gin**, a kind of colliery gin (E.D.D.); † **macaroni stake** (see quot.); **macaroni tool**, a square-cutting tool used in wood-carving.

1781 *Westm. Mag.* IX. 71 A supple-jack or a *macaroni cane, embellished with silk and gold tassels. [**1769** E. RAFFALD *Experienced Eng. Housekeeper* xii. 261 To dress Macaroni with Permasent Cheese... Boil it.., pour it on a Plate, lay all over it Permasent Cheese toasted.] **1877** TROLLOPE *Is he Popenjoy?* (1878) I. i. 2 It is as though one were asked to eat boiled mutton after woodcocks, caviare, or *maccaroni [macaroni, 1877 *serial publ.*] cheese. **1934** A. RANSOME *Coot Club* iii. 40 Tell her we won't be late. Macaroni cheese to-night. **1972** B. NILSON *Pears Bk. Light Meals* xii. 184 Macaroni cheese with ham. **1851** in *Illustr. Lond. News* 5 Aug. (1854) 119/1 Occupations of the People, ..*Maccaroni-dealer. **1772** FOOTE *Nabob* I. (1778) 26 The waiter at Almack's has just brought him home his *macaroni dress for the hazard table. **1777** MME. D'ARBLAY *Early Diary* Apr.-July (1889) II. 185 First came a French horn, —..then a violin,—a bass,—a bassoon,—a *Macaroni fiddle. **1789** BRAND *Hist. Newcastle* II. 684 There is a sort of gins called 'whim gins', and a kind known by the name of '*macaroni gins'. **1769** *Public Advert.* 18 May 4/2 Thy Paper is the *Macarony Intelligencer. **1859** THACKERAY *Virgin.* xcii. (1878) 758, I never bargained to have a *Maccaroni Marquis to command me. **1797** *Monthly Mag.* III. 92 In this fanciful æra, when *macaroni philosophers hold flirtation with science. **1861** MRS. BEETON *Bk. Househ. Managem.* xxvii. 654 *Sweet *macaroni pudding*... Put the macaroni, with a pint of the milk, into a saucepan with the lemon-peel. **1963** N. HEATON *Puddings* II. 56 *Macaroni Pudding*... When cool, add the beaten egg and the sugar. **1775** MME. D'ARBLAY *Early Diary* 21 Nov., 'It is not at all the ton to like her':..(with a *Macarony shrug). **1845** E. ACTON *Mod. Cookery* (ed. 2) i. 11 **Maccaroni soup*. Throw four ounces of fine fresh mellow maccaroni into a pan of fast-boiling water. **1949** H. SMITH *Master Bk. Soups* xv. 198 *Thick Macaroni Soup*. Prepare 3 pints of good gravy... Garnish with 6 ozs. macaroni cooked in salted water. **1823** 'JON BEE' *Dict. Turf*, **Macaroni stakes*, those ridden by gentlemen, not jockies. **1814** *Sporting Mag.* XLIV. 103 You dash among the pots of a *macaroni-stall. **1867** G. A. ROGERS *Wood Carving* 2 A *maccaroni tool. **1890** C. G. LELAND *Wood Carving* 10 The Macaroni Tool..is for removing wood on each side of a vein or leaf, or similar delicate work. *Ibid.* 42 The so-called 'macaroni-tool'..is really very little used, owing to the great difficulty of keeping it sharp, and its liability to break. **1773** GOLDSM. *Stoops to Conq.* Epil., Ye travell'd tribe, ye *macaroni train. **1901** *Westm. Gaz.* 23 July 7/3 The *macaroni wheat crop (a new venture in the United States).

† **maca'ronian**, *a. Obs.* [f. prec. + -AN.]

1. = MACARONIC *a.* 1.

1727–41 CHAMBERS *Cycl.*, *Macaronic*, or *Macaronian*, a kind of burlesque poetry... We have little in English in the Macaronian way. **1751** CAMBRIDGE *Scribleriad* II. 184 *note*, The Macaronian is a kind of burlesque poetry, consisting of a jumble of words of different languages, with words of the vulgar tongue latinized, and latin words modernized.

2. = MACARONIC *a.* 3.

1788 R. GALLOWAY *Poems* (1792) 16 Give ear ilk Macaronian beau, 'Tween George's Square an eke Soho.

macaronic (mækəˈrɒnɪk), *a.* and *sb.* Also 7 **makeronick**, 8 **maccaronic**. [ad. mod.L. *macarōnic-us* = It. (†*macaronico*) *maccheronico*, f. (†*macaroni*) *maccheroni* MACARONI.

The word seems to have been invented by Teofilo Folengo ('Merlinus Cocaius') whose 'macaronic' poem (*Liber Macaronices*) was published in 1517. He explains (ed. 2, 1521) that the 'macaronic art' is so called from macaroni, which is 'quoddam pulmentum farina, caseo, botiro compaginatum, grossum, rude, et rusticanum'.]

A. *adj.* **1.** Used to designate a burlesque form of verse in which vernacular words are introduced into a Latin context with Latin terminations and in Latin constructions. Also, applied to similar verse of which the basis is Greek instead of Latin; and *loosely* to any form of verse in which two or more languages are mingled together. Hence of language, style, etc.: Resembling the mixed jargon of macaronic poetry.

1638 SIR J. BEAUMONT in *Jonsonus Virbius* 12 He Latin Horace found..Translated in the Macaronicke toung, Cloth'd in such raggs as [etc.]. **1711** *Drumm. of Hawth.'s Wks.*, *Life* 5 For diverting himself and his Friends, he wrote a Sheet which he called *Polemo-Middinia*; 'Tis a sort of Macaronick Poetry, in which the Scots Words are put in Latin Terminations. **1778** JOHNSON 14 Apr. in *Boswell*, Maccaronick verses are verses made out of a mixture of different languages. **1837** HALLAM *Hist. Lit.* I. vi. §31 I. 519 Maillard..whose sermons, printed if not preached in Latin, with sometimes a sort of almost macaronic intermixture of French. **1897** DOWDEN *Fr. Lit.* II. i. 90 The macaronic poet Folengo. **1898** STEVENSON *St. Ives* 236 Grace was said..in a macaronic latin.

† **2.** Of the nature of a jumble or medley. *Obs.*

1611 (*title*) Coryats Crambe, or his Colwort Twise Sodden, And Now serued in with other Macaronicke dishes, as the second course to his Crudities. **1806** J. DALLAWAY *Obs. Eng. Arch.* 222 Those Travellers who have seen the new buildings of Edinburgh and Glasgow will look on the architecture of Bath, as belonging to the maccaronick order. **1816** G. COLMAN *Br. Grins, Lament.* xiv. (1872) 271 My coarse, macaronic style may here and there excite a smile.

3. Pertaining to a macaroni. *rare*⁻⁰.

1828–32 WEBSTER, *Macaronic*, pertaining to or like a macaroni; empty; trifling; vain; affected.

B. *sb.*

1. a. Macaronic language or composition. **b.** *pl.* Macaronic verses.

a **1668** DENHAM *Dialogue* 33 You that were once so œconomick, Quitting the thrifty style Laconick, Turn Prodigal in Makeronick. **1693** *Apol. Clergy Scot.* 31 When some of his Party mounts the Desk and declaims their Maccaronicks. **1727** BAILEY vol. II, *Macaronicks* [among the Italians], a sort of Burlesque Poetry made out of their Language, and the Scraps and Terminations of divers other. **1839** HALLAM *Introd. Lit. Europe* II. v. 267 *note*, Folengo.. sat down for the rest of his life to write Macaronics. *a* **1864** LUCY AIKIN in *Mem.* etc. 77 Our own people were turning Scotch without knowing it. We began to allow the macaronic of the Edinburgh Review for actual English!

† **2.** A jumble or medley. *Obs.*

1611 COTGR., *Macaronique*, a Macaronick; a confused heape, or huddle of many seuerall things.

† **maca'ronical**, *a. Obs.* Also 6 **macheronicall**. [See prec. and -ICAL.] = MACARONIC *a.*

1585 E. D. *Prayse of Nothing* H j b, The macheronicall phantasies of Merlinus Cocaius. **1596** NASHE *Saffron Walden* F, Who..hath translated my *Piers Pennilesse* into the Macaronicall tongue.

maca'ronically, *adv.* [f. MACARONIC: see -ICALLY.] In the macaronic manner.

1821 W. TAYLOR in *Monthly Rev.* XCVI. 82 That strange mixture of Portuguese, Spanish,..[etc.] names with which most European maps of South America are macaronically diversified. **1900** G. W. E. RUSSELL *Conferences* ii. 24 The earliest pieces..are in the learned language, sometimes macaronically interspersed with the vernacular.

macaronicism (mækəˈrɒnɪsɪz(ə)m). [f. MACARONIC + -ISM.] Macaronic style.

1830 *Gentl. Mag.* C. II. 123 Moliere gives an amusing specimen of macaronicism, in the *troisième intermede* of Le Malade Imaginaire. **1845** *Encycl. Metrop.* XXI. 629/2 It may be doubted, however, whether the Ancients would be very solicitous to establish a prior claim to Macaronicism.

macaronism (mækəˈrəʊnɪz(ə)m). Also 8 **macaronyism**, 9 **maccaroni-ism**. [f. MACARONI + -ISM.] Behaviour characteristic of a macaroni; dandyism.

1775 MME. D'ARBLAY *Early Diary* 21 Nov, He is a good deal in the present ton, which is not Macaronyism. **1835** *Tait's Mag.* II. 20 His colonel..requited his maccaroni-ism by a week's arrest. **1863** SALA *Capt. Dangerous* II. viii. 252 We would have thought it vile poltroonery and macaronism to have worn wigs. **1868** C'TESS MINTO *Mem. H. Elliot* i. 28 His maccaronism seems to have been a subject of jest among his friends.

maca'ronyish, *a. rare*⁻¹. [f. MACARONI + -ISH.] Characteristic of dandyism.

1859 SALA *Tw. round Clock* (1861) 288 There is something supercilious, pragmatical, macaronyish, un-English, in the announcement, 'No half-price'.

macaroon (mækəˈruːn). Also 7 **makeron(e, maquaroon, mackroom, mackroon**, 7–8 **mackeroon(e, mackaroon(e, macaron**, 8 **makeroon, macron**, 7–9 **maccaroon**. [a. F. *macaron* (16th c.), ad. It. *maccarone* (now *maccherone*) sing. of *maccaroni*: see MACARONI.]

1. A small sweet cake or biscuit consisting chiefly of ground almonds, white of egg, and sugar.

1611 COTGR., *Macarons*, Macarons; little Fritter-like Bunnes, or thicke Losenges, compounded of Sugar, Almonds, Rosewater, and Muske. **1611** MARKHAM *Country Content.* II. ii. (1668) 98 To make Jumbals more fine and curious..and nearer to the taste of the Macaroon. **1630** J. TAYLOR (Water P.) *Gt. Eater Kent* Wks. I. 146/1 Whether it bee..Fritter, or Flapiacke, or Posset, Galley-Mawfrey, Mackeroone, Kickshaw, or Tantablin. **1688** R. HOLME *Armoury* III. 83/2 Mackrooms, a kind of roul of sweet Bread. **1725** BRADLEY *Fam. Dict.* s.v. *Tourte*, You may also put a pounded Macaroon into the Artichoke Cream. **1747** MRS. GLASSE *Cookery* xv. 141 To make Maccaroons. **1848** J. GRANT *Adv. Aide-de-C.* xxviii. (Rtldg.) 227 Little maccaroons, sweet as sugar and almonds could make them. **1875** A. R. HOPE *My School-boy Fr.* 138 We were regaling on macaroons.

attrib. **1783** MME. D'ARBLAY *Diary* 9 Dec., I had no more power to prevent it than this macaroon cake in my hand. **1836** T. HOOK *G. Gurney* I. 297 A Jew boy, selling macaroon cakes. **1898** GULLY in *Daily News* 21 July 7/5 A Marchpane is an edifice in macaroon work.

† **2.** = MACARONI 1. *Obs.*

1704 J. PITTS *Acc. Mahometans* iii. (1738) 24 What they call Mackaroon is some Paste made only with Flour and Water. **1738** [G. SMITH] *Curious Relat.* II. 302 A Sort of Pudding, which they [in Malta] call *Macron*. **1753** CHAMBERS *Cycl. Supp.*, *Macaron*, the name of a sort of vermicelli, a paste made of flour and water, and formed into the shape of the barrel of a quill, or the guts of small fowls.

† **3.** A buffoon; a blockhead, dolt. Also *dial.* a fop (= MACARONI 2). *Obs.* [Cf. It. *maccherone*.]

a **1631** DONNE *Sat.* iv. 117 Like a bigge wife, at sight of lothed meat..; so I sigh and sweat To heare this Makeron talke in vaine. *a* **1633** R. B. *In Mem., Donne's Poems* 401 A Macaroon And no way fit to speake to clouted shoone. *a* **1825** FORBY *Voc. E. Anglia*, *Macaroon*, a fop.

Macartney (məˈkɑːtnɪ). [The name of George, Earl *Macartney* (1737–1806).] **a.** Used in ***Macartney cock, pheasant***, and in shortened form ***Macartney***: A pheasant of the genus *Euplocamus*, esp. *E. ignitus*; a fireback.

[**179.** DR. SHAW in Sir G. Staunton *Macartney's Embassy to China* (1797) I. 248 It may be called the *fire-backed pheasant*. **1813** TEMMINCK *Hist. Nat. des Pigeons* etc. II. 273 Houpifère Macartney. Gallus Macartneyi. Mihi...Cette belle espèce de Gallinacé..a été indiquée..par sir Georges Staunton, d'après un individu qui fut offert à Lord Macartney, Ambassadeur Anglais auprès de l'Empereur de la Chine.] **1834** SIR W. JARDINE *Nat. Hist. Gallinaceous Birds* I. 214 The Macartney Cock. *Euplocamus ignitus*. Fire-backed Pheasant of Java. **1840** BLYTH tr. *Cuvier's Anim. Kingd.* (1849) 227 The Macartneys.

b. Macartney rose, an evergreen white-flowered climbing rose, *Rosa bracteata*, introduced in 1795 by Lord Macartney.

1811 *Curtis's Bot. Mag.* XXXIV. 1377 Macartny's [*sic*] Rose... Native of China, whence it was introduced by Lord Macartny [*sic*], on his return from his embassy to that country. **1837** [see ROSE *sb.* 3]. **1908** H. H. ROBBINS *Our First Ambassador to China* p. viii, The design on the cover of the book is one adapted from a sprig of the original Macartney rose, growing in the North of Ireland. **1955** C. C. HURST in G. S. Thomas *Old Shrub Roses* ix. 93 So many different species have been concerned in the nineteenth and twentieth centuries... Macartney Roses from *R*[*osa*] *bracteata* [etc.]. **1974** *Country Life* 21 Mar. 631/1 The Macartney Rose, *Rosa bracteata*, belongs essentially to late summer..an exquisite creature with large white blooms and golden stamens.

macary bitter. 'A West Indian name for *Picramnia Antidesma*' (*Treas. Bot.* 1866).

a **1726** H. BARHAM *Hortus Americanus* (1794) 96 Majoe... It is also called Macary bitter from its growing in great plenty in the bay of Macary.

Macassar (məˈkæsə(r)). [The name (in the native form *Mangkasara*) of a district in the island of Celebes.] **1. Macassar ebony**, the dark-coloured wood of *Diospyros celebica* and related species from Celebes and the Andaman Islands. **Macassar oil**, an unguent for the hair, grandiloquently advertised in the early part of the 19th century, and represented by the makers (Rowland and Son) to consist of ingredients obtained from Macassar. The name has subsequently been given commercially to various natural products imported from the East, e.g. to the oils expressed from the seeds of *Schleichera trijuga*, *Carthamus tinctorius*, and the berries of *Stadtmannia Sideroxylon*. (Hence **Macassar-oiled** *a.*, anointed with this oil.) **Macassar poison**, the gum of a tree, with which the Malays poison their arrows.

1666–7 *Phil. Trans.* II. 417 Whether it be true, that the onely Antidote hitherto known, against the..Macassar-poison, is humane Ordure, taken inwardly? **1797** *Encycl. Brit.* (ed. 3) X. 357/1 *Macassar Poison*,..called *ippo* in the Macassar and Malayan tongue. **1809** ALEX. ROWLAND jun. (*title*) Essay on..the Human Hair, with Remarks on the Virtues of the Macassar Oil. **1819** BYRON *Juan* I. xvii, In virtues nothing earthly could surpass her, Save thine 'incomparable oil,' Macassar! **1831** TRELAWNY *Adv. Younger Son* III. 280 [The author professes to have met in Celebes with] the oleaginous extract from a fruit-tree, since that period become so notorious in Europe, (by name I mean,)—Macassar oil. **1842** S. LOVER *Handy Andy* x. 99 He ran his fingers through his Macassar-oiled ringlets. **1889** G. S. BOULGER *Uses of Plants* vii. 177 Those [sticks] most commonly cut out of the solid log are Oak..home-grown; Ceylon or Macassar Ebony..; and the Palmyra Palm. **1896** BRANNT *Fats & Oils* (ed. 2) II. 82 Macassar oil..is obtained from the seed of *Schleichera trijuga*..Considerable quantities of the oil were formerly imported, but what at present comes into commerce under the name of 'macassar oil' is mostly a mixture of cocoa-nut oil and ylang-ylang extract, coloured red with alkannin. **1920** A. L. HOWARD *Man. Timbers of World* 76 (*heading*) Ebony, macassar... This wood is imported in large billets and round logs... The colour ranges from dark brown to black, and a large proportion of the logs are streaked with yellow or yellowish brown, some very handsomely figured pieces being occasionally found. **1936** *Nature* 9 May 790/2 Counter front ..in finely figured macassar ebony. **1947** J. C. RICH *Materials & Methods of Sculpture* x. 288 Macassar ebony, or Coromandel,..is considered by many wood carvers to be inferior to African ebony. **1972** *Handbk. Hardwoods* (Building Res. Establishment) (ed. 2) 68 In Macassar ebony pale to medium brown zones contrast with black wood.

2. Also **Macasar, Makasar, Makassar, Mangkasar, Mungkasar**. A native or inhabitant of Macassar; the name of their language. Also *attrib.* or as *adj.*

1808 *Asiatick Researches* X. 194 The dialect of Mungkásar or Macassar, the bravest and most renowned of the Búgis tribes, differs..from the Búgis proper... I have formed a short radical vocabulary of the Búgis and Mungkásar [languages]. **1816** T. S. RAFFLES *On Malayu Nation* 125 To the collection that has already been made of the various laws and usages of the Malays, Sumatrans, Javanese, Bugis, Macasars and Sulus, may be added the compendium of the Muhammedan law of inheritance. **1817** —— *Hist. Java* II. xi. 162 By the aid of the Dutch..the Makásar chief was driven from his post. **1840** J. BROOKE *Jrnl.* 14 Feb. in R. Mundy *Narr. Events Borneo & Celebes* (1848) I. vii. 106 From his residence at Tetiagi..he transmits information to the Makassar government. **1886** *Misc. Papers relating to Indo-China* (Straits Branch R. Asiatic Soc.) I. xii. 108 The

descriptive catalogues of the extensive Bugis and Makassar literature..may now be consulted. **1911** *Encycl. Brit.* V. 598/1 The Macassars are well-built and muscular, and have in general a dark-brown complexion. **1968** *Ibid.* V. 132/2 They [*sc.* the Toradja tribe] came under a Bugis and Makasarese civilizing influence... The Bugis and Makasars ..came into touch with Hindu culture in southern Celebes ..and later were converted to Islam. *Ibid.* XIV. 654/1 Gaily coloured, plaited basketry is an outstanding feature of Makasarese markets... The people, the Mangkasaras or Makasars, are a branch of the Malay people, similar to but not identical with the Bugis, who inhabit the same region.

Macassarese (məkæsəˈriːz). Also **Makas(s)arese**. **a.** The Macassar people. **b.** Their language. Also *attrib.* or as *adj.*

1880 [see DYAK]. **1948** D. DIRINGER *Alphabet* vii. 430 The Macassarese and the Buginese..are the most important and the most advanced peoples of the island [*sc.* Celebes]... Macassarese is spoken nowadays in all the districts from Balu Kumba to Segere. **1959** *Chambers's Encycl.* III. 211/1 The peoples of the south (Buginese and Macassarese) are Moslems. **1968** [see MACASSAR 2].

macauco, variant of MACACO.

Macaulayism (məˈkɔːlɪɪz(ə)m). [f. the name of Thomas Babington (Lord) *Macaulay* (1800–1859) + -ISM.] The characteristic historical method or literary style of Macaulay; an instance of this. So **Maˈcaulayan**, **Macaulayˈesque**, **Maˈcaulayish** *adjs.*, pertaining to or modelled upon Macaulay's method or style. **Macaulayˈese** (erron. *Macaulese*), Macaulay's kind of diction.

1846 POE *Cary* Wks. 1864 III. 68 Models of style in these days of rhodomontades and Macaulayisms. **1859** NAPIER *Life Visct. Dundee* I. 4 *note*, How often does he give us Macaulese for history! **1865** *Spectator* 492 Lord Derby does not talk leading articles after this Macaulayish fashion. **1871** M. ARNOLD *Friendship's Garland* 71 Why do you call Mr. Hepworth Dixon's style middle-class Macaulayese? **1884** *Pall Mall G.* 26 Sept. 3/1 There is something quite Macaulayesque in the description..of the way in which [etc.]. **1887** *Spectator* 27 Aug. 1159 Macaulayan and other historical—or at least other historians'—incrustations. **1892** *Athenæum* 11 June 758/3 Dressing up platitudes in a sort of faded Macaulayese.

macaw[1] (məˈkɔː). Also 7 machao, 7–8 macao, 7–9 maccaw, 8 maccau, 8–9 mackaw. [a. Pg. *macao*, of obscure origin; a Tupi name for the bird is *macavuana*.

Cf. Sp. '*máca*, a Bird in the Province of Quito, in South-America, less than our Cocks, with a long Bill Red and Yellow, and its Feathers of such Variety of Colours as is admirable' (Pineda, 1740).]

1. The name for several species of large long-tailed birds of the parrot kind constituting the genus *Ara*; they inhabit tropical and subtropical America and are remarkable for their gaudy plumage.

1668 CHARLETON *Onomasticon Zoicon* 66 Great blew and yellow Parrat called the *Machao*, or *Cockatoon*. *a* **1672** WILLUGHBY *Ornithol.* II. xi. (1676) 73 Psittacus maximus alter Aldrov. Angl. Maccaw, sev Macao & Cockatoon. **1703** DAMPIER *Voy.* (1729) III. I. 405 The Red Maccaw. **1707** FUNNELL *Voy.* iv. 70 The Maccaw..is about the bigness of a Hawk. **1788** *New Lond. Mag.* 61 The larger Psittaci are called Macaos. **1802** BINGLEY *Anim. Biog.* (1813) II. 75 The Brasilian Green Macaw. **1821–30** LD. COCKBURN *Mem.* v. (1874) 257 [He] was walking..dressed like a mackaw, as the Commissioner's purse-bearer. **1870** DISRAELI *Lothair* xxxv, Upon gilt and painted perches also there were..macaws.

†**2.** Applied (?erron.) to some oriental bird. *Obs.*

1699 DAMPIER *Voy.* II. I. 128 In the [Achin] Woods there are many sorts of wild Fowls, viz. Maccaws, Parrots [etc.].

3. *attrib.*, as ***macaw tribe***; † ***macaw-fish***, some brightly coloured fish (cf. *parrot-fish*).

1753 CHAMBERS *Cycl. Supp.* s.v., With some it [cockatoon] is made the synonymous name of all the Macaw tribe. **1792** MAR. RIDDELL *Voy. Madeira* 69 The parrot-fish, the macaw-fish.

macaw[2] (məˈkɔː). Also 7 macow, 7–8 maccaw, 8–9 mackaw, 9 macca-. [Prob. repr. one or more Carib words; cf. Arawak (Guiana) *mocaya*, *macoya*, the macaw-palm.] The West Indian name for palms of the genus *Acrocomia*; formerly also †the fruit of these palms. Now only *attrib.* in ***macaw-berry***, ***-palm***, ***-tree***; also **macaw-bush**, a West Indian plant, *Solanum mammosum* (Treas. Bot. 1866); **macaw-fat**, a West Indian name for the Oil Palm, *Elæis guineensis*.

1657 LIGON *Barbados* 72 The Macow is one of the strangest trees the Iland affords. **1672** R. BLOME *Jamaica*, etc. 73 [Descr. Barbadoes] Limes, Lemons, Macows, Grapes [etc.]. **1697** DAMPIER *Voy.* (1698) I. ii. 20 We got Macaw-berries..wherewith we satisfied ourselves this day, though coursly. **1699** L. WAFER *Voy.* 16 We found there a Maccaw tree, which afforded us berries, of which we eat greedily. *Ibid.* 20 This being the 7th Day of our Fast, save only the Maccaw-berries before related. **1756** P. BROWNE *Jamaica* 343 The Mackaw Tree..is very common in most of the sugar-colonies. **1858** SIMMONDS *Dict. Trade*, *Macaw-fat*, a West Indian name for oil palm, *Elais Guineensis*. *Macaw-palm*, the *Acrocomia sclerocarpa* of Martius. **1864** GRISEBACH *Flora W. Ind.* 785 Mackaw Tree, *Acrocomia sclerocarpa*. **1882** J. SMITH *Dict. Pop. Names Plants*, Macaw Palm or Gru-Gru (*Acrocomia fusiformis*). **1894** *Outing* (U.S.) XXIII. 380/2 The oil palm or macca-fat.

McBurney's point (məkˈbɜːniːz). *Surg.* and *Anat.* Also **McBurney point**. [f. the name of Charles *McBurney* (1845–1913), U.S. surgeon, who described it in 1889.] A point on the surface of the abdomen situated along a line from the umbilicus to where the anterior superior spine of the right ilium can be felt and at a distance of 1½ to 2 inches from this spine, which point normally lies directly above the appendix and is the point of maximum tenderness in appendicitis.

1890 L. A. STIMSON in *N.Y. Med. Jrnl.* 25 Oct. 449/2, I found him..very weak, with marked tenderness and slight deep induration at a point midway between the umbilicus and the right anterior superior spine of the ilium... For the sake of brevity, and as a proper recognition of the value of this symptom, I shall speak of this point as 'McBurney's point'. *Ibid.* 450/1 The McBurney point was well marked. **1910** *Practitioner* Feb. 261 In peritonitis the pain is situated over the inflamed viscus, *e.g.* at McBurney's point in appendicitis. **1972** *Sci. Amer.* Aug. 122/2 Draw a line from the navel to the frontal protuberance of the right hipbone. Place your finger about one and a half inches from the bony end. That is McBurney's point.

macca (ˈmækə). [f. MACAW[2].] **1.** A Jamaican name for the palm *Acrocomia sclerocarpa*, distinguished by its prickles; hence, used for the prickles of other plants and animals. Also *attrib.*

1873 [implied in sense 2]. **1910** ANDERSON & CUNDALL *Jamaica Anancy Stories* 31 De man dat hab on boot must go befo' so' mash macca. **1946** E. N. BURKE *Stories told by Uncle Newton* I. 17 There was soft grease—applied warm—for prickles ('macca' to us children) in the fingers or toes. **1956** J. HEARNE *Stranger at Gate* xvii. 131 They went through the bush..the dry *macca* crunching beneath their shoes. *Ibid.* xxxi. 239 If I have to walk a hundred mile on macca thorn, I am going to be dere. **1961** F. G. CASSIDY *Jamaica Talk* i. 7 A thoroughly Jamaican word..is *macca*, which now means any kind of prickle, thorn, bur, or sharp spine on plants or animals... It is used in many combinations too, like *macca breadfruit*, *macca yam*, *macca fern*.

2. macca-fat, a Jamaican name for the fruits of certain oil-yielding palms, esp. those of the genus *Acrocomia* and the oil palm, *Elæis guineensis*; **macca-fat palm**, one of these trees. Cf. *macaw-fat* (MACAW[2]).

1873 C. J. G. RAMPINI *Lett. from Jamaica* 71 Clumps of wild ginger, Macca-fat palms,—surely the most graceful of all that graceful tribe. **1961** F. G. CASSIDY *Jamaica Talk* i. 7 The *macaw tree* [is]..also called the *macca-fat palm* in Jamaica. *Ibid.*, The two most prominent features of these trees [are]—the fruits (not dates, but a similar nut-like berry with an edible rind, the *macca-fat* of today) and the thorns.

Maccabean, -æan (mækəˈbiːən), *a.* and *sb.* [f. MACCABEE + -AN.] **A.** *adj.* Of or pertaining to Judas Maccabæus or the Maccabees. **B.** *sb.* = MACCABEE.

1821 R. LAURENCE *Bk. of Enoch* 207 Between the period of the captivity, and the rise of the Maccabæan dynasty. **1840** J. H. HOWLETT *Metrical Chronol.* (ed. 3) 16 Under the Maccabaean princes, what did the Jews become? **1845** [see MACCABEE]. **1890** CHURCH & SEELEY (*title*) The hammer, a story of Maccabean times. **1920** *Q. Rev.* July 4 His [*sc.* Disraeli's] party reaped the benefit of his Maccabean courage. **1952** GERTH & MARTINDALE tr. *Weber's Anc. Judaism* IV. xiv. 360 The high priest Onias, who in the confusion of Maccabean party struggles had escaped to Egypt..had not scrupled to build a temple there. **1973** [see HASMONEAN *sb.* and *a.*].

Maccabee (ˈmækəbiː). *Jewish Hist.* [ad. L. *Maccabæ-us*, Gr. Μακκαβαῖος, the epithet of the Jewish patriot Judas.

'The source of the name is uncertain, but it is most natural to connect it with *maqāb*, "hammer".' 1883 *Encycl. Brit.* XV. 130/2.]

A supporter or successor of Judas Maccabæus, the leader of a religious revolt against Antiochus IV, 175–164 B.C., as recorded in the Books of the Maccabees.

1375 BARBOUR *Bruce* I. 465 Thai was lik to the Machabeys, That, as men in the bibill seys [etc.]. *a* **1420** WYCLIF *1 Macc.* (*heading*) Here biginnith the firste book of Machabeies. **1550** *Briefe & Compendiouse Table, Concordaunce Bible* Title-page, The thirde boke of the Machabees. **1614** RALEGH *Hist. World* I. II. x. 377 Then Modin the Natiue Citie of the Macchabees. **1702** R. L'ESTRANGE tr. *Josephus' Works* 1058 Flavius Josephus, his discourse of the Maccabees. **1845** *Encycl. Metrop.* IX. 643/2 Hence, all who fought under that standard were called Maccabees, or Maccabeans. **1920** H. F. HENDERSON *Relig. in Scotl.* i. 16 The patriotism of the Jew, especially in the age of the Maccabees, was an ardent passion that enabled him to overcome enemies four times his number. **1956** W. R. FARMER (*title*) Maccabees, Zealots, and Josephus. An inquiry into Jewish nationalism in the Greco-Roman period.

transf. and *attrib.* **1865** *Sunday at Home* 194/2 But at length one of the Maccabee princes..subdued them. **1883** *Encycl. Brit.* XV. 131/1 The Vatican [MS.] does not contain the Maccabee books. **1959** *Listener* 20 Aug. 292/2 The Maccabees of this small but resolute movement..were the Aaronsohn family.

Maccabiah (mækəˈbiːə). [f. *Maccabi*, the name of an Israeli sporting organization + *-ah* Heb. adj. ending.] In full, ***Maccabiah Games***. A sporting contest, modelled on the Olympic Games, for Jewish athletes, and held at four-yearly intervals in Israel.

[**1962** *New Jewish Encycl.* 299/1 The major project of the Maccabi is the organization of Maccabiads, or 'Jewish Olympics'.] **1963** J. COMAY *Introducing Israel* viii. 129 The Maccabiah, an 'Olympic Games' for Jewish athletes..takes place in the huge Ramat Gan Sports Stadium. **1969** *National Herald* (New Delhi) 29 July 10/3 The kindling of the Maccabiah flame was followed by the release of hundreds of doves. **1973** *Black Panther* 11 Aug. 12/3 Israel has declared that athletes from Rhodesia who took part in the so-called Maccabiah Games had no official status.

†**maccarib.** *Obs.* [App. cogn. w. *caribou*, a. Micmac *kaleboo*, lit. 'shoveller' (N. & Q. 9th Ser. IX. 465). Cf. F. *macaribo* (Littré).]
= CARIBOU.

1672 JOSSELYN *New Eng. Rarities* 20 The *Maccarib*, *Caribo*, or *Pohano*, a kind of Deer, as big as a Stag, round hooved, smooth hair'd and soft as silk.

maccaroni: see MACARONI.

McCarthyism (məˈkɑːθɪɪz(ə)m). [f. the name of Joseph R. *McCarthy* (1908–57), U.S. senator + -ISM.] The policy of hunting out (suspected) Communists and removing them from Government departments or other positions. Hence **Mc'Carthyist** *a.*, of or pertaining to McCarthyism; **Mc'Carthyite**, one who gave support to such a policy; also *attrib.* and *transf.*

1950 *N.Y. Post* 5 Apr. 44/1 To call McCarthyism a fascist atmosphere would be descriptive enough. **1951** [see *big lie* (BIG *a.* B. 2)]. **1952** *N.Y. Times* 26 Oct. I. 70/7 McCarthyism breeds fear, suspicion and unrest. It turns neighbor against neighbor and makes every American a suspected traitor until and unless he can prove his innocence by McCarthyite standards. **1952** *San Francisco Examiner* 18 Sept. 3/6 The McCarthyites unquestionably have an appeal, Senator Lehman conceded, since they come before the people as super-patriots. **1953** *Ibid.* 23 July 20/8 The editorial denounced a House committee investigation of Communistic clergymen... The 'Daily Worker' called it 'the new McCarthyite drive against the integrity and independence of the church'. **1954** *Encounter* Aug. 10/1 For the unlucky rest of us, McCarthy and McCarthyism—the proper noun and the common one—are familiar to excess. **1954** RORTY & DECTER *McCarthy & Communists* 118 They are not so much *pro*-McCarthyites as anti-anti-McCarthyites (opponents of all who oppose McCarthy). **1955** H. READ *Grass Roots of Art* (rev. ed.) iv. 85 We are at once struck by the fact that whatever the political ideology may be—socialist, fascist, communist, or MacCarthyist—..all express one opinion about art. **1957** *Times Lit. Suppl.* 27 Dec. 782/2 Has this book been written to add fuel to McCarthyist flames that have long been dying away in the United States? **1959** *Ibid.* 6 Nov. p. xix/3 The whole academic community is only now emerging from the shock of the assault on the academies that was one of the most sinister results of 'McCarthyism'. **1960** *20th Cent.* June 578 People who were not active McCarthyites..were none the less sources of strength for him. **1971** *Guardian* 19 Jan. 10/2 Once people start..wondering about their neighbours, a McCarthyite infection could take hold. **1973** *Ibid.* 18 June 4/4 A tradition of paranoia out of which grew McCarthyism and many earlier witch-hunts. **1973** *Times Lit. Suppl.* 6 July 765/1 The tendency is timeless—and by no means sinister or subversive even in McCarthyite terms.

maccase(e)ne, maccaw: see MOCCASIN, MACAW.

macche, obs. form of MATCH.

‖**macchia** (ˈmakia). [Corsican It.] = MAQUIS I.

[**1868** J. A. SYMONDS *Let.* 4 May (1967) I. 805 The sea shore [of Corsica]..is a tangle of sweet & splendid flowers. .. The whole air is fragrant with multitudinous scents wafted from these 'macchi', as the natives call them.] **1924** A. HUXLEY *Let.* 3 Dec. (1969) 238 The mountain is covered with woods of cork trees and a kind of macchia or bush of fragrant shrubs. **1936** *Nature* 2 May 735/2 Such characteristic native vegetation as the beautiful 'fijnbos' (the macchia or maquis of the south-west Cape) may be irretrievably damaged by fire. **1962** *Times* 24 Mar. 11/4 A cottage lost in the *macchia*. **1966** C. MACKENZIE *My Life & Times* V. 133 One looked down..into the *macchia* of Ventrosa.

Macciavelian: see MACHIAVELLIAN.

macco (ˈmækəʊ). ? *Obs.* [? A variant spelling of MACAO.] A gambling game; = MACAO.

1809 BYRON in Moore *Life* (1875) 143 When macco (or whatever they spell it) was introduced. **1825** *Sporting Mag.* XVI. 277 A rubber of whist, or a game of Macco. **1859** THACKERAY *Virgin.* xli, He dines at White's ordinary, and sits down to macco and lansquenet afterwards.

attrib. **1825** T. HOOK *Man of Many Fr.*, *Say. & Doings* Ser. II. II. 18 His uncle was still at the Macco table. **1859** THACKERAY *Virgin.* xliv, I..left it at the Macco-table.

maccoboy (ˈmækəbɔɪ). Also 8 **macabao**, **macauba**, 9 **maccaboy**, **maccubau**, **mac(c)ouba**, **mackabaw**, *Sc.* **macabaa**, **-baw**, **maccaba(w.** [Named from *Macouba*, a district in Martinique.] A kind of snuff, usually scented with attar of roses.

1740 *Wimble's List of Snuffs* in Fairholt *Tobacco* (1859) 269 Macabao. **1799** *Hull Advertiser* 27 July 4/4 You are famous..For having the best Macauba [*rime* draw]. **18..** G. WUSHART in Mactaggart *Gallovid. Encycl.* (1824) 223 Ye maun bring me a teat o' this same Macabaa. **1823** J. BADCOCK *Dom. Amusem.* 99 The snuff of Martinico, celebrated under the term 'Macouba'. **1849** THACKERAY *Pendennis* II. ii. 14 [He] pocketted his snuff-box, not desirous that Madame Brack's dubious fingers should

plunge too frequently into his Mackabaw. **1858** SIMMONDS *Dict. Trade, Maccoboy, Maccubau*, a kind of snuff. **1893** STEVENSON *Catriona* xix. 218 Him I found already at his desk and already bedabbled with maccabaw. **1896** E. MARRIAGE tr. *Balzac's Old Goriot* 21 His snuff-box is always likely to be filled with maccaboy.

McCoy (mə'kɔɪ). In the colloq. phr. ***the real McCoy*** (or ***Mackay, McKie***): the 'genuine article', the real thing.

Its origin remains uncertain: see, for example, *Amer. Speech* (1958) XXXIII. 297 f.

1883 R. L. STEVENSON *Lett. to C. Baxter* (1956) 123 For society, there isnae sae muckle; but there's myself—the auld Johnstone, ye ken—he's the real Mackay, whatever. **1922** *Collier's* 7 Oct. 26/2 'At's the real McCoy you got there, brother!.. Comes right down from Canada! **1930** *Amer. Mercury* Dec. 456/2 *McCoy*, genuine liquor. 'This is McCoy. You can't fake Quebec wrappers.' **1934** M. ALLINGHAM *Death of Ghost* v. 68 There's something very attractive about the real McKie when you meet it. **1935** R. C. WOODTHORPE *Shadow on Downs* xii. 298 It looks like the real Mackay. A lovely colour. **1940** *Penguin New Writing* I. 73 'You look the real McCoy, now,' he said. **1942** C. BARRETT *On Wallaby* v. 103 It's the real Mackay we've got, Chas.; didn't it spring out of the wall? **1949** N. MARSH *Swing, Brother, Swing* vi. 140 If I could pick my work I'd be in an outfit that went for the real mackay. **1952** W. R. BURNETT *Vanity Row* (1953) v. 43 A real gentleman... Not a phony... He was the real McCoy. **1959** L. BERNSTEIN *Joy of Mus.* (1960) 167 The operetta score..was musically elaborate, closer to opera, even containing finales, with everybody *singing* his way through the plot, vocalizing different sentiments at the same time—the real contrapuntal McCoy. **1972** *Guardian* 17 Feb. 10/3 Sadler's Wells is playing host to the regal offspring Royal Ballet, and not, please note, a second eleven but the real Macoy.

mace (meɪs), *sb.*[1] Also 4-5 **mas**, 4-7 **mase**, 5-6 **mais**, (5 **maas, mass, meyce**, 6 **maysse**, 6-7 **masse**). [a. OF. *masse, mace* = Pr. *massa*, It. *mazza*, Sp. *maza*, Pg. *maça*:—L. type **mat(t)ea* (prob. the origin of the rare *mat(t)eola* ? mallet).]

1. a. A heavy staff or club, either entirely of metal or having a metal head, often spiked: formerly a regular weapon of war. (Also called †***mace of arms*** = F. *masse d'armes*.) †In early use also, a club of any kind.

1297 R. GLOUC. (Rolls) 4219 Þis geant..bigan is mace adrawe. *c* **1320** *Sir Beues* 3800 Þei leide on..Wiþ swerdes and wiþ maces. *a* **1330** *Otuel* 1112 He cam wiþ a mase of bras. **1375** BARBOUR *Bruce* XI. 600 The Ynglis men..Kest emang thame swerdis and mas. *c* **1386** CHAUCER *Knt.'s T.* 1753 With myghty maces the bones they tobreste. **1390** GOWER *Conf.* III. 359 And Hercules..Was ther, berende his grete Mace. **1426** LYDG. *De Guil. Pilgr.* 22171 And with this ylke sturdy Maas, I putte hem out a ffull greet paas. *Ibid* 23160 Then cam Treason with hir mas Hevy as a clobbe of leed. **1555** EDEN *Decades* 161 Laton whereof they make such maces and hammers as are vsed in the warres. **1585** T. WASHINGTON tr. *Nicholay's Voy.* III. v. 78 Vppon their saddle bow, their roundel & the Busdeghan (being the mase of armes). **1678** WANLEY *Wond. Lit. World* v. ii. §86. 473/1 He would cast a Horseman's Mace of nine or ten pounds weight farther than any other of his Court. **1728** POPE *Dunc.* I. 85 Pomps without guilt, of bloodless swords and maces. **1825** SCOTT *Talism.* i, A steel axe, or hammer, called a mace-of-arms. **1834** PLANCHÉ *Brit. Costume* 244 The pistol superseded the mace in the hands of officers during this reign [Hen. VIII].

†**b.** Applied to the trident of Neptune. *Obs.*

1582 STANYHURST *Æneis* II. (Arb.) 63 Thee wals God Neptune, with mace threeforcked, vphurleth. **1590** SPENSER *Muiopotmos* 315 The God of Seas..strikes the rockes with his three-forked mace. **1791** COWPER *Iliad* XII. 29 Neptune with his tridental mace himself Led them.

c. *fig.*

1601 SHAKS. *Jul. C.* IV. iii. 268 O Murd'rous slumber! Layest thou thy Leaden Mace vpon my Boy? **1667** MILTON *P.L.* x. 294 The aggregated Soyle Death, with his Mace petrific, cold and dry, As with a Trident smote. **1840** LONGF. *Sp. Stud.* I. v, Hark! how the loud and ponderous mace of Time Knocks at the golden portals of the day! **1878** BROWNING *La Saisiaz* 385 As..Beethoven's Titan mace Smote the immense to storm.

2. a. A sceptre or staff of office, resembling in shape the weapon of war, which is borne before (or was formerly carried by) certain officials. †Also formerly = the sceptre of sovereignty.

For *sergeant at* (or *of*) *mace*, see SERGEANT. The mace which lies on the table in the House of Commons when the Speaker is in the chair is viewed as a symbol of the authority of the House (cf. b).

c **1440** *Promp. Parv.* 319/1 Mace of a seriawnt, *s[c]eptrum, clava*. **1471** RIPLEY *Comp. Alch.* v. xxviii. in Ashm. (1652) 155 Wyth Sylver Macys..Sarjaunts awayting on them every owre. **1526** *Pilgr. Perf.* (W. de W. 1531) 253 They gaue hym a rede in his hande for a septer or a mace. **1559** *Mirr. Mag., Jas. I* xx. 5 My murdring uncle..That longed for my kingdome and my mace. **1580** *Nottingham Rec.* IV. 195 Payd to Towley for the other ij. maces mendyng. **1593** SHAKS. *2 Hen. VI*, IV. vii. 144 With these borne before vs, in steed of Maces, Will we ride through the streets. **1623-4** in Swayne *Churchw. Acc. Sarum* (1896) 177 The Iron wch holds the Mase at the end of Mr. Maiors pewe. **1677** E. SMITH in *12th Rep. Hist. MSS. Comm.* App. v. 37 Some mischievous persons to dishonour my Lord Chancellour.. stole the mace and the two purses. **1708** J. CHAMBERLAYNE *St. Gt. Brit.* I. II. xiii. (1710) 100 The Mace, while the Speaker is in the Chair, is always upon the Table, except when sent upon any extraordinary Occasion into Westminster-Hall, and Court of Requests, to summon the Members to attend. **1758** JOHNSON *Idler* No. 96 ¶1 He.. read the Gothick characters inscribed on his brazen mace. **1856** EMERSON *Eng. Traits, Ability* Wks. (Bohn) II. 45 The chancellor carries England on his mace. **1877** J. D. CHAMBERS *Div. Worship* 186 A Beadle, or other official, with a wand or mace, clearing the way.

b. ***by (warrant of) the mace***: in House of Commons use, said of occasions when the Serjeant-at-Arms is sent with the mace as his warrant for demanding obedience to a command of the House.

1576 *Jrnl. Ho. Comm.* 22 Feb. I. 107 The said Committees found no Precedent for setting at large by the Mace any Person in Arrest; but only by Writ. *Ibid.* 27 Feb. I. 108 It is Resolved, That Edward Smalleye..shall be brought hither To-morrow, by the Serjeant; and so set at Liberty, by Warrant of the Mace, and not by writ.

c. A mace-bearer.

1663 *Flagellum or O. Cromwell* (1672) 26 And here upon a Mace was sent to bring Cromwell into the Court. **1670** MARVELL *Let.* 21 Mar. *Wks.* (Grosart) II. 315 Sir Thomas Clifford carryed Speaker and Mace, and all members there, into the King's cellar, to drink his health. **1753** GRAY *Long Story* iii, My grave Lord-Keeper led the brawls; The seals and maces danc'd before him. **1855** MACAULAY *Hist. Eng.* XI. III. 1 Garter King at arms..was followed by the maces of the two Houses, by the two Speakers [etc.].

3. a. *Billiards.* A stick with a flat square head, formerly used for propelling the balls; now superseded by the cue. (Cf. MAST *sb.*[3]) **b.** A similar instrument used in *Bagatelle*.

1727 BOYER *Fr. Dict., Masse*, (Billard dont on joue) Mass, or Billiard Stick. **1734** R. SEYMOUR *Compl. Gamester* III. (ed. 5) 84 If a Person breaks a Stick, or the Mace, he must pay Six-pence for the Stick and two Shillings for the Mace. **1744** J. LOVE *Cricket* 4 The dull Ball trails before the feeble Mace. **1797** *Encycl. Brit.* (ed. 3) III. 229 [Billiards] is played with sticks, called *maces*, or with cues; the first consist of a long straight stick, with a head at the end, and are the most powerful instruments of the two... In England the mace is the prevailing instrument, which the foreigners hold in contempt. **1814** COL. HAWKER *Diary* (1893) I. 119 We.. enjoyed the novelty of playing with the Emperor's favourite cue, and Maria Louisa's mace. **1856** 'CAPT. CRAWLEY' *Billiards* (1859) 8 The Mace, by the way, is seldom or never used by the present generation of billiard players. **1873** BENNETT & 'CAVENDISH' *Billiards* 4 Maces (called 'masts') only were used, made of lignum vitæ or some other weighty wood, and tipped with ivory. **1883** *Cassell's Sports & Past.* 329 [*Bagatelle*]. The balls are struck with either a cue or a mace; of these two the latter will be found the easier.

4. *Tanning.* (See quots.)

1839 URE *Dict. Arts* 378 The chief operations of the currier are four:—1. Dipping the leather, which consists in moistening it with water, and beating it with the mace, or a mallet upon the hurdle. **1852** MORFIT *Tanning & Currying* (1853) 462 The leather may either be beaten out with the feet, or with an instrument called the mace.

5. *attrib.* and *Comb.*, as ***mace-blow, head***; †**mace-proof** *a.*, *nonce-wd.*, safe from arrest; **mace-reed** = REED-MACE.

1879 G. MEREDITH *Egoist* II. v. 104 The effect..was to produce an image of surpassingness in the features of Clara that gave him the final, or *mace-blow. **1899** *Daily News* 12 Sept. 7/2 Sargon of Accad..of whom a *mace head bearing his name is to be seen in the British Museum. **1633** SHIRLEY *Bird in a Cage* II. D 3 b, You shall..come vp to the face of a Sergiant,..and be *mace proofe. **1901** G. MEREDITH *Reading of Life* 126 A hundred mares, all white! their manes Like *mace-reed of the marshy plains Thick-tufted, wavy.

mace (meɪs), *sb.*[2] Forms: α. 4-5 **macys**, 4-6 **macis, maces**, (4 **macz**, 5 **macez, masis**, 6 **mases**). β. 4- **mace**, (6 **mase**). [ME. *macis*, a. F. *macis* (14th c. in Godef.), of unknown origin; cf. F. (16th c.) *massia*, ? cinnamon flower. The form *macis* being in Eng. apprehended as a plural, the new singular *mace* was formed from it.

It is not likely that the word has any connexion with L. *maccis* (accus. *maccida*) occurring once in Plautus in a bombastic list of unknown and perhaps imaginary spices.]

1. A spice consisting of the dried outer covering of the nutmeg.

a **1377** *Abingdon Acc.* (Camden) 38 In farina xxviijs. In croco xls. In macys ijs. xd. [etc.]. **1398** TREVISA *Barth. De P.R.* XVII. ii. (1495) 595 The Mace is the flowre, and the Notmygge is the fruyte. *Ibid.* cix. 672 The rynde of Nux musticata, the notmygge, hight Macis. *c* **1400** MAUNDEV. (Roxb.) xxi. 94 Þe macez er Þe huskes of Þe nutemug. *c* **1420** *Liber Cocorum* (1862) 13 Fors hit with clowes or macys gode. **1471** *Paston Lett.* III. 25 Sende me word qwat price a *li.* of peppyr, clowys, masis, gingyr [etc.]. **1527** R. THORNE in *Hakluyt's Voy.* (1589) 252 The Islands are fertile of Cloues, Nutmegs, Mace, and Cinnamom. **1544** PHAER *Regim. Lyfe* (1553) E j a, Mithridatum..wel tempered in a littel white wine with a fewe maces. **1594** BLUNDEVIL *Exerc.* v. xi. (1636) 554 But when the Nut waxeth dry, the Mace do sever from the Nut. *Ibid.* xii. 557 From the Ile Banda doth come Nutmegs and Maces. **1732** ARBUTHNOT *Rules of Diet* 259 Spices, as Cinnamon, Mace, Nutmeg. **1747** MRS. GLASSE *Cookery* ii. 32 Add some..Pepper and Salt, and a little beaten Mace. **1811** A. T. THOMSON *Lond. Disp.* (1818) 262 Oil of Mace. **1871** C. KINGSLEY *At Last* v, The nutmegs, the mace still clinging round them, lie scattered on the grass.

2. *attrib.*: †**mace-ale**, ale spiced with mace.

1611 BEAUM. & FL. *Four Pl., Triumph of Love* iv, She had more need of mace-ale..than your aged Discipline. **1676** WISEMAN *Surg.* IV. v. 318 That night she took an anodyne Syrup in a draught of Mace-ale.

mace (meɪs), *sb.*[3] Forms: 6 **mase**, 7 **mas(se, maz, mess**, 8 **masscie**, 8- **mace**. [a. Malay *mās* (also *emās*); said to be repr. Skr. *māsha* a weight of about 17 grains.]

1. In Malay countries: A small gold coin weighing 9 grains. Also, 'a weight used in Sumatra, being according to Crawfurd 1-16th of a Malay tael, or about 40 grains' (Y.).

1598 W. PHILLIP tr. *Linschoten's Voy.* 44 A Tael of Malacca is 16 Mases. **1600** J. DAVIS in Purchas *Pilgrimage* (1614) I. III. i. 117 That [coin] of Gold is named a *Mas*, and is nine pence halfe penie neerest. Those of Lead are called *Caxas*: whereof a thousand sixe hundred make one *Mas*. **1699** DAMPIER *Voy.* II. I. 132 Of these [cash] 1500 make a *Mess*, which..is a small thin piece of Gold... It is in value 15 pence English. **1727** A. HAMILTON *New Acc. E. Ind.* II. xli. 109 At Atcheen they have a small Coin of Leaden Money called Cash, from twelve to sixteen hundred of them goes to one Mace, or Masscie. **1813** MILBURN *Oriental Comm.* (1825) 348 The currency here [Tringano, Malay Peninsula] consists also of the following:..16 mace equal to 1 tale. *Ibid.* 360 [Sumatra] The lesser weights are as follow:—4 Copangs equal to 1 Mace.

2. A Chinese money of account equivalent to one-tenth of a silver liang or tael.

1615 R. COCKS *Diary* (1883) I. 1 We bought 5 greate square postes..cost *2 mas 6 condrins* per peece. **1796** MORSE *Amer. Geog.* II. 531 Although the terms candereen and mace are employed to certify a certain quantity of caxees, there are no coins..which bear that specific value. **1802** CAPT. ELMORE in *Naval Chron.* VIII. 382 At seven mace two candereen per head. **1896** *Blackw. Mag.* Apr. 580/2 The [poppy] tax is stated to be one mace or six-tenths of a mace the plot.

mace (meɪs), *sb.*[4] *slang.* Swindling, robbery by fraud. ***on mace***: on credit, 'on tick'.

1781 G. PARKER *View Soc.* II. 34 The mace is a man who goes to any capital tradesman..in an elegant vis-à-vis [etc.]. **1879** J. W. HORSLEY in *Macm. Mag.* XL. 502 The following people used to go in there—toy-getters (watch-stealers).. men at the mace (sham loan offices). **1893** P. H. EMERSON *Signor Lippo* xxii. 100 Letting 'em have the super and slang on mace, for he gets to know their account and he puts the pot on 'em settling day.

b. *Comb.*: **mace-cove, -gloak, -man** = MACER[2].

1812 J. H. VAUX *Flash Dict., Mace-gloak*, a man who lives upon the mace. **1823** 'J. BEE' *Dict. Turf* s.v. *Mace*, The mace-cove is he who will cheat, take in, or swindle, as often as may be. **1859** SALA *Tw. round Clock* (1861) 160 The nightside of London is fruitful in 'macemen', 'mouchers', and 'go-alongs'. **1865** M. COLLINS *Who is the Heir?* II. 245 What is a maceman?.. A person who buys anything he can get without paying for it, and sells it again at once for anything he can get. **1884** *Daily News* 5 Jan. 5/2 The victim appears to have entered an omnibus and to have been at once pounced upon by two 'macemen', otherwise 'swell mobsmen'.

Mace (meɪs), *sb.*[5] In full, ***Chemical Mace***. The proprietary name of a chemical preparation used as a disabling weapon by being sprayed at a person's face; also *attrib.* Hence (usu. with small initial) as *v. trans.*, to attack with this liquid.

1966 *Official Gaz.* (U.S. Patent Office) 22 Nov. TM 174, SN 233,338. General Ordnance Equipment Corp., Pittsburgh. Pa. Filed Nov. 26, 1965. Chemical Mace. The word 'Chemical' is disclaimed apart from its use with the mark. For Non-Explosive Defensive Weapons in the Nature of Tear Gas Packaged in Aerosol Containers. **1966** *Law & Order* June 50/3 The development..of the Chemical Mace, a liquid, long range, selective, tear gas projector is an event of considerable importance to law enforcement. **1967** *N.Y. Times* 3 Aug. 17/2 The gas is called Mace and it comes in a small black aerosol container like a hair spray can. **1968** *Listener* 9 May 595/3 A new anti-riot chemical called Mace. Sprayed like tear gas it turns the victim temporarily blind. **1968** *Sun* (Baltimore) 18 Sept. A.14/6 Scores of innocent adult bystanders..were clubbed, maced, arrested. **1969** E. AMBLER *Intercom Conspiracy* (1970) vii. 143 The stuff was..some kind of chemical Mace or nerve gas. **1970** W. WAGER *Sledgehammer* (1971) xvi. 103 Williston raised the can of Mace, aimed for his enemy's eyes and nose. **1971** *Harper's Mag.* Sept. 63 He responded to foul and abusive language by Macing an old woman's hot dog. **1972** J. ROSSITER *Rope for General Dietz* i. 16 The two pen-shaped aerosols of Mace chemical gas I invariably carried. **1973** *Black Panther* 25 Aug. 2/2 They feel that because they are in power they can call ten or 20 pigs for just one man, mace him, beat him up and call him profane names.

mace, *v.*[1] *rare*$^{-1}$. [f. MACE *sb.*[1]] *trans.* To strike as with a mace.

1840 DICKENS *Barn. Rudge* iv, The 'prentices no longer carried clubs wherewith to mace the citizens.

†**mace**, *v.*[2] *Obs. rare*$^{-1}$. [f. MACE *sb.*[2]] *trans.* To season with mace. In quot. *fig.*

a **1640** DAY *Peregr. Schol.* (1881) 70 If anie of you come vnder there clowches theile pepper you and mace you with a vengeance.

mace, *v.*[3] *slang.* [f. MACE *sb.*[4]] *trans.* and *intr.* To swindle. Hence '**macing** *vbl. sb.*

1790 POTTER *New Dict. Cant.* (1795) *Mace*, to cheat. **1812** *Sporting Mag.* XXXIX. 138 A..party of inferior pugilists had been macing in the southern towns. **1819** J. H. VAUX *Mem.* I. 53, I sometimes raised the wind by..obtaining goods on credit, called in the cant language maceing. **1885** *Daily Tel.* 18 Aug. 3/2 Fancy him being so soft as to give that jay a quid back out of the ten he'd maced him of!

'**mace-bearer.** One who carries a mace; *spec.* an official whose duty it is to carry a mace, as a symbol of authority, before some high functionary.

1552 HULOET, Mace bearer, *cliduchus*. **1683** *Addr. fr. Oxford* in *Lond. Gaz.* No. 1863/5 Our respective Mayor, Bayliffs,.. Town-Clerk, Mace bearer or any other Officers. **1687** WOOD *Life* 3 Sept., Afterwards the macebearer put the mace into the mayor's hands. **1763** H. WALPOLE *Catal. Engravers* (1765) 20 John bishop of Lincoln, with purse-bearer, mace-bearer [etc.]. **1823** DE QUINCEY *Incognito* Wks. 1862 X. 2 The chief-burgomaster..turned the mace-bearer out of the room. **1835** *1st Munic. Corp. Comm. Rep.* App. III. 1686 Other officers of the Corporation [of Preston]

are, Mace-Bearer, Beadle [etc.]. **1841** ELPHINSTONE *Hist. Ind.* II. 349 A mace-bearer called out to him, with mock solemnity, to receive the salutations of his servants. **1870** BRYANT *Iliad* I. VII. 210 The mace-bearer Areithous.

Macedo- (ˈmæsɪdɒ), combining form of MACEDONIAN *a.*[1] in the names of dialects spoken in Macedonia, an area in the central Balkans (see MACEDONIAN *a.*[1] and *sb.*[1]), as ***Macedo-Bulgarian, -Illyrian, -Rumanian, -Rumanic.***

1861 MAX MÜLLER *Lect. Sci. of Lang.* v. 182 This Romance language is spoken in Wallachia and Moldavia, and in parts of Hungary, Transylvania, and Bessarabia... It is divided by the Danube into two branches: the Northern or Daco-romanic, and the Southern or Macedo-romanic. **1880** A. H. SAYCE *Introd. Sci. of Lang.* II. vii. 120 The Danube divides it [*sc.* Rumanian] into two branches, the northern or Daco-Rumanic, and the southern or Macedo-Rumanic, the latter of which abounds with Albanian and Greek words. **1908** T. G. TUCKER *Introd. Nat. Hist. Lang.* 240 A southern division [of Rumanian]..is formed by the *Macedo-Roumanian* (or *Vlach*) of parts of Roumelia, Macedonia, and Thessaly. **1937** J. ORR tr. *Iordan's Introd. Romance Ling.* ii. 95 The current forms in Macedo-Rumanian. *Ibid.* iii. 267 The five Macedo-Rumanian, the two Megleno-Rumanian, and the two Istro-Rumanian localities. **1948** L. SPITZER *Linguistics & Lit. Hist.* 3 Meyer-Lübke would quote.. Macedo-rumanian. **1949** ENTWISTLE & MORISON *Russ. & Slavonic Lang.* vii. 370 It is the pronunciation current in Macedo-Bulgarian dialects. *Ibid.* 374 The forms in *-m* are widely distributed in Bulgarian dialects, and are universal in Macedo-Bulgarian. **1959** G. NANDRIS *Handbk. Old Church Slavonic* I. 20 It [*sc.* epenthetic *l*] is dropped as a rule in Macedo-Bulgarian. **1960** R. AUTY *Ibid.* II. 10 The researches of Vatroslav Oblak showed the affinities of O[ld] C[hurch] S[lavonic] with present-day Macedo-Bulgarian dialects. **1965** G. Y. SHEVELOV *Prehist. Slavic* 611 There are also two small peripheral areas with a tendency to self-isolation from the other Slavs.. : West Baltic and Macedo-B[ul]g[arian]. **1966** E. G. POLOMÉ in Birnbaum & Puhvel *Anc. Indo-European Dial.* 70 Pisani preferred to consider the former as Macedonian,..without, however, connecting *siiri-* with 'Macedo-Illyrian' Σίρρας. **1966** H. BIRNBAUM *Ibid.* 161 We can..assume here the existence of certain C[ommon] Sl[avic] dialect groups... These dialect groups will be shown to correspond to East Slavic.., Lekhitic.., Sorbian.., Czechoslovak.., Sloveno-Serbocroatian.., and Macedo-Bulgarian. **1967** D. S. PARLETT *Short Dict. Lang.* 103 Macedo-Rumanian (or Arumanian), in Albania, Thessaly, Macedonia. **1972** W. B. LOCKWOOD *Panorama Indo-European Lang.* 45 Macedo-Rumanian or Aromunian ..is the language of the Aromuni, the Rumanians of the south.

macédoine (masedwan). [Fr., f. *Macédoine* Macedonia, with reference to the diversity of peoples in the Macedonian empire of Alexander the Great] **1.** Mixed fruit or vegetables cut up into small pieces. Also *attrib.*

1846 C. E. FRANCATELLI *Mod. Cook* 32 White macedoine of vegetables. *Ibid.*, Garnish of brown macedoine. Prepare the vegetables for the *Macedoine* according to the directions given in the preceding recipe. **1855** E. ACTON *Mod. Cookery* (rev. ed.) xxiii. 453 Jelly of two colours, with *macedoine* of fruit. **1894** L. HERITAGE *Cassell's New Universal Cookery Bk.* 67 Soup with Macédoines. *Ibid.* 1127 Macédoine of Fruits. **1895** 'M. RONALD' *Century Cook Bk.* 378 Macédoine salad. **1960** *Good Housek. Cookery Bk.* (rev. ed.) 313/2 Macédoine of fruit.

2. *fig.* A medley or mixture of unrelated things.

1820 H. LUTTRELL *Advice to Julia* 18 Such is the tattle of our beaus. These simple elements compose..The *Macedoine* of London-talk. **1857** G. C. MUNDY *Our Antipodes* (ed. 4) 10 Now for a *macédoine* of advertisements, word for word as entered. **1925** *Glasgow Herald* 3 Nov. 10 Europe contains as many different types of features,..as India. But there are few parts of Europe which present such a mosaic, or macédoine, of contrasts side by side. **1974** *Times* 30 Apr. 8/5 Ann Buck designs in what I call the *macedoine* style, with all sorts of bits and pieces of fabric welded into a garment.

Macedon (ˈmæsɪdən). [ad. L. *Macedon-em* (*Macedo*), Gr. Μακεδόν-α (-ών).]

†**1. a.** One of the people (to which Alexander the Great belonged) that inhabited ancient Macedonia. *Obs.*

[**1382** WYCLIF *2 Cor.* ix. 4 When Macedonyes schulen come with me.] *a* **1400-50** *Alexander* 934, 1179, 1253, etc., Messadones, Messedones, -edoyns, Mas(s)idons. **1594** KYD *Cornelia* I. 63 Macedons or Medes. **1632** MASSINGER *City Madam* IV. ii, The valiant Macedon..Lamented that there were no more [worlds] to conquer. **1700** DRYDEN *Fables, To Duchess of Ormond* 133 As once the Macedon, by Jove's decree, Was taught to dream an herb for Ptolemy.

†**b.** *appos.* or quasi-*adj.* = Macedonian. *Obs.*

1710 *The Tipling Philosophers* 17 Diogenes, Surly and Proud, Who Snarl'd at the Macedon Youth.

2. Anglicized name of ancient Macedonia. *arch.*

1584 C. ROBINSON *Handf. Ples. Delites* (Arb.) 46 The famous Prince of Macedon. **1625** BACON *Ess., Prophecies*, Phillip of Macedon. **1871** S. J. STONE *Hymn*, Through midnight gloom from Macedon. **1940** A. H. M. JONES *Greek City* i. 8 As king of Macedon he [*sc.* Alexander] could draw as he wished on the resources of Macedonia. **1969** A. TOYNBEE *Some Probl. Greek Hist.* IV. ii. 426 The invaders found the entire manpower of Macedon arrayed against them. **1969** 'M. RENAULT' *Fire from Heaven* (1970) vi. 275 In Athens, the marble tablet which witnessed the peace with Macedon had been torn down, in formal declaration of war. **1972** F. W. WALBANK *Polybius* i. 26 Polybius describes with amazement Demetrius of Phalerum's prophecy of the future downfall of Macedon.

Macedonian (mæsɪˈdəʊnɪən), *a.*[1] and *sb.*[1] [f. L. *Macedoni-us* (= Gr. Μακεδόνιος, f. Μακεδών: see prec.) + -AN.] **A.** *adj.* Pertaining to Macedonia, an ancient country north of Greece; now, a geographical area in the central Balkans lying astride the frontiers of southern Yugoslavia, northern Greece, and southwestern Bulgaria; also, the name of a province in Yugoslavia.

Macedonian parsley: see PARSLEY.

1607 TOPSELL *Four-f. Beasts* 196 At one time is giuen them nine Macedonian Bushels, but..of drinke eyther wine or water thirty Macedonian pintes at a time. **1707** *Curios. in Husb. & Gard.* 257 To make Celery, and Macedonian Parsly grow very fast. **1844** THIRLWALL *Greece* lxvi. VIII. 419 It had received a Macedonian admiral in its port. **1946** [see B. c below]. **1958** *Listener* 4 Dec. 912/2 The first Macedonian dictionary is being prepared, there are newspapers in the Macedonian language, and Skopje has acquired a brand-new Macedonian university. **1974** *Encycl. Brit. Micropædia* VI. 442/1 Yugoslav Macedonia contains the great majority of the Macedonian people.

B. *sb.* **a.** A native of Macedonia.

1582 N. T. (Rhem.) *2 Cor.* ix. 2, I know your prompt minde: for the which I glorie of you to the Macedonians. **1834** LYTTON *Pompeii* II. i, I will teach thee, young braggart, to play the Macedonian with me. **1840** *Penny Cycl.* XVIII. 75/2 He was stabbed by a young Macedonian of his own body-guard. **1844** [see EPIROT]. **1897** W. E. GLADSTONE *Let.* 19 Jan. in *Macedonian Question* (1902) 3 Why not Macedonia for the Macedonians as well as Bulgaria for the Bulgarians and Servia for the Servians? **1902** N. BUXTON *Ibid.* 44 There is, moreover, a certain enmity in Bulgaria towards the Macedonians. **1935** S. CHRISTOWE *Heroes & Assassins* vii. 116 The Macedonians took as their motto 'Liberty or Death'. **1950** E. BARKER *Macedonia* ii. 23 After King Alexander instituted his dictatorship in January 1929 ..the Macedonians began to settle down and to accept Yugoslav rule passively. **1966** D. DAKIN *Greek Struggle in Macedonia* xii. 307 There seems also to have been some conflict between the National Greeks and the Greek Macedonians over the question of leadership. **1971** PALMER & KING *Yugoslav Communism & Macedonian Question* iv. 64 Evidently there was no attempt by the Macedonians to proclaim an independent or autonomous state, as the Croatians did. **1974** *Encycl. Brit. Micropædia* VI. 442/1 In the Greek province are Slavic speakers, Macedonians, and Pomaks, or Bulgarian-speaking Muslims.

b. The language of ancient Macedonia, recorded in fragmentary remains, and usually regarded as a variety of Greek within the Indo-European family.

1556 *Robinson's tr. More's Utopia* Printer to Reader (Arb.) 168 Seyng it is a tongue to vs muche straunger then the Indian,..the Macedonian,..etc. **1933** C. D. BUCK *Compar. Gram. Greek & Latin* 14 Languages for which Illyrian origin is claimed or disputed are Venetic and Messapian in ancient Italy, Macedonian, and Albanian. Macedonian, that is, the native speech of the Macedonians as distinguished from the Attic κοινή which they came to adopt as their official language, is known from proper names and rather numerous glosses. **1939** L. H. GRAY *Foundations of Lang.* 330 The relation of Macedonian to Greek is uncertain. **1966** E. G. POLOMÉ in Birnbaum & Puhvel *Anc. Indo-European Dial.* 70, σιβύνη and σιγύνη are both occasionally ascribed to Macedonian by scholiasts and lexicographers. **1972** W. B. LOCKWOOD *Panorama Indo-European Lang.* 6 Since Macedonian was in contact with Illyrian and Thracian, borrowings from these languages could account for the exotic strain... It is to be assumed that the Macedonian dialect (or language) succumbed to Attic Greek..during the Hellenistic Age.

c. The modern language of the province of Macedonia in Yugoslavia and adjacent areas of Bulgaria and Greece. Also *attrib.* So ***Macedonian-speaking.***

1946 R. CAPELL *Simiomata* II. 85 A Macedonian nationalist, one Gotchi, has been leading a band of Macedonian-speaking Andartes. **1955** R. JAKOBSON *Slavic Lang.* (ed. 2) 15 Still preserved is the nasal component in.. some border dialects of Slovenian and Macedonian. **1964** M. PARTRIDGE *Serbo-Croatian* 13 Together with Bulgarian, Macedonian and Slovene, Serbo-Croatian belongs linguistically to the southern branch of the Slavonic group. **1972** W. B. LOCKWOOD *Panorama Indo-European Lang.* 162 The greatest concentration of Macedonian speakers was found in that part of the province which passed to Serbia. In 1945, this area became the Macedonian Constituent Republic of Yugoslavia with Macedonian as its official language. The number of speakers exceeds one million. **1974** *Encycl. Brit. Micropædia* VI. 442/2 Macedonian became the official language of the People's Republic of Macedonia, an autonomous area in Yugoslavia, when it was established in the 1940s.

Macedonian (mæsɪˈdəʊnɪən), *a.*[2] and *sb.*[2] [ad. Eccl. L. *Macedoniān-us*, f. *Macedonius*: see -AN.] A follower of Macedonius, a heretical Bishop of Constantinople in the 4th century.

1559 [see EUNOMIAN *sb.* (*a.*)]. **1577** VAUTROUILLIER *Luther on Ep. Gal.* 18 Arians, Eunomians, Macedonians, and such other heretikes. **1701** tr. *Le Clerc's Prim. Fathers* 252 He [Gregory] disputes about the Consubstantiality of the Holy Spirit against the Macedonians. **1727-52** CHAMBERS *Cycl.* s.v. *Semi-Arians*, A new branch of Macedonian Semi-arians, or Pneumatomachi. **1882-3** *Schaff's Encycl. Relig. Knowl.* II. 1578 They are Macedonians, esteeming the Holy Spirit as no person, but only an influence or emanation.

Hence **Maceˈdonianism.**

1642 HALES *Schism* 9 Manichanisme, Valentinianisme, Macedonianisme, Mahometisme, are truly and properly Heresies. **1646** BP. MAXWELL *Burd. Issach.* 21 The grossest Heresies, Arianisme, Arminianisme, Macedonianisme [etc.].

Macedonic (mæsɪˈdɒnɪk), *a.* [a. L. *Macedonic-us*, Gr. Μακεδονικ-ός Macedonian.] = MACEDONIAN *a.*[1]

1859 E. MASSON tr. *Winer's Gram. New Testament Diction* I. 33 The previously distinct dialects..were blended into a popular spoken language, with a predominance of the Macedonic variety.

[**macegriefs**, 'such as willingly buy stolen flesh' (Cowell 1607, whence in later Law Dicts.), is a spurious word, due to misunderstanding of the AF. text of Britton I. xxx. §3, which speaks of 'butchers (*macegriers*) who knowingly sell stolen flesh'.]

macelency, obs. form of MACILENCY.

†**maceˈllarious**, *a.* *Obs.*⁻⁰ [f. L. *macellāri-us* (f. *macellum* meat market) + -OUS.]

1656 BLOUNT *Glossogr.*, *Macellarious*, pertaining to the Butchers Row or Shambles.

macer[1] (ˈmeɪsə(r)). Also *Sc.* 5-6 **maser(e, masar,** 6 **messer, measer, masser,** 6-7 **maissar, -er.** [a. OF. *maissier, massier*, f. *masse* MACE *sb.*[1]: see -ER[2].] A mace-bearer; *spec.* in Scotland, an official who keeps order in courts of law.

13.. *St. Erkenwolde* 143 in Horstm. *Altengl. Leg.* (1881) 269 Þe maire with mony maȝti mene & macers before hyme. **1377** LANGL. *P. Pl.* B. III. 76 Meires and maceres that menes ben bitwene The kynge and the comune to kepe the lawes. *c* **1440** *Promp. Parv.* 319/1 Macer, or he þat berythe the mace, *scept(r)iger.* *c* **1470** HENRY *Wallace* VII. 304 Thar folowed him fyfteyn Wicht, wallyt men..With a maser [*ed.* 1570 maissar], to tach him to the law. **1535** STEWART *Cron. Scot.* III. 275 Sextie that tyme quhilk war summond aw Be ane masar for to cum to the law. **1546** *Reg. Privy Council Scot.* I. 26 Heraldis, pursevantis, masseries, and utheris officiaris of armes. **1550** *Ibid.* 105 Ane messer or uthir officiar of armes. **1583** *Leg. Bp. St. Androis* 1065 A measʳ vpon the gait him mett. **1679** *Royal Proclam.* in *Lond. Gaz.* No 1406/1 Charles by the Grace of God [etc.]..To Our Lyon King at Arms, and his Brethren Heraulds, Macers, or Messengers at Arms. **1709** STRYPE *Ann. Ref.* I. xxi. 237 Thomas Lever, S.T.B. formerly of S. John's College and sometime macer (as was the Bishop himself). **1710** *Chamberlayne's St. Gt. Brit.* II. iii. (ed. 23) 662 Macers of Exchequer. Sal. 50*l.* per Ann. each. **1752** J. LOUTHIAN *Form of Process* (ed. 2) 7 The Justice-Court has three Macers... The Macer's chief Business is, to execute all Indictments, Criminal Letters, &c. **1818** SCOTT *Hrt. Midl.* v, *Non omnia*—as Mr. Crossmyloof said, when he was called by two macers at once, *non omnia possumus—pessimus—possimis.* **1893** STEVENSON *Catriona* 189 And the very macer cried 'Cruachan'.

b. *attrib.*: †**macer wand**, a mace.

1535 STEWART *Cron. Scot.* II. 677 [He] Arreistit thame, syne with ane maissar wand, Or tha passit out of Northumberland, Richt mony thousand of thame thair wes slane.

Hence **ˈmacership.**

1883 *Edinb. Daily Rev.* 6 June 2/5 Mr. G. G. has been appointed..to the vacant macership in the Court of Session.

macer[2] (ˈmeɪsə(r)). *slang.* [f. MACE *v.*[3] + -ER[1].] A swindler.

1819 *Sporting Mag.* V. 123 The cup-and-ball Macers. **1870** STEINMETZ *Gaming Table* II. vii. 220 A well known macer, who was celebrated for slipping an 'old gentleman' (a long card) into the pack.

†**ˈmacerable**, *a.* *Obs. rare.* [as if ad. L. **mācerābilis*, f. *mācerāre* to MACERATE.] That may be macerated.

a **1631** DONNE *Six Serm.* i. (1634) 30 Miserable, unexpressible, unimaginable macerable condition, where the sufferer would be glad to be but a devil. **1742** EAMES in *Phil. Trans.* XLII. 33 The Auditory Bones are of a tartareous kind of friable and easily macerable Substance.

maceral (ˈmæsərəl). *Geol.* [f. L. *mācer-āre* MACERATE *v.* + -AL, after MINERAL *sb.*] Any of the microscopic structural constituents of coal.

1935 M. C. STOPES in *Fuel in Sci. & Pract.* XIV. 11/1 To ..construct an acceptable petrological classification, therefore, a prime need became obvious, viz., a word to cover all petrological units seen in microscopic sections of coals, as distinct from the visible units seen in hand specimens... I now propose the new word 'Maceral' (from the Latin, macerare, to macerate)... The word 'macerals' will, I hope, be accepted as a pleasantly sounding parallel to the word 'minerals', conveying the suggestions of the fundamental difference between them. *Ibid.*, The concept behind the word 'macerals' is that the complex of biological units represented by a forest tree which crashed into a watery swamp and there partly decomposed and was macerated in the process of coal formation, did not in that process become uniform throughout but still retains delimited regions optically differing under the microscope, which may or may not have different chemical formulae and properties. These *organic* units, composing the coal mass I propose to call *macerals*, and they are the descriptive equivalent of the *inorganic* units composing most rock masses and universally called *minerals.* **1970** *Nature* 11 July 194/2 The petrographic components (macerals) of coals possess different stability ranges.

†**ˈmacerate**, *ppl. a.* *Obs.* [ad. L. *mācerāt-us*, f. *mācerāre* to MACERATE.] Wasted, weakened: = the later MACERATED.

1540-1 ELYOT *Image Gov.* 30 Macerate with labours, and made feeble with age. **1632** *Womens Rights* 332 Shee chuse ..not a man macerate and dryed vp with study.

macerate (ˈmæsəreɪt), *v.* Also 6-7 **masserate,** 7 **mascerate.** [f. L. *mācerāt-*, ppl. stem of

mācerāre, f. root *māc-*, perh. cogn. w. Gr. *μάσσειν* (:—**maky-*, *mn̥ky-*) to knead. For the suffix cf. *tolerāre*, *recuperāre*. Cf. F. *macérer*.]

1. *trans.* To soften by steeping in a liquid, with or without heat; to wear away or separate the soft parts of, by steeping. Also with *away*. Applied also to the treatment of food in the process of digestion.

1563 T. GALE *Antidot.* II. 10 Macerate them [*sc.* lard and rose leaves] and let them stand together seuen dayes. **1620** VENNER *Via Recta* vii. 133 They [*sc.* Pine-Apple or Nut] must first be macerated the space of an houre in warme water, and then eaten. **1660** R. COKE *Power & Subj.* 129 Iron macerated with vinegar, so as it should be inflexible. **1691** RAY *Creation* (1714) 27 It is by the Heat thereof concocted macerated and reduced into a Chyle or Cremor. **1759** BROWN *Compleat Farmer* 79 The gizzard that macerates their food. **1773** COOK *Voy.* (1790) IV. 1418 The bark is rolled up, and macerated for some time in water. **1822** IMISON *Sci. & Art* II. 178 Soak, or macerate the rags sufficiently. **1835–6** TODD *Cycl. Anat.* I. 479/1 More complete mastication is performed after the food has been long macerated in the paunch. **1875** DARWIN *Insectiv. Pl.* vi. 88 The leaves were macerated for some hours. **1899** *Allbutt's Syst. Med.* VIII. 558 In the axillary, anal and scrotal region, where the scales are often macerated away. *fig.* **1829** LANDOR *Imag. Conv.* Wks. 1846 II. 211 A good writer will not..macerate things into such particles that nothing shall be remaining of their natural contexture.

b. *intr.* for *pass.* To undergo maceration.

1610 B. JONSON *Alch.* II. v, Let 'hem macerate, together. **1641** FRENCH *Distill.* ii. (1651) 48 Beat the spices small and bruise the Hearbs, letting them macerate twelve houres. **1755** B. MARTIN *Mag. Arts & Sci.* III. viii. 329 The ignorant Farmer cuts down his Corn and his Hay..and leaves them to macerate..in the soaking Showers. **1816** ACCUM *Chem. Tests* (1818) 81 Suffering the whole to macerate for a few hours. **1889** J. M. DUNCAN *Lect. Dis. Wom.* v. (ed. 4) 22 If the liquor amnii is not discharged it is absorbed, and the contents of the uterus either macerate or become mummified.

2. *trans.* To cause (the body, flesh, etc.) to waste or wear away, esp. by fasting.

1547 BOORDE *Brev. Health* i. 7 Fastynge to much it dryeth and macerateth the body. **1613** PURCHAS *Pilgrimage* v. xiv. 442 To..macerate his body for his owne sinnes. **1647** CLARENDON *Contempl. Ps.* Tracts (1727) 415 Macerating our bodies with imprisonments and torments. **1712** STEELE *Spect.* No. 282 ¶5 The Happiness of him who is macerated by Abstinence. **1830** D'ISRAELI *Chas. I*, III. vii. 135 Her frame was macerated by her secret sorrows. **1860** T. MARTIN *Horace* 24 The fierce unrest, the deathless flame, That slowly macerates my frame. **1877** C. GEIKIE *Christ* xxxiii. (1879) 385 Men who lodged in tombs and macerated themselves with fasting.

†**b.** *fig.* To oppress, 'crush'. *Obs.*

1637 BASTWICK *Litany* I. 4/1 They greatly dishonour his Cesarean Maiestie, & miserably afflict and macerate [*printed* macecrate] his poore subiects. **1640** H. PARKER *Case Ship Money* 46 Civill wars have..infected and macerated that goodly Country.

†**c.** *intr.* for *pass.* To waste, pine away. *Obs.*

1599 MARSTON *Sco. Villanie* I. ii. 176 Once to be pursie fat Had wont be cause that life did macerate.

†**3.** In immaterial sense: To fret, vex, worry. *Obs.*

1588 SPENSER *Virg. Gnat* 94 No such sad cares, as wont to macerate And rend the greedie mindes of covetous men. **1591** *Troub. Raigne K. Iohn* (1611) 14 A viper, who with poysoned words Doth masserate the bowels of my soule. *a* **1695** Z. CRADOCK *Serm. on Charity* (1740) 8 Why do some Christians..macerate and torment themselves? **1761** STERNE *Tr. Shandy* III. iv, A city so macerated with expectation.

macerate (ˈmæsəreɪt), *sb.* [f. the vb., after *precipitate*, *filtrate*, etc.] A product obtained by maceration.

1961 in WEBSTER. **1974** *Nature* 27 Sept. 294/2 In scanning electron microscopical (SEM) investigations of Precambrian sedimentary rocks, the risk of contamination during the preparation of rock macerates is extremely high. **1975** *Ibid.* 20 Mar. 184/2 Nitrate production was depressed when *Hyparrhenia* root macerate was added to soils.

macerated (ˈmæsəreɪtɪd), *ppl. a.* [f. MACERATE *v.* + -ED[1].] In senses of the vb.

1587 FLEMING *Contn. Holinshed* III. 1399/1 Whether it were possible to find a bodie more withered, afflicted, macerated,..or pale. **1659** *Gentl. Calling* (1696) 98 It need not doubt to maintain the Field against poor macerated Chastity. **1706** HEARNE *Collect.* 4 Mar. (O.H.S.) I. 197 What might recruit his macerated Body. **1899** *Allbutt's Syst. Med.* VIII. 611 This application is repeated, and the macerated skin cleansed, every forty-eight hours.

absol. **1694** MOTTEUX *Rabelais* (1737) V. 232 Th' Opime you'd linquish for the Macerated.

macerating (ˈmæsəreɪtɪŋ), *vbl. sb.* [f. MACERATE *v.* + -ING[1].] The action of MACERATE *v.*

1600 SURFLET *Country Farme* III. lxiii. 575 Infusion is nothing else but a macerating or steeping of the thing intended to be distilled in some licour. **1630** BRATHWAIT *Eng. Gentlem.* (1641) 183 It is macerating of the flesh that fattens the spirit. **1775** in ASH, Suppl.

macerating (ˈmæsəreɪtɪŋ), *ppl. a.* [f. MACERATE *v.* + -ING[2].] That macerates (see the vb.).

1689 HARVEY *Curing Dis. by Expect.* xiv. 113 The Jesuit Confessor redoubles his macerating penance. **1836** J. M. GULLY *Magendie's Formul.* (ed. 2) 132 The disgusting odour arising from the macerating intestines. **1899** *Allbutt's Syst. Med.* VIII. 605 The macerating action of a plaster.

maceration (mæsəˈreɪʃən). [ad. L. *mācerātiōn-em*, n. of action f. *mācerāre* to MACERATE.]

1. The action or process of softening by steeping in a liquid; also, the state of being subjected to this process; an instance of this.

1612 WOODALL *Surg. Mate* Wks. (1653) 272 Maceration is preparation of things not unlike to Humectation. *a* **1652** J. SMITH *Sel. Disc.* iv. 75 The very grass..may,..after many refinings, macerations, and maturations..spring up into so many rational souls. **1691** RAY *Creation* I. (1692) 121 For the maceration and dissolution of the Meat into a Chyle. **1794** SULLIVAN *View Nat.* II. 157 Decomposed by long maceration in water. **1861** BUMSTEAD *Ven. Dis.* (1879) 591 The constant maceration of the mucous membrane of the mouth. **1880** HUXLEY *Crayfish* iii. 100 When the exoskeleton is cleaned by maceration.

attrib. **1898** *Rev. Brit. Pharm.* 34 The maceration tinctures are not to be made up to a prescribed volume with the menstruum.

b. In smelting iron ore (see quot.).

1868 *Rep. to Govt. U.S. Munitions War* 120 It [the ore] is then allowed to remain exposed to the air for a time long enough to permit the small traces of sulphur to be dissipated, [etc.]... This process is termed maceration.

c. quasi-*concr.* A product of maceration.

1836 J. M. GULLY *Magendie's Formul.* (ed. 2) 153 He collects the different spirituous macerations in an alembic.

2. The process of wasting or wearing away (the body, flesh, etc.); mortification; an instance of this; also the condition of being macerated.

1491 CAXTON *Vitas Patr.* (W. de W. 1495) I. xl. 57 b/2 She gaaf..her body..to were the hayre, and other maceracyons of the flesshe. **1605** BACON *Adv. Learn.* II. ix. §3. 37 Fastings, abstinences, and other macerations and humiliations of the bodie. **1628** BP. HALL *Serm.* 30 Mar., Wks. 1808 V. 361, I speak of a true and serious maceration of our bodies by an absolute and total refraining from sustenance. **1827** HARE *Guesses* Ser. I. (1873) 178 The voluptuousness and the macerations of Oriental religions. **1856** EMERSON *Eng. Traits, Race* Wks. (Bohn) II. 31 In describing the poverty and maceration of Father Lacey. **1881** STEVENSON *Virg. Puerisque* 167 It should be a place for nobody but hermits dwelling in prayer and maceration.

†**3.** In immaterial sense: Fretting, vexation, worry; an instance of this. *Obs.*

1616 *Rich Cabinet* 142 b, Sorrow is the cause of..many melancholike maladies and macerations. **1645** BP. HALL *Remedy Discontents* 163 What maceration is there here with feares, and jealousies. **1669** CLARENDON *Ess.* Tracts (1727) 174 This maceration,..is a sawcy contradiction of God's wisdom in the creation.

macerator (ˈmæsəreɪtə(r)). Also **macerater**. [agent-n. f. MACERATE *v.*: see -OR.] **a.** One who macerates or mortifies (the body). *rare.*

1891 AUGUSTA T. DRANE *Hist. St. Dominic* 167 A man of rare abstinence, the frequent macerator of his own body.

b. A vessel used for the process of maceration (*Cent. Dict.* 1891).

c. A pulping machine. *U.S.*

1912 *Publishers' Circular* 12 Oct. 503 Then the macerator, the greatest consumer of contemporary literature, takes them [*sc.* books] to its bosom.

†**ˈmacery.** *Obs.* In 6 **masarie.** [f. MACER + -Y.] The functions of a macer.

1545 *Reg. Privy Council Scot.* I. 7 Dischargis all the saidis masseris of all using of thair offices of masarie in all tymes cuming.

macˈfarlanite. *Min.* [Named by A. H. Sibley, 1880, after T. *Macfarlane*, who described it: see -ITE.] 'A mixture of huntilite, animikite and other minerals, which constitutes the ore of the mines at Silver Islet, Ontario' (A. H. Chester).

Mach (mɑːk, mæk, ‖maːx). The name of Ernst *Mach* (1838–1916), Austrian physicist and philosopher: **a.** Used, usu. *attrib.*, to designate certain concepts associated with his work on aerodynamics, as **Mach('s) angle**, the angle between a generator of the Mach cone and its axis; **Mach cone**, a cone that extends backwards from a body moving at supersonic speed and coincides with the shock wave it produces, separating a region affected by the motion (inside the cone) from a region unaffected by it (outside the cone); **Mach('s) number**, the ratio of the relative speed of a body and a fluid to the speed of sound at the same point; so ***Mach one, two*** (or *1, 2*), etc., a speed corresponding to a Mach number of one, two, etc.

1930 DOUGALL & DEANS tr. *Ewald's Physics Solids & Fluids* v. 262 During a small interval of time τ, a point source of disturbance expands to a sphere of radius $c\tau$, the centre of which has moved through a distance $q\tau$. The cone touches this sphere, so that $\sin a = c\tau/q\tau = c/q$... a is called Mach's angle. **1933** *Proc. R. Soc.* A. CXXXIX. 307 The Mach cone $x = y$ and $z = 1$ would satisfy the required conditions. **1937** DODGE & THOMPSON *Fluid Mech.* xiii. 370 The ratio V/c will be found to appear in all flow problems where compressibility is an important factor. It is known as Mach's number..in honor of the Austrian scientist. **1938** *Jrnl. R. Aeronaut. Soc.* XLII. 194 The part of the wave at a distance from the shell moves normal to itself with the speed of sound and this fact determines the angle it makes with the direction of motion of the shell (the 'Mach angle'). **1947** *Time* 8 Sept. 76/2 During both flights it reached 'mach ·828'. **1948** 'N. SHUTE' *No Highway* 34 It was diving at round about Mach unity, and the wings came off. **1953** *Sci. News* XXIX. 93 The non-dimensional quantity $M = V/a$ is defined as the 'Mach Number' of the flow. **1957** *Spaceflight* I. 51/1 In a rocket exhaust where the gases are moving at 6,000 ft./sec.,..the velocity of sound is 2,000 ft./sec., so the Mach No. is 3. **1967** *Technology Week* 23 Jan. 29/2 (Advt.), McDonnell testing and development facilities range from man-rated space chambers to Mach 28 wind tunnels.

b. Used, usu. *attrib.*, to designate an optical illusion first investigated by Mach (in *Sitzungsber. der K. Akad. der Wissensch. (Math.-Natur. Cl.)* (1865)), in which a place where the spatial rate of variation of surface brightness abruptly increases or decreases (as at the inner and outer edges of an indistinct shadow) may appear extra dark or bright to an extent that cannot be accounted for simply in terms of the objective variation in brightness.

1932 W. M. DEANS tr. *Pohl's Physical Princ. Mech. & Acoustics* i. 4 Mach's bands have led to much trouble in the carrying out of physical observations. **1936** *Brit. Jrnl. Psychol.* XXVII. 103 The same generalizations can be made about the Mach effect on a rotating colour wheel. **1965** GRAHAM & BROWN in C. H. Graham et al. *Vision* xvi. 474/2 Mach rings with spatial variations in color. **1965** F. RATLIFF *Mach Bands* ii. 43 The Mach bands appear at once in the shadow cast on a piece of white paper by the edge of a card held under a fluorescent desk lamp, which provides an extended source of light. Covering the ends of the lamp, which usually are not uniformly bright, somewhat enhances the effect. **1970** —— in Cohen & Seeger *Ernst Mach* 32 The Mach bands are one of the most compelling of all the visual 'illusions', and have been mistaken for objective physical phenomena.

mach, obs. form of MATCH *sb.* and *v.*

machærodont (məˈkɪərədɒnt), *a.* (and *sb.*) *Zool.* Also **machairodont.** [f. Gr. *μάχαιρα* sword, sabre + *ὀδοντ-*, *ὀδούς* tooth.] Characterized by teeth like those of the genus *Machairodus*; sabre-toothed.

1883 FLOWER in *Encycl. Brit.* XV. 435/2 Many modifications of this commonly-called 'machærodont' type have been met with. *Ibid.*, The sabre-toothed or machærodont dentition, the most specially carnivorous type of structure known. **1889** NICHOLSON & LYDEKKER *Man. Palæont.* (ed. 3) II. 1448 The extinct Machærodonts or Sabre-toothed Tigers. **1925** C. R. EASTMAN tr. *Zittel's Text-bk. Palaeont.* III. 75 A possible derivation of both Felines and Machairodonts may be from Dinictis. **1973** *Nature* 3 Aug. 311/2 A minimum of twenty-three large mammal species were represented, including at least five extinct forms—a large baboon (?*Simopithecus*), a sabretooth cat (machairodont), [etc.].

†**machæromancy.** *Obs. rare*[−1]. [f. Gr. *μάχαιρα* sword + *μαντεία* divination.] (See quot.)

1652 GAULE *Magastrom.* 165 Macharomancy [*sic*], [divining] by knives or swords.

machair (ˈmaxər). *Sc.* Also **machaire, machar, machir, machirr.** [Gael. *machair*, Ir. *machaire*.] A flat or low-lying coastal strip of arable or grassland usually overlying shell sand. Also *attrib.*

1684 A. SYMSON in A. Mitchell *Geogr. Coll. relating to Scotl.* (1907) II. 86 These three parishes last described..are commonly called the Machirrs or Machirrs of Whithern, which word Machirrs, as I am informed, imports white ground, and indeed those parishes, contain by far much more arable and white land, than up in the Moors, though the parishes there be much larger. **1878** *Q. Jrnl. Geol. Soc.* XXXIV. 848 Benbecula..has only one hill; and if we except the 'Machair', as the 'good land' along the west coast is called, all the rest of the island consists of low-lying moor, bog, and lake, with long shallow inlets of the sea straggling in. *Ibid.* 849 Adjoining the sandy shores are the delightful 'machairs', with their wealth of bright colour; while inland from the 'machairs' stretch the brown sombre peat and moorland. **1899** *Blackw. Mag.* Feb. 423/2 The burial-ground..occupied a little knoll in the middle of the 'machar', close to the sea (*machar* is the fine sweet pasture or links lying along the shore). **1924** *Glasgow Herald* 15 Mar. 4 In Highland glens or by the machirs of the Western Isles a crone..will still be consulted as if she were the Delphic sibyl. **1930** J. BUCHAN *Castle Gay* xvii. 271 The machars, yellowing with autumn, stretched for miles before him. **1955** F. F. DARLING *West Highland Survey* 21 There is a sufficiency of shell among the sand to encourage a fairly typical *machair* flora. *Ibid.* 51 The introduction of rabbits in the nineteenth century has gone a long way towards ruining the agricultural potential of the island, as these animals have created several small deserts on the *machair*. **1958** *Irish Times* 7 June, The term 'machaire' is used by English-speakers here to denote 'coastal strips of pasture land'. **1971** *Country Life* 24 June 1606/1 Her parents complained of attempts to put holiday caravans and a public lavatory on the machair. **1973** *Stornoway Gaz.* 3 Mar. 6/2 We are appealing to any reader (rugby enthusiast or not) who might be able to suggest (or lend) any reasonably flat area of ground—a stretch of machair or croftland—within, say, five miles of Stornoway.

‖**Machairodus** (məˈkaɪərədəs). *Palæont.* Also **Machærodus.** [mod.L. (Kaup 1833), f. Gr. *μάχαιρα* sword, sabre + *ὀδούς* tooth.] A genus of extinct animals of the cat family, having the upper canines enormously developed.

1836 BUCKLAND *Geol. & Min.* (1837) I. 91 *note.* **1839** *Penny Cycl.* XIV. 244/1 The canine teeth of Machairodus are very far from those of the bears. **1880** DAWKINS *Early Man* 31 The *Machairodus*, or sabre-toothed lion.

†**macham.** *Obs. rare*[−1]. (See quot.)

1689 [FAREWELL] *Irish Hudibras* 35 Some play the Trump, some trot the Hay, Some at Macham, some Noddy play. *marg. note* A Game at Cards.

Machamete, -ote, -yte, obs. ff. MAHOMET.

‖**machan** (mʌˈtʃɑːn). Also 9 **muchán, mucharn.** [Hindi *machān.*] An elevated platform; a scaffolding erected to watch for a tiger, etc.

1886 YULE *Hobson-Jobson, Muchán.* **1887** J. C. FIFE-COOKSON *Tiger Shooting* 41 W. at once arranged for a machan, or platform, to be made in a neighbouring tree from which he could watch the kill. **1890** SIR S. W. BAKER *Wild Beasts* I. 153 Branches..so arranged as to form a screen that will conceal the watcher... This arrangement is called a 'mucharn'. **1902** *Speaker* 6 Sept. 600/2 We struggle up the ravine to our machans or rather the trees they are to be slung in.

machance: see MAYCHANCE *adv.*

machanic, obs. form of MECHANIC *a.*

Machavil(l)ian, obs. form of MACHIAVELLIAN.

mache, obs. form of MATCH *sb.* and *v.*

mâche (mɑʃ). Also **mache.** [Fr.] = CORN-SALAD.

1830 [see *lamb's lettuce* s.v. LAMB *sb.* 7 b]. **1961** *Harper's Bazaar* June 84/2 Other salad greens..watercress, and French *mache.* **1962** S. COMBES *Dict. Cuisine French* 44/2 *Mâche,* lamb's lettuce, corn-salad. **1964** *Harper's Bazaar* Sept. 125/2, I like a green salad..lettuce or *mâche* or endive.

macheat, variant of MATCHET.

†**machecole,** *v. Obs.* Also 5 **magecolle, matchecole.** [a. OF. *machecoller,* connected with MACHICOULIS.] *trans.* To machicolate. Chiefly in *pa. pple.*

1412–20 LYDG. *Chron. Troy* II. ii, The walles were.. Magecolled without for sautes and assaye. **1470–85** MALORY *Arthur* VII. x. 226 They sawe a toure as whyte as ony snowe wel matchecold al aboute. *c* **1500** *Melusine* xix. 103 Fortyfyed round aboute with grete toures machecolyd. **1530** PALSGR. 616/2, I mage colle (Lydgate).

machecollate, obs. form of MACHICOLATE *v.*

machecoulis: see MACHICOULIS.

macheer (məˈtʃɪə(r)). *Western U.S.* Also **machere.** [Corruptly ad. Sp. *mochila.*] A leather flap attached to a saddle. Also *attrib.*

1847 *Calif. Star* (San Francisco) 21 Aug. 2/3 [A] man declares his *macheres* (saddle cover) was stolen from under him, although seated upon his horse and his horse in motion. **1853** G. D. BREWERTON *Overland with Kit Carson* (1930) 49 Our saddles were of the true Mexican pattern, wooden trees covered with leathers called *macheers.* *a* **1861** T. WINTHROP *John Brent* (1883) v. 45 Showers shrank his buckskins and soaked the macheers of his saddle to mere pulp. **1873** J. MILLER *Life amongst Modocs* 50 The Prince unfastened his cloak from the macheers behind my saddle. **1927** C. M. RUSSELL *Trails plowed Under* 166 I've seen bronc riders use an old macheer saddle with a Texas tree.

‖**macher** (ˈmæxə(r)). *U.S.* [Yiddish, f. G. *macher* maker, doer.] A man of importance, a bigwig; a braggart. Often *derogatory.*

1930 *Amer. Speech* VI. 126 A *Macher*..from the German word... Literally translated the word means 'maker' and idiomatically..is used derisively, referring to a braggart. **1964** S. BELLOW *Herzog* 87 He's a fine fellow... Not like that *macher,* Alexander. Always some scandal about him. **1964** W. MARKFIELD *To Early Grave* (1965) ii. 29 A man who sat on every board and committee, a powerful *macher* in Jewish communal affairs, who had passed around word that he needed a speech-writer. **1969** D. S. DAVIS *Where Dark Streets Go* (1970) i. 10 His father's a big *macher* in the union. **1973** *Jewish Chron.* 2 Feb. 19/3 It doesn't matter a tinker's cuss whether you amend the constitution to call the chairman president, macher or grand panjandrum.

†**maches.** *Obs.* Also 8 **masches, maschets, maskets.** [a. F. *mâche.*] The plant corn-salad (*Valerianella olitoria*).

1693 EVELYN *De la Quint. Compl. Gard.* II. 197 Maches, are a sort of little Sallet..seldom..brought before any noble Company. They are multiplied by Seed which is gathered in July, and are only used towards the end of Winter. **1704** *Dict. Rust. & Urb.,* Maches or Maschets. **1706** PHILLIPS (ed. Kersey), *Maches* or *Masches,* a kind of Corn-Sallet. **1719** LONDON & WISE *Compl. Gard.* 221 Maches.

machete (məˈtʃɛtɪ). Forms: α. 7 **matcheat,** 7–9 **machette,** 9 **matchet, -ett(e,** 9– **machete.** β. 7 in quasi-Sp. form **macheto.** [ad. Sp. *machete.*] A broad and heavy knife or cutlass, used, esp. in Central America and the West Indies, both as a tool and a weapon.

1598 HAKLUYT *Voy.* I. 414 A dozen of machetos to minch the whale. **1648** GAGE *West Indies* 129 They have no weapons but a Machette, which is a short Tuck. **1685** WAFER *Voy.* (1729) 278 Having no tool with us except a Macheat or long knife. **1697** DAMPIER *Voy.* (1729) I. 13 We tempted him with Beads, Money, Hatchets, Matcheats, or long knives. **1831** J. HOLLAND *Manuf. Metal* I. 142 These tools consist of matchets, canebills and hoes. **1832** M. R. MITFORD *Lights & Shadows Amer. Life* III. 215 The monteros drew their *machetes,* the sharp broad-swords they usually carry about with them. **1854** J. L. STEPHENS *Centr. Amer.* 70 The Machete, or chopping-knife..varies in form in different sections of the country. **1863** R. F. BURTON *Abeokuta* II. 92 Little things here means matchets and mirrors, kerchiefs and blue baft, rum and tobacco. **1897** MARY KINGSLEY *W. Africa* 161 A wall made up of strong tendrils and climbing grasses, through which the said atom has to cut its way with a machette. **1956** H. G. DE LISSER *Cup & Lip* v. 66 A dozen black men rushed forward, two with upraised machetes. **1958** J. COPE *Golden Oriole* xxiii. 131 On the far side of the wooden building an old man hired by Chipi was slowly chopping with a machete at the tropical growth. **1962** S. WYNTER *Hills of Hebron* ii. 29 The shadow of a man flung across the dirt track as he stalked along, one hand swinging free, the other with his machete held at the ready. **1973** *Black World* Sept. 12/2 The blade of the machete has a deeper significance in the song of the cane cutter.

attrib. **1881** *Instr. Census Clerks* (1885) 44 Matchett Maker. **1887** MOLONEY *Forestry W. Afr.* 233 The vines.. are being used only for matchet handles.

Machian (ˈmɑːkɪən), *a.* and *sb.* [f. MACH + -IAN.] **A.** *adj.* Of, pertaining to, or characteristic of Ernst Mach (see MACH) or his theories or ideas. **B.** *sb.* A follower or adherent of Mach or his ideas.

1927 D. KVITKO tr. *Lenin's Materialism & Empirio-Criticism* i. 69 We shall confine ourselves to those opinions which reveal the 'subjective' ignorance of our Machians. *Ibid.* ii. 85 Your statement..is utterly fallacious, and follows only from your Machian position. **1938** A. FINEBERG tr. *Lenin's Materialism & Empirio-Criticism* i. 82 Karl Pearson, the English Machian, who avoids all philosophical artifices. *Ibid.* iii. 169 James Ward... does not controvert Mach, but ..utilises the entire Machian trend in physics in his fight against materialism. **1941** *Mind* L. 82 The Machian positivists of Peirce's day denied that there are 'really' any natural laws. **1958** *Victorian Stud.* I. 253 Russell's own theory of knowledge underwent an increasingly Machian development from *Our Knowledge of the External World*..to the *Analysis of Mind,* in which a full-blooded neutral monism of Mach's variety is expounded. **1963** K. R. POPPER *Conjectures & Refutations* vi. 173 In our own day essentialism has been dethroned; a Berkeleian or Machian positivism or instrumentalism has..become fashionable. **1974** *Nature* 11 Jan. 99/2 Relation (8) may be looked upon either as an equipartition between the gravitational energy and the energy of expansion according to Einstein's equations or as a Machian relation determining the gravitational constant in terms of the matter content of the Universe.

Machiavel (ˈmækɪəvɛl). Also 6 **Machivell,** 6–8 **Machiavell,** 7–8 **-vil(l,** 7–9 **Macchiavel.** [Anglicized name of Niccolò *Machiavelli,* a celebrated Florentine statesman, who advocated in his work *Del Principe* the pursuit of statecraft at the expense of morality.] One who acts on the principles of Machiavelli; an intriguer, an unscrupulous schemer. † Also *appositive.*

1570 BUCHANAN *Admonitioun* Wks. (S.T.S.) 24 Proud contemnpnars or machiavell mokkaris of all religioun and vertew. **1597** J. PAYNE *Royal Exch.* 11, I wyshe you bannishe from your tables suche Atheists and machivells. **1598** SHAKS. *Merry W.* III. i. 104 Am I politicke? Am I subtle? Am I a Machiuell? **1632** B. JONSON *Magn. Lady* I, The very Agat Of State and Politie: cut from the Quar of Macchiavel. **1691** NORRIS *Pract. Disc.* 20 Intreaguers and Projectors, the very Machiavels of their age. **1712** ADDISON *Spect.* No. 305 ⁋ 15 These young Machiavils will, in a little time, turn their College upside-down with Plots and Stratagems. **1775** SHERIDAN *Duenna* II. iv, Oh, this little cunning head! I'm a Machiavel—a very Machiavel. **1863** READE *Hard Cash* xxix, This artful man, who had now become a very Machiavel.

Hence †**Machiavelize** *v. intr.* = *Machiavellianize.* †**Machiavelizing** *vbl. sb.*

1611 COTGR., *Machiavelizer,* to Machiauelize it; to practise Machiauellisme. **1617** MINSHEU *Ductor, Macheualize.* **1656** BLOUNT *Glossogr., Machevalize* or *Machiavellianize.* **1775** ASH, Suppl., *Machiavelizing,* the act of practising the politics of Machiavel.

Machiavellian (ˌmækɪəˈvɛlɪən), *a.* and *sb.* Forms: 6 **Macciavelian,** 6–7 **Mac(h)avil(l)ian, Machevelian, -vilian, Machivil(l)ian,** 7 **Macchiavilian, Matchia-, Matchievil(l)ian,** 7–8 **Machiavil(l)ian,** 7–9 **-velian,** 6– **Machiavellian.** [f. MACHIAVEL or *Machiavelli* + -(I)AN.]

A. *adj.* Of, pertaining to, or characteristic of Machiavelli, or his alleged principles; following the methods recommended by Machiavelli in preferring expediency to morality; practising duplicity in statecraft or in general conduct; astute, cunning, intriguing.

1579 J. STUBBES *Gaping Gulf* C viij, Thys absurd manner of reasoning is very Macciauelian logick. **1592** GREENE *Groat's W. Wit* (1617) 35 Is it pestilent Machiuilian policie that thou hast studied? **1613** CHAPMAN *Revenge Bussy D'Ambois* Plays 1873 II. 159 These are your Macheuilian Villaines. **1631** GOUGE *God's Arrows* I. xix. 26 What got that Machivillian politician Achitophell. **1637–50** ROW *Hist. Kirk* (1842) 162 *Divide et regna* is an old Matchiavilian maxime and trick. **1653** A. WILSON *Jas. I* 185 The true way of Treaties is with Christian, not Machiavelian policy. **1722** W. BOND *Ded. to Hartcliffe's Virtues* 5 The refined Matchiavillian thinkers have..altered the very nature of ethicks. **1790** BURKE *Fr. Rev.* Wks. V. 158 Where men follow their natural impulses, they would not bear the odious maxims of a Machiavelian policy. **1848** THACKERAY *Van. Fair* xxiii, So this Machiavellian captain of infantry cast about him for some..stratagem. **1878** E. JENKINS *Haverholme* 63 Conducting his party with Machiavellian subtlety.

B. *sb.* A follower of Machiavelli; one who adopts Machiavelli's principles in statecraft or in general conduct.

1568 *Satir. Poems Reform.* ix. 113 This false Machivilian. **1598** MARSTON *Pygmal.* II. 145 A damn'd Macheuelian Holds candle to the deuill for a while. **1608** WILLET *Hexapla Exod.* 320 Protagoras with the Machiauellians..were doubtful whether there were any God. **1647** *Husbandman's Plea agst. Tithes* 91 Never any Machivilian, or cruell State Politician..could never have devised a more effectuall way. **1668** R. STEELE *Husbandman's Calling* vii. (1672) 187 He hath need of discretion..that he be neither monk nor Matchevillian. **1710** STEELE *Tatler* No. 193 ⁋3 During this Retreat the Machiavilian was not idle, but secretly fomented Divisions. **1814** SCOTT *Let. to J. B. S. Morritt* 30 Apr., An awful lesson to sovereigns that morality is not so indifferent to politics as Machiavellians will assert.

Hence ˌ**Machiaˈvellianism,** the principles and practice of Machiavelli or of the Machiavellians, the employment of cunning and duplicity in statecraft or in general conduct; an instance of this. †**Machiaˈvellianize** *v.,* to practise Machiavellianism (Blount *Glossogr.* 1656). †**Machiaˈvellianly** *adv.,* in a Machiavellian manner.

1626 BERNARD *Isle of Man* (1627) 104 The Bills of Inditement framed by those false informers..Formalitie.. Machiavillianisme, Statisme..against Christian Conference. **1640** HOWELL *Dodona's Gr.* 173 Behold a notable peece of machiavillianisme. **1660** EVELYN *News fr. Brussels* Misc. Writ. (1805) 198 This impress he hath so Machiavelianly, and with such art and cunning, besprinkled and scattered over the whole paper. **1711** W. KING tr. *Naude's Ref. Politics* i. 19 The courts..where these Machiavilianisms are so common. **1882** PALGRAVE in Grosart *Spenser's Wks.* IV. p. xxv, The Machiavellianism of the sixteenth century.

Machiavellic (ˌmækɪəˈvɛlɪk), *a.* Also **-velic.** [formed as prec. adj. + -IC.] Machiavellian.

1838 *Blackw. Mag.* XLIII. 510 The Whigs indeed had concocted their schemes beforehand with all the Machiavelic forecast of veterans in the art of creating family broils. **1879** FARRAR *St. Paul* (1883) 350 The astute and machiavellic policy of Rome.

†**Machiaˈvelline,** *a. Obs. rare*⁻¹. In 7 **Machiaveline.** [formed as prec. + -INE.] = prec.

1602 PATERICKE tr. *Gentillet* 312 They have so well profited in their Machiaveline philosophie, that [etc.].

Machiavellism (ˌmækɪəˈvɛlɪz(ə)m). Also 6–7 **Machiavilisme,** 7 **-velism(e, matchiavellisme,** 9 **Mac(c)hiavelism.** [formed as prec. + -ISM.] = MACHIAVELLIANISM.

1592 NASHE *P. Penilesse* (Shaks. Soc.) 68, I comprehend.. vnder hypocrisie, al Machiavilisme. **1607** WALKINGTON *Opt. Glass* 66 b, A brocher of dangerous matchiauellisme. **1617** BP. HALL *Quo Vadis?* §21 Where had we..the art of dishonestie in practicall Machiauelisme, in false equiuocations? **1810** BENTHAM *Offic. Apt. Maximized, Def. Econ.* (1830) 57 A Government, in which, under the guidance of upstart Machiavelism, titled and confederated imbecility should lord it over King and people. **1897** *Daily News* 3 June 6/1 What..is the history of the Italian Republics..but the history of Machiavellism before Machiavelli?

ˌ**Machiaˈvellist.** Also 6 **Machivelist,** 7 **Matchi(a)vel(l)ist,** 8–9 **Machiavelist.** [formed as prec. + -IST.] One who practises or favours the principles of Machiavelli.

1589 NASHE *Martins Months Minde* To Rdr., I meddle not here with the Anabaptists, Famely louists, Machiauellists, nor Atheists. *Ibid.* H, Yee Machiuelists, Athiests, and each mischieuous head. **1640** R. BAILLIE *Canterb. Self-Convict.* 7 The contrarie maximes of the Turkish Empire, wherewith Matchivelists this day every where are labouring to poyson the eares of all Christian Princes. **1799** *Hull Advertiser* 6 July 1/4 A profound Machiavelist. **1829** SOUTHEY *Sir T. More* II. 80 The art of directing enthusiasm..is the most difficult which the Machiavellists of Papal Rome have ever been called upon to practise.

machicolate (məˈtʃɪkəleɪt), *v.* Also 8–9 **machecollate, matchicolate.** [f. ppl. stem of med.L. *machicol(l)āre* = OF. *machecoller*: see MACHECOLE *v.*] *trans.* To furnish with machicolations. Chiefly in **maˈchicolated** *pa. pple.* and *ppl. a.*

1773 *Gentl. Mag.* XLIII. 536 The gate-house..is fortified with a port-cluse or port-cullis, and machecollated. **1814** BRITTON *Archit. Antiq.* IV. 181 Cæsar's-tower..is surmounted by a bold machicolated parapet. **1842** BARHAM *Ingol. Leg., Bloudie Jacke,* With iron it's plated And machecollated, To pour boiling oil or lead down. **1860** HAWTHORNE *Marble Faun* (1879) I. vi. 61 A mediaeval tower,..battlemented and machicolated at the summit. **1890** *Times* 8 Apr. 11/3 The machicolated towers of Raglan Castle.

transf. **1848** W. S. MAYO *Kaloolah* (1887) 7, I could see every stone of the towers, matchicolated with stork's nests.

machicolation (mətʃɪkəˈleɪʃən). *Arch.* [f. prec.: see -ATION.]

1. An opening between the corbels which support a projecting parapet, or in the vault of a portal, through which combustibles, molten lead, stones, etc., were dropped on the heads of assailants. Also, a projecting structure containing a range of such openings.

1788 GROSE *Milit. Antiq.* II. 336 The grand entrance was mostly through a gate flanked by two large and strong towers, with a projection over the passage, called a machicolation. **1806** DALLAWAY *Observ. Eng. Archit.* 92 Lofty embattled walls..crested with hanging galleries and macchicolations which served the double purpose of military defence and great external beauty. **1832** G. DOWNES *Lett. Cont. Countries* I. 521 The antique castle is furnished with a machicolation. **1848** RICKMAN *Archit.* 119 Wakefield steeple..is singular for its machicolations in the top of the tower. **1871** MISS BRADDON *Lovels* v. 87 The

crenellated roof, with its machicolations, is considered a great success.

2. The action of discharging missiles, etc., through such apertures. *rare*—⁰; perh. an error.

1828–32 in WEBSTER; and in later Dicts.

‖**machicoulis** (mɑːʃɪˈkuːlɪ). Also 9 machecoulis, machicouli, and in quasi-anglicized form machicoule. [F. *mâchecoulis*, *mâchicoulis*, OF. *maschecoulis*.] = MACHICOLATION 1.

1793 SMEATON *Edystone L.* Introd. 4 A lodgment, in fortification called a Machicoulis, is built upon the wall over the stairs. **1802** JAMES *Milit. Dict.* s.v., When a place is besieged, detached parties of the garrison may be posted in the several machicoulises. **1851** *Fraser's Mag.* XLIII. 154 A large granite block, formed like a machicoule, and projecting from the front wall of the castle. **1859** PARKER *Dom. Archit.* III. i. 5 The bastions carried upon corbels, with open intervals between them for throwing down..missiles, and commonly known by the name of *machecoulis*. **1865** STREET *Gothic Archit. Spain* 193 A parapet boldly corbelled out on machicoulis from the walls. **1885** LADY HERBERT tr. *Lagrange's Life Dupanloup* I. 340 This picturesque old château, with its postern gate, its portcullis, and machicoulis.

attrib. **1834–47** J. S. MACAULAY *Field Fortif.* (1851) 151 The machicoulis gallery is made to project 2 feet from the wall. **1860** TRISTRAM *Gt. Sahara* xi. 180 Guardrooms with loopholes..and machicouli gallery.

‖**machila** (maˈʃila). Also machilla. [Pg., perh. f. Tamil *macil*, *mañcil* stage in a journey, f. Hindi *manzil*, f. Arabic.] A conveyance, usually for one person, used in Africa, consisting of a hammock slung between two poles, carried by two or more bearers.

1884 MRS. M. A. PRINGLE *Towards Mountains of Moon* vii. 89 The Portuguese [in Quilliman] go from house to house in a sort of palanquin, called here a *machilla* (pronounced *masheela*). **1897** H. H. JOHNSTON *Brit. Cent. Afr.* iv. 91 We then started for Kotakota, Jumbe's men insisting on carrying me in a machilla. **1900** GROGAN & SHARP *From Cape to Cairo* 168 [He] obtained..a team of boys to carry me in a machila to the highlands of Kivu. **1944** J. C. HEENAN *Cardinal Hinsley* 64, I have now travelled in Africa in every kind of conveyance—ox carts, glorified perambulators, machilla. **1952** S. CLOETE *Curve & Tusk* (1953) iv. 38 We will carry you, Lord, we will carry you in a machila, a hammock.

b. *attrib.*, as ***machila-carrier***, etc.

1900 GROGAN & SHARP *From Cape to Cairo* vi. 57 [He] utilized the bandsmen when off duty as machila-carriers. **1906** R. C. F. MAUGHAM *Portuguese E. Afr.* 14 Machilla-travelling on the Frontier.

‖ˈ**machina**. *Obs.* Pl. machinas. [L. *māchina* MACHINE.] = MACHINE in various senses.

1612 SHELTON *Quix.* I. v. I. 32 The Labourer grew almost mad for Anger to hear that Machina of Follies. **1622** MABBE tr. *Aleman's Guzman d'Alf.* II. 97 So great a Machina, and such a masse of things. **1640** GLAPTHORNE *Hollander* IV. G 3, If I doe not second you confidently, may my tongue be cramped,..and the machina of my invention ruind perpetually. **1653** H. MORE *Antid. Ath.* III. xi. (1712) 124 To assert that Animals themselves were Machinas. **1676** HALE *Contempl.* I. 220 One poor unthought of accident..breaks all to shivers the whole elaborate Machina.

machinability (məʃiːnəˈbɪlɪtɪ). [f. MACHIN(E *v.* + -ABILITY.] The ability to be cut by machine tools.

1921 *Glasgow Herald* 22 Sept. 5 The influence of lead on the greater possibility of liquation from gun metal castings, the easier machinability, expected minimised corrosion and improvement for bearings. **1940** [see GRAPHITIZER]. **1941** F. T. SISCO *Mod. Metall. for Engin.* x. 159 It is impossible to evaluate the machinability of ferrous or non-ferrous materials by a single laboratory test. **1961** *Jrnl. Iron & Steel Inst.* CXCVII. 171/1 The machinability of nodular cast iron is compared with that of steels of similar microstructure and mechanical properties. **1968** A. KOBAYASHI in *Encycl. Polymer Sci. & Technol.* VIII. 349 The machinability of polyester cast resin is relatively poor.

machinable (məˈʃiːnəb(ə)l), *a.* [f. MACHIN(E *v.* + -ABLE.] Capable of being cut by machine tools.

1917 *Sci. Amer. Suppl.* 16 June 374/2 If well handled in the cupola the product will be strong and machinable. **1930** *Engineering* 23 May 676/2 The resistor of a new electric furnace..is a new machinable alloy of iron with several other metals. **1951** WOLDMAN & GIBBONS *Machinability & Machining of Metals* i. 1 The most machinable metal is the one which will permit the fastest removal of the greatest amount of material per grind.

†**machinal**, *a.* *Obs.* [ad. L. *māchināl-is*, f. *māchina* MACHINE. Cf. F. *machinal*.] Of or pertaining to a machine or machines; mechanical.

1680 MOXON *Mech. Exerc., Turning* 236 But to make it move thus..there are required several Machinal Helps. **1685** BOYLE *Enq. Notion Nat.* 330 Man is..like a Mann'd Boat, where, besides the Machinal Part,..there is an Intelligent Being. **1760** *Projects* in *Ann. Reg.* 147/1 In the erection of the machinal crane-works.

†**machinament**. *Obs.* [ad. L. *māchināment-um*, f. *māchinārī* (see next).] A contrivance, engine, machine, vehicle.

1413 *Pilgr. Sowle* (Caxton) IV. xxix. (1859) 60 At the last I saw before me a wonder machynament, and meruaylous! *c* **1425** *Found. St. Bartholomew's* 37 And skippynge forth with all Iryne machynamentis he came to the doer. **1658** BROMHALL *Treat. Specters* IV. 255 A very stormy South-wind did..palsie and shoulder-shake..machinaments and fortifications. **1674** PETTY *Disc. Dupl. Proportion* 7 Materials applied..to Carts, or any other Machinaments intended for strength. **1727** in BAILEY vol. II.

machinate (ˈmækɪneɪt), *v.* Also 7 machinat. [f. L. *māchināt-*, ppl. stem of *māchinārī* to contrive, f. *māchina* MACHINE.]

1. *intr.* To lay plots; to intrigue, scheme.

1600 W. WATSON *Decacordon* (1602) 243 Such persons as shall machinate and deuise to execute such outragious designements against their prince. **1689** *Def. Liberty agst. Tyrants* 130 A Tyrant conspires, machinates, and lays his plots and practises. **1830** *Fraser's Mag.* I. 101 The blackest treason may lurk and machinate at his very threshold. **1858** FABER *Bartoli & Maffei's Life Xavier* 312 Whilst the Portuguese had been preparing for their departure, the bonzes had been machinating against them.

2. *trans.* To contrive, plan, plot. Now *rare*.

1602 FULBECKE *2nd Pt. Parallel* 23 *Dolus bonus*, is when a man doth machinate or deuise anie thing to entrap a thiefe, or a traytour. **1643** PRYNNE *Romes Masterpeece* 14 He thought fit, that a desperate Treason, machinated against so many soules was to be revealed. **1651** HOWELL *Venice* 187 Which makes Urban the 8...to machinat violent means for to invest his Nephews in another Princes Estate. **1760–72** H. BROOKE *Fool of Qual.* (1809) I. 122 The..robberies, massacres, and assassinations, that the violent machinate against the peaceful. **1822** T. TAYLOR *Apuleius* 359 [He] injures himself in a greater degree than he injures him against whom he machinates destruction.

machinating (ˈmækɪneɪtɪŋ), *ppl. a.* [-ING².] That machinates or plots; given to plotting.

1748 RICHARDSON *Clarissa* (1811) III. 355 Willingness to think well of a spirit so inventive, and so machinating. **1754** —— *Grandison* (1781) V. xlii. 261 It was all open day, no dark machinating night, in the heart of the undissembling Olivia. **1900** O. ONIONS *Compl. Bachelor* v. 57 The machinating married woman! No bachelor is safe with her.

machination (mækɪˈneɪʃən). Also 7 matchination. [ad. L. *māchinātiōn-em* (either directly, or through F. *machination*), n. of action f. *māchinārī* to contrive, MACHINATE.]

1. The action or process of contriving or planning; contrivance, intrigue, plotting. Now *rare*.

1549 *Compl. Scot.* xi. 90 There liberte..vas ane lang tyme in captiuite, be the machination of ȝour ald enemes. **1605** SHAKS. *Lear* v. i. 46 If you miscarry, Your businesse of the world hath so an end, And machination ceases. **1651** HOBBES *Leviath.* I. xiii. 60 By secret machination, or by confederacy with others. **1667** MILTON *P.L.* VI. 504 Some one..inspired With dev'lish machination, might devise Like instrument. **1835** I. TAYLOR *Spir. Despot.* iv. 159 The machination in closets of interests that ought to be openly discussed is a treason against the community.

2. An instance of plotting or contrivance; an intrigue, plot, scheme. Usually in bad sense.

c **1477** CAXTON *Jason* 77 b, Some welwillars of the king.. tolde to him the machinacion of Zethephius. **1539** CROMWELL *Let.* 286 in Merriman *Life & Lett.* (1902) II. 168 Albeit his highnes dothe in no wise feare any of his Censures attemptates or other malicious & devilishe machinacions. **1656** J. HAMMOND *Leah & R.* (1844) 24 His Highnesse, (not acquainted with these matchinations), had [etc.]. **1678** WOOD *Life* 29 Sept., This machinacion fayling, another.. was put on foote. **1713** STEELE *Englishman* No. 12. 81 Such Men would stand up..against the Machinations of Popery and Slavery. **1749** FIELDING *Tom Jones* XVI. iv. To defeat my wisest machinations by your blunders. **1855** MACAULAY *Hist. Eng.* xiii. III. 306 Ludlow escaped unhurt from all the machinations of his enemies. **1867** FREEMAN *Norm. Conq.* (1876) I. iv. 224 The French and German writers know nothing of these machinations of Arnulf.

†**3.** The use or construction of machinery. *Obs.*

1641 EARL MONM. tr. *Biondi's Civil Warres* IV. 50 Hoping that time and hunger might effect that, which..by all their machinations and assaults they could not doe. **1711** W. SUTHERLAND *Shipbuild. Assist.* 21 Machination, or the forming Machines or Engines.

†**4.** Something contrived or constructed; *esp.* in material sense, e.g. a mechanical appliance for war, a framework or apparatus. *Obs.*

1605 BACON *Adv. Learn.* I. vi. 14 The Edict..was.. accounted a more pernitious engine and machination against the Christian faith, than [etc.]. **1613** R. CAWDREY *Table Alph.* (ed. 3), *Machinations*, war-like weapons. **1652** GAULE *Magastrom.* 108 Will not then their whole machination, or fabrick of judiciall Astrologie fall to the ground? **1680** MOXON *Mech. Exerc., Turning* 235 If the Puppet be made to it with the Machination described in Plate 17.

machinator (ˈmækɪneɪtə(r)). [a. L. *māchinātor*, agent-n. f. *māchinārī* to contrive, MACHINATE.] One who contrives or schemes; a contriver, intriguer, plotter, schemer; usually in bad sense.

1611 COTGR., *Machinateur*, a machinator, framer, deuiser, (especially of bad things). **1627** H. BURTON *Baiting Pope's Bull* 26 Their art infernall,..infused into them by that.. chiefe machinator of all mischiefe. **1760** C. JOHNSTON *Chrysal* (1822) II. 152 Not only escape the ruin meditated against him, but also retort it on the machinators. **1839** I. TAYLOR *Anc. Chr.* I. Pref. 7 Certain wary machinators around us. **1862** LATHAM *Channel Isl.* III. xvi. (ed. 2) 381 There were intrigues and divisions of all sorts: Lord Digby being the chief machinator. **1892** *Pall Mall G.* 3 May 2/2 The machinators of the Union..destroyed nearly every document bearing on that shameful transaction.

machine (məˈʃiːn), *sb.* Also 7–8 machin. [ad. F. *machine* (= Sp. *maquina*, Pg. *maquina*, *machina*, It. *macchina*), ad. L. *māchina*, ad. Gr. μηχανή, f. μῆχος contrivance, cogn. w. Teut. **magan* to be able (see MAY *v.*).

The Fr. word has passed into all the mod. Teut. langs.: G. *maschine*, Du. *machine*, Da. *maskine*, Sw. *maskin*.

In 17–18th c. the word was often stressed on the first syll.]

1. a. A structure of any kind, material or immaterial; a fabric, an erection. Now *rare* exc. in ***machine-for-living(-in)*** [tr. F. *machine à habiter* ('Le Corbusier' *Vers une Architecture* (1923) p. ix)], a house, and in imitative phrases.

1549 *Compl. Scot.* Ep. to Queen 3 The maist illustir potent prince of the maist fertil & pacebil realme, vndir the machine of the supreme olimp. **1599** A. HUME *Hymnes* ii. 38 Be his wisdome..so wondrouslie of nocht, This machin round, this vniuers, this vther world he wrocht. **1674** PLAYFORD *Skill Mus.* Pref. 2 Disposing the whole Machine of the World. **1674** HICKMAN *Quinquart. Hist.* (ed. 2) 225 They that asserted Universal redemption by the death of Christ destroyed the whole Machine of the Calvinian predestination. **1682** N. O. tr. *Boileau's Lutrin* I. 239 Behind this Machine [a pulpit], cover'd as with a skreen, The Sneaking Chanter scarce could then be seen. **1687** A. LOVELL tr. *Thevenot's Trav.* III. 23 They put fire next to a Machine which seemed to be a blew Tree when it was on fire. **1697** DRYDEN *Æneid* II. 25 With inward Arms the dire Machine [*sc.* the wooden horse] they load. **1753** HANWAY *Trav.* (1762) I. v. lxii. 286 Her imperial majesty is drawn.. in a large machine, which contains her bed, a table, and other conveniences... This machine is set on a sledge, and drawn by twenty-four post horses. **1784** J. BARRY in *Lect. Paint.* v. (1848) 196 Had the whole of this great machine of the Fontana di Trevi been committed to any one of those sculptors. **1791** CHARLOTTE SMITH *Celestina* (ed. 2) I. 129 Her new laylock bonnet..for the safety of which she was so solicitous that she would have taken the great machine in which it was contained into the coach, had it not been opposed by the coachman. **1829** R. HALL *Wks.* (1832) VI. 457 The mind casts its eye over the whole machine of society. **1878** BROWNING *La Saisiaz* 279 To each mortal peradventure earth becomes a new machine. **1931** A. HUXLEY *Music at Night* 217 In Le Corbusier's phrase, a house is a 'machine for living in'. **1934** —— *Beyond Mexique Bay* 132 Le Corbusier himself could hardly have done the trick better: King's is the perfect machine-for-praying-in. **1960** R. W. MARKS *Dymaxion World of B. Fuller* 22/1 The house was actually the world's first tangible embodiment of what one French architect hopefully designated as a 'Machine-for-Living'. **1966** 'J. MELVILLE' *Nell Alone* vii. 75 The whole house was..a machine for Mrs Richier to live in.

b. *spec.* A vehicle of any kind (usually wheeled). In the 18th and part of the 19th centuries commonly applied to a stage-coach or mail-coach. *Obs.* exc. *Sc.* Also short for *bathing-machine*.

1687 A. LOVELL tr. *Thevenot's Trav.* III. 54 They make use of an Engine which they call Palanquin... This Machine hangs by a long Pole [etc.]. **1704** SWIFT *Mech. Operat. Spirit* Misc. (1711) 275 Tho' there is not any other Nation in the World so plentifully provided with Carriages for that Journey..yet there are abundance of us who will not be satisfy'd with any other Machine besides this of Mahomet. **1709** *Lond. Gaz.* No. 4545/1 His Serenity, accompanied by ..the Boy who drew the Balls for the Election [of Doge] sitting in the same Machine, was carried out of the Church. **1769** *De Foe's Tour Gt. Britain* III. 106 A Machine going out to, and coming in from, London three Times a Week in the Summer. **1759** ADAM SMITH *Mor. Sent.* (1781) 267 The poor man's son..sees his superiors carried about in machines. **1772** BURKE *Corr.* (1844) I. 372 Your very kind letter of the 15th,..I received by the machine. **1788** E. SHERIDAN *Jrnl.* (1960) iv. 114, I went down to the bathing House where I found a great Number of Ladies and Gentlemen waiting to take their turn in the Machines. **1791** MRS. GRANT *Lett. fr. Mountains* (1813) II. xxxvii. 184, I came in a little open machine we keep for these journeys. **1822** *Acc. Establ. Gen. P.-O.* 8 in *Parl. Pap.* XVIII. 175 To loss by death of two horses before the machine commenced running. **1825** E. WEETON *Jrnl.* 14 June (1969) II. 384 Southport..is sadly exposing..and the modest complain much, gentlemen's and ladies' machines standing promiscuously in the water! **1832** *Massachusetts Stat.* c. 75 §4 Every cart, wagon, or other machine, drawn by two or four oxen. **1859** *All Year Round* No. 19. 446, I got into the wrong machine [*sc.* a bathing-machine] first. **1870** G. MEREDITH *Lett.* (1970) I. 426 We have a flat sandy shore, and you see half a dozen fat men at a time scampering out of the machines. **1893** H. JOYCE *Hist. Post Office* xii. 215 In that year [1784], and for some little time afterwards, coaches which carried the mails were called diligences or machines, and the coachmen were called machine-drivers. **1894** BLACK *Highland Cousins* I. 37, I would bring a machine and drive you up to the Drill-Hall.

†**c.** Applied to a ship or other vessel. *Obs.*

1637 HEYWOOD *Royal Ship* 27 Shee [Pallas] hath (no doubt) raptured our Undertaker This Machine to devise first, and then make her. **1702** S. PARKER tr. *Cicero's De Finibus* v. 320 In vain upon the Canvas plays A wanton Gale. The Machin stays Becalm'd with Harmony. **1717** W. SUTHERLAND (*title*) Britain's Glory or Ship-building Unveil'd, being a General Director for Building and Compleating the said Machines. **1782** CREVECOEUR *Lett.* 220 [Slaves] carried in a strange machine over an ever agitated element, which they had never seen before. **1807** SOUTHEY *Espriella's Lett.* II. 155 We..embarked upon the canal in a stage boat bound for Chester... The shape of the machine resembles the common representations of Noah's ark.

d. (See quot.) (Cf. sense 3.)

1883 S. PLIMSOLL in *19th Cent.* July 147 The box..is called by many names, as 'van', 'machine', 'tank', 'trunk', &c. *Ibid.* 162 The 'kit' haddocks are put loose into what are called machines. These machines are long boxes lined with lead..divided internally into four equal spaces.

e. A motor car. *U.S.*

1901 *McClure's Mag.* XVIII. i. 21/2 His assistant crouching at his feet out of range of the swift-flying currents of air produced by the mad flight of the machine. **1912** *Collier's* 21 Sept. 37/2 Leslie, Lanagan, and I hurried in the chief's machine to the Swanson home. **1915** *Sat. Even. Post*

3 Apr. 62/2 The reliability of the machine was so amazing that, in seven years of business, not a single breakdown had been reported. **1919** *Ibid.* 25 Jan. 45/3 As I neared my own house I slowed the machine.

2. A military engine, siege-tower, or the like. Now *rare*. Chiefly *Anc. Hist.* (= L. *machina*).

1656 Blount *Glossogr.*, *Machine*, an instrument or engine of War. **1674** *Ch. & Court of Rome* 4 These are the goodly Machines..recommended to batter down the Protestant Cause. **1732** Lediard *Sethos* II. ix. 277 He [raised] enormous machines round about the city. **1839** Thirlwall *Greece* VI. xlix. 165 The besieged made many vigorous sallies for the purpose of setting fire to the machines.

3. a. An apparatus, appliance, instrument.

1650 Bulwer *Anthropomet.* 92 In the curious Machin of speech, the Nose is added as a Recorder. **1707** *Curios. in Husb. & Gard.* 27 The Microscope..has been but lately discover'd: for the Naturalists..were not aided by that Machine. **1727–41** Chambers *Cycl.*, *Racket* is also a machine, which the savages of Canada bind to their feet, to enable them to walk more commodiously over the snow. **1941** G. Marx *Groucho Lett.* (1967) 48 They will wind up at Las Vegas playing the machines. **1962** *Gloss. Terms Automatic Data Processing* (*B.S.I.*) 92 *Tabulator* (*accounting machine*), a machine which reads data from a medium..and produces lists, tables or totals. **1968** *Times* 11 Oct. 8/2 Thorpe has analysed the fish-calls of 40 sandwich terns by means of a sound spectrograph, a machine which analyses sounds, in terms of their pitch and loudness and produces a graphical representation of the sound. **1970** *Washington Post* 30 Sept. B.14/1 The stoves, the refrigerators and other machines. **1973** *Black Panther* 14 Apr. 6/1 The Visiting Room containing tables and chairs and machines for snacks and soft drinks.

†**b.** In immaterial sense: A device, machination. *Obs.*

1595–6 Q. Eliz. *Let. to Jas. VI* (Camden Soc.) 113 In wordz..of such waight, as, in honest dimars, hit may mar the façon of diuelische machines, and crase the hartz of treason-mynding men. *Ibid.* 173 And how I mynde to kipe my owne dores from my ennemis malice; and so do wische that our solide amitie may overthawrt thes develische machines.

4. a. In a narrower sense: An apparatus for applying mechanical power, consisting of a number of interrelated parts, each having a definite function.

In recent use the word tends to be applied esp. to an apparatus so devised that the result of its operation is not dependent on the strength or manipulative skill of the workman; thus the term *printing-machine* does not in ordinary language include the hand-press, but is reserved for those apparatus of later invention in which manual labour is superseded by the action of the mechanism.

1673 Ray *Journ. Low C.* 5 This kind of Machin is generally used..for raising up Water. **1756–7** tr. *Keysler's Trav.* (1760) II. 250 For raising this obelisk out of the ground,..Fontana contrived forty-one machines. **1822** Robison *Syst. Mech. Philos.* II. 48 It is certain that the account given in the 'Century of Inventions' could instruct no person who was not sufficiently acquainted with the property of steam to be able to invent the machine himself. **1851** Carpenter *Man. Phys.* iii. (ed. 2) 96 Examining the component parts of the Machine,—its springs, wheels, levers, cords, pulleys, &c. **1881** Sir W. Thomson in *Nature* No. 619. 434 Windmills as hitherto made are very costly machines. **1888** *Pall Mall G.* 12 Apr. 12/1 An Automatic Gas Machine... The machine is charged with one of the first products of petroleum, or gasolene.

fig. **1749** Fielding *Tom Jones* vi. ii, The great state wheels in all the political machines of Europe. **1801** Wellington in Gurw. *Desp.* (1837) I. 342 More experience than we have yet had of the operation of the court (of the manner in which the machine works). **1809–10** Coleridge *Friend* xv. (1887) 64 To expose the folly and the legerdemain of those who have thus abused the blessed machine of language. **1876** L. Stephen *Eng. Th. in 18th Cent.* II. ix. iii. 19 The Church was excellent as a national refrigerating machine.

b. Used *spec.* for the particular kind of machine with which the speaker is chiefly concerned; e.g. short for *sewing-machine*, *printing-machine*, (Austral. and N.Z.) *shearing-machine*. Also, in recent use, a bicycle or tricycle; a flying-machine, an aircraft; a mechanical printing press; a fire-engine (U.S.); a typewriter; a calculating machine or computer.

1659 T. St. Serf tr. *Cyrano de Bergerac's Govt. World in Moon* sig. D3v, I caused a Machine to be made of Iron..and being well seated in the seat, I cast my Magnetique Bowl into the Air. **1679** R. Hooke in *Phil. Coll. R. Soc.* I. 15 A Machin newly Invented for Flying in the Air. **1751** R. Morris *Narr. Life J. Daniel* xii. 170 He had brought his machine to absolute perfection, and..had been making an experiment for flying in it. **1809** *Nicholson's Jrnl. Nat. Philos.* Nov. 172 It may be of some amusement to some of your readers to see a machine rise in the air by mechanical means. *Ibid.* 173 The little machine is completed. **1825** T. C. Hansard *Typographia* 699 The machine being put in motion, the paper which is to be printed is laid upon a board, passed through, and receives the impression on one side. *Ibid.* 700 One machine was to perform the work of eight presses. *Ibid.* 712 My machine has had a trial of six months: its ordinary speed is..at an average of two thousand impressions, or one thousand perfected sheets per hour. **1832**, etc. [see *calculating machines* s.v. calculating *vbl. sb.*]. **1833** *Penny Mag.* Monthly Suppl. Nov.–Dec. 508/2 One thousand perfect copies..could only have been daily produced at one press by the labour of two men. The machine produces sixteen thousand copies. **1841** *Penny Cycl.* XIX. 20/1 A sheet of paper is..put into the machine by one attendant and taken out printed on both sides by the other attendant. *c* **1848** B. A. Baker *Glance at N.Y.* (*c* 1857) 9 I've made up my mind not to run wid der machine any more. **1859** Bartlett *Dict. Amer.* (ed. 2) 259 *Machine*, the name for a fire-engine among the New York 'b'hoys'. **1871** *Porcupine* 29 July 276/1 Tantalising the toll-bar keepers on a 'machine'. **1883** Sturmy *Tricyclist's Ann.* (ed. 3) 126 A glance at the tricycle trade..with full description of upwards of 250 machines. *Ibid.* 190 A well-made machine, and the easiest..folded tricycle in the market. **1891** W. D. Howells in 'Twain' & Howells *Mark Twain-Howell's Lett.* (1960) II. 639 The machine with which this letter is written is a Hammond. **1892** A. Powell *Southward's Pract. Printing* (ed. 4) ii. 11 Presses..are of two kinds, (a) hand presses and (b) mechanical presses. The latter are, in England, usually called 'machines' or 'printing machines'. *Ibid.* xlviii. 429 The one-side, single-cylinder machine, which is generally referred to when a cylinder machine, or, indeed, 'a machine', is mentioned among printers. **1899** *Northern Times* (Golspie, Sutherland) 22 June 1/1 (Advt.), Splendid cycles... Boys' machines at £5 10s. **1900** F. M. Ford *Let.* Oct. (1965) 10 My dear Galsworthy, Excuse my writing by machine; Christine at this moment monopolizes the only pen there is in the house. **1909** *Aeronautics* Dec. 151 Any machine—'plane or dirigible. **1915** *Southward's Mod. Printing* (ed. 3) II. i. 1 In the printing office the hand press is spoken of as the 'press' and the machine press as the 'machine'... The press can be worked by hand power only; the machine may be driven by steam, gas, or other motive power. **1919** 'Boyd Cable' *Old Contemptibles* viii. 124 He paid more attention now to watching for enemy machines, and never failed..to rush his pilot to a machine and into the air if a German was reported in sight. **1927** H. Crane *Let.* 30 Mar. (1965) 295 I'm *so* unhappy without a machine. Hope I get my new one soon. **1940** *Bulletin* (Sydney) 10 Jan. 16/1 'Anyone,' [Old Harry] declared, 'could put up tallies with machines. With the tongs now—'..Harry produced half a dozen pairs of tongs and some sheep. **1944** 'N. Shute' *Pastoral* iv. 89 The machine before them opened out and trundled down the runway. **1946** V. S. Ganderton in H. Whetton *Pract. Printing & Binding* x. 114/2 Work on the principle of matching the new sheet to the machine, not the machine to the sheet. **1946** *Ann. Computation Lab. Harvard Univ.* I. Foreword, Harvard University's need for a machine such as the IBM Automatic Sequence Controlled Calculator has long been a matter of discussion. **1954**, etc. [see *machine code*, *instruction*, etc., in sense 10]. **1956** G. Bowen *Wool Away!* (ed. 2) i. 9 Relative quality of workmanship between blades and machines is a debatable point. **1957** D. D. McCracken *Digital Computer Programming* ii. 14 The first two digits [of the instruction]..tell the machine what to do. **1960** N. R. Scott *Analog & Digital Computer Technol.* v. 170 Instructions to the machine consist of combinations of these addresses with code numbers designating the arithmetical operations to be performed. **1970** E. A. D. Hutchings *Survey of Printing Processes* iv. 58 The inking unit is situated at the top of the machine, above the type-bed. **1970** O. Dopping *Computers & Data Processing* xix. 306 A company which changes computers normally changes to a machine which is considerably faster than the old one. **1972** *Daily Tel.* 5 Aug. 9/3 For us, it was back to our bicycles. We stacked our machines in the back of the car and set off for gently contoured Norfolk.

c. Applied to the human and animal frame as a combination of several parts. (Cf. sense 1.)

Now chiefly with metaphorical intention.

1602 Shaks. *Ham.* ii. ii. 124 Thine euermore most deere Lady, whilst this Machine is to him. **1687** *Death's Vis.* ix. 130 What Nobler Souls the Nobler Machins Wear. **1699** Garth *Dispens.* v. 54 And shall so useful a Machin as I Engage in civil Broyls, I know not why? **1712** Addison *Spect.* No. 387 ⁋2 Cheerfulness is..the best Promoter of Health. Repinings..wear out the Machine insensibly. **1722** Quincy *Lex. Phys.-Med.* (ed. 2) 17 Until some Authors..have demonstrated the Laws of Circulation in an Animal Machine. **1804** Wordsw. '*She was a Phantom of delight*' 22 And now I see with eye serene The very pulse of the machine. **1805** *Med. Jrnl.* XIV. 181 When a product of diseased action has been effected,..in consequence of which the machine becomes again sensible to the impressions of ordinary causes. **1876** Preece & Sivewright *Telegraphy* 114 The human machine tires, and as a consequence not only is the speed of working reduced, but [etc.].

d. A combination of parts moving mechanically, as contrasted with a being having life, consciousness and will. Hence applied to a person who acts merely from habit or obedience to rule, without intelligence, or to one whose actions have the undeviating precision and uniformity of a 'machine'.

1692 Bentley *Boyle Lect.* 59 If brutes be supposed to be bare engins and machins. **1779** A. Hamilton *Wks.* (1886) VII. 565 The nearer the soldiers approach to machines, perhaps the better. **1809–10** Coleridge *Friend* (1865) 119 Man must be free; or to what purpose was he made a spirit of reason, and not a machine of instinct? **1820** Byron *Mar. Fal.* i. ii. 302 They are..mere machines, To serve the nobles' most patrician pleasure. **1830** Carlyle in Froude *Life* (1882) II. 90 Wherefore their system [Utilitarianism] is a machine and cannot grow or endure. **1866** Geo. Eliot *F. Holt* (1868) 18 I'll have old Hickes. He was a neat little machine of a butler. **1890** 'L. Falconer' *Mlle. Ixe* (1891) 108, I believe women think horses are machines, and made of cast-iron too. **1895** *Outing* (U.S.) Dec. 248/2 Too much preparation..makes a man a mere machine, set to go off at a particular day.

e. *slang.* The penis; a condom (see also quot. 1896).

1749 J. Cleland *Mem. Woman Pleasure* I. 200 Coming out with that formidable machine of his, he lets the fury loose. **1785** Grose *Dict. Vulgar T.*, *Machines*,..See *Cundum*. *c* **1863** Philo cunnus *Festival of Passions* II. 12, I then seized his stiff machine in my grasp. **1896** Farmer & Henley *Slang* IV. 262/2 *Machine*,..1. The female *pudendum*... 2. The *penis*.

f. *N.Z. colloq.* A totalizator.

1889 G. P. Williams in A. E. Woodhouse *N.Z. Farm & Station Verse* (1950) 26 What a lot [of money] you left behind in the 'machine'. **1891** Williams & Reeves *In Double Harness* 8 When racing was developed by the aid of the 'machine'. **1900** J. Scott *Tales Colonial Turf* 218 The bookmakers would not pay 30–1 as the machine is doing.

5. *Mech.* Any instrument employed to transmit force, or to modify its application. ***simple machine***: one in which there is no combination of parts, e.g. a lever, or any other of the so-called *mechanical powers*. ***compound machine***: one whose efficiency depends on the combined action of two or more parts.

[An artificial extension of sense 4, the notion of complexity implied in that sense being treated as unessential.]

1704 J. Harris *Lex. Techn.*, *Machine*, or *Engine*, in Mechanicks, is whatsoever hath Force sufficient either to raise or stop the Motion of a Body... *Simple Machines* are commonly reckoned to be Six in Number, viz. the Ballance, Leaver, Pulley, Wheel, Wedge, and Screw... *Compound Machines*, or *Engines*, are innumerable. **1831** Lardner *Hydrost.* ii. 10 By this singular power of transmitting pressure, a fluid becomes, in the strictest sense of the term, a machine. **1839** G. Bird *Nat. Philos.* 60 By means of these simple machines it must not be supposed that we beget or increase force. **1866** Dk. Argyll *Reign Law* ii. (ed. 4) 90 A man's arm is a machine.

6. *Theatr.* [= L. *machina*.] A contrivance for the production of stage-effects. Also in *pl.* = *stage-machinery*. *Obs.* exc. in occasional allusion to the ancient stage.

1658 *Hist. Q. Christina* 225 This play succeeded very well, especially for the admirable beauty and finenesse of the machins. **1681** Cotton *Wond. Peak* (ed. 4) 9 Like a Machine which, when some god appears, We see descend upon our Theaters. **1687** Settle *Refl. Dryden* 56 The Poet if he had thought on't, might have introduced her by a Machin. **1712–14** Pope *Rape Lock* iv. 46 Now lakes of liquid gold, Elysian scenes, And crystal domes, and angels in machines. **1720** De Foe *Duncan Campbell* (1895) 177 She..descended into that room full of company, as a miracle appearing in a machine from above. **1741** Betterton *Eng. Stage* i. 9 Adorned..with all the Machines and Decorations, the Skill of those Times could afford. *a* **1845** Hood *Vauxhall* vii, Time's ripe for the Ballet, Like bees they all rally Before the machine! **1873** Browning *Red Cott. Nt.-cap* 124 Forth steps the needy tailor on the stage, Deity-like from dusk machine of fog.

b. [A Gallicism.] A painting of large size.

1932 R. Fry *Characteristics French Art* iii. 62 He was too poor in spirit ever to try, himself, to paint one of the big machines which made one an historical painter. **1965** *Listener* 28 Oct. 672/1 The small pictures and the *machines* appear to be the different sides of the same coin.

7. Hence in literary use: A contrivance for the sake of effect; a supernatural agency or personage introduced into a poem; the interposition of one of these.

1678 Dryden *Œdipus* Epil. 10 Terror and pity this whole poem sway; The mightiest machines that can move a play. **1693** —— *Juvenal* Ded. (1697) 13 His [Milton's] Heavenly Machines are many, and his Human Persons are but two. **1700** —— *Fables* Pref., Wks. (Globe) 498 Virgil never made use of such machines, when he was moving you to commiserate the death of Dido. **1705** Addison *Italy* 425 The Apparition of Venus comes in very properly..for without such a Machine..I can't see how the Heroe could..leave Neoptolemus triumphant. **1712** —— *Spect.* No. 351 ⁋5 The changing of the Trojan fleet into Water-Nymphs..is the most violent Machine of the whole Æneid. **1713** Steele *Guardian* No. 130 ⁋20, I come now to consider the machines; a sort of beings that have the outside and appearance of men, without being really such. **1715** Pope *Iliad* I. Pref. B4b, The Marvelous Fable includes whatever is supernatural, and especially the Machines of the Gods. **1716** Lady M. W. Montagu *Let. to Pope* 14 Sept., The story of the opera..gives opportunities for a great variety of machines. **1727** Pope, etc. *Art of Sinking* 120 [Recipe] for the Machines; Take of deities, male and female, as many as you can use. **1756–82** J. Warton *Ess. Pope* (ed. 4) I. iv. 230 These machines are vastly superior to the allegorical personages of Boileau and Garth. **1765** H. Walpole *Otranto* (ed. 2) Pref., The actions, sentiments, conversations, of the heroes and heroines of ancient days were as unnatural as the machines employed to put them in motion. **1774** Warton *Hist. Eng. Poetry* III. xxiii. 83 It has nothing, except the machine of the chime, in common with Fabyll's Ghoste. **1897** W. P. Ker *Epic & Romance* 36 The episodes of Circe, of the Sirens, and of Polyphemus, are machines.

8. orig. *U.S.* The controlling organization of a political party. Hence applied, with disparaging emphasis, to organizations of more or less similar character in England. Also *transf.*

1876 H. V. Boynton in *N. Amer. Rev.* CXXIII. 327 In a word he encountered the combinations inside politics,—the machine. **1884** *L'pool Mercury* 18 Feb. 5/5 An election which gives to Lord Randolph Churchill the practical control of the Conservative electioneering machine. **1884** *Tit-Bits* 28 June 164/3 The Business Machine was furious. He said that [etc.]. **1888** Bryce *Amer. Commw.* II. iii. lxvi. 498 The officials..in whose gift this patronage lies place it at the disposal of the leaders of the Machine. Now there are three Machines in New York; two Democratic, because the Democratic party..is divided into two factions.., and one Republican. **1890** *Review of Rev.* II. 602/1 His followers in Ireland, the men of the machine, the members whom he nominated to their constituencies,..set about making noisy demonstrations in his favour. **1892** *Boston* (Mass.) *Jrnl.* 29 Nov. 3/1 (*heading*) The Machine Drops Senator Wm. S. McNary. **1901** *N. Amer. Rev.* Feb. 255 The Nationalist Party..are working the machine with unflagging energy. **1941** *Ann. Reg. 1940* 281 Britain unaided could not hold out against the spectacular German machine. **1942** *R.A.F. Jrnl.* 18 Apr. 13 It dared to oppose the Nazi war machine. **1948** P. D. Whitting in M. Beloff *Hist.* xvi. 338/1 Hitler, backed by a finely organized propaganda machine, could rouse the German nation to frenzied hatred of one country after another. **1965** *New Statesman* 7 May 706/1 To some people who have observed the scope and method of operations at Transport House, the question is not simply one of finding new custodians to mind the party machine. It is whether

that machine ought not to be taken apart and entirely reconstructed. **1972** *Guardian* 28 Oct. 13/4 The Labour machine had failed to pick up..the magnitude of the swing towards Cyril Smith. **1973** *Black Panther* 20 Oct. 17/3 The 'Miracle Mets'..surprised everyone by..swamping the 'Big Red' Cincinnati machine in the National League playoffs.

9. *attrib.* and *Comb.* **a.** simple attributive, as (sense 3) ***machine aesthetic, art, form, sculpture***; (sense 4) ***machine-action, -drill, -electricity, -horse, house, part, -power, -process, -room, -strap***; (sense 4 b) ***machine embroidery, lace, stitch***; (sense 4 d) ***machine-society***; (sense 8) ***machine candidate, party, -politician, -politics, power***; also ***machine-like*** adj.

1882 *Rep. to Ho. Repr. Prec. Met. U.S.* 593 The first of these conditions..is the strains of *machine action. **1945** H. Read *Coat of Many Colours* lxvii. 320 (*heading*) *Machine aesthetic. **1967** *Listener* 8 June 745/3 The Bauhaus is one thing, and the machine aesthetic..is another. **1973** *Times* 8 Aug. 10/4 In Léger's writings of the Twenties, it is not so much speed as the mass-produced object and the 'machine aesthetic' which occupies his attention. He saw the mass-produced object as the surfacing of an anonymous natural beauty of man-made forms independent of the self-conscious architect-designer. **1945** H. Read *Coat of Many Colours* lxvii. 323 What the critics of *machine art object to ..is not the fact of standardization, but rather the failure to reproduce certain qualities which they regard as essential to art. **1959** —— *Conc. Hist. Mod. Painting* vi. 213 [The Bauhaus] established for the first time a course in basic design that could serve as a training for the machine art of an industrial civilization. **1950** *Economist* 9 Dec. 1004/1 The two *machine candidates in New York City. **1877** Raymond *Statist. Mines & Mining* 292 The company has also determined to use *machine drills in the mine. **1843** Mill *Logic* III. ix. §2 (1856) I. 450 Common, or *machine electricity. **1960** G. Lewis *Handbk. Crafts* 66 The word 'machine', perhaps, makes this sort of embroidery sound dull and mechanical, but in actual fact *machine embroidery is decorative, exciting and creative, and has the added advantage that it is relatively quick to do. **1973** 'E. Ferrars' *Foot in Grave* vi. 104 I'll write and I'll paint, and I'll take up machine embroidery. **1909** W. R. Sorley *Interpretation of Evolution* 29 Instinct..impresses the *machine-form upon portions of the external world, as in the bird's nest or beaver's dam. **1955** P. Heron *Changing Forms of Art* 70 They are the crystallized thoughts of an inventor, but one who is aware of the beauty of the machine-forms which come to him out of the blue. **1860** Geo. Eliot *Mill on Fl.* I. viii, The depressed, unexpectant look of a *machine-horse. **1808** J. Steele *Let.* 31 Aug. in *Papers* (1924) II. 562, I bought them [*sc.* steelyards]..last winter for the use of my *Machine house. **1913** J. Vaizey *College Girl* xxvi. 360 'A neck arrangement', composed of the cheapest of *machine lace. **1698–1712** Shaftesbury *Philos. Regimen* (1900) 114 *Machine-like to be moved and wrought upon, wound up and governed exteriorly, as if there were nothing that ruled within or had the least control. **1880** L. Wallace *Ben-Hur* 117 The machine-like unity of the whole moving mass. **1932** E. Bowen *To North* xv. 151 Machine-like efficiency is not, she had been given to understand, compatible with high intelligence. **1944** *Horizon* Feb. 97 What society wants is the *machine-part which does the job. **1972** *Sci. Amer.* June 122/3 A distributor of bearings and similar machine parts. **1858** *N.Y. Daily Tribune* 1 Nov. 7/6 Both of these alleged swindlers are prominent members of the '*Masheen' party of the First Ward. **1888** Bryce *Amer. Commw.* III. iv. lxxix. 44 Committees are often formed in cities to combat the *Machine politicians in the interests of municipal reform. **1893** *Times* 26 Apr. 9/5 Irishmen exhibit a faculty for assimilating the baser elements in the *machine politics of America. **1924** *Army Q.* Oct. 38 The replacement of muscle-power by *machine-power is the cardinal fact in every department of material life. **1937** B. H. L. Hart *Europe in Arms* xxiii. 312 As was inevitable, machine-power overcame an ill-equipped opponent. **1951** S. Spender *World within World* v. 284 The new phase of domination, and threat by machine-power politics. **1968** *Brit. Med. Bull.* XXIV. 189/1 The first industrial revolution is largely the history of enlisting machine power in the performance of many thousands of tasks. **1935** *Burlington Mag.* July 48/2 One familiar with *machine-processes. **1970** *New Scientist* 12 Mar. 513 The ultimate comment on technology came from the American artist Tinguely who built *machine-sculptures that could be exhibited only once—because they destroy themselves. **1757** Mrs. Griffith *Lett. Henry & Frances* (1767) I. 8 When I am confined to such *machine society..I fancy I am got into Powell's commonwealth. **1934** Webster, *Machine stitch. **1964** *McCall's Sewing* vii. 98/2 Use a fine machine-stitch..and a fine machine needle. **1858** Simmonds *Dict. Trade*, **Machine-strap maker*, a manufacturer of leather and other connecting bands.

b. objective, as ***machine-breaking, -drawing, -maker, -minder, -monger, -operator, -overseer, -owner, -tender***.

1832 Miss Mitford *Village* Ser. v. 11 Several men had been arraigned together for *machine-breaking. **1887** D. A. Low *Machine Draw.* Pref., *Machine drawing is simply the application of the principles of descriptive geometry to the representation of machines. **1813** *Examiner* 26 Apr. 262/1 B. Roberts, Pudsey, Yorkshire, *machine-maker. **1858** Simmonds *Dict. Trade*, *Machine-maker*..a constructive builder, who designs or supplies machines..to order. **1835** Ure *Philos. Manuf.* 213 From the hand-openers the flax is carried to the heckling machines. Young boys, called *machine-minders,..tend them. **1876** J. Gould *Letterpress Printer* (1893) 130 The machine-minder must examine every sheet for some time. **1840** Gen. P. Thompson *Exerc.* (1842) V. 9 Every man is a *machine-monger when the question is of himself. **1896** *Indianopolis Typogr. Jrnl.* 16 Nov. 407 The man is a *machine-operator on a city daily. **1899** *Daily News* 23 May 10/6 Letterpress *machine overseer..seeks permanency. **1817** Cobbett *Wks.* XXXII. 363 Violences against *machine owners. **1890** *Spectator* 8 Feb., The Emperor..forgets the *machine-tenders altogether.

c. instrumental, with sense 'by or with a machine', esp. in contradistinction to what is done by hand, as ***machine-driller, -knitter, -printer; machine-darning, -drilling, -knitting, -moulding, -printing, -production, -riveting, -stitching, -switching; machine-closed, -coated, -cut, -divided, -driven, -finished, -generated, -ginned, -glazed, -knitted, -made, -planed, -printed, -processable, -readable, -ruled, -set, -sewed, -stitched, -tooled, -welted, -wrought*** adjs.; ***machine-darn, -knit, -mould*** vbs.

1862 *Catal. Internat. Exhib.* II. xxvii. 55 *Machine-closed uppers. **1963** R. R. A. Higham *Handbk. Papermaking* ix. 228 To the papermaker, the term **machine-coated* signifies a paper which has been coated on the paper machine as an integral part of the papermaking process. To the printer, however, machine-coated means a class of paper. **1897** *Daily News* 29 Mar. 8/7 A supply of large files..to be hand cut, *machine cut, or partly hand and partly machine cut. **1900** *Ibid.* 2 Nov. 9/1 Machine-cut tobacco is affected adversely by the heat engendered. **1932** D. C. Minter *Mod. Needlecraft* 182/2 This type of tear may also be *machine-darned. *Ibid.* 177/2 *Machine-darning is suitable for table-linen. **1967** E. Short *Embroidery & Fabric Collage* i. 17 (*caption*) Motif on net with machine darning and cut work. **1902** Marshall *Metal Tools* 7 A *machine-divided steel rule. **1906** *Westm. Gaz.* 11 Jan. 3/1 The wages of *machine-drillers on the surface are 10s. a day. **1902** *Westm. Gaz.* 13 Oct. 7/3 Fine dust given off during the *machine-drilling operations. **1901** *Daily Chron.* 29 May 3/7 A *machine-driven vehicle naturally needs restrictions that do not apply to horse-driven vehicles. **1892** W. W. Greener *Breech-Loader* 52 The machine-made and *machine-finished gun may be distinguished: First, by [etc.]. **1960** *Gloss. Paper, Stationery* (*B.S.I.*) 17 *Machine-finished* (*M.F.*) *paper*, paper treated mechanically on a paper-machine to obtain a smoother and more uniform appearance on both sides than on the unfinished paper. **1973** S. Jennett *Making of Bks.* (ed. 5) xi. 182 Machine-finished Papers (or M.F.) have the normal finish of the paper-making machine. The surface is moderately smooth and shiny, but not glossy. **1961** F. Kaufman *Electronic Data Processing & Auditing* vii. 117 The loss of a *machine-generated decision is surely no worse than the failure of careless or overburdened people to make such decisions. **1883** *Times* 27 Aug. 9/6 Fine *machine-ginned Broach [cotton]. **1914** *Machine-glazed [see *M.G.* s.v. M 5]. **1959** *Gloss. Packaging Terms* (*B.S.I.*) 66 *Machine glazed* (*M.G.*) *paper or board*, paper or board which has had one side made smooth and glossy by drying on a heated, polished metal cylinder, forming part of the drying section of the machine. The other side remains relatively rough. **1962** F. T. Day *Introd. to Paper* iv. 44 The M.G. high-speed single-cylinder paper making machine illustrated here is a standard type of equipment employed in the mill for making thin machine glazed papers. A popular name for the M.G. or cylinder machine is the 'Yankee'. **1927** T. Woodhouse *Artificial Silk* 83 Enormous lengths were *machine-knitted into hose and half-hose. *Ibid.* 79 The utilization of artificial silk yarn for hand-knitted and machine-knitted articles. *Ibid.* 83 If a *machine-knitter does not wind the yarns in his own mill, he can have them supplied in the form of bottle bobbins. **1886** *Family Friend* Jan. 87/1 *Machine-knitting. **1927** T. Woodhouse *Artificial Silk* 86 In machine-knitting several courses are formed simultaneously. **1858** Greener *Gunnery* 431 Enfield *machine-made arms. **1899** *Daily News* 27 Nov. 3/1 Above the level of what are known in America as 'machine-made plays'. **1922** *Encycl. Brit.* XXX. 36/1 By 1915–6 cast-iron cylinders were cast from metal patterns and *machine-moulded. **1888** *Lockwood's Dict. Mech. Engin.* 217 **Machine-moulding*,..embraces the moulding of wheels and ordinary work by the aid of special machines. **1949** F. Bowers *Princ. Bibliogr. Descr.* x. 355 It seems necessary for the purposes of descriptive bibliography to draw a chronological line after which the methods of description for *machine-printed books will in general hold. **1963** *Times Lit. Suppl.* 26 Apr. 312/1 Machine-set and machine-printed books. **1909** *Westm. Gaz.* 24 Sept. 8/1 An old man.. described as a *machine-printer. **1825** T. C. Hansard *Typographia* 714 *Machine printing will..be only applicable to works of extensive sale. **1892** A. Powell *Southward's Pract. Printing* (ed. 4) liii. 467 (*heading*) Some difficulties in machine printing. **1897** *Chiswick Press* 4 They have obtained..greater facilities for Machine Printing. **1972** P. Gaskell *New Introd. Bibliogr.* 260 Inks for machine printing differed little from those for the hand-press period. **1967** Cox & Grose *Organiz. Bibliogr. Rec. by Computer* vii. 185 The B.N.B. *machine-processable records. **1971** J. B. Carroll et al. *Word Frequency Bk.* p. ix, Machine-processable data for lexicography. **1898** J. A. Hobson *John Ruskin* ix. 217 The 'driving' tendency of modern *machine-production. **1931** L. Watt *Future of Capitalism* iv. 42 This 'dilemma' of technological unemployment (unemployment resulting from the development of machine-production) would..face any form of economic organisation. **1961** *Times* 30 Oct. (Computer Suppl.) p. ix/6 The three basic types of *machine-readable document. **1971** *Computers & Humanities* V. 301 To collect in machine-readable form a million-character corpus of modern vernacular literature. **1888** *Lockwood's Dict. Mech. Engin.* 217 **Machine-riveting*, riveting performed by a single application of steady pressure at the same instant upon the tail and the head of a rivet. **1878** Sala in *Gentl. Mag.* May 565 Much of his [G. Cruikshank's] ..foreground work was..'*machine-ruled', instead of being free-handed. **1908** Kipling *Lett. of Travel* (1920) 154 The brittle pulp-paper, the *machine-set type, are all as standardised as the railway cars of the Continent. **1967** Karch & Buber *Offset Processes* iii. 47 The layout man may choose to use proofs (also called proof-press prints). These proofs may be hand-set, machine-set or both. **1900** *Daily News* 19 May 6/5 White silk *machine-stitched in a pattern. **1899** *Ibid.* 28 Oct. 7/3 The coatbodice has *machine-stitching all round the outlines. **1922** Glazebrook *Dict. Appl. Physics* II. 834/1 Several types of *machine switching or automatic exchange systems have been devised, but in each of them the principle is to move the terminal of the calling line to that of the called line, which is fixed. **1950** J. Atkinson *Herbert & Procter's Telephony* II. i. 1/1 The idea of automatic or machine switching is by no means new. **1962** *Times* 3 Mar. 11/3 Hook-making..is a high-speed *machine-tooled operation. **1895** *Daily News* 16 Mar. 6/5 *Machine-welted work. **1867** W. Felkin (*title*) A History of the *Machine-Wrought Hosiery and Lace Manufactures.

10. Special combs.: **machine age**, a name given to an era notable for its extensive use of mechanical devices; also *attrib.*; **machine-bolt**, a bolt with a thread, and a square or hexagonal head (Knight 1884); **machine-boy**, a boy who attends to a machine; **machine code**, a code (code *sb.*[1] 3 b or 3 c) prepared by or for the use of a machine; *spec.* = *machine language*; so, ***machine-coded*** adj.; †**machine-driver**, the driver of a mail-coach; **machine finish**, a moderately smooth finish that paper has after leaving the machine on which it was made (see quots. 1937, 1960); **machine-head**, a head for a double-bass or guitar, having worms and pinions, instead of pegs, for tightening the strings; **machine-holder** (see quot.); **machine-hours**, hours during which a machine operates; **machine instruction** *Computers*, an instruction (instruction 4 c) in a machine language; **machine language** *Computers*, a language (language *sb.* 1 d) that a particular computer can handle or act on directly, without further translation; **machine-man**, one who works a machine (esp. a printing-machine); also, a manager of the political machine (see 8), a 'wire-puller'; **machine-oriented** *a. Computers*, (of a computer language) devised in the light of the requirements of a particular kind of computer; **machine-pistol**, a submachine gun; **machine proof** = *press-proof* (press *sb.*[1] 16 b); **machine-room** *Printing*, the room in which printing presses are operated; **machine-ruler**, a machine for ruling lines on paper (Ogilvie, 1882); **machine-shop**, a workshop for making or repairing machines or parts of machines; also *attrib.*; **machine-time**, time during which a computer is in use; **machine-tool**, a machine for cutting or shaping wood, metals, etc., by means of a tool, esp. one designed for use in a machine-shop; **machine translation**, translation by a computer; **machine-twist** *U.S.*, a kind of silk twist, made especially for the sewing-machine (Knight *Suppl.* 1884); †**machine-vessel**, a fireship; **machine-whim** (see quot.); **machine word** see word *sb.*; **machine-work**, †(*a*) poetic 'machinery' (see sense 7) as represented in art; (*b*) work done by a machine, as distinguished from that done by hand, esp. with reference to printing..

1922 L. Mumford in H. E. Stearns *Civilization in U.S.* 11 These buildings..shall embody all that is good in the *Machine Age. **1934** H. Read *Art & Industry* I. i. 6 Has he [*sc.* the artist] any function in a machine-age society? **1967** Singha & Massey *Indian Dances* i. 36 Shaivism itself, under the impact of the new materialistic machine age had lost its religious fervour. **1875** Southward *Dict. Typogr.*, **Machine-boy*, a boy engaged in the machine-room for laying-on and taking-off the sheets. **1954** *First Gloss. Programming Terminol.* (Assoc. Computing Machinery) 4 *Computer code* (**Machine code*), the code representing the operations built into the hardware of the computer. **1958** G. Greene *Our Man in Havana* I. iv. 45 Of course it's [a book-code] not so hard to break as a machine-code. **1971** Lowe & Hidden *Computer Control in Process Industries* v. 108 The machine language, or machine code,..is the repertoire of instructions for the basic operations that the central processor is designed to perform. **1964** F. L. Westwater *Electronic Computers* ix. 144 A special routine called a 'compiler'..produced an efficient *machine-coded program from the pseudo-code. **1893** *Machine-driver [see 1 b]. **1907** Cross & Bevan *Text-bk. Paper-Making* (ed. 3) x. 270 The mill or *machine finish is one which can be varied within wide limits. **1937** E. J. Labarre *Dict. Paper* 170/1 Machine finish is the surface of the paper (1) as it leaves the last drying cylinder of the paper machine; (2) as it leaves the calenders immediately following the paper-machine. **1960** G. A. Glaister *Gloss. Bk.* 245/1 *Machine-finish*, paper made smooth, but not glossy, by receiving the normal finish of a Fourdrinier paper-making machine which completes its process by passing the paper over heated drums and through steel calendering rolls. These smooth the surface to the required degree. **1844** G. Dodd *Textile Manuf.* vii. 213 He lets them [lace making machines] out at so much a day to middlemen called '*machine-holders'. **1921** Eggleston & Robinson *Business Costs* 377 Direct labor and overhead... *Machine Hours 30. **1966** A. Battersby *Math. in Managem.* vii. 173 For the sake of simplicity, we may choose to use a measure such as 'idle machine-hours', on the grounds that a reduction in idleness will automatically bring down operating costs. **1956** *Machine instruction [see language *sb.* 1 d]. **1970** Machine instruction [see microprogrammer]. **1949**, etc. *Machine language [see language *sb.* 1 d]. **1967** A. Hassitt *Computer Programming* ii. 41 There are a series of programs..which accept Fortran statements as data and produce machine language statements as output. *Ibid.*, Although there are many different machine languages, many concepts are common to all of these languages. Some of the common ideas are binary arithmetic, index registers, memory addresses, [etc.]. **1968** *Brit. Med. Bull.* XXIV. 192/1 The user prepared his program in a..computer language..which the computer itself translated into its own basic machine language. **1876** J. Gould *Letterpress Printer* (1893) 125 My remarks must be taken as those of a workman,..not as those of a *machine-

man proper. **1883** *Nation* 21 June 520/3 The Republican Machine men are in possession of the regular party organization. **1890** *Daily News* 17 Feb. 3/3 For the last ten years I have been employed as machine man at the London and Tilbury Railway Works. **1897** *Literature* 13 Nov. 124/1 The 'machine-men' of the printing-houses of Edinburgh. **1901** *Daily Chron.* 10 Sept. 9/7 Pork and Beef Butcher.—Young man wants Situation as machineman. **1967** D. WILSON in Wills & Yearsley *Handbk. Managem. Technol.* iii. 47 These programs are often referred to as problem-oriented languages, as opposed to the lower-level assembly or auto-coder languages which are more commonly used at present and are *machine-oriented. **1970** O. DOPPING *Computers & Data Processing* xiv. 227 When problem-oriented programming languages..are used instead of simple machine-oriented languages, programming time is often reduced drastically. **1940** *Illustr. London News* CXCVI. 786 (*caption*) Much has been heard of the *machine-pistols used by Nazi parachutists. **1962** *Spectator* 1 June 710/1 A Police State that tries to stop runaway schoolboys with machine-pistol fire. **1973** M. WOODHOUSE *Blue Bone* xiv. 153 A man with red hair and a machine pistol. **1951** S. JENNETT *Making of Bks.* vi. 88 The *machine proof ..is pulled immediately before the forme goes on the press, or while it is actually on the press. **1961** T. LANDAU *Encycl. Librarianship* (ed. 2) 233/1 *Machine revise*, a proof printed when the forme is on the printing machine... Also called machine proof. **1833** *Penny Mag.* Monthly Suppl. Nov.-Dec. 510/1 We will conduct our readers to Mr. Clowes's printing establishment, where there are more printing machines at work than at any other office in the world... Upon entering the *machine-room the stranger will naturally feel distracted by the din of so many wheels and cylinders in action. **1904** *Brit. Printer* Feb. 6/2 One of the strong points of the establishment—its machine-room accommodation—is examined. **1946** V. S. GANDERTON in H. Whetton *Pract. Printing & Binding* x. 128 (*caption*) A fine example of a modern letterpress machine room. **1972** P. GASKELL *New Introd. Bibliogr.* 294 The machine-room overseer, an important man who ran the hand-press department as well as the machine-room. **1827** *Aurora* (Philadelphia) 25 July 1/3 A *Machine Shop, from 60 to 70 feet long and 20 feet wide, two stories high. **1856** EMERSON *Eng. Traits, Wealth* Wks. (Bohn) II. 70 'Tis a curious chapter in modern history, the growth of the machine-shop. **1898** *Engineering Mag.* XVI. 38 A pile of machine-shop scrap containing 149 different things. **1968** *New Scientist* 12 Sept. 548 In my environment the majority of user time, not *machine time but user time, is spent in writing and running short programs. **1973** *Computers & Humanities* Mar. 198 The operation that consumes most machine time is the verification of Rule II, where we test that each sentence is contained in the union of at most three others. **1861** W. FAIRBAIRN *Address to Brit. Assoc.* 64 It is to the exactitude and accuracy of our *machine tools that our machinery of the present time owes its smoothness of motion and certainty of action. **1949** W. WEAVER in Locke & Booth *Machine Transl. of Lang.* (1955) 20 Mr. Max Zeldner, in a letter to the *Herald Tribune* on June 13, 1949 [*published* June 26], stating that the most you could expect of a *machine translation of fifty-five Hebrew words which form the 23d Psalm would start out Lord my shepherd no I will lack [etc.]. **1956** *Nature* 7 Jan. 1/1 Dr. Booth is optimistic that even the problems of machine-translation of literary work may prove less complex than they at present appear. **1960** E. DELAVENAY *Introd. Machine Transl.* 123 Machine translations today are still very imperfect. **1968** J. LYONS *Introd. Theoret. Ling.* iv. 159 The automatic analysis of written texts for the purpose of machine-translation. **1694** LUTTRELL *Brief Rel.* (1857) III. 342, 2 *machine vessells, wherein were lodged some 100 chests of powder to tear up all before it. **1811** *Self Instructor* 587 Vessels of war are..a ketch, a machine-vessel. **1860** *Eng. & For. Mining Gloss.* (Cornwall Terms), **Machine-whim*, a rotary steam-engine employed for winding. **1711** SHAFTESB. *Charact.* (1737) III. 384 The separate ornaments, independent both of figures and perspective; such as the *machine-work or divinitys in the sky. **1861** B. HEMYNG in H. Mayhew *London Labour* (1862) Extra vol. 222/1 She then supported herself and her child by doing machine-work for a manufacturer. **1867** A. D. WHITNEY *Summer in L. Goldthwaite's Life* i. 10 No machine-work, but all real dainty finger-craft.

machine (məˈʃiːn), *v.* Also 5–6 **machyne.** [In early use a. F. *machiner*, ad. L. *māchinārī*: see MACHINATE *v.* In later use f. MACHINE *sb.*]

†**1. a.** *trans.* To contrive, plot; also, to resolve *that*. **b.** *intr.* To plot, devise schemes (*against* a person). *Obs.*

c **1450** *St. Cuthbert* (Surtees) 523 Sho..machynd in hir mynde for thy þat it was best for hir to fly. **1456** SIR G. HAYE *Law Arms* (S.T.S.) 64/6 The traytouris that had his dede machynit had ordanyt [etc.]. **1484** CAXTON *Curial* 12 Somme shal machyne by somme moyen to deceyue the. **1530** PALSGR. 616/1 He hath not onely machyned agaynst me to make me lese my good, but also he hath machyned my dethe. **1679** GAVAN in *Speeches Jesuits* 7 As I never in my life did machine, or contrive either the deposition or death of the King.

2. a. *trans.* To form, make, or operate upon (e.g. to cut, engrave, make, and esp. to print, to sew) by means of a machine. Also with *in*.

1878 SALA in *Gentl. Mag.* May 565 Some of the..plates.. seem to be..machined. **1881** GREENER *Gun* 246 The work is fitted into slots machined under the body of breech-action. **1886** BESANT *Childr. Gibeon* II. xxv, Making shirts, machining men's coats [etc.]. **1892** *Times* 31 Dec. 12/4 A book put in type in America, and only 'machined' by them. **1894** J. E. DAVIS *Elem. Mod. Dressmaking* 47 Tacking is not strong enough to hold sleeves well to the arm-hole for machining-in. **1896** *Living Topics Cycl.* (N.Y.) II. 260, 5 [rifled guns] were well advanced, and the parts for the remainder were nearly all forged and some of them machined. **1901** *Census Schedule, Instructions*, Sewing machinists should name the article they machine—as Boot Machinist.

b. *absol.* To manufacture things by machinery.

1916 H. G. WELLS *Mr. Britling* I. i. 16 They had standardized and machined wholesale, while the British were still making the things one by one.

3. To place (a tree) on the transplanting machine.

1827 STEUART *Planter's G.* (1828) 247 It is a material consideration so to machine the Tree, as that its lee-side branches,..should, if possible, be uppermost on the pole.

4. *fig.* **a.** To manage, work (a project, etc.) like a machine. **b.** To furnish (a tale) with the machinery of a plot. **c.** To render mechanical; to treat as if machinery.

1881 H. LABOUCHERE in *Daily News* 22 Mar. 6/3 The paper was machined by your father. **1889** *Academy* 1 June 374/2 It is not, as a story, very cunningly machined. **1916** F. M. FORD *Let.* Sept. (1965) 72 The French Press..continues to blaze and coruscate about my gifts... Of course these salvos are a little machined by the French Govt. **1916** H. G. WELLS *Mr. Britling* I. ii. 67 The reality of life is adventure, not performance. What can be ruled about can be machined. **1919** J. L. GARVIN *Econ. Found. Peace* 183 As they drilled under arms or machined their Socialism. **1959** *Listener* 19 Nov. 868/2 'The new poets,' Apollinaire wrote in 1917, 'will one day machine poetry (*machiner la poésie*) as the modern age has machined the world.'

†**5.** *intr.* To appear, as a god, from a 'machine'; to serve the function of a poetic 'machine'. *Obs.*

1697 [see MACHINING *ppl. a.*].

Hence **maˈchined** *ppl. a.*

1891 R. BUCHANAN *Coming Terror* 149 Highly finished, perfectly machined. **1891** *Wheeling* 25 Feb. 399 All sorts of lamps, bells, spanners, and machined parts. **1893** *Daily News* 13 June 5/6 The mechanically machined amendments not evoking any interest.

machineel, -elle: see MANCHINEEL.

machineful (məˈʃiːnfʊl). *nonce-wd.* [See -FUL 2.] As much as a machine will hold.

1890 'R. BOLDREWOOD' *Miner's Right* (1899) 66/2 Enough to complete a machineful of wash-dirt.

machine-gun, *sb.* A mounted gun which is mechanically loaded and fired, delivering a continuous fire of projectiles. Also *fig.*, *attrib.*, and *Comb.*

Some more recent types of machine-gun can be fired from the hip and are adaptable for firing single shots.

1870 *Jrnl. R. United Service Inst.* XIV. 504 Machine Guns: The 'Gatling Battery'—The Agar and Claxton Guns—The French and Montigny Mitrailleurs. **1882** *Army & Navy Mag.* Dec. 195 Machine-guns, which have an effective range not differing materially from that of small arms, would ..have to advance with infantry. **1890** W. J. GORDON *Foundry* 26 We may as well say something here about the machine guns. **1906** *Westm. Gaz.* 4 Oct. 2/3 Motor-bicycles, those machine-gun terrors of the road. **1909** *Ibid.* 9 Dec. 5/1 Experiments carried out with the machine-gun fitted aeroplane. **1915** R. W. CAMPBELL *Private Spud Tamson* xix. 288 Z-r-r-p—Z-r-r-p—Z-r-r-p spat the machine-gun batteries behind the little knolls. **1919** 'BOYD CABLE' *Old Contemptibles* ix. 146 The steady postman's-knock *rat-tat-tat* of machine-guns. *Ibid.* xvi. 255 The rifle and machine-gun fire rose again. **1928** H. LASKI in *Holmes-Laski Lett.* (1953) II. 1077 They cross-examined me with machine-gun rapidity. **1937** KOESTLER *Spanish Testament* v. 104 Militiamen were frequently obliged to smoke out the machine-gun nests set up in the monasteries. **1941** *Ann. Reg. 1940* 154 [France] sent..5,000 machine-gun rifles. **1955** S. SPENDER *Coll. Poems 1928–53* 99 Machine-gun anger quickly scythed the grasses. **1970** *Toronto Daily Star* 24 Sept. 3/3 They put their machine-gun nests on roofs and in the rooms and gardens of private houses. **1972** 'E. LATHEN' *Murder without Icing* (1973) iii. 30 Convulsions on one level or another could be expected with..machine-gun rapidity. **1973** *Times* 14 Nov. 8/1 The Israelis..have reinforced their machinegun posts beside the road.

So **machine-gun** *v. trans.*, to turn a machine-gun on, to fire at with a machine-gun; **machine-gunning** *vbl. sb.*; **machine-gunner**, one who operates a machine-gun. Also *fig.*

1915 R. BROOKE *Let.* 29 Jan. (1968) 658 There's a good chance of my going to Hythe for a fortnight to learn machine-gunning. **1915** 'I. HAY' *First Hundred Thousand* xix. 279 The machine-gunner is a more or less accepted nuisance by this time. **1917** 'CONTACT' *Airman's Outings* 185 Other guerilla work is done by craft which..machine-gun whatever worth-while objects they spot. **1918** E. M. ROBERTS *Flying Fighter* 38 Whatever they saw was sure to be machine-gunned. **1930** J. B. PRIESTLEY *Angel Pavement* ii. 76 They sweep, lash, and machine-gun the streets with rain. **1942** *R.A.F. Jrnl.* 2 May 5 Our work was mainly bombing and machine gunning, to weaken the will of the enemy. *Ibid.* 16 May 21, I..maintained my course to machine-gun the decks. **1955** *Times* 25 June 6/3 He said that a conspiracy was hatched last November for a military revolt... The aim was to murder the President of the Republic through air bombardment or land action and to intimidate civilians by air bombing or machine-gunning the streets. **1967** B. PATTEN *Little Johnny's Confession* 17 The last young thigh.. machineguns you down. **1970** T. HUGHES *Crow* 24 The face Of a machine-gunner a long burst not long enough. **1972** *Daily Tel.* 1 June 2/8 This was followed by a machine-gunning of the Spanish Embassy on December 3. **1973** D. LEES *Rape of Quiet Town* vi. 102, I aimed at one of the machine-gunners.

maˈchineless, *a.* [f. MACHINE *sb.* + -LESS.] That does not use or does not require a machine or machines. Spec. ***machineless waving*** (see quot. 1966); also *ellipt.* as *sb.*

1909 in WEBSTER. **1926** *United Free Ch. Miss. Rec.* May 201/1 It was a machineless age, the world moved at a slow pace. **1933** *Catholic Med. Guardian* Apr. 90 Catholic Law Associations..advocate the return to machineless handicrafts. **1942** *Horizon* July 58 One of Thelma's ladies was settin' over yonder..gitting a machineless. **1966** J. S. COX *Illustr. Dict. Hairdressing* 93/1 *Machineless waving*, (1) Hot permanent waving in which the required heat is either generated chemically in a pad applied to the hair, or by means of a pre-heated metal clamp. (2) Cold Permanent Waving.

machiner (məˈʃiːnə(r)). [f. MACHINE *sb.* + -ER[1].]

1. One who works a machine **a.** for transplanting trees; **b.** for sewing; a sewing-machine.

1827 STEUART *Planter's G.* (1828) 246 Whom [*sc.* the planter] I have ventured to denominate the Machiner... The Machiner..at once ascertains the side, upon which the Tree can be best laid along the pole. **1888** *Times* 20 Sept. 7/4 Mr. M. never knew a good machiner who would work for less than six shillings a day.

2. A horse employed to draw a 'machine' or vehicle; a post-, stage-, coach-, or van-horse.

1835 SIR G. STEPHEN *Adv. Search Horse* xv. (1841) 210 Machiners, as they are called, that is, post-horses, or stage-horses. **1854** KNIGHT *Once upon a Time* I. 156 Hence stage-coach horses were called 'Machiners'. **1857** MUSGRAVE *Pilgr. into Dauphiné* I. xiii. 293 The Poncheron horse..is.. the favourite 'machiner' in this part of the country. **1875** 'STONEHENGE' *Brit. Sports* II. III. i. §2. 518 The ordinary hunter..comprehends every variety between the one described above and the heavy machiner.

machinery (məˈʃiːnəri). Also 8 **machinary.** [f. MACHINE *sb.* + -ERY. Cf. F. *machinerie*.]

1. *Theatr.* and *literary.* †**a.** Stage appliances and contrivances. (Cf. MACHINE *sb.* 6.) *Obs.* exc. as in 2. **b.** The assemblage of 'machines' (MACHINE *sb.* 7) employed in a poem; supernatural personages and incidents introduced in narrative or dramatic poetry.

1687 WINSTANLEY *Lives Poets* 216 Vying with the Opera's of Italy, in the Pomp of Scenes, Marchinry [*sic*] and Musical performance. **1713** STEELE *Englishman* No. 52. 336 His Machinary is not a Jargon of Heathenism and Christianity. **1714** POPE *Rape Lock* Ded., The Machinery, Madam, is a term invented by the Critics, to signify that part which the Deities, Angels, or Dæmons, are made to act in a Poem. **1756–82** J. WARTON *Ess. Pope* (ed. 4) I. iv. 226 The insertion of the machinery of the sylphs..is one of the happiest efforts of judgment and art. **1799** HAN. MORE *Fem. Educ.* (ed. 4) I. 40 Those who most earnestly deny the immortality of the soul are most eager to introduce the machinery of ghosts. **1848** MRS. JAMESON *Sacr. & Leg. Art* (1850) 129 The angels always allowable as machinery, have here a particular propriety. **1861** O'CURRY *Lect. MS. Materials Irish Hist.* 242 The rules of these compositions permitted the introduction of a certain amount of poetic machinery.

2. Machines, or the constituent parts of a machine, taken collectively; the mechanism or 'works' of a machine or machines.

1731 in BAILEY vol. II. **1765** A. DICKSON *Treat. Agric.* (ed. 2) 219 The more machinery there is in any instrument, it is the more liable to be broken. **1776** ADAM SMITH *W. N.* I. xi. (1869) I. 256 In consequence of better machinery..a much smaller quantity of labour becomes requisite. **1803** *Med. Jrnl.* IX. 291 The communication is then formed and interrupted alternately by means of machinery. **1872** YEATS *Techn. Hist. Comm.* 180 Lock-making was undoubtedly the parent of much of our machinery. **1878** JEVONS *Prim. Pol. Econ.* 73 Spinning machinery, which can do an immense quantity of work compared with the number of hands employed.

b. *transf.* and *fig.*

1770 *Junius Lett.* xl. 206 *note*, Luttrell,..for whom the whole machinery is put in motion, becomes adjutant-general. **1788** GIBBON *Decl. & F.* l. (1846) V. 12 The nice and artificial machinery of the Greek and Roman republics. **1818** HALLAM *Mid. Ages* (1872) I. 461 The terrible and odious machinery of a police. **1855** MACAULAY *Hist. Eng.* xiv. III. 409 The whole machinery of government was out of joint. **1859** DARWIN *Orig. Spec.* iv. (1878) 65 She [Nature] can act on the whole machinery of life. **1876** FREEMAN *Norm. Conq.* V. xxiv. 464 Nor does the machinery of the court seem to have been greatly altered.

c. A system or a kind of machinery. *lit.* and *fig.*

1849 MACAULAY *Hist. Eng.* iii. I. 290 The beacons..were regarded rather as curious relics of ancient manners than as parts of a machinery necessary to the safety of the state. **1864** *Spectator* 438 The County franchise..is..a machinery for returning anybody the local peers choose to nominate. **1866** CARLYLE *Remin.* (1881) I. 138 Little..sea villages, with their ..rude innocent machineries.

3. *attrib.*

1887 *Daily News* 8 July 2/5 There is now..a machinery hall, an agricultural hall, and an armoury. **1898** *Engineering Mag* XVI. 100 A machinery installation..should be one source of energy.

maˈchine-wash, *v.* [f. MACHINE *sb.* + WASH *v.*] *trans.* To wash in a washing-machine. So **maˈchine-ˈwashable** *a.*

1960 *Farmer & Stockbreeder* 26 Jan. (Suppl.) 4/3 Some drip-drys can be successfully machine-washed. **1962** *N.Y. Post* 9 Oct. 54 Stretch-ever elastic made without rubber so you can machine-wash it. **1963** *New Yorker* 8 June 87 Guaranteed machine-washable. **1970** *Guardian* 28 May 11/5, I doubt if you would really machine-wash a child's walking shoe. *Ibid.* 16 June 13/2 In Welsh peasant cotton, machine washable. Jacket with inset waistband. **1975** *Country Life* 13 Mar. 673/3 Machine-washable continental quilts.

machining (məˈʃiːnɪŋ), *vbl. sb.* [f. MACHINE *v.* + -ING[1].] The action of MACHINE *v.* in various senses; also *attrib.*

1560 ROLLAND *Crt. Venus* II. 173 We Intend on vther machyning, In Musicall Airt, and diuers science. **1678**

DRYDEN *Kind Keeper* Prol. 8 Now our machining lumber will not sell, And you no longer care for Heaven or Hell. **1714** POPE *Let. to Blount* 27 Aug., Wks. 1737 I. 140 The machining part of poetry. **1827** STEUART *Planter's G.* (1828) 246 The Tree, being in readiness..for removal to its new site, the Machining of it (if I may be permitted the expression), is a work deserving of..particular attention. **1887** G. R. SIMS *Mary Jane's Mem.* 298 Many girls give up service..to work at shops and factories, and do machining. **1889** *Athenæum* 5 Oct. 453/2 The mistake..of supposing that anything will do for the sixpenny public—old type, bad paper, and slovenly machining. **1890** *Nature* 11 Sept., The sole machining..consisting in the formation of the bore and the drilling of the vent. **1891** *Econ. Jrnl.* I. 638 The machining of trousers and waistcoats in London is performed exclusively by women.

machining (məˈʃiːnɪŋ), *ppl. a.* [f. MACHINE *v.* + -ING².] That machines; †appearing, as a god, from a 'machine'; serving the function of a poetic 'machine'.

1697 DRYDEN *Æneid* Ded. (a) 3 b, If there had not been more Machining Persons than Humane in his Poem. *a* **1700** —— *Ovid's Art of Love* I. 120 The stage with rushes or with leaves they strew'd, No scenes in prospect, no machining god.

machinist (məˈʃiːnɪst). Also 8–9 *erron.* **machinest.** [orig. ad. F. *machiniste*, f. *machine*; but prob. re-formed on MACHINE *sb.* + -IST.]

1. One who invents, makes or controls machines or machinery; an engineer.

1706 PHILLIPS (ed. Kersey), *Machinist*, an Inventer, or Manager of Engines. *a* **1774** GOLDSM. *Surv. Exp. Philos.* (1776) II. 29 The machinist that directed the whole was at a loss, till a countryman taught him to shorten the cords by the affusion of water. **1788** in *Titles Patents* (1854) I. 302 A grant unto Andrew Meikle..engineer and machinist, of his new invented mill or machine for separating corn..from the straw. **1817** J. BRADBURY *Trav. Amer.* 311 Prohibiting the emigration of manufacturers and machinists to the United States. **1873** J. RICHARDS *Wood-working Factories* 81 An operator of wood machinery should be a machinist. Good operators are generally able to do ordinary repairs. **1895** *Booth's Life & Labour* V. 86 The machinist's shop, for planing, moulding, mortising, and turning, being now an *annexe* of every large joinery works.

b. esp. with reference to the theatre: one who constructs or manages the mechanical appliances used for the production of scenic effects. Now *rare.*

1739 CIBBER *Apol.* (1756) II. 67 A manager is to direct and oversee the painters, machinists, musicians, singers, and dancers. **1751** *Beau-philosopher* 227 The Machinest of the Opera and his Wife, who were her Relations. *a* **1800** STEEVENS *Note on Macb., Plays Shaks.* (1803) X. 324 Has the insufficiency of machinists hitherto disgraced the imagery of the poet? **1806–7** J. BERESFORD *Miseries Hum. Life* (1826) v. Concl., The accumulated crimes of author, composer, machinist. **1837** HALLAM *Hist. Lit.* I. I. iii. §107. 299 The decorations of this theatre must have appeared splendid... Nor was the machinist's art unknown. **1863** KIRK *Chas. Bold* I. 471 'Histories'—a kind of dramatic representation, in which the poet..was forced to follow the inspirations of the machinest.

c. *fig.* (Cf. MACHINE 4 *fig.*)

1799 G. WAKEFIELD in *Mem.* (1804) II. 409, [I] am no political machinist, nor was ever occupied in..the fraudulent intrigues of rival partisans.

2. One who works a machine, esp. a sewing-machine.

1879 *St. George's Hosp. Rep.* IX. 577 The laundress, the machinist, the signalman may be persons who work hard on scanty diet. **1888** *Times* 20 Sept. 7/4 A tailor's machinist. **1890** *Anthony's Photogr. Bull.* III. 349 Such..hardly rank as photographers—they are machinists. **1901** *Census Schedule, Instructions*, Such terms as..Machinist..must not be used alone. Sewing Machinists should name the article they machine.

3. A painter who works mechanically and by rule.

c **1801** FUSELI in *Lect. Paint.* v. (1848) 461 Though the first and greatest, Correggio was no more than a machinist. **1879** *Encycl. Brit.* IX. 687/1 Franceschini..is reckoned among those painters of the decline of art to whom the general name of 'machinist' is applied.

4. *U.S.* **a.** An engine-room artificer or attendant.

1890 in *Century Dict.*

b. A 'machine' politician (see MACHINE *sb.* 8).

1883 *Nation* 21 June 520/3 While the Machinists may be willing to nominate 'good men', the Independents are reminded of the fact that [etc.]. **1884** GOLDW. SMITH in *Contemp. Rev.* Sept. 320 The machine once fairly constructed and installed in power, the country is in the hands of the machinists. **1892** —— in *19th Cent.* Sept. 347 There was a struggle between the thoroughly 'machinist' section of the party and the section less loyal to the machine.

machinize (məˈʃiːnaɪz), *v.* [f. MACHINE *sb.* + -IZE.] *trans.* To make into a machine; to reduce to the form and semblance of a machine. Hence **machiniˈzation**, the action or process of making into a machine; the result of the process.

1856 EMERSON *Eng. Traits* iii. 41 The traveller..reads quietly the Times newspaper, which, by its immense correspondence and reporting, seems to have machinized the rest of the world for his occasion. **1890** *Jrnl. Educ.* 1 Aug. 423/2 [Their] admirable discipline and organization almost amount to Machinization.

machinofacture (məʃiːnəʊˈfæktjʊə(r), -tʃʊə(r)). [f. MACHINE *sb.* + -O + FACTURE.] The making of articles by machine; mechanization.

1903 L. F. WARD *Pure Sociol.* 26 The invention of tools, instruments, utensils, missiles, traps, snares, and weapons comes under this head, crowned by the era of machinofacture, artificial locomotion, and electric intercommunication. **1928** E. & C. PAUL tr. *Marx's Capital* xiii. 403 An organised system of working machines which are one and all set in motion by the transmitting mechanism from a central automaton, constitutes the fully developed form of machinofacture.

† **machinous,** *a. Obs. rare*⁻¹. [f. MACHINE *sb.* + -OUS. Cf. L. *māchinōsus*.] Cunningly contrived.

1633 MARMION *Fine Companion* v. ii. K 2 b, Ile..stand in his defence against all machinous Engines that shall bee planted for the battery of his wit and fortune.

machinule (ˈmækɪnjuːl). [As if ad. L. **māchinula*, dim. of *māchina* MACHINE *sb.*: see -ULE. Cf. F. *machinule* little machine.] A surveyor's instrument for obtaining a right angle.

In some mod. Dicts.

machir(r), varr. MACHAIR.

Machism (ˈmɑːkɪz(ə)m, -x-). [f. name of Ernst *Mach* (see MACH) + -ISM.] The theories of Ernst Mach, esp. his concept of empirio-criticism.

1927 D. KVITKO tr. *Lenin's Materialism & Empirio-Criticism* i. 69 In philosophical literature, writers of various tendencies have long since discovered the chief sin of Machism in spite of all its covering. **1949** P. FRANK *Mod. Sci. & its Philos.* x. 194 A logical contradiction exists only between a metaphysically conceived Machism, which is then subjective idealism, and a metaphysically conceived materialism, which accepts only matter as having existence. **1968** *Listener* 14 Nov. 648/3 Lenin was particularly incensed at Machism, and wrote his *Materialism and Empiriocriticism* against Mach and Avenarius. **1972** J. T. BLACKMORE *Ernst Mach* xiv. 214 If we may define 'pure Machism' as a phenomenalism hostile to atomism and theoretical physics, [etc.].

machismo (məˈtʃiːzməʊ). [Mexican-Sp., f. *mach(o* masculine + *-ismo* -ISM.] The quality of being MACHO; male virility, masculine pride. Also *attrib.*

1948 B. GRIFFITH *Amer. Me* 50 Machismo makes a boy swear big round oaths as a youngster. **1962** *Listener* 12 Apr. 649/1 The Mexican obsession with the concept of *machismo*, of masculinity. **1967** MCCORMICK & MASCAREÑAS *Compl. Aficionado* iii. 74 To bite the cape like an animal while folding it is false machismo. **1969** J. MANDER *Static Society* i. 56 The exaggerated masculinity, the famous *machismo*, of the Mexican. **1969** A. MARIN *Rise with Wind* v. 63 The bus driver..drove with Latin *machismo* through a tangle of narrow streets. *Ibid.* x. 125 A eunuch was without *machismo*, that peculiar combination of pride and virility that was the essence of manliness. **1971** *Guardian* 20 July 11/8 The contradictions, hypocrisy, and 'machismo' ideal in Puerto Rican culture. **1973** GAGNON & SIMON *Sexual Conduct* (1974) viii. 251 In the prison, toughness may substitute for intercourse as a measure of *machismo*.

machit, var. of MESQUITA².

Machivell, obs. form of MACHIAVEL.

Machmeter (ˈmɑːk-, ˈmækmiːtə(r), ˈmɑːx-). *Aeronaut.* Also **Mach meter.** [f. MACH + METER *sb.*³] An air-speed indicator that reads directly in Mach numbers.

1947 *Jrnl. R. Aeronaut. Soc.* LI. 734/1 An instrument known as a Mach meter, which indicates the Mach number of flight at any height, has already been developed and is now being fitted in certain high-speed aircraft. **1948** 'N. SHUTE' *No Highway* xii. 305 What was the Machmeter showing? **1958** 'P. BRYANT' *Two Hours to Doom* 118 He watched the Machmeter carefully as it moved up from point nine. **1964** J. E. D. WILLIAMS *Operation of Airliners* xx. 320 The indication of the Mach meter is not..instantaneously responsive to changes of engine thrust. **1975** L. J. CLANCY *Aerodynamics* iii. 32 A Machmeter..depends on measurements of total and static pressure by the pitot-static tube.

‖ **macho** (ˈmatʃo), *sb.*¹ *U.S.* [Sp. *macho* mullet.] The California mullet (see quot.).

1882 JORDAN & GILBERT *Fishes N. Amer.* (Bulletin U.S. Nat. Mus. no. 16) 403 *Mugil mexicanus* Steindachner. California Mullet; Macho..Pacific coast.

‖ **macho** (ˈmatʃo, ˈmɑːtʃəʊ, -æ-), *sb.*² and *a.* orig. *U.S.* [Mexican-Sp. *macho*, a male animal or plant; *adj.*, masculine, vigorous.] **A.** *sb.* A man; *spec.* a 'tough guy'; also, manliness, virility; an impression of this. **B.** *adj.* Ostentatiously or notably manly and virile.

1928 *Nation* 29 Feb. 233/2 The Machos (Americans) have taken El Chipote. *Ibid.* 11 Mar. 288/1 Here was I in their midst, a Macho Yankee Gringo, yet treated with consideration. **1951** *Sat. Rev. Lit.* 22 Sept. 15/2 In the Continente, men were supposed to be *machos*—males—and the women were supposed to bear their children, besides keeping their houses, and awaiting with patience their returns from the beds of their mixed-breed mistresses, or the battlefield. **1959** N. MAILER *Advts. for Myself* (1961) 19 Every American writer who takes himself to be both major and *macho* must sooner or later give a *faena* which borrows from the self-love of a Hemingway style. *Ibid.* 418 'Man, you can take care of yourself,' he said with glee. 'I don't know about that,' I answered, obeying the formal minuet of the *macho*. **1964** *Punch* 25 Mar. 444/1 A quality much prized in Mexico called *macho*, namely 'masculinity, virility'. **1964** S. BELLOW *Herzog* 157 Provided that he remain *macho* she would listen with glistening eyes. *Ibid.* 186 A province of the erotic Renaissance, in his *macho* garments. **1968** T. HOWARD *Black Light* xix. 163 The medical practitioner had to salvage a little of that all-important Latin-American *macho*—or manliness. **1972** *Publishers' Weekly* 23 Oct. 40/2 Reveals the *macho* of the sport for what it is: gridiron Darwinism, young athletes psyched out of their skulls. **1972** *New Yorker* 2 Dec. 159/3 And so we have separate cultures—black-*macho* movies and white-*macho* movies, equally impoverished, equally debased. **1975** *Ibid.* 14 July 65/1 She [*sc.* Greta Garbo] played opposite Clark Gable once, and the collision, though heated, didn't quite work; his macho directness—and opacity—reduced her from passionate goddess to passionate woman.

Machomet, -an, etc.: see MAHOMET, -AN, etc.

machopolyp (ˌmækəʊˈpɒlɪp). *Zool.* Also **-polype.** [f. Gr. μάχη fight + POLYP.] A zooid modified to serve a defensive function. (See quots.)

1883 W. S. DALLAS [tr. Von Lendenfeld] in *Ann. & Mag. Nat. Hist.* Oct. 250 Hamann explains the contents of the nematophore as a modified polyp, for which he proposes the designation 'machopolyp'. **1888** ROLLESTON & JACKSON *Forms Anim. Life* (ed. 2) 758 The structures known as nematophores, sarcothecæ, guard-polypes or macho-polyps [*sic*] which are confined to the..Plumularidæ. *Ibid.*, In the genus *Aglaophenia*..the machopolypes are usually disposed in a median and two lateral rows.

machoun, obs. form of MASON.

Machoun(d, obs. form of MAHOUND.

machree (məˈkriː). *Ir.* Also **Machree, ma chree, mochree.** [Ir.-Gaelic *mo chroidhe* (of) my heart, my dear.] My dear! Often in phr. ***Mother Machree.***

1829 G. GRIFFIN *Collegians* (ed. 2) II. xx. 92 Coax him, *ma chree, ma lanuv*, to gi' me the price o' the whiskey. *Ibid.* xxiv. 195 Oh, ma chree, m'asthora... What ails you? **1831** S. LOVER *Legends & Stories Ireland* p. xxiii, *Machree*, my dear. *Ibid.* 89 They wint to the wine-cellar, but, jew'l machree, they soon run back into his room. **1866** MRS. GASKELL *Wives & Daughters* II. xvi. 160 Thanks to you, little Molly—cuishla ma chree, pulse of my heart. **1918** N. MUNRO *Jaunty Jock* 159 'I could live on the berries.., I love them!' 'Doubtless, mochree,' would he answer her, laughing. **1918–19** *T. Eaton & Co. Catal.* Fall & Winter 389/2 Vocal Records... Mother Machree (Tenor). **1952** E. O'NEILL *Moon for Misbegotten* (1953) 132 In a minute you'll start singing 'Mother Machree'! **1970** M. KENYON *100,000 Welcomes* iv. 32 'You ever been to Ireland, Louie?'..'Every year... Ol' Mother Machree. And see the Micks get stoned.' **1973** *Listener* 1 Mar. 277/2 The Celtic Revival, born as it was of romantic nationalism—Mother Machree, Kathleen ni Houlihan and the whole pack of Gaelic Norns started calling to us.

macht, obs. Sc. f. MIGHT *sb.* and *v.*, MAUGH *sb.*

‖ **macht-politik** (ˈmaxtpɔlitiːk). Also **macht politik, machtpolitik.** [G., f. *macht* power, strength + *politik* policy, politics.] Power politics; strength as a potential factor to use in gaining a desired result.

1916 J. W. HEADLAM in Prince von Bülow *Imperial Germany* (rev. ed.) p. xxiii, Let us consider these things purely as a balance-sheet of loss and gain according to the undiluted principles of 'Macht-Politik'. **1940** *Horizon* May 326 Our leaders display not the qualities of *Macht-politik*, but the caution of the peaceful negotiator. **1958** *Times Lit. Suppl.* 11 Apr. 190/4 Indeed, the uniformly cynical *Machtpolitik* practised by every leading actor in the drama is profoundly depressing. **1964** P. MEADOWS in I. L. Horowitz *New Sociol.* II. 456 A space age revolution..in which the technological *Machtpolitik* of space conquest is also serving as a relatively moral equivalent for war. **1969** J. MANDER *Static Society* vi. 179 Naked *machtpolitik*..calls countervailing forces into being. **1973** *Times* 26 Oct. 20/1 The Chinese, in a gesture of fastidious distaste, abstained from the Security Council resolution on the reasonable grounds that although it was in effect a blatant example of Soviet-American *macht politik* it would be perverse to vote against it simply on that account.

Machumetan, -ist: see MAHOMETAN, -IST.

-machy, in actual use **-omachy** (ˈɒməkɪ), represents the ending -μαχία of certain Gr. sbs. with the general sense 'fighting, warfare', which are derivatives of adjs. in -μάχος with the general sense 'that fights'; the root is that of μάχεσθαι to fight, μάχη battle. Of the Eng. words with this ending, some are adoptions of actual Gr. words, as *logomachy*; others have been formed from Gr. elements on Gr. analogies, as *angelomachy*; the ending has not been employed in hybrid formations.

Machzor (ˈmɑːxzɔː(r)). Also **Machsor, Mahzor.** Pl. **-im.** [Heb. *maḥzor* a cycle.] In Jewish liturgy, the name for the books of prayers and readings used on various occasions in the liturgical year; usu. used *spec.* for the book of prayers for use at festivals.

1864 *Chambers's Encycl.* VI. 155 Later, the term [sc. *Siddurim*] was restricted to the weekday ritual, that for festivals being called *Machsor* (Cycle). **1883** *Encycl. Brit.* XV. 292/2 The *Maḥzor*, meaning prayer-book, is capable of division..into..the Smaller and the Larger. The Smaller Maḥzor contains ordinary prayers,..with the poetical

insertions and lessons from the Pentateuch and the Prophets... The Larger Maḥzor..embodies the ordinary prayers..for the whole year, and the lessons..for all feasts and fasts and..other occasions. **1891** M. FRIEDLÄNDER *Jewish Relig.* 391 The *Machzor*..or Prayer-book for the Holy-days contains numerous additions to the ordinary prayers. **1892** I. ZANGWILL *Childr. Ghetto* I. 276 Three sets of Machzorim, or Festival Prayer-Books. **1893** —— *Ghetto Tragedies* 66 She bent her eyes downwards on her neighbour's *Machzor*. The woman immediately pushed the prayer-book more towards Rebecca. **1973** *Synagogue Light* Sept. 42/2 The festival prayer book, the Machzor, is used during the High Holidays because many additional prayers not recited throughout the year are read on these days. **1974** *Encycl. Brit. Micropædia* VI. 505/3 *Maḥzor*.., originally a Jewish prayer book arranged according to liturgical chronology and used throughout the whole year... *Maḥzor* has come to mean the festive prayer book, as distinguished from the Jewish prayer book (Siddur) used on ordinary sabbaths and on week-days.

†**maci'ation.** *Obs.* [n. of action f. late L. *maciāre*, f. *maciēs* (see next): cf. EMACIATION.] 'A making lean' (Bailey 1727 vol. II).

‖**macies** ('meɪsiiːz). *Path.* [L.] Emaciation.
1801 *Med. Jrnl.* V. 65 The leading circumstance in diabetes is the macies. **1889** in *Syd. Soc. Lex.*

‖**macigno** (ma'tʃiɲɲo). *Geol.* [It. *macigno.*] An Eocene sandstone from the Italian Alps.
1832 DE LA BECHE *Geol. Man.* (ed. 2) 325 It [brown sandstone]..is one of the *macignos* of the Italians.

macilence ('mæsɪləns). *rare.* [as if ad. L. **macilentia*, f. *macilentus* MACILENT: cf. F. *macilence.*] Thinness, leanness.
1852 *Fraser's Mag.* XLV. 31 A certain gentility of style.. derived from the excessive macilence of his face and figure. **1889** *Syd. Soc. Lex.*, *Macilence*, extreme thinness of the whole or part of the body.

macilency ('mæsɪlənsɪ). Now *rare.* [See prec. and -ENCY.] Leanness. *lit.* and *fig.*
1632 SANDYS *Ovid's Metam.* XIV. *Notes* 484 His [*sc.* a Heron's] vigilant feare,..macilency, and pittiful screamings. **1633** T. ADAMS *Exp. 2 Peter* i. 6 These effects [of intemperance] are,..2. Macilency of grace. **1798** C. CROWTHER in Beddoes *Contrib. Phys. & Med. Knowl.* (1799) 350 From a state of extreme macilency [she] became obese. **1822** *Blackw. Mag.* XII. 525 On recollecting the macilency of the Parisians, he justly inferred, that double the number of French people might inhabit London.. without inconvenience.

macilent ('mæsɪlənt), *a.* Now *rare.* Also 6 **macilente.** [ad. L. *macilent-us* lean.] Lean, shrivelled, thin; **a.** in material sense.
1535 STEWART *Cron. Scot.* (1858) II. 512 With sic abundance of exceidand sweit, His cumlie cors..lene wes maid, and macilent. **1607** TOPSELL *Four-f. Beasts* (1658) 181 If they [goats] be fat, they are lesse venereous then being macilent or lean. **1647** LILLY *Chr. Astrol.* clxxvi. 747 Other Significators represent a body somewhat dry, macilent, erect and straight. **1683** W. HARRIS *Pharmacologia* xiv. 260 By reason of the exanguious macilent condition of the Junctures after Feavers. **1755** in JOHNSON. **1865** *Reader* 28 Jan. 93/2 George I. seated at supper with the tall, macilent, and ill-favoured Duchess of Kendal standing bolt upright behind him. **1871** M. COLLINS *Inn Strange Meetings* 4 Not Mephistophiles is macilenter Than the man.
b. *fig.* Of verses: Jejune, poor.
1624 BP. MOUNTAGU *Gagg* 252 That jejune and macilent conceit of Zwinglius. **1658** J. R. tr. *Mouffet's Theat. Insects* 898 Balm: concerning which Macer sang these macilent verses. **1702** J. HOWE *Liv. Temple* II. xi. Wks. 1724 I. 240 So copious an effusion of the Holy Spirit, as will..make it spring up, out of its macilent wither'd State, into its primitive Liveliness and Beauty.

McIntosh ('mækɪntɒʃ). Also **MacIntosh, Mackintosh.** The name of John *McIntosh* (b. 1777), Canadian farmer, used *attrib.* in **McIntosh Red** to designate a red-skinned variety of eating apple or the tree producing it, first developed on his farm. Also *absol.*
1878 *Canad. Horticulturalist* Mar. 42 Winter apples; here my list will be small, but I think reliable: Talman's Sweet, Pomme Grise, American Golden Russet, and McIntosh Red. **1908** *Busy Man's Mag.* Feb. 89 The First McIntosh Red Tree in Canada. **1910** L. WOOLVERTON *Canad. Apple Grower's Guide* 190 McIntosh [is] a very fine dessert apple for early winter use. **1932** [see DELICIOUS *a.* 2 b]. **1933** M. DE LA ROCHE *Master of Jalna* xii. 136 He extracted a large, perfectly shaped MacIntosh Red from his pocket. **1965** MRS. L. B. JOHNSON *White House Diary* 15 Jan. (1970) 221 Our best brands are Northern Spies and MacIntosh Reds. **1969** *New Yorker* 20 Dec. 76/2 Already on our six acres..we have planted..a MacIntosh apple. **1970** *Globe & Mail* (Toronto) 28 Sept. 5/2 (*caption*) Alison Loates..found a bright-red McIntosh was her fancy.

macintosh: see MACKINTOSH.

macis: obs. form of MACE *sb.*[2]

†**mack** *sb.*[1] *Obs.* Some game at cards.
1548 FORREST *Pleas. Poesye* 221 At ale howse too sitt, at mack or at mall. **1592** CHETTLE *Kind-Harts Dr.* F, Macke, Maw, Ruffe, Noddy, and Trumpe. **1602** WARNER *Alb. Eng.* IX. xlvi. 217 Hence arrant Preachers, humming out a common-place or two, With bad, ill, naught, Pope, pots, play, mack, keeping of fowle adoe.

mack (mæk) *sb.*[2] *Obs.* exc. *dial.* Also 6 **meke,** 9 **macks.** [An unmeaning word, suggested either by 'by *Mary*' or by 'by the Mass' (see MASS *sb.*[1]). Cf. 'by the matte' (Udall *Roister D.* IV. vii. 118), also MACKINS and dial. *megs.*] In the phrase *by* (*the*) *mack!* (also simply *mack!* as quasi-*int.*), an exclamatory form of asseveration.
c **1560** *Misogonus* IV. i. 55 (Brandl) Bith meke, Isbell. **1598** B. JONSON *Ev. Man in Hum.* III. iv, Humour? mack, I thinke it be so, indeed. **1599** *Sir John Oldcastle* (1600) C 4, Now by the macke, a prettie wench indeed. **1638** WHITING *Hist. Albino* 130 Is not my daughter Maudge as fine a mayd, And yet, by mack, you see she troules the bowle. **1664** COTTON *Scarron.* I. 105 By the Mack.

†**Mack** *sb.*[3] *Obs.* Variant of MAC[1]. Used contemptuously for: A Celtic Irishman. Also *attrib.*
[**1596** SPENSER *State Irel.* Wks. (Globe ed.) 677/1 The Oes and Macks, which the heads of the septs have taken to theyr names.] **1617** MORYSON *Itin.* II. 138, I cannot dissemble how confident I am, to beate these Spanish Dons, as well as euer I did our Irish Macks and Oes. **1681** LUTTRELL *Brief Rel.* (1857) I. 91 Another of these Mack Irish papists has sworn that [etc.]. *c* **1688** *New Letany* iii. in *Third Collect. Poems* 8/1 Who's Rid, and Impos'd on, by many a score Of Priests, Macks, and Footmen, his Q. and his Wh—.

mack (mæk), *sb.*[4] *slang.* Also **mac.** [Short for MACKEREL[2].] A pander.
1887 W. E. HENLEY *Villon's Straight Tip* ii. (F.), Fiddle, or fence, or mace, or mack. **1894** STEAD *If Christ came to Chicago* 372 The procurers, the souteneurs and the 'macs'. **1926** MAINES & GRANT *Wise-Crack Dict.* 11/1 *Mac*, man who lives off the earnings of a woman. **1931** G. IRWIN *Amer. Tramp & Underworld Slang* 125 *Mac*, a pander; a lover or associate of lewd women. No doubt from the French word for this class, 'maqereau'.., although the shorter word has been in use in America for years. **1950** BLESH & JANIS *They all played Ragtime* (1958) ii. 39 The dapper, foppish 'macks'..in their Stetsons, box-back coats, and St. Louis 'flat' shoes got their gambling stakes from the girls. **1972** T. KOCHMAN *Rappin' & Stylin' Out* 243 'Pimp', or 'mack man'..a person of considerable status in the street hierarchy, who, by his lively and persuasive rapping ('macking' is also used in this context), has acquired a stable of girls to hustle for him and give him money. **1973** *Washington Post* 21 Apr. D 7/2 Now comes 'The Mack', a movie about the rise and fall of a sweet pimp named Goldie.

mack (mæk), *sb.*[5] Also **mac.** A common abbrev. of MACKINTOSH 2 and 3.
1901 'R. ANDOM' *Troddles & Us & Others* xxi. 245 It rained pretty steadily... Murray and Wilks, having left their 'macs.' behind, were constrained to spend one solid day loafing about the..inn premises. **1902** *Captain* VII. 468/1 Who said you might wear my mackintosh?.. Suppose you give it up... Buck up. It looks like rain... Mack up, please. I want it. **1917** A. G. EMPEY *From Fire Step* 170 In front of the door stood an officer in a mack (macintosh). **1923** *Daily Mail* 12 Feb. 12 (Advt.), Girls' Mack Capes with Hoods... All guaranteed waterproof. **1929** GALSWORTHY *Roof* iii. 54 'Have we got to dress?'.. 'No; bung on your mack and shoes.' **1963** *Times* 15 May 14/6 Small knots of mac-clad farmers. **1973** A. BEHREND *Samarai Affair* viii. 85 Richardson slipped on his mack and went round to India buildings. **1974** D. WINSOR *Death Convention* ii. 10, I had dug my hands in my mac pockets.

Mack (mæk), *sb.*[6] [f. *Mack*, name of manufacturer.] The proprietary name of several types of heavy vehicle, as lorries, tractors, etc. Also *attrib.*
1913 *Hand Bk. Gasoline Automobiles* (U.S. Automobile Board of Trade) 165 (*caption*) Mack 2-ton truck. **1921** *Official Gaz.* (U.S. Patent Office) 4 Jan. 192/1 International Motor Company, New York, N.Y... Mack..[for] Motor-Trucks. Claims use since about Oct. 13, 1911. **1930** J. DOS PASSOS *42nd Parallel* v. 401 Charley..started to help clean the parts of the carburetor of a Mack truck. **1948** PARTRIDGE *Dict. Forces' Slang* 114 *Mack*, a ten-ton lorry. (Army.) **1959** E. K. WENLOCK *Kitchin's Road Transport Law* (ed. 12) 85/1 Mack type N.M. heavy artillery tractors may be used for snow ploughing, or grit or salt distribution on frosty roads, notwithstanding their excess width. **1962** *Times* 27 Nov. 13/3 A fleet of 'Macks'—snow-shifters. **1971** M. TAK *Truck Talk* 103 *Mack*, a popular, economical and long-wearing make of tractor, the one best known to the public... The Mack engine has a characteristic sound... The Mack trademark is a bulldog. **1972** MARSHALL & BISHOP *Lorries, Trucks & Vans* 123 No other name can surely be more autonomous with the US truck industry than Mack. 'Built like a Mack' is still a phrase used by Americans to signify something solid or sturdy. **1973** *Trade Marks Jrnl.* 13 June 1141/2 Mack... Commercial motor road vehicles and parts and fittings therefor..Mack Trucks, Inc..., Allentown, State of Pennsylvania, United States of America; manufacturers.

†**mack,** *a.* Also 5 **make,** 5, 9 **mak.** [a. ON. *mak-r* (found in compar. only). Cf. MACKLY *adv.*, and dial. *mackerly*, *mackly* adj., *mack-like*, *macky* seemly, etc.] **a.** Apt, convenient. **b.** Neat, tidy.
c **1440** *Promp. Parv.* 321/1 Make, or fyt, and mete (*MS. K.* mak, fyt, or esy), *aptus, conveniens.* **1825-80** JAMIESON, *Mack, mak*, neat, tidy; Roxb.

mack: see BLACK-MACK.

mack, obs. f. MAKE.

mackabaw, variant of MACCOBOY.

†**mackabroin.** *Obs. rare*[−1]. [Derived from *macabree*: see MACABRE.] An old hag.
1546 J. HEYWOOD *Prov.* (1867) 61 Such an olde witche, suche a mackabroyne, As euermore like a hog hangeth the groyne, On hir husbande, except he be hir slaue.

†**mackallow.** *Sc. Obs.* Also 7 **mac(k)helve,** 8 **macalive.** [Gael. *macaladh* fostering.] Something handed over to a foster-parent along with a child for the benefit of the latter. Also *attrib.*
1580 in *Black Bk. Taymouth*, etc. (Bannatyne Club) 224 The said father and foster father giving between them of makhelve guddis in donation to the said bairn at Beltane thereafter the value of two hundred merks of ky [etc.]. **1671** *Contract* in *Proc. Soc. Ant. Scot.* XXX. (1896) 22 The makhelve is 9 ky. **1678** *Ibid.* 20 Whilk wholl mackallow goods..the said Duncan and Margret oblidges them..to gress and pastur and hird to the behoofe of ther said foster. **1775** JOHNSON *Western Isl.* Wks. X. 484 These beasts are considered as a portion and called Macalive Cattle.

mackar, obs. Sc. form of MAKER.

mackarel(l, variant of MACKEREL[1].

mackaroon: see MACAROON.

mackassin, obs. form of MOCASSIN.

mackaw: see MACAW.

Mackay: see MCCOY.

mackayite (mə'kaɪaɪt). *Min.* [f. the name of John W. *Mackay* (see quot. 1944[2]) + -ITE[1].] A green hydrated tellurite of ferric iron, perhaps $Fe_2(TeO_3)_3.xH_2O$.
1944 FRONDEL & POUGH in *Amer. Mineralogist* XXIX. 217 The new mineral described here under the name mackayite was found in specimens from two deposits in Goldfield, Nevada. *Ibid.* 218 At the instance of Mr. C. D. Woodhouse, the writers propose the name mackayite for the species after John W. Mackay (1831-1902), a mining operator who in a few years amassed a great fortune on the Comstock Lode, Nevada. The name is intended to recognize Mackay's financial endowment of the School of Mines of the University of Nebraska. **1968** I. KOSTOV *Mineral.* 518 Mackayite is tetragonal.., found as short prismatic green crystals.

†'**mackeler.** *rare*[−1]. [ad. Du. *makelaar*, f. *makelen* to negotiate. Cf. MACKLE *v.*[2]] A broker.
1682 SCARLETT *Exchanges* 9 Exchange is concluded, either by the Mackelers or Brogers, alone betwixt themselves, or by bringing the parties face to face.

†**mackeleredge.** *Obs. rare*[−1]. [ad. Du. *makelarij*, f. *makelaar* MACKELER.] Brokerage.
1682 SCARLETT *Exchanges* 177 The Factor..must place his Principal to account Courtagie and Mackeleridge.

†**mackenboy.** *Obs.* Also 7 **mackenbory, mackinboy, makimboy,** 7-9 **makinboy.** [a. Irish *meacan buidhe* (*an t-s'eibhe*) 'yellow root (of the mountain)'.] An Irish spurge (*Euphorbia hiberna*) said to have powerful purgative properties.
1652 *Hartlib's Legacie* (ed. 2) App., Interrogatory, *Maccamboy.* Whether there be such a thing at all, that this herb should purge the body meerly by external touch, or whether it be a fable, [etc.]? **1670** RAY *Catal. Plant. Angliæ* 299 *Tithymalus Hibernicus*, Makinboy. **1672** PETTY *Pol. Anat.* (1691) 111 What is said of the Herb Mackenbory is fabulous. **1678** PHILLIPS, *Mackenboy*, or *Makimboy*, a kind of Spurge with a knotty Root, growing naturally in Ireland, which being but carried about one, causeth the party to go often to stool. **1687** ASHE in *Phil. Trans.* XX. 294 The famous Irish Herb called Mackenboy. **1816-20** T. GREEN *Univ. Herbal* I. 543 Euphorbia Hibernica, *Irish Spurge*... Native of Ireland..where it is known by the name of *makinboy.*

McKenney (mə'kenɪ). [f. the name of W. E. *McKenney* (1891-1950), who popularized it.] The name given to a suit preference signal in Bridge, devised by the American player Lavinthal in 1934. Freq. as ***McKenney convention.***
1952 I. MACLEOD *Bridge is Easy Game* xiii. 158 You should study and play what is called the 'McKenney' suit preference signal. *Ibid.* 159 East must make a 'McKenney' by throwing the Jack of Diamonds calling for a Spade switch. There is a danger that a McKenney signal may be confused with the ordinary demand for the suit to be continued. **1959** *Listener* 20 Aug. 298/3 Many partnerships, therefore, have a rule, 'No McKenney at trick 1'—McKenney being an alternative name for a suit preference signal. **1964** *Official Encycl. Bridge* 341/2 *McKenney*, standard term in Great Britain for the suit preference signal... McKenney's support..caused the convention to be called in European countries the McKenney convention. **1965** *Listener* 3 June 842/1 The convention known as the McKenney convention is a form of suit-preference signalling, publicized by McKenney, but invented by another American player, Hy. Lavinthal. It differs from other suit-signalling conventions in as much as the signals relate to suits other than that played.

mackerel[1] ('mækərəl). Forms: 3-6 **makerel(l,** 5 **makerelle, makyrelle,** 4-7 **macrel(l, makrel(l,** 5 **macrelle,** 6 **macquerell,** 7 **maquerel,** 7-8 **macril(l, maycril,** 6-8 **mackrell,** 7-9 **mackrel,** 4-9 **mackerell,** 7-9 **mackarel,** 8 **mackarell,** 7- **mackerel.** [a. OF. *makerel* (F. *maquereau*) of unknown origin.]
1. a. A well-known sea-fish, *Scomber scombrus*, much used for food, that approaches the shore in shoals in summer-time for the purpose of spawning. Also used for other fishes of similar appearance belonging to the family Scombridæ.
c **1300** *Havelok* 758 Keling he tok, and tumberel, Hering, and þe makerel. *a* **1377** *Abingdon Acc.* (Camden) 38 In

makerell, xxxiijs. *c* **1425** *Voc.* in Wr.-Wülcker 642/2 *Hic megarus*, makyrelle. *c* **1460** J. RUSSELL *Bk. Nurture* 558 Merlynge, makerelle. **1530** PALSGR. 241/2 Macquerell a fysshe, *macquerel*. **1573** TUSSER *Husb.* xii. (1878) 28 When Mackrell ceaseth from the Seas, John Baptist brings grassebeafe and pease. **1601** CHESTER *Love's Mart., Dialogue* lxxix, Sommer louing Mackrell. **1623** MIDDLETON & ROWLEY *Sp. Gipsy* III. ii, Bad fortunes are like mackerel at mid-summer. *a* **1658** CLEVELAND *Poor Cavalier* 51 Thou shalt.. Bait Fishes Hooks to couzen Mackrels Lips. **1704** SWIFT *T. Tub* Conclus., A book that misses its tide, shall be neglected.. like mackarel a week after the season. **1741** *Compl. Fam.-Piece* I. iii. 214 Slit your Mackrel in halves, take out the Roes, gut and clean them. **1789** MRS. PIOZZI *Journ. France* I. 2 Shoals of maycril. **1838** J. S. POLACK *New Zealand* I. ix. 322 The *pátiki*.. is equally excellent with the European fish [sole], as are also the *mackarel*, of which there are several varieties. **1843** E. DIEFFENBACH *Trav. N.Z.* II. 209 *Scomber loo*.. (*Scomber scombrus*, Solander, Pisc. Austr., p. 31.) Solander observed this mackerel in Queen Charlotte's Sound. **1870** YEATS *Nat. Hist. Comm.* 321 Mackerel will bite at almost any bait. **1886** R. A. SHERRIN *Handbk. Fishes N.Z.* 61 In season mackerel are often found between Cape Colville and the Great Barrier. **1951** T. C. ROUGHLEY *Fish Austral.* 96 Common mackerel (Slimy mackerel—*Pneumatophorus australasicus*). The common mackerel (of the family Scombridæ) is found in all Australian States and occurs in great numbers, particularly round the southern half of the continent where it inhabits ocean waters no great distance from the coast. **1960** DOOGUE & MORELAND *N.Z. Sea Anglers' Guide* 250 Common mackerel.. is the mackerel of English-speaking countries... Other names: *Pneumatophorus japonicus*; southern mackerel, English mackerel, frigate mackerel; tawatawa (Maori).

b. In proverbs and proverbial expressions.

1760 FOOTE *Minor* I. Wks. 1799 I. 238 You can be secret as well as serviceable?.. Mute as a mackrel. **1819** *Metropolis* III. 154 We were as mute as mackarel for exactly seven minutes and a half. **1890** HALL CAINE *Bondman* II. xiii, Was he throwing a sprat to catch a mackerel?

c. Phr. ***holy mackerel***, an exclam. expressing wonder or astonishment.

1899 ADE *In Babel* (1903) 111 Hot? Holy sufferin' mackerel! Me pushin' up the lid.. to get a little fresh air. **1944** T. RATTIGAN *While Sun Shines* II. 218 Holy mackerel! A Duke! **1958** 'J. BROGAN' *Cummings Report* xviii. 189 Holy mackerel! What a way to run an army! **1961** *Amer. Speech* XXXVI. 40 *Holy Mary* is probably the idea underlying *holy Moses* and *holy mackerel*.

2. Applied with qualifying word to other fishes. †***great mackerel***, ? the tunny. ***Spanish mackerel***, †(*a*) the tunny, (*b*) in England the *Scomber colias*, (*c*) in U.S. the *Scomberomerus maculatus*. See also HORSE-MACKEREL.

a **1672** WILLUGHBY *Icthyogr.* (1686) Tab. M. 1 *Thynnus sive Thunnus Gesn.* Spanish Mackerel. **1709** DAMPIER *Voy.* (1729) III. I. 414 The Great Mackarell is 7 Foot long. **1832** COUCH in *Mag. Nat. Hist.* V. 22 Spanish Mackarel (*Scomber maculatus*). **1880** GÜNTHER *Fishes* 457 *S*[*comber*] *colias*.. often called 'Spanish' Mackerel.

3. *Angling*. Short for *mackerel-fly*.

1799 G. SMITH *Laboratory* II. 311, 1. Mackarel. Dubbing, of light brown camel's hair. **1864** *Intell. Observ.* VI. 152 A fly known to anglers as the mackerel.

4. *attrib.* and *Comb.*, as ***mackerel-catcher***, ***-fishery***, ***fleck***, ***-fleet***, ***-gaff***, ***-smack***; † **mackerel-back** *sb.* (see quot. *a* 1700); **mackerel-back**, **-backed** *adjs.*, †(*a*) *slang*, long-backed; (*b*) said of clouds, sky: see *mackerel-sky*; **mackerel-bait**, a fisherman's name for jelly-fish (*Cent. Dict.*); **mackerel-bird**, local name for the wryneck and the young kittiwake (see quots.); **mackerel-boat**, a boat for mackerel-fishing; 'a stout clinch-worked vessel, with a large fore-sail, spritsail, and mizen' (Smyth *Sailor's Word-bk.*); **mackerel-bob**, a four-pointed fish-jig, for catching mackerel; **mackerel-breeze**, a breeze that ruffles the water, so as to favour the catching of mackerel (cf. *mackerel-gale*); hence **mackerel-breezy** *a.*; **mackerel-clouds** (see *mackerel-sky*); **mackerel-cock**, a local name for the Manx Shearwater (Newton); **mackerel-cry**, the hawker's cry of 'new mackerel'; **mackerel-fly** *Angling*, a species of May-fly, also an artificial fly imitating this; **mackerel-gale**, a strong breeze such as mackerel are best caught in; **mackerel-guide**, a local name for the gar-fish; **mackerel-gull**, a name in U.S. for the tern; **mackerel-midge**, the young of the rockling (*Motella*) (Günther); † **mackerel-mint**, common mint (*Mentha viridis*); **mackerel-pike**, any fish of the genus *Scombresocidæ*; a saury (*Cent. Dict.*); **mackerel-plough**, a knife used for creasing the sides of lean mackerel in order to improve their appearance (Knight *Dict. Mech.* 1884); **mackerel-scad**, an American fish, *Decapterus macarellus*; **mackerel-scout** = *mackerel-guide*; **mackerel shark**, a shark of the family Lamnidæ, esp. a mako shark (MAKO[1]) or the porbeagle, *Lamna nasus*; **mackerel-skied** *a.*, having, or characterized by, a mackerel-sky; **mackerel-sky**, a sky dappled with small white fleecy clouds (cirro-cumulus); **mackerel-sture**, a northern name for the tunny.

a **1700** B. E. *Dict. Cant. Crew*, **Mackarel-back*, a very tall, lank Person. **1844** H. STEPHENS *Bk. of Farm* I. 249 At other times it is.. mottled like a mackerel's back, when it is called the 'mackerel-back sky'. **1888** *Pall Mall G.* 22 Sept. 1/2 In some places the clouds were what we sailors call 'mackerel back'. **1785** GROSE *Dict. Vulg. Tongue*, **Mackarel backed*, long backed. **1865** *Intell. Observ.* VIII. 257 *Cirro-cumulus*, or a 'mackerel-backed' sky. **1879** CECIL SMITH *Birds of Guernsey* 94 The Wryneck.. arriving.. about the same time as the mackerel, wherefore it has also obtained the local name of '*Mackerel Bird'. **1882-4** YARRELL *Brit. Birds* (ed. 4) III. 654 Mr. Cordeaux says that the Flamborough fishermen call the young Kittiwakes 'Mackerel-birds', because they usually appear at sea with their parents in August when the fish are approaching the coast. **1768** *Ann. Reg.* 120 A premium.. for encouraging the *mackerel-boats to bring their fish to market. **1883** *Fisheries Exhib. Catal.* 195 *Mackerel bob formerly used by New England fishermen for the capture of mackerel without the use of bait. **1751** SMOLLETT *Per. Pic.* (1779) II. xiv. 209 They tacked to and fro in the river under the impulse of a *mackerel breeze. **1843** LE FEVRE *Life Trav. Phys.* III. III. i. 89 It was blowing a mackarel breeze only. **1834** R. MUDIE *Brit. Birds* (1841) I. 2 It is one of those *mackerel-breezy days on which the surface of the water just dances and dimples. **1614** *Eng. way to wealth* in *Harl. Misc.* (Malh.) III. 244 The fishermen-*mackarel-catchers. **1830** N. S. WHEATON *Jrnl.* 510 *Mackarel clouds.. are hung around the horizon. **1772** RUTTY *Nat. Hist. Co. Dublin* I. 329 The *Mackarel-Cock.. a bird of passage coming to us in June and July, about the time of the Mackarels... It is commonly as big as a Cormorant [etc.]. **1714** GAY *Trivia* II. 310 Ev'n Sundays are prophan'd by *Mackrell Cries. **1883** HUXLEY *Addr. Fishery Congress* 18 June 16, I believe then that the ..*mackerel-fishery, and probably all the great sea-fisheries, are inexhaustible. **1940** R. GIBBINGS *Sweet Thames run Softly* xx. 182 Tall nimbus clouds reared their heads towards the *mackerel flecks in the upper air. **1894** HALL CAINE *Manxman* 425 The *mackerel fleet were leaving for Kinsale. **1829** *Glover's Hist. Derby* I. 177 Lesser hackle fly, *mackerel fly [etc.]. **1883** *Fisheries Exhib. Catal.* 195 *Mackerel gaff.. used by New England fishermen. **1577-87** HARRISON *England* I. x. in *Holinshed* I. 45/1 Scarse comparable to the *makerell gale. **1687** DRYDEN *Hind & P.* III. 456 The wind was fair, but blew a mackrel gale. **1769** PENNANT *Zool.* III. 222 This fish [mackrel] is easily taken by a bait, but the best time is during a fresh gale of wind, which is thence called a mackrel gale. **1835** JENYNS *Man. Brit. Vert. Anim.* 419 *Belone vulgaris*... From its usually preceding the Mackerel, is sometimes called the *Mackerel-Guide. **1796** NEMNICH *Polygl.-Lex. Nat. Hist.* v. 820 *Mackarel gull *Larus ridibundus*. **1883** *Century Mag.* Sept. 653/1 Among the most common birds are the.. tern or mackerell-gull. **1832** COUCH in *Mag. Nat. Hist.* V. 16 It is the *mackerel midge of our fishermen, to whom it is well known. **1860** GOSSE *Rom. Nat. Hist.* 149 The mackerel-midge.. never surpasses an inch and a quarter in length. **1597** GERARDE *Herbal* II. ccxv. 553 The third [Mint] is called ..in English Speare Mint,.. Browne Mint, and *Macrell Mint. **1880-4** F. DAY *Brit. Fishes* II. 148 In Ireland horn-eel (Belfast Bay); *mackerel-scout (Strangford Lough). **1819** *Plough Boy* I. 135 The revenue cutter brought in two very strange fish, found eating a dead horse, supposed to be *mackerel sharks. **1959** A. HARDY *Fish & Fisheries* iv. 73 The inclusion here [*sc.* in the British list] of the mako or mackerel shark, *Isurus oxyrinchus*, is a surprise. **1971** *Islander* (Victoria, B.C.) 17 Oct. 6/1 A.. fisherman.. found a drift bottle inside a mackerel shark. **1921** W. DE LA MARE *Mem. Midget* xxxviii. 255 One *mackerel-skied afternoon, Mrs. Monnerie and I and Susan were returning across the Park. **1669** WORLIDGE *Syst. Agric.* (1681) 295 In a fair day, if the sky seem to be dapled with white Clouds, (which they usually term a *Mackarel-sky) it usually predicts Rain. **1883** R. H. SCOTT *Elem. Meteorol.* 126 Small detached rounded masses [of cloud].. like the markings of a mackerel, whence the name 'mackerel sky'. **1697** *Lond. Gaz.* No. 3295/3 An open Pinnace.. came into the Downes,.. put on Board a *Mackrel Smack, and carried away the Master. **1772** BARRINGTON in *Phil. Trans.* LXII. 310 *note*, The tunny fish [are caught] on the coast of Argyleshire,.. where they are called *mackrel sture.

†'**mackerel**[2]. *Obs.* Forms: 5-6 **makerel(l**, **makrel(l**, 5-7 **ma(c)querel**, 7 **maquerell(e**, **mackarel(l**, **-erel(le**, **macrell**; also in quasi-Italian form **maquerel(l)a**. [ad. OF. *maquerel* (F. *maquereau*, *maquerelle*) of unknown origin; possibly the same word as MACKEREL[1]; some have conjectured that it is from Du. *makelaar* broker.] One who ministers to sexual debauchery; a bawd, pimp, procurer or procuress.

1426 LYDG. *De Guil. Pilgr.* 13478 *Glotonye*: Yiff thow me calle.. Lyk as I am, A Bocheresse, Or in ffrench.. I am callyd a Makerel, Whos offyce.. Ys in ynglysshe bauderye. **1483** CAXTON *Cato* B vij, Nyghe hys hows dwellyd a maquerel or bawde. **1513** DOUGLAS *Æneis* IV. Prol. 192 Sic poyd makrellis for Lucifer bene leche. **1585** JAS. I *Ess. Poesie* (Arb.) 27, I no wais can, vnwet my cheekes, beholde My sisters made by Frenchemen macquerelsolde. *a* **1600** MONTGOMERIE *Sonn.* lxx. 8 Quhy maks thou makrels of the modest Muses. *a* **1613** SIR T. OVERBURY *A Wife*, etc. (1638) 142 A Maquerela, in plaine English, a Bawde. **1630** J. TAYLOR (Water P.) *Gt. Eater Kent* Wks. I. 143/1 Some get their liuing.. by tayles, as Maquerellaes, Concubines, Curtezanes [etc.]. *c* **1645** HOWELL *Lett.* II. xxiv, The Pander did his Office, but brought him a Citizen clad in Damoisells apparell, so she and her Maquerell were paid accordingly. **1658** in PHILLIPS. *a* **1700** in B. E. *Dict. Cant. Crew.*

† **mackerelage.** *Obs.* In 7 **maquorelage**. [a. F. *maquerelage*, f. **maquerel*, *maquereau*: see prec.] The services of a bawd or pander.

1602 FLORIO *Montaigne* II. vii. (1632) 211.

mackereler ('mækərələ(r)). [f. MACKEREL[1] + -ER[1].] **a.** One who goes mackerel-fishing. **b.** A boat used in mackerel-fishing.

1883 *Chamb. Jrnl.* 272 Here is a model of that vast net used by the mackereler. **1886** *Century Mag.* XXXII. 824 The mackerelers do not keep together so much as formerly.

mackereling ('mækərəlɪŋ), *vbl. sb.* Also **mackerelling** [f. MACKEREL[1] + -ING[1].] **a.** Fishing for mackerel.

1856 J. REYNOLDS *Peter Gott* xiv. 167 When fishermen can make as much in a few weeks at mackerelling, as in as many months at codfishing,.. they prefer to run their chance in the former. *Ibid.*, Mackerelling is often called a lottery. **1880** *Harper's Mag.* Sept. 510/1 Among the rest are two of the singular 'porgy steamers' turned to mackereling. **1881** S. P. MCLEAN *Cape Cod Folks* iii. 62, I was going mackerellin' with ye myself that time. **1887** GOODE, etc. *Fisheries of U.S.* v. II. 604 Men who go mackereling. **1952** *Gloucester* (Mass.) *Daily Times* 20 Mar. 8/7 His present seiner is the Jean and Patricia which stays with mackereling only.

b. A mackerel-like effect.

1866 G. M. HOPKINS *Jrnls. & Papers* (1959) 139 Scud spots etc, and some very faintly made out mackerelling... Bright, with mackerelling now and then. **1883** —— *Let.* 21 Dec. in Hopkins & Dixon *Corr.* (1955) 165, I have further noticed streamers, fine ribbing or mackerelling, and other.. textures.

mackeroon, variant of MACAROON.

McKie: see MCCOY.

Mackinaw ('mækɪnɔː). Also **Mackinac**, **Macinaw**, **Mackina**, and with lower-case initial. The name of an island in the strait between Lakes Huron and Michigan; occurring in the following collocations: **Mackinaw blanket**, also simply **Mackinaw**, a thick blanket, such as used to be distributed to the Indians of the North-west by the U.S. government; **Mackinaw (boat)**, (*a*) a large flat-bottomed sharp-ended boat, used on the Great Lakes; (*b*) a schooner-rigged boat formerly used on the Great Lakes; **Mackinaw coat** (or **jacket**), a thick double-breasted jacket; also *ellipt.*; **Mackinaw shirt**, a plaid woollen shirt; **Mackinaw skiff** = *Mackinaw (boat)*; **Mackinaw trout**, the *lake-trout* (see TROUT); also, a North American char, *Cristivomer namaycush*. Also *absol.*, a heavy woollen cloth, now usu. with a plaid design; *pl.*, garments made of this cloth.

1812 J. G. LUTTIG *Jrnl. Expedition Upper Missouri* (1920) 54 The Mackina Boat took 5 hunters to the Island. **1822** L. CASS *Let.* 4 Oct. in *Wisconsin State Hist. Soc. Coll.* (1911) XX. 287 The heavy Mackinac blankets are almost impervious to the rain, and are universally worn by the Indians in this quarter. **1826** T. FLINT *Recoll.* 102, I have seen a Mackinaw skiff, carrying five tons, which came from the lakes into the Chicago of Michigan. **1836** in *Mass. Hist. Soc. Proc.* (1892) 2nd Ser. VII. 276 Covering, a cotton counterpane, a sheet.., besides my own great coats and green Mackinaw. **1840** *Southern Lit. Messenger* VI. 604/1 The celebrated Mackinaw trout, so called after the town, near which they are found, is generally caught by the hook. **1841** CATLIN *N. Amer. Ind.* (1844) I. x. 73 A mackinaw-boat, capable of carrying 50 or 100 casks. **1841** *Western Herald & Farmers' Mag.* (Sandwich, Ontario) 31 Mar. 3/2 They have also a large assortment of blankets.. of the real Mackinaw. **1842** *Southern Lit. Messenger* VIII. 586/2 A party of six.. had occasion.. to ascend the Missouri, in a Mackinaw [boat], with the purpose of trading. **1851** MAYNE REID *Scalp Hunt.* iii. 22 My 'Mackinaw'.. makes my bed by night and my great coat on other occasions. **1872** Mackinaw blanket [see *blanket coat* s.v. BLANKET *sb.* 7]. **1876** G. B. GOODE *Anim. Resources U.S.* 41 Lure-fish used in taking Mackinaw trout. **1887** *Rep. U.S. Comm. Fisheries* 24 At Duluth, Minnesota, the mackinaw boats average about 32 feet in length. **1900** *Atlantic Monthly* LXXXV. 102/1 It is then the woodsman dons his Mackinaw jacket. **1901** *Longm. Mag.* Jan. 218 Sedate family boats with three pairs of oars, mackinaws with white sails light in the fresh breeze. **1902** J. LONDON *Daughter of Snows* 316 He was interrupted by a warm-complexioned man clad in faded mackinaws. **1902** S. E. WHITE *Blazed Trail* 16 They all wore heavy blanket Mackinaw coats. *Ibid.* 375 A tall.. individual dressed in a faded mackinaw and a limp slouch hat. **1912** J. SANDILANDS *Western Canad. Dict.* 28 *Mackinaw*, a heavy woolen cloth much in favour among lumberjacks. A lumberjack speaks of his thick winter jacket as his mackinaw. **1916** H. KEPHART *Camping & Woodcraft* I. 147, I usually discard the sweater in favor of a mackinaw shirt. **1920** S. LEWIS *Main St.* 230 He had given up.. wearing red mackinaws in lumber-camps. **1930** J. DOS PASSOS *42nd Parallel* I. 101 A young man, his head and ears huddled into the collar of a mackinaw. **1938** E. HEMINGWAY *Fifth Column* (1939) 479 He wore.. a mackinaw shirt. **1941** L. D. BALDWIN *Keelboat Age* 50 The Mackinaw boat in use on the Missouri was an adaptation of the flatboat and of the Mackinaw skiff. **1945** R. W. SERVICE *Ploughman of Moon* 157, I couched on the floor, lying on a buffalo-robe and wrapped in a mackinaw blanket. **1956** J. S. GOWLAND *Sikanaska Trail* 44 A guard in plain clothes brought along my mackinaw jacket. **1961** E. HUNTER *Mothers & Daughters* I. 9 She had hardly ever seen him without his hooded Mackinaw. **1961** *Vancouver Sun* 17 Aug. 23/1 The laker (mackinaw trout) is a record. Largest Canadian sport-caught lake char.. is an 87 pounder. **1964** *Atlantic Advocate* July 77/1 William M... was operating the mill and producing a large red and black check design for Mackinaw or cruiser cloth. **1968** R. F. ADAMS *Western Words* (ed. 2) 187 The Mackinaw was a flat-bottomed boat with a pointed prow and a square stern... A large Mackinaw was as much as 50 or 60 feet long. **1971** J. MCDOUGALL *Parsons on Plains* i. 1 My first recollections are of stumps, log heaps,.. bateaux, Mackinaw boats. **1973** D. MACKENZIE *Postscript to Dead Let.* 9 He was.. wearing a red-and-grey mackinaw over a shirt without a tie. **1973** J. RYDER *Trevayne* (1974) xxxiv. 264 A man in a mackinaw coat and a fur cap.

mackinawite ('mækɪnɔːaɪt). *Min.* [f. *Mackinaw*, the name of a mine in Snohomish

County, Washington + -ITE[1].] A black tetragonal iron sulphide.

1962 H. T. EVANS et al. in *Program Ann. Meetings Geol. Soc. Amer.* 47A Recently, another iron sulfide mineral, mackinawite, very similar in physical properties, to valleriite, but containing no copper.., has been identified from the Mackinaw Mine, Snohomish County, Washington. **1969** *Amer. Mineralogist* LIV. 1190 Information about the occurrence, optical properties, microhardness and cell-size is given for a nickelian mackinawite (Fe 38·1%, Co 3·3%, Ni 18·7%) from Vlakfontein in the Transvaal. *Ibid.*, This mackinawite was examined in reflected light in both air and oil. It shows the very strong pleochroism and anisotropy characteristic of this mineral. **1970** *Nature* 15 Aug. 700/1 Modern surface sediments containing H_2S are often coloured black by fine grained, iron monosulphide minerals such as mackinawite, $Fe_{1+x}S$, and greigite, Fe_3S_4.

mackinboy, variant of MACKENBOY *Obs.*

mackins (ˈmækɪnz). *Obs.* exc. *dial.* Also 6 **meckinse, 7 makin(g)s, 7–8 mackings, 8 maakins,** 9 *dial.* **macklins, makkers,** etc.: see E.D.D. [Formed as MACK[2] with suffix -KIN frequent in similar words.] Used in the asseverative exclamation *by (the) mackins.* (Cf. MACK *sb.*[2])

c **1560** *Misogonus* III. iii. 73 (Brandl) Bith meckinse. **1605** *Lond. Prodigal* II. ii. C, A by the mackins, good syr Lancelot. **1654** GAYTON *Pleas. Notes* III. ii. 75 'Twas well thought on, by the mackins. **1694** ECHARD *Plautus* 12 By the Mackins, I believe Phebus has been playing the Good-Fellow. **1697** VANBRUGH *Relapse* IV. i. (1708) 40 *Fashion.* Pray accept of this small Acknowledgement. *Nurse.* (Aside.) Gold, by makings, your Honour's goodness is too great. **1887** *S. Cheshire Gloss.* s.v. *By*, By the makkins.

mackintosh (ˈmækɪntɒʃ). Also †**Mackintosh, macintosh.**

1. The name of Charles *Macintosh* (1766–1843), applied *attrib.* to designate garments made of the waterproof material invented by him (patent no. 4804, 17 June 1823), consisting of two or more layers of cloth cemented together with india-rubber. Now viewed as an attributive use of 3, and written with small initial.

1836 *Murray's Handbk. N. Germ.* p. xx, A Mackintosh cloak is almost indispensable. **1849** *Brit. Q. Rev.* Feb. 5 Old port, tender mutton and Mackintosh capes are excellent things, no doubt. **1853** READE *Chr. Johnstone* 227 A fisherman's long mackintosh coat. **1859** W. COLLINS *Q. of Hearts* (1875) 39 Jessie put on my mackintosh cloak. **1895** *Montgomery Ward Catal.* 296/3 Men's Double Texture Mackintosh Box Coats, double breasted, all wool black tricot.., fancy plaid lining, silk velvet collar.

2. Short for *mackintosh cloak, coat,* etc. Now freq. used to designate any type of rain-proof coat. Also *Comb.*, as *mackintosh-maker.*

1836 FRITH *Let.* 18 Oct. in *Autobiog.* (1888) III. 61, I like the mackintosh very much. **1840** LONGF. in *Life* (1891) I. 365 Sumner striding down Hancock Street in his white mackintosh. **1842** BARHAM *Ingol. Leg., Misadv. Margate* xiv, I could not see my Macintosh..Nor yet my best white beaver hat. **1851** *Illustr. Lond. News* 5 Aug. (1854) 119/1 Macintosh-maker. **1871** CARLYLE in *Mrs. Carlyle's Lett.* I. 141 Wrapt in an old dressing-gown with mackintosh buttoned round it. **1897** *Sears, Roebuck Catal.* 188/2 Ladies' Single Military Cape Mackintosh. Made from extra fine all wool Scotch mixed cheviot, with fine, soft dressy finish. **1900** *Q. Rev.* July 56 The bodies of officers having been buried in mackintoshes had not so disappeared. **1956** A. S. C. Ross in N. Mitford *Noblesse Oblige* 30 *Burberry* and *raincoat* are of the same genre, *macintosh* or *mac* being normal.

3. The material of which 'mackintosh' garments are made; now applied to any cloth made waterproof by a coating of india-rubber. Also *attrib.*

1880 MACCORMAC *Antisept. Surg.* 170 The mackintosh should be dipped, shortly before use, in carbolic solution. **1889** *Lancet* 27 Apr. 830/1 The bed is covered with a mackintosh sheet. **1896** *Allbutt's Syst. Med.* I. 429 If necessary, a square of mackintosh is placed under the draw-sheet. **1899** *Ibid.* VIII. 579 India-rubber or mackintosh coverings are certainly effectual.

mackintoshed (ˈmækɪntɒʃt), *a.* Also **macintoshed.** [f. MACKINTOSH + -ED[2].] Wearing, or protected by, a mackintosh.

1904 J. VAIZEY *More about Pixie* xxiv. 257 The cloaked and mackintoshed figures..seemed all black, all the same. **1927** *Daily Mail* 30 June 9/4 Mackintoshed enthusiasts occupied them [*sc.* boats]. **1962** *Punch* 21 Nov. 751/1 Macintoshed ruthless plainclothesmen. **1963** *Times* 25 Apr. 6/1 They sauntered self-consciously off, mackintoshed and blackbooted, to mingle with the unsuspecting crowd.

Mackintosh Red: see MCINTOSH.

mackintoshy (ˈmækɪntɒʃɪ), *a.* [f. MACKINTOSH + -Y[1].] Of, belonging to, or suggestive of mackintoshes; characterized by or given to wearing mackintoshes.

1939 'G. ORWELL' *Coming up for Air* IV. vii. 279 The gas-bill and the school-fees, and the mackintoshy smell. **1941** E. BOWEN *Look at Roses* 253 'They're mackintoshy sort of people,' she said.

mackle, macle (ˈmæk(ə)l), *sb. Printing.* [ad. F. *macule*, ad. L. *macula* spot. Cf. G. *makel* spot, stain.] A blur in printing; a doubling of the impression; also, a blurred sheet. (Cf. MACULE *sb.*)

1706 PHILLIPS (ed. Kersey), *Maculature*, or *Macle*, a waste Sheet of printed Paper. **1825** HANSARD *Typographia* 928 *Mackle*, when part of the impression on a page appears double, owing to the platten's dragging on the frisket. **1871** *Amer. Encycl. Printing* (ed. Ringwalt) s.v., If the frame of the tympan rubs against the platen, it will cause a slur or mackle. **1888** JACOBI *Printers' Vocab.*, *Mackle*, a printed sheet with a slurred appearance.

mackle, macle (ˈmæk(ə)l), *v.*[1] *Printing.* [f. MACKLE *sb.*] **a.** *trans.* To blur, spot, or spoil (a sheet of paper); also (now usually) to print (a page) blurred or double. **b.** *intr.* Of the paper: To become blurred or spoiled. (Cf. MACULE *v.*) Hence **ˈmackled** *ppl. a.*, **ˈmackling** *vbl. sb.*

1594 R. ASHLEY tr. *Loys le Roy* 22 On a double tympan or parchmin (hauing a wollen cloth betwixt them) and a moyst linnen cloth to keepe the leafe from mackling. **1724** BAILEY, *Mackled*, blotted or daub'd in Printing. **1867** FRY *Playing-Card Terms* in *Philol. Soc. Trans.* 56 *To Mackle, To Macule*, v. a. To spot, stain, soil; to set off newly printed or painted work. *Mackled*, adj. Spotted, stained, soiled. *Macklings, Mackling-paper, Mackling-sheets*, soiling-paper; sheet of paper put between printed sheets of playing-cards, to prevent rubbing, setting-off, and soiling.

†**ˈmackle,** *v.*[2] *Obs.*—[0] [ad. Du. *makelen* to offer for sale.] *intr.* 'To sell weavers' goods to shop-keepers' (Bailey 1724).

Hence †**ˈmackler**, a seller of weavers' goods (Bailey 1731 vol. II).

mackless, variant of MAKELESS *a.*[1] and [2].

†**ˈmackly,** *adv. Obs.* In 5–6 **makly.** [f. MACK *a.* + -LY[2].] Evenly, aptly, easily.

c **1440** *Promp. Parv.* 322/2 Makly, or esyly, *faciliter* (P. *apte*). **1513** DOUGLAS *Æneis* V. xiv. 32 The windis blawis full evin and rycht makly.

†**mackˈninny.** *Obs. rare*—[1]. [a. It. *machinine*, pl. dim. of *macchina* MACHINE *sb.*] ? A puppet-show.

a **1734** NORTH *Exam.* III. viii. §12 (1740) 590 He..could..represent emblematically the Downfall of Majesty; as in his Raree-Show and Mackninny.

mackrel, -ell, obs. forms of MACKEREL.

macle (ˈmæk(ə)l). See also MASCLE. [a. F. *macle*, ad. L. *macula* spot, mesh.]

1. *Cryst.* A hemitropic or twin crystal. Also *attrib.* [After Romé de L'Isle's use of F. *macle*, 1783.]

1801 *De Bournon's Acc. certain Minerals* in *Phil. Trans.* XCI. 185 Whence results a kind of macle, the form of which is a rhomboidal tetraedral prism. **1829** *Nat. Philos., Polaris. Light* xvi. 60 (U.K.S.) The irregularities of crystallisation, which are known by the name of *Macle*, or *Hemitrope* forms. **1860** MAURY *Phys. Geog. Sea* ix. §442 Crystals of ice, like macles of snow, were observed to form near the bottom. **1883** *All Year Round* 17 Nov. 535 A diamond at last, of macle shape, weighing some twenty carats!

2. *Min.* (See quot. 1865.)

1839 URE *Dict. Arts, Macle*, is the name of certain diagonal black spots in minerals, like the ace of diamonds in cards. *a* **1852** MACGILLIVRAY *Nat. Hist. Dee Side* (1855) 454 Orthoclase..forms large macles in Rubislaw quarries, near Aberdeen. **1865** WATTS *Dict. Chem.*, *Macle* is the name given to certain spots in minerals of a deeper hue than the rest; sometimes proceeding from difference of aggregation, sometimes from the presence of a foreign substance; clay-slate, for example, may be macled with iron pyrites. **1872** PAGE *Adv. Text-Bk. Geol.* vii. 118 Felspar with large macles of mica.

3. = CHIASTOLITE.

[**1821** JAMESON *Man. Mineral.* 318 Chiastolite, Macle, Haüy.] **1821** MAWE *Catal. Minerals* (ed. 4) 99 Chiastolite—*Macle*, is of a yellowish white colour. **1822** CLEAVELAND *Mineral. & Geol.* I. 427 The term Macle, as the name of a distinct species, applies to the whitish prisms only. **1862** DANA *Man. Geol.* §60. 58 [Andalusite] often having the interior tesselated with black, in which case it is usually called macle or chiastolite. **1896** CHESTER *Dict. Min.*, *Macle*, a syn. of chiastolite, alluding particularly to the black centre which a crystal often shows when cut transversely, similar to the mascle of heraldry.

4. *Her.* = MASCLE.

1727–41 CHAMBERS *Cycl.*, *Mascle*, or *Macle.* **1828–40** BERRY *Encycl. Her.* I, *Macles* or *Mashes.* These terms occur in ancient books of armory, meaning the same as Mascles. **1847** *Gloss. Heraldry*, *Macle*, see *Mascle.*

macle, *Printing*: see MACKLE.

macled (ˈmæk(ə)ld), *ppl. a.* Also mackled. [f. MACLE + -ED.] **a.** Of a crystal: Hemitropic. **b.** Marked like chiastolite (Webster Suppl. 1880). **c.** *Her.* = MASCLED (Webster 1897).

1822 CLEAVELAND *Mineral. & Geol.* II. 793 Macled Crystal, a hemitrope crystal is sometimes thus called. *a* **1852** MACGILLIVRAY *Nat. Hist. Dee Side* (1855) 455 Garnet..In pentagonal dodecahedrons, single or macled. **1858** MAURY *Phys. Geog. Sea* xiii. §761 Organisms as delicate as the macled frost. **1862** G. P. SCROPE *Volcanos* 33 *note*, The crystals being..many of them mackled. **1865** [see MACLE 2].

McLeod (məˈklaʊd). Also erron. **Macleod.** [Name of Herbert *McLeod* (1841–1923), English scientist, who invented the instrument in 1874 (*Phil. Mag.* XLVIII. 110).] *McLeod gauge*: a type of mercury-in-glass manometer for the absolute measurement of low pressures, in which a fixed large volume of the gas to be measured is compressed by the mercury into a small volume and the resulting pressure found from the height of the column of mercury it supports, the desired pressure then being obtained by multiplying this by the ratio of the smaller to the larger volume in accordance with Boyle's law.

1880 J. E. H. GORDON *Physical Treat. Electr. & Magn.* II. xxxv. 83 The apparatus is in connection with a McLeod gauge, by means of which pressures to 0·00005 millim. can be determined. **1923** *Proc. Cambr. Philos. Soc.* XXI. 505 The residual pressure of the gas in the box was measured by a Macleod gauge. **1971** *Sci. Amer.* Aug. 114/2 Although the McLeod gauge indicates absolute pressure and is universally used for calibrating other instruments, it is inconvenient to operate.

maclock, var. MUCKLUCK.

McLuhanism (məˈkluːənɪz(ə)m). The social ideas of the Canadian writer H. Marshall *McLuhan* (1911–80), such as that the effect of the introduction of the mass media is to deaden the critical faculties of individuals. Hence **McLuhaˈnesque** *a.*; **Mcˈ Luhanite** *a.* and *sb.*, of or pertaining to, an adherent of, McLuhan; **Mcˈ Luhanize** *v. trans.*, to convert to McLuhanism; to render in a manner typical of McLuhan.

1967 *Punch* 4 Oct. 520/1 Most of us 20th-century electric circuitry villagers by now have got at least the drift of McLuhanism. **1967** *Spectator* 10 Nov. 571/2, I am leaving on one side all McLuhanite arguments that books are on the way out. **1967** *Observer* 10 Dec. 24/3 A suitably McLuhanesque fanfare. **1968** *Listener* 4 Jan. 8/1 Then there is Father Walter Ong, whom Martin Dodsworth once McLuhanised into 'the Ong with the numinous prose'. *Ibid.* 6 June 722/3 The demolition of fashionable McLuhanite myths about television has been another of the year's benefits. *Ibid.* 751/1 It was really a kind of McLuhanesque exercise in the depiction of the influence of media on people's lives. **1968** *Punch* 17 July 100/3 Mr. Turner and director Peter Hammond had bravely attempted to McLuhanise the intractably literary. **1970** *Times* 31 Mar. (Australian Suppl.) p. vi/8 The thesis of Australia in the seventies as a model McLuhanized society is fervently denied by publishers. **1971** *Guardian* 14 Jan. 7/1 McLuhanites and Orwellians are likely to block our view of their masters' arguments. *Ibid.* 1 Nov. 9/1 One occasionally wonders whether the image—as in some McLuhanesque lens—is not more important than its object. **1972** *Ibid.* 8 Feb. 4/6 It is on the basis of evolution..and not instant McLuhanism that the Swiss delegation has opened negotiations at Brussels. **1973** *Ibid.* 19 Feb. 8/6 Designers on a newspaper—whatever McLuhanesque horror next?

maclura (məˈkl(j)ʊərə). [mod.L. (T. Nuttall, 1818), f. the name of William *Maclure* (1763–1840), American geologist.] A deciduous North American tree, *Maclura pomifera*, of the genus so called, belonging to the family Moraceæ and bearing an inedible fruit resembling an orange; the Osage orange or bow-wood. Also *attrib.*

1818 T. NUTTALL *Genera N. Amer. Plants* II. 233 Maclura. (Bow-wood, Yellow-wood.) **1857** *Trans. Illinois Agric. Soc.* II. 222 A few Maclura hedges are growing. *Ibid.* 302 Mr. Tisdell has two hedges of the maclura growing on his farm. **1858** J. A. WARDER *Hedges & Evergreens* 21 The division of the prairies into twenty-acre lots, by the dense hedges of maclura. *Ibid.* 52 The cost of the maclura hedge.

maˈclur(e)ite. *Min.* [Named after W. Maclure, U.S. geologist: see -ITE.] A name independently proposed in 1822 for two different minerals, now identified respectively with augite and chondrodite.

1822 NUTTALL in *Amer. Jrnl. Sci.* V. 246 Maclurite. **1822** SEYBERT *ibid.* 344 Maclureite. **1822** CLEAVELAND *Mineral. & Geol.* II. 783.

Macˈmillanite. [Named after John Macmillan (*died* 1753), the founder of the body: see -ITE.] A member of the body known as the Reformed Presbyterian Church of Scotland.

1799 *Statist. Acc. Scotl.* XXI. Index 1, Macmillanites. **1818** SCOTT *Hrt. Midl.* xvii, I only meant to say that you were a Cameronian, or MacMillanite.

M'Naghten rules (məkˈnɔːt(ə)n). Also **McNaghten, MacNaughten, Macnaughton,** etc., **rules (or case,** etc.). [Named after Daniel *M'Naghten* who was tried for murder in 1843 and acquitted on a plea of insanity.] Name applied to the answers given in the House of Lords in 1843 after the trial of Daniel M'Naghten for the murder of Sir Robert Peel's secretary, Edward Drummond, when five questions were put respecting crimes alleged to have been committed by persons suffering from insanity; subsequently used as criteria for judging an accused person's responsibility for his actions.

[**1843** *Times* 14 Mar. 4/3 Last night the Lord Chancellor ..brought forward the circumstances of M'Naughten's trial for the consideration of the Peers... He proceeded to caution their Lordships against supposing that, even if the

verdict in M'Naughten's case should appear to have been given upon faulty or inconclusive evidence, it would be necessary to alter the law upon the subject.] **1892** D. H. TUKE *Dict. Psychol. Med.* I. 318/1 Juries are never, at the present day, charged strictly in conformity with the McNaghten rules. [**1902** *Encycl. Brit.* XXIX. 491/2 The answers [by Chief Justice Tindal] to these questions are commonly called 'The rules in Macnaughton's case' and they still nominally contain the law of England as to the criminal responsibility of the insane.] **1958** B. HAMILTON *Too Much of Water* xii. 271 So long as the McNaughton rules run, I don't think he's got a *chance* of Broadmoor. **1959** JOWITT *Dict. Eng. Law* II. 1122/2 In *R.* v. *McNaghten* or *M'Naghten* or *Macnaughten* (1843)..a discussion took place in the House of Lords upon the direction to the jury..and as a result a series of questions was put to the judges. The answers of the majority constitute the 'McNaghten Rules', and have been accepted as laying down the law as to insanity with reference to criminal responsibility. **1959** *Listener* 24 Sept. 481/1 Insanity in this context was until lately very narrowly defined by the McNaghten rules. **1962** *Lancet* 1 Dec. 1148/1 Giving the background to present-day legal views on diminished responsibility, the McNaughten rules, uncontrollable impulse, and psychopathy. **1968** N. WALKER *Crime & Insanity in Eng.* vi. 105 It is difficult to find a clear statement of the medical objections to the M'Naghten Rules at this date. *Ibid.* 107 Mr Justice Bray explained the M'Naghten Rules to the Gloucester jury. **1971** *Reader's Digest Family Guide to Law* 773/1 The McNaughten Rules can be applied to all offences, but they are rarely used in anything but murder cases. **1973** *Times* 24 May 12/7 What emerges clearly from the Canadian trial is the immense benefit to both doctors and lawyers in *this* country from the subsidence of the McNaughten rules and the introduction of the plea of diminished responsibility.

macock, var. MAYCOCK, kind of pumpkin.

Macomet, -it(e, -yt(e, obs. ff. MAHOMET.

Mâcon[1] (mɑkɔ̃). [Name of a city in the department of Saône-et-Loire, France.] A wine of Burgundy, produced in the district around Mâcon.

[**1699** M. LISTER *Journey to Paris* 161 The White Wines of value are those of *Mascon* in *Burgundy*.] **1863** T. G. SHAW *Wine* viii. 258 A bottle of the homely Mâcon, instead of the elegant Beaujolais, had to be called for. **1908** CHESTERTON *Man who was Thursday* viii. 155 Draining a glass of Mâcon. **1963** *Spectator* 1 Mar. 275, I chose a Macon from the wine-list and subsequently paid £1 for it. **1967** A. LICHINE *Encycl. Wines* 336/2 A slightly lesser amount [of wine] will be sold simply as Mâcon with no other indication of source. **1972** H. W. YOXALL *Enjoyment of Wine* xv. 117 A glass or two of cool, light, dry wine—a young moselle, a muscadet, a mâcon blanc..—is a first-rate aperitif.

macon[2] (ˈmeɪkən). [f. M(UTTON + B)ACON.] During the 1939–45 war: mutton salted and smoked like bacon.

1939 *Daily Express* 22 Nov., *Macon* has now been adapted by other newspapers as a name for mutton bacon. This is only the latest of many words and phrases originally coined in this office which have later been used generally. **1939** *News Rev.* 30 Nov. 15 Macon, the Scottish dish which may eke out any wartime shortage of bacon. Macon is mutton cured in the same way as bacon. **1939** *Times* 7 Dec. 10/4 Macon was introduced..at the Savoy Hotel yesterday... Mr. Cecil Rodd, introducing macon..said he did not pretend to know how the word macon came into being; it just happened. **1968** *Punch* 7 Feb. 177/2 The Ministry of Food then stood in for Mrs. Beeton, instructing them how to..work wonders with such unlikely raw materials as macon (bacon made from mutton, children)..and..coelacanth.

macon, obs. form of MAHOUND, MASON.

maconite (ˈmeɪkənaɪt). *Min.* [f. *Macon* name of a county in Georgia, U.S.A.: see -ITE.] A hydrous silicate of aluminium, iron, and magnesium.

1873 F. A. GENTH in *Proc. Amer. Philos. Soc.* XIII. 396 Maconite, (a new species [of corundum]).

Maconochie (məˈkɒnəkɪ). *colloq.* [The name of the makers, *Maconochie* Brothers, of London.] **1.** Meat stewed with vegetables and tinned, esp. as supplied to soldiers on active service; a tin of such meat. Also ***Maconochie ration***.

1901 'LINESMAN' *Words by Eyewitness* i. 9 The hungry shelterers trooped back to their 'dixies', and wasted not a thought upon them [*sc.* shells], until the 'Maconochie' had vanished. **1915** F. H. LAWRENCE in T. E. Lawrence *Home Lett.* (1954) 689 We have found several tins of Maconochie Rations & also Jam in the house. **1917** 'I. HAY' *Carrying on* viii. 220 How would a Maconochie apiece suit your boys? **1940** 'GUN BUSTER' *Return via Dunkirk* II. xix. 225 He manages to scrape together two tins of Maconochie (stew), a tin of cold potatoes,..and some 'issue biscuits'. **1954** W. FAULKNER *Fable* 61 His company commander was shaving out of a Maconochie tin.

2. *joc. slang.* The stomach. Also ***Maconochie Cross, Medal*** (see quots.).

1919 W. H. DOWNING *Digger Dial.* 32 *Maconochie*, ..stomach. *Ibid.*, *Maconochie Cross*, Military Cross. *Maconochie Medal*, Military Medal. **1925** FRASER & GIBBONS *Soldier & Sailor Words* 149 *Maconochie*..was also sometimes used for stomach, *e.g.*, 'He got hit in the Maconochie'. **1965** BROPHY & PARTRIDGE *Long Trail* 147 *Maconochie Medal*, the Military Medal; *Maconochie Cross*, the Military Cross.

‖**macoumère** (makumɛr). *West Indies.* Also **macomère, macoumere.** [French Creole.] A god-mother, or the mother of one's godchild; more generally applied to any female friend of a family, or as a derogatory term for an old woman or gossip.

1942 H. C. GORDON *West Indian Scenes* xix. 217 *Macomère Crab*, who was a kind soul, complied with her request. **1952** S. SELVON *Brighter Sun* vi. 95 And is why yuh looking at me so, *macoumère*? **1960** *Tamarack Rev.* XIV. 22 This time so, they ain't bothering about the other people in the queue at all, they mauvalanging and bursting out in some loud kya-kya laugh like them macoumere in the market in..Trinidad.

macoute, variant of MACUTE.

macquerel(l, obs. form of MACKEREL.

‖**macquignon.** *Obs.* [F. *maquignon.*] A horse-dealer.

1798 CHARLOTTE SMITH *Yng. Philos.* III. 126 'Lord who?' said the macquignon* in a surly tone. [*Foot-n.*] *A sort of jobber in horses who still calls himself a gentleman. [**1834** JAMES *J. Marston Hall* x, I remember his turning off his chief ecuyer for merely whispering in the street with a maquignon, who was bringing him a horse for sale.]

macramé (məˈkrɑːmeɪ). Also **macrami.** [App. a. Turk. *maqrama* towel, napkin, handkerchief, a. Arab. *miqramaʰ* ? striped cloth.] A fringe or trimming of knotted thread or cord; knotted-work; the art of making this. Also *attrib.*

1869 MRS. PALLISER *Lace* iv. 65 This art is principally applied to the ornamenting of huckaback towels, termed Macramé, a long fringe of thread being left at each end, for the purpose of being knotted together in geometrical designs. **1881** *Daily News* 16 July 2/7 Macrami laces continue to attract some attention. **1882** CAULFEILD & SAWARD *Dict. Needlewk.* 331 The basis of all Macramé Lace is knots... Macramé is celebrated for its durability and excellence. **1898** *Daily News* 8 Dec. 3/2 The girls had the result of their deft labours in woolwork, needlework, macramiwork.

‖**macrauchenia** (ˌmækrɔːˈkiːnɪə). Also in anglicized form **macrauchene.** [mod.L. *Macrauchēnia* (Owen 1838), generic name f. Gr. μακραύχην long-necked, f. μακρ-ός long + αὐχήν neck.] A fossil animal of the order *Pachydermata* having some resemblance to a camel.

1838 OWEN *Fossil Mamm.*, *Zool. Voy. Beagle* (1840) I. 35 The animal—which..I propose to call Macrauchenia. *Ibid.* 42 The Macrauchene. **1859** DARWIN *Orig. Spec.* vii. (1878) 178 The camel, guanaco, and macrauchenia. **1903** *Q. Rev.* Jan. 59 The macrauchenia, a three-toed ungulate of the size and proportions of a camel.

macrell, obs. form of MACKEREL[2].

macrergate (mæˈkrɜːgeɪt). *Ent.* Also **macroërgate.** [ad. G. *makroergate* (E. Wasmann 1895, in *Biol. Centralbl.* XV. 606), f. Gr. μακρ-ός large + ἐργάτης worker.] A large worker ant.

1901 W. M. WHEELER in *Amer. Naturalist* XXXV. 879 The larger macroërgates are nearly eight times as large as the normal workers. **1910** —— *Ants* vi. 97 The *macrergate* is an unusually large worker form which in some species is produced only in populous or affluent colonies. **1915** H. ST. J. K. DONISTHORPE *Brit. Ants* 40 The macrergate is larger in stature than the normal worker of the species in question.

†**ˈmacrio.** *Obs. rare*⁻¹. [? altered from F. *maquereau.*] = MACKEREL[2].

a **1627** MIDDLETON *Anything for Quiet Life* v. ii. (1662) G 3, Pander, Wittoll, Macrio, basest of knaves.

†**ˈmacritude.** *Obs.*⁻⁰. [ad. L. *macritūdo*, f. *macer* lean.] Leanness.

1623 in COCKERAM (*machr-*). **1656** in BLOUNT *Glossogr.*

macro (ˈmækrəʊ), *sb.* [f. the prefix MACRO-.] **1.** *Computers.* A macro-instruction. Freq. *attrib.*

1959 *Jrnl. Assoc. Computing Machinery* VI. 132 The built-in system macro instructions in SCAT presently consist of (1) two macros for generating the..standard entry and exit from subroutines, (2) a set of debugging macros [etc.]. **1961** LEEDS & WEINBERG *Computer Programming Fund.* iv. 103 The assembly program can be instructed to recognize this instruction sequence through the use of a single form called a macro-instruction... Recognition of the 'macro' form causes the assembly program to assemble the corresponding sequence of one or more machine instructions. **1963** L. SCHULTZ *Digital Processing* xi. 240 To avoid having to write the groups repeatedly, the programmer..instructs the machine to establish a table in which it stores the group of instructions. To identify the group, he assigns a code name, called a macro name. *Ibid.*, The programmer writes one instruction (a macro) and the machine 'generates' several. **1966** *New Scientist* 27 Oct. 162/3 In the ICT command language it is possible to define new commands in the language in terms of those already defined. An example of this 'macro' facility is given here... The effect is to allow the user to condense a long and complicated job description into a shorthand phrase of his own choice. The use of 'macros' in this way makes it extremely easy for the user to set up his own conventions. **1970** O. DOPPING *Computers & Data Processing* xix. 324 As an advantage of automatic coding, it is pointed out that the macros and subroutines are tested and error-free, in contrast to home-made subroutines. **1972** J. J. DONOVAN *Systems Programming* iv. 111 In employing a macro, the programmer essentially defines a single 'instruction' to represent a block of code. For every occurrence of this one-line macro instruction in his program, the macro processing assembler will substitute the entire block.

2. *Photogr.* (See MACRO- 2 c.)

macro- (ˈmækrəʊ), before a vowel **macr-**, repr. Gr. μακρο-, comb. form of μακρός long, large, used in many scientific terms (see also the main words).

a. *Phys.* and *Path.*, in sbs. of mod.L. form in *-ia* compounded with Gr. names for different parts of the body, and signifying excessive development of the part in question, as **ˌmacroceˈphalia** [Gr. κεφαλή head] (also anglicized **macroˈcephaly**), excessive length or size of the head. **ˌmacroˈcheilia** [Gr. χεῖλος lip], an enlargement and thickening of the lips. **ˌmacroˈglossia** [Gr. γλῶσσα tongue], a progressive enlargement of the tongue, with protrusion from the mouth. **ˌmacroˈmelia** [Gr. μέλος limb], abnormal development of a limb. **ˌmacroˈstomia** [Gr. στόμα mouth], abnormal extension of one or both angles of the mouth.

1889 *Syd. Soc. Lex.*, **Macrocephalia, Macrocephaly.* **1883** *Ashhurst's Internat. Encycl. Surg.* III. 34 **Macro-chilia.* **1899** *Allbutt's Syst. Med.* VI. 455 Macrocheilia is a similar condition to macroglossia. **1862** *Syd. Soc. Yearbk.* 117 Case of *Macroglossia. **1870** *Holmes' Syst. Surg.* (ed. 2) IV. 216 Macro-glossia. **1899** *Allbutt's Syst. Med.* VI. 452 They.. may occur on the limbs, giving rise to *macro-melia. **1854** JONES & SIEV. *Pathol. Anat.* (1874) 535 *Makro-stomia, is prolongation of the corners of the mouth.

b. in sbs. in which the combining form *macro-* is prefixed to a sb. to indicate either that the individual is of unusual size, or that it contains a number of smaller individuals (for the signification see the second member in each case); chiefly formed for antithesis with words beginning with *micro-* of earlier or simultaneous formation, as ***macrochromosome, macrococcus, macroconidium, macrocyst, macro-farad, macrogamete, macrogametocyte, macrogonidium, macromerozoite, macro-nucleus, macro-septum, macrosomite*** (hence ***-somitic*** adj.), ***macro-stylospore, macro-vegetation, macrozoogonidium, macrozoospore***; **ˈmacroform** (see quot.); **ˈmacrofossil** *Palæont.*, a fossil discernible to the naked eye; **ˈmacro-instruction** *Computers*, an instruction in a programming or source language which is equivalent to a specified set of ordinary instructions in an object language (which may be the source language or machine language); freq. as two words (cf. MACRO *sb.* 1); **maˈcrophagous** *Zool.* [-PHAGOUS], feeding on relatively large pieces of food; **macroˈtrichium** *Ent.* [Gr. θρίξ, τριχ- hair], usu. in pl. **macroˈtrichia**, in certain insects, the larger hairs on the body, esp. those on the surface of the wings.

1905, 1969 *Macrochromosome [see *microchromosome* s.v. MICRO- 1]. **1887** GARNSEY & BALFOUR tr. *De Bary's Fungi* 458 Cocci..are distinguished..according to their dimensions into *micrococci*, **macrococci*, and *monad-forms.* **1874** COOKE *Fungi* 175 As early as 1860 he [Tulasne] recognized the large..vesicles which originate the fertile tissue, but did not comprehend the part which these *Macrocysts were to perform. **1884** H. M. WARD in *Q. Jrnl. Microscop. Sci.* XXIV. 279 Each pair consists of a macrocyst and a so-called paracyst. **1967** *Anglo-Amer. Catal. Rules: Brit. Text* 267 **Macroform*, a reproduction large enough to be easily read by the unaided eye. Used in contradistinction to 'microform'. **1937** G. D. HANNA in Camp & Hanna *Methods in Paleont.* II. 79 Under the term *macrofossils it will be desirable to treat together many of the larger groups of invertebrates such as the Mollusca, Brachiopoda, Echinodermata, Bryozoa, and Crustacea... All forms more than 10 mm. in diameter will be treated as macrofossils. **1969** BENNISON & WRIGHT *Geol. Hist. Brit. Isles* ii. 34 The larger fossils (macrofossils) of the Chalk are largely neritic. **1974** A. HUXLEY *Plant & Planet* ii. 9 Tertiary and Cretaceous sediments in Venezuela and Borneo..yielded a detailed pollen record but virtually no macro-fossils. **1899** *Allbutt's Syst. Med.* VIII. 945 The female gametocyte, consisting of a single *macrogamete. **1903** E. A. MINCHIN *Sporozoa* in Ray Lankester *Zool.* I. *Protozoa* 215 Since..the gametes are differentiated into male elements or *microgametes*, and female elements or *macrogametes*, their mother cells must be distinguished further into *microgametocytes* and **macrogametocytes.* **1853** HENFREY [tr. *Braun's Rejuvenesc.*] *Bot. & Physiol. Mem.* (Ray Soc.) 137 Plants with two kinds of moving germ-cells, large (**macrogonidia*) and small (*microgonidia*). **1959** *Macroinstruction [see MICROINSTRUCTION]. **1959, 1961** [see MACRO *sb.* 1]. **1961** *Times* 3 Oct. (Computer Suppl.) p. x/5 Through the use of these macro-instructions the computer can be given the semblance of being a much more powerful machine than it really is. **1970** O. DOPPING *Computers & Data Processing* xix. 312 By introducing macro instructions in the source language, the designer can bring about the same ease of programming as could be achieved by giving the computer a more powerful operation list than it really has. But naturally, one does not get the same advantages in terms of economy of memory space and computer time as would be obtained if the more powerful instructions were really built into the machine. **1972** Macro instruction [see MACRO *sb.* 1]. **1903** E. A. MINCHIN *Sporozoa* in Ray Lankester *Zool.* I. *Protozoa* 256 Within the cytocyst the schizont may break up into smaller micromerozoites or larger *macromerozoites. **1892** J. A. THOMSON *Outlines of Zoology* 101 In the ciliated Infusorians there are two nuclear bodies... The smaller or micro-nucleus lies by the side of the larger or *macro-nucleus. **1949** I. F. & W. D. HENDERSON *Dict. Sci. Terms* (ed. 4) 240/1 *Macrophagous.

..Feeding on relatively large masses of food; *opp.* microphagous. **1951** M. ABERCROMBIE et al. *Dict. Biol.* 130 All land animals are macrophagous. **1964** *Oceanogr. & Marine Biol.* II. 396 He [*sc.* A. R. Fontaine] finds both microphagous and macrophagous mechanisms are used in this species [sc. *Ophiocomina nigra*]. **1888** *Amer. Nat.* XXII. 942 The head..is divided into..the primitive head-segment..and the gnathophorous *macrosomite. *Ibid.* 941 The..primary or *macrosomitic segmentation of the primitive body. **1934** C. H. CURRAN *Families & Genera N. Amer. Diptera* 487 *Macrotrichia—The larger microscopic hairs on the surface of the wings. **1957** RICHARDS & DAVIES *Imms's Textbk. Ent.* (ed. 9) I. 12 Setae or Macrotrichia are commonly known as hairs and each arises from a cup-like pit or alveolus. *Ibid.* 38 Macrotrichia or true setae..are found on the main veins and their branches,..less frequently on the wing-membrane. **1970** E. F. RIEK in *Insects of Australia* (Commonwealth Sci. & Industr. Res. Organization) xxxvii. 875/2 Hooked macrotrichia may occur over most of the fore margin of the hind wing [in Hymenoptera]. **1958** *Jrnl. du Conseil Internat. Explor. de la Mer* XXIV. 32 Samples of *macrovegetation were collected in the spring. **1960** *Oikos* XI. 183 (*heading*) Subaquatic macrovegetation in Ösbysjön, Djursholm. **1880** BESSEY *Botany* 223 The protoplasmic contents of certain cells [of *Hydrodictyon*] break up into a large number of daughter-cells (*macrozoogonidia). **1875** *Q. Jrnl. Microscop. Sci.* XV. 396 *Macrozoospores (which germinate asexually).

c. *Cryst.* **macro-axis** = *macrodiagonal* sb. **ˌmacrodiˈagonal** *sb.* the longer of the diagonals of a rhombic prism; also *adj.*, pertaining to this diagonal. **ˈmacrodome**, a dome (see DOME 5 b) parallel to the macrodiagonal; hence **macrodoˈmatic** *a.*, pertaining to the macrodome. **macroˈpinacoid**, a pinacoid parallel to the vertical and macrodiagonal axes. **ˈmacroprism**, a prism of an orthorhombic crystal between the macropinacoid and the unit prism. **ˌmacroˈpyramid**, a pyramid corresponding to the macroprism.

1898 DANA *Mineral.*, *Macro-axis. **1848** WEBSTER, **Macro-diagonal.* **1858** THUDICHUM *Urine* 143 The planes ..of the macrodiagonal prism [are inclined] at an angle of 85° 14′. **1883** HEDDLE in *Encycl. Brit.* XVI. 360/1 To the greater lateral axis the name macrodiagonal is given. *Ibid.* 360/2 When n = ∞ a *macrodome results. *Ibid.*, The limiting *macropinacoid. *Ibid.*, On the one side originate numerous *macroprisms. *Ibid.*, A new pyramid is produced, named a *macropyramid. **1878** LAWRENCE tr. *Cotta's Rocks Classified* 29 Cleavage prismatic, very perfect, *Macrodomatic perfect.

d. in adjs., with sense 'containing or possessed of some object in a largely developed form', as **macroˈcranial** *a.*, having a long skull; macrocephalic. **maˈcrandrous** *a. Bot.* [Gr. ἀνδρ-, ἀνήρ man], having elongated male plants. **macroˈdactyl** *a.* = MACROBIAN *a.*; *sb.* (see quot.). **macrodacˈtylic, -ˈdactylous** *adjs.* [Gr. δάκτυλος finger, toe], having long fingers or toes. **ˈmacrodont** *a.* [Gr. ὀδοντ-, ὀδούς tooth], having long teeth. **ˌmacroˈpetalous** *a.* [Gr. πέταλον leaf], having long or large leaves or petals (Mayne *Expos. Lex.* 1856). **macroˈphallic** *a.*, having a large phallus. **macroˈphylline, -ˈphyllous** *adjs.* [Gr. φύλλον leaf], having long or large leaves. **ˌmacroˈpleural** *a.* [Gr. πλευρά rib, side], having long pleuræ. **ˌmacroˈstylous** *a. Bot.*, having a long style (Mayne *Expos. Lex.* 1856). **maˈcrotous** *a.* [Gr. ὠτ-, οὖς ear], having long ears. **ˈmacrotypous** *a. Min.* [TYPE], having a long form.

1882-4 COOKE *Brit. Fresh-w. Algæ* I. 148 Male plants, dwarf (nannandrous)..or elongated (*macrandrous). **1902** *Biometrika* Aug. 462 Dolichocephaly and chamaecephaly in both races are associated with *macrocranial characters. **1907** *Practitioner* Aug. 318 The population of the south-west of Scotland, exclusive of Glasgow, is longheaded or macrocranial. **1837** PARTINGTON *Brit. Cycl. Nat. Hist.* III. 73 **Macrodactyles*, long toes. The last of the regular families into which Cuvier divides the stilt birds or waders. **1836** —— *Ibid.* II. 886 Cuvier's *Macrodactylic, or long-toed family of *Echassiers*, or stilt birds. **1848** MAUNDER *Treas. Nat. Hist.* Gloss., **Macrodactylous*, furnished with long toes adapted for traversing floating leaves and aquatic herbage. **1891** FLOWER & LYDEKKER *Mammals* 745 [Negroid type.] Thick, everted lips; prognathous jaws; large teeth (*macrodont). **1970** F. SNOWDEN *Blacks in Antiquity* 23 The circumcised and *macrophallic Ethiopians. **1972** *Sunday Times* 23 Apr. 43 Commercial porn..with its inevitable distortions, brutalised women and macrophallic faceless men. **1871** W. A. LEIGHTON *Lichen-flora* 55 Thallus *macrophylline. **1856** MAYNE *Expos. Lex.*, *Macrophyllus* ..*macrophyllous. **1881** in *Academy* 22 Oct. 315 The *macropleural and brachypleural types. **1886** FORD in *Amer. Jrnl. Sci.* Ser. III. XXXII. 475 Reasons for believing that the Brachypleural species of the genus *Paradoxides* are more recent than the Macropleural. **1887** WARD tr. *Sachs' Physiol. Plants* 790 The pollen of the *macrostylous flowers is transferred to the microstylous stigma of another plant. **1840** SMART, **Macrotous*, long-eared. **1821** JAMESON *Man. Mineral.* 55 *Macro-typous Limestone.

e. Terms in which *macro-* indicates subject-matter treated on a larger scale, or more comprehensive phenomena or levels of treatment, than is implied either by the word to which *macro-* is attached or by the corresponding term beginning *micro-*, as ***macro-planning***, ***-sociology*** (hence *-sociological* adj.); ***macro-historical*** adj.; **ˈmacroclimate**, the general climate of a relatively large area; so **ˌmacrocliˈmatic** *a.*; **ˌmacro-evoˈlution**, evolutionary change over a long period, leading to the appearance of new groups of plants or animals; **ˈmacrophysics**, the part of physics that is concerned with bodies and phenomena on a macroscopic scale; so **macroˈphysical** *a.*

1939 *Geogr. Jrnl.* XCIII. 463 As in all local climates strong departure from the *macroclimate develops in the climates of cities in calm cloudless weather. **1967** M. J. COE *Ecol. Alpine Zone Mt. Kenya* 59 This remarkable contrast between the micro- and macroclimates of these areas is expressed even more clearly by Mani. **1971** J. Z. YOUNG *Introd. Study Man* xxxviii. 544 The British..move with less protection in their damp but equable macroclimate. **1939** *Ecology* XX. 30 Microclimate..makes it possible for smaller groups of preclimax vegetation to persist as relict colonies long after *macroclimatic changes have shifted formations. **1946** S. A. WILDE *Forest Soils* iii. 21 Macro-climatic soil-forest zones. **1939** *Ann. Reg. 1938* 369 The gene theory was applied increasingly to problems of *macro-evolution. **1940** R. GOLDSCHMIDT *Material Basis of Evolution* iii. 8 Microevolution..has been used..for evolutionary processes observable within the span of a human lifetime as opposed to macroevolution, on a geological scale. **1972** *Listener* 3 Aug. 138/2 There may be a different mechanism for grand heroic macro-evolution and for ordinary humdrum everyday evolution at species or sub-species level. **1955** *Bull. Atomic Sci.* Feb. 42/2 There are some who profess to see in matters of culture, in matters precisely of the arts and sciences, a certain *macro-historical pattern, a grand system of laws which determines the course of civilization and gives a kind of inevitable quality to the unfolding of the future. **1902** MANN & MILLIKAN tr. *Drude's Theory of Optics* p. vii, Pure electromagnetic experiments lead to conclusions in what may be called the domain of *macrophysical properties only. For the explanation of optical dispersion a hypothesis as to the microphysical properties of bodies must be made. **1956** E. H. HUTTEN *Lang. Mod. Physics* v. 179 Two micro-physical events are connected in a different way from two macro-physical events. **1960** *Times* 15 Mar. 2/2 A study of the relationships between the macro-physical properties of soils and the physical chemistry of their colloidal constituents. **1909** *Cent. Dict.* Suppl., *Macrophysics. **1936** *Discovery* Mar. 96/2 Thirteen unsolved problems are listed, ranging from those concerning the creation of the universe..to the structure of the atom, from macrophysics and astronomy *via* biology..back to physical science again. **1956** *Nature* 18 Feb. 321/1 Mr. F. H. Ludlam..pointed out that the partitioning (into micro-, macro- and synoptic-physics) of cloud studies..must not be made too rigid. **1966** *Economist* 11 June 1206/1 To mention only a few [contributions], largely concerned with *macro-planning: welfare-theoretical problems and planner's and consumer's sovereignty are the theme of Joan Robinson. **1973** *Financial Times* 26 Mar. 16/4 The macro-planning functions of the metropolitan county (mainly transport and town and country planning, together with fire and police, consumer protection, [etc.]). **1951** R. FIRTH *Elem. Social Organiz.* i. 18 If the distinguishing feature of the anthropologist is micro-sociological technique, his theory is *macro-sociological. **1970** *New Society* 5 Feb. 232/3 The approach, the initiated will recognise, is essentially macrosociological. **1941** G. GURVITCH in *Jrnl. Philos.* XXXVIII. 486 *Macrosociology is the study of the world of groups and of global societies, each of which are microcosms of the forms of sociality. **1958** W. STARK *Sociol. of Knowl.* i. 20 It might be useful..to call the one the macrosociology of knowledge, because it fixes its attention on the inclusive society.

2. Combs. in which *macro* can be regarded as a separable element having adjectival force, with the meaning: macroscopic, large-scale; overall, comprehensive; large. Hence used as an independent word not preceding the sb. it qualifies.

1934 WEBSTER, *Macro* adj. = *macro-*. **1937** *Mind* XLVI. 327 Quantum mechanics, moreover, claims applicability not only to micro-processes; it also contains laws of mechanics which are applicable to macro-processes. **1954** *Gloss. Terms Iron & Steel* (*B.S.I.*) I. 19 *Macro etch test*, etching with acids or other reagents to reveal the macro structure, flow lines and/or defects. **1957** C. DAY LEWIS *Poet's Way of Knowl.* 14 Until recently the scientist has sought for general laws governing macro-events, and has drawn from them inferences about individual events. **1959** K. R. POPPER *Logic Sci. Discovery* II. viii. 196 Observable physical effects are interpreted as 'macro laws'. **1961** G. H. ORCUTT et al. *Microanalysis Socioecon. Syst.* p. xv, Given the possibility of experimentation at both micro- and macrolevels, it has been possible for the physical sciences to achieve great successes at both levels without the necessity of predicting aggregate behavior on the basis of knowledge about microbehavior. **1962** J. T. MARSH *Self-Smoothing Fabrics* xv. 263 This type of staining test..does, however, demonstrate irregularity of distribution on a macro-basis as distinct from a micro-basis, and provide useful evidence of uneven impregnation during padding, or of resin migration during drying. **1966** *McGraw-Hill Encycl. Sci. & Technol.* XI. 143/2 The instruments and apparatus used in microanalytical work are to some extent miniature replicas of macro instruments and apparatus. **1967** COX & GROSE *Organiz. Bibliogr. Rec. by Computer* v. 107 Before I move from the macro-level of the overall design of a MARC service to the minutiae of record data content and file organization. **1967** D. WILSON in Wills & Yearsley *Handbk. Managem. Technol.* iii. 47 The logic for the individual programs is expressed in terms of macro and micro block-diagrams. The macro block-diagrams show the main logic for a particular program and may be prepared by the systems analyst; the micro block-diagrams show the detailed logic for program coding and will be prepared by the programmer. **1970** *Guardian Weekly* 18 Apr. 15 Revolutions, including the Russian one, made the mistake of insisting that the macro-change, of the whole system, should come before micro-change, of the life style. **1971** *New Scientist* 21 Jan. 100/1 Undoubtedly a number of serious macro-problems face the Ulster community. *Ibid.* 100/2 In the absence of a knowledge of these macro-changes, systems will continue to evolve on the basis of year-to-year crisis decisions. **1971** *Good Motoring* Sept. 9/2 As vehicle speeds rise from 25–30 mph to 60–70 mph, however, tyre grip in wet weather diminishes unless there is also 'macro' or large-scale roughness of the surface. **1973** A. E. WILKERSON *Rights of Children* 307 These issues..reflect the necessity for a macro-approach to child welfare. **1974** *Times Lit. Suppl.* 8 Mar. 242/5 The forms and methods of economic management, both micro and macro.

b. *Chem.* Of or pertaining to macroanalysis. Cf. MACRO-SCALE.

1933 *Biochem. Jrnl.* XXVII. 434 The present micro-method for urea in 0·2 cc of blood compares very favourably with the comparatively macro-method of Van Slyke and Cullen. **1938** ARTHUR & SMITH *Semi-Micro Qualitative Analysis* I. 3 Dealing with samples of only 3 to 5 mg. (compared with the usual 0·5 to 1·0 g. macro sample), the micro method consumes much less time for reactions..and in many other ways proves superior to the macro methods. **1946** MELDRUM & DAGGETT *Textbk. Qualitative Analysis* i. 2 The two..generally applicable methods of qualitative analysis of inorganic materials are the macro and the semimicro methods. **1974** [see MICRO- 8 b].

c. *Photogr.* Denoting apparatus or procedures used in macrophotography, as **macro lens** (also *ellipt.* as *macro*), a lens suitable for taking photographs unusually close to the subject.

1956 *Focal Encycl. Photogr.* 688/1 A camera with back focusing is a great advantage in macro work. **1961** L. A. MANNHEIM tr. *Croy's Camera Close Up* 85 The maximum aperture of a macro-lens depends..on its design. *Ibid.* 88 Macro-exposures. Exposures in close-up work have to allow for..the subject and its lighting..and the scale of reproduction. **1968** GAUNT & PETZOLD *Pict. Cycl. Photogr.* 425/2 The main requirement for a macro-camera is adequate lens extension. **1971** *Amat. Photographer* 13 Jan. 80/1 (Advt.), 50 mm f/3·5 Macro. **1974** *Ibid.* 29 May 8/1 The picture on the left could only have been taken with a macro lens. *Ibid.*, It's impossible to combine macro and telephoto in one lens.

macroanalysis (mækrəʊæˈnælɪsɪs). *Chem.* [f. MACRO- 1 e + ANALYSIS.] Quantitative analysis of samples of the size for which the older chemical techniques were usually developed, commonly 0·1–1 gramme.

1938 MELDRUM & FLOSDORF *Qualitative Analysis Inorg. Materials* 1. 7 Microanalysis may be applied when the amount of material available..is very small... Many of the reactions are essentially the same as those used in the systematic macroanalysis. **1955** [see MICRO- 8 b]. **1966** *McGraw-Hill Encycl. Sci. & Technol.* XI. 143/1 Methods of quantitative analysis vary with the amount of sample taken and of constituent being determined. A macro-analysis (decigram analysis) uses a sample of about 0·1–0·5 gram.

macrobian (məˈkrəʊbɪən), *a.* [f. Gr. μακρόβιο-ς (f. μακρό-ς long + βίος life) + -AN.] Long-lived.

[**1727** BRADLEY *Fam. Dict.* s.v. *Age*, The Macrobian Pills ..have their Name from a Greek Word which signifies long Life.] **1859** R. F. BURTON *Centr. Afr.* in *Jrnl. Geogr. Soc.* XXIX. 323 The race is still macrobian, arriving late at maturity.

macrobiote (-ˈbaɪəʊt). *rare*$^{-1}$. [ad. Gr. μακροβίοτος, f. μακρό-ς long + βίοτος life.] A long-liver.

1882 F. L. OSWALD in *Pop. Sci. Monthly* XXI. 590 The Thessalian mountaineers were the macrobiotes, the long-livers, par excellence, of the Roman Empire.

macrobiotic (ˌmækrəʊbaɪˈɒtɪk), *a.* and *sb.* [Formed as prec. + -IC.] **1.** *a. adj.* Inclined or tending to prolong life; relating to the prolongation of life. **b.** *sb. pl.* The science of prolonging life.

1797 *Hufeland's Art Prolong. Life* Pref. (1853) 11 Hence arises a particular science, the Macrobiotic, or the art of prolonging it [life], which forms the subject of the present work. **1822** *New Monthly Mag.* V. 351 Any of your readers ..of macrobiotic tendencies. **1862** DE QUINCEY *Wks.* X. 251 *note*, A Greek work on the subject of macro-biotics. **1879** *Punch* 1 Nov. 201/2 Dr. Richardson..is a great makrobiotic sage.

2. *adj.* Of or pertaining to a Zen Buddhist dietary system intended to prolong life, comprising pure vegetable foods, brown rice, etc. Also as *sb.*, a follower or adherent of this system; **macrobiotics** *sb. pl.* (const. as *sing.*), the use or theory of such a dietary system.

1936 L. P. WEAVER tr. *Székely's Cosmos, Man & Society* III. ii. 207 (*heading*) Macrobiotics, the optimal and omnilateral correlations of longevity. **1965** W. DUFTY *You are All Sanpaku* (Eng. version of *Y. Sakurazawa's Zen Macrobiotics*) 178 Macrobiotics is not the kind of vegetarianism which is merely sentimental. **1968** *New Yorker* 10 Feb. 22 Macrobiotic. That means she'll eat fish. **1969** *Listener* 17 July 79/3 Macrobiotics is a life science discovered in Japan by Georges Ohsawa and it's based on the two pillars of philosophy and diet—the staple food being brown rice. **1970** M. SPARK *Driver's Seat* 48 Rice, unpolished rice is the basis of macrobiotics... It is a cleansing diet. Physically, mentally and spiritually. **1970** *Time* 16 Nov. 59 Most macrobiotics, as Ohsawa's devotees call themselves, try to follow his other nine diets, which are graduated from six to minus three to include increasing amounts of fish and vegetables—organically grown—along with brown rice. **1971** *Courier-Mail* (Brisbane) 10 May 9/4 Macrobiotic nibblers of seeds, bean curd, kale, other seaweeds and brown rice, are spreading their message of love and peace by feeding. **1971** *Daily Tel.* 18 Oct. 4/6 The macrobiotic diet, a rigid system based on vegetables and cereals..is denounced..by the American Medical Association as bad for health and even potentially lethal. **1972** *Guardian* 1 Dec. 11/2 Right now she is into the Zen macrobiotic brown-rice bit. **1973** 'P. REID' *Harris in Wonderland* vii. 55 Supper..was macrobiotic, leeks and brown rice on a wooden plate. **1975** *Listener* 1 May 589/3

Macrobiotics crumbling to death in the name of good health.

macrocarpa (ˌmækrəˈkɑːpə). [mod.L., specific epithet of *Cupressus macrocarpa* (T. Hartweg 1847, in *Jrnl. Hort. Soc.* II. 187), f. Gr. μακρό-ς large + καρπός fruit.] An evergreen tree, *Cupressus macrocarpa*, native to the Monterey peninsula of California and widely cultivated elsewhere, esp. as a fast-growing hedge or windbreak; = *Monterey cypress*. Also *attrib.*

[**1866** 'SENILIS' *Pinaceæ* 73 It [*sc.* large-coned cypress] is to be found in two forms. *Macrocarpa*, when raised from seed, has a distinct, continuous, and erect leader with the side branches regularly disposed and gracefully drooping.] **1905** *Daily News* 12 Feb. 4/6 The Bird only moved from a macrocarpa tree to the cypress and lime trees. **1922** *N.Z. Jrnl. Agric.* 20 Mar. 176 The macrocarpa is very rapid in its growth. **1935** *Discovery* Dec. 375/1, I have found macrocarpa hedges a very popular breeding place for various species. **1937** 'R. HYDE' *Persephone in Winter* 42 The faint wet tang of macrocarpa leaves. **1948** J. BETJEMAN *Sel. Poems* 78 Those macrocarpas still survive the gales They must have had last winter. **1950** *N.Z. Jrnl. Agric.* Feb. 163 Good, well-kept shelter belts of macrocarpa. **1959** A. MCLINTOCK *Descr. Atlas N.Z.* p. xiii, Plantations and shelter belts of introduced (exotic) trees, mainly radiata pine and macrocarpa, break up the farm-lands. **1966** G. W. TURNER *Eng. Lang. Austral. & N.Z.* iv. 82 Children..grew up among the pine and macrocarpa hedges or bleak unsheltered paddocks which replaced the bush.

macrocephalic (ˌmækrəʊsɪˈfælɪk), *a.* [f. Gr. μακροκέφαλ-ος (f. μακρό-ς long + κεφαλή head) + -IC.] **a.** Pertaining to persons with long or large heads. **b.** Of a person: Having a long or large head.

1851 D. WILSON *Preh. Ann.* (1863) I. ix. 236 The macrocephalic skulls of the Crimea. **1877** BURNETT *Ear* 25 In macrocephalic heads we find large massive ears. **1898** TUNNICLIFFE in *Nature* 15 Dec. 150/1 To the physician the professional athlete is neither more nor less interesting than the macrocephalic dwarf.

macrocephalous (ˌmækrəʊˈsɛfələs), *a.* [f. Gr. μακροκέφαλ-ος (see prec.) + -OUS.] Long-headed. **a.** Having or pertaining to a long head. **b.** *Bot.* Said of dicotyledonous embryos whose cotyledons are consolidated.

1835 LINDLEY *Introd. Bot.* I. ii. (1839) 251 Those embryos which..Richard [called] macrocephalous. **1865** THURNAM in *Nat. Hist. Rev.* V. 266 The macrocephalous skulls of the Crimea.

macrochoanite (ˌmækrəʊˈkəʊənaɪt). *Palæont.* [f. MACRO- + Gr. χοάν-η funnel + -ITE[1] 2 a.] A nautiloid cephalopod once included in a suborder Macrochoanites, in which each septal neck reaches back into the preceding one. Hence ˌ**macrochoaˈnitic** *a.*, (having septal necks) characteristic of a macrochoanite.

1883 A. HYATT in *Proc. Boston Soc. Nat. Hist.* XXII. 260 We, therefore, divide the Ellipochoanoida into the true Microchoanites,..and the Macrochoanites. *Ibid.*, In the more complicated forms of Goniatitinæ, while the young are quite generally macrochoanitic, the later larval stages and the adults are universally short funnelled. **1964** C. TEICHERT in R. C. Moore *Treat. Invertebr. Paleont.* K 39/1 Macrochoanitic necks are found only in the Endocerida. *Ibid.* 95/1 Hyatt distinguished the Bactritidae as 'Macrochoanites'.

macrocosm (ˈmækrəʊkɒz(ə)m). Also rarely in L. and quasi-Gr. forms: 7 **macrocosmus**, 9 **-cosmos**. [ad. F. *macrocosme* (*c* 1300), ad. med.L. *macrocosmus*, repr. Gr. *μακρὸς κόσμος (μακρός long, great, κόσμος world). (Cf. MEGACOSM.)

Although med.L. *macrocosmus* has not been found earlier than in Higden (*c* 1350) it must be the source of the Fr. form recorded *c* 1300, and it seems to imply the prior existence of a Gr. phrase *μακρὸς κόσμος formed in imitation of μικρὸς κόσμος MICROCOSM. For the idea expressed, cf. Macrobius *in Somn. Scip.* I. xii, 'Ideo physici mundum magnum hominem, et hominem brevem mundum esse dixerunt'. From the use of *brevem* here, and the gloss 'Microscosmum ..*petit monde, c'est l'homme qui pou dure*' (Du Cange), it may be suspected that μακρός was at first intended in the sense of 'long', interpreted with regard to duration; though the inference is not absolutely necessary, as the formal similarity of the word to μικρός would sufficiently account for its selection in an antithetic phrase. However this may be, the relation of the words *macrocosm* and *microcosm* has suggested the use of MACRO- with the sense 'on a large scale', in many modern words antithetic to words beginning with *micro-*.]

1. The 'great world' or universe, in contradistinction to the 'little world' or MICROCOSM, i.e. to man viewed as an epitome of the universe.

The earliest instances of the word in Eng. occur in Lydgate's *Assembly of the Gods* (*c* 1420; oldest MS. *a* 1500), where however it is a mistake (either on the part of Lydgate or of the scribe) for *microcosm*. (See, e.g., line 1828: And as for Macrocosme, hit ys no more to say But the lesse worlde.)

1600 W. WATSON *Decacordon* (1602) 274 Throughout all this vaste Macrocosme, they finde not one patterne..like to ours. **1794** G. ADAMS *Nat. & Exp. Philos.* IV. xlix. 353 Applied and determined by an Infinite Mind in the macrocosm or universe. **1867** FROUDE *Short Stud., Sci. Hist.* 9 He desires, first, to see the spirit of the Macrocosmos. **1881** HUXLEY in *Nature* No. 615. 346 The microcosm repeats the macrocosm.

2. *transf.* In various occasional applications, denoting some great whole, the structure of which is conceived to be imaged on a smaller scale by that of some constituent portion of it.

1851 SIR F. PALGRAVE *Norm. & Eng.* I. 347 No population ..is absolutely inert in the macrocosm of humanity. **1875** *N. Amer. Rev.* CXX. 256 The macrocosm of society can be inferred from the microcosm of individual human nature. **1896** J. R. HARRIS *Union with God* iii. 59 His life is the great life, and all our little lives are involved in it, Christ being the macrocosm, and ourselves the microcosm.

Hence ˌ**macroˈcosmic** *a.* [-IC], of or pertaining to the macrocosm or universe. †**macroˈcosmical** *a.* [-IC + -AL], = MACROCOSMIC *a.* **macrocosˈmology** [-(O)LOGY], a description of the macrocosm.

1625 GILL *Sacr. Philos.* IV. 53 There is some powerfull principle, for sending up such waters which naturally doe flee from heat, as this macrocosmicall Sun is for drawing of them upward. **1690** W. Y. *Artif. Wines* To Rdr. A ij b, When the Macrocosmical World was finished. **1856** MAYNE *Expos. Lex.*, *Macrocosmical, Macrocosmology.* **1871** TYLOR *Prim. Cult.* I. 316 It forms part of that macrocosmic description of the universe well known in Asiatic myth.

macroˈcosmically, *adv.* [f. MACROCOSMIC *a.*: see -LY[2].] In relation to the macrocosm.

1881 [see MICROCOSMICALLY *adv.*]. **1939** C. WILLIAMS *Descent of Dove* 128 Considered macrocosmically or microcosmically.

macrocyclic (mækrəʊˈsaɪklɪk), *a.* [f. MACRO- + CYCLIC *a.*] **1.** *Bot.* Of a rust fungus: having a long life cycle.

1926 ARTHUR & KERN in *Mycologia* XVIII. 90 The vegetative body is either long-cycle (macrocyclic), consisting of two unlike and discontinuous generations, or short-cycle (microcyclic), consisting of one continuous generation. *Ibid.* 91 We are indebted to Dr. G. Lagerheim, of Stockholm, for the suggestion of the terms macrocyclic and microcyclic which seem to us to be very appropriate and satisfactory. **1929** [see ÆCIUM]. **1950** E. A. BESSEY *Morphol. & Taxon. Fungi* xii. 396 Rusts possessing such a cycle are called macrocyclic or long-cycle rusts. **1970** J. WEBSTER *Introd. Fungi* 376 It is also believed that forms with shorter life cycles arose..from macrocyclic ancestors.

2. *Chem.* Containing or being a ring composed of a relatively large number of atoms.

1947 R. L. WAKEMAN *Chem. Commercial Plastics* xi. 225 Macrocyclic esters can thus be formed, containing even as many as 16 or more members in the ring. **1960** [see MACROLIDE]. **1964** M. HYNES *Med. Bacteriol.* (ed. 8) x. 137 These substances, as well as erythromycin, have a macrocyclic lactose ring, and are sometimes termed macrolides. **1972** BANTHORPE & CHARLWOOD in A. A. Newman *Chem. Terpenes* vii. 377 The macrocyclic compound cembrene..is probably derived from GGPP.

Hence (as a back-formation) ˈ**macrocycle**, a macrocyclic compound or molecule.

1956 *Nature* 14 Jan. 70/1 Synthesis of azaporphins and related macrocycles. **1971** *Ibid.* 17 Sept. 183/1 Several [antibiotics] have structures made up of two types of chemical entity; for example..the macrolides (macrocycles attached to carbohydrate residues). **1974** *Chem. Rev.* LXXIV. 351/2 Christensen and coworkers have discussed for several classes of macrocycles their unique ion binding properties.

macrocyte (ˈmækrəsaɪt). *Path.* [f. MACRO- + -CYTE.] An abnormally large red blood-corpuscle found in some forms of anæmia. Hence **macrocythæmia, -emia** (-sɪˈθiːmɪə) [Gr. αἷμα blood], the presence of macrocytes in the blood; **macrocytic** (-ˈsɪtɪk) *a.*, typical or characteristic of a macrocyte; characterized by macrocytes; **macrocytosis** (-saɪˈtəʊsɪs) = MACROCYTHÆMIA.

1889 *Syd. Soc. Lex.*, *Macrocyte.* **1893** DUNGLISON *Dict. Med. Sci.* (ed. 21) 656/2 *Macrocytosis*, condition in which the red corpuscles are increased in size, becoming macrocytes. **1894** GOULD *Illustr. Dict. Med.*, *Macrocythemia.* **1897** *Allbutt's Syst. Med.* II. 750 If..a further examination of the blood be made,..both microcytes and macrocytes will have practically disappeared. **1898** *Ibid.* V. 414 This condition, named *macrocythæmia*, is apt to occur..in any case of severe anæmia. **1930** DAVIDSON & GULLAND *Pernicious Anæmia* xi. 237 We would describe the condition as a macrocytic hæmolytic anæmia. **1930** M. M. WINTROBE in *Proc. Soc. Exper. Biol. & Med.* XXVII. 1072 The first and most obvious group [of anemias], which can be called macrocytic, includes the cases of pernicious anemia, sprue, and a case of pernicious anemia of pregnancy. **1932** *Jrnl. Exper. Med.* LVI. 551 Evidence that a normal red corpuscle could change into a macrocytic or a microcytic form. **1947** *Radiology* XLIX. 289/2 Macrocytic anemias appeared in certain animals on chronic exposure to doses in the range under discussion. **1962** *Lancet* 12 May 1004/2 Clinical and hæmatological examinations..showed anæmia with.. macrocytosis, and reticulocytosis. *Ibid.* 1 Dec. 1142/2 The peripheral blood is not strikingly macrocytic. **1968** J. H. BURN *Lect. Notes Pharmacol.* (ed. 9) 79 In pernicious anaemia there is enough haemoglobin but too few red cells. The red cells are swollen (macrocytic) and hyperchromic.

ˌ**macro-ecoˈnomics**, *sb. pl.* (usu. const. as *sing.*). Also **macroeconomics**. [f. MACRO- + ECONOMIC B. *sb.* 2 c.] The science or study of the economy as a whole. Opp. MICRO-ECONOMICS *sb. pl.* So ˌ**macro-ecoˈnomic** *a.*

1948 *Econometrica* XVI. 309 (*heading*) Some conditions of macroeconomic stability. **1948, 1949** [see MICRO-ECONOMICS *sb. pl.*]. **1957** *Economist* 5 Oct. 36/3 The macroeconomic prophets, having seen their forecasts repeatedly falsified, have lost something of their confidence. **1961** G. ACKLEY *Macroecon. Theory* i. 4 Macroeconomics deals with economic affairs 'in the large'. It concerns the over-all dimensions of economic life. **1966** *Listener* 3 Mar. 312/2 Even within the field of what we call macro-economics—the study of what determines the over-all level of activity and other aspects of the economy as a whole—there have been considerable elements of continuity. **1969** *Daily Tel.* 1 Nov. 10 The Government may be difficult to challenge in matters of macro-economics or high finance. When it comes to the practical mechanics of daily life, however, in which a convenient coinage matters a great deal, the public is the best judge. **1971** *New Scientist* 15 Apr. 147/1 The pundits argue about the overall, macro-economic effects of the budget. **1975** *Times* 16 July 15/5 The wonderful world of established macro-economics—no serious unemployment, no intolerable inflation, no controls.

macroërgate, var. MACRERGATE.

macrogametophyte (mækrəʊgæˈmiːtəʊfaɪt). *Bot.* [f. MACRO- + *gametophyte* (s.v. GAMETE).] = MEGAGAMETOPHYTE.

1931 *Bot. Gaz.* XCII. 23 (*heading*) Development of the macrogametophyte and embryo of *Daucus carota*. **1938** G. M. SMITH *Cryptogamic Bot.* II. vii. 193 The developing embryo of *Selaginella* always pushes deeply into the macrogametophyte by means of a suspensor.

macroglobulin (mækrəʊˈglɒbjʊlɪn). *Biochem.* [ad. G. *makroglobulin* (attributed to Pedersen and Waldenström by Waldenström 1948, in *Schweiz. Med. Wochenschr.* 25 Sept. 928/2): see MACRO- b and GLOBULIN.] Any of the immunoglobulins of very high molecular weight (about 1,000,000 or more).

1952 J. WALDENSTRÖM in *Adv. Internal Med.* V. 408 Pedersen compared this normally occurring macromolecule with the pathologic so-called 'macroglobulin' found in the disease described by us as macroglobulinemia. **1961** [see *macroglobulinæmia* below]. **1967** *Times* 21 Nov. 3/6 As well as these small antibody molecules, the body produces much larger antibodies, called macroglobulins.

So ˌ**macroglobuliˈnæmia** [ad. G. *makroglobulinämie* (J. Waldenström 1948, in *Schweiz. Med. Wochenschr.* 25 Sept. 928/2)], an excess of macroglobulins in the blood; esp. (more fully ***Waldenström's macroglobulinæmia*** or ***syndrome***) a disease similar to myelomatosis but less often fatal; ˌ**macroglobuˈlinæmic** *a.*

1949 K. PEDERSEN in *Jrnl. Franklin Inst.* CCXLVIII. 570 In a few rare cases of essential macroglobulinemia.., a very high concentration of the 20 S component has been found. **1961** *Lancet* 5 Aug. 289/2 While there can be no doubt that Waldenström's syndrome exists, it seems that such increases in macroglobulins are not confined to a single disease entity. The term macroglobulinæmia will therefore be used in this paper to refer to the presence in the serum of increased amounts of macroglobulins, regardless of the clinical associations. *Ibid.* 290/1 On paper electrophoresis, macroglobulinæmic sera yield patterns which are indistinguishable from those found in multiple myeloma. **1971** D. HAWKINS in S. O. Freedman *Clin. Immunol.* vi. 179 Patients with Waldenström's [*sic*] macroglobulinemia may have proteinuria and even nephrotic syndrome.

macrognathic (ˌmækrəʊˈgnæθɪk), *a.* [f. MACRO- + Gr. γνάθ-ος jaw + -IC.] Having long or protruding jaws. So **macrognathism** (məˈkrɒgnəθɪz(ə)m), the peculiarity or fact of being macrognathic; protrusion of the jaws. **macrognathous** (məˈkrɒgnəθəs) *a.* = MACROGNATHIC.

1856 MAYNE *Expos. Lex.*, *Macrognathous.* **1864** HUXLEY in *Reader* 5 Mar., The jaws..project more forward than in man, so that the chimpanzee is both macrognathous and prognathous. **1864** —— *ibid.* 19 Mar. 364/3 The macrognathism and prognathism are carried to about the same extent. **1874** DAWKINS *Cave Hunt.* vi. 193 The entire maxillary apparatus is so largely developed, that the term 'macrognathic', introduced by Professor Huxley, is particularly applicable.

macrography (mæˈkrɒgrəfɪ). [f. MACRO- + Gr. -γραφία writing.] Abnormally large writing (as a symptom of nervous disorder). Hence ˌ**macroˈgraphic** *a.*

1899 *Pop. Sci. Monthly* June 203 The macrography alternating with the micrography. *Ibid.* 205 Fig. 3, Macrographic and micrographic writing by the same epileptic.

ˌ**Macrolepiˈdoptera**, *sb. pl. Ent.* [f. MACRO- + LEPIDOPTERA *sb. pl.*] A collective term for the larger butterflies and moths.

1882 W. F. KIRBY *European Butterflies & Moths* p. iii, The present work is designed to provide entomologists.. with a comprehensive illustrated guide to the study of European Macro-Lepidoptera. **1907** R. SOUTH *Moths Brit. Isles* 1st Ser. 6 Quite a number of the species included in that division [*sc.* Micro-lepidoptera] are actually larger than the many kinds that were placed in the other contingent styled Macro-lepidoptera. **1946** *Nature* 12 Oct. 498/2 A well-worked group of insects such as the Macrolepidoptera affords admirable material for faunistic comparisons. **1955** E. B. FORD *Moths* p. xv, The Macro-Lepidoptera are an artificial assemblage, consisting of an arbitrary selection of certain families, and parts of families, without scientific validity. **1972** L. E. CHADWICK tr. *Linsenmaier's Insects of World* 226/2 These families [*sc.* Microlepidoptera] consist of very small species, yet they are in no way separated from the others (the 'Macrolepidoptera').

macrolide ('mækrəlaɪd). *Pharm.* [ad. Polish *makrolid* (Z. Katula 1958, in *Postepy Hig. i Med. Dosiviadczalnej* XII. 491): see MACRO- and LACTIDE.] Any of a class of antibiotics containing macrocyclic lactone rings.

1960 *Biol. Abstr.* XXXV. 4202/2 From the fermentation products of various strains of *Streptomyces* there have been isolated several dozen antibiotics, whose common characteristic is a macrocyclic lactic ring. These antibiotics are called macrolides. **1967** [see ERYTHROMYCIN]. **1968** *New Scientist* 28 Mar. 678/2 Tylosin is a macrolide antibiotic, and organisms resistant to it are often cross-resistant to other macrolides, such as erythromycin, oleandomycin, and spiromycin.

macrology (mæ'krɒlədʒɪ). [ad. L. *macrologia*, a. Gr. μακρολογία, f. μακρολόγος speaking at length, f. μακρό-ς long + -λόγος speaking.] **a.** As a rhetorical figure: The use of redundant words or phrases. **b.** *gen.* Prolixity of speech.

[**1586** A. DAY *Eng. Secretary* II. (1595) 82 *Macrologia* where a clause is finally added to the matter going before, in seeming more then needed.] **1616** BULLOKAR *Eng. Expos.*, *Macrologie*, long and tedious talke. **1656** BLOUNT *Glossogr.*, *Macrology*, prolixity in speaking. **1727** POPE, etc. *Art of Sinking* 105 The Macrology and Pleonasm are as generally coupled, as a lean rabbit with a fat one.

macromere ('mækrəʊmɪə(r)). *Embryology.* [f. Gr. μακρό-ς long + μέρος part.] The larger of the two masses into which the vitellus of the developing ovum of *Lamellibranchiata* divides: cf. MICROMERE. Hence **macro'meral, macro'meric** *adjs.*, of or pertaining to the macromere.

1877 HUXLEY *Anat. Inv. Anim.* viii. 483 Those [blastomeres] which proceed from the macromere long remain larger and more granular than those which proceed from the micromere. *Ibid.* 484 The macromeral hemisphere next undergoes invagination. *Ibid.* 499 The macromeric part of the vitellus. **1895** J. A. THOMSON *Outlines Zool.* (ed. 2) 417 The third cleavage..gives rise to four larger cells (or macromeres),..and to four smaller cells (or micromeres).

macromeritic (ˌmækrəmə'rɪtɪk), *a.* [f. MACRO- + Gr. μέρ-ος part + -ITE + -IC.] Of granitoid rocks: Having a structure discernible by the naked eye; opposed to *micromeritic*.

[**1882** GEIKIE *Text-book Geol.* II. II. iii. 90 This structure is characteristic of many eruptive rocks. Though usually distinctly recognizable by the naked eye ('macromerite' of Vogelsang), it sometimes becomes very fine ('micromerite').] In mod. Dicts.

macrometer (mæ'krɒmɪtə(r)). [f. MACRO- + -METER.] An instrument for measuring distant or inaccessible objects.

1825 W. HAMILTON *Handbk. Terms Arts & Sci.*, *Macrometer*, in Mathematics, an instrument contrived to measure the distance of inaccessible objects by means of two reflectors on a common sextant. **1888** *Encycl. Brit.* XXIII. 126/1 Porro's telemeter, Elliott's telescope, and Nordenfelt's macrometer illustrate the principle.

macromolecule (ˌmækrəʊ'mɒlɪkjuːl, -'məʊlɪkjuːl). *Chem.* [f. MACRO- + MOLECULE.] †**a.** A group of chemical molecules in a crystal bound together in a characteristic shape, which was once believed to account for the symmetry of the crystal. *Obs.*

1886 G. J. STONEY in *Rep. Brit. Assoc. Adv. Sci. 1885* 989 In iron pyrites, FeS_2, the hemihedral form which is characteristic of this mineral..can be traced on from the chemical molecule FeS_2 through a macromolecule which includes six of these as sub-molecules, and which is connected with the other similar macromolecules in a regular way.

b. [ad. G. *makromolekel* (Staudinger & Fritschi 1922, in *Helv. Chim. Acta* V. 788).] A molecule composed of a very large number of atoms and having a high molecular weight (e.g. a molecule of a polymer, a protein, or a nucleic acid).

1935 *Nature* 19 Oct. 626/1 The now generally accepted view that the polymers and condensates must be regarded as constituted of macromolecules formed by the polymerization or condensation of single units. **1957** *New Biol.* XXIII. 66 Proteins are macromolecules normally built up from hundreds or thousands of individual amino acid molecules, and possessing molecular weights in the range of 10,000 to several millions. **1959** *Sunday Times* 5 Apr. 8/6 The macromolecules that are thought to have been the progenitors of living matter. **1969** *Sci. Jrnl.* Nov. 15/3 The two key macromolecules of living things, proteins and nucleic acids, principally play the parts of catalyst and information carriers respectively.

So ˌ**macromo'lecular** *a.*, of, pertaining to, or consisting of a macromolecule or macromolecules.

1931 *Chem. Rev.* VIII. 409 The physical properties of rubber..indicate..that it is macromolecular. **1958** *New Scientist* 26 June 256/2 We know how the macromolecular mechanism of the chromosomes reshuffles the genes when the sperm and the eggs are formed. **1964** G. H. HAGGIS et al. *Introd. Molecular Biol.* iv. 80 The helix is emerging today as a fundamental feature of macromolecular structure at several levels. **1970** *New Statesman* 20 Mar. 406/3 Otto Wichterle, director of Macromolecular Chemistry in Prague.

macromyelon (ˌmækrəʊ'maɪlɒn). *Anat.* [f. MACRO- + MYELON.] Owen's name for the medulla oblongata. Hence **macro'myelonal** *a.*

1846 OWEN *Lect. Anat. Vertebrate Anim.* Contents 9 'Macromyelon' or Medulla Oblongata. **1868** —— *Anat. Vertebrates* III. 83 The floor of the expanded macromyelonal canal.

‖**macron** ('mækrɒn, 'meɪkrɒn). [a. Gr. μακρόν, neut. of μακρός long.] A straight horizontal line (¯) placed over a vowel to indicate that it is 'long'.

1851 G. BROWN *Gram. of Gramm.* 810 *note*, The different uses made of the breve, the macron, and the accents. **1891** H. BRADLEY *Stratmann's M.-E. Dict.* Pref. viii, In my notation the macron is placed over an original long vowel which remained long in Middle-English.

macronutrient (ˌmækrəʊ'njuːtrɪənt). *Plant Physiol.* [f. MACRO- + NUTRIENT *sb.*] Any of the chemical elements (as potassium, nitrogen, calcium, sulphur, phosphorus, or magnesium) which are normally taken up by plants as inorganic salts and which are required for growth and development in relatively large amounts (rather than trace amounts).

1942 *Bot. Gaz.* CIII. 651 An extensive experiment in plant nutrition was designed in order to examine the effects of varying concentrations of macro-nutrient elements in the nutrient medium on the ascorbic-acid content of tomato fruits. **1970** *Nature* 25 July 376/1 The lack of macronutrients especially N, P and K, and sometimes micronutrients.

macropædia (ˌmækrəʊ'piːdɪə). [f. MACRO- + Gr. παιδεία learning.] The main section of the 15th edition of the *Encyclopædia Britannica* (published in 1974) in which information is presented in the form of extended articles. (Cf. MICROPÆDIA, PROPÆDIA.) Hence **macro'pædic** *a.*

1974 *Times* 12 Jan. 12/1 Finally, there is macropaedia, 19 volumes of substantive essays ranging the world of learning, with articles from 750 to 250,000 words each. Twelve articles are book length. *Ibid.* 16 Jan. 14/4 The *Encyclopaedia Britannica*..proclaimed the imminent publication of a new edition..the macropaedia, supplying knowledge in depth, with 19 volumes. **1974** *Times Lit. Suppl.* 11 Oct. 1120/4 Some sorts of item, those needing more than 750 words but less than full-scale Macropaedic attention,..get Procrustean treatment.

macrophage ('mækrəʊfeɪdʒ). *Phys.* [ad. mod.L. *macrophagus*, f. Gr. μακρό-ς long + φαγεῖν to devour.] A name given to certain large leucocytes, from their supposed power of devouring other organisms, especially pathogenic microbes. Hence **macro'phagic** *a.*

1890 RUFFER in *Q. Jrnl. Microsc. Sci.* Feb. 483 Cells to which he [Metschnikoff] has given the name of macrophages and microphages. **1897** *Allbutt's Syst. Med.* II. 7 These macrophages can destroy the tubercle bacilli. **1904** *Brit. Med. Jrnl.* 10 Sept. 562/1 The lymph glands and other macrophagic organs. **1971** *Nature* 5 Feb. 412/2 A sparse scattering of cells, presumably macrophagic or inflammatory.

macrophagocyte (ˌmækrəʊ'fægəsaɪt). *Phys.* [f. MACRO- + PHAGOCYTE *sb.*] = prec.

1896 *Allbutt's Syst. Med.* I. 79.

ˌ**macropho'tography.** [f. MACRO- + PHOTOGRAPHY.] Photography in which objects are reproduced larger than or at their actual size but without the degree of magnification that use of a microscope would give.

1889 E. J. WALL *Dict. Photogr.* 114 *Macro-photography*, a term used to denote the enlargement of the negative. **1940** A. L. M. SOWERBY *Wall's Dict. Photogr.* (ed. 15) 438 *Macro-photographs*, term applied to photographs of small objects reproduced at or about natural size. Macro-photography occupies a position intermediate between ordinary photography, in which objects are much reduced, and photo-micrography, in which objects are shown greatly enlarged. **1958** *Newnes Compl. Amat. Photogr.* xiv. 147 Macrophotography, showing all the colour variations of a natural subject in close-up, is a fruitful field. **1964** *Times Rev. Industry* Apr. 42/2 Representatives..demonstrating photomicrography, oscillography, macrophotography and general industrial photography to present or potential Polaroid users in industry. **1967** *Pix* 6 May 24 It might be said that photomacrography (or macro-photography) is that area of close-up photography which lies between what can be done by a simple dioptre lens (close-up attachment lens) and what requires the attachment of the camera to a microscope (i.e., photomicrography).

So ˌ**macro'photograph**, a photograph produced by macrophotography.

1900 DORLAND *Med. Dict.* 370/1 *Macrophotograph*, an enlarged photograph. **1933** *Burlington Mag.* Jan. 15/2 A wealth of information is recorded by the X-rays, macro-photographs, micro-photographs and details. **1940** [see above]. **1973** *Sci. Amer.* Feb. 63/2 (Advt.), Macrophotographs (formerly up to 10 times actual size) can now be made up to 14·8 times actual size.

macropicide (mæ'krɒpɪsaɪd). *nonce-wd.* [See next and -CIDE I.] A slayer of kangaroos.

1866 *Cornh. Mag.* Dec. 744 The stockmen..were decidedly the most efficient macropicides.

macropine ('mækrəpaɪn), *a.* [f. mod.L. *macropus* (ad. Gr. μακρόπους: see next) kangaroo + -INE.] Of or pertaining to the kangaroo.

1888 O. THOMAS *Catal. Marsupialia Brit. Mus.* 122 The macropine characters of its lower jaw. **1891** FLOWER & LYDEKKER *Mammals* 162 The macropine characters of the mandible preponderate.

macropod ('mækrəpɒd), *a.* and *sb.* [a. Gr. μακροποδ-, μακρόπους long-footed, f. μακρό-ς long + ποδ-, πούς foot.] **a.** *adj.* Long-footed. **b.** *sb.* A long-footed animal, e.g. a spider-crab. (In recent Dicts.) **ma'cropodal** *a. Bot.*, of a monocotyledonous embryo: Having the radicle large in proportion to the cotyledon. **macro'podian** *Zool.*, one of a tribe of brachyurous decapod crustaceans. **ma'cropodous** *a.* = MACROPODAL.

1830 LINDLEY *Nat. Syst. Bot.* 253 The plants belonging to Alismaceæ..and Butomeæ, have all a disproportionally large radicle, whence the embryos of such were called by the late M. Richard, macropodal. **1839** *Penny Cycl.* XIV. 256/2 *Macropodians.* **1852** HENSLOW *Dict. Bot. Terms*, *Macropodous.* **1887** GARNSEY & BALFOUR tr. *Goebel's Classif. & Morphol. Plants* 431 In the Helobiae the axial portion forms the larger part of the embryo (macropodous embryo).

macropsia (mæ'krɒpsɪə). *Ophthalm.* [f. MACRO- + *-opsia*, as in MEGALOPSIA.] = MEGALOPSIA.

1890 BILLINGS *Med. Dict.* II. 96/1 *Macropsia*, a condition of vision in which objects appear abnormally increased in size. **1899** [see MICRO- 3]. **1961** A. HUBER *Eye Symptoms in Brain Tumors* i. 24 The usual hallucinations and the phenomena of micropsia and macropsia actually bring us to the symptomology of disturbances of the higher visual functions.

macropterous (mæ'krɒptərəs), *a.* [f. Gr. μακρόπτερ-ος (f. μακρό-ς long + πτερό-ν wing) + -OUS.] Long-winged.

1835-6 TODD *Cycl. Anat.* I. 280/2 Macropterous Sea-birds.

macro-scale ('mækrəʊskeɪl). Also **macro scale, macroscale.** [f. MACRO- + SCALE *sb.*[3]] A large or macroscopic scale; *spec.* in *Chem.*, the scale of macroanalysis.

Macro is freq. apprehended as an adj. qualifying *scale* (cf. MACRO- 2).

1931 J. W. BROWN in C. A. Mitchell *Recent Adv. Analytical Chem.* II. xv. 304 Developments in the application of general macro-scale chemical methods of qualitative and quantitative analysis to amounts of material 50, 100 or 1,000 times smaller. **1941** J. H. REEDY *Elem. Qualitative Analysis* (ed. 3) 2 Formerly chemical analysis was carried out on a 'macro' scale, using considerable amounts of material. **1964** N. G. CLARK *Mod. Org. Chem.* xxiv. 496 Quantitative analysis was originally designed to be performed on a sample of 0·4–1·0 g for each elemental determination (only carbon and hydrogen are estimated on the same sample); this is called the macro-scale. **1968** C. A. DOXIADIS *Between Dystopia & Utopia* 52 Also, we should not forget that projecting in the macro-scale..is easier than in the micro-scale. It is easier to predict where the future population will settle in one generation than what type of house, or dress, a certain lady is going to like next year. **1970** *Interior Design* Dec. 767/1 Nevertheless, changes will occur, of course, but on a micro- not macro-scale. **1972** *Physics Bull.* Nov. 668/1 A polymer crystallized from the melt will show, on a macroscale, random crystalline orientation.

macroscian (mə'krɒʃɪən), *a.* and *sb.* [f. Gr. μακρόσκιος, f. μακρό-ς long + σκία shadow. Cf. ANTISCIAN.] **a.** *adj.* Having a long shadow. **b.** *sb.* One having a long shadow, an inhabitant of the polar regions.

In some mod. Dicts.

macroscopic (ˌmækrəʊ'skɒpɪk), *a.* [f. MACRO- + -SCOPIC.] Visible to the naked eye, in opposition to MICROSCOPIC. Also *fig.*, general, comprehensive, concerned with large units.

1872 PEASLEE *Ovar. Tumours* 31 The macroscopic character of these two forms of cystoma depends on the number and size of their constituent cysts. **1897** *Athenæum* 7 Aug. 194/3 The structure of lavas, microscopic and macroscopic. **1931** M. DOBB in W. Rose *Outl. Mod. Knowl.* II. xiv. 623 Those macroscopic, as distinct from microscopic, issues of the economic order. **1960** E. DELAVENAY *Introd. Machine Transl.* 132 Macroscopic study concentrates on large-scale aspects of phenomena—for instance macroscopic linguistics bears on very general statistical rules of language. **1963** *Listener* 10 Oct. 536/2 The problem is to explain *macroscopic individuality* (in common usage) in terms of microscopic non-individuals, rather than the other way round. **1964** I. L. HOROWITZ *New Sociol.* 3 The rationalists, or 'macroscopic' tendency, concerned with developing 'general theories' of human behavior.

Hence ˌ**macro'scopical** *a.* = MACROSCOPIC *a.*; ˌ**macro'scopically** *adv.*, by the naked eye, as studied by the naked eye without the aid of a lens.

1877 *Q. Jrnl. Microsc. Sci.* XVII. 228 Macroscopically and microscopically the retina, exposed to yellow light, behaves in the same way as after the operation of red light. **1878** T. BRYANT *Pract. Surg.* I. 388 Its macroscopical appearance was that of a fibrous tumour. **1879** DANA *Man. Geol.* (ed. 3) 66 A rock may be studied microscopically or macroscopically. **1899** *Allbutt's Syst. Med.* VII. 236 At the autopsy, nothing pathological was found macroscopically. *Ibid.* 837 Macroscopical examinations of the central nervous system in uncomplicated cases of chorea.

macrosegment (ˈmækrəʊsɛgmənt). *Linguistics.* [f. MACRO- + SEGMENT *sb.*] A continuous unit of speech between two pauses, with a single intonation.

1958 C. F. HOCKETT *Course in Mod. Ling.* iv. 38 The stretch of material spoken with a single intonation is called a *macrosegment*. *Ibid.* 41 Though the center of an intonation is by definition the most prominent syllable in the macrosegment, it need not carry the highest pitch. **1963** [see MICROSEGMENT]. **1964** K. L. PIKE in D. Abercrombie et al. *Daniel Jones* 430 The total phonemic phrase (i.e., the macrosegment including the sum of units between primary juncture,..) in unemotional speech has an overall intonation contour. **1965** *Language* XLI. 244 A major segment (..Hockett's macrosegment) consists of a series of pitch levels terminated by a major juncture. **1971** *Ibid.* XLVII. 739 In the nucleus column for macro-segment and mega-segment, a O symbol occurs with no explanation given.

macroseism (ˈmækrəʊsaɪz(ə)m). *Geol.* [f. MACRO- + SEISM.] A major earthquake; in mod. use (*rare*), any earthquake, as opposed to an imperceptible earth tremor (cf. MICROSEISM).

1903 *Sci. Amer.* Suppl. 2 May 22855 Prof. Milne pointed out the distinction which exists between macroseisms, or large earthquakes, and microseisms, or small earthquakes. The former he described as world-shaking disturbances. **1907** *Jrnl. Geol.* XV. 401 Great confusion exists because of the different uses of the terms 'macroseism' and 'microseism', as well as the adjectives derived from them. The usage here is that of both Milne and de Montessus, which makes 'macroseism' apply to the greater disturbance on the ground. **1924** *Bull. Seismol. Soc. Amer.* XIV. 29 Various useful compounds [of *seism*] have been suggested, such as..*macroseism*, de Montessus, 1907, for an ordinary sensible earthquake. **1972** *Gloss. Geol.* (Amer. Geol. Inst.) 424/1 *Macroseism*, a syn. of *earthquake*, as opposed to *microseism*.

Hence **macroˈseismic** *a.*, of or pertaining to a macroseism or (in mod. use) those effects of an earthquake that are perceptible without the aid of instruments; **macroˈseismically** *adv.*

1903 *Nature* 9 July 235/1 This is probably true for other phases of motion, and it has also been shown to exist for macro-seismic disturbances. **1907** *Jrnl. Geol.* XV. 408 Macroseismic origins. **1938** *Nature* 1 Oct. 624/1 The region over which the shock was felt macroseismically extended as far as the island. **1940** *Ibid.* 6 Jan. 14/1 On the basis of the macroseismic data, the accompanying sketch map showing the isoseismal lines has been constructed. **1947** K. E. BULLEN *Introd. Theory Seismol.* xv. 252 Macroseismic data ..usefully supplement the data obtained from seismographs. **1973** *Nature* 17 Aug. 384/2 Fairly complete pictures of what are now termed the macroseismic aspects of Britain's larger earthquakes.

macrosˈmatic, *a.* [irreg. f. MACRO- + Gr. ὀσμή smell.] *Zool.* Having well-developed olfactory organs. Also *fig.*

1890 W. TURNER in *Jrnl. Anat. & Physiol.* XXV. 106, I propose..to arrange the Mammalia in relation to the development of the olfactory apparatus into three groups:—(a) Macrosmatic, where the organs of smell are largely developed, a condition which is found..in the majority of mammals. [Etc.] **1894** *Proc. Zool. Soc.* 9 *Echidna* ..is, to use Turner's nomenclature, 'macrosmatic'. **1899** *Allbutt's Syst. Med.* VI. 753 All that remains in man of the great rhinencephalon of macrosmatic mammals is the olfactory bulb and tract. **1924** *Jrnl. Comparative Neurol.* XXXVII. 318 Even macrosmatic animals like dogs and fishes locate odorous substances by random seeking reactions, not by direct orientation. **1962** *Science Survey* III. 260 Cats and dogs, most of the predators, rodents and deer, and many others are called macrosmatic because a large part of their nasal labyrinths are covered with a special olfactory epithelium. **1968** *Times* 5 Oct. 20/7 [Orwell is] a macrosmatic writer tracking down the stench of hypocrisy or the gangrene of intellectual treachery. **1971** *Nature* 16 Apr. 432/1 Groddeck argued that man is as macrosmatic as the dog.

macrosporange (ˌmækrəʊspɒˈrændʒ). Also in mod.L. form **-sporangium**. [f. MACRO- + SPORANGE.] The sporange or capsule containing the macrospores. (Cf. MEGASPORANGE.)

1875 BENNETT & DYER *Sachs' Bot.* 396 If a microsporangium is about to be formed, each of the mother-cells is broken up into four tetrahedral spores, which all develope into microspores; in the macrosporangium, on the contrary, the mother-cells remain, with one exception, undivided. **1882** *Gard. Chron.* XVIII. 40 Four of these macrospores occur in each macrosporange.

macrospore (ˈmækrəʊspɔə(r)). [f. MACRO- + SPORE.] **a.** *Bot.* = *megaspore* (s.v. MEGA-). **b.** *Zool.* One of the spore-like parts into which a monad subdivides.

1859 TODD *Cycl. Anat.* V. 243/1 The development of the prothallium commences..several months after the macrospore has been sown. **1870** HOOKER *Stud. Flora* 469 The macrospores of Selaginella and Isoetes develop a cellular prothallus. **1875** BENNETT & DYER *Sachs' Bot.* 335 The separation of the sexes is already prefigured by the two kinds of spores, the Macrospores being female, in so far as they develope a small prothallium. **1955** G. M. SMITH *Cryptogamic Bot.* (ed. 2) II. x. 281 The heterospory was pronounced [in the fossil fern *Archaeopteris*], the macrospores having a diameter about ten times that of microspores. **1965** [see *megaspore* s.v. MEGA-]. **1974** *Mycopathologia et Mycologia Applicata* LIII. 56 Some fungi ..produce two spore states which are similar in type but differ in size. The large septate spores are frequently referred to as macrospores and the smaller, nonseptate spores as microspores. The term macrospore is also used infrequently as synonymous with chlamydospore... This latter usage seems undesirable.

macrosporophyll (ˌmækrəʊˈspɒrəfɪl). *Bot.* [f. MACRO- + *sporophyll* (s.v. SPORO-).] = *megasporophyll* (s.v. MEGA-).

1888 *Encycl. Brit.* XXIV. 130/2 Carpel = leaf bearing macrosporangia (macrosporophyll). **1955** G. M. SMITH *Cryptogamic Bot.* (ed. 2) II. viii. 201 According to the nature of their sporangia, the sporophylls are called macrosporophylls and microsporophylls.

ˈmacrostructure. Also **macro-structure**. [f. MACRO- + STRUCTURE *sb.*] Large-scale or overall structure; *spec.* the structure of a metal that is visible (on polished and etched surfaces) to the naked eye or under low magnification.

1920 *Glasgow Herald* 18 Dec. 4 The lecturer spoke of microscopical methods, of macro-structure, and dealt with the variation of physical properties of steel. **1930** *Engineering* 14 Mar. 357/1 Macrostructure of cast alloys. **1960** E. H. GOMBRICH *Art & Illusion* xi. 365 Van Gogh's own [accent] can be forged with relative ease. But then his swirling lines still belong to the macrostructure of his style. **1964** *English Studies* XLV. (Suppl.) 180 Bogard also rejects the possibility of Shakespeare having influenced the macro-structure of Webster's tragedies.

b. *concr.*

1956 *Nature* 14 Jan. 81/1 The protein and its associated copper bonds..are stable or protected in highly organized macrostructures such as mammalian melanin granules.

So ˌ**macroˈstructural** *a.*

1893 [see MICROSTRUCTURAL *a.*]. **1963** J. WIESENFARTH *Henry James & Dramatic Analogy* i. 15 One of the principles of James's dramatized novel is that it should always represent. Such macrostructural devices as scenes and pictures..are integral elements by which this ideal is realized. **1964** *English Studies* XLV. (Suppl.) 188 It is strange that no one appears to have taken much interest in the macro-structural relations between his plays and those of other Elizabethan and Jacobean dramatists. **1974** B. JESSOP *Traditionalism, Conservatism & Brit. Political Culture* ii. 42 This requires macrostructural analysis as well as survey analysis.

macrothere (ˈmækrəθɪə(r)). Also in L. form **macrotherium**. [ad. mod.L. *macrothērium*, f. Gr. μακρό-ς long + θηρίον wild beast.] A member of an extinct European genus of the sloth tribe.

1862 DANA *Man. Geol.* iv. 528 The Macrothere..was related to the African Pangolin (the Anteater) but was six or eight times its size. **1884** G. ALLEN in *Longm. Mag.* June 192 The macrotherium, a monstrous ant-eater.

ˈmacrotone. *rare*$^{-0}$. [? f. MACRO- + TONE. Cf. Gr. μακρότον-ος stretched out.] = MACRON.

1880 in WEBSTER; and in later Dicts.

macrurous, macrourous (məˈkrʊərəs), *a.* *Zool.* [f. mod.L. *macrūra* neut. pl. (f. Gr. μακρό-ς long + οὐρά tail) + -OUS.] Pertaining to the *Macrura*, or long-tailed tribe of the Decapod Crustacea, which includes the lobster and its congeners.

1826 KIRBY & SP. *Entomol.* xlviii. IV. 452 *Exochnata* (Macrurous Decapod Crustacea, Latr.). **1839–47** TODD *Cycl. Anat.* III. 445/1 The Macrourous Decapods..are all organized for swimming. **1890** *Nature* 11 Sept., The descent of crabs from macrurous ancestors.

So **maˈcrural, -ˈoural** *a.* (also *sb.* one of the *Macrura*); **maˈcruran, -ˈouran** *a.* and *sb.*

1842 BRANDE *Dict. Sci.* etc., Macrourans. **1851** *Brit. Assoc. Rep., Sections* 81 On the Antennæ of the Annulosa, and their Homology in the Macrourals. By Dr. W. Macdonald. **1852** DANA *Crust.* I. 33 Corresponding precisely in its course to that of the Macroural suture. **1877** HUXLEY *Anat. Inv. Anim.* vi. 340 Nor are the antennules capable of being folded back into distinct chambers in any Macruran at present known. **1902** *Edin. Rev.* Jan. 202 It is not technically a crab but a Pagurid, a macruran hermit.

† **mactate,** *v. Obs.*$^{-0}$ [f. L. *mactāt-*, ppl. stem of *mactāre* to slay.] *trans.* To kill or slay.

1623 in COCKERAM.

mactation (mækˈteɪʃən). [ad. L. *mactātiōn-em*, f. *mactāre* to slay.] The action of killing, *esp.* the slaughtering of a sacrificial victim.

1640 SIR E. DERING *Prop. Sacr.* (1644) 57 He..neither sacrificed by mactation or killing of beasts. **1711** HICKES *Treat. Christ. Priesth.* (1847) II. 111 To sacrifice or offer animals by slaughter, or mactation. **1838** M. RUSSELL *Hist. Egypt* vi. (1853) 192 The deity before whom the mactation is about to be performed. **1888** *Ch. Times* 24 Aug. 720 The view gained ground that each Mass is a separate mactation.

† **macˈtator.** *Obs. rare*$^{-0}$. [a. L. *mactātor*, agent-n. f. *mactāre* to slay.]

1656 BLOUNT *Glossogr.*, *Mactator*, a killer or murderer. (In recent Dicts.)

‖ **macula** (ˈmækjʊlə). Pl. **-æ**. [L.] **1.** A spot or stain. Chiefly in scientific use: *Astron.* one of the dark spots in the sun; *Min.* a spot in a mineral due to the presence of particles of some other mineral; *Ent.* (see quot. 1826); *Path.* a spot or stain in the skin, now *esp.* one which is permanent; *Anat.* any of various structures which have the appearance of a spot; *spec.* the *macula lutea* (see below).

c **1400** *Lanfranc's Cirurg.* 247 Macula is a wem in a mannys ȝȝe. **1690** T. BURNET *Th. Earth* III. xi. 97 The Body of the Sun may contract..some Spots or *Maculæ* greater than usual. **1722** QUINCY *Lex. Physico-Med.* (ed. 2) Macula, is applied by Physicians to express any Spots upon the Skin, whether those in Fevers, or scorbutick Habits. **1766** *Ann. Reg.* 92/2 The spot or macula on the sun, mentioned to have appeared lately. **1802** PLAYFAIR *Illustr. Hutton. Theory* 298 Rectangular maculæ of feltspar. **1826** KIRBY & SP. *Entomol.* IV. 285 Macula (*Macula*), a larger indeterminately shaped spot. **1849** SAXE *Times* 152 Their honoured name Bears.. some maculae of shame. **1867–77** G. F. CHAMBERS *Astron.* I. i. 7 In the equatorial zones of the Sun dark spots or maculae. **1877** ROBERTS *Handbk. Med.* (ed. 3) I. 111 The maculæ on the skin which are observed during life are frequently persistent after death. **1899** *Allbutt's Syst. Med.* VIII. 640 In all cases a deeply pigmented macula remains. **1901** *Phil. Trans. R. Soc.* B. CXCIV. 74 Fundus oculi (right eye) of the Lemurine Douroucouli. The macula is present, but the macula ring has disappeared. **1932** S. ZUCKERMAN *Social Life Monkeys* x. 153 Since the eyes of the lower mammal are usually set more to the sides than to the front of the head.. a specially sensitive area or macula is not developed. **1952** *Sci. News* XXIII. 73 When an object is fixed, the eyes are directed towards it in such a way that it is focused on the central spot of the retina—the area for acute vision, known as the macula. **1964** [see CRISTA].

2. *Anat.* and *Path.* Used in various mod.L. collocations, as **macula densa** [(K. W. Zimmermann 1929, in *Zeitschr. f. mikrosk.-anat. Forschung* XVIII. 529), f. L. *densus* thick, dense], a small mass of cells of uncertain function closely associated with the juxtaglomerular cells; **macula lutea** [L. *luteus* yellow], an oval, yellowish area near the centre of the retina, where visual acuteness is most pronounced; the yellow spot.

1836–9 R. B. TODD *Cycl. Anat. & Physiol.* II. 530/1 Its bottom..presents a sieve-like spot, *macula cribrosa*. **1848** DUNGLISON *Dict. Med. Sci.* (ed. 7) 370/1 *Foramen centrale et limbus luteus retinæ*; the central foramen and yellow spot of the retina; discovered by Sömmering. Macula lutea. **1857** *Ibid.* (rev. ed.) 560/2 *Maculæ albæ*, white spots, seen on serous membranes..and which appear to be the result of previous inflammatory action. **1942** *Lancet* 3 Oct. 394/2 Zimmerman [*sic*] first recognised the different appearance of the cells of the distal tubule most closely applied to the afferent arteriole in its juxtaglomerular portion. In this part, the ordinary tubular cells seem aggregated, and become in some species much higher and more columnar. Because of this grouping together of nuclei, and the impression of increased density of epithelial cells produced, Zimmerman called this the macula densa. **1952** Macula densa [see JUXTAGLOMERULAR *a.*]. **1962** *Gray's Anat.* (ed. 33) 1302 The pyramid and adjoining part of the elliptical recess [of the internal ear] are perforated by a number of holes (macula cribrosa superior). **1967** G. M. WYBURN et al. *Conc. Anat.* viii. 206/2 In the centre of the retina is the yellow spot, the macula lutea. **1968** Macula densa [see JUXTAGLOMERULAR *a.*].

macular (ˈmækjʊlə(r)), *a.* *Biol.* and *Path.* [f. MACULA + -AR.] Of or pertaining to maculæ; characterized by the presence of maculæ; *spec.* of or pertaining to the *macula lutea*.

1822 GOOD *Study Med.* IV. 679 Macular skin. **1826** KIRBY & SP. *Entomol.* IV. 289 Macular Fascia (*Fascia macularis*), a band consisting of distinct spots. **1880** J. W. LEGG *Bile* 468 The macular eruption was thought to be cured. **1897** *Brit. Birds* II. 175 Slightly macular along its inferior margin. **1898** P. MANSON *Trop. Diseases* xxvi. 389 The primary exanthem or macular stage. **1900** J. HUTCHINSON *Arch. Surg.* XI. 46 Macular leprosy. **1909** M. GREENWOOD in L. Hill *Further Adv. Physiol.* 397 If there is a good deal of macular pigmentation the mixed light undergoes selective absorption. **1932** S. ZUCKERMAN *Social Life Monkeys* x. 166 Monkeys have hands and, what the handed prosimiæ lack, macular vision to guide their manipulations. **1961** R. D. BAKER *Essent. Path.* iv. 49 In Tay-Sachs disease..lipids are collected in ganglion cells.. and in the macula of the retina (macular star).

maculate (ˈmækjʊleɪt), *ppl. a.* [ad. L. *maculāt-us*, pa. pple. of *maculāre*, f. *macula* spot.] = MACULATED; in early use occas. *pa. pple.* Now chiefly *lit.* and *poet.*, in expressed or implied antithesis to *immaculate*.

1490 CAXTON *Eneydos* iv. 20 So departe thou thenne fro this londe, maculate, and full of fylthe and ordure. **1509** BARCLAY *Shyp of Folys* (1570) 144 The places that ye haue edified, Are nowe disordred, and with vices maculate. **1549** *Compl. Scot.* xiii. 150 That the honour of verteous gentil men be nocht maculat vitht the vice ande inciuilite of vicius pretendit gentil men. **1575–85** ABP. SANDYS *Serm.* vii. 122 Hauing cloathed ourselves with the maculate coate of sinne. **1612** *Two Noble K.* v. iii, Thy rare greene eye..never yet Beheld things maculate. **1756–7** tr. *Keysler's Trav.* (1760) I. 74 The cardinal of St. Clemente hurt himself by declaring for the maculate conception. **1878** *N. Amer. Rev.* CXXVII. 296 Unfortunately for her already maculate reputation. **1887** STEVENSON *Misadv. J. Nicholson* ii, Foul walls and maculate table linen. **1919** T. S. ELIOT *Sweeney among Nightingales* in *Poems*, The zebra stripes along his jaw Swelling to maculate giraffe. **1932** W. FAULKNER *Light in August* (1933) xiii. 300 Leaning in the window, breathing the hot still rich maculate smell of the earth. **1964** C. S. LEWIS *Discarded Image* vii. 161 In Shakespeare's *Lucrece* we need to know fully who the 'spotted princess' (719–28) is: Tarquin's Reason, rightful sovereign of his soul, now maculate. **1965** E. BISHOP *Questions of Travel* 22 House, open house..Darkened and tarnished By the warm touch Of the warm breath, Maculate, cherished, Rejoice!

maculate (ˈmækjʊleɪt), *v.* Now *rare*. *Pa. t.* 5 **maculate**. [f. L. *maculāt-*, ppl. stem of *maculāre*, f. *macula* spot.] *trans.* To spot, stain, soil, defile, pollute.

1432–50 tr. *Higden* (Rolls) V. 235 Whiche commynge to Affrike wastede hit, and maculate [*Trevisa* defouled] the feithe in hit. **1481** CAXTON *Godfrey* clxxxvii. 274 The hethen men..whiche had fowled and shamefully had maculated [the place] with theyr mahometry. **1490** —— *Eneydos* viii. 35 Hir innocente blood whiche maculate & bysprange all

theym that stode by. **1513** BRADSHAW *St. Werburge* I. 2791 A sensuall prynce..Purposed to maculate this vyrgyn gloryous. **1531** ELYOT *Gov.* I. xxvi, They wolde nat maculate the honour of their people. ? *a* **1550** *Schole-house of Wom.* 914 in Hazl. *E.P.P.* IV. 140 Whose drops vncleen dooth maculate The finest vesture that any man weres. **1632** J. HAYWARD tr. *Biondi's Eromena* 28 Thou hast done too much in maculating our bloud. **1719** D'URFEY *Pills* (1872) IV. 166 They maculate Men's Blood, and make them silly. **1737** A. BAXTER *Inquiry Human Soul* (ed. 2) II. 202 *Lucretius* tells us maculating dreams accompany youth. *a* **1945** E. R. EDDISON *Mezentian Gate* (1972) ii. 21 That were to maculate the purity of your own proper nature.

maculated (ˈmækjʊleɪtɪd), *ppl. a.* [f. MACULATE *v.* + -ED¹]

1. Spotted, stained, defiled, polluted.

1646 SIR T. BROWNE *Pseud. Ep.* v. xxi. 272 For Warts we ..commit any maculated part unto the touch of the dead. *a* **1661** FULLER *Worthies, Merionethsh.* (1662) IV. 43 Who being casually cast into bad company..keep their own innocency entire, not maculated with the mixture of their bad manners. **1841** D'ISRAELI *Amen. Lit.* (1867) 660 A maculated man seeking to shelter himself in dejection and in shade. **1883** *Fortn. Rev.* Feb. 158 A variegated record of profitless extravagance and maculated victory.

2. In scientific use: Marked with maculæ.

1676 DE GARENCIERES *Coral* 15 Red coral will grow.. maculated with several spots. **1819** G. SAMOUELLE *Entomol. Compend.* 110 Body cinereous, maculated with fuscous. **1875** H. C. WOOD *Therap.* (1879) 373 The gastric mucous membrane is..maculated with patches of a deep-crimson.

maculation (mækjuːˈleɪʃən). [ad. L. *maculātiōn-em* agent-n. f. *maculāre* MACULATE *v.* Cf. F. *maculation.*]

1. The action of spotting or staining; the condition of being spotted or defiled.

a **1450** *Cov. Myst.* xiv. (Shaks. Soc.) 138 If he be gilty, sum maculacion Pleyne in his face xal shewe it owth. *Ibid.* 141, I nevyr knew of mannys maculacion, But evyr have lyved in trew virginite. **1606** SHAKS. *Tr. & Cr.* IV. iv. 66, I will throw my Gloue to death himselfe, That there's no maculation in thy heart. **1772** NUGENT tr. *Hist. Fr. Gerund* I. 531 The nigrescent maculation of their pristine niveous candour. **1853** G. J. CAYLEY *Las Alforjas* I. 34, I waged a blind and ineffectual warfare all night, to the loss of my rest and the maculation of my countenance. **1887** STEVENSON *Mem. & Portraits* vi. 102 It was from the maculation of sheep's blood that he had come..to cleanse himself.

2. In scientific use: The state of being marked with maculæ; a particular arrangement or pattern of maculæ.

1826 KIRBY & SP. *Entomol.* xxxv. III. 650 Numerous Libellulinæ emulate the Heliconian butterflies by their maculation. **1879** PROCTOR *Pleas. Ways Sci.* ii. 40 The doctrine that an intimate association exists between solar maculation (or spottiness) and terrestrial meteorological phenomena. **1884** *Science* IV. 44/2 The maculation is normally noctuidous, and the wings are ample. **1888** *Amer. Nat.* XXII. 642 Patches of vividly red Poppies, with fine black maculations, like eyes, edged with white.

†**maculatory**, *a.* *Obs. rare*⁻¹. [f. L. *maculāt-*, ppl. stem. + -ORY.] Apt to spot or defile.

1614 T. ADAMS *Devil's Banquet* 17 The lutulent, spumy, maculatorie waters of Sinne.

maculature. [f. L. *maculāt-*, ppl. stem of *maculāre* to stain + -URE. Cf. F. *maculature* (Cotgr.), G. *makulatur.*] **1.** (See quots.) *Obs.*⁻⁰

1656 BLOUNT *Glossogr., Maculatures*, blotting or waste papers. **1706** PHILLIPS (ed. Kersey), *Maculature* or *Macle*, a waste Sheet of printed Paper. **1721** BAILEY, *Maculature*, a Waste or blotting Paper.

2. *Engraving* (see quots.).

1904 *Burlington Mag.* V. 70 One of these [impressions of the Hundred Guilder Plate]..is a 'maculature', an impression on a sheet of ordinary paper passed over the plate to remove the ink. **1914** *Brit. Mus. Guide Processes of Engraving* 52 A maculature is another form of weak impression. A copper plate needs to be inked between each impression. Sometimes a second impression is taken from the plate before re-inking, as a means of extracting the remainder of the ink from the lines. This is called a maculature.

macule (ˈmækjuːl), *sb.* Also 6 *Sc.* macull, makle. [f. L. *macula*, either directly or through F. *macule.*] A blemish, spot. *Obs.* in general sense.

1483 CAXTON *G. de la Tour* K v b, It is a perle whiche is.. without macule or spotte. **1490** —— *Eneydos* xxix. 113 The throte quycke, and without spotte or macule. **1500–20** DUNBAR *Poems* xlviii. 152 But ony spot or macull doing spring. *Ibid.* lxxxv. 22 Haile, moder and maid but makle!

b. *Path.* = MACULA.

1863 *Edinb. Med. Jrnl.* Jan. 599 Skin diseases..1. Macules and Deformities. **1899** *Allbutt's Syst. Med.* VIII. 465 The eruption commonly consists of macules.

c. *Printing.* A blur causing the impression of a page to appear double; = MACKLE *sb.*

1841 SAVAGE *Dict. Printing* 775 Instead of its being a macule, it is nothing more than [etc.].

macule (ˈmækjuːl), *v.* [f. F. *maculer*, f. *macule* a spot.] *trans.* To spot, stain. *Obs.* in general use.

1484 CAXTON *Fables of Alfonce* (1889) 261, I byleue not that this poure [man] may be maculed ne gylty of the blame.

b. *Printing* = MACKLE *v.* (*trans.* and *intr.*).

1841 SAVAGE *Dict. Printing* s.v., If the joints of the tympan, or the head, or the nut of the spindle be loose, or any accident happen in pulling, so that the impression be somewhat doubled, and not clear, it is said to be maculed. *Ibid.* 775, I have heard many complaints of the middle pages of a twelves form maculing at a two-pull press.

maculiferous (ˌmækjuːˈlɪfərəs), *a.* [f. MACULE + -(I)FEROUS.] Bearing or marked by spots, spotty.

1853 HERSCHEL *Pop. Lect. Sci.* II. xxxv. (1873) 77 The maculiferous belts of the sun.

maculopapule (ˌmækjʊləʊˈpæpjuːl). *Med.* [f. MACUL(A + -O + PAPULE.] A maculopapular lesion. So **ˌmaculoˈpapular** *a.*, having characteristics of both a macule and a papule; characterized by such lesions.

1900 DORLAND *Med. Dict.* 370/2 Maculopapule. **1905** GOULD *Dict. New Med. Terms* 347/1 Maculopapular. **1912** H. FRENCH *Index Differential Diagn. Main Symptoms* 424 If a macule takes on a slight degree of elevation it is sometimes styled a maculo-papule. *Ibid.* 528 If the lesions, originating as erythematous macules, do not take on the full character of papules, they are said to be maculo-papular. **1928** C. P. EMERSON *Physical Diagn.* iii. 82 There may be some maculopapules or true papules on the palms or soles. **1962** *Lancet* 12 May 998/2 He had a scattered maculopapular rash over the trunk. **1968** *Biol. Abstr.* XLIX. 4986/2 The scales are grayish in appearance in chronic squamous maculopapular dermatoses.

maculose (ˈmækjʊləʊs), *a.* [ad. L. *maculōs-us*, f. *macula* spot.] Full of spots; spotted.

1727 in BAILEY vol. II. **1819** G. SAMOUELLE *Entomol. Compend.* 124 A..maculose, dentated band. **1861** HAGEN *Syn. Neuroptera N. Amer.* 341 (Smithsonian Collect. IV.).

ˈmaculous, *a. rare*⁻⁰. [See -OUS.] = prec.

1688 R. HOLME *Armoury* II. 366/1 A Masculous [*sic: in the 'Table'* Maculous], or spotted Cramp-fish, hath the Eyes turned into black round spots. **1735** DYCHE & PARDON *Dict.*, *Maculous* or *Maculose*, troubled or affected with Spots, Defects, or natural Deformities. **1856** in MAYNE *Expos. Lex.*

macumba (məˈkʊmbə). Also **makumba**. [Pg.] A religious cult-practice of the Negro population of Brazil characterized by sorcery, ritual dancing, and the use of fetishes. Also *attrib.*

1939 *Peabody Bull.* Dec. 8 The frenzy of a *macumba* or the tropical sensuality of a son. **1941** *Survey Graphic* Mar. 181 The religious *macumba* or *candomblé* found in the morros (the hills) combines Catholicism with African and Indian magic rituals. **1948** H. MIELCHE *From Santos to Bahia* vii, Once a year..for four days the city surrenders to the spell of Makumba. **1951** SMITH & MARCHANT *Brazil* v. 145 Brazilian *macumbas* and *candomblés* are undergoing rapid changes. There is a curious fusion..with other religions and cults, especially with Catholicism and Spiritualism. **1963** *Guardian* 4 June 7/1 Some of the most striking scenes are depictions of the macumba rites. **1964** *Listener* 6 Aug. 211/1 They had penetrated a *macumba* temple in Rio de Janeiro. **1969** J. MANDER *Static Society* vii. 211 The Brazilian North-East, where Voodoo or *makumba* cults flourish. **1971** *Daily Colonist* (Victoria, B.C.) 23 May 33/3 The people of Bahia are..devotees of Macumba, that unique north east Brazilian blend of voodoo and Christianity.

Macushi (məˈkuːʃɪ). Also **Macusi**. **a.** A Carib Indian people inhabiting Guyana (formerly British Guiana) and Brazil; a member of this people. **b.** The language of this people. Also *attrib.* or as *adj.*

1881 *Encycl. Brit.* XII. 828/2 In British Guiana the Carib tribes are the Ackawais and Caribisi of the coast and forest regions, the Arecunas and Macusis of the savannah region. **1934** E. WAUGH *Handful of Dust* v. 273 She Macushi woman. All these people Macushi people. *Ibid.* 274, I wish I could speak Macushi. **1934** —— *Ninety-two Days* iii. 78 There was a large Indian village. These were sophisticated Macushis who were in constant contact with the ranches. *Ibid.* 89 He was at work on a translation of the scriptures into Macushi. **1974** H. MACINNES *Climb to Lost World* iv. 57 A Macusi Indian had been taken to England by some missionaries.

macushla (məˈkʊʃlə). *Anglo-Ir.* [f. Ir. *mo* my + *cuisle* vein, pulse (of the heart). Cf. ACUSHLA.] (My) dear heart; darling. (Used as a term of address.)

1887 W. B. YEATS *Dawn-Song* in *Irish Fireside* 5 Feb. 83/3 Wake, *ma cushla*, sleepy-headed. **1918–19** *T. Eaton & Co. Catal.* Fall & Winter 369/2 Vocal Records... Macushla (Tenor). **1946** A. SETON *Turquoise* viii. 115 Sure, and ye're a foine figger of a woman yourself, macushla. **1950** O. NASH *Family Reunion* (1951) 89 In a word, Macushla, There's a scad o' things that to make a house a home it takes.

macute (məˈkjuːt). Also 8 **maccuta**, **maccute**, **macoute**, 8–9 **macuta**. [ad. native African *makuta*.

The Rev. W. Holman Bentley, writing from the Congo Free State, informs us that *makuta* is the plural of **ekuta*, and denotes a bundle of ten mats of palm-fibre, still used as currency north of the Congo near the French frontier. Elsewhere the word survives only as the name of the Angola 'penny' piece or its value. Mr. Bentley says that it is derived from a Congo verb *kuta* to tie, now obsolete, but preserved in the reversing form *kutulula* to untie (N.E.D.).]

At the beginning of the 18th c., said to be the name for one of the pieces of cloth used as money by the Negroes of the Congo. Subsequently used in the W. African trade as the name for a money of account (= 2000 cowries), and hence adopted by the Portuguese at Angola as a denomination in their local coinage (= 50 reis); the Sierra Leone Company also issued (1791–1805) pieces of 1, 2, 5 and 10 macutes, the silver macute being worth about 4¾*d.* sterling. The account given by Montesquieu (quot. 1748), and adopted by Mill and other English writers on political economy, appears to be based on misapprehension.

1704 tr. *Merolla's Voy. Congo* in *Churchill's Voy.* I. 740 The current Coins here are the Maccuta's, being certain pieces of Straw-Cloth of about the largeness of a Sheet of Pastboard each. **1704** tr. *Acc. Gattina's Voy. Congo* ibid. I. 620 There is but little Mony passes in that Country, but instead of it they buy and sell with Maccutes... The Maccutes are pieces of coarse Cotton Cloth..five Ells long, and cost 200 Reys the Piece. *Ibid.*, Two thousand of them [Zimbis] are worth a Maccute. **1748** NUGENT tr. *Montesquieu's Spirit Laws* XXII. viii. (1752) 77 The negroes on the coast of Africa have a sign of value without money. It is a sign merely ideal... A certain commodity or merchandise is worth three macoutes; another six macoutes; another ten macoutes... The price is formed by a comparison of all merchandises with each other. They have therefore no particular money; but each kind of merchandise is money to the other. **1823** CRABB *Technol. Dict., Macuta.* **1848** J. S. MILL *Pol. Econ.* III. vii. §1.

†**mad**, *sb.*¹ *Obs.* (? exc. *dial.*) [var. of MATHE.]

1. A maggot or grub; *esp.* the larva of the blowfly, which causes a disease in sheep. Also *pl.*, the disease so caused.

1573 TUSSER *Husb.* l. (1878) 109 Sheepe wrigling taile hath mads without faile. **1641** BEST *Farm. Bks.* (Surtees) 6 Lambes that wriggle theyre tayles..are to bee..searched, for fear of maddes breedinge. **1669** WORLIDGE *Syst. Agric.* 273 Madds, a Disease in Sheep. **1688** R. HOLME *Armoury* III. 268/1 Keep Sheeps Tails from Maggots and Mads.

2. An earthworm.

1586 WARNER *Alb. Eng.* II. ix. 41 Content thee, Daphles, mooles take mads. **1592** *Ibid.* VII. xxxvii. 180 Here maiest thou feast thee with a Made. **1601** HOLLAND *Pliny* II. 361 Earth-worms or mads stamped and laid too are verie good to cure the biting of scorpions. **1674–91** RAY *S. & E.C. Words, Mad*, an earth-worm.

mad (mæd), *sb.*² *dial.* and *U.S. slang.* [subst. use of MAD *a.*] Madness, fury, anger.

1834 in J. S. Bassett *Southern Plantation Overseer* (1925) 65, I will be darnde if I can do anythinge with them and they all ways in the mads. **1847–89** HALLIWELL, *Mad*, madness, intoxication. *Glouc.* **1867** W. L. GOSS *Soldier's Story* xiv. 258 The Colonel has got his mad up. **1878** E. B. TUTTLE *Border Tales* 50 A grizzly will stand in the middle of the road, growling and getting his mad up. **1884** *Century Mag.* Nov. 57/2 His mad was getting up. **1897** *Outing* (U.S.) XXX. 487/2 Let the pony get his mad up. **1916** H. L. WILSON *Somewhere in Red Gap* ii. 57 She kept her mad down better. She set there as nice and sweet as a pet scorpion. **1950** J. D. MACDONALD *Brass Cupcake* (1955) iii. 25 When I want a personality course, friend, I'll go to someone who hasn't a mad on at the world. **1973** M. & G. GORDON *Informant* xxxiii. 128 Well, thanks a lot! I go through hell for you and you take your mad out on me.

mad (mæd), *a.* Forms: 1 **ȝemǽd(e)d**, 3–4 **med(d, medde**, 3–6 **madd(e**, (5 **made**, **maad**), 3– **mad.** [Aphetic repr. OE. *ȝemǽd(e)d* (see AMAD), pa. pple. of **ȝemǽdan* to render insane, f. *ȝemád* insane ('*vecors*, ȝemaad', Corpus Gl.), corresponding to OS. *gimêd* foolish, OHG. *gameit*, *kimeit*, foolish, vain, boastful (MHG. *gimeit* merry, stately, handsome), Goth. *gamaiþs* crippled:—OTeut. **gamaiđo-*, f. **ga-* prefix (Y-) + **maiđo-*:—pre-Teut. **moitó-*, pa. pple of the Indogermanic root **mei-* to change (cf. L. *mūtāre*). The primary sense of **maiđo-* changed, appears in the derivative Goth. *maidjan* to change, adulterate (*in-maideins* exchange); the corresponding ON. *meiða* means to cripple (cf. the sense of the Goth. adj. above). The OE. *mád* adj., without prefix, app. occurs once in the compound *mádmód* folly.

It is commonly stated that the OE. (*ȝe*)*mád* survived into ME. in the form *mād*, *mǭd*. The examples cited are the following. *c* **1310** in Wright *Lyric P.* viii. 31 For-thi on molde y waxe mot (riming with *blod* in the next line but one, with *wot*, *lot* in the previous quatrain). *c* **1425** *Seven Sages* (P.) 2091 To sla the childe he was ful rade, He ferde as man that was made. *c* **1460** *Lybeaus Disc.* (Ritson) 2001 Lybeaus began to swete, Ther he satte yn hys sete, Maad as he were (the earlier texts read quite differently). In the first quot. the text is certainly corrupt (? read *wod*: *blod*); the later quots. do not prove the length of the vowel.]

1. a. Suffering from mental disease; beside oneself, out of one's mind; insane, lunatic. In mod. use chiefly with a more restricted application, implying violent excitement or extravagant delusions: Maniacal, frenzied.

The word has always had some tinge of contempt or disgust, and would now be quite inappropriate in medical use, or in referring sympathetically to an insane person as the subject of an affliction.

a **1000** *Riddles* xii. 6 Ic þæs nowhit wat þæt heo swa ȝemædde mode bestolene Dæde ȝedwolene deoraþ mine Won wisan ȝehwam. *c* **1050** *Voc.* in Wr.-Wülcker 347/19 *Amens*, ȝemæd. *c* **1050** *Gloss.* ibid. 513/33 *Uecordem*, ȝemædedne. **1390** GOWER *Conf.* I. 46 For certes such a maladie..It myghte make a wisman madd. *Ibid.* II. 144 And if..hir list noght to be gladd, He berth an hond that sche is madd. *c* **1440** *Promp. Parv.* 319/1 Madde, or wood, *amens, demens, furiosus.* **1489** CAXTON *Faytes of A.* III. xx. 213 Whyche duke or erle happeth to wex madde so that al alone as a fole he gothe renning by wodes and hedges. **1500–20** DUNBAR *Poems* xix. 12 Gife I be sorrowfull and sad, Than will thay say that I am mad. **1590** SHAKS. *Com. Err.* II. ii. 11 Wast thou mad, That thus so madlie thou didst

answere me? **1590** SWINBURNE *Treat. Test.* 37 They did see him hisse like a goose or barke lyke a dogge, or play such other parts as madfolks vse to doo. **1611** BIBLE *John* x. 20 And many of them said, He hath a deuill, and is mad, why heare ye him? **1664–5** PEPYS *Diary* 25 Jan., He told me what a mad freaking fellow Sir Ellis Layton hath been, and is, and once at Antwerp was really mad. **1726** SWIFT *Gulliver* II. viii, Some of them, upon hearing me talk so wildly, thought I was mad. **1791** BOSWELL *Johnson* an. 1729 (1847) 15/1 If a man tells me that he 'sees' this [a ruffian with a drawn sword] and in consternation calls to me to look at it I pronounce him to be mad. **1855** TENNYSON *Maud* II. v. i, And then to hear a dead man chatter Is enough to drive one mad.

absol. **1728** POPE *Dunc.* I. 106 She saw slow Philips creep like Tate's poor page, And all the mighty Mad in Dennis rage.

b. Phrases, ***to †fall, go, run mad.***

1589 RIDER *Bibl. Schol.*, Running madde, *Bacchatus.* **1596** SHAKS. *1 Hen. IV*, III. i. 212 Nay, if thou melt, then will she runne madde. **1605** SHAKS. *Lear* II. iv. 289 O Foole, I shall go mad. **1654** R. CODRINGTON tr. *Iustine*, etc. 567 Being troubled in his Conscience he did fall mad. **1670** G. H. *Hist. Cardinals* II. III. 191 Seeing Nini preferr'd, [he] was ready to run mad. *c* **1709** LADY M. W. MONTAGU *Let. to Mrs. Hewet* 12 Nov., You have not then received my letter? Well! I shall run mad. **1782** COWPER *Poems* I. 314 What! hang a man for going mad? Then farewell British freedom. **1795–1804** W. BLAKE *Vala* I. in *Compl. Writings* (1972) 265 Thou wilt go mad with horror if thou dost Examine thus Every moment of my Secret hours. **1839** in *Amer. Speech* (1965) XL. 130 O dear, I shall go mad, My husband is so crazy. *a* **1850** ROSSETTI *Dante & Circ.* I. (1874) 27 A perversion of gospel-teaching which had gained ground in his day to the extent of becoming a popular frenzy. People went literally mad.

fig. **1735** POPE *Prol. Sat.* 188 It is not Poetry, but Prose run mad. **1762** WESLEY *Jrnl.* 6 Nov., That manner of writing, in prose run mad, I cordially dislike. **1901** G. B. SHAW *Three Plays for Puritans* Pref. p. xxix, Besides, I have a technical objection to making sexual infatuation a tragic theme. Experience proves that it is only effective in the comic spirit .. but .. to worship it, deify it, and imply that it alone makes our lives worth living, is nothing but folly gone mad erotically. **1914** —— *Parents & Children* in *Misalliance* p. cii, The sort of Rationalism which says to a child 'You must suspend your judgment until you are old enough to choose your religion' is Rationalism gone mad. **1923** L. W. REESE *Wild Cherry* 21 The weather has gone mad with white. **1949** T. RATTIGAN *Playbill* 56 The lighting for this scene has gone mad.

c. ***like mad***: literally, in the manner of one who is mad; hence, furiously, with excessive violence or enthusiasm. Also † ***like any mad***, †***for mad.***

c **1420** *Anturs of Arth.* 110 (Thornton MS.) It marrede, it mournede, it moyssede for made. [**1530** PALSGR. 572/1, I go madde, I go up and downe lyke a madde body, *je cours les rues.*] **1653** H. MORE *Antid. Ath.* III. vii. (1712) 108 For she was then seen .. in her fetters, running about like mad. **1663** PEPYS *Diary* 13 June, Thence by coach, with a mad coachman, that drove like mad. **1732** FIELDING *Covent Gard. Trag.* II. xii, My reeling head! which aches like any mad. **1742** RICHARDSON *Pamela* IV. 118 Several Harlequins, and other ludicrous Forms, that jump'd and ran about like mad. **1745** C. J. HAMILTON in *Academy* 18 Nov. (1893) 410/3 They were Shooting at yᵉ Standards Like Mad. **1824** LADY GRANVILLE *Lett.* (1894) I. 262 We are writing like mad for the post. **1893** FORBES-MITCHELL *Remin. Gt. Mutiny* 101 We .. heard our fellows cheering like mad.

d. *transf.* of the effects of alcoholic drink.

1743 BULKELEY & CUMMINS *Voy. S. Seas* 19 Being drunk and mad with Liquor, they plunder'd Chests and Cabins.

†**e.** Causing madness. *Obs. rare.*

1567 MAPLET *Gr. Forest* 41 b, There is another kind of the self same name which is called mad Dwale. Which being drunken sheweth wonders by a certain false shewe of imagination. **1658** ROWLAND tr. *Moufet's Theat. Ins.* 909 There is also another kinde of pernicious honey made, which from the madness that it causeth, is termed Mad-honey. **1676** DRYDEN *Aurengz.* IV. i. 1890 Pow'r like new Wine, does your weak Brain surprize, And it's mad Fumes, in hot Discourses rise.

2. Foolish, unwise. Now only in stronger sense (corresponding to the modern restricted application of sense 1): Extravagantly or wildly foolish; ruinously imprudent.

c **725** *Corpus Gloss.* (Hessels) I. 412 *Ineptus*, ʒemedid. *Ibid.* U. 36 *Uanus*, ʒemaeded. *a* **1300** *Body & Soul* (MS. Laud 108) 100, I þolede þe and [dude] as mad to be maister and i þi cnaue. **13..** *E.E. Allit. P.* A. 267 Me þynk þe put in a mad porpose, & busyez þe aboute a raysoun bref. *c* **1400** *Destr. Troy* 1864 Me meruellis of þi momlyng & þi mad wordes. *a* **1540** BARNES *Wks.* (1573) 349/1 Is not this a madde manner of prayer that men vse to our Lady? **1600** SHAKS. *A.Y.L.* III. ii. 438, I draue my Sutor from his mad humor of loue to a liuing humor of madnes. **1608** MIDDLETON (*title*) A Mad World my Masters. **1611** BIBLE *Eccl.* ii. 2, I saide of laughter, It is mad: and of mirth, What doeth it? **1743** BULKELEY & CUMMINS *Voy. S. Seas* Pref. 14 Our Attempt for Liberty in sailing .. with such a number of People, stow'd in a Long Boat, has been censur'd as a mad Undertaking. **1849** MACAULAY *Hist. Eng.* v. I. 643 The chief justice .. was not mad enough to risk a quarrel on such a subject. **1864** BROWNING *Confessions* ix, How sad and bad and mad it was—But then, how it was sweet! **1878** B. TAYLOR *Deukalion* I. ii. 27 Was I mad, To fear, one moment, thou couldst ever die?

quasi-adv. **13..** *E.E. Allit. P.* A. 1166 Hit payed hym not þat I so flonc, Ouer meruelous merez so mad arayed.

†**3.** Stupefied with astonishment, fear, or suffering: dazed. *Obs.*

a **1300** *Cursor M.* 10310 For þat bright-nes was he sa radd, þat he stode still als he war madd. *Ibid.* 10851 Sant gabriel .. said her till, 'Maria, quarfor es þou madd? Es þe na nede to be radd'. *Ibid.* 24886 All þaa þat in þat ferr cost fard War medd [*Gött.* mad; *Edin.* med] quen þai him [*sc.* the angel] sagh and herd. *c* **1400** *Destr. Troy* 11542 þus in pouert am I pyght, put vnder fote, þat makes me full mad, & mournes in my hert.

4. a. Carried away by enthusiasm or desire; wildly excited; infatuated. Const. *about, after, for, †of, on, upon.*

c **1330** R. BRUNNE *Chron. Wace* (Rolls) 7604 Out of mesure was he glad, Opon þat mayden he wax al mad. **1601** SHAKS. *All's Well* v. iii. 260 He loued her, for indeede he was madde for her. **1611** BIBLE *Jer.* l. 38 It is the land of grauen images, and they are madde vpon their idoles. **1614** B. JONSON *Barthol. Fair* I. (1631) 9, I thought he would ha' runne madde o' the blacke boy in Bucklers-bury. **1678** RYMER *Trag. Last Age* 7, I cannot be perswaded that the people are so very mad of Acorns, but that they could be well content to eat the Bread of civil persons. **1690** W. WALKER *Idiomat. Anglo-Lat.* 283 He began to be mad on her. **1692** DRYDEN *Cleomenes* Pref. A 4, The World is running mad after Farce,—the Extremitie of bad Poetry. **1700** —— *Cinyras & Myrrha* 128 Mad with desire, she ruminates her Sin And wishes all her Wishes o'er again. **1719** DE FOE *Crusoe* II. ix. (1840) 208 They were mad upon their journey. **1744** H. WALPOLE *Corr.* (ed. 3) I. cv. 350 We are now mad about tar-water. **1849** MACAULAY *Hist. Eng.* ii. I. 175 The people were mad with loyal enthusiasm. **1868** FREEMAN *Norm. Conq.* (1876) II. vii. 42 When all the world seemed mad after monks. **1881** TENNYSON *Heavy Brigade* iii, O mad for the charge and the battle were we.

b. Wildly desirous *to* do something. Now *rare.*

a **1627** MIDDLETON *Wom. beware Wom.* III. ii, This makes me madder to enjoy him now. **1732** SWIFT *Jrnl. Mod. Lady* 178 All mad to speak, and none to hearken. **1794** MISS GUNNING *Packet* IV. ix. 166 Every honest cottager was so mad to pursue it after his own mode, that [etc.]. **1814** SOUTHEY *Roderick* I, Mad to wreak His vengeance for his violated child On Roderick's head.

c. Frequently used as the second element in combinations, as ***music-mad, poetry-mad.***

1776 [see *music-mad* s.v. MUSIC *sb.* 13 b]. **1825** H. WILSON *Mem.* I. 41 One of her new admirers, who, being flute-mad, and a beautiful flute player, was always ready. **1848** [see *woman-mad* adj. s.v. WOMAN *sb.* 7]. **1904**, etc. [see *man-mad* adj. s.v. MAN *sb.*¹ 20]. **1943** E. M. ALMEDINGEN *Frossia* ii. 58 Look at all this promiscuity... They have all gone sex-mad. **1946** K. TENNANT *Lost Haven* (1947) 8 All the family were horse-mad. **1974** 'P. B. YUILL' *Bornless Keeper* xiii. 129 Perhaps you can save her from a sex-mad rabbit and win her undying love.

5. 'Beside oneself' with anger; moved to uncontrollable rage; furious. Now only *colloq.* (In many dialects in Great Britain and the U.S. the ordinary word for 'angry'.)

a **1300** *Cursor M.* 17595 For-þi þaa Iuus war full medd, þair sandes come again vn-spedd. *c* **1330** R. BRUNNE *Chron. Wace* (Rolls) 608 þys lady Venus was al glad, þe oþere were for wrayth al mad. **14..** *Arthur* 234 Whan þis lettre was open & rad, þe bretouns & alle men were mad, And wolde þe messager scle. **1539** BIBLE *Ps.* cii. 8 They that are mad vpon me, are sworne together agaynst me. [Similarly, **1611**; the Heb. word literally means 'insane'.] **1577** HANMER *Anc. Eccl. Hist.* 75 They which for familiarity sake used moderation before, now were exceedingly moved and mad with us. *a* **1604** —— *Chron. Irel.* (1633) 125 Roderic was mad, and in his rage, caused his pledges head .. to be cut off. **1622** MABBE tr. *Aleman's Guzman d'Alf.* II. 155 Whereat the merchant was so mad, and so transported with passion, that he knew not what to say. **1705** HICKERINGILL *Priest-cr.* III. Wks. 1716 III. 184 That makes them so mad at me, when I touch the Craft by which they get their Wealth. **1707** *Reflex. upon Ridicule* 350 You are mad to hear other's Works commended. **1766** GARRICK *Neck or Nothing* I. ii, He was damned mad that he could not be at the wedding. **1806** *Simple Narrative* II. 9 I'll pump out of her how she got the book;—how deuced mad she will be. **1847** MARRYAT *Childr. N. Forest* vii, He thought .. you would be mad at the idea of this injustice. **1867** TROLLOPE *Last Chron. Barset* (1869) II. i. 4, I am sometimes so mad with myself when I think over it all,—that I should like to blow my brains out. **1887** F. FRANCIS *Saddle & Mocassin* 111 The more he studied it [*sc.* the bill] the madder he got. **1902** W. JAMES *Varieties Relig. Experience* xi. 264 He can't 'get mad' at any of his alternatives; and the career of a man beset by such an all-round amiability is hopeless. **1925** E. WALLACE *King by Night* viii. 32 Don't get fresh with that girl of mine... You just get mad at her. **1939** [see CHISEL *v.*¹ 4]. **1956** M. DUGGAN in C. K. Stead *N.Z. Short Stories* (1966) 90 Are you mad at me? Simpson asked. **1962** H. HOOD in R. Weaver *Canad. Short Stories* (1968) 2nd Ser. 210 'Why is Daddy mad?' said Deedee. '*I'm not mad!*' **1973** *Black World* June 57/1 Gloria mad at me three days now.

6. a. Of an animal: Abnormally furious, rabid. Often said of bulls; also, in a more specific sense, of dogs, horses, etc. suffering from rabies.

The sense appears to be of late emergence; before the 16th c. it was expressed by WOOD *a.*

1538 [implied in MADNESS 1]. **1565** COOPER *Thesaurus* s.v. *Furibundus, Canis furibundus*, a madde dogge. *Taurus furibundus*, a madde bull. **1579** FULKE *Heskins' Parl.* 463 Dogges after they had eaten the sacrament, .. ranne madde. **1590** SHAKS. *Com. Err.* v. i. 70. **1702** in *12th Rep. Hist. MSS. Comm.* App. III. 7 A great Mad Bull to be turned loose in the Game-place, with Fire-works all over him. **1766** GOLDSM. *Elegy Mad Dog* 20 The dog, to gain some private ends, Went mad, and bit the man. **1769** PENNANT *Zool.* III. 315 Fish thus affected the Thames fishermen call mad bleaks. **1800** *Med. Jrnl.* IV. 58 Keep the dogs, or other animals, supposed mad, shut up safely in a convenient place for five or six weeks. **1848** DICKENS *Dombey* vi, A thundering alarm of 'Mad Bull' was raised.

†**b.** ***mad dog***: another name for HUFF-CAP. *Obs.*

1577 [See HUFF-CAP B 1].

7. a. Uncontrolled by reason; passing all rational bounds in demeanour or conduct; extravagant in gaiety; wild.

1597, 1635 Mad Greeke [see GREEK *sb.* 5]. **1598** MARSTON in *Shaks. C. Praise* 29 Why, how now, currish, mad Athenian? **1605** CAMDEN *Rem.* (1637) 377 A merry mad maker as they call Poets now, was he, which .. made this for John Calfe. **1655** *Nicholas Papers* (Camden) II. 338 You will heare mad work shortly, for the Jesuit is at worke. *a* **1715** BURNET *Own Time* (1724) I. 244 He .. was engaged in a mad-ramble after pleasure and minded no business. **1732** BERKELEY *Alciphr.* II. §10 The mad sallies of intemperance and debauchery. **1777** MME. D'ARBLAY *Early Diary* 7 Apr., The sweet little thing was quite in mad spirits. **1862** G. MEREDITH *Marian* iii, She is steadfast as a star, And yet the maddest maiden. **1873** OUIDA *Pascarè l* I. 69 They would play me all sorts of sweet little mad *canzoni.*

b. *transf.* Of storm, wind: Wild, violent.

1836 MRS. BROWNING *Poet's Vow* I. xiii, Mad winds that howling go From east to west. **1863** WOOLNER *My Beautiful Lady* 50 Here the mad gale had rioted and thrown Far drifts of snowy petals.

8. Proverbs. ***as mad as a buck, a hatter, a March hare*** (see HARE *sb.* 1 b), etc. Also (***as***) ***mad as a cut snake*** (Austral.), † ***Ajax, a hornet*** (U.S.), ***a meat axe*** (chiefly Austral. and N.Z.), ***a wet hen.***

a **1529** SKELTON *Replycacion* 35 Thou madde Marche hare. **1529** [see HARE *sb.* 1 b]. **1588** SHAKS. *L.L.L.* IV. iii. 7 By the Lord this Loue is as mad as Aiax, it kils sheepe. **1590** SHAKS. *Com. Err.* III. i. 72 It would make a man mad as a Bucke to be so bought and sold. **1607** CHAPMAN *Bussy d'Ambois* III. 468 Murther market folkes, quarrell with sheepe, And runne as mad as Aiax. **1609** *Ev. Wom. in Humor* I. in Bullen *Old Plays* IV. 314 If he were as madde as a weaver. **1626** FLETCHER *Noble Gent.* I. ii, Monsieur Shattillion's mad... Mad as May-butter, And which is more, mad for a wench. **1732** T. FULLER *Gnomologia* 140 Love is as mad as Ajax; it kills Sheep, so it kills me. **1823** J. DODDRIDGE *Dialogue of Backwoodsman & Dandy* in *Logan* 42 Every body that was not ax'd was mad as a wet hen. **1855** T. C. HALIBURTON *Nat. & Hum. Nat.* I. 85, I feel as mad as a meat axe. **1837–40, 1857** [see HATTER 1]. **1849** THACKERAY *Pendennis* x, We were .. chaffing Derby Oaks—until he was as mad as a hatter. **1901** T. RATCLIFFE in *N. & Q.* 9th Ser. VIII. 501/2 In Derbyshire .. there is no commoner saying to express anger shown by any one than to say that he or she was 'as mad as a tup'. **1902** W. N. HARBEN *Abner Daniel* 54 The Colonel is as mad as a wet hen about the whole thing. **1919** MENCKEN *Amer. Lang.* 80 In the familiar simile, *as mad as a hornet*, it [*sc.* the word *mad*] is used in the American sense. **1923** WODEHOUSE *Inimitable Jeeves* xviii. 249 My uncle will be as mad as a wet hen when he finds out that he has been fooled. **1927** *Amer. Speech* II. 360 He was as mad as a hornet when he heard how the election went. **1932** 'W. HATFIELD' *Ginger Murdoch* 30 'But you're mad!' said Mick, 'mad as a cut snake!' **1946** J. FOUNTAIN in *Coast to Coast 1945* 252 The cow's mad—mad as a meat axe! **1951** S. MACKENZIE *Dead Men Rising* 203 'Mad as a cut snake,' Johnson said admiringly, 'and there's not a better feller in the whole camp.' **1963** *Moderna Språk* LVII. I. 10 *As mad as a cut snake*: 'mad' is used in the sense of 'angry', and the phrase means 'extremely angry'. **1970** D. M. DAVIN *Not Here, Not Now* v. iii. 263 She's mad as a meataxe anyway about the whole idea. **1971** *Wall St. Jrnl.* 22 July W. 1/4 The chicken farmers of Quebec .. are as mad as, well, a wet hen.

9. *Comb.*, parasynthetic, as ***mad-blooded, -humoured, -mooded, -pated*** adjs.; with adjs., indicating some condition that proceeds from, resembles, or results in madness, as ***mad-afraid***, †***mad-angry***, ***-blazing***, ***-drunk***, †***-hardy*** (hence †***mad-hardiness***), †***-hungry***, ***-keen***, †***-merry***, †***-proud***, †***-red*** adjs.; also ***mad-like*** adj. and in attributive combinations of the adj. used *absol.*, as **mad minute** *Army slang*, a minute of rapid rifle-fire or frenzied bayonet-practice (see quots.); **mad money** *colloq.*, money for use in an emergency; *spec.* (see quot. 1922); **mad nurse** (*colloq.*) a nurse attending on insane patients; **mad scientist**, a scientist who is mad or eccentric, esp. so as to be dangerous or evil: a stock figure of melodramatic horror-stories; freq. *attrib.* See also MAD-DOCTOR, MADHOUSE.

1895 KIPLING *Seven Seas* (1896) 90 When the steers are *mad-afraid. **1589** RIDER *Bibl. Schol.*, *Madde angrie, or raging madde, *sævus, furiosus.* **1632** J. HAYWARD tr. *Biondi's Eromena* v. 142 Whose Prince mad angry for being discovered, assayling with a sudden furie the Granadan Galley, easily tooke her. **1837** CARLYLE *Fr. Rev.* III. v. vii, *Mad-blazing with flame of all imaginable tints. **1885** RUNCIMAN *Skippers & Sh.* 84 He was a *mad blooded rip that cared for nothing. **1653** BAXTER *Chr. Concord* 32, I have neighbours that go *mad-drunk about the streets. **1871** *Routledge's Ev. Boy's Ann.* 33 He was mad drunk, and did not know what he was doing. **1534** WHITINTON *Tullyes Offices* I. (1540) 28 Of the hye pride of herte whiche is in reproche, and maye be called *madhardynesse. *Ibid.* 35 *Madhardy men of our cyte of Rome. **1665** PEPYS *Diary* 6 Dec., Knipp, who is .. the most excellent *mad-humoured thing, and sings the noblest that ever I heard. **1608** CHAPMAN *Byron's Conspir.* Plays 1873 II. 233 Such *mad-hungrie men, as well may eate Hote coles of fire. **1949** A. CHRISTIE *Crooked House* xvi. 126 She's *mad keen on this detecting stuff. **1974** L. LAMB *Man in Mist* xiii. 88 Derek Boots was not exactly the type to join us here... I was not so mad keen on him. **1836** [G. E. INMAN] *Sir Orfeo* 6 With a *mad-like dreaminess crying. **1887** P. M'NEILL *Blawearie* 144 The mad-like act would never have been heard of. **1599** *Sir John Oldcastle* (1600) C 4, Ye olde *mad merry Constable, art thou aduisde of that? **1609** BOYS *Wks.* (1629) 30 The wicked are often merrie, sometime mad-merry. **1917** A. G. EMPEY *Over Top* 298 **Mad minute*, firing fifteen rounds from your rifle in sixty seconds. A man is mad to attempt it, especially with a stiff bolt. **1942** in Baker *Austral. Lang.* (1945) viii. 155 *The mad minute*, bayonet drill. **1945** C. H. B. PRIDHAM *Superiority of Fire* vi. 57 By 1914, many men in each regiment could exceed even twenty rounds in the 'mad minute'. **1964** C. FALLS in S. Nowell-Smith *Edwardian England* xiv. 537 Reservists and young soldiers alike could shoot steadily and accurately at a relatively slow rate for long periods, or in emergency fire what they called their 'mad minute'. **1965** BROPHY & PARTRIDGE *Long Trail* 147 *Mad minute*, a newspaper phrase for British rapid fire during the Retreat from Mons... The name was also

applied to the frenzied minute spent charging down the assault course, bayoneting straw-filled dummies, representing enemy soldiers. **1922** *Dialect Notes* V. 148 **Mad money*, money a girl carries in case she has a row with her escort and wishes to go home alone. **1933** PARTRIDGE *Slang To-day & Yesterday* v. 285 *Mad money*, return fare, it being very generally believed by the New Zealand troops . . that every English girl infallibly carried her return fare in case her soldier friend became *mad*, i.e., acted with an excessive freedom of manner. **1943** J. STEINBECK *Once there was War* (1959) 136 He has a nest egg or mad money. **1962** L. DEIGHTON *Ipcress File* x. 61, I think he grabs an S. I. now and again when he needs some mad money. **1970** 'D. SHANNON' *Unexpected Death* (1971) ix. 135, I haven't even a dime of mad money with me, hope I don't need it. **1972** O. SELA *Bearer Plot* i. 15, I reached for the wad of notes Keith kept as mad money. **1583** T. WATSON *Centurie of Loue* lii. Poems (Arb.) 88 *Mad mooded Loue vsurping Reasons place. **1753** *The World* No. 23 ¶7 After such hospitals are built, . . and doctors, surgeons, apothecaries and *mad nurses provided. **1771** T. HULL *Sir W. Harrington* (1797) II. 223 Your *mad-pated Julia. **14..** *Voc.* in Wr.-Wülcker 605/15 *Produculus*, *madprud. **1614** LODGE *Seneca, Life* ix, This Prince waxed *mad red with anger. **1940** 'N. BLAKE' *Malice in Wonderland* III. xviii. 282 A sort of *mad-scientist motive for the whole series of outrages. **1963** 'G. BAGBY' *Murder's Little Helper* (1964) iv. 36 The whole idea smacked too much of some mad-scientist fable out of a comic strip. **1972** B. TURNER *Solden's Women* ix. 82 He would have passed for the mad scientist in one of those films which star giant insects.

mad (mæd), *v.* [f. MAD *a.*]

1. *trans.* To make mad, in various senses of the adj.; to madden, make insane; †to render foolish; †to bewilder, stupefy, daze; to infuriate, enrage. Now *rare* exc. *U.S. colloq.*, to exasperate.

1399 LANGL. *Rich. Redeles* I. 63 And no soule persone to punnyshe þe wrongis; And þat maddid þi men. *Ibid.* II. 132 With many derke mystis þat maddid her eyne. *c* **1400** *Destr. Troy* 8061 So full are þo faire fild of dessait, And men for to mad is most þere dessyre. **1561** T. NORTON *Calvin's Inst.* IV. 125 The deuell hath with horrible bewitchyng madded their myndes. **1593** NASHE *Christ's T.* (1613) 44 Nothing so much doth macerate and mad mee. **1600** HOLLAND *Livy* XXVIII. XV. 679 The Elephants also affrighted and madded . . ran from the wings. **1621** BURTON *Anat. Mel.* II. iii. VII. 425 He plaid on his drumme and by that meanes madded her more. **1682** SOUTHERNE *Loyal Brother* IV. i, O Hell! it mads my reason but to think on't. **1810** CRABBE *Borough* viii, Again! By Heav'n, it mads me. **1850** BLACKIE *Æschylus* I. 22 Sin . . Mads the ill-counsell'd heart. **1863** J. WEISS *Life T. Parker* I. 191 You have madded Parker and in this way he shews his spite. **1873** M. HOLLEY *My Opinions* 249 At the same time it madded some of the Republicans. **1893** 'O. THANET' *Stories Western Town* 31, I madded him first; I was a fool. **1916** H. L. WILSON *Somewhere in Red Gap* vi. 268, I think to find him all madded up and mortified; but he's strangely cheerful for one who has suffered. **1924** W. M. RAINE *Troubled Waters* vi. 59 O' course, it ain't that any of them's afraid to mad that crazy gunman, Tait.

2. a. *intr.* To be or to become mad; to act like a madman, rage, behave furiously. Now *rare*.

a **1366** CHAUCER *Rom. Rose* 1072 Richesse a robe of purpre on hadde, Ne trowe not that I lye or madde. **1382** WYCLIF *Acts* xxvi. 24 Festus with greet vois seyde, Poul, thou maddist, or wexist wood. *c* **1386** CHAUCER *Miller's T.* 373 Suffiseth thee, but if thy wittes madde To han as greet a grace as Noe hadde. *c* **1394** *P. Pl. Crede* 280 'Alas!' quaþ þe frier 'almost y madde in mynde, To sen hou3 þis Minoures many men begyleth!' *c* **1412** HOCCLEVE *De Reg. Princ.* 930, I . . muse so, that vn-to lite I madde. *c* **1440** *Promp. Parv.* 319/2 Maddyn, or dotyn, *desipio*. Maddyn, or waxyn woode, *insanio, furio*. **1529** LUPSET *Charity* (1539) 23, I maye loue for my sensuall luste, as when . . I madde or dote vppon women. **1530** PALSGR. 616/1, I madde, I waxe or become mad, *je enraige*. I holde my lyfe on it the felowe maddeth. **1574** HELLOWES *Gueuara's Fam. Ep.* (1577) 310 He brawleth and maddeth with the maids. **1873** M. ARNOLD *Lit. & Dogma* (1876) 148 The unclean spirits . . came raging and madding before him.

†**b.** Phrase, *to go* or ***run madding***. *Obs.*

a **1619** FOTHERBY *Atheom.* II. ii. §5 (1622) 205 Wee runne madding after Gold. **1621** T. WILLIAMSON tr. *Goulart's Wise Vieillard* 25 Ouer violent passions of the minde . . ouerwhelme the soule, . . making it to goe gadding and madding heere and there to and fro. **1650** HOWELL *Giraffi's Rev. Naples* I. 79 Going thus arming daily more and more, and madding up and down the streets. *a* **1691** POCOCK *Theol. Wks.* (1740) II. 195/1 A . . mad-headed, unruly heifer, that . . runs wantonly madding about.

†**c.** To become infatuated. Const. *after*, *upon*. *Obs.*

1594 KYD *Cornelia* I. 60 A martiall people madding after Armes. **1624** F. WHITE *Repl. Fisher* 555 The practise of your people . . madding vpon the merits of Saints, and contemning the merits of Christ . . is intollerable.

Madagascan (mædə'gæskən), *a.* and *sb.* [irreg. f. *Madagascar* (see next) + -AN.] **A.** *adj.* Of or pertaining to Madagascar. **B.** *sb.* A native or inhabitant of Madagascar.

1886 *Ibis* 135 The alternative hypothesis . . that the Madagascan and Columbian species [of Snipes] have changed. **1890** *Cent. Dict., Madagascan*, . . a native or an inhabitant of Madagascar. **1953** L. D. STAMP *Africa* XX. 511 Every Madagascan farm has a few pigs. **1973** *Listener* 20 Sept. 369/1 The Madagascan revolt, in which eighty thousand were killed. **1973** *Country Life* 20 Dec. 2122/2 The Japanese . . have developed a real yen for it [*sc.* Beaujolais]. So have the Madagascans, the Tahitians and the Nationalist Chinese.

Madagascar (mædə'gæskə(r)). The large island off the east coast of Africa, used *attrib.* in special collocations, as **Madagascar cat**, the ring-tailed lemur, *Lemur catta*; **Madagascar (clove) nutmeg, manna** (see quots.); **Madagascar periwinkle**, a tropical plant (*Vinca rosea*) with white or rose-coloured flowers.

1900 H. A. BRYDEN *Animals Afr.* 12 Some of these curious lemurs, which are usually known as 'Madagascar Cats'. **1866** LINDLEY & MOORE *Treas. Bot.* I. 28/2 One species, *A*[*gathophyllum*] *aromaticum*, grows in Madagascar. . . The fruit . . encloses a kernel of an acrid caustic taste, known as Madagascar clove nutmegs. **1889** *Cent. Dict., Dulcitol*, . . is commercially obtained from an unknown plant in Madagascar, and in the crude state is called *Madagascar manna*. **1821** M. BROWNE *Diary* (1905) 104 There were . . myrtles, beautiful campanulas, geraniums, Madagascar periwinkles, etc.

Madagascarian (mædəgæ'skɛəriən), *a.* [f. prec. + -IAN] = MADAGASCAN *a.* Also **Mada'gascarene, Mada'gascrian** *sbs.* = MADAGASCAN *sb.*

1824 M. A. HEDGE *Radama* iv. 78 The first order is usually composed of those termed the white Madagascrians. **1856** C. NORDHOFF *Merchant Vessel* xix. 246 The natives . . are mostly black, the descendants of Madagascarenes. **1875** *Encycl. Brit.* III. 758/2 Madagascar, the Comoros, and the widely-scattered Mascarene Islands constitute a fifth Subregion, . . and for this we may most reasonably use the name 'Madagascarian'. **1893** A. NEWTON *Dict. Birds* II. 347 Those [genera] belonging to the insular or Madagascarian Subregion.

Madagass. Also **Madegass, Madecass.** [Variant of MALAGASH.]

1. A native or inhabitant of Madagascar.

1793 TRAPP tr. *Rochon's Voy. Madagascar* 33 The inhabitants of Madagascar call themselves indistinctly Malegashes, or Madecasses. **1815** A. BURN *Mem.* v. (1816) 208 It is lamentable that some attempts are not made to convert the Madagasses to Christianity. **1839** *Penny Cycl.* XIV. 259/2 The Madegasses have made considerable progress in the arts of civilization.

2. A Jamaican Black, having skin less dark and hair less crisped than is typical among African peoples.

1873 GARDNER *Hist. Jamaica* II. iv. 97 The term Madagass is still applied to certain light complexioned negroes, especially those whose hair is less woolly than common.

‖**madal** (mə'dɑːl). Also **madāla, maddale.** A double-headed drum used in Nepal and eastern India. Cf. MRIDANGAM.

1914 A. H. F. STRANGWAYS *Mus. Hindostan* IX. 228 The *maddale* (*mṛdānga*-shape) hollowed out of a tree. **1954** J. MASTERS *Bhowani Junction* 329 My Birkhe beat cheerfully on a madal, which is a deep and narrow Gurkha drum. **1960** S. PRAJÑĀNANANDA *Hist. Devel. Indian Mus.* i. 7 The different musical instruments of folk-music like *ekatāra*, . . *madāla*, . . etc. bear testimony to . . the cultural taste and outlook of the peoples of Bengal. **1969** *Illustr. Weekly India* 27 July 33/1 They assemble . . and dance—both men and women—to the accompaniment of the *madal* (the Santali drum). **1971** K. KENT in C. Bonington *Annapurna South Face* App. H. 314 Most boys [in Nepal] learn to play the flute and *madal*—a double-ended drum, with one end slightly smaller than the other.

madam ('mædəm), *sb.* Forms: 3–6 **madame,** 4–5 **madaum** *Sc.* **madem(e, 5 maydame,** 6 **maddame,** 4–9 **madame,** 4– **madam.** [a. OF. *ma dame* (in mod.Fr. written MADAME), literally, 'my lady' (see DAME, DAM), corresp. etymologically to It. *madonna, monna*, med.L. *mea domina*.

The spelling *madame* is still preferred by some writers, but the more general and convenient practice is to write *madam* when the word is used as English, and MADAME when it is used as a foreign title. For the plural (in sense 1) MESDAMES is now used; the Eng. plural is obs. exc. in sense 3.]

1. a. A form of respectful or polite address (substituted for the name) originally used by servants in speaking to their mistress, and by people generally in speaking to a lady of high rank; subsequently used with progressively extended application, and now capable of being (in certain circumstances) employed in addressing a woman of whatever rank or position. (Corresponding to SIR.)

The early occurrence of DAME in the sense of mother suggests that in AF. and early ME. *ma dame* was very commonly used by children to their mother; but in the extant examples the mother so addressed is a queen or a lady of very high rank. In Chaucer's time (*C.T. Prol.* 376) to be addressed as *madame* was one of the advantages which a citizen's wife gained by her husband's being made alderman; this probably indicates the lowest social grade in which at that time the title could be claimed as a matter of customary right. In poetry of the 14th and 15th c. the lover often addresses his mistress as *madame*. Nuns (originally only the elder ones: see quot. *c* 1400) were called *madame* down to the Reformation.

While in France the title has (with certain customary exceptions) been confined to married women, in England no such rule has been generally adopted, though there are traces of a tendency in the 16–17th c. to address matrons as 'madam' and spinsters as 'mistress'.

From the 17th c. *madam* has been the title normally used in beginning or subscribing a letter to a woman of any station, except where the use of the name (as in 'Dear Mrs. A.' etc.) is permitted ('my lady', etc. not being admitted in epistolary usage). In oral use the title now rarely occurs; from the 18th c. it has been, except in very formal use, largely superseded by the contracted form MA'AM, which has itself in recent years been greatly restricted in currency; however, *madam* is in London and other towns still the word commonly used by salesmen to their female customers, and by persons in the position of servants to the public.

1297 R. GLOUC. (Rolls) 832 Heo [*sc.* Cordeille] sede . . Mid hou mani kni3tes is he come, þe oþer a3en sede, Ma dame bote mid o man. *Ibid.* 5858 Certes ma dame quaþ þe king [to his stepmother] so ne may it no3t be. *a* **1300–1400** *Cursor M.* 4340 (Gött.) In chamber hendely he [Joseph] hir grett, And said, 'madam [*Cott.* lauedi], cum to 3our mett'. *c* **1330** *Arth. & Merl.* 4644 (Kölbing) Þo bispac Wawain curteys [addressing his mother] Madame, purvaieþ ous harnais. *c* **1375** *Sc. Leg. Saints* l. (*Katerine*) 658 [T]hane purphir sad till hir [*sc.* the queen] alsone: 'dred nocht, mademe! It sall be done'. **1390** GOWER *Conf.* I. 47 Ma dame, I am a man of thyne, That in thi Court have longe served. *a* **1400–50** *Alexander* 229 'Haile, modi qwene of Messidoyne' he maister-like said; þare deyned him na daynte 'madame' hire to call. *Ibid.* 874 Þen airis him on Alexander to his awen modire; 'Bees not a-glopened, madame ne greued at my fadire'. *c* **1400** *Rule St. Benet* 2210 'Damisel' þe 3ongest [nun] es, þe elder 'madaum' & 'mastres'. Þe Priores als principall Es 'lady' & leder of þam all. *a* **1440** *Sir Degrev.* 785 'Maydame!' sche seid, 'gramercy of thi gret cortesy'. *c* **1470** HENRY *Wallace* v. 1030 'Grace', scho cryit, 'for hym that deit on tre'. Than Wallace said; 'Mademe, your noyis lat be'. **1513** BRADSHAW *St. Werburge* II. 1393 'Alas', he sayd, 'ma dame and patronesse, For sorowe I can nat my peynes expresse'. **1547** EARL SUSSEX in Ellis *Orig. Lett.* Ser. I. II. 137 [To his wife.] Madame . . thies be to signifie [etc.]. *Ibid.* 138 Thus, good Madame albeit [etc.]. **1552** LYNDESAY *Monarche* III. 4664 The seilye Nun wyll thynk gret schame, Without scho callit be Madame. **1597** SHAKS. *2 Hen. IV*, II. i. 109 And didst not thou . . desire me to be no more familiar with such poore people, saying, that ere long they should call me Madam? **1602** —— *Ham.* II. ii. 96 *Qu.* More matter, with lesse Art. *Pol.* Madam, I sweare I vse no Art at all. **1609** B. JONSON *Silent Woman* v. (1620) O 2, *Tru.* You see, what creatures you may bestow your fauours on, Madames. **1648** MILTON *Sonn.* x. 11 *To the Lady Margaret Ley*, Though later born, than to have known the dayes Wherein your Father flourisht, yet by you Madam, me thinks I see him living yet. **1696** PHILLIPS (ed. 5), *Madam*, a Title of Honour, which is given as well in Writing as Speaking, to Women of Quality, as Princesses, Dutchesses, and others; but grown a little too common of late. **1749** FIELDING *Tom Jones* XVII. vi, 'If you will have patience, madam', answered Mrs. Miller, 'I will acquaint you who I am' . . 'I have no curiosity, madam, to know anything', cries Sophia. **1851** TENNYSON *To the Queen*, Take, Madam, this poor book of song. **1884** J. QUINCY *Figures of Past* 325 'So you've been over the farm, Colonel Pickering', said my mother. . . 'Why, yes, Madame', was the reply, 'I have been all over the farm, and a weary tramp I've had of it'. **1901** *Daily Chron.* 10 Dec. 5/2 The street-car conductors of Boston are compelled to address all their women passengers as 'madam'.

b. Non-vocatively, substituted for the name of a lady entitled to be addressed as 'madam'. ?*Obs.*

c **1500** *Melusine* 11 Sire, Madame the quene Pressyne your wyf . . is delyuered of thre doughtirs. **1605** SHAKS. *Lear* I. ii. 9 Why Bastard? . . When my Dimensions are as well compact . . As honest Madams issue? **1716** SWIFT *Phillis* Wks. 1755 III. II. 159 Old madam, who went up to find What papers Phil had left behind. **1720** —— *Fates Clergym.* ibid. II. II. 28 He kept a miserable house, but the blame was laid wholly upon madam; for the good doctor was always at his books. **1762** BICKERSTAFFE *Love in Village* I. ix. (1765) 18, I know what makes you false hearted to me, that you may keep company with young madam's waiting woman. **1839–41** WARREN *Ten Thous. a Year* xvii. II. 93 It's very hard ma'am, that madam's maid is to go with her, and I'm not to go with *you*! ['Madam' is the lady of the house; the speaker is her sister-in-law's maid.]

c. Used in contempt or anger. Chiefly *dial.*

1854 MISS BAKER *Northampt. Gloss.*, I'll give it you, madam, if you don't do as you're bid.

2. As a prefixed title. †**a.** Prefixed to a first or sole name. *Obs.*

c **1386** CHAUCER *Prol.* 121 She [the prioress] was cleped madame Eglentyne. **1591** SHAKS. *Two Gent.* II. i. 9 Goe to, sir, tell me: do you know Madam Siluia? *Ibid.* II. v. 8 But sirha, how did thy Master part with Madam Julia? **1613** HEYWOOD *Brazen Age* II. ii, *Iason.* Madam Medea. *Medea.* Leaue circumstance, away. **1749** FIELDING *Tom Jones* VIII. viii, etc. [An unmarried young lady is referred to by servants and inferiors as 'Madam Sophia'.]

b. Prefixed to a surname: (*a*) Now in U.S., and perh. formerly in England, the style of a woman who has a married son (whose wife has the style of 'Mrs.'). (*b*) *dial.* The style of a married woman of position, such as the squire's wife. (*c*) *U.S.* (See quot. 1809).

1703 PETIVER *Musei Petiver.* 94 Madam Elizabeth Glanville. To this Curious Gentlewoman I am obliged for an hundred Insects. **1705** *Lond. Gaz.* No. 4106/4 Madam Clark of Yeovil, Mrs. Jervice of Favent. *a* **1774** GOLDSM. *Elegy on Mrs. Blaize*, Good people all, with one accord Lament for Madam Blaize. **1809** KENDALL *Trav.* II. XXXVIII. 44 It has been, and still is the practice, to prefix to the name of a deceased female of some consideration . . the title of madam. *a* **1825** FORBY *Voc. E. Anglia, Madam*, a term of respect to gentlewomen; below *lady*, but above *mistress*. In a village, the Esquire's wife . . must have *madam* prefixed to her surname. The parson's wife, if he be a doctor, or a man of . . genteel figure, must be *madam* too. **1849** LYELL *2nd Visit U.S.* I. ix. 162 The title of Madam is sometimes given here [in Boston], and generally . . in the South, to a mother whose son has married, and the daughter-in-law is then called Mrs.

†**c.** ***madame regent*** = queen regent. Also *fig.* *Obs.*

1523 SKELTON *Garl. Laurel* 53 [to Pallas] Prynces moost pusant . . All other transcendyng . . Madame regent of the seyence seuyn. *Ibid.* 951. *a* **1562** G. CAVENDISH *Wolsey* (1893) 84 Nowe was there lodged also Madame Regent, the kyng's mother, and all hir trayn of ladys and gentillwomen.

†**d.** In playful or derisive uses. *Obs.*

1603 SHAKS. *Meas. for M.* I. ii. 43 Behold, behold, where madam Mitigation comes. **1624** HEYWOOD *Captives* IV. i. in

Bullen *O. Pl.* IV, Naye, make his honest and chast wyfe no better Then a madam makarell. **1633** FORD *'Tis Pity* II. ii, 'Tis not your new Mistresse, Your goodly Madam Merchant, shall triumph On my deiection. **1670** EACHARD *Cont. Clergy* 28 After a lad has taken his leave of Madam University,..he is not likely to deal..with much Latine. **1687** DRYDEN *Hind & P.* II. 250 But madam Panther, you, though more sincere, Are not so wise as your adulterer. *a* **1806** H. K. WHITE *My Study*, The ideal flights of Madam Brain.

3. A woman who is addressed as 'madam'.

†**a.** A lady of rank or station. Also *fig. Obs.*

1543 BALE *Yet a Course* 38 b, She [holy church] became a gloryouse madame of the earth. **1550** —— *Image Both Ch.* Pref. A vj b, They have alwaies for lucres sake, gloriouslye garnished their holy mother, the madame of mischiefe and proude synagog of Sathan w^t golde, siluer [etc.]. **1576** FLEMING *Panopl. Epist.* Epit. Preceptes A ij b, His grandmother a sober matrone and vertuous old maddame. **1589** PUTTENHAM *Eng. Poesie* III. i. (Arb.) 149 As we see in these great Madames of honour. **1616** R. C. *Times' Whistle*, etc. (1871) 134 'Tis certaine he had been a knight a[t] lest, And made his wife (what she hath lookt for long) A Madame. *appositively.* **1632** MASSINGER *City Madam* I. i, The want of one [*sc.* a male heir] Swells my young Mistresses, and their madam mother With hopes above their birth, and scale.

b. The mistress of a house. Now only *U.S. vulgar.*

1824 GALT *Rothelan* II. xv, We shall..use a little more freedom with the madam of the mansion. **1879** TOURGEE *Fool's Err.* xv. 75 Well, Colonel,..I've brought back the books I borrowed of the madam the other day.

c. In derisive or opprobrious use. (*a*) An affected fine lady. †(*b*) A kept mistress, a courtesan, prostitute (*obs.*). (*c*) Used as a general term of contempt for a female: a 'hussy', 'minx'. (*d*) A brothel-keeper; cf. MADAME 4. (*e*) Nonsense, humbug. *slang.*

These uses may perhaps, so far as origin is concerned, belong partly to MADAME, as being more or less due to prejudice against foreign women. Cf. '*Madam Van* [?i.e. a Dutchwoman: cf. MADAME 1] a whore' (*Dict. Cant. Crew, a* 1700).

(*a*) **1598** MARSTON *Sco. Villanie* In Lect. B 2, Let me alone, the Madams call for thee Longing to laugh at thy wits pouertie. **1623** MASSINGER *Dk. Milan* III. ii, Fine meeters To tinckle in the eares of ignorant Madams. **1664** POWER *Exp. Philos.* I. 11 Ovid's Lydian-Spinstresse, that proud Madam which Pallas, for her Rivalship transform'd into the Spider. **1682** O. N. *Boileau's Lutrin* I. Argt. 11 Thus Queasie Madams meat forbear Untill they read, The Bill of Fare. **1725** *New Cant. Dict., Mistress Princum-Prancum*, such a stiff, over-nice, precise Madam. **1803** MARY CHARLTON *Wife & Mistress* III. 57 What should I care what those fine Madams says of me! **1840** HOOD *Kilmansegg, Honeymoon* xxii, She was far too pamper'd a madam.

(*b*) **1719** D'URFEY *Pills* IV. 139 Hide-Park may be term'd the Market of Madams, or Lady-Fair. **1721** AMHERST *Terræ Fil.* No. 28 (1754) 152 At Oxford..several of our most celebrated and right beautiful madams would pluck off their fine feathers, and betake themselves to an honest livelihood. **1747** *Gentl. Mag.* 96 On a Gentleman who mistook a Kept Madam for a Lady of Fashion. **1761** *Ann. Reg.* II. 66 He indulged himself and madam with green peas at five shillings a quart.

(*c*) **1802** WOLCOT (P. Pindar) *Middlesex Elect.* ii. Wks. 1816 IV. 183 I'd make the madams squall. **1874** S. BEAUCHAMP *Grantley Grange* I. 68 'I do not think they [hop-pickers] are troubled with much shyness'. 'O, not a bit of it, Sir Charles..they're brazen madams, and quite above my hands'.

(*d*) *a* **1911** D. G. PHILLIPS *Susan Lenox* (1917) I. xxi. 393 The madam fixes things so that every girl always owes her money. **1912** T. DREISER *Financier* xlvi. 510 In a few moments the 'madam', as the current word characterized this type of woman, appeared. **1918** C. GARNETT tr. *Dostoevsky's White Nights* 117 Before me was standing a person with a stupid smile, the 'madam' herself. **1926** J. BLACK *You can't Win* iv. 30 The following week I called at Madam Kate Singleton's... In a minute the madam came down. **1959** N. MAILER *Advts. for Myself* (1961) 279 A rather remarkable woman who had been the madam of a whorehouse. **1960** AUDEN *Homage to Clio* 85 Henry Adams Was mortally afraid of Madams: In a disorderly house He sat quiet as a mouse. **1962** *Punch* 30 May p. xiii/1 Barbara Stanwyck as Lesbian madam of New Orleans brothel. **1975** *Daily Tel.* (Colour Suppl.) 18 July 7/1 The oldest girl is a woman, maybe Czechoslovakian, maybe the madam.

(*e*) **1927** E. WALLACE *Feathered Serpent* xvii. 218 'I was getting a hundred quid for this job..and I couldn't turn him down.' 'The usual "madam"!' sneered the inspector. 'It's not "madam", Mr. Brown,' said Jerry earnestly, 'though I admit it sounds as likely as cream in skilly; but it's true.' **1932** A. GARDNER *Tinker's Kitchen* 284 Madam = made up story; flattery. **1936** J. CURTIS *Gilt Kid* ii. 18 'What did the old boy say?' 'Just the usual madam.' **1965** *Sunday Times Mag.* 11 July 21 Both sides are expert with the madam—a form of kidology which seems to come naturally to most Merseysiders. **1973** J. WAINWRIGHT *Touch of Malice* 130 It was not the sort of place conducive to putting over a spot of old madam. The normally glib flannel tended to stick in his throat and the guff and eye-wash hadn't enough elbow-room to..sound..feasible.

4. †**a.** *Comb.* (*appositive*). *Obs.*

1593 G. HARVEY *Pierce's Super.* 174 Floorishing London, the Staple of Wealth, & Madame-towne of the Realme.

b. madam-shop [MADAM *sb.* 3], a small shop which sells ready-to-wear clothes for the fashionable woman of mature taste.

1952 *Times Lit. Suppl.* 28 Nov. 778 The juggling with couture dressmakers..and owners of 'madam shops' in order to keep them contented with their share of reporting. **1963** *Harper's Bazaar* Feb. 20/3 The sight of two assistants in one of those little madam shops fitting girdles on to plastic models. **1965** *Guardian* 16 July 8/5 Boutiques are nothing new in Manchester. There is a stalwart 'madam shop' tradition; little shops for women of substance. **1966** H. W. YOXALL *Fashion of Life* viii. 68 The contemporary Madam Shops, so aptly named,..are enjoying a new popularity. **1967** *Guardian* 30 Mar. 5/1 The madam shops... Shops catering for women over 25 who want to dress in fashion, and can afford to.

Hence (*nonce-wds.*) **'madamish** *a.*, like a 'fine lady'; †**'madamship**.

1620 *Swetnam Arraigned* (1880) 62, I thanke your Madame-ship, Ime glad o' this. **1881** J. YOUNGER *Autobiog.* xv. 171 The mistress at home grew quite madamish.

madam ('mædəm), *v.* [f. MADAM *sb.*] *trans.* To address as 'madam'. †Also with *up.*

1622 ROWLANDS *Good Newes & B.* 7 She..would be Madam'd, Worship'd, Ladifide. **1668** DRYDEN *Evening's Love* III. i. (1671) 33 Madam me no Madam. **1741** RICHARDSON *Pamela* (1824) I. 58 In came the coachman..and madamed me up strangely. **1748** —— *Clarissa* Wks. 1883 VIII. 447, I am..Madam'd up perhaps to matrimonial perfection. **1829** *Examiner* 116/1 The sparring scene between her and Mrs. Chatterley, wherein they 'Madam' each other with genteel petulance.

‖**madame** (madam; often mə'dɑːm, or anglicized 'mædəm). Also **madam.** Pl. MESDAMES; †**madames.** [Fr.: see MADAM *sb.*

The uses in which the word is meant to represent a foreign title are treated in the present article, although in early examples the spelling is often *madam*. For *madame*, when it is a mere variant spelling of the Eng. word, see MADAM.]

1. a. The title prefixed to the surname of a French married woman (corresponding to the Eng. 'Mrs.', 'Lady', etc., according to degree of rank). Abbreviated *Mme.*; in Eng. books and newspapers *Mdme.* often occurs.

In English use it is very commonly applied to a married woman belonging to any foreign nation (substituted, e.g., for the Ger. *Frau* or the Du. *Mevrouw*). It is also frequently assumed (instead of 'Mrs.') by English or American professional singers or musicians, and by women engaged in businesses such as dressmaking, in which native taste or skill is reputed to be inferior to that of Frenchwomen.

a **1674** CLARENDON *Hist. Reb.* xv. §155 One day he visited madam Turyn. **1699** PETIVER *Musei Petiver.* 46 Madam Margaretha Hendrina van Otteren, Widow to..Dr. Oldenland. **1706** LUTTRELL *Brief Rel.* 18 May (1857) VI. 46 Mrs. Skelton, daughter to Madam Orfeur. **1838** DICKENS *Nich. Nick.* x, 'The Lady's name', said Ralph,..'is Mantalini—Madame Mantalini'. **1871** E. C. G. MURRAY *Member for Paris* I. 258 One of Madame Roderheim's plushed footmen. *Ibid.* 296 'Father Glabre never talks politics', answered Mdme. de Margauld. **1877** J. GRANT *Six Yrs. Ago* II. 188 Madame von Hohenthal. **1888** MAPLESON *Mem.* (ed. 2) I. 193 Mdme. Christine Nilsson.

b. Used (both vocatively and otherwise) with omission of the name, or in substitution for it.

1853 BRONTE *Villette* xiv, As soon as Georgette was well, Madame sent her away into the country. **1894** S. J. WEYMAN *Man in Black* 198 Presently madame followed her example.

†**2.** The title given to female members of the French royal family; a French princess; *spec.* the eldest daughter of the French king or of the dauphin; in the reign of Louis XIV, the wife of MONSIEUR, the king's only brother. *Obs.*

1670 G. H. *Hist. Cardinals* I. I. 14 In the presence of Madam Royall in Turin. **1679** *Marriage Charles II*, 7 Next to her followed Madam. **1701** *Lond. Gaz.* No. 3714/3 Madame does not yet give Audience. *a* **1715** BURNET *Own Time* (1724) I. 302 The King of France had courted Madame Soissons, and made a shew of courting Madame [*sc.* the Duchess of Orleans]. **1765** *Ann. Reg.* 112 Don Philip, duke of Parma,..has left issue, by the late madame of France, a prince and a princess. **1766** *Ibid.* II. 4 The Madames of France were much devoted to reading in their private apartments. **1798** R. C. DALLAS tr. *Cléry's Jrnl. Occur. Louis XVI* 40 A small antichamber almost without light, was occupied by Madame Royale and Madame Elizabeth.

†**3.** A French married woman; a Frenchman's wife. *Obs.*

1599 SHAKS. *Hen. V*, I. i. 23 The Madams too, not vs'd to toyle, did almost sweat to beare The Pride vpon them. *Ibid.* III. v. 28 *Dolphin.* By Faith and Honor, Our Madames mock at vs. **1599** B. JONSON *Cynthia's Rev.* IV. i, I would tell you, which Madame lou'd a Monsieur. **1627** DRAYTON *Agincourt* cxlvii, In which [a Chariot] they meane to Paris him to bring, To make sport to their Madames and their Boyes. **1765** BICKERSTAFFE *Maid of Mill* I. vi. 11 When I was on my travels, among the madames, and signoras, we never saluted more than the tip of the ear.

4. = MADAM *sb.* 3 c (*d*).

1871 *N.Y. Herald* 29 July 6/2 The Madame..sent her to an infamous den in Forsyth Street kept by a Mrs. Hines. **1922** V. WOOLF *Jacob's Room* ix. 171 Only Madame herself ..had about her that leer, that lewdness. **1934** A. WOOLLCOTT *While Rome Burns* 157 Visiting the local Maison Tellier..and taking the madame and all her girls out duck-shooting. **1961** M. JONES *Potbank* xxvi. 111 Her behaviour..made me think of a *madame* in the more discreet sort of brothel. **1969** G. GREENE *Trav. with my Aunt* I. viii. 83 There was a discipline in the old-time brothels. The madame..played a rôle similar to that of the headmistress of Roedean. **1975** *Sunday Times* 12 Jan. 37/2 She plays the part of the notorious Xaviera Hollander, New York call-girl and *madame*.

madamoiselle, obs. variant of MADEMOISELLE.

madane, obs. form of MAIDEN.

madapollam (mædə'pɒləm). Also **-polland, -polam.** [From *Madapollam* (*Mādhava-palam*), a suburb of Narsapur, Madras presidency.] A kind of cotton cloth, orig. manufactured at Madapollam, and afterwards imitated on the British looms, and exported in great quantities to India.

1832 in M. Russell *Egypt* viii. (1853) 327 He intends to send long-cloths, madapollams [etc.]. **1858** SIMMONDS *Dict. Trade, Madapollam*, a kind of fine long cloth, shipped to the Eastern markets. **1882** CAULFEILD & SAWARD *Dict. Needlework, Madapolams*, a coarse description of calico cloth, of a stiff, heavy make, originally of Indian manufacture, where it was employed for Quilts. **1885** *Manch. Exam.* 31 Dec. 4/4 Buff-end madapollams.

'mad-apple. [A translation of mod.L. *mālum insānum*, a corruption of the oriental word which appears variously as *melongena*, *badingan*, BRINJAL. Also called *raging* (*love*) *apple*: see RAGING *ppl. a.* 2.] The fruit of the EGG-PLANT.

1597 GERARDE *Herbal* II. liv. 274 Madde or raging Apples. **1688** R. HOLME *Armoury* II. 82/2 An Assirian Made Apple. The pod is whitish green, and the cup jagged [etc.]. **1760** J. LEE *Introd. Bot.* 318 Mad Apple, *Solanum.* **1785** MARTYN *Rousseau's Bot.* xvi. (1794) 202 Mad-Apple is also of this genus. **1864** GRISEBACH *Flora W. Ind.* 785 Mad-apple, *Solanum Melongena.*

madar: see MUDAR.

‖**madarosis** (mædə'rəʊsɪs). *Med.* [mod.L., a. Gr. μαδάρωσις, f. μαδαρός bald: see -OSIS.] Loss of hair; esp. of that of the eyebrows.

1693 in *Blancard's Physical Dict.* (ed. 2). **1706** in PHILLIPS (ed. Kersey). In mod. Dicts. **1902** GOULD & WARREN *Internat. Text-bk. Surg.* (ed. 2) II. xxvii. 864 The affection may go on until nearly all the eye-lashes are lost and the lids left bald—madarosis. **1956** 'H. MACDIARMID' *Stony Limits & Scots Unbound* 39 Nor..can we..Shut our eyes despite their madarosis of the sun. **1972** A. SORSBY *Mod. Ophthalm.* (ed. 2) II. xx. 557 (*caption*) Leprosy showing lagophthalmos and madarosis of brows and lashes.

'madbrain, *sb.* (and *a.*)

A. *sb.* A mad-brained person; a 'scatter-brain'.

c **1570** *Marr. Wit & Sci.* v. i. E 1 b, Thou art some mad braine, or some foole. **1608** MIDDLETON *Mad World* I. A 3 Heer's a mad-braine a'th first, whose prankes scorne to haue presidents. **1616** J. DEACON *Tobacco Tortured* 57 Alas poore Tobacco..thou that hast bene hitherto accompted..the mad-braines merriment,..and the vnthrifts pasport. **1876** G. MEREDITH *Beauch. Career* II. xvi. 285 He began to think her lost beyond hope, embarked for good and all with the madbrain.

†**B.** *attrib.* or *adj.* = MAD-BRAINED. *Obs.*

1592 G. HARVEY *Four Lett.* 45, I haue..seene the mad-braynest Roister-doister in a countrey dashte out of countenaunce. **1596** SHAKS. *Tam. Shr.* III. ii. 10, I must forsooth be forst To give my hand..Vnto a mad-braine rudesby. **1605** ROWLANDS *Hell's Broke Loose* 33 With..mad-braine heat, Munster they enter. **1631** WEEVER *Anc. Funeral Mon.* 295 That wilde madbraine Falques.

mad-brained ('mædbreɪnd), *a.* Having or manifesting a mad brain; hot-headed, uncontrolled.

1577 G. HARVEY *Letter-bk.* (Camden) 57 And Skelton that same madbraynd knave Look how he knawes a deade horse boane. **1596** SHAKS. *Tam. Shr.* III. ii. 165 This mad-brain'd bridegroome tooke him such a cuffe, That downe fell Priest and booke. **1607** —— *Timon* v. i. 177 Giuing our holy Virgins to the staine Of contumelious, beastly, mad-brain'd warre. **1649** G. DANIEL *Trinarch., Hen. IV*, cxlvii, The Mad-Brain'd Spartacus. **1751** ELIZA HEYWOOD *Betsy Thoughtless* I. 104 The heedless levities of the one sex, and the mad-brained passions of the other. **1819** SHELLEY *Peter Bell* VI. xx, A mad-brained goblin for a guide. **1894** G. M. FENN *Real Gold* 379 Your father's mad-brained ideas.

madcap ('mædkæp), *sb.* and *a.* [f. MAD *a.* + CAP *sb.*; cf. *fuddlecap*, *huffcap*.]

A. *sb.* †**a.** In early use, a madman, maniac (*obs. rare*). **b.** One who acts like a maniac; a reckless, wildly impulsive person. In recent use often applied playfully to young women of lively and impulsive temperament.

1589 GREENE *Sp. Masquerado* C 3 b, This crue of popish Madcaps. **1591** SHAKS. *Two Gent.* II. v. 8 Come-on you mad-cap: Ile to the Ale-house with you. **1599** HAYWARD *1st Pt. Hen. IV* 19 There was..Sir Hugh Linne, a good souldier, but a very mad-cap. **1607** DEKKER *Northward Hoe* IV. Wks. 1873 III. 57 What mad-caps haue you in your house [Bedlam]. **1667** DRYDEN *Secret Love* III. i. (1668) 34 Lord, that such a Mad-Cap as I should ever live to be jealous! **1711** *Countrey-Man's Let. to Curat* 12 There were ..some Mad-caps *alias* High-Flyers, in the Council that opposed the granting of it. **1861** THACKERAY *Four Georges* ii. (1876) 53, I should like to have seen that noble old madcap [Peterborough]. **1869** PHILLIPS *Vesuv.* ii. 12 To be singing when Vesuvius was thundering..was not unfitting the imperial madcap. **1885** MABEL COLLINS *Prettiest Woman* i, On the boards she was the merriest, gayest, madcap in the world.

B. *attrib.* and *adj.* Mad, 'crack-brained'; reckless, wildly impulsive.

1588 SHAKS. *L.L.L.* II. i. 215 That last is Beroune, the mery mad-cap Lord. **1598** E. GUILPIN *Skial.* (1878) 27 When thou hast read this mad-cap stuffe. **1619** FLETCHER *M. Thomas* I. iii, *Dor.* And is your hate so mortall? *Mar.* Not to his person, But to his qualities, his mad-cap follies. **1807** W. IRVING *Salmag.* (1824) 274 The thoughtless flow of mad-cap spirits. **1852** THACKERAY *Esmond* III. ii, The mad-cap girl ran up to her mother. **1887** BOWEN *Virg. Ecl.* IX. 43 Let the madcap billows in thunder break on the shore. **1893** VIZETELLY *Glances Back* II. xxxiii. 233 Madcap republicans bent on disturbing the emperor's pleasure.

madcapery (ˈmædkæpərɪ). Also **madcappery.** [f. MADCAP *sb.* + -ERY.] The behaviour of a madcap; mischievous or reckless conduct.

1905 D. SLADEN *Playing Game* xii. 139, I wondered what madcapery Rich had been up to. **1966** *Punch* 20 April 586/2 Seeing the two plays in such quick succession..does provide an opportunity to follow in one long sweep the two stages of Prince Hal's progress from madcappery to maturity.

madded (ˈmædɪd), *ppl. a.* Now *rare.* [f. MAD *v.* + -ED¹.] Rendered mad, in various senses of the adj. **a.** Deprived of reason or intelligence. **b.** Excited to fury, enraged.

c **1580** SIDNEY *Ps.* XXII. vii, I am enclos'd with yong bulls madded rowt. **1611** SHAKS. *Cymb.* IV. ii. 313 All Curses madded Hecuba gaue the Greekes. *a* **1641** BP. MOUNTAGU *Acts & Mon.* (1642) 290 The two Confitents..were by the madded multitude stoned to death. **1681** WHARTON *Disc. Soul World* Wks. (1683) 647 But Tycho-Brahe..shall..unfold to us this matter far different from the Madded Nursery of Peripateticks. **1766** NICOL *Poems* 240 Shall I so besotted be And madded, as to sell My soul to flames..? **1872** BLACKIE *Lays Highl.* 101 Downward Sheer the madded torrent pours.

madden (ˈmæd(ə)n), *v.* [f. MAD *a.* + -EN⁵.]

1. *intr.* To become mad.

1735 POPE *Prol. Sat.* 6 They rave, recite, and madden round the land. **1796** MRS. M. ROBINSON *Angelina* I. 8 My mind would madden at the retrospect of her injuries. **1802** *Noble Wanderers* II. 85, I saw her strength wasting..and maddened at the view! **1811** W. R. SPENCER *Poems* 19 My fierce steed maddens to be gone. **1855** MILMAN *Lat. Chr.* IX. vii. (1864) V. 369 Whole populations maddening to avenge the cause of the injured Son of God. **1858** H. LAW *Christ is All, Numbers* 79 Malignant passions maddened in opposing breasts.

2. *trans.* To make mad; to drive out of one's mind; to excite to frenzy or uncontrollable anger; (esp. as the *ppl. adj.*: see below) to irritate, annoy, vex.

1822 GOOD *Study Med.* IV. 167 Opium maddens the head. **1833** HT. MARTINEAU *Loom & Lugger* II. v. 105 It was enough to madden the most gentle. **1849** MACAULAY *Hist. Eng.* ii. I. 267 Fierce spirits, unrestrained by principle, maddened by fanaticism. **1879** FARRAR *St. Paul* (1883) 119 The raging passion which maddens a crowd of Eastern fanatics.

Hence ˈ**maddened** *ppl. a.*, ˈ**maddening** *ppl. a.* and *vbl. sb.* Also ˈ**maddeningly** *adv.*, in a maddening manner.

a **1743** SAVAGE *To J. Powell* 35 Calm, on the beach while maddening billows rave, He gains Philosophy from every wave. **1775** ASH Suppl., *Maddening*, the act of making mad. **1806** SURR *Winter in Lond.* III. 79 The shrieks..of its maddened mother..did not arouse the sleeping nurse. **1822** GOOD *Study Med.* IV. 624 The burning and maddening pain..can rarely be alleviated but by opium. *a* **1861** MRS. BROWNING *From Nonnus* Poems 1890 V. 85 She named her hero, and raged maddeningly Against the brine of waters. **1863** WOOLNER *My Beautiful Lady* Introd. 3 The wind Heaving the ocean into maddened arms That clutch and dash huge vessels on the rocks. **1891** T. HARDY *Tess* (1900) 117/2 There never was such a maddening mouth since Eve's! **1896** A. BEARDSLEY *Let. c* 25 Oct. (1971) 188 Dent must be simply maddening. **1925** N. COWARD *Vortex* II. 55 'Have you only one set, Florence?'.. 'Yes, isn't it maddening? Clara promised to bring hers down but forgot.' **1944** —— *Middle East Diary* 36 So many of my Naval friends are here and it's maddening that I shall have no time to go and visit them. **1947** A. HUXLEY *Let.* 19 Jan. (1969) 565 There will still be revisions to do on the screen play..maddening work, resembling jig saw puzzles rather than literature.

madder (ˈmædə(r)), *sb.*¹ Forms: 1 **mædere, mæddre, mæderu,** 3–7 **mader,** 4–5 **madyr,** (5 **madur, maddyre, madre**), 5–6 **maddre,** 6–7 **mather,** (8 **maddar**), 4– **madder.** [OE. *mædere* wk. fem. corresp. to ON. *maðra* in place-names (Sw. *madra*, dial. *mådra, måra*, Norw. *modra, maure*); app. related in some way are MDu., MLG. *mêde* (mod.Du. *mede, mee*), madder.

The word in OE. and ON. could not originally have denoted the exotic *Rubia*, but probably belonged to various species of the allied genera *Asperula* and *Galium*, some of which are still used as substitutes for madder. In Iceland, Sweden, and Norway, it is now applied chiefly to *Galium boreale*; in Sweden also to *Asperula tinctoria* (Dyer's Woodruff), while *Rubia tinctorum* is called *röd madra* and *krapp*. In the mod. Wiltshire dialect *madder* is used for the Sweet Woodruff (*Asperula odorata*); the *madder(s* or *mather* applied in several dialects to the Stinking Camomile is prob. a distinct word (see MAYTHE).]

1. a. A herbaceous climbing plant, *Rubia tinctorum*, having rough hairy stems and bearing panicles of small yellowish flowers: cultivated, esp. in Holland and France, for the dye obtained from it (see 2). Called also *dyer's madder.*

c **1000** *Sax. Leechd.* I. 154 Ðeos wyrt þe man gryas & oðrum naman mædere nemneð byð cenned fyrmust in lucania. *c* **1050** *Herbarium* in *Sax. Leechd.* I. 24 Herba gryas þæt is mæderu [*v.r.* mædere]. *c* **1265** *Voc. Plants* in Wr.-Wülcker 608/27 *Rubea*, mader. **14..** *Voc.* ibid. 576/22 *Cressula*, Mader. *c* **1440** *Promp. Parv.* 319/1 Madyr, herbe. **1562** TURNER *Herbal* II. 118 The stalkes of madder are foure squared, longe, rough lyke vnto the stalkes of gooshareth. **1688** R. HOLME *Armoury* II. 76/2 The Garden Madder hath a long rough leaf. **1758** P. MILLER (*title*) The Method of cultivating Madder, As it is now practised by the Dutch in Zealand. **1846** MCCULLOCH *Acc. Brit. Empire* (1854) I. 109 Madder has been attempted to be raised [in England], but without success. **1882** HOLDEN *Hum. Osteol.* (ed. 6) 33 The colouring principle of the madder (*Rubia tinctorum*) has a strong affinity for phosphate of lime.

b. With specific qualification, applied to other plants. **Bengal madder,** *Rubia cordifolia* (Treas. Bot. 1866). **field madder** (see FIELD *sb.* 20). **hog's madder** (see HOG *sb.*¹ 13 d). **Indian madder,** (*a*) *R. cordifolia*; (*b*) *Oldenlandia umbellata* (Treas. Bot.). **petty madder,** the genus *Crucianella.* **wild madder,** (*a*) *R. peregrina*, native to the south-west of England; (*b*) *Galium Mollugo.*

14.. *Voc.* in Wr.-Wülcker 570/10 *Candeo*, wylde madur. **1578** LYTE *Dodoens* IV. lxxiii. 537 There be two sortes of Madder, the tame Madder..and the wild Madder. **1597** GERARDE *Herbal* 961, 1 *Rubia tinctorum*, Red Madder. 2 *Rubia syluestris*, Wilde Madder. 3 *Rubia marina*, Sea Madder. **1760** J. LEE *Introd. Bot.* App. 318 Petty Madder, *Crucianella.* **1776** WITHERING *Bot. Arrangem. Vegetables* I. 81 Madder. Mollugo. Goosegrass... Wild Madder, Great Bastard Madder. **1813** AINSLIE *Mat. Med. Hindostan* 87 Bengal Madder, *Rubia Manjith* Roxb.

2. a. The root of this plant, employed medicinally or as a source of colouring matter; the dye-stuff or pigment prepared from this.

The chief colouring matters contained in madder are alizarin and purpurin. The 'Turkey red', used in dyeing cotton, is prepared from madder.

1347–8 *Rolls of Parlt.* II. 215/2 Come il ait fait avenir en Engleterre XI pokes de madder a Lenn. *c* **1374** CHAUCER *Former Age* 17 No mader [*v.rr.* madyr, madder], welde, or wood no litestere Ne knew. **1389** in *Eng. Gilds* (1870) 358 Euerych a cart y'lade wᵗ mader, þᵗ comeþ to selle, twey pans. **1436** *Pol. Poems* (Rolls) II. 180 Yit marchaundy of Braban and Selande, The madre and woode that dyers take on hande To dyne wyth. **1579** LANGHAM *Gard. Health* (1633) 377 Madder. The root is sharp and bitter, and therefore purgeth the liuer and the milt. **1581** *Act 23 Eliz.* c. 9 §3 Wherein no Mather shalbe used. **1601** R. JOHNSON *Kingd. & Commw.* (1603) 28 It bringeth forth great quantitie of mather, very perfect woade, but no great store. **1747** COOKE in Hanway *Trav.* (1762) I. IV. lv. 258 These Tartars trade..with the Russians with their madder. **1846** J. BAXTER *Libr. Pract. Agric.* (ed. 4) II. 311 Sulphur and madder are the best alterants in foulness of the skin or habit. **1882** W. T. SUFFOLK in *Sci. Gossip* Mar. 50 Avoid..cochineal colours; the madders are the only safe substitutes.

b. With defining word, indicating a special kind or quality, as *bale-, bunch-, fat-, pipe-madder*; sometimes with designation adopted from Du., as *mull, umbro madder*; **crap-madder** [CRAP *sb.*²], corruptly *crop-, grape-madder*, the best quality of madder.

1640 in Entick *London* (1766) II. 168 Crop madder, and all other bale madder..Fat madder..Mull madder. *a* **1661** FULLER *Worthies, Kent* II (1662) 57 Madder..there are three kinds thereof. 1. Crop-Madder. 2. Umber-Owe. 3. Pipe or Fat-Madder. **1765** *Museum Rust.* IV. 176 The best umbro madder, imported from Holland. **1797** *Encycl. Brit.* (ed. 3) X. 400/2 The commodity, when manufactured, is distinguished into different kinds, as grape-madder, bunch-madder, &c. The grape-madder is the heart of the root.

3. The colour produced by madder dyes or pigments; also with defining word, as *crimson madder.* Also *attrib.* or *adj.*

1861 THORNBURY *Turner* I. 30 Of the yellow and madder sails..he took careful note. **1863** KINGSLEY *Water-Bab.* 12 A crimson madder petticoat. **1886** RUSKIN *Præterita* I. 396 Shade cobalt through pink madder into yellow ochre for skies.

4. *attrib.* and *Comb.*, as *madder-bath, -croft, -crop, -dye, -dyeing, -field, -grinder, -ground, -miller, -pit, -plant, root, -stove, style, tribe*; *madder-printed* adj. Also in names of colours produced by dyes or pigments in which madder is an ingredient, as *madder-black, -brown, -lake, -purple, -red*, etc. Also **madder-bleach,** a special method of bleaching cotton; **madder-print,** madder-printed cloth or cotton (*Cent. Dict.* 1890); **madderwort** *Bot.*, Lindley's term for a plant of the N.O. *Galiaceæ.*

1763 W. LEWIS *Philos. Comm. Arts* 420 The colour hence produced [*sc.* by madder upon blue cloth] is called *madder-black. **1909** L. A. OLNEY *Textile Chem. & Dyeing* II. 58 The *Madder Bleach... In calico printing..where a particularly clear and white ground is desired this form of bleach is used. **1897** ANNE PAGE *Afternoon Ride* 63 Ineffaceable *madder brown—a pigment lost to art. **1...** *Newminster Cartul.* (1878) 237 Juxta pontem de le *Madercroft. **1816** J. SMITH *Panorama Sci. & Art* II. 536 The use of archil gives a..bloom to the *madder dye. **1899** MACKAIL *W. Morris* II. 34 Water..required for *madder-dyeing. **1901** *Westm. Gaz.* 30 Aug. 3/1 The *madder fields of Alsace, of Southern France, and of Algeria have practically ceased to exist. **1851** in *Illustr. Lond. News* 5 Aug. (1854) 119/1 *Madder-grinder. **1758** P. MILLER *Cultiv. Madder* 35 The Dutch always sow Grain upon their *Madder Ground. **1822** IMISON *Sci. & Art* II. 411 *Madder-lake. **1851** in *Illustr. Lond. News* 5 Aug. (1854) 119/1 *Madder-miller. **1616** BROWNE *Brit. Past.* II. iii. 59 The bowels of our mother were not ript For *Mader-pits. **1758** P. MILLER *Cultiv. Madder* 7 A *Madder Plant, that has many of these [side] Roots, is called a well bearded Madder Plant. **1881** W. MORRIS in Mackail *Life* (1899) II. 53 The best hanging would be the inclosed *madder-printed cotton. **1838** T. THOMSON *Chem. Org. Bodies* 392 Sulphuric acid..throws down the *madder-purple. **1727–52** CHAMBERS *Cycl.* s.v. *Red*, *Madder red is dyed with madder. **1744** *Phil. Trans.* XLI. 390 These Callicoe-printers make use of the *Rubia Tinctorum*, or *Madder-root. **1757** *Act 31 Geo. II*, c. 35 §5 For preventing the stealing or destroying of Madder roots. **1758** P. MILLER *Cultiv. Madder* 12 In the *Madder Stoves, the People work more by Night than Day. **1839** URE *Dict. Arts* 224 The *madder style [of calico-printing]..in which the mordants are applied to the white cloth..and the colours are afterwards brought up in the dye-bath. **1836** LINDLEY *Nat. Syst. Bot.* 249 Order cxxxix. Stellatæ, or Galiaceæ. The *Madder Tribe. **1845** —— *Sch. Bot.* (ed. 14) 77 Order xxxiv. Galiaceæ—*Madderworts, or Stellates.

madder (ˈmædə(r)), *sb.*² *Anglo-Irish.* Also **meadar, mether.** [a. Irish *meadar.*] A square wooden drinking vessel.

1720 SWIFT *Irish Feast* in *Misc.* (1735) V. 14 Usquebagh to our Feast In Pails was brought up, An hundred at least, And a Madder our Cup. **1832** LADY MORGAN *Mem.* (1862) II. 337 The 'madder' so often mentioned in Irish song was a wooden Tankard, made square. **1886** WOOD-MARTIN *Lake Dwellings Irel.* I. v. 103 'Meadar', or 'Mether', is the Irish designation for a species of drinking-cup.

madder (ˈmædə(r)), *v.* [f. MADDER *sb.*¹] *trans.* To treat or dye with madder.

c **1461** *E.E. Misc.* (Warton Club) 90 To a dosyne of violettes viij pownde of Madyre..and loke ȝe madere theme as ȝe do ȝour redys. **1464** *Rolls of Parlt.* V. 562/1 That the same Wolle and Cloth be perfitly boyled and madered. **1530** PALSGR. 616/1, I madder clothe to be dyed... Your vyolet hath nat his full dye but he is maddered. **1763** W. LEWIS *Comm. Philos. Techn.* 405 The..regulations for the French Dyers..require the cloth, after it has been blued, to be maddered. **1811** *Self Instructor* 539 They are maddered higher than black.

Hence ˈ**maddered** *ppl. a.*, ˈ**maddering** *vbl. sb.*

c **1461** *E.E. Misc.* (Warton Club) 88 At ȝoure Maderynge ȝe schall take of the same wateris. **1581** *Act 23 Eliz.* c. 9 §2 Where Clothes Karsies & Hosen..have been died with..a galled & mathered Black. **1808** *Nicholson's Jrnl.* XXI. 44 On the maddering of Cotton and Linen Thread. **1839** URE *Dict. Arts* 787 There next follows..the galling, the aluming, the maddering.

ˈ**madderish,** *a.* [f. MADDER *sb.*¹ + -ISH.] Resembling the colour of madder.

1888 *Harper's Mag.* July 212 Some..seem..to be made of gold vapor; others have a madderish tone.

†ˈ**madderlen.** *Obs. rare*⁻¹. [f. MADDER *sb.*¹ + *-len* (? = -LING¹).] A name (perh. invented by Hill) for the genus *Sherardia.*

1770 HILL *Herb. Brit.* II. 153 *Sherardia.* Madderlen. *Ibid.* 154 *Sherardia arvensis.* Field Madderlen.

maddery (ˈmædərɪ), *a. nonce-wd.* [f. MADDER *sb.*¹ + -Y¹ 2.] = MADDERISH *a.*

1873 G. M. HOPKINS *Note-bks. & Papers* (1937) 186 Its dewlaps and bellyings painted with a maddery campion-colour.

madding (ˈmædɪŋ), *vbl. sb.* [f. MAD *v.* + -ING¹.] The action of the vb. MAD; becoming or being mad, madness; mad behaviour. Now only in phrases (*arch.* or *dial.*) to *go*, †*run, set a-madding* (or †*on madding*).

13.. *E.E. Allit. P.* A. 1153 My manez mynde to maddyng malte. *a* **1400–50** *Alexander* 3546 Madding marrid has þi mode & þi mynd changid. **1526** SKELTON *Magnyf.* 288 It is but a maddynge, these wayes that ye vse. **1565** CALFHILL *Answ. Treat. Cross* Pref. 5 They..went a madding after their Idols. *a* **1586** SIDNEY *Arcadia* IV. (1598) 394 Poore Dametas began now to thinke, that..a generall madding was falne. **1600** HOLLAND *Livy* XXXVII. xli. 969 The dromedarie camels..were unruly and set a madding. **1611** SPEED *Hist. Gt. Brit.* IX. xiii. (1623) 733 [They] forced sundry principall Gentlemen to attend them in their madding. **1614** BP. HALL *Contempl., O. T.* VII. iii, All the world would be glad to runne on madding after their bait. **1627–77** FELTHAM *Resolves* I. xxix. 49 Our error of opinion, ..and our madding after unnecessary gold, have brambled the way of Vertue. **1712** ARBUTHNOT *John Bull* I. viii, John had not run on a madding so long, had it not been for an extravagant bitch of a wife. **1775** MME. D'ARBLAY *Early Diary* 21 Nov., Lady Edgecumbe..declared she was set a-madding. **1857** MRS. MATHEWS *Tea-Table Talk* I. 205 Men ..whose crazed brains go a madding after forbidden fruit. **1865** MRS. WHITNEY *Gayworthys* viii. (1879) 79 To set all the urchins' brains a madding.

†**b.** *attrib.*, as *madding-day, month, time.*

16.. I. T. *Grim the Collier of Croydon* III. (1662) 50 Why how now man! is this your madding month! **1625** *Gonsalvio's Sp. Inquis.* 34 In all her madding time shee had nothing else in her mouth. **1691** LUDLOW *Let. to Sir E. S.* title-p., Occasioned by the reading Dr. Pelling's Lewd Harangues upon the 30th of Janvary, being the Anniversary, or General Madding-Day. **1717** (*title*) A Rebuke to the High Church Priests for turning the 30ᵗʰ of January into a Madding-Day.

madding (ˈmædɪŋ), *ppl. a.* Now *poet.* or *rhetorical.* [f. MAD *v.* + -ING².]

1. Becoming mad; acting madly; frenzied. Esp. in phrase *far from the madding crowd* (see quot. 1749), a conventional phrase denoting a secluded place removed from public notice.

1579 SPENSER *Sheph. Cal.* Apr. 26 But now from me hys madding mynd is starte, And woes the Widdowes daughter of the glenne. **1582** T. WATSON *Centurie of Loue* lxxvi. *heading*, The Author being, as it were, in halfe a madding moode. **1614** DRUMM. OF HAWTH. *Sonn.* '*Deare Wood*' Farre from the madding Worldling's hoarse discords. **1635** BRATHWAIT *Arcad. Pr.* 171 Observe the madding motion of his eyes. **1667** MILTON *P.L.* VI. 210 The madding Wheeles Of brazen Chariots rag'd. **1697** DRYDEN *Æneid* VII. 539 She ..mixing with the throng Of madding matrons, bears the bride along. **1714** ADDISON *To Princess of Wales, with Cato* 38 Bid impious discord cease, And sooth the madding factions into peace. **1749** GRAY *Elegy* 73 Far from the madding crowd's ignoble strife. [Cf. quot. 1614 above.] **1802** *Eng. Encycl.* VIII. 308/1 These [words] are poetical, but were never in common use..shook (shaken), madding [etc.]. **1822** WORDSW. *Eccl. Sonn.* II. xx. *Monastic Volupt.*,

High conceits to madding Fancy dear. 1874 Hardy (*title*) Far from the madding crowd. 1889 J. K. Jerome *Three Men in Boat* i. 9, I..suggested that we should seek out some retired and old-world spot, far from the madding crowd, and dream away a sunny week among its drowsy lanes. 1944 F. Clune *Red Heart* 14 People..far from the madding crowds, west of the Darling River. 1952 G. Sarton *Hist. Sci.* I. xvi. 397 He [*sc.* Plato] did not want to teach in the streets and markets, but on the contrary in a place that was sufficiently distant from the madding crowd and secluded.

2. That makes mad; maddening.

c1600 Shaks. *Sonn.* cxix, How haue mine eyes out of their Spheares bene fitted In the distraction of this madding feuer. 1644 Maxwell *Prerog. Chr. Kings* 67 Superstition is a mad and madding thing. 1650 Baxter *Saints' R.* iv. vi. §7 (1651) 154 Are these such sadding and madding thoughts? 1871 R. Ellis tr. *Catullus* lxiv. 94 O thou cruel of heart, thou madding worker of anguish.

Hence †**'maddingly** *adv.*

a1625 Fletcher *Women Pleased* iv. i, Your poor neighbours Run maddingly affrighted through the Villages.

maddish ('mædɪʃ), *a.* [f. mad *a.* + -ish[1].] †a. Having the manner or ideas of a madman; like a madman in behaviour; appropriate to or befitting a madman (*obs.*). b. Somewhat mad.

1573 Tusser *Husb.* etc. (1580) 83 What with voluptuousnes, and other maddish toies. c1638 Strafford in Browning *Life* (1891) 208 'Hypochondriack humours'..is to be civilly and silently maddish. 1642 Bp. Morton *Presentm. Schismatic* 6, I have reserved for the last place a Character..called by Austen maddish obstinacy. 1655 M. Casaubon *Enthus.* iii. (1656) 109 Some..became (in a degree) maddish of the stage, and were perpetually acting some part of a Tragedy. 1740 tr. *De Mouhy's Fort. Country-Maid* (1741) II. 141 Do you know I am a little maddish. 1778 *Learning at a Loss* II. 161 A maddish looking Gentleman. 1815 Lamb *Let. to Wordsw.* in *Final Mem.* vi. 244 Excuse this maddish letter. 1829 Scott *Jrnl.* 20 Apr., [The] wit..of Lord Erskine was moody and maddish.

maddle ('mæd(ə)l), *v. Obs.* exc. *dial.* [f. mad *a.*: see -le 3.] a. *intr.* To be or become crazy; to be confused in mind; to be dotingly fond *of*. b. *trans.* To craze; to confuse in mind, bewilder.

c1540 tr. *Pol. Verg. Eng. Hist.* (Camden No. 29) 205 He was becoome feble by reason of sore and dayly siknes and began to maddle. 1570 Levins *Manip.* 8/18 To Maddle, *delirare, dissipere*. *Ibid.* 126/40 To Maddil, *delirare*. 1691 Ray *N.C. Words* 47 To *Maddle*; to be fond. She *maddles* of this Fellow, she is fond of him. 1829 J. Hunter *Hallamsh. Gloss.*, *Maddle*, to cause distraction of thought, confusion of mind, as by long continued and loud talking. *Ibid.* App., *Maddled*, puzzled. 1850 *Tales of Kirkbeck* Ser. ii. 79 I'm afraid she's quite maddled. 1855 Robinson *Whitby Gloss.*, To *Maddle*, to be fond of to the extent of losing one's wits. 1864 T. Clarke in *Kendal Mercury* 30 Jan., A wes faer maddl't amang em.

†**maddock** ('mædək). *Obs.* Also 3 **maðek**. See also mawk. [Early ME. *maðek*, a. (or corresponding to) ON. *maðk-r* (Da. *madike*, Sw. *mask*), MLG. *medeke*, dim. (with *-k-* suffix: see -ock) of the word which appears in OE. as *maðu*, *maða*: see mathe. There may have been an OE. **maðuc*.]

1. a. An earthworm. b. A maggot.

a1240 *Sawles Warde* in *Cott. Hom.* 251 As meaðen [*MS. Titus* maðekes] in forrotet flesch. c1400 *Lanfranc's Cirurg.* 44 Maddockis—þat ben wormes of þe erþe. 14.. *Voc.* in Wr.-Wülcker 594/3 *Lumbricus*, a maddock. c1450 *ME. Med. Bk.* (Heinrich) 210 Item Euytes eyron & maddolkes, & openes, & wasche hem clene. c1450 *Alphita* (Anecd. Oxon.) 87/30 Uermes siue lumbrici terreni... Angl. angeltwychches uel maddokkes. 1684 G. Meriton *Praise Yorks. Ale*, etc. Clavis, Mawks are Maddocks.

2. *north. dial.* A whim (Grose 1790). Cf. maggot.

'mad-'doctor. [f. mad *a.* used subst.] A physician who specializes in disorders of the mind; a psychiatrist.

1703 Farquhar *Inconstant* iv. iv, No mad-doctor in Christendom could have done it more effectually. 1818 Cobbett *Pol. Reg.* XXXIII. 363 His father was a mad-doctor. 1852 Dickens & Wills *Curious Dance round Curious Tree* in *Househ. Words* 17 Jan. 385/1 Nothing was too wildly extravagant, nothing too monstrously cruel, to be prescribed by mad-doctors. 1877 J. M. Granville *Care & Cure of Insane* I. 2 It must never be forgotten that the so-called 'mad doctors' have been the first to press this truth on the profession. 1881 W. S. Gilbert *Foggerty's Fairy* 111, Clearheaded, logical men of sense, these mad-doctors. 1890 (*title*) Mad doctors by one of them, being a defence of asylum physicians. 1972 C. Achebe *Girls at War* 9 That humble practitioner who did the miracle became overnight the most celebrated mad-doctor of his generation.

†**'maddy,** *a. Obs.* [f. mad *a.* + -y.] Somewhat mad.

1719 D'Urfey *Pills* II. 159 They must be..drunk or maddy.

made (meɪd), *ppl. a.* [pa. pple. of make *v.*[1]]

I. Produced or obtained by 'making' as distinguished from other modes of origin or acquisition.

1. a. Artificially constructed or produced, artificial as opposed to 'natural'. So ***made earth, ground***: solid ground that has been 'made' by filling up a marsh, embanking a river, etc.

a1578 Lindesay (Pitscottie) *Chron. Scot.* (S.T.S.) II. 301 It was conclwdit that na salt nor wictuallis nor na maid wark sould be convoyit of the realme. 1590 Spenser *Muiopotmos* 166 Arte..doth aspire T'excell the naturall, with made delights. 1596–7 S. Finche in Ducarel *Hist. Croydon* App. (1783) 153 Findinge that grounde made and false, digged the trenche alonge the door. 1643 Twyne in *Wood's Life* (O.H.S.) I. 96 The earth allso beinge found to be made ground all there abouts. 1687 B. Randolph *Archipelago* 65 Where formerly was a made-way in the sea for people to pass over. 1691 T. H[ale] *Acc. New Invent.* p. lxxi, It was all such as we call made Earth, and had been gain'd out of the Thames. 1699 R. L'Estrange *Erasm. Colloq.* (1711) 76 How comes it that all your made-Hedges are green too? 1719 De Foe *Crusoe* ii. xii. (1840) 252 This canal is a navigable made stream. 1878 Huxley *Physiogr.* xvii. 277 The successive beds of made ground. 1884 T. Brown *Ann. Disruption* iv. (1890) 37 There was not a made road in the parish. 1895 *Outing* (U.S.) XXVI. 16/2 They were most of them gentlemen—I mean gentlemen born. 'And you', said Miss Harriman pleasantly, 'are a gentleman made'. 1897 Mrs. Lynn Linton *Geo. Eliot* in *Women Novelists* 114 Her whole life and being were moulded to an artificial pose, and the 'made' woman could not possibly be the spontaneous artist. 1902 A. E. W. Mason *Four Feathers* xii. 112 The hedged fields and made roads.

b. Of a story: Invented, fictitious. Of a word: Invented, 'coined'. Of an errand: Invented for a pretext. ?*Obs.* (Cf. *made-up*.)

1387 Trevisa *Higden* (Rolls) II. 195 Hit is no made tale, but hit is sooþ as þe lettre is i-write. 1607 Norden *Surv. Dial.* ii. 41 The word [mannor] is used among our Lawyers, as many other made words are, which haue bin termes raised by our Lawes, & are not elsewhere in use. 1629 *Orkney Witch Trial* in *County Folk-Lore* III. (1903) 78 Christane Reid in Clett cam in ane maid errand. 1655 *Nicholas Papers* (Camden) II. 273 These are but made stories to delude fooles. 1687 Miege *Gt. Fr. Dict.* ii. s.v., A made Word, *Un Mot factice, imaginé, ou fait à plaisir*. 1843 J. H. Newman *Miracles* 124 It reads like a made story.

c. Brought about by contrivance.

1594 Lyly *Mother Bombie* i. iii. 49 (Bond) She forsooth will choose her own husband; made marriages proue mad marriages. 1802–12 Bentham *Ration. Judic. Evid.* Wks. 1843 VII. 306 Made offices are partly the effects, partly the causes, of made business. Create useless work, you create the necessity of useless hands for the performance of it.

2. Formed by composition. In certain specific applications. a. Cookery. ***made dish***: a dish composed of several ingredients; so †***made meat***. ***made gravy***: a 'gravy' artificially compounded, as opposed to one consisting only of the juices exuding from meat in cooking.

1598 *Epulario* D j b, To make a kind of made meat in flesh time. 1621 Burton *Anat. Mel.* i. ii. ii. i. 96 An infinite number of compound artificiall made dishes. 1622 Mabbe tr. *Aleman's Guzman d'Alf.* i. 106 What made dishes; what hot, what cold, what boyld, what rost? 1632 B. Jonson *Magn. Lady* i. (1640) 17 A farragoe, Or a made dish in Court. 1747 Mrs. Glasse *Cookery* ii. 13 Force-Meat Balls are a great Addition to all Made-Dishes. 1796 *Ibid.* viii. 142 You may use made-gravy, if you have not time to use the bones. 1852 Dickens *Bleak Ho.* xlix, The made-gravy acquiring no flavor, and turning out of a flaxen complexion. 1858 Mayhew *Upper Rhine* ii. §1 (1860) 48 The subtle nicety of a French made-dish.

b. Naut. ***made mast***: one composed of several pieces of timber. ***made block***: a pulley-block composed of several parts joined together. ***made eye***: 'synonymous with flemish eye' (Adm. Smyth).

1627 Capt. Smith *Seaman's Gram.* iii. 15 If it be a made Mast, that is greater than one Tree. 1794 *Rigging & Seamanship* I. 1 Masts..made of several trees joined together [are called] *made-masts*. *Ibid.* 153 Very large..blocks are formed of separate pieces,..when thus made, they are termed *made-blocks*. 1867 Smyth *Sailor's Word-bk.*, *Made Masts*, the large masts made in several pieces. A ship's lower mast is a made spar... *Made block* is one having its shell composed of different pieces.

3. a. Said occas. of articles of domestic or local manufacture, in contradistinction to those obtained from a distance. ***made wines***: a term applied to the so-called 'British wines' (as currant, ginger, gooseberry, etc. wine).

1750 T. Short (*title*) Discourses on Tea, Sugar, Milk, Made Wines, Spirits, Punch, Tobacco, &c. 1805 Pike *Sources Mississ.* (1810) 7 Gave them one quart of *made* whiskey, a few biscuit and some salt. 1806–7 J. Beresford *Miseries Hum. Life* (1826) xix. ii. 216 Brewing at home what are curiously called 'made wines', (as if all foreign wines were self-existent!). 1884 S. Dowell *Hist. Taxation* II. 289 The beverages termed British wines or made wines.

b. Of bills of exchange: (see quots.).

1868 E. Seyd *Bullion & Foreign Exch.* 89 The foregoing Foreign Bills of Class 2 are called *drawn* Bills, being usually negotiated from the Drawer direct to a London Foreign Banker; but where such drafts are made in the Country, and sent up to a correspondent in London, who then negotiates the same with his own Indorsement on them, they are called *made* Bills. *Ibid.* 90 Bills drawn abroad and payable abroad, but negotiated in the United Kingdom, are also *made* Bills.

II. Of which the making has taken place.

4. Already framed or produced. *rare* in attributive use.

a1635 Corbet *Poems* (1807) 121 Made lawes were uselesse growne To him, he needed but his owne.

5. a. That has undergone the process of manufacture. Also *occas.* prepared for use (cf. senses of make *v.*). *rare*.

1428 *Burgh Recs. Edinb.* (1869) I. 3 Of the last of maid irne viij*d*. 1545 *Rates Custome Ho.* a vj, Corke made the laste, xl*s*. Corke made the barell, iii.*s*. iiii.*d*. 1582 *Ibid.* B iv b, Cork made for diers the last..iiij*l*... Cork made for shoomakers. 1795 J. Aikin *Manchester* 239 The raw materials come from Manchester..and the made goods are sent thither. 1806 A. Hunter *Culina* (ed. 3) 209 A tea-spoonful of made mustard.

b. ***made to measure***: see measure *sb.* 2 a; also (usu. with hyphens) *attrib.*; ***made to order***: see order *sb.* 24 c; also (usu. with hyphens) *attrib.*; so ***made-to-order-ness***, the state or condition of being made to order.

1960 *Sunday Express* 24 July 12/6 Made-to-measure tweed skirt. 1973 *Guardian* 26 Feb. 3/3 Good lighting is made-to-measure lighting..the result of applying a lighting engineer's expertise to your particular office problem. 1974 *Country Life* 3–10 Jan. 58/1 Made-to-measure..corsets, brassieres, maternity foundation. 1921 *Daily Colonist* (Victoria, B.C.) 3 Apr. 9/1 (Advt.), Ladies' and gents' smart made-to-order spring suits made with particular care to every detail. 1947 'G. Orwell' *England your England* (1953) 8 There was the made-to-order stuff which I produced quickly. 1973 *Amer. Speech 1969* XLIV. 277 Or the phrase used in a television advertisement for 'Sentry—the made-to-order insurance'. 1973 R. Stout *Please Pass the Guilt* (1974) ii. 11 He sat..in his made-to-order chair. 1923 *Glasgow Herald* 8 Nov. 4 There is an air of cynical made-to-order-ness about the second [poem].

6. Of soldiers, also of horses, hounds, etc.: Fully trained.

1673 Boyle *Ess. Effluviums* iii. iv. 28 To make a tryal whether a young Blood-hound was well instructed, (or as the Huntsmen call it, *made*) he caus'd one of his Servants..to walk to a Country-town [etc.]. 1796 *Campaigns* 1793–4 I. i. vi. 45 None but made soldiers and serviceable horses would be employed. 1901 *Daily Chron.* 29 Apr. 6/2 In the 'made' class the best pony was Mr. Matherson's Lotus.

7. a. Of a person: Having his success in life assured. Chiefly in phr. ***a made man***.

c1590 Marlowe *Faust* (1631) F 3 b, O, joyfull day, now am I a made man for euer. 1605 S. Rowley *When You See Me* C 3, Hele lafe, and be as merie as a magge pie, and thow't bee a mayd man by it. 1708 *Brit. Apollo* No. 38. 2/2 You are a Made Man. 1871 Smiles *Charac.* ii. (1876) 54 Teach a boy arithmetic thoroughly, and he is a made man.

b. *Golf.* (See quot.)

1897 *Encycl. Sport* I. 473 (Golf) *Made*, a player is said to be made when he is within a full shot of the green.

c. ***to have (got) it made***, to be sure of success; to have it easy, to have no more obstacles to overcome. *colloq.* (orig. *U.S.*).

1955 in *Amer. Speech* May 118. 1960 J. Updike *Rabbit, Run* (1961) 108 Say. You really think you have it made. 1961 J. Heller *Catch-22* (1962) vi. 51, I had it made, I tell you. Fifty grand a year I was knocking down, and almost all of it tax-free. 1967 A. Diment *Dolly Dolly Spy* vi. 85 The money you earn is fantastic... You've got it made, mate. 1968 —— *Gt. Spy Race* iii. 45 She had..big, well-proportioned hips. I tell you, if the derrière gets with-it again this bird had it made. 1972 'H. Howard' *Nice Day for Funeral* iii. 49 This was the kind of set-up half the dames I know would've given their back teeth for. I had it made. 1974 *Times Lit. Suppl.* 8 Mar. 227/2 The abstentions of 1972 were due not to this disillusionment but to an overwhelming conviction that Mr Nixon had it made, so why take time..to go out and vote?

III. Combinations.

8. With prefixed sb., adj., or adv., forming combinations usually hyphened when used attributively, and in some instances also when used predicatively. a. With sb. in locative or instrumental relation, or adj., giving the general sense 'Made in a certain locality or by a certain class of agents', as in ***country-, foreign-, English-, German-, London-, Swiss-made***, home-made; ***God-, man-, self-, state-, tailor-made***. b. With adv. (or sometimes adj.) giving the sense 'made in a certain manner, having a certain quality or kind of make', as in ***badly-, neatly-, well-made***; often with reference to the 'make' or 'build' of the body (= *-built*), as in ***loosely-, powerfully-, stoutly-, strong(ly)-made***. Most of these combs. are treated under their first element, or in their alphabetical place as Main words.

9. In Comb. with adv. (hyphened in attributive use) corresponding to the similar combinations of make *v.*, as ***made-out, made-over***; **made-up**, †(*a*) consummate, accomplished (*obs.*); (*b*) put together; composed of parts from various sources; (*c*) artificially contrived or prepared, esp. for the purpose of deception or producing a favourable impression; (*d*) of a person's 'mind', resolved, decided; (*e*) of articles of trade, ready-made, not made to measure; also **made-up tie**, a tie, esp. a bow-tie, with a fixed bow or knot; (*f*) of stakes, arranged after the original programme of races is drawn up; (*g*) of a book, with its deficiencies made good by the insertion of a leaf, etc., from another copy of the same edition.

1607 Shaks. *Timon* v. i. 101 Know his grosse patchery..Yet remaine assur'd That he's a made-vp Villaine. 1677 Hubbard *Narrative* (1865) I. 82 They defended themselves under a small hastily made up Defence. 1725 M. W. Montagu *Let.* c 10 June (1966) II. 53, I wish you would lay out part of my Money in a made up Mantua and petticoat. 1773 Goldsm. *Stoops to Conq.* ii. (*near end*), Yes, you must allow her some beauty. *Tony*. Bandbox! She's all a made-up thing, mun. 1789 Charlotte Smith *Ethelinde* (1814) IV. 115 And as to that made-up antiquity, Mrs. Maltravers, she hates you. 1806 Surr *Winter in Lond.* (ed. 3) II. 95 Yours will be considered as a made-up character. 1820 T. Chalmers *Congregat. Serm.* (1838) II. 14 The logical process which leads..to the ultimate and made-out conclusion. 1849 *Theatrical Programme* 16 July 55 (Advt.),

The immense patronage they have received this season in their made-up skirt-rooms. **1859** *Eng. Cookery Bk.* 156 Chap. xiii.—Warmed-up Meats and Made-up Dishes or Entrées. **1863** Mrs. Gaskell *Sylvia's Lovers* xx. II. 105 In a forced made-up voice she inquired aloud [etc.]. **1871** Howells *Wedd. Journ.* (1892) 246 She bought and bought of the made-up wares. **1873** L. Wallace *Fair God* v. viii. 311 Ye.. are of made-up minds. **1876** *Coursing Calendar* 110 In the made-up stakes for puppies Mr. Farmer's brace.. made a good display. **1883** *Graphic* 14 Apr. 395/4 (Advt.), A full assortment of made-up articles of the best and most suitable description. **1895** *New Rev.* June 631 It is an odious fact that this country spends about a million and a half a year in the purchase of made-up clothes from Germany. **1896** A. Dobson *18th Cent. Vign.* Ser. III. i. 14 This made-up face was not produced by stage paint. **1900** Ld. Roberts in *Daily News* 4 May 5/2 Hamilton speaks in high terms of the good service performed by.. a made-up regiment of Lancers. **1912** R. A. Wason *Friar Tuck* xxx. 208 When Jim came back he was a made-over man, and everyone asked him if he had religion. **1913** C. Mackenzie *Sinister St.* I. II. ii. 171 The boys.. bought made-up bow-ties of purple and pink that were twisted round the stud with elastic. **1913** R. B. McKerrow in *Trans. Bibliogr. Soc.* XII. 303 The cruder sort of made-up copies that one often finds in the second-hand market. **1916** J. E. Wells *Man. Writings Middle Eng.* 294 A copy, and perhaps a somewhat made-over copy of an earlier text. **1929** W. K. Gregory *Our Face from Fish to Man* II. 153 Even the most imposing human faces are but made-over fish traps. **1929** J. Buchan *Courts of Morning* 25 Sandy in a greasy dress suit and a made-up black tie. **1952** J. Carter *Bks. & Bk.-Collectors* (1956) vi. ii. 195 The.. language of book-collectors.. is thickly encrusted with jargon... 'Made-up,' says one, with a sniff. 'Q6 is a cancel as usual,' says another. **1967** A. Lewin *Unaltered Cat* I. ii. 24 A place very like her own, a made-over brownstone only two blocks away. **1972** M. Gilbert *Body of Girl* v. 52 He was wearing a blue suit,.. a flannel shirt and a made-up bow tie.

IV. 10. Colloq. phr. ***made of money***, extremely rich, very wealthy.

1849 D. W. Jerrold (*title*) A man made of money. **1855** Mrs. Gaskell *North & South* I. xii. 143 'I shall order horses.' 'Nonsense, John. One would think you were made of money.' **1876** Trollope *Prime Minister* III. xv. 254 You're living here in a grand house, and your father's made of money. **1895** Mrs. H. Ward *Story B. Costrell* ii. 35 You don't care, not you!—one 'ud think yer were made o' money. **1918** C. Mackenzie *Early Life Sylvia Scarlett* II. ii. 292 He asked if I thought he was made of money and could buy top-hats like matches. **1967** E. Coxhead *Thankless Muse* iv. 103 'Then why don't we keep it?' 'You think Clare's made of money, I suppose?' **1975** C. Egleton *Skirmish* x. 104 Book him into a hotel.. but nothing fancy, we're not made of money.

made, obs. form of maid *sb.*

†**madefacient**, *a.* *Obs.* *rare*$^{-0}$. [ad. L. *madefacient-em*, pr. pple. of *madefacĕre*, to madefy.]

1727 Bailey vol. II, *Madefacient*, making moist, wetting.

madefaction (mædɪˈfækʃən). Now *rare* or *Obs.* [a. F. *madéfaction*, ad. L. *madefactiōn-em*, n. of action f. *madefacĕre*: see madefy.] A wetting; the action or process of making wet or moist.

1581 E. Campion in *Confer.* III. (1584) U iij, If it please God to take away the substance of water, and leaue the qualitie of madefaction, what hurt were it? **1626** Bacon *Sylva* §865 To all Madefaction there is required an Imbibition. **1657** Tomlinson *Renou's Disp.* 121 Such parts.. are hurt with fluent madefactions.

humorously pedantic. **1859** Thackeray *Virgin.* lxxvii, Aunt Lambert (who was indulging in that madefaction of pocket-handkerchiefs which I have before described).

†ˈ**madefy**, *v.* *Obs.* Also **modify(e, -ie**. [a. F. *madéfier*, ad. L. *madefacĕre*, f. *madēre* to be wet: see -fy.] *trans.* To make wet; to moisten.

c **1420** *Pallad. on Husb.* IV. 145 Her seed yf me reclyne In baume.. other in masticyne, Or madific it so in oil lauryne. **1597** A. M. tr. *Guillemeau's Fr. Chirurg.* 18 b/2 A sponge which is madefied and wetted in wyne. **1599** —— tr. *Gabelhouer's Bk. Physicke* 2/2 Madefye it with Rosewater. **1618** T. Adams *Rage Oppression* Wks. (1629) 609 The Bonners.. rode ouer the faces of Gods Saints, and madefied the earth with their bloods. **1671** J. Webster *Metallogr.* xvi. 235 Being madefied, it doth most easily contract a rust.

Hence †**madefiˈcation** [see -fication], 'a moistening or wetting' (1727 Bailey vol. II, spelt *modification*); ˈ**madefied**, ˈ**madefying** *ppl. adjs.*

1597 A. M. tr. *Guillemeau's Fr. Chirurg.* 31 b/1 With wett and madefyed cloutes. **1599** —— tr. *Gabelhouer's Bk. Physicke* 84/1 Dipp therin a madefyed finger. **1646** Sir T. Browne *Pseud. Ep.* VI. xii. 334 Any kind of vaporous or madefying excretion.

Madeira[1] (məˈdɪərə). Also 6–8 **Madera**. [a. Pg. *Madeira*; the island was so called because formerly thickly wooded (Pg. *madeira* = Sp. *madera* wood timber:—L. *māteria*: see matter *sb.*).]

1. The name of an island situated in the Atlantic Ocean, about 400 miles from the N. W. coast of Africa. Used *attrib.* in the designations of various things produced in or connected with the island, as ***Madeira lace, laurel, orchis, pear, tea, work*** (see quots.); **Madeira chair**, a kind of wicker or cane chair; **Madeira mahogany**, Canary wood, the wood of *Persea* (formerly *Laurus*) *indica*; **Madeira nut** *U.S.* [perh. belongs to 2 c], the common European walnut, esp. the 'Titmouse' or thin-shelled variety (*Juglans regia tenera*); **Madeira wine** = sense 2; **Madeira wood** (see quot.; cf. madeira[2]).

1889 Rider Haggard *K. Solomon's Mines* 16 Sir Henry was sitting opposite to me in a *Madeira chair. **1882** Caulfeild & Saward *Dict. Needlework*, **Madeira lace*. The lace made by the natives of Madeira is not a native production... The laces made are Maltese, Torchon, and a coarse description of Mechlin. **1796** Nemnich *Polygl. Lex. Nat. Hist.* v. 820 *Madeira laurel, *Laurus foetens*. *Ibid.* 955 *Madeira mahogany, *Laurus indica*. **1829** Loudon *Encycl. Plants* 334 *Laurus indica*.. The wood.. is called *Vigniatico* in the island of Madeira, and is probably what is imported into England under the name of Madeira mahogany. **1866** *Treas. Bot.*, Mahogany, Madeira, *Persea indica*. **1845–50** Mrs. Lincoln *Lect. Bot.* App. 116 *Juglans regia* (*madeira nut). **1882** *Garden* 11 Feb. 89/2 The *Madeira Orchis (*O. foliosa*) is remarkable.. for the readiness with which it doubles its bulb. **1664** Evelyn *Kal. Hort.* June (1679) 18 Pears, The Maudlin (first ripe), *Madera, Green-Royal [etc.]. **1892** Walsh *Tea* 33 Regular shipments of '*Madeira tea' are now being made to the London market. **1687** Congreve *Old Bach.* IV. ix, Why this same *Madera-wine has made me as light as a grasshopper. **1705** *Lond. Gaz.* No. 4131/4, 69 Pipes and 9 Hogsheads of White Madera Wines, 13 Hogsheads of Red Ditto. **1839** *Penny Cycl.* XIV. 262/1 The importation of Madeira wine into England in 1833 was 301,057 gallons. **1796** Nemnich *Polygl. Lex. Nat. Hist.* v. 820 *Madeira wood, *Cedrela odorata*. **1882** Caulfeild & Saward *Dict. Needlework*, **Madeira work*. This is white Embroidery upon fine linen, or cambric.. made by the nuns in Madeira.

2. a. (Also *Madeira wine*: see 1.) A white wine produced in the island of Madeira.

It is of a deep amber tint, full body, and some sweetness, resembling a well-matured full-bodied brown sherry.

1596 Shaks. *1 Hen. IV*, I. ii. 128 A Cup of Madera, and a cold Capons legge. **1612** *Sc. Bk. of Rates* in *Halyburton's Ledger* (1867) 335 Sackes Canareis Malagas Maderais.. Teynts and Allacants. **1708** S. Sewall *Diary* 12 Apr., We drank a Bottle of Madera together. **1787** M. Cutler in *Life*, etc. (1888) I. 235 You cannot please him more than by praising his Madeira. **1823** Byron *Juan* XIII. v, But then they have their claret and Madeira. **1861** Dutton Cook *P. Foster's D.* viii, I think I could eat a chop.. and a glass of Madeira.

b. with various qualifying prefixes.

East Indian madeira was madeira which had been sent on a sea voyage to the East Indies, to improve its quality.

1723 *Lond. Gaz.* No. 6173/3 There will be no other Malmsey Madera Wine landed this Year. 31 Pipes.. of.. White Vidonia Madera Wine. **1819** Shelley *Peter Bell the Third* IV. xviii. 5 Venison,.. And best East Indian madeira.

c. *Comb.*, as ***Madeira glass***; ***Madeira-drinking*** adj.; **Madeira cake**, a kind of sponge-cake; **Madeira sauce**, a rich brown sauce made with Madeira and served with braised or roast meats.

1800 *Asiat. Ann. Reg., Chron.* 123/2 A tea spoonful of the alkali in a Madeira glass half filled with water. **1845** Miss Acton *Mod. Cookery* 515 A good Madeira Cake. **1872** R. C. Smith *Madeira & its Associations*, The lively Frenchman.. dwells upon the virtues of delicious Madeira. He offers at once to despatch his grandfather in Madeira sauce. *A la Sauce Madère on mangerait son grandpère.* **1877** *Cassell's Dict. Cookery* 57/1 *Beef, Lumber, in Madeira Sauce*.. Prepare a sauce with brown stock or broth, some butter, flour, cayenne pepper, salt, pepper, and a glass of Madeira. **1902** *Munsey's Mag.* XXVI. 522/1 The interruptions.. from the Madeira-drinking men of letters overhead. **1946** G. Millar *Horned Pigeon* xix. 305 She followed this with kidneys and a Madeira sauce. **1956** L. Diat *French Cooking for Home* 43 Boiling spoils the flavour of Madeira Sauce.

madeira[2] (məˈdɪərə). In 7–8 **madera**. [a. Sp. *madera* wood (= Pg. *madeira*: see prec.). The usual spelling is due to assimilation to Madeira[1].] A West Indian name for Mahogany (*Swietenia Mahagoni*). Also ***madeira wood***.

1663 Gerbier *Counsel* 108 Precious Woods are to be had.. in the West-Indies, some.. hard as Marble; besides rare Madera, and other variously figured. **1736** Mortimer in *Phil. Trans.* XXXIX. 254 It is next in Beauty to what is here called Madera, which is the Mahogany of Jamaica. **1829** Loudon *Encycl. Plants* 352 The trees on the Bahama islands.. are known in Europe as Madeira wood.

madeleine (ˈmædleɪn). Also **madeline**. [F., prob. f. name of *Madeleine* Paulmier, 19th-c. French pastry-cook.] A (kind of) small rich cake baked in a shell-shaped tin. Sometimes (with allusion to Proust, quot. 1922) taken as typical of something that strongly evokes memories or nostalgia. Also, in English cooking, a kind of baked pudding or small fancy cake.

1845 E. Acton *Mod. Cookery* xviii. 473 (*heading*) Madeleine puddings. (To be served cold.) **1846** C. E. Francatelli *Mod. Cook* 404 Madeleines.. are made with the same kind of batter as Genoese cakes, to which currants, dried cherries, candied peel or angelica, may be added. **1902** G. H. Ellwanger *Pleasures of Table* vi. 169 Dumas tells the story of the excellent cake called madeleine, an entremets which all who have been in France will remember. **1922** C. K. S. Moncrieff tr. *Proust's Swann's Way* I. 61 And suddenly the memory returns. The taste was that of the little crumb of madeleine.. my aunt Léonie used to give me, dipping it first in her own cup of.. tea. **1939** O. Lancaster *Homes Sweet Homes* 42 The flavour of Bordeaux pigeon summons with all the completeness of Proust's tea-soaked madeleine an unforgettable cloud of Mons. Doré's angels hovering over the Colosseum. **1948** *Good Housek. Cookery Bk.* 577 Dip a cherry in a little jam, place on top of each madeleine and put on 2 leaves of angelica. **1958** *Spectator* 1 Aug. 174/1 We all have our little fragment of *madeleine* that brings back a dearly remembered but half-forgotten past. **1960** E. David *French Provincial Cooking* 32 At the little town of Commercy originated the small, fragile, shell-shaped cakes called madeleines so beloved of French children... (How the English madeleine, a sort of castle pudding covered in jam and coconut, with a cherry on the top, came by the same name is something of a mystery.) **1962** *Punch* 21 Mar. 462/1 It may be said—if it may then Proust has certainly said it—that the intensity of nostalgic emotion has little to do with the quality of the material which evokes it. (I dare say that madeleine cakes are very nasty.) **1972** 'M. Innes' *Open House* I. ii. 12 He might have been Proust's Marcel, hard upon imbibing the displeasing little sopped *madeleine* which brought his childhood flooding back to memory.

‖**mademoiselle** (madmwazɛl; often anglicized mædəmᵊˈzɛl). Also 7–8 **madamoiselle**, (7 **-ella**). [Fr.; orig. two words *ma* my (fem.), *demoiselle* (see damsel).]

1. The title (prefixed to the surname or the Christian name, or used *absol.* as a substitute for the name) applied to an unmarried Frenchwoman. In English use very often applied to unmarried women of foreign nationality other than French, instead of using the equivalent prefix (e.g.) in Dutch or Swedish, or substituting the English 'Miss'. Often used *absol.* as the designation of a French governess or the French teacher in a girls' school. Abbreviated *Mlle.*, in English often incorrectly *Mdlle.* Plural, **mesdemoiselles** (medmwazɛl), abbreviated *Mlles.*

In early Fr. use, the prefix *mademoiselle* was applied also to married women whose husbands were below the rank of knighthood.

a **1450** *Knt. de la Tour* (1868) 126 Madamoiselle! y praie you that ye ansuere not vnto this fole. **1696** Phillips (ed. 5), *Mademoiselle*, a Title of Honour given to the Daughters and Wives of born Gentlemen; much us'd in France. *a* **1734** North *Exam.* III. vi. §76 (1740) 479 The beautiful Mademoiselle Carwell, afterwards Duchess of Portsmouth. **1753** Smollett *Ct. Fathom* ix. Wks. 1872 V. 47 She [the maid] took the first opportunity of going to mademoiselle, and demanding money for some necessary expense. **1794** Mrs. Radcliffe *Myst. Udolpho* vii, Our cottage may be envied, sir, since you and Mademoiselle have honoured it with your presence. **1840** Barham *Ingol. Leg. Spectre of Tappington*, Mademoiselle boxed Mr. Maguire's ears, and Mr. Maguire pulled Mademoiselle upon his knee. **1850** Julia Kavanagh *Nathalie* ix. 213 Mademoiselle Dantin coughed, by way of opening the conversation. **1880** *Theatre* Feb. 118 Mademoiselle Lido sang well and tunefully as Irene. **1888** Mapleson *Mem.* (ed. 2) I. 306 The duty, therefore, of singing fell to Mdlle. Dotti.

2. *French Hist.* The title (used as a substitute for the name) of the eldest daughter of 'Monsieur', the eldest brother of the king. Subsequently applied to the eldest daughter of the king, or, if he had no daughter, to the first princess of the blood, so long as she remained unmarried.

1679 *Marriage Chas. II* 3 It was.. time for her to bring Madamoiselle to him. **1768** *Ann. Reg.* 192/2 His Danish majesty handed mademoiselle to her place. **1783** *Ibid.* 240 Deaths... At Versailles, mademoiselle of France, aged five years, only daughter of the French king.

3. *occas.* A person usually referred to as 'mademoiselle', an umarried Frenchwoman; *spec.* †a (foreign) serving-maid (*obs.*); a French governess.

Occas. in forms representing uneducated pronunciation.

1642 Milton *Apol. Smect.* Wks. 1851 III. 268 Prostituting the shame of that ministery.. to the eyes of Courtiers and Court-Ladies, with their Groomes and Madamoisellaes. **1765** Bickerstaffe *Maid of Mill* I. i. 2 She sits there all day.. dressed like a fine madumasel. **1833** M. Scott *Tom Cringle* xvi. (1842) 439 'De tout mon cœur', said a buxom brown dame, about eighteen stone... The extensive mademoiselle, suiting the action to the word, started up [etc.]. **1861** Mrs. H. Wood *East Lynne* III. iii, When I heard that Mrs. Carlyle had engaged a madmoselle for these children.

transf. **1712** Budgell *Spect.* No 277 ¶2 This Wooden *Madamoiselle* [a dressmaker's lay-figure].

4. *U.S.* A sea fish (see quot.).

1882 Jordan & Gilbert *Syn. Fishes N. Amer.* 570 (*Bull. U.S. Nat. Mus.* No. 16) *Sciæna punctata*.. Silver Perch; Yellow-tail; Mademoiselle.

maden, obs. and dial. f. maiden *sb.*

†**madent.** *Obs.* *rare*$^{-0}$. [ad. L. *madent-em*, pres. pple. of *madēre*, to be wet.] Wet, moist (Bailey vol. II, 1727).

‖**madérisé** (maderize), *a.* [Fr.] Of wine, affected with maderization (see below). So ˈ**maderize** [F. *madériser*] *v. intr.*, to become *madérisé*.

1941 Schoonmaker & Marvel *Amer. Wines* 219 The French also describe a white wine which has been too long in barrel.. as *madérisé*, or 'madeiraed'. **1950** O. A. Mendelsohn *Earnest Drinker* xx. 189 When a white wine starts to go a brownish colour and gets a curious.. musty smell about it, it is called *Madérisé* and means that the wine is on the road downhill. **1958** A. L. Simon *Dict. Wines* 105/2 *Madérisé*, the polite French word to use to describe the bottle stink of a wine which has been kept too long. **1961** W. E. Massee *Wines & Spirits* 10 A white table wine that has maderized is undrinkable. **1972** H. W. Yoxall *Enjoyment of Wine* v. 39–40 White wine deepens its tone with age and becomes what they call maderisé, though not all white wines that are so darkened acquire the musty taste of a truly maderized wine.

maderization (mædɪəraɪˈzeɪʃən). [ad. F. *madérisation* (also used), f. MADEIRA[1] 2 + -IZATION.] A brown discoloration in white wines often appearing after overlong or unsuitable storage.

1951 R. POSTGATE *Plain Man's Guide to Wine* iv. 76 The only noticeable change is an occasional darkening of colour, called *madérisation*. **1952** H. W. ALLEN *White Wines & Cognac* ii. 53 Still without a hint of *madérisation* and golden as sunlight. **1952** A. LICHINE *Wines of France* i. 7 A characteristic called maderization after Madeira wine, whose colour they take. **1959** W. JAMES *Word-bk. Wine* 113 *Maderization*, a flaw in white wines caused by their absorption of too much oxygen during vinification or maturation; the wine turns rusty in the bottle, and takes on a brown colour and a musty, flat, taste; when much advanced there may be some resemblance to a very poor madeira. **1971** *Times Lit. Suppl.* 12 Mar. 297/2 Such a bouquet suggests maderization, and I cannot believe that a lover of German wines would enjoy this very much. **1973** *Vogue* 15 Apr. 153/3 Old champagne can be great. It goes brown with age, and turns sweeter and heavier—a condition known as 'maderization'.

madeus, variant of MAIDEUX *Obs.*

† **ˈmadful**, *a. Obs. rare*$^{-1}$. [f. MAD *a.* + -FUL.] Mad.

14.. *Pol. Rel. & L. Poems* 245 A madful mone may men make Quan þat suete Ihesu was take!

madge[1] (mædʒ). [app. identical with *Madge*, pet-name for *Margaret*.]

1. The Barn-Owl, *Aluco flammeus*. Also ***madge-howlet, -owl, -owlet***.

1591 SYLVESTER *Du Bartas* I. v. 767 Thou lasie Madge That, fearing light, still seekest where to hide. **1598** B. JONSON *Ev. Man in Hum.* II. i, Ile sit in a barne, with Madge-howlet, and catch mice first. **1603** HARSNET *Pop. Impost.* 108 This must needes make the poore Madge Owlets cry out. **1606** DAY *Ile of Guls* II. iv. (1881) 54 The black swan of beauty and madg-howlet of admiration. **1635** SWAN *Spec. M.* (1670) 359 Ulula..which we call the Howlet, or the Madge. **1637** B. JONSON *Sad Sheph.* II. i, Thou shoul'dst ha' given her a Madge-Owle. **1694** MOTTEUX *Rabelais* v. ix, Under his Cage he perceived a Madge howlet. **1823** LAMB *Lett.* xii. *To B. Barton* 119 A silent meeting of madge-owlets. **1848** *Zoologist* VI. 2191 The barn owl..in Warwickshire..is generally called a 'madge' or 'madge owlet'.

2. The Common Magpie, *Pica caudata*.

1823 MOOR *Suffolk Words*, *Madge, Mag, Meg*, a magpie. **1828** J. FLEMING *Hist. Brit. Anim.* 87 *P. caudata*. Common Magpie... *E.* Pianet, Madge. **1894** NEWTON *Dict. Birds* 720 *note*, 'Magot' and 'Madge', are names frequently given in England to the Pie.

madge[2] (mædʒ). A leaden hammer covered thickly with stout woollen cloth, used in hard solder plating.

1870 *Eng. Mech.* 25 Feb. 573/1 A leaden hammer, clothed with kersey or woollen cloth, called a madge.

† **ˈmadhead**[1]. *Obs.* [See -HEAD.] Madness.

c **1375** *Cursor M.* 22865 (Fairf.) Þat to wene is bot madhede [*older texts* sothede]. *a* **1450** MYRC 1657 Lest þow do oȝt on madhede.

† **ˈmadhead**[2]. *Obs.* exc. *dial.* [f. MAD *a.* + HEAD *sb.*[1]] A mad person. Also *appos.* or *attrib.*

1600 BRETON *Pasquils Fooles-cap* (Grosart) 22/1 Such Madhead fellowes are but Fooles indeede. **1602** —— *Merry Wonders* To Rdr., Hoping that some mad-head in the world might have as much leysure to read as I haue had [to] write. **1959** *New Statesman* 26 Dec. 904/3 He'd quietened down now though, and butter wouldn't melt in his mouth, he said ..after all his stories about him being a madhead. **1959** I. & P. OPIE *Lore & Lang. Schoolch.* ix. 170 Red heads attract a barrage of nicknames..glow-worm, mad head [etc.].

mad-headed, *a.* [f. MAD *a.* + HEADED *a.*] = MAD-BRAINED.

1567 R. EDWARDS *Damon & Pithias* (1571) Eiv, For well I knewe it was some madheded chylde That inuented this name. **1596** SHAKS. *1 Hen. IV*, II. iii. 80. **1599** BRETON *Praise Vertuous Ladies* (Grosart) 56 For a few mad-headed wenches, they seek to bring..almost all women in contempt. **1793** SOUTHEY *Lett.* (1856) I. 20 Nor does it become a young mad-headed enthusiast to judge. **1809–10** COLERIDGE *Friend* (1865) 216 The inflammatory harangues of some mad-headed enthusiast. **1897** HENTY *On the Irrawaddy* 37 It seems to me a mad-headed thing to begin at the present time.

madhouse (ˈmædhaʊs). Now *rhetorical* or *derisive*. [f. MAD *a.* (used *subst.*) + HOUSE *sb.*]

a. A house set apart for the reception and detention of the insane; a lunatic asylum.

1687 LUTTRELL *Brief Rel.* (1857) I. 407 He was severely reprimanded, and told he was fitter for a mad house. **1695** *Par. Reg., S. James, Clerkenwell* (Harl. Soc. V. 171) Burials. .. Ann Pallmer, widow, from Dr. Newton's Mad house. **1774** *Act 14 Geo. III*, c. 49 (title), An Act for regulating Madhouses. **1828** CARLYLE *Misc.* (1857) I. 234 Tasso pines in the cell of a madhouse. **1833** MARRYAT *P. Simple* lxiv, I was a prisoner in a madhouse. **1901** *Scotsman* 29 Nov. 5/4 The American Eagle screams like a madhouse. **1916** G. B. SHAW *Androcles & Lion* Pref. p. lxiii, One person in every five dies in a workhouse, a public hospital, or a madhouse. **1922** JOYCE *Ulysses* 358 The nobleman with the foreign name..had to have her put into a mad-house, cruel only to be kind. **1929** F. N. HART *Hide in Dark* v. 182 It seems fairly essential to get at what facts are available..if some of us aren't to wind up in a mad-house. **1955** G. WILLANS *Fasten your Lapstraps!* i. 23 There is a dull sound of barley sugar being crunched and gum chewed—the whole place..is like a Victorian mad-house. **1971** J. NAMIER *Lewis Namier* xiii. 234 To L insanity was man's ultimate degradation; a madhouse, however well appointed, was hell.

b. *fig.* A scene of uproar or confusion bewildering to the onlooker.

1919 G. B. SHAW *Heartbreak Ho.* III. 95 Is this England, or is it a madhouse? **1929** H. CRANE *Let.* 7 Feb. (1965) 335 This City [*sc.* Paris], as you know, is the most interesting madhouse in the world. **1946** E. O'NEILL *Iceman Cometh* (1947) III. 160 God, I'm glad I'm leaving this madhouse! **1956** R. BRADDON *Nancy Wake* xiv. 155 The Moulins railway junction was a mad-house of torn and tangled lines and shattered rolling stock. **1973** *Radio Times* 26 Apr. 48/1 They [*sc.* chefs] roast and stew and bake in a kind of madhouse of shouted commands, cancelled orders and frayed tempers.

‖ **madia** (ˈmeɪdɪə). [a. mod.L. *madia*, a. Chilean *madi*.] The plant *Madia sativa*, a coarse, hairy, erect annual, allied to the Sunflowers. It is a native of Chile, and is cultivated for its seeds, which yield a valuable oil, and are made into cake for cattle. Also *attrib.* in ***madia oil***

[**1809** (Italian original 1787) tr. *Molina's Hist. Chili* I. iii. 111 The madi (madia. gen. nov.). Of this plant there are two kinds, the one wild, the other cultivated. The cultivated, which I have called *madia sativa*, has a branching hairy stalk.] **1839** *Gardener's Mag.* XV. 143, 100 parts of the Madia oil consist of 45 parts of oleine [etc.]. **1846** LINDLEY *Veget. Kingd.* 707 Madia oil, expressed without heat, is described as transparent, yellow, scentless. **1855** STEPHENS *Bk. of the Farm* (ed. 2) II. 106 The madia is in the same botanical position as the sunflower.

madid (ˈmædɪd), *a.* Now *rare*. Also 7 maddid. [ad. L. *madid-us*, f. *madēre* to be wet.] Wet, moist.

1615 CROOKE *Body of Man* 425 Auicen..saith they [*sc.* the lungs] are not soft but maddid. **1627–77** FELTHAM *Resolves* I. lxii. 95 The madid South, sorrowful, and full of tears. **1657** TOMLINSON *Renou's Disp.* 146 No where save in wine cellars or such madid places. **1720** WELTON *Suffer. Son of God* I. v. 98 The very Ground..is madid and Bedew'd with Drops that distil from thine Eyes. **1762** FALCONER *Shipwr* I. 356 Full from the madid south the winds arise. **1844** DISRAELI *Coningsby* I. iii, His large deep blue eye, madid and yet piercing. **1881** J. E. H. THOMSON *Upland Tarn* I. 92 The evening with its madid mantle grey Had shrouded all the sky.

† **ˈmadidate**, *v. Obs.*$^{-0}$ [f. late L. *madidāt-*, ppl. stem of *madidāre*, f. *madid-us* moist.] *trans.* 'To wet or moisten' (Blount *Glossogr.* 1656).

† **ˈmadidity.** *Obs.*$^{-0}$ [f. MADID + -ITY.] 'Moisture or fulness of moisture' (Blount *Glossogr.* 1656).

† **ˈmadidness.** *Obs.*$^{-0}$ [f. MADID + -NESS.] 'Moistness, wetness'.

1731 BAILEY vol. II.

madifie, -fy(e, variant forms of MADEFY *Obs.*

madin, obs. form of MEDINE.

madin(e, madinne, obs. forms of MAIDEN.

madinhad, -heid, variants of MAIDENHEAD.

ˈMadison. orig. *U.S.* [Origin unknown.] A group dance, popular in the 1950s and 1960s.

1962 *Listener* 27 Dec. 1074/2 Girls in traditional Kimono dancing the twist or the Madison. **1966** *Punch* 25 May 768/2 We found the Bishop and Dolly Girl an hour later. She was teaching him the rudimentary technique of The Madison. **1968** M. & J. STEARNS *Jazz Dance* 4 Before and during Presley's initial success, the first wave of dances became popular. Group dances such as the Madison and the Birdland arrived first. **1969** C. BOOKER *Neophiliacs* vii. 177 In the same month of October [1962]..the unknown Beatles first joined the fashionable beat of the Madison in the charts.

Madison Avenue (ˈmædɪsən ˈævɪnjuː). The name of a street in New York City, which is the centre of the American advertising business; hence *allusively*, (American) advertising generally, the advertising business; *collect.*, American advertising agents. Also *attrib.*

1955 H. KURNITZ *Invasion of Privacy* (1956) v. 39 A tall, lean young man..dressed in the dark grey and neat stripes of a Madison Avenue advertising executive. **1957** J. BLISH *Fallen Star* ii. 33 We had..Madison Avenue gossip..for lunch. **1958** J. K. GALBRAITH *Affluent Society* xviii. 200 The violent mores of Hollywood and Madison Avenue. **1959** N. MAILER *Advts. for Myself* (1961) 404, I kept expecting him to go Madison Avenue, I was certain he would sell out sooner or later. **1959** V. PACKARD *Status Seekers* (1960) i. 12 Madison Avenue has been busily trying to understand our tastes and buying behaviour. **1960** *Guardian* 15 Oct. 6/5 An Eisenhowerish vocabulary which..sometimes has more of a Madison Avenue ring. **1961** [see HARLEY]. **1970** *Times* 24 Aug. 15/5 Britain's Madison Avenue widely predicted that after a decent interval, *Ad Weekly* would also attempt something spectacular. **1972** *Jazz & Blues* Sept. 9/2 We know what's wanted. I had something to offer Madison Avenue.

madjoon, -oun, variant forms of MAJOON.

madle, obs. variant of MALE *a.*

madlie, variant of MAIDLY *a. Obs.*

madling (ˈmædlɪŋ), *sb.*[1] [f. MAD *a.* + -LING[1].] A mad creature; one who acts wildly or foolishly.

c **1648–50** BRATHWAIT *Barnabees Jrnl.* I. (1818) 19 There another wanton madling Who her hog was set a sadling. **1841** *Let.* in R. Oastler *Fleet Papers* I. viii. 58 Poor madlings! they are killing the goose, to get at the golden eggs. **1847** E. BRONTE *Wuthering Heights* xiii. 120 Gooid-for-nowt madling!..flinging t' precious gifts uh God under fooit i' yer flaysome rages.

† **ˈmadling**, *sb.*[2] [? Corruption of F. *Madeleine* a kind of small cake.] *attrib.* in ***madling cake***.

1747 MRS. GLASSE *Cookery* xv. 141 Madling Cakes.

† **ˈmadling**, *a. Obs.* [? attrib. use of MADLING *sb.*[1] or *adv.*; ? or = *maddling* f. MADDLE *v.*] Mad.

1608 T. MORTON *Preamb. Encounter* 126 Why doe I trouble my selfe with these my Aduersaries madling conceits?

† **ˈmadling**, *adv. Obs.* [? f. MAD *a.* + -LING[2]: cf. *darkling*.] = MADLY.

1584 HUDSON *Du Bartas' Judith* VI. (1608) 93 Some madling runnes, some trembles in a traunce.

madly (ˈmædlɪ), *a. rare*$^{-1}$. [f. MAD *a.* + -LY[1].] Characteristic of a mad person.

1816 BYRON *Parisina* xviii, It was a woman's shriek and ne'er In madlier accents rose despair.

madly (ˈmædlɪ), *adv.* [f. MAD *a.* + -LY[2].]

1. a. In a mad, insane or foolish manner.

a **1225** *Leg. Kath.* 2083 Hwi motestu se mediche? *c* **1375** *Cursor M.* 14608 (Fairf.) Als witles men madli þai lete. *c* **1475** *Rauf Coilȝear* 22 Amang thay myrk Montanis sa madlie thay mer. **1535** COVERDALE *Ps.* lxxiv. 4, I sayde vnto the madde people: deale not so madly. **1590** SHAKS. *Mids. N.* II. i. 171 The iuyce of it, on sleeping eye-lids laid, Will make or man or woman madly dote. **1606** —— *Tr. & Cr.* II. ii. 116 Or is your bloud So madly hot, that [etc.]? **1654** *Martini's Conq. China* 9 The men, though madly, use it [horse-hair] in tying up their hair. *a* **1717** PARNELL *Elegy Old Beauty* 33 And all that's madly wild, or oddly gay, We call it only pretty Fanny's way. **1778** MME. D'ARBLAY *Let.* 6 July, Half the flattery I have had would have made me madly merry. **1849** MACAULAY *Hist. Eng.* ix. II. 463 The help of that single power he had madly rejected. **1874** GREEN *Short Hist.* iii. §5. 139 The young King drew his sword, and rushed madly on the Justiciary.

b. *Comb.*, as ***madly-used, -wrested*** adjs.

1601 SHAKS. *Twel. N.* v. i. 319 The madly us'd Maluolio. **1656** EARL MONM. tr. *Boccalini's Advts. fr. Parnass.* I. xxviii. (1674) 30 The madly-wrested Reason of State which was now practised by many.

2. Colloq. uses. **a.** Passionately, fervently (cf. quot. 1590).

1767 BOSWELL *Let.* 30 Mar. (1924) I. 108, I was so madly in love as to think of marrying her. **1880** O. C. STONE *Few Months New Guinea* iv. 55 The natives..seem madly fond of *kuku* [*sc.* tobacco], and would pawn their very clothes for it if they wore any. **1888** W. S. GILBERT *Trial by Jury* 12, I love him—I love him—with fervour increasing, I worship and madly adore. **1924** A. CHRISTIE *Man in Brown Suit* ii. 19, I could never marry a man unless I loved him madly. **1959** [see BEETLE *sb.*[2] 2 b]. **1974** M. CECIL *Heroines in Love* v. 151 Upper-class heroines..were never 'in love', always 'madly in love'.

b. Extremely, very, 'awfully'.

1888 H. JAMES *Reverberator* II. i. 16, I was not madly impatient to see you married. **1902** G. BELL *Lett.* (1927) I. vii. 130 It is a madly interesting place. **1935** N. MARSH *Enter Murderer* ii. 31 She's madly keen on criminology. **1937** C. CONNOLLY in L. Russell *Press Gang!* 79 Hubert said Balliol was perfect for case-histories like mine, but I realised I should find it madly ungay. **1945** N. MITFORD *Pursuit of Love* ix. 73 It's madly wearing to the optic nerve centres. **1954** J. B. PRIESTLEY *Magicians* i. 20 Mavis..brightened up like a touched-off firework and was at once, in her own phrase, 'madly gay'. **1967** [see DRAGGY *a.* b]. **1974** *Radio Times* 3 Jan. 5/4 Mr Williams's facial mobility is *madly* impressive.

madman (ˈmædmən). [Originally two words: see MAD *a.* and MAN *sb.*] One who is insane; a lunatic. Also *transf.* and *hyperbolically*, one who behaves like a lunatic, a wildly foolish person.

1377 LANGL. *P. Pl.* B. IX. 69 Faderelees children; And wydwes,..Madde men, and maydenes, þat helplees were. *c* **1475** *Rauf Coilȝear* 441, I am bot ane mad man. ? *a* **1500** *Chester Pl.* (Shaks. Soc.) II. 168 Madmen, maddmen, leeve on me, That am on god, so is not he. *a* **1533** LD. BERNERS *Huon* xxiii. 68 He wyll come after vs lyke a madd man. **1601** SHAKS. *Twel. N.* I. v. 115 Fetch him off I pray you, he speakes nothing but madman. **1611** BIBLE *1 Sam.* xxi. 15 Haue I need of mad-men, that ye haue brought this fellow to play the mad-man in my presence? **1648** BOYLE *Seraph. Love* xiv. (1700) 84 The wicked's spite against God is but like a madman's running his head against the wall. **1674** MARVELL *Corr.* Wks. 1872–5 II. 424 Carleton the B[ishop] of Bristol hath played the madman in that City. **1796** MORSE *Amer. Geog.* I. 547 This hospital is the general receptacle of lunatics and madmen. **1810** SCOTT *Lady of L.* II. xxxiv, Madmen, forbear your frantic jar! **1843** BETHUNE *Sc. Fireside Stor.* 75, I have been a madman and a fool. **1885** *Manch. Exam.* 16 May 5/1 Policemen who find a half-naked madman howling at midnight.

† **madme.** *Obs.* Forms: 1 **máð(ð)um, máðm, mádm**, 3 *pl.* **maðmes, madmes**, *Orm.* **maddmess**. [OE. *máðm* masc. corresponds to OS. *mēðmos* pl. gifts, MHG. *meidem*, ON. *meiðmar* pl., gifts, presents, Goth. *maiþm-s* gift (δῶρον):—O.Teut. **maiþmo-z*:—pre-Teut. type **moitmo-s* f. **moit-* to exchange (as in L. *mūtāre*:—**moitāre*).] A precious thing, treasure, valuable gift.

a **1000** *Boeth. Metr.* xxi. 20 Gylden maðm, sylofren sincstan..modes eaȝan æfre ne onlyhtað. *a* **1000** *Gnomic verses (Exeter Bk.)* 155 Maþþum oþres weorð, gold mon sceal ȝifan. *c* **1200** ORMIN 6471 & illc an king oppnede þær Hiss

hord off hise maddmess. *c* **1205** LAY. 896 ȝeue us þe king & al his gold, & þa maðmes of his lond. *a* **1250** *Prov. Ælfred* 384 in *O.E. Misc.* 126 Vyches cunnes madmes to mixe schulen i-Multen.

†**'madnep.** *Obs.* Also -nip. [f. MAD *a.* (cf. quot. 1686) + *nep, nip,* NEEP.] The Cow Parsnip, *Heracleum Sphondylium.*

1597 GERARDE *Herbal* II. ccclxxvii. 856 Spondylium..is called..in English Cow Parsnep, meddowe Parsnep, and Madnepe. **1601** HOLLAND *Pliny* II. 181 Spondylium, a kind of wild Parsnep or Madnep. **1652** CULPEPPER *Eng. Physic.* 161 The seed of the wilde Parsnipe being ripe about the beginning of August, and if they do flower for seed in the first year of sowing the Countrey people call them 'Madneps'. **1686** RAY *Hist. Plant.* I. 410 Nostrates asserunt Pastinacas ipsas vetustiores & annosas delirium..inducere, unde eas Mad-neps..vocant. **1712** tr. *Pomet's Hist. Drugs* I. 30 The Peasants call it the Mad Nip.

madness ('mædnɪs). [f. MAD *a.* + -NESS.] The quality or condition of being mad.

1. Mental disease, insanity; now applied *esp.* to insanity characterized by wild excitement or extravagant delusions; mania. Also (in animals) rabies.

1398 TREVISA *Barth. De P.R.* VII. vi. (1495) 226 And thise passions ben dyuers madnesse that hyghte Inania [*read* Mania] & madnesse that hyghte Malencolonia [*sic*]. *c* **1440** *Promp. Parv.* 319/2 Maddenesse, *amencia, demencia.* **1538** ELYOT *Dict., Rabies,* Madnesse of a dogge. **1567** MAPLET *Gr. Forest* 46 Henbane, hath the name to be a cause of madnesse or furie. **1602** SHAKS. *Ham.* III. iv. 187 Let him..Make you to rauell all this matter out, That I essentially am not in madnesse But made in craft. **1611** BIBLE *Zech.* xii. 4, I will smite euery horse with astonishment, and his rider with madnesse. **1687** MAYERN in *Phil. Trans.* XVI. 408 Doggs are Subject to these several sorts of Madness or rather diseases. **1753** CHAMBERS *Cycl. Supp.* s.v. *Mania,* Madness arising from immaterial causes is much more difficult to cure. **1849** MACAULAY *Hist. Eng.* iv. I. 524 This delusion becomes almost a madness when many exiles..herd together. **1879** LINDSAY *Mind in Lower Anim.* I. 16 Madness in lower animals may mean any one of several very different affections, including especially insanity and rabies.

2. Imprudence or delusion resembling insanity; extravagant folly.

1382 WYCLIF *Hos.* ix. 7 Yrael, wite thou thee a fool, a wood prophete,..for the multitude of thi wickidnesse, and multitude of madnesse. **1560** DAUS tr. *Sleidane's Comm.* 368 What madnes were this, with his own mony..to maintaine the force of his adversarye. **1697** DRYDEN *Virg. Georg.* IV. 642 What Madness cou'd provoke A Mortal Man t'invade a sleeping God? **1721** R. KEITH tr. *T. à Kempis' Solil. Soul* x. 173 Wander not forth, O my Soul, after Vanities, nor after lying Madnesses. **1849** MACAULAY *Hist. Eng.* v. I. 602 To advance towards London would have been madness. **1862** G. LONG *Thoughts of Antoninus* (1877) 113 To seek what is impossible is madness. **1885** J. PAYN *Talk of Town* II. 69 It would have been madness indeed to have any altercation.

3. Ungovernable anger, rage, fury.

1665 MANLEY *Grotius' Low C. Warres* 273 The baser sort of people cover'd nothing of their Madness, but shew'd their Fury in their Speeches. **1698** VANBRUGH *Prov. Wife* II. i, Now could I cry for madness, but that I know he'd laugh at me for it. **1781** GIBBON *Decl. & F.* xxx. III. 157 The madness of the people soon subsided. **1802** MRS. J. WEST *Infidel Father* III. 45 Sir Bronze absolutely stamped for madness at this intelligence.

transf. **1697** DRYDEN *Virg. Georg.* III. 367 Not with more Madness, rolling from afar, The spumy Waves proclaim the watry War. **1884** W. C. SMITH *Kildrostan* 87 Then I see..the waves Lashed into madness.

4. Extravagant excitement or enthusiasm; ecstasy.

1596 SHAKS. *Merch. V.* I. ii. 21 Such a hare is madness the youth, to skip ore the meshes of good counsaile the cripple. **1607** NORDEN *Surv. Dial.* I. 9 A kind of madness, as I may call it, but in the best sence it is a kind of ambitious..emulation. **1775** JOHNSON *Tax. no Tyr.* 55 The madness of independence has spread from Colony to Colony. **1799** CAMPBELL *Pleas. Hope* I. 160 The smiling Muse..Shall..breathe a holy madness o'er thy mind. **1820** SHELLEY *Skylark* 103 Such harmonious madness From my lips would flow. **1822** LAMB *Elia* Ser. I. *On Some Old Actors,* None..possessed even a portion of that fine madness which he threw out in Hotspur's famous rant. **1879** SYMONDS *Shelley* 195 The Muses filled this man with sacred madness.

mado ('mɑːdəʊ). *Austral.* [Aboriginal name.] A small marine fish, *Atypichthys mado* (or *A. strigatus*), found in southern Australian and northern New Zealand waters.

1898 E. E. MORRIS *Austral Eng.* 277/2 *Mado,* a Sydney fish, *Therapon cuvieri,* Bleek; called also *Trumpeter-Perch.* **1906** D. G. STEAD *Fishes of Australia* 134 The mado is a handsome little fish, having alternate brown and yellow longitudinal stripes along the body. **1958** *Austral. Encycl.* V. 458/2 *Mado,* a small fish (*Atypichthys mado*) very common round wharf-piles and in inlets along the coasts of the southern half of Australia. **1960** DOOGUE & MORELAND *N.Z. Sea Anglers' Guide* 229 Mado..yellow with longitudinal brown streaks..Distribution: North Island south to about East Cape. Also occurs in Australian waters.

Madonna (mə'dɒnə). Also 7 **Maddona,** 6–9 **madona.** [a. It. *madonna,* orig. two words (*ma* OIt. unstressed form of *mia* fem., my; *donna* = F. *dame*:—L. *domina* lady) corresponding to F. *ma dame*: see MADAM.]

‖ **1. a.** As an Italian form of address or title: My lady, madam. *Obs.*

1584 R. W. *Three Ladies Lond.* I. B ij b, *Merca.* Madona, me be a Merchant and be cald senior Merkadorus. **1592** NASHE *P. Penilesse* 20 b, They drawe out a dinner with sallets,..& make Madona Nature their best Caterer. **1601** SHAKS. *Twel. N.* I. v. 72 Good Madona, why mournst thou? *a* **1626** MIDDLETON *More Dissemblers* v. i. (1657) 67 *Crotch.* (Here they sing Prick-song) How like you this Madona? *Celia.* Pretty. **1632** MASSINGER *Maid of Hon.* v. ii, Gracious Maddona, Noble Generall, Brave Captaines, and my quondam rivalls, wear 'em. **1827** MACAULAY *Song* Misc. Writ. (1860) II. 417 Oh stay, Madonna! stay.

†**b.** An Italian lady. *Obs.*

1602 MIDDLETON *Blurt* II. ii. C 2 b, *Hip.* Well Sir, you know..the flea-bitten fac'd Ladie. *Doit.* Oh Sir, the freckle cheeke Madona, I know her Signior, as well— *Hip.* Not as I doe, I hope Sir. *a* **1625** FLETCHER *Fair Maid of Inn* III. i, A dancer..that by teaching great Madonnas to foot it, has miraculously purchast a ribanded wastcote. **1639** SHIRLEY *Gent. Ven.* v. ii. (1655) 64 De'e think to mount Madonas here, and not Pay for the sweet Carreere.

2. a. An Italian designation of the Virgin Mary; usually with *the*; occas. used vocatively. **b.** A picture or statue (esp. Italian) of the Virgin Mary.

1644 EVELYN *Diary* (1879) I. 122 A faire Madona of Pietro Perugino, painted on the wall. **1645** *Ibid.* I. 203 The miraculous shrine of the Madona wch Pope Paul III. brought barefooted to the place. **1717** LADY M. W. MONTAGU *Let. to Abbé Conti* 29 May, They shewed me..a picture of the Virgin Mary, drawn by the hand of St. Luke,..the finest Madonna of Italy is not more famous for her miracles. **1816** BYRON *Siege Cor.* xxx, Madonna's face upon him shone, Painted in heavenly hues above. **1825–9** MRS. SHERWOOD *Lady of Manor* V. xxxii. 338 A beautiful madonna in white marble which I had seen in a church in Rome. **1833** TENNYSON *Mariana in South* 22 'Ave Mary' was her moan, 'Madonna, sad is night and morn'. **1849** JAMES *Woodman* ii, A very early painting of the Madonna and Child. **1853** FROUDE *Eng. Forgotten Worthies* Short Stud. (ed. 2) 305 Whose pretences to religion might rank with the devotion of an Italian bandit to the Madonna. **1855** BROWNING *One Word More* ii, Rafael made a century of sonnets,..Else he only used to draw Madonnas.

3. A mode of dressing a woman's hair, with the parting down the middle, and the hair arranged smoothly on each side. (Cf. 4.)

a **1839** T. H. BAYLY *Songs & Ball.* I. 139 I've tried all styles of hair dressing, Madonnas, frizzes, crops.

4. *attrib.* and *Comb.* (esp. with reference to pictures of the Madonna and the mode of dressing the hair), as ***Madonna braid, coiffure, face, front, lid, style***; ***Madonna-like*** adj.; ***Madonna-wise*** adv.; **Madonna blue,** a shade of deep blue; **Madonna-braided** *a.,* (of the hair) arranged in smooth braids on each side of the face, after the manner of Italian representations of the Madonna; **Madonna lily,** the White Lily, *Lilium candidum,* often represented with the Madonna in pictures.

[**1930** MAERZ & PAUL *Dict. Color* 198/2, 1917 Madonna.] **1932** A. CHRISTIE *Peril at End House* vii. 85 She was wearing a gown of *Madonna blue. **1935** *Times* 2 Oct. 17/4 A Madonna-blue lining. **1971** N. FREELING *Over High Side* II. 110 Twilight had fallen, of a pure madonna blue. **1829** *Souvenir* II. 317/2 (Stant.) The hair is beautifully arranged in a *Madonna braid in front. **1849** AYTOUN *Poems, Buried Flower* 83 Raven locks, *Madonna-braided O'er her sweet and blushing face. **1890** *Pall Mall G.* 26 Nov. 1/3 Her fair hair..is simply parted in the centre, in the way which is now often playfully called the '*madonna coiffure'. **1790** HEL. M. WILLIAMS *Julia* I. i. 3 She had a *madona face. **1849** THACKERAY *Pendennis* I. xvi. 143 She returned a rather elderly character with a *Madonna front and a melancholy countenance. **1863** WOOLNER *My Beautiful Lady* 95 O wan girl-mother with *Madonna lids Downcast. **1850** MRS. GASKELL *Let.* 24 Jan. (1966) 101 She was a *madonna-like person with a face..full of thought and gentle love. **1895** G. B. SHAW *Let.* 20 Mar. (1965) 502 You must..be sweet..and Madonna like. **1909** M. DIVER *Candles in Wind* I. iv. 40 The soft brown hair..giving a Madonna-like air of purity to the oval face. **1966** 'R. STANDISH' *Widow Hack* vi. 65 She has large, generous features which compose themselves in a Madonna-like serenity. **1877** E. S. PHELPS *Story of Avis* ix. 172 An exquisite motion which an artist..would not have wasted..on anything less than a *Madonna lily. **1900** *Field* 23 June 903/3 The Madonna lily (*Lilium candidum*). **1902** *Daily Chron.* 1 Apr. 2/1 Large branches of Madonna lilies. **1963** W. BLUNT *Of Flowers & Village* 173 My whole room is scented by a great pot of Madonna lilies. **1974** *Country Life* 21 Mar. 632/1 A child in a bonnet creeps shyly down the path, dwarfed by the Madonna lilies. **1818** *La Belle Assemblée* XVII. 86 The hair is worn more in the *Madona style. **1830** TENNYSON *Isabel* i., Locks not wide-dispread, *Madonna-wise on either side her head.

Hence **Ma'donnahood,** the character or quality of a Madonna. **Ma'donnaish** *a.,* like a Madonna.

1860 RUSKIN *Mod. Paint.* V. IX. iv. 236 Brown gleams of gipsy Madonnahood from Murillo. **1891** *Athenæum* 24 Oct. 547/1 She is too Madonnaish in one way, too languishing and sentimental in another.

madoqua ('mædəʊkwə). [Amharic.] A tiny antelope of Abyssinia, *Neotragus saltianus* (*N. madoqua*), of about the size of a hare.

[**1681** J. LUDOLF *Hist. Aethiop.* I. x. ¶73 Amharice Madakua; animalia quae capris assimilabat Gregorius. Rupicaprae vel Ibices esse videntur.] **1790** BRUCE *Trav. Source Nile* V. 83 Among the wild animals are prodigious numbers of the gazel or antelope kind; the bohur, sassa, feeho, and madoqua. **1885** *Cassell's Nat. Hist.* III. 18.

‖**'mador.** *Med. Obs.* Also 7 **madour.** [L. *mador* moisture, f. *madēre*: see MADID.] Sweat.

1620 VENNER *Via Recta* (1650) 296 If in sleep the body..be sometimes in a little mador or light sweat. **1658** PHILLIPS, *Madidity* or *Madour,* moistness or wetness. **1705** *Phil. Trans.* XXV. 2105 Without any offensive Smell, or fastidious Mador. **1856** MAYNE *Expos. Lex., Mador,*..Moisture that is superfluous or unnatural. Old term for that kind of sweat which takes place in syncope, whether warm or cold.

mador, variant of MADAR.

†**madpash.** *Obs.* [f. MAD *a.* + PASH head.] A crack-brained person. Also *attrib.*

1611 COTGR., *Mat,* a foole, fop, gull; mad-pash, harebrained ninnie. *a* **1693** *Urquhart's Rabelais* III. xxv, Let us leave this Madpash Bedlam, this hair-brained Fop.

Madras (mə'drɑːs, -æ-).

1. The name of a city of India and the province of which it is the capital; used *attrib.* in the names of things produced there or originally connected therewith: **Madras cotton,** cotton fabric produced in Madras, *esp.* the brightly checked or striped cottons the colours of which run together in laundering. Also *ellipt.* as **Madras. Madras lace, (net) muslin** (see quots. 1882); **Madras stucco** = CHUNAM; **Madras work** (see quot.).

1864 *Chamb. Encycl.* VI. 251/1 Madras stucco, or *chunam,* is largely employed in the decoration of public buildings. **1882** CAULFEILD & SAWARD *Dict. Needlewk., Madras Lace,* A school for lace making has lately been founded in Madras. The lace made is the black and white silk Maltese guipure. *Madras-net Muslin,* This is a handsome, but coarse make of Muslin, produced in several varieties..They are all 72 inches wide. *Madras Work,* This is so called from its being executed upon the brightly coloured silk handkerchiefs that are known as Madras handkerchiefs. **1890** L. HEARN *Two Years in French West Indies* 216 The making-up of the Madras into a turban is called 'tying a head'. **1895** *Army & Navy Co-oper. Soc.* Price List 1105/1 Frilled Madras Muslin. **1897** *Sears, Roebuck Catal.* 216/3 French Madras is a fine soft finished fabric with the colors woven through...Light colors, plaids or stripes. **1921** *Daily Colonist* (Victoria, B.C.) 22 Oct. 7/2 (Advt.), 50-Inch Colored Madras at $1.50 a Yard..this Madras will make beautiful side curtains. **1942** J. HOYE *Staple Cotton Fabrics* vii. 148 When made in fancy weaves and of fine yarns, they are known as Madras ginghams. **1962** L. DEIGHTON *Ipcress File* xxviii. 177 A bright Madras jacket. **1964** HOLLEN & SADDLER *Textiles* (ed. 2) 153/2 The imported Indian madras, today, is handwoven with white warp and colored filling 'guaranteed to bleed'. **1968** H. WAUGH *Con Game* iii. 34 Three pairs of men's shoes and one wrinkled Madras jacket. **1972** *Vogue* Feb. 86 Madras checked safari jacket, unlined seersucker.

2. In full ***Madras handkerchief***: A bright-coloured handkerchief of silk and cotton worn by the West Indian Blacks as a head-dress, 'formerly exported from Madras' (Yule).

1833 M. SCOTT *Tom Cringle* xvi. (1842) 437 The black officers, in general, covered their woolly pates with Madras handkerchiefs. **1881** CABLE *Mad. Delphine,* etc. 97 Old Charlie..was sitting on his bench under a China-tree, his head, as was his fashion, bound in a Madras handkerchief. **1888** —— *Bonaventure, Au Large* i. 146 A black woman in red-and-yellow Madras turban,..crouched against the wall.

3. = *Madras-net muslin* (see 1).

1902 *Westm. Gaz.* 27 Aug. 8/1 The shirt, a fine madras, plaited *négligé* with square point narrow link cuffs.

‖**madrasah** (mə'dræsə), **medresseh** (me'drɛseɪ). Also 7 **mandresa,** 9 **madrasa, madrassah, -asseh, -assee, -essé, medressé,** 20 **medarsa, medersa,** *Dicts.* **madressah, -issa(h.** [The various forms represent Indian, Turkish, Persian and Arabic regional pronunciations of Arab. *madrasaʰ,* f. *darasa* to study.] A Muslim college.

1662 J. DAVIES tr. *Olearius' Voy. Ambass.* 214 We..found that it was a School or College, which they call Mandresa, of which kind there are very many all over Persia. *Ibid.* 333 They [the Persians] have their Colleges, or Universities, which they call Medressa. **1687** A. LOVELL tr. *Thevenot's Trav.* II. 80 Lodging Rooms for the Scholars of the Medrese. **1819** T. HOPE *Anastasius* (1820) III. xi. 271 His fortune was spent in placing me in a Medressé. **1834** MORIER *Ayesha* I. xii. 269 The *medresseh,* or school, which adjoined the principal mosque. **1841** *Penny Cycl.* XX. 375/2 (*Samarcand*) The mesids (lower schools) and medresses (high schools or colleges). **1876** A. ARNOLD in *Contemp. Rev.* June 47 The Madrassee or mosque school of Ispahan. **1881** HUNTER in *Encycl. Brit.* XII. 774/2 The Calcutta *madrasa* for Mahometan teaching. **1882** O'DONOVAN *Merv Oasis* xvi. I. 276 Within sight are three *medressés,* or collegiate institutions, for the instruction of Turcoman students for the priesthood. **1920** *Blackw. Mag.* Dec. 750/1 The 'universities'—'Medarsas'—of Fez and Marrakesh..are now open once more to the Christian visitor. **1923** G. CASSERLEY *Algeria To-Day* iii. 58 There is a finely-built Medersa or theological college for Mahommedans. **1935** *Times Lit. Suppl.* 3 Jan. 4/3 President of a *medersa*—that is, an Arabic University—and commandant of the neighbouring fort of Gouridam. **1968** *Vogue* 15 Apr. 124/2 Fès, the ancient university city of Morocco..this crowded ancient place of mosques and medersas.

Madrasi (mə'dræsɪ), *a.* and *sb.* Also **Madrassi, -assee.** [Urdu *Madrasī,* f. *Madras* the city in southern India.] **A.** *adj.* Of or pertaining to Madras. **B.** *sb.* A native or inhabitant of Madras.

1878 *Chambers's Jrnl.* Feb. 115/1 English, after the rickety fashion of a Madrassee, Sam spoke fairly enough. **1879** H. HARTIGAN *Stray Leaves* 2nd Ser. 129 While ruminating, a Madrasi servant came out. **1921** *Contemp. Rev.* Sept. 291 'Western civilisation,' said an eminent Madrasi the other day, 'has led to war.' **1924** *Blackw. Mag.* Aug. 227/2 The officer commanding..Madrasi Christians, will not admit this. **1971** R. RUSSELL tr. *Ahmad's Shore & Wave* v. 49 His

partner, a solemn-looking, bald Madrasi, was suffering all this in silence.

† **madrean.** *Obs.* Also 4 madryan, -am. [a. OF. *madrian* 'sorte de fruit' (Godef.).] A spice, ? a kind of ginger.

1357–8 *Durham Acc. Rolls* (Surtees) 124 In 4 cofynes de Anys comfeyt, madryan, et aliarum specierum. *Ibid.* 560 In diversis speciebus..videlicet..anys Comfett, et Madryam, vijs. iiijd. **1390–1** *Earl Derby's Exped.* (Camden) 19 Pro ijlb. ginger madrean, ijs. iiijd. *a* **1400** in Henslow *Med. Wks. 14th C.* (1899) 122 To make conserue of madrian.

madregal ('mædrɪgæl). Also med-. [Of unknown origin.] A fish of the genus *Seriola*.

1884 G. B. Goode etc. *Nat. Hist. Aquatic Anim.* 331 *Seriola fasciata*, This fish, called in Cuba the 'Medregal' and in Bermuda the 'Bonito', has been observed in South Florida. **1896** Jordan & Evermann *Fishes N. & Mid. Amer.* 904 (*Bull. U.S. Nat. Mus.* No. 47) *Seriola fasciata* (Medregal). *Ibid.* 905 *Seriola falcata*..(Madregal: 'Rock Salmon'.)

madre-perl. *rare*$^{-1}$. [ad. It. *madreperla*, f. *madre* mother + *perla* PEARL.] Mother-of-pearl.

1878 Longf. *Kéramos* 175 Nor less Maestro Giorgio shines With madre-perl and golden lines Of arabesques.

madreporacean (ˌmædrɪpɒˈreɪʃən). *Zool.* [f. mod.L. *Madreporacea*, f. *Madrepora*: see -ACEAN.] A coral of the group *Madreporacea* or *Madreporaria*.

1878 *Encycl. Brit.* VI. 380/1 In the great coralliferous deposits of the Carboniferous, again, no representative of the group [*Perforata*] is known, save the single genus *Palæacis*, which appears to be a *Madreporacean*.

madreporarian (ˌmædrɪpɔəˈrɛərɪən), *a.* and *sb.* *Zool.* [f. mod.L. *Madreporāria* (f. *Madrepora* MADREPORE) + -AN.]

A. *adj.* Pertaining to the group *Madreporaria* (the madrepores and related corals). B. *sb.* A coral of this group.

1881 *Athenæum* 6 Aug. 181/1 The true or Madreporarian corals. **1893** G. Brook (*title*), Catalogue of the Madreporarian Corals in the British Museum.

madrepore ('mædrɪpɔə(r)). [ad. mod.L. *madrepora* or F. *madrépore* (1710), ad. It. *madrepora*.

The Italian naturalist Ferrante Imperato (*Hist. Nat.*, 1599) uses *poro* as a name for 'a kind of vegetable the substance of which resembles that of coral, but differs in being porous'. He evidently regarded this word as identical with the ordinary It. *poro*, ad. L. *porus* PORE *sb.*; but perh. it really represented late L. *pōrus*, a. Gr. πῶρος calcareous stone, stalactite. Among the species of 'poro' he enumerates *millepora*, *frondipora*, and 'those plants by some called madrepores (here *madripore*, but elsewhere *madrepora* occurs), which are tubular growths, issuing from a common stem, and attached together at their roots, so that they resemble a honeycomb'. The word *madrepora* (which Imperato app. did not invent) seems to be f. *madre* mother + *poro*, the ending of the latter being changed to suit the gender of the sb. prefixed in apposition; on this view, the other words, *millepora*, *frondipora*, etc., must have been formed later in imitation of *madrepora*. A comparison of Imperato's woodcut of the 'madrepores' with those of the other species of *poro* seems to suggest that the prefix 'mother' may refer to the appearance of prolific growth characteristic of this 'plant'.]

1. Formerly applied loosely to most or all of the perforate corals (which, however, were not originally classed as corals); now usually in more restricted use, a polypidom of the genus *Madrepora* (or family *Madreporidæ*).

1751 Stack (tr. from French) in *Phil. Trans.* XLVII. 449 The several species of vermicular tubes found in the sea, the madrepores, millepores, lithophytons, corallines, sponges. *Ibid.* 460 They have denominated pora that class of them, which seem'd pierc'd with holes. Of these they found some, the holes of which were large; and these they call'd madrepora. **1802** Bingley *Anim. Biog.* (1813) III. 475 The Branching and Prickly Madrepore. **1832** Lyell *Princ. Geol.* II. 111 The madrepores or lamelliferous polyparia, are found in their fullest development only in the tropical seas of Polynesia and the West Indies. **1840** Blyth, etc. tr. *Cuvier's Anim. Kingd.* (1849) 658 When the Madrepore is branched, and the stars are confined to the extremities of each branch, it is the *Caryophyllia* of Lamouroux... *Madrepora*, or Madrepores properly so called, have the whole surface roughened by little stars. **1875** Huxley in *Encycl. Brit.* I. 130/2 In some madrepores the whole skeleton is reduced to a mere network of dense calcareous substance. **1882** *Cassell's Nat. Hist.* VI. 297 The common so-called Madrepore of the Devonshire coast, and those which are dredged up out of moderately deep water in the North Atlantic, are common examples of the genus Caryophyllia.

2. The animal producing the madrepore coral.

1841 Emerson *Address, Method Nature* Wks. (Bohn) II. 224 Nature turns off new firmaments..as fast as the madrepores make coral. **1875** Merivale *Gen. Hist. Rome* xxiii. (1877) 160 The..instinct with which the madrepore extends his empire over the bottom of the ocean.

3. Limestone composed of fossil madrepores.

1809 Valentia *Voy.* III. 309 The houses in Jidda are far superior to those at Mocha. They are built of large blocks of very fine madrapore [*sic*].

4. *attrib.*, as ***madrepore coral, hole, island***; **madrepore marble**, = sense 3.

1866–7 Livingstone *Last Jrnls.* (1873) I. iv. 85 The yellow plains..look like yellow hæmatite with madrepore holes in it. **1869** tr. *Pouchet's Universe* (1871) 76 Twenty-six madrepore islands. **1876** Page *Adv. Text-Bk. Geol.* iii. 67 A branch of the common madrepore coral. **1879** *Cassell's Techn. Educ.* II. 87 Many blocks are almost entirely formed of fossil corals, and known as madrepore marbles.

madreporic (mædrɪˈpɒrɪk), *a.* [f. mod.L. *Madrepora* or MADREPORE + -IC.]

1. Pertaining or related to, consisting or characteristic of, madrepore coral.

1817 *Q. Rev.* XVII. 240 The madriporic [*sic*] productions which have been found to exist..above the present level of the sea. **1833** Lyell *Princ. Geol.* III. 133 Part of the madreporic rock has been converted into silex and calcedony. **1887** H. H. Howorth *Mammoth & Flood* 360 The madreporic calcareous deposits surrounding Havana.

2. The distinctive epithet of certain structures in echinoderms (***madreporic body, canal, plate, tubercle***), so called because perforated with small holes like a madrepore.

1861 Dana *Man. Geol.* 160 To one side of the dorsal centre..in the regular Echinoids, there is a small porous prominence on the shell, often called the madreporic body, from a degree of resemblance in structure to coral. **1862** Thomson in *Q. Jrnl. Microscop. Sci.* II. 139 The madreporic tubercle gradually increases in size and distinctness. **1870** Nicholson *Man. Zool.* 123 The madreporic canals and their tubercles depending freely from the circular canal into the perivisceral cavity. **1878** Bell *Gegenbaur's Comp. Anat.* 204 One of these [genital plates of the Desmosticha] is the madreporic plate.

madreporid (mædrɪˈpɔərɪd), *sb.* and *a.* *Zool.* [ad. mod.L. *Madreporidæ*, f. *madrepora*: see MADREPORE and -ID.] **a.** *sb.* An animal of the family *Madreporidæ*, including the genus *Madrepora*. **b.** *adj.* Pertaining to the *Madreporidæ*. Hence **madreˈporidan** *a.*, characteristic of the *Madreporidæ*.

1899 Bernard in *Jrnl. Linn. Soc., Zool.* XXVII. 130 Porites is..related to the Madreporids. *Ibid.* 141 An exclusively Madreporid origin. *Ibid.* 142 There is no reason why further growth should not simply enlarge it without necessarily running it into ancestral Madreporidan lines.

madreporiform (mædrɪˈpɔərɪfɔːm), *a.* [f. mod.L. *Madrepora* + -FORM.] Having the form or characters of madrepore coral; *spec.* = MADREPORIC 2.

1843 Forbes in *Proc. Berw. Nat. Club* II. No. 11. 79 Madreporiform tubercle nearer the margin than centre. **1870** Nicholson *Man. Zool.* 125 One of the genital plates is larger than the others, and supports a spongy tubercle, perforated by many minute apertures..and termed the 'madreporiform tubercle'. **1877** C. W. Thomson *Voy. Challenger* II. iv. 237.

madreporigenous (ˌmædrɪpɔəˈrɪdʒɪnəs), *a.* *rare.* *Zool.* [f. mod.L. *Madrepora* MADREPORE + -GENOUS.] Producing madrepore coral.

1847–9 Todd *Cycl. Anat.* IV. 33/1 Madreporigenous polypes can only exist at depths where they enjoy the influences of light and air.

madreporite (mædrɪˈpɔəraɪt). [f. MADREPORE + -ITE. Cf. G. *madreporit*, F. *madréporite*.]

1. *Palæont.* Fossil madrepore.

1828–32 in Webster. **1843** Humble *Dict. Geol.*, etc., *Madreporite.* 1. Fossil madrepore.

2. *Min.* A calcareous rock of columnar structure marked by radiated prismatic concretions.

1802–3 tr. *Pallas's Trav.* (1812) I. 147 Its cells and tubes extend, as is the case with mäandrites, or madreporites, in a parallel line from the surface. **1821** Ure *Dict. Chem.* s.v. *Limestone*, It [prismatic lucullite] was at one time called madreporite. **1839** *Penny Cycl.* XIV. 271/2 *Madreporite.*—Anthraconite; Columnar Carbonate of Lime.

3. *Zool.* The madreporic tubercle in echinoderms.

1877 Huxley *Anat. Inv. Anim.* ix. 554 The madreporic tubercle or madreporite. **1884** Sladen in *Q. Jrnl. Microscop. Sci.* XXIV. 31 The madreporite or water-pore in Asterids usually punctures a basal plate.

‖ **madrier** ('mædrɪə(r)). *Fortif.* [Fr.] (See quot. 1704.)

1704 J. Harris *Lex. Techn.*, *Madrier*, in Fortification, is a thick Plank arm'd with Plates of Iron, and having a Concavity sufficient to receive the Mouth of the Petard when charged, with which it is applied against a Gate, or any thing else that you design to break down. This term is also appropriated to certain flat Beams, which are fix'd at the bottom of a Moat, to support a Wall. There are also Madriers lined with Tin, which are cover'd with Earth, to serve as a Defence against Artificial Fires. **1758** J. Watson *Milit. Dict.* (ed. 5). **1826** Scott *Woodst.* xxxiii, The petard ..is secured with a thick..piece of plank, termed the madrier.

madrigal ('mædrɪgəl), *sb.* Also 6–7 -ale, -all. [ad. It. *madrigale* (whence Fr., Sp. *madrigal*).

The origin of the It. word is obscure. On the ground of the occurrence in early It. of the variant forms *madriale*, *mandriale* (cf. obs. Sp. *mandrial*, *mandrigal*), Diez (followed by most later etymologists) accepts Ménage's derivation from It. *mandria* herd, f. L. *mandra*, a. Gr. μάνδρα fold; the primitive sense according to this view would be 'pastoral song' (cf. quots. 1597, 1614 in 3).]

1. A short lyrical poem of amatory character; chiefly, a poem suitable for a musical setting such as is described below (see 2).

1588 (*title*) Mvsica Transalpina, Madrigales translated of foure, fiue, and sixe parts, chosen oute of diuers excellent Authors. *Ibid.* A ij, I had the hap to find in the hands of some of my good friends, certaine Italian Madrigales, translated most of them fiue yeeres agoe by a Gentleman for his priuate delight. **1621** Burton *Anat. Mel.* II. ii. vi. iii. (1651) 299 How to make Jigs, Sonnets, Madrigals in commendation of his Mistress. *a* **1637** B. Jonson *Underwoods* (1640) 209 He That chanc'd the lace, laid on a Smock, to see And straight-way spent a Sonnet; with that other That (in pure Madrigall) unto his Mother Commended the French-hood [etc.]. **1736** Sheridan in *Swift's Lett.* (1768) IV. 167, I know you love Alexandrines; for which reason I closed the above madrigal with one. I think it is of a very good proportion, which I hope you will set to musick. *a* **1771** Gray *Metrum* Wks. 1843 V. 250 Madrigals of Eight [lines], on Three Rhymes. Sir T. Wyatt. **1774** Warton *Hist. Eng. Poetry* (1840) III. 142 He [Clément Marot] was the inventor of the rondeau, and the restorer of the madrigal. **1888** *Murray's Mag.* July 43 Poetically speaking a madrigal may be defined as the shortest form of lyrical poetry.

2. *Mus.* A kind of part song for three or more voices (usually, five or six) characterized by adherence to an ecclesiastical mode, elaborate contrapuntal imitation, and the absence of instrumental accompaniment; also applied loosely to part songs or glees not bound by these conditions.

See *Encycl. Brit.* (ed. 9) XV. 192/1, XVII. 84/1.

1588 [see 1]. **1593** Nashe *Christ's T.* 34 b, Their merry-running Madrigals, and sportiue Base-bidding Roundelayes. **1594** Morley (*title*) Madrigalles to foure Voyces, the first Booke. **1597** —— *Introd. Mus.* 180 The light musicke hath beene of late more deepely diued into.. the best kind of it is termed Madrigal..it is a kinde of musicke made vpon songs and sonnets...As for the musicke it is next unto the Motet, the most artificial and to men of vnderstanding most delightfull. **1644** Milton *Areop.* (Arb.) 50 And who shall silence all the airs and madrigalls, that whisper softnes in chambers? **1674** Playford *Skill Mus.* I. 59 Your Madrigals or Fala's of five and six Parts, which were composed for Viols and Voices by many of our excellent English Authors, as Mr. Morley, Wilks, Wilbey, Ward, and others. **1789** Burney *Hist. Mus.* (ed. 2) III. ii. 201 The most chearful species of secular Music..was that of madrigals, a style of composition, that was brought to its highest degree of perfection about the latter end of the 16th century. **1811** L. M. Hawkins *C'tess & Gertr.* I. 31 A little club, where catches, glees, motets, and madrigals, with the canon 'Non nobis' *in finale*, were 'done' in plain correctness. **1879** E. Prout in Grove *Dict. Mus.* I. 306 The only difference between the canzona and the madrigal being that the former was less strict in style. **1879** J. Hullah *ibid.* 598 The glee differs from the madrigal..in its tonality, which is uniformly modern.

3. *transf.* and *fig.* A song, ditty.

1589 Greene *Menaphon* (Arb.) 25 If a wrinckle appeare in her brow, then our shepheard must put on his working day face, and frame nought but dolefull Madrigals of sorrowe. *a* **1593** Marlowe *Pass. Sheph. to his Love* ii, By shallow Rivers, to whose fals Melodious birds sing Madrigals. **1597** Middleton *Wisdom of Solomon* xvii. 16 The merry shepherd..Tuning sweet madrigals of harvest's joy. **1614** Sir W. Alexander *Alexis to Damon* in Drumm. of Hawth. *Poems*, Those Madrigals we song amidst our Flockes. **1634** Milton *Comus* 495 Thyrsis? Whose artful strains have oft delaid The huddling brook to hear his madrigal. *a* **1640** Jackson *Creed* x. xxiii. §8 Changing their late joyful hymns of Hosanna to the Son of David into sad madrigals of Crucifige, crucifige. **1800–24** Campbell *O'Connor's Child* iii, And oft amidst the lonely rocks She sings sweet madrigals. **1821** Clare *Vill. Minstr.* I. 178 Thrushes chant their madrigals. **1848** Dickens *Dombey* xli, Gentle Mr. Toots..hears the requiem of little Dombey on the waters, rising and falling in the lulls of their eternal madrigal in praise of Florence.

4. *attrib.* and *Comb.*

1611 Florio, *Madrigáli, Madriáli*, Madrigall songs. **1877** W. A. Barrett (*title*) English Glee and Madrigal Writers. **1880** Mackeson in *Grove's Dict. Mus.* II. 192 Founded in 1741 by John Immyns, a member of the Academy of Ancient Music, the Madrigal Society enjoys the distinction of being the oldest musical association in Europe. **1883** *Encycl. Brit.* XV. 192/1 The art of madrigal composition was never practised in Germany, and it died out in other countries early in the 17th century. **1888** J. A. F. Maitland in *Dict. Nat. Biog.* XVI. 327/1 The madrigal form as used by the Italians.

Hence **ˈmadrigal** *v.* (*rare*) *intr.*, to write, compose, or sing madrigals. Also with *it*.

1593 G. Harvey *Pierce's Super.* 48 When Elderton began to ballat, Gascoine to sonnet, Turberuile to madrigal, Drant to versify [etc.]. **1742** Jarvis *Quix.* II. lxviii. 272 Madrigal it as much as your worship pleases.

madrigalesque (mædrɪgəˈlɛsk), *a.* [f. MADRIGAL *sb.* + -ESQUE; cf. F. *madrigalesque* f. It. *madrigalesco*.] Having the features or characteristics of madrigals.

1911 *Encycl. Brit.* XVII. 295/2 Long afterwards we occasionally meet with the word again, when a 17th or 18th century composer sets to some kind of accompanied singing a poem of madrigalesque character. **1924** W. H. Hadow *Music* iv. 99 A pleasant light comedy set to madrigalesque music with a real sense of characterization.

madrigalian (mædrɪˈgeɪlɪən), *a.* [f. MADRIGAL *sb.* + -IAN.] Pertaining to, consisting or characteristic of, or dealing with madrigals.

1848 (*title*) Madrigalian Feast, a collection of twenty Madrigals. **1869** Ouseley *Counterp.* xiv. 89 The old madrigalian composers. **1879** E. G. Monk in Grove *Dict. Mus.* I. 72 Anthems of the Madrigalian era. **1882** *Athenæum* No. 2854. 58 The English madrigalian writers being represented solely by a few songs and unimportant pieces.

madrigalist ('mædrɪgəlɪst). [f. MADRIGAL *sb.* + -IST.] A writer or composer of madrigals.

1789 Burney *Hist. Mus.* III. 123 The best madrigalists of our country. **1888** J. A. F. Maitland in *Dict. Nat. Biog.* XVI. 328/1 In the next few years [after 1596] nearly all the masterpieces of the English madrigalists were issued.

'madrigaller. [f. MADRIGAL *v.* + -ER¹.] = prec.
a **1704** T. BROWN *Lett. Dead to Living* II. (1707) 33 Sonniters, Songsters, Satyrists, Panegyrists, Madrigallers. **1710** WYCHERLEY in *Pope's Lett.* (1735) I. 46 No Madrigaller can entertain the Head, unless he pleases the Ear.

madrilene (mædrɪ'liːn, -'lɛn), *sb.* Also **madrilène**. [ad. F. (*consommé à la*) *madrilène*, f. Sp. *Madrileño, -leña* of Madrid.] A clear soup which is usually served cold (see quot. 1907).
1907 G. A. ESCOFFIER *Guide Mod. Cookery* xiii. 224 *Consommé a la madriléne*. Add four oz. of raw tomato and one oz. of capsicum to the consommé per every quart of the latter. Mix these ingredients with the clarification, and serve as cold as possible. **1931** J. BERJANE *French Dishes for Eng. Tables* i. 13 Consommé Froid aux Tomates, or Madrilène. **1952** S. KAUFFMANN *Philanderer* (1953) xi. 183 He found a lot of food in the icebox and had fixed some madrilène and a big salad and some fruit cup by the time she arrived. **1955** E. BOWEN *World of Love* v. 96 Terence.. began to spoon up liquidly-jellied madrilene. **1956** A. L. SIMON *Wine & Food Menu Bk.* 182 Consommé madrilène..should be rather highly seasoned and its colour should be not more than just a maiden's blushing pink. **1964** A. LAUNAY *Caviare & After* 135 *Madrilène (à la Madrilène)*, dishes flavoured with tomato juice or clear soups flavoured with tomato juice and usually served chilled.

Madrilenian (mædrɪ'liːnɪən), *a.* and *sb.* Also **Madrileñan, Madrilene, Madrilenean.** [f. Sp. *Madrileño, -leña* of Madrid, the capital of Spain.] **A.** *adj.* Of or pertaining to Madrid. **B.** *sb.* A native or inhabitant of Madrid.
1841 BORROW *Zincali* I. II. ii. 241 The Madrilenian Gypsy women are indefatigable in the pursuit of prey. **1846** R. FORD *Gatherings from Spain* xviii. 254 This bit of land was taken possession of by a worthy Madrilenian. **1873** BROWNING *Red Cott. Nt.-Cap* I. 42 Father Miranda, goldsmith of renown: By birth, a Madrilene. **1882** F. R. MCCLINTOCK *Holidays in Spain* 20 The carriages and horses of the Madrilenian high-life are as good as anything to be seen in Hyde Park. **1889** M. S. VAN DE VELDE *Cosmopolitan Recoll.* II. iv. 135 One of the unsavoury apartments is occupied by Señor de Castellan—a gentleman, a scholar, and an officer in the navy—who was once the most conspicuous figure in the Madrilene world of fashion. **1909** *Daily Chron.* 2 July 3/1 A far better opportunity..of seeing the inner life of a Madrilenean family of distinction. **1921** J. B. TREND *Pict. Mod. Spain* 65 Some critics have accused Baroja of distorting the Madrileñan character. **1957** A. MACNAB *Bulls of Iberia* xii. 129 Vicente Pastor... A Madrilenian born and bred,..had the dry, dominating, Castilian style in the ring. **1972** *Times* 11 May (Spain Suppl.) p. vii/2 Madrilenians take their bullfighting seriously. **1974** *Times* 2 May 17/2 Madrid's residents are crowded... Few Madrilenians live in one-family homes.

Madrileño (madri'leɲo). Fem. **Madrileña** (-'leɲa). [Sp.] = MADRILENIAN *sb.*
1832 E. C. WINES *Two Yrs. in Navy* (1833) I. x. 307 The tragedian was a *Madrileno*, as nearly all the actors on the Spanish stage are. **1866** MRS. W. P. BYRNE *Cosas de España* I. viii. 180 The Madrileños and Madrileñas were already sunning themselves in the bright morning air. **1903** L. WILLIAMS *Toledo & Madrid* II. i. 117 Both were *Madrileños*, and taught the sciences at Toledo and Granada. **1932** E. HEMINGWAY *Death in Afternoon* v. 50 Madrileños love the climate. **1943** E. A. PEERS *Spain in Eclipse* I. iv. 85 'Han pasado, han pasado..' shouted crowds of Nationalist Madrileños. **1950** G. BRENAN *Face of Spain* v. 101 Mr. Washbrook is a New Englander.. his wife is a handsome and vigorous Madrileña. **1965** C. D. EBY *Siege of Alcázar* (1966) i. 28 Swarms of Madrileños of the lower classes were arguing along the curbs. **1975** *Times* 19 Apr. 12/4 Do as the Madrileños do: punctuate your perambulations at the various bars.

‖**madroño** (ma'droɲo). Also **madrona, madrone.** [Sp.] A handsome evergreen tree of western North America, *Arbutus Menziesii*, having a very hard wood and bearing yellow berries. Also *attrib.*
1850 B. TAYLOR *Eldorado* xiii. (1862) 130 Clumps of the madrono—a native evergreen,..filled the ravines. **1882** J. HAWTHORNE *Fort. Fool* I. xxvi, The whisper of the breeze in the madroño. **1883** STEVENSON *Silverado Sq.* 71 Woods of oak and madrona, dotted with enormous pines. **1888** *Amer. Humor.* 5 May 12/1 Here and there a madrona tree grows, with its bark peeling off in its own peculiar way, leaving the tree bright red and as smooth as satin.
Comb. **1900** R. KIPLING *From Sea to Sea* xxvi, There were the pines and the madrone-clad hills.

madryam, -an, var. forms of MADREAN *Obs.*

†**'madship.** *Obs.* In 3 **mad-, med-, meadschipe.** [f. MAD *a.* + -SHIP.] Madness.
a **1225** *Leg. Kath.* 327 Hwat is mare madschipe þen for to leuen on him & seggen þ he is Godes Sune? *c* **1230** *Hali Meid.* 52 Ha is..mare amead, ȝef ha mei, þen is meadschipe seolf.

madstone ('mædstəʊn). *U.S.* [f. MAD *a.* used subst. + STONE *sb.*] A stone supposed to have the power of allaying or curing the madness caused by the bite of a 'mad' animal.
1864 *Round Table* 18 June 2/2 We are not so ready with an explanation of the 'mad-stone' used to obviate ill effects from the bites of rabid animals. **1888** *Boston* (Mass.) *Jrnl.* 9 Aug. 2/4 The Orlando (Fla.) Record tells a remarkable story of the effects of a madstone in a case of snakebite.

Madura ('mædʊrə). The name of a district of Madras, used *attrib.* in **Madura foot**, a disease of the foot common in Madura and other parts of India; = MYCETOMA. Also ***Madura disease.***
1863 W. T. FOX *Skin Dis. Parasitic Orig.* 15 In the Transactions of the Medical and Physical Society of Bombay for 1860, is a description by Dr. H. V. Carter, of a disease occurring in many parts of India, called variously 'Ulcus grave', 'Morbus tuberculosis pedis', 'Madura foot', 'Podelkoma', 'Mycetoma'. **1868** J. H. NELSON *Madura Country* I. iv. 91 Its classical name is *morbus pedis entophyticus*; but it is better known in this District by the name of 'the Madura foot'. **1871** BRISTOWE in *Trans. Pathol. Soc. Lond.* XXII. 326 The fungus of the Madura foot. **1874** *Q. Jrnl. Microscop. Sci.* XIV. 263 On the Etiology of Madura-foot.

Madurese (mædjʊ'riːz), *a.* and *sb.* [f. *Madur(a* + -ESE.] **A.** *adj.* Of or belonging to Madura, an island lying off the north-east coast of Java. **B.** *sb.* **a.** A native or inhabitant of Madura. **b.** The Austronesian language of Madura. Also **Ma'duran.**
1817 T. S. RAFFLES *Hist. Java* I. ii. 59 The Madurese.. display a more martial and independent air..than the natives of Java. *Ibid.* viii. 359 In the provinces east of Surabáya, the language partakes much of the Madurese. **1853** J. R. LOGAN in *Jrnl. Indian Archipelago* VII. 33 Anam heads are common in eastern Java and especially amongst the..Madurans. **1878** R. N. CUST *Sk. Mod. Lang. E. Indies* ix. 137 The Javanese is the chief Language of the island of Java... Its Character..is used by the Sundanese, Balinese, Madurese, and the people of Lombok. *Ibid.* 138 The Madurese..has one Dialect, the Sumanap. **1880** *Encycl. Brit.* XIII. 607/1 The limits of the Madurese area are not so easily given. **1933** L. BLOOMFIELD *Lang.* iv. 71 The languages of the great islands of the East, such as.. Maduran. **1969** *Language* XLV. 685 Although there is still much of Madurese morphology which requires further description, this study goes far beyond anything done for Madurese heretofore.

maduro (ma'duro). [Sp., = ripe, MATURE *a.*] A dark-coloured cigar.
1889 L. FRIEDLANDER *Tobacconist* (ed. 5) 28 M..Maduro—very dark brown. **1908** S. FORD *Side-Stepping with Shorty* vii. 106 The spots of him that you could see..was the colour of a twenty-cent maduro cigar. **1939** C. GRAVES *Cigars & Man* 16 The two remaining darker shades, Colorado-Maduro and Maduro are seldom met with in England. **1957** C. MACKENZIE *Sublime Tobacco* xiv. 240 '1 pound full Cabañas'... These may have been Maduro, the darkest of all, which are never seen to-day.

maduromycosis (,mædʊrəʊmaɪ'kəʊsɪs). *Path.* [mod.L., f. MADUR(A + -O + MYCOSIS.] A chronic destructive infection of the foot (rarely of other parts) that is accompanied by many discharging sinuses and is caused by various actinomycetes and fungi; also called *Madura foot* when appropriate.
1916 CHALMERS & ARCHIBALD in *Ann. Trop. Med. & Parasitol.* X. 170 But confusion may arise between the terms 'Mycetoma' and 'True Mycetoma', and, therefore..we suggest the word 'Maduromycosis' instead of True Mycetoma. **1937** *Nature* 27 Feb. 377/2 Maduromycosis, a fungus disease affecting the legs of human beings. **1961** R. D. BAKER *Essent. Path.* ix. 213 Maduromycosis or mycetoma is an infection of an extremity, usually the lower, as the result of a puncture wound.

'madwoman. [f. MAD *a.* + WOMAN, after MADMAN.] An insane woman.
1622 T. SCOTT *Belg. Pismire* 15, I remember a witty mad-woman..told a friend of hers [etc.]. **1842** DICKENS *Amer. Notes* iii, The rest of the madwomen seemed to understand the joke perfectly. **1844** MARG. FULLER *Wom. in 19th C.* (1862) 105 She..will not be pitied as a mad-woman, nor shrunk from as unnatural.

madwort ('mædwɜːt). [Cf. quot. 1597; the name is perh. a transl. of L. *alyssum*, a. Gr. ἄλυσσον, f. ἀ- (privative particle) + λύσσα rabies.]
1. A herb of the genus *Alyssum.*
Britten and Holland (*Plant-n.*) consider Gerarde's 'madwort' to be of doubtful identity, and assign his 'German madwort' to the genus *Stachys* or *Sideritis.*
1597 GERARDE *Herbal* II. cxviii. 379 The Germaine Madwoort bringeth foorth from a fibrous roote, two broad, rough, and hoarie leaues; between which riseth vp a hoarie brittle stalke, diuided into sundrie small branches, whereupon do growe long, narrow leaues..; from the bosome of which leaues come foorth small roundles of purple flowers like those of the dead Nettle. *Ibid.* 380 Madwoort or Moonewort is called..of the Latines *Alyssum*: in English Galens Madwoort: of some Heale dog; and it hath the name thereof, bicause it is a present remedie for them that are bitten of a mad dog. **1611** COTGR., *Alysson*, the hearbe Madwort, Moonewort, heale dog. **1640** PARKINSON *Theatr. Bot.* 590 *Alyssum montanum Columnæ.* Mountaine Mad-wort of Columna. **1760** J. LEE *Introd. Bot.* App. 313 Mad-wort, *Alyssum.* **1861** MISS PRATT *Flower. Pl.* I. 105 Alyssum, which is the Mad-wort of the ancients, and the plants of which were supposed to allay anger.
2. The Trailing Catchweed, *Asperugo procumbens.* (Also called ***German madwort.***)
1760 J. LEE *Introd. Bot.* App. 318 German Mad-wort, *Asperugo.* **1806** GALPINE *Brit. Bot.* 79 *Asperugo*, Madwort.

madyn(e, -ynne, obs. forms of MAIDEN.

mae (mɛː), *v. dial.* [Onomatopœic. Cf. *bae*, BA.] *intr.* Of a lamb: To utter its peculiar cry.
1728 RAMSAY *Robert, Richy, & Sandy* 124 While ewes shall bleat, and little lambkins mae.

mae, variant of MO, more.

mæander, etc.: see MEANDER, etc.

Mæcenas (miː'siːnæs). Pl. **Mæcenases,** †**Mæcenates** (-eɪtiːz). Also 6–7 **Mecenas,** 6– *erron.* **Mecænas.** The name of a Roman knight, the friend of Augustus and the patron of Horace and Virgil. Hence used for: A generous patron of literature or art; † occas. *gen.* a patron.
c **1561** VERON *Free-will* 7 This my rude labor, whiche..I offer unto youre honoure, as unto the Mecenas and patron of all godlye learninge. **1590** SPENSER *F.Q.* Verses addr. to Noblemen, This lowly Muse,..Flies for like aide unto your Patronage, That are the great Mecænas of this age. **1597** MORLEY *Introd. Mus.* III. 179 The composers of musick who otherwise would follow the depth of their skill,..are compelled for lacke of mæcenates to put on another humor. **1611** CORYAT *Crudities* Ep. Ded., My illustrious Mecænas Sir Edward Philips Master of the Rolles. *c* **1620** T. ROBINSON *Mary Magdalene* Ded. 105 Yet some Mœcenases this age hath left vs. **1663** GERBIER *Counsel* b viij b, A Mecenas to all vertues. **1711** SHAFTESB. *Charact.* (1737) I. 216 The Muses..., with or without their Mæcenas's, will grow in credit and esteem. **1779** SHERIDAN *Critic* I. i, Are you not called..a mock Mæcenas to second-hand Authors? **1812** L. HUNT in *Examiner* 14 Dec. 787/2 This Mecænas of the Age. **1827** LYTTON *Pelham* xlvi, See what it is to furnish a house differently from other people; one becomes a *bel esprit*, and a Mæcænas, immediately. **1875** ESCOTT in *Belgravia* XXV. 80 The Mæcenas of the last century did influence literature and art; the Mæcenas of to-day cannot.
Hence **Mæ'cenas** *v. trans.*, to act as a patron to. **Mæ'cenasship,** the position of a Mæcenas.
1832 CARLYLE *Ess.* (1872) IV. 101 Neither..was the new way of Bookseller Mecænasship worthless. **1837** MARRYAT *Olla Podr.* xxx, Literary men are not *Mæcenased* by..the.. aristocracy.

†**Mæ'cenatism.** *Obs. rare*⁻¹. [f. *Mæcēnāt-*, MÆCENAS + -ISM.] Patronage.
1606 BIRNIE *Kirk-Buriall* Ded., I strong-hold myself under your Marqueships Mecenatisme.

maeht, obs. form of MIGHT.

mael(e, Sc. form of MOLE (spot).

maelstrom ('meɪlstrəm). Also 7 [**malestrand,**] **male stream,** 8 **malestrom,** 9 **maelström,** and in Ger. form **mahlstrom.** [a. early mod.Du. *maelstrom* (now *maalstroom*), whirlpool, f. *malen* to grind, also to whirl round + *stroom* stream.
The use of *maelstrom* as a proper name (also in Fr.) seems to come from Du. maps, e.g. that in Mercator's *Atlas* (1595). Dutch philologists are of opinion that the word is native. It is true that it is found in all the mod. Scandinavian langs. as a common noun, but it is purely literary, and Danish scholars regard it as adopted from Du. or LG. The earliest known instance of Da. *malstrøm* (formerly also written *malestrøm*) occurs in 1673 in Debes *Færoa reserata*, the author of which was a pastor in the Færöe Islands. Cf. Norw. dial. *malstraum* (admitted by Aasen to be 'little used', which prob. means that he had never heard it in actual popular use), Sw. *malström*, Færoic *mal(u)streymur* (Hammershaimb *Færøsk Anthologi*, Glossary; the vb. *mala* in Færoic means 'to grind', 'to whirl round').
The form *Malestrand* in quot. *c* 1560 can only be a blunder; probably Jenkinson hearing the name *Malestrøm* confused it with the name of Malestrand (? meaning 'pebbly shore'), now Marstrand, in South Sweden.]
A famous whirlpool in the Arctic Ocean on the west coast of Norway, formerly supposed to suck in and destroy all vessels within a long radius. Also *transf.* a great whirlpool.
[*c* **1560** A. JENKINSON in *Hakluyt's Voy.* (1589) 334 There is between the said Rost Islands, and Lofoote, a whirle poole, called Malestrand, which..maketh such a terrible noise, that it shaketh the rings in the doores of the inhabitants houses of the said Islands, ten miles of.] **1682** R. BURTON *Wond. Curios.* (1684) 229 Between the coast of Cathness and Orkney is a dreadful Frith or Gulf, in the North end of which, by reason of the meeting of 9 contrary Tides or Currents, is a Male Stream or great Whirlpool. **1701** C. WOLLEY *Jrnl. New York* (1860) 47 A dangerous Current,..as dangerous and as unaccountable as the Norway Whirl-Pool or Mael-strom. **1755** tr. *Pontoppidan's Nat. Hist. Norway* I. 77 There is another kind of current.. in the sea of Norway,..namely the Malestrom, or Moskoestrom [orig. 1752 *den vidtbkiendte Male-strøm eller Moske-strøm*],..near the island Moskoe. *a* **1844** POE (*title*) A descent into the Maelström. **1856** W. E. AYTOUN *Bothwell* (1857) 56 And if a ship should chance to pass within the maelstrom's sweep. **1860** MISS BRADDON *Trail Serpent* I. i, Every gutter in every one of these streets was a little Niagara, with a maelstrom at the corner.
b. *fig.*
1831 CARLYLE *Sart. Res.* I. iv. (1858) 19 Some single billow in that vast World-Mahlstrom of Humour. **1854** J. S. C. ABBOTT *Napoleon* (1855) II. iv. 69 An accumulated mass, in one wild maelstrom of affrighted men, struggling in frantic eddies. **1883** *Harper's Mag.* July 956/1 In the wild and glittering maelstrom of luxury and extravagance.

maemae, var. MAIMAI.

mænad ('miːnæd). [ad. L. *Mænad-*, *Mænăs*, a. Gr. Μαιναδ-, Μαινάς, f. μαίν-εσθαι to rave.] A Bacchante.
1579 E. K. *Gloss. Spenser's Sheph. Cal.* Oct. 111 The Mænades (that is Bacchus franticke priestes). *c* **1620** T. ROBINSON *Mary Magdalene* 795 Like to yᵉ Menades yᵗ Euhœ crie. **1638–48** G. DANIEL *Eclog* iii. 153 The Women.. Like yauling Mænades, their Ioo's send To the full-fraught, lest drinking there should end. **1820** SHELLEY *Ode Liberty* vii, Like a wolf-cub from a Cadmæan Mænad, She drew the milk of greatness. **1882** *Athenæum* 7 Jan. 22/2 Another

[nymph], furious as a mænad, is about to whirl on high the headless body of a kid.

Hence **mæ'nadic** *a.*, characteristic of a Mænad; resembling a Mænad, infuriated.

1830 CARLYLE *Misc.* (1872) III. 2 Phallophori and Mænadic women. 1830 *Fraser's Mag.* I. 587 There is a clapping of hands, and shouts of Mænadic glorification.

maende, obs. form of MEND.

mæne: see MEAN, MENE.

maenial(l, obs. form of MENIAL.

maer, mære, obs. forms of MORE, MERE.

maes, maesse, obs. forms of MAIZE, MASS.

maest, obs. form of MOST.

mæstive, variant of MESTIVE.

‖**maestoso** (maes'toso). *Mus.* [It. = majestic.] A direction denoting that a composition is to be executed majestically.

1724 *Expl. For. Words Music, Maestoso*, or *Maestuoso*. 1815 *Europ. Mag.* LXVIII. 154 Var. 8 (*Maestoso*) in minor.

maëstral, variant of MISTRAL.

maestrale (maɪ'strɑːleɪ). Also **maestral, maestro** ('maɪstrəʊ). [It. *maestrale*, f. L. *magistrāl-is*, f. *magister* MASTER *sb.*¹] The name of a wind experienced in the Mediterranean (see quot. 1944). Cf. MISTRAL.

1766, 1813 [see MISTRAL]. 1902 *Encycl. Brit.* XXX. 622/1 In summer a north-west 'trade' wind, the Maestro occurs in the Adriatic. 1920 *19th Cent.* Aug. 288 The waves..on the beaches of Corfu..come in with a pleasant surge when the northerly *maestro* is blowing. 1944 *Italy* (Geogr. Handbk. Ser. B.R. 517, Admiralty, Naval Intelligence Div.) I. v. 415 The *maestro* (or *maestrale*), although bearing the same name as the mistral of the Rhône valley, is not to be confused with it. The name is given to NW. winds in the Adriatic, and NW., N., and NE. winds in Liguria and Tuscany. In the west the maestrale is a winter wind (Genoa), but is less cold and dry than the mistral proper. In the Adriatic it is a summer wind. 1967 D. S. WALKER *Geogr. Italy* (ed. 2) iii. 224 The influence of persistent winds (especially the *maestrale*) is apparent in the tortured shapes of the trees.

‖**maestria** (maes'tria). [It.] Skill, mastery.

1876 STAINER & BARRETT *Dict. Mus. Terms* 279/1 *Maestria* (It.), skill, address, authority. 1921 R. FRY *Let.* 15 Mar. (1972) II. 505 He [*sc.* Derain]'s becoming more and more Baroque... It may be dangerous with his incredible *maestria*. 1928 *Daily Express* 16 Jan. 4 Sir Charles..can occasionally be persuaded to render the 'Volga Boatmen's Song', which he sings with incomparable maestria. 1938 *Daily Tel.* 25 July 9/1 While admiring the maestria of this piece of writing by Mr. Shaw I find in it..several inaccuracies. 1955 TAYLOR & KERR *Mus. Lovers' Encycl.* 633/1 Maëstria.

Maestrichtian (mɑː'strɪçtɪən), *a.* *Geol.* Also **Maastrichtian.** [ad. F. *maestrichtien* (A. Dumont 1849, in *Bull. de l'Acad. R. d. Sci.*, etc., *de Belgique* XVI. II. 360), f. *Maestricht* (now *Maastricht*), the name of a city in SE. Holland; see -IAN.] Of, pertaining to, or designating a division of the Upper Cretaceous in Europe that is now regarded as a stage lying next below the Danian. Also *absol.*

1885 A. GEIKIE *Text-bk. Geol.* (ed. 2) 834 In the Cotentin, a limestone with *Baculites anceps, Scaphites constrictus*, and other fossils has been paralleled with the Maestricht chalk (Maestrichtian sub-stage). 1931 GREGORY & BARRETT *Gen. Stratigr.* xi. 171 The Senonian deposits in the N.E. of France and Belgium were those of a shallow sea, such as the phosphatic chalks of the Campanian and the limestone 'tuffau' of the Maastrichtian. 1967 D. H. RAYNER *Stratigr. Brit. Isles* x. 337 Maastrichtian chalk is rare in Britain but small remnants of the lower zone (*Belemnitella lanceolata*) are known from the Norfolk coast and north-eastern Antrim. 1971 *Nature* 19 Feb. 553/2 Although disputed by some, the latest Cretaceous and earliest Tertiary (Maestrichtian and Danian stages) have generally been recognized as a brief interval during which many organisms underwent a severe attenuation in diversity or became extinct. 1975 *Ibid.* 6 Mar. 50/1 By about 70 Myr ago (late Cretaceous: Maastrichtian) there seems to have been a gap large enough to have prevented east-west migration of marine reef colonies.

maestriss, obs. Sc. form of MISTRESS.

‖**maestro** (ma'ɛstro, 'maɪstrəʊ). Pl. **maestri, maestros.** [It. = 'master'.] **a.** A master in music; a great musical composer, teacher, or conductor.

1797 MRS. RADCLIFFE *Italian* vii, He might be a ghost, by his silence, for aught I know, Maestro. 1845 E. HOLMES *Mozart* 79 The archduke and his bride..inclined their heads from their box and applauded the maestro. 1884 F. M. CRAWFORD *Rom. Singer* I. 22, I went to the Maestro's house and sat for two hours listening to the singing. 1891 *Speaker* 2 May 528/1 The performance of some musical maestro on an instrument that almost seems part of himself. 1947 *Penguin Music Mag.* IV. 44 The maestros on the rostrum. 1952 J. K. SHERMAN (*title*) Music and maestros.

b. *transf.* A master or leader in any art, profession, etc.

1938 M. ALLINGHAM *Fashion in Shrouds* xv. 238 The old *maestro* allows beautiful suspect to slip through nicotine-stained fingers. 1942 BERREY & VAN DEN BARK *Amer. Thes. Slang* § 629 Coach; trainer; manager..*maestro*. 1945 R. CHANDLER in *Atlantic Monthly* Nov. 51/3 There is no reason to expect from the anonymous toilers of the screen a quality which we are very obviously not getting from..the sulky maestri of the little magazines. 1945 S. LEWIS *Cass Timberlane* (1946) xix. 114 Reverence for jazz and familiarity with such contemporary maestri as Benny Goodman and Pee-wee Russell. 1952 PHILLIPS & REESE *Bridge with Mr. Playbetter* xxix. 123 'Perhaps, if you lead a low Diamond originally,' answered the maestro. 1953 *Proc. Geologists' Assoc.* LXIV. 139 That maestro of Highland tectonics, Sir Edward Bailey. 1958 *Listener* 2 Oct. 537/3 The 'Ted Ray Show' came back with the maestro in full hilarity. 1960 V. NABOKOV *Invitation to Beheading* xix. 193 We beseech you, be calm, maestro. If something was not just right, it was the result of an oversight. 1964 L. NKOSI *Rhythm of Violence* 64, I deman' an explanation why my bottle is being impounded... Ah, the maestro needed a shot in the arm too! 1971 *Sunday Nation* (Nairobi) 11 Apr. 26/1 Anyone willing to part with a work of the maestro is asked to contact the Society.

maestro: see MAESTRALE.

‖**maestro di cappella** (ma'ɛstro di kap'pɛlla, 'maɪstrəʊ —). *Mus.* Also **maestro di capella.** [It., lit. 'master of the chapel'.] = *kapellmeister* (see KAPELLE); choir-master; musical director, conductor.

1724 *Short Explication Foreign Words in Musick Bks.* 44 *Maestro*, is Master. Thus, *Maestro de capella*, is Master of the Chapel Musick or Master of Musick only, meaning thereby one of the first Rank. 1774 'J. COLLIER' *Mus. Trav.* 16 All the musicians of Britain..together with every *Maestro di Capella* in Italy. 1880 J. H. SHORTHOUSE *John Inglesant* xxiii. 316 The elder, whose name was Giacomo Andria, was maestro di capella of one of the churches. 1947 C. GRAY *Contingencies* 98 In 1850, Raimondi became *maestro di cappella* at St. Peter's in Rome. 1964 *Conc. Oxf. Dict. Opera* 238/2 The *Maestro di cappella* was orig. the equivalent of the German Kapellmeister..but today the term is used only with reference to religious music.

Maeterlinckian (meɪtə'lɪŋkɪən, 'mɑːtə -), *a.* [f. *Maeterlinck* (see below) + -IAN.] Of, pertaining to, or having the characteristics of Maurice Maeterlinck, Belgian author (1862–1949), or his writings.

1895 G. B. SHAW *Our Theatres in Nineties* (1932) I. 189 The Maeterlinckian treatment of Pelléas et Mélisande. 1904 W. L. COURTNEY *Devel. M. Maeterlinck* 35 It is hardly a characteristic example of the Maeterlinckian drama. 1909 *Times Lit. Suppl.* 22 Apr. 150/2 Conflicting with the spirit of mystery and fascinating Maeterlinckian unreality. 1933 *Ibid.* 5 Oct. 657/2 The old haunted house of the Harveys on the Quay, with its Maeterlinckian terrors for a sensitively imaginative child. 1974 P. DE VRIES *Glory of Hummingbird* (1975) xiii. 173 On the one hand, flocks of Maeterlinckian bluebirds fresh descended from heaven; on the other, a passel of pubescent near-villains queuing up for release from hell.

Mae West (meɪ wɛst). *slang* (orig. *R.A.F.*). [f. the professional name of an American film actress and entertainer (1892–1980), with reference to her curvaceous figure (see quot. 1941).] An inflatable life-jacket, orig. issued to R.A.F. men in the war of 1939–45, later in more general use where the risk of drowning is involved.

1940 *Reader's Digest* May 31/2 The aviators have adopted amusing novelties. For example..*Mae West* for a life jacket. 1941 *N.Y. Times Mag.* 27 July 21/2 One can understand.. why an airman's life-belt should be a 'Mae-West'. It..gives the wearer a somewhat feminine figure. 1942 *R.A.F. Jrnl.* 16 May 33 A second more determined pull opened it [*sc.* the parachute] at about 400–500 feet. The pilot did not inflate his Mae West. 1945 *Daily Mirror* 15 Aug. 3/3 McGarvey discarded his Mae West and swam to the vessel. 1952 T. J. MULVEY *These are your Sons* v. 100 When you are flying over the hills of Korea, Mae Wests are a poor substitute for parachutes. 1958 M. DICKENS *Man Overboard* x. 152 I'm glad I wasn't in your submarine, Ben. I'd have worn a Mae West all the time. 1971 *Daily Tel.* 16 Jan. 21/8 He was burned about the face and floated in his 'Mae West' until rescued by the Air-Sea Rescue Service. 1974 *Times* 4 Sept. 1/8 One of them had a Mae West on with the words, 'Morning Cloud' written across it.

maez, obs. form of MAIZE.

ma fal (= *may fall*, perhaps): see MAY *v.*¹

‖**mafeesh** (mə'fiːʃ), *a.* and *int.* Also **mafish, mefeesh.** [ad. colloq. Eastern Arab. *mā fī-š* there is nothing.] (See quot. 1925.)

1855 R. F. BURTON *Pilgrimage to El-Medinah & Meccah* I. i. 11 When a little boy, presuming that the occasion might possibly open the hand of generosity, looked in my face and exclaimed 'Bakhshish', he obtained in reply 'Mafish'; which convinced the bystanders that the sheep-skin contained a real sheep. 1897 A. CONAN DOYLE *Tragedy of Korosko* (1898) viii. 225 'But what..about the three ladies?' The black soldier shrugged his shoulders. 'Mefeesh!' ['Mafeesh!', 1897 serial publ.] said he. 'One of them is old, and..there are plenty more women if we get back to Egypt.' 1916 C. J. DENNIS *Moods of Ginger Mick* (1918) 135 *Mafeesh*, finish; I am finished. 1919 W. H. DOWNING *Digger Dial.* 32 Mafish..,finish, finished. 1924 KIPLING *Debits & Credits* (1926) 318 As soon as he reached the place it was *mafeesh* with him, as usual... You never noticed him. *Ibid.* 320 House, two ricks an' stable *mafeesh*, the big glasshouse with every pane smashed. 1925 FRASER & GIBBONS *Soldier & Sailor Words* 150 *Mafeesh*, (*Arabic*). Dead. Done with. Finished. Used colloquially everywhere on Eastern Fronts. .. It had other meanings: 'I can't', 'I know', 'Get out', 'Go to hell', [etc.]. 1931 T. R. G. LYELL *Slang* 497 *Mafeesh*, old lad—nothing doing! I gave away the last of them a week ago.

†**mafey**, *int. Obs.* Also 5 mai-, mayfay, maffay, ma(f)fay, ma fa; maffeith, -feyth. [a. OF. *ma fei!* (mod.F. *ma foi!*) 'my faith': see FAY *sb.*¹] An asseveration, lit. = 'my faith!' Cf. MA FOI *int.*

c1374 CHAUCER *Troylus* III. 3 (52) Mafey þought he þus wole I sey. c1400 *Pride of Life* (Brandl 1898) 451 Nou, maifay, hit schal be sene. 1401 *Pol. Poems* (Rolls) II. 75 A, Iak, mafey, me merveilith moche of thin lewidheed! c1412 HOCCLEVE *De Reg. Princ.* 3283 Maffeith! your lif stood þere in iupartie. c1440 *Promp. Parv.* 319/2 Mafey, othe (*MS. S.* maffeyth), *medius fidius*. c1460 *Towneley Myst.* xxiii. 564 Ma-fay, I tell his lyfe is lorne.

maffaisour, maffia, var. ff. MALFEASOR, MAFIA.

maffick ('mæfɪk), *v.* [Back-formation from *mafficking* (i.e., the proper name '*Mafeking* treated jocularly as a gerund or pres. pple.).] *intr.* Originally used to designate the behaviour of the crowds (in London and other towns) that celebrated with uproarious rejoicings the relief of the British garrison besieged in Mafeking (17 May 1900). Hence *gen.* to indulge in extravagant demonstrations of exultation on occasions of national rejoicing. Hence **'mafficking** *vbl. sb.* and *ppl. a.*; **'mafficker**, one who 'mafficks'; **'maffick** *sb.*, an act of 'mafficking'.

The words appear to be confined to journalistic use; but we have a large number of examples from newspapers of all shades of political opinion.

1900 *Pall Mall G.* 21 May 2/2 We trust Cape Town..will 'maffick' to-day, if we may coin a word, as we at home did on Friday and Saturday. 1900 *Westm. Gaz.* 25 May 2/3 The feathers..are sold for a penny each to enable 'Mafficking' revellers to tickle other revellers' noses. 1902 *Daily Chron.* 9 July 6/5 We have no wish to advocate the hysteria of which the name is 'mafficking'. 1902 *Westm. Gaz.* 4 June 7/3 The Peace 'maffick' has not yet been completely worked off. 1902 *Times* 11 June 12/1 [The 'Merry Wives of Windsor'] is..'a pure anticipated cognition', as Shelley would have said, of the mafficking spirit. 1910 *Blackw. Mag.* July 9/2 The 'mafficker' may hereafter come within sight of the enemy.

†**'mafflard.** *Obs.* [f. MAFFLE *v.* + -ARD.] A stammering or blundering fool.

c1450 *Pol. Poems* (Rolls) II. 225 The churche of Chester, whiche crieth, alas! That to suche a mafflarde marryede she was.

maffle ('mæf(ə)l), *v.* *Obs.* exc. *dial.* Also 7 **maffell.** [Cf. early mod.Du. *maffelen* to move the jaws (Kilian). The Eng. word has a wide dialectal currency in several senses (see E.D.D.).]

1. *intr.* To stammer; to speak indistinctly, mumble. † Also with an obj.

1387 TREVISA *Higden* (Rolls) II. 91 ȝif Alfrede seiþ nay in þat, he wot nouȝt what he maffleþ. *Ibid.* V. 215. 1399 LANGL. *Rich. Redeles* IV. 63 Somme mafflid with þe mouþ and nyst what þey mente. 1565 COOPER *Thesaurus, Balbutio*, to maffle in the mouth, as not able to sounde his wordes. 1603 HOLLAND *Plutarch's Mor.* 34 Those disciples who..would needs stut, stammer and maffle as Aristotle did. 1623 COCKERAM, *Maffell*, to stammer. 1875 *Lanc. Gloss.*, *Maffle*, to hesitate, to falter, to stammer, to mumble.

2. To blunder, bungle; to delay, waste time.

1781 HUTTON *Tour to Caves*. 1837 [see MAFFLING *vbl. sb.*].

3. *trans.* To confuse, bewilder, muddle (see E.D.D. and MAFFLED *ppl. a.*).

Hence **'maffling** *vbl. sb.* and *ppl. a.*, **'mafflingly** *adv.* Also **'maffler**, one who 'maffles'.

1552 ELYOT *Dict.*, *Balbus*, that can not well pronounce wordes in speakyng, a mafflar. 1565 COOPER *Thesaurus*, *Balbe*, obscurely: mafflyingly: with no perfit sowne. 1577–87 HOLINSHED *Chron.* II. 13/1 It [Aqua Vitæ] keepeth ..the toong from lisping, the mouth from maffling. 1586 J. HOOKER *Hist. Irel.* in *Holinshed* II. 88/2 He deliuered his speeches by reason of his palseie, in such staggering and mafling wise, that [etc.]. 1603 HOLLAND *Plutarch's Mor.* 653 They..go too far in their commandements..who enjoine stutters, stammerers and mafflers to sing. 1608 TOPSELL *Serpents* 252 They make a maffeling with their mouth and stammer so that they cannot distinctly be understood. 1609 BIBLE (Douay) *Isa.* xxxii. 4 The tongue of mafflers shal speake readely and plaine. *Ibid.* xxxii. Comm., This prophecie of maffling or unperfect tongues, to speake readily, is fulfilled in the Church of Christ. 1611 COTGR., *Bredouillement*, a faultering, or maffling; an ill-fauoured speaking, imperfect pronunciation. 1837 CARLYLE *Let. to Margaret* 22 Jan. in Froude *Life* (1884) I. iv. 94 After much higgling and maffling, the printers have got fairly afloat.

maffled ('mæf(ə)ld), *ppl. a. dial.* [f. MAFFLE *v.* + -ED¹.] Confused, muddled.

1820 SOUTHEY *Lett.* (1856) III. 186 She was, what they call in the country, maffled; that is, confused in her intellect. 1845 DE QUINCEY *Coleridge & Opium-eating* Wks. 1859 XII. 92 The Westmorland people..expounded his condition to us by saying that he was 'maffled'; which word means 'perplexed in the extreme'. 1886 MRS. LYNN LINTON *Paston Carew* II. x. 211 She did not smell of drink, and was sober though decidedly maffled.

mafia (ma'fiːa, now usu. 'mæfɪə, 'mɑːfɪə). Also **maffia.** [Sicilian.] In Sicily, the spirit of hostility to the law and its ministers prevailing among a large portion of the population, and manifesting itself frequently in vindictive crimes; the body of those who share in this anti-legal spirit. In the U.S. and elsewhere, an organized secret society

existing for criminal purposes. Also *attrib.* and *transf.* Hence **maf(f)i'oso** (pl. **-osi**), **mafi'osa** (fem.), **'Mafiaist**, a member or supporter of the mafia; **'Mafiaism**, the doctrines or practices of the mafia.

1875 *Times* 9 June 5/4 The malevolent influence and oppression of the *Mafia* and the *Mafiosi*. **1902** *Encycl. Brit.* XXXI. 163/1 (art. *New Orleans*) He had been active in proceedings against certain Italians accused of crime, and it was popularly believed that his death was the work of a *maffia*, or sworn secret society. **1902** G. MOSCA *Ibid.* XXXII. 618/1 (art. *Sicily*) The Maffia is not, as is generally believed, one vast society of criminals, but is rather a sentiment akin to arrogance which imposes a special line of conduct upon persons affected by it... The *maffioso* considers it dishonourable to have recourse to lawful authority to obtain redress for a wrong or a crime committed against him. **1924** A. CHRISTIE *Poirot Investigates* iii. 92 Suddenly they learn that one of these secret societies, the Mafia, or the Camorra..is on their track. **1927** *Daily Tel.* 22 Nov. 7 Thuggism meant an end to human life; Mafiaism poisoned every department of it. **1948** *Oxf. Jun. Encycl.* I. 135/2 Through a secret society called the Mafia, they [*sc.* the Czechs and Slovaks] gave help to the Allies against the Austrians and Germans. **1948** E. L. IREY *Tax Dodgers* (1949) vii. 145 His gunmen shot the Mafiaists out of the top rung of the underworld. **1959** *Times Lit. Suppl.* 9 Oct. 575/1 Mr. Maxwell also prints statements by members of the ruling classes and outsiders: a nun, a priest, a semi-*mafioso* doctor, a Tuscan *carabiniere*. **1965** J. WAINWRIGHT *Death in Sleeping City* I. 75 She was born into the Mafia. She was a Mafiosa... He was a lousy Mafioso—because he wasn't all rotten. **1967** *Times* 28 Feb. (Canada Suppl.) 29 Their Mafia-conscious compatriots south of the border. **1967** *Listener* 20 Apr. 529/2 He [*sc.* J. F. Kennedy] was constantly personalizing the office he held, filling the White House with his 'Irish mafia',..extending the influence of the Kennedy court to cover the whole range of American cultural and intellectual activity. **1969** C. DRUMMOND *Odds on Death* v. 118 No law enforcement agency had ever learned to cope with *mafiosi*. **1970** *New Yorker* 3 Jan. 44 The composers' Mafia, with its dedication to atonality and the production of new noises, holds no terrors for him. **1970** E. TIDYMAN *Shaft* (1971) vi. 92 If a Mafia don was breaking his kid into the business today, he would break him in through the Harvard Business School. **1971** M. MCCARTHY *Birds of America* 263 I'm prepared for attacks, naturally, from the academic Mafia. **1971** P. ZIEGLER *King William IV* xiii. 162 It was the turn of the Ultra Tories. This mafia of malcontents..pledged themselves to destroy the Duke [of Wellington]. **1972** 'J. RIPLEY' *My Word you should have seen Us* 88 The F.B.I. know Joseph Colombo as a Capo Mafioso. **1973** *Guardian* 16 Feb. 13/8 British Brussels is..split on the issue of the TUC's participation in Europe. The Labour Party mafia is oversensitive about the TUC. **1974** *Sumter* (S. Carolina) *Daily Item* 24 Apr. 12A/4 Another top Mafioso, Aniello Dellacroce, just finished an income tax sentence in the Atlanta pen. A few days before his release, another Mafioso leader, Frank Valenti, was locked behind federal bars.

mafic ('mæfɪk), *a. Min.* [f. MA(GNESIUM + L. *f-errum* iron + -IC.] Pertaining to, containing, or designating the dark-coloured minerals of igneous rocks, which are predominantly ferromagnesian in character. Opp. FELSIC *a.*

1912 W. CROSS et al. in *Jrnl. Geol.* XX. 561 We suggest the term..*mafic* for the group of modal ferromagnesian minerals of all kinds. **1920** [see FEMIC *a.*]. **1926** [see ANKARAMITE]. **1969** *Nature* 20 Dec. 1153/1 The lavas are intruded by ultramafic and mafic bodies and dyke swarms. **1970** *Ibid.* 31 Oct. 413/1 The African rifts are sites of under-saturated, predominantly mafic volcanics erupted in comparatively small volume from single vents. **1971** I. G. GASS et al. *Understanding Earth* v. 83/1 The oceans, with their thin (about 5 km) mafic crust.

mafioso: see MAFIA.

mafish, var. MAFEESH *a.* and *int.*

‖**ma foi** (ma fwa), *int.* [Fr., lit. 'my faith'.] On, upon my word (see WORD *sb.* 15 a). Cf. †MAFEY *int.*

c **1400** *Brut* 17 'Ma foy,' quod þe fader, 'y may no more axen.' **1778** F. BURNEY *Evelina* I. xiv. 76 '*Ma foi*, Sir,' answered she, '..none of my acquaintance is in town.' **1791** J. LEARMONT *Poems* 143 Mafoy! ye'll dwindle to a den. **1842** BARHAM *Ingol. Leg.* Ser. II. *Black Mousquetaire*, Stay! I have it—ma foi! **1868** C. M. YONGE *Chaplet of Pearls* II. xxxvi. 159 [He] had the civility to give me a guide and an escort... *Ma foi*! I believe they were given to..take me by indirect roads. **1906** BARONESS ORCZY *I will Repay* xvii. 197 'A splendid combination, *ma foi*!' said Merlin. **1928** A. CHRISTIE *Mystery of Blue Train* xxvii. 221 This time, *ma foi*, I thought we had got him.

mafoo ('mɑːfuː). Also **ma-fu.** [ad. Chinese *ma-fu*, f. *ma* horse + *fu* servant, labourer.] A Chinese groom, stable-boy, or coachman.

1863 G. FLEMING *Trav. Mantchu Tartary* ii. 16 Ma-foo, as he was soon christened, from his occupation as horse-keeper. **1880** W. GILL *River of Golden Sand* II. viii. 310, I at first rode a hired pony, and my new Ma-Fu walked on in front leading the grey. **1890** BARRÈRE & LELAND *Dict. Slang* II. 37/2 *Mafoo* (pidgin), horse-boy, groom. **1924** *Blackw. Mag.* Feb. 232/2 Let them send word to the mafoo to have the ponies saddled. *Ibid.* Aug. 265/2 He borrowed Cantegril's famous two-horse barouche, all complete, with its variegated *mafoos*. **1939** 'A. BRIDGE' *Four-Part Setting* xxiii. 313 They dismounted and left the mafoos and ponies in an open grassy space.

mafortune: see MAY *v.*[1]

mag (mæg), *sb.*[1] *colloq.* [f. MAG *v.*] **a.** Chatter, talk. **b.** A chatterbox.

a. 1778 MME. D'ARBLAY *Diary* Sept., *Mrs. Thrale*: Oh, if you have any mag in you, we'll draw it out! **1875** MRS. LYNN LINTON *Patricia Kemball* II. iv. 78 Hold your mag on things you don't understand. **1885** E. C. SHARLAND *Ways Devonsh. Village* ii. 26 You go away for a while, my dear, and let me have a little mag with Emma.

b. 1892 F. ANSTEY *The Talking Horse*, etc. 46 'Alick does call me a "mag",' said Priscilla; 'but that's wrong, because I never speak without having something to say'.

Mag (mæg), *sb.*[2] Cf. MEG. [Playful shortening of the female name *Margaret*.]

1. Used as a personal name in various proverbial phrases. †***Mag('s tales***: nonsense, trifling. ***Mag's diversion*** (also *Meg's*: see MEG).

c **1410** LOVE *Bonavent. Mirr.* xxxix. 85 (Sherard MS.) [The Lollard] scorneth..suche miracles haldynge hem but as magges tales [*B.N.C. MS.* magge tales, *W. de W.* (eds. 1517–30) madde tales] and feyned illusiouns. **1834** M. G. DOWLING *Othello Travestie* I. iii, The galley slaves Are playing mag's diversion on the waves. [**1837** SOUTHEY *Doctor* IV. cxxv. 250 Who was Magg? and what was his diversion?] **1849** DICKENS in Forster *Life* (1872) II. xx. 432 Mag's Diversions. Being the personal history of Mr. Thomas Mag the Younger, Of Blunderstone House.

2. Used as a proper name for a magpie. Also as a common noun = MAGPIE.

1802 G. MONTAGU *Ornith. Dict.* (1833) 311. **18..** CLARE *Life & Rem.* (1873) 245 While mag's on her nest with her tail peeping out. **1885** SWAINSON *Prov. Names Birds*, Magpie (*Pica rustica*)... Familiar names. Mag, or Madge.

3. *Rifle-shooting.* = MAGPIE.

1895 *Pall Mall G.* 29 July 11/2 If Winans made a 'mag' with his first shot he would probably cease firing.

4. ***long-tailed mag*** (dial.): the Long-tailed Titmouse, *Acredula rosea*.

1851 MORRIS *Hist. Brit. Birds* I. 275.

mag (mæg), *sb.*[3] *slang.* Also **meg.** [Of obscure origin: cf. the synon. MAKE *sb.*] A halfpenny.

1781 G. PARKER *Life's Painter* 129 Mag is a halfpenny. *Ibid.* 161 Halfpenny—A meg. **1813** *Sporting Mag.* XLII. 219 Neither of these forsaken damsels had one single mag, or piece of any kind of coin. **1852** DICKENS *Bleak Ho.* xxiii, It can't be worth a mag to him. **1862** H. KINGSLEY *Ravenshoe* I. ix. 111 As long as he had a 'mag' to bless himself with, he would always be a lazy, useless humbug.

b. *Comb.* **'magflying** *vbl. sb.*, playing 'pitch and toss'; **'magflyer.**

1882 *Standard* 8 Aug. 3/7 There were usually three or four in a gang, one acting as the 'magflyer', the 'mag' being the coin, another as the caller of the odds or amounts, a third as treasurer. **1883** *Daily Tel.* 26 Mar. 2/8 (Farmer) Of the twenty-nine 'night-charges', by far the greater number were of..boys for mag flying, i.e., 'pitch and toss'.

mag (mæg), *sb.*[4], abbrev. of MAGAZINE (sense 5 b).

1801 WOLCOT (P. Pindar) *Tears & Smiles* Wks. 1812 V. 55 Who wrote in mags for hire. **1869** *Chamb. Jrnl.* 8 May 303/2 Why don't you fellows write something for the mags? **1888** JACOBI *Printer's Voc.*, *Mag*, an abbreviation very generally used by printers for 'magazine'.

mag (mæg), *sb.*[5] *Astr.* Also **mag.** (with point). Abbrev. of *magnitude(s)* (MAGNITUDE 3 a).

1840 *Mem. R. Astron. Soc.* XI. 283 (*heading*) Relative order of mag. as observed. **1851** *Monthly Notices R. Astron. Soc.* XI. 187 A double star..appearing to the naked eye as a bright 4 mag., and designated by A as 3·4. **1918** *Astrophysical Jrnl.* XLVII. 264 The absolute magnitudes of the bulk of the A stars lie within a range of 2·6 mags. **1972** *Nature* 22 Dec. 439/2 The distribution of galaxies brighter than 16 mag is..not especially isotropic.

mag (mæg), *sb.*[6] Also **mag.** (with point). Colloq. abbrev. of MAGNETO.

1920 *Blackw. Mag.* Nov. 562/2 Having wrestled for an hour with the mags., they were eventually induced to give forth reluctant sparks. **1930** [see DIFFERENTIAL *a.* and *sb.* B 4]. **1943** *R.A.F. Jrnl.* Aug. 11, I could see her eyes intent on the rev counter as she cut out first one mag, then the other. **1958** 'CASTLE' & HAILEY *Flight into Danger* i. 16 Each engine has two magnetos... In the run-up each engine in turn is opened to full throttle and each of the mags tested separately. **1973** E. ARNOLD *Proving Ground* (1974) iv. 61 Sayers pulled off the throttle and cut off the mag.

mag (mæg), *sb.*[7] Also **mag.** (with point). Colloq. abbrev. of MAGNESIUM, often used for *magnesium alloy*.

1969 C. TRICKEY *Building & Racing 850 Mini* i. 10/2 While, naturally, mag. alloy wheels are highly desirable from other points of view, the steel ones are obviously the best choice for a formula which is trying to keep costs to a minimum. **1970** *Telegraph* (Brisbane) 8 Dec. 14 Many 'mag' wheels sold as extras for hotted-up cars are made of cast aluminium. They cost about $40 each. Genuine magnesium alloy wheels, as used on racing cars, cost about $120 each. **1973** D. J. ABODAHER (*title*) Mag wheels and racing stripes.

mag (mæg), *v.* Also **meg.** [f. MAG *sb.*[2]] *intr.* To chatter; also with *away*.

1810 *Splendid Follies* I. 68 Don't you think she magged away pretty sharply! That's the worst of the young ones —they will cackle so confoundedly. **1885** RUNCIMAN *Skippers & Sh.* 248 I'll snap your backbone across my knee if you meg half a second more.

Maga ('mægə). [Shortened form of MAGAZINE.] A familiar abbreviation for Blackwood's Magazine.

1825 *Blackw. Mag.* XVII. 384 Two Numbers of Maga, you dog. **1886** SAINTSBURY *Ess. Eng. Lit.* (1891) 301 The monkey tricks of mannerism which..were incumbent on a reviewer in 'Maga'. **1899** *Literature* 4 Feb. 123 With more than the lightness and speed of the Quagga, She'll..show them a clean pair of heels, will our Maga!

†**magade.** *Obs. rare.* Also 5 **magada.** [ad. med.L. *magada* fem., f. Gr. μαγάς (accus. μαγάδα).] The bridge or fret of a stringed instrument.

1432–50 tr. *Higden* (Rolls) III. 211 The wire extendede on a holowe body is distreynede diametrally by an instrumente restreynenge the wyre to a certeyne acorde callede magada [L. *magada*]. **1609** DOWLAND *Ornith. Microl.* 22 That shall be the first Magade of the Instrument. *Ibid.* 23 In the extreame point of the Magades, set little props.

‖**magadis** ('mægədɪs). *Ancient Music.* [Gr. μάγαδις.] An instrument with twenty strings, arranged in octaves. Also, the Lydian flageolet (Liddell & Scott).

1721 A. MALCOLM *Treat. Mus.* 473 The Psalterium, Trigon, Sambuca, Pectis, Magadis, Barbiton. **1763** J. BROWN *Poetry & Mus.* v. 69 One Instrument they [the Ancients] used, which had two Strings to every Note..called the Magadis. **1864** ENGEL *Mus. Anc. Nat.* v. 200 Of the Magadis it is even not satisfactorily ascertained whether it was a stringed or a wind instrument. **1884** *Encycl. Brit.* XVII. 79/1 Anacreon (540 B.C.) sang to the accompaniment of the magadis (doubling bridge), an instrument imported from Egypt to Greece.

magadize ('mægədaɪz), *v. Ancient Mus.* [ad. Gr. μαγαδίζειν, f. μάγαδις MAGADIS: see -IZE.]

a. *intr.* To play or sing in octaves. **b.** To play upon the magadis. Hence **'magadized** *ppl. a.*, **'magadizing** *vbl. sb.*

1776 BURNEY *Hist. Mus.* (1789) I. viii. 132 It appears that the union of two voices in octaves was called Magadizing from a treble instrument of the name of Magadis, strung with double strings tuned octaves to each other. **1898** STAINER & BARRETT *Dict. Mus. Terms* s.v., To Magadize. (1) To play upon the magadis. (2) To play in octaves. **1901** H. E. WOOLDRIDGE *Oxf. Hist. Mus.* I. 44 The Greek practice of magadizing, in which..lay the fundamental principle of Polyphony. *Ibid.* 47 In addition to the old magadized octave the consonances of the fourth and fifth were now sung in parallel movement.

†**magar**[1]. *Obs. rare*[−1]. Some kind of ship.

1590 GREENE *Orl. Fur.* (1599) 4 Stately Argosies, Caluars, and Magars, hulkes of burden great.

Magar[2] ('mɑːgɑː(r)). Also **Muggur. a.** A member of one of the tribes of western Nepal, of Mongol origin and noted for their prowess in fighting. **b.** The language spoken by this tribe. Also *attrib.* or as *adj.*

1811 W. KIRKPATRICK *Acct. Kingdom Nepal* vii. 220 Besides the Sanskrit,..the principal vernacular languages of this country are, the Purbutti, the Newar, the Dhenwar, the Muggur, [etc.]. **1833** B. H. HODGSON in *Jrnl. Bengal Asiatic Soc.* II. 219 Both Gúrúngs and Magars still maintain their own vernacular tongues, Tartar faces, and careless manners. *Ibid.* 221 The attachment of the Magars to the house of Gorkhá is but recent, and of no extraordinary or intimate nature. **1859** R. G. LATHAM *Descriptive Ethnol.* II. xlii. 403 Gorkha, so far as it was other than Hindu, seems to have been chiefly Magar. **1877** L. H. MORGAN *Anc. Society* III. vi. 513 If the organizations..of..the Magars of Nepaul..were examined upon the original evidence, it is highly probable that they would be found exactly analogous to the Iroquois tribes. **1911** *Encycl. Brit.* XIX. 379/2 The Gurkhalis, Magars, and Gurungs are Hindus, but..the Magars will eat pork but not buffalo's flesh. **1950** T. LONGSTAFF *This My Voyage* v. 93 Besides speaking Khaskura..he was familiar with the peculiar dialects of the Magars and Gurungs, two of the most redoubtable of the fighting clans. **1971** C. BONINGTON *Annapurna South Face* iv. 47 Our porters were recruited in the main from two different tribes, the Magars and the Gurungs. **1971** J. PEMBLE *Invasion of Nepal* i. 9 Lévi thought that the Mongolian Magar tribesmen were the earliest inhabitants of the western hills.

magaseine, -sin, -son, obs. ff. MAGAZINE.

†**ma'gastromancy.** *Obs. rare.* [f. L. *mag-us* (see MAGE, MAGIC, MAGUS) + ASTROMANCY.] A name invented by Gaule for: 'Magical astrology'.

1652 GAULE *Magastrom.* 202 If there were any congruity or consistency betwixt prophecy and magastromancy.

So **ma'gastro,mancer**, one who practises 'magastromancy'. **ma'gastro,mantic** *a.*, pertaining to 'magastromancy'.

1652 GAULE (*title*) Πυς-μαντία. Mag-astro-mancer, or the Magicall-Astrologicall-Diviner Posed, and Puzzled. *Ibid.* 223 To what end serve the feigned mirables of nature but to feigne the magastromantick art for the greatest mirable? *Ibid.* 369 Examples of the magastromancers fatall miseries.. are too many to be instanc't in at large.

magatapie, obs. form of MAGGOT-PIE.

magazan, erron. form of MAZAGAN.

†**magazinage.** *Obs. rare*[−0]. (See quot.)

1730–6 BAILEY (folio) Pref., *Magazinage*..the Hire or Rent of a Warehouse or Place for laying up Goods or Stores; also the Warehouse, &c. itself.

magazinary (mægə'ziːnərɪ). *nonce-wd.* [f. MAGAZINE *sb.* + -ARY.] The office or place of production of a magazine.

1825 *Blackw. Mag.* XV. 445 He In editorial gloom, In Colburn's magazinary, Gives each his destined room.

magazine (mægəˈziːn), *sb.* Forms: 6 **magason, magosine,** 6–7 **magasin, -zin,** 7 **magazen,** (**maggezzine, magazin(e, magaseine, magozin**), 7–8 **magazeen(e,** 6– **magazine.** [a. F. *magasin* (OF. *magazin*), It. *magazzino* (Sardinian *magasinu*, metathetically *camasinu*), Sp. *magacen*, a. Arab. *makhāzin*, pl. of *makhzan* storehouse, f. *khazana* to store up. The Arab. word, with prefixed article *al-*, appears as Sp. *almagacen, almacen*, Pg. *armazem* warehouse.]

1. a. A place where goods are laid up; a storehouse or repository for goods or merchandise; a warehouse, depot. Now *rare.*

1583 J. NEWBERY *Let.* in Purchas *Pilgrims* (1625) II. 1643 That the Bashaw, neither any other Officer shall meddle with the goods, but that it may be kept in a Magosine. **1588** T. HICKOCK tr. *Frederick's Voy.* 27 The merchants haue all one house or Magason..and there they put all their goods of any valure. **1613** PURCHAS *Pilgrimage* VI. x. 511 Vnder which Porches or Galleries [of the Church] are Magazines or Store-houses, wherein are kept lampes, oile, mats, and other necessaries. **1731** *Gentl. Mag.* I. Introd., This Consideration has induced several Gentlemen to promote a Monthly Collection to treasure up, as in a Magazine, the most remarkable Pieces on the Subjects abovemention'd. **1768** STERNE *Sent. Journ.* (Rtldg.) 304 (*The Remise*) Mons. Dessein came up with the key of the remise in his hand, and forthwith let us into his magazine of chaises. **1793** BURKE *Corr.* (1844) IV. 143 No magazine, from the ware-houses of the East India Company to the grocer's and the baker's shop, possesses the smallest degree of safety. **1808** PIKE *Sources Mississ.* III. App. 23 A public magazine for provisions, where every farmer brings whatever grain and produce he may have for sale. **1875** STANLEY in *Contemp. Rev.* XXV. 489 Imported..from the magazines of France and of Belgium, according to the last fashions of Brussels or Paris.

fig. **1599** B. JONSON *Ev. Man out of Hum.* II. iii, What more than heauenly pulchritude is this? What Magazine, or treasurie of bliss? *a* **1610** HEALEY *Theophrastus* (1636) To Rdr., That great Magazine or Storehouse of all learning M. Cassaubon. **1738** [G. SMITH] *Curious Relat.* II. 216 My Friend! the Rich are the Poor Man's Magazine. **1817** *Parl. Debates* 352 A magazine of petitions had been opened in Scotland.

b. *transf.* esp. of a country or district with reference to its natural products or of a city, etc., as a centre of commerce.

1596 RALEIGH *Discov. Gviana* 3 Guiana (the Magazin of all rich mettels). **1632** LITHGOW *Trav.* IV. 165 Constantinople..Aleppo..and grand Cayro..are the three Maggezzines of the whole Empire. **1640** DIGBY in *Lismore Papers* Ser. II. (1888) IV. 133 He conceaued that the City of London was the Magazine of money. **1650** FULLER *Pisgah* III. i. 410 Timber they fetched from Mount Libanus (the magazeen of cedars). **1705** ADDISON *Italy* (1767) 196 (*Rome*) The great magazine for all kinds of treasure, is supposed to be the bed of the Tiber. **1787** *Gentl. Mag.* LVII. II. 1115/2 The Dutch islands of Curaçoa and St. Eustatius are now converted into complete magazines for all kinds of European goods. **1833** L. RITCHIE *Wand. by Loire* 109 The..bourg of Chouzé, set down in a perfect magazine of fruit and vegetables, grain and wine.

c. A portable receptacle containing articles of value. Now *rare.*

1768 STERNE *Sent. Journ.* (Rtldg.) 341 (*Case Conscience*) She opened her little magazine, and laid all her laces.. before me. **1779–81** JOHNSON *L.P., Thomson*, He had recommendations..which he had tied up carefully in his handkerchief; but..his magazine of credentials was stolen from him. **1861** HOLLAND *Less. Life* viii. 120 The great army of little men that is yearly commissioned to go forth into the world with a case of sharp knives in one hand, and a magazine of drugs in the other.

2. *Mil.* **a.** *gen.* A building in which is stored a supply of arms, ammunition and provisions for an army for use in time of war. **b.** *spec.* A place in which gunpowder and other explosives are stored in large quantities; a powder magazine.

1596 SPENSER *State Irel.* Wks. (Globe) 669/2 Then would I wish that there should be good store of howses and magasins erected in all those greate places of garrison, and in all great townes, as well for the vittayling of souldiours and shippes, as for..preventing of all times of dearthe. **1644** NYE *Gunnery* (1647) 72 A barrell of the best powder in the Magazine. **1667** MILTON *P.L.* IV. 816 A heap of nitrous Powder, laid Fit for the Tun som Magazin to store Against a rumord Warr. **1709** POPE *Ess. Crit.* 671 Thus useful arms in magazines we place. *a* **1744** SWIFT *Epigram* Wks. 1824 XIV. 399 Here Irish wit is seen! When nothing's left that's worth defence, We build a magazine. **1769** FALCONER *Dict. Marine* (1780), *Magazine*, a..store-house, built in the fore, or after-part of a ship's hold, to contain the gunpowder. **1800** WELLINGTON in Gurw. *Desp.* (1837) I. 213, I have no power to order the repair of magazines, storerooms, &c. **1849** PRESCOTT *Peru* (1850) II. 23 In another quarter they beheld one of those magazines destined for the army, filled with grain and with articles of clothing. **1868** *Regul. & Ord. Army* ¶1238 The reserve Ammunition will be kept in the Magazine. **1877** A. B. EDWARDS *Up Nile* ix. 239 To provide a safe underground magazine for gunpowder.

fig. **1653** R. SANDERS *Physiogn.* 25 The Heart is the Magazine and Arsenal of Life. **1715–20** POPE *Iliad* XII. 332 As when high Jove his sharp artillery forms, And opes his cloudy magazine of storms. **1750** JOHNSON *Rambler* No. 76 ¶6 He has stored his magazine of malice with weapons equally sharp. *a* **1764** LLOYD *Law Student* Poet. Wks. 1774 I. 23 While armed with these, the student views with awe His rooms become the magazine of Law.

3. a. *Mil.* The contents of a magazine; a store. Also *collect. pl.* († rarely *collect. sing.*): Stores, provisions, munitions of war; armament, military equipments.

1589 *Voy. Spaine & Portingale* 17 Abundant store of victualls..which was confessed..to be the beginning of a *Magasin* of all sorts of prouision for a new Voiage into England. **1591** RALEIGH *Last Fight Rev.* (Arb.) 16 Of which [Armada] the number of souldiers..with all other their magasines of prouision, were put in print. *a* **1613** OVERBURY *Observ. Trav.* (1626) 11 Megazins of powder. **1644** in Rushw. *Hist. Coll.* III. II. 670 The Kings forces..marcht away with their Artillery and Magazeen towards Oxford. **1666** DRYDEN *Ann. Mirab.* cclxxi, And bade him swiftly drive the approaching fire From where our naval magazines were stored. **1671** MILTON *Samson* 1281 Thir Armories and Magazins. **1774** T. WEST *Antiq. Furness* (1805) 48 They took most part of their arms..with a coup laden with magazeen, drawn by six oxen. **1781** GIBBON *Decl. & F.* xxxi. III. 259 He used, with so much skill and resolution, a large magazine of darts and arrows, that [etc.]. **1810** WELLINGTON in Gurw. *Desp.* (1838) VI. 27 A corps of 5000 men..had carried away a magazine of arms. **1813** *Ibid.* X. 419 Whenever a magazine of provisions shall be taken from the enemy by the troops.

fig. **1638** BAKER tr. *Balzac's Lett.* (vol. III.) 242, I take not upon me to contend with you in complements..who..have whole magasins of good words. **1663** COWLEY *Misc., Chronicle*, The Lace, the Paint, and warlike things That make up all their Magazins. **1742** YOUNG *Nt. Th.* II. 478 Speech burnishes our mental magazine; Brightens, for ornament; and whets for use. **1836** EMERSON *Nature, Language* Wks. (Bohn) II. 154 That which was unconscious truth, becomes..a new weapon in the magazine of power.

b. *gen.* A store, heap (of provisions, materials, etc.); † a stock of clothing, wardrobe.

1615 H. CROOKE *Body of Man* 61 Next vnder the Skin lyeth the Fat..a Stowage or Magazine of nourishment against a time of dearth. **1624** HEYWOOD *Captives* II. ii. in Bullen *O. Pl.* IV. 145 That have no more left of a magazine Then these wett cloathes upon mee. **1637** —— *Lond. Mirr.* Wks. 1874 IV. 314 By which small mites to Magazines increase. **1661** EVELYN *Fumifugium* To Rdr., The Deformity of so frequent Wharfes and Magazines of Wood, Coale, Boards, and other course Materials. **1669** J. ROSE *Eng. Vineyard* (1675) 34 A load of lime, to every ten loads of dung, will make an admirable compost..but your magazine will require the maturity of two, or three years. **1712** ARBUTHNOT *John Bull* II. iv, She [Usury] had amassed vast magazines of all sorts of things. **1714** GAY *Fan.* I. 243 Should you the Wardrobe's Magazine rehearse, And glossy Manteaus rustle in thy Verse. **1719** DE FOE *Crusoe* I. x. (1840) 182 A..magazine of flesh, milk, butter, and cheese. **1771** GOLDSM. *Hist. Eng.* III. 165 A magazine of coals were usually deposited there. **1790** BEWICK *Hist. Quadrupeds* (1807) 419 Each Beaver forms its bed of moss, and each family lays in its magazine of winter provisions. **1828** SYD. SMITH *Wks.* (1859) II. 21/1 Distillation, too, always insures a magazine against famine... It opens a market for grain. **1849** MACAULAY *Hist. Eng.* ix. II. 437 In every asylum were collected magazines of stolen or smuggled goods.

fig. **1709** SACHEVERELL *Serm.* 15 Aug. 15 What a Magazine of Sin, what an Inexhaustible Fund of Debauchery,..does any Author of Heresie..set up! **1795** BURKE *Let. to W. Elliot* Wks. VII. 348 The magazine of topicks and common-places which I suppose he keeps by him. **1836–7** SIR W. HAMILTON *Metaph.* (1877) I. ii. 23 An individual may possess an ample magazine of knowledge, and still be little better than an intellectual barbarian.

†**4.** A ship laden with stores, a victualling ship; more fully ***magazine(s ship.*** (Cf. F. *magasins*, 'the store-ships which attend on a fleet of men of war', Falconer *Dict. Marine, Fr. Sea-Terms* 1780.)

1624 CAPT. SMITH *Virginia* IV. 155 Some pety Magazines came this Summer. *Ibid.* v. 189 About this time arriued the *Diana* with a good supply of men and prouision, and the first Magazin euer seene in those Iles. *Ibid.* 194 The Magazin ship..came into the Harbour. *Ibid.* 195 He made..a large new storehouse of Cedar for the yeerely Magazines goods. *Ibid.* 196 The Magazins ship. *Ibid.* 198 Constrained to buy what they wanted, and sell what they had at what price the Magazin pleased.

5. †**a.** Used in the titles of books, with the sense (*fig.* from 1 and 2): A storehouse of information on a specified subject or for a particular class of persons. *Obs.*

1639 R. WARD, Animadversions of Warre; or, a Militarie Magazine of the trvest rvles..for the Managing of Warre. **1669** STURMY, The Mariners Magazine. **1705** G. SHELLEY, The Penman's Magazine: or, a New Copy-book, of the English, French and Italian Hands. **1719** R. HAYES, Negociator's Magazine. **1802** J. ALLEN, Spiritual Magazine, or Christian's Grand Treasure.

b. A periodical publication containing articles by various writers; *chiefly*, a periodical publication intended for general rather than learned or professional readers, and consisting of a miscellany of critical and descriptive articles, essays, works of fiction, etc.

1731 (*title*) The Gentleman's Magazine: or, Monthly Intelligencer. [Cf. quot. 1731 in sense 1.] **1742** POPE *Dunc.* I. 42 Hence Journals, Medleys, Merc'ries, Magazines;..and all the Grub-street race. **1748** LADY LUXBOROUGH *Let. to Shenstone* 28 Apr., Nothing can be more just than the criticism upon the Play in the Magazine. **1758–65** GOLDSM. *Ess., Spec. Mag.*, It is the life and soul of a magazine never to be long dull upon one subject. **1798** A. TILLOCH (*title*) The Philosophical Magazine. **1819** BYRON *Juan* I. ccxi, All other magazines of art or science, Daily, or monthly, or three monthly. **1823** (*title*) The Mechanics' Magazine. **1857** MRS. MATHEWS *Tea-Table T.* I. 2 A Magazine is the fancy fair of literature—a reader's veritable bazaar. **1860** (*title*) Baily's Monthly Magazine of Sports and Pastimes. **1880** MCCARTHY *Own Times* IV. lix. 304 He wrote largely on the subject in reviews and magazines.

c. = *magazine programme.*

1936 *Radio Times* 30 Oct. 88/2 'Picture Page'. A Magazine of Topical and General Interest. **1949** *Ibid.* 15 July 12/2 Music Magazine. A weekly review. **1953** *Ann. Reg. 1952* 360 The establishment of the radio magazine *New Soundings*. **1957** *B.B.C. Handbk.* 153 *Family affairs*: a weekly magazine for mothers with children. **1975** *ITV Evidence to Annan Committee* 46 A thirty-minute news magazine is taking shape for 6 pm transmission.

6. In various transferred uses of sense 2. †**a.** A chamber for a supply of bullets in a 'magazine wind-gun'. **b.** A chamber in a repeating rifle, machine-gun, etc., containing a supply of cartridges which are fed automatically to the breech. **c.** A case in which a supply of cartridges is carried. **d.** A reservoir or supply-chamber in a machine, stove, battery, etc. Also, in a camera, projector, etc. **e.** ***magnetic magazine***: see quot.

a. 1744 DESAGULIERS *Exper. Philos.* II. 399 The small or shooting Barrel, which receives the Bullets one at a time from the Magazine, being a serpentine Cavity, wherein the Bullets..nine or ten, are lodged.

b. 1868 *Rep. to Govt. U.S. Munitions War* 28 Drop the cartridges into the outer magazine, ball foremost, to the number of seven. **1884** H. BOND *Treat. Small Arms* 89 Magazine arms in which the cartridges are placed in a tube or magazine under the barrel. **1890** HENTY *With Lee in Virginia* 153 Many of the men carried repeating rifles, and the magazines were filled before these were slung across the riders' shoulders. **1915** 'I. HAY' *First Hundred Thousand* vii. 77 Pumpherston graciously accepted the charger of cartridges.., rammed it into the magazine, adjusted the sights,..and fired his first shot. **1919** 'BOYD CABLE' *Old Contemptibles* xvii. 277 Carruthers..took a box of cartridges from a niche in the wall, and proceeded to recharge his magazine. **1964** H. L. PETERSON *Encycl. Firearms* 255/1 This turret system was revived many years later as a practical magazine for the Lewis machine gun.

c. 1892 GREENER *Breech Loader* 184 Cartridges are best carried in a magazine of solid leather.

d. 1873 J. RICHARDS *Wood-working Factories* 45 Exhausting the air from the magazine by fans. **1884** KNIGHT *Dict. Mech., Suppl.* 570/2 As in the Daniells' battery, which has a magazine of sulphate of copper crystals. **1889** *Judge* (U.S.) 22 June 180/2 Every operator can develop and print his own negatives and refill his magazine. **1893** BOTHAMLEY *Ilford Man. Photogr.* xix. 136 Hand-cameras..in which the plate-reservoir or magazine is detachable. **1958** *Amat. Photographer* 31 Dec. 3/2 (Advt.), The Hanomatic slide changer is complete with a plastic magazine holding 36 slides. **1964** C. WILLOCK *Enormous Zoo* v. 77 John Buxton used up one magazine of film and then reloaded with terrible precision. **1967** H. M. R. SOUTO *Technique Motion Pict. Camera* i. 13 The first mechanism has the task of drawing the unexposed film (or raw stock) from the storage chamber, called a *magazine*, and after exposure, driving it into a similar magazine.

e. 1870 ATKINSON tr. *Ganot's Physics* (ed. 4) 602 A magnetic battery or magazine consists of a number of magnets joined together by their similar poles.

7. *attrib.* and *Comb.*, as (sense 5 b) ***magazine article, -editor, -monger, paper, rack, -reader, table, verse, world, -writer, writing***; (senses 1, 2) †***magazine house,*** †***storehouse***; (sense 1 c) †***magazine bag***; (sense 6 b) ***magazine arms, rifle, slot, weapon***; **magazine battery**, a voltaic battery with a magazine containing crystals to keep the solution saturated (Knight *Dict. Mech.* Suppl. 1884); **magazine camera**, a camera in which the plates for exposure are put in in batches; **magazine clothing**, woollen clothing to be put on before entering a powder magazine; **magazine cover**, the cover, freq. pictorial, of a magazine; **magazine day**, the day upon which periodical magazines are issued to the trade; **magazine gun**, † (*a*) (see quot. 1744), also called ***magazine wind-gun*** (obs.); (*b*) a gun (i.e. either a cannon or a rifle etc.) provided with a 'magazine' (sense 6 b); **magazine programme**, a periodical broadcast programme comprised of varied items of entertainment linked together as a single series (see quot. 1941); **magazine rights**, the rights of publishing matter in a magazine; **magazine section**, a section included in some newspapers the contents of which resemble a magazine; † **magazine ship** (see 4); **magazine story**, a story written for publication in a magazine; **magazine stove** (see quot.); **magazine work**, (*a*) writing for magazines; (*b*) *Printing*, setting up type for magazines.

1868 *Rep. to Govt. U.S. Munitions War* 19 These cartridges cannot with safety be used in *magazine arms. **1884** [see 6 b]. **1854** S. LOVER *Handy Andy* (ed. 4) Pref., The early pages were written..as a *magazine article. **1681** CHETHAM *Angler's Vade-m.* xxxiv. (1689) 185 The Angler must always have in readiness a large *Magazine Bag or Budget plentifully furnished with the following materials. **1893** *Beginner's Guide to Photogr.* (ed. 5) 130 The ..*Magazine Camera was highly extolled..as least complicated of Reservoir Cameras. **1876** VOYLE & STEVENSON *Milit. Dict.* 558 All persons employed in magazines..will..change their own clothes and boots for *magazine clothing and slippers. **1938** *Toronto Daily Star* 30 Dec. 12/6 Famous Hollywood Glamour Girls. *Magazine cover models. **1942** E. PAUL *Narrow St.* xvi. 124 Mireille was not the most attractive, from the magazine-cover standpoint. **1951** M. MCLUHAN *Mech. Bride* (1967) 120/2 The feminine images of our ads and magazine covers. **1858** SIMMONDS *Dict. Trade*, **Magazine-day*. **1872** FORSTER *Life Dickens* I. 129 The magazine-day of that April month, I remember, fell upon a Saturday. **1877** W. T. THORNTON *Word for Word fr. Horace* Pref. 8 Failing to discover a *Magazine-Editor good-natured enough to print any of my versions. **1744** DESAGULIERS *Exper. Philos.* II. 399 An ingenious Workman call'd L. Colbe has very much improv'd it [*sc.* the old Wind-Gun], by making it a *Magazine Wind-Gun; so that 10 Bullets are so lodg'd in a Cavity..that they may be..successively shot. *Ibid.*, The

Magazine-Gun, as he calls it. **1880** *Encycl. Brit.* XI. 284/2 The Vetterli gun..is a repeater or magazine gun. *a* **1649** DRUMM. OF HAWTH. *Consid. to Parlt.* Wks. (1711) 185 That ..the town's *magazine-houses be furnished with arms. **1767** S. PATERSON *Another Trav.* II. 134 A noted book-maker, *magazine-monger, and anti-critic of the eighteenth-century. **1833** *Fraser's Mag.* VIII. 482/1 He had written some smart *magazine papers, bound up in a volume called *Pelham*. **1941** *B.B.C. Gloss. Broadcasting Terms* 18 **Magazine programme*, programme made up of miscellaneous items (e.g. talks, interviews, musical acts), loosely related one to the other by a compère or by other means of presentation. **1970** *Times* 23 Feb. 25/3 B.B.C. Newcastle..will have its own budget which will be sufficient to allow the production of another 30-minute weekly magazine programme. **1972** P. BLACK *Biggest Aspidistra* III. iv. 175 Godfrey Bazely, a Midland Region broadcaster..loved the world of farming... The BBC gave him a new magazine programme aimed at farmers and their families. **1917–18** *T. Eaton & Co. Catal.* Fall & Winter 416/1 Morris Chair... Paper and *magazine rack under arm. **1955** E. BOWEN *World of Love* ii. 42 One or two ruched taffeta cushions and a magazine-rack..survived from her few attempts to bring the room into line with her ideas. **1969** *House & Garden* Apr. 160/2 Magazine rack in Afrormosia. **1833** MILL *Let.* 24 Sept. in *Works* (1963) XII. 179 They would not be attractive to the bulk of *Magazine-readers. **1882** W. JAMES *Will to Believe* (1897) 109 Thousands of innocent magazine readers lie paralyzed and terrified in the network of shallow negations which the leaders of opinion have thrown over their souls. **1876** VOYLE & STEVENSON *Milit. Dict.* 344/2 The best known *magazine rifles are the Spencer, the Winchester, and the Vetterli rifles. **1909** *Westm. Gaz.* 14 July 11/2 In America '*magazine rights' did not necessarily mean publication by instalments. The term was used to distinguish magazine rights from newspaper syndicate rights. **1959** N. MAILER *Advts. for Myself* (1961) 158 Sam throws the *Magazine Section away... Sam is enraged at editorial dishonesty. **1969** *Listener* 30 Jan. 148/1 Leavis did not apologise that his terms of reference should be the Robbins Report and Harold Wilson and the magazine sections of the English Sundays. **1910** KIPLING *Land & Sea Tales* (1923) 178 The tiny twenty-two cartridge had dropped into the *magazine-slot. *a* **1654** in Wotton *Lett.* (1654) II. 91 To erect and set up..a Company, to be called The East Indian Company of Scotland, making their first *Magazin Storehouse..in some parts of our Realm of Ireland. **1858** J. A. FROUDE *Let.* 17 Jan. in J. W. Cross *George Eliot's Life* (1885) II. viii. 4, I had made acquaintance with 'Janet's Repentance', and had found there something extremely different from general *magazine stories. **1885** C. M. YONGE *Nuttie's Father* II. ii. 23 The hero of many a magazine story. **1932** Q. D. LEAVIS *Fiction & Reading Public* I. iii. 47 The magazine story is almost without exception a commercial article. **1942** Magazine story [see EXCLUSIVE A. *adj.* 9]. **1875** KNIGHT *Dict. Mech.*, **Magazine-stove*, one in which is a fuel-chamber which supplies coal to the fire as that in the grate burns away. **1966** H. ROTH *Button, Button* (1967) I. 15 A small, locked safe.. unnoticeable..because the top was extended to make it look like a *magazine table. **1967** A. DIMENT *Dolly Dolly Spy* xi. 145 The magazine table caught them neatly behind the naked knees and..they overbalanced. **1891** E. PEACOCK *N. Brendon* I. 49 Please don't quote silly *magazine verses. **1884** *Pall Mall G.* 28 Aug. 5/1 The information as to *magazine or repeating weapons is very meagre. **1831** CARLYLE in Froude *Life* (1882) II. 151 *Magazine work is below street sweeping as a trade. **1891** *Labour Commission Gloss., Magazine Work*, printing work paid by the 100 lines. **1833** *Fraser's Mag.* VIII. 482/1 He [Bulwer] came into our *magazine world with an impertinent swagger. **1787** P. MATY tr. *Riesbeck's Trav. Germ.* II. xlv. 206 Reviewers, *magazine-writers. **1835** MARRYAT *Olla Podr.* xxx, *Magazine writing..is the most difficult of all writing.

maga'zine, *v.* Now *rare*. [f. MAGAZINE *sb.*]

1. *trans.* To lay up in or as in a magazine or storehouse. Also with *up*.

1643 *Let.* in Boys *Sandwich* (1792) 754 Those arms..shall be magazined up, in such convenient place as shall be thought fit. **1651** R. CHILD in *Hartlib's Legacy* (1655) 93 It is a great Deficiency in England, that we do not magazine or store up Corn. **1656** S. H. *Golden Law* 97 Thus the Sweden King, so the great Alexander, ..did contract and magazine al the Honour &c. in their own names, which..their Commanders, Officers, and Souldiery had a great share in. *a* **1734** NORTH *Exam.* I. iii. (1740) 222 Such Secrets..that, being magazined up in a Diary, might serve for Materials, as ..might serve to build up his Plot.

2. *intr.* To conduct a magazine.

a **1763** [implied in the *ppl. a.* below].

Hence **maga'zining** *vbl. sb.* and *ppl. a.*

a **1763** BYROM *Pass. Particip. Petit.* i. Poems 1773 I. 106 Urban or Sylvan,..thou foremost in the Fame Of Magazining Chiefs. **1862** DANA *Man. Geol.* iv. 747 The Vegetable Kingdom is a provision for the storing away or magazining of force for the Animal Kingdom.

magazinedom (mægə'ziːndəm). [f. MAGAZINE *sb.* 5 b + -DOM.] The world or sphere of magazines.

1890 *Review of Reviews* I. 9/1 Such a guide to magazinedom as you propose to establish would be extremely useful. **1902** *Tablet* 22 Sept. 448 It is the very romance of magazinedom. **1907** *Daily Chron.* 19 Feb. 3/2 It is true that magazinedom is very crowded, but there is always room at the top.

magaziner (mægə'ziːnə(r)). *rare.* [f. MAGAZINE *sb.* + -ER[1].] One who writes articles for a magazine.

1758–65 GOLDSM. *Ess., Spec. Mag.*, If a magaziner be dull upon the Spanish war, he soon has us up again with the Ghost in Cock-lane. **1834** *Fraser's Mag.* IX. 124 Considering Macaulay as a magaziner, his papers in Knight's *Quarterly* were in general full of talent.

maga'zinery. *rare.* [f. as prec. + -ERY.] The profession of a magazine-writer.

1833 *Fraser's Mag.* VIII. 482/1 We, the old long-trained veterans of magazinery.

magazinish (mægə'ziːnɪʃ), *a.* [f. as prec. + -ISH.] Having the characteristics of what is usually found in magazines.

1794 COLERIDGE *Lett.* (1895) I. 117 The mediocrity of the eight first lines is most miserably magazinish. **1883** BLACK *Shandon Bells* xxvi, 'It is very magazinish', he said. 'Why should the magazines monopolize literature?' she answered.

magazinism (mægə'ziːnɪz(ə)m). [f. as prec. + -ISM.] The profession of writing for magazines.

1882 *Spectator* 22 Apr. 533 Magazinism..is threatening now-a-days to become merely journalism writ large. **1889** *Sat. Rev.* 22 June 761/1 Is editing and conducting a magazine magazinism?

magazinist (mægə'ziːnɪst). [f. as prec. + -IST.] One who writes for magazines.

1821 *Blackw. Mag.* X. 557 Christopher, Cock of the North, Prince of Periodicals, and Monarch of Magazinists. **1823** DE QUINCEY *Lett. Yng. Man* iii. Wks. 1890 X. 43 Reviewer, magazinist and author of all work. **1880** M. COLLINS *Th. in Garden* I. 102 The modern magazinist is a pitiable poetaster.

magaziny (mægə'ziːnɪ), *a.* Also **magaziney**. [f. as prec. + -Y[1].] Of the nature of, or suitable for, a magazine.

1885 *Sat. Rev.* 9 May 621/2 Not unamusing, though a little 'magaziny', to use a word of reproach. **1894** *Athenæum* 22 Sept. 383/2 We have heard his writings called 'shallow' and 'magaziny'. **1938** *New Statesman* 8 Jan. 56/2 Nor is *The Best Poems* negligible. It is magaziney, but contains respectable work by De la Mare [etc.]. **1941** *Scrutiny* IX. 379 He [*sc.* Mr. Plomer] attempts also pseudo-ballads made to the Auden formula, which are amusing in a magaziny way. **1961** *Times Lit. Suppl.* 23 Jun. 385/1 Of these fourteen pieces at least eight are almost defiantly magaziny. **1966** *Punch* 9 Mar. 362/3 The violence seems somehow bookish and the literary chat magaziney.

Magdala ('mægdələ). The name of a town in Abyssinia, where a victory was gained in 1868 by General Napier. Used *attrib.* for the name of a red aniline dye.

1875 *Ure's Dict. Arts* (ed. 7). **1890** THORPE *Dict. Appl. Chem.* I. 233/2 Magdala red... This old and very beautiful colouring matter is the saffranine of the naphthalene series.

Magdalen, Magdalene ('mægdələn, -liːn). [ad. Eccl. Latin (*Marīa*) *Magdalēna*, *-lēnē*, a. Gr. (Μαρία ἡ) Μαγδαληνή, (Mary) of Magdala (a town on the Sea of Galilee). The vernacular form of the word (adopted through Fr.) is MAUDLIN; the pronunciation ('mɔːdlɪn) represented by this spelling is still current for the names of Magdalen College, Oxford, and Magdalene College, Cambridge.]

1. a. *the Magdalen(e*: the appellation of a disciple of Christ named Mary, 'out of whom went seven devils' (Luke viii. 2). She has commonly been supposed to be identical with the unnamed 'sinner' of Luke vii. 37, and therefore appears in Western hagiology as a harlot restored to purity and elevated to saintship by repentance and faith. (In the full designation *Mary Magdalen(e* the article is omitted.) For early examples see also MAUDLIN *sb.*

c **1386** CHAUCER *Pars. T.* ¶428 As Iudas grucched ayeines the Magdalene. **1500–20** DUNBAR *Poems* xxxvii. 18 The Magdalene and Mare Salamee Abasit wer in spirit. **1850** S. DOBELL *Roman* ii, Heaven, Where angels hail the Magdalen. **1865** PLUMPTRE *Master & Scholar* 93 The twain, The sinner and the Magdalene, they joyed To think that [etc.].

b. A representation of Mary Magdalen in art.

1661 EVELYN *Diary* 9 Aug., Many excellent pictures, especialy the Magdalen of Caracci. **1851** RUSKIN *Stones Ven.* (1894) I. 160 But a smooth Magdalen of Carlo Dolci with a tear on each cheek..rarely fails of being verily, often deeply, felt for the time.

2. *transf.* One whose history resembles that of the Magdalen; *esp.* a reformed prostitute.

1697 DENNIS *Plot & no Plot* Epil., I, your young, buxom Magdalens despise, She-Saints, that have sev'n Devils in their eyes. [**1737** BAILEY vol. II, *Magdalens*, an order of nuns, or rather worn out and penitent courtesans at Rome, upon whom a revenue was settled by Pope Clement VIII.] **1758** *Plan for establishing Magdalen-Charity* 36 The General Committee shall empower three of their number to visit the wards, to enquire into the behavior of the Magdalens [etc.]. **1777** SHERIDAN *Trip Scarb.* Prol., Those writers well and wisely use their pens Who turn our wantons into Magdalens. *a* **1882** TROLLOPE *Autobiog.* xviii. (1883) II. 180 A poor abased creature..with very little of the Magdalene about her—because though there may be Magdalenes they are not often found.

3. A home for the refuge and reformation of prostitutes. [Short for *Magdalen hospital*.]

1766 ENTICK *London* IV. 311 In Prescot-street..we find a modern institution..founded by the name of the Magdalen. **1792** MARY WOLLSTONECR. *Rights Wom.* iv. 155 Many innocent girls..are..'ruined' before they know the difference between virtue and vice... Asylums and Magdalenes are not the proper remedies for these abuses. **1859** C. BARKER *Assoc. Princ.* i. 1 The numerous temples, hospitals,..and magdalens which then covered our land.

4. The name of a kind of peach. [Cf. MAUDLIN.]

1706 LONDON & WISE *Retir'd Gard'ner* I. I. viii. 38 The White Magdalen has a..sugar'd winy Taste. **1719** —— *Compl. Gard.* p. viij, There are sometimes..but scurvy Peaches among the Minions, Magdalens, Violets, Admirables, &c. **1765** *Museum Rusticum* IV. iv. 17 The magdalene is generally a vigorous tree.

†**5.** Some plant. *Obs.* [Cf. MAUDLIN.]

c **1590** J. ELDRED in *Hakluyt's Voy.* (1599) II. I. 270 These camels will liue very well two or three dayes without water: their feeding is on thistles, worme-wood, magdalene, and other strong weeds.

6. *attrib.* and *Comb.*, as (sense 1) ***Magdalen-like*** adj., ***-look***, ***-style***; **Magdalen day**, the feast of St. Mary Magdalen, 22 July; **Magdalen asylum, charity, home, hospital, house** = sense 3; **Magdalen pear**, some variety of pear = MAUDLIN *sb.* 4; **Magdalen ward**, the ward (in a hospital) devoted to the reception of 'Magdalens'.

1869 LECKY *Europ. Mor.* iv. (1877) II. 98 *Magdalen asylums and foundling hospitals. **1758** (*title*) A plan for establishing a Charity-House..for the reception of repenting Prostitutes, to be called the *Magdalen Charity. **1485** *Certificate* in *Surtees Misc.* (1890) 46 The Sunday after þe *Magdaleyne day. **1901** *Daily Chron.* 14 Aug. 5/7 These institutions are *Magdalene homes. **1758** *Ann. Reg., Chron.* 10 Aug. (1783) 104/2 The *Magdalen hospital in Goodman's fields..was opened. **1758** (*title*) The plan of the *Magdalen House for the reception of penitent Prostitutes. **1776** *Carlisle Mag.* 21 Sept. 169 Obtaining admittance into the Magdalen-house. **1794** CHARLOTTE SMITH *Wandering of Warwick* 169 With all her penitent looks, and *Magdalen-like graces. **1752** SIR H. BEAUMONT *Crito* 11 That *Magdalen-look in some fine Faces after weeping. **1741** *Compl. Fam.-Piece* II. iii. 388 And these Pears: [Aug.].. Gross Oignonet, *Magdalen Pear, Cassolette. **1765** *Ann. Reg., Charac.* 59/1 She wrote a letter to her husband d'Estiolles, in the true *Magdalen style; intreating him to receive her again.

Magdalenian (mægdə'liːnɪən), *a.* and *sb.* *Archæol.* Also **Madelainean, Madelenian**. [ad. F. *magdalénien* (G. de Mortillet, *c* 1867), f. the place-name *La Madeleine* in the department of Dordogne, France: see -AN.] **A.** *adj.* Of or belonging to the Lower Palæolithic culture represented by remains found at La Madeleine. **B.** *sb.* A man or woman of this culture.

1885 A. GEIKIE *Text-bk. Geol.* (ed. 2) vi. 914 Those [deposits] which contain well-finished implements associated with carved bone and ivory, as at the caves of La Madeleine (Périgord), have been called Magdalenian. **1896** A. H. KEANE *Ethnol.* 87 Madelenian or Third Cave Age. **1904** [see SOLUTRIAN, SOLUTREAN *a.*]. **1911** W. J. SOLLAS *Anc. Hunters* 323 The Magdalenians were quite capable of making respectable buckles or fibulæ. **1920** *Q. Rev.* Oct. 376 We are moved by a greater number of artistic qualities than were the Magdalenian reindeer men. **1956** H. READ *Art of Sculpture* ii. 28 This highly stylized figure anticipates the schematic character of the later Magdalenian figures. **1963** *Field Archaeol.* (Ordnance Survey) (ed. 4) 21 From the period of the Magdalenians who were hunting and making their wonderful cave paintings in France round about 20,000 B.C...there is very little in Britain... A few typical Magdalenian objects have been found in Mendip caves. **1973** *Listener* 10 May 606/2 The Magdalenian hunters of southern Europe fifteen thousand years ago invented the harpoon.

†**magdaleon.** *Pharmacy. Obs.* [ad. med.L. *magdaleōn-em*, *magdaleo* (whence F. *magdaléon*, 16th c.), also *magdalium*, f. Gr. μαγδαλιά, dough or bread-crumb (Galen), later form of ἀπομαγδαλιά soft bread to wipe one's hands upon at table, f. ἀπομάσσειν to wipe.] A cylindrical roll of plaster, salve, or any medicinal substance.

c **1450** *ME. Med. Bk.* (Heinrich) 182 When þou hast medled al þy poudre, þen forme þer of þy magdaleones in newe wyt leþer or in good pauper. **1646** SIR T. BROWNE *Pseud. Ep.* II. iii. 74 Applying the magdaleon or roale unto the Needle it would both stir and attract it. **1670** W. SIMPSON *Hydrol. Ess.* 108 We..melted it, and in small lead pipes cast it into magdaleons..resembling common sulphur. **1673** E. BROWN *Trav. Germ.* etc. (1677) 168 We saw also the manner of casting the Brimstone into Rolls, or Magdaleons. **1725** BRADLEY *Fam. Dict.* s.v. *Sulphur*, They ..liquify it [sulphur] by Fire, then pour it into Moulds, and form it into Sticks or Pieces, call'd abroad Magdaleons. **1731** BAILEY vol. II, *Magdaleon*, a roll of salve or plaister.

Magdeburg centuries, hemispheres: see CENTURY 8, HEMISPHERE 1 b.

mage (meɪdʒ). *arch.* [Anglicized form of MAGUS. Cf. F. *mage* (OF. had *mague*).]

1. A magician; *transf.* a person of exceptional wisdom and learning.

c **1400** *Apol. Loll.* 95 We callen þe magis, þoo þat calculun bi þe sternis þingis to cum, wening as þei were Goddis gouernours. **1586** T. B. *La Primaud. Fr. Acad.* I. 157 Plato, after he was well instructed by Socrates, sought out the mages and wise men of Egypt, by whose meanes he saw the bookes of Moises. **1590** SPENSER *F.Q.* III. iii. 14 The hardy Mayd..the dreadfull Mage there fownd Depe busied bout worke of wondrous end. **1611** DONNE *Anat. World* 390 Th' Egyptian Mages. **1860** FORSTER *Gr. Remonstr.* 68 Though such circumstances worked well for the Mage [Henry VII] upon the English throne, he did not with all his craft [etc.]. **1869** TENNYSON *Coming of Arthur* 279 And there I saw mage Merlin.

2. One of the magi: see MAGUS 1.

1585 T. WASHINGTON tr. *Nicholay's Voy.* IV. ii. 115 Their Mages..annoynted their sacrifice with oyle. **1594** R. ASHLEY tr. *Loys le Roy* 31 b, As we will declare hereafter when we speake of the Persians, and of their Mages. **1877** SMITH & WACE *Dict. Christian Biogr.* I. 477/2 The author of that superstition was Masdec,..a mage, who gathered the credulous around him.

magecolle, variant of MACHECOLE *v. Obs.*

mageirics, -istic: see MAGIRICS, -ISTIC.

†**magel.** *Obs.* (Only in Trevisa.) Also **mag(g)ed, magil, magyl.** ?Fictitious, fabulous.
1387 TREVISA *Higden* (Rolls) V. 337 Here William telleþ a magel [*v.r.* maged] tale wiþ oute evidence. *Ibid.* 339 Madde men telle magel [*v.rr.* magil, magged] tales.

Magellan (mə'gɛlən). The Eng. form of the name of a famous Portuguese navigator, Fernão de Magalhães (?1470–1521), the first European discoverer who passed through the channel now called the Straits of Magellan into the Pacific Ocean; used *attrib.* (or in possessive) = MAGELLANIC.
1638 J. CHILMEAD *Treat. Globes* II. vii. (Hakl. Soc.) 67 Our mariners used to call them Magellanes Clouds. **1671** OGILBY *Amer.* 474 *marg.*, Description of the Magellan Straights. **1696** PHILLIPS (ed. 5), *Magellan's Clouds*, two small Clouds of the same colour with *Via Lactea*, not far distant from the South Pole. **1840** R. H. DANA *Bef. Mast* v. 9 The Magellan Clouds consist of three small nebulæ in the southern part of the heavens. **1867** SMYTH *Sailor's Word-bk.*, *Magellan Jacket*, a name given to a watch-coat with a hood, worn in high latitudes.
b. = 'Magellan's Straits', ? *nonce-use.*
1787 BURNS *To W. Simpson* vii, Or whare wild-meeting oceans boil Besouth Magellan.
Hence †**Mage'llanian** *a.* = next.
1698 FRYER *Acc. E. India & P.* 1. The Magellanian Clouds.

Magellanic (mægɪ'lænɪk), *a.* [ad. mod.L. *Magellanic-us*, f. MAGELLAN: see -IC.] Pertaining to or named after Magellan (see prec.), used in the appellations of regions discovered by him, nautical objects, etc.
Magellanic bark, a kind of Peruvian bark. **Magellanic clouds**, two large globular cloudy spots formed of vast numbers of nebulæ and clusters of stars, visible in the southern hemisphere. **Magellanic fox** (see quot.). **Magellanic jacket**, a sailor's watch-coat with a hood. **Magellanic regions**, those regions of Patagonia visited by Magellan. †**Magellanic Sea**, the South Pacific Ocean. **Magellanic Straits**, the straits through which Magellan passed from the Atlantic to the Pacific.
1775 SIR E. BARRY *Observ. Wines* 221 An equal quantity of the Peruvian and *Magellanic bark. **1685–6** MACKRITH *Let.* 5 Feb. in *Boyle's Wks.* (1744) V. 651 The *Magellanick clouds..consist of a greater and a lesser. **1880** PROCTOR *Poetry Astron.* xii. 434 The Magellanic Clouds are roughly spherical in shape. **1837** J. E. GRAY in *Mag. Nat. Hist.* Nov. 578 *Vulpes magellanica* (*Magellanic Fox). Greyish, varied with black on the back [etc.]. Inhabits Magellan's Straits. **1773** HAWKESWORTH *Voy.* II. 40 Each of them received what is called a *Magellanic jacket and a pair of trowsers. The jacket is made of a thick woollen stuff called Fearnought. **1771** *Ann. Reg.* 2/2 That..right which they [the Spaniards] pretend to all the *Magellanic regions. **1602** *Metamorph. Tabacco* (1863) 17 The *Magellanick sea her visions brought. **1708** *Brit. Apollo* No. 91. 2/2 The Magellanic Sea. **1696** J. EDWARDS *Demonstr. Exist. & Provid. God* I. 231 The people about the *Megallanick Streights are white.

Magen David (mɑː'gɛn dɑː'viːd). Also **Mogen David** ('mɒgən 'dɒvɪd). [Heb. *māghēn Dāwīdh* shield of David, f. *Dāwīdh* David, king of Judah and Israel, d. circa 973 B.C.] A six-pointed star symbolizing Jewishness or Zionism.
1904 *Jewish Encycl.* VIII. 251/2 *Magen Dawid* ('David's Shield'), the hexagram formed by the combination of two equilateral triangles. **1934** *Encycl. Jewish Knowl.* 324/2 *Magen David*... During the World War it was used..as equivalent to the Red Cross, such organizations described themselves as the 'Red Magen David'. **1964** W. MARKFIELD *To Early Grave* (1965) vi. 109 During the Sinai campaign she beat two Egyptians to death with a *Mogen David* she herself welded together from a pair of captured gasoline drums. **1972** C. RAPHAEL *Feast of Hist.* (dust-jacket), The 'square' Magen David on the jacket appears in some Jewish manuscripts from late-fifteenth-century Portugal. **1975** *Jewish Chron.* 7 Feb. 21/5 Can anyone explain why Jewish greetings cards should be so expensive?.. Why should the addition of a..Magen David make them so much dearer than their non-denominational counterparts?

magenta (mə'dʒɛntə). The name of a town in Northern Italy where, in 1859, the Austrians were defeated by the French and Sardinians. Used for the name of a brilliant crimson aniline dye, discovered shortly after the date of the battle.
1860 *R. Smith's Patent* 11 Aug. in *Newton's Lond. Jrnl. Arts & Sci.* (1861) XIII. 225 What is called 'Magenta red', ..may be obtained as follows. **1861** R. HUNT in *St. James's Mag.* I. 43 The much-admired tones of the Mauve and Magenta. **1863** W. ROBERTS in *Proc. Roy. Soc.* XII. 481 On Peculiar Appearances exhibited by Blood-corpuscles under the influence of Solutions of Magenta and Tannin. **1891** *Truth* 10 Dec. 1240/2 Velvet of a peculiarly bright and daring tone of dahlia red, almost a magenta.
b. *attrib.* passing into *adj.*
1875 HUXLEY & MARTIN *Elem. Biol.* (1877) 7 Run in magenta solution under the cover-glass. **1877** READE *Wom. Hater* ix. I. 208 He wore..a magenta tie that gave Zoe a pain in the eye. **1896** BARRIE *Marg. Ogilvy* ix. 178, I used to wear a magenta frock and a white pinafore.
c. Qualifying other designations of colour.
1882 *Garden* 29 Apr. 288/2 Tulips..Proserpine, magenta-pink. *Ibid.* 298/3 The flowers..a glowing magenta-crimson.

mager, variant of MAUGRE.

mageram, obs. form of MARJORAM.

magery, obs. form of MAUGRE.

mageship ('meɪdʒʃɪp). [See -SHIP.] The position or function of a mage.
1875 E. DOWDEN *Shakspere: his Mind & Art* i. 37 Prospero must forever have remained somewhat apart and distinguished from other Dukes..by virtue of the enchanted island and the marvellous years of mageship.

magest-: see MAGIST-.

mageste, -ical, obs. ff. MAJESTY, MAJESTICAL.

†**magg**, *v.*[1] *Obs. rare*[−1]. [Cf. MAGGLE.] *trans.* To mangle.
a **1400–50** *Alexander* 1268 (Ashm. MS.) Þen mournes all þe Messedones..For maistris & mynistris menere & grettir, Þat was in morsels magged [*Dublin MS.* made] & martrid a hundreth.

magg (mæg), *v.*[2] *Sc.* [? f. MAG *sb.*[2], magpie.] *trans.* To pilfer.
1818 SCOTT *Hrt. Midl.* xlii, I hae made a clean house o' Jenny Balchristie and her niece. They were a bad pack—steal'd meat and mault, and loot the carters magg the coals.

magged (mægd), *a. Naut.* **a.** (See quot.)
1867 SMYTH *Sailor's Word-bk.*, *Magged*, worn, fretted, and stretched rope, as a magged brace.
b. Irritated; exhausted, jaded.
1839 F. TROLLOPE *Fragment in Dom. Manners Amer.* (ed. 5) 272 Mrs. Rapp... We shall be right down magged without her... Angelina... It won't convene for me to be mixing doe cakes..all day. **1903** *Eng. Dial. Dict.* IV. 7/2 I'm quite magged with my day's glanin'.

magger, magget, variants of MAUGRE, MAGGOT.

maggezzine, obs. form of MAGAZINE.

Maggid ('mɑːgɪd). Also **Magid**, **m-**. Pl. **Maggidim**. [Heb. *maggīdh* narrator.] An itinerant Jewish preacher.
1892 I. ZANGWILL *Childr. Ghetto* I. 35 The central place of honour which befits a Maggid. **1902** H. HAPGOOD *Spirit of Ghetto* x. 289 He was sitting opposite an old 'magid', or wandering preacher. **1941** G. G. SCHOLEM *Major Trends Jewish Mysticism* ix. 329 Rabbi Baer the *Maggid*, or popular preacher. **1960** L. P. GARTNER *Jewish Immigrant* iv. 105 Hirsch Dainow (1833–1877), a recently arrived Maggid of some note.

maggie ('mægɪ). [f. MAG *sb.*[2] + -IE.]
1. *Sc.* A girl.
1603 *Philotus* cxxxvi, ȝe trowit to get ane burd of blisse, To haue ane of thir Maggies. **1819** G. BEATTIE *Ketty Pert* Poems (1826) 83 Troth, little profit has she made By fisher maggies.
2. a. *Sc.* Local name for the Common Guillemot (*Alca troile*).
1885 in SWAINSON *Provinc. Names Birds.*
b. *dial.* and *Austral.* A magpie.
1825 J. T. BROCKETT *Gloss. North Country Words* 131 *Maggy*, a magpie. **1878** *Zoologist* Sept. 332/1 Magpie. *Piet*; *Maggie*. **1934** *Bulletin* (Sydney) 19 Sept. 21/2 Out maggie went backwards through the door, arguing every inch of the ground. **1965** *Jrnl. Lancs. Dial. Soc.* Jan. 7 *Maggie*: Tunstall, Burton, Hornby, Bentham, [etc.].
3. *Rifle-shooting.* = MAGPIE 7, MAG *sb.*[2] 3.
1901 *Daily Chron.* 22 July 7/2 The Englishman fired again, and once more it was only a 'maggie'.
4. In full, ***Maggie Ann*** (also ***Maggy Anne***). Margarine. *colloq.*
1933 PARTRIDGE *Slang To-day & Yesterday* 385 *Maggie Ann.* Margarine: C20. **1959** I. & P. OPIE *Lore & Lang. Schoolch.* ix. 163 Margarine or 'marg' is 'Maggy Anne'. **1971** D. LEES *Rainbow Conspiracy* vi. 91 Sam never paid him enough to put maggy on his bread.

magging (mægɪŋ), *vbl. sb. slang.* [f. MAG *v.* + -ING[1].] Chattering, talking.
1814 PEGGE *Suppl. to Grose*, *Magging*, prating, chattering. *a* **1845** HOOD *Sweep's Complaint* 34 But I'm bound the members as silenced us, in doing it had plenty of magging. **1849** ALB. SMITH *Pottleton Leg.* vii. 48 'It's a pity she's so deaf'.. 'Oh, it's a great comfort, sir... It stops all magging'. **1864** E. YATES *Broken to Harness* xxx, The chatter and magging of these silly women.

†'**maggle**, *v. Sc. Obs.* Also 6 **maggill, magel**, 7 **maigle.** [Of obscure etymology: connexion with MANGLE *v.* is difficult to justify.] *trans.* To mangle, maul, damage.
1456 SIR G. HAYE *Law Arms* (S.T.S.) 278 Gif it hapnyt ony..man to be slayn in felde, and sa magglit that his visage mycht nocht be knawin. **1500–20** DUNBAR *Poems* lix. 3 A refyng sone of rakyng Muris Hes magglit my making. **1513** DOUGLAS *Æneis*, *Time, etc. of Transl.* 24 Bot redis leill, and tak gud tent in tyme, Ȝhe nowder maggill nor mismetir my ryme. **1570** LEVINS *Manip.* 10/26 To Maggle, *mactare, excarnificare*. *Ibid.* 127/24 To Maggil, *mactitare*.
Hence '**maggled** *ppl. a.*
1513 DOUGLAS *Æneis* VI. viii. 39 King Priamus son, with body tore and rent, Thair he beheld, and creuell maglit face. *a* **1555** LYNDESAY *Tragedie* 385 Lyke doytit Doctoris new cum out of Athenis, And mummyll ouer ane pair of maglit matenis. **1603** *Philotus* cliii, My maiglit face maks mee to feill, That myne man be the same [i.e. a devil].

maggot[1] ('mægət). Forms: 4, 6 **magotte**, 5 **magat, maked**, 5–6 **mag(g)ote**, 5–7, 9 **magot**, 6 **mag(g)ette, magot(t)e**, 7 **magget**, 6– **maggot.** [Prob. related in some way to the synonymous ME. *maðek* MADDOCK; but the exact formation is not easy to determine.
The 15th c. form *maked* (only once, in a glossary) may be a metathetic alteration of *maðek, madek*; but even if so, it may be only an individual blunder, and in any case it seems unlikely to be the source of the mod. form; more probably it represents an occasional pronunciation of *maggot* (cf. mod. Somerset *macket* for MAGGOT[2]). Possibly the form *mak*, MAWK (a variant of MADDOCK) may have suggested a jocular application of the female nickname *Maggot* for Margaret (cf. MAGGOT[2] and the north midland dial. *dick* for a louse).]
1. A worm or grub of the kind formerly supposed to be generated by corruption; chiefly applied to the larva of a dipterous fly, *esp.* those of the cheese-fly and the flesh-fly or 'blue-bottle'. ***red maggot***: the larva (destructive to corn) of the wheat-midge.
1398 TREVISA *Barth. De P.R.* XVIII. cxv. (1495) 856 Magottes ben wormes that brede of corrupt and rotyd moysture in flesshe. *c* **1440** *Promp. Parv.* 321 (s.v. *Make*) *Winchester MS.*, Magat, may, or math, *tarmus, cimex* [*Phillipps MS. and Pynson c* 1500 *have* magot]. *c* **1475** *Pict. Voc.* in Wr.-Wülcker 767/5 *Hic tarinus* [read *tarmus*], *hic simax* [? = *cimex*], a maked. **1496** *Fysshynge w. Angle* (1883) 29 In Juyll take..the codworme & maggotes vnto Mighelmas. *c* **1515** *Cocke Lorell's B.* 2 His hosen gresy upon his thyes, That place for magottes was very good. **1542** BOORDE *Dyetary* xiii, In High Alemen the chese whiche is full of magotes is called there the best chese. **1602** SHAKS. *Ham.* IV. iii. 24 Your worm is your onely Emperor for diet. We fat all creatures else to fat vs, and we fat our selfe for Magots. **1663** BUTLER *Hud.* I. iii. 1276 But I deny they are the same, More then a Maggot and I am. **1698** G. THOMAS *Pensilvania* (1848) 22 Sheep..are generally free from those infectious Diseases..the Rot, Scab, or Maggots. **1774** GOLDSM. *Nat. Hist.* (1776) VIII. 4 Caterpillars may be easily distinguished from worms or maggots, by the number of their feet. **1859** DARWIN *Orig. Spec.* xiv. (1873) 387 The larva or maggot of a fly, namely the Cecidomyia, producing asexually other larvæ. **1867** F. FRANCIS *Angling* i. (1880) 27 Maggots, or gentles, as they are more commonly called by metropolitan anglers. **1871** TYNDALL *Fragm. Sci.* (1879) II. xiii. 293, I jumped to the conclusion that these maggots had been spontaneously generated in the meat. **1886** *Times* 18 Aug. 10/6 The wheat midge..produces the red maggots which so seriously damage the ripening ears of corn.
fig. **1649** G. DANIEL *Trinarch.*, *Hen. IV* ccclxxi, The Maggots of the Court Eate into favour; where they bred, they bite. **1780** COWPER *Progr. Err.* 326 Ye pimps..Who fasten without mercy on the fair, And suck, and leave a crawling maggot there. **1809** E. S. BARRETT *Setting Sun* II. 125 The disgusting scene of the maggots of avarice, corruption, and meretricious influence preying on the state.
2. A whimsical or perverse fancy; a crotchet.
a **1625** FLETCHER *Women Pleased* III. iv, Are not you mad, my friend?.. Have not you Maggots in your braines? *c* **1645** HOWELL *Lett.* (1688) II. 328 There's a strange Magot hath got into their Brain. **1678** DRYDEN *Limberham* v. 1, What new maggot's this; you dare not, sure, be jealous! **1685** S. WESLEY (*title*) Maggots; or Poems on several subjects. **1693** SHADWELL *Volunteers* v. Wks. 1720 IV. 480 *Blunt.* Ha Fellow! what dost thou mean by a maggot? *Hop.* Sir, a little concern of mine in my way, a little whim, or so, Sir. **1717** PRIOR *Alma* I. 400 Your Horace owns, he various writ, As wild or sober maggots bit. **1784** BURNS *Common Pl. Bk.* August, One who spends the hours..with Ossian, Shakspeare,..&c.; or, as the maggot takes him, a gun, a fiddle, or a song to make or mend. **1802** WOLCOT (P. Pindar) *Pitt & his Statue* Wks. 1812 IV. 501 Soon as a maggot crept into my head I caught a stump of pen and put it down. **1816** SCOTT *Antiq.* xxxviii, For a' the nonsense maggots that ye whiles take into your head, ye are the maist wise and discreet o' a' our country gentles. **1898** D. C. MURRAY *Tales* 255 She's got some maggot in her head about being loved for her own sake.
†**b.** Fancifulness. *Obs. rare.*
1701 COLLIER *M. Anton.* etc. 257 A handsome young Lady..dress'd like Quality, but not to any degree of Magot or Curiosity.
c. *Proverb.*
1687 MIEGE *Gt. Fr. Dict.* II. s.v., I shall do it, when the maggot bites. *Je le ferai, quand il m'en prendra envie.*
†**d.** Used in the names of many dance-tunes. *Obs.*
1716 *Dancing-Master* (ed. 16) 179 Betty's Maggot. *Ibid.* 180 Mr. Beveridge's Maggot. *Ibid.* 191 Huntington's Maggot. *Ibid.* 203 Drapers Maggot. *Ibid.* 211 Mr. Lane's Maggot. *Ibid.* 224 Captain's Maggot. *Ibid.* 245 My Lord Byron's Maggot. *Ibid.* 258 Carpenters Maggot. *Ibid.* 264 George's Maggot [etc.]. **1719** *Ibid.* II. 75 [ten similar titles].
3. A whimsical or capricious person.
1681 T. FLATMAN *Heraclitus Ridens* No. 39 (1713) I. 259 Whose britch has most Fire in it, Harry's, or the Maggots and Whigs? *a* **1700** B. E. *Dict. Cant. Crew*, *Maggot*, a whimsical Fellow, full of strange Fancies. **1725** BAILEY *Erasm. Colloq.* (1733) 230 You were as great a Maggot as any in the World when you were at Paris. **1735** DYCHE & PARDON *Dict.*, *Maggot*,..a whimsical Fellow that is full of strange freakish Fancies.
4. *attrib.* and *Comb.*, as ***maggot ostentation***; ***maggot-eaten***, (sense 2) ***-headed, -pated*** adjs.; **maggot-boiler** *slang*, a tallow-chandler; **maggot-fishing**, angling with a maggot for bait; †**maggot-monger**, a crotcheteer; †**maggot-pate**, a silly whimsical person; **maggot-pimple**, a form of acne (*Acne punctata*); **maggot-race**, a race between maggots or grubs.

1796 *Grose's Dict. Vulgar Tongue*, **Maggot-boiler*, a tallow chandler. **1621** BURTON *Anat. Mel.* Democr. to Rdr. (1651) 28 Going barefoot to..our Lady of Lauretts..to creep to those counterfeit and *Maggot-eaten Reliques. **1804** *Kentish Angler* title-p., Worm, Minnow, Cadis, and *Maggot Fishing. *a* **1695** WOOD *Life* (O.H.S.) I. 273 A *maggot-headed person and humourous. **1660** *Bibliotheca Fanatica* 2 Jeremy Ives, the gifted *Maggot-Monger. **1588** SHAKS. *L.L.L.* v. ii. 409 These summer flies, Haue blowne me full of *maggot ostentation. **1622** FLETCHER *Sp. Curate* IV. v, Did you thinke, had this man been rich,..He would have chosen such a Wolfe, a Cancker, A *Maggot-pate, to be his whole Executor. **1681** T. FLATMAN *Heraclitus Ridens* No. 39 (1713) I. 259 The *Maggot-pated Whigs, who would ..set us all on Fire at Home. **1687** KIRBY & BISHOP *Marrow of Astrol.* I. 60 Nice conclusions, and maggot pated whimsies, to no purpose. *a* **1700** B. E. *Dict. Cant. Crew, Bully-fop*, a Maggot-pated, huffing, silly, ratling Fellow. **1822** GOOD *Study Med.* II. 292 It is necessary to make the pressure harder than for the discharge of the mucus in the *maggot-pimple. **1856** MAYNE *Expos. Lex.*, *Maggot Pimple*, a common name for the *Varus punctatus*. **1792** W. ROBERTS *Looker-on* No. 28 (1794) I. 400 To run a *maggot-race with Jack Smoaky. **1810** *Sporting Mag.* XXXV. 69 Lost fifty pounds with Jack Frolic on a maggot race.

maggot[2] (ˈmægət). [A use of *Magote* (Cursor M. 25455), a. F. *Margot*, pet name for *Marguerite* Margaret.] † **a.** Applied as a proper name to (*a*) a magpie; (*b*) a sow. *Obs.* **b.** A magpie (see also MAGGOT-PIE). Now *dial.*

1573, etc. [see MAGGOT-PIE]. **1608** H. CLAPHAM *Errour on Left Hand* 49 Maggot my sow. **1791** WOLCOT (P. Pindar) *Magpie & Robin* Wks. 1812 II. 475 All on a sudden, Maggot starts and stares. **1848** *Zoologist* VI. 2290 The magpie is a 'maggot' [in Worcestershire].

'maggotiness. [f. MAGGOTY + -NESS.] Maggoty condition.

1727 BAILEY vol. II, *Maggottiness.*

†**'maggotish,** *a. Obs.* [f. MAGGOT[1] 2 + -ISH.] Crotchety.

a **1700** B. E. *Dict. Cant. Crew, Whimsical*, maggotish. **1731** BAILEY, *Freakish, freaked*, whimsical, maggottish.

'maggot-pie. *Obs.* exc. *dial.* Forms: 6 **magget the py,** 6–7 **mag(g)ot-a-pie,** 7 **magot o' pie, magata-, meggata-, maggotte-, maggoti-pie, pye, maggot-pie, -pye,** 9 *dial.* **maggotty-pie.** [f. MAGGOT[2] (as quasi-proper name) + PIE; the middle syllable of some forms represents *the*; cf. F. *Margot la pie.*] A magpie.

1573 TUSSER *Husb.* (1878) 108 If gentils be scrauling, call magget the py. **1598** FLORIO, *Garzetta*, a magot a pie, or piot... *Gazzotto*, a maggot-a-pie. **1604** BRETON *Grimellos Fortunes* D 4 b, His wife..had in her house a young Pie; (which we call a Magot-a-Pie). **1605** SHAKS. *Macb.* III. iv. 125 Maggot Pyes, & Choughes, & Rookes. **1605** CAMDEN *Rem.* (1637) 166 So an Hare on a bottle for Harebottle; a Maggot-pie upon a Goate for Pigot [etc.]. **1611** COTGR., *Agasse*, a Pie, Piannet, or Magatapie. *Ibid.*, *Pie*, a Pye, Pyannat, Meggata-pye. **1632** CHAPMAN & SHIRLEY *Ball* I. i, At the Maggot-a-pie in the Strand, Sir. **1681** HICKERINGILL *Black Non-Conf.* Introd., Wks. 1716 II. 2 Did you never see a Crow or a Maggottepye sit pecking, and cawing..upon an Asses back? **1893** *Wilts. Gloss.*, *Maggotty-pie*..still in use.

†**'maggotry.** *Obs.* [f. MAGGOT[1] + -RY.] Folly, absurdity.

1706 *Reflex. upon Ridicule* 326 The maggotry of some people is inconceivable. **1731** MEDLEY *Kolben's Cape G. Hope* I. 309 The magotry is this.

maggoty (ˈmægətɪ), *a.* [f. MAGGOT[1] + -Y.]

1. Full of maggots.

1727 BAILEY vol. II, *Maggotty*, full of Maggots. **1787** FARLEY *Lond. Art Cookery* (ed. 4) 13 If it [cheese] be..full of holes, it will give reason to suspect that it is maggotty. **1844** *P. Parley's Ann.* V. 293 Jack..was fed with maggoty biscuit and bilge water. **1867** *Morn. Star* 9 Sept., A man was let off lightly for working up maggoty meat into polonies.

2. a. Full of whims and foolish fancies; freakish.

1678 NORRIS *Coll. Misc.* (1699) 136 To pretend to work out a neat Scheme of Thoughts with a maggoty unsettled Head is..ridiculous. **1706** FARQUHAR *Recruiting Officer* II. ii, Then should I have some rogue of a builder... Transform my noble oaks and elms into cornices..to adorn some maggotty, new-fashioned bauble upon the Thames. **1707** *Reflex. upon Ridicule* 304 He borrows an apish and magotty Carriage. **1816** KIRBY & SP. *Entomol.* (1843) I. 126 The common saying that a whimsical person is maggoty.. perhaps arose from the freaks the sheep have been observed to exhibit when infested by their bots. **1834–43** SOUTHEY *Doctor* xxiv. (1862) 62 His son proved as maggoty as the father. **1864** R. REID *Old Glasgow* 381 A maggoty fancy.

b. *Comb.*, as ***maggoty-headed, -pated*** adjs.

1667 WOOD *Life* 31 Aug., He [Aubrey] was a shiftless person, roving and magotie-headed. **1850** *N. & Q.* 1st Ser. II. 173/2 A maggoty-pated fellow is often used to express a whimsical man.

3. *Austral.* and *N.Z.* Also **maggotty**. Angry, bad-tempered, esp. in phr. ***to go maggoty***, to lose one's temper.

Dialectal evidence of this use is presented in *Eng. Dial. Dict.*

1919 W. H. DOWNING *Digger Dial.* 33 *Maggotty*, angry. **1936** F. SARGESON *Conversations with Uncle* 24 There was a shearer who used to go maggoty if a lamb wouldn't sit still. **1951** D. STIVENS *Jimmy Brockett* 31, I didn't need to, but I shaved every day and my old man made me maggotty by asking me one day, 'Do you shave up or down?' **1959** D. FORREST *Last Blue Sea* 74 He's down there..going maggotty about doctors and Japs and boongs.

magh(e, variant of MAUGH, MAW.

†**magha.** *Obs. rare*[−1]. [App. misspelling of L. *maga*, fem. of MAGUS.] A sorceress.

1609 DANIEL *Civ. Wars* VIII. cv, And doth with idle rest deforme vs more Than any Magha can or sorceresse.

maghemite (mægˈhiːmaɪt). *Min.* [f. MAG(NETITE + *hem-atite* (var. HÆMATITE) + -ITE[1].] A modification of ferric oxide, Fe_2O_3, belonging to the spinel family, which is found as brown isometric crystals, is highly ferromagnetic, and is principally an alteration product of magnetite.

1927 P. A. WAGNER in *Econ. Geol.* XXII. 846 The interesting form of ferric oxide under discussion appears to be identical in atomic structure with magnetite, but has the chemical composition and the physical properties of hematite... It is desirable that it should have a distinctive designation... I would suggest *maghemite*. **1944** *Trans. Geol. Soc. S. Afr.* XLVI. 30 Maghemite is the commonest and most widely distributed mineral in the Bushveld magnetic iron ores. **1962** W. A. DEER et al. *Rock-Forming Min.* V. 73 Maghemite is metastable, and inverts to haematite (α-Fe_2O_3) on heating.

Maghoore, obs. variant of MOGUL.

Maghribi (mæˈgrɪbiː), *sb.* and *a.* Also **Maghrabee, Maghrabi, Maghrebi.** [Arab. *maġribī*, lit. 'western'.] **A.** *sb.* **a.** A native or inhabitant of the Maghrib, a region of north-western Africa, including Morocco, Algeria, and Tunisia. **b.** The Arabic spoken in this region. **B.** *adj.* Of or pertaining to the Maghribi or their language.

1840 E. W. LANE tr. *Arabian Nights' Entertainments* II. xviii. 600 The people of Western Africa... Called by the Arabs 'El-Maghrib'. This name is generally given to the districts of Northern Africa west of Egypt. The inhabitants of those parts are called 'Maghrabees'. **1855** R. F. BURTON *Pilgrimage to El-Medinah & Meccah* I. viii. 228 We lay down upon the sand, to rest among a party of Maghrabi pilgrims travelling to Suez. **1898** A. J. BUTLER tr. *Ratzel's Hist. Mankind* III. v. v. 196 The Islamite world witnessed a great struggle for supremacy between..the Maghrebin in the west, the Mashrikin in the east. **1948** D. DIRINGER *Alphabet* II. iv. 272 Kufic gave rise to a number of varieties, ..in northern (known as Maghribi, or western) and central Africa. **1969** *Word* XXV. 116 In many varieties of Maghribi Arabic when it co-occurs with a sibilant in the same word.

maght, maȝt, etc.: see MIGHT, etc.

Maghzen (ˈmɑːxzən). Also **Maghasen, Makhzen, -an.** [Arab. *makzan*.] The Moroccan government; the dominant official class in Morocco; irregular Algerian horsemen in the service of France. Also *transf.*

1854 J. R. MORELL *Algeria* xxi. 392 Immediately that the tribes were subdued, the victors required them to supply irregular horsemen, called *makhzen* or *goum*, to attack the refractory. **1874** tr. *G. Rohlfs's Adventures Morocco* ix. 193 Every day at midday on his return from the Maghasen (palace of the Sultan and seat of government) I was called. **1894** G. MONTBARD *Among Moors* 169 A knot of soldiers of the Maghzen are plunging their horses into the stream. **1901** *Chambers's Jrnl.* 6 July 504/1 Laraiche, once offered to the British Maghzen (Government) in return for help against the enemies of the Sultan. **1930** *Economist* 24 May 1179/1 This loan of 62,500,000 francs was originally contracted by the Maghzen of Morocco. **1973** R. E. DUNN in Gellner & Micaud *Arabs & Berbers* 92 At the 'national' level it influenced foundation of the *makhzan's* policies towards the Saharan region, especially in relation to the southward expansion of French Algeria.

Magi (ˈmeɪdʒaɪ), *sb. pl.*: see MAGUS.

Magian (ˈmeɪdʒɪən), *a.* and *sb.* [f. L. MAG-US + -IAN.] **A.** *adj.* **a.** Of or pertaining to the Magi.

1716 PRIDEAUX *O. & N. Test. Connect.* I. iv. (1718) 170 Another reformation which he [Zoroaster] made in the Magian religion, was [etc.]. **1796** BP. WATSON *Apol. Bible* 160 Addicted to the magian superstition of two independent Beings. **1875** LIGHTFOOT *Comm. Coloss.* 151 It was then.. that the magian system took root in Asia Minor.

b. Magical. (*poet. rare.*)

1818 KEATS *Endym.* III. 264 Will he..keep me as a chosen food to draw His magian fish through hated fire and flame?

B. *sb.* One of the Magi; a follower of or believer in the Magi; a magician, wizard.

1578 *Bk. Com. Prayer* New Calendar 6 Jan., The Magians as vpon this day..worshipped Christ. **1716** PRIDEAUX *O. & N. Test. Connect.* I. iv. (1718) 174 It is not to be understood that all Magians, that is, all of the sect, were thus learned. **1768–74** TUCKER *Lt. Nat.* (1834) II. 471 His star appeared in the East, filling the Magians there with exceeding great joy. **1817** BYRON *Manfred* II. iv. 31 A Magian of great power, and fearful skill! **1861** GOLDW. SMITH *Lect. Mod. Hist.* 61 It little avails the king to rule the people if the Magian is to rule the king. **1877** *Outlines Hist. Relig.* 165 The Magians were ..a pre-Semitic and pre-Aryan priestly tribe in West Asia.

Magianism (ˈmeɪdʒɪənɪz(ə)m). [f. MAGIAN + -ISM.] The tenets or doctrines of the Magi.

1716 PRIDEAUX *O. & N. Test. Connect.* I. iv. (1718) 171 His [Zoroaster's] reformation of Magianism. **1841** *Blackw. Mag.* XLIX. 233 Some..were so deeply tainted..with mysticism and Magianism, as to retain but little trace of the primitive doctrines of Islam. **1864** PUSEY *Lect. Daniel* vi. 325 He had the..prejudice, that the Bible was indebted to Magianism for the belief in the life to come. **1880** HUXLEY in *19th Cent.* June 932 His mode of divination was fraught with danger to magianism in general.

magic (ˈmædʒɪk), *sb.* Forms: 4–6 **magike, magyke,** (5 **malgyk,** 6 **magict, magika**), 4–7 **magique,** 7–8 **magick,** 7 **magic.** [ad. OF. *magique*, ad. late L. *magica* (Pliny has *magicē* = Gr. *μαγική* sc. *τέχνη*), subst. use (by ellipsis of *ars* art) of the fem. of *magicus* MAGIC *a.*

In the mod. Rom. langs. the place of the word is taken by the cognate F. *magie*, It., Sp., Pg. *magia*, ad. med.L. *magia*, a. Gr. *μαγεία* f. *μάγος* MAGUS.]

1. a. The pretended art of influencing the course of events, and of producing marvellous physical phenomena, by processes supposed to owe their efficacy to their power of compelling the intervention of spiritual beings, or of bringing into operation some occult controlling principle of nature; sorcery, witchcraft. Also, the practice of this art.

The 'magic' which made use of the invocation of evil or doubtful spirits was of course always regarded as sinful; but *natural magic*, i. e. that which did not involve recourse to the agency of personal spirits, was in the Middle Ages usually recognized as a legitimate department of study and practice, so long as it was not employed for maleficent ends. Of 'natural magic' as understood by mediæval writers, typical examples are the making of an image, under certain astrological conditions, in order to injure or benefit the health of the person represented; and the application of a medicament to a weapon in order to heal the wound made by it. These things, if now practised, would still be called 'magic', though the qualification 'natural' would seem quite inappropriate. On the other hand, the 'natural magic' of the Middle Ages included much that from the standpoint of modern science is 'natural', but not 'magical', the processes resorted to being really, according to the now known laws of physical causation, adapted to produce the intended effects.

c **1386** CHAUCER *Man of Law's T.* 116 They speken of Magyk and Abusion. **1390** GOWER *Conf.* III. 46 Magique he useth forto winne His love. **1447** BOKENHAM *Seyntys* (Roxb.) 268 The myht of malgyk or enchauntement. **1490** CAXTON *Eneydos* xxiv. 88 She inuoqued..the moder of magyque in her triple proporcyon. **1509** HAWES *Past. Pleas.* xxxvi. (Percy Soc.) 189 My swerde..set with magykes arte. **1569** BP. PARKHURST *Injunctions* Articles to be inquired of ¶29 Whether ye know any that vse any sorcerie Inchantments, Magika [etc.]. **1581** N. BURNE *Disput.* xxii. 102 b, As for the practeis of magict I micht obiect vnto you Willox, quhais sone raised the deuil. *c* **1590** MARLOWE *Faust* Prol., Nothing so sweete as magicke is to him. **1642** FULLER *Holy & Prof. St.* II. x. 89 When they cannot flie up to heaven to make it a Miracle, they fetch it from hell to make it Magick. **1776** GIBBON *Decl. & F.* xxiii. (1869) I. 649 The arts of magic and divination were strictly prohibited. **1867** W. W. SMYTH *Coal & Coal-mining* 194 It is like an effect of magic to pass, with the safety-lamp in hand, into a fiery stall. **1884** H. JENNINGS *Phallicism* ii. 8 Magic, which means the unnatural interference with nature.

b. With defining adj. ***black magic*** [= F. *magie noire*]: a designation given by modern writers to the kind of magic that was supposed to involve the invocation of devils; opposed to ***white magic*** [= F. *magie blanche*]. ***natural magic***: see above.

c **1384** CHAUCER *H. Fame* III. 176 And Clerkes eke which konne wel Alle this magikes naturel That craftely doon her ententes To maken in certeyn ascendentes Ymages, lo, thrugh which magike To make a man ben hool or syke. *c* **1386** —— *Prol.* 416. **1477** NORTON *Ord. Alch.* i. in Ashm. (1652) 21 And also of Magique naturall. **1605** BACON *Adv. Learn.* I. iv. § 11 Natural magic pretendeth to call and reduce natural philosophy from variety of speculations to the magnitude of works. **1718** BP. HUTCHINSON *Witchcraft* ii. (1720) 34 White Magic, that pretends to deal only with Good Angels. **1871** TYLOR *Prim. Cult.* I. 125 What with slavery and what with black-magic, life is precarious among the Wakhutu.

†**c.** A magical procedure or rite; also *concr.* a magical object, a charm, fetish. *Obs.*

c **1386** CHAUCER *Sqr.'s T.* 210 It is rather lyk An apparence ymaad by som Magyk. **1573** L. LLOYD *Pilgr. Princes* 37 There are diuers kindes of these Magicks, whereby they bragge and boast that they are able to do any thing, and that they know herebye all things. **1603** DRAYTON *Bar. Wars* II. xi, To sing..Of gloomie Magiques, and benumming Charmes. **1814** BRACKENRIDGE *Jrnl.* in *Views Louisiana* 256 Besides their public resident lodge, in which they have a great collection of magic, or sacred things, every one has his private magic in his lodge about his person. *Ibid.* 257 On these occasions, each one suspends his private magic on a high pole before his door.

d. ***like magic***: without any apparent explanation; with incredible rapidity. (Cf. LIKE *a.*, etc. B. I b.)

1857 *Knickerbocker* Jan. 98 Broiled chicken and oysters.. disappeared from before us like magic. **1900** *Congress. Rec.* 9 Jan. 704/2 Germany's Chinese trade is increasing like magic.

2. *fig.* A secret and overmastering influence resembling magic in its effects.

1611 SHAKS. *Winter T.* v. iii. 39 Oh Royall Peece: There's Magick in thy Maiestie. *a* **1631** DONNE *Poems* (1650) 19 All such rules, loves magique can undoe. **1702** *Eng. Theophrast.* 104 Civility is a strong Political magick. **1792** S. ROGERS *Pleas. Mem.* II. 26 The Moon..gilds the brow of night With the mild magic of reflected light. **1805** FOSTER *Ess.* IV. v. 192 A transforming magic of genius. **1822** W. IRVING *Braceb. Hall* iii. 28 The work of the house is performed as if by magic, but it is the magic of system. **1837** DISRAELI *Venetia* I. xviii, What mourner has not felt the magic of time? **1869** FREEMAN *Norm. Conq.* (1876) III. xi. 60 Won over by the magic of his personal presence.

3. *transf.* The art of producing (by legerdemain, optical illusion, or devices suggested by knowledge of physical science)

surprising phenomena resembling the pretended results of 'magic'; conjuring.

1831 Brewster (*title*) Natural Magic. *Mod. Advt.*, Professor —'s Home of Magic and Mystery.

4. *Comb.*, as ***magic-monger***; ***magic-gifted***, ***-like***, ***-planted***, ***-tempered*** adjs.; **magic-man**, a magician, sorcerer; also *fig.*

1811 W. R. Spencer *Poems* 49 [Painting's] *magic-gifted hand. **1862** Lytton *Str. Story* II. 223 That wand, of which I have described to you the *magic-like effects. **1905** *Westm. Gaz.* 6 Apr. 3/2 Disease was thought to be a visitation of supernatural wrath, to be appeased by offerings to the priests and *magic-men of the time. **1923** R. Graves *Whipperginny* 51 Time and Space, folly's wonder, Three-card shufflers, magic-men! **1959** Halas & Manvell *Technique Film Animation* v. 62 Magic-men, mummers and actors wore masks in earlier times to typify..the farcical, the comic, the eccentric, the pathetic, the tragic and the insane in human portraiture. **1635–56** Cowley *Davideis* I. 519 *note*, Which Texts..are ill produc'd by the *Magick-mongers for a Proof of the Power of Charms. **1852** J. H. Newman *Callista* (1856) 168 Mere atheists and magic-mongers. **1759** Mason *Caractacus* 2 These mighty piles of *magic-planted rock. **1777** Warton *Poems* 71 The monarch's massy blade Of *magick temper'd metal made.

magic ('mædʒɪk), *a.* [a. F. *magique* (= Pr. *magic*, Sp. *mágico*, It., Pg. *magico*), ad. L. *magicus*, ad. Gr. *μαγικός*, lit. pertaining to the Magi, f. *μάγος*: see Magus.]

1. a. Of or pertaining to magic (freq. in phr. † ***art magic***, ***magic arts***, etc.). Also, working or produced by enchantment. Not in predicative use.

1390 Gower *Conf.* II. 259 Jason..Upon Medea made him bold, Of art magique, which sche couthe. *a* **1547** Surrey *Æneid* iv. (1557) F iij, To magike artes against my will I bend. *c* **1590** Greene *Fr. Bacon* iv, Set him but Nonplus in his magicke spels. **1591** Shaks. *1 Hen. VI*, I. i. 26 Sorcerers..By Magick Verses haue contriu'd his end. **1634** Milton *Comus* 798 Till all thy magick structures rear'd so high, Were shatter'd into heaps o're thy false head. **1658** Waller *Æneis* iv. Poems (1664) 189 With loose hair The Magick Prophetess begins her prayr. **1679** Dryden *Troilus & Cr.* II. iii, He may know his man without art magic. **1695** Ld. Preston *Boeth.* iv. 175 Whilst into various Forms her Magick Hand Doth turn those Men. **1736** Gray *Statius* I. 54 The sun's pale sister, drawn by magic strain. **1767** Sir W. Jones *Seven Fount.* in *Poems* (1777) 41 A..joyless place, A scene of nameless deeds, and magick spells. **1830** Pusey *Hist. Enq.* II. 289 By some magic process [to] form the dissevered members into a frame of more youthful vigour.

b. Of a material object, a diagram, etc.: Employed in magic rites, endued with magic powers, enchanted. ***magic glass***, ***mirror***: one in which the spectator is supposed to see the representation of future events or distant scenes; often *fig.*

1697 Dryden *Virg. Georg.* III. 446 This..With noxious Weeds..Dire Stepdames in the Magick Bowl infuse. **1712** Steele *Spect.* No. 332 ⁋1 They describe a sort of Magick Circle. **1786** Burns *To J. S.* xii, Where Pleasure is the Magic-wand, That, wielded right, Maks Hours like Minutes [etc.]. **1792** S. Rogers *Pleas. Mem.* I. 91 Memory—What softened views thy magic glass reveals. **1843** Carlyle *Past & Pr.* II. i, And in this manner vanishes King Lackland; traverses swiftly our strange intermittent magic-mirror. **1870** L'Estrange *Life Miss Mitford* I. vi. 185 The possessor of a magic crystal ball. **1877** W. Jones *Finger-ring* 107 A portrait of Hadrian, engraved with Mercury in a magic ring. **1903** F. W. H. Myers *Human Personality* I. 158 Just as the magic mill of the fable continues magical.

†**c.** Addicted to magic. *Obs. rare.*

1634 Sir T. Herbert *Trav.* 24 A Magique Nation.

2. Producing wonderful appearances or results, like those commonly attributed to sorcery. ***magic box***: applied *colloq.* to various, esp. electronic, devices; ***magic carpet***: a legendary carpet on which a person could be transported wherever he wished; also *transf.* and *fig.*; ***Magic Marker***: the proprietary name of an instrument, consisting of a tube of quick-drying ink and a felt-tipped pen, used for marking objects; also ***magic marker***.

1696 [see magic lantern]. **1744** Akenside *Pleas. Imag.* I. 16 The glances of her magic eye, She blends and shifts at will. **1826** Scott *Rev. Life Kemble* in *Lockhart* ii. (1839) 22/1 The vain longings which we felt that..the magic curtain [would] once more arise. **1842** Tennyson *Day Dream, Arrival* iv, The Magic Music in his heart Beats quick and quicker. **1877** C. Geikie *Christ* xlix. (1879) 589 Water at all times is a magic word in a sultry climate like Palestine. **1897** Kipling *Capt. Cour.* ix. 189 From San Diego to Sixteenth Street, Chicago, let the magic carpet be laid down. Hurry! oh, hurry! **1909** H. G. Wells *Tono-Bungay* IV. i. 434, I had to come off my magic carpet and walk once more in the world. **1931** *Times Lit. Suppl.* 20 Aug. 625/2 His Magic Carpet is a book of travels, by means of which he is transported into lands that he is fated never to see. **1935** A. J. Pollock *Underworld Speaks* 74/2 *Magic box*, crooked farobank box in which 53 instead of 52 cards are manipulated by dealer. **1935** J. Hargan *Gloss. Prison Lang.* 5 *Magic-box*, coil arrangement which starts any car—without the aid of key. **1936** *Daily Tel.* 15 Aug. 15/5 (*heading*) Nicknames of the freight expresses... The Magic Carpet is not from Arabia, but Kidderminster, bringing fine weaves to London's floors. **1945** *Daily Mirror* 15 Aug. 4/2 Most sensational development was the 'Magic Box', which gave our pilots a picture of the ground beneath them even though it was hidden by darkness and cloud. **1956** *Official Gaz.* (U.S. Patent Office) 4 Dec. TM5/2 Speedry Products, Inc., Richmond Hill, N.Y.... *Magic Marker*. Applicant disclaims the term 'Marker' apart from the mark as a whole. For Felt Nib Marking Pens Comprising Small Containers for Such Ink, Equipped with Caps and having Felt Nibs at their Ends for Marking. First use on or about Sept. 1, 1952. **1959** *20th Cent.* Nov. 325 Both radio receivers and television sets have been known and called for brief periods 'magic boxes'. **1960** *Guardian* 22 Mar. 10/4 The job of the 'magic boxes' in the wheelhouse is to take some of the chance out of trawling. **1960** D. Lessing *In Pursuit of English* vi. 204 The yapping..of the..puppies distracted Flo from her magic box. **1960** L. Meynell *Bandaberry* viii. 127, I had suddenly an immense desire to get on a magic carpet and float away..to some carefree place. **1962** L. Deighton *Ipcress File* xxxii. 209 A slim green file; on the cover it said 'Henry' in magic-marker lettering. **1964** 'S. Forbes' *Long Hate* (1966) ii. 16 Block letters. Magic Marker, unquestionably. Children used Magic Markers in school these days. **1971** R. Russell tr. *Ahmad's Shore & Wave* vii. 59 Nur Jahan felt as though she were on a magic carpet soaring towards the sky. **1971** C. Bonington *Annapurna South Face* App. B 255 Magic markers 20. **1973** 'J. Patrick' *Glasgow Gang Observed* xiii. 120 With chalk, magic markers, but most often with..aerosol spray paint, the pitch was marked out with slogans. **1974** D. Mackenzie *Zaleski's Percentage* iv. 94 That restaurant's his magic carpet. If they take it away from him, he'll never stop falling.

3. ***magic square***: a diagram consisting of a square divided into smaller squares, in each of which a number is written, their position being so arranged that the sum of the figures in a row, vertical, horizontal, or diagonal, is always the same. ***magic circle***: (*a*) an arrangement of numbers in concentric circles with radial divisions, with arithmetical properties similar to those of the magic square; invented by Benj. Franklin in 1749; (*b*) the title of a society of conjurers; (*c*) a circle used in magic as a protection against evil; (*d*) a small group of people who are privileged to receive confidential information, make important decisions, etc.

1704 J. Harris *Lex. Techn.*, *Magick Square*. **1749** Franklin *Let.* Wks. 1887 II. 159 You will readily allow this square of sixteen to be the most magically magical of any magic square ever made by any magician. **1797** *Encycl. Brit.* (ed. 3) X. 422 Dr. Franklin..has constructed, not only a magic square of squares, but likewise a magic circle of circles. [Description follows.] **1892** Barnard Smith & Hudson *Arithm. for Sch.* 19 Magic and nasik squares. **1912** *Magic Wand* Aug. 377/2 (*heading*) 'The Magic Circular'.—A monthly review of the magic art, issued for private circulation only amongst members of the Magic Circle. **1934** Webster, *Magic circle*, 1. a. A circle drawn by a magician about any person or place, within which demons raised by incantations were believed to have no power. b. A clearly defined place, group, or the like, entrance into which is regarded as desirable, pleasing, etc. **1955** *Radio Times* 22 Apr. 32/3 All this week magicians from all over the world are gathering to celebrate the Golden Jubilee of the Magic Circle. **1965** *Listener* 10 June 859/1 Kaiser wrote a series of plays centred on the love of two people. The pattern is throughout the same: the lovers are enclosed in a kind of magic circle which isolates them from the rest of the world. **1971** G. Mitchell *Lament for Leto* ii. 51 He..was an amateur conjuror and..was 'on the fringe of the Magic Circle'. **1973** *Jrnl. Genetic Psychology* CXXII. 168 The complete, circular form of the Ufos is reminiscent of the mandala or 'magic circle': i.e., totality. **1974** E. Ambler *Dr. Frigo* I. 65 Could he have concluded belatedly that letting me into the magic circle had been a mistake..? **1974** *Times* 13 Nov. 16/7 The Tories..would be making a profound mistake if they were to take the right to decide their leader out of the exclusive hands of the elected MPs and put it back into those of some kind of new-furbished Magic Circle.

4. ***magic (chain-)stitch*** (see quot. 1900).

1900 Day & Buckle *Art in Needlework* 41 A playful variation upon chain-stitch..is effected by the use of two threads of different colour... The light thread disappears, and comes out again to the left of the dark one... This 'magic stitch'..is to be found in Persian, Indian, and Italian Renaissance work. **1934** M. Thomas *Dict. Embroidery Stitches* 34 *Chain stitch—chequered*, also known as *magic stitch* and *magic chain stitch*. **1957** M. B. Picken *Fashion Dict.* 329/2 *Magic Chain-stitch*... Chain-stitch worked with two threads of different colors in one needle.

5. *Nuclear Physics.* Applied to a set of numbers which correspond to nuclei of exceptional stability when either the number of protons or the number of neutrons in it is equal to one of the set (now taken to be 2, 8, 20, 28, 50, 82, 126, and perhaps 184); hence applied to nuclei containing such a number of protons or neutrons; ***doubly magic***, containing a magic number of protons and also a magic number (not necessarily the same) of neutrons. Occas. extended to an analogous set of numbers (see quot. 1974) for electrons in atoms.

1949 O. Haxel et al. in *Physical Rev.* LXXV. 1766/1 A simple explanation of the 'magic numbers' 14, 28, 50, 82, 126 follows at once from the oscillator model of the nucleus. **1956** *Nature* 28 Jan. 159/1 The current work on fast-neutron capture..refines the earlier studies by D. J. Hughes of the variation of cross-section with atomic weight which..throws more light on the magic-number nuclei. **1969** *Physics Lett.* XXVIIIb. 544/2 Since the nucleon shells at $Z = 114$, $N = 184$ are not as 'magic' as those at $Z = 82$, $N = 126$, we would not expect an unusually small capture cross section for $^{294}110$. **1969** *Nature* 27 Dec. 1253/2 In calcium-40 which, like lead-208, is doubly magic and so a suitable isotope for nuclear structure calculations, the protons have been found to bunch together towards the centre of the nucleus. **1971** *Ibid.* 12 Feb. 451/2 One complication is that for heavier nuclei, the magic numbers probably differ for neutrons and protons. **1971** *Physics Bull.* Dec. 711/2 Much interest has been aroused by the prediction that the nucleus ($A = 298$, $Z = 114$) may be a doubly magic nucleus.., which could involve an island of stability in the mass region around 300. **1974** *Encycl. Brit. Micropædia* VI. 484/1 The magic numbers for atoms are 2, 10, 18, 36, 54, and 86.

6. In weakened use as an enthusiastic term of commendation: superlatively good, excellent, 'fantastic'. *colloq.*

1956 R. Barr *Long Arm* (*unpubl. film-script*) 100 *Ward*: Good with locks too, eh? *Thomas*: Magic! **1975** *Guardian* 26 May 11/3 Finally we ate in a pizza parlour. 'What's this pisser?' asked Jimmy. 'It's magic,' Gordon told him. **1976** *Scotsman* 24 Dec. (Weekend Suppl.) 5/1 'Oh, aye,' said Jock graciously, 'he's magic with that mashie.' **1987** *Weekend Tel.* 15 Aug. p. i/7 As I watched the rushes with diminishing anxiety, I found myself agreeing with our producer's favourite comment: magic.

magic ('mædʒɪk), *v.* [f. the sb.] *trans.* To transform, make, etc., (as if) by magic; also ***to magic*** (something) ***away***, to cause, as if magically, to disappear.

1906 Kipling *Puck of Pook's Hill* 304 There was Oak and Ash and Thorn enough in that year-end shower to magic away a thousand memories. **1909** L. M. Montgomery *Anne of Avonlea* xxiv. 282, I actually have a half-guilty feeling as if I had 'magicked' it [*sc.* a storm] up. **1925** W. de la Mare *Miss Jemima* 31, I discovered, as if the Fairy Creature herself had magicked it there..a large hay-wain. **1952** A. Grimble *Pattern of Islands* v. 104 A steel hook bought from a trade-store could only be magicked once, as a finished article. **1957** J. Frame *Owls do Cry* ix. 38 It was to have these things sitting in their head, like a charm, to magic away the drudgery. **1966** *New Statesman* 25 Nov. 792/2 Children, who are still capable of being magicked, will, I hope, get it for Christmas. Though it's not a children's book. **1972** *Times* 16 Feb 13/3 We cannot magic them away. **1973** D. Francis *Slay-Ride* iv. 56 He magicked some huge open sandwiches on about a foot of French loaf.

magical ('mædʒɪkəl), *a.* [f. magic *a.* + -al^{1}.]

1. a. Of or pertaining to magic; = magic *a.* 1.

1555 Eden *Decades* 181 They..vsed certeine secreate magicall operations. *c* **1590** Marlowe *Faust* i, Come, shewe me some demonstrations magical. *c* **1610** *Women Saints* 146 The superstition of the Christians, whose magicall artes do make them verie bragge. **1665** Glanvill *Def. Vanity Dogm.* 35 Those strange operations are not Mechanical but Magical. **1692** Locke *Toleration* III. x. Wks. 1727 II. 427 To confound the magical delusions of the Hereticks of that time. **1727** De Foe *Syst. Magic* I. iii. (1840) 63 Two things ..naturally made way for these magical studies. **1762–71** H. Walpole *Vertue's Anecd. Paint.* (1786) III. 253 Some thought his musical assembly only a cover..for magical purposes. **1863** Froude *Hist. Eng.* VII. 74 The service of God was asserted to be a reasonable service of the mind and heart, and not a magical superstition.

†**b.** = magic *a.* 1 b. *Obs.*

1623 Webster *Duchess Malfi* IV. i, It wastes me more, Than were't my picture, fashion'd out of wax, Stucke with a magicall needle, and then buried. **1624** Middleton *Game at Chess* III. ii, This is the room he did appear to me in; And, look you, this the magical glass that show'd him. **1652** Ashmole *Theat. Chem.* Prol. 8 By the Magicall or Prospective Stone it is possible to discover any Person in what part of the World soever. **1750** tr. *Leonardus' Mirr. Stones* 100 Fastened over the heart with magical bands.

†**c.** = magic *a.* 1 c. *Obs.*

1634 Sir T. Herbert *Trav.* 24 They [of Mohelia] are superstitious and Magicall.

2. Resembling magic in action or effect. Also, produced as if by magic.

1606 Shaks. *Ant. & Cl.* III. i. 31 Ile humbly signifie what in his name, That magicall word of Warre we haue effected. ? **1750** Franklin *Lett.* Wks. 1840 VI. 103 The most magically magical of any magic square. **1818** Byron *Ch. Har.* IV. xxix, All its hues Their magical variety diffuse. **1824** Miss Mitford in L'Estrange *Life* (1870) II. ix. 183 Some little hay was got in in a magical sort of way between the showers. **1851** Nichol *Archit. Heav.* 13 The almost magical velocity of light. **1877** Black *Green Past.* ii. (1878) 14 The magical disappearance of about fifty or sixty rabbits. **1884** *Nonconf. & Indep.* 12 June 577/2 The warm and abundant rain-showers..have already had a magical effect upon the face of the country.

†**3.** ***magical circle***, ***square***: see magic *a.* 3. *Obs.*

1749 Franklin *Lett.* Wks. 1887 II. 160, I am glad the perusal of the magical squares afforded you any amusement. I now send you the magical circle. **1915** *Encycl. Relig. & Ethics* VIII. 322/1 The famous constituent of the mediaeval magical circle.

Hence **magi'cality**, magical power or quality; **'magicalize** *v. trans.*, to give a magical character to.

1867 M. Arnold *Celtic Lit.* 161 The landscape..is suddenly magicalised by the romance touch. **1924** W. J. Locke *Coming of Amos* iv. 43 An untouched cheque-book of whose magicality he was innocently certain.

magically ('mædʒɪkəlɪ), *adv.* [f. magical + -ly^{2}.] In a magical manner; by or as if by magic.

1605 Camden *Rem.* (1657) 244 A ring magically prepared. **1701** Grew *Cosm. Sacra* IV. viii. 269 It was believed, that unless they were Magically used, they would do more hurt, than good. **1707** J. Stevens tr. *Quevedo's Com. Wks.* (1709) 454 Others more Superstitious, and Magically inclined. **1727–52** Chambers *Cycl.* s.v. *Magic Square*, This done, with the first progression repeated, he fills the square of the root 7 magically. **1870** Huxley *Lay Serm.* xiv. 352 There are other men who attain greatness because they embody the potentiality of their own day, and magically reflect the future. **1879** Farrar *St. Paul* (1883) 680 The stratagem was for the time almost magically successful.

magic eye. [f. magic *a.* + eye *sb.*^{1}] **a.** A miniature cathode-ray tube used as a tuning indicator on a radio receiver, or to indicate the

correct adjustment of other electrical equipment.

Magic Eye is registered as a proprietary name in the U.S. [**1936** *Official Gaz.* (U.S. Patent Office) 6 Oct. 21/1 RCA Manufacturing Company, Inc.,..*Magic eye* for radio receiving sets of the type equipped with cathode ray tubes for resonance indication and accessories and parts thereof.] **1937** *Night & Day* 26 Aug. 28/1 Should one..plump for the [wireless] set with a 'mystic eye', or are those which boast a 'magic eye' or an 'electric eye' to be preferred? **1939** *Proc. IRE* XXVII. 631/2 The ground wave alone was introduced into a receiver which had a 'magic eye'. With this wave, the 'eye' remained exactly fixed in deflection. **1962** A. NISBETT *Technique Sound Studio* v. 100 A 'magic eye' is a useful guide, but should not be relied on unless the recordist is quite sure of what its indications mean in terms of the particular programme material. **1968** *Radio Communication Handbk.* (ed. 4) ii. 20/2 Magic-eye tubes are often used as voltage indicators in a.f and r.f. measuring equipment and also widely as indicators of signal level for tape recorders.

b. A photo-electric cell or similar electrical device used for identification, detection, or measurement.

1938 *Sun* (Baltimore) 22 Feb. 20/3 Eleven pairs of 'magic eyes'..have counted approximately 7,000,000 motor vehicles during the last year. **1945** *Nature* 15 Sept. 320/2 The aids to the bombing of invisible targets which were variously called 'H_2S', the 'gen-box', 'Mickey' and the 'Magic Eye'. **1958** *Times* 2 May 7/2 The large radio antenna carried on the superstructure of the Victorious..was a form of 'magic eye'. **1962** *Daily Tel.* 26 Oct. 17/7 The 'magic eye' records the wagon numbers of freight vehicles moving at speeds up to 100 mph. **1974** *Country Life* 6 June 1449/1 An automatic 'magic eye' lets in exactly the right amount of light every time you want to take a picture.

magician (məˈdʒɪʃən). Forms: 4 **magicien**, 6 (*Sc.*) -7 **magitian**, 6 **magission**, 7- **magician**. [a. F. *magicien*, f. L. *magic-a* MAGIC *sb.*] One skilled in magic or sorcery; a necromancer, wizard. Also *occas.* a practitioner of legerdemain, a conjuror.

c **1384** CHAUCER *H. Fame* III. 170 Ther saugh I pley Magiciens and tregetours. **1390** GOWER *Conf.* II. 230 Protheüs..was an Astronomien And ek a gret Magicien. *c* **1560** *Misogonus* III. iii. 43 (Brandl), I am also a very scilfull southsaier and magission. **1596** DALRYMPLE tr. *Leslie's Hist. Scot.* I. 122 Burne ane and al Juglaris, magitianis, familiars wᵗ wicked and euill spirits. **1611** BIBLE *Exod.* viii. 18 The Magicians did so with their enchantments. **1687** DRYDEN *Hind & P.* III. 721 The dire magicians threw their mists around. **1780** HARRIS *Philol. Enq.* Wks. (1841) 499 Virgil himself had been foolishly thought a magician. **1822** BYRON *Werner* III. i. 341 A wise magician who has bound the devil. **1831** BREWSTER *Nat. Magic* vi. (1833) 148 Even the most ignorant beholder regards the modern magician as but an ordinary man. **1878** MACLEAR *Celts* ii. 25 The monarch of Ireland..having in his service his..magicians.

b. *fig.* One who exercises a power compared to that of magic.

18.. LOCKHART *Life Scott* (1869) IV. xxv. 40 A set of beautiful stanzas, inscribed to Scott by Mr. Wilson [in 1812] under the title of the 'Magic Mirror', in which..he designated him [Scott] for the first time by what afterwards became one of his standing titles, that of 'The Great Magician'. **1831** CARLYLE *Sart. Res.* III. ix, The Magician, Shakespeare. **1877** LD. W. P. LENNOX *Celebrities* Ser. II. II. 22 All have done equal justice to the genius of the Magician of the North [i.e. Walter Scott].

Hence †**maˈgicianess**, a female magician. *rare*⁻¹.

1651 J. F[REAKE] *Agrippa's Occ. Philos.* 74 Which the Egyptians seeing called Nature a Magicianess.

‖**magicienne**. *Obs. rare*⁻¹. [Fr., fem. of *magicien*: see prec.] A female magician.

1490 CAXTON *Eneydos* xxiv. 88 The vierge dyane, wherof maketh her Inuocacion this lady olde magicienne.

ˈmagic ˈlantern. [transl. of mod.L. *lāterna magica*: cf. F. *lanterne magique* (also, †*lanterne vive*), G. *zauberlaterne*.

De Chales *Curs. Math.* 1674 II. 655, 665, says that in 1665 'a learned Dane' exhibited at Lyons a contrivance 'sub nomine Laternæ magicæ', which his description shows to be identical with the instrument now so called. The common statement that the magic lantern is described by Kircher *Ars Magna Lucis et Umbræ* (1646) appears to be incorrect.]

An optical instrument by means of which a magnified image of a picture on glass is thrown upon a white screen or wall in a darkened room. Also *fig.*

1696 PHILLIPS s.v. *Lanthorn*, A *Magic Lanthorn*, a certain small Optical Macheen, that shews by a gloomy Light upon a white Wall, Spectres and Monsters so hideous, that he who knows not the Secret, believes it to be perform'd by Magick Art. **1753** SMOLLETT *Ct. Fathom* (1784) 172/2 The travelling Savoyards who stroll about Europe, amusing ignorant people with the effects of a magick-lanthorn. **1775** *Morning Chron.* 29 May 1 (Advt.), At Marylebone Gardens, To-morrow..will be presented The Modern Magic Lantern.. being an attempt at a Sketch of the Times in a variety of Caricaturas. **1840** C. FOX *Jrnl.* 21 July (1972) 100 We are all shadows in the magic lanthorn of Time. **1894** *Engineer* 23 Nov., The first to make magic lanterns in this country was Philip Carpenter, about 1808. **1933** S. SPENDER *Poems* 28 Where magic-lantern faces skew for greeting.

attrib. **1784** J. BARRY in *Lect. Paint.* v. (1848) 183 That appearance of magic-lanthorn-like..contrivance which sometimes offends in the works of Rembrandt. **1802** MAR. EDGEWORTH in A. J. C. Hare *Life* I. 105 Push on the magic-lanthorn slide. **1817** KEATS *Wks.* (1889) III. 4 To him they are mere magic-lantern horrors. **1874** W. CORY *Lett. & Jrnls.* (1897) 368 The jerky magic-lantern-slide manner of introducing scenes.

Hence **ˈmagic-ˈlanternist**, one who gives an exhibition with a magic lantern; **magic-lantern** *v.*, to exhibit as in a magic lantern.

1859 *Athenæum* 12 Feb. 219 That devil, whom the monks magic-lanterned till he grew so large as to be [etc.]. **1891** S. MOSTYN *Curatica* 165 After the tea they were handed over to a Punch, a Magic Lanternist, and a Conjuror. **1935** W. EMPSON *Poems* 29 All those large dreams by which men long live well Are magic-lanterned on the smoke of hell.

†**ˈmagicly**, *adv. Obs. rare*⁻¹. [f. MAGIC *a.* + -LY².] = MAGICALLY.

1683 E. HOOKER *Pref. Pordage's Mystic Div.* 79 Wisdom doth sometimes as it were magicly transfigure a man.

magico- (ˈmædʒɪkəʊ). Combining form of MAGICAL *a.* with other adjs. as ***magico-erotic***, ***-oriental***, ***-profane***, ***-religious***.

1915 *Encycl. Relig. & Ethics* VIII. 258/2 These are of a magico-erotic nature, and, like similar rites among savages, are founded on the belief that the ghost can cause fruitfulness, or perhaps may incarnate himself in the barren woman who performs the rite. **1930** *Times Lit. Suppl.* 27 Nov. 1004/3 As against the 'magico-oriental' view of the image maintained by the Iconoclast stands the Platonism of the image-worshipper. **1941** *Jrnl. R. Anthrop. Inst.* LXXI. 85/2 Numerous acts and ceremonies..which the European ..would place under the category of magico-profane, magico-religious or superstition. **1908** *Man* VIII. 46 The magico-religious ideas and practices of savage and proto-historic man. **1922** *Nature* 29 Apr. 540/2 The complex and inexorable system of magico-religious *gennas*. **1967** C. L. WRENN *Word & Symbol* 17 Anglo-Saxon magico-religious arts.

Magid, var. MAGGID.

†**magie**. *Obs. rare*⁻¹. [? ad. late L. *magīa* (whence F. *magie*): see MAGIC *sb.* (But perh. only a misprint.)] = MAGIC *sb.*

1592 G. HARVEY *Four Lett.* 56 Naturall Magie.

magilp, variant of MEGILP.

‖**magilus** (ˈmædʒɪləs). *Conch.* Pl. **magili**. [mod. Latin (D. de Montfort, 1810; the authorities cited by him do not contain the name, the origin of which is unexplained).] A gasteropod mollusc (*Magilus antiquus*) found in the Red Sea, parasitic upon living coral.

1824 DUBOIS *Epit. Lamarck's Arrangem. Testacea*, 21 The animal of the Magilus. **1851-6** WOODWARD *Mollusca* 12. **1876** *Beneden's Anim. Parasites* 38 A mollusc called *Magilus*, which naturalists considered for a long time to be the calcareous tube of an annelid. *Ibid.*, All conchologists know the shell of the Magili, so valued by collectors.

†**maginate**, *v. Obs. rare*⁻⁰. [? Shortened form of IMAGINATE *v.*] (See quot.)

1623 COCKERAM, *Maginate*, to trifle.

†**magine**, *v. Obs.* Aphetic variant of IMAGINE.

1530 PALSGR. 616/2, I magyne, declared in 'I ymagyn'.

Maginot (‖maʒino, ˈmædʒɪnəʊ). The name of a French minister of war, André *Maginot* (1877-1932), used to designate the line of fortifications (***Maginot Line***) built before the war of 1939-45 along the north-eastern borders of France, and in which the French placed excessive confidence. Also *transf.* (designating other similar lines of defence) and *fig.*

1936 *Times* 30 Oct. 15/4 The Maginot Line. M. Daladier ..inspected the recently completed frontier fortifications between Maubeuge and Valenciennes. **1937** A. VAGTS *Hist. Militarism* xii. 457 The American coast is the Maginot Line of the United States. **1938** *Nation* (N.Y.) 23 July 78 Little Steel's Maginot Line against unionism. *Ibid.* 83/2 Along the border the Czech Maginot Line is artfully concealed. **1940** *Economist* 27 July 118/1 Sea-power is no Maginot Line to lull us again into lethargy. **1940** L. B. NAMIER in *19th Cent.* Nov. 468 Her [*sc.* France's] system of alliances in East-Central Europe was as imperfect and as deceptive as her Maginot line later on. **1947** C. S. LEWIS *Miracles* xiv. 146 The belief that nothing but Nature exists and that if anything else did she is protected from it by a Maginot Line. **1972** *Times* 14 Nov. 17/2 The Dow has still to close above what is jestfully known on Wall Street as the 'Maginot Line' of 1,000. **1973** B. FREEMANTLE *Goodbye to Old Friend* i. 14 He..lifted out his tray containing pens..and set it..at the head of the blotter. My Maginot Line, he thought. Behind the tray, I'm safe. **1975** *Guardian* 27 Jan. 4/3 Casemate 35/3, a key heavy gun emplacement in the Maginot Line.

Hence *attrib.* and *Comb.*, as **Maginot-minded** *a.*, obsessed with the inviolability of the Maginot Line; ***Maginot(-Line) complex***, ***mentality***, etc.: indicating an obsession with defence (of the status quo, etc.) as an attitude of mind.

1940 *Economist* 13 July 37/1 The efficacy of blockade is a mirage, a delusion comparable to the Maginot-complex that bemused and enervated France. **1942** *Ann. Reg. 1941* 79 People began to wonder whether the Government had not become 'Maginot-minded'. **1955** *Bull. Atomic Sci.* Mar. 81/1 Maginot-line mentality..denotes..a one-sided preoccupation with putting all reliance on a single strategy. **1962** *Listener* 24 May 893/1 Defence is only relevant to my present argument as evidence of the Maginot attitude of the old and Great Powers. **1962** *Observer* 1 July 7/1 There is also the danger that a national shelter programme could lead to a Maginot Line psychology. **1973** *New Society* 13 Sept. 632/2 The NGA has been attacked by the non-craft unions for having a 'Maginot line mentality'.

magir, variant of MAUGRE.

magiric (məˈdʒaɪrɪk), *a.* and *sb. rare.* Also **mageiric**. [ad. Gr. μαγειρικός, f. μάγειρος cook.]

A. *adj.* Of or pertaining to cookery.

1853 SOYER *Pantroph.* 173 The magiric science, therefore, began in the year of the world 1656.

B. *sb. pl.* The art of cooking.

1889 *Syd. Soc. Lex.*, *Mageirics*.

magirist (məˈdʒaɪərɪst). *rare*⁻¹. [f. Gr. μάγειρ-ος cook + -IST.] An expert in cookery. So **magiˈristic** *a.* (in quot. *mageir-*), pertaining to cookery. **maˌgiroˈlogical** *a.*, skilled in cookery. **magiˈrologist** = MAGIRIST. **magiˈrology** [see -OLOGY], the art or science of cookery.

1814 *Sch. Gd. Living* 53 To their Magirists was given an appointment of culinary artists. *Ibid.* 59 From the very first appearance of magirology in Greece, it produced effects absolutely magical. *Ibid.* 72 Peace to your shades, ye noble magirologists. *Ibid.* 107 Roberto da Nola, a magirological artist of the most transcendent genius. **1892** *Punch* 21 May 249/1 Immortal contributions to mageiristic lore.

Magism (ˈmeɪdʒɪz(ə)m). [f. L. *mag-us* + -ISM.] The beliefs, principles and practices of the Magi.

1844 W. KAY *Fleury's Eccl. Hist.* III. 232 *note*, This may be another trace of Magism: for Mithra had his 'oblation of bread'. **1852** BADGER *Nestorians* I. 331 The connection of some of their doctrines and rites with Sabianism and Magism. **1864** PUSEY *Lect. Daniel* 539 It is then a mere myth, to speak of the relative purity of early Magism.

‖**magister** (məˈdʒɪstə(r)). [L.: see MASTER *sb.*] A mediæval and modern Latin title of academic rank, usually rendered by MASTER, but occas. employed *Hist.* or in speaking of foreign universities.

1756-7 tr. *Keysler's Trav.* (1760) I. 125 The first two years are again employed in..exercises, introductory to the degree of *magister*. **1864** BURTON *Scot Abr.* I. v. 255 Of old, when every *magister* was entitled to teach in the university, the regents were persons selected from among them.

magisterial (ˌmædʒɪˈstɪərɪəl), *a.* Also 7 **mages-**, **magisteriall**. [ad. med.L. *magisteriālis*, f. late L. *magisterius*, f. L. *magister* MASTER *sb.*] Of or pertaining to a master or a magistrate.

†**1.** Of or pertaining to a master-workman; displaying a master's skill; also, having the qualifications of a master. *Obs.*

1643 SIR T. BROWNE *Relig. Med.* I. § 34 These are certainly the Magisterial and master-pieces of the Creator. **1664** EVELYN tr. *Freart's Archit.* II. i. 90 Though it concede somewhat to it in the execution and magisterial handling. **1683** PETTUS *Fleta Min.* I. (1686) 343 These [Engravings] are not designed for Magisterial Artists.

2. Of, pertaining, or proper to a master or teacher, or one qualified to speak with authority. Of opinions, utterances, etc.: Authoritative. Of persons: Having the bearing of a master; invested with authority. Sometimes in unfavourable sense: Assuming authority, dictatorial.

1632 SANDERSON *Serm. ad Pop.* (1681) 293 [They] exercise a spiritual Lordship over their disciples..by imposing upon their consciences sundry Magisterial conclusions. **1644** MILTON *Judgm. Bucer* To Parlt., Wks. 1851 IV. 299 Where they thought to be most Magisterial, they have display'd their own want, both of reading, and of judgment. *c* **1645** HOWELL *Lett.* (1650) I. 427 Not to make any one's opinion so magisterial and binding, but that I might be at liberty to recede from it. **1690** LOCKE *Hum. Und.* III. ix. § 23 It would become us to be..less magisterial, positive, and imperious, in imposing our own Sense and Interpretations. **1697** COLLIER *Ess. Mor. Subj.* II. (1698) 86 These Magisterial Propositions don't Dispute for Belief, but demand it. **1699** BENTLEY *Phal.* Pref. 101 A Magisterial Air and too much Heat and Passion appear in their Writings. **1819** BYRON *Juan* II. lvi, For Juan wore the magisterial face Which courage gives. **1838-9** HALLAM *Hist. Lit.* III. III. vi. § 54. 317 There is something magisterial in the manner wherein he dismisses each play like a boy's exercise. **1903** *Class. Rev.* XVII. 131/2 His magisterial method of criticism as exhibited in the castigation of Thucydides.

3. Of, pertaining to, or proper to a magistrate or magistrates. Of persons: Holding the office of a magistrate. Of an inquiry: Conducted by magistrates.

1660 R. COKE *Power & Subj.* 31 When the laws or higher powers enable such men to nominate their magistrate, there the nominators are the instruments by which the law does transfer this magisterial power. **1711** SHAFTESB. *Charac.* VI. iii. (1737) III. 363 We need give her only in her hand the.. Magisterial Sword. **1775** ADAIR *Amer. Ind.* 288 While this military man acted in the magisterial office. **1795** COLERIDGE *Plot Discovered* 27 Any man, whom a magisterial neighbour chooses to insult under pretext of suspicion. **1883** *Fortn. Rev.* May 693 The progressive extension of magisterial jurisdiction. **1885** *Manch. Exam.* 20 Feb. 4/6 The magisterial inquiry into the charge of arson.

†**4.** *Alch.* and *Med.* Pertaining to a magistery; also, = MAGISTRAL 2. *Obs.*

1658 PHILLIPS *s.v.*, A pill or plaister, &c. prepared after the best manner is called Magisterial. **1683** PETTUS *Fleta Min.* II. 3 It [the word *kern*] may intend also that magisterial pouder of Projection. **1722** QUINCY *Lex. Physico-Med.* (ed. 2), *Magisterial Remedy*, is yet sometimes retained in the Cant of Empiricks, more for its great Sound than any Significancy.

†**5.** quasi-*sb.* or *sb.* = MAGISTERY 3. *Obs.*

1638 H. SHIRLEY *Mart. Soldier* III. iv. in Bullen *O. Pl.* I. 217 With it was dissolv'd the Magisteriall Made of the Horne Armenia so much boast of. **1657** TOMLINSON *Renou's Disp.* Pref., Every man must have his own Compositions and Magisterials. **1658** OSBORN *Jas. I*, Wks. (1673) 533 This Monster in excess, eat..a whole Pie..composed of Amber-Greece, Magesterial of Pearl, Musk, &c. **1662** J. CHANDLER *Van Helmont's Oriat.* 215 Magisterials among Chymists, do indeed melt the body of a thing, and do open it with a seperating of some certain dregs also.

†**magisteriality.** *Obs.* Also 7 **majesterialty.** [f. prec. + -ITY.] The quality or condition of being magisterial; mastership, authoritative position.

1655 FULLER *Ch. Hist.* IX. iv. § 11 When these Statutes were first in the state, or magisteriality thereof, they were severely put in practice on such offendours as they first lighted on. *a* **1661** —— *Worthies, Leicestersh.* II. (1662) 132 He [William de Leicester] was also known by the name of Mr. William an evidence..sufficient to avouch his Majesterialty in all Learning.

magisterially (ˌmædʒɪˈstɪərɪəlɪ), *adv.* [-LY².] In a magisterial manner.

1. In the manner of a master: **a.** like a schoolmaster; with superior knowledge or the assumption of it; authoritatively (now the dominant sense); **b.** like a lord over subjects; domineeringly.

1647 CLARENDON *Hist. Reb.* VI. § 126 Whilst the King was at Nottingham..they gave orders Magisterially for the War. **1651** in E. D. Neill *Virginia Carolorum* (1886) 213 The reason why they talk so Magisterially to us, is this, we are forsooth their worships slaves. **1693** EVELYN *De la Quint. Compl. Gard., Refl. Agric.* 50, I do not pretend Magisterially to Determine, whither of the two Opinions has the more of ..Reason on its side. **1729** BUTLER *Serm. Hum. Nat.* ii. Wks. 1874 II. 24 Conscience..without being advised with, magisterially exerts itself. **1761–2** HUME *Hist. Eng.* (1806) III. xlv. 645 He [James I] was employed in dictating magisterially to an assembly of divines. **1865** M. ARNOLD *Ess. Crit.* i. (1875) 40 When Protestantism..gives the law to criticism too magisterially. **1963** *Times* 4 Mar. 14/2 M. Planchon, who wrote every word of the text and was responsible for every step of the choreography, rarely stumbles and magisterially weaves the disparate threads into one homogeneous pattern. **1972** *Times* 15 June 7/3 These dons, judges and headmasters..who moved so magisterially within their cathedral closes, [etc.]. **1975** *Gramophone* Oct. 633/3 The new Karajan reading is certainly magnificent, magisterially played by the finest orchestra in the world.

2. In the capacity of a magistrate; also, by a magistrate or magistrates.

1875 POSTE *Gaius* I. (ed. 2) 138 A magisterially appointed guardian is called by modern commentators tutor dativus. **1883** *Pall Mall G.* 30 May 8/2 The men arrested..were magisterially examined at Castlebar to-day.

†**magi'sterialness.** *Obs.* [-NESS.] The quality or condition of being magisterial; assumption of authority.

1651 H. MORE *Second Lash* in *Enthus. Tri.*, etc. (1656) 168 Those two famous Philosophers..whom your Magisterialnesse has made bold to use at least as coursely as I seem to have used you. **1674** *Govt. Tongue* xi. §1 A magisterialness in matters of opinion. **1713** NELSON *Life Dr. Bull* 225 He chargeth him with too much precipitancy and magisterialness in judging.

†**magi'sterical,** *a. Obs. rare.* Also 7 **majesterical, -ycall.** [f. L. *magister* + -IC + -AL¹.] Pertaining or proper to a magistrate.

1646 LILBURNE & OVERTON *Out-cryes Oppressed Comm.* (ed. 2) 16 In case of Forfiting the Majesterycall trust, the trusters (the people) are disobleged from their obedience. **1670** BAXTER *Cure Church-div.* 288. **1680** HICKERINGILL *Meroz* 31 A Style..more Magisterical, Dictator-like.

†**magi'sterious,** *a. Obs.*—⁰ [f. late L. *magisterius* (see MAGISTERIAL) + -OUS.] Exercising the authority of a master. Hence †**magi'steriously** *adv.*, with an assumption of authority. †**magi'steriousness,** assumption of authority.

1650 R. HOLLINGWORTH *Exerc. Usurped Powers* 54 He delivering it (as he doth other odd and unsound stuffe) with a pythagoricall magisteriousnesse. **1673** *Lady's Call.* I. i. §9 He that ingrosses the talk, enforces silence upon the rest, and so is presumed to look on them only as his Auditors and Pupils, whilst he magisteriously dictates to them. **1684** N. S. *Crit. Enq. Edit. Bible* xv. 148 He censures the generality of Divines, who take upon them Magisteriously to judge of the matter in hand.

‖**magisterium** (ˌmædʒɪˈstɪərɪəm). [L.: = next.]

†**1.** *Alchemy.* = MAGISTERY 3 a. *Obs.*

1593 G. HARVEY *Pierce's Super.* 30 Hee is a Pythagorean, and a close fellow of his tongue, and pen, that hath the right *magisterium* indeede. **1610** B. JONSON *Alch.* I. iv, This is the day, I am to perfect for him The magisterium, our great worke, the stone. **1654** GAYTON *Pleas. Notes* II. ii. 39 Which without doubt hath a villanous *contagium* upon the grand *magisterium* of the Stone.

2. *R.C. Theol.* The teaching function of the Church.

1866 *Dublin Rev.* Apr. 422 Roman Catholics, throughout the world, are instructed in certain *doctrines*; are exhorted to certain *practices*; are encouraged and trained in certain *tempers* and *dispositions*. The Church's office in providing for this is called her 'magisterium'. **1893** *Tablet* 11 Feb. 205 Catholic obedience is due to the Church's magisterium, namely, the authoritative teaching of the Pope and the Bishops. **1899** *Dublin Rev.* Apr. 262 Opposed to the ordinary teaching magisterium of the Catholic Church.

magistery (ˈmædʒɪstərɪ). *Obs.* exc. *Hist.* Also 7 **majestery,** 9 **magestry, magistry.** [ad. L. *magisterium,* (1) in classical L. the office of a master, (2) in med.L. the philosopher's stone; f. *magister* MASTER *sb.*]

†**1. a.** = MAGISTRACY 2. **b.** = MAGISTRACY 4. *Obs.*

1566 PAINTER *Pal. Pleas.* (1575) I. 18 A goodlie document to men of like calling, to moderate them selues, and their magisterie with good and honest life. **1585** STUBBES *Anat. Abus.* I. 16 It is lawfull for the nobilitie, the gentrie, and the magisterie, to weare riche attire.

†**2. a.** The quality or functions of a master; mastership, authority, authoritative appearance. **b.** The office of a (Grand) Master. *Obs.*

1642 *Fuller Answ. to Dr. Ferne* 1 Blowing aside the Magistery of the Title, Author, Style of this Treatise, as but the pindust of it, that gilds but intercepts the Letter. **1644** J. GOODWIN *Innoc. Triumph.* (1645) 7 Resigne up his..conscience to be ordered, obliged, and tied, by the meere authority and magistery of men. **1660** JER. TAYLOR *Duct. Dubit.* III. iv. rule 22 §1 To give them [General Councils] a legislative power and magistery in faith. **1670** G. H. *Hist. Cardinals* II. II. 142 Francisco began..to manage it [the Church] with great Magistery and Dominion. **1706** PHILLIPS (ed. Kersey), *Magistery*, Mastership; especially the Office of the great Master of Maltha.

3. *Alchemy, Medicine,* etc. **a.** A master principle of nature; a potent transmuting or curative quality or agency; *concr.* a substance that has the power of transmuting or changing the nature of other substances, e.g. the philosopher's stone.

1594 PLAT *Jewell-ho., Chem. Concl.* 37, I wil not..discover any magistery upon so base an occasion. **1601** HOLLAND *Pliny* II. 165 Moreouer, they made proofe of the said floures dried, and this high magistery they found, That being beaten to pouder, they cured [etc.]. *c* **1645** HOWELL *Lett.* VI. xli. (1650) 232 He that hath water turn'd to ashes, hath the Magistery, and the true Philosophers stone. **1670** *Moral State Eng.* 43 That great Magistery of Nature (as they call it) the Philosophers stone. **1678** R. R[USSELL] *Geber* II. i. I. v. 31 For there is one Stone, one Medicine in which the Magistery consists. **1723** *(title)* The Hermetical Triumph, or, Victorious Philosophical Stone: a Treatise..concerning the Hermetical Magistery. **1837** WHEWELL *Hist. Induct. Sci.* (1857) I. 232 There existed preparations which possessed the power of changing the whole of a body into a substance of another kind: these were called magisteries.

fig. a **1677** HALE *Contempl.* II. 179 This is the great Engine of a Christian, a Magistery, that was never attained by the most exquisite Philosopher.

b. A product or result of transmutation.

1605 TIMME *Quersit.* I. i. 3 Which meale or flower we mixe with water, we leaven and bake; whereof ariseth a great magistery, namely bread. **1655** in Hartlib *Ref. Commw. Bees* 35 Honey is a Vegetable Magistery, in part perfected by the Specifick virtue of the flour,..compleated by the peerlesse virtue of the Bee, which doth transmute that sweetnesse into a new Creature, which is Honey. **1671** J. WEBSTER *Metallogr.* xii. 190 By this solvent the whole Metal is brought into another disposition, (which he calls a magistery).

c. The concentrated essence of a substance.

1641 FRENCH *Distill.* i. (1651) 26 Thou shalt have the true magistery or Spirit of Wine. **1658** tr. *Porta's Nat. Magic* x. xiv. 270 A Magistery..is what can be extracted out of things without separation of the Elements. **1668** *Phil. Trans.* III. 787 The volatile Salt, Spirit, Oyle, Magistery, made of the several parts of the Stagg.

d. The residuum obtained by precipitation from an acid solution, e.g. ***magistery of bismuth, pearls,*** etc.; a precipitate. Applied also to a resinous extract.

1602 F. HERING *Anatomyes* 15 Vnicornes horne,..Magistery of Pearles, and Forreine Bugges and Drugges. **1663** BOYLE *Usef. Exp. Nat. Philos.* II. ii. 159 The magistery prepared by dissolving them [pearls] in acid spirits. **1678** SALMON *Lond. Disp.* 852/1 Magisteries of Bones... They are dissolved with Acids..and precipitated with Alkalies. **1712** tr. *Pomet's Hist. Drugs* I. 29 The Resin or Magistery of Jalap is made with Spirit of Wine. **1756** C. LUCAS *Ess. Waters* I. 60 The metals are suddenly precipitated in the form of a magistery. **1794–6** E. DARWIN *Zoon.* IV. 96 A calx, or magistery, of bismuth. **1822** IMISON *Sci. & Art* II. 116 The magistry of bismuth, or pearl white. **1861** HULME tr. *Moquin-Tandon* II. III. ii. 89 The old practitioners..made use of a magestry or precipitate of coral.

e. A specially prepared medicine; a specific.

1669 W. SIMPSON *Hydrol. Chym.* 162 It would have proved a very good magistery for a horse. *c* **1720** W. GIBSON *Farrier's Dispens.* III. II. (1734) 112 There is a magistery made from Calamine.

†**4.** An art, craft, or employment. *Obs.*

1647 LILLY *Chr. Astrol.* lxxxiv. 450 These two Planets are the Significators of Magistery, Trade or Profession. **1669** *Addr. hopeful young Gentry Eng.* 72 These mistresses of the Magistery of dissimulation are the greatest enemies to the convers of the world.

5. = MAGISTERIUM 2.

1899 C. B. PALLEN tr. *Sarda y Salvany's What is Liberalism?* xxxii. 105 The Church alone possesses supreme doctrinal magistery in fact and in right.

magistracy (ˈmædʒɪstrəsɪ). Also 6–7 **magistracie,** 7 **magistratie.** [f. MAGISTRATE: see -ACY.]

†**1.** The existence of magistrates; the condition of being a magistrate. *Obs.*

c **1585** R. BROWNE *Answ. Cartwright* 3 As for the Maiestracie of Byshops there is no lawe to warrant it. **1587** *T. Norton's Calvin's Inst.* IV. xx. 496 *marg.*, Magistracy [is] not taken away by the libertie which is promised in the gospell. **1612** T. TAYLOR *Comm. Titus* ii. 12 We..in magistracie and subjection, must shew what price we set on Gods mercie. **1644** A. BURGESSE *Magistr. Commiss. fr. Heaven* 2 He was convinced the state of Magistracie he lived in to be pleasing to God. **1693** DRYDEN *Persius* (1697) 455 Young Noblemen..were too forward in aspiring to Publick Magistracy.

2. The office of the magistrate; magisterial power or dignity; *occas.* conduct in office as a magistrate. Now *rare.*

1577 tr. *Bullinger's Decades* (1592) 169 The Magistracie (that I may henceforwarde vse this worde of the magistrates power and place) is an office, and an action in executing the same. **1697** C. LESLIE *Snake in Grass* (ed. 2) 131 Their..open Contempt of Magistracy and the Laws. **1765** BLACKSTONE *Comm.* I. ii. 142 In all tyrannical governments the supreme magistracy, or the right both of making and of enforcing the laws, is vested in one and the same man. **1782** *Gentl. Mag.* LII. 597 [They] were both committed to New Bridewell..for contempt of magistracy. **1835** I. TAYLOR *Spir. Despot.* III. 112 A principal portion of the..spiritual magistracy had been usurped. **1849** MACAULAY *Hist. Eng.* viii. II. 277 Literature and science were, in the academical system of England,..armed with magistracy. **1875** JOWETT *Plato* (ed. 2) V. 169 All magistrates..must give an account of their magistracy.

3. The office, dignity, and functions of some magistrate (e.g. a consul, justice of the peace, etc.) contextually indicated.

1600 HOLLAND *Livy* X. xv. 361 To plucke the Consulship out of the mire..and to restore the auncient majestie..to the Magistracie. **1695** LD. PRESTON *Boeth.* I. 17, I had no other end in aspiring to the Magistracy, than that one, of doing good to all. **1715** LEONI *Palladio's Archit.* (1742) II. 65 The Candidates, who put in for any Magistracy. **1790** BURKE *Fr. Rev.* 18 A popular choice is necessary to the legal existence of the sovereign magistracy. **1849** MACAULAY *Hist. Eng.* I. 74 The public regarded them merely as eminent citizens invested with temporary magistracies. **1868** FREEMAN *Norm. Conq.* (1876) II. vii. 136 A town over which he exercised the powers of the highest civil magistracy.

4. Magistrates collectively; the whole body of magistrates.

1601 DENT *Pathw. Heaven, Morn. Prayer* (1631) Dd 5 b, We pray thee blesse Magistracie, Ministerie, & Commonalty. **1651** BIGGS *New Disp.* Pref. 9 So grave a Magistracie sitting in Parliament. **1755** MAGENS *Insurances* II. 276 A just Valuation, which must be confirmed by a Sentence of the nearest Magistracy or other competent Tribunal. **1758** J. BLAKE *Plan Mar. Syst.* 52 Our sea-ports, to the shame of magistracy, abound with lewd..women. **1800** COLQUHOUN *Comm. Thames* viii. 265 Checks established under the control of a vigilant magistracy. **1849** MACAULAY *Hist. Eng.* x. II. 555 The peers repaired to Guildhall, and were received there with all honor by the magistracy of the city. **1883** *Fortn. Rev.* May 700 Guardians have come to be regarded with almost as much respect as the magistracy.

5. a. A district under the government of a magistrate. **b.** A magistrate's residence or station.

1888 *Athenæum* 7 Apr. 439/1 Dividing the country into magistracies, and instituting local courts and officials. **1895** SCULLY *Kafir Stories* 189 The Kwesa clan of Pondos dwelt ..within thirty miles of the Magistracy.

magistral (məˈdʒɪstrəl), *a.* and *sb.* Also 6–7 **magistrall.** [a. F. *magistral* or ad. L. *magistrālis,* f. *magister* MASTER *sb.*] **A.** *adj.*

1. a. Of or pertaining to, or befitting a master; authoritative, dogmatic. Now *rare.*

1605 BACON *Adv. Learn.* I. v. §9 Another Error is in the manner of the tradition and deliuerie of knowledge, which is for the most part Magistrall and peremptorie; and not ingenuous and faithfull. **1626** T. H[AWKINS] *Caussin's Holy Crt.* 149 We must haue an authority mouing, magistrall, and decisiue. **1641** *Answ. Vind. Smectymnuus* 27 Your assertion..is more Magistrall, then true. **1862** RUSKIN *Munera P.* (1872) 110 Magistral powers, of the More over the less, and the forceful and free over the weak and servile elements of life. **1942** PARTRIDGE *Usage & Abusage* (1947) 5, I obtained permission from..eminent scholars..to quote at length from their magistral works.

†**b.** Of a problem, a point of instruction: ? Handed down from the masters of a science; forming part of the accepted course of teaching. *Obs.*

1572 DEE *Math. Pref.*, Which thing, I leaue to your consideration: making hast to despatch an other Magistrall Probleme: and to bring it, nerer to your knowledge,..then the world (before this day) had it for you. **1644** BULWER *Chiron.* 80 This action is Magistrall in Rhetorique, but grounded upon Nature.

2. *Pharmacy.* **a.** Of a remedy, a formula: Devised by a physician for a particular case; not included in the recognized pharmacopœia; opposed to OFFICINAL.

1605 BACON *Adv. Learn.* II. x. §8 Here is the deficience which I finde, that Physitians haue not..set downe and deliuered ouer, certaine Experimentall Medicines, for the Cure of particular Diseases; besides their own Coniecturall and Magistrall Descriptions. **1635** A. READ *Tumors & Vlcers* 271 Some magistrall compositions are required in the curation of these griefes. **1638** RAWLEY tr. *Bacon's Life & Death* (1651) 29 Some Magistrall Opiate weaker than those that are commonly in use. **1710** T. FULLER *Pharm. Extemp.* 409 The Magistrall Decoction of Mallows. **1831** J. DAVIES *Manual Mat. Med.* Pref. 11 Some magistral formulæ to serve as examples of the manner of prescribing it. **1875** H. C. WOOD *Therap.* (1879) 582 Cacao Butter..is..very largely used in the preparation of suppositories, both officinal and magistral. **1878** tr. *von Ziemssen's Cycl. Med.* VIII. 419 *note,* The curious magistral formula for this tincture is the following.

†**b.** By some writers app. taken to mean: 'Sovereign', supremely effective. *Obs.*

1592 G. HARVEY *Pierce's Super.* 37 Who knoweth not that Magistrall vnguent [cf. *magistralis unctio* in Du Cange], knoweth nothing: and who hath that magistral vnguent, feareth no gunshott. **1641** SHIRLEY *Cardinal* v. iii, Receive This ivory box; in it, an antidote 'Bove that they boast the great magistral medicine. **1678** SALMON *Lond. Disp.* 645/2 A magistral pouder against worm.

3. *Fortification.* Leading, principal, 'master-'.

1828 J. M. SPEARMAN *Brit. Gunner* (ed. 2) 302 The principal or magistral gallery runs all round the work, under the banquette of the covered-way. **1838** *Penny Cycl.* X. 375/2 The line which on the plan indicates the directions of the faces, flanks, etc., of the works is called the magistral line. **1872** VOYLE & STEVENSON *Mil. Dict., Magistral line*.. In field fortifications, this line is the interior crest line. In permanent fortifications, it is usually the line of the top of the escarp of each work.

4. In occasional uses: Having the title of 'Master'; of or pertaining to a 'master' or 'masters' (in various applications of the word).

1837 G. S. FABER *Prim. Doctr. Justif.* 268 Thomas Aquinas.. and his magistral predecessor [*sc.* the Master of the Sentences]. **1878** RUSKIN *Fors Clav.* lxxxvi, The men are rebuked, in the magistral homilies, for their ingratitude in striking. **1881** F. E. HULME *Town, College, & Neighb. Marlborough* 91 The magistral staff is composed of the Master and about thirty assistant masters. **1882** *Gentl. Mag.* May 570 According to the masters [*sc.* the Meistersingers], the institution of the school of magistral song was of the remotest antiquity.

5. Used for: Masterly. [So in Fr.] *rare*$^{-1}$.

1889 J. M. ROBERTSON *Ess. Crit. Method* 256 Magistral as Milton at his greatest, but subtle beyond his scope.

B. *sb.*

†**1.** *Pharmacy.* A magistral preparation or formula. *Obs.*

1621 BURTON *Anat. Mel.* II. iv. I. v, Every Citty, Towne, almost euery priuate man hath his owne.. receits, magistralls, precepts, as if hee scorned antiquity. **1654** WHITLOCK *Zootomia* 103 Hee pretendeth to Magistralls, that none but his Apothecary and he must understand. **1670** *Lex Talionis* 29 He shall.. prescribe so many of his Nostrums and Magistrals, as he calls them.

fig. **1647** HAMMOND *Serm.* x. Wks. 1683 IV. 535 But for the magistrals of nature and art, such are Gods smitings and punishments, which cost God dear, as it were, he is fain to fetch them from far.

2. *Fortification.* = *magistral line.* (See A. 3.)

1853 STOCQUELER *Milit. Encycl., Magistral*, the tracing or guiding line in fortification.. from which the position of all the other works is determined. In field fortification the crest line of the parapet is the magistral; in permanent fortification the cordon.. is the guide.

‖**3.** *Eccl.* A Spanish cathedral priest, with special duties as a preacher.

1772 NUGENT tr. *Hist. Friar Gerund* II. 83 The Magistral .. had purposely seated himself in the confessional of the parson of the parish.

‖**4.** *Min.* [Sp. (maxis'tral).] (See quot.)

1839 URE *Dict. Arts, Magistral*, in the language of the Spanish smelters of Mexico and South America, is the roasted and pulverized copper pyrites, which is added to the ground ores of silver.. for the purpose of decomposing the horn silver present. **1881** in RAYMOND *Mining Gloss.*

†**magi'strality.** *Obs.* [f. prec. + -ITY.] The quality or condition of being magistral. **a.** The standing of a master or mistress; the right to lay down the law or to dogmatize; authoritative character. **b.** quasi-*concr.* a dogmatic utterance; in *Med.* a special prescription.

a. 1603 *North's Plutarch, Seneca* (1612) 1213 Agrippina.. thinking she could by her magistralitie remedie this well inough. **1605** BACON *Adv. Learn.* II. viii. §5 To those that seeke truth and not Magistralitie it cannot but seeme a Matter of great profit. **1641** J. JACKSON *True Evang. T.* I. 71 The authority and magistrality of the first assertor of it. **b. 1605** BACON *Adv. Learn.* II. x. §8 The phisitians haue frustrated the fruite of tradition & experience by their magistralities. **1691** WOOD *Ath. Oxon.* II. 572 Humane Magistralities, self-weaved Ratiocinations,.. have laid.. claim to the highest advance of humane learning.

†**ma'gistrally,** *adv. Obs.* [f. as prec. + -LY^2.] In a magistral manner; authoritatively, dogmatically.

a **1603** T. CARTWRIGHT *Confut. Rhem. N.T.* (1618) 172 You haue put that magistrally which Ambrose maketh a *perhaps* of. **1656** HOBBES *Liberty, Necess.*, etc. (1841) 257 To assume.. a licence to control so magistrally.. the doctors of the Church in general.

magistrand ('mædʒɪstrænd). *Sc.* Also 7 **magestrand.** [ad. med.L. *magistrand-us*, gerundive pple. of *magistrārī* to become a Master (of Arts).] Originally, in Scottish Universities, an Arts student in the fourth or highest class; subsequently, one in the fourth year. Now retained, in official use, only at Aberdeen. At St. Andrews it has recently been revived, among the students, as an unofficial designation. Also *attrib.* in ***magistrand-class***.

16.. in *Crauford's Hist. Univ. Edin.* (1808) 24 The Magestrands (as now) conveened in the high hall. **1642** *Statutes Visitation* 8 Aug. (St. Andrews), The whole Magistrandes and Doctaloures in the two Colledges of Philosophy.. sall only haue voice in choyseing the Rector of the University. **1708** J. CHAMBERLAYNE *St. Gt. Brit.* II. III. x. (1710) 470 This is the last Year, after which they go out Masters of Arts; and for that reason this is called the Magistrand Class. **1812** W. TENNANT *Anster F.* II. xiv. (1871) 25 Up from their mouldy books and tasks had sprung Bigent and Magistrand to try the game. **1879** G. MACDONALD *Sir Gibbie* III. ix. 153 Although now a magistrand—that is, one about to take his degree of Master of Arts. **1889** *Univ. News Sheet* (St. Andrews) 11 Jan. 7 With us at St. Andrews the words *semi, tertian*, and *magistrand*,.. have long since entirely gone out of use. **1891** *College Echoes* (St. Andrews) 15 Jan., The present designations—Second-year man, Third-year man, and Fourth-year-man are colourless and awkward. Why should not Bejants become Semis, then Tertians, and close their career with the melancholy glory of Magistrand?

magistrate ('mædʒɪstrət), *sb.* Forms: 4–6 **magestrat(e, maiestrat(e,** 4–7 **magistrat,** 5– **magistrate.** [ad. L. *magistrātus* (*u*-stem), orig. a magisterial rank or office, a magistracy; hence a person holding such an office; f. *magister* MASTER *sb.* (see -ATE^1 1 a). Cf. F. *magistrat.*]

†**1.** The office and dignity of a magistrate; magistracy. *Obs.*

c **1374** CHAUCER *Boeth.* III. pr. iv. 57 (Camb. MS.) That thow woldest beren the magestrat with decorat. **1530** PALSGR. 241/2 Magistrate dignyte, *magistrat.*

2. A civil officer charged with the administration of the laws, a member of the executive government. ***chief magistrate, first magistrate***: in a monarchy, the sovereign: in a republic, usually the president.

1382 WYCLIF *Luke* xxiii. 14 The magestratis of the peple clepid to gidere, Pilat seide to hem. **1432–50** tr. *Higden* (Rolls) III. 255 The peple of Rome not suffrenge.. the sedicion of þe magistrates, ordeynede x. men to write þe lawes. **1550** CROWLEY *Epigr.* 27b, Woulde God the maiestrates woulde se men set a-worke. **1581** PETTIE *Guazzo's Civ. Conv.* II. (1586) 101 A discreet Magistrate ought not to.. alter his manners in respect of his dignitie. **1592** DAVIES *Immort. Soul* XXIX. iv, The Common's Peace the Magistrates preserve. **1614** RALEIGH *Hist. World* III. (1634) 72 Every Estate.. were governed by Lawes,.. and by their owne Magistrates. **1681** DRYDEN *Hind & P.* I. 489 Suppose the magistrate revenge her cause, 'Tis only for transgressing human laws. **1761** HUME *Hist. Eng.* III. liv. 175 The king was too eminent a magistrate to be trusted with discretionary power. **1791** JEFFERSON in *Washington's Writ.* (1892) XII. 20 *note*, It is fortunate that our first chief magistrate is purely and zealously republican. **1821** BYRON *Mar. Fal.* I. ii, Health and respect to the Doge Faliero, Chief magistrate of Venice. **1857** TOULMIN SMITH *Parish* 372 The Coroner himself is an elected Magistrate.

attrib. **1602** PATERICKE tr. *Gentillet* 26 The Paynim Lawyer may serve for a goodly example to condemne many Magistrate Lawyers of our time.

fig. **1612** BACON *Ess., Custom* (Arb.) 370 Custome is the principal Magistrate of mans life.

3. *spec.* In England and Ireland, a more frequent synonym for 'justice of the peace' (see JUSTICE *sb.* 10); also applied (chiefly with prefixed word, as in ***police, stipendiary magistrate***, and, in Ireland, ***resident magistrate***) to salaried officials having, like the justices of the peace, criminal jurisdiction of the first instance. In Scotland, applied to the provost and bailies of a burgh, as forming a court for police jurisdiction and the granting of licences. ***magistrates' court***: a court for the trial of minor offences and small civil cases and for the preliminary hearing of more serious cases.

The mayor of a town is sometimes referred to as its 'chief' or 'first magistrate'.

a **1688** G. DALLAS *Stiles* 12 The said M. R... and the remanent Magistrats of the said Burgh.. The said R. M. Bailie of the said Burgh, and the Provost and remanent Bailies of the same. **1727** in Quincy *Hist. Harvard* (1840) I. 567 The signification of magistrate in England, and even now in New England, extends to every one of his Majesty's Justices of the Peace; but in the time when the act above-said was made [1642],.. the known signification extended only to those who were Assistants to the Governor in Council. **1752** FIELDING *Amelia* I. ii, The worthy magistrate submitted to hear his defence. **1867** T. W. SAUNDERS *Practice in Magistrates' Courts* (ed. 3) i. 1 The various kinds of magistrates' courts—petty and special sessions—quarter sessions—clerk to the justices. *Ibid.*, It is.. the design of the following pages to treat of the *practice* of the magistrates' courts as we find these courts established. **1889** DOYLE *Micah Clarke* xxiii. 237 This fellow would make two of the gauger, and leave enough over to fashion a magistrate's clerk. **1904** J. F. & B. E. CRUMP *Magistrate's Pocket Manual* xii. 47 There is perhaps even greater need to observe the spirit of these instructions in the Magistrates' Courts, because.. rough and uncultivated manners.. make so great a strain on the patience and self-control of the Bench. **1952** *Act 1 Eliz. II* c. 55 § 38 Where a person is taken into custody for an offence without a warrant and is retained in custody, he shall be brought before a magistrates' court as soon as practicable. **1959** JOWITT *Dict. Eng. Law* II. 1341/2 *Petty sessional court*, a court of summary jurisdiction consisting of two or more justices.. now known as the magistrates' court. **1965** *New Statesman* 10 Dec. 920/2 The police courts, reborn as magistrates' courts in 1952, are still police courts not only to those who never frequent them but also to the old lags who frequent them most.

4. *Sc. slang.* In full, ***Glasgow magistrate.*** A herring.

1833 *Chambers's Edin. Jrnl.* 2 Nov. 314/2 My neighbour, thinking it absurd to mince such a matter as a *Glasgow Magistrate*, handed up a whole one to the chairman. **1874** HOTTEN *Slang Dict.* 177 *Glasgow Magistrate*, a salt herring. When George IV. visited Scotland, a wag placed some salt herrings on the iron guard of the carriage belonging to a well-known Glasgow magistrate, who made one of a deputation to receive his Majesty. **1890** BARRÈRE & LELAND *Dict. Slang* II. 38/1 *Magistrate* (Scotch slang), a herring. **1895** J. NICHOLSON *Kilwuddie* (ed. 4) 119 Ham's unco dear, sae, if ye like, we's hae a 'magistrate'. **1950** *Scots Mag.* Dec. 171 Herring were cured there by Walter Gibson, a merchant of Glasgow and Provost of that city in 1688, and it is perhaps because of Provost Gibson that salt herring acquired their nickname of 'Glasgow Magistrates'.

†**magistrate,** *v. Obs.*$^{-0}$ [f. ppl. stem of L. *magistrāre*: see MAGISTRATION.] *intr.* To play the master (Cockeram 1623).

'**magistrateship.** [f. MAGISTRATE *sb.* + -SHIP.] The dignity, office, and functions of a magistrate; also, the term of a magistrate's office.

1574 *Life Abp. Parker* B viij b, He was wonte to rubbe his minde with the memorye off that sentence, that all fame,.. all magistratshippes.. shall perishe, and decaye. *a* **1656** USSHER *Ann.* (1658) 595 Rullus,.. in the beginning of his magistrateship, published the Agrarian Law. **1884** J. PAYNE *1001 Nights* VIII. 93 'Tis one of the duties of magistrateship, To hang up the chief of police o'er his door. **1886** *Athenæum* 10 July 47/2 He was something of a soldier, and (which was much rarer at the time than either soldiership or magistrateship) he was a bibliophile.

†**magi'stratial,** *a. Obs. rare*$^{-1}$. [f. as prec. + -IAL.] = MAGISTERIAL 3.

1774 *Poetry* in *Ann. Reg.* 208 Hast thou.. seen.. In the plain hall the magistratial chair?

†**magi'stratic,** *a. Obs.* Also 7 **magistratique.** [f. as prec. + -IC.] = prec.

1653 GAUDEN *Hierasp.* 458 Onely to look exactly to civill interests and safety; is to make Magistratick power,.. to concurre with the malice of the Divels. **1667** WATERHOUSE *Fire Lond.* 79 Publick places of Magistratique dispatch. **1677** GALE *Crt. Gentiles* IV. 206 Clemence also ought to be illustrious in magistratic administrations.

magistratical (ˌmædʒɪ'strætɪkəl), *a.* [f. prec. + -AL^1.] Of or pertaining to, or befitting a magistrate or magistrates. (Cf. MAGISTERIAL 3.)

1638 *Div. & Pol. Observations* 55 A stile no lesse Magistrale, if not so Magistraticall as this Speech. **1644** J. WINTHROP *New Eng.* (1826) II. 205 Whether the deputies in the general court have judicial and magistratical authority? *a* **1683** SIDNEY *Disc. Govt.* (1714) 383 The original of Magistratical Power. **1752** FIELDING *Amelia* I. ii, Mr. Thrasher.. had some few imperfections in his magistratical capacity. **1769** *De Foe's Tour Gt. Brit.* II. 324 They are allowed the highest Marks of magistratical Honour. **1848** P. MACFARLANE in *Mem. R. Craig* x. (1862) 244 God is the fountain, the first source of human magistratical power. **1850** *Tait's Mag.* XVII. 556/1 The magistratical and clerical orders. **1893** M. HUTCHISON *Ref. Presb. Ch. Scot.* v. 121 With such conceptions of magistratical powers.. the Revolution settlement would appear to be deserving only of condemnation.

Hence **magi'stratically** *adv.*, in a magistratical or magisterial manner.

1650 R. HOLLINGWORTH *Exerc. Usurped Powers* 82 That such things should be maintained Magistratically by a Tyrant. **1872** J. WALKER *Theology & Theologians Scot.* v. (1888) 147 Unless.. he acted in this sovereign way, with the sword behind all his enactments and injunctions, he did not act in the proper sense magistratically.

†**magi'stration.** *Obs. rare*$^{-1}$. [ad. late L. *magistrātiōn-em*, n. of action f. *magistrāre* to rule, f. *magister* MASTER *sb.*] Command, direction.

1490 CAXTON *Eneydos* i. 11 Agamenon.. hadde the magystracyon.. of alle thexcersite and hoost to-fore Troye.

magistrative ('mædʒɪstrətɪv), *a. rare*$^{-1}$. [f. *magistrāt-*, ppl. stem of *magistrāre* (see prec.) + -IVE.] Proper to a magistrate, requisite for ruling.

1865 BUSHNELL *Vicar. Sacr.* III. iii. 241 A want of system and magistrative firmness.

magistrature ('mædʒɪstrətjʊə(r)). [a. F. *magistrature*, f. *magistrat* MAGISTRATE *sb.*]

1. The dignity or office of a magistrate; magisterial office; occas. the exercise of the office; with *a* and *pl.* an individual office. (Cf. MAGISTRACY 3.)

1672 *Essex Papers* (Camden) 23 That noe person whatsoever bee admitted into any Place of Magistrature or Government.. till [etc.]. **1791** *State Papers* in *Ann. Reg.* 183 *In case.. of a collision between magistratures. **1824** LANDOR *Imag. Conv., Marcus Tullius & Quinctus Cicero* Wks. 1853 I. 238/1 Finding all our magistratures in the disposal of the senate. **1829** *Ibid., Diog. & Plato* ibid. 504/1 Giving to this one rightly what that one would hold wrongfully, is justice in magistrature. **1833** *New Monthly Mag.* XXXVII. 465 The family rose to the dignities of the magistrature. **1833** *Fraser's Mag.* VII. 650 With these some of the magistratures are now filled.

fig. **1796** BURNEY *Mem. Metastasio* II. 325 Does music aspire at this supreme magistrature?

b. The term of a magistrate's office.

1720 OZELL *Vertot's Rom. Rep.* I. I. 59 The two Consuls, whose Magistrature was expiring, appointed the Assembly for the Election of their Successors. **1824** LANDOR *Imag. Conv., Leopold & Presid. du Paty* Wks. 1853 I. 68/2 A.. man, who can reproach himself with no perversion or neglect of justice, in a magistrature of twenty years.

2. *collect.* The body of magistrates; = MAGISTRACY 4.

1679 EVELYN *Diary* 21 Nov., I dined at my Lord Mayor's .. Such a.. splendid magistrature does no city in the world show. **1830** *Examiner* 548/1 The magistrature continued. The very men who had opposed the liberty of the press.. continued in their positions. **1859** *Sat. Rev.* VII. 273/2 That illustrious magistrature which, in former days, guided France by their counsels. **1898** A. W. WARD in *Eng. Hist.*

Rev. Jan. 175 The conservative tendencies of the Belgian magistrature.

ma'gistricide. *nonce-wd.* [f. as if L. **magistricīda* (after *parricīda*, etc.: see -CIDE 1), f. *magister* master.] A murderer of one's master or teacher.

1670 LASSELS *Voy. Italy* II. 172 Nero the Magistricide, who put this rare man his master to death.

magitian, obs. form of MAGICIAN.

Maglemose (mæglə'məʊsə). [The Danish place-name *Maglemose* (great moss) near Mullerup on the west coast of Sjælland.] Used *attrib.* to designate the Mesolithic culture of northern Europe represented by bone implements and microliths found at Maglemose.

1915 W. J. SOLLAS *Anc. Hunters* (ed. 2) 544 The Maglemose industry is widely distributed around the Baltic. **1921** M. C. BURKITT *Prehistory* xii. 155 These..formed the Maglemose culture along the shores of the Baltic. **1931** *Times Lit. Suppl.* 8 Jan. 23/1 Azilian and Maglemose man. **1932** *Antiquity* VI. 218 It proves..that during the Maglemose period, there was fresh water at a spot now many feet below the sea. **1948** A. L. KROEBER *Anthropol.* (rev. ed.) xvi. 668 For the first time we find European habitation sites along beaches (Ertebølle and Asturian phases of Mesolithic culture), river mouths (Azilian), on lake and bog shores (Maglemose).

Maglemosian (mæglə'məʊsɪən), *a.* and *sb.* Also **-ean.** [f. prec. + -IAN.] **A.** *adj.* = prec. **B.** *sb.* A person of the Maglemosian culture; the culture itself.

1918 in WEBSTER Add. **1921** M. C. BURKITT *Prehistory* xiii. 163 The first culture found is the so-called Maglemosean. **1925** V. G. CHILDE *Dawn European Civilization* i. 9 The Maglemosians had axes and adzes and their command over nature was thereby enormously extended. **1943** J. & C. HAWKES *Prehist. Brit.* i. 26 The Maglemosians probably crossed the area now covered by the North Sea as fishers and fowlers. **1949** W. F. ALBRIGHT *Archaeol. of Palestine* iii. 62 If we allow the Tahunian a time spread of between one and two thousand years (say about 6000–4500 B.C.) it would have been roughly contemporary with the late Maglemosean. **1954** S. PIGGOTT *Neolithic Cultures* i. 14 The Star Carr discoveries in Yorkshire have shown that cultures of Maglemosean affinities were established in what is now eastern England at least as early as the beginning of Boreal times. **1970** *Guardian* 5 Aug. 18/4 An almost complete skeleton of an elk..unearthed near Blackpool..belongs to the early mesolithic period which began around 8000 B.C... This new find is the first evidence that this maglemosian culture extended to what is now the North-west of England.

maglev ('mæglɛv). Also **mag-lev.** Abbrev. of *magnetic levitation* (see LEVITATION 1 c).

1973 *Financial Times* 7 Sept. 25/7 Krauss-Maffei expects to be running a 20-passenger 'maglev' vehicle capable of speeds up to 250 mph later this autumn. **1973** *Sci. Amer.* Oct. 18/3 Two entirely different approaches to magnetic levitation (which is often shortened to 'maglev') are being pursued. **1974** *Globe & Mail* (Toronto) 16 May 4/4 The Canadian program is aimed at the development of mag-lev vehicles which will travel at 300 miles an hour, carrying about 100 passengers each.

magma ('mægmə). [a. L. *magma* (sense 1), Gr. *μάγμα*, f. root of *μάσσειν* to knead.]

†**1.** The dregs that remain from a semi-liquid substance after the more liquid part has been removed by pressure or evaporation. *Obs.*

c **1420** *Pallad. on Husb.* XI. 351 Taak aloen & mirre & magma with Saffron [L. *crocomagma* lees of saffron], of yche yliche. *a* **1648** DIGBY *Closet Open.* (1677) 18 You may squeze out the clear juyce and hang the Magma in a bag in the bung. **1694** SALMON *Bate's Dispens.* (1713) 38/2 By another Distillation, reduce the Magma at bottom, to the Consistency of Honey. **1730** STACK in *Phil. Trans.* XXXVI. 271 The Eggs..resemble a Magma of a brown Colour. **1737** BRACKEN *Farriery Impr.* (1756) I. 310 Apply the Magma (or Herbs after they are squeezed out of the Liquor) to the Wound. **1856** MAYNE *Expos. Lex.*, *Magma*,..a squeezed mass of a certain consistence.

2. 'Any crude mixture of mineral or organic matters, in a thin pasty state' (Ure *Dict. Arts* 1839).

1681 tr. *Willis' Rem. Med. Wks.* Vocab., *Magma*, the blended dross and fæces of several metals, as also of chymical extractions. **1782** KIRWAN in *Phil. Trans.* LXXIII. 17 [They] afford no crystals, but only a magma or mother liquor. **1806** HATCHETT *ibid.* XCVI. 111 It formed with sulphuric acid a thick black magma. **1838** T. THOMSON *Chem. Org. Bodies* 688 A concentrated solution of potash forms with bird-lime a whitish magma, which becomes brown by evaporation. **1854** J. SCOFFERN in *Orr's Circ. Sci., Chem.* 24 A magma of dark-coloured sugar. **1875** H. C. WOOD *Therap.* (1879) 93 It..should be so moist as to constitute a magma. **1894** HUXLEY *Wks.* IX. 8 Our earth may once have formed part of a nebulous cosmic magma.

3. *Geol.* **a.** One of two or more supposed strata of fluid or semi-fluid matter lying beneath the solid crust of the earth. In mod. use: A hot, fluid or semi-fluid material beneath the earth's crust from which igneous rocks are believed to be formed by cooling and solidification and which erupts as lava. **b.** The amorphous basis of certain porphyritic rocks.

1865 HAUGHTON *Man. Geol.* 3 According to Durocher.. the first and second layers of the globe are composed of totally different materials. The outer layer, which he calls the Acid Magma, corresponds with the granites; and the inner or second layer, which he calls the Basic Magma, corresponds with the trap rocks and the greenstones. **1869** PHILLIPS *Vesuv.* xii. 336 Whether these rocks..constitute practically a solid basis, or float in a magma of slow fluidity. **1874** DAWKINS in *Ess. Owen's Coll. Manchester* V. 148 Two distinct layers or magmas beneath the stratified rocks. **1882** GEIKIE *Text-bk. Geol.* II. II. iii. 87 Many crystalline rocks consist..of a magma or paste, in which the crystalline particles are..embedded. **1897** —— *Anc. Volcanoes Gt. Brit.* I. 12 There will thus be a constant pressure of the molten magma into the roots of volcanoes. **1944** A. HOLMES *Princ. Physical Geol.* iii. 28 A volcano is essentially a rift or vent through which magma (molten rock material highly charged with gases) from the depths is erupted at the surface. **1955** *Sci. News Let.* 19 Mar. 187/3 The liquefied material forms a fluid mass, called magma, that is lighter than the overlying rocks and tends to rise at an opening. Magma is called lava when it reaches the earth's surface. **1971** I. G. GASS et al. *Understanding Earth* xxi. 310/2 At the close of volcanism, the magma in these chambers will also solidify to coarse-grained rocks having the same composition as the lavas which previously were being erupted.

4. *Pharmacy.* An ointment or confection of a softish consistence. (*Syd. Soc. Lex.* 1889.)

1855 DUNGLISON *Med. Lex.* (ed. 12), *Magma*..also, a salve of a certain consistence.

5. *fig.*

1928 R. A. S. MACALISTER *Archæol. of Ireland* iv. 219 A conglomerate of lazy abbreviations..studded in a repulsive magma of exotic gibberish. **1933** H. G. WELLS *Shape of Things to Come* III. §1. 261 The need for a planned 'renucleation' in the social magma that arose out of this dissolution.

6. *attrib.*, as (sense 3) ***magma reservoir.***

1909 A. HARKER *Nat. Hist. Igneous Rocks* ii. 36 At the depth at which we suppose a large magma-reservoir to be situated the conditions would be quite different. **1971** I. G. GASS et al. *Understanding Earth* xxi. 303/1 Because these volcanoes are large and their volcanic history is long, the magma reservoirs beneath them..have fractionated, giving rise to diversified lava assemblages.

Hence **mag'matic** *a.*, of or pertaining to the magma (sense 3).

1890 in *Cent. Dict.* **1903** GEIKIE *Text-bk. Geol.* (ed. 4) II. 808 (*heading*) Magmatic ores. **1910** *Encycl. Brit.* III. 513/2 The modifications of the granite are ascribed to magmatic segregation (chemical and physical processes which occasioned diffusion of certain components towards the cooling surfaces). **1933** *Geogr. Jrnl.* LXXXI. 332 Magmatic movement, however caused, has been a factor in the formation of the Rift Valleys. **1957** G. E. HUTCHINSON *Treat. Limnol.* I. i. 33 Intermittent volcanic activity.. repeatedly drew off material from the magmatic reservoir. **1971** I. G. GASS et al. *Understanding Earth* i. 24/1 Quartz and nepheline if brought into contact at magmatic temperatures react to give albite.

magmatism ('mægmətɪz(ə)m). *Geol.* [f. L. *magmat-*, *magma* (see MAGMA) + -ISM.]

a. The theory advocated by magmatists.

1948 *Q. Jrnl. Geol. Soc.* CIII. 140 Dr. Reynolds 'tolls the knell' of the passing theory of 'magmatism' as an all-embracing explanation of the origin of all plutonic rocks. *Ibid.* 141 A new era in petrogeny, an era in which 'magmatism' will become incorporated with 'transformism', plutonic processes will become closely linked with metamorphic processes, and petrogenesis..will become an integral part of a wider science of geochemistry.

b. Motion or solidification of magma; magmatic activity.

1952 H. RAMBERG *Orig. Metamorphic & Metasomatic Rocks* 3 (*heading*) Natural boundary between metamorphism and magmatism. **1970** CLIFFORD & GASS *Afr. Magmatism & Tectonics* p. vii, Studies..to illustrate the relationship between two important geological processes —magmatism and tectonics. **1974** *Nature* 19 Apr. 650/1 Seismicity, tectonism and magmatism are now concentrated near plate margins.

magmatist ('mægmətɪst). *Geol.* [f. as prec. + -IST.] One who believes that many granitic rocks, or plutonic rocks in general, were formed from magma.

1944 *Proc. Geologists' Assoc.* LV. 86 The inability of the magmatists to interpret the plain field-facts arises..from the inertia of a century of belief in the magmatic origin of all granitic rocks. **1947** *Geol. Mag.* LXXXIV. 209 Much of the disagreement..arises from a belief on the part of the Magmatists that Hutton proved the magmatic origin of granite. **1947** *Q. Jrnl. Geol. Soc.* CII. 443 He agrees with the 'magmatists' that 'the now classical views of Sederholm, put forth in explanation of the pre-Cambrian granite phenomena of Finland, are reasonable and may be applied ..to other Archaean formations, such as the Canadian Shield'.

†**'magment.** *Obs. rare*⁻⁰. [ad. L. *magmentum.*] Great increase.

1623 in COCKERAM.

magmoid ('mægmɔɪd), *a.* *Bot.* [f. MAGMA + -OID.] (See quot.)

1879 W. A. LEIGHTON *Lichen-flora* (ed. 3) 516 *Magmoid*, like an alga, consisting of spherical green cells.

Magna Charta, Magna Carta ('mægnə 'kɑːtə). Also 7 *pl.* **magna chartaes.** [med.L., signifying 'great charter'.] The Great Charter of English personal and political liberty, obtained from King John in 1215, repeatedly confirmed, and appealed to in all disputes between the sovereign and his subjects, till the establishment of constitutional government.

[**1279** *Rolls of Parlt.* I. 224 Quod tollatur magna carta de foribus Ecclesiarum.] **1568** GRAFTON *Chron.* II. 118 This Parliament king Edwards lawes were again restored, & Magna carta confirmed. **1641** LD. J. DIGBY *Sp. in Ho. Comm.* 19 Jan. 15 An Accumulation of all the publique Grievances since *Magna Carta*. **1766** BLACKSTONE *Comm.* II. v. 74 John was obliged to consent, by his magna carta, that [etc.]. **1865** DICKENS *Mut. Fr.* I. v, Considered to represent the penn'orth appointed by Magna Charta.

transf. and *fig.* **1630** B. JONSON *New Inn* I. i, It is against my freehold, my inheritance, My Magna Charta.. To drink such balderdash, or bonny-clabber. **1643** PRYNNE *Sov. Power Parl.* I. (ed. 2) 22 Which you may read in ancient Magna Chartaes. *a* **1686** T. WATSON *Body Divin.* (1692) 460 The Covenant of Grace is our Magna Charta, by vertue of which God passeth himself over to us to be our God. **1879** G. G. SCOTT *Lect. Mediæv. Archit.* II. 181, I have called the use of diagonal ribs the *Magna Charta* of the art of vaulting.

‖**magna cum laude** ('mægnɑː kʌm 'lɔːdiː, 'mægnɑː kʊm laʊdiː), *phr.* Chiefly *U.S.* [L., 'with great praise'.] With great distinction: designating a degree, diploma, etc., of a higher standard than the average (though not the highest). Also *transf.* and *fig.*

1900 *Dialect Notes* II. 13 A few words or phrases of direct Latin importation used at some of the older institutions... more commonly *cum laude*, *magna* or *summa cum laude* for the degree of honor attained in studies. **1933** BALMER & WYLIE *When Worlds Collide* i. 22 He was graduated from Harvard with a *magna cum laude*. **1963** M. MCCARTHY *Group* v. 102 He was angry because Helena had failed to get *magna cum laude*, when a lot of the Jewish girls had. **1973** *Physics Bull.* Feb. 116/3 From 1911 to 1914 he was an 1851 Exhibition research scholar in physics, and spent the period in Göttingen taking special advanced courses in a variety of subjects and carrying out research on *Die Struktur des Gels der Kieselsäure*, for which he was awarded the degree of PhD 'magna cum laude'. **1973** E. PACE *Any War will Do* (1974) I. 47 The minute I heard poor Ollie shout, I knew you had passed. And when the counter splintered, you got magna cum laude.

†**mag'nævous,** *a.* *Obs. rare*⁻⁰. [as if f. L. **magnæv-us* (f. *magn-us* great + *ævum* age) + -OUS.] Of great age. = GRANDEVOUS.

1727 in BAILEY vol. II.

magnaflux ('mægnəflʌks). Also **Magnaflux.** [f. *magna-*, taken as comb. form of MAGNETIC *a.* + FLUX *sb.*] A method of testing metal parts for internal or surface defects by magnetizing the metal and observing the pattern assumed by a magnetic powder that is applied to it (either directly, or in oil that is used as a bath or sprayed on the metal). Usu. *attrib.*

1938 *S.A.E. Jrnl.* May 36/1 Another method of magnetic testing..involves the use of Magnaflux in which the parts to be inspected are first longitudinally or circularly magnetized... When properly magnetized, defects result in local flux leakage. Magnaflux powder, being of high magnetic permeability..adheres along the lines of flux leakage. **1940** CRUMP & MAUL *Our Airliners* vii. 139 Every piece is measured and checked for wear and many of the parts go to the magnaflux tank. **1946** *Jrnl. R. Aeronaut. Soc.* L. 535/2 Japanese designers considered that all important parts should be hardness-tested after heat treatment; that welded primary structures should be magnaflux tested; and casting radiologically examined. **1963** JONES & SCHUBERT *Engin. Encycl.* (ed. 3) 783 Although the Magnaflux method of inspection has been universally adopted throughout the aircraft industry it is by no means confined to it.

‖**mag'nale.** *Obs.* [as if a. L. **magnāle*, sing. of MAGNALIA.] A great or wonderful thing, a wonder.

1623 COCKERAM, *Magnalls*, great things to be wondered at. [**1626** BACON *Sylva* §747 To restore Teeth in Age, were Magnale Naturæ.] **1646** J. HALL *Horæ Vac.* 115 'Tis great art in dissimulation to dissemble the art of dissimulation, greater to performe that Magnale in Perspective. **1650** CHARLETON *Paradoxes* Ep. Ded. A4b, In the discovery of some Magnale in Knowledg. **1665** GLANVILL *Scepsis Sci.* vi. 24 We'l examine these Accounts of the Magnale.

‖**mag'nalia,** *sb. pl.* *Obs.* Also 7 *erron.* **magnalia's** [L. *magnālia* neut. pl., f. *magnus* great.] Great or wonderful works; wonders.

c **1645** HOWELL *Lett.* (1892) II. 663 In Natures Cabinet.. there are divers mysteries and Magnalia's yet unknown. **1649** G. DANIEL *Trinarch., Hen. IV*, cvii, These the Magnalia, wᶜʰ but some can find In Nature, Earth by Earth only Calcin'd. **1681** GLANVILL *Sadducismus* 82 He made no discovery of the Magnalia of Art or Nature.

†**mag'nality.** *Obs.* [f. MAGNALIA + -ITY.] A great or wonderful thing.

1646 SIR T. BROWNE *Pseud. Ep.* II. iii. 70 Too greedy of magnalities, we are apt to make but favourable experiments concerning welcome truths. **1682** —— *Chr. Mor.* III. §14 Fill thy Spirit..with the mysteries of Faith, the magnalities of Religion.

magnalium (mæg'neɪlɪəm). [f. MAGN(ESIUM + AL(UMIN)IUM.] A light aluminium-based alloy containing some magnesium.

1900 *Motor-Car World* I. 90/1 Magnalium is a new alloy of aluminium with from ten to thirty per cent. of its weight of magnesium. **1910** *Encycl. Brit.* I. 708/2 This alloy, under the name of magnalium, is coming into use for small articles in which lightness and rigidity have to be combined. **1948** J. J. STEVENS tr. *A. von Zeerleder's Technol. Aluminium* ii. 20 The binary aluminium-magnesium alloys, which were developed in 1899 by Mach under the name 'Magnalium',

exhibit rising mechanical properties with rising magnesium content... After 1910 these alloys fell out of favour owing to low corrosion resistance.

‖**magna mater** (ˈmægnə ˈmeɪtə(r), ˈmægnə ˈmɑːtə(r)). [L., lit. great mother.] A mother-goddess, a fertility deity; also *transf.*

1728 [see GREAT A. *adj.* 12 b]. **1845** *Encycl. Metrop.* XVII. 481/2 *Cybele*, otherwise known as Ops, Rhea, Vesta,.. Idæa Mater, Magna Mater, Mater Deorum, Bona Dea, and Tellus. **1896** [see FIELDSTONE]. **1919** J. BUCHAN *Mr. Standfast* xxi. 356 There was a strange cult in the ancient world, the worship of *Magna Mater*—the Great Mother. **1962** 'M. INNES' *Connoisseur's Case* viii. 92 She was a kind of *magna mater* whose true sphere was a teeming nursery. **1974** *Times Lit. Suppl.* 13 Sept. 977/3 In Frieda [von Richthofen]'s case this was a straightforward matter. Like other *magnae matres* of the time (Mr. Green discusses Alma Mahler, Isadora Duncan, Lou Andreas-Salome and Mabel Dodge Luhan), she sought to enhance life by erotic love.

‖**magnanerie** (maɲanri). [F., f. *magnan* silkworm.] A silkworm house.

1887 PATON in *Encycl. Brit.* XXII. 59/2 Small educations reared apart from the ordinary magnanerie, for the production of graine alone, were recommended. **1888** E. A. BUTLER *Silkworms* 53 In large establishments, or magnaneries, as they are called.

† **magˈnanimate**, *v. Obs. rare*⁻¹. [f. L. *magnanim-us* (see MAGNANIMOUS) + -ATE.] *trans.* To render high-souled; to cheer, inspirit.

1640 HOWELL *Dodona's Gr.* 9 Present danger magnanimats them, and inflames their courage.

† **magnanime**, *a. Obs.* Also 6 **magnanyme**. [a. F. *magnanime*, ad. L. *magnanimus*: see MAGNANIMOUS.] High-souled, lofty, magnanimous.

1523 CROMWELL in Merriman *Life & Lett.* (1902) I. 30 This high and Magnanyme enterpryse. **1549** *Compl. Scot.* Ep. Queen 2 Illustir princes, engendrit of magnanime genoligie. **1590** R. HITCHCOCK *Quintess. Wit* 1 b, Neither to profitte, but to most magnanime and hautie endes.

magnanimious, obs. form of MAGNANIMOUS.

magnanimity (ˌmægnəˈnɪmɪtɪ). [a. F. *magnanimité*, ad. L. *magnanimitāt-em*, f. *magnanimus* MAGNANIMOUS.]

†**1.** Used (with somewhat vague meaning) as the name of one of the virtues recognized in mediæval ethics. *Obs.*

Primarily this represented the Aristotelian μεγαλοψυχία (see 3), but in scholastic descriptions the notion was modified in accordance with Christian ideals, and blended with elements suggested by the etymology of the L. word (*animus* being capable of the sense 'courage'); hence 'magnanimity' is often classed as a subdivision of 'fortitude' (so Aquinas, following Macrobius *In Somn. Scip.* I. viii. §7).

1340 *Ayenb.* 164 Magnanimite is heȝnesse gratnesse and noblesse of wylhede.. þis uirtue heþ tuo delles: greate þinges onworþi, and wel grater to nime an hand. *c* **1386** CHAUCER *Sec. Nun's T.* 110 Right so men goostly in this mayden free Seyen of feith the magnanymytee. *c* **1412** HOCCLEVE *De Reg. Princ.* 3900 Off magnanimite now wole I trete, þat is to seyn, strong herte or grete corage. **1526** *Pilgr. Perf.* (W. de W. 1531) 136 Magnanimity is the vertue, wherby man or woman hath a discrete doughtynesse.. to speke or to do that thynge that they ought to do by right and reason for the loue of god.

†**2.** Lofty courage; fortitude. *Obs.*

(In some examples perh. the Aristotelian sense: see 3.)

1509 BARCLAY *Shyp of Folys* (1570) 206 For his strength and magnanimitie.. Of one founde on grounde like to him can not be. **1560** DAUS tr. *Sleidane's Comm.* 322 This.. magnanimiti in so great adversity [L. *in rebus adversis animi fortitudo*] got him great love every wher amongs al men. **1576** GASCOIGNE *Steele Gl.* Ded. (Arb.) 43 Shall I yelde to mysery as a iust plague apointed for my portion? Magnanimitie saith no. **1610** WILLET *Hexapla Daniel* 62 In courage and magnanimitie superiour to Hercules. **1744** HARRIS *Three Treat.* Wks. (1841) 107, I can bear whatever happens with manlike magnanimity. **1801** MAR. EDGEWORTH *Angelina* ii. (1832) 13 The courage and magnanimity with which she had escaped from her aristocratic persecutors.

3. In the Aristotelian sense of μεγαλοψυχία (see below). Also, loftiness of thought or purpose; grandeur of designs, nobly ambitious spirit. Now *rare*.

In Aristotle the word (by modern translators rendered 'greatsouledness', 'highmindedness') expresses the attitude of one who, rightly conscious of his own great merits, is indifferent to praise except from those whose approval is valuable, regards the chances of fortune with equanimity, and, while ready to confer benefits, will seldom condescend to accept them.

1598 BARCKLEY *Felic. Man* (1631) 167 Carolus Martellus shewed great magnanimitie in refusing principalitie. *c* **1651** HOBBES *Rhet.* (1840) 437 Magnanimity.. is a virtue by which a man is apt to do great benefits. **1717** L. HOWEL *Desiderius* 74 We are indued with a spiritual Magnanimity, that sets us above the Desire of temporal Goods. **1761** HUME *Hist. Eng.* II. xliv. 499 The queen's magnanimity in forming such extensive projects was the more remarkable. **1769** ROBERTSON *Chas. V*, XI. Wks. 1813 III. 267 That magnanimity of soul which delights in bold enterprizes.

4. Nobility of feeling; superiority to petty resentment or jealousy; generous disregard of injuries.

1771 BURKE *Lett., to Bp. of Chester* (1844) I. 271 It may be magnanimity in Lord Mansfield to despise attacks made upon himself. **1785** PALEY *Mor. Philos.* Wks. 1825 IV. 9 Forgiveness of injuries is accounted by one sort of people magnanimity, by another meanness. **1841** ELPHINSTONE *Hist. India* II. 219 The mean spirit of Mahmúd was incapable of imitating the magnanimity of his enemy. **1868** E. EDWARDS *Ralegh* I. xiii. 258 Ralegh.. on former occasions had shown towards Essex a wise and noble magnanimity. **1900** J. H. MUIRHEAD *Chapters fr. Aristotle's Ethics* 243 With regard to honour and dishonour, there is a mean called magnanimity, or high-mindedness, a species of excess called vanity, and a defect called pusillanimity or little-mindedness.

b. *pl.* Instances of magnanimity.

a **1639** WOTTON in *Reliq.* (1672) 241 Some seeming Magnanimities being indeed (if you sound them well) at the bottom, very Impotencies. **1844** MRS. BROWNING *Drama of Exile* Poems 1850 I. 73 Aspire Unto the calms and magnanimities,.. To which thou art elect.

†**5.** In occasional use: Affectation of grandeur; magnificence. *Obs.*

1658 SIR T. BROWNE *Hydriot.* 48 Pyramids, Arches, Obelisks, were but the irregularities of vain-glory and wilde enormities of ancient magnanimity.

†**6.** *water of magnanimity*: any gently stimulating remedy. (*Syd. Soc. Lex.*) *Obs.*

1861 HULME tr. *Moquin-Tandon* II. III. 65 Distilled Ants (Water of Magnanimity).

magnanimous (mægˈnænɪməs), *a.* Also 6–7 **magnanimious**. [f. L. *magnanim-us* (f. *magnus* great + *animus* soul: corresponding in formation to Gr. μεγαλόψυχος, and in scholastic Latin used as its translation) + -OUS. Cf. F. *magnanime*.]

1. Great in courage; nobly brave or valiant. Of qualities, actions, etc.: Proceeding from or manifesting high courage. ? *Obs.*

1584 *Mirr. Mag.* 1 b, The incouragement, that the magnanimious Cesar gaue vnto his souldiours. **1589** WARNER *Alb. Eng.* Prose Add. (1612) 332 Elisa (whom the Phœnicians for her magnanimious dying, did afterwardes name Dido). **1665** G. HAVERS *P. della Valle's Trav. E. India* 196 The first course seem'd safest and most considerate; the latter was more magnanimous, but with-all temerarious. *a* **1719** ADDISON *Evid. Chr. Relig.* iii. (1733) 25 The irreproachable lives and magnanimous sufferings of their followers. **1761** HUME *Hist. Eng.* II. xli. 430 When she saw an evident necessity she braved danger with magnanimous courage. **1770** *Junius Lett.* xxxviii. 189 *note*, All their magnanimous threats ended in a ridiculous vote of censure. **1828** SCOTT *F. M. Perth* xxxiv, The Douglas.. was too magnanimous not to interest himself in what was passing. **1858** LONGF. *M. Standish* iii, For he was great of heart, magnanimous, courtly, courageous.

2. High-souled; nobly ambitious; lofty of purpose; noble in feeling or conduct. Now chiefly: Superior to petty resentment or jealousy, loftily generous in disregard of injuries. (Cf. MAGNANIMITY 3, 4.)

1598 HAYDOCKE tr. *Lomazzo* II. 30 Ivstice being.. a masculine vertue, hath manlie, magnanimious, considerate and moderate actions. **1604** T. WRIGHT *Passions* v. §4. 225 It cannot but proceede from a noble magnanimous minde to contemne all base iniuries offered. **1633** G. HERBERT *Temple, Ch. Porch* lvi, Pitch thy behaviour low, thy projects high; So shalt thou humble and magnanimous be. *c* **1665** MRS. HUTCHINSON *Mem. Col. Hutchinson* (1846) 33 He was so truly magnanimous, that prosperity could never lift him up in the least. **1769** BLACKSTONE *Comm.* IV. xxxiii. 416 Richard the first, a brave and magnanimous prince, was a sportsman as well as a soldier. **1802** WORDSW. *Sonn.*, '*Great men have been among us*', They knew.. what strength was, that would not bend But in magnanimous meekness. **1847** DISRAELI *Tancred* II. i, They think they are doing a very kind and generous and magnanimous thing. **1849** MACAULAY *Hist. Eng.* II. 167 The magnanimous frankness of a man who had done great things, and who could well afford to acknowledge some deficiencies.

Hence **magˈnanimously** *adv.*; **magˈnanimousness** *rare* = MAGNANIMITY.

1606 W. W[OODCOCKE] *Hist. Ivstine* XVIII. 71 They should.. see he had the like liberallity and magnanimousnesse of mind. **1611** COTGR., *Magnanimement*, magnanimously. **1614** EARL STIRLING *Domes-day* IV. lxxvii. (1637) 88 Who first from death by deeds redeem'd their names, And eminent magnanimously grew. **1796** BURKE *Regic. Peace* i. Wks. VIII. 159 With Hannibal at her gates, she [Holland] had nobly and magnanimously refused all separate treaty. **1851** D. WILSON *Preh. Ann.* (1863) II. III. iv. 126 A golden treasure which they magnanimously resolved should be equitably divided. **1862** MRS. OLIPHANT *Last of Mortimers* II. 257, I am not sure my great magnanimousness did not have a root in what Harry called 'feeling extravagant'. **1885** *Manch. Exam.* 7 Feb. 5/2 The French journals magnanimously drop their querulous tone.

magnase. *rare*⁻⁰. A workman's corrupt form of MANGANESE. (Cf. MAGNUS.) Only *attrib.* in *magnase black*.

1849–50 *Weale's Dict. Terms*, *Magnase black* is the best of all blacks for drying in oil without addition, or preparation of the oil. **1854** in FAIRHOLT *Dict. Terms Art.*

magnate (ˈmægneɪt). Chiefly *pl.* Also 8–9 **magnat**. [ad. late L. *magnāt-*, *magnās* (also *magnātus*), f. *magnus* great.]

1. A great man; a noble; a man of wealth or eminence in any sphere.

Not in Johnson or Todd. It is possible that all the examples before the 19th c. represent the L. plural *magnātēs*.

1430–40 LYDG. *Bochas* IX. xxxiv. (1558) 35 The greatest states rulers of the toun Called Magnates. **1590** SIR J. SMYTH *Disc. Weapons* Ded. 15 Your Lordships (being the Nobilitie and Magnates of the Kingdome). **1654** TRAPP *Comm. Job* iii. 322 For Magnates are Magnetes, they draw many by their example. **1790** BURKE *Fr. Rev.* 39 The popular representative and.. the magnates of the kingdom. **1814** BYRON *Lara* I. vii, Born of high lineage.. He mingled with the Magnates of his land. **1844** LD. BROUGHAM *Brit. Const.* i. (1862) 5 A patrician body accustomed to consider themselves as the magnates in a country. **1850** W. IRVING *Goldsmith* xx. 220 The associate of Johnson, Burke, Topham Beauclerc, and other magnates. **1874** L. STEPHEN *Hours in Library* (1892) I. iv. 167 Unlike the irritable race of literary magnates.. [Scott] never lost a friend. **1883** *Fortn. Rev.* 1 Nov. 609 The small class of territorial magnates who possess the soil of the country.

transf. **1853** KANE *Grinnell Exp.* xxxiii. (1856) 290 The stars, except one or two of the northern magnates, invisible at noonday.

2. *spec.* In Hungary and Poland, a member of the Upper House in the Diet. *Hist.*

1797 *Encycl. Brit.* (ed. 3) XV. 290/1 The bishops of Cracow and Kiow.. and several magnats declared that they would never consent to the establishment of such a commission. **1845** S. AUSTIN *Ranke's Hist. Ref.* I. 181 In Hungary some magnates and cities were quickly reduced to obedience. *Ibid.* II. 461 A few magnates collected around the king.

magnateship (ˈmægneɪt-ʃɪp). [See -SHIP.] The dignity or position of a magnate.

1916 W. J. LOCKE *Wonderful Year* i. 4 The vast, original Margett had retired.. to county magnateship. **1937** *Sat. Rev. Lit.* 24 Apr. 14 The Ball Brothers glass jar magnateship.

† **magnatical**, *a. Obs.* [f. MAGNATE + -ICAL.] ? Lordly, domineering.

1608 H. CLAPHAM *Errour on Left Hand*, To Rdr. A 2 b, Their magnaticall one-eard Inuectiues were set on fire from hell, for destroying the Church peace.

magne- (ˈmægniː) an irregular combining form used instead of MAGNETO-, in certain scientific terms introduced by Faraday:—

ˌmagne-ˈcrystal, a crystal acted upon by magnetism. **ˌmagnecryˈstallic** *a.*, pertaining to the effect produced by magnetism upon a crystalline body. **ˌmagneˈlectric** *a.* = MAGNETO-ELECTRIC. **ˌmagne-ˈoptic** *a.*, pertaining to the relation between the optic axis of a crystal and the line of magnetic force through it.

1831 FARADAY [see MAGNETO-ELECTRIC]. **1848** —— in *Phil. Trans.* CXXXIX. 4 They [*sc.* results] appear to present to us a new force.. which.. I will conventionally designate by a new word, as the magnecrystallic force. *Ibid.* 33, I.. could perceive no traces of any phenomena having either magne-optic, or magnecrystallic, or any other relation to the crystalline structure of the masses. **1870** BENCE JONES *Life Faraday* II. 348 The action of heat on magne-crystals. **1879** NOAD & PREECE *Electricity* 300 An impelling force distinct from the magnetic and the diamagnetic, and which he [Faraday] called the *magne-crystallic force*. **1881** MAXWELL *Electr. & Magn.* II. 46 Magnecrystallic phenomena.

magnefy, obs. form of MAGNIFY.

magnelle, obs. form of MANGONEL.

† **magnes**. *Obs.* Also 4 *erron.* **magnas**. [L. *magnēs* = Gr. ὁ Μάγνης λίθος, the Magnesian stone, MAGNET.] A magnet, loadstone.

1398 TREVISA *Barth. De P.R.* XVI. vii. (1495) 557 Though the magnas drawyth yren to itself: the admas drawyth it away fro the magnas. *Ibid.* lxii. 573 It semyth that the ymage hangyth in the ayre by the myghte and vertue of the stone magnes. **1559** W. CUNNINGHAM *Cosmogr. Glasse* 161 Thys is a merveilous nedle, whiche beinge touched, (as I heare) onlye with the Magnes shoulde knowe to turne alwaye to the North pole. *a* **1586** SIDNEY *Arcadia* II. (1590) 113 b, As a perfect Magnes, though put in an iuorie boxe, will thorow the boxe send forth his imbraced vertue to a beloued needle. *a* **1677** HALE *Prim. Orig. Man.* IV. iv. 329 In this lower World there seems many things directed to the special use of Mankind.. the Metals of Silver, Gold, Copper, the very Situation of the Seas, the Magnes. **1750** tr. *Leonardus' Mirr. Stones* 206.

b. *attrib.*: **magnes-stone**, in the same sense.

1398 TREVISA *Barth. De P.R.* XVI. lxii. (1495) 573 There ben mountayns of suche magnes stones and they drawe to them and breke shippes that ben nayled with yren. *a* **1586** SIDNEY *Arcadia* III. (1590) 267 As if the sight of the enimie had bene a Magnes stone to his courage. **1590** SPENSER *F.Q.* II. xii. 4. **1625** PURCHAS *Pilgrims* II. 1487 There is neither Iron or Steele, or the Magnes Stone that should so make the Tombe of Mahomet to hang in the Ayre.

c. *transf.* Magnetic virtue.

1664 EVELYN *Sylva* 33 There is such a Magnes in this simple Tree as does manifestly draw to it self some occult, and wonderful virtue.

d. Applied to each of the poles.

a **1653** G. DANIEL *Idyll* v. 164 His temper'd Earth, whips (as you Agitate The Ayre) to either Magnes, This, or That.

† **magnesane**. *Chem. Obs.* [f. MAGNES-IA: see -ANE².] Chloride of magnesium.

1812 SIR H. DAVY *Chem. Philos.* 353 It is evident that there exists a combination of magnesium and chlorine; though this body, which may be called magnesane, has never been examined in a separate state.

magnesia (mægˈniːʃ(ɪ)ə). Also 4 **magnasia**, 5 **magnetia**. [a. med.L. *magnēsia*, a. Gr. ἡ Μαγνησία λίθος, 'the Magnesian stone', a designation of two different minerals: (1) the loadstone; (2) a stone shining like silver, perhaps talc (Liddell & Scott).

It is not clear which of these two senses gave rise to the alchemical use; the brilliant lustre ascribed by the alchemists to 'magnesia' favours the latter view, and the substance seems not to have been identified with the loadstone, in spite of the resemblance of its name to the familiar word *Magnes*.]

†**1.** *Alchemy.* A mineral alleged by some alchemists to be one of the ingredients of the philosopher's stone. *Obs.*

c **1386** CHAUCER *Can. Yeom. Prol. & T.* 902 Take the stoon that Titanos men name. Which is that quod he. Magnasia is the same, Seyde Plato. *Ibid.* 905 What is Magnasia, good sire, I yow preye. It is a water that is maad, I seye, Of elementes foure, quod Plato. **1472** RIPLEY *Comp. Alch.* Pref. in Ashm. (1652) 133 Our Stone ys callyd the lesse World one and three, Magnesia also of Sulphure and Mercury Proportionate by Nature most perfytly. **1477** NORTON *Ord. Alch.* iii. ibid. 42 Another Stone..you must have withall..A Stone glittering with perspecuitie..The price of an Ounce Conveniently Is twenty shillings;..Her name is Magnetia, few people her knowe. **1610** B. JONSON *Alch.* II. iii, Your marchesite, your tutie, your magnesia. *fig.* **1651** BIGGS *New Disp.* Pref. b 2 b, We catch at onely painted Butter-flyes, and speculate not the Magnesia or substantiality of Physicks, but rather its Umbrage; not the Body, but the Bark, and superficial out side.

†**b.** Used by Paracelsus for: AMALGAM. *Obs.*

1641 FRENCH *Distill.* vi. (1651) 185 Hang plates of gold over the fume of Argent vive, and they will become white, friable, and fluxil as wax. This is called the Magnesia of gold, as saith Paracelsus.

†**2.** = MANGANESE 1. Also ***black magnesia.*** *Obs.*

[This use prob. arose from the notion that manganese was a form of the 'magnesia' of alchemy. There may, however, have been some early confusion of manganese with loadstone: Pliny *N. H.* XXXVI. lxvi says that loadstone (*magnes lapis*) was used in making glass. In the Latin of early chemistry the word was applied to various other substances: e.g. *magnesia opalina* was a red sulphide of antimony (? = KERMES 3).]

1677 PLOT *Oxfordsh.* 79 Magnesia (in the Glass-houses, called Manganese). **1712** tr. *Pomet's Hist. Drugs* I. 103/2 The last ingredient [*sc.* of Cristalline Glass] is Manganese, or Magnesia, so called from its Likeness in Colour, Weight and Substance to the Load-Stone. **1753** CHAMBERS *Cycl. Supp.* s.v. *Magnissa*, Many have supposed the Magnissa to be the same with magnesia, that is, manganese, but this is an error. **1797** *Encycl. Brit.* (ed. 3) X. 427/1 *Black Magnesia.* See Manganese.

3. (In early use often †***white magnesia*** = mod.L. *magnesia alba*, in contradistinction to ***black magnesia***: see 2.) **a.** Originally, and still in popular language, applied to hydrated magnesium carbonate, a white earthy powder, used in medicine as an antacid and cathartic. ***calcined magnesia***: magnesium oxide (pure 'magnesia': see b) prepared by heating the carbonate. **b.** In modern *Chemistry*, an alkaline earth, now recognized as the oxide of magnesium (MgO).

[This application of the word seems not to be connected with the use in sense 1, but to have been suggested by the mod.L. *magnes carneus* 'flesh-magnet', applied *c* 1550 by Cardan (*De Subtilitate* VII, Opera III. 475) to a white earth resembling osteocolla, because it was found to adhere strongly to the lips, and was therefore supposed to have the same attraction for flesh that the loadstone has for iron. The mod.L. term *magnesia alba* seems to have been first employed by Hoffmann in 1722 (*Opera* 1740 IV. 479/2).]

1755 J. BLACK *Exper. Magnesia Alba* etc. (1893) 7, I have had no opportunity of seeing Hoffman's first magnesia. *Ibid.* 8 Those who would prepare a magnesia from Epsom salt may use the following process. **1794** SULLIVAN *View Nat.* I. 240 It exists in a state of combination, in lime-stone, common magnesia, alkalis, &c. **1799** *Med. Jrnl.* II. 206 Magnesia has long been a celebrated remedy for these [stomachic] complaints. **1812** SIR H. DAVY *Chem. Philos.* 48 Hoffman, in the beginning of the 18th century, pointed out magnesia as a peculiar substance. **1823** BYRON *Juan* X. lxxiii, These sodas and magnesias Which form that bitter draught, the human species. **1878** HUXLEY *Physiogr.* 80 The metal combines with the oxygen of the air to form oxide of magnesium or magnesia.

c. *attrib.*

1846 G. E. DAY tr. *Simon's Anim. Chem.* II. 133 The magnesia salts would..answer this purpose better. **1876** PREECE & SIVEWRIGHT *Telegraphy* 34 A solution of the magnesia sulphate ($MgSO_4$. Epsom salts).

magnesian (mæg'niːʃ(ɪ)ən), *a.* [f. MAGNESIA + -AN.]

1. a. Of or pertaining to, or containing magnesia.

1794 SULLIVAN *View Nat.* I. 434 The five simple earths are, the calcareous, the ponderous, the magnesian or muriatic, the argillaceous, and the siliceous. **1799** TENNANT in *Phil. Trans.* LXXXIX. 309 Magnesian limestone may be easily distinguished from that which is purely calcareous, by the slowness of its solution in acids. **1807** T. THOMSON *Chem.* (ed. 3) II. 476 Magnesia has a very marked affinity for alumina... This affinity was first pointed out by Mr. Chenevix in his analysis of magnesian stones. **1812** SIR H. DAVY *Chem. Philos.* 33 In 1756 Dr. Black published his admirable researches on calcareous, magnesian, and alkaline substances. **1876** PAGE *Adv. Text-bk. Geol.* v. 102 Dolomite is a granular or crystalline variety of magnesian lime-stone. **1882** *Rep. to Ho. Repr. Prec. Met. U.S.* 622 This earth has a magnesian or chalky aspect.

b. magnesian limestone *Geol.*, a name for the lower division of the New Red Sandstone rocks, now known as 'Permian'.

1836 T. THOMSON *Outl. Min., Geol., & Min. Anal.* II. 142 The magnesian limestone begins at Tynemouth, and extends..as far as Nottingham. **1865** LYELL *Elem. Geol.* (ed. 6) 456 For the lower, or Magnesian Limestone division of English Geologists, Sir R. Murchison proposed, in 1841, the name of Permian.

2. *Min.* [See -IAN 2.] Of a mineral: having a (small) proportion of a constituent element replaced by magnesium.

1930 W. T. SCHALLER in *Amer. Mineralogist* XV. 571/2 Magnesium-magnesian. **1951** C. PALACHE et al. *Dana's Syst. Min.* (ed. 7) II. 503 Cuprian melanterite and pisanite are obtained from solutions containing added copper sulfate; and magnesian and other compositional variants may be similarly obtained by appropriate additions. **1968** I. KOSTOV *Mineral.* II. ix. 498 Kirovite a magnesian variety [of melanterite].

†**mag'nesiated,** *a. Chem. Obs.* [f. MAGNESIA + -ATE + -ED[1].] Combined with magnesia.

1796 KIRWAN *Elem. Min.* (ed. 2) II. 386 After dissolving the Magnesiated Iron in any acid.

magnesic (mæg'niːsɪk), *a.* [f. MAGNES-IA and MAGNES-IUM + -IC.]

a. Containing magnesia. **b.** In names of salts: Of or pertaining to magnesium.

1877 KINGZETT *Alkali Trade* 208 This tendency to fuse on the part of the mixture is due to the magnesic chloride. **1881** S. P. THOMPSON in *Nature* XXIV. 465 Magnesic platino-cyanide. **1894** *U.S. Tariff* in *Times* 16 Aug. 6/2 Magnesic fire-brick.

magnesiferous (mægniː'sɪfərəs), *a.* [f. mod.L. *magnēsi-a*: see -FEROUS.] Containing magnesia.

1856 MAYNE *Expos. Lex.*

magnesioferrite (mæg,niːsɪəʊ'fɛraɪt). *Min.* [f. *magnesio-*, taken as combining form of MAGNESIA + FERRITE.] Black octahedral crystals of magnesia and oxide of iron, from Vesuvius.

1868 DANA *Min.* (ed. 5) 152.

magnesite ('mægniːsaɪt). *Min.* [f. MAGNES-IA + -ITE[1].] Carbonate of magnesium, occurring commonly in compact white masses, but occasionally crystalline.

Formerly applied also to the hydrous silicate of magnesium (sepiolite or meerschaum).

1815 W. PHILLIPS *Outl. Min. & Geol.* (1818) 27 Magnesia is combined with the carbonic acid in the magnesite. **1862** DANA *Elem. Geol.* 63. **1877** KINGZETT *Alkali Trade* 207 Neutralising the acid liquor..with Greek stone or very nearly pure magnesite (carbonate of magnesium).

magnesium (mæg'niːsɪəm, -'iːʃ(ɪ)əm). *Chem.* [f. MAGNESIA, on the type of other names of metals in -UM, -IUM.]

†**1.** = MANGANESE. *Obs.*

1808 SIR H. DAVY in *Phil. Trans.* XCVIII. 346, I shall venture to denominate the metals from the alkaline earths barium, strontium, calcium, and magnium: the last of these words is undoubtedly objectionable, but magnesium [*footnote refers to* Bergman *Opusc.* II. 200] has been already applied to metallic manganese.

2. A chemical element, one of the 'metals of the alkaline earths', being the base of magnesia.

Though one of the most widely diffused of elements it is found in nature only in composition, and was discovered by Sir H. Davy in 1807 and first successfully separated by Bussy in 1830, as a light silvery metal, ductile and malleable, which is stable in dry air but tarnishes when exposed to moisture, and burns with a blinding white light when held in a flame. Symbol Mg.

1812 SIR H. DAVY *Chem. Philos.* 352 That magnesia consists of magnesium and oxygene, is proved both by analysis and synthesis. **1841** BRANDE *Man. Chem.* (ed. 5) 705. **1880** *Nature* XXI. 289 On the dichroitic fluorescence of magnesium-platinum-cyanide. **1881** LOCKYER in *Nature* No. 617. 394 The spectra are as distinct as the spectrum of magnesium.

3. *attrib.*: **magnesium lamp**, a lamp constructed to burn magnesium; **magnesium light**, a brilliant light produced by the combustion of magnesium; **magnesium ribbon, thread, wire**, a thin strip or wire of magnesium prepared for burning.

1860 *Photogr. News* 8 June 70/2 A rival..to the strong lights hitherto used is like to spring up in Bunsen's *magnesium-lamp. **1871** M. COLLINS *Mrq. & Merch.* I. vi. 204 A magnesium lamp stood on the table. **1860** *Photogr. News* 8 June 70/2 The excellence of the *magnesium-light. **1871** KINGSLEY *At Last* vi, My host,..by the help of the magnesium light, had penetrated further into the cave. **1890** *Anthony's Photogr. Bull.* III. 126 *Magnesium ribbon. **1860** *Photogr. News* 8 June 70/2 Notwithstanding the high price of the *magnesium thread. **1864** *Proc. Amer. Phil. Soc.* IX. 458 *Magnesium wire. **1878** H. S. WILSON *Alp. Ascents* iii. 94 The intense flame of the magnesium wire.

magnet ('mægnɪt). Also 5-7 **magnete**, 6 **magnnet**. [a. OF. *magnete* (also *manette*), or directly ad. L. *magnēta*, accus. of *magnēs*: see MAGNES.

The word has been superseded in mod. F. by *aimant*, but is current in the other Rom. and Teut. langs.: It., Sp., Pg. *magnete*, Ger., Da., Sw. *magnet*, Du. *magneet*.]

1. *Min.* = LOADSTONE; a variety of magnetite (proto-sesquioxide of iron) characterized by its power of attracting iron and steel, and by certain other associated properties (see 2).

c **1440** *Promp. Parv.* 325/1 Magnete, precyowse stone, *magnes.* **1447** BOKENHAM *Seyntys* (Roxb.) 14 Hym thowte that nevere in so lytyl space He had more seyn, wych his herte drow As the magnet doth iryn. **1555** EDEN *Decades* 322 The Ilande of Magnete that is the Iland of the lode stone which is vnder or near abowte the northe pole. **1601** HOLLAND *Pliny* II. 515 Dinocrates began to make the arched roufe of the temple of Arsinoe all of Magnet or this Loadstone. *a* **1674** MILTON *Hist. Mosc.* iii. Wks. 1851 VIII. 487 In midst of this white City stands a Castle built of Magnet. **1728** PEMBERTON *Newton's Philos.* 13 That any stone should have so amazing a property, as we find in the magnet [etc.]. *c* **1860** FARADAY *Forces Nat.* v. 130 There are some curious bodies in nature..which are called magnets or loadstones—ores of iron. **1861** C. W. KING *Ant. Gems* (1866) 60 On Magnet, a black compact and hard iron-ore, I have seen rude intagli of the Lower Empire.

2. a. A piece of loadstone; also, a piece of iron or steel to which the characteristic properties of loadstone have been imparted, either permanently or temporarily, by contact with another magnet, by induction, or by means of an electric current. A magnet has an axis, at the extremities of which (the 'poles') the attractive power is greatest, and at the middle of which it becomes *nil.* When suspended freely, a magnet assumes such a position that one of its poles (hence called the north pole) points approximately north, and the other (the south pole) approximately south; the like poles of two magnets repel each other, while the unlike poles attract each other.

bar magnet, a polarized rod of iron, now much used in the construction of electro-magnetic apparatus. ***horse-shoe magnet***, a magnet made of steel in the form of a horse-shoe. ***natural magnet***: one consisting of loadstone; opposed to ***artificial magnet.*** See also ELECTRO-MAGNET.

1625 N. CARPENTER *Geog. Del.* I. iii. (1635) 57 Let there bee cut out of a rocke of Load-stone, a Magnet of reasonable quantity. **1727** DE FOE *Syst. Magic* I. ii. (1840) 58-9 What would have been said, to see him make a piece of iron dance round a table, while the agent held the Magnet underneath. **1777** PRIESTLEY *Matt. & Spir.* (1782) I. xiii. 151 We are not ..able to conceive how it is that a magnet attracts iron. **1832** *Nat. Philos.* II. *Magnetism* v. 53 (U.K.S.) These horse-shoe magnets..may be rendered magnetic by the same process as a straight bar. **1839** G. BIRD *Nat. Philos.* 146 Each portion will become a perfect magnet, each of the fractured ends exhibiting a polar state, as perfect as the entire magnet. **1894** BOTTONE *Electr. Instr. Making* (ed. 6) 156 A bar-magnet, around one pole of which is coiled about a hundred feet of ..copper wire. *Ibid.* 231 It is easily seen, that if (as in bell magnets, horseshoe magnets) the winding is not carried on [etc.].

b. In extended sense: A body possessing the properties characteristic of a magnet.

1797 *Encycl. Brit.* (ed. 3) X. 435/2 [Cavallo's hypothesis] is, that the earth itself is a magnet.

3. *fig.* Something which attracts.

1655 H. VAUGHAN *Silex Scint.*, *Starre* vi, These are the Magnets which so strongly move And work all night upon thy light and love. **1687** DRYDEN *Hind & P.* III. 368 Two magnets, heaven and earth, allure to bliss, The larger load-stone that, the nearer this. **1691-8** NORRIS *Pract. Disc.* (1711) III. 12 God is the true great Magnet of our souls. **1777** MISS BURNEY *Evelina* xxi, They know the attraction of the magnet that draws me. **1800** MRS. HERVEY *Mourtray Fam.* II. 64 The lovely Emma was the magnet that attracted them both. **1821** JOANNA BAILLIE *Metr. Leg., Columbus* i, The magnet of a thousand eyes. **1868** LYNCH *Rivulet* CXLI. iii, Let love your magnet be To draw him back to you.

4. *attrib.* and *Comb.*, as ***magnet-drawn***, ***-like*** adjs.; ***magnet-wise*** adv.; **magnet core**, the rod or bar of soft magnetized iron placed in the middle of an electro-magnet; **magnet-cylinder**, a metal cylinder, containing magnets, used for generating electricity; **magnet helix**, a coil of wire such as surrounds the core of an electro-magnet; **magnet house**, a house in which magnetic apparatus is kept.

1894 BOTTONE *Elect. Instr. Making* (ed. 6) 231 This is true whatever be the form of the *magnet core. **1866** H. WILDE in *Phil. Trans.* CLVII. 91 A compound hollow cylinder of brass and iron, hereafter called the *magnet-cylinder. **1923** R. GRAVES *Whipperginny* 43 She was *magnet-drawn by his least wish. **1952** R. CAMPBELL tr. *Baudelaire's Poems* 67 When to a cherished cat my gaze Is magnet-drawn. **1879** PRESCOTT *Sp. Telephone* 23 Whenever one part of a circuit is brought in proximity to another, as is the case in *magnet helices. **1900** *Daily News* 3 July 5/2 The *magnet house of the Observatory. **1821** SHELLEY *Prometh. Unb.* IV. 466 Borne beside thee by a power Like the polar Paradise, *Magnet-like of lovers' eyes. **1849** MOZLEY *Ess.* (1878) II. 201 The obliquity of this visible system is..the one theme, which is ever drawing them *magnet-wise.

†**magnetarian,** *a. Obs. rare*$^{-1}$. [f. MAGNET + -ARIAN.] Conversant with the magnet.

1654 CHARLETON *Physiol. Epic.-Gass.-Charltoniana* 388 The Speculations and Observations of our Modern Magnetarian Authors, Gilbert, Cabeus, Kircher, &c.

magnetarium (mægnɪ'tɛərɪəm). [quasi-Latin, f. MAGNET + -ARIUM.] An instrument for the illustration of the phenomena of the earth's magnetism.

1894 H. WILDE in *Proc. Roy. Soc.* LV. 210 By means of some electro-mechanism, new to experimental science, which [in a paper read in June 1890] I termed a magnetarium, the period of backward rotation [etc.]. **1902** *Encycl. Brit.* XXX. 463/1 Wilde had succeeded in reproducing some of the most conspicuous features of the earth's magnetization by a contrivance called a magnetarium.

‖**mag'netes.** *Obs.* [L., a. Gr. μαγνήτης = μάγνης MAGNET.] = MAGNET.

c **1581** LODGE *Repl. Gosson's Sch. Abuse* (Shaks. Soc. 1853) 21 As the magnetes draweth iorne..so Musik [etc.].

magnetic (mæg'nɛtɪk), *a.* and *sb.* [ad. mod.L. *magnētic-us* (F. *magnétique*, Sp. *magnético*, It. *magnetico*), f. *magnēt-*: see MAGNET and -IC.]

A. *adj.*

1. a. Having the properties of a magnet; pertaining to a magnet or to magnetism; producing, caused by, or operating by means of, magnetism. See also sense 5).

Frequently forming phraseological combs. with sbs., as in *magnetic amplitude, azimuth, compass, core, declination, dip, equator, field, fluid, meridian, needle, north, pole, potential, separator, storm, telegraph, zenith*: see the sbs.

1634 HABINGTON *Castara* I. (Arb.) 23 Why doth the stubborne iron prove So gentle to th' magnetique stone? **1635** QUARLES *Embl.* I. xiii. (1718) 53 Like as the am'rous needle joys to bend To her magnetick friend. **1647** H. MORE *Philos. Poems* 385 Let the arrow K keep in BC the same line of the air or earthly magnetick spirit. **1656** BLOUNT *Glossogr.*, *Magnetick*, belonging to the Lodestone. **1796** H. HUNTER tr. *St.-Pierre's Stud. Nat.* (1799) I. 64 Metals, which have magnetic powers, most of which are still unknown to us. **1796** KIRWAN *Elem. Min.* II. 158 Common Magnetic Iron Ore. *Ibid.* 161 Magnetic Sand. **1851** CARPENTER *Man. Phys.* (ed. 2) 12 *note*, When iron rails, pokers, &c. become magnetic by the influence of the earth. **1884** A. DANIELL *Princ. Physics* xvi. 609 When an iron or cobalt bar is magnetised it..emits a slight sound—a 'magnetic tick'. **1926** *Jrnl. Iron & Steel Inst.* CXIV. 112 The concentrate from the magnetic separation is always mixed with much water, and cannot on that account be directly used. **1964** F. L. WESTWATER *Electronic Computers* iv. 65 If we now suppose that we have another electro-magnet which we can call a 'reading' magnet or magnetic head as it is more usually termed, when the magnetised spot of wire passes under the reading head there will be a change of magnetic flux through the coils on the head. **1964** T. W. MCRAE *Impact of Computers on Accounting* i. 6 The current vogue is to use magnetic storage devices which employ the principle of magnetic hysteresis or retained magnetism. The more popular of these devices are: 1. Magnetic tape. 2. Magnetic drum. 3. Magnetic disks. 4. Magnetic cards. 5. Magnetic core (i.e. ferrite core). **1966** A. BATTERSBY *Math. in Managem.* viii. 200 An alternative to optical scanning is to use characters printed in magnetic ink. The MICR system (Magnetic Ink Character Recognition) is mainly used by banks, and the specially designed characters are now becoming a familiar feature of our cheque-books. **1967** D. WILSON in Wills & Yearsley *Handbk. Managem. Technol.* iii. 42 Many data processing installations are now planning to use magnetic disks or magnetic cards for the first time. **1970** *Sci. Amer.* Feb. 29/2 By 1972, if not sooner, it should be economic to replace the standard magnetic-core memory of the computer (the type of memory in which tiny magnetic rings of ceramic are threaded on a matrix of thin wires) with a series of LSI memory modules. **1971** J. H. SMITH *Digital Logic* vi. 126 A variation of the drum is the magnetic disc, very much like a long playing record, but again coated with magnetic material. A whole stack of these discs are normally assembled to give a reasonably fast memory of very large capacity.

†**b.** Formerly applied to a healing plaster of which 'magnet' or loadstone formed an ingredient, and which was regarded as possessing occult attractive power similar to that of the magnet. *Obs.*

1658 A. FOX *Wurtz' Surg.* II. x. 86 Then is it requisite, that you have a good Medicine, which penetrate with its vertue, and that is the Magnetick plaister. **1658** tr. *Bergerac's Satyr. Char.* xii. 47, I teach them to find..the magnetique plaster. **1671** SALMON *Syn. Med.* III. lxxvii. 675 Apply the magnetick Emplaster..till it [the wound] is sufficiently cleansed.

†**c.** Said with reference to other attractive forces formerly confused with magnetism. *Obs.*

1667 MILTON *P.L.* III. 583 They [the Constellations] towards his all-chearing Lamp Turn swift their various motions, or are turnd By his Magnetic beam.

2. *fig.* **a.** Having powers of attraction; very attractive or seductive. Now often with some mixture of sense 4.

1632 B. JONSON (*title*) The Magnetick Lady. **1638** SIR T. HERBERT *Trav.* (ed. 2) 55 Turk, Jew, and others, drawne thither by the magnetick power of gaine. **1658** ROWLAND *Topsell's Four-f. Beasts* Pref., There is such a magnetick force in Goodness, that it draws the hearts of men after it. **1778** MISS BURNEY *Evelina* xxiii, The magnetic power of beauty. **1845** M. PATTISON *Ess.* (1889) I. 9 That magnetic influence which irresistibly draws our feet to spots on which our imagination has long fed. **1880** *Spectator* 3 Nov. 1437 The Americans have invented, and Englishmen are slowly adopting into their political vocabulary, a new word, intended to account for the otherwise unaccountable popularity of some politicians. They say they are 'magnetic'. **1888** BRYCE *Amer. Commw.* II. III. lxxiv. 612 If he can join to them a ready and winning address, a geniality of manner if not of heart, he becomes what is called magnetic. **1901** *Scotsman* 7 Oct. 2/7, I found him one of the most magnetic and companionable of men.

b. Const. *to*, †*of*.

1667 WATERHOUSE *Fire Lond.* 107 Whose appositeness for Trade, was Magnetique of all Nations and Merchandises to it. **1864** TENNYSON *Aylmer's F.* 626 His face magnetic to the hand from which Livid he pluck'd it forth.

3. Applied to those bodies, as iron, nickel, cobalt, which are capable of receiving the properties of the loadstone, or of being attracted by it; also, = PARAMAGNETIC.

1837 BREWSTER *Magnet.* 9 He [Gilbert *c* 1600] applies the term magnetic to all bodies which are acted upon by load-stones and magnets. **1843** PORTLOCK *Geol.* 225 Magnetic pyrites occurs in considerable quantity in a greenstone dike. **1846** [see DIAMAGNETIC *a.*]. **1871** ROSCOE *Elem. Chem.* 239 Ferrous oxide and the ferric salts are magnetic.

4. Pertaining to animal magnetism; mesmeric.

1800 *Med. Jrnl.* IV. 130 The magnetic influence of Mesmer. **1834** *Penny Cycl.* II. 33/1 The mode of bringing the magnetised under the influence of the magnetic fluid was peculiar. **1838** DICKENS *Nich. Nick.* vii, As if he had been in a magnetic slumber. **1855** SMEDLEY *Occult Sci.* 222 The magnetic awakening in the body.

5. Special collocations (see also sense 1): **magnetic anomaly**, a local deviation from the general pattern of the earth's magnetic field; **magnetic bottle**, a magnetic field that confines a plasma inside it to a restricted region; **magnetic brake**, a friction brake that is actuated magnetically; **magnetic bubble**, a small, mobile region of reverse magnetization in a very thin sheet of magnetic material in which the magnetization is perpendicular to the sheet and predominantly in one direction; **magnetic drum** *Computers*, a cylinder that can be rotated and has a magnetizable outer surface on which data can be recorded on circular tracks by means of a set of fixed heads (one opposite each track); **magnetic induction** (see INDUCTION 10 b); **magnetic lens**, (a device producing) a magnetic field capable of focusing a beam of charged particles; **magnetic memory**, (*a*) a dependence of the magnetic state of a body on its previous magnetic history; (*b*) *Computers*, a memory (sense 2 d) that employs the magnetic properties of bodies; **magnetic mine**, a submarine mine that is detonated by the approach of a magnetized body such as a ship; **magnetic mirror**, (*a*) a magnetized surface that reflects light; (*b*) a magnetic field that causes approaching charged particles to be reflected; **magnetic moment** (see MOMENT *sb.* 8 c); **magnetic quantum number**, the quantum number *m* (see M 5 b); **magnetic resonance accelerator** = CYCLOTRON; **magnetic stripe** (see STRIPE *sb.*[3]); **magnetic tape**, tape (now usu. of plastic) coated or impregnated with a magnetic material, or made of magnetic material, for use as a recording medium.

1899 *Jrnl. Brit. Astron. Assoc.* IX. 134 (*heading*) Magnetic anomalies in Russia. **1929** EVE & KEYS *Appl. Geophysics* ii. 38 Three auxiliary magnets of different strengths are usually carried in order to provide for the measurement of large magnetic anomalies and thus extend the range of measurement. **1971** *Nature* 5 Feb. 374/2 The magnetic evidence for seafloor spreading is based on the pattern of the linear magnetic anomalies which lie over and to the sides of mid-oceanic ridges. **1957** *Sci. Amer.* Aug. 80/2 Since no conceivable material will withstand the temperature of these [thermonuclear] reactions, the hope is to contain them in a 'magnetic bottle' that will take advantage of the plasma's response to electromagnetic forces. **1967** *Science Year* 341 No one yet knows how to confine a hot plasma in a 'magnetic bottle' long enough for the energy liberated by relatively infrequent thermo-nuclear reactions to overcome the inevitable loss from electromagnetic radiation and from plasma escaping from the bottle. **1899** *Sci. Abstr.* II. 572 Using a magnetic brake, which acts upon the fly-wheel of the driving engine. **1922** GLAZEBROOK *Dict. Appl. Physics* II. 323/1 In magnetic brakes..an electromagnet..is held just above the rail to which it is attracted upon excitation. **1970** *Nature* 10 Oct. 114/1 Magnetic bubbles, small stable regions of reverse magnetization in a highly anisotropic ferrimagnetic sheet, were described by Dr. F. C. Rossol. **1971** *Sci. Amer.* June 78/1 A promising alternative.. exploits a new technology in which data bits are stored in the form of magnetic 'bubbles' moving in thin films of magnetic material... The bubbles are stable over a considerable range of conditions and can be moved from point to point at high velocity. **1950** W. W. STIFLER *High-Speed Computing Devices* xiv. 304 A rotating magnetic drum..is a static storage system, according to this definition, because data recorded on the drum are static with respect to the surface of the drum. **1955** *Sci. Amer.* June 98/2 For the larger, intermediate-speed memory of a computer the favorite device at present is the magnetic drum. **1968** *Brit. Med. Bull.* XXIV. 192/1 Different users require..different combinations of back-up storage (magnetic tape units,.. magnetic drum units, and so on). **1919** *Phil. Mag.* XXXVIII. 709 Such a 'magnetic lens' is not of much immediate value as the magnetic spectrum of positive rays is very complex. **1966** *McGraw-Hill Encycl. Sci. & Technol.* VIII. 33/2 Magnetic lenses are employed as condensers, objectives, and projection lenses in magnetic electron microscopes, as final focusing lenses in the electron guns of cathode-ray tubes, and for the selection of groups of charged particles of specific velocity in velocity spectrographs. **1887** *Jrnl. Soc. Telegr. Engin.* XVI. 523 No matter how treated, a piece of soft iron has a 'magnetic memory'. **1947** L. B. LOEB *Fund. Electr. & Magn.* (ed. 3) xvii. 242 A continuous curve is retraced that never restores the magnetic material back to its zero value. This behavior can be ascribed to a sort of 'magnetic memory' of the substance. **1957** *Economist* 30 Nov. 797 The electronic valves, transistors and magnetic memories used in the modern computer have been developed from knowledge gained from other spheres of electronic applications. **1939** *News Rev.* 30 Nov. 13/1 We already know the secrets of the magnetic mine. **1939** *War Weekly* 1 Dec. 185/1 The new magnetic mine is said to be in use by the Germans at the present time. **1974** *Encycl. Brit. Micropædia* VI. 910/2 Three common types of naval mine are in use, classed by their method of detonation: magnetic mines, pressure mines, and acoustic mines. **1894** *Jrnl. Inst. Electr. Engin.* XXIII. 448 (*heading*) Researches on the reflection of polarised light from magnetic mirrors. **1952** R. F. POST in *Classified Conf. Thermonucl. Reactors held at Denver June 28, 1952* (AEC Rept. Wash.-115) 83 A second possible attack on the problem of containment of a linear discharge at its ends is through the use of what might be called an 'enhanced magnetic mirror'. The ordinary 'magnetic mirror' effect has been known for some time. **1956** L. SPITZER *Physics of fully Ionized Gases* i. 11 The constancy of the magnetic moment has the immediate result that gyrating particles will tend to be reflected from regions of increasing magnetic field... Such a reflecting region may be called a 'magnetic mirror'. **1966** *McGraw-Hill Encycl. Sci. & Technol.* X. 388/1 The 'mirror machine' (invented by R. F. Post) allows confinement [of the plasma] in a tube with ends 'plugged' by magnetic mirrors... A magnetic mirror is merely a localized region where the magnetic field is made much stronger than average, so that charged particles tend to be reflected as they approach the mirror. **1923** Magnetic quantum number [see M 5 b]. **1961** POWELL & CRASEMANN *Quantum Mech.* x. 355 Since the single electron in these atoms has zero angular momentum in the ground state, the magnetic quantum number must be *m* = 0. **1935** Magnetic resonance accelerator [see CYCLOTRON]. **1968** F. KERTESZ *Lang. Nucl. Sci.* (Oak Ridge Nat. Lab. TM 2367) 17 A number of the accelerators..have names ending in '... tron', recalling the generic term *cyclotron* or magnetic resonance accelerator. **1937** *Bell Syst. Techn. Jrnl.* XVI. 165 (*heading*) Sound recording on magnetic tape. **1942** *Jrnl. R. Aeronaut. Soc.* XLVI. 68 This paper described an electro-magnetic method of producing and controlling reverberation by the use of a magnetic tape recording system. It consists of recording a sound pattern magnetically on steel tape. **1957** *Economist* 30 Nov. 807/2 The computer, in turn, produces the instructions on magnetic tape which is read by the control apparatus of the cutting machine. **1958** *Listener* 16 Oct. 605/1 Stereophonic magnetic tape recordings have been available for some time. **1967** C. BERNERS-LEE in Wills & Yearsley *Handbk. Managem. Technol.* i. 6 It may well be that the data already exists on magnetic tape in a computer installation.

B. *sb.*

†**1.** = MAGNET, *lit.* and *fig. Obs.*

1654 H. L'ESTRANGE *Chas. I* (1655) 60 They [alliances between princes] are not souldered by any magnetique of Love. **1658** J. WEBB *Cleopatra* VIII. II. 20 Retiring her eyes from a magnetick which even forceably attracted them. **1671** MILTON *P.R.* II. 168 Such object hath the power to.. lead At will the manliest, resolutest brest, As the Magnetic hardest Iron draws.

2. a. 'Any metal, as iron, steel, nickel, cobalt, &c., which may receive the properties of the loadstone' (Webster 1847–54 citing *Dana*). **b.** A paramagnetic body (*Cent. Dict.* 1890).

3. magnetics: the science of magnetism.

1786 CAVALLO in *Phil. Trans.* LXXVII. 11 It is a proposition well established in magnetics, that soft iron, or soft steel, acquires magnetism very easily. **1881** MAXWELL *Electr. & Magn.* I. 12 In electrostatics and magnetics. **1971** *Nature* 26 Nov. 187/2 Gravity and magnetics have theorems which limit the amount of interpretation which can be applied to observations of potentials and in general geophysicists work within the confines of these restrictions.

4. *pl.* Magnetic devices or materials.

1965 *IEEE Trans. Magnetics* Mar. 3/1 The name became Magnetics Group, and its scope:..treatment of all matters in which the dominant factors are the fundamental developments, design, and certain applications of magnetic devices. **1971** *Physics Bull.* Nov. 646/1 The size of the magnetics market however does not hold any reassurances for research.

5. *pl.* Magnetic properties or phenomena collectively.

1972 *Nature* 22 Dec. 438/1 They have recorded bathymetry, magnetics and gravity along a profile over a ridge striking N 50° W. **1974** *Ibid.* 4 Jan. 9/1 A new geophysical model for the Red Sea is presented in Fig. 5... The synthetic magnetics is compared with the observed. The fit of the anomalies for the older crust is not quite so good as for the Gulf data.

magnetical (mæg'nɛtɪkəl), *a.* Now *rare.* [f. mod.L. *magnĕtic-us* (see prec.) + -AL[1].]

1. = MAGNETIC *a.* 1.

1581 BOROUGH (*title*) A Discours of the Variation of the Cumpas, or Magneticall Needle. **1581** —— *Disc. Var. Compass* i. Bj, The magneticall meridian. **1625** N. CARPENTER *Geogr. Del.* I. iii. (1635) 46 A Magneticall Body by some is defined to bee that which seated in the Aire doth place it selfe in one place naturall, not alterable. **1633** T. JAMES *Voy.* Q ij b, The Magneticall Azimuths. **1696** WHISTON *Th. Earth* II. (1722) 109 Dr. Halley..has discover'd at least two Magnetical Poles. **1773** BRYDONE *Sicily* xi. (1776) I. 231 The needle..entirely lost its magnetical power, standing indiscriminately at every point of the compass. **1794** G. ADAMS *Nat. & Exp. Philos.* IV. l. 382 You will find the iron appear more magnetical than the steel. **1797** *Encycl. Brit.* (ed. 3) X. 435/2 The variation of the compass first showed..that the earth had two magnetical poles by which the needle is influenced. **1876** DAVIS *Polaris Exp.* App. 639 The Coast Survey..has contributed astronomical and magnetical instruments.

†**b.** = MAGNETIC 1 c. Also const. *of*. *Obs.*

1626 BACON *Sylva* §75 There is an Opinion, that the Moone is Magneticall of Heat, as the Sun is of Cold, and Moisture. **1642** H. MORE *Song of Soul* II. i. II. xxvi, All these be substances self-moveable: And that we call virtue magneticall..I comprehend it in the life plantall. **1671** GREW *Anat. Plants* I. iii. §21 It will in its own magnetical tendency to ascend, reduce the Cortical Body to a compliance with it. **1686** GOAD *Celest. Bodies* II. i. 124 For who, almost, grants not..that the Planets are Magnetical Bodys touched by the Sun,..and thereupon move faster when in ☌ with him, direct.

†**c.** Of a writer: That treats of magnetism. *Obs.*

1676 BOYLE *Mech. Orig. divers Qual., Magnetism* 20 But Magnetism is so fertile a Subject, that if I had now the leisure and conveniency to range among Magnetical Writers, I should scarce doubt of finding [etc.].

¶**d.** In the 17th c. often applied to remedies for which a magical or occult virtue was claimed.

1628 BURTON *Anat. Mel.* II. i. I. i. (ed. 3) 209 Whether by these diabolical meanes..this disease and the like may be cured? and if they may whether it bee lawfull to make vse of them, those magneticall cures? **1632** *Ibid.* ii. IV. (ed. 4) 281 Balsomes, strange extracts, elixars, and such like magico-magneticall cures. **1621** *Ibid.* III. ii. v. iv. 651 Cardan.. reckons up many magneticall remedies. **1630** HALES *Gold. Rem.* I. (1673) 289 He tells of a great Person, who usually

works such Magnetical Cures of that disease. **1663** BOYLE *Usef. Exp. Nat. Philos.* II. v. 226 Eminent physicians have both made use of and commended magnetical remedies. **1722** QUINCY *Lex. Physico-Med.* (ed. 2), *Magnetism*, and *Magnetical Virtues*, are much used by some who find their Account more in Amusement than useful Knowledge: and some affect to explain or recommend by such Terms, those Remedies, for the Application and Operation of which, they have no better Reasons at hand.

2. *fig.* = MAGNETIC *a.* 2.

a **1649** DRUMM. OF HAWTH. *Hist. Jas. V*, Wks. (1711) 96 That the king had a magnetical affection towards him. **1675** TRAHERNE *Chr. Ethics* 468 Modesty..preferreth another above it self, and in that its magnetical and obliging quality much consisteth. *a* **1792** HORNE *Wks.* (1818) III. iii. 34 The virtue of his death, and the consequent 'power of his resurrection'..compose a divine magnetical influence.

3. Pertaining to animal magnetism.

1794 GODWIN *Cal. Williams* 112 There was a magnetical sympathy between me and my master. **1797** *Encycl. Brit.* (ed. 3) X. 449/2 The room where the patients underwent the magnetical operations. **1802** ACERBI *Trav.* I. 273 The proficiency of the Baron in the magnetical science has not met with very great success.

†**B.** *sb. pl.* Magnetic properties. *Obs. rare.*

1646 SIR T. BROWNE *Pseud. Ep.* II. iii. 71 Men that ascribe thus much unto rocks of the north, must presume or discover the like magneticals in the south.

magnetically (mæg'nɛtɪkəlɪ), *adv.* [f. prec. + -LY[2].] In a magnetic manner; by means or in respect of magnetism.

1621 BURTON *Anat. Mel.* I. ii. III. ii. 126 Many greene wounds magnetically cured. **1682** SIR T. BROWNE *Chr. Mor.* I. §9 Stand magnetically upon that Axis, when prudent simplicity hath fixt there. *c* **1790** IMISON *Sch. Art* II. 166 The operator ought not to stop longer on the first bar than is necessary to open the pores, and to arrange them magnetically. **1873** MAXWELL *Electr. & Magn.* II. 45 Iron which is magnetically hard is..more apt to break. **1878** C. STANFORD *Symb. Christ* ii. 44 On a sudden they became magnetically conscious of supernatural presence.

†**mag'neticalness.** *Obs. rare*⁻¹. [-NESS.] Magnetic quality or condition.

1757 BIRCH *Hist. R. Soc.* IV. 253 It related not to the instances of the magneticalness of lightning.

magnetician (mægnɪ'tɪʃən). [f. MAGNETIC + -IAN.] One skilled in magnetism; a magnetist.

1838 *Ann. Electr. Magn. & Chem.* II. 53 Had Mr. Clarke, the 'magnetician', known that fact, he might have saved himself the trouble. **1846** C. FOX *Jrnl.* 13 Oct. (1972) 168 Mineral veins, however, a quite different case; infinite scope therein for Papa and all Magneticians. **1854** *Pereira's Polarized Light* (ed. 2) 65 The electrician and the magnetician have assumed, respectively, an electric and a magnetic fluid. **1897** *Proc. R. Soc.* LX. p. x, His first paper on that subject..was completely overlooked by magneticians. **1939** *Geogr. Jrnl.* XCIII. 157 Gilbert the magnetician. **1966** *McGraw-Hill Encycl. Sci. & Technol.* IV. 20/1 One of these [components], called variation by the navigator and magnetic declination by the magnetician, is the angle between magnetic and geographic meridians. **1970** *Nature* 29 Aug. 982/2 He found that magneticians were far readier to collect than to interpret data, and set himself to analyse geomagnetic variations.

†**mag'neticness.** *Obs. rare*⁻¹. [f. MAGNETIC *a.* + -NESS.] = MAGNETICALNESS.

1663 WATERHOUSE *Comm. Fortescue* 187 They fortified themselves against all incursions,..which the Magnetiqueness of their external success..might..occasion them.

magnetico- (mæg'nɛtɪkəʊ), used (*rarely*) as combining f. MAGNETIC to denote 'magnetic and ..'.

1816 BENTHAM *Chrestomathia* Wks. 1843 VIII. 145 There are—1. The Magnetic or Magnetico-spastic. 2. The Electric or Electrico-spastic [etc.].

magne'tiferous, *a.* [f. MAGNET + -IFEROUS.] Producing or conducting magnetism.

1832 WEBSTER (citing *Journal of Science*). In mod. Dicts.

†**mag'netify,** *v. Obs.* [f. MAGNET + -IFY.] *trans.* = MAGNETIZE. Hence **mag'netified** *ppl. a.*

1650 CHARLETON *Paradoxes* Prol. 2 Like the Aguish magnetified Needle, reels to and fro. **1797** *Encycl. Brit.* (ed. 3) X. 450/1 Several persons in a higher sphere of life were magnetified and felt nothing. *Ibid.* XVIII. 621/1 The south pole of a small magnetified needle.

†**magne'timeter.** *Obs.* [f. MAGNET + -METER, after *calorimeter*.] = MAGNETOMETER.

1821 W. SCORESBY Jun. in *Trans. Roy. Soc. Edinb.* (1823) IX. 243 Description of a Magnetimeter, being a New Instrument for Measuring Magnetic Attractions, and Finding the Dip of the Needle.

magnetine ('mægnɪtɪn). [f. MAGNET + -INE.]

†**1.** A hypothetical imponderable substance regarded as the principle of magnetism. *Obs. rare*⁻¹.

1848 *Lond. Jrnl. Arts*, etc. XXXII. 64 [where also other related terms (*magnetide* etc.) are proposed].

2. A mixture of some magnetized material and cement, used in making magnetic belts, etc.

1890 in *Century Dict.*

magnetipolar (,mægnɪtɪ'pəʊlə(r)), *a.* [f. MAGNET + POLAR *a.*] Having the property of magnetic polarity.

1890 in *Century Dict.*

†**magnetish,** *a. Obs.* [f. MAGNET + -ISH.] = MAGNETIC.

1683 PETTUS *Fleta Minor* I. 317 Some of these Iron-stones are Magnetish, and draw the Iron apparently, which proceeds from their hidden heat.

magnetism ('mægnɪtɪz(ə)m). [ad. mod.L. *magnētismus* (F. *magnétisme*, 1724 in Hatz.-Darm.), f. *magnēt-*: see MAGNET and -ISM.]

1. The characteristic properties of the magnet; magnetic phenomena and their laws. Also, the natural agency or principle concerned in the production of magnetic phenomena; formerly often supposed to be an 'imponderable fluid', but now regarded as a modification of energy.

terrestrial magnetism: the magnetic properties of the earth, considered as a whole.

1616 W. BARLOWE *Magn. Aduert.* Ep. Ded. A 2, What I had built vpon his foundation of the Magnetisme of the earth. **1664** POWER *Exp. Philos.* III. 160 You shall thereby give it a most powerful Magnetisme, so that it will then as actively move the Needle..as the Loadstone it-self. **1775** HARRIS *Philos. Arrangem.* Wks. (1841) 376 Are we to speak of those other motive powers, the powers of magnetism and electricity? **1816** J. SMITH *Panorama Sci. & Art* II. 164 A peculiar species of attraction, exerted by bodies called magnets or loadstones, receives the appellation of magnetism. **1837** WHEWELL *Hist. Induct. Sci.* (1857) III. 38 The subject of terrestrial magnetism forms a very important addition to the general facts. **1839** *Penny Cycl.* XIV. 288/1 The mutual relations of the two magnetisms [Austral and Boreal], and those of positive and negative electricity. *c* **1865** J. WYLDE in *Circ. Sci.* I. 249/2 The magnetic effect remains for some time; and this is called *residuary magnetism*. **1871** TYNDALL *Fragm. Sci.* (1879) II. xvi. 423 A blue flame, which being usually bent by the earth's magnetism, received the name of the Voltaic Arc.

†**b.** In the 17th c. often confused with various phenomena of attraction not now recognized as immediately related to it. *Obs.*

1646 SIR T. BROWNE *Pseud. Ep.* II. iii. (1658) 85 Many other Magnetisms may be pretended, and the like attractions through all the creatures of Nature. **1671** GREW *Anat. Plants* I. ii. §25 The two Contrary Tendencies of the Lignous and Cortical Bodies..(being most probably external, and a kind of Magnetisme).

c. *fig.* Attractive power or influence, esp. personal charm or ascendancy. Sometimes with allusion to sense 3.

1655 H. VAUGHAN *Silex Scint.* II. *Cock-crowing* i, Their magnetisme works all night And dreams of Paradise and light. **1662** GLANVILL *Lux Orient.* xiv. 13 The bodies they have contracted..may by a kind of fatal magnetisme be chained down to their proper element. **1671** MARVELL *Corr.* Wks. 1872–5 II. 393 The magnetism of two souls, rightly touched, works beyond all natural limits. **1691** NORRIS *Pract. Disc.* 172 Nothing is more common than to see Men of singular Strictness..who yet..stoop and yield to the Magnetism of this dirty Planet. *a* **1711** KEN *Preparatives* Poet. Wks. 1721 IV. 64 The Magnetism of Heav'nly Love, Draws some to God above. **1753** RICHARDSON *Grandison* (1781) III. ix. 67 There is a kind of magnetism in goodness. **1859** KINGSLEY *Misc.* I. 28 He could draw round him..by the spiritual magnetism of his genius, many a noble soul. **1888** BRYCE *Amer. Commw.* II. III. lxxiv. 612 Now, magnetism is among the highest qualities which an American popular leader can possess.

2. The science which is concerned with magnetic phenomena.

1828–32 in WEBSTER. **1885** S. P. THOMPSON (*title*) Lessons in Electricity and Magnetism.

3. Short for *animal magnetism* (see ANIMAL C. 1) = MESMERISM.

[**1784**, etc.; see ANIMAL C. 1.] **1785** *Mesmer's Aphorisms* 13 It cannot be determined how long a tree may preserve the magnetism. **1797** *Encycl. Brit.* (ed. 3) X. 450/1 The principal application of magnetism..was by pressure of the hands..on the hypochondria. **1855** SMEDLEY *Occult Sci.* 224 Magnetism by the eye is indeed often more powerful than by the hands.

magnetist ('mægnɪtɪst). [f. MAGNET + -IST.]

1. One skilled in the science of magnetism.

1761 T. H. CROKER *Syst. Magn.* 7 A noted Magnetist's Pretence of making steadier compasses. **1859** BACHE *Discuss. Magn. & Meteorol. Observ.* I. 14 The same distinguished magnetist.

2. One who practises 'animal magnetism'; a mesmerist. Also ***animal magnetist*** (see ANIMAL C. 1).

1802–12 BENTHAM *Ration. Judic. Evid.* (1827) V. 189 The operations..of the magnetist..in the expulsion of non-existent diseases. **1807** SOUTHEY *Espriella's Lett.* II. 397 The animal magnetists kept up this unnatural state of attention long enough..to produce..insensibility. **1846** *Blackw. Mag.* LX. 235 The magnetist..made the usual passes along the arm. **1855** SMEDLEY *Occult Sci.* 224 The will, after all, is the real power exercised by the magnetist.

magnetite ('mægnɪtaɪt). *Min.* [ad. G. *magnetit* (Haidinger 1845): see MAGNET and -ITE.] Protosesquioxide of iron, which is readily attracted by the magnet; magnetic oxide of iron.

1851 D. WILSON *Preh. Ann.* (1863) II. 19 The most important iron ore wrought in Norway and Sweden is Magnetite. **1879** RUTLEY *Stud. Rocks* x. 153 Magnetite is frequently titaniferous.

magnetizability (,mægnɪtaɪzə'bɪlɪtɪ). [f. next: see -ITY.] Capacity of being magnetized.

1880 *Nature* XXIII. 210 The magnetisability of iron at very high temperatures. **1881** MAXWELL *Electr. & Magn.* II. 412 Not exactly proportional to its diamagnetic or ferromagnetic magnetizability.

magnetizable ('mægnɪtaɪzəb(ə)l), *a.* [f. MAGNETIZE + -ABLE.] Capable of being magnetized.

1797 *Encycl. Brit.* (ed. 3) XVIII. 623/2 These intervening masses of magnetisable iron-ore. **1837** BREWSTER *Magnet.* 92 The continuous parts of a magnetizable body. **1881** *Times* 11 Apr. 4 Diamagnetism, which gave indications that 'space'..is magnetizable.

magnetization (,mægnɪtaɪ'zeɪʃən). [f. MAGNETIZE + -ATION.]

1. The action of magnetizing or the condition of being magnetized.

1801 *Encycl. Brit.* Suppl. II. 133/2 The striking it with a key will..make the process of magnetization very quick. **1832** *Nat. Philos.* II. *Electro-Magnet.* x. 56 (U.K.S.) We shall call the action which produces an arrangement of poles similar to that resulting from a voltaic current, positive magnetization. **1845** TODD & BOWMAN *Phys. Anat.* I. 239 Further tests of the presence of galvanic action are found in the magnetization of a steel needle placed within a coil. **1849** S. R. MAITLAND *Illustr. Mesmerism* 74 M. Swedenborg being present, she begged him to increase the efficacy of the water, by joining in the magnetisation. **1868** *Athenæum* 14 Mar. 390/2 Dr. Tyndall repeated Faraday's marvellous experiment—the magnetization of light. **1871** TYNDALL *Fragm. Sci.* (1879) I. xiii. 373 Previous to magnetization, a dipping needle..stands accurately level.

2. Special Comb.: **magnetization curve**, a graph of magnetic induction against magnetic field strength in the same region.

1890 J. HOPKINSON in *Proc. R. Soc.* XLVIII. 2 A magnetisation curve is all that I have obtained free from doubt; the sample was heated and its magnetisation determined at various temperatures for a force of 0·50. **1968** C. G. KUPER *Introd. Theory Superconductivity* v. 86 Figure (5.5) shows a typical magnetization curve for a small cylinder in a transverse field.

magnetize ('mægnɪtaɪz), *v.* [f. MAGNET + -IZE.]

1. *trans.* To charge or supply with magnetic properties.

1801 *Encycl. Brit.* Suppl. II. 133/2 The most simple method of magnetising a steel bar. **1831** BREWSTER *Optics* x. 92 The violet rays..had the power of magnetising small steel needles. **1894** BOTTONE *Electr. Instr. Making* (ed. 6) 215 If, therefore, we wind our field magnets with about 6 lbs. No. 20 = 12·5 ohms, we shall get a sufficient number of turns on to magnetise them efficiently.

2. *intr.* To become magnetic.

In mod. Dicts.

3. *trans.* To attract as a magnet does. Chiefly *fig.* (with mixture of sense 4), to subdue or win by personal charm.

1836 *Edin. Rev.* LXII. 310 The noblest associations, thus insensibly introduced into the mind, magnetize it anew. **1842** TENNYSON *Talking Oak* 255, I kiss it twice, I kiss it thrice, The warmth it thence shall win To riper life may magnetise The baby-oak within. **1847** DISRAELI *Tancred* IV. iii, You will magnetise the Queen as you have magnetised me. **1876** MOZLEY *Univ. Serm.* vi. 141 External Nature is..an enchantress who magnetises the human spirit.

4. To influence by 'animal magnetism'; to mesmerize. Also *fig.*

1785 *Mesmer's Aphorisms* 11 The operation must be repeated, till you have magnetized every side of the plant. **1797** *Encycl. Brit.* (ed. 3) X. 450/1 Seven of Deslon's patients were magnetised at Dr. Franklin's house. **1849** S. R. MAITLAND *Illustr. Mesmerism* 74 M. Renard..had requested that Adèle the clairvoyante might, while in her sleep, magnetise a little bottle of water for him. **1864** LOWELL *Fireside Trav.* 189 You must magnetize him many times to get him *en rapport* with a jest.

Hence **'magnetized** *ppl. a.* (also *absol.*); **'magnetizing** *vbl. sb.* and *ppl. a.*

1787 MME. D'ARBLAY *Diary* 19 June, He whispered..that..he intended to introduce magnetizing. **1797** *Encycl. Brit.* (ed. 3) X. 450/1 A magnetised tree was said to produce convulsions. **1830** HERSCHEL *Stud. Nat. Phil.* 57 Masks of magnetized steel wire are..adapted to the faces of the workmen. **1834** *Penny Cycl.* II. 33/1 The mode of bringing the magnetised under the influence of the magnetic fluid was peculiar. **1843** *Rep. Brit. Assoc.* 27 The magnetizing action of transitory electric currents. **1877** *Academy* 3 Nov. 428/1 In an article on the magnetising of animals, Herr Preyer investigates the physiological effects [etc.]. **1880** J. E. H. GORDON *Electr. & Magn.* I. 147 The magnetized bar.

magnetizer ('mægnɪtaɪzə(r)). [f. MAGNETIZE + -ER[1].]

1. One who magnetizes; in quots. one who practises 'animal magnetism', a mesmerist.

1802 ACERBI *Trav.* I. 270, I saw my fellow traveller..fall into a profound sleep by the mere motion of the magnetiser's fingers. **1834** *Penny Cycl.* II. 32/2 Hundreds were ready to attest the wonderful cures wrought upon their own persons by the great magnetizer [Mesmer]. **1867** CARLYLE *Remin.* (1881) II. 269 Two magnetisers, first a man, then a quack woman. **1886** *Pall Mall G.* 7 July 3/2 The Italian magnetizer Donato.

2. That which imparts magnetism.

In mod. Dicts.

magneto (mæg'ni:təʊ), *sb.* **a.** Used colloq. as an abbreviation for MAGNETO-ELECTRIC MACHINE; *spec.* one in an internal-combustion engine employing spark ignition.

1882 *Daily News* 27 Jan. 2/1 Various curious forms of early telegraphs are shown,..for instance..Highton's gold-leaf and horseshoe needle, Henley's magneto, and others. **1893** PREECE & STUBBS *Man. Telephony* 129 For such a purpose commutated magnetos are made. **1902** J. E. HUTTON in A. C. Harmsworth et al. *Motors* viii. 154 The magneto is driven off the main shaft of the engine..by means of a chain. **1929** A. HUXLEY *Let.* 22 Feb. (1969) 307

At Albengo on the Italian riviera, our magneto suddenly gave out. Short circuit, something fused. **1959** *Motor Man.* (ed. 36) vi. 169 Special equipment is needed to develop the high tension required for ignition... There are two systems. One, commonly known as coil ignition, takes in low tension current from the battery and converts it to high tension. The other depends upon a magneto-electric machine—a magneto, for short—which is driven by the engine and generates high-tension current. **1971** *Arable Farmer* Feb. 49/1 On external types of magneto.. the points are normally accessible by removing the end cover.

b. *attrib.*, as **magneto ignition**, in some internal-combustion engines, ignition by means of a voltage generated by a magneto that is driven by the engine.

1902 J. E. HUTTON in A. C. Harmsworth et al. *Motors* viii. 159 The magneto ignition system, which is applied to all the new model motor-engines of M. Mors, consists of a magneto-electric rotary machine, combined with a series of mechanical contact-breakers. **1905** *Westm. Gaz.* 12 Dec. 4/2 The all but universal use of magneto-ignition. *c* **1933** E. MOLLOY *Mod. Motor Repair* III. 877/1 The distance of the gaps..should be adjusted as accurately as possible to between ·015 to ·018 in.; if the engine is fitted with magneto ignition. **1966** *McGraw-Hill Encycl. Sci. & Technol.* VIII. 52/2 The higher cost of magneto ignition is not warranted in modern automobiles, where storage batteries are required for other electrically operated equipment.

magneto- (mæg'niːtəʊ), formally repr. the combining form of Gr. μάγνητ-, μάγνης MAGNET, first occurring in quasi-Greek derivatives like MAGNETOMETER, and now used without restriction to form combinations (chiefly written with hyphen) denoting processes carried on by magnetic means, or the application of magnetism to particular departments of art or industry, as in ***magneto-electro-telluric***, ***-induced***, ***-inductive***, ***-optic***, ***-optical*** adjs.; ***magneto-generator***, ***-induction***, ***-rotation***. Also in the following: **magneto-bell**, **magneto-call-bell**, an electric bell in which the armature of the electro-magnet is polarized; **mag͵neto'caloric** *a.* [ad. F. *magnétocalorique* (Weiss & Piccard 1918, in *Compt. Rend.* CLXVI. 352)], applied to the reversible change of temperature that accompanies a change in the magnetization of a paramagnetic or ferromagnetic material; **mag͵neto'cardiogram** *Med.*, a record of the variations in the magnetic field of a patient's body that occur as a result of the beating of the heart; so **mag͵neto'cardiograph**, an instrument used to make such records; **mag͵netocardio'graphic** *a.*, **-cardi'ography**; **mag͵neto'chemistry**, the branch of science concerned with the relation between magnetism and chemical phenomena, molecular and atomic structure, etc.; so **mag͵neto'chemical** *a.*; **magneto-dynamo** (see quot.); **mag͵neto-ex'ploder**, a magneto-electric apparatus for firing an explosive charge; **magneto-instrument** (*Cent. Dict.* 1890), **-machine**, a magneto-electric machine; **mag͵neto-i'onic** *a.*, of or pertaining to the joint effect of a magnetic field and ionized gas (e.g. in the ionosphere) on the propagation of radio waves; **mag͵neto-me'chanical** *a.*, pertaining to the interrelation of magnetic and mechanical properties, esp. the magnetic moment and angular momentum of an atom or particle; *spec.* applied to the ratio of these quantities (or its reciprocal); **magneto-optics**, the branch of physics which deals with the optical effects of magnetic fields; **magneto-phonograph**, a sound-recording and producing instrument worked by means of magnetic electricity; **magneto-pointer** (in mod. Dicts.), the index of a magneto-electric dial telegraph; **magneto-printer** (in mod. Dicts.), a recording telegraph worked by magneto-electricity; **mag͵netore'sistance**, dependence of the electrical resistance of a body on an external magnetic field; **mag͵neto'sonic** *a.*, pertaining to or designating a type of magnetohydrodynamic wave that has two speeds of propagation (both functions of the magnetic field strength and the speed of sound in the fluid), can travel in any direction relative to that of the field, and is characterized by a displacement of the fluid in any direction in the plane defined by the directions of propagation and of the field except the direction normal to the former; **mag͵neto'static** *a.*, **-'statically** *adv.*; **mag͵neto'statics** [after ELECTROSTATICS], the branch of physics dealing with unchanging magnetic fields; so **mag'netotail** [TAIL *sb.*[1]], the broad, elongated part of the magnetosphere that extends from the vicinity of the earth in a direction away from the sun; **magneto-telegraph** (in mod. Dicts.), a telegraph worked by magneto-electricity; **magneto-telephone**, a magneto-electric sound transmitter; **mag͵netote'lluric** *a.*, pertaining to or designating a technique for investigating the electrical conductivity of the earth by measuring simultaneously fluctuations in its magnetic and electric fields at the surface; hence **mag͵netote'llurics** [-IC 2], the branch of geophysics concerned with this; **magneto-therapy**, the treatment of disease by the external application of metal plates inducing magnetic electricity (*Syd. Soc. Lex.* 1889); **magneto-transmitter** (in mod. Dicts.), a magneto-electric machine for the transmission of (*a*) electric force, (*b*) sound.

1889 PREECE & MAIER *Telephone* Index, *Magneto Bell. **1884** KNIGHT *Dict. Mech.* Suppl., **Magneto Call-bell*, the sounder of a telephone circuit. **1921** *Sci. Abstr.* A. XXIV. 724 (*heading*) *Magneto-caloric effect. **1937** J. W. T. SPINKS tr. *Herzberg's Atomic Spectra & Atomic Struct.* vi. 211 The magnetocaloric effect [in paramagnetic substances] is so small at room temperature that it cannot be observed. **1965** A. H. MORRISH *Physical Princ. Magn.* iii. 83 Since for a normal paramagnetic salt $(\partial M/\partial T)_H$ is negative, an increase in the field produces a heating and conversely decreasing H gives rise to a temperature drop. This is often called the magnetocaloric effect. The important application of this effect is in the production of temperatures below 1°K. **1963** BAULE & MCFEE in *Amer. Heart Jrnl.* LXVI. 95/1 The electromotive forces of the heart set up currents in the torso which in turn produce magnetic fields. These fields are exceedingly small... Nevertheless, they may be detected, as is shown by the *magnetocardiogram. **1971** *New Scientist* 10 June 631/2 As well as being more convenient, a magnetocardiogram (MKG) is faster to take than an electrocardiogram. **1963** *Amer. Heart Jrnl.* LXVI. 96/2 The *magnetocardiograph offers the potentiality of detecting otherwise 'silent' components of the electromotive forces of the heart. **1967** *N.Y. Times* 6 May 33 Dr. Cohen said.. it is ..too early to assess the long-range potential of the magnetocardiograph. **1970** *Amer. Heart Jrnl.* LXXIX. 231/2 Since the electromotive surface representing the activation boundaries lies in the heart, electrocardiographic or magnetocardiographic lead fields need only be known within this region. **1967** *Bull. Exper. Biol. & Med.* LXIV. 1024 *Magnetocardiography is also valuable as an addition to electrocardiography. **1911** *Jrnl. Chem. Soc.* C. II. 367 (*heading*) *Magneto-chemical researches on the atomic structure of the halogens. **1943** P. W. SELWOOD *Magnetochem.* iii. 58 The dimerization of free radicals and of other paramagnetic molecules is one of the most fruitful fields for magnetochemical research. **1972** *Indian Jrnl. Chem.* X. 726/2 A magnetochemical study of these derivatives has also been carried out to get some information about the nature of bonding of the metal ions with the polyphosphate chain. **1914** *Chem. Abstr.* VIII. 2648 (*heading*) *Magneto-chemistry. **1937** *Nature* 20 Mar. 489/1 By magnetochemistry is meant the examination of the problems of chemical structure in the light of magnetic measurements and modern magnetic theory. **1969** *Jrnl. Leeds Univ. Union Chem. Soc.* XI. 42 The earliest significant work on magnetochemistry was probably by Faraday who devised a method for measuring susceptibility which is still used today. **1973** *Nature* 31 Aug. p. xi (Advt.), Magnetochemistry, especially the study of metal-metal interactions in paramagnetic clusters. **1884** S. P. THOMPSON *Dynamo-Electr. Machinery* 199 In *magneto-dynamos, in which the field is due to permanent magnets of steel. **1846** J. JOYCE *Sci. Dial.* VI. 423 The machine in this case has been termed the *magneto-electro-telluric machine. **1869** *Chambers's Jrnl.* Apr. 271/2 A *magneto-exploder..was shewn, which will fire a fuse, and consequently a cannon. **1908** *Installation News* II. 149/2 Water-tight bells and magneto exploders for blasting purposes. **1893** PREECE & STUBBS *Man. Telephony* 125 The Ericsson-Bell Company's *magneto generators. **1871** *Eng. Mechanic* 3 Feb. 480/1 He is referring to a galvanic, and not a *magneto-induced current. **1892** S. P. THOMPSON *Magneto-Electr. Machinery* 8 Within a few months machines on the principle of *magneto-induction had been devised by Dal Negro and by Pixii. **1879** G. PRESCOTT *Sp. Telephone* 259 The *magneto-inductive waves were superposed. **1925** APPLETON & BARNETT in *Electrician* 3 Apr. 398/1 The same theory (for which we propose the name *magneto-ionic theory) has also been independently put forward by Messrs. Nicholls and Schelling ('Nature', March 7th, 1925). **1932** E. V. APPLETON in *Jrnl. Inst. Electr. Engin.* LXXI. 645/2 It is highly probable that interference between the various magneto-ionic components of singly- and multiply-reflected downcoming waves is partly responsible for resultant intensity fading. **1973** *Physics Bull.* May 291/3 A first start is made to the problem of the transfer of radio emission in a pulsar magnetosphere by applying the method of magnetoionic theory. *c* **1865** G. GORE in *Circ. Sci.* I. 229/1 The *magneto-machine being in some cases employed. **1891** S. P. THOMPSON tr. *Guillemin's Magn. & Electr.* 415 Gramme's magneto-machine. **1925** *Sci. Abstr.* A. XXVIII. 611 *Magneto-mechanical anomaly of the atom. **1930** Magneto-mechanical [see GYROMAGNETIC *a.* 1]. **1950** W. FINKELNBURG *Atomic Physics* iii. 153 The magnetic moment of paramagnetic atoms is due to the electron rotating in its orbit or to the spin of the electron. The so-called magnetomechanical parallelism enables us to distinguish between these two contributions to the atomic magnetism. **1953** [see GYROMAGNETIC *a.* 1]. **1958** CONDON & ODISHAW *Handbk. Physics* IV. viii. 136/1 Because of the magnetomechanical interactions.., internal stresses due to cold-working, impurities, precipitates, etc., contribute a spatially varying component of the short-range energy. **1881** S. P. THOMPSON *Elem. Electr. & Magnet.* §387. 350 *Magneto-optic Rotation of the Plane of Polarisation of a Ray of Light. **1913** P. ZEEMAN *Res. Magneto-Optics* p. xi, To the memory of this sage [*sc.* Faraday]—..the pioneer in *magneto-optics as in so many things, I have ventured to dedicate this volume. **1960** *Physical Rev. Lett.* IV. 357 (*heading*) Photon momentum effects in the magneto-optics of excitons. **1848** FARADAY in *Phil. Trans.* CXXXIX. 35 Plücker's *magneto-optical results. **1850** TYNDALL in *Rep. Brit. Assoc., Sections* (1851) 23 On the Magneto-Optical Properties of Crystals. **1902** J. J. THOMSON in *Encycl. Brit.* XXX. 464 *Magneto-Optics. **1902** *Harper's Mag.* Feb. 496 It has been variously designated as the 'telegraphone', the 'microphonograph' and the '*magneto-phonograph' in Europe. **1930** L. W. MCKEEHAN in *Physical Rev.* XXXVI. 949 The *magneto-resistance effect in non-ferromagnetics is only measurable with accuracy in very intense magnetic fields. **1961** *Engineering* 22 Dec. 823 One of the first practical devices to use the phenomenon of magnetoresistance is a voltage regulator. **1966** *New Scientist* 3 Feb. 286/2 The magnetoresistance effect in semiconductors, which has recently been shown to exist at frequencies well up into the microwave region. **1889** *Syd. Soc. Lex.*, **Magneto-rotation.* **1962** W. B. THOMPSON *Introd. Plasma Physics* v. 84 There is remarkably little evidence for the propagation of *magnetosonic waves through a plasma. *Ibid.* 91 In the magnetohydrodynamic case, there are three possible parametrizing velocities C_s, C_A and the magnetosonic speed $C_T = \sqrt{(C_A^2 + C_s^2)}$. **1971** *Nature* 13 Aug. 443/3 The Crab pulsar.. seems to be associated with a series of wisps of gas. .. Wisps 2, 3 and 4 have been generated by the magnetosonic waves which this motion of Wisp 1 produces. **1893** *Notices Proc. R. Inst. Gt. Brit.* XIII. 348 *Magneto-static screening by soft iron would follow the same law as electrostatic screening, if the magnetic susceptibility of the iron were infinitely great. **1950** *Physical Rev.* LXXV. 156 The domain patterns..represent configurations of low magnetostatic energy. **1969** M. A. UMAN *Lightning* 101 The magnetostatic field present during a lightning discharge is directly proportional to the discharge current. **1960** *Physical Rev. Lett.* V. 47/1 The figure of 10^{-8} erg/cm^3 represents.. a solar wind flux sufficient to compress the geomagnetic field *magnetostatically to $\sim 9R_e$ if we utilize the usual model. **1897** A. G. WEBSTER *Theory Electr. & Magn.* ix. 353 (*heading*) Parallel treatment of electrostatics and *magnetostatics. **1952** E. G. RAMBERG tr. *Sommerfeld's Electrodynamics* I. 40 In most treatments the analogy between electrostatics and magnetostatics is emphasized. **1968** J. C. ANDERSON *Magnetism* i. 10 In magnetostatics it is convenient to define a magnetic pole strength, q, analogous to electric charge. **1971** *Daily Tel.* 4 Aug. 4/3 This region's outlines become distorted by a varying stream of electrified atomic particles from the Sun called solar wind. It sweeps part of the magneto-sphere..into a tear-drop shape which scientists would now refer to as the Earth's *magnetotail. **1973** *Nature* 9 Mar. 79/2 The multiple satellite mission will help unravel the spatial and temporal variations of the radiation belt, the magnetopause, the bow shock and magnetotail. **1883** S. P. THOMPSON *P. Reis* 9 In 1877, when the *Magneto-Telephones of Graham Bell began to make their way into Europe. **1953** L. CAGNIARD in *Geophysics* XVIII. 605 (*heading*) Basic theory of the *magneto-telluric method of geophysical prospecting. **1967** L. R. ALLDREDGE in Matsushita & Campbell *Physics of Geomagn. Phenomena* I. I. ii. 55 Smith et al...describe instrumentation for magneto-telluric experiments for which simultaneous measurements of geomagnetic micropulsations and telluric currents are made. **1971** *Nature* 3 Sept. 13/1 To learn something about the behaviour of the upper mantle.. Tammemagi and Lilley..have made four magnetotelluric soundings at 150 km intervals roughly along the latitude of Canberra. **1960** *Jrnl. Geophysical Res.* LXV. 4202/1 Useful field results have not been numerous in the literature, and field *magnetotellurics is still in the developmental stage. **1967** A. T. PRICE in Matsushita & Campbell *Physics of Geomagn. Phenomena* I. II. iii. 295 There is, at present, much activity in the theory and practice of magnetotellurics, which should greatly help the task of unravelling and interpreting many geomagnetic phenomena.

magneto-crystallic (mæg͵niːtəʊkrɪ'stælɪk), *a.* [f. MAGNETO- + CRYSTALLIC.] Of or relating to the magnetic properties possessed by crystals.

1848 FARADAY in *Phil. Trans.* CXXXIX. 30 In that case the word magnetocrystallic ought probably to be applied to this force, as it is generated or developed under the influence of the magnet. *Ibid.* 40 Both the magnetic and magneto-crystallic forces are at the same time doubled or quadrupled.

† **magnetod.** *Obs.* [See OD[2].] (See quot. 1889.)

1850 ASHBURNER tr. *Reichenbach's Dynamics* 224 We may name this product *crystallod*,..that from electricity briefly as *elod*, from light *photod*, and so on, *magnetod*, *chymod*, *heliod* [etc.]. **1889** *Syd. Soc. Lex.*, *Magnetod*, Reichenbach's term for the odylic force found in magnets.

mag͵neto-e'lectric, *a.* Pertaining to electric phenomena involving electric currents induced in conductors by the relative motion of these conductors with respect to either permanent magnets or electro-magnets.

Introduced, in 1831, by Faraday, who employed it in its most general sense for describing the currents induced by motion of conduction in conjunction with any of the following kinds of magnet: permanent steel magnets, ordinary loadstones, electro-magnets, the earth. He used it tentatively at first in contradistinction to the term *volta-electric*, which he applied to the induction of electricity by turning on or turning off an electric current in a stationary coil.

1831 FARADAY in *Phil. Trans.* (1832) CXXII. 139 As a distinction in language is still necessary, I propose to call the agency thus exerted by ordinary magnets, *magneto-electric* or *magnelectric* induction. *Ibid.* 173 Upon the supposition that the rotation of the earth tended, by magneto-electric induction, to cause currents in its own mass. **1833** *Ibid.* CXXIII. 44, I had the pleasure..of making an experiment, for which the great magnet [a loadstone] in the museum.. and the magneto-electric coil described in my first paper, were put in requisition. **1834** —— in *Philos. Mag.* V. 349 When I first obtained the magneto-electric spark it was by the use of a secondary magnet... My principal was an electromagnet; Nobili's was, I believe, an ordinary magnet; others have used the natural magnet. **1839** J. F. DANIELL *Introd. Chem. Philos.* 489 Magneto-electric is the converse to electro-magnetic action. **1854** G. BIRD & C. BROOKE *Elem. Nat. Philos.* xvii. (ed. 4) 421 *note*, Similarly, electro-magnetic induction would mean the development of magnetism by a current, and magneto-electric induction, that of a current by magnetism. **1881** MAXWELL *Electr. & Magn.* II. 208 This is the electromotive force which must be

supplied from sources independent of magneto-electric induction.

b. magneto-electric current. Used by Faraday to distinguish currents generated mechanically by magneto-electric induction from those generated in a voltaic battery.

1851 FARADAY in *Phil. Trans.* CXLII. (1852) 137 On the employment of the Induced Magneto-electric Current as a test and measure of Magnetic Forces.

c. magneto-electric machine. First used by Faraday, in 1831, to denote a machine generating currents by magneto-electric induction. By later writers employed in variously limited senses.

The appellation continued to be used in Faraday's wide sense by various writers down to about 1867, when the improvements of Wilde, Wheatstone, Siemens, Ladd, Varley and others attracted much attention, and the term 'dynamo-electric machine' was introduced by Brooke. This term was defined by Brooke himself to denote in general a machine 'in which dynamic energy is employed to produce an electric current' (*Proc. Roy. Soc.* XV. 409, *footnote*); by others, however, it has been applied to signify only such machines as embodied the principle of self-excitation and did not contain any permanent magnets. Those who adopted the latter usage limited the meaning of 'magneto-electric machine'; some including under that term only the machines with permanent magnets of steel, while others included under the name both these and the machines with separately-excited electro-magnets. The present tendency is to confine the term strictly to the machines with permanent steel magnets. Some writers define magneto-electric machines as simply old-fashioned or rudimentary kinds of dynamos; others treat the terms as synonymous. On the other hand some writers treat 'magneto-electric machine' as a generic term, of which dynamo-electric machines form a sub-class.

1831 FARADAY in *Phil. Trans.* (1832) CXXII. 160 Two rough trials were made with the intention of constructing magneto-electric machines. *Ibid.* 163 [Under heading *Terrestrial Magneto-electric Induction*, describes as magneto-electric machines discs of copper caused to revolve, and thereby generate electric currents under the magnetic influence of the earth.] **1866** CROOKES in *Q. Jrnl. Sci.* XII. 504 Magneto-electric machines, with revolving armatures, in which electro-magnets had been substituted for permanent magnets, had been constructed. **1867** WHEATSTONE in *Proc. Roy. Soc.* XV. 369 The magneto-electric machines which have been hitherto described are actuated either by a permanent magnet or by an electro-magnet. **1878** *Proc. Inst. Civ. Engin.* LII. 63 M. Alfred Niaudet remarked that he did not agree with..the distinction between dynamo-electric and magneto-electric machines. In all these instruments mechanical power was converted into electricity by the action of magnetism; consequently all were both magneto-electric and dynamo-electric. **1878** J. N. SHOOLBRED *Pres. State Electric Lighting* 6 For the older form, where permanent magnets are employed, the term 'magneto-electric' machine has been retained. **1880** A. SIEMENS in *Jrnl. Soc. Telegr. Engin.* IX. 93 A constant and permanent magnetic-field is, therefore, of paramount importance, and it can be produced in the way proposed by Mr. Wilde in 1863 for magneto-electric machines by employing a separate machine for exciting the field-magnets of one or more similar machines. **1882** S. P. THOMPSON in *Jrnl. Soc. Arts* XXXI. 120 The arbitrary distinction between so-called magneto-electric machines and dynamo-electric machines fails when examined carefully. In all these machines a magnet, whether permanently excited, independently excited, or self-excited, is employed to provide a field of magnetic force. And in all of them dynamic power is employed. **1887** W. B. ESSON *Magneto- & Dynamo-electric Machines* 22 In all the machines yet described, the electric currents were induced by means of steel magnets, or, as in Wilde's machine, by magnets that were magnetised by the current produced in another machine. Such machines are usually called 'magneto-electric' machines, to distinguish them from the 'dynamo-electric' machines. **1889** *Chambers's Encycl.* IV. 146/2 The term 'dynamo-electric' was at first applied to distinguish those machines which were self-exciting from 'magneto-electric' machines, which had permanent magnets to give the field; but this distinction is no longer maintained. **1891** J. W. URQUHART *Dynamo-Constr.* 2 A magneto-electric machine—an apparatus in which steel magnets are used to furnish the 'magnetic field'—is not strictly by common consent called a dynamo.

So **magˌneto-eˈlectrical** *a.*, in the same sense.

1836 MULLINS in *Lond. & Edinb. Philos. Mag.* Aug. 120 On certain Improvements in the Construction of Magneto-electrical Machines. **1873** F. JENKIN *Electr. & Magn.* xx. § 1. 280 It is convenient to retain the name magneto-electrical apparatus for those arrangements in which powerful electric currents are induced in wires moved across a magnetic field produced by permanent magnets or electro-magnets.

magˈneto-elecˈtricity. Electricity generated by the relative movement of electric conductors and magnets of any kind. Also the branch of science concerned with this.

1832 FARADAY in *Phil. Trans.* (1833) CXXIII. 44, I have made many endeavours to effect chemical decomposition by magneto-electricity. **1842** W. R. GROVE *Lect. Progr. Phys. Sci.* 21 Here originates the Science of Magneto-electricity, the true converse of Electro-magnetism. **1845** JOULE in *Electr. Mag.* I. 138 The magneto-electricity developed in the coils of the revolving electro-magnet. **1853** F. C. BAKEWELL *Electric Sci.* 143 Electro-magnets..have been sometimes used instead of permanent magnets for the induction of magneto-electricity. **1866** H. WILDE in *Phil. Trans.* CLVII. 92 Waves of magneto-electricity were generated.

magnetogram (mæɡˈniːtəʊɡræm). [f. MAGNETO- + -GRAM.] The automatic record of magnetic needles.

1884 C. MELDRUM in *Erupt. Krakatoa* (ed. Symons 1888) 473, I forwarded copies of magnetograms. **1902** *Encycl. Brit.* XXX. 460/2 Any number of examples are afforded by the magnetograms from stations such as Kew and Falmouth.

magnetograph (mæɡˈniːtəʊɡrɑːf, -æ-). [f. MAGNETO- + -GRAPH.]

1. An instrument arranged to record automatically the movements of the magnetometer. Also *attrib.*

1847 RONALDS in *Phil. Trans.* CXXXVII. 113 The applicability of this system of self-registration to a magnetograph was sufficiently obvious. **1883** C. CARPMAEL in *Erupt. Krakatoa* (ed. Symons 1888) 474 The three magnetograph traces were unusually steady. **1902** *Encycl. Brit.* XXX. 460/2 The records from ordinary Kew pattern magnetographs not infrequently show a repetition of..small rhythmic movements.

2. = MAGNETOGRAM. (In recent U.S. Dicts.)

3. (See quot.)

1896 *Current Hist.* (Buffalo, N.Y.) VI. 467 Professor John S. McKay..has obtained interesting pictures, which he calls 'magnetographs'; resembling X-ray prints in being silhouettes of objects excluded from light.

Hence **magˌnetoˈgraphic** *a.*, of or belonging to the magnetograph.

1887 *Science* (U.S.) 20 May 499/1 The earthquake was recorded automatically upon the magnetographic traces in the observatory.

magnetogyric (mæɡˌniːtəʊˈdʒaɪərɪk), *a. Physics.* [f. MAGNETO- + Gr. γῦρ-ος ring, circle + -IC.] **1.** Pertaining to or exhibiting the Faraday effect (FARADAY 1).

1904 A. SCHUSTER *Introd. Theory Optics* xii. 272 All substances turn the plane of polarization when they are traversed by light in the direction of a magnetic field. They become therefore 'magneto-gyric'. *Ibid.* 290 A simple and rational connexion between the Zeeman effect and magneto-gyric properties.

2. Applied to the ratio of the magnetic moment of an atom or particle to its angular momentum.

1965 M. G. SCROGGIE *Electron in Electronics* ix. 204, γ_s, the magnetogyric ratio for spin, is different from the orbital γ, being practically twice as large. **1967** CONDON & ODISHAW *Handbk. Physics* (ed. 2) VIII. ix. 113/1 The term $g_N(e/2Mc)$ is often replaced by γ, the magnetogyric ratio; hence, $\mu = \gamma hI$. **1972** *Science* 27 Oct. 364/1 As long as $\mathbf{H}_1$ is applied, **M** precesses..at a frequency given by the Larmor relation $\omega_R = \gamma H_1$ (in radians per second) where γ is the magnetogyric ratio of the nucleus. **1974** *McGraw-Hill Yearbk. Sci. & Technol.* 314/2 Compared to H^1, the C^{13} nuclei are much weaker magnets. The magnet strength (magnetogyric ratio γ) is only about $\frac{1}{4}$ that of protons.

magnetohydrodynamic (mæɡˌniːtəʊhaɪdrəʊdaɪˈnæmɪk), *a.* [f. MAGNETO- (repr. *electromagnetic*) + HYDRODYNAMIC *a.*] = HYDROMAGNETIC *a.* Abbrev. MHD (see M 5).

1943 [see HYDROMAGNETIC *a.*]. **1950** H. ALFVÉN *Cosmical Electrodynamics* iv. 76 This coupling between mechanical and electromagnetic forces produces a type of wave motion, called magneto-hydrodynamic waves. **1960** *Times* 14 Apr. 2/2 (Advt.), Central Electricity Generating Board... Teams are being formed to work on the following projects:— .. Magnetohydrodynamic generation. Fundamental research on (relatively) low temperature plasmas and their interactions with magnetic fields [etc.]. **1961** *Engineering* 16 June 817/3 The magnetohydrodynamic prospect, direct generation by passing hot gas through a magnetic field. **1962** F. I. ORDWAY et al. *Basic Astronautics* vi. 287 In a binary system, the angular momentum of the main star seems to have been transferred to the orbital motion of the second star. The means by which the angular momentum was shuffled off is not entirely clear, but magnetohydrodynamic or viscous effects could have played the key role. **1971** I. G. GASS et al. *Understanding Earth* vi. 94/2 Runcorn has re-examined the possibility of exciting the wobble [of the rotating earth] by the effects of magnetohydrodynamic turbulence in the fluid outer core.

Hence **magˌnetohydrodyˈnamical** *a.*, **-dyˈnamically** *adv.*

1953 L. H. ALLER *Astrophysics* ix. 354 Alfvén suggested a theory of sunspots based on magneto-hydrodynamical waves. **1959** *Jrnl. Geophysical Res.* LXIV. 1220/1 The entire medium can..be stirred up without requiring any magnetohydrodynamical work. **1962** W. B. THOMPSON *Introd. Plasma Physics* iv. 58 The possibility of producing a magnetohydrodynamically confined plasma has stimulated an enormous research effort in plasma physics.

magnetohydrodynamics (mæɡˌniːtəʊhaɪdrəʊdaɪˈnæmɪks), *sb. pl.* (const. as *sing.*). [f. prec.: see -IC 2.] The more usual name for HYDROMAGNETICS *sb. pl.*

1950 *Sci. Amer.* Oct. 39/3 Among these [theories] one can mention the magneto-hydrodynamics of charged particles proposed by the Swedish cosmologist H. Alfven. **1958** *Observer* 7 Sept. 13/5 'Magnetohydrodynamics', a branch of theoretical physics which combines classical theory of the behaviour of water and of magnetic fields, ..is becoming one of the most elaborate and enthralling branches of science. **1973** M. HARWIT *Astrophysical Concepts* vi. 194 Magnetohydrodynamics..tells us that the presence of a force, such as a gravitational or electrostatic force, acting normal to the magnetic field, can produce a drifting motion.

Hence **magˌnetohydrodyˈnamicist**, one who studies magnetohydrodynamics.

1955 *Sci. Amer.* Feb. 41/1 How the corpuscles travel through space is still in dispute. The Alfvén school of 'magneto-hydrodynamicists', for instance, maintains that the Chapman–Ferraro theory is basically incorrect, and that the solar corpuscles, as well as cosmic rays, are accelerated by magnetic and electrical fields in space.

magnetoid (mæɡˈniːtɔɪd), *a.* [f. MAGNET + -OID.] Resembling, or having the characteristics of, a magnet.

1851 RUTTER (*title*) Magnetoid Currents, their forces and directions; with a description of the Magnetoscope.

magnetology (mæɡnɪˈtɒlədʒɪ). [f. MAGNET + -OLOGY. Cf. F. *magnétologie*.] A treatise on the magnet and magnetism.

1856 MAYNE *Expos. Lex.*

magnetometer (mæɡnɪˈtɒmɪtə(r)). [ad. F. *magnétomètre*, f. *magnéto-* MAGNETO- + *-mètre*, ad. Gr. μέτρον measure, -METER.] An instrument for measuring magnetic forces, esp. the force of terrestrial magnetism at any point.

1827 EATON in *Amer. Jrnl. Sci.* XII. 15 Delicately suspended needles, which might be called a suit of magnetrometers [*sic*]. **1839** *Proc. Amer. Phil. Soc.* I. 154 A magnetometer for the declination. **1902** *Encycl. Brit.* XXX. 453/1 Under Wilde's auspices a variety of forms of magnetometers and earth-inductors have been used.

Hence **magˌneto-ˈmetric, -ˈmetrical** *adjs.*, of, pertaining to, or measured by the magnetometer. **magneˈtometry**, the measurement of magnetic force by means of the magnetometer (*Cent. Dict.*).

1847 SIR J. C. ROSS *Voy. S. & Antarctic Reg.* I. 91 A valuable series of hourly magnetometric observations was continued. **1902** *Encycl. Brit.* XXX. 433/2 A magnetizing coil such as is used in magnetometric experiments.

magˌnetoˈmotive, *a.* [f. MAGNETO- + MOTIVE *a.*] ***magnetomotive force***: a term introduced by R. H. M. Bosanquet to denote the line integral of the magnetizing forces exerted around a magnetic circuit by an electric current interlinked with it.

1883 BOSANQUET in *Philos. Mag.* XV. 205, I shall use the expression 'magnetomotive force' to indicate the analogue of electromotive force. It is a difference of magnetic potential. **1896** S. P. THOMPSON *Dynamo-electric Machinery* (ed. 5) 119 The total magnetomotive-force in a magnetic circuit is the sum of the magnetomotive-forces separately produced by each coil of wire.

magˌnetoˈmotor. [f. MAGNETO- + MOTOR.] 'A voltaic series of two or more large plates which produce a great quantity of electricity of low intensity, adapted to the exhibition of electro-magnetic phenomena' (Knight *Dict. Mech.* 1875).

1823 T. GILL *Techn. Repos.* III. 313 On the Magnetomotor;—a new form of the Voltaic Apparatus. By Mr. Pepys.

magneton (ˈmæɡnɪtɒn). *Physics.* [ad. F. *magnéton* (P. Weiss 1911, in *Compt. Rend.* CLII. 189), f. *magnéti-que* MAGNETIC *a.*: see -ON[1].] Any of several units of magnetic moment used in atomic and nuclear physics: ***Bohr magneton*** [BOHR], a unit that arises naturally in Bohr's theory of the atom, equal to $eh/4\pi m$ (where e and m are the charge and mass of the electron, and h is Planck's constant, in S.I. units), i.e. about $9{\cdot}27 \times 10^{-24}$ joule per tesla; ***nuclear magneton***, a unit used for expressing nuclear magnetic moments, defined analogously to the Bohr magneton with the mass of the proton replacing that of the electron and equal to about $5{\cdot}05 \times 10^{-27}$ joule per tesla; ***Weiss magneton*** [named after P. *Weiss* (see above)], a disused unit (equal to approximately one-fifth of a Bohr magneton) arrived at as the highest common factor of the measured magnetic moments of the atoms of various elements.

At first often regarded as a 'particle' or 'atom' of magnetism.

1911 *Sci. Abstr.* A. XIV. 191 The author [*sc.* P. Weiss] is led to postulate the existence of a common constituent of magnetic materials—the elementary magnets of [*sic*] which he terms *magnétons*, and which are to be found in the atoms of all magnetic substances. *Ibid.* 243 (*heading*) Size of the magneton deduced from the coefficients of magnetisation of solutions of iron salts. **1915** *Proc. Physical Soc.* XXVII. 430 A further comparison with experimental determinations is rendered possible by assuming that the magnetic moment of an electron revolving with the unit of angular momentum is equivalent to 5 magnetons. **1917** R. W. HUTCHINSON *Adv. Textbk. Magn. & Electr.* II. 313 This fundamental magnet he calls the 'magneton'. Calculation shows that iron, nickel and magnetite contain 11, 3, and 7 of these magnetons per molecule respectively. **1919** *Nature* 6 Nov. 227/2 The suggestion, first proposed by Weiss, that there exists a natural unit of magnetism called the magneton, analogous in some respects to the atom of electricity, still lacks definite proof. **1923** Bohr magneton [see BOHR]. **1927** N. V. SIDGWICK *Electronic Theory of Valency* 208 The Bohr magneton..is almost exactly five (4·96) times the Weiss magneton. **1932** J. H. VAN VLECK *Theory Electr. & Magn. Susceptibilities* ix. 228 Although many molecules are still found to have moments which are integral multiples of the Weiss magneton within the experimental error, this is probably fortuitous, for there are many reasons for believing the Weiss magneton phenomenon to be spurious. **1935** *Physical Rev.* XLVII. 745/2 Using the value 3/2 for the spin of K^{39} and 0·0152 for $\Delta\nu$ we get 0·39 nuclear Bohr magnetons for the magnetic moment of the K^{39} nucleus. *Ibid.* 801/1 We obtain a value of 3·14 nuclear magnetons for the magnetic moment of the Li^7 nucleus. **1962** H. D. BUSH *Atomic &*

Nucl. Physics iii. 60 For all nuclei, including the proton the magnitude of the moment is not an integral multiple of the nuclear magneton. **1973** *Nature* 26 Jan. 239/1 Quantum fluctuations of the electromagnetic field close to the particle [*sc.* a free electron] imply an apparent increase in its magnetic moment beyond the value of one Bohr magneton implied by the unmodified Dirac theory.

magnetopause (mæg'niːtəʊpɔːz). [f. MAGNETO- + PAUSE *sb.*] The outer limit of a magnetosphere.

1963 SONETT & ABRAMS in *Jrnl. Geophysical Res.* LXVIII. 1243/2 We call the region discussed in this paper the magnetopause (the transition region between the magnetosphere proper and the interplanetary medium). **1969** *Physics Bull.* Feb. 54/1 The third spacecraft..is intended to investigate the 'solar wind' of low energy protons and electrons together with the geomagnetic cavity or magnetopause, where these particles are just in balance with the earth's magnetic field. **1971** I. G. GASS et al. *Understanding Earth* xviii. 259/2 The solar wind protons are reflected at the magnetopause, and so never enter the magnetosphere.

magnetophone (mæg'niːtəʊfəʊn). [f. MAGNETO- + Gr. φωνή sound.]

1. A magnetic instrument used for the production of musical tones.

1883 CARHART in *Science* II. 394 The intensity of the sounds obtained by the magnetophone is sometimes so great as to be painful to the ear when the telephone is held closely against it.

2. An early form of moving-coil microphone.

1922 *Encycl. Brit.* XXXII. 528/1 The behaviour of microphones in this respect was often unsatisfactory, and telephone earpieces, or magnetophones, were frequently substituted for them. This results in diminished sensitivity, but the binaural effects are much improved. **1929** J. A. RATCLIFFE *Phys. Princ. Wireless* v. 73 A microphone of quite a different type is much used at the present day for broadcasting. It is known as the magnetophone, and consists of a small coil of very light aluminium wire attached to the back of a freely moving diaphragm. The coil is placed between the poles of an electro-magnet. **1931** *B.B.C. Year-Bk.* 445/2 The magnetophone is relatively insensitive, and its output requires considerable amplification. **1962** *Listener* 8 Nov. 765/3 Two of the earliest [*sc.* BBC microphones] are to be seen..: Round-Sykes 'magnetophone', [etc.].

3. Also **-phon.** [a. G. *magnetophon.*] A tape recorder. (Used chiefly as a rendering of the German or with reference to German machines.)

1946 *Wireless World* Feb. 53/1 The equipment, known as the magnetophone, uses a thin plastic tape, about 0·25 in. wide, coated with a metallic powder film. **1949** *Electronic Engin.* XXI. 124/3 Sound recorders of the magnetophone type make use of two oscillatory currents in the recording head. **1953** F. SPANDÖCK in E. G. Richardson *Technical Aspects Sound* I. xv. 410 After the Second World War magnetophones were built in many countries in many different forms. **1954** *Sci. Abstr.* B. LVII. 245/1 The various tests carried out on magnetophones, microphones and amplifiers are enumerated. **1974** *Encycl. Brit. Macropædia* XVII. 55/2 The Magnetophon Company of Germany succeeded in producing a magnetic film-coated tape that constituted a low-cost recording medium. During World War II the magnetophon, using the coated tape, served the Nazi propaganda organizations well.

magnetoplumbite (mæg,niːtəʊ'plʌmbaɪt). *Min.* [ad. G. *magnetoplumbit* (G. Aminoff 1925, in *Geol. För. i Stockholm Förh.* XLVII. 289), f. Gr. μάγνητ-, μάγνης MAGNET + L. *plumb-um* lead: see -ITE[1].] A strongly magnetic greyish black oxide of manganese, lead, titanium, and ferric iron occurring as acute dipyramidal crystals.

1926 *Chem. Abstr.* XX. 1194 (*heading*) A new oxide mineral from Långban, magnetoplumbite. **1944** C. PALACHE et al. *Dana's Syst. Min.* (ed. 7) I. 728 Adelsköld,..(1938), gives *C6/mmc* as the space group of an artificial material supposedly the same as magnetoplumbite... The supposed composition $PbFe_{12}O_{19}$, by analogy with so-called β-alumina, proposed by Adelsköld (1938) is not indicated by analysis. **1968** I. KOSTOV *Mineral.* II. iv. 259 Magnetoplumbite has a perfect {0001} cleavage.

magnetoscope (mæg'niːtəʊskəʊp). [f. MAGNETO- + -SCOPE.]

†**1.** An instrument used by mesmerists for detecting the supposed magnetism of the human body.

1851 [see MAGNETOID]. **1852** LD. CARLISLE *Let.* 19 May in *Macaulay's Life & Lett.* (1878) II. 309 We talked a good deal about the magnetoscope.

2. 'A person supposed to see, or a thing supposed to aid in seeing, by means of magnetism; a clairvoyant, or a clairvoyant's device' (*Cent. Dict.*).

3. *Physics.* An apparatus for indicating the presence of magnetic force without measuring its amount.

(In recent Dicts.)

magnetosphere (mæg'niːtəʊsfɪə(r)). [f. MAGNETO- + SPHERE *sb.*] The region surrounding the earth or a heavenly body in which its magnetic field is effective and prevails over magnetic fields due to other causes (in the case of the earth not spherical but much elongated on the side away from the sun).

1959 T. GOLD in *Jrnl. Geophysical Res.* LXIV. 1219/1 The region above the ionosphere in which the magnetic field of the earth has a dominant control over the motions of gas and fast charged particles..is known to extend out to a distance of the order of 10 earth radii; it may appropriately be called the magnetosphere. **1962** *Flight Internat.* LXXXI. 222 Instead of distinct inner and outer [radiation] belts, the picture now appears to be of one large region in which particles of different characteristics are trapped. Different types of particles have been observed at 1½ Earth radii (from the centre of the Earth), three radii, four radii (the older concept of the outer belt) and between six radii and the outer edge of the magnetosphere, as the region is now known. The outer limit varies from day to day but is at approximately 8–12 Earth radii. **1967** *New Scientist* 26 Jan. 198/1 Like the Earth, Jupiter is expected to have a 'magnetosphere' with a 'tail' pushed away from it by the solar wind. **1971** I. G. GASS et al. *Understanding Earth* xviii. 260/1 The Van Allen belts are zones of stably trapped particles within the magnetosphere. **1971** *Nature* 13 Aug. 443/3 Much work needs to be done to investigate the kinds of plasma instabilities that can occur in the magnetospheres of neutron stars.

Hence **magneto'spheric** *a.*

1961 *New Scientist* 19 Jan. 167/2 What have been termed 'magnetospheric waveguides' may provide new methods of radio communication between the northern and southern hemispheres. **1969** *Physics Bull.* June 223/1 Instabilities.. occur in both laboratory and magnetospheric and interplanetary plasmas. **1974** *McGraw-Hill Yearbk. Sci. & Technol.* 277/2 The so-called whistlers in the kilohertz frequency range, as well as the long-period waves,..have become important tools in magnetospheric exploration both from the ground and from satellites.

magnetostriction (mæg,niːtəʊ'strɪkʃən). [f. MAGNETO- + L. *strictiōn-em* drawing or pressing together (f. *stringere* to draw together, draw tight).] A dependence of the state of strain of a body (and hence its dimensions) on its state of magnetization. Freq. *attrib.*

1896 *Phil. Mag.* XLI. 454 (*heading*) On the effects of magnetic stress in magnetostriction. **1926** *Jrnl. Iron & Steel Inst.* CXIII. 657 A reciprocal relation between magneto-striction and the effect of stress on magnetisation was investigated experimentally. **1937** *Nature* 18 Dec. 1068/2 A magnetostriction oscillator has been developed which produces intense audible vibrations of frequencies of 8000 cycles per second, capable of fracturing glass. **1959** H. BARNES *Oceanogr. & Marine Biol.* 74 The magneto-striction effect depends upon the fact that when certain metals, notably nickel, are placed in a varying magnetic field they undergo mechanical changes; nickel itself contracts in an increasing and expands in a decreasing magnetic field. As with the mechanical changes brought about by the piezo-electric effect, these also may be transmitted to a medium and, if they are sufficiently rapid, ultrasonic waves are produced. **1966** C. R. TOTTLE *Sci. Engin. Materials* vi. 138 Iron crystals expand along the direction of magnetization and contract at right-angles to it, whereas nickel contracts along the magnetization direction and expands perpendicular to it. This phenomenon is known as magnetostriction.

Hence **mag,neto'strictive** *a.*, of, exhibiting, or employing magnetostriction.

1911 *Chem. Abstr.* V. 1550 (*heading*) A study of the Joule and Wiedemann magnetostrictive effects in steel tubes. **1939** *Nature* 11 Mar. 416/1 Pierce and the late J. H. Vincent independently developed similar oscillators based upon the magnetostrictive properties of iron and nickel and their alloys. **1951** *Electronic Engin.* XXIII. 16 The maximum dimensional change is obtained when the magnetostrictive element is excited at its natural resonant frequency. **1964** T. W. MCRAE *Impact of Computers on Accounting* i. 6 The Ferranti 'Pegasus' introduced the so-called magnetostrictive delay line store, whereby a mechanical stress wave passing along a wire represents a bit.

magnetron ('mægnɪtrɒn). *Electronics.* [f. MAGNET(IC *a.* + -TRON] A diode with a cylindrical anode surrounding a coaxial cathode in which the flow of electrons is controlled by a magnetic field applied parallel to the axis, and now usu. designed to produce microwave pulses of high power.

1924 *Sci. Monthly* XVIII. 650 As the negatively charged grid cuts off the current of the three-element tube, so an external magnetic field will also do it in the two-element tube... Such a device, called a magnetron, was shown. **1945** *Times* 15 Aug. 2/1 In July 1940, Professor J. T. Randall, of Birmingham, produced a magnetron which was the first high-power generator of centimetric waves in the world. The magnetron remains the heart of every modern Radar equipment. **1958** *Engineering* 7 Feb. 174/3 The machine [*sc.* a linear accelerator] is of the travelling-wave type, using radio-frequency power generated by a magnetron valve operating at a frequency of 3,000 Mc/s. **1971** *New Scientist* 1 Apr. 36/1 Outred is developing microwave cavity sources using very high-powered (kilowatts) magnetrons for the infrared spectroscopy programme.

magnicaudate (mægnɪ'kɔːdeɪt), *a.* *Zool.* [a. mod.L. *magnicaudāt-us*, f. *magn-us* great + *cauda* tail: see -ATE[2].] 'Having a long tail' (Mayne *Expos. Lex.* 1856). So **magnicau'datous** *a.* (*ibid.*).

magnifiable ('mægnɪfaɪəb(ə)l), *a.* *rare.* [f. MAGNIFY + -ABLE.] Capable of being magnified.

1646 SIR T. BROWNE *Pseud. Ep.* IV. xii. 208 Thus is it not improbable it hath also fared with number; which though wonderfull in it self, and sufficiently magnyfiable from its demonstrable affections [etc.].

magnific (mæg'nɪfɪk), *a.* Now *literary* and *arch.* Also 5–7 **magnifique**; see also MAGNIFIQUE. [a. F. *magnifique*, ad. L. *magnific-us* (whence also Sp., Pg., It. *magnifico*), f. *magnus* great: see -FIC.]

†**1.** Renowned, glorious. (Cf. MAGNIFICENT 1.)

1490 CAXTON *Eneydos* vi. 25 This gentylman was..of name magnyfyque. **1512** *Helyas* in Thoms *E.E. Pr. Rom.* (1858) III. 38 The magnifike and excellent lignage. **1513** BRADSHAW *St. Werburge* Bal. to St. W. 13 Diuers of thy kynne magnifique Redact in the catholique papall. **1622** J. TAYLOR (Water P.) *Mem. Monarchs* (1630) F 8, In peace and warre, Magnifique, Glorious. **1669** GALE *Crt. Gentiles* I. II. vii. 85 This Adramelech signifies a magnific King.

†**2.** Nobly lavish or munificent; = MAGNIFICENT 2. *Obs.*

1611 SPEED *Hist. Gt. Brit.* VIII. iii. §13. 385 And that this Kings zeale might be further seene, by his magnificke workes [etc.]. **1617** MURE *Misc. Poems* xxi. 45 A liberall hand, a most magnifick hart. **1655** SIR W. LOWER tr. *de Ceriziers' Innoc. Lord* 141 He [God] is just, if he ordain us punishment; he is magnifick, if he doth us good.

3. Sumptuous, splendid: = MAGNIFICENT 3, 4.

1490 CAXTON *Eneydos* xvi. 60 For whome folke of Moryenne haue..made an assemble magnyfyque of metes and of wynes for to a solempnelle feste. **1541** ELYOT *Image Gov.* 78 Finally the saied foure hospitalles..were builded on the riuer of Tyber, in the most ample and magnifike facion. **1550** J. COKE *Eng. & Fr. Heralds* (1877) 116 Considre the magnifique and decorate churches [of London]. *a* **1631** DONNE *Serm.* lvi. (1640) 569 Cover not thy extortions with magnifique buildings and sumptuous furniture. **1654** tr. *Scudery's Curia Pol.* 38 Tis true, thy life must be short, but thy Hearse shall be the more Magnificke. **1730–46** THOMSON *Autumn* 134 The pillared dome magnific heaved Its ample roof. **1742** YOUNG *Nt. Th.* IX. 852 And dare Earth's bold Inhabitants deny The sumptuous, the magnific Embassy A Moment's Audience? **1861** I. TAYLOR *Spir. Heb. Poetry* 239 Objects held forth in vision, for a symbolic purpose, may be stupendous, or they may be magnific or splendid.

4. Imposing by vastness or dignity. Of language, ideas, etc.: Exalted, sublime; *occas.* in derisive sense, pompous, grandiloquent.

1558–66 *Hist. Est. Scotl.* in *Wodrow Soc. Misc.* (1844) 56 The Bishop sang a magnifick Mass. **1589** PUTTENHAM *Eng. Poesie* III. v. (Arb.) 164 They be matter stately and high, and require a stile to be lift vp..by choyse of wordes..high, loftie, eloquent, and magnifik in proportion. **1628** LE GRYS tr. *Barclay's Argenis* 57 A man of no common presence, which a mighty confidence made appeare more magnifique. **1676** GLANVILL *Ess.* III. 16 Astronomy, one of the grandest and most magnifique of all those that lie within the compass of Natural Inquiry. **1744** AKENSIDE *Pleas. Imag.* III. 140 He stalks, resounding in magnific phrase The vanity of riches. **1807** WORDSW. *Wh. Doe* III. 150 Magnific limbs of withered state; A face to fear and venerate. **1817** COLERIDGE *Satyrane's Lett.* i. in *Biog. Lit.* etc. (1882) 240 He commenced the conversation in the most magnific style. **1837** T. C. GRATTAN in *New Monthly Mag.* LI. 333 The magnific hill shooting far up above the clouds! **1864** *Gd. Words* 11/1 This magnific heaving of the bosom of the ocean. **1880** BROWNING *Clive* 34 Power..God's gift magnific, exercised for good or ill.

†**5.** Of compositions, also (with mixture of sense 4) of titles, expressions, etc.: Serving to magnify or extol; highly honorific or eulogistic. *Obs.*

1548 UDALL *Erasm. Par. Mark* xii. 84 What with theyr magnifike and hye titles. **1641** MILTON *Ch. Govt.* Wks. 1738 I. 30 Those magnific Odes and Hymns wherin Pindarus and Callimachus are in most things worthy, some others in their frame judicious, in their matter most an end faulty. **1644** MAXWELL *Prerog. Chr. Kings* 23 To say..that Soveraignty in the King is immediately from God by approbation or confirmation onely..doth not sort well with the magnifick expressions of Holy Scripture. **1649** EARL MONM. tr. *Senault's Use Passions* (1671) 355 The magnifique titles which Historians would give him in their Writings. **1667** MILTON *P.L.* v. 770 Thrones, Dominations, Princedomes, Vertues, Powers, If these magnific Titles yet remain Not meerly titular.

magnifical (mæg'nɪfɪkəl), *a.* Also 6–7 **magnificial**. [f. prec. + -AL[1].]

†**1.** Eminent, renowned, glorious. *Obs.*

1557 N.T. (Genev.) Epistle *iv, The magnifical and triumphing Kyng Solomon. **1574** *Life Abp. Parker* To Rdr. C vj b, The magnifiienge of that magnifical seignorie and Archipiscopall territorie off Canterburye. **1579** TWYNE *Phisicke agst. Fort.* I. xxxvii. 51 Pompeius..being then great in deede and magnificiall.

†**2.** 'Royally' liberal or bountiful, munificent.

1586 T. B. *La Primaud. Fr. Acad.* I. 624 Neither must he be onely liberal, but magnifical also & sumptuous, provided alwaies that of magnificall, he become not prodigall. **1597** A. M. tr. *Guillemeau's Fr. Chirurg.* 3 What is more magnificall and more divine, then to recreate the afflicted. **1623** in *Crt. & Times Jas. I* (1849) II. 357 Sheriff Hawford hath been very magnifical, and feasted all the king's servants.

3. Splendid, stately, sumptuous; = MAGNIFICENT 3, 4. *arch.*

1538 STARKEY *England* II. i. 176 Gudly cytes and townys, wyth magnyfycal and gudly housys. **1560** BIBLE (Genev.) *1 Chron.* xxii. 5 We must buylde an house for the Lord, magnifical [**1611** exceeding magnificall], excellent and of great fame. *a* **1577** SIR T. SMITH *Commw. Eng.* (1609) 26 August and Magnifical apparell both of stuff and fashion. **1599** SANDYS *Europæ Spec.* (1632) 152 Very magnificall and ceremoniall in his outward comportement. **1604** EDMONDS *Observ. Cæsar's Comm.* 25 Their funerals..are magnificall and sumptuous. *a* **1619** FOTHERBY *Atheom.* II. xi. §3 (1622) 314 They daunce a most stately and magnificall daunce. **1890** Æ. PRINCE *Of Joyous Gard* iii. 363 The sight magnifical, beyond desire.

4. = MAGNIFIC 4. *arch.* †Also, = MAGNIFIC 5.

1572 tr. *Buchanan's Detection* I j b, Now you luke to heare how this magnificall boaster of valiantnesse did acquit hymselfe. **1581** J. BELL *Haddon's Answ. Osor.* 453 These be lofty, glorious, & magnificall speeches, but besides the bare sounde of wordes, no matter at all. **1582** BENTLEY *Mon. Matrones* III. 321 A magnificall Vow of a Queene consecrated to the King of heauen. **1582** G. MARTIN *Corrupt. Holy Script.* xiv. 214 What..could be spoken more magnifical of

any Sacrament? **1600** HOLLAND *Livy* VI. xli. 247 A man that in the hearing of his souldiours, could onely make goodly and magnificall Orations. *a* **1626** BP. ANDREWES *Serm.* (1661) 429 We (no doubt) will rise straight in our magnifical, lofty style and say [etc.]. **1867** *Tracts for the Day, Purgatory* 2 A truly magnifical and stupendous act of worship. **1895** W. PATER *Wks.* (1901) VIII. 71 Certain distinguished, magnifical, or elect souls, vessels of election.

magnifically (mæg'nɪfɪkəlɪ), *adv. arch.* [f. MAGNIFICAL + -LY².] In a 'magnific' manner; magnificently, splendidly: in eulogistic terms.

1555 EDEN *Decades* 139 They frendely & magnifycally enterteyned owr men. **1578** T. N. tr. *Conq. W. India* 361 The Emperour received Cortes magnificially. **1579** FULKE *Conf. Sanders* 668 Chrysostome..speaketh magnifically of the crosse. **1609** BIBLE (Douay) *Ps.* cxxv[i]. 2 Our Lord hath done magnifically with them. **1617** MORYSON *Itin.* III. 113 The Venetians live sparingly. The Siennesi magnifically. **1651** tr. *De-las-Coveras' Don Fenise* 247 Treating him magnifically, he began to qualifie him with the name of sonne-in-law. **1889** *Sat. Rev.* 11 May 562/1 A paragraph magnifically headed 'Mr. Harrison's Return to Oxford'.

‖**Magnificat** (mæg'nɪfɪkæt). [L.; 3rd pers. sing. pres. ind. of *magnificāre* to MAGNIFY.]

1. The hymn of the Virgin Mary in *Luke* i. 46–55 (in the Vulgate beginning *Magnificat anima mea Dominum*), used as a canticle at evensong or vespers. Also, a musical setting of this canticle.

c **1200** *Vices & Virtues* 55 Ðe hali woordes ðe ic habbe iwriten on *magnificat*. *c* **1380** WYCLIF *Wks.* (1880) 169 Gret criynge & ioly chauntynge þat..lettiþ men fro þe sentence of holy writt, as Magnyficat, sanctus & agnus dei, þat is so broken bi newe knackynge. ? **14..** *Stasyons of Jerus.* 724 in Horstm. *Altengl. Leg.* (1881) 365 Sche [Mary] knelyd after onne a stone Magnificat sche made anone. **1552** *Bk. Com. Prayer* Even. Pr. (Rubric), After that, *Magnificat*, in Englishe as foloweth. **1597** HOOKER *Eccl. Pol.* v. xl. §1 Of reading or singing..*Magnificat, Benedictus*, and *Nunc Dimittis* oftener than the rest of the Psalms. **1862** LONGF. *K. Robt. of Sicily* 6 Robert of Sicily..at vespers, proudly sat And heard the priests chant the *Magnificat*.

2. *transf.* A song of praise; a 'pæan'.

1614 JACKSON *Creed* III. ix. 179 The lauish Magnificates of present times. **1707** HEARNE *Collect.* 13 June (O.H.S.) II. 20 His magnificat upon Plato is a disparagement to his Cause. *a* **1711** KEN *Sion* Poet. Wks. 1721 IV. 422 Philothea, Mary-like, in Jesus joy'd And in Magnificats her days employ'd. **1896** *Daily News* 23 Apr. 5/4 M. Beurdeley delivered himself of a magnificat in honour of the Orleans and MacMahon families.

3. In various proverbial phrases (translated from Fr.: see Littré and Hatz.-Darm.). ***to correct Magnificat***: a byword for presumptuous fault-finding. ***to correct Magnificat before one has learnt Te Deum***: to attempt that for which one has no qualifications. ***Magnificat at matins***: something out of place.

1533 ELYOT *Knowledge* Pref., Accomptyng to be in me no lyttell presumption, that I wylle in notynge other mens vices correct Magnificat. **1540** PALSGR. tr. *Acolastus* B iij, Thou Philyp fynde faute (which takest vppon the to correct Magnificat). **1542** UDALL *Erasm. Apoph.* 342 b, Suche..yᵗ will take vpon theim to bee doctours in those thynges in whiche theimselfes haue no skille at all, for whiche wee saie in Englyshe, to correcte Magnificat before he haue learned Te Deum. **1588** BP. ANDREWES *Serm. at Spital* (1629) 24 The note is heere all out of place..and so, their note comes in like Magnificat at Matins. **1622** MABBE tr. *Aleman's Guzman D'Alf.* II. 75 To looke to heare a Magnificat at Mattens, or to seeke after the man in the Moone. **1694** R. L'ESTRANGE *Fables* cccxiii. (1714) 329 Where Subjects take upon them to Correct the Magnificat, and to prescribe to their Superiors.

†**mag'nificate**, *ppl. a. Obs. rare.* [ad. L. *magnificāt-us*, pa. pple. of *magnificāre* to MAGNIFY.] Made unduly great, exaggerated.

a **1592** H. SMITH *Serm.* (1592) 443 A magnificate opinion of themselues and an ouerweening of their owne gifts.

†**mag'nificate**, *v. Obs.* [f. ppl. stem of L. *magnificāre* to MAGNIFY.] *trans.* = MAGNIFY *v.*

1598 MARSTON *Pygmal.* etc. *Sat.* ii. 42 [He] With that depaints a church reformed state, The which the female tongues magnificate. **1599** —— *Sco. Villanie* II. Proem. 192, I cannot with swolne lines magnificate Mine owne poore worth. **1672** MARVELL *Reh. Transp.* I. 295 To Magnificate the Church with triumphal Pomp and Ceremony.

magnification (ˌmægnɪfɪ'keɪʃən). [f. L. *magnificātiōn-em*, n. of action f. *magnificāre*: see MAGNIFY and -ATION.] The action of magnifying; the condition of being magnified.

1. The action of representing as great or greater; laudation, extolling.

1625 JACKSON *Creed* V. xxxii. §3 The distempered zeale which the one bare vnto a Moses of his owne making and magnification did empoyson his soule [etc.]. **1663** JER. TAYLOR *Fides formata* Wks. 1850 VIII. 292 Those words so often used in scripture, for the magnification of faith, 'The just shall live by faith'. **1670** G. H. *Hist. Cardinals* I. I. 3 Of the Rodomontadoes which the Roman Theologues write in magnification of the Pope. *Ibid.* 25 Loosing themselves some times in magnifications of their virtues, as false as tedious. **1802–12** BENTHAM *Ration. Judic. Evid.* (1827) IV. 196 The unfeigned love and indefatigable magnification of that sham law. **1863** LYTTON *Caxtoniana* I. 60 That magnification which proverbially belongs to the unknown. **1879** CHR. ROSSETTI *Seek & F.* 62 Frost and cold..are invoked to render blessing, praise, and magnification, to the Lord their Ordainer. **1899** *Q. Rev.* Jan. 82 Next to the glorification of himself [Dumas], his mission was the magnification of his country.

2. The apparent enlargement of an object as seen through a lens.

1672 GREGORY in Rigaud *Corr. Sci. Men* (1841) II. 245 Neither is it probable to me that the errors of the object speculum are made more sensible (the magnification being always the same) by a concave or convex speculum and an eyeglass. *c* **1790** IMISON *Sch. Art* I. 253 If the diameters be multiplied into one another, the product will express the magnification of the whole visible area. **1867** J. HOGG *Microsc.* I. ii. 78 The Kelner eye-piece, while it increases the magnification detracts from the definition. **1881** LOCKYER in *Nature* No. 614. 319 A perfect photograph will bear a very considerable amount of magnification. **1896** *Allbutt's Syst. Med.* I. 83 Two giant-cells seen under high magnification (× 1515 diam.).

b. *transf.* Also quasi-*concr.* a magnified reproduction.

1833 COLERIDGE *Table-t.* 10 Apr., America would then be ..Great Britain in a state of glorious magnification! **1858** HAWTHORNE *Fr. & It. Note-bks.* (1871) I. 60 They looked like a magnification of some exquisite piece of Tunbridge ware. **1874** M. ARNOLD *God & the Bible* (1875) Introd. 21 Its divinities are magnifications of nothing unworthy.

magnificative (mæg'nɪfɪkətɪv). *Gram. rare.* [f. MAGNIFICATE *v.* + -IVE.] = AUGMENTATIVE *sb.*

1875 WHITNEY *Life Lang.* xi. 214 Distinguishing always the large, the medium, and the small individuals of a kind, by diminutives and magnificatives.

magnificence (mæg'nɪfɪsəns). Also 4, 6 magnifecence. [a. F. *magnificence* (OF. also *magnifiance*), ad. L. *magnificentia*, f. *magnificent-*: see MAGNIFICENT and -ENCE.]

1. As the name of one of the 'moral virtues' recognized in Aristotelian and scholastic ethics; rendering Gr. μεγαλοπρέπεια, explained by Aristotle to mean liberality of expenditure combined with good taste.

1340 *Ayenb.* 168 Þe zixte stape of prouesse hi clepieþ magnificence. Þise uirtue hi descriueþ þous. Magnificence is hi ziggeþ of heȝe nyede y-blissede bleuinge. *c* **1386** CHAUCER *Pars. T.* ¶ 662 Thanne comth Magnificence, that is to seyn, whan a man dooth and perfourneth grete werkes of goodnesse. **1506** [see MAGNIFICENTIAL]. *a* **1679** HOBBES *Rhet.* ix. (1681) 22 Magnificence; which is a Vertue, by which a man is apt to be at great cost. **1691** HARTCLIFFE *Virtues* 103 Magnificence..is a Virtue, that teaches us how to observe a Decorum in the managing of great and costly Expences. **1879** MORLEY *Burke* 36 The noble mean of magnificence, standing midway between the two extremes of vulgar ostentation and narrow pettiness.

†**2.** Sovereign bounty or munificence. *Obs.*

14.. in *Tundale's Vis.* (1843) 122 Graunt vs thys day of thi magnyfycence The gold of love the franke of innocence. **1473** *Proclam. Edw. IV* 10 Nov. (Pat. Roll 13 Edw. IV, Pt. 2), For which we thank most humbly His infinite magnificence. *c* **1502** *Joseph Arim.* (E.E.T.S.) 51/456 Vnto the whiche god bryng bothe you & me Of his fauour, grace, and magnyfycence. **1508** KENNEDIE *Flyting w. Dunbar* 421 Traistand to haue of his magnificence Guerdon, reward, and benefice bedene. **1631** MASSINGER *Emperor East* III. ii, His exorbitant prodigality, How ere his..flatterers call it Royall magnificence. **1647** COTTERELL *Davila's Hist. Fr.* 10 That magnificence, he [Francis I] showed towards men.

†**3.** Glory; greatness of nature or reputation.

c **1386** CHAUCER *Prioress' T.* 22 Lady thy bountee, thy magnificence,..Ther may no tonge expresse in no science. **1509** BARCLAY *Shyp of Folys* (1570) 104 God by his power and hye magnificence Made him a beast. **1545** *Primer, Third Hour* E iij, Let tong & hart, strength and sense, Commende thy magnificence. **1611** BIBLE *Acts* xix. 27 So that..the Temple of the great goddesse Diana should be despised, and her magnificence should be destroyed. **1667** MILTON *P.L.* VIII. 101 And for the Heav'ns wide Circuit, let it speak The Makers high magnificence.

4. Sumptuousness or splendour of surroundings or appointments.

1382 WYCLIF *Dan.* iv. 33 [36], I am ordeyned in my kingdam, and my magnyfience [*sic*: *gloss* or gretenesse], is addid to me. *c* **1460** FORTESCUE *Abs. & Lim. Mon.* vii. (1885) 125 It shall nede þat the kyng..mey make new bildynges whan he woll, ffor his pleasure and magnificence. **1500–20** DUNBAR *Poems* lxxvii. 28 Thow gart the orient kingis thrie Offer to Chryst..Gold, sence, and mir,..Schawand him king with most magnificence. **1553** EDEN *Treat. Newe Ind.* (Arb.) 25 In what pompe & triumphant magnificence he sheweth him self when he goeth to hauke or hunt. **1671** MILTON *P.R.* IV. 111 Nor doth this grandeur and majestic show Of luxury, though call'd magnificence,..allure mine eye. *a* **1720** SHEFFIELD (Dk. Buckhm.) *Wks.* (1753) I. 269 By these refin'd diversions, we perceive This town retains its old magnificence. **1796** MORSE *Amer. Geog.* II. 17 The fur [of the ermine] forms a principal part even of royal magnificence. **1841** TRENCH *Parables* xii. (1877) 236 It was and is part of the magnificence of Oriental princes..to have vast stores of costly dresses laid up. **1859** TENNYSON *Enid* 296 His dress a suit of fray'd magnificence, Once fit for feast of ceremony.

†**b.** An instance or particular display of magnificence; a splendid ceremony. *Obs.*

a **1533** LD. BERNERS *Gold. Bk. M. Aurel.* (1546) C vij, It is a greatte magnifience to a man, to haue diuers sortes of meates. **1615** tr. *De Monfart's Surv. E. Indies* 10 At this his entrie they made him a great triumph, with a long magnificence. **1652** J. WRIGHT tr. *Camus' Nat. Paradox* XII. 365 Such Pomp, Tiltings, Masks, Banquets, and other Magnificences. **1670** COTTON *Espernon* II. VIII. 415 The Ceremony of this Marriage was perform'd in the Marquis de Saint-Chaumont's House,.. but the Magnificences at the Duke's own Lodgings. **1674** *Govt. Tongue* ix. § 6 (1684) 151 With what gust and sensuality will they tell how such a jest of theirs took, or such a magnificence was admired?

5. Grandeur or imposing beauty of appearance. †Also *pl.* features constituting magnificence. *Obs.*

c **1430** LYDG. *Min. Poems* (Percy Soc.) 11 This tabernacle of most magnyfycence Whas of his byldyng. **1555** EDEN *Decades* To Rdr. (Arb.) 49 They..whiche in buyldynge of cities..haue so ioyned magnificence with profecte. **1645** EVELYN *Diary* 6 May, That Cittie [Rome], with its Amphitheaters, Naumachia..and other magnificences. **1667** MILTON *P.L.* I. 718 Not Babilon, Nor great Alcairo such magnificence Equal'd in all thir glories. *a* **1703** POMFRET *Eleazar's Lament. Jerus.* i. 10 Where's now the vast Magnificence, which made The Souls of Foreigners adore Thy [Jerusalem's] wond'rous Brightness? **1860** TYNDALL *Glac.* I. xxiv. 175 The weather had been fine, and towards evening augmented to magnificence. **1879** W. H. BARTLETT *Egypt to Pal.* xxvii. 537 These ruins are remarkable, both for their great extent and magnificence [etc.].

b. of language or speech.

1697 DRYDEN *Virg. Georg.* III. 456 The mean Matter which my Theme affords, To embellish with Magnificence of Words.

6. As a title of honour, applied to kings and other distinguished persons. *Obs.* exc. *Hist.* and as rendering of a foreign title.

[**1278** *Rolls of Parlt.* I. 1/2 Magnificentie Regis monstrant Abbas et Conventus Bordesleg'.] *c* **1420** LYDG. *Assembly of Gods* 82 Pluto to thy magnyfycence I shall reherse what thys creature Eolus hath doon to me out of mesure. **1598** HAKLUYT *Voy.* I. 150 The said Master generall therefore maketh no doubt, that al the aboue written damages..be altogether vnknown vnto your magnificence. *a* **1604** HANMER *Chron. Irel.* (1633) 107 Your magnificence hath beene very carefull and studious how you might enlarge the Church of God here on earth. **1755** MAGENS *Insurances* I. 300 Illustrious Lords, Respected Patrons! We the underwritten skillful Calculators, chosen and appointed by your Magnificences [etc.]. **1901** *Times* 20 June 5/4 In reply to the toast of his health, proposed by the Burgomaster, the [German] Emperor..spoke as follows:—Your magnificence ..gave us a sketch of the development of German yachting [etc.].

mag'nificency. Also 6 -centie, manyfycency. [ad. L. *magnificenti-a*: see prec. and -ENCY.]

†**1.** = MAGNIFICENCE in various senses. *Obs.*

1538 in *Lett. Suppress. Monasteries* (Camden) 243, I commend me unto your good lordship, ever more thanckyng you of your manyfycency and gret goodnes. *c* **1540** tr. *Pol. Verg. Eng. Hist.* (Camden No. 36) 219 In number of schollers and magnificentie of colliges it is not superior. **1604** T. WRIGHT *Passions* v. § iv. 244 The necessity of the gift declared the magnificency of hir mind. **1668** *Lond. Gaz.* No. 283/1 She has been since entertained with much State and Magnificency. **1686** F. SPENCE tr. *Varillas' Ho. Medicis* 113 His humour was naturally prone to magnificency.

2. With *a* and *pl.* A magnificent or imposingly beautiful object, ceremony, etc. *Obs.* or *arch.*

1585 T. WASHINGTON tr. *Nicholay's Voy.* I. xxi. 27 The castle, where for a magnificency were set vp 2. faire pauillions. **1645** EVELYN *Mem.* (1819) I. 178 This canopy or arch of water, I thought one of the most surprizing magnificiencies I had ever seene. **1653** H. COGAN tr. *Pinto's Trav.* xxiii. 86 The Portugals..could not sufficiently commend the excellent order and Gentilenesse of these Magnificencies. **1670** G. H. *Hist. Cardinals* II. III. 192 He delights in certain magnificencies and pastimes. **1670–98** LASSELS *Voy. Italy* II. 52 It deserves to be mentioned among the rare Magnificencies of ancient Rome. **1839** J. WILSON in *Blackw. Mag.* XLV. 564 This Christian poet journeyed religiously among the magnificencies of nature.

magnificent (mæg'nɪfɪsənt), *a.* and *sb.* Also 7 *erron.* -ficient. [a. OF. *magnificent*, f. L. *magnificent-*, altered stem (found in the comparative *magnificentior*, after *benevolentior* from *benevolens* = *benevolus*) of *magnificus*, lit. doing great deeds, f. *magn-us* great: see -FIC. All the senses below were already approximately developed in Latin.]

A. *adj.*

1. Characterized by greatness of achievement or by the conduct befitting lofty position. *Obs.* exc. in the titular epithet ***the Magnificent*** (= L. *magnificus*) historically attached to the names of certain distinguished rulers, as Eadmund I of England, Sultan Solyman, Lorenzo de' Medici.

1513 MORE in *Grafton's Chron.* (1568) II. 878 Yet the King [Hen. VII] of his magnificent minde, pardoned the innocent and rurall people. **1602** WARNER *Alb. Eng.* Epit. (1612) 356 Of whom many, and some of them heere-borne Incolents, became afterwards the most magnificent of the Emperors. **1656** BLOUNT *Glossogr.*, *Magnificent*,..that achieveth worthy acts,..acting great matters. **1717** *Hist. Acc. Hungary* 332 This was formerly the Bulwark of Hungary, 'till taken by Soliman the Magnificent. **1795** W. ROSCOE (*title*) The Life of Lorenzo de' Medici, called The Magnificent. **1875** FORTNUM *Maiolica* xi. 107 Lorenzo the magnificent.

†**b.** As the rendering of the customary title (usually L. *magnificus*) of certain foreign officials and official bodies. *Obs.*

1763 *Ann. Reg.* 86 The proceedings of the magnificent council [of Geneva].

†**c.** Proud, arrogantly ambitious. *Obs.*

1603 KNOLLES *Hist. Turks* (1621) 732 This Perenus was one of the greatest peeres of Hungarie, but of a most haughtie and magnificent mind.

2. Characterized by expenditure or munificence on a great scale; 'royally' lavish or munificent. Now *rare*.

1579 G. HARVEY *Lett. to Spenser* (1580) 65 Your lauishe, and magnificent liberalitie. *a* **1586** SIDNEY *Arcadia* II. (1590) 169 b, If he were magnificent, he spent much with an aspiring intent. **1593** R. HARVEY *Philad.* Ded. 21 Thus trusting to your Lordships magnificent..fauour. **1631**

MASSINGER *Emperor East* II. i, A Prince is neuer so magnificent, As when hee's sparing to inrich a few With th'iniuries of many. **1647** CLARENDON *Hist. Reb.* I. §126 Nor had his Heir cause to complain,.. though his Expences had been very magnificent,.. considering the wealth he left in Jewels, Plate, and Furniture. *a* **1661** FULLER *Worthies* (1840) II. 313 Hampton Court was built by.. Cardinal Wolsey; once so magnificent in his expenses. **1667** MILTON *P.L.* IX. 153 Man he made, and for him built Magnificent this World, and Earth his seat. **1737** WHISTON *Josephus, Antiq.* xv. ix. § 5 Herod.. bestowed presents on every one.. using his magnificent disposition, so as his kingdom might be the better secured. **1855** MACAULAY *Hist. Eng.* xi. III. 24 He received from the private bounty of the magnificent Chamberlain a pension equal to the salary which had been withdrawn. **1868** MILMAN *St. Paul's* 332 He was munificent, almost magnificent.

3. Of conditions of life: Characterized by grandeur or stateliness. Of persons: Living in splendour; characterized by display of wealth and ceremonial pomp.

1526 *Pilgr. Perf.* (W. de W. 1531) 203 Delapsed and commynge downe from his magnyfycent glory. **1585** T. WASHINGTON tr. *Nicholay's Voy.* I. ix. 12 b, Such was the beginning of the magnificent estate of Cariedin Barberousse. **1706** PHILLIPS (ed. Kersey), *Magnificent*, that lives in great State; stately, noble, great, fine, costly, lofty. **1709** ATTERBURY *Serm.* (*Luke* x. 32) 4 Whether we are not too Magnificent and Sumptuous in our Table and Attendance. **1849** MACAULAY *Hist. Eng.* vii. II. 183 The magnificent king who, in more than one sense, represented France.

4. Sumptuously constructed or adorned; also, in wider sense, imposingly beautiful, splendid.

a **1540** BARNES *Wks.* (1573) 357 That magnificent Temple of Salomon. **1658** *Hist. Christina Alessandra Q. Swedland* 109 Of a modern structure and one of the magnificentest fabriques of Europe. **1667** MILTON *P.L.* III. 502 Farr distant hee descries Ascending by degrees magnificent Up to the wall of Heaven a Structure high. **1687** T. BROWN *Lib. Consc.* in *Dk. Buckingham's Wks.* (1705) II. 122 She did not delight in gaudy Liveries, and what the World calls a Magnificient Equipage. **1701** ADDISON *Let. fr. Italy* 72 When Rome's exalted beauties I descry, Magnificent in piles of ruine lye. **1725** DE FOE *Voy. round World* (1840) 268 Two rooms.. very magnificent in their way. **1756** BURKE *Subl. & B.* II. xiii, A great profusion of things which are splendid or valuable in themselves, is magnificent. **1841** LANE *Arab. Nts.* I. 107 She then arose, and attired herself in the most magnificent of her apparel. **1894** J. T. FOWLER *Adamnan* Introd. 51 Lord Dunraven's magnificent work entitled *Notes on Irish Architecture*.

5. Of immaterial things, conceptions, language, etc.: Imposing, exalted.

1639 N. N. tr. *Du Bosq's Compl. Woman* I. 3 There needes but a pleasing voice, a magnificent tone, a sweet accent,.. to charme those who hearken. **1665** BOYLE *Occas. Refl. Disc. Occas. Medit.* (1848) 76 Making good that magnificent Assertion of the Apostle, That all things work together for good to them that love God. **1701** *Stanley's Hist. Philos.* Biog. 4 Thales was thought to deserve the Magnificent Title of Wise for his Noble Discoveries. **1748** HUME *Ess.* ix. *Brit. Govt.* 72 These Considerations are apt to make one entertain a very magnificent Idea of the British Spirit and Love of Liberty. **1781** COWPER *Truth* 412 The song magnificent—the theme a worm! **1781** —— *Table-t.* 593 Language.. Was natural as is the flowing stream, And yet magnificent, a God the theme.

6. Used to express enthusiastic admiration: 'Splendid', wonderfully fine.

a **1704** T. BROWN *Praise of Drunkenness* Wks. 1730 I. 37 Pray take notice of his belly, how plump and round it is, of what a magnificent circumference. **1704** YALDEN *On Sir Willoughby Aston* 348 Methinks I see a pompous tomb arise, Beauteous the form, magnificent the size. **1858** RUSKIN *Arrows of Chace* (1880) I. 130 All the drawings so kept are in magnificent preservation. **1860** TYNDALL *Glac.* I. xii. 90 The day was magnificent. **1867** W. W. SMYTH *Coal & Coal-mining* 91 At Lehigh Summit mine the great coal-bed is a magnificent seam of 50 feet.

B. *sb.*

†**1.** An eminent personage. *Obs.*

1612 W. PARKES *Curtaine-Dr.* (1876) 20 The Courts and mansions of the Potentates and Magnificents of the World.

2. *pl. slang.* A mood of haughty indignation.

1836 MARRYAT *Midsh. Easy* xxvi, Nevertheless, Jack walked his first watch in the 'magnificents', as all middies do when they cannot go on shore.

Hence †**mag'nificent** *v.* (*nonce-wd*), *trans.* to make or proclaim great. **mag'nificentness**, the state or condition of being magnificent (1727 in Bailey vol. II).

1656 S. H. *Golden Law* 2 His mercy is above all his works, and doth magnificent him.

†**magnifi'cential**, *a.* *Obs. rare*$^{-1}$. [f. L. *magnificentia* MAGNIFICENCE + -AL^{1}.] Magnificent.

1506 *Kalender Sheph.* (1892) 98 Magnyfycens is a Ioyeous clerenes of courage admynystrynge thynges laudable & magnyfycencyall, that is to saye, hye or grete.

magnificently (mæɡ'nɪfɪsəntlɪ), *adv.* [f. MAGNIFICENT *a.* + -LY^{2}.] In a magnificent manner.

1. With great splendour or stateliness.

1538 LELAND *Itin.* I. 97 The Castel stondith magnificently and strongely on a Rok. **1599** *Life Sir T. More* in Wordsw. *Eccl. Biog.* (1853) II. 93 Charles the fifth.. was most magnificentlie received by the cittee of London. **1659** HAMMOND *On Ps.* lxxiii. 6 They set themselves out most magnificently. **1709** STEELE *Tatler* No. 49 ¶ 7 No Persian Prince was ever so magnificently bountiful. **1717** LADY M. W. MONTAGU *Let. to C'tess Mar* 10 Mar., Her house was magnificently furnished. **1725** POPE *Odyss.* VIII. 494 And to the feast magnificently treads. **1816** BYRON *Ch. Har.* III. xxviii, The Battle's magnificently stern array! **1849** MACAULAY *Hist. Eng.* vi. II. 69 She loved to adorn herself magnificently. **1884** *Law Times* LXXVII. 402/1 The business meetings will be held in the magnificently furnished council chamber.

b. With grandeur or impressiveness.

1818 SHELLEY *Let. to Mr. & Mrs. Gisborne* 10 July, Scenery magnificently fine. **1856** KANE *Arct. Expl.* II. xxiv. 245 How magnificently the surf beats against its sides. **1877** LADY BRASSEY *Voy. Sunbeam* xv. (1878) 268 It was all terribly grand, magnificently sublime.

c. After a great or noble fashion.

1831 LAMB *Elia* Ser. II. *Ellistoniana*, Waiving his great loss as nothing, and magnificently sinking the sense of fallen material grandeur.

2. With reference to expression: In an elevated manner. †Also, in highly laudatory terms.

1630 *R. Johnson's Kingd. & Commw.* A iij, In like manner hath Botero.. beene suspected to have had a feeling of the Spanish Pistolets, for that hee hath written so magnificently of that Nation. **1651** BAXTER *Inf. Bapt.* 340 So that the Scripture speaks more magnificently of the Church of Christ for the extent of it, then Mr. T. doth. **1710** DR. WHITBY *Disc.* III. i. §2 (1735) 209 That Duty of which the Scripture speaketh so magnificently. **1835** J. H. NEWMAN *Par. Serm.* (1842) II. v. 61 Writers.. talk magnificently about loving the whole human race.

‖**Magnificet.** *Obs.* [L.; 3rd pers. sing. pres. subj. of *magnificāre* to MAGNIFY.] (See quot.)

1841 HAMPSON *Medii Ævi Kalend.* II. 254 *Magnificet*, a name of Midlent Thursday, taken from the first word of the collect.

magnificial, obs. form of MAGNIFICAL.

†**magnificie.** *Obs. rare*$^{-1}$. [f. MAGNIFIC *a.* + *-ie*: see -Y.] Greatness, importance.

1570 *Satir. Poems Reform.* xix. 109 And he that is of maist Magnificie ȝour baner sall display.

†**mag'nificly**, *adv.* *Obs.* [f. MAGNIFIC + -LY^{2}.] = MAGNIFICALLY.

1538 ELYOT *Dict.* Addit., *Ampliter*, largely, abundantly, magnifikely. **1591** SYLVESTER *Ivry* 273 That.. can, as King, magnifikly advance His faithfull Servants. **1609** HUME *Admonit.* in *Wodrow Soc. Misc.* (1844) 572 Ye were not aschamed to ryde to parliament magnifickly mounted and apparrelled.

‖**magnifico** (mæɡ'nɪfɪkəʊ). [It. *magnifico* adj. = MAGNIFIC.] An honorary descriptive title bestowed upon the magnates of Venice: *transf.* any person in an exalted position.

1573 G. HARVEY *Letter-bk.* (Camden) 175 A cumpanie of sutch Italian magnificoes. **1591** SPENSER *M. Hubberd* 665 Where the fond Ape.. stalketh stately by, As if he were some great Magnifico. **1596** SHAKS. *Merch. V.* III. i. 282 The Duke himselfe, and the Magnificoes Of greatest port haue all perswaded with him. **1630** *R. Johnson's Kingd. & Commw.* 476 Hee must turne himselfe about, and not dare to looke this Magnifico in the face. **1745** ELIZA HEYWOOD *Female Spect.* No. 16 (1748) III. 183 The mechanics forsake their shops, to ride about the town in state like so many magnificoes. **1845** DISRAELI *Sybil* (1863) 15 Rockingham, a virtuous magnifico,.. resolved to revive something of the pristine purity.. of the old whig connection. **1891** *Spectator* 11 July, The reception.. by the populace has been.. cordial, though it is doubtful if.. they know who the magnificoes are.

b. *attrib.* or *adj.* = Magnificent, 'grand'.

1654 WHITLOCK *Zootomia* 41 It is a Magnifico gate of spirit.. not to mend, or slack our pace, for all the barking Curs, great or small. **1808** SOUTHEY *Lett.* (1856) II. 75 The magnifico book-case is greatly increased in *ricosity*.

mag'nificous, *a.* *rare*$^{-0}$. [f. L. *magnific-us* MAGNIFIC + -OUS.] = MAGNIFICENT.

In mod. Dicts.

Hence †**mag'nificously** *adv.* *rare*$^{-1}$.

1683 E. HOOKER *Pref. Pordage's Mystic Div.* 103 How magnificously soever wee bragg.. of our Reason, or Faith.

magnified ('mæɡnɪfaɪd), *ppl. a.* [f. MAGNIFY + -ED^{1}.]

†**1.** Extolled, lauded. *Obs.*

1646 SIR T. BROWNE *Pseud. Ep.* I. vi. 22 The magnified Virgil. **1660** WATERHOUSE *Arms & Arm.* 190 The illustrious Copies drawn by their fair and magnified hands. **1664** H. MORE *Synopsis Proph.* To Rdr. 185 Those worthily magnified elucubrations of Mr. Joseph Mede. **1690** LOCKE *Hum. Und.* IV. vii. §11 They are far enough from receiving any help from the Contemplation of these, or the like magnify'd Maxims.

2. Enlarged to the sight. *lit.* and *fig.*

1839 *Penny Cycl.* XV. 177/2 An instrument for enabling the eye.. to see magnified images of small objects. **1852** ROBERTSON *Serm.* Ser. III. xii. 151 This is but prudence after all, it is but magnified selfishness carried on into eternity. **1876** GEO. ELIOT *Dan. Der.* II. xxviii. 217 Her hands showing curves and dimples like a magnified baby's. **1899** J. CAIRD *Fundamental Ideas Chr.* I. iii. 57 Ordinary thought finds no impossibility in representing to itself a personality who is simply a magnified man.

magnifier ('mæɡnɪfaɪə(r)). [f. MAGNIFY *v.* + -ER^{1}.]

1. One who or something which magnifies.

1550 J. COKE *Eng. & Fr. Heralds* v. (1877) 58 The Frenchemen be great braggers, bosters, and magnyfyers of them selves. **1570–6** LAMBARDE *Peramb. Kent* (1826) 281 These Monks were marveylous and monstruous magnifiers, of such deceivable trumperie. **1621** BURTON *Anat. Mel.* II. ii. VI. iv. (1676) 189 *Mens hilaris, requies, moderata diæta*.. is a great magnifier of honest mirth. *a* **1763** SHENSTONE *Ess.* (1806) 238 Imagination is a great magnifier and causes the hopes we conceive to grow too large for their object.

2. A lens or combination of lenses used to increase the apparent size of objects.

1665 BOYLE *Exp. Hist. Cold* ix. 249 One of our Microscopes.. has been counted.. as good a Magnifier, as perhaps any is in the world. **1759** KNIGHT in *Phil. Trans.* LI. 296 Some of them, when viewed with a microscope, required a third or fourth magnifier to see them distinctly. **1830** HERSCHEL *Stud. Nat. Phil.* 297 No examination with magnifiers is.. sufficient to detect the ingredients. **1856** KANE *Arct. Expl.* I. xiii. 144 We barely succeeded by magnifiers in reading the verniers.

fig. **1791** WASHINGTON *Lett.* Writ. 1892 XII. 56 Each of whom.. looking through a magnifier, would speak of the greatest extent to which there was any probability of their numbers reaching. **1813** *Examiner* 22 Mar. 186/2 His Lordship may be permitted to examine the gallant Chieftain's actions through a magnifier. **1818** HAZLITT *Eng. Poets* iv. (1870) 95 The wrong end of the magnifier is, to be sure, held to everything.

‖**magnifique.** *Obs.* [Fr. = MAGNIFIC.] Profuse in expenditure.

1759 *Compl. Let. writer* (ed. 6) 225 The Considerable and the Magnifique in such Sorts of Assemblies. **1775** MME. D'ARBLAY *Early Diary* (1889) II. 110 He is handsome, tall, fat, upright, and *magnifique*. **1823** BYRON *Juan* x. lxx, Juan, though careless, young, and magnifique And rich in rubles, diamonds, cash, and credit.

magnify ('mæɡnɪfaɪ), *v.* Also 4, 6 **magnifye**, 4–6 **magnefie, magnyfye**, 4–7 **magnifie**, 6 **magnifi, mangnify**, 4- **magnify**. [ad. L. *magnificāre* (partly through F. *magnifier*; cf. It. *magnificare*, Sp. *magnificar*), f. *magnificus*: see MAGNIFICENT and -FY. Sense 4 is purely Eng.; the Rom. langs. have the word chiefly in the biblical sense 'to extol'.]

1. *trans.* To speak or act for the honour or glory of (a person or thing); to glorify, extol. *arch.*

c **1380** WYCLIF *Sel. Wks.* II. 2 For þei maken Cristis wordis unworshipid and magnifien þer owne wordis. *a* **1400–50** *Alexander* 2838 Obey þe to þe baratour þe best I con rede; Magnifie him with þi mouthe. **1430–40** LYDG. *Bochas* IX. ii. (1554) 197 b, This was the ende of false Machomete,.. whom Sarazins so greatly magnifie. **1508** DUNBAR *Poems* viii. 14 Quhois force all France in fame did magnifie. **1553** EDEN *Treat. Newe Ind.* (Arb.) 29 Columbus.. was.. greatlye magnified with innumerable glorious tittles. **1568** GRAFTON *Chron.* II. 524 After this victorie, the Lorde Scales.. returned to the siege, where he was.. highly magnified and praysed. **1605** BACON *Adv. Learn.* I. viii. §6 If the invention of the ship was thought so noble,.. how much more are letters to be magnified, which as ships pass through the vast seas of time. **1668–9** PEPYS *Diary* 10 Feb., Here he dined, and did mightily magnify his sauce. *a* **1715** BURNET *Own Time* (1724) I. 248 He had magnified him highly to the King, as much the greatest man in the Scottish Clergy. **1837** HT. MARTINEAU *Soc. Amer.* III. 64 Sunday-school teachers admire their pupils; and the scholars magnify their teachers. **1849** MACAULAY *Hist. Eng.* ii. I. 191 Everywhere men magnified his valour, genius, and patriotism.

b. *esp.* To praise, render honour to (God). *arch.*

1382 WYCLIF *Luke* i. 46 And Marie seide, My soule magnyfieth the Lord, and my spirit hath gladid in God, myn heelthe. *c* **1420** LYDG. *Assembly of Gods* 2102 With heuynly spyrytes, hys name to magnyfy. **1535** COVERDALE *Ecclus.* xliii. 30 Prayse the Lorde, and magnifie him as moch as ye maye. **1864** SKEAT tr. *Uhland's Poems* 91 When on your knees ye humbly fell And magnified a Higher Power.

2. To make greater in size, status, importance, or qualities; to enlarge, augment. Now *rare.* †Also, to render magnificent. *Obs.*

1382 WYCLIF *Matt.* xxiii. 5 Forsothe thei alargen her filateries, and magnifie hemmys. **1390** GOWER *Conf.* I. 143 Thanne he gan to syke For cloth of gold and for perrie, Which him was wont to magnefie. *c* **1430** LYDG. *Compl. Bl. Knt.* 428 And can hemselve now best magnify With feyned port and false presumption. **1535** COVERDALE *Job* xx. 6 Though he be magnified vp to the heauen. **1598** GRENEWEY *Tacitus, Ann.* XII. vii. (1622) 162 Agrippina also was magnified [L. *augetur*] with the surname of Augusta. **1611** BIBLE *Job* xix. 5 If indeed yee will magnifie your selues against me, and plead against me my reproch. **1701** GREW *Cosm. Sacra* II. v. 53 The least error in a Small Quantity, as in a Small Circle: will, in a great one, as in the Circles of the Heavenly Orbs, be proportionably Magnify'd. **1715** ADDISON *Freeholder* No. 10 ¶ 3 Arbitrary Power.. creates [in a man] an Ambition of magnifying Himself, by the Exertion of such a Power in all its Instances. **1726** BUTLER *Serm. Rolls Chap.* ix. 159 The imagined Dignity of the Person offended would scarce ever fail to magnifie the Offence. *a* **1729** CONGREVE *To Cynthia* 54 Speak, ere my Fancy magnifie my Fears. **1784** COWPER *Task* IV. 542 Her head, adorned with lappets pinned aloft, And magnified beyond all human size. **1841** MYERS *Cath. Th.* IV. §37. 369 The spirit of law is also represented as magnified by the very act of superseding its letter. **1860** TYNDALL *Glac.* I. xxvii. 210 The oblique arrangement of the crevasses also magnified the labour by increasing the circuits.

b. *intr.* To become greater. *nonce-use.*

1814 J. RANDOLPH 22 Mar. in *Life of Jos. Quincy* 350 The curse of slavery, however,—an evil daily magnifying, great as it already is,—embitters many a moment of the Virginian landholder.

3. *trans.* To represent (persons, actions, or things) as great or greater than they are; to exaggerate. Now often associated with sense 4.

1759 ROBERTSON *Hist. Scot.* VI. Wks. 1813 I. 399 Fame magnified the number and progress of their troops. **1766** GOLDSM. *Vic. W.* xvi, It must be owned my wife.. used every art to magnify the merit of her daughter. **1784** COWPER *Tiroc.* 476 Each vainly magnifies his own success, Resents his fellows, wishes it were less. **1838** THIRLWALL *Greece* xxv. III. 397 But his enemies at home magnified the

danger of Argos. **1839** Yeowell *Anc. Brit. Ch.* ix. (1847) 93 Fame magnified his labours. **1841** Myers *Cath. Th.* iv. 19. 276 Unquestionably external evidences .. have been unduly magnified. **1862** Sir B. Brodie *Psychol. Inq.* II. iii. 81 Small evils which cannot be avoided are magnified into great ones.

4. To increase the apparent size of an object by artificial means (as with a lens or microscope). Also *absol.* (often with advb. accusative, ***to magnify ten, twenty,*** etc. ***diameters***).

1665 *Phil. Trans.* I. 60 It would magnifie but 600 times in Diameter. **1726** Swift *Gulliver* iii. iii, Although their largest Telescopes do not exceed three Feet, they magnify much more than those of an hundred among us. **1776–96** Withering *Brit. Plants* (ed. 3) IV. 3 When magnified they appear like ill-formed warts. **1812–16** J. Smith *Panorama Sci. & Art* I. 407 It is supposed that the ancient engravers used glass globes to magnify their figures. **1837** Goring & Pritchard *Microgr.* 57 You only wish to know exactly how much it magnifies. **1868** Lockyer *Elem. Astron.* iii. (1879) 91 A powerful telescope will magnify an object 1,000 times. *fig.* **1853** Kane *Grinnell Exp.* xiv. (1856) 110 The effects of fogs upon our estimation of dimension .. are well known: men are magnified to giants. **1862** Mrs. H. Wood *Mrs. Hallib.* iii. xii. 155 Ill reports never lose by carrying: the two cats on the tiles, you know, were magnified into a hundred.

5. *intr.* 'A cant word for *to have effect*' (J.); to signify. Now *dial.*

1712 Steele *Spect.* No. 431 ⁋3 My Governess .. told him I was continually eating some Trash or other... But this magnified but little with my Father. **1733** *Gentl. Mag.* III. 532 Now may hap, zir, what doez ael this magnify? **1880** *Antrim & Down Gloss.* s. v., That hurt won't magnify.

magnifying ('mægnɪfaɪɪŋ), *vbl. sb.* [f. MAGNIFY *v.* + -ING^{1}.] The action of the verb MAGNIFY.

c **1380** Wyclif *Wks.* (1880) 162 þei meyntenen anticristis prestis and here lawis .. & magnifyenge of mennus lawis & dispisynge of goddis lawis. **1382** —— *Jude* 25 To God aloone oure sauyour, bi Jhesu Crist oure Lord, glorye and magnyfiying. *c* **1384** Chaucer *H. Fame* i. 306 Of oon he wolde have fame In magnifying of his name. **1612** Bacon *Ess.*, *Praise* (Arb.) 354 Too much magnifying of man or matter, doth irritate contradiction. **1651** Hobbes *Leviath.* ii. xxxi. 189 Praise, and Magnifying are signified but by Words, and Actions. **1868** J. M. Campbell in *Mem.* (1877) II. xiii. 203 A growing magnifying of their office on the part of the clergy.

b. *attrib.*, in ***magnifying power***.

c **1705** Berkeley *Commonpl. Bk.* Wks. 1871 IV. 481 The magnifying power of glasses. **1774** M. Mackenzie *Maritime Surv.* 110 Write down .. what Sort of Telescope you observed with, and its length and magnifying Power. **1807** J. E. Smith *Phys. Bot.* 14 By the help of the highest magnifying powers.

magnifying ('mægnɪfaɪɪŋ), *ppl. a.* [f. MAGNIFY *v.* + -ING^{2}.] That magnifies, in various senses.

1650 Ashmole *Chym. Collect.* Proleg. 17 The airy and empty glory of Magnifying-Fame. **1901** *Munsey's Mag.* (U.S.) XXV. 641/1 The microbes of disease are such minute .. germs of life .. under the microscopist's three-hundred magnifying lens.

b. magnifying glass. A glass lens, or combination of lenses, used to increase the apparent size of any object seen through it.

1665 Boyle *Occas. Refl.* Disc. Occas. Medit. (1848) 28 Attention, like a magnifying glass, shews us .. divers particularities undiscerned by those who want that advantage. **1705** Pope *Let. to Wycherley* 23 June, 'Tis certain, the greatest magnifying Glasses in the World are a Man's own Eyes. **1859** Reeve *Brittany* 187 With a strong magnifying-glass the words .. may be distinctly read.

magniloquence (mæg'nɪləkwəns). [f. MAGNILOQUENT: see -ENCE.] The quality of being magniloquent; loftiness of speech or expression.

1623 Cockeram, *Magniloquence*, proud speeches. **1656** Blount *Glossogr.*, *Magniloquence*, .. a lofty manner of speaking, or a discourse of great matters. *a* **1670** Hacket *Abp. Williams* ii. (1692) 65 He [Buckingham] magnified himself to serve the King, who did not foresee the envy that his magniloquence bred. **1713** Bentley *Rem. Disc. Freethink.* ii. §44. 28 And our Author might have seen, how all the Sects ridiculed this Magniloquence of Epicurus. **1859** I. Taylor *Logic in Theol.* 179 We must discharge a mass of magniloquence and affectation. **1863** Cowden Clarke *Shaks. Char.* xviii. 455 Cibber .. foisted his own bombast into the company of Shakespeare's magniloquence. **1872** Spurgeon *Treas. Dav.* Ps. lxxiii. 8 Their language is colossal, their magniloquence ridiculous.

So † **mag'niloquency**, in the same sense.

1615 A. Stafford *Heav. Dogge* 38 Neyther was this onely Stoicall Magniloquency: hee did the great things he spake.

magniloquent (mæg'nɪləkwənt), *a.* [f. L. *magniloqu-us* (of the same meaning), f. *magnus* great + *-loquus* speaking + -ENT.] Of persons, hence of utterances or compositions: Lofty or ambitious in expression, grandiloquent. Also, *occas.*, 'talking big', boastful.

1656 Blount *Glossogr.*, *Magniloquent*, that useth a stately manner of speaking or writeing. **1659** Gauden *Slight Healers* (1660) 10 Really they are no other than imperious Hypocrites, magniloquent Montebanks. **1849** Longf. *Kavanagh* xxi. Pr. Wks. 1886 II. 345 A large basket, containing what the Squire .. in Don Quixote, called his 'fiambreras',—that magniloquent Castilian word for cold collation. **1854** Thackeray *Newcomes* I. xxiii. 222 She was a trifle more magniloquent than usual, and entertained us with stories of colonial governors and their ladies. **1891** Lounsbury *Stud. Chaucer* I. iv. 426 If he meant intentionally to describe so slight a performance in so magniloquent a manner.

¶ **b.** Misused for: Pompous, 'mouthing'.

1850 Kingsley *Alt. Locke* viii, I read my verses aloud in as resonant and magniloquent a voice as I could command.

Hence **mag'niloquently** *adv.*

1849 *Fraser's Mag.* XL. 12 So he, magniloquently, as was his wont [etc.]. **1892** Stevenson *Across the Plains* iii. 141 To finish a study and magniloquently ticket it a picture.

† **mag'niloquous**, *a. Obs.*$^{-0}$ [f. L. *magniloqu-us* (see prec.) + -OUS.] = MAGNILOQUENT.

1727 in Bailey vol. II.

magniloquy (mæg'nɪləkwɪ). *rare.* [ad. L. *magniloqui-um.*] Magniloquence.

1656 Blount *Glossogr.* **1889** *Buck's Handbk. Med. Sci.* VIII. 520 Of many anatomical terms the chief characteristics are antiquity, magniloquy, and unintelligibility.

magniot, obs. form of MANIOC.

† **magnipend**, *v. Obs.*$^{-0}$ [ad. L. phrase *magnī pendĕre* (*magnī* at a great price, *pendĕre* to esteem, lit. to weigh).] 'Much to esteeme or set by' (Cockeram 1623).

mag'nipotence. *rare*$^{-1}$. [f. L. *magnipotent-em*: see next and -ENCE.] The quality of being 'magnipotent'; mighty power.

1861 Patmore in *Macm. Mag.* V. 114 Jehovah's mild magnipotence Smiles to behold His children play.

† **mag'nipotent**, *a. Obs. rare.* [ad. L. type **magnipotent-em*, f. *magn-us* great + *potent-em*: see POTENT *a.*] Possessing great power.

1680 *Observ. 'Curse Ye Meroz'* 8 Though this be so magnipotent and all-sufficient a Sermon. **1727** De Foe *Syst. Magic* i. iii. (1840) 84 Satan, as he is a spirit, is magnipotent, but he never was omnipotent.

magnirostrate (mægnɪ'rɒstrət), *a.* [ad. mod.L. *magnirostrāt-us*, f. *magn-us* great + *rostr-um* beak: see -ATE^{2}.] 'Having a long and strong beak' (Mayne *Expos. Lex.* 1856).

magnisonant (mæg'nɪsənənt), *a. rare.* [ad. late L. *magnisonant-em*, f. *magn-us* great + pr. pple. of *sonāre* to SOUND.] High sounding.

a **1843** Southey *Doctor*, *Cats Greta Hall* (1847) VII. 589 Rumpelstilzchen .. that strange and magnisonant appellation. **1843** Cardl. Wiseman *Ess.* (1853) III. 442 A new city just starting from the mud, with some magnisonant name from Egypt or Greece.

magnitude ('mægnɪtjuːd). [ad. L. *magnitūdo*, f. *magn-us* great, cogn. w. Gr. μέγας, OTeut. **mikilo-*: see MUCH. Cf. OF. *magnitude.*]

1. The quality or fact of being great, in various senses; = GREATNESS.

† **a.** Greatness of character, rank, or position. Also *jocularly*, as a title of address. *Obs.*

1398 Trevisa *Barth. De P.R.* i. (1495) 3 Our wytte maye be led to the consyderacyon of the gretnesse, or magnytude, of the moost excellent bewteuous clarete dyuyne & Inuysyble. **1432–50** tr. *Higden* (Rolls) III. 117 This Nabugodonosor transcendede in magnitude and fortitude Hercules in his actes. **1609** B. Jonson *Masque Queens* Wks. 1616 I. 961 [Boadicea's] orations .. wherein is expressed all magnitude of a spirit, breathing to the libertie and redemption of her Countrie. **1620** Shelton *Quix.* III. xxxii. 231 And, for proof of this, let me tell your Magnitudes [etc.]. **1647** Clarendon *Hist. Reb.* i. §141 The two Secretaries of State (which were not in those days officers of that magnitude they have been since ..) were [etc.]. **1665** Manley *Grotius' Low C. Warres* 741 The United States did not omit forthwith to send an Embassy to congratulate him [King James] for his new access of magnitude.

b. In physical sense: Greatness of size or extent. †Of sound: Loudness. *Obs.*

c **1420** *Pallad. on Husb.* i. 1066 To bey thy been biholde hem riche and fulle, Or preve hem by their murmurs magnitude. **1432–50** tr. *Higden* (Rolls) I. 127 Profitable waters and wholsome, whiche be callede sees what for the magnitude of theyme and for the copious multitude of fissches. **1640** Wilkins *New Planet* ii. (1684) 149 'Tis said, that Magnitude does always add to the swiftness of a violent motion. **1650** Bulwer *Anthropomet.* xxi. 230 That which fails in magnitude is called smal. **1727** De Foe *Syst. Magic* i. i. (1840) 9 The height, and strength, and magnitude of their building could only serve to make its fall .. more terrible. **1817** Chalmers *Astron. Disc.* i. (1852) 22 We have something more than the mere magnitude of the planets to allege in favour of the idea that they are inhabited. **1860** Tyndall *Glac.* i. xi. 82 And as our eye ranged over the broad shoulders of the mountain, .. the conception of its magnitude grew upon us.

c. Of immaterial things: Great amount or importance.

1432–50 tr. *Higden* (Rolls) II. 343 He [Saturnus] was .. namede as godde of alle goddes for the magnitude of his power. **1526** *Pilgr. Perf.* (W. de W. 1531) 268 b, And how the effectes y^{t} suche ioye of ye spiryt leueth behynde it, sheweth ye magnitude or greatnes therof. **1769** *Junius Lett.* xxiii. 108 A great man, .. even in the magnitude of his crimes, finds a rescue from contempt. *a* **1806** Horsley *Serm.* I. iv. (1816) 70 We commonly find in the ambitious man a superiority of parts, in some measure proportioned to the magnitude of his designs. **1844** Thirlwall *Greece* lx. VIII. 29 The preparations .. were .. on a scale proportioned to the magnitude of the object he had in view. **1861** Stanley *East. Ch.* vi. (1869) 189 No conversion of such magnitude [as that of Constantine] had occurred since the Apostolic age.

2. a. Size whether great or small; in geometrical use, the measure or extent of a particular line, area, volume, or angle.

1570 Billingsley *Euclid* i. i. 1 A signe or poynt .. is the beginning of magnitude. **1599** A. M. tr. *Gabelhouer's Bk. Physicke* 74/1 Mixe of this poulder the magnitude of a hasell-nutte amongst a little Cotten. **1615** Crooke *Body of Man* 355 It is a Membrane enclosing the whole cauity of the Chest, wherefore his Figure and magnitude is answerable to that cauity. **1658** Rowland tr. *Moufet's Theat. Ins.* 1080 It is a small creature, and contemptible for its magnitude. **1725** De Foe *Voy. round World* (1840) 284 As to the magnitude of those rivers, he could say little. **1754** Sherlock *Disc.* (1759) I. iv. 159 Reason can measure the Magnitudes and Distances of the heavenly Bodies. **1840** Lardner *Geom.* v. 59 We can never obtain an arc of the precise value of any one of the usual denominations of angular magnitude. **1854** Brewster *More Worlds* v. 94 The creations of the material world, whether they be of colossal or atomic magnitude. **1885** Watson & Burbury *Math. Th. Electr. & Magn.* I. 119 Two infinite series of images, the magnitudes or values of which converge.

b. quasi-*concr.*

1570 Dee *Math. Pref.* 3 What Magnitude so euer, is Solide or Thicke, is also broade, and long... A long magnitude, we terme a Line. **1570** Billingsley *Euclid* v. ix. 141 Magnitudes which haue to one and the same magnitude one and the same proportion: are equall the one to the other. **1859** Barn. Smith *Arith. & Algebra* (ed. 6) 192 The term Magnitude or Quantity is used in Mathematics to express whatever is capable of increase or diminution. Thus a sum of money is a magnitude or quantity. **1864** Bowen *Logic* iv. 66 A Concept is a magnitude or Quantity.

c. The intrinsic size of an earthquake or underground explosion (as distinguished from the intensity of its effects at any particular place), usu. expressed by a number that is a logarithmic function of the maximum resulting seismometric deflection adjusted to allow for distance.

The use shown in quot. 1830 under sense 3 c is unrelated.

1935 C. F. Richter in *Bull. Seismol. Soc. Amer.* XXV. 1 In the course of historical or statistical study of earthquakes in any given region it is frequently desirable to have a scale for rating these shocks in terms of their original energy, independently of the effects which may be produced at any particular point of observation. On the suggestion of Mr. H. O. Wood, it is here proposed to refer to such a scale as a 'magnitude scale'. *Ibid.* 2 The requirements of research .. call for some estimate of the magnitude, in the sense here used, of each important shock in the California region. **1947** K. E. Bullen *Introd. Theory Seismol.* xiv. 234 The smallest earthquakes reported felt are of magnitude 1·5; .. those of magnitude 4·5 are capable of causing slight damage near the epicentre. **1959** B. F. Howell *Introd. Geophysics* ix. 125 Values of magnitude calculated at different observatories, using different seismometers at one observatory, or even different phases (body or surface waves) on the same seismogram, may be different. **1971** *Daily Colonist* (Victoria, B.C.) 7 Feb. 1/1 The quake had a magnitude of 6·7 on the Richter scale. **1972** *Sci. Amer.* Jan. 14/3 Underground explosions in the megaton range can have a body-wave magnitude of 6·5 to 7.

3. A class in a system of classification determined by size. **a.** Each of the classes into which the fixed stars have been arranged according to their degree of brilliancy. Now regarded as a number on a continuous scale representing the negative logarithm of the brightness, such that a decrease of five magnitudes represents a hundred-fold increase in brightness and a decrease of one magnitude an increase of 2·512 times.

The stars 'of the first magnitude' are the most brilliant; the 'sixth magnitude' includes those that are barely visible to the naked eye; the seventh and lower magnitudes are telescopic only. The classification into 'magnitudes', originally somewhat loose, as depending on the estimate formed by the individual observer, is now a matter of photometric measurement. The word *magnitude* in this application is a literal rendering of the Gr. μέγεθος, used by Ptolemy. Formerly often denoted by the symbol m, as 2.m, 3.m.

Before decimal or fractional numbers were used there was an intermediate stage illustrated by quots. 1796, 1826 (and also 1851).

[**1594** Blundevil *Exerc.* iv. xxxi. (1636) 485 The fift sheweth the magnitude or greatnesse of the starre, whether it be of the first, second, or third bignesse.] *a* **1641** Bp. Mountagu *Acts & Mon.* (1642) 121 In the firmament of heaven be many Starres; .. of the first, second, third magnitude, as they use to speak. **1667** Milton *P.L.* vii. 357 He form'd the Moon Globose, and everie magnitude of Starrs. **1690** Leybourn *Curs. Math.* 383 A star of the 1 Magnitude may be seen when the Sun is but 12 deg. below the Horizon. **1796** W. Herschel in *Phil. Trans. R. Soc.* LXXXVI. 168, 1.2m for instance, denotes that a star so marked is between the first and second magnitude. 2.1 signifies the same thing, with an intimation that the star so marked is nearly at the second magnitude, but partakes still something of the lustre of a star of the first order. **1826** J. F. W. Herschel in *Mem. R. Astron. Soc.* II. 444, I shall extend the examination to all stars of the 8th and (8·9) magnitudes; those of the 9th however not included. **1851** *Monthly Notices R. Astron. Soc.* XI. 187 The differences .. clearly show that widely different *scales* of magnitude have been adopted. *Ibid.*, This triple star .. is designated by Argelander .. as of magnitude 5·4 (or about 4·7). **1893** Sir R. Ball *Story of Sun* 13 A star of about the eighth magnitude. **1897** D. P. Todd *New Astron.* xvi. 423 Even the surpassing brilliancy of the sun can be indicated on the same scale; the number − 25·4 expresses his stellar magnitude. **1902** *Daily Chron.* 11 Aug. 6/7 Eros will be detected by the naked eye as a sixth magnitude star. **1930** R. H. Baker *Astron.* i. 20 The magnitude of the brightest star, Sirius, is − 1·6; Canopus is − 0·9. **1967** C. M. Huffer et al. *Introd. Astron.* xvii. 248/2

The photoelectric photometer, under the best conditions and by averaging several observations, can make measures down to 0·001 magnitude in accuracy.

†**b.** *Numismatics. Obs.*

1705 HEARNE *Collect.* 19 Dec. (O.H.S.) I. 133 The said Coyns are all Brass of the 3d magnitude.

c. Occas. in other applications. *Phr.* ***of the first magnitude*** (fig.): of the utmost greatness or importance.

1693 G. STEPNY *Juvenal Sat.* VIII. 47 Whatever be your Birth, you're sure to be A Peer of the First Magnitude to me. **1830** LYELL *Princ. Geol.* I. 413 In the following year there were one hundred and fifty-one [*sc.* earthquake shocks: they were registered in four classes], of which ninety-eight were of the first magnitude. *Mod.* To do this would be a blunder of the first magnitude.

magnitudinous (mægnɪˈtjuːdɪnəs), *a.* [f. L. *magnitūdin-* (*-tūdo*) MAGNITUDE + -OUS.] Characterized by magnitude; involving greatness of scale.

1803 W. TAYLOR in *Monthly Mag.* XVI. 223 The inference..is.., in its possible consequences, too magnitudinous, to be lightly stated in words. **1826** *Examiner* 120/1 His designs were bold, severe, magnitudinous. **1893** *Age* (Melbourne) 19 May, It has gone abroad..that directors..may plead positive ignorance of magnitudinous transactions.

†**ˈmagnity**, *a. Obs. rare*⁻¹. [ad. L. *magnitās* f. *magn-us* great: see -ITY.] = MAGNITUDE 1 b.

1790 *Bystander* 198 A fool..excites no wonder though he commit every moment follies of the greatest magnity.

†**magnium.** *Obs.* [f. MAGN(ESIA) + -IUM.] = MAGNESIUM; a name applied to the metal by Sir H. Davy in 1808 and withdrawn in 1812.

1808 [See MAGNESIUM 1]. **1812** —— *Chem. Philos.* 348.

magnolia (mægˈnəʊlɪə). [a. mod.L. *magnōlia*, f. name of Pierre Magnol (latinized *Magnōlius*), professor of botany at Montpellier, 1638–1715.]

a. A genus of large (rarely shrubby) trees (the typical genus of the N.O. *Magnoliaceæ*), cultivated for the beauty of their foliage and flowers.

1748 *Phil. Trans.* XLV. 166 The Magnolia..tho' scarce in Virginia, has been since found to grow in great plenty in the North-West Parts of Pensylvania. **1751** BARTRAM *Observ. in Trav. Pensilv.* etc. 67 A great hill, cloathed with large Magnolia, 2 feet diameter and 100 feet high. **1799** WORDSW. *Ruth* xi, He told of the magnolia spread High as a cloud, high over head! **1823** RUTTER *Fonthill* 90 Here and there the beautiful magnolia displayed the exquisite whiteness of its large blossoms. **1858** HOGG *Veg. Kingd.* 24 The bark and fruit of all the Magnolias are possessed of the same medicinal properties.

b. 'The pharmacopœial name (U.S.A.) for the bark of several species of Magnolia' (Mayne *Expos. Lex.* 1856).

c. The colour of magnolia blossom, usu. a shade of pale pink. Hence *attrib.* passing into *adj.*, of the colour of magnolia blossom.

1931 *Daily Chron.* 21 May 6/1 A gown of pale magnolia-pink satin. **1963** *Times* 25 Apr. 6/6 For her wedding yesterday Princess Alexandra chose..a traditional dress..fine cotton lace..faintly tinted with magnolia. **1971** R. FULLER in *Listener* 28 Oct. 583/1 My study has been repainted 'Magnolia'... Magnolia shows bright enough, if really Only off-white. **1974** 'S. HARVESTER' *Forgotten Road* xii. 137 The pale blue cotton shirt had been replaced by one of a droopy magnolia tint.

d. *attrib.* and *Comb.*

a **1821** SHELLEY *Fragm. Unfinished Drama* 146 Holding a cup like a magnolia flower. **1897** PULLEN-BURRY *Blotted Out* 11 Mrs. Aylesbury's magnolia-covered house.

magnoliaceous (mægnəʊlɪˈeɪʃəs), *a. Bot.* [f. mod.L. *Magnōliace-æ*, f. MAGNOLIA: see -ACEOUS.] Of or belonging to the N.O. *Magnoliaceæ*.

1852 TH. ROSS tr. *Humboldt's Trav.* I. vi. 213 *note*, Magnoliaceous plants.

magˈnoliad. *Bot.* [f. MAGNOLIA + -AD.] Lindley's name for: A plant of the N.O. *Magnoliaceæ*.

1846 LINDLEY *Veg. Kingd.* 417 Wintereæ, which do not seem to possess any solid distinction from Magnoliads.

magnolious (mægˈnəʊlɪəs), *a. slang.* [Humorously f. MAGNOLIA + -OUS.] Magnificent, splendid, large. Hence **magˈnoliousness** [see -NESS], the fact or quality of being magnolious.

1865 G. A. SALA *My Diary in Amer.* 114 But..she might be the sheriff's daughter.., accustomed to go out on Sundays with a 'magnolious' parasol and a 'spanglorious' crinoline. **1913** *Dialect Notes* IV. 19 *Magnolious*, very fine, magnificent. Used in Wyoming. 'How do you like my suit?' 'It's *magnolious.*' **1921** JOYCE *Lett.* (1957) I. 173 With many thanks again and wishes for your magnolious expansiveness. *Ibid.* 175 Best wishes for your continued magnoliousness. **1942** BERREY & VAN DEN BARK *Amer. Thes. Slang* §29/5 *Magnificent*,..magnolious, phenomenal, red-hot.

magnolite (ˈmægnəlaɪt). *Min.* [f. the place-name *Magnolia* + -ITE.] A white tellurate of mercury found in minute acicular crystals, in the Magnolia district of Colorado.

1877 F. A. GENTH in *Proc. Amer. Philos. Soc.* XVII. 118 Magnolite, a new Mineral. This highly interesting mineral is the product of the oxydation of coloradoite.

magnon (ˈmægnɒn). *Physics.* [f. MAGN(ETIC *a.* or MAGN(ETISM + -ON[1].] The quantum or quasiparticle associated with a spin wave in a magnetic material.

1941 *Jrnl. Physics* (Moscow) IV. 358/1 Such magnetic excitations will be called..'magnons' (this name was suggested by L. Landau). **1971** *Nature* 18 June 424/2 Light scattering research has been revolutionized by the introduction of the laser... Scattering from magnons or spin waves has furthered understanding of antiferromagnetic materials and their phase transitions. **1973** *Sci. Amer.* Jan. 91/1 Phonons and magnons are typical examples of quasiparticles that are bosons.

magnoperate (mægˈnɒpəreɪt), *v. rare.* [Two formations: (1) f. L. *magnopere* greatly (short for *magnō opere*) + -ATE[3]; (2) f. L. *magn-us* great + *oper-*, *opus* work: after *operate*.]

†**1.** *trans.* To make greater. *Obs.*

1610 HOPTON *Baculum Geod.* Ep. Ded. (1614), Which will not a little magnoperate the splendour of your well knowne Honour, to these succeeding times.

2. *intr.* (*nonce-use.*) To work at a 'magnum opus'.

1821 BYRON *Let.* 22 June, That is right; keep to your magnum opus—magnoperate away.

3. *intr.* (*nonce-use.*) To act in a grand manner.

1926 J. AGATE *Contemporary Theatre 1925* 18 Everything about Richard is magnificent... He may be said not to act, but to magnoperate.

Also (as *nonce-wds.*) **magnopeˈration**, a great 'operation', a *magnum opus*; **magˈnoperator**, a great 'operator'; **magˈnoperous** *a.*, ? operating in a grand manner.

1928 BEERBOHM *Seven Men & Two Others* (1950) 230 Mr. Nat Heinz, the famous 'Firsts Agent', had recently come over from New York... I wrote at once a respectful note to this magnoperator. **1930** *Times* 28 Mar. 15/4 Not until the very last volume did Sir John Fortescue seek the help of a 'devil' in any part of his 'magnoperation'. **1939** JOYCE *Finnegans Wake* I. 57 The shadow of the huge outlander,..magnoperous, had bulked at the bar of a rota of tribunals.

magnox (ˈmægnɒks). *Nuclear Engin.* Also **Magnox.** [f. *mag*nesium *no ox*idation.] Any of various magnesium-based alloys containing a small proportion of aluminium that were developed for the containers of the fuel in nuclear reactors. Freq. *attrib.*

1953 *Technical Memorandum Min. of Supply, Div. of Atomic Energy (Production), Res. & Devel. Branch, Metall. Lab.* 30 Dec. 1 A magnesium alloy 'Magnox E'. **1955** *U.K. Atomic Energy Authority Rep. SCS-M-301* (*title*) The spectrographic determination of aluminium and beryllium in magnox alloys. **1957** *Financial Times Ann. Rev. Brit. Industry* 15/3 Materials able to stand up to much higher temperatures than..the present metallic uranium fuel and Magnox cans. **1962** *Economist* 2 June 913/1 Assumptions about the cost of nuclear generation of electricity by the magnox systems are unduly conservative. **1971** *Nature* 28 May 233/1 The UK had then just announced plans for its first nuclear power programme based on magnox reactors.

magnum (ˈmægnəm), *sb.* [sb. use of neut. sing. of L. *magnus* great.]

1. A bottle containing two quarts of wine or spirits; also, the measure of liquor contained in such a bottle.

1788 BURNS *Prose Wks.* 40 If you add a tankard of brown stout, and superadd a magnum of right Oporto. **1816** SCOTT *Antiq.* ii, Bearing in his hand an immense double quart bottle, or magnum, as it is called in Scotland. **1855** LD. HOUGHTON in *Life* (1891) I. xi. 505 Tell my father we had four magnums of 1841 claret on the table. **1893** VIZETELLY *Glances back* I. xvii. 328 [His] weakness was a too great partiality for..magnums of old port. **1895** *Strand Mag.* X. 556/2 The party broached a magnum of whisky.

b. *nonce-use.* A large glass (of spirits).

1837 DICKENS *Pickw.* xix, They..ordered a glass of brandy and water all round, with a magnum of extra strength, for Mr. Samuel Weller.

2. Short for MAGNUM BONUM 2.

1889 *Daily News* 25 Nov. 7/6 Potatoes at wholesale Prices —112 lb. Floury Magnums, 3*s.* 6*d.*

magnum (ˈmægnəm), *a.* [Cf. MAGNUM.] (Freq. with capital initial.) Of a cartridge: adapted so as to be more powerful than its calibre suggests. Of a gun: designed to fire such cartridges. Also *absol.*

Magnum is registered as a proprietary name in the U.S.

1935 *Official Gaz.* (U.S. Pat. Office) 26 Mar. 718/2 Smith & Wesson, Inc., Springfield, Mass. Filed Feb. 20, 1935. *Magnum* for Revolvers. Claims use since Dec. 28, 1934. **1937** P. B. SHARPE *Compl. Guide Handloading* xxx. 286/1 A Magnum load..is anything which is 'stepped up' in power and should be so treated by the handloader. **1962** *Amer. Speech* XXXVII. 267 A ·357 Magnum bullet. **1970** *New York* 16 Nov. 50/1 A picture of Huggins and his Magnum on the floor of UCLA. **1971** V. CANNING *Firecrest* xiii. 188 Guards who carried twelve-bore shotguns and ·375 Magnum rifles. **1973** *Black Panther* 31 Mar. 6/3 It was a magnum type revolver bullet that killed Carr. **1973** G. C. NONTE *Firearms Encycl.* 157 While magnum cartridges are legion in the rifle field, there are currently only three used in handguns.

magnum bonum (ˈmægnəm ˈbəʊnəm, ˈbɒnəm). [neut. sing. of L. *magnus* great and *bonus* good.]

1. A particular kind of large yellow cooking-plum. Also ***magnum bonum plum.***

1721 MORTIMER *Husb.* II. 298 The Bonum Magnum a fair yellowish green Plumb. **1769** MRS. RAFFALD *Eng. Housekpr.* (1778) 230 To preserve Magnum Bonum Plums. **1813** SIR H. DAVY *Agric. Chem.* (1814) 257 Two fruits can scarcely be conceived more different in colour, size, and appearance, than the wild plum and the rich Magnum bonum. **1879** MISS YONGE *Magnum Bonum* I. 183 A basket of plums..as unlike magnum bonums as could well be.

2. A kind of potato.

1882 *Garden* 4 Feb. 75/2 In..1879 my employer wished me to plant half a rood of ground with Magnum Bonums.

†**3.** *Sc.* (Meaning not clear: ? = MAGNUM *sb.* 1.)

1790 BURNS *Ball. Dumfries Election*, While Welsh, who ne'er yet flinched his ground High wav'd his magnum-bonum round With Cyclopean fury.

4. A large-barrelled steel pen.

1851 MAYHEW *Lond. Labour* (1864) I. 287 The street-stationers do not go beyond 2*s.* the gross, which is for magnum bonums.

‖**magnum opus.** See OPUS *sb.* 2.

†**ˈmagnus.** *Obs.* [var. of MANGANESE: cf. MAGNASE.] Black oxide of manganese, used in the Staffordshire potteries.

1640 *Rates* in Noorthouck *London* (1773) 838/2 Malt, the quarter ½*d.* Magnus, the cwt. 1*d.* **1686** PLOT *Staffordsh.* 123 The Motley-colour..is procured by blending the Lead with Manganese, by the Workmen call'd Magnus.

Magnus effect (ˈmægnəs ɛˈfɛkt). [Named after Heinrich G. *Magnus* (1802–70), German scientist, who first described it.] The effect of rapid spinning on a cylinder or sphere moving through a fluid in a direction at right angles to the axis of spin, which results in a sideways force at right angles to both the direction of motion and the axis of spin and towards the side where the peripheral motion of the body is in the opposite direction to its overall motion.

1921 tr. *Cranz & Becker's Handbk. Ballistics* I. 314 A quantitative theory of the deviation of a sphere under the influence of the adhering air (Magnus effect) was attempted ..by Tait. **1925** *Flight* 8 Jan. 14/1 It does not appear to be until quite recently that the idea of applying the Magnus effect has occurred to anyone. **1943** R. C. BINDER *Fluid Mech.* xi. 143 The Flettner rotor, which employs the Magnus effect, has been applied to the propulsion of marine vessels. Vertical cylinders are extended some distance above the deck. Each cylinder is rotated about its axis by a small motor, and an air force is produced for moving the craft. **1973** *Sci. Amer.* Apr. 121/2 The drag of the turbulent wake and the sidewise forces of the Magnus effect (the name given the transverse forces produced by the flow pattern around a spinning ball) are carefully considered. They are at the heart of baseball, tennis, golf and high-quality soccer.

†**mago-chemical**, *a. Obs. rare*⁻¹. [f. *mago-*, comb. form of Gr. μάγο-ς: see MAGUS, MAGIC.] Pertaining to magic and chemistry.

1652 GAULE *Magastrom.* 307 Magicall or mago-chymicall arts, &c.

magoll, obs. form of MOGUL.

magonell, magonneaul, obs. ff. MANGONEL.

magophony (məˈgɒfənɪ). *rare.* [ad. Gr. μαγοφονία, f. μάγο-ς MAGUS + φόνος slaughter.] The Massacre of the Magi, a famous event in Persian history. Hence *transf.* or *fig.*

1711 SHAFTESB. *Charac.* I. 86 Much less wou'd you (my Friend!) have carry'd on this Magophony, or Priest-Massacre, with such a barbarous Zeal.

magor(e, magosine, obs. ff. MOGUL, MAGAZINE.

Magosian (məˈgəʊsɪən), *a. Archæol.* [f. the place-name *Magosi* in Uganda + -AN.] Of, pertaining to, or designating a stone-age culture in Uganda.

1932 WAYLAND & BURKITT in *Jrnl. R. Anthrop. Inst.* LXII. 369 The Magosian Culture of Uganda... Magosi, an outpost of the King's African Rifles in Karamojo (North-East Uganda), is situated 160 miles due north of the centre of Mount Elgon and less than 5 miles to the west of the.. escarpment that forms the boundary between Uganda and ..Kenya Colony. **1946** *Ibid.* LXXVI. I. 60/1 The Magosian culture was first noticed at Sawmills..by Jones in 1924. At that time..it was not even given a name. **1959** J. D. CLARK *Prehist. S. Afr.* ii. 40 We find a similar link between the Middle and the Later Stone Ages. These are the various forms of the Magosian Culture and they are now placed in the Second Intermediate stage. This culture is named from the small rock cistern in north-eastern Uganda, excavated by Wayland. **1968** *Encycl. Brit.* II. 232/2 In the final stages of the Middle Stone Age, known as the South African Magosian, microlithic elements appear, just as in the case of east Africa. **1970** BRAY & TRUMP *Dict. Archaeol.* 120 The sequence continued with Sangoan, followed by Early Middle Stone Age (Lupemban) industries related to those of the Congo, then Magosian.

‖**magot** ('mægət, mago). [Fr.]

1. A species of ape (*Macacus inuus*); the 'tailless' Barbary Ape of Gibraltar and North Africa.

1607 Topsell *Four-f. Beasts* 12 There was at Paris another beast called a Tartarine, and in some places a Magot (much lyke a Baboun). **1774** Goldsm. *Nat. Hist.* (1862) I. vii. i. 498 The Cynocephalus, or the Magot of Buffon. **1882** A. R. Wallace in *Contemp. Rev.* Mar. 423 In some few this stump is so very short that there appears to be no tail, as in the magot of North Africa and Gibraltar.

2. A small grotesque figure of porcelain, ivory, wood, etc. of Chinese or Japanese workmanship.

1844 Thackeray *Barry Lyndon* xiii, Her rooms were crowded with hideous China magots. **1881** Saintsbury *Dryden* ii. 35 This [see *Ann. Mirab.* st. 29] cannot be considered the happiest possible means of informing us that the Dutch fleet was laden with spices and *magots*.

magot, magozin, obs. ff. maggot, magazine.

magpie ('mægpaɪ). Also 7 **magge pye, megpye.** [f. Mag *sb.*[2] + pie[1]. Cf. maggot-pie, maw-pie.]

1. a. A common European bird, *Pica caudata*, of the family *Corvidæ*, having a long pointed tail and black-and-white plumage. It is well known for its noisy chatter, and is often taught to speak; its habits of pilfering and hoarding are proverbial, and it is popularly regarded as a bird of ill omen.

1605 S. Rowley *When You See Me* C 3 As merie as a magge pie. **1634** Peacham *Gentl. Exerc.* ii. i. 108 Dissimulation. A Lady wearing a vizard of two faces,..in her right hand a magpye. **1647** R. Stapylton *Juvenal* 62 The nine daughters of Pierus..were for that saucy ambition transformed into meg-pyes. **1664** H. More *Myst. Iniq.* 333 The Loquacity of the Magpie. **1720** Gay *Poems* (1745) I. 70 No magpie chatter'd, nor the painted Jay. **1751** in Hone *Every-day Bk.* II. 1457 No horseshoe nor magpye shall baffle our skill. **1821** Clare *Vill. Minstr.* I. 159 And magpies that chattered, no omen so black. **1855** Tennyson *To F. D. Maurice* 19 And only hear the Magpie gossip Garrulous under a roof of pine. **1859** Darwin *Orig. Spec.* viii. (1873) 209 The magpie, so wary in England, is tame in Norway.

b. *Austral.* Applied to the black-and-white Crow-shrike (*Gymnorrhina*); also, in Tasmania, to the genus *Strepera*.

1859 H. Kingsley *G. Hamlyn* xviii. II. 4 A magpie was chanting his noble vesper hymn from a lofty tree. *Ibid.* xxxiii. II. 314 *note*, Magpie, a large, pied crow. Of all the birds I have ever seen, the cleverest, the most grotesque, and the most musical. **1886** I. Henry *Fortunate Days* 47 The magpie swells from knoll or silent brake His loud sweet tune. **1898** Morris *Austral Eng.* 277.

2. *transf.* An idle or impertinent chatterer.

1632 Massinger & Field *Fatal Dowry* iv. i, I haue waited, sir, Three houres to speake w'ee, and not take it well, Such magpies, are admitted, whilst I daunce Attendance. **1791** Burke *Let. to Chev. de Rivarol* (1844) III. 211 He will not care what..the whole flight of the magpies and jays of philosophy, may fancy and chatter. **1838** *Lett. fr. Madras* (1843) 189 The Moonshee..is not the little talkative magpie who told me about the language of the planets. **1895** Scully *Kafir Stories* 132 He was so fond of talking that his comrades nicknamed him 'magpie'.

3. †**a.** A derisive term for an Anglican bishop, from the black chimere and white rochet forming his ordinary ceremonial attire (*obs.*). **b.** In recent use, a jocular name for the episcopal costume consisting of these vestments.

[*c* **1645** Howell *Lett.* Verses to Rdr., Prelats, like magpies, in the Ayr had flown. **1663** Killigrew *Parsons Wedd.* iii. v. 114 Have you not heard of the Scriveners Wife that..was deliver'd of a Mag-Pie;..the Mid-wife cri'd out, 'twas born a Bishop, with Tippet and white-sleeves] *a* **1704** T. Brown *Wks.* (1730) I. 107 Root out of them all Anti-Christian Tyranny of most abominable Bishops; let not those Silk-worms and Magpies have dominion over us. *a* **1904** *Mod.* Did he wear a cope, or only his magpie? **1917** G. W. E. Russell *Politics & Personalities* ix. 357 The most hideous of all known costumes—the episcopal 'Magpie'—costs £100. *Ibid.* 360 Carrying with his own apostolic hands the sacred appliances of Mitre or Magpie. **1920** P. Dearmer *Ornaments of Ministers* (new ed.) plate 29 (*caption*) The..figures of the two bishops well illustrate the 'magpie' dress. **1923** *Brewer's Dict. Phr. & Fable* (new ed.) 700/2 Formerly bishops were humorously or derisively called magpies because of their black and white vestments.

4. A kind of potato.

1794 Billingsley *Agric. Somerset* (1797) 116 The sorts [of potatoes] cultivated are the kidney,..magpie, rough red [etc.]. **1829** *Jrnl. of Naturalist* 31 Our chief sorts [of potato] are pink eyes,..magpies, and china oranges.

5. A name given to a particular variety of the domestic pigeon.

1868 Tegetmeier *Pigeons* xxi. 174 Magpies are another variety of German Toys that are well known in England. **1895** *Times* 16 Jan. 11/6 For the rest, the Magpies, black, red, yellow, and blue..deserve to be mentioned. **1898** *Daily News* 5 Jan. 2 Mr. F. Warner has some excellent magpies.

6. *slang.* A halfpenny. (Cf. mag *sb.*[3])

1838 Dickens *O. Twist* viii, I'm at low-water-mark my self—only one bob and a magpie.

7. *Mil. slang.* A shot from a rifle which strikes the outermost division but one of a target, and is signalled by a black and white flag.

1884 *Times* 23 July 8/1 After running through the scoring gamut with an outer, a magpie, and a miss. **1894** *Ibid.* 14 July 10/1 He followed his first two bull's eyes with two more, then came a magpie.

8. a. *attrib.* and *Comb.*, as ***magpie-like, -minded*** adjs.: **magpie diver**, (*a*) the Golden-eye Duck, *Clangula glaucion*; (*b*) the Smew, *Merganser albellus*; **magpie finch**, a bird of the genus *Spermestes*; **magpie goose** (see quot.); **magpie lark**, a small Australian bird, *Grallina picata*; **magpie-maki**, a species of lemur, *Lemur macaco* (Cent. Dict.); **magpie moth**, a white moth, patched with black and some yellow spots, *Abraxas grossulariata*; **magpie perch** (see quot.); **magpie robin** = dial-bird; **magpie shrike**, a South American bird, *Cissopis leverianus*.

1796 Nemnich *Polygl. Lex. Nat. Hist.* v. 820 *Magpie diver, the smew. **1882** Payne-Gallwey *Fowler in Irel.* 107 Another local name [of the Goldeneye] is the 'Magpie Diver', a very descriptive one by reason of the black and white plumage of the adult male. **1869–73** T. R. Jones *Cassell's Bk. of Birds* I. 158 The *Magpie Finch is an inhabitant of the countries in the vicinity of the river Gambia. **1898** Morris *Austral Eng.* 278 **Magpie-Goose*, a common name for the Australian Goose, *Anseranus melanoleuca*. **1888** *Cassell's Pict. Australasia* II. 235 The little *magpie-lark. **1805** T. Harrol *Scenes of Life* III. 104 What was before black had now assumed a *magpie-like appearance. **1955** G. A. N. Lowndes *Brit. Educ. Syst.* iii. 49 Satisfying his curiosity..with unrelated snippets of knowledge which may lead to his becoming *magpie-minded. **1796** Nemnich *Polygl. Lex. Nat. Hist.* v. 820 The large *Magpie moth, *Phal. grossulariata*. The small Magpie moth, *Phal. urticata*. **1819** G. Samouelle *Entomol. Compend.* 252 Magpie moth (*Abraxas grossulariata*). **1890** E. A. Ormerod *Injur. Insects* (ed. 2) 310 The caterpillars of the Magpie Moth sometimes do a great deal of mischief. **1898** Morris *Austral Eng.* 278 **Magpie-Perch*, a West Australian, Victorian, and Tasmanian fish, *Chilodactylus gibbosus*. **1839** Jerdon in *Madras Jrnl.* X. 263 Dial bird... Large or *Magpie Robin. **1781** Latham *Gen. Syn. Birds* I. 192 *Magpie Shrike. Size of a Song-thrush: length ten inches.

b. *attrib.* and quasi-*adj.*: with allusion to the acquisitiveness, curiosity, etc., of the magpie.

1808 M. Wilmot *Russ. Jrnls.* (1934) iii. 371 He deplores ..the Magpye mingle of foreign expressions with the language of the Country. **1901** G. B. Shaw *Caesar & Cleopatra* ii. 114 He maintains an air of magpie keenness and profundity. **1936** P. Fleming *News from Tartary* iii. ii. 116 All our actions..were closely scrutinized..by the Chinese with ill-concealed amusement and a magpie curiosity. **1940** *Proc. Prehist. Soc.* VI. 120 Beaker people.. showed a magpie acquisitiveness for other people's chattels. **1953** R. Lehmann *Echoing Grove* ii. 32 Where does she get this magpie streak from?.. But Mother hoarded, didn't she? **1962** G. K. Hunter *John Lyly* iv. 162 A variety of elements which would appeal to the magpie taste for classical motifs. **1974** 'J. Le Carré' *Tinker, Tailor* xv. 125 That whole magpie collection of tattered hotel junk.

c. Used *attrib.* of something with black and white colouring.

1885 Kipling *Phantom 'Rickshaw* (1889) 9 My eye was arrested by the sight of four *jhampanies* in 'magpie' livery... Was it not enough that the woman was dead.., without her black and white servitors re-appearing? **1923** *Daily Mail* 28 Mar. 11 *Magpie Millinery*. Black and white millinery is popular at all seasons. **1932** *Daily Tel.* 25 Apr. 4/5 Black and white is to continue its long reign this summer. Charming examples of this smart, practical 'magpie' fashion will be found at most inexpensive prices. *Ibid.* (Advt.), Ermine that imparts the fashionable magpie effect. **1942** H. J. Massingham *Field Fellowship* ii. 58 Moreton Old Hall in Cheshire is the conventional example of the magpie style. *Ibid.*, We find the wood-workmanship of the Avon Valley carried to the utmost pitch of elaboration and complexity... This is the country of the 'magpie' timber-framing. **1971** J. S. Gunn *Opal Terminol.* 26 *Magpie*, black and white patch formed together.

Hence (*nonce-wds.*) **'magpied** *ppl. a.*, made like a magpie; **'magpieish** *a.*, magpie-like.

1845 E. Warburton *Crescent & Cross* I. 64 Black slaves, magpied with white napkins round their head and loins. **1880** *Daily News* 9 Aug. 2/2 Money, which..had been abstracted and disposed of in a magpieish spirit of mischief.

magpiety (mæg'paɪɪtɪ). *nonce-wd.* [jocular f. magpie, after *piety*.] (Cf. quots.)

a **1845** Hood *Jarvis & Mrs. Cope* ii, Not pious in its proper sense, But chattring like a bird, Of sin and grace—in such a case Mag-piety's the word. **1891** *Blackw. Mag.* CL. 400/2 Conceive the agony of suppressed speech when a man is as garrulous as a magpie by nature; and my friend is that, though his magpiety is of an elevated sort.

magre, variant of maugre.

magrei, -rey, -rie, -ry: see maugre.

magryme, obs. form of megrim.

magslip ('mægslɪp). [said to be f. mag(netic *a.* + *slip*(-*ring*.] A kind of electric motor designed so that, when it is operating as a receiver, the angular position of its rotor is maintained the same as that of the rotor of a similar motor electrically connected to it and operating as a transmitter; *orig.* applied to a particular design of receiver in which the rotor is a simple magnetic member without windings polarized by a fixed coil and moved by a three-phase stator.

1947 *Electronic Engin.* XIX. 259/1 Small instruments of the magslip or selsyn type, in which shaft position corresponds to the angular datum of the input quantity. **1950** *Engineering* 29 Dec. 557/3 The forces developed by the gyroscopes are..small and therefore have to be amplified. This is achieved by means of a sensitive hydraulic-motor unit developed by the Admiralty, the signals being transmitted from the gyroscope to the hydraulic unit by a system of 'magslips'. The magslip is, of course, well known as a device for the electrical transmission of angular displacements. **1954** *Jrnl. Brit. Interplanetary Soc.* XIII. 281 Running up the axis of the life compartment and projecting through the nose is the coelostat tube topped by a semi-elliptical mirror which can be tilted and rotated by a servo magslip motor thus allowing viewing in all directions. **1962** J. Bell in G. A. T. Burdett *Automatic Control Handbk.* iv. 11 Magslips were developed for use in the Royal Navy for transmission of bearing, range and elevation data between observing instruments, calculating tables, searchlights and guns. **1967** M. Healey *Princ. Automatic Control* xiv. 261 Some confusion existed over terminology, but military specifications have led to standardisation of sizes, voltages, frequencies, etc., so that older units such as Selsyns and Magslips are similar in principle but different in size.

magsman ('mægsmən). *slang.* [f. mag *sb.*[1]]

1. A street swindler, 'confidence man'.

1838 *The Town* 27 Jan. 276 A *magsman* must of necessity be a great actor and a most studious observer of human nature. **1866** Dickens *Reprinted Pieces, Detective Police* (1868) 241 Tally-ho Thompson was a famous horse-stealer, couper, and magsman. **1897** M. Davitt in *Westm. Gaz.* 30 Sept. 2/1 Almost every possible kind of convict, from the sneak-thief..to professional magsmen.

2. *Austral.* A story-teller, raconteur.

1944 W. E. Harney *Taboo* (ed. 3) 56 We were discussing dreams... It was the Doc's subject and he was..'giving it hell'. I let him go—with his complexes and repressions, but I was itching to have my say, for I too am a good 'magsman'. **1963** —— *To Ayers Rock & Beyond* v. 45 We would sit around the camp-fire to sing songs or recite our favourite poems... I am pretty sure that this bush school of oral teaching was the starting point with many a bush-poet and magsman, such as I, who kept up the yarning into later days. **1967** *Telegraph* (Brisbane) 8 Apr. 4/1 Hardy..became the official yarn-spinning champion of Australia today. He won the magsman's championship in Darwin.

‖**magtig** ('maxtix), *int. S. Afr.* [Afrikaans, shortened form of *allamagtig* almighty *a.*] An exclamation of astonishment, awe, etc.

1891 B. Mitford *Weird of Deadly Hollow* viii. 77 *Magtag*! It's all through the *vrouw-menschen*. Whoever heard of bringing *vrouw-menschen* out springbok-hunting! **1925** W. Plomer *Turbott Wolfe* iii. 141 '*Magtig*!' he said, 'supposing Jacop dies—.' **1927** —— *I Speak of Afr.* i. 53 Magtig! but he's a strong man! **1943** 'B. Knight' *Covenant* (1944) ii. iii. 64 A hundred and fifty! *Magtig*, that is a lot to lose. **1948** *Sunday Times* (Johannesburg) 17 Oct. 21 If only Oom Piet were a reasonable man. But, magtig, what's the good of wishing that? **1973** S. Cloete *Company with Heart of Gold* 126 *Magtig*, what is a farm if there is no one to leave it to?

‖**maguari** (mə'gwɑːrɪ). [Tupi *mbaguári* (Ruiz de Montoya *Tesoro de la Lingua Guarani* 1639).] A South American Stork, *Euxenura maguari*, with a forked tail.

1678 Ray *Willughby's Ornith.* 287 The American Stork, called by the Brasilians Maguari of Marggrave. **1824** Latham *Gen. Hist. Birds* IX. 54 The Spaniards call it Cicogne; the Guarinis Baguari and Maguari. **1889** P. L. Sclater *Argentine Ornith.* II. 107 The Maguari Stork is a well-known bird on the pampas.

maguder, variant of magydare. *Obs.*

‖**maguey** ('mægweɪ; Sp. ma'gej). Forms: 6 **magueans, magueis, -eiz, -aiz, maguay,** 7 **manguay, mangouay,** 8 **ma(y)quey.** [Sp., a. Haitian.] The American aloe, *Agave Americana*.

1555 Eden *Decades* 135 Magueans which is an herbe muche lyke vnto that which is commonly called Sengrene or Orpin. [The Latin has *palmarum puta Magueiorum, quæ est herba*, etc.] **1586** *Chilton's Voy.* in *Hakluyt*, About Mexico..there groweth a certeine plant called magueis which yeeldeth wine [etc.]. **1589** Parke tr. *Mendoza's Hist. China*, etc. 320 A plant called Maguey... They take out of this plant wine, which is that which the Indians doo drinke ordinarily, and the Negros. **1604** E. G[rimstone] *D'Acosta's Hist. Indies* v. xxix. 420 They strewd round about a great quantitie of the boughes of Manguay, the leaves whereof are large and pricking. **1660** F. Brooke tr. *Le Blanc's Trav.* 363 There are some that furiously lash their bare shoulders with thorns of Mangouay. **1706** Phillips (ed. Kersey), *Maquey* or *Mayquey*, an admirable Tree in New Spain, in the West-Indies. **1712** W. Rogers *Voy.* (1718) 318 Their most remarkable plant is that call'd Maguey. **1899** *Atlantic Monthly* LXXXIII. 758/1 He who has once slept upon a mass of the shredded fibres of the maguey, or Spanish bayonet, will not be envious of the down couches of kings.

b. *attrib.*, as ***maguey fibre, leaf, tree***.

1745 P. Thomas *Jrnl. Anson's Voy.* 128 They call it a Maguey Tree, and from it they get Wine, Vinegar, Honey, Thread, Needles, Stuffs for cloathing, or Sails for Canoes and Small Boats, and Timber for building. **1893** *Outing* (U.S.) XXII. 111/1 A small roll made from the fiber of the maguey leaf. **1901** *Westm. Gaz.* 21 Oct. 5/1 All the maguey fibre Mexico can produce will be taken at good prices.

‖**Magus** ('meɪgəs). Pl. **Magi** ('meɪdʒaɪ); also 4 **magy.** [L., a. Gr. μάγος, a. OPersian *magu-s*.]

1. *Hist.* A member of the ancient Persian priestly caste, said by ancient historians to have been originally a Median tribe. Hence, in wider sense, one skilled in Oriental magic and astrology, an ancient magician or sorcerer.

sing. [*c* **1384** Chaucer *H. Fame* iii. 184 Ther saugh I Hermes Ballenus, Lymote, and eek Simon Magus.] **1621** Quarles *Div. Poems, Esther* (1638) 93 Tyrant Cambyses being dead and gone,..Mounts up a Magus, with dissembled right. **1638** Sir T. Herbert *Trav.* 214 Let me rather busie my brains in quest of what a Magus was..under which Title, many Witches, Sorcerers..and other

Diaboliques have cloakt their trumperies. **1742** POPE *Dunc.* IV. 516 Thy *Magus*, Goddess! shall perform the rest. **1805** H. K. WHITE *Let.* 10 Nov. *Remains* (1816) I. 207, I have as much expectation of gaining it, as of being elected supreme magus over the mysteries of Mithra. **1821** SHELLEY *Prometh. Unb.* I. 192 The Magus Zoroaster.

plur. [*c* **1400** *Three Kings Cologne* 49 Seynt Austyn seiþ þat þis word Magi in the tung of Chaldee is as moche to seye as a Philosophre.] **1555** WATREMAN *Fardle of Facions* II. vii. K iv b, [In Persia] their Magi (that is to say men skylfull in ye secretes of nature). **1609** HOLLAND *Amm. Marcell.* XXIII. vi. 231 In these tracts lye the fertile fields of the Magi. **1614** SYLVESTER *Bethulias Rescue* v. 301 You Parthians, Cossians, and Arabians too, By your sad Magi's deep prophetlike Charms Sacredly counsell'd. **1711** POPE *Temp. Fame* 97 There in long robes the royal Magi stand, Grave Zoroaster waves the circling wand. **1864** PUSEY *Lect. Daniel* vii. 418 Among the Persians, those who are wise as to the Deity, and are its ministers, are called Magi.

b. Applied by Irish historians to the heathen sorcerers who opposed St. Patrick.

1822 LANIGAN *Eccl. Hist. Irel.* I. 224 Leogaire..set out..with a considerable number of followers and one or two of the principal Magi. **1845** PETRIE *Round Towers Irel.* II. ii. 132 Quoted as the composition of a certain magus of the name of Con, in the ancient Life of St. Patrick. **1887** SIR D. O. HUNTER BLAIR tr. *A. Bellesheim's Hist. Cath. Ch. of Scotl.* I. 72 Thereupon the Magi, or *Druadh*, bitterly reproached the parents for their adoption of Christianity. *Ibid.* I. 73 Broichan, the Magus of King Brude.

c. *transf.*

1851 CARLYLE *Sterling* II. ii. (1872) 94 His Father,..the magus of the *Times*, had talk and argument ever ready.

2. *spec.* ***the*** **(*three*)** ***Magi***: the three 'wise men' who came from the East, bearing offerings to the infant Christ.

1377 LANGL. *P. Pl.* B. XIX. 81 Wherfore and whi wyse men that tyme, Maistres and lettred men Magy [*C.* Magi] hem called. **1652** GAULE *Magastrom.* 13 The Magi that came to Christ. **1656** BLOUNT *Glossogr., Balthasar*,..one of the *Magi*, or wise-men, vulgarly called the three Kings of Collein. **1756-7** tr. *Keysler's Trav.* (1760) I. 405 A golden medal, said to be among the offerings of the eastern *magi* to Jesus Christ. **1839** *Penny Cycl.* XIV. 281 Whence the wise men of the East who came to see Christ are called simply Magi.

† **magusian.** *Obs. rare*^−1^. [f. prec. + -IAN.] A magian; a follower of the magi.

1587 GOLDING *De Mornay* xxxiii. 530 The Magusians..are giuen to Incest after the custome of their Mother country Persia.

Magyar ('madjar, 'mægjɑː(r)), *sb.* and *a.* [The native name.]

A. *sb.*

1. An individual of that Mongoloid race, now forming, numerically and politically, the predominant section of the inhabitants of Hungary.

1797 TOWNSON *Trav. Hungary* 141 An old Magyar to be *obliged* to learn, and to learn the *German* language! **1828** *Foreign Q. Rev.* III. 29 That the Magyars settled in Hungary during the ninth century is certain. **1864** *Spectator* 438 The moment it [a British fleet] threatens Trieste the Magyar will be in arms. **1878** *N. Amer. Rev.* CXXVI. 557 The Magyars received the knowledge of southern products and of agriculture from their Turkic neighbors.

2. The language of the Magyars; Hungarian.

1828 *Foreign Q. Rev.* III. 73 Volumes written in Latin, German and Magyar. **1866** CHARNOCK in *Anthrop. Rev.* IV. 172 In the Magyar there is only one conjugation for all regular verbs. **1884** EM. DE LAVELEYE in *Contemp. Rev.* Dec. 820 He..translated Stuart Mill's 'Liberty' into Magyar.

Comb. **1886** W. J. TUCKER *E. Europe* 231 The Hungarian stage, being thus limited to the Magyar-speaking population..can never enjoy European fame.

B. *adj.*

1. Of or pertaining to the Magyars, or to the language of the Magyars.

1828 *Foreign Q. Rev.* III. 34 The letters of the Magyar alphabet which require particular notice are ö [etc.]. *Ibid.* 39 Scarcely a fragment remains of old Magyar minstrelsy. **1851** MAYHEW *Lond. Labour* I. 25 The Magyar noblesse. **1888** L. OLIPHANT *Episodes in Life Adventure* 180 Divers hospitable Magyar country-houses.

2. *Dressmaking.* Of or pertaining to a style of blouse, bodice, etc., in which the sleeves are cut in one piece with the main part of the garment. Also *ellipt.* as *sb.*

1911 *Daily Colonist* (Victoria, B.C.) 5 Apr. 24/1 (Advt.), Evening gown of grey chiffon..with low neck and magyar sleeves. **1912** *Home Chat* 13 Apr. 112/2 Take away the lace insertion, and you get a quite plain little Magyar of white muslin. **1912** A. J. REEVE *Elem. Dress Pattern-Making* 17 The Empire yoke may be cut Magyar style if preferred. *Ibid.* 19 Magyar Blouse. Cut from Blouse Pattern. **1923** *Daily Mail* 19 June 15 A tight-fitting bodice which buttons down the back, the bolero bodice, and cross-over magyar. **1952** *Woman's Jrnl.* June 73/3 Asta's interpretation is in white fleecy wool, with..magyar sleeves and immensely wide cuffs. **1958** V. CLIFFE *Making your own Clothes* iii. 42 It is not at all difficult, especially if you begin with what is known as a Magyar blouse. **1964** N. BRAY *More Dress Pattern Designing* xiii. 150 (*heading*) The kimono or magyar block. **1968** W. CLARK *Dressmaking Techniques for Trade Students* 33 The magyar is not to be confused with a Dolman sleeve which, although cut in one with the bodice, is closer fitting. **1972** H. STANLEY *Modelling & Flat Cutting for Fashion* viii. 93 Variations of style in category (b) are limited to the Kimono (or Magyar) and to styles with gussets of differing shapes.

Hence '**Magyarism**, the principles of Magyar patriotism; '**Magyarize** *v. trans.*, to assimilate to the Magyar type; to translate (names) into Magyar; hence '**Magyarized** *ppl. a.*; '**Magyarization**; '**Magyarizing** *vbl. sb.*

1862 *Sat. Rev.* 8 Feb. 158 Magyarism once meant a tyranny of race. **1879** W. R. MORFILL in *Westm. Rev.* Oct., How long this small nationality [of Slovaks] will be able to resist Magyarisation is doubtful. **1880** *Echo* 23 Oct. 1/5 The Chauvinist agitators for the 'Magyarising of Commerce'. **1884** EM. DE LAVELEYE in *Contemp. Rev.* Dec. 826 Austria Hungary can neither Magyarize nor Germanize Bosnia. **1886** W. J. TUCKER *E. Europe* 48 Those amongst us bearing German names Magyarise them. *Ibid.* 133 Government, in the frenzy of its Magyarizing hallucinations, heralds the Magyarizing of the name with applause. **1889** *Daily News* 21 Nov. 5/3 The..completely Magyarised family of the Archduke Joseph. **1897** *Contemp. Rev.* Jan. 13 The Roumanian subjects..refuse to be Magyarised.

† **magydare.** *Obs.* Also 6 **maguder.** [ad. L. *magudaris, magydaris, -deris*, a. Gr. μαγύδαρις.] The root of the plant laserwort; the plant itself.

1530 PALSGR. 241/2 Maguder a stalke of an herbe, *chion.* **1597** GERARDE *Herbal* II. ccclxxv. 854 It is called in Latin *Laserpitium*: in English Laserwoort and Magydare: the gum or liquor that issueth out of the same is called Lacer. **1706** PHILLIPS (ed. Kersey), *Magydare*, a sort of Herb.

mah (mɑː, unstressed mə), var. MY *poss. adj.* Common in written Black English. Cf. *ma* s.v. MY *poss. adj.*

1933 J. M. BREWER in *Publ. Texas Folklore Soc.* XI. 101 Yuh kin sow in mah fiel' ef yuh wants to. **1935** Z. N. HURSTON *Mules & Men* I. i. 31 Nobody don't want to buy *mah* ole rusty toe. **1938** C. HIMES *Black on Black* (1973) 168 Mah belly feels lak mah throat wus cut. **1953** S. A. BROWN in A. Dundes *Mother Wit* (1973) 41/2 Ah wuz settin' in de do' wid mah pipe. **1966** E. BULLINS *Theme is Blackness* (1973) 25 Now, brothers and mah good sisters, now are we really honest? **1966** M. THELWELL in A. Chapman *New Black Voices* (1972) 141 Ah *kno-o-ows* in mah heart she would. **1968** *Esquire* Apr. 88/2 To those so blessed as to have had bestowed upon them at birth the lifetime gift of soul, these are the most communicative and meaningful sounds..: the familiar 'mah' instead of 'my'.

Mahabharata (mɑːhə'bɑːrətə). Also **Mahābhārata, Mahabharat.** [Skr., 'the great history of the Bharata dynasty'.] An ancient Hindu epic.

1784 W. HASTINGS *Let.* 4 Oct. in C. Wilkins tr. *Bhăgvăt-Geetă* (1785) 6 The Măhābhārăt contains the genealogy and general history of the house of Bhaurut, so called from Bhurrut its founder. *Ibid.* 11 The Măhābhārăt..is said to consist of more than one hundred thousand metrical stanzas, of which he [*sc.* Wilkins] has at this time translated more than a third. **1788** *Asiatick Researches* I. 351 The next in celebrity [to the *Ramayana*], if it be not superior in reputation for holiness, was the Mahábhárata of Vyása. **1795** C. WILKINS (*title*) The story of Dooshwanta and Sakoontalā extracted from the Mahābhārata, a poem in the Sanskreet language. **1863** M. WILLIAMS *Indian Epic Poetry* 16, I come now to the Mahá-bhárata or Great Bharateid, that is, the great poem which describes the achievements, mutual rivalries, and contests of the descendants of Bharata. **1894** J. C. OMAN *Gt. Indian Epics* II. i. 91 Of the one hundred thousand verses of the *Mahabharata* not more than a fourth part is concerned with the main story of the epic. **1901** E. W. HOPKINS *Gt. Epic of India* ii. 63 The later Rāmāyana..unquestionably betrays acquaintance with the Mahābhārata. **1931** E. J. THOMAS *Song of Lord* 22 In Book VI of the *Mahābhārata* begins the account of the great battle, probably a real event of prehistoric times. **1948** S. RADHAKRISHNAN *Bhagavadgītā* 14 The authorship of the *Gītā* is attributed to Vyāsa, the legendary compiler of the *Mahābhārata*. **1967** SINGHA & MASSEY *Indian Dances* II. viii. 88 Plays were written with themes from other sacred works such as the *Mahabharata*, the *Shiva Purana* and the *Bhagavad Purana*. **1972** P. HOLROYDE *Indian Mus.* iii. 75 Musical instruments had already been mentioned in the *Upanishads* (*c.* 600 BC) and in the *Mahabharat* (*c.* 500 BC–AD 200). **1972** M. SHEPPARD *Taman Indera* 69 The patrons of the Javanese and Balinese shadow plays seem always to have preferred the Mahabharata, with its plethora of gods and heroes. **1973** J. A. B. VAN BUITENEN *Mahābhārata* I. p. xiii, The central story of *The Mahābhārata* takes its matter from the legitimacy of the succession to the kingdom of Kuruksetra in northern India.

Mahadee, obs. form of MAHDI.

mahaila (mə'haɪlə). Also **mahailah, maheila, maheileh, mahela(h), mehala.** [App. f. Arab *safīna mahīla* ship treated with bitumen; cf. Arab. *muhl(a)* liquid pitch.] A large river sailing-boat used in Iraq.

1904 H. V. GEERE *By Nile & Euphrates* vi. 86 On the Shatt el-Arab many varieties of native craft are to be seen, *dhows, mehalas.* **1916** T. E. LAWRENCE *Home Lett.* (1954) 319 The bellam is the passenger boat..and the Mahaila the cargo boat. Mahailas sit on the water like the scooped third of a melon-rind. **1922** *Blackw. Mag.* Jan. 10/2 They were..waiting for a mahaila to pass on her way upstream. **1952** E. F. DAVIES *Illyrian Venture* iii. 44 The Nile showed up.., and mahelas with their lateen rig were sailing downstream. **1969** R. MILLAR *Kut* i. 9 Townshend..improvised a mock fleet from the few available river steamers and disguised *mahailas* (small river dhows).

‖ **mahajun** (mə'hɑːdʒʌn). [Hindī *mahājan*, repr. Skr. *mahājana* great man, head of tribe or caste.] A money-lender, usurer.

1858 J. B. NORTON *Topics* 245 The mahajun kindly undertakes to advance the money. *c* **1861** A. C. LYALL *Old Pindaree* (Y.), Down there lives a Mahajun—my father gave him a bill, I have paid the knave thrice over, and here I'm paying him still.

‖ **mahal** (mə'hɑːl). *Indian.* Also 7 **mahael, mohol(l,** 8–9 **mahl,** 9 **muhal.** [Urdū (Arab.) *maḥall*, f. Arab. root *ḥalla* to lodge.]

1. Private apartments or lodgings.

1638 SIR T. HERBERT *Trav.* 71 Who..leads him into the Mahael (or private lodging). **1662** J. DAVIES tr. *Mandelslo's Trav.* 76 He went to the *Mahael*, or Queens Lodgings. **1793** T. MAURICE *Ind. Antiq.* I. 67 The mahls, the courts, the galleries, the rooms of state, are almost endless. **1799** WELLINGTON *Suppl. Desp.* (1858) I. 322, I beg that you will desire my moonshee to write a letter to the ladies in the mahal. **1800** *Asiat. Ann. Reg., Misc. Tracts* 294/1 These inner apartments are said to have been the mahl, or private chambers of Gundrufsein.

2. A summer house or palace.

1625 PURCHAS *Pilgrims* I. IV. 428 A Garden, and Moholl or Summer house of the Queene Mothers. **1638** SIR T. HERBERT *Trav.* 159 An even delicate street..bestrew'd with Moholls or Summer houses. **1800** *Asiat. Ann. Reg., Misc. Tracts* 162/2 Rajah Ragonaut's old mahal or house under Goosapahar. **1834** *Baboo* I. xi. 200 This old dwelling is not like the ancient Muhal of my fathers.

3. A territorial division in India; a ward of a town. Also, a division of an estate or tract of land for farming or hunting purposes.

1793 T. MAURICE *Ind. Antiq.* I. 106 The soobah of Bengal is said to consist of twenty-four circars and seven hundred and eighty-seven mahls. **1800** *Asiat. Ann. Reg., Char.* 3/1 Colar is a mahl of Sera. **1815** SIR J. MALCOLM *Hist. Persia* II. 177 *note*, He was made magistrate of all the Hyderee mâhâls, or wards termed Hyderee, which included more than half the city. **1823** —— *Mem. Central India* I. 146 *note*, The first grants of twelve Mahals to Mulharjee Holkar. **1883** *19th Cent.* Sept. 424 The supervisors were instructed to prepare rent-rolls of each mahal, or farm. **1885** SIR W. HUNTER *Imp. Gaz. India* I. 349 The elephant hunting-grounds..are divided into several mahals, which are leased out.

4. (With capital initial.) The name of a type of coarse-woven carpet made in villages near Arak, Iran. Also *attrib.*

1911 G. G. LEWIS *Pract. Bk. Oriental Rugs* xiii. 201 Mahal is but a trade name. **1913** W. A. HAWLEY *Oriental Rugs* 286 If the field has concentric medallions, the rug may be a..Mahal. **1931** A. U. DILLEY *Oriental Rugs & Carpets* iv. 121 With us Mahal means the lowest grade of Sultanabad weaving. **1967** K. LARSON *Rugs & Carpets of Orient* 104/1 *Mahal*, made in: the districts of Mahallat, Muskabad and Dulakhoo. **1972** P. L. PHILLIPS tr. *Formenton's Oriental Rugs & Carpets* 150 Mahal carpets are easily recognizable because of their large knots and their softness.

mahaleb ('mɑːhəlɛb). Also 6–8 **macaleb,** 8 **mahalep,** 9 **mahlib, melub.** [a. F. *macaleb, -lep* (Cotgr.), a. Arab. *maḥlab.* Cf. It. *macalepo* 'a kinde of perfume or sweete smell' (Florio 1598).] A kind of cherry, *Prunus Mahaleb*, the kernels of which are used by perfumers; the tree itself is used as a dwarf grafting-stock for cherries.

1558 WARDE tr. *Alexis' Secr.* 50 Take the Macaleb, whiche are litle soote and odoriferous graynes so called. **1597** GERARDE *Herbal* III. lv. 1211 This shrubbie tree called Macaleb or Mahaleb is also one of the Priuets. **1656** BLOUNT *Glossogr., Macaleb*, the bastard Coral or Pomander; of whose sweet and shining black berries, chains, and bracelets are made. **1712** tr. *Pomet's Hist. Drugs* I. 13 Mahalep is the Kernel of a small Berry, almost like a Cherry-Stone. **1858** SIMMONDS *Dict. Trade, Mahlib, melub*, the fragrant kernels of *Prunus Mahaleb* of Linnæus, strung as necklaces, which are much valued by the women of Sinde and other parts of India. **1892** J. WRIGHT *Fruit Grower's Guide* II. 120 The Mahaleb is the principal dwarfing stock.

Mahamad ('mɑːhəmɑːd). Also **Ma'amad** and with small initial. [mod. Heb. *ma'umud.*] The body of trustees ruling a Sephardic synagogue; freq. in phr. ***gentlemen of the Mahamad.*** Also *attrib.*

1831 *Ascamot, or Laws & Regulations Jewish Congregation* v. 37 The institution of the *Mahamad* in this congregation is very ancient... The *Mahamad*..is composed of the four *Parnassim* and a *Gabay*, elected annually. **1893** I. ZANGWILL *Childr. Ghetto* (ed. 3) I. 8 The blue-blooded Dons, 'the gentlemen of the Mahamad', who ruffled it with swords and knee-breeches in the best Christian Society. **1904** *Jewish Encycl.* VIII. 259 The mahamad exercised over the members of the congregation a despotic control which degenerated into a sort of police supervision. **1923** *Public Opinion* 17 Aug. 161/1 The gentlemen of the Mahamad had sent a call to members of the Spanish and Portuguese Jews' Congregation of London to assemble at their ancient burial-ground in Mile-end Road. **1944** *New Judaea* May 125/2 The Sephardim were to learn that..the Haham..would brook no trespass by the *Mahamad.* **1971** *Encycl. Judaica* XI. 638/1 One of the characteristic features of *ma'amad* policy was that on completion of its term of office the *ma'amad* itself appointed its successors.

Mahammudan, obs. form of MUHAMMADAN.

mahan, obs. form of MAUND, Indian weight.

‖ **mahant** (mə'hʌnt). *Indian.* Also 9 **mehunt.** [Hindī.] A religious superior.

1800 *Asiat. Ann. Reg., Misc. Tr.* 247/1 The ruling power was..held by the priests of the Goosaigns, distinguished by the appellation of Mehunts. **1896** MRS. B. M. CROKER *Village Tales* 160 A venerable Mahant, or high-priest of the Gosains, now advanced.

‖**maharaj** (mɑːhəˈrɑːdʒ). [Hindī *mahārāj*, f. *mahā* great + *rāj* sovereignty, (in compounds) sovereign.] = next.

1826 Hockley *Pandurang Hari* I. 11 A small tent through which all must pass before they could enter the presence of the Ma,ha,raj. **1903** *Westm. Gaz.* 13 Aug. 8/2 Calcutta Corporation..the following resolution was proposed by the Maharaj Kumar Prodyat Tagore.

‖**maharaja(h)** (mɑːhəˈrɑːdʒə). Also 7 **mau raja(h**. [Hindī *mahārājā* great king, f. *mahā* great + *rājā* RAJA(H.] The title of certain Indian princes.

1698 Fryer *Acc. E. India & P.* 76 Seva Gi..is preparing to be install'd Mau Raja, or Arch Raja, at his Court at Rairee. *Ibid.* 174 Mau Rajah. **1776** *Trial of Joseph Fowke* 2/1, I went to Maha Rajah Nundocomar. **1859** Lang *Wand. Ind.* 38 The Maharajah with his suite appeared.

maharana (mɑːhəˈrɑːnə). [Hindi, f. *mahā* great + *rānā* (dial. var. of *rājā*) RAJA(H.] = MAHARAJA(H), *spec.* in the title of the Maharana of Udaipur.

1823 J. Malcolm *Mem. Cent. India* I. viii. 342 The old chief immediately unbuckled his sword, which..he laid at the feet of the Maha Rana... Maha Rana means Great Prince, the title by which the rulers of Odeypoor are always distinguished. **1876** L. Rousselet *India & Native Princes* xiv. 168 In my conversations with the Maharana I learnt several curious particulars concerning the fauna of the country. **1899** Kipling *From Sea to Sea* I. 65 To return.. to modern Udaipur... The Maharana and the Prime Minister..divide the power of the State. **1906** W. Crooke *Things Indian* 398 Udaypur, the greatest of all, who claims descent from the god Ráma, and has a pedigree dating back to 144 A.D., calls himself Mahárána. **1971** *Femina* (Bombay) 2 Apr. 65/2 A former palace of the Maharana of Udaipur, the Lake Palace Hotel is presently run by the Maharana himself.

‖**maharanee** (mɑːhəˈrɑːniː). Also **maharani**. [Hindī *mahārānī*, f. *mahā* great + *rānī* queen.] The wife of a maharajah.

1855 H. H. Wilson *Gloss. Judicial & Revenue Terms* 318/1 *Mahárání*,..the principal wife of a Rájá, or a queen in her own right: applied also in courtesy to Hindu ladies of rank, although not of princely dignity. **1862** Beveridge *Hist. India* III. viii. vi. 472 The maharajah was..childless. His wife, the maharanee, was..only twelve years of age. **1924** J. Buchan *Ld. Minto* x. 280 The Maharani sang Scots songs to him from behind the *purdah*. **1938** W. V. Grigson *Maria Gonds of Bustar* i. 3 The late Chief, Maharani Prafulla Kumari Devi, at her accession in 1924 was the last legitimate survivor of one of the most ancient royal families of southern India. **1971** R. Russell tr. *Ahmad's Shore & Wave* ix. 110 God knows how many maharanis' hearts he had conquered.

Maharashtri (mɑːhəˈrɑːʃtriː). Also **Maharastri** (-st-). [Skr. *Mahārāshṭrī* f. *Mahārāshṭra* Great Kingdom.] The Prakrit language of the Maharashtra region of India, the modern descendant of which is Marathi (Mahratti).

[**1803** H. T. Colebrooke in *Asiatick Researches* VII. 227 The Maháráshtra or Mahrátta is the language of a nation which has in the present century greatly enlarged its antient limits.] **1880** A. F. R. Hoernle *Compar. Gram. Gaudian Lang.* p. xviii, There are in reality only two varieties of Prákrit. One includes the Ṣaurasenī and the (so-called) Mahárásḥṭrí. **1900** R. B. Joshi *Comprehensive Marathi Gram.* i. 35 Our present Marathi is derived from the Maharashtri through the Apabransha form of that Prakrit language. **1903** *Indian Antiquary* XXXII. 189 It will be seen that Marâthî occupies exactly the same position within the modern Indo-Aryan vernaculars as Mâhârâshṭrî among the Prâkrits. **1968** *Encycl. Brit.* XVIII. 429/1 Later, Māhārāṣṭrī was especially used in composing lyric poetry, possibly on the basis of a popular oral lyric in the dialect; it began to flourish in the 3rd-4th centuries A.D.

Maharashtrian (mɑːhəˈrɑːʃtriən), *a.* and *sb.* Also **Mahrashtrian**. [f. *Maharashtra* a region of India + -IAN.] **A.** *adj.* Of, pertaining to, or characteristic of Maharashtra. **B.** *sb.* A native or inhabitant of Maharashtra. Cf. Maharashtri.

1957 *Ann. Reg. 1956* 103 Maharashtrian demonstrations took place outside Parliament House in Delhi. **1958** A. Toynbee *East to West* xxxii. 99 But how is one to dispose of a great city in which labour is Maharashtrian while capital is Gujerati? **1965** P. Robinson *Pakistani Agent* i. 8 Parulekar was a slightly-built Mahrashtrian in his late twenties. *Ibid.* viii. 106 The brassière, worn high in the Mahrashtrian style. **1969** *Capital* (Calcutta) 27 Feb. 358/1 In Bombay, the Shiv Sena, in its attempt to drive out all the non-Maharashtrians from the city, committed atrocities on them. **1969** *Enactment* (Delhi) Nov. 12/1 He is an 'invader' in Bombay just as the Maharashtrian is an 'invader' in Ahmedabad. **1971** *Hindustan Times Weekly Rev.* (New Delhi) 4 Apr. p. iv/5 A Maharashtrian girl married to a Saraswat..felt that 'marriage is mostly give and take'. **1971** *Femina* (Bombay) 30 Apr. 7/1, I was sitting and chatting with a group of friends, all of whom were Maharashtrians.

maharee, mahari, varr. MEHARI.

maharishi (mɑːhəˈriːʃɪ). Also 9 **Maharshi**. [Skr. *mahārshi*, f. *mahā* great + *ṛishi* inspired sage.] The title of a Hindu sage or holy man. Also in more general use: (the title of) a popular leader of spiritual thought or opinion. Cf. GURU.

1785 C. Wilkins tr. *Bhăgvăt-Gēētā* 144 *Māhārshēēs*, great saints, of whom there are reckoned seven, who were at the creation produced from the mind of Brāhmā. **1810** E. Moor *Hindu Pantheon* 94 The terms *Devarshi, Rajarshi, Maharshi*, are nearly synonymous with *Rishi*; meaning saint, deified saint, great saint, or great sage. **1855** H. H. Wilson *Gloss. Judicial & Revenue Terms* 318/1 Maharishi. **1966** C. F. Lutes in Mahesh Yogi *Sci. of Being* (rev. ed.) 13 It was in Madras, in 1958, that Maharishi founded the Spiritual Regeneration Movement. **1968** *Listener* 4 Jan. 8/1 The Dial Press..have published as 'A Brahmin Book' *McLuhan hot & cool*, the new 'critical symposium' on Maharishi McLuhan. **1970** K. Platt *Pushbutton Butterfly* (1971) ix. 107 Testimonials of faith and gratitude to Guru Maharishi Viparina. **1972** *Guardian* 1 Nov. 10/6 The Beatles..turned to the Maharishi, but he let them down.

mahaseer, -sur, variants of MAHSEER.

mahatma (məˈhætmə). [ad. Skr. *mahātman* 'great-souled', f. *mahā* great + *ātman* soul.]

1. In 'Esoteric Buddhism', one of a class of persons with preternatural powers, imagined to exist in India and Tibet.

1884 *Pall Mall G.* 19 Aug. 1/1 One of Madame Blavatsky's Mahatmas. **1855** *Daily News* 14 Feb. 5/2 Teacups are found by Mahatmas where no teacups should have been, unless they were either miraculously created or surreptitiously introduced. **1888** Mme. Blavatsky *Secr. Doctr.* II. 173 The Third Race had thus created the so-called Sons of Will and Yoga, or the 'ancestors'..of all the subsequent and present Arhats, or Mahatmas, in a truly immaculate way. **1909** [see HIGHER *a.* 2]. **1961** A. H. Nethercot *First Five Lives of Annie Besant* v. 295 (*heading*) The Chela of the Mahatmas.

2. (With capital initial.) A title indicative of love and respect conferred on revered persons in India; applied freq. to Mohandas Karamchand Gandhi (1869–1948).

1931 *Manch. Guardian* 11 Aug. 8/2 The great soul in the insignificant-looking body is the distinguishing mark of the Mahatma. **1948** C. Leslie *Goat to Kali* v. 203 His casual mention of great names convinced her that he was an intimate friend of them all: of the Mahatma, of Nehru, of Subhas Bose. **1949** H. N. Brailsford in H. S. L. Polak et al. *Mahatma Gandhi* viii. 96 On 9 January, 1915,..Gandhi landed in Bombay... Soon after..in a published letter, the poet Rabindranath Tagore conferred on him the title of 'Mahatma', of which the literal meaning is 'great soul'. It is the custom among Indians to bestow such distinctions on leaders whom they love and admire. *c* **1949** P. Yogananda *Autobiogr. Yogi* xliv. 352 Mr. Desai led us..to the writing-room where, cross-legged, sat Mahatma Gandhi... He never refers to himself as 'Mahatma'. He has made some humble, and witty, protests about the title. **1973** J. Ferguson *Politics of Love* iv. 104 This is why Mahatma Gandhi said 'If you Christians rely on soldiers for your safety, you are denying your own doctrine of the Cross.'

Mahayana (mɑːhəˈjɑːnə). [Skr. *mahāyāna*, f. *mahā* great + *yāna* vehicle.] The 'Great Vehicle', a name given to the more general form of Buddhism practised in northern Asia. Cf. Hinayana. Also *attrib.* So **Mahaˈyanian** *a.*, **Mahaˈyanism**, **Mahaˈyanist** *a.* and *sb.*, **Mahayaˈnistic** *a.*

1868 [see Hinayana]. **1883** Max Müller *India* iii. 87 The Northern conquerors..seem to have made a kind of compromise with Buddhism, and it is probably due to that compromise, or to an amalgamation of Saka legends with Buddhist doctrines, that we owe the so-called Mahâyâna form of Buddhism. **1891** W. W. Rockhill *Land of Lamas* 105 A curious perversion of the Mahāyānist doctrine of the *Kāyatraya*. **1907** [see Hinayana]. **1907** D. T. Suzuki *Outl. Mahayana Buddhism* 21 The idea is distinctly Mahayanistic. **1927** A. Huxley *Proper Stud.* v. 187 In the first century of our era..the Mahayana or Great Vehicle was created, and Buddhism became an entirely new religion. **1945, 1951** [see Hinayana]. **1956** A. Toynbee *Historian's Approach to Relig.* i. vii. 89 The Mahayanian Buddhists in China. **1961** J. Masters *Road past Mandalay* xiii. 162 They worshipped God according to the rites of the Mahayana and Hinayana. **1971** *Sun* (Ceylon) 17 Sept. 5/6 This impact of Japan and Mahayana Buddhism on him opened a further avenue for his missionary zeal. **1973** *Times* 14 Apr. (Nepal Suppl.) p. ii/3 Although several early statues of the historic Buddha Sākyamuni survive, the favourite motifs of Mahāyāna art were the five Celestial or Dhyāni Buddhas and the Bodhisattvas, whose images became the centres of devotional cults.

mahayme, obs. form of MAIM.

‖**Mahdi** (ˈmɑːdɪ). Also 9 **mohdi, mahadi, -dee, mehdi, mehdee**. [Arab. *mahdīy*, lit. 'he who is guided aright', passive pple. of *hadā* to lead in the right way.] A spiritual and temporal leader expected by the Muslims to appear in the latter days. In recent use chiefly applied to certain insurrectionary leaders in the Sudan from about 1880, who are alleged to have claimed to be the predicted 'Mahdi'.

1800 *Asiat. Ann. Reg., Misc. Tr.* 125/1 Mahommed, who was proclaimed Khalif at Medina in the year of the Hejira 145, and who assumed the title of Mohdi or Mahadi. **1803** T. Winterbottom *Sierra Leone* I. xiv. 246 Some years ago a celebrated impostor, who called himself Mahadee,..made his appearance among the Soosoos and Mandingos. **1868** J. P. Brown *Dervishes* ii. 74 It is from among the descendants of 'Alee that the more devout Moslems expect the Mehdee. **1885** *Times* 20 Mar. 5/5 The desert Arabs state that a new Mahdi has appeared in Kordofan.

Hence **ˈMahdiship**, the dignity or position of a Mahdi; **ˈMahdism, ˈMahdi-ism**, the rebel movements in the Sudan about 1880–1885, and subsequently, under leaders claiming to be the Mahdi; **ˈMahdian, ˈMahdist, ˈMahdi-ist**, an adherent of a pretended Mahdi.

1884 *19th Cent.* May 816 The impostor who has..laid claim to the Mahdiship. **1884** *Times* (weekly ed.) 29 Aug. 1 Mâhdism is essentially a Shiya doctrine. **1885** *Pall Mall G.* 10 June 3/1 Mahdi-ism is in his eyes a real danger. **1885** *Daily Tel.* 19 Feb. 5/2 A demonstration..was..made against Metemneh, in order to draw the Mahdists off. **1885** *Ibid.* 21 Mar. 5/1 No hardy Mahdian got nearer than twenty yards. **1891** *Daily News* 18 Dec. 6/1 The invasion of Egypt by the Mahdiists in August, 1889. **1897** *Ibid.* 22 Sept. 6/4 Gordon, and Sir Samuel Baker..were even more responsible for the rise of Soudanese Mahdism than the Mahdi himself.

mahe, mahem, obs. ff. MAW *sb.*[1], MAIM.

mahen, maheym, obs. ff. MAY *v.*, MAIM.

mahiz, obs. form of MAIZE.

mah jong, mah-jong (mɑː ˈdʒɒŋ). Also **mah jongg, mah jongh**, etc., and as one word. [Chinese *ma-ch'iao* (Shanghai dial. *-tsiang*) sparrows (f. *ma* hemp + *tsiang* small birds), the name of the game.] An old Chinese game resembling certain card games, introduced into Europe and America in the early 1920s. The 136 or 144 pieces used in the game are known as tiles, and they are divided into five or six suits. The object of the players, usually four in number, is to build a hand containing four sets of three tiles and a pair. Also *attrib.*

1922 R. E. Lindsell (*title*) Ma-Cheuk or Mah-Jongg. **1923** Chiang Lee *Mah Jong* 7 Mah Jong, or Mah Tsiong (Sparrows), as it is pronounced in the city of Ning Po where it received its name and modern form, has been in vogue in China as a card game for about eight centuries. **1923** *Daily Mail* 23 June 6 There will be..demonstrations of Mah Jongg, the wonderful Chinese game which threatens to oust Bridge. **1923** Joyce *Let.* 2 Nov. (1966) III. 82, I have prepared a nice intricate Mah Jongg puzzle for myself. **1931** *Times Lit. Suppl.* 7 May 365/2 Particularly interesting are his snapshots of modern China's methods of civil warfare (hireling warriors firing harmless fusillades in the intervals of their mah jongh). **1963** J. Kirkup *Tropic Temper* 63 Two old men were playing mah-jong. **1967** *Guardian* 16 Aug. 6/6 Following the traditional 'Cleansing of the Tiles' the North Cotswold Mah-Jongg Canton started another session last Wednesday at their Stow-on-the-Wold tryst. **1967** D. & E. T. Riesman *Conversations in Japan* 116 The favourite pre-war game, mah-jongg, still popular with many. **1971** K. Hopkins *Hong Kong* 246 The interests of these 'unions' centre on..mahjong. **1972** *Straits Times* (Malaysian ed.) 22 Nov. 21/7 The $10,000 hold-up of mahjong players at the Keong Kee sawmill's recreation club.

Hence **mah jong** *v. intr.*, to complete one's hand at the game of mah jong.

1923 J. Bray *How to play Mah Jong* 12 Each player in turn draws a tile and discards one in place of this until some player completes his hand; i.e. 'Mah Jongs'. *Ibid.* 21 None of the following tiles in the hand assist so far in Mah Jonging (completing the hand)..and may be discarded. **1924** M. C. Work *Mah-Jongg Up-to-Date* i. 32 The Chinese word 'Woo' (meaning peace) has been extensively used by many American writers in the same sense as it is used by Chinese players; viz., to Mah-Jongg, to win the game, to go out. **1933** E. Talbot *Mah-Jong made Easy* 31 Sometimes a player collects tiles that will give a small mah-jong to oneself and discards those of high value that give another player the opportunity of making a big hand, even if he does not mah-jong. **1966** 'Han Suyin' *Mortal Flower* i. 24 Everyone.. shopping, tea-ing, mahjonging or donkey-riding.

Mahlerian (mɑːˈlɪərɪən), *a.* and *sb.* [-IAN.] **A.** *adj.* Of, pertaining to, or characteristic of the Austrian composer Gustav Mahler (1860–1911) or his music. **B.** *sb.* An admirer or adherent of Mahler; an exponent of Mahler's music. Also **ˈMahlerish** *a.*, resembling the classical-romantic style of Mahler; **ˈMahlerite** *sb.* = Mahlerian *sb.*

1947 D. Newlin *Bruckner, Mahler, Schoenberg* v. 130 The typically Mahlerian direction..sets the stage for a mysterious march-like beginning, likewise typically Mahlerian. **1948** *Penguin Music Mag.* VI. 132, I am no ardent Mahlerite. **1959** *Listener* 27 Aug. 333/2 He [*sc.* a conductor] was a great Mahlerian. *Ibid.* 10 Dec. 1052/3 Almost a Mahlerish work. **1962** *Times* 2 Feb. 13/2 Mahlerites are likely to owe their allegiance to the prewar gramophone records conducted by Dr. Bruno Walter. **1962** *Listener* 25 Oct. 695/1 We hear an eclectic, youthful style penetrated by what we recognize as the unmistakable and emerging Mahlerian voice. **1963** *Times* 7 Mar. 8/3 Emotionally the music lacks the concentrated intensity of anguish to win it Mahlerian popularity. **1971** *Guardian* 17 Apr. 8/1 Does he then consider that composer's [*sc.* Shostakovitch's] expiatory fifth symphony better music than his weird Mahlerian fourth? **1974** *Times* 18 Apr. 7/7 Blaukopf has heeded the lesson and his essay has a proper Mahlerian sharpness to it.

mahlstick, variant of MAULSTICK.

mahlstrom, Ger. form of MAELSTROM.

‖**mahˈmudi**. *Obs.* Also 7 **mammothee, mamudee, mahomedee, mamoodo, mammo(o)da, mam(m)oodee, mahmoudi, -y**, 7–8 **mamooda**, 8 **mahmoodee, mahmudie, mahmoude**. [Pers. *maḥmūdī*, f. the name of Shah *Maḥmūd*.] A Persian money of account, orig. a silver coin of the approximate value of twelve pence. Also, a gold coin formerly circulating in India.

1612 R. Coverte *True Rep.* etc. 34 A Mammothee..being nine pence English. **1625** Purchas *Pilgrims* I. 523 Their moneyes in Persia of Siluer, are the Abacee, the Mahomedee [etc.]. **1687** A. Lovell tr. *Thevenot's Trav.* ii. 63 An Abassi and a Mahmoudi, which is asmuch as a Chai, and a Para. *Ibid.* iii. 18 There is also a Mogole Silver-Coin, called

Mahmoudy, which is worth about eleven Sols and a half. **1783** GLADWIN *Ayeen Akbery* I. 17 The Mahmoodee and Mozuffery of Guzerat and Malwah. **1797** *Encycl. Brit.* (ed. 3) XIV. 176/1 An abassee is worth two mahmoudes. **1878** *Note* in *Hawkins' Voy.* (Hakluyt Soc.) 407 The Mahmudi was a gold coin of Gujrát.

Maho, variant of MAHU. *Obs.*

‖**mahoe**[1] (məˈhəʊ). *Bot.* Also 7–8 **mahot, maho,** 8 **moho,** 9 **mohoe, mohaul, mohaut.** [Carib *mahou*; the early spelling *mahot* is Fr.]

1. The name of several trees. (Also ***mahoe-tree***.) **a.** A sterculiaceous tree or large shrub (*Sterculia caribæa*), a native of the West Indies. **b.** A malvaceous shrub or tree (*Paritium tiliaceum* and *P. elatum*), with a wide range through tropical countries. **c.** Applied with qualifications to similar plants of various genera. (See quot. 1866.)

1666 J. DAVIES *Hist. Carib. Isl.* I. viii. 49 [tr. Rochefort 1658] Of the Tree called Mahot there are two kinds, Mahot-franc, and Mahot d'herbe. **1671** OGILBY *America* 348 The Mahot-Tree, of the Bark of which are made Laces and Points. **1697** DAMPIER *Voy.* (1729) I. iii. 37 They make their Lines both for fishing and striking with the Bark of Maho. **1756** P. BROWNE *Jamaica* 284 The Mountain Mohoe.. grows to a considerable size,.. and is generally reckoned an excellent timber-tree. **1774** GOLDSM. *Nat. Hist.* (1824) III. 162 Having fed upon the flowers of the mahot..it [the iguana] goes to repose upon the branches of the trees. **1838** *Penny Cycl.* XII. 193/1 In the West Indies the whips with which the slaves are lashed are made from the fibres of *H[ibiscus] arboreus* (mohoe or mohaul). **1845** LINDLEY *Veg. Kingd.* (1846) 369 The plant [*sc.* Hibiscus] is called Mohoe or Mohaut. **1866** *Treas. Bot.* 711/1 Mahoe, blue or common, *Paritium elatum*. —, bombast, *Ochroma Lagopus*. —, Congo, *Hibiscus clypeatus*. —, grey or mountain, *Paritium elatum*. —, seaside, *Thespesia populnea*.

2. The wood or the fibre of some of these trees.

1897 *Daily News* 10 Mar. 6/3 In rods alone there was an almost endless variety, whether of built cane,.. blue mahoe, ..or any other material.

3. *attrib.*, as ***mahoe bush***; **mahoe-piment**, *Daphnopsis caribæa* (Grisebach *Flora W. Ind.* 1864, p. 785).

1827 ROBERTS *Voy. Centr. Amer.* 127 Some of the very low land is covered with water..producing only rank coarse grass and Mohoe bushes.

‖**mahoe**[2] (ˈmɑːhɔe, məˈhəʊɪ). [Maori.] The New Zealand Whitewood-tree, *Melicytus ramiflorus*

1835 W. YATE *Acc. N. Zealand* (ed. 2) 49 Mahoe (*Melicytus ramiflorus*)..grows to a height of not more than fifty feet. **1866** *Treas. Bot.* s.v. *Melicytus*, M. *ramiflorus* is the Mahoë of the New Zealanders, which must not be confounded with the Mahoe of the West Indies.

†**maˈhoganite.** *slang. Obs.* [f. MAHOGANY + -ITE.] (See quot.)

1825 *Sporting Mag.* XVI. 9 *note*, A mahoganite is one who rides at a most infernal pace about the introduction of the second bottle..with his knees under any semicircular mahogany fire table.

mahoganize (məˈhɒgənaɪz), *v. U.S.* Also mahoganyize. [f. MAHOGANY + -IZE.] *trans.* (See quot.)

1848–59 BARTLETT *Dict. Amer.*, *Mahoganyize*, to paint wood in imitation of mahogany. **1855** OGILVIE, *Mahoganize*. (American.)

mahogany (məˈhɒgənɪ). Also 7 **mohogeney,** 8 **mohog(g)ony, mahogena, mahogon(e)y.** [Written *mohogeney* in 1671; of unknown origin. The Eng. word was adopted into botanical Latin by Linnæus (1762) as *mahagoni*, and is prob. the source of the continental forms: F. *mahagoni*, *mohogon* (rare), It. *mogano* (*mogogane*, *mogogon*, etc.), Pg. *mogno*, G. *mahagoni*, Du. *mahonie*, Sw. *mahogny*, Da. *mahogni*.

The statement that the word is Carib is founded on a misreading by Von Martius: see J. Platt, Jr. in *N. & Q.* 9th Ser. VIII. 201. The only known name in the Carib language is *caoba*, which has been adopted in Sp.]

1. a. The wood of *Swietenia Mahagoni* (N.O. *Cedrelaceæ*), a tree indigenous to the tropical parts of America, esp. Mexico, Central America, and the West Indies. It varies in colour from yellow to a rich red brown, is remarkably hard and fine-grained, and takes a high polish. Also with qualification denoting the special variety or place of origin, as ***baywood, Cuba, Honduras, Jamaica, Spanish mahogany***.

1671 OGILBY *America* 338 Here [in Jamaica] are..the most curious and rich sorts of Woods, as Cedar, Mohogeney, Lignum-vitæ, Ebony [etc.]. **1703** *Lond. Gaz.* No. 3891/3 On Wednesday.., will be..exposed to Publick Sale.., the Cargo of the Galeon called the Tauro.., consisting of..Cocoa,..Brazelletto, Mohogony. **1733** BRAMSTON *Man of Taste* 15 Say thou that do'st thy father's table praise, Was there Mahogena in former days? *a* **1746** T. WARTON *Poems* (1748) 109 Odious! upon a walnut-plank to dine! No—the red-vein'd Mohoggony be mine! **1817** BYRON *Beppo* lxx, He was a Turk, the colour of mahogany. **1842** GWILT *Archit.* (1859) 487 The variety called Spanish Mahogany, and imported from Cuba, Jamaica, Hispaniola, and other West India islands [etc.]. *Ibid.* 996 The Jamaica mahogany is the hardest and most beautiful. **1860** JEAFFRESON *Bk. about Drs.* I. 185 He [Gibbons] brought into domestic use the mahogany with which one has so many pleasant associations. **1875** *Carpentry & Join.* 15 Oak, teak, and mahogany should find a place in the workshop more often than they do, the mahogany being what is often called cedar, to distinguish it from the very hard Spanish wood. The softer and more common kind is from Honduras. **1892** *Mod. Trade Circular*, Mahogany, Mexican, 5*d* to 6*d*. per foot, superficial. Do., Tobasco, 5½*d*. to 7*d*. per foot, superficial.

b. The tree itself.

1759 MILLER *Gard. Dict.* (ed. 7) s.v. *Cedrus*. The second Sort is the Mahogony, whose Wood is now well known in England. **1846** LINDLEY *Veg. Kingd.* 462 The bark..of Mahogany (*Swietenia Mahagoni*) is also accounted febrifugal.

2. *transf.* Applied, chiefly with qualification, to various woods resembling mahogany, and to the trees producing them. In Australia mainly used for various species of *Eucalyptus*, esp. the Jarrah (*E. marginata*), and for *Tristania conferta* (N.O. *Myrtaceæ*): see Morris *Austral Eng.* (1898) 278–9.

African mahogany, *Khaya Senegalensis*; **bastard mahogany**, *Matayba* (*Ratonia*) *apetala*; also *Eucalyptus botryoides* and *E. marginata*; **East India mahogany**, *Soymida febrifuga*; **forest mahogany**, *Eucalyptus resinifera* and *E. microcorys*; **Indian mahogany**, *Cedrela Toona*; **Madeira mahogany**, *Persea indica* (see MADEIRA[1] 1); **mountain mahogany**, *Betula lenta* and *Cerco-carpus ledifolius*; **red mahogany**, *Eucalyptus resinifera*; **swamp mahogany**, *Eucalyptus robusta* and *E. botryoides*; **white mahogany**, (in Jamaica) *Stenostomum bifurcatum*; (in Australia) *Eucalyptus robusta*; also *E. pilularis*. (See *Treas. Bot.* 1866.)

1842 *Penny Cycl.* XXIII. 404/2 *S[wietenia] Senegalensis* has also been formed into a new genus, Khaya, and is the tree yielding African mahogany. **1846** STOKES *Discov. Australia* II. iv. 132 Mahogany—Jarrail—Eucalyptus—grows on white sandy land. **1884** *Pall Mall G.* 22 Aug. 3/1 The main saloon is finished in white mahogany throughout.

3. *colloq.* **a.** A table, esp. a dining-table.

1840 DICKENS *Old C. Shop* lxvi, I had hoped..to have seen you three gentlemen..with your legs under the mahogany in my humble parlour. **1846** THACKERAY *Bk. Snobs* xxxi, Other families did not welcome us to their mahogany. **1848** —— *Van. Fair* xiii, George was going..to bring the supply question on the mahogany. **1850** *Florists' Jrnl.* 149 Nearly forty gathered round Mr. Lidgard's mahogany after the exhibition. **1891** MRS. WALFORD *Mischief of Monica* III. 90, I could have put my feet under his mahogany..with the very greatest satisfaction.

b. = BAR *sb.*[1] 28.

1936 N. COLLINS *Trinity Town* i. 18 From the moment Mr. Primrose appeared behind his own mahogany and superseded the barmaid, he dominated everything. **1955** *Punch* 4 May 557/1 Every interval sees twenty orchestral players with their elbows on the mahogany and off-duty singers in full fig on high stools being selectively sweet about their rivals.

4. *slang* and *dial.* **a.** A Cornish beverage compounded of gin and treacle. **b.** A strong mixture of brandy and water.

1791 BOSWELL *Johnson* an. 1781, 30 Mar., They [the Cornish fishermen] call it Mahogany; and it is made of two parts gin and one part treacle well beaten together. **1816** 'QUIZ' *Grand Master* II. 54 *note*, It is believed that drinking mahogany (a strong description of brandy pauny) is the best preventive against the sun's heat. The remedy is in general repute in Bombay. **1823** T. BOND *Hist. E. & W. Looe* 82 *note*, At a trial at the Cornish Assizes some years ago, a witness..puzzled his lordship and the council, by telling them he was..'eating Fair maids and drinking Mahogany'. **1852** C. J. MATHEWS *Little Toddlekins* 20 *Capt. Littlepop.* I've been obliged to..diet myself on stiff brandy and water. *Brownsmith.* Mahogany? I have got some,..black as coffee, strong as mustard.

5. A kind of moth, *Noctua tetra*.

1819 G. SAMOUELLE *Entomol. Compend.* 370 *Noctua tetra*, the Mahogany.

6. *attrib.* and *quasi-adj.* **a.** Made of mahogany.

1730 W. WARREN *Collectanea* in Willis & Clark *Cambridge* (1886) I. 225 Mohogany window Seats: A Marble Table for yᵉ Side-board on a Mohogany Stand. **1763** *Museum Rusticum* (ed. 2) I. 179 The world of England has been, for some years past, running mad after mahogany furniture. **1773** GOLDSM. *Stoops to Conq.* IV, Then there's a mahogany table. **1864** SALA *Quite Alone* I. v. 75 In a recess were three handsome mahogany desks. **1885** R. BUCHANAN *Annan Water* ix, At one side of the room stood a large mahogany bed.

b. Of the colour of polished mahogany, reddish-brown. Also *absol.*

1737 W. SALMON *Country Builder's Estim.* (ed. 2) 101 Chocolate-Colour, Mahogony-Colour, Cedar and Walnut-tree-Colour. **1751** SMOLLETT *Per. Pic.* II. lxix, Their natural colour..degenerated into a mahogany tint. **1761** *Brit. Mag.* II. 44/2 To stain Wood of a Mahogony Colour. **1823** *Spirit Publ. Jrnls.* (1825) 292 Molly Lowe, suffused with mahogany blushes. **1834** *Tait's Mag.* I. 384/1 His testy temper and mahogany complexion obtained him credit for being an American. **1839** tr. *Lamartine's Trav. East* 103/1 Their legs and hands were..painted a mahogany colour. **1855** DICKENS *Dorrit* I. xxiv, Travelling people usually get more or less mahogany. **1893** STEVENSON *Catriona* 359 We saw he was a big fellow with a mahogany face.

7. *attrib.* and *Comb.*: simple attrib., as ***mahogany-dust, -plank, -trade, -wood; mahogany-brown, -red*** adjs.; parasynthetic, as ***mahogany-coloured, -faced*** adjs. Also **mahogany birch** *U.S.*, *Betula lenta*; **mahogany cutter**, a workman employed in felling and trimming mahogany; **mahogany flat** *slang*, a bed-bug; **mahogany gum**, *Australian*, the jarrah; **mahogany scrub**, *Australian*, a tract thickly covered with 'mahogany' or jarrah trees; **mahogany tree**, (*a*) the *Swietenia Mahagoni*, or any of the trees to which the name is transferred (see 2); (*b*) *jocularly*, a dining table.

1813 H. MUHLENBERG *Catal. Plant.* 88 *Betula lenta*..soft birch,..black birch,..sweet birch,..or *mahogany birch. **1908** N. L. BRITTON *N. Amer. Trees* 256 The cherry birch, or Black birch,..is also called Sweet birch and Mahogany birch. **1850** CHALONER & FLEMING *Mahogany Tree* 42, 1st of April, when the *Mahogany Cutters' harvest may be said to commence. **1875** *Carpentry & Join.* 79 By *mahogany dust and glue a nail hole may be partially hidden. **1864** HOTTEN *Slang Dict.* 176 **Mahogany flat*, a bug. **1942** BERREY & VAN DEN BARK *Amer. Thes. Slang* § 120/60 *Bedbugs*,..flats, mahogany flats. **1952** *New Biol.* XIII. 86 The abdomen [of the bed-bug] when empty is flat (hence the name 'mahogany flat'). **1959** SOUTHWOOD & LESTON *Land & Water Bugs* 188 Bedbug. Also known as 'wall lice', 'mahogany flats' and 'crimson ramblers' these insects have been carried all round the world. **1967** B. J. BANFILL *Pioneer Nurse* v. 61 Until two months ago we had only a log shanty. Somehow the Mahogany Flats took over and we had to burn it. **1739** *Will* in Payne *Eng. Cath.* (1889) 53 My coffin to be of *mahogany plank. **1843** PORTLOCK *Geol.* 513 The paste,..is of a dark red, frequently *mahogany-red, felspar. **1846** STOKES *Discov. Australia* II. vi. 231 Part of our road lay through a thick *mahogany scrub. **1850** CHALONER & FLEMING *Mahogany Tree* Pref., The promotion of the interests of the *Mahogany trade. **1747** MORTIMER in *Phil. Trans.* XLIV. 599 He begins this Set with the *Mahogony-Tree. **1847** THACKERAY *Mahogany Tree* i, Little we fear Weather without, Sheltered about The Mahogany Tree. **1875** T. LASLETT *Timber & Timber Trees* 189 The Jarrah or Mahogany tree..is also found in Western Australia. **1703** *Lond. Gaz.* No. 3891/3 On Wednesday.., will be exposed to Publick Sale Goods..consisting of..Nicaragua and *Mohogony Wood,..&c.

mahoganyize: see MAHOGANIZE.

†**mahoitre.** *Obs.* [ad. OF. *mahustre*, *-hoitre*, *-heutre*.] A padding placed in the upper part of the sleeve of a garment for the purpose of increasing the apparent breadth of the shoulders.

1834 PLANCHÉ *Brit. Costume* 201 The shoulders were padded out with large waddings called mahoitres. **1860** FAIRHOLT *Costume* (ed. 2) Gloss., *Mahoitre*,..the wadded and upraised shoulders in fashion during the fifteenth and sixteenth centuries.

†**mahomery.** *Obs.* In 4 **mameri,** 5 **mahom(m)erye.** [a. OF. *mahomerie*, f. *Mahom* MAHOUND.] A mosque.

c **1320** *Sir Beues* 1350 Aboute þe time of middai Out of a mameri a sai Sarasins come gret foisoun, þat hadde anoured here Mahoun. **1481** CAXTON *Godfrey* civ. 157 Our barons had aduysed to make a grete fortresse..in a mahommerye that the turkes had. *Ibid.* cvi. 162 Oute of theyr graues in the mahomerye.

Mahomet (məˈhɒmɪt; in verse occas. ˈmeɪhəʊmɛt). Forms: 4 **Macamethe,** 4–5 **Machamete, Mac-, Makomete, Makametc,** 4 6 **Machomete,** 5–6 **Machomet,** 6 **Machamyte, Macomit(e, -yt(e, Mahomet(t)e, -ite,** 6–7 **Mahumet,** 6– **Mahomet.** See also MAHOUND, MAUMET. [Cf. F. *Mahomet*, med.L. *Machometus*, *Mahumetus*, *Mahometus*.]

1. The popular rendering of the Arabic name *Muḥammad*, borne by the founder of the religion of Islam (*died* 632). In literary use superseded by the more correct form MOHAMMED, and more recently MUHAMMAD.

c **1380** WYCLIF *Wks.* (1880) 301 þe secte of macamethe. *c* **1380** —— *Sel. Wks.* III. 364 Alȝif þe fende..medle good wiþ þe yvel; for þus dide Machamete in his lawe. *c* **1386** CHAUCER *Man of Law's T.* 235 The hooly lawes of oure Alkaron, Yeuen by goddes message Makomete [*v.r.* Makamete]. *Ibid.* 238 Makometes lawe [*v.r.* Macometis]. **1387** TREVISA *Higden* (Rolls) I. 33 þe fifte leuynge [L. *ritus*] of Sarazynes bygan vndir Makomete [**1432–50** Machomete]. *c* **1400** MAUNDEV. (1839) xii. 131 Alkaron..the whiche Book Machamete toke hem. *Ibid.* 135 Machomet. **1547** BOORDE *Introd. Knowl.* xxxvii. (1870) 214, I am a Turk, and Machamytes law do kepe. [Also: Macomyt(e, -it(e.] **1600** J. PORY tr. *Leo's Africa* III. 151 Mahumets law affirmeth all kinde of diuinations to be vaine. **1625** BACON *Ess.*, *Of Boldness* (Arb.) 519 If the Hill will not come to Mahomet, Mahomet wil go to the hil. **1678** BUTLER *Hud.* III. ii. 605 To hang, like Mah'met in the air, Or St. Ignatius, at his prayer. **1821** SHELLEY *Hellas* 221 The moon of Mahomet Arose, and it shall set. **1881** SIR W. HUNTER in *Encycl. Brit.* XII. 792/1 Muhammad commonly known as Mahomet.

†**2.** A quasi-deity. *Obs. rare*$^{-1}$.

1553 EDEN *Treat. Newe Ind.* (Arb.) 25 Whom they honoure & reuerence as a great God & mighti Mahumet.

†**3.** An idol. *Obs.* (Cf. MAUMET.)

[*c* **1205** etc.: see MAUMET.] ? *a* **1500** *Chester Pl.* x. 285 For Mahometis, both one and all, that men of Egipt Gods can call, at your coming downe shall fall. *c* **1530** LD. BERNERS *Arth. Lyt. Bryt.* (1814) 147 At the laste..Arthur founde two ymages of coper..and whan Arthur sawe them, he toke his swerde in his hande, & layde on with all his myght on these mahomettes. **1553** BECON *Reliques of Rome* (1563) 88 Afterwarde thys doung-hel of Idolatry..set vp agayne her Idoles and mahomets. *Ibid.* 93* Brought into our Churche Idolles and Mahomettes.

†**4.** = MAHOMETAN, MUHAMMADAN. *Obs.* (Cf. MAHOMITE.)

1508 KENNEDIE *Flyting w. Dunbar* 526 Sarazene, symonyte,..Mahomete, manesuorne. **1533** GAU *Richt Vay* (1888) 105 The machometis and the turkis, the iowis and oder infidelis. **1601** W. PARRY *Trav. Sir A. Sherley* 10 They are damned Infidels and Zodomiticall Mahomets. **1747** *Mem. Nutrebian Crt.* II. 197 From all parts of the

neighbouring kingdom had drawn mahomets, coptics, and idolaters.

5. A kind of pigeon. ? *Obs.*

[So called in allusion to the story that Muhammad had a pigeon which used to peck corn out of his ear, in order to make his followers believe that he received communication from the Holy Ghost in the form of a dove.]

[**1678**: see MAUMET.] **1735** J. MOORE *Columbarium* 51 *Columba Numidica Alba.* The Mahomet. This Pigeon is no more in Reality than a white Barb. **1765** *Treat. Dom. Pigeons* 141 It is the opinion of many fanciers, that the Bird called a mahomet is nearly of a cream colour.

Mahometan (mə'hɒmɪtən), *a.* and *sb.* Also 6 **Machometan, Machumetan,** 7–8 **Mahumetan(e,** 6– **Mahometan.** [ad. med.L. *Machometān-us, Mahometānus*, f. *Machumetus, Mahometus*: see prec. Cf. F. *mahométain.*]

A. *adj.* **1.** = MUHAMMADAN *a.*

1600 J. PORY tr. *Leo's Africa* I. 10 The Mahumetan priestes alwaies forbad the Arabians to passe over Nilus with their armies. *Ibid.* III. 165 No Mahumetan king or prince may weare a crowne. **1714** *Spect.* No. 631 ⁋ 7 The Jewish Law, (and the Mahometan, which in some things copies after it) is filled with Bathings..and other Rites. **1777** WATSON *Philip II* (1839) 161 Putting to death..all the priests and other Christians who refused to embrace the Mahometan religion. **1850** ROBERTSON *Serm.* Ser. III. ii. (1872) 25 The anticipated rewards and punishments must be of a Mahometan character.

†**2.** = TURKISH. *Obs.*

1600 R. CARR (*title*) The Mahumetane or Turkish Historie, in three Bookes.

B. *sb.* A MUHAMMADAN.

1529 MORE *Dyaloge* IV. Wks. 260/1 The Machometanys beyng a sensual sect, dyd in fewe yeres draw the great part of the world vnto it. **1600** J. PORY tr. *Leo's Africa* III. 160 In old Fez neither gold nor siluer is coined, nor any Mahumetans are suffered to be goldsmiths. **1727–41** CHAMBERS *Cycl.* s.v. *Mahometanism*, The Mahometans account all such as own anything of number in the divinity, to be infidels or idolaters. **1841** ELPHINSTONE *Hist. Ind.* I. 147 It is these three descriptions of persons, together with others who have risen under the Mahometans [etc.].

Hence †**Mahome'tanical** *a.* = MUHAMMADAN *a.*; **Ma'hometanize** *v. trans.*, to convert to Muhammadanism.

1632 LITHGOW *Trav.* IV. 147 The Alcoran,..whereupon dependeth the whole Mahometanicall Law. **1779** SWINBURNE *Trav. Spain* xliv. 419, I am inclined to suspect that our old structures have been new-named, and Mahometanised without sufficient proof of their Arabic origin.

Mahometanism (mə'hɒmɪtənɪz(ə)m). Also 7 **Mahumetanism.** [f. MAHOMETAN + -ISM. Cf. F. *mahométanisme.*] = MUHAMMADANISM.

1612 BREREWOOD *Lang. & Relig.* x. 83 In Africk, all the regions in a manner, that Christian religion had gained from idolatry, Mahumetanism hath regained from Christianity. **1632** LITHGOW *Trav.* IV. 144 They were..initiated in Mahometanisme. **1756–7** tr. *Keysler's Trav.* (1760) I. 103 Even Mahometanism was preferable to Calvinism. **1840** CARLYLE *Heroes* (1853) 216 Mahometanism among the Arabs.

†**Ma'hometant.** *rare*$^{-1}$. Corrupt form of MAHOMETAN, after sbs. in -ANT. = MUHAMMADAN. So †**Ma'hometantism** (also *Mahu-*) = MUHAMMADANISM.

1635 PAGITT *Christianogr.* I. ii. (1636) 46 The Mahometants have but three Temples or Meskites. **1656** BLOUNT *Glossogr.*, *Mahumetism*, or *Mahumetantism*, the Religion and profession of Mahumet and the great Turk.

†**Mahometic,** *a. Obs. rare.* Also 7 **Mahumetic.** [a. med.L. *mahometic-us*, f. *Mahomet-us.* Cf. OF. *mahométique.*] Muslim.

1585 T. WASHINGTON tr. *Nicholay's Voy.* 165 Doctours of the lawe Mahometicke. **1648–99** J. BEAUMONT *Psyche* XVII. xii. (Grosart) II. 96 The Land of Milk and Honey lay.. overflown With Mahumetick Poison.

†**Maho'metical,** *a. Obs.* [f. med.L. *mahometic-us* (see prec.) + -AL¹.] = prec.

1561 DAUS tr. *Bullinger on Apoc.* (1573) 126 The Papisticall and Mahometicall conception, wickednes and tyranny. **1601** R. JOHNSON *Kingd. & Commw.* (1603) 227 The slaughter of the Moores by the Christians spoken of in their Mahometicall legend. **1647** FARINGDON *Serm.* iv. 72 A Mahometical Paradise of all sensual delights. **1713** *Gentl. Instr.* III. viii. (ed. 5) 435 Those Obscenities that make up here the Mahometical Elysium of Libertines.

†**Mahome'tician.** *Obs.* [f. MAHOMET: see -ICIAN. Cf. OF. *mahommeticien.*] A MUHAMMADAN.

1588 J. HARVEY *Disc. Probl.* 49 There continue euen to this day..certaine furious creatures, or mad rauing wizardes amongst the Mahometicians.

†**Mahometish,** *a. Obs. rare*$^{-1}$. [f. MAHOMET + -ISH.] = MUHAMMADAN *a.*

1583 STOCKER *Civ. Warres Lowe C.* II. 42 a, To the ende the Mahometishe and Jeweshe religion, myght not any way derogate from the Catholique Religion.

†**Ma'hometism.** *Obs.* Also 6–7 **Mahumetism(e, Mahumatism.** [f. MAHOMET + -ISM.] = MUHAMMADANISM.

1597 BEARD *Theatre God's Judgem.* (1612) 158 Their detestable Mahumetisme and Turkish religion. **1600** W. WATSON *Decacordon* (1602) 301 This is right Mahumetisme, and tendeth to the ouerthrow of the Gospel and church Catholike. **1615** G. SANDYS *Trav.* 59 Mahometisme had not yet vtterly extinguished all good literature. **1715** J. CHAPPELOW *Rt. way Rich* (1717) 164 Far more frightful.. than popery, slavery, mahometism, or the devil himself. **1793** TRAPP tr. *Rochon's Voy. Madagascar* 48 It is surprising that Mahometism should not have made more progress in this island.

†**Ma'hometist.** *Obs.* Also 6 **Machumetiste, -hometiste,** 6–7 **Mahumetist,** 7 **Mohammetist, Mahumatist.** [f. MAHOMET + -IST.] A MUHAMMADAN.

1553 EDEN *Treat. Newe Ind.* (Arb.) 27 Amonge certayne Mahumetistes are found a few Christian men. **1555** —— *Decades* 226 If they had byn Moores (that is Machumetistes). **1594** BLUNDEVIL *Exerc.* v. viii. (1636) 549 Now as touching their religion they be Mahometists. **1602** FULBECKE *1st Pt. Parall.* Introd. 21 The Portugallians make villaines of the Mahometistes. **1603** FLORIO *Montaigne* II. xxix. (1632) 398 The Assassines..are esteemed among the Mahometists of a soveraigne devotion and puritie of manners. **1650** BULWER *Anthropomet.* 205 They educate them very delicately, and afterwards sell them to the Persians and other Mahumatists. **1654** VILVAIN *Epit. Ess.* III. 37 Christians, Mahometists.

†**Ma'hometize,** *v. Obs.* Forms: see MAHOMET; also **Mahemat-, Mehemetize.** [f. MAHOMET + -IZE.] **a.** *trans.* To convert to Muhammadanism. **b.** *intr.* To act like a Muslim.

1585 T. WASHINGTON tr. *Nicholay's Voy.* I. viii. 8 The most part..are Christians renied, or Mahumetised. *Ibid.* II. xxi. 58 In Constantinople as also in all the other cities Mahematised in Græcia. **1656** H. MORE *Enthus. Tri.* 22 Though born a Christian, yet he did Mahomitise [*ed.* 1712 Mahometize] in this that he also did indulge plurality of wives.

Hence †**Ma'hometized** *ppl. a.*

1585 T. WASHINGTON tr. *Nicholay's Voy.* II. xxi. 59 The Turks, Moors, and generally al the Mehemetised frequent thither most often.

Mahometry (mə'hɒmɪtrɪ). *Obs.* exc. *arch.* See also MAUMETRY. [f. MAHOMET + -RY.] = MUHAMMADANISM. In the 16th c. sometimes misused for 'false religion', 'idolatry'.

1481 CAXTON *Godfrey* clxxxvii. 274 Theyr mahometry and fowle lawe of machomet. **1530** TINDALE *Answ. More's Dial.* Wks. (1573) 256/1 The sacrifices which God gaue Adams sonnes were no dumme popetrie or superstitious Mahometrie. **1561** DAUS tr. *Bullinger on Apoc.* (1573) 121 b, The sixt conflict or fight is of Mahometrie by the Saracenes, Turkes, and Tartarians. **1579** FULKE *Ref. Rastel* 752 It is wholesome diuinitie, to iustifie all superstition, Mahometrie and Idolatrie in the world..to be excusable. **1804** SOUTHEY in Robberds *Mem. W. Taylor* I. 502 Fatalism is the corner-stone of Mahometry. **1890** E. JOHNSON *Rise Christendom* 339 Their mission was to..denounce destruction against Mahometry and Jewry.

†**Mahomite.** *Obs.* [f. MAHOM(ET + -ITE.] A Muslim. (Cf. MAHOMET 4.)

1559 W. CUNNINGHAM *Cosmogr. Glasse* 197 Christians, Turkes, Mahomites, Caffranans, Idolaters. **1564** tr. *Jewel's Apol. Ch. Eng.* H ij, The Mahomytes at this day..chuse rather to be caled Saracenes, as though they came of Sara, the free woman, and Abraham's wyfe. *a* **1618** SYLVESTER *Mirac. Peace* Sonn. xxxviii, The Mahomite..His mooned Standards hath already pight.

‖**mahone.** *Obs.* Also 6 **mahume,** 7 **mahoon,** 9 **maon, mahonna.** [Occurs as F. *mahonne*, Sp. *mahona*, It. *maona*, Turk. *māwuna.*] A flat-bottomed sailing vessel formerly used by the Turks.

1572 MALIM in *Hakluyt's Voy.* (1599) II. I. 122 Great Hulkes called Maones. **1585** T. WASHINGTON tr. *Nicholay's Voy.* I. xxi. 27 The gallies, foists and gallions.., besides the great gallion and 2. Mahumez [Fr. *Mahomez*]. **1651** HOWELL *Venice* 197 Meeting with a great Fleet of Turkish Gallies and Mahoons in the Egean Sea. **1658** EARL MONM. tr. *Paruta's Wars Cyprus* 204 Vluzzali, and Piali Bashaw, put to sea..with 150 Gallies, 30 Fliboats, and ten Mahones. **1696** PHILLIPS (ed. 5), *Mahoon.* **1858** SIMMONDS *Dict. Trade.* **1867** SMYTH *Sailor's Word-bk.*, *Mahone, Mahonna,* or *Maon.*

Hence †**ma'honnet** [see -ET].

a **1599** *Hakluyt's Voy.* II. 78 The number of the ships were these: 30 galliasses, 103 gallies, as well bastards as subtill mahonnets.

‖**mahonia** (mə'həʊnɪə). *Bot.* [mod.L., f. the name of Bernard McMahon, an American botanist + -IA.] A genus of *Berberidaceæ*, having evergreen pinnate leaves; a plant of this genus.

1829 LOUDON *Encycl. Plants* 1055 The Berberises.. especially the species with pinnated leaves, which are sometimes called Mahonias. **1883** *Harper's Mag.* Apr. 731/1 Mahonias from Japan.

mahoohoo, var. MOHOOHOO.

mahoot, mahot(e: see MAHOE, MAHOUT.

mahorka (mə'hɔːkə). Also **makharka, makhorka.** [Russ. *makhórka* shag.] A coarse tobacco smoked in Russia mostly by soldiers and peasants. Also *attrib.*

1902 R. N. BAIN tr. *Tales from Gorky* ix. 263 The chums were going along the high-road smoking *makharka* cigars of their own manufacture. **1949** I. DEUTSCHER *Stalin* i. 22 The circles met in the workers' own overcrowded slum-dwellings and filled the air with the biting smoke of *makhorka.* **1951** KOESTLER *Age of Longing* iv. 68 The tall old man with the dignified stoop, the mahorka smell and the sparkling, close-set eyes. *Ibid.* vi. 94 Old Arin sat down on the foot of the bed, smoking his mahorka cigarettes. **1962** *Listener* 2 Aug. 182/2 The sights and sounds of St Petersburg—..the smell of Mahorka tobacco and of the droshkies. **1964** *Sunday Mail Mag.* (Brisbane) 22 Nov., Villagers in the Caucasus have been smoking a mossy mixture known as mahorka.

Mahound (mə'huːnd, mə'haʊnd). Forms: *α.* 3 **Mahum, Mahun,** 4, 6 **Mahoune,** 4–6, 8 **Mahoun,** 5 **Mahon(e, Mawhown, Machoun,** 5, 7 **Mahown(e,** 6–7 **Macon;** *β.* 4 **Mahount,** 6 **Mahownd(e, Machound,** 7 **Mauhound,** 6– **Mahound.** [Early ME. *Mahun, Mahum*, a. OF. *Mahun, Mahum, Mahom*, shortened form of *Mahomet.* Cf. MAHOMET, MAUMET.]

1. The 'false prophet' Muhammad; in the Middle Ages often vaguely imagined to be worshipped as a god. (Cf. MAHOMET 1.) Now only *arch.*

c **1290** *S. Eng. Leg.* 187/101 þes þef us wole ouer-come; Mahun, ȝware is þi miȝte? *a* **1300** *Cursor M.* 7458 Moght i euer wit me wit him ming..I suld him sla, bi sir mahun! [*Gött.* saint mahoune]. *c* **1380** *Sir Ferumb.* 4939 þe ymage of Mahoun y-mad of golde Wiþ þe axe smot he oppon þe molde. *a* **1400** *Octouian* 1092 The Sarsyns cryde all yn fere To hare God Mahone To help her geaunt in that fyght. **1460** *Towneley Myst.* xxii. 408 Now by mahowne, oure heuen kyng. *c* **1540** J. REDFORD *Mor. Play Wit & Sci.* (Shaks. Soc.) 11 By Mahowndes bones,..by Mahowndes nose. **1591** HARRINGTON *Orl. Fur.* XVI. liv. 125 By Macon and Lanfusa he doth sweare. **1596** SPENSER *F.Q.* VI. vii. 47 The Carle did fret And fume..And oftentimes by Turmagant and Mahound swore. **1600** FAIRFAX *Tasso* XII. x. 215 Praised (quoth he) be Macon, whom we serue. **1605** *Tryall Chev.* v. ii. in Bullen *O. Pl.* (1884) III. 344 And Mahound and Termagant come against us, weele fight with them. **1735** POPE *Donne Sat.* iv. 239 The Presence seems, with things so richly odd, The mosque of Mahound, or some queer Pagod. **1825** SCOTT *Talism.* iii, Down with Mahound, Termagaunt, and all their adherents. **1849** JAMES *Woodman* iv, The very approach of a follower of Mahound, however, was an abomination to the good nun.

†**2.** *gen.* A false god; an idol. (Cf. MAUMET.) *Obs.*

c **1205** LAY. 230 Ah heo nom þene mahum [*c* **1275** mahun], þe heo tolden for godd. *Ibid.* 8079 þer stoden in þere temple ten þusend monnen..bi-foren heore mahun. *c* **1400** *Destr. Troy* 4312 The false goddes in fere fell to þe ground; Bothe Mawhownus & maumettes myrtild in peces. **1426** LYDG. *De Guil. Pilgr.* 17224 [Avarice *loq.*] Ley doun thy skryppe and thy bordoun, And do homage to my Mahown! *c* **1450** *Mirour Saluacioun* 1554 A grete dragon Wham alle that landes folk held god and thare mahon.

†**3.** A monster; a hideous creature. *Obs.*

c **1400** *Destr. Troy* 7758 There met hym þis Mawhown, þat was so mysshap, Euyn forne in his face, as he He wold. **1598** FLORIO, *Mamau*, a machound, a bugbeare, a raw-head and bloodie bone.

†**4.** *Sc.* Used as a name for the devil. Also *transf.* as a term of execration applied to a man. *Obs.* (? exc. *dial.*).

1377 LANGL. *P. Pl.* B. XIII. 82 And wisshed..That disshes and dobleres bifor this ilke doctour, Were molten led in his maw and Mahoun amyddes. **1500–20** DUNBAR *Poems* xxvi. 6 Me thocht, amangis the feyndis fell, Mahoun gart cry ane dance Off schrewis. *Ibid.* xxvii. 3 Nixt that a turnament wes tryid, That lang befoir in hell wes cryid, In presens of Mahoun. **1578** N. BAXTER *Calvin on Jonah* Ep. Ded. 3 In the pestilent pollicies of that Mahound Matchiavile. **1794** BURNS *The De'il's awa* 3 The De'il cam fiddling thro' the town, And danc'd awa wi' the Exciseman; And ilka wife cry'd, 'Auld Mahoun, We wish you luck o' your prize, man'.

†**5.** *attrib.* or *adj.* Muslim, heathen.

1624 FLETCHER *Rule a Wife* IV. iii, My pagan cozen, My mighty Mahound kinsman, what quirk now? *Ibid.* v. v, Who's this? my Mauhound cousin?

‖**mahout** (mə'haʊt). *Indian.* Also 9 **mahote, mohout, mahouht, mohout.** [Hindī *mahāut, mahāwat.*] An elephant-driver.

1662 J. DAVIES tr. *Mandelslo's Trav.* 81 The *Serriewan* hath the oversight of the Camels, and the *Mahout*, that of the Elephants. **1799** CORSE in *Phil. Trans.* LXXXIX. 36 *note*, I sent for the driver [*note*, Or *Mahote*, as he is generally called] to ask some questions concerning this elephant. **1819** *Sporting Mag.* IV. 174 The scuffle between the elephant and the Mahout. **1826** HOCKLEY *Pandurang Hari* I. 6 A *Mahouhut*, or elephant driver. **1859** LANG *Wand. India* 90 The mahoot, or elephant-driver, was attired in the most gorgeous manner. **1891** R. KIPLING *Life's Handicap* 307 The very best of the elephants belonged to the very worst of the drivers or mahouts.

mahova, mahower, var. forms of MAHWA.

‖**Mahratta** (mə'rætə). Also 8 **Moratta, Maharattor, Morattoe, Mar(h)atta, Merhattah,** 8–9 **Mharatta,** 9– **Maratha.** [Hindī *Marhaṭṭa.*]

1. One of a Scytho-Dravidian race occupying the central and south-western parts of India.

1763 SCRAFTON *Indostan* (1770) 36 He was suddenly alarmed with an invasion of eighty thousand Mharattas. **1765** HOLWELL *Hist. Events Bengal* I. (1766) 105 These united princes and people are those which are known by the general name of Maharattors. **1778** R. ORME *Hist. Milit. Trans.* II. I. 32 An army of 80,000 Morattoes. **1844** H. H. WILSON *Brit. India* I. 3 In the outset of the contest, native opinion had inclined to the Mahrattas. **1925** S. N. SEN *Administrative Syst. Marathas* (ed. 2) p. vii, The Marathas ..engaged in a life and death struggle. **1971** R. RUSSELL tr. *Ahmad's Shore & Wave* i. 10 The Mughal Empire fell and the Marathas overspread the land.

2. The language of the Mahrattas. = MAHRATTI.

1837 COLEBROOKE *Misc. Ess.* II. 29 The Maháráshtra, or Mahrátta, is the language of a nation which has in the present century greatly enlarged its ancient limits.

3. *attrib.* or *adj.* Pertaining to the Mahrattas. ***Mahratta Ditch*** (or ***Entrenchment***): a ditch made in 1742 to protect Calcutta from invasion by Mahrattas; a similar ditch made at Madras in 1780.

1758 *Ann. Reg.* 285 There was a man who carried a large Moratta battle-ax on his shoulder. **1778** R. ORME *Hist. Milit. Trans.* II. I. 45 The Morattoe ditch. **1782** *Indian Gaz.* 10 Aug. (Y.), To the Proprietors and Occupiers of Houses.. within the Mahratta Entrenchment. **1797** *Encycl. Brit.* (ed. 3) X. 563/2 Rajah Sahou, who considerably extended the Marhatta dominions. **1823** SIR J. MALCOLM *Mem. Central India* II. 115 The Mahratta Brahmins. **1842** TENNYSON *Locksley H.* 155 Where in wild Mahratta-battle fell my father evil-starr'd. **1858** J. M. MITCHELL *Mem. R. Nesbit* iii 65 The Maratha chiefs soon claimed to be the lords paramount of India. **1874** LAL BEHARI DAY *Govinda Samanta* I iv. 25 The Calcutta cockney, who glories in the Mahratta Ditch. **1886** KIPLING *Departmental Ditties* (ed. 2) 7 Rajah Rustum.. Roused his Secretariat to a fine Maratha fury. **1913** E. M. FORSTER *Let.* 1 Jan. in *Hill of Devi* (1953) 21 Cocked rakishly over one ear was a Maratha Turban of scarlet and gold. **1942** *R.A.F. Jrnl.* 13 June 4 The Maratha heirs of Sivalji. **1973** *Times* 16 Jan. 12/2 For years.. the cry of economic exploitation by the dominant Maratha caste to the south has been raised.

‖**Mahratti** (mə'rætɪ). Also 7 moratty, 9- marathi, -ee, murathee. [Hindī *Marhaṭṭī*, f. *Marhaṭṭa*: see prec.] The language of the Mahrattas. Also *attrib.*

1698 FRYER *Acc. E. India & P.* 174 They tell their Tale in Moratty. **1827** R. NESBIT in *Mem.* iii. (1858) 82, I attended the Marathi worship... I performed worship with the servants in Marathi. **1831** J. T. MOLESWORTH (*title*) A Dictionary Murathee and English. **1868** BELLAIRS & LAKSHMAN (*title*) A Grammar of the Marathi Language. **1875, 1880** [see KANARESE *a.* and *sb.*]. **1878** G. SMITH *Life J. Wilson* ii. (1879) 34 The New Testament in the Vernacular Marathee. **1908** T. G. TUCKER *Introd. Nat. Hist. Lang.* 187 Marāthi in the north-west Deccan. **1925** S. N. SEN *Administrative Syst. Marathas* (ed. 2) 2 Next in importance, are the *bakhars* or Marathi prose chronicles. **1933** L. BLOOMFIELD *Lang.* iv. 63 Such great languages as Marathi. **1949** 'G. ORWELL' *Note-Bk.* in *Coll. Ess.* (1968) IV. 513 We always had difficulty with the Marathi newsletter. **1953** E. M. FORSTER *Hill of Devi* 41 He could recall his father reciting in Marathi the ballads and epics of their race. **1958** A. TOYNBEE *East to West* xxxii. 99 If the city [*sc.* Bombay] had been merged in a separate Marathi-speaking state, [etc.]. **1967** 'W. HAGGARD' *Conspirators* ii. 20 His parents had spoken Marathi, beautiful Brahmin's Marathi. **1971** *Illustr. Weekly India* 25 Apr. 21/2 The personal feelings of eminent Marathi poet P. S. Rege. **1971** *Femina* (Bombay) 30 Apr. 16/2 (Advt.), In four languages: English, Hindi, Gujarati and Marathi. **1971** H. R. F. KEATING *Inspector Ghote goes by Train* II. ix. 211 He ordered in Hindi. He ordered in Marathi. He ordered in crude English.

‖**mahseer** ('mɑːsɪə(r)). Also mahase(e)r, mahsir, marseir, *Dicts.* mah(a)sur, maseer. [Hindī *mahāsir*, believed to represent Skr. *mahāçiras* 'bighead'. Another Hindī name is *mahāsaula*, of obscure origin.] A large Indian freshwater cyprinoid fish, *Barbus tor*, resembling the barbel.

1854 HOOKER *Himalayan Jrnls.* I. xvii. 398 A fine 'Mahaser' (a very large carp). **1858** SIMMONDS *Dict. Trade*, *Mahaseer.* **1859** LANG *Wand. India* 3 In the broad tributaries to the Ganges and the Jumna, may be caught [with a fly] the mâhseer, the leviathan salmon. **1880** GÜNTHER *Fishes* 594 The 'Mahaseer' of the mountain streams of India. **1894** POLLOK *Incid. For. Sport* 355 Mahseer Fishing. *Ibid.* 366, I got 277 pounds of mahseer.

Mahsud ('mɑːsuːd). Also Mahsood. A member of one of the principal tribes of Waziristan in north-west Pakistan, noted for their bellicosity. Also as *adj.*

1873 E. BALFOUR *Cycl. India* (ed. 2) V. s.v. *Wazira*, The Wazeeri are divided into three great divisions, or Usman kheyl, Ahmedzye, and Mahsood. **1882** H. B. ROWNEY *Wild Tribes India* II. i. 120 The Wuzeerás... are a bold and ferocious people... The principal tribal divisions among them are: the Máhsuds, Áhmedzyes, Othmánzyes, and Bithunnees. **1895** *Blackw. Mag.* July 79 The Mahsud headmen solemnly bound themselves to renounce looting the Powindah caravans. **1898** H. W. MILLS *Pathan Revolt N.-W. India* (ed. 3) iv. 22 Even after the Mahsuds had attacked Wano, Waziristan was not permanently occupied. **1909** *Daily Chron.* 2 June 1/7 The Mahsuds, who have been causing trouble on the Indian frontier, are said to have secured 10,000 rifles. **1920** *Blackw. Mag.* Oct. 445/1 You take the road to Mahsudland. *Ibid.* 457/2 The half-veiled, unfriendly, grey Mahsud hills. **1924** [see BRAHUI *sb.* and *a.*]. **1957** R. HILTON *N.-W. Frontier* x. 133 The 20th Punjabis.. hustled the mob of Mahsuds out of the camp at the points of their bayonets. **1963** *Listener* 10 Jan. 96/2 A column was out against refractory Mahsuds.

†'**Mahu.** *Obs.* Also 7 Maho. [Perh. suggested by MAHOUND.] Used as the name of a devil.

1603 HARSNET *Popish Impost.* x. 50 Maho was generall Dictator of hell: and yet for good manners sake, hee was contented of his good nature to make shew, that himselfe was vnder the check of Modu. **1605** SHAKS. *Lear* III. iv. 149 The Prince of Darknesse is a Gentleman. Modo he's call'd and Mahu. *Ibid.* IV. i. 63 (1608 Qo.) Hobbididence Prince of dumbnes, Mahu of stealing, Modo of murder.

mahume, variant of MAHONE *Obs.*

Mahumetan(e, variant of MAHOMETAN.

‖**mahwa** ('mɑːwə). Also 7 mahova, mahoua, máwee, 8-9 mahwah, 9 mowah, mahva, mhowa, mahúa, muohwa, mahower, 20 moa, mohua, mohur, mohwa, mowra, mowrah. [Hindī *mahwa*, also *mahūa*, repr. Skr. *madhūka*, f. *madhu* sweet.]

1. A large tree, *Madhuca latifolia*, native to India and belonging to the family Sapotaceæ, which bears fleshy, edible flowers and is used as a timber-tree; also, a smaller, related tree, *Madhuca butyracea*, the Indian butter tree, native to Nepal, whose seeds yield an oily, butter-like substance. Also *mahwa-tree.*

1687 A. LOVELL tr. *Thevenot's Trav.* III. 73 Manguiers, Mahova, Quieson, Caboul, and other sorts of Trees. *Ibid.* 94 They are Trees which they call Mahoua. **1785** C. HAMILTON in *Asiat. Researches* (1799) I. 300 There is a very curious and useful tree called by the Natives of Bahar.. the Máhwah or Máwee.. the Sanscrit name is Madhúca or Madhudruma. *Ibid.*, A description of the Mahwah tree. **1803** J. T. BLUNT *ibid.* VII. 58 We encamped at a tank and grove of Mowah trees. **1813** J. FORBES *Orient. Mem.* II. 451 The mowah (*bassia butyracea*).. attains the size of an English oak. **1854** SIMMONDS *Commerc. Prod. Veget. Kingd.* 538 Mahower (*Bassia latifolia*) is common in most parts of the Bengal Presidency. The oil a good deal resembles that last described. **1879** E. ARNOLD *Lt. Asia* VI. (1881) 140 Beneath broad-leaved mahúa trees. **1889** G. S. BOULGER *Uses of Plants* III. 139 The Mahwa, besides its saccharine flowers, yields 33 per cent. of a butter from its seeds, used in India as food, and now imported for soap and candle making. **1895** MRS. B. M. CROKER *Village Tales* (1896) 177 Drink—drink, from the fatal mowra-tree. **1907** B. M. CROKER *Company's Servant* xii. 108 A sickly tamarind and two frail gold mohur trees. **1922** W. SCHLICH *Man. Forestry* (ed. 4) I. II. 134 Mention should be made of the flowers of.. the 'mohwa' tree, the corolla of which is eaten fresh or dried, or distilled into intoxicating liquor. **1934** 'G. ORWELL' *Burmese Days* ii. 20 Gold mohur trees like vast umbrellas of bloodred bloom. **1951** *Dict. Gardening* (R. Hort. Soc.) III. 1229/2 *M*[*adhuca*] *latifolia.* Mahwah or Moa... The fl[owers] are edible and the wood valuable. **1954** J. MASTERS *Bhowani Junction* xxvii. 234 There was a gold mohur tree in bloom, its branches leaning out. **1964** R. PERRY *World of Tiger* x. 142 The oak-like mohua tree.. carries a tremendous weight of flowers—a hundredweight or more on a single tree.

2. An ardent spirit distilled from the flowers of the Mahwa tree.

1810 V. M. WILLIAMSON *E. India Vade Mecum* II. 153 Shops where.. Mowah, Pariah Arrack, &c., are served out. **1866** *Treas. Bot.*, *Mowra*, a kind of arrack obtained from *Bassia latifolia.*

3. *attrib.*, as ***mahwa-arrack, -butter, -flower, -liquor, -oil, -spirit***; **mowrah meal**, the dried and powdered residue of the seeds of the mahwa tree, after the oil has been extracted, used as a pesticide to kill worms in turf.

1813 J. FORBES *Orient. Mem.* II. 451 This by way of distinction is called mowah-arrack. **1854** SIMMONDS *Commerc. Prod. Veget. Kingd.* 511 Illiepie oil.. and Muohwa oil. **1873** DRURY *Usef. Plants India* 70 In 1848 a quantity of Mahwah oil was forwarded to the Secretary of the E. I. and China Association. **1876** *Cornh. Mag.* Sept. 321 A great cup of liquor distilled from the Mhowa flower. **1889** *Syd. Soc. Lex.*, *Mahwah butter*, a greenish or yellowish concrete oil obtained from the seeds of *Bassia latifolia.* **1920** *Nature* 1 Apr. 147/1 The possibility of utilising the mowra flowers of India for the purpose [of manufacturing alcohol] is discussed... They are used by the natives as a foodstuff, and especially for the preparation by fermentation of an alcoholic liquor called daru or mohwa spirit. **1939** R. B. DAWSON *Pract. Lawn Craft* xxv. 180 Mowrah meal.. does not maintain the turf in worm-free condition for longer than about two years. **1948** I. G. LEWIS *Turf* xii. 121 The residue of an Indian bean after the oil has been extracted for commercial purposes, Mowrah Meal is a material which is entirely safe to use. **1971** *Illustr. Weekly India* 18 Apr. 35/1 Toddy and mohua liquor are also sometimes drunk. **1973** R. GROUNDS *Perfect Lawn* viii. 73 Mowrah meal applied in summer or autumn.. will effectively reduce the worm population.

Mahzor, var. MACHZOR.

mai (maɪ). Shortened form of MATAI.

1831 G. BENNETT in *London Med. Gaz.* 12 Nov. 184/2 *Podocarpus Species*... This tree, the Mai or Matai of the natives of New Zealand, is an unpublished species of Podocarpus. **1845** [see HINAU]. **1855** R. TAYLOR *Te Ika a Mani* 440 Matai, mai.., a tree with a fine thick top, and leaf much resembling that of the yew. **1874** LINDLEY & MOORE *Treas. Bot.* II. Suppl. 1315/1 Mai (N. Zeal.), *Podocarpus spicata.* **1946** *Jrnl. Polynesian Soc.* LV. 145 Matai, a tree (*Podocarpus spicatus*), black-pine: often shortened to mãi.

‖**maia** ('meɪə, 'maɪə). *Zool.* [L. *maia*, Gr. *μαῖα.*] A spider-crab.

1706 PHILLIPS (ed. Kersey), *Maia*,.. a kind of Sea Crab-fish. **1865** GOSSE *Land & Sea* (1874) 81 The spider-crab, or maia; of little value as food, though occasionally eaten.

maian ('meɪən). *Zool.* [f. prec. + -AN.] A crustacean of the family *Maiidæ.* (Cf. MAIOID.)

1839 *Penny Cycl.* XIV. 296 *Maiidæ* or *Maians*, the second tribe of the family of *Oxyrhynchi*, according to the system of M. Milne Edwards.

maich, Sc. form of MAUGH.

maid (meɪd), *sb.*[1] Forms: 2 meide, 2–3 mede, 3 mæide, 3–6 meyde, mayde, 3–7 maide, 5–7 mayd, (6 mayed, 7 made), 6- maid. [Shortened from MAIDEN: not identical with OE. *mægeð* = G. *magd.*]

1. a. A girl; a young (unmarried) woman. = MAIDEN 1. Now only (exc. *dial.*) *arch.* or *playful.*

c **1205** LAY. 256 þa þis child was feir muche þa luuede he a maide. **1297** R. GLOUC. (Rolls) 297 þis mayde ispoused was of so heye blode. *c* **1320** *Sir Tristr.* 2702 þe maide answerd in lede, 'þer of haue þow no care'. *c* **1407** LYDG. *Reas. & Sens.* 151 Faire and fresh of hewe, As a mayde in hir beaute. **1546–7** *Test. Ebor.* (Surtees Soc.) VI. 252 Desiringe her to be good ladie to my litle meyde, her god doughter. **1571** ABP. GRINDAL *Articles* § 54 Legacies giuen.. to other .. godly vses as to.. poore Maydes marriages. **1596** SPENSER *F.Q.* VI. xii. 20 She found.. That this young Mayd.. Is her owne daughter. **1629** MILTON *Hymn Nativ.* xxii, In vain the Tyrian Maids their wounded Thamuz mourn. **1782** COWPER '*Sweet stream*', Sweet stream.. Apt emblem of a virtuous maid! **1800** COLERIDGE *Christabel* II. 238 Sweet maid,.. Thy sire and I will crush the snake! **1830** TENNYSON *Poems* 142 There are no maids like English maids, So beautiful as they be. **1886** KIPLING *Departm. Ditties*, etc. (1888) 64 'By all I am misunderstood!' if the Matron shall say, or the Maid.

b. *poet.* in personifications. (Freq. in the 18th c.)

1742 GRAY *Adversity* 27 Melancholy, silent maid, With leaden eye. **1747** COLLINS *Ode Passions* 1 When Music, heavenly maid, was young.

2. a. A virgin; *spec.* of the Virgin Mary (†*maid Mary*); = MAIDEN 2. *Obs.* or *arch.*

a **1175** *Cott. Hom.* 227 To ane mede þe was Maria ȝehaten. *c* **1175** *Lamb. Hom.* 77 þet halie meide [*sc.* Maria]. *c* **1275** *Passion our Lord* 597 in *O.E. Misc.* 54 Vre louerd ihesu crist þe wes ibore of þe meyde. *c* **1290** *S. Eng. Leg.* 79/57 I-bore of mayde marie. *c* **1320** *Sir Beues* 2197 þat i ne tok neuer wif, Boute ȝhe were maide clene. *c* **1386** CHAUCER *Knt.'s T.* 1470 Thou art mayde and kepere of vs alle.. And whil I lyue a mayde I wol thee serue. *c* **1410** HOCCLEVE *Moder of God* 11 Humble lady mayde modir and wyf. *c* **1483** CAXTON *Dialogues* 48/17 Who serueth our lord, And the mayde marye. **1500–20** DUNBAR *Poems* lxx. 4 Thow.. Gabriell send with the salutatioun On-to the mayd of maist humilite. *a* **1529** SKELTON *Replyc.* 47 Wks. 1843 I. 210 Wotte ye what ye sayed Of Mary, mother and mayed? **1697** DRYDEN *Virg. Georg.* IV. 479 Cydippe with Licorias, one a Maid, And one that once had call'd Lucina's Aid. **1834** SIR H. TAYLOR *2nd Pt. Philip van Artevelde* v. i. (*song*), Quoth tongue of neither maid nor wife To heart of neither wife nor maid.

b. *Hist.* As a title of Joan of Arc, ***the Maid*** (***of God, of Orleans***), a rendering of F. *la Pucelle.*

a **1548** HALL *Chron., Hen. VI* (1809) 157 This wytch or manly woman, (called the maide of God) the Frenchemen greatly glorified. **1691** J. HEATH *Eng. Chron.* 164 Joan, called by the French, the Maid of God. **1762** HUME *Hist. Eng. to Hen. VII*, II. 335 *marg.*, The maid of Orleans. **1849** LINGARD *Hist. Eng.* (1855) IV. i. 17/2 The maid of Orleans ..led the assailants. **1875** J. GAIRDNER *Lancaster & York* vii. (ed.2) 130 Rumours of the.. miracles of the Maid were repeated even in the English camp.

†**c.** *transf.* A man that has always abstained from sexual intercourse. (Cf. Gr. *παρθένος* and patristic L. *virgo.*) *Obs.*

1340 *Ayenb.* 230 Saint Ion þe ewangelist þet wes mayde wes amang þe apostles þe meste belouede of oure lhorde. **1387** TREVISA *Higden* (Rolls) I. 365 A preost þat is clene mayde. **1460** CAPGRAVE *Chron.* (1858) 5 Abel,.. a mayde, a martire, killid of his brothir of pure envy. **1525** LD. BERNERS *Froiss.* II. cxv. [cxi.] 331 He was swete, courtesse, meke, and a mayde of body. **1601** SHAKS. *Twel. N.* v. i. 270 You are betroth'd both to a maid and man. **1606** B. JONSON *Hymenæi* 94 View two noble Maids Of either sexe, to Union sacrificed. *a* **1641** BP. MOUNTAGU *Acts & Mon.* (1642) 542 Joseph was .. a maid, never knowing woman, as never being married before. **1710** *Brit. Apollo* III. No. 60. 2/2 He Dy'd a *Maid.*

3. An unmarried woman, spinster. †***to stand on the maid***: (of a woman) to remain single. (Now *rare* exc. in OLD MAID.)

1603 DEKKER *Wonderfull Yeare* E, To die maides! O horrible! **1615** CHAPMAN *Odyss.* VI. 52 Because thou shalt no more stand on the Maid [*ἐπεὶ οὔτοι ἔτι δὴν παρθένος ἔσσεαι*]. **1648** *Par Reg. St. John Maddermarket, Norwich* (MS.), A maid almost a hundred yeare old, buried 14 Nov. Anno dni 1648. **1700** DRYDEN *Sigis. & Guisc.* 16 For this, when ripe for marriage, he delayed Her nuptial bands, and kept her long a maid. **1747** *General Advertiser* 4 July, The Match [at Cricket].. between the Maids of Charlton and the Maids of Singleton.. will be play'd in the Artillery-Ground. **1814** SCOTT *Wav.* v, Miss Lucy St. Aubin lived and died a maid for his sake.

4. a. A female servant or attendant; a MAID-SERVANT; often with defining word prefixed as ***bar-, chamber-, farm-, house-, nurse-, servant-maid***, etc., q.v.; ***lady's maid*** (see LADY 18).

1390 GOWER *Conf.* I. 128 Sche.. goth to chambre and hath compleigned Unto a Maide which she triste. **1513** MORE *Rich. III* (1883) 59 That it was not princely to mary hys owne subiect,.. onely as it were a rich man that would mary his mayde. **1567** *Gude & Godlie B.* ix. (S.T.S.) 9 Thy nychtbouris wyfe.. Thow couet not to the,.. his oxe, his maide nor page. **1658** EVELYN *Diary* 27 Jan., He [a child] would.. select the most pathetic psalms,.. to reade to his mayde during his sicknesse. **1698** WANLEY in *Lett. Lit. Men* (Camden) 258 The maid told me that Dr. Smith had been there since I went. **1794** MRS. RADCLIFFE *Myst. Udolpho* xxv, You must dismiss your maid, lady. **1835** *Gentl. Mag.* Nov. 491 We kept no maid:—and I had much to do. **1860** Q. VICTORIA *Life Highl.* (1868) 138 The two maids had driven over by another road in the waggonette. **1880** OUIDA *Moths* I. 39 My maid must run up something for you to wear by to-morrow.

b. ***maid-of-all-work***, a female servant who does all kinds of house-work.

1809 MALKIN *Gil Blas* IV. vii. ¶8 An old abigail, whom I had formerly known as maid-of-all-work to an actress. **1848** THACKERAY *Trav. Lond.* Wks. 1886 XXIV. 350 The red-haired maid-of-all-work coming out with yesterday's paper. **1887** *Spectator* 16 Apr. 534/2 First she is a maid-of-all-work in the family of a poor clergyman.

transf. **1858** HUXLEY in *Life* (1900) I. xii. 158 Non-official maid-of-all-work in Natural Science to the Government.

5. In certain American universities used as a degree-title in correspondence to *Bachelor*. Now *Hist.*

1885 *Pall Mall G.* 5 Mar. 3/2 The Americans..talk of Miss Bluestocking..as 'Maid of Philosophy', 'Maid of Science', 'Maid of Arts'. **1888** BRYCE *Amer. Commw.* III. VI. cii. 445 *note*, Mr. D. C. Gilman..mentions the following among the degree titles awarded in some institutions to women..Laureate of Science, Proficient in Music, Maid of Philosophy.

6. Applied *dial.* to various inanimate objects (see also E.D.D.). **a.** = MAIDEN *sb.* 5. **b.** = MAIDEN *sb.* 6. **c.** A clothes-horse; = MAIDEN *sb.* 7b. **d.** A washerwoman's dolly; = MAIDEN 7c.

a. *a* **1700** B. E. *Dict. Cant. Crew, Kissing the Maid*, an Engine in Scotland, and at Halifax in England.

b. **1786** *Har'st Rig* cxlii. (1794) 43 Lang was the Har'st and little corn! And, sad mischance! the Maid was shorn After sunset.

c. **1795** *Lond. Chron.* 23 July 78 As if a horse, or maid for clothes, had been thrown with violence to the ground.

d. **1882** *W. Worc. Gloss.* 36.

7. A name given to the Skate and Thornback (*Raia batis* and *R. clavata*) when young. Also to the Twait Shad, *Alosa finta* (in Fr. similarly called *pucelle*). Cf. MAIDEN *sb.* 8.

1579 J. JONES *Preserv. Bodie & Soule* I. xiv. 26 Of fishes, ..Whiting, Smelt, Maids, Loch, Sammon. **1598** *Epulario* F iiij, Take out the guts of maids or Thornebackes by the gils with a forke or string. **1655** MOUFET & BENNET *Health's Improv.* 157 Maides are as little and tender Skates. **1714** GAY *Trivia* II. 292 The golden-belly'd Carp, the broad-finn'd Maid. **1769** PENNANT *Brit. Zool.* III. 70 Their [the thornbacks'] young..which (as well as those of the skate) before they are old enough to breed, are called maids. **1851** MAYHEW *Lond. Labour* I. 65 Piles of huge maids, dropping slime from the counter, are eagerly examined and bartered for. **1862** COUCH *Brit. Fishes* IV. 122 Twait Shad. Maid.

8. *Comb.*: **a.** appositive, as ***maid-attendant***, ***-mother***, ***-nurse***, ***service***, ***-slave***, ***-widow***, **†*-woman***; **b.** attributive, as ***maid-face***; **c.** originative, as ***maid-birth***, ***-born*** adjs.; **d.** parasynthetic, as ***maid-faced*** adj.; **e.** similative, as ***maid-like***, ***-pale*** adjs.; also **maid-fish** = sense 7; **† maids' ale**, the festival of the maidens' guild; **† maid's hair**, *Galium verum*; **maid's sickness** = GREEN-SICKNESS.

1896 *Daily News* 30 Oct. 10/7 *Maid-Attendant to an elderly or invalid lady. **1855** BAILEY *Mystic*, etc. 91 The pearl conceived of dew and lightning, type Of that pure *maid birth yet to bless the world. *a* **1649** DRUMM. OF HAWTH. *Poems* Wks. (1711) 24 Mild creatures, in whose warm crib now lies That..holy *maid-born Wight. *c* **1407** LYDG. *Reas. & Sens.* 3629 Euerych hath a *mayde face Of syghte lusty to enbrace. **1610** HEALEY *St. Aug. Citie of God* 686 Sphinx *maid-fac'd, fetherd-foule, foure-footed beast. **1810** *Splendid Follies* I. 130 Distorting her countenance to the semblance of a *maid-fish. **1606** SYLVESTER *Du Bartas* II. iv. II. *Magnif.* 1417 A Mars-like Courage in a *Maid-like blush. **1839** BAILEY *Festus* iii. (1852) 28 Seven fair maidlike moons attending him Perfect his sky. **1830** TENNYSON *Palace of Art* xxiv, The *maid-mother..Sat smiling, babe in arm. **1895** *Daily News* 15 May 10/6 Mrs. H. wishes to recommend her maid..as *Maid-Nurse. **1593** SHAKS. *Rich. II*, III. iii. 98 Ten thousand bloody crownes of Mothers Sonnes Shall..Change the complexion of her *Maid-pale Peace To Scarlet Indignation. **1547** *Croscombe Ch.-wardens' Accts.* (Som. Rec. Soc.), [Received from] The *maydes ayll xxijs vjd. **1597** GERARDE *Herbal* II. ccccxlviii. 968 In English our Ladies Bedstraw, Cheese renning, *Maides Haire, and petie Mugwet. **1657** COLES *Adam in Eden* cccxliii, It is called..in English Ladies Bedstraw, and sometimes Maids haire, from the finenesse of the Leaves. **1951** *N.Y. Times* 28 Oct. VIII. 19 (Advt.), Shamrock apartment hotel... *Maid service. **1968** *Globe & Mail* (Toronto) 17 Feb. 49/1 (Advt.), Prince Carlton Hotel Ltd. Rooms. Maid service, telephones. **1969** 'O. BLEECK' *Brass Go-Between* (1970) vi. 69 In addition to daily maidservice, the Adelphi offered a restaurant and bar. **1971** *Country Life* 23 Dec. 1814/4 [Villa]..Sleep 10, c.h.w., refrigerator, maid service. **1973** H. NIELSEN *Severed Key* v. 60, I wonder if this place provides maid service. **1633** FORD *'Tis Pity* III. ii, May bee, 'tis but the *Maides sicknesse, an ouer-flux of youth. **1603** *North's Plutarch, Camillus* (1612) 150 Faire *maide slaues dressed vp like gentlewomen. **1655** FULLER *Ch. Hist.* II. ii. §92 He stayed so long, that his Church presumed him dead, and herself a *Maid-Widow, which lawfully might receive another Husband. *c* **1320** *Sir Beues* (MS. A) 2203 And boute þe finde me *maide wimman..Send me aȝen to me fon.

† maid, *sb.*² Corrupt form of MEDINE, Egyptian coin. *Obs.*

1674 JEAKE *Arith.* (1696) 134 At..Alexandria, They accompt by Ducats, either Ducat de Pargo, of 120 Maids,.. or Italian Ducat of 35 Maids.

maid, *v.* [f. MAID *sb.*¹]

1. *intr.* To do maids' work; to act as a maid.

1900 PINERO *Gay Ld. Quex* I. 14 And when I got sick of maiding, I went to Dundas's opposite, and served three years at the hairdressing. **1936** M. MITCHELL *Gone with Wind* iv. 63 My Prissy been maidin' fo' Miss India fo' a year now. **1958** V. P. JOHNS *Servant's Probl.* i. 11 During the two months I've been maiding for Mr. Atterbury, one or the other of them have been in every day.

2. *dial.* = MAIDEN *v.* 2.

1882 *W. Worc. Gloss.*

3. *trans.* To wait on (a person) as a maid.

1909 R. HICHENS *Bella Donna* xxi. 228, I must learn to maid you. **1929** 'R. OKE' *Frolic Wind* v. 83 It was, of course, certainly untrue that she had a fourth to maid her. **1934** A. CHRISTIE *Murder on Orient Express* III. iv. 219 Susanne.. used to look after my clothes and maid me. **1949** C. H. B. KITCHIN *Cornish Fox* xi. 164 What would happen to the Colonel after the wedding?.. Upton wouldn't be at all pleased if Delia continued to 'maid' her father from Southview.

Hence **'maiding** *vbl. sb.*

1882 *W. Worc. Gloss.* 36 Maiding-tub. **1900** [see MAID *v.* 1]. **1921** *Chambers's Jrnl.* 1 Jan. 73/1 If you require 'maiding', you tell the lady of the bureau of your floor, and she supplies you with an attendant. **1955** 'C. H. ROLPH' *Women of Streets* vi. 78 Maiding to a prostitute is a definite job.

maid, obs. pa. t. and pa. pple. of MAKE *v.*

‖**maidan** (maɪ'dɑːn). *Indian.* Also 7 **maydan, medon, mei-, m(e)ydan,** 7,9 **midan,** 9 **maidaun.** [Pers. *maidān*.] An open space in or near a town; an esplanade or parade-ground.

1625 PURCHAS *Pilgrims* I. IV. 423 The Medon, which is a pleasant greene, in the middest whereof is a May-pole to hang a light on. **1662** J. DAVIES tr. *Olearius' Voy. Ambass.* v. (1669) 172 The Meydan, that is the great Market-place. *Ibid.* 178 The Market-place, or Maydan, is large and noble. **1698** FRYER *Acc. E. India & P.* 249 The Midan, or open space before the Caun's Palace. **1845** STOCQUELER *Handbk. Brit. India* (1854) 189 Dum Dum..is a spacious cantonment, with an extensive maidaun, or esplanade. **1879** A. FORBES *Camps, Quarters*, etc. (1896) 283 Before me on the maidan is the plain monument to Sir Mountstuart Jackson. **1882** MRS. B. M. CROKER *Proper Pride* II. i. 14 He..was galloping away over the moonlit midan.

† maid-child. *Obs.* = MAIDEN-CHILD.

c **1205** LAY. 14378 He bad Hengest his dring ȝiuen him þat maide-child. *Ibid.* 24529 Moni mæide child wes þere. *c* **1375** *Cursor M.* 11299 (Laud) For maide child [*other texts* maiden child] as long also. *c* **1386** CHAUCER *Shipman's T.* 95 A mayde child cam in hire compaignye. *a* **1450** MYRC 217 Also thys mote ben hem sayde, Boþe for knaue chyldere & for mayde, That [etc.]. **1535** COVERDALE *Lev.* xii. 5 But yf she beare a maydechilde [**1611** maid child]. **1608** SHAKS. *Per.* v. iii. 6 [She] brought forth a Mayd child calld Marina.

maiden ('meɪd(ə)n), *sb.* and *a.* Forms: 1 **mægden, mæden,** *Northumb.* **mai(ʒ)den,** 2 **mæȝdon,** 2–3 **mei-, meyden,** 3 **mæiden,** *Orm.* **maȝȝdenn,** 4–7 **mayden,** (4 **maþen,** 4–6 **ma-, mai-, maj-, maydan, -din(e, -don, -dun, -dyn,** 6 **madne,** 9 **maden),** 3– **maiden.** [OE. *mægden* str. neut. = OHG. *magatîn*, (MHG. *magetîn*; the mod.G. *mädchen* is not identical):—OTeut. type **magadînom*:—pre-Teut. **moghwotîno-m*, a dim. formation (see -EN) from **moghwóti-s* maiden, girl, represented by Goth. *magaþ-s*, OHG. *magad* (MHG. *maget*, mod.G. *magd*, maidservant), OS. *magath* (MDu. *maghet*, Du. *maagd*), OE. *mæȝeð*, *mæȝð* maid, virgin; related to pre-Teut. **moghu-s* boy, young man (OIrish *mug* slave, Avestic *magu* young man), whence Goth. *magu-s*, ON. *mǫg-r*, OS., OE. *magu*. Cf. MAY *sb.*¹]

A. *sb.*

1. a. A girl; a young (unmarried) woman; = MAID 1. (Not now in colloquial use exc. *dial.*)

c **1000** *Ags. Gosp.* Matt. ix. 24 Gað heonun nys þys mæden [*c*1160 *Hatton* mæȝdon] dead soðlice ac heo slæpð. *a* **1100** *Voc.* in Wr.-Wülcker 310/9 *Puella*, mæden, oððe ȝeong wifman. *c* **1205** LAY. 2214 He nom of þan monkunne þreo swiðe feire mæidene. *c* **1250** *Gen. & Ex.* 2749 Hirdes wulden ðe maidenes deren, Oc moyses ðor hem gan weren. **1340** HAMPOLE *Pr. Consc.* 4966 Alle men sal ryse þan þat ever had life, Man and woman, mayden and wyfe. *c* **1375** *Sc. Leg. Saints* vi. (*Thomas*) 58 A madyne com amange þam all of hebrow borne In-to þe land. *c* **1400** *Destr. Troy* 1363 Maydons for mornyng haue þere mynde loste. *c* **1470** HENRY *Wallace* v. 580 In Lanryk duelt a gentill woman thar, A madyn myld. **1559** *Mirr. Mag., Dk. Clarence* vii, A maiden of a noble house and old. **1601** SHAKS. *All's Well* I. iii 155 (Gods mercie maiden) dos it curd thy blood To say I am thy mother? **1710** *Tatler* No. 252 ¶5 We..have a Boy and a Girl: The Lad Seventeen, the Maiden Sixteen. **1853** M. ARNOLD *Scholar-Gipsy* ix, Maidens, who from the distant hamlets come To dance around the Fyfield elm in May. **1855** *Cornwall* 227 'Maidens', as the Cornish people term girls from 16 to 17 years of age. **1860** TYNDALL *Glac.* I. xxiv. 173 A vigorous English maiden might have ascended the [ice] fall without much difficulty. **1887** BOWEN *Virg., Æneid* II. 238 Round it advance in procession unwedded maiden and boy.

b. A female child. *Obs.* exc. *dial.*

c **1200** ORMIN 4107 To clippen swa þe cnapess shapp, & toffrenn lac forr maȝȝdenn.

c. ***the answer to a maiden's prayer***, an eligible bachelor. Also *transf.*

1935 *Mademoiselle* Aug. 15 Here, you Freshmen, Seniors, et al, is the answer to a maiden's prayer. **1957** J. FLEMING *Maiden's Prayer* II. 109 You're the answer to a maiden's prayer, dear heart. No need for you to do a stroke of work, you can marry money and live the life of a gentleman. **1971** J. BRUNNER *Honky in Woodpile* xi. 83, I was still in college. Thought he was the greatest..answer to a maiden's prayer! **1974** A. PRICE *Other Paths* II. i. 112 You're the answer to a maiden's prayer.

2. a. A virgin; *spec.* of the Virgin Mary (**†** ***maiden Mary***); = MAID 2. Now *rare.*

a **1035** *Laws of Cnut* II. c. 52 (53) Gif hwa mæden nydnæme, *si quis violenter virginem opprimat.* *a* **1175** *Lamb. Hom.* 77 Þet halie meiden onswerede and seide Quomodo [etc.]. *c* **1200** ORMIN 2102 Þeȝȝ wenndenn þatt ȝho wære wif, Acc ȝho wass maȝȝdenn clene. *c* **1290** *S. Eng. Leg.* 3/68 I-bore he was of þe maydene Marie! *c* **1300** *Cursor M.* 28483 (Cott.), I..forced sum woman with nede, and maþens reft þair maþenhede. **1387** TREVISA *Higden* (Rolls) VI. 319 Þe kyng ȝaf here lond for to bulde tweie abbayes of maydons. *c* **1400** *Destr. Troy* 2940 Þat comes but to harme, Gers maidnes be mart, mariage fordone. *a* **1400** *Relig. Pieces fr. Thornton MS.* 27 Goddes sone tuke flesche and blode of þe blyssed maydene Marie. **1470–85** MALORY *Arthur* XVIII. xix. 760 A clene mayden I am for hym and for alle other. **1599** SHAKS. *Much Ado* IV. i. 88 Why then you are no maiden.

b. *transf.* A man that has always abstained from sexual intercourse; = MAID 2c. *Obs.*

c **1300** *Havelok* 995 Of bodi was he mayden clene. **1377** LANGL. *P. Pl.* B. IX. 173 Maydenes and maydenes macche ȝow togideres. *c* **1440** *Jacob's Well* 277 He was a munk and priour of his hows, & a clene mayden. **1470–85** MALORY *Arthur* XI. xiv, Syre Percyuale..was a parfyte clene mayden. **1497** BP. ALCOCK *Mons Perfect.* D iij, Yᵉ grete nombre of his apostles were maydens.

3. An unmarried woman, spinster; = MAID 3. *Obs.* exc. *dial.* ***old maiden*** (rare) = OLD MAID. ***to go maiden***: to remain single.

1775 *Tender Father* I. 139 This gentlewoman was an old maiden, and possessed many particularities. *a* **1802** *Cruel Sister* xiv. in Child *Ballads* I. 128/2 Your cherry cheeks and your yellow hair Garrd me gang maiden evermair.

4. A maid-servant, a female attendant. (Cf. MAID 4.) *arch.* and *dial.* **†** ***maiden of honour*** = MAID OF HONOUR.

971 *Blickl. Hom.* 159 Forþon þu nu sceawa þines mæȝ(d)enes eaþmodnesse. **1297** R. GLOUC. (Rolls) 8965 Hire maidens broȝte hire clene water euere wanne heo lete. **13..** *Coer de L.* 880 The kynges doughter lay in her bower, With her maydenys of honour. **1377** LANGL. *P. Pl.* B. v. 630 Charite and Chastite ben his chief maydenes. **1434** *E.E. Wills* (1882) 97 To Aneys hir mayden, a russet kyrtell. *a* **1550** *Freiris of Berwik* 251 in *Dunbar's Poems* 293 He bad the madin kindill on the fyre. **1596** DALRYMPLE tr. *Leslie's Hist. Scot.* II. 113 He requyres in mariage ane of the Quenes madnes. **1611** BIBLE *Ps.* cxxiii. 2 As the eyes of a maiden [looke] vnto the hand of her mistresse. **1631** WEEVER *Anc. Funeral Mon.* 446 The Ladies of the Court, and Maydens of Honor.

5. The instrument, similar to the guillotine, formerly used in Edinburgh for beheading criminals; applied occas. to the *Halifax gibbet* (see GIBBET 1c).

1581 in Row *Hist. Kirk* (1842) 86, June 2, 1581.—The Earle of Morton was beheaded with the axe of the Maiden he himself had caused make. **1721** RAMSAY *Genty Tibby* iii, My wyzen with the maiden shore. **1722** WODROW *Hist. Suffer. Ch. Scot.* II. 545 Falling down on his Knees upon the Stool, [the Earl of Argyle] embraced the Maiden..very pleasantly. **1810** BENTHAM *Packing* (1821) 121 The Guillotine..(a French edition of our Halifax Maiden). **1849** MACAULAY *Hist. Eng.* v. I. 565 The rude old guillotine of Scotland, called the Maiden.

6. *Sc.* **a.** The last handful of corn cut in the harvest-field, often rudely shaped into the figure of a girl and decorated with ribbons (cf. KIRN-BABY). Also ***harvest maiden***.

1786 *Har'st Rig* cxxxvi. (1794) 42 For now the Maiden has been win, And Winter is at last brought in. **1797** *Statist. Acc. Scotl.* XIX. 550 The fortunate lass who took the maiden was the Queen of the feast. **1814** J. TRAIN *Mountain Muse* 95 A former neighbour.. Who had with them for wedding bruises run, And from them oft the harvest maiden won.

b. The harvest-home and the feast with which it was celebrated.

1806 A. DOUGLAS *Poems* 144 (Jam.) The master has them bidden Come back again, be't foul or fair 'Gainst gloamin', to the Maiden. **1899** *Westm. Gaz.* 13 Mar. 2/1 We speak always of our Harvest Homes as 'Maidens'.

7. † a. (See quot. 1688.) **b.** *dial.* A clothes-horse. **c.** *north. dial.* A washerwoman's dolly.

a. **1688** R. HOLME *Armoury* III. 286/2 The Maidens or Damsels, the two Stands in which the Spindle turns.

b. **1859** E. WAUGH *'Come whoam to thi Childer & Me'* 28 Poems 55 So aw iron't o my clooas reet weel, An' aw hang'd 'em o' th maiden to dry. **1881** [see *maiden-maker* in 10].

c. **1752** *Gentl. Mag.* XXII. 32 A Machine for washing of Linnen, called a Yorkshire Maiden. **1781** REES *Cycl.*, *Maiden*..the name of a machine first used in Yorkshire, and since introduced into other places, for washing of linen. [The apparatus as described consists of a dolly fitted to a covered wooden tub. This use of the name has app. not survived.] **1829** J. HUNTER *Hallamsh. Gloss.*, *Maiden*, an instrument used in the laundry. **1888** *Sheffield Gloss.* s.v., The maiden is sometimes called a peggy or dolly.

† 8. The name of a fish. (? = MAID *sb.* 8.) *Obs.*

1555 EDEN *Decades* 269 Dryed fysshe as soles maydens playces. [**1624** HEYWOOD *Captives* II. ii. in Bullen *Old Plays* (1885) IV. 145 For whom weare you a fishinge? *Mild.* Marry, for maydens;..But, my gutts, Howe they are sweld with sea brine!]

9. a. Short for *maiden horse, over, race, tree* (see B).

1807 SIR J. MALCOLM in *Life* (1856) I xiv. 379 *note*, Grant and I have two horses for the two first maidens. **1880** *Times* 28 Sept. 11/5 [Cricket] Shaw joined Selby, and when a couple of maidens had been sent down luncheon intervened. **1894** *Field* 9 June 850/2 A plantation of young apple trees, ..mostly maidens and two-year-olds, was badly attacked by green aphis. **1898** *Stratford-on-Avon Herald* 11 Feb. 4/4 The Warwickshire Hunt Cup... For horses five years old and upwards, maidens at the time of closing.

b. A strawberry plant bearing its first crop. Also *attrib.*

1928 *Daily Express* 28 May 5/3 The 'runners' are laid from the 'maidens' or last year's [strawberry-]beds. **1974** *Times* 13 July 11/3 Another advantage of growing only maiden strawberries is that it gives us one more crop to work into our programme of crop rotation... I have now decided..to grow only maidens—that is, to take one crop off a plant and then discard it.

c. Short for *maiden bell* (see sense B. 4 f).

1909 *Daily Chron.* 1 Oct. 7/5 The High Wycombe 'tenor' ..thus issues proudly from the Whitechapel Foundry a 'maiden'.

10. a. *attrib.* and *Comb.*, as ***maiden-blush***; ***maiden-catching***, ***-eyed***, ***-faced***, ***-folded***, ***-furled***, ***-hued***, ***tongued*** adjs.; ***maiden-maker***, ***-monger***; **maiden-bark**, ? the bark of saplings; **maiden-feast**, the feast after cutting the maiden (sense 6); †**maiden-gear**, †**-gem**, virginity; †**maiden-heart**, a variety of pear; **maiden-meek** *a.*, meek as befits a maiden; †**maiden-nut** (see quot.); **maiden-rip** *Sc.* = 6; **maiden-servant** = sense 4; **maiden-skate** *Sc.* (see quot.); †**maidens' light**, a light (in a church) maintained by maidens; †**maidens' milk** = LAC VIRGINIS; **maiden-thought** *poet.*, Keats's term for the stage of human development after 'the infant or thoughtless Chamber', one of innocent, untarnished hope; **maiden-widowed** *a.*, *nonce-wd.*, widowed while still a maiden.

1832 *Planting* 92 in *Lib. Usef. Knowl., Husb.* III, Tiller or Tellar, a shoot selected.. to stand.. for *maiden bark. **1605** BRETON *Soules Immort. Crowne* (Grosart) 7/2 She shewes her there the *Maiden-blush complection, Betwixt the cherrie Red, and snowie White. **1655** GURNALL *Chr. in Arm.* verse 14. ix. (1669) 36/2 His Maiden-blush modesty will not suffer him to declare his sin. **1861** J. RUFFINI *Dr. Antonio* i, The maidenblush clearness of the skin. **1957** AUDEN & KALLMAN *Magic Flute* I. i. 28 Had I a *maiden-catching net, Fair maids by dozens I should daily get. **1930** J. MASEFIELD *Wanderer of Liverpool* 24 The *maiden-eyed morning. **1567** GOLDING *Ovid's Met.* VII. (1593) 151 Boreas sonnes had chaste Away the *maiden-faced foules that did the vittels waste. **1797** *Statist. Acc. Scotl.* XIX. 550 It was, till very lately, the custom to give what was called a *Maiden Feast, upon the finishing of the harvest. **1916** D. H. LAWRENCE *Amores* 100 Then lets her black hair loose, the darkness fall About her from her *maiden-folded bands. **1876** G. M. HOPKINS *Wreck of Deutschland* xxxiv, in *Poems* (1967) 62 The heaven-flung, heart-fleshed, *maiden-furled Miracle-in-Mary-of-flame. **1719** D'URFEY *Pills* I. 130 My father takes me for a Saint, Tho' weary of my *Maiden Geer. **1612** DRAYTON *Poly-olb.* x. 148 Chaste Winifrid: who chose Before her *mayden-gem she forcibly would lose [etc.]. **1721** MORTIMER *Husb.* II. 295 The Lewis Pear, or by some the *Maiden-heart. **1913** E. F. BENSON *Thorley Weir* i. 21 The dog-rose spread its *maiden-hued face skywards. **1881** *Instr. Census Clerks* (1885) 143 *Maiden Maker (Clothes Horse). **1847** TENNYSON *Princess* III. 118 Yet *maiden-meek, I prayed Concealment. *a* **1625** FLETCHER *Custom of Country* I. i, This thing you study to betray your child to. This *Maiden-monger. **1884** KNIGHT *Dict. Mech.* Suppl., **Maiden Nut*, the inner one of two nuts on the same screw; the outer is the jam-nut. **1882** J. WALKER *Jaunt to Auld Reekie*, etc. 12 She grips some stalks and twists the *maiden-rip In triple strands. **1533** GAU *Richt Vay* (1888) 11 Thou sal noth desir thy nichtburs wiff *madin seruand beist or ony thing quhilk pertenis to hime. **1741** RICHARDSON *Pamela* (1824) I. iv. 19 If the wench, (for so she calls us maiden-servants) takes care of herself she'll improve. **1810** NEILL *List Fishes* 28 (Jam.) The young both of the Thornback and the Skate are denominated *Maiden-skate. **1547–8** in Swayne *Sarum Church-w. Acc.* (1896) 275 For viij li. of wex for the *Maydens light vs. *a* **1400–50** *Stockh. Med. MS.* 4 A water þat is clepyd *maydinis mylke. **1818** KEATS *Let.* 3 May (1958) I. 281 We no sooner get into the second Chamber, which I shall call the Chamber of *Maiden-Thought, than we become intoxicated with the light and the atmosphere. **1954** L. MACNEICE *Autumn Sequel* 22 The Customs Office of Maiden-thought. **1597** SHAKS. *Lover's Compl.* 100 *Maiden tongu'd he was, and thereof free. **1592** —— *Rom. & Jul.* III. ii. 135, I a Maid, die *Maiden-widowed.

b. In various plant-names; †**maiden-lip(s**, *Echinospermum Lappula*; †**maiden mercury**, a name for male plants of *Mercurialis annua*; **maiden oak**, *Quercus sessiliflora*; **maiden pink**, *Dianthus deltoides*; **maiden plum (tree)**, a name given to two West Indian trees, *(a) Comocladia integrifolia*, *(b) Chrysobalanus*; **maiden rose** = MAIDEN'S BLUSH; †**maidens' honesty**, *Clematis vitalba*; **maiden's wreath**, a perennial herb of the genus *Francoa*, bearing pink or white flowers in spikes or racemes; cf. *bridal wreath* (BRIDAL *a.* 2 c). Also MAIDENHAIR, MAIDENWEED.

1589 RIDER *Bibl. Schol.* 1748 *Maiden lips, or tasil, *lappago*. **1578** LYTE *Dodoens* I. lii 78 This kinde may be called in English.. Daughters Phyllon, or *Mayden Mercury. **1848** *Phytologist* III. 883 *note*, The Quercus sessiliflora they [woodmen] call White Oak and *Maiden Oak. **1755** B. STILLINGFL. *Cal. Flora* 7 July, Pinks, *maiden, *Dianthus deltoides*. **1776–96** WITHERING *Brit. Plants* (ed. 3) II. 410 *Maiden Pink*. Sandy meadows, pastures, and heaths. **1882** J. HARDY in *Proc. Berw. Nat. Club* IX. 476 At Makerstoun Crags.. the spindle-tree, maiden-pink,.. and the common feverfew grew. **1725** SLOANE *Jamaica* II. 131 The *Maiden-Plumb-Tree. **1760** J. LEE *Introd. Bot.* App. 318 Maiden Plumb, *Chrysobalanus*. **1864** GRISEBACH *Flora W. Ind.* 785 Maiden-plum, *Comocladia integrifolia*. **1827** G. DARLEY *Sylvia* 102 Here's a garland of red *maiden-roses for you. **1832** MISS MITFORD *Village* Ser. v. 89 She has just as much colour as any woman ought to have—the maiden-rose tint. *a* **1691** AUBREY *Nat. Hist. Wilts* (1847) 49 Wild vetch, *maiden's honesty, polypodium [etc.]. **1691** RAY *Ibid.* 50 Calver-keys, hare's-parseley, mayden's-honesty, are countrey names unknown to me. **1893** W. ROBINSON *Eng. Flower Garden* (ed. 3) 419/1 Francoa (*Maiden's Wreath).—Chilian plants of the Saxifrage family... They are rather tender. **1908** G. JEKYLL in *Colour Flower Garden* xiii. 116 Maiden's Wreath (*Francoa ramosa*) is a plant for many uses. The foliage, though sparing in quantity, is distinct and handsome. The long flower-stems are flung out with a kind of determination of character. **1952** A. G. L. HELLYER *Sanders' Encycl. Gardening* (ed. 22) 198 Francoa (Maiden's Wreath; Bridal Wreath).

B. *adj.* (from appositive and attributive uses of the sb.). Cf. VIRGIN.

I. Literal uses.

1. Appositive uses. **a.** Unmarried; now chiefly in ***maiden lady, sister***: see also MAIDEN AUNT. †**b.** Of a child: Female; see MAIDEN-CHILD (*obs.*). **c.** Virgin; sometimes said of men (*obs.*).

a **1300** *Cursor M.* 5546 (Cott.) þe knau barns.. þai suld.. sla, þe maiden barns þai suld lat ga. **1300–1400** *Ibid.* 21019 (Gött.) Iohn, maiden saint, iam broþer, [was] mar luued wid crist þan ani oþer. **1303** R. BRUNNE *Handl. Synne* 6080 ȝyf an husbond chyldryn haue, One or two, mayden or knaue. *c* **1314** *Guy Warw.* (A.) 196 And euerich kniȝt [ches] his leman Of þat gentil maiden wiman. **1585** T. WASHINGTON tr. *Nicholay's Voy.* I. viii. 8 b, The Moorishe women and mayden slaues. **1589** PUTTENHAM *Eng. Poesie* III. (Arb.) 192 To blazon foorth the Brytton mayden Queene. **1591** SHAKS. *1 Hen. VI*, IV. vii. 38 Thou Maiden youth, be vanquisht by a Maide. **1640** *Wits Recreat.* § 166 She will.. sit at dinner like a mayden-bride. **1647** TRAPP *Comm. Matt.* xxvii. 60 A new tomb it was, and fit it should be for that virgin body, or maiden-corpse, as one calls it. **1765** in Waghorn *Cricket Scores* (1899) 59 A cricket-match was played.. by eleven married against eleven maiden women. **1777** SHERIDAN *Sch. Scand.* IV. i, Here, now, is a maiden sister of his. **1798** *Monthly Mag.* VI. 75 [Died] At Windsor Castle, Mrs. Hannah Corbett, a maiden lady. **1852** ROCK *Ch. of Fathers* III. I. 269 The girl-like maiden-mother bowed down before the crib.

2. Of or pertaining to a maiden, or to maidenhood; befitting a maiden, having the qualities of a maiden. ***maiden name***: the surname borne by a married woman before her marriage.

1591 SHAKS. *1 Hen. VI*, II. iv. 47, I pluck this pale and maiden blossom here. *Ibid.* v. iv. 52 Joan of Arc.. Whose Maiden-blood, thus rigorously effus'd, Will cry for Vengeance at the Gates of Heauen. **1592** —— *Rom. & Jul.* II. ii. 86 The maske of night is on my face, Else would a Maiden blush bepaint my cheeke. **1601** —— *Twel. N.* v. i. 262 Ile bring you to a Captaine in this Towne, Where lye my maiden weeds. **1613** —— *Hen. VIII*, IV. ii. 169 Strew me ouer With Maiden Flowers, that all the world may know I was a chaste Wife, to my Graue. **1648** HERRICK *Hesper.*, *To Anne Soame*, The meanest part of her Smells like the maiden-pomander. **1689** S. SEWALL *Diary* (1878) I. 305 Visited Cousin Powers, and Cous. Lapworth, whose maiden name was Ann Lee. **1700** DRYDEN *Cinyras & Myrrha* 113 The tender sire who saw her blush and cry Ascrib'd it all to maiden-modesty. **1773** *Life N. Frowde* 5, I was baptized by her [the mother's] maiden Name Neville. **1814** SCOTT *Ld. of Isles* I. iv, Wake, Maid of Lorn! the moments fly, Which yet that maiden-name allow. **1844** DISRAELI *Coningsby* v. vi, Not.. a word that could call forth a maiden blush. **1862** BORROW *Wild Wales* III. v. 41, I asked her her maiden name. **1922** JOYCE *Ulysses* 366 Her maiden name was Jemima Brown And she lived with her mother in Irishtown.

3. Of female animals: Uncoupled, unmated.

1840 *Boston Advertiser* 30 June 3/4, I killed two sheep; one was a maiden ewe, and the other a wether. **1885** *Bell's Life* 15 June 1/1 To be Sold, Two Maiden Three Year Old Fillies. **1892** *Stratford-on-Avon Herald* 18 Nov. 4/1 To the owner and feeder of the best Pair of.. Maiden Sows.

II. Figurative uses.

4. That has yielded no results. **a.** Of an assize, circuit, session: Formerly, one at which no prisoner was condemned to death; now, one at which there are no cases for trial.

a **1700** B. E. *Dict. Cant. Crew*, *Maiden-sessions*, when none are Hang'd. **1742** *Gentl. Mag.* July 386 Ended the sessions at the Old Bailey, which proved a maiden one, none having been capitally convicted. **1826** SCOTT *Jrnl.* 17 Apr., The judge was presented with a pair of white gloves, in consideration of its being a maiden circuit. **1847** HALLIWELL s.v., Maiden-assize. **1868** *Daily Tel.* 16 Apr., It is nearly half a century since there has been a maiden sessions at Oxford.

b. Of a game, esp. *Cricket* of an over: One in which no runs are scored.

1598 FLORIO s.v. *Marcio*,.. a lurch or a maiden set at any game. **1851** J. PYCROFT *Cricket Field* iv. 58 In point of style the old players did not play the steady game with maiden overs as at present. **1864** *Daily Tel.* 16 May, Half-a-dozen 'maiden overs' in succession, every ball dead on the middle stump, and yet played steadily back again to the bowler. **1893** W. S. GILBERT *Utopia* 11, An occasional 'maiden over'.

c. Of a tide: One on which no vessels enter or leave the dock.

1897 *Daily Tel.* 30 Nov. 10/2 Hull.—There was to-day a maiden tide, no vessel being able either to enter or to leave, owing to the storm and flood.

d. (See quot.)

1900 *New Cent. Rev.* VII. 374, 7 was called the maiden number, because within the decade it has no factors or product.

e. Of a horse, etc.: That has never won a prize. Hence of a prize or a race: Offered or open to maiden horses, etc.

1760 R. HEBER *Horse Matches* ix. 40 All Maiden Horses favoured 2 lb. **1856** 'STONEHENGE' *Brit. Sports* II. I. xiii. (ed. 2) 364 A Maiden horse or mare is one that has never won. **1886** *York Herald* 10 Aug. 7/5 Two Miles Maiden Bicycle Handicap. **1896** *Daily News* 17 July 3/4 The maiden class for horses that have never won a first prize before.

f. In Bell-founding: (see quots.).

1901 H. E. BULWER *Gloss. Technical Terms Bells* 2 *Maiden bell*, a bell that requires no tuning after it comes from the mould. **1910** *Encycl. Brit.* III. 688/1 The metal is then boiled and run molten into the mould... When extricated it ought to be scarcely touched and should hardly require tuning. This is called its maiden state. **1912** H. B. WALTERS *Church Bells Eng.* ii. 47 Sometimes a whole peal used to be turned out so nearly correct that no tuning was needed; such bells were known as a 'maiden peal'.

5. That has not been conquered, tried, worked, etc. **a.** Of a town, castle, fortress, etc.: That has never been taken, 'virgin'.

The appellation *Maiden Castle* (quot. 1639) given to Edinburgh prob. did not originally mean 'virgin fortress', as in Geoffrey of Monmouth (12th c.) it appears as *Castrum Puellarum*, 'maidens' castle'. Several ancient earthworks in England are also called Maiden Castle: the sense may possibly be 'a fortress so strong as to be capable of being defended by maidens'; there may have been an allusion to some forgotten legend. Cf. the equivalent Ger. name *Magdeburg*.

1593 SHAKS. *Lucr.* 408 Her breasts.. A paire of maiden worlds vnconquered. **1601** J. WHEELER *Treat. Comm.* 30 Tournay.. at that time termed the Maiden Citie. **1631** J. TAYLOR (Water P.) *Turn Fort. Wheel* (Halliw.) 9 Victorie forsook him for ever since he ransacked the maiden town of Magdenburg. **1639** DRUMM. OF HAWTH. *Sp. for Edinburgh* Wks. (1711) 216 Relieving king James III. when he was beleaguer'd in his maiden-castle. **1648** J. BOND *Eschol* 27 Those parts of the Kingdome which had hitherto been untoucht, the Mayden Counties, as they call them, have been now most of all defloured. **1756** NUGENT *Gr. Tour, France* IV. 26 [Abbeville] is called *The maiden town*, because it was never taken by an enemy. **1802** WORDSW. *Sonn. Extinct. Venet. Repub.*, She was a maiden City, bright and free.

b. Of a plant or tree: *(a)* That has grown from seed, not from a stock; *(b)* That has not been budded, lopped, pruned, or transplanted.

a **1649** DRUMM. OF HAWTH. *Poems* Wks. (1711) 22/1 Though envy, avarice, time, your tombs throw down, With maiden-lawrells nature will them crown. **1655** MOUFET & BENNET *Health's Improv.* (1746) 320 The unset Leek, or Maiden-leek, is not so hot as the knopped ones. **1763** BURN *Eccl. Law* II. 413 Maiden trees of beech proceeding from stools above 20 years growth. **1805** R. W. DICKSON *Pract. Agric.* 1095 In cutting-wood one *maden* standard is left to each *lugg* or forty-nine square yards. **1832** *Planting* 91 in *Lib. Usef. Knowl., Husb.* III. Maiden-plant.—A young tree raised from seed, in opposition to one produced from an old root or stub. **1900** *Brit. Med. Jrnl.* No. 2080. 1367 The child so suffering [from congenital hernia] is passed naked through a cleft maiden ash on a Sunday morning at sunrise.

c. Of soil, metals, etc.: That has never been disturbed, ploughed, or worked. Also **maiden-wax**, 'virgin' wax (= F. *cire vierge*, Du. *maagdenwas*), wax taken from the comb without melting.

1622 MALYNES *Anc. Law-Merch.* 259 There is Mayden-gold so called because it was never in the fire. **1726** LEONI *Alberti's Archit.* I. 50/2 Cramps done over with Maiden-wax.. never rot. **1776** G. SEMPLE *Building in Water* 34 You work on fresh maiden Ground, that has not been fouled or incumbered with Stones. **1812** SIR R. HOARE *Anc. South Wilts.* 16 Maiden downs, by which I mean all land untouched by the plough. **1849** *Florist* 43 Refreshing my beds annually with a few barrowfuls of maiden earth mixed with pig or horse dung. **1878** *Archæol. Cantiana* XII. 8 I found the earth was almost entirely maiden soil. **1897** *Daily News* 23 Apr. 3/1 Much of it [coal] was in its 'maiden state'—that is, had not been worked over in the past.

d. Of a soldier, etc.; also of a weapon: Untried.

1596 SHAKS. *1 Hen. IV*, v. iv. 132 Full bravely hast thou flesht thy Maiden sword. **1603** DRAYTON *Odes* xvii. 102 Though but a Maiden Knight. **1647** CLARENDON *Hist. Reb.* VI. § 291 The Horse he put under the Command of his Brother, the Lord John Somerset, a maiden Soldier too. **1834** L. RITCHIE *Wand. by Seine* 15 He had not as yet fleshed his maiden sword. **1838** LYTTON *Alice* IV. v, The air rather of a martyr than a maiden placeman. **1842** TENNYSON *Sir Galahad* 61 A maiden knight—to me is given Such hope, I know not fear.

6. That is the first of its kind; made, used, etc. for the first time. Occas. in sense *early*, *earliest*. ***maiden speech***: the first speech delivered in the House by a Member of Parliament.

1555 W. WATREMAN *Fardle Facions* Pref. 20 He but borowyng their woordes, bryngeth it foorthe for a mayden booke. **1622** CULLIS *Stat. Sewers* v. (1647) 219 Your Reader took in hand to read upon a Maiden-law, which never before this time abide [*sic*] his Exposition in any Inns of Court. *c* **1645** HOWELL *Lett.* (1650) II. 122, I send one of the maiden Copies heerwith to attend you. **1786** WOLCOT (P. Pindar) *Odes to R. A.'s* ii. But not a single maiden dish, poor gentleman, of flesh or fish. **1794** *Hist.* in *Ann. Reg.* 61 Mr. Canning, in his maiden speech (according to the technical language of the house) said [etc.]. **1798** *Sporting Mag.* XII. 4 A maiden deer was turned out at Tower Hill. **1799** G. SMITH *Laboratory* II. 261 The usual baits are the tail-part of a maiden lob-worm. *a* **1813** A. WILSON *Foresters* Poet. Wks. (1846) 211 Fresh on his maiden cruise to see the world. **1813** VANCOUVER *Agric. Devon* 213 The maiden bite of the artificial grasses and white clover. **1825** COL. HAWKER *Diary* (1893) I. 284 This was my maiden day at English black game shooting. **1842** H. ROGERS *Ess.* (1874) I. i. 4 The same year was signalised by his maiden publication. **1843** LE FEVRE *Life Trav. Phys.* I. I. i. 20 It was at this time.. that I took my maiden fee. **1883** *Cassell's Fam. Mag.* Aug. 527/2 In the second year the planter gets a very small crop called the maiden-crop. **1884** *Times* (weekly ed.) 31 Oct. 19/4 The.. new steamship.. sailed from Plymouth.. on her maiden trip to the Antipodes. **1901** *Scotsman* 11 Mar. 8/7 The.. steamer.. was on her maiden voyage from London to China.

maiden ('meɪd(ə)n), *v.* [f. MAIDEN *sb.*]

†**1.** In phr. *to maiden it*: to act like a maiden; to be coy. *Obs.*

1597–8 BP. HALL *Sat.* III. iii. 5 For had I mayden'd it, as many use, Loath for to graunt, but loather to refuse.

2. *trans.* (*dial.*) To wash clothes with a 'maiden'. Hence ***maidening-pot***, ***-tub***.

1839 BYWATER *Sheffield Dial.* 132 Salla do yo pull toud maidnin tub tot table. **1890** *Sheffield Daily Tel.* 11 Apr. 7/1 The child was standing near a maidening pot half full of water.

maiden aunt ('meɪd(ə)n ɑːnt). [f. MAIDEN *a.* 1 + AUNT.] An unmarried aunt. Hence

ˌ**maiden-ˈauntishly** *adv.*, in a manner characteristic of maiden aunts; primly.

1709 PRIOR *Henry & Emma* in *Poems on Several Occasions* 244 The ancient Maiden Aunt. **1711** [see AUNT 1 a]. **1758** JOHNSON *Idler* No. 24 ⁋5 Maiden aunts with small fortunes. **1847** C. M. YONGE *Scenes & Characters* xiii. 158 That worst of plagues, a prying maiden aunt. **1917** T. S. ELIOT *Prufrock* 33 Miss Helen Slingsby was my maiden aunt. **1928** *Observer* 22 July 7 Camberley..was rather like a shocked maiden aunt, who had been forced to look on at something not quite 'nice'. Maiden-auntishly she took up again the knitting of the Franco-German War. **1938** W. S. MAUGHAM *Summing Up* 176, I..ask myself whether in another forty years the bright young things of current letters will appear as jejune as do now their maiden aunts of The Yellow Book. **1975** *Harper's & Queen* May 137/3 As for aged relations, maiden aunts in whose name so much is suffered, Miss Charlton hasn't got any.

†**maiden-child**. *Obs.* A female child. (Cf. MAID-CHILD.)

*c***893** K. ÆLFRED *Oros.* I. x. §2 Eft þonne þa wif heora bearn cendon, þonne feddon hie þa mædencild. *c***1200** ORMIN 7897, & maȝȝdennchild bitacneþþ uss Wac mahht i gode dedess. *c***1250** *Gen. & Ex.* 2574 Ðo bad monophis pharaun..leten ðe mayden childre liuen. *c***1440** *Bone Flor.* 31 A feyre lady he had to wyfe, That..dyed of a maydyn chylde. **1587** FLEMING *Contn. Holinshed* III. 1999/1 Leaving but one maiden-child and princesse. **1643** J. STEER tr. *Exp. Chyrurg.* ix. 42 There was a Maiden childe, of the age of two yeares.

maidenhair (ˈmeɪd(ə)nhɛə(r)). Also 6–7 **maiden's hair.** [f. MAIDEN *sb.* + HAIR.]

1. The name of certain ferns having fine hair-like stalks and delicate fronds. **a.** *Adiantum Capillus-veneris*, called also ***black*** or ***true maidenhair***; formerly much used in medicine.

*c***1450** *ME. Med. Bk.* (Heinrich) 102 Take..verueyne, maydenher [etc.]. **1549** *Compl. Scot.* vi. 67, I sau madyn hayr, of the quhilk ane sirop maid of it is remeid contrar the infectione of the melt. **1562** TURNER *Herbal* II. 157 b, Trichomanes (that is our English Maydens heare) is supposed to haue the same vertue that the Lumbardy Maydens heare hath. **1597** GERARDE *Herbal* II. cccclvii. 982–3 True Maiden haire... The right Maiden haire groweth vpon wals..it is a stranger in Englande... In English black Maiden haire, and Venus haire. **1697** TRYON *Way to Health* xv. (ed. 3) 368 Take..a pint and half, Tincture of Saffron, and Syrup of Maidenhair. **1785** MARTYN *Rousseau's Bot.* xxxii. (1794) 491 True Maiden-hair..is used or supposed to be so, in the syrup of capillaire. **1887** E. LYALL *Knight-Errant* (1889) 87 A little lizard..plunged into the maidenhair that fringed the altar.

b. *Asplenium Trichomanes*, called also ***common*** or ***English maidenhair***.

*a***1400–50** *Stockh. Med. MS.* 176 Maydenheer or watir-wourt, *capillus virginis*. **1562** [see a]. **1579** LANGHAM *Gard. Health* (1633) 379 Tricomanes, Polytricon or English Maiden-haire hath yᵉ same vertues that Capillus Veneris hath. **1597** GERARDE *Herbal* II. cccclviii. 984 Of English or common Maiden haire. **1634** PEACHAM *Gentl. Exerc.* III. II. vii. 144 June in a mantle of darke grasse greene, upon his head a garland of Bents, King-cups, and Maidens haire. **1688** R. HOLME *Armoury* II. 74/1 The English Maiden-hair is a small spiry stalk with two round leaves fixed to the side [etc.]. **1760** J. LEE *Introd. Bot.* App. 318 Maiden-hair, English black, *Asplenium*.

c. ***white maidenhair***: *Asplenium Ruta-muraria*.

1597 GERARDE *Herbal* II. cccclvii. 983 Wall Rue, or Rue Maiden haire..White Maiden haire. **1718** QUINCY *Compl. Disp.* 115 White Maidenhair.—It is used in Decays of the Lungs. **1760** J. LEE *Introd. Bot.* App. 318 Maiden-hair, White, *Asplenium*. **1861** MISS PRATT *Flower. Pl.* VI. 213.

2. In other plant-names. **a.** ***golden maidenhair***, the moss *Polytrichum commune*.

1578 LYTE *Dodoens* III. lxxi. 412 Goldylockes, *Polytrichon*, or Golden Maydenheare. **1785** MARTYN *Rousseau's Bot.* xxxii. (1794) 493 Greater Golden Maidenhair..is a large sort of moss and abundant in woods, heaths and bogs.

b. The Lancashire Asphodel, *Narthecium ossifragum* (see quot.).

1633 JOHNSON *Gerarde's Herbal* I. lxxi. 96 Another water Asphodill, which..in Lancashire is vsed by women to die their haire of a yellowish colour, and therefore by them it is termed Maiden-haire, if we may beleeue Lobell.

c. Yellow Bedstraw, *Galium verum*.

1548 TURNER *Name of Herbes* (E.D.S.) 39 Galion or gallion is named in English in the North countrey Maydens heire. **1562** —— *Herbal* II. 6 b.

d. Ground Ivy, *Nepeta Glechoma*.

1657 COLES *Adam in Eden* xxvi. 53 Some Country people that would have the barren Ivy to be the true Ground-Ivy, call the other Maiden-hair.

†**3.** Some textile fabric. *Obs.*

1359 *Will of Agnes Selby* in *Test. Ebor.* (Surtees) I. 71 Lego Anabillæ quondam servienti meæ..unam tunicam de maydenhare.

†**4.** ? Some kind of marking on flowers. *Obs.*

? **1607** DAY *Parl. Bees* xi. (1641) G 3 b, July-flowers, and Carnations weare Leaves double streakt with Maiden haire.

¶**5. a.** In literal sense: A maiden's hair. *rare*$^{-1}$.

1648 HERRICK *Hesper., Dissuas. fr. Idleness*, Play not with the maiden-haire For each ringlet there's a snare.

b. A woman's pubic hair.

1928 D. H. LAWRENCE *Lady Chatterley* xv. 265 That's where to put forget-me-nots, in the man-hair, or the maiden-hair. *a***1930** —— *Last Poems* (1932) 14 The dim blotch of black maidenhair like an indicator, Giving a message to the man.

6. *attrib.* and *Comb.*, as †*maidenhair-syrup*; **maidenhair fern** = 1; **maidenhair grass**, *Briza media*; **(golden) maidenhair-moss** = 2 a; **maidenhair-spleenwort**, a book-name for various plants of the genus *Asplenium* (see quot. 1837); **maidenhair-tree**, a name for the GINKGO.

1833 *Penny Cycl.* I. 120/1 The A[diantum] Capillus Veneris, or the *maiden-hair fern. **1640** PARKINSON *Theatr. Bot.* 1165 *Gramen tremulum medium*. *Maidenhaire grasse, or the lesser quaking grasse. **1597** GERARDE *Herbal* III. clvii. 1371 *Muscus capillaris*..Goldilocks, or Golden *Maiden haire Mosse. **1837** MACGILLIVRAY *Withering's Brit. Plants* 383 *Asplenium Trichomanes*. Common *Maidenhair Spleenwort... *A. viride*. Green Maidenhair Spleenwort... *A. Adiantum-nigrum*. Black Maidenhair Spleenwort. **1862** ANSTED *Channel Isl.* II. viii. (ed. 2) 183 The *a. trichomanes* or maiden-hair spleen-wort, is the most delicate of the group. **1711** *Lond. Gaz.* No. 4845/4, 200 half pint Bottles of *Maidenhair Sirrup. **1773** *Gentl. Mag.* XLIII. 338 The Ginkgo, or *Maiden-hair tree, from China,..has been propagated by Mr. Gordon, of Mile-End. **1882** *Garden* 12 Aug. 145/3 The leaves bear a good deal of resemblance to those of the Maidenhair tree.

maidenhead[1] (ˈmeɪd(ə)nhɛd). *arch.* [f. MAIDEN *sb.* + -HEAD.]

1. The state or condition of a maiden; virginity; said occas. of a man (see MAIDEN *sb.* 2 b). Also = HYMEN[2] 1.

*a***1300** *Cursor M.* 10880, I herd it neuer in lijf ne ledd Womman ber barn in maiden-hedd. *Ibid.* 12706 Sent Ion, þe wangelist..he liued in maiden-hede. **1357** *Lay Folks Catech.* 125 Iesu crist..was sothefastely consayued of the maiden mari,..Withouten ony mynnyng of hir maidenhede. **1423** JAS. I *Kingis Q.* 55 Pitee was to here The crueltee of that vnknyghtly dede, Quhare was fro the bereft thi maidenhede. **1535** COVERDALE *Judg.* xi. 38 Then wente shee with her playefeeres, and bewayled hir mayden heade vpon the mountaynes. **1592** SHAKS. *Rom. & Jul.* I. i. 23, I will bee civill with the Maids, and cut off their heads..the heads of the Maids, or their Maiden-heads. **1613** SHAKS. *Hen. VIII*, II. iii. 23 By my troth, and Maidenhead, I would not be a Queene. **1697** DRYDEN *Virg. Georg.* Ded., He who carries a Maidenhead into a Cloyster, is sometimes apt to lose it there. **1749** FIELDING *Tom Jones* XVIII. xiii, A merry song which bore some relation to matrimony and the loss of a maidenhead. **1796** PEGGE *Anonym.* (1809) 457 To be able to look upon the sun, they say, is a sign of one's having a maidenhead. **1867** R. G. LATHAM *Dict. Eng. Lang.*, *Maidenhead*,..Virginity..the hymen, or virginal membrane. **1885–94** R. BRIDGES *Eros & Psyche* Feb. xxiv, His earthly bride, Who won his love, in simple maidenhead. **1928** F. W. S. BROWNE tr. *T. H. van de Velde's Ideal Marriage* II. iv. 57 Within this space is the sexual orifice... In maidens this is closed by the *hymen*..or virginal membrane, popularly called 'maidenhead'.

†**b.** Phrases: ***to enjoy, get, have, prove, take, win (a woman's) maidenhead***; also of a woman (*rarely* of a man), ***to keep, lose*** (Sc. ***tine***) ***one's maidenhead***. *Obs.*

*c***1250** *Gen. & Ex.* 1852 Sichem tok hire maiden-hed. *c***1320** *Sir Tristr.* 2134, Y loued neuer man wiþ mode Bot him þat hadde mi maidenhede. *c***1330** *Amis & Amil.* 767 So thai plaid in word and dede, That he wan hir maidenhede. *c***1375** *Sc. Leg. Saints* xviii. (*Egipciane*) 446 Myn madynned quhow I first tynt þar. *c***1400** *Destr. Troy* 3997 Most was hir mynde hir maidonhede to kepe. *c***1450** *St. Cuthbert* (Surtees) 204 Sho wepid..þat wyked dede þat made hir lose hir maydenhede. **1567** *Gude & Godlie B.* (S.T.S.) 146 Zit keipit scho hir madinheid vnforlorne. **1591** LYLY *Sappho* II. i, Phœbus in his godhead sought to get my maidenhead. **1663** DRYDEN *Wild Gallant* Prol., As some raw squire, by tender mother bred, 'Till one-and-twenty keeps his maidenhead. **1697** VANBRUGH *2nd Pt. Æsop* iii. 51 *Æsop.* How long did you stay? *Beau.* Till I had lost my maidenhead.

†**2.** *transf.* and *fig.*, *esp.* the first stage or first-fruits of anything; the first example, proof, trial, or use; also in phrases (see 1 b). *Obs.*

*c***1412** HOCCLEVE *De Reg. Princ.* 3036 þou..þe maydenhede of this Iuel Shalt preue anone. *a***1550** *Tales & Quick Answ.* xcv. (1814) 98 That he wolde gyue him leaue to haue the maidenheed of the pyllory. **1591** FLORIO *2nd Fruites* Ep. Ded., The maiden head of my industrie I yeelded to a noble Mecenas (renoumed Lecester) the honor of England. *a***1592** H. SMITH *Serm.* (1599) 536 God requiring the first labours of his seruants, and (as I may say), the maidenhead of euery man. **1612** (*title*) Parthenia, or the Maydenhead of the first musicke that euer was printed for the Virginalls. *a***1687** PETTY *Pol. Arith.* i. (1691) 20 One sort of Vessels, and Rigging, where haste is requisite for the Maidenhead of a Market. **1755** SMOLLETT *Quix.* (1803) I. 19 Others affirm, that the windmills had the maidenhead of his valour. **1775** S. J. PRATT *Liberal Opin.* cxxxvii. (1783) IV. 260 He had received a present, of which, he insisted upon it, we should have the maidenhead.

†ˈ**maidenhead**[2]. *Obs.* [f. MAIDEN *sb.* + HEAD.] A representation of the head or bust of the Virgin Mary. **a.** As an ornamental finish to the handle of a spoon; *occas.*, the spoon itself.

[**1446** *Wills & Inv.* (Surtees Soc.) I. 92 In Promptuario sunt ij Coclearia argentea et deaurata..cum ymaginibus Beatæ Mariæ in fine eorundem.] **1495** in Wadley *Notes Wills in Gt. Orphan Bk. Bristol* (1886) 170 [Six silver spoons] cum Maidenheddis. [Six silver spoons] de Maidenheddis. **1522** *Test. Ebor.* (Surtees) V. 162 Mariæ Evers sex cocliaria de arg. cum le madynheddes. **1538** *Bury Wills* (Camden) 134 Allso I bequeth to Nycholas Esthaw my syluer pece and iij syluer sponys wᵗ mayeden hedes. **1567** *Richmond Wills* (Surtees Soc.) 198, xiij postle spones..½ dossone lyones and ½ doss. madinehedes.

b. *Her.* As a bearing on a shield, etc.

1615 HEYWOOD *Foure Prentises* Wks. 1874 II. 229 Godfreyes shield, hauing a Maidenhead with a Crowne in it. **1618** J. TAYLOR (Water P.) *Pennyless Pilgr.* A 4 b, I..went that night as farre as Islington, There did I finde..A Maydenhead of twenty fiue yeeres old, But surely it was painted,..And for a signe or wonder, hang'd at' dore. **1728** S. KENT *Banner Display'd* II. 764 Crest, on a Torce of his Colours, a maidenhead proper, enclos'd in a Ring of Gold.

maidenhood (ˈmeɪd(ə)nhʊd). Forms: see MAIDEN *sb.* and -HOOD. [OE. *mæȝdenhád*, f. *mæȝden* MAIDEN + *-hád* -HOOD.] The condition of being a maiden; the time of life during which one is a maiden. Formerly also = MAIDENHEAD[1] 1 b and 2, in phrases ***to have, hold, keep, lose,*** etc. (***one's***) ***maidenhood***.

*a***900** CYNEWULF *Crist* 1419 þa ic sylf ȝestaȝ maȝa in modor, þeah wæs hyre mæȝdenhad æȝhwæs onwalȝ. *c***1200** *Vices & Virtues* 55 Þat hie ne behiet hire maidenhad æure mo to healden. *c***1200** ORMIN 46 Forr maȝȝdenhad & widdwesshad & weddlac birrþ ben clene. *a***1225** *Ancr. R.* 54 Heo leas hire meidenhod, & was imaked hore. *c***1290** *S. Eng. Leg.* 380/137 For ȝe habbez ȝeot ouwer Maidenhod. **1362** LANGL. *P. Pl.* A. I. 158 Ʒe naue no more merit In Masse ne In houres þen Malkyn of hir Maydenhod, þat no Mon desyreþ. **1388** WYCLIF *Luke* ii. 36 [She] hadde lyued with hir hosebonde seuene ȝeer fro hir maydynhod. *c***1450** LONELICH *Grail* xxix. 150 For Maydenhod is In this maner trewly, that felte neuere man fleschly,..but virginite is An heighere thing. *c***1575** *Balfour's Practicks* 678 The Lord of the ground sall have the maidenhood of all maidenis..dwelland on the ground. **1591** SHAKS. *1 Hen. VI*, IV. vi. 17 The irefull Bastard Orleance, that drew blood From thee my Boy, and had the Maidenhood Of thy first fight, I soone encountred. *a***1603** [see MAIDENLESS]. **1641** EARL MONM. tr. *Biondi's Civil Warres* II. 83 No maidenhood was undeflowred, nor marriage bed unviolated. **1846** C. G. PROWETT *Prometheus Bound* 40 In loveless maidenhood outworn. **1858** HAWTHORNE *Fr. & It. Jrnls.* I. 226 There is..a very pleasant atmosphere of maidenhood about her. **1863** WOOLNER *My Beautiful Lady* Introd. 5 A man..who has found His..daughter..Fallen from her maidenhood.

maidenish (ˈmeɪd(ə)nɪʃ), *a.* [f. MAIDEN *sb.* + -ISH.] Resembling a maiden, characteristic of a maiden. Used in depreciatory sense.

1749 FIELDING *Tom Jones* VI. vii, 'Come, come', says Western, 'none of your maidenish airs'. **1815** *Zeluca* I. 172 Do not let one word of this rhodomontade come within ken of your maidenish aunts. **1825** *New Monthly Mag.* XV. 299 A pretty affectation of maidenish coyness.

Comb. **1789** ANNA SEWARD *Lett.* (1811) II. 250 But, Lord! what a pale, maidenish-looking animal for a voluptuary!

maidenism (ˈmeɪd(ə)nɪz(ə)m). *rare.* [f. MAIDEN *sb.* + -ISM.] Maidenish bearing and behaviour; a maidenish notion or peculiarity.

1790 ANNA SEWARD *Lett.* (1811) III. 38 When he confessed these maidenisms, I despaired of his suiting the pleasant, prancing, pop-gun situation of butler at Prior's Lea. **1825** *Gentl. Mag.* XCV. I. 626 The elegant simplicity and delicate maidenism of the pretty Miriam Gray.

†ˈ**maidenkin**. *Obs.*$^{-1}$ [f. MAIDEN *sb.* + -KIN.] = MAIDKIN.

*c***1330** *Arth. & Merlin* 671 (Kölbing) To ligge bi a maidenkin & biȝeten a child her in. *c***1440** [see MAIDKIN].

†ˈ**maidenless**, *a.* *nonce-wd.* [f. MAIDEN *sb.* + -LESS.] Not truly 'maiden'.

*a***1603** T. CARTWRIGHT *Confut. Rhem. N.T.* (1618) 39 The Greeke Church, which neuer liked of the maidenlesse maidenhood of their Priests.

ˈ**maidenlike**, *a.* and *adv.* [f. MAIDEN *sb.* + -LIKE.] **a.** *adj.* Such as is usual with maidens; befitting a maiden. †**b.** *adv.* After the manner of maidens. *Obs.*

15.. *Robin Conscience* 318 in Hazl. *E.P.P.* III. 246 To clatter and flatter is no maidenlike way. *a***1548** HALL *Chron., Hen. VI* 183 The yong erle of Rutland..scace of yᵉ age of .xii. yeres, a faire gentleman and a maydenlike person. **1589** FLEMING *Virg. Georg.* I. 15 If she overcast vpon hir face a virgins rednesse Or blushing maidenlike. **1632** LITHGOW *Trav.* III. 96 He was maiden-like brought vp amongst the Kings daughters. **1825** J. NEAL *Bro. Jonathan* II. 179 Our boy contrived..to do a multitude of..pretty, maiden-like things. **1834** LYTTON *Pompeii* 23 Her manners are not maidenlike. **1847** TENNYSON *Princess* IV. 73 And maidenlike as far As I could ape their treble, did I sing.

maidenliness (ˈmeɪd(ə)nlɪnɪs). [f. MAIDENLY + -NESS.] The quality of being maidenly; the behaviour proper to a maiden.

1555 W. WATREMAN *Fardle Facions* App. 326 Any man of a shamefaced maindenlines [*sic*]. **1583** BABINGTON *Commaundm.* (1615) 42 Silence is ignorance, modesty is too much maidenlinesse. **1617** *Rider's Dict.*, *Virginalitas*, Maidenlinesse. **1868** PUSEY *Serm. Pharisaism* 13 Those who used to furnish our ideal of maidenliness and purity. **1879** G. MEREDITH *Egoist* I. x. 193 That fair childish maidenliness had ceased.

maidenly (ˈmeɪd(ə)nlɪ), *a.* and *adv.* [f. MAIDEN *sb.* + -LY.] **A.** *adj.*

1. Of or pertaining to a maiden, or to maidenhood. In early use = VIRGIN *a.*

1450–1530 *Myrr. our Ladye* 112 Whyche shulde be conceyued and borne of thy maydenly body. **1582** BENTLEY *Mon. Matrones* Pref. Bj, Even from their tender and maidenlie yeeres, to spend their time..in the studies of noble and approved sciences. **1871** R. ELLIS tr. *Catullus* lxiv. 78 Taxed of her youthful array, her maidenly bloom fresh-glowing. **1892** *Temple Bar* May 114 The maidenly curve of her bust.

b. *nonce-use.* (Cf. MAIDEN *a.* 6.)

1823 BYRON *Juan* XIII. xc, An orator,..Who had deliver'd well a very set Smooth speech, his first and maidenly transgression.

†**2.** Of persons: Resembling a maiden in action or bearing. Characterized by a maiden's

qualities, e.g. gentleness, modesty, timidity. *Obs.*

1523 SKELTON *Garl. Laurel* 865 Lyke to Aryna maydenly of porte. **1549** CHALONER *Erasmus on Folly* A ij, Shall one of those shamefast and maidenly men not sticke than to displaie his pecockes fethers? **1592** GREENE *Groatsw. Wit* (1617) D 3 b, My brother is a maidenly Batcheler. **1597** SHAKS. *2 Hen. IV*, II. ii. 82 Wherefore blush you now? what a Maidenly man at Armes are you become? **1655** GURNALL *Chr. in Arm.* verse 14. iii. (1669) 8/2 They..were so maidenly and fearful, as not to venture down their hills, for fear of drowning. **1672** MARVELL *Reh. Transp.* I. 4 Our author is very maidenly, and condescends to his Bookseller not without some reluctance.

3. Of qualities, actions, etc.: Proper to, or characteristic of a maiden.

1532 MORE *Confut. Tindale* Wks. 626/1 To learne of hys lemman some very maidenly shamefastenes. **1590** SHAKS. *Mids. N.* III. ii. 217 And will you rent our ancient loue asunder, To ioyne with men in scorning your poore friend? It is not friendly, 'tis not maidenly. **1748** RICHARDSON *Clarissa* (1811) II. 68 A confession, that all your past behaviour was maidenly reserve only. **1849** JAMES *Woodman* xxii, She..with maidenly modesty retired till she had the sanction of her guardian's presence. **1884** *Contemp. Rev.* Oct. 547 The manner in which Miss Victoria Dare.. captures Lord Dunbeg..is not exactly maidenly.

B. *adv.* After the fashion of a maiden; in a maidenly manner.

1596 HARINGTON *Metam. Ajax* (1813) 20, I that maidenly to write was wont. **1625** *Gonsalvio's Sp. Inquis.* 59 Bending her head downeward maidenly. **1844** MRS. BROWNING *Crowned & Wedded*, Her looks turned maidenly to ground. **1889** F. M. CRAWFORD *Greifenstein* I. ii. 39 She was..away from the world,..and maidenly ignorant of all it contained.

† **'maidenman.** *Obs.* [f. MAIDEN *sb.* + MAN *sb.*¹] A maiden, virgin.

c **893** K. ÆLFRED *Oros.* I. xiv. §1 Mesiane noldon ðæt Læcedemonia mæȝdenmenn mid heora ofreden. *c* **1000** *Sax. Leechd.* III. 42 Ga þænne an mæden man to and ho hit on his sweoran. *c* **1200** ORMIN 2085 Sannte Marȝe..wass æfre maȝȝdennmann. *a* **1310** in Wright *Lyric P.* 82 For nou thou wost of moder fare thou thou be clene mayden mon.

maiden's blush.

1. Used as a name for a delicate pink colour. Hence, a rose of this colour; also ***maiden-blush rose.***

Cf. *maiden blush*, s.v. MAIDEN A. 10.

1648 HERRICK *Hesper., Epithal. Sir C. Carew*, But for prick-madam, and for gentle-heart, And soft maidens-blush, the bride Makes holy these. **1661** PEACHAM *Compl. Gent.* (ed. 3) 156 Of the signification of Colours. Maidens-blush, [signifieth] Envy. **1750** G. HUGHES *Barbadoes* 226 From which Place rise several many-leav'd Flowers, of a Maiden's-blush. **1861** C. M. YONGE *Stokesley Secret* ii. 35 The standard maiden-blush rose. **1882** *Garden* 19 Aug. 168/2 The Maiden's Blush Rose, once so popular, but now seldom met with. **1928** D. H. LAWRENCE *Let.* 14 Nov. (1962) II. 1100 Those maiden-blush roses.

2. A small geometrid moth, *Ephyra punctaria.*

1869 E. NEWMAN *Brit. Moths* 73.

3. Either of two Australian trees with pinkish wood, *Sloanea australis*, of the family Elæocarpaceæ, or *Euroschinus falcatus*, of the family Anacardiaceæ.

1884 A. NILSON *Timber Trees New South Wales* 54 *E[chinocarpus] Australis.*—Maiden's Blush.—A beautiful tree, sometimes attaining a height of 150 feet. **1965** *Austral. Encycl.* I. 174/2 It [sc. *Euroschinus falcatus*] is variously known as pink poplar, ribbonwood, Donnelly's cedar and most generally perhaps as maiden's blush, though this last vernacular is now retained for a very different tree, *Sloanea australis. Ibid.* III. 364/2 *S[loanea] australis* (maiden's blush or bush alder) is a small tree with showy flowers, found in the coastal brush forests from Illawarra in southern New South Wales to Queensland.

4. *Austral.* (See quots.)

1941 BAKER *Dict. Austral. Slang* 45 *Maiden's blush*, ginger beer and raspberry. **1961** PARTRIDGE *Dict. Slang* Suppl. 1177/1 *Maiden's blush*, ginger beer and raspberry cordial: Australian. **1966** G. W. TURNER *Eng. Lang. Austral. & N.Z.* vi. 116 *Maiden's blush* (a drink, either of port and lemonade or rum and raspberry).

maidenship ('meɪd(ə)nʃɪp). [f. MAIDEN *sb.* + -SHIP.] The personality of a maiden; chiefly in ***Your Maidenship***, as a playful form of address.

1602 ROWLANDS *Tis Merrie* 22 Your Mayden-ship takes Liquor in too nice. **1637** HEYWOOD *Royall King* III. i. E 2 b, Yes if it please your Maidenship. **1756** MRS. F. BROOKE *Old Maid* No. 9. 64 Your maidenship has opened a channel, through which my thoughts may flow. **1831** *Fraser's Mag.* IV. 183 We trust that their chaste maidenships the Muses will not suffer much of this metrical rubbish to fall in our way.

† **maidenweed.** *Obs.* [In sense 1 for **maythen-weed* (see MAYTHEN); in sense 2 f. MAIDEN *sb.*]

1. = MAIDWEED.

1499 *Promp. Parv.* (Pynson) [see MAIDWEED quot. *c* 1440]. **1530** PALSGR. 241/2 Maydenwede. **1591** PERCIVALL *Sp. Dict.*, *Ervato*, maidenweeds, hogfenell, *Peucedanum.* **1592** R. D. *Hypnerotomachia* 29 A garland..of bitter alisander commixt with dead leaves of maydenweede. **1607** TOPSELL *Four-f. Beasts* (1658) 39 Castoreum..procureth sleep, they being anointed with it, maiden-weed, and conserve of roses. **1718** ROWE tr. *Lucan* 404 Wound-wort and Maiden-weed perfume the Air.

2. = MAIDENHAIR 1 a.

1524 *Grete Herball* xxxvii, Adianthos. Maydenweede.

† **maideux.** *Obs.* Also 5 **madeus, maydese, ma aydeus.** [OF. *m'aide deus* 'God help me'.] In phrase *so maideux* = 'so help me God'.

a **1400–50** *Alexander* 729 'So madeus' [*Ashm. MS.* Sa ma aydeus], quod þis oþer man. *Ibid.* 4446 And maydese ȝit. *Ibid.* 5024 'So maideux', quod þe mone-tree.

maidfeloun, obs. variant of MATFELLON.

† **'maidhead.** *Obs.* [f. MAID *sb.* + -HEAD.] = MAIDENHEAD¹.

1390 GOWER *Conf.* II. 341 The beaute of his face streited He hath, and threste out bothe hise yhen, That alle wommen whiche him syhen Thanne afterward, of him ne roghte. And thus his maidehiede he boghte. **1567** *Gude & Godlie B.* (S.T.S.) 146 *note*, Yet keipit shee her maid-heid vnforlorne.

maidhood ('meɪdhʊd). [f. MAID *sb.* + -HOOD. In the earliest examples repr. OE. *mæȝ(e)þ-hád*, f. *mæȝ(e)þ* (see MAIDEN *sb.*).] = MAIDENHOOD.

a **900** *O.E. Martyrol.* 31 May 88 Heo on mæȝðhade hire lif geendade. *c* **1200** ORMIN 2497 Baþe leddenn i maȝȝþhad All þeȝȝre lif till ende. *c* **1200** *Trin. Coll. Hom.* 21 Ne hire maidhod ne was awemned. *a* **1225** *St. Marher.* 3 Ich habbe a deore ȝimstan ant ich hit habbe iȝeuen þe mi meidhad ich meane. **1601** SHAKS. *Twel. N.* III. i. 162. **1604** —— *Oth.* I. i. 173 Is there not Charmes, By which the propertie of Youth, and Maidhood May be abus'd? **1800** HELENA WELLS *Constantia Neville* (ed. 2) II. 159 As by a matron the airs and graces of maidhood would be relinquished. **1881** W. WILKINS *Songs of Study* 154 The innocence of her maidhood.

maidie: see MAIDY.

maiding: see under MAID *v.*

maidish ('meɪdɪʃ), *a.* [f. MAID *sb.* + -ISH.] = MAIDENISH.

1872 GROSART *Donne's Poems* I. 22 *note*, The delays of maidish indecision. **1895** CROCKETT *Men of Moss Hags* xxxvi. 258 From a maidish and natural liking for a young and unmarried man.

† **'maidkin.** *Obs.*⁻⁰ In 5 **maydekin.** [f. MAID *sb.* + -KIN.] A little maid.

c **1440** *Promp. Parv.* 319/2 Maydekin, or lytylle mayde (*H., P.*, maydyn kyn), *puella.*

maidless ('meɪdlɪs), *a.* [f. MAID *sb.*¹ + -LESS.] Not having or without a maid-servant.

1892 C. M. YONGE *That Stick* I. xi. 117 My Lady could not well be allowed to go maidless. **1909** *Daily Chron.* 19 Aug. 7/3 The clever housekeeper knows the value of saying to the cook—or family, if maidless—'It is going to be so hot that we'll have cold meals.' **1926** *Public Opinion* 23 Apr. 410/3 The maidless mother is the chief victim of the storm. **1973** *Sci. Amer.* June 10/1 My outside interests are those one acquires in raising four children (a geologist, an astronomer, a mathematician and a violinist) and running a busy, exciting, maidless household.

maidling ('meɪdlɪŋ). *nonce-wd.* [f. MAID *sb.* + -LING.] A little maid.

In quot. 1831 coined to render MHG. *magetlein*, which is not really equivalent in formation.

1831 CARLYLE *Misc. Ess.* (1857) II. 226 She let it [her hair] flow down, The lovely maidling. **1896** *Pall Mall Mag.* Sept. 30 The dissonant pipings of ten charity maidlings.

† **'maidly,** *a. Obs.* [f. MAID *sb.* + -LY¹.] Resembling a maid.

1563 B. GOOGE *Eglogs*, etc. (Arb.) 71 O Cowards all, and maydly men of Courage faynt and weake. **1565** *Satir. Poems Reform.* i. 376 Howe the Frenshe Kinge in marag did endowe me wth Royall right, a madlie wydowe.

Maid Marian. Also 6 **mayd(e-, mawd-, -marion,** 7 **-marrian, -marrion, -morion.** A female personage in the May-game and morris-dance. In the later forms of the story of Robin Hood she appears as the companion of the outlaw, the association having prob. been suggested by the fact that the two were both represented in the May-day pageants.

c **1525** BARCLAY *Eclog* iv. (1570) C vj, Yet would I gladly heare nowe some mery fit Of mayde Marion, or els of Robin hood. **1575** LANEHAM *Let.* (1871) 22 A liuely morisdauns according too the auncient manner, six daunserz, Mawd-marion, and the fool. **1589** *Pasquil's Ret.* B iij b, Martin..is the Mayd-marian, trimlie drest vppe in a cast Gowne, and a Kercher. **1596** SHAKS. *1 Hen. IV*, III. iii. 129 For Wooman-hood, Maid-marian may be the Deputies wife of the Ward to thee. **1652** C. B. STAPYLTON *Herodian* 65 Train'd Bands are Pamp'red like unto Maidmarians. **1656** BLOUNT *Glossogr.* s.v., *Morisco*, a Boy dressed in a Girles habit, whom they call the Maid Marrian. **1696** PHILLIPS, *Maid Marrion*, or *Morion.* *a* **1699** TEMPLE *Of Health & Long Life* Wks. 1720 I. 277 A Sett of Morrice Dancers, composed of Ten Men who danced, a Maid Marian, and a Tabor and Pipe. [Misquoted by Johnson, who in consequence explains *Maidmarian* as 'a kind of dance', an error which is copied in later Dicts.]

maid of honour.

1. An unmarried lady, usually of noble birth, who attends upon a queen or princess.

c **1586** C'TESS PEMBROKE *Ps.* XLV. vii, Her maides of honor shall on her attend. **1646** CRASHAW *Sosp. d'Herode* xlii, The foul queen's most abhorred maids of honour..stand to wait upon her. **1711** STEELE *Spect.* No. 109 ¶4 The Action at the Tilt-yard you may be sure won the fair Lady, who was a Maid of Honour. **1756–7** tr. *Keysler's Trav.* (1760) IV. 189 Another court-festivity is at the marriage of one of the empress's maids of honour. **1842** TENNYSON *Day Dream* 80 The maid-of-honour blooming fair.

2. A kind of cheesecake orig. sold at Richmond, Surrey.

1769 *Public Advertiser* 11 Mar. 3/3 Almond and Lemon Cheesecakes, Maid of Honour, Sweetmeat Tarts. **1836** T. HOOK *G. Gurney* I. 110 What are called cheesecakes elsewhere, are here called maids of honour. **1865** *Reader* 16 Sept. 311/2 A maid-of-honour, fresh from the *cuisine* of the Star and Garter, is relishable with its adjuncts. **1942** MRS. BELLOC LOWNDES *Let.* 19 Nov. (1971) 235 There were lobster patties, and queer looking Maid of Honour cakes. **1960** *Good Housek. Cookery Bk.* (rev. ed.) 394/1 Maids of Honour..3 oz. butter, 2 eggs,..1 oz. blanched almonds.. puff pastry, [etc.]. **1966** J. DOS PASSOS *Best Times* (1968) i. 11, I had so many little cheesecakes called Maids of Honor that I felt a bit sick.

3. The principal unmarried female attendant on the bride at a wedding; a bridesmaid. Also *fig.*

1895 in *Funk's Stand. Dict.* **1906** M. E. FREEMAN *Light of Soul* 348 Lily asked Maria to be her maid of honor. She planned to be married in church. **1911** H. S. HARRISON *Queed* xxi. 267 A victoria containing two lovely young girls sponsor and maid of honor for South Carolina. **1922** JOYCE *Ulysses* 321 The maids of honour..sisters of the bride, wore very becoming costumes. **1974** 'R. B. DOMINIC' *Epitaph for Lobbyist* x. 90 The maid of honour and the bridesmaids passed by...Betty Jo appeared on the arm of her father.. floating in a cloud of white.

Hence **maid-of-honourship** *nonce-wd.*

1896 A. DOBSON in *Longm. Mag.* Sept. 456 Her Maid-of-Honourship came to an end with her marriage.

'maidservant. [f. MAID *sb.* + SERVANT.] A female servant, usually a domestic servant.

1526 *Pilgr. Perf.* (W. de W. 1531) 83 A mayde seruaunt, thrall and bonde, all naked, fylthy, and deformed. **1600** J. PORY tr. *Leo's Africa* vii. 287 All the women of this region except maid-seruants go with their faces couered. *a* **1687** PETTY *Pol. Arith.* (1690) 101 The Wages given to the poorest Maid-Servant in the Countrey..is 30*s.* per annum. **1849** MRS. CARLYLE *Lett.* II. 68 The maid-servant met me at the front door. **1876** T. HARDY *Ethelberta* (1890) 395 One of the pretty maid-servants.

maidsweet: see MEADSWEET.

† **maidweed.** *Obs.* Also 5–6 **mayde-,** 6 **mayd-, made-.** [For **maithe-*, **maythe-weed*: see MAYTHE.] **a.** Stinking Camomile, *Anthemis Cotula.* **b.** ***red maidweed***, Red or Purple Camomile, *Adonis autumnalis.* (Cf. MAYWEED.)

c **1440** *Promp. Parv.* 319/2 Mayde wede, herbe, or maythys (*MS. S.* maydewode, *P.* maydenwede), *melissa, amarusca.* **1548** TURNER *Names of Herbes* (E.D.S.) 14 They call it in Englishe red mathes, alij, red mayde wed, alij purple camomyle. *Ibid.* 60 Stynkyng maydweede. **1551** —— *Herbal* I. D ij, Dyuers thynke, that heranthemon is the herbe: whych is called of the herbaryes, amarisca rubra: and of oure countre men, red mathe, or red made wede. **1660** LUPTON *1000 Notable Things* VIII. §46. 202 Which Maid-weed is a stinking herb, having a flower like a Daysie.

maidy ('meɪdɪ). *dial.* Also **maidie.** [f. MAID *sb.*: see -IE and -Y.] A little maid.

1880 T. HARDY *Trumpet-Major* I. iii. 57 You and maidy Anne must come in, if it be only for half an hour. **1882** W. S. GILBERT *Iolanthe* (1886) 32 If you go in You're sure to win—Yours will be the charming maidie. **1891** T. HARDY *Tess* (1900) 47/2 'Is it so, maidy?' he said.

maied, obs. f. MEAD *sb.*¹; pa. ppl. of MAY *v. Obs.*

maierom(e, obs. form of MARJORAM.

maiest-: see MAJEST-.

maiester, obs. form of MASTER.

maieutic (meɪ'juːtɪk), *a.* (and *sb.*) Also 7 **majeutic.** [ad. Gr. *μαιευτικ-ός* (*lit.* 'obstetric': used *fig.* by Socrates), f. *μαιεύεσθαι* to act as a midwife, f. *μαῖα* midwife.] Pertaining to (intellectual) midwifery, *i.e.* to the Socratic process of assisting a person to bring out into clear consciousness conceptions previously latent in his mind.

1655 STANLEY *Hist. Philos.*, *Plato* xv. 46 Of Platonick Discourse there are two kinds, Hyphegetick and Exegetick [of which a sub-division is called] Majeutick. **1856** W. A. BUTLER *Hist. Anc. Philos.* I. 374 The method of Socrates is ..essentially a 'maieutic' or obstetric method. **1868** *Contemp. Rev.* VII. 12 Teaching botany..by what he truly calls a *maieutic* process, drawing out intelligence before communicating knowledge. **1882** *Sat. Rev.* 23 Sept. 415/2 Examples of Mr. Cory's stimulating and maieutic method of dealing with history. **1886** SYMONDS *Renaiss. It., Cath. React.* (1898) VII xi. 176 Their maieutic ingenuity was vain.

b. *sb. pl.* The maieutic method.

1885 W. H. PAYNE tr. *Compayré's Hist. Pedagogy* 23 Maieutics, or the art of giving birth to ideas.

† **maieutical**, *a. Obs. rare*⁻¹. [f. prec. + -AL¹.] = prec. adj.

1678 CUDWORTH *Intell. Syst.* I. v. 693 Yet is all humane teaching but maieutical or obstetricious.

maigne, maigné, -ie, obs. ff. MAIN *a.*, MEYNIE.

maigre ('meɪgə(r)), *sb.* Also 9 **meagre.** [a. F. *maigre.*] A large fish, *Sciæna aquila*, common in the Mediterranean.

The *megyr* of *Promp. Parv.* is prob. unconnected.

1835 JENYNS *Man. Brit. Vert. Anim.* 352 *Sciæna Aquila* Cuv. (Maigre). **1836** YARRELL *Brit. Fishes* I. 90 The Maigre. *Ibid.* 92 Three fishermen once took twenty Maigres by a single sweep of their net. **1880** GÜNTHER *Fishes* 430 *Sciæna*

aquila..not rarely reaches the British coasts, where it is known as 'Meagre'. **1883** *Fisheries Exhib. Catal.* (ed. 4) 118 Skeleton of Maigre or Royal Fish.

‖**maigre** (mɛgr, 'meɪgə(r)), *a.* [F. *maigre*, lit. lean: see MEAGRE *a.*]

1. Of articles of diet, esp. soup: Not containing flesh or the juices of flesh; proper for 'maigre' days.

1787 P. BECKFORD *Lett. fr. Italy* (1805) I. 365 A common maigre dish in this country. **1806** H. HUNTER *Culina* (ed. 3) 58 For want of this precaution, the soup has a maigre taste. *Ibid.* 122 In this receipt for a maigre soup, much is left to the taste of the Cook. **1831** SCOTT *Q. Durw.* Introd. 57 The soup, although bearing the term *maigre*,..was most delicately flavoured.

2. Applied to those days on which, in the Roman Church, abstinence from flesh is enjoined.

1683 ROBINSON in *Ray's Corr.* (1848) 132 Most of the inhabitants here, do generally eat it in Lent, and upon maigre days. **1768** PENNANT *Zool.* I. 68 The Romish church permits the use of it [otter] on maigre-days. **1879** R. LUBBOCK *Fauna of Norfolk* 77 Sustenance upon maigre days.

†**3.** *to eat, keep, live maigre*: to live on 'maigre' diet. *Obs.*

1739 H. WALPOLE *Corr.* (1820) I. 18 A greater penance than eating maigre. **1764** —— *Lett., to G. Montagu* 18 June (1846) IV. 429, I must keep maigre. **1764** SMOLLETT *France & Italy* xxii. (1766) 340 A good catholic, who lives *maigre* one half of the year. **1778** HAN. MORE *Let.* in W. Roberts *Mem.* (1834) I. 136 At last he [the doctor] consented on condition that I should..live maigre and drink no wine.

maigre, obs. form of MEAGRE.

maii, -ij, obs. forms of MAY (the month).

maik, maikless, Sc. ff. MAKE *sb.*, MAKELESS.

‖**maiko** ('maikɒ). [Jap.] A girl who is being trained to become a geisha.

1904 R. J. FARRER *Garden of Asia* xii. 111 They are but Maiko—geisha so young and untried as to be beneath Japanese consideration. *Ibid.* 113 She rises.., flanked by the two Maiko. **1938** BUSH & KAGAMI *Japanalia* 69/1 Young apprentice geisha are called *Maiko* in Kyōto and *Hangyoku* in Tōkyō. **1966** P. S. BUCK *People of Japan* (1968) vii. 93 Young geisha, or *maiko*, usually dance with some gaiety. **1971** *Vogue* Dec. 92/1 An apprentice Geisha is a Maiko—a girl usually between seventeen and twenty.

mail (meɪl), *sb.*[1] Forms: 4–7 **maill(e, maile**, 4–5 **mayll(e**, *Sc.* **mailȝe**, (5 **mailye**, 6 *Sc.* **mailyie**), 5 **mayl**, 5–8 **mayle**, 4– **mail**; *pl.* 4 **mailez**, 5 **maylez, -is, -us, malys**, *Sc.* **maily(h)eis**, 5–6 **mailȝeis, -ȝies**. [a. F. *maille* (whence MDu. *maelge*, Du. *malie*):—L. *macula* spot, mesh of a net.]

†**1.** One of the metal rings or plates of which mail-armour was composed. *Obs.*

c **1320** *Sir Beues* 2836 Al to-brosten is ventaile, And of his hauberk a þosend maile. *c* **1330** R. BRUNNE *Chron. Wace* (Rolls) 13807 Ne hauberk [was þer] non, wyth maille gret, þat his spere ne þorow schet. *c* **1420** *Anturs of Arth.* (Camden Soc.) xl, Syxti maylis and moe, The squrd squappes in toe. **1460** *Lybeaus Disc.* 252 (Kaluza) And an hauberk briȝt þat richely was adiȝt With mailes þikke and smale. **1513** DOUGLAS *Æneis* v. ii. 91 As golden mailȝeis hir scalis glitterand brycht. **1597** A. M. tr. *Guillemeau's Fr. Chirurg.* 13 b/2 To drawe out any..Mayles which mighte remayne stitckinge [*sic*] in the Wounde. **1611** COTGR., *Annelet*, a mayle, or a ring of mayle. **1706** PHILLIPS (ed. Kersey), *Mail*, a little Iron-ring for Armour.

fig. **1549** COVERDALE, etc. *Erasm. Par. Eph.* vi. 10–17 For the breste plate, put on innocencie and righteousnes, to kepe the inward partes of your mynd safe and sure with the mayles of vertue and godlines.

†**b.** *Proverb.* (Literally from OFr.) *Obs.*

1597 SKENE *De Verb. Sign.* s.v. *Hawbert*, The common proverb, manie mailzies makis an haubergion, monie littles makis an meikle.

†**c.** *transf. pl.* The scales (of a fish). *Obs. rare.*

1484 CAXTON *Fables of Poge* v. (1889) 303 And at the bothe his elbowes he [the monstre] hadde wynges ryght brode and grete of fysshes mayles wherwith he swymmed.

2. *collect.* Armour composed of interlaced rings or chain-work or of overlapping plates fastened upon a groundwork. *coat of mail*: see COAT *sb.* 5. (Cf. CHAIN-*mail*, PLATE-*mail*, RING-*mail*.)

c **1374** CHAUCER *Troylus* v. 1559 Achilles thorwgh the maylle, And thorwgh the body gan hym for to ryve. *c* **1386** —— *Clerk's T.* 1146 Though thyn housbonde armed be in maille. *c* **1400** *Destr. Troy* 11107 Sho was bare of hir breast to þe bright mayll. **1460** *Lybeaus Disc.* 1230 (Kaluza) Hys fomen wer well boun, To perce his acketoun, Gipell, maile and plate. **1465** MARG. PASTON in *P. Lett.* II. 190 A standard of mayle. **1513** DOUGLAS *Æneis* XII. ii. 95 Abowt his schuldris assais his hawbryk fyne, Of burnist maill. **1552** *Reg. Privy Council Scot.* I. 130 A jack of plett, steilbonet, splent slevis, of mailyie or plait. **1600** J. PORY tr. *Leo's Africa* 21 Their armour..certaine shirts of male verie long and streight. **1667** MILTON *P.L.* VI. 368 Mangl'd with gastly wounds through Plate and Maile. **1810** CAMPBELL *Ballads* vii, Every bosom shook Beneath it's iron mail. **1838** LYTTON *Leila* v. i. 49 The king was armed *cap-a-pied* in mail. **1877** MORRIS *Sigurd* 4 Through the glimmering thicket the linked mail rang out.

†**b.** A piece of mail-armour. *Obs.*

1606 SHAKS. *Tr. & Cr.* III. iii. 152 To hang Quite out of fashion, like a rustie male. **1607** TOPSELL *Four-f. Beasts* 200 The trunk of the elephant was couered with a maile for defence. **1617** MORYSON *Itin.* III. 25 They presently arme al their bodies, and..their very shinbones, and hinder parts, with males of Iron.

c. *transf.* of the protective shell or scales of certain animals.

1714 GAY *Fan* III. 179 For this..His clouded Mail the Tortoise shall resign. **1833** TENNYSON *Two Voices* iv, Today I saw the dragon-fly... From head to tail Came out clear plates of sapphire mail. **1849** M. ARNOLD *Forsaken Merman*, Where the sea-snakes coil and twine, Dry their mail and bask in the brine. **1885** R. L. & F. STEVENSON *Dynamiter* 106 The mail of a boiled lobster.

d. *fig.*

1813 J. N. BREWER *Beaut. Eng.* II. 77 The antiquaries who have entered the lists, have come cased up in the mail of prejudice. **1866** B. TAYLOR *Poems, Autumnal Vespers* 38 In stiff December's mail. **1866** G. MACDONALD *Ann. Q. Neighb.* xxxii. (1878) 547 She was clad in the mail of endurance.

3. A 'web' in the eye. [So F. *maille* (Cotgr.); cf. MACULA quot. *c* 1400.] *Obs.* exc. *dial.*

1601 HOLLAND *Pliny* (1634) II. 312 Which eie-salue they say, serues also for the mailles or spots [L. *argema*]..in the eies. **1847** HALLIWELL, *Mail*, a defect in vision. *Devon.*

†**4.** A hole for the passage of a lace, clasp, or other fastening of a garment; an eyelet-hole, 'eye'. Also *fig. Obs.*

c **1470** HENRYSON *Garm. Gude Ladeis* 15 Poems (1865) 8 Hir kirtill suld be of clene constance, Lasit with lesum lufe, The mailyheis of continuance For nevir to remufe. **1530** PALSGR. 241/2 Mayle that receyveth the claspe of a gowne into it, *porte.* **1572** *Satir. Poems Reform.* xxxiii. 25 My Sleifis wer of to borrow and len glaidlie; My Lais and Mailzies of trew permanence. **1588** THOMAS *Dict.* (1606), *Orbiculus*, the male or rundle thorough which the latchet of the shoe passeth. **1607** *Barley-Breake* (1877) 16 And day by day this lace a mayle doth bate.

b. *spec.* in *Weaving.* (See quots.)

1731 MORTIMER in *Phil. Trans.* XXXVII. 106 Every Thread of the Warp goes through a small Brass Ring called a Male. **1831** G. R. PORTER *Silk Manuf.* 216 A modern improvement substitutes for the loops small metallic eyes, through which the warp threads are passed,..these eyes are called mails. **1835** WEBSTER *Rhymes* 152 (E.D.D.) Temper yer ilka thrum and thread, Yea, whether they wimple thro' a head, Or thro' a mail.

5. *Hawking.* The breast-feathers of a hawk when the feathers are full-grown. Occas. applied to the plumage of other birds.

1486 *Bk. St. Albans* A vij, Hawkes haue White maill, Canuas maill or Rede maill. And som call Rede maill Iren mayll. White maill is soone knawe. Canuas maill is betwene white maill and Iron maill. And Iron maill is varri Rede. *Ibid.* A vij b, A Goshawke nor a tercell in thare sore aage haue nott thair mayles named bot it is calde their plumage, and after the cote it is calde theyr Maill. **1530** PALSGR. 241/2 Mayle of a hauke, *greuelure.* **1575** [see MAILED *ppl. a.* 4]. **1614** MARKHAM *Cheap Husb.* (1623) 135 His [a dunghill cock's] eyes round and great, the colour answering the colour of his plume or male. **1655** WALTON *Angler* (1661) 107 The wings made of the blackish mail of the Drake. **1678** *Willughby's Ornithol.* App. 398 The Mail of a Hawk is the Breast or Plumage of the Breast in reference to its colour: So they say a Hawk changes the mail, or is white-maild, &c. **1686** BLOME *Gentl. Recr.* II. 182/1 The little Dun-flye hath his Body made of Dun-Wooll, and his Wings of the Mayle of a Partridge. **1852** R. F. BURTON *Falconry Valley of Indus* viii. 76 Full breast, covered with regular mail. *Note.* The 'mails' are the breast feathers.

b. (See quot.: cf. MAILED *ppl. a.* 4 b.)

1727 PHILLIPS (ed. Kersey), *Mail*, a Speck on the Feathers of Birds.

6. *Rope-making.* (See quot. 1794.)

1750 BLANCKLEY *Nav. Expositor*, *Mails*, are made of Iron, and interwoven, not unlike a Chain; they are for rubbing off the loose Hemp which remains on Lines or white Cordage after it is made. **1794** *Rigging & Seamanship* 55 *Mail*, to rub off the loose hemp that remains on white cordage, is a kind of steel chain-work, flat, and fastened upon leather, about nine-inches long and seven-inches broad. **1867** SMYTH *Sailor's Word-bk.*

7. *attrib.* and *Comb.*, as *mail-armour, -coat, -plate, -quilt, -sark, -shirt, -work*; instrumental, as *mail-clad, -covered, -sheathed* adjs.; **mail net** (see quot.); **mail-shell**, a name for the genus *Chiton* (Smyth *Sailor's Word-bk.* 1867).

1868 G. STEPHENS *Runic Mon.* I. 184 The ring-like dots—which I take to be a conventional representation of *mail-armour. **1777** R. POTTER tr. *Æschylus, Persians* 515 Thy *mail-clad horse. **1805** SCOTT *Last Minstr.* I. v, Ten squires, ten yeomen, mail-clad men. **1862** ANSTED *Channel Isl.* I. ii. (ed. 2) 24 Should an attack be made with mail-clad ships. **1653** URQUHART *Rabelais* I. xi, He..would have the *Mail-coats to be made link after link. **1803** BYRON *On Leaving Newstead Abbey* ii, The *mail-cover'd Barons. **1773** J. CAMPBELL *Mod. Falconry* 262 **Male-feathers*, those on the breast. **1875** KNIGHT *Dict. Mech.*, **Mail-net*, a form of loom-made net, which is a combination of common gauze and whip-net in the same fabric. **1771** MICKLE tr. *Camoens' Lusiad* III. (1776) 128 Vain were the *mail-plates of Granada's bands. *Ibid.* I. 47 There clasping greaves, and plated *mail-quilts strong. **1838** LONGF. *Beowulf's Exp. Heort* 76 The Weather people..their *mail-sarks shook. **1850** OGILVIE, **Mail-sheathed.* **1817** SCOTT *Harold* I. ix. 16 Wilt thou..Lay down thy *mail-shirt for clothing of hair. **1869** BOUTELL *Arms & Arm.* vii. 107 This mail shirt, or hauberk, was fitted almost tightly to the person. *Ibid.* ii. 18 The cuirass..was formed..of interwoven *mail-work.

mail (meɪl), *sb.*[2] Now only *Sc.* Forms: 1–3 **mal**, 3 **mol**, 3–6 **male**, 5 **maile**, 7 **maille**, 7–8 **meal**, 5–7, 9 **maill**, 6– **mail**. [Late OE. *mál*, a. ON. *mál* neut., speech, agreement = OE. (poet.) *mæl* speech; prob. a contracted form of the word which appears as OHG., OS. *mahal* assembly, judgement, treaty, OE. *mæðel* meeting, discussion, Goth. *maþl* meeting-place. (Cf. MALLUM.) In sense, however, the Eng. word seems rather to represent the ON. derivative *máli* wk. masc., contract, stipulation, stipulated pay; cf. Ormin's *måle* accus.

The word has survived only in Sc. and northern dialects, and hence its phonetic form is northern. If it had come down in midland or southern use its form would have been *mole* (məʊl).]

1. Payment, tax, tribute, rent. ***mails and duties*** (see quot. 1861). Cf. BLACKMAIL *sb.*

O.E. Chron. an. 1086 Se cyng sealde his land swa deore to male swa heo deorost mihte. *c* **1200** ORMIN 10188 Forrþi badd hemm Sannt Johan..sammnenn laȝhelike & rihht þe kingess rihhte måle. *c* **1200** *Trin. Coll. Hom.* 179 And giet ne wile þe louerd ben paid mid his rihcte mol. *c* **1275** *XI Pains Hell* 161 in *O.E. Misc.* 151 Of heom hi token vnriht mol. *a* **1300** *Cursor M.* 5376, I giue him woningsted to wale For euer-mare, wit-outen male. **1396** in *Scottish Antiq.* XIV. 217 The forsayd Scher Jone sal haf the malys of Ouchtyrtyre. **1430–31** *Rolls of Parlt.* IV. 376/1 That no maile of siche certificate made..put to ony prejudice..any persone. *c* **1480** HENRYSON *Mor. Fab.* XII. (*Wolf & Lamb*) xx, Scantlie may he purches by his maill To leif vpon dry breid. **1549** *Compl. Scot.* xv. 123 The malis and fermis of the grond..is hychtit to sic ane price. **1746–7** *Act 20 Geo. II*, c. 43 §17 Recovering and uplifting from the vassals..the mails and duties or rents and profits thereof. *a* **1768** ERSKINE *Inst.* III. vii. §20 (1773) 529 The arrears of rent, or, in our law-style, of mails and duties, prescribe, if [etc.]. **1824** SCOTT *Redgauntlet* Let. xi, The rental-book..bore evidence against the Goodman of Primrose-Knowe, as behind the hand with his mails and duties. **1861** W. BELL *Dict. Law Scot.* s.v., Mails and Duties are the rents of an estate, whether in money or grain; hence, an action for the rents of an estate..is termed an action of maills and duties. **1900** CROCKETT *Little Anna Mark* viii, He carried a great sum about with him, being the rents and mails of all his New Milns property.

b. With word prefixed, as ***borough, feu, grass, house mail***; **land mail**: see LAND *sb.*[1] 12; **silver mail**, rent paid in money.

1424 *Sc. Acts Jas. I*, c. 8 All þe gret and smal custumys & burovmaills of þe Realme. **1479–1752** Grass mail [see GRASS *sb.*[1] 12]. **1566–67** *Reg. Privy Council Scot.* I. 499 He..wes in possessioun..of the hous maill occupiit be the saidis tennentis. **1585** *Reg. Privy Council Scot.* Ser. I. IV. 14 To mak pament of his few maills. **1597** SKENE *De Verb. Sign.*, s.v. *Firmarius, Firma* signifies the duty quhilk the tennent paies to the landis-lord, quhidder it be siluer-maill, victuall, or vther duetie. **1609** —— *Reg. Maj.* 125 Gif thy mail-man will not pay to thee the house maill at the terme. **1640** BAILLIE *Lett.* (1841) I. 272 Our house maills everie week above eleven pound Sterling.

c. *fig.* ***to pay the mail*** = to pay the penalty.

1807 HOGG *Mount. Bard* 199 Poet. Wks. (1838) II. 263 My sister..By Lairistan foully was betrayed, And roundly has he payed the mail.

2. *attrib.* and *Comb.*, as ***mail-payer, paying***; **mail-duty**, rent; **mail-free** *a.* and *adv.*, free of rent, exempt from payment of rent; **mail garden**, 'a garden, the products of which are raised for sale' (Jam.) (hence ***mail-gardener***); **mail-man**, one who pays rent, a tenant; **mailmart**, a cow sent in payment of rent; **mail-rooms** *pl.*, rented rooms.

1638 *Extracts Burgh Rec. Glasgow* (1876) I. 392 That na burges..sett or promeis to sett for *maill dewtie or vtherwayes,..wntill [etc.]. **1818** SCOTT *Hrt. Midl.* viii, Deans..contrived to maintain his ground upon the estate by regular payment of mail-duties. **1471** *Acta Dom. Audit.* 10/2 *Male fre fore þe formale pait be him to þe said Alexander. **1638** RUTHERFORD *Lett.* iii. (1664) 14 Many..of you..have been like a tennent that sitteth mealfree. **1798** J. NAISMYTH *Agric. Clydesd.* vi. 101 The *mail gardens around the city of Glasgow. **1820** SCOTT *Abbot* xxxv, The candle shines from the house of Blinkhoolie, the *mail-gardener. *c* **1480** HENRYSON *Mor. Fab.* XII. (*Wolf & Lamb*) xiv, The pure people..As *maill-men, marchandis, and all lawboreris. **1609** SKENE *Reg. Maj.* 113 Na Mail-man, or Fermour, may thirle his Lord of his frie tenement. **1445** *Exch. Rolls Scot.* V. 213 Lez *mailmartis insule de Bute. **1597** SKENE *De Verb. Sign.*, *Firmarius*, ane *mail-payer, ane mailer, or mail-man. **1724** RAMSAY *Vision* ix, Mailpayers wiss it to the devil. **1581** *Reg. Privy Council Scot.* Ser. I. III. 417 Throw the quhilk waist, *maill-paying, and tyning of the proffites of the saidis landis, he is utterlie wrakkit. *c* **1626** in W. K. Tweedie *Sel. Biog.* (1845) I. 351 He warned me from the rest of my *mail-rooms in Salt-coats and East Mains.

mail (meɪl), *sb.*[3] Forms: 3–8 **male**, 5 **maylle**, 5–6 **mayle, malle**, 6 **maale**, 6– **mail**. [ME. *male*, a. OF. *male* (F. *malle*) = Pr., Sp., Pg., It. *mala*; of Teut. origin: cf. OHG. *malha* (MHG. *malhe*), MDu. *male* (Du. *maal*).]

1. a. A bag, pack, or wallet; a travelling bag. Now only *Sc.* and *U.S.* in *pl.* = baggage.

c **1205** LAY. 3543 Ich þe wulle bi-tache a male riche. *c* **1300** *Havelok* 48 A man that bore..gold upon hijs bac, In a male with or blac. *c* **1320** *Sir Beues* 1297 Inouȝ a leide him before, Bred and flesc out of is male. *c* **1386** CHAUCER *Can. Yeom. Prol.* 13 A male tweyfold on his croper lay. **1489–90** *Plumpton Corr.* 89 Robart, my servant..is large to ryde afore my male, and ouer weyghty for my horse. **1552** *Act 5 & 6 Edw. VI*, c. 15 §2 Such as make Males, Bougets, Leather Pots,..or any other Wares of Leather. **1567** R. EDWARDS *Damon & Pithias* Fij, Who inuented these monsters [breeches] first, did it to a gostly ende, To haue a male readie to put in other folkes stuffe. **1609** BIBLE (Douay) *1 Kings* ix. 7 The bread is spent in our males. **1632** DELONEY *Thomas of Reading* xi. G 4, They..take away the mans apparell, as also his money, In his male or cap-case. **1670** COTTON *Espernon* II. VII. 335 His Jewels..were lock'd up in a little iron Chest, and carried in a Male. **1706** PHILLIPS (ed. Kersey), *Mail*,..also a kind of Port-mantle, Sack or Trunk

to travel with. **1820** SCOTT *Abbot* xxxviii, They charged me with bearing letters for the Queen, and searched my mail. **1893** STEVENSON *Catriona* xvii. 190 He..emptied out his mails upon the floor that I might have a change of clothes.

†**b.** As a measure of quantity. *Obs. rare*$^{-1}$.

1502 ARNOLDE *Chron.* (1811) 191 Wulle is bought by the sacke by the tod by the stone and by the mayle.

†**c.** *transf.* and *fig. Obs.*

c **1250** *Gen. & Ex.* 22 Quhu lucifer..[Broȝte mankinde in sinne and bale] And held hem sperd in helles male. *c* **1386** CHAUCER *Parson's Prol.* 26 Vnbokele and shewe vs what is in thy Male. *c* **1430** LYDG. *Bochas* IX. iii. (1494) E vij/1 If ye shall tell youre owne tale..Ye wyll vnclose but a lytyll male, Shewe of youre vices but a small parcele. **1450** MYRC 1343 Art thou I-wonet to go to the ale To fulle there thy fowle male.

2. a. A bag or packet of letters or dispatches for conveyance by post, more fully ***mail of letters***; †thence, the letters or dispatches so conveyed (*obs.*). ***the mail***, the postal matter, collectively, conveyed from office to office; also (orig. *U.S.*) without article.

1654 *Ord. Office Postage Lett.* §8 To have in readiness one good Horse or Mare to receive and carry the Male of Letters. .. That no other person (besides the Post that carrieth the Male) be suffered to ride Post with the Male. **1684** *Lond. Gaz.* No. 1900/2 Our Pacquet-Boats put to Sea yesterday with the Mails for Calais. **1692** LUTTRELL *Brief Rel.* (1857) II. 489 Yesterday a Flanders mail of an old date, confirms the several repulses of the enemy. **1746** SMOLLETT *Reproof* 160 With all the horrors of prophetic dread That rack his bosom while the mail is read. **1767** COLMAN *Eng. Merch.* I. i, I collect the articles of news from the other papers,.. translate the mails, write occasional letters [etc.]. **1776** C. CARROLL *Jrnl.* (1845) 53 Dr. Franklin found in the Canada mail, which he opened, a letter for General Schuyler. **1782** COWPER *Expostulation* 606 Now think,..If the new mail thy merchants now receive, Or expectation of the next, give leave. **1792** *Stat. U.S.* I. vii. §17 (1856) I. 237 That if any person..shall rob any carrier of the mail..of such mail, or if any person shall rob the mail, in which letters are sent to be conveyed by post..or shall steal such mail. **1794** *Ibid.* I. xxiii. §26 (1856) I. 365 And the letters so received shall be formed into a mail, sealed up, and directed to the postmaster of the port. **1838** *Act 1 & 2 Vict.* c. 98 §5 The Mails or Post Letter Bags so to be carried..by Railways. **1852** HAWTHORNE *Amer. Note-Bks.* (1883) 424 The regular passenger-boat is now coming in, and probably brings the mail. **1873** BLACK *Pr. Thule* vii, Everything will be as right as the mail. **1873** J. H. BEADLE *Undevel. West* xxii. 441, I think this office gives us three times as much mail as that at Salt Lake. **1883** *Whitaker's Almanack* 384 [Postal Guide.] India.—Mails made up every Friday evening at the rate of 5*d.* per ½ oz. **1893** *Daily News* 22 Sept. 6/5 Little incidents of camp life in the East, as the arrival and distribution of a mail of letters. **1913** *U.S. Official Postal Guide* July 12 The postage on fourth-class mail may be prepaid by..ordinary postage stamps. **1941** *Men Only* Sept. 12 Forwarding mail is another job that usually falls to the Mess Secretary.

b. orig. *U.S.* (A person's) batch of letters.

a **1844** M. C. FIELD in S. F. Smith *Theatr. Apprenticeship* (1846) 204 He walks as if he had the missing mail in his pocket and an extra to issue immediately. **1873** T. B. ALDRICH *Marj. Daw* 163, I go over to K— for my mail. **1890** T. L. JAMES in *Railways Amer.* 319 That official was opening his mail. **1901** *Harper's Mag.* CII. 784/1 Stormfield in his mail that day..found a despatch: 'Unexpectedly called home'. **1941** *Men Only* Sept. 12 Although the addressee has made half a dozen moves since leaving the Mess, he expects his mail to reach him without delay. **1953** *Manch. Guardian Wkly.* 3 Sept. 7/4 Mr. Lattimore..had his personal mail forwarded to the White House.

c. Used as the name of a newspaper.

1789 (*title*) The Evening Mail. **1823** (*title*) Waterford Daily Mail. **1896** (*title*) The Daily Mail. **1896** LLOYD GEORGE *Family Lett.* (1973) 108 There are excellent reports in the Mail & S.W. Daily News of Saturday's meeting at Barry. **1922** JOYCE *Ulysses* 242 Look here Martin, John Wyse Nolan said, overtaking them at the *Mail* office. **1975** *Times* 10 Apr. 17/4 The tremendous financial support that the *Daily Mail* has received..from its readers for its Vietnam Orphans Fund.

3. a. The person, vehicle, or train that carries the mail or postal matter; often short for *mail coach*, *mail train*, etc. Hence, the method or system of transmission of letters by post; the official conveyance or dispatch of postal matter; the POST.

So used now in *U.S.* In England the word in ordinary use is limited to the dispatch of letters abroad, as the ***Indian mail***, etc., or as short for mail-train, as the ***down mail, night mail***. It is retained as the official word for the dispatch and delivery of inland letters where the general public use POST.

1654 *Ord. Office Postage Lett.* §2 The said John Manley.. shall..safely and faithfully carry all.. Letters and Dispatches..and that by the Common, Ordinary Male or other speedy and safe passage. **1692** LUTTRELL *Brief Rel.* (1857) II. 489 One letter by the last mail sayes, the king intended to fight the enemy Saturday 7 night last. **1720** *Lond. Gaz.* No. 5850/2 The Bristol Mail was robbed. **1778** ABIGAIL ADAMS in *Fam. Lett.* (1876) 343 Four or five sheets of paper, written to you by the last mail, were destroyed when the vessel was taken. **1794** COLERIDGE *Lett.* 26 Sept. (1895) I. 86, I..sent them off by the mail directed to Mrs. Southey. **1822–56** DE QUINCEY *Confess.* Wks. 1890 III. 348 The mails were..made so strong as to be the heaviest of all carriages. **1831** in *Parl. Papers* (1831–2) XLV. 128 b, When it is permitted in England for the mails to take parcels on the road. **1842** TENNYSON *Walking to the Mail* 102, I fear That we shall miss the mail. **1864** J. H. NEWMAN *Apologia* 96 While waiting for the down mail to Falmouth. **1880** *Print. Trades Jrnl.* No. 30. 34 Tender and brittle, and hardly bears its journey through the mail. **1886** P. ROBINSON *Valley Teetotum Trees* 71 Just in time to catch the night-mail to London. **1888** *Amer. Humorist* 2 June 3/2 Why didn't he send his poem by mail? **1891** *37th Rept. Postm.-General* 5 Sixty-four additional direct Parcel Mails between London and other places have been established in the year. **1900** *Post Office Guide* 1 Jan. 14 When intended for despatch by a particular mail they should..be presented for registration half an hour before the closing of the letter-box for that mail.

b. Short for *mail coach* or *van* (on a railway).

1862 *Building News* 6 June 389/2, 555 Locomotives and Tenders. 494 First Class Mails.

4. *attrib.* and *Comb.*: **a.** (sense 1) simple attrib., chiefly obsolete, as ***mail-band, -girt, -girth, -horse, -lock, -man, -panel, -pillion, -saddle, -trunk***; also objective, as ***mail-maker***.

1515 *Test. Ebor.* (Surtees) V. 69 A male wyth ij *male bandys. **1607** TOPSELL *Four-f. Beasts* (1658) 155 The females [*sc.* elephants] carry over their calves upon their snowts,..binding them fast with their truncks, like as with ropes or *male girts. **1673** *12th Rep. Hist. MSS. Comm.* App. VII. (1890) 384 For a *male-girth and tabbs 1*s.* 6*d.* *c* **1440** *Promp. Parv.* 323/1 *Male horse, *gerulus*. **1469** *Househ. Ord.* (1790) 97 A maile horse and a botell horse whiche the maile-man shall keepe. **1673** *12th Rep. Hist. MSS. Comm.* App. VII. (1890) 384 For a *male-lock and a letter, 8*d.* **1311** *Cal. Lett.-Bks. Lond., Lett-Bk.* D. (1902) 74 [The same day, John Morice] *melmakere, [admitted]. *c* **1515** *Cocke Lorell's B.* 9 Masones, male makers, and merbelers. **1469** *Maile-man [see *mail horse*]. **1392** *Earl Derby's Exp.* (Camden) 152 Pro iij capistris et *male panel. **1639** T. DE GREY *Compl. Horsem.* 216 A galled backe commeth..with the..pack-saddle or *male-pillion. **1686** *Lond. Gaz.* No. 2130/4 A black Gelding..a little hurt of his back with a Mail-pillion. **1833** M. SCOTT *Tom Cringle* xi. (1842) 257 His portmanteau behind him on a mail-pillion. **1378–9** *Durh. Acc. Rolls* (Surtees) 388 In una *malesadill empt. ixs. iijd. **1414–15** *Ibid.* 184, j Malesadil. *a* **1726** VANBRUGH *Journ. Lond.* I. i. 81 My lady..laid on four *mail-trunks, besides the great deal-box.

b. (sense 2) simple attrib., e.g. in the names of vehicles employed to carry the mail, as ***mail boat, carriage, diligence, gig, -hack, packet, -plane, schooner, ship, steamer, -van, wagon***; also ***mail-boy, mail-carrier, letter, matter, room, time; mail-carrying*** adj.; **mailbag**, a large bag in which the mail is carried; **mail-box**, (*a*) a box in which the mail-bags were placed on a mail-coach; (*b*) *U.S.*, a letter-box; **mail-car**, (*a*) a railway car in which the mail is carried; (*b*) *Ireland*, an 'outside car' used for conveyance of the mails; (*c*) *Austral.* and *N.Z.*, a motor vehicle used for the conveyance of the mail (and also sometimes of passengers); **mail-cart**, (*a*) a vehicle in which the mail is carried by road; also *attrib.*; (*b*) a light vehicle to carry children, made with shafts to be drawn or pushed by hand; **mail-catcher** *U.S.* (see quot. 1890); **mail-contract**, a contract for the conveyance of postal matter; **mail contractor**, one who contracts with the government for the conveyance of the mail; **mail cover** *U.S.*, the monitoring of all mail sent to a specified address; **mail-day**, the day on which mails are dispatched or received; **mail drop** [DROP *sb.* 17 d], a place where mail may be left to be collected by another person; **mail-guard**, the guard of a mail-coach; **mail horn**, a long horn used by the guard of a mail-coach; †**mail-maker**, an official in the General Letter-Office; **mail-man**, one who carries the mail; **mail-master** *U.S.*, **-officer** (see quot. 1855); **mail order** orig. *U.S.*, an order for goods sent to a business house by post; hence as *v. trans.*; also **mail-order firm**, **house**, one transacting business mainly by post; so ***mail-order business, catalogue***; **mail-phaeton**, a high two-seated phaeton (q.v.) drawn by a pair of horses; **mail-pouch** (*U.S.*), a locked leather mail-bag; **mail-rack** (*U.S.*), a letter-rack; **mail-rider**, a mail-carrier; **mail-road, -route**, the road or route by which the mail is regularly conveyed; **mail run** *Austral.* and *N.Z.*, = *mail-route*; **mail-runner**, a mail-carrier (in India); **mail sack** (*U.S.*), a canvas bag used for the conveyance of the mail; †**mail-setting** *a.*, that robs the mail; **mailshot** = *mailing shot* s.v. MAILING *vbl. sb.*[2]; **mail-slot** *U.S.*, = *letter-slit*; **mail stage** (*U.S.*) = MAIL-COACH; **mail-time**, the time mails take to pass between two places; **mail-train**, a fast train which carries the mails; **mail truck**, a motor vehicle used for the conveyance of mail. Also MAIL-COACH.

1812 *Theatrical Inquisitor* I. 273 The majority of readers ..ramble through books as post-boys ride through towns.. and..can tell you as little of the contents as those who carry the *mail-bags can of the letters. **1840** LONGF. in *Life* (1891) I. 358 There were three insides besides myself, and a dozen mail-bags. **1795** in R. Putnam *Mem.* (1903) 397 It has been suggested to me that the *mail boats are much too heavy for pushing with the requisite speed. **1855** HYDE CLARKE *Dict.*, *Mail-boat.* **1895** A. H. NORWAY *P.-O. Packet Service* i. 3 The Post-Office selected Falmouth in 1688 as the point of embarkation..for the..mail boats. **1933** L. A. G. STRONG *Sea Wall* 1 He did not even heed the mailboat, as she glided gracefully in..to the harbour. **1810** in J. W. Hyde *Roy. Mail* iii. (1885) 34 The bags of letters..were stolen from the *mail-box..whilst the horses were changing. **1872** *Rep. Comm. Patents 1870* (U.S.) II. 751/1 In a mail-box, the arrangement herein shown and described..for the purpose of guiding and holding the mail matter. **1922** M. B. HOUSTON *Witch-Man* xix. 260 She stopped now at the foot of Little Glory to look in the mail-box. Always she brought him his mail now. **1973** 'H. HOWARD' *Highway to Murder* x. 128 One of the mail boxes said Miss Thorpe's flatlet was on the third floor. **1842** in J. S. Buckingham *E. & W. States Amer.* II. 118 [I] saw descending the hill..the *mail-boy on his horse at full speed. *a* **1861** T. WINTHROP *John Brent* (1883) xvii. 159 Jake Shamberlain aint a hog, and his mail boys aint of the pork kind. **1874** *Congress. Rec.* 15 Apr. 3099/1 Hitherto seven [officers] were known as mail-boys and the others as mail-messengers. **1907** N. MUNRO *Daft Days* i. 3 The tune of the mail-boy's song. **1842** S. C. HALL *Ireland* II. 77 *Mail-cars. **1889** *Ch. Times* 27 Dec. 1227 The regular train consists of two sleepers,..and enough mail-cars to contain the mail. **1942** C. ASTON in *N.Z. New Writing* I. 55 Martin heard the mailcar go past. **1945** C. MANN in Murdoch & Drake-Brockman *Austral. Short Stories* (1951) 261 Sent by the mail-car up to Town. **1947** 'A. P. GASKELL' *Big Game* 48 She had returned from town..in the mailcar. **1860** J. G. HOLLAND *Miss Gilbert's Career* x. 166 The Crampton line of public travel and *mail carriage was only one of the many tributaries to the great trunk lines. **1799** *Stat. U.S.* III. xliii. §13 (1856) I. 736 The receipt and delivery of letters on the way, between post-offices, shall not be required of the *mail-carriers. **1901** *N. Amer. Rev.* Feb. 289 The usefulness of fast steamships as mail-carriers. **1909** *Westm. Gaz.* 1 June 8/3 The various lines of passenger and *mail-carrying steamers. **1837** *Act 7 Will. IV & 1 Vict.* c. 33 §18 No Mail Coach, Mail Diligence, or *Mail Cart conveying..any Mail or Bag of Letters in Ireland. **1893** H. JOYCE *Hist. Post Office* xiii. 316 The London Mail-Cart and Van Service. **1903** *G.W.R. Time Tables*, Parcels and Goods Arrangem., Perambulators and Children's Mail Carts. **1875** *Chicago Tribune* 18 Sept. 5/3 The Post-Office Department has introduced the use of a '*mail-catcher'. **1884** KNIGHT *Dict. Mech.* Suppl., *Mail-catcher*. **1890** T. L. JAMES in *Railways Amer.* 326 The letter car is provided with a 'mail catcher', which is placed at a small door through which mail pouches are snatched from conveniently placed posts at wayside stations where stops are not made. *a* **1861** T. WINTHROP *John Brent* (1883) vi. 50 His ranch is down the valley, towards Pravo. He owns half the United States *mail contract. **1830** *Act 11 Geo. IV & 1 Will. IV*, c. 68 *Mail Contractors, Stage Coach Proprietors [etc.]. **1837** *Mail Diligence [see *mail-cart*]. **1965** *N.Y. Times* 24 Feb. 26 When a person is subjected to a *mail cover, the Post Office records the name and address of anyone sending mail to him, as well as the postmarking and the class of mail. **1974** *Daily Tel.* 29 Jan. 17/4 The FBI began its investigation of Miss Paton as a result of a 'mail cover' on the New York headquarters of the party. **1855** J. EVANS *Let.* 15 June in G. N. Jones *Florida Plantation Rec.* (1927) 131 People will be there [*sc.* at the post office] every *Mail day. **1926** [see BACK BLOCKS, BACKBLOCKS *sb. pl.*]. **1933** B. WILLOUGHBY *Alaskans All* 102 Everywhere in the land mail-day is the most longed-for, the most important day the Alaskan knows. **1972** *Time* 17 Apr. 45/1 It is hiring a full-time employment counselor to help them find new jobs if they are fired, and even has a special *mail drop to receive anonymous tips. **1973** *Sat. Rev. World* (U.S.) 4 Dec. 46/2 Today's students traveling abroad use American Express offices as a mail drop. **1887** C. F. HOLDER *Living Lights* 119 John Stewart, who for many years drove a *mail-gig between Dunkeld and Aberfeldy. **1790** WOLCOT (P. Pindar) *Advice to Future Laureat* Wks. 1812 II. 341 The *Mail guard To load his blunderbuss and blow his horn. **1844** Mail Guard [see *mail-train*]. **1909** 'O. HENRY' *Roads of Destiny* x. 165 One afternoon Jimmy Valentine..climbed out of the *mail-hack. **1852** R. S. SURTEES *Sponge's Sp. Tour* (1893) 299 The shrill twang, twang, twang, of the now almost forgotten *mail-horn. **1799** *Stat. U.S.* III. xliii. §15 (1856) I. 737 If any person..shall secrete, embezzle or destroy any such *mail letter or packet. **1735–55** J. CHAMBERLAYNE *St. Gt. Brit.* II. iii, List of Officers in General Letter-Office. [Two] *Mail-makers. **1881** MRS. C. PRAED *Policy & P.* I. i. 9 Tom Dungie, the *mail-man,..had just removed his saddle with its load of brown leather post-bags. **1889** *Westm. Gaz.* 5 Sept. 8/1 The mails are still conveyed for the most part upon the heads and backs of native mailmen. **1855** HYDE CLARKE *Dict.*, *Mail-master*, officer having charge of the mail. **1875** *Atlantic Monthly* XXXV. 98/1 The *mail matter can be classified into letters, daily papers [etc.]. **1906** *Churchman* 10 Nov. 724 All mail matter for the secretary of the convention should be addressed to [etc.]. **1882** FLOYER *Unexpl. Baluchistan* 138 The *mail-officer passed us with the mails [in a boat]. **1867** *Commercial & Financial Chron.* V. 26/2 *Mail and telegraph orders will receive our personal attention. **1875** *Chicago Tribune* 8 July 6/3 Few buyers were present and the 'mail order' business also was light. **1897** *Sears, Roebuck Catal.* 579 There was a time when the consumer paid what was asked... [This] is radically changed,—changed by the Mail Order Business. **1906** S. E. SPARLING *Introd. Business Organiz.* 318 The mail order is based almost exclusively upon circular advertising, and while the mail-order firms employ general publicity, they rely almost exclusively upon circularization in developing and holding the trade. **1916** H. L. WILSON *Somewhere in Red Gap* v. 175 Hetty Daggett.. orders this [skirt] by catalogue,..from the mail-order house in Chicago. **1928** *Collier's* 29 Dec. 7/1 Wasn't it my suggestion that marriage be turned over to the mail-order houses? **1930** J. B. PRIESTLEY *Angel Pavement* iv. 167 He read all the advertisements in his newspaper, which specialised on Saturdays in the mail-order business. **1968** 'N. BLAKE' *Private Wound* iv. 64 A brand-new suite of furniture which looked as if it had been mail-ordered out of a catalogue. **1969** *Times* 7 Nov. 14/7 The sophisticated stores—even the better mail order catalogues—want to know what is happening. **1972** *Guardian* 23 Feb. 11/3 Allcraft..mail-order a candle-making kit. **1844** ROWLAND HILL *State Penny Postage* 16 The net expense of the *Mail packets to these Islands..amounted in 1840–41 to about 7000*l.* **1857** G. A. LAWRENCE *Guy Livingstone* viii. 64 We were driving over in his *mail-phaeton. **1926** *Daily Colonist* (Victoria, B.C.) 2 July 1/5 Vessel expected to arrive here on July 12—Mr. Wells and Mr. Evans then to leave on *mail plane. **1931** C. KELLY *U.S. Postal Policy* vii. 137 At the great airports may be seen the alert, efficient, young eagles who pilot the mail planes. **1940** *Jrnl. R. Aeronaut. Soc.* XLIV. 743 The design of a high-speed mailplane for overnight trans-Atlantic services. **1890** T. L. JAMES in *Railways Amer.* 312 The *mail pouch just thrown from the car. **1896** *Cosmopolitan* XX. 406 Near one of the doors..is ..the *mail-rack. **1801** in C. Cist *Cincinnati in 1841* (1841) 177 The *mail-rider..from the upper route. **1846** *Knickerbocker* XXVI. 52 The mail-rider sank down

apparently through the solid ground with his horse and saddle-bags. **1897** *Outing* (U.S.) XXIX. 385/1 These Turkish mail-riders.. drive two horses loaded with the mail-bags at a gallop in front of them. **1944** F. CLUNE *Red Heart* 81 The far-western mail-rider who, once a fortnight, jogged over the red-soil plains. **1818** in H. B. Fearon *Sk. Amer.* 430 About three miles from the great *mail road to Cincinnati. **1837** ROWLAND HILL *P.O. Reform* 29 The cost of transit along the mail-roads.. being so trifling. **1882** OGILVIE, **Mail-room*. **1891** *Pall Mall G.* 27 Aug. 7/2 The mail-room occupies the place of what was formerly the second saloon. **1911** *Daily Colonist* (Victoria, B.C.) 7 Apr. 7/2 Came before the police magistrate yesterday to answer to the charge of wrecking the mail room of the steamer, throwing mail bags over board, and generally making things interesting. **1968** *Punch* 21 Feb. 270/3 The Mail Rooms (I believe you call them Dispatch Rooms).. were crowded. **1840** *Penny Cycl.* XVIII. 457/2 Sorting [letters] according to the different *mail-routes. **1946** M. TRIST in Murdoch & Drake-Brockman *Austral. Short Stories* (1951) 418 A mail run used to be a *mail run in those days. **1961** B. CRUMP *Hang on a Minute* 88 [He was] doing the Whenuaroa mail-run in a flash new truck. **1892** R. KIPLING *Barrack-r. Ballads* 121 Up the hill to Simoorie.. The bags on his shoulder, the *mail-runner trudges. **1822** *Acc. Establ. Gen. P.O.* Parl. Pap. XVIII. 166b, Hire of Seven *Mail Schooners in the West Indies £5,100. *c* **1688** *New Letany* viii. in *Coll. Poems Popery* (1689) 8/1 A Turncoat, *Mail-setting, King-killing Rascal. **1891** *Act 54 & 55 Vict.* c. 31 §2 The master of a British *mail ship.. when carrying mails to or from any port [etc.]. *Ibid.* §10 This Act may be cited as the Mail Ships Act, 1891. **1963** *Times* 8 May 17/6 (Advt.), Posters, brochures, *mailshots—these things we love at Tillotsons. **1983** *Buses* Feb. 63/3 A mailshot to all 100,000 households in the city comprising well-produced and comprehensive literature outlining the changes. **1957** J. KEROUAC *On Road* (1958) 183 He peeked down through her *mail-slot. **1803** M. CUTLER in *Life, Jrnls. & Corr.* (1888) II. 135 At 8 o'clock at night, set out in the *mail stage. **1821** T. NUTTALL *Jrnl. Trav. Arkansa* i. 35 On the morning of the second of October 1818, I took my departure from Philadelphia in the mail stage. **1834** *Southern Lit. Messenger* I. 181, I took my seat in the mail stage, and travelled three hundred miles without once going to bed. **1866** SALA *Let.* 11 Apr. in Frith *Autobiog.* (1888) III. 255 All the wonderful people you see on board the *mail-steamer. **1841** THACKERAY *Fatal Boots* xi, In the evening, after *mail-time, I [a letter-carrier] went back to my mamma and sister. **1912** *Chambers's Jrnl.* Jan. 5/2 The mail-time between that town [*sc.* Villa Rica] and London will be reduced from thirty days to about eighteen. **1844** *Act 7 & 8 Vict.* c. 85 §11 It shall be also lawful for the Postmaster General to send any Mail Guard with Bags.. by any Trains other than a *Mail Train. **1961** L. VAN DER POST *Heart of Hunter* I. vii. 112 Catch the fortnightly *mail truck to Ghanzis. **1963** A. LUBBOCK *Austral. Roundabout* 44 Twice a week, the mail-truck from Bourke brought out their stores and fresh vegetables. **1909** *Chambers's Jrnl.* June 343/2 *Mail-vans in large numbers.. are now being driven by mechanical power. **1959** *Times* 2 Apr. 10/4 A Post Office spokesman said that the mailvan had previously collected three bags from a firm in Bell Street. **1831** *Boston Even. Transcript* 23 June 2/1 We.. were carted thence in the *mail waggon to Sandwich. **1871** E. EGGLESTON *Hoosier Schoolmaster* (1872) xvii. 135 You can git on the mail-wagon that passes there about five o'clock. **1890** T. L. JAMES in *Railways Amer.* 325 The big lumbering mail wagons which are familiar sights in the streets of the metropolis [New York].

mail, *sb.*[4] *Obs.* exc. *Hist.* Also 6 *Sc.* **malȝe**, 9 **maille**. [a. AF. *mayle*, OF. *maille*, *meaille* (whence MDu. *maelge*):—late L. **metallea*: see MEDAL.]

1. A halfpenny.

[**1292** BRITTON I. xxxi. §2 Quant a ii. s. vi. d. dunc soit le poys liiii. s. iiii. d. mayle ferling. **1379** *Rolls of Parlt.* III. 64/2 De faire ordeiner Mayles & Ferthinges, pur paier pur les petites mesures. **1415** *Act 3 Hen. V*, Et ces quest trove bon argent pr estre illoeques ferrez & coynez en mayls Engleys.] **1570** *Satir. Poems Reform.* xiii. 125 Ȝe left him nocht ane Malȝe or Deneir. **1707** FLEETWOOD *Chron. Prec.* Pref., Till about 1544, the Silver Money of England consisted of Groats, Half-Groats, Pence, Half-Pence (called, of old, Mails) and Farthings. **1890** SERVICE *Thir Notandums* ix. 67 Gold Pennies and Mailles, Lozenge Lions [etc.].

2. ***maille noble***: a gold coin of the reign of Edw. III; a half-noble.

[**1344** in Rymer *Fœdera* (1708) V. 416/1 Et une autre Monoie d'Or, Currante la piece pur Quarante Deners d'Esterlings, que serra appelle Maille Noble.] **1884** KENYON *Gold Coins* 18.

† **mail**, *sb.*[5] *Obs.* exc. as alien word (mɑj). Also 7 **maill(e**; and see MALL. [a. F. *mail*:—L. *malleus* hammer. Cf. Du. *malie*.] The game of pall-mall; a place where the game was played; hence (from the 'Mail' at Paris), a public promenade bordered by trees. ***the Mail*** (in St. James's Park, London): now called the MALL.

1644 EVELYN *Diary* 8 May, Recreating myself sometimes at the maill, and sometymes about the towne. [See *ante*, 2 May, where the word appears as *mall*.] **1670** LASSELS *Voy. Italy* I. 29 Going out of the house, you find a handsome Mail, and rare Ponds of water. **1705** ADDISON *Italy* 217 A Highway.. near as long and as broad as the Mail in St. James's Park. [**1903** *Westm. Gaz.* 11 Feb. 1/3 A long *mail* of elms looks down into the gulf.]

b. ***High Mail***: = *High Mall* (see MALL *sb.*[1] 4).

1676 ETHEREDGE *Man of Mode* III. iii, 'Tis now but high Mail, Madam, the most entertaining Time of all the Evening.

mail (meɪl), *v.*[1] [f. MAIL *sb.*[1]; partly back-formation from MAILED *a.*] *trans.* To clothe or arm with or as with mail.

1795 SOUTHEY *Joan of Arc* v. 4 The martial Maid arose. She mail'd her limbs; The white plumes nodded o'er her helmed head. **1848** LYTTON *Harold* (1862) 58, I will.. ask what Englishmen are there who will aim shaft or spear at this breast, never mailed against England. **1858** LONGF. *Warden Cinque Ports*, A single warrior, In sombre harness mailed.

mail (meɪl), *v.*[2] *Sc.* [f. MAIL *sb.*[2]] *trans.* To rent, pay rent for. Hence **mailed** *ppl. a.*

1425 *Sc. Acts Jas. I* (1814) II. 12/2 Ande gif it be a man at malis þe hous & birnis it reklesly he sal amende þe scaith efter his power. **1877** ALEXANDER *Notes & Sk.* 8 (E.D.D.) A lone woman or two in a 'mailt-house'.

mail (meɪl), *v.*[3] [Of obscure origin: sense 2 may possibly be the original use. Cf. MAIL *sb.*[1] and *sb.*[3]]

†**1.** *trans.* To tie (*up*), wrap up (goods, a parcel, etc.); to envelop. Also *fig. Obs.*

In the early 17th c. often in expressions like 'mailed in armour', with allusion to MAIL *sb.*[1]

[**1548–78** implied in MAILING *vbl. sb.*[1]] **1570** FOXE *A. & M.* (ed. 2) III. 1644/1 It [gold and silver] was matted about with mattes and mayled in littell bundels about ij. foote long. **1588** PARKE tr. *Mendoza's Hist. China* 209 [A present] was mailed and sealed and so sent vnto the viceroy of Aucheo. **1593** SHAKS. *2 Hen. VI*, II. iv. 31 Me thinkes I should not thus be led along, Mayl'd vp in shame, with Papers on my back. **1598** DRAYTON *Heroic. Ep.* xiii. 59 How could it be, those that were wont to stand, To see my pompe.. Should after see mee mayld vp in a sheete, Doe shamefull penance. **1601** WEEVER *Mirr. Mart.* C iv, Then ledde I warre mailde vp in sheetes of brasse. **1619** *Let. fr. Factors at Surat to the E.I.C.* in *Embassy Sir T. Roe* (Hakl.) 517 To whom wee have delivered a box sealed, maled, and covered. **1653** in T. Fowler *Hist. C.C.C.* (O.H.S.) 228 A basket mal'd up with Cords. **1657** TRAPP *Comm. Ezra* ix. 11 Who.. do miserably mail themselves in the filthiness of leudnesse. **1660** F. BROOKE tr. *Le Blanc's Trav.* 225 Three hundred Elephants follow richly mail'd with Sea-wolf skins.

2. *spec.* in *Hawking.* (See quot. 1883).

1575 TURBERV. *Faulconrie* 295 Mayle your hawke fast. *c* **1610** BEAUM. & FL. *Philaster* v. iv, Prince, by your leave I'le have a Sursingle, And Male you like a Hawke. **1623** FLETCHER & ROWLEY *Maid in Mill* III. iii, If you had.. handled her as men do unmand Hawks, Cast her, and malde her up in good clean linnen. **1883** HARTING *Gloss. Perf. Bk. Kepinge Sparhawkes* 44 To mail a hawk, i.e. to wrap her up in a handkerchief.. either to tame her,.. or to keep her quiet during an operation.

mail (meɪl), *v.*[4] orig. *U.S.* [f. MAIL *sb.*[3] (senses 2, 3).] *trans.* To send by post, to post.

The usual word in the U.K. is still *post*.

1828–32 WEBSTER, *Mail*, to inclose in a wrapper and direct to a post-office. We say, letters were *mailed* for Philadelphia. **1850** OGILVIE, *Mail*, to post letters, papers, &c. **1862** *Morn. Star* 14 Oct., The Federal Post-office department has issued a notice that any letter mailed with stamps at all soiled or defaced will be treated as unpaid. **1872** O. W. HOLMES *Poet Breakf.-t.* iii. 89 Those creatures.. who mail the newspaper which has the article we had much better not have seen. **1875** *Atlantic Monthly* XXXV. 98/2 They mail 244,000,000 letters a year. **1948** H. T. MOORE in D. H. Lawrence *Lett. to B. Russell* 8 Lawrence is telling Lady Ottoline that Russell, who has mailed him the synopsis of his lectures.. still needs to break away. **1968** M. RICHLER in R. Weaver *Canad. Short Stories* 2nd Ser. 170 Once more Mervyn mailed off his novel.

mail, dial. var. MEAL; Sc. f. MOLE (spot).

maila'bility. *U.S.* [f. MAILABLE *a.*] The quality or fact of being mailable.

1883 *U.S. Official Postal Guide* Jan. 664 Mailability of Doubtful Matter. **1903** *Publishers' Circular* 3 Mar. 275/3 As the card does not bear on the address side the words 'United States of America', its mailability is not affected by my circular of the 16th ult. **1944** *Newsweek* 29 May 72 Manhattan's postmaster, Albert Goldman, doubtful as to the mailability of 'Strange Fruit'. **1968** *U.S. Postal Bull.* LXXXIX. No. 20226, 2/1 (*heading*) Mailability of concealable firearms.

mailable ('meɪləb(ə)l), *a.* *U.S.* [f. MAIL *v.*[4] + -ABLE.] That may be sent through the post.

1845 *Stat. U.S.* II. xliii. §10 (1856) V. 736 Any letter.. or other mailable matter whatsoever. **1886** *Pall Mall G.* 3 Sept. 14/1 Any one in the United States can send any mailable matter to any post-office.. for immediate delivery.

'mail-coach. [MAIL *sb.*[3] 2.]

1. A stage-coach used primarily for the conveyance of the mail; subsequently *spec.* a coach employed by the Post Office for carrying parcels by road.

The mail-coach system was introduced by John Palmer in 1784, and was superseded by the railway.

1787 HAN. MORE *Let. Walpole* July *Mem.* (1834) II. 77 Mail coaches, which come to others, come not to me. **1797** *Encycl. Brit.* (ed. 3) V. 86/2 Mail-coaches, are stage-coaches of a particular construction to prevent overturns; and for a certain consideration carry his majesty's mails. **1813** *Act 53 Geo. III*, c. 68 §6 All letters and Packets which he shall convey, carry or send Post, in or by any Mail Coach or Carriage. **1896** *42nd Rept. Postm.-General* 5 There has been no extension this year of the system of night mail coaches for the conveyance of parcels. **1899** *Cassell's Mag.* 404/2 The mail-coaches [for 'road-borne' parcels].. with their swiftly trotting teams and armed guards.

attrib. **1813** BYRON *Let. to Moore* 22 Aug., In a 'mail-coach copy' of the *Edinburgh*, I perceive *The Giaour* is second article. The numbers are still in the Leith smack. **1815** *Ibid.* 10 Jan., Scott's 'Lord of the Isles' is out—'the mail-coach copy' I have, by special licence, of Murray. **1822** *Acc. Establ. Gen. P.-O.* Parl. Pap. XVIII. 175 To eight pair of best mail coach lamps £12 12s. **1885** J. W. HYDE *Roy. Mail* iii. (ed. 2) 65 Yet the mail-coach days had charms and attractions for travellers.

2. A railway carriage carrying the mail.

1838 *Act 1 & 2 Vict.* c. 98 §12 If the Company.. shall refuse to carry on their Railway any Mail Coaches [etc.]. **1890** T. L. JAMES in *Railways Amer.* 335 The fifth.. car is the last mail coach on the train.

mailed (meɪld), *a.* [f. MAIL *sb.*[1] + -ED[2].]

1. Covered with or composed of mail or plates of metal.

1382 WYCLIF *1 Sam.* xvii. 5 And he was clothid with a maylid [Vulg. *squamata*] hawberioun. —— *1 Macc.* vi. 35 A thousand men stoden niȝ in mailid to gidre hauberiownes [Vulg. *in loricis concatenatis*]. **1450** W. LOMNER in *Paston Lett.* I. 125 Oon.. toke awey his gown of russet, and his dobelette of velvet mayled. **1513** DOUGLAS *Æneis* IX. xi. 92 The dowbyll malyt traste hawbryk. **1582** STANYHURST *Æneis* III. (Arb.) 85 A shirt mayled with gould. **1597** A. M. tr. *Guillemeau's Fr. Chirurg.* 7/2 We muste consider, if it be a mayled doublete, how manye mayles are wantinge. **1856** R. A. VAUGHAN *Mystics* (1860) I. 170 The mailed glove [is] manfully hurled in his teeth. **1922** JOYCE *Ulysses* 305 With his mailed gauntlet he brushed away a furtive tear.

2. Armed with mail, mail-clad. Of a vessel: Iron-clad. ***mailed fist***, (a threat of) armed force or superior might.

1596 SHAKS. *1 Hen. IV*, IV. i. 116 The mayled Mars shall on his Altar sit Vp to the eares in blood. **1607** —— *Cor.* I. iii. 38 His bloody brow With his mail'd hand, then wiping, forth he goes. **1773–83** HOOLE *Orl. Fur.* XLVI. 1001 He.. stands with point addrest To pierce the mailed side or plated brest. **1827** KEBLE *Chr. Y.* Adv. Sund., A crown'd monarch's mailèd breast. **1860** TENNENT *Story Guns* III. i. (1864) 229 None of the mailed gun-boats.. were ready in time. **1863** WOOLNER *My Beautiful Lady* 137 When Norman William.. with charge of mailèd horse and showers Of steel won England. **1897** *Times* 17 Dec. 7/1 [tr. Emp. Will. II of Germany] But should any one essay to detract from our just rights or to injure us, then up and at him with your mailed fist [G. *fahre darein mit gepanzerter Faust*]. **1898** *19th Cent.* Jan. 164 Japan is a foe who will not be terrified by the mailed fist of Germany. **1898** *Review of Reviews* Mar. 214 Prince Henry of the mailed fist has by this time reached his destination. **1920** M. BEER *Hist. Brit. Socialism* II. III. i. 16 The first rude contact with the mailed fist brought him back to the sober realities of life.

fig. **1799** CAMPBELL *Pleas. Hope* II. 10 In self-adoring pride securely mail'd. **1850** BLACKIE *Æschylus* II. 230 With constancy mailed for the fight. **1870** BRYANT *Iliad* I. I. 9 Thou mailed in impudence [I. 149 ἀναιδείην ἐπιειμένε].

3. *transf.* of animals, etc.: Having a skin or protective covering resembling mail-armour.

mailed-cheeks, the family *Sclerogenidæ* of fishes.

1681 GREW *Musæum* 117 The Mailed-fish, *Cataphractus Schonveldi*. **1828** STARK *Elem. Nat. Hist.* I. 489 *Centriscus*, Lin. Back mailed with long scaly plates. **1834** McMURTRIE *Cuvier's Anim. Kingd.* 195 Buccæ Loricatæ. The family of the Mailed-Cheeks. **1838** SWAINSON *Nat. Hist. Fishes*, etc. I. 330 The *Loricarinæ* or mailed cat-fish. **1839** *Ibid.* II. 21 The *Holocentrinæ*, or mailed-perches. **1854** OWEN *Skel. & Teeth* 3 The ball-proof character of the skin of the largest of these mailed examples. **1860** GOSSE *Rom. Nat. Hist.* 290 The mailed and glittering beings that shoot along like animated beams of light.

4. a. Of a hawk: Having mail or breast-feathers (of a specified colour).

1575 TURBERV. *Faulconrie* 34 They are ordinarily of foure mayles, eyther blancke, russet, browne, or turtle maylde, and some pure white maylde. **1672** JOSSELYN *New Eng. Rarities* 11 The Osprey, which in this Country is white mail'd. **1683** *Lond. Gaz.* No. 1799/4 A large black Mayled, whole Feathered, and thorough mewed Falcon.

†**b.** Speckled or spotted. *Obs.*

1611 COTGR. s.v. *Maillé*, *Perdrix maillée*, a maylde, menild, or spotted Partridge. **1706** PHILLIPS (ed. Kersey), *Mailed*, full of Specks, or speckled, as the Feathers of Hawks, Partridges, &c. or as the Furrs of some wild Beasts are. [So 1726 *Dict. Rust.* (ed. 3); 1727 Bailey vol. II.]

mail eiss, Sc. variant of MALEASE *Obs.*

mailer[1] ('meɪlə(r)). *Sc.* Also 5–6 **mailler, malar**, 8 **mealler**. [f. MAIL *sb.*[2] + -ER[1].]

1. One who pays rent; also, see quots. 1792–3.

1452 in Tytler *Hist. Scot.* (1864) II. 387 All the tenants and maillers being within my lands quatsomever sall remane with their tacks and maling quhile Whitsonday come a year. *c* **1470** HENRYSON *Mor. Fab.* XII. (*Wolf & Lamb*) xix, Lordis, that hes land be goddis lane, And settis to the mailleris ane village. **1565** *Reg. Privy Council Scot.* I. 358 Gif ony malaris, takkismen, rentalaris or commonis sal happin to be slane. **1597** SKENE *De Verb. Sign.*, *Firmarius*, ane mail-payer, ane mailer. **1792** *Statist. Acc. Scotl.* II. 560 A species of cottagers, here [*sc.* co. Ross] called meallers, who build a small house for themselves, on a waste piece of ground, with the consent of the proprietor, and there, are ready to hire themselves out as day-labourers. **1793** *Ibid.* VII. 254 Two classes, tenants and cottagers; or, as the latter are called here [co. Ross and Inverness] mailers. **1894** *Liberal* 1 Dec. 69 His farm stock was better cared for than those of any other mailer in Netherclugh.

†**2.** ? = Landlord. *Obs.*

1456 SIR G. HAYE *Law Arms* (S.T.S.) 103 Cristin men that ar duelland in the mistrowand menis housis under malis suld be lele to thair malaris and obeisand.

mailer[2] ('meɪlə(r)). [f. MAIL *v.*[4] and *sb.*[3] + -ER[1].]

1. *U.S.* One who mails or dispatches by post.

1884–94 J. T. PERRY in W. F. Crafts *Sabb. for Man* (ed. 7) 328 Editors and compositors are kept up until the small hours on Sunday morning; pressmen and mailers for an hour or two later. **1887** *Bureau Statist. Labour, New York* 490 Newspaper mailers.

2. *U.S.* A boat which carries the mail; a mail-boat.

1883 *Century Mag.* Nov. 160/1 Showing the skill and good control On Transatlantic Mailers.

3. *U.S.* = *mailing machine*.

1902 in WEBSTER *Suppl.*

4. *S. Afr.* A person who purchases liquor from a bottle-store and resells it to an illicit liquor dealer or shebeener.

1950 *Cape Times Week-end Mag.* 17 June 5 As soon as the bottlestore opens, the *mailer* is there. He gets his regulation two bottles and takes this to the shebeen. Then he goes to another bottlestore for a further two bottles. And so he goes on the whole day. **1950** [see DOP *sb.*[3] 2]. **1959** *Cape Argus* 14 Nov. 2/9 When we stopped the delivery the shebeens arranged for mailers to get the liquor for them.

mail ess, Sc. variant of MALEASE *Obs.*

mailet, obs. form of MALLET.

mailhouris, Sc. variant of MALEUROUS *Obs.*

mailing ('meɪlɪŋ), *sb. Sc.* Also 5 **malyn,** 5–7 **mailling,** 6 **maling,** 8 **mealing,** 8–9 **mailin, mailen.** [f. MAIL *sb.*[2] + -ING[1].]

1. A rented farm.

1452 [see MAILER[1] 1]. **1459** *Peebles Charters*, etc. (1872) 132 That neuir nan of hym na his sed com in that malyn agan. *c* **1470** HENRYSON *Mor. Fab.* XII. (*Wolf & Lamb*) xvii, Thay gif na rak, Bot ouer his heid his mailling will thay tak. **1562** *Reg. Privy Council Scot.* I. 222 Thair landis, fischeingis, malingis, rowmes, and possessionis. **1674** W. CUNNINGHAM *Diary* 24 Aug. (1887) 3 John Murdie who dwells in a mailling neir by. **1725** RAMSAY *Gentle Sheph.* v. iii, And to your heirs, I give, in endless feu, The mailens ye possess. *a* **1818** MACNEILL *Poems* (1844) 78 Greenswaird hows, and dainty mealing. **1824** SCOTT *Redgauntlet* ch. xx, I had two or three bonnie bits of mailings amang the closes. **1843** HARDY in *Proc. Berw. Nat. Club* II. No. 11. 64 The farmer and his family.. managed their limited mailings, without extrinsic aid.

2. The rent paid for a farm.

1725 RAMSAY *Gentle Sheph.* II. i, Nor shor'd to raise Our mailens when we put on Sunday claes. **1768** Ross *Helenore* I. 13 Our house is happed, an' our mailen paid. **1818** SCOTT *Hrt. Midl.* viii, Let the creatures stay at a moderate mailing.

3. The term during which a tenant possesses a farm (Jam.).

1609 SKENE *Reg. Maj.* 113 Nor ȝit is he prejudged in his right be the deed of his Fermour, done be him in the time of his mailling.

†'**mailing,** *vbl. sb.*[1] *Obs.* [f. MAIL *v.*[3] + -ING[1].] The action of tying or wrapping up. (*attrib.*)

1531 *Privy Purse Exp. Hen. VIII* (1827) 159 Item for mayling Clothes and Cordes to trusse the same stuf. **1548** *Ludlow Churchw. Acc.* (Camden) 35 Item, for iij. maylinge coordes to hange up the vaile in the quyre afore the alter. **1558** *Lanc. Wills* (1857) I. 177 On malinge sheete of canvas xij[d]. **1569** *Bury Wills* (Camd. Soc.) 155 A malyn lyne withe my woadfat coveryings. **1578** *Richmond Wills* (Surtees) 282 A capp case, a malynge cover.

mailing ('meɪlɪŋ), *vbl. sb.*[2] *U.S.* [f. MAIL *v.*[4]] The action of sending by mail; posting. Also *attrib.*, as *mailing machine, table*; **mailing list** orig. *U.S.*, a register of addresses to which goods and postal matter may be sent; **mailing shot** *Advertising*, material dispatched to potential customers as part of an advertising campaign.

1871 *Amer. Encycl. Print.* (ed. Ringwalt) 292/2 *Mailing Machines*, contrivances.. to facilitate the operation of directing newspapers. **1884** KNIGHT *Dict. Mech.* Suppl., *Mailing Table*, a table at which mail matter is distributed to the mail bags. **1900** *Daily News* 8 Jan. 3/1 Up to the time of mailing no particulars are to hand. **1909** *Daily Chron.* 12 Oct. 4/5 In the States there are 600,000 farmers on the mailing list. **1928** *Publishers' Weekly* 26 May 2201 It is proposed that the booksellers of the country place in this Clearing House.. duplicates of their mailing lists. **1961** *Lebende Sprachen* VI. 70/1 Office furniture, machines and supplies.. mailing list. **1968** *Heidelberg News* (Heidelberg Printing Machinery Co.) Sept. 3/3 The primary aim of a mailing shot is to obtain sales leads. So include a reply paid card and only as much information as is needed to provoke interest. **1969** *Times* 5 Nov. 21/2 A gift offer of a beauty pack with a new bathroom cleaner, real shillings back in an off-pack offer for the bleach, mailing shots, and trade press advertising. **1972** *Times* 30 Nov. 23/5 They decided to go ahead with a 10,000 mailing shot, coupled with.. advertisements. **1973** *Sat. Rev. Society* (U.S.) May 68/2 Ask to be put on the mailing list for Selected U.S. Government Publications.

maill(e, obs. f. MAIL, MALE; obs. Sc. f. MEAL.

‖**maillechort** (mɑjʃɔr). [Fr.; said to be f. the names of the inventors, Maillot and Chorier.] An alloy of zinc, copper, and nickel.

1851 WATTS tr. *Gmelin's Handbk. Chem.* V. 497. **1895** *United Service Mag.* Feb. 456 Bullet, No. 12. Material, Maillechort.

mailless ('meɪllɪs), *a.* [f. MAIL *sb.*[1] + -LESS.] Without mail-armour; not protected with mail.

1817 SCOTT *Harold* III. viii, Unshielded, mail-less, on he goes. **1848** LYTTON *Harold* IX. iii, Let each shaft be aimed at whatever space in my mailless body I leave unguarded.

maillet, obs. form of MALLET.

†**maill(e)y.** *Obs.* [Cf. OF. *maillie gravele* (? fine gravel), *mail* marl, *maillier* to marl (land).]

1747 HOOSON *Miner's Dict.* s.v. *Stone*, Mailly Stone... *Mailley*, is a softer sort of Lime very dusty, and will cut pritty well.

maill eys, Sc. variant of MALEASE *Obs.*

‖**maillot** (majo). [Fr. (13th c. in Robert, but the undermentioned senses are not recorded in Fr. before the 19th c.), lit. 'swaddling clothes'; prob. alteration of *maillol*, *maille* mesh, mail (see MAIL *sb.*[1]).] **1.** Tights.

Romance etymologists mention, but have not verified the existence of, the Maillot referred to in quot. 1936.

1888 H. JAMES in *Cent. Mag.* Apr. 872 The hungry conjurer, the gymnast whose *maillot* is loose, have something of the glamour of the hero. [**1936** A. HASKELL *Prelude to Ballet* 101, 1801.. An important development of costume affecting the dance is the invention of tights by Maillot, costumier of the Paris Opera.] **1939** in WEBSTER Add.

2. A tight-fitting, usu. one-piece, swimming costume.

1928 *Daily Express* 30 June 5/3 Dressmakers have prepared for these holiday-makers most delightful bathing outfits, and mannequins walk in maillots, bathing caps and wraps. **1928** *Daily Mail* 9 Aug. 3/4, I have heard of a wonderful eelskin maillot. **1960** 'J. & E. BONETT' *No Grave for Lady* v. 79 Lumina, in a white maillot, was.. wincing as her bare feet met the sharp stones. **1974** F. SELWYN *Cracksman on Velvet* II. 80 She was dressed in the latest Parisian *maillot*... It was hardly to be imagined that so fragile a costume would survive a single immersion in sea-water.

3. A jersey, 'top'.

1948 A. WAUGH *Unclouded Summer* iv. 65 At a gala evening where the men would discard their *maillots* for starched linen. *Ibid.* 78 His heart was thudding against the cotton of his *maillot*. **1955** *Times* 29 July 9/4 This is the *maillot jaune*, the yellow jersey which the rider, who is so far ahead on aggregate, is privileged to wear as the emblem of leadership. **1955** D. BARTON *Glorious Life* vi. 74 In a not quite clean maillot and a seersucker skirt.

mailteth, var. MELTITH *Sc.*

†**mailure.** *Obs. rare*[−1]. [f. MAIL *sb.*[1] + -URE, after OF. *emmailleure*.] Mail-armour, mail.

c **1430** *Pilgr. Lyf Manhode* I. cxx. (1869) 62 Thou shuldest wite that this armure [the gorgeer] is maad of double mailure [1426 *Lydg.* maylle; F. *emmailleure*].

†**maily,** *a. Obs. rare*[−1]. [? a. OF. *maillié* speckled. But cf. MEALY *a.*] (Sense uncertain.)

1610 MARKHAM *Masterp.* I. x. 27 His [the horse's] colour is.. darke bay, with mayly nose [edd. 1636–75 mayly mouth].

mailyeis, obs. form of MALICE.

maim (meɪm), *sb. Obs.* or *arch.* Forms: α. 4 **maheym,** 4, 6–8 **maime,** 5 **maym,** 5–7 **mayme,** 6 **mame, mahayme,** 6– **maim;** β. 5–6 **mayne,** 6–7 **maine.** See also MAYHEM and MANYIE. [ME. *maheym*, *mayne*, a. OF. *mayhem*, *mahaing*, *main*, etc. (for the forms see Godef.), also fem. *meshaigne*, *maaigne*; vbl. sb. related to *mahaignier* MAIM *v.* Cf. It. *magagna*.] An injury to the body which causes the loss of a limb, or of the use of it; a mutilation, or mutilating wound. †In early use more widely, any lasting wound or bodily injury.

c **1475** *Partenay* 6356 That mariage no mahyme to his kinred. **1340** *Ayenb.* 135 He is ase þe y-maymed ate porche of þe cherche þet ne heþ none ssame uor to sseawy alle his maimes to alle þon þet þer guoþ. *c* **1430** *Syr Gener.* (Roxb.) 3432 In werre somtyme a wound had he, A mayme in the hamme behind the kne. *c* **1440** *Promp. Parv.* 320/1 Mayne, or hurte (*H.*, *P.*, mayme), *mutilacio*. *a* **1450** *Knt. de la Tour* (1868) 9 Thorughe whiche misauenture the lady was one-yed. And for that foule mayme her husbonde kiste away his herte from his wyff. **1496** *Dives & Paup.* (W. de W.) v. xviii. 221/2 Ther sholde no man serue at goddes aulter that had ony greate foule mayme. **1519** HORMAN *Vulg.* 14 b, No man that.. hath a mahayme or a blemmysshe, that maketh hym vngoodly, shall take orders. **1552** ELYOT *Dict.*, *Coloboma*, the mayme or lacke of any membre of the body. *a* **1568** ASCHAM *Scholem.* II. (Arb.) 148 As a foote of wood is a plaine shew of a manifest maime. **1601** HOLLAND *Pliny* I. 170 His Colleagues.. would not permit him to be at the solemne sacrifices, because he had a maim, and wanted a lim. **1653** HOLCROFT *Procopius* I. 26 The Law excluded him, for his mayme of an eye. **1712** STEELE *Spect.* No. 474 ¶3 The more Maims this Brotherhood [of huntsmen] shall have met with, the easier will their Conversation flow. **1741** RICHARDSON *Pamela* (1824) I. 87 These bruises and maims that I have gotten. **1764** FOOTE *Mayor of G.* I. Wks. 1799 I. 162 Maims, bruises, contusions, dislocations,.. may likely ensue.

b. In generalized sense: Loss or permanent disablement of a limb. In early use, any serious bodily injury.

c **1386** CHAUCER *Pars. T.* ¶551 For peyne is sent by the rightwys sonde of god,.. be it Meselrie, or Maheym or maladie. **14..** in *Tundale's Vis.* (1843) 91 Hyt cureth sores hyt heleth euery wownd And saveth men fro maym of swyrd and sper. *c* **1450** *Merlin* 161 God vs deffende fro deth this day and fro mayme. **1529** in *Vicary's Anat.* (1888) App. xiv. 255 Persones.. whiche ys in perell of deth or mayne. **1876** BANCROFT *Hist. U.S.* I. x. 326 A crowd gathered round the scaffold when Prynne and Bastwick and Burton were to suffer maim.

c. *transf.* and *fig.* Mutilation or loss of some essential part; a grave defect, blemish, or disablement; an injury or hurt of any kind.

1543 GRAFTON *Contn. Harding* Pref. xii, Whiche bookes, if they had neuer been set out, It had been a greate maime to our knowlage. **1577** HARRISON *England* II. v. (1877) I. 111 It is accounted a maime in anie one of them [the cleargie] not to be exactlie seene in the Greeke and Hebrue. **1594** HOOKER *Eccl. Pol.* IV. xii. §6 It was a weakenes in the Christian Iewes, and a maime of iudgement in them, that they thought the Gentiles polluted by the eating of those meates [etc.]. **1596** SHAKS. *1 Hen. IV*, IV. i. 42 *Wor.* Your Father's sicknesse is a mayme to vs. *Hotsp.* A perillous Gash, a very Limme lopt off. **1602** MARSTON *Antonio's Rev.* I. iv, Cast my life In a dead sleepe, whilst lawe cuts off yon maine, Yon putred ulcer of my roiall bloode. **1610** HOLLAND *Camden's Brit.* I. 679 This without any maime of the name is called at this day Bod-vari, that is Mansion-Vari. *a* **1627** HAYWARD *Edw. VI* (1630) 47 A noble writer in our time esteemes it to be a mayme in historie that acts of Parliament should not bee recited. *a* **1661** FULLER *Worthies* (1840) I. xxv. 99 They are so eminent in their generations, that their omission would make a maim in history. **1689–90** TEMPLE *Ess.*, *Learning* Wks. 1731 I. 168 The last Maim given to Learning, has been by the Scorn of Pedantry. **1704** SWIFT *T. Tub* i, But the greatest Maim given to that general reception, which the writings of our society have formerly received.. hath been a superficial vein among many readers.

maim (meɪm), *a. rare.* Also 5 **mayn,** 7 **maime.** [Related to prec.: cf. OF. *mehaigne*, mod.F. dial. *mécaigne* (Godef.).] = MAIMED.

Not in any Eng. Dict.

c **1475** *Pict. Voc.* in Wr.-Wülcker 791/18 *Hic mutulatus*, a mayn. **1653** HOLCROFT *Procopius* Pref. A 3, It hath since been the fate of this.. to be exposed maime, and mangled to the world. **1687** MIÉGE *Eng.-Fr. Dict.*, Maim, curtailed of any member, *manchot, estropié*. **1760** BARETTI *Eng.-Ital. Dict.* **1865** tr. *Strauss's New Life Jesus* I. I. 352 Such a thing could not properly be expected of the poor and the maim. **1880** *World* 19 May 6 Refuges for the halt, the maim, the sick, and the blind. **1881** STEVENSON *Moral. Profess. Lett.* in *Fortn. Rev.* Apr., His own life being maim, some of them are not admitted in his theory.

maim (meɪm), *v.* Forms: α. 3–7 **mayme,** 4 **mahayme,** 5 **mayheime,** 5–6 **maym, meyme,** 6 **meyheme, mayhime, mayhme,** 6–7 **maihme,** 5– **maim.** β. 4 **maynhe,** 5 **meygne,** 5–7 **mayn(e,** 6–7 **main(e;** see also Sc. MANYIE *v.* [ME. *maynhe*, *mayn*, etc. (and, with assimilation to MAIM *sb.*, *mahayme*, *mayme*, etc.), a. OF. *mahaignier*, *mayner*, etc. (see Godef. for forms) = Pr. *maganhar*, It. *magagnare*, med.L. *mahemiare*. The ulterior origin is uncertain: the conjectures of Diez and others have little probability.] *trans.* To deprive of the use of some member; to mutilate, cripple. †In early use more widely, to disable, wound, cause bodily hurt or disfigurement to.

1297 R. GLOUC. (Rolls) 5833 Hii velle & to brusede some anon to deþe & some ymaymed [*v.r.* maymed] & some yhurt. *c* **1330** R. BRUNNE *Chron.* (1810) 305 Was no man Inglis maynhed no dede þat day. *a* **1350** *St. Andrew* 38 in Horstm. *Altengl. Leg.* (1881) 132 And eghen sight þai toke fro sum, And sum croked, þat þai might noght ga: And all þat thai mahaymid swa [etc.]. **1393** LANGL. *P. Pl.* C. XXI. 387 Ho so hitteth out a mannes eye.. Othere eny manere membre maymeth other hurteth. *c* **1400** *Lanfranc's Cirurg.* 313 A mannes nose is sumtyme to-broken,.. & if it be longe or he haue ony help, þanne he schal be maymed for euermore. *c* **1400** *Destr. Troy* XXV. 10012 Mony of þo Mirmydons maynet for euer. *c* **1450** *St. Cuthbert* (Surtees) 7843 Some þai hedid, some þai mayne. **1470–85** MALORY *Arthur* II. x, Kynge Arthur slewe that daye xx knyghtes & maymed xl. **1528** MORE *Dial. Heresyes* IV. xiv. Wks. 277/2 And destroy as that sect hath done many a good religious house, spoyled, meyhemed, & slaine many a good vertuous man [etc.]. **1530** PALSGR. 617/1, I mayne, or I mayne one, I take the use of one of his lymmes from hym. **1574** tr. *Littleton's Tenures* 40 b, The Lorde maye not mayme hys villayne. **1604** SHAKS. *Oth.* v. i. 27, I am maym'd for euer: Helpe hoa: Murther, murther. **1622** R. HAWKINS *Voy. S. Sea* lix. 137 Sometimes the winde of the shott ouerthroweth one, and the splinters.. mayne and hurt others. **1635** R. N. *Camden's Hist. Eliz.* Introd., Better it is that a member be joyned to the head, though it be maymed, then quite cut off. *a* **1674** CLARENDON *Hist. Reb.* XIV. §140 Who had lost his father and had been himself maimed in the King's service. **1769** BLACKSTONE *Comm.* IV. xv. 206 By the antient law of England he that maimed any man, whereby he lost any part of his body, was sentenced to lose the like part. **1792** BURKE *Let. Sir H. Langrishe* Wks. 1842 I. 546 Nocturnal assemblies for the purpose of pulling down hedges,.. firing barns, maiming cattle. **1867** LADY HERBERT *Cradle L.* i. 26 They maim themselves in every way to escape it [conscription]. **1868** *Rep. to Govt. U.S. Munitions War* 182 Thousands who have lost limbs altogether,.. have done the State.. good service after they were maimed.

b. *fig.* To mutilate, cripple, render powerless or essentially incomplete; †to deprive *of*.

c **1386** CHAUCER *Wife's T.* 276 For of oure eldres may we no thyng clayme, But temporel thyng, þat man may hurte and mayme. *c* **1400** *Rom. Rose* 5317 For it maymeth, in many wyse, Syke hertis with coveityse. **1562** COOPER *Answ. Def. Truth* iii. 21 b, Hee that altereth or taketh away any doth alter and maime christes institution. **1563** B. GOOGE *Eglogs*, etc. (Arb.) 102 A Creature maymde of Reasons parte. **1593** SHAKS. *2 Hen. VI*, IV. ii. 172 Thereby is England main'd And faine to go with a staffe. **1613** —— *Hen. VIII*, III. ii. 312 You wrought to be a Legate, by which power You maim'd the Jurisdiction of all Bishops. **1682** DRYDEN *Religio Laici* 279 For since the original Scripture has been lost, All copies disagreeing, maimed the most. **1759** FRANKLIN *Ess.* Wks. 1840 III. 399 To abridge would be to maim one of the most lively pieces that liberty ever inspired. **1767** HARTE *Medit. T. à Kempis* 117 But ah! their neighbour's pittance maims their field. **1823** SCOTT *Peveril* xv, That.. act of royalty and supreme jurisdiction, the consequences of which maimed my estate so cruelly. **1868** M. PATTISON *Academ. Org.* 6 The House passed the Government Bill, maiming it in vital points in its passage through Committee.

maimai ('maɪmaɪ). *N.Z.* Also **maemae, mai mai, mimi.** [Alteration of Austral. Aboriginal

mia-mia MIA-MIA.] A makeshift Maori shelter of sticks, grass, etc. (see quots. 1863, 1873). Hence, in more recent use, a duckshooter's hide or stand.

1863 S. BUTLER *First Year in Canterbury Settlement* v. 72 The few Maories that inhabit this settlement.. always go on foot, and we saw several traces of their encampments—little *mimis*, as they are called—a few light sticks thrown together, and covered with grass, affording a sort of half-and-half shelter for a single individual. **1873** J. H. H. ST. JOHN *Pakeha Rambles through Maori Lands* ix. 153 In the days of bush fighting it used to be a common occurrence at the end of a day's march, when the maemae's had been knocked up by the side of a stream, to see three or four of the men gravely set to work with pannikin.. and 'wash' for a prospect. **1963** *Weekly News* (Auckland) 15 May 27 W. Porter operated successfully from a well-made maimai in the shallows of the Waikato River. **1966** J. K. BAXTER *Pig Island Lett.* 43 He needs the maimai's breast of shade.

maimed (meɪmd), *ppl. a.* [f. MAIM *v.* + -ED¹.] Mutilated, crippled, injured: see the verb.

a **1400–50** *Alexander* 4544 Lo, to so many mayned gods ȝour menbris ȝe dele. **1578** *Nottingham Rec.* IV. 176, iiij. meymed men that cum fourth of Eyrland. **1591** SPENSER *M. Hubberd* 272 But my late maymed limbs lack wonted might To doo their kindly services. **1625** BACON *Ess.*, *Greatness Kingd.* (Arb.) 491 Hospitals for Maimed Soldiers. **1638** JUNIUS *Paint. Ancients* 42 They stand and stare upon such maimed creatures as want either legges or armes. **1720** DE FOE *Capt. Singleton* xi. (1840) 198 This maimed man. **1864–7** GEO. ELIOT *Sp. Gipsy* I. (1868) 4 A maimed giant in his agony.

b. *fig.*

1570 BILLINGSLEY *Euclid* VII. Introd. 183 Geometrie boroweth of it [Arithmetic] principles,.. and is as it were maymed without it. **1602** SHAKS. *Ham.* v. i. 242 Who is that they follow, And with such maimed rites? **1877** J. D. CHAMBERS *Divine Worship* 308 In such a maimed and dislocated form. **1900** S. PHILLIPS *Paolo & Francesca* I. 26 All these maimèd wants and thwarted thoughts.

c. *absol.*

1340 *Ayenb.* 135 [see MAIM *sb.*]. *Ibid.* 141 Þo he hedde y-preched and y-ued þet uolk and þe zike and þe ymamed y-held. *c* **1420** *Chron. Vilod.* 1098 For leuer here was þe pore to fede, Þe maymot, þe seke to wasshe & hele. **1526** TINDALE *Matt.* xv. 31 In so moche that the people wondred, to se.. the maymed whole. **1764** FOOTE *Mayor of G.* I. Wks. 1799 I. 162 Is it your Worship's will that I lend a ministring hand to the maim'd? **1848** MRS. JAMESON *Sacr. & Leg. Art* II. 298 The sick and maimed who are healed by her intercession.

†'**maimedly**, *adv. Obs.* [-LY².] In a maimed manner.

1596 NASHE *Saffron Walden* Wks. (Grosart) III. 47 Being aboue 2 yeres since maimedly translated into the French tongue. **1598** *Hakluyt's Voy.* I. 614, I rather leaue it out altogether, then presume to doe it maymedly. **1680** H. MORE *Apocal. Apoc.* 154 Some strictures there were,.. but hinted very maimedly, obscurely and interruptedly.

maimedness ('meɪmɪdnɪs). [-NESS.] The condition of being maimed (*lit.* and *fig.*).

1607 HIERON *Wks.* I. 122 He will see such weakenesse,.. such maimednesse, such imperfection, in his best performances. **1613** PURCHAS *Pilgrimage* II. vii. (1614) 135 The conditions required in the High Priest, as that he should not haue the bodily defects of Blindnesse, lamenesse, maymednesse, &c. **1886** RUSKIN *Præterita* I. xii. 425 So much did its sullenness and maimedness pollute the meagre sacrifice.

maimer ('meɪmə(r)). [f. MAIM *v.* + -ER¹.] One who maims or mutilates.

1530 PALSGR. 241/2 Maymer of men, *mvtilatevr.* **1769** BLACKSTONE *Comm.* IV. 13 If a man maliciously should put out the remaining eye of him who had lost one before, it is too slight a punishment for the maimer to lose only one of his. **1884** *Athenæum* Feb. 182/1 Terrorists and maimers of cattle.

maiming ('meɪmɪŋ), *vbl. sb.* [-ING¹.] The action of the verb MAIM.

a **1400–50** *Alexander* 4088 Þan wald his pepill & his princes haue past ouir þe bourne, And miȝt noȝt for þe morsure & maynyng of bestis. *a* **1568** ASCHAM *Scholem.* II. (Arb.) 99 To the marring and mayning of the Scholer in learning. **1602** FULBECKE *1st Pt. Parall.* 78 The opinion of M. Brooke is that hee may beate him if hee cannot otherwise escape without stripes or wounds or mayming. **1727** SWIFT *Let. Eng. Tongue* Wks. 1755 II. I. 188 Another cause.. which hath contributed.. to the maiming of our language, is a foolish opinion,.. that we ought to spell exactly as we speak. **1768–74** TUCKER *Lt. Nat.* (1834) II. 43 Inevitable evils are.. such as sudden deaths, maimings, or other bodily hurts by the stroke of lightning.

Maimonidean, Maimonidian (maɪmɒnɪ'diːən, maɪməʊ'nɪdɪən), *a.* (*sb.*) [f. L. *Maimonidēs* + -AN, -IAN.] **a.** Pertaining to the Jewish theologian *Maimonides* (*Mōshe^h ben Maymōn* 1135–1204). **b.** *sb.* An adherent of Maimonides.

1864 *Chambers's Encycl.* VI. 273 The.. spiritualistic Maimonidian and the 'literal Talmudistic' schools. **1876** SCHILLER-SZINESSY *Catal. Hebr. MSS. Cambr.* I. 187 The so-called Maimonidean school. **1882–3** SCHAFF *Encycl. Relig. Knowl.* II. 1388 Judaism was soon divided into the Maimonidians and Anti-Maimonidians. **1886** *Encycl. Brit.* XX. 283/2 The Maimonidean controversy.

Maimonist ('maɪmənɪst). [f. *Maimon-ides* (see prec.) + -IST.] An adherent of Maimonides.

1881 FRIEDLÄNDER *Maimonides' Guide of Perplexed* I. Life 35 The controversy between Maimonists and anti-Maimonists.

main (meɪn), *sb.*¹ Forms: 1 **mæȝen, mæȝn,** 2–4 **mein,** (3 *Lay.* **mæin**), 3–4 **meyn,** 3–6 **mayn,** 4–6 *Sc.* **mane,** 4–7 **maine, mayne,** 3– **main.** [OE. *mæȝen*, = OS. *megin*, OHG. *magan*, *megin*, ON. *magn*, *megn*, *megin*, f. root **mag-*: see MAY *v.*, MIGHT *sb.*]

I. 1. a. Physical strength, force, or power. *Obs.* exc. in phr. ***with might and main*** (see 2).

Beowulf 789 Se þe manna wæs mæȝene strengest. *c* **1205** LAY. 26698 Þer he finden mihte þe his main wolde fondien hond aȝan honde. *c* **1275** *Luue Ron* 69 in *O.E. Misc.* 95 Ector wiþ his scharpe meyne. ? *c* **1325** *Old Age* x. in *E.E.P.* (1862) 149, I spend, an marrit is mi main. **1375** BARBOUR *Bruce* I. 444 The king.. went till Ingland.. With mony man off mekill mayn. *Ibid.* VI. 318 Thair chiftane Wes of sic hert and of sic mane, That [etc.]. **1460** *Lybeaus Disc.* (Kaluza) 560 He nadde main ne miȝt. *c* **1470** HENRY *Wallace* I. 320 Hyr eldest son, that mekill was of mayn. **1501** DOUGLAS *Pal. Hon.* III. lxxvi, Thay with speir, with swordis, and with kniues, In just battell war fundin maist of mane. **1590** SPENSER *F.Q.* I. vii. 11 He gan aduaunce With huge force and insupportable mayne.

†**b.** *fig.*, and in immaterial applications. *Obs.*

a **1300** *Cursor M.* 21051 (Cott.) O treind wandes gold he wroght.. And efter-ward wit crists main þam turnd to þair kind egain. **1390** GOWER *Conf.* III. 4 Love is of so gret a main, That.. Ther mai nothing his miht withstonde. *c* **1440** *York Myst.* xx. 123 Þou arte nowthir of myght ne mayne To kenne it as a clerke may knawe. **1549–62** STERNHOLD & H. *Ps.* xciii. 1 And he to shew his strength and maine, hath girt himselfe with might.

†**c.** *transf.* Of things: Power, virtue, efficacy.

c **1000** *Sax. Leechd.* I. 94 Þonne ys seo ærre [wyrt] hwitre, & heo hæfð þas mæȝnu. *c* **1320** *Sir Tristr.* 1581 Sche com wiþ adrink of main.

2. Phrases. †***with*** (***mid***) or ***in all one's main, with main, with all, great*** or ***mickle main*** (in ME. poetry often used as a metrical stopgap or tag): with the utmost strength or vigour one is capable of. †***to set one's main to***: to apply all one's energies to. †***to do one's main***: to do one's utmost, one's best. ***with might and main,*** †***with main and might,*** †***with mood and main,*** etc.: see MIGHT *sb.*, MOOD *sb.* See also AMAIN.

c **1175** *Lamb. Hom.* 123 Luuian we hine mid alre heorte.. mid alle meine. *c* **1290** *S. Eng. Leg.* I. 104/113 A þousend men with al heore main on hire gonne drawe. *c* **1314** *Guy Warw.* (A.) 884 Gii.. þe stede toke bi the reyn, & lepe vp wiþ gret meyn. *c* **1320** *Sir Tristr.* 1083 Tristrem smot wiþ main. *c* **1375** *Sc. Leg. Saints* iv. (*Jacobus*) 299 He gert fele knychtis.. pryk efter þame in al þar mayne. *Ibid.* xxvii. (*Machor*) 8, I wald fayne,.. set my mayne sume thing to say of sancte moryse. *c* **1375** *Cursor M.* 1076 (Fairf.) Quen he [*sc.* Cain] had his broþer slayne To hide him he dide his mayne. *c* **1450** *St. Cuthbert* (Surtees) 4048 He thanked god with all his mayne. *c* **1460** *Towneley Myst.* xv. 101 Tell me, Ioseph, with mayn, youre red. **1542** BECON *Potat. Lent* D iv b, That ye cleue stedfastly with all mayne to the promyses which [etc.]. *a* **1568** *Wyfe of Auchtermuchty* vii, Than owt he ran in all his mane.

†**3.** A host of men; a (military) force. *Obs.*

a **1000** *Andreas* 876 We ðær heahfæderas haliȝe oncneowon & martyra mæȝen unlytel. **10..** *O.E. Chron.* an 1004 Ðær wærð East Engla folces seo yld of slaȝen, ac ȝif þet fulle mæȝen þære wære, ne eodan hi næfre eft to scipon swa hi sylfe sædon. **1297** R. GLOUC. (Rolls) 8999 William courtehese he made of þe verste wardein & in þe oþer bihinde he was him sulf mid al is main.

II. Senses arising from absol. uses of MAIN *a.*

4. a. *ellipt.* for *main land*, MAINLAND. *arch.*

1555 EDEN *Decades* 351 At three leaques off the mayne, there is xv. fadome. **1577–87** HOLINSHED *Chron.* I. 43/2 This Iland, which for the quantitie thereof maie well be called a maine, although it be inuironed about with the Ocean sea. **1600** J. PORY tr. *Leo's Africa* 50 Not far from the main are certaine dry and rockie isles. **1698** FRYER *Acc. E. India & P.* 14 The most traded Empories here, are St. Augustine on the Island [Madagascar], and Mosambique on the Main. **1711** STEELE *Spect.* No. 11 ¶5 The *Achilles*, in some distress, put into a Creek on the Main of America. **1823** BYRON *Juan* VII. xxxi, Their Delhis mann'd some boats and.. tried to make a landing on the main. **1839** THIRLWALL *Greece* VI. l. 196 The island.. was separated from the main by a channel half a mile broad. **1891** J. WINSOR *Columbus* xiii. 290 He was anxious to make a thorough examination of Cuba, which was a part of the neighboring main of Cathay, as he was ready to suppose.

b. Short for SPANISH MAIN, q.v.

1890 CORBETT *Sir F. Drake* iii. 33 Drake.. sailed once more for the Main. **1897** HENLEY *Hawthorn & Lavender*, etc. (1901) 95 The trim Slaver.. Held.. Her musky course from Benin to the Main, And back again for niggers.

5. a. *ellipt.* for MAIN SEA: The high sea, the open ocean. Now *poet.*

1579–80 NORTH *Plutarch*, *C. Marius* (1595) 468 The winde stoode full against them comming from the maine [F. *le uent se tourna du costé de la pleine mer*]. **1601** R. JOHNSON *Kingd. & Commw.* (1603) 211 They dare not venter into the maine, but houering by the shore, timerously saile from one place to another. **1695** WOODWARD *Hist. Earth* I. 27 The Tides and Storms.. affect only the superficial parts of the Ocean,.. but never reach the greater Depths, or disturb the bottom of the Main. **1698** FROGER *Voy.* 65 A gentle Breeze came off from the Main [F. *du large*]. **1731** POPE *Ep. Burlington* 198 Bid the broad Arch the dang'rous Flood contain, The Mole projected break the roaring Main. **1764** GOLDSM. *Trav.* 410 To traverse climes beyond the western main. **1847** TENNYSON *Princess* VII. 21 As one that climbs a peak to gaze O'er land and main.

fig. **1597** R. JOHNSON *Champions* (1608) II. Addr., But having better hope I boldly leade thee to this mayne from this doubtfull floude where I rest. **1602** MARSTON *Ant. & Mel.* IV. Wks. 1856 I. 46 Launched out Into the surgy maine of government. **1839** LONGF. *Ps. of Life* viii, Sailing o'er life's solemn main.

†**b.** *transf.* A broad expanse. *poet. Obs.*

c **1600** SHAKS. *Sonn.* lx. 5 Natiuity once in the maine of light, Crawles to maturity. **1667** MILTON *P.L.* x. 257 Adventrous work,.. to found a path Over this Maine from Hell to that new World Where Satan now prevailes.

6. a. The most important part of some business, subject, argument, or the like; the chief matter or principal thing in hand. (Cf. MAIN *sb.*³ 1 b.)

1602 SHAKS. *Ham.* II. ii. 56, I doubt it is no other, but the maine, His Fathers death, and our o'er-hasty Marriage. **1615** tr. *De Monfart's Surv. E. Indies* Pref. B iij, Neyther doth he stand vpon any other vayne particulars, but directly goeth to the maine. **1650** BAXTER *Saints' R.* I. ii. §1 (1651) 192 If I should here enter upon that task.. I should make too broad a digression, and set upon a work as large as the main, for whose sake I should undertake it. **1663** COWLEY *Country-Mouse* 5 Frugal, and grave, and careful of the Main. **1702** *Eng. Theophrast.* 132 We let the Main go, while we grasp at the accessories. **1716–20** *Lett. fr. Mist's Jrnl.* (1722) I. 244 She complied with your last Advice, as to the Main.

b. Phrases: ***in,*** †***for,*** †***on,*** †***upon the main***: for the most part; in all essential points; mainly.

a **1628** PRESTON *New Covt.* (1634) 12 Holy men have that apprehension in the maine, but not in a constant tenour at all times. **1639** FULLER *Holy War* I. xvi. (1840) 28 As long as they agree in the main, we need not be much moved with their petty dissensions. **1662** H. MORE *Philos. Writ.* Pref. Gen. p. vi, Being carried captive by the power of reason into a true belief of things for the main. **1697** J. SERGEANT *Solid Philos.* 80 Whence, upon the main, is clearly discovered, how all true Philosophy is nothing but the knowledge of Things. **1699** BENTLEY *Phal.* 49 Generally and for the main he resided at Crotona. **1711** STEELE *Spect.* No. 118 ¶3, I do not know whether in the main I am the worse for having loved her. **1748** RICHARDSON *Clarissa* (1811) II. 145 If Nancy did not think well of you upon the main. **1799** in *Spirit Pub. Jrnls.* III. 394 John is, upon the main, no fool. **1832** J. C. HARE *Philol. Mus.* I. 163 *note*, Since writing the above I have found a reading agreeing on the main with mine in the edition of Asconius by Paulus Manutius. **1840** DICKENS *Old C. Shop* lvi, Mr. Swiveller being in the main a good-natured fellow. **1893** R. WILLIAMS in Traill *Social Eng.* i. 31 In the main, therefore, the leading ideas of the heathen Celt were those of heathen nations generally.

c. Const. *of.* The chief or principal part (*of* some whole, material or immaterial); the important or essential point. Phr. † ***the main of all.***

1595 DANIEL *Civ. Wars* III. xxxvii, I know you know how much the thing doth touch The maine of all your states, your blood, your seed. **1601** SIR W. CORNWALLIS *Disc. Seneca* (1631) M m 2, It is no charity to giue so violently as may waste the maine of an estate. **1631** HEYWOOD *2nd Pt. Maid of West* II. Wks. 1874 II. 363 Why that's the main of all: all without his freedome That we can aime at's nothing. **1647** MAY *Hist. Parl.* I. viii. 104 It was not onely agreed that their Ships.. should be restored.. but for the maine of all, it was resolved upon by both houses, to give the full summe of £300000. **1653** HOLCROFT *Procopius* II. 38 But the maine of all: studies he not [etc.]? **1683** CAVE *Ecclesiastici*, *Chrysostom* 501 The main of the Church was destroyed [by fire] in three hours space. **1693** *Mem. Cnt. Teckely* IV. 49 He assaulted them in the Front with the main of his Army. **1711** ADDISON *Spect.* No. 47 ¶9 The Persons we laugh at may in the main of their Characters be much wiser Men than our selves. **1750** JOHNSON *Rambler* No. 68 ¶3 The main of life is composed of small incidents. **1781** WESLEY *Wks.* (1872) IV. 215 He has sufficiently proved the main of his hypothesis. **1845** STEPHEN *Comm. Laws Eng.* (1874) I. 119 If a lord had a parcel of land detached from the main of his estate. **1880** BLACKMORE *Mary Anerley* II. xvi. 279 The main of their cargo was landed. **1880** ANNIE R. ELLIS *Sylvestra* II. 275 She told him the main of the morning's news. **1903** *Contemp. Rev.* Feb. 190 The main of us have never set eyes upon a Dane before.

†**7.** The object aimed at; end, purpose. *Obs.*

Perh. orig. a term of archery. Cf. MAIN *sb.*³ 2.

a **1610** HEALEY *Epictetus' Man.* (1636) 6 The ayme of appetite, is to attaine what it affecteth, and the maine of dislike is to avoide what it disliketh. **1610** W. FOLKINGHAM *Art of Survey* To Rdr. 3, I ayme not at the Racke nor the Slack, the qualified Meane is the Maine of my Marke. **1623** WEBSTER *Duchess Malfi* II. i, *Bos.* You say you would fain be taken for an eminent courtier? *Cast.* 'Tis the very main of my ambition. **1633** B. JONSON *Tale of a Tub* III. iv, Wee have by this meanes disappointed him, And that was all the maine I aimed at. **1652** R. BOREMAN *Countrymans Catech.* i. 1 This Happinesse (or the Salvation of our Soules) being the maine of all our enlarged desires. **1657** SPARROW *Bk. Com. Prayer* 173 Therefore differing so much in the main of the Feast, they would not comply with them.

8. a. A principal channel, duct, or conductor for conveying water, sewage, gas, or electricity, e.g. along the street of a town. (Cf. *main drain*, 1707–12 s.v. MAIN *a.* 8 b.) The pl. *mains* is freq. used, esp. *attrib.* and in *Comb.*, in a collective sense: the public supply, esp. the electricity supply.

1727 BRADLEY *Fam. Dict.* s.v. *Building*, Where any Stock-Blocks of Wood with Plugs, or any Fire-Cocks, were made and fix'd on any Mains [etc.]. **1762** *Ann. Reg.* 120/1 Wooden pipes were inserted into the mains in almost every street. **1808** MURDOCH in *Phil. Trans.* XCVIII. 125 The gas.. is conveyed by iron pipes into.. gazometers,.. previous to its being conveyed through other pipes, called mains, to the mill. **1825** LOUDON *Encycl. Agric.* 658 The use of both the large and small mains is to feed the various trenches with water, which branch out into all parts of the meadow. **1871** TYNDALL *Fragm. Sci.* (1879) II. xvi. 449 The electric main carrying the outgoing current. **1894** *Nat. Observer* 189/2 Take the case of a lead-pipe led into a block of houses from the iron main. **1895** S. P. THOMPSON & E. THOMAS *Electr. Tab. & Mem.* 4 In factory wiring it is often preferred to keep the positive and negative mains far apart. **1929** *Radio Times* 8 Nov. 433/1 Faultless Radio, coupled to an all-mains system of current supply, operating.. without mains hum. **1930** *Morning Post* 18 Aug., With any good receiver, costing from about £12 for a battery-operated model, to £30 for a

mains-model, several foreign stations may be regularly well received. **1936** *Discovery* July 203/1 It is still safer to switch off the current at the mains. **1959** *Times* 26 Aug. 5/4 A transistor radio receiver will soon be a serious challenge to the mains-driven sound radio receiver. **1962** *Which?* Aug. 261/1 The voltage will probably be fixed—a mains voltage of 200 to 250 volts. **1968** *Listener* 22 Aug. 239/1 At the airport there were lights—not from the mains, but from a generator. **1969** *Soviet Weekly* 13 Sept. 12 You rent a cottage with mains water and a gas cooker for 32 to 38 roubles a month. **1971** 'H. CALVIN' *Poison Chasers* xii. 161 There was an old-fashioned mains radio on the sideboard, and I switched it on. **1975** *Daily Tel.* 13 June 13/4 Villages on high ground at the end of the mains system have been temporarily without supplies, the South West Water Authority announced.

fig. **1865** MASSON *Rec. Brit. Philos.* i. 15 It is not only Britain.. that the writer accuses of this folly of not drawing its philosophy from the main.

b. In jocular phr. ***to turn on the main***, to begin to weep copiously.

1837 DICKENS *Pickw.* xvi, Blessed if I don't think he's got a main in his head as is always turned on. **1857** BRADLEY (C. Bede) *Verdant Green* III. xi. 90 You've no idea how she turned on the main, and did the briny! **1878** M. C. JACKSON *Chaperon's Cares* I. x. 128 The mains were turned on, and tears flowed until weeping became infectious.

9. Short for *mainsail* (obs.), *mainmast*.

1535 STEWART *Cron. Scot.* I. 373 Tha led thame in with musall, fuk, and mane. **1894** *Times* 7 Apr. 7/3 All the ships .. were gaily decked with bunting, the German flag flying at the main. **1903** *Blackw. Mag.* Apr. 523/1 Skiffs with well-reefed mains scudded for sheltering creeks.

10. *techn.* **a.** ? A principal vein of mineral. **b.** A main line of railway.

1867 MUSGRAVE *Nooks & Corners* II. 2 A wide main of this mineral lies beneath the stupendous masses of dark blueish rock. **1892** *Daily News* 8 June 2/3 The railway will be a double main.

main (meɪn), *sb.*² *Sc.* and *north.* Also 5 **mayn**; *pl.* 6 **maynis, manis, maines,** 7 **maynes, mainnes,** 8 **mainse.** [Aphetic f. DOMAIN, DEMESNE.]

†**1.** ***mains*** or ***main lands*** = demesne lands. *Obs.*

1454 in *14th Rep. Hist. MSS. Comm.* App. III. 10 The sayde Androw Ker sal gyff..tyl the sayde Thom Robson.. his mayn landis of Hownum. **1577–95** *Descr. Isles Scot.* in Skene *Celtic Scot.* III. App. 436 The said John Stewart hes it all under maynes.

2. *pl.* The farm attached to a mansion house; a home farm. (Now esp. retained in Scotland in the names of farms, e.g. the Mains of Forthar.)

1533 CLYFFORD in *St. Papers Hen. VIII*, IV. 633 Wher we brynt theis townes that is to wite, Sesfurth.. Sesfurth Mayns, Mows Mayns.. Cavertone Mayns [etc.]. **1573–4** *Reg. Privy Council Scot.* Ser. I. II. 320 The landis mains and cornis of Sanct Thomas Chapell. *a* **1578** LINDESAY (Pitscottie) *Chron. Scot.* (S.T.S.) I. 226 3e sall haue the manis of Kirkforther for it. **1589** *Wills & Inv. N.C.* (Surtees 1860) 164, I geue to Mathew Forster,.. Edderstoun east hall, and the maynis thairoff. **1597** SKENE *De Verb. Sign.*, *Manerivm*,.. ane mainnes, or domaine landes,.. Because they ar laboured and inhabited be the Lorde, and proprietar of the samin. **1606** in *North Riding Rec.* (1884) I. 48 John Dodsworth of Massam Maynes. **1766** W. GORDON *Gen. Counting-ho.* 468 The tenants and Mainse fall now to be debited for crop 1765. **1769** *De Foe's Tour Gt. Brit.* IV. 72 Every Nobleman's House [in Scotland] hath what they call the Mains, where their Land-labourers, Grooms, and every Body belonging to the Stable and Poultry, reside. **1814** SCOTT *Wav.* xv, That the Bailie should send his own three milk cows down to the mains for the use of the Baron's family. **1834** H. MILLER *Scenes & Leg.* xxvii. (1857) 398 He was employed.. at the Mains of Invergordon.

main (meɪn), *sb.*³ Also 6–7 **maine, mayne.** [Of obscure history.

From the early use in antithesis with *by* (which seems in the game of hazard to have meant the same as *chance* in the later language) the word would appear to be an absolute or elliptical application of MAIN *a.* (Cf. MAIN CHANCE.) The usual view that the word is a. F. *main* 'hand' has no evidence; quot. *c* 1685–8 in sense 3 prob. embodies a mere etymological speculation.]

1. In the game of hazard, a number (from five to nine inclusive) called by the 'caster' before the dice are thrown.

'If he "throws in", or "nicks", he wins the sum played for from the banker or "setter"... If the caster "throws out" by throwing aces, or deuce, ace (called crabs), he loses... If the caster neither nicks nor throws out, the number thrown is his "chance", and he keeps on throwing till either the chance comes up, when he wins, or till the main comes up, when he loses' (*Encycl. Brit.* s.v. *Hazard*).

1580 LD. OFFALEY in Stanyhurst *Æneis*, etc. (Arb.) 153, I loathe too see them [*sc.* dice-players] sweare.., When they the mayne haue lost; Forgetting al thee byes, that weare With God and holye goast. **1580** LYLY *Euphues* (Arb.) 289 Not vnlyke the vse of foule gamesters, who hauing lost the maine by true iudgement, thinke to face it out with a false oath. **1598** BARCKLEY *Felic. Man* Pref., Diceplayers, that gaine more by the bye then by the maine. *a* **1635** CORBET *Poems* (1807) 128 Amongst the gamsters, where they name thee [the pox] thicke At the last maine, or the last pocky nicke. **1665** EARL DORSET *Song written at Sea* vii, To pass our tedious Hours away, We throw a merry Main. **1684** OTWAY *Atheist* III. i, The Main was Seven, and the Chance Four. **1726** *Art & Myst. of Gaming Exposed* 29 Loaded or Scooped Dice are..changed as often as the Main and Chance, or Occasion requires. **1731** FIELDING *Mod. Husb.* II. x, *La. Char.* Eleven mains together, Modern; you are a devil. *Mr. Gaywit.* She has always great luck at Hazard. **1777** COLMAN *Epil. Sheridan's Sch. Scand.* (1883) 76 Seven's the main. **1837** THACKERAY *Ravenswing* viii, He likes to throw a main of an evening. **1881** SHORTHOUSE *J. Inglesant* (1882) II. 306 Come and take your chances in the next main. **1894** MASKELYNE *Sharps & Flats* 255 The first throw made by the player is called the 'main'.

†**b.** *fig.* esp. coupled with or in antithesis to *by* (see BY *sb.*² 1). *Obs.*

1567, **1580** [see BY *sb.*² 1]. **1589** WARNER *Alb. Eng.* Prose Addit. 155 Whatsoeuer thy play be in Affrick, let henceforth the Mayne be Italie. **1593** SHAKS. *2 Hen. VI*, I. i. 208 Then lets make hast away, And looke vnto the maine. **1595** *Maroccus Ext.* (Percy Soc.) 12 *Horse.* No, no, his minde was on the twentieth daie of the moneth following, when his money was due. *Bankes.* Tis good to haue an eie to the maine. **1596** SHAKS. *1 Hen. IV*, IV. i. 47 To set so rich a mayne On the nice hazard of one doubtfull houre. **1602** DANIEL *Civ. Wars* VII. xxv, The doubtful Dye of War cast at the Main Is such as one bad Chance may lose you all. **1612** R. DABORNE *Chr. turn'd Turke* 8 Deale Merchant-like, put it vpon one maine, And throw at all. **1676** TOWERSON *Decalogue* 462 Recreations.. must consequently be.. used as things on the by and not as the main. **1781** *Westm. Mag.* IX. 604 When each grave Senator the sport promotes, And throws the main with—cogg'd and loaded votes.

†**2.** A match (at archery, boxing, bowls). *Obs.*

Cf. MAIN *sb.*¹ 7. But in the first quot. *a maine* may possibly be AMAIN *adv.*

1589 NASHE *Martins Months Mind* To Rdr. C 3 b, To shoote a maine for the vpshot, at the fairest markes of all. **1812** *Sporting Mag.* XXXIX. 19 The champion has won a main, and certainly Molineux could have no chance in any combat with him. **1886** *Cheshire Gloss.* s.v., A main at bowls is a match played by a number of couples, the winners again playing in couples against each other till one man is left the victor. [Cf. *Welsh main* in 3.]

3. A match fought between cocks. Hence *occas.* a number of cocks engaged in a match. ***Welsh main*** (see quot. 1770); *transf.* (see quot. 1886).

[*c* **1685–8** *MS. Life of Alderman Barnes* in Brand *Pop. Antiq.* (1813) I. 481 His chief Recreation was Cock-fighting. .. One Cock particularly he had, called 'Spang Counter', which came off victor in a great many battles *a la main*. **1716** *Lond. Gaz.* No. 5429/4 There will be By-Battles,.. And in the Afternoon will begin the main Match.] **1760** R. HEBER *Horse Matches* ix. 154 A Main of Cocks were fought between the D. of Cleveland and Ld. Northumberland. **1770** S. PEGGE in *Archæologia* (1775) I. 149 The Welsh-main consists, we will suppose of sixteen pair of cocks; of these the sixteen conquerors are pitted a second time; the eight conquerors of these are pitted a third time; the four conquerors the fourth time; and lastly, the two conquerors of these are pitted a fifth time. **1828** SCOTT *F.M. Perth* xxi, Laying schemes for massacring men on Palm Sunday, as if he were backing a Welsh main, where all must fight to death. **1855** MACAULAY *Hist. Eng.* xvii. IV. 57 The dexterity with which he.. turned conversation away from matters of state to a main of cocks or the pedigree of a racehorse. **1880** JEFFERIES *Gr. Ferne F.* 59 He could swear and drink no more, nor fight a main of cocks every Sunday afternoon on his dining room table. **1886** *Cheshire Gloss.* s.v., There is also the term *Welsh main*, applied in a secondary sense to voting: voting until two only are left in, and then for those two alone. **1890** H. FREDERIC *Lawton Girl* 33, I've seen dog-fights and cock-mains in England.

main (meɪn), *sb.*⁴ Also 7 **meane.** [a. F. *main*.]

†**1.** *Her.* The hand. *Obs.*

1688 R. HOLME *Armoury* I. 103/2 Our old English terms were.. Maine for Hand. Meane Dexter for R. Hand.

2. 'A banker's shovel for coin' (Knight 1875).

Cf. F. *main*, 'pelle de tôle, à manche de bois très-court' (Littré).

main (meɪn), *a.* Forms: [1 **mæȝen-**], 3 **mæin,** 4–7 **mayn,** 5 *Sc.* **mane,** 5–7 **mayne,** 6–7 **maine, maigne,** 5– **main.** [Prob. partly repr. OE. *mæȝen-* (MAIN *sb.*¹) in compounds, and partly an adoption of the cognate ON. *megenn, megn* adj., strong, powerful; in some uses (e.g. in MAIN SEA = ON. *megensjór*) it seems to represent ON. *megen-* (= MAIN *sb.*¹) in compounds.

It is doubtful whether the development of the Eng. word owes anything to the influence of OF. *maine, maigne* great:—L. *magnus*. The OFr. word is purely poetical, and occurs chiefly as an epithet of kings and nobles; it may prob. have influenced the use of *main* by ME. poets, but the only unequivocal evidence of its adoption is the 15th c. Sc. *Alexandir the mane, Charlis the mane* (see MANE *a.*).]

1. Strong, vigorous, mighty; possessed of, manifesting, or exerting, great physical strength or force. †**a.** Said of acts or activities which imply force or energy. *Obs.*

[*Beowulf* 1519 (Gr.) Mæȝenræs forȝeaf hildebille.] **13..** *Gaw. & Gr. Knt.* 336 No more mate ne dismayd for hys mayn dintez. *c* **1400** *Destr. Troy* 6915 He myst of þe mon with his mayn dynt. *c* **1600** in *Boys' Wks.* (1629) 626 Jesu thy loue within me is so maine,.. That with thy loue my heart is well nigh rent. **1629** MAXWELL tr. *Herodian* (1635) 273 If they be driven to fly, or pursue the enemie, their long loose garments are a maine let to them. **1641** BAKER *Chron.* (1660) 87 This was a main blow to Prince Lewis, and the last of his battels in England. **1644** DIGBY *Mans Soul* (1645) 33 These two powerfull motives.. have so maine an influence in mens actions. **1653** H. MORE *Antid. Ath.* II. viii. (1712) 62 Without main violence done to our Faculties we can in no wise deny it. **1667** MILTON *P.L.* VI. 243 Soaring on main wing. **1671** —— *Samson* 1634 Those two massie Pillars That to the arched roof gave main support. **1870** H. FOULIS *Hist. Rom. Treasons* III. ii. 136 She also gave a main stroke against Cecchino.

b. As an epithet of *force, strength*, etc.: Exerted to the full, sheer. Esp. in phr. *by* (or †*with*) ***main force***; †similarly, ***by*** or ***with main strength, dint, power, courage, importunity, labour.*** †***with main logic*** = by sheer force of reasoning.

[*Beowulf* 2678 (Gr.) þa ȝen guðcyning mærða ȝemunde, mæȝenstrengo, sloh hildebille. *a* **1000** *Guthlac* 1105 (Gr.) þæs weres stihtung, mod & mæȝencræft.] **1542** BECON *Christmas Banq.* F viij, Therfore ought all men.. with all mayne & francke courage to apply themselues to the diligent practyse of good workes. **1579** LYLY *Euphues* (Arb.) 111 Loue creepeth into the minde by priuie craft, and keepeth his holde by maine courage. **1579** FULKE *Ref. Rastel* 734 M. R. hath gotten the day, and that with maine logike. **1593** SHAKS. *2 Hen. VI*, I. i. 208 That Maine, which by maine force Warwicke did winne. **1605** VERSTEGAN *Dec. Intell.* iii. (1628) 56 By meere valour and maine force of armes they attained vnto their desired habitation. **1613** SHAKS. *Hen. VIII*, II. ii. 7 A man of my Lord Cardinalls, by Commission, and maine power tooke 'em from me. **1651** HOBBES *Govt. & Soc.* iii. §9. 43 Each one.. is suppos'd, with all his main might, to intend the procurement of those things which are necessary to his own preservation. **1655** FULLER *Ch. Hist.* II. v. §46 Next Night they on afresh; and, with main Force, plucked up the ponderous Coffin upon the Pavement. *a* **1680** BUTLER *Rem.* (1759) II. 68 To prosecute his suit, till he recover it against him by main Importunity. **1687** LOVELL tr. *Thevenot's Trav.* I. 18 They [old Galleys] were carried by main strength over the Isthmus of Corinth. **1697** tr. *Le Comte's Mem. & Rem. China* iv. (1737) 103 By main labour they drained the water. **1755** SMOLLETT *Quix.* (1803) II. 182 We were.. by main dint of rowing kept from running a-ground. **1810** SCOTT *Lady of L.* I. xxiv, Yet with main strength his strokes he drew. **1849** MACAULAY *Hist. Eng.* i. I. 123 To restrain his musqueteers and dragoons from invading by main force the pulpits of ministers.

†**c.** Of motion, etc.: Swift, speedy, rapid. ***a main pace*** or ***speed*** = at full speed. *Obs.*

1577–87 HOLINSHED *Chron.* (1807–8) II. 254 They were constraind.. to run awaie a maine pase. **1581** SAVILE *Tacitus, Hist.* IV. xi. (1591) 175 With a maine course [he] drewe the whole manage of affaires into his owne handes. **1607** MARKHAM *Caval.* III. x. 51 Some Horsemen.. wil.. breake into a maine chace and so giue their Horse a sweate. **1609** DEKKER *Raven's Alm.* C, Citizens, Schollers and Saylers thinke a horse neuer goes fast enough though he run a maine gallop. *a* **1625** FLETCHER *Cust. Country* I. i, We saw e'm Making with all maine speed to 'th port. **1632** J. HAYWARD tr. *Biondi's Eromena* 4 Gallopping a maine speede out of the Quirie.

†**d.** ***by*** or ***with main hand***: with a strong hand, forcibly. *Obs.*

1567 FENTON *Trag. Disc.* Ep. Ded., Yet, brydlinge wythe maine hand, the humour of theyr inordinate luste. **1583** GOLDING *Calvin on Deut.* lxxii. 444 God therefore must be faine to ouermaster vs, and to tame vs by maine hande.

†**e.** Of drink: Potent. Of a voice or cry: Loud. Of a fit, a storm: Violent. *Obs.* or *arch.*

13.. *Gaw. & Gr. Knt.* 497 þaȝ men ben mery in mynde, quen þay han mayn drynk. **1582** STANYHURST *Æneis* III. (Arb.) 72 With mayne noise lifted to the slayne soule lastlye we shouted. **1611** SPEED *Hist. Gt. Brit.* IX. xv. (1623) 810 [He] made towards his Pages with a maine cry. **1627** ABP. ABBOT *Narr.* in Rushw. *Hist. Coll.* (1659) I. 449 My main fit of the Stone did call upon me to get me to the Countrey. **1628** DIGBY *Voy. Medit.* (1868) 51 It was a maine storme. **1922** JOYCE *Ulysses* 339 And he answered with a main cry: *Abba! Adonai!*

†**2.** Of an army, host, multitude: Great in numbers; numerous; 'mighty'; powerful in arms. In 16–17th c., the usual epithet distinctive of a complete and equipped army, as opposed to small or irregular forces. ***main battle***: a pitched battle, as opposed to mere skirmishing. *Obs.*

[*a* **900** CYNEWULF *Crist* 877 (Gr.) Swa on syne beorȝ somod up cymeð mæȝenfolc micel.] *a* **1400–50** *Alexander* 3018 He had of men out of mynde many mayn hundreth. **1529** MORE *Dyaloge* III. Wks. 227/2 That company, wherof there is such a main multitude. *c* **1540** tr. *Pol. Verg. Eng. Hist.* (Camden No. 29) 42 Returned againe with a mayne hoste to relieve his people. **1555** EDEN *Decades* 116 They goo foorth.. with a mayne armye of purpose to hunt for men. **1568** GRAFTON *Chron.* II. 497 And first the warre beganne by light skirmishes, but after it proceeded into mayne battles. **1583** STOCKER *Civ. Warres Lowe C.* I. 29 King Philip .. determined.. to come downe.. with a mayne force. **1602** MARSTON *Ant. & Mel.* III. Wks. 1856 I. 33 Huge troups of barbed steeds, Maine squares of pikes, millions of harguebush. **1602** CAREW *Cornwall* (1769) 149 To withstand any great Navie or maigne invasion. **1612** DAVIES *Why Ireland*, etc. 19 This young Prince.. with a traine of yong Noblemen and Gentlemen,.. but not with any maine army, came ouer to take possession of his new Patrimony. **1620** SHELTON *Quix.* IV. iii. II. 34 My Father knew that this Giant .. would pass with a main power into my Land.

3. a. Of material things, animals, etc.: Of great size or bulk. (Sometimes connoting strength, resisting power, or the like.) *Obs.* exc. *dial.*

[*Beowulf* 3091 (Gr.) Ic on ofoste ȝefeng micle mid mundum mæȝenbyrðenne hordȝestreona. *a* **1000** *Boeth. Metr.* v. 16 Oð him on innan felð muntes mæȝenstan.] *c* **1205** LAY. 15292 Æne muchelne mæin clubbe he bar an his rugge. **13..** *Gaw. & Gr. Knt.* 187 þe mane of þat mayn hors. *c* **1400** *Destr. Troy* 8748 The triet stones.. lemet so light, þat ledes might se Aboute midnyght merke as with mayn torches. *a* **1400–50** *Alexander* 3932 þan mys out of þis marras as any mayn foxes Come furth. **1604** E. G[RIMSTONE] *D'Acosta's Hist. Indies* IV. iv. 212 In their Temples they set vppe maine Images of pure golde. **1607** WALKINGTON *Opt. Glass* 125 Hoist vp to the ridge of a maine billow. *c* **1630** RISDON *Surv. Devon* §329 (1811) 340 A man of extraordinary strength and stature. A main stone,.. by him thrown a far distance, witnesseth the one. **1667** MILTON *P.L.* VI. 654 Themselves invaded next, and on thir heads Main Promontories flung. **1850** *Gower Dial.* in *Proc. Philol. Soc.* IV. 222 *Main*, strong, fine (of growing crops). **1883** *Hampshire Gloss.* s.v., 'What a great main pond!'

b. Of quantity or amount: Large. *Obs.* exc. *dial.*

1609 HOLLAND *Amm. Marcell.* XXII. vii. 199 A maine deale of water breaketh forth. **1868** in *N. & Q.* 4th Ser. II. 287 My vowles eat a main deal of barley. **1894** RAYMOND *Love & Quiet Life* iv. 34 He axed a main lot o' questions.

4. a. Said of a considerable, uninterrupted stretch of land or water; occas. also of void space. See MAINLAND, MAIN SEA.

a **1548** HALL *Chron., Hen. VIII* (1550) 258 The army..so returned home by land, through all the mayn contry of Scotlande. **1553** EDEN *Treat. Newe Ind.* (Arb.) 7 The mayne South sea. **1577** R. WILLES *Eden's Decades* Pref. 1 The discouery of Peru, in the maigne west Indish lande. **1630** *R. Johnson's Kingd. & Commw.* 119 Upon the West, the South, and the North, the maine Ocean incompasseth it. **1660** tr. *Amyraldus' Treat. conc. Relig.* III. viii. 481 An infinite essence..diffus'd infinitely in the mane space, beyond the world. **1667** MILTON *P.L.* III. 83 Whom no bounds Prescrib'd, no barrs of Hell..nor yet the main Abyss Wide interrupt can hold. *Ibid.* VII. 279 Over all the face of Earth Main Ocean flow'd. **1867** SMYTH *Sailor's Word-bk., Main-ice*, a body of impenetrable ice apparently detached from the land, but immovable.

†**b.** Of earth, rock: Forming the principal or entire mass; 'solid'. *Obs.*

1538 LELAND *Itin.* V. 79 Penbroke..standith on a veri maine Rocki Ground. **1586** WARNER *Alb. Eng.* I. vi. (1589) 18 The entrance is so straite, Cut out the rough maine stonie Rocke. **1615** G. SANDYS *Trav.* 174 In the vineyards are sundry places of buriall hewne out of the maine rocke. **1632** LITHGOW *Trav* II. 56 The large promontore..eight miles in length, being the face of a square and maine Rocke. **1638** JUNIUS *Paint. Ancients* 68 Fountaines gushing forth out of a main rock. **1647** SPRIGGE *Anglia Rediv.* III. i. (1854) 133 Sir Charles Lloyd..had added to the strength of its natural situation..having cut out of the main earth several works.

†**c.** *of main white*: mainly of white. *Obs.*

1523 FITZHERB. *Husb.* §68 Put..to your coloured mares of mayne whyte, a horse of colour of mayn whyte.

†**5. a.** Of an affair, event, etc.: Highly important; having great results or important consequences; momentous. Rarely const. *to*. *Obs.*

1581 MULCASTER *Positions* Ep. Ded. (1887) 4 Many and maine affaires of your estate. **1602** WARNER *Alb. Eng.* Epit., Hasten we to our purposed prosecution of State matters, mainer, and of more note. **1613** SHAKS. *Hen. VIII*, III. ii. 215 What croste Diuell Made me put this maine Secret in the Packet I sent the King? *a* **1619** FLETCHER *Mad Lover* III. i, 'Tis a maine worke and full of feare. *a* **1626** BACON *New Atl.* (1900) 19 So you see, by this maine Accident of Time, wee lost our Traffique with the Americans. **1643** MILTON *Divorce* II. ix. Wks. 1851 IV. 85 In competition with higher things, as religion and charity in mainest matters. **1667** —— *P.L.* VI. 471 That, which thou aright Beleivst so main to our success. **1671** —— *P.R.* I. 112 They all commit the care And management of this main enterprize To him their great Dictator.

b. Of a person: Great, mighty (in power, rank or position). *rare.*

[*a* **900** CYNEWULF *Crist* 917 (Gr.) Waldendes cyme, mægen-cyninges.] *c* **1400** *Destr. Troy* 10290 The Mirmydons hade mynd of þe mayne troiell. *Ibid.* 10294 But mony of þo Mirmydons þe mayn knight slogh. **1623** FLETCHER & ROWLEY *Maid in Mill* III. ii, How dare you (Sirrha), 'gainst so main a person, A man of so much Noble note and honour, Put up this base complaint?

6. a. Of things in general, qualities, conditions, actions, etc.: Very great (in degree, value, etc.); highly remarkable (for some quality indicated by the sb.); very great or considerable of its kind. (Occas. in *superlative*.) *Obs.* exc. *dial.*

[*c* **1000** *Ags. Gosp.* Matt. xxv. 31 þonne mannes sunu cymð on hys mægen-þrymme.] **13..** *Gaw. & Gr. Knt.* 94 Of sum mayn meruayle, þat he myȝt trawe. *c* **1400** *Destr. Troy* 8807 þen þos maisters gert make, all with mayn crafte, Fovre lampis full light. *a* **1400-50** *Alexander* 3777 þai wiȝtly him sente..Of mony & of mekill quat mayn giftis. **1565** JEWEL *Def. Apol.* (1611) 41 And this he reckoneth for a great maine lie. **1573** G. HARVEY *Letter-bk.* (Camden) 23 Main evils you know must have main remmedies. **1600** HEYWOOD *1st Pt. Edw. IV*, Wks. 1874 I. 32 Affaires, I mean, of so maine consequence. *a* **1619** FLETCHER *Mad Lover* II. ii, And to purchase This day the company of one deare Custard, Or a messe of Rice ap Thomas, needs a maine wit. **1634** *Relat. Ld. Baltimore's Plantat.* (1865) 8 The losse of much linnen, and amongst the rest, I lost the best of mine which is a very maine losse in these parts. **1638** FEATLY *Strict. Lyndom.* II. 11 And indeed this is one of our mainest exceptions against the Roman Church. *a* **1656** USSHER *Ann.* vi. (1658) 96 Cyaxares and Cyrus, march against the Babylonian King and Croesus, and gain a main Victory against them. **1668** H. MORE *Div. Dial.* II. 437 He professes he understands clearly the truth of severall Prophecies of the mainest concernment. **1672** MARVELL *Reh. Transp.* I. 80 We shall find ere we have done that there is still a mainer reason. **1815** SCOTT *Guy M.* v, It's a main untruth. **1883** STEVENSON *Treas. Isl.* II. xii. (1886) 95 It [the island] were a main place for pirates once.

b. With sb. indicating a person or agent: Great, remarkable, or pre-eminent for the quality or characteristics indicated. *Obs.* exc. *dial.*

c **1400** *Destr. Troy* 12260 Thelamon..manast hom mightily as his mayn fos. **1642** ROGERS *Naaman* 346 That carnall reason is a maine enemy to all the matters of revealed truths. **1654** WHITLOCK *Zootomia* 497 Many a one that in his own conceit is a main Husband, and is forward enough to call some..prodigall, will bee found to live, as I said, but in another Street of it. **1691** WOOD *Ath. Oxon.* II. 328 Mathew Hazard..a main Incendiary in the Rebellion. **1777** SHERIDAN *Trip Scarb.* v. ii, I am a main bungler at a long story. **1860** PENRUDDOCKE *Content* 31 (E.D.D.) Yow be a main fool.

¶ **c.** *main and...* = MAIN *adv.* (Cf. *fine and..*, *nice and...*) *dial.*

1762 COLLINS *Misc.* 13 (Halliw.) Observing Dick looked main and blue. **1863** MRS. GASKELL *Sylvia's L.* xxi. II. 121 T'shop is doing main an' well. **1895** 'ROSEMARY' *Chilterns* v. 163 He's a main an' bad, and I believe as 'ee's took for death.

7. a. Chief in size or extent; constituting the bulk or principal part; the chief part of (that which is denoted by the sb). ***main body***, † ***battle***, the body of troops which form the bulk of an army or armed force, marching between the vanguard and the rear.

1593 SHAKS. *3 Hen. VI*, I. i. 8 Lord Clifford and Lord Stafford all a-brest Charg'd our maine Battailes Front. **1600** —— *A.Y.L.* III. v. 103 To gleane the broken eares after the man That the maine haruest reapes. **1603** KNOLLES *Hist. Turks* (1621) 195 In the maine battell he stood himselfe; the vauntgard was conducted by Temurtases. **1640** FULLER *Joseph's Coat* (1867) 11 The apostle, commending the Corinthians, meaneth the main and general body of the church, though there might be many stragglers justly to be reproved. **1642** ROGERS *Naaman* To Rdr., Into which the maine sap of the root is carried. **1670** COTTON *Espernon* I. III. 111 The King of Navarre commanded the Vant-Guard of the Army, and his Majesty himself the main Battel, reserving the command of the Rear for the Duke of Espernon. **1687** T. BROWN *Saints in Uproar* Wks. 1730 I. 78 Whether you march'd in one main body, or in several columns. **1761** HUME *Hist. Eng.* II. xxvii. 131 Lord Howard led the main body of the first line. **1775** JOHNSON *Let. to Mrs. Thrale* 1 Aug., Our business is to pursue their main army, and disperse it by a decisive battle. **1807** SOUTHEY *Espriella's Lett.* I. 277 Of the baptismal names the main proportion are Saxon and Norman. **1812** WELLINGTON *Disp.* 28 July in *Examiner* 24 Aug. 535/2 The main body of the allied army is..on the Adaja and Zapardiel rivers. **1849** MACAULAY *Hist. Eng.* iv. I. 456 The sturdy country gentlemen who formed the main strength of the Tory party.

†**b.** Referring or pertaining to all or the majority; general. *Obs.*

1599 SHAKS. *Hen. V*, I. ii. 144 We do not meane the coursing snatchers onely, But feare the maine intendment of the Scot. **1602** —— *Ham.* I. iii. 28 Which is no further, Then the maine voyce of Denmarke goes withall. **1613** —— *Hen. VIII*, IV. i. 31 By the maine assent Of all these Learned men, she was diuorc'd. *c* **1618** FLETCHER *Queen of Corinth* II. iii, For I am nothing now but a maine pestilence Able to poyson all. *a* **1638** MEDE *Wks.* (1672) 761 There may be some Præludia of some particulars converted upon other motives, as a forerunner of the great and main Conversion.

8. a. Great or important above others of the kind; of pre-eminent importance; principal, chief, leading.

1588 J. UDALL *Demonstr. Discipl.* (Arb.) 42 They fight hard against this, because it striketh at a maine pillar of their kingdome. **1594** HOOKER *Eccl. Pol.* IV. i. §2 In every grand or main public duty which God requireth at the hands of his Church. **1602** SHAKS. *Ham.* I. i. 105 And this (I take it) Is the maine Motiue of our Preparations. **1618** BOLTON *Florus* (1636) 47 Capua..once accounted after Rome, and Carthage, the third maine City of the World. **1633** BP. HALL *Occas. Medit.* 138 Every parcell thereof shall seeme maine and essentiall. **1651** HOBBES *Leviath.* III. xxxiv. 210 Submission to that main Article of Christian faith, that Jesus is the Christ. **1667** MILTON *P.L.* II. 121 If what was urg'd Main reason to perswade immediate Warr, Did not disswade me most. **1732** LAW *Serious C.* i. (ed. 2) 15 They are like Heathens in all the main and chief articles of their lives. **1779** SHERIDAN *Critic* II. ii, Let your under-plot have as little connection with your main-plot as possible. **1852** H. ROGERS *Ecl. Faith* (1853) 166, I went carefully over all the main points of the argument. **1860** TYNDALL *Glac.* II. xxi. 341 Mr. Thomson's main thought was familiar to me long before his first communication..appeared. **1865** LECKY *Ration.* II. v. 178 The main champions of tyrannicide were the Jesuits. **1867** FREEMAN *Norm. Conq.* (1876) I. App. 779 The statements may be grouped under two main heads.

b. Chief or principal in permanent relation to others of the same kind or group. In many collocations, e.g. ***main drain, road, street*** (see also MAIN STREET), ***sewer, pipe, root***.

a **1490** BOTONER *Itin.* (Nasmith 1778) 260 The hyest toure called the mayn, id est myghtyest toure aboue all the iiii towres. **1551-60** *Inv.* in H. Hall *Eliz. Soc.* (1887) 151 Twoo great standing chestes withe one mayne cheste. **1568** GRAFTON *Chron.* II. 23 The maine roofe of the great Church of Sarisbury was consumed and brent with lightnyng. **1598**, etc. [see MAIN STREET]. **1610** W. FOLKINGHAM *Art of Survey* II. v. 55 Plant not the Table at euery Angle, but,..extend from some fewe Maine Angles..Base lines..for Boundaries. **1615** W. LAWSON *Country Housew. Gard.* (1626) 15, I vtterly dislike the opinion of those great Gardiners, that..would haue the maine roots cut away. **1617-18** in Swayne *Sarum Church-w. Acc.* (1896) 167 Mendinge one of the maine pypes of the Organ. **1707-12** MORTIMER *Husb.* (1721) I. 23 Make your main Drains wide and deep enough to carry off the Water from the whole Level. **1818** SCOTT *Hrt. Midl.* vii, Opening..the wicket of the main-gate. **1820** W. IRVING *Sketch Bk.* I. 50 After turning from the main road up a narrow lane. **1840** DICKENS *Barn. Rudge* lxvii, They meant to cut off the main-pipes, so that there might be no water. **1858** LYTTON *What will he do* I. i, The main street was lined with booths. **1876** *Encycl. Brit.* IV. 467/2 A rate of fall of 1 in 120..is desirable..for a main sewer. **1878** *Act 41 & 42 Vict.* c. 77 §15 Where it appears to any highway authority that any highway..ought to become a main road by reason of its being a medium of communication between great towns [etc.]. **1879** SIR G. SCOTT *Lect. Archit.* I. 195 An eastern transept, in addition to that at the main crossing. **1884** BOWER & SCOTT *De Bary's Phaner.* 357 The subsidiary roots..in this class..usually far exceed the main-roots in thickness. **1889** *Spectator* 9 Mar. 331/2 The burglar who leaves the back-door open for escape in case the policeman should enter by the main entrance.

†**9.** ***main flood***: **a.** High water. **b.** A large or full-flowing body of water. Also ***main tide*** (in quot. *fig.*). **c.** The ocean or MAIN SEA. *Obs.*

c **1303** *Reg. Pal. Dunelm.* (Rolls) III. 40 Et eadem aqua mensurari debet a le mainflod, quando eadem aqua ita fluit ut sit plena de bank' en bank'. **1311** *Ibid.* I. 8 Eadem aqua mensurari debet ad mayne flod. **1549-62** STERNHOLD & H. *Ps.* cxiv. 8, I meane the God which from hard rocks Doth cause mayne flouds appeare. **1555** W. WATREMAN *Fardle Facions* Pref. 11 Riuers, and maigne floudes, whiche..ouerflowed the neighboured aboute. **1596** SHAKS. *Merch. V.* IV. i. 72 You may as well go stand vpon the beach, And bid the maine flood baite his vsuall height. **1596** DALRYMPLE tr. *Leslie's Hist. Scot.* I. 35 Quhatevir land is betueine thir twa mane fludes Forth southward, and Tai northward, Fife is called. **1605** CAMDEN *Rem.* (1637) 13 If I should but enter into consideration thereof, I should be over-whelmed with maine tides of matter.

10. *Naut.* in the sense 'pertaining to, connected with, or near the mainmast or mainsail', as ***main-bonnet, -boom, -bowlines, -bridles, -capstan, -chains***, †***-drynge*** (?), ***-hatch, -hatchway, -hold, -jeers***, †***-knight, -lifts, -parrels, -pendant, -rigging, -royal, -royal-mast, -shrouds, -spencer, studding sail, -tack, -tackle, -truck, -truss, -tyes***. Also MAIN-BRACE, etc.

1485 *Naval Acc. Hen. VII* (1896) 37 Mayne shrowdes. *Ibid.* 39 Maine perells. *Ibid.* 47 Mainestaies..Maynetyes. *Ibid.* 48 Mayne trusses. *Ibid.*, Mayne takkes. *Ibid.*, Mayne lyfts. *Ibid.*, Mayne Bowlynes. *Ibid.* 53 Mayne drynges. **1495** *Ibid.* 198 Mayne Jeres. **1626** CAPT. SMITH *Accid. Yng. Seamen* 14 The maine-shroudes and chaines. *Ibid.* 15 The maine bowling and bridles. **1635** BRERETON *Trav.* (Chetham Soc.) 125 The Sailors did in all haste take down the lower part of the main-sail and the foresail, which they call the main-bowline or main bonnet. **1678** PHILLIPS (ed. 4) s.v., *Fore-knight and Main-knight*, in Navigation are two short thick pieces of Wood carved, with the head of a Man fast bolted to the Beams upon the second Deck. **1712** W. ROGERS *Voy.* 34 He was lash'd to the Main-Gears and drub'd. **1748** *Anson's Voy.* I. viii. 80 Two of our main-shrouds..broke. *Ibid.* x. 99 We..lost a main studding-sail-boom. **1769** FALCONER *Dict. Marine* (1780) Bbb 3 b, The main-boom of a brig, sloop, or schooner. **1772-84** COOK *Voy.* (1790) V. 1914 The main-tack of the Discovery gave way. **1833** MARRYAT *P. Simple* xv, The second lieutenant went up the main-rigging. **1835** SIR J. ROSS *Narr. 2nd Voy.* vi. 87 The main and fore hatchway. **1858** SIMMONDS *Dict. Trade, Chain-plates*..take their name from the mast and are hence called fore-chains, main-chains, or mizen-chains. **1861** *Sat. Rev.* 22 June 635 Entire freedom from dizziness..is possessed by every sailor who mounts to the maintruck of a man-of-war. **1867** SMYTH *Sailor's Word-bk., Main-tackle*, a large and strong tackle, hooked occasionally upon the main pendant. **1872** BLACKMORE *Maid of Sker* (1881) 46 The ship had no canvas left, except some tatters of the fore-topsail, and a piece of the main-royals. **1897** R. KIPLING *Captains Courageous* iii. 62 Uncle Salters..sat stiffly on the main-hatch.

11. Special collocations in technical use (mostly hyphened): **main-bar** (see quot.); **main beam**, (*a*) *Building* (see quot. 1940); (*b*) the undipped beam of the headlights of a motor vehicle; **main-breadth, main half-breadth** (see quots.); **main centre** (see quot.); **main chancer** [CHANCER *sb.*], an opportunist, one who has an eye to the main chance; **main couple** *Arch.*, the principal truss in a roof; **main course, dish**, one of a number of substantial dishes in a large menu; the principal dish of a meal; also *fig.*; **main crop**, the chief crop, excluding the early and late varieties or sections; also *attrib.* (usu. as one word); **main drag** (see DRAG *sb.* 3 e); **main earth**, the chief 'earth' in which the fox kennels; **main frame** *Computers* (now usu. as one word): (see quots. 1964, 1970); also, any large or general-purpose computer, esp. one supporting numerous peripherals or subordinate computers; †**main-holder** (see quot.); **main keel**, the principal keel of a ship, as distinguished from the false keel and the kelson; **main man** *U.S. slang* (see quot. 1970); **main-master** (? supposed by Disraeli to be a miner's word for a colliery owner); **main-piece** *Shipbuilding*, (*a*) 'the principal piece of timber in a rudder'; (*b*) 'the strong horizontal beam of a windlass' (Smyth *Sailor's Word-bk.* 1867); (*c*) 'the principal piece of the head' (Knight 1875); **main plane** *Aeronaut.*, a principal supporting surface of an aircraft (as distinguished from a tail plane); also ***mainplane***; **main-plate**, the principal plate of a lock; **main-post** *Shipbuilding*, the stern-post; **main range** *Austral.* and *N.Z.*, the principal ridge of a chain of mountains; **main sequence** *Astr.*, in the Hertzsprung–Russell diagram of stellar magnitude against spectral type or decreasing surface temperature, a continuous band of star types extending from the upper left of the diagram (hot, bright stars) to the lower right (cool, dim stars) to which most of the stars in the neighbourhood of the sun belong; freq. *attrib.* (usu. hyphenated); †**main-shire**, ? an old name for Warwickshire; **main squeeze** *U.S. slang*, an important person; also (with pun on SQUEEZE *sb.* 2 b) a man's principal woman friend (see also quot. 1941); **main-transom** *Shipbuilding* = wing-transom (Smyth); **main-wale** *Naut.*, the lower wale (Smyth); **main-way**, the gangway or principal passage in a mine; **main word**, the term adopted in this dictionary to designate a word of sufficient importance to be regarded as

a principal word, as distinguished from a subordinate word or a combination; **main-work** *Fortif.*, 'the enceinte or principal works inclosing the body of the place' (Knight *Dict. Mech.* 1875).

1897 *Encycl. Sport* I. 341 (Driving), **Main-bar*, the cross timber fixed to the pole-head, from which hang the swing-bars or leading bars. **1940** *Chambers's Techn. Dict.* 522/1 **Main beam*, in floor construction, one of the principal beams transmitting loads direct to the columns. **1964** *Which?* Apr. 47/2 Our drivers particularly liked the headlamps of the *BMC Bluebird* and *Commer* on main beam and also found their dipped beam better than the other caravans. **1967** *Autocar* 28 Dec. 2/2 The little trio of warning lights—red for ignition, green for blinkers and blue for main-beam—are set..into the walnut of the facia. *c* **1850** *Rudim. Navig.* (Weale) 130 **Main-breadth*, the broadest part of the ship at any particular timber or frame. **1797** *Encycl. Brit.* (ed. 3) XVII. 378/1 **Main half breadth*, is a section of the ship at its broadest part. *c* **1850** *Rudim. Navig.* (Weale) 130 *Main half-breadth*, half of the main breadth. **1858** R. MURRAY *Marine Engines* (ed. 3) 231 **Main centre*, in side-lever engines, is the strong shaft upon which the side levers vibrate. **1940** 'N. BLAKE' *Malice in Wonderland* I. vii. 95 There was a terrific row on the local council... Beauty-snobs versus *main-chancers. **1974** *Publishers Weekly* 5 Aug. 57/1 Candid but never mean-spirited, O'Brien comes across as a deeply dedicated party man who is far more than a main-chancer. **1842** GWILT *Archit.* Gloss. 958 The *main couples answer to the trusses. **1889** A. FILIPPINI *Table* 21 French dinners are generally served in three *main courses, viz., *Relevés*, *Entrées*, and *Rotis*; all the rest are considered side courses. **1936** E. CRAIG *Woman, Wine & Saucepan* i. 17 If the courses are few, choose one wine, red or white, according to what you are serving as the main course. **1967** *Guardian* 22 July 4/5 As low as 5s for a main course (meat balls, potato salad). **1970** 'M. UNDERWOOD' *Silent Liars* II. xii. 134 How many more main courses to come? **1782** MAWE & ABERCROMBIE *Every Man his own Gardener* (ed. 9) 119 Onions or leeks for the *main crop should be sown the beginning or middle of this month. **1859** R. THOMPSON *Gardener's Assistant* 249 The main crop of the Long Horn, Altrincham, and other large sorts [of carrots] for winter use, should be sown [etc.]. **1877** S. HIBBERD *Amateur's Kitchen Garden* 49 The second early and main crop sorts [of peas]. **1883** *Culture of Vegetables & Flowers* (Sutton & Sons) 147 Potatoes for main crops should now be got in. **1908** *Daily Chron.* 2 Oct. 3/5 The 'White City' potato..is confidently expected to surpass all the maincrop varieties hitherto produced. **1942** *R.A.F. Jrnl.* 18 Apr. 8 There should be full scale raking down of land and sowing of maincrop Carrots, Onions..and Lettuce. **1962** *New Scientist* 12 Apr. 31/2 Arran Pilot, an early potato, which develops more rapidly than main-crop varieties. **1971** *Arable Farmer* Feb. 35/2 Maris Piper. Early maincrop. **1957** A. MACNAB *Bulls of Iberia* viii. 81 Three modes: the high spectacular curtain-raisers, the low dominating 'benders', and the *main dish or *natural* passes with the breast pass as their natural complement. **1972** J. BALL *Five Pieces Jade* x. 118 A small, intimate meal was waiting in basic Japanese style... There was no evident main dish as in Western dining. **1897** *Encycl. Sport* I. 582 (Hunting), **Main earth*, the fox's own lair and breeding place. **1964** *Gloss. Data Processing & Communication Terms* (Honeywell Inc.) 27/1 **Main frame*, (1) the central processor of the computer system. It contains the main storage, arithmetic unit and special register groups... (2) All that portion of a computer exclusive of the input, output, peripheral and in some instances, storage units. **1970** A. CHANDOR et al. *Dict. Computers* 245 *Main frame.* Originally implied the main framework of a central processing unit on which the arithmetic unit and associated logic circuits were mounted, but now used colloquially to refer to the central processor itself. **1973** *Ann. N.Y. Acad. Sci.* CCXI. 282 The development of small main-frame computers called 'minicomputers'. *Ibid.* 283 Their chief advantages are small size, low price—as low as $2500 for a main frame. **1974** *Sci. Amer.* Apr. 79/1 The laboratory station mainframe has the essentials built-in (power supply, logic state indicators and programmers, and pulse sources to provide active stimulus for the student's circuits). **1975** *Nature* 25 Dec. 654/2 ICL sells 'mainframe' computers which are general purpose systems. **1979** *Computers in Shell* (Shell Internat. Petroleum Co.) 1 Computers now range from huge main frames, requiring a specially-equipped computer centre with complex and expensive air conditioning and power supplies and highly-trained staff, to desk-top devices powered by pocket-size batteries. **1984** *Economist* 11 Aug. 77/2 Mainframes, which are used by big businesses for their centralised data processing, are slower than supercomputers (though still very fast). **1688** R. HOLME *Armoury* II. 84/1 In the Root there is The *Main-holder, which is that part of the root next the tree. **1769** FALCONER *Dict. Marine* (1780) s.v. *Keel*, The false-keel, which is also very useful in preserving the lower side of the *main keel. **1967** I. A. BARAKA in W. King *Black Short Story Anthol.* (1972) 126 'Hey, man, I saw that d' fagit Bobby Hutchens down in the lobby with a real D.C. queer.' .. 'Hey man you cats better cool it... You talkin' about Ray's *main man. You dig?' **1970** C. MAJOR *Dict. Afro-Amer. Slang* 79 *Main man*, favorite male friend; one's hero. **1845** DISRAELI *Sybil* III. i, It's as easy for a miner to speak to a *main-master, as it is for me to pick coal with this here clay. *c* **1850** *Rudim. Navig.* (Weale) 144 It [the rudder] is formed of several pieces of timber, of which the *main piece is generally of oak. **1867** SMYTH *Sailor's Word-bk.*, *Main-piece*, the strong horizontal beam of the windlass. **1910** R. FERRIS *How it Flies* xx. 464 **Main plane*, the principal supporting surface of an aeroplane. In the biplane, or the multiplane type, it denotes the lowest surface, unless some other is decidedly larger. **1913** A. E. BERRIMAN *Aviation* iii. 21 The presence of the two main planes as the distinguishing feature of biplanes. **1946** *Happy Landings* (Air Ministry) July 5/1 The aircraft..was seen..minus the port outer mainplane and engine. **1973** *Nature* 14 Sept. 95/1 A further important observation was of a 20 cm ball which appeared at a height of about 50 cm over the trailing edge of the mainplane of an aircraft in flight. **1677** MOXON *Mech. Exerc.* 22 Cut out of an Iron plate with a Cold Chissel the size and shape of the *Main-Plate. *c* **1850** *Rudim. Navig.* (Weale) 131 **Main post.* **1888** 'R. BOLDREWOOD' *Robbery under Arms* II. iii. 52, I say,..we haven't made any mistake—crossed over the *main range and got back to the coast, have we? **1950** *N.Z. Jrnl. Agric.* Jan. 19/1 The barren and unproductive land consists of bare mountain tops, and native bush areas on the slopes of the main ranges. **1971** *N.Z. Listener* 19 Apr. 56/4 A *main range* is the major backbone of any individual group of mountains. [**1926** A. S. EDDINGTON *Internal Constitution of Stars* vii. 151 The three stars belong to what is now called the 'main series' running from types *O* and *B* down the dwarf series to type *M*.] **1927** P. DOIG *Outl. Stellar Astron.* I. i. 10 The dwarf branch is now more frequently referred to as the '*main sequence', a name due to Eddington. **1962** F. I. ORDWAY et al. *Basic Astronautics* vi. 284 A new star not yet hot enough to initiate thermonuclear reactions obtains its luminosity from gravitational contraction. Later, as the star heats up, thermonuclear reactions commence; and it joins the main sequence. **1966** *McGraw-Hill Encycl. Sci. & Technol.* XIII. 106/2 Stars that do not belong to the main sequence fall into two main groups: red giants..and white dwarfs... Modern theoretical work indicates that red giants and white dwarfs began their stellar careers as normal main-sequence stars and owe their distinctive properties to evolutionary changes incident on the exhaustion of nuclear energy sources. **1626** B. JONSON *Masque of Owls*, Though that have been a fit Of our *main-shire wit. **1896** ADE *Artie* vii. 63, I went in and asked the *main squeeze o' the works how much the sacque meant to him. **1927** D. HAMMETT in *Black Mask* Feb. 12/2 Vance seems to be the main squeeze. **1941** J. SMILEY *Hash House Lingo* 36 *Main squeeze*, hostess. **1970** H. E. ROBERTS *Third Ear* 9/2 *Main squeeze*, a man's closest woman friend. **1769** FALCONER *Dict. Marine* (1780) s.v. *Wales*, They are usually distinguished into the *main-wale and the channel-wale. **1881** RAYMOND *Mining Gloss.*, **Mainway*, a gangway or principal passage. **1892** *Daily News* 3 Mar. 5/7 Counting 'mainways', passages, and cuttings of all descriptions. **1833** STRAITH *Fortif.* 3 Detached works are those which it sometimes becomes necessary to construct beyond the range of the defensive musketry of the *main works.

main (meɪn), *adv.* Now *dial.* [f. MAIN *a.* Cf. similar use of *mighty*; also the use of ON. *megen-* (= MAIN *sb.*[1]) in *megenkátr* very cheerful, *megenmildr* very mild, *megenvel* very well.] Very, exceedingly. (After the 17th c. chiefly in representations of rustic or illiterate speech.)

1632 *St. Papers Chas. I*, 17 May No. 216 fol. 56 I (Hampsh. Gloss.), Sparing the Toppes of the Trees, which yeeld maine good knees. **1647** LILLY *Chr. Astrol.* xxxviii. 220 A maine strong argument. *a* **1700** B. E. *Dict. Cant. Crew* s.v., *Main-good*, very good. **1741** RICHARDSON *Pamela* I. 201 Ay, said the Idiot, she is main good Company, Madam; no wonder you miss her. **1754** FOOTE *Knights* II. i. (1765) 40 *Waiter.* Would you chuse any refreshment? *Suck.* A draught of ale, friend, for I'm main dry. **1794** GODWIN *Cal. Williams* 40, I know, your honour, that it is main foolish of me to talk to you thus. **1828** SCOTT *Jrnl.* II. 149, I was main stupid indeed, and much disposed to sleep. **1872** *Punch* 31 Aug. 91/1 Beg your pardon, sir; but I be main deaf, to be sure. **1897** BARING-GOULD *Bladys of the Stewponey* viii, The Stewponey is a great house, and ours is a main little one.

main (meɪn), *v.* [f. *main road* (MAIN *a.* 8 b).]

1. *trans.* To convert into a main road.

1927 *Daily Tel.* 7 June 11/3 The widening and 'maining' of the road leading to the Royal Hotel corner. **1930** *Jrnl. Town Planning Inst.* XVI. 102/1 It is reported that the process of 'maining' roads has been steady and continuous. **1969** A. BIRD *Roads & Vehicles* iii. 40 The new county councils were made responsible for maintaining all 'main' roads in their counties, though it was left to them to determine which should be 'mained'.

2. *slang.* To insert (heroin or a similar drug) into a vein; to mainline.

1970 *Time* 16 Mar. 17 All my friends were on heroin. I snorted a couple of times, skinned a lot, and after that I mained it. **1972** J. BROWN *Chancer* v. 69 The bastard, he maimed me. I said to skin it, but he mained it. First time. **1973** *Daily Mail* 3 Apr. 19/4 *Maining*, injecting straight into the vein.

main, obs. f. MANE, MOAN.

maina, var. MINA[2].

'main-brace[1]. *Naut.* [See MAIN *a.* and BRACE *sb.*[3]] The brace attached to the main-yard.

1487 *Naval Acc. Hen. VII* (1896) 67 Mayne brases. **1626** CAPT. SMITH *Accid. Yng. Seamen* 28 Ease your mayne brases. **1801** COL. STEWART *Narr.* in Nicolas *Disp. Nelson* (1845) IV. 309 By another shot several of the Marines, while hauling on the main-brace shared the same fate. **1840** R. H. DANA *Bef. Mast* xxiii. 69 All the rest of the crew..tallied on to the main brace.

b. *Naut. slang. to splice the main-brace*: to serve out 'grog'; hence, to drink freely.

1805 *Naval Chron.* XIII. 480 Now splice the main brace. **1833** MARRYAT *P. Simple* xv, Mr. Falcon, splice the main-brace, and call the watch. **1836** HT. MARTINEAU *Autobiog.* (1877) II. App. 480 Yesterday the captain shouted, for the first time, 'Splice the main-brace'.

'main-brace[2]. [See MAIN *a.* and BRACE *sb.*[2]] A principal brace; *Mech.* in a system of braces, that which resists the main strain.

1680 SIR J. FOULIS *Acct. Bk.* 13 Aug. (Sc. Hist. Soc.) 487 To James Wilson, sadler, for..helping y^{e} main braces. **1794** W. FELTON *Carriages* (1801) I. 210 Main braces..Are what the body [of the coach] hangs by. **1870** *Spon's Dict. Engin.* II. 679 (*Bridges*) In Fig. 1394, U is the upper chord..M, main-brace.

main chance. [MAIN *a.*]

†**1.** A term in the game of Hazard; = MAIN *sb.*[3] 1. In quots. only *fig.* or *allusive.* **a.** The venture or course of action from which most is hoped; the likeliest course to obtain success. *to stand to the main chance*: ? to take one's own risk. *to look, have an eye*, etc., *to the main chance*: to use one's best endeavours, be solicitous (for some object). **b.** The general probability with regard to a future event or the success of an undertaking. **c.** The most important point risked or at stake; also, the general outcome of a series of events; the whole fortunes of a person, a nation, etc. *Obs.*

1579 LYLY *Euphues* (Arb.) 104 Good Father either content your selfe with my choice [*sc.* of a husband], or lette mee stande to the maine chaunce. **1587** HOLINSHED *Chron. Scot.* 300 Nothing could be either more fond or foolish, than to fight at pleasure of the enimie, and to set all on a maine chance at his will and appointment. **1591** GREENE *Disc. Coosnage* (1592) C 3 When their other trades fail..then to maintaine the main chance, they vse the benefite of their wiues or friends. **1593** NASHE *Four Lett. Confut.* 84 Haue an eie to the maine-chaunce, for so sooner shall they vnderstand what thou hast said by mee of them, but theyle goe neere to haue thee about the eares for this geare. **1597** SHAKS. *2 Hen. IV*, III. i. 83 A man may prophecie With a neere ayme, of the maine chance of things, As yet not come to Life. **1600** HOLLAND *Livy* IX. xviii. 327 Every one should have lived and died according to the fatall course of his owne severall destinie, without the hazard of the whole and maine chance [L. *summa rerum*]. *Ibid.* XXI. xvi. 402 So ashamed in themselves they were,..and so mightily feared the losse of the verie maine chance at home, as if the enemie had beene already at the gates of the cittie. **1610** —— *Camden's Brit.* I. 22 With whom the Romans for many yeeres maintained war, ..for the very main-chance of life and living. **1625** PURCHAS *Pilgrims* II. 1822 It behoued the Bashaw to looke to the main chance for the quenching of the Fire. **1655** FULLER *Ch. Hist.* III. i. §5 Yet withall he was carefull of the main chance to keep the essentials of his Crown. **1703** COLLIER *Ess.* II. 67 None so fit to prescribe, to direct the enterprise, and secure the main-chance.

2. That which is of principal importance in life; now *esp.* the opportunity of enriching oneself or of getting gain; one's own interests. (Often in phr. *to have an eye to, be careful of, the main chance.*)

1584 R. W. *Three Ladies Lond.* I. E ij b, Trust me thou art as craftie to haue an eye to the mayne chaunce: As the Taylor that out of seuen yardes stole one and a halfe of durance. **1644** BP. HALL *Serm.* Rem. Wks. (1660) II. 136 Shall we be lesse carefull of the main-chance, even of the eternal inheritance of Heaven? **1693** DRYDEN *Persius* vi. (1697) 497 Be careful still of the main Chance, my Son. **1698** COLLIER *Ess. Mor. Subj.* II. (ed. 3) 136 Wise men will..take care of the main Chance, and provide for Accidents and Age. **1751** JOHNSON *Rambler* No. 116 ¶6 My Master..had all the good qualities which naturally arise from a close and unwearied attention to the main chance. **1767** GRAY in *Corr. w. Nicholls* (1843) 69 Come quickly, if the main chance will suffer you, or I will know the reason why. **1828** *Lights & Shades* II. 159 A Scotchman looks only to the main-chance. **1902** L. STEPHEN *Stud. Biographer* IV. i. 36 It..cannot be said that an eye for the main chance is inconsistent with the poetical character.

maincheat, obs. form of MANCHET.

main-course. *Naut.* ? *Obs.* [See MAIN *a.* and COURSE *sb.* 33.] = MAINSAIL.

c **1515** *Cocke Lorell's B.* (Percy Soc.) 12 Some y^{e} longe bote dyde launce, some mende y^{e} corse, Mayne corfe [*read* corse] toke in a refe byforce. **1610** SHAKS. *Temp.* I. i. 38 Down with the top-Mast; yare, lower, lower, bring her to Try with Maine-course. **1626** CAPT. SMITH *Accid. Yng. Seamen* 16 The maine course or a paire of courses. **1687** B. RANDOLPH *Archipelago* 102 Towards break of day we handed our main course, but before it was well secured the storm came. **1719** DE FOE *Crusoe* (1858) II. ii, Having no sails to work the ship with, but a main course [etc.]. **1867** SMYTH *Sailor's Word-bk.*

main-deck. *Naut.* [See MAIN *a.* and DECK *sb.*[1] 2, 2 b.] **a.** In a man-of-war, the deck next below the spar-deck. **b.** In a merchantman, that part of the upper deck which lies between the poop and the forecastle.

1748 *Anson's Voy.* III. vii. 360 The crew..were drawn up under arms on the main-deck. **1798** *Anti-Jacobin* No. 33 (1852) 189 We walk the main-deck. **1824** W. IRVING *T. Trav.* (1849) 416 There was a shout of victory from the main-deck. **1833** MARRYAT *P. Simple* vi, Washing down the main-deck.

attrib. **1868** *Rep. to Govt. U.S. Munit. War* 267 That part of the ship supported by and below the main-deck beams.

c. *fig.* Used for: The main body or chief representatives (of).

1847 DE QUINCEY *Secret Societies* Wks. 1863 VI. 258 No round-robins, signed by the whole maindeck of the Platonic Academy.

†**maine**, *sb.*[1] *Obs.* Also 5–6 **mayne**, *Sc.* **mane**, 6–7 **mayn.** [Aphetic f. *demaine* in PAIN-DEMAINE, DEMEINE. (Cf. MANCHET.)] Used attrib. in the following terms: **a. maine bread**, occas. (Sc.) *breid of mane* (? also simply *mane*, quot. *c* 1470), bread of the finest quality; = PAIN-DEMAINE, DEMEINE. (The city of York was once famous for a kind of bread so called.)

1443 *Burgh Rec. Edinb.* (1869) I. 7 It is..ordanit that na baxter baik na mayne breid to sell fra hine furthwart, saiffing allenarly at Witsounday [etc.]. *c* **1470** HENRYSON *Mor. Fab.* II. xviii. (ed. Laing), And mane full fyne scho brocht in steid of geill. **1509** *Test. Ebor.* (Surtees) V. 5 And at tharbe skallapis of mayne breid. ? *a* **1550** *Freiris Berwik* 160 in *Dunbar's Poems* (1893) 290 And eik ane creill full of breid of mane. *Ibid.* 376 Mayne breid. **1572** J. JONES *Bathes Buckstone* 9 b, But these and all other the mayne bread of York excelleth, for that it is of the finest floure of the Wheat well tempered. *a* **1578** LINDESAY (Pitscottie) *Chron. Scot.*

(S.T.S.) I. 337 Quhyte breid, maine breid, and gingebreid. **1584** COGAN *Haven Health* iv. (1636) 25 Good bread is made thereof, especially that of Yorke, which they call Maine bread. **1622** in J. J. Cartwright *Chapt. Hist. Yks.* (1872) 281 Bakers..disobedient in not bakeinge of mayn bread beinge an auncient mistery used in this cittie and in no other citties of this kingdome.

b. maine flour, flour of the finest quality. **maine multure**, the portion of 'maine flour' payable as multure.

a **1483** *Liber Niger* in *Househ. Ord.* (1790) 70 One yoman in this office [of Bakehouse] for the kinge's mouthe recevyng the mayne floure of the Sergeaunt, by tayle. **1523** *Burgh Rec. Edinb.* (1869) I. 217 The baillies and counsall ordanis all the maisteris of the baxter craft till content and pay to the fermoraris thair mayne mutter, that is to say, of ilk iiij laid that thai brek aboue ane pek of mayne flour, and gif thai brek les to pay na thing. **1524–5** *Ibid.* 220 Als thai ordane the saidis baxteris to pay the mayne flour to the saidis fermoraris as vs and wont hes bene in tymes bygane.

Maine (meɪn), *sb.*² *U.S.* **a.** The name of the State of *Maine* used in ***Maine (liquor) law***, a law forbidding the manufacture or sale of intoxicating liquors; hence applied to similar laws (see quot. 1897).

1852 *Lantern* (N.Y.) I. 119/2 Does the Maine Law, in abolishing the use of liquors, include the Cotton-Gin? **1853** *Illustr. London News* 26 Nov. 438/1 The Earl of Harrington approves of a Maine law for England. **1855** *Knickerbocker* XLV. 479 They have the Maine Law down below. **1860** W. L. SARGANT *Robert Owen & his Social Philos.* xix. 216 Nor had he had recourse to a Maine law. **1864** T. H. NICHOLS *40 Yrs. Amer. Life* I. 76 But drunkenness becoming common, ..spirits were banished, the apple orchards cut down, ..'Maine Laws' were finally passed. **1871** *Scribner's Monthly* I. 673 Its special suggestiveness resides in the fact that it originates with the friends of the Maine law. **1897** *Encycl. Social Reform* 1107/1 A prohibitory law was passed in Maine in 1846, and in 1851 a more stringent one, including the provision for the seizure and destruction of intoxicating liquors (known as the 'Maine Law'..) was enacted... Vermont in 1852, New Hampshire in 1855, and Connecticut in 1854, passed the Maine law. **1960** R. K. WEBB *H. Martineau* xi. 346 She saw the Maine Law..as the exercise of the will of a democratic people.

b. ***Maine law man***: a prohibitionist.

1858 *Leisure Hour* 3 June 352/2 Upon the extensive mines ..are large numbers of teetotallers and Maine Law men.

† **maine**, *v. Naut. Obs.* Also **mayne.** [Aphetic f. AMAIN(E *v.*] *trans.* To lower (a sail).

1517 TORKINGTON *Pilgr.* (1884) 59 He made vs to mayne, that ys to sey stryk Downe ower sayles. **1579** T. STEVENS in *Hakluyt's Voy.* (1599) II. II. 99 When it is tempest almost intollerable for other ships, and maketh them maine all their sailes, these hoise vp, and saile excellent well.

maine, obs. form of MANE, MEINIE.

maineath, variant of MANATH *Obs.*

main'ferre. *Obs.* exc. *Hist.* Also 5 **maynefere,** 7 **mainefeere, mainefaire,** (8–9 *Hist.* **mane-, manifaire**). [Perh. repr. F. *main ferrée* (iron-clad hand) or *main-de-fer* (hand of iron): the latter occurs in this sense in Viollet-le-Duc *Dict. Mobilier français* (1874) V. 449.] Some piece of armour; prob. the gauntlet for the left arm, of which examples are preserved.

c **1470** in *Archæologia* XVII. 292 A maynefere with a ryngge. *a* **1548** HALL *Chron., Hen. IV* 12 Some had the mainferres, the close gantlettes the quissettes the flancardes dropped & gutted with red. **1631** in *Archæologia* XXXVII. 486 The horse's furniture being a saddle, barbe, crinett,.. and for the man 2 grangardes, 2 pasgardes, 2 mainefeeres, 2 peer of vambraces [etc.]. **1660** *Surv. Armoury Tower* in *Archæologia* XI. 99 Masking armor complete, reported to be made for king Henry the Seventh... Mainefaires, russet, white. **1786** GROSE *Anc. Armour* 30 [Writes the word as *manefaire*, and erroneously refers it to MANE *sb.*; hence he treats it as synonymous with CRINIERE. So in MEYRICK **1824**.] **1830** JAMES *Darnley* x, With his chanfron, snaffle-bit, manifaire, and fluted poitrel. **1844** —— *Agincourt* I. 77.

† **mainful**, *a. Obs.* In 3 **meinful(e,** 4 **maynful.** [f. MAIN *sb.*¹ + -FUL.] Powerful, mighty.

a **1225** *Leg. Kath.* 1097 þurh þ he is drihtin meinful & almihti. *a* **1225** *Juliana* 35 Lef me þat ich mote mihti meinfule godd iseon him isscheomet. **13..** *E.E. Allit. P.* A. 1093 Ryȝt as þe maynful mone con rys, Er þenne þe day glem dryue al doun. *Ibid.* B. 1730.

main-guard.

1. *Fortif.* The keep of a castle; also, the building within a fortress in which the 'main-guard' (sense 2 b) is lodged. Also *fig.*

1653 E. WATERHOUSE *Apol. Learn.* Pref., Nothing..is so great a security to the main-guard of Religion, as well to provide for her out-ports & lines of learning. **1662** PEPYS *Diary* 19 Dec., With the Lieutenant's leave set them to work in the garden, in the corner against the mayneguard. **1690** *Lond. Gaz.* No. 2544/2 They passed the Ditch, and made themselves Masters of the Main-guard. **1778** *Eng. Gazetteer* (ed. 2) s.v. *Marlborough*, The keep or main guard of the castle. **1902** *Daily Chron.* 3 Mar. 3/1 The hideous new main-guard which has been built close to the White Tower.

2. *Mil.* **a.** = GRAND GUARD 2. **b.** (See quot. 1876.)

1706 PHILLIPS (ed. Kersey) s.v. *Guard, Main Guard*, (in the Field) is a considerable Body of Horse sent out to the Head of the Camp to secure the Army, by diligently guarding all the Avenues or Passages that lead to it. **1797** *Encycl. Brit.* (ed. 3) VIII. 170/2 *Main Guard*, is that from which all other guards are detached. **1876** VOYLE & STEVENSON *Milit. Dict.* (ed. 3) s.v., Large forts or fortresses have a main guard chosen from the troops garrisoning them, under which guard all disturbers of the peace, drunkards, &c., are placed.

maingy, obs. form of MANGY *a.*

mainland ('meɪnlənd, -lænd). Forms: see MAIN *a.* and LAND *sb.*¹; also 4–5 *Sc.* **manland.** [See MAIN *a.* 4. Cf. ON. *megenland.*]

1. a. That continuous body of land which includes the greater part of a country or territory, in contradistinction to the portions outlying as islands or peninsulas. †Formerly *occas.* = land as opposed to sea, *terra firma*; also in ME. poetry, great extent of country, wide territory.

1375 BARBOUR *Bruce* III. 389 And then he thocht, but mar delay, In-to the manland till arywe. ? *a* **1400** *Morte Arth.* 427 And merke sythene over the mounttez in-to his mayne londez. *Ibid.* 4071 This was a mache vn-mete,..To melle with that multitude in thase man londis. *c* **1470** HENRY *Wallace* x. 1015 Na man was left all this mayn land [= Scotland] within. *a* **1490** BOTONER *Itin.* (Nasmith 1778) 153 Insula Prestholm..distat a le mayn lond circa spacium duarum arcuum. **1511** GUYLFORDE *Pilgr.* (1851) 11 There be ij. stronge castelles stondynge upon two rokkes..and the Turkes mayne lande lyeth within .ij. or .iij. myle of theym. **1527** R. THORNE in Hakluyt *Voy.* (1589) 253 It appeareth the said land that we found and the Indies to be all one maine land. **1530** PALSGR. 242/1 Mayne-land, *terre ferme.* **1535** STEWART *Cron. Scot.* (1858) I. 100 Befoir wes medow and mane land, Quhair now is nocht bot salt water and sand. **1600** E. BLOUNT tr. *Conestaggio* 2 It contains in circuit 850 miles, whereof 400 run along the Sea shore, the rest is maine land. **1604** E. G[RIMSTONE] *D'Acosta's Hist. Indies* I. vi. 20 The Isles of Acores, Cape Verd and others,..are not above three hundred leagues or five hundred from the Mayne land. **1719** DE FOE *Crusoe* I. xv, Friday, the weather being very serene, looks very earnestly towards the main land. **1838** THIRLWALL *Greece* II. xii. 83 The ancient Æolian cities on the main-land..amounted to eleven. **1878** HUXLEY *Physiogr.* 168 Pillars of chalk have thus been separated from the mainland.

b. Applied to the largest island of the Shetlands and to the largest island of the Orkneys (Pomona).

1596 DALRYMPLE tr. *Leslie's Hist. Scot.* I. 63 Pomonia, quhilke is of sik a boundes that the inhabitouris calles it the mayne land. **1822** SCOTT *Pirate* i, That long, narrow, and irregular island, usually called the Mainland of Zetland. **1846** MᶜCULLOCH *Acc. Brit. Empire* (1854) I. 315 There are about a dozen principal islands: Pomona, or the mainland, being decidedly the largest.

c. *Canad.* That part of British Columbia on the mainland of Canada, as opposed to Vancouver Island.

1921 *Daily Colonist* (Victoria, B.C.) 26 Mar. 5/4 Vancouver Island has done a great deal to support the Mainland in the past, and is doing so at present. The Mainland is no good to us.

d. The continent of Australia, as opposed to Tasmania.

1934 T. WOOD *Cobbers* xiii. 164 They are tied to Australia —'the mainland', they call it... 'The mainland' is an object of suspicion, envy, and dislike. **1944** *Living off Land* v. 102 So far as malaria is concerned, there's not much of it on the mainland. **1958** C. KOCH *Boys in Island* 15 He lived in an island. At six years old he knew about that. He heard it at school, and knew about it from Uncle Charlie's talk about the Mainland, Australia. **1968** G. DUTTON *Andy* 200 Soon as I blew from the boob, I headed down for the Old Tassy. .. I'll get over on the Mainland soon, or up the islands.

e. *N.Z. colloq.* The South Island.

1949 *Journeys* XXXIV. 56 I'm sure South Islanders are right in claiming that they live on the 'mainland'. **1965** *Weekly News* (Auckland, N.Z.) 10 Feb. 3/1 Greater numbers of adventurous North Islanders than ever before have crossed the seas this summer to the 'mainland'.

2. a. *attrib.*

1810 SCOTT *Lady of L.* III. xii, When it [*sc.* the boat] had neared the mainland hill. **1867** *Syme's Eng. Bot.* (ed. 3) VII. 49 Extending east to Sussex and mainland Hants. **1895** *Westm. Gaz.* 24 Oct. 4/2 The possible recognition by mainland Powers of the Cubans as belligerents.

b. Special combs., as **mainland China**, the People's Republic of China, as opposed to Taiwan; hence ***mainland Chinese.***

1967 *Guardian* 14 July 5/3 She lived in Hongkong and.. visited Japan, Korea, and what is known as 'Mainland China'. **1972** *Korea Herald* 17 Nov. 2/2 (*caption*) Chiao Kuanhua, first vice foreign minister of mainland China is greeted Tuesday by David Scotfox on behalf of Alec Douglas-Home at London airport. **1973** J. GOODFIELD *Courier to Peking* iii. 42 Teh Chang..went to mainland China... He was from Hong Kong. **1975** *Times* 3 Mar. 14/5 Mainland China is about to fight back against..the degenerate Hong Kong cult of violence, *Kung fu.* **1966** C. ISRAEL *Hostages* 38 World War III won't begin..until everyone has a chance to see what happens when the Mainland Chinese take their seat in the General Assembly. **1972** W. GARNER *Ditto, Brother Rat!* xxi. 159 Chinese, right? Mainland Chinese, too, I'd say.

†**3.** (See quot.) *Obs.*

1686 PLOT *Staffordsh.* ix. 341 A mixt sort of land, either of Clay and Gravel, or Clay and Sand..this..they call in the Moorelands their Main-land, which is indeed the best they have.

Hence **'mainlander**, a dweller on the mainland.

1860 PALFREY *Hist. New Eng.* II. 359 The mainlanders and the islanders. **1882** A. J. EVANS in *Archæologia* XLVIII. 17 We find a self-governing community, waging war with the Illyrian mainlanders. **1897** MARY KINGSLEY *W. Africa* 56 A thing that differentiates them more than any other characteristic from the mainlanders. **1941** BAKER *Dict. Austral. Slang* 45 *Mainlander*, a person living on the Aust. continent, in contrast to one living in Tasmania or an island dependency. **1966** *Tribune* (Palmerston North, N.Z.) 1 Apr. 8/7 It's great what a pause in the wrong place does to the meaning of a phrase. Judging by a news announcer on Tv. the other night we can now lay claim to being Mainlanders. The news item doesn't matter but in the script were the words 'Palmerston, North Otago'. **1969** *Times* (Taiwan Suppl.) 9 Dec. p. iii/2 Taiwan's population today is 13.6m. —10.1m. native-born Taiwanese and 3.5m. mainlanders. **1971** *Guardian* 5 Nov. 21/3 If the mainlanders do not deliver on the current promises, the Taiwanese will be further disillusioned.

ma-in-law, colloq. abbrev. of MOTHER-IN-LAW.

1961 in PARTRIDGE *Dict. Slang* Suppl. **1971** R. RENDELL *One Across* v. 45 We've got some old tab coming here... Pal of my ma-in-law's. **1971** J. TYNDALL *Death in Lebanon* x. 181 So Ma-in-law has been quick to take her revenge. **1974** *People's Jrnl.* (Inverness & Northern Counties ed.) 29 June 4/2 My ma-in-law used to say..'Fierce is the light which beats upon the throne.'

†**'mainless**, *a. Obs.* [f. OE. *mæȝenléas*, f. *mæȝen* MAIN *sb.*¹ + *-léas* -LESS.] Powerless.

c **1000** ÆLFRIC *Gloss.* in Wr.-Wülcker 162/24 *Eneruis*, mæȝenleas. *c* **1220** *Bestiary* 128 He is lene and mainles.

‖**main levee.** [Fr. = (literally) 'raised hand'.] Replevin.

1653 SIR R. BROWNE in *Evelyn's Diary*, etc. (1879) IV. 291 Captain Anthonio hath..by this means obtained main-levee of all the goods arrested.

main line. [f. MAIN *a.* + LINE *sb.*² 26 b.]

1. The principal line of a railway.

1841 [see LINE *sb.*² 26 b]. **1865** TROLLOPE *Belton Est.* vii. 74 At Taunton there branched away from the main-line that line which was to take her to Perivale. **1880** *Harper's Mag.* July 196/2 The main line will soon have reached the Rio Grande Valley. **1959** *Chambers's Encycl.* XI. 488/2 The first lengthy main line, the Grand Junction, was opened in 1837. **1970** O. S. NOCK *Rail, Steam & Speed* i. 17 A 'Gladstone' gliding effortlessly down one of the 1 in 264 banks of the Brighton main line.

b. *transf.* A principal route, connection, conduit, family, etc. *U.S.*

1845 *Hunt's Merchant's Mag.* XIII. 127 The main line of state works of Pennsylvania extends from the city of Philadelphia..to the city of Pittsburg. **1925** *Amer. Speech* I. 136/1 The cable that hauled the logs was called 'the main line'. **1945** S. J. PERELMAN *Crazy like Fox* 124 Why not follow the example of glamorous Mrs Barney Kessler, socially prominent matron of the Main Line. **1952** *Sunday Times* 3 Feb. 5/4 'Main line'..in America..is widely applied to important roads or conduits or arteries of one kind or another.

c. A large or principal vein, into which drugs can readily be injected; hence, an intravenous injection of drugs; the act or habit of making such an injection. *slang* (orig. *U.S.*).

1933 *Amer. Speech* VIII. II. 27/2 The *main line* is the blood vessel into which the injection is made. **1938** *Amer. Speech* XIII. 182/2 From my dropper I'll shake the dust, From my spike I'll scrape the rust, And my old main-line I'll bust. **1953** W. BURROUGHS *Junkie* (1972) iii. 33, I began shooting in the main line to save stuff and because the immediate kick was better. **1959** 'E. MCBAIN' *Pusher* iv. 36, I gave him a snort... He got on mainline a couple of weeks later. **1968** 'J. WELCOME' *Hell is where you find It* xiv. 165 What about the purple hearts? Gone on main line yet? **1970** *Sunday Times* 8 Mar. 1/2 She was taking big doses of heroin ..by mainline-injection into a vein—every four hours.

2. *attrib.* or quasi-*adj.* (often with hyphen).

a. Of or pertaining to the main line of a railway.

1879 E. J. SIMMONS *Mem. Station Master* (1974) viii. 124, I couldn't take charge of this main-line station if you gave me all the world. **1884** R. PIKE *Railway Adventures & Anecdotes* 93 A gentleman..got into a first-class carriage.. with the intention of proceeding home by one of the main line down trains. **1926** *Daily Express* 11 May 1/1 Great improvements in the main line train services continue to be made throughout the country. **1958** *New Statesman* 11 Oct. 484/2 Wuhsi..apparently sees a foreigner rarely although it is a large main-line city. **1969** M. GILBERT *Etruscan Net* I. i. 13 At main line stations they have a nose for these things.

b. *transf.* and *fig.* Principal; occupying a principal or important position; also, 'middle-of-the-road', 'mainstream'.

1941 BLUNDEN *Thomas Hardy* iii. 42 Here he wrote one of his main-line novels. **1941** *Time* 20 Jan. 77 High life in Philadelphia's Main Line society. **1958** *Listener* 13 Nov. 775/1 Asimov's two books..in addition to being main-line science fiction, are also 'whodunits' in the classic tradition. **1963** *Guardian* 29 Apr. 9/1 She is from a wealthy main-line Philadelphia family. **1965** P. FREUND *Spymaster* 114 His family, though not Main Line, was acceptable. **1968** *Punch* 11 Sept. 378/3 The enthusiasm of American main-line politicians for TV is said to be waning. **1972** *Times* 15 Apr. 16/4 The 'mainline Christian churches', says these young folk, have sold out to the 'establishment'.

c. Of, pertaining to, or characterized by the intravenous injection of drugs. Also *fig.*

1938 *Amer. Speech* XIII. 187/2 *Main-line shooter*, a vein-shooter. **1944** R. A. MOORE *Textbk. Path.* xlvii. 522 On occasion, as in 'main-line' drug addicts, the fungus may be introduced directly into the blood. **1957** J. KEROUAC *On Road* (1958) 173 A big shot of heroin in the main-line vein. **1969** *Daily Tel.* 29 Jan. 21/7 He was allowed a daily prescription of three grains—18 pills—of heroin. These were dissolved and injected directly into the bloodstream, which was known as the 'mainline' method. **1969** *Punch* 26 Feb. 295/3 Flattery is the mainline drug of the theatre—there is no one connected with that ridiculous institution who does not need his fix. **1972** *Times* 10 Apr. 10/4 As a mainline addict of BBC news..it has taken a week of comparing news on the two channels..to push me into the

ranks of the deserters. **1974** G. Jenkins *Bridge of Magpies* iii. 46 Then you'll be like that poor bugger coming off now in the boat. Started smoking grass. Grew the stuff..in a potty in his cottage... He's on to mainline stuff now.

main-line, *v. slang* (orig. *U.S.*). Also (without hyphen) **mainline**. [f. prec.] *trans.* and *intr.* To inject (a drug or drugs) intravenously. So **main-liner**; **main-lining** *vbl. sb.*

1934 *Detective Fiction Weekly* 21 Apr. 113/2 The addict who shoots stuff into the veins is said to be a gutter, or mainliner. **1938** *Amer. Speech* XIII. 187/2 If you can main-line a cube of that stuff, it is on the house. **1950** R. Chandler *Let.* 18 May in *R. Chandler Speaking* (1966) 79, I don't think any writer could think up an expression like 'mainliner' for a narcotic addict who shoots the stuff into a vein. **1951** *N.Y. Times* 27 June 19/1 An intravenous injection of the drug.. is called 'mainlining'. **1959** A. Bestic *Girl Outside* xiii. 213 She took to the needle. She's what they call a mainliner. **1959** 'E. McBain' *Pusher* viii. 77 Snorting?.. Skin pops?.. Larry, Larry, are you mainlining? **1964** B. Ellis *I came back from Hell* iii. 24 She was only skin-popping in those days (injecting her arms), not mainlining (injecting her veins). **1967** M. M. Glatt et al. *Drug Scene* v. 58, I don't know how much longer I would have lasted before I would have tried to mainline. *Ibid.* 59 Peter was revolted by the sight of someone else 'mainlining hard drugs' yet, whilst under the influence of hashish, he thought that he might go on to try mainlining for a bigger kick. **1970** N. Marsh *When in Rome* v. 126 The big leap. Pothead to main-liner. **1971** *Nature* 5 Nov. 14/3 The serious possibilities were raised of teratogenicity, tachycardia (especially if main-lining ever started), brain damage, [etc.]. **1972** M. Pereira *Singing Millionaire* vii. 71 He made himself a fix..and he mainlined it. **1974** D. Gray *Dead Give Away* ii. 23 What about the ones that can't cope in the rat race?.. The meths drinkers, the mainliners?

mainly ('meɪnlɪ), *adv.* Forms: 3 **mainliche**, 5 **maineliche, manly**, 4–7 **maynly**, 5–6 **maynely, -lie**, 6–7 **mainely**, 7– **mainly**. [f. MAIN *a.* + -LY^{2}.]

†**1.** Of physical actions: With force, vigour, or violence; mightily, vigorously, violently. *Obs.*

c **1275** Lay. 1915, I grop hine bi þan gurdle, and hine mainliche heof. *Ibid.* 14705 To-gadere hii come and mainliche on-slowe. *a* **1400–50** *Alexander* 2042 Fra morne to þe mirke niȝt maynly þa cocken [*Dubl. MS.* manly] þai feghtyn]. **1582** Stanyhurst *Æneis* iv. (Arb.) 103 Not to the sky maynely, but neere sea meanelye she [*sc.* a bird] flickreth. **1586** Marlowe *1st Pt. Tamburl.* ii. i. (1590) B 2 b, Such breadth of shoulders as might mainely beare Olde Atlas burthen. **1590** Spenser *F.Q.* i. vii. 12 The geaunt strooke so maynly mercilesse, That could have overthrowne a stony towre. **1603** Holland *Plutarch's Mor.* 163 When he would rid the ground of some wilde bushes,..he laieth at them mainely with his grubbing hooke or mattocke. **1621** Lady M. Wroth *Urania* 553 A terrible, fierce and mighty boare, issued out of the wood, running mainly at Amphilanthus. **1640** tr. *Verdere's Rom. Rom.* III. 50 One of them took his Scimitar..and..strook so mainly at his head, that [etc.]. **1656** M. Ben Israel *Vind. Judæorum* in *Phenix* (1708) II. 396 Every day the Jews [they] mainly strike, and buffet, shamefully spitting on them.

b. Of the production of sound: Lustily, loudly.

c **1275** Lay. 808 He..his horn mainliche bleu. **13..** *E.E. Allit. P.* B. 1427 Maynly his marschal þe mayster vpon calles. **1563** *Homilies* ii. *Passion* ii. (1640) 184 He cried mainely out against sinners. **1631** Weever *Anc. Funeral Mon.* 15 They..cried out mainly. **1881** Slow *Wiltsh. Rhymes* 123 Mainly he did roar.

†**c.** Of expression, thought: Vehemently, strongly; earnestly, eagerly. *Obs.*

c **1400** *Destr. Troy* 13860 This mild of his moder so mainly dessiret, þat [etc.]. *a* **1400–50** *Alexander* 1217 Þan was ser Meliager moued & maynly [*Dubl. MS.* manly] debatis. *Ibid.* 3424 My mekill miȝtfull gods I maynly ȝow swere. **1588** J. Udall *Demonstr. Discipl.* (Arb.) 76 Men mainly suspected of notorious transgressions. **1611** Speed *Hist. Gt. Brit.* ix. xvi (1623) 847 His..opinion..was as mainely opposed by the Cardinall.

†**2.** In a great degree; greatly, considerably, very much, a great deal. Also *occas.* entirely, perfectly. *Obs.*

c **1400–50** *Alexander* 934 His men & all þe Messadones full maynly ware stourbed. **1562** J. Heywood *Prov. & Epigr.* (1867) 111 Thou fleest that vice not meanly nor barely, But mainely, scrupulously. **1602** Shaks. *Ham.* iv. vii. 9 As by your Safety, Wisedome, all things else, You mainly were stirr'd vp. **1605** —— *Lear* iv. vii. 65, I am mainely ignorant What place this is. **1616** Beaum. & Fl. *Scornful Lady* ii. i, The people are so mainely giuen to spoonemeate. **1617** Fletcher *Mad Lover* iii. iv, Still she eyes him mainlie. **1628** Digby *Voy. Medit.* (1868) 6 Perceiuing she [*sc.* a ship] gott mainely of vs wee gaue ouer our chace. **1702** Farquhar *Inconstant* ii. i, I like her mainly. **1772** Foote *Nabob* iii. Wks. 1799 II. 318 Things are mainly changed since we were boys. **1800** Lamb *Lett.* vi. *to Manning* 51, I think we should suit one another mainly.

†**b.** Abundantly, copiously; lavishly. *Obs.*

1618 J. Bullokar in Farr *S.P. Jas. I* (1847) 291 This precious liquor..Whose sweet-distilling drops full mainly showres Adowne his neck. **1632** Lithgow *Trav.* i. 25 This Prouince is mainely watered through the middle with stately Po. *Ibid.* ix. 381 Danser tooke the presence of the Bashaw for a great fauour, and mainely feasted him with good cheare.

c. Used as an intensive with adjs. and advs. = Very, exceedingly. = MAIN *adv.* Now *dial.*

1670 Eachard *Cont. Clergy* 127 This invention pleases some mainly well. **1684** Bunyan *Pilgr.* ii. 191 She loveth Banqueting, and Feasting mainly well. **1718** D'Urfey *Grecian Heroine* v. ii, I like mine mainly well, faith. **1748** Smollett *Rod. Rand.* xxiv. (1760) I. 193 The captain was mainly wroth, and would certainly have done him a mischief. **1890** *Glouc. Gloss.*, *Main, Mainly*, very, exceedingly.

3. For the most part; in the main; as the chief thing, chiefly, principally.

1667 Milton *P.L.* xi. 519 Ungovern'd appetite,..a brutish vice, Inductive mainly to the sin of Eve. **1695** Woodward *Nat. Hist. Earth* iv. 188 The metallick..matter ..was..originally..interspersed..amongst the..Matter, whereof the said Strata mainly consist. **1820** Marshall *Const. Opin.* (1839) 218 The cause depends mainly on the validity of this act. **1874** Green *Short Hist.* iv. §3. 183 The body of commissioners which the King nominated were mainly Scotch. **1894** J. T. Fowler *Adamnan* Introd. 15 It is with Ireland that we are mainly concerned.

mainmast ('meɪnmɑːst, -æ-, -məst). [f. MAIN *a.* (sense 10) + MAST.] The principal mast in a ship.

15.. [see b]. **1596** Spenser *Pres. St. Ireland* Wks. (Globe) 666/2 So that he might sitt, as it were, at the very mayne mast of his shipp. **1611** Shaks. *Wint. T.* iii. iii. 94 The Shippe boaring the Moone with her maine Mast. **1634** Brereton *Trav.* (Chetham Soc.) 169 The main-mast which is placed almost in the middle of the ship. **1748** *Anson's Voy.* ii. iv. 161 We converted the fore-mast of the Victualler into a main-mast for the Tryal Sloop. **1764** Veitch in *Phil. Trans.* LIV. 287 Sometimes the name of main-mast is applied to all the three pieces as they stand erected, and sometimes to the lower piece, or part of the mast only: and when they are distinguished severally, they are called the main-mast, main top-mast, and main-top-gallant-mast. **1855** Browning *By the Fireside* iii, Out we slip To cut from the hazels by the creek A mainmast for our ship.

b. *attrib.*, as ***mainmast-top, -tree***.

15.. *Sir Andrew Barton* xxii. in *Surtees Misc.* (1888) 70 I'le hange them al on my mayn mast tree. **1768–74** Tucker *Lt. Nat.* (1834) II. 18 A sailor ordered up the main-mast top to descry ships.

†**mainmission.** *Obs. rare*$^{-1}$. [a. OF. *mainmission* (1461), refashioning of *manumission* after *main* hand.] = MANUMISSION.

c **1500** Medwall *Nature* (Brandl) 166 Thou hast now lybertye and nedest no mayn-myssyon.

†**main-'mizen.** *Naut. Obs.* [f. MAIN *a.* (sense 10) + MIZEN.] **a.** ? A spanker. **b.** The foremost of the two mizen masts formerly in use. (Also ***main mizen mast, sail***.)

1486 *Naval Acc. Hen. VII* (1896) 14 A Mayne Meson mast for the said Ship. *Ibid.* 43 Mayne meson sailes. *c* **1515** *Cocke Lorell's B.* (Percy Soc.), Some pulde at the beryll, some sprede y^{e} mayne myssyll. **1704** J. Harris *Lex. Techn.* s.v. *Missen-Mast*, Some great Ships require two [mizens]; then that next the Main-mast is the Main-missen.

†**mainmort.** *Obs.* [a. F. *mainmorte* = DEADHAND.] **a.** = MORTMAIN. **b.** *French Feudal Law* (see quot. 1727–41).

1387 Trevisa *Higden* (Rolls) VIII. 265. **1598** Dallington *Meth. Trav.* E iij b, Nominations of Chappels, goods of Main-mort, fifts of Lands sold. [**1727–41** Chambers *Cycl.*, *Main-Morte*, a term in some antient customs, still obtaining in Burgundy, signifying a right which the lord has, on the death of the chief of a family that is *Mainmortable*, of taking the best moveable in the house.]

mainmortable (meɪn'mɔːtəb(ə)l), *a.* and *sb. Hist.* [a. F. *mainmortable*, f. *mainmorte*: see prec.] **A.** *adj.* Applied to serfs (in France) who were not at liberty to alienate their possessions if they died childless; also to their possessions.

[1727–41: see prec.] **1779** *Gentl. Mag.* XLIX. 544 The mainmortable heritages, situated in our lands and signiories. **1889** M. Betham-Edwards *Introd. A. Young's Trav. France* 21 These bond-servants..were up to that time mainmortable.

B. *sb.* A 'mainmortable' serf.

1779 *Gentl. Mag.* XLIX. 545 We ordain that the Droit de Suite over mainmortables shall henceforth be abolished and suppressed. **1882** W. B. Weeden *Soc. Law Labor* 84 The lords..held the right to pursuit, by which they could follow a mainmortable who had abandoned the land.

'mainour, 'manner. *Obs.* exc. *Hist.* or *arch.* Forms: 5 **menowr, manor**, 6–8 **maner**, (6 **mayner, -ure**, 6–7 **maynour**, 7 **manoir**), 7–8 *Law Dicts.* **manour, meinor, -our(e**, 6– **mainour, manner**. [a. AF. *meinoure, mainoure, mainoevere*, a. OF. *maneuvre*, lit. 'hand-work': see MANŒUVRE.

From the etymology, it would seem probable that the original sense was 'the act or fact (of a crime)', as in 2 below. The AFr. examples, however, already show the concrete sense as in 1. The phrase *pris ov mainoure* ('taken with the mainour'; = *capta cum manuopere*, Fleta, *c* 1290) seems to have been framed to render the OE. *æt hæbbendre handa ȝefangen*: see HAND-HABEND *a.* Since the 16th c. the word has in non-technical use often been confused with MANNER *sb.*, and assimilated to that word in spelling.]

1. *Law.* The stolen thing which is found in a thief's possession when he is arrested: chiefly in phr. ***taken, found with the mainour***.

[**1275** *Act 3 Edw. I, Stat. Westm.* i. c. 15 Toz que sunt pris ov meinoure. **1311** *Act 5 Edw. II, Ordin.* c. 19 Qe desormes nul ne soit pris ne enprisone pur vert ne pur veneson, si il ne soit trove ove mainoure. **1399** *Liber Cust.* 487 Et quod prædictus Dux..haberet quæcunque bona et catalla vocata 'manuopera' capta vel capienda cum quacunque persona infra..feoda prædicta.] ? **1472** *Plumpton Corr.* (Camden) 26 One Richard of the Burgh, that had take and led away feloniously certaine ky and other cattell..was take and arested with the said manor att Spofford, whearat they yett remaine. **1481** Caxton *Reynard* (Arb.) 8 Yet al had he courtoys hanged whan he fonde hym with the menowr, he had not moche mysdon he trespaced. **1550** Latimer *Serm. bef. Edw. VI*, D iv, Euen as a theefe that is taken with the manner when [*ed.* 1584 that] he stealeth. **1551** Robinson tr. *More's Utop.* i. (1895) 69 Moneye fownde abowte them shoulde betraye the robberye. They shoulde be no soner taken wyth the maner, but furth wyth they shoulde be punysshed. **1597** Shaks. *2 Hen. IV*, ii. iv. 347 O Villaine, thou stolest a Cup of Sacke eighteene yeeres agoe, and were taken with the manner. **1607** Cowell *Interpr.*, *Mainour*, alias *Manour*, alias *Meinoure*, signifieth in our common lawe, the thing that a theefe taketh away or stealeth. **1769** Blackstone *Comm.* IV. 303 When a thief was taken with the mainour, that is, with the thing stolen upon him, *in manu*. **1838–42** Arnold *Hist. Rome* (1846) I. xiv. 293 *note*, No power could bail a thief taken with the manner, that is, with the thing stolen upon him. **1867** Pearson *Hist. Eng.* I. 274 The thief overtaken with the mainour might be killed.

2. ***with*** (later ***in***) ***the mainour*** (usually ***manner***): in the act of doing something unlawful, 'in flagrante delicto'.

1530 Palsgr. 752/1, I take with the maner, as a thefe is taken with thefte, or a person in the doyng of any other acte, *je prens sur le faict*. **1566** *Pasquine in a Traunce* 107 Whether fryers..hauing bene so often taken with the maner to vse deceyte,..be therefore any more to be trusted afterwarde. **1579** *Termes of the Lawe* 144 b (s.v. *Maynour*), We commonlye vse to saye when we finde one doing of an vnlawfull act, that wee tooke him wyth the mainour, or manner. **1597** Beard *Theatre God's Judgem.* (1612) 46 Being taken in the manner, the Christians stoned him to death. **1609** Holland *Amm. Marcell.* xxi. ii. 168 [He] committed those and such like outrages..but being taken with the manoir and convict, he forbare and abstained. **1611** Bible *Num.* v. 13 If..a man lye with her carnally,..and there be no witnesse against her, neither she be taken with the maner [etc.]. **1615** Crooke *Body of Man* 282 They feigne that when Venus and Mars were in bed together, they were deprehended or taken in the manner, as we say, by Mercury. **1760–72** H. Brooke *Fool of Qual.* (1809) IV. 124, I held it beneath me to be caught in the manner. **1828** Scott *F.M. Perth* xii, 'Ha! my jolly Smith', he said, 'have I caught thee in the manner?' **1866** *Chamb. Jrnl.* No. 28. 261 If he were taken in the act or mainour.

mainpast ('meɪnpɑːst, -æ-). *Law. Obs.* exc. *Hist.* [ad. AF. *meynpast*, f. med.L. *manupastus*, f. L. *manū* abl. of *manus* hand + *pāstus*, pa. pple. of *pāscere* to feed (cf. PASTURE *sb.*).] A man's household; a domestic; a dependant.

Anglo-Norman examples are cited in *Mod. Lang. Notes* (1932) June 375–6.

1865 F. M. Nichols tr. *Britton* I. i. ii. 13 Let the coroner inquire of whose tithing or whose mainpast such fugitive was. **1891** Maitland & Baildon tr. *Court Baron* (Selden Soc.) 53 Thy son who is thy mainpast entered the lord's garden. **1895** Pollock & Maitland *Hist. Eng. Law* I. ii. iii. 555 The head of a household answers for the appearance in court of the members of his household, his servants, his retainers, those whom his hand feeds, his *manupastus* or *mainpast*. **1909** W. S. Holdsworth *Hist. Eng. Law* III. ii. 295 We can see traces of the older principles under which he was held to be liable in the rule which made him responsible for the doings of his household or 'mainpast'. **1961** R. F. Hunnisett *Medieval Coroner* iv. 64 They [*sc.* the coroners] had to inquire in whose tithing or mainpast the outlaw had been and enrol it, in order that it might be amerced at the eyre for his flight.

†**mainpernable**, *a. Obs.* [a. AF. *mainpernable*, **mainprenable*, f. *mainprendre*: see MAINPRIZE *sb.*] Capable of being mainprized.

[**1330** *Act 4 Edw. III*, c. 2 Sils ne soyent meynpernables par la lei.] **1487** *Act 3 Hen. VII*, c. 3 Dyverse persones such as wer not maynp^{r}nable ware oftymes leten to baille and maynprise. **1630** in Rushw. *Hist. Coll.* (1659) I. 27 Although he did nothing, he is not main-pernable until the King sent his pleasure, because he was armed and furiously disposed. **1647** Sir R. Holbourne *Freeholders' Grand Inquest* 34 The penalty for detaining a Prisoner that is mainpernable is a Fine at the Kings Pleasure. **1772** *Junius Lett.* lxviii. 342 In the two preceding statutes, the words bailable, replevisable, and mainpernable, are used synonymously.

mainpernor. *Law. Obs.* exc. *Hist.* or *arch.* Forms: 3–4 **meynpernour**, 4 **mein-, menepernour**, 4, 7, 8 **mainpernor**, 5 **maynpernour, meynpurnour**, 5–7, 9 **mainpernour**, 6 **mayneperner**, 6–7 **mainperner**, 7 **mainepernour, manipernor**. [a. AF. *mainpernour* = OF. **mainprenor, -preneur*, agent-n. f. *mainprendre*: see MAINPRIZE *sb.* Cf. MANUCAPTOR.] A surety for a prisoner's appearance in court on a specified day; one who gives mainprize for another. (Also *fig.*)

For the alleged distinction between *mainpernor* and *bail* see quot. 1768. With regard to the etymological misapprehensions in quots. 1607 and 1768, see MAINPRIZE 2.

[**1292** Britton i. ii. §6 Les nouns des meynpernours, solom ceo qe il troverunt par le verdit, face enrouler. **1326–7** *Act 1 Edw. III, Stat.* i. c. 8, & le nouns des meinpernours face liverer a mesmes les verders, a respoundre en eir devant Justices.] **1362** Langl. *P. Pl.* A. iv. 99 That Meede moste be meynpernour Reson heo bi-souȝte. *c* **1412** Hoccleve *De Reg. Princ.* 2399 And to prison he gooth; he gette no bettre, Til his mainpernour his arrest vnfettre. **1459** *Rolls of Parlt.* V. 368/1 Unto the tyme that they have founde suerte of iiii Meynpurnours. *a* **1548** Hall *Chron.*, *Hen. IV* 12 b, Thou knowest wel enough that I am thy pledge borowe and mayneperner, body for body, and land for goodes in open parliament. **1586** J. Hooker *Hist. Irel.* in *Holinshed* II. 72/1 [They] became mainpernours for the said earle of Desmond, that he should come into England, and abide such triall as the law would award. **1607** Cowell *Interpr.* s.v. *Mainprise*, They that do thus vndertake for any, are called Mainpernours, because they do receiue him into their hands. **1647** N. Bacon *Disc. Govt. Eng.* i. liii. (1739) 94 Mainperners are not to be punished as Principals, unless they be parties or privies to the failing of the Principal. **1768** Blackstone *Comm.* III. 128 Mainpernors differ from bail, in that a man's bail may imprison or surrender him up

before the stipulated day of appearance; mainpernors can do neither, but are barely sureties for his appearance at the day: bail are only sureties, that the party be answerable for the special matter for which they stipulate; mainpernors are bound to produce him to answer all charges whatsoever. **1857** SIR F. PALGRAVE *Norm. & Eng.* II. 691 If any friend had pledged himself to the assurance that..the fine young Duke had always conducted himself with strictly edifying propriety we should say..a bold mainpernour was he.

¶ See quot. (Prob. some error.)

1631 WEEVER *Anc. Funeral Mon.* 342 Officers belonging to these Staples, were Maiors, Constables, Manipernors.

† **mainport.** *Obs.* Also 7 **manport, maineporte, maynport.** [Of obscure origin: possibly f. F. *main*, L. *manus* hand, and F. *porter*, L. *portāre* to carry.] (See quot. 1670–91.)

1664 SPELMAN *Gloss.* s.v., Vicaria de Wragby consistit in toto Altaragio & in ceragio vulgariter dict. *Waxshot*, in panibus vulgariter dict. Manport. *Ibid.*, Mainport. **1670–91** BLOUNT *Law Dict.*, *Maine-porte (in manu portatum)*, is a small tribute (commonly of Loaves of Bread) which in some places the Parishioners pay to the Rector of their Church, in recompence for certain Tythes. **1677** THOROTON *Antiq. Nottingh.* 474 They also..assigned him [the Vicar of Blyth] many small matters in which the Vicarage was to consist, as ..in the Bread which is called Maynport.

mainprize ('meɪnpraɪz), *sb. Obs.* exc. *Hist.* Forms: 4 **meynprize**, 4–5 **meyn-**, **maynprise**, **-pryse**, 5 **main-**, **maympris**, **maynprice**, ? **maunprese**, 5–6 **maynpris(e**, 6 **-prize**, **mempris**, 6–7 **main(e)prise**, 7– **mainprize**. [a. AF., OF. *mein-*, *mainprise*, n. of action f. *mainprendre* (f. *main* hand + *prendre* to take: see PRIZE *sb.*), the equivalent of the med.L. *manūcapĕre*, lit. 'to take in the hand', hence 'to assume responsibility, pledge oneself'.

The Latinized form *meinprisa*, in the general sense 'undertaking, promise under penalties', is cited by Du Cange from an English charter of 1174.]

1. *gen.* The action of making oneself legally responsible for the fulfilment of a contract or undertaking by another person; suretyship.

1447 *Waterf. Arch.* in *10th Rep. Hist. MSS. Comm.* App. v. 297 No citsayn or freman shal receve none estraungers in pledge or maynprice for ony bargaine. ? *a* **1500** in ARNOLDE *Chron.* (1811) 24 That..an English Marchaunt bee not amytted into the fraunches of yᵉ cite of any crafte but be Mempris of vi good men and sufficyent of the crafte.

2. *spec.* The action of procuring the release of a prisoner by becoming surety ('mainpernor') for his appearance in court at a specified time. Chiefly in phr. ***to let*** or ***receive to*** (or ***in***) ***mainprize***, ***to deliver upon*** (or ***by***) ***mainprize***, ***to nim under mainprize*** [= AF. *laisser par*, *mettre par meynprise*]. ***without bail or mainprize***: with no permission to obtain release by finding sureties. ***writ of mainprize***: see quot. 1768.

By the legal antiquaries of the 16th c., the 'taking in hand' etymologically implied by AF. *mainprise*, med.L. *manucaptio*, was supposed to denote the act of 'receiving into friendly custody' the person who would otherwise have been committed to prison (cf. BAIL *sb.*¹ 3), and the later definitions of *mainprize* and *mainpernor*, e.g. those of Cowell and Blackstone (see MAINPERNOR) are worded in accordance with this misapprehension.

[**1292** BRITTON I. xviii. §1 Les aloygneours soint mis par meynprise jekes en heyre des Justices.] **1377** LANGL. *P. Pl.* B. xx. 17 Nede anon riȝte nymeth hym vnder meynpryse. *a* **1400** *Pride of Life* (Brandl, 1898) 379 þer [in hell] ne fallit ne maynpris ne supersidias. *c* **1400** *Gamelyn* 744, I bidde him to maynpris [*v.r.* maympris] that thou graunte him me Til the nexte sitting of deliveraunce. **1414** *Rolls of Parlt.* IV. 57/2 Sith the tyme that I was resseyved to meynpryse. **1423** *Ibid.* 258/2 Imprisenment of a moneth, withoute baille or mainpris. **1444** *Ibid.* V. 107/1 To abide in Prison..withoute lettyng to maynprise, or in any other wise to go at large. **1509** BARCLAY *Shyp of Folys* (1570) 4 There shall be no bayle nor treating of mainprise. **1554** *Act 1 & 2 Phil. & Mary* c. 13 §1 The same Justices to be presente together at the tyme of the said Bailement or Mayneprise. **1577** NORTHBROOKE *Dicing* (1843) 137 They should bee committed to the gaole without bayle or mainprise, for the space of three monethes. **1586** J. HOOKER *Hist. Irel.* in *Holinshed* II. 71/2 He afterward deliuered him vpon mainprise of these suerties whose names insue. **1612** DAVIES *Why Ireland*, etc. 202 Though the Earle of Desmond were left [*sic*] to Mainprize, vpon condition hee should appeare before the King by a certain day. *a* **1625** SIR H. FINCH *Law* (1636) 446 At writ of mainprise to set at liberty one baileable finding baile. **1655** FULLER *Ch. Hist.* IV. ii. §4 (Petit. agst. Lollards) That they ..be..put in Prison, without being delivered in Bail, or otherwise, except by good and sufficient mainprise, to be taken before the Chancellour of England. **1744** *Act 17 Geo. II*, c. 40 §10 There to remain without Bail or Mainprize, until Payment be made. **1768** BLACKSTONE *Comm.* III. 128 The writ of mainprize..is a writ directed to the sheriff.. commanding him to take sureties for the prisoner's appearance, usually called mainpernors, and to set him at large. *a* **1845** BARHAM *Ingol. Leg.* Ser. III. *House Warming*, Taken to jail..without mainprize or bail.

b. *fig.* and in fig. contexts.

1412–20 LYDG. *Chron. Troy* III. xxv, That of the death stode tho vnder a reste, Without maynpryse sothly as of lyfe. **1631** HEYLIN *St. George* 42 Without hope of Bayle, or any mercie of mainprise; he must be in Hell. **1636** FEATLY *Clavis Myst.* xxii. 290 No baile or mainprize from this common prison of all mankinde, the grave. **1663** COWLEY *Cutter Colman St.* II. iv, Come on; I'll send thee presently to Erebus; Without either Bail or Main-prize. **1698** FRYER *Acc. E. India & P.* 13 Had she [the ship] given way never so little, we must have sunk without Bail or Mainprize.

3. *concr.* One's mainpernor or mainpernors.

1362 LANGL. *P. Pl.* A. IV. 75 And he amendes make let meynprize him haue. **1678** BUTLER *Hud.* III. i. 60 He therefore..Resolv'd to leave the Squire for Bail And Mainprize for him to the Goal. **1847** SIR H. TAYLOR *Eve of Conquest* Wks. 1864 III. 211 He greatly grudged This mainprize of my loyalty to let loose.

† **'mainprize**, *v. Law. Obs.* exc. *Hist.* Forms: 4 **maynpris**, 4–5 **-prise**, **-pryse**, **meynprise**, (5 **maynprice**, **-prese**, **meyme-**, **maym-**, **mempryse**, **mem-**, **menprise**, **maynsprise**), 7 **mainprise**, **-prize**. [f. prec.] *trans.* To procure or grant the release of (a prisoner) by mainprize; to accept mainpernors for the appearance of. Often *fig.*

c **1330** R. BRUNNE *Chron.* (1810) 138 Bot if he to þer baylifes mak his sikernesse, þat þei wille him maynp[r]is. **1377** LANGL. *P. Pl.* B. IV. 179 Mede shal nouȝte meynprise ȝow bi the Marie of heuene! **1393** *Ibid.* C. XXI. 189 God hath ..graunted to al mankynde, Mercy, my suster, and me to maynprise hem alle. *c* **1440** *Promp. Parv.* 320/1 Maynprysyd, or menprisyd (*MS. K.* maynsprisid, *MS. S.* maymprysyd, or memprisyd), *manucaptus*, *fidejussus.* *a* **1500** MEDWALL *Nature* (Brandl) II. 1123 God..Dyd vs..wyth hys own blode maynpryce And vs redemed fro paynes endles. **1598** MANWOOD *Lawes Forest* I. 167. **1681** W. ROBERTSON *Phraseol. Gen.* (1693) 857 To mainprize, *vadimonio obstringere.* **1865** S. DOBELL *Life & Lett.* (1878) II. iii. 272 Not Moses only or Elias, But Heaven mainprized, and every standing saint Astonied into marble. **1895** POLLOCK & MAITLAND *Hist. Eng. Law* II. II. ix. 582 If a man was arrested he was usually replevied (*replegiatus*) or mainprised (*manucaptus*), that is to say, he was set free so soon as some sureties (*plegii*) undertook (*manuceperunt*)..his appearance in court. **1904** M. BATESON *Borough Customs* (Selden Soc.) I. 99 If distress be delivered by pledge or mainprise of any one, if he who is..mainprised does not come to justify himself..let his..mainpernours be distrained to produce him.

¶ Erroneously used for MISPRIZE.

[The error prob. arose from association of the first syllable with OF. *meins*, *moins* less; cf. the spelling *maynsprisid* in the King's College MS. of *Promp. Parv.*]

c **1450** LYDG. & BURGH *Secrees* 2219 He is so trewe no good man may hym mempryse.

Hence † **'mainprizing** *vbl. sb.* = MAINPRIZE *sb.* Also † **'mainprizer** = MAINPERNOR.

c **1440** *Promp. Parv.* 320/2 Maynprisynge, *manucap(t)io. Ibid.*, Maynprisowre, *mancipator* [? *manucaptor*], *fide-jussor.* **1610** *Holland's Camden's Brit.* II. 176 There was the Earle of Vlster enlarged, who..found mainprisers or sureties to answer the writs of law.

mainrent, mains *Sc.*: see MANRED, MAIN *sb.*³

mainsail ('meɪnseɪl, 'meɪns(ə)l). *Naut.* [See MAIN *a.* 10.] The principal sail of a ship.

a. In square-rigged vessels, the sail which is bent to the main-yard. **b.** In fore-and-aft rigged vessels, the sail which is set on the after part of the mainmast.

1485 *Naval Acc. Hen. VII* (1896) 40 Mayne sailes. *c* **1515** *Cocke Lorell's B.* (Percy Soc.) 12 Some howysed the mayne sayle. **1526** TINDALE *Acts* xxvii. 40 They..hoysed vppe the mayne sayle to the wynde. **1626** CAPT. SMITH *Accid. Yng. Seamen* 6 The Younkers are the yong men called Fore-mast men, to..Furle, and Sling the maine Saile. **1772–84** COOK *Voy.* (1790) I. 151 It blew a storm from the east,..which compelled us to bring the ship to, under her mainsail. **1783** WOLCOT (P. Pindar) *Odes to R. A.'s* vii. Wks. 1812 I. 65 Broad as the Mainsail of a man of war. **1794** *Rigging & Seamanship* II. 319 Raise tacks and sheets, and main sail haul. **1835** SIR J. ROSS *Narr. 2nd Voy.* iii. 33 The close-reefed mainsail. **1873** BLACK *Pr. Thule* (1874) 5 There was just enough wind to catch the brown mainsail.

attrib. **1549** *Compl. Scotl.* vi. 40 Hail out the mane sail boulene.

fig. **1579** FULKE *Heskins' Parl.* 29 He inueyeth with mayn sayle of open rayling against the people.

mainschot, Sc. variant of MANCHET.

main sea. *arch.* [See MAIN *a.* 4. Cf. ON. *megensió-r.*] The high sea; = MAIN *sb.*¹ 5.

1526 *Pilgr. Perf.* (W. de W. 1531) 181 b, No more..than a particular ryuer is to be compared to yᵉ mayne see. **1573** TUSSER *Husb.* (1878) 30 At change or at full, come it late or else soone, Maine sea is at highest, at midnight and noone. **1617** MORYSON *Itin.* I. 212 In the maine Sea, greater Dolphins, and in greater number, did play about our ship. **1623** COCKERAM, *Ocean*, the vniuersall maine Sea. **1695** WOODWARD *Nat. Hist. Earth* 27 The *Pelagiæ*, or those kinds of Shells which naturally have their abode at mainsea, and which therefore are now never flung up upon the Shores. **1709** STEELE *Tatler* No. 12 ⁋22 The starving Wolves along the main Sea prowl. **1876** SWINBURNE *Erechtheus* 1699 Who shall meet The wind's whole soul and might of the main sea Full in the face of battle.

fig. **1570–6** LAMBARDE *Peramb. Kent* 236 The maine Seas of sinne and iniquitie, wherein the worlde..was almost whole [*sic*] drenched. **1575–85** ABP. SANDYS *Serm.* xviii. 211 Through the middest of sundrie maine seas of troubles and afflictions.

main-sheet, 'mainsheet. *Naut.*

1. The rope which secures the mainsail when set.

1485 *Naval Acc. Hen. VII* (1896) 48 Mayne shetes. *a* **1637** B. JONSON *Discov.*, *De orationis dign.*, The main-sheet and the boulin. **1694** *Acc. Sev. Late Voy.* I. (1711) 163 We.. veered out the main-Sheet to ware the Ship. **1762** FALCONER *Shipwr.* II. 27 Let the main-sheet fly! **1862** MARSH *Eng. Lang.* xi. 164 A sailor will not be likely to interlard his go-ashore talk with clew-lines, main-sheets, and halliards.

fig. *a* **1575** GASCOIGNE *Dan Bartholomew* Posies *Flowers* 80 Yet hauld I in the mayne-sheate of the minde.

b. *attrib.*, as ***main-sheet-block***, ***-horse***.

1867 SMYTH *Sailor's Word-bk.*, *Mainsheet-horse*, a kind of iron dog fixed at the middle of a wooden beam, stretching across a craft's stern, from one quarter stanchion to the other; on it the mainsheet-block travels.

2. *Jamaica slang.* (See first quot.)

1882 *Pall Mall G.* 20 May 4/2 Main-sheet is weak rum-and-water..and it seems to derive its quaintly expressive name from the native habit of taking constant pulls at it all day long. **1890** *Blackw. Mag.* June 784 An old man invited to have a drink of mainsheet.

mainspring ('meɪnsprɪŋ). [MAIN *a.* 8 b.]

1. A principal spring in a piece of mechanism.

a. In a gun-lock, the spring which drives the hammer. (Also *fig.*)

a **1616** BEAUM. & FL. *Custom of Country* III. iii, Hee's foule i'th touch-hole; and recoiles againe, The main spring's weakned that holds up his cock. **1824** COL. HAWKER *Instr. Yng. Sportsm.* (ed. 3) 42 The mainspring to be well regulated should at first pull up very hard. **1828** SCOTT *F.M. Perth* vi, How now, Smith, is thy mainspring rusted?

b. The principal coiled spring of a watch, clock, or other piece of mechanism.

1591 SYLVESTER *Du Bartas* I. vii. 162 God's the main spring, that maketh every way All the small wheels of this great Engin play. **1763** T. MUDGE *Th. Improv. Watches* (1799) 12 The wheel that communicates the force of the main-spring to the balance. **1830** KATER & LARDNER *Mech.* xiv. 195 In watches and portable chronometers,..a spiral spring, called the mainspring, is the moving power. **1869** NOAD *Electricity* 381 Levers are released, and the machinery of the telegraph worked by mainsprings, are [*sic*] left free to rotate.

2. *fig.* The chief motive power; the main incentive.

c **1695** J. MILLER *Descr. New York* (1843) 30 It being proposed that the bishop himself who shall be sent over be the main-spring and mover in this work. **1799** NELSON 21 Apr. in Nicolas *Disp.* (1846) VII. p. clxxx, I am here the mainspring which keeps all things in proper train. **1823** BYRON *Juan* IX. lxxiii, Some heathenish philosophers Make love the main-spring of the universe. **1850** MERIVALE *Rom. Emp.* (1865) I. i. 23 The cupidity which animated individuals was..the mainspring of the political factions of the time. **1888** BURGON *12 Gd. Men* II. x. 287 Truth..was the very mainspring..which actuated everything he thought, or said, or did.

3. *attrib.*, as ***mainspring cramp*** (in a gun-lock), ***hook***, ***punch***, ***winder*** (in a watch).

1844 *Regul. & Ord. Army* 96 *note*, One Main-Spring Cramp. **1884** F. J. BRITTEN *Watch & Clockm.* 165 Main Spring Hook..Main Spring Punch..Main Spring Winder.

mainstay ('meɪnsteɪ). [See MAIN *a.* 8, 10.]

1. *Naut.* The stay which extends from the main-top to the foot of the foremast.

1485 *Naval Acc. Hen. VII* (1896) 37 Cablettes for the mayne stay. **1626** CAPT. SMITH *Accid. Yng. Seamen* 14 The tacklings are the fore stay, the maine stay. **1709** *Lond. Gaz.* No. 4521/2 Having..our Shrouds and Back-stays cut to pieces; as also our Main and False-stay.

b. *attrib.*: **mainstaysail**, a storm-sail set on the mainstay.

1742 WOODROOFE in *Hanway's Trav.* (1762) I. II. xxiii. 100 We furled the foresail, and lay to under a mainstaysail. **1867** SMYTH *Sailor's Word-bk.*, *Main-staysail.*

2. Chief support; that on which one mainly relies.

1787 JEFFERSON *Writ.* (1859) II. 163 The points of contact and connection with this country, which I consider as our surest mainstay under every event. **1839–40** W. IRVING *Wolfert's R.* (1855) 207 This maxim, which has been pretty much my mainstay throughout life. **1861** HUGHES *Tom Brown at Oxf.* iv. (1889) 30 The host..was one of the main-stays of the College boat-club. **1865** TYLOR *Early Hist. Man.* vii. 150 Direct record is the mainstay of History. **1867** FREEMAN *Norm. Conq.* (1876) I. vi. 458 The Norman Duke was the mainstay of the French kingdom.

main stem. [MAIN *a.* 8 b.] The principal stem; also *transf.* and *fig.* in various (chiefly *U.S. slang*) senses, as a main street, main line of a railway, pre-eminent person, etc.

1832 *Amer. Railroad Jrnl.* I. 804/2 The western fork.. connects it with the main stem. **1900** ADE *Fables in Slang* iv. 24 To grow up and be the Main Stem, like Mr. Jeffries. **1900** 'FLYNT' & WALTON *Powers that Prey* x. 250 Investigations that have been begun in 'the main stem'. **1907** J. LONDON *Road* (1914) vii. 218 The kids began 'battering' the 'main-stem'. **1923** D. H. LAWRENCE *Birds, Beasts & Flowers* 42 Each single twig, Each one setting off straight to the sky As if it were the leader, the main-stem, the fore-runner. **1928** [see FOLD *v.*¹ 5]. **1931** [see DRAG *sb.* 3 e]. **1941** J. SMILEY *Hash House Lingo* 36 *Main stem*, principal street of a city. **1945** E. T. WALLACE *Barington* 62 The hog bounced us around and finally got back on the main stem. **1959** *Times Lit. Suppl.* 6 Nov. p. xxii/1 London audiences were listening to a play called *Broadway*..typical of drama at that time in and around the Main Stem.

main stream. Also **mainstream**, **main-stream**. [MAIN *a.* 8 b.] The principal stream or current (of a river, etc.). Also *transf.* and *fig.*, the prevailing direction of opinion, fashion, society, etc.; *spec.* of jazz: see quot. 1960². Also *attrib.* Hence **'mainstreamer**, a musician, etc., who is in the 'main stream' of his profession.

1667 MILTON *P.L.* IV. 233 The neather Flood,..now divided into four main Streames. **1831** CARLYLE in *Foreign Q. Rev.* VIII. 355 But after Luther's day, the Didactic Tendency again sinks to a lower level; mingles with manifold other tendencies; among which, admitting that it still forms the main stream, it is no longer so pre-eminent, positive, and universal, as properly to characterize the whole. **1865** M. ARNOLD *Ess. in Crit.* 171 Byron and Shelley

will be long remembered..for their..Titanic effort to flow in the main stream of modern literature. **1938** F. M. Ford *Let.* Oct. (1965) 302 The very considerable influence that Mr. Pound..exercised on literary mainstreams. **1952** *New World Writing* Apr. 33 Negro artists, in moving out into the mainstream of American culture, should gain a sense of solidarity with both the national and the general world of art. **1957** S. Dance in S. Traill *Concerning Jazz* 55 Mainstream jazz, typified by musicians like Basie, Ellington..Armstrong. **1957** *Jazz News* Apr. 2/3 Rising like a Pheonix [*sic*] from the dying embers of the British modern jazz world is a musical form that has been tagged 'Mainstream'. **1958** 'E. Crispin' *Best SF Three* 9 Mainstream fiction..has been almost uniformly catatonic in its withdrawal from environment. **1960** W. Naylor *Silver Birch Anthol.* 7 Ask him a question on a comparatively minor issue and time and time again he will use it as a tributary through which to return to the mainstream of his philosophy. **1960** *Sunday Times* 11 Sept. 37/1 Very broadly you can break up jazz asymmetrically into the big, simple, driving noise of the traditionalists and the smaller, sophisticated, elegiac sound of modern jazz. In between, there is a discernible third group of 'mainstream' enthusiasts. **1961** *New Left Rev.* July–Aug. 42/2 Humph is authentic mainstreamer: he's been influenced by everything in jazz up to the moment. **1966** R. Ellison in A. Chapman *New Black Voices* (1972) 407 The main stream of American literature is in me, even though I am a Negro, because I possess more of Mark Twain than many white writers do. **1969** *Listener* 26 June 904/3 Gesualdo..belongs less to the mainstream of music than to one of its smaller and more wayward canals. **1973** C. Bonington *Next Horizon* xxii. 297 A climber who had always been on the outside of the mainstream British climbing scene. **1974** *Listener* 10 Jan. 54/2 Dick Taverne..possesses a rigid habit of mind, so far quite alien to mainstream British politics.

Main Street, main street. [MAIN *a.* 8 b.]

a. The principal street of a town, esp. in the U.S.; freq. used as a proper name.

In quots. 1598–1743 preceded by an article and not a special collocation.

[**1598** Florio *Worlde of Wordes* 327/2 *Rióne*, a maine streete, a high way. **1687** S. Sewall *Diary* (1878) I. 183 At night a great Uproar and Lewd rout in the Main Street. **1698** *Rec. East Hampton, N.Y.* (1887) II. 434 Ten Acres of Land..[bound] on the west with the Maine Street of the said Town. **1717** in *Narragansett Hist. Reg.* (1884–5) III. 279 In or through the Main street, called Hope street, in this town [*sc.* Bristol, R.I.]. **1741–3** Wesley *Extract of Jrnl.* (1749) 117 They made no more stop 'till they had carried me thro' the main-street, from one end of the town to the other.] **1810** F. Cuming *Sk. Tour Western Country* 194 Main street, parallel to Water street, is one hundred feet wide. **1817** S. Brown *Western Gazetteer* 92 Main street presents to the traveller as much wealth, and more beauty than can be found in most of the Atlantic cities. **1855** *Knickerbocker* XLVI. 328 Louisville is an imposing, wealthy city. Main-street, in its entire extent would do honor to any metropolis in America. **1888** 'R. Boldrewood' *Robbery under Arms* II. iii. 54 Go on down Main Street (the first street in a diggings is always called Main Street). **1889** W. D. Howells *Hazard of New Fortunes* I. I. xi. 106 You know the kind of street Main Street always used to be in our section—half plank-road..and the rest mud-hole. **1892** Kipling *Lett. of Travel* (1920) 8 Every..thing, is reported, digested, discussed, and rediscussed up and down Main Street [in Vermont]. **1961** L. Mumford *City in Hist.* iii. 74 It was rather a Broad Ways ..it served as the classic 'Main Street'. **1968** *Michelin Guide N.Y. City* 78 Before the Revolution..Greenwich Street, which then bordered the Hudson and its warehouses, was 'Main Street'. *Ibid.* 82 Mulberry Street is the Italian 'Main Street': colorful shops offer national specialities. **1973** A. Broinowski *Take One Ambassador* vii. 86 You should see this station in rush hour. It's like Main Street Christmas Eve.

b. Used allusively, esp. since the publication in 1920 of Sinclair Lewis's novel *Main Street*, as a symbol of mediocrity, parochialism, or materialism in small-town life. Also *attrib.*

[**1855** *N.Y. Tribune* 31 Dec. 4/4 It has risen to its present position of bloated arrogance and swaggering insolence by the liberal and unstinting patronage it has received from the full purses and free hands of Eastern men in Main street and elsewhere.] **1916** 'B. M. Bower' *Phantom Herd* i. 5 You'll have to let me weed out some of these Main Street cowboys. **1920** S. Lewis (*title*) Main Street. **1931** *Times Lit. Suppl.* 9 Apr. 282/3 He dislikes uniformity, mass-control, Main-street and Rotarian ideals. **1948** *Time* 6 Dec. 20/3 Harry Truman has never lost his great respect for Marshall, nor is he unmindful of the prestige and authority Marshall carries on Main Street as well as in Moscow. **1972** B. Garfield *Line of Succession* (1974) 11. 126 The President..was an amalgam of liberal traditions..and the values of Main Street. **1973** T. H. White *Making of President 1972* (1974) ix. 231 From faculty club to student union, from bar to parlor, from Wall Street to Main Street, all wanted out of Vietnam.

Hence **Main Streeter, 'Mainstreeter**, a typical inhabitant of a small American town; one who shares the values of Main Street (sense b). Also **main-street** (*N. Amer.*) *v. intr.*, to campaign in main streets during an electoral campaign; hence **main-streeting** *vbl. sb.*

1934 Webster, Main Streeter. **1945** *Sat. Rev.* (U.S.) 6 Oct. 8/2 His books started some Americans laughing at others and made it possible for people to realize that somebody else was a Main Streeter. **1947** *Time* 27 Jan. 4/3 It has raised the hope of this Mainstreeter from Podunk to its highest ebb since the era of Wendell Willkie's 'One World'. **1966** *Maclean's Mag.* 1 Jan. 31 Though she [*sc.* Olive Diefenbaker] refuses to speak in public she mainstreets better than The Chief [*sc.* John Diefenbaker]. **1967** *Canad. Ann. Rev. 1966* 133 Duff Roblin, whose rural main-streeting, recorded bagpipe accompaniment, and unflagging oratory had won him his fourth personal victory in a row. **1971** *Time* 14 June 20 Boston has witnessed a merry binge of mainstreeting, leafletting and parties with some of the excitement of a mayoral election. **1974** *Globe & Mail* (Toronto) 5 June 8/3 New Democratic Party Leader David Lewis traded polemics with Parti Quebecois supporters in Montreal's working-class St. Jacques district yesterday before doing some mainstreeting not far from the area where he lived as a young immigrant half a century ago.

†**mainstrong**, *a. Obs.* [OE. *mæȝenstrang*: see MAIN *sb.*[1] and STRONG *a.*] Strong in power.

a **1000** *Riddles* lxxxvii. 3 (Gr.) þeȝn folȝade mæȝenstrong & mundrof. *c* **1205** Lay. 27731 þeos weoren on moncunne eorles main stronge.

mainswear, obs. form of MANSWEAR.

maint (meɪnt), *a. rare. (pseudo-arch.)* [a. F. *maint.*] Many, numerous.

1706 Phillips (ed. Kersey), *Maint*,..an old Word for many, several. **1801** Moore *Ring* 170 Now Austin was a reverend man, Who acted wonders maint. **1866** J. B. Rose *Ecl. & Georg. Virg.* 79 View the wide world and races maint of man. —— tr. *Ovid's Met.* 77 Ah me, ah me, there's maint an honest dame, Brought by fictitious Joves to grief and shame.

†**maintain**, *sb. Obs.* In 5 maynten(e, -teyn(e, -teygne, -tyen(e, -tiene, 6 maintene, -taine. [f. next vb., after F. *maintien.*]

1. Bearing, deportment, behaviour.

1470–85 Malory *Arthur* v. ii. 163 He..holdeth the most noble courte of the world, alle other kynges ne prynces maye not compare vnto his noble mayntene. **1471** Caxton *Recuyell* (ed. Sommer) 124 He had not the maynteygne of a yoman or of a seruaunt. *Ibid.* 130 [She] began to wexe reed and to lese her mayntyene and contenance whan she sawe hym. **1481** —— *Myrr.* III. x. 153 Atte longe, Nature may not suffre dyuerse mayntenes vnresonable. *c* **1500** *Melusine* 202 The king recomforted his peuple by his wo[r]þy contenaunce & valyaunt maynten. **1578** *Proctor's Gorg. Gallery* N iv, Joy were to here their prety wordes, and sweet mamtam [? *read* maintain] to see, And how all day they passe the time, til darknes dimmes the skye.

2. Maintenance, support.

1483 in Rymer *Foedera* XII. (1711) 174/1 To the upholde, maynteyne and encrease of their both Estatis against alle Persones. **1599** Porter *Angry Wom. Abingt.* (Percy Soc.) 16 The mettell of our minds, Having the temper of true reason in them, Affoordes a better edge of argument For the maintaine of our familiar loues Then the soft leaden wit of women can.

maintain (meɪnˈteɪn, mənˈteɪn), *v.* Forms: 3–6 mainten(e, maynten(e, 4–5 maynetene, 4–6 mein-, meyntene, 4–5 meynetene, 4–6 mantene, 6 *Sc.* manteane, 4–5 mentene, -teene; 3–7 main-, mayntein(e, -teyn(e, 5–6 mainteigne, 4–6 mein-, meyntein(e, -teyn(e, 4–5 meyneteyne, 3–6 mantein(e, -teyn(e, 6 manteigne, 4–6 menteyn(e, -teine; 4–5 mayntyn(e, maintiene, meintiene, 6–7 *Sc.* mantine; 4–6 *Sc.* man-, mayneme, -teym(e; 5 mayntan; 5–7 main-, mayntayn(e, -taine, 6 man-, mainetayne, 4–6 mentayne, 8 *Sc.* mentain, 6 maintain. [ME. *maintene, -teine*, a. F. *maintenir* (OF. 3 sing. pres. ind. *-tient, -tent*, subj. *-teigne, -tiegne*), = Pr. *mantener, mentener*, Sp. *mantener*, Pg. *manter*, It. *mantenere*:—L. phrase *manū tenēre*, lit. 'to hold in one's hand' (*manū* abl. of *manus* hand; *tenēre* to hold). Cf. Du. *mainteneeren* (from Fr.).]

†**1.** *trans.* To practise habitually (an action, a virtue or vice); to observe (a rule, custom). *Obs.*

a **1250** *Owl & Night.* (Cotton) 759 Ich kan wit and song manteine [*Jesus MS. reads* mony eine] Ne triste ich to non oþer maine. **1303** R. Brunne *Handl. Synne* 6558 þou art vnbuxum, And mainteynest an euyl custum. *a* **1340** Hampole *Psalter* xxvii. 5 þa sall þai be punyst þat first fyndes þaim, and all þat oyses þaim & mayntens þaim [*sc.* ill deeds]. *c* **1375** *Cursor M.* 2454 (Fairf.) þa folk ware fulle of misdede and maynteined wrang and wikkedhede. *c* **1400** *Destr. Troy* 2049 How þai maintene þere malis with manas & pride. **1550** Crowley *Last Trumpet* 1287 Thou wilt.. mayntayne outragiouse playe, Tyl thou haue spent both lande and fee. **1611** Bible *Titus* iii. 14 And let ours also learne to maintaine good workes [Gr. καλῶν ἔργων προΐστασθαι] for necessarie vses, that they be not vnfruitfull.

2. † **a.** *gen.* To go on with, continue, persevere in (an undertaking). Also *occas.* to go on with the use of (something). *Obs.*

1375 Barbour *Bruce* II. 189 Frendis, and frendschip purchesand, To maynteym that he had begunnyn. *c* **1386** Chaucer *Knt.'s T.* 920 A proud despitous man That wol maynteyne that he first bigan. **1526** *Pilgr. Perf.* (W. de W. 1531) 14 Lest they sholde waxe feble afterwarde, and so to be not able to mayntayne theyr iourney. **1545** Ascham *Toxoph.* To Gentlem. Eng. (Arb.) 19 Some shooters take in hande stronger bowes, than they be able to mayntayne.

b. To carry on, keep up, prosecute (a war, fight, siege, contest).

c **1350** *Will. Palerne* 3002 How here walles were broke ..þat þei mi3t no more meintene þe sege. **1375** Barbour *Bruce* x. 184 Quhill at thar rout,..Cum for to maynteme the melle. *Ibid.* XIII. 280 Thai that wicht war and hardy,..At gret myschef mantemyt the ficht. *a* **1400** *R. Brunne's Chron. Wace* (Rolls) 5464 Y schal vndertake [*Petyt MS.* sall maynten forþe] þys were. *c* **1400** *Rom. Rose* 3550, I pray you ..For to mayntene no lenger here, Such cruel werre agayn your man. **1560** Daus tr. *Sleidane's Comm.* 137 Than had Charles Duke of Savoye, a certen space maynteyned warre against the Citie of Geneva. **1665** Manley *Grotius' Low C. Warres* 277 To..raise a Siege which is so strongly setled and maintained. **1697** Dryden *Virg. Georg.* IV. 128 Long the doubtful Combat they maintain, 'Till one prevails (for one can only Reign). **1828** Scott *F.M. Perth* xxix, It is false.. I..will maintain the combat with him that shall call it true.

c. To carry on (an action at law); to have ground for sustaining (an action).

1463–4 *Rolls of Parlt.* V. 506/2 To haue and maynten Action or Actions of Dette. **1512** *Act 3 Hen. VIII*, c. 1 §4 Any maner of accion..to be..mayntened ayenst any of the Kingis Subgiettes. **1620** J. Wilkinson *Coroners & Sherifes* 67 No sherife shall suffer a Barreter to maintaine any actions or quarrels in their countie courts. **1818** Cruise *Digest* (ed. 2) II. 417 This Court granted an injunction against him, though no action whatsoever could be maintained at law. **1892** *Law Times Rep.* LXVII. 142/1 In order to maintain an action of deceit there must be moral delinquency on the part of the person proceeded against.

d. To continue in, preserve, retain (a physical or mental condition, a position, attitude, etc.), in spite of disturbing influences.

1837 Disraeli *Venetia* I. x, Lady Annabel for some time maintained complete silence. **1856** Froude *Hist. Eng.* (1858) I. i. 10 The old English organization maintained its full activity. **1869** Freeman *Norm. Conq.* (1876) III. xi. 3 The English writers maintain a sort of sullen silence. **1879** R. K. Douglas *Confucianism* iii. 72 The Sage..maintains a perfect uprightness and pursues the heavenly way without the slightest deflection. **1898** [G. W. E. Russell] *Coll. & Recoll.* x. 131 Amidst all this hurly burly Pitt maintained a stately..reserve.

e. To keep up (friendly relations, correspondence).

1622 Bacon *Hen. VII* 240 When they [*sc.* ambassadors] were returned, they did commonly maintaine Intelligence with him. **1706** Hearne *Collect.* 2 Apr. (O.H.S.) I. 215 He is..much addicted to maintain Correspondence. **1718** *Freethinker* No. 79 ¶5 A brotherly Correspondence was maintained with all the Foreign Protestant Churches.

†**3.** To keep a stock of. *Obs. rare*⁻¹. [A frequent sense in OFr.]

c **1483** Caxton *Dialogues* 6/29 Who wyne wyll mayntene Behoueth to haue selers And a lowe chambre.

4. a. To keep up, preserve, cause to continue in being (a state of things, a condition or activity, etc.); to keep vigorous, effective, or unimpaired; to guard from loss or derogation.

c **1330** R. Brunne *Chron.* (1810) 60 Eldolf, bisshop of Bath, þe pes mayntend & helde. *c* **1350** *Will. Palerne* 2676 Meyntenes 3it 3oure manchip manli a while. **1375** Barbour *Bruce* xx. 605 The law sa weill mantemyt he, And held in pess swa the cuntre. *c* **1440** *York Myst.* xvii. 310, I rede we reste a thrawe, For to maynteyne our myght. *a* **1535** More *Edw. V.* (1641) 29 He..had holpe to maintaine a long continued grudge. **1581** Mulcaster *Positions* vi. (1887) 42 How health is maintained, and disease auoided. **1651** Hobbes *Leviath.* II. xxx. 175 It is the Office of the Soveraign, to maintain those Rights entire. **1675** H. Nevile tr. *Machiavelli's Prince* iii. (1883) 16 Maintaining to them their old condition. **1742** Hume *Ess.* I. v. (1777) I. 35 All men are sensible of the necessity of justice to maintain peace and order. **1855** Bain *Senses & Int.* II. i. §6 (1864) 77 Nervous influence is required for maintaining the breathing action. **1855** Macaulay *Hist. Eng.* xi. III. 43 All that was necessary for the purpose of maintaining military discipline. **1875** Jowett *Plato* (ed. 2) I. 28 As he had a reputation to maintain.

b. With concrete obj.: To preserve in existence.

1659 Pearson *Creed* (1839) 220 We are still preserved by his power, and as he made us, so doth he maintain us. **1715** De Foe *Fam. Instruct.* I. i. (1841) I. 17 And the same power preserves and maintains all things.

5. a. To cause to continue in a specified state, relation, or position, †to secure the continuance of (a possession) *to* a person (*obs.*); to secure (a person) *in* continued possession of property.

1300–1400 *R. Gloucester's Chron.* (Rolls) App. XX. 70 þe amperesse..made him oþ swere To meinteini engelond to hure. *c* **1380** Wyclif *Wks.* (1880) 24 To procure, norische, & meyntene cristen soulis in good gouernaile and holy lif. **1800** Addison *Amer. Law Rep.* 274 Young contended that McCulloch..ought to be maintained in possession of the land. **1874** Carpenter *Ment. Phys.* I. ii. §68 (1879) 71 The limb was maintained in this state of tension for several seconds. **1879** *Cassell's Techn. Educ.* IV. 72/2 That the tools shall be maintained in proper position upon the rest.

b. *Comm.* To keep (stock) from decline in price.

1881 *Daily News* 8 July 6/1 American railroads are not quite maintained. **1892** *Daily Tel.* 5 Sept. 4/6 Consols rose ⅛ per cent. and English railways were maintained.

†**6.** To keep in good order, to rule, sway (a people, country); to preserve *in* (a state of peace, etc.). *Obs.*

c **1375** *Lay Folks Mass Bk.* (MS. B.) 365 þat þai be wele mayntenande hore states in alle godnesse, and reule þo folk in rightwisnesse. **1375** Barbour *Bruce* XIII. 709 God grant that thai..maynteyme the land, And hald the folk weill to warrand. *Ibid.* XVI. 34 Vardanis in [his] absens maid he, For till manteym weill the cuntre. *a* **1533** Ld. Berners *Huon* lxvi. 228, I haue..maynteyned the countre in peace & rest and good iustyce. **1535** Coverdale *Ecclus.* xxxviii. 32 Without these maye not the cities be manteyned, inhabited ner occupied. **1602** S. Patericke (*title*) A Discovrse vpon the meanes of wel governing and maintaining in good peace, a Kingdome, or other Principalitie.

†**7.** *refl.* **a.** To bear or conduct oneself (in a specified manner). *Obs.*

1375 Barbour *Bruce* II. 486 Bot always, as A man off mayn, He mayntemyt him full manlyly. *c* **1400** Maundev. (1839) xiv. 155 Thei gon often tyme in sowd, to help of other Kynges, in here Werres..: and thei meyntenen hem self right vygourously. **1481** Caxton *Godfrey* lxxvi. *heading*, How Tancre mayntenyd hym moche wel in conqueryng contrees. **1530** Palsgr. 617/1 You shall se me mayntayne my selfe so honestly that you shall prayse me.

†**b.** To continue *in* an action or state; to keep oneself resolutely in a specified state (indicated by adj. complement). *Obs.*

1481 CAXTON *Godfrey* clxxviii. 262 They shold alle goo vnto the mount of Olyuet, And they shold mayntene them this day in fastyng. **1597** BACON *Ess., Faction* (Arb.) 76 Great men that haue strength in themselues were better to maintaine themselues indifferent and neutrall.

8. a. To support (one's state in life) by expenditure, etc. **b.** To sustain (life) by nourishment.

1375 BARBOUR *Bruce* x. 779 The king,..to manteym his stat, him gaff Rentis and landis fair eneuch. *c* **1386** CHAUCER *Knt.'s T.* 583 Of his chambre he made hym a Squier And gaf him gold to mayntene his degree. **1495** *Act 11 Hen. VII*, c. 39 He hath not yerely revenues to maynteyn honorably and convenyently the astate of a Duke. **1584** COGAN *Haven Health* iii. (1636) 23 Nature hath taught all living creatures to seeke by sustenance to maintaine their lives. **1592** *Nobody & Someb.* in Simpson *Sch. Shaks.* I. 289 Nobody takes them in, provides them harbor, Maintaines their ruind fortunes at his charge. **1593** SHAKS. *2 Hen. VI*, VI. x. 24 Sufficeth, that I haue maintaines my state. **1614** EARL STIRLING *Doomes-day* VIII. xii. (1637) 169 Whil'st old (and poore perchance) with toyle and strife, Glad (by his labour) to maintaine his life. **1647–8** COTTERELL *Davila's Hist. Fr.* (1678) 11 Finding the narrowness of his fortune could not maintain the greatness of his Birth. **1856** FROUDE *Hist. Eng.* (1858) I. i. 52 The first condition of a worthy life was the ability to maintain it in independence. **1856** SIR B. BRODIE *Psychol. Inq.* I. v. 187 Food is required because life cannot be maintained without it.

†**c.** To bear the expense of, afford. *Obs.*

? *a* **1366** CHAUCER *Rom. Rose* 1144 And Richesse mighte it wel sustene And hir dispenses wel mayntene. **1596** SHAKS. *Tam. Shr.* v. i. 79 What cernes it you, if I weare Pearle and gold: I thank my good Father, I am able to maintaine it. **1605** *Lond. Prodigal* I. i, But honesty maintains not a French hood, Goes very seldom in a chain of gold.

9. a. To provide with livelihood; to furnish with means of subsistence or necessaries of life; to bear the expenses of (a person) for living, education, etc. Also, †to keep (a person) *in* (clothing).

a **1400** *Cursor M.* 28961 (Cott. Galba) For ay þe more man is of elde, þe more men aw..for to do him almus dede and mayntene him for sawl mede. **1487** *Dietary* 60 in *Barbour's Bruce*, etc. (1870) 539 Eftir thi power maynteme ay thi houshald. **1546** *Supplic. Poore Commons* (E.E.T.S.) 80 Suche possessioners as..vsed to maintain their owne chyldren, and some of ours, to lernyng. **1582** N. LICHEFIELD tr. *Castanheda's Conq. E. Ind.* I. ii. 6 These people doe mainteine themselues with rootes of hearbes,..and whale fish. **1676** LADY CHAWORTH in *12th Rep. Hist. MSS. Comm.* App. v. 31 [It] frights Sir Carr Scrope..from marying her, saying his estate will scarce maintaine her in clothes. **1709** *Tatler* No. 101 ¶1, 150*l.* per Annum, which would very handsomely maintain me and my little family. **1749** FIELDING *Tom Jones* XVIII. vii, I believe you bred the young man up, and maintained him at the university. **1770** GOLDSM. *Des. Vill.* 58 A time there was, ere England's griefs began, When every rood of ground maintained its man. **1816** SCOTT *Antiq.* xxvi, I maun hae a man that can mainteen his wife. **1838** JAMES *Robber* vii, Sufficient to maintain me in comfort and independence as a gentleman.

†**b.** To provide for the 'keep' of (an animal).

1576 FLEMING tr. *Caius' Dogs* iv. (1880) 28 And therfore were certain dogges founde and maintained at the common costes and charges of the Citizens of Rome in the place called *Capitolium*. **1672** PETTY *Pol. Anat.* (1691) 53 An Ox of 6 or 7 years old..will be maintained with two Acres of good Pasture.

c. To give a drug to (an individual, esp. a drug addict) in maintenance doses so as to sustain a particular therapeutic effect. Cf. MAINTENANCE 7c.

1957 *Jrnl. Amer. Med. Assoc.* 14 Dec. 1970/1 The current discussion..can be reduced to the desirability and feasibility of treating the addict as a total person,.. withdrawing drugs.., or of maintaining him on an appropriate amount of drugs if it is determined he cannot be successfully cured of his addiction. **1971** *Nature* 22 Oct. 558/2 The recipient dogs were anaesthetized with intravenous thiopentone and maintained with halothane, nitrous oxide and oxygen through an endotracheal tube. **1972** *Science* 26 May 881/1 In April 1971, a program was inaugurated to maintain at least 20,000 addicts on methadone in New York State alone.

10. a. To pay for the keeping up of, bear the expense of; to keep supplied or equipped (e.g. a ship, a garrison); to keep (a light) burning by supply of fuel; to keep (a road, building) in repair.

1389 in *Eng. Gilds* (1870) 27 þis light þey hoten & a-vowed to kepyn & myntenyn [*sic*]. *Ibid.* 62 To meyteyn [*sic*] wit-al a lythe brennynge in ye chyrche of sent Jame. **1533–4** *Act 25 Hen. VIII*, c. 8 Euerie person..hauinge anie of the saide landes..shall..sufficiently meintein the pauement of the said waye. *a* **1578** LINDESAY (Pitscottie) *Chron. Scot.* (S.T.S.) I. 227 Witht tua schipis weill mantenitt and artaillzeit. **1600** J. PORY tr. *Leo's Africa* v. 237 Here is an hospitall maintained at the common charges of the towne, to entertaine strangers that passe by. **1611** BIBLE *1 Esdras* iv. 52 Tenne talents yeerely, to maintaine the burnt offerings vpon the Altar euery day. **1617** MORYSON *Itin.* I. 55 The States maintained some men of warre in this Inland Sea. *a* **1687** PETTY *Pol. Arith.* (1690) 77 The annual charge of maintaining the Shipping of England, by new Buildings and Preparations. **1707** J. CHAMBERLAYNE *St. Gt. Brit.* III. ix. 341 They..maintain Lectures upon the Holy Sacrament of the Lord's Supper, almost every Lord's Day Evening. **1725** DE FOE *Voy. round World* (1840) 280 Strong forts erected.. and strong garrisons maintained in them. **1846** J. BAXTER *Libr. Pract. Agric.* (ed. 4) II. 233 Stone, wood, and iron, are the materials principally employed in making and maintaining roads. **1861** M. PATTISON *Ess.* (1889) I. 48 The Germans..maintained in it [this church] an altar.

b. To furnish the means for conducting (a suit or action at law). Cf. 12d.

[*c* **1380**: see 11.] **1540** *Act 32 Hen. VIII*, c. 9 §3 That no maner of personne..doo herafter unlaufully maineteyne or cause or procure any unlaufull mayntenaunce in any action. **1769** BLACKSTONE *Comm.* IV. 134 A man may however maintain the suit of his near kinsman, servant, or poor neighbour, out of charity and compassion, with impunity. **1843** *Meeson & Welsby's Excheq. Rep.* (1844) XI. 676 The defendants resisted and maintained, supported, &c. such defences and resistance.

11. To back up, stand, give one's support to, defend, uphold (a cause, something established, one's side or interest, etc.).

c **1320** *Sir Beues* (A.) 4123 We redeþ meintene ȝour parti. *c* **1330** R. BRUNNE *Chron. Wace* (Rolls) 6528 þe Frensche.. rysen aȝeyn Conan to fight; Bot Conan meyntende wel his right. **1375** BARBOUR *Bruce* x. 289 He hyet honor and largess, And ay mantemyt richtwisnes. *c* **1380** WYCLIF *Sel. Wks.* III. 322 Alle þat taken and meyntenen false causes ben cursed grevously... Also lordis holdynge grete lovedaies, and bi here lordischip meyntenenge þe fals pert, for money frendischip or favour, fallen opynly in þis curs, and so don men of lawe, wiþ alle false witnesses þat meyntenen falsenesse aȝenst treuþe, wityngly or unwityngly. *c* **1420** LYDG. *Assembly of Gods* 747 Vertew dyd hys besy peyne Pepyll to reyse hys quarell to menteyne. *c* **1440** *York Myst.* xxxviii. 11, 13 þat we mayntayne and stand þerby þat werke all-way. *Cayph.* ȝis, sir, þat dede schall we mayntayne, By lawe it was done all be-dene. **1482** *Surtees Misc.* (1888) 40 Every trew Cristen man..is bunden forto supporte and maynteyn ye trewth. **1513** DOUGLAS *Æneis* XI. xii. 114 By hurtis feill for to manteym thar rycht. **1535** COVERDALE *Ps.* ix. 4 For thou hast manteyned my right and my cause. **1558** KNOX *First Blast* (Arb.) 8 Suche as oght to mainteine the truth and veritie of God. **1560** DAUS tr. *Sleidane's Comm.* 122 The true & holsome doctrine is..every where oppressed,..and open crymes mainteined. **1638** R. BAKER tr. *Balzac's Lett.* (vol. II.) 16 The cause I maintaine is the cause of my Prince and Country. **1667** MILTON *P.L.* VI. 30 Who single hast maintaind Against revolted multitudes the Cause Of Truth. **1678** BUTLER *Hud.* III. iii. 584 H' had.. us'd two equal ways of gaining: By hindring Justice, or maintaining. **1792** BURKE *Let. to Sir H. Langrishe* Wks. 1842 I. 548 First, the king swears he will maintain, to the utmost of his power, 'the laws of God'.

12. a. To uphold, back up, stand by, support the cause of (a person, party, etc.); to defend, protect, assist; to support or uphold *in* (an action). *arch.*

a **1300** *Cursor M.* 7374 His sede and his barntem Ouer al men i sal maintein. *c* **1330** R. BRUNNE *Chron. Wace* (Rolls) 16661 Cadwaladre bad Iuor his sone, & Iny his neuew, 'wende & wone In to Bretaigne, & meintene efte þo þat were of Bretons lefte'. **1340** HAMPOLE *Pr. Consc.* 1108 Or he sal þe tane of þam mayntene And þe tother despyse [Matt. vi. 24]. *c* **1350** *Will. Palerne* 2698 Sche..preyed ful pitousli to þe prince of heuene,..to mayntene hire & help, þat hire foos for no cas wiþ fors hire conquerede. *c* **1460** *Towneley Myst.* xxvi. 96 To mayntene vs euermore ye aw. **1470–85** MALORY *Arthur* xv. i, To mayntene his neuewe ageynst the myghty Erle. **1530** PALSGR. 438/2, I assyste, or stande by, or mayntayne a person in doynge of a dede. *a* **1553** UDALL *Royster D.* v. v. (Arb.) 84 We must to make vs mirth, maintaine hym all we can. **1576** FLEMING *Panopl. Epist.* 383 One frend to take another frendes part, to defend and maintaine him against backbiting. **1593** SHAKS. *2 Hen. VI*, I. i. 161 Iesu maintaine your Royall Excellence. *a* **1604** HANMER *Chron. Irel.* (1633) 31 His three sonnes..formerly went into Ireland to maintaine one of the factions. **1625** BACON *Ess., Friendship* (Arb.) 171 He..would often maintaine Plantianus, in doing Affronts to his Son. **1883** GARDINER *Hist. Eng.* II. xix. 328 In spite of all, James was still ready to maintain Somerset against his ill-willers in public, if he expostulated with him in private.

†**b.** In bad sense: To give support or countenance to evil-doers; to aid or abet *in* (wrong-doing); to back up *in* (error or wickedness). *Obs.*

1362 LANGL. *P. Pl.* A. III. 232 To meyntene misdoers meede thei taken. **1377** *Ibid.* B. III. 90 Of alle suche sellers syluer to take,..Ringes or other ricchesse, the regrateres to maynetene. *c* **1380** WYCLIF *Sel. Wks.* III. 323 Officeris þat meyntenen oþere men in synne. **1399** LANGL. *Rich. Redeles* III. 311 Thus is the lawe louyd thoru myȝhty lordis willys, That meyneteyne myssdoers more than other peple. *c* **1400** MAUNDEV. (Roxb.) xxxiv. 155 A fende..tellez þam many thinges,..for to mayntene þam in þaire mawmetry and þaire errour. *c* **1430** *Freemasonry* 255 To lere him so that for no mon No fals mantenans he take hym apon Ny maynteine hys felows yn here synne For no good that he myȝht wynne. **1528** NORTHUMBERLAND in *St. Papers Hen. VIII*, IV. 514 Also I can not perceyve that any redresse can be maid uppon the Borders, for the Kyng of Scottes doth maynteyn all the theves and rebelles of the same. **1552** LATIMER *Serm. Lincolnsh.* iii. (1562) 81 O crafty deuil: he went away, not for feare of the holy water, but because he would mayntaine men in errour and foolishnes.

†**c.** With *inf.*: To assist, encourage, incite (to do something, *esp.* something evil), to support or uphold (in doing it). *Obs.*

c **1325** *Poem times Edw. II* (Percy Soc.) xxxvii, He shal be maintend full wel To lede a sory life. **1362** LANGL. *P. Pl.* A. III. 145 Prouendreres, persuns, preostes heo meynteneth, To holde lemmons and lotebyes al heor lyf-dayes. *Ibid.* A. IV. 42 He meynteneth his men to morthere myn owne. **1393** *Ibid.* C. XVIII. 234 The pope..That with moneye menteyneth men to werren vp-on cristine. **1546** J. ALEN in *St. Papers Hen. VIII*, III. 577 The Justices nephew maynteyned the burgesses of the Newcastell, to take from me a parcell of pasture. **1626** *Scogin's Jests* in Hazl. *Shaks. Jest-bks.* (1864) 124 When the king's servants had espied him, they did maintaine their dogges to runne at Scogin.

d. *Law.* To give support to (a suitor) in an action in which one is not concerned. Cf. 10b; also MAINTENANCE 6.

1716 W. HAWKINS *Pleas Crown* I. 249 Of this second kind of Maintenance there seem to be three Species:..2. Where one maintains one Side, to have Part of the Thing in Suit, which is called Champerty. *Ibid.* 252 A Man may lawfully maintain those who are infeoffed of Lands in Trust for him in any Action concerning those Lands. **1836** *Bingham's New Cases Comm. Pleas* II. 650 The Defendant..has voluntarily and officiously undertaken to maintain the Plaintiff in a suit with which the Defendant has no connection. **1886** *Law Rep. 17 Q.B.D.* 504 The present action was brought by the plaintiff against the defendant to recover the 118*l.* on the ground that he had 'maintained' Nailer in the former action.

13. To hold, keep, defend (a place, position, possession) against hostility or attack, actual or threatened. Phr. ***to maintain one's ground*** (often *fig.*). Also *refl.* = to make a stand, defend one's position; similarly †***to maintain one's own.***

c **1350** *Will. Palerne* 3642 William say þer oþer side of fers & so breme, þat his men miȝt nouȝt meyntene here owne. *a* **1400–50** *Alexander* 1972 Miȝt þou þe marches so Messedoyne mayntene þi-selfe. **1513** DOUGLAS *Æneis* IV. v. 81 And now that secund Paris,..By reif mantemys hir suld ouris be. **1595** DANIEL *Civ. Wars* IV. xlvi. 75 b, Bedford who our onely hold maintaind. **1595** SHAKS. *John* III. iv. 136 A Scepter snatch'd with an vnruly hand Must be as boysterously maintain'd as gain'd. **1599** —— *Hen. V*, III. vi. 95 *Flu.* The Duke of Exeter ha's very gallantly maintain'd the Pridge. **1615** G. SANDYS *Trav.* 217 A fort maintained by a small garrison of Moores. **1624** FLETCHER *Rule a Wife* III. v. (1640) 37 *Leon...* I stand upon the ground of mine own honor, And will maintaine it. **1660** F. BROOKE tr. *Le Blanc's Trav.* 15 There are four avenues cut through the Mountain, easie to be maintained. **1736** BUTLER *Anal.* I. iii. Wks. 1874 I. 63 In this case then, brute force might more than maintain its ground against reason. **1748** GRAY *Alliance* 88 An Iron-race the mountain cliffs maintain. **1792** *Anecd. W. Pitt* I. xviii. 283 The King of Prussia, though surrounded by his numerous enemies, maintained himself with astonishing skill and valour. **1849** JAMES *Woodman* iv, She maintained her ground, although the Moor rode close up to her with his companions. **1853** J. H. NEWMAN *Hist. Sk.* (1873) II. I. iv. 178 Venice..by a system of jealous and odious tyranny,.. continued to maintain its ground. **1893** SIR L. GRIFFIN in *19th Cent.* Nov. 684 Our subsidies and open support have enabled Abdur Rahman Khan to maintain himself against his many enemies.

14. a. To support or uphold in speech or argument; to defend (an opinion, statement, tenet, etc.); to assert the truth of, contend to be true or right.

1340 HAMPOLE *Pr. Consc.* 3080 Yhit has men herd som clerkes maynte[ne] Swilk an opinion, als I wene, þat a saule [etc.]. *c* **1380** WYCLIF *Sel. Wks.* III. 323 Clerkis þat don evyl and meyntene it bi sotilte of word. *c* **1449** PECOCK *Repr.* I. i. 5 Alle the othere vntrewe opiniouns and holdingis..muste needis..lacke it wherbi thei miȝten in eny colour or semyng be mentened, holde, and supported. *c* **1450** *Pistill of Susan* (MS. I) 220 þies wordes þat we say, On þis womman verray, þat wil we mayntan for aye. **1512** *Act 4 Hen. VIII*, c. 19 *Preamble*, The seid Frensche Kyng..alway erronyously defendyng & mayntenynyng his seid obstynate opynyons agayne the unitye of the holye Churche. **1530** PALSGR. 617/1 And he ones saye a thyng, he wyll mayntayne it to dye for it. **1616** R. C. *Times' Whistle* v. 2120 What phisitian..would.. such a lye maintaine? **1651** HOBBES *Leviath.* II. xxx. 180 The doctrines maintained by so many Preachers. **1686** HORNECK *Crucif. Jesus* xi. 205 This point they do so stiffly, and so uncharitably maintain. **1772–84** COOK *Voy.* (1790) V. 1649 They also, in some degree, maintain our old doctrine of planetary influence. **1856** WHATELY *Bacon's Ess.* i. 10 It is not enough to believe what you maintain; you must maintain what you believe, and maintain it *because* you believe it.

b. With clause: To affirm, assert, or contend (*that*). With obj. and infin.: To assert (something) *to be* (etc.); †also in passive.

c **1380** WYCLIF *Wks.* (1880) 10 ȝif þei seyn and meyntenen in scole and oþere placis þat þe wordis of holy writt ben false. **1594** HOOKER *Eccl. Pol.* III. viii. §13 Because we maintaine that in scripture we are taught all things necessary vnto saluation. **1605** SHAKS. *Lear* I. ii. 77, I haue heard him oft maintaine it to be fit, that [etc.]. **1646** SIR T. BROWNE *Pseud. Ep.* III. xxiv. 169 Some [animals] there are in the Land which were never maintained to be in the Sea, as Panthers, Hyæna's [etc.]. **1652** NEEDHAM tr. *Selden's Mare Cl.* 203 It is mainteined by divers learned Men that these were the ruins of the same Tower. **1682** DRYDEN *Medal* 86 He.. Maintains the Multitude can never err. **1729** BUTLER *Serm.* Wks. 1874 II. Pref. 24 The Epicureans..maintained that absence of pain was the highest happiness. **1849** MACAULAY *Hist. Eng.* ii. I. 195 The country, he maintained, would never be well governed till [etc.]. **1875** JOWETT *Plato* (ed. 2) V. 222 Pleasure and pain I maintain to be the first perceptions of children.

†**15.** ? To hold upright. *Obs. rare*$^{-1}$.

1661 MORGAN *Sph. Gentry* III. vi. 61 Vert, a Flower-pot Argent maintaining Gilliflowers Gules.

†**16.** ? To stand for, represent. *Obs. rare*$^{-1}$.

1588 SHAKS. *L.L.L.* v. ii. 902 This side is *Hiems*, Winter, This *Ver*, the Spring: the one maintained by the Owle, Th' other by the Cuckow.

Hence **maintained** *ppl. a.* **maintained school** (see quots.).

1944 in *Parl. Papers 1943–4* (Cmd. 6523) (*title*) Principles of government in maintained secondary schools. **1960** *Where?* iii. 15/1 *Maintained school*, a school maintained by a local education authority, including county, voluntary aided, and voluntary controlled schools. **1966** *Rep. Comm. Inquiry Univ. Oxf.* I. 74 It is also likely that the swing to science has played some part in raising the rate of recruitment from maintained schools. **1973** *Guardian* 25 Apr. 15/4 The 12-man governing board of Sacred Heart (a Catholic maintained school).

maintainability (meɪn-, mənˌteɪnəˈbɪlɪtɪ). [f. MAINTAINABLE *a.*; see -BILITY.] The quality of being easily maintained; capability of being maintained.

1943 *Sci. Amer.* June 250 Engineering . . determines the serviceability and maintainability of new types of equipment. **1971** *New Scientist* 3 June 574/3 Every project should have goals for reliability . . and 'maintainability'. **1974** *Daily Colonist* (Victoria, B.C.) 9 Oct. 3/2 It demonstrates the maintainability of the Candu reactor system.

maintainable (meɪn-, mənˈteɪnəb(ə)l), *a.* Also 5 **mayntenable**, 6 **mayn-**, **mainteinable**, 7 **maintenable**. [f. MAINTAIN *v.* + -ABLE.]

1. That can be maintained, kept up, held, defended, etc.; *esp.* of an opinion, an action at law.

1439 *Rolls of Parlt.* V. 22/1 No action to be mayntenable ayenste the seid named Executours. **1541** *Act 33 Hen. VIII*, c. 21 §1 Wordes vttered by them . . not mainteinable in your lawes. **1559** in Strype *Ann. Ref.* (1824) I. II. App. viii. 427 No suite for any cause rysinge within the realme, maynteinable in any place out of the realm. **1586** A. DAY *Eng. Secretary* I. (1625) 88 A matter sinisterly suggested unto you against mee without any maintainable reason. **1602** FULBECKE *1st Pt. Parall.* 68 Your exception is good, and maintenable by our Law. **1648** tr. *Senault's Paraphr. Job* 338 Doe you thinke that your Propositions are maintaineable? **1680** *Lond. Gaz.* No. 1522/3 His Excellency called a Council of War, where it was judged, That the Out Forts were not maintainable. **1777** HAMILTON *Wks.* (1886) VII. 483 To effect this would require a chain of posts, and such a number of men at each as would never be practicable or maintainable, but to an immense army. **1826** SOUTHEY *Lett.* (1856) III. 527, I think he extends the inspiration of Scripture further than is maintainable. **1837** SIR N. C. TINDAL in *Bingham's New Cases* I. 99, I think this action is maintainable against the husband and wife jointly. **1873** M. ARNOLD *Lit. & Dogma* (1876) 350 It is a maintainable thesis that the allegorising of the Fathers is right.

†**2.** Affording a livelihood. *Obs. rare.*

1583 STUBBES *Anat. Abus.* II. (1882) 84 May a pastor . . (having a maintainable liuing allowed him of his flock) preach in other places for monie? *Ibid.* 88.

Hence **main'tainableness**.

1727 in BAILEY vol. II. **1865** *Pall Mall G.* 11 Nov. 6 The point in favour of the maintainableness of the action . . had been argued by two able counsel.

maintainer (meɪn-, mənˈteɪnə(r)). Forms: 4–5 **mayn-**, **meyntenour(e**, 4–6 **-tener**, 5 **-tenowre**, **-tenor**, **-tynour**, **-teynour**, 6 **maintener**, **-tenour**, **main-**, **mayntayner**, **-teinour**, **-teiner**, **-teyner**, *Sc.* **main-**, **man-**, **menteiner**, **-teinar**, **-tenar**, **-teaner**, 7 *Sc.* **mainteener**, 9 (*Law*) **maintainor**, 6– **maintainer**. [ME. *mayntenour*, a. AF. *mayntenour*, OF. *maintenëor*, agent-n. f. *maintenir* MAINTAIN *v.*; the mod. word is a new formation on MAINTAIN *v.* + -ER[1].]

1. One who upholds, defends, guards, keeps in being, preserves unharmed (a cause, right, state of things, etc.).

c **1420** LYDG. *Assembly of Gods* 918 Mayntenours of ryght, . . Distroyers of errour. **1447** BOKENHAM *Seyntys* (Roxb.) 186 Of crystene feyth a meynteynour. **1514** BARCLAY *Cyt. & Uplondyshm.* (Percy Soc.) 34 O where be rulers meynteyners of justyce. **1526** TINDALE *Matt.* v. 9 Blessed are the mayntayners of peace. **1579** E. K. in *Spenser's Sheph. Cal.* Ep. Ded., Ma. Phi. Sidney, a special fauourer & maintainer of all kind of learning. *c* **1635** MURE *Ps.* xvi. 6 Mainteener of my lote thow art. **1639** COKAINE *Masque* Dram. Wks. (1874) 11 A great maintainer Of our great-grand-father's virtue—hospitality. **1749** FIELDING *Tom Jones* III. iii, The maintainers of all the different Sects in the world. **1781** JOHNSON *Life Cave* Wks. IV. 529 A tenacious maintainer, though not a clamorous demander of his right. **1824** MISS MITFORD *Village* Ser. I. 66 She a school-mistress, a keeper of silence, a maintainer of discipline! **1840** THIRLWALL *Greece* lix. VII. 321 Polysperchon . . appears as the maintainer of the rights of Hercules. **1875** JOWETT *Plato* (ed. 2) III. 124 The maintainer of justice . . is aiming at strengthening the man.

b. In bad sense: One who fosters or supports (wrong-doing, sedition, false quarrels, etc.).

1393 LANGL. *P. Pl.* C. IV. 288 Mede ys euermore a meyntenour of gyle. **1413** *Pilgr. Sowle* (Caxton 1483) III. iv. 53 Ye laweours and maynteners of wrong. *c* **1420** LYDG. *Assembly of Gods* 677 Meyntenours of querelles, horryble lyers. **1502** ARNOLDE *Chron.* (1811) 90 Mayntener of quarels . . or other comon mysdoers. **1545** BRINKLOW *Complaynt* 19 b, Thei be maynteyners of discord for their priuate lukers sake. **1567** *Satir. Poems Reform.* iv. 88 Fostararis of falset . . Mantenaris of murther. **1575–85** ABP. SANDYS *Serm.* iv. 74 All breeders and maintainers of sedition.

c. Something which maintains or preserves.

1574 NEWTON *Health Mag.* 23 Breade and Wyne, two of the cheefest mainteiners of mans life. **1655** MOUFET & BENNET *Health's Improv.* (1746) 374 Outward Heat draweth out their inward Moisture, which should be the Maintainer and Food of their Heat natural. **1696** TRYON *Misc.* i. 3 The Volatile Spirit . . is the Essential Life of every thing, and is the maintainer of its Colour.

2. One who upholds or supports in speech or argument, one who contends for the truth or validity of (a doctrine, assertion, tenet, etc.).

1560 DAUS tr. *Sleidane's Comm.* 82 The maynteners of that doctrine, are nother called nor hearde. **1561** T. NORTON *Calvin's Inst.* III. 306 This opinion . . hath had greate mainteiners. **1691** WOOD *Ath. Oxon.* I. 349 He was . . a principal maintainer of Protestancy. **1738** WARBURTON *Div. Legat.* I. 404 The Maintainers of the Immateriality of the Divine Substance were likewise divided into two Parties. **1754** EDWARDS *Freed. Will* IV. xii. 275 Epicurus . . maintained no such Doctrine of Necessity, but was the greatest Maintainer of Contingence. **1845** JEBB *Gen. Law* in *Encycl. Metrop.* (1847) II. 702/1 To quiet the violent contest of two honest maintainers of contrary opinions. **1868** M. PATTISON *Academ. Org.* v. 154 The conservative maintainers of the 'status in quo' ought to have been called upon to justify . . what had actually taken place.

†**3.** One who gives aid, countenance, or support to another; a defender and helper. *Obs.*

c **1330** R. BRUNNE *Chron. Wace* (Rolls) 3222 Now þou comest to reue vs our [socour], þat scholdest ben oure mayntenour. *c* **1400** *Laud Troy Bk.* 17056 For now lesen thei her mayntenoure And alle the gode that thei owe. *c* **1440** *Promp. Parv.* 320/2 Mayntenowre, *manutentor*, *defensor*, *supportator*, *fautor*. **1535** COVERDALE *Ezek.* xxx. 6 The maynteyners of the londe of Egipte shal fall. **1578** *Chr. Prayers* in *Priv. Prayers* (1851) 504 Thou, Lord, art my maintainer, and the holder up of my head. **1686** GOAD *Celest. Bodies* I. ix. 28 Seeing he acts by dependance on Him, as all the Rest do, we must compare None of them to their Maintainer.

†**b.** In bad sense: One who aids and abets another in wrong-doing or error. *Obs.*

c **1330** R. BRUNNE *Chron.* (1810) 255 Edward þei cald & teld, þat he was mayntenoure, þe robbed he all held, as a resceyuour. *c* **1380** WYCLIF *Sel. Wks.* III. 318 Alle ressettours and meynteneris of siche [*sc.* thieves] wityngly ben cursed. *c* **1440** *Jacob's Well* 59 Heretykes . . & alle here mayntenourys or fauourerys. **1495** *Act II Hen. VII*, c. 10 §2 The mayntenours of him or theym so mysdoing. **1560** DAUS tr. *Sleidane's Comm.* 456 b, The counsell of Calcedonie deposed Dioscorides the maynteyner of Eutyches from his Byshoprike. **1566–7** *Reg. Privy Council Scot.* I. 497 Ane mantenar of wickit and brokin men. **1570** *Act 13 Eliz.* c. 2 §2 All . . Aydors, Comforters, or Maynteyners of anye the said . . Offendors. **1588** A. KING tr. *Canisius' Catech.* 141 Maintenars and patrons of euil doars. **1614** RALEIGH *Hist. World* II. (1634) 467 The Conspirators had neither any mighty partakers in their fact, nor strong maintainers of their persons. **1660** R. COKE *Power & Subj.* 233 The aiders, maintainers and concealers, who shall not within twenty daies . . disclose the same to some Justice of Peace.

4. *Law.* One who unlawfully supports a suit in which he is not concerned. Cf. MAINTENANCE 6.

1399 LANGL. *Rich. Redeles* II. 78 That no manere meyntenour shulde merkis bere, Ne haue lordis leuere the lawe to apeire. **1503** *Act 19 Hen. VII*, c. 13 Punishment of the Maintainers and Embracers of the Jurors. **1531–2** *Act 23 Hen. VIII*, c. 3 Vnlawfull maintenours embrasours and Jurours. **1875** STUBBS *Const. Hist.* (1896) III. xxi. 550 The maintainers of false causes, whether they were barons or lawyers, became very early the object of severe legislation. **1898** *Encycl. Laws Eng.* (ed. Renton) VIII. 74 The maintainor must have some special interest other than that of the public at large.

5. One who provides (a person) with the requisites of life; †one who keeps a mistress.

1632 MASSINGER *City Madam* IV. ii, Be assur'd first Of a new maintainer e're you cashire the old one. **1650** BULWER *Anthropomet.* 199 The Clergie, who are the chief maintainers of these Ganimedes. **1692** WASHINGTON tr. *Milton's Def. Pop.* iii. Wks. 1851 VIII. 76 Plato would not have . . the People [called] Servants, but Maintainers of their Magistrates, because they give Meat, Drink, and Wages to their Kings themselves. **1870** *Echo* 12 Nov., Every thief his own maintainer, every prisoner his own reformer.

†**6.** ? A mine-owner. *Obs.*

1747 HOOSON *Miner's Dict.* Y iij, I could wish that some of the Cross Carping Maintainers might try the difference of these two Airs.

7. *Watch-making.* An apparatus for keeping the movement of a clock or watch from being interrupted during the process of winding.

1884 F. J. BRITTEN *Watch & Clockm.* 167 In some of Arnold's watches is a continuous maintainer.

main'taining, *vbl. sb.* [-ING[1].]

1. The action of the verb MAINTAIN; maintenance, support, etc.

c **1330** R. BRUNNE *Chron.* (1810) 100 Þorgh Anselm may[n]tenyng was þe contek ent. *c* **1380** WYCLIF *Sel. Wks.* III. 322 In alle þis fals meyntenyng þei holden wiþ þe fend aȝenst God. **1395** PURVEY *Remonstrance* (1851) 87 Vnworthi to haue ony benefice othir mayntenynge in the rewme. **1490–91** in Swayne *Sarum Church-w. Acc.* (1896) 37 To the maynteynynge of the light before the rode, xxij*s.* j*d.* ob. **1592** GREENE *Art Connycatch.* III. 2 Except they applied themselues to such honest trades . . as might witnesse their maintaining was by true and honest meanes. **1643** MILTON *Divorce* viii. Wks. 1851 IV. 21 To the strict maintaining of a generall and religious command. **1794** S. WILLIAMS *Vermont* 232 They were at all times ready . . to contribute their full proportion towards the maintaining the present just war. **1890** 'R. BOLDREWOOD' *Col. Reformer* (1891) 107 The reaching and maintaining of an independent pastoral position.

†**2.** Bearing, demeanour, behaviour. *Obs.*

c **1477** CAXTON *Jason* 5 The broder of kyng Eson . . there beyng present could not holde ne kepe his mayntening. **1483** —— *G. de la Tour* Prol., A fayr wyff . . whiche had knowleche of alle honoure, alle good, and fayre mayntenyng. **1530** PALSGR. 241/2 Mayntenyng, *port*.

3. *attrib.*: **maintaining power**, in a watch or clock, the power which keeps the motion continuous (cf. MAINTAINER 7); so **maintaining wheel** = *going-wheel* (Knight *Dict. Mech.* Suppl. 1884).

1766 A. CUMMING *Clock & Watch Work* 138 Care is to be taken to acquire in all watches as great a maintaining power as circumstances can admit. **1825** J. NICHOLSON *Operat. Mechanic* 519 The swing-wheel . . is constantly urged forward by the maintaining power, which is supplied by a small weight. **1884** F. J. BRITTEN *Watch & Clockm.* 123 Another feature of Huyghens' clock is the maintaining power.

†**maintainment.** *Obs. rare.* [f. MAINTAIN *v.* + -MENT.] Maintenance.

c **1485** *Digby Myst.* (1882) v. 708 Therfor thei be expedient to these meny of maynte[n]ment. **1543** *Plumpton Corr.* (Camden) 244 Sir Christopher Bird, person, who honestly did kepe the cure under the forsaid late person, and the maintenment of God service.

maintenance (ˈmeɪntɪnəns). Forms: 4–5 **meyn-**, **meintenaunce**, **-ance**, **meyntynaunce**, **menteynaunce**, 4–6 **mayntenaunce**, **-ance**, 5 **mayntenanse**, **mayntnaunce**, **mantenans**, 5–6 **maynetenaunce**, 6 **maintaynance**, **main-**, **mayn-tenans**, **-tennance**, **-tennence**, **mantei(g)nance**, 6–7 **mantenance**, 6–8 **maintainance**, 4– **maintenance**. [a. F. *maintenance*, f. *maintenir*: see MAINTAIN *v.* and -ANCE. Cf. Pr. *mantenensa*, Sp. *mantenencia*, Pg. *mantença*, It. *mantenenza*.]

†**1.** Bearing, deportment, demeanour, behaviour.

c **1369** CHAUCER *Dethe Blaunche* 834 She had so stedfaste countenaunce, So noble porte and meyntenaunce. **1430–40** LYDG. *Bochas* VIII. (1494) D v b, Where there be summe that wrongly it werrey, Holde therageyne by frowarde maynte[n]aunce. **1579** SPENSER *Sheph. Cal.* Sept. 169 For all their craft is in their countenaunce, They bene so graue and full of mayntenaunce. **1596** SHAKS. *1 Hen. IV*, v. iv. 22, I saw him hold Lord Percy at the point, With lustier maintenance then I did looke for Of such an vngrowne Warriour.

2. The action of upholding or keeping in being (a cause, right, state of things, government, etc.); the state or fact of being upheld or sustained; †that which upholds, means of sustentation.

1413 *Pilgr. Sowle* (Caxton 1483) IV. xxxii. 81 Neither of them shalle be the lift hand to mayntenaunce of wrong. **1529** MORE *Dyaloge* I. Wks. 109/1 For the maintenaunce of theyr authorite. **1538** STARKEY *England* I. i. 25 To apply and indeuur myselfe to the mayntennance and setting forward of the true commyn wele. **1548–9** (Mar.) *Bk. Com. Prayer, Communion*, The maintenaunce of Goddes true religion and vertue. **1570** *Homilies* II. *Agst. Rebellion* IV. (1640) 302 So hath a frantick Religion need of such furious maintenances as is Rebellion. **1579** LYLY *Euphues* (Arb.) 111 Idlenesse is . . ye sole maintenaunce of youthful affection. **1591** SPENSER *Teares of Muses* 338 So every where they rule and tyrannize, For their usurped kingdomes maintenaunce. **1681** *Addr. fr. Helstone* in *Lond. Gaz.* No. 1629/7 Whatever we can do for and towards the Support, Preservation, and maintainance of the just Rights and Prerogative of Your Majesty. **1871** EARLE *Philol. Eng. Tongue* §88 Where there is a central literature, there is a constant provision for the maintenance of uniformity even though words are changing their sense.

3. The action of keeping in effective condition, in working order, in repair, etc.; the keeping up of (a building, light, institution, body of troops, etc.) by the supply of funds or needful provision; the state or fact of being so kept up; means or provision for keeping up. Freq. *attrib.*

c **1460** FORTESCUE *Abs. & Lim. Mon.* vi. (1885) 120 It is necessarie that the kynge be alway riche, wich may not be withowt he haue revenues sufficiant for the yerely mayntenance of his estate. **1481–90** *Howard Househ. Bks.* (Roxb.) 149 For the mayntenanse of the lampe . . spent xiiij. quartes of oyle iij.*d.* ob. **1546** *Mem. Ripon* (Surtees) III. 23 Certen landes belongynge . . to the Maynetenaunce of divers and syndrye Chauntriez in the same Churche. **1587** FLEMING *Contn. Holinshed* III. 1537/1 That which was doone . . made an excellent rode or harborough for the time it continued, and had maintenance. **1611** BIBLE *Transl. Pref.* ¶2 Against Church-maintenance and allowance, in such sort, as the Embassadors and messengers of the great King of Kings should be furnished. **1616** SURFL. & MARKH. *Country Farm* 10 Your House . . will be . . of greatest maintenance, preseruation, and safetie, if you enuiron it round about with water. **1665** BUNYAN *Holy Citie* 250 Having thus shewed us this City . . he now comes to shew us her Provision and Maintenance, wherewith she is kept in safety, life, peace and comfort. **1775** BURKE *Concil. Amer.* Wks. III. 100 Secondly, that they had acted legally and laudably in their grants of money, and their maintenance of troops. **1844** H. H. WILSON *Brit. India* III. 407 A further sequestration was subsequently authorised, in order to ensure the maintenance of the contingent horse, which the Gaekwar was bound by treaty to keep up for the service of the British Government. **1861** M. PATTISON *Ess.* (1889) I. 47 The maintenance and repair of the northern gate, Bishopsgate, was assigned to them. **1884** *List of Subscribers* (London & Globe Telephone Co.), In case of unsatisfactory service . . send complaint in writing . . to London and Globe Telephone and Maintenance Company, Limited. **1942** *Aeronautics* May 40/1 The public does not hear very much about the Maintenance Command of the Royal Air Force. **1957** *Ann. Reg. 1956* 67 A prolonged ban on overtime working by the maintenance men. **1958** *Listener* 23 Oct. 650/1 Maintenance engineers at London Airport vote unanimously to continue their strike. **1970** *E. Afr. Standard* (Nairobi) 23 Jan. 18/2 (Advt.), Applicants . . should have at least five years' experience, either in a supervisory capacity or as a maintenance engineer in sole charge of a plant. **1974** *Times* 7 Mar. 1/1 Maintenance workers will be allowed into the pits during the weekend.

†**4.** The carrying on (of a war) by furnishing supplies. *Obs.*

1496–7 *Act 12 Hen. VII*, c. 12 §6 The seid xvme . . shalbe . . levyed and paied for mayntenance of the same Werre. **1543–4** *Act 35 Hen. VIII*, c. 12 Inestimable costes charges and expences . . for the maintenaunce of his warres.

†**5.** The action of giving aid, countenance, or support to (a person in what he does). *Obs.*

13.. *E.E. Allit. P.* B. 186 For marryng of maryagez & mayntnaunce of schrewez. **1377** LANGL. *P. Pl.* B. v. 253 Lentestow euere lordes for loue of her mayntenaunce?

c **1425** *Eng. Conq. Irel.* 20 Al oure enemy..hath I-broght vnked folk vp-on vs, that the harme wich he had no power to don vs hym-self, throgh helpe of ham & mayntenaunce, the better myght brynge to end. **1592** GREENE *Upst. Courtier* E, Sildome was there any pleas put in before that vpstart veluet breeches, for his maintaynance inuented strange controuersies. *a* **1600** MONTGOMERIE *Misc. Poems* xxv. 14 And I sall be thy seruand, in sik sort To merit thy mantenance, if I may.

6. The action of wrongfully aiding and abetting litigation; *spec.* sustentation of a suit or suitor at law by a party who has no interest in the proceedings or who acts from any improper motive. (Cf. MAINTAIN *v.* 2 d.)

[**1321–2** *Rolls of Parlt.* I. 398/2 Q'il voille enquerre coment p la mayntenaunce le dit Conte ele pert son Manoir.] **1389** in *Eng. Gilds* (1870) 39 þei shullen makyn no meyntenaunce ne confideracie ageyn þe kyngis right ne þe comoun lawe. **1399** *Rolls of Parlt.* III. 452/2 Some men..have taken mych more by extorsion..and by mayntenance of quereles. *c* **1420** LYDG. *Assembly of Gods* 659 Hoordam, Bawdry, False Mayntenaunce, Treson, Abusion, & Pety Brybry. *c* **1430** *Freemasonry* 254 That for no mon, No fals mantenans he take hym apon. **1447** *Rolls of Parlt.* V. 130/1 By grete might, mayntenaunce, and other undue meones. **1460** *Ibid.* 374/2 In an action of mayntenaunce. **1467** in *Eng. Gilds* (1870) 400 Alle the attorners..truly to execute ther office as the lawe requirith w^t^out mayntenaunce, or champertye, or conseilynge ther cliauntoʳˢ to vse eny fals accyons. **1591** LAMBARDE *Archeion* (1635) 127 That he shall not by himselfe, or by any other, commit Maintenance, or other thing, which may disturbe the course of the Common Law. **1628** COKE *On Litt.* 368 b, Maintenance..signifieth in Law, a taking in hand, bearing vp or vpholding of quarrels and sides, to the disturbance or hindrance of common right. **1787** BENTHAM *Def. Usury* xii. 118 Champerty is but a particular modification of this sin of Maintenance. **1836** *Bingham's New Cases Comm. Pleas* II. 639 If the Defendant was not privy to the publication of the libel, he was a stranger to the action brought against the Plaintiff, and in undertaking to indemnify the Plaintiff against the costs was guilty of maintenance. **1875** POSTE *Gaius* IV. (ed. 2) 611 Unless the assignment savour of Maintenance, i.e. be made with the design of fomenting litigation. **1883** *Law Rep.*, *11 Q.B.D.* 1 Bradlaugh v. Newdegate... The action was for maintenance. **1886** *Law Rep.*, *17 Q.B.D.* 504 The action was brought to recover damages occasioned to the plaintiff by reason of the defendant's 'maintenance' of one Nailer in an action which he had brought against the plaintiff. **1901** SIR F. POLLOCK *Law of Torts* 321 The wrong of maintenance, or aiding a party in litigation without either interest in the suit, or lawful cause of kindred, affection, or charity for aiding him, is..akin to malicious prosecution and other abuses of legal process... Actions for maintenance are in modern times rare though possible.

7. a. The action of providing (a person) with the requisites of life; the fact or state of being so provided. Also, that which supports or maintains a person with livelihood, means of subsistence; the amount provided for a person's livelihood.

1389 in *Eng. Gilds* (1870) 4 He schal ȝeue somwhat in maintenance of þe bretherhede. *a* **1400–50** *Alexander* 1179 Rather to thole þe mayntenance of the Messedoyns & of þe meri Grekis, þan þaim of Persy to pay. **1540** *Act 32 Hen. VIII*, c. 14 The nauy..is..the maintenaunce of many masters mariners and sea men. **1581** MULCASTER *Positions* xxxvii. (1887) 148 Will ye haue the multitude waxe, where the maintenance waines? **1591** SHAKS. *Two Gent.* I. iii. 68 What maintenance he from his friends receiues, Like exhibition thou shalt haue from me. **1592** BABINGTON *Notes Genesis* i. Wks. (1622) 6 The pride of some, who cannot abide to haue any..come neere them in any circumstance of life or maintenance. **1600** HAKLUYT *Voy.* (1810) III. 555 This Maiz is the greatest maintenance which the Indian hath. **1612** WOODALL *Surg. Mate* Wks. (1653) Ep. Salut. 2, I was forced for my maintenance to follow the practice of the cure of the Plague. **1645** FEATLY *Dippers Dipt* (1646) 133 Some lands, profits, and emoluments..assigned for the maintenance of the Ministry. *c* **1701** CIBBER *Love Makes a Man* II. i. 22 Enough to give him Books, and a moderate Maintainance. **1709** SWIFT *Adv. Relig.*, They are not under a necessity of making learning their maintenance. **1732** LAW *Serious C.* viii. (ed. 2) 114 The parish allowance to such people, is very seldom a comfortable maintenance. **1818** CRUISE *Digest* (ed. 2) VI. 117 In case he should have any children by her, to provide for their maintenance. **1840** MACAULAY *Ess.*, *Clive* (1887) 560 The civil servants were clearly entitled to a maintenance out of the revenue. **1863** MARY HOWITT *F. Bremer's Greece* II. xxi. 297 The Greek convent-houses are chiefly houses of maintenance for poor men and women.

b. ***separate maintenance***: support given by a husband to a wife when the parties are separated. ***maintenance order***: a court order, in the case of a broken marriage, compelling the husband to pay the wife a regular fixed sum for her maintenance.

1722 DE FOE *Col. Jack* (1840) 211 She demanded a separate maintenance. **1777** SHERIDAN *Sch. Scand.* I. i, She has been the cause of six matches being broken off,..nine separate maintenances, and two divorces. **1803** G. COLMAN *John Bull* IV. 42 I'll settle a separate maintenance upon ould mother Brulgruddery [*sc.* his wife]. **1866** *Act 29 & 30 Vict.* c. 32 §1 It shall be lawful for the Court to make an order on the husband for payment to the wife during their joint lives of such monthly or weekly sums for her maintenance..as the Court may think reasonable. **1907** *Act 7 Edw. VII* c. 12 §1 The court may..make an order on the husband for payment to the wife..for her maintenance. **1920** *Act 10 & 11 Geo. V* c. 33 §10 The expression 'maintenance order' means an order other than an order of affiliation for the periodical payment of sums of money towards the maintenance of the wife or other dependants of the person against whom the order is made. **1960** M. SPARK *Bachelors* vi. 88 But there's usually a question of maintenance orders. I distinctly recall his being described as a bachelor. **1971** *Reader's Digest Family Guide to Law* 265/2 In many cases a wife will be left, after a separation, with insufficient money for her own day-to-day expenses. Her need for maintenance will be even more urgent if she is taking care of any children of the marriage... She can apply to the local magistrates' court or to a divorce court for a maintenance order. **1973** *Times* 14 Mar. 20/4 To qualify for maintenance a wife does not have to ask for a divorce.

c. The action of providing (a person) over a period of time with doses of a drug sufficient to maintain its effect on the body while usu. being less than the dose given initially; usu. *attrib.*, as ***maintenance dose***.

1936 STEDMAN *Med. Dict.* (ed. 13) 319/2 *Maintenance dose*, the dose given in a protracted case of illness, to keep the patient under the influence of the drug after this has been attained by the initial dosage. **1963** *Brit. Pharmaceutical Codex* 683 Dose [of propylthiouracil]. Controlling dose, 200 to 600 milligrams daily; maintenance dose, 50 to 200 milligrams daily. **1965** *Jrnl. Amer. Med. Assoc.* 23 Aug. 648/1 Addicts coming to a maintenance program usually fear that physicians will not prescribe enough medication. **1971** *Nature* 29 Jan. 290/2 The committee believes that the British system of maintenance, in which an addict is supplied with daily doses of heroin, and the methadone maintenance treatment,..both have their advantages and drawbacks.

8. The act of supporting or upholding in speech or argument; assertion of the truth or validity of (an opinion, plea, tenet).

1533 MORE *Debell. Salem* Wks. 990/2 For herein see I none other shyft for this good man, but for the maintenance of his matter to say, that in the common law [etc.]. **1560** DAUS tr. *Sleidane's Comm.* 22 b, The Duke..aunswereth, that it was never his intent to defende Luthers doctrine by his maintenaunce. **1562** *Child-Marriages* 195 This deponent did colourably declare (for the maintenaunce of his matter) that he had sondry witnesses. **1691** T. H[ALE] *Acc. New Invent.* 29 What has been severally offered and asserted..in Maintenance of their different Conceptions touching the Evil now enquired into. **1875** H. R. REYNOLDS in *Expositor* I. 308 He could never have appealed, as he did, to the authority of Paul in maintenance of his own peculiar opinions.

9. a. ***cap*** (or †***hat***) ***of maintenance***: a kind of hat or cap formerly worn as a symbol of official dignity or high rank, or carried before a sovereign or a high dignitary in processions.

The sense of *maintenance* here is obscure. Cf. the app. equivalent *cap of estate, cap of dignity* (see CAP *sb.* 4 g). In the earliest example (*c* 1485) the *hat of maintenance* is worn by the members of the Holborn Quest. Afterwards the *cap of maintenance* is mentioned by contemporaries as having been given by the Pope thrice to Henry VII and once to Henry VIII; in 1551 it is referred to as one of the insignia of a prince. In the 17th c. and later it appears chiefly as borne, together with the sword, before the Lord Mayor, and before the Sovereign at his coronation. A kind of cap, with two points like horns behind, borne in the arms of certain families either as a charge or in the place of a wreath, is described by heralds as a 'cap of maintenance': cf. quot. 1700.

c **1485** *Digby Myst.* (1882) v. 727 (*Stage direct.*) Here entrithe vj. Iorours in a sute gownyde with hoodes a-bowte her nec[kes], hattes of mayntenaunce ther-vpone. **1489** WRIOTHESLEY *Chron.* (1875) I. 2 A capp of mayntenaunce brought from Rome to the Kinge. **1551** ROBINSON tr. *More's Utop.* II. (1895) 233–4 Nor the prince hymselfe is not knowen from the other..by a crown or diademe or cappe of maintenaunce. **1577–87** HOLINSHED *Chron.* III. 1122/1 They had two caps of maintenance likewise borne before them: whereof the earle of Arundell bare the one, and the earle of Shrewesburie the other. **1614** R. TAILOR *Hog hath lost Pearl* III. E 3 b, As if a females fauour could not be obteyn'd by any, but he that weares the Cap of maintenance. **1622** J. TAYLOR (Water P.) *Very Merry Wherry-Ferry Voy.* Wks. (1630) II. 13/2 A Sword, a Cap of maintenance, a Mace ..Are borne before the Maior, and Aldermen. **1632** MASSINGER *City Madam* IV. i, I see Lord Mayor written on his forehead; The Cap of Maintenance and Citie Sword Born up in state before him. **1639** MAYNE *City Match* I. iii, Think, man, how it may In time..raise thee To the sword and cap of maintenance. **1656** in Jewitt & Hope *Corporation Plate* (1895) I. p. lxxviii, [Cromwell granted to Salisbury that the Sword-bearer should bear a sword and] weare a Cap of Mayntenance before the Maior of the said Citie for the tyme being. **1698** FRYER *Acc. E. India & P.* 358 A high Red Velvet Cap, plaited at Top like a Cap of Maintenance. **1700** CONGREVE *Way of World* III. xviii, They [a pair of horns] may prove a cap of maintenance to you still. **1714** MANDEVILLE *Fab. Bees* (1725) I. 177 If my lord mayor had nothing to defend himself but his great two-handed sword, the huge cap of maintenance, and his gilded mace. **1736** DRAKE *Eboracum* I. vi. 223 The sword-bearer hath a hat of maintenance, which he wears only on Christmas day,..and on the high days of solemnity. **1808** SCOTT *Marm.* IV. vii, His cap of maintenance was graced With the proud heron's plume. **1875** STUBBS *Const. Hist.* III. xx. 434 It became the rule for a duke to be created by the girding on of the sword, the bestowal of a golden rod, and the imposition of a cap of maintenance and circlet of gold. [Under Edw. III; but the document cited has *per impositionem cappæ*.]

†**b.** *jocularly* (with allusion to sense 7). *Obs.*

1597 *1st Pt. Return fr. Parnass.* I. i. 389 Take us with thee; for wee muste provide us a poore capp of mantenance.

† **maintenant**, *adv.* *Obs.* Forms: 4 **meigntenaunt**, 5 **meyn-**, **mayntenaunt(e**, 6 **manteynent**, **maintenant**. [a. OF. *maintenant* in the same sense (in mod.F. = now), f. *main* hand + *tenant*, pr. pple. of *tenir* to hold.] At once, immediately.

13.. *K. Alis.* 5302 That on lep on a lyoun, And to ground hym threw adoun, And hym astrangled meigntenaunt. ? *a* **1400** *Arthur* 383 [They] broute Arthour Meyntenaunt Euen byfore þe gyant. *a* **1470** TIPTOFT *Cæsar* iv. (1530) 6 They delyvered mayntenaunte one parte and the remnaunt wyth in few dayes. *a* **1548** HALL *Chron.* (1809) 660 The Frenchmen..alighted as though they would geve assaut maintenaunt. **1592** WEST *1st Pt. Symbol.* §44 C, Euerie estate is either executed maintenant, or executorie by limitation of vse. **1598** *Child-Marriages* 166, 2 packetes,..which were maintenaunt..deliuered to Mr. John Francis to be posted hens.

† **maintenantly**, *adv.* *Obs.* [-LY².] = prec.

1528 *St. Papers Hen. VIII*, IV. 497 If thaye maye chace theim ons out of Scotland, thoughe thaye..manteynentlie retourne again after he be departed, yet [etc.]. **1577–87** HOLINSHED *Chron.* III. 822/1 Monsieur de la Palice, and monsieur de Imbrecourt..were put to their ransomes, and licenced maintenantlie to depart vpon their word.

¶ Used with etymological allusion.

1552 HULOET, Sell a thing before wytnesse, or by delyuerynge possession mayntenantly to the buyer.., *mancipio dare.*

‖**Maintenon** (mɑ̃tənɔ̃). The name of the Marquise de Maintenon, secretly married to Louis XIV in 1685; used *attrib.* in names of things arbitrarily called after her, as ***Maintenon bonnet, chop, cutlet***; **Maintenon cross** [= F. *maintenon*], a cross with a diamond at the extremity of each limb, worn as an ornament.

[**1710** SWIFT *Jrnl. to Stella* 8 Oct., We had a neck of mutton dressed *à la Maintenon*, that the dog could not eat.] **1805** *Sporting Mag.* XXV. 226 Veal cutlets, haricoed mutton, maintenon chops. **1836** MARRYAT *Three Cutters* v, 'And what else, sir?' 'Maintenon cutlets, my lord.' **1836–7** DICKENS *Sk. Boz*, *Tales* viii, Mr. Alexander Trott sat down to a fried sole, maintenon cutlet, Madeira, and sundries. **1884** *West. Daily Press* 13 June 7/6 The popular form of bonnet is that called 'Maintenon'.

maintenous (ˈmeɪntɪnəs), *a.* *Law. rare.* [irreg. f. MAINTEN(ANCE) + -OUS.] Relating to, or of the nature of, maintenance.

1898 *Encycl. Laws Eng.* (ed. Renton) VIII. 75 A maintenous agreement is illegal and therefore void.

† **maintenue.** *Obs. rare*⁻¹. [a. F. *maintenue*, f. *maintenir* to MAINTAIN.] = MAINTENANCE 6.

1390 GOWER *Conf.* III. 380 To seche and loke how that it is Touchende of the chevalerie,.. That of here large retenue The lond is ful of maintenue, Which causith that the comune right In fewe contrees stant upright.

‖**maintien** (mɛ̃tjɛ̃). [Fr.] Bearing, deportment.

1849 GEO. ELIOT *Let.* 4 Oct. (1954) I. 313 Those happy souls..who do really effect much good, simply by their calm and even *maintien*. **1889** G. B. SHAW *London Music 1888–89* (1937) 73 Josabeth had the *maintien* of the French stage in a degree that would have enraptured A. B. Walkley.

main-top (ˈmeɪntɒp). *Naut.* [See MAIN *a.* 10.] The TOP of a mainmast; a platform just above the head of the lower mainmast. Often used loosely for ***main-topgallant-masthead***.

1485 *Naval Acc. Hen. VII* (1896) 48 Mayne toppes. **1582** N. LICHEFIELD tr. *Castanheda's Conq. E. Ind.* I. xxviii. 70 b, The king with his owne hand did deliver it unto the Captaine Generall, for to bestowe it in his maine toppe. **1627** CAPT. SMITH *Seaman's Gram.* xiii. 62 The Admirall of each squadron..doth carry in their maine tops, flags of sundry colours. **1725** DE FOE *Voy. round World* (1840) 308 The man at the main-top, who was ordered to look out. **1835** MARRYAT *Jac. Faithf.* xvii, When I was captain of the main-top in the La Minerve. **1887** *Standard* 21 Sept. 5/7 The war vessels..each flying the British ensign at the maintop.

b. *attrib.* (sometimes = 'belonging to the main-topsail'), as ***main-top bowline, -man, shroud***.

1626 CAPT. SMITH *Accid. Yng. Seamen* 14 The maine top shroudes. *c* **1860** H. STUART *Seaman's Catech.* 79 The duties of fore or main-topmen in their respective tops are much the same. **1867** SMYTH *Sailor's Word-bk.*, *Main-top Bowline*, the bowline of the main-topsail. **1882** *Standard* 1 Dec. 3/6 There were no maintopmen on deck.

main-topgallant (ˌmeɪntɒpˈgælənt). *Naut.* [See MAIN *a.* 10 and TOPGALLANT.] Used *attrib.* in **main-topgallant-mast**, the mast above the main-topmast; similarly in ***main-topgallant-masthead, -sail*** (***-yard***), ***-yard***, etc.

1626 CAPT. SMITH *Accid. Yng. Seamen* 13 The maine top gallant sayle yeard. **1693** OLIVER in *Phil. Trans.* XVII. 912 Our Main Top-Gallant Mast was split in pieces. **1748** *Anson's Voy.* II. x. 239 One of the Captains..carries the royal standard of Spain at the main-top gallant mast-head. **1760** C. JOHNSTON *Chrysal* (1822) II. 233 To hand the main-top-gallant sail in a storm at midnight. **1790** BEATSON *Nav. & Mil. Mem.* II. 411 The man on the main-top-gallant-yard of the Rochester. **1876** *Encycl. Brit.* XXI. 153/1 On the main-mast we have the main-course or main-sail, main-top-sail, main-top-gallant-sail, and the main-royal.

main-topmast (meɪnˈtɒpmɑːst, -æ-, -məst). *Naut.* Also 5 **mane-**. [See MAIN *a.* 10 and TOPMAST.] The mast next above the lower mainmast.

1495 *Naval Acc. Hen. VII* (1896) 269 The mane toppe maste. **1626** CAPT. SMITH *Accid. Yng. Seamen* 12. **1634** BRERETON *Trav.* (Chetham Soc.) 169 Upon the mainmast.. there is also placed..the main top mast. **1762** FALCONER *Shipwr.* III. 584 While, in the general wreck, the faithful stay Drags the main-topmast from its post away. **1833** M. SCOTT *Tom Cringle* xvi. (1859) 424 Her maintopmast was gone close by the cap.

b. *attrib.*: ***main-topmast-head, -staysail***.

1672 *Lond. Gaz.* No. 683/3, 3 English Seamen ran up to his Main-top-mast-head, and took down his Pendant. **1779** F. HERVEY *Nav. Hist.* II. 157 He is said to have passed through the Channel, with a broom at his main-top-mast

head. **1866** *Daily Tel.* 6 Feb. 3/3 At eight o'clock the maintopmast-staysail was carried away.

main-topsail (meɪn'tɒpseɪl, -s(ə)l). *Naut.* [See MAIN *a.* 10.] The sail above the mainsail.

1618 *News of Rauleigh* (1844) 16 If the Maister..bid heaue out the maine Top-saile. **1748** *Anson's Voy.* II. v. 170 The weather proved squally, and we split our maintop-sail. **1884** PAE *Eustace* 137 Her main topsail is shivering.

b. *attrib.*, as ***main-topsail bowline, brace, halyard, rigging, sheet, tye, yard.***

1626 CAPT. SMITH *Accid. Yng. Seamen* 12 The maine top sayle yeard. *Ibid.* 14 The maine top sayle hallyards,..the maine top sayle sheats,.. the maine top sayle braces. *Ibid.* 15 The maine top sayle bowlin. **1800** *Asiat. Ann. Reg., Chron.* 66/1 Our maintop-sail tye was shot away. **1813** *Examiner* 26 Apr. 261/2 The [American frigate] Constitution suffered severely,.. having.. both main-topsail-yards..badly shot. **1854** MRS. GASKELL *North & S.* xiv, Some sailors being aloft in the maintopsail rigging.

main-ward, mainward. [MAIN *a.*]

†**1.** The main body of an army. *Obs.*

1563-87 FOXE *A. & M.* (1596) 46/2 As well my vaward, main-ward, as rereward. **1581** STYWARD *Mart. Discipl.* II. 122 The which..are to be diuided into three battailes: the Voward, the Maineward, and the Rereward battaile. **1591** *Garrard's Art Warre* 184 When the fronts were wearied the Mainward and Rereward succeeded.

2. The principal ward of a lock, fastened to the main-plate.

1677 MOXON *Mech. Exerc.* No. 2. 23 The true Place of the Main-ward. **1688** R. HOLME *Armoury* III. 301/2 The Maine ward [of a key] is that on the lower side the Bit. **1875** KNIGHT *Dict. Mech.* 1339/1, G is a ward-lock key..The various parts are,—*a*, the main-ward, or bridge-ward.

mainy, variant of MEINIE, company.

main-yard ('meɪnjɑːd). *Naut.* [See MAIN *a.* 10.] The yard on which the mainsail is extended.

1485 *Naval Acc. Hen. VII* (1896) 37 Brasse pendaunts for the mayne yerdes. *c* **1572** GASCOIGNE *Mask* Posies (1575) *Flowers* 48 His eares cut from his head, they set him in a chayre, And from a maine yard hoisted him aloft into the ayre. **1627** CAPT. SMITH *Seaman's Gram.* iii. 16 Suppose the ship be 76. foot at the Keele, her maine yard must be 21. yards in length, and in thicknesse but 17. inches. **1824** J. SYMMONS tr. *Æschylus' Agam.* 59 Ship against ship, with crashing mainyards roll'd. **1840** R. H. DANA *Bef. Mast* xvii. 46 We got a whip on the main-yard.

b. *attrib.*, as ***main-yard-arm, -rope***; **main-yard man** *Naut. slang* (see quot.).

1497 *Naval Acc. Hen. VII* (1896) 307, ij mayne yerde Ropes. **1762** FALCONER *Shipwr.* III. 665 Some, from the main-yard-arm impetuous thrown. **1867** SMYTH *Sailor's Word-bk.*, *Main-yard Men*, those in the doctor's list.

maioid ('meɪɔɪd), *a.* and *sb. Zool.* [f. MAIA + -OID.] **A.** *adj.* Of or pertaining to the genus *Maia* or family *Maiideæ* or superfamily *Maioidea* of crabs. **B.** *sb.* A maioid crab.

1851 DANA in *Amer. Jrnl. Sci.* Ser. II. XI. 425 On the Classification of the Maioid Crustacea or Oxyrhyncha. **1852** —— *Crust.* I. 48 Small antennary space, as in the Maioids.

Hence **mai'oidean** *a.* and *sb.* = prec.

1852 DANA *Crust.* I. 51 The Maioidean series passes down from the Parthenopinea.

Maioli (mɑː'jɒlɪ). The name of Thomas Mahieu (fl. 1549–72), latinized as *Maiolus*, French book-collector and secretary to Catherine de Médicis, used *attrib.* to designate a French style of book-binding with elaborate gold tooling, used for some of the books in his library. Also *absol.*

[**1837** 'J. A. ARNETT' *Inquiry into Nature & Form of Bks. of Ancients* vi. 142 Another patron, of the name of Maioli, is well known, from his bindings, though of his personal history no traces are left.] **1890** *Catal. Exhib. Recent Bk.-Bindings 1860–9* (Grolier Club) 37 [Book] Brown morocco ..Sides decorated with a Maioli design. **1894** W. S. BRASSINGTON *Hist. Art of Bookbinding* xiii. 178 (*caption*) Maioli binding, Italian, early sixteenth century. **1928** E. P. GOLDSCHMIDT *Gothic & Renaissance Bookbindings* I. 105 Both the Groliers and the Maiolis were made by the same binders and gilders at the same time. **1961** J. P. HARTHAN *Bookbindings* (ed. 2) 12 The 'atelier au trèfle' which supplied bindings to Grolier and Henri II is probably the source also of these fine Maioli bindings.

maiolica, var. form of MAJOLICA.

maior, obs. form of MAJOR and MAYOR.

maioral, -alitie, obs. ff. MAYORAL, -ALTY.

maioram, -ane, -on, obs. forms of MARJORAM.

maiosis, maiotic, obs. varr. MEIOSIS 3, MEIOTIC *a.* 2.

maiour, obs. form of MAJOR and MAYOR.

mair, northern form of MORE, and (NIGHT)MARE.

mair, mair-: see MAYOR, MAYOR-.

†**mairatour,** *adv. Sc. Obs.* Forms: see ATOUR. [f. *mair* MORE + ATOUR.] Moreover.

1513 DOUGLAS *Æneis* III. vi. 148 And mairatour, gif outhir wit, or fame, Or traist may be [etc.]. **1552** LYNDESAY *Monarche* 6155 And, mairattour, thay sall feill sic ane smell Surmountyng far the fleure of earthly flowris. **1596** DALRYMPLE tr. *Leslie's Hist. Scot.* IV. 225 He mairattour honouret christe in his Preistes. **1819** W. TENNANT *Papistry Storm'd* (1827) 77 And mairattour,..He did dislike baith Pape and Deil.

mairch, obs. Sc. form of MARCH *sb.* and *v.*

‖**maire**[1] ('maire). Also **mairi.** [Maori.] A name for several New Zealand trees with heavy close-grained wood: **a.** *Santalum cunninghami*; **b.** *Olea* of various species; **c.** *Eugenia maire.*

1835 W. YATE *Acc. N. Zealand* (ed. 2) 41 Mairi—a tree of the Podocarpus species, growing from forty to sixty feet high. **1883** J. HECTOR *Handbk. N. Zealand* 132, 133 (Morris) Maire—a small tree ten to fifteen feet high;..wood hard, close-grained, heavy..Black maire, N.O. *Jasmineæ*; also Maire-rau-nui, *Olea Cunninghamii.*

‖**maire**[2] (mɛr). [Fr.; see MAYOR.] A mayor; the chief municipal officer of a French town or of one of the arrondissements or districts of Paris.

1790 H. WALPOLE *Let.* 30 Aug. (1905) XIV. 289 At Marseilles..a Monsieur Cazalet..had been invited to dine with the *maire*! *a* **1861** A. H. CLOUGH *Poems* (1862) 239 Their *maire*, he said, could neither write nor read. **1900** C. M. YONGE *Modern Broods* xiii. 121 She gabbled away most eloquently to the Maire, almost as fluently as a born Frenchwoman. **1955** *Times* 22 Aug. 8/6 As a record of continuous office-holding it is overshadowed by that of Edmond Mathis, maire of Ehuns in the Haute-Savoie from 1878 to 1953. **1964** C. MACKENZIE *My Life & Times* III. i. 31 Monsieur Boeuf the *maire*, who looked exactly like his name. **1974** S. SHELDON *Other Side of Midnight* ii. 55 Let's get married by some *maire* in the country.

maire, obs. form of MAYOR, MORE.

‖**mairie** (meri). [Fr., f. *maire* mayor (see MAIRE[2]).] In France, a town hall; a public building housing the municipal offices of a town or arrondissement and often also serving as the official residence of the mayor.

1864 DICKENS *Mrs. Lirriper's Legacy* i, in *All Year Round* Extra Christmas No., 1 Dec. 8/2 The Major went down to the Mairie. **1896** E. DOWSON *Let.* *c* 25 Apr. (1967) 359 In his official capacity I cannot reach him, although I call daily at the mairie & at his house. **1925** E., O., & S. SITWELL *Poor Young People* 13 Outside the mairie of this country place. **1935** W. FORTESCUE *Perfume from Provence* 82 The mysteries in the Mairie having been performed, the procession..went into the church, where the Marriage Mass was celebrated. **1966** N. FREELING *King of Rainy Country* 96 A real French country mairie with grandiose pillars outside to support the dignity of the Republic. **1974** *Times* 16 Apr. 5/1, I found M. Jarrot at the *mairie* of Montceau-les-Mines.

mairmaid, mairman: see MERMAID, -MAN.

mairouer, -ir, obs. Sc. forms of MOREOVER.

mairt: see MART.

mais, maischloch, obs. ff. MESS, MASHLOCH.

maise, variant of MEASE *sb.*[3]

maise, maisels, obs. ff. MAIZE, MEASLES.

‖**maison** (mɛzɔ̃). Also 6 **maisoun.** [a. F. *maison.*]

1. A house. Now usu. in the sense of a business (esp. a fashion) house or firm.

The early (16th–17th c.) use of the word was *Sc.*

1570 *Satir. Poems Reform.* x. 412 With all foull vice thou hes defylde yair Maisoun. *a* **1625** SIR J. SEMPLE *Picktooth for Pope* in *Harp Renfrew.* Ser. II. (1873) 19, I can but..seek my meat through many an unknown Maison. **1922** JOYCE *Ulysses* 165 He went on by la Maison Claire. **1932** 'E. M. DELAFIELD' *Thank Heaven Fasting* I. ii. 32 The tall, yellow-headed assistant from the Maison Leroy in Sloane Street.. twisted the hot irons in and out of her hair. **1935** A. CHRISTIE *Death in Clouds* xiii. 138 I'll easily get what I want from Henri's or the Maison Richet. **1966** J. S. COX *Illustr. Dict. Hairdressing* 94 *Maison*... A mode of address used by many fashionable hairdressers of the Victorian and Edwardian periods... The intention was to convey to the public that the firm had a knowledge of French hair styles... An example was *Maison Stephens et Cie.*, Queen's Road, Clifton. **1968** *Listener* 29 Aug. 280/2 The *spécialité* of this particular *maison* is the primal bourgeois myth, the Dick Whittington legend brought up to date. **1970** 'J. & E. BONETT' *Sound of Murder* ix. 112 In gold letters on a heart-shaped label were the words 'Maison Petronelle—Nail Lacquer'. **1971** D. AYERST *Guardian* xxiii. 330 Dresses by 'Maison N'Importe' and all the rest of it.

2. *Comb.* **maison close** [lit. 'closed house'], a brothel; **maison de couture,** a fashion house; **maison de passe** [lit. 'house of passage'], a brothel (see quot. 1967); **maison de santé** [lit. 'house of health'], a nursing home; also, *euphem.*, a home for the mentally sick; **maison tolérée** [lit. 'tolerated house'], a licensed brothel.

1939 E. AMBLER *Mask of Dimitrios* vii. 126 Your *maison close* must have proved disappointing. The inevitable Armenian girls, of course. **1950** *Landfall* IV. 124 The squalid harlot in the *maison close.* **1961** *Guardian* 10 Feb. 9/4 Toulouse-Lautrec..became..an inhabitant of the *Maisons Closes* where the girls regarded him as an amiable..mascot. **1927** E. HEMINGWAY in *Scribner's Mag.* Apr. 359/2 The American lady had bought her own clothes for twenty years now from the same maison de couturier [*sic*] in the Rue Saint Honoré. **1933** A. CHRISTIE *Lord Edgware Dies* xii. 107 The name of Lao Tse would suggest to her a prize Pekingese dog, the name of Molière a *maison de couture.* **1964** A. ADBURGHAM *Shops & Shopping* xxi. 247 Paul Poiret.. described..a visit paid to his *maison de couture* by Margot Asquith. **1970** S. J. PERELMAN *Baby, it's Cold Inside* 53 The rigors of squiring her through a score of *maisons de couture*, jewelers', and millinery shops were..unimaginable. **1960** B. MARSHALL *Divided Lady* xxix. 99 The hotel we drew up at eventually reminded me of a *maison-de-passe* I used to know in Barcelona. **1967** L. DEIGHTON *Expensive Place to Die* x. 71 It's not a brothel... It's a *maison de passe.* It's a house that people go to when they already have a girl with them. **1841** POE *Murders in Rue Morgue* in *Tales* (1845) 142 Some raving maniac escaped from a neighbouring *Maison de Santé.* **1859** *Times* 5 Feb. 5/6 (Advt.), Maison de Santé, or Residence for Invalids. **1910** W. J. LOCKE *Simon* xxiv. 337 He seemed to be happy enough at the *maison de santé.* **1940** JOYCE *Let.* 3 Nov. (1966) III. 496, I had arranged for the reception at a Swiss *maison de santé.* **1942** 'A. BRIDGE' *Frontier Passage* vii. 125 We don't want him shut up in a *maison de santé* for spy mania. **1893** G. B. SHAW *Let.* 12 Dec. (1965) 412 A woman of bad character, proprietress of two *maisons tolérées* in Brussels. **1927** *Observer* 11 Dec. 20/2 Agreement on that point [*sc.* that abolition of the licensed houses of prostitution decreases the white slave traffic] greatly strengthens the hands of the League in working for the abolition of the maison tolérée. **1970** K. CHESNEY *Victorian Underworld* x. 343 Conditioned by her existence in a *maison tolérée*,..she was very much in the hands of the bawd to whom she was consigned.

maison, obs. form of MASON.

maison-dieu: see MEASONDUE *Hist.*, hospital.

‖**maisonette** (meɪzə'nɛt). Also **maisonnette.** [ad. Fr. *maisonnette*, diminutive of *maison* house. The correct spelling with *-nn-* is rarely found.]

1. A small house.

1818 LADY MORGAN *Autobiog.* (1859) 27 The Charlevilles have exchanged their maisonette in Berkeley Square for Queensberry House. **1880** OUIDA *Moths* I. 234 They all lived in a little maisonette in the park.

2. A part of a residential building which is let separately, usu. distinguished from a flat by not being all on one floor.

1912 *Chambers's Jrnl.* Feb. 144/2 Flats or maisonettes, such as Queen Anne's Mansions, Westminster, London. **1919** T. S. ELIOT *Whispers of Immortality* in *Poems*, Grishkin has a maisonette. **1923** A. HUXLEY *Antic Hay* ix. 129 'It's a dr-dreadful little maisonnette,' she explained. 'Full of awful things. We had to take it furnished.' **1957** *New Yorker* 5 Oct. 171/1 Le Corbusier wisely utilized the type of apartment the English call the maisonette, with a narrow private stairs to connect upper and lower rooms. **1959** *Times* 28 May 13/5 To-day one sees maisonnettes advertised as such but also covering a range of separate living accommodation from the hotch potch of the converted house to the modern slab block of flats. **1961** L. MUMFORD *City in Hist.* Note to plate 51, The London County Council's Roehampton estate, with its mixture of tower apartments and lower houses and maisonettes. **1975** J. SYMONS *Three Pipe Problem* iii. 22 Why did wretched house agents insist upon using not the word rooms, nor apartment, nor even flat, but the atrocious *maisonette*?

maiss, variant of MEASE *v. Sc.*, to soothe.

maist, northern form of MOST.

maister: see MASTER.

†**maisterel(l.** *Obs. rare*[−1]. [f. *maister*, MASTER + -EL[2].] An imp or familiar.

1652 GAULE *Magastrom.* 25 Who is a consulter with familiar spirits? What? he that hath..confariation with a petty Maisterell? *Ibid.* 179 How many magicians,..have had their..maisterels, and minstrels, their imps, and familiars.

maisteresse: see MAISTRICE *Obs.*, MISTRESS.

maistery, maistir: see MASTERY, MASTER.

maistre, obs. form of MASTER, MASTERY.

maistres(se, obs. form of MISTRESS.

maistri, obs. form of MASTERY.

†**maistrice.** Chiefly *Sc. Obs.* Forms: 4–5 **mastrice, -is, mais-, maystries, -yes, -yse,** 5–6 **mastres,** 4–6 **maistres,** 5–6 **maistrice,** 7 **maisteresse.** [a. OF. *maistrise* (mod.F. *maîtrise*), f. *maître* MASTER. In 16–17th c. confused with the pl. of MASTERY, q.v.] = MASTERY in various senses; superiority, superior force or skill; a deed of might or skill, a feat. ***to make maistrice***: to display one's power or skill.

a **1300** *Cursor M.* 14611 Quar es nu..þis prophete..Nu sal he sceu vs his maistris. **13..** *K. Alis.* 5591 By maistres, be werres he conquerde. **1375** BARBOUR *Bruce* IV. 524 And it, that ouris suld be of richt, Throu thair maistrice thai occupy. *Ibid.* VI. 566 The hund did than sa gret mastris, That he [etc.]. *a* **1400** *Pistill of Susan* 227 He was..More miȝti mon þen we his Maistris to Make. *c* **1400** *Sowdone Bab.* 3117 Lenger durste thay no maystryes make, Thai were so sore agaste. *c* **1400** *Rom. Rose* 4172 And eek amidde this purpryse Was maad a tour of gret maistryse. *a* **1400–50** *Alexander* 333 þe renke..Gase him doune..Furthe to make his maistryse and mose in his arte. *c* **1460** *Towneley Myst.* xxv. 232 Tell me in this tyde what mastres thou makys here. *c* **1470** HENRY *Wallace* x. 696 Quhat Sotheroun thai ourtak Contrar the Scottis com neuir maistrice to mak. **1526** TINDALE *1 Cor.* ix. 25 Every man that proveth mastres abstaineth from all thynges. *c* **1560** A. SCOTT *Poems* (S.T.S.) vi. 8 So luve garris sober wemen small Get maistrice our grit

men of gud. **1680** AUBREY in *Lett. Emin. Persons* (1813) III. 566 Notwithstanding his great witt and maisteresse in rhetorique etc. he will oftentimes be guilty of mispelling in English.

† **'maistrie**, *v. Obs.* [ad. OF. *maistrier*, f. *maistre* MASTER *sb.*] *trans.* = MASTER *v.*

c **1412** HOCCLEVE *De Reg. Princ.* 1845 Naght is his goost maistried With daunger. *Ibid.* 4603 Of so seekly a condicioun, That it may by no cure be maistryed. **1481** CAXTON *Myrr.* I. v. 26 They [*sc.* unlearned clerks] be called maistres wrongfully, for vanyte maistryeth them. *c* **1532** DU WES *Introd. Fr.* in Palsgr. 950 *Maistrier*, to mastry.

maistrie, obs. form of MASTERY.

maistry ('meɪstrɪ). *Indian.* Also **maistri, mistry.** [Hindī *mistrī*, corruption of Pg. *mestre* master.] A master-workman, a foreman; applied also to a skilled workman, e.g. a cook, a tailor.

1798 WELLINGTON in Owen *Mrq. Wellesley's Desp.* (1877) 765 These are to be had in any number by making advances to the bullock owners or maistries. **1849** E. B. EASTWICK *Dry Leaves* 135 The head maistri, or builder, had discovered.. that some of the workmen had deserted. **1880** C. R. MARKHAM *Peruv. Bark* 362 The usual method of obtaining labourers is to employ a native *maistry*, who engages to enlist a fixed number of coolies.

maistry(e, maistur, obs. ff. MASTERY, MASTER.

mait, Sc. form of MATE *sb.*, *a.*, and *v.*

maiter, maith, obs. ff. MATTER, MAIZE.

maith, Sc. variant of MATHE, maggot.

maithen, maithes: see MAYTHEN, MAYTHE.

Maithili ('maɪtɪlɪ). The name of a dialect of Bihari, one of the Indo-Aryan group of languages; also, the name of its script.

1881 G. A. GRIERSON *Introd. Maithili Lang. of N. Bihar* I. i. 5 The Maithilí character is nearly the same as Bangálí, differing only in one or two letters. *Ibid.* ii. 8 Words derived direct from the Saṃskṛit, which were originally neuter, become masculine in Maithili. **1928** *Funk's Stand. Dict.* 1494/3 Many lyrics in Maithili script date from the 15th century. **1948** D. DIRINGER *Alphabet* II. vi. 365 The Oriya, Maithili and Early Manipuri characters seem...to be somewhat connected with the Bengali script. **1962** D. C. SWANSON in Householder & Saporta *Probl. Lexicogr.* I. 74, I have been unable to elicit any ['diminutive' suffixes] from speakers of.. Maithili. **1968** *Encycl. Brit.* III. 606/1 Maithili is the dialect of the old country of Mithila or Tirhut, famous from ancient times for its learning... The only dialect which has any real literature is Maithili.

maitles, obs. variant of MIGHTLESS.

‖**Maitrank** ('maɪtraŋk). [G., f. *Mai* May + *trank* drink, beverage.] = *May-drink* (MAY *sb.*[3] 5 a).

1858 GEO. ELIOT *Jrnl.* in J. W. Cross *George Eliot's Life* (1885) II. viii. 41 Delicious *Mai-trank*, made by putting the fresh *Waldmeister*—a cruciferous plant with a small white flower..into mild wine, together with sugar. **1897** G. DU MAURIER *Martian* 273 You might sit for sixpence in a pretty garden and drink coffee, beer, or Maitrank. **1899** G. JEKYLL *Wood & Garden* vi. 60 The pretty little Woodruff..revives memories..of Maitrank, that best of the 'cup' tribe of pleasant drinks, whose flavour is borrowed from its flowering tips.

‖**maître** (mɛtr). [Fr., = master.] **1.** *slang.* Also **maître d', maitre de** (mɛtr də or di). Used *ellipt.* for MAÎTRE D'HÔTEL 2.

1899 R. WHITEING *No. 5 John St.* xviii. 188 But the viands! Some of them, as the maître is so good as to tell me ..come straight from Paris. **1953** P. ADLER *House is not Home* (1954) i. 16 Hat-check girls, waiters, the maître d', some nicely-dressed people..all spoke to Harry. **1959** *Guardian* 12 Dec. 3/1 The maître de (they do not bother about the 'hotel' bit) ushered..parties..to tables. **1967** C. DRUMMOND *Death at Furlong Post* iv. 56 A very large steak ..made with great blobs of butter by a spivvy little *maître* with a spirit stove. **1969** A. GLYN *Dragon Variation* vii. 208 The *maître d'*, who knew her well, greeted her and led her to her usual table on the north side. **1973** M. CATTO *Sam Casanova* iv. 74 With the help of the *maître* who looked after the cellar they chose a fabulous Chateau d'Yquem. **1973** W. MCCARTHY *Detail* iii. 161 I've just brought over a new maître de, a young Italian fellow who will be running the place [*sc.* a restaurant]. **1974** *Publishers Weekly* 17 June 10/1 The sort of lady who is instinctively escorted to corner tables by *maitres d'*.

2. The title and form of address of a French lawyer.

1883 C. M. YONGE *Stray Pearls* I. xvi. 211 Technically he [*sc.* a lawyer] was only Maître Darpent, and his mother only would have been called Mademoiselle. Monsieur and Madame were much more jealously limited to nobility than ..now. **1910** BARONESS ORCZY *Lady Molly of Scotland Yard* vi. 148, I hear from Maître Vendôme that he has safely received my letter. *Ibid.* 165 He was met by his late aunt's lawyer, Maître Vendôme. **1957** D. DU MAURIER *Scapegoat* xxiii. 305 The lawyer bowed. 'You will have the kindness, Maître, to see that notification of the death goes to the newspapers.' **1971** *Guardian* 15 Sept. 2/6 Maître Nicolet then said in court that the centre of the European gang was a Frenchman.

3. a. maître d'armes (mɛtr darm) [lit. 'master of arms'], a fencing instructor.

1896 G. A. HENTY *Through Russian Snows* vii. 143 The veterans were always ready to give him lessons with the sabre or rapier in addition to those he received from the *maître d'armes* of the regiment. **1932** *Times Lit. Suppl.* 24 Mar. 220/2 He will by then be lost in a maze of technical terms..and will fly to a *maître d'armes* for instruction. **1956** J. D. AYLWARD *Eng. Master of Arms* ix. 110 He was.. abreast of the progress made during the seventeenth century by the great French *maîtres d'armes*. **1961** F. C. AVIS *Sportsman's Gloss.* 194 *Maître d'Armes*, a master of arms or fencing master.

b. maître de ballet (mɛtr də balɛ) [lit. 'ballet-master'], originally one who composed and superintended the production and performance of a ballet; now, a trainer of ballet dancers; hence **maîtresse de ballet**, the female counterpart.

1823 T. CREEVEY *Let.* in *Creevey Papers* (1903) II. iii. 64 Yesterday I spent a very amusing hour with Sefton at the Opera House, seeing the *maitre de ballet* manœuvre about 50 *figurantes* for the approaching new ballet of *Alfred*. **1828** J. EBERS *Seven Yrs. King's Theatre* xii. 351 An amiable and able individual..has experienced the common fate of mortality; I mean M. Boisgerard, the second Maître de Ballet. **1845** *Morning Post* 9 Apr. 5/5 *Maîtres de ballet* have to begin a new course of study. **1913** A. E. JOHNSON *Russ. Ballet* 3 But though his [*sc.* Noverre's] ambition as a *maître de ballet* outran his perceptions as an artist,..he initiated and firmly established a new form of art. **1915** M. E. PERUGINI *Art of Ballet* xxxiii. 278 A wise choice was made in the selection of the late Madame Katti Lanner as *maîtresse de ballet*. **1959** *Times* 1 Sept. 11/3 Under its *maître de ballet*.. it has reached international standards. **1975** *Times* 27 May 11/5 Hu's fight master is a former Peking *maître de ballet*.

‖**maître d'hôtel** (mɛtr dotɛl). Also 6 maistre d'hostell. [Fr. phrase = 'house-master'.]

1. A head domestic, a major-domo, a steward or butler.

1540 in Ellis *Orig. Lett.* Ser. III. III. 252 Tannagel, the maistre d'hostell with vij persons. **1695** EARL OF PERTH *Lett.* (Camden) 64 A marquise who is his maître d'hôtelle [Meant for a fem.!]. **1704** ADDISON *Italy* (1705) 488 His chief Lay-Officer is the Grand *Maître d'Hôtel* or High Steward of the Houshold. **1769** *Ann. Reg.* 104 His royal highness gave to the maitre de hotel who was charged with it [a present] a gold snuff-box. **1849** THACKERAY *Pendennis* lxxv (*init.*), Frederic Lightfoot, formerly *maître d'hôtel* in the service of Sir Francis Clavering.

2. A hotel manager; now usually the manager of a hotel dining-room, a head waiter.

1891 R. H. SAVAGE *My Official Wife* iv. 43 The attentive *maître d'hôtel* flew past us and threw open the door of a splendid apartment. **1907** E. GLYN *Three Weeks* i. 17 Her red wine the *maître d'hôtel* poured into her glass himself. **1923** M. ARLEN *These Charming People* 85 The agreeable and polished M. Risotto, prince of *maitre d'hôtels*, chanced by our table. **1959** T. S. ELIOT *Elder Statesman* I. 9 The *maître d'hôtel* And the waiters all seem to be your intimate friends. **1973** D. MILLER *Chinese Jade Affair* xvii. 157 The 'canard aux navets' was brought to the table by the Maître d'Hotel himself.

3. *attrib.* (See quots.)

1845 E. ACTON *Mod. Cookery* (ed. 2) iv. 107 *French Maitre d'Hotel*, or *Steward's Sauce*. Add to half a pint of rich, pale veal gravy,..salt, minced parsley, and lemon-juice. **1861** MRS. BEETON *Bk. Househ. Managem.* x. 223 *Maître d'Hôtel Butter*, for putting into Broiled Fish just before it is sent to Table. *Maître d'Hôtel Sauce* (*Hot*), to serve with Calf's Head, Boiled Eels, and different Fish. **1951** *Good Housek. Home Encycl.* 543/2 Simply prepared dishes garnished with maître d'hôtel butter. **1965** *House & Garden* Dec. 84/2 *Maître d'hôtel*. If given this name, a dish will probably be fairly quickly and simply cooked—a grill or something like that—and it will include parsley in some form or other. When used to describe butter, it means that the butter has been seasoned, has chopped parsley and lemon juice worked into it and is then put to get cold so that it can be made into pats. **1974** *Times* 6 Nov. 14/8 My salmon steak with maître d'hotel butter was good.

‖**maîtresse** (mɛtrɛs). [Fr., mistress.] Used in phrases, as **maîtresse en titre** [lit. 'mistress in name'], an official or acknowledged mistress; **maîtresse femme**, a strong-willed or domineering woman.

1839 THACKERAY *Catherine* in *Fraser's Mag.* July 104/1 We had a great mind to make..Mrs. Catherine *maîtresse en titre* to Mr. Alexander Pope. **1853** C. BRONTË *Villette* III. xxxii. 83 Ah! I know you well..cette maîtresse-femme, my cousin Beck herself. **1876** C. M. YONGE *Womankind* xxii. 179 There are four kinds of wives—the cowed woman, the dead-weight, the *maîtresse femme*, and the helpmeet. **1925** W. J. LOCKE *Great Pandolfo* xix. 240 She had been the *maîtresse en titre* of one of his friends. **1929** S. RUNCIMAN *Emperor Romanus Lecapenus* ii. 42 At first Leo did not dare to marry her: though he took her to the Palace as an acknowledged *maîtresse en titre*. **1929** C. L. THOMSON *Jane Austen* i. 50 The wonderful heroine [of *Corinne*], a *maîtresse femme* like Mme de Staël herself. **1931** *Times Lit. Suppl.* 9 July 544/1 She tells of..dwarf, and cicisbeo, and maîtresse en titre. **1936** G. B. SHAW *Millionairess* Pref. 105 In the humblest cabin that contains a family you may find a *maîtresse femme* who rules in the household by a sort of divine right. *Ibid.* 107 Queen Elizabeth was a *maîtresse femme*. **1953** M. STEEN *Anna Fitzalan* iii. 72 For two and a half years Anna fulfilled..the functions of a nurse, as well as those of a *maîtresse en titre* of Evan's household. **1964** *Guardian* 26 Oct. 16/8 An accredited speech-writer is, like a 'maitresse en titre', an offence to public morals. **1973** D. CHANDLER *Marlborough* i. 5 Arabella [Churchill] was.. combining the roles of maid-of-honour to the Duchess and *maîtresse-en-titre* to the Duke, to whom she bore several children. **1973** E. HYAMS *Final Agenda* viii. 98 The widow was a *maîtresse femme* whose place in the hierarchy was three steps higher than that of her..husband.

Maitreya (maɪ'treɪjə). [Skr., f. *maitrī* friendship.] In Buddhist theology, the name of the Buddha who will appear in the future; also, an artistic representation of this future Buddha.

1889 M. MONIER-WILLIAMS *Buddhism* iv. 135 Gautama is the fourth Buddha of the present age... He is to be followed by the fifth Buddha, Maitreya (a name meaning 'full of love towards all beings'). **1923** A. B. KEITH *Buddhist Philos.* xvii. 289 We have the Buddha's own authority for the advent of Maitreya. **1933** E. J. THOMAS *Hist. Buddhist Thought* xiii. 168 As a part of this doctrine of a succession of Buddhas arose the belief in a future Buddha, Metteyya, or Maitreya. **1961** *Guardian* 23 Mar. 11/3 A seated Maitreya in gilt bronze, Silla—early seventh century. **1972** P. M. BARTZ *S. Korea* 142/1 The figures are *miroks*, images of Maitreya, the Buddha of the future. **1972** D. BLOODWORTH *Any Number can Play* iii. 17 The guru strikingly resembled the Maitreya who would one day come to herald an age of happiness.

† **maitrise**, *v. Obs. rare*[−1]. [ad. F. *maîtriser*, f. *maîtrise*: see MAISTRICE.] *trans.* To make oneself master of, to conquer.

1636 BRATHWAIT *Rom. Emp.* 125 Hee recovered France newly over-run and maitrised by the Barbarians.

maize (meɪz). Forms: 6 **maith, mayis, 6–8 mais, maiz,** (7 **maes, maix, maijs, maze, mass, 8 maez**), **7–8 mayz(e, 7–8 mays,** (9 **mais(e**), 7– **maize.** Also 6 in mod.L. form **maizium.** [a. Sp. *maiz* (formerly also *mahiz, mahis, mayz*), a word of the Cuban dialect, the pronunciation of which is rendered by Oviedo in Sp. orthography as *maisi* or *majisi*; prob. identical with the Arawak (Guiana) *marisi*, and the Carib '*márichi*, bled d'Inde' (Breton, *Dict. Caraïbe*, 1665). Cf. F. *maïs*, in 16th c. *mahiz* (1555 in Hatz.-Darm.).]

1. An American graminaceous plant (*Zea Mays*) or the grain produced by it; = INDIAN CORN.

a. The plant.

1585 T. WASHINGTON tr. *Nicholay's Voy.* I. xviii. 21 In steed of corn they sow Maith [Fr. *ils sement du Maith*], which is a kind of grosse Mill. **1613** PURCHAS *Pilgrimage* VI. i. 561 The fields of Mais the great stalkes whereof were trodden downe. **1613** R. HARCOURT *Voy. to Guiana* 28 There is a kind of great wheat, called Maix, of some it is called Guinea wheat. **1672** JOSSELYN *New Eng. Rarities* 17 They [Racoons] feed upon Mass, and do infest our Indian Corn very much. **1674** —— *Voy. New Eng.* 73 Maze, otherwise called Turkie-wheat, or rather Indian-wheat, because it came first from thence. **1742** COLLINS *Ecl.* iii. 6 'Tis sweet..to..scent the breathing maize at setting day. **1861** TYLOR *Anahuac* ix. 228 The Mexicans were cultivating maize and tobacco when the Spaniards invaded the country.

b. The grain.

1555 EDEN *Decades* 3 This kynde of grayne they call maizium. *c* **1565** SPARKE *Sir J. Hawkins' 2nd Voy.* in *Hakluyt* (1589) 540 Mayis maketh good sauory bread. **1594** R. ASHLEY tr. *Loys le Roy* 15 b, Throughout the western Islands they make bread of a kind of wheat called Mahiz. **1596** RALEIGH *Discov. Gviana* 3 It hath also for bread sufficient Mais, Cassaui. **1600** HAKLUYT *Voy.* (1810) III. 602 A corne called Maiz, in bignesse of a pease, the eare whereof is much like to a teasell. *a* **1626** BACON *Med. Rem.* Wks. 1857 III. 828 Take of Indian maiz half a pound. **1732** ARBUTHNOT *Rules of Diet* i. 250 Mays is not so easily brought to Fermentation. **1832** *Veg. Subst. Food* 101 Maize is said to contain no gluten, and little..saccharine matter. **1855** LONGF. *Hiaw.* XVII. 159 They..Beat to death poor Pau-Puk-Keewis, Pounded him as maize is pounded. **1894** *Century Mag.* Apr. 849 The first generations of English-Americans subsisted mainly on maize.

2. water maize [Sp. *maiz del agua*], the *Victoria regia*, so called because of its farinaceous seeds (*Treas. Bot.* 1866); **mountain maize**, the genus *Ombrophytum* (Miller *Plant-n.* 1884).

3. Adopted as the name of one of the coal-tar colours, a pale yellow resembling that of maize. Freq. denoting a colour of cloth or dress-material.

1838 E. GROSVENOR *Jrnl.* 9 June in G. Huxley *Lady Elizabeth & the Grosvenors* (1965) iii. 78 Succeeded in finding..a maize and silver gown. **1853** MRS. GASKELL *Cranford* xiii. 244 If a happy sea-green could be met with, the gown was to be sea-green; if not she inclined to maize. **1858** GEO. ELIOT *Scenes Clerical Life* I. ii. 32 Maize is a colour that decidedly did *not* suit his complexion. **1890** THORPE *Dict. Appl. Chem.* I. 263 The sodium salt of azoxystilbene-disulphonic acid..known in commerce as 'sun yellow' or 'maize'. **1923** *Daily Mail* 15 June 6 (Advt.), Crepe de Chine..newest shades, including: Pale Pink,.. Maize, Lemon. **1970** *Cape Times* 28 Oct. 19/3 (Advt.), Rambler Rogue, 1970, 5500 miles, maize with cognac trim. **1975** *New Yorker* 26 May 54/1 (Advt.), Our all silk honan tie... Navy, red, brown, maize, rust, bottle green.

4. *attrib.* and *Comb.*, as ***maize-beer, -bread, -cob, -colour, -cutter, -ear, -field, -flour, -garden, -grain, -grits, -harvest, -meal, -oil, -plant, -stalk, -starch, -straw, -trough, -whiskey***; ***maize-coloured, -fed*** adjs.; ***maize-husking, maize-poisoning*** vbl. sbs.; **maize-bird**, an American blackbird of the subfamily *Agelæinæ*, esp. *Agelæus phœniceus*, so called from its fondness for maize; **maize-cream**, a decoction or gruel of maize or maize-meal; **maize-eater**, a South American maize-bird; **maize-smut**, a destructive fungus (*Ustilago Maydis*) attacking the maize-plant; **maize-thief** = *maize-bird*; **maize-yellow**, a yellow like that of maize.

1887 MOLONEY *Forestry W. Afr.* 450 In South America a kind of beer called Chica or *Maize beer is made from the

grain. **1837** SWAINSON *Nat. Hist. Birds* II. 100 The Agelainæ, or *maize-birds. **1855** KINGSLEY *Westw. Ho!* xxv, Baskets.. freighted with.. *maize-bread. **1890** O. CRAWFURD *Round Cal. Portugal* 197 Now the broad fields of maize are cut and the *maize-cobs garnered. **1862** O'NEILL *Dict. Calico Printing*, etc., **Maize colour*, a low toned yellow orange. **1861** *Englishwom. Dom. Mag.* III. 263/1 One skein of gold or *maize-coloured Russia braid. **1626** BACON *Sylva* §49 Indian Maiz.. must be throughly boyled, and made into a *Maiz-Creame, like a Barley Creame. **1855** LONGF. *Hiaw.* XIII. 41 Wagemin, the thief of cornfields! Paimosaid, who steals the *maize-ear! **1894** *Times* (weekly ed.) 2 Feb. 89/3 The wheat-fed pork of the North West may yet compete with the *maize-fed pork of Chicago. **1771** J. R. FORSTER tr. *Kalm's Trav. N. Amer.* II. 77 They [birds] assemble by thousands in the *maize-fields, and live at discretion. **1855** LONGF. *Hiaw.* XIII. 21 All around the happy village Stood the maize-fields. **1843** PRESCOTT *Mexico* (1850) I. 131 Pastry, for which their *maize-flour and sugar supplied ample materials. **1899** WERNER *Capt. of Locusts* 263 They.. carried her to the grove beyond the *maize-gardens. **1880** C. R. MARKHAM *Peruv. Bark* 479 The grains [of Cuzco maize] are four or five times the size of ordinary *maize grains. **1901** *Oxford Times* 9 Mar. 7/1 [The advertisers] have never used any.. *maize-grits, or any other substitute for either malt or hops. **1828** P. CUNNINGHAM *N. S. Wales* (ed. 3) II. 22, I chanced to stop for the night at the house of a gentleman during the *maize-harvest. *Ibid.* 293 Their diet.. [should] consist principally of *maize meal. **1871** KINGSLEY *At Last* xvi, The Red Indians looked on Mondamin, the *maize-plant, as a gift of god. **1897** *Allbutt's Syst. Med.* II. 801 The special characters of *maize poisoning may be due to some peculiarity in the chemical structure of this grain itself. **1896** P. A. BRUCE *Econ. Hist. Virginia* I. 167 Except the juice sucked from the crushed fibre of the *maizestalk, they had no knowledge of any spirits. **1887** MOLONEY *Forestry W. Afr.* 450 The finer qualities of *Maize starch are largely used as a substitute for arrowroot. **1886** W. J. TUCKER *E. Europe* 299 A hole in the *maize-straw thatched roofs served as chimney. **1772** J. R. FORSTER tr. *Kalm's Trav. N. Amer.* I. 372 The laws of Pensylvania.. have settled a premium of three-pence a dozen for dead *maize thieves. **1853** F. O. MORRIS *Hist. Brit. Birds* III. 9 Red-winged maize-bird... Maize-thief. **1851** MAYNE REID *Scalp Hunt.* xiii. 98 Your horse is standing at the *maize-trough. **1893** LELAND *Mem.* I. 13 *Maize-whiskey could be bought then for fifteen cents a gallon. **1897** C. T. DAVIS *Manuf. Leather* (ed. 2) 607 Light ochre yellow, *maize yellow to dark gold ochre yellow.

maizena (meɪˈziːnə). [Arbitrarily f. MAIZE.] Maize-starch prepared for use as food. Also *attrib.*

1862 in *Rep. Juries Exhib.* 1862 (1863) III. A. 13. **1862** MRS. HAWTHORNE in *N. Hawthorne & Wife* (1885) II. 326, I carried to Mrs. Alcott early this morning some maizena blanc-mange. *a* **1875** F. OATES *Matabele Land* (1889) 24 Made into a pudding with maizena.

ˈmaizer. [f. MAIZE + -ER¹.] A maize-bird.

1837 SWAINSON *Nat. Hist. Birds* II. 275 Subfam. *Aglainæ* [i.e. *Agelæinæ*] Maizers.

‖**maja** (ˈmaxa). [Sp., fem. of MAJO¹.] A Spanish woman who dresses gaily. Also *attrib.*

1832 [see MAJO¹]. **1840** LONGF. *Sp. Stud.* II. i, Now bring me, dear Dolores, my basquiña, My richest maja dress.

majerom, obs. form of MARJORAM.

majeˈstarian, *a.* *nonce-wd.* [f. MAJESTY + -*arian*.] Used humorously for: (Her) Majesty's.

1857 CLOUGH *Poems*, etc. (1869) I. 115 He is to have a deer-stalking party to-morrow, Lord Adolphus Fitzclarence, and other majestarian officers.

†**majestate.** *Obs. rare*⁻¹. [ad. L. *mājestātem* MAJESTY.] Majesty.

1533 GAU *Richt Vay* (1888) 32 Thir iii persons ar equal in power maiestate and in ewer lestyng.

majestatic (mædʒɪˈstætɪk), *a.* Now *rare.* [ad. med.L. *mājestātic-us*, f. *mājestāt-* MAJESTY.] Pertaining to the majesty of God. Cf. MAJESTICAL 2.

1659 HAMMOND *On Ps.* lxxxv. 9 The glorious majestatick presence or inhabitation of God. **1695** BP. PATRICK *Comm. Gen.* iii. 8 They heard the Voice of the Lord... The Sound of the Majestatick Presence, or the Glory of the Lord. *a* **1711** KEN *Hymns Evang.* Poet. Wks. 1721 I. 14 To gain a transient beatifick sight, Of Jesus rob'd in Majestatick Light. **1756** AMORY *Buncle* (1770) II. 53 We must distinguish.. between the essential and the majestatic presence of God.

So †**majeˈstatical** *a.*, in the same sense.

a **1694** J. SCOTT *Wks.* (1718) II. 493 He placed a great Part of the Glory of his Majestatical Presence in the Tabernacle.

†**majestative,** *a.* *Obs.*⁻⁰ [ad. late L. *majestativ-us*, f. *mājestāt-* MAJESTY: see -IVE.] Majestic.

1656 in BLOUNT *Glossogr.*

Hence †**majestativeness.** *Obs.*⁻⁰

1727 in BAILEY vol. II.

majesterialty, majesterycall: see MAGIST-.

majestic (məˈdʒɛstɪk), *a.* [f. MAJESTY + -IC.] Possessing or characterized by majesty; of imposing dignity or grandeur. **a.** Of persons, their attributes, etc.

1610 G. FLETCHER *Christ's Vict.* I. xvi, Bowing her self with a majestique air. *a* **1652** BROME *Queene's Exch.* I. i. Wks. 1873 III. 458 Your no less prudent than Majestick Father With power & policy enricht this Land. *a* **1700** DRYDEN *Flower & Leaf* 176 But in the midst was seen A lady of a more majestic mien. **1725** DE FOE *Voy. round World* (1840) 132 He was grave and majestic, and carried it something like a king. **1807** CRABBE *Par. Reg.* III. 812 His stride majestic and his frown severe. **1856** FROUDE *Hist. Eng.* (1858) I. ii. 173 Amidst the easy freedom of his address, his manner remained majestic. **1866** LIDDON *Bamp. Lect.* v. (1875) 225 St. John is spiritually as simple as he is intellectually majestic. **1871** R. ELLIS tr. *Catullus* lxxxvi. 1 Lovely to many a man is Quintia; shapely, majestic, Stately, to me.

Comb. **1870** L'ESTRANGE *Miss Mitford* I. vi. 168 A fine majestic-looking old woman of sixty.

b. Of things material and immaterial.

1601 SHAKS. *Jul. C.* I. ii. 130 It doth amaze me, A man of such a feeble temper should So get the start of the Maiesticke world. **1610** —— *Temp.* IV. i. 118 This is a most maiesticke vision. **1664** EVELYN *Sylva* iv. (1679) 33 No Tree whatsoever, becoming long Walks and Avenues, comparably to this Majestick plant [the Elm]. *a* **1704** T. BROWN *Prol. 1st Sat. Persius* Wks. ed. 1730 I. 51 Virgil's great majestick lines. **1742** YOUNG *Nt. Th.* III. 193 This Heav'n-assum'd majestic Robe of Earth, He deign'd to wear. **1794** MRS. RADCLIFFE *Myst. Udolpho* i, The view was bounded by the majestic Pyrenees. **1833–6** J. H. NEWMAN *Hist. Sk.* (1873) I. IV. i. 360 There they [Ambrosian chants] are in use still, in all the majestic austerity which gave them their original power. **1879** GEO. ELIOT *Theo. Such* ii. 32 Clad in the majestic folds of the *himation.*

Hence †**maˈjesticness,** majesty.

a **1643** CARTWRIGHT *To C'tess Carlisle* 24 Such a.. Lovely, self-arm'd, naked Majesticness. **1685** H. MORE *Illustr.*, etc. 263 Which is a marvellous manner of Transition.. sutable to the usual Majestickness of this Book of the Apocalypse.

Maˈjestic, *sb.* [f. the adj.] A variety of potato, producing light-skinned, kidney-shaped tubers.

1917 T. W. SANDERS *Bk. Potato* (ed. 3) xviii. 99 *Majestic*, tubers, oval-shaped; hardy, strong grower; enormous cropper; fine quality and appearance. **1926** R. N. SALAMAN *Potato Varieties* xxvi. 285 Majestic has attained great popularity, and today is one of the most widely grown field crop potatoes in the country. **1956** S. M. GAULT *Vegetables* x. 203 *Main Crop.* Majestic, a heavy cropping white kidney, with shallow-eyed large tubers. **1963** *Times* 22 Apr. 2/6 Majestic, which takes up over 50 per cent of the maincrop acreage, was introduced in 1912.

majestical (məˈdʒɛstɪkəl), *a.* Now chiefly *poet.* [Formed as MAJESTIC *a.*: see -ICAL.]

1. = MAJESTIC. **a.** Of persons, their attributes, etc. (*occas.* ironical).

1589 HORSEY *Trav.* (Hakl. Soc.) App. 295 Kynore [? *read* Kyuore = cover] my good lord, with thy princely wisdome and majestyecall clemency this unwillinge faulte comytted. **1593** NASHE *Christ's T.* Ded. 2 All those maiesticall wit forestalling worthies of your sexe. **1617** MORYSON *Itin.* II. 99 His person and carriage was most comely, and (if I may use the word) Maiesticall. **1652–62** HEYLIN *Cosmogr.* I. (1682) 207 Their gate is.. very stately and majestical. **1663** COWLEY *Ess., Greatness* (1688) 121 If I were ever to fall in love again.. it would be, I think, with Prettiness, rather than with Majestical Beauty. **1781** JUSTAMOND *Priv. Life Lewis XV*, II. 214 His entrance.. was splendid and majestical. **1821** BYRON *Sardan.* II. i. 532 His marble face majestical Frowns. **1866** J. H. NEWMAN *Gerontius* iv. 30 And therefore is it, in respect of man, Those fallen ones show so majestical. **1876** BANCROFT *Hist. U.S.* I. iv. 101 A grave and majestical countenance.

b. Of things material and immaterial.

1579 LYLY *Euphues* (Arb.) 161 What can we beholde more noble then the world..? what more maiesticall to the sight, or more constant in substance? *a* **1586** SIDNEY *Apol. Poetrie* (Arb.) 65 Theyr Playes.. thrust in Clownes by head and shoulders, to play a part in maiesticall matters. **1621** BURTON *Anat. Mel.* I. i. II. iv. (1651) 17 Suppose you were now brought into some.. Majestical Palace. **1651** N. BACON *Disc. Govt.* II. xi. (1739) 58 War is ever terrible, but if just and well governed, majestical. **1693** DRYDEN *Ess., Orig. Satire* (ed. Ker) II. 107 The first six lines of the stanza seem majestical and severe. **1851** LONGF. *Gold. Leg.* v. *Inn at Genoa* 4 It is the sea,.. Silent, majestical and slow. **1867** M. ARNOLD *Celtic Lit.* 61 An older architecture, greater, cunninger, more majestical.

†**2.** = MAJESTATIC. *Obs.*

1581 E. CAMPION in *Confer.* III. (1584) R ij, S. Augustine excludeth not by maiestical presence al bodily presence. **1597** HOOKER *Eccl. Pol.* v. lv. §6 If his Maiesticall body haue now any such new property. **1633** BP. HALL *Hard Texts, O. T.* 291 It pleased the Lord to represent unto me a cleare signe of the majesticall presence of the Sonne of God, sitting on high, upon a glorious throne. *a* **1638** MEDE *Wks.* (1672) 639 The proper place where the Majestical Glory is revealed, is the Heavens. **1675** BROOKS *Gold. Key* Wks. 1867 V. 526 The presence of God with his people is very majestical. *a* **1680** CHARNOCK *Attrib. God* (1682) 257 [Heaven] 'Tis the Court of his Majestical presence.

Hence †**maˈjesticalness,** majesty.

1613 *Decl. Arriv. C. Haga at Constantinople* 14 The Maiesticalnesse of Our Royall and Princely State. **1652** KIRKMAN *Clerio & Lozia* 78 This splendid greatness of a maid surpassed the magesticalness of the purest French Lillies of King Henry the third. **1727** BAILEY vol. II. **1905** *Westm. Gaz.* 19 Apr. 1/3 The majesticalness of this masterwork of human genius and human sorrows.

majestically (məˈdʒɛstɪkəlɪ), *adv.* [f. MAJESTIC, -ICAL: see -ICALLY.] In a majestic manner; with majesty, imposing dignity or grandeur.

1596 SHAKS. *1 Hen. IV*, II. iv. 479 If thou do'st it halfe so grauely, so majestically [etc.]. **1670** CLARENDON *Contempl. Ps.* Tracts (1727) 568 If princes would.. majestically suppress haughty and impetuous transgressors. **1697** DRYDEN *Æneid* IX. 35 Silent they move; majestically slow, Like ebbing Nile, or Ganges in his flow. **1725** POPE *Odyss.* VI. 158 He bends his way Majestically fierce, to seize his prey. **1853** J. H. NEWMAN *Hist. Sk.* (1873) II. I. iii. 126 The great stream of the Po.. flows majestically through its length. **1896** *Law Times* C. 489/2 Inglis.. stalked majestically out of Court, looking neither to the right hand nor to the left.

†**maˈjestify,** *v.* *Obs. rare*⁻¹. [f. MAJESTY + -FY.] *trans.* To make majestic.

1616 LANE *Cont. Sqr.'s T.* XII. (1887) 24 Vppon his helme a plume of white and redd maiestifyed his pace.

maˈjestuous, *a.* *rare.* Also ? majestious. [a. F. *majestueux*, f. *majesté* MAJESTY, after *voluptueux* VOLUPTUOUS.] Majestic.

1685 *Gracian's Courtiers Orac.* 65 The other [employments] are more majestuous, and as such, attract more veneration. **1864** CARLYLE *Fredk. Gt.* IV. 252 That voice 'sombre and majestious'.

majesty (ˈmædʒɪstɪ). Forms: 4–5 **magestee,** 4–6 **mai-, maj-, mageste,** (5 **maiestee, magiste**), 5–6 **magestie, -y,** 5–7 **maiesty, majestie,** (6 **maiestye, majistye**), 6–7 **maiestie,** (7 **majiste**), 6– **majesty.** [a. F. *majesté*, ad. L. *mājestāt-em*, *mājestās*, f. **mājes-*, ablaut-var. of **mājos-* (*mājus*, *mājōr-em* greater: see MAJOR) + *-tāt-*: see -TY. Cf. Pr. *mai-*, *majestat*, It. *magestà*, *maestà*, Sp. *majestad*, Pg. *magestade*; also G. *majestät*, Du. *majesteit*.]

1. a. The dignity or greatness of a sovereign; sovereign power, sovereignty. Also *concr.* or semi-*concr.* The person or personality of a sovereign.

1375 BARBOUR *Bruce* I. 431 [Edward I loquitur] Hys fadyr.. wes agayne my maieste. *c* **1400** *Destr. Troy* 2632 A! nobill kyng & nomekowthe!.. Let mene to your maiesty þe mynde of my tale. *c* **1460** FORTESCUE *Abs. & Lim. Mon.* vii. (1885) 125 He [*sc.* the king] woll.. bie also horses off grete price.. and do other suche nobell and grete costes, as bisitith is roiall mageste. **1489** CAXTON *Faytes of A.* I. vi. 13 The subget fereth to offende the mageste of his souerayn lorde. **1523** LD. BERNERS *Froiss.* I. ccxliii. 362 By our ryall magesty and segnory, we commaunde you [etc.]. **1528** ROY *Rede me*, etc. (Arb.) 29 Fye apon his maieste and renowne Clayminge on erthe to be in Christis stead. **1595** SHAKS. *John* II. i. 480 Why answer not the double Maiesties, This friendly treatie of our threatned Towne. **1606** —— *Ant. & Cl.* III. iii. 2 Good Maiestie: Herod of Iury dare not looke vpon you. **1726–31** TINDAL *Rapin's Hist. Eng.* (1743) II. xvii. 126 She was a sovereign queen and would do nothing prejudicial to Royal Majesty. **1782** WOLCOT in J. J. Rogers *Opie & Works* (1878) 22 The King came in after, with a skip; (not a very proper pace I think for Majesty). **1849** MACAULAY *Hist. Eng.* iv. I. 508 A man who was daily seen at the palace, and who was known to have free access to majesty. **1883** EARL ROSEBERY *Sp. at Edinb.* 21 July, The buried paraphernalia of dead majesty.

b. *spec.* The greatness and glory of God. (The earliest use in Eng.)

a **1300** *Sarmun* lvi. in *E. E. P.* (1862) 7 Boþe god and man in mageste þe heiȝ king aboue vs alle. *a* **1340** HAMPOLE *Psalter* xx. 5 He sall appere in mageste. ? *a* **1366** CHAUCER *Rom. Rose* 1339 God that sit in magestee. **1390** GOWER *Conf.* I. 195 O hihe mageste, Which sest the point of every trowthe. **1470–85** MALORY *Arthur* XVII. xxi. 721 To see the blessid Trynyte.. and the mageste of oure lord Ihesu Cryst. **1526** *Pilgr. Perf.* (W. de W. 1531) 18 b, He yᵗ wyll serche the secrete Maiestye of God by naturall reason. **1611** BIBLE *Heb.* viii. 1. **1629** MILTON *Christ's Nativ.* ii, That far-beaming blaze of Majesty. **1695** BP. PATRICK *Comm. Gen.* iii. 8 The Voice of the Lord... The Sound of the Divine Majesty's approach. *a* **1729** S. CLARKE *Serm.* lxxxiii. Wks. 1738 I. 517 The Supereminent Glory and Majesty of God. **1881** BIBLE (R. V.) *Luke* ix. 43 And they were all astonished at the majesty [*Gr.* μεγαλειότητι, TINDALE, etc. mighty power] of God. **1892** WESTCOTT *Gospel of Life* Pref. 22 The incomprehensible majesty of God and His infinite love.

c. *transf.* and *fig.*

1567 *Gude & Godlie B.* (S. T. S.) 78 Christ come full humill and full low, Us to exalt in Maiestie. **1596** DALRYMPLE tr. *Leslie's Hist. Scot.* x. 382 To contemne the Maiestie, diminise the authoritie of the Kirk. **1663** CHARLETON *Chor. Gigant.* 13 So great devotion and reverence toward the majesty of Truth. **1668** CULPEPPER & COLE *Barthol. Anat.* II. vi. 106 It were contrary to the Majesty of the principal Part, to be moved by another whether it will or no. **1712** ADDISON *Spect.* No. 327 ⁋14 The natural Majesty of Adam. **1863** WOOLNER *My Beautiful Lady* 135 The worth and majesty of England's name.

d. *Rom. Hist.* Used to render the equivalent L. *majestas* in the sense: The sovereign power and dignity of the Roman people, *esp.* considered with reference to offences against it. (Cf. LESE-MAJESTY.)

1565 COOPER *Thesaurus*, *Actio maiestatis*, an action for the breakyng of the honour and maiestie of any great or heade officer. **1581** SAVILE *Tacitus, Hist.* I. lxxvii. (1591) 43 Crime of Majesty and treason. **1862** MERIVALE *Rom. Emp.* xliv. (1865) V. 248 Under the empire the law of majesty was the legal protection thrown round the person of the chief of the state.

2. Preceded by a possessive, *your, his, her, the king's, the queen's*; sometimes with a qualifying epithet, as (*most*) *sacred, gracious, †royal.* Used as an honorific title in speaking to or of a king, queen, emperor, or empress. In this use ***Your Majesty*** is a respectful substitute for the pronoun *you*, and ***His, Her Majesty*** (abbreviated H.M.) may be either prefixed to such designations as *the King, the Queen, King Edward VII*, etc., or substituted for them; so, in modern use, ***Their Majesties***, when more then one royal person is meant. Also, with distinguishing epithet: ***His, Her Imperial Majesty*** (abbreviated H.I.M.), said of an emperor or empress; ***His Britannic Majesty*** (abbreviated H.B.M.), the King of Great Britain (and Ireland); ***His Catholic Majesty***, the

King of Spain; ***His Most Christian Majesty*** (Hist.), the King of France; in jocular language, ***His Satanic Majesty***, the Devil, Satan; also ***his sable majesty*** (see SABLE *a.*).

This use, common to all the Rom. langs., and from them adopted into all the living Teut. langs., descends from the Latin of the later Roman empire (*tua, vestra majestas*). In England it occurs, in its Latin form, from the 12th c., though examples of the vernacular form are not met with before the 15th c. It was not until the 17th c. that *your majesty* entirely superseded the other customary forms of address to the sovereign. Henry VIII and Queen Elizabeth were often addressed as 'Your Grace' and 'Your Highness', and the latter alternates with 'Your Majesty' in the dedication of the Bible of 1611 to James I.

The English syntax of this word (as of the other abstract nouns similarly employed as titles, e.g. *highness, lordship, grace, excellency*) is somewhat inconsistent. Although *Your Majesty*, like *His, Her Majesty*, requires the following verb to be in the 3rd person sing. to agree with the sb., this principle of concord is not applied to the pronouns, as in Fr. and some other langs. The neuter pronouns *it, its, which*, cannot be used with reference to a foregoing (*Your, His, Her*) *Majesty*; either the titular phrase must be repeated, or the pronoun must be the same as if the simple form ('you', or 'the king', 'the queen') had been used instead of the periphrastic form.

[**1171** *Addr. King's Clerks to Hen. II* in *Mat. Hist. T. Becket* (1885) VII. 471 Noverit vestra Majestas, quod (etc.).] **1433** *Rolls of Parlt.* IV. 444/2 Plese it to your Rial Mageste. **1536** in Speed *Hist. Gt. Brit.* (1632) 1025 The Kings most roiall Magesty. **1585** WHITGIFT in Fuller *Ch. Hist.* IX. vi. §24 To the Queens most excellent Majesty. May it please your Majesty to be advertised that notwithstanding the charge of late given by your Highness to the lower House of Parliament [etc.]. **1596** SPENSER *State Irel.* (Globe) 661/1 The great good which shall growe to her Majestie, should.. readely drawe on her Highnes to the undertaking of the enterprise. **1624** in *Archæologia* XLVIII. 211 Given by the King's Matie.. to one Bonner. **1660** BLOUNT (*title*) Boscobel or the History of His Sacred Majesties most miraculous preservation after the Battle of Worcester. **1678** BUNYAN *Pilgr.* I. 143 One of his Majesties Judges. **1751** RICHARDSON *Clarissa* (ed. 4) IV. 126 To be sure, Jack, she means to do great despight to his Satanic Majesty in her hopes of reforming me. **1761** CRUDEN *Conc. Bib.* Ded. to King, I doubt not but your Majesty will pardon my forbearing to enter upon your valuable personal accomplishments. *c* **1777** BURKE *Addr. to King* Wks. IX. 183 Your Majesty was touched with a sense of so great a disaster. **1804** M. CUTLER in *Life, Jrnls. & Corr.* (1888) III. 171 This morning, paid the high homage of my respects to his Democratic Majesty, the President. **1881** JAS. GRANT *Cameronians* I. ii. 23 Before summoning his sable majesty. **1884** G. FLEMING (Julia Fletcher) *Vestigia* I. iv. 131 His Majesty, King Humbert, will hold a grand review of his troops. **1888** MAPLESON *Mem.* (ed. 2) I. 295 His Majesty the King of Hawaii. **1922** JOYCE *Ulysses* 325 The priests and bishops of Ireland doing up his room in Maynooth in his Satanic Majesty's racing colours.

†**3.** The external magnificence befitting a sovereign. *Obs.*

1481 CAXTON *Godfrey* xxxix. 77 Themperour satte in his mageste, and the barons aboute hym. **1667** MILTON *P. L.* II. 266 Heav'ns all-ruling Sire.. with the Majesty of darkness round Covers his Throne.

4. a. Kingly or queenly dignity of look, bearing, or appearance; impressive stateliness of aspect or demeanour.

1531 ELYOT *Gov.* II. ii, The fountaine of all excellent maners is Maiestie, which.. is proprelie a beautie or comelynesse in his countenance, langage and gesture apt to his dignite, and accomodate to time, place, and company. **1549** COVERDALE, etc. *Erasm. Par. 2 Cor.* 58 A weake bodye, wherin there is no maiestye. **1603** KNOLLES *Hist. Turks* (1621) 1161 With a faire countenance, and a majestie full of mildnesse. **1667** MILTON *P. L.* XI. 232, I descrie.. One of the heav'nly Host, and by his Gate.. some great Potentate.. such Majestie Invests him coming. **1710** STEELE *Tatler* No. 115 ¶1 [Nicolini] commanded the Attention of the Audience with the Majesty of his Appearance. **1836** KINGSLEY *Lett.* (1878) I. 34 His looks were majesty, and his tongue justice. **1848** DICKENS *Dombey* xxx, Edith was there in all her majesty of brow and figure.

b. *transf.* Of natural objects, buildings, etc.

1555 EDEN *Decades* To Rdr. (Arb.) 50 The contemplation of goddes workes & maiestie of nature. **1565** COOPER *Thesaurus* s.v. *Maiestas*, the maiestie and goodly sight of a place. **1570–6** LAMBARDE *Peramb. Kent* (1826) 281 A shrine, of golde and of great Maiestie. **1667** MILTON *P. L.* IV. 607 The Moon Rising in clouded Majestie. **1822** BYRON *Heaven & Earth* I. iii, Your rugged majesty of rocks And toppling trees. **1830** J. G. STRUTT *Sylva Brit.* 6 The funereal majesty of the cedar or the yew. **1879** JENKINSON *Guide Eng. Lakes* (ed. 6) 159 At the foot of Skiddaw, which stands forth in all its majesty.

c. *sarcastically.*

1588 GREENE *Pandosto* (1607) 21 The goodman seeing his wife in her maiestie, with her mace in her hand, thought it was time to bowe for feare of blowes.

5. Impressive stateliness of character, expression, or action.

1597 MORLEY *Introd. Mus.* 114 Those *per arsin & thesin*, which of all other Canons carie both most difficultie, and most maiestie. **1662** STILLINGFL. *Orig. Sacr.* III. i. §2 Hence it is that Moses with so much Majesty and Authority begins the History of the Creation, with, In the beginning [etc.]. **1709** FELTON *Classics* (1718) 16 The Romans have left no Tragedies behind them, that may compare with the Majesty of the Grecian Stage. **1809–10** COLERIDGE *Friend* (1865) 131 Imposing only by the majesty of plain dealing. **1871** H. MACMILLAN *True Vine* vi. (1872) 260 Every thing in nature partakes of the majesty of measured progressiveness and slowness.

6. A canopy over a hearse. *Obs.* exc. *Hist.*

1483 *Funeral of Edw. IV* in *Lett. Rich. III* (Rolls) I. 7 A blacke magestie, clothe of sarsenet drawen with vj coursers traped with blacke velvet. **15..** *MS. Cott. Tib.* E viij. in Strutt *Mann. & Customs* (1776) III. 162 If he be an earle he must have a majeste and valence fringed. **1546** in Strype *Eccl. Mem.* II. II. App. A. 6 [A] stately herse of nine principals with double stories and a costly Majesty. **1849** ROCK *Ch. of Fathers* II. vii. 498 This tester-like covering [of the hearse] was known as the 'majesty'. **1850** *Gloss. Terms Archit.* I. 250.

7. *Religious Art.* (See quots.)

Cf. med.L. *majestas* (see Du Cange), OF. *maysté*, 'image de la Vierge' (Godefroy), It. *maestà*.

1485 CAXTON *Paris & Vienne* (Roxb. Libr. 1868) 27 A lytel chamber whyche.. was an oratory, where as was the mageste [F. *la maiesté*] of our Lord Ihesu Cryst vpon a lytel aulter. **1847** EASTLAKE *Mater. Hist. Oil Painting* I. 171 *note*, The only existing document relating to Cimabue shows that he was employed in 1301.. on a mosaic 'Majesty' in the tribune of the Duomo at Pisa. *Ibid.* 480 The central picture .. generally represented a 'Majesty', or enthroned Madonna. **1850** NEALE *East. Ch.* Introd. I. 238 The dome [of St. Sophia at Constantinople] was covered with mosaic of glass: the summit, as usual, representing a Majesty. **1854** FAIRHOLT *Dict. Terms Art, Majesty*,.. a representation of the Saviour seated in glory on a throne, and giving his benediction, encompassed with the nimbus called *Vesica Piscis*, and surrounded by cherubim and the four evangelistic symbols, with the *A* and *Ω*. **1872** *Gloss. Eccl. Terms* (ed. Shipley), *Majesty*, a picture of God the Father enthroned as a pope, with a tiara on His head, and with the other persons of the Blessed Trinity portrayed or symbolized. **1883** J. G. WALLER in *Archæologia* XLIX. 200 'The Majesty', a term of ancient use, is given to the figure of Our Lord seated within an aureole, holding up the right hand in act of benediction, in the other a book or orb.

8. *Her.* (See quot.)

1828–40 BERRY *Encycl. Her.* I, *Majesty*, this term is applied to the eagle when crowned, and holding a sceptre. It is then blazoned an eagle in her Majesty.

9. *attrib.*: †**majesty scutcheon**, (app.) an escutcheon bearing the royal arms.

1722 *Lond. Gaz.* No. 6084/2 A Chair of State.. with a Majesty Scutcheon over it.

Hence †**majestyship** *nonce-wd.* = MAJESTY 2.

1594 LODGE & GREENE *Looking Glasse* (1598) E 3 b, Nay and please your maiesti-ship for proofe he was my childe, search the parish booke.

majeutic, variant of MAIEUTIC.

maji, variant of *magi*, pl. of MAGUS.

majlis (mædʒ'lɪs). Also **madjlis, majlas, majliss, medjelis, medjliss, mejliss, mezlis.** [Arab. *majlis.*] An assembly or council; *spec.* the national assembly in Iran; also, a reception-room.

1821 G. F. LYON *Narr. Trav. N. Afr.* vi. 261, I found Mukni sitting in the greatest agitation, pale, and alone in the Mezlis, or Court of his Castle, and scarcely able to welcome me. **1830** J. L. BURCKHARDT *Notes on Bedouins & Wahábys* 291 At his evening assemblies (*madjlis*), everybody sat down where he could find a convenient place. **1855** R. F. BURTON *Pilgrimage* II. xv. 36 The Shaykh.. led me up to the *majlis*, which was swept and garnished with all due apparatus for the forthcoming reception ceremony. **1870** *Once a Week* 7 May 303/2 'To-morrow,' we said, 'at the *Medjliss* hour, we will be punctual.' **1885** E. BALFOUR *Cycl. India* (ed. 3) II. 799/1 *Majlas*, Arab., is an assembly. **1911** *Encycl. Brit.* XXI. 198/2 By a rescript dated the 5th of August [1906] Muzza-far-ud-Dīn Shah gave his assent to the formation of a national council (*Majlis i shora i milli*). **1920** *Glasgow Herald* 29 Nov. 11/2 The British Government expects the Mejliss to meet within a month to decide whether it wishes to ratify the Anglo-Persian agreement. **1925** *Lit. Digest* 27 June 19/2 Premier Riza Khan replied in the Medjelis that.. he would proclaim Persia a republic. **1940** F. STARK *Winter in Arabia* 160 There in the Mansabi majliss they sit. **1955** *Times* 22 June 11/3 The lead.. has been taken up by the Majlis, where a strong group of Government supporters has been formed. **1964** *Ann. Reg. 1963* 296 The Majlis was opened on 6 October, thus bringing to an end a period of some two and a half years during which the Constitution had been suspended. **1972** *Daily Colonist* (Victoria, B.C.) 12 Mar. 28/1 [Bahrein] There is an air of desert democracy mixed with a certain noblesse oblige about the majlis, the formal Arab court session in which the ruler sits on his throne. **1973** *Nat. Geographic* Feb. 227/2, I found him presiding over the *majlis*, the open meeting attended by petitioners and friends each day [in Oman]. **1974** *Christian Science Monitor* 5 Dec. 3F/2 Colorful Arab dhows sail past concrete skyscrapers outside the windows of the Majlis.

‖**majo**¹ ('maxo). [Sp.; cf. MAJA.] A Spanish dandy of the lower classes. Also *attrib.*

1832 W. IRVING *Alhambra* (1896) 134 (*The Balcony*), *Majos* and *majas*, the beaux and belles of the lower classes, in their Andalusian dresses. **1845** FORD *Handbk. Spain* I. 146 The *Majo*, the *Figaro* of our theatres, is entirely in word and deed of Moorish origin;.. he is the local dandy... The *Majo* glitters in velvets and filigree buttons, tags and tassels. **1883** LD. SALTOUN *Scraps* I. ii. 192, I had bought a full Spanish *majo* costume.. and at a distance might have been mistaken for a Spanish dandy.

majo² ('meɪdʒəʊ). Also 8 **murjoe**, 8–9 **majoe**. A West Indian shrub, *Picramnia Antidesma*. ***majo bitters*** (see quot. 1866).

a **1726** H. BARHAM *Hortus Americanus* (1794) 96 Majoe, or Macary Bitter. This admirable plant hath its name from Majoe, an old negro woman,.. who, with a simple decoction, did wonderful cures. **1797** *Encycl. Brit.* (ed. 3) XIV. 727/2 There is only one species [of Picramnia], viz. the antidesma, or murjoe bush. **1866** *Treas. Bot.* 886/2 In the West Indies the negroes use an infusion of *Picramnia Antidesma*, a shrub about eight feet high, as a cure for colic and other complaints, under the name of Majo-bitters.

majolica, maiolica (mə'dʒɒlɪkə, mə'jɒlɪkə). Also 6 **maiolique**. [a. It. *maiolica* (whence F. *majolique, maïolique*).

According to J. C. Scaliger *Exoteric. Exercit.* (1557) 136, the best ware of this kind was said to be made in the island of Majorca (called *Majolica* in the 14th c.: see Du Cange); if this statement be correct, the word is prob. derived from the name of the island.]

1. A term applied originally to a fine kind of Italian pottery coated with an opaque white enamel ornamented with metallic colours; but later applied to all kinds of glazed Italian ware, beautifully ornamented and richly coloured, also called *faience* and *Raffaelle* ware. Also, a modern imitation ware coated with a coloured enamel and decorated.

1555 EDEN *Decades* 238 The fine whyte earthe cauled Porcellana, of the which are made the earthen dysshes of the woorke of Maiolica. **1585** T. WASHINGTON tr. *Nicholay's Voy.* I. xi. 13 Two great platters of Maiolique [*printed* Macolique]. **1856** J. C. ROBINSON *Soulages Collect.* 50 The pieces.. which, in the fifteenth century, were curtly termed by the Italians 'Majorca' or 'Majorica', and thence by corruption 'Majolica', a term which.. ultimately obtained a place in the language, and was applied indiscriminately to all kinds of glazed earthenware. **1875** FORTNUM *Maiolica* 20 The general term 'Maiolica', also spelt 'Majolica', has long been and is still erroneously applied to all varieties of glazed earthenware of Italian origin. We have seen that it was not so originally but that the term was restricted to the lustred wares.

attrib. **1861** *Our English Home* 153 Majolica dishes were every day more in request. **1862** *Catal. Internat. Exhib.* II. xxv. 120/2 Modern Majolica Ware. **1873** MRS. PALLISER tr. *Jacquemart's Ceramic Art* 245 In the first years of the sixteenth century, a Florentine artist carried the majolica art into Spain.

†**b.** (See quot.) *Obs.*

1598 R. HAYDOCKE tr. *Lomazzo* III. iv. 99 Reddes are made.. of the red earth called Maiolica, otherwise browne of spaine.

2. (See quot.)

1866 LAWRENCE tr. *Cotta's Rocks Class.* 283 Majolica, a white compact limestone.

‖**majoon** (mə'dʒuːn). Also 8 **majum**, 9 **majun, madjoon, -oun.** [(Urdū and Turk.) a. Arab. *maᶜjūn.*] An intoxicating confection made of the leaves of the Indian hemp, poppyseed, nux vomica, and other ingredients.

1781 *Let.* in Ld. Lindsay *Lives Lindsays* (1840) IV. 222 Our ill-favoured guard brought us a dose of majum each, and obliged us to eat it. **1819** T. HOPE *Anast.* (1820) I. xi. 216 The ample dose of madjoon he had just swallowed. **1858** SIMMONDS *Dict. Trade, Majoon.* **1883** H. H. KANE in *Harper's Mag.* Nov. 946/1 Small black lozenges, consisting of the resin of hemp, henbane, crushed datura seeds, butter, and honey, and known in India as *Majoon*, amongst the Moors as *El Mogen*.

major ('meɪdʒə(r)), *sb.*¹ [a. F. *major*, short for *sergent-major*, SERGEANT-MAJOR, which like some other military titles originally designated a much higher grade than at present.]

1. a. In the army: An officer next below the rank of a lieutenant-colonel and above that of a captain. ***major of (a) brigade*** = brigade-major.

[**1579** DIGGES *Stratiot.* 105 Item, the Sergeant Maior, by his office, is to appoint euerie Captayne his place.] **1643** WHITELOCKE *Mem.* 70 Major Gunter was shot dead in the place. **1647** CLARENDON *Hist. Rebell.* VII. §34 Whereof the lord Digby.. colonel Wagstaffe, and major Legg, were the chief of the wounded. *a* **1671** LD. FAIRFAX *Mem.* (1699) 88 Major Fairfax, who was Major to his regiment, had at least 30 wounds, of which he dyed at York. **1675** BAXTER *Cath. Theol.* II. XIII. 294 Major Danvers, an Anabaptist. **1706** PHILLIPS (ed. Kersey), *Major of a Brigade*, an Officer, either of Horse or Foot, who receiving Orders, and the Word from the Major General, gives them to the Major of each Regiment. **1781** T. SIMES *Milit. Guide* (ed. 3) 9 The Majors of Brigade go every day to receive the orders from the Adjutant-general. *Ibid.* 11 When the encampment is to be formed, the General Officers, Brigade-majors, Aid-de-camps, &c. are appointed in public orders to their several posts and stations. **1833** MARRYAT *P. Simple* xx, The major commandant and the officers retired to consult. **1844** *Regul. & Ord. Army* 69 No Officer shall be promoted to the Rank of Major, until he has been six years in the Service.

b. ***brigade-, fort-, town-major***, etc.: see the prefixed words.

c. An officer in the Salvation Army.

1907 G. B. SHAW (*title*) Major Barbara. **1970** C. BRAMWELL-BOOTH *Catherine Booth* vi. 377 The Army Mother gave colours to.. Major Rose Clapham and her assistants who were to establish the work in South Africa. **1975** *Times* 30 Apr. 9/3 Major Eva den Hartog, of the Dutch Salvation Army, has spent the last 17 years at the disaster centres of the world.

d. Major Mitchell *Austral.* = *Leadbeater's cockatoo* (LEADBEATER¹).

1898 E. E. MORRIS *Austral Eng.* 280/1 *Major Mitchell*, vernacular name of a species of Cockatoo, *Cacatua leadbeateri*... It was called after the explorer, Major (afterwards Sir Thomas) Mitchell, who was Surveyor-General of New South Wales. The cry of the bird was fancifully supposed to resemble his name. **1911** C. E. W. BEAN '*Dreadnought' of Darling* xvii. 169 We came across a flock of 'Major Mitchells',.. white and pink, and exceedingly pretty when they fly and show the whole expanse of their pink feathers. **1953** A. MOOREHEAD *Rum Jungle* iii. 40 Two of the Major Mitchells lighted on my shoulder. **1966** *Times* 28 Mar. (Austral. Suppl.) p. xvi/5 The Major Mitchell or pink cockatoo.

e. (See quot. 1919.)

1910 R. Blatchford *My Life in Army* xvii. 52 The 'major' meant well. **1919** *Athenæum* 25 July 664/1 '*Major*', for Sergeant-major—a polite form of address by an N.C.O. **1925** Fraser & Gibbons *Soldier & Sailor Words* 150 *Major, the*, the usual name among N.C.O.'s colloquially for the Sergeant Major.

2. A kind of wig (see quot. *c* 1770). Also ***major wig***. *Obs.* exc. *Hist.*

1753 Smollett *Cnt. Fathom* (1784) 162/1 His tye-wig degenerated into a major. ***c* 1770** *J. Granger's Lett.* (1815) 280 A full wig tied back in one curl is a Major, in two curls is a Brigadier. **1785** Mackenzie *Lounger* No. 4 An embroidered waistcoat with very large flaps, a major wig, long ruffles nicely plaited. **1823** *Mirror of Lit.* 12 July II. 115/1 Lander made his [the poet Thomson's] majors and bobs.

3. *Angling.* The name of an artificial salmon fly.

1867 F. Francis *Angling* x. 302.

major ('meɪdʒə(r)), *a.* and *sb.*[2] Also 4 **maiour**, 6–7 **maior**. [a. L. *mājor* nom. sing. masc. and fem. (neut. *mājus*; declension stem *mājōr-*), used as comparative of *magnus* great, to the root of which it is referred by most philologists, though the phonology is not quite clear.

Cf. OF. *maire*, obj.-case *maor*, *maiour*, Pr. *majer*, *maer*, obj.-case *major*, Sp. *mayor*, Pg. *major*, *mor*, It. *maggiore*; also the learned forms F. *majeur*, *major*, used in certain specific senses, and perh. the proximate source of some of the Eng. uses below. Cf. mayor.]

A. *adj.*

I. = greater in certain applications. (Not followed by *than*.)

1. a. Used as the distinctive epithet of the greater (in various senses) of two things, species, etc., that have a common designation; also applied to those members of a class that form a subdivision on the ground of being greater than the rest; opposed to *minor*. Chiefly in certain special collocations which originated in med. or mod.L.; in most of these *greater* may be substituted, e.g. in *major excommunication*, *orders*, *prophets* (see those sbs.). † ***Major Fellow*** (Cambridge): a senior Fellow. ***major epilepsy***: epilepsy proper, as distinguished from the 'petit mal'. ***major road***, esp. in phr. ***major road ahead*** used on traffic signs (until 1967).

Much less common than the corresponding use of minor. Occasional uses (as 'major poet') are sometimes suggested by antithesis with the recognized collocations of *minor*.

***a* 1400** *Stac. Rome* 475 At seinte Marie þe maiour [= Santa Maria Maggiore, Rome] þer is a chirche of gret honour. **1597** Skene *De Verb. Sign.* s.v. *Homagium*, [Homage] sulde be maid be the vassall being *minor*, or *maior*, to his ouerlorde. **1660** Trapp (*title*) A Commentary or Exposition upon The four Major Prophets. **1670** Walton *Lives* iv. 21 He was made Minor Fellow in the year 1609... Major Fellow of the Colledge, March 15. 1615. **1727–41** Chambers *Cycl.* s.v. *Orders*, Sacred, or Major Orders, we have already observed, are three: viz. those of deacon, priest, and bishop. **1883–5** *Catholic Dict.* (ed. 3) s.v. *Excommunication*, The major excommunication deprives of all ecclesiastical communion, and is equivalent in substance to *anathema*. *Ibid.* s.v., The superior ranks of the sacred ministry—bishops, priests, deacons, and subdeacons—are said to have major orders. Before the thirteenth century the subdiaconate was one of the minor orders. **1887** Freeman *Exeter* iii. 63 There is not much to note in the nomenclature of these churches... Saint Mary Major..takes also the English shape of St. Mary More. **1898** *Allbutt's Syst. Med.* V. 846 An increased circulation in the cutaneous area and sweating, as we see in the major epilepsy. **1901** *Scotsman* 9 Sept. 7/1 Miller made a declaration before the sheriff, but will probably have to make another on the major charge of causing Durham's death. **1930** *Highway Code* 7 It is the duty of a driver on a minor road when approaching a major road *to go dead slow*. **1937** R. F. Broad *Motor Driving made Easy* (ed. 6) v. 61 The *Halt at Major Road Ahead* sign.. enforces a definite standstill upon road users. **1950** *N.Y. Times* 20 Apr. 1/5 Railroad firemen and engineers called a strike against four major roads for Wednesday. **1967** L. Meynell *Mauve Front Door* xi. 137 Sidney Street runs into Falloden Street at right angles; there isn't any sort of traffic sign ('Halt' 'Major Road Ahead' or anything like that). **1968** *Highway Code* 14 You must..be ready to stop to let traffic on the major road go by first. **1972** A. Draper *Death Penalty* v. 37 Hudson drove the car at full speed, not even bothering to halt at the major road ahead.

b. *Prosody.* Used to distinguish the longer of two types of verse bearing a common name.

1883 G. A. Simcox *Hist. Lat. Lit.* II. 356 St. Agnes, whose legend is given in very spirited major alcaics.

c. *Football.* ***major point***: a goal (opposed to *minor point*, i.e. a try).

1896 *Field* 4 Jan. 22/2 McIlwaine registered a try and Boas bringing off the major point, Belfast left off winners by a goal and a try to a goal.

d. In Bridge. ***major suit***: spades or hearts (tricks taken by the declarer when these are trumps score more points than when clubs or diamonds are trumps). Also *ellipt.*

1916 R. F. Foster *Auction Bridge for All* vii. 27 High cards, two sure tricks, are just as necessary in the major suits as in the minor suits. **1927** M. C. Work *Contract Bridge* ii. 11 Many find it easier to remember 20 for Minors, 30 for Majors and 35 for No Trump. **1958** *Listener* 9 Oct. 572/3 It would give an exaggerated picture to reverse by following One Diamond with Two of a major. **1973** *Country Life* 13 Dec. 2048/1 Many pairs reached Six Diamonds, which is an inferior contract... It scores less than the major suit slam. **1974** *Times* 27 Apr. 10/3 After opening a strong No Trump without a four-card major, I rarely know how much strength to read into my partner's second response.

e. N. Amer. ***major league***, the highest division of teams in baseball, etc. Also *attrib.*

1942 *Sun* (Baltimore) 3 Apr. 18/6 The pitching machine now used in several major league training camps. **1947** *Partisan Rev.* XIV. 258 He concealed his fear most of all from himself by means of his devotion to professional sports, major league baseball especially. **1963** C. Anderson *Young Sportsman's Guide Baseball* ii. 17 A vast number of the current major league players had participated in the American Legion sponsored Leagues. **1968** *Globe & Mail* (Toronto) 17 Feb. 35 (Advt.), Start with the finest beaches in Florida, add great fishing,..major league baseball, greyhound and horse racing. **1971** H. Seymour *Baseball* II. p. vi, I..scouted unofficially..for two major-league clubs.

2. *Logic.* ***major term***: the term which enters into the predicate of the conclusion of a syllogism. ***major premiss***, ***proposition***: that premiss of a syllogism that contains the major term.

***a* 1533** Frith *Wks.* 147/1 Now of this maior or first proposition thus vnderstand, doth the conclusion folowe directly. **1661** Cowley *Verses & Ess., Cromwell* (1669) 66 Your last argument is such (when reduced to Syllogism) that the Major Proposition of it would make strange work in the World if it were received for truth. **1860** Abp. Thomson *Laws Th.* §93. 164 That premiss in which the predicate (major term) is compared with the middle, was formerly called the Major premiss. **1871** Morley *Crit. Misc.* Ser. I. *Carlyle* (1878) 168 A man of genius is at liberty to assume all his major premisses.

3. *Math.* and *Astron.* †**a.** (See quot. 1571.) *Obs.* **b.** ***major axis***: the axis (of a conic section) which passes through the foci; also called *transverse axis*. † ***major circle*** = great circle (see circle 2).

1571 Digges *Pantom.* iv. Xiv b, If the side of Icosaedron be a line rationall, the dimetient of the comprehending sphere shalbe an irrationall line called *Maior*. *Ibid.*, The semi-dimetiente of that circle wheron the body is framed will be an irrationall, called of Euclide *Maior*. **1646** Sir T. Browne *Pseud. Ep.* ii. ii. 62 The true meridian is a major circle passing through the poles of the world, and the Zenith or Vortex of any place, exactly dividing the East from the West. **1854** Moseley *Astron.* lxxxviii. (ed. 4) 231 The larger axis of the ellipse, which is the orbit of a planet, being called its axis major. **1862** *Catal. Internat. Exhib.* II. xi. 15 The difference between major and minor axis being ·012 of an inch. **1885** Leudesdorf *Cremona's Proj. Geom.* 275 The polar reciprocal of an ellipse (hyperbola) with respect to a circle having its centre at a focus and its radius equal to half the minor (conjugate) axis is the circle described on the major (transverse) axis as diameter.

4. *Mus.* **a.** Applied to intervals greater by a chromatic semitone than those called *minor*, i.e. to the normal or perfect intervals; as ***major third***, ***sixth***, ***seventh*** (and, in occasional recent use, ***major fourth*** and ***fifth***, commonly called *perfect fourth* and *fifth*). Hence also applied to the note distant by a major interval from a given note. Also, in acoustical theory, applied to the larger of two intervals differing by a minute quantity, as ***major tone*** (vibration-ratio $\frac{9}{8}$, being greater by a comma than the *minor tone*, $\frac{10}{9}$). **b.** Applied to a common chord or triad containing a major third between the root and the second note; hence to a cadence ending on such a chord. **c.** Denoting those keys, or that mode, in which the scale has a major third (and also a major sixth or seventh). (In naming a key, *major* follows the letter, as *C major*.)

1694 W. Holder *Harmony* (1731) 49 If A to B be as 5 to 4, they sound a Ditone, or Third Major. *Ibid.* 50, $\frac{4}{5}$ sound a Third Major,..$\frac{3}{5}$ a Sixth Major. *Ibid.* 114 In Diatonic Music there is but one sort of Hemitone..call'd Hemitone Major, whose Ration is 16 to 15... There are two sorts of Tones; viz. Major, and Minor. *Ibid.* 130 Seventh Major, 15 to 8. ***a* 1734** North *Lives* (1742) 298 He makes great Ado about dividing Tones Major, Tones Minor, Dieses and Commas, with the Quantities of them. **1806** Callcott *Mus. Gram.* ii. i. 98 The Major Second..does not consist of two equal parts. **1811** Busby *Dict. Mus.* s.v. *Key*, The natural keys of C major and A minor. **1848** Rimbault *First Bk. Piano.* 37 Every Major Key has its relative Minor; that is to say, a piece with the same signature may be written either in a Major or a Minor mode, according to the position of the Key-note. **1866** Engel *Nat. Mus.* ii. 25 The major and minor scales. **1887** Browning *Parleyings, Ch. Avison* xiii, Blare it forth, bold C major! **1898** Stainer & Barrett *Dict. Mus. Terms* s.v. *Interval*, The pertinacity with which professors adhere to the expression *perfect* fifth and *perfect* fourth, and abhor the term *major* fifth and *major* fourth.

5. That constitutes the majority or larger part; now only with *part*, *portion*, or other sbs. of like meaning. Formerly (*rare*) in predicative use: †Preponderating in quantity.

1594 Hooker *Eccl. Pol.* iv. xiii. §9 When they are the major part of a general assembly. **1599** B. Jonson *Cynthia's Rev.* ii. iii, The more generall, or maior part of opinion goes with the face, and (simply) respects nothing else. **1621** Elsing *Debates Ho. Lords* (Camden) 85 The House to debate the doubte,..and, if the major part doubte, yt may be re-comitted. **1630** *R. Johnson's Kingd. & Commw.* 118 For the Major part it is barren. **1649** N. Bacon *Disc. Govt. Eng.* i. xlvii. (1739) 79 That they all had votes, and that the major number concluded the matter. **1703** Maundrell *Journ. Jerus.* (1732) 26 The major part of the City lies between two Hills. **1743** *Lond. & Country Brew.* iii. (ed. 2) 243 Not only the *Fæces*, but the whole Body of the Drink will consequently oppose the Remedy, and if they be Major, the Attempt will prove abortive. **1774** T. Hutchinson *Diary* 3 Oct. (1884) I. 254 A person had the major vote for Alderman... Another person..had the minor vote in the election. **1790** Umfreville *Hudson's Bay* 16 After wandering about..for the major part of the day. **1818** Jas. Mill *Brit. India* I. v. ii. 374 The major party deemed it an important article of the duty of the Supreme Council. **1866** Crump *Banking* i. 25 It will be found, in by far the major part of these failures.

†**6.** Used for: Paramount to all other claims.

1606 Shaks. *Tr. & Cr.* v. i. 49 My maior vow lyes heere; this Ile obay.

7. Following the sb. qualified. **a.** In certain combinations adopted from Fr., as in ***quart***, ***quint***, ***tierce major***: see quart *sb.*[3], quint *sb.*[2], tierce, and in military titles, as drum-major, sergeant-major, ***surgeon-major***. So (jocularly) ***poet-major***. **b.** ***bob major*** (Bell-ringing): see bob *sb.*[5] **c.** In boys' schools, appended to a surname to distinguish the elder (or the one who has been longest in the school) of two namesakes.

1616 B. Jonson *Ev. Man in Hum.* i. i, One is a Rimer sir, o' your owne batch, your owne leuin; but doth think himselfe Poet-maior, o' the towne. **1866** *Routledge's Ev. Boy's Ann.* Mar. 146 Brown major had a trick of bringing up unpleasant topics.

II. 8. a. Of full age; out of (one's) minority.

1646 Howell *Lewis XIII* 27 [It] was an open..attempt upon his authoritie now that he is declar'd *Major*. ***a* 1649** Drumm. of Hawth. *Hist. Jas. II*, Wks. (1711) 21 A king of France is declared to be of full years and major the fourteenth of his age. **1745** *De Foe's Eng. Tradesman* (1841) I. ii. 12 At which time I arrived to Man's estate, and became Major. **1787** Charlotte Smith *Rom. Real Life* I. 162 The Chevalier de Villiers being major, might marry Julie de Lalande. **1840** Thackeray *Yellowplush Mem., Mr. Deuceace at Paris* viii, We are both major, you know; so that the ceremony of a guardian's consent is unnecessary. **1892** Gillespie *Bar's Priv. Intern. Law* (ed. 2) 312 A Dutch minor, who is by the law of Belgium major, cannot dispose of his real property in Belgium without [etc.].

b. *fig.* in *Sc. Proverb.*

1808 Forsyth *Beauties Scotl.* V. 220 The double stone dike or wall..makes at once a complete fence, or, as is sometimes said, 'it is major the day it is born'.

B. *sb.*

1. In occasional uses: A 'major' individual of a specified class. Cf. A. 1.

1626 Bacon *Sylva* §839 *marg.*, Experiment Solitary, touching Alterations, which may be called Maiors. **1660** *Trial Regic.* 12 If He [the King] be Supreme, there is neither Major, nor Superior. **1897** *Daily News* 20 Mar. 5/2 The minors [*sc.* poets], and many who esteem themselves majors, are constantly on offer.

2. *Logic.* The major premiss in a syllogism.

1530 Palsgr. 467/1 Of that major graunted he brought in foure or fyve conclusions. **1532** More *Answ. Frith* Wks. 840/2 In this argument hee begynneth with (shoulde) in the maior, and than in the minor and the conclusion turneth into (can). **1634** Canne *Necess. Separ.* 91, I need not here take D. Laitons compasse, to fetch the Bishops Major, and the Separatists minor, to make vp an entire Syllogisme of separation. **1696** Vanbrugh *Relapse* v. iii, Thou art out in thy logic. Thy major is true, but thy minor is false. **1717** Prior *Alma* iii. 78 Can syllogism set things right? No: majors soon with minors fight. **1849** Macaulay *Hist. Eng.* x. II. 629 They cared little whether their major agreed with their conclusion.

3. *Mus.* Short for *major key*, *mode*, etc.: see A. 4.

1797 *Encycl. Brit.* (ed. 3) XII. 547 *note*, Such another piece [is]..upon C, with sol, ut, and its major. **1818** Busby *Gram. Mus.* 360 The transition..from any Minor key to its relative Major. *Ibid.* 363 A Minor key [may be said to be related] to the same key in the Major.

4. One who has 'come of age'.

1616 J. Castle in *Crt. & Times Jas. I* (1848) I. 431 Every man that is once knighted is *ipso-facto* made a major, and *sui juris*. **1754** Shebbeare *Matrimony* (1766) II. 280 In France ..the Major, whether Man or Woman, who marries a Minor, is punished with Death. ***a* 1845** Hood *Sniffing a Birthday* vii, I'm free to give my I O U, Sign, draw, accept, as majors do.

5. As an official title. (Cf. major *sb.*[1]) ‖**a.** The (Latin) designation of the superior in certain brotherhoods. **b.** The designation of some university official at Oxford. *Obs.* exc. *Hist.*

a. 1882–3 Schaff *Encycl. Relig. Knowl.* II. 1025 Even the smaller ones [brotherhoods] had their superior or major.

b. 1726 Amherst *Terræ Fil.* No. 10. 51 Having saunter'd a pretty while along the quadrangle, impatient of the lecturer's delay, I ask'd the *major* (who is an officer belonging to the schools) whether it was usual now and then to slip a lecture or so.

6. In some universities, a subject to which special attention is given during a certain period of study. Also, this subject seen as a qualification. Also, a student thus specializing. orig. *U.S.*

1890 in T. W. Goodspeed *Hist. Univ. Chicago* (1916) 142 A subject taken as a major requires eight or ten hours classroom work or lecture work a week. **1907** *Columbia Univ. Catal.* Mar., Open only to students taking a major in the Department of English. **1926** [see elective *sb.* 2]. **1948** *Democrat* 5 Aug. 1/7 Mr. Gray will receive the Bachelor of Science degree with a major in business administration. **1949** *Daily Ardmoreite* (Ardmore, Okla.) 25 Jan. 6/6 McLaurin is a Negro education major at the University of Oklahoma who is receiving instruction in a separate classroom. **1953** *Manch. Guardian Weekly* 24 Dec. 14/3 Courses for the 'English major'. These are courses in phases of English literature designed largely..for those who are 'majoring' in English. **1959** *Times* 8 Sept. 3/2 (Advt.), Royal Australian Air Force. Education Officers required with Majors in Maths or Physics. **1961** *New Statesman* 3 Mar. 338 In English Studies the 'major' could be English

literature. **1964** L. Nkosi *Rhythm of Violence* II. ii. 38 She has been campaigning among Afrikaner students... Sarie is a Social Science major! **1972** *Jrnl. Social Psychol.* LXXXVII. 91 Three female upperclass psychology majors served as experimenters. **1972** *N.Y. Times* 3 Nov. 22/4 The regulars are unhappy..that the McGovern organization has selected as its two district coordinators a shaggy-headed political-science major at Brooklyn College who sometimes tours the neighborhood in dungarees, [etc.]. **1973** *Black World* Mar. 62 He is presently a theater-arts major at Los Angeles Community College.

7. *Sport. ellipt.* for *major penalty*, *score*, etc.

1951 *Football Record* (Melbourne) 8 Sept. 18 They opened with four behinds, and then rattled on sixteen majors. **1962** *Kingston* (Ontario) *Whig-Standard* 28 Dec. 9/7 Kingston took 21 penalties and Gananoque sat out 14 sentences, including a misconduct to James McGlade for incurring his second major of the game. **1969** *Sun-Herald* (Sydney) 13 July 48/2 Goals by Brian Douge and Ray Wilson seemed to put the seal on the match for Hawthorn until a last-minute burst by the Dons took them to within a straight goal, with two majors by Blethyn. **1970** *Toronto Daily Star* 24 Sept. 17/5 Peter Murray of Jarvis raced 23 yards for a third-quarter major, then quarter-back Mike Chrzan sneaked from three yards in the fourth, Lang converting. **1970** *Globe & Mail* (Toronto) 25 Sept. 33/3 Parkdale quarterback Rich Chudziak tossed a 38-yard pass to Wally Lytwynec, who ran 30 yards for the major.

8. A major company, organization, etc.

1968 *Wall St. Jrnl.* 24 Apr., Says a Columbia Pictures Corp. screen writer: 'You can be sure what Russ is doing today will be done by the majors tomorrow.' **1968** *Blues Unlimited* Sept. 29 Apart from Goldstar, the major outputs were from the majors in Hollywood. **1973** *Time* 25 June 85/2 In some cases, asserted his Connecticut counter-part, Robert Killian, 'the majors are taking over the choice locations, putting up giant 20-pump stations with 24-hr. service and are replacing the small dealers'. **1974** *ITV 1974* 10/2 The [Independent Television] Authority..created a system made up of several large so-called 'network companies' (sometimes also called the 'majors') and a number of smaller 'regional companies' (sometimes called the 'minors')... The five major companies..are the main providers of network programmes to be used by the whole service. **1974** *Spartanburg* (S. Carolina) *Herald* 24 Apr. A2/2 Of the four majors reporting so far, only Exxon showed a decline from the fourth-quarter profits, while Amoco's net rose 81 per cent.

major (ˈmeɪdʒə(r)), *v. dial.* [f. MAJOR *sb.*[1]]

1. *intr.* To walk with an important air; to strut. Also with *about*, *up and down*.

1814 Scott *Wav.* xlii, Mr. Waverley's wearied wi' majoring yonder afore the muckle pier-glass. **1822** —— *Pirate* xxx, She..majors up and down my house as if she was mistress of it. **1832** —— *St. Ronan's* xx, Can it be for the puir body M'Durk's health to major about [1824 to gang about] in the tartans like a tobacconist's sign in a frosty morning? **1892** *Monthly Packet* May 548 The African dove..goes 'majoring' about to very lively tunes of its own.

2. *trans.* To bully, domineer over.

1829 *Examiner* 17/1 In majoring, hectoring, and bullying subalterns, he will be found peremptory enough.

3. *intr.* Of a university student: to take, or qualify *in*, a major course of study. Also *transf.* orig. *U.S.*

1924 P. Marks *Plastic Age* xvii. 185 Having decided to major in English, he found that he was required to take a composition course the second half of his sophomore year. **1927** *Brit. Weekly* 1 Sept. 470/2 It is a thesis for the Th.D. degree, for which he has already stood the examination, 'Majoring' in Greek New Testament at Louisville. **1929** *Publishers' Weekly* 20 July 252 Bulbous-headed adolescents who have majored in English descend in shoals. **1955** W. Gaddis *Recognitions* I. i. 7 As a youth in a New England college he had..majored in classical poetry. **1958** *Times Lit. Suppl.* 5 Sept. 502/2 He majored in forgery and illegal entry inside several specially recommended prisons. **1965** *Listener* 25 Feb. 290/2 A student who in the School of Social Studies 'majors'—Sussex seems to revel in this transatlantic noun-verb—in history also reads various 'contextual' subjects. **1971** *Progress* (Cape Town) May 1/2 He majored in Afrikaans at Witwatersrand University. **1972** *Daily Tel.* 12 June 21/2, I am studying A levels in geography, English and art, with a view to majoring in geography. **1973** *Amer. N. & Q.* 83/1 For both B.A. and M.A., Eliot majored in literature.

major, -al(i)ty, obs. ff. MAYOR, MAYORALTY.

majoram, -an(e, obs. ff. MARJORAM.

‖**majorat** (maʒɔra). *Continental Law.* [Fr., ad. med.L. *mājōrātus* (*u*-stem), f. L. *mājōr-em* MAJOR *a.* in the sense 'elder': see -ATE[1].] The right of primogeniture; also, an estate attached to the right of primogeniture.

1841 W. Spalding *Italy & It. Isl.* III. 83 That restoration of hereditary aristocracy which was effected in France, took place in Italy likewise, by a decree of 1808, bestowing on the sovereign the power of conferring titles, and allowing the nobles so created to institute majorats, or devises of lands in favour of their eldest sons, or others whom they might select to transmit their honours. **1853** Whewell *Grotius* I. 379 The same rule holds with regard to the majorats in that kingdom [Castile]. **1879** Baring-Gould *Germany* I. 54 In Bavaria, the noble families are allowed by law to found fresh majorats, *i.e.* fresh families with entailed estates.

majorate (ˈmeɪdʒəreɪt), *sb. rare*$^{-0}$. [f. MAJOR *sb.*[1] + -ATE[1]; cf. F. *majorat* in the same sense.] The rank or office of a major; a majority.

1822 Booth *Analyt. Dict.* 127 That [*sc.* the rank or office] of a Major is a Majorate, or a Majority.

†**majorate**, *v. Obs. rare*$^{-1}$. [f. med.L. *mājōrāt-*, ppl. stem of *mājōrāre*, f. L. *mājōr-em* greater: see MAJOR *a.*] *trans.* To make greater; to cause to increase or develop.

1656 Blount *Glossogr.*, *Majorate*, to make greater. **1660** Howell *Parley* 142 The Embryo..proceeds to majoration and augmentation accordingly; And it is..an absurdity to think, that the Infant after conception should be majorated by the influence of any other Soul then that from whom he received his formation.

†**majoˈration.** *Obs.* [a. med.L. *mājōrātiōn-em*, n. of action f. *mājōrāre*: see prec.] The action of increasing or intensifying; *esp.* in *Med.*

1626 Bacon *Sylva* §154 So that there be five wayes.. of Majoration of Sounds. **1659** *Gentl. Calling* viii. §16 The Physicians indeed talk of a method of curing some Diseases by Majoration. **1660** [see MAJORATE *v.*]. **1673** *Lady's Call.* II. ii. §9 Some..as if they thought Jealousy were to be cured by majoration, have..don things to inflame it.

Majorcan (məˈdʒɔːkən, məˈjɔːkən), *sb.* and *a.* Also 7 **Majorkine.** [f. *Majorca* the name of one of the Balearic Islands + -AN.] **a.** *sb.* A native or inhabitant of Majorca. **b.** *adj.* Of or pertaining to Majorca. Cf. MALLORCAN *sb.* and *a.*, MALLORQUIN *sb.* and *a.*

1697 H. Maundrell *Jrnl.* 27 Apr. in *Journey from Aleppo* (1703) 123 We..were very courteously receiv'd by the Guardian, Father Raphael, a Majorkine by birth. **1848** E. J. Sabine tr. *A. von Humboldt's Cosmos* II. 147 One maritime people after another, Phoenicians,.. Majorcans,.. and Spaniards, made successive efforts to penetrate onwards in the Atlantic Ocean. **1858** *Leisure Hour* 18 Feb. 103/2 This Majorcan driver said he had always thought a Protestant meant 'somebody who does not accept the Bible'. **1873** *Gentl. Mag.* Feb. 219 The family of Napoleon I. was originally native of that island *i.e.* Majorcan. **1876** C. T. Bidwell *Balearic Islands* 105 Myrtle-covered posts, in the use of which the Majorcans display natural skill. *Ibid.* 111 Majorcan carpets and matting cover the floors. **1935** J. A. Fraser *Spain & W. Country* ix. 106 The five following treatises of the great Majorcan [*sc.* Ramon Lull]. **1965** *New Statesman* 14 May 766/3 There is some farcical reporting of Majorcan dialogue. *Ibid.* 767/1 The Majorcans believe in being 'formal' as the Spaniards also do. **1973** *Times* 2 June 13/7 A Majorcan official remarked that the British went about as though they owned the country.

major-domo (ˈmeɪdʒəˈdəʊməʊ). Forms: 6 **maiordome, -domo, mayordome, 7 mayordomo, (7 major-dome, mayordom), 7– major domo.** [ad. Sp. *mayordomo*, It. *maggiordomo* (whence F. *majordome*), ad. med.L. *mājor domūs* 'chief of the house' (*mājor* subst. use of *mājor* greater, MAJOR *a.*; *domūs* gen. of *domus* house), the title of the highest official of the royal household under the Merovingians, commonly rendered 'mayor of the palace' (see MAYOR).] **a.** In early use, the chief official of an Italian or Spanish princely household, often discharging some of the functions of a minister of state. Subsequently applied also (in accordance with later It. and Sp. use) to the head servant of a wealthy household in foreign countries, and in more or less playful use to an English house-steward or butler.

1589 Puttenham *Eng. Poesie* III. iv. (Arb.) 20 How was it possible that Homer..should so exactly set foorth..as some great Princes maiordome..the order..of royal bankets [etc.]? *Ibid.* 158 *Maior-domo*: in truth this word is borrowed of the Spaniard and Italian, and therefore new and not vsuall, but to them that are acquainted with the affaires of Court... A man might haue said in steade of *Maior-domo*.. the right English word (*Lord Steward*). **1598** Barret *Theor. Warres* Gloss. 251 Mayordome, is with the Italian and Spaniard, the steward of a house; but in warr he is the steward and Guardian of the munition for warre. *c* **1645** Howell *Lett.* III. viii. (1650) 50 He is *Mayor-domo* Lord steward to the *Infante* Cardinall. *Ibid.* III. xv. 60 As one to be his Mayordom (his Steward), another to be Master of the Horse. **1674** *Govt. Tongue* viii. §11 Whose designs are so humble, as not to aspire above a major-domo, or some such domestic preferment. **1692** *Lond. Gaz.* No. 2820/3 The Marquis de la Puebla, Major-Dome to the King of Spain. **1725** De Foe *Voy. round World* (1840) 253 He and his major-domo would go along with me. **1814** Scott *Wav.* ix, The major-domo, for such he was, and indisputably the second officer of state in the barony,..laid down his spade. [**1823** Byron *Juan* x. lxx, His Maggior Duomo, a smart, subtle Greek. **1845** Darwin *Voy. Nat.* xii. 255 The mayor-domo of the Hacienda was good enough to give me a guide.] **1855** Motley *Dutch Rep.* (1861) II. 260 His Major-domo had previously been permitted to furnish his master's table with provisions dressed by his own cook. [**1876** *N. Amer. Rev.* CXXIII. 45 A king, averse to marriage, commanded his maggiordomo to remain single.]

¶**b.** In etymological sense 'chief of the house'.

1649 Jer. Taylor *Gt. Exemp.* Pref., [Mankind] were forced to divide their dwellings, and this they did by families especially, the great Father being the Major domo to all his minors. *Ibid.* II. vii. 34 God was the Major domo, the Master of those assemblies. *a* **1716** South *12 Serm.* (1727) VI. 340 Let him have nothing to do with any House or Family (tho' never so great and so much in Power) where the Devil is Major Domo and governs all.

c. *U.S.* In south-western states, an overseer on a farm or ranch; also, the water-master or official in charge of irrigation in New Mexico.

1834 in *Calif. Hist. Soc. Q.* (1929) VIII. 228 Four ranchos, each one made up of an Indian village, a house for the *mayordomo* directing it, [etc.]. **1836** D. B. Edward *Hist. Texas* ix. 291 Having thus glanced at the Major domo, we shall take a peek at his Locum tenens. **1902** F. H. Newell *Irrigation in U.S.* 107 He is usually known as the 'water master' or 'ditch-rider'; or, in Spanish-speaking communities as majordomo. **1910** J. Hart *Vigilante Girl* xiv. 195 Arthur's chair was taken to the *portal*, where they found the major-domo and a group of *vaqueros* waiting. **1948** P. Johnston *Lost & Living Cities Calif. Gold Rush* p. ii, The precious metal was found..by Francisco López, majordomo of San Gabriel Mission, in Placerita Canyon.

Hence **ˈmajor-ˈdomoship**, the office of major-domo.

1772 Nugent tr. *Hist. Friar Gerund* I. 87 When the uncle of the house served any majordomoship [Sp. *servia alguna mayordomia*]. **1889** *Pall Mall G.* 30 Jan. 6/1 A successor to whom he could hand over the Imperial Major-domoship.

majoress, obs. form of MAYORESS.

majorette (meɪdʒəˈrɛt). orig. *U.S.* [f. MAJOR *sb.*[1] + -ETTE.] = DRUM-MAJORETTE.

1941 *San Francisco Examiner* 20 Apr. (Amer. Weekly Section) 4/1 During the past few years the drum major..has given way to the so-called majorette. **1951** M. McLuhan *Mech. Bride* (1967) 122/1 The majorette is no man beater. **1959** *Times* 30 Nov. (Canada Suppl.) p. xx/4 Each club has a band and a corps of bare-legged prancing girls called majorettes. **1960** *Wanganui* (N.Z.) *Photo News* 13 Feb. 30 (*caption*) Coach of the Wanganui Majorettes. **1973** *Sat. Rev. Society* (U.S.) May 64/1 A bubbly ex-majorette named Linda.

ˈmajor-ˈgeneral. *Mil.* [a. F. *major-général*, where *major* is the sb. and *général* the adj. Cf. G. *generalmajor*. The fuller form *sergeant-major general* is earlier in Eng. use; *sergeant major major* occurs in Sir J. Smyth *Instr. Observ. & Orders Milit.* (1595) 60, 61.]

1. An officer of the lowest grade of general officers, ranking below a lieutenant-general.

1642 Whitelocke *Mem.* 65 The city bands marched forth ..under the command of major-general Skippon. **1647** Clarendon *Hist. Rebell.* VII. §86 James Chudleigh, the major general of the rebels. **1710** *Lond. Gaz.* No. 4723/2 The Brigadiers Juel and Daa were created Majors-General. **1806** *Gazetteer Scotl.* (ed. 2) Introd. 35 The military establishment of Scotland consists of a lieutenant general, three major generals [etc.]. **1849** W. Irving *Goldsmith* 279 He had..been promoted to the rank of major-general in 1745.

2. *Hist.* The title given to the officers placed in command of the twelve administrative districts into which England was divided in Cromwell's system of military government (1655–1657).

1655 Whitelocke *Mem.* 634 The protector told them [the mayor and common council] the reasons of his appointing major-generals in the several counties, as a means to preserve the peace, to suppress wickedness [etc.]. **1655** Cromwell in *Thurloe's St. Papers* (1742) III. 486 We..do hereby constitute..you the said major general Disbrowe to be major general of all the militia forces raised and to be raised within the counties of Cornwall, Devon, Somerset, Dorset, Wilts, and Gloucester.

Hence **ˈmajor-ˈgeneralcy**, the office or rank of major-general; **ˈmajor-ˈgeneralship** = prec.; also *Hist.* the district commanded by a major-general.

1670 Hobbes *Behemoth* IV. (1682) 307 He [Cromwell] divided England into eleven Major-Generalships. **1845** Carlyle *Cromwell* (1871) IV. 245 Now their Major Generalcies have all proved failures. **1885** U. S. Grant *Mem.* II. xlv. 98, I..strongly recommended him for a major-generalcy. **1898** *Daily News* 28 Nov. 5/1 His bravery on the field of Omdurman has won him his Major-Generalship.

majoris, obs. form of MAYORESS.

Majorism (ˈmeɪdʒərɪz(ə)m). [f. *Major* (see below) + -ISM.] The opinions held by Georg Major (1502–74), a German Protestant, who maintained that good works are necessary for salvation. So **ˈMajorist**, a follower of Major. **Majoˈristic** *a.*, pertaining to Majorism or to the Majorists.

1845 *Encycl. Metrop.* XIII. 475/1 These which are called the *Majoristic* and *Synergistic* controversies greatly agitated the Lutheran body. **1857** Pusey *Doctr. Real Presence* (1869) 77 At the Conference at Worms A.D. 1557,.. Flacius wrote to Christiern King of Denmark: 'another maintains Majorism on the necessity of works to salvation'. **1874** Blunt *Dict. Sects* etc., *Majorists*, the followers of Major in his controversy with Amsdorf. **1882–3** Schaff *Encycl. Relig. Knowl.* III. 1827 The Weimar *Confutatio* (1559) in which synergism, majorism, adiaphorism, etc., are confuted.

majoritarian (məˌdʒɒrɪˈtɛərɪən), *a.* [f. MAJORIT(Y + *-arian* as in *libertarian*, etc.] Governed by or believing in decision by a majority; supporting the majority party. Also as *sb.*

1918 J. Buchan *Nelson's Hist. War* XX. 118 Early in June came the delegation of the German Majority Socialists, which included—besides Scheidemann, the Majoritarian leader—that Hermann Müller who, on the eve of the declaration of war, had invited the French Socialists to vote against war credits. **1957** *Britannica Bk. of Year* 512/1 Some new words arose from politics and world affairs... Majoritarian was an adjective meaning ruled by the beliefs of the majority. **1964** Gould & Kolb *Dict. Social Sci.* 484/2 The idea of party responsibility..aims at facilitating the practice of majoritarian democracy. **1965** *Listener* 21 Jan. 113/3 The fateful divide in the pre-revolutionary Russian Social-Democratic movement between the Mensheviks (i.e., minoritarians) and the Bolsheviks (i.e., majoritarians) ..went far deeper than a purely political argument. **1971** P. Worsthorne *Socialist Myth* viii. 196 The idealistic disillusion with majoritarian democracy. **1972** *Mod. Law Rev.* XXXV. I. 73 In exercising their discretion the courts

have normally adopted a posture which is both 'legalistic' and 'majoritarian'.., majoritarian in the sense that the views of the majority have been treated as the most probative..factor.

Hence **majori'tarianism**, belief in, or the existence of, rule or decisions by a majority.

1961 in WEBSTER. **1968** A. LIJPHART *Politics of Accommodation* vii. 125 In short, the rule is majoritarianism tempered by the spirit of concurrent majority. **1968** *Internat. Encycl. Social Sci.* IX. 537/2 Opponents of strict majoritarianism advance numerous arguments. First, they point out that the majoritarian principle might be used to destroy the conditions of its own existence, such as freedom of association and expression. **1975** *N.Y. Times* 28 Mar. 27/3 The public interest defined as the greatest happiness for the greatest number..has hardened into an increasingly impervious 'majoritarianism'.

majority (mə'dʒɒrɪtɪ). [a. F. *majorité*, ad. med.L. *mājōritāt-em*, f. L. *mājōr-em* MAJOR *a.* Cf. Sp. *mayoridad*, Pg. *maioridade*, It. *maggiorità.*]

†**1.** The state or fact of being greater; superiority; pre-eminence. *Obs.*

1552 LATIMER *Serm. SS. Simon & Jude's Day* (1584) 267 Nowe abideth fayth, hope, and loue, euen these three; but the chiefe of these is loue. There be some learned men whiche expound this maioritie of which S. Paule speaketh here for diuturnitie. **1577** tr. *Bullinger's Decades* (1592) 866 It may be prooued that that maiority [i.e. the primacy of Rome] as they call it, hath not the originall from the sonne of God. **1596** SHAKS. *1 Hen. IV*, III. ii. 109. **1597** BACON *Colours Good & Euill* v. E 5 b, It is not plurality of partes without maiority of partes that maketh the totall greater. **1641** 'SMECTYMNUUS' *Answ.* (1653) 53 This particularization of Peter did not import any singular preheminence or majoritie of power to Peter more then to the other Apostles. **1677** GALE *Crt. Gentiles* IV. 280 In Eternitie there is no divisibilitie: no majoritie or minoritie. **1690** LEYBOURN *Curs. Math.* I. 335 Of Algebra. Symbols of Majority >, Minority <, Æquality = [etc.]. **1727–41** CHAMBERS *Cycl.* s.v. *Character*, > Is the sign of majority, or of the excess of one quantity beyond another.

2. The state of being major or of full age. Also *transf.*

1565 *Reg. Privy Council Scot.* I. 370 Quhen we ar at oure full majoritie, sall we be brocht bak to the stait of pupillis and minoris. **1579** FENTON *Guicciard.* I. (1599) 19 At what time Phillip being risen to his maioritie, might in good validitie confirme the accord past. **1632** LITHGOW *Trav.* A 2 b, [These] being begunne in Your hopefull Infancy, are now finally accomplished in the fulnesse of Your thrice blessed Majority. **1842** J. D. CHAMBERS *Jurisd. High Crt. Chancery over Infants* III. 506 So where the settlement executed is the completion of a treaty entered into during minority, without the sanction of the Court, there is jurisdiction to control that after majority. **1867** *John Bull* 7 Sept. 628/2 The Majority of Mr. C. L. A...has been celebrated during the week in the good old English style at the family seat. **1892** GILLESPIE *Bar's Priv. Intern. Law* (ed. 2) 311 A Cuban of twenty-two years of age, who by the law of his own country would not attain majority till twenty-five. **1909** *Westm. Gaz.* 28 Sept. 5/1 The majority celebration of the pneumatic tyre promises to be the biggest trade function on record. **1939** F. M. FORD *Let.* 25 May (1965) 324 If it [*sc.* the book] did not see the light until its majority it will become almost a historical novel. **1965** *Listener* 1 July 10/1 It is sad that, as it approaches its majority, this organisation should have run into deep waters.

3. a. The greater number or part; a number which is more than half the whole number; *spec.* the larger party voting together in a deliberative assembly or electoral body.

absolute majority: A number of votes received by one candidate which is more than half the total number polled, or than half the number of electors.

1691 NORRIS *Pract. Disc.* 102 Measures of Right and Wrong are not always to be concluded from the consent of Majority; for you see here, that Vice has by much the Majority of its side. *c* **1714** POPE, etc. *Mem. M. Scriblerus* xii. Wks. 1741 II. 47 In a House of Commons all things are determin'd by a Majority. **1714** SWIFT *Pres. State Affairs* Wks. 1751 IV. 264 The Queen, finding herself and the Majority of her Kingdom grown weary of the Avarice and Insolence..of her former Ministers. **1759** ROBERTSON *Hist. Scot.* VI. Wks. 1813 I. 413 War was chosen by a majority of voices. **1793** *Blackstone's Comm.* I. 181 In the house of commons the speaker never votes but when there is an equality without his casting vote, which in that case creates a majority. **1821** BYRON *Two Foscari* I. i, The majority In council were against you. **1844** LD. BROUGHAM *Brit. Const.* xv. (1862) 228 A majority of seven to five soon after [1640] decided that the levying ship money was legal. **1856** FROUDE *Hist. Eng.* (1858) I. iii. 247 The clergy commanded an actual majority in that [Upper] House from their own body. **1860** MILL *Repr. Gov.* (1865) 16/1 At some period..almost every people, now civilized, have consisted, in majority, of slaves. **1882** *Nature* XXVI. 389 The majority of the coral which I [Haeckel] collected was obtained by divers. **1888** J. BRYCE *Amer. Commonwealth* I. v. 55 Neither Polk in 1844, nor Taylor in 1848,..had an absolute majority of the popular vote. **1971** G. K. ROBERTS *Dict. Political Analysis* 120 In politics..the number of votes constituting a majority is equal to 50 per cent plus one of votes cast (sometimes referred to as an 'absolute majority').

b. with adj., as *great*, *vast*, etc.

1710 HOADLY *Orig. Civ. Govt.* 154 The People of the Earth, that is, a vast Majority of Mankind, are represented by Moses, as voluntarily journeying from one part of the Earth to another. **1759** ROBERTSON *Hist. Scotl.* I. II. 97 A considerable majority declared for the treaty. **1818** CRUISE *Digest* V. 244 It was determined by a great majority of all the Judges..that [etc.]. **1849** MACAULAY *Hist. Eng.* II. 315 In the great majority of those towns..no courtly candidate could dare to show his face. **1875** SCRIVENER *Lect. Text N. Test.* 5 Nor in the vast majority of instances does it exist. **1903** JOS. CONN *Fulness of Time* xi. 161 What supported.. the claims of Holy Church did not to the great majority require proof.

c. ***the majority***: the dead. Chiefly in the phrases ***to join the majority***, ***to go*** or ***pass over to the majority***. [After L. phrase *abiit ad plures.*]

1719 YOUNG *Revenge* IV. i, Life is the desart, life the solitude; Death joins us to the great majority. **1764** *Lond. Mag.* Nov. 581 'Oh, no, it is all over with me; I am going, as fast as possible, to join the majority.'—*Ad plures.* **1837** CARLYLE *Misc. Ess.*, *Mirabeau* (1840) V. 200 This Mirabeau's work then is done... He has gone over to the majority: *Abiit ad plures.* **1883** *Longm. Mag.* Dec. 179 He had passed over to the majority..we should see his face no more. **1889** T. A. TROLLOPE *What I remember* III. 61 He, too, alas! has joined the majority.

4. The number by which, in voting, the votes cast on one side exceed those cast on the other.

a **1743** LD. HERVEY *Mem.* (1848) II. 253 All the lists made by the Prince's people gave him a majority of near forty. **1765** *Ann. Reg.* 41/1 This motion..passed in the negative by a very large majority. **1775** *Ibid.* 118*/2 The motion..was carried upon a division..by the majority of sixty. **1838** THIRLWALL *Greece* xxx. IV. 135 This motion was carried,.. by a very small majority. **1879** MCCARTHY *Own Times* II. xix. 59 A majority of forty-six was given for the resolution.

†**5.** Ancestry. [After L. *majores* ancestors.]

1646 SIR T. BROWNE *Pseud. Ep.* III. xvi. 146 Of evill parents, an evill generation, a posterity not unlike their majority.

6. [Properly a distinct word: ad. F. *majorité*, f. *major* MAJOR *sb.*[1]] The rank or office of a major.

1776 in *Harper's Mag.* (1883) Sept. 546/2 Appointed to the Majority in the 2[d] Reg[t]. **1800** *Asiat. Ann. Reg.*, *Char.* 45/2 M. D'Auband had been named to a Majority in the isle of Bourbon. **1814** SCOTT *Wav.* xli, I am surprised that the Prince should have offered you a majority, when he knows very well that nothing short of lieutenant-colonel will satisfy others. **1900** *Daily News* 11 Sept. 5/7 He was..promoted to a half-pay majority.

7. *attrib.* and *Comb.* ***majority-rule***, ***-vote***; **majority calling**, in Bridge (see quot. 1964); **majority carrier** *Electronics*, a charge carrier of the kind carrying the greater proportion of the electric current in a semiconducting material (i.e. an electron in *n*-type and a hole in *p*-type material); **Majority-Socialist**, one who, after the division of the German Socialists during the 1914–18 war, acted with the larger party; **majority verdict**, the verdict of the majority of a jury; also *transf.*

1927 *Daily Express* 28 June 1/7 The system of 'majority calling' at auction bridge, the adoption of which in this country was first advocated by the 'Evening Standard'. **1929** *Laws Contract Bridge Portland Club* 6 While, at the Portland Club, 'value calling' is invariably played at 'Auction', 'majority calling' is being used at 'Contract'. **1964** *Official Encycl. Bridge* 343/1 *Majority calling*, the principle by which any bid outranks any other bid at a lower level, regardless of scoring value. **1951** W. SHOCKLEY et al. in *Physical Rev.* LXXXIII. 151/2 The density of minority carriers is much smaller than the density of majority carriers in each region. **1962** SIMPSON & RICHARDS *Physical Princ. Junction Transistors* vi. 100 Using equation (1.11) with the assumption that the conductivities in emitter and base are decided practically entirely by their majority-carrier densities, we obtain γ_0 = [etc.]. **1891** W. S. LILLY *Shibboleths* 113 Party politics..are mere majority-mongering. **1903** *Daily Chron.* 17 Jan. 3/2 A majority dinner at which our hero..is entertaining the élite of London. **1893** B. R. TUCKER *Instead of Bk.* 169 Rule is evil, and..it is none the better for being majority rule. **1959** *Chambers's Encycl.* XI. 701/1 When such deep and permanent cleavages are absent, majority rule seems more likely to secure more equal freedom than any other, at least if free discussion and airing of grievances are presupposed. **1968** J. R. PENNOCK in *Internat. Encycl. Social Sci.* IX. 536 The term 'majority rule' stands for a rule of decision making within a specified group. At its simplest, the rule requires that the votes of each member shall be counted as equal to that of every other and that no vote or decision by a minority may override that of a majority. By extension, majority rule is sometimes contrasted with any rule requiring that decisions be unanimous or by any number larger than a simple majority. **1972** *Guardian* 28 Jan. 10/1 The Smith regime..is proving ..how slender is the hope of orderly progress towards majority rule. **1918** J. BUCHAN *Hist. War* XX. 125 The great governing parties, apart from the Conservatives on the extreme right and the Minority Socialists on the extreme left, were the Catholic Centre, the Radicals, the National Liberals, and the Majority Socialists. **1923** E. A. ROSS *Russ. Soviet Republic* 20 At this time [*sc.* 1918] a Soviet was formed in Berlin, to which members of even the Majority Socialists adhered. **1972** S. DELMER *Weimar Germany* i. 6 Ebert and his 'Majority' Socialists called on him [*sc.* Prince Max] to hand over power to them. **1905** *Westm. Gaz.* 7 Apr. 5/2 The jury..sent in to court to inquire if the parties would accept a majority verdict. **1966** H. KALVEN et al. *Amer. Jury* xxxvi. 461 Numerous states allow for a majority verdict in civil cases. **1973** 'D. HALLIDAY' *Dolly & Starry Bird* vi. 82 We can all go home and finish our knitting if the majority verdict prefers it. **1927** *Chambers's Jrnl.* 602/2 Now he had the majority vote. **1953** B. M. CROSS *Legislative Struggle* xviii. 380 In committee sessions, disputed questions are decided by a majority vote. **1965** *Wireless World* Sept. 419 This is a triplicated system with a majority vote scheme for ensuring correct operation. **1973** *Listener* 20 Dec. 841/2 [An] impeachment resolution..requires a simple majority vote.

majorize ('meɪdʒəraɪz), *v.* [f. MAJOR *sb.*[2] + -IZE.]

1. *intr.* To attain (one's) majority; to come of age.

1896 C. F. KEARY *Herbert Vanlennert* i. 5, I didn't know you had regularly come of age..I imagined that you didn't majorize till twenty-five or something of that sort.

2. *Rugby Football.* To convert a try into a goal, i.e. to increase the points from three to five.

majorlame, majoron, obs. ff. MARJORAM.

majorship ('meɪdʒəʃɪp). [f. MAJOR *sb.*[1] + -SHIP.] The office or rank of a major; majority.

1717 *New Hampsh. Prov. Papers* (1868) II. 710 Majr Peter Wear..asked pardon for his so doing: whereupon the Govr pronounced him restored to his Major-ship. **1865** *Cornh. Mag.* Aug. 172 This provost of Dublin is said, in a political crisis, to have squeezed from Lord Townshend a majorship of dragoons. **1875** HOWELLS *Foregone Concl.* xviii. 294 The colonelcies are..inaccessible,..and so are the lieutenant-colonelcies; but a majorship, now—.

¶ Used jocularly as a title.

1795 *Jemima* I. 108 What I know must not be known to man..until his Majorship..has had some sport with his son.

majum, majun: see MAJOON.

majuscular (mə'dʒʌskjʊlə(r)), *a. Palæogr.* [f. L. *mājuscul-us*: see next and -AR.] Of the nature of a majuscule; composed of majuscules.

[**1825** L. HUNT *Redi's Bacchus in Tuscany* 21 In the beverage bold Let's renew us and grow muscular; And for those who're getting old, Glasses get of size majuscular (orig. *vetri majusculi*).] **1864** W. H. BLACK *Anc. Bibl. Chronogr.* 8 The great or (as they are called by critics) majuscular letters. **1895** H. REYNOLDS *Anc. Dioc. Exeter* iv. 111 It is impossible to mistake that firm majuscular sign manual.

majuscule (mə'dʒʌskjuːl), *a.* and *sb.* [a. F. *majuscule*, ad. L. *mājuscula* (sc. *littera*), fem. of *mājusculus* somewhat larger, dim. of *mājor* (neut. *mājus*): see MAJOR *a.*]

A. *adj.* †**a.** *Printing.* Of a letter: Capital. *Obs.* **b.** *Palæogr.* Of a letter: Large (whether capital or uncial). Also, written in majuscules.

1727–41 CHAMBERS *Cycl.* s.v. *Letter*, Printers distinguish their letters into capital, majuscule, initial or upper-case letters..and minuscule, small, or under-case letters. **1850** MADDEN tr. *Silvestre's Univ. Palæogr.* I. 140 To the first class [inscriptions] belong the capital or square majuscule characters; to the second [books], the uncial characters (which are majuscules intermixed with rounded letters); and to the third [documents], the conjoined, cursive writing. **1885** E. M. THOMPSON in *Encycl. Brit.* XVIII. 145 In Latin majuscule writing there exist both capitals and uncials. **1892** —— *Gr. & Lat. Palæogr.* xiv. 196 Early majuscule MSS.

B. *sb.* †**a.** *Printing.* A large or capital letter. *Obs.* **b.** *Palæogr.* A large letter, whether capital or uncial.

1825 W. HAMILTON *Dict. Terms Arts & Sci.*, *Majuscules*, in *Printing*, large letters, sometimes ornamented, usually placed at the beginning of chapters. **1850** [see A above]. **1851** SIR F. PALGRAVE *Norm. & Eng.* I. 433 A few firm majuscules inscribed by Roman Power. **1892** E. M. THOMPSON *Gr. & Lat. Palæogr.* viii. 117 In both Greek and Latin palæography, large letters are called 'majuscules'; small letters, 'minuscules'.

mak, obs. and dial. variant of MAKE *sb.* and *v.*

makable ('meɪkəb(ə)l), *a.* Also **makeable.** [f. MAKE *v.* + -ABLE.] That can be made.

c **1449** PECOCK *Repr.* II. i. 134 It is a treuthe doable or makeable. **1678** CUDWORTH *Intell. Syst.* I. ii. §9. 70 The Accidents..are all makeable and destroyable, generable and corruptible. **1832** *Westm. Rev.* XVII. 22 The quantity of goods makeable, is quite a distinct thing from the quantity of goods saleable. **1865** CARLYLE *Fredk. Gt.* XVI. xi. (1872) VI. 273 Plenty of editions made or makable by a little surreptitious legerdemain.

mak-a-doo: see MAKE-A-DO *Obs.*

makadowe, variant of MOCKADO *Obs.*

makak, var. MOCOCK.

‖**makan** ('makan). *Malaysia.* [Cf. Malay *makan* to eat; *makanan* food.] Food.

1927 R. J. H. SIDNEY *In Brit. Malaya To-Day* 233 His stomach may become distended with some of the weird mixtures..from the School *makan* shop. **1963** J. KIRKUP *Tropic Temper* 101, I wander back to the hotel for my makan. (Cold turkey.) **1971** *Carry Singapore in your Pocket* (Singapore Tourist Promotion Board) (ed. 3) 29 Watch a meal of noodles being fried in 5 minutes at the 'makan' (food) stall.

†'**makande.** *Obs.* [a. ON. *makindi*; cf. mod. Icel. *í makindum* at one's ease.] Comfort, ease.

a **1400** *Parlt. 3 Ages* 278 And aftir irkede me with this and ese was me leuere As man in his medill elde his makande wolde haue.

makar(e, obs. form of MAKER.

‖**makara** ('mʌkərə). Also **Makara.** [Skr.] A mythical Hindu sea-animal, variously represented in Indian art; the equivalent of Capricorn in the signs of the zodiac.

1873 E. BALFOUR *Cycl. India* (ed. 2) III. M 58/2 Kama.. bears on his banner the fish Makara, an aquatic monster something like the sign of the zodiac Capricornus. **1901** A. C. GIBSON tr. *Gruenwedel's Buddhist Art India* ii. 57 The sea-elephant, Makara, a creature formed of the fore-part of an elephant with the body and tail of a fish..has been retained everywhere in Indian art. **1934** *Burlington Mag.* Oct. 164/1 But essentially Indian is the Makara, a phantastic animal which, since the days of King Asoka, has played a part in Indian art; it is seen on toranas of all times;..it

followed the spread of Indian art to the islands, .. whilst it lives a prolific life on all sorts of minor objects in Ceylon. **1969** A. K. COOMARASWAMY *Introd. Indian Art* (ed. 2) ix. 42 Decorative work with *makaras* and other marine monsters [is] represented. **1971** *Illustr. Weekly India* 11 Apr. 67/2 (*December 21 to Jan. 19*) *Capricorn* (*Makara*). Frankness with friends may make you happy till midweek. **1972** *Oxf. Univ. Gaz.* CII. Suppl. No. 3. 54 A fine terracotta relief in the form of a *makara*.., formerly part of an architectural frieze.. was also acquired.

Makassar, Makas(s)arese: see MACASSAR, MACASSARESE.

makdome: see MAKEDOM *Sc.*

make (meɪk), *sb.*¹ *Obs.* exc. *dial.* Forms: α. 1 **ȝemaca**, 2 **ȝemace**, 3 **imake**. β. 2– **make**; also 4–9 *north.* **mak**, (5 **mac**, 6 **mack, maike**), 6–9 *Sc.* **maik.** [OE. *ȝemaca* wk. masc. corresponds to OS. *gimaco*, fellow, equal, OHG. *gimahho* 'socius' (fem. *gimahha* wife):—OTeut. type **gamakon-*, subst. form of **gamako-* adj. (OE. *ȝemæc* equal, well-matched, OHG. *gimah* fit, matched, convenient, MHG. *gemach* appertaining, belonging, like, mod.G. *gemach* easy, comfortable, MDu. *gemac* appertaining, also agreeable, quiet, calm), f. **ga-* Y- *prefix* (expressing the notions of conjunction and mutual relation) + **mako-*, app. primarily meaning 'fit, suitable', whence **makôjo-* MAKE *v.* The simple stem occurs (though perh. through loss of the prefix) in ON. *mak-r* (only in compar. and superl.) fitting, easy, comfortable, *make* wk. masc., mate, match, equal (Sw. *make*, Da. *mage* consort, like), mod.Du. *mak* tame, docile, gentle. The root has not been traced outside Teut.

As the prefix *y-* of sbs. was universally lost in early ME., the mod. form is the normal representative of OE. *ȝemaca*. The currency of the word may, however, esp. in northern dialects, be due to adoption of ON. *make*. Cf. the cognate MATCH *sb.*]

1. An (or one's) equal, peer, match; (one's) like. In ME. freq. in phr. ***but (any) make.***

α. *c* **1000** ÆLFRIC *Gram.* ix. (Z.) 43 *Hic et hæc et hoc par*, ȝemaca. *a* **1300** *Floriz & Bl.* 77 (Cott. Vitell. MS.) In worle nes nere non þine imake of no wimmon.

β. *a* **1300** *Cursor M.* 19656 O preching had he [*sc.* Saul of Tarsus] na mak. *c* **1375** *Sc. Leg. Saints* xviii. (*Egipciane*) 543 For I wes gyrne but ony mak þat sawlis put to lestand vrak. *c* **1460** *Towneley Myst.* ii. 442 Yit knew I neuer thi make. **1509** BARCLAY *Shyp of Folys* (1874) II. 235 Lo yonder same is he Whiche without make thynketh hym wyse to be. **1596** DALRYMPLE tr. *Leslie's Hist. Scot.* I. 45 Elgin, quhair is sa noble and notable a kirke in beutie and decore that with vs it hes na make. *c* **1620** MURE *Sonn.* i, Admir'd, but maik, euin in a thowsand thingis. **1717** RAMSAY *Elegy on Lucky Wood* ix, She has na left her mak behind her. **1724** —— *Tea-t. Misc.* (1733) I. 28 Your Tocher it sall be good There's nane sall hae it's maik. **1893** *Northumbld. Gloss., Make*, an equal, one that is matched or mated with another.

†**b.** ***the make***: the like. *Sc. Obs.*

1535 STEWART *Cron. Scot.* III. 436 Traist weill.. sen God can do the maik Onto ȝour self. **1539** *Extracts Aberd. Reg.* (1844) I. 160 Gif euer scho dois the maik in tyme cumyng. **1560** ROLLAND *Crt. Venus* II. 896 In mappamond the maik is not perchance.

2. An image. *rare.*

α. *c* **1205** LAY. 18206 þe king lette wurchen tweien imaken [*c* 1275 ymages], tweien gulden draken.

β. **1890** J. SERVICE *Thir Notandums* xiv. 101 They made wee maiks oot o' clay.. of them that had thortered them.

3. A mate, companion. (*occas.* applied to the opponent with whom a fighter is matched.)

α. *a* **1175** *Cott. Hom.* 221 Uton wircan him ȝemace him to fultume and to froure.

β. *a* **1225** *Ancr. R.* 114 Ne beo þu nout Gius fere ne Gius make uorte birlen him so. *c* **1386** CHAUCER *Knt.'s T.* 1698 And if so be the chieftayn be take On outher syde or elles sleen his make. *a* **1400–50** *Alexander* 5430 A turne þai turnay to-gedire, Ilkane mellis with his make & so þare many dies. **1598** FLORIO, *Sótio*, a companion, a fellow, a make. **1721** RAMSAY *Answ. Burchet* 18 When honour'd Burchet and his maikes are pleas'd.. With my corn-pipe. **1886** *Cheshire Gloss., Make*, a mate or companion.

4. Of animals, esp. birds: A mate (male or female).

α. *c* **1000** ÆLFRIC *Gen.* vi. 19 And of eallum nytenum ealles flæsces twegen ȝemacan þu lætst in to þam arce. *a* **1175** *Cott. Hom.* 225 Ic ȝegaderi.. of fugel cynne simle ȝemacan þat hi eft to fostre bien.

β. *c* **1200** ORMIN 1276 Fra þatt hire make iss dæd Ne kepeþþ ȝho [þe turrtle] nan oþerr. **1390** GOWER *Conf.* I. 45 That was in the Monthe of Maii, Whan every brid hath chose his make. *c* **1430** LYDG. *Min. Poems* (Percy Soc.) 153 Nyghtynggales al nyght syngen and wake, For long absence .. of his make. **1542–5** BRINKLOW *Lament.* (1874) 117 The vypar.. destroyeth her make or male in the concepcyon. **1579** LYLY *Euphues* (Arb.) 97 The Wolfe chooseth him for hir make that hath or doth endure most travayll for hir sake. **1611** COTGR. s.v. *Muge*, The female Mullet will rather be caught by fishermen then abandon her Make.

5. Of human beings: A mate, consort; a husband or wife, lover or mistress.

a **1240** *Lofsong* in *Cott. Hom.* 209 Iesu.. of þe eadie meiden iboren Maria þet is meiden and bute make moder. *a* **1250** *Owl & Night.* 1159 Oþer þat wif leost hire make. *a* **1300** *Cursor M.* 4668 þe king him did a wijf to tak, Hight assener, a doghti mak. *c* **1374** CHAUCER *Compl. Mars* 154 God yif every wyghte joy of his make! *c* **1380** *Sir Ferumb.* 2086 Wolde he be my worldly make & wedde me to wyue. *c* **1460** *Towneley Myst.* i. 187 A rib I from the take, therof shall be maide thi make. *a* **1586** SIDNEY *Arcadia* I. (1590) 4 b, Like a widdow hauing lost her make. **1596** SPENSER *F.Q.* IV. ii. 30 And each not farre behinde him had his make, To weete, two ladies of most goodly hew. **1626** B. JONSON *Masque of Owls*, Where their Maides, and their Makes, At dancings, and Wakes, Had their Napkins and poses. **1725** RAMSAY *Gentle Sheph.* I. ii, Whensoe'er they [*sc.* men] slight their maiks at hame. **1890** *Glouc. Gloss., Make*, mate, companion, lover. **1893** *Northumbld. Gloss., Maik, make*, .. a companion, consort, mate.

make (meɪk), *sb.*² Also (*Sc.* and *north.*) 4–9 **mak**, 6 **mayck**, 7–9 **mack**, 9 **maik.** [f. MAKE *v.*¹]

†**1.** Doing, action; *esp.* (*Sc.*) manner, style (of action, behaviour, speech). *Obs.*

a **1300–1400** *Cursor M.* 18788 (Gött.) His kin ne will he noght forsake, Bot it be thoru vr auen make [*Cott.* sake]. *c* **1375** *Sc. Leg. Saints* iii. (*Andreas*) 790 Quhen scho saw þe haly man one þat mak de. *c* **1470** HENRY *Wallace* x. 554 To rewll the ost on a gud mak. **1500–20** DUNBAR *Poems* xiii. 1 Ane morlandis man of vplandis mak. **1535** STEWART *Cron. Scot.* I. 614 Commanding him opone the samin mak [etc.].

2. The manner in which a thing is made. **a.** Of a product of art or manufacture: Style of construction, kind of composition. *spec.* with implied reference to the manufacturer or source of manufacture; = BRAND *sb.* 6.

c **1375** *Sc. Leg. Saints* ix. (*Bertholomeus*) 224 Bundyne with chenȝeis of fule mak. **1390** GOWER *Conf.* II. 204 He let tuo cofres make Of o semblance and of o make. *a* **1400–50** *Alexander* 3218 [He] was on þe mark of þat mote noȝt mervalled a litill. *a* **1500** MEDWALL *Nature* 1065 (Brandl) A doublet of the new make. **1699** L. WAFER *Voy.* (1729) 306 The other houses and churches are pretty handsome after the Spanish make. **1710** HEARNE *Collect.* 7 May (O. H. S.) II. 387 The make of the Letters.. appear not.. ancient. **1760** BROWN *Compl. Farmer* II. 8 This depends much upon the make of the plough. **1833** HT. MARTINEAU *Brooke Farm* viii. 104 The caps and bonnets were of quite a new make. **1854** W. COLLINS *Hide & Seek* III. 186 After suggesting that the candle might have gone out through some defect in the make of it. **1868** JOYNSON *Metals* 32 A great variety of what are technically called 'makes' of iron are produced in a wide range of degrees of hardness. **1889** *Anthony's Photogr. Bull.* II. 80 Use a slow make of bromide paper. **1909** WEBSTER, *Make*,.. often referring to quality or origin of a manufactured article; as, whose *make* is it? **1937** *Discovery* Feb. 61/2, I tested the records on four different makes of gramophone. **1937** J. BETJEMAN *Continual Dew* 5 Talk of sports and makes of cars In various bogus Tudor bars. **1975** 'D. CRAIG' *Dead Liberty* xix. 108 It would be better not to park the same.. vehicle in that street again... He wished now he had not mentioned the make.

b. Of a natural object: Form or composition, structure, constitution. Often of the body: 'Build'.

14.. *How Good Wife taught Dau.* 126 in *Barbour's Bruce*, etc. (1870) 529 Flawm nocht na fluriss that vill fade, To mend the mak that god has made. *a* **1600** MONTGOMERIE *Misc. Poems* li. 37 Gif she had bene into the dayis auld, Quhen Jupiter the schap of bull did tak.. Sum greater mayck, I wait, he had gart mak, Hir to haue stollin be his slichtis quent. **1665** BOYLE *Occas. Refl.* Disc. (1848) 64 The Leaves.. of a Tree,.. are of a more solid Texture.. than the Blossoms, which seem to be of a slighter make. **1697** DAMPIER *Voy.* (1729) I. 537 Their Faces are of a flat oval Figure, of the Negro make. **1719** *Freethinker* No. 148 ¶2 A Greek virgin, of exquisite Make and Feature. **1742** YOUNG *Nt. Th.* IX. 868–9 Nature.. gave A Make to Man directive of his Thought; A Make set upright. **1751** D. JEFFERIES *Treat. Diamonds* (ed. 2) 23 A right knowledge of the true make of Diamonds. **1792** BURNS *Lady Mary Ann* iv, Young Charlie Cochran was the sprout of an aik, Bonie, and bloomin' and straught was its make. **1812** BYRON *Juan* v. xi, He had an English look; that is, was square In make, of a complexion white and ruddy. **1822–34** *Good's Study Med.* (ed. 4) III. 32 The apparently isolated molecules found in the make of the polype and various worms. **1832** HT. MARTINEAU *Life in Wilds* iv. 46 Look at his delicate hands and slight make. **1886** RUSKIN *Præterita* I. 291 The Jura rock, balanced in the make of it between chalk and marble. **1894** MRS. H. WARD *Marcella* II. 301 A huge man, with the make and muscles of a prize-fighter.

c. Of immaterial things: Form, fashion; hence, sort, character, nature (passing into 4).

1660 COWLEY *Ode Restoration* xiv, All the Weapons malice e'r could try, Of all the sev'ral makes of wicked Policy. **1673** *Lady's Call.* I. iv. §9 Mutual visits.. should flow from a real kindness, but if those now in use be sifted, how few will be found of that make? **1679** J. GOODMAN *Penit. Pard.* I. i. (1713) 15 The make and fabrick of a Parable. **1857** BUCKLE *Civiliz.* I. vii. 397 A corresponding change, in the very form and make of our literature. **1890** *Harper's Mag.* Mar. 524/2, I did not know just the make and manner of his trouble.

†**d.** ***all of a make, of one make***: of the same character throughout. *Obs.*

1674 N. FAIRFAX *Bulk & Selv.* 72 There being nothing in the Tube to hinder, Why should not the man fall further, the air of the Well being all of a make? **1682** GREW *Exp. Luctation* Introd., The Experiments may seem too numerous to be of one make. **1684** N. S. *Crit. Enq. Edit. Bible* xxvii. 241 St. Jerom's Translation.. is not all of a make, but hath some little mixture of the Ancient or Italian.

3. Mental or moral constitution, disposition, or character.

1674 N. FAIRFAX *Bulk & Selv.* To Rdr., Deeming there were more in the World of my make. **1676** TOWERSON *Decalogue* 89 A gesture.. us'd even by good men towards those of the same make with themselves. **1713** STEELE *Guard.* No. 13 ¶4 Mr. William, the next brother, is not of this smooth make. **1748** RICHARDSON *Clarissa* IV. 153, I, who, as to my will, and impatience, and so forth, am of the true lady-make! **1765** LD. HOLLAND *Let.* 19 July in Jesse *G. Selwyn* (1843) I. 387 You are not of a make to be a confidant there. **1806–7** J. BERESFORD *Miseries Hum. Life* (1826) I. x, You are happily of a hardy and contentious make. **1877** RUSKIN *Fors Clav.* vii. 106 Giotto was, in the make of him, and contents, a very much stronger.. man than Titian.

4. Kind, sort, species. *dial.*

1740 J. COLLIER (Tim Bobbin) *View Lanc. Dial.* Wks. (1862) 62 I'r freetn't aw macks o weys. **1785** *Span. Rivals* 8 Why, mun, he's of all macks of sorts. **1788** W. MARSHALL *Yorksh.* II. 341 Gloss., *Mack*, sort, species; as, what mack of corn, or stock? **1829** BROCKETT *N. C. Gloss.* (ed. 2), *Macks*, sorts, fashions—makes. 'A little o' a' macks'.

5. a. The action or process of making or manufacture. Now *rare* exc. *techn.*

1743 J. MORRIS *Serm.* ii. 38 He created the vast universe, that he might impart such degrees of happiness and perfection to the several orders of beings, as are suitable to the end of their make. **1805** W. TAYLOR in *Ann. Rev.* III. 47 It appears that the make of linen began in Spain. —— in *Monthly Mag.* XX. 147 One of your correspondents inquired concerning the make of marbled soap. **1879** BROWNING *Ned Bratts* 132 He taught himself the make Of laces, tagged and tough. **1890** JACOBI *Printing* xxxi. 250 Papers.. torn or broken in the 'make'— as the manufacture is technically termed.

b. Qualified by an adj. or possessive denoting the source of manufacture or the manufacturer, often with mixture of sense 2 a implying the style or quality associated with such an origin.

1873 *Athenæum* 19 Apr. 508/3 A cast-iron chain of the old Sussex make. **1884** *Times* (weekly ed.) 29 Feb. 5/7 A pocket .. of American make. *Mod.* Are these shoes your own make?

6. Amount manufactured; quantity produced.

1865 *Pall Mall G.* 27 June 5 The make of puddled iron has been materially reduced at many of the works. **1884** W. H. GREENWOOD *Steel & Iron* viii. 174 The economy in fuel and increased make per furnace, effected by the introduction of the hot blast. **1886** *Times* 20 Aug. 11/2 The make of pig iron in the United Kingdom over the first six months of the year shows a decrease of 270,321 tons.

7. *slang.* 'A successful theft or swindle' (*Slang Dict.* 1860). Cf. MAKE *v.*¹ 29 b.

8. ***on the make***: intent on profit or advancement; also, intent on winning someone's affections; seeking sexual pleasure; improving, advancing, getting better. *slang* (orig. *U. S.*).

1869 J. R. BROWNE *Adventures Apache Country* 507 'Oh, you're on the make, are you?'.. 'Why, yes, to be candid, I'd like to make fifty thousand or so.' **1874** HOTTEN *Slang Dict.* 221 Any one is said to be 'on the make' who asks too high a price for his goods, or endeavours in any way to overreach. **1890** *Pall Mall G.* 6 Sept. 2/1 Suppose.. that I am a man, as our American cousins say, 'on the make'—suppose that I have parliamentary ambitions. **1893** *Nation* (N. Y.) 9 Mar. 172/2 The men who wanted offices rather than the triumph of great principles, those who were 'on the make' in politics. **1898** HENLEY *Lond. Types, Bus-driver*, Being stony broke, Lives lustily; is ever on the make. **1918** BARRIE *What Every Woman Knows* II. 55 There are few more impressive sights in the world than a Scotsman on the make. **1929** J. P. MCEVOY *Hollywood Girl* (1930) 41 Jimmy.. said Buelow was on the make for me or he wouldn't have wasted that much time on me. **1934** J. O'HARA *Appointment in Samarra* (1935) vii. 212 It's the first time I ever knew of you going on the make for some dame. **1955** *Times* 12 May 7/3, I think we are on the make and that, on balance, the tide is running in our favour. **1967** N. FREELING *Strike Out* 77 He struck me always as a sly nasty fellow, a bootlicker, always on the make. **1973** 'A. BLAISDELL' *Crime by Chance* vii. 126 You mean he was still on the make? At his age? **1973** W. M. DUNCAN *Big Timer* xxii. 150 Riordan was on the make. He'd found out something he could use. **1974** R. ADAMS *Shardik* li. 426 Insinuating, dandified, with the manners, at once familiar and obsequious, of a presuming servant on the make.

9. *Electr.* The action of making contact in an electric circuit; the position in which contact is made (in phr. ***at make***).

1875, etc. [see MAKE-AND-BREAK]. **1892** *Gloss. Electrical Terms* in *Lightning* 7 Jan. (Suppl.), *Make* and *Break*... The words are sometimes used as substantives denoting the action of making or breaking contact thus 'at make', 'at break'.

10. = DECLARATION 8 b (see also quot. 1964).

1902 J. B. ELWELL *Bridge* 13 In considering a heart make, the dealer should be influenced by the general strength of his hand and by the number of honours he holds in the trump suit. **1905** R. F. FOSTER *Compl. Bridge* 316 The declaration is often called the make. **1964** *Official Encycl. Bridge* 343/1 *Make*... As a noun, it means a successful contract, but usually a hypothetical one in the post-mortem: 'Five diamonds would have been a make.' **1974** *Country Life* 17 Jan. 98/3 Four Spades is a make, but Five Clubs is the safer sacrifice.

11. A (sexual) conquest; *spec.* a woman of easy virtue. Cf. MAKE *v.*¹ 65. *slang* (orig. *U.S.*).

1942 BERREY & VAN DEN BARK *Amer. Thes. Slang* §439/1 Woman of easy morals.. *make*. **1951** *Landfall* V. 98 'A widow's an easy make,' He said, 'you pedal and let her steer.'

12. An identification of, or information about, a person or thing from police records, fingerprints, etc. *slang* (orig. *U.S.*).

1950 in Wentworth & Flexner *Dict. Amer. Slang* (1960) 332/1 We got a make on his prints. **1959** 'E. MCBAIN' *Pusher* vii. 62 Couldn't get a make on those fingerprints. **1965** 'L. EGAN' *Detective's Due* (1966) vii. 71, I think this is too good to be true, but we'll get a make on it just for fun. *Ibid.* 80 The D.M.V. just came through with a make on that plate number... It belongs to a fifty-five two-door Ford. **1967** W. PINE *Protectors* ix. 82 We've got a make on Beth Paget. She's on our files. **1972** R. K. SMITH *Ransom* IV. 175 We got a make on the Chevvy... Stolen last week. **1973** *Daily Colonist* (Victoria, B.C.) 6 Sept. 4/5 For years authorities have been trying to get a better 'make' on motorists who sidestep the law by picking up a licence in a nearby state after theirs has been revoked.

13. ***make and mend***: the action of making and repairing clothes; spec. *Naut.*, a period set apart

for seamen to repair their clothes; hence, a period of leisure; a half-holiday; also *attrib.* and as vb.

1884 W. D. HOWELLS *Rise S. Lapham* (1885) i. 5 She cooked, swept, washed, ironed, made and mended from daylight till dark. **1899** *Navy & Army Illustr.* 14 Oct. 107 (*caption*) Thursday has been in the Navy, ever since King William IV.. first instituted the practice, regularly observed as 'make and mend' day. **1903** KIPLING *Traffics & Discov.* (1904) 154 I'm going to ask this young gentleman to breakfast, and then we'll make and mend clothes till the umpires have decided. **1916** 'TAFFRAIL' *Pincher Martin* xv. 273 Th' navy's 'avin' its make an' mend, an' carn't be disturbed. **1925** FRASER & GIBBONS *Soldier & Sailor Words* 150 *A make and mend*, a naval holiday. In old days.. usually on a Thursday. Now-a-days.. the weekly half holiday (often transferred to a Saturday) continues to be known as a 'Make and Mend'. **1935** *New Survey London Life* IX. IV. xiii. 423 On Tuesday afternoon I go to the make-and-mend class. **1942** F. G. HACKFORTH-JONES *One-One-One* xxi. 193 Saturday too, when all on board H.M.S. *Empire* were supposed to be enjoying a well-earned 'make and mend'. **1943** *Our Towns* (Women's Group on Public Welfare) ii. 60 Any 'Make and Mend' organisation evolved during the war should form the basis of a permanent service. **1955** *Times* 12 July 9/6 They.. move out to their 'sun-porch', usually a clearing in the forest where they spend their time in 'make-and-mend'.

make, *sb.*[3] *slang* and *dial.* Also 6 meke, 9 *Sc.* maik, maick. [Cf. MAG *sb.*[3]] A halfpenny.

a **1547** *Hye Way to Spyttel-ho.* in Hazlitt *E.P.P.* IV. 69 Docked the dell for a coper meke. **1567** HARMAN *Caveat* G iij, A make, a halfepenny. **1618** B. HOLYDAY *Technogamia* II. vi, Good Sir, if you be a *Gentry coue*, vouchsafe some small *Win* or but a *Make*, for wee haue neither *Lowre*, nor *Libbeg*, nor *Libkin*. **1826** SCOTT *Woodst.* xxxvi, I take it; for a make to a million. **1852** in Beveridge *Poets Clackmannan.* (1885) 66 That was ca'd threepence, twa maiks frae a groat. **1880** JAMIESON, *Maik*,.. still a cant term in the West of S., especially among boys when bargain-making.

make (meɪk), *v.*[1] Pa. t. and pa. pple. made (meɪd). Forms: *Inf.* α. 1 macian, (1 macan, 2 macen, macie), 2–3 makian, -ie(n, 3–4 maky(ȝ)e, -iȝe, maki, (*imper.* mac), 3–5 maken (*Ormin* makenn), 4–6 (9 *dial.*) mak, (5 makyn, also 9 *dial.* maak), 5–6 mack, (6 *Sc.* maik(e, mek), 3– make. β. 4–6 ma, (4 man), 9 *dial.* maa, may. *Pres. ind. 2nd and 3rd sing.*; and *pl.* (contracted northern forms) 4–5 mas(s, mays(s, maiss, 4–6 mais, (5 mase, mace, maise). *Past. ind.* α. 1–2 macode, 2–3 makede, (2 mac(h)ede, 3 makode), 2–5 maket, 3–5 (7) maked, (4 makked). β. 3– made; also 3 maude, 4–5 mad, maad(e, 4–6 *Sc.* maid, (3 mede, 4 madde, 6 mayd). *Pa. pple.* α. 1 ȝemacod, 2–3 imaked(e, (2 ȝemaked, imacad, 3 imaket), 3–5 ymaked, (4 -yd, imake); 2 makiet, 3 *Ormin* makedd, 3–5 maked, (4 maket, *strong* makyn), 4–5 makid. β. 3–4 imad, ymad, 4–5 ymaad, 4–5 (7) ymade; 3–5 mad, 4–5 maad, 4–6 *Sc.* maid, (5 madde, 6 *Sc.* maed, maide), 4– made. [Com. WGer.: OE. *macian* = OFris. *makia*, OS. *macon* (LG., Du. *maken*), OHG. *mahhôn* (MHG., mod.G. *machen*), app. f. **mako-* fit, suitable (see MAKE *sb.*[1]). On this view the primary sense would be 'to fit, arrange'; but in the earliest known stages of the WGer. tongues the verb corresponded generally to the L. *facere* in such of its senses as were not expressed by DO. The MSw. *maka* to make, construct (mod.Sw. *make* to move), Da. *mage* to manage, arrange, appear to have been adopted from LG.

Many senses which later Eng. shares with continental Teut. are not recorded in OE., or not until near the end of that period; possibly the vb. originally had some of these meanings, but was displaced in the literary dialect by synonyms. Materials are wanting for a genealogical arrangement of the senses; the order of the main branches in the following scheme has been adopted on grounds of convenience. The word is not very frequent in OE.; the most prominent uses are in causative and factitive applications (see 48, 49, 52) and in the phrase *hit macian* 'to make it' = to act, behave (see 68).]

I. Senses in which the object of the verb is a product or result.

* To bring into existence by construction or elaboration. (Not common until late in OE.; the L. *facere* is usually rendered by *ȝewyrcan*.)

1. *trans.* **a.** To produce (a material thing) by combination of parts, or by giving a certain form to a portion of matter; to construct, frame, fashion.

Formerly common in various applications in which vbs. of more specific meaning are now almost universally employed; used, e.g. for to build or erect a house, town, column, ship, to paint a picture, to carve or sculpture a statue.

1056–66 *Inscr. Kirkdale Ch., Yks.*, He hit let macan newan from grvnde. *a* **1100** *Gerefa* in *Anglia* (1886) IX. 261 Fiscwer and mylne macian. *c* **1154** *O.E. Chron.* an. 1137 In mani of þe castles wæron lof & grin.. þat was sua maced [etc.]. *c* **1205** LAY. 1937 Heo makeden tunes. *Ibid.* 27876 He .. lette makien beren riche and swiðe maren. *c* **1250** *Gen. & Ex.* 3541 Mac vs godes foren us to gon. *c* **1320** *Sir Tristr.* 2765 Þis forest wil y felle And castel wil y ma. *c* **1330** R. BRUNNE *Chron.* (1810) 336 He mad a coruen kyng. **1375** BARBOUR *Bruce* XI. 368 Ane vax-cayme that beis mais. **1377** LANGL. *P. Pl.* B. VI. 191 An heep of heremites.. ketten here copes and courtpies hem made. **1382** WYCLIF *Ps.* ciii. [civ.] 17 There sparewis shul make nestis. *a* **1400–50** *Alexander* 2587 He.. mas a brig ouire þe bourne of Barges with cheynes. **1432–50** tr. *Higden* (Rolls) I. 163 Men off Phenicia .. made [L. *condiderunt*] the cites of Sidon and of Tyrus. **1470–85** MALORY *Arthur* Table (II. vii.), Kyng Marke.. maad a tombe ouer them. **1530** PALSGR. 617/1, I make hym a gowne, a house, a cappe, or suche lyke. *Ibid.* 621/2, I make cockes of haye. **1571** *Satir. Poems Reform.* xxviii. 99 To Magnifie my name I maid ane Stepill. **1687** A. LOVELL tr. *Thevenot's Trav.* I. 208 The Franciscan Friars had made some Rooms there for the convenience of Pilgrims. **1686** AGLIONBY *Painting Illustr.* Explan. Terms s. v. *Antique*, All the Works of Painting, Sculpture, and Architecture that have been made in the Time of the Antient Greeks. **1751** R. PALTOCK *P. Wilkins* xlv. (1883) 132/2 One of the colambs being making a house to reside in. *a* **1774** GOLDSM. *Hist. Greece* I. 172 They caused a statue of Jupiter to be made at the general expence. **1774** —— *Nat. Hist.* (1776) VIII. 41 As birds sometimes are seen to make their nests. **1849** *Chambers's Inform.* II. 719/2 The machine being.. composed of the parts in ordinary use, only made circular. **1852** ROBERTSON *Serm.* Ser. III. xii. 147 The beaver makes its hole, the bee makes its cell. **1865** M. ARNOLD *Ess. Crit.* vi. 195 That dress, made full, as you've got it, suits you.

¶ An apparent sense 'to represent by graphic or plastic art' occasionally arises from the practice of applying the name of the thing portrayed to its representation.

a **1300–1400** *Cursor M.* 23216 (Gött.) Na mar.. þan painted fire.. þat on wagh wit man war mad right [*Cott.* þat apon awagh war wroght]. **1850** DICKENS *Dav. Copp.* xx, It was a startling likeness... The painter hadn't made the scar, but *I* made it. **1859** TENNYSON *Vivien* 329, I took his brush and blotted out the bird, And made a Gardener putting in a graff.

b. Const. *of, out of, with* (the material or component parts). See also 4.

13.. *Coer de L.* 2648 Torches maad with wex ful cleer. **1382** WYCLIF *Exod.* xxxii. 4 He.. made of hem a ȝotun calf. **1633** P. FLETCHER *Poet. Misc.* 62 My little pipe of seven reeds ymade. *a* **1774** GOLDSM. *Surv. Exp. Philos.* (1776) II. 239 Burning instruments.. are usually made with glass. —— tr. *Scarron's Com. Romance* (1775) I. 31 A.. pair of breeches .. which he had given to this botcher, to make out of them a more fashionable suit. **1791** J. TOWNSEND *Journ. Spain* (1792) III. 118 Buskins.. which are made with the esparto rush. **1859** H. T. ELLIS *Hong Kong to Manilla* 148 An Indian can make almost anything out of bamboo.

c. *absol.* in phr. ***make or mend***. Also, of a craftsman: To make the article which he produces *for* specified persons.

1851 MAYHEW *Lond. Labour* (1864) II. 34/1 Those who make or mend, and who must make or mend so cheaply that the veriest vagrant may be their customer [etc.]. **1856** *Househ. Words* XIV. 420/2, I do not make, or mend, or mar. **1862** *Temple Bar* VI. 482 He makes for Count This and Prince That, and they never want their coats altered.

d. *colloq.* ***as good*** (or ***clever***, etc.) ***as they make them***: as good (etc.) as possible.

187. *Broadside Ball.* title (Farmer), As good as they make 'em. **1889** G. ALLEN *Tents of Shem* iii. I. 51, I like them —thorough ladies,.. and as clever as they make them. **1934** T. S. ELIOT *Rock* i. 13, 'e was a fine fellow on one side and as bad as they make 'em on the other.

e. In various trades, applied *spec.* to some one of the operations constituting the process of manufacture.

1888 *Arts & Crafts Catal.* 82 The volume passes into the hands of the 'forwarder', who 'makes' the back. **1900** *Eng. Dial. Dict.*, *Make*, to put the soles on boots or shoes.

2. a. With a substance as object: To produce by the combination of ingredients, by extraction from a source, or by the modification of some other substance by mechanical or chemical processes. Const. *from, out of* (the source or original substance), *of*, †*with* (the ingredients).

c **1200** ORMIN 1480 Ʒiff þatt tu willt makenn laf, þu þresshesst tine shæfess. *c* **1230** *Hali Meid.* 33 Hit greueð þe se swiðe þat tu wilt.. makien puisun. *c* **1386** CHAUCER *Can. Yeom. Prol. & T.* 259 Cley maad with hors and mannes heer, and oille Of Tartre. *c* **1400** *Lanfranc's Cirurg.* 14 A medicyn maad in oon maner þat worchiþ dyuers effectis. **1471** RIPLEY *Comp. Alch.* Adm. viii. in Ashm. (1652) 191 Many Amalgame dyd I make. **1552** HULOET, Make mortar, *concinnare lutum.* **1585** T. WASHINGTON tr. *Nicholay's Voy.* I. xiv. 15 A small round fruite.. Of which the Inhabitants.. make oyle. **1611** BIBLE *Ecclus.* xlix. 1 The perfume yt is made by the art of the Apothecarie. **1669** STURMY *Mariner's Mag.* v. xii. 67 To make Red Powder. **1698** *Phil. Trans.* XX. 291 The way of making Pitch, Tarr, Rosin and Turpentine. **1710** HEARNE *Collect.* (O. H. S.) III. 30 Mr. William Stallenge.. was the first Author of making silk in England. **1853** URE *Dict. Arts*, etc. II. 728 The patent plan of Mr. William Onions of making cast steel seems worthy of adoption.

b. *spec.* To produce (an article of food or drink) by culinary or other operations. ***to make meat*** (obs. exc. dial.): to prepare food.

Some of the examples placed here might appear to belong to branch II; but originally *meat* was taken to mean the food as prepared. (Similarly in *to make tea* or *coffee*.)

c **1000** ÆLFRIC *Gen.* xxvii. 9 Bring me twa þa betstan tyccenu, þæt ic maciȝe mete þinum fæder þær of [Vulg. *ut faciam ex eis escas patri tuo*]. **1297** R. GLOUC. (Rolls) 8339 Wo þat miȝte.. seþe & Make potage. *a* **1300** *Cursor M.* 3497 Þe hus to kepe and ma þe mett. **13..** *E. E. Allit. P.* B. 625 Þre mettez of mele menge & ma kakez. *c* **1440** in *Househ. Ord.* (1790) 461 As men maken ruschewes. **1463** *Bury Wills* (Camden) 32 In leeffull tyme to make her mete in the chymeny. *a* **1589** R. TOMSON in *Hakluyt's Voy.* 581 The bread they make there, is certaine cakes made of rootes. **1603** DEKKER & CHETTLE *Grissil* IV. ii. (Shaks. Soc.) 59 Grissil shall go make pap, and I'll lick the skillet. **1747** MRS. GLASSE *Cookery* (1767) 215 To make a boiled loaf. **1846** DICKENS *Cricket* i. 15 Only let me make the tea first, John. **1850** —— *Dav. Copp.* xxiii, I then made her.. a glass of hot white wine and water, and a slice of toast cut into long thin strips. **1886** BESANT *Children Gibeon* II. xix, The cloth was spread, and she was making the tea.

3. a. Said of God as Creator; with reference both to material and to spiritual objects. Also *occas.* of Nature, and in *passive* with the agent unspecified.

c **1175** *Lamb. Hom.* 139 Sunnendai weren engles makede of godes muðe. *c* **1200** *Trin. Coll. Hom.* 222 He makeð þe fisses in þe sa þe fueles on þe lofte. *c* **1230** *Hali Meid.* 45 Ich chulle halde me hal þurh þe grace of godd, as cunde me makede. **1297** R. GLOUC. (Rolls) 478 Þre þousend & four score & þre ȝer Fram þat þe world was verst imad. *a* **1300** *Cursor M.* 345 He þat mad [*c* **1375** *Fairf.* maket] al thing o noght. **1382** WYCLIF *Gen.* i. 16 And God made two greet liȝt ȝyuerys. *c* **1449** PECOCK *Repr.* II. 146 God that made the world and alle thingis that ben in it. **1609** BIBLE (Douay) II. Index, Light, an accident made the first day. **1660** tr. *Amyraldus' Treat. conc. Relig.* II. vi. 241 Nature ha's not made us of Iron. **1667** MILTON *P. L.* IX. 137. **1742** YOUNG *Nt. Th.* IV. 828 Truth, eldest Daughter of the Deity; Truth, of his Council, when he made the Worlds. **1852** MRS. STOWE *Uncle Tom's C.* xx. 205 'Do you know who made you?' 'Nobody, as I knows on,' said the child... 'I spect I grow'd. Don't think nobody never made me.'

b. With compl. or advb. phrase denoting the form or condition of the creature, or the purpose or object of creation. Hence in *passive*, to be naturally fitted or destined (const. *for, to* with inf.). ***to be made for each other*** (or ***one another***): to be such as to harmonize perfectly or form an ideal combination; to be ideally suited: usu. of a specified man and woman.

c **1175** *Lamb. Hom.* 79 Þo þet weren imakede engles in houene, and fellen ut for hore wrechede. *c* **1250** *Gen. & Ex.* 122 Of euerilc ouȝt, of euerilc sed, Was erðe mad moder of sped. *a* **1300–1400** *Cursor M.* 12370 (Gött.) Ʒe þat he has made to men,.. And þat eftir his aunen ymage. **1382** WYCLIF *Mark* ii. 27 The Sabote is maad for man, and nat a man for the Sabote. *c* **1430** LYDG. *Min. Poems* (Percy Soc.) 121 Highe and lowe were made of oo nature. *a* **1533** LD. BERNERS *Huon* lix. 206 We be all made to dye. **1593** SHAKS. *2 Hen. VI*, v. i. 7 This hand was made to handle nought but Gold. **1607** —— *Cor.* I. i. 211 They said.. that dogges must eate, That meate was made for mouths. **1697** DRYDEN *Virg. Georg.* III. 259 The Calf, by Nature.. made To turn the Glebe. **1712** STEELE *Spect.* No. 515 ⁋6 Indeed, Gatty, we [*sc.* women] are made for Man. **1715** DE FOE *Fam. Instruct.* I. i. (1841) I. 13 Did God make me to serve him? **1732** POPE *Ess. Man* I. 39 Ask.. why oaks are made Taller or stronger than the weeds they shade. **1751** RICHARDSON *Clarissa* (ed. 3) III. 328 Her features are all harmony, and made for one another. **1784** BURNS (*title*) Man was made to mourn. **1822** COBBETT *Weekly Reg.* 30 Mar. 778 It is true enough, that God made all the women; but he did not make them all players. **1854** BREWSTER *More Worlds* xiii. 202 Man was not made for the planet—but the planet was made for man. **1857** DICKENS *Let.* Sept. (1938) II. 887 Poor Catherine and I are not made for each other, and there is no help for it. **1870** DICKENS *E. Drood* ii, She.. said that she had become your pupil, and that you were made for your vocation. **1927** J. N. MCILWRAITH *Kinsmen at War* xvii. 172 She and Stephen were made for one another. **1971** D. CLARK *Sick to Death* iv. 82 When two people—what's the popular phrase?—are made for each other, these things happen.

c. *pass.* ***to be*** (***well***, etc.) ***made***: said of the bodily frame.

a **1310** in Wright *Lyric P.* 36 Heo hath.. Body ant brest wel mad al. **1375** BARBOUR *Bruce* I. 385 Bot off lymmys he wes weill maid. *a* **1400–50** *Alexander* 3921 Then come a beste.. Mad & merkid as a Meere. *c* **1402** LYDG. *Compl. Bl. Knt.* 163 Of brede and lengthe So wel y-mad by good proporcioun. **1483** CAXTON *G. de la Tour* (1868) 168 To seme to the folkes syght better maad and fayrer of body. **1886** ADEL. SERGEANT *No Saint* I. i. 3 His frame was broad and strongly made.

4. a. ***to be made of***: to have been fashioned (whether by art or nature) out of (certain materials); to have as its material, constituents, or component parts; to consist or be composed of.

c **1200** *Trin. Coll. Hom.* 145 Ane box ȝemaked of marbelstone. *c* **1290** *St. Michael* 666 in *S. Eng. Leg.* I. 318 Of þis foure elemenz ech quic þing I-make is. **1307** *Elegy Edw. I*, viii, The holy crois ymad of tre. *c* **1374** CHAUCER *Boeth.* I. pr. i. 2 (Camb. MS.) Hyr clothes weren maked of riht delye thredes. *c* **1400** MAUNDEV. (Roxb.) ii. 6 Þe table.. was made of olyue. **1449** PECOCK *Repr.* I. 8 An argument if he be ful and foormal, which is clepid a sillogisme, is mad of twey proposicions. **1500–20** DUNBAR *Poems* xxi. 46 Toungis now are maid of quhyte quhaill bone, And hairtis ar maid of hard flynt stone. **1530** PALSGR. 318/1 Made of cristall, *cristalin.* **1542** UDALL *Erasm. Apoph.* 255 b, I found Rome made but of bricke, and I will leaue it of marble. **1633** MASSINGER *Guardian* I. i, I am made of other clay. **1669** STURMY *Mariner's Mag.* v. xii. 66 Cords made of Hemp. **1827** *Mirror* II. 164/1 Books aren't made of Stilton cheese. **1892** *Argosy* Oct. 312 The drums were made of metal.

†**b.** To be 'compact' of (certain qualities). *Obs.*

c **1374** CHAUCER *Boeth.* II. pr. iv. 27 (Camb. MS.) A man maked alle of sapyence and vertu. **1611** SHAKS. *Cymb.* III. v. 33 She looke[s] vs like A thing more made of malice, then of duty.

5. a. To compose, write as the author (a book, poem, or other literary work, †a letter). Formerly often (now only as a rare archaism) with the title of a work as obj.; in mod. use chiefly in the phrase to ***make verses*** (***poetry***, etc.). Also said with reference to musical composition.

The mod. usage is difficult to reduce to rule. It is common to speak of 'making' a sonnet or an epigram; but it would sound odd to speak of 'making' a tragedy or a novel, except

with some added phrase, as in 'Some one has made a tragedy on this subject'.

c **1175** *Lamb. Hom.* 125 Ða songes .. boð makede of þere heouenliche blisse þe us wes iopenad on þisse timan. *c* **1200** *Trin. Coll. Hom.* 71 On þe godspelle þe sein lucas makede. *c* **1205** LAY. 32 He nom þa Englisca boc þa makede seint Beda. *a* **1300** *Cursor M.* 87 Of hir to mak bath rim and sang. **1375** BARBOUR *Bruce* I. 33 Off thaim I thynk this buk to ma. **1377** LANGL. *P. Pl.* B. v. 415 I haue leuere here an harlotrie .. þan al þat euere Marke made, Mathew, John, & lucas. **1485** CAXTON in *Malory's Arthur* Pref. 2 Alle suche bookes as been maad of hym ben fayned and fables. **1508** DUNBAR *Poems* iv. 66 Clerk of Tranent .. That maid the anteris of Gawane. **1530** PALSGR. 617/2, I make a booke, as a clerke dothe... Is your boke made yet? *Ibid.* 625/1, I wyll go make a letter. *Ibid.* 630/2, I make the dytie of a songe. **1612** BACON *Ess., Beauty* (Arb.) 210 As a Musitian that maketh an excellent aire in Musick. **1612** BRINSLEY *Lud. Lit.* xiv. (1627) 190 How to make Verses with delight and certainety. **1650** HOWELL *Giraffi's Rev. Naples* I. 127 Cavalier Cosmo Fonseca .. who us'd to make epitaphs. **1699** BENTLEY *Phal.* 211 *Philoctetes*, which was not made till sixscore years after Phalaris's death. **1787** J. RAMSAY in *Burns' Wks.* II. 117 He has made words to one or two of them [*sc.* tunes]. **1803** tr. *P. Le Brun's Mons. Botte* I. 6 Would you .. have me marry a woman that makes verses? **1819** CRABBE *T. of Hall* x, I penn'd some notes, and might a book have made, But I had no connection with the trade. **1889** D. HANNAY *Capt. Marryat* 100 Travellers who came to spy out the land, and make a book about it. **1894** W. MORRIS *Wood beyond World* colophon, Here ends the tale of the Wood beyond the World made by William Morris.

†**b.** *absol.* or *intr.* To compose verses; to write poetry; to rime. (Cf. MAKER 5.) *Obs.*

1377 LANGL. *P. Pl.* B. XII. 22 To solacen hym sum tyme as I do whan I make. *c* **1385** CHAUCER *L. G. W.* Prol. 69 Ye lovers that can make of sentement. *c* **1392** —— *Compl. Venus* 82 Graunson, flour of hem that make in Fraunce. **1500–20** DUNBAR *Poems* lxxviii. 2 My heid did ȝak ȝester-nicht, This day to mak that I na micht. **1579** SPENSER *Sheph. Cal.* Apr. 19 And hath he skill to make so excellent? **1612** DRAYTON *Poly-olb.* iv. 59 Those who scarce have seene a booke Most skilfully will make. **1622** WITHER *Mistr. Philar.* Postscr. N 8, I make to please my selfe, and not for them. **1864** DASENT *Jest & Earnest* (1873) II. 303 Thou art a good skald .. if thou canst 'make' no worse than Glum.

†**c.** *to make Latin* or *Latins*: to write Latin composition. *Obs.*

c **1500**, *a* **1568**, **1607** [see LATIN *sb.* 4]. **1612** BRINSLEY *Pos. Parts* (1669) 130 Directions to make Latine. **1675** E. COLES (*title*) Nolens volens, or you shall make Latin whether you will or no.

d. To draw up (a legal document).

1362 LANGL. *P. Pl.* A. II. 58 Now Simonye and Siuyle stondeþ forþ boþe, Vn-Foldyng þe Feffement þat Falsnes made. **1476** *Surtees Misc.* (1890) 35 Made in the yere of our Lorde millesimo cccclxxvj. **1484** CAXTON *Fables of Poge* vi, Whanne he was .. at the poynt of dethe he wold make his testament. **15..** *Doun by ane Rever as I red* 71 in *Dunbar's Poems* 307 Quhill Deid he hint him be the back, .. And lute him nocht his testment mack. **1519** *Rec. Allhallows' Barking* in Rimbault *Hist. Organ* 56 This endenture made the yere of our lorde god m[l]v[c] xix. **1658–9** *Burton's Diary* (1828) IV. 45 Put the case, that none but servants be at making their master's will. **1697** G. DALLAS *Syst. Stiles* I The foresaid Clause made anent payment of Annual rents. *Ibid.* 7 [A] Writ made by way of Contract. **1797** *Encycl. Brit.* (ed. 3) XVIII. 395/1 If he recovers, he may alter his dispositions, and have time to make a written will. **1823** GREVILLE *Mem.* (1875) I. 64 In 1810 the King made another will, but .. he always put off signing it. **1903** *Spectator* 31 Oct. 704/2 Daulac .. and his companions made their wills, confessed, and received the sacrament.

6. To put together materials for (a fire) and set them alight.

c **1205** LAY. 1186 He makede bi þon weofede a swiðe wunsum fur. **1375** BARBOUR *Bruce* IV. 561 Luk on na viss the fyre he ma. **1565** COOPER *Thesaurus* s.v. *Facere, Bustum*, to make a funeral fyer. ? *c* **1558** [see FIRE *sb.* 3]. **1603** DEKKER & CHETTLE *Grissil* I. i. (Shaks. Soc.) 15 Master, I have made a good fire. **1687** A. LOVELL tr. *Thevenot's Trav.* I. 225 They made great Fires all along the Coast. **1844** E. WARBURTON *Cresc. & Cross* II. 101, I .. ordered the other [Arab] to make a fire instantly.

7. To set apart and prepare the site for (a garden, park, road, etc.).

1382 WYCLIF *Amos* ix. 14 Thei shuln make gardyns. **1727–41** CHAMBERS *Cycl.* s.v. *Road*, Artificial Road is that made by labour of the hand, either of earth or masonry. **1804** CHARLOTTE SMITH *Conversations*, etc. I. 93 We had made gardens of our own. **1818** *Order* in Willis & Clark *Cambridge* (1886) I. 573 The making a walk from the New Bridge along the new Plantation. **1866** M. ARNOLD *Thyrsis* i, How changed is here each spot man makes or fills!

** In wider sense: To cause to exist, to produce.

8. a. To cause the existence of (a material thing or a physical phenomenon) by some action; to inflict (a wound); to produce (a hole, a mark, a sound, etc.). So *to make melody, minstrelsy; to make a note*, etc.: see the sbs.

c **1200** *Trin. Coll. Hom.* 33 þe wundes þat hie on him makeden. *a* **1300** *Cursor M.* 17288 + 101 þe erthe quoke & made sown. *c* **1420** *Anturs of Arth.* 125 (Douce MS.) þe grisly goost made a gryme bere. **1530** PALSGR. 617/2 The droppes of water with ofte fallynge make the hole in a marbyll stone. *Ibid.*, What a cherme these byrdes make. **1589** PUTTENHAM *Eng. Poesie* II. x[i]. (Arb.) 103 Make me .. so many strokes or lines with your pen as ye would haue your song containe verses. **1601** SHAKS. *Jul. C.* I. i. 49 Haue you not made an Vniuersall shout? **1680** COTTON *Compl. Gamester* x. (ed. 2) 85 Although the best of other eyes shall not discern where any mark was made. **1687** A. LOVELL tr. *Thevenot's Trav.* I. 111 Great claps of Thunder, which .. made with the beating of the waves, a fearful noise. **1820** J. GIFFORD *Compl. Eng. Lawyer* II. xiii. 219 If any person shall make a hole in such ship. **1842** TENNYSON *Morte d'Arthur* 137 The great brand Made lightnings in the splendour of the moon. **1886** *Pall Mall G.* 15 July 6/1 To make his cross upon the ballot paper.

†**b.** *impers.* with reference to weather. [Cf. F. *il fait chaud, il fait obscur.*] *Obs. rare.*

a **1300** *Cursor M.* 11658 Gret hete in wildernes it made. **1654** WHITELOCKE *Swed. Ambassy* (1772) I. 165 Yett made it darke before they were from table.

9. a. To produce by action, bring about (a condition of things, a state of feeling).

For *to make ado*, †*a coil*, (*a*) *commotion, fun, a fuss, game, an impression*, †*a matter, a pother, a row, a sensation, sport, a stir*: see the sbs.

c **1122** *O.E. Chron.* an. 1052 (MS. E.) Hi macodon mæst þet unseht betweonan Godwine eorle & þam cynge. **1352** MINOT *Poems* viii. 34 þe Franche men .. mase grete dray when þai er dight. *c* **1386** CHAUCER *Sqr.'s T.* 210 It is rather lyk An apparence y-maad by som Magyk. *c* **1400** *Destr. Troy* 4213 Lamydon .. was fader to the freike that offens mas. *c* **1449** PECOCK *Repr.* Prol. 3 Tho blamers .. han therbi maad ful miche indignacioun. *c* **1475** *Rauf Coilȝear* 172 Mak na mair stryfe. **1530** PALSGR. 619/1, I make a revell, I make a do. **1573** BARET *Alv.* M 48 To make strife and debate, *concire vel concitare lites.* **1611** COTGR., *Faire le Diable de vauvert*, .. to make a hurlyburly. **1650** BAXTER *Saints' R.* IV. (1651) 36 The sufferings which we do make our selves, have usually issues answerable to their causes. **1813** BYRON *Br. Abydos* II. xx, He makes a solitude, and calls it—peace! **1897** A. D. INNES *Macaulay's Ess. Clive* (Pitt Press) 128 Buying up all the rice—in the trade-jargon of to-day 'making a corner'.

†**b.** Const. dat. of the person or with *to, unto*: To cause (something) to happen to or fall to the lot of (a person); to cause (a person) to experience (something); to bring into a person's possession or power. *Obs.*

a **1000** *Cædmon's Gen.* 755 (Gr.) Eac is hearm gode modsorȝ ȝemacod. *c* **1000** ÆLFRIC *Judg.* xvi. 25 þa bædon hiȝ sume þæt Samson moste him macian sum gamen. **1303** R. BRUNNE *Handl. Synne* 3939 ȝyf þou make one so hard stresse þat hys godnesse wexe þe lesse. *a* **1310** in Wright *Lyric P.* 31 Al wrong y wrohte for a wyf, that made us wo in world ful wyde. *c* **1375**, *c* **1386** [see GAME *sb.* 1]. *a* **1400** *Cursor M.* 28630 (Cott. Galba) Two maners of mending makes men mede. **1483** CAXTON *G. de la Tour* F vij, This quene .. made unto the peple grete dyuersytees. **1590** SPENSER *F.Q.* I. viii. 34 He .. Then .. from his arme did reach Those keyes, and made himselfe free enterance. **1610** B. JONSON *Alch.* III. ii, Euen the med'cinall vse shall make you a faction, And party in the realme. **1629** R. HILL *Pathw. Piety* I. 184 If we have made them any offence. **1690** LOCKE *Govt.* II. v. §39 Labour could make Men distinct titles to several parcels of it [*sc.* the World]. **1725** RAMSAY *Gentle Sheph.* II. iii, The last wind made Glaud a roofless barn.

c. *to make peace*, †*grith*, †*sib*: (*a*) to bring about a condition of peace; (*b*) to conclude a treaty of peace.

c **1122** *O.E. Chron.* an. 1086 (MS. E.) Betwyx oðrum þingum nis na to forgytane þæt gode frið þe he macode on þisan lande. *c* **1154** *Ibid.* an. 1140 ¶ 11 He dide god iustise & makede pais. *a* **1175** *Cott. Hom.* 243 Wið wam we ne muȝe grið ne sibbe macie. *a* **1310** in Wright *Lyric P.* 100 Jesu Crist, thou be mi bote, so boun icham to make my pees. **1390** GOWER *Conf.* I. 12 To make pes betwen the kynges After the lawe of charite. *c* **1410** HOCCLEVE *Mother of God* 78 By thee, lady, y-makid is the pees Betwixt Angels and men. **1590** SPENSER *F.Q.* II. iii. 9 So happy peace they made and faire accord. **1651** HOBBES *Leviath.* III. xl. 253 The Supreme Power of making War and Peace, was in the Priest. **1849** MACAULAY *Hist. Eng.* vii. II. 224 He now made his peace, and went as far in servility as he had ever done in faction. **1863** H. COX *Instit.* III. ii. 596 The sole prerogative of the Crown of making peace and war.

d. *to make place, room, way*: see the sbs.

¶ **e.** In the 14–15th c. the passive often renders L. *fieri* 'to begin to exist', 'to take place', or (after Hellenistic Gr. γίγνεσθαι) 'to be'. Cf. 48 f, 49 e.

1382 WYCLIF *Luke* iii. 3 The word of the Lord is maad on John. *c* **1400** MAUNDEV. (1839) v. 40 That gret Babyloyne, where the Dyversite of Langages was first made.

10. a. To give rise to; to have as a result or consequence; to be the cause of. Very common in proverbs. Also in phrases *to make a difference*, †*a wonder. to make work*: to occasion the necessity for work to be done; to give trouble.

c **1175** *Lamb. Hom.* 103 *Auaricia* .. heo macað reaflac .. and lesunge. *c* **1230** *Hali Meid.* 17 Eise makeð þeof. **1375** BARBOUR *Bruce* II. 330 God may rycht weill our werdis dele; For multitud maiss na victory. **1533** ELYOT *Cast. Helthe* (1539) 54 The meate that shall make syckenesse, muste nat a lyttell excede the exquisite measure. **1565** COOPER *Thesaurus* s. v. *Facere*, Vse maketh a custome. **1573** BARET *Alv.* M 49 Old age maketh wrinckles. **1597** BACON *Coulers Good & Evill* (Arb.) 154 The second blow makes the fray, The second word makes the bargaine. **1630** B. JONSON *New Inn* I. (*init.*) A heavy purse makes a light heart. **1655** WOOD *Life* 12 Oct. (O.H.S.) I. 199 It made a great wonder, that a maid should be in love with such a person as he. **1662** GERBIER *Principles* 14 Too many Staires and back-Doores makes Thieves and Whores. **1668** R. STEELE *Husbandman's Calling* vi. (1672) 176 Except infants that make work, he will have all the rest do some work or other. **1738** SWIFT *Pol. Conversat.* 39 One Fool makes many. **1759** BROWN *Compl. Farmer* 91 Dry weather makes plenty of honey. **1791** *Gentl. Mag.* 22/2 It makes very little difference, with which of the acids the ether is composed. **1834** *Brit. Husb.* I. 56 (U.K.S.) A very common opinion among farmers, that 'high rents make good farmers'.

†**b.** With *it* as obj.: To be the cause of the fact stated or supposed. *Obs.*

c **1375** *Cursor M.* 18788 (Fairf.) His kin ne wille he noȝt forsake bot if þai hit ham-seluen make [*Cott.* bot it be thoru þair aun sake]. **1362** LANGL. *P. Pl.* A. x. 55 In Monnes Brayn .. he [*sc.* Inwit] is Bremest, But ȝif blod hit make. **1377** *Ibid.* B. v. 420, I nam nouȝte shryuen some tyme but if sekenesse it make. **1393** *Ibid.* C. XI. 157 Man is .. semblable in soule to god bote yf synne hit make. *Ibid.* XXI. 326.

11. *Gram.* Of a word: To 'form' (a certain case, tense, etc.) in a specified manner; to change into (a specified form) when inflected. [After L. *facere.*]

c **1000** ÆLFRIC *Gram.* viii. (Z.) 21 Seo forme declinatio .. macað hire genitivvm on *ae.* **1886** T. LE M. DOUSE *Introd. Gothic* 167 *Wahsja* .. makes in the present 2 p[erson] s[ingular] *wahseis.*

12. a. To establish (a rule, ordinance); to enact (a law); to impose (a rate); †to found, institute (a religious order, etc.).

c **1124** *O.E. Chron.*, an. 963 (Laud MS.) He macode þær twa abbotrice, an of muneca oðer of nunna. *a* **1225** *Ancr. R.* 6 þeos riwle is imaked nout of monnes fundleas, auh is of godes hestes. *c* **1300** *Havelok* 31 Gode lawes He dede maken, an ful wel holden. *a* **1300** *Cursor M* 11189 Ouer al þe werld he mad statut. *c* **1380** WYCLIF *Wks.* (1880) 2 Here ordris maad of synful men. **1423** *Rolls of Parlt.* IV. 257/2 To graunte, ordeyne, and mak by estatut. **1542** UDALL *Erasm. Apoph.* 275 [They] made a lawe that [etc.]. **1568** GRAFTON *Chron.* II. 517 Certeine ordinaunces, made by the Maior and Aldermen of London. **1765** BLACKSTONE *Comm.* I. ii. 142 In all tyrannical governments .. the right of both making and enforcing the laws, is vested in one and the same man. **1845** STEPHEN *Comm. Laws Eng.* II. 356 Poor rates made in respect of the premises. **1875** STUBBS *Const. Hist.* (1896) II. xvii. 614 The theory that the laws were made or enacted by the king with the consent of the lords and at the petition of the commons. **1898** *Encycl. Laws Eng.* VIII. 70 A receiving order is 'made' on the day it is pronounced, not when it is drawn up.

†**b.** To arrange, fix the time and place for (a match); to institute (games). *Obs.*

a **1568** ASCHAM *Scholem.* II. (Arb.) 125 The games running, wrestling, and shoting, that Achilles maketh in Homer, with the selfe same games that Æneas maketh in Virgil. **1676** LADY CHAWORTH in *12th Rep. Hist. MSS. Comm.* App. v. 32 They have made four matches to be run at Newmarket. **1703** *Lond. Gaz.* No. 3905/4 There is a Cock-Match made between the Counties of Surrey and Sussex. **1752** AINSWORTH *Lat. Eng. Dict.* s.v., To make a match for fighting, *Certamen instituere.*

13. Uses arising from ellipsis of obj. in the factitive senses (branch III). **a.** To create by election, appointment, or ordination; to appoint (an officer), ordain (a priest, etc.).

1297 R. GLOUC. (Rolls) 58 Voure kinges hii made þo in þis kinedom. **1340** *Ayenb.* 42 Dingnetes þet me makeþ be chyezinge. *c* **1400** *Rule St. Benet* 145 The Method of makeing a Nunn. *a* **1400–50** *Alexander* 3441 þe prouynce piȝt is in pes & princes ere maked. **1422** *Rolls of Parlt.* IV. 176 Such officers, and all othre, be maad by advys. **1500–20** DUNBAR *Poems* xiv. 46 Sa mony jugeis and lordis now maid of lait. **1552** *Bk. Com. Prayer* Ordination, The fourme and maner of makynge and consecratynge, Bishoppes, Priestes, and Deacons. **1585** *Act 27 Eliz.* c. 2 § 1 Priestes, which have bene .. made .. beyonde the Seas, by or according to the Order .. of the Romishe Church. **1641** BAKER *Chron.* (1660) 148 He [Rich. II] then made nine Knights, and created four Earls. **1762** GOLDSM. *Cit. W.* lxxiv, When the Tartars make a Lama, their first care is to place him in a dark corner of the temple. **1810** WELLINGTON *Let. to Lt. Col. Torrens* in Gurw. *Desp.* (1838) VI. 326, I .. have not the power of making even a Corporal.

b. *Naut.* To promote in rank: occas. *into* a particular ship.

1795 NELSON 26 Dec. in Nicolas *Disp.* (1845) II. 123 My late First-Lieutenant is now a Captain, made by the Admiralty, for the services of the Agamemnon. **1798** JANE AUSTEN *Lett.* (1884) I. 190 Frank is made. He was yesterday raised to the rank of Commander. *a* **1817** —— *Persuas.* I. 256 When he came home from the Cape,—just made into the Grappler. **1833** MARRYAT *P. Simple* xxxviii, I had now served my time as midshipman, .. and I thought that I had a better chance of being made in England than abroad. **1867** SMYTH *Sailor's Word-bk.*, *Made*, a professional term for having obtained a commission, or being promoted.

c. *gen.* To cause a person or persons to become (what is specified by the object).

to make friends is first recorded in idiomatic phrases (see FRIEND *sb.* 6 b) in which the (presumably) original force of the verb is obscured.

1594 HOOKER *Eccl. Pol.* III. i. § 9 If they be no Christians, how make they Christians [by baptism]? **1597** SHAKS. *2 Hen. IV*, I. i. 214 Get Posts, and Letters, and make Friends with speed. **1610** B. JONSON *Alch.* III. ii, There you haue made a friend. **1711** ADDISON *Spect.* No. 47 ¶ 7 For these Ten Years successively he has not made less than an Hundred April Fools. **1720** OZELL *Vertot's Rom. Rep.* I. VI. 343 [He] made a great Number of Prisoners. **1849** MACAULAY *Hist. Eng.* VI. II. 97 He .. tried .. to make as few enemies as possible. **1859–60** J. H. NEWMAN *Hist. Sk.* (1873) III. II. ii. 237 He was .. a man to make both friends and enemies.

†**d.** To translate, 'render'. *Obs.* (Cf. *make English*, 48.)

1529 MORE *Dyalogue* III. Wks. 233/2 The clergie hath not forboden the byble to bee made and readde in englishe. **1612** BRINSLEY *Pos. Parts* (1669) 130 This word *of*, coming after a verb, is made by a Preposition.

e. To fix (a price). Now only *Comm.*

1567 *Gude & Godlie Ball.*, '*The Wind blawis cauld*', The theif Judas did greit trespas, That Christ for siluer sauld: Bot Preistis will tak, and his price mak, For les be mony fauld. **1752** AINSWORTH *Eng.-Lat. Dict.* s.v., To make a price, *Pretium alicui rei facere vel indicere.* **1895** A. J. WILSON *Gloss. Terms Stock Exch.*, *To make a Price.* A dealer is said to 'make a price' when he states the price at which he is prepared to buy and the one at which he is ready to sell a particular security.

14. To prepare or provide (a meal, feast) for guests; to give (a dinner, etc.). *Obs.* exc. *arch.*

c **1000** *Ags. Gosp.* Matt. xxii. 2 Heofona rice ys ȝelic ȝewurden þam cyninge þe macude hys suna gyfata [*qui fecit nuptias filio suo*]. *c* **1205** LAY. 14425 þe king makede ueorme, swiðe store [*c* **1275** feste]. *c* **1380** WYCLIF *Sel. Wks.* III. 416 In his two feestis þat he maked by myracle, he fed þo puple.

1382 —— *Luke* xiv. 12 Whanne thou makist a mete, ether souper. *a* **1400–50** *Alexander* 831 þou mas þe slike a mangery & macchis changis. **1483** CAXTON *G. de la Tour* G viij b, She made grete dyners to the poure peple. *a* **1548** HALL *Chron., Hen. VIII* 21 So he made them a banket and thei departed. **1682, 1814** [see FEAST *sb.* 3]. **1762** GOLDSM. *Nash* Wks. (Globe) 525/1 People of fashion make public breakfasts at the assembly-houses, to which they invite their acquaintances. **1867** M. ARNOLD *Obermann once more*, He made a feast, drank fierce and fast, And crown'd his hair with flowers.

15. To form by collection of individuals.

†**a.** To get together (a party, a force); to muster or raise (troops). Also ***to make a head***: see HEAD *sb.*¹ 57 b. *Obs.*

13.. *Coer de L.* 1251 The kyng comaundyd.. At London to make a parlement. **1387** TREVISA *Higden* (Rolls) VII. 111 At Oxenforde he made a parlement. *a* **1400–50** *Alexander* 2210 Alexander.. all a-boute þe cite, Makis foure thousand with flanes & bowis. *c* **1420** LYDG. *Assembly of Gods* 1055 He seyde pleynly he Vertu wold forsake, And in Vyce hys quarell all hys power make. **1470–85** MALORY *Arthur* XXI. xxii. 839 Wherfore Syr Mordred made a parlemente and called the lordes togyder. **1523** LD. BERNERS *Froiss.* I. xxviii. 42 These lordes be thei that may make moost men of warre in short space of any that I know. **1594** SHAKS. *Rich. III*, IV. iv. 449 The greatest strength and power that he can make. **1607** —— *Cor.* v. i. 37. **1617** MORYSON *Itin.* III. 266 The Sweitzers can make six score thousand foote for the defence of their owne Country. **1647** COTTERELL tr. *Davila's Hist. Fr.* I. 50 The Duke of Guise sent forth Jaques d'Aubon.. and James Savoy.. with all the horse they could make. *a* **1715** BURNET *Own Time* (1724) I. 407 Lord Danby saw his error, of neglecting the leading men, and reckoning upon a majority, such as could be made.

b. In parliamentary phrase, ***to make a House***: to ensure the presence of the number (now 40) of members required for a regularly constituted sitting of the House (of Commons). Also said of the members. Similarly, ***to make a quorum***.

1648 DR. DENTON 7 Dec. in F. P. Verney *Mem. Verney Family* (1892–9) II. 395 Most of the secured members lay in Hell last night, and are now gone to the generall. There is scarce enough left free to make a house. **1775** [see HOUSE *sb.*¹ 4 d]. **1830** *Examiner* 409/2 Twice this week have Ministers failed to make a House of Commons. **1864** *Spectator* 7 May 529 A Bill which.. will before long interest every taxpayer, was interrupted by mere official carelessness as to 'making a House'. **1884** *Manch. Exam.* 15 May 5/4 A House was made to-day promptly at a quarter-past 12 o'clock.

c. *Sporting.* ***to make a bag***: to kill a number of game on a shooting expedition. ***to make the bag***: said of the sportsman who contributes most to the total of game killed.

1863, 1867 [see BAG *sb.* 9]. **1889** *Cornhill Mag.* XIII. 209 Sir Allan is making the bag. That is the third time he has wiped Sir Joseph's eye.

d. *Betting.* ***to make a book***: to arrange a series of bets referring to one and the same race or 'event', with odds calculated with a view to a probable gain on the whole transaction.

1828 HOOD *Miss Kilmansegg, Honeymoon*, Of making a book how he made a stir. **1856** 'STONEHENGE' *Brit. Rural Sports* II. I. xiii. §137 It does not always happen that the person laying the odds makes a book. **1892** *Cassell's Sat. Jrnl.* 28 May 859/1 There certainly is a way of 'making a book' by which the layer of odds must win.

† **16. a.** To bring forth (fruit, blossom); to have as a product. *Obs.*

1375 BARBOUR *Bruce* v. 9 The treis begouth to ma Burgeonys and brycht blwmys alsua. **1382** WYCLIF *Matt.* vii. 17 So euery good tree makith good fruytis. *c* **1380** —— *Serm.* Sel. Wks. I. 166. *c* **1400** *Apol. Loll.* 4. **1604** E. G[RIMSTONE] *D'Acosta's Hist. Indies* IV. xxxii. 296 In new Spaine, there are some vignes which beare grapes, and yet make no wine.

b. ***to make water***, †***urine*** [= F. *faire de l'eau*]: to urinate. (See the sbs.)

†**17.** Of a mother: To give birth to (young). Of a father: To beget. *Obs.* [So F. *faire.*]

1362 LANGL. *P. Pl.* A. x. 164 þe cursede blod þat Caym haþ I-maket. **1483** CAXTON *G. de la Tour* G viij b, This good lady Rachel as she had made a child she forthwith.. gaf thankyngis of it to god. **1484** —— *Fables of Æsop* II. iv, A sowe whiche wepte.. for the grete payne that she felte by cause she wold make her young pygges. *c* **1500** *Melusine* 102 She made a fayre child that was her second sonne.

18. a. Used with const. *of* or *out of* (by extension of the notion in sense 1 b), to designate the action of causing what is denoted by the regimen of the prep. to become what is denoted by the object of the verb.

So in many phrases, as ***to make a business, practice, trade of; to make an example, a fool of; to make an ass, a beast, an exhibition of oneself***: for illustration see the sbs.

c **1175** *Lamb. Hom.* 103 þa.. scinne.. þet is ihaten *fornicatio*.. maceð of cristes leoman heoranna leoman. *c* **1200** *Vices & Virtues* 137 Of here wombe hie makieð here godd. *c* **1205** LAY. 13674 Heo.. wulleð.. makien king of ane Peohte. *a* **1300** *Cursor M.* 13419 Vr drightin.. made þam of þair water win. *Ibid.* 18790 þat we vr fa mak of vr freind. *c* **1330** *Assump. Virg.* 671 Ihesu crist.. Of a wilde hounde haþ made a lomb. **1530** TINDALE *Pract. Prel.* C iij, And thus of one empyre was made twayne. **1563** FOXE *A. & M.* 1711/1 There was no more behinde, to make a very Iphigenia of her, but her offeryng vp vpon the aultar of the scaffolde. **1610** SHAKS. *Temp.* I. ii. 101, 169. **1611** COTGR., *Faire estat de*.. to vse, or make a practise of. **1667** MILTON *P. L.* I. 255 The mind.. Can make a Heav'n of Hell, a Hell of Heav'n. **1686** HORNECK *Crucif. Jesus* xiv. 331 Such a person must not make a trade of repenting and sinning. **1707** *Curios. in Husb. & Gard.* Pref. 5 The Heathens, who made Gods of the very Onions that grew in their Gardens. **1759** STERNE *Tr. Shandy* II. ii, I beg only you will make no strangers of yourselves. **1859** TENNYSON *Lancelot & Elaine* 912 Such service have ye done me, that I make My will of yours. **1889** J. K. JEROME *Three Men in Boat* 206 Montmorency made an awful ass of himself. **1892** MRS. H. WARD *D. Grieve* II. vii, He was making a friend of her. **1894** EMILY LAWLESS *Maelcho* I. ii. 32 He was not going to make a show of himself.

b. in *indirect passive*.

1715 [see FOOL *sb.*¹ 3]. **1742** RICHARDSON *Pamela* III. 92 I will attend you,.. altho' I doubt I am to be made a Shew of. **1766** GOLDSM. *Vic. W.* xxxi, She was now made an honest woman of. **1803** *Pic Nic* No. 4 (1806) I. 140 They must be made an example of.

c. With idiomatic *of it.*

1660 INGELO *Bentiv. & Ur.* I. (1682) 55 They were going to make a Day of it in Sports and Musick upon the Water. **1752** AINSWORTH *Eng.-Lat. Dict.* s.v., You have made a good day's work of it. **1789** CHARLOTTE SMITH *Ethelinde* (1814) III. 162 A bad history, a bad history, I am afraid, that young man has made of it. **1809** MALKIN *Gil Blas* IV. vi. ¶8 He is going to make a night of it. *Ibid.* x. x. ¶12, I made but one nap of it all night. **1844** DICKENS *Mart. Chuz.* v, I always supposed that Mrs. Lupin and you would make a match of it. **1855** COSTELLO *Stor. Screen* 90, made a clean breast of it to Desirée. **1856** WHYTE MELVILLE *Kate Cov.* vi, I.. had a great mind to make a bolt of it and run up-stairs.

d. ***to make*** (***much, little, something, nothing,*** etc.) ***of***: to derive (much or little) advantage from; to turn to (much or little) account.

to make the best, the most of: see BEST *sb.*, MOST *sb.*

1643 TRAPP *Comm. Gen.* xxxii. 12 A flye can make little of a flower; but a bee will not off, till he hath the sweet thyme out of it. **1687** A. LOVELL tr. *Thevenot's Trav.* I. 229 They Boarded her again the third time, but could make nothing on't. **1707** *Curios. in Husb. & Gard.* 202, I set about the work.. resolv'd to.. be certain whether I could make anything of it or not. **1732** LD. TYRAWLY in *Buccleuch MSS.* (Hist. MSS. Comm.) I. 381 Unless you have two Molettamen.. you won't be able to make anything at all of her [*sc.* a boat], with any hands you'll get. **1870** ROGERS *Hist. Gleanings* Ser. II. 246 Calumny made something of his relations with William Tooke. **1884** W. C. SMITH *Kildrostan* 59 They hold the place which once the chieftain held, And what have they made of it?

e. ***to make a hash, mess, muddle of***: to fail grossly in, bungle (a business). See the sbs.

f. ***to make.. of***: to do.. with. *Sc.* [Cf. F. 'qu'avez-vous fait *de*..'.]

1824 MISS FERRIER *Inher.* lxxiii, It was inconceivable, too, what he made of himself all day.

*** To frame in thought or representation.

19. To form within the mind; to give conceptual existence to. **a.** To entertain (doubt, scruple, question, etc.) in the mind; to formulate mentally; to form (a judgement).

to make conscience: see CONSCIENCE ii. ***to make a difference***: see DIFFERENCE *sb.* 5.

1375 BARBOUR *Bruce* I. 249 Than mayss clerkis questioun,.. That [etc.]. *a* **1425** *Cursor M.* 23846 (Trin.) From hit may we no way scape for no wile þat we con make. **1565** COOPER *Thesaurus* s.v. *Facere, Controuersiam*, to propose as doubtfull: to make doubt of. **1583–1875** [see QUESTION *sb.* 5]. **1586–1875** [see DOUBT *sb.*¹ 4 a]. **1661** BOYLE *Style of Script.* (1675) 228 The more scruple I would make to rob them. **1709** BERKELEY *Th. Vision* §3 The estimate we make of the distance of objects. **1721** PERRY *Daggenh. Breach* 4 Persons, who may be able to make a Judgment of the Truth of what I relate. **1844** *Fraser's Mag.* XXX. 98/1, I make no doubt every one.. has practised similar stratagems. **1870** LOWELL *Study Wind.* 229 The judgement of him [Chaucer] which we make from his works. **1885–94** R. BRIDGES *Eros & Psyche* May xiii, She made no wonder how the wonder was.

b. ***to make*** (***great,*** etc.) ***account,*** †***count,*** †***esteem,*** †***estimation,*** †***reckoning,*** †***regard,*** †***store of***: to have a high opinion of, set store by. (Chiefly *obs.* or *arch.*)

1393, etc. [see ACCOUNT *sb.* 12]. **1484**, etc. [see COUNT *sb.*¹ 5]. **1539** CROMWELL in Merriman *Life & Lett.* (1902) II. 244 His Maieste wold neither make store of them ne bestowe a two penys for their conveyance hither. **1576** FLEMING *Panopl. Epist.* 95, I would haue you make ful reckoning of al my counsel. *c* **1586** C'TESS PEMBROKE *Ps.* CXIX. ii, Such regard of thee I make, For feare of thee my flesh doth quake. **1605** BACON *Adv. Learn.* II. xv. §2, I make no more estimation of repeating a number of names or words upon once hearing.. than [etc.]. **1652** J. WRIGHT tr. *Camus' Nat. Paradox* XI. 308 The same cause made Amiclea disdain the esteem which Liante made of her. **1654–66** EARL ORRERY *Parthen.* (1676) 508 You will demonstrate how little esteem you make of a Wife. **1877** SPURGEON *Serm.* XXIII. 402 What fools we were to make such count of momentary, transient pleasures! **1884** MRS. OLIPHANT *Sir Tom* II. vii. 114 A poor girl.. unnoticed, made no more account of than the chair upon which she sat.

c. To recognize in classification (a certain number of kinds, species, etc.).

1562 WINȜET *Cert. Tractates* Wks. 1888 I. 12 The wickit dum pastour, of the quhilk we mak thre kyndis. **1617** MORYSON *Itin.* I. 90 It aboundeth with sea birds, whereof the Venetian writers make two hundred kinds. **1621** BURTON *Anat. Mel.* I. ii. I. ii. (1676) 26/2 Our School-men.. make nine kinds of bad Spirits. **1678** CUDWORTH *Intell. Syst.* 37 Anaxagoras.. made Bony and Fleshy Atoms,.. which he supposed to exist.. alwaies immutably the same.

d. *legal.* To formulate, set out (a case, title).

1883 COTTON in *Law Rep.*, 9 *Prob. Div.* 25 It would be better.. for the party alleging undue influence to.. shew with reasonable particularity the nature of the case he intends to make. **1891** *Law Rep.*, *Weekly Notes* 77/2 The new trustees were therefore validly appointed, and could make a good title.

20. Used with const. *of* (cf. 18, of which this may be viewed as a figurative application): To regard (what is denoted by the regimen of the prep.) as being (what the object of the verb denotes); to arrive at (a particular amount or quantity) as the result of calculation or estimation; to assign (a meaning) to a statement, expression, representation, etc., or (a cause, motive, or reason) for actions or phenomena. Often with interrog. or indef. pronoun as obj.

For ***to make head or tail*** (also ***top or tail***) ***of, to make sense of***, see the sbs.

1531 TINDALE *Exp.* I *John* v. (1538) 59 b, Yf thou burnest bloude and fat together to please God, what other thynge doest thou make of God, than one that had lust to smell to burnt flotesse? **1565** RANDOLPH in Ellis *Orig. Lett.* Ser. I. II. 203 Suspicious men, or suche as are geven of all thyngs to mayke the worst. **1609** HOLLAND *Amm. Marcell.* 316, I wote not wel what to make of this: the text I suspect be faultie. *a* **1654** SELDEN *Table-t.* (Arb.) 20 When it comes among the Common People, Lord, what Gear do they make of it! **1776** C. LEE in Sparks *Corr. Amer. Rev.* (1853) I. 157, I know not what to make of this apathy on so important a subject. **1833** D. MACMILLAN in *Life* ii. (1882) 16 He has gone to Edinburgh now. I don't know what to make of him. **1861** DICKENS *Gt. Expect.* xxiv, What do you make of four times five? **1887** L. CARROLL *Game of Logic* i. §1. 10 What would you make of such a Proposition as 'The Cake you have given me is nice'? Is it Particular or Universal?

21. a. ***to make*** (much, little, nothing, etc.) ***of***: to have a (high, low, etc.) opinion of; to value at a (high, low, etc.) rate; to treat with (much, no, etc.) consideration. ***to make much of***: often, to treat with marked courtesy and show of affection; also in *indirect passive*. ***to make nothing of*** (doing something): to find no difficulty in or feel no scruples at (cf. 51 c).

to make light of, † ***to make slight of***: see LIGHT *a.*¹ 13 d (*b*), SLIGHT.

a **1300** *Cursor M.* 23860 Quen noght es mad of crists word. *c* **1305** *St. Dunstan* 46 in *E.E.P.* (1862) 35 A gret ordeynour he was And makede moche of gode reule. **1470–85** MALORY *Arthur* IX. xviii. 365 The more she made of hym, the more was his payne. *c* **1500** *Melusine* 302 Whan geffray with the grete toth herd that the geaunt made so lytel of hym. *a* **1548** HALL *Chron., Edw. IV* 220 She had nothyng more to be beloved, nothyng more derer, nor nothynge to be made more of. **1610** SHAKS. *Temp.* I. ii. 333. **1612** SHELTON *Don Quix.* IV. i. (1620) 282, I was one of the most made of and cherished daughters that euer father brought vp. **1622** BACON *Hen. VII* (ed. Lumby) 40 He was very honourably entertained, and extremely much made on by the Pope. **1711** ADDISON *Spect.* No. 57 ¶3 She talks of Hounds and Horses, and makes nothing of leaping over a Six-bar Gate. **1823** BYRON *Juan* x. lvi, Whate'er the cause, the church made little of it. **1838** LYTTON *Alice* II. ii, No queen could be more made of. **1888** W. J. KNOX LITTLE *Child of Stafferton* i. 12 The child was petted and made much of.

b. intr. ***to make of***: † (*a*) To esteem (well or ill); to treat *as if*... *Obs.* (*b*) To value highly; to treat with great consideration; = ***to make much of***; also in indirect passive. *Obs.* exc. *dial.*

1375 BARBOUR *Bruce* XVI. 592 The king aucht weill to ma Of ȝow. *c* **1449** PECOCK *Repr.* I. xiii. 69 Thouȝ the oold lawe was good to the kepers therof, ȝit was not so good as thei maden therof. *a* **1529** SKELTON *Magnyf.* 174, I am Lyberte, made of in euery nacion. *a* **1533** LD. BERNERS *Gold. Bk. M. Aurel.* (1546) KK j b, And that that some setteth littell by, other make of. *a* **1546** BALE *Latter Exam. A. Askew* (1547) 22 b, It was an abhomynable shame vnto hym to make no better of the eternall worde of God, than of his slenderlye conceyued fantasye. **1601** DENT *Pathw. Heaven* 77 An.. Hawke, which a man holdeth upon his fist, stroketh her, maketh of her. **1607** SHAKS. *Cor.* IV. v. 203. **1631** *Celestina* (1894) 142 You make of me, as if I had been borne but yesterday. **1725** RAMSAY *Gentle Sheph.* I. ii, Their greatest wish, Is to be made of, and obtain a kiss. *a* **1825** FORBY *Voc. E. Anglia* s.v., To make on, to caress, to distinguish by particular attention. **1828** MRS. CARLYLE 20 Aug. in *New Lett.* (1903) I. 29 Everyone here is trying to make my stay agreeable to me! Indeed, I have not been so made of since very long ago.

22. *Naut.* To descry or discern as from the top of a mast or tower; to come in sight of; = ***make out*** (91 l). † ***to make*** (an object) ***for***: to discern it to be (something). †Also ***to make.. to be***.

c **1565** SPARKE in *Hakluyt's Voy.* (1589) 536 Wee had sight of an Island, which we made to be Iamaica. *c* **1600** NORDEN *Spec. Brit., Cornw.* (1728) 96 A place whence they discouer ships at sea which they call makinge a sayle. **1628** DIGBY *Voy. Medit.* (1868) 4 Which afterwardes wee made to be a small Frenchman. *Ibid.* 33, I descryed a sayle which I made for a sattie. **1666** PEPYS *Diary* 3 June, At his coming into port, he could make another ship of the King's coming in. **1669** STURMY *Mariner's Mag.* To Rdr., The Lizard being.. the first Land made at their return home. *Ibid.* IV. i. 139 [He] at last made the Coasts of Brasilia. **1708** *Lond. Gaz.* No. 4422/7 It was thought proper that this Ship should go down to make them perfectly. **1712** W. ROGERS *Voy.* (1718) 292, I order'd the pinnace to be mann'd and arm'd, and sent her away to make what she was. **1725** DE FOE *Voy. round World* (1840) 7 We.. made the Coast of Galway, in Ireland, the 10th. **1760** C. JOHNSTON *Chrysal* (1822) II. 250 The man at the masthead had made the land. **1833** MARRYAT *P. Simple* li, We made Barbadoes without any further adventure, and were about ten miles off the bay. **1840** R. H. DANA *Bef. Mast* xxxii. 124 If we could make land, we should know where we were. **1890** 'R. BOLDREWOOD' *Col. Reformer* (1891) 171 Poor Grant made the light, sometime after nightfall.

**** Said of constituent parts or material.

23. To amount to. Also, of the latest item in an enumeration, to bring up the sum to (a certain amount).

a **1225** *Ancr. R.* 96 (Corpus MS.) þreo halpenes makeð a peni. *c* **1386** CHAUCER *Parson's T.* ¶288 The proverbe seith: that manye smale maken a greet. *c* **1400** MAUNDEV. (Roxb.) xx. 90 Of whilke mynutes LX. makez a degre. **1545** *Rates of Custome Ho.* d iij b, One Flemisshe elle makithe iii. quarters of a yarde englisshe. **1589** PUTTENHAM *Eng. Poesie* II. x[i.]

(Arb.) 99 These ten litle meeters make but one Exameter at length. **1596** SHAKS. *1 Hen. IV*, IV. ii. 6 This Bottle makes an Angell. **1601** ? MARSTON *Pasquil & Kath.* I. 66 Many a small make a great. **1672** VILLIERS (Dk. Buckhm.) *Rehearsal* III. i. (Arb.) 69 Nine Taylors make but one man. **1724** DE FOE *Mem. Cavalier* (1840) 35 All which did not make thirty thousand men. **1825** *New Monthly Mag.* XIV. 330 How many birds would this make in the course of the day? **1875** J. SOUTHWARD *Dict. Typogr.* s.v., In casting-off copy or matter it is said that it 'makes' so much—a galley, a stickful, &c.—that is occupies so much space. **1892** *Sat. Rev.* 12 Nov. 562/1 Twice one makes two. **1897** FL. MARRYAT *Blood Vampire* iv, 'E's a regular business man and knows 'ow many beans make five!

24. Of an adjunct or feature: To be sufficient to constitute; to be the essential criterion of. In proverbial or quasi-proverbial uses, mainly in negative contexts.

1340 *Ayenb.* 165 Þe cloþinge ne makeþ naȝt þane monek, ne þe armes þane knyȝt. *c***1430** *Freemasonry* 726 Gode maners maken a man. **1546** HEYWOOD *Prov.* (1867) 57 One swalowe maketh not sommer. **1611** COTGR. s.v. *Moine*, The Cowle makes not the Monke. **1649** LOVELACE *Poems* (1864) 119 Stone walls doe not a prison make, Nor iron bars a cage. **1734** POPE *Ess. Man* IV. 203 Worth makes the man, and want of it, the fellow. **1859** TENNYSON *Guinevere* 479 And courtliness, and the desire of fame, And love of truth, and all that makes a man. **1861** *Temple Bar* III. 256 A long beard does not make a philosopher. **1893** *National Observer* 7 Oct. 531/2 One actress does not make a play.

25. a. To amount to, count as, avail, signify (much, little, nothing, etc.) in relation to the question under consideration. (Cf. 74.) Const. *for*, *to*. Now *rare*. ***to make no matter*** (somewhat *arch.*): to make no difference, not to matter. †***what maketh matter but that..?*** = 'What hinders that..?'

1456 SIR G. HAYE *Law Arms* (S. T. S.) 283 And suppos sum ignoraunt men wald say gold is metall and na coloure, that makis nocht. **1478** W. PASTON in *P. Lett.* III. 237, I beseche yow to sende me a hose clothe,..how corse so ever it be it makyth no matyr. **1535** STEWART *Cron. Scot.* II. 383 Quhat makis that to the? **1549** LATIMER *Serm. Ploughers* (Arb.) 18 In deede it toucheth not monkerie, nor maketh any thyng at all for any such matter. **1563** MAN *Musculus' Commonpl.* 284 What maketh matter but that the Jewe, which is so often washed in the lawe, might be washed agayne if he come to Christ? **1574** WHITGIFT *Def. Answ.* ii. 106 Those things which..make something to exhort vnto a better life. **1606** SHAKS. *Ant. & Cl.* II. vi. 126, I thinke the policy of that purpose, made more in the Marriage, than the loue of the parties. **1611** BIBLE *Transl. Pref.* ¶3 The course which he intended made much for the glory of God. **1631** GOUGE *God's Arrows* III. §9. 202 Circumstances make much to the goodnesse or badnesse of an action. **1697** C. LESLIE *Snake in Grass* (ed. 2) 299 That he was a Loose Man, &c. which makes nothing to the business. **1728** RAMSAY *Last Sp. Miser* xxix, Away his wretched spirit flew, It maksnae where. **1768** STERNE *Sent. Journ.* (1778) II. 70 (*Passport*) By what magic he could [etc.] makes nothing in this account. **1768** ROSS *Helenore* (1789) 85 Maksna, quo she, gin I my hazard tak. **1808–80** JAMIESON s.v. *Mak*, *It makes na*, it does not signify, it is of no consequence; sometimes as one word, *maksna*. **1862** TRENCH *Mirac.* xxxiii. 456 It makes something for the current opinion that..Nathanael..is Bartholomew.. thus to find him named..in the midst of some of the very chiefest Apostles.

†**b.** Of arguments or evidence: To avail (much, little, etc.) *for*, *against* (an opinion or a disputant).

1579 FULKE *Heskins' Parl.* 333 These..sentences..make nothing for him, but much against him. *a***1649** CHARLES I. *Wks.* 177, I believe this argument makes little for you. **1660** tr. *Amyraldus' Treat. Religions* III. ii. 331 That makes nothing against us. **1690** LOCKE *Hum. Und.* I. iii. §3 Wks. 1727 I. 13 But this makes nothing for Innate Characters on the Mind.

26. To count as, have the position of, 'form', be (a part or unit in an aggregate, a particular member in an ordinal series). ***to make one*** (***of***): often, to take part in a combined action, be present at a meeting, etc.; also, to assimilate oneself to the company one joins.

1375 BARBOUR *Bruce* XI. 340 He said, the rerward he vald ma. **1523** FITZHERB. *Husb.* §120 Whan these three be mette, if ye hadde a potycarye to make the fourthe [etc.]. **1542** UDALL *Erasm. Apoph.* 86 He would..not refuse to make one at a mannes table. **1634** FORD *P. Warbeck* II. iii, There have been Irish hubbubs, when I have made one too. **1658** JER. TAYLOR *Let.* in *12th Rep. Hist. MSS. Comm.* App. v. 5 Her duty to you..does apparently make a very great part of her religion to God. **1711** BUDGELL *Spect.* No. 77 ¶5, I always make one of the Company I am in. **1826** KIRBY & SP. *Entomol.* III. xxxiv. 485 It is marked out into three triangles, the *postnasus* making a fourth. **1850** DICKENS *Dav. Copp.* xx, It would be worth a journey..to see that sort of people together, and to make one of 'em. **1869** FREEMAN *Norm. Conq.* (1876) III. xii. 179 To make one of the illustrious gathering. **1892** *Cornh. Mag.* Dec. 566, I was number thirteen, and you came in and made the fourteenth.

27. a. To be the material or components of; to be made or converted into; to serve for.

1620–55 I. JONES *Stone-Heng* (1725) 45 The Stones making the Portico within. **1661** BOYLE *Style of Script.* (1675) 53 Where there's nothing but choice flowers,..they will make a good posie. **1699** T. BROWN in R. L'Estrange *Erasm. Colloq.* 20 She was fit to have made a Spouse for Jupiter himself. **1703** MOXON *Mech. Exerc.* 114 Pieces that are intended to make the Frames for small Pictures. **1712** ADDISON *Spect.* No. 414 ¶4 Fields of Corn make a pleasant Prospect. **1724** SWIFT *Stella's Birthday*, Merry folks, who want by chance A pair to make a country dance. **1768** GOLDSM. *Good-n. Man* I. (end), I am told he makes a very handsome corpse and becomes his coffin prodigiously. **1797** *Encycl. Brit.* (ed. 3) VIII. 485/2 Such as are kept to make red herrings are washed in great vats in fresh water. **1838** LYTTON *Leila* III. iii, One of the vaults which made the mighty cemetery of the Monarchs of Granada. **1887** A. BIRRELL *Obiter Dicta* Ser. II. 70 Poor authors..with their pockets full of the bad eggs that should have made their breakfasts. **1890** 'R. BOLDREWOOD' *Col. Reformer* (1891) 94 He's steady enough to make a wheeler in a coach. **1890** *Standard* 5 Nov. 5/1 [He] had much to say that will make unpleasant reading for the Liberal wirepullers.

b. To admit of being made into.

*c***1420** *Palladius on Husb.* IV. 457 The gourde is good this citur nygh to sowe, Whos vynes brent maath askes for hem sete. **1577** B. GOOGE *Heresbach's Husb.* III. (1586) 152 Neither is their..a beast that makes more dishes. **1592** KYD *Sp. Trag.* III. vi. 69 Doost thou think to liue till his olde doublet will make thee a new trusse? **1598** SHAKS. *Merry W.* I. iii. 18 An old Cloake makes a new Ierkin. **1605** *1st Pt. Jeronimo* III. i. 43 My hose will scarse make thee a standing coller. **1646** SIR T. BROWNE *Pseud. Ep.* II. v. 87 A pint of salt of tartar, exposed unto a moist aire,..will make far more liquor..then the former measure will contain. **1787** BECKFORD *Lett. fr. Italy* (1805) I. 365 They [frogs] make a good soup, and not a bad fricassée.

28. Of persons: To become by development or training. Also, with obj. a sb. qualified by *good*, *bad*, or other adj. of praise or the contrary: To perform (well, ill, etc.) the part or function of.

1572 MIDDELMORE in Ellis *Orig. Lett.* Ser. II. III. 8, I think he [the Duke of Anjou] will make as rare a prince as any is in Christendome. **1591** SHAKS. *1 Hen. VI* IV. vii. 44 Doubtlesse he would haue made a noble Knight. **1677** MIEGE *Eng.-Fr. Dict.* s.v., These men might make good Soldiers if they were well disciplined. **1726–7** POPE *Th. var. Subj.* in *Swift's Wks.* (1751) V. 262 For a King to make an amiable character, he needs only to be a man of common honesty, well advised. **1736** BERKELEY *Disc. to Magistr.* Wks. III. 412 The young rake makes an old infidel. **1828** *Examiner* 244/1 Mr. Kean, jun. will never make so great an actor as his father. **1844** H. STEPHENS *Bk. of Farm* II. 89 The shepherd knowing the flock makes their best drover. **1870** E. PEACOCK *Ralf Skirl.* III. 25 As the times then went, Mr. Earl made a very fair pastor. **1885** J. PAYN *Luck of Darrells* I. viii. 125 She will make him a good wife.

***** To gain, acquire.

29. a. To gain, acquire, or earn (money, reputation, etc.) by labour, business, or the like. Const. *of*, *out of*. Phr. †***to make*** (***one's***) ***advantage*** (see ADVANTAGE *sb.* 5 b), ***increment of***; ***to make a*** (or ***one's***) ***fortune*** (see FORTUNE *sb.* 6); ***to make capital out of*** (see CAPITAL *sb.* 3 d); ***to make a living*** (see LIVING *vbl. sb.* 3); ***to make a name*** (for oneself). See NAME *sb.*

*c***1315** SHOREHAM iii. 294 In londe suche his many a þef Þat y-now hym makeþ. **1382** WYCLIF *Jer.* xxxii. 20 Thou madist to thee a name. **1472** *Paston Lett.* III. 71, I truste be Ester to make of money..at the leest l. marke. **1546** O. JOHNSON in Ellis *Orig. Lett.* Ser. II. II. 175 Besides the monney that I shal make of the said wares. **1583** STOCKER *Civ. Warres Lowe C.* II. 64 [They] furnished him with all the money they were able to make. **1588** PARKE tr *Mendoza's Hist. China* 45 Then may the husband afterwardes sell his wife for a slave, and make money of her for the dowrie he gaue her. **1604** SHAKS. *Oth.* I. iii. 361. **1632** LITHGOW *Trav.* I. 64 This little Ile maketh yearely..onely of Currants 160000 Chickins [= sequins]. **1632** SHERWOOD, To make money of, *vendre*. **1706** E. WARD *Wooden World Diss.* (1708) Advt., Making a Profit at the Expence of other Men. **1821** BYRON *Juan* III. lxxxv, His muse made increment of anything, From the high lyric down to the low rational. **1823** J. BADCOCK *Dom. Amusem.* 28 More than he could probably hope to make by any transaction in the Alley. **1840** MACAULAY *Ess.*, *Clive* (1887) 555 A great quantity of wealth is made by English functionaries in India;..and what is made is slowly, hardly, and honestly earned. **1842** BORROW *Bible in Spain* xiii. (Pelh. Libr.) 97 [They] had buried..a great booty which they had made in Portugal. **1863** *Edin. Rev.* CXVII. 417 The men complain that without it [*sc.* blasting] they cannot 'make wages'. **1887** RUSKIN *Præterita* II. 332 [He] would often, for the mere pleasure of playing a trick, lose a customer without making a penny by him. **1889** T. GIFT *Not for the Night-time* 83, I..made a name as a successful artist. **1895** *Bookman* Oct. 16/2, I know several gentlemen in Paris..who make a very good living by hawking these nightingales round the cafés.

b. *slang* and *dial.* To steal. Also, in milder sense, to 'acquire', manage to get. (See also quots. 1926, 1953.)

*a***1700** B. E. *Dict. Cant. Crew*, *Made*, Stolen. *I Made this Knife at a beat*, I stole it cleaverly. **1740** DYCHE & PARDON *Dict.*, *Make*..also to steal or convey privately away. **1865** *Daily Tel.* 27 Oct. 5/1 'The same day', he continued, 'we only made [*i.e.* stole] a leg of pork from 12, Harrow-road' [etc.]. **1866** MANSFIELD *Sch. Life* (1870) 46 In the matter of certain articles..supplied by the College [Winchester], we used to put a liberal interpretation on the eighth commandment..and it was considered fair 'to make' (*i.e.* take) them if you could. **1881** *Leicestersh. Gloss.* **1914** D. O. BARNETT *Lett.* (1915) 13 The company made a dog the other day, but it was claimed almost at once, so we haven't got a mascot. **1926** J. BLACK *You can't Win* i. 5, I was an expert house burglar..carefully choosing only the best homes... I 'made' them in the small hours of the night. *Ibid.* vi. 74 Better wait till night if you want to make a train. **1928** KIPLING *Limits & Renewals* (1932) 53 I've made a temp'ry collar and lead off Probert. **1946** G. MILLAR *Horned Pigeon* ii. 16 Skinner and I were both good at what the Army calls 'making things', which is what the civilian would call 'finding' or even 'stealing' things. *Ibid.*, Potatoes and onions I had 'made' from the food-dumps round Alexandria. **1953** W. BURROUGHS *Junkie* (1972) iii. 34 Taking junk hidden by another junkie is known as 'making him for his stash'. *Ibid.* 158 *Making Cars*... Breaking into parked cars and stealing the contents.

c. To fetch (a certain price).

1868 *Jrnl. R. Agric. Soc.* Ser. II. IV. II. 289 One [bullock]..made 60*l.* in a Woburn auction. **1896** *Athenæum* No. 3569. 382/1 Matthew's Bible, 1537, made 11*l.* 15*s.*

30. a. *Cards.* To win or 'take' (a trick); to play to advantage (a certain card). Also *intr.* of a card: to take a trick.

1608 L. MACHIN *Dumb Knight* IV. H 4 You are a double game, and I am no lesse, theres an hundred, & all cards made but one knaue. **1742** HOYLE *Whist* 39 In the third round you make your Queen. *Ibid.* 50 You probably make two Tricks in it by this Method of Play. **1876** 'CAPT. CRAWLEY' *Card Players' Man.* 61 If your partner hold the ace and another, you have a good chance of making the entire suit. **1878** H. H. GIBBS *Ombre* 24 He will endeavour to make one trick only. **1879** CAVENDISH *Card Ess.*, etc. 160 His partner..has his last trump drawn, and the ace and king of diamonds make. *Ibid.* 197 The fourth hand made the king.

b. Various uses in games: To secure (a certain score); to score (a point in the game); to perform (a particular stroke) successfully.

1680 COTTON *Compl. Gamester* (ed. 2) 78 You may make Pairs, Sequences, Flush, Fifteens, Pair-Royals, [etc.] *Ibid.* 89 If one and thirty be not made, then he that play'd last and is nearest one and thirty without making out, must set up one. **1825** HONE *Every-day Bk.* I. 868 Give him a foot of wall, and he was sure to make the ball. **1849** *Chambers's Inform. People* II. 652/1 The game is determined by the number of runs made in two innings by each player. **1857** HUGHES *Tom Brown* II. viii, Johnson's batting [is] worthy of the occasion. He makes here a two, and there a one, managing to keep the ball to himself. **1873** BENNETT & 'CAVENDISH' *Billiards* 339 To make the hazard, play at the shoulder of the pocket. **1874** J. D. HEATH *Croquet Player* 53 It being much easier to roll up to and make the peg, than to get into position for a hoop, from a long distance. **1890** *Field* 31 May 784/3 He made ten fours, six threes, and two twos.

31. To gain, 'put on' (weight). Also of a tree, to produce a growth of (timber). ***to make water*** (Naut.): to take in water by a leak: see WATER *sb.*

1832 WITHERS in *Planting* (L. U. K.) vii. 78 *note*, The manured tree made..one foot one-third of timber in each year. **1846** *Jrnl. R. Agric. Soc.* VII. II. 393 Two of them made twenty stones each in sixteen weeks.

II. To subject to operation; to elaborate; to put in order.

†**32.** To handle, manage, use (OE. only); to treat, deal with in a particular way. *Obs.*

*c***1000** ÆLFRIC *Gen.* iv. 21 Iubal, þe wæs fæder..þæra þe organan macodun [Vulg. *canentium cithara et organo*]. *c***1175** *Lamb. Hom.* 121 Þet folc þe hine þus makede knewede to-foren him on bismer. *c***1250** *Gen. & Ex.* 2515 Hise liche was spice-like maked, And longe egipte-like waked.

†**33.** To bring *to* a specified condition, reduce *to*. Phr. ***to make to death***; ***to make away*** (see 84 a–c), ***make out of the way***, ***make hence*** = make away with. *Obs.*

*c***1175** *Lamb. Hom.* 85 Hwense we habbeð imaked þene licome to þer saule bihoue. *c***1220** *Bestiary* 154 Redi..to deren er to ded maken. **1390** GOWER *Conf.* I. 13 Whan thei to thilke astat ben made. *a***1400–50** *Alexander* 2741 Þare mas þou þe to malicole. **1530** PALSGR. 631/1, I make to the bowe, as we make a yonge persone to our mynde. **1535** COVERDALE *2 Chron.* xxxiv. 4 Molten ymages brake he in peces and made them to dust. **1551** ROBINSON tr. *More's Utop.* II. vii. (1895) 230 If they should hastiely put them to death, and make them out of the waye. **1603** B. JONSON *Sejanus* II. ii, It is as daungerous to make them hence, If nothing but their birth be their offence. **1605** —— *Volpone* IV. v, Haue they made you to this! **1692** R. L'ESTRANGE *Josephus*, *Antiq.* XII. xv. (1733) 325 [He] told him that..that Man must be made out of the way.

34. †**a.** *refl.* To set oneself, get ready (*to do* something); to prepare *for*. *Obs.* (Chiefly *Sc.*)

1362 LANGL. *P. Pl.* A. VII. 103 Vche mon in his maner made him to done. **1375** BARBOUR *Bruce* XII. 252 Thai.. Mais thame to ficht. **1390** GOWER *Conf.* I. 188 And to the bed with that he yede..And made him there forto seche. *c***1470** HENRY *Wallace* VII. 846 The Irland folk than maid thaim for the flycht. **1500–20** DUNBAR *Poems* liii. 46 To the danceing soun he him maid. **1535** COVERDALE *Ps.* cxix. [cxx.] 7, I laboured for peace, but when I spake therof, they made them to battayl. —— *Ezek.* xx. 8 Then I made me to poure my indignacion ouer them. *a***1572** KNOX *Hist. Ref.* Wks. 1846 I. 175 Whill the portar maid him for defence, his head was brokin. **1630** RUTHERFORD *Lett.* (1862) I. 64 Christ is putting on His clothes and making Him, like an illhandled stranger, to go to other lands.

b. *intr.* To attempt or 'offer' (*to do* something).

1880 *Antrim & Down Gloss.* s.v., He made to strike me. **1889** *Universal Rev.* Oct. 256 The beauty of this blossom drew the man's soul, and he made to pluck it. **1900** S. PHILLIPS *Paolo & Franc.* II. ii. (*Stage dir.*), He makes to follow, then stops. **1902** *Daily Chron.* 25 Aug. 9/3 He got very excited, and made to catch hold of her dress.

35. With ellipsis of verb of motion: To prepare to go; to proceed in a certain direction. †**a.** *refl.*

1535 COVERDALE *1 Sam.* xvii. 41 The Philistyne wente forth, and made him to Dauid. —— *Nahum* ii. 3 His charettes are as fyre, when he maketh him forwarde. **1632** LITHGOW *Trav.* VI. 261 At the breach of day, we sixe made vs for the mountaine.

b. *intr.* for *refl.*, with adv. or advb. phr. (Often, ***to make towards*** —.) See also *make away*, *make forth*, etc.

1488 [see *make over*, 92 e]. **1542** [see *make upon*, 81]. **1558** [see *make out*, 91 m]. **1570** *Satir. Poems Reform.* xii. 174 Mak of the towne. **1573** *Ibid.* xlii. 16 Thir twa vnto Sanctandrois maid. **1586–93** MARLOWE *Dido* I. ii, There is a place, Hesperia..Thither made we. **1588** *Housh. Philos.* in *Kyd's Wks.* (1901) 242 But making neerer to his Father, he whispred to him [etc.]. **1611** BIBLE *Acts* xxvii. 40 They.. made toward shore. **1639** FULLER *Holy War* II. xxviii. (1647) 80 Hence Conrade made forward to Iconium. **1645** R. BAILLIE *Lett. & Jrnls.* (Bannatyne Club) II. 305 Our army ..is in good case. They are now making over the Severne. **1694** *Lond. Gaz.* No. 2961/1 The Weymouth..left the rest of the homeward bound..Fleet..off the Lizard, making up the Channel. **1760–72** H. BROOKE *Fool of Qual.* (1809) II. 93

Let us make home the best we can. **1790** Beatson *Nav. & Milit. Mem.* II. 194 Notwithstanding that the ship of the line and the frigate..were now within a league of him, and making to his assistance. **1812** Capt. Hillyar in *Examiner* (1813) 18 Jan. 43/2 Twelve..were thrown over-board when making from us. **1840** Dickens *Barn. Rudge* lix, He..made straight towards a distant light. **1878** W. Black *Green Past.* xliv. 356 We see an immense flock of geese making up the stream. **1883** Stevenson *Treas. Isl.* III. xiv. 112, I made steadily but slowly towards them.

36. To prepare (a bed) for sleeping in.

[Cf. G. *ein bett machen*, F. *faire un lit*. In this use the vb. had originally the sense of branch I, as the sb. meant not a permanent article of furniture, but a prepared place for repose, which does not exist until 'made'.]

c **1290** *S. Brendan* 128 in *S. Eng. Leg.* I. 223 Beddes þer were al ȝare ymaked er here soper were ido. *c* **1300** *Havelok* 658 Hwan he hauede eten, and was fed, Grim dede maken a ful fayr bed. *c* **1385** Chaucer *L.G.W.* Prol. 205, I bad men shulde my couche make. *c* **1440** *York Myst.* xlviii. 298 Ȝe brought me of þe beste, And made my bedde full esyly. **1530** Palsgr. 617/2 Make your bedde a dayes or you go out of your chamber. **1750** J. Ray *Rebell.* (1758) 145 After I was gone..the Chambermaid went to make my Bed. **1784** Abigail Adams *Lett.* (1848) 157 Not one of us could make her own bed, put on or take off her shoes, or even lift a finger. **1889** Mrs. E. Kennard *Landing a Prize* III. iv. 78 She knows how to make a bed..and cook a dinner.

37. To shut, close, bar (a door). Now *arch.* and *dial.*

c **1290** *Beket* 2062 in *S. Eng. Leg.* I. 165 Some wolden makien þe doren þo heo þat folk i-seiȝe. **1590** Shaks. *Com. Err.* III. i. 93 Why at this time the doors are made against you. **1600** —— *A.Y.L.* IV. i. 162 Make the doores vpon a womans wit, and it will out at the casement. **1613** Chapman *Rev. Bussy D'Ambois* Plays 1873 II. 175 All dores are sure made. **1641** Hinde *J. Bruen* lxiii. 210 Leaving neither Cooke nor Butler behinde him, nor any of his servants, but two or three to make the doores, and tend the house. **1871** R. Ellis tr. *Catullus* xxxii. 5 See no jealousy make the gate against me.

38. In the phrase ***to make hay***, primarily used in sense 2, but also applied *spec.* to that part of the operation which consists in turning over and exposing to the sun the grass after it is mown. (See hay *sb.*[1] 3 for the phrase and its uses.) Hence by extension, to subject (certain kinds of crops) to this treatment. Also *intr.* for *passive*.

1523 Fitzherbert *Husb.* §25 Good teddynge is the chiefe poynte to make good hey. **1546, 1673, 1703** [see hay *sb.*[1] 3]. **1707–12** Mortimer *Husb.* (1721) I. 35 They seldom have Weather good enough to make the last Crop well. **1778** [W. Marshall] *Minutes Agric.* 26 July 1775 Perhaps, hay makes faster in heaps..than is generally imagined. *a* **1825** Forby *Voc. E. Anglia* s.v. *Make, sb.*, We..talk of '*making* the crop of peas'. Indeed, every crop, howsoever severed from the soil, and left upon it to dry, is said to be *made* when it is in a fit state to be carried. **1847** *Jrnl. R. Agric. Soc.* VIII. II. 300 If it is not made too much, it will be pretty good hay. **1862** *Ibid.* XXIII. 63 The swampy meadows are chiefly 'made' in that month. **1865** *Ibid.* Ser. II. I. II. 248 The straw must be carefully 'made'. **1892** *Field* 19 Mar. 424/2 The man who expects one variety of corn, to 'make'—*i.e.*, to get fit for stacking exactly as another would, will be rewarded by a 'rick afire'.

39. To prepare (fish) for the market, by curing or packing. (See also *Dict. Canadianisms.*)

1555 *Sc. Acts Mary* (1814) II. 498/1 The haill burrowis of the west cuntrie..hes..resortit to the fisching of Loch Fyne ..for making of hering..certaine cuntrie men..hes rasit ane greit custume of euerie last of maid hering that ar tane in the said Loch. **1690** Child *Disc. Trade* (1694) 3 The fish which our English make in Newfoundland..often prove false and deceitfully made; and our pilchards from the West-Country false packed. **1809** [see making *vbl. sb.*[1] 2]. **1856** J. Reynolds *Peter Gott* 43 Since the last war with England, the fishermen from the States have not been allowed to make their fish upon the shores of the British Provinces. **1909** E. C. Robinson *In Unknown Land* 30 A fisherman comes here to 'make' fish, not to catch them. **1923** *Canad. Fisherman* 243/1 It is a new departure for Newfoundland green fish to be taken to Europe to be 'made'. **1971** S. E. Morison *European Discovery Amer.: Northern Voy.* xiv. 491 In our times 'making fish', as the Maine people call curing cod, haddock, and pollock in the sun, is simple enough... You simply soak the gutted, split, and washed fish in brine for two or three days, slack-salt them, and spread them on home-made flakes to be cured in the sun. **1974** *Nat. Geographic* Jan. 122/1 Many south coast men [in Newfoundland] have to 'make' fish—that is, preserve their own.

†**40.** ***to make a man's beard***: see beard *sb.* 1 e.

41. *dial.* To hew or shape (timber); to cut up (wood) into faggots or for firewood.

14.. *Voc.* in Wr.-Wülcker 582/6 *Faculo*, to make faget. **1466** *Yatton Church-w. Acc.* (Som. Rec. Soc.) 104 For makyng tymbyr, and makyng of steches. **1607** T. Cocks *Diary* (1901) 2/1 Payde to Wm. Tybbold..for felling and making my wood, xv*s*. **1886** in Elworthy *W. Som. Word-bk.* **1891** *Hartland Gloss.*, *Make wood*, to make wood into faggots.

42. *Eccl.* To 'mix' (the chalice) at the offertory in the Eucharist.

? **1540** *Bk. Ceremonies* (MS. Cott. Cleop. E. 5. lf. 280) Offertory..at which tyme the Mynyster..maketh the chalice, myxyng the water with the wyne. **1892** J. Wickham Legg in *Trans. St. Paul's Ecclesiol. Soc.* III. 78 The liturgical moment of the making of the chalice in certain western rites.

43. *Cards.* To shuffle. [Cf. F. *faire.*]

1876 A. Campbell-Walker *Correct Card* (1880) Gloss. p. xii, *To make the cards* means to shuffle. **1902** Ld. Aldenham *Game of Ombre* 85 The Baron makes the cards, and hands them to Belinda.

44. Naut. ***to make sail***: (*a*) to spread a sail or sails; hence, to start on a voyage; to set sail, to sail; (*b*) to spread additional sails in order to increase the ship's speed. (See also sail *sb.*) Also †***to make the tackling***.

c **1450** *Pilgrims' Sea-Voy.* in *Rel. Ant.* I. 2 The mastyr commaundeth..To hys shypmen..To dresse hem sone about the mast, Theyr takelyng to make. **1517** Torkington *Pilgr.* (1884) 15 We mad sayle with scace Wynde. **1634** Sir T. Herbert *Trav.* 182 Both rowing and making large saile. **1890** Clark Russell *Ocean Trag.* I. iii. 50 The men..were making sail upon the yacht nimbly.

45. a. To train (a hawk, dog, horse). Also with defining phr., as ***for the river***, ***to the hood***. †Also (in Turbervile) ***to make*** (a hawk) ***flying*** (cf. the factitive sense 48).

c **1400** *Master of Game* (MS. Digby 182) xiii, Forto entre and make houndes. *c* **1450** *Bk. Hawkyng* in *Rel. Ant.* I. 297 Then is your hawke made as towchyng to perteriches. **1530** Palsgr. 645/1, I have nosylled my yonge dogge to daye at a beare, he his made for ever. **1575** Turberv. *Faulconrie* 121 If you would make your hawke to the Crane, take a Nyasse Falcon gentle... And when you would make hir fleeing, lette hir flee from the fiste, and succour hir quickely. For you muste haue dogges made for the purpose, whiche may helpe and succoure hir sooner than a man can doe. *Ibid.* 122 If you woulde make your hawke fleing to the Partridge, or Feasant, when she is reclaimed and made, then [etc.]. **1590** Cokaine *Treat. Hunting* B j b, Stopping all the holes, saving two or three, which must be set with Foxe pursenets, to take a yong Cubbe, to make your Terriars withall. **1673** Boyle *Ess. Effluviums* III. iv. 29 A studious person that was Keeper of a Red-dear-park and vers'd in making Blood-hounds. **1696** Sir W. Hope tr. *Solleysell's Compl. Horsem.* title-p., The best method of Breeding and Backing of Colts, Making their Mouths [etc.]. **1711** Addison *Spect.* No. 108 ¶3 A Setting-dog that he has *made* himself. **1797** *Encycl. Brit.* (ed. 3) VIII. 345 If she [a hawk] be made for the river. **1879** Jefferies *Wild Life in S.C.* vii. 136 Some of the lesser men who 'make' hunters, and ride not only for pleasure but possible profit from the sale. **1897** *Encycl. Sport* I. 373 (Falconry) *Make to the Hood*, to accustom a hawk to the hood.

transf. **1526** Skelton *Magnyf.* 1592 Wolde money, trowest thou, make suche one to the call? *c* **1600** Bacon *Disc. Helps Intell. Powers* Wks. (Spedding) VII. 100 It was many degrees too hot for any man, not made to it, to breathe or take in.

†**b.** To prepare (a person) for a business; to make acquainted, initiate, 'prime'. *Obs. rare.*

1598 B. Jonson *Ev. Man in Hum.* IV. ix, Come, let's before, and make the Iustice, Captaine. **1603** —— *Sejanus* II. i, But let Drusus drug Be first prepar'd. *Evd.* Were Lygdus made, that's done. **1624** *Nero* II. in Bullen *O. Pl.* I. 41 Rufus, the Captaine of the Guard, 's with us, And divers other oth' Prætorian band Already made.

46. a. To effect or secure the success or advancement of; to 'be the making of'; *chiefly*, to endow (a person) with fortune or prosperity; to render independent, set up (*esp.* in *pass.*; cf. made *ppl. a.* 7). Phr. ***to make one's day***: to render a day delightful or redeem it from routine, dullness, or banality. Similarly, ***to make one's evening***, etc.

1375 Barbour *Bruce* I. 510 And rycht mayss oft the feble wycht. **1460** *Paston Lett.* I. 535 That yf the Lords..now discessid myte haf standyn in governans, that Fortesku.. and he, schuld be made for evir. **1579** Lyly *Euphues* (Arb.) 104 It is the eye of the master that fatteth the horse, and the loue of the woeman, that maketh the man. **1598** B. Jonson *Ev. Man in Hum.* II. ii, *Veni, vidi, vici*, I may say with Captayne Caesar, I am made for euer, ifaith. **1604** Shaks. *Oth.* V. i. 127. *a* **1614** D. Dyke *Myst. Self-deceiving* (ed. 8) 51 If riches bee that that makes men happy (according to the foolish phrase men vse when such things befall one, *O he is made*!). **1675** Brooks *Gold. Key* Wks. 1867 V. 182 If you embrace him, you are made for ever; but if you reject him, you perish for ever. **1732** Berkeley *Alciphr.* II. §2 [That] what one man loses another gets, and that, consequently, as many are made as ruined. **1854** J. S. C. Abbott *Napoleon* (1888) II. xxi. 396 Victory made Napoleon, Victory unmade him. **1888** B. W. Richardson *Son of a Star* II. ii. 6 Let him take up a person, and that person is made. **1890** *Sat. Rev.* 8 Feb. 161/2 Bismarck has made Germany. **1903** A. Bennett *Leonora* vi. 168 The conductor..told her..that she had simply made the show. **1909** F. Barclay *Rosary* xxiv. 252, I knew her presence made my day and her absence meant chill night. **1935** Wodehouse *Luck of Bodkins* i. 15 That.. will be great. That will just make my day. **1942** M. Dickens *One Pair of Feet* ix. 194 If she could put you in the wrong in front of Sister, her day was made. **1942** T. Rattigan *Flare Path* I. 113 We've got some nice cheerful news for you boys. It's going to make your evening. **1953** X. Fielding *Stronghold* 220 For Ioanna, the evening had been made. **1958** *Listener* 16 Oct. 623/2 What made the programme was the alternation of argument with recorded extracts from the conference itself. **1959** *Ibid.* 6 Aug. 223/3 It [*sc.* a play] didn't make my day. **1970** H. McLeave *Question of Negligence* (1973) xviii. 141 Get him to..show us his scar... Go on, dare him. It'll make the evening.

b. Proverbial phrase. ***to make or mar*** (occas. ***make or break***): to cause either the complete success or the ruin of (a person or thing). Also *absol.*

c **1420** Lydg. *Assembly of Gods* 556 Neptunus, that dothe bothe make & marre. **1542** Udall *Erasm. Apoph.* 267 b, Declaring that he was vtterly mynded to put al in hasards to make or marre, & to bee manne or mous. **1591** Harrington *Orl. Fur.* v. xix. 33 In vaine I seeke my dukes oue to expound, The more I seeke to make the more I mard. **1596** Spenser *F.Q.* IV. i. 29 That one did make the other mard againe. **1613** Day *Festivals* vii. (1615) 206 That Part of a Woman which either makes all, or marres all, I meane her Tongue. **1650** Trapp *Comm. Lev.* xvi. 33 It beeing the manner that either make's, or mar's an action. **1840** Dickens *Barn. Rudge* iii, I always tell my girl to make sure beforehand that she has a good man and true, and the chance will neither make her nor break her. **1885** Mrs. C. Praed *Affinities* II. xii. 5 As for Lady Romer's scheme, it is not my business to make or mar it. **1889** Stevenson *Master of B.* x. 267 Not that you should make and mar behind my back. **1892** *Chamb. Jrnl.* 2 Apr. 216/1 A man is made or marred by his wife.

c. *dial.* To bring up, provide for children.

1725 Ramsay *Gent. Sheph.* I. ii, To mak' them brats then ye maun toil and spin. **1893** *Eng. Dial. Dict.*, *Make* 23, to foster (Warwicksh.).

47. ***to make one's soul*** (Anglo-Irish): to devote one's efforts to the saving of one's soul; to repent and be converted.

1836 in C. Forster *Life Bp. Jebb* II. (ed. 2) 112 'Make your soul; there is no time to lose; you will die next November.' **1851** Mayhew *Lond. Labour* (1864) II. 51 'What's all you can get here compared to making your sowl?'

III. To cause to be or become (something specified).

48. a. With adj. as compl.: To cause to be, render.

to make English: to translate into English. For *to make even*, *fast*, *good*, *ready*, *sure*, *unready*, *void*, *waste*; *to make it hot*, *warm*, *make things lively*: see the adjs.

c **1000** Ælfric *Hom.* II. 88 Hi..heora lufiȝendne ȝemaciaþ weliȝne ecelice. *c* **1175** *Lamb. Hom.* 101 þe oferlifa on hete and on wete macað þene mon unhalne. *c* **1200** Ormin 995 Smeredd wel wiþþ elesæw & makedd fatt & nesshe. *c* **1205** Lay. 10591 Al þat lond heo makeden west. **1297** R. Glouc. (Rolls) 412 þo hii adde al bar imad þe contrei al aboute. *c* **1330** R. Brunne *Chron. Wace* (Rolls) 11567 Idelnesse makeþ man ful slow. *c* **1386** Chaucer *Pars. T.* ¶75 Thrugh synne ther he was free now is he maked bonde. **1483** Caxton *G. de la Tour* F vij b, At theyr requeste god maad her hole ageyne. **1530** Palsgr. 617/2 He made me more a frayde than I was these twelve monethes. **1549** Latimer *Serm. Ploughers* (Arb.) 20 Making them supple herted. **1620** T. Granger *Div. Logike* A iv b, Each Reader may this Garden make his owne. **1664** Evelyn (*title*) Parallel of the Antient Architecture with the Modern, written by Roland Freart, made English for the benefit of builders by J. Evelyn. **1693** Dryden *Juvenal* (1697) Ded. 54 In making these two Authors English. **1709** Berkeley *Th. Vision* §119 Any theories of vision hitherto made public. **1768** Goldsm. *Good-n. Man* III, What makes the bread rising?.. What makes the mutton fivepence a pound? **1781** Gibbon *Decl. & F.* xviii. (1869) I. 496 The elephants, made furious by their wounds, encreased the disorder. **1829** Scott *Jrnl.* 8 June, God make me thankful for so cheering a prospect! **1847** Marryat *Childr. N. Forest* xvii, On that score you may make your mind easy. **1883** *Century Mag.* XXVI. 239/1 You'll only make bad worse.

b. with pa. pple. as compl. Now chiefly with ***known***, ***acquainted***, ***felt***, ***heard***, ***understood***; a pa. pple. which implies the performance of an action is now rarely used without a preceding *to be*.

a **1300** *E. E. Psalter* cii[i]. 7 Kouthe made he to Moises his waies wele. *a* **1300** *Cursor M.* 26666 Propre þat es þat þou ma knaun nan oþer plightes bot þin aun. *c* **1384** Chaucer *H. Fame* I. 155 The greke Synon With his fals forsweryngе.. Made the hors broght in-to troye. **1387** Trevisa *Higden* (Rolls) V. 391 He made alle þe hedes and lymes of mawmettes i-kut of. *c* **1500** *Melusine* (1895) 153 Thus makyng his wounde opend. **1647** W. Browne *Polexander* II. IV. ¶¶¶ 2 b, Polexander.. going away, as if afraid, strove to make it believed he had had no advantage ore Almanzor. *a* **1641** Bp. Mountagu *Acts & Mon.* (1642) 263 She.. secretly made Cleopatra acquainted with it. **1759** Johnson *Rasselas* xvi, His generosity made him courted by many dependents. **1812** Sir H. Davy *Chem. Philos.* 24 Glauber at Amsterdam about 1640 made known several neutral salts. **1818** Hobhouse *Italy* (1859) II. App. B. 319 The opposition of a whole life against the nobles made him regarded by all the lower classes, as the great partizan of the democracy. **1827** Southey *Hist. Penins. War* II. 208 The neighbourhood of Ferrol has made it [Vigo] neglected as a naval station. **1836** J. H. Newman *Lett.* (1891) II. 202 Their coming from you will make them [*sc.* sermons] read. **1891** *Leeds Merc.* 27 Apr. 4/4 If the miners made their power felt.

†**c.** with predicative phr. as compl. ***to make*** (a place) ***in one's way***: to direct one's journey so as to pass by or through it. *Obs.*

a **1300** *Cursor M.* 2605 Agar was made wit child in hi. *Ibid.* 9744 For sothfastnes algat sal i At an a-cord mak wit merci. **1470–85** Malory *Arthur* XVIII. xx. 761 Now hath dethe made vs two at debate for your loue. **1523** Ld. Berners *Froiss.* I. cl. 73 b, I thynke he neuer made the frenche kyng of knowledge therof. **1530** Palsgr. 627/1 It were a good dede by policye to make them of affynite. **1560** Daus tr. *Sleidane's Comm.* 428 He was not as yet made at one with him. **1601** Lyly *Loues Metam.* V. iv. 12 (Bond) You might haue made me a [= of] counsell of your loues. **1611** Bible *Rom.* iv. 14 Faith is made voide, and the promise made of none effect. **1673** Newton in Rigaud *Corr. Sci. Men* (1841) II. 361 Mr. Gregory is at London, and intends to make Cambridge in his way into Scotland. **1676** Hale *Contempl.* I. 186 This makes him at a point with these sollicitations, peremptory to conclude [etc.]. **1767** S. Paterson *Another Trav.* I. 51, I made every bookseller's shop in my way. **1800** Lamb *Let. to Manning* 16 Oct. (Ainger 1888) I. 144, I wish you had made London in your way.

d. *absol.* or with obj. omitted. (For idiomatic phrases with adjs., as *make ready*, †*short*, *sure*, see these words.)

c **1330** *Spec. Gy de Warewyke* 835 Anoþer manere wasshing Makeþ clene of alle þing. **1398** Trevisa *Barth. De P. R.* XIX. lxiii. (1495) 899 The substaunce of wheye is watry and makyth thynne. *c* **1400** *Lanfranc's Cirurg.* 6 Of resolueres & manere of vndoynge & makynge nessche. **1535** Coverdale *Prov.* x. 4 An ydle hande maketh poore, but a quycke laboringe hande maketh riche. **1754** Richardson *Grandison* IV. iv. 29 Make happy; and be happy.

e. with refl. pron. as obj. ***to make oneself scarce***: see scarce *a.*

a 1175 *Cott. Hom.* 233 Se hlaford .. dranc and macede hine wel bliðe mid his. *c* 1250 *Gen. & Ex.* 1591 For-ði he maked him stið & strong. *c* 1320 *Sir Trist.* 144 Þai busked and maked hem boun. 13.. *Gaw. & Gr. Knt.* 1885 He mace hym as mery among þe fre ladyes, .. As neuer he did bot þat daye. 1496 *Dives & Paup.* VII. iv. (W. de W.) 280/1 Make the plesaunt in speche to the congregacyon of poore folke. 1621 T. WILLIAMSON tr. *Goulart's Wise Vieillard* Ep. Ded. A iij, That I may not make my selfe otherwise knowne vnto your worship, then by [etc.]. 1632 LITHGOW *Trav.* III. 199 I'me there arriud, and eftsoones made me bound For the Venetian Consul. 1647 W. BROWNE *Polexander* I. II. 54 Concealing his .. Countrey, [he] made himselfe taken for a kinsman of the last Cacique. 1773 GOLDSM. *Stoops to Conq.* IV, With cunning and malice enough to make himself merry with all our embarrassments. 1779 SHERIDAN *Critic* I. ii, Here are two very civil gentlemen trying to make themselves understood. 1846 DICKENS *Cricket* i. 15 Take the precious darling, Tilly, while I make myself of some use. *a* 1859 DE QUINCEY *Posth. Wks.* (1891) I. 108 This Parker had a 'knack' at making himself odious. 1876 A. S. PALMER *Leaves fr. Wordhunter's Notebk.* xi. 266 Many diseases first make themselves felt in the 'dead of night'. 1888 B. W. RICHARDSON *Son of a Star* II. v. 72 They make themselves quite at home.

¶**f.** In *passive* as a literalism for L. *fieri* = to become. (Cf. 9e, 49e.)

a 1300 *E. E. Psalter* ci. 7 Like am I made to pellicane of annesse. 13.. *Prose Psalter* lii. 4 Hij ben made inprofitable.

49. With sb. as complement. **a.** To cause (a person or thing) to be or become (what is denoted by the complement).

c 1000 ÆLFRIC *Hom.* II. 82 Þone ðe he ær ehtende martyr ȝemacode. *c* 1200 *Trin. Coll. Hom.* 61 Þo þe was turnd fro him and makede him fleme þere he hadde er louerd iben. *a* 1225 *Ancr. R.* 54 Heo leas hire meidenhod, & was imaked hore. *c* 1305 *St. Andrew* 5 in *E.E.P.* (1862) 98 Come, he seide, after me and ic wole ȝou make Manfischers. 1362 LANGL. *P. Pl.* A. Prol. 36 Bote Iapers and Iangelers Iudas Children, Founden hem Fantasyes and fooles hem maaden. 1382 WYCLIF *Matt.* xxi. 13 Forsothe ȝe han made it a denne of thefes. *c* 1430 LYDG. *Chichev. & Byc.* vii, These husbandes, whiche theyr wyfes Maken maystresses of theyr lives. 1571 *Reg. Gild Co. Chr. York* (1872) 230 *note*, That if he may bringe him upp, and maike him a man. 1583 STOCKER *Civ. Warres Lowe C.* IV. 6 The true enheritors .. are disturbed, made no bodies, or vtterly dishenerited of their due succession. 1603 DEKKER & CHETTLE *Grissil* v. ii. (Shaks. Soc.) 81 It's pity that fellow was not made a soldier. *a* 1708 BEVERIDGE *Thes. Theol.* (1711) III. 298 To make onesself a slave for he knows not whom. 1849 MACAULAY *Hist. Eng.* ii. I. 171 The defeat which made him again a wanderer. 1890 T. F. TOUT *Hist. Eng. fr.* 1689, 26 This sentence made the noisy doctor a popular hero.

b. *spec.* To appoint to the office of; to raise to the dignity of; to create (a person) a noble, etc.

c 1200 *Trin. Coll. Hom.* 59 He hadde maked adam louerd ouer þis middelherd. *c* 1290 *Beket* 241 in *S. Eng. Leg.* I. 113 He makede him chaunceler. *c* 1374 CHAUCER *Boeth.* II. pr. iii. 25 (Camb. MS.) The remenbraunce of thilke day þat thow saye thi two sones makyd conseileres. 1470–85 MALORY *Arthur* Table (IX. ix), How .. Syr Launcelot .. was made knyght of the rounde table. 1564 *Child Marr.* 132 He askid hym .. whom he wold make his executour. *a* 1568 ASCHAM *Scholem.* II. (Arb.) 136 Therefore did som .. cause hedge priestes fette oute of the contrie, to be made fellowes in the vniuersitie. *a* 1715 BURNET *Own Time* (1724) I. 147 One Sir George Mackenzie, since made Lord Tarbot and Earl of Cromarty. 1849 MACAULAY *Hist. Eng.* iv. I. 447 He was made Chamberlain to the Queen. 1890 T. F. TOUT *Hist. Eng. fr.* 1689, 18 She made Marlborough a duke.

c. To determine (a thing, occas. a person) to be (what is expressed by the compl.); to establish or set down as (a law, penalty, etc.). Often with the compl. qualified by a possessive: To take as (one's business, boast, prey, abode, object, etc.).

Sometimes with *it* as formal obj., explained by a following inf. or clause.

1500–20 DUNBAR *Poems* xi. 46 Thy Ransonner, with woundis fyve, Mak thy plycht anker. 1594 HOOKER *Eccl. Pol.* I. xi. §2 Unless the last good of all .. be also infinite, we do evil in making it our end. 1611 BIBLE *Gen.* xlvii. 26 And Ioseph made it a law .. that Pharaoh should haue the fift part. 1630 USSHER *Lett.* (1686) 434 If he fail, I must make you my last refuge. 1659 *Burton's Diary* (1828) IV. 442 No reasoning by scripture will convince them; for they make that but a nose of wax. 1663 *Flagellum or O. Cromwell* (ed. 2) 10 He made it no Punctilio to invite his Roysters to a Barrel of Drink, and give it them at the charge of his Host. 1683 *Apol. Prot. France* Pref. 1 They .. make it the utmost penalty .. so much as to attempt a departure. 1738 GRAY *Imit. Propertius* II. i. 14 That the soft Subject of my Song I make. 1821 CLARE *Vill. Minstr.* I. 177 Make my cot thy home. 1842 BORROW *Bible in Spain* xii. (Pelh. Libr.) 88, I am not one of those who .. make it a constant practice to disparage the higher orders. 1882 STEVENSON *New Arab. Nts.* (1884) 179, I made it my pride to keep aloof. 1885 EDGAR *Old Ch. Life Scotl.* 273 The malediction of a parent was made a capital offence. 1893 LIDDON, etc. *Life Pusey* I. xv. 342 To make the reality and value of sacramental grace a main interest of his life.

d. To transform, transmute, or fashion into something else. Chiefly in *passive*, after L. *fieri*. *Obs.* or *arch.*: the notion is usually expressed by *to make .. into* (see 50), or, with reversed construction, *to make .. of* (see 18).

c 1200 ORMIN 19201 Godess Word iss makedd flæsh. 1382 WYCLIF *Matt.* iv. 3 Ȝif thou be Goddis sone, say that these stoons be made looues. *c* 1386 CHAUCER *Knt.'s T.* 1207 There saugh I Attheon an hert ymaked. 1611 BIBLE *Isa.* xlii. 15, I will make the riuers Ilands. *a* 1708 BEVERIDGE *Thes. Theol.* (1710) II. 222 The Word .. how made flesh?

¶**e.** In *passive* as a literalism for L. *fieri* = to become. (Cf. 9e, 48f.)

1382 WYCLIF *1 Cor.* xiii. 11 Whanne I was maad man.

†**f.** In early use, a dative preceded by *to* (in OE. rarely a simple dative) occurs in place of the complementary accusative. *Obs.*

c 1000 ÆLFRIC *De Vet. Test.* (Gr.) 2 [Lucifer] wolde .. þurh modiȝnesse hine macian to gode. —— *Gen.* xii. 2 Ic maciȝe þe mycelre mæȝðe [Vulg. *faciam te in gentem magnam*]. *c* 1175 *Lamb. Hom.* 103 Heo [*sc.* pride] macode englas to ateliche deoflan. *c* 1200 *Trin. Coll. Hom.* 193 Talewise men .. maken wrong to rihte and riht to wronge. *c* 1205 LAY. 29985 Heo makeden to kinge Cadwan þene kene. 13.. *K. Horn* 522 (Ritson) Horn .. made hem alle to knyhte.

50. a. Const. *into*. To convert by process of manufacture or otherwise into something else; to work upon (materials) so as to produce (something).

1583 *Leg. Bp. St. Androis* 568 He causit an talyeour turne it [a cloak] and mak it Into wich maill [= 'into the said portmanteau']. 1617 MORYSON *Itin.* III. 115 Fresh curds newly pressed, and made into little cheeses. 1710 PRIDEAUX *Orig. Tithes* ii. 76 The Grapes made into Wine, the Olives into Oyl. 1791 in R. W. Dickson *Pract. Agric.* (1805) I. 486 Mowing the first crop 0 2 6. Making it into hay 0 2 6. 1820 W. IRVING *Sketch Bk.* (1849) 286 *note*, Sometimes it [the peacock] was made into a pie. 1895 *19th Cent.* Aug. 329 You think that *The Wages of Sin* might be made into a play. 1900 JENKS *Hist. Politics* vii. (ed. 2) 60 The wife and daughters of the shepherd .. make the milk of the herds into butter and cheese.

intr. for *passive*. 1893 *Illustr. Sport. & Dram. News* 8 Apr. 165/2 A little corner flap-table which makes into a good-sized square when the flap is up.

b. To arrange, divide, or combine so as to form.

1849 *Jrnl. R. Agric. Soc.* X. I. 134 The wheaten straw is carefully made into bundles. 1879 MISS YONGE *Cameos* Ser. IV. xvi. 169 Worcester was suppressed and made into an archdeaconry. 1888 G. GISSING *Life's Morning* III. xix. 110 The shopman put them aside, to be made into a parcel.

51. To regard as, consider or compute to be; to describe or represent as (so-and-so); to cause to appear as. (Cf. 56.) **a.** with sb. as compl.

a 1225 *Ancr. R.* 224 Seinte Powel cleopeð hine 'angelum lucis' þet is, engel of liht vor swuch he makeð him ofte. *a* 1400 *Sir Perc.* 1086 What knyghte es that, .. That thou mase of thy menynge? 1500–20 DUNBAR *Poems* xxii. 36 Thocht I in court be maid refuss. 1560 DAUS tr. *Sleidane's Comm.* 3 In graunting of the same [he] maketh the byshop of Rome a great Prince. 1649 MILTON *Eikon.* v. Wks. (1847) 289/1 Was this becoming such a saint as they would make him? 1699 T. BAKER *Refl. Learning* xiii. 161 He is not that Goose and Ass that Valla would make him. *a* 1700 DRYDEN *Ovid's Met.* xv. Argt. *Fables* (1700) 503 Ovid .. makes Numa the Schollar of Pythagoras. 1707 *Curios. in Husb. & Gard.* Pref. 5 The Peripateticks .. made Nature a Goddess. 1849 *Tait's Mag.* XVI. 279/2 Some argue that they are Picts, and some make them Northmen. 1865 DICKENS *Mut. Fr.* III. xiii, What time may you make it, Mr. Twemlow? 1892 *Field* 27 Feb. 302/1 The distance travelled I make by the map five miles.

b. with adj., †pa. pple., or †phrase as compl.

1581 PETTIE *Guazzo's Civ. Conv.* I. (1586) 17 b, To saie, y^t euerie man should haue an eie onelie to his owne affaires, is nothing else but to make man like to beasts. 1599 THYNNE *Animadv.* (1875) 32 Not withstandinge that Hollybande, in his frenche-Englishe dictionarye, make yt of the valewe of a duckett. 1676 HOBBES *Iliad* Pref. (1686) 4 Homer begins not his Iliad with the injury done by Paris but makes it related by Menelaus. *a* 1687 PETTY *Pol. Arith.* x. (1690) 117 The King's Subjects are not in so bad a condition as discontented Men would make them. 1736 LEDIARD *Life Marlborough* II. 201 The Enemy's Army is not so numerous as they make it. 1868 LOCKYER *Guillemin's Heavens* (ed. 3) 493 This climate .. is not so bad .. as some Anglophobes would make it. 1879 M. J. GUEST *Lect. Hist. Eng.* xiv. 128 Macbeth is not half so bad as the play makes him.

c. *to make nothing* (*to do* something): to look upon it as no great thing, not to stick at it. (Cf. 21.)

1675 H. MORE in R. Ward *Life* (1710) 245 If a Man make nothing to halt and faulter in the first .. Sin. *a* 1716 SOUTH *Serm.* (1843) II. vii. 105 One of the greatest .. courage, who makes nothing to look death and danger in the face. 1720 DE FOE *Capt. Singleton* v. (1840) 89 Ten men .. took up one of the canoes, and made nothing to carry it.

†**d.** *refl.* with sb. or adj. as compl.: To maintain or pretend that one is (so-and-so). *Obs.* (Cf. *make out*, 91 j.)

a 1225 *Ancr. R.* 128 Ant te valse ancre .. makieð ham [*sic*] oðre þen ha beoð. *a* 1300 *Cursor M.* 14684 Þou mas þe godd, and þou art man. 1382 WYCLIF *John* viii. 53 Whom makist thou thi silf? *c* 1440 *Floris & Bl.* 76 (Trentham MS.) Y rede eke þat þe maydens moder make hur seek. 1533 in Strype *Eccl. Mem.* (1721) I. I. xxi. 152 The same Act may be .. set up on every church door .. to the intent that no parson .. nor any other of the king's subjects, shall make themselves ignorant thereof. 1535 COVERDALE *2 Sam.* xiii. 6 So Ammon layed him downe, and made him sicke. 1648 JENKYN *Blind Guide* i. 13 He makes himself a ballad-maker.

e. *make it so* (Naut. phr.): see quot. 1867. Also *to make noon*, etc.

1835 MARRYAT *Olla Podr.* xiv, The master reported that the heavens intimated that it was twelve o'clock; and .. I ordered him to 'make it so'. 1867 SMYTH *Sailor's Word-bk.*, *Make it so*, the order of a commander to confirm the time, sunrise, noon, or sunset, reported to him by the officer of the watch. 1892 STEVENSON & OSBOURNE *Wrecker* xii. 203 Noon was made; the captain dined.

f. *U.S. Underworld slang.* To recognize or identify (a person, etc.). Cf. MAKE *sb.*[2] 12.

1906 A. H. LEWIS *Confessions of Detective* 222 You wouldn't have come within a block of him. In the language of the guild, Sorg, he would have 'made you' and got away. 1908 J. M. SULLIVAN *Criminal Slang* 16 *Make one*, identify a person. 1914 JACKSON & HELLYER *Vocab. Criminal Slang* 57 You had better ring up (disguise) so he won't make you. 1955 *Publ. Amer. Dial. Soc.* XXIV. 81 The victim then can possibly identify, or *make*, the tool if he is arrested. 1971 'O. BLEECK' *Thief who painted Sunlight* (1972) xiv. 127 I'm a pretty good tail. You didn't make me. 1973 'D. SHANNON' *Spring of Violence* (1974) vi. 107 'Have you made the gun?' 'Right off. It's a Hi-Standard revolver.'

IV. Causative uses.

52. With dependent clause: To cause (something to happen); to bring it about (*that* something happens). *Obs.* exc. *arch.*

c 1000 ÆLFRIC *Exod.* v. 21 Ðe habbað .. ȝemacod þæt hiȝ wyllað us mid hyra swurdum ofslean. *c* 1122 *O.E. Chron.* an. 1075 Þæt landfolc him toȝeanes comen & ȝemacodon þæt he naht ne dyde. *c* 1200 *Trin. Coll. Hom.* 31 Ðus deuel eggeð ælch man on his herte, and macað þat he wule do þat he him to teihte. *c* 1386 CHAUCER *Sompn. T.* 176 The clennesse and the fastynge of vs freres Maketh þat crist accepteth oure preyeres. *c* 1470 HENRY *Wallace* x. 141 This makis it, thow art cled with our men. *c* 1485 *Digby Myst.* v. 581 That mase, that all vnkunnynge I disdeyne. 1526 TINDALE *John* xi. 37 Coulde not he which openned the eyes of the blynde have made also that this man shulde not haue deyed? 1632 LITHGOW *Trav.* IX. 381 This .. maketh that the Hennes with them are so innumerable. 1674 MARVELL *Corr.* Wks. 1872–5 II. 418 Sir Jeremy being out of town .. makes that I can not returne any proper or perfect answer. *a* 1715 BURNET *Own Time* (1724) I. 197 The Convocation being no more necessary to the Crown, this made that there was less regard had to them afterwards. 1885 MRS. LYNN LINTON *Chr. Kirkland* III. viii. 271 That well-known law, so disastrous to stock-raisers, which makes that, when the breed has been brought to the highest possible point of perfection, it stops.

53. With obj. and inf.: To cause a person or thing to do something; to have something done to a person or thing. **a.** const. inf. without *to*: now normally used only when both *make* and the dependent verb are in the active voice; otherwise *arch.*

c 1175 *Lamb. Hom.* 159 Swa makeð þe halie gast þe Mon bi-halden up to houene. *a* 1225 *Juliana* 38 Ich makede þen wittie ysaye beon isahet þurh ant þurh to deaðe. 1297 R. GLOUC. (Rolls) 7669 King willam adauntede þat folc of walis & made hom bere him truage. *a* 1300 *Cursor M.* 8795 Als a fische þou made me fere. 1340 *Ayenb.* 47 Hy .. diȝteþ ham þe more quaynteliche .. uor to maki musi þe foles to ham. 1390 GOWER *Conf.* I. 202 At Knaresburgh be nyhtes tuo The kinges Moder made him duelle. *c* 1450 *Merlin* 29 The kynge made hem alle be Shett in a stronge house. 14.. in *Hist. Coll. Citizen Lond.* (Camden) 194 The carre was made stonde stylle. 1502 *Ord. Crysten Men* (W. de W. 1506) I. iii. 21 Our lorde y^t .. this present worlde shall make brenne by fyre. 1567 *Gude & Godlie B.* (S.T.S.) 64 Trew Faith, Lord, mak vs fang. 1600 W. WATSON *Decacordon* (1602) 343 Pius Quintus .. was made beleeue that the Duke of Norfolke was a Catholike. 1650 BAXTER *Saints' R.* IV. (1651) 36 What made Peter deny his Lord? 1680 BURNET *Rochester* 142 He had made it be read so often to him that he had got it by heart. 1736 BUTLER *Anal.* I. v. ¶8 Their character is formed and made appear. 1738 SWIFT *Pol. Conversat.* 23, I wonder what makes these Bells ring. 1814 MRS. J. WEST *Alicia de Lacy* IV. 275 He made quail the courage of the heroic prince. 1847 MARRYAT *Childr. N. Forest* iii, Now I'll cut up the onions, for they will make your eyes water. 1896 A. E. HOUSMAN *Shropshire Lad* iii, You will .. make the foes of England Be sorry you were born.

b. const. inf. with *to*, †*for to*: now normally used only when *make* is in the passive voice; otherwise somewhat *arch.*

c 1200 *Trin. Coll. Hom.* 11 Þe deuel .. makeð þe unbilefulle man to leuen swilche wiȝeles. *a* 1225 *Ancr. R.* 224 Of þen oðer holie monne þet he makede uorte ileuen þet he was engel. 1377 LANGL. *P. Pl.* B. Prol. 113 Miȝt of þe comunes made hym [a king] to regne. *c* 1386 CHAUCER *Pars. T.* ¶540 Flaterye .. maketh a man to enhauncen his herte. *c* 1449 PECOCK *Repr.* Prol. 2 [They] han therbi maad ful miche indignacioun .. forto rise and be contynued in manie persoones. *c* 1489 CAXTON *Blanchardyn* xlviii. 185 He shal to morowe make hym to be hanged. *a* 1533 LD. BERNERS *Huon* lviii. 196 He made to be cryed through the cyte, that euery man shulde make him redy. 1597 HOOKER *Eccl. Pol.* v. xxxv. 72 He therefore which made vs to liue hath also taught vs to pray. 1603 SHAKS. *Meas. for M.* III. ii. 254, I am made to vnderstand, that you haue lent him visitation. 1616 S. WARD *Coale fr. Altar* (1627) 62 Violent affections haue made the dumbe to finde a tongue. 1746 W. LEWIS *Chem.* 31 *note*, Many such phænomena may be easily made to appear .. by exposing solutions of .. metals [etc.]. 1859 F. E. PAGET *Curate of Cumberworth* 153 Making the dust to fly in all directions. 1889 FROUDE *Two Chiefs Dunboy* ix. 110 A bath .. made the lame to walk and the blind to see. 1893 *Graphic* 29 Apr. 458/1 A Budget which maketh the Opposition to jeer. 1896 A. E. HOUSMAN *Shropshire Lad* xxxiii, I think the love I bear you Should make you not to die. *Mod.* The two statements can hardly be made to agree.

c. In proverbial phrases: ***to make both ends meet*** (END *sb.* 24), ***one's hair stand on end***, etc.

1534 MORE *Comf. agst. Trib.* II. v. (1847) 100 He made my own hair stand up upon my head. 1623 HEMINGE & CONDELL *1st Folio Shaks.* To Rdr., Censure will not driue a Trade, or make the Iacke go. 1748 RICHARDSON *Clarissa* IV. 92 And thus went he on for twelve years, and tho' he had a good estate, hardly making both ends meet. *Ibid.* 187 Money makes the mare to go. 1809 MALKIN *Gil Blas* VI. ii. ¶1 With such a sum .. it might be said, without boasting, that we knew how to make both ends meet. 1825 J. NEAL *Bro. Jonathan* I. 94 He'd make the feathers fly .. I believe.

†**d.** with ellipsis of an indef. obj. (e.g. *one*). (Cf. DO *v.* B. 23, GAR *v.* 2d.) *Obs.*

c 1302 *Pol. Songs* (Camden) 191 We shule flo the Conyng, ant make roste is loyne. *c* 1385 CHAUCER *L.G.W.* 2166 (*Ariadne*) He made his ship a londe for to sette. *a* 1425 *Cursor M.* 6615 (Trin.) Þis golden calf he made [*other texts* did, gart] to brest to peces. *a* 1450 *Knt. de la Tour* (1868) 6 Whanne her fader wost she was with childe, he made cast her in to the riuer. 1500–20 DUNBAR *Poems* lxiv. 14 This gentill herte .. Quhois petewous deithe dois to my hart sic pane That I wald mak to plant his rute agane. 1560

WHITEHORNE *Arte Warre* (1573) 71 Many times the saying backe, backe, hath made to ruinate an armie.

e. ***to make believe***: † (*a*) [after F. *faire croire*] to cause people to believe (chiefly with clause) (*obs.*); (*b*) in mod. use, to pretend *to do* something; to simulate a belief *that*; now often (said, e.g., of children in play), to subject oneself voluntarily to the illusion *that*. (Now often hyphened.)

1390 GOWER *Conf.* I. 231 And thus Fa crere makth believe So that fulofte he hath deceived. **1643** TRAPP *Comm. Gen.* xix. 2 If Solomon sinned not in making beleeve he would do that which was unlawful to be done. **1716** C'TESS COWPER *Diary* (1864) 64 Some Passages were wrote on purpose to make believe it was Sir R. Steele. **1738** tr. *Guazzo's Art Conversation* 31 Solitude..makes believe Things that have no Existence but in the Brain. **1748** RICHARDSON *Clarissa* (1811) III. 250 A false letter..macking believe as how her she-cuzzen..was coming to see her. **1773** GOLDSM. *Stoops to Conq.* IV, You were so nice and so busy with your Shake-bags and Goose-greens, that I thought you could never be making believe. **1806** SURR *Winter in Lond.* I. 141 He makes believe to work a little now and then, when he's well enough. **1840** DICKENS *Barn. Rudge* xvii, When I shut my eyes and make-believe to slumber. **1862** KINGSLEY *Water-Bab.* ii, We will make believe that there are fairies in the world. **1874** MICKLETHWAITE *Modern Par. Churches* 99 Do not make-believe with a shabby-genteel substitute. **1890** *Spectator* 15 Mar., To make believe that the country is excited about a discussion which [etc.]. **1902** G. B. SHAW *Mrs. Warren's Profession* Pref. p. xxiii, At such plays we do not believe: we make-believe. **1904** KIPLING *Traffics & Discov.* 334, I did all that..just to make believe. **1925** S. LEWIS *Martin Arrowsmith* xxxii. 386, I make believe read my French books. **1951** G. GREENE *End of Affair* I. vi. 37 As long as I could make-believe that love lasted, I was happy. **1974** J. WAINWRIGHT *Hard Hit* 38, I make-believe I am giving it careful thought.

f. ***to make do***: to manage *with* (what is available, esp. an inferior substitute). Also *absol.*, esp. in phr. ***to make do and mend***: to repair for continued use (cf. MAKE *sb.*² 13); also as *sb. phr.* See also MAKE-DO.

[**1899** E. WHARTON *Greater Inclination* 87 She had..accepted it [*sc.* marriage] as a provisional compensation,—she had made it 'do'.] **1927** *Observer* 28 Aug. 16/4 The listener who was content to receive only the programmes from his local station..could make do with a very simple and inefficient form of direct-coupled tuning arrangement. **1934** J. MARSTON *Andromeda* xii. 156 She had already had experience..in 'making do' on a small income. She 'made do' now, with a skill which impressed.. Letty. **1941** *New Statesman* 26 Apr. 431/1 It should be no great hardship for the community to make do with the same housing accommodation that it enjoyed in 1938. **1947** I. BROWN *Say Word* 105 This age of bits and pieces, queues, rationing, and make-do-and-mend. **1958** *Technology* Jan. 375/4 We may put all our energy into making real the ideal technical schools of 1944, or we may make do and mend by integrating technical studies in..grammar..schools. **1961** NEW ENG. BIBLE *Luke* iii. 14 No bullying; no blackmail; make do with your pay! **1967** A. WILSON *No Laughing Matter* IV. 414 You *are* lucky. Having a family to make do and mend for. **1968** M. WOODHOUSE *Rock Baby* vi. 51 Rasmussen had to make do with four eggs and only half a dozen rounds of toast because I was there.

54. a. To constrain (a person) *to do* something, by an exercise of influence, authority, or actual or threatened violence; to compel, force. (*To* is now always omitted before the inf. when *make* is active; in 16–17th c. this rule was not always followed.)

c **1592** MARLOWE *Jew of Malta* IV. iv, I'le make him send me half he has, & glad he scapes so too. **1592** GREENE *Upst. Courtier* Wks. (Grosart) XI. 227, I will make thee do me homage. **1593** SHAKS. *3 Hen. VI*, I. i. 142 He rose against him, being his Soueraigne, And made him to resigne his Crowne perforce. **1646** FULLER *Wounded Consc.* (1841) 311 Man can neither make him to whom he speaks, to hear what he says, or believe what he hears. **1662** STRYPE in *Lett. Lit. Men* (Camden) 179 He made me stay and sup with him. **1721–2** WODROW *Suffer. Ch. Scot.* (1837) II. II. xiii. §5. 456/2 Sir, we will cause a sharper thing make you confess. **1852** THACKERAY *Esmond* I. v, Harry..made her bring a light and wake my lady. **1879** M. J. GUEST *Lect. Hist. Eng.* x. 89 The Church made him do penance for it.

b. with ellipsis of the inf. Common *colloq.*

1888 *Times* 11 Aug. 9/5 The enemy will not play the game according to the rules, and there are none to make him.

†**55.** With ellipsis of the vb. of motion: To send or cause to go in a specified direction. *Obs. rare.* Cf. *make forth* 87 b, *make out* 91 a (*c*).

13.. *Evang. Nicod.* 86 in Herrig *Archiv* LIII. 393 Tyll Alexander..In message was I made. **1601** HOLLAND *Pliny* I. 195 Anniball..made [L. *misit*] after him certaine light horsemen to ouertake him.

56. a. To consider, represent, or allege *to* be or do something. (Cf. 51.)

1594 HOOKER *Eccl. Pol.* I. viii. §5 This did the very heathens themselves obscurely insinuate, by making Themis..to be the daughter of heaven and earth. **1662** STILLINGFL. *Orig. Sacr.* I. i. §20 Parius..makes his coming to Greece to be in the time of Hellen. **1687** BURNET *Repl. Varillas* 144 Varillas must be Sublime in every thing, so he makes him to have lived till he was 99. **1724** RAMSAY *Some Contents of 'Evergreen'* i, Balantyne..Makis Vertew triumph. **1825** *New Monthly Mag.* XIV. 543 Your sight is better than mine, what do you make that bird to be? **1868** FREEMAN *Norm. Conq.* (1876) II. App. 631 Most of the Chronicles make Richard die in 1026. **1875** SAYCE in *Encycl. Brit.* III. 182/2 Even the estimate of Ctesias, however, would make Babylon cover a space of about 100 square miles.

†**b.** To show or allege *that* something is the case.

1555 WATREMAN *Fardle of Facions* I. v. 50 All whiche their doynges, dooe manifestly make, that thei came of the Aethiopes. **1586–7** Q. ELIZ. *Let. to Jas. VI* (Camden Soc.) 44 Yet the[y] wyl make that her [Mary's] life may be saved and myne safe, wiche wold God wer true.

V. To do, perform, accomplish.

57. From the 12th c. *make* (corresponding to L. *facere*, F. *faire*) has been extensively used with a noun of action as object, where the older language would have used the verb *ȝewyrcan* (WORK) or *dón* (DO). †**a.** In various obsolete uses: To work (a miracle); to commit (a sin, crime, fault), 'tell' (a lie); to do (justice, mercy); to give (alms). *Obs.*

c **1000** ÆLFRIC *Jos.* ii. 12 Sweriað me..þæt ȝe don eft wið me swilce mildheortnisse, swa ic macode wið eow [L. *quomodo ego misericordiam feci vobiscum*]. *c* **1154** *O. E. Chron.* an. 1137 ⁊ 7 He maket þur ure Drihtin wunderlice & manifældlice miracles. *c* **1200** *Trin. Coll. Hom.* 29 þenne þu almesse makest. **1297** R. GLOUC. (Rolls) 163 Telle me ssal herafterward of þes wondres..& hou hii were verst imaked. *a* **1300** *Cursor M.* 28120 And titter wald i lesyng make, þan man my worde vn-treu to take. *Ibid.* 28777 Vnnait is þat almusthing þat þou þe mas of reuid thing. *c* **1320** *Sir Tristr.* 343 A tresoun þer was made. **1377** LANGL. *P. Pl.* B. v. 73 On owre lady he cryed, To make mercy for his mis-dedes. *c* **1400** *Laud Troy Bk.* (E.E.T.S.) 10478 He made Achilles leue his chace, That he no lenger mordur mace. *c* **1400** MAUNDEV. (1839) xxv. 261 That was a gret Myracle, that God made for hem. **1459** *Peebles Charters* etc. (1872) 133 Thai haf ordanit..for the faut that he made, that he pay to the tolbuth *xs.* **1483** CAXTON *G. de la Tour* F v b, That such justyce should be made of Aman as [etc.]. **1500–20** DUNBAR *Poems* xlix. 43 The murtherer ay mvrthour mais. *a* **1533** LD. BERNERS *Huon* xxxvii. 116 Huon thus beyng in dyspleasure with hym selfe for the lye that he made. **1621** BOLTON *Stat. Irel.* 16 The Sheriffe of the county shall..make levy of the money aforesaid. *a* **1715** BURNET *Own Time* (1724) I. 149 His design being..to..save himself from the malice and lies of others, and not to make lies of any.

b. To wage (WAR). So ***to make †battle, (a) fight, † an army*** (= expedition). Also, †to serve or take part in (a campaign).

c **1205** LAY. 627 Stal fiht heo makeden. *c* **1460** FORTESCUE *Abs. & Lim. Mon.* vi. (1885) 123 For the brekynge off an armye when any shall be made ayen hym apon þe see. **1530** PALSGR. 620/1 He made batayle agaynst hym tenne yeres. **1542** UDALL *Erasm. Apoph.* 262 b, Sylla..who made ciuile battail wᵗ Marius. **1594** KYD *Cornelia* IV. i. 131 These Nations did he purposely prouoke, To make an Armie for his after-ayde Against the Romans. **1647** [see CAMPAIGN *sb.* 3]. **1749** FIELDING *Tom Jones* VII. xi, [He] told the latter many entertaining stories of his campaigns, though in reality he had never made any. **1814** SCOTT *Wav.* x, Mr. Bradwardine..made some campaigns in foreign service. **1858** THACKERAY *Virgin.* vii, To make the campaign was the dearest wish of Harry's life.

c. To perform (a bodily movement or gesture, e.g. one expressive of respect or of contempt).

For *to make a* (or *one's*) *bow*, *make courtesy*, *make a curtsy*, *make a face* (*at*), *make horns at*, *make a leg*, *make* (*an*) *obeisance*, *a salaam*, see the sbs.

c **1400** MAUNDEV. (Roxb.) xxvi. 122 Þai do grete wirschepe also to þe sonne, and mase many knelinges þerto. **1484**, etc. [see OBEISANCE 3]. **1508** DUNBAR *Tua Mariit Wemen* 117 Quhen I heir nemmyt his name, than mak I nyne crocis. **1570**, etc. [see FACE *sb.* 6 b]. **1583** GOLDING *Calvin on Deut.* clxii. 1003 They make but a figge at it. **1632** MASSINGER & FIELD *Fatal Dowry* v. ii, The people, apt to mocke calamity, ..made no hornes at me. **1719–1805** [see HONOUR *sb.* 5 b]. **1734** tr. *Rollin's Anc. Hist.* (1827) I. 66 Jumping, skipping and making variety of strange unnatural motions. **1776** *Trial of Nundocomar* 70/2 I..made my salam to him. **1847** MARRYAT *Childr. N. Forest* xxvii, The King..made a low obeisance to the window where they were standing.

d. To enter into, conclude (a bargain, contract). So, ***to make a marriage*** (now only *legal*).

c **1250** *Gen. & Ex.* 1269 He had him maken siker pliȝt Of luue and trewðe. *a* **1300** *Cursor M.* 10781 þe spusail þat was mad þar. **1362** LANGL. *P. Pl.* A. II. 26 To-Morwe worth þe Mariage I-mad. **1508** DUNBAR *Tua Mariit Wemen* 56 God gif matrimony were made to mell for ane yeir. **1530** PALSGR. 586/2, I holde it, as we saye whan we make bargen. **1535** COVERDALE *1 Kings* iii. 1 Salomon made mariage with Pharao the kynge of Egipte, & toke Pharaos doughter. **1606** SHAKS. *Ant. & Cl.* II. iii. 39 Though I make this marriage for my peace. **1651** HOBBES *Leviath.* Rev. & Concl. 391 A Contract lawfully made, cannot lawfully be broken. *a* **1715** BURNET *Own Time* (1724) I. 562 The marriage that was now made with the brother of Denmark. **1722** DE FOE *Relig. Courtsh.* I. i. (1840) 8 Have you been both making your bargains? **1845** STEPHEN *Comm. Laws Eng.* (1874) II. 261 Having thus shown how marriage may be made.

e. *Eccl.* in certain phrases, as ***to make*** (***one's***) ***confession***. †***to make the sacrament***: to celebrate the Eucharist (*obs.*). ***to make one's Communion***: to communicate. Also, to perform, 'do' (penance).

[*c* **1320** R. BRUNNE *Medit.* 196 He seyd, 'makeþ þys yn my mende'.] *c* **1380** WYCLIF *Wks.* (1880) 327 Confessioun þat man makiþ of synne is made of man in two maners. Summe is mad oonly to god... And sum confessioun is made to man. *c* **1400** MAUNDEV. (1839) vii. 80 Thei maken here Sacrement of the Awtier, seyenge, *Pater noster*, and other Preyeres. *c* **1511** *1st Eng. Bk. Amer.* (Arb.) Introd. 31/1 They make the sacrament in broune brede. **1585** T. WASHINGTON tr. *Nicholay's Voy.* IV. xix. 133 b, Making their sacrament according to the Roman maner, with a round cake. **1705** BP. WILSON in Keble *Life* vii. (1863) 233 To make one Sunday's penance apiece in penitential habit in Kirk Michael Church. **1888** W. J. KNOX-LITTLE *Child of Stafferton* xii. 151 He intended to make his confession that night and to make his Communion in the morning.

f. With reference to locomotion or travel, in phrases ***to make an excursion, an expedition, a journey, a pace, a passage, a progress, a step*** (now rare), ***a tour, a trip, a voyage***, †***to make one's course***, †***to make return*** (= to come back), ***to make one's way, to make a circuit***: see the sbs.

English idiom is app. capricious in excluding many locutions which would seem to be parallel with these; we cannot, e.g. use *make* with obj. *a ride, a walk* (cf. G. *einen Spaziergang machen*).

c **1290** [see COURSE *sb.* 2]. **1340** HAMPOLE *Pr. Consc.* 6377 Þe son and þe mone þair course mas. *a* **1548** HALL *Chron. Edw. IV* 209 And as the kyng with sayle and ower was makynge his course as fast as coulde be possible. **1646** SIR T. BROWNE *Pseud. Ep.* VI. v. 291 If we imagine the Sun to make his Course out of the Eclyptick. **1828** J. H. MOORE *Pract. Navig.* (ed. 20) 102 A ship from the Lizard makes her course S. 39° W.

g. To deliver orally. Now only ***to make a speech, an oration***; formerly also † ***to make (a) sermon***. (See the sbs.)

†**h.** ***to make memory (min, mind, minning)***: to commemorate, record (see the sbs.). *Obs.*

†**i.** ? *absol.* To have effect, operate. *Obs.*

1303 R. BRUNNE *Handl. Synne* 557 Beleue wyl make þere þe wurde no myȝt may take.

58. a. In questions introduced by an objective *what*, e.g. ***what make you here?*** = What are you doing here? What is your business, right, or purpose? Now *arch.* (Common in 16–17th c.)

13.. *Cursor M.* 10990 (Cott.) Þe folk... Thoght ferli quat wit þis he madde [*Fairf.* Wondird what he was a-bowte]. *a* **1400–50** *Alexander* 2908 Bedis buske þe to batell quat makis [*v. r.* mase] þou here? *c* **1435** *Torr. Portugal* 2151 What makist thou in this contre? **1535** COVERDALE *Judg.* xviii. 3 Who broughte yᵉ hither? What makest thou here? **1601** MARSTON *Pasquil & Kath.* II. 66 Alas, good aged sir, what make you vp? **1602** KYD *Sp. Trag.* III. xii. (A). 24 *Hier.* What make you with your torches in the darke? *a* **1616** BEAUM. & FL. *Cust. Country* III. iii, What made you wandring So late i' th' night? **1677** WOOD *Life* (O.H.S.) II. 399 The proctor met him and ask'd him what he made out so late. **1693** DRYDEN *Persius* v. (1697) 482 Friend, What dost thou make a Shipboard? **1715–20** POPE *Iliad* XVI. 247 If that dire fury must for ever burn, What make we here? **1823** SCOTT *Quentin D.* xxi, What should my daughter make here at such an onslaught? **1842** BARHAM *Ingol. Leg.* Ser. II. *Misadv. Margate*, I saw a little vulgar Boy—I said, 'What make you here?'

b. Hence, by inversion of the preceding construction: ***what makes you here?*** taken as if = 'What causes you to be here?' (Cf. branch IV.)

1658 R. FRANCK *North. Mem.* (1694) 28 What makes him there? **1676** ETHEREDGE *Man of Mode* v. i, *Footman.* Madam, Mr. Dorimant! *Lov.* What makes him here? **1688** SHADWELL *Sqr. Alsatia* I, What makes you abroad so early? **1797** COLERIDGE *Christabel* I, What makes her in the wood so late A furlong from the castle gate?

59. With sbs. expressing the action of vbs. (whether etymologically cognate or not), *make* forms innumerable phrases approximately equivalent in sense to those verbs. In some of these phrases the obj.-noun appears always without qualifying word; in others it may be preceded by the indefinite article, or by a possessive adj. relating to the subject of the sentence. When standing alone, the combination of *make* with its object is equivalent to a verb used *intr.* or *absol.*; but in many instances the obj.-noun admits or requires construction with *of*, and this addition converts the phrase into the equivalent of a transitive verb. In this Dictionary these phrases are usually illustrated (and if necessary explained) under their respective sbs.; but a selection of them is given here in order to exhibit the variety of applications. (For the illustration of those phrases which are enumerated without quotations, see the sbs.)

Many of the ME. phrases of this type are literal renderings of phrases with L. *facere* or F. *faire*, the sb. being often adopted from one of those languages. In early use a gerund in *-ing* was often the obj. of *make*, but this is now rare.

a. The following are still more or less in use: *to make an abatement*, *(one's) abode*, *abstraction*, *an acknowledgement*, *an acquisition*, *an address*, *an advance*, *(an) affirmation*, *an allegation*, *(an) allowance*, *an animadversion*, *(an) answer*, *an appeal*, *an* (also *one's*) *appearance*, *(an) application*, *an ascent*, *an assault*, *an assay*, *an assertion*, *(an) assurance*, *atonement*, *an attack*, *an attempt*, *(an) avowal*, *an award*, *a beginning*, *a bid*, *a blunder*, *(a, one's) boast*, *a calculation*, *a call*, *a challenge*, *a change*, *(a) choice*, *(a) claim*, *a climb*, *a comment*, *a comparison*, *a complaint*, *a computation*, *a cut*, *a dash*, *a defence*, *delay*, *a demonstration*, *a discovery*, *a donation*, *an endeavour*, *an entrance*, *an error*, *an essay*, *an excavation*, *(an) exception*, *(an) exchange*, *(an) excuse*, *an experiment*, *an explanation*, *a find*, *a gift*, *a grant*, *haste*, *an incision*, *(an) inquiry*, *inquisition*, *intercession*, *a joke*, *lamentation*, *a landing*, *mention*, *a mistake*, *a motion*, *mourning*, *a move*, *narration*, *(an) oath*, *(an) objection*, *an*

observation, an offer, an offering, a (one's) petition, pretence, pretension, (a) proclamation, (a) profession, a proffer, progress, a promise, proof, a proposal, a proposition, a protest, provision, a recovery, a remark, (a) reply, reprisals, (a) request, resistance, restitution, (a) retreat, a sacrifice, a sale, (a) search, (a) shift, a shot, slaughter, a slip, a stand, a start, a stay, a surrender, a transition, a translation, (a) trial, use, one's vaunt, a venture, a vow.

a **1225** *Ancr. R.* 6 Non ancre bi mine read ne schal makien professiun..bute þreo þinges. *c* **1320** *Sir Beues* 215 (MS. A.) A prikede out be-fore is ost, For pride and for make bost. *c* **1384** CHAUCER *H. Fame* II. 416 For whom was maked moch compleynt. **1500–20** DUNBAR *Poems* ix. 85 To proper curat to mak confessioun trew. **1530** PALSGR. 621/1, I make clayme to a thyng by processe of the lawe. *a* **1533** LD. BERNERS *Huon* xxxii. 96 Agaynst that Gyaunt thou canst make no resystence. **1563–4** *Reg. Privy Council Scot.* I. 256 In presence of the Queins Majestie..comperit Johne Erle of Athole, and maid this offer underspecifit. **1616** R. C. *Times' Whistle* v. 1886 Let's make a challenge. **1640** HABINGTON *Edw. IV* 3 Hee..lookt about, where he might on the best advantage make experience of his fortune. **1660** INGELO *Bentiv. & Ur.* II. (1682) 164 The obedient Theoprepians made appearance at the time appointed. **1669** STURMY *Mariner's Mag.* I. ii. 25 This Observation was first made by Thales Milesius. **1680** AUBREY in *Lett. Eminent Persons* (1813) III. 386 'Twas a minute watch, wth wch he made his experiments. *a* **1687** SIR W. PETTY in *Hale's Acc. New Invent.* 132 We shall..make some animadversions upon each of the three great branches of that Expence. **1711** ADDISON *Spect.* No. 1 ⁋5 There is no Place of general Resort, wherein I do not make my Appearance. *a* **1715** BURNET *Own Time* (1724) I. 361 The House of Commons resolved..to make an address to the King. **1796** NELSON 11 Sept. in Nicolas *Disp.* (1846) VII. p. cxi, To make reprisals for the value of the property. **1836** CALHOUN *Sp.* 9 Mar., Wks. 1864 II. 483 Whenever the attempt shall be made to abolish slavery. **1842** BORROW *Bible in Spain* xxvii. (Pelh. Libr.) 192 He advised me to..obtain permission to make excavations. **1849** MACAULAY *Hist. Eng.* iii. I. 340 *note*, I have made allowance for the increase. **1867** MILL *Subj. Women* (1869) 98 Let us at first make entire abstraction of all psychological considerations tending to show, that [etc.]. **1870** E. PEACOCK *Ralf Skirl.* III. 199 No explanation had been made. **1870** DICKENS *E. Drood* iii, The rest [of the streets] being mostly disappointing yards with..no thoroughfare—exception made of the Cathedral-close. **1879** M. ARNOLD *Mixed Ess.* 340 That astonishing recovery which France has made since her defeat. **1883** *Century Mag.* XXVI. 245/1 [He] made a cut at something in the water. **1887** RIDER HAGGARD *Jess* xxviii, Still the old man made no comment.

† **b.** The following are examples of the obsolete uses: *to make abode* (but cf. *to make one's abode*), *abstinence, (an) assembly, one's avaunt, avauntment, baptizing, bodeword, a boon* (= prayer), *cease, delaying, ending, experience, an exposition, one's flitting, a gathering, greeting, hesitation, a hunt, information, an invitation, a kneeling, a meeting, menace, mourning, muster, ockering, an operation, (one's) orison, overdoing, parlage, plaint, prayer, process, procession, ransoming, one's recourse, refuge, residence, revenge, roos, rosing, show, showing, sojourn, spare, speaking, store, supply, supplying, tarrying, watch, witnessing, yelp* (ȝelp = boast).

c **1154** *O.E. Chron.* an. 1137 ⁋2 þa macod he his gadering æt Oxene ford. *c* **1200** *Trin. Coll. Hom.* 91 Elhc cristene man makeð þis dai procession fro chirche to chirche. *c* **1205** LAY. 26451 For æuere heo ȝelp makieð. *a* **1300** *Cursor M.* 8126 þei ..made ilkan þair orison. *Ibid.* 12274 Quen þe angell hir bodeword made. *Ibid.* 12518 þai..to bethleem þair flitting made. *Ibid.* 12776 þat he now suilk baptiszing mass. *Ibid.* 13194 For to mak ending o mi tale. *Ibid.* 14334 Til fader his he made a bon. *Ibid.* 28817 þou þat okering mas wit man. *c* **1330** R. BRUNNE *Chron.* (Rolls) 11669, & of þis þey make auauntement. **1340** *Ayenb.* 240 Sobrete lokeþ mesure ine mete and ine drinke þet me ne maki overdoinge. **13..** *Childh. Jesus* 1527 þat noman ne miȝte make delayingue Of þing þat he wolde don. *c* **1375** *Sc. Leg. Saints* xxxiii. (*George*) 797 Ambrose to þis mais witnesing. *c* **1400** MAUNDEV. (1839) v. 44 There he made the Expositioun of Dremes. **1449** *Rolls of Parlt.* V. 147/2 Of the which offenses, they hadde be.. required..to make cesse. **1483** CAXTON *G. de la Tour* H iij, They..fasted and made abstynence. **1535** COVERDALE *Ps.* xl. 17 Make no longe tarienge o my God. **1563** *Homilies* II. *Rogat. Week* II. (1859) 480 The Wise Man..made his recourse to God for it. **1632** HOLLAND *Cyrupædia* 102 As touching the money in coine..they would then make partage thereof. **1715** DESAGULIERS *Fires Impr.* 137 Make several Chymical Operations. *a* **1715** BURNET *Own Time* (1724) I. 595 The Pope..made great returns of money into Germany. **1769** GOLDSM. *Hist. Rome* (1786) I. 106 Veturia, the mother of Coriolanus, at first made some hesitation to undertake so pious a work. **1771** —— *Hist. Eng.* IV. 161 A French officer, who had made some useful informations relative to the affairs of France. **1821** J. FOWLER *Jrnl.* (1898) 69 To morrow the Indeans make a Hunt.

60. To eat (a meal).

1542 UDALL *Erasm. Apoph.* 127 On a tyme Diogenes made al his dyner with Olives onely. **1577** B. GOOGE *Heresbach's Husb.* I. (1586) 15 That they make not to great meales, but eate little and often. **1662** J. DAVIES tr. *Olearius' Voy. Ambass.* 270 Some times our people made but one meal a day. **1742** YOUNG *Nt. Th.* v. 465 There take large draughts; make her chief banquet there. **1859** JEPHSON *Brittany* xix. 311 As I made my delicious and refreshing luncheon of green figs. **1864** LEMON *Loved at last* I. vi. 145, I never made a better dinner in my life. **1890** *Longm. Mag.* July 254 He made his simple morning meal.

61. a. To offer, present, render. †Formerly in many specific applications: to 'do' (homage, fealty); to 'pay' (some mark of respect); to render (support, aid); to present (a person's 'compliments'); to propound (a question); to give (an instance, notice, a reason, warning) (*obs.*). Also in ***to make amends***, †***asseth, satisfaction***: see the sbs. Const. *to* or *dative*.

The phr. *to make love* (see LOVE *sb.*[1] 6 g) may perh. be referred to this sense.

a **1300** *Cursor M.* 20620 Al heuen court sal serue þe, To mak þe manred. *c* **1330** R. BRUNNE *Chron. Wace* (Rolls) 6461 Conan made hym þer fewte. **1375** BARBOUR *Bruce* v. 297 And he him-self first homage maid. *Ibid.* 502 Thai maid him mony tyme varnyng. *c* **1375** *Sc. Leg. Saints* xxxvi. (*Baptista*) 352 He bad þaim..sic demand hym ma [etc.]. *c* **1400**, etc. [see FEALTY 2]. **1426** LYDG. *De Guil. Pilgr.* 3298 Makynge to hyr thys questyoun. **1450** *Rolls of Parlt.* V. 212/1 Therof made notice to the seid Evan Aprice. **1473** SIR J. PASTON in *P. Lett.* III. 84, I made yowr answer to the ffrends off Mestresse Jane Godnoston accordyng to yowr instrucions. **1500–20** KENNEDIE *Flyting w. Dunbar* 410 Homage to Edward Langschankis maid thy kyn. **1523** LD. BERNERS *Froiss.* I. ccxxxviii. 344 They..came..and made homage to kynge Dampeter. **1539** CROMWELL 21 Jan. in Merriman *Life & Lett.* (1902) II. 169 To make supporte subvention and confort unto them to resist his malice. **1582** G. MARTIN *Discov. Corrupt. Script.* ii. 29 And make vs a good reason why you put the word, traditions, here. **1599** B. JONSON *Ev. Man out of his Humour* II. i, Why Ile make you an Instance: your Citie wiues [etc.]. **1654–66** EARL ORRERY *Parthen.* (1676) 660 He had but one desire more to make me. **1719** JAMES (the Pretender) *Let.* in *Pearson's 76th Catal.* (1894) 33 Pray make him my kind compliments. **1761** HUME *Hist. Eng.* II. xxvii. 127 He made warning of the danger to his master. **1800** ADDISON *Amer. Law Rep.* 286 Brackenridge.. made two questions.

b. ***to make head*** [= F. *faire tête*]: see HEAD *sb.*[1]

a **1569** KINGESMYLL *Confl. Satan* (1578) 8 If thou couldest make head against him. **1577–87**, etc. [see HEAD[1] *sb.* 57 a].

c. *Law.* Of a court, a judge: To render, give (a decision, judgement).

'Now unusual in England; still common in America' (Sir F. Pollock).

1804 LD. ELDON *Vesey's Rep.* X. 121, I am not aware that such a decision has been made since that case.

†**62. a.** To entertain or manifest (certain emotions). ***to make gladness, glee, joy, merriment, mirth***: to rejoice, be merry. ***to make care***: to be careful or anxious. ***to make dole, sorrow***: to mourn. *Obs.*

c **1205** LAY. 1795 Muchel wes þa murðe þe þat folc makode. **1297** R. GLOUC. (Rolls) 7820 He him sulf deol inou & sorwe made al so. *a* **1300** *Cursor M.* 11031 (Cott.) Again him [he] mad gladnes an glu. *a* **1300–1400** *Ibid.* 17974 (Gött.) Ful mekil ioy þai made i-wis. *c* **1400** *Laud Troy Bk.* (E.E.T.S.) 9957 Knyȝtes kene that ben of Troye, Now make murthe and mochel Ioye. *c* **1489** CAXTON *Sonnes of Aymon* vi. 140 The grete sorowe that the poure Knightes made for theyr brother. **1513** DOUGLAS *Æneis* x. i. 107 As for Ene, forsuyth, I mak na cayr. **1570** *Satir. Poems Reform.* xii. 200 The Feynd mak cair, I say na mair. **1590** SPENSER *F.Q.* III. i. 57 Some to make loue, some to make meryment.

b. ***to make*** (***a***) ***mock***, †***scorn*** (***at, of***): see the sbs.

63. To put forth (an effort). Also, †***to make labour, pain.*** †***to make force*** (***at***, etc.): see FORCE *sb.*[1] 22 b.

1456 SIR G. HAYE *Law Arms* (S.T.S.) 38 He maid grete payne to ger that langage of Latyne sprede. *c* **1489**, etc. [see EFFORT *sb.* 2]. **1491**, etc. [see LABOUR *sb.* 5 b]. **1596** DALRYMPLE tr. *Leslie's Hist. Scot.* I. 6 Gif mair labour and industrie war maid. **1597** BEARD *Theatre God's Judgem.* (1612) 297 The dog..instantly made force at him..as a man would doe at his mortall enemie. **1871** SMILES *Charac.* i. (1876) 11 Every honest effort made in an upward direction.

64. a. In certain phrases, used for: To incur, suffer (something undesirable). So ***to make*** †***expense***, †***wreck, shipwreck*** (arch.), ***a loss*** (?obs. exc. in commercial use: cf. sense 29).

For *to make (good* or *bad) weather* (Naut.), see WEATHER.

1453 *Rolls Parlt.* V. 268/1 All theire costes, expenses and lostez, made and suffred by hem in this partie. **1526** TINDALE *1 Tim.* i. 19 Some..as concernynge fayth have made ship-wracke. **1563** *Reg. Privy Council Scot.* I. 239 All expensissis maid in..pleying of the said caus. **1577–87** HOLINSHED *Chron.* (1807–8) II. 218 Everie person making wrecke by sea, and comming alive to land. **1609** G. BENSON *Serm. 7 May* 5 If you..make wrack neyther vpon the Rockes, nor vpon the Sandes, neyther vppon open nor secret sinnes. **1626** C. POTTER tr. *Sarpi's Hist. Quarrels* 99 They could not continue to make such expence, nor to furnish so many persons with Vestiments. **1640** tr. *Verdere's Rom. Rom.* III. 199 They could not learn any news of the losse they had made. *a* **1715** BURNET *Own Time* (1724) I. 251 Both England and Holland had made a great loss both in ships and treasure.

† **b.** Hence (chiefly *Sc.*), to defray, provide for (expenses, costs). *Obs.*

c **1460** FORTESCUE *Abs. & Lim. Mon.* v. (1885) 118 Yff a kynge be pore, he shall bi nescessite make his expences..by creaunce and borowynge. **1473** *Ld. Treas. Acc. Scot.* (1877) I. 46 Gevin to Wil Oliphant..to mak his expensis xx *li.* **1574** *Reg. Privy Council Scot.* II. 388 The said Robert oblist him to mak the said Williames reasonable expenssis, and to pay the same to him.

65. a. To accomplish (a distance) by travelling, etc.

1564–5 N. WOTTON in Burgon *Life Gresham* (1839) II. 70, I made a-foote vi myles ere I came to Dunkerke. **1662** J. DAVIES tr. *Olearius' Voy. Ambass.* 2 It's violence hindred us not from keeping on our course, and making fifteen Leagues that night. **1687** A. LOVELL tr. *Thevenot's Trav.* I. 270 When the Wind blew so hard, that we made nine or ten Miles an hour. **1768** BOYER *Eng.-Fr. Dict.* s.v., They make sometimes ten fathom at one leap. **1856** OLMSTED *Slave States* 16 The boat makes 55 miles in $3\frac{1}{4}$ hours. **1899** *Pall Mall Mag.* Mar. 373, I could get no boat farther than Kirkcaldy, so I must make the distance on foot.

b. orig. *Naut.* To reach (a place) in travelling, come to, arrive at; *slang* to catch (a train, etc.). Also *fig.*, to achieve, accomplish, reach. Freq. ***to make it***, to reach a certain place; to succeed in traversing a specified distance; to achieve a desired object; to be successful; *spec.* to achieve sexual intercourse.

c **1624** WALLER *Pr. Charles at Sant' Anders* 148 From the stern of some good ship appears A friendly light... New courage..they take, And, climbing o'er the waves, that taper make. **1641** EVELYN *Diary* 12 Oct., Tho' not far from Dover, we could not make the Peere till 4 in the afternoon. **1697** DRYDEN *Æneid* I. 227 The weary Trojans ply their shatter'd Oars To nearest Land, and make the Libian Shoars. **1708** *Lond. Gaz.* No. 4481/3 The West-India Fleet and Coasters,..not being able to make Torbay,..were all forced..to the Westward. *a* **1774** GOLDSM. tr. *Scarron's Com. Romance* (1775) II. 103 We forced open the prison gates, and..made the mountains on the borders of Valentia. **1805** PIKE *Sources Mississ.* (1810) 39, I determined to attempt to make the river, and for that purpose took a due south course. **1827** J. F. COOPER *Prairie* I. xvii. 245 It will be wise to make a cover, lest the Sons of the Squatter should be out skirting on our trail. **1828** *Sporting Mag.* XXI. 322 She [a coach]..started at ten, and made the White Horse, Fetter Lane, at four precisely. **1882** SALA *Amer. Revis.* (1885) 360 We made Chicago at 7.30 on Sunday morning. **1885** HOWELLS *Silas Lapham* (1891) I. 137 He..jumped on board the steamboat..'Just made it', he said. **1885** [see BULLOCKY *a.* 2]. **1905** R. BEACH *Pardners* (1912) ii. 56 We can't make it over into Mexico without being caught up. **1912** R. A. WASON *Friar Tuck* xxvi. 187 Badger-face tried to raise himself on his elbow, but he couldn't quite make it. **1916** H. L. WILSON *Somewhere in Red Gap* i. 25, I hurried home to get a bite to eat and dress and make the party. **1925** E. HEMINGWAY *In Our Time* (1926) ix. 121 It looked like him or the bull and then he finally made it. **1928** [see BEST *adv.* 3 b]. **1935** L. A. G. STRONG *Seven Arms* 46 No matter if they can't make it in the day, sleeping out won't hurt them. **1938** G. GREENE *Brighton Rock* I. i. 20 'Will you be there?' 'No,' Hale said. 'I can't make it.' **1951** N. M. GUNN *Well at World's End* xviii. 148 He had..found out that we could make Pamplona that day and asked if we were game. **1955** W. GADDIS *Recognitions* I. vii. 266 But I have to make a train, he said. **1957** J. KEROUAC *On Road* III. viii. 225 They went to a parking lot in broad daylight..and there, he claims, he made it with her in nothing flat. **1959** N. MAILER *Advts. for Myself* (1961) 217, I knew *The Deer Park* had damn well better make it or I was close to some serious illness. *Ibid.* 295 The hipster's belief that when he really makes it, he will be able to turn his hand to anything. **1967** *Field & Stream* June 96/3, I hope he makes it through the winter. **1968** *Observer* 28 Jan. 12/3 A flood of letters has convinced us that we are providing a useful service and this view was confirmed a week ago when we 'made it' in the House of Commons. **1970** G. GREER *Female Eunuch* 159 His wife, who had been a trendy catch ten years before, was not making it so well. **1970** G. F. NEWMAN *Sir, You Bastard* viii. 202 Billie would eventually get the sheet changed..or Mrs Basil, whoever made the scene first. **1970** *Observer* 20 Sept. 26/1 Bombers ..lurching along the runway like a swarm of crippled insects, until finally they make it into the air. **1973** *Weekly News* (Glasgow) 11 Aug. 3/1 She's been a member [of the Glasgow Police Judo Club] for the past three years and managed to make the team which gave a display at the last Police Tattoo. **1973** *Times* 12 Nov. 15/7 Only those undergraduates most likely to make the team are engaged. **1973** *Times Lit. Suppl.* 16 Nov. 1389/2 He finally makes it with long-desired Rachel.

c. To be successful in advances to (a member of the opposite sex); to win the affection of; *spec.* to persuade (a person) to consent to sexual intercourse; to seduce. *slang* (orig. *U.S.*).

1918 H. C. WITWER in *Amer. Mag.* June 110/3 Look at that big stiff tryin' to make the dame! **1921** *Sat. Even. Post* 1 Oct. 17/1 She give up trying to make me and got off at Albany. She was a good looker but I have no time for gals that tries to make strangers on a train. **1926** ANDERSON & STALLINGS *What Price Glory* I, in *Three Amer. Plays* (1926) 7 God! I guess even Lippy could make a kid if she slept on the other side of a paper wall. *Ibid.* 8 This broad I was trying to make insisted on riding on the merry-go-round. **1926** S. LEWIS *Mantrap* xii. 155 The guys..think they can make you P.D.Q. [*sc.* pretty damn quick], even if they're old and fat. **1930** E. RICE *Voy. to Purilia* ii. 27 Never before had I seen a face so disfigured by unbridled lust! 'Looks as if he's trying to make her,' shouted Johnson. **1952** L. A. G. STRONG *Darling Tom* xiv. 116, I don't say I'd always have been content with thoughts of you, or that, if you'd stayed lost, I mightn't have tried to make you. **1959** P. H. JOHNSON *Humbler Creation* xxvi. 187 Young Fraser tried to make her once. **1969** E. GOFFMAN *Where Action Is* 200 James Bond makes the acquaintance of an unattainable girl and then rapidly makes the girl.

66. In phrases like ***to make long hours*** (i.e to work many hours in the day). Also, ***to make good time***: to accomplish a distance in a short time. ***to make time*** (***with***) (a person): to make advances to (a member of the opposite sex); to court or flirt with; also = sense 65 c above. *N. Amer. slang.*

1887 I. R. *Ranche Life Montana* 140 We drove to Three Forks..in an hour and twenty minutes. Jem calls it fourteen miles, so I think we made good time. **1890** *Standard* 17 Mar. 3/1 At present..the colliers..make very short time. *a* **1904** *Mod.* I made a very long day last Friday. **1934** G. & S. LORIMER *Stag Line* iv. 122 'You can't make any time with me,' I said giving him a lazy smile. 'I belong to another.' **1953** W. BURROUGHS *Junkie* (1972) xiv. 141 At another table two young men were trying to make time with some Mexican girls. **1962** E. LUCIA *Klondike Kate* viii. 171 The ranchers and cowpokes came in for a peek, and to make time if they could. **1962** J. POTTS *Evil Wish* xii. 159 She decided that Joe was lying... Probably making time with some kid half Marcia's age. **1971** E. BULLINS in W. King *Black Short*

Story Anthol. (1972) 82 Say, are ya makin' much time with mah little sister? There was a guarded flash in his eyes. **1971** 'D. SHANNON' *Ringer* (1972) viii. 140 Frankly, he'd have liked to make time with that girl, but she'd turned up her nose at him. **1973** D. HUGHES *Along Side Road* (1974) ii. 16 Which I'll bet he did if he wanted to make time with her, eh?

¶**67.** †**a.** To 'play' (the fool) (*obs.*). **b.** = DO *v.* 11 j, in ***to make the agreeable*** (? *obs.*). [After F. *faire.*]

1529 LYNDESAY *Complaynt* 236 Sum maid the fule, and sum did flatter. **1841** LEVER *C. O'Malley* vi. 31 Sir George Dashwood was 'making the agreeable' to the guests. **1867** H. KINGSLEY *Silcote of S.* xviii, The best thing you can do is to ..begin to make the agreeable to the eldest Miss Granby.

VI. To behave, act, or move (in a specified way).

†**68. a.** ***to make it*** (with adv. or advb. phr. denoting manner): to act, behave. *Obs.*

c **888** K. ÆLFRED *Boeth.* Tit. vii, & sæde him bispell hu he hit macian sceolde ȝif he heora þeȝen beon sceolde. *c* **1000** ÆLFRIC *Hom.* II. 354 Swa he hit macode on his life. **1387** TREVISA *Higden* (Rolls) VII. 27 Þe kyng..made it as þey were nouȝt wrooþ [L. *dissimulato odio*]. ? *a* **1500** *Peblis to the Play* viii, Quhat neidis you to maik it sua?

†**b.** With adj. as complement. ***to make it coy, nice, proud, quaint, stout, strange, tough***: to behave in a coy, proud, etc., manner (see the adjs.). ***to make it goodly***: to give oneself airs.

1611 COTGR., *Faire la petite bouche*, to mince, or simper it; to make it goodly.

69. Hence *intr.* (the obj. *it* being omitted); in OE. with *adv.*; later with adj., in ***to make bold, free,*** †***glad, merry,*** †***nice,*** †***strange*** (see the adjs.).

a **1000** *Institutes of Polity* xv. in Thorpe *Laws* II. 322 Riht is þæt mynecena mynsterlice macian.

70. a. ***to make as if, as though*** (arch. *as*): to behave as if; hence, to pretend that. Cf. 34 b.

[**1387**: see 68.] *a* **1450** *Knt. de la Tour* (1868) 77 The prince ..made as they he hadde take none hede therof. **1530** PALSGR. 655/2, I patter with the lyppes, as one dothe that maketh as though he prayed and dothe nat. *a* **1533** LD. BERNERS *Huon* lxv. 222 Make as though ye were dyspleasyd with hym. *a* **1553** UDALL *Royster D.* I. ii. (Arb.) 13, I wyll make as I sawe him not. **1603** KNOLLES *Hist. Turks* (1621) 41 Which reproachfull speech the Emperour put up in silence, making as if hee had not heard it. **1611** BIBLE *Josh.* viii. 15 And Ioshua and all Israel made as if they were beaten before them, and fled. **1720** DE FOE *Capt. Singleton* xvii. (1840) 290 Thou makest as if those poor savage wretches could do mighty things. **1752** CHESTERF. *Lett.* (1792) III. 264, I am very glad (to use a vulgar expression) that *you make as if you* were not well, though you really are. **1851** LONGF. *Gold. Leg.* III, He..beckons, and makes as he would speak. **1889** *Dict. Nat. Biog.* XVII. 59/2 Edward at first intended, or made as though he intended, to [etc.] **1919** V. WOOLF *Night & Day* iv. 53 Denham..made as if he were tearing up handfuls of grass..from the carpet. **1957** 'M. YOURCENAR' *Coup de Grace* 86 With her foolish bundle she looked like a discharged servant-girl; shifting it from one arm to the other she made as if to escape. **1971** *Leader* (Durban) 7 May 9/2 The girls want to look like boys and the boys make as if they are girls.

b. ***to make like***: to pretend (to be), to behave like or as if; to imitate. *colloq.* (orig. *U.S.*). Cf. sense 73 a.

a **1881** S. LANIER *Poems* (1892) 179 Then he..made like he neither had seen nor heerd. **1928** J. PETERKIN *Scarlet Sister Mary* x. 100 Mary made like she was nearly dead. **1939** J. STEINBECK *Grapes of Wrath* xxiii. 396 This rich fella ..makes like he's poor. **1953** P. FRANKAU *Winged Horse* III. i. 177 Couldn't make like nice when the old boy said he knew I'd be..ready for my native land again. **1956** B. HOLIDAY *Lady sings Blues* (1973) iii. 34 The next time around she made like a big shot and started the ball rolling by handing me a big tip. **1968** W. WARWICK *Surf-riding in N.Z.* 20/3 On a large wave it is also possible to spread your arms and legs out and make like a bird in flight. **1968** M. WOODHOUSE *Rock Baby* xxiii. 227 Well, you aren't making much noise... For a guy who was making like an avalanche an hour back.

71. To have to do *with* (a person or thing); to interfere *in* (a matter); chiefly in collocation with *meddle. dial.*

1564 *Child Marr.* (1897) 123, I will neither make nor medle with her. **1661** PEPYS *Diary* 7 Nov., Pegg Kite now hath declared she will have the beggarly rogue the weaver; and so we are resolved neither to meddle nor make with her. **1662** LIVINGSTONE in *Wodrow Sel. Biog.* (1845) I. 208 He thinks he will only preach against Poprie, and not make with other controversies. **1756** TOLDERVY *Hist. 2 Orphans* I. 146 And so, Sir, pray don't meddle nor make with the maids. **1834** LANDOR *Exam. Shaks.* Wks. 1853 II. 298/1 The business is a ticklish one: I like not overmuch to meddle and make therein. **1849** C. BRONTË *Shirley* xxi, Moore may settle his own matters henceforward for me; I'll neither meddle nor make with them further.

72. a. *Naut.* Of the flood or ebb tide (†in early use *passive*, or perh. *intr.* conjugated with *be*): To begin to flow or ebb respectively; also, to be in progress. Hence of the tide: To flow towards the land; to rise; also, to flow in a specified direction.

1651 CHAS. II in Hone *Every-day Bk.* I. 1716 Just as the tide off ebb was made. **1708** *Lond. Gaz.* No. 4422/7 The Tide of Flood being made, and there proving little Wind, we were oblig'd to Anchor. **1719** DE FOE *Crusoe* I. xiii, The tide made to the westward. *Ibid.*, The tide beginning to make home again. **1776** C. CARROLL *Jrnl.* (1845) 40 About nine o'clock at night, the tide making, we weighed anchor. **1840** MARRYAT *Poor Jack* I, The flood tide made. *a* **1861** CLOUGH *'Say not the Struggle'* 11 Far back, through creeks and inlets making, Comes silent, flooding in, the main. **1875** BEDFORD *Sailor's Pocket Bk.* v. (ed. 2) 169 When the stream makes to the Eastward at Spithead, the water falls at Southampton. **1883** STEVENSON *Treas. Isl.* IV. xvii. (1886) 135 The ebb was now making. **1910** BELLOC *Verses* 3 The tide is making over Arun Bar. **1956** C. WILLOCK *Death at Flight* viii. 104 We shall build this into a platform..in order to give us a little extra height when the tide makes.

b. Of ice: to form. *N. Amer.*

1784 N. WEBSTER in E. E. Ford *Notes Life N. Webster* (1912) I. 88 Cold; ice makes in the river. **1817** *Montreal Herald* 8 Feb. 2/5 The ice having made in the bay, has added greatly to the gaiety of the place. **1888** J. MCDOUGALL *George Millward McDougall* 114 As soon as the snow falls and ice makes, dogs will become the means of transport for the most part. **1890** *N.Y. Tribune* 12 Dec. 3/3 Several good guides..will assist him in an attempt to reach Kadiak Island by crossing Alaska Peninsula before the ice makes. **1933** E. MERRICK *True North* 11. 86 A gray day, ice making everywhere. **1971** J. MCDOUGALL *Parsons on Plains* iv. 31 After ice makes, the fish freeze almost as soon as you take them out of the water.

73. Of land, landscape, etc.: †**a.** *Naut.* To have a certain form or appearance; to look *like* (*obs.*). **b.** *U.S.* and *Colonial.* To extend in a certain direction. (Cf. 91 n.)

1743 BULKELEY & CUMMINS *Voy. S. Seas* 151 Two Ledges of Rocks, running two Leagues out from a Point of Land which makes like an old Castle. **1748** *Anson's Voy.* II. xii. 260 There appears a hummock, which at first makes like an island. **1770** SIR J. BANKS *Jrnl.* 17 May (1896) 270 At sunset the land made in one bank, over which nothing could be seen. **1787** JEFFERSON *Writ.* (1859) II. 136 Spurs, or ramifications of high mountains, making down from the Alps. **1808** PIKE *Sources Mississ.* II. (1810) 192 A copse of woods, which made down a considerable distance from the mountains. **1890** *Melbourne Argus* 16 June 6/1 Wherever slides are abundant, or two make from east and west.

74. Of arguments, evidence, influences: To be effective, 'tell' (on one side or the other). (Cf. 25, 25 b.) Chiefly with *for* (†*to, with*), *against* (see 76 a, 78 a, 79 a, 82 a). [Cf. L. *facere cum, facere contra.*]

1892 *Sat. Rev.* 2 Jan. 1/1 He had the highest opinion of.. precedents—when they made in his own favour. **1893** *Sketch* 1 Feb. 14/1 All these things..make in favour of Mr. Gladstone.

VII. With prepositions in specialized senses (all intransitive).

75. make after ——. To go in pursuit of, to pursue, follow. *arch.* (Cf. 35 b.)

1590 GREENE *Orpharion* Wks. (Grosart) XII. 54 Acestes ..made after the King of Lidia, as fast as his men were able to march. **1600** ABP. ABBOT *Exp. Jonah* 177 When they were so pursued and made after by the chariots and horsemen of the Egyptians. **1688** BUNYAN *Heav. Footman* (1886) 148 There is never a poor soul that is going to heaven, but the devil, the law, sin, death and hell makes after that soul. **1748** *Anson's Voy.* III. v. 336 His people made after them, in hopes of finding out their retreat. **1856** VAUGHAN *Mystics* (1860) I. VI. viii. 261 As he flounders about, out tumbles the book; he lets go his staff, and makes after it.

76. make against ——. **a.** To be unfavourable to; to militate or 'tell' against. (Cf. 74.)

a **1540** BARNES *Wks.* (1573) 315/1 The texte maketh agaynst the Pope. **1648** MILTON *Observ. Art. Peace* Wks. 1738 I. 355 The third Reason which they use, makes against them. **1668** CULPEPPER & COLE *Barthol. Anat.* I. xxviii. 65 Ocular Experience makes against this. **1713** BERKELEY *Hylas & Phil.* iii. Wks. 1871 I. 345 That which makes equally against two contradictory opinions can be a proof against neither. **1855** PRESCOTT *Philip II*, I. II. iii. 179 He sought out whatever could make against the orthodoxy of the new prelate. **1890** *Sat. Rev.* 8 Feb. 165/2 Figures, if you carefully select those which make for you, and as carefully ignore those which make against you, can..be made to prove anything.

†**b.** To make a hostile movement towards; to go to attack. *Obs.* (Cf. 35 b.)

1628 HOBBES *Thucyd.* I. (1629) 26 The Corcyræan's vnderstanding that they [the Corinthians] made against them [ὡς ᾔσθοντο αὐτοὺς προσπλέοντας].

77. make at ——. To approach in order to or as if to attack or seize; to make a hostile movement towards. (Cf. 35 b.) Now somewhat *arch.*

1637 R. ASHLEY tr. *Malvezzi's David Persecuted* 247 There hath beene one, that seeing no other remedy, made at the soveraignty it selfe. **1671** *Hatton Corr.* (Camden) 61 Immediately, the cowe made at him. **1698** FRYER *Acc. E. India & P.* 162, I was made at by an unsizable Snake. **1712** STEELE *Spect.* No. 450 ⁋1 All men..make at the same common thing, Mony. **1787** BEST *Angling* (ed. 2) 24 When you dip for chub, roach, and dace, move your fly very slow when you see them make at it. **1858** THOREAU *Maine W.* ii. (1869) 153 A very small black puppy rushed into the room and made at the Governor's feet. **1867** J. B. ROSE tr. *Virgil's Æneid* 261 Volscens..with his unsheathed sword Made at Euryalus. **1889** FR. A. KEMBLE *Far Away* vi. 55 He made at me with an evident intention of striking me.

78. make for ——. **a.** To operate in favour of, be favourable to; to tend to the advancement or progress of; to favour, further, aid. (Cf. 74.)

1517 TORKINGTON *Pilgr.* (1884) 59 The wynde made well for vs in ower way. **1526** *Pilgr. Perf.* (W. de W. 1531) 1 b, Ioynynge also therto the goostly exercyse and experyence of goostly fathers, as I thought them to make moost for my purpose. **1526** TINDALE *Rom.* xiv. 19 Let vs folowe tho thinges which make for peace. **1593** NASHE *Foure Lett. Conf.* Wks. (Grosart) II. 201 But, say wee should beleeue it, what doth it make for thee? **1612** BACON *Ess., Atheism* (Arb.) 332 None denie there is a God, but those for whom it maketh that there were no God. **1639** N. N. tr. *Du Bosq's Compl. Woman* I. Pref. F iv b, Is there any thing that makes more for him, then that they upbrayd him with? **1684** T. GODDARD *Plato's Demon* 273 How our Author augments, or diminisheth..the truth of things, as they make most convenient for his purpose. **1690** NORRIS *Beatitudes* (1694) I. 103 A Doctrin..such as makes neither for the Honour of God, nor for the Safety of Man. **1711** STEELE *Spect.* No. 158 ⁋1 Out of a firm Regard for Impartiality I print these Letters, let them make for me or not. **1754** RICHARDSON *Grandison* (1781) II. xxi. 219 The behaviour makes not for your honour. **1831** T. L. PEACOCK *Crotchet C.* vii. 140 Your story makes for my side of the question. **1881** STEVENSON *Virg. Puerisque* 24 Whatever makes for lounging and contentment, makes just so surely for domestic happiness. **1890** [see *make against* 76 a]. **1894** *Times* 25 May 9/5 The forces and conditions which make for sea power.

b. To proceed or direct one's course towards; to go in the direction of; also, to assail, 'go for'.

Not frequent before the 19th c.

1590 MARLOWE *Edw. II*, IV. vi, I see our soules are fleeting hence; Make for a new life, man. **1633** P. FLETCHER *Elisa* I. xli, And glorious Angels on their wings it [*sc.* a soul] taking, ..for heaven making. **1748** *Anson's Voy.* II. v. 170 One of these [ships]..made directly for us. **1791** MRS. INCHBALD *Simple Story* IV. xii. 151 Sandford,..without a word in reply, made for the door. **1831** CARLYLE *Sart. Res.* II. vi, The wounded eagle is said to make for its own eyrie. **1859** H. KINGSLEY *G. Hamlyn* xxii. (1860) 169 Don't..get frightened; make for the shore. **1874** GREEN *Short Hist.* iii. §6. 145 They had hardly landed at Dover before they made straight for London. **1878** BROWNING *La Saisiaz* 55 We made for home together. **1893** *Chamb. Jrnl.* 15 July 434/1 They will at once 'make for' each other's eyes.

†**c.** To pretend, assert. (In quots. *absol.* and in *indirect pass.*) *Obs.*

1522 MORE *De quat. noviss.* Wks. 72/2 This medicyne thoughe thou make a sowre face at it, is not so bytter as thou makeste for. **1529** —— *Dyaloge* III. Wks. 222/1 Whyther Luthers matters bee so madde as they bee made for, that shall we see hereafter.

79. make to ——. †**a.** To tend or contribute to; to be favourable or conducive to; to go to support. (Cf. 74.) *Obs.*

1528 GARDINER in Pocock *Rec. Ref.* I. li. 124 Such reasons as seemed to make to the contrary. **1561** DAUS tr. *Bullinger on Apoc.* (1573) 97 All thynges that may make to life and saluation. **1585–7** T. ROGERS *39 Art.* xix. (1625) 92 This maketh to the strengthning of vs against those Popish assertions of Viguerius. **1638** RAWLEY tr. *Bacon's Life & Death* (1651) 12 In every corruptible Body, Quantity maketh much to the Conservation of the whole. **1732** NEAL *Hist. Purit.* I. 159 Making more to seemliness..or edification.

†**b.** To be pertinent or applicable to. *Obs.*

c **1645** HOWELL *Lett.* I. I. xxxi, That Hair is but an excrementitious thing, and makes not to this purpose. **1726** LEONI tr. *Alberti's Archit.* II. 84/2 Those things which are most obvious, and make more immediately to the subject in hand.

†**c.** To go in the direction of, proceed towards.

a **1568** *Wyfe of Auchtermuchty* 114 Then vp scho gat ane mekle rung, And the gudman maid to the dur. **1600** *Disc. Gowrie Consp.* in Moyses *Mem.* (1755) 266 The court making to their horses, as his highnesse selfe was. **1602** MARSTON *Antonio's Rev.* I. i, Maria, Genoas dutchesse, makes to court. **1694** *Acc. Sev. Late Voy.* II. (1711) 20 When the Ice comes floating in too hard,..then the Ships make to the Harbours. **1780** COXE *Russ. Disc.* 192 He cut his way through the troops..and made to the banks of the Irtish.

make toward(s ——: see 35 b.

80. make unto ——. = *make to*, 79 c.

1570–6 W. LAMBARDE *Peramb. Kent* (1826) 131 Since Dover is not many myles off..let us make unto it. **1592** SHAKS. *Ven. & Ad.* 5 Sick-thoughted Venus makes amaine vnto him. **1603** DRAYTON *Heroic. Ep.* xxi. 31 Unto the Ship she makes, which she discovers.

†**81. make upon** ——. = ***make at***, 77. *Obs.*

1542 UDALL *Erasm. Apoph.* 264 b, He made vpon these pirates, whom..he tooke and subdued. **1606** G. W[OODCOCKE] *Hist. Ivstine* II. 8 The king vnderstanding.. that they made vpon him in such speedy manner, fledde for feare. **1727** *Philip Quarll* (1816) 37 Seeing themselves made upon by a pirate.

82. make with ——. †**a.** To side with, make common cause with. Of things: To tell in favour of. (Cf. 74.) *Obs.*

1559 MORWYNG *Evonym.* 250 The description following maketh with me [L. *mecum ferè facit*]. **1597** HOOKER *Eccl. Pol.* v. vii. §3 Antiquity, custom, and consent..making with that which law doth establish, are themselves most sufficient reasons to uphold the same. **1600** HOLLAND *Livy* VIII. xxxiv. 306 There made with young Fabius, and tooke his part, the majestie and countenance of the Senat [L. *stabat cum eo senatus maiestas*]. **1608** D. T. *Ess. Pol. & Mor.* 19 b, It is the nature, and propertie of Passions, euen to make those thinges make with them. *a* **1617** BAYNE *Lect.* (1634) 273 So farre as outward things make with salvation.

†**b.** To grapple with, select as one's adversary.

a **1548** HALL *Chron., Hen. VIII* 21 b, The Lorde Admirall made with the greate ship of Depe, and chased her stil. *Ibid.* 122 The vj shippes perceiuyng that, left their chace & made with the Barke of Sandwyche.

†**c.** (See sense 71.) *Obs.*

d. [tr. Yiddish *mach mit.*] To bring into operation; to use, affect; to concern oneself with. *slang* (orig. *U.S.*).

1940 J. O'HARA *Pal Joey* 131 The poor man's Bing Crosby is still making with the throat here in Chi. **1943** *Amer. Speech* XVIII. 46 'To make with the mouth', meaning 'to give the bird, to give forth a Bronx cheer'. *Ibid.*, Come, Baby, make with your hands. **1959** W. BURROUGHS *Naked Lunch* 80 A. J., surrounded and fighting against overwhelming odds, throws back his head and makes with the hog-call. **1962** L. DEIGHTON *Ipcress File* xviii. 114 Dalby had changed into a red Hawaiian shirt... 'You're making with the native costume?' **1964** 'C. E. MAINE' *Never let Up* xv. 149 Don't be a Smart Alick. Make with the alcohol. I haven't got all night. **1972** 'H. HOWARD' *Nice Day for Funeral* xi. 148 Make with the feet into your bathroom. **1972** D. LEES *Zodiac* 118 When people like Zodiac make with the dreams you have to listen. **1974** 'A. GILBERT' *Nice Little*

Killing i. 6 Make with the feet, sugar... You're embarrassing Jim. Time his place closed.

VIII. With adverbs in specialized senses.

†**83. make again.** *trans.* To make good, repair, restore. *Obs.*

c1433 in Willis & Clark *Cambridge* (1886) II. 429 That [they]..do make ayein the grete pipe of the said conduyt in wyse as was afore. 1471 CAXTON *Recuyell* (ed. Sommer) 149 The harnoys broken was made agayn and amended. 1565 COOPER *Thesaurus, Reparator*, one that repayreth or maketh agayne.

84. make away. (Now superseded in the transitive senses by *make away with*.) †**a.** *trans.* To put (a person) out of the way, put to death; also, to put an end to (a person's life). (Cf. 33.) *Obs.*

Common in 16–17th c.

1566 *Pasquine in Traunce* 58b, Saint Dominick..was treating with them for the burning of Heretiques, or how by some other deuise to make them away. 1590 MARLOWE *Edw. II*, II. ii, Why then weele haue him priuily made away. 1593 SHAKS. *2 Hen. VI*, III. i. 167 To make away my guiltlesse Life. 1621 BURTON *Anat. Mel.* III. ii. v. i. (1651) 544 Constantine Despota, made away Catharine his wife..for the love of a base Scriveners daughter. a1656 BP. HALL *Rem. Wks.* (1660) 415 Wicked harlots who..have made away their stolen birth. 1713 ADDISON *Guard.* No. 105 ¶4 What Multitude of Infants have been made away by those who brought them into the World. 1760–72 H. BROOKE *Fool of Qual.* (1809) I. 142 They would..make him away by pistol, or poison.

refl. 1581 PETTIE *Guazzo's Civ. Conv.* I. (1586) 4b, Other sortes..that haue made themselues awaie by the meanes either of water, or fire, or sword. 1654 GATAKER *Disc. Apol.* 58, I was there told by the Physician, that I must whollie forbear Preaching, unless I would wilfullie make away my self. c1684 *Roxb. Ball.* (1886) VI. 621 She, for love of the Groom, fell into Despair, and in conclusion made herself away. 1698 *Christ Exalted* §61. 50 They would make away themselves immediately, if possible.

†**b.** To destroy (a thing). *Obs.*

1566 in Peacock *Eng. Ch. Furniture* (1866) 66 A Mass book wth all such books of papistrie ar abolished made awaie and defaced. c1600 SHAKS. *Sonn.* xi, If all were minded so, the times should cease And threescore yeare would make the world away. 1650 TRAPP *Comm. Lev.* xiii. 47 Instruments of idolatrie..are to bee destroied, and made awaie.

†**c.** To alienate or transfer to another's possession; to dispose of, get rid of. *Obs.*

1580 HOLLYBAND *Treas. Fr. Tong, Alienation*, alienation or making away. 1600 J. PORY tr. *Leo's Africa* Introd. 41 Their slaues which they cannot make away for a good round price, they sell vnto the butchers. a1640 WALLER *On Friendship betw. Sacharissa & Amoret* 16 Debters..When they never mean to pay,..To some friend make all away. 1741 RICHARDSON *Pamela* II. 21 Will you, said he, on your Honour, let me see them uncurtail'd, and not offer to make them away? 1855 MILMAN *Lat. Christ.* XIV. i. (1864) IX. 15 If usurped, or its usufruct, if not the fee, fraudulently made away, it [Church property] had in many cases widely extended itself by purchase.

d. *intr.* To go away suddenly or hastily, run away; = *make off*, 89d.

1600 B. JONSON *Cynthia's Rev.* I. i, Deare sparke of beautie, make not so fast away. 1639 FULLER *Holy War* v. v. (1640) 237 If there be five to one, it is interpreted wisdome not cowardlinesse, to make away from them. 1787 'G. GAMBADO' *Acad. Horsemen* 42 His horse made away with him whilst Gimcrack was running a match. 1883 BLACK *Yolande* II. xii. 217 Then they set out for home; Duncan and the gillies making away for a sort of ford. 1891 *Cornh. Mag.* Jan. 108 The people..are making away as fast as they can.

85. make away *with*. **a.** To put out of the way; = 84a. Often *euphemistic* for: To kill.

1502 TOWNLEY in *Plumpton Corr.* (Camden) 164 There was a servant of yours, and a kynsman of myne, was myschevously made away with. 1583 STUBBES *Anat. Abus.* II. (1882) 55 For mony I am persuaded they [physicians] can make away with any whom they haue accesse vnto. 1628 tr. *Mathieu's Powerf. Fav.* 11 Tiberius had resolued to make away with Germanicus. 1756–7 tr. *Keysler's Trav.* (1760) I. 108 His relations pretend that he was made away with by poison. 1862 *Jrnl. R. Agric. Soc.* XXIII. 242 The owl nightly makes away with more mice than the very best of cats. 1886 STEVENSON *Dr. Jekyll* viii, He was made away with, eight days ago, when we heard him cry out upon the name of God.

refl. 1666–7 PEPYS *Diary* 24 Feb., It seems she..hath endeavoured to make away with herself often. 1768 GOLDSM. *Good-n. Man* I, These were the very words of Dick Doleful to me not a week before he made away with himself. 1856 READE *Never too Late* xii, He was a lunatic, and would have made away with himself anywhere.

b. To remove from its rightful place or ownership; to get rid of; to dissipate, squander (= 84c); to destroy fraudulently.

1691 tr. *Emilianne's Frauds Rom. Monks* (ed. 3) 407 It will not be difficult to conceive, how the Roman Clergy can make away with these vast Revenues they are possessed of. 1760–72 H. BROOKE *Fool of Qual.* (1809) I. 142 They would ..make away with the effects. 1781 D. WILLIAMS tr. *Voltaire's Dram. Wks.* II. 132, I will make away with my castle and dowry to support the cause. 1843 CARLYLE *Past & Pr.* II. i, 'Thirteen pence sterling', this was what the Convent got from Lackland, for all the victuals he and his had made away with. 1849 MACAULAY *Hist. Eng.* x. II. 572 He had burned the writs, made away with the seal [etc.]. 1873 *Act 36 & 37 Vict.* c. 77 §26 If any person designedly makes away with..any thing issued to him as a volunteer. 1883 KATH. S. MACQUOID *Her Sailor Love* III. VII. iv. 115 It's an ugly thing to make away with a letter. 1892 *Temple Bar* Nov. 298 Hendrik had made away with his stepbrother's money.

86. make down. a. Sc. *to make down a bed*: 'to fold down the bed-clothes, so as to make it ready for being entered' (Jam.).

1816 SCOTT *Antiq.* xxv, We'se mak ye down a bed at the lodge. a1835 HOGG *Tales & Sk.* (1837) III. 199 Betty, my dear, make down the bed.

b. *colloq.* To refashion so as to fit a smaller wearer.

1877 'S. TYTLER' *Childhood 100 Yrs. Ago* i. 19 Old clothes of their seniors carefully kept and 'made down' for their descendants. a1904 *Mod.* The eldest girl's frocks can be made down for her sisters.

87. make forth. †**a.** *trans.* To complete the preparation or equipment of. *Sc.*

1496 *Ld. Treas. Acc. Scot.* (1877) I. 261 Item, gevin be the Lard of Balgony to maik furth this coit, iij ellis of vellous. 1497 *Ibid.* 339 Item, giffin to Thom Barkar and Johne Lam to pas to Home, to mak furth the artailȝery there iiij lib. iiij s.

†**b.** To send forth. (Cf. sense 55.) *Obs.*

c1470 *Gaw. & Gol.* 120, I rede ye mak furth ane man, mekar of mude.

†**c.** To issue (a commission, debenture). *Obs.*

1640 tr. *Verdere's Rom. Rom.* III. 213 This great Monarch ..made forth Commissions. 1666 in *10th Rep. Hist. MSS. Comm.* App. v. 6 His Majestie's Auditor-Generall shall make forth debentures for what is due to the petitioner.

†**d.** *intr.* To go forward, advance, set out; (of a boat) to put out. *Obs.*

1594 KYD *Cornelia* v. 241 When Wolues..Make forth amongst the flock. 1599 SHAKS. *Hen. V*, II. iv. 5. 1601 —— *Jul. C.* v. i. 25. a1610 HEALEY *Cebes* (1636) 149 As shippes doe, that having unlaided their fraught make presently forth for a new voiage. 1625 BACON *Ess., Usury* (Arb.) 542 To prouide, that while we make forth, to that which is better, we meet not, with that which is worse. a1626 —— *New Atl.* (1900) 2 Ther made forth to us a small Boate.

88. make in. †**a.** *trans.* ? To carry in. (Cf. *make out*, 91a.) *Obs.*

a1483 *Liber Niger* in *Househ. Ord.* (1790) 25 Lett it alwey be remembered to make in the Kinges doggettes..as often as it pleseth the King the prince to come or goe.

b. *intr.* To go in towards a particular point; to intervene in an action; to join in a fray; †to strike in in a conversation; in *Hawking* (see quot. 1897).

1575 TURBERV. *Faulconrie* 161 Unhood your Hawke, to the end that when she espieth the Hearon she may flee hir: and if she do so, make in apace to succour hir. c1611 CHAPMAN *Iliad* XV. 492 While these made-in [Gr. εἰσάσθην], to spoyle his armes. 1612 DRAYTON *Poly-olb.* viii. 456 Small Marbrooke maketh-in, to her [*sc.* the Severn's] inticing Deepe. 1622 BEAUM. & FL. *Sea Voy.* I. i, We have discover'd the land, sir; pray let's make in! 1634 MASSINGER *Very Woman* v. iii, Make in, loggerhead; my son fights like a dragon. 1656 EARL MONM. tr. *Boccalini's Advts. fr. Parnass.* II. lvii. (1674) 209 To the succor whereof, all the inhabitants along the River side made in. 1828 SCOTT *F.M. Perth* xxx, During this moment of delay, Ramorney whispered to Dwining, 'Make in, knave, with some objection'. 1865 G. F. BERKELEY *Life* II. 281 It is ever a gallant gentleman who thus makes in. 1891 *Longm. Mag.* Sept. 500 The larger galleons made in at once for Corunna. 1897 *Encycl. Sport* I. 373 (Falconry) *Make in* (of the falconer), to go up to a hawk after it has killed.

89. make off. †**a.** *trans.* To dispose of. *Obs.*

a1649 WINTHROP *New Eng.* (1853) II. 15 He could not subsist here, and thereupon made off his estate.

b. *Whaling.* (See quot.)

1820 SCORESBY *Arctic Reg.* II. 304 The operation of *making-off*..consists of freeing the fat from all extraneous substances,..then cutting it into small pieces, and putting it in casks through the bung-holes.

c. *Farming.* To fatten (lambs) for the market.

1851 *Jrnl. R. Agric. Soc.* XII. II. 395 Whenever farmers make off their own flock instead of selling their lamb-hogs to feeders, they choose a small breed. 1852 *Ibid.* XIII. I. 60 The lambs are..made off fat, early in the summer. 1868 *Ibid.* Ser. II. IV. II. 264 No store stock..is ever sold, everything being made off for the butcher.

d. *intr.* To depart or leave a place suddenly, often with a disparaging implication; to hasten or run away; to decamp, 'bolt'.

1709 STEELE *Tatler* No. 85 ¶5 My Sister took this Occasion to make off. 1787 'G. GAMBADO' *Acad. Horsemen* (1809) 29 Should your horse prove, what is properly termed too many for you, and make off. 1805 *Log of H.M.S. Belleisle* 21 Oct. in Nicolas *Disp. Nelson* (1846) VII. 164 *note*, Several of the Enemy's ships making off to leeward. 1847 MARRYAT *Childr. N. Forest* xi, [He] perceived that the bull had not made off with the rest of the cattle. 1889 G. GISSING *Nether World* I. xii. 272 He..made off at a run.

e. ***to make off with***: to decamp with (something) in one's possession. Also, ***to make off with oneself*** = d.

1820 J. GIFFORD *Compl. Eng. Lawyer* II. xiii. 216 Although the thief do not quite make off with them. 1856 J. H. NEWMAN *Callista* xxviii. 249 He was quite easy about Agellius, who had, as he considered, successfully made off with himself. 1865 DICKENS *Mut. Fr.* III. vii, Mr. Wegg had seen the minion surreptitiously making off with that bottle. 1890 *Standard* 14 Apr. 2/6 The girl had made off with her employer's money.

90. make on. a. *trans.* To make (a fire). *dial.*

1634 RUTHERFORD *Lett.* (1862) I. 110 The Lord is making on a fire in Jerusalem. 1777 SIR M. HUNTER *Jrnl.* (1894) 26 We had got..a fire made on in our little room. 1885 HOWELLS *Silas Lapham* (1891) I. 65 I'll be the death of that darkey..if he don't stop making on such a fire. 1893 *Illustr. Lond. News* Christm. No. 23/2 To 'make on' a good fire at nightfall.

b. *intr.* To go forward, proceed; to hasten on.

1608 *Yorksh. Trag.* I. viii. 214 Up, up and struggle to thy horse; make on. 1622 BACON *Hen. VII* 33 The Earle of Lincolne..resolued to make on where the King was, and to giue him battaile. a1677 BARROW *Serm.* Wks. 1716 I. 2 He that knows his way..makes on merrily and carelessly..to his journey's end. 1719 DE FOE *Crusoe* I. iii, We made on to the southward. 1849 M. ARNOLD *Sick King Bokhara*, Send him away, Sirs, and make on. 1890 *Graphic* Summer No. 24/2 He made on in his headlong flight.

91. make out. †**a.** *trans.* In various physical senses: (*a*) tr. L. *exstruere*, to build up; (*b*) to take or carry out (cf. *make in*, 88a); (*c*) to send out (cf. sense 55); (*d*) to throw out (cards) from one's hand = *lay out* (LAY *v.*[1] 56k). *Obs.*

1382 WYCLIF *Prov.* xiv. 1 The wise womman bildeth vp hir hous; the vnwise the maad out [Vulg. *exstructam*]..shal destroȝe. a1483 *Liber Niger* in *Househ. Ord.* (1790) 71 Noe yoman of this office..to bere or make oute of this office any breade but by knowledge of the brevour. 1560 DAUS tr. *Sleidane's Comm.* 109 He fel into the lappes of our horsemen, which were made out [L. *fuerant emissi*] to kepe hym from the spoyle. 1568 GRAFTON *Chron.* I. 142 The Londoners hearing of their doings, made out a certaine number of men of armes, who..put the Danes from that Tower. 1603 HOLLAND *Plutarch's Mor.* 343 He..made out certaine pinnaces..for to observe what..landing places there were. 1680 COTTON *Compl. Gamester* viii. (ed. 2) 76 He that deals makes out the best Cards he can for his Crib, and the other the worst.

b. To draw up (a list, a document, etc.); to make a draft of; to write out (a bill, cheque, etc.).

1465 MARG. PASTON in *P. Lett.* II. 218 They have mad oute bothe warantes and *supersedias*. 1472–3 *Rolls of Parlt.* VI. 42/1 So alwey that every of the seid Writtes be made oute xx daies or more, afore the seid day of apparaunce lymyted. 1770 P. BURTON *Pract. Crt. Excheq.* 18 The Inquiry is made out by the Clerk in Court, who pays only Two Shillings to the Master for signing, &c. 1793 SMEATON *Edystone L.* §278, I was myself forming and making out the necessary designs for..the balcony. 1801 tr. *Gabrielli's Myst. Husb.* I. 125 His Lordship..inquired whether he had paid the bill. 'It is being made out, I am informed, Sir.' 1825 *New Monthly Mag.* XVI. 557 The Duke had obliged the Duchess to receive Lady Denham as one of her ladies of the bedchamber; but just before her appointment was made out, she died. 1885 MRS. C. L. PIRKIS *Lady Lovelace* I. xvi. 237 The cheque which I had made out. 1893 *Law Times* XCV. 34/2 The accounts generally took some three or four weeks to make out.

c. (*a*) To succeed in accomplishing; to effect, achieve. Now *Sc.* Also *absol.* in certain games: To make the score prescribed by the rules as bringing the game to an end.

1535 COVERDALE *Ecclus.* xxxviii. 28 He hath set his minde there vpon, that he wyll make out his worke. 1634 MASSINGER *Very Woman* III. v, Now she is at a cold scent. Make out your doubles, Mistress. O well hunted, That's she. 1680 COTTON *Compl. Gamester* (ed. 2) 89 And if one and thirty be not made, then he that play'd last and is nearest one and thirty without making out, must set up one. 1706 DE FOE *Jure Div.* I. 17 *note*, To implore the Gods that he might never enter that City, which they foresaw he would act the Fury in, and fill it with Blood and Slaughter, which he effectually made out. 1774 KAMES *Hist. Man* II. xi. II. 65 People there [in a populous city] seldom make out the usual time of life. 1824 MISS FERRIER *Inher.* xxiv, I shall make out my visit to you yet. 1827 *Examiner* 246/1 Harley, as too frequently happens to this mercurial comedian, has to make out his own part of a roguish innkeeper as well as he is able. 1840 CARLYLE *Heroes* v. (1858) 309 Byron, born rich and noble, made-out even less than Burns, poor and plebeian.

(*b*) To manage, make shift, *to do* something. Also *absol.* to make shift, get along; to succeed, thrive; to get on (well, badly). Also ***to make it out***.

1609 JONSON *Silent Woman* v. i, It is the price and estimation of your vertue only, that hath embarqu'd mee to this adventure; and I could not but make out to tell you. 1776 ABIGAIL ADAMS in *Fam. Lett.* (1876) 180, I would not have you anxious about me. I make out better than I did. 1776 J. ADAMS *ibid.* 231 Amidst these interruptions, how shall I make out to write a letter? 1807 P. GASS *Jrnl.* 92 We ..made out to get enough of drift wood to cook with. 1809 W. IRVING *Knickerb.* (1861) 42 She made out to accomplish her voyage in a very few months, and came to anchor at the mouth of the Hudson. 1820 —— in *Life & Lett.* (1864) II. 30, I wish you would..let me know..how you and Murray make out together. 1851 HAWTHORNE in *N. Hawthorne & Wife* (1885) I. 396 To whom is Dora married, and how is she making out? 1861 DICKENS *Gt. Expect.* xxi, I am rather bare here, but I hope you'll be able to make out tolerably well till Monday. 1861 W. COLLINS *Tom Tiddler's Ground* iv, in *All Year Round* Extra Christmas No., 12 Dec. 22/1 They were artisans and farm-labourers who couldn't make it out in the old country. 1891 *Harper's Mag.* Mar. 574/1, 'I don't believe you will be satisfied in heaven; you will find it too monotonous'. 'Oh, I shall make out, I'm sure'. 1894 *Outing* (U.S.) XXIV. 253/2, I have made out to sleep with tolerable comfort in a cave. 1916 'BOYD CABLE' *Action Front* 7, I took a fancy to seein' how the engines made out under war conditions. 1931 W. G. MCADOO *Crowded Yrs.* v. 55 Without my wife's..help I could not have made out at all. 1932 WODEHOUSE *Hot Water* x. 170 'How did you make out?' 'Oke. I'm in the Château.' 1935 M. M. ATWATER *Murder in Midsummer* vii. 64 Uncle Will can go to hell; we'll make out somehow. 1939 D. PARKER *Here Lies* 116 With that big yard and all, I think we'll make out all right. 1942 J. DILL in W. S. Churchill *Second World War* (1951) IV. II. xxv. 397 Leaving us with limited American assistance to make out as best we can against Germany. 1951 E. PAUL *Springtime in Paris* ii. 37 We made out all right, with a hare paté, onion soup, a rare sirloin steak.., a slice of Port Salut, [etc.]. 1959 *Observer* 17 May 1/1 Whitsun seemed a good occasion to learn how Shakespeare and tourism were making out. 1965 *Listener* 16 Sept. 433/3 Sibelius might not have made out very well as an opera composer had he chosen to do so. 1966 BEREITER & ENGELMANN *Teaching Disadvantaged Children* i. 2 How do you think they'll make out there?

(*c*) *spec.* To gain sexual satisfaction; to have sexual intercourse (*with*). *slang* (orig. *U.S.*). Cf. MAKING *vbl. sb.*[1] 10b.

1939 I. Baird *Waste Heritage* vii. 99 Oh, say, how'd you make out with Hazel? 1961 *Times* 27 Apr. 17/2 The detailed accounts of how he 'made out' sexually and emotionally with some sixteen different girls. 1962 *Amer. Speech* XXXVII. 39 When I was young, if one 'made out', his accomplishment was a good deal more total than was implied by either *to neck* or *to pet*, or both.

d. †To compensate (a lack, defect, disadvantage); to supply (what is wanting); to supply the deficiencies of, to eke out. *Obs.* Also *intr.* (? rare) to make up, compensate *for*.

1629 Earle *Microcosm., Insolent Man* (Arb.) 85 Such men are of no merit at all: but make out in pride what they want in worth. 1642 Sir T. Browne *Relig. Med.* i. (1896) 19 Our wills must be our performances, and our intents make out our Actions. 1649 Milton *Eikon.* xxiv. 196 One mans defects cannot be made out..by another mans abilities. 1665 Dryden *Ind. Emp.* iv. i. (1668) 39 Make out the rest,—I am disorder'd so I know not farther what to say or do:—But answer me to what you think I meant. 1699 T. Brown in R. L'Estrange *Erasm. Colloq.* 42 And if such a Disaster happen'd to him, he did not fail to make it out one way or other at Home. 1700 Tyrrell *Hist. Eng.* II. 847 When the Lyon's Skin alone would not serve turn, he knew how to make it out with that of the Fox. 1709–10 Steele *Tatler* No. 128 ¶5 What I want in Length, I make out in Breadth. 1801 tr. *Gabrielli's Myst. Husb.* III. 104 [She] only lamented she had not something better to offer them, but promised to make it out at dinner. 1850 L. Hunt in *Tait's Mag.* XVII. 570/2 Conscious of not having all the strength he wished, he endeavoured to make out for it by violence and pretension. 1891 *Leeds Merc.* 3 Oct. 3/7 [They] are becoming listless and indifferent, supposing that someone will make out for them.

†**e.** Of an item in a series: To complete (a certain total); also, of several items, to amount collectively to. *Obs.*

1535 Coverdale *Ezek.* i. 2 The fifth daye off the Moneth made out the fyfth yeare off kynge Ioachims captiuyte. 1571–2 *Reg. Privy Council Scot.* Ser. i. II. 112 The sowme of fyve hundrith and fifty merkis, with the thrid of the provestrie of Methven, makand out in the haill V^m merkis.

f. To make complete; to get together with difficulty or by degrees.

1791 Burke *App. Whigs* Wks. VI. 48 They..must make out a scanty subsistence with the labour of their hands. 1828–32 Webster s.v., He promised to pay, but was not able to make out the money or the whole sum. 1861 Dickens *Gt. Expect.* xxxvii, He by little and little made out this elegant and beautiful property. 1879 M. Pattison *Milton* xii. 162 Adding to them, with a view to make out a volume, his college exercises.

g. To fill up or while away (the time) with some occupation. ? *Obs.*

1809 Malkin *Gil Blas* iii. vi. ¶1 To make the most of the precious moments, and..to make out the time agreeably. 1813 Jane Austen *Lett.* (1884) II. 196 We were obliged to saunter about anywhere..to make out the time. 1849 Alb. Smith *Pottleton Leg.* (repr.) 76 To doze, or otherwise make out the time, until the first train went back.

h. To represent or delineate clearly or in detail; now only in *Art.* †Also of things: To form the figure of (*obs.*).

1646 Sir T. Browne *Pseud. Ep.* iii. xxiv. 170 Hippopotamus..so little resembleth an horse, that..in all, except the feet, it better makes out a swine. 1647 Saltmarsh *Spark. Glory* (1847) 127 God..would make out himself in an image in this Creation. 1674 N. Fairfax *Bulk & Selv.* 117 It may be objected, That a wheel of manifold rims whirl'd upon its axletree, would make out uneven bows of circles. 1784 J. Barry in *Lect. Paint.* v. (1848) 179 All the parts of objects exposed to the light..appear more made out and determined, than the parts in shadow. 1825 *New Monthly Mag.* XV. 534 Its dumb show is very eloquent and impressive; its story is fully made out to the eye. 1862 Thornbury *Turner* I. 199 The foliage of the ash-trees in the foreground is not at all made out, but is washed in..with hardly any details. 1875 Tyrwhitt *Handbk. Pict. Art* (ed. 2) 194 Proceed to make out the two distant hills by putting in quick triangular touches. *Ibid.*, That want is expressed by the words 'making out'. That is to say, you want additional facts, principally of form.

i. To establish by evidence, argument, or investigation; to demonstrate, prove. Also *colloq.* esp. in ***how do you make that out?*** = By what process do you arrive at that conclusion? Also with clause as obj.

1658 Sir T. Browne *Hydriot.* i. ¶5 If it could be made out that Adam was buried near Damascus. 1660 tr. *Amyraldus' Treat. conc. Relig.* ii. iii. 197 They are..at a loss..to make out whence they learn't that God is powerful. 1662 Stillingfl. *Orig. Sacr.* iii. iv. §13 What they only touch at, we shall endeavour to make out more at large. 1664 Power *Exp. Philos.* i. 29 That all Vegetables have a constant perspiration, the continual dispersion of their odour makes out. 1794 Paley *Evid.* ii. vi. §36 (1817) 165 That in truth it was so, is made out by a variety of examples which the writings of Josephus furnish. 1803 *Pic Nic* No. 4 (1806) I. 144 How do these gentlemen make out their case? 1883 *Law Rep. 11 Q. Bench Div.* 597 A subordinate judge is liable to an action for slander, if malice is clearly made out. 1887 L. Carroll *Game of Logic* iv. 93 'That lets me into a little fact about you, you know!' 'Why, how do you make that out? You never heard me play the organ?' 1892 *Sat. Rev.* 8 Oct. 419/2 It would be easy to make out a strong case for the contention.

j. To claim to have proved, or to try to prove (something to be true); to make to appear, to represent, pretend. With clause as obj., or with obj. and complement, or *inf.*

1658–9 *Burton's Diary* (1828) IV. 43 There is a Petition in some person's hands touching this business. They make it out that their right was in the time of Henry VI. 1832 *Examiner* 17/2 What, Sir, would you make me out a Radical? 1855 Prescott *Philip II*, iv. (1857) 65 Making him out..as much of an Englishman as possible. 1861 Mrs. H. Wood *East Lynne* iii. xiii, It seems they want to make out now that Dick never murdered Hallijohn. 1872 Butler *Erewhon* viii. 68, I certainly did not make myself out to be any better than I was. 1873 Black *Pr. Thule* xi. 177 She is not nearly so soft as she tries to make out. 1891 *Spectator* 30 May, Mr. Hutton was certainly careless as to figures, though not so careless as Dr. Abbott makes out. 1902 A. E. W. Mason *Four Feathers* xiv. 133, 'I was not thinking of that', Ethne exclaimed, 'when I asked why we must wait. That makes me out most selfish'.

k. To find out the meaning of; to discover the drift of; to arrive at an understanding of; to interpret for oneself; to decipher, succeed in reading; †to understand or 'take' (an author) in a particular way (*obs.*); to understand the behaviour of (a person). Also (with clause or obj. and inf.), to discover, find out.

1646 Sir T. Browne *Pseud. Ep.* vi. i. 277 By this Chronology are many Greeke authors to be understood; and thus is Martinus Crusius to be made out, when [etc.]. 1688 Boyle *Final Causes Nat. Things* iv. 141 To suppose Him to have made such things for a particular end, which we cannot make out to be in any considerable measure worthy of his wisdom. 1709 Felton *Dissert. Classicks* (1718) 145 Your Antiquaries make out the most ancient Medals from a letter and some Pieces of Letters,..with great Difficulty to be discerned upon the Face or Reverse. 1773 Goldsm. *She Stoops to Conq.* iv. (Globe) 669/1, I would not lose the rest of it [*sc.* a letter] for a guinea. Here, mother, do you make it out. 1794 'G. Gambado' *Ann. Horsemen* xvii. (1809) 135 His shouts (which, from what I can make out from the Girl's imitations of them, much resembled the war-hoops of the Indians). 1859 Jephson *Brittany* iii. 35 He could not make out what the police wanted. 1863 Bagehot *Biog. Stud.* 208 To those who had an opportunity of accurately observing Sir George Lewis there was no difficulty in making him out. 1867 Freeman *Norm. Conq.* (1876) I. vi. 528 As far as it is possible to make out anything from the tangled mazes of history and legend. 1875 Jowett *Plato* (ed. 2) I. 193, I made out, as I thought, that he was a stranger with whom you were talking. 1883 Sir N. Lindley in *Law Times Rep.* (1884) XLIX. 727/1 They are clearly inviting the public to come and buy, both wholesale and retail, as far as I can make out.

l. To discern or discover visually; to succeed in perceiving or identifying (something not easily visible). Also with clause as obj., and with obj. and inf. or complement. (Cf. 22.)

1754 Richardson *Grandison* (1776) VI. 193, I always think when I see those badgerly virgins fond of a parrot,..or a lap dog, that their imagination makes out husband and children in their animals. 1805 Sir E. Berry 13 Oct. in Nicolas *Disp. Nelson* (1846) VII. 117 *note*, The ship that bore down to us I soon made out to be a Three-decker. 1847 Marryat *Childr. N. Forest* xi, At last he thought that he could make out a human figure lying at the bottom [of the pit]. 1872 Black *Adv. Phaeton* xxx. 406 Minute dots that you can make out to be sheep. 1889 Doyle *Micah Clarke* xxxi. 325 By the aid of a glass I was able to make out their lines and camp. 1891 *Temple Bar* Dec. 581 In the darkness he made out a shed by the path.

m. *intr.* To go, start, or sally forth; to get away, to escape. ? Now only *dial.*

1558 Phaer *Æneid* iv. (1573) L ij b, Set sailes aloft, make out with ores, in ships, in boates, in frames. c1583 Hayes in *Hakluyt's Voy.* (1589) 692 Making out from this danger, we sownded one while seuen fathome, then fiue fathome, then [etc.]... At last we recouered..in some despaire, to sea roome enough. 1601 Shaks. *Twel. N.* ii. v. 65 Seauen of my people with an obedient start, make out for him. a1632 T. Taylor *God's Judgem.* i. ii. xviii. (1642) 240 The Lion made out for his prey. a1703 Burkitt *On N.T., Luke* ii. 20 A gracious soul no sooner hears where Christ is, but instantly makes out after him. 1847 L. Hunt *Men, Women, & B.* I. ix. 153 Poor Abbott..rushes forth for the second time, and makes out as fast as he can for a third coffee-house. 1884 'R. Boldrewood' *Melb. Memories* xxii. 157 The ruder portion of the herd 'made out' that way.

n. To extend in a particular direction or for a specified distance. (Cf. 73 b.) *rare.*

1743 Pococke *Descr. of East* I. 25 From the north end..the foot of the hill makes out to the river. 1860 *Merc. Marine Mag.* VII. 198 At the N. W. end of San Nicolas heavy breakers make out 2½ miles.

92. make over. **a.** *trans.* To hand over (*properly*, by a formal agreement); to transfer the possession of (a thing) from oneself *to* another.

1546 O. Johnson in Ellis *Orig. Lett.* Ser. ii. II. 178 When she doeth intend to occupie her monney she will lett me knowe for to write to Robert Androwe to make it over. 1651 Baxter *Inf. Bapt.* 13 The mercies that Christ hath purchased for their Children, and made over to them. 1762–71 H. Walpole *Vertue's Anecd. Paint.* (1786) III. 270 Being persuaded to make it [a fortune] over to his son. 1879 M. J. Guest *Lect. Hist. Eng.* xxi. 206 He made over the whole free kingdom of England to the Pope. 1883 Black *Yolande* III. xiii. 249 It is all settled now, and the land made over to its rightful possessor. 1893 Forbes-Mitchell *Remin. Gt. Mutiny* 180 My prisoner had no sooner been made over to me than [etc.].

†**b.** *spec.* 'To settle in the hands of trustees' (J.); also *absol.* *Obs.*

1650 May *Old Couple* iv. (1658) 33 All your widowes of Aldermen, that marry Lords, of late, Make over their estates, and by that meanes, Retaine a power to curbe their lordly husbands. 1678 Butler *Hud.* iii. i. 670 And Widows, who have try'd one Lover, Trust none again, 'till th'have made over. *Ibid.* 1193.

†**c.** To remove from one place to another. *Obs.*

1713 Addison *Guard.* No. 121 ¶5 My waist..is reduced to the depth of four inches by what I have already made over to my neck.

d. To remake, refashion.

1698 Collier *Ess. Mor. Subj.* ii. (1703) 59 Age and youth can never be made over or adjusted. Nothing but time can take away years or give them. 1883 Howells *Woman's Reason* xii. II. 4 She made over all her bonnets and dresses. 1884 Lowell *Democr.*, etc. (1887) 26 We have taken from Europe..the most turbulent of her people, and have made them over into good citizens. 1899 R. W. Trine *In Tune with the Infinite* (1903) 50 That the entire human structure can be completely changed, made over, within a period of less than one year. 1903 H. James *Ambassadors* viii. 111 The new quantity was represented by the fact that Chad had been made over. 1928 R. Macaulay *Keeping Up Appearances* ix. 94 Feeling..in need of restoration, she..had a small port. That's better, she agreed with herself..makes you feel quite made over. 1936 'J. Tey' *Shilling for Candles* xvi. 180 She..never recognized Chris... She'd heard that they made you over in Hollywood. Perhaps that was it. 1958 *Technology* Jan. 375/4 Had we better do what we can to 'make over' the traditional grammar school for an age of scientific industry? 1972 *Daily Tel.* (Colour Suppl.) 8 Sept. 26/1 A sewing machine stands on a table with a limp-looking dress, in the process of being 'made over', hanging on a nearby chair.

†**e.** *intr.* = *come over* (come 70 a). *Obs.*

1488 *Paston Lett.* III. 344 And they had nott seylyd not paste vj. leges butt they aspied a Frencheman, and the Frencheman mad over to them.

†**93. make through.** *intr.* To go through. *Obs.*

1606 Marston *Sophonisba* ii. ii. Wks. 1856 I. 172 Then amaine Make through to Scipio; he yields safe abodes. 1628 Rutherford *Lett.* (1862) I. 42, I doubt not but that, if hell were betwixt you and Christ, as a river which ye behoved to cross ere you could come at Him, but ye would willingly put in your foot and make through to be at Him. 1825–80 Jamieson, *To Mak throw wi'*, to finish, to come to a conclusion, after surmounting all difficulties; as, 'He maid throw wi' his sermon after an unco pingle'.

†**94. make to.** *intr.* To set to work. *Sc. Obs.*

1563 Winȝet *Wks.* (1890) II. 4 Quhilkis being done..makis he to without delay. 1570 *Satir. Poems Reform.* xii. 91 First on the feildis mak schortly to. 1572 *Ibid.* xxxi. 12 How sone I vnderstude the cace, I maid me to frahand. a1662 R. Baillie *Lett.* (1775) II. 36 (Jam.) Sundry other shires are making to.

†**95. make together.** *trans.* To compound.

1535 Coverdale *Ecclus.* xlix. 1 Whan the Apotecary maketh many precious swete smellynge thinges together.

96. make up. †**a.** *trans.* To build, erect (a tower, city, etc.). *Obs.*

c1400 *Destr. Troy* 275 Argus made vp a mekyll ship. c1400 *Rom. Rose* 7060 And he couthe thurgh his sleight Do maken up a tour of height. c1450 *Merlin* 39 Than comaunded Vortiger the werkemen to make vp the toure the strengest that myght be devised. 1490 Caxton *Eneydos* xvi. 63 He fonde eneas..all ocupyed for to make vp the cytee of cartage.

†**b.** To build up (a bank, etc.) again where it has fallen away; to repair (an earthwork, fence, etc.) by filling up gaps. *Obs.*

1468 *Peebles Charters* etc. (1872) 158 Mychell of Forest sall mak wp hys syd dyk fra his bern to the yet wythin viij dayis. 1553 Wriothesley *Chron.* (Camden) II. 102 The worke..was begun to be made up agayn with breke. 1576 in W. H. Turner *Select. Rec. Oxford* 385 By the default of the..Cytie in not meakinge up the..bancks. 1585 T. Washington tr. *Nicholay's Voy.* I. xix. 22 b, That whiche was beaten downe..the assieged made vp againe. 1603 Knolles *Hist. Turks* (1621) 863 The Christians in the meane time made up their breaches with earth, [etc.] 1611 Bible *Ezek.* xiii. 5 Yee haue not gone vp into the gaps, neither made vp the hedge for the house of Israel.

c. To supply (deficiencies); to make complete. (*a*) To fill up what is wanting to; to supply the deficiencies of; to complete (a given number, quantity, period, etc.). †Also pass. ***to be made up***, to be completed in form or growth.

a1568 Ascham *Scholem.* ii. (Arb.) 138 Now to know, what Author doth medle onelie with some one..member of eloquence, and who doth perfitelie make vp the whole bodie. 1594 Hooker *Eccl. Pol.* i. xiv. §2 Before the full and complete measure of things necessarie be made vp. *Ibid.* ii. viii. §5 Whatsoeuer to make vp the doctrine of mans saluation is added, as in supply of the scriptures vnsufficiencie, we reiect it. 1579 Beard *Theatre God's Judgem.* (1612) 490 [He] passing that night in great distresse, the next day made vp his wicked and miserable end. 1594 Shaks. *Rich. III*, i. i. 21 Sent before my time Into this breathing World, scarse halfe made vp. 1611 —— *Cymb.* iv. ii. 109 Being scarse made vp, I meane to man. 1612 Bacon *Ess., Beauty* (Arb.) 212 For no youth can be comely, but by pardon, and considering the youth, as to make vp the comlinesse. 1629 Milton *Hymn Nativ.* xiii, And with your ninefold harmony Make up full consort to th' Angelike symphony. 1641 J. Jackson *True Evang. T.* ii. 137 Lastly, I will make up the Decade with a meaner person,..Elizabeth Folks. 1651 *Life Father Sarpi* (1676) 28 Not only from being verst, but consummate, and made up in all sorts of Learning. 1656 Cowley *Davideis* i. Note 14 There are some Places in him [Virgil], which I dare almost swear have been made up..by the putid Officiousness of some Grammarians. 1793 *Regal Rambler* 47 Paper is thrown in to make up the weight. 1879 'Cavendish' *Card Essays*, etc. 189 When people are asked to make up a rubber. 1888 J. Payn *Myst. Mirbridge* I. v. 84 He will make up our game of lawn tennis..three is always an awkward number. 1892 *Monthly Packet* May 575 They..decided to sell the cow in order to make up the rent. 1894 R. Bridges *Feast of Bacchus* i. 234 'Twill make our numbers up.

(*b*) †To bring up to (a given number, expressed by numeral compl.) (*obs.*). Also, to raise (a sum) *to* a larger sum.

1629 J. Cole *Of Death* 195 His deceased children were alive still in heaven; and the ten more given him here, made them up twenty. 1719 De Foe *Crusoe* (1840) II. vi. 124 At first, I distributed linen sufficient to make every one of them four shirts; and, at the Spaniard's request, afterwards made them up six. 1890 *Illustr. Lond. News* 28 June 814/3 He makes up the income of his wife..to £2000 per annum.

(*c*) To make good, to compensate for (something that is wanting); to supply (a deficiency). Phrases, ***to make up (lost) ground, leeway***.

1538 ELYOT *Dict., Suppleo*..To make vp that whiche lacketh. 1660 INGELO *Bentiv. & Ur.* I. (1682) 27 This he performed with such accurate Skill, that it made up whatsoever he wanted of Force. 1688 BURNET *Lett. Pres. St. Italy* 122 The Clergy..had neither learning nor vertue but made up all Defects by a slavish Obsequiousness. 1711 ADDISON *Spect.* No. 127 ⁋2 What they have lost in Height they make up in Breadth. 1766 GOLDSM. *Vic. W.* iv, What the conversation wanted in wit was made up in laughter. 1812 L. M. HAWKINS *C'tess & Gertr.* IV. lxviii. 25 [The Almighty] never forgets us; it's all made up to us one time or the other. 1837 *Ord. & Reg. Harvard Univ.* 10 Recitations omitted may be made up with the assent of the Instructer, at any time within the term, in which they occur. 1862 *Temple Bar* VI. 397 Should the confessor order him to make up the injury done to the treasury? 1882 EDNA LYALL *Donovan* xlii, He had large arrears of sleep to make up. 1890 *Sat. Rev.* 31 May 668/2 After getting a very indifferent start, she made up ground at the Bushes. 1890 *Illustr. Sport. & Dram. News* 10 May 279/2 The huntsman..is now rapidly making up lost ground.

(*d*) *intr.* To compensate *for*, atone *for*.

1711 STEELE *Spect.* No. 33 ⁋1 Daphne..found her self obliged to acquire some Accomplishments to make up for the want of those Attractions. 1774 FOOTE *Cozeners* III. ii. (1778) 70 You may renew hostilities and make up for lost time, as soon as you are out of the house. 1856 J. H. NEWMAN *Callista* (1885) 274 If we have been wanting in due consideration for him, we now trust to make up for it. 1859 JEPHSON *Brittany* ii. 16 A lovely view made up to me for the sights and smells. 1879 DOWDEN *Southey* v. 132 Southey made up in weight for what was wanting in measure. 1889 MRS. E. KENNARD *Landing a Prize* I. xi. 191 She does not attempt to make up for lost ground.

d. *trans.* To fill up (an opening or gap); to stop up (a hole or passage); to shut or fasten up (a door, a house). Now chiefly *dial.*

1582 in W. H. TURNER *Select. Rec. Oxford* 435 Nayles and woorkmanshippe to make uppe the hole in the walle. 1603 B. JONSON *Sejanus* I. ii, We must make up our eares 'gainst these assaults Of charming tongues. 1655 STANLEY *Hist. Philos.* (1687) 12/2 Some say that the old channel was quite made up. 1719 DE FOE *Crusoe* I. iv, I made up the entrance, which till now I had left open. 1841 TRENCH *Parables* (1893) 334 The house is made up for the night, barred and bolted. 1886 *Chesh. Gloss., Make up*..(3) to repair, to close up. 'You mun mak yon gap up'. 1886 *S. W. Linc. Gloss.* s.v.,'The silt soon maks up the pipes'. 1889 *N. W. Linc. Gloss., Make up.* (1) To fasten up. To shut up. 1891 *Law Times* XC. 395/1 The hind proceeded to make up the gap by placing wooden rails on the side next the glebe land.

e. †To close up (a letter); to wrap up (an article); to put together (a parcel) *of* goods.

1626 MASSINGER *Rom. Actor* IV. i, I brib'd the boy that did conuey the letter, And, hauing perus'd it, made it vp againe. 1709 *Brit. Apollo* II. No. 70. 3/2 [Paper] to make up Soap in. 1823 *Examiner* 802/2, I was making up a parcel. 1832 *Ibid.* 617/1 Mails will be made up at the Post-office for..Lisbon every Tuesday. 1889 STEVENSON *Master of B.* x. 277 Making up his portmanteau for a voyage.

f. To put together, construct, compound.

(*a*) To put together a substance or material into a particular form: the obj. being either the word denoting the substance or that denoting the form.

1530 PALSGR. 632/1 Nowe that I have made up my cockes I wyll carye in as fast as I can. 1727 ARBUTHNOT *Tables Anc. Coins* etc. 304 A Catapotium is a Medicine that is..most commonly made up in Pills. 1852 *Jrnl. R. Agric. Soc.* XIII. I. 40 If proper care is taken in 'making up' the butter formed from cream slightly acescent. 1859 *Ibid.* XX. I. 45 The hay is sometimes made up into bundles. 1861 *Temple Bar* III. 250 Some curious tricks of the trade are practised in making up false hair. *Ibid.* 254 The best *coiffeurs*..having a secret of making up a lady's head to last for three months.

(*b*) To make (a garment, etc.) by fitting and sewing pieces of material cut out for the purpose; also, to fit together (pieces of material) to form a garment, etc.; to make (cloth) into clothing.

1672 in Willis & Clark *Cambridge* (1886) II. 295 For making up ye Sarcenet Curtain. 1672 VILLIERS (Dk. Buckhm.) *Rehearsal* III. i. (Arb.) 69 [A tailor says] If I can't make up all the work I cut out, I shan't want Journey-men to help me. 1709 *Lond. Gaz.* No. 4577/4 A wrought Gown stitch'd upon East-India Dimety,..not..made up. 1789 MRS. PIOZZI *Journ. France* I. 184 A skeleton wire upon the head, such as we use to make up hats. 1789 WOLCOT (P. Pindar) *Expost. Odes* xi, Like mercers had variety of stuff For such whose turn it was to be made up. 1855 MRS. CARLYLE *Lett.* II. 268 Took the black silk..to Catchpool..that it might be made up. 1863 EARL LYTTON *Ring of Amasis* vii. (1890) 135 Mother was making up some bandages for his hand. 1879 M. J. GUEST *Lect. Hist. Eng.* xxx. 301 They pay twenty-five times as much for making up the dress as the cloth cost at first.

(*c*) quasi-*passive*. To admit of being made up.

1861 MRS. H. WOOD *E. Lynne* II. vii, Her striped silk, turned, will make up as handsome as ever. 1892 *Sat. Rev.* 10 Dec. 682/1 It is a modest, unobtrusive stone, and makes up so well with diamonds, that [etc.].

(*d*) *trans.* To compound (a substance, medicine, etc.) of different ingredients; to mix (dough).

1649 CULPEPPER (*title*) Physical Directory; a Translation of the Dispensatory..imposed upon all the Apothecaries of England to make up their Medicines by. 1699 EVELYN *Acetaria* 18 Omlets, made up with Cream. 1718 *Freethinker* No. 97 ⁋8, I make up my own Medicines. 1824 *Examiner* 10/1 [She] is in the habit of making up medicines for the poor. 1829 *Ibid.* 589/2 The prescription was made up by Mr. Snow's assistant. 1844 *Jrnl. R. Agric. Soc.* V. I. 3 A description of flour called 'cowens,' used by the bakers for making up their dough. 1852 MRS. STOWE *Uncle Tom's C.* xiii. 115 Rachel now took down a snowy moulding-board, and..proceeded quietly to make up some biscuits. 1883 HOWELLS *Woman's Reason* xi. I. 216 I'll give you a tonic. Make you up a bottle and send it to you.

(*e*) To get together, collect (a company, a sum of money); to furnish by contributions from different sources.

1593 SHAKS. *2 Hen. VI*, II. i. 40 Make up no factious numbers for the matter. 1654 tr. *Scudery's Curia Pol.* 106 To imbezell the treasure of the State, and so make up Bankes for private uses. 1691 LOCKE *Consid. Lower. Interest* (1692) 92 How will the Farmer be able to make up his Rent at Quarter Day? *c* 1718 PRIOR *Ladle* 158 The miser must make up his plum. 1837 *Penny Cycl.* IX. 435/1 Nor was this an expensive company made up for the new house; for all, or nearly, all of the performers..had belonged to the old one. 1846 C. ST. JOHN *Wild Sports Highl.* 27 It requires quick shooting and good walking to make up a handsome bag. 1855 MACAULAY *Hist. Eng.* xv. III. 547 To contribute of their substance in order to make up a purse for Jeffreys. 1880 GOLDW. SMITH *Cowper* ii. 22 His relations..combined to make up a little income for him. 1887 BARING-GOULD *Gaverocks* II. xxv. 59 We used to make up parties to read plays, each taking a part.

(*f*) *Printing.* To arrange into columns or pages.

1771 LUCKOMBE *Printing* 380 Having made up the Head of the first page, we cut it off by a rule. *Ibid.*, The first page being made up to the length of the number of lines of which it is to consist. 1896 T. L. DE VINNE *Moxon's Mech. Exerc., Printing* 421 The compositor was required to make up his page as soon as it was composed.

(*g*) To put (coaches, etc.) together to form a train; also, to put (a train) together.

1864 *Jrnl. R. Agric. Soc.* XXV. II. 372 The waggons..were made up into trains. 1889 *Scribner's Mag.* May 581/2 The train once made 'up',..its progress..is comparatively simple.

(*h*) †Formerly, to lay and light (a fire). Now, to add fuel to (a fire already burning) so as to keep it at a proper 'height'.

1785 MRS. FLETCHER in *Wesley's Serm.* lvii. Wks. (1827) IX. 28 The servant came in to make up the fire. 1801 CHARLOTTE SMITH *Lett. Solit. Wand.* I. 93 The usual hour of bringing candles, and making up the fire, was certainly past. *Ibid.* II. 168 The daughter of the poor man under whose roof she was made up a fire in the wretched room assigned to her. 1861 DICKENS *Gt. Expect.* liii, I made up the fire which was still burning. 1889 MRS. OLIPHANT *Poor Gentleman* II. x. 172, 'I might at least find a decent fire.' 'I'll make it up in a moment, Edward. A little wood will make it all right'.

g. To compose, compile.

(*a*) To put together in due form; to compile, draw up (a list, document, etc.).

c 1374 CHAUCER *Troylus* III. 291 (340) And day is set, the chartres up to make. 1552 HULOET, Make vp, *scribo.* 1613 SHAKS. *Hen. VIII*, I. i. 75 He makes vp the File Of all the Gentry. 1662 GRAUNT *Bills of Mortality* 11 On Wednesday the general Accompt is made up, and Printed. 1885 *Act 48 Vict.* c. 16. §6 Every future valuation roll to be made up in any county. 1891 *Sat. Rev.* 8 Aug. 163/1 The averages of the season, made up to Saturday last.

(*b*) To compose (a book, sermon). *Obs.* or *dial.*

1630 USSHER *Lett.* (1686) 434 The History of Gotteschalcus,..which I am now a making up. 1825–80 JAMIESON, *To mak up*..4. To compose; as, 'The minister's thrang makin' up his sermon.'

(*c*) To concoct, invent, fabricate (a story, lie). Also, to compose (verses, etc.) impromptu; to improvise.

1825–80 in JAMIESON. 1847 MARRYAT *Childr. N. Forest* xiv, Well, the story was not badly made up. 1879 M. J. GUEST *Lect. Hist. Eng.* iv. 28 People began to make up a history of the Britons. 1889 MRS. H. L. CAMERON *Lost Wife* II. iv. 47 One can easily make up some plausible reason. 1891 MRS. S. EDWARDS *Secr. Princess* II. i. 2 He sang his verses as he made them up. 1891 *Strand Mag.* II. 502/2 Make it up out of your head. 1893 R. KIPLING *Many Invent.* 98, I made up a whole lot of new things to go into the story.

h. Said of component parts. (*a*) Of quantities, individuals: To form (a certain sum or total) either by themselves or with others. Now *rare.*

1504 in *Bury Wills* (Camden) 96 As mych lond more as shall makuppe the valor of xj marc by yeer wt the seid londes in Watton. 1542–3 *Act 34 & 35 Hen. VIII*, c. 5. §12 As muche of the two partes residue, as shall accomplishe and make vp a full thirde parte. 1588 SHAKS. *L.L.L.* IV. iii. 207 That you three fooles, lackt mee foole, to make vp the messe. 1602 MARSTON *Ant. & Mel.* II. Wks. 1856 I. 27, I have nineteene mistresses alreadie, and I not much disdeigne that thou shold'st make up the ful score. 1641 BROME *Jov. Crew* I. Wks. 1873 III. 358 Cash; which added Unto your former Banck, makes up in all..Twelve thousand and odd pounds. 1662 STILLINGFL. *Orig. Sacr.* I. v §2 Reckoning three Generations to make up a century. 1748 RICHARDSON *Clarissa* III. 321 These four [gentlemen], with Mrs. Sinclair, Miss Partington,..Mr. Lovelace, and myself, made up the company. 1860 *Jrnl. R. Agric. Soc.* XXI. II. 450 The sums..do not quite make up 100.

(*b*) To form the components of; to constitute, compose; to contribute to the formation of; to go to form or produce. Freq. in passive ***to be made up*** (of certain parts).

1592 SHAKS. *Rom. & Jul.* v. i. 48 Old cakes of Roses Were thinly scattered, to make vp a shew. 1593 —— *3 Hen. VI*, I. iv. 25 The Sands are numbred, that makes vp my Life. 1634 SIR T. HERBERT *Trav.* 2 Men and manners, which make up a Librarie to themselves. 1660 F. BROOKE tr. *Le Blanc's Trav.* 63 The River..is pleasant and large, and helps to make up a good haven. 1688 BURNET *Lett. Pres. St. Italy* 129, I have writ you a very loose sort of a Letter, all made up of digressions. 1693 DRYDEN *Disc. Satire* Ess. (ed. Ker) II. 45 Satyrus, that mixed kind of animal,..made up betwixt a man and a goat. 1711 STEELE *Spect.* No. 152 ⁋3 These are the People who make up the Gross of the Soldiery. 1711 SWIFT *Let. conc. Sacram. Test* Misc. 335 The Parties among us are made up on one side of Moderate Whigs, and on the other, of Presbyterians. 1712 BERKELEY *Pass. Obed.* Wks. III. 107 An audience almost wholly made up of young persons. 1713 ADDISON *Cato* IV. iii. 48 He was all made up of Love and Charms. 1834 J. H. NEWMAN *Par. Serm.* (1837) I. xxi. 316 Soul and body make up one man. 1849 MACAULAY *Hist. Eng.* i. I. 131 The few members who made up what was contemptuously called the Rump of the House of Commons. 1861 MRS. CARLYLE *Lett.* III. 81 Ramsgate..is made up of narrow, steep, confused streets. 1867 FREEMAN *Norm. Conq.* (1876) I. App. 756 The force was made up of men of all nations. 1889 KATH. S. MACQUOID *Roger Ferron* I. 122 Life is made up of tiny trifles. 1890 *Temple Bar* Feb. 168 All in short that goes to make up..an Englishman's ideal of felicity.

i. To prepare.

†(*a*) To attire (a person) suitably for receiving guests, etc. *Obs.*

1602 DEKKER *Satirom.* K 4 b, Wat Terrill, th'art ill suited, ill made vp, In Sable collours. 1633 B. JONSON *Tale of Tub* i. iv, The bravest, richest, and the properest, man A Taylor could make up. 1634 MASSINGER *Very Woman* I. i, *Ped.* 'Morrow sister, Do I not come unseasonably? *Al.* Why good brother? *Ped.* Because you are not yet fully made up, Nor fit for visitation.

(*b*) (esp. *Theatr.*) To prepare (an actor) for the impersonation of a character by dressing him in an appropriate costume and disguising his features by means of false hair, cosmetics, etc. Of a woman: to apply cosmetics to (one's face). Chiefly *refl.* and *pass.*

1808 *Monthly Pantheon* I. 346/1 Yes, she produces a good effect!—she's well *made up*! 1809 MALKIN *Gil Blas* III. ix. ⁋2, I made myself up,..with the barber's aid, as a sort of middle man between Don Cæsar and Gil Blas. *Ibid.* IV. vii. ⁋5 Just as he had done making himself up [said of an old beau at his toilette]. *a* 1817 JANE AUSTEN *Persuasion* (1818) IV. x. 222 Morning visits are never fair by women at her time of life, who make themselves up so little. If she would only wear rouge. 1844 *Puck* 30 (Farmer) My young ambition sadly I resign,—My mind and face made up for first old men. 1859 LANG *Wand. India* 362 The General was very old, close upon eighty; but he was 'made up' to represent a gentleman of about forty. 1862 *Temple Bar* VI. 339 His face is marvellously 'made up'. 1891 *New Rev.* Aug. 176 They have no teeth; they have skins that would make a lemon look white;..But the maid makes them up; and people say how handsome they are. 1926 GALSWORTHY *Silver Spoon* III. vi. 258 Marjorie Ferrar stepped into the Box, not exactly nervous, and only just 'made-up'. 1930 V. SACKVILLE-WEST *Edwardians* i. 15 She was heavily but badly made-up, with a triangle of red on either cheek. 1945 S. LEWIS *Cass Timberlane* (1946) xlvii. 333 Small white wool socks..to be worn with bare legs that were made-up to look tanned. 1968 A. MUNRO in R. Weaver *Canad. Short Stories* 2nd Ser. 295 The women's faces in the room, made up some time before, have begun to show the effects of heat.

(*c*) *intr.* for *refl.*

1838 DICKENS *Nich. Nick.* xxv, Mr. Crummles..had..'made up' for the part by arraying himself in a theatrical wig [etc.]. 1862 *Temple Bar* VI. 340 Mr. Sothern 'makes up' so very darkly as to appear almost Jewish. 1879 SALA *Paris herself again* (ed. 4) II. ii. 28 He had 'made up' for the part of a distressed poet. 1890 *Sat. Rev.* 22 Nov. 591/2 When she went off with Paris, he had by magic arts made up as Menelaus, and she thought he was her husband. 1901 C. MORRIS *Life on Stage* v. 26 Of course when you are making up for a character part you go by a different rule. 1931 *Daily Tel.* 21 May 13/3 She came to a car in which one girl was smoking a cigarette and two others were busily 'making up'.

(*d*) To arrange (the features) so as to produce a particular expression. ***to make up one's mouth***: see MOUTH *sb.* Now *U.S.*

1641 BROME *Jovial Crew* IV. i, Make up your face quickly. [The person addressed has been weeping.] Here comes one of the Servants, I suppose. 1828–32 WEBSTER s.v., To assume a particular form of features; as, to make up a face; whence, to make up a lip, is to pout.

(*e*) To get (a horse, etc.) into good condition for selling; to fatten. Also *intr.* for *pass.* (Cf. *make off*, 89 c.)

1794 *Sporting Mag.* IV. 208 He thoroughly understands (what is termed by dealers) *making up a horse.* 1842 *Jrnl. R. Agric. Soc.* III. II. 217 All the lambs being made up for the butcher. 1857 *Ibid.* XVIII. I. 19 The majority..buy them as colts; when fit for the collar,..make them up for the London brewers. 1867 *Ibid.* Ser. II. III. II. 533 If they [fowls] have been 'sent along' with Indian corn [etc.],..they will make up to nearly 2 lbs. heavier.

(*f*) To prepare, put in order (a bed) for a particular occasion. Also, to put (a room) in order; to 'do up' (? *local*).

1824 *Examiner* 45/2 [She] desired witness to make up the bed in her room. 1879 MISS YONGE *Cameos* Ser. IV. xxxii. 346 She had a couch made up for her on deck. 1889 W. WESTALL *Birch Dene* I. xiii. 178 We might..make you up a bed on the office floor. 1891 *Blackw. Mag.* CL. 506/2 'Where have you made up Mr. Smith's room'? 'In the north wing, sir'. 1894 G. MOORE *Esther Waters* 102 Esther said she would make up her room, and when that was done she insisted on helping her mother with the house-work.

(*g*) To get up (linen). *rare.*

1890 *Blackw. Mag.* CXLVIII. 56/1 They can make up linen execrably.

(*h*) To bring (spirits) to a required degree of strength by adding water; to 'lower'.

1725 G. SMITH *Distilling* 77 When you have made up your goods to the quantity and quality you intend. 1731 P. SHAW *Ess. Artif. Philos.* 89 To keep out of the Spirit the grosser Oil of the Faints; and instead of these, to *make up*, as they call it, to Proof, with pure distill'd or simple water. 1753 CHAMBERS *Cycl. Supp.* s.v. *Making-up*, When it is necessary to make up waters lower than proof, they are generally cloudy.

j. To set out the items of (an account) in order; to add up and balance (an account).

1472 J. PASTON in *P. Lett.* III. 32, I porpose to make up my byllys clere, and send yow the copyse. **1607** SHAKS. *Cor.* I. i. 148 Yet I can make my Awdit vp, that [etc.]. *a* **1729** J. ROGERS 19 *Serm.* ii. (1735) 33 He was to make up his Accounts with his Lord. **1742** RICHARDSON *Pamela* III. 250 A Desk, at which sometimes Mr. Jonathan makes up his running Accounts to Mr. Longman. **1749** FIELDING *Tom Jones* v. viii, Who but an atheist could think of leaving the world without having first made up his account? **1858** *Jrnl. R. Agric. Soc.* XIX. I. 123 A farmer's accounts should be made up once a year. **1889** MARY E. CARTER *Mrs. Severn* I. I. i. 27 Her husband.. made up the tradesmen's books. **1892** J. ADAM *Commerc. Corresp.* 22 It is customary for the banker to make up, or balance, the current account at the end of each half-year.

k. (*a*) ***to make up one's mind***: to come to a decision or conclusion; often const. inf. or clause. Also (nonce-uses), ***to make up one's resolution***, † ***a determination***. Hence, with extended meaning, ***to make up one's mind for***, *to*, or *to do* (something): to be reconciled to the thought of, to be prepared for. †Also in *passive*: ? = 'to have one's mind made up' *for*.

1595 SHAKS. *John* II. i. 541, I know she is not for this match made vp. [Otherwise in modern editions.] **1606** —— *Tr. & Cr.* II. ii. 170 To make vp a free determination 'Twixt right and wrong. **1821** *Examiner* 363/1 In winter people make up their minds for the worst and go. **1830** *Ibid.* 663/2 The King has quite made up his mind to the loss of Belgium. **1847** MARRYAT *Childr. N. Forest* xiv, Edward made up his resolution to join the army. **1849** MACAULAY *Hist. Eng.* i. I. 107 He.. had wisely made up his mind to what could no longer be avoided. **1859** MILL *Liberty* v. (1865) 62/2 If the government would make up its mind to require for every child a good education. **1883** STEVENSON *Treas. Isl.* IV. xvii, We had all quietly made up our minds to treat him like one of ourselves. **1887** RUSKIN *Præterita* II. 189, I believe he made up his mind that I was heartless and selfish.

†(*b*) *absol.* ? 'To come to a decision' (Schmidt).

1605 SHAKS. *Lear* I. i. 209 Pardon me, Royall Sir, Election makes not vp in such conditions.

l. To settle, arrange. (*a*) To arrange, settle (a marriage, etc.); to conclude (a treaty).

1562 *Child-Marr.* (1897) 75 Bie the consent of their frendes, who made vp the mariage betwixe them. **1607** SHAKS. *Cor.* v. iii. 140 Be Blest For making vp this peace. **1879** M. J. GUEST *Lect. Hist. Eng.* xxxviii. 384 Edward tried to make up a kind of peace between them. **1890** *Univ. Rev.* Feb. 282 The best marriages are those which are made up by sympathetic and understanding friends.

(*b*) To settle (a dispute, etc.); to end (a quarrel) by reconciliation.

1699 T. BROWN *Erasm. Colloq.* 67 What passes between two People is much easier made up, than when once it has taken Air. **1727** A. HAMILTON *New Acc. E. Ind.* II. xxxvii. 62 Mediators in making up Cases of Debate and Contention. **1773** FOOTE *Bankrupt* III. Wks. 1799 II. 133 And now this difference is whole and compos'd, let me try if I can't make up the other. **1828** SCOTT *F. M. Perth* xxi, Perhaps the feud may be made up without farther fighting or difficulty. **1855** MACAULAY *Hist. Eng.* xix. IV. 301 That two.. gentlemen should be deputed to wait on Her Majesty and try to make matters up. **1870** ROGERS *Hist. Gleanings* Ser. II. 230 He had made up his differences with Fox.

(*c*) *intr.* (also often ***to make it up***). To be reconciled after a dispute; to become friends again.

1669 R. MONTAGU in *Buccleuch MSS.* (Hist. MSS. Comm.) I. 441 You had made up with the Duke of York without his knowledge. **1748** RICHARDSON *Clarissa* IV. 26 If I should be obliged to make up with him again, I shall think I am always doing myself a spight. **1749** FIELDING *Tom Jones* VII. v, I beseech you.. that you will endeavour to make it up with my aunt. **1837** THACKERAY *Yellowplush* i, There we were, quarrelling and making up.. by turns. **1887** MRS. C. L. PIRKIS *Dateless Bargain* II. xviii. 232 We've kissed and made it up again. **1892** STEVENSON & L. OSBOURNE *Wrecker* xix. 288 We.. had quarrelled and made up.

m. To make the fortune of, enrich. *dial.*

1786 *Scotland's Glory & Shame* II. 53 He'll make you up for ever. **1829** HOGG *Sheph. Cal.* viii. I. 230 Your master will soon be sic a rich man now, that we'll a' be made up.

n. *intr.* (*a*) To advance in a certain direction; now only in ***to make up to***, to draw near to, approach. Also *occas.* of the tide: To flow up a river (cf. 72).

1595 SHAKS. *John* III. ii. 5 Philip make vp. **1596** *Edw. III*, IV. vii. 31 Make up once more with me; the twentieth part Of those that liue, are men inow to quaile The feeble handfull on the aduerse part. **1611** HEYWOOD *Gold. Age* v. Wks. 1874 III. 75 Let's make vp to his rescue. **1622** FLETCHER *Span. Cur.* I. i, There I would follow you as a guid to honour, Though all the horrours of the Warre made up To stop my passage. **1632** MASSINGER *Maid of Hon.* IV. i, Hell, stoppe their brawling throats; againe! make up And cudgel them into jelly. **1678** BUNYAN *Pilgr.* I. 38 He espied two Men come tumbling over the Wall,.. and they made up a pace to him. **1725** DE FOE *Voy. round World* (1840) 104 With intent to have endeavoured to make up into the latitude of 50 or 60°. **1809** MALKIN *Gil Blas* x. viii. ⁋9 Impatient to know,.. he made up to me immediately. **1855** COSTELLO *Stor. Screen* 87, I saw her make up to the lady I have described. **1898** *Daily News* 25 March 8/3 There was very little water in the river as the tide was only just beginning to make up.

(*b*) ***to make up to*** (fig.): to make advances to (a person); to pay court or make love to.

1781 D. WILLIAMS tr. *Voltaire's Dram. Wks.* II. 25 She ogles me still, or I'm mistaken; I'll e'en make up to her. **1809** MALKIN *Gil Blas* VII. i. ⁋2 They made up to Don Cæsar or his son at once, without currying my favour as the channel of all good graces. **1842** S. LOVER *Handy Andy* ii. 22 Tom's making up to the widow. **1848** THACKERAY *Van. Fair* xii, Young Bullock,.. who had been making up to Miss Maria the last two seasons. **1889** STEVENSON *Master of B.* i. 8, I have it by all accounts that Mr. Henry was more made up to from that hour.

☛ *Key to phrases, etc.*

Uses of *passive* 3, 3 b, 3 c, 4; (= L. *fieri*) 9 e, 48 f, 49 d, e; *refl.* (with *for* or inf.) 34 a, 35; *impers.* (of the weather) 8 b; (it) maksna *Sc.* 25; *intr.* (= compose poetry) 5 b, (= go) 35 b; see also 69–74.

What make you here? 58; what do you make of..? 20. ¶Make or mar, make or break 46 b; make or mend 1 c; meddle or make with 71. ¶Proverbs and proverbial phrases occur in senses 1 d, 10, 24, 53 c.

Make account of 19 b; *m* acquainted 48 b; *m* ado 9; *m* after 75; *m* again 83; *m* against 76; *m* the agreeable 67; *m* alms 57 a; *m* amends 61; *m* an army 57 b; *m* as if, as though 70; *m* an ass of oneself 18; *m* asseth 61; *m* at 77; *m* away 84; *m* away with 85; *m* a bag 15 c; *m* a bargain 57 d; *m* battle 57 b; *m* one's beard 40; *m* a beast of oneself 18; *m* a bed 36; *m* believe 53 e; *m* the best of 18 d; *m* bold 69; *m* a book 5, 15 d; *m* a (or one's) bow 57 c; *m* a business of 18; *m* (it) one's business 49 c; *m* a campaign 57 b; *m* capital out of 29; *m* (= score with) a card 30; *m* the cards 43; *m* care 62; *m* a case 19 d; *m* the chalice 42; *m* a child 17; *m* a circuit 57 f; *m* coffee 2 b; *m* a coil, a commotion 9; *m* one's Communion 57 e; *m* one's compliments 61; *m* (one's) confession 57 e; *m* conscience 19 a; *m* a contract 57 d; *m* a corner (in) 9; *m* count of 19 b; *m* one's course 57 f; *m* a covenant 57 d; *m* it coy 68 b; *m* a decision 61 c; *m* a difference 10, 19 a; *m* (= eat) a dinner 60; *m* (= train) a dog 45; *m* dole 62; *m* (= shut) a door 37; *m* (no) doubt 19 a; *m* down 86; *m* an effort 63; *m* English 48; *m* esteem, estimation (of) 19 b; *m* even 48; *m* an example of 18; *m* an excursion 57 f; *m* an exhibition of oneself 18; *m* an expedition 57 f; *m* expense 64, one's expenses 64 b; *m* a face (at) 57 c; *m* fast 48; *m* a fault 57 a; *m* fealty 61; *m* a feast 14; *m* felt 48 b; *m* (a) fight 57 b; *m* a fire 6; *m* (= prepare) fish 39; *m* a fool of 18; *m* for 25, 25 b, 78; *m* force (at) 63; *m* forth 87; *m* a fortune 29; *m* free 69; *m* friends 13 c; *m* (something) from 2; *m* (= bring forth) fruit 16; *m* fun, a fuss, game 9; *m* games 12 b; *m* a garden 7; *m* glad 69; *m* gladness, glee 62; *m* good 48; *m* it goodly 68 b; *m* a hash of 18 e; *m* (= train) a hawk 45; *m* hay 38; *m* head 61 b; *m* a head 15 a; *m* head or tail of 20; *m* heard 48 b; *m* hence 33; *m* a hole 8; *m* homage 61; *m* horns 57 c; *m* (= train) a horse 45; *m* it hot 48; *m* (long) hours 66; *m* a House 15 b; *m* an impression 9; *m* in 88; *m* in one's way 48 c; *m* (= give) an instance 61; *m* (something) into 50, 50 b; *m* it (= cause it to be so) 10 b; *m* it one's boast, business, etc. 49 c; *m* it (coy, etc.) 68, 68 b; *m* it so 51 e; *m* a journey 57 f; *m* joy 62; *m* a judgement 19 a, 61 c; *m* known 48 b; *m* labour 63; *m* Latin(s 5 c; *m* a law 12; *m* a leg 57 c; *m* a lie 57 a; *m* light of 21; *m* like (= look like) 73 a; *m* little of 18 d, 21; *m* things lively 48; *m* a living 29; *m* a loss 64; *m* love 61; *m* a mark 8; *m* a marriage 57 d; *m* (= arrange) a match 12 b; *m* (no) matter 25; *m* a meal 60; *m* (= prepare) meat 2 b; *m* melody 8; *m* memory 57 h; *m* mercy 57 a; *m* merriment 62; *m* merry 69; *m* a mess of 18 e; *m* mind 57 h; *m* minstrelsy 8; *m* a miracle 57 a; *m* mirth 62; *m* (a) mock (of) 62 b; *m* money 29; *m* the most of 18 d; *m* much of 18 d, 21; *m* a muddle of 18 e; *m* a name (for oneself) 29; *m* (it) nice 68 b, 69; *m* a noise, a note 8; *m* nothing of 18 d, 21; *m* nothing to do (= not to hesitate) 51 c; *m* (= give) notice 61; *m* (an) obeisance 57 c; *m*.. of 1 b, 2, 4, 4 b, 18; (= esteem) 21 b; *m*.. of it 18 c; *m* off 89; *m* on 90; *m* one (of) 26; *m* an oration 57 g; *m* an order, ordinance 12; *m* out 91; *m*.. out of 1 b, 2, 18; *m* out of the way 33; *m* over 94; *m* a pace 57 f; *m* pain 63; *m* a park 7; *m* a passage 57 f; *m* peace 9 c; *m* penance 57 e; *m* place 9 d; *m* a practice of 18; *m* a profit 29; *m* a progress 57 f; *m* it proud, quaint 68 b; *m* question 19 a; *m* (= propound) a question 61; *m* a quorum 15 b; *m* (= impose) a rate 12; *m* ready 48, 48 d; *m* (= give) a reason 61; *m* reckoning, regard of 19 b; *m* (a) reputation 29; *m* return (= come back) 57 f; *m* a road 7; *m* room 9 d; *m* a row 9; *m* a rule 12; *m* runs 30 b; *m* the sacrament 57 e; *m* sail 44; *m* a salaam 57 c; *m* satisfaction 61; *m* oneself scarce 48 e; *m* a score 30 b; *m* scorn (of) 62 b; *m* scruple 19 a; *m* a sensation 9; *m* sense of 20; *m* a sermon 57 g; *m* shipwreck 64; *m* short 48 d; *m* slight of 21; *m* something of 18 d; *m* sorrow 62; *m* one's soul 47; *m* a sound 8; *m* a speech 57 g; *m* sport 9; *m* a step 57 f; *m* a stir 9; *m* store of (= value highly) 19 b; *m* (it) stout, strange 68 b, 69; *m* sure 48, 48 d; *m* the tackling 44; *m* tea 2 b; *m* that.. (= bring it about that) 52, (= show or allege that) 56 b; *m* through 93; *m* timber 31, 41; *m* (good, short, etc.) time 66; *m* a title 19 d; *m* to (*prep.*) 79, (*adv.*) 94; *m* (= bring or reduce) to (a condition) 33; *m* (one) to (king, etc.) 49 e; *m* (= attempt) to do 34 b; *m* together 95; *m* top or tail of 20; *m* it tough 68 b; *m* a tour 57 f; *m* towards 35 b; *m* a trade of 18; *m* a trick 30; *m* a trip 57 f; *m* understood 48 b; *m* unready 48; *m* unto 80; *m* up 96; *m* upon 81; *m* urine 16 b; *m* verses 5; *m* void 48; *m* a voyage 57 f; *m* war 57 b; *m* it warm 48; *m* (= give) warning 61; *m* waste 48; *m* water 16 b, 31; *m* way 9 d; *m* one's way 57 f; *m* weight 31; *m* a will 5 d; *m* with 82, 71; *m*.. with 1 b, 2; *m* a wonder 10; *m* wood 31, 41; *m* work 10; *m* a wound 8; *m* wreck 64.

For many other phrases, with nouns expressing the action of a verb, see the lists in 59 and 59 b.

† **make**, *v.*² *Obs.* Also 6 *Sc.* **maik**. [f. MAKE *sb.*¹] *trans.* and *intr.* To mate, pair, match.

1463 *Bury Wills* (Camden) 23, I wille she haue.. my flat pece enchased to make with a salt saler of sylver. **1513** DOUGLAS *Æneis* IV. Prol. 53 The snaw quhite dow oft to the gray maik will. **1522** *Mundus et Infans* (Manly) 262 So fell a fyghter in felde was there neuer yfounde. To me no man is makyde.

make: see MAWK, MEAK, MEEK.

make-, the stem of MAKE *v.*¹ in combination, chiefly with a sb. as the second element, occas. with an adj. or adv., as in the following (chiefly nonce-wds.): † **make-braser** [? f. BRACE *v.*²], ? one who domineers or blusters; † **make-debate** = MAKE-BATE; **make-faith** *nonce-wd.*, something that serves for faith; **make-falcon** = MAKE-HAWK; † **make-fire**, an incendiary; † **make-fray**, a raiser of quarrels; † **make-God** *a.*, applied as a derisive term to Romish priests; † **make-king** = KING-MAKER; † **make-law** *a.*, law-giving; † **make-mirth** = MAKE-SPORT; **make-play** = MAKE-SPORT; **make-queen**, a queen-maker; **make-rime**, a phrase introduced merely for the sake of rime; **make-shame** *a.*, causing shame; † **make-strife** = MAKEBATE; **make-talk**, something said for the mere sake of talking; **make-wages** (see quot.); **make-way**, an event which leads up to another.

c **1515** *Cocke Lorell's B.* 11 Surmowsers, yll thynkers, and *make brasers. **1741** RICHARDSON *Fam. Lett.* lv. (ed. 7) 68 The busy Whisperings of officious *Make-debates. **1825** COLERIDGE *Aids Refl.* (1848) I. 336 Thousands of sober, and in their way pious, Christians will echo the words,.. and adopt the doctrine for their *make-faith. **1575** TURBERV. *Faulconrie* 160 By.. calling of them to the lewre with other *make Falcons, that is to say, a cast at once, to the end they may accustom and aquaint themselues one with another. **1560** DAUS tr. *Sleidane's Comm.* 179 The seuerall confession of euery one of these *make fyers [L. *incendiarii*]. **1598** BP. HALL *Sat.* IV. iv. 31 If brabling *Make-fray, at ech Fayre and Sise, Picks quarrels for to shew his valiantise. **1705** HICKERINGILL *Priest-cr.* I. (1721) 12 Not only the *Make-God Pope, but the Make-God Priest. **1611** SPEED *Theat. Gt. Brit.* xxvii. (1614) 53/1 That stout *make-king Richard Nevil Earle of Warwicke. **1631** WEEVER *Anc. Funeral Mon.* 705 Warwicke (the Mars and Make-King of England). **1582** STANYHURST *Æneis* IV. (Arb.) 96 First to Ceres *Makelaw [L. *legiferæ*], too Phoebus, then to Lyæus. **1656** EARL MONM. tr. *Boccalini's Advts. fr. Parnass.* 258 Court officers, princes favorits, *make-mirths, flatterers. **1592** NASHE *P. Penilesse* Wks. (Grosart) II. 69 Our Poets and Writers about London whome thou hast called piperly *Make-plaies and Make-bates. **1655** FULLER *Hist. Camb.* (1840) 186 As Neville earl of Warwick was the make-king, so this Dudley earl of Warwick.. was the *make-queen. **1893** *Athenæum* 14 Oct. 516/2 The sorry *make-rhymes 'I wis', 'I trow', 'I weet', make their appearance now and again. **1850** S. G. OSBORNE *Glean.* 78 This make-shift, *make-shame system. **1617** MINSHEU *Ductor* s.v., A Make-bate, *make-strife, or contentious person. **1856** ARCHD. ALLEN *Lect. Ladies* 211 A sort of complimentary observation, mere words of course, an unreal piece of *make-talk. **1884** H. SPENCER in *Contemp. Rev.* Apr. 463 There had grown up the practice of paying out of the rates a part of the wages of each farm-servant—'*make-wages', as the sum was called. **1894** CREIGHTON *Hist. Papacy* (1897) V. v. xv. 151 The intrigues of Cardinal Rovere.. led to the election of Pius III as a *make-way to his own election.

† **make-a-do.** *Obs.* [f. MAKE *v.*¹ + ADO.]

1. A 'to-do', uproar, stir.

1575 *Gamm. Gurton* I. iii, What deuill make-a-doe is this betweene our dame and thee?

2. One who is fond of making a to-do.

1589 R. HARVEY *Pl. Perc.* (1590) 8, I will nicke-name no bodie: I am none of these tuft mockadoo mak-a-dooes.

ˌmake-and-ˈbreak. Also without hyphens. [f. the vbs. as used in *to make contact* (MAKE *v.*¹ 8), *to break contact* (BREAK *v.* 29): see CONTACT 1 c.]

a. The alternate making and breaking of electrical contact. Freq. *attrib.*

1857 *Chambers's Jrnl.* 22 Aug. 121/1 The transmission of the current having.. to be made through a make and break key of metal. **1875** F. GUTHRIE *Magn. & Electr.* §235 The automatic make and break. **1898** *Engin. Mag.* XVI. 120/2 The interruptions corresponding to the make and break of a telegraph key. **1904** A. B. F. YOUNG *Compl. Motorist* (ed. 2) 197 The time of firing is controlled by a simple 'make-and-break' commutator placed on the half-time shaft. **1911** *Encycl. Brit.* XXVI. 520/2 In Squier and Crehore's 'Synchronograph' system 'sine waves' of current, instead of sharp 'makes and breaks',.. are employed for transmitting signals. **1938** *Archit. Rev.* LXXXIII. p. lviii, A semi-rotary quick make-and-break switch. **1958** *Newnes Compl. Amat. Photogr.* 120 To charge a large capacitor from accumulators requires a more complex power pack which includes a make-and-break coil, transformer and rectifier.

b. An apparatus for automatically making and breaking electrical contact.

1908 *Daily Chron.* 7 Nov. 3/3 The 'make and break' or commutator.. is.. frequently placed in an inaccessible position. **1911** A. B. SMITH *Mod. Amer. Telephony* xxv. 689 The circuit consisted of an induction coil.. and mechanical 'make and break' that gave 10,000 sparks per second. **1929** *Times* 5 Nov. 7/5 The distributor and make-and-break are easily seen. **1970** K. BALL *Fiat 600, 600D Autobook* xi. 138/2 Failure of the horn to operate may be due to.. dirty contacts on the horn make-and-break.

makebate (ˈmeɪkbeɪt). Also 8 **makebait.** [f. MAKE *v.*¹ + BATE *sb.*¹.]

1. One who or something which creates contention or discord; a breeder of strife. (Common in 16th–17th cent.) *arch.*

1529 MORE *Suppl. Soulys* Wks. 296/2 They agree better together, then to fal at variaunce for yͤ wild wordes of suche a malicious make-bate. *a* **1586** SIDNEY *Arcadia* II. (1590) 221 Disdaining this fellow should play the preacher, who had bin one of the chiefest make-bates. **1613** PURCHAS *Pilgrimage* VI. iv. 576 It was not likely they would joyne in conspiracie, whom Religion (the most mortall make-bate) had disioyned. **1655** GURNALL *Chr. in Arm.* I. 145 Satan, who is the great make-bate between God and the soul. *a* **1703** BURKITT *On N.T., Jas.* iv. 1 Lust within is the make-bait of all societies and communities without. **1710** SWIFT *Examiner* No. 15 ⁋5 Like a couple of makebates, who inflame small quarrels by a thousand stories. **1821** SCOTT *Kenilw.* xxxvi, I thank Heaven, I am no make-bate or informer. **1849** MACAULAY *Hist. Eng.* vi. II. 22 Barillon was.. directed to act, with all possible precautions against detection, the part of a makebate. **1896** SAINTSBURY *Hist. 19th Cent. Lit.* iv. 185 He [Hazlitt] appears to have played the part of fire-brand and makebate in the John Scott duel referred to.

†**2.** The breeding of quarrels, mischief-making.

1626 BERNARD *Isle of Man* (1627) 207 Selfeloue, Makebate, and Vnmercifulnesse.

†**3. a.** Gerarde's name for the Yellow Jasmine, *Jasminum fruticans*. **b.** A book-name for Greek Valerian, *Polemonium cœruleum*. *Obs.*

1597 GERARDE *Herbal* III. xiv. 1128 Of the shrub Trefoile, called also Makebate. **1611** COTGR. s.v. *Polemoine*. **1866** *Treas. Bot.* 711/2 Makebate, *Polemonium cœruleum*.

†**4.** *attrib.* passing into adj. *Obs.*

1582 STANYHURST *Æneis* II. (Arb.) 62 Thee bane of vs Troians, of Greeks thee mak bate Erinnys. **1622** ROWLANDS *Gd. Newes & Bad* 31 Which she in memorie would still retaine, And cross the deuill in his make-bate veine. **1675** T. TULLY *Let. to Baxter* 14 Your own make-bate Novelties.

'make-beˌlief. = next.

Substituted by some writers for MAKE-BELIEVE; the formation of the latter, being misunderstood, was imagined to be incorrect.

1833–40 J. H. NEWMAN *Ch. of Fathers* (1842) 372 Evil Spirits..are but actors in a play, changing their appearance and frightening children by their tumult and their make-belief. **1854** *Lett. of American* (ed. Landor) 17 Creeds and lichens grow in the extremities of his [the Tzar's] frozen regions; farther to the southwest, beliefs are make-beliefs. **1858** FREEMAN *Hist. Ess.* Ser. II. ii. (1873) 85 The early institutions of a nation may fail of fully carrying out their ends, but there is no make-belief as to what those ends are. **1873** HAMERTON *Intell. Life* VII. i. (1876) 229 A sort of make-belief lady. **1909** *Westm. Gaz.* 20 Aug. 4/1 The contempt with which all things are remembered, to which cling suggestions of the theatrical and the make-belief. **1960** J. RAE *Custard Boys* II. xix. 212 He had been my guide through the days of make-belief and blinkered memory. **1971** *Daily Tel.* 11 Oct. 9/1 That great reservoir of make-belief which lies hidden in so many children.

'make-beˌlieve. [The phr. *make believe* (see MAKE *v.*[1] 53 e) used subst. (Cf. FACRERE.)]

1. Pretence.

1811 L. M. HAWKINS *C'tess & Gertr.* (1812) IV. 62, I was drest like Minerva,..and then the little ones came and worshipped me: 'twas all make-believe, you see. **1811** *Morn. Chron.* 9 Apr., Her mourning is all make-believe, She's gay as any linnet. **1818** LAMB *Three Friends*, Not that she did really grieve It was only make-believe. **1855** H. ROGERS *Ess.* (1874) II. vii. 331 This great empire is rotten..ceremony, etiquette, conventionality, insincerity,—'make believe', in short,— constitute it. **1888** *Times* 23 June 17/2 The public does not object to magic in small quantities. It is quite ready to join in the game of 'make-believe'.

b. in particularized sense.

1825 COLERIDGE *Aids Refl.* (1848) I. 56 [To practise praying] as a species of animal-magnetism to be brought about by..a temporary make-believe on the part of the self-magnetizer! **1862** SALA *Accepted Addr.* 191 The world is full of make-believes. **1887** JESSOPP *Arcady* viii. 234 That old-fashioned place of resort..the village green, has become a mere make-believe now.

2. One who makes believe or pretends.

1863 S. WILBERFORCE *Sp. Missions* (1874) 2 Do not be an idler and make-believe in the work. **1865** TROLLOPE *Belton Est.* xv. 171 The ordinary make-believes of society, saying little civil speeches and not going beyond them.

3. *attrib.* passing into *adj.* Of the nature of make-believe.

1824 MISS MITFORD *Village* Ser. I. 248 That was a make-believe thing, compared with this. **1852** GLADSTONE *Glean.* IV. xlii. 96 Here again I am met with a make-believe reply. **1877** T. A. TROLLOPE *Life Pius IX*, II. III. iii. 3 The republicans and their make-believe government. **1890** 'R. BOLDREWOOD' *Col. Reformer* (1891) 138 The hour's talk and make-believe school.

So **make-believer, -believing** [f. phrase *make believe*].

1884 *N. Amer. Rev.* CXXXVIII. 443 A volume which believers, unbelievers, misbelievers, and make-believers would unite in neglecting or condemning. **1899** MISS HARRADEN *Fowler* 125 Children..not tiring easily of their many make-believings. **1907** G. B. SHAW *Major Barbara* Pref. 149 The romantic make-believer lay outside the pale of sympathy in literature. **1909** *Times Lit. Suppl.* 18 Mar. 105/2 A little make-believing girl, not unlike..the make-believing child of the 'Child's Garden of Verses'. **1954** T. S. ELIOT *Confid. Clerk* I. 40 It begins as a kind of make-believe And the make-believing makes it real. **1957** L. MACNEICE *Visitations* 17 Coral islands of first love Where makebelieving boy and girl Assume the music of the spheres.

make-do (ˌmeɪk'du:). [f. *to make do*: see MAKE *v.*[1] 53 f.] A makeshift; a temporary expedient. Also *attrib.* or quasi-*adj.*, characterized by makeshift methods. So *make-do-and-mend* (cf. MAKE *v.*[1] 53 f).

1895 *Dialect Notes* I. 372 These 'ere make-dos are no 'count. **1916** KIPLING *Tales of 'Trade'* 13 The full tale of their improvisations and 'make-do's' will probably never come to light. **1923** *Daily Mail* 12 Feb. 4 When..prices steadily mounted to their peak, thousands of careful housewives adopted what was known as a 'make-do' policy. **1944** in R. W. Zandvoort et al. *Wartime English* (1957) 151 This garment is being made in the Make-do-and-Mend Department of the store from an old costume. **1948** *Times* 19 Aug. 5/2 Large schemes..must be ruled out; make do and mend must take their place. **1961** L. MUMFORD *City in Hist.* xiv. 420 The spirit of make-shift and make-do too often prevailed.

'makedom. *Sc.* ? *Obs.* Also 5–6 **makdome.** [App. f. either MACK *a.* or MAKE *sb.*[1] + -DOM; but the formation is somewhat anomalous, esp. for so early a period.] Form, shape; *esp.* elegant form, shapeliness, comeliness; rarely *concr.*

c **1470** HENRY *Wallace* IX. 358 Bathe statur and curage, Maner, makdome, thar fassoun and thar wesage. **1508** DUNBAR *Tua Mariit Wemen* 73 To manifest my makdome to multitude of pepill. **1535** STEWART *Cron. Scot.* II. 125 Without makdome vther of lym or lith. **1585** JAS. I, *Ess. Poesie* (Arb.) 65 Be warre ze descryue zour Loues makdome, or her fairnes. *a* **1586** MONTGOMERIE *Misc. Poems* I. 13 Fair forme, and face angelicall,..Makdome, and proper memberis all Sa perfyte. *a* **1810** FINDLAY in Ford *Harp Perthsh.* (1893) 419 Yon stalwart makedom I ken richt weel.

†**make-fare.** *Obs.*—0 An alleged name for the hare.

c **1300** *Names of Hare* in *Rel. Ant.* I. 134.

'make-game. [Cf. MAKE-SPORT.] One who or that which furnishes matter for amusement; hence, a laughing-stock, butt.

1762 BICKERSTAFFE *Love in Village* II. x. (1765) 44, I am the make-game of the whole village upon your account. **1797** MRS. M. ROBINSON *Walsingham* I 280, I thought myself the mere make-game of a giddy girl. **1806** *Sporting Mag.* XXVII. 197 A new discovery or invention, by way of make-game I suppose. **1817** GODWIN *Mandeville* I. 263 I was treated as nothing, a flouting-stock and a make-game.

'make-hawk. *Falconry.* [See MAKE *v.*[1] 45.] A hawk employed to teach young ones.

1575 TURBERV. *Faulconrie* 113 If at þe first you inure hir with a make hawke a good Hearoner. **1674** N. COX *Gentl. Recreat.* (1677) 205 Never fly your Faulcon again at a Hern unless with a Make-hawk well entred. **1773** J. CAMPBELL *Mod. Falconry* 262. **1852** R. F. BURTON *Falconry in Valley Indus* v. 61 *note*, A make-hawk is a staunch bird, or one accustomed to fly at a particular kind of game, used to 'head the pack' when more than a cast are thrown up at once. **1891** HARTING *Bibl. Accipitr.* 226.

'makeless, *a.* *Obs.* exc. *dial.* Forms: see MAKE *sb.*[1] [f. MAKE *sb.*[1] + -LESS.]

1. Without an equal; matchless, peerless.

a **1225** *St. Marher.* 17 Þis is ure cunde, makelese meiden. *a* **1300** *Cursor M.* 12119 And þof þou wen make-less to be, þat nan in lare sal teche þe. *c* **1374** CHAUCER *Troylus* I. 116 (172) In bewte erst so stood she makeles. *c* **1450** HOLLAND *Howlat* 902 He thocht him maid on the mold makless of mycht. **1470–85** MALORY *Arthur* x. lxxiii. 540 It is quene Isoud that oute taken my lady your quene she is makeles. **1500–20** DUNBAR *Poems* lxxv. 52 Wylcum! my golk of maireland, My chirrie and my maikles munȝoun. **1563** *Mirr. Mag., Buckingh.* xiii, A makeles prynce in ryches and in myght. *c* **1615** MURE *Misc. Poems* ii. 33 Mackles dame, quhom all ye world admires. **1674–91** RAY *N.C. Words, Make*, match; *makeless*, matchless. **1829** BROCKETT *N.C. Gloss.* (ed. 2), *Makeless*, matchless, without an equal.

2. Mateless; wifeless, husbandless, widowed.

c **1425** *Seven Sag.* (P.) 3307 The ȝonge that helpe hyr for to lyve, He schal have that he ches, And the holde go makeless. **1513** DOUGLAS *Æneis* VIII. Prol. 32 To mak her maikles of hir man. *c* **1600** SHAKS. *Sonn.* ix, The world will waile thee like a makelesse wife. **1825–80** JAMIESON, s.v. *Maikless*, The mother's a makeless bird.

'make-peace. [See MAKE *v.*[1] 9 c.] One who or something which makes peace; a peace-maker. Also *attrib.*

1516 FABYAN *Chron.* (1811) II. 439 It was not longe after or the Scottis..callyd hir Iane make peace. **1552** T. BARNABE in Ellis *Orig. Lett.* Ser. II. II. 202, I knowe a towne in Normandye..is now a second Rone, & yt is the verye gulfe, gulet and mouthe of the See, and a make-peace yf we hadde yt. **1593** SHAKS. *Rich. II*, I. i. 160. **1601** DANIEL *Civ. Wars* VI. xliv. (1609) 154 When make-peace Hymen shall Bring the conioyned aduerse powers to bed. **1657** W. COLES *Adam in Eden* cccxx. 594 The civill uses whereunto the Birch tree serveth are many, as for the punishment of Children..for it hath an admirable influence upon them, to quiet them when they are out of Order, and therefore some call it Make-peace. **1836** [G. E. INMAN] *Sir Orfeo* 13 Sir Orfeo might have gone To seek his make-peace wife alone. **1855** MISS SEWELL *Cleve Hall* I. 388 Fanny, who was the make-peace of the family, found a place for him at the table.

maker ('meɪkə(r)). Also (4 **makiere, -yere**), 4–5 **macare, makare, -ere,** 4–6 **makar,** (6 *Sc.* **mackar, makkar, makker**). [f. MAKE *v.*[1] + -ER[1].]

1. One who fashions, constructs, prepares for use, or manufactures; a manufacturer, *spec.* in certain trades (see, e.g., quot. 1892).

a **1300** *Cursor M.* 11036 Hijs lauerd he kneu welwel biforn þat he was of his moder born [cf. *Luke* i. 41],..þe makere kneu his hand-werc. *c* **1374** CHAUCER *Troylus* I. 685 (741) It is seyd man maketh ofte a yerde With which þe makere is hym self beten. *c* **1375** *Sc. Leg. Saints* xxxiii. (*George*) 403 Þi godis..ar mad bot of handis of men..þar makaris noþir gifand na hele. *c* **1440** *Promp. Parv.* 319/1 Macare, *factor, plasmator.* **1511–2** *Act 3 Hen. VIII*, c. 6 §3 The maker merchaunt or byer of eny wollen clothes called Bastardes. **1530** PALSGR. 242/1 Maker of haye to cockes. *Ibid.*, Maker of naylles. **1550** LATIMER *Last Serm. bef. Edw. VI* (1562) 129 They be bothe Woodmongers and makers of cooles. **1611** BIBLE *Isa.* xlv. 16 Makers of idoles. **1672** PETTY *Pol. Anat.* (1691) 65, I valued an Irish Cabbin at the number of days food, which the Maker spent in building of it. **1726** tr. *Gregory's Astron.* I. 259 The Makers of these Instruments have fitted an Ecliptic to it. **1858** GREENER *Gunnery* 314 The display of artistically constructed guns by the French makers in their Great Exposition of 1855. **1859** LANG *Wand. India* 384 We procured some honey, which is taken from its makers in a very singular manner. **1873** J. H. NEWMAN *Idea University Def.* 47 The maker of a bridle or an epaulet. **1892** *Labour Commission Gloss.*, *Makers*, the workmen who receive the tops and then complete the making of hand-sewn boots and shoes. The term is also applied to those who make the bottom (with the exception of the finishing) of a rivetted or machine-made boot.

b. with prefixed sb., forming many compounds, q.v. under the first element or as Main words.

14.. *Nom.* in Wr.-Wülcker 685/15 *Hic campanarius*, a belmaker. *Ibid.* 686/35 *Hic anularius*, a ryngmaker. **1502** in *Cov. Corp. Chr. Plays* (E.E.T.S.) App. ii. 104 The wholl body of the craft of the tylmakers of Stoke. **1696** W. DERHAM (*title*) The Artificial Clock-maker. **1711** *Lond. Gaz.* No. 4833/3 Tho. Morse,..a Mathematical Instrument-maker. **1902** *Daily Chron.* 17 Sept. 6/6 The necktie-makers and the artificial-flower-makers.

2. Qualified by *the*, a possessive, or an attrib. phr.: Applied to God as the Creator of the universe. (Now with capital M.)

a **1300** *Cursor M.* 17875 Þis ilke liȝt forsoþe is he þat maker is of lastyng liȝt. **1340** *Ayenb.* 251 Þe herte..y-ziȝþ hire zelue and hire makiere. *Ibid.* 262, I leue ine god uader almiȝti makere of heuene and of erþe. *c* **1400** *Destr. Troy* Prol. 1 Maistur in mageste, maker of Alle. *c* **1440** *Promp. Parv.* 319/1 Macare of noghte, as God only, *creator*. *c* **1470** HENRY *Wallace* v. 229 Flayt by him self to the Makar off buffe. ? **1507** *Communyc.* (W. de W.) Bij, I was made to knowe my maker And to loue hym ouer all thynge. **1535** COVERDALE *Ps.* xciv. [xcv.] 6 Let vs knele before the Lorde oure maker. **1599** SIR J. DAVIES *Nosce Teipsum* 54 O what is man (great maker of mankind). **1629** MILTON *Hymn Nativ.* ii, Confounded, that her Makers eyes Should look so neer upon her foul deformities. **1718** WATTS *Hymn* i, Nature with open volume stands, To spread her Maker's praise abroad. **1827** KEBLE *Chr. Y., Septuag.* iii, The glorious sky embracing all Is like the Maker's love. **1871** CARLYLE in *Mrs. C.'s Lett.* II. 221 Pious to God the Maker and to all He had made.

†**b.** *to receive one's Maker*: to receive the Communion. Hence applied to the consecrated Host in the mass. *Obs.*

1539 T. PERY in Ellis *Orig. Lett.* Ser. II. II. 145 That hys Grace..recewythe hys maker yerlye acording to the lawdebwll usse..of owr holly mother Chwrche. **1634** *Malory's Morte Arthur* (1816) II. 100 Then he received his Maker [*Malory* x. lxii. 520 his creatoure]: and, when he was dead [etc.]. **1635** PAGITT *Christianogr.* 51 Henry Stephens writeth of a Dogge, that did eat 80 of their Hoasts, or Makers, in one morning.

3. One who composes a book, draws up a document, frames a law, or the like.

a **1340** HAMPOLE *Psalter* xvii. 13 Þe haly gast..þat is makere of haly writ. *c* **1375** *Sc. Leg. Saints* x. (*Mathou*) 566 Makare of þe saltere. **1485** *Act 1 Hen. VII*, c. 7 The Maker of any such Warrant. **1495** *Act 11 Hen. VII*, c. 8 Which acte ..is so obscure..that the true entent of the makers therof cannot..be undrestond. **1594** HOOKER *Eccl. Pol.* III. ix. §1 Lawes for the Church are not made as they should be, vnles the makers follow such direction as they ought to be guided by. **1818** CRUISE *Digest* (ed. 2) V. 229 The makers of the act.

b. with prefixed sb. (Cf. 1 b.)

1678 BUTLER *Hud.* III. ii. 274 Sp'ritual Affidavit makers. **1719** DE FOE *Crusoe* II. xv, Our map-makers..do not agree. **1902** GREENOUGH & KITTREDGE *Words* 181 A controlling effect on the action of the early language-makers.

4. In various immaterial senses: One who brings about or produces a condition, effect, state of mind, etc.; a creator or producer (*of*); †one who appoints to an office; †a contriver.

c **1430** *Syr Gener.* (Roxb.) 2682, I dar wel swere That Malachias is chief maker With som treason vs to betray. *c* **1522** BP. FOX in Ellis *Orig. Lett.* Ser. II. II. 6 The Kyng that was my maker and promotor to the dignytie that I..doo occupye. *a* **1568** ASCHAM *Scholem.* I. (Arb.) 68 You be in deed, makers or marrers, of all mens maners within the Realme. *Ibid.* 85 The greatest makers of loue, the daylie daliers. **1568** GRAFTON *Chron.* II. 751 They..perceiuyng that the Castell of Barwicke was the onely maker of the peace. **1617** MORYSON *Itin.* I. 205 The maker of the bargaine. *a* **1625** SIR H. FINCH *Law* (1636) 409 All mainteyners, conspirators, makers of confederacie. **1714** POPE *Let. to Mrs. T. Blount* Lett. (1737) 133 Her makers of visits and complements. **1858** LONGF. *M. Standish* II. 66, I am a maker of war, and not a maker of phrases. **1871** SMILES *Charac.* i. 22 Great workers and great thinkers are the true makers of history.

b. with prefixed sb. (Cf. 1 b.)

1601 SIR W. CORNWALLIS *Disc. Seneca* (1631) 56 Death or destiny or any of those period makers. **1719** D'URFEY *Pills* II. 341 Who dully think all Foreigners Man-makers, Send out their Booby Sons to France, to Dress. **1827** HONE *Every-day Bk.* II. 12 Drink is..the widow-maker of their wives. **1876** OUIDA *Winter City* ii. 16 The calumny-makers.

5. A poet. *Obs.* exc. *arch.* (Cf. Gr. ποιητής.)

1387–8 T. USK *Test. Love* III. iv. (Skeat) I. 258 In wit and in good reason of sentence, he [Chaucer] passeth al other makers. *c* **1400** *Beryn* 2462, I woll nat feyn oon woord, as makers doon to ryme. **1470–85** MALORY *Arthur* x. lxxxiv. 562 There is no maker can reherce the tenthe parte. **1500–20** DUNBAR *Poems* iv. 45, I see that makaris amang the laif Playis heir ther pageant, syne gois to graif. *Ibid.* liii. 22 Than cam in Dunbar the Mackar [*v.r.* makker]. **1577–87** HOLINSHED *Chron.* II. 42/2 Owen Odewhee, a preacher, and a maker in Irish. **1581** SIDNEY *Apol. Poetrie* (Arb.) 24 Wherein I know not, whether by lucke or wisedome, wee Englishmen haue mette with the Greekes, in calling him a maker. **1756–82** J. WARTON *Ess. Pope* II. 98 Here all is in life and motion; here we behold the true Poet or Maker. **1876** BESANT & RICE *Gold. Butterfly* iii. 27 'You find your pleasure in reading divine poetry', said the Maker softly. **1878** GROSART *Introd. H. More's Poems* 46/1 To reinscribe the venerable name of Henry More among our real Makers and Singers.

†**6.** *Cards.* (See quot. 1754.) *Obs.*

1753 *Scots Mag.* XV. 74/2 You'd rather hold—two aces and a maker. **1754** 'GYLES SMITH' *Refl. Card-playing* 14 (Brag) Here the Power of the Knave is so great, that he is usually called a Maker. The Meaning is, that, whatever Company he comes into, he is enabled to make himself one of them. He is a Queen, with Queens; a King, with Kings; and an Ace, with Aces.

7. 'The person who signs a promissory note' (Wharton *Law Lex.* 1848).

8. With an adv.: **maker-up**, one who 'makes up' in various senses (esp. in technical use).

1535 COVERDALE *Isa.* lviii. 12 Thou shalt be called the maker vp of hedges. **1846** TRENCH *Mirac.* xxix. (1862) 412

A maker-up of the narrative from later and insecure traditions. **1884** W. S. B. McLaren *Spinning Woollen & Worsted* 64 One or two men, called 'makers-up', are employed for each box to keep drawing the wool through their hands, making it into a kind of 'lap'. **1891** *Daily News* 16 Jan. 8/4 Wanted, overseer, in country printing office... Good maker-up. **1892** *Labour Commission Gloss.* s.v., After the bodies and parts of Britannia metal goods have been shaped..the maker-up puts them together.

Hence (nonce-wds.) **'makeress**, a female maker of something (in comb. ***brick-makeress***); **'makership**, the office of a maker or creator.

1857 *Househ. Words* XVI. 411/2 Brick-makers and brick-makeresses jolting up and down on planks. **1863** F. Hall in *Reader* 24 Jan. 95 We should much like to know..whether the Magian sage [Zoroaster] seems to have had any idea of Makership apart from a material cause.

make-ready. [f. phr. *to make ready* (see READY *a.* III).]

1. = READY C. 2.

1830 Marryat *King's Own* ii, The captain..brought his men to the 'make ready', and they were about to present.

2. *Printing.* The operation of 'making ready' (see READY *a.* 15 b); the result thereby obtained; the sheet on which the overlays are pasted for printing a particular form of type. Also *attrib.*

1887 *Sci. Amer.* 25 June 405/1 It is a safe rule to keep the make-ready of every type job until the job has been distributed. **1915** *Southward's Mod. Printing* (ed. 3) II. iii. 39 As a preventive against slurring through baggy tympans as much of the make-ready as is practicable should be done at the back of the forme. **1946** *N. & Q.* 9 Mar. 93/1 Most early books are marked by bad paper, brownish ink, poor typography, lack of care in 'make-ready', and crude illustrations. **1959** *Times* 14 Jan. 12/4 A saving of 50 hours' make-ready time. **1967** Karch & Buber *Offset Processes* ii. 24 Makeready can be mechanical..with the 3 M makeready machine. **1970** E. A. D. Hutchings *Survey of Printing Processes* 200 *Make-ready*, specifically, all operations carried out on the production machine from receipt of the job to the start of the production run.

makerell(e, obs. form of MACKEREL.

makeshift ('meɪkʃɪft). [f. phr. *to make shift* (see SHIFT *sb.*).]

A. *sb.*† **1.** One who is given to making shifts; a shifty person, a rogue. *Obs.*

1565 J. Halle *Hist. Expost.* B bb iij, Not longe after came thither a makeshifte, with two men wayghting on hym,.. bragging that he was a profounde phisicien. **1573** Tusser *Husb.* (1878) 43 At night if it shine, out trudgeth Hew make shift, with hooke and with line. **1598** Barret *Theor. Warres* I. i. 7 The subtill make-shift, is preferred before the silent man. **1602** F. Herring *Anatomyes* 23 The Colledge is now become the Common Inne of Make-shifts and Impostors. **1608** Middleton *Trick to catch Old one* II. i, [He] whom but last day he proclaimed rioter, penurious make-shift, despised brothel-master.

2. That with which one makes shift; a temporary substitute of an inferior kind. (Cf. B. 2.) Also *transf.*, of a person.

Quot. 1848 may belong to sense 1.

1802–12 Bentham *Ration. Judic. Evid.* (1827) V. 408 Jurisprudential law is the miserable makeshift of inexperienced ages. **1822** Lamb *Elia* Ser. I. *Roast Pig*, The cottage was a sorry antediluvian make-shift of a building. **1848** [see WIRE-PULLER]. **1850** W. Irving *Goldsmith* xiii. 153 Goldsmith continued to consider literature a mere make-shift. **1873** Burton *Hist. Scot.* I. i. 27 They hated patchwork and makeshifts. **1899** Baring-Gould *Bk. of West* I. xiii. 230 The Maypole is a makeshift for an actual tree. **1912** [see GAWD]. **1920** H. Crane *Let.* 22 Dec. (1965) 50, I..hope that I have not been relinquished as one of Akron's temporary 'make-shifts' or 'reliefs'. **1951** E. Paul *Springtime in Paris* ix. 162 Dr. Thiouville..completed his studies under the De Gaulle régime and the first few Middle-of-the-Road makeshifts.

3. The action of making shift.

1870 *Daily News* 27 Oct., There is..so much clever make-shift to be accomplished that [etc.].

B. *attrib.* or as *adj.*

† **1.** Of persons: Shifty, roguish. *Obs.*

1592 Greene (*title*) Groatsworth of Witte: bovght with a million of Repentance: Describing the Folly of Youth, the falshood of Make-shift Flatterers.

2. a. With which one makes shift; serving as a temporary and inferior substitute.

1683 Moxon *Mech. Exerc., Printing* x. *ad init.*, A make-shift slovenly contrivance. **1757** Mrs. Griffith *Lett. Henry & Frances* (1767) III. 44, I readily grant, that these make-shift Pleasures fall short..of mutual Delight. **1809** Malkin *Gil Blas* VII. v. ¶5 After our make-shift dinner..I will treat you with a couple of bottles. **1876** Geo. Eliot *Dan. Der.* I. iii, With..everything make-shift about us,..what was the use of my being anything?

b. *transf.* Characterized by makeshifts.

1824 Lamb *Elia* Ser. II. *Capt. Jackson*, Your honest aims at grandeur, your makeshift efforts of magnificence. **1854** Mrs. Gaskell *North & S.* xvi, How will Margaret bear our makeshift poverty after the thorough comfort and luxury in Harley Street? **1887** Hissey *Holiday on Road* 333 Patched and repaired in a happy makeshift way.

Hence **'make-shiftness**, the condition of being a makeshift; **'make-shifty** *a.*, of the nature of or characterized by makeshift; whence **'make-ˌshiftiness.**

1858 Lady Canning in Hare *Two Noble Lives* (1893) II. 422 The hospitals at Allahabad are rather make-shifty. **1866** *Q. Rev.* July 224 The make-shifty and hap-hazard looseness with which some 800,000 black semi-barbarians were.. admitted to the full civil rights of English citizens. **1887** Ruskin *Præterita* II. 267 Partly through laziness and make-shiftiness..I never opened the midmost wall, though it considerably fretted me. **1892** *Black & White* 12 Mar. 346/1 He hated..the make-shiftness of poverty.

† **make-sport.** *Obs.* [See MAKE *v.*[1] 9.] One who or something which provides sport for others; hence, a laughing-stock.

1611 Speed *Hist. Gt. Brit.* VIII. ii. §12. 381 To adventure himselfe among the Danish Host, as a base Minstrell and contemptible Make-sport. *a* **1625** Fletcher *Chances* III. i, My patience..must be your make-sport now. **1640** Quarles *Enchirid.* III. xliv, Let not mirth be thy profession, lest thou become a Make-sport. *a* **1661** Fuller *Worthies* (1840) II. 455 Being made the make-sport in all plays for a coward.

b. *attrib.* or as *adj.* Providing sport; mocking.

1582 Stanyhurst *Æneis* I. (Arb.) 41 Let make sport Bacchus [L. *lætitiae Bacchus dator*]..be present. **1600** T. Weelkes *Madrigals of 5 & 6 Parts* ix. C i, The make sport Cuckow, and the Quaile. **1621** Bp. Mountagu *Diatribæ* 11 No..mad prankes playd by any toyish or make-sport diuels in the vault.

'make-up. [f. phr. *make up* (see MAKE *v.*[1] 96).]

1. a. The manner in which something is made up, put together, or composed; composition, constitution. *spec.* The character or temperament of a person (cf. quot. 1821). Also *transf.*

1821 *Examiner* 708/1 Some national distinctions in the make-up of French and English minds. **1864** H. Spencer *Illustr. Univ. Progr.* 62 Something in the pattern or make-up of their clothes. **1891** *Field* 5 Dec. 865/3 Our Cambridge correspondent describes the practice..and gives the make up of the crews. **1896** *Allbutt's Syst. Med.* I. 169 There may be an inherited defect in the 'make-up' of one particular tissue. **1898** [see GET *v.* 81 b]. **1908** W. McDougall *Introd. Social Psychol.* iv. 117 Constitutional conditions..that exert a constant influence..responsible for much in the mental make-up of the adult. **1928** *Morning Post* 23 Mar. 15 M. Poincaré..works alone, and has nothing of the people's tribune in his make-up. **1942** *R.A.F. Jrnl.* 13 June 5 The lack of conscience in the make-up of the Japanese. **1965** G. N. Garmonsway in Bessinger & Creed *Medieval & Ling. Stud.* 140 He becomes the prototype of the more ruthless type of Germanic hero, with a touch in his make-up of the berserk or ruffian. **1975** *Country Life* 6 Feb. 343/1 Dogs possessing faults in their make-up..are liable to pass them on to their offspring.

b. The balancing of accounts at the end of a certain period; cf. MAKE *v.*[1] 96 j. Also *attrib.*

1952 *Economist* 21 June 839 Electricity repayments by B.E.A. completed by the date of the May make-up. **1975** *Guardian* 20 Jan. 12/2 On the latest make-up date, the banks' acquisitions of interest-bearing liabilities were.. higher.

2. a. Chiefly *Theatr.* An appearance of face, dress, etc. assumed in order to impersonate a character.

1858 Geo. Eliot in Cross *Life* (1885) II. 61 The Zouaves, with their wondrous make-ups as women. **1862** Dickens *Lett.* 16 Mar. (1880) II. 177 Add to this a perfectly picturesque and romantic 'make up'..and you have the leading virtues of the impersonation. **1872** *Punch* 19 Oct. 163/1 His make-up was admirable, his playing of the first and last act well-nigh faultless. **1882** Besant *Revolt of man* iii. 61 In her make-up she studiously affected..the vigour and strength of middle life.

b. *concr.* Cosmetics, paint, etc. used by actors in making up. Also used by women generally.

1886 *All Year Round* 28 Aug. 78 The whole tribe of Cosmetics, curtly designated in theatrical parlance as 'make-up'. **1888** *Pall Mall G.* 27 Jan. 2/1, I..asked for a towel and soap to wash my make-up off. **1932** 'N. Shute' *Lonely Road* vii. 135 She had made herself look quieter than before. It may have been that she had less make-up on. **1959** J. Braine *Vodi* xxi. 229 Her mother would..put on a little makeup. The lipstick and rouge seemed to give the large face..not less but more dignity. **1974** *Listener* 7 Nov. 603/3 We've all got our 'titfers' on, four layers of make-up, every jewel we can find.

c. Style of costume, get-up. *rare.*

1883 *Daily News* 6 Sept. 2/2 The mongrel cross-country make-up indulged in for the Spa promenade.

d. The action or process of 'making up' with cosmetics, etc.

1890 *Cent. Dict.*, *Make up*,..the preparation of an actor for impersonating the character assigned to him, including dress, painting and altering the appearance of the face, etc. **1922** J. Erskine *Coll. Poems* 120 If this world be a stage, what hours we give To tedious make-up in the tiring-room. **1930** *Punch* 8 Jan. 47/2 One 'make-up' each morning, says Popkin, is plenty. **1951** *Good Housek. Home Encycl.* 20/2 It is a good idea to have also a magnifying mirror for shaving or make-up. **1974** *Country Life* 28 Nov. 694/3 A cleanse and make-up from £2.50, a make-up lesson £5.

e. A make-up room; the place where an actor or the like is 'made up'; the work of such a place. *colloq.*

1960 *Guardian* 5 May 9/4, I..lost no time phoning Groucho, who was 'in make-up'. **1967** M. Shulman *Kill 3* III. viii. 146 'She's been to make up?' 'Only a bit of powder. We thought the wan look was best.' **1972** *New Statesman* 28 Apr. 554/3 There are still important women in BBC TV. They have four of the top 70 jobs, to do with planning, education and children's programmes. And Head of Make-up, of course. **1973** *Listener* 20 Dec. 838/3 They've got a new girl in make-up here and I'm not sure whether she has caught the Ronnie Corbett look.

3. *Printing.* The process of making up type into columns or pages; the matter so made up. Also, an editor's selection of articles to form a number of a periodical.

1852 Smedley *L. Arundel* xv, That is the 'make-up', as we call it, of the third and fourth sheets of the Magazine. **1884** in *Cassell's Encycl. Dict.* **1899** *Daily News* 23 May 10/5 Compositor (Society) seeks situation. All-round jobbing, posters, make up, etc.

4. a. A made-up story; an invention or fiction.

1844 Alb. Smith *Adv. Mr. Ledbury* lv. (1886) 167 The whole story is one of the most singular make-ups that ever attained universal credence. **1877** Spurgeon *Serm.* XXIII. 101 Have you undergone a great transformation? The necessity for it is no make-up of mine, remember.

b. *colloq.* or *dial.* Something (esp. food) made up from odds and ends. Also *attrib.*

1854 A. E. Baker *Gloss. Northamptonshire Words* II. 6 *A make-up dinner*, a dinner composed of scraps and remnants. **1877** J. M. Neilson *Poems* 48 The treacle mak'-up on the candyman's stand. **1924** 'L. Malet' *Dogs of Want* v. 129 The sort of refreshments caterers supply at a public entertainment like this—left-overs and make-ups, from the local restaurants.

5. a. A compensation. *rare.*

1859 W. Chadwick *Life De Foe* vi. 309 He was taken into diplomatic service by Harley, as a make-up..for his forced neglect of his pamphleteer while confined in Newgate.

b. Replacement of the water lost from a boiler or the like by evaporation, leakage, etc.; water added for this purpose.

1930 *Engineering* 10 Jan. 56/1 Others..treat the entire boiler feed water, including condensate and make-up, [etc.]. **1971** *Sci. Amer.* May 71/2 The amount of water required for 'makeup' in a large cooling tower is considerable. **1972** R. G. Kazmann *Mod. Hydrol.* (ed. 2) iv. 133 A 500 megawatt plant will use 500,000 gallons of water an hour for makeup purposes.

6. *attrib.* as (sense 2 a) ***make-up girl, man, room***; (sense 2 b) ***make-up box, kit, tray***; (sense 2 d) ***make-up mirror***; (sense 3) ***make-up copy, editor, hand, man***; **make-up bed**, a bed that can be set up temporarily.

1911 A. Bennett *Hilda Lessways* IV. i. 276, I quite forgot about the *make-up bed for Florrie. **1885** J. K. Jerome *On the Stage* 93 A '*make-up' box, a dressing-case, writing-case, etc., etc., made a pretty big pile. **1960** G. A. Glaister *Gloss. Bk.* 249/1 **Make-up copy*, i.e., a set of folded sheets and plates put in the correct order as a pattern. **1903** J. Ralph *Making of Journalist* xiii. 153 Around the walls are the desks..that of the night or '*make-up' editor, and that of the managing editor. **1972** H. Evans *Editing & Design: Newsman's English* i. 8 In the composing room..an editorial man watches... He may be called a production editor, a make-up editor or a stone sub or stone editor. **1957** *Times* 28 Aug. (Radio & T.V. Suppl.) p. xix/2 Ordeal by Television.. under the impersonal inspection of..camera-men, *make-up girls. **1971** 'W. Haggard' *Bitter Harvest* vii. 74 A make-up girl had powdered his bald patch... Now he sat..in the sweaty studio. **1949** R. Hostettler *Technical Terms Printing Industry* 122/2 *Make-up hand. **1955** A. Huxley *Genius & Goddess* 51 Ruth..squandered a year's accumulated savings on a *make-up kit and a bottle of cheap perfume. **1896** *Living Topics Mag.* (N.Y.) Jan. 105 The best stage manager in England, as well as the best *make-up man and character delineator. **1922** S. A. Cuneo *From Printer to President* 43 It was necessary for the owner to be a typesetter, a make-up man, a press feeder, in fact an all 'round printer. **1959** Make-up man [see *goose pimples*]. **1973** W. McGivern *Reprisal* (1974) 116 A part in a picture..a make-up man to fuss over her. **1964** *Harper's Bazaar* Nov. 99 The *make-up mirror..in black opaline and ormolu, £27. **1966** H. Nielsen *After Midnight* (1967) vi. 86 A make-up mirror on the bedside table. **1900** *Daily News* 15 Nov. 6/1 Some curious illustrations are derived from the '*make-up room'. **1889** *Pall Mall G.* 29 Oct. 3/1 On it are placed candles, a looking-glass, a '*make-up' tray [etc.].

make-weight, makeweight ('meɪkweɪt). [See MAKE *v.*[1] 23.]

1. A comparatively small quantity added to make up a certain weight; *spec.* a small candle. (See early quots.)

1695 Kennett *Par. Antiq.* Gloss. s.v. *Putta*, In the North a Puttock-candle is the least in the pound, put in to make weight, call'd..in Kent a make-weight. **1764** *Oxf. Sausage* 56 Dire Want of..chearful Candle (save the Make-Weight's Gleam Haply remaining). **1787** Grose *Prov. Gloss.*, *Make-weight*, a small candle thrown in to complete the pound. N. **1866** Jevons *Coal Quest.* (ed. 2) 261 A large part of our shipping would thus have to leave our ports half empty, or in ballast, unless there were some makeweight or natural supply of bulky cargo as back carriage.

transf. **1785** Grose *Dict. Vulg. Tongue*, *Make weight*, a small candle, a term applied to a little slender man.

2. *fig.* A person or thing of insignificant value thrown in to make up a deficiency or fill a gap.

1776 Paine *Com. Sense* (1791) 33 By her dependence on Britain she [America] is made the make-weight in the scale of British politics. **1796** Burke *Regic. Peace* iii. Wks. VIII. 418 The mines..are now thrown in as a make-weight in the scale. **1809** Malkin *Gil Blas* VII. vii. ¶21 She praised me up to the skies, and held all the actresses in Madrid as mere makeweights in the scale. **1825** Coleridge *Aids Refl.* (1848) I. 188 Those semi-pagan Christians who regarded revelation as a mere make-weight to their boasted religion of nature. **1838** Dickens *Nich. Nick.* xix, The colonel was in conversation with somebody, who appeared to be a make-weight, and was not introduced at all. **1838–9** Hallam *Hist. Lit.* IV. IV. vi. §43. 284 An incestuous passion brought forward as the make-weight of a plot, to eke out a fifth act. **1864** Pusey *Lect. Daniel* vi. 393, I cannot..use Divine authority as a makeweight to human proof.

3. A counterbalancing weight, counterpoise.

1787 Jefferson *Writ.* (1853) II. 108 His devotion to the principles of pure despotism, renders him unaffectionate to our governments. His fear of England makes him value us as a make weight. **1855** Kingsley *Westw. Ho!* xxviii, 'But the prize?' 'Ah! that was no small make-weight to our disasters, after all'. **1886** Symonds *Renaiss. It., Cath. React.* II. xi. 307 Perhaps it may be argued that the fulsome promises on which those miserable vassals found their hopes, are make-weights for such miseries.

4. *attrib.* or as *adj.* Serving as a make-weight.

1701 J. PHILIPS *Splendid Shilling* 98 The glimmering light Of make-weight candle. 1793 ANNA SEWARD *Lett.* (1811) III. 248 It is no custom of Shakespeare's to give us merely makeweight epithets. 1852 R. S. SURTEES *Sponge's Sp. Tour* xl. 219 Men..admit of no makeweight, or merely ornamental dishes.

make-work ('meɪkwɜːk). orig. *U.S.* [f. MAKE- + WORK *sb.*] Work or activity of little or no value devised mainly to keep someone busy. Also *attrib.*

1937 *Political Q.* VIII. 608 A nation-wide organization of relief work, including..genuine public works and a host of make-work projects of questionable merit. 1947 *Yale Law Jrnl.* Dec. 182 Community development subordinated to make-work and pump-priming. 1957 [see *cost-accounted* ppl. a. s.v. COST *sb.*² 6]. 1972 *Guardian* 13 Sept. 12/1 Still the old make-work continues, the mailbags and the excessive cleaning, which..occupy almost a quarter of the prison population.

Makhzen, -an: see MAGHZEN.

maki ('meɪkɪ, 'mækɪ). [repr. Malagasy '*maka*, a species of lemur' (Richardson *Malag. Dict.* 1885).] The French name of the LEMUR, formerly current in English. (Cf. MACACO².)

1774 GOLDSM. *Nat. Hist.* (1824) II. 160 The maki kind in some measure seems to unite the fox and the monkey. 1797 *Encycl. Brit.* (ed. 3) IX. 785/2 The catta, or ring-tailed maki, inhabits Madagascar and the neighbouring isles. 1839 *Penny Cycl.* XIII. 419/1 The Makis, or Macaucos, properly so called, *Lemur*.

makiere, obs. form of MAKER.

makim-, makinboy: see MACKENBOY.

‖**makimono** (maki'moːno). Also **emakimono**, **makemono**, (with hyphen) **maki-mono**. [Jap., something rolled up, a scroll. The form *emakimono* contains the element *e* picture, painting.] A Japanese scroll containing pictures, usually with explanatory writing, to form a continuous narrative, designed to be examined progressively from right to left as it is unrolled.

1882 G. A. AUDSLEY *Ornamental Arts Japan* I. plate 16 (*caption*), She appears to be rising out of the mist at her feet bearing a *makimono* covered with writing. 1884 SATOW & HAWES *Handbk. for Travellers Cent. & N. Japan* (ed. 2) 554/2 *Maki-mono*, a long roll graphic or pictorial. 1889 S. BING in *Artistic Japan* III. 161 All the paintings..are executed..on rolls of silk or paper, which are known in the Japanese language as *Kakémono* (that is to say, a thing to hang up) when the subject is upright, and under the word *Makimono* when it stretches itself out in a horizontal manner. 1901 L. HEARN *Jap. Misc.* 243 The shrine contained a *makémono*, or scroll, inscribed with the spirit-names of many ancestors. 1911 L. BINYON *Flight of Dragon* x. 81 The makimono, or continuous long scroll-paintings of landscapes, admirably fulfilled the aim of Taoist art. 1926 A. WALEY tr. *Sacred Tree* 31 The first painted makimonos.. were regarded merely as a succession of topographical records, joined together more or less fortuitously. 1958 Y. YASHIRO *2,000 Yrs. Jap. Art* iv. 161 The finest expression and the fullest development of *Yamato-e* are the *e-makimono* (scroll-paintings). 1966 J. ROSENFIELD tr. *Noma's Arts Japan* vi. 122 These long horizontal paintings, the *emakimono*, are sometimes said to be peculiarly Japanese in form, but similar scrolls have been made by the Chinese as well.

making ('meɪkɪŋ), *vbl. sb.*¹ [OE. *macung*, f. *macian*: see MAKE *v.*¹ and -ING¹.]

1. a. The action of MAKE *v.*¹ in its various senses: fabrication, production, preparation; institution, appointment; doing, performance (of a specified action); conversion into, causing to become something; etc. (See the vb.) Also occas. the process of being made.

a 1123 *O.E. Chron.* an. 1101 þurh þes macunge..se eorl Rotbert..þis land mid unfriðe ȝesohte. *a* 1300 *Cursor M.* 1551 Quen sa fele yeier ar wroken oute..þe planetes all ar went again O þair first making in to þe state. 1377 LANGL. *P. Pl.* B. III. 62, I shal..Wowes do whitten and wyndowes glasen, Do peynten and purtraye and paye for þe makynge. *c* 1440 HYLTON *Scala Perf.* (W. de W. 1494) II. xxxiv, We be beholde to loue Ihũ moche for oure makynge but more for our ayenbyenge. 1483 *Rolls of Parlt.* VI. 254/1 Sith the tymes of makynge of the seid Acts of Atteinders. 1529 RASTELL *Pastime of People* (1811) 148 The makynge of Westmyster halle. 1553 CRANMER *Let. to Q. Mary* in Coverdale *Lett. Martyrs* (1564) 1 If by any meanes it had bene in me to haue letted the makyng of that will. 1578 LYTE *Dodoens* I. vii. 13 Of this herbe they make Axsen, which is vsed for the making of glasses. 1611 BIBLE *Transl. Pref.* 1 To motion the making of a new Law for the abrogating of an old. 1625 HART *Anat. Ur.* II. i. 55 Whether the vrine were thinne at the first making or not. 1662 STILLINGFL. *Orig. Sacr.* III. iv. §5 Many causes concurred to the making of this Deluge. 1667 MILTON *P.L.* III. 113. 1703 MOXON *Mech. Exerc.* 239 Most Counties in England afford Earth for the making of Bricks. *a* 1715 BURNET *Own Time* (1724) I. 320 They set it..up for a maxim, that the making of a Stadtholder was the giving up their liberty. 1738 SWIFT *Pol. Conversat.* 52, I think she was cut out for a Gentlewoman, but she was spoil'd in the making. 1823 J. BADCOCK *Dom. Amusem.* 29 Whitening and plaister of Paris..whiten the flour, and contribute to its adhesion in making. 1828 in Picton *L'pool Munic. Rec.* (1886) II. 343 In the making of the purchases. 1842 TENNYSON *Morte D'Arthur* 203 Since the making of the world. 1875 F. GUTHRIE *Magn. & Electr.* §236 If it be desired to get a still more nimble making and breaking of the circuit. 1891 *Law Rep.* Weekly Notes 138/1 The making of the Codicil. 1897 *Daily News* 4 Jan. 3/4 There was a general move up in all the ranks of the force, accompanied by the 'making' of several engineers.

b. Often used gerundially as the second member of an objective combination, as ***biscuit-, carpet-, debate-, gift-, ice-, imposition-, war-making***, etc. See also BOOK-MAKING, HAYMAKING, etc.

c 1400 *Laud Troy-bk.* 3113 In sorwe and dele-makyng Lenges non honour. *Ibid.* 14538 With-oute any debate-makyng. *c* 1449 PECOCK *Repr.* (Rolls) II. 552 With this trust thei helden hem content and paied in her ȝifte making. 1523 LD. BERNERS *Froiss.* I. clv. 187 Such as were at the imposicion makyng. 1560 DAUS tr. *Sleidane's Comm.* 116 b, They take in hande also an other peace making. 1614 T. GODWIN *Moses & Aaron* (1641) 142 Their Apotheosis, or god-making Ceremonies. 1768 STERNE *Sent. Journ., Montriul* iii, His talents of drum-beating and spatterdash-making. 1863 TREVELYAN *Compet. Wallah* (1866) 182 An early effort of the Public Works Department in the canal-making line. 1880 MORRIS in Mackail *Life* (1899) II. 5 The art of Carpet-making is dead, or dying fast. 1891 T. HARDY *Tess* xxix, At skimmings, at butter-makings, at cheese-makings.

c. Qualified by a possessive, in phr. *of* (so-and-so's) *making* = made by (so and so). In predicative use sometimes with omission of *of*.

1470–85 MALORY *Arthur* x. lxii. 519, I kyng Hermaunce.. am slayn..thurȝ two knyghtes..of myn own bryngyng vp and of myn owne makyng. 1500–20 DUNBAR *Poems* xlvi. 55 His creature of his awin making. ? *c* 1526 FRITH *Disput. Purgat.* To Rdr. (?1533) A iv b, I haue sent you such bokes as you wrote for, and one moo of Rastels makinge. 1611 BIBLE *Transl. Pref.* ¶13 [They] doe either make new Translations themselues, or follow new ones of other mens making. *a* 1654 SELDEN *Table-t.* (Arb.) 35 The Laws of the Church are most Favourable to the Church, because they were the Churches own making. 1676 LADY CHAWORTH in *12th Rep. Hist. MSS. Comm.* App. v. 28 'Twas a match of his friends and not his owne making. *a* 1700 DRYDEN *Cinyras & Myrrha* 52 Man a Slave of his own making lives. 1709 STEELE *Tatler* No. 44 ¶3 The Statuary, who fell in Love with the Image of his own making. 1828 CARLYLE *Misc.* (1857) I. 206 A poet of Nature's own making. 1894 HALL CAINE *Manxman* III. xvii. 183 The marriage was not of her making.

d. (*to be*) *in making*, *a-making*, now usually *to be making*: (to be) in course of being made.

c 1430 *Pilgr. Lyf Manhode* (1869) 19 All manere of fardelles maad and in makinge. 1480 CAXTON *Chron. Eng.* ccviii. 190 That bisshop had in london a fayre toure in makynge. 1535 COVERDALE *2 Macc.* i. 23 All the prestes prayed, whyle the sacrifice was a makynge. 1605 SHAKS. *Macb.* III. iv. 34 The Feast is sold That is not often vouch'd, while 'tis a making. 1702 *Royal Proclam.* 8 Mar. in *Lond. Gaz.* No. 3790/4 Corn or Grain making into Malt. 1761 HUME *Hist. Eng.* III. liv. 171 Provisions of arms were making beyond the sea. 1767 MRS. S. PENNINGTON *Lett.* III. 177 This..gentleman..informed her of the use that was making of her letters. 1791 WASHINGTON *Lett.* Writ. 1892 XII. 54 Those changes, which are either making, or contemplated. 1793 *Copper-Plate Mag.* No. 22 This ancient place..is watered by the River Soar,..now making navigable. 1816 SHELLEY *Lett.* Pr. Wks. 1888 I. 341 The hay was making under the trees. 1857 KINGSLEY *Misc.*, *Th. Gravel-pit* II. 381 When the South-Western Railway was in making. 1891 *Graphic* 31 Oct. 526/3 That good prices are making for English cheese argues good quality.

e. ***in the making***: used adjectively (in imitation of Milton) to designate something as existing in an undeveloped state.

1644 MILTON *Areop.* (Arb.) 69 Opinion in good men is but knowledge in the making. 1876 GEO. ELIOT *Dan. Der.* lxiv, His opinion..may be our virtue in the making. 1879 MAUDSLEY *Pathol. Mind* vi. 282 Evil is good in the making as vice is virtue in the making. 1889 D. HANNAY *Capt. Marryat* vii. 99 Unless the [newspaper] correspondent has seen history in the making. 1890 *Guardian* 26 Nov. 1892/3 It is a great soul in the making.

2. *spec.* in technical uses: The training or bringing to the required condition (of an animal); the preparation (of hay); the curing (of fish).

1390 GOWER *Conf.* II. 161 He tawhte men..the makinge Of Oxen, and of hors the same. 1523 FITZHERB. *Husb.* §25 A man maye speke of makynge of hey, and gettynge of corne, but god disposeth and ordreth all thynge. 1615 LATHAM *Falconry* (1633) 12 Forget not all this time of her making.. to walke round about her, using your voice, and giving her many bits with your hand. 1809 KENDALL *Trav.* II. xlvii. 154 The curing, or as it is called, the making of the fish. 1893 *Field* 17 June 904/3 The light swath is converted from grass to hay in a few hours without any 'making'. 1902 *Daily Chron.* 21 July 3/1 Ponies that only require 'making' in order to become valuable.

†**3.** Poetical composition; poetizing, versifying. Also *pl.* = poetical compositions, poems. *Obs.*

c 1330 R. BRUNNE *Chron. Wace* (Rolls) 129 For þis makyng I will no mede bot gude prayere when ȝe it rede. *c* 1374 CHAUCER *Troylus* v. 1789 But litel bok no makyng þow nenuye But subgit be to alle poesye. *c* 1375 *XI Pains Hell* 352 in *O. E. Misc.* 222 Meruel ȝe not of þis makyng. 1377 LANGL. *P. Pl.* B. XII. 16 þow medlest þe with makynges and myȝtest go sey þi sauter. *c* 1430 LYDG. *Min. Poems* (Percy Soc.) 128, I the refreyn tooke, Of hym that was in makyng soverayne, My maister Chaucier. 1567 DRANT *Horace, Ep.* To Rdr. *v, Flim flames, and gue gawes,..are soner rapte vp thenne are those which be lettered and Clarkly makinges. 1589 PUTTENHAM *Eng. Poesie* III. xix. (Arb.) 247 A noble gentleman and much delighted in vulgar making. 1614 J. DAVIES *Eclogue* 19 (Grosart) For, fro thy Makings, milke, and mellie, flowes To feed the Songster-swaines with Arts soot-meats.

†**4.** Testamentary disposition. [= MDu. *makinge.*] *Obs.*

1621 in *Brasenose Coll. Muniments* (MS.) 22/12, I charge myne executors that the same [money] bee payed according to my makinge.

5. Advancement, success. *Obs.* exc. in phr. ***to be the making of***: to be what ensures the success of (a person or thing).

c 1470 G. ASHBY *Active Policy* 731 A man to be preferred to honour Of fee or office to his grete makyng. 1496–7 *Plumpton Corr.* (Camden) 124 Your good and discret answere may be my making. 1622 MABBE tr. *Aleman's Guzman d'Alf.* II. 215 They [women] are the making or the marring of their house. *a* 1680 BUTLER *Rem.* (1759) II. 31 A lucky Repartee hit upon by Chance may be the making of a Man. 1749 FIELDING *Tom Jones* VIII. xi, The fine gentleman, ..who doth so much honour to his family and is to be the making of it. 1871 SMILES *Charac.* xi. (1876) 324 A wife may be the making or the unmaking of the best of men.

†**6. a.** The way in which a thing is made; style of construction; conformation, form, shape, build, 'make'. *Obs.*

1393 LANGL. *P. Pl.* C. XIV. 193 þer-fore meruaileþ me for man, as in makynge, Is most yliche þe in wit and in werkes, Whi [etc.]. 1398 TREVISA *Barth. De P. R.* XVIII. ix. (1495) 763 Congres and Elys ben lyke to serpentes in makynge. *c* 1400 *Destr. Troy* 9774, I..am febiller be fer þen þe fre prinse, Both of myght, & of makyng, & of mayn strenkith. 1466 in Willis & Clark *Cambridge* (1886) III. 93 The same dores and wyndowes shalbe like of strength and makyng of the dores and wyndowes of the other new scoles. 1494 in *Somerset Medieval Wills* (1901) 323 A newe mete-cloth of Lankeshire making. 1523 FITZHERB. *Husb.* §2 There be plowes of dyuers makynges in dyuers countreys. 1534 MORE *On Passion* Wks. 1304/1 That oyntment truly made was veri costly: which was the cause that the true making was lesse vsed. 1599 HAKLUYT *Voy.* II. I. 103 In colour, eating, and making like a Makarell. 1642 SHIRLEY *Sisters* v. i. (1652) 49, I see the greatest men are flesh And blood, our souls are much upon a making. 1656 HEYLIN *Surv. France* 54 There are erected..[nine] hansome Crosses of stone; all of a making. 1660 *Act 12 Chas. II*, c. 4. Sched. s.v. *Buckrams*, Buckrams of French making. 1662 J. DAVIES tr. *Olearius' Voy. Ambass.* 263 Another sort of insect of a making much like a Spider. 1669 STURMY *Mariner's Mag.* II. 45 A general and particular Description, Making, and Use of all the.. Instruments.

†**b.** with reference to a literary production; in quots. = version, edition. *Obs.*

1382 WYCLIF *Prov.* Prol., Masloch, that Ebrues Parablis, the comun making [St. Jerome *vulgata editio*] Prouerbis clepeth. 1482 CAXTON *Higden's Polychron.* Prohemye, Polychronicon..emprynted & sette in forme by me William Caxton and a lytel embelysshed fro tholde makyng.

†**c.** Of persons: Bodily form or appearance; build, 'make'. *Obs.*

c 1430 *Generydes* 4555 By his making He is ful like to my derling. 1587 FLEMING *Cont. Holinshed* III. 355/1 Some.. esteemed him a man for making well proportioned. 1590 SHAKS. *Com. Err.* IV. ii. 22 Stigmaticall in making worse in minde. 1609 HOLLAND *Amm. Marcell.* 282 Bigge he was of making, and withall verie tall. *c* 1640 *Lovely North. Lasse* iii. in Child *Ballads* IV. 208/2, I was so greatly taken with his speech, and with his comely making.

†**d.** Mental or moral character; = MAKE *sb.*² 3.

1647 CLARENDON *Hist. Reb.* I. §120 William earl of Pembroke was next, a man of another mould and making.

7. *concr.* **a.** Something that has been made; †a created thing, creature (*obs.*); a product of manufacture. Also, the quantity made at one time.

1340 *Ayenb.* 92 þet þet body of man is þe meste poure makynge..and þe spirit of man..ys..þe heȝeste sseppe þet may by. 1645 *Shetland Witch Trial* in Hibbert *Descr. Shetl. Isles* (1822) 594 You did thereby marr and undo twa whole makings of the said bear, quhilk never did good. 1823 J. BADCOCK *Dom. Amusem.* 139 Whatever quantity is required for any particular job of work should be made all at one time; no two makings coming away alike, but depending entirely upon accident. *Ibid.* 150 Cut your making into cakes. 1882 OGILVIE, *Making*..2. What has been made, especially at one time; as, the whole making is before you. 1890 *Century Dict.* s.v., A making of bread.

b. *pl.* Earnings, profits. *colloq.*

1837 HT. MARTINEAU *Soc. Amer.* III. 122 That a wife shall possess half, or a large part, of her husband's earnings or makings. 1892 *Cassell's Sat. Jrnl.* 21 Sept. 13/3 My makings in the way of tips bringing in on an average about twice that sum. 1900 *Daily News* 10 Feb. 2/4 'Makings', in the way of tips, had been very poor.

8. a. The material out of which something may be made; the potentiality of becoming something; in phr. ***to have*** or ***be the making***(***s of***...

1613 SHAKS. *Hen. VIII*, IV. i. 87 She had all the Royall makings of a Queene. 1837 DICKENS *Pickw.* xxxvii, He seemed to have the makings of a very nice fellow about him. 1857 LAWRENCE *Guy Liv.* iii. 17 There was the making of a good rider in many of them. 1858 TROLLOPE *Dr. Thorne* I. v. 124 He's the making of a very nice horse, I don't doubt. 1861 W. H. RUSSELL in *Times* 24 Sept., They are not an army, but they are the making, as we say, of a splendid one. 1886 *American* XII. 134 This Bavarian king was the making of a fine man when he was young. 1887 H. SMART *Cleverly won* ii. 16 There was possibly the makings of a great cross-country horse in her.

b. *pl.* Paper and tobacco for rolling a cigarette. *N. Amer.*, *Austral.*, and *N.Z. colloq.*

1905 'O. HENRY' in *Everybody's Mag.* Dec. 817/1 He took out his 'makings' and rolled a cigarette. 1907 S. E. WHITE *Arizona Nights* I. ix. 161 'Well,' agreed Rogers, 'pass over the "makings" and I will.' 1910 R. W. SERVICE *Trail of '98* (1911) I. iv. 15 'Got the makings?' 'No, I'm sorry; I don't smoke.' 1912 *Collier's* 21 Dec. 23/2 A revelation to any man who doesn't know a real 'makin's' cigarette. 1930 J. DEVANNY *Bushman Burke* 26 He grinned and took out the 'makings'. 1940 *Amer. Speech* XV. 213/1 The day before payday, the camp's 'smoking' has become scarce and

'rollings' or 'makings' are at a premium. **1941** *Coast to Coast* 207 We rolled our makings, lit them and stood about waiting for someone to start talking about something. **1949** S. P. LLEWELLYN *Troopships* 7 The normal Kiwi..his clothes in a heap beside him, the 'makings' handy. **1963** B. PEARSON *Coal Flat* iv. 70 Rogers offered him a cigarette but McKenzie shook his head and pulled out the makings in a way that seemed to suggest that tailor-mades were a stigma of middle-class ideology. **1963** H. GARNER in R. Weaver *Canad. Short Stories* (1968) 2nd Ser. 30, I gave McKinnon enough money to get me a package of makings.

9. *pl.* in *Coal-mining.* (See quots.)

1851 GREENWELL *Coal-trade Terms Northumb. & Durh.* 36 *Makings.*—The small coals hewed out in kirving. **1883** GRESLEY *Gloss. Coal Mining, Makings,* the slack and dirt made in holing.

10. *Comb.* **a.** attributive: **making-cylinder,** in a paper-making machine, the cylinder on which the pulp is felted into a sheet (distinguished from the *beating cylinder* and the *drying cylinder*); **making-felt,** 'that felt of a cylinder paper-machine on which the web of pulp is taken from the making-cylinder' (Knight); **making-iron** (now often confused with *meaking-iron*: see MEAKING), a kind of grooved chisel used by caulkers to finish off seams.

1769 FALCONER *Dict. Marine* (1780) II, *Calfat double,* a caulker's making-iron. **1846** YOUNG *Naut. Dict.* s.v. *Caulk.*

b. With following adv. or adj., forming nouns of action corresponding to phrasal combinations of the sb., as ***making-off, -out, -over,*** MAKING-UP; ***making-good;*** **making-merry** *rare* = MERRY-MAKING; **making-out,** the action of the vbl. phr. *to make out* (MAKE *v.*[1] 91 c (*c*)); **making-ready,** preparation (for technical uses see READY *a.* III); also *attrib.* Also **making-as-if** *nonce-wd.* (cf. MAKE *v.*[1] 70), pretence, make-believe.

1382 WYCLIF *John* xix. 14 It was the makinge redy, or euyn, of pask. **1530** PALSGR. 242/1 Makyng redy, *parure.* **1674** N. FAIRFAX *Bulk & Selv.* 118 For the better making out of which, we are to bethink our selves, that [etc.]. *Ibid.* 129 We shall find that begetting the like, is making over of springs. **1813** L. HUNT in *Examiner* 3 May 273/2 That ordinary and vulgar state-cunning,—that wretched *making-as-if.* **1815** J. LAING *Voy. Spitzbergen* (1822) 99 The process of paring and barrelling up the blubber, is termed *making off.* **1822** SCOTT *Peveril* iv, A making-merry in the house of Tirzah. **1846** YOUNG *Naut. Dict.* s.v. *Flensing,* The blubber ..is cut into square pieces and stowed in the hold; afterwards, these are..cut into smaller pieces to be stowed away in casks; this latter process is termed *making-off.* **1874** SOUTHWARD *Pract. Print.* xlv. (ed. 4) 413 Place the sheet [of paper]..on the making-ready board. **1881** YOUNG *Every Man his own Mechanic* §1386 All *making good* as it is technically called—i.e. patching up holes in old plastering —used to be done with plaster. **1887** GOODE, etc. *Fisheries U. S.* Sect. v. II. 286 Paring and barreling blubber, termed making-off. **1957** F. KOHNER *Gidget* vii. 76 'No sweaty hands, no making out in drive-in movies.' 'Making out?' My God, Larry, where've you been living. I guess you still call it necking.' **1964** C. NICOLAI *Murder in Fine Arts* xxviii. 248 He had a violent aversion to necking or 'making out' as the current expression had it. **1967** 'J. H. ROBERTS' *February Plan* I. iv. 113 She had been..putting him off when it came to making out (how many evasive phrases were there for the act of sexual intercourse?). **1969** E. GOFFMAN *Where Action Is* 157 Adult males may define a female as an object to initiate a sexually potential relationship with... This action is sometimes called 'making out'. In our society there are special times and places set aside for making out.

†**'making,** *vbl. sb.*[2] *Obs.* [f. MAKE *v.*[2] + -ING[2].] Mating, matchmaking.

1608 MIDDLETON *Trick to Catch Old One* III. iii, My Vncle comes with Gentlemen, his friends, And tis vpon a making.

making ('meɪkɪŋ), *ppl. a. rare.* [f. MAKE *v.*[1] + -ING[1].] That makes (in various senses); †productive, creative; †money-making, prosperous.

1434 MISYN *Mending Life* 126 With swetnes of þe godhede & warmnes of Makand lyght. **1592** WEST *1st Pt. Symbol.* §46 A, Instruments..of their effects be either constitutiue and making, or remissorie and liberatorie. **1760–72** H. BROOKE *Fool of Qual.* (1809) III. 118 You are an industrious and a making young man. *a* **1774** GOLDSM. *Surv. Exp. Philos.* (1776) I. 31 When artificial magnets are made by rubbing, each pole in the making magnet begets its sympathetic pole of a different name in the newly made magnet. **1903** *Daily Chron.* 18 Nov. 8/6 Artificial Florist. —Wanted a good making forewoman.

makings, obs. form of MACKINS.

making-up. a. In the various senses of *make up* (see MAKE *v.*[1] 96); completion; compounding, composition; reconciliation; dressing up and disguising for the impersonation of a character; the balancing of accounts at the end of a certain period.

1593 ABP. BANCROFT *Daung. Posit.* IV. x. 168 Of purpose to haue drawen Lancaster vnto them, for the making vp of a quaternion. **1620** MASSINGER & FIELD *Fatal Dowry* III. i, Thy Taylor,..Can bring more to the making vp of a man, Then can be hop'd from thee. **1671** BLAGRAVE *Astrol. Physick* (title-p.), Directing the way to Distil and Extract their Vertues and making up of Medicines. **1674** N. FAIRFAX *Bulk & Selv.* 39 The finites that go to the making up of an infinite. **1753** CHAMBERS *Cycl. Supp., Making Up,* a term used by the distillers to express the bringing spirits up to a certain standard of strength by the addition of water. **1808** C. STOWER *Printer's Gram.* 467 As soon as the first person brings him his matter, he [*sc.* the clicker] counts off the number of lines,..then gives him another taking of copy, and proceeds with the making up [of the type pages]. **1816** JANE AUSTEN *Emma* I. xii. 206 She hoped they might now become friends again... Making-up indeed would not do. *She* certainly had not been in the wrong. **1827** L. T. REDE *Road to Stage* 40 My readers will call to mind the excellent 'making up' of Mr. T. P. Cooke, in the Monster, 'Frankenstein'. **1838** DICKENS *Let.* 15 Nov. (1965) I. 453 On the other side I forward you a copy of the making-up. **1840** CARLYLE *Heroes* ii, Any making-up of his mind. **1841** W. SAVAGE *Dict. Art of Printing* 470 When a compositor in a companionship has composed his copy to within the quantity of a page of the work, he gives the overplus of the copy, after having completed his own last page, to him who is composing the copy that follows his matter... This is called *giving the making-up.* **1864** D. W. THOMPSON *Day Dreams Schoolm.* (ed. 2) 231 Then will we promise to be good; we will throw tiny arms half round papa's neck..O the bliss of making up! **1869** MRS. H. WOOD *R. Yorke* xxv. II. 226 That lady..had absolute need of artistic aid in the matter of making-up. **1878** E. C. MADDISON *Speculation on Stock Exchange* 15 The process known as 'making-up' settles many bargains before the arrival of the settling-day. Making-up commences on the contango-day and is continued on the ticket-day. **1884** MCLAREN *Spinning Woollen & Worsted* 65 The master should therefore insist on his 'making up' being done thoroughly. **1890** *Daily News* 23 Dec. 5/4 The herring boats came in from sea at Lowestoft last week, and the process of 'making-up' being now concluded [etc.]. **1892** *Ibid.* 10 May 7/3 From ten to twenty millions have been added to the market value of Stock Exchange securities since the last making-up. **1894** BEERBOHM in *Yellow Bk.* I. Apr. 73 'Making-up' is an art. **1905** J. C. LINCOLN *Partners of Tide* iv. 74 His worst quarrel with Gus and her friend, Clara Hopkins—the quarrel that lasted two weeks without a making up—came about because the new member refused to tell what the initials 'stood for'. **1913** *Trans. Bibliogr. Soc.* XII. 303 There seems to have been a good deal of very clumsy making-up of copies in the early part of last century.

b. *attrib.*

1875 *Encycl. Brit.* I. 92/1 The price at which such transactions are adjusted is the 'Making-Up' price of the day. **1883** HOWELLS *Woman's Reas.* x. I. 206 I've written him a making-up letter. **1887** *Pall Mall G.* 12 Oct. 12/1 The following table shows the drop since the last making-up price. **1890** *Ibid.* 8 Sept. 7/2 Since the last 'making up' day most of the movements in the Home Railway market have been favourable to operators for the rise. **1895** A. J. WILSON *Gloss. Terms Stock Exch., Making up Prices,* the prices fixed on the first and second days of the settlement for the purposes of continuing or carrying over transactions. The prices at which transactions continued to the following account are settled. **1900** *Daily News* 3 Dec. 2/5 The shirt and making-up factories are..very well engaged. **1969** *Jane's Freight Containers 1968–69* 195/1 Three rail sidings are available for making-up trains.

makins, obs. form of MACKINS.

makkar, -er, obs. Sc. forms of MAKER.

makkers, dial. form of MACKINS.

‖**makkoli** ('mækəlɪ). [Korean.] A popular alcoholic beverage in Korea.

1972 P. M. BARTZ *S. Korea* 73/1 Domestic production [of wheat] is one-quarter the volume of imports and is used mainly for noodles and *makkoli,* the common alcoholic beverage. **1972** E. FODOR *Japan & E. Asia* 477 These are both cloudy and light-tan colored and are known together as *makkoli.*

mako[1] ('makɔ). [Maori.] In full, ***mako shark.*** A large blue shark of the genus *Isurus,* esp. *I. oxyrinchus;* also called mackerel shark.

1727 J. G. SCHEUCHZER tr. *Kæmpfer's Hist. Japan* I. I. 133 *Mako* never exceeds three or four fathom in length. **1848** R. TAYLOR *Leaf from Nat. Hist. N.Z.* 14 *Mako,* a shark, peculiar to this latitude, teeth prized as ear ornament. **1872** F. W. HUTTON *Fishes N.Z.* 77 *Lamna Glauca.* Tiger Shark. Mako... The shark from which the Maoris obtain the teeth with which they decorate their ears. **1936** 'R. HYDE' *Check to Your King* xiii. 153 They wore pieces of *mako* tooth in the lobe of the ear. **1938** *Times Lit. Suppl.* 24 Sept. 619/1 Giant mako in New Zealand waters. **1952** E. HEMINGWAY *Old Man & Sea* 100 He was a very big Mako shark built to swim as fast as the fastest fish in the sea. **1959** *Manch. Guardian* 13 July 5/1 The sharks come to Cornwall..blue sharks, makos, porbeagles. **1969** A. WHEELER *Fishes Brit. Isles & N.-W. Europe* 53/1 The mako has no commercial value beyond its angling appeal. **1970** *E. Afr. Standard* (Nairobi) 2 Jan. 19/4 The big item of fishing news last week..was the capture of Kenya's first mako shark. **1972** *Shooting Times & Country Mag.* 27 May 17/1 The four British species of shark are blue, mako, porbeagle and thresher.

mako[2], var. MAKOMAKO[2].

Makololo (mækɔ'ləʊləʊ), *sb.* and *a.* Also **Makalolo, Ma Kololo. A.** *sb.* A Negro people of Africa now living in Zambia near the junction of the Zambesi and Kafue rivers; a member of this people. **B.** *adj.* Of or pertaining to this people.

1857 D. LIVINGSTONE *Missionary Trav. & Res. S. Afr.* ix. 179 Mamochisane..said she would never consent to govern the Makololo so long as she had a brother living. *Ibid.* x. 204 The Makololo chiefs pride themselves on eating with their people. **1867** [see SJAMBOK *sb.* *y*]. **1871** J. MACKENZIE *Ten Yrs. North of Orange River* ii. 34 Both the Matebele and Makololo countries were far beyond the territories of the Transvaal. **1871** C. M. YONGE *Pioneers & Founders* xi. 306 There was no choice but to have recourse to the Makololo, and thus let loose one set of savages against another. **1900** A. H. KEANE *Boer States* vii. 101 The Makololos and other Basutos..founded a powerful State about the middle Zambesi. **1932** C. FULLER *Louis Trigardt's Trek* 21 The foundation of the Ma Kololo nation. **1974** J. R. BAKER *Race* xx. 371 By far the largest group of houses recorded by any of the explorers was at Linyanti, in Makololo territory. *Ibid.* 389 Among the Bakuena and Makololo..there was no despotic cruelty.

makomako[1] ('makɔ'makɔ). *N.Z.* [Maori.] = KORIMAKO.

1848 R. TAYLOR *Leaf from Nat. Hist. N.Z.* 8/2 Makomako, a bird. Syn. with korimako. **1873** W. L. BULLER *Hist. Birds N.Z.* 91 *Anthornis Melanura* (Bell-Bird).. Native names. Mako, Makomako..Korimako..Kopara. Of the above names, Korimako is most generally used by the northern and Makomako by the southern tribes. **1875** W. E. ATKINSON *Let.* 16 Aug. in *Richmond-Atkinson Papers* (1960) II. 399, I have also the mako mako, silver-eye, [etc.].., and besides the birds a great many shells. **1911** *Encycl. Brit.* XIX. 626/2 The tui and makomako rank high as songsters. **1966** [see KORIMAKO].

makomako[2] ('makɔ'makɔ). *N.Z.* Also **mako.** [Maori.] A small New Zealand tree, *Aristotelia serrata* (or *A. racemosa*), of the family Elæocarpaceæ, which bears clusters of small pink flowers and dark red berries; also called wineberry.

1848 R. TAYLOR *Leaf from Nat. Hist. N.Z.* 20/2 *Mako,* a tree; the bark used as a black dye. *Makomako,* a tree (*Friesia racemosa*). **1861** A. S. ATKINSON *Jrnl.* 24 Mar. in *Richmond-Atkinson Papers* (1960) I. 696 Just before the fireplace were a few makos which they had been sleeping on. **1866** LINDLEY & MOORE *Treas. Bot.* II. 92/1 The berries of *Aristotelia racemosa,* the Mako-Mako of the natives, are eaten. **1883** J. HECTOR *Handbk. N.Z.* (ed. 3) 130 Mako, a small handsome tree, six to twenty feet high, quick-growing, with large racemes of reddish nodding flowers. **1949** P. BUCK *Coming of Maori* (1950) II. ix. 239 The spears were formed of..rods of light *mako* wood. **1966** *Encycl. N.Z.* II. 670/1 (*caption*) *Aristotelia serrata,* mako-mako or wineberry, is a small tree of graceful appearance.

Makonde (mə'kəʊndiː), *sb.* and *a.* **A.** *sb.* A Bantu-speaking people of Tanzania and Mozambique; a member of this people. **B.** *adj.* Of or pertaining to this people.

1911 *Encycl. Brit.* I. 330/2 Bantu negroids... Ma-konde. *Ibid.* III. 359/1 The archaic *Makonde* or *Mabiha* [language] of the lower Ruvuma, and the coast between Lindi and Ibo. **1948** D. DIRINGER *Alphabet* 26 The Makonde people, an important tribe of Tanganyika Territory. **1973** *Times* 17 Feb. (Mozambique Suppl.) p. iv/3 (Advt.), The Makondes were more given to tattooing. **1974** *Times* 2 May 5/2 Mr Simon Makada, a Makonde..and a Frelimo youth leader. **1974** *Afr. Encycl.* 317/3 The Makonde are traditionally an agricultural people... In Mozambique many Makonde and Makua people are involved in war against the Portuguese administration.

makoré (mækɔ'reɪ). Also **makora, makori.** [Native name in West Afr.] A large West African tree, *Tieghemella* (or *Mimusops*) *heckelii,* of the family Sapotaceæ; also, the dark red-brown wood produced by it.

1915 J. H. HOLLAND *Useful Plants Nigeria* III. 422 *Dumoria Heckeli*... Vernac[ular] names... Mako, Makoré, Makerou. **1936** *Nature* 9 May 791/1 Skirting and dado in specially cut logs of Makoré with small marquetry banding in the Makoré doors of maple burr. **1947** J. C. RICH *Materials & Methods of Sculpture* x. 292 Makore is also known as Makori, Makora, and African cherry. The wood is beautifully figured. **1972** *Handbk. Hardwoods* (Building Res. Establishment) (ed. 2) 121 Marine plywood of makoré is also widely used in boat-building.

makrel(l, obs. form of MACKEREL[1] and [2].

†**makrelty.** *Obs.* Also **makrellty, maclarte.** [Metathetic alteration of MDu. *makelardie,* f. *makelare* broker: see MACKELER.] Brokerage.

1495 in *Halyburton's Ledger* (1867) 106 Item makrellty 8 g. **1498** *Ibid.* 124 Item for makrelty of the 2 sekis to Peter Rekeyr, 5s. **1499** *Ibid.* 225 Item for maclarte, ilk sek xxx g.

†**makron.** *Obs.*—[0] [? corruption of MALKIN.] = MALKIN 3.

1573 BARET *Alv.* M 56 A Makron or colerake. *Rutabulum.*

maktuk, var. MUKTUK.

makuk, var. MOCOCK.

makumba, var. MACUMBA.

makuta: see LIKUTA.

makutu (mɑː'kʊtʊ). *N.Z.* [Maori.] Sorcery, witchcraft; a magic spell. Also as *v. trans.,* to bewitch.

1846 J. WHITE *Jrnl.* (MS.) 1 If anyone..offended us..we should try to kill them by makutuing them to see if makutu was true. **1905** W. B. *Where White Man Treads* 41 Another decimating tool in the hands of spite and revenge was makutu (witchcraft)... Let one fear that a makutu spell had been laid upon him,.. he would..die! **1938** R. D. FINLAYSON *Brown Man's Burden* 70 She was sure someone had put a makutu spell on her and the evil spirit was eating her life away. **1943** N. MARSH *Colour Scheme* i. 25 'I'll tell my great-grandfather..and he'll *makutu* you.' 'Kid-stakes! Nobody's going to put a jinx on me.' **1963** *Evening Post* (Wellington, N.Z.) 16 Dec., The true tohunga whiawhia, who had gained complete mastery of the powers of makutu, was able to project his spirit in such a manner as to kill men and women. **1971** *N.Z. Listener* 29 Mar. 11 A number of modern case histories of patients whose illness or death has been connected with makutu.

makyere, obs. form of MAKER.

‖**mal.** *Obs.* [F. and It. *mal.*] = EVIL *sb.*[1] 7 b.

1745 Pococke *Descr. East* II. i. 151 Among the English it [a disorder in which blotches break out on the body] goes by the name of the Mal of Aleppo. **1756** A. Russell *Nat Hist. Aleppo* [262 A cutaneous disease..has acquired the name of *Il mal d'Aleppo* or *Aleppo evil*.] 264 The third kind of Mal.. begins like the two others, but [etc.].

Mal, var. Maler *sb.* and *a.*

mal- (mæl), *prefix*, formerly often written **male-** (but pronounced as one syll.), chiefly represents the F. *mal* adv.:—L. *male* ill, badly; rarely, as in *maltalent*, it represents the OF. *mal* adj.:—L. *malus* bad. In its advb. use the prefix occurs in many adoptions from Fr., which are sometimes combinations with vbs., as *maltreat*; sometimes nouns of action formed from such combinations, as *malfeasance*; and sometimes combinations with adjs., where the prefix serves to reverse the favourable connotation of the word, as *maladroit*, *malcontent*. In imitation of these adopted words, *mal-* has from the 16th c. been prefixed to many Eng. words, to convey the sense 'ill', 'wrong', 'improper(ly)'. The words thus modified are chiefly nouns of action, as in *malpractice*, and many physiological terms, as *malassimilation*, *malformation*; occasionally adjs. and vbs., as in *malodorous*, *malappropriate*. The formations that have a permanent character are treated in their alphabetical places; examples of the frequent use of the prefix in the creation of nonce-words are ***mal-accident***, ***-application***, ***-appointment***, ***-association***, ***-cultivation***, ***-development***, ***-direction***, ***-feeling***, ***-hygiene***, ***-identification***, ***-institution***, ***-instruction***, ***-operation***, ***-performance***, ***-publication***, ***-reasoning***, ***-use***, ***-volition***; ***mal-conceited***, ***-created***, ***-discontented***, ***-shapen*** adjs.

1608 H. Clapham *Errour on Left Hand* 29 Master Malcontent, me thinks you are malconceited. **1692** *Rhode Island Col. Rec.* (1858) III. 288 Some male-discontented persons. **1714** J. Fortescue-Aland *Fortescue's Absol. & Lim. Mon.* Pref. 13 It is owing to Passion and Interest, and not to the Male-Institution of the Law. **1715** M. Davies *Athen. Brit.* I. 10 The Expression and Malepublication of the respective criminal Contents of such Scandalous Libels. **1799** R. Warner *Walk* (1800) 6 There are no limits to the vicious conceptions, malassociations, and wild incongruities of false taste. **1803** *Spirit Pub. Jrnls.* VII. 22 If, however, it so happens that either mal-accident or your own discretion ..has prevented [etc.]. **1808** E. S. Barrett *Miss-led General* 125 These malappointments took place..when the army had ceased to be a matter of mere parade. **1822** Mrs. E. Nathan *Langreath* I. 81 This maloperation of the affections ..may be best prevented..by that wholesome species of dissipation. **1824** *Examiner* 423/2 A man I never saw, and therefore could have no malfeeling towards. **1839** *Blackw. Mag.* XLV. 812 Fearful gropings to imitate what they render malcreated and hideous. **1840** Mill *Diss. & Disc.* (1859) I. 94 The question often is, what is least prejudicial to the intellect, uncultivation or malcultivation. **1841** Gen. P. Thompson *Exerc.* (1842) VI. 161 That mal-reasoning which makes men expect [etc.]. **1843** *Jrnl. R. Agric. Soc.* IV. i. 192 The abuse, however, or rather mal-use, of an article is no argument against it. *a* **1849** Poe *Wks.* 1864 III. 369 The heart is stirred, and the mind does not lament its mal-instruction. **1855** Miss Cobbe *Intuit. Mor.* 155 He proceeds ..to guard against its malapplication by arguing that [etc.]. **1870** O. W. Holmes *Mechanism in Th. & Mor.* in *Old Vol. Life* (1893) 305 So to rate the gravity of a mal-volition by its consequences is the merest sensational materialism. **1887** *Harper's Mag.* May 952 Beggars abound, hideously malshapen. **1888** T. Gill in *Amer. Naturalist* Oct. 926 Incredible as such a malidentification on the part of Pictet must appear. **1898** *Allbutt's Syst. Med.* V. 614 Intensified and fostered by conditions of malhygiene. **1899** *Ibid.* VII. 116 The maldirection of movement is much increased when the aid of the sight is denied. *Ibid.* 732 The altered shapes of cells, regarded by Sachs as evidence of congenital maldevelopment. **1938** R. G. Collingwood *Princ. Art* xii. 283 It is the malperformance of the act which converts what is merely psychic (impression) into what is conscious (idea). **1964** M. Critchley *Developmental Dyslexia* ix. 60 Dyslexics show only a mild tendency towards a malperformance of higher order right-left orientation exercises.

Malabar ('mæləbɑː(r)). [The name of a sea-board district in the S.W. of Hindostan.]

1. An inhabitant of the Malabar coast.

1582 N. Lichefield tr. *Lopez de Castaneda's Hist. Conquest E. Indias* f. 37ᵛ They asked of the Malabars which went with him what he was? **1681** R. Knox *Hist. Relation Ceylon* iv. ix. 159 This Plain is..inhabited by Malabars, a distinct People from the Chingulayes. **1753** Chambers *Cycl. Supp.* App., *Malabar-nut*,..the English name of a genus of plants, called by botanists *Adhatoda*. **1787** tr. *Linnæus' Fam. Plants* I. 202 *Basella.* Malabar Nightshade. **1813** Ainslie *Mat. Med. Hindostan* 99 Malabar Cat Mint. *Nepeta Malabarica*. Lin. **1816–20** T. Green *Univ. Herbal* I. 162 *Basella Rubra*, Red Malabar Nightshade. *Ibid.* 777 *Justicia Adhatoda*, Malabar Nut. **1840** Paxton *Bot. Dict.*, Malabar Leaf, see *Cinnamomum Malabatrum*... Malabar Rose, see *Hibiscus Rosa malabarica*. **1855** Ogilvie *Suppl.*, *Malabar Plum*. **1867** C. J. Boyle *Far Away* 72 Started on foot up the gorge, our bags on the shoulders of Malabars. **1882** *Garden* 1 Apr. 215/1 Melastoma malabathrica..is a common plant in Malabar, where it is used in much the same way as the common Laurel is here; hence the name Malabar Laurel. **1883** Simmonds *Dict. Usef. Anim.*, *Malabar Oil-Sardine* (*Clupea longiceps*). Large quantities of oil are made from this fish on the coast of Malabar. **1931** M. Yeo *St. Francis Xavier* xii. 155 One night his faithful Malabar..woke to the sound of blows. *Ibid.*, The Malabar told his tale.

2. The language spoken on the Malabar coast.

1801 T. Munro in G. R. Gleig *Life T. Munro* (1830) I. 322 From Miliserum to the Chandergeery river no language is understood but the Malabars of that coast. **1837** T. Bacon *First Impr. Hindostan* I. 99 He was compelled to fall back upon his only two words of Malabar. **1872** [see Tamulic *a.*]. **1931** M. Yeo *St. Francis Xavier* x. 124 Tamil, the pre-Aryan language of southern India, which Francis, Portuguese-fashion, calls Malabar.

3. A kind of handkerchief (see quots.).

1882 Caulfeild & Saward *Dict. Needlework* 340 *Malabars*, cotton handkerchiefs, printed in imitation of Indian handkerchiefs, the patterns of which are of a peculiar and distinctive type, and the contrasts of colour brilliant and striking. **1957** M. B. Picken *Fashion Dict.* 218/2 *Malabar*, cotton handkerchief printed in brilliant colors and designs of East Indian type.

4. *attrib.*; esp. in the names of various plants, vegetable products, etc. **Malabar bark**, the genus *Ochna* (*Cassell's Encycl. Dict.* 1885); **Malabar catmint**, a labiate plant, *Anisomeles malabarica*, used in India as a tonic and febrifuge; **Malabar laurel**, *Melastoma malabathrica* (see quot.); **Malabar leaf**, *Cinnamomum malabathrum*; **Malabar night-shade**, the chenopodiaceous genus *Basella*; **Malabar nut**, an acanthaceous plant, *Justicia Adhatoda*; **Malabar-oil**, an oil obtained from the livers of various fishes found on the Malabar coast; **Malabar plum**, the jamrosade or rose-apple, *Eugenia jambos* (*Jambosa vulgaris*); **Malabar rose**, a shrubby East Indian rose-mallow, *Hibiscus rosa-malabarica*.

1696 J. Ovington *Voy. Suratt* 213 Many of their Women by their usual Custom in these cases..have gain'd the Name of Malabar Quills. **1778** Malabar language [see Tamil]. **1872** tr. *St. Francis Xavier's Lett.* in H. J. Coleridge *Life & Lett. St. Francis Xavier* II. 73 Enrico Enriquez..writes and speaks the Malabar tongue.

Hence **Malaba'rese** *a.* [-ese], of or pertaining to the Malabar coast or its inhabitants; **Mala'barian** *a.* and *sb.*; **Mala'baric** *a.* and *sb.*; **Mala'barish** *a.* and *sb.*

1709 A. W. Boehm *Propagation of Gospel in East* 17 This place [*sc.* Tranquebar] is altogether stocked with Malabarian Heathens. *Ibid.* 28, I will set down here..the Malabarick Letters. *Ibid.*, I caused..The Lord's-Prayer.. to be put into Malabarick. **1717** J. T. Philipps *Acct. People Malabar* i. 2 According to the Malabarish way of Reasoning. *Ibid.* 8 The chief Reasons why the Malabarians refuse to embrace the Christian Religion. *Ibid.* v. 53 There are some things..writ in Malabarish. **1718** Ziegenbalg & Grundler *Let.* in R. Millar *Hist. Propagation of Christianity* (1731) II. viii. 505 We catechise..every Friday in Malabarian. **1788** Malabaric [see Tamil]. **1808** C. Stower *Printer's Gram.* Index, Malabaric alphabet. **1922** *Blackw. Mag.* May 612/1 The Moplahs..are the descendants of Arab fathers and Malabarese mothers. **1922** O. Jespersen *Language* ii. 39 He [*sc.* Rask] was also the first to see that the Dravidian (by him called Malabaric) languages were totally different from Sanskrit.

‖**malabathrum** (mælə'bæθrəm). *Hist.* Also **malobathrum, mala-, malobathron.** [L. *mălа-*, *mălobathrum*, *-on*, a. Gr. μᾶλά-, μαλόβαθρον, a. Skr. *tamālapattra*, f. *tamāla* (Hindī *tamāl*) the name of various trees (see below) + *pattra* leaf.] An aromatic leaf mentioned by ancient writers; a perfumed ointment prepared from this.

The Hindī *tamāl*, Skr. *tamāla* (which is the source of the Gr. and L. word), is applied to the tree *Xanthochymus pictorius*, and also to various species of *Cinnamomum*, two of which have been named *C. Malabathrum* and *C. Tamala*. The 'malabathrum' of antiquity was prob. the leaf of one or more species of *Cinnamomum*. The identification with the betel leaf (Skr. *tāmbūla*, Hindī *tambōl*) is erroneous.

1601 Holland *Pliny* I. 378 We are beholden moreover to Syria for Malobathrum... Ægypt is more fruitfull of this hearbe than Syria. And yet there commeth a better kind thereof from India than both of these countries. *Ibid.* 379 The perfume or smell that Malobathrum or the leafe yeeldeth when it is boiled in wine, passeth all others. **1625** Purchas *Pilgrims* I. i. i. 43 Amomum, Ginger, Malabathrum, Ammoniake. **1706** Phillips (ed. Kersey), *Malobathrum*. **1885** tr. *Wellhausen's Proleg. Hist. Israel* 391 The cultivation of the malabathron in Syria. **1886** Sheldon tr. *Flaubert's Salammbô* 16 For your enjoyment bread, meat, oil, and malobathrum were provided from the store-houses.

malable, obs. form of malleable.

,malab'sorption. *Physiol.* [f. mal- + absorption.] Imperfect absorption (of food material by the body).

1932 Dorland *Med. Dict.* (ed. 16) 739/2 *Malabsorption*, disorder of normal nutritive absorption; disordered anabolism. **1962** *Lancet* 2 June 1168/2 The rickets of cœliac disease is commonly attributed to malabsorption of vitamin D. **1974** Passmore & Robson *Compan. Med. Stud.* III. xix. 58/1 The term malabsorption syndrome is applied to a number of conditions that affect the gut or digestive glands and which result in disturbance of the absorption of one or more nutrients.

†**malaca'donian.** *Obs.* [app. f. some corruption of melocoton + -ian.] = myrobalan.

1608 *Closet for Ladies* 4 To preserue Mirabolans or Malacadonians. Take your Malacadonians and stone them.

malaca-tawney, obs. f. mulligatawny.

malacaton, -catoon, var. ff. melocoton.

Malacca (mə'lækə). The name of a town and district on the Malay peninsula in the S.E. of Asia; used *attrib.* in some names of plants and vegetable products. **Malacca apple** = *Malay apple* (see Malay *a.*); **Malacca bean**, the fruit of the *Semecarpus Anacardium* or marking-nut of India (see also Molucca); **Malacca cane** (also simply *Malacca*), a walking-cane of a rich brown colour, often clouded or mottled, made of the stem of the palm *Calamus Scipionum*.

1611 Cotgr., *Anacarde*, th' East Indian fruit called Anacardium, or Beane of Malaca. **1844** *Ainsworth's Mag.* VI. 501 He..struck the pavement..with the brass-shod point of his Malacca cane. **1846** A. J. H. Duganne *Daguerrotype Miniature* 7 He held..a musk cigar, and twirled in his right..a unique and delicate Malacca cane. **1855** Ogilvie *Suppl.*, *Malacca bean*. **1856** Seemann *Hist. Palms* 131 The well-known 'Malacca Canes'..do not occur about Malacca itself, but are imported from Siak, on the opposite coast of Sumatra. **1871** *Good Words* XII. 431 It takes an expert to detect a real from a painted Malacca. **1871** Kingsley *At Last* xvi, That with..bright flesh-coloured fruit, [is] a Malacca-apple, or perhaps a Rose-apple. **1885** Lady Brassey *The Trades* 135 The malacca apple with its bright magenta flowers. **1963** J. Kirkup *Tropic Temper* 83 There were some stalls selling..the famous Malacca Canes, stout walking-sticks with carved and decorated handles. **1965** C. Shuttleworth *Malayan Safari* vi. 88 Malacca cane grows in clumps in the jungle.

†**malace.** *Obs. rare*⁻⁰. [ad. L. *malacia* a calm at sea, a. Gr. μαλακία; cf. malacia.] 'A calme at Sea' (Cockeram 1623).

malachatauni, variant of mulligatawny.

malachite ('mæləkaɪt). Forms: α. 4 **melochites**, 8 **malachites, molochites.** β. 6 **molochite**, 6–7 **melochite**, (8 **malachquite**), 7– **malachite**. [a. OF. *melochite*, F. *malachite*, ad. L. **malachītēs*, *molochītēs*, Gr. *μαλαχίτης, *μολοχίτης, a stone (perh. our malachite) resembling the leaf of the mallow in colour, f. μαλάχη, μολόχη the mallow.]

1. a. Hydrous carbonate of copper, occurring as a mineral of a beautiful green colour, susceptible of a high polish; it is often made into ornamental articles. Also, an example or specimen of this mineral.

1398 Trevisa *Barth. De P.R.* xvi. lxvii. (1495) 574 Melochites is a grene stone lyke to Smaragdus and hath that name of the colour of malewes. **1567** Maplet *Gr. Forest* 15 b, The Melochite is a greene Gem, much like to the Smaragde. **1585** T. Washington tr. *Nicholay's Voy.* iv. xi. 123 b, In this place are also found the Sardonique stones, Molochite, and those which are called Iris. **1656** Blount *Glossogr.*, Malachite (*malachites*), a stone of a dark green colour. **1756–7** tr. *Keysler's Trav.* (1760) I. 56 Remarkable stones,..as crystal, dragons-blood, malachites, asteria's. **1844** Disraeli *Coningsby* i. iv, Colossal vases of malachite presented by emperors.

b. ***blue malachite*** = azurite i.

1821 Jameson *Man. Mineral.* 98 Blue Malachite, or Blue Copper.

c. *attrib.*; sometimes quasi-*adj.* = of the colour of malachite. **malachite-green**, (*a*) = malachite; (*b*) a dye of the colour of malachite.

1880 Friswell in *Soc. of Arts Jrnl.* 445 The well-known methyl green..is now..replaced by the malachite green, discovered by Oscar Doebner. **1899** Cagney tr. *Jaksch's Clin. Diagn.* v. (ed. 4) 157 Köster has recently employed malachite-green with good results as a test for hydrochloric acid. **1900** F. Anstey *Brass Bottle* i. 3 Against a background of lapis lazuli and malachite sea.

2. malachite kingfisher, a small blue, green, and red kingfisher, *Corythornis cristata*, found in Africa south of the Sahara; **malachite sunbird**, a blue and green sunbird, *Nectarinia johnstoni*, found in parts of southern and eastern Africa.

[**1875** *Ibis* V. 68 Malachite-crested Kingfisher. This charming little Kingfisher is found invariably frequenting the small streams and ditches close to Durban.] **1903** A. C. Stark *Birds S. Afr.* III. 82 The Malachite Kingfisher is found throughout the greater part of Africa south of the Sahara. **1906** *Daily Chron.* 10 Feb. 7/7 A great rarity is a Malachite sun bird, a most wonderfully-formed bird with a bill as long as its body and as fine as a piece of wire. **1947** J. Stevenson-Hamilton *Wild Life S. Afr.* xxxiv. 300 The beautifully coloured malachite kingfisher (*Corythornis cristata*)..likes to sit on an over-hanging branch, whence he scrutinizes the water beneath. **1966** E. Palmer *Plains of Camdeboo* xii. 197 The male malachite sunbirds would be flashing their astonishing green and gold. **1971** *Country Life* 28 Oct. 1127/2 Tiny malachite kingfishers, brilliant red and blue, sped among the tall rushes.

‖**malacia** (mə'leɪʃ(ɪ)ə). *Path.* [L. *malacia* (*stomachi*), Gr. μαλακία softness, f. μαλακός soft.]

a. Morbid softening of a tissue or part. **b.** Depraved or fanciful appetite, as in chlorosis or pregnancy or dirt-eating. (*Syd. Soc. Lex.* 1889.)

1657 *Physical Dict.*, *Malacia*,..a corrupt appetite,.. which is the cause of longings in women. **1706** Phillips, *Malacia*,..a queasiness, or squeamishness of Stomach... Also a tenderness of Body. **1866** A. Flint *Princ. Med.* (1880) 511 Malacia denotes a morbid craving for certain articles of food or articles which are not devoid of nutrition, whereas pica denotes a desire for innutritious substances.

malacic (mə'læsɪk), *a.* [f. MALAC-IA + -IC.] Of or pertaining to malacia.
1890 in *Century Dict.*

† **mala'cissant**, *a. Obs. rare.* [ad. L. *malacissant-em*, pres. pple. of *malaciss-āre*, ad. Gr. μαλακίζ-ειν, f. μαλακός soft.] Softening.
1638 RAWLEY tr. *Bacon's Life & Death* (1651) 64 The Diet Malacissant or Suppling. **1640** G. WATTS tr. *Bacon's Adv. Learn.* IV. ii. 203 Malacissant and mollifying Qualities.

† ,**malaci'ssation.** *Obs. rare.* [ad. L. *malacissātiōn-em*, n. of action f. *malacissāre*: see prec.] The action of making soft or supple.
1638 RAWLEY tr. *Bacon's Life & Death* (1651) 48 As touching the Malacissation, or Mollifying of the Members, we shall speake afterward. *Ibid.* 50.

malacoderm ('mæləkəʊdɜːm), *a.* and *sb. Nat. Hist.* [f. Gr. μαλακό-ς soft + δέρμα skin.]
A. *adj.* Having a soft skin. B. *sb.* A soft-skinned animal; an animal of any of the various groups called *Malacodermata* (*-derma, -dermi*), viz.: a. one of the two divisions of Reptiles, opposed to *Sclerodermata*; b. a tribe of beetles, including the fireflies; c. the sea-anemones.
1835 KIRBY *Hab. & Inst. Anim.* II. xxii. 414 Though the Malacoderm, or soft-coated Reptiles, appear the legitimate successors of the Fishes. **1866** *Intell. Observ.* No. 56. 134 This curious elongate Malacoderm [an insect]. **1880** PASCOE *Zool. Classif.* (ed. 2) 139 The Malacoderms [= Telephoridæ].

malacodermatous (mæləkəʊ'dɜːmətəs), *a. Nat. Hist.* [f. mod.L. *Malacodermata* neut. pl. (f. Gr. μαλακός soft + δέρμα skin) + -OUS.] Pertaining to the *Malacodermata*, in any of the applications of the term: see prec.
1856 in MAYNE *Expos. Lex.*; and in recent Dicts.

malacodermous (mæləkəʊ'dɜːməs), *a. Nat. Hist.* [f. Gr. μαλακόδερμος soft-skinned (f. μαλακός soft + δέρμα skin) + -OUS.] Soft-skinned; = MALACODERM A.
1856 in MAYNE *Expos. Lex.*; and in recent Dicts.

malacolious, variant of MELANCHOLIOUS *Obs.*

malacolite ('mæləkəlaɪt). *Min.* [ad. F. *malacolithe* (Abildgaard 1800 in *Ann. de Chimie* xxxii. 196: 'pierre molle'), f. Gr. μαλακό-ς soft + λίθος stone: see -LITE.] A synonym of diopside.
1823 PHILLIPS *Mineral.* Index, *Malacolite.* **1859** PAGE *Handbk. Geol. Terms, Malacolite*, known also as Sahlite; a variety of augite of various shades of green, and of a vitreous or sub-pearly lustre.

malacology (mælə'kɒlədʒɪ). [a. F. *malacologie* (De Blainville 1825, who says that it is short for *malacozoologie*), f. Gr. μαλακό-ς soft + -LOGY.] The science which treats of the formation and habits of soft-bodied animals or molluscs.
1836 *Blackw. Mag.* XXXIX. 306 We have also seen your book upon shells, or rather upon malacology. **1857** WOOD *Comm. Obj. Sea-shore* 14 This branch of Natural History has leaped at once out of the mere childish toy of conchology into the maturer science of malacology.
b. *humorously.* The substance of a mollusc.
1854 BADHAM *Halieut.* 38 Men took a great pride..in fattening their different coquillages, not so much..with a view to the increase of the malacology within, as to produce enormous shells. **1855** *Fraser's Mag.* LI. 548 Sometimes after mousing a snail till it has put its head out..they fly at and peck off a little mouthful of its malacology.
Hence **malaco'logical** *a.*, pertaining to malacology. **mala'cologist**, one versed in malacology.
1847–54 WEBSTER, *Malacologist.* **1881** *Amer. Naturalist* Sept. 704 Papers bearing on malacological topics. **1895** *Edin. Rev.* Oct. 358 The recently instituted Malacological Society of London. *Ibid.*, A malacologist is concerned first with the molluscous animal.

malacon ('mæləkən). *Min.* Also † **malacone.** [ad. G. *malakon* (T. Scheerer 1844, in *Ann. d. Physik* LXII. 436), f. Gr. μαλακόν, neut. of μαλακός soft.] A soft brown altered form of zircon.
1854 DANA *Syst. Min.* (ed. 4) III. ii. 196 Malacone. **1868** *Ibid.* (ed. 5) 275 The following tetragonal zircon-like minerals are probably altered zircon... Malacon. **1921** *Mineral. Abstr.* I. 173 The malacon of Madagascar shows a higher degree of radioactivity than is accounted for by its content of thorium. **1941** *Amer. Jrnl. Sci.* CCXXXIX. 306 The third type of [zircon] is characteristic of the younger granite in the Oxford House Area, and of the late pre-Huronian and Huronian granites of the Lake Superior region. This variety is malacon, a form of zircon with relatively low refringence, weak birefringence and a dirty, altered appearance. **1968** I. KOSTOV *Mineral.* II. v. 294 Malacon is a metamict zircon.

malacopterygian (,mæləkɒptə'rɪdʒ(ɪ)ən), *a.* and *sb.* [f. mod.L. *malacopterygi-ī* (f. Gr. μαλακό-ς + πτέρυγ-, πτέρυξ wing) + -AN.]
a. *adj.* Of or pertaining to the *Malacopterygii* or soft-finned fishes. b. *sb.* One of the *Malacopterygii.*
1835 KIRBY *Hab. & Inst. Anim.* II. xxi. 392 Malacopterygian or soft-rayed Fishes. *Ibid.*, Apode Malacopterygians. **1843** LOWE *Fishes Madeira* Introd. 13 The second series of the true fishes, called Malacopterygians or Soft-finned. **1876** *Beneden's Anim. Parasites* 7 A sea anemone living on good terms with a Malacopterygian fish.

malacopterygious (,mæləkɒptə'rɪdʒəs), *a.* [formed as prec. + -OUS.] = MALACOPTERYGIAN *a.*
1753 CHAMBERS *Cycl. Supp.* s.v. *Ammodytes*, The fish is of the malacopterygious or soft-finned kind. **1875** *Encycl. Brit.* I. 31/1 *Abdominales* or *Abdominal Fishes*, a subdivision of the Malacopterygious Order.

‖ **malacosteon** (mælə'kɒstɪɒn). *Path.* [mod.L. f. Gr. μαλακ-ός soft + ὀστέον bone.] = OSTEOMALACIA.
1801 *Med. Jrnl.* V. 50 In..cases where malacosteon has made such dreadful ravages in the female constitution. **1877** tr. *von Ziemssen's Cycl. Med.* XVI. 226.

malacostomous (mælə'kɒstəməs), *a.* [f. mod.L. *malacostom-us* (Ray's *Willughby* 1686; f. Gr. μαλακό-ς soft + στόμ-α mouth) + -OUS.] Of fishes: Having a soft mouth (i.e. toothless jaws); leather-mouthed.
1753 in CHAMBERS *Cycl. Supp.* **1775** in ASH; and in mod. Dicts.

malacostracan (mælə'kɒstrəkən), *a.* and *sb.* [f. mod.L. *malacostraca* pl., Gr. μαλακόστρακα, neut. pl. of μαλακόστρακος softed-shelled (f. μαλακός soft + ὄστρακον shell) + -AN.] a. *adj.* Of or belonging to the *Malacostraca*, one of the orders of the *Crustacea*. b. *sb.* An individual of this order.
1835 KIRBY *Hab. & Inst. Anim.* II. xiv. 18 He [Dr. Leach] further subdivides..the Crustaceans into Entomostracans and Malacostracans. **1859** DARWIN *Orig. Spec.* xiv. (1878) 390 The whole great malacostracan order. **1893** SHIPLEY *Zool. Invertebrata* 280 The characteristic Malacostracan excretory gland is found opening on the second antennæ.

malacostracology (,mæləkəstrə'kɒlədʒɪ). [f. mod.L. *malacostraca* (see MALACOSTRACAN) + -OLOGY.] The science which treats of the *Malacostraca.*
1847–54 in WEBSTER. **1855** in OGILVIE *Suppl.*
Hence **mala,costraco'logical** *a.*, pertaining to malacostracology; **mala,costra'cologist**, one versed in this science.
1890 in *Century Dict.*

malacostracous (mælə'kɒstrəkəs), *a.* [f. mod.L. *malacostraca* (see MALACOSTRACAN) + -OUS.] = MALACOSTRACAN *a.*
1845 *Encycl. Metrop.* XXV. 2 The Malacostracous Crustaceans of Latreille and Edwards. **1877** HUXLEY *Anat. Inv. Anim.* vii. 375 A malacostracous crustacean.

malacotomy (mælə'kɒtəmɪ). [f. Gr. μαλακό-ς soft + -τομία cutting.] The anatomy of soft-bodied animals, e.g. the Mollusca.
1879 in ROSSITER *Dict. Sci. Terms.*
Hence **malaco'tomic** *a.*, pertaining to malacotomy; **mala'cotomist**, one versed in malacotomy.
In some recent Dicts.

malacoton, -oon, -oun, var. MELOCOTON.

malacozoic ('mæləkəʊ'zəʊɪk), *a.* [f. mod.L. *malacozōa* (f. Gr. μαλακό-ς soft + ζῷον an animal) + -IC.] Of or pertaining to the *Malacozoa* or soft-bodied animals, e.g. the Mollusca. *malacozoic series*: Huxley's term for the series of animals from the lowest *Polyzoa* to the highest molluscs.
1877 HUXLEY *Anat. Inv. Anim.* xii. 679.

,**malaco'zooid.** [formed as prec. + -OID.]
1862 DANA *Man. Geol.* (1863) 749 Malacozoöids; or Mollusk-like Protozoans, as the Rhizopods.

malaco-zoology (,mæləkəzəʊ'ɒlədʒɪ). [a. F. *malacozoologie* (De Blainville 1825), f. mod.L. *malacozōa* (see MALACOZOIC and -OLOGY); cf. ZOOLOGY.] = MALACOLOGY.
1856 in MAYNE *Expos. Lex.* **1902** *Catal. Lib. Univ. Museum, Oxford.*

† **ma'lactic**, *a.* and *sb.* ? *Obs.* [ad. Gr. μαλακτικ-ός, f. μαλακ-, stem of μαλάσσειν to soften, cogn. w. μαλακός soft.] a. *adj.* Adapted to soften; emollient. b. *sb.* An emollient medicine. Hence **ma'lactical** *a.*, in the same sense.
1541 R. COPLAND *Galyen's Terap.* 2 C ij, A salue malactyke. **1657** TOMLINSON *Renou's Disp.* 35 Some [purge] by mollifying as most malacticks. *Ibid.* 200 A malactical and mollitive medicament and a Malagm do not at all differ. **1684** tr. *Bonet's Merc. Compit* VII. 253 Ammoniack, or some other Malactick, must be applied. **1727** BRADLEY *Fam. Dict.* s.v. *Gargarism*, Others [Gargarisms]..are malactick and digestive. **1889** in *Syd. Soc. Lex.*

† **malacy**, anglicized form of MALACIA.
1656 in BLOUNT *Glossogr.* **1658–96** in PHILLIPS.

maladaptation (,mælædæp'teɪʃən). [f. MAL- *prefix* + ADAPTATION.] Faulty adaptation. Hence **mala'daptive** *a.*; **mala'daptively** *adv.*
1877 W. K. CLIFFORD *Lect. & Ess.* (1879) II. 273 The silly maladaptations in organic nature are seen to be steps towards the improvement or discarding of imperfect organs. **1931** *Brit. Jrnl. Psychol.* Jan. 334 Prof. Fisher begins his study of the abnormal by considering..how maladaptive the responses of the normal individual often are, when he is faced with a difficult situation. *Ibid.* Oct. 132 Both images and symbols function maladaptively [in mental defectives]. **1957** P. LAFITTE *Person in Psychol.* v. 58 Three modes of adaptive and eight modes of maladaptive behaviour that are used in response to frustration. **1969** *Sci. Jrnl.* Nov. 70/3 Long fingers are..generally maladaptive in terrestrial primates. **1971** *Sci. Amer.* Sept. 132/3 Some aspects of what we have called progress or social evolution may be maladaptive. **1974** *Times Lit. Suppl.* 30 Aug. 923/1 Man's instincts..have become seriously maladaptive. *Ibid.* 923/5 The hypertrophied human brain has become as maladaptive as the dinosaur's armour.

maladdress, anglicized form of MALADRESSE.

† **malade.** *Obs.* [a. F. *malade*: see MALADY.] A sick person, an invalid.
1483 CAXTON *Gold. Leg.* 271 b/2 And the malades and seke men refused their medycyne and heler. **1651** tr. *De-las-Coveras Don Fenise* 8 They carried the Malade unto Poleron's house.

‖ **malade imaginaire** (malad imaʒinɛr). [Fr. (after the title of Molière's play, 1673); cf. MALADE.] A person suffering from an imaginary illness.
1818 LADY MORGAN *Florence Macarthy* IV. v. 202, I trust you will not think I am playing the *Malade Imaginaire*, when I assign indisposition as an excuse for my absence. **1888** *Athenæum* 15 Dec. 811/1 A *malade imaginaire*..who sacrifices her daughter to her own comfort. **1911** G. B. SHAW *Doctor's Dilemma* Pref. p. xxviii, Doctors..nurse the delusions of the *malade imaginaire.* **1958** M. STEWART *Nine Coaches Waiting* v. 60 Enough pills and boluses to satisfy the most highly-strung *malade imaginaire.* **1974** E. AMBLER *Dr. Frigo* II. 80 He's..inclined to worry about his health. If you mean do I think him a malade imaginaire, no I don't.

maladerie. *Obs.* exc. *Hist.* In 5 **maledery, mallardri.** [a. OF. *maladerie* (mod.F. corruptly *maladrerie*, after *ladre* leper), f. *malade* sick.] A hospital, esp. for lepers.
A leper hospital near Sandwich is mentioned in various 15th c. wills as 'le Maldrye' (1408), 'the Maldery' (1492), 'the Mullery' (1499); a modern lease has 'Mauldry'.
1461 *Rolls of Parlt.* V. 472/2 The Hospitall of the holy Innocentes called the mallardri. **1494** FABYAN *Chron.* VII. 470 The maledery of Le Longe Iumell. **1903** JEANS *Murray's Handbk. Lincsh.* (ed. 2) 64 Just outside the gate [*sc.* Bar Gate, Lincoln] is 'Malandery field', so called from the Maladerie, or Hospital for lepers, founded by Remigius.

maladichte, -dicte: see MALEDIGHT.

‖ **maladif** (maladif), *a.* [Fr.; cf. MALADIVE *a.*] = MALADIVE *a.*
1859 QUEEN VICTORIA *Let.* 8 Jan. in R. Fulford *Dearest Child* (1964) 157, I thought he was too maladif to marry. **1886** *Portfolio* 51/2 Standing in the corner..a fragile, *maladif* little figure, with a disproportionately impressive head. **1911** D. H. LAWRENCE *Let.* 30 Dec. (1962) I. 90 You'll find it [*sc.* the story], perhaps, thin—*maladif.* **1950** D. GASCOYNE *Vagrant* 55 For a maladif, mandarin-miened, mauve melody-man.

† **ma'ladious**, *a. Obs.* [f. MALADY + -OUS; cf. OF. *maladieux.*] = next.
1607 WALKINGTON *Opt. Glass* 18 The soule her selfe as maladious feeles some want of her excellencie.

maladive ('mælədɪv), *a.* Also 5 **-if.** [a. F. *maladif, -ive*, f. *malade*: see MALADY.] Of, pertaining to, or affected with sickness, sickly. Cf. MALADIF *a.*
1481 BOTONER *Tulle on Old Age* (Caxton) C j, They haue their bodyes seke & maladif. **1605** DANIEL *Queen's Arcadia* I. i. (1606) B, Our holesome climate growne more maladiue. **1865** *Argosy* I. 33 He can confound nervousness with indigestion, and make it odious by maladive associations innumerable. **1879** FARRAR *St. Paul* II. 216 *note*, The Arminian [theory], which regards hereditary corruption not as sin or guilt, but as infirmity, a maladive condition. **1907** R. BROOKE *Let.* Oct. (1968) 112 Lippo Lippi's girl-Madonna's, with the maladive sensuality of their tired faces. **1940** *Horizon* Mar. 171 There is the road to Newchurch-on-Arrow, up which Kilvert..used to stride to see his sweet but *maladive* Emmeline. **1953** *Economist* 6 June 641 The most dangerous trend in post-war Britain..the tendency..to indulge in maladive self-attention.

† **maladize**, *v. Obs. rare*$^{-1}$. [f. MALADY *sb.* + -IZE.] *trans.* To affect with a malady or maladies. Only in *pa. pple.*
1790 J. WILLIAMS *Shrove Tuesday* in *A Cabinet*, etc. (1794) 28 In Courts or Camps, or Maladis'd or Sound.

mala'djusted, *a.* [f. MAL- + ADJUSTED *ppl. a.*] Inadequately adjusted; exhibiting or characterized by psychological maladjustment.
1886 W. GRAHAM *Soc. Problem* 18 Society..maladjusted and 'out of joint' in its social relations and parts. **1930** R. S. WOODWORTH *Psychol.* (ed. 8) xiii. 564 Ways of helping maladjusted individuals. **1931** E. WILSON *Axel's Castle* iv. 93 Only thirty at the time of his death, Tristan Corbière had been an eccentric and very maladjusted man. **1953** R. LEHMANN *Echoing Grove* 32 Where did she get this magpie streak from? Can she be maladjusted? **1957** P. LAFITTE *Person in Psychol.* vi. 75 Persistence is characteristic of the maladjusted person, who cannot change because he is unable to learn by getting to grips with his situation. **1970** R. C. CARSON *Interaction Concepts of Personality* vi. 203 The families from which maladjusted persons emerge.

maladjustment (mælə'dʒʌstmənt). [f. MAL- + ADJUSTMENT.] Faulty adjustment. *spec.* in

Psychol., unsuccessful adaptation to one's social environment.

1833 CHALMERS *Const. Man* I. vii. (1834) II. 7 This maladjustment between the voice that nature gives forth on the right of property, and the voice that arbitrary law gives forth upon it. **1878** NEWCOMB *Pop. Astron.* III. iii. 297 They may also arise from a slight maladjustment of the lenses of the eye-piece. **1899** *Allbutt's Syst. Med.* VIII. 274 Whether the maladjustment is corrigible. **1909** E. T. DEVINE in *Fabian News* Dec. 94/1 Not poverty and not punishment explains the misery of our modern commercial and industrial communities, but rather social maladjustment. **1923** J. S. HUXLEY *Ess. Biologist* i. 55 Whatever overstress and maladjustment the complexity of modern civilization has brought with it. **1930** R. S. WOODWORTH *Psychol.* (ed. 8) xiii. 565 This..picture of the situation in which the maladjustment arose is of value to the troubled adult. **1949** E. JENKINS *Six Criminal Women* 166 Cook did not take to the road through want, but rather from what the psychiatrists call 'maladjustment'. **1965** J. R. WITTENBORN in B. B. Wolman *Handbk. Clin. Psychol.* 1039/1 Evidence of periodic or constant maladjustment of varying degree from early life. **1970** R. C. CARSON *Interaction Concepts of Personality* vi. 203 Processes that appear to be implicated in the acquisition of maladjustment within the family.

maladminister (ˌmælæd'mɪnɪstə(r)), *v.* [f. MAL- *prefix* + ADMINISTER.] *trans.* To administer, execute, or manage inefficiently or badly.

1705 HARCOURT in Ld. Campbell *Chancellors* (1857) V. cxviii. 365 The government is mal-administered by corrupt persons. **1808** G. EDWARDS *Pract. Plan* iii. 45 As those interests might be mal-administered. **1895** ROOSEVELT in *Atlantic Monthly* Feb. 245 We will never allow the cry of party to be used as a shield in the defense of a man who maladministers the law.

maladministration (ˌmælædmɪnɪ'streɪʃən). Also 7–9 **male-**. [f. MAL- *prefix* + ADMINISTRATION.] Faulty administration; inefficient or improper management of affairs, *esp.* public affairs.

1644 HEYLIN *Stumbling-block* Tracts (1681) 681 The people had not only power to elect their Magistrates, but to call them also to accompt, in case of mal-administration. **1647** SALTMARSH *Spark. Glory* (1847) 161 Independency, Presbytery, Baptism,..and all other male-administrations. **1735** BOLINGBROKE *Lett. Hist.* ii. (1752) 36 King James's mal-administration rendered a revolution necessary and practicable. **1809** KENDALL *Trav.* I. iv. 26 Call any court or magistrate..to an account for any misdemeanor or male administration. **1863** H. COX *Instit.* III. viii. 711 The maladministration of the army had been the subject of complaints.

b. *occas.* The irregular administration of a religious rite.

a **1655** VINES *Lord's Supp.* (1677) 259 So that their mal-administration bring not epidemick judgements upon us.

So **maladministrator**, one who is guilty of maladministration.

1866 *Q. Rev.* Oct. 547 Maladministration in every department begins..the moment the maladministrators can say, 'Blame us as you please, but you cannot supplant us'.

‖**maladresse** (mælə'drɛs). Also in anglicized form **maladdress**. [a. F. *maladresse*, noun of quality to *maladroit*: see MALADROIT.] Want of dexterity or tact; awkwardness.

1804 EUGENIA DE ACTON *Tale without Title* II. 192 Without the least *maladresse*, they visited in the family, as if nothing material had occurred. **1862** MERIVALE *Rom. Emp.* xlii. (1865) V. 149 His behaviour was in striking contrast both with the reserve of Augustus and the mal-address of Tiberius. **1870** MISS BROUGHTON *Red as Rose* I. viii. 158 An unlucky footman..had the *maladresse* to drop three spoons that he was carrying upon a tray.

maladroit ('mælədrɔɪt), *a.* [a. F. *maladroit*: see MAL- and ADROIT *a.*] Wanting in adroitness or dexterity; awkward, bungling, clumsy.

1685 COTTON tr. *Montaigne* I. xxiv. (1711) I. 179 When he comes back from School..there is nothing so aukward and maladroit. **1731** in BAILEY vol. II. **1845** CARLYLE *Cromwell* (1871) IV. 79 Maladroit ship-carpenters. **1848** CLOUGH *Amours de Voy.* I. 205 My bookish and maladroit manners. **1898** J. E. C. BODLEY *France* II. IV. iv. 380 The fortunes of a maladroit faction.

Hence **'maladroitly** *adv.*, **'maladroitness**.

1673 DRYDEN *Marr. à la Mode* II. i, Doing all things so *mal a droitly* [sic]. **1781** JUSTAMOND *Priv. Life Lewis XV*, II. 212 His maladroitness was soon the cause of his Sovereign's losing the castles. **1827** CARLYLE *Misc.*, *Richter* (1869) 4 They rather testify, however maladroitly, that the Germans have felt their loss. **1862** MERIVALE *Rom. Emp.* xlv. (1865) V. 318 With his usual maladroitness, the terms he used were such as seemed to imply a feeling of jealousy.

† **malad'venture.** *Obs.* Also 5 **male aventure**, 9 **mal-aventure**. [OF. *malaventure*: see MAL- and ADVENTURE *sb.*] **a.** A lawless proceeding, an escapade. **b.** An unlucky undertaking; a misadventure.

c **1470** HARDING *Chron.* CLXVII. iii, Ryotous lyuyng and male auentures. **1471** CAXTON *Recuyell* (Sommer) I. 293 [He] ran vnto the rescouse to his maleauenture. **1592** NASHE *P. Penilesse* (Shaks. Soc.) 33 Trye if you can tempt Enuie to embark himselfe in the maladuenture. **1800** A. CARLYLE *Autobiog.* 305 Youth and good spirits made us convert all maladventures into fun. **1815** *Zeluca* II. 2 Charged with all the mal-aventures, it seemed to be considered in the duties of her post to have overcome.

malady ('mælədɪ). Forms: 3–7 maladi(e, -ye, (5 malade, -idy), 4–6 maledie, -dy(e, 6 melady, 6– malady; *pl.* 5 maledius, 6 maladeis, 4– maladies. [a. F. *maladie*, f. *malade* sick = Pr. *malapte*, *malaute*:—late L. *male habitus* (L. *male* ill, *habitus* pa. pple. of *habēre* to have); cf. the Vulgate *male habens* (= Gr. κακῶς ἔχων) Luke vii. 2.]

1. †**a.** Ill health, sickness, disease (*obs.*). **b.** A specific kind of ill health, an ailment, a disease.

c **1250** *Kent. Serm.* in *O. E. Misc.* 31 He was i-warisd of his maladie. *c* **1320** *Sir Beues* (MS. A.) 3921 God..heled him of his maladie. **1340** HAMPOLE *Pr. Consc.* 701 Fevyr, dropsy, and Iaunys, Tysyk, goute, and other maladys. *a* **1400–50** *Alexander* 2127 Amendid of hire malidy his moder he fyndis. **1433** *Rolls of Parlt.* IV. 424/1 For maladie, or for any other resonable cause. *c* **1440** LONELICH *Grail* xxxvi. 200 They knew not fulliche his Malade. **1480** CAXTON *Chron. Eng.* v. (1520) 44 b/1 He sayd he wolde helpe the kynge of his malady. *a* **1533** LD. BERNERS *Huon* lx. 210 She tooke there such a maladye that she dyed therof. **1549** *Compl. Scot.* vi. 57 In dangeir of diuers maladeis, as of fluxis, caterris, collic, and gut. **1588** SHAKS. *L. L. L.* IV. iii. 295 Abstinence ingenders maladies. **1647** TRAPP *Marrow Gd. Authors* in *Comm. Ep.* 614 Q. Elizabeth..knew, that much meat, much malady. **1789** W. BUCHAN *Dom. Med.* (1790) 137 Those who breathe the impure air of cities, have many maladies to which the more happy rustics are entire strangers. **1871** NAPHEYS *Prev. & Cure Dis.* III. ii. 619 The vast number of maladies which may attack our bodies.

personified. **1563** SACKVILLE *Induct. Mirr. Mag.* xlix, And fast by him pale Maladie was plaste, Sore sicke in bed, her colour al forgone.

2. *fig.* A morbid or depraved condition (e.g. of mind, morals, social arrangements, etc.); something that calls for a remedy. (Cf. DISEASE 2.)

13.. *Minor Poems fr. Vernon MS.* 239/686 To helen vs of seuen Maledius. *c* **1385** CHAUCER *L. G. W.* 1379 *Hypsip.*, Thow ne feltist malady Sa[v]e foul delyt. **1390** GOWER *Conf.* II. 142 That ilke unsely maladie, The which is cleped Jelousie. *c* **1410** HOCCLEVE *Mother of God* 117 Beeth leches of our synful maladie. **1500–20** DUNBAR *Poems* xxii. 56 May nane remeid my melady Sa weill as ȝe, schir, veraly. **1563** *Homilies* II. *Rebellion* I. (1859) 555 Such lewd remedies being far worse than any other maladies and disorders that can be in the body of a commonwealth. **1647** MAY *Hist. Parlt.* I. iv. 41 Not hoping..so quick a call of a nationall Synod, as the present malady required. **1687** DRYDEN *Hind & P.* III. 69 The matron was not slow to find What sort of malady had seized her mind. **1751** JOHNSON *Rambler* No. 87 ¶6 The cure of our intellectual maladies. **1786–7** BONNYCASTLE *Astron.* i. 5 Astrology is another malady of weak minds. **1829** CARLYLE *Misc.* (1857) II. 116 Our spiritual maladies are but of Opinion. **1891** E. KINGLAKE *Australian at H.* 17 A clerk's calling is not the only one overdone. That of the governess suffers from the same malady.

† **malaë'ration.** *Med. Obs.* [f. MAL- + AERATION.] Imperfect aeration (of the blood).

1843 R. J. GRAVES *Syst. Clin. Med.* xx. 245 Her countenance exhibits no proof of malaëration of the blood. **1908** *Practitioner* Mar. 321 Such cyanosis may..indicate lack of propelling power in the circulation, with consequent malaëration.

‖**mala fide** ('meɪleɪ 'faɪdiː), *adv.* and *a.* [L. *malā fidē* = 'in bad faith'. Cf. BONA FIDE.]

A. *adv.* In bad faith. **B.** *adj.* Chiefly with agent nouns: Acting in bad faith; pretended, not genuine, sham. ***mala fide possessor***: one who holds by a title which he knows to be bad.

[**1561** *Reg. Privy Council Scot.* I. 180 The said Thomas was in mala fide be intrometting with the gudis libellit.] **1681** VISCT. STAIR *Instit.* I. vii. (1693) 64 It extends to the Fruits which he hath enjoyed, *mala fide*. **1808** BENTHAM *Sc. Reform* 7 On the part of malâ fide suitors (suitors conscious of being in the wrong). **1875** POSTE *Gaius* II. (ed. 2) 203 The mala fide possessor..acquires no property in the consumed fruits. **1901** *Scotsman* 2 Oct. 9/3 The authorities of the Excise have taken no action..to deal with the mala-fide and proprietary clubs.

‖**mala fides** ('meɪlə 'faɪdiːz). *Law.* [L. *mala fidēs* bad faith.] Bad faith, intent to deceive.

1681 VISCT. STAIR *Instit.* II. xii. (1693) 354 *Bona fides* is presumed, unless a contrary Probation, or vehement Presumption be for *mala fides*. **1802–12** BENTHAM *Ration. Judic. Evid.* (1827) III. 623 At the peril of extra costs in case of mala fides. **1885** LD. COLERIDGE in *Law Rep.* 15 Q. Bench Div. 137 Absence of mala fides..is not enough.

malafiges, *sb. pl.* ? *U.S.* [a. Du. *malefijtje*, *malefietje*, dim. of *malefijt*, of obscure origin: ? connected with F. *maléfique* MALEFIC *a.*] 'A sailors' name for a small sea-bird supposed to appear before a storm: apparently, the stormy petrel or Mother Carey's chicken' (*Cent. Dict.*).

Malaga ('mæləgə). Also 7 **malaca**, **mal(l)igo**, **mallago(e**, **-egoe**, **-igo(e**, 8 **malago**. The name of a seaport in the south of Spain. Used *attrib.*, as in ***Malaga raisins***, ***sack***, ***wine***. Also as *sb.* (short for *Malaga wine*), a white wine exported from Malaga.

1608 DAY *Law Trickes* I. ii. (1881) 21 Ile put al my loue into one quart of Maligo. **1623** J. TAYLOR (Water P.) *Praise Hempseed* Wks. (1630) III. 65/1 Braue Wine Merchants, little were your gaine, By Mallegoes, Canaries Sacke from Spaine. **1623** MIDDLETON & ROWLEY *Span. Gipsy* III. i. (1653) E I b, Peter see me shall wash thy nowle, And Malligo Glasses fox thee. **1656** BLOUNT *Glossogr.*, *Malaga* or *Malaca Sack*. **1686** WOOD *Life* (O.H.S.) III. 199 Before the warr nothing but sack and mallagoes were drunk and claret not at all. **1698** *Phil. Trans.* XX. 291 A Grocer's Basket, such as they put up their Malaga Raisins in. **1768** PIGOTT in *Phil. Trans.* LXI. 287, I exposed..a wine glass half full of Malaga wine. **1806** A. HUNTER *Culina* (ed. 3) 45 To each gallon put two pounds of Malaga raisins a little chopped. **1887** PATER *Imag. Portr.* 2 The lad..left untasted the glass of Malaga which was offered to him.

Comb. **1898** P. MANSON *Trop. Diseases* ii. 64 His urine has become very dark in colour, perhaps malaga-coloured.

malagas (mælə'gæs). *S. Afr.* Also 8 **malagos**; **malagash**, Afrikaans **malgas** (mal'xas). [Afrikaans, f. Du. *mallegas*, a. Pg. *mangas(-de-velludo)*, 'velvet-sleeves', the wandering albatross.] The Cape gannet, *Morus* (or *Sula*) *capensis*.

1731 G. MEDLEY tr. *Kolb's Present State Cape Good-Hope* II. 143 As soon as the *Malagos* 'spies a Fish under her, she pops her Head nimbly into the Water. **1906** STARK & SCLATER *Birds S. Afr.* IV. 17 *Sula capensis*. Malagash. *Ibid.* 19 The Malagash is found along the coasts of South Africa. **1936** E. L. GILL *First Guide S. Afr. Birds* 186 Malagas, Malgas, Cape Gannet; *Morus capensis*. This is the gannet of the South African guano islands. **1944** M. DE B. NESBITT *Road to Avalon* (1949) xxi. 163 The malagas seabird..is prolific here. **1964** A. L. THOMSON *New Dict. Birds* 330/1 The Cape Gannet (or Malagash) *S*[*ula*] *capensis* (with dark tail), breeding off South Africa and migrating northwards. **1970** MCLACHLAN & LIVERSIDGE *Roberts's Birds S. Afr.* (ed. 3) 21 Cape Gannet. Malgas. *Morus capensis*... These birds may be picked up at some distance by their conspicuous whiteness. **1974** *Eastern Province Herald* 7 Nov. 22 There are vast colonies of malgas (gannets) and other birds which live off the shoals of fodder fish in our waters.

Malagash ('mæləgæʃ), *a.* and *sb.* Also **Mal(l)egass**, 8–9 **Malegash**. See also MADAGASS. [var. of next. Cf. F. *Malgache*.] **a.** *adj.* Of or pertaining to Madagascar. **b.** *sb.* A native of Madagascar; also as *plural*.

1711 tr. *Cauche's Voy. Madagascar* 40 In the Province of Matatan, Neighbouring on that of the Mallegasses or Madegasses. *Ibid.* 56 The Malegasses. **1793** TRAPP tr. *Rochon's Voy. Madagascar* 40 The Malegashes know but two ways of dressing their meat. *Ibid.* 52 The Malegash language. **1833** OWEN *Voy. Afr., Arabia & Madagascar* II. ix. 100 A large population of Malegash and Arabs. *Ibid.*, The style of their buildings..is one-half Arab and the other Malegash.

Malagasy (mælə'gæsɪ), *a.* and *sb.* [Used in the native lang., but believed to be an altered form of a foreign appellation (of obscure origin) represented by the variants *Madecass*, *Madagass*, whence the name *Madagascar*.

In the Malagasy language the unstressed vowels are 'whispered', and the *s* before *i* or *y* approaches the sound of (ʃ); hence the European form MALAGASH.]

A. *adj.* Of or pertaining to Madagascar, its inhabitants, language, etc. **B.** *sb.* **a.** A native of Madagascar; also as *plural*. **b.** The language spoken there.

1835 J. J. FREEMAN (*title*) A Dictionary of the Malagasy language. **1839** W. ELLIS *Hist. Madagascar* I. 112 The floors of the Malagasy houses are generally covered with red and yellow rush mats. *Ibid.* 145 The physical, moral and intellectual peculiarities of the Malagasy. *Ibid.* 184 This..conveys as much to a Malagasy as the heartiest thrice-repeated cheer does to an Englishman. **1839** J. J. FREEMAN *ibid.* 496 A prefix, in Malay, *pen*, in Malagasy, *mpan*. **1878** W. E. COUSINS *Malagasy Lang.* in *Phil. Soc. Trans.* 311 The Malagasy is undoubtedly a genuine member of the Malayo-Polynesian family. **1882** *Illustr. Miss. News* Mar. 27 The Malagasy Christians may truly be called 'Bible Christians'. Show the Malagasy chapter and verse..and they are satisfied. **1898** A. LANG *Making of Relig.* v. 92 The Malagasies..divine by crystals.

malagatany, -tawny, obs. ff. MULLIGATAWNY.

† **ma'lagma.** *Med. Obs.* Pl. **malagmata**. Also in anglicized form 6–7 **malagme**, 7 **malagm**. [late L., a. Gr. μάλαγμα, f. μαλάσσειν to assuage.] An emollient plaster.

1541 R. COPLAND *Galyen's Terap.* 2 C ii, A malagme (that is to wyt a salue malactyke). **1643** TUCKNEY *Balme of G.* 12 Their Malagmata and Lenitives. **1657** TOMLINSON *Renou's Disp.* 200 A malactical and mollitive medicament and a Malagm do not at all differ. **1748** tr. *Veg. Renatus' Distemp. Horses* 188 You should make use of a Malagma, or of a Caustick. **1753** CHAMBERS *Cycl. Supp.*, *Malagma*,..very often the malagma's consisted only of gums dissolved in wine.

mala'grug(o)rous, *a. jocular.* [? Distortion of It. *malaguroso*, unfortunate. But cf. Sc. *malagruized* 'rumpled, disordered' (E.D.D.).] Dismal, lugubrious. Hence **mala'grugrously** *adv.*

1818 LOCKHART in *Blackw. Mag.* III. 407 He writes more malagrugrously than Dante. **1826** *Ibid.* XX. 327 He looketh malagrugorous and world-wearied. **1839** LOCKHART *Ballantyne-humbug* 106 A certain malagrugrous exposition of his own views..drawn up by James Ballantyne in..1826.

Malagueña (mælə'geɪnjə). [Sp. (see MALAGA).]

1. A woman of Malaga.

1845 R. FORD *Hand-bk. for Travellers Spain* I. 352/1 Teresita, the daughter, is a pretty specimen of a *Malagueña*. **1868** H. O'SHEA *Guide to Spain & Portugal* (ed. 3) 312/2 The Malagueñas are considered to be the prettiest women in all Spain.

2. (Also with small initial.) A Spanish dance resembling the fandango; also, a song accompanying this dance.

1883 GROVE *Dict. Mus.* III. 599/2 The dance-songs—*fandangos, rondeñas,* and *malagueñas,*..have..more symmetry and more animation. *Ibid.*, Songs and dances often derive their names from the provinces or towns in which they are indigenous; thus..*malagueña* from Malaga. **1922** J. HERGESHEIMER *Bright Shawl* (1923) 69 The ceaseless playing of the guitars, strains of jotas and malagueñas. **1925** *Blackw. Mag.* Jan. 80/2 Hansson sang a queer malagueña which he had heard often in Andalucia. **1968** K. BIRD *Smash Glass Image* ix. 113 The next dance was slow, nostalgic. A *malagueña* perhaps? **1973** *Times* 6 Jan. 14/4 One typical dance [in the Canaries], the *malagueña*, reveals its peninsular origin in its name.

malaguetta (mælə'gɛtə). Forms: 6 **manguetta, manegete,** 7 **mellegette,** 7–8 **malegutta,** 8 **malaget, malaghetta, malagato, malegetta,** 8–9 **malaguette,** 9 **maniguette, malaguet(a, meleguet(t)a,** 7– **malaguetta.** [Of obscure origin.

App. identical with the med.L. *melegeta*, the name of a spice mentioned *c* 1214 in connexion with cloves and cardamoms, and said *a* 1331 to be among the productions of Java (see Du Cange). Both the authors cited are Italian, and in 1486 Simon a Cordo (*Clavis Sanationis*) explains the word as a diminutive of It. *melica* millet, remarking that the grains resemble those of millet. This seems probable; but if the word be of European origin, it has either been adopted in a corrupt form into some West African langs., or confused with a native word, the source of the earliest Eng. form and of the F. *maniguette*. In 1599 Towrson (Hakl. *Voy.* II. ii. 27), in a list of phrases from the lang. of Guinea, gives '*manegete afoye*, graines ynough'. Miss M. Kingsley, *West Afr. Studies* (1899) ii. 57, says that in the native lang. at Cape Palmas the name is *emanequetta*, but that as the name is very local (the more usual word is *waizanzag*), a European origin is possible.]

The capsules or seeds of *Amomum Meliguetta* of West Africa, used as a spice and in medicine; also known as *grains of paradise* and *Guinea grains.* (Cf. CARDAMOM.)

1568 M. HACKET tr. *Thevet's New Found World* 26 In Ginney the fruit that is most rife and common..is named Manguetta. **1670** OGILBY *Africa* 413 Graines of paradise.. which the natives call Mellegette. **1670** tr. *Villaut's Guinea* 101 They call not Pepper..Grain, with the Hollanders, but Malaguetta, with us. **1705** BOSMAN *Guinea* xiii. (1721) 216 Malaget, otherwise called the Grains of Paradise. *Ibid.* xvi. 285 Malagueta, otherwise called Paradice-Grains, or Guinea Pepper. **1788** CLARKSON *Impol. Slave Tr.* 13 The first [pepper] that was discovered or imported, was malaguetta, or grains of Paradise.

b. *attrib.*, as ***malaguetta pepper.***

1745 *Astley's Voy.* II. 520 The Malaghetta, Grain, or Pepper Coast. **1788** J. MATTHEWS *Sierra Leone* 58 The Malagato Pepper, or Grains of Paradise. **1863** R. F. BURTON *Wand. W. Afr.* II. 37 By the Dutch they were called Guinea Grains; by the trade Malaguetta Pepper. **1877** R. H. MAJOR *Discov. Pr. Henry* xi. 170 The natives.. brought Malaguette pepper in grain and in its pods as it grew. **1899** MARY KINGSLEY *West Afr. Stud.* ii. 57 Meleguetta pepper.

malahack ('mæləhæk), *v. dial. trans.* To cut or carve badly.

a **1825** FORBY *Voc. E. Anglia*, *Malahack v.*,..to cut or carve in an awkward and slovenly manner. **1866** LOWELL *Biglow P.* Introd., [Words New Eng. dial.] *Malahack*, to cut up hastily or awkwardly. **1893** *Broad Norf.* (ed. Cozens-Hardy) 54, I heard of a donkey purchased for little money on account of some injury; but 'it was not so malahacked as to be jammucked for all that'.

‖**malahane.** *Obs. rare*⁻¹. [Irish *mulachán* a kind of soft cheese.]

1656 S. HOLLAND *Zara* 17 Stewd Prunes, bread made of Malahane [*margin*, Bread made of Cruds. See the Irish Dictionary], And Honey fetcht from Sugar Cane.

‖**malaise** ('mæleɪz, Fr. malɛz). [F. *malaise*, f. OF. *mal* adj., bad, ill + *aise* EASE *sb.*] A condition of bodily uneasiness or discomfort, esp. a condition of bodily suffering or lassitude, without the development of specific disease. (Cf. MALEASE.)

1768 LD. CHESTERF. *Let. to Bp. Chenevix* 25 June *Misc. Wks.* (1777) II. 532, I feel what the French call a general *mal-aise*, and what we call in Ireland an *unwellness*. **1857** *G. Bird's Urin. Deposits* (ed. 5) 211 A young man..who.. became a patient of Dr. Garrod's for general malaise. **1870** *Holmes' Syst. Surg.* (ed. 2) IV. 218 Loss of appetite and a general sensation of *malaise*. **1899** *Allbutt's Syst. Med.* VII. 740 The illness begins..with general malaise and feverishness.

b. *fig.*

1883 *St. James's Gaz.* 27 Dec. 3/1 There will be, first, a universal *malaise*; then the loss of the faculties of government and self-defence. **1885** *Wool Trade Circular*, The Wool Market has not escaped the influence of an almost universal commercial malaise.

malakatoon(e, variant of MELOCOTON.

Malakoff ('mæləkɒf). [The name of a fortification erected by the Russians at Sevastopol, and captured by the French, 8 Sept., 1855.]

†**1.** A crinoline. *Obs.* [So in Fr.: see *Le Figaro* 22 Sept. 1885, 1/3.]

1861 LADY CHATTERTON *Mem. Ld. Gambier* I. ii. 27 Englishwomen have witnessed the superior circumference of their Gallic sisters, in the palmy days of 'Malakoffs'.

2. A particular form of four-handed dominoes.

1870 *Routledge's Ev. Boy's Ann.* Nov. 671 Calling the restricted game the 'Malakoff', leaving the wider game the old title of Sebastopol.

3. (See quot.)

1883 SIMMONDS *Dict. Usef. Anim.*, *Malakoff*, a small round cream cheese made in Gournay, France.

malaky, var. MALARKEY.

malambo (mə'læmbəʊ). The aromatic bark of *Croton malambo*, a euphorbiaceous shrub of Venezuela and New Granada, used in medicine and perfumery. Also ***malambo bark.***

1816 *Jrnl. Sci. & Arts* I. 59 The Malambo bark, which the French have lately introduced into their materia medica.

malamute ('mæləmjuːt). Also **malemut(e).** [The name of an Eskimo people living on the Alaskan coast.] A large grey or black and white dog with a thick coat, pointed ears, and a plumed tail curling over its back, belonging to the spitz breed so called, which first developed in Alaska. Also *attrib.*

[**1874** *Ann. Rep. Board of Regents Smithsonian Inst.* 27 Maglemut.] **1898** *Klondike Nugget* (Dawson, Yukon Territory) 20 July 3/2 After appointing a committee to keep stray Malamoots and donkeys off the diamond, the game was called. **1898** *Yukon Midnight Sun* (Dawson, Yukon Territory) 1 Oct. 2/5, I have the first man to find in the country who owns a dog, it matters not whether he is malamute, husky,..or little mongrel. **1908** *St. Nicholas* Mar. 387/2 Few pure malamutes..are now employed in the mail service. **1913** *Outing* Feb. 521/1 Sitting among a litter of Malamute puppies. **1922** G. C. F. PRINGLE *Tillicums of Trail* 84, I first picked on a big grey-muzzled malemute named Steal as a likely fellow to lead... All malemutes are born thieves, some men think. **1934** *Times Educ. Suppl.* 15 Sept. p. iv/2 These Arctic or sub-Arctic dogs—huskies, malamutes, Samoyeds..are wonderful in their strength, powers of endurance, and stoutness of heart. **1948** *Chicago Tribune* 23 Feb. IV. 1/6 Along with the Eskimos will be a representation of the Malemute sled dogs that provide the only motive power available to Eskimos. **1952** M. K. WILSON tr. *Lorenz's King Solomon's Ring* x. 117 The purest wolf-dogs that exist are certain breeds of Arctic America, particularly the so-called malemuts, huskies etc. **1955** *Reader's Digest* (Austral.) Dec. 122/2 This malemute was bitten by a mad red fox. **1962** M. E. MURIE *Two in Far North* I. vi. 51 Long strings of Malemutes lope down the streets. **1971** F. HAMILTON *World Encycl. Dogs* 569 The Malamute must give an impression of great strength and tremendous propelling power.

malancolius, malanc(h)oly(e, obs. ff. MELANCHOLIOUS, MELANCHOLY.

malander, mallender ('mæləndə(r)). Now only *pl.* Forms: 5 **malawnder,** 6 **malandre, malandrie,** 6–8 **malender,** 7 **mallander,** 8 **mallendar,** 6– **malander,** 7– **mallender.** [a. F. *malandre* a sore in a horse's knee, ad. L. *malandria* (neut. pl. and fem. sing.).] A dry scabby eruption behind the knee in horses.

†**a.** *sing. Obs.*

c **1400** *Promp. Parv.* 323/1 Malawnder, sekeness, *morbus*. **1523** FITZHERB. *Husb.* §94 A malander is an yl sorance..and appereth..in the bendynge of the knee behynde. **1530** PALSGR. 176 *Malendre*, a malandre, a sore. *Ibid.* 242/1 Malandrie, sicknesse, *malandre*. **1607** TOPSELL *Four-f. Beasts* (1658) 313 A Malander is a kinde of Scab growing.. overthwart the bent of the knee. **1614** MARKHAM *Cheap Husb.* 32 Of the Mallandar, Sellander... Crowne-scabs, and such like. **1639** T. DE GREY *Compl. Horsem.* 6 Subject to mainge, mallender, sellender..or any other the like sorances. **1759** BROWN *Compl. Farmer* 18 For a Mallendar. Take bay-salt, gunpowder [etc.]. **1835** *Penny Cycl.* III. 422/1 Spavin and mullender [*sic*] are of very rare occurrence.

attrib. **1688** *Lond. Gaz.* No. 2408/4 The hair clipped close on the Mallender place of the near Leg.

b. *pl.*

1601 HOLLAND *Pliny* II. 335 *marg.*, Lichenes: some take them for the Malanders. **1607** MARKHAM *Caval.* I. (1617) 20 The best keepers cannot preserve them from scratches, paines and mallanders. **1762** *Crazy Tales* 74 Withouten splint, or malanders, or grease. **1884** *Sat. Rev.* 5 July 27/2 It is a breach of a warranty of soundness if the warranted horse suffers from..mallenders.

Hence **'malandered** *ppl. a.*, affected with malanders.

1696 *Lond. Gaz.* No. 3248/4 A strong..Rigil Horse,.. malender'd on the near leg.

†**malandryn.** *Obs. rare*⁻¹. [a. F. *malandrin* = It. *malandrino.*] A highwayman, a robber.

1460 CAPGRAVE *Chron.* (Rolls) 309 Jon was broute to the Councelle in the same aray thei toke him, in schort clothis, lich a Malandryn.

malapert ('mæləpɜːt), *a.* and *sb. Obs.* exc. *arch.* Forms: 5 **maleapert, maleperte,** 5–7 **malapart,** 6 **malaperte, malepeirt, maloperte, mallaparte,** 6–7 **malepart, malipert, malipart, mallapert,** 6–8 **malepert,** 7 **maleparte, mallepart, mallipart, mally part, malapart,** 5– **malapert.** [a. OF. *malapert*, used by E. Deschamps as the contrary of *appert* = *espert* clever, able (:—L. *expertus* EXPERT *a.*). Here *mal* has (as in *maladroit, malcontent*) the effect of reversing a favourable signification; but the Eng. sense of the compound points to its having been apprehended as if f. *mal* (in the sense 'improperly') + *apert* bold, outspoken, insolent (see APERT *a.* 5).]

A. *adj.* Of persons, their qualities, actions, etc.: Presumptuous, impudent, 'saucy'.

c **1420** LYDG. *Assembly of Gods* 503 They swere gret othes for the noonys Her lawe to dyspyce, that was so malapert. *c* **1430** — *Min. Poems* (Percy Soc.) 166 Maleapert of chiere and of visage. *c* **1440** *Jacob's Well* 148 þe secunde is veyn woordys, male-apert, in iangeling. **1513** DOUGLAS *Æneis* IX. i. 7 Hir madyne Iris from hevin sendis sche To the bald Turnus, malapert and stout. **1529** MORE *Dyaloge* III. Wks. 227/1 His malepert boldnes might peraduenture be punished. **1567** DRANT *Horace, Ep.* I. xviii. F vj, Be perte, and cleare in countinaunce, not malipert, and light. **1601** SHAKS. *Twel. N.* IV. i. 47, I must haue an Ounce or two of this malapert blood from you. **1609** BIBLE (Douay) *Prov.* vii. 15 Taking the yong-man she kisseth him, and with malepert countenance speaketh fayre. **1633** T. STAFFORD *Pac. Hib.* I. iii. (1810) 253, I haue uterly rooted those malepart bowes out of the orchard of my country. **1640** BROME *Sparagus Garden* II. iii. Wks. 1873 III. 141 With dry jests to maule the mallipart'st lesser ones..out o' the pit of wit. *Ibid.* II. v. 148 Yes Malipert Jack, I have heard that he has seene her. **1671** H. FOULIS *Hist. Rom. Treas.* VI. iii. 382 In the mean time the Presbyterian Kirk grow very mallypart. **1738** tr. *Guazzo's Art Conversation* 151 b, They ought not to suffer the Honour and Degree of Gentry to be disgraced by the Presumption of malapert Clowns. **1763** *Brit. Mag.* IV. 296 The officer who uttered the first malapert sentence, was put under arrest. **1825** SCOTT *Betrothed* viii, You are too malapert for a young maiden. **1884** W. C. SMITH *Kildrostan* 40 If I was malapert, 'Twere fitter to rebuke than second me.

quasi-*adv.* **1609** B. JONSON *Sil. Wom.* IV. iv, It angred me to the soule, to heare 'hem beginne to talke so malepert.

B. *sb.* A presumptuous or 'saucy' person.

1622 R. HAWKINS *Voy. S. Sea* (1847) 165 Such malaperts deserve..to have their spoyle taken from them. **1709** STEELE *Tatler* No. 143 ¶1 The Malapert knew well enough I laughed at her. **1765** G. COLMAN *Comedies of Terence* 292 Away, you malapert! Your frowardness Had well nigh ruined me.

'malapertly, *adv. Obs.* exc. *arch.* [f. as prec. + -LY².] In a malapert manner.

1447 BOKENHAM *Seyntys* (Roxb.) 252 How darst thou..so malapertly Hym nemelyn ageyn in my presence. *c* **1460** *Play Sacram.* 637 Syr thu art ontawght..to pere in my presence thus malepertly. **1563–87** FOXE *A. & M.* (1596) 38/1 He, not reuerentlie, but more malipertlie than was requisite.. rushed into the judgment place. **1643** BURROUGHES *Exp. Hosea* i. (1652) 152 They should..not speak mallapertly, but with all reverence and submission. **1725** KIRKPATRICK *Relig. Ord. Norwich* (1845) 191 They talked malapertly to several prelates.

'malapertness. *Obs.* exc. *arch.* [f. MALAPERT *a.* + -NESS.] The quality of being malapert.

1430–40 LYDG. *Bochas* IV. xv. (1494) p vi b, Moost cruelte and vengeaunce in lowe blode with malapertnesse and indiscrecion. **1563** N. WINZET *Wks.* (1890) II. 24 The malepeirtnes of prophane noueltie. **1579–80** NORTH *Plutarch, Alex. Gt.* (1595) 745 Clitus..would not giue ouer his impudencie and malapertenesse. **1657** THORNLEY tr. *Longus' Daphnis & Chloe* 17 Daphnis was vext to see the horn broke, and that kind of malepertnesse of the Goat. **1682** BUNYAN *Holy War* 92 Yet he had for his malapertness, one of his legs broken. **1752** CARTE *Hist. Eng.* III. 422 Such was their malapertness that great disorders would have ensued.

malapplication: see MAL- *prefix.*

malappropriate (mælə'prəʊprɪət), *a.* [f. MAL- + APPROPRIATE *a.*] Ill-suited, inappropriate.

1851 DE QUINCEY *Ld. Carlisle on Pope* Wks. 1859 XIII. 13 If a prize had been offered for a bad and malappropriate subject, none worse could have been suggested. **1883** *St. James's Gaz.* 28 Apr. 4 Much eloquent (if rather malappropriate) language about religious liberty.

malappropriate (mælə'prəʊprɪeɪt), *v.* [f. MAL- + APPROPRIATE *v.*] *trans.* To misapply.

1847 E. BRONTE *Wuthering Heights* xxxii. (1850) 268 She thrust the hearth-brush into the grates in mistake for the poker, and mal-appropriated several other articles of her craft.

malappropriation (mælə'prəʊprɪ'eɪʃən). [f. MAL- + APPROPRIATION.] The action of malappropriating; misapplication.

1848 LYTTON *Harold* XI. vi. 283 A charge of mal-appropriation, whether of pay or of booty, was brought against him. **1855** MILMAN *Lat. Chr.* IX. vii. IV. 132 The mal-appropriation of a large sum deposited in another quarter.

‖**mala praxis** ('meɪlə 'præksɪs). *Law.* [mod.L. *mala*, fem. of *malus* bad, wrong + *prāxis*: see PRAXIS. Cf. MALPRAXIS.] = MALPRACTICE 1 a.

a **1733** RAYMOND *Cases King's Bench* (1775) I. 214 The court resolved, that *mala praxis* is a great misdemeanor and offence at common law..because it breaks the trust which the party has placed in the physician, tending directly to his destruction. **1768** BLACKSTONE *Comm.* III. 122. **1865** A. S. TAYLOR *Pract. Med. Jurispr.* (1873) I. 15 A charge of malapraxis is sometimes raised against a medical man in consequence of the death of a patient.

malaprop ('mæləprɒp), *sb.*, *a.*, and *v.* [from the name of Mrs. *Malaprop* (suggested by MALAPROPOS), a character in Sheridan's play of *The Rivals* (1775), remarkable for her misuse of words.] **a.** *sb.* = MALAPROPISM. **b.** *adj.* = MALAPROPIAN. **c.** *v. intr.*, to utter a malapropism; *trans.*, to make a malapropism of (a word).

1823 *Edin. Rev.* XXXIX. 171 An agreeable intermixture of malaprops. **1840** DE QUINCEY *Style* I. Wks. 1860 X. 152 But observe..the total absence of all malaprop picturesqueness that might have defeated its deadly action upon the nervous system. **1878** BAIN *Educ. as Science* ix. 329 A malaprop use of words. **1887** *Athenæum* 5 Feb. 189/1 The

expression 'on suffrage', a delightful malaprop for 'on sufferance'. **1959** I. JEFFERIES *Thirteen Days* v. 67 The usage was so wild that I thought he was malapropping. **1970** M. TRIPP *Man without Friends* iii. 27 She malaprops any word of more than two syllables.

malapropian (mælə'prɒpɪən, -'prəʊpɪən), *a.* [f. prec. + -IAN.] Of the nature of a malapropism; given to malapropisms.

1860 GEO. ELIOT in Cross *Life* (1885) II. 263 Mr. Lewes is sending what a Malapropian friend once called a 'missile' to Sara. **1898** *Spectator* 16 Apr. 539/2 There is a latent shrewdness in his malapropian talk which is quite delightful.

malapropism ('mæləprɒpɪz(ə)m). [f. MALAPROP + -ISM.] Ludicrous misuse of words; an instance of this.

1849 C. BRONTE *Shirley* II. vi. 145 A malapropism which rumour had not failed to repeat. **1887** *Spectator* 9 Apr. 492/1 That mental haziness which has its outcome in malapropism. **1890** *Harper's Mag.* Apr. 664/1 Lemaître has reproached Shakespeare for his love of Malapropisms.

malapropoism (mælæprə'pəʊɪz(ə)m). *nonce-wd.* [f. next + -ISM.] Ludicrous misapplication of language; an instance of this; = MALAPROPISM.

1834 MAR. EDGEWORTH *Helen* xxv, Sadly annoyed he is sometimes by her mal-apropoisms. **1893** A. DOBSON in *Longm. Mag.* Aug. 371 Not even the Malapropoism of Sheridan or Dickens is quite as riotously diverting.

‖**malapropos** (malaprɔpo, mælæprə'pəʊ), *adv.*, *a.*, and *sb.* Variously written **mal à propos, mal a propos, mal a-propos, †malapropo, mal apropos, malapropos.** [F. *mal à propos*, f. *mal* ill + *à* to + *propos* purpose: see MAL- and APROPOS.]

A. *adv.* In an inopportune or awkward manner; unseasonably, inappropriately.

1668 DRYDEN *Ess. Dram.* 28 They do it not so unseasonably, or *mal a propos* as we. **1673** —— *Marr. à la Mode* v. i, How durst you interrupt me so *mal a propos*. **1679** MRS. BEHN *Feign'd Curtizan* IV. i, Thou dost come out with things so malapropo. **1750–1** MRS. DELANY *Let. to Mrs. Dewes* 5 Jan., Family affairs..sometimes will break in malapropos. **1823** BYRON *Juan* VI. lxxxiv, One who had no sin to show Save that of dreaming once 'mal-à-propos'. **1831** PRAED *Bridal of Belmont* Poems (1864) I. 175 Some people have a knack, we know, Of saying things mal-à-propos.

B. *adj.* Inopportune, inappropriate.

1711 BUDGELL *Spect.* No. 77 ¶5 Doing and saying an hundred Things which..were somewhat *mal a propos* and undesigned. **1735** FIELDING *Eurydice* Wks. 1771 III. 219 Considering where the scene lies, I think these sentiments are not *mal-à-propos*. **1802** MRS. J. WEST *Infidel Father* II. xi. 4 His malapropos answers indicated that one important subject engrossed his thoughts. **1894** H. NISBET *Bush Girl's Rom.* 41 Feeling very bitter..towards this intruder for coming at such a *mal-à-propos* moment.

C. *sb.* Something inopportune or inappropriate.

1868 BAIN *Ment. & Mor. Sci.* 488 Aristotle is happily unembroiled with the modern controversy. The *mal-apropos* of 'Freedom' had not been applied to voluntary action.

‖**malapterurus** (mælæptə'rʊərəs). *Zool. Pl.* -**uri** (-'ʊəraɪ). [mod.L. (Lacépède 1803), badly f. Gr. μαλακός soft + πτερόν wing + οὐρά tail.] A genus of catfishes, certain species of which (esp. *M. electricus* of the Nile) have the property of giving an electric shock when handled.

1834 tr. *Cuvier's Anim. Kingd.* II. 187. **1848** CARPENTER *Anim. Phys.* ix. (1872) 341. **1892** *Daily News* 11 Jan. 3/2 Malapteruri, or 'thunder fishes' as they are called by the Arabs.

malar ('meɪlə(r)), *a.* (and *sb.*) *Anat.* [ad. mod.L. *mālār-is*, f. L. *māla* jaw, cheek bone, cheek, prob. related to the synonym *maxilla* as *āla* (:—**ak-slā*) to *axilla*. Cf. F. *malaire.*]

A. *adj.* Of or belonging to the cheek. ***malar bone***, the cheek bone.

1782 A. MONRO *Anat.* 97 A very rough triangular surface is extended downwards and outwards, to be connected to the cheek-bone; and therefore may be called the *malar* process. **1840** G. V. ELLIS *Anat.* 99 The nerve divides into two branches, a malar and temporal. **1870** ROLLESTON *Anim. Life* 6 The whole length of the malar arch. **1892** MIVART *Elem. Ornithol.* 142 At the lower margin of the cheek is a narrow linear space known as the malar region.

B. *sb.* (or *absol.*) The cheek bone.

1866 HUXLEY *Preh. Rem. Caithn.* 120 The facial bones short and small; the malars flat. **1881** MIVART *Cat* 74 The malar is a rather small, lamellar bone which forms the most prominent part of the cheek.

malar, variant of MAILER[1] *Sc.*

malard(e, obs. form of MALLARD.

malaria (mə'lɛərɪə). [a. It. *mal'aria* for *mala aria*, lit. 'bad air'.] **a.** The unwholesome condition of the atmosphere which results from the exhalations of marshy districts. Hence used as the name of a class of intermittent and remittent fevers formerly supposed to proceed from this cause, but now known to be caused by the bite of a mosquito of the genus *Anopheles*, by which the germs of the disease are conveyed.

1740 H. WALPOLE *Corr.* (1820) I. 68 A horrid thing called the mal'aria, that comes to Rome every summer and kills one. **1801** CHARLOTTE SMITH *Lett. Solit. Wand.* II. 56 He had prolonged our stay at the season of the mal-aria. **1813** J. FORSYTH *Rem. Excurs. Italy* 266 This mal'aria is an evil more active than the Romans, and continues to increase. **1843** PRESCOTT *Mexico* III. i. (1864) 131 The same burning sun..calls forth the pestilent malaria, with its train of bilious disorders. **1866** A. FLINT *Princ. Med.* (1880) 110 Periodical fever, commonly known as malaria. **1875** MERIVALE *Gen. Hist. Rome* lxxviii. (1877) 656 The malaria of the Campagna..induced the citizens..to reside permanently within their walls.

b. *transf.* and *fig.*

1829 SOUTHEY *Sir T. More* II. 94 Practical irreligion is thus produced even in those who escape the malaria of infidelity. **1855** THACKERAY *Newcomes* II. 19 She was a malaria to him, poisoning his atmosphere. **1862** T. C. GRATTAN *Beaten Paths* II. 350 A sort of moral malaria pervading society and carrying off many victims.

c. *attrib.* and *Comb.*, as ***malaria season***, etc.; ***malaria bearing***, ***-carrying***, ***infected*** adjs.; **malaria fever**, an intermittent or remittent fever prevalent in marshy or swampy districts, esp. in tropical countries; **malaria germ**, a protozoal organism capable of becoming parasitic and causing the disease known as malaria; so **malaria parasite**.

1899 *Allbutt's Syst. Med.* VIII. 947 The *malaria-bearing mosquito. **1916** *Brit. Mus. Econ. Ser.* IV. 8 This group [of mosquitoes]..includes also several of the *malaria-carrying *Anopheles*. **1946** *Nature* 10 Aug. 202/2 The experimental infection of laboratory-hatched larvæ of the malaria-carrying *Anopheles gambiæ* Giles with a fungus of the genus *Cœlomyces* Keilin. **1818** SHELLEY *Ess. & Lett.* (1852) II. 106 A *malaria fever, caught in the Pontine Marshes. **1832** *Blackw. Mag.* Oct. 525/2 Life [in Padua] creeps away..in having the Malaria fever in summer, and the pleurisy in winter [etc.]. **1898** P. MANSON *Trop. Dis.* v. 97 The mosquito,..the alternative host of the *malaria germ. **1899** *Allbutt's Syst. Med.* VIII. 947 Mosquitoes reared from the eggs of *malaria-infected insects. **1898** P. MANSON *Trop. Dis.* i. 1 The *malaria parasite. This organism is by far the most important disease agency in tropical pathology. **1821** BYRON *Let.* 1 Oct. in Moore *Lett. & Jrnls.* (1830) II. 542, I staid out too late for this *malaria season.

malarial (mə'lɛərɪəl), *a.* and *sb.* [f. prec. + -AL[1].] **A.** *adj.*

1. Infected with malaria; malarious.

1847 in WEBSTER. **1870** *Pall Mall G.* 26 Aug. 5 The malarial plains of India. **1883** *Harper's Mag.* Feb. 419/1 Malarial swamps made it unsafe for him to stay there. **1900** *Brit. Med. Jrnl.* No. 2041. 301 In this circulation of the contagion the presence of malarial man is indispensable.

2. Belonging to, or of the nature of, malaria.

1861 H. MACMILLAN *Footn. Nature* 222 Malarial and epidemic fevers. **1871** NAPHEYS *Prev. & Cure Dis.* I. iii. 100 The malarial poison in the atmosphere. **1875** H. C. WOOD *Therap.* (1879) 75 The wonderful power quinia has upon all forms of malarial disease.

B. *sb.* One who suffers from or is subject to attacks of malaria.

1898 P. MANSON *Trop. Dis.* iii. 86 In many malarials depressing influences..are sufficient to provoke relapse of fever.

malarialist (mə'lɛərɪəlɪst). *rare.* [f. prec. + -IST.] One who studies malarial diseases.

1884 *Harper's Mag.* Aug. 441/2 According as one is a sanitarian, a chemist, or a malarialist.

malarian (mə'lɛərɪən), *a.* [f. MALARIA + -AN.] Pertaining to or causing malaria; malarial.

1834 *Good's Study Med.* (ed. 4) I. 573 The peculiar effect of a malarian poison. **1870** TENNYSON *Golden Supper* 151 A flat malarian world of reed and rush! **1887** RUSKIN *Præterita* II. 256 There was no malarian taint or other malignity in it [the fever].

malariated (mə'lɛərɪeɪtɪd), *ppl. a.* [f. MALARIA + -ATE[3] + -ED[1].] Infected with malaria.

1897 *Allbutt's Syst. Med.* II. 729 *note*, He has succeeded in giving malarial fever to healthy men by administering to them water in which malariated mosquitoes had died.

mala'rigenous, *a. rare.* [Badly f. MALARIA + -GEN + -OUS.] That carries or spreads malaria.

1900 *Brit. Med. Jrnl.* No. 2041. 301 The malarigenous mosquitos.

ma'larioid, *a. rare*[-0]. [f. MALARIA + -OID.] 'Resembling malaria' (*Syd. Soc. Lex.* 1889).

malari'ologist. [f. MALARIA + -(O)LOGIST.] One who studies malaria.

1900 *Brit. Med. Jrnl.* No. 2041. 324 The importance of these labours of the Roman malariologists is beginning to be appreciated by the Italian Government. **1944** *Living off Land* v. 115 Sir Ronald Ross, of the Indian Medical Service ..became the world's foremost malariologist. **1966** *New Scientist* 18 Aug. 374/3 Malariologists are seeking to add to the established methods for controlling the disease. **1971** *Nature* 5 Mar. 65/1 For many years he was a 'wet-foot' malariologist in some of the most difficult countries in the world.

malariology (mə,lɛərɪ'ɒlədʒɪ). [f. MALARI(A + -OLOGY.] The scientific study of malaria.

1925 *Science* 9 Oct. 320/2 In the field of malariology Dr. Carter has long held..the same position of preeminence that he enjoyed in relation to yellow fever. **1936** *Discovery* Nov. 353/1 Instruction in malariology was given to a number of medical practitioners. **1967** D. F. CLYDE *Malaria in Tanzania* p. x, Britain provided..grants with which the research units in Dar es Salaam and Tanga were enabled to lay the scientific foundations of modern malariology in this country. **1974** *Nature* 1 Feb. 318/3 His fleeting acquaintance with the discipline of malariology and with the realities of malaria control.

malarious (mə'lɛərɪəs), *a.* [f. MALARIA + -OUS.] Infected with malaria; of the nature of or producing malaria.

1834 *Cycl. Pract. Med.* III. 61/1 Jungle-fever is as common a name for malarious disease in southern latitudes as marsh-fever is in Europe. **1847** WEBSTER, *Malarious*, pertaining to, or infected by malaria. **1861** MISS BEAUFORT *Egypt. Sep. & Syr. Shr.* I. vii. 153 Deadly the fever of the malarious plain on which the little town stands. **1864** *Gd. Words* Feb. 123 F. E. Barnard caught a malarious fever. **1871** KINGSLEY in *Life* (1877) II. 370 To enforce..a sanitary reform in town and country..till there is not a fever alley or a malarious ditch left in any British city. **1897** *Allbutt's Syst. Med.* II. 1085 If..the patient [is]..neither malarious, anæmic nor scorbutic. **1899** *Ibid.* VIII. 942 When a mosquito ingests the blood of a malarious subject.

fig. **1870** LOWELL *Among my Bks.* Ser. I. 341 In judging Rousseau, it would be unfair not to take note of the malarious atmosphere in which he grew up.

malarkey (mə'lɑːkɪ). *slang* (orig. *U.S.*). Also **malaky, malarky, mullarkey.** [Origin unknown.] Humbug, nonsense, foolishness.

1929 J. P. MCEVOY *Hollywood Girl* vii. 102 It's a wonder you notice me, I told him. That's a lot of malaky, says he. **1930** *Variety* 29 Oct., The song is ended but the Malarkey lingers on. **1934** *Esquire* Dec. 49/3 Daughter of Mrs. Sally Alden, father unknown! What malarkey! All hooey, even protected by the official records of a friendly republic. **1938** *Down Beat* Mar. 5/4 We've got to say to the recording companies..'Cut out the Mullarkey and give us some down-home stuff!' **1945** J. STEINBECK *Cannery Row* xiii. 55 He knew God damn well the story was so much malarky. **1958** *Sunday Times* 20 Apr. 31/1, I will only give you the politician's malarky about imponderables and changing circumstances. **1960** G. M. WILSON *It rained that Friday* xi. 107 Somebody's passed the word round that the island's haunted. I told them it was a lot of malarkey. **1963** J. MITFORD *Amer. Way of Death* iii. 139 The malarkey that surrounds the usual kind of funeral. **1964** *Punch* 23 Dec. 964/3 Any mullarkey from ratting to potato picking. **1965** *Sunday Mail Mag.* (Brisbane) 15 Aug. 5/3 Here was a man who didn't give you the old malarky. **1971** [see FLOPSY BUNNY]. **1973** *Observer* 25 Mar. 12/2 Tall stories..of rattlesnakes bringing up a nestful of baby robins,..or some such malarkey.

mala'rrangement. [f. MAL- + ARRANGEMENT.] Faulty arrangement.

1853 F. W. NEWMAN *Odes of Horace* Pref. 7 Nothing but the fact that Horace is chiefly read..for the mere language ..can make the existing malarrangement endurable. **1865** *Athenæum* 16 Sept. 365/1 Here is another specimen of malarrangement [of facts].

†**malasade.** *Cookery. Obs.* Also 5 **malesade, mes(e)lade.** [f. OF. *malaxé*, f. *malaxer* 'to blend, and beat together, as egges' (Cotgr.: see MALAXATE *v.*) + -ADE.] An old dish composed chiefly of fried eggs softened with butter.

c **1430** *Two Cookery-bks.* 42–3 Meselade. Take Eyroun [etc.]... An to euery good meslade take a þowsand [*read* dd = 12] Eyroun or mo. *c* **1450** *Ibid.* 83–4 Malasade... And to euery malesade, take [etc.]. [Cf. quot. 1753 s.v. MALAX *v.* 2.]

'malassimi'lation. [f. MAL- + ASSIMILATION.] Imperfect assimilation; *esp.* in *Path.* imperfect absorption of nutriment into the system.

1865 *Reader* 29 July 125/2 Viewed in the light of the science of nature or a true physiology, it [the doctrine of substitution] is at best only mal-assimilation. **1875** B. MEADOWS *Clin. Observ.* 10 'Eczema',..associated with dyspepsia, mal-assimilation, and hepatic disorder. **1897** *Allbutt's Syst. Med.* II. 484 A malassimilation of oxygen by the nervous system.

malasso(e)s, -assus, obs. forms of MOLASSES.

malate ('meɪlət). *Chem.* Also 8–9 **-at.** [f. MAL-IC *a.* + -ATE[4].] A salt of malic acid.

1794 G. ADAMS *Nat. & Exp. Philos.* I. App. 547 Malats —but little known. **1801** *Med. Jrnl.* V. 198 Cit. Vaquelin has discovered in the common house leek..a great quantity of malat of lime (*malate de chaux*). **1807** THOMSON *Chem.* (ed. 3) II. 309 Malic acid..forms salts known by the name of *malates*. **1876** HARLEY *Mat. Med.* (ed. 6) 214 Malate of Iron is..prescribed in the old Prussian Pharmacopœia.

malathion (mælə'θaɪən). [The substance is manufactured from diethyl *mal*eate (an ester of MALEIC acid) and a *thio*-acid (see s.v. THIO-).

The name orig. proposed was *malathon* (see quot. 1953[2]). Later *malathion* was registered in the U.S. both as a generic (i.e. non-proprietary) name and as a trade-mark of the American Cyanamid Co.]

An organophosphorus insecticide which is relatively harmless to plants and animals; in commercial preparations it is a brownish liquid with a strong smell of garlic and is also used in the form of a powder.

1953 *Official Gaz.* (U.S. Patent Office) 14 Apr. 322/2 American Cyanamid Company... *Malathion* For Insecticide. **1953** *Substitution of Malathion for Malathon as a Coined (Generic) Name for the Insecticidal Chemical O,O-Dimethyl Dithiophosphate of Diethyl Mercaptosuccinate* (Interdepartmental Comm. Pest Control, Bureau Entomol. & Plant Quarantine, U.S. Dept. Agric.), On January 30, 1952 the Interdepartmental Committee on Pest Control approved the name 'malathon' as coined name for *O,O*-dimethyl dithiophosphate of diethyl

mercaptosuccinate. Because of difficulty encountered in the trade-marking of the name selected at first the commercial sponsor, American Cyanamid Co., decided to change the name to 'malathion'. The American Chemical Society and the American Medical Association are agreeable to the change. Malathion has been registered with the Trade-Mark Division and released for general use. On March 27, 1953, the Interdepartmental Committee on Pest Control approved the name 'malathion' as a coined (generic) name for the chemical in question. **1955** *Sci. News Let.* 3 Sept. 157/1 The insecticides DDT, EPN, heptachlor and malathion have been tested in granular forms. **1960** *Farmer & Stockbreeder* 19 Jan. 119/3 However, as a cure [for red mite in woodwork], it is best to use a B.H.C. or malathion preparation. **1964** *Which?* Apr. 114/1 The organophosphorus compounds, such as dimethoate, malathion, menazon, are mainly poisonous to sucking insects, such as greenfly. **1968** M. PYKE *Food & Society* viii. 119 It is reckoned that whereas 0·5, 0·06, 9 and 1·2 micrograms of DDT, lindane, malathion and carbaryl are ingested for each kilogram of human body weight, the least amounts of these pesticides likely to be harmful are 10, 12, 14 and 20 micrograms respectively.

malato, obs. form of MULATTO.

Malawi (mə'lɑːwɪ), *a.* and *sb.* [Name of a Central African state, formerly Nyasaland.]

A. *adj.* Of or pertaining to Malawi or its inhabitants. **B.** *sb.* A native or inhabitant of Malawi. Also **Ma'lawian** *sb.* and *a.*

1960 *Economist* 15 Oct. 252/1 Dr. Banda's Malawi Congress party. **1963** *Ibid.* 6 July 23/2 His [*sc.* Dr. Banda's] Malawians have lost from the absence of a Nyasa delegation. **1964** *Times* 6 July (Suppl.) 1/2 He [*sc.* Dr. Banda]..has invited the Prime Minister of Southern Rhodesia, Mr. Ian Smith, to the Malawi independence celebrations. **1964** *Observer* 12 July 13/2 The brand-new Malawi flag with a red rising sun. **1965** *Guardian* 4 Oct. 9/6 A brawl at a nightclub between a young British bank clerk and a Malawian. **1966** *Listener* 5 May 637/2 In Rhodesia..Malawis are regarded as the best employees. **1970** *Times* 26 Mar. (Malawi Suppl.) p. i/6 As for Rhodesia, it is inconceivable that the Malawians should adhere strictly to sanctions. *Ibid.* p. iv/4 At Fort Johnston we..acquired the company of a Malawian student hitching a ride home to see his parents. **1971** *Rand Daily Mail* 4 Dec. 1/4 The tiny Malawi Defence Force. *Ibid.* 3/8 Terrorists might enter Malawi purely to embarrass the Malawian Government. **1972** *Whitaker's Almanack 1973* 756/2 In 1970 a 70-mile line was opened..linking the Malawi rail system with the Mozambique network. **1973** *Guardian* 17 Apr. 12/2 Dr. Banda..believed passionately that grammar was what the Malawians most needed.

†**malax**, *v. Obs.* Also 5–7 **malaxe**. [ad. L. *malax-āre*: see MALAXATE. Cf. F. *malaxer*.]

1. *trans.* To rub or knead (a plaster, etc.) to softness.

c **1400** *Lanfranc's Cirurg.* 132 Whanne þin hondis ben anoyntid wiþ oile of rosis, malaxe it [*sc.* a plaster] longe tyme togidere. **1543** TRAHERON *Vigo's Chirurg.* III. i. vi. 93 Strayn them, and make a cerote wyth whyte waxe, and malaxe it in cowes mylke. **1597** LOWE *Chirurg.* (1634) 322 Using on the wound the emplaister Diacalciteos malaxed in wine. **1639** J. W. tr. *Guibert's Char. Physic.* II. 117 Powder all the medicaments severally, then mixe..and beate and malaxe them into a mass. **1693** N. STAPHORST tr. *Rauwolf's Trav. East* in *Ray's Journ. Low C.* (1738) II. 21 He..toucheth and stretcheth your joints again in such a manner, as if he did malax a plaister. **1754–64** SMELLIE *Midwif.* I. Introd. 36 A poultice of barley-meal malaxed with oil must be applied.

2. To soften. (Said of a material agent.)

1634 T. JOHNSON *Parey's Chirurg.* XXVI. xiii. (1678) 637 A mollifying Medicin..malaxeth or softeneth hardned bodies. **1753** SMOLLETT *Ct. Fathom* (1784) 116/1 The major, who complained that his appetite had forsaken him, amused himself with some forty hard eggs, malaxed with salt butter.

Hence †**malaxing** *ppl. a.*

1638 A. READ *Chirurg.* ii. 12 Unlesse fomentation with some moystning and malaxing liquor be used.

†**malaxable**, *a. Obs.* [f. MALAX *v.* + -ABLE.] That may be softened.

1762 tr. *Busching's Syst. Geog.* I. 41 These are firm, compact bodies, which are not malaxable in water or oil.

‖**malaxage** (malaksaʒ). [Fr.; f. *malaxer* MALAX *v.*] 'The operation of kneading and working the unbaked clay of which pottery is to be made' (*Cent. Dict.* 1890).

malaxate ('mælækseɪt), *v.* [f. ppl. stem of L. *malaxāre*, ad. Gr. μαλάσσειν, to make soft, related to μαλακός soft: see -ATE.]

1. *trans.* To knead to softness; to make soft by mixing or rubbing.

1657 TOMLINSON *Renou's Disp.* 126 Materials malaxated in honey. **1755** in JOHNSON. **1853** SOYER *Pantroph.* 172 As soon as it has been malaxated..it is put into brown freestone pots.

†**2.** To soften by means of an emollient. *Obs.*

1735 FERGUSON in *Phil. Trans.* XL. 426 The Abdomen was stuped twice a Day.., and after stuping it was always malaxated with an emollient Liniment.

malaxation (mælæk'seɪʃən). [ad. L. *malaxātiōn-em*, n. of action f. *malaxāre* to MALAXATE. Cf. F. *malaxation*.] **a.** The action of reducing to a soft mass by kneading or rolling.

1657 TOMLINSON *Renou's Disp.* 126 Being by malaxation coagulated. **1706** PHILLIPS (ed. Kersey), *Malaxation*, the working of Pills, and especially Plaisters, with other things, with the hand; a Pestle, or other Instrument. **1894** *Times* 1 Feb. 5/4 He said 'malaxation', or mixing by rolling, was practically the same as kneading.

b. *Ent.* (See quot.)

1898 PECKHAM *Solitary Wasps* 11 The stinging being completed, she [a wasp] proceeded to the process known as *malaxation*, which consists in repeatedly squeezing the neck of the caterpillar, or other victim [to be used as living food for young wasps], between the mandibles.

c. A form of massage.

1887 D. MAGUIRE *Art of Massage* (ed. 4) 46 Malaxation is the same movement [as pétrissage], differing only on account of the flat of the hand being applied with more or less strength before bringing the fingers together to exercise the pétrissage. **1961** *Brit. Med. Dict.* 870/1 *Malaxation*, pétrissage, one of the movements carried out in massage, in which the muscles are grasped in the masseur's hands and rolled and pressed; kneading.

malaxator ('mælækseɪtə(r)). [f. MALAXATE *v.* + -OR.] 'A mixing-mill. A cylinder having a rotating shaft and stirring arms to incorporate materials' (Knight *Dict. Mech.* 1875).

1884 in *Cassell's Encycl. Dict.* **1890** in *Century Dict.*

malaxe, variant of MALAX *Obs.*

Malay (mə'leɪ), *sb.* and *a.* Also 6 **Malayo**, **Melayo**, 8 **Malaya**. [repr. the native name, Malay *malāyu*.] **A.** *sb.*

1. a. One of a race predominating in Malacca and the Eastern Archipelago, a Malayan; more strictly one of those who call themselves by this name and speak the Malay language.

1598 W. PHILLIPS tr. *Linschoten* xviii. 31/2 The Malayos [Du. *De Malayos*] of Malacca say, that the first originall or beginning of Malacca hath bene but of late yeares. **1727** A. HAMILTON *New Acc. E. Ind.* II. xliii. 121 The Natives of the Island are, as most other Malayas, very treacherous. **1840** *Penny Cycl.* XVIII. 328/1 In person the Malays are short, squat, and robust. **1847** TENNYSON *Princess* II. 142 The highest is the measure of the man, And not the Kaffir, Hottentot, Malay. **1867** *Spectator* 26 Jan. 101/1 As.. murderous as a quick-tempered Malay. **1883** MISS BIRD *Golden Chersonese* Introd. 17 The Malays proper inhabit the Malay Peninsula, and almost all the coast regions of Borneo and Sumatra.

b. *spec.* in S. Afr. One of the Muslim community of Cape Town and adjoining districts (see quots. 1944 and 1972). In full, *Cape Malay*.

1785 tr. *Sparrman's Voyage to Cape of Good Hope* I. 12 The burial grounds of the Chinese and free Malays that live at the Cape. **1812** A. PLUMPTRE tr. *Lichtenstein's Trav. S. Afr.* I. i. ii. 28 This practice receives great encouragement from the natural inclination that the slaves, particularly the Malays, have to music. **1844** J. BACKHOUSE *Narr. Visit Mauritius & S. Afr.* v. 82 The religion of the False Prophet was introduced into the Colony by the importation of Malacca slaves, by the Dutch. Hence the terms Malay and Mahomedan became synonymous in the Colony. **1944** I. D. DU PLESSIS *Cape Malays* i. 1 Strictly speaking 'Malay' stands for that section of the local Muslim community in which the descendants of Malay slaves and political exiles are to be found. **1972** *Standard Encycl. S. Afr.* VII. 145/2 Coming from Java and the neighbouring Indonesian islands, the Cape Malays belong essentially to the Javanese and Balinese section of the Malay race.

2. The language spoken by the Malays; the Malay language. (Cf. MALAYS.)

1598 W. PHILLIPS tr. *Linschoten* xviii. 31/2 And this speech called Melayo [Du. *Malayo*] is reported to be the most courteous and seemelie speech of all the Orient. **1883** MISS BIRD *Golden Chersonese* Introd. 19 Malay is the *lingua franca* of the Straits Settlements. **1883** *Encycl. Brit.* XV. 325/1 Malay is essentially..a dissyllabic language.

3. Short for *Malay fowl*.

1830 'B. MOUBRAY' *Dom. Poultry* (ed. 6) 17 The Chittagong or Malay, another Indian variety. **1867** TEGETMEIER *Poultry Bk.* 76 The plumage in Malays is short and close.

B. *adj.* **a.** Of, pertaining to, or characteristic of, the Malays or their country.

1779 FORREST *Voy. N. Guinea* 8 They knew not a word of the Malay tongue. **1840** *Penny Cycl.* XVIII. 328/1 Words.. derived from the Malay language. **1850** GORDON CUMMING *S. Africa* (1902) 34/2 Handkerchiefs..of a striped red and green colour, usually called Malay handkerchiefs. **1883** MISS BIRD *Golden Chersonese* Introd. 23 Cock-fighting..is the popular Malay sport.

b. In the names of plants, animals, etc. native in the Malay Peninsula, e.g. **Malay apple**, a myrtaceous tree, *Jambosa* (*Eugenia*) *malaccensis*, with an edible fruit; **Malay camphor**, Borneo camphor (see BORNEO); **Malay cat** (see quot. 1881); **Malay fowl**, a large variety of domestic fowl introduced from the Malay peninsula; **Malay porcupine**, *Atherura fasciculata*; **Malay tapir**, the Asiatic or Indian Tapir, *Tapirus malayanus*.

1820 SIR S. RAFFLES in *Trans. Linnean Soc.* (1822) XIII. 270 The Malay Tapir resembles in form the American. **1829** LOUDON *Encycl. Plants* 416 *Eugenia malaccensis*. Malay Apple-tr. **1833** W. B. DICKSON *Poultry* (1847) 9 The Malay, or Chittagong Fowl. These fowls have remarkably long legs, and large bones... The colour of the feathers is black, or very dark brown, streaked with yellow. **1837** *Penny Cycl.* IX. 163/1 It is commonly called Malay Camphor, or Camphor of Barus, from the port of Sumatra whence it is mostly shipped. **1840** PAXTON *Bot. Dict.*, Malay Apple, see *Jambosa malaccensis*. **1849** D. J. BROWNE *Amer. Poultry Yard* 37 The Kulm, or Great Malay Fowl. **1873** L. WRIGHT *Illustr. Bk. Poultry* xxi. 297 The finest breed of Malay Game cock (using the word Malay in this case to express locality, and *not* the breed now so-called). **1881** MIVART *Cat* i. 7 In Pegu, Siam, and Burmah, there is a race of cats—the Malay Cat—with tails only of half the ordinary length.

c. Of, pertaining to, or characteristic of the Cape Malays.

1881 *Cape Monthly Mag.* Mar. 192 A Malay hat. **1953** DU PLESSIS & LÜCKHOFF *Malay Quarter* 9 A Malay wedding. **1974** *S. Afr. Panorama* Mar. 7 The oldest of its two gables, dated 1800, is..reputedly the work of a Malay craftsman.

Malayalam (mælə'jɑːləm). Also 9 **Malayalma**, **Malayalim**. [Native name; cf. next.] A Dravidian language, closely related to Tamil, spoken in southern India. Also *attrib.* or as *adj.*

1837 H. HARKNESS *Anc. & Mod. Alphabets Pop. Hindu Lang.* p. i, Under the head of Malayalma are also included the Characters of..Tuluva. **1839** F. SPRING (*title*) Outlines of a grammar of the Malayalim language. **1864** A. J. ARBUTHNOT (*title*) Malayalam selections. **1902** [see DRAVIDIAN A. *adj.*]. **1908** T. G. TUCKER *Introd. Nat. Hist. Lang.* 136 *Malayālam*, occupying a comparatively small area of the west or Malabar coast south of Mangalore. **1911** *Encycl. Brit.* XVII. 466/1 *Malayalam*, a language of the Dravidian family, spoken on the west coast of southern India. **1960** *Universe* 14 Apr. 24/2 Malayalam, a vernacular language of Southern India, was used for the first time as the liturgical language in an ordination in the Syro-Malabar rite at Ernakulam. **1971** *Leader* (Durban) 7 May 8/4 He wrote in Malayalam, which is the mellifluous, if impossibly difficult language of Kerala... His directness and his Malayalam-accented English were always irresistible.

Malayali (mælə'jɑːlɪ). Also **Malayalee**. [Native name, f. Dravidian *mala* mountain + *āḷ* possess.] A member of a Malayalam-speaking people inhabiting the state of Kerala on the Malabar coast of southern India. Cf. MALAYALAM. Also *attrib.*

1856 R. CALDWELL *Compar. Gram. Dravidian Lang.* 491 The higher castes are styled 'Hindus', or else 'Tamilians', 'Malayâlis', &c., according to their language and nation. **1889** L. J. FROHNMEYER *Progressive Gram. Malayalam Lang.* p. xii, The Malayalees have not a few Folk Songs. *Ibid.* xvi. 133 The Malayali..prefers to divide in two or three activities, what Europeans would express by one Verb. **1928** *Chambers's Jrnl.* XVIII. 244/1 Chetwynd managed to hold the Malayalees together for another three days. **1961** P. SPEAR *India* vii. 91 The southern Dravidian people were articulated in four groups..the Tamils,..the Telugus or Andhras,..the Malayalis along the west coast in the modern state of Kerala; and the Kanaras. **1971** *Hindustan Times Weekly Rev.* (New Delhi) 4 Apr. p. iv/5 We celebrate both Malayali and Bengali festivals.

Malayan (mə'leɪən), *a.* and *sb.* [f. MALAY + -AN.] **A.** *adj.*

1. a. Of or pertaining to the Malays or the Malay archipelago.

1668 WILKINS *Real Char.* I. ii. 10 That which seems to be the newest Language in the World, is the Malayan. **1668** T. HYDE *Let. to Boyle* 23 Feb. in *B.'s Wks.* (1744) V. 592/2 The printing of St. Luke and the Acts in the Malayan letter, would make about thirty sheets. **1842** PRICHARD *Nat. Hist. Man* 22 The Malayan or Polynesian race. **1847** TENNYSON *Princess* 21 The cursed Malayan crease, and battle-clubs From the isles of palm. **1864** — *Aylmer's F.* 463 My lady's cousin..Ran a Malayan amuck against the times.

b. in the names of various animals, products, etc. of the Malay archipelago, as **Malayan (sun) bear**, *Helarctos* (*Ursus*) *malayanus*; **Malayan camphor, porcupine, tapir** = *Malay camphor*, etc.

1824 T. HORSFIELD *Zool. Researches Java, Tapirus Malayanus*... In the month of September, 1820, the first specimen of the Malayan Tapir was received in England from Sir Thomas Stamford Raffles. **1826** — in *Zool. Jrnl.* II. 222 In the year 1819 a specimen of the Malayan Bear, obtained at Bencoolen, was brought to England. **1855** W. S. DALLAS *Zool.* II. 486 The Malayan Sun Bear.

2. Of or belonging to the variety of domestic fowl known as the Malay.

1885 TEGETMEIER in *Encycl. Brit.* XIX. 645/1 *Malayan Fowls*.—The Malayan type has been long recognized as of Eastern origin.

B. *sb.* **1.** = MALAY *sb.* 1.

1598 W. PHILLIPS tr. *Linschoten* xviii. 31/2 And all the Malaiens [Du. *die Malayen*], as well men as women, are very amorous... And hee that dwelleth in India, and can not speake the Malayans [Du. *dese Malayen men*] speach, wil hardly with vs learne the French tongue. **1796** MORSE *Amer. Geog.* II. 561 The inhabitants..go under the name of Malayans. **1902** *Blackw. Mag.* Nov. 620/2 The one Malayan who has ever displayed commanding ability.

2. = MALAY *sb.* 2.

1688 T. HYDE *Let. to Boyle* 25 Oct. in *B.'s Wks.* (1744) V. 592/1 We have in Dutch and Malayan a grammar and two vocabularies. **1883** MISS BIRD *Golden Chersonese* Introd. 15 There is a very strong resemblance between their dialects and pure Malayan.

3. During the existence of the Federation of Malaya (from 1948 until 1963), an inhabitant of Malaya (regardless of race or creed).

1954 V. BARTLETT *Rep. from Malaya* ii. 23 A Malayan is anybody—be he Malay, Chinese, Tamil, Eurasian or European—whose home is in Malaya, whereas a Malay is a member of a large race of whom about 3,000,000 live in Malaya, and more than 70,000,000 in Java, Sumatra and the other islands of Indonesia. **1958** G. MIKES *East is East* 114 A *Malayan* is an inhabitant of Malaya, irrespective of race or creed. **1961** L. D. STAMP *Gloss. Geogr. Terms* 304/2 Since the independence of Malaya..Malayan has a political significance as a citizen of Malaya.

Malayanize (mə'leɪənaɪz), *v.* [f. MALAYAN *a.* and *sb.* + -IZE.] *trans.* To make Malayan in character or composition. So **Ma,layani'zation**.

1955 *Times* 24 Aug. 5/5 With regard to Malayanization of the Civil Service, there were good men among Malayan

members of the Civil Service. **1956** *Times* 22 Nov. 9/5 The Government [of Singapore] would begin to put its Malayanization scheme into effect next January. **1960** *Times* 25 Nov. 13/2 Singapore had better get ahead with 'malayanizing' its university. **1965** R. McKie *Company of Animals* i. 15 'Malayanization'—the replacement of Europeans in government services by local-born people. **1971** N. Barber *War of Running Dogs* iii. 46 Everything would change with independence and Malayanization. **1972** *Accountant* 5 Oct. 420/2 It was contended for the taxpayer that there was no evidence..that he had accepted any variation of the agreement because of the policy to Malayanize the staff.

Malayic (mə'leɪɪk), *a. rare.* Also 8 **Malaic**. [See -IC.] = Malayan *a.*

1723 R. Millar *Hist. Propagation Christianity* II. viii. 478 Sermons..in the Malaic Tongue. **1890** D. G. Brinton *Races & Peoples* 230 The Malayic stock.

Ma'layo-, used as combining form of Malay; chiefly in **Malayo-Polynesian** *a.*, the designation of the race to which the Malays and most of the Polynesians belong, and of the group of allied languages including Malay and the Polynesian dialects.

1842 Prichard *Nat. Hist. Man* 327, I shall term these people the Malayo-Polynesian..race. **1876** *Encycl. Brit.* V. 288/1 Their [*sc.* the Macassars'] language..belongs to the Malayo-Javanese group. **1878** W. E. Cousins *Malagasy Lang.* in *Trans. Phil. Soc.* 303 The Malayo-Polynesian languages. *Ibid.* 426 ff. **1879** A. H. Keane in A. R. Wallace *Australasia* 607 Papûans proper in the centre; Malayo-Papûans in the Indian Archipelago. **1880** A. H. Sayce *Introd. Sci. of Lang.* II. viii. 188 The agglutinated adjuncts ..may be almost wholly dispensed with, as in Malayo-Polynesian. **1887** A. Featherman *Social Hist. Races Mankind* II. I. 251 The Malayo-Melanesians are the most important branch of the Melanesian stock. **1896** A. H. Keane *Ethnol.* 285 The Negroid Malayo-Malagasy peoples of Madagascar. *Ibid.* 331 Semi-cultured and rude Malayo-African populations. *Ibid.* 333 The Philippine half-castes may be roughly classed as..Malayo-Indonesians, Malayo-Europeans, and Malayo-Chinese. **1911** Webster, Malayo-Negrito. **1933** [see Austric *a.*]. **1934** Priebsch & Collinson *German Lang.* I. ii. 35 A Creolized language, in this case a blend called Malayo-Portuguese, which was used by the whites in dealing with slaves.

Malayo, obs. form of Malay.

†**Malays.** *Obs.* [a. Du. *Maleisch.* Cf. F. *malais.*] The Malay language.

1779 Forrest *Voy. N. Guinea* 8 They soon learnt to speak Malays.

Malaysian (mə'leɪsɪən), *a.* and *sb.* [f. *Malaysia*, a name given by some geographers to the Malay archipelago + -AN.] **A.** *adj.* Of or belonging to Malaysia. Recently in the narrower sense: of or pertaining to the Federation of Malaysia (formed in 1963 from the states of Malaya, Sabah, Sarawak, and (until 1965) Singapore).

1883 *Encycl. Brit.* XV. 324/2 This astonishing expansion of the Malaysian peoples throughout the Oceanic area. **1884** *Q. Rev.* Apr. 332 The principal..actors in the life drama of the Malaysian stage. **1962** *Times* 9 Jan. 9/3 English is to remain as an 'international language' in the proposed Malaysian Federation. **1963** *Daily Tel.* 12 Sept. 21/7 The agreement covers the question of sovereignty for Singapore and arrangements as between the Singapore Government and the Malaysian Government for emergency security measures. **1963** *Guardian* 16 Sept. 9/4 The Malaysian Government is fully aware that recognition is not a right but a privilege. **1971** *Ibid.* 22 Feb. 3/1 About ninety bills face the Malaysian Parliament when it re-opens tomorrow after 21 months. **1973** J. M. White *Garden Game* 97 A crumpled fistful of Malaysian money.

B. *sb.* A native or inhabitant of the Malay archipelago (quot. 1625) or of Malaysia.

1625 Purchas *Pilgrimes* I. III. xiv. 321, I cannot imagine what the Hollanders meane to suffer these Maleysians, Chinesians, and Moores of those countries. **1955** *Times* 15 June 9/6 The population of the Malay States comprises roughly 50 per cent. Malaysians, 40 per cent. Chinese, 10 per cent. others. **1965** *Guardian* 24 July 8/6 His efforts to overrun the Malaysians in Borneo. **1970** *Daily Tel.* 16 June 2/8 (*heading*) Malaysian jailed for blackmail. **1974** 'G. Black' *Golden Cockatrice* v. 93 You are as good a Malaysian as I am a Taiwanese.

malaysianite (mə'leɪzɪənaɪt). *Geol.* [f. Malaysian *a.* + -ITE[1].] Any tektite from the tektite field of the Malay peninsula.

1940 *Pop. Astron.* XLVIII. 45 Malaysianites tend to show irregular and heavily etched surfaces. **1964** *New Scientist* 16 Jan. 160/2 The widespread Australasian strewn field.. consisting of the australites, the javanites, the malaysianites, billitonites and philippinites.

†**mal-behaviour.** *Obs. rare.* In quots. *male-*. Improper behaviour.

1721 Amherst *Terræ Fil.* No. 45 (1726) 247, I am the only person..who has forfeited his fellowship for male-behaviour. **1736** *Enq. into Frauds of Factors of S. S. Co.* 56 And as to the present Directors, the Male Behaviour of Mr. Woolley, and others, plainly declare, that [etc.].

malbouche, variant of malebouche *Obs.*

malchus ('mælkəs). *Antiq.* [a. F. *malchus*, in both senses a use of the name of *Malchus* (John xviii. 10) whose ear St. Peter cut off with a sword.]

1. 'A short cutting-sword' (*Cent. Dict.* 1890).

2. (See quot.)

1883 Mollett *Dict. Art & Archæol.*, *Malchus*, an old term for a confessional having only one stool for penitents; it signified that which has only one ear, from the fact that Malchus, Caiaphas' servant, was deprived of his right ear by Peter.

malconduct (mæl'kɒndəkt), *sb.* Also 8 **male-**. [f. MAL- + conduct *sb.*] Improper conduct; *esp.* improper or dishonest administration of an office, business, etc.

1741 Johnson *Parl. Deb.* in *Gentl. Mag.* XI. 414 The Male-conduct of the Right Hon. Gentleman. **1757** *Monitor* No. 92 II. 395 To distinguish between men disgraced for mal-conduct; and ministers displaced who [etc.]. **1778** Gouv. Morris in Sparks *Life & Writ.* (1832) I. 201 He must be convicted of malconduct, before he can be removed. **1798** Nelson 13 Nov. in Nicolas *Disp.* (1845) III. 171 Instances of the greatest mal-conduct of persons in office. **1799** *Ibid.* 4 Feb. 255 The malconduct of the Maltese has caused the enterprise to fail. **1804** M. Cutler in *Life*, etc. (1888) II. 157 Some evidence, of mal-conduct or specific charges, was called for.

Hence †**malconduct** *v. intr. rare*, to be guilty of malconduct.

1801 E. Gerry in *N. Eng. Hist. & Gen. Register* (1896) L. 27 Its own government..having removed from office, such as it conceived had malconducted.

,mal,confor'mation. [See MAL-.] Bad or faulty conformation.

1776 T. Percival *Ess.* III. 282 The disease is neither owing to inflammation, nor to any mal-conformation of the parts. **1851** Sir F. Palgrave *Norm. & Eng.* I. 136 The inherent malconformation of the Carlovingian Empire. **1858** De Quincey *Language* Wks. IX. 91 A sentence..is capable of multiform beauty, and liable to a whole nosology of malconformations. **1871** Darwin *Desc. Man* I. i. 9 Is man subject to similar malconformations?

,malcon'struction. [See MAL-.] Faulty construction.

1809 in *Spirit Pub. Jrnls.* XIII. 65 'A roarer'; that is, a horse, which, owing to a mal-construction of the organs, makes a roaring noise. **1858** Greener *Gunnery* 105 The only failures Mr. Krupp has made..have arisen from mal-construction. **1897** *Trans. Amer. Pediatric Soc.* IX. 110 There is a very material malconstruction of the diaphragm.

malcontent ('mælkəntɛnt), *a.* and *sb.* Also 6–9 **malecontent**. [a. OF. *malcontent*: see MAL- and content *a.*]

A. *adj.* Discontented, dissatisfied. Now chiefly in political use: Actively discontented; indisposed to acquiesce in the existing administration of affairs (e.g. of the state, of a party, etc.); inclined to rebellion or mutiny; restless and disaffected.

1586 B. Young *Guazzo's Civ. Conv.* IV. 201 b, If the Ape is malecontent for want of a taile. **1593** Shaks. *3 Hen. VI*, IV. i. 10 How like you our Choyce, That you stand pensiue, as halfe malecontent? **1601** F. Godwin *Bps. of Eng.* 116 He quickly began to grow malcontent, and..entred at last into a conspiracie. **1673** Temple *Observ. United Prov.* Wks. 1731 I. 19 At this time began to be form'd the Male-content Party in the Low-Countries. **1679** J. Goodman *Penit. Pard.* I. iv. (1713) 86 He presently grows male-content with his condition. **1769** *Ann. Reg.* 4/2 This malcontent temper of the Grecian Christians. **1816** Scott *Old Mort.* vii, Lady Margaret Bellenden had returned, in romantic phrase, male-content, and full of heaviness. **1827** Hallam *Const. Hist.* (1876) III. xv. 146 The malecontent whigs were now [1701] so consolidated with the tories as in general to bear their name. **1892** Stevenson *Across the Plains* 234 He has ever since been malcontent with literature.

B. *sb.*

1. A malcontent person (see A).

1581 L. Aldersey in Hakluyt *Voy.* (1589) 177 Besides the perill of the Malcontents, who were vpon both sides of the riuer [Rhine]. **1581** Pettie *Guazzo's Civ. Conv.* III. (1586) 152, I thinke they haue iust cause to be mal contents, who knowing themselues to be sufficient men..are..used by their father like children. **1587** Holinshed *Chron.* III. 10/2 The onelie place wherein all the mal-contents [*ed.* 1577 Rebels] of his realme had their refuge. **1668** R. Steele *Husbandman's Calling* v. (1672) 67 No, sayes the male-content, if things had sorted to my mind, it had been far better than it is. **1687** Dryden *Hind & P.* III. 662 Your sons are male-contents, but yet are true, As far as non-resistance makes 'em so. **1759** Robertson *Hist. Scot.* III. Wks. 1813 I. 258 The malecontents had not yet openly taken up arms. **1841** Trench *Parables* (1860) 416 He expostulates with the malcontent. **1874** Green *Short Hist.* ix. §7. 662 The leading malcontents..were already calling on him to interfere in arms.

†**2.** The state of being discontented. *Obs.*

[Really a distinct word: see content *sb.*]

1591 *Troub. Raigne K. John* (1611) 39 We must obscure this mone with melodie, Least worser wrack ensue our male-content. **1632** Lithgow *Trav.* I. 6 Let me enter into consideration of the intractable passage of my malecontents past. **1643** Milton *Divorce* II. xx. Wks. 1851 IV. 119 A necessity of sadnesse and malecontent. **1658** Sir T. Browne *Hydriot.* v. 25 Content to be nothing, or never to have been, which was beyond the *male*-content of Job, who cursed not the day of his life, but his nativity. **1663** *Flagellum or O. Cromwell* (1672) 29 Rash and blind Furies, that made way to the unobserved advancement of this private Male-content.

†**malcon'tented,** (*pa. pple.* and) *a. Obs.* Also **male-**. [Partly f. prec. adj. + -ED[1]; partly f. MAL- + contented *a.*]

1. As *pa. pple.* Made malcontent. *rare*$^{-1}$.

1584 *Leycesters Commw.* (1641) 150 Noble men of the Realm, who live abroad..much iniured and malcontented by his insolencie.

2. = malcontent *a.*

c **1586** C'tess Pembroke *Ps.* LXXIII. vi, For what purpose was it..For me to fume with malecontented heart? **1593–4** Sylvester *Profit Imprisonm.* 541 Murmuring 'gainst the Lord, with male-contented voyce. **1600** Heywood *1st Pt. Edw. IV* (1613) A 4, To him the malcontented commons flocke, From euery part of Sussex. **1614** Jackson *Creed* III. xxxii. §3 If men male-contented with this present, may haue sweete promises of euerlasting happinesse in the life to come. **1622** Bacon *Hen. VII* 39 For the better securing of his estate, against mutinous and malcontented Subiects. **1696** Luttrell *Brief Rel.* (1857) IV. 119 The restlesse attempts of the malecontented party. *a* **1716** South *Serm. Sev. Occas.* (1744) VII. 289 To satisfy or silence this malecontented Enquiry.

Hence †**malcon'tentedly** *adv.*

1630 *R. Johnson's Kingd. & Commw.* 231 The Portugals.. live male-contentedly under his obedience and government. **1755** Johnson, *Malecontentedly*.

†**malcon'tentedness.** *Obs.* Also **male-**. [See -NESS.] The state of being malcontented.

1601 Deacon & Walker *Spirits & Divels* 349 In an onelie malcontentednes, rather against the persons of some in authoritie then in any true mindednes towards reformation. *a* **1639** Wotton in *Reliq.* (1685) 659 The Pope appear'd not publickly,..for a kind of malecontentedness with his own action. **1712** Addison *Spect.* No. 445 ¶5, I fear they would ascribe the laying down my Paper, on such an Occasion, to a Spirit of Malcontentedness.

Personified. **1626** Bernard *Isle of Man* (1627) 67 Where sullen Male-contentednesse sits.

'malcontentism. *rare*$^{-1}$. [-ISM.] = prec.

1813 *Examiner* 3 May 288/1 A sign of malcontentism.

'malcontently, *a. rare*$^{-0}$. [f. malcontent *a.* + -LY[2].] In a malcontent manner.

In some recent Dicts.

†**malcontentment.** *Obs.* Also **male-**. [a. OF. *malcontentement*: cf. MAL- and contentment.] The condition of being malcontent.

1587 Holinshed *Scot. Chron.* 446/2 They had..by vniuersall male-contentment of the people..procured a great distraction of the kings leeges hearts. **1588** Kyd *Househ. Phil.* Wks. (1901) 252 Vppon the malcontentment of the minde followes the..weakenes of the bodie. **1606** Bp. W. Barlow *Serm.* 21 Sept. E, Their ground was Malecontentment,..because they could not be made Bishops. **1637–50** in Row *Hist. Kirk* (1842) 288 So he put in fifty merks with shame and great malcontentment.

mal-'convenance. *rare.* [quasi-Fr., f. phr. *mal convenir* to be unsuitable.] Defective adaptation.

1835 Chalmers *Nat. Theol.* (1849) I. II. iii. 266 Any mal-convenance which is incompatible with life cannot..be presented to observation.

‖**mal-crasis** (mæl'kreɪsɪs). *Path. rare.* [f. MAL- + crasis.] A faulty combination of constituents.

1854 Jones & Siev. *Pathol. Anat.* 115 Inflammations which arise in consequence of a mal-crasis of the blood.

†**maldathait.** *Obs.* Also 4 **maldat**. [a. OF. *maldehait*: see MAL- and dahet.] 'May he have misfortune'; = dahet.

a **1300** *Cursor M.* 16290 (Cott.) For þi mis-sau þat all has herd maldathait [*Gött.* maldat] qua þe spare.

‖**mal de flanc.** *Obs.* [Fr.] Disease of the side.

c **1290** *Becket* 901 in *S. Eng. Leg.* 132 þe bischop thomas lay, In þe syknesse of maldeflanke.

‖**mal de mer.** [Fr.] Sea-sickness.

1778 J. Adams *Diary* 19 Feb., Wks. 1851 III. 98 The *mal de mer* seems to be merely the effect of agitation. **1899** Godley *Lyra frivola* 6 He notes his qualms with care, And bids the public know 'em In 'Thoughts on Mal de Mer' Or 'Nausea: a Poem'.

malde'scended, *a. Med.* [f. MAL- + descended *ppl. a.*] Of a testis: not having descended all the way into the scrotum from the abdominal cavity during development of the fœtus, or having descended ectopically.

1908 *Ann. Surg.* XLVIII. 321 (*heading*) Treatment of the undescended or maldescended testis. **1933** *Post-Graduate Med. Jrnl.* IX. 248 There is a widespread..belief that if a young boy with a mal-descended testis is left alone the organ will drop..at puberty. **1936** H. Bailey *Dis. Testicle* ii. 11 A maldescended testis is one which cannot be made to touch the bottom of the scrotum. **1962** *Lancet* 19 May 1059/1 A few weeks ago we attempted to evaluate the dangers of malignancy arising in undescended and maldescended testes.

malde'scent. *Med.* [f. MAL- + descent.] The state (of a testis) of being maldescended; incomplete or ectopic descent.

1908 *Ann. Surg.* XLVIII. 324 The different types of maldescent of the testis. **1948** L. Martin *Clin. Endocrinol.* viii. 159 In cryptorchidism the testes remain in the abdomen, in maldescent they lie in the inguinal canals or unduly high in the scrotum. **1954** G. I. M. Swyer *Reproduction & Sex* vi. 65 Sometimes maldescent is present on one side only, the testicle on the other side being situated in the normal position. **1964** *Arch. Dis. Childhood* XXIX. 607/1 Any testis not in the scrotum, that is, 4 cm. or less from the pubic crest in infants and boys is undescended. If it is more than this distance but not as low as it should be it is incompletely descended. The terms mal-descent and imperfect descent have no useful meaning.

†**maldisant.** *Obs.* Also 6 **maledizant.** [a. F. *maldisant*, f. *mal* ill + *disant*, pr. pple. of *dire* to say.] An evil-speaker, slanderer.

1598 FLORIO *Ital. Dict.* a 6 He is to blame..that will be wittie in another mans booke. How then will scoffing readers scape this marke of a maledizant? **1617** MINSHEU *Ductor* s.v., A Maldisant or euill speaker. **1661** BLOUNT *Glossogr.* (ed. 2), *Maldisant*, an evil speaker, a backbiter.

maldistribution (ˌmældɪstrɪˈbjuːʃən). [f. MAL- + DISTRIBUTION.] Faulty distribution. Hence ˌ**maldiˈstributed** *ppl. a.*

1895 *U.S. Dept. Agric. Farmers' Bulletin* XXXIII. 22 This ruinous state of affairs is not attributable to over-production, but to maldistribution. **1928** *Britain's Industr. Future* (Liberal Industr. Inquiry) III. xix. 243 We agree with the Socialists in thinking that a distribution so uneven as is at present found is maldistribution. **1931** *Times Trade & Engin. Suppl.* 24 Jan. 431/2 We are suffering from maldistribution of gold. **1933** *Planning* 6 June 1 Unemployment has grown..to a world-wide problem of maldistributed leisure. **1935** *Discovery* Jan. 14/1 Poverty persists and populations become maldistributed. **1957** *Economist* 23 Nov. 694/2 The chronic maldistribution of wealth. **1969** *Listener* 6 Mar. 318/1 The story which began in the wilderness ends..in automated (if maldistributed) affluence. **1971** *Daily Tel.* 3 July 12 Summer is the time when maldistribution of business at the start of the session catches up with the Lords.

Maldivian (mɒlˈdɪvɪən, -ɔː-), *sb.* and *a.* Also 9 **Maldivan.** A. *sb.* A native or inhabitant of the Maldive Islands in the Indian Ocean; their language. B. *adj.* Of or pertaining to the Maldive Islands or their inhabitants.

1836 *Trans. Bombay Geogr. Soc.* I. 77 The Maldivans have a written, as well as an unwritten law. **1841** *Jrnl. R. Asiatic Soc.* VI. 42 (*title*) Vocabulary of the Maldivian language. **1959** *Times* 19 Mar. 6/3 He was able to learn something of the Maldivian language. **1970** *Trans. Philol. Soc.* 148 The Maldivian numerals are lexically related to the Indic numeral systems. **1972** *Guardian* 15 Mar. 13/5 The Maldivians are hopefully extending the runway. **1972** *Language* XLVIII. 464 The only language closely related to Sinhalese is Maldivian, spoken in the Maldive Islands and on the island of Minicoy, which is part of India.

maldonite (ˈmɔːldənaɪt). *Min.* [Named in 1876 by Ulrich, from *Maldon*, Victoria, its locality: see -ITE.] A variety of gold, containing bismuth.

1870 *Amer. Jrnl. Sci.* Ser. II. L. 272 Maldonite, or Bismuthic Gold.

malduck (ˈmældʌk). [? f. *mall* = MAW *sb.*² + DUCK *sb.* But cf. MALLEMUCK.] A name, in the Shetland Isles, for the Fulmar.

1802 G. MONTAGU *Ornith. Dict.* (1833) 315 *Malduck.* **1806** P. NEILL *Tour Orkney & Shetl.* 198 Malmock, Mallemock, or Mallduck, Fulmar, Procellaria glacialis.—Appears in the friths of Orkney, and voes of Shetland.

‖**mal du siècle** (mal dy sjɛkl(ə)). [Fr.] World-weariness, weariness of life, deep melancholy because of the condition of the world.

In French with specific reference to the early 19th-c. Romantic poets.

1926 A. HUXLEY *Essays New & Old* 38 The *mal du siècle* was an inevitable evil. **1932** *Times Lit. Suppl.* 16 June 439/1 We have the sentimental and practical romanticism, the *mal du siècle*. **1957** G. SMITH *Friends* ii. 36 A bijou house in Chelsea, premature obesity, *mal du siècle* and incipient gout. **1963** R. WELLEK in N. Frye *Romanticism Reconsidered* 109 Little has been accomplished by calling familiar states of mind—*Weltschmerz, mal du siècle*, pessimism—'negative' romanticism.

maldy. *Sc.* ? *Obs.* 'A coarse woollen cloth of grey or mixed colour' (Jam. *Suppl.*). Also *attrib.*

1588–9 *Extracts Rec. Glasgow* (1876) 128 In the first, ane cloik of maldy, price thrie pundis:..ane pair of maldy schankis [etc.].

†**male**, *sb.*¹ *Obs.* Also MELE. [ad. L. *māl-us* apple-tree, *māl-um* apple.] An apple; an apple-tree. Also *Comb.* as *male-apple*, *-apple-tree*.

a **1400** *Song Solomon* [ii. 3] in *Rel. Ant.* I. 40 As the male is plentiuouse of apples..so is my derlyng among sones. *c* **1420** *Pallad. on Husb.*, Tabula, Male appeltreen. Male applis. *Ibid.* XI. 259 This mone also the male [orig. *mali*] is sett to sprynge; This male is sette in londis hoot & drie.

male (meɪl), *a.* and *sb.*² Forms: 5, 7 **masle**, 4 **madle, mawl, maal, maule**; *Sc.* 5–6 **maill**, 6 **mail**, 7 **maile**; 4– **male.** (See also MASCLE *a.*) [a. OF. *male, masle* (mod.F. *mâle*), earlier *mascle*:—L. *masculus* (f. *mās* male person, male), whence MASCULINE *a.* Cf. Pr. *mascle*, Sp., Pg. *macho*, It. *maschio*.

The spelling *masle* was the prevailing one in Law French, and in legal use appears in Eng. down to the 17th c. Sir T. Browne is the only non-legal writer of the 17th c. who uses it: doubtless as suggesting the original Latin etymon.]

A. *adj.*

I. Of or belonging to the sex which begets offspring, or performs the fecundating function of generation.

1. a. of persons. In *Law*: *heir, issue, line, tail male.* (In early, *esp.* legal use, often pl. *males.*)

1375 BARBOUR *Bruce* XX. 130 Gif it fell that his sone Davy Deit but air male of his body Gottyn. **1377** LANGL. *P. Pl.* B. XVI. 236, I circumcised..my meyne and alle þat male were. **1382** [see FEMALE *a.* 1]. *c* **1450** *Merlin* 88 She is now leide down in his bedde of a childe male. **1450** *Rolls of Parlt.* V. 188/1 To hym and to his heires masles of his body lawfully begoten. **1463** *Bury Wills* (Camden) 25 And for defawte of yssew male of the seid Robert than I wil John Baret..haue it, to hym and to his eyres male. ? *a* **1500** *Sir Beues* 3392 (Pynson) Yonge male chyldren two. *c* **1500** *Melusine* 18 He begate on her many children males. **1563** WINȜET *Four Scoir Thre Quest.* Wks. 1888 I. 82 The maill barne nocht circumcidit the auchtin day. **1595** SHAKS. *John* III. iv. 76 Caine, the first male-childe. **1613** —— *Hen. VIII*, II. iv. 189 My Ladies wombe..conceiu'd a male-child by me. **1614** SELDEN *Titles Hon.* 196 Reseruing..the reuersion to themselues in default of heires masles. **1647–8** COTTERELL *Davila's Hist. Fr.* (1678) 6 In the male-line of their Predecessors. **1752** HUME *Pol. Disc.* x. 166 All masters discourage the marrying of their male servants. **1818** CRUISE *Digest* (ed. 2) VI. 315 An estate in tail male was vested in Edmund Hicks, as heir male of the body of Launcelot Hicks. **1847** TENNYSON *Princess* Prol. 151, I would make it death For any male thing but to peep at us.

b. of animals.

c **1400** *Master of Game* xxxiv. (MS. Digby 182), She [the hare] oþer while is male..and oþere while is female. *c* **1440** *Promp. Parv.* 323/1 Male, best or fowle, no femel, *masculus*. *a* **1500** [see FEMALE *a.* 1 b]. **1530** PALSGR. 242/1 Male gote, *bovc.* **1607** SHAKS. *Cor.* v. iv. 30 There is no more mercy in him, then there is milke in a male-Tyger. **1797** *Encycl. Brit.* (ed. 3) VII. 258/1 This operation [castration] may be performed both on male and female fish. **1855** W. S. DALLAS *Syst. Nat. Hist.* I. 348 In the autumn, male and female insects are found, furnished with perfect generative organs. **1902** *Oxford Times* 22 Feb. 2/1 For sale..3 hens and 1 male bird.

absol. **1390** GOWER *Conf.* II. 45 Sche sih the bestes in her kinde,..The madle go with the femele.

c. In *male †kind* (also *attrib.*), *sex* (see SEX).

1382 WYCLIF *Luke* ii. 23 For ech male kynde openynge the wombe to go out, schal be clepid hooly to the Lord. **1530** PALSGR. 318/1 Male of the male kynde, *masle*. **1598** GUILPIN *Skial.* Sat. iv. (Grosart) 51 A male-kind sparrow once mistooke his nest And fled for harbour to faire Liuias breast. **1611** COTGR., *Masculeyté*, Manhood, or the male kind. **1681** R. KNOX *Hist. Ceylon* 41 The Malekind may come and see him, but no Women are admitted. *a* **1682** SIR T. BROWNE *Tracts* 119 A smaller bird Tercellene or Tassel of the masle sex. **1727** BAILEY vol. II, *Male-kind*.

d. Said of the reproductive organs of this sex.

1607 TOPSELL *Four-f. Beasts* (1658) 254 They took from them [stoned horses] their male parts. **1836–9** TODD *Cycl. Anat.* II. 140/1 The male-duct..terminates at the anterior extremity of the body. **1888** ROLLESTON & JACKSON *Anim. Life* 472 *Neomenia carinata* [a mollusc] has been said to possess lateral male ducts.

e. Used jocularly to qualify female designations, e.g. **male aunt** = uncle; **male bawd** = pander, etc.; also to qualify female conditions, as **male widowhood**, the condition of being a widower. Also used, not jocularly, in referring to professions that are usually considered to be predominantly female, as ***male midwife, model, nurse, prostitute.***

1597 SHAKS. *2 Hen. IV*, IV. iii. 100 They fall into a kinde of Male Greene-sicknesse. **1607** TOURNEUR *Rev. Trag.* I. ii, When base male-Bawdes kept Centinell at staire-head. **1681** OTWAY *Soldier's Fort.* II. i, Your Go-between, your Male-Baud there. **1712** STEELE *Spect.* No. 288 ¶1 Which has given me Encouragement to describe a certain Species of Mankind under the Denomination of Male Jilts. *Ibid.* ¶2 They whom my correspondent calls Male Coquets, shall hereafter be called Fribblers. *Ibid.* No. 320 ¶1 You have published the Term Male-Coquets. **1712** FRANCHAM *ibid.* No. 520 ¶1, I cannot but recommend the Subject of Male Widowhood to you. **1755** J. SHEBBEARE *Lydia* (1769) I. 59 When a new work is advertised, the male and female ladies ..immediately conclude it cannot be worth the reading. **1770–93** [see COQUETTE 1 c]. **1781** MME. D'ARBLAY *Diary* II. 87 He is an actual Male prude! **1821** LAMB *Elia* Ser. I. *My relations*, Male aunts, as somebody calls them, I had none —to remember. **1878** TROLLOPE *John Caldigate* (1879) II. iv. 45 He took the child very gently... He had already assumed for himself the character of being a good male nurse. **1915** MRS. BELLOC LOWNDES *Diary* 12 Mar. (1971) 58 It is very difficult to get the right type of man to be a male nurse. **1948** A. KINSEY et al. *Sexual Behavior in Human Male* vi. 216 Some male prostitutes ejaculate five, six, or more times per day with regularity over long periods of years. **1961** S. BAKER *Visual Persuasion* ii. 47/2 Male model agencies and actors' guilds always have a few personalities on hand. **1972** 'W. HAGGARD' *Protectors* vi. 71 The man in the chair..was kept alive by two male nurses. **1974** *Mother & Baby* Feb. 44 (*heading*) Would you like a male midwife? **1974** H. WAUGH *Parrish for Defence* (1975) xix. 321 He is presently serving as a male prostitute for other males. **1975** *Times* 11 Mar. 4/8 It would be wrong to rule out male midwives as a matter of principle. **1975** 'G. BLACK' *Big Wind* vii. 114 He looked like a male model in one of those ads for expensive men's knitwear.

f. *Comb.*

1587 GOLDING *De Mornay* vi. 63 God..who is also Minde, & life and Light, and Malefemale [*marg.* ἀρρενόθηλυς], begat or bred Logon the Speach. **1603** B. JONSON *Sejanus* II. ii. (1605) D 3 b, That male-spirited Dame, Their Mother. **1774** *Westm. Mag.* II. 453 You will see behind a Perfumer's counter..a Male-Female Thing of this sort.

2. With reference to the vegetable kingdom.

a. Said of certain plants (of diœcious genera) the flowers of which contain only the fecundating organs. Subsequently said also of the fecundating organs of plants, and of flowers containing only organs of this kind. **male-sterile** *a.*, (of a hermaphrodite plant) incapable of producing fertile pollen; so **male-sterility.**

1398 TREVISA *Barth. De P. R.* XVII. ii. (1495) 597 Yf..the rynde of a male palme be put to the leuys of the female..the fruyte..shall be the sooner rype. *a* **1400** *Stockh. Medical MS.* ii. 715 in *Anglia* XVIII. 324 In a vessell..Putte hem, & þou schalt sene Wyche is femel & wyche is male. **1600** J. PORY tr. *Leo's Africa* VI. 268 Of date-trees some are male and some are female. **1789** G. WHITE *Selborne* v. (1853) 209 This is a male tree, which in the spring sheds clouds of dust, and fills the atmosphere around with its farina. **1791** *Gentl. Mag.* 2/2 The catkins which appear in January are the male parts of a nut-tree. **1796** WITHERING *Brit. Pl.* (ed. 3) I. 188 In the Ribes alpinum, the male and female flowers are sometimes found on different plants. **1871** KINGSLEY *At Last* i, In the midst of the yard grew, side by side,..a male and female Papaw. **1875** BENNETT & DYER tr. *Sachs' Bot.* 448 The resemblance of the male flowers to the inflorescence of Equisetum is as striking [etc.]. **1880** GRAY *Struct. Bot.* vi. § 1. 165 The Stamens are the male or fertilizing organs of a flower. **1921** *Jrnl. Genetics* XI. 269 (*heading*) Male-sterility in flax, subject to two types of segregation. *Ibid.* 271 In the breeding work it was not thought necessary to emasculate the male-sterile flowers. **1946** *Nature* 21 Sept. 422/2 Further tabulation of male-sterility genes in varieties of the onion is given. **1959** *New Biol.* XXVIII. 75 Certain willow-herb crosses which produce male-sterile progeny.

b. Applied to certain plants to which sex was formerly attributed on account of some peculiarity of habit, colour, etc. **male fern**, *Asplenium* (*Nephrodium*) *Filix-mas*; also *attrib.*

1562 TURNER *Herbal* II. 3 The vertues of the male ferne. **1597** GERARDE *Herbal* II. cclxix. (1633) 773 The male Mullein or Higtaper hath broad leaves. **1639** T. DE GREY *Compl. Horseman* 319 Take the root of male brake or fearn. **1718** QUINCY *Compl. Disp.* 133 Paul's Betony or Male Speedwell. **1779** M. UNDERWOOD *Dis. Childr.* (ed. 4) I. 147 The male fern alone is reckoned a specific [for worms]. **1838** LINDLEY *Flora Med.* 512 Purga Macho, or Male Jalap. **1871** KINGSLEY *At Last* v, Here and there a young one [palm] springing up like a gigantic crown of male-fern. **1877** tr. *von Ziemssen's Cycl. Med.* VII. 702 Male fern-root.

II. 3. a. Of or pertaining to a man or men, or to male animals; peculiar to or characteristic of men; composed or consisting of men.

a **1631** DONNE *Progr. Soul* I. 12 By thy male force is all wee have begot. **1682** R. BURTON *Admir. Curios.* (1684) 67 It was after altered into a Male-Nunnery. **1684** T. BURNET *Th. Earth* I. 198 The ancients..have suppos'd that there was something of an æthereal element in the male-geniture. **1710–11** SWIFT *Jrnl. to Stella* 26 Feb., They keep as good female company as I do male. **1784** COWPER *Task* VI. 233 Profaned,..under various names, Female and male. **1804–5** WORDSW. *Prelude* III. 56 Trinity's loquacious clock..told the hours Twice over with a male and female voice. **1871** DARWIN *Desc. Man* (1888) 393 The common drake..after the breeding season is well known to lose his male plumage for a period of three months. **1900** *Daily News* 18 Sept. 4/6 A case filled with moths whose right wings belong to the male coloration. **1903** *Westm. Gaz.* 3 Feb. 9/1 It is intended to form a male voice choir.

b. Appropriate or adapted to the use of a man.

1788 J. WARE in *Mem. Med. Soc.* II. 336 Strictures on the Use of the Male Catheter. **1828** SIR A. HALLIDAY *Pres. St. Lunatics* 98, 1 Matron for Male Hospital. **1898** *Allbutt's Syst. Med.* V. 986 A large soft rubber male catheter.

III. *transf.* Applied to various material and immaterial things, denoting superiority, strength, greatness, or the like.

†**4.** In occasional applications. *Obs.*

c **1645** HOWELL *Lett.* (1650) I. 371 As in France, so in all other wine countries, the white is called the female, and the claret or red wine is called the male, because commonly it hath more sulphur, body, and heat in it. **1649** BLITHE *Eng. Improv. Impr.* ix. (1653) 48, I shall provoke unto the best Improvement, and where there can be a Male-Improvement offer not to the Common-Wealth a Female. **1667** MILTON *P. L.* VIII. 150 Other Suns perhaps With their attendant Moons thou wilt descrie Communicating Male and Female Light.

†**5. a.** Said of precious stones, on account of depth, brilliance or other accident of colour; also of other stones, with reference to their hardness or other esteemed qualities. [Gr. ἄρρην, L. *masculus*.]

c **1400** MAUNDEV. (1839) xiv. 158 Thei [the dyamandes] growen to gedre, male and femele. **1681** GREW *Musæum* 290 The Sardius or Cornelian,..The best, by some called The Male. *Ibid.* 297 The Florid Male Eagle-Stone. **1726** LEONI *Alberti's Archit.* I. 58/2 The Stones found in Rivers, which are call'd Male ones,..grow dry immediately when..taken out of the water. **1855** BROWNING *Saul* viii, Lordly male-sapphires.

†**b.** Used to distinguish the harder and more compact kind of sand or gravel. *Obs.*

1601 HOLLAND *Pliny* II. 409 The hard and compact gravell called the Male gravell [L. *sabulum masculum*]. **1610** W. FOLKINGHAM *Art of Survey* IV. Concl. 87 A faire Pond.. springing from the West forth of a male grauell. **1726** LEONI *Alberti's Archit.* II. 105/2 The male-sand [It. *sabbione maschio*] and the hard grit are sure to afford the best of water. **1813** VANCOUVER *Agric. Devon* 65 The male or bastard tin-stone is found..on Dartmoor.

†**6. male incense.** [So in L. and Fr.] A superior quality of incense, known by the greater size of the 'tears' in which it is collected; frankincense. *Obs.*

1598 W. PHILLIP tr. *Linschoten's Voy.* I. lxxii. 119 Frankinsence is of two sorts, one white, that is round and like vnto drops, which is the best, and called the masle; the other blacke. **1647** HERRICK *Noble Numb.*, *Dirge Jephthah's Dau.* xiii, May Virgins, when they come to mourn, Male-Incense burn Upon thine Altar! **1727–41** CHAMBERS *Cycl.* s.v. *Frankincense, Male incense*, or *olibanum*.

7. Of rime: = MASCULINE.

1581 SIDNEY *Apol. Poetrie* (Arb.) 71 The French..hath both the Male [ryme], as *Bon, Son*, and the Female, as *Plaise, Taise*. **1841** *Penny Cycl.* XIX. 486/1 These mono-syllable or last-syllable rhymes are called male rhymes. **1896** S. W. BARNUM *Vocab. Eng. Rhymes* (ed. 2) Introd. 16 Part I consists of single or male rhymes.

8. Said of the external layer of bark on a tree.

1884 [see FEMALE A. 8].

IV. 9. a. A distinctive epithet for that part of an instrument or contrivance which is adapted to penetrate or fill the corresponding female part.

a **1856** H. MILLER in *Footpr. Creator* (1874) 342 The male half of the hinge belongs to the head, and the female half to the jaw. **1884** BRITTEN *Watch & Clockm.* 274 Steel runners with male centres are handy when turning bouchons. **1889** *Mayne's Med. Voc., Female*..the part of a double-limbed instrument which receives the male or corresponding part.

b. (See quot.)

1688 R. HOLME *Armoury* III. xii. 433/1 There is no difference between the male and female Trepan, but for the pin in the middle which the female wants.

c. ***male gauge***: the outer gauge or screw of a printing press. ***male screw***: the spiral pin or rod which fits the spirally bored circular socket of the 'female' screw.

1669 BOYLE *Contn. New Exp.* II. (1682) 11 A Female Screw, to receive the Male-screw of the Stop-cock. **1683** MOXON *Mech. Exerc., Printing* xix. 170 So as the Male-Gages may fall into the Female-Gages. **1822** IMISON *Sci. & Art* I. 48 The first is called the Male or outside screw. **1827** FARADAY *Chem. Manip.* xv. 361 Their use is to connect together stop-cocks..terminated by male screws. **1856** C. CAREY in *Abr. Specif. Patents, Writ. Instr.* (1869) 210 At each of the four angles of one is fixed an upright male screw.

B. *sb.*

1. A male animal.

13.. *E.E. Allit. P.* B. 337 Ay þou meng with þe malez þe mete ho-bestez. **1398** TREVISA *Barth. De P. R.* VI. xii. (1495) 196 In all kynde of beestes the male is more crafti. **1590** SHAKS. *Com. Err.* II. i. 19 The beasts, the fishes, and the winged fowles Are their males subjects. **1596** NASHE *Saffron Walden* Ep. Ded. A 2, Musing Dick, that studied a whole yeare to know which was the male and female of red herrings. **1688** R. HOLME *Armoury* II. 236/1 A Boccaret [Hawk] is the Male of a Boccarell. **1697** DRYDEN *Virg. Georg.* III. 420 The furious Mare, Barr'd from the Male, is frantick with Despair. **1774** GOLDSM. *Nat. Hist.* (1776) III. 314 There are some of the males who attach themselves to the female. **1802** PALEY *Nat. Theol.* xix. (ed. 2) 363 The glow-worm is a female caterpillar; the male of which is a fly. **1857** *Househ. Words* 19 Dec. 16 No less than sixteen of these little animals (all males).

fig. **1871** MORLEY *Crit. Misc.* Ser. I. *Carlyle* (1878) 175 Carlylism is the male of Byronism.

2. a. A male person; a boy or man. Only in expressed or implied antithesis with *female*.

13.. *E. E. Allit. P.* B. 695 Vch male mas his mach a man as hymseluen. **1375** BARBOUR *Bruce* I. 60 For thar mycht succed na female, Quhill foundyn mycht be ony male. **1382** WYCLIF *Rom.* i. 27 The mawlis [*gloss* or men] the kyndeli vss of womman forsakyn. *c* **1412** HOCCLEVE *De Reg. Princ.* 565 The ende is deþ of male & of femele. **1593** SHAKS. *3 Hen. VI*, II. i. 42 You loue the Breeder better than the Male. **1609** SKENE *Reg. Maj.* 36 Sic heires being mailes, the perfite age is twentie ane zeares. **1614** SELDEN *Titles Hon.* 73 That [crown] of Pharaoh was only for masles, not for feminin capacitie. **1667** MILTON *P. L.* XII. 168 Whence of guests he makes them slaves Inhospitably, and kills their infant Males. **1809** in *Earl Malmesbury's Lett.* (1870) II. 204, I am the only male here that is not gone hunting. **1855** MACAULAY *Hist. Eng.* xv. III. 574 Every male in the kingdom who had attained the age of sixteen. **1868** FREEMAN *Norm. Conq.* (1876) II. x. 481 Every male who resisted was put to the sword.

b. *occas.* A male plant. (Cf. A. 2, 2 b.)

1548 TURNER *Names of Herbes* (E.D.S.) 12 [Pimpernel.] The male hath a crimsin floure, & the female hath a blewe floure. **1600** J. PORY tr. *Leo's Africa* VI. 268 The flowers of the female will not open, vnlesse the boughes and flowers of the male be ioined vnto them. **1646** SIR T. BROWNE *Pseud. Ep.* II. vi. 94 Herbalists..naming that the masle, whose leaves are lighter.

3. A 'male' precious stone. (Cf. A. 5 a.)

1727–41 CHAMBERS *Cycl.* s.v. *Sapphire*, ..Different colours constitute different kinds thereof; the deepest blues being esteemed males, and the whitest females. **1750** tr. *Leonardus' Mirr. Stones* 152 A milder flame is assigned to the females, but a yellower and more fervent to the males.

4. Comb. ***male climacteric, menopause, pill, supremacist*** (also *attrib.*), ***supremacy***; ***male-determining, -dominated*** adjs.; **male chauvinism**, an attitude attributed to men of excessive loyalty to members of the male sex and of prejudice against women; hence **male chauvinist**, one who adopts this attitude; also *attrib.*, esp. in phr. ***male chauvinist pig***; **male impersonator**, a female who impersonates a male on the stage.

1970 *Time* 17 Aug. 23 European women have accepted their lot much more readily than their American counterparts. Recently, however, growing numbers..have launched their attack on male chauvinism. **1973** O. LANCASTER *Littlehampton Bequest* 84 Their marriage has always been a completely unselfish relationship, both taking an active part in the struggle against Imperialism, Neo-Colonialism and Male Chauvinism. **1970** *New Yorker* 5 Sept. 27/1 Hello, you male-chauvinist racist pig. *Ibid.*, Repent Male Chauvinists. **1972** *Southerly* XXXII. 75 The male chauvinist aspects of mateship have come in for considerable discussion since the spread of women's liberation critiques. **1972** *Punch* 1 Mar. 289/1, I know, I know; me male chauvinist pig, you Jane. But the exercise has finally woken me up to ask—why should there be separate magazines for men and women at all? **1974** J. HELLER *Something Happened* 333, I enjoy fucking my wife. She lets me do it any way I want. No Women's Liberation for her. Lots of male chauvinist pig. **1966** G. B. MAIR *Kisses from Satan* vii. 78 I've got a male climacteric and I don't like it. **1972** *Daily Colonist* (Victoria, B.C.) 8 Feb. 2/1 Men may experience a certain slackening in sexual interest that may be related to what medical literature calls 'male climacteric' (a retrogression of the sex glands). **1931**, **1957** Male-determining [see FEMALE B. *sb.* 3]. **1958** W. J. H. SPROTT *Human Groups* 65 The home..is in certain important respects male-dominated. **1964** W. MCCORD in I. L. Horowitz *New Sociol.* xxv. 434 The city is a male-dominated area (more men enter the city seeking jobs than women). **1973** I. SINGER *Goals of Human Sexuality* i. 33 She submits to the relationship as a way of conforming to the demands of a male-dominated society. **1895** STUART & PARK *Variety Stage* 222 Serio-comics, sisters, dancers, male impersonators, and ballad and character vocalists. **1930** *Bulletin* 14 May 5 That popular male impersonator and pantomime principal boy, Miss Nora Delany. **1972** *Times* 29 Sept. 16/8 To the connoisseurs of the music hall there have been only two great male impersonators, one of whom was Vesta Tilley, the other Hetty King. **1949** ERNST & LOTH *Sexual Behaviour & Kinsey Report* viii. 93 Another reason which has sometimes been given is that many men reach in middle age a climacteric which is dubbed a male menopause. **1963** E. LANHAM *Monkey on Chain* xii. 195 You think dirty, you act dirty—like a dirty old man. What is it? Male menopause? **1971** J. WAINWRIGHT *Last Buccaneer* II. 187 Middle-aged men get odd ideas. It's a sort of male menopause—a change of life. **1966** *New Statesman* 27 May 767/1 Techniques like the 'male pill', tying of the spermatic cords..are in use or under investigation. **1971** *Black Scholar* Dec. 7/2 Excepting the woman's role as caretaker of the household, male supremacist structures could not become deeply embedded in the internal workings of the slave system. **1973** J. JONES *Touch of Danger* xxviii. 167 You just don't want to understand Jane... She's a threat to all you male supremacists. **1908** CHESTERTON *Man who was Thursday* i. 12 Most of the women were of the kind vaguely called emancipated, and professed some protest against male supremacy.

† **male**, *sb.*[3] *Obs.* A word of obscure origin and meaning, occurring in certain phrases. ***the male wryes*** or ***wrings***: something is wrong, there is a state of hardship. ***to wring*** (a person) ***on the males***: to cause trouble to. (Quot. *a* 1500 is obscure, perh. textually corrupt.)

c **1430** LYDG. *Min. Poems* (Percy Soc.) 43 The male so wryes, That no kunnyng may prevayl.. Ayens a wommans wytt. ? *a* **1500** *Wisdom* 669 in *Digby Myst.* 163 Ther pouert is the male wry, though right be, he shall neuer renewe. *c* **1522** SKELTON *Why nat to Court* 75, The countrynge at Cales Wrang vs on the males. —— *Colyn Cloute* 688 And so they blere your eye, That ye can not espye Howe the male dothe wrye. —— *Phyllyp Sparowe* 700 Yet there was a thyng That made the male to wryng.

male, obs. form of MAIL, MEAL, MOLE.

Male, var. MALER *sb.* and *a.*

male-, *prefix*: see MAL-.

maleadministration, maleapert, etc.: see MALA-.

malease. Forms: 3 **malees, malisce**, 3–4 **maless**, 3–5 **males**, 4 **malis, male-ese**, *Sc.* **mail eiss, mail ess**, 4–5 **mal ese**, 5 **male eese, mayll easse, male ease**, 6 *Sc.* **maill eys.** [a. OF. *malaise*: see MALAISE.]

1. Absence of ease; uneasiness, discomfort; inconvenience, annoyance; disquiet; distress, trouble.

a **1300** *Cursor M.* 6300 Wit þair danger, sir moyses, Oft þai did him haue malees. *Ibid.* 6788 Widues ne barns faderles Do yee na wrang, ne na males. *c* **1300** *K. Alis.* 7366 Beter is, lyte to have in ese, Then muche to have in malese. **1377** LANGL. *P. Pl.* B. XIII. 76 What myschief and malese Cryst for man tholed. *a* **1400** *Relig. Pieces fr. Thornton MS.* 18 Euer mare when þou erte at male-ese þan he comforthes þe. **1470–85** MALORY *Arth.* VIII. xli. 338 A syr yet shalle I shewe you faueour in your male ease.

1923 *S.P.E. Tract* XIII. 35 All French loan-words that are sufficiently naturalized to be considered as English should be treated as English... We should be glad if London editors would..print as follows:..*malease* for *malaise.* **1929** R. BRIDGES *Testament of Beauty* I. 231 [St.] Francis climbed—rather his gentle soul had learn'd From taste of vanity and by malease of the flesh. **1930** *Times Lit. Suppl.* 4 Dec. 1022/2 Yet her achievement was muted by excess of ardour and by a subtle, fundamental malease. **1938** L. P. SMITH *Unforgotten Yrs.* vi. 165 My tutor gave it unusual praise, in which praise I was conscious of the mingling of a curious malease.

†**2.** Disease, sickness. *Obs.*

a **1300** *Cursor M.* 23161 Oft i was wit malisce [*other texts* malese] mette, Bot for you was me neuer bett. **1375** BARBOUR *Bruce* xx. 73, 75 Ane male ess tuk hym so sare,.. His mail eiss of ane fundyng Begouth. **1388** WYCLIF *Matt.* iv. 24 Thei brouȝten to hym alle that weren at male ese. **1500–20** DUNBAR *Poems* xxix. 34 This malice, That with sic panis prickillis me. **1513** DOUGLAS *Æneis* XII. i. 114 Quha wald wyth cuyr of medycyne hym meys, The moir encressys and growis his maill eys.

maleate (məˈliːeɪt). *Chem.* [f. MALE(IC *a.* + -ATE[4].] A salt or ester, or the anion, of maleic acid.

1853 H. WATTS tr. *Gmelin's Hand-bk. Chem.* VIII. 153 The Salts of Maleic acid, the Maleates, are all soluble in water. **1925** *Jrnl. Amer. Chem. Soc.* XLVII. 1073 First, association occurs between permanganate ion or molecule with maleate or fumarate ion. **1970** R. W. MCGILVERY *Biochem.* xi. 220 Fumarate is a *trans* compound (maleate is the corresponding *cis* isomer), and hydrates to yield the L-enantiomorph.

male aventure: see MALADVENTURE.

‖ **malebolge** (maleˈboldʒe). [It. *Malebolge*, f. *male* pl. fem. of *malo* evil + *bolge* pl. of *bolgia* lit. 'budget'. (The sing. form malebolgia has occasionally been used by Eng. writers.)] The name given by Dante to his eighth circle in Hell, consisting of ten rock-bound concentric circular trenches, designated 'bolge'. Used *transf.*, chiefly with allusion either to the pool of filth in the second 'bolgia' (Canto xviii), or to the boiling pitch in the fifth 'bolgia' (Canto xxi).

1861 BERESF. HOPE *Eng. Cathedr. 19th C.* vii. 250 The malebolge of stock-brick and cement in which we have been so long wandering. **1884** *Q. Rev.* Apr. 350 We..look down into a boiling malebolgia of steam and sulphur. **1894** *Scotsman* 12 July, The channels that feed this devouring malebolge are the newspapers and the telegraph offices.

Hence **maleˈbolgian, maleˈbolgic** *adjs.*, of or resembling the malebolge.

1883 *Harper's Mag.* June 121/1, I confess having felt a.. reluctance to immerse myself in this malebolgian mass of peat mud. **1883** *Pall Mall G.* 16 Oct. 1/2 This Malebolgic pool of London's misery.

† **malebouche.** *Obs.* Also 6 **Male boush.** [a. OF. *Malebouche* (lit. 'evil mouth'), the name of an allegorical personage in *Le Roman de la Rose* (*c* 1200–30); called 'Wikkid-Tonge' in *Rom. Rose* 7357.] Evil speaking personified.

1390 GOWER *Conf.* I. 172 Malebouche, Whos tunge neither pyl ne crouche Mai hyre, so that he pronounce A plein good word. *c* **1402** LYDG. *Compl. Bl. Knt.* 260 And Male-bouche gan first the tale telle. *c* **1460** SIR R. ROS *La Belle Dame* 741 Male-bouche in courte hath gret comaundement. **1593–4** CHURCHYARD *Rebuke to Rebellion* in Nichols *Progr.* III. 239 Ne wit nor skill, can scape the scowling scorne Of bold male boush, that like ban-dog doth ball.

malece, obs. form of MALICE.

malecontent, etc.: see MALCONTENT, etc.

malecoto(o)n, variant of MELOCOTON.

maledery, variant of MALADERIE.

† **maleˈdicency.** *Obs. rare.* [f. next: see -ENCY.] The practice or habit of speaking evil.

1653 R. BAILLIE *Dissuas. Vind.* (1655) 57 *marg.*, One ground of my patience of M. Ts. maledicency. **1723** ATTERBURY *Answ. Consid. Spirit Luther* 69 We are now to have a Tast of the maledicency of Luther's Spirit from his Book against Henry the 8th.

maledicent (mælɪˈdaɪsənt), *a.* and *sb.* Now *rare.* Also 7 *erron.* **-dicant.** [ad. L. *maledīcentem*, pr. pple. of *maledīcĕre* to speak evil of, orig. two words, *male* ill + *dīcĕre* to speak, say.]

A. *adj.* Given to evil-speaking. Also, of utterances: Of the nature of evil-speaking, slanderous.

1599 SANDYS *Europæ Spec.* (1632) 93 Possessed with..so furious, so maledicent, and so slovenly spirits. **1678** CUDWORTH *Intell. Syst.* I. iv. §16. 284 You can boldly insert into her Verses, Many, and those Maledicent things of your own. **1837** CARLYLE *Fr. Rev.* I. VII. x, The maledicent Bodyguard, getting..better malediction than he gave. **1846** HARE *Mission Comf.* Pref. (1850) 12 Ignorance..when it is maledicent, is sure to find a credulous auditory.

B. *sb.* One who speaks evil of another.

1657 HAWKE *Killing is M.* Pref. 1 Tiberius..who otherwise was merciful to Male-dicants.

maledict (ˈmælɪdɪkt), *a.* (*sb.*) *arch.* [ad. L. *maledictus*, pa. pple. of *maledīcĕre*: see prec.] Accursed. Also as *sb.*, an accursed person.

a **1550** *Image Hypocr.* in *Skelton's Wks.* (1843) II. 441/1 For some be Benedictes With many maledictes. **1867** LONGF. tr. *Dante's Inferno* v. 42 As the wings of starlings bear them on In the cold season in large band and full, So doth that blast the spirits maledict.

maledict (ˈmælɪdɪkt), *v.* [f. L. *maledict-*, ppl. stem of *maledīcĕre*: see MALEDICENT.] *trans.* To address with maledictions, curse, execrate.

1780 in F. Moore *Songs Amer. Rev.* (1856) 333 Thy name should now be maledicted. **1898** T. HARDY *Wessex Poems* 36, I can but maledict her. **1901** *Contemp. Rev.* Mar. 425 Their gods were..to be crushed, broken, maledicted.

maledicted (ˈmælɪdɪktɪd), *ppl. a.* [f. prec. + -ED[1].] Accursed; evil-spoken of.

1727 BAILEY vol. II, *Maledicted*, cursed or banned. **1864** SALA in *Daily Tel.* 19 Oct., The scurvy maledicted money which never did any one any good. **1890** *Daily News* 13 Oct. 6/5 This much maledicted article of attire.

maleˈdictine, *a.* and *sb.* Parody of BENEDICTINE, after *malediction.*

1641 R. BAILLIE *Parall. Liturgy w. Massbk.* Pref. 5 Till that cruell maledictine Monk..had massacred 2000.. opposers. **1654** GAYTON *Pleas. Notes* I. viii. 31 And left poor Sancho..a Monke, but of the order of the Maledictines.

malediction (mælɪˈdɪkʃən). Also 5 **malediccyoun, -dyccion**, 5–6 **-diccion**, 6 **-diccyon.** [ad. L. *maledictiōnem*, n. of action f. *maledīcĕre*: see MALEDICENT *a.* Cf. MALISON.]

1. The utterance of a curse; the condition of being under a ban or curse.

1447 BOKENHAM *Seyntys* (Roxb.) 49 Tyl assoylled thou be Of this legal malediccyoun. **1483** CAXTON *Gold. Leg.* 179/2 He was moche angry & gaue his malediccion & curse to the temple. **1526** TINDALE *Gal.* iii. 10 For as many as are under the dedes of the lawe are vnder malediccion. **1528** MORE *Dyalogue* I. xvii. Wks. 139 And after he sheweth the maledicciouns that shall fall therevpon. **1599** HAKLUYT *Voy.* II. I. 93 He gaue his malediction or curse to his children and successours. **1605** SHAKS. *Lear* I. ii. 160 (1608 Qo.) Menaces

and maledictions against King and nobles. **1671** MILTON *Samson* 978. **1796** H. HUNTER tr. *St.-Pierre's Stud. Nat.* (1799) III. 485 They tried to persuade her to pronounce a malediction upon Alcibiades. **1828** SCOTT *F. M. Perth* xix, I taunted him, ridiculed him, loaded him with maledictions. **1851** LONGF. *Gold. Leg.* I, The malediction Of my affliction Is taken from me. **1855** MILMAN *Lat. Chr.* IX. vi. (1864) V. 292 His progress instead of being a blessing to the land was deemed a malediction.

2. Reviling, slander; the condition of being reviled or slandered.

1526 *Pilgr. Perf.* (W. de W. 1531) 182 b, Thou art and euer hast ben free from all malediccyon and opprobry. **1659** STANLEY *Hist. Philos.* XIII. (1701) 618/2 Giving no man a just cause of contumely or malediction. **1885** EDGAR *Old Ch. Life Scotl.* 273 In the year 1661 the malediction of a parent was made a capital offence in Scotland.

maledictive (mælɪ'dɪktɪv), *a.* [f. L. *maledict-* (see MALEDICTION) + -IVE.] Characterized by cursing or curses; uttering maledictions.

1865 S. FERGUSON *Lays of Western Gael* 54 Daily in their mystic ring They turn'd the maledictive stones. **1905** K. MEYER *Cáin Adamnáin* p. vii, A poem on the maledictive psalms selected by Adamnan. **1922** JOYCE *Ulysses* 326 Seats of learning and maledictive stones.

maledictory (mælɪ'dɪktərɪ), *a.* [f. L. *maledict-* (see MALEDICTION) + -ORY.] Of the nature of, or resembling a malediction.

1822 *Blackw. Mag.* II. 593 This manful and maledictory Manifesto. **1887** *Temple Bar* Apr. 478 With maledictory groans and ejaculations.

† **maledight**, *a.* and *pple. Obs.* Also 3 **maledith**, 4–5 **malediht**, 5 **maladichte, maledi3t, maladicte.** [ad. L. *maledictus*, pa. pple. of *maledīcĕre*: see MALEDICENT. The form is perh. influenced by association with ME. *diht*, pa. pple. of *dihten* DIGHT *v.*] Cursed, accursed.

a **1300** *Cursor M.* 891 (Cott.) þou worm, þou sal be maledight. *Ibid.* 2074 þu art and sal be maledith [*rime-word* sith = sight]. *Ibid.* 2136 Cham þe maledight. *Ibid.* 10266 Biclepis þat man for maledight [*c* **1375** *Fairf.* maladicte; *a* **1300–1400** *Gött.* maledihτ] þat has na barn. *Ibid.* 13336 Na wrenches o þe maledight [*c* **1375** *Fairf.* maladicte]. *Ibid.* 22034 Maledight [*a* **1400** *Edinb.* maledicht].

Hence † **maledight** *v.* (in pa. t. *maledight*), *trans.* to curse.

a **1300** *Cursor M.* 2478 þai war put in a fole plight þat god and man þam maledight.

maledius, obs. pl. of MALADY.

maledizant, variant of MALDISANT *Obs.*

mal-edu'cation. *rare.* [See MAL-.] Imperfect or misdirected education.

1848 tr. *Richter's Levana* 8 Mere establishments for mal-education. **1867** EMERSON *Lett. & Soc. Aims, Progr. Cult.* Wks. (Bohn) III. 233 The obstructions of their mal-formation and mal-education shall be trained away.

male ease, eese, variants of MALEASE *Obs.*

male engin(e, engyne, var. ff. MALENGIN *Obs.*

† **male entente.** *Obs.* [a. OF. *male entente*: see MAL- *prefix* and INTENT *sb.*] Evil intention.

c **1450** *Guy Warw.* (Camb.) 5370 That the dewke in hys parlement Hym forgeue hys maleentente.

malees, male-ese, variants of MALEASE *Obs.*

maleesh ('mɑːliːʃ), *int.* Also **ma(a)lesh.** [ad. colloq. Eastern Arab. *mā 'ale-š* no matter.] No matter! never mind! Also as *sb.*, indifference, slackness.

1913 'S. ROHMER' *Mystery of Dr Fu-Manchu* iv. 44 '*Ma 'alesh!*' came her soft whisper; 'but I am afraid to trust you —yet.' **1919** W. H. DOWNING *Digger Dial.* 33 *Maleesh*, it doesn't matter. **1925** FRASER & GIBBONS *Soldier & Sailor Words* 151 *Maleesh*: Never mind. It doesn't matter. Used colloquially on Eastern Fronts. **1946** *Happy Landings* (Air Ministry) July 12/1 The manpower problem will solve itself in time, but there is no excuse for the *maleesh* attitude. **1947** *Landfall* I. 162 Not so much of the *ma lesh!* **1958** L. DURRELL *Mountolive* xvi. 315 *Ma-alesh!* Let it be forgiven! Nothing avails our grief! **1971** *Guardian* 22 June 3/3 The general air of 'malesh', Arabic for 'never mind', or 'forget it', continues to hang over the police force.

† **malefact.** *Obs.* [ad. L. *malefactum*, neut. pa. pple. of *malefacĕre* to do wrong, f. *male* ill + *facĕre* to do.] A malefaction, offence.

1534 *Act 26 Hen. VIII*, c. 6 §1 Wilful burning of houses, & other scelerous dedes and abhominable malefactis. **1556–7** *Act 3–4 Phil. & Mary* in Bolton *Stat. Irel.* (1621) 256 Brought to answer to the law for that malefact. **1632** LITHGOW *Trav.* x. 457 Hee demanded me . . what malefact I was guilty of?

malefaction (mælɪ'fækʃən). [ad. L. *malefactiōnem*, n. of action f. *malefacĕre*: see prec.] Evil-doing; an instance of evil-doing, a criminal act.

1602 SHAKS. *Ham.* II. ii. 621 Guilty Creatures . . Haue . . Bene strooke so to the soule, that presently They haue proclaim'd their Malefactions. **1624** HEYWOOD *Captives* III. ii. in Bullen *O. Pl.* IV. 162 And all thy malefactions crownd with lyes. **1793** J. WILLIAMS *Mem. W. Hastings* 20 That overbearing tide of prejudice, which would . . come rushing down even upon innocence when charged with malefactions. **1805** T. HOLCROFT *Bryan Perdue* I. 70 The vice of gaming was not the only malefaction of my father. **1900** *Daily Tel.* 27 Aug. 6/2 The misery caused by their malefaction.

b. *occas.* An act of wrong or injury *to* a person.

1879 H. SPENCER *Data of Ethics* xi. §72. 194 Such disregard of self as brings on suffering, bodily or mental, is a malefaction to others.

† **malefactious**, *a. Obs.*$^{-0}$ [f. MALEFACTION + -OUS.] Wicked, criminal.

1660 HEXHAM, *Misdadigh*, Ill-doing, Malefactious, Offensive, or Criminall.

malefactor ('mælɪfæktə(r)). Also 5 **malfacteur**, 5–7 **malefactour**, 6 **mallefactore.** Cf. MALFETOUR. [a. L. *malefactor*, agent-n. f. *malefacĕre*: see MALEFACT.]

1. One guilty of a heinous offence against the law; a felon, a criminal.

c **1440** *Gesta Rom.* I. xvi. 56 (Add. MS.) Anon thei entred the forest and sone the malefactours mette hem. **1471** CAXTON *Recuyell* (Sommer) I. 16 He dyde iustyce on malfacteurs. **1582** BIBLE (Rheims) *Luke* xxiii. 32 And there were led also other two malefactours with him, to be executed. **1585** T. WASHINGTON tr. *Nicholay's Voy.* I. xvi. 17 The great place . . wher the malefactors are punished. **1606** SHAKS. *Ant. & Cl.* II. v. 53. **1649** BP. REYNOLDS *Hosea* iv. 88 Leade them forth . . as . . malefactours to execution. **1719** DE FOE *Crusoe* I. iii, A Malefactor, who has the Halter about his Neck. **1796** MORSE *Amer. Geog.* II. 27 For the most atrocious crimes . . the malefactor is broken upon the wheel. **1862** H. SPENCER *First Princ.* II. xix. §153 (1875) 421 By a malefactor, we now understand a convicted criminal, which is far from being the acceptation of evil-doer.

transf. **1693** DRYDEN *Juvenal* vi. (1697) 144 If their Barking Dog disturb her ease . . Th'unmanner'd Malefactor is arraign'd. **1697** —— *Virg. Georg.* II. 523 For this the Malefactor Goat was laid On Bacchus' Altar, and his Forfeit paid.

2. An evil-doer; one who does ill towards another; esp. in antithesis with *benefactor*.

1483 CAXTON *Cato* G vj, Hit is better that the malefactour juge hym selfe than that another shold juge hym. **1603** SHAKS. *Meas. for M.* II. i. 52 Benefactors? Well: What Benefactors are they? Are they not Malefactors? **1634** W. TIRWHYT tr. *Balzac's Lett.* (vol. I) 45 God . . doth sometimes punish Malefactors, without observing the formes of justice. **1655** FULLER *Hist. Camb.* v. §19 *margin*, King Edward the fourth a malefactour to this Colledge. **1760–72** H. BROOKE *Fool of Qual.* xi. (1792) II. 121 Goodman Warmhouse . . rode much at his ease by the chariot of his malefactor. **1860** EMERSON *Cond. Life, Considerations* Wks. (Bohn) II. 414 Mankind divides itself into two classes,—benefactors and malefactors. **1864** PUSEY *Lect. Daniel* vi. 296 That later king, who . . was called from his deeds, Kakergetes, 'malefactor'.

malefactory (mælɪ'fæktərɪ), *a. rare*$^{-1}$. [As if ad. L. **malefactōrius*, f. *malefactor*: see prec. and -ORY.] Evil-doing.

1871 G. MEREDITH *H. Richmond* III. 122 The Grange lived on its own solid substance, defying malefactory Radical tricksters.

malefactress ('mælɪfæktrɪs). [f. MALEFACTOR + -ESS.] A female malefactor.

1647 FANSHAWE tr. *Pastor Fido* (1676) 123 She dies a Malefactress. **1797** MARK NOBLE *Mem. Ho. Medici* xv. 285 Bianca [was buried] with the ignominy and contempt of a malefactress, and a beggar. **1850** HAWTHORNE *Scarlet L.* ii. (1883) 71 We women . . should have the handling of such malefactresses as this Hester Prynne.

† **malefacture.** *Obs.* [f. L. *malefact-*, *malefacĕre*: see MALEFACT and -URE.] = MALEFACTION.

1635 HEYWOOD *Hierarch.* VII. 412 The Putred Fountaine and bitumenous Well, From whence all Vice and Malefactures swell. **1652** GAULE *Magastrom.* 57 Whether it be in all their Art to elude them, as concerning the obnoxiousness of guilt, crime, offence or malefacture?

malefeazance, -fesour: see MALFEASANCE, -OR.

† **mal-e'ffect.** *Obs.* [See MAL-.] Evil effect.

1686 GOAD *Celest. Bodies* III. iii. 473 The Mal-Effects of Discord being Infinite.

malefic (mə'lɛfɪk), *a.* and *sb.* Also 7, 9 **malefick**, 7 **malefique.** [ad. L. *malefic-us* (also *malificus*), f. *male* ill + *-ficus*: see -FIC. Cf. F. *maléfique*, Sp. *maléfico*, Pg., It. *malefico*.]

A. *adj.* Productive of disaster or evil; baleful in effect or purpose. Said *esp.* of stellar influences and magical arts or practices.

1652 GAULE *Magastrom.* 263 Neither could the malefick starres impell the Brachmans to malefice or malefacture. **1686** GOAD *Celest. Bodies* III. i. 388 We shall point out . . Constellations . . that are Malefique. **1796** H. HUNTER tr. *St.-Pierre's Stud. Nat.* (1799) I. 584 Whether the embryons of their fruits do not disclose . . harsh oppositions, which give warning of their malefic characters. **1809** A. HENRY *Trav.* 124 A man who charged him with having brought his brother to death by malefic arts. **1841** BORROW *Zincali* I. viii. i. 145 Practices equally malefic as the crime imputed to them. **1851** MAYHEW *Lond. Labour* I. 105 The slackness of certain periodic trades . . [and] want of employment . . have a doubly malefic effect. **1879** FARRAR *St. Paul* I. 385 It belonged to the malefic arts of which they may well have heard from Roman visitors.

B. *sb.* **a.** *Astrol.* A malefic aspect or body. † **b.** One who practices malefic arts; a malign wizard. *Obs.*

1652 GAULE *Magastrom.* 139 A conjunction of all the maleficks that are named in their [planetarians] art. *Ibid.* 174 Most arrant inchanters, sorcerers, veneficks, maleficks, wizzards, and witches in the world. **1819** J. WILSON *Dict. Astrol.*, *Malefics*, doers of evil: Saturn and Mars. *Ibid.*, A retrograde malefic would be rendered by it [*sc.* retrogradation] more innoxious.

Hence † **ma'leficness.**

1727 BAILEY vol. II, *Malefickness*, injuriousness.

† **ma'lefical**, *a. Obs. rare.* [Formed as prec. + -AL[1].] = MALEFIC *a.*

1615 CROOKE *Body of Man* 342 The threatnings of the Starres and their maleficall influence. **1647** LILLY *Chr. Astrol.* lxvii. 411 Whether there arise . . any maleficall fixed Starres. **1652** GAULE *Magastrom.* 349 A certaine maleficall sorcerer . . made all the locks fall off and doors fly open.

Hence **ma'lefically** *adv.*, in a malefic manner.

1652 GAULE *Magastrom.* 279 Magicians . . malefically imprecating, and venefically murdering [etc.]. **1881** R. A. PROCTOR in *Cornh. Mag.* Dec. 700 Believing . . that comets act malefically by their direct influence on the air.

maleficate (mə'lɛfɪkeɪt), *v. rare*$^{-1}$. [f. MALEFIC *a.* + -ATE; cf. med.L. *maleficāre*. Cf. MALEFICIATE *v.*] *trans.* To bewitch.

1827 SIR H. TAYLOR *Isaac Comnenus* II. iv. 87 What will not a man do when once he is maleficated?

malefice ('mælɪfɪs). Also 5 **-fyce.** [ad. L. *maleficium*, f. *malefic-us* MALEFIC. Cf. F. *maléfice*.]

1. A wicked enchantment; sorcery. *arch.*

c **1374** CHAUCER *Boeth.* I. pr. iv. 12 (Camb. MS.) They trowen þat I haue had affinite to malefice or enchauntement [L. *affines fuisse videmur maleficio*]. **1483** CAXTON *Gold. Leg.* 203/2 Seynt Peter . . disclosed all his [Simon Magus'] malefyces. **1652** GAULE *Magastrom.* 100 Malefice and sorcery. **1700** DR. HICKES *Let.* 19 June *Pepys' Diary* (1879) VI. 202 The discovery of witches, and their malefices and enchantments. **1865** *Cornh. Mag.* XI. 471 That he should die by the malefice of a sorcerer.

2. An evil deed; mischief. *Obs.* or *arch.*

1591 SPENSER *M. Hubberd* 1153 He crammed them with crumbs of Benefices, And fild their mouthes with meeds of malefices. **1611** J. DAVIES (Heref.) *Sco. Folly* (Grosart) 38/1 So to the curat tis a malefice, But to the patron still a benefice. **1689** tr. *Buchanan's De Jure Regni* 52 They use to be highly offended with robbers, and that very justly, if any of them in their malefices pretend the King's name. **1867** P. B. ST. JOHN *Snow Ship* v. 47 Of man, his tricks and malefices, there was no sign.

† **3.** In astrological sense: Malefic character. *Obs.*

1652 GAULE *Magastrom.* 77 Made to consist by the stars, and to thrive, or dwindle away, according to the benefice, or malefice, of their influence.

maleficence (mə'lɛfɪsəns). [ad. L. *maleficentia*, f. *maleficus* MALEFIC: cf. MAGNIFICENCE.]

1. Evil-doing; *rarely*, an act of evil-doing.

1598 J. KEEPER tr. *Romei's Court. Acad.* 252 Povertie bringeth foorth seditions and maleficences. *a* **1670** HACKET *Abp. Williams* II. (1692) 85 The Bishop of Lincoln . . fell into trouble . . for want of a parliament to keep him from maleficence. **1830** BENTHAM *Offic. Apt. Maximized* Pref. 25 *note*, The correspondent closeness of connection between maleficence . . and punishment. **1865** J. GROTE *Treat. Mor. Ideas* xi. (1876) 244 By 'maleficence' I mean the attempt to give pain, as such, to others. **1865** CARLYLE *Fredk. Gt.* XIX. viii. (1872) VIII. 249 Who the perpetrator of this Parisian maleficence was, remained dark.

2. Malefic character; harmfulness.

1796 H. HUNTER tr. *St.-Pierre's Stud. Nat.* (1799) II. 32 In order to express the maleficent character of a venomous plant, she combines in it clashing oppositions of the forms and colours which are the indications of that maleficence. **1830** *Westm. Rev.* XIII. 428 He takes in hand Matchless Constitution's plan. Not sufficient for him is its maleficence —he adds to it [etc.]. **1897** *Allbutt's Syst. Med.* II. 884 There is still in such [formerly malarious] districts some remnant of maleficence.

maleficent (mə'lɛfɪsənt), *a.* [f. L. *maleficent-*, altered stem (cf. MAGNIFICENT) of *maleficus* MALEFIC *a.*]

1. Of things and spiritual agencies: Working harm, hurtful, malefic. Const. *to*.

1678 CUDWORTH *Intell. Syst.* I. iv. §13. 219 That before the . . Formation of the World, there was Unformed and disorderly Matter existing (from Eternity) together with a Maleficent Soul. **1786** tr. *Beckford's Vathek* (1868) 107 Our people have fled, and left us at the mercy of maleficent spirits. **1793** *Hist.* in *Ann. Reg.* 182 Principles maleficent to all government and order. **1835** KIRBY *Hab. & Inst. Anim.* II. xvi. 86 Whether these animals are really as venomous and maleficent as they were said to be of old . . seems very doubtful. **1846** GROTE *Greece* I. xvi. I. 565 Beneficent and maleficent demons. **1867** SALA *Fr. Waterloo to Penins.* I. 255 It dispenses maleficent gases, and is always going out at the wrong time. **1900** W. L. COURTNEY *Idea Trag.* 67 The mundane sphere in which the beneficent and maleficent forces are warring.

2. Of persons, their acts and dispositions: Wrong-doing, criminal.

1760 tr. *Vattell's Law Nat.* II. v. §70 Let us apply to the unjust, what we have said above of a mischievous, or maleficent nation. **1811–31** BENTHAM *Ess. Lang.* Wks. 1843 VIII. 316 The sort of act thus described is a maleficent act. **1829** —— *Justice & Cod. Petit.* 50 No man is maleficent without a motive.

† **male'ficial**, *a. Obs.* [f. L. *malefici-um* (see MALEFICE) + -AL[1].] Malefic, maleficent.

1601 HOLLAND *Pliny* II. 231 Such sorceries and maleficiall poisons, as men haue deuised . . to the mischiefe of their own kind. **1655** FULLER *Ch. Hist.* III. vi. §14 A law so maleficial unto them. **1811–31** BENTHAM *Ess. Lang.* Wks. 1843 VIII. 319/1 Formation of new words on the ground of analogy. Example . . from beneficial, maleficial.

† **maleficiate**, *ppl. a. Obs.* [a. med.L. *maleficiāt-us*, pa. pple. of *maleficiāre*: see next.] Bewitched; *spec.* rendered impotent by spells.

a **1613** OVERBURY *A Wife*, etc. (1638) 317 This cures the Maleficiate. **1626** RAWLEY in *Bacon's Sylva* To Rdr., Mens mindes, being bound; and (as it were) Maleficiate, by the Charmes of deceiuing Notions and Theories. **1649** J. H. *Motion to Parl. Adv. Learn.* 4 You being loosed from those charmes wherewith you..were maleficiate, began to act powerfully. **1653** R. SANDERS *Physiogn.* 171 Unable for Venery, cold and maleficiate as to generation.

† **male'ficiate**, *v. Obs.* [f. med.L. *maleficiāt-*, ppl. stem of *maleficiāre*, f. L. *malefici-um* MALEFICE.] *trans.* To bewitch; *spec.* to render impotent by spells. Hence † **maleficiated** *ppl. a.*, † **maleficiating** *vbl. sb.* and *ppl. a.*

1621 BURTON *Anat. Mel.* I. iii. I. ii, A third..fears all old women as witches,..every person comes near him is maleficiated. **1626** BACON *Sylva* §888 *marg.*, Experiment Solitary touching Maleficiating. **1646** GAULE *Cases Consc.* 174 Not only in regard of their Maleficiating mischiefes, but also of Gods judgments. **1651** BIGGS *New Disp.* 179 To maleficiate a humor in any part of the Head. *a* **1693** *Urquhart's Rabelais* III. xxxi. 257 Drugs..which make the Taker cold, maleficiated.

† **malefici'ation**. *Obs.* [n. of action f. prec. vb.: see -ATION.] The action of 'maleficiating'.

1649 BP. HALL *Cases Consc.* (1650) 379 A preceding, irremediable impotency,..whether by way of perpetuall maleficiation, or casualty. **1902** KONRATH *Shoreham's Poems* 214 [Accidental impotence] was generally ascribed to maleficiation.

† **male'ficious**, *a. Obs. rare.* [f. L. *malefici-um* MALEFICE + -OUS.] Of the nature of witchcraft. Hence † **male'ficiousness**.

1547 BOORDE *Brev. Health* §119 Which herbe..doth repell suche malyfycyousnes or spirites. **1684** tr. *Bonet's Merc. Compit.* IX. 326 If any thing superstitious or maleficious come from the wickedness of the Devil.

† **male-fidian**. *nonce-wd.* [f. L. *male* amiss + *fid-ēs* faith + -IAN.] A misbeliever.

1659 H. L'ESTRANGE *Alliance Div. Off.* 447 Against male-fidians, as well as against nulli-fidians, and soli-fidians heaven's gates are certainly kept close barred.

malefique, obs. form of MALEFIC *a.*

† **male fortune**. *Obs.* [a. F. *male fortune* (*male* fem. of *mal* adj., evil).] = MISFORTUNE.

1470–85 MALORY *Arthur* IX. xii. 356 Somtyme he was putte to the werse by male fortune. *Ibid.* IX. xxxiv. 392 Syr launcelot by male fortune stroke sir Tristram on the syde.

† **malegerent**, *a. Obs. rare*$^{-0}$. [f. L. *male* ill + *gerent-*, pr. pple. of *gerĕre* to conduct (oneself).]

1727 BAILEY vol. II, *Malegerent*, ill-behaving, unthrifty, improvident.

malegetta, -gutta, obs. ff. MALAGUETTA.

malegrefe, -greve: see MAUGRE.

ma-lé-grubbles, obs. form of MULLIGRUBS.

maleheur(e, variant of MALHEUR *Obs.*

maleheureux, variant of MALEUROUS *Obs.*

maleheurte, -hurte, var. ff. MALEURTE *Obs.*

maleic (mə'liːɪk), *a. Chem.* Also † **malæic**. [ad. F. *maléique* (Pelouze 1834); formed by alteration of *malique* MALIC, to indicate that this acid was related to malic acid.] ***maleic acid***: a product of the dry distillation of malic acid; ***maleic anhydride***, the anhydride, $C_4H_2O_3$, of maleic acid which is a crystalline compound that forms addition compounds with substances containing conjugated carbon—carbon double bonds; ***maleic*** (***anhydride***) ***value***, a measure of the number of conjugated double bonds in a substance (e.g. an oil) obtained by reaction with maleic anhydride.

1838 T. THOMSON *Chem. Org. Bodies* 55. **1857** W. A. MILLER *Elem. Chem.* III. v. 335 Hydrated malæic acid when maintained in a state of fusion at 300°, is converted into a crystalline mass of fumaric acid. If distilled by a temperature suddenly elevated to 460°, malæic anhydride is formed. **1873** WATTS *Fownes' Chem.* (ed. 11) 725 The volatile acid produced with fumaric acid is called maleic acid. **1898** *Jrnl. Chem. Soc.* LXXIV. I. 177 Maleinoid chlorobromosuccinic acid is prepared by saturating with chlorine a solution of bromine in chloroform, adding maleic anhydride, again passing chlorine into the liquid, which is then exposed to bright sunlight. **1936** ELLIS & JONES in *Analyst* LXI. 814 The calculation of the 'maleic anhydride value' (M.A.V.) or, more shortly, 'maleic value' is given... At the moment the term 'maleic value' is suggested for this figure in preference to 'diene value'. **1944** H. G. KIRSCHENBAUER *Fats & Oils* v. 46 The theoretical Maleic Anhydride Value of trielaeostearin is 87·2. **1950** K. A. WILLIAMS *Oils, Fats & Fatty Foods* (ed. 3) iii. 116 The maleic anhydride value is given by the expression: 12·692 × ml. of alkali used ÷ weight of sample taken in grams. **1964** N. G. CLARK *Mod. Org. Chem.* xix. 389 A purely aliphatic compound, maleic anhydride, an intermediate for alkyd resins..is obtained from benzene by passing its vapour, mixed with air, over a vanadium pentoxide catalyst at 450°. **1972** *Materials & Technol.* IV. xiii. 465 The peculiar structure of maleic anhydride, in which a C = C double bond is in conjugation with a C = O double bond, makes it the most important and widely used dienoph[i]lic component in the Diels-Alder reaction with 1,3-dienes to produce non-aromatic six-membered ring compounds.

Also **male'inic** = MALEIC. (Cf. G. *maleïnsäure*.)

1889 in *Syd. Soc. Lex.*

male ingine, ingyne, var. ff. MALENGIN *Obs.*

maleinoid, obs. var. MALENOID *a.*

male-institution: see MAL- *prefix*.

† **male journey**. *Obs.* [a. OF. *male journee* 'evil day'.] An unfortunate battle.

1455 *Paston Lett.* I. 345 The Lord Cromwell wold have excused hym self of all the steryng or moevyng of the male journey of Seynt Albones. **1461** *Rolls of Parlt.* V. 492/1 Your true Liegemen..which were not ayen..youre.. Fader, at the Felde and male journey of Wakefeld.

malekin, variant of MALKIN.

‖ **mal élevé** (mal elәve), *adj. phr.* Also fem. **mal élevée**. [Fr., lit. 'badly brought up'.] Of a person: bad-mannered, ill-bred. Of an object or situation: lacking in refinement.

1878 H. JAMES *Europeans* II. v. 198 Even that *mal-élevée* little girl..makes him do what she wishes. **1924** A. D. SEDGWICK *Little French Girl* III. v. 263 It was odd..but not *mal élevé*. **1949** E. BOWEN *Encounters* p. xi, If I was *mal élevée* ..so were my betters. **1964** A. WILSON *Late Call* 24 She echoed her mother's horror at all things *mal élevées*. **1974** E. AMBLER *Dr. Frigo* I. 34 The wives of certain French officials have expressed disapproval [of her]. *Mal elevée* is their verdict.

† **male morte**. *Obs.* [? a. AF. **mal mort* lit. 'dead evil'.] = MORMAL.

c **1400** *Master of Game* (MS. Digby 182) xii, Houndes.. haue þe male morte in hir nosethrylles.

malemut(e, varr. MALAMUTE.

malenc(h)olye, -li(e, -lia, obs. ff. MELANCHOLY.

malencoleous, malencolious, obs. ff. MELANCHOLIOUS.

malender, obs. form of MALANDER.

maleness ('meɪlnɪs). [f. MALE *a.* + -NESS.] **a.** 'Masculine' or vigorous character; masculinity; also = virility. **b.** The quality of being of the male sex.

1663 SIR G. MACKENZIE *Relig. Stoic* 144 The vatican of paganism cannot, for the male-ness of its stile, match that matchless Book of Genesis. **1889** GEDDES & THOMSON *Evol. Sex* xiii. 179 The [parthenogenetic] female cell has a certain maleness about it. **1900** *Pop. Sci. Monthly* Feb. 486 The differences are the external expression of maleness and femaleness. **1925** *New Yorker* 27 June 17/2 Her strongest reason was the fascination of St. Mawr's terrific 'maleness'. **1929** D. H. LAWRENCE *Pansies* 126 So it is with Englishmen. They are all double roses And their true maleness is gone. **1937** *Discovery* Oct. 315/1 His [*sc.* the stag's] maleness reigns supreme. **1975** A. FRASER *Whistler's Lane* xi. 173 His jacket smelt of horses and tobacco and general maleness.

† **malengin**. *Obs.* Forms: 4–7 **malengin**, 5 **male ingyne**, 5–6 **male engyne, malengyne**, 5, 7 **malengyn**, 6 **male engin, mallengyn, malingen, male-ingine, malengine**, 6–7 **male engine**. [a. OF. *malengin*, f *mal* evil (see MAL-) + *engin* contrivance, ENGINE *sb.*] Evil machination, ill-intent; fraud, deceit, guile.

1390 GOWER *Conf.* II. 138 So mai men knowe, how the florin Was moder ferst of malengin. **1426** in *E.E. Wills* (1882) 70 Withoute fraude or male engyne. **1470–85** MALORY *Arthur* XVIII. v. 733 For good loue she bad vs to dyner and not for no male engyne. **1502** ARNOLDE *Chron.* 88 b/1 He was a good & an honest marchaunt without fraude or malengyne. **1529** *Act 21 Hen. VIII*, c. 13 By any Manner of Means, Fraud, or Male Engine. *c* **1540** tr. *Pol. Verg. Eng. Hist.* (Camden No. 36) 226 Whoe, preventinge his Male Engine, invaded his bowndes. **1590** SPENSER *F. Q.* III. i. 53 Priefe Of such malengine and fine forgerye. **1611** SPEED *Hist. Gt. Brit.* IX. vii. §5. 514 The same in good faith keepe, and without mal-Engyn. **1641** MILTON *Reform.* I. Wks. 1851 III. 8 When the Protectors Brother..through private malice and mal-engin was to lose his life. **1726** AYLIFFE *Parergon* 315 All Presumption of Fraud and Male-engine ceases through the authority of the Judge.

¶ **b.** Misused for: ? Ruin; ? evil genius.

1601 BP. W. BARLOW *Defence* 59 An opinion which is the verie male-engine of all sound diuinitie.

malenoid ('mælәnɔɪd), *a. Chem.* Formerly also **ma'leinoid**. [f. MALEIN(IC *a.* + -OID.] Resembling maleic acid in having a *cis* configuration in geometrical isomerism.

1895 [see FUMAROID *a.*]. **1898** [see MALEIC *a.*]. **1907** [see CIS- 3]. **1938** [see FUMAROID *a.*]. **1964** *Internat. Encycl. Chem. Sci.* 709/2 *Malenoid form*, the *cis* form of geometrical isomerism.

‖ **mal-entendu** (malɑ̃tɑ̃dy), *a.* and *sb.* [Fr., f. *mal* ill + *entendu* understood.] † **a.** *adj.* Mistaken, misapprehended. *Obs.* **b.** *sb.* A misunderstanding.

? **1616** RALEIGH *Let.* in E. Edwards *Life* (1868) II. Introd. p. lxii, I take it..for a libertie mal entendu to be removed out of this steddy Tower into a rowling shipp. **1780** H. WALPOLE *Lett.* (1858) VII. 448 By some mal-entendu it was packed up in his heavy baggage. **1824** HEBER *Narrative* (1828) II. xvi. 127, I suspect that several mal-entendus of this kind have occurred. **1893** F. ADAMS *New Egypt* 217 Things culminated in a stupid mal-entendu with the *Times* correspondent.

‖ **maleo** ('mælɪәʊ). [Native name, applied to various megapode birds in the Malay Archipelago. Written by Valentijn 1726 in Du. spelling *moeleoe, malleoe*.] A megapode bird, *Megacephalon maleo*, inhabiting Celebes.

1869 A. R. WALLACE *Malay Archip.* I. 413 One specimen of the large and interesting Maleo.

† **maleolent**, *a. Obs. rare*$^{-1}$. [ad. L. *male olent-em* (*male* ill + pr. pple of *olēre* to smell).] 'That hath an ill smell' (*Phys. Dict.* 1657).

1657 TOMLINSON *Renou's Disp.* 212 Those that are not familiar, unpleasant and maleolent. **1727** in BAILEY vol. II.

male-ominous, variant of MAL-OMINOUS.

Maler ('mɑːlә(r)), *sb.* and *a.* Also **Mal, Male, Moler, Muler.** [Native word = 'hillmen', ult. f. Dravidian *mala* mountain.] **A.** *sb.* **a.** A Dravidian people living in the Rajmahal hills of northern India; a member of this people. **b.** The language spoken by this people (also called MALTO, RAJMAHALI). **B.** *adj.* Of or pertaining to the Maler people or their language.

1811 F. BUCHANAN *Jrnl. Survey Bhagalpur* (1930) 133 The Not Pahariyas..eat and intermarry with the Moler... Many of the men speak the Moler language. *Ibid.* 138 The interpreter tribe is here called Desi Moler... Many of them speak the Muler language, and they eat and can intermarry with the Muler of the hills. **1853** J. R. LOGAN in *Jrnl. Indian Archipelago* VII. 50, I infer that the Male and Kol resemble the coarser Binua tribes of the Malay Peninsula more than the Burmans. **1872** E. T. DALTON *Descriptive Ethnol. Bengal* viii. 264 The Málers were the first of the aboriginal tribes of Bengal that were prominently noticed by the officers of the East India Company. **1873** E. BALFOUR *Cycl. India* III. s.v. *Male*, The Male or Rajmahali are described as mostly very low in stature, but stout and well proportioned. **1885** G. C. WHITWORTH *Anglo-Indian Dict.* 262/1 *Rájmaháli*, the name of a tribe called also Pahári. Also the name of their language, which is Dravidian. These people call themselves Maler. **1892** H. H. RISLEY *Tribes & Castes Bengal: Ethnogr. Gloss.* II. 54 In 1782..one of the archers murdered a Mâlē woman, and in order to punish this..Mr. Cleveland proposed the formation of a district tribunal. **1906** G. A. GRIERSON *Ling. Survey India* IV. 446 In former days the Maler made frequent raids on the plains. **1915** *Encycl. Relig. & Ethics* VIII. 344/2 *Māl, Mālē, Māl Pahāriā*, a non-Aryan tribe, containing various groups... The inter-relations of the North and South groups have not been clearly ascertained, but they seem to be, to a large extent, pure Dravidians, and those in the Rājmahāl Hills in Bengal are closely allied to the Orāons. **1930** C. E. A. W. OLDHAM in F. Buchanan *Jrnl. Survey Bhagalpur* 138 Here we find Bhuiyās still speaking the Maler or Malto language. **1938** S. S. SARKAR *Mālērs of Rajmahal Hills* i. 8 The dress of the womenfolk of the Mālērs and the Orāons differs greatly from one another. *Ibid.* 15 The Mālér country is bounded by the Ganges in the north. **1963** L. P. VIDYARTHI *Maler* i. 11 To a Maler, the pleasure or wrath of spirits and supernatural powers controls the nature of happenings in the Maler family, village,..field or ..forests.

malerde, obs. form of MALLARD.

‖ **malerisch** ('mɑːlәrɪʃ), *a.* [G., 'painterly', f. *maler* painter.] After H. Wölfflin's use (1915 *Kunstgeschichtliche Grundbegriffe*): of or pertaining to a manner of painting characterized more by the merging of colours than by the more formal linear style; painterly.

1933 *Burlington Mag.* Dec. 269/2 Ruskin somewhere draws a distinction between drawing with a brush and painting with a brush—a distinction which in our time has been further elaborated by Heinrich Wölfflin. In Wölfflin's sense, the English water-colourists are always linear, and never malerisch. **1937** *Ibid.* Oct. 168/1 The most splendid examples of Raphael's draughtsmanship... They are '*malerisch*'. **1955** *Times* 2 Aug. 10/2 This is..a resuscitation of the great malerisch tradition, which was rejected by those who thought they were following Cézanne. **1961** *Times* 1 Mar. 15/3 The *malerisch* flow and swirl of the paint itself.

malerous(e, variant of MALEUROUS *Obs.*

males, malescun: see MALEASE, MALISON.

mal ese, variant of MALEASE *Obs.*

maleson(e, -esoune, obs. forms of MALISON.

maless, malesse: see MALEASE *Obs.*, MALICE.

male stream, -strom, obs. ff. MAELSTROM.

† **malesuete**, *a. Obs. rare*$^{-0}$. [ad. quasi-L. **male suēt-us* (*male* ill, *suētus* accustomed).]

1727 BAILEY vol. II, *Malesuete*, that has contracted an ill Habit or Custom.

malesun, obs. form of MALISON.

malet, variant of MALLET.

maletalent, -if, var. ff. MALTALENT, -IVE.

[**maletent**, bad reading for next in the transl. (1543) of *Act 25 Edw. I*, c. 7 (the AF. orig. has *male toute*); thence copied into various Law Dicts.]

† **maletolt.** *Law. Obs.* Forms: 6 maltot, 6, 9 maltote, 7 maletot, 7, 9 maltolt, 7 maletool, 8–9 maletolt, maltolte, 9 maletote, maletoute. [a. AF. *maletoute*, OF. *maltolte*, *maletoute* (mod.F. *maltôte*; hence Du. *maltoot*), repr. med.L. *mala tolta* (*mala* fem., evil, *tolta* tax, f. *tolt-*, med.L. ppl. stem of L. *tollĕre*, OF. *tolir*, *toudre* to take); cf. It. *malatolta*, OPg. *malatosta*.] An unjust or burdensome tax.

1514 *Mem. Constables Tournay* in Strype *Eccl. Mem.* (1721) I. App. iv. 8 In Calais..no maltot is demaunded..: wheras we of the king's garrison of Tournay pay for every tun of wine 40*s.* sterling maltot. *a* **1618** RALEIGH *Prerog. Parl.* (1628) 32 The King [Richard II] had giuen him a subsedy upon wools, called a Maletot. **1627** SIR R. COTTON *View Reign Hen. III* 23 They blame him..to haue vndone the trade of Merchants by bringing in Maletools and heauy customes. **1844** LD. BROUGHAM *Brit. Const.* xiii. (1862) 180 [Richard II] had recourse to forced loans, and to..the Maletolte of his grandfather. **1884** DOWELL *Taxation* v. ii. I. 133 The King and counsel authorised an impost; but this subsequently formed the subject of complaint as a maletoute. **1901** ROSA GRAHAM *S. Gilbert of Sempringham* 126 The maltôtes..levied on the export of wool by the Crown.

maleure, variant of MALHEUR *Obs.*

† **maleured,** *a. Obs.* In 6 male vryd. [f. *maleur MALHEUR + -ED².] Ill-fortuned.

a **1529** SKELTON *Agst. Scottes* 111 Wks. 1843 I. 185 Male vryd was your fals entent.

maleureus, maleurite: see MALEUROUS, MALEURTEE.

† **maleurous,** *a. Obs.* Forms: 5 maleureus, malewreus, malerouse, maleurouse, 5–6 malerous, maleheureux, 6 *Sc.* malewrus, mailhouris, malheurius. [a. OF. *maleuros*, *-eus*, *-ous* (mod.F. *malheureux*), f. *maleur* (mod.F. *malheur*): see MALHEUR. Cf. BENEUROUS.] Unhappy, unfortunate.

1471 CAXTON *Recuyell* (Sommer) I. 162 The maleureus & vnhappy saturne. *c* **1475** *Partenay* 6473 All glorius patriarkes in breue,..Iff I thaim for-gatte I were malerous. *c* **1477** CAXTON *Jason* 17 The right malerouse king was constrayned to..calle his knightes unto his ayde. *Ibid.* 110 What wil ye don with this malerous and pyteus childe. **1513** DOUGLAS *Æneis* XI. Prol. 150 Rycht so, quha vertuus was, and fallis tharfro, Of verray ressoune malewrus hait is he. **1533** BELLENDEN *Livy* I. viii. (S.T.S.) I. 47 Vtheris sa mailhouris þat na felicite mycht follow be þare operacioun. **1553** KENNEDY *Compend. Tract.* in *Wodrow Soc. Misc.* (1844) 152 The malheurius prince sall warie the tyme.

† **maleurtee.** *Obs.* Also 5 maleurte, maleh(e)urte, maluerte, 6 mallewrite, maleurite, -itie, malurit(e. [OF. *maleurté* misfortune, f. *maleur*: see MALHEUR and -TY.] Misfortune.

1471 CAXTON *Recuyell* (Sommer) II. 690 Hys malehurte and grete vnhappynesse. **1474** —— *Chesse* II. v. D viij b, This cyte of rome..is peruerted and torned in to maleheurte and thyse euylles. *Ibid.* III. vii. Ij, Thys drede surmounteth alle other maleurtees and euylles, for it is maleurte of drede nyght and day. **1481** —— *Godfrey* (1893) 203 They vnderstonde not yet the maluerte that they be in. **1533** BELLENDEN *Livy* IV. xii. (S.T.S.) II. 86 Dredand þe sammyn chance & mallewrite [*v.r.* maleurite] to fall to þare tovn. *Ibid.* 96 Repreving þame þat þai loist þare curage for sa small trubill and maluritee [*v.r.* malurite] of fortoun. **1546** THIRLBY in *St. Papers Hen. VIII*, XI. 397 This is my maleuritie.

malevesyn, obs. variant of MALVOISIE.

malevolence (mə'lɛvələns). Also 5–6 mali-, malyvolence, 6 malevolens. [a. OF. *mali-*, *malevolence*, ad. L. *mali-*, *malevolentia*, f. *malevolentem*: see MALEVOLENT.] The attribute of being malevolent; the wishing or the disposition to wish evil to others; ill-will.

c **1489** CAXTON *Blanchardyn* xli. 153 The grete malyuolence or euyll wylle that he had. **1509** BARCLAY *Shyp of Folys* (1570) 16 Wo be to them who by maliuolence Slaunder or defame any creature. **1575** LANEHAM *Let.* 65 Too him that..either of ignorauns..or els of maleuolens woold make any doout. **1605** SHAKS. *Macb.* III. vi. 28 The maleuolence of Fortune. **1688** NORRIS *Theory Love* I. ii. 15 A willing evil to some person or thing, which we call Malice or Malevolence. **1712** STEELE *Spect.* No. 422 ¶4 The Malevolence, which is too general towards those who excell. **1789** BELSHAM *Ess.* II. xl. 510 The reputation of Hooker..rises far above the reach of Mr. Burke's malevolence. **1838** LYTTON *Calderon* i, This prudent frankness disarmed malevolence on the score of birth. **1885** *L'pool Daily Post* 1 June 5/3 Every obstacle which partisan malevolence could create he has had to encounter.

b. Sarcastically suggested as a more appropriate term for BENEVOLENCE 4.

[*a* **1548** HALL *Chron., Edw. IV.* 226 b, The kyng..called this graunt of money a benevolence, not withstanding that many with grudge and maleuolence gave great summes toward that new founde benevolence.] **1592** STOW *Ann.*, an. 1473. 701 The king..called this grant of money a Beneuolence, notwithstanding that many grudged therat and called it a Maleuolence. **1640** LD. J. DIGBY *Sp. in Ho. Com.* 9 Nov. 4 The granting of Subsidies, and that under so preposterous a name as of a *Benevolence*, for that which is a *Malevolence* indeed.

† **malevolency.** *Obs.* [ad. L. *malevolentia*: see prec. and -ENCY.] = MALEVOLENCE.

a **1662** HEYLIN *Laud* I. III. (1668) 240 This was the first taste which they gave the King of their malevolency towards his Person. **1714** POPE *Let. to Addison* 10 Oct., May I hope that some late malevolencies have lost their effect?

malevolent (mə'lɛvələnt), *a.* and *sb.* Also 6 maly-, malivolent. [a. OF. *malivolent*, ad. L. *mali-*, *malevolent-em*, f. *male* ill + *volent-em* willing, pr. pple. of *velle* to will, wish.]

A. *adj.*

1. Of persons, their feelings and actions: Desirous of evil to others; entertaining, actuated by, or indicative of ill-will; disposed or addicted to ill-will.

1509 BARCLAY *Shyp of Folys* (1874) II. 216 The honour of hym that is absent..Is hurt and distayned by worde malyuolent. **1528** ROY *Rede me*, etc. (Arb.) 118 Iudas the traytour malivolent Whiche betrayed Christ to the Iues. **1593** NASHE *Christ's T.* 66 Malicious and maleuolent are they, that will exclude any one Arte..from bearing witnesse of God. **1645** PAGITT *Heresiogr.* (1661) 72 They are as malevolent to Dutch and French Churches as to us. **1664** H. MORE *Myst. Iniq., Apol.* 561 [To] disenable malevolent men from doing the free and ingenuous undeserved mischief. **1689** in *Wood's Life* 21 Nov. (O.H.S.) III. 314 Some malivolent people have lately defaced King William's picture in the Guild-hall. **1751** JOHNSON *Rambler* No. 172 ¶4 Whoever rises..will have many malevolent gazers at his eminence. **1833** KEBLE *Serm.* vi. (1848) 143 The..malevolent feeling of disgust,..which is apt to lay hold on sensitive minds. **1841** MACAULAY *Ess.*, *W. Hastings* (1851) 599 The keen, severe, and even malevolent scrutiny to which his whole public life was subjected. **1894** S. WEYMAN *Under Red Robe* v. (1897) 133 His lean malevolent face..chilled me.

† **b.** *transf.*

1719 LONDON & WISE *Compl. Gard.* xxv, For securing of..tender Greens and Plants from malevolent Winds.

† **2.** *Astrol.* Exercising an evil or baleful influence.

1593 R. HARVEY *Philad.* 56 Some infortunate and malevolent configuration of mouable skies and starres. **1691** DRYDEN *K. Arthur* v. 44 At length I have thee in my Arms; Tho our Malevolent Stars have strugled hard, And held us long asunder. **1696** PHILLIPS (ed. 5), *Malevolent Planets*, Saturn and Mars.

b. *transf.* and *fig.*

1596 SHAKS. *1 Hen. IV*, I. i. 97 This is Worcester, Maleuolent to you in all Aspects. **1672** SIR T. BROWNE *Lett. Friend* §4 Death hath not only particular Stars in Heaven, but Malevolent Places on Earth. **1685** BOYLE *Enq. Notion Nat.* iv. 83 The malevolent aspect, that the vulgar notion of nature..may have on religion.

B. *sb.*

† **1.** A person of evil wishes or designs. *Obs.*

1595 DANIEL *Civ. Wars* IV. xxxi. (1609) 95 They durst not..present..their defences, in respect He was incenst by some maleuolent. **1637** LAUD *Sp. in Starr Chamber* Ded. a 2, Mr. Prinn..[will] scarce find such a Malevolent as himselfe against State and Church. **1654** H. L'ESTRANGE *Chas. I* (1655) 127 Notwithstanding..these close insinuations by these turbulent malevolents, the Act passed. **1670** in Somers *Tracts* I. 3 Which his malevolents affirmed to be an emblem of himself.

† **2.** *Astrol.* An evil influence. *Obs.*

1651 CULPEPPER *Astrol. Judgem. Dis.* (1658) 150 They are both afflicted by malevolents, the Moon by Conjunction of Saturn, and the Sun by Conjunction of Mars.

malevolently (mə'lɛvələntlı), *adv.* [f. prec. + -LY².] In a malevolent manner.

1615 T. ADAMS *White Devill* 16 If a levy..wold force your benevolence it comes malevolently from you. **1640** HOWELL *Dodona's Gr.* 114 The gracious Oke..did vindicat him from those aspersions malevolently cast upon him. **1792** GEDDES tr. *Bible* Pref. 7 The serpent..malevolently persuaded the woman to eat of the fruit. **1897** MARY KINGSLEY *W. Africa* 585 They stagger about on the ground, buzzing malevolently.

ma'levolentness. *rare*⁻⁰. [f. MALEVOLENT + -NESS.] = MALEVOLENCE.

1727 in BAILEY vol. II.

† **malevolo.** *Obs. rare*⁻¹. [a. It. *malevolo*, ad. L. *malevolus*: see next.] A malevolent person.

1648 *Brit. Bellman* 2 Many Plots were discovered..in which..ye Malevolos, might have claimed the chiefest Livery, as Beelzebubs nearest Attendants.

† **ma'levolous,** *a. Obs.* Also 6 malivolus, malyvolus. [f. L. *malevol-us* (f. L. *male* ill + *vol-*, *velle* to wish) + -OUS.] = MALEVOLENT 1.

1536 BELLENDEN *Cron. Scot.* (1821) II. 274 Ane wickit and malivolus man, namit Edrik. **1547** BOORDE *Brev. Health* lxix. 29 b, This impediment doth come..of some malyvolus humoure. **1588** J. HARVEY *Disc. Probl.* 108 We neede not greatly recke, or care for his maleuolous intention. **1652** GAULE *Magastrom.* 223 They caution straitly to observe the planet, benevolous or malevolous. **1679** C. NESSE *Antid. agst. Popery* 102 Satan is a malevolous adversary. **1727** WARBURTON *Tracts* (1789) 128 These malevolous Critics.

malewe, obs. form of MALLOW.

malewr(e)us, variant of MALEUROUS *a. Obs.*

malexecution. Also 7 male-execution. [See MAL-.] Bad execution or administration.

1689 *Trial Pritchard v. Papillon* 6 Nov. an. 1684. 9 That were a Misfesance, or a Male-execution of their Office. **1848** in CRAIG. *a* **1852** D. WEBSTER cited in Webster 1854.

maleyce, -ys, obs. forms of MALICE.

malfeasance (mæl'fi:zəns). Also 7 malefeazance, 8 malefeasance, 8–9 malfaisance, 9 malfesance. [a. AF. **malfaisance* (cf. mod.F. *malfaisance*), f. OF. *malfaisant*: see next.]

1. *Law.* Evil-doing; *spec.* official misconduct on the part of one in public employment.

1696 *Lond. Gaz.* No. 3242/4 Special Bars in Case, viz... Slander,..Mis feazance, Male-feazance [etc.]. **1765** BLACKSTONE *Comm.* I. 393 Statutes, which declare the benefice void, for some nonfeasance or neglect, or else some male-feasance or crime. **1827** HALLAM *Const. Hist.* (1876) II. viii. 32 Thus corruption, breach of trust, and malfeasance in public affairs..came..under the cognizance of the star-chamber. **1839** J. STORY *Law Bailments* 123 The same rule which is applied by the common law to cases of malfesance, governs also cases of negligent execution of a gratuitous trust or agency. **1885** *Spectator* 8 Aug. 1041/1 The protection of Hastings, whom he had charged with various malfeasances. **1892** *Times* (weekly ed.) 4 Nov. 4/1 Various charges of malfeasance.

2. *gen.* Wrong-doing; an instance of this. *rare.*

1856 EMERSON *Eng. Traits* xv. 260 A relentless inquisition..turns the glare of this solar microscope [the newspaper] on every malfaisance. **1860** —— *Cond. Life, Consid.* Wks. (Bohn) II. 415 Nature turns all malfaisance to good.

malfeasant (mæl'fi:zənt), *a.* and *sb.* Also 9 malfaisant. [a. F. *malfaisant*, f. *mal* ill, MAL-, + *faisant*, pr. pple. of *faire* to do.] **a.** *adj.* Evil-doing. **b.** *sb.* An evil-doer, a criminal.

1809 E. S. BARRETT *Setting Sun* I. 31 Christians (soi-disant but mal-faisant followers of the mild doctrines of Christ). **1882** MORLEY *R. Cobden* xxiv. (1902) 84/1 Malfeasants on board a British ship should not be seized but..demanded from the Consul.

† **malfeasor.** *Obs.* Forms: 4–5 mal(e)fesour, mau-, mawfesour, 5 maffaisour. [a. OF. *malfaisor*, agent-n. f. *mal faire*: see prec.] An evil-doer, a malefactor.

c **1330** R. BRUNNE *Chron.* (1810) 211 þe maufesours ateynt, & cursed ouer þe nape. **14..** in *Hist. Coll. Citizen London* (Camden) 99 Hoolye for to forgevyn alle the malefesourys or evylle doers of hem dwellynge in the same cytte. **1401** *Pol. Poems* (Rolls) II. 85 Al maner mawfesours shulden ben unponnishid. **1424** *Paston Lett.* I. 12 Certeyns maffaisours, felons, and brekeres of the kynges peas vnknowyn.

† **malfetour.** *Obs.* [a. OF. *malfetor* (mod.F. *malfaiteur*):—L. *malefactōr-em*.] = MALEFACTOR.

c **1450** LONELICH *Grail* xxxvi. 335 They supposide Everychon..that it hadde be sum Malfetour that was for-Iogged.

malfor'mation. [f. MAL- + FORMATION.] Faulty or anomalous formation or structure of parts, esp. of a living body.

1800 *Med. Jrnl.* III. 397 Case of extraordinary Malformation in a Foetus by T. Pole. **1844** DUTTON *Deafness* 116 Where the auditory nerve is perfect, and there is no congenital malformation. **1872** T. BRYANT *Pract. Surg.* 126 A malformation of the septum nasi.

fig. **1855** MACAULAY *Hist. Eng.* xiii. III. 377 It [the army] ceased to exist,..not in consequence of any great blow from without, but by a natural dissolution, the effect of internal malformation.

mal'formed, *a.* [f. MAL- + FORMED *ppl. a.*] Badly formed; marked by malformation.

1817 LAWRENCE *Lect.* (1823) 110 It is admitted that an ideot with a malformed brain has no mind. **1836–9** TODD *Cycl. Anat.* II. 633/1 Children with hearts so malformed live three, four, or five days. **1872** O. W. HOLMES *Poet Breakf.-t.* viii. (1885) 205 Malformed salmon..can be supplied. **1879** *St. George's Hosp. Rep.* IX. 631 Both the teeth were malformed, hollow, and smaller than natural.

b. *transf.* and *fig.*

1867 SWINBURNE *Ess. & Stud.* (1875) 112 These first poems of Mr. Morris were not malformed. **1872** O. W. HOLMES *Poet Breakf.-t.* viii. 264 You do not get such a malformed character as that without a long chain of causes. **1899** *Daily News* 21 July 8/6 Malformed and tainted human nature.

malfunction (mæl'fʌŋkʃən), *sb.* [f. MAL- + FUNCTION *sb.* 3.] Faulty functioning. So **mal'function** *v. intr.*; **mal'functioning** *vbl. sb.* and *ppl. a.*

1928 E. BAGBY *Psychol. of Personality* xi. 154 Conditions of this sort are usually found to be *symptoms* of a malfunctioning of fundamental bodily processes. **1941** JOHNSON & HAVEN *Automatic Arms* 128 The slide on an automatic pistol may fail to remain open after the last shot, due to a malfunction of the catch... The use of the term 'malfunction' conveys nothing unless we know *what malfunctioned.* **1957** *New Scientist* 9 May 38/2 As an ophthalmic optician I was entertained by 'Geminus' (25 April) on his visits to his optician and his own experiments at correcting the malfunctions of his extra-ocular muscles. **1957** *New Biol.* XXII. 83 They [*sc.* psychosomatic disorders] come to the attention of patient and physician through some malfunctioning of an organ. **1958** *Times* 14 Mar. 10/1 Through 'mechanical malfunctioning', a B-47 bomber aircraft dropped what is described as 'an unarmed nuclear device'. *Ibid.* 17 Oct. 15/2 Eyes whose tear-ducts were malfunctioning because of the absence of gravity. **1961** *New Scientist* 7 Dec. 617/1 Some tiny valves in the spaceship's plumbing system failed to function properly... This malfunction has been brushed off in the newspapers. **1966** T. PYNCHON *Crying of Lot 49* i. 14 A dented, malfunctioning version of himself. **1972** *Daily Tel.* 22 Jan. 17/2 An investigation was being made to discover why the warm-air heating system at the house..had malfunctioned. *Ibid.*, Recommendations would be made to the house

builders when the cause of the malfunction had been discovered. **1973** *Sci. Amer.* Oct. 69/3 An instrumental malfunction at the crucial time can spoil the results of months of preparation.

malgas, var. MALAGAS.

† **mal'governance.** *Obs. rare*⁻¹. In 7 male-governance. [f. MAL- + GOVERNANCE.] = next.
1673 H. STUBBES *Further Vind. Dutch War* App. 92 They saw disorders to encrease there upon the male-governance of that pretended Parliament.

mal'government. Also 7 male-. [f. MAL- + GOVERNMENT.] Bad government.
a **1653** GOUGE *Comm. Heb.* xi. 32 Yet doth not that phrase intend, that he gave over the whole government to them, much lesse that he justified them in their male-government. **1848** *Fraser's Mag.* XXXVII. 146 Any degree of mal-government and misery. **1880** V. L. CAMERON *Our Future Highway* II. xv. 340 The country is much richer.. notwithstanding its mal-government.

malgrace (mæl'greɪs). [Orig. two words, a. OF. *male grace* (*male* fem. of *mal* evil, *grace* GRACE *sb*).]
† **1.** Disfavour. *Obs.*
c **1425** *Seven Sag.* (P.) 2108 And he answerd ryght in the place, 'Maugré have thou and male grace!' **1639** SPOTTISWOOD *Hist. Ch. Scot.* VI. (1677) 326 The Rebels or others known to be in his Majesties mal-grace. **1714** FORTESCUE-ALAND Note in *Fortescue's Abs. & Lim. Mon.* 75 *Magre*.. signifies the same as mal-grace, disfavour, or ill-will.
2. Something unbecoming. *pseudo-arch.*
1882 G. MACDONALD *Weighed & Wanting* iv. I. 57 May these not see in us some malgrace which it needs the gentleness of Christ to get over and forget?

† **mal'gracious,** *a.* *Obs. rare.* Also 5 maugracious. [a. OF. *malgracieux, maugracieux*: see MAL- and GRACIOUS *a.*] **a.** Ill-favoured, uncomely. **b.** Ungracious, disobliging.
1390 GOWER *Conf.* II. 149 His [Vulcanus'] figure Bothe of visage and of stature Is lothly and malgracious. *c* **1430** *Pilgr. Lyf Manhode* II. lxxxv. (1869) 106 A vile old oon, and maugracious [F. *maugracieuse*] and hideous, that j sih not bifore. **1471** CAXTON *Recuyell* (ed. Sommer) I. 68 The moo prayers that they made vnto Tytan, the more fonde they hym vncourtoys felon and malgracyous. *a* **1500** *Colkelbie Sow* 131 A malgratious millare, A berward, a brawlar.

‖ **mal'grado,** *prep.* *Obs.* [It. *malgrado*: see MAUGRE and cf. next.] In spite of. Also with *of*.
1590 MARLOWE *Edw. II*, II. v, Malgrado all your beards. **1590** LODGE *Rosalind* (1887) 166 To force Phoebe to fancy the shepherd, malgrado the resolution of her mind. **1590** GREENE *Orl. Fur.* (1599) H, What I haue said, Ile pawne my sword, To seale it on the shield of him that dares Malgrado of his honour, combate me.

‖ **malgré** (malgre), *prep.* [Fr.: see MAUGRE.]
1. In spite of, notwithstanding. (In first quot. without regimen.)
1608 BP. HALL *Epist.* IV. iv. 363 Woe were vs, if our safetie depended vpon your hopes, or his [*sc.* the pope's] mercies. Blessed be that God, which malgrè hath made and kept vs happie. *a* **1734** NORTH *Exam.* I. i. §29 (1740) 28 Our late Sovereign, who, malgre all his endeavours to the Contrary is yet..of glorious Memory. **1769** HIRST in *Phil. Trans.* LIX. 232 To..acknowledge conviction, *malgré* all prejudice and preconceived opinion. **1814** SIR R. WILSON *Priv. Diary* (1861) II. 302, I went..to the opera, *malgré* the gutters and spouts. **1815** BYRON in Moore *Life* (1838) 281/2, I went (*malgré* that I ought to have stayed at home in sackcloth..) to..my private box. **1878** L. W. M. LOCKHART *Mine is Thine* II. xxxv. 313 The 'fowler'..went forth, accordingly, *malgré* his sister's remonstrances.
2. Freq. followed by a pronoun, as **malgré lui** (lɥi), in spite of himself or herself; also **malgré elle, eux, moi,** etc., in spite of herself, themselves, myself, etc. Also **malgré tout,** despite everything.
1830 C. C. F. GREVILLE *Mem.* (1874) II. xi. 38 This was my first dinner at Dudley's, brought about *malgré lui* by Lady Glengall. **1843** THACKERAY *Confessions of G. Fitz-Boodle*: *Mr. & Mrs. Berry* in *Fraser's Mag.* Mar. 359/2 We obliged the Frenchman to drink *malgré lui.* **1852** GEO. ELIOT *Let.* 24–25 July (1954) II. 50, I congratulate you on your ability to be cheerful *malgré tout.* **1883** G. BLOOMFIELD *Reminisc.* II. xiii. 45 They say that, *malgré eux*, they cannot yield. **1904** WODEHOUSE *Gold Bat* xiii. 142 He could imagine their feelings when the prodigal strolled into their midst—an old Wrykinian *malgré lui.* **1929** A. HUXLEY *Holy Face* 26 That too, too merry laughter of clergymen who want to prove that, *malgré tout*, they can be good fellows. **1932** *Mind* XLI. 24 He [*sc.* Callicles] stands revealed as a moralist *malgré lui.* **1933** *Times Lit. Suppl.* 26 Jan. 56/2 The Bulpington as a warrior *malgré lui*, whose conduct in action might..have brought him to the execution squad. **1943** WYNDHAM LEWIS *Let.* 15 Aug. (1963) 363 As you know I am here malgré moi; but I attempt to put to some serious use my prolonged immersion in this N. American civilisation. **1950** A. HUXLEY *Let.* 11 Aug. (1969) 629 One likes him, *malgré tout.* **1963** *Economist* 28 Dec. 1318/1 These central bankers ..have created, almost *malgré eux*, a code of practice. **1970** *Guardian* 11 Dec. 10/6 The weight of the acting fell mostly on Anna Cropper as the fertility goddess *malgré elle.*

malgyk, obs. form of MAGIC.

‖ **malheur.** *Obs.* Also 5 maleheure, maleure, malure, 6 mallure, 7 malheure, maleheur. [Fr., earlier *maleur*, f. *mal* evil + *eur* fortune:—L. *augurium* AUGURY.] Misfortune.
1471 CAXTON *Recuyell* (Sommer) I. 268 Yf my maleheure and mysauenture renne vpon me. *Ibid.* II. 490, I haue maleure and myshappe. *a* **1500** *Chaucer's Dream* 601, I wofull wight full of malure, Am worse than dead. **1560** A. SCOTT *Poems* xvi. 3 The mornyng and the grit mallure Can nane devyne. **1602** J. CECIL in *Archpriest Controv.* (Camden) II. 206 We recurred to God and our blessed ladye that they woulde diverte this malheure from vs. **1673** DRYDEN *Marr. à la Mode* v. i, Ay, 'tis long of you that this *Malheur* is fall'n upon me. **1682** C. IRVINE *Hist. Scott. Nomencl.* Ded. *vj b, Seldome ever any Maleheur befell them. **1770** FITZPATRICK in J. H. Jesse *G. Selwyn & Contemp.* (1843) II. 396, I am heartily sorry for your *malheur.* **1792** *Elvina* II. 65, I had no opportunity to acquaint her with my malheur.

malheurius, Sc. variant of MALEUROUS *Obs.*

‖ **mali** ('mɑːliː), *sb.*¹ *Anglo-Indian.* Also 8–9 molly, 9 mollie, mollee, mallee, mallie, maul(ly). [Hindi *mālī*.] One of the gardener caste in India; hence any native gardener.
1759 *Wages tariff* in Long *Sel. Rec. Ft. William* (1869) 182 (Y.) House Molly..2 Rs. **1810** T. WILLIAMSON *E. Ind. Vade Mecum* I. 261 The Mauly, or gardener, next claims attention. *Ibid.* 263 It would surprize an European to see with what precision maullies sow and cover their seeds. *a* **1825** D. JOHNSON *Observ. Dis. India* in Good *Study Med.* (1825) III. 425 Such people as have their feet and hands frequently in cold water or earth, such as..Dobys (washerwomen) and Mollies (gardeners) in the upper provinces of India. **1879** MRS. A. E. JAMES *Ind. Househ. Managem.* 63 We soon got a mallee, or gardener, and a garden-coolie. **1886** R. KIPLING *Departm. Ditties* (1899) 34 He shall see the mallie steals the slab For currie-grinder, and for goats the grass. **1908** C. SORABJI *Between Twilights* xii. 150 While my *Mali* and I did tidyings in the Garden, I spoke to him gently about the plant. **1934** 'G. ORWELL' *Burmese Days* ii. 20 A nearly naked mali, watering-can in hand. **1971** *Hindustan Times Weekly* (New Delhi) 4 Apr. 10/7 The groundsmen and malis were being paid from the University Sports Fund.

Mali ('mɑːlɪ), *a.* and *sb.*² Also **Melle, Melli.**
A. *adj.* Of or pertaining to Mali, an ancient empire (of the 13th and 14th centuries) and a modern republic (founded in 1960) in west Africa. **B.** *sb.* A native or inhabitant of Mali. So **'Malian** *a.* and *sb.*
1906 H. H. JOHNSTON *Liberia* II. xxvii. 896 The Melli.. empire..arose and flourished in Nigeria before the foundation of Timbuktu. **1911** *Encycl. Brit.* XVII. 565/1 It is not known by whom the Melle (Mali) state was founded. .. The first king whose name is preserved was Baramindana, believed to have reigned from 1213 to 1235. **1960** *Times* 28 Mar. 6/1 The Mali folklore is less unfamiliar to Parisians than that of its sister republic. **1960** *Daily Tel.* 24 Aug. 1/1 The Mali force..was due to be withdrawn from the Congo. *Ibid.*, Irish troops of the U.N. were to have taken over from the Malis. **1960** *Economist* 31 Dec. 1367/2 The Malians themselves (or Soudanese, as they used to call themselves) have only lately emerged from black Africa's first working experiment of a sovereign federation. **1967** S. KNIGHT *Window on Shanghai* xv. 65, I especially like the beautifully robed Malians... They are all members of the Malian government. **1970** P. OLIVER *Savannah Syncopators* 106 Mali lutes, Senegal *kora.* **1973** *Times* 15 Oct. 8/8 Police today charged a 31-year-old Malian with illegal entry into Italy after the deaths yesterday of three young Africans believed to have been involved in illegal traffic of African labourers to Europe. **1974** *Black World* Feb. 56 West African elements, in particular the Malians, were installed in America before the arrival of the Europeans.

Malibu, malibu ('mælɪbuː). Chiefly *Austral.* and *N.Z.* [The name of *Malibu* Beach in California.] In full, ***Malibu board.*** A short light-weight surf-board.
1962 *Austral. Women's Weekly* Suppl. 24 Oct. 3/3 *Malibu*, type of surfboard made from foam, balsa, or fibre-glass and under 10 ft. long. **1965** *N.Z. Listener* 17 Dec. 4/4 Australia had its first look at the Malibu board when film star Peter Lawford took one 'down under' in 1954. **1969** *Times* 25 July 5/2 Worried by the number of thefts of malibu boards, police have issued leaflets in the surfers' own language. **1970** *N.Z. News* 8 Apr. 16/3 A. Griffin won both the ski and malibu board races.

malic ('meɪlɪk), *a.* *Chem.* [a. F. *malique*, f. L. *māl-um* apple.] ***malic acid***: an acid ($C_4H_6O_5$) derived from the apple, the berries of the mountain-ash, and many other fruits. Applied to enzymes whose substrate is malic acid, as ***malic dehydrogenase***; ***malic enzyme*** (see quot. 1951).
1797 *Encycl. Brit.* (ed. 3) XVIII. 871/1 The citric and malic acids which I have found in wine. **1801** *Encycl. Brit.* Suppl. (ed. 3) I. 326/1 Scheele discovered a peculiar acid.. which, because it is found most abundantly in apples, has been called malic acid. **1813** SIR H. DAVY *Agric. Chem.* (1814) 107 Malic Acid may be obtained from the juice of apples, barberries, plums, elderberries [etc.]. **1897** *Allbutt's Syst. Med.* II. 843 Cider contains malic acid. **1937** H. TAUBER *Enzyme Chem.* vii. 170 Malic dehydrogenase may be prepared by washing frog or ox muscle with *M*/15 phosphate buffer. **1948** *Jrnl. Biol. Chem.* CLXXIV. 997 There might be a mechanism for fixation of CO_2 by pyruvate other than that involving the 'malic' enzyme. **1951** *Physiol. Rev.* XXXI. 86 Enzymes catalyzing the reversible oxidative decarboxylation of *l*-malic acid are widely distributed. These enzymes are distinct from malic dehydrogenase, which catalyzes the reversible oxidation of *l*-malic acid, and are referred to as 'malic' enzymes. The majority of the known malic enzymes function specifically with TPN as coenzyme. **1972** *Biochem. Genetics* VII. 303 Polymorphic variation of the human mitochondrial malic enzyme was detected in Caucasians and Negroes.

malice ('mælɪs), *sb.* Forms: 4 malyes, maleys, 4–5 malis, malece, 4, 6 maliss, maleyce, 4–6 malys, malyce, 5 malyhs, mailyeis, 5–6 malesse, malise, malles, 6 mallyce, maleis(e, 6–7 mallice, 3– malice. [a. F. *malice* (recorded from 12th c.), ad. L. *malitia*, f. *mal-us* bad. (Cf. Sp., Pg. *malicia*, It. *malizia*.)
Some of the early forms are coincident with those of MALEASE; in some senses the two words seem to have been sometimes confused.]
† **1.** Bad quality, badness; chiefly in moral sense, wickedness. *Obs.*
a **1300** *Cursor M.* 1555 Mikel malice was first in man Bot neuer forwit sua mikel as þan. *a* **1340** HAMPOLE *Psalter* v. 1 Halykirke þat prayes to be departid fra þe malice of þe warld. **13..** *E.E. Allit. P.* B. 518 Al is þe mynde of þe man to malyce enclyned. *c* **1375** *Sc. Leg. Saints* l. (*Katerine*) 74 Scho ȝed and sad..sir king, Resone requeris..þat þu knaw þi malyes & with-draw now sic seruice fra þis goddis fals, þat þe dissawis. **1398** TREVISA *Barth. De P.R.* XVII. ii. (1495) 596 To make a wylde tree chaunge out of malyce in to goodnes. *c* **1400** MAUNDEV. (Roxb.) ix. 33 Þai er..full of all maner of wickedness and malice. *c* **1420** *Pallad. on Husb.* I. 264 The malice of that lond, or cause of drede, That wyntir with his shouris may of dryue. **1477** EARL RIVERS (Caxton) *Dictes* 14 Make your children lerne good in their youthe or they falle to malice. **1594** CAREW *Huarte's Exam. Wits* (1596) 278 In man there is no power which hath tokens to descry the goodnesse or malice of his object. **1600** ABP. ABBOT *Exp. Jonah* 19 When..they returned to their malice as a dog to his vomit, it [Nineveh] was destroyed. **1605** BACON *Adv. Learn.* I. v. §1 It seemeth the children of time do take after the nature and malice of the father.
† **2.** Power to harm, harmfulness; harmful action or effect. Of a disease, a poison, etc.: Virulence.
c **1380** WYCLIF *Wks.* (1880) 457 Neþer þe word of þer prelat ne þe word of þer somenour han so myche maliss wiþ hem þat [etc.]. **1390** GOWER *Conf.* I. 266 The water of a welle Of fyr abateth the malice. **1432–50** tr. *Higden* (Rolls) I. 339 Venym and poysoun..leseþ his malys anon as he passeþ þe myddel of þe see. **1528** PAYNEL *Salerne's Regim.* O iv b, Suche wyne doth alay the malice of yᵉ meate. **1544** PHAER *Regim. Lyfe* (1560) S viij b, It is a singular remedy, to remove yᵉ malice [of a canker] in a short while. **1555** W. WATREMAN *Fardle Facions* II. i. 114 Myrrhe, whose smoke is so unholsome, that excepte thei withstode the malice therof with the perfume of styrax [etc.]. **1595** SHAKS. *John* II. i. 251 Our Cannons malice vainly shall be spent. **1614** RALEIGH *Hist. World* II. v. iii. §6. 374 The malice of a great Armie is broken..in a great Siege. *a* **1619** FOTHERBY *Atheom.* II. v. §4 (1622) 242 The malice of the sicknesse surpassing all the helpe of the most approved medicines. **1655** CULPEPPER, etc. *Riverius* IV. vii. 116 These Evacuations..come..from the malice of the matter of the Disease. **1685** DRYDEN *Threnod. August.* 177 Undaunted Cæsar underwent The malice of their [*sc.* the physicians'] art.
† **3.** *Astrol.* The baleful influence of certain stars.
1398 TREVISA *Barth. De P.R.* VIII. xxii. (Helmingham MS.), Þe malice of a malicious sterre is y-temprid..by presence of a goodly sterre. **1563** HYLL *Art Garden.* (1593) 20 Throgh some malice of the celestial bodies.
4. The desire to injure another person; active ill-will or hatred. In mod. use sometimes in weaker sense: Sportively 'mischievous' intent, desire to tease (cf. F. *malice*).
1297 R. GLOUC. (Rolls) 12027 He ne dude it vor non vuel ne malice bi speke er. **1390** GOWER *Conf.* I. 62 He that was a Lomb beforn Is thanne a Wolf, and thus malice Under the colour of justice Is hid. *c* **1430** LYDG. *Min. Poems* (Percy Soc.) 23 The wolf of malys..Upon the lambe complenynd ageyn reson. **1477** *Surtees Misc.* (1890) 35 A man..was notyd and diffamyd..be veray malesse, yᵗ he shud be a Skotte. **1500–20** DUNBAR *Poems* lix. 3 A refyng sone of rakyng Muris Hes magellit my making, throw his maliss. **1593** SHAKS. *2 Hen. VI*, III. ii. 23 God forbid any Malice should preuayle. **1601** BP. W. BARLOW *Serm. Paules Crosse* Pref. 7 Malice marres logike and charitie both. **1691** HARTCLIFFE *Virtues* 381 When we think of..the malice of our Spiritual Adversaries; we are apt to despond. **1781** GIBBON *Decl. & F.* xix. II. 132 He furnished the malice of his enemies with the arms of truth. **1825** COLERIDGE *Aids Refl.* xxxi. (1836) 100 The slanders..may be the implements, not the inventions of Malice. **1849** MACAULAY *Hist. Eng.* ix. II. 495 Then the archbishop, with that gentle and temperate malice which inflicts the deepest wounds, said [etc.]. **1871** MORLEY *Voltaire* (1886) 5 The rank vocabulary of malice and hate.
b. Occas. personified.
1601 SHAKS. *Twel. N.* I. v. 196 Yet (by the verie phangs of malice, I sweare) I am not that I play. **1781** COWPER *Hope* 559 The blot For every dart that malice ever shot.
c. Phrase. *to bear malice*: to feel ill-will; now usually, to cherish revengeful or unfriendly feelings on account of some injury. Const. *to* or dative; also † *against*, † *toward*.
1530 PALSGR. 450/1, I beare grutche or malyce agaynst a person, *je porte malice.* **1560** DAUS tr. *Sleidane's Comm.* 112, I have tolde you..howe Duke George of Saxony, bare malice. **1572** *Lament. Lady Scot.* 43 in *Satir. Poems Reform.* xxxiii, The malice greit, that ilk to vther beiris. **1613** SHAKS. *Hen. VIII*, II. i. 62 The Law I beare no mallice for my death. **1838** LYTTON *Calderon* iii, I bear no malice to him for that, your highness. *a* **1846** LANDOR *Imag. Conv.* Wks. I. 15, I never bear malice toward those who try to reduce me to their own dimensions. **1875** MRS. RANDOLPH *W. Hyacinth* I. 72, I believe you bear malice still.
d. *fig.* Attributed to fortune, or impersonal agencies.
1660 F. BROOKE tr. *Le Blanc's Trav.* 268 Often exposed to the malice of weather, but more to the malice of men. **1797** MRS. RADCLIFFE *Italian* ii. (1826) 15 He defied the utmost malice of future fortune. *a* **1859** DE QUINCEY *Dream Fugue*

Wks. 1897 XIII. 320 The deeps opened ahead in malice to receive her.

¶ **e.** Misused for: Anger. *Obs. rare*⁻¹.

1538 BALE *God's Promises* in Dodsley *O. Pl.* (1780) I. 19 Tell me, blessed Lorde, where wyll thy great malyce light.

† **5.** Malicious conduct; a malicious act or device.

1390 GOWER *Conf.* III. 207 A thousendfold welmore he soghte Thanne afterward to do malice. **14..** *Story of Alexander* 7 in *Wars Alex.* (E.E.T.S.) 279 But I schewe to you þat I hate frawdez & maleces. **1413** *Pilgr. Sowle* (Caxton 1483) I. ii. 3 The performyng of malyce standyth nought in thy power, but the purposyng of malyce is thyne owne properte. *c* **1440** *York Myst.* xvii. 317 Herowde the kyng has malise ment. **1454** *Paston Lett.* I. 273 Thes vengeable malics don to hir and me. *c* **1470** HENRY *Wallace* IX. 562 He..now agayn begynnys a malice new. **1607** SHAKS. *Cor.* II. ii. 36 To report otherwise, were a Mallice, that..would plucke..rebuke from euery Eare that heard it. **1669** R. MONTAGU in *Buccleuch MS.* (Hist. MSS. Comm.) I. 449 The French look upon this as an art and malice of the Spaniard to destroy the trade.

6. *Law.* **a.** Wrongful intention generally. **b.** That kind of evil intent which constitutes the aggravation of guilt distinctive of certain offences (*esp.* of murder), or which deprives some act, on the face of it unlawful, of a justification or excuse that might otherwise have been allowed.

The first meaning mentioned under b was originally expressed by the AF. phrase *malice purpensé* or *prepense*, which in modern legal language appears as ***malice prepense*** (see PREPENSE *a.*) and in the translated form ***malice aforethought***. In early use the phrase occurs in many anglicized forms: ***malice prepensed, purpensed, pretensed*** (also ***prepensed***, etc. ***malice***); occasional variants found in non-technical writers are ***malice propense*** (17th c.), ***malice prepensive*** (Fielding), ***malice perpended*** (Charles Lamb). For examples see the various adjs.

See also quots. 1825–1901 below, and quot. 1889 s.v. MALICIOUSLY 4. It is not possible to frame any such general definition as would show what legally constitutes 'malice' or proof of 'malice' in particular kinds of cases.

1547 *Act 1 Edw. VI*, c. 12 §9 No parsone..convicted of murder of malyse prepensed. *Ibid.*, Or shall stande willfullie or of malyce muett. *a* **1625** SIR H. FINCH *Law* (1636) 215 Murder is Man-slaughter upon former malice: which wee call prepensed malice. **1670–1** *Act 22 & 23 Chas. II*, c. 1 §6 If any person..on purpose and of malice forethought..shall [etc.]. **1716** W. HAWKINS *Pleas Crown* I. 88 The Murther of a Person by one who was his Servant, upon Malice conceived during the Service. **1817** W. SELWYN *Law Nisi Prius* (ed. 4) II. 997 To support this action, malice..must be alleged and proved. **1825** JUSTICE BAYLEY *Barnewall & Cresswell Rep.* IV. 255 Malice in common acceptation means ill-will against a person, but in its legal sense it means a wrongful act done intentionally without just cause or excuse. **1871** MARKBY *Elem. Law* (1874) §226 In the best known definitions of malice it is scarcely distinguishable from intention. **1898** W. F. CRAIES in *Encycl. Laws Eng.* VIII. 77 The meaning of the term malice (*malitia*) in English law has been a question of much difficulty and controversy... It certainly has different meanings with respect to responsibility for civil wrongs and responsibility for crime. **1901** SIR F. POLLOCK *Law of Torts* (ed. 6) 24 Such abuse [of privilege allowed by law on special occasions and for special purposes, where the act is done not in good faith or for the advancement of justice, but from evil motives such as personal enmity] is called 'malice' or 'express malice', and deprives the act of justification... The words 'malice', 'malicious', and 'maliciously' were formerly used in pleading, and thence in forensic and judicial language, in many places where they were superfluous.

† **'malice**, *a.* *Obs. rare.* [f. prec. Cf. OF. *malicement* maliciously.] Full of wrath or ill-will.

c **1475** *Partenay* 3446 So inly malice, full of wrath and yre. *Ibid.* 3537 But Raymounde malice And full angry was.

† **'malice**, *v.* *Obs.* [f. MALICE *sb.*]

1. *trans.* To regard with malice; to seek or desire to injure.

a **1547** SURREY *Compl. louer that defied loue* in *Tottel's Misc.* (Arb.) 8 Thou blinded god (quoth I) forgeue me this offense, Vnwillingly [*ed.* 2 Vnwittingly] I went about to malice thy pretense. **1552** LATIMER *Serm. 3rd Sund. aft. Epiph.* (1584) 314 They would not beleue in hym, but despised and maliced him. **1599** B. JONSON *Ev. Man out of Hum.* v. vii. (1600) Q iiij b, I am so farre from malicing their states That I begin to pittie them. **1600** HOLLAND *Livy* XLII. xv. 1124 But above all other he maliced Eumenes most [L. *Eumeni ante omnes infestus erat*]. **1621** LADY M. WROTH *Urania* 183 At last his sister grew to malice his respect to me. **1653** BAXTER *Chr. Concord* 47, I know they will malice our Union in this Country. **1659** FULLER *App. Inj. Innoc.* (1840) 299 For the Papists, though I malice not their persons,..yet I do..dislike their errors. **1686** W. DE BRITAINE *Hum. Prud.* xvi. 80 None are less Maliced or more applauded than he, who is thought rather happy than able. **1694** E. ELYS in *Lett. Sev. Subj.* 94 To have an Aversion to the Notion..is to Malice or Hate God.

2. *intr.* To entertain malice. Also const. *at*.

1587 TURBERV. *Trag. T.* (1837) 243 Yet fortune seemde to grutche And malice at her featurd shape. **1592** KYD *Sp. Trag.* III. i, My guiltles death will be aueng'd on thee,..that hath malisde thus.

Hence **'maliced** *ppl. a.*, **'malicing** *vbl. sb.*

1601 B. JONSON *Poetaster* Induct. 10 Your forc't stings Would hide them selues within his malic't sides. **1604** DANIEL *Funeral Poem Earl Devonsh.*, Without any private malicing, Or public grievance. *a* **1640** W. FENNER *Sacrifice Faithf.* (1648) 50 Go on in drinking, whoring,..and dicing, hating and malicing, fretting and chafing. **1643** 'F. GREVILLE' *Five Yrs. Jas. I* 73 It concerneth not onely the destruction of the maliced man, but of every man.

malice, variant of MALEASE *Obs.*

maliceful ('mælɪsfʊl), *a.* Chiefly *dial.*: see E.D.D. [f. MALICE *sb.* + -FUL.] = MALICIOUS.

1839 POE *Fall Ho. Usher* Wks. 1864 I. 306 The hermit..was of an obstinate and maliceful turn. **1893** *Nat. Observer* 25 Mar. 468/1 Being maliceful of humour I praised that smile.

† **'maliceless**, *a.* *Obs.* [f. MALICE *sb.* + -LESS.] Without malice.

a **1618** SYLVESTER tr. *Panaretus* 827 Wks. (Grosart) II. 131 When..bad advice (though malice-lesse) Ruins the Friend to whom it meant Redresse. *a* **1684** LEIGHTON *Comm. 1 Pet.* (1850) 204 How few there are that have truly maliceless hearts.

malicho: see MICHING MALICHO.

malicious (mə'lɪʃəs), *a.* Forms: 3 malicius, 4 malycyouse, 4, 6 maliciouse, 5 malicous, malycyowse, maleciouse, 5–6 malycyous, malitius, 5–7 malycious, 6 malysyous, malyciouse, malycieux, malicyous, 6–7 malitious, 4– malicious. [a. OF. *malicius* (mod.F. *malicieux*), ad. L. *malitiōsus*, f. *malitia*: see MALICE *sb.* and -OUS. Cf. Sp. *malicioso*, It. *malizioso*.]

1. Of persons, their dispositions, etc.: Given to malice; addicted to sentiments or acts of ill-will. Now sometimes in milder sense: Given to sportive mischief; inclined to tease.

a **1225** *Ancr. R.* 210 þe attri neddre [sleað] alle þeo ontfule, & alle þeo luðere iðoncked [*MS. Titus* þat beon malicius & liðere aȝain oðere]. *a* **1325** in Horstm. *Altengl. Leg.* (1878) 143 Why artow so malicious Toward god & toward ous. *c* **1440** *Jacob's Well* 90 þe angry, fell, & malycyous man wayteth his leysere, to wrekyn his tene at wylle. **1551** T. WILSON *Logike* (1580) 17 When one for lucre beareth a faire face outwardly, and feedeth inwardly a malicious stomacke. **1607** SHAKS. *Cor.* I. i. 91 Either you must Confesse your selues wondrous Malicious, Or be accus'd of Folly. **1623** BINGHAM *Xenophon* 20 In case any man shewed him kindnesse, or were malitious against him, he would doe all he could, to goe beyond him in either of both. **1667** MILTON *P. L.* IX. 253 Thou knowst..what malicious Foe..seeks to work us woe and shame By sly assault. **1689–90** WOOD *Life* 12 Mar. (O.H.S.) III. 327 Two malitious fellowes were found sticking up a libell reflecting on the fast. **1727** DE FOE *Hist. Appar.* iii. (1840) 23 He is still in being, and still the same malicious Devil. **1880** OUIDA *Moths* xiii. II. 57 She was not very clever, but she was very malicious, which is more successful with society.

Comb. **1642** VICARS *God in Mount* (1644) 55 A most impious and malicious-hearted fellow. **1842** BORROW *Bible in Spain* xxi, A..malicious-looking urchin of about fifteen.

† **b.** Wicked, evil-disposed. *Obs.*

13.. *E. E. Allit. P.* C. 508 So mony malicious mon as mournez þer-inne. *c* **1440** *Alph. Tales* (E.E.T.S.) 38 Amicus hard tell þat his fadur was dead, & att malicious men wold take his heritage fro hym. *c* **1477** CAXTON *Jason* 43 Women one and other properly to speke ben malicious in her werkes.

c. *absol.*

1535 COVERDALE *Ps.* ix. [x.] 15 Break thou yᵉ arme off the vngodly and malycious, search out the wickednesse which he hath done. **1563** *Homilies* II. *Disobedience* v. (1859) 585 A few ambitious and malicious are the authors..of rebellion. **1581** PETTIE tr. *Guazzo's Civ. Conv.* I. (1586) 17 The high judgement of God wil not faile you,..against the malitious. **1745** H. WALPOLE *Lett.* (1846) II. 27 A few malicious, who would have countenanced her to vex him. **1814** CARY *Dante's Purgatory* VI. 84 While now thy living ones In thee abide not without war; and one Malicious gnaws another.

2. Of things, qualities, etc.: Proceeding from or characterized by malice. In early use often: † Evil, wicked. Now sometimes used in a weakened sense: Sportively 'mischievous'. (Cf. MALICE *sb.* 4.)

a **1340** HAMPOLE *Psalter* iii. 7 þe tethe of synful ere þe malycyouse gnawyngs of bakbiters. *c* **1380** WYCLIF *Sel. Wks.* III. 21 þe malicious bisynes of þis world. *c* **1400** *Destr. Troy* 4894 We..manast his messanger with malicous pride. *a* **1533** LD. BERNERS *Huon* lxxxiii. 261 Gerarde, who by his malysyous entent hath done this treason. **1573** G. HARVEY *Letter-bk.* (Camden) 48 A mani of sutch glorius brags and malitius words, utterid of purpose. **1591** SHAKS. *1 Hen. VI*, IV. i. 7 Esteeme none..your Foes, but such as shall pretend Malicious practises against his State. **1651** *Nicholas Papers* (Camden) 273 The private whisper of a malicious groundlesse lye. **1727** DE FOE *Syst. Magic* I. iv. 97 We are sure the Devil does communicate his malicious Proposals of Mischief to Mankind. **1855** MACAULAY *Hist. Eng.* xxii. IV. 733 Those who felt this had learned with malicious delight that the First Lord of the Treasury was named in the confession.

† **b.** Stern, fierce. *Obs.*

1485 CAXTON *Chas. Gt.* 26 He..had hys syght and regarde fyers & malycyous.

3. *Law.* Characterized by 'malice prepense', as in ***malicious damage, mischief, prosecution, slander, striking, waste.***

[**1312** *Rolls of Parlt.* I. 282/2 Qi amercient les malicious Pleintifs.] **1530–1** *Act 22 Hen. VIII*, c. 11 Every suche perverse & malicyous cuttyng downe & brekyng up of any parte or partes of the sayde Dykes. **1541–2** *Act 33 Hen. VIII*, c. 12 §1 Murders manslaughters and other malicious strikinges. **1765** BLACKSTONE *Comm.* I. viii. 126 A special action on the case for a false and malicious prosecution. **1769** *Ibid.* IV. xiv. 243 Malicious mischief, or damage, is the next species of injury to private property. **1785** PALEY *Mor. Philos.* III. II. xii. 236 Malicious slander is the relating of either truth or falshood, with a conscious purpose of creating misery. **1818** CRUISE *Digest* (ed. 2) I. 156 Cutting down trees planted for shelter or ornament; or any other kind of malicious waste. **1839** *Penny Cycl.* XIV. 333/1 Injuries to private property..committed with the malicious intention of injuring the owner of such property. **1866** MR. BARON MARTIN in *L'pool Merc.* 18 Aug., Any wrongful act, done intentionally, without just cause or excuse, was a malicious act.

† **4.** *Astrol.* Of baleful promise. *Obs.*

1413 *Pilgr. Sowle* (Caxton 1483) v. xi. 102 These seuen signes were malicious to oure glorious sonne.

† **5.** *Med.* Malignant, virulent. *Obs.*

c **1400** *Lanfranc's Cirurg.* 207 þere comeþ manie pustulis, & summe þerof ben ful malicious after þe malice of þe matere. **1559** MORWYNG *Evonym.* 58 Thinges..destilled in lead I judge them altogether to be disalowed; because of the ..malicious qualities of the leade. **1598** FLORIO, *Tumore*,..a rising of flesh by some malicious matter or ill humour. *a* **1720** WOODWARD in *Stow's Surv.* (1720) I. I. xxviii. 240/2 Infested by those so fatal and malicious Maladies.

† **6.** Clever, artful. *Obs.*

a **1450** *Knt. de la Tour* (1868) 8 And thus she leued tille she was weddid to a knight, wyse and malicious, that had knowlache of her maners. **1590** SPENSER *F. Q.* I. viii. 23 As a Castle..By subtile engins and malitious slight Is undermined.

maliciously (mə'lɪʃəslɪ), *adv.* [f. prec. + -LY².]

1. In a spirit of malice or ill-will; *occas.* with sportive 'malice'. In early use also: † Wickedly.

1382 WYCLIF *Dan.* xiii. 43 These thingus, whiche these maliciously maken to gydre aȝeinus me. *c* **1440** *Jacob's Well* 14 We denounce acursed alle þo þat malycyously depriue of here ryght..holy cherche. **1555** W. WATREMAN *Fardle Facions* Pref. 15 It hadde been much better for them, neuer ..to haue knowen the waie of truthe, then..so rashely and maliciously to haue forsaken it. **1619** DALTON *Country Just.* lxxv. (1630) 191 Taunts or songs malitiously repeated or sung. **1710** *Tatler* No. 235 ¶2 This kind Parent..is maliciously thankful that none of her Girls are like any of her Neighbours. **1838** DICKENS *Nich. Nick.* xiii, 'Well Nickleby', said Squeers, eyeing him maliciously, 'you think he has run away'. **1849** MACAULAY *Hist. Eng.* viii. II. 381 Wright maliciously told the counsel for the defence that they had only themselves to thank.

† **2.** Violently. *Obs.*

c **1470** *Lament. Mary Magd.* xviii, Thei him assailed so malicioaslie With their scourges and strokes beastiall. **1606** SHAKS. *Ant. & Cl.* III. xiii. 179, I will be trebble-sinewed, hearted, breath'd, And fight maliciously. **1611** —— *Wint. T.* I. ii. 321 A lingring Dram, that should not worke Maliciously, like Poyson.

† **3.** Unpropitiously, unfavourably. *Obs.*

1677 EARL ORRERY *Art of War* 100 Unless the Wind blows maliciously.

4. *Law.* With 'malice prepense'.

1421 in *Calr. Proc. Chanc. Q. Eliz.* I. (1827) Introd. 17 John Wethy..malycyouslych ymagenyd him to slee. **1530–1** *Act 22 Hen. VIII*, c. 11 Dyvers evyll dysposed personnes..maliciously at dyverse and sondry tymes hathe cutte cast downe and broken up dyvers parties of the Dyke. **1670–1** *Act 22 & 23 Chas. II*, c. 7 §1 Where..any person.. shall in the night time malitiously unlawfully and willingly burne..any Ricks [etc.]. **1716** W. HAWKINS *Pleas Crown* I. 106 He may be indicted as having maliciously burned the House of B. **1885** *Law Rep.* Weekly Notes 72/1 The maliciously procuring a bankruptcy is not actionable unless the adjudication is set aside. **1889** LD. JUSTICE BOWEN 23 *Q. B. Div.* 612 'Maliciously'..implies an intention to do an act which is wrongful, to the detriment of another.

maliciousness (mə'lɪʃəsnɪs). [f. MALICIOUS *a.* + -NESS.] The quality or condition of being malicious; malevolence, spitefulness. † Of wounds or poison: Virulence, malignity.

a **1450** *Paston Lett.* I. 97 Other cause he had non to him as fer as I kan knawe, bot awnly for the malissiousness that he hath unto me. **1535** COVERDALE *1 Macc.* vii. 42 Punysh him, acordinge to his maliciousnesse. **1555** EDEN *Decades* 53 The maliciousnes of the veneme consumed. *Ibid.* 122 The malyciousnesse of the venemous wounde. **1600** SURFLET *Country Farm* VI. xiii. 751 If there be many bay trees planted ..all the maliciousnes of the mists will fall vpon their boughes. **1682** LUTTRELL *Brief Rel.* (1857) I. 238 The court being fully satisfied with..the maliciousness of the prosecution. **1791–1823** D'ISRAELI *Cur. Lit.* (1866) 291/1 Who seems much embarrassed by their tiny maliciousness.

malicole, -coly, obs. forms of MELANCHOLY.

‖ **mali'corium.** *Obs.* [L., f. *māl-um* apple + *corium* skin, leather.] The rind of the pomegranate fruit (used medicinally and in the arts).

1727–41 in CHAMBERS *Cycl.* s.v. *Pomegranate.* **1866** in *Treas. Bot.* 712/1. In mod. Dicts.

maliferous (mə'lɪfərəs), *a.* [f. L. *mal-us* bad: see -FEROUS.] Bringing, or producing evil; unwholesome, insalubrious.

1727 BAILEY vol. II, *Maliferous.* **1860** RUSSELL *Diary India* I. 72 That gallant, fine-hearted soldier who..fell a victim to the maliferous climate of China. **1890** A. F. BAILLIE *Kurrachee* vii. 116 He is gazetted to another appointment..in some other District, where the climate is maliferous, and life is a misery. **1894** *Ten Yrs.' Work Outcast London* (Lond. Congreg. Union pamphlet) 44 Poor children..being fortified against the maliferous influences in the midst of which they have to live.

maliform ('meɪlɪfɔrm), *a.* [a. F. *maliforme* apple-shaped, f. L. *māl-um* apple: see -FORM.] Having the form of an apple.

1856 in MAYNE *Expos. Lex.* **1889** in *Syd. Soc. Lex.*

† **maligar.** *Obs.* [Cf. F. *malingre.*] A choice kind of apple. Also *attrib.*

1600 SURFLET *Country Farm* III. xlix. 528 Apples..of a pleasant smell and delightsome taste,..the heroet,.. maligar, rambur [etc.]. **1611** COTGR. (s.v. *Malingre*), *Pomme de malingre*, a sowrish apple, tearmed, the Maligar apple.

1664 EVELYN *Kal. Hort., May* (1679) 16 Apples...Pepins, ..Gilly-flower-apples, the Maligar, &c. **1707–12** MORTIMER *Husb.* (1721) II. 369.

malign (mə'laɪn), *a.* Forms: 4–7 **maligne**, 5 **malyng**, 6 **malygne**, 7– **malign**. [a. OF. *maligne*, *malin* (mod.F. *malin*), ad. L. *malignus* evil-disposed, f. *mal-us* evil. Cf. BENIGN *a.*]

1. Of persons and their dispositions: Characterized by ill-will; desiring, or rejoicing in, the suffering of others; malignant, malevolent. Now *rare*.

c **1450** *Mirour Saluacioun* 1602 Synnere vile & maligne. *c* **1485** *Digby Myst.* III. 428 Spirits malyngny. [? Meant for L. *spiritus maligni*.] *Ibid.* 434 How, how, spirits malyng. **1583** STUBBES *Anat. Abus.* I. Ep. Ded. (1877) 6 Whose gentle fauour..shall counterpoyse..the maligne stomacks and stearn countenances of the other. **1667** MILTON *P. L.* IV. 503, VII. 189. **1674** *Govt. Tongue* VI. §10 Some tempers are so malign, that they wish ill to all, and believe ill of all. **1747** WESLEY *Char. Methodist* 9 The Love of God has purified his heart..from every unkind Temper or malign Affection. **1790** COWPER *Odyss.* XX. 344 Guiltless of heart piercing scoffs Malign. **1862** LYTTON *Str. Story* I. 190 Or whether he was actuated by a malign and impish desire to upset the established laws of decorum.

absol. **1557** *Sarum Primer, Dirige* I j, The maligne [L. *malignus*; Ps. v. 6] shall not dwell neare thee.

2. Of things: Evil in nature and effects; baleful, gravely injurious. †Of sin: Heinous.

c **1315** SHOREHAM *Poems* i. 411 So feawe stondeþ styf To fytte aȝenis senne Maligne. *Ibid.* 1999 Treuþe hys, þat þer no gile be þourwe spousebreche maligne. **1500–20** DUNBAR *Poems* lxxxv. 17 All thing maling we dovne thring, Be sicht of his signakle. **1594** PLAT *Jewell-ho.* III. 18 We shall finde the hop farre to exceede the wormwood in his maligne qualitie. **1603** FLORIO *Montaigne* III. xii. (1632) 586 It [War] is of so ruinous and maligne a Nature; that together with all things els, she ruineth her selfe. *a* **1716** SOUTH *Serm.* (1717) V. 434 A dark malign Shade always obscuring and eclipsing them. **1693** SIR T. P. BLOUNT *Nat. Hist.* 116 Meconium is the courser and weaker [Gum], yet the more malign. **1727** HARTE *Ps.* cvii. 13 Poems 236 The broad expance of heav'n Their canopy, the ground of damp malign, Their bed nocturnal. **1854** LONGF. *Catawba Wine* ix, A poison malign Is such Borgia wine. **1871** R. ELLIS tr. *Catullus* lxviii. 101 Tomb'd in Troy the malign, in Troy the unholy reposing. **1888** BRYCE *Amer. Commw.* III. cxv. 663 A struggle between two forces, the one beneficent, the other malign.

3. Of diseases: Malignant.

1541 R. COPLAND *Galyen's Terap.* 2 D ij b, Suche an vlcere. I call it entyerly malygne & cacoethes. **1563** T. GALE *Antidot.* II. 12 This vnguent is good against old and maligne vlcers. **1622** BACON *Hen. VII* (1876) 12 A malign vapour flew to the heart, and seized the vital spirits. **1671** SALMON *Syn. Med.* III. xxii. 415 It quencheth thirst, and abates the heat of Malign Feavers. **1899** *Allbutt's Syst. Med.* VIII. 813 In cases of so-called 'precocious malign' syphilis.

4. *Astrol.* Having a baleful influence or effect.

1626 BACON *Sylva* §353 Saturn which is a planet Maligne. **1652** GAULE *Magastrom.* 85 Whether the planets have.. those prime elementary qualities..in such different measures..as to make some of them benign, others of them malign in their influences [etc.]. **1667** MILTON *P. L.* VI. 313 Two Planets rushing from aspect maligne Of fiercest opposition. **1738** WESLEY *Ps.* CXXI. v, Thee the Moon's malignest Ray Shall never blast by Night.

b. *transf.*

1605 BACON *Adv. Learn.* II. Ded. §8 This dedicating of foundations and dotations to professory learning hath..had a malign aspect and influence upon the growth of sciences. **1842** S. LOVER *Handy Andy* xvi. 147 The Genius of Disaster, with aspect malign, waved her sable wand.

malign (mə'laɪn), *v.* Forms: 5 **malyngne**, 5–6 **-ygne**, 5–7 **-igne**, 6 *Sc.* **malligne, malyng**, 6–7 *Sc.* **maling**, 6– **malign**. [a. OF. *malignier*, *maliner* to plot, deceive, ad. L. *malign-āre* to do or contrive maliciously, f. *malignus* MALIGN *a.*]

†**1.** *intr.* To speak evil, inveigh (*against*). *Obs.*

1426 LYDG. in *Pol. Poems* (Rolls) II. 135 Ageins which noman may maligne, But that he stondith in the veray ligne, ..as descendid is Of the stok and blode of seint Lowys. —— *De Guil. Pilgr.* 20391 And who that euere ageyn malygnes, They be but markys [etc.]. **1526** *Pilgr. Perf.* (W. de W. 1531) 223 Luther and his adherentes, that moost of all maligneth agaynst this present article. **1549** *Compl. Scot.* iv. 30 Parchance sum inuyful detrakkers vil maling contrar me, sayand that [etc.].

†**2.** To entertain malice or ill-will. Const. *against*, *at*. *Obs.*

1494 FABYAN *Chron.* v. cxxiv. 103 Euer after they malygned agayne Theodobert. **1530** PALSGR. 632/1, I malygne agaynst one, I beare hym malyce. **1577–87** HOLINSHED *Chron.* III. 865/1, I nothing maligne for that you haue doone to me. **1652** C. B. STAPYLTON *Herodian* XVII. 142 Maligning much at this her Daughters Honour.

†**3.** To plot; to contrive (*against*). *Obs.*

1430–40 LYDG. *Bochas* IX. i. (1494) E v b, Whan any kingdom fyll in rebellyon Or gan malygne ageyn rome toun. *a* **1450** *Paston Lett.* I. 96 Hugh Wythom hath said he wold be in rest and peese with me, and not to maligne agayn me otherwise than lawe and right wold. **1494** FABYAN *Chron.* v. cii. 77 Thyse .ii. Bretherne newely maligned agayn theyr neuwe Theodobert,..and entendyd by theyr malyce to byreue hym of the Lordshyp of Austracy. **1539** CROMWELL in Merriman *Life & Lett.* 21 Jan. (1902) II. 168 The said bishop..contynually studyeth and maligneth, howe he might annoye or greve hym. *a* **1578** LINDESAY (Pitscottie) *Chron. Scot.* (S. T. S.) II. 85 They..still mallignit aganis the quene.

†**4.** *trans.* To regard with hatred or bitter dislike. Also, to resent, take amiss. *Obs.*

1513 MORE *Rich. III* Wks. 37/1 The Queene and the Lordes of her bloode whiche highlye maligned the kynges kinred. **1560** BECON *Catech.* Wks. 1564 I. 411 b, S. Stephen ..did so litle malign his enemies, that he did not only frely forgeue them, but he also prayed vnto God for them. *a* **1594** KYD *Sp. Trag.* III. ii. 34 What cause had they Horatio to maligne? **1604** R. CAWDREY *Table Alph.*, *Maligne*, to hate, with purpose to hurt. **1611** SPEED *Theat. Gt. Brit.* xlvi. (1614) 92/1 The people of Dublin sent for him, and made him their king, which Mure-card King of Ireland maligning raised war. **1662** STILLINGFL. *Orig. Sacr.* II. i. §4 Can we think that a Nation and religion so maligned as the Jewish were, could have escaped discovery, if [etc.]. **1667** SOUTH *Twelve Serm.* (1697) II. 35 An ungrounded, odious, detestable Interest, so heartily, and so justly maligned.

†**5.** To regard with envy; to grudge, begrudge. Very frequent during the 17th c.

1590 NASHE *Almond for Parrat* 3 Didst thou so muche malign the successeful thriuings of the Gospell, that thou shouldst filche thyselfe..into our gouernement? **1594** KYD *Cornelia* IV. ii. 75 And rendring thanks to heauen as we goe, For brideling those that dyd maligne our glory, Lets to the Capitoll. **1599** HAKLUYT *Voy.* II. I. 285 The King of Spaine, ..maligning the quiet trafique which they vsed to and in the dominions..vnder the obedience of the Great Turke, had [etc.]. **1611** BIBLE *Ecclus.* xlv. 18 Strangers conspired together against him, and maligned [Gr. ἐζήλωσαν] him in the wildernesse. **1638** H. SHIRLEY *Mart. Souldier* III. iv. in Bullen *O. Pl.* I. 218 No, no; the envious Gods Maligne our happinesse. **1645** MILTON *Colast.* Wks. (1847) 228/2 This odious fool..maligning that anything should be spoke or understood above his own genuine baseness. **1653** H. COGAN tr. *Pinto's Trav.* lvi. 220 They reap no benefit by their maligning the prosperity of others. **1706** PHILLIPS (ed. Kersey), To *Malign*, to envy; as *To malign one's Happiness*.

†**b.** *fig.* *Obs.*

1601 ? MARSTON *Pasquil & Kath.* II. 165 But now no more, bright day malings our loue. **1613** PURCHAS *Pilgrimage* III. i. 188 The scarcitie of wood and water, with the barrennesse of the Soyle..shew how it is maligned of the Elements. **1661** BOYLE *Style of Script.* (1675) 87 Those Grounds, whose Surface bears no Fruit-Trees, (too much malign'd by the Arsenical and resembling fumes).

6. To speak ill of (one), to traduce, slander.

1647 CLARENDON *Hist. Reb.* I. §189 He was always maligned and persecuted by those who were of the Calvinian faction. **1718** *Entertainer* No. 30. 205 He is represented as a Tyrant and his Ministers malign'd of Persecution. *a* **1758** J. EDWARDS *Hist Redempt.* III. ii. (1793) 350 No religion ever was so maligned, age after age. **1831** BREWSTER *Newton* (1855) II. xv. 47 The party who had first disturbed the tranquillity of science by maligning its most distinguished ornament. **1882** MISS BRADDON *Mt. Royal* II. x. 238, I don't want to malign a man who has treated me with exceptional kindness and cordiality.

malignance (mə'lɪgnəns). [f. MALIGNANT *a.*: see -ANCE.] = MALIGNANCY.

1641 MILTON *Ch. Govt.* II. iii. Wks. 1851 III. 171 The minister..speeds him betimes to overtake that diffus'd malignance with some gentle potion of admonishment. **1743** FIELDING *J. Wild* III. x, They discharge all their malignance outwardly. **1804** ANNA SEWARD *Lett.* (1811) VI. 157 Its satire, which gratifies human malignance. **1895** *Chamb. Jrnl.* XII. 696/2 This is on a piece with Brant Dalton's cowardly malignance toward one who is fighting for him.

malignancy (mə'lɪgnənsɪ). [f. MALIGNANT *a.*: see -ANCY.] The quality of being malignant.

1. Disaffection to rightful authority. *Obs.* exc. *Hist.* as the hostile designation for sympathy with the royalist cause. (Cf. MALIGNANT B.)

1644 (*title*) Medicine for Malignancy: or Parliament Pill serving to Purge out the Malignant humours of men disaffected to the Republic. **1645** in Greenshields *Annals Lesmahagow* (1864) 153 The Lady Marquesse of Douglasse, ..being gravely examined anent her malignancie and obstinate continewance in the profession of poperie. **1647** MAY *Hist. Parl.* II. i. 3 The malignancy, which at that time began to appear in people. **1649** MILTON *Eikon.* ix. Wks. 1851 III. 404 Many of the Lords and some few of the Commons, either intic'd away by the King, or overaw'd by the sence of thir own Malignancy not prevailing, deserted the Parlament. **1660** BURNEY *Κέρδ. Δῶρον* Ep. Ded. (1661) 2 Each holy text that mentioned a king, was then a note of Malignancy.

2. *Path.* Of a disease, morbid growth, etc. (Cf. MALIGNANT A. 2.)

1685 EVELYN *Mrs. Godolphin* 148 There now appearing a kind of Erisypulus..the malignancy grew desperate. **1706** PHILLIPS (ed. Kersey), *Malignancy*, malignant Nature or Quality; as *The Malignancy of a Feaver*. **1724** DE FOE *Mem. Cavalier* (1840) 26 A slow..fever..turned to a burning malignancy. **1826** S. COOPER *First Lines Surg.* (ed. 5) 202 It cannot be cured without an operation; but it is quite free from malignancy. **1898** J. HUTCHINSON in *Arch. Surg.* IX. 295 The tumour..was..so suggestive of malignancy that amputation was contemplated.

3. Malign or baleful character; unpropitiousness; noxiousness, deleteriousness.

1601 SHAKS. *Twel. N.* II. i. 4 My starres shine darkely ouer me; the malignancie of my fate, might perhaps distemper yours. **1656** STANLEY *Hist. Philos.* v. (1701) 207/2 Jupiter [is placed] next Saturn, to abate his Malignancy. **1727** SWIFT *What passed in London* Wks. 1755 III. I. 187 There might be a pestilential malignancy in the air, occasioned by the comet.

4. Malignant or intensely malevolent disposition; envenomed hostility; desire to inflict injury or suffering.

1640 HOWELL *Dodona's Grove* 109 His eldest Graff succeeded him a while in Royall favour; but he quickly fell, by the malignancie of great ones. **1683** DRYDEN *Life Plutarch* 43 The meer malignancy of a spirit delighted naturally in mischief. **1706** *Reflex. upon Ridicule* 390 Penetration gives her more artifice and malignancy. **1782** ELIZ. BLOWER *Geo. Bateman* III. 118 The malignancy of disappointed playwrights. **1856** FROUDE *Hist. Eng.* (1858) I. i. 17 A war unequalled in history for its fierce and determined malignancy. **1897** MARY KINGSLEY *W. Africa* 505 If a man were..shot with an arrow, the cause of death is clearly the malignancy of the person using these weapons.

5. An instance of malignancy; a malignant quality.

1652 BP. HALL *Myst. Godl.* §7. 34 O Saviour, abundantly justified in the spirit against all the malignancies of men and Devils! **1672** GREW *Idea Philos. Hist. Plants* §8 What may best correct their Malignancies, or inforce their Virtues. **1869** BUSHNELL *Wom. Suffrage* vii. 141 They let in also little malignancies that are poisonous. **1899** *Daily News* 29 May 8/5 The merits of whose members compensate for the malignancies of their [golf] course.

malignant (mə'lɪgnənt), *a.* and *sb.* [ad. late L. *malignant-em*, pr. pple. of *malignāre*, *-ārī* to do mischief, injure maliciously (see MALIGN *v.*). Cf. OF. *malignant*.

Sense 1 is derived from the use of *malignantes* in the Vulgate as the rendering of Heb. *m'rē'īm*, pr. pple. of *hērēaʿ* to do evil (to): see MALIGN *v.* Senses 2–4 represent uses of the L. *malignus*: see MALIGN *a.*]

A. *adj.*

†**1.** Disposed to rebel against God or against constituted authority; disaffected, malcontent. *Obs.*

the church malignant: a patristic designation for the followers of antichrist, often applied by the early Protestants to the Church of Rome. Cf. F. *église malignante* in Godefroy. (Alluding to Ps. xxv[i]. 5, Vulg. *ecclesiam malignantium*, Eng. Bible 'the congregation of euill doers'.)

1542–5 BRINKLOW *Lament.* (1874) 116 Your other brethern of the Romishe churches, or church malygnant. **1548** UDALL *Erasm. Par.* Pref. to Rdr., Whosoeuer is not of an extreme malignaunt stomake against the due settyng forth of Goddes woorde. **1553** KENNEDY *Compend. Tract.* in *Wodrow Soc. Misc.* (1844) 115 The Kirk malignant. *a* **1563** BECON *God's Word & Man's Inv.* Wks. 1563 III. 394 Mans inuention is the execrable rule of the children of Satans kingdome, that is, of yᵉ Church malignant. **1604** SHAKS. *Oth.* V. ii. 353 In Aleppo once, Where a malignant, and a Turbond-Turke Beate a Venetian, and traduc'd the State. **1621** BP. MOUNTAGU *Diatribæ* 312, I have good cause to ranke you with the formost of those malignant ones. **1659** J. ARROWSMITH *Chain Princ.* 173 Logicians say of this particle Not, that it is of a malignant nature; Divines know that the malignant Church is much built up by such negatives.

absol. **1778** BP. LOWTH *Transl. Isaiah* xxix. 24 (ed. 12) 54 The malignant [A.V. They that murmured] shall attend to instruction. **1846** J. BAXTER *Libr. Pract. Agric.* (ed. 4) I. p. xvii, Excesses in which the malignant indulged under the guise of patriotism [*c* 1832].

b. *spec.* Applied between 1641 and 1660 by the supporters of the Parliament and the Commonwealth to their adversaries. (See B. b.)

1641 *Remonstr. St. Kingd.* 11 The unexpected reconciliation was most acceptable to all the Kingdome, except to the malignant partie, whereof the Archbishop and the Earle of St[r]afford being heads, they and their faction begun [etc.]. *Ibid.* 24 Thus with Eliah, we are called by this malignant party the troublers of the State. **1642** J. M[ARSH] *Argt. conc. Militia* 28 The Parliament defend the king and kingdom; and the malignant party use all their skill to make both miserable. **1659** *Clarke Papers* (Camden) IV. 169 Mannaged wholly by the Cavaleere Malignant party. **1708** SWIFT *Sacram. Test* Wks. 1755 II. I. 133 In those times, when the church of England was malignant.

c. In 1642 Charles I retorted the application of the epithet upon the Parliamentary party.

1642 CHAS. I *Sp.* 27 Sept. in Rushw. *Hist. Coll.* (1721) V. 21 How I have been dealt with by a Powerful malignant Party in this Kingdom, whose Designs are no less than to destroy my Person and Crown. **1642** *Declar. Lords & Com.* ibid. 42 Whereas the Parliament, under the Name of a Malignant Party, is charged with an Endeavour to..corrupt the Allegiance of the King's Subjects.

2. Of a disease: Characterized by extreme virulence; exceptionally contagious or infectious. Now chiefly used as the distinctive epithet of a definite variety of a disease, as in ***malignant cholera***, ***malignant small-pox***, etc.

malignant growth, tumour: in mod. use applied to carcinomata and sarcomata, forming a class 'characterized by their rapidity of growth,..by the extension to the lymphatic glands, and by their recurrence in situ and in distant organs after removal' (*Syd. Soc. Lex.*).

1568 SKEYNE *The Pest* A iij, Quhilk is generit within vs, or of vther causis [than the air] is callit ane Malignant feuer. **1601** SHAKS. *All's Well* II. i. 114 Hearing your high Maiestie is toucht With that malignant cause. **1608** TOPSELL *Serpents* (1658) 629 The malignant symptomes were all evacuated. **1706** PHILLIPS (ed. Kersey), *Malignant Disease*, is that which rages more vehemently, and continues longer than its Nature seems to incline. *Ibid.* s.v. *Tumour*, Malignant Tumours, those that are always accompany'd with extraordinary and dreadful Symptoms. *a* **1776** R. JAMES *Diss. Fevers* (1778) 130 That species of sore throat which is ridiculously called malignant. **1799** *Med. Jrnl.* II. 499 The malignant small-pox, which prevailed..during the year 1798. **1804** ABERNETHY *Surg. Obs.* 45 The wound degenerated into a malignant ulcer. **1807–26** S. COOPER *First Lines Surg.* (ed. 5) 60 The malignant or gangrenous erysipelas. **1873** T. H. GREEN *Introd. Pathol.* (ed. 2) 108 The malignant properties of a tumour may manifest themselves either in the tissues immediately adjacent to it or..in more distant parts. *Ibid.* 157 'Cancerous' and 'malignant' have come to be regarded by many as synonymous terms. **1885** *West. Daily Press* 19 Jan. 7/5 The woolsorters' disease, known also as splenic fever, malignant pustule, and Siberian plague. **1897** *Allbutt's Syst. Med.* II. 104 Several forms of malignant measles are met with. **1898** J. HUTCHINSON in *Arch. Surg.* IX. 327 There was no definite history of tuberculosis or of malignant growths in the family.

b. *absol.* A malignant fever.

1825 GOOD *Study Med.* (ed. 2) II. 164 It is the *febris gastrico-nervosa* of Professor Frank, who justly regards it as

an intense variety of the ordinary autumnal malignant of temperate climates.

3. Having an evil influence. Chiefly *Astrol.* and with reference to magical agencies = MALIGN (whence *transf.* in ***malignant aspect***). Formerly also of material substances, plants, etc.: Poisonous, deleterious.

1591 SHAKS. *1 Hen. VI*, IV. v. 6 O malignant and ill-boading Starres. —— *Two Gent.* III. i. 238 No more: vnles the next word that thou speak'st Haue some malignant power vpon my life. **1608** D. T. T[UVIL] *Ess. Pol. & Mor.* 21 b, The malignant aspect of any person in authority towards his inferiour, is thought a sufficient warrant for euery man to wrong him. **1654** BRAMHALL *Just Vind.* vi. (1661) 146 Where the influence of Religion is malignant. **1667** MILTON *P.L.* x. 662 Taught the fixt Thir influence malignant when to showre. **1691** RAY *Creation* I. (1692) 103 The noxious and malignant Plants. **1692** —— *Disc.* ii. (1732) 106 Melted Snow which gives it [the water] that malignant Quality. **1704** SWIFT *Batt. Bks.* Wks. 1751 I. 210 An atramentous Quality of most malignant Nature was seen to distil from his Lips. **1752** YOUNG *Brothers* I. i, A comet, with malignant blaze, Denouncing ruin. **1756** BURKE *Vind. Nat. Soc.* Wks. I. 70 The close vapour of these malignant minerals. **1765** T. HUTCHINSON *Hist. Mass.* I. 150 A witch ..charged with having..a malignant touch. **1799** CAMPBELL *Pleas. Hope* I. 34 Every woe, Shot from malignant Stars to earth below. **1822** GOOD *Study Med.* II. 221 Attended by nurses or midwives, who had previously attended the latter [i.e. puerperal patients] without sufficiently changing their malignant dress. **1876** FREEMAN *Norm. Conq.* V. xxiv. 381 The malignant genius of Flambard. **1887** RUSKIN *Præterita* II. 38 The bise, now first letting one feel what malignant wind could be.

absol. **1800** COLERIDGE *Piccolom.* I. ii, This is your Venus! and the sole malignant [orig. *der Maleficus*], The only one that harmeth you, is Doubt.

4. Characterized by malignity or intense ill-will; keenly desirous of the suffering or misfortune of another, or of others generally.

1592 tr. *Junius on Rev.* ix. 3 The malignant spirits invading the world. **1594** SHAKS. *Rich. III*, II. ii. 52 Two Mirrors of his Princely semblance, Are crack'd in pieces, by malignant death. **1613** —— *Hen. VIII*, I. ii. 141 His will is most malignant, and it stretches Beyond you to your friends. **1625** BACON *Ess., Envy* (Arb.) 513 Cains Enuy, was the more vile, and Malignant, towards his brother Abel. **1667** MILTON *P. L.* XII. 538 So shall the World goe on, To good malignant, to bad men benigne. **1751** JOHNSON *Rambler* No. 87 ¶12 An author cannot..be often suspected of any malignant intention to insult his readers with his knowledge or his wit. **1778** JOHNSON in Boswell *Life* (1831) IV. 140 An old gentleman who was absolutely malignant. He really wished evil to others, and rejoiced at it. **1792** BURKE *Lett., to R. Burke* (1844) III. 368 It is full of the most malignant insinuations. **1866** DK. ARGYLL *Reign Law* vi. (1871) 278 The loving may become malignant: the simple-minded may become suspicious. **1897** MARY KINGSLEY *W. Africa* 505 Death was always the consequence of the action of some malignant spirit.

†**b.** Wickedly disposed, obstinately criminal.

1784 COWPER *Task* II. 158 But where all Stand chargeable with guilt,..God..May punish, if He please, the less, to warn The more malignant.

B. *sb.* One who is disaffected towards rightful authority, a malcontent. †In early use also: One who is ill-disposed toward true religion.

1597 HOOKER *Eccl. Pol.* v. ii. §4 There are of these wise malignants some, who have vouchsafed it [religion] their marvellous favourable countenance. **1617** HALES *Serm.* 29 Diverse malignants there are, who lie in wait to espie where our reasons on which we build are weake. **1716** ADDISON *Freeholder* No. 8 ¶2 One may..discover, among the Malignants of the Sex, a face that seems to have been naturally designed for a Whig lady... Would the pretty Malcontent be persuaded to love her King and Country, it would [etc.]. **1776** TRUMBULL in Sparks *Corr. Amer. Rev.* (1853) I. 269 Our internal malignants may be permitted to do many injurious and insidious things. **1862** MERIVALE *Rom. Emp.* (1865) VII. lix. 243 Once more he charged Josephus to summon the malignants. **1884** J. COLBORNE *Hicks Pasha* 115 It is suggested to us by the Egyptian officers that these woods are full of malignants.

b. Used by opponents as a designation for a member of the party which supported Charles I against the Parliament; a Royalist, Cavalier. Also, in religious sense, applied by Puritans and Covenanters to their ecclesiastical adversaries. (The two applications are often coincident.) Now *Hist.*

1642 CHAS. I *Declar.* in Rushw. *Hist. Coll.* (1721) V. 76 That to be a Traitor (which is defined, and every Man understands) should be no Crime; and to be called a Malignant (which no Body knows the Meaning of) should be Ground enough for close Imprisonment? **1642-3** EARL OF NEWCASTLE *Declar.* ibid. 134 The second Charge is, That my Army consists of Papists and other Malignants. **1644** QUARLES *Barnabas & B.* 128 His studied prayers shew him to be a high malignant. **1644** *Weekly Intell.* No. 68. 548 The country is full of Malignants. **1651** BAXTER *Inf. Bapt.* 233, I undertake..to defend the..Dominion of my Lord, whose name is King of Kings..(not onely the greatest of Kings, as some Malignants do interpret it, as if others were, though lesser, yet not subordinate). **1670** —— *Cure Ch. Div.* Pref. II. §6 He was no Malignant nor intended to gird at Godliness. **1743** J. GLAS *Treat. Lords Supper* II. iii. 34 The holy One of God passed for a Deceiver and a Samaritan, or malignant. **1874** GREEN *Short Hist.* viii. §10. 567 Catholics and 'Malignants', as those who had fought for the King were called, were alone excluded from the franchise.

malignantly (məˈlɪgnəntlɪ), *adv.* [f. MALIGNANT *a.* + -LY^2.] In a malignant manner.

1606 WARNER *Alb. Eng.* XVI. ci. 401 Nor beate we here malignantly at sacred Beauties Luster. **1607** SHAKS. *Cor.* II. iii. 191 If he should still malignantly remaine Fast Foe toth' Plebeij. **1634** SIR T. HERBERT *Trav.* 211 [One tree] I tasted of, which..malignantly bit and wronged my mouth and lips. **1745** W. THOMPSON *Sickness* I. 337 Malignantly delighted, dire Disease Surveys the glittering pest, and grimly smiles. **1855** MACAULAY *Hist. Eng.* xvii. IV. 50 Her powers of seduction and intimidation were malignantly extolled.

b. In the manner of a malignant.

1645 *Answ. Prynne's Quest. Ch. Govt.* in Prynne *Irish Discov. Wand. Blazing Stars* 42 The greatest part..are thought to be Popishly or Malignantly inclined.

†**maˈlignantness.** *Obs.*$^{-0}$ [f. MALIGNANT *a.* + -NESS.] = MALIGNANCY.

1727 BAILEY vol. II, *Malignantness*, hurtfulness, mischievousness, malignant nature or quality, ill-will.

malignation (mælɪgˈneɪʃən). Also 5 **malignacion, malynacyon.** [n. of action f. late L. *malignāre*: see MALIGN *v.*]

†**1.** Feeling of dislike or ill-will. *Obs.*

c **1470** HARDING *Chron.* VI. i, So stronge then was this generacion None durst it noye for theyr malignacion. *c* **1485** *Digby Myst.* (1882) III. 128 þat..ony moteryng aȝens me make with malynacyon.

†**2.** ? A malefic incantation. *Obs.*

1652 GAULE *Magastrom.* 269 Carpocrates..used.. malignations, inductions, illictations, &c.

3. The action of maligning or slandering. *rare.*

1836 MRS. GORE *Mrs. Armytage* III. 21 Mrs. Armytage.. suffered him to proceed with his malignations. **1843** G. S. FABER *Sacr. Calend. Prophecy* (1844) I. p. xvi, An Extensive Suppression of Evidence which stood opposed to the author's purpose of malignation.

†**maligne.** *Obs.* Forms: 5 **malygny, malynge, malyngne.** [a. OF. *maligne* sb., f. *maligne* MALIGN *a.*] Malice, wickedness.

a **1460** *Gregory's Chron.* in *Hist. Coll. Citizen Lond.* (Camden) 125 Welle and trewly whythe owte any fraude or malygny [*Chron. in Julius B.* i *reads* malengyne]. *Ibid.* 150 With owte fraude, desepsyon, and malynge. *c* **1485** *Digby Myst.* (1882) III. 720 þat we may com to your blysse gloryfyed from malyngne.

maligner (məˈlaɪnə(r)). Also 5 **malyngnour.** [f. MALIGN *v.* + -ER^1.] One who maligns, in various senses of the vb.; †one who bears ill-will (*obs.*); a traducer, slanderer.

c **1425** *Found. St. Bartholomew's* (E.E.T.S.) 16 [He] ȝaue sharpe sentence aȝenste contrary malyngnours. **1526** *Pilgr. Perf.* (W. de W. 1531) 218 b, I have hated the congregacyon of maligners [= Ps. xxv. 17 Vulg. *ecclesiam malignantium*]. *c* **1557** ABP. PARKER *Ps.* xxxvii. 102 Maligners all shall haue a fall, They shall be all deepe rooted out. [Cf. Vulgate: *qui malignantur, exterminabuntur.*] **1621** BP. MOUNTAGU *Diatribæ* 483 Maligners at, and detayners of the Church-Portion in Tithes. **1624** CAPT. SMITH *Virginia* III. xi. 86 A most crafty fellow and his ancient Maligner. **1742** RICHARDSON *Pamela* IV. 220 In a better Sense I speak it than the Maligner spoke it of Job. **1889** *Sat. Rev.* 23 Mar. 335/1 He might handle the maligners of quiet women and men as they deserve.

malignify (məˈlɪgnɪfaɪ), *v. rare.* [f. L. *malign-us* malign + *-ficāre*: see -FY.] *trans.* To render malign.

1613 JACKSON *Creed* I. xxx. §4. 206 Stubbornenesse is but a strong hope malignified, or..growne wilde and out of kinde. **1638** CHILLINGW. *Relig. Prot.* I. Answ. Pref. §29 As they [errors] were qualified or malignified with good or bad circumstances. **1829** SOUTHEY *Sir T. More* I. 258 So dreadful are the effects of a strong faith malignified.

maˈligning, *ppl. a.* [f. MALIGN *v.* + -ING^2.] That maligns (see the vb.).

c **1425** *Found. St. Bartholomew's* (E.E.T.S.) 49 The malignyng ennemy went his way. **1687** SHADWELL *Juvenal* x. 171 Vows from the maligning Gods obtein'd. **1871** R. ELLIS tr. *Catullus* v. 2 Sour severity, tongue of eld maligning.

†**maˈlignious,** *a. Obs. rare*$^{-1}$. [f. MALIGN *a.* + -IOUS. Cf. It. *malignoso.*] Of malicious speech.

1578 FLORIO *1st Fruites* Ep. Ded., Being bold under your honours patronage to shield me with defence against such carping, blustering, and malignious tongues.

malignity (məˈlɪgnɪtɪ). Also 4 **malignitee, malygnitee,** 6 **malygnyte, malignite, malygnitie,** 7 **malignitie.** [a. OF. *malignité*, ad. L. *malignitās*, f. *malignus* MALIGN *a.*: see -ITY.]

1. Wicked and deep-rooted ill-will or hatred; intense and persistent desire to cause suffering to another person; propensity to this feeling.

c **1386** CHAUCER *Pars. T.* ¶439 Thanne comth malignitee thurgh which a man anoyeth his neighebor priuely. **1533-4** *Act 25 Hen. VIII*, c. 12 Persons..whiche beare malice and malignite to al the kinges procedinges in the said deuorse. **1593** R. HARVEY *Philad.* 17 Jealousie and malignity are two blinde guids. **1611** BIBLE *Transl. Pref.* ¶3 Neither is there any likelihood, that enuie and malignitie died, and were buried with the ancient. **1641** *Remonstr. St. Kingd.* 3 The Commons..do yet finde an abounding Malignity, and opposition in those parties, and factions, who have been the cause of those evils. **1775** JOHNSON *Let. to Mrs. Thrale* 21 July, There are few things that are worthy of anger, and still fewer that can justify malignity. **1797** MRS. RADCLIFFE *Italian* iv. (1826) 25 A dark malignity overspread the features of the monk. **1803** WELLINGTON in Gurw. *Desp.* (1837) II. 300 The falsehood and malignity of the charge. **1818** HAZLITT *Eng. Poets* iii. (1870) 84 Satan is not the principle of malignity, or of abstract love of evil. **1849** MACAULAY *Hist. Eng.* i. I. 87 He..felt towards those whom he had deserted that peculiar malignity which has, in all ages, been characteristic of apostates. **1862** STANLEY *Jew. Ch.* (1877) I. v. 92 His flight is occasioned rather by the malignity of his countrymen than by the enmity of the Egyptians.

b. *pl.* Malignant feelings or actions.

a **1529** SKELTON *Col. Cloute* 541 Raylynge haynously And dysdaynously Of preestly dygnytes, But theyr malygnytes. **1607** CARPENTER *Plaine Mans Plough* 212 Nor would the Diuell..surcease..his cursed malignities against Christ. **1861** HOLLAND *Less. Life* xv. 220 If they..clothe these black malignities in silken phrases we hear them with a certain kind of pleasure.

2. Wickedness, heinousness. *arch.*

1534 MORE *Comf. agst. Trib.* II. Wks. 1199/2 We..are consumed & wasted & come to nought in our malygnitie. **1654** BRAMHALL *Just Vind.* iii. (1661) 33 A title..laid aside by Protestants, not so much for any malignity that was in it, as for the ill sounds sake. **1684** *Contempl. St. Man* II. x. (1699) 235 So great is the Malignity of a Mortal Sin. **1702** *Eng. Theophrast.* 180 We imitate the good out of emulation, and the bad out of our natural corruption and malignity. **1860** PUSEY *Min. Proph.* 178 The more God reveals to any, what He Is,..the more utter malignity it is..to have indeed said to Him, 'On Thy terms I will have none of Thee'.

3. Noxiousness, deleteriousness. *arch.*

1605 TIMME *Quersit.* I. xv. 77 Coagulated salts or tartar.. doe reach to the uppermost degree of their malignity. **1617** MORYSON *Itin.* I. 250 They say, that the Owes of the Sea doe here much increase the malignitie of the aire. **1626** BACON *Sylva* §74, I conceive that Opium and the like, make the Spirits flie rather by Malignity, than by Cold. **1656** EVELYN *Diary* (1850) I. 316 Cinders..deprived of their sulphur and arsenic malignity. **1705** ADDISON *Italy* 230 The Sides of the Grotto are mark'd with Green, as high as the Malignity of the Vapour reaches. **1712** —— *Spect.* No. 457 ¶3 The Lady Blast..has such a particular Malignity in her Whisper, that it blights like an Easterly Wind. **1707-12** MORTIMER *Husb.* (1721) I. 251 Some propose to Macerate them [acorns] in Water first, to extract their Malignity. **1777** BURKE *Lett. to Sheriffs of Bristol* Wks. III. 136 The other [statute] (for a partial suspension of the *Habeas Corpus*) appears to me of a much deeper malignity. **1858** HAWTHORNE *Fr. & It. Note-Bks.* (1872) I. 54 The atmosphere certainly has a peculiar quality of malignity.

4. Of diseases or wounds: Malignant character, malignancy.

1646 SIR T. BROWNE *Pseud. Ep.* II. iii. 73 Wounds which are made with weapons excited by the Loadstone, contract a malignity, and become of more difficult cure. **1670** WALTON *Lives* III. 225 He fell into a long and sharp sickness ..from the malignity of which he was never recovered. **1747** BERKELEY *Tar-water in Plague* Wks. III. 481 An erysipelas, which sheweth a degree of malignity nearest to the plague. **1759** ROBERTSON *Hist. Scot.* IV. Wks. 1813 I. 300 The vigour of his constitution surmounted the malignity of his disease. **1806** *Med. Jrnl.* XV. 311 The natural small-pox, which almost every year desolated Mexico and Peru, has lost its malignity in those climates. **1865** *Cornh. Mag.* XI. 599 Typhus fever..has assumed unwonted activity and malignity. **1897** *Allbutt's Syst. Med.* IV. 836 Early implication of neighbouring portions of the larynx..points to malignity.

malignly (məˈlaɪnlɪ), *adv.* [f. MALIGN *a.* + -LY^2.] In a malign manner.

1. With malicious or evil intention.

1543 BALE *Yet a Course Rom. Fox* 52 Soche are euermore the vnworthye wayes of thys worlde, malygnelye to blame menne for ther wele doynge. **1670** MILTON *Hist. Eng.* v. *Ethelwolf*, The Eastern and worst part was malignly afforded to the Father. **1737** POPE *Hor. Epist.* II. i. 339 Yet lest you think I..praise malignly Arts I cannot reach, Let me [etc.]. **1741** SHENSTONE *Judgm. Hercules* 117 Her thoughts, to other's charms malignly blind. **1876** G. MEREDITH *Beauch. Career* II. v. 74 The object malignly called the Briton. **1881** MRS. C. PRAED *Policy & P.* II. 36 The old man chuckled malignly.

2. Unpropitiously, perniciously.

1828 in WEBSTER.

malignment (məˈlaɪnmənt). *rare.* [f. MALIGN *v.* + -MENT.] The act of maligning.

1885 *Century Mag.* XXX. 675 That recrimination and malignment of motive.

†**maˈlignous,** *a. Obs. rare*$^{-1}$. [f. L. *malign-us* MALIGN *a.* + -OUS.] = MALIGNANT.

1610 BARROUGH *Meth. Physick* v. xi. (1617) 294 It mightily discusseth the malignous humour which exciteth the Carbuncle.

malihini (mɑːlɪˈhiːnɪ). [Hawaiian *malihini* stranger.] In Hawaii, a stranger, a newcomer; a beginner, a novice.

1914 *Outing* LXIV. 26/1 A couple of canoes are launching ..where the neophytes, the 'malihini', learn their first lessons in riding the rollers. **1966** *Surfer* VII. 39 Hawkshaw rode tandem with two malihinis (beginners) on his shoulders. **1967** J. SEVERSON *Great Surfing* Gloss., *Malihini*, a newcomer to the Hawaiian Islands. Newcomers to the sport of surfing are also referred to as malihinis.

‖**malik** (ˈmælɪk). Also **melik.** [Arab. *mālik*, pr. pple. of *malaka* to possess, rule.] The chief or headman of a village or other community in parts of India and Central Asia.

1855 H. H. WILSON *Gloss. Judic. & Rev. Terms*, *Malik*,.. a master, an owner,..or a person having a beneficial and hereditary interest in the revenue paid by the cultivators, and responsible to the government for its share; hence considered applicable, in Bengal, to Zamindars, and in the north-west provinces to the head man of a village. **1897** *Daily News* 14 June 5/7 Two maliks were sent ahead by him to Maizar. **1901** *Scotsman* 11 Mar. 9/1 Government has been giving a good round sum to the Maliks yearly. **1920** *Blackw. Mag.* Nov. 669/1 Each hilla, or village, has its sheik, each group of hillas is under a melik.

Hence ‖**malikana** (mælɪ'kɑːnə), a pension or retaining fee paid to an Indian chief or headman.

1846 H. H. WILSON *Brit. India* II. 140 He was accordingly allowed to reside at Puri,..upon a yearly malikana.

malilla, malillio, variant forms of MANILLE.

malincolia, -coly(e, obs. ff. MELANCHOLIA, -LY.

malincolyous, obs. form of MELANCHOLIOUS.

Malines (mæ'liːn). [The name of a town (also called MECHLIN) in Belgium.] **1.** In full ***Malines lace*** = Mechlin lace. In full ***Malines*** (also ***Maline***) ***net***, a net made for millinery or veils.

1833 CARLYLE *Sart. Res.* I. iv. in *Fraser's Mag.* Nov. 590/2 To Teufelsdröckh the highest Duchess is respectable..but nowise for her pearl bracelets, and Malines laces. **1842** THACKERAY *Fitz-Boodle's Confessions* in *Fraser's Mag.* June 713/1, I thought she would not let the evening pass without talking of her Malines lace. **1850** *Harper's Mag.* Aug. 431/2 Another pattern is..embroidered and trimmed with *malines*. **1897** *Sears, Roebuck Catal.* 318/1 A 27 inch Maline net veiling..in black, brown, cream or navy blue. **1909** *Daily Chron.* 4 Mar. 4/5 Lady Anne Lambton was the wearer of Malines net, the skirt panelled with lace. **1911** J. MASEFIELD *Jim Davis* iii. 30 It contained a dozen yards of very beautiful Malines lace. **1912** *Queen* 13 Apr. 613/1 This coat..had long sleeves slit up at the wrist, and edged with white net bordered with Malines. **1964** MRS. L. B. JOHNSON *White House Diary* 12 Mar. (1970) 89, I dressed early this morning, in solid black, with my mantilla draped over my maline hat, and set out..for the Requiem Mass for King Paul.

2. A Belgian breed of the domestic fowl. Also *attrib.*

1906 E. BROWN *Races Domestic Poultry* viii. 117/1 The birds which are known as *poulets* and *poulardes de Bruxelles* are entirely Malines. **1910** *Encycl. Poultry* II. 295 The Malines fowl is of the Asiatic type, and is large in size... There are two varieties—the Coucou and the white. **1938** T. NEWMAN *Princ. & Pract. Poultry Husbandry* i. 23 The Maline..was the result of a cross between the Langshan and Campine, and the Antwerp Brahma.

mal-'influence. [See MAL-.] Evil influence.

1792 ANNA SEWARD *Lett.* (1811) III. 117 The mal-influence upon your nerves from marine damps. **1796** *Ibid.* IV. 289 The mal-influence of a violent cold. **1822** DE QUINCEY *Confess.* App. 199 Opium..having left the body weaker..and thus predisposed to any mal-influence whatever.

†**mal-in'fortuned**, *ppl. a. Obs.* [f. MAL- + (?) ENFORTUNE *v.* + -ED¹.] Ill-fortuned.

1475 *Bk. Noblesse* (Roxb.) 17 The male-infortuned journey at Bougée. [Cf. MALE-JOURNEY.]

maling, obs. f. MAILING *Sc.*, MALIGN *v.*

malingen, variant of MALENGIN *Obs.*

malinger (mə'lɪŋgə(r)), *v.* [f. F. *malingre* sickly, ailing (formerly 'sore, scabbie, ouglie, loathsome', Cotgr.); of obscure origin.] *intr.* To pretend illness, or to produce or protract disease, in order to escape duty; said *esp.* of soldiers and sailors.

1820 E. T. LUSCOMBE *Pract. Obs. Means Preserv. Health Sold.* 88 Formerly, it was ulcers of the legs, which were most usually produced by artificial means by soldiers..disposed to malinger. **1844** MACAULAY *Ess.*, *Chatham*, Some were half inclined to suspect that he was, to use a military phrase, malingering. **1872** BROWNING *Fifine* lxxvi, Be sick by stealth, Nor traffic with disease—malingering in health! **1899** *Allbutt's Syst. Med.* VII. 150 The question comes to be, whether the patient..is malingering.

malingerer (mə'lɪŋgərə(r)). [f. MALINGER *v.* + -ER¹.] One who malingers.

1785 GROSE *Dict. Vulg. Tongue*, *Malingeror*, a military term for one who under pretence of sickness evades his duty. **1843** GAVIN *Feigned & Factitious Dis.* 13 Soldiers and sailors feigning disease are commonly designated as malingerers or skulkers. **1899** *Allbutt's Syst. Med.* VIII. 157 The crew of incapables and malingerers who infest our hospitals, our asylums, and our gaols.

malingering (mə'lɪŋgərɪŋ), *vbl. sb.* [See -ING¹.] The action of the verb MALINGER.

1861 T. J. GRAHAM *Pract. Med.* 602 There are three conditions from which it is important to distinguish it—from apoplexy, from hysteria, and..from malingering. **1899** *Allbutt's Syst. Med.* VII. 150 Malingering is generally easily detected by one who is accustomed to examine nervous cases.

ma'lingering, *ppl. a.* [f. MALINGER *v.* + -ING².] That malingers.

1865 CARLYLE *Fredk. Gt.* XIV. viii (1872) V. 261 Karl Edzard, Prince of East Friesland, long a weak malingering creature, died, rather suddenly. **1894** H. NISBET *Bush Girl's Rom.* 60 [He] mopes about like a malingering lag.

malingery (mə'lɪŋgərɪ). [f. MALINGER *v.* + -Y.] = MALINGERING *vbl. sb.*

1847–54 in WEBSTER; and in later Dicts.

Malinke (mə'lɪŋkeɪ). The name of a people of western Africa and their language. Also *attrib.* or as *adj.* Cf. MANDINKA *sb.* and *a.*

1883 *Encycl. Brit.* XV. 475/2 *Mandingoes*, otherwise known as *Wangawara*, *Malinkes*, or *Wakore*..are one of the most widely distributed and important peoples of Western Africa to the north of the equator. **1911** F. W. H. MIGEOD *Lang. W. Afr.* I. i. 33 Among the tribes whose languages furnish evidence of the extent of Mandingo influence are the Malinke, Bambara, Susu, [etc.]. *Ibid.* viii. 202 Malinke, Susu, and Soninke take suffixes to the verb. **1913** *Ibid.* II. xxi. 332 The Malinke held in the past a less leading position than many other branches of the Mandingos. **1950** D. JONES *Phoneme* xxviii. 206 Variphones consisting of r-like and l-like sounds would also appear to occur in some languages of Africa, for instance, in Bambara and Malinke. **1970** P. OLIVER *Savannah Syncopators* 106 Lobi and Malinke xylophones. *Ibid.* 112 *Malinke*, extensively distributed tribe occupying large areas of Senegal, Guinea and western Ivory Coast. **1970** *Western Folklore* XXIX. 241 Among the Kissi and Malinké of Liberia..*banga* has the specialized meaning of a children's instrument of several strings.

Malinois (malɪnwa). [Fr., f. *Malinois* of or from Malines in Belgium.] A wire-haired variety of the Belgian Sheepdog.

1947 C. L. B. HUBBARD *Working Dogs of World* 104 The Malinois forms one of the three main groups of Belgian Sheepdogs... The breed takes its name from the district of Malines, where it probably originated. **1948** B. VESEY-FITZGERALD *Bk. Dog* 564 The Malinois represents the wire-haired Belgian Sheepdog. **1971** F. HAMILTON *World Encycl. Dogs* 56 The Malinois is short-haired,..generally fawn in colour, with dark tips to the hairs on back and sides, giving a 'blackened' or shaded effect, and with a black mask.

Malinowskian (ˌmælɪ'nɒfskɪən), *a.* [f. the name of Bronislaw Kasper *Malinowski* (1884–1942), Polish-born anthropologist + -AN.] Of, pertaining to, or characteristic of Malinowski and his works.

1954 *Amer. Anthropologist* Oct. 915 A fascinating personality—a Malinowskian anthropologist and a classical Confucian scholar rolled into one. **1955** HOMANS & SCHNEIDER *Marriage, Authority & Final Causes* 15 We may also call it Malinowskian functionalism. **1956** L. A. FALLERS *Bantu Bureaucracy* 129 It is rather in the nature of a 'mythical charter', in the Malinowskian sense. **1960** *Guardian* 19 Feb. 6/2 Malinowskian methods of field investigation. **1968** *Listener* 9 May 614/3 Interminable guest-shows communicated nothing (though even that laughing, wisecracking phatic stuff has its Malinowskian place).

malinowskite (mælɪ'nɒvskaɪt). *Min.* [Named in 1876 by A. Raimondi after E. *Malinowski*.] A variety of tetrahedrite, containing lead and silver.

1882 DANA *Man. Mineral. & Lithol.* (ed. 4) 136.

mal-in'sertion. *Anat.* [f. MAL- + INSERTION.] Abnormal insertion (INSERTION 3).

1904 E. H. FENWICK *Handbk. Clin. Electr.-Light Cystoscopy* xxi. 439 Some form of ureteric obstruction—either an acute bend of the ureter, due to adhesion or mal-insertion in movable kidney,..or a stone impacted low down in the ureter. **1964** S. DUKE-ELDER *Parsons' Dis. Eye* (ed. 14) xxix. 460 It occurs chiefly in cases of congenital origin—probably mal-insertion of the muscles—but has been met with after interference with the pulley of the superior oblique in frontal sinus operations.

†**mal-intentionee.** *Obs.* In quot. male-. [ad. F. *mal-intentionné*, f. *mal* (see MAL-) + *intentionné* intentioned.] An evil-intentioned person.

a **1734** NORTH *Exam.* III. vii. §41 (1740) 532 There was another Agent..qualified to treat with the Male Intentionees in England.

malipart, -pert, variant forms of MALAPERT.

malipede ('mælɪpiːd). *Zool.* [f. mod.L. *māla* jaw + *ped-*, *pēs* foot.] Any one of the last two pairs of cephalic appendages in the chilopods.

1883 PACKARD in *Proc. Amer. Phil. Soc.* June 201 The second pair of malipedes, or last pair of mouth-appendages, are the poison fangs. —— in *Ann. & Mag. Nat. Hist.* Nov. 342 We therefore propose the term malipedes..for the fourth and fifth pair of cephalic appendages.

Hence **malipedal** (mə'lɪpɪdəl), *a. Zool.*, pertaining to the malipedes of chilopods.

1883 PACKARD in *Proc. Amer. Phil. Soc.* June 201 The tergum of the fourth segment, or second malipedal segment. —— in *Ann. & Mag. Nat. Hist.* Nov. 343 The second malipedal tergite.

‖**malis** ('meɪlɪs). *Path. Obs.* [mod.L. *mālis*, a. Gr. μᾶλις a disease in horses and asses (the late L. *malleus* 'glanders', may perh. be identical). In medical Latin, *malis* has been used as a generic term (with various specific designations) for parasitic skin diseases.] = GLANDERS.

1607 TOPSELL *Four-f. Beasts* (1658) 60 The Malis or Glaunders... The humors which annoy the body of oxen are many. The first is a moist one called Malis, issuing at the nose.

malis, malisce, variant ff. MALEASE *Obs.*

malis(e, obs. form of MALICE.

malism ('meɪlɪz(ə)m). [f. L. *mal-us* bad, evil + -ISM, after *pessimism*.] The doctrine that this world is an evil one.

1883 EDGEWORTH in *Academy* 17 Mar. 182/3 Mr. Barlow decides in favour of Pessimism, or rather 'Malism', the preponderance of evil over good. **1883** H. GOODWIN *Sci. & Faith* 243 Malism, to use a convenient expression, is acknowledged on all hands; while against pessimism [etc.]. **1887** CHEYNE *Job & Solomon* 201 Koheleth, though theoretically perhaps an optimist, constantly relapses into a more congenial 'malism'. **1896** TOLLEMACHE *Jowett* 91 Jowett's optimism verges on pessimism, or, let us say, his bonism verges on malism.

malison ('mælɪsən), *sb. arch.* and *dial.* Forms: 4 **malisun(e, malysun, malesun, maliscun, malescun, malicun, malicoun, 4–5 malyson(e, malisoun(e, 4–6 malysoun, 5–6 maleso(u)n(e, 6 malisone, 7 mallison, 4– malison.** [a. OF. *maleison*:—L. *maledictiōn-em* MALEDICTION.]

1. A curse, malediction.

a **1300** *Cursor M.* 2051 His malison on þam he laid. *c* **1300** *Havelok* 426 Haue he the malisun to-day Of alle þat eure speken may! *c* **1320** *Sir Beues* 3696, I praie Mahoun þar fore ȝeue þe is malisoun. *c* **1450** *Mirour Saluacioun* 580 The malison of oure for-modere shuld torne to benedictionne. **1583** *Leg. Bp. St. Androis* 283 Scho endit, And left hir malisone, consider, To Lowrie, and the land together. **1586** *Durham Depos.* (Surtees) 319 He answered, God's malison light on him, for he haith beggered me. **1691** RAY *Coll. Words, Gloss. Northanhymb.* 146 *Mallison*, q.d. *Malediction*, v. *Bennison*. **1721** RAMSAY *Lucky Spence* xvi, My malison light..On them that drink and dinna pay. **1808** SCOTT *Marmion* v. xxv, A minstrel's malison is said. **1861** GOLDW. SMITH *Irish Hist.* 43 Their malison was almost as terrible as the curse of a priest. **1865** KINGSLEY *Herew.* xiii, Farewell, and my malison abide with thee!

†**2.** The state or condition of being cursed. *Obs.*

c **1375** *Sc. Leg. Saints* xliii. (*Cecile*) 277 Sa man, þat ves in malysone, mycht þar chese lestand benysone.

3. *dial.* A plague, torment. Also with sb. prefixed, as ***cat-malison*** (see CAT *sb.* 18), ***horse-malison*** one who is cruel to horses. (See E.D.D.)

†**malison** ('mælɪsən), *v. Sc. Obs.* [f. prec. sb.] *trans.* To curse; to pronounce a malediction upon.

1588 A. KING tr. *Canisius' Catech.* in *Cath. Tract.* (S.T.S.) 215 To malesone any, by geuing thame to the deuil, in visching thame sicknes, deathe or any euill. **1675** in Edgar *Old Ch. Life Scotl.* (1885) 273 *note*, [A woman confessed that she] malinsount [another woman].

maliss, obs. form of MALICE.

malist ('meɪlɪst). [f. L. *mal-us* bad, evil + -IST.] One who holds the doctrine of malism.

1882 J. W. BARLOW *Ultim. Pessimism* 5 So we see that Optimist and Pessimist are no longer suitable names..; and the positive forms Bonist and Malist would certainly be more appropriate. **1887** CHEYNE *Job & Solomon* 202 Bad as things are, he does not believe that the world is getting worse and worse..he is a 'malist'.

malistic (mə'lɪstɪk), *a.* [f. MALIST + -IC.] Pertaining to or favouring malism.

1896 TOLLEMACHE *Jowett* 95 After putting side by side the bonistic and malistic sayings of Jowett.

maliti(o)us, obs. form of MALICIOUS.

malivolence, -ent, -us: see MALEVOLENCE, etc.

malke, obs. form of MAWK.

malkin, mawkin ('mɔːkɪn). *Obs.* exc. *dial.* Forms: α. 3 **malekin, 4–7 malkyn, 5 malkyne, 6–8 maulkin, 7 maulken, malkine, malking, mol-kin, 4– malkin.** β. 6 **maukyn, mawkine, 6–9 maukin, 6–8 mauking,** 8 *Sc.* **mawking, 6– mawkin.** [A familiar diminutive of *Matilda*, *Maud* (ME. *Maalde*, *Malde*): see -KIN.]

†**1.** Used as a female personal name; applied typically to a woman of the lower classes, esp. in various proverbial expressions. *Obs.*

c **1275** *Lutel Sermun* 54 in *O. E. Misc.* 188 Ne þeos prude ȝungemen þat luuieþ malekin, And þeos prude maidenes þat luuieþ Ianekin. **1362** LANGL. *P. Pl.* A. I. 158 ȝe naue no more movit in masse ne in houres Then Malkyn of hire maydenhod that no mon desyreth. *c* **1386** CHAUCER *Man of Law's Prol.* 30 It wol nat come agayn with outen drede Na moore than wole Malkynes maydenhede Whan she hath lost it in hir wantownesse. *c* **1440** *Promp. Parv.* 323/2 Malkyne, or Mawt, propyr name..*Matildis*. **1546** J. HEYWOOD *Prov.* (1867) 26 Whan I wyld the any other where to go, Tushe, there was no mo maydes but malkyn tho. **1564** MARTIALL *Treat. Cross* IV. 67 A goodly reason by S. Mary, not much vnlieke to an old mother Maukyns talk. **1579** GOSSON *Sch. Abuse* (Arb.) 37 There are more houses then Parishe Churches, more maydes then Maulkin. **1602** BRETON *Wond. worth Hearing* (Grosart) 8/2 Holding out her chinne and drawing in her mouth (lyke Malkins olde Mare). **1670** RAY *Prov.* 118 There are more maids then maukin.

†**b.** The proper name of a female spectre or demon. (In 17th. c. app. associated with sense 5 a.)

c **1207** RAD. DE COGGESHALL *Chron. Angl.* (Rolls) 120–1 [A spectre in the form of a female child said that it was called 'Malekin']. **1604** MIDDLETON *Witch* III. iii, *Fire.* Hark, hark, the Catt sings a brave treble in Her owne language. *Hec.* (going up) Now I goe, now I flie, Malkin my sweete spirit and I. **1605** SHAKS. *Macb.* I. i. 9, I come, Gray-Malkin!

†**c.** = MAID MARIAN. *Obs.*

1619 FLETCHER *M. Thomas* II. ii, You must turne tippet, And suddenly..Put on the shape of order and humanity, Or you must marry Malkyn the May Lady.

2. An untidy female, esp. a servant or country wench; a slut, slattern, drab; *occas.* a lewd woman.

a. **1586** WARNER *Alb. Eng.* II. ix. (1612) 41 Euen Carters Malkines will disdaine when Gentrie will digest. **1604**

MIDDLETON *Ant & Night.* To Rdr., None can iustly except at me but some riotous vomiting Kit, or some Gentleman-swallowing Mol-kin. **1607** SHAKS. *Cor.* II. i. 224 The Kitchin Malkin pinnes Her richest Lockram 'bout her reechie necke. **1652** J. WRIGHT tr. *Camus' Nat. Paradox* VI. 114, I should bee too long if I should relate in what manner those subtile Wits inveagled the simplicity of those silly Maulkins. For I haue heard these Court-Ladies allow Large pensions to their Paramors. **1762** *Lond. Mag.* Apr. 205/1 Now monst'rous in hoop, now trapish, and walking With your petticoats clung to your heels, like a maulkin. **1871** TENNYSON *Last Tourn.* 629 The swineherd's malkin.

β. **1600** BRETON *Pasquill's Mad-Cappe* (1626) B, The Chuffe that sits and champes upon his chaffe May have his Mawkin kisse him like a mare. *a* **1625** FLETCHER *Chances* III. i, Thou took'st me up at every word I spoke, As I had been a Mawkin, a flurt Gillian. **1702** VANBRUGH *False Friend* I. i, The dull heavy-tail'd maukin melts him down with her modesty. *a* **1745** SWIFT *Ballyspellin* (Answ.) viii. Wks. 1765 XIV. 231 Your mawkins there, smocks hempen wear. **1847** TENNYSON *Princess* v. 25 A draggled mawkin, .. That tends her bristled grunters in the sludge.

attrib. **1642** MILTON *Apol. Smect.* vi. 33 Her maukin knuckles were never shapen to that royall buskin.

†**b.** An effeminate man. *Obs.*

1468 *Medulla Gram.* in *Promp. Parv.* 323/2 *Gallinacius, i. homo debilis,* a malkyn, and a capoun.

3. A mop; a bundle of rags fastened to the end of a stick; *esp.* that used to clean out a baker's oven. *Obs.* exc. *dial.*

α. **14..** *Voc.* in Wr.-Wülcker 616/12 *Tersorium,* a swepelles (a malkyn). *c* **1440** *Promp. Parv.* 323/2 Malkyne, mappyl, or oven swepare, .. *dossorium, tersorium.* **1590** [TARLTON] *News Purgat.* (Shaks. Soc.) 59 He helde betweene both his hands a durty malkin, such as Bakers sweepe their ovens withall. **1596** NASHE *Saffron Walden* 135 Shee will .. haue a handfull of his beard .. for a maulkin or wispe to wype her shooes with. **1611** COTGR., *Vuaudrée,* a maulkin, or the clowt wherewith an Ouen is made cleane. **1620** MARKHAM *Farew. Husb.* (1625) 96 Blacke, foule, and ugly like bakers malkins. **1792** WOLCOT (P. Pindar) *Royal Tour* Wks. 1812 III. 324 Of Royalty the Purple Robe so grand They to a Malkin turn, to wipe their shoes. **1796** *Grose's Dict. Vulg. Tongue* (ed. 3), *Malkin* or *Maulkin,* .. also a parcel of rags fastened to the end of a stick, to clean an oven. **1880** JEFFERIES *Gt. Estate* 153 The malkin, being wetted, cleaned out the ashes [from the oven].

β. **1580** HOLLYBAND *Treas. Fr. Tong., Waudrée,* or *escouillon,* the clout wherewith they clense or sweepe the Ouen, called a Maukin. **1598** R. BERNARD tr. *Terence, Eunuch* IV. vii, Dost thou think to fight with a mauking that thou bringst it hither. **1607** DEKKER *Knts. Conjur.* (1842) 42 A beard filthier then a bakers mawkin that he sweepes his ouen. **1630** J. TAYLOR (Water P.) *Jacke-a-Lent* Wks. I. 115/1 An Ensigne made of a piece of a Bakers mawkin fixed vpon a Broome-staffe. **1694** BURNABY *Sat. Petronius Arbiter* 84 Do you remember .. the Story of Ulysses, how a Cyclop put his Thumb out of Joint with a Mawkin? **1727** BRADLEY *Fam. Dict.* s.v. *Bake-house,* Peels, Cole-Rakes, Maukins.

b. *Naut.* 'A joint-staff sponge, for cleaning out a piece of ordnance' (Smyth *Sailor's Word-bk.*).

4. A scarecrow (also *fig.*); a ragged puppet or grotesque effigy; a 'guy'. *Obs.* exc. *dial.*

α. **1633** T. ADAMS *Exp. 2 Peter* ii. 7 I. 632 A Malking frights a child, a man contemnes it. **1638** NABBES *Cov. Gard.* v. vi. 71, *Ralph.* .. What are you Sir? *Spruce.* A Gentleman Vsher. *Ralph.* You're a Malkin of mock-Gentry, made up of silke and vaine-glory. **1640** —— *Bride* I. iv, You malkin of suburb authority set up only to fright crows. *a* **1700** B. E. *Dict. Cant. Crew, Malkin* or *Maukin,* a scarecrow. *a* **1734** NORTH *Exam.* II. iv. §5 (1740) 233 Then he mounted up the Maulkin to be viewed round, though nothing was to be seen or understood of it from him, more than of a scare Crow, that is the Rags and Trumpery it was garnished with. **1748** *Earthquake Peru* i. 82 A Basket from which issued a Puppet, or Maulkin. **1866** KINGSLEY *Herew.* II. iv. 65 He must fight it out henceforth not with a straw malkin like thee.

β. **1687** CONGREVE *Old Bach.* III. vi, Thou Maukin, made up of the Shreds and Pairings of his [thy Master's] superfluous Fopperies. **1710** *Brit. Apollo* II. No. 86. 3/1 Were you hang'd for a Mauking on a Tree. **1710** SWIFT *Jrnl. to Stella* 13 Dec., Dressing up a hat on a stick and calling it Harley; then .. discharging a pistol with the other [hand] at the maukin. **1712** *Pol. Ball.* (1860) II. 121 You for your bonfires mawkins dress'd On good Queen Bess's day. **1742** H. WALPOLE *Lett. H. Mann* (1834) I. 124 The first thing I beheld was a Mawkin in a chair, with three footmen and a label on the breast inscribed *Lady Mary.* **1776** S. J. PRATT *Pupil Pleas.* (ed. 2) I. lviii. 236 And Dost thou, after all, boggle at a shadow—a maukin—at conscience? **1791** BECKFORD tr. *Pop. Tales Germans* II. 82 Just .. a mawkin suspended amongst pease to scare away the voracious sparrows. **1818** LAMB *Inconven. fr. being Hanged,* Like a maukin, fit only to scare away birds. **1859** GEO. ELIOT *A. Bede* vi, You knew no more .. than the mawkin i' the field. **1898** RIDER HAGGARD in *Longm. Mag.* Dec. 127 Hood promises to set up some mawkins to fright them.

Comb. *a* **1700** B. E. *Dict. Cant. Crew* s.v., Hence *Malkin-trash,* for one in a rueful Dress, enough to Fright one.

5. As a designation for certain animals: sometimes as quasi-proper name. **a.** A cat. *dial.*

Grimalkin occurs in Baldwin's *Beware the Cat,* 1561-82.

1673 COTTON *Voy. Irel.* II. Poems (1689) 182 We went, and e'er Malkin could well lick her ear .. forsooth, we were there. **1785** GROSE *Dict. Vulg. Tongue, Malkin,* or *Maulkin,* a general name for a cat. **1876** *Whitby Gloss.*

b. *Sc.* and *north. dial.* A hare.

1724 RAMSAY *Tea-t. Misc.* (1733) I. 61 Skipping like a mawking. **1785** BURNS *Vision* I. i, The sun had clos'd the winter day, .. An' hunger'd Maukin taen her way To kail-yards green. **1786** —— *Tam Samson's Elegy* vii, Ye Maukins, cock your fud fu' braw, Withouten dread. **1793** in Lockhart *Scott* vii, I'll send ye a maukin the morn, man. **1818** *Blackw. Mag.* IV. 65 He [a sportsman] would probably be as much gratified by the discovery of mawkin, as the Astronomer would be by the discovery of a constellation. **1895** CROCKETT *Men of Moss Hags* xlvii, Once they raised, as it had been a poor maukin, a young lad that ran from them.

Malkite, var. MELCHITE.

mall[1] (mɔːl). Also 7 **mell,** 8 **maul.** [A special application of *mall,* MAUL *sb.*[1], in the 17th c. taken to represent certain contemporary senses of the F. *mail,* which is etymologically identical with the Eng. word. Cf. PALL-MALL.]

1. The mallet (cf. MAUL *sb.*[1] 2) used in the game of 'mall' or 'pall-mall'; = PALL-MALL 1.

1662 *Order-bk. Gen. Monck* 26 Apr. in *N. & Q.* 9th Ser. VIII. 14/2 That noe persons shall after play carry their malls out of S. James's Parke without leave of the said keeper. **1706** PHILLIPS (ed. Kersey), *Mall,* .. the Instrument with which the Ball is struck is also called a Mall. **1711** ADDISON *Spect.* No. 195 ⁋1 He took an hollow Ball of Wood .. He likewise took a Mall. **1884** J. PAYNE *Tales fr. Arabic* I. 123 The king's son was playing in the exercise-ground with the ball and mall.

2. a. A certain game; = PALL-MALL 2.

1646 EVELYN *Diary* (Chandos ed.) 193 Having seene this field and play'd a game at Mall. **1675** COTTON *Scoffer Scoft* 103 But playing with the Boy at Mall, .. I strooke the Ball .. A pretty height into the Air. **1796** MORSE *Amer. Geog.* II. 154 The diversion [goff] .. resembles that of the Mall, which was common in England in the middle of the last century. **1868** W. J. WHITMORE *Croquet Tact.* 4 The Mall received its name from having been appropriated to the purpose of playing at mall.

†**b.** Applied to polo; = PALL-MALL 2b. *Obs.*

1662 J. DAVIES tr. *Olearius' Voy. Ambass.* 297 A certain Game, which the Persians call Kuitskaukan, which is a kind of Mall. **1687** A. LOVELL tr. *Thevenot's Trav.* II. 79 There are two Banks .. which serve for playing at the mall on horse back, and the bowl must go betwixt those Banks.

3. The alley in which the game of 'mall' was played. = PALL-MALL 3.

1644 EVELYN *Diary* 2 May, The mall [at Tours] without comparison is the noblest in Europe... Here we play'd a party or two. *a* **1687** WALLER *On St. James's Park* 64 No sooner has he touched the flying ball But 'tis already more than half the Mall. **1687** R. FERRIER *Jrnl.* 34 (Camd. Soc. Misc. IX.), There are several handsome walks, one whereof .. is a decayed Mell. **1706** PHILLIPS (ed. Kersey) s.v., The Instrument .. is also termed a Mall, and the Place where the Gamesters play. **1812** COBBETT in *Examiner* 19 Oct. 671/1 Noble Ladies, who graciously condescended to become housekeepers and sweepers of malls.

4. a. Now usu. pronounced (mæl). *the Mall*: a walk bordered by trees in St. James's Park, London, which was originally a 'mall' in sense 3, and was a fashionable promenade in the 17–18th c. †*High Mall*: the time when the throng of promenaders in the Mall was at its height; also *transf.,* ? a fashionable assembly in the open air.

1674 J. D. (*title*) The Mall: or the Modish Lovers. A Comedy. *Ibid.* I. ii, I will be in the Mall, as soon as it begins to be dark, if I can get from my husband. **1676** D'URFEY *Mad. Fickle* III. i, You may repair that inconvenience in the Mall to night Sir. **1706** *Reflex. upon Ridicule* 128 We see them in the Maul and in the Park walking, giggling, with their sparks. **1710** PALMER *Proverbs* 203 The intrigues of the mall and the playhouse. **1712** *Spect.* No. 437 ⁋4 Were you to see Gatty walk the Park at high Mall. **1727** FIELDING *Love in Sev. Masq.* I. iv, Well, gentlemen, are you for the Mall this morning? **1752** A. MURPHY *Gray's Inn Jrnl.* No. 9 In St. James's Park, at high Mall, on Sunday next. *Ibid.,* High Mall at the Bedford Coffee-House To-morrow Evening. **1775** SHERIDAN *Rivals* II. i, I've travelled like a comet, with a tail of dust .. as long as the Mall. **1778** [W. MARSHALL] *Minutes Agric., Digest* 5 She resembles a .. cottage-bred Country-housewife .. parading the Mall of Taste amidst modern Petits-Maitres. **1816** J. SCOTT *Vis. Paris* (ed. 5) 64 He appeals to the smooth and level mall, and the carefully preserved canal of St. James's Park.

b. *transf.* A sheltered walk serving as a promenade; in some towns adopted as a proper name. Also, a shopping-precinct.

[Cf. F. *mail,* used in various towns for a shaded walk, which in many instances was orig. an alley for playing mall.]

1737 EARL OF OXFORD in *Portland Papers* (Hist. MSS. Comm.) VI. 169 The churchyard is well planted, the walks gravelled; this is the Mall for the beaux and belles of Chelmsford. **1752** MRS. DELANY *Lett., to Mrs. Dewes* 134 It is the mall of Drogheda. **1808** *Norfolk Tour, Norwich* (ed. 6) 248 The new walk or mall from the bars by the work-house to Gannock-gates. **1838** LONGF. in *Life* (1891) I. 298 Afterwards walked in the Mall [Boston, U. S.] in the cool of the evening. **1883** F. M. CRAWFORD *Mr. Isaacs* i. 7 Such of the changing crowd on the verandah and on the mall [at Simla] as caught my attention. **1914** JOYCE *Dubliners* 24 All the branches of the tall trees which lined the mall were gay with little light green leaves. **1963** *Observer* 15 Sept. 23/6 The central paved avenue, or 'mall' [in a shopping-centre], wider than any street, with booths in the middle. **1969** *Daily Tel.* 19 Aug. 13/2 Basically, the housewife is demanding more comfort and convenience in shopping. This means covered and heated 'malls' with car-parking facilities adjacent. **1974** *Economist* 21 Dec. 47/1 The developers have discovered an even more potent device for generating sales: the rigidly controlled 'shopping environment' of the enclosed malls... Woodfield Mall, near Chicago .. includes 235 stores in a roofed-over area of 191 acres. **1975** *Times* 19 Feb. 4/8 Malls smoke danger. Special fire precautions are needed in single-storey shopping malls.

5. *Comb.,* as (sense 1) ***mall-maker***; (sense 3) ***mall-keeper.***

1708 LUTTRELL *Brief Rel.* (1857) VI. 354 Mrs. Masham, mall keeper of St. James's Park, worth 500*l.* per ann. **1901** T. J. JEAKES in *N. & Q.* 9th Ser. VII. 353/1 The mall-maker's shop was on the same road.

mall[2]. *Hist. rare*[−1]. [ad. med.L. *mallum, -us*: see MALLUM and MAIL *sb.*[2]] A convention or assembly among the Franks.

1855 MILMAN *Lat. Chr.* IV. x. (1864) II. 441 Councils, which had been as frequent as diets or malls, ceased.

mall: see MAUL, MAW.

Mallaby-Deeley (ˌmæləbɪˈdiːlɪ). [f. Harry *Mallaby-Deeley* (1863–1937), an English clothing manufacturer.] A cheap suit of clothes (see quots.). Also *transf.*

1920 *Punch* 10 Mar. 196 Oo, Lumme! Wot price Reginald in 'is Mallaby-Deeleys? **1937** *Evening Standard* 5 Feb. 3/1 In 1920 he [*sc.* Mallaby-Deeley] became the leader of cheap mass-production tailoring... A 'Mallaby-Deeley' soon became another name for a suit. **1959** R. POSTGATE *Every Man is God* xxiii. 218 'You don't know what a Mallaby Deeley is?' said his one time Major... David Roddman learned that a Mallaby Deeley was a cheap mass-produced suit invented by a smart M.P. Ex-officers, out of work, for the use of. **1962** GRANVILLE *Dict. Sailors' Slang* 74/2 *Mallaby-Deeley's,* plain clothes worn by Naval officers and men on shore leave.

mallagatoon, obs. form of MELOCOTON.

‖ **mallam** (ˈmæləm). [ad. Hausa *mālam(i)* (often used as a title).] A learned man, scribe, teacher.

1932 J. CARY *Aissa Saved* viii. 44 The white mallam put his hand on her head. *Ibid.* x. 53 She went to all the priests and mallams and juju men for a hundred miles round and commanded them to give the baby medicine. **1936** —— *Afr. Witch* xxii. 329 The old *mallam* went into his own room, which was the late Emir Aliu's office. **1939** —— *Mister Johnson* 82 He has been described .. as a hamfish or *mallam* judge—that is, an office keeper. **1965** A. NICOL *Truly Married Woman* 88 'What foolishness is this?' the Mallam said sternly.

mallan, obs. form of MALM.

mallancoly, obs. form of MELANCHOLY.

mallander, mallany: see MALANDER, MALMY.

mallard (ˈmæləd). Forms: 4 **maular,** 4–5 **mawlard, maulard(e,** 4–6 **malarde,** 4, 8 **malard,** 5 **malerde, mavelard, maud-, mawdelard(e,** 5–6 **mallarde,** 6 **mallert, mallerde,** 7 **mallerd, mallet,** 4– **mallard.** [a. OF. *malart, mallart* wild drake; of obscure origin.

The conjecture given in Hatz.-Darm. that it represents the OHG. male proper name *Madelhart* is remarkably supported by the evidence of the Eng. form *maud-, mawdelard,* which, however, has not been found in OF. The bird may under this name have figured as a personage in some lost example of the Germanic 'beast-epic'. Another hypothesis is that the word is f. OF. *masle, male* MALE *a.* + *-art,* -ARD; but against this there is the objection that the form *maslart* does not occur until late, though the word is recorded from the 12th c.]

1. The male of the wild duck (*Anas boscas*). †Formerly often applied also to the male of the domesticated variety; = DRAKE[2].

c **1330** *Arth. & Merl.* 4140 Þe cherl bent his bowe sone & smot a doke mididone, & wiþ a bolt afterward Anon he hitt a maulard. **14..** *Voc.* in Wr.-Wülcker 563/46 *Anatus,* a mallard. **1533–4** *Act 25 Hen. VIII,* c. 11 §1 Duckes, mallardes, wigeons, teales, wildgeese and diuers other kinde of wildfowle. **1601** HOLLAND *Pliny* II. 383 To stay a flux of the belly, the bloud of Mallards or Drakes is thought also to be singular good. **1606** SHAKS. *Ant. & Cl.* III. x. 20 The Noble ruine of her Magicke, Anthony, Claps on his Sea-wing, and (like a doting Mallard) .. flyes after her. **1776** *Ann. Reg.* 152 The old duck left them [the eggs], but soon after returned with the mallard. **1861** G. F. BERKELEY *Sportsm. W. Prairies* xx. 337, I walked to within shot of some straggling wild ducks, and killed a very fine mallard. **1893** NEWTON *Dict. Birds* 168 Technically the term Duck is restricted to the female, the male being called Drake, and in one species Mallard.

2. a. Used for either sex: A wild drake or duck. †Formerly also applied to the domestic variety.

1314 in *Wardr. Acc. 8 Edw. II* 21/12, 1 mallard 4½*d.* **1348** *Durham Acc. Rolls* (Surtees) 43 In v Mallard domestic. et v Mallard de Ryuer et xiiij perdicibus, iiijs. *xd.* ob. *c* **1400** *Siege of Troy* 1070 in *Archiv neu. Spr.* LXXII. 38 Plover, partriche and wyld Bores .. With Malardes wylde and fesaunt. *c* **1400** *Lanfranc's Cirurg.* 181 Anoynte þe place wiþ grece of a maulard. *c* **1420** *Liber Cocorum* (1862) 27 With þo grece of þo mawdelarde þou sethe hom. *c* **1440** *Promp. Parv.* 323/1 Malarde, byrde (or mavelarde). **1486** *Bk. St. Albans* d ij b, Take a tame Malarde and set hym in a fayr playn. **1502** ARNOLDE *Chron.* 91 Also yf ony persone kepe or norrysh hoggis oxen kyen or mallardis with in the ward in noyng of ther neyhbours. **1657** TOMLINSON *Renou's Disp.* I. viii. 13 The Mallet [rendering of L. *anas*]. **1751** JOHNSON *Rambler* No. 138 ⁋8 Shooting mallards in the fens. **1774** GOLDSM. *Nat. Hist.* III. 283 The Mallard is probably the stock of which our tame breed is the product. **1860** GOSSE *Rom. Nat. Hist.* 199 Our own wild-duck or mallard is a shy bird. **1894** J. SKELTON *Table-t. Shirley* (1895) 64 The frost is so hard that woodcock and mallard are driven from inland copses and marshes to the open springs.

b. The flesh of this bird.

c **1440** *Douce MS.* 55 lf. 14 Cast it in a pott and fressh broth .. and of canell and [dropping *Harl.* 4016] of the malarde & lete hem buille. **14..** in *Househ. Ord.* (1790) 441 Sause neyger for Maudelard roasted. **1513** *Bk. Keruynge* in *Babees Bk.* 278 In the fyrst course, potage, befe, .. with goose, capon, mallarde, swanne, or fesande. **1555** W. WATREMAN *Fardle Facions* I. v. 53 Quaile, and mallard, are not but for the richer sorte. **1607** DEKKER & WEBSTER *Westw. Hoe* I. i, They .. loue Mallard and Teale in the fall, and Woodcocke in winter.

c. *attrib.*, as ***mallard call, decoy, drake, duck, -shooting***.

1772 J. R. FORSTER in *Phil. Trans.* LXII. 419 Anas. 53 Boschas.. Mallard Drake. **1852** R. GLISAN *Jrnl. Army Life* (1874) ix. 102 A fine mallard duck suddenly flew up. **1874** J. W. LONG *Amer. Wild-Fowl Shooting* xiv. 186 Morning and evening mallard-shooting. *Ibid.* xix. 214 They decoy exceedingly well to mallard decoys, and come readily to the mallard call.

3. ***the Mallard***: a festival celebrated on the 14th Jan. at All Souls College, Oxford (see quots.). Also *attrib.*

1632 ABP. ABBOT in M. Burrows *Worthies All Souls* viii. (1874) 126 Civil men should never so far forget themselves under pretence of a foolish Mallard as to do things barbarously unbecoming. **1722-3** HEARNE *Diary* 18 Jan., Last Monday, the 14th inst... was All Souls college Mallard, at which time 'tis usual with the fellows and their friends to have a supper, and to sit up all night drinking and singing. Their song is the mallard, and formerly they used to ramble about the college with sticks and poles, &c. in quest of the mallard... They tell you the custom arose from a swinging old mallard, that had been lost at the foundation of the college, and found many years after in the sink. **1801** BP. HEBER *Let.* 15 Jan. in *Life* (1830) I. 25 A very severe cold which I caught by getting out of bed.. to see the celebration of the famous All Souls' mallard feast... I had thus a full view of the Lord Mallard and about forty fellows, in a kind of procession on the library roof. **1899** C. G. ROBERTSON *All Souls Coll.* 102 The song of the mallard (which is still sung at the college Gaudies).

mallardite ('mælədaɪt). *Min.* [Named by A. Carnot, 1879, after E. *Mallard*: see -ITE.] A hydrous sulphate of manganese, found in colourless, fibrous masses (Chester *Dict. Names Min.* 1896).

1883 HEDDLE in *Encycl. Brit.* XVI. 401/2.

mallassus, obs. form of MOLASSES.

mallatto, obs. form of MULATTO.

malle, obs. f. MAIL *sb.*[3], MAUL *sb.*[1], *sb.*[2] and *v.*

malleability (ˌmælɪə'bɪlɪtɪ). [f. MALLEABLE + -ITY.] The property of being malleable.

1690 LOCKE *Hum. Und.* III. vi. §6. 210 Supposing the nominal Essence of Gold, to be a Body of such a peculiar Colour and Weight, with Malleability and Fusibility. **1762** tr. *Busching's Syst. Geog.* I. 45 The Noble metals are bodies of the greatest Malleability. **1830** HERSCHEL *Stud. Nat. Phil.* 238 Malleability is again another quality of solids, especially metals, quite distinct from toughness. **1890** SIR F. ABEL *Pres. Addr. Brit. Assoc.* in *Nature* 4 Sept., The existence in steel of proportions [of manganese] ranging from 0·1 up to about 2·75 per cent. improves its strength and malleability.

b. *fig.* Capacity for being fashioned or adapted.

1877 BURROUGHS *Taxation* 402 Malleability.. is one of the ..characteristics of the common law. **1880** OUIDA *Moths* I. viii. 190 You are old-fashioned, pedantic, unpleasant,.. you have no malleability.

malleable ('mælɪəb(ə)l), *a.* Also 4-6 **malliable**, 5 **malyable, mallyable**, 7 **malable**, 8 **mallable**. [a. OF. *malleable*, ad. L. **malleābil-is*, f. L. *malleāre* to MALLEATE: see -ABLE.]

1. Having the property (possessed by certain substances, esp. metals) of being deprived of form by hammering or pressure, without a tendency or capacity to return to it, or to fracture.

malleable iron: iron which has been decarburized by oxidation under prolonged heat and rendered capable of being malleated in a slight degree.

c **1386** CHAUCER *Can. Yeom. Prol. & T.* 577 Make as good siluer and as fyn As ther is any in youre purse or myn.. and make it malliable. *c* **1407** LYDG. *Reas. & Sens.* 6814 Men kan nat maken yt plicable Nor forge yt to be Malliable. *c* **1450** LYDG. & BURGH *Secrees* 2125 Science nor Crafft to hym was delectable, but to forge malyable mataylle. **1568** GRAFTON *Chron.* I. 123 A certeyn craftes man had found out the Art of.. melting of Glasse in such sort, as he made the same malliable. **1692** LUTTRELL *Brief Rel.* (1857) II. 365 An invention to melt and make malleable a sort of oar found among the tinn mines. **1794** SULLIVAN *View Nat.* I. 469 Metals are malleable or ductile under the hammer. **1822** IMISON *Sci. & Art* II. 95 Zinc is very little malleable, except when heated. **1825** J. NICHOLSON *Operat. Mechanic* 650 The ease with which cast-iron can be made into any required shape has.. given to rails of that material a decided superiority over those of malleable-iron. **1881** SIR J. EVANS *Anc. Bronze Impl.* 11 One alloy of copper and tin is rendered most malleable by rapid cooling. **1889** G. FINDLAY *Eng. Railway* 40 The first malleable iron rail was patented by J. Birkenshaw, in 1820. **1898** *Engineering Mag.* XVI. 105 Examples.. are found in malleable-iron castings.

¶ **b.** In etymological sense. Of stone: That may be dressed with a hammer.

1665 J. WEBB *Stone-Heng* (1725) 209 When the Stones were once down,.. Men might, as they found them more or less malleable, for their own Advantage.. make Use of them.

2. *transf.* and *fig.* Capable of being fashioned or adapted.

1612 LD. ROCHESTER in *Buccleuch MSS.* (Hist. MSS. Comm.) I. 119 Your enemies have objected.. that you are too violent, which signifies in Court language not malleable to their use. **1663** BUTLER *Hud.* I. i. 182 He.. could tell.. Who first made Musick malleable. **1796** BURKE *Regic. Peace* iii. 32 We grow more malleable under their blows. **1802** WOLCOT (P. Pindar) *Horrors Bribery* Wks. 1812 V. 211 Courtiers.. Were made of very malleable matter. **1849** H. ROGERS *Ess.* (1874) I. 227 To seize a language in its rude state, and compel it.. to become a malleable material of thought, is the exclusive prerogative of the highest species of minds. **1882** *Times* 21 July 10 The Chancellorship of the Duchy so remoulded would cease to be malleable; it would cease to be capable of discharging unappropriated duties.

malleableize, malleablize ('mælɪəb(ə)laɪz), *v.* [f. prec. + -IZE.] *trans.* To render malleable.

1882 in OGILVIE. **1884** C. G. W. LOCK *Workshop Receipts* Ser. III. 251/2 The castings will be full of small holes after they have been malleableized.

malleableness ('mælɪəb(ə)lnɪs). [Formed as prec. + -NESS.] = MALLEABILITY.

1644 *Prerogative Anatomized* 6 It was conceiv'd that the tame Kingdome of England.. would quickly coole again, and be reduc'd to its former malleablenesse. **1690** LOCKE *Hum. Und.* III. x. (1695) 283 Malleableness.. is inseparable from the real Essence of Gold. **1731** in BAILEY (vol. II.).

mallear ('mælɪə(r)), *a.* [ad. mod.L. *malleāris*, f. MALLEUS.] Pertaining to the malleus.

1889 in *Syd. Soc. Lex.*

malleate ('mælɪət), *a.* *Zool.* [ad. mod.L. *malleāt-us*, f. MALLEUS.] Furnished with a malleus.

1884 C. T. HUDSON in *Q. Jrnl. Microsc. Sci.* XXIV. 351. **1886** HUDSON & GOSSE *Rotifera* I. 31 *Hydatinadæ*.. trophi malleate.

malleate ('mælɪət), *v.* Now *rare.* [f. L. *malleāt-*, ppl. stem of *malleāre*, f. *malle-us* hammer.] *trans.* To beat with a hammer; *spec.* to beat (metal) thin or flat.

1597 A. M. tr. *Guillemeau's Fr. Chirurg.* 51/1 Allthoughe the same [corslet] be beaten and malleated smothe agayne. **1599** —— tr. *Gabelhouer's Bk. Physicke* 113/2 Take it out, and malleate it till it wexe as thin as the backe of a knife. **1659** GAUDEN *Slight Healers* (1660) 55 A crackt silver vessell, is sooner sodered and new burnished, then a new one malleated out of the rough mass or wedge of metal. **1713** DERHAM *Phys.-Theol.* v. i. 307 Tubal-Cain was.. the first that found the Art of Melting and Malleating Metals.

absol. **1659** STANLEY *Hist. Philos.* XIII. (1701) 580/1 Some Metals,.. by reason of the solidity they had acquired, might be made fit to malleate, or to strike, or for other uses.

fig. **1627-47** FELTHAM *Resolves* II. xcix. 447 Many have been abused, by being malleated in their troublesome fear. **1660** GAUDEN *God's Gt. Demonstr.* 18 Some points may by long Orations be (like gold) malleated and extended to such great latitudes of diffused expressions, as make them very combersom. **1647** FARINGDON *Serm.* (1672) I. 413 We cannot find one [circumstance] which was not as a hammer to malleate and soften his stony heart. **1647** H. MORE *Song of Soul* III. App. xxx, And pox and pestilence do malleate.

malleated ('mælɪeɪtɪd), *ppl. a. rare.* [f. prec. + -ED[1].] Wrought with a hammer; also, marked or dented as with a hammer.

1656 BLOUNT *Glossogr.*, *Malleated*,.. wrought or beaten with the hammer or beetle. **1881** WATSON in *Jrnl. Linn. Soc.* XV. 246 The surface is faintly malleated in a somewhat disorderly fashion.

malleation (mælɪ'eɪʃən). [ad. late L. *malleātiōn-em*, f. *malleāre*: see MALLEATE *v.*]

1. The action of malleating or condition of being malleated. Now *rare.*

1596 PLAT *Jewell-ho.* III. 85 Abiding both the touch, malleation, and coppell. **1610** B. JONSON *Alch.* II. v, *Svb.* What's the proper passion of Mettalls? *Fac.* Malleation. **1696** J. EDWARDS *Demonstr. Exist. God* I. 139 An ounce of it may be so extended by malleation, that it will take up ten acres. **1796** KIRWAN *Elem. Min.* (ed. 2) II. 104 An agglutinated mass susceptible of Malleation.

fig. **1654** GAYTON *Pleas. Notes* III. i. 67 His Squire, who by often malleations.. and threshings, might in good time be beaten out into the forme of a gentileman. **1792** SIR P. FRANCIS *Let.* 21 Jan. in *Burke's Corr.* (1844) III. 377 Some of us.. have been humming our brains for an inscription; but what signifies malleation without fire?

2. A mark or dent resembling one produced by hammering on metal.

1881 WATSON in *Jrnl. Linn. Soc.* XV. 246 Besides the larger system of malleations there is a second system a good deal smaller and more irregular.

3. *Path.* A convulsive disorder characterized by the hammering one part of the body against another; occurring as a symptom in chorea and insanity.

1822-34 *Good's Study Med.* (ed. 4) III. 394 The convulsion is often accompanied with a peculiar kind of percussion.. resembling the malleation we have already had occasion to describe. **1899** *Allbutt's Syst. Med.* VIII. 106 A patient may be constantly making bowing movements (salutation spasm), or hammering (malleation).

mallecho: see MICHING MALICHO.

mallee ('mæli:). Also **malle**. [Native Australian.] Any one of several scrubby species of eucalyptus which flourish in the desert parts of South Australia and Victoria; esp. *Eucalyptus dumosa* and *E. oleosa*. Also, the 'scrub' or thicket formed by these trees. **mallee bird, fowl, hen**, an Australian mound-bird, *Leipoa ocellata*; **mallee root** *slang* (see quot. 1941).

1848 W. WESTGARTH *Austral. Felix* 73 Laap, a sweet exudation from the leaf of the mallee (*Eucalyptus dumosa*). **1857** HOWITT *Tallangetta* xii. II. 2 This Mallee scrub.. consists of a dense wood of a dwarf species of gum-tree. **1898** 'R. BOLDREWOOD' *Rom. Canvass Town* 37 Far off, amidst the sea-like expanse of the mallee.. rise sombre, sharply-defined peaks and ranges. **1911** E. M. CLOWES *On Wallaby* ix. 249 On the Wimmera Plains is massed the dwarf eucalyptus known as the Mallee Scrub, the roots of which make such ideal firewood. **1936** I. L. IDRIESS *Cattle King* ii. 10 They passed through the mallee belt, then out on to plain country. **1941** BAKER *Dict. Austral. Slang* 45 *Mallee root*, a prostitute. **1944** A. RUSSELL *Bush Ways* xxii. 104, I think of the mallee scrubs and red gum fringes of the lower Murray River. **1958** E. O. SCHLUNKE *Village Hampden* 127 'They're going to lynch you, Regerson,' Harry told him, grinning. 'You'd better take to the mallee before they come for you.' **1963** *Times* 12 Mar. p. x/7 The mallee fowl is one of the megapodiidae or mound-building birds of the dry interior. **1966** G. DURRELL *Two in Bush* v. 166 Mallee scrub consists of a small species of eucalyptus between six and twenty feet high, and in places the trees grow very close together, their branches entwining and forming a continuous canopy. **1973** *Sun-Herald* (Sydney) 26 Aug. 85/2 (*caption*) A mallee fowl on its mound.

mallee, var. MALI.

mallei, pl. of MALLEUS.

malleiform ('mælɪ:ɪfɔ:m), *a.* [ad. mod.L. *malleiform-is*, f. *malleus* hammer: see -FORM.] Having the form of a hammer.

1856 in MAYNE *Expos. Lex.* **1877** HUXLEY *Anat. Inv. Anim.* v. 238 In some species of Polynöe, the parapodia give rise.. to large, richly ciliated, malleiform tubercles.

mallein ('mælɪ:ɪn), *sb.* Also **-ine**. [f. L. *malle-us* glanders + -IN.] A sterilized culture of the bacillus of glanders, used for the inoculation of that disease.

1892 *Daily News* 29 Sept. 6/6 They [*sc.* glandered horses] are inoculated by him with a virus called malleine. **1902** G. S. WOODHEAD in *Encycl. Brit.* XXXI. 532/1 The glanders bacillus grows best in the presence of oxygen;.. it then appears to have the power of forming toxin... This poison (mallein) is used for the purpose of diagnosing the presence of glanders. *Ibid.*, The mallein test.

mallein ('mælɪ:ɪn), *v.* [f. the sb.] *trans.* To inoculate (a horse or mule) against glanders.

1915 *Punch* 4 Aug. 101/2 All mules on joining units will in future be malleined.

mallema'roking. *Naut.* [f. Du. *mallemerok* foolish woman, tomboy, f. *mal* foolish + *merok*, *marok*, *marot*, a. F. *marotte* 'object of foolish affection' (Littré).] (See quot.)

1867 SMYTH *Sailor's Word-bk.*, *Mallemaroking*, the visiting and carousing of seamen in the Greenland ships.

mallemuck, var. MOLLYMAWK.

mallender, obs. form of MALANDER.

mallengyn, variant of MALENGIN *Obs.*

malleo-incudal ('mælɪəʊɪn'kju:dəl), *a.* *Anat.* [f. *malleo-*, MALLEUS + L. *incūd-em* INCUS + -AL[1].] Pertaining jointly to the malleus and the incus.

1877 BURNETT *Ear* 75 The articulating surfaces for the malleo-incudal joint.

malleolar (mæ'li:ələ(r), 'mælɪələ(r)), *a.* *Anat.* [f. MALLEOL-US + -AR.] Pertaining to the malleolus.

1842 E. WILSON *Anat. Vade M.* (ed. 2) 325 The malleolar arteries are distributed to the ankle-joint. **1890** GRAY *Anat.* (ed. 12) 591 The malleolar arteries supply the ankle-joint.

‖**malleolus** (mæ'li:ələs). Pl. **-i**. Also in Anglicized form **malleol**. [L. *malleolus*, dim. of *malleus* hammer.]

1. *Anat.* Either of the two bony eminences of the leg bone at the ankle. (The ***internal malleus*** belongs to the tibia, the ***external m.*** to the fibula.)

1693 *Blancard's Phys. Dict.* (ed. 2), *Malleolus* or *Malleus*, is Twofold, *external*,.. Or *internal*,.. these make the Ancle. **1758** J. S. tr. *Le Dran's Observ. Surg.* (1771) 355 The external Malleol remained very large. **1879** *St. George's Hosp. Rep.* IX. 742 It is also very bad.. behind the malleoli, especially the internal malleolus. **1893** A. S. ECCLES *Sciatica* 9 Between the inner malleolus and the heel.

2. *Hort.* A layer which when separated from the parent stem presents a hammer-shape.

1706 PHILLIPS (ed. Kersey), *Malleolus*,.. a Sprout growing out of a Branch, which grew out it self but the Year before. **1839** LINDLEY *Introd. Bot.* (ed. 3) 84 The layer was called malleolus, which literally signifies a hammer.

†**3.** *Antiq.* A kind of fire-dart. *Obs.*

1706 PHILLIPS (ed. Kersey), *Malleoli*, were certain Devices made of combustible Matter. **1753** CHAMBERS *Cycl. Supp.* **1797** *Encycl. Brit.* (ed. 3) X. 480/2.

malleoramate (mælɪəʊ'reɪmət), *a.* *Zool.* [f. *malleo-*, used as comb. form of MALLEUS + RAM-US + -ATE[3].] In rotifers: Having the mallei fixed by unci to the rami.

1884 C. T. HUDSON in *Q. Jrnl. Microsc. Sci.* XXIV. 352. **1886** HUDSON & GOSSE *Rotifera* I. 30 *Melicertidæ*.. trophi malleo-ramate.

malles, obs. form of MALICE.

mallet ('mælɪt), *sb.*[1] Forms: 5 **mailȝet, mailet, maylet(te, -leot, -lat**, 5-6 **maillet**, 6 **mayllet, mallette**, 6-7 **malet**, 6- **mallet**. [a. F. *maillet* wooden hammer, dim. of *mail* MAUL *sb.*[1]]

1. a. A kind of hammer, normally of wood, but sometimes of other materials, smaller than a

maul or beetle. It has many diverse forms, according to the purpose for which it is used.

The mason's mallet is a broad, nearly cylindrical mass of wood, with a short handle set perpendicularly in the middle of the upper surface, and is used for driving a cold chisel; a similar implement is used for driving wedges. The carpenter's mallet for driving a chisel or gouge has usually a massive square or barrel-shaped head.

c **1425** WYNTOUN *Chron.* III. i. 104 Þe nayl þan til his hewide scho set, And straik on fast wiþe þat mailȝet. *c* **1440** *Promp. Parv.* 323/1 Malyet, betyl. *c* **1475** *Pict. Voc.* in Wr.-Wülcker 805/16 *Hic porticulus*, a maylat. **1523** FITZHERB. *Husb.* §136 A mallet to dryue the knyfe and thy wedge in-to the tree. **1560** DAUS tr. *Sleidane's Comm.* 343 b, The bishop striketh on the gate with a golden mallet. **1577** B. GOOGE *Heresbach's Husb.* II. (1586) 108 b, For Pullies..and Mallettes, the meetest are the wilde Oliue, the Boxe. **1600** HOLLAND *Livy* XXVII. xlix. 664 A carpenters chissell and a mallet. **1660** BOYLE *New Exp. Phys. Mech.* xx. 146 The Vessel..was warily..struck in divers places with a Wooden Mallet. **1666** DRYDEN *Ann. Mirab.* cxlvi, Their left hand does the caulking-iron guide, The rattling mallet with the right they lift. **1683** MOXON *Mech. Exerc.* II. 30 Printers Mallets have a Cilindrick Head, and a round Handle. **1720** GAY *Poems* (1745) I. 34 The weighty mallet deals resounding blows. **1828** SCOTT *Tales Grandfather* Ser. II. xviii, Mitchell..endured nine blows of the mallet with the utmost firmness. **1844** H. STEPHENS *Bk. Farm* 1269 The stake *e* is driven into the ground by the wooden mallet. **1860** *Eng. & For. Min. Gloss.* (Cornw. Terms), *Mallet*, an instrument used with the borer. **1875** KNIGHT *Dict. Mech.* II. 1749 s.v. *Plugger*, The electric mallet is an automatic dental instrument for condensing the filling or plug in a tooth by a rapid succession of strokes imparted by means of electro-magnetism. **1895** ARNOLD & SONS *Catal. Surg. Instr.* 107 Mallet for use with Osteotomy Chisel, boxwood.

b. *Games.* (*a*) The wooden hammer used for striking the balls in the game of croquet; also *transf.* (with qualifying adj.), one who wields the mallet, a croquet-player. (*b*) The 'stick' used at polo.

1868 *Chambers's Encycl.* X. 483/2 [Croquet] The Mallets should be light and handy; with ash shafts, and boxwood or ash heads. The heads of the mallets are of various shapes—as the dice-box, which is the most common shape; the plane-convex, the hammer-head, and the cue-shape. **1877** MAR. M. GRANT *Sun-Maid* ix, Bébé was the 'crack' mallet of the [croquet] club. **1868** HOLME LEE *B. Godfrey* lxi, She ..dropped her mallet. **1897** *Outing* (U.S.) XXX. 483/1 The mallets or sticks [in Polo] are generally of malacca cane.

c. *slang.* The fist.

1821 *Sporting Mag.* VIII. 234 Powel..went to work with his mallets at a tremendous rate.

†**d.** Phrase. ***as sad*** (i.e. dull) ***as any mallet.***

1645 MILTON *Colast.* Wks. 1851 IV. 357, I amaze me, though the fancy of this doubt be as obtuse and sad as any mallet, how the Licenser could sleep out all this.

†**e.** *fig.* A person or agency that smites, beats down or crushes. *Obs.* [After L. *malleus*, F. *maillet*: cf. HAMMER *sb.* 1 b.]

1525 LD. BERNERS *Froiss.* II. clxxxvi. [clxxxii.] 232 The malettes were laide downe, to the entent to kepe vnder the parisyence. **1561** T. NORTON *Calvin's Inst.* II. v. (1634) 138 Sometimes like a mallet, to strike the Israelites. **1577–87** HOLINSHED *Chron.* (1807–8) II. 430 A verie mallet of such strangers as sought preferment in this realme by the popes provisions. **1584** R. SCOT *Discov. Witchcr.* XVI. i. (1886) 396 The booke called A Mallet to braine witches. **1823** [see MALLETER].

f. *Mus.* A light hammer used for playing the vibraphone, xylophone, or similar instrument.

1930 *Melody Maker* Jan. 69/2 You should use at least three different 'hardnesses' of mallets for solo playing. **1968** *Ibid.* 23 Nov. 18 Having started with four mallets right from the beginning, I found myself playing the instrument in piano style.

†**2.** A mace. *Obs.*

c **1475** *Partenay* 4698 A [s]quare maillet the Geant gan hold. *Ibid.* 4716 No-thyng was he wurth, right noght myght he do, Where cursedly had done with his maillet soo. *c* **1500** *Melusine* 329 The Geaunt..held in his hand a gret mayllet. **1523** LD. BERNERS *Froiss.* I. cccxcvii. 278 b, Also they had seruantes right well harnessed, bearynge great malettes of yron and stele, to confounde helmes.

†**3.** *Antiq.* = MALLEOLUS 3. *Obs.*

1541 PAYNEL *Catiline, Cicero's Orat.* xviii. 32 b, Let them leaue lying in awayte about the consuls house,..to prepare mallettes and torches to set fyre on the citie. *Ibid. note*, Mallettes were lyke arrowes whiche were caste burnynge.

4. A distemper in cattle. ? *Obs.*

1600 SURFLET *Country Farm* I. xxiii. 132 The stithie, hapning to the oxe, being otherwise called a mallet or hammer. **1688** R. HOLME *Armoury* II. 172/2 Diseases in Cows... The Stithie, or the Mallet, or Hammer.

5. *Anat.* = MALLEUS 1.

1796 in NEMNICH *Polyglotten-Lex.* v. **1877** BURNETT *Ear* 68 The malleus, or mallet, received its name from Vesalius.

6. *attrib.* and *Comb.*, as ***mallet-form, -head, -pate, -paw***; ***mallet-shaped*** adj.; **mallet finger** *Med.*, a condition in which a finger is permanently flexed at the distal joint, usu. resulting from a blow to the tip of the extended finger, which ruptures the extensor tendon; a finger so affected; †**mallet-fish** (see quot.); **mallet-flower**, any plant of the genus *Tupistra* (Cent. Dict.); **mallet-headed** *a.*, (*a*) applied to a chisel made to be struck with a mallet; (*b*) having a head shaped like that of a mallet; **mallet-headed oyster**, an oyster of the genus *Malleus*; **mallet-shoot**, a hammer-shaped slip of a tree or shrub for planting.

1894 GOULD *Dict. Med.* 472/2 **Mallet finger*, a deformity of a finger characterized by deficient extension or undue flexion of the terminal phalanx. **1934** KEY & CONWELL *Managem. Fractures* xx. 718 (*heading*) Drop or mallet finger (baseball finger). **1956** *Jrnl. Amer. Med. Assoc.* 21 July 1135 (*heading*) New technique for treatment of mallet fingers and fractures of distal phalanx. **1967** *Punch* 29 Mar. 458/3 Less heroically, women can contract Mallet Finger by 'tucking the bed-clothes under the mattress when bed-making'. **1611** COTGR., *Cagnole*, the rauenous, and ougly dogfish, called (of the fashion of his head) the *Mallet-fish. *a* **1697** AUBREY *Lives, Hobbes* (1898) I. 348 His head was..of a *mallet-forme (approved by the physiologers). **1707–12** MORTIMER *Husb.* (1721) II. 59 Which Wood is useful for..*Mallet-heads [etc.]..being very hard and durable. **1897** *Outing* (U.S.) XXX. 483/1 The mallet-head now used [in Polo] is generally cigar-shaped, 2 inches thick and 8 or 9 inches long. **1906** E. JOHNSTON *Writing & Illuminating* xvii. 396 The chisels are either *Hammer-headed* or **Mallet-headed.* **1909** *Westm. Gaz.* 26 Oct. 5/2 The announcement made by the Rules of Golf Committee on the subject of mallet-headed clubs will have far-spreading consequences. **1753** CHAMBERS *Cycl. Supp.* s.v. *Ostrea*, The malleum, or brachiated oister; called the *mallet-headed oister. **1823** *Blackw. Mag.* XIV. 520 As for the *mallet-pate, pig-eye Chinese. **1902** N. HOWARD *Kiartan* 50 What! Art thou mum? Old tramp, old *mallet-paw [*addressing Thor*]. **1901** *N. & Q.* 9th Ser. VIII. 215/1 A *mallet-shaped head for driving in the stakes of the sheepfold. **1745** tr. *Columella's Husb.* III. xvii, They so planted the *mallet-shoot, that some part of the old branch did stick to the young one. **1879** LEWIS & SHORT *Lat. Dict.*, *Malleolus*,..a mallet-shoot for planting.

†**'mallet**, *sb.*[2] *Obs. rare*[−1]. In mod. Dicts. malet. [ad. Sp. *maleta* = F. *mallette*, dim. of *malle* MAIL *sb.*[3]] A little bag or portmanteau.

1612 SHELTON *Quix.* III. ix. (1620) 207 Sancho past ouer the mallet, without leauing a corner of it, or the cushion vnsearched. **1847** WEBSTER (citing Shelton), *Malet*, a little bag or budget; a portmanteau.

mallet ('mælɪt), *v. Obs.* exc. *arch.* [f. MALLET *sb.*[1]] *trans.* To beat, hammer; *lit.* and *fig.*

1594 LYLY *Mother Bombie* II. i. 59 (Bond) My head is full of hammers, and they haue so maletted my wit, that I am almost a malcontent. *a* **1633** AUSTIN *Medit.* (1635) 108 They Malletted him with their cruell Fists; as if he had bin Brasse indeede. *c* **1840** MRS. BROWNING *Lett. to R. H. Horne* (1877) I. iii. 19 Your Elizabethan fashion of malleting down your metaphors..produces a diction of extraordinary power.

mallet, erron. form of MALLARD.

malleted ('mælɪtɪd), *ppl. a.* [f. MALLET *v.* + -ED[1].] **a.** Fixed as if by hammering. **b.** Struck with a mallet.

1582 STANYHURST *Æneis* III. (Arb.) 91 His oane light, That stood in his lowring front gloommish malleted onlye. **1833** MRS. BROWNING *Prometh. Bound* Poems 1850 I. 145 The clank of the iron, the malleted blow.

malleter ('mælɪtə(r)). *nonce-wd.* [f. MALLET *v.* + -ER[1].] One who beats, as with a mallet.

1823 *Blackw. Mag.* XIV. 212 You ask me to be the..reviewer of the reviews—the mallet of the malleters.

malleting ('mælɪtɪŋ), *vbl. sb.* [f. MALLET *v.* + -ING[1].] The action of striking with a mallet.

1872 L. P. MEREDITH *Teeth* (1878) 87 In filling very large cavities requiring a great deal of pressure and malleting, there is [etc.].

malleurite, variant of MALEURTE *Obs.*

‖**malleus** ('mælɪəs). *Anat.* Pl. **-ei** (-ɪaɪ). [L.: lit. 'hammer'.]

1. The outermost of the three small bones (*malleus*, *incus*, and *stapes*) in the ear of mammals, which transmits the vibrations of the tympanum to the incus or 'anvil': = HAMMER 2 d.

1669 HOLDER *Elem. Speech* 162 The Malleus lies along fixed to the Tympanum. **1705** *Phil. Trans.* XXV. 1982 The head of the Malleus lyes hid in the beginning of the *Sinus Mastoideus*. **1761** P. MORANT *ibid.* LII. 264 A young lad..had the malleus of each ear..dropt out. **1840** G. V. ELLIS *Anat.* 284 The laxator tympani, or great external muscle of the malleus. **1881** MIVART *Cat* 299 One such suspends the Malleus from the wall of the tympanum.

2. One of two organs of the 'trophi' or mouth-apparatus in *Rotifera*, which work upon the incus.

1850 GOSSE in *Trans. Microscop. Soc.* (1852) III. 94 The implements of mastication..consist of two bent jaws, which work upon a central table, and have been likened to a pair of hammers working on an anvil; I shall therefore name the working arms the *mallei*, and the central table the *incus*. **1877** HUXLEY *Anat. Inv. Anim.* iv. 188. **1888** ROLLESTON & JACKSON *Anim. Life* 633.

3. *Zool.* A genus of molluscs of the family *Aviculidæ* (Hammer-shells or Hammer-oysters).

1839 *Penny Cycl.* XIV. 334/2. **1878** BELL *Gegenbaur's Comp. Anat.* 329 Malleus, Avicula, [etc.]..have an organ [byssus-secreting gland] of this kind.

mallice, obs. form of MALICE.

mallico: see MICHING MALICHO.

malligo, mallilla, obs. ff. MALAGA, MANILLE.

Malling ('mɔːlɪŋ). The names of two villages, East and West *Malling*, in Kent, used to designate: **1.** English pottery of the late sixteenth century in the form of tin-enamelled jugs, one of which was found at West Malling; = *tiger-ware*.

[**1903** *Times* 11 Feb. 10/6 The West Malling Elizabethan jug..will be sold [on]..February 19th.] **1933** W. B. HONEY *Eng. Pott. & Porc.* iii. 36 A 'Malling jug' of 1550..was sold for five hundred and sixty guineas. **1968** A. RAY *Eng. Delftware Pott.* xi. 91 The 16th century 'Malling' jugs are the earliest tin-glazed pottery.

2. A rootstock for fruit trees developed at the East Malling Research Station. Also *attrib.*

1927 *Gardeners' Chronicle* 19 Mar. 199/2 Present-day planters have the advantage of being able to buy trees on the East Malling stocks. *Ibid.* There is a very strong demand amongst market growers for dessert Apples on Jaune de Metz (Type IX), the most dwarfing of the Malling selections. **1928** A. H. HOARE *Eng. Grass Orchard* v. 73 It is good news for orchard planters that it has been found possible to select and propagate by layering the most desirable of the seedling crabs and the very vigorous types of 'Paradise' stocks, as they are called. These are known as Malling Types XII., XIII. and XVI., and Bristol No. 5... They are not yet plentiful. **1936** H. V. TAYLOR *Apples Eng.* p. iii (Advt.), Selected trees on Malling stocks. **1966** A. G. BROWN in *Fruit Present & Future* (R. Hort. Soc.) 18 East Malling has continued to work with rootstocks and has recently introduced a new dwarfing stock Malling 26. **1973** *Pears Encycl. Gardening: Fruit & Vegetables* 23 Trees on Malling IX, which are planted closer than those of other rootstocks..will ensure the largest weight of fruit from a small garden, in the quickest possible time.

†**mallok(e.** *Obs.* [repr. Irish *mallacht*, a. L. *maledict-* (see MALEDICTION): cf. ON. *bjannak* (once) from Irish *bennacht* benediction.] Cursing.

a **1300** *E. E. Psalter* ix. 28 Of whas mallok [*v. r.* malloke, malloc] his mouth ful is. *Ibid.* xiii. 3, cviii. 16.

mallophagan (mæ'lɒfəgən), *a.* and *sb. Zool.* [Formed as next: see -AN.]

a. *adj.* = next. **b.** *sb.* An individual of the group *Mallophaga*.

In mod. Dicts.

mallophagous (mæ'lɒfəgəs), *a. Ent.* [f. mod.L. *mallophag-us*, pl. (f. Gr. μαλλός lock of wool + -φάγος that eats) + -OUS.] Of an insect: Devouring wool, hair, feathers, etc.; applied to the *Mallophaga*, a group of apodous parasitic insects.

1890 *Athenæum* 11 Oct. 487/3 A specimen of *Ornithomyia avicularia*,..to which there were firmly adhering..several specimens of a mallophagous insect.

Mallorcan (mə'lɔːkən, mə'ljɔː-), *sb.* and *a.* [ad. Sp. *Mallorca* Majorca + -AN.] = MAJORCAN *sb.* and *a.* Also, the language of the Mallorcans.

1868 H. O'SHEA *Guide to Spain & Portugal* (ed. 3) 341/1 The inhabitants, especially the Mallorcans, are an honest, interesting..people. *Ibid.* 342/2 There is great similarity between Mallorcan and the Languedocian patois of Montpellier. *Ibid.* 343/1 The learned Scaliger expatiates on the excellence of the Mallorcan pottery. **1927** N. L. DURYEA *Mallorca* i. 6 Oriental eyes brood in Mallorcan faces. **1934** *Scottish Geogr. Mag.* L. 136 A great proportion of the Mallorcan trees are exceedingly old. **1937** W. FORTESCUE *Sunset House* ix. 162 A little red Mallorcan sausage. **1954** T. MAYNARD *Long Road of Father Serra* (1956) i. 13 Not all Mallorcans were so pious as the Serras. *Ibid.* 17 The beauty of the Mallorcan scene. **1972** A. LOWE *Catalan Venegeance* 140 The *Carta Catalana*, the commercial map of oriental trade drawn in 1375 by the Mallorcan Jew Abraham Cresques.

Mallorquin (mə'lɔːkɪn, mə'ljɔː-), *sb.* and *a.* Also **-quine**. [Sp. *Mallorquín*, f. *Mallorca* Majorca: see MAJORCAN *sb.* and *a.*] = MAJORCAN *sb.* and *a.* Also, the language of the Mallorquins.

1839 *Penny Cycl.* XIV. 339/1 In character the Mallorquines somewhat resemble the Catalans. **1868** H. O'SHEA *Guide to Spain & Portugal* (ed. 3) 342/2 The 'Mallorquin' is a corruption of the Catalan dialect. **1869** H. W. BATES *Illustr. Trav.* I. 267/2 The women of Soller are..by no means so plain in their appearance as the majority of the Mallorquine females. **1875** *Encycl. Brit.* III. 277/2 A railway is in course of construction from Palma by Inca to Alcudia, and the stock is all held by Mallorquins. **1926** R. MACAULAY *Crewe Train* I. i. 4 As..his knowledge of the Mallorquin idiom improved..he discovered that Mallorquins are almost the kindest and most sociable people in the world. **1929** D. H. LAWRENCE *Let.* 26 May (1932) 806 The Mallorquin servants cooked Spanish rice over a fire. **1952** [see IBIZAN *a.*]. **1954** T. MAYNARD *Long Road of Father Serra* (1956) i. 2 They have their own language, Mallorquin, even if this is no more than a dialect of Catalan. **1973** *Times* 3 Mar. 26/2 *Mallorquin*, the local dialect of the native Catalan language, runs a poor second. **1974** R. JEFFRIES *Mistakenly in Mallorca* iii. 24 A Mallorquin inlaid sideboard. *Ibid.* v. 34 She was not..a Mallorquin or a Spaniard.

mallow ('mæləʊ). Forms: 1 **mealuwe, malwa, mealwe, mealewe,** 1, 5 **malwe,** 3–5 **malue,** 4–5 **malve,** 5 **maloo, malewe,** 6 **mallo, malew, malowe,** 6–7 **mallowe,** 6– **mallow**. [OE. *mealuwe* wk. fem., a. L. *malva*; prob. related in some way to the synonymous Gr. μαλάχη, μολόχη. Cf. Du. *malve*, *maluwe*, G. *malve*, OF. *malve* (mod.F. *mauve*), It., Sp., Pg. *malva*. Cf. MAUL *sb.*[2], MAW.]

1. (Also *pl.*, const. as *sing.*) A common wild plant, *Malva sylvestris* (N.O. *Malvaceæ*), having hairy stems and leaves and deeply-cleft reddish-purple flowers; it is very mucilaginous. Also

called *common, field, wild mallow*. In extended use, any plant of the genus *Malva*.

c **1000** ÆLFRIC *Gloss.* in Wr.-Wülcker 135/27 *Malua*, malwe, uel ȝeormenletic. *c* **1000** *Sax. Leechd.* II. 194 Leahtric & mealwan & hænne flæsc. *Ibid.* 214 Eft wildre mealwan seawes þry lytle bollan fullan. *c* **1265** *Voc. Names Pl.* in Wr.-Wülcker 559/3 *Malua*, malue. *c* **1380** WYCLIF *Serm.* Sel. Wks. II. 194 It growiþ to a tree, as done malues in sum contre. *c* **1420** *Liber Cocorum* (1862) 47 Redde nettel crop and malues grene. *c* **1450** *M E. Med. Bk.* (Heinrich) 151 Tak bausones grece, wylde malwe..& pimpernel. **1573** TUSSER *Husb.* (1878) 72 Dig garden, stroy mallow. **1573–80** BARET *Alv.* M 77 Mallowes, this herb groweth in gardens, and in vntilled places. **1597** GERARDE *Herbal* II. cccxxxvii. 784 The wilde Mallowe hath broade leaues somewhat rounde [etc.]. **1605** B. JONSON *Volpone* I. i, A thresher.. dares not taste the smallest graine, But feedes on mallowes. **1610** SHAKS. *Temp.* II. i. 144. **1611** COTGR. s.v. *Maulve*, The white Mallow... The field Mallow, wild Mallow; our ordinarie Mallow. **1783** CRABBE *Village* I, Hardy and high ..The slimy mallow waves her silky leaf. **1855** TENNYSON *Brook* 46 Many a fairy foreland set With willow-weed and mallow. **1855** E. SMITH *Bot.* in *Syst. Nat. Hist.* I. 117 In the Geranium and the Mallows the whole [of the stamens] are united. **1876** HARLEY *Mat. Med.* (ed. 6) 709 The Mallow is found in most parts of Europe.

2. With qualification applied to various malvaceous plants: †**crisp(ed, curled(-leaved) mallow**, *Malva crispa*; †**cut mallow** = *vervain mallow*; **dwarf mallow**, *M. rotundifolia*; **French mallow**, *Lavatera Olbia*; **Indian mallow**, (*a*) *Abutilon Avicennæ*; (*b*) any plant of the genera *Urena* or *Sida*; **rose mallow**, (*a*) see 5; (*b*) the genus *Hibiscus*, esp. *H. Moscheutos*; **shrub** (†**shrubbed**, †**shrubby**) **mallow**, *Hibiscus syriacus*; †**thorny mallow**, *Hibiscus Sabdariffa*; **tree mallow**, *Lavatera arborea*; **Venetian, Venice mallow**, *Hibiscus Trionum*; **vervain mallow**, *M. Alcea*; **yellow mallow** = INDIAN MALLOW. See also JEWS' MALLOW (JEW 3 d), MARSHMALLOW, MUSK MALLOW.

c **1265** *Voc. Names Pl.* in Wr.-Wülcker 558/1 *Malua cri[s]pia*, screpemalue [*sic*]. *c* **1450** *ME. Med. Bk.* (Heinrich) 225 Tak þe rote of altea,..& þe crysp malwe, & boile alle in wyn or in ale. **1548** TURNER *Names of Herbes* (1881) 10 It may be named Veruen mallowe, or cut mallowe. *Ibid.* 50 It is called in englishe french Mallowe. **1578** LYTE *Dodoens* V. xxiv. 581 The small wilde Hocke, or Dwarffe Mallowe. **1597** GERARDE *Herbal* II. cccxxxviii. 788 *Althæa arborescens.* Tree Mallowe. *Ibid.*, *Althæa frutex Clusii.* Shrubbed Mallowe. *Ibid.*, The shrubbie Mallowe riseth vp like vnto a hedge bush. *Ibid.* II. cccxxxix. 790 *Althæa lutea.* Yellow Mallowe. .. It is called *Abutilon*. *Ibid.* cccxl. 791 *Alcea Peregrina.* Venice Mallowe. *Sabdarifa.* Thorney Mallowe. **1611** COTGR., *Maulve grande*, the great Mallow, or tree Mallow. **1620** VENNER *Via Recta* vii. 144 The best and wholsomest of them is the curled Mallow. **1707–12** MORTIMER *Husb.* (1721) II. 180 *Althæa Fruticosa*, or Shrub-Mallow. **1754** *Catal. Seeds* in *Fam. Rose of Kilravock* (Spalding Club) 427 Tree-mallow, a shrub. *Ibid.* 428 Curled-leaved mallow... Abutilon, (Indian mallow). **1760** J. LEE *Introd. Bot.* App. 318 Mallow, Yellow, *Sida*. **1785** MARTYN *Rousseau's Bot.* xxiv. 344 Dwarf Mallow. *Ibid.* 345 Vervain Mallow. **1846–50** A. WOOD *Class-bk. Bot.* 207 *M[alva] Crispa.* Curled or Crisped-leaved Mallow. **1866** *Treas. Bot.*, *Hibiscus*, the Rose-mallow family. *Ibid.* 665/1 *L[avatera] arborea*, the Sea or Tree Mallow, is a common south-west European plant.

3. = MARSH MALLOW, *Althæa officinalis*. Called also ***water, white mallow***.

14.. in *Rel. Ant.* I. 53 Tak the white malue, and bryn hit. **1483** *Cath. Angl.* 226/2 A Malue, *altea*. **1548** TURNER *Names of Herbes* (E.D.S.) 11 Althea..in Englishe marish mallowe or water mallowe. **1597** GERARDE *Herbal* II. cccxxxviii. 789 In English marsh Mallowe, moorish Mallowe, and white Mallowe.

4. The Syrian Mallow, *Hibiscus syriacus*.

a **1387** *Sinon. Barthol.* (Anecd. Oxon.) 24 *Herba siriaca*, i. malve. *c* **1450** *Alphita* (Anecd. Oxon.) 111 *Malua siriaca*, ..malewe. **1754** *Catal. Seeds* in *Fam. Rose of Kilravock* (Spalding Club) 427 Ketmia, (Syrian mallow). **1797** *Encycl. Brit.* (ed. 3) VIII. 498/2 *Hibiscus*, Syrian mallow.

5. ***garden*** or ***rose mallow***, the hollyhock, *Althæa rosea*.

1577 B. GOOGE *Heresbach's Husb.* II. (1586) 61 It is Hollioke, or Garden Mallow. **1597** GERARDE *Herbal* II. cccxxxvi. 782 Of the garden Mallow called Hollihocke. **1707–12** MORTIMER *Husb.* (1721) II. 229 Mallows of the Garden, is a fair large Flower,..the time of its flowering is in August and September. **1753** CHAMBERS *Cycl. Supp.* s.v. *Malva*, The rose Mallow, or, as we call it, the hollyoak.

6. The leaf or fibre of the mallow used for writing upon.

1656 COWLEY *Davideis* I. Note 54 They did anciently write too upon Mallows. [**1797** *Encycl. Brit.* (ed. 3) X. 504/1 Paper from the mallows may be used.]

7. *attrib.* and *Comb.*, as ***mallow colour, family, flower, leaf, plant, tribe, water***; ***mallow-flowered*** adj.; **mallows red** (see quot.); **mallow rose**, *Hibiscus Moscheutos*; **mallow tree** = *tree mallow* (see 2); **mallow wort**, a plant of the N. O. *Malvaceæ*.

1611 COTGR., *Presme d'Esmaraude*, a..course Emerauld; ..some..of a thicke, or troubled *mallow colour. **1857** A. GRAY *First Less. Bot.* (1866) 109 In the corolla of Geranium ..and of the *Mallow Family. **1611** COTGR., *Gris violant*, *Mallow-flower colour. **1871** KINGSLEY *At Last* xvi, Ochro —a purple-stemmed *mallow-flowered plant. *c* **1400** *Lanfranc's Cirurg.* 56 Take *malowe leues & leues of violet. **1816** BENTHAM *Chrestom.* 325 A *mallow plant, with a flower on it. **1862** O'NEILL *Dict. Calico Printing*, etc. s.v. *Mallow*, The ordinary '*mallows red' is exactly the same as dark crimson. **1840** PAXTON *Bot. Dict.*, *Mallow rose, see *Hibiscus moschatus* [sic]. **1741** *Compl. Fam.-Piece* II. iii. 374 Trees and Shrubs which are now in Flower, as..*Mallow Tree, *Arbor Judæ* [etc.]. **1846** J. BAXTER *Libr. Pract. Agric.* (ed. 4) I. 125 The *mallow tribe are characterized by containing..mucilaginous matter. **1852** HENSLOW *Dict. Bot. Terms* (1856), *Malvaceæ*..the Mallow Tribe. **1898** EVA LÜCKES *Gen. Nursing* x. (1900) 122 *Mallow water and camomile flower water are made in the same way. **1845** LINDLEY *Sch. Bot.* 45 *Mallowworts, or Malvads. **1866** *Treas. Bot.* 665/1 Like the rest of mallowworts the Tree Mallow contains..mucilaginous matter.

‖**mallum** ('mæləm), **mallus** ('mæləs). *Hist.* [med.L. *mallum*, *-us*, ad. OFrankish **mall-*, contracted form of OTeut. **maþlo-* (Goth. *maþl* meeting-place, OE. *mæðel* meeting, discussion, OHG., OS. *mahal* assembly, judgement, speech). Cf. MAIL *sb.*[2], MALL[2].] The hundred-court among the Franks. (By modern historians sometimes used as the name of a common Germanic institution, and so attributed to the Anglo-Saxons.)

1844 LD. BROUGHAM *Brit. Const.* iii. (1862) 54 There was a popular infusion occasionally in the King's mallum, or council. **1851** SIR F. PALGRAVE *Norm. & Eng.* I. 400 The mallum, the Shire-moot, could not be convened. **1874** STUBBS *Const. Hist.* I. iii. §25. 55 From the decisions of the mallus there is no appeal, except to the king himself.

mallure, variant of MALHEUR *Obs.*

†**mally**, *a.* *Obs.* [Cf. Du. 'een regte malle moeder', 'malle, ouwe vader' (*Wb. d. nederl. Taal*, s.v. *Mal* adj.).] Foolishly fond.

1592 BABINGTON *Notes Genesis* xxxiv. 5 (1596) 253 *Blanda patrum segnes facit indulgentia natos.* A mallie father maketh a wicked childe.

mallyce, obs. form of MALICE.

malm (mɑːm), *sb.* Also 4, 9 **malme**, 6 **maund** (?), 7 **maume, mawme, mame, maln**, 8 **maum, mallan**. [OE. *mealm-*, in comb. *mealmstán* (see 3) and in the deriv. *mealmiht* sandy; cogn. w. ON. *malm-r* (Icel. *málmr*, OSw. *malmber*, Sw., Da. *malm*) ore, metal, Goth. *malma* masc., sand; a parallel formation from another grade of the root is OS., OHG. *melm* dust; f. root **mel-*, *mal-* to grind: see MEAL *sb.*]

1. a. A soft friable rock consisting largely of chalky material. **b.** The light loamy soil formed by the disintegration of this rock.

1477 *Rolls of Parlt.* VI. 189/2 The Vaynes called the Malme or Marle and Chalke, liyng comenly in the grounde. **1579–80** NORTH *Plutarch, Alexander* (1595) 737 The earth spued out continually a kind of maund or chalkie clay somewhat lyquid. **1607** J. NORDEN *Surv. Dial.* v. 229 In part of Hamshire they haue another kind of earth,..the slub of the riuer of Auon, which they call Mawme. **1670** J. SMITH *Eng. Improv. Reviv'd* 15 You shall lay or bestow 200 Cartload of the best slimy or fattest Marle or Mame on each or every Acre of Land. **1677** PLOT *Oxfordsh.* iv. 69, I found a soft stone there-about called Maume, of a whitish colour. *a* **1697** AUBREY *Nat. Hist. Wilts* (1847) 107 The soile of the downes I take generally to be a white earth or mawme. **1697** *View Penal Laws* 239 It shall likewise be tryed and severed from Stones, Maln, Marle, and Chalk. **1719** STRACHEY in *Phil. Trans.* XXX. 969 These Clives vary much in Hardness, in some places being little harder than Malm or Loom. **1743** NEEDHAM *ibid.* XLII. 634 This Bed of Malm lies in a Valley, at the Foot of a long Ridge of Chalky Downs. **1747** HOOSON *Miner's Dict.* M ij, *Mallan*, this is of divers Colours,..and always Soft. **1787** G. WHITE *Selborne* i. 2 The gardens..consist of a warm, forward, crumbling mould, called black malm. *Ibid.* 4 A range of fair enclosures, consisting of what is called white malm. **1825** COBBETT *Rur. Rides* (1853) 207 The lanes were very deep; the wet malme just about the colour of rye-meal mixed up with water. **1851** *Jrnl. R. Agric. Soc.* XII. II. 481 *Marme*, a white marl containing an admixture of clay. **1881** WHITEHEAD *Hops* 21 A peculiar fertile clay, known locally as 'malm'. **1885** HINDE in *Phil. Trans.* CLXXVI. 413 The beds..have been described under the local names of malm, firestone [etc.].

2. Short for *malm-brick*.

1858 *Skyring's Builders' Prices* (ed. 48) 66 Points to groins of common stocks..Ditto of Malms. **1881** YOUNG *Every Man his own Mechanic* §1152 Malms are made of a finer clay. **1895** *Oracle Encycl.* I. 500/1 'Marls' or 'Malms' is the name given to the best bricks.

3. *attrib.*: **malm-brick**, the best kind of brick (so ***malm cutter, pavior, stock***); **malm-rock** = sense 1 a; also *Geol.* = GREENSAND 1 c; **malm-stone** = sense 1 a.

c **893** K. ÆLFRED *Oros.* IV. xiii. §5 Mon heardlice gnide þone hnescestan mealmstan æfter þæm [etc.]. **1824** *Mech. Mag.* No. 33. 77 Bricks..which are used for facing buildings, called malm stock Bricks. *Ibid.* 78 The earth and other ingredients, with which the soil for malm Bricks are composed. **1833** LYELL *Princ. Geol.* III. 292 The upper green-sand ('firestone', or 'malm rock', as it is sometimes called) is almost absent. **1842** Malm cutter [see CUTTER *sb.*[1] 7]. **1843** *Mech. Mag.* XXXIX. 192 The difference between malm paviors and stocks was fifteen or twenty shillings per thousand. **1858** *Skyring's Builders' Prices* (ed. 48) 65 Picked stock facings..Seconds malm ditto. **1859** A. C. RAMSAY *Catal. Rock Spec.* (1860) 53 A very fine..sandstone, locally termed 'Malm-rock'. **1876** PAGE *Adv. Text-bk. Geol.* xviii. 349 'Malm rock', a soft silicious substance, containing a large percentage of soluble silica. **1889** *Q. Jrnl. Geol. Soc.* XLV. 406 In the more siliceous malmstones fragments of siliceous sponge-spicules are abundant. **1894** *Jrnl. Royal Agric. Soc.* June 391 The persistence of the Malmstone over a very wide extent of the Upper Greensand of England is a noteworthy fact.

malm (mɑːm, mɔːm), *a.* *dial.* Forms: 7–8 **moam**, 9 **mome**, 7–9 **mawm**, 7– **maum**. [f. root of MALM *sb.*; for the sense cf. the cognate MELCH, MELLOW adjs.] Mellow, soft.

1691 RAY *N. Cy. Words* (E.D.S.), *Moam*, vel *Maum*, maturomitis, mellow. **1788** MARSHALL *Rural Econ. E. Yks.* (E.D.S.), *Maum*, mellow, attended with a degree of dryness. **1829** BROCKETT *Gloss. N. Cy. Words* (ed. 2), *Maum, Maumy*, mellow, soft. *Mome*, soft, smooth, conjoining the idea of sweetness. **1869** *Lonsdale Gloss.*, *Maum, Mawm*, (1) mellow. (2) Gentle, quiet. **1876** *Whitby Gloss.*, *Maum, Mome*, or *Maumy*, mellow; insipid.

malm (mɑːm), *v.*[1] Also 7 **marm**. [f. MALM *sb.*] *trans.* †**a.** To treat (land) with malm (*obs.*). **b.** To convert (clay) into artificial malm for brick-making; to cover (brick-earth) with artificial malm. Hence **malmed** *ppl. a.*, '**malming** *vbl. sb.*

1619–21 *Norden's Surv., Duchy of Lanc.* in *North Riding Rec. Soc.* (1894) I. 24 Fra Scapphow till the west ende of Langhow Bran even suth til the nether syde marmed land. **1850** DOBSON *Manuf. Bricks & Tiles* I. 26 The malm or malmed brick-earth..is turned over with the spade. *Ibid.* II. 3 The brick-earth.. may be malmed, i.e. covered with artificial malm. **1876** A. B. MACDOWALL *Brick* in *Encycl. Brit.* IV. 280/1 The most common mode of preparing the clay, in the London district, is that of *malming*..an artificial malm is made by mixing chalk and clay, previously reduced to pulp, and allowing the mixture to consolidate by evaporation.

†**malm**, *v.*[2] *Obs.* In 7 **mawme**, 9 **maum**. [f. MALM *a.*] *intr.* To become soft.

1641 BEST *Farm. Bks.* (Surtees) 107 Then they water it [earth], and lette it lye three or fower dayes to mawme. **1825** JAMIESON, *Maum*, to soften and swell by means of rain, or from being steeped in water; to become mellow. Malt is said to *maum*, when steeped.

‖**malmag** ('mælmæg). [Appears as *malmay* in Blumentritt's vocabulary of the Sp. dialect of the Philippines, 1882.] The Spectre, *Tarsius spectrum*, a small lemuroid animal, native of Borneo and the Philippines.

1838 CUMING in *Zool. Soc. Proc.* VI. 67 The Malmag is a small animal living under the roots of trees [in the Philippines]. **1871** *Cassell's Nat. Hist.* I. 248 The Spectre Tarsier, or Tarsius. The Malmag.

Malmaison (mæl'meɪzɒn). *Hort.* [Short for *Souvenirs de Malmaison* (Fr. 'recollections of Malmaison', the palace at which the empress Josephine held her court), originally (and still) the name of a delicate variety of blush rose, and transferred to the carnation from some notion of resemblance.] A variety of the carnation.

1892 *Carnation Manual* 149 The Malmaison Carnations can be classed with the tree or perpetual types. **1896** ASHBY-STERRY *Tale Thomas* (1903) 53/2 The three ladies in their fresh crisp morning dresses, their Malmaison carnations, and their warm-coloured wraps. **1900** *Bk. Gardening* 708 Carnations are divided into three groups: (1) Show, (2) Tree or Perpetuals, and (3) Malmaisons. *Ibid.* 709 Malmaisons.. Sorts: These are all varieties obtained from the original Souvenir de la Malmaison. **1901** *Daily Chron.* 20 July 10/3 [The bridesmaids] carried conventional bouquets of pink and sulphur malmaisons.

†**malmarsh**. *Obs. dial.* [? var. or corruption of MALLEMUCK.] = FULMAR.

1833 *Montagu's Ornith. Dict.* 315.

malmaset, obs. form of MARMOSET.

†**malmeny**. *Obs.* Forms: 4 **mawmenny, -menee**, 5 **momene, maumen(y)e, mawmene, -many, -meny, malmany(e, menye, malmens, mammenye, -ony, mameny**, 5–6 **mamony**. [Of obscure origin. Connexion with F. *malmener* 'to maltreat' seems unlikely. The receipt might suggest derivation from MALMSEY or its source.] A dish in old cookery.

? *c* **1390** *Forme of Cury* xx. (1780) 19 Mawmenee. Take a pottel of wyne greke and ii pounde of sugar [etc.]. *Ibid.* cxciv. 88 For to make Mawmenny. *c* **1420** *Liber Cocorum* (1862) 26 For to make momene. *c* **1430** *Two Cookery-bks.* 22 Maumenye ryalle... Mammenye bastarde. *Ibid.* 48 Malmenye Furnez...with the wete dyssche ley þe malmenye & þe cofyns. *a* **1450** *Tourn. Tottenham, Feest* v. in Hazl. *E.P.P.* III. 94 Ther was gryndulstones in gravy And mylstones in mawmany. **1513** *Bk. Keruynge* in *Babees Bk.* (1868) 275 And the seconde course, Iussell with mamony.

malmignatte (mælmɪ'njæt). [ad. mod.L. *malmignattus*, ad. Corsican *malmignatto*, f. It. *malo* bad + *mignatto* (cf. '*mignatta* a horse-leach, a bloud-sucker, *mignatti* a kind of silke-wormes', Florio 1611).] A spider, *Theridion* (*Latrodectus*) *malmignattus*.

[**1699** RAY in *Phil. Trans.* XXI. 57 The Island of Corsica ..breeds venemous Spiders, called by the Inhabitants Tarantola or Malmignatto.] **1882** *Cassell's Nat. Hist.* VI. 176 The Malmignatte..is almost half an inch long [etc.]. *Ibid.* 383 Index, Malmignatte Spider.

†'**malmish**, *a.* *Obs.* [f. MALM (? *sb.* or *a.*) + -ISH.] ? Resembling malm; ? somewhat 'malm' or soft.

a **1722** LISLE *Observ. Husb.* 99 (E.D.S.) A heavy malmish sort of clay.

malmoutrye, variant of MAUMETRY *Obs.*

malmsey (ˈmɑːmzɪ). Forms: 5 **malmesyne**, 5–6 **malmasye**, 5–7 **malmesey**, 6 **malmesay**, **malmyse**, **malmesye**, **mammesey**, **malmesee**, **mamulsye**, **mawlmsey**, 6–7 **malmesie**, **malmsie**, 7 **malmesy**, 5– **malmsey**. [ad. (? through OF. or Pr. **malmesie*: cf. Béarnais *marmusie*) med.L. *malmasia* (Diefenbach), a corruption of the Gr. place-name *Μονεμβασία* (Monemvasia); cf. MDu. *malemeseye*, MLG. *malmesie*, MHG. *malmasier* (in 15th c. latinized *malmasetum*), MDa. *malmesye*. The parallel corruption *Malvasia* has given rise to the OF. and ME. *malvesie* as a name for the wine: see MALVOISIE.]

1. A strong sweet wine, originally the product of the neighbourhood of Monemvasia (Napoli di Malvasia) in the Morea; but now obtained from Spain, the Azores, and the islands of Madeira and the Canaries, as well as from Greece.

14.. *Mann. & Househ. Exp.* (Roxb.) 456 A bote of malmesey and a federbed. ? *c* **1475** *Sqr. lowe Degre* 754, Ye shall haue rumney and malmesyne [*rime* wyne]. **1513** MORE *Hist. Rich. III* Wks. 37/1 Attainted was hee by parliament and judged to the death, and thereupon hastely drouned in a Butt of Malmesey. **1531–2** *Act 23 Hen. VIII*, c. 7 No malmeseis Romeneis sackes nor other swete wynes..shalbe reteiled aboue xii.d. the gallon. **1549–50** in Fowler *Hist. C.C.C.* (O.H.S.) 356 Several small charges for mammesey. **1572** J. JONES *Bathes Buckstone* 10 With Sugar, or whyte Mamulsyes of Madera, a myas of good Ale, a cawdell or Alebury. **1621** BURTON *Anat. Mel.* I. ii. I. i. 93 All black Wines..as Muscadine, Malmesie,..Broune bastard, Metheglen, and the like. **1772–84** *Cook's Voy.* (1790) IV. 1223 Canary sack..which the French call Vin de Malvesie, and we..name Malmsey. **1814** W. M. LEAKE *Researches in Greece* 197 *note*, The place [Monemvasia] being celebrated for the fine wines produced in the neighbourhood, Malvasia changed to Malvoisie in French, and Malmsey in English, came to be applied to many of the rich wines of the Archipelago, Greece, and other countries. **1843** *Penny Cycl.* XXVII. 465/2 The original Malmsey of the Grecian Archipelago, that of Madeira [etc.]. **1871** E. C. G. MURRAY *Member for Paris* III. 115 A second brother statesman..had just been treating himself to a glass of Malmsey. **1880** *Macm. Mag.* XLI. 236 Malmsey was formerly the produce of those parts only [Candia and Greece]. **1895** *Army & Navy Co-op. List* 166 Choice Old Malmsey.

b. *attrib.*, as ***malmsey-butt***, ***-cup***; **malmsey-face**, a face inflamed by drink; **malmsey madeira**, a malmsey wine made in Madeira; **malmsey-nose** (see quots. 1597, *a* 1700).

1588 *Lanc. & Chesh. Wills* III. 138 One Mawlmsey cupp wth cover all guylt. **1594** SHAKS. *Rich. III*, I. iv. 161 Throw him into the Malmesey-Butte. **1597** —— *2 Hen. IV*, II. i. 42 Yonder he comes, and that arrant Malmesey-Nose Bardolfe. **1611** COTGR. s.v. *Visage*, A mustulent, or maumsie face. **1684** OTWAY *Atheist* V. i, This Malmsey nose of minc. *a* **1700** B. E. *Dict. Cant. Crew*, *Malmesey-nose*, a jolly, red Nose. **1723** *Lond. Gaz.* No. 6173/3 There will be no other Malmsey Madera Wine landed this Year. **1858** HOMANS *Cycl. Comm.* 1974/1 Malmsey Madeira.

2. A kind of grape, from which the wine Malmsey was originally made.

1511 GUYLFORDE *Pilgr.* (Camden) 12 Vpon that hyll is a cyte called Malsasia, where firste grewe Malmasye, and yet dothe. **1603** KNOLLES *Hist. Turks* (1621) 868 It is now most famous..for the good Malmesey which there groweth. **1615** G. SANDYS *Trav.* 224 Muscadines and Malmesies, those kindes of grapes brought hither first from Arabia.

malmy (ˈmɑːmɪ), *a.*[1] Also 7–8 **maumy**, 8 **mallany**, 9 **maulmy**. [f. MALM *sb.* + -Y[1].]

1. Of a loamy character.

1677 PLOT *Oxfordsh.* ix. 240 If the Land be of that sort they call Maumy, consisting of a mixture of White-clay and Chalk, and somwhat of Sand. **1744–50** W. ELLIS *Mod. Husbandm.* I. i. ii. 36 The Chalk and Mould are so mixed together that in Hertfordshire we call it a Maumy Earth. **1858** *Jrnl. R. Agric. Soc.* XIX. II. 279 Parts of Norfolk—particularly the white malmy soils—were unkind for turnips. **1880** *Encycl. Brit.* XI. 430/2 The eastern portion [of Hampshire]..is a grey sandy loam provincially called 'malmy' land.

†**2.** Resembling a stratum or vein of malmstone.

1747 HOOSON *Miner's Dict.* M ij, Ore lying in it [mallan] is as Bullets and naked Lumps..and rare to be seen after the manner of a Rib; hence we say Mallany Gear, or Stuff, when the vein inclines to that kind.

malmy (ˈmɑːmɪ, ˈmɔːmɪ), *a.*[2] *dial.* Also **maumy**. [f. MALM *a.* + -Y.] Mellow; soft and insipid; †also *fig.*

1728 *Wodrow Corr.* (1843) III. 403 You'll probably think I am too soft and malmy now. **1825** JAMIESON, *Maumie*, mellow. **1829**, **1876** [see MALM *a.*].

maln, obs. form of MALM.

mal'nourished, *a.* [f. MAL- + NOURISHED *ppl. a.*; cf. MALNUTRITION.] Suffering from or provided with insufficient nutrition or nourishment; undernourished.

1928 *Daily Tel.* 11 Dec. 17/1 He [*sc.* Lord Eustace Percy] had emphasised the importance of local authorities making adequate provision for mal-nourished children. **1963** *Economist* 29 June 1348/1 Half the world's population is still hungry or malnourished or both. **1972** *Lancet* 22 July 143/1, 200 randomly selected malnourished children under the age of five years.

mal'nourishment. [f. MAL- + NOURISHMENT.] = MALNUTRITION.

1932 *N.Y. World-Telegram* 16 June 22/7 The inroads of starvation, diseases and malnourishment. **1936** E. P. O'DONNELL *Green Margins* 222 Many of them were tuberculous from malnourishment. **1969** N. W. PIRIE *Food Resources* iii. 99 There will be protein malnourishment unless food, averaged over a day, contains a reasonable percentage of protein.

malnutrition (mælnjuːˈtrɪʃən). [f. MAL- + NUTRITION.] Insufficient nutrition.

1862 *Cornh. Mag.* VI. 323 Diseases of which the starting point is mal-nutrition. **1899** *Allbutt's Syst. Med.* VIII. 183 Mental disorder may arise from temporary malnutrition of the fore-brain.

malobathrum, variant of MALABATHRUM.

mal-ob'servance. [f. MAL- + OBSERVANCE.] Observance of a wrong kind.

1822 P. BEAUCHAMP (G. Grote) *Anal. Infl. Nat. Relig.* (1875) 75 Mal-observance, like unbelief, includes non-observance. **18..** DR. BEGG in Crafts *Sabb. for Man* (1894) 182[Working men] wish for something more pungent than a museum in their malobservance of the Sabbath.

mal-obser'vation. Defective observation.

1843 MILL *Logic* II. v. iv. 387 It is mal-observation, when something is not simply unseen, but seen wrong; when the fact or phenomenon..is mistaken for something else. **1886** MAUDSLEY *Nat. Causes & Supernat. Seemings* 50 The common malobservation which, taking note of agreeing, takes no note of contradicting, instances. **1895** J. N. MASKELYNE in *Daily Chron.* 29 Oct. 3/4 A charge of either mal-observation or collective hallucination on the part of a large number of eminent men. **1895** A. LANG in R. M. Dorson *Peasant Customs* (1968) II. 444 If he denies it, if he says with Lord Kelvin that hypnotism is all imposture and malobservation, I am silenced. **1922** *Encycl. Brit.* XXXII. 199/2 Repression of the truth would have to be added as a third to mal-observation and forgetfulness, as a very subtle source of error in testimony to the occurrence of the supernormal.

maloca (məˈləʊkə). Also 9 **malocca**. [Pg., a large hut, f. Amer. Sp., raid, attack, f. Araucanian *malocan* to fight (Webster).] A large hut in certain Indian settlements in South America.

1860 MAYNE REID *Odd People* 122 The Mundrucus build the *malocca*..only in their case it is not used as a dwelling, but rather as a grand arsenal, a council-chamber,..and, if need be, a fortress. *Ibid.* 47 Three or four hundred individuals not unfrequently assemble under the roof of a single *malocca*. **1944** S. PUTNAM tr. *E. da Cunha's Rebellion in Backlands* II. iii. 175 The ruins of the *malocas*, or native villages. **1951** J. C. FENNESSY *Sonnet in Bottle* III. v. 81 The village consisted only of three large malocas, with palm-thatched roofs reaching nearly to the ground. **1962** N. MAXWELL *Witch-Doctor's Apprentice* xiv. 171 In the Colombian Amazon, a maloca is the traditional dirt-floored, round or oval Indian house whose walls are made of the same thatch as its roof.

malo'cclusion. *Dentistry.* [f. MAL- + OCCLUSION.] Faulty occlusion (of the teeth).

1888 J. N. FARRAR *Treat. Irregularities Teeth* I. lv. 563 (*heading*) Mal-occlusion of the anterior teeth.—Treatment. **1937** *Times* 22 Nov. 9/4 A constant stream of visiting dentists..inspected their malocclusions. **1968** *New Scientist* 12 Sept. 538/2 Malocclusion of the jaws, with resulting pyorrhoea, was the pharaohs' biggest dental problem.

malocotoon, variant of MELOCOTON.

malodorous (mæˈləʊdərəs), *a.* [f. MAL- + ODOROUS.] Evil-smelling, *lit.* and *fig.*

1850 CARLYLE *Latter-d. Pamph.* ii. 27 This malodorous phosphorescence of *post-mortem* sentimentalism. **1856** G. WILSON *Gateways Knowl.* (1859) 83 If..some mal-odorous body had been mixed with the incense. **1889** J. ASHTON *Fleet* xviii. 230 The river retaliated in such kind, as to become a malodorous and offensive nuisance. **1891** *Law Times* XC. 459/2 This malodorous litigation.

Hence **ma'lodorously** *adv.*, **ma'lodorousness**.

1886 GUILLEMARD *Cruise Marchesa* II. 124 As for malodourousness, it is perhaps one of the few points in which the resemblance between the two cities fails. **1903** *Blackw. Mag.* July 19/1 The missile malodorously discharged itself.

malodour (mæˈləʊdə(r)). [f. MAL- + ODOUR.] An evil smell, a stench.

1825 SOUTHEY in *Q. Rev.* XXXI. 380 In vain did the fair traveller hope to escape from that omnipresent mal-odour. **1858** CARLYLE *Fredk. Gt.* v. ii. I. 544 Putrid fermentation ending, after the endurance of much malodour, in mere zero to you and to every one.

†**mal-'ominous**, *a. Obs.* In 7 **male-ominous**. [f. MAL- + OMINOUS.] Of evil omen.

1658 tr. *Bergerac's Satyr. Char.* xii. 42, I saw it encompasst by a million of male-ominous creatures.

malonate (ˈmæləneɪt). *Chem.* [f. MALON(IC *a.* + -ATE[4].] The anion, or an ester or salt, of malonic acid.

1862 W. A. MILLER *Elem. Chem.* (ed. 2) III. v. 367 The malonates of potash and ammonia are deliquescent, but uncrystallizable. **1898** J. WADE *Introd. Study Org. Chem.* xxv. 153 Ethyl malonate, $CH_2(COOEt)_2$, is a heavy, colourless liquid, which has a pleasant aromatic odour, and boils at 198°. **1951** A. GROLLMAN *Pharmacol. & Therapeutics* xxix. 676 Both malonate and succinate of sodium are absorbed only slowly from the intestine, and act as saline cathartics. **1962** *Times* 1 May 4/1 (Advt.), They'll be available later in an attractive bound volume scented with perfumes based on certain allyl esters such as salicylate and malonate. **1962** H. A. KREBS in A. Pirie *Lens Metabolism Rel. Cataract* 351 The effects of malonate on the oxidation of succinate.

malonic (məˈlɒnɪk), *a. Chem.* [a. F. *malonique* (Dessaignes 1858 in *Comptes Rendus* XLVII. 76), arbitrarily altered from *malique* MAL-IC.] In ***malonic acid***: an acid obtained by the oxidation of malic acid; ***malonic ester***, the diethyl ester, $CH_2(COOC_2H_5)_2$, of malonic acid, which is a liquid widely used in synthesis, as of carboxylic acids $RR'C(COOH)_2$ or $RR'CHCOOH$ by alkylation with alkyl halides (***malonic ester synthesis***).

1859 WATTS tr. *Gmelin's Handbk. Chem.* XIII. 560. **1881** *Chem. News* 28 Jan. 47/1 (*heading*) Syntheses by means of malonic ester. **1888** REMSEN *Org. Chem.* 204 Treated with an alkali, barbituric acid breaks up into malonic acid and urea. **1906** J. J. SUDBOROUGH *Bernthsen's Text-bk. Org. Chem.* (rev. ed.) x. 238 This so-called 'malonic ester' synthesis is an important method for the preparation of higher dibasic acids. **1968** R. O. C. NORMAN *Princ. Org. Synthesis* x. 330 The use of malonic ester considerably increases the versatility of this general method [of amino-acid synthesis]. **1971** N. ALLINGER et al. *Org. Chem.* xxiv. 665 In the malonic ester synthesis, diethyl malonate is converted by sodium ethoxide into its sodium salt, which is then allowed to react with an alkyl halide.

Hence **'malonyl**, the radical $-CO{\cdot}CH_2{\cdot}CO-$ derived from malonic acid by removal of the two hydroxyl groups.

1889 G. M'GOWAN tr. *Bernthsen's Text-bk. Org. Chem.* 282 Barbituric acid, malonyl urea, $C_4H_4N_2O_3$, is a dibasic acid. **1931** *Jrnl. Chem. Soc.* 273 The Friedel-Crafts reaction has now been extended to the coupling of malonyl chloride ..with methyl ethers of resorcinol. **1970** R. W. MCGILVERY *Biochem.* xvi. 317 The butyryl group can be displaced onto the neighboring cysteinyl group by an incoming malonyl group. **1971** *Nomencl. Org. Chem.* (I.U.P.A.C.) (ed. 2) C. 313 Malonyl (preferred to propanedioyl) $-CO{\cdot}CH_2{\cdot}CO-$.

mal-organi'zation. [f. MAL- + ORGANIZATION.] Faulty organization.

1841 GRESLEY *C. Lever* 130 He will not be condemned for his mal-organisation..but because he did not act according to his conscience. **1862** HELPS *Organiz. Daily Life* 37. **1889** *20th Century* (N.Y.) Apr. 13 The root of the evil is in the malorganization of society.

mal-'organized, *a.* [f. MAL- + ORGANIZED *ppl. a.*] Faultily organized.

1862 HELPS *Organiz. Daily Life* 112 Of course a thing may be elaborate but yet mal-organized.

Malo-Russian (meɪləʊˈrʌʃ(ɪ)ən), *sb.* and *a.* [f. Russ. *Malorossíya* Little Russia, or ad. *Malorós(s)*, *-rús* or *Malorossiyánin* Little Russian.] **A.** *sb.* A member of the Little Russian race inhabiting the south of Russia; their language. **B.** *adj.* Of or pertaining to the Little Russians, Ruthenian.

1862 [see RUTHENIAN *sb.* 2]. **1880** W. R. MORFILL *Russia* 74 The Malo-Russian is very rich in Skazki (national tales) and in songs. *Ibid.* 75 The Malo-Russian philologists. **1923** E. A. ROSS *Russ. Soviet Republic* 58 Between Great Russia and the Black Sea live the Ukrainians or Little Russians (Malo-Russians).

malosses, malotto, obs. ff. MOLASSES, MULATTO.

malpais (mælpɑːˈiːs). *U.S.* [Sp., f. *malo* bad + *país* country, region.] Rugged or difficult country of volcanic origin.

1844 G. W. KENDALL *Narr. Santa Fé Expedition* II. 384 We had crossed the *mal pais*, or bad country, as it is called. **1847** G. A. F. RUXTON *Adventures Mexico & Rocky Mts.* xi. 79 The tract of country known as the *Mal Pais*, a most interesting volcanic region. **1896** *Nat. Geogr. Mag.* VII. 295 Bench mesas may be classified by structure into bolson mesas, stream-terrace mesas, talus-fan mesas, and malpais mesas. **1918** C. E. MULFORD *Man from Bar-20* xvii. 178 Slipping on the treacherous malpais and loose stones. **1942** KEARNEY & PEEBLES *Flowering Plants Arizona* 17 Some of these are limestone areas, whereas others are volcanic, locally known as 'mallapy' (*mal pais*).

malpighiaceous (mælpɪgɪˈeɪʃəs), *a. Bot.* [a. mod.L. *Malpighia* a genus of plants (f. name of Marcello *Malpighi* (1628–94) an Italian physician) + -ACEOUS.] Pertaining to or characteristic of the N. O. *Malpighiaceæ*.

1835 LINDLEY *Introd. Bot.* (1848) I. 156 Malpighiaceous and glandular hairs. **1839** *Penny Cycl.* XIV. 341/1 In many species [of Malpighiaceæ] the hairs are attached to the leaves, &c. by the middle; so that hairs of that description have acquired the name of Malpighiaceous.

mal'pighiad. *Bot.* [See prec. and -AD.] Lindley's term for: A plant of the N.O. *Malpighiaceæ*.

1846 LINDLEY *Veg. Kingd.* 388.

Malpighian (mælˈpɪgɪən), *a. Anat.* and *Bot.* [f. *Malpighi* (see MALPIGHIACEOUS) + -AN.]

1. *Anat.* The distinctive epithet of certain structures discovered by Malpighi, and of others connected with these.

Malpighian bodies, corpuscles: certain minute bodies in the substance of the kidney. ***Malpighian corpuscles of the spleen***: the lymphatic corpuscles of that organ. ***Malpighian capsules*** (see quot. 1866). ***Malpighian layer***: the inner layer of the epidermis. ***Malpighian pyramids***: the

medullary substance of the kidney, consisting of palish red-coloured, striated conical masses. ***Malpighian tubules***: the uriniferous tubes of which the kidney is for the most part made up. ***Malpighian tuft***: a vascular glomerule of convoluted capillary blood-vessels in the kidney.

1847–9 TODD *Cycl. Anat.* IV. 244 The Malpighian bodies consist of a rounded mass of minute blood-vessels. **1848** *Quain's Anat.* (ed. 5) II. 1088 These little vesicles or capsules, formerly known as the Malpighian corpuscles of the spleen, were discovered in the pig by Malpighi. *Ibid.* 1191 These [small round dark red points] are the Malpighian bodies or corpuscles of the kidney. *Ibid.* 1196 Others look on a Malpighian tuft as merely an example of an artery breaking up into a rete mirabile. **1866** HUXLEY *Phys.* v. §9 The tubules [of the kidney]..terminate in dilatations ..called Malpighian capsules. **1877** —— *Anat. Inv. Anim.* vii. 393 The intestine is provided with Malpighian tubules. **1878** FOSTER *Bk. Phys.* II. (1889) 687 The epidermis consists of..an inner soft layer, the Malpighian layer [etc.]. **1890** H. GRAY *Anat.* (ed. 12) 942 The *tubuli uriniferi*..finally terminate at the apices of the Malpighian pyramids.

2. *Bot.* in ***Malpighian cells***: see quot.

1900 B. D. JACKSON *Gloss. Bot. Terms* 152/1 *Malpighian Cells*, those which compose the outer layer of the seed in Malpighiaceae.

†**malpleasant**, *a. Obs.* [f. MAL- + PLEASANT, after F. *malplaisant*.] Unpleasant, disagreeable.

c **1532** DU WES *Introd. Fr.* in Palsgr. 1077 Nat to be tedious nor malpleasant, I remitte it to an other tyme. **1592** CONSTABLE *Sonn.* VIII. ii, But I, that nowe haue draune Malpleasant breath [etc.].

malposed (mæl'pəʊzd), *ppl. a.* [f. MAL- + *-posed*, after *transposed*, etc. Cf. next.] Wrongly placed.

1900 *Lancet* 31 Mar. 939/2 Mr. George J. Goldie demonstrated the usefulness of the x rays in..the regulation of teeth malposed in the jaw.

malpo'sition. [f. MAL- + POSITION.] Misplacement; the condition of being wrongly placed.

1862 TROLLOPE *N. Amer.* I. 145 There are edifices.. which cry aloud to the gods by the force of their own ugliness and malposition. **1868** PEARD *Water-farm.* xi. 110 These..curiosities were often rendered..useless by malposition.

b. *spec.* in *Obstetrics.* Faulty position of a part or organ, *esp.* of the fœtus in the uterus.

1836–9 TODD *Cycl. Anat.* II. 631/1 The apex of the heart adhered to the palate; but..the malposition appears to have been owing to a morbid adhesion of the umbilical cord to the head. **1859** *Ibid.* V. 683/2 An extreme degree of anti-version [of the uterus]... This malposition materially impedes labour. **1881** LE CONTE *Sight* 20 Malpositions of the eye, such as squinting. **1899** *Allbutt's Syst. Med.* VII. 735 The length and difficulty of the labour, due to deformity in the mother or to malposition of the child.

mal'practice. [f. MAL- + PRACTICE.]

1. *Law.* **a.** Improper treatment or culpable neglect of a patient by the physician.

1671 MAYNWARING *Anc. & Mod. Pract. Phys.* 20 Well then, you Prescriber in the mode of male-Practice. **1694** W. SALMON *Bate's Dispens.* (1713) 252/1, I give this Relation.. to convince..those Homicides [Pretenders to Physick] of their Barbarity and Mal-Practice. **1751** SMOLLETT *Per. Pic.* (1779) II. lxx. 250 The malpractice of a surgeon. **1816** A. C. HUTCHISON *Pract. Obs. Surg.* (1826) 181 This boy is dangerously ill, and likely to die, in consequence of such malpractice. **1863** HOLLAND *Lett. Joneses* xx. 286 A professional brother, prosecuted for malpractice, is always sure you will do what you can to clear him.

b. Illegal action by which a person seeks to benefit himself at the cost of others, while in a position of trust.

1758 *Ann. Reg.* 85 He was charged for male-practices in the management of his command abroad. **1768** BLACKSTONE *Comm.* III. 408 King Edward..found it necessary..to prosecute his judges for their corruption and other malpractices. **1773** *Gentl. Mag.* XLIII. 199 Charges of extortion, and other mal-practices, had been brought against a British subject. **1855** MACAULAY *Hist. Eng.* xv. III. 528 The mal-practices, which had done more than the exhalations of the marshes of Dundalk to destroy the efficiency of the English troops, were [etc.]. **1895** *Pop. Sci. Monthly* Sept. 717 Malpractices begin with the prospectus and continue till liquidation.

2. *gen.* A criminal or overtly mischievous action; wrong-doing, misconduct.

1772–84 *Cook's Voy.* (1790) I. 136 When another canoe was struck for their mal-practices, the natives behaved in the same manner. **1812** *Chron.* in *Ann. Reg.* 19 The outrages.. have assumed a more decided character than at any period since the commencement of the malpractises. **1848** CLOUGH *Amours de Voy.* II. 273, I tremble for something factitious, Some malpractice of heart and illegitimate process. **1851** THACKERAY *Kickleburys on Rhine* (ed. 2) 73 Fanny was almost ready to tell fibs to screen her brother's malpractices from her mamma. **1884** J. COLBORNE *Hicks Pasha* 79 We took pains..to correct the malpractice of the men.

ˌ**mal-prac'titioner.** [MAL- + PRACTITIONER.] A corrupt or culpably incompetent practitioner (of law or medicine).

1800 DIBDIN *Jew & Doctor* I. i, The wisdom of our ancestors has provided a remedy for the mistakes of malpractitioners in..an English jury.

malpraxis (mæl'præksɪs). [f. MAL- + Gr. πρᾶξις PRAXIS. Cf. MALA PRAXIS.] **a.** = MALPRACTICE 1 a. **b.** = MALPRACTICE 1 b.

1860 *N. Syd. Soc. Year-bk. Med. & Surg. for 1859.* 431 A midwife and an accoucheur were accused of malpraxis. **1866** ARNOULD *Mar. Insur.* II. iii. (ed. 3) II. 594 Such malpraxis as amounts to a denial of justice. **1891** *Lancet* 3 Oct. 758 Served with a legal process by some scoundrelly man or woman for an alleged malpraxis.

ˌ**malpresen'tation.** *Obstet.* [f. MAL- + PRESENTATION.] Abnormal presentation at childbirth.

1852 *Lancet* 2 Oct. 299/2 The proportion of malpresentations is increased in cases in which labour comes on at the full term. **1899** *Ibid.* 14 Oct. 1021/1 If a malpresentation were diagnosed it might be necessary to correct it by manipulation. **1962** R. H. SMYTHE *Anat. of Dog Breeding* v. 104 There is always the possibility of malpresentation or malformation of an individual puppy.

malpro'priety. [f. MAL- + PROPRIETY *sb.*] Want of proper condition; disorderliness.

1888 E. EGGLESTON *Graysons* xvii. 188 The whole interior had a harmonious air of sloth, stupidity, and malpropriety.

malrotation (mælrəʊ'teɪʃən). *Med.* [f. MAL- + ROTATION.] Faulty or abnormal rotation of a part of the body, esp. of the intestines during development.

1932 *New Eng. Jrnl. Med.* CVI. 280 At operation a distended stomach was found... There was no evidence of mal-rotation. **1961** *Lancet* 9 Sept. 598/1 There was also malrotation and severe mesenteric lymphadenitis.

malscre, obs. form of MASKER *v.*

†'**malshave.** *Obs.* Forms: 1 **mælsceafa**, 2 **mæslesceafa**, 4 **malschave**, 5 **malschawe**. [OE. *mælsceafa* (? *mǽl-*); the first element may, if the vowel be short, be cogn. w. ON. *mǫl-r* (Sw. *mal-*, Da. *møl*), Goth. *malô* moth; the second element (cf. *sceafa* plane) is cogn. w. SHAVE *v.*, but the intended sense of the compound is not clear.] A caterpillar.

c **1000** ÆLFRIC *Gram.* Gloss. (Z.) 310 *Eruca*, mælsceafa. *c* **1150** *Voc.* in Wr.-Wülcker 544/13 *Eruca*, mæslesceafa. **1387** TREVISA *Higden* (Rolls) VI. 19 Þanne as þe grete flye folweþ þe tras of þe malschave [*MS. B* malschawe, *Caxton* malshawe, L. *erucam*] so after oþer woo com þe pestilence of þe Ismaelites.

malshrag ('mælʃræg). *Obs.* exc. *dial.* Forms (see E.D.D.): 9 **maleshag, malley-, mallishag, maltshag, moleshag**, 5, 9 *Yorksh.* **malshrag**. [App. a corruption of prec., after SHRAG. Other corrupt forms in mod. dialects, influenced by SCRAWL *v.* (= *crawl*) are *mawl-scrawl*, *malscral*, *maskell*.] A caterpillar.

1398 TREVISA *Barth. De P.R.* XVIII. xviii. (1495) 777 A malshrag that gnawyth caul leuys. *Ibid.* xlvii. 808 Of malshragges comyth and bredyth butterflyes. **1881** *Isle of Wight Gloss.*, *Mallishag*, a caterpillar. **1883** *Hampsh. Gloss.*, *Maleshag*, a caterpillar. **1890** *Glouc. Gloss.*, *Moleshag*, a sort of grub or caterpillar.

malskre, obs. f. MASKER *v. dial.*, to bewilder.

malstick, variant of MAULSTICK.

malt (mɒlt, -ɔː-), *sb.*[1] Forms: 1 **mealt**, 6–8 (9 *Sc.*) **mault**, 6 **maulte**, 5–6 **malte**, (7 **mawlt**), 8–9 *Sc.* and *north. dial.* **maut**, 1– **malt**. [Com. Teut.: OE. *mealt* = OS. *malt* (Du. *mout*), OHG. (MHG., mod.G.) *malz*, ON. (Sw., Da.) *malt*:—OTeut. **maltos-* neut., whence Finnish *mallas* (from which the declension of the OTeut. word is inferred) and OSl. *mlato*; related to the adj. OTeut. **malto-* or **maltu-* (= Skr. *mṛdu*) represented in OHG., MHG. *malt* soft, ON. *malt-r* rotten; from the root of MELT, SMELT *vbs.*]

1. a. Barley or other grain prepared for brewing or distilling by steeping, germinating and kiln-drying, or by gelatinization, etc.

a **700** *Epinal Gloss.* 136 *Bratium*, malt. **835** *Charter* in *O.E. Texts* 448, Ic bidde & bebeode swælc monn se ðæt min lond hebbe ðæt he ælce ȝere aȝefe ðem hiȝum æt folcanstane L ambra maltes. **11..** *Voc.* in Wr.-Wülcker 548/44 *Bracium*, malt. **1375** BARBOUR *Bruce* v. 398 All the vittale..As quhet, flour, meill, and malt, In the vyne-sellar gert he bryng. **1377** LANGL. *P. Pl.* B. Prol. 197 For many mannus malt we mys wolde destruye. *c* **1386** CHAUCER *Sompn. T.* 38 Yif hym a busshel whete, Malt, or Reye. **1455** *Rolls of Parlt.* V. 324/2 All Bruers..bought their malt in ye open marketts. **1535** STEWART *Cron. Scot.* III. 61 The starkest aill of malt that mycht be browin. **1589** *Pappe w. Hatchet* C ij, As honest a woman as euer burnt malt. **1605** SHAKS. *Lear* III. ii. 82 When Brewers marre their Malt with water. *a* **1618** SYLVESTER *Tobacco Battered* 748 Taverns, Tap-houses!..Most sinfully hath Mault been sunken heer In nappy Ale, and double-double-Beer. **1696–7** *Act 8 & 9 Will. III*, c. 22 (*title*) An Act for granting to His Majesty certain Duties upon Malt [etc.]. **1712** ADDISON *Spect.* No. 269 ¶8, I allow a double Quantity of Malt to my small Beer. **1725** RAMSAY *Gentle Sheph.* II. i, Yestreen I brew'd a bow of maut. **1818** SCOTT *Hrt. Midl.* xlii, They were a bad pack—steal'd meat and mault, and loot the carters magg the coals. **1871** TYNDALL *Fragm. Sci.* (1879) II. xii. 256 The malt is crisp to the teeth, and decidedly sweeter to the taste then the original barley. **1885** H. STOPES *Malt & Malting* xii. 168 Gelatinised Malt. Until very recently malt was made, commercially, by germination solely, and almost exclusively from barley. Since the repeal of the Malt Duties numerous other methods of manufacture have been attempted,..and many other varieties of grain have been malted.

b. with qualifying word, as ***barley, oat, wheat malt***; ***brown***, etc., ***malt*** (see quot. 1839); ***patent malt*** (see quot. 1830). ***blown malt*** (see quot. 1876).

1532 *Test. Ebor.* (Surtees) VI. 34 A quarten barley mault. **1568** in W. H. Turner *Select. Rec. Oxford* (1880) 325 Ne any brewer..grinde their wheate malte in..any other mill. **1707** MORTIMER *Husb.* xii. 278 In Kent, where they commonly Brew with one half Oat-malt, and the other half Barly-malt. **1743** *Lond. & Country Brew.* III. (ed. 2) 179 It is a common Saying, that there is brought to London the worst of brown Malt, and the best of Pale. **1830** M. DONOVAN *Dom. Econ.* I. 87 The deep brown malt, now in use under the name of patent malt, is made by roasting malt..in the same manner as coffee is roasted, until it become blackish brown. **1839** URE *Dict. Arts* 95 According to the colour and the degree of drying, malt is distributed into three sorts; pale, yellow, and brown... The black malt used by the porter brewer..is partially charred. **1876** *Encycl. Brit.* IV. 270/1 Brown or porter malt..is sometimes called 'blown malt', from its distended appearance. *Ibid.* 271/1 Americans are now making beer largely from maize meal and maize malt.

c. ***extract of malt***, a preparation of malt used as a food for invalids. See ***malt extract*** in 5.

1872 W. AITKEN *Sci. & Pract. Med.* (ed. 6) II. 913 The extract of malt..may be prepared by any pharmaceutical chemist. **1889** *Syd. Soc. Lex.* s.v., *Extract of Malt*..is prepared by digesting malt with water, straining, and evaporating the product to the consistency of thick honey. It contains diastase, and so acts as a digestive ferment, as well as being itself nutritious.

2. *Proverbs* and *Phrases.* ***the malt is above the meal*** (†rarely ***wheat, bere, water***), said of a person under the influence of drink. ***soft fire makes sweet malt***, an admonition to be gentle or merciful.

1546 J. HEYWOOD *Prov.* (1867) 5 Soft fire maketh sweete malte. *Ibid.* 25 Malt is aboue wheate with him, market men saie. **1601** DENT *Pathw. Heaven* 249 Soft and faire, sir... Soft fire maketh sweet mault. **1626** BRETON *Fantastickes* B 3 Haruest. Malt is now aboue wheat with a number of mad people. **1670** RAY *Prov.* 295 [Scottish Proverbs.] The malt is above the beir. **1678** *Ibid.* (ed. 2) 87 Proverbiall Periphrases of one drunk... The malt is above the water. **1721** KELLY *Scot. Prov.* 320 The Malt's above the Meal with you. That is, you are drunk. **1816** SCOTT *Old Mort.* iv, When the malt begins to get aboon the meal..they are like to quarrel. **1858** M. PORTEOUS *Souter Johnny* 10 He was a sturdy stalwart chiel,..Fond o' his maut aboon his meal.

3. *transf.* Used for: Malt liquor. Now usu. = *malt whisky*. *slang* or *colloq.*

1718 RAMSAY *Christ's Kirk Gr.* III. xi, The bauld billy took his maut, And scour'd aff healths anew. **1823** 'JON BEE' *Slang*, *Malt*, the chief ingredient of beer, has been used figuratively for the beer itself. 'A shovel of malt', is a pot of porter. **1828** LYTTON *Pelham* xxiii, I rejected malt with the air of his majesty, and formed a violent affection for maraschino. **1861** HUGHES *Tom Brown at Oxf.* i, I am naturally a thirsty soul, and cannot often resist the malt myself. **1861** LEVER *One of Them* xxvi, 'And will again, old boy', cried Hawke, finishing off the other's malt. **1925**, etc. [see BALL *sb.*[4]]. **1967** A. DIMENT *Dolly Dolly Spy* iv. 39 He.. poured himself a big shot of the finest Malt. **1972** A. ROSS *London Assignment* 32, I had put plenty of Malvern water into the malt, figuring to make it last. **1974** *Times Lit. Suppl.* 11 Jan. 38/5 Ross Wilson ignores the religious divisions of the trade ('malts' are the Catholic whiskies). **1975** *Scottish Field* Jan. 13/2 Hugh MacDiarmid, a whisky drinker for 60 years, expounds on the great malts.

4. *attrib.* and *Comb.* **a.** *attrib.* quasi-*adj.* in the sense 'brewed' or 'distilled from malt', as ***malt-drink, -spirits, whisky***.

1707 MORTIMER *Husb.* xii. 276 To improve our English Liquors..in our Southern Parts where they have generally very bad Malt-drink. **1714** MANDEVILLE *Fab. Bees* (1725) I. 118 A beggar may make himself as drunk with stale-beer or malt-spirits, as a lord with Burgundy. **1731** P. SHAW *Ess. Artif. Philos.* 97 Malt-Low-wines, prepared in the common way, are exceeding nauseous. **1839** URE *Dict. Arts* 402 The distiller of malt whiskey calculates on obtaining two gallons of proof spirits from one bushel of malt. **1968** *Scottish Field* Nov. 56 (Advt.), Chivas Regal is blended with the softest Glenlivet malt whiskies. **1970** SIMON & HOWE *Dict. Gastron.* 389/1 About a hundred years ago it became the custom to blend straight malt whisky with neutral grain whisky.

b. Simple attrib., as ***malt-bag, -barn, -barrow, -cellar, -chamber, -corn, -garner, (tea-)loaf, -market, -meal, -rake, -shovel, -skep, †-spout, -store, -trade***.

1415–16 *Durham Acc. Rolls* (Surtees) 612 Item pro factura de lez *maltbagges, 1*s.* 6*d.* **1753** W. MAITLAND *Hist. Edinb.* II. 151/1 *Malt-barns, Breweries [etc.]. **1885** H. STOPES *Malt & Malting* xvi. 264 *Malt-barrows vary considerably in shape, manufacture, and use. **1576** *Reg. Privy Council Scot.* Ser. I. II. 578 To sell thair malt..in thair *malt sellaris at hame. **1676** in Taylor *Wakefield Manor* (1886) 109 Cum ..brasio, anglice *malt chambers. **1581** W. STAFFORD *Exam. Compl.* ii (1876) 46 It pleaseth vs..nothing at all, which buy most both breade-corne and *malt-corne for our peny. **1453–4** *Durham Acc. Rolls* (Surtees) 634 [Operantibus] super reparacionem..de le Whetgarner et le *Maltgarner. **1901** B. S. ROWNTREE *Poverty* viii. 288/2 *Malt loaf. 3d. **1969** E. GÉBLER *Shall I eat you Now?* 98 They drank tea and ate slices of a sticky malt tealoaf. **1455** *Rolls of Parlt.* V. 324/2 Thus is ye *Malt markett lost. **1622** MALYNES *Anc. Law-Merch.* 231 Casting *Mault meale, or Beane meale vpon the same. **1884** KNIGHT *Dict. Mech.* Suppl., **Malt Rake*, a hand tool used in stirring malt on the kiln floor. **1688** R. HOLME *Armoury* III. 331/1 He beareth Gules, a..*Malt Shovel, Argent. **1577** in Rogers *Agric. & Prices* (1866) III. 580 *Malt skep. **1334–5** *Durham Acc. Rolls* (Surtees) 526 In 1 coreo equino empt. pro le *Maltspout in Bracina. **1885** H. STOPES *Malt & Malting* xiii. 183 *Malt-stores, and granaries. **1707** MORTIMER *Husb.* xii. 276, I shall..for the Conveniency of the *Malt Trade, add a particular sort of Mill that [etc.].

c. objective, as ***malt-making, -roasting***; ***malt-carrier, -seller***. Also MALT-MAKER.

1708 *Lond. Gaz.* No. 4447/4 A *Malt-Carrier. **1455** *Rolls of Parlt.* V. 324/2 People..nowe..for noon occupation of

*Malt makynge be in grete idelnesse. **1885** H. STOPES *Malt & Malting* xvii. 292 The monopoly of *malt-roasting, created by the numerous stringent Acts of Parliament.

d. instrumental (sense 3), as †***malt-conceived, -inspired, -mad*** adjs.

1579 G. HARVEY *Letter-bk.* (Camden) 67 Sum newe devisid interlude, or sum *Maltconceived Comedye. **1838** RODGER *Poems* (1897) 24 (E.D.D.) A set o' *maut-inspired whims That end in perfect smoke. **1621** FLETCHER *Pilgrim* III. vi, Peace, thou heathenish Drunkard, Peace for shame. These English are so *Malt-mad;..when they have a Fruitful Year of Barly there, the whole Island's thus.

5. Special comb.: †**malt-book**, an account-book for the collections of malt-tax; †**malt boud** = MALT-WORM 1; **malt-bree** *Sc.*, malt liquor; **malt-bruiser**, a mill for bruising or crushing malt; †**malt-bug** = MALT-WORM 2; **malt-crusher**, a small crusher for testing samples of malt; **malt-distiller**, one who distils spirits from malt; so **malt-distillery**, †(*a*) the action or art of the malt-distiller (*obs.*); (*b*) a place where malt spirits are distilled; **malt-dryer** (see quot.); **malt extract**, a saccharine and mucilaginous substance obtained from wort; also = *extract of malt* (see 1 c); **malt-factor**, a dealer in malt; **malt-floor**, (*a*) a floor upon which the malt is spread to germinate; (*b*) (see quot. 1858); **malt food**, food composed of or combined with extract of malt; †**malt-gavel** = *malt shot*; **malt grid, grinder** (see quots.); **malt-kiln**, a kiln in which the malt is dried after 'steeping' and 'couching'; **malt liquor**, liquor made from malt by fermentation as opposed to distillation, as ale, beer, stout, etc.; **malt-loft**, the place where prepared malt is stored; **malt-lottery**, a lottery promoted by authority of Parliament in 1697 with the malt duty as security; †**malt-mare** (cf. MALT HORSE); †**malt master** = MALTSTER; **malt-mill**, a mill for grinding or crushing malt; †**malt-money**, money paid as a tax on the making of malt; **malt office**, a malt house, malting; †**malt-officer**, a collector of malt-tax; **malt-oil** (see quot.); †**malt-penny** = *malt money*; †**malt pie** *jocular*, drink, liquor; **malt plough**, an implement for turning the malt when upon the malt-floor; **malt poultice** (see quot.); **malt-querns** *sb. pl.*, *dial.* (see quot. 1877); **malt roaster**, a machine for roasting malt on a small scale; **malt roller** (see quot.); **malt sack**, a sack of or for malt; **malt-screen**, a utensil for screening or sifting malt; **malt shop** *U.S.*, a shop where malted milk is sold; †**malt shot**, a duty paid for the privilege of making malt [OE. *mealtȝescot* (Wulfstan)]; **malt-sieve** = *malt screen*; **malt-silver**, (*a*) = *malt-money*; (*b*) *Sc.* (see quot. 1825–80); †**malt-stiller** = *malt distiller*; **malt-sugar** = MALTOSE; **malt-surrogate**, 'any substitute..used in the manufacture of beer in place of a part of the malt' (*Cent. Dict.*); **malt-tails**, the roots and shoots of dried malt, = MALT-COMES; **malt-tap** (see quot.); **malt-tax**, a tax on malt, imposed by Parliament in 1697, repealed and superseded by the beer-duty in 1880; **malt tea**, 'the liquid infusion of the mash in brewing' (*Cent. Dict.* 1890); **malt ticket**, a ticket for a share in the malt-lottery; also *attrib.*; **malt trader, -turner** (see quots.); **malt vinegar**, vinegar made from the fermentation of malt; **malt wash**, the wash or wort obtained in distilling from grain. Also MALT DUST, MALT HORSE, etc.

1710 J. CHAMBERLAYNE *St. Gt. Brit.* II. III. 505 Edward, chief Examiner of the Country Officers *Malt-Books. *c* **1440** *Promp. Parv.* 323/2 *Malte bowde (or wevyl), *gurgulio*. **1780** W. FORBES *Dominie* 6 Keep very far frae Bacchus' reach, He drowned a' my cares to preach Wi' his *ma't-bree. **1796** *Encycl. Brit.* (ed. 3) X. 490/1 *Malt-bruiser, or Bruising-mill. **1577** HARRISON *England* I. II. xi. 85 b/2 It is incredible to say how our *Maultbugges lug at this liquor. **1885** H. STOPES *Malt & Malting* xvii. 284 Small *malt-crushers are very generally used. **1753** *Scots Mag.* Feb. 96/2 The *malt-distillers advertised, Feb. 19, that they would not receive or pay them [counterfeit halfpence] for the future. **1753** CHAMBERS *Cycl. Supp.*, *Malt Distillery... The art is to convert fermented Malt liquors into a clear inflammable spirit. **1839** URE *Dict. Arts* 401 The..produce of malt distilleries. **1875** KNIGHT *Dict. Mech.*, **Malt-dryer*, a device to hasten the drying of malt by artificial heat. **1839** URE *Dict. Arts* 100 The specific gravities of solutions of *malt extract. **1897** ROBERTS *Digest. & Diet* 223 Malt extracts are essentially infusions of malt concentrated by evaporation to the consistency of a thick treacle. **1704** *Lond. Gaz.* No. 4035/4 Richard Haley and Samuel Wallis, *Mault-factors. **1707** MORTIMER *Husb.* xii. 259 Empty the Corn from the Cistern into the *Malt-floor. **1858** SIMMONDS *Dict. Trade*, *Malt-floor*, a perforated floor in the..malt-kiln, through which the heat ascends from the furnace below, and dries the barley laid upon it. **1896** *Allbutt's Syst. Med.* I. 403 If milk be rejected, *malt food is generally available. **1...** *Custumal Mepham, Kent* in Somner *Treat. Gavelkind* (1660) 27 De xxj. sum. iiij. bush. de *Maltgavel. **1889** BARNARD *Noted Breweries* I. 62 The malt receiving room..contains two *malt grids..with strong wire screens at the bottom, through which the malt passes to the mills in the room below. **1858** SIMMONDS *Dict. Trade*, **Malt-grinder*, a machine for crushing or cutting malted barley. **1538** LAYTON in Ellis *Orig. Lett.* Ser. III. III. 212 Therbe here.. many *malte kylnes. **1855** MACAULAY *Hist. Eng.* xiii. III. 324 Four or five hundred houses, two churches, twelve maltkilns, crowded close together. **1693** *Lond. Gaz.* No. 2868/2 An Additional Excise upon *Malt Liquors. **1786** COWPER *Let. to Unwin* Wks. (ed. Southey) VI. 5 Government is too much interested in the consumption of malt-liquor to reduce the number of venders. **1897** *Allbutt's Syst. Med.* II. 228 To those in the habit of drinking malt liquors, stout and bitter ale may be given. **1682** *True Protest. Mercury* No. 162. 2/1 *Mault-Lofts, Hop-Lofts [etc.]. **1839** URE *Dict. Arts* 110 The malt for the supply of the brewery is stored in vast granaries or malt-lofts. **1697** *Lond. Gaz.* No. 3316/4 Lost.., two 10*l.* Tickets belonging to the *Malt Lottery. **1594** LYLY *Moth. Bomb.* IV. ii, It was a verie good horse... If one ranne him, he woulde simper and mump, as though he had gone a wooing to a *maltmare at Rochester. **1612** T. ADAMS *White Devil* (1613) 49 The markets are hoysed vp, if the poore cannot reach the price, the *Mault-master wil. **1607** NORDEN *Surv. Dial.* III. 108 Any customarie Water-mill,..Griest-mill, *Mault-mill..or any other kind of mill. **1707** *Lond. Gaz.* No. 4293/3 Malt-Milne, and all Conveniencies fit for a Common Brewer. **1600** in *N. & Q.* 6th Ser. (1882) V. 88/2 Here followeth a general Rate of the *Malte Money due to the Church. **1800** *Hull Advertiser* 12 July 2/3 A..brick and tiled *Malt-office.. capable of steeping and drying at once fourteen quarters. **1737** J. CHAMBERLAYNE *St. Gt. Brit.* (ed. 33) II. 84 The Excise and *Malt-Officers Country Books. **1753** CHAMBERS *Cycl. Supp.* s.v. *Malt*, The odious taste of the *Malt oil will be distinguished. **1...** *Rental Eastry Manor, Kent* in Somner *Treat. Gavelkind* (1660) 27 *Malt-peny. **1600** HEYWOOD *1st Pt. Edw. IV* (1613) Bjb, See how S. Katherines smokes, wipe slaues your eies, And whet your stomackes for the good *mault pies. **1885** H. STOPES *Malt & Malting* xvii. 289 Several forms of *malt-ploughs are known and used. **1856** MAYNE *Expos. Lex.*, **Malt Poultice*, common name for the *Cataplasma bynes*. **1586** SPENSER *Will* in Grosart *S.'s Wks.* I. p. xvii, I give and bequethe unto Johon Spenser..one payre of *malt wyrnes. **1877** *N.W. Linc. Gloss.*, *Malt-quearns*, (1) stones for grinding malt; (2) a mill with steel crushers for the same purpose. **1858** SIMMONDS *Dict. Trade*, **Malt roaster Maker*, a manufacturer of machines for roasting barley on a small scale. **1885** H. STOPES *Malt & Malting* xii. 164 Every brewer in Germany has his own malt-roaster. **1839** URE *Dict. Arts* 113 The *malt-rollers, or machines for bruising the grains of the malt. **1530** PALSGR. 601/2 She layde upon him lyke a *maulte sacke. **1885** H. STOPES *Malt & Malting* xvii. 293 Malt- and barley-sacks usually hold one comb or four bushels. *Ibid.* 295 *Malt-screens for separation of all combes and other matters, and also for grading. **1943** D. BAKER *Trio* II. 88 She was out of the gate and into a little section of bright lights—college clothes,..*malt shops. **1949** *Time* 26 Sept. 25/1 The word was relayed through the drive-ins, malt shops and garages. **1...** *Rental Eastry Manor, Kent* in Somner *Treat. Gavelkind* (1660) 27 De *Malt-shot termino circumcisionis Domini xxd. **1388–9** *Abingdon Rolls* (Camden) 57, ij *maltsyues. *a* **1472** in *Cartul. Walt. de Norvico MS.* (White Kennett MS. note in *Cowell's Interpr.* 1701 (Bodl. copy) s.v. *Molsilver*, Dabit pro ..*Maltsilver ad festum Nat. Domini III *d* ob. **1825–80** JAMIESON, *Maut-siller.* 1. Literally, money for malt. 2. Most frequently used in a figurative sense; as, 'That's ill paid maut-siller'; a proverbial phrase signifying, that a benefit has been ill requited. **1731** P. SHAW *Ess. Artif. Philos.* 99 Which should encourage the *Malt-Stiller to be careful and intelligent in this business. **1862** MILLER *Elem. Chem.* III. 83 *Malt sugar ($C_{12}H_{12}O_{12}$). **1900** R. HUTCHISON *Food* 263 The remaining sugars of this group are malt-sugar, or maltose, and milk-sugar, or lactose. **1743** *Lond. & Country Brew.* III. (ed. 2) 179 By that and the Help of the *Malt Tails, he [the Maltster] fills the Bushel with a great deal of Show and little good Malt. **1854** MISS BAKER *Northampt. Gloss.*, **Malt-tap*, the wicker strainer that is put in the mash-vat, to prevent the grains passing through the tap. **1711** *Let. to Sacheverel* 11 The levying the Land-Tax and *Malt-Tax. **1840** THACKERAY *Jolly Jack* iv, When village Solons cursed the Lords, And called the malt-tax sinful. **1697** *Lond. Gaz.* No. 3318/4 Lost or mislaid..four *Malt-Tickets. **1880** *Act 43 & 44 Vict.* c. 20 Interpretation of terms. '*Malt trader' means and includes a maltster or maker of malt, a dealer in malt, a roaster of malt, a brewer of beer for sale, and a vinegar maker. **1884** KNIGHT *Dict. Mech.* Suppl., **Malt Turner*, a mechanical arrangement for turning the malt while being heated in the kiln. **1858** SIMMONDS *Dict. Trade*, **Malt-vinegar*. **1729** G. SMITH *Fermentation* 27 The practice of fermenting all Molosses and *Malt-wash, without any previous boiling. **1839** URE *Dict. Arts* 91 A peculiar volatile oil of a concrete nature, which is obtained during the process of distilling fermented malt wash.

Malt (mɒlt, -ɔː-), *sb.*[2] *slang.* = MALTESE *sb.* 1 a.

1959 C. MACINNES *Absolute Beginners* 40 A sickly simper, ..that she turned on like a light for the two beefo Malts. **1969** *Sunday Mail* (Brisbane) 16 Mar. 10 A new and frightening power is suddenly emerging in the Sydney underworld. It is called by those who know about it 'The Malts'. Police fear it is taking the form of a Maltese 'Mafia'. **1971** *Guardian* 6 July 11/6 The 'Malts', as one used to refer to them, or sometimes 'yellow-bellied bastards'.

malt (mɒlt, -ɔː-), *v.* [f. MALT *sb.*[1]]

1. *trans.* To convert (grain) into malt. Also *absol.*

c **1440** *Promp. Parv.* 324/1 Maltyn, or make malt, *brasio*. **1608** *Nottingham Rec.* IV. 289 Order to be gyven to euerie maltster..to forbeare buyinge of barley to mawlt. **1616** SURFL. & MARKH. *Country Farm* 559 These Oates being maulted, as you mault Barley, make a verie good mault. **1636** in *Buccleuch MSS.* (Hist. MSS. Comm.) I. 275 Sundry abuses by them in buying barley..and in malting it at unseasonable times. **1753** CHAMBERS *Cycl. Supp.* s.v., The whole grain [of maize] will not this way be malted or rendered tender or floury. **1889** BARNARD *Noted Breweries* I. 56 [These brewers] malt every week 7,600 quarters..of barley.

b. *intr.* To admit of being malted.

1766 *Compl. Farmer* s.v., Old barley, mixed with that of the last harvest, does not malt well. **1870** YEATS *Nat. Hist. Comm.* 48 Scotch barley..does not malt well.

2. *transf.* (*pass.* and *intr.*). Of seeds: To come to the condition of malt owing to germination being checked by drought.

1733 TULL *Horse-Hoeing Husb.* xiv. 166 If they [St. Foin seeds] are not cover'd, they will be Malted. *Note.* We say it is Malted when it lies above Ground, and sends out its Root, which is killed by the Air. **1763** *Museum Rust.* (ed. 2) I. 210 Turnep-seed..if it is not covered as soon as sown..will sprout prematurely, malt, or mould. **1861** *Jrnl. R. Agric. Soc.* XXII. II. 418 After the seeds have become saturated with moisture, the dry weather returns, and they become 'malted'. **1873** MOGGRIDGE *Ants & Spiders* I. 26 The seeds are thus in effect malted, the starch being changed into sugar.

3. *trans.* To make (liquor) with malt.

1605 CAMDEN *Rem.* 235 A man of worship, whose beere was better hopped than maulted. **1621** J. TAYLOR (Water P.) *Taylors Goose* Wks. (1630) I. 105/1 She is..better two dayes salted For then she'll try if Ale or Beere be malted.

4. *intr.* To drink malt liquor. *vulgar.*

1813 COL. HAWKER *Diary* (1893) I. 68 We..stopped to malt at all the hedge alehouses. **1825** *New Monthly Mag.* XIV. 180 Lord U— too declares he saw her malting the same evening. **1835** MARRYAT *Jac. Faithf.* xxv, 'Well, I malts', said Tom, reaching a pot of porter, and taking a long pull. **1840** HOOD *Kilmansegg, Birth* xxi, She drank nothing lower than Curaçoa,..And, on principle, never malted.

malt, obs. pa. t. of MELT *v.*

Malta ('mɒltə, -ɔː-). The name of an island in the Mediterranean, formerly a dependency of Great Britain and now an independent republic. Used *attrib.*, as †**Malta cross** = *Maltese cross*; **Malta fever**, a complicated fever of long duration, common in Malta and other places in the Mediterranean; **Malta fungus** (see quot. 1870; cf. MALTESE MUSHROOM).

1651 Malta cross [see CROSS *sb.* 19]. **1725** J. COATS *Dict. Her.*, *Malta-cross*, so call'd because worn by the Knights of that Order. **1866** WOOD in *Edin. Med. Jrnl.* I. 60 Malta Fever. **1870** H. SEDDALL *Malta* 340 *Cynomorium coccineum* (L.) *Ærk el generàl* (Malt.), the curious so-called Malta fungus, which grows abundantly on the General's Rock, off Gozo. **1897** *Allbutt's Syst. Med.* II. 463 *note*, Some nosologists object to the term Malta Fever.

†'**maltalent.** *Obs.* Forms: 4–5 **mautalent**, 5 **mautelent**; 5–6 **matalent**, 5 **matelent**, 6 **matilent**, **matulat**; 5 **maltalente**, 5–7 **maletalent**, (5 **male talente**, 6 *Sc.* **mailtalent**), 4–7 (9 *arch.*) **maltalent**. [a. OF. *maltalent* (*maut-*, *mat-*), f. *mal* evil (see MAL-) + *talent* disposition, temper (see TALENT).] Ill-will, malevolence.

c **1320** *Sir Beues* (MS. A) 3978 Sire Beues þo, veraiment For-ȝaf him alle is mautalent. **13..** *K. Alis.* 906 To his ost oone he went, Ful of ire and maltalent. *c* **1440** *Partonope* 4499 That my lady hath hyr maletalent Me forgyfen. *c* **1450** *Merlin* 339 The Geaunte..gnasshed his teth and rolled his iyen, that were grete swollen for ire and mautelent [*printed* mantelent] that he had. *c* **1470** HENRY *Wallace* IV. 465 Vpon the hed him straik in matelent. **1481** CAXTON *Godfrey* clxxviii. 262 And how they pardonned eche other theyr mal talentes and euyll wylles. **1513** DOUGLAS *Æneis* I. i. (*title*), Junois wraith and mailtalent. **1560** ROLLAND *Crt. Venus* II. 332 Thay grew in matilent. **1590** SPENSER *F.Q.* III. iv. 61 With heavy look, and lumpish pace, that plaine In him bewraid great grudge and maltalent. *a* **1648** LD. HERBERT *Hen. VIII* (1683) 103 But not on this part only did the French shew their Mal-Talent. *a* **1649** DRUMM. OF HAWTH. *Jas. I* Wks. (1711) 14 He had ever a male-talent against the king since the adjudging of the earldom of Strathern from his nephew Miles. **1828** SCOTT *F.M. Perth* xii. That is the lot of them that the Black Douglas bears mal-talent against.

¶**b.** As *adj.* Ill-tempered.

a **1578** LINDESAY (Pitscottie) *Chron. Scot.* (S.T.S.) II. 43 King Harrie brunt as fyre and grew so matulat in anger that [etc.].

†**maltalentive**, *a. Obs. rare.* In 5 **maletalentif**, **matelentif**. [a. OF. *maltalentif*, f. *maltalent*: see prec. and -IVE.] Bearing 'maltalent'; malevolent.

c **1450** *Merlin* 219 Thei rode in a-monge theire enmyes wroth and matelentif. *Ibid.* 338 And ronne to-geder wroth and maletalentif that oon a-gein that other.

maltase ('mɒlteɪs, -ɔː-). *Chem.* [f. MALT *sb.*[1] + *-ase*, after *diastase*.] Any enzyme which hydrolyses maltose and other α-glycosides.

1890 *Jrnl. Chem. Soc.* LVIII. 998 The author starts with the assumption that the diastase of malt is composed of a mixture of two enzymes—maltase and dextrinase. **1899** *19th Cent.* No. 265. 412 *note*, It [sucrase] is now named maltase, the termination in *-ase* being reserved for the names of all liquid ferments, or rather enzymes. **1946** *Thorpe's Dict. Appl. Chem.* (ed. 4) VII. 481/2 Maltase also hydrolyses ..α-glycosides but not β-glycosides. **1964** N. G. CLARK *Mod. Org. Chem.* xvi. 327 Hydrolysis with dilute hydrochloric acid yields two molecular proportions of glucose, and the glycosidic linkage is established as α by the fact that similar hydrolysis occurs with the enzyme maltase (which is specific for α-glycosides). **1968** A. WHITE et al. *Princ. Biochem.* (ed. 4) xviii. 387 Maltases IV and V account for about two-thirds of the total maltase activity.

maltate ('mɒltət, -ɔː-). *Chem.* [f. MALT *sb.*[1] + -ATE[1].] (See quot.)

1885 H. STOPES *Malt & Malting* xi. 140 Maltose combines with lime to form calcic maltate, the solution of which is lævo-rotatory as are those of other maltates.

malt-comes, *sb. pl.* (rarely *sing.*) The dried radicles which are separated from the grain in the kiln-drying process of malting; = COME *sb.*[2]
c **1440** *Promp. Parv.* 324/1 Malte comys. **1770-4** A. HUNTER *Georg. Ess.* (1803) I. 427, I manured a piece of land with maltcombs. **1787** MARSHALL *E. Norfolk* (1795) I. 35 Rapecake is also in good esteem [as manure]..as are Malt-coombs. **1874** W. WILLIAMS *Vet. Med.* 555 Flatulent colic. .. Its causes are—food..such as..a mixture of maltcums and brewers grains. **1877** *N.W. Linc. Gloss.*, *Malt-comb*, the dried sprouts, refuse used by some people to pack bacon in to keep flies away.

So **malt-comings** *dial.* (in the same sense).
a **1728** KENNETT *Lansd. MS.* 1033 (Promp. Parv. 324 *note*), Malt comes, or malt comings, the little beards or shoots, when malt begins to run, or come; *Yorkshire.* **1893** *Northumberld. Gloss.*, *Malt-cummins.*

malt-dust. The refuse, consisting chiefly of the dried radicles or 'comes', which falls from the grain in the process of malting.
1512 *MS. Acc. St. John's Hosp., Canterb.*, Payd for malt dowst for to dobe wyth. **1620** MARKHAM *Farew. Husb.* xiv. 110 Some are perswaded that this come or malt dust, is a great breeder of the worme or weeuell. **1707** MORTIMER *Husb.* vi. 94 Mault-dust is an enricher of barren Land. **1849** COBDEN *Speeches* 20 One of the ablest farmers in the country ..told me he bought great quantities of malt-dust, which he mixes..with the food he gives to his lambs. **1875** WATTS *Dict. Chem.* 2nd Suppl. 765 The malt is..screened to remove the radicle and plumule, which constitute malt-dust.

malte, obs. pa. t. MELT.

malted ('mɒltɪd, -ɔː-), *ppl. a.* (and *sb.*) [f. MALT *v.* + -ED[1].]
1. Made into malt; *rarely* in narrower sense, that has germinated in the process of malting.
1676 GREW *Anat. Flowers* ii. §15 As we use to dry Maulted Barly over a warm Kiln. **1692** W. Y-WORTH *Distillation* 9 Others Ferment Malted Wheat and Malt, and so Distill. **1702** LUTTRELL *Brief Rel.* (1857) V. 249 The commons read a 2d time, and committed the bill for encouraging the consumption of malted corn. **1745** DODSLEY *Agric.* I. 131 Trifles II. 104 To mash the malted barley, and extract Its flavour'd strength. **1844** T. J. GRAHAM *Dom. Med.* 180 Beer made from an infusion of malted groats, or malted rye. **1846** J. BAXTER *Libr. Pract. Agric.* (ed. 4) I. 133 Saccharine..may be extracted either from malted or raw grain.
2. Combined with extract of malt.
1887 *Official Gaz.* (U.S. Patent Office) XLI. 358 Trade-Marks..Food preparation for infants and invalids.—Horlick's Food Company, Mount Pleasant and Racine, Wis.,..'The words *Malted Milk* and the letters "M.M."' **1896** YEO *Food* 536 And first, with regard to the use of Malt extracts and Malted food in general. **1898** *Daily News* 11 Aug. 5/6 A few jars of beef extract, malted milk, &c. **1920** [see BEEZER 2]. **1930** BELLOC *New Cautionary Tales* 41 He gave him medicine by the pail And malted milk, and nutmeg ale. **1960** A. E. BENDER *Dict. Nutrition* 82/1 Malted milk —liquid separated from mash of ground barley malt and wheat flour mixed with milk and the mixture dried. **1974** *Times* 16 Mar. 11/6 My palate has reverted to childhood and adores American food—sandwiches, malted milk,..jello.
b. as *sb.* A drink of malted milk.
1945 *Newsweek* 8 Jan. 84 The couple..went into a Walgreen drugstore for ice cream. There, high above the ads for malteds, they noticed Vedovelli's paintings. **1949** A. MILLER *Death of Salesman* 11. 117 Let's go downstairs and get you a malted. **1953** *Manch. Guardian Weekly* 13 Aug. 7 The soda fountain serves such luxuries as candy and malteds. **1969** GISH & PINCHOT *Lillian Gish* xiv. 202 Order her a malted and a cheese sandwich.

malten ('mɒlt(ə)n, -ɔː-), *v. Sc. rare.* [f. MALT *sb.*[1] + -EN[5].] *intr.* To undergo malting, to malt.
1806 FORSYTH *Beauties Scotl.* IV. 67 When barley and common bear or big have been cultivated for some time in a mixed state, they spring and ripen and malten equally. **1825-80** JAMIESON, To *Mauten, Mawten*, to begin to spring; a term applied to grain, when steeped in order to be converted into malt.

'**malter.** *Obs.* exc. *dial.* Also 5 **maltar**, 7 **maulter.** [f. MALT *v.* + -ER[1].] A maltster.
c **1440** *Promp. Parv.* 324/1 Malstere, or maltestere (*H., P.*, maltar), *brasiatrix, brasiator.* **1630** in J. Hutchins *Hist. Dorset* (ed. 3) II. 338/2 Brewers. Maulters. Bakers. **1848** W. BARNES *Poems Rur. Life* (ed. 2) Gloss., *Malter*; rightly used instead of *maltster*, which is properly a *woman malter.*

Maltese (mɒl'tiːz, -ɔː-), *a.* and *sb. sing.* and *pl.* Also 9 *sing.* **Maltee** (*vulgar*), 7 *pl.* **Malteses.** [f. MALTA + -ESE. Cf. It. *maltese.*] **A.** *adj.*
1. a. Of or pertaining to Malta and its inhabitants. **b.** Pertaining to the Knights of Malta.
1797 *Encycl. Brit.* (ed. 3) X. 491/1 At the first landing of the Maltese knights. *Ibid.* 401/2 The attempt..proved unsuccessful through the base avarice of the Maltese forces. **1837** G. C. LEWIS *Lett.* 3 Apr. (1870) 77 The vulgar adjective from Malta, used by sailors and others in the island is Maltee. **1839** *Penny Cycl.* XIV. 350/1 The Maltese people at length obtained the fulfilment of their wishes. **1869** ROGERS *Hist. Gleanings* I. 97 The legend of the Maltese money ran—*non æs sed fides.*
2. Special collocations: **Maltese cat**, a fancy variety of the domestic cat (see quot. 1902); **Maltese cross**, (*a*) see CROSS *sb.* 18; also, see quots. 1884 and 1890; (*b*) *Philately*, name given to the postmark used on British postage stamps from their introduction in 1840 until 1844; (*c*) *Cinemat.* = *Geneva mechanism*; **Maltese dog**, = sense B. 4; **Maltese guipure, lace** (see quots.); **Maltese mushroom**, the fungus *Cynomorium coccineum* (formerly *Fungus melitensis*), found in the islands of Malta and Gozo; **Maltese orange, stone, vulture** (see quots.); **Maltese terrier** = sense B. 4.
1857 in *N. & Q.* 2nd Ser. IV. 247 A New York merchant recently sent for a cargo of *Maltese cats from that celebrated island. **1902** 'DICK WHITTINGTON' *Cat Manual* ii. 32 There is a strain of short-haired blue cats known as Maltese cats, which used to be extremely popular in America. **1877** W. JONES *Finger-ring* 373 A *Maltese cross in red on a black ground. **1881** PHILBRICK & WESTOBY *Postage & Telegr. Stamps Gt. Brit.* 291 Several obliterating marks are found: 1. The Maltese cross, or *croix patée*, as then in use. **1884** F. J. BRITTEN *Watch and Clockm.* 247 The wheel of the going barrel stop work..is called indifferently a star wheel or a Maltese cross. **1890** BILLINGS *Nat. Med. Dict.*, *Maltese cross*, square compress cut out at the corners in form of a Maltese cross. **1909** J. G. HENDY *Hist. Postmarks Brit. Isles 1840-76* 9 The Maltese Cross or *croix patée* obliterator —the latter is really the correct term to apply to it from a heraldic point of view—varied a good deal in shape in different places. **1917** C. N. BENNETT *Guide to Kinematogr.* ix. 127 Modern Maltese cross movements are descendants of the 'Geneva stop' by which overwinding of watches is prevented. **1934** J. B. SEYMOUR *Stamps Gt. Brit.*: *Line-Engraved Issues 1840-53* 9 The design generally used for obliterating the British stamps from 1840 to 1844 has been called, incorrectly, a Croix Patée or Maltese Cross; it is neither one nor the other. But it is so well known as the Maltese Cross that it is deemed advisable to call it so for the purpose of this work. *Ibid.* 102 The stamps from the first forty plates [*sc.* of the one penny red imperforate] are usually obliterated with the Maltese Cross. **1949** P. C. LITCHFIELD *Guide Lines to Penny Black* 16 Stamps with the red Maltese Cross are more likely to have come from one of the early plates. **1953** Maltese cross [see GENEVA[2] b]. **1963** *Gt. Brit.*: *Specialised Stamp Catal.*: *Queen Victoria* (Stanley Gibbons Ltd.) 23 The Maltese Cross is a valuable plating aid for collectors of the Penny Red imperf. Its presence on a stamp is strong evidence that that stamp is from a plate put to press before 1845. **1796** NEMNICH *Polyglotten-Lex.* v, The hairy *Maltese dog. *Canis Melitaeus.* The small Maltese dog ..*Canis brevipilis.* **1864** *Chambers's Encycl.* VI. 287/1 Maltese Dog, a small kind of spaniel, with roundish muzzle, and long, silky, generally white hair. **1913** V. SHAW *Encycl. Kennel* 130 Many people persist in calling the delicate little Maltese dog a terrier, whereas he is nothing of the kind, but a fragile member of the toy family. **1902** *Mrs. Palliser's Hist. Lace* 392 At this time [1851] was introduced the *Maltese guipures,..a variety grafted on the old Maltese. **1882** CAULFEILD & SAWARD *Dict. Needlework* 340 The manufacture of *Maltese Lace is not confined to Malta. **1900** MRS. F. N. JACKSON *Hand-made Lace* 180 Maltese Lace. A bobbin-made lace, which has been made in Malta ever since the commencement of the sixteenth century. **1902** *Mrs. Palliser's Hist. Lace* 87 *note*, There is no corroboration of Mrs. Palliser's statement above that lace was ever made in Malta; if so, it would have been of the Genoese geometrical kind, of which Lady Hamilton Chichester adapted the designs and evolved what is now known as Maltese lace. **1816-20** T. GREEN *Univ. Herbal* I. 320/1 It is commonly said that the *Maltese red oranges are budded on the pomegranate. **1884** *Encycl. Brit.* XVII. 812/1 'Maltese' or 'Blood' oranges, much grown in southern Italy, are distinguished by the deep-red tint of the pulp. **1858** SIMMONDS *Dict. Trade*, **Maltese stone*, a soft stone quarried in Malta, used for carving, and for making large jars, &c. **1880** H. DALZIEL *Brit. Dogs* III. viii. 430 Whether the dog we now call a *Maltese terrier be a descendant more or less pure from the breed Strabo wrote of, it is now impossible to say. **1954** M. K. WILSON tr. *Lorenz's Man meets Dog* iv. 42 They [*sc.* two large dogs] nearly pulled a Maltese terrier in half. **1781** LATHAM *Gen. Synopsis Birds* I. 15 *Maltese Vulture... This bird inhabits many parts of Europe, chiefly the island of Malta. **1843** *Penny Cycl.* XXVI. 472/1 *Neophron percnopterus*... This is the.. Maltese Vulture of Latham.
B. *sb.*
1. a. A native or an inhabitant of Malta. **b.** A Knight of Malta.
1615 G. SANDYS *Trav.* 227 With him a Maltese, whose father was an English man. *Ibid.* 234 The Malteses are little lesse tawnie then the Moores. **1624** MASSINGER *Renegado* II. v, Your fellow Pirats Sir, the bold Malteze Whom with your lookes you thinke to quell. **1651** HOWELL *Venice* 195 The Malteses [the Knights of Malta] having made prize of them, arriv'd afterwards in Candy. **1797** *Encycl. Brit.* (ed. 3) X. 492/2 The Maltese still continued to behave with their usual valour against the Turks. **1838** J. L. STEPHENS *Trav. Greece*, etc. 41/1 An old Maltese, who spoke French and Italian.
2. The language of the natives of Malta, a corrupt Arabic.
1828 *Foreign Q. Rev.* III. 321 The affinity between the Maltese and the languages of the neighbouring continent. **1839** *Penny Cycl.* XIV. 346/1 The mother-tongue of the people, the Maltese, has continued in use.
3. Short for MALTESE LACE.
1900 MRS. F. N. JACKSON *Hand-made Lace* 180 In Ceylon the natives work a kind of Maltese. **1902** *Mrs. Palliser's Hist. Lace* 88 Much Maltese is made in the orphanage in..Gozo.
4. A very small, long-coated, white dog of the breed so called, formerly known as *Maltese dogs* or *Maltese terriers* (sense A. 2).
1867 MRS. F. LEHMANN *Let.* 22 Jan. in Geo. Eliot *Lett.* (1956) IV. 336 The Lewes's were enchanted with Chang. They say he is a real Maltese. **1950** A. C. SMITH *Dogs since 1900* 318 The Maltese. This, one of the oldest of the toy breeds in Europe, at one time had 'Terrier' added to its name. **1972** *Country Life* 10 Feb. (Suppl.) 21/1 'Floriana Maltese'..good straight white coats, with black points.
Hence †**Mal'tesian** *sb.*, a Maltese.
1656 BLOUNT *Glossogr.*, *Maltesian*, an Inhabitant of the Island Malta.

maltha ('mælθə). Also anglicized 5 **malthe.** [a. L. *maltha*, a. Gr. μάλθα, μάλθη mixture of wax and pitch.]
1. A kind of cement made by mixing pitch and wax, or lime and sand, with other ingredients.
c **1420** *Pallad. on Husb.* I. 1115 Conuenyent hit is to knowe, of bathis..what malthis hote & colde Are able,..To make hit hool and watir wel to holde. **1601** HOLLAND *Pliny* II. 595 Concerning Maltha, it was wont to be made of quicke and new lime: for they tooke the limestone and quenched it in wine, which done, presently they punned it with swines grease and figs. **1703** MOXON *Mech. Exerc.* 243 There is other Morter..very hard and durable, as may be seen at Rome,..which is called Maltha, from a kind of Bitumen Dug there;..But their Cement differs from both the Malthas in Composition and use. **1847** SMEATON *Builder's Man.* 123 Maltha, or Greek Mastic. This is made by mixing lime and sand..and making it into a proper consistency with milk or size, instead of water.
2. The name anciently given to some viscid form of bitumen; applied by Kirwan to the 'semi-compact' variety of 'mineral pitch' or asphaltum, and by later mineralogists variously to 'mineral tar' and to ozocerite (Kirwan's 'mineral tallow').
1601 HOLLAND *Pliny* I. 46 In a citie of Comagene, named Samosatis, there is a pond, yeelding forth a kind of slimie mud (called Maltha) which will burne cleare. **1727-41** CHAMBERS *Cycl.* s.v., Natural maltha is a kind of bitumen, wherewith the Asiatics plaster their walls. **1796** KIRWAN *Elem. Min.* II. 46 Species IV. Mineral Pitch, Asphaltum... Second Variety. Semi Compact. Maltha. Erdiges Erdpech of Werner. Its colour dark reddish, or blackish brown... I shall denote it by the name of Maltha. **1799** W. TOOKE *View Russian Emp.* I. 292, A watery vapour..which collected in pitchers is..so richly impregnated with naphtha, but still more with maltha, that the inhabitants take both and use the latter as tar. **1807** T. THOMSON *Chem.* (ed. 3) II. 455 Sea wax, or maltha, is a solid substance found on the Baikal lake in Siberia. **1865** WATTS *Dict. Chem.*, *Maltha*, the mineral tallow of Kirwan, said to have been found on the coast of Finland. It resembles wax. **1868** *Proc. Amer. Philos. Soc.* X. 455 Maltha, or mineral tar,..is more nearly allied to tar.. than to oil.

malthacite ('mælθəsaɪt). *Min.* Also **malthazite.** [ad. G. *malthazit* (A. Breithaupt 1837), f. Gr. μαλθακ-ός soft: see -ITE.] A variety of fullers' earth (Chester *Dict. Min.* 1896).
1849 WATTS tr. *Gmelin's Handbk. Chem.* III. 419. **1883** *Encycl. Brit.* XVI. 424/2 Malthazite, from Steindörfel near Bautzen.

malthoid ('mælθɔɪd). *Austral.* and *N.Z.* [f. MALTHA + -OID.] The proprietary name of a bituminous material made from wood fibre and used as a roof- or floor-covering or for covering other surfaces.
1936 *Patent Office Jrnl.* (N.Z.) 3 Dec. 367/1 *Malthoid.* Pabco Products (Australia), Limited... Paints, varnishes, coatings, and paint compounds, [etc.]. **1959** *Numbers* IX. 9 The malthoid roof. **1960** B. CRUMP *Good Keen Man* 76 When all the boards were on [the hut] we covered the whole structure with malthoid and tacked it into place. **1960** J. FINGLETON *Four Chukkas to Austral.* 7 An odd sort of trial upon a malthoid pitch.

† '**malt-horse.** *Obs.* A heavy kind of horse used by maltsters; used occas. as a term of abuse.
1561 T. HOBY tr. *Castiglione's Courtyer* I. E iij, To carie a mans head so like a malthorse for feare of ruffling his hear. **1590** SHAKS. *Com. Err.* III. i. 32 Mome, Malthorse, Capon, Coxcombe, Idiot. **1596** —— *Tam. Shr.* IV. i. 132. **1598** B. JONSON *Ev. Man in Hum.* I. iii, Why he has no more iudgement then a malt horse. **1603** HARSNET *Pop. Impost.* 82 A stiffe resty spirit, of kin (as seemes) to a malt-horse of Ware, that wil not out of his way. *c* **1616** S. WARD *Coal from Altar* (1627) 57 Such as hold onely a certaine stint of daily duties as malt-horses their pace, or mill-horses their round.

malt-house ('mɒlthaʊs, -ɔː-). A building in which malt is prepared and stored; a malting.
c **1050** *Suppl. Ælfric's Gloss.* in Wr.-Wülcker 185/24 *Brationarium*, mealthus. **1360-1** *Durham Acc. Rolls* (Surtees) 563 Johanni lepemaker pro..4 sportis pro le Malthous. **1429** *Munim. Magd. Coll. Oxf.* (1882) 16 Item, j bakhous cum j malthous et le brewhous. **1577** HARRISON *England* I. III. i. 95 b/2 Beare with me gentle reader..that leade thee..from a table delicately furnished, into a mustye mault house. **1692** *Lond. Gaz.* No. 2800/4 A Large and convenient Brew-house and Malthouse. **1776** ADAM SMITH *W. N.* v. ii. 507 The opportunities of defrauding the revenue being much greater in a brewery than in a malt-house. **1885** H. STOPES *Malt & Malting* xiii. 183 Malt-houses (or maltings).

Malthusian (mæl'θjuːzɪən), *a.* and *sb.* [f. the proper name *Malthus* + -IAN.] **A.** *adj.*
1. Pertaining to T. R. Malthus (1766–1835) or his teaching (see MALTHUSIANISM).
1821 SHELLEY *Lett.* Pr. Wks. 1880 IV. 195 In the comparison of Platonic and Malthusian doctrines. **1839** CARLYLE *Chartism* x. (1840) 109 How often have we read in Malthusian benefactors of the species: 'The working people have their condition in their own hands'. **1872** W. R. GREG *Enigmas* 56 Terms on which alone, according to the Malthusian theory, plenty can be secured for all.
2. Befitting or characteristic of a Malthusian.
1891 T. HARDY *Tess* I. v. I. 65 She felt Malthusian vexation with her mother for thoughtlessly giving her so many little brothers and sisters.
B. *sb.* A follower or supporter of T. R. Malthus in his views on population.
1812 R. SOUTHEY in *Q. Rev.* VIII. 324 The Malthusians observe..that the new discovery is matter of science. **1845**

MILL *Diss. & Disc.* (1875) II. 187 We need not wonder that the epithets of 'Malthusians' and 'Political Economists' are so often considered equivalent to hard-hearted, unfeeling, and enemies of the poor. **1885** J. BONAR *Malthus* I. i. 4 A Malthusian is supposed to forbid all marriage.

Malthusianism (mæl'θjuːzɪənɪz(ə)m). [formed as prec. + -ISM.] The teaching of Malthus and his followers on the question of population.

T. R. Malthus in his *Essay on Population* (1798) contended that the rate of increase of the population being out of proportion to the increase of its means of subsistence, it should be checked, mainly by moral restraint. This has often been popularly viewed as a proposal to check marriage.

1848 MILL *Pol. Econ.* (ed. 5) I. 450 Even Boards of Guardians.. will seldom hear patiently of anything which they are pleased to designate as Malthusianism. **1892** *Nation* (N.Y.) 21 Apr. 311/3 This religious Malthusianism is calculated to please the economists who think that the world is too small for mankind.

Mal'thusianize, *v.* [f. MALTHUSIAN + -IZE.] *intr.* To adopt the principles of Malthus.

1893 *National Observer* 1 Apr. 485/2 If Britain had Malthusianised, where were our colonies?

maltin ('mɒltɪn, -ɔː-). *Chem.* [ad. F. *maltin*, f. MALT *sb.*^{1}: see -IN^1.] (See quot. 1872.)

1871 WATTS tr. *Gmelin's Handbk. Chem.* XVIII. 455. **1872** —— *Dict. Chem.* Suppl., *Maltin*, a nitrogenous ferment existing, according to Dubrunfaut, in malt, and much more active than diastase. **1883** *Encycl. Brit.* XV. 339/1.

maltine ('mɒltiːn, -ɔː-). [f. MALT *sb.*^{1} + -INE.]

1889 *Syd. Soc. Lex.*, *Maltine*, a name given in commerce to an extract of malt which contains dextrin, glucose, and a variable quantity of diastase.

malting ('mɒltɪŋ, -ɔː-), *vbl. sb.* [f. MALT *v.* + -ING^1.]

1. The action or process of making malt or of converting into malt.

c **1440** *Promp. Parv.* 324/1 Maltynge, *brasiatura* (P. *brasiacio*). **1467**, **1585** [see 3]. **1626** BACON *Sylva* §647 Barley, (as appeareth in the Malting,) being steeped in Water three dayes.. will sprout. **1714** MANDEVILLE *Fab. Bees* (1725) I. 90 The variety of labour, required in husbandry, in malting, in carriage and distillation. **1813** VANCOUVER *Agric. Devon* 172 Malting is generally a business of itself. **1839** URE *Dict. Arts* 105 Maize.. has also been employed to make beer; but its malting is somewhat difficult. **1885** H. STOPES *Malt & Malting* xiv. 224 A comparatively new form of malting is known as the 'pneumatic system'.

2. A MALT-HOUSE.

1846 M. A. RICHARDSON *Local Hist. Table Bk.* V. 30 A spacious malting.. belonging to Mr. Richard Robinson, brewer. **1870** *Daily News* 18 June, An old malting, situated about nine miles from Cambridge, was burned down. **1887** W. RYE *Norfolk Broads* 77 A strange.. village.. chiefly composed of maltings and other buildings connected with beer brewing.

3. *attrib.* and *Comb.*, as ***malting barley, business, district, sample, time***, etc.; **malting-floor, house, kiln, office** = *malt floor, house*, etc.

1467 *Bury Wills* (Camden) 46 That the seid Denys haue.. esement in the maltynghows joyned therto. *Ibid.*, Duryng maltyng tyme. **1585** *Abingdon Rolls* (Camden) 167 The Maltinge House. **1637** *Documents agst. Prynne* (Camden) 84 The maulting business goes on, but with some restrictions. **1641** MILTON *Animadv.* 58 Though they keep back their sordid sperm.. and turne them to their malting-kils. **1723** *Lond. Gaz.* No. 6196/5 A large Malting Office. **1764** *Museum Rust.* III. li. 219 Many of the farms have malting-offices annexed to them. **1813** *Examiner* 12 Apr. 240/2 Fine Malting Barley. **1834** *Brit. Husb.* I. 146 Inferior malting samples frequently fetch little more than feed oats of good quality. **1840** *Cottager's Man.* 10 in *Libr. Usef. Knowl. Husb.* III, The bruised grain.. is said to be as complete as if it had lain a fortnight on the malting-floor. **1846** McCULLOCH *Acc. Brit. Empire* (1854) I. 189 The malting business is extensively prosecuted at Ware.

maltless ('mɒltlɪs, -ɔː-), *a.* [f. MALT *sb.*^{1} + -LESS.] Without malt, deficient in malt.

1828 *Blackw. Mag.* XXIV. 352 Weak small-beer, frothy and maltless.

'maltlong. *dial.* Also **moltlong, -ling.** = ANBURY 1, ANGLEBERRY.

1610 MARKHAM *Masterp.* II. cviii. 390 The maltlong, or as some Farriers call it, the maltworme, is a cankerous soarrance aboue the hoofe, iust vpon the cronet. **1649** *Eng. Farrier* B 2 b, Molt-long, is the pinching of a straight-hoofe. **1704** *Dict. Rust.* **1847** HALLIWELL, *Moltling.* **1895** *E. Anglian Gloss.*, *Moltlong*, a sore or disease between or rather above the clees of cattle (Johnson).

'malt-maker. A maltster.

1455 *Rolls of Parlt.* V. 324/2 Thus is.. ye seid commen peple that were wonte to be Malt makers grevously hurt. **1551** *Reg. Privy Council Scot.* I. 115 The maltmakaris, sellaris of malt, baxtaris. **1593** NORDEN *Spec. Brit., M'sex* II. 14 Baldock.. yeeldeth malt-makers not a few. **1691** TRYON *Art Brewing* (ed. 3) 52 These ill customs all Mault-Makers ought to understand and avoid. **1753** CHAMBERS *Cycl. Supp.* s.v. *Malt*, Our barley Malt-makers have tried all their skill to make good Malt of it [maize].

maltman ('mɒltmən, -ɔː-). A maltster.

1408 *E.E. Wills* (1882) 14 Iohn plot, Citaysyn and Malt-man of london. **1500–20** DUNBAR *Poems* xxxiv. 51 The maltman sais, 'I God forsaik,.. Gif ony bettir malt may be'. **1576** GASCOIGNE *Steele Gl.* H iij b, When maltemen make vs drinke no firmentie. *a* **1627** MIDDLETON *No Wit like Woman's* III. i, Let each man look to his part now, and not feed Upon one dish all four on's, like plain maltmen. **1724** DE FOE *Fort. Mistress* (1854) 5 He found money in cash to pay the malt-man and the excise. **1737–8** *Manch. School Reg.* (1866) I. 8 William son of Ellis Farmer of Salford, maltman. **1889** BARNARD *Noted Breweries* I. 55 A messroom and lavatory, etc., for the malt-men.

†**b.** *Proverbial phrases. Obs.*

c **1530** *Hye Way Spyttell House* 62 in Hazl. *E.P.P.* (1866) IV. 55 Make we Mery as longe as we can, And drynke a pace: the deuill pay the malt man! **1600** ROWLANDS *Lett. Humours Blood* Sat. vi. 53 For he that is in Malt-mans Hall inrolde, Cares not a poynt for hunger nor for colde.

Malto ('mæltəʊ), *sb.* [Native word = 'language of the Maler': see MALER *sb.* and *a.*] A Dravidian language spoken by the Maler people living in the Rajmahal hills of northern India. Also called RAJMAHALI. Also as *adj.*

1884 E. DROESE *Introd. Malto Lang.* p. i, Malto is the language of one of the aboriginal races of India who call themselves Maler *i.e.* men, and go among their Aryan neighbours by the name of Paharias (Hill people). **1906** G. A. GRIERSON *Ling. Survey India* IV. 446 Malto is almost exclusively spoken in the Rajmahal Hills in the north-east of the Sonthal Parganas... Malto is the name used by the people themselves in order to denote their language. The word simply means 'the language of the Maler', and *maler* in Malto means 'men' and is the name the people apply to themselves... It is.. probable that Malto like Malayāļam is derived from the common Dravidian *mala*, mountain, so that the original meaning of 'maler' would be 'hillmen'. *Ibid.* 447 Malto does not possess a literature of its own... The Malto language very closely agrees with Kuruḳh. **1938** S. S. SARKAR *Mālers of Rajmahal Hills* i. 18 The Mālers speak *Mālto*. **1955** T. BURROW *Sanskrit Lang.* viii. 387 The Dravidian languages Kurukh and Malto are preserved even now in Northern India, and may be regarded as islands surviving from a once extensive Dravidian territory. **1963** L. P. VIDYARTHI *Maler* iv. 57 The Maler.. call themselves 'Male' in their native Malto language which means hill-man. **1972** W. B. LOCKWOOD *Panorama Indo-European Lang.* 224 Malto, the vernacular of 100,000 tribesmen, is found in the Rajmahal Hills.

,malto-'dextrin. *Physiol. Chem.* (See quot.)

1900 GOULD *Dict. Med.*, *Maltodextrin* $C_6H_{10}O_5$. A carbonhydrate, intermediate between starch and maltose.

maltol ('mɒltɒl, -ɔː-). *Chem.* [a. G. *maltol* (J. Brand 1894, in *Ber. d. Deut. Chem. Ges.* XXVII. 810): see MALT *sb.* and -OL.] A crystalline compound, $C_6H_6O_3$, which occurs in larch bark and chicory and is formed by roasting malt; 3-hydroxy-2-methylpyran-4-one.

1894 *Jrnl. Chem. Soc.* LXVI. I. 271 Beer, prepared from caramel malt, gives a violet coloration with ferric chloride; this is not due to salicylic acid, but to the presence of a compound termed maltol, which is distinguished from salicylic acid by giving no reaction with Millon's reagent. **1945** *Jrnl. Amer. Chem. Soc.* LXVII. 2276 Hydrolysis of streptomycin chloride with *N* sodium hydroxide... yields a weakly acidic substance, m.p. 161–162°, which has been characterized as maltol. **1972** *Sci. Amer.* Mar. 16/2 In recent years the use of maltol, which can intensify or modify the flavor of preserves, desserts, fruit, soft drinks and foods generally high in carbohydrates, has expanded greatly.

maltolt, variant of MALETOLT *Obs.*

maltose ('mɒltəʊs, -ɔː-). *Chem.* [a. F. *maltose* (Dubrunfaut), f. MALT *sb.*^{1}: see -OSE.] (See quot.)

1862 WATTS tr. *Gmelin's Handbk. Chem.* XV. 338 Maltose. The sugar produced from starch-paste by the action of malt (or diastase) is, according to Dubrunfaut, different from dextro-glucose. **1883** *Standard* 29 Nov. 3/2 Maltose is the best.. of the sugar compounds. **1885** H. STOPES *Malt & Malting* xi. 140 Maltose, when free from glucose sugars, crystallises like cane-sugar or sucrose.

maltot(e, variant of MALETOLT *Obs.*

†**maltout.** *slang. Obs.* (See quot.)

1785 GROSE *Dict. Vulg. Tongue*, *Maltout*, a nickname for a marine, used by sailors and soldiers of other corps, probably a corruption of matelot, the French word for a sailor.

†**maltreat**, *pa. pple. Obs. rare*$^{-1}$. In 6 **maletrait.** [? a. OF. *maltrait*, pa. pple. of *maltraire* to suffer.] ? Suffered.

1592 WYRLEY *Armorie, Ld. Chandos* 36 News him was brought.. How Lord Clisson had lost his head they told And maletrait, the French kings ire t' appease.

maltreat (mæl'triːt), *v.* Also 8 **maltrait, maletreat.** [a. F. *maltraiter*: see MAL- and TREAT *v.*] *trans.* To abuse, ill-use; to handle roughly or rudely; to ill-treat.

1708 COLLIER *Further Vind. View Stage* 32 The Doctor [Filmer] agrees.. the Clergy ought by no means to be *maltraited* [Dr. Filmer had used the word 'abus'd'] and ridicul'd on the Stage. **1739** CIBBER *Apol.* (1756) I. 61 This indignity cast upon a gentleman only for having maltreated a player was [etc.]. **1759** STERNE *Tr. Shandy* II. xvii, Yorick, indeed, was never better served in his life!—but it was a little hard to male-treat him after, and plunder him after he was laid in his grave. **1859** HOLLAND *Gold F.* iv. 49 It is against the law that she turn them out of doors, or kill them, or maltreat them in any way. **1868** MISS YONGE *Cameos* I. xxxiv. 290 The jurymen.. were often liable to be beaten and maltreated in revenge. **1881** SAINTSBURY *Dryden* 172 The metre, though a well-known English critic has maltreated it of late, is a very fine one.

Hence **mal'treated** *ppl. a.*

1829 CARLYLE *Misc.* (1857) II. 28 The cheerful thraldom of this maltreated philosopher. **1864** *Reader* IV. 477/2 We cannot take leave of this maltreated book without [etc.]. **1901** *Spectator* 20 July 94/2 An unskilful physician was imprisoned by the family of a maltreated patient.

maltreater (mæl'triːtə(r)). [f. MALTREAT *v.* + -ER^1.] One who maltreats or ill-uses.

1902 O. WISTER *Virginian* iv. 57 A maltreater of hawsses [horses]. **1906** B. VON HUTTEN *What became of Pam* I. ii, Tyrants,.. drunkards, maltreaters [of women]. **1965** M. SPARK *Mandelbaum Gate* iii. 55 Much as the timid spinsters of the old days, while abroad, would be moved to violence against the maltreater of the donkey.

maltreatment (mæl'triːtmənt). Also 8 **maletreatment.** [ad. F. *maltraitement*, f. *maltraiter*: see MALTREAT *v.* and -MENT.] The action of maltreating; the state of being maltreated.

1721 AMHERST *Terræ Fil.* Pref. (1754) 14 Nature will sometimes rebel against principle, when it is long and grievously provoked by male-treatment and oppression. **1768** BLACKSTONE *Comm.* III. viii. 140 If the beating or other maltreatment be very enormous.. the law then gives him a separate remedy. **1816** COLERIDGE *Lay Serm.* (1817) 379 [They] after much contumely.. and cruel maltreatment on all sides, rushed out of the pile. **1845** CARLYLE *Cromwell* I. i. 8 From this source has proceeded our maltreatment of it [the 17th cent.], our miseditings, miswritings [etc.]. **1882** J. HAWTHORNE *Fort. Fool* I. xxxv, Thus had his deliberate maltreatment of another man's soul resulted in the loss of his own moral free-will.

maltster ('mɒltstə(r), -ɔː-). Forms: 4–5 **maltestere, malstere,** 6 **maultster,** 7 **maulster,** 7–8 **malster,** 7– **maltster.** [f. MALT *sb.*^{1} + -STER.] One whose occupation it is to make malt.

c **1370–80** *Durham Acc. Rolls* (Surtees) 328 Johannes Molend' Malstere. *c* **1440** *Promp. Parv.* 324/1 Malstere, or maltestere (*H., P.* maltar), *brasiatrix, brasiator.* **1577** HARRISON *England* I. III. i. 95 b/2 Ye making wherof [mault] I will her set in such order, as my skill therein may extend vnto, (for I am scarse a good maultster). **1608** *Nottingham Rec.* IV. 289 Euerie maltster in the towne to forbeare buyinge of barley. **1656** S. HOLLAND *Zara* (1719) 141 Dukes and Marquisses fall by the Bullet or the Ax, when Dunghil-Rakers and Maulsters out-live themselves. **1683** LUTTRELL *Brief Rel.* (1857) I. 262 The 23d [June] also came out a proclamation.. for the apprehending.. Richard Rumbold, malster [etc.]. **1729** SWIFT *Grand Question* Wks. 1751 X. 124 Sir Arthur the Malster! how fine it will sound! **1776** ADAM SMITH *W.N.* v. ii. (1869) II. 489 For the maltster to get back eighteen shillings in the advanced price of his malt. **1830** M. DONOVAN *Dom. Econ.* I. 79 The brewer or distiller who is his own maltster can always protect himself. **1863** FAWCETT *Pol. Econ.* IV. ii. (1876) 537 The Malt Duty is nominally paid by maltsters.

'malt-worm.

†**1.** A weevil which infests malt. *Obs.*

c **1440** *Promp. Parv.* 46/1 Bowde, malte-worme (*P.* boude of malte), *gurgulio.*

2. *transf.* One who loves malt-liquor; a toper.

c **1550** *Drinking Song* in *Skelton's Wks.* (1843) I. p. x, Then dothe she troule To me the bolle As a goode malte worme sholde. **1580** G. HARVEY *Three Lett.* 29 A morning bookeworm, an afternoone maltworm. **1596** SHAKS. *1 Hen. IV*, II. i. 83 Mustachio-purple-hu'd Maltwormes. **1605** *Tryall Chev.* III. i, The whorson Mault-worm has a throat like the burning Clyme. **1859** R. F. BURTON *Centr. Afr.* in *Jrnl. Geog. Soc.* XXIX. 367 Many a gallon must be drunk by the veteran maltworm before intoxication. **1876** *Whitby Gloss.*, *Maut-worm*, a lover of beer.

†**3.** = MALTLONG. *Obs. rare*$^{-1}$.

1610 [see MALTLONG].

malt-wort ('mɒltwɜːt, -ɔː-). Forms: 1 **mealtwurt, maltwyrt,** 7 **mault-,** 8– **malt-wort.** [f. MALT *sb.*^{1} + WORT^2.] = WORT^2.

c **1000** ÆLFRIC *Gloss.* in Wr.-Wülcker 129/6 *Acinum*, mealtwurt. *c* **1050** *Voc.* ibid. 356/33 *Acinum*, maltwyrt. **1630** J. TAYLOR (Water P.) *Wit & Mirth* Wks. II. 181/2 He ..dipped some small quantity of the Lye, which he supposing to be mault-wort, dranke vp. **1731** P. SHAW *Ess. Artif. Philos.* 41 The boiling down Malt-Wort to a Treacle. *c* **1796** SIR J. DALRYMPLE *Observ. Yeast-cake* 4, I can make molasses-worts as easily into cakes as malt-worts.

malty ('mɒltɪ, -ɔː-), *a.* [f. MALT *sb.*^{1} + -Y.] *jocular.* Addicted to, affected by, or containing malt (in the form of malt liquor). Also *slang*, drunk.

1819 *Metropolis* III. 144 'Tis degrading to see.. our malty ladies of quality. **1823** 'JON BEE' *Slang* 117 'Malty'; drunk, with beer, or drunkish any how, stupidly so. **1852** DICKENS *Bleak Ho.* xl, Those particular parts of the country on which Doodle is at present throwing himself in an auriferous and malty shower.

b. Of the nature of or resembling malt.

1830 M. DONOVAN *Dom. Econ.* I. 361 The bread would be soft, clammy, greyish, and malty. **1892** WALSH *Tea* (Philad.) 100 Japan Pekoe.. smooth in liquor and 'malty' in flavor.

maluerte, malure: see MALEURTEE, MALHEUR.

‖**malum in se** ('mæləm ɪn siː). Pl. **mala in se.** [med.L.] Something intrinsically evil or wicked. Also as *adj. phr.*

1623 J. WILLIAMS *Let.* 30 Aug. in J. Hacket *Scrinia Reserata* (1693) I. 157 But to grant a Pardon even for a thing that is *malum in se.* **1811** *Edin. Rev.* Feb. 275 That corruption is not.. a *malum in se*, as Mr Windham has been pleased to assert. **1826** *Ibid.* Feb. 331 Whether there be.. any solecism which is a *malum in se*, as distinct from a *malum prohibitum.* **1856** *Sat. Rev.* 26 July 290/1 It is the bargaining intention, and this is *malum in se.* The *malum prohibitum* is the contract. **1893** [see HYPERTENSION 1 a]. **1959** JOWITT *Dict. Eng. Law* II. 1130/1 *Mala in se*, acts which are wrong in themselves, such as murder, as opposed to *mala prohibita.* **1961** *Times* 18 Mar. 12/6 That part of the criminal law which covered offences *mala in se.*

malurine (ˈmæljʊraɪn), *a. Ornith.* [ad. mod.L. *Malūrīn-us*, f. *Malūrus* (see below).
The name *Malurus* (Vieillot 1816) was app. intended to mean 'soft-tailed (bird)', repr. Gr. μάλουρος (Hesych.), f. μαλλός (Theocr., once) variously conjectured to mean 'white', 'shaggy', or 'soft' + οὐρά tail.]
Belonging to the *Malurinæ*, a small group of birds (chiefly Australian) of which the typical genus is *Malurus*, the Superb Warbler.
1862 Wood *Illustr. Nat. Hist.* II. 274 Perhaps the most curious example of the Malurine birds is the beautiful little Emeu Wren of Australia.

malurit(e, variant of MALEURTEE *Obs.*

malva (ˈmælvə). [L. *malva* mallow; adopted by Linnæus in his *Genera Plantarum* (1737) 308 as the name of a genus.] = MALLOW.
[**1548** W. Turner *Names of Herbes* sig. E3 Malva is called in greeke Malache, in englishe a Mallowe or a Mallo.] **1883** W. Robinson *Wild Garden* (ed. 3) xiv. 150 Some of the Malvas are..vigorous-growing plants. **1959** W. Strache *Forms & Patterns in Nature* 35 (*caption*) Malva flower. **1966** E. Palmer *Plains of Camdeboo* xvii. 277 The early settlers... used..the Malva to bathe sore eyes.

malvaceous (mælˈveɪʃəs), *a. Bot.* [f. late L. *malvāceus* (whence mod.L. *Malvāce-æ*), f. *malva* mallow: see -ACEOUS.] Pertaining to the genus *Malva* (the Mallow), or to the N.O. *Malvaceæ*.
1699 *Phil. Trans.* XXI. 64 An exact Division of Mallows, or Malvaceous Plants. **1727** Bailey vol. II, *Malvaceous*, like, belonging to, or made with mallows. **1861** Bentley *Man. Bot.* 209 *Althæa rosea*, and some other Malvaceous Plants. **1880** C. & F. Darwin *Movem. Pl.* 232 The leaves in several Malvaceous genera sink at night.

ˈmalvad. *Bot.* [f. L. *malva* mallow + -AD.] Lindley's term for a plant of the N.O. *Malvaceæ*.
1845 Lindley *Sch. Bot.* 45 Mallowworts, or Malvads.

malvady, corrupt form of MARAVEDI.

malval (ˈmælvəl), *a. Bot.* [f. L. *malva* MALLOW + -AL[1].] Only in ***malval alliance, exogens***: in Lindley's classification, an 'alliance' embracing the N.O. *Malvaceæ* and other orders.
1836 Lindley *Nat. Syst. Bot.* (ed. 2) 92 The highest alliances in regard to structure are the Malval and Melial. **1846** —— *Veg. Kingd.* 368 Malval exogens, with columnar stamens.

‖**malvasia** (malvaˈsia). Also **malvoisia.** [It.: see MALMSEY. Cf. Sp., Pg. *malvasia*, F. *malvoisie*: see MALVOISIE.] = MALMSEY. Also *attrib.*, as ***malvasia sack***, and in Pg. phr. ***malvasia de Madeira*** (cf. *malmsey madeira*, s.v. MALMSEY).
1839 *Penny Cycl.* XIV. 262/1 The wine exported is Madeira wine and Malvasia de Madera. **1851** Borrow *Lavengro* xciii. (1893) 360 There is Malvoisia sack,..and partridge, and beccafico. **1895** *Chamb. Jrnl.* XII. 627/2 We entered the shanty and drank malvasia.

malveisyn, variant of MALVOISIE.

Malvern (ˈmɒlvən, -ɔː-). The name of a town in Hereford and Worcester, used *attrib.* and *ellipt.* to designate alkaline mineral water obtained from springs there.
1757 J. Wall *Exper. & Observations Malvern Waters* (ed. 2) App. 68 She was last Year perswaded to try Malvern Water,..and..the Water has been constantly sent to London all the Winter for her Use. **1907** *Yesterday's Shopping* (1969) 27 Malvern water... Bots. 6/0 [per doz.]. **1930** A. Bennett *Imperial Palace* lxiv. 525 She watched over his flowers and his Malvern water. **1965** *New Statesman* 14 May 753/1 One of the lackeys will carry a 10-day supply of Malvern water. **1967** *Observer* (Colour Suppl.) 28 May 38/2 Malvern. The one British mineral water that is sold on a national scale. **1974** J. Stubbs *Painted Face* iv. 70 A picnic basket, complete from cold capon..to Malvern water.

Malvernian (mɒlˈvɜːnɪən, -ɔː-), *a. Geol.* [f. the name of the *Malvern* Hills, a range in England between Hereford and Worcester: see -IAN.] Of, pertaining to, or characteristic of the Malvern Hills; *spec.* (*a*) applied to a Pre-Cambrian series of plutonic rocks that forms most of the hills; also *absol.*; (*b*) applied to a north-south orientation like that of the hills.
1879 *Q. Jrnl. Geol. Soc.* XXXV. 654 The contained pebbles..consist of quartzite, quartz, gneiss, mica-schist, red felspar, and granitoid rock. This assemblage strongly suggests derivation from the Malvernian series represented at Primrose Hill. **1899** *Proc. Geologists' Assoc.* XV. 426 The strike of the axes of the main folding of the country [around Stourbridge] is first north and south, in continuation of the main axes of the Malvern ridge (Malvernian folding), but at Abberley Hill it swings round almost at right angles to this direction, the axes now striking from west to east (Hercynian or Mercian folding). **1948** L. J. Wills *Palaeogeogr. Midlands* ii. 7 The distribution of the Malvernian away from Malvern itself is quite unknown. **1969** Bennison & Wright *Geol. Hist. Brit. Isles* iii. 68 The Malvernian is composed predominantly of metamorphosed igneous rocks, diorites and gabbros. *Ibid.* x. 248 (*heading*) Structures of Malvernian trend.

malversate (mælˈvɜːseɪt), *v.* [Back-formation from MALVERSATION.] *trans.* To use (funds) for purposes other than those for which they were intended.
1881 S. Butler *Family Lett.* (1962) 198 If I malversated these funds or lost them, my co-trustee might come down on the company for having regarded the order of one trustee to the disregard of a joint order. **1928** G. B. Shaw *Intelligent Woman's Guide Socialism* 417 The public school (meaning a very exclusive private school malversating public endowments).

malversation (mælvəˈseɪʃən). [a. F. *malversation*, f. *malverser*: see MALVERSE *v.*] Corrupt behaviour in an office, commission, employment, or position of trust; an instance of this.
1549 *Compl. Scot.* xix. 160 Quhen the pepil disobeyis thy gude doctryne throucht the euyl exempil of thy maluersatione, thou sal be mair doubil puneist nor the sal be. **1669** Marvell *Let. to Mayor of Hull* Wks. 1776 I. 121 The criminal part of what is reported by the commissioners concerning his malversation in his office. **1776–83** Justamond tr. *Raynal's Hist. Indies* I. 370 The malversations that prevail in the manufactures, magazines, docks and arsenals at Batavia..are scarcely to be paralleled. **1811** Wellington *Let. to Gordon* 12 June in Gurw. *Desp.* (1838) VIII. 6 Those malversations in office; those neglects of duty..are passed unnoticed. **1874** Green *Short Hist.* viii. §ix. 561 Charges of malversation and corruption were hurled at the members of the House.
b. Corrupt administration *of* something.
1706 De Foe *Jure Div.* Pref. 8 Bringing in a Foreign Power to question him for Malversation of Government. **1818** Hallam *Mid. Ages* (1872) I. 229 The kingdom was reduced to the utmost danger..as much by malversation of its government, as by the armies of Edward III. **1839** James *Louis XIV*, III. 133 The inquiry into the malversation of the finances. **1852** Thackeray *Esmond* III. v, Cardonnel was turned out of the House of Commons..for malversation of public money. **1881** Black *Sunrise* III. xi. 172 Malversation of justice amongst those in a high grade.
†**c.** *gen.* Evil conduct. *Obs. rare.*
1752 J. Macsparran *Amer. Dissected* (1753) 12 Though some of the Felons do reform, yet they are so few, that their Malversation has a bad Effect upon the Morals of the lower Class of Inhabitants.

†**malverse**, *v. Obs. rare.* [ad. F. *malverser*, ad. L. *male versārī* (*male* wrongly, ill, *versārī* to behave, conduct oneself, passive freq. of *vertĕre* to turn).] *intr.* To act corruptly in a position of trust.
1671 *True Nonconf.* 13 He could not, *impunè*, without danger of punishment, mal-verse, much less subvert Religion. **1714** W. Forbes *Jrnl. Session* Pref. 8 The advocates are subject to the authority of the Lords, who.. may censure, fine, or debar them from their imployment for disobedience or malversing in their office. **1733** P. Lindsay *Interest Scot.* 95 If any Judge shall neglect or refuse to execute the Law,..or Malverse in the Exercise of it, he is [etc.].

Malvi (ˈmɑːlvɪ). Also **Malwi.** A dialect of Rajasthani.
1883 *Census of Central Provinces 1881* (India Census) II. 91 (*table*) Languages and dialects amalgamated therein... Urdú, Málvi, Nimári, [etc.]. **1901**, **1957** [see JAIPUR]. **1968** B. Walker *Hindu World* I. 586 Other Rājasthāni dialects are *Mārwāri*.., *Jaipuri*.., *Mālvi*.., *Mewāri*.., *Udaipuri*.

malvoisia: see MALVASIA.

malvoisie (ˈmælvɔɪzɪ). *Obs.* exc. *arch.* Forms: 4 **malvesin, mauvesyn**, 4–6 **malvesye**, 4–7 **-vesie**, 5 **-veisyn, mal(e)vesyn, malveseye, -vaset**, 5–6 **-vasy, -vesey**, 6 **-vesy, -ie, -vase, -vese, -veseie, -vesyne, -weysy**, *Sc.* **mavasy, mawissie, mavasie**, 7 **malvasie, -ey, -vesie**, 9 **malvoisie.** [a. OF. *malvesie*, ad. It. *malvasia*: see MALMSEY. The forms with final *n* seem to represent an adj. formation in OFr.: cf. med.L. *vinum malvasinum*. The 19th c. form *malvoisie* is that of mod.Fr.]
1. = MALMSEY 1.
1379–80 *Durham Acc. Rolls* (Surtees) 389 In uno pipe de Malvesin. *c* **1386** Chaucer *Shipman's T.* 70 With hym broghte he a Iubbe of Maluesye And eek another, ful of fyn vernage. *a* **1440** *Sir Degrev.* 1415 And evere sche drow hom the wyn, Bothe the Roche and the Reyn, And the good Malvesyn. **1500–20** Dunbar *Poems* xl. 14 All wyne to test scho wald disdane Bot mavasy [*v.rr.* mawissie, mavasie], she bad nane vder. **1508** *Extracts Aberd. Reg.* (1844) I. Pref. 21, ½ gallone of Maluasy, price iiiis. viiid. **1584** Cogan *Haven Health* (1636) 310 You shall take Rose water, white Rosevineger, Strong white Wine or Malvasie, of each like much; &c. **1828** Scott *F.M. Perth* viii, I hope you have no more grave errand than to try if the malvoisie holds its flavour. **1861** Dora Greenwell *Poems* 24 Flowing of the Malvoisie And largesse clinking loud.
2. = MALMSEY 2.
1517 Torkington *Pilgr.* (1884) 20 Ther groweth the Voyne that ys callyd Malweysy and muskedell. **1883** Stevenson *Silverado Sq.* (1886) 21 He had broken ground up here with his black malvoisies.

‖**mal vu** (mal vy). [Fr.] Held in very poor esteem, or in no esteem, looked down upon. Also *attrib.*
1904 H. O. Sturgis *Belchamber* iii. 42 There is nothing so easy as to get rid of me. I am horribly *mal vu* by the authorities. **1958** L. Durrell *Mountolive* ii. 62 He is.. rather an old-fashioned reactionary in his outlook, and is consequently rather *mal vu* by his brother craftsmen. **1958** *Times Lit. Suppl.* 21 Nov. 672/3 Her daughter Elsie's marriage to a clever but socially *mal vue* [*sic*] research scientist.

malwe, obs. form of MALLOW.

maly(e)s, -ysyous, etc.: see MALICE, -ICIOUS.

maly(n)coli, etc., obs. forms of MELANCHOLY.

malyvolus, variant of MALEVOLOUS *Obs.*

mam[1] (mæm). *colloq.* Also 6 **mame**, 6–7 **mamme.** [Not recorded before the 16th c., the instance in one MS. of the Chester Plays being almost certainly due to a late alteration of the text. It is improbable that the word is adopted from the Welsh *mam* (:—Protoceltic **mammā*); it seems rather to have originated independently from a sound instinctively made by young children; similar words for 'mother' exist in many languages. See MAMMA[1].] A childish (formerly also a familiar or vulgar) word for mother; corresponding to DAD *sb.*[1], but now more strictly confined to infantine use or allusions to this. †***mam's loll***: see LOLL *sb.* 3.
?*a* **1500** (*MS.* **1592**) [see DAD *sb.*[1]]. **1573** Tusser *Husb.* (1878) 186 Yet cocking Mams, and shifting Dads from schooles, Make pregnant wits to prooue vnlearned fooles. *c* **1580** Jefferie *Bugbears* I. ii. 99 in *Archiv Stud. neu. Spr.* XCVIII. (1897) 309 Oh, thies mammes are exigent, thier daughters prankes to hide. **1590** Greene *Never too late* I. (1600) H 2, When the boy sayes, Mam, where is my Dad, when will he come home? **1611** Cotgr., *Mammam* (the voice of infants), Mam. **1675** Cotton *Scoffer Scoft* 80 Then of this Child hee's Syre and Dam, And it may call him Dad and Mam. **1710** E. Ward *Brit. Hud.* III. 26 It stroaks Pappa, and beats the Mam. **1757** Eliz. Griffith *Lett. betw. Henry & Frances* (1767) II. 160 Has it [a child] a broad, good-humoured countenance, like dad; or a lively eye,..and saucy look, like mam? **1816** 'Quiz' *Grand Master* Argt. I. 1 The hero of the tale appears, Leaving his dad and mam in tears. **1872** Hartley *Yorks. Ditties* Ser. II. 112 Whear is thi' Daddy doy? Whear is thi' mam?
†**b.** reduplicated. *Obs.*
1606 Sylvester *Du Bartas* II. iv. III. *Schism* 777 And smiling sweet Mam-mam, mam-mam he cries [F. *crie me a mé me*].
†**c.** *attrib.* and *Comb. Obs.*
1599 Nashe *Lenten Stuffe* Wks. (Grosart) V. 269 The nurse or mother Mampudding..down she sunk to the earth. **1653** R. Carpenter *Anabapt. Washt* 21 These..Censurers know no other Language than Mam-English, or, their mother tongue.

†**mam**[2]. *Obs. rare*$^{-0}$. [ad. L. *mamma* breast.]
1611 Florio, *Mamma*, a pap, a dug, a mam, a breast.

mam, obs. form of MA'AM.

mama, variant of MAMMA[1].

‖**mamaku** (ˈmamakʊ). *N.Z.* [Maori.] A tree fern, *Cyathea medullaris*, or the starchy food formerly prepared from its pith.
1846 C. Heaphy *Jrnl.* 15 May in N. M. Taylor *Early Travellers in N.Z.* (1959) 232 Encamped in order to collect and bake *mamaku*, the stem of the fern tree, which was to constitute our provisions. **1882** W. D. Hay *Brighter Britain!* II. 152 The inner stems of mamaku or tree-fern. **1905** W. B. *Where White Man Treads* 16, I have forgotten 'mamaku' (the tree fern)—fanning itself in the mid-heat of summer. **1949** P. Buck *Coming of Maori* (1950) I. iii. 34 Tree fern pith (*mamaku*), and fern root (*aruhe*) were placed before them. **1966** *Encycl. N.Z.* II. 785/1 Mamaku or black tree fern (*Cyathea medullaris*) was an important source of starch food. .. The pith [of the trunk] was steamed for about two days ..and the resulting sago-like substance could be eaten cold or dried for future use.

‖**mamaliga** (məməˈliːgə). [Rumanian *mămăligă.*] = POLENTA c; maize porridge: a staple food in Rumania.
1878 J. W. Ozanne *Three Years in Roumania* 121 Maize forms the staple food of the lower classes. Every day a portion is boiled for the use of the family. It is called *mamaliga*, and is usually eaten alone; a little milk or a piece of salt fish being, however, sometimes added. **1925** J. A. Hammerton *Countries of World* XXXIV. 3425/1 The peasants live for the most part on mamaliga. **1970** *Sat. Rev.* (U.S.) 12 Sept. 107/3 In Rumania, unfermented grape juice or must is sold at wooden stalls..with slices of hot *mamaliga*, the national dish of of cornmeal mush.

mamaloi (ˈmamalwa). Also **mamanloi.** Pl. **mamaloi, mamalois.** [ad. Haitian Creole *mamalwa*, f. *mama* mother + *lwa* LOA[2].] A voodoo priestess.
1884 S. St. John *Hayti, or Black Republic* v. 194 The Haytians have corrupted the compounds Papa Roi and Maman Roi into Papaloi and Mamanloi. **1935** R. A. Loederer *Voodoo Fire in Haiti* The priests are called 'Papaloi' by their followers, and the priestesses 'Mamaloi', both words being Creole corruptions of 'Papa Roi' and 'Mama Roi'.

†**Mamalone.** *Obs. rare*$^{-1}$. [Obscure; perh. a misreading for *mamalouc* (see MAMELUKE).]
1799 Jane Austen *Lett.* 8 Jan. (1884) I. 192, I am to wear a mamalone cap instead... It is all the fashion now.

Mamalucco, etc.: see MAMELUCO, MAMELUKE.

‖**Mamamouchi.** The mock-Turkish title pretended to have been conferred by the Sultan upon M. Jourdain, in Molière's play *Le Bourgeois Gentilhomme*, IV. iii. Hence occas. used for: A pompous-sounding title; also, one

assuming such a title; a ridiculous pretender to elevated dignity.

1672 DRYDEN *Assign.* Prol. 30 You must have Mamamouchi, such a Fop As would appear a Monster in a Shop. *a* **1734** NORTH *Exam.* II. iv. §5 (1740) 233 So then he drops his mammamouchi Outside of Oates's Plot in the dark, no more to be heard of in that Reign. **1749** H. WALPOLE *Lett.* (1846) II. 287 This ridiculous Mamamouchi [The Duke of Newcastle, Chancellor of Cambridge University].

Comb. **1673** *Mem. Madam Charlton* 12 Charlton fancies nothing less than to be made a Duke, or some strange Mammamouchy-Titulado.

mamanite ('meɪmənaɪt). *Min.* [f. *Maman*, in Persia, its locality + -ITE: so named by A. Goebel in 1865.] 'A sulphate similar to polyhalite, but somewhat different in composition' (Chester *Dict. Names Min.* 1896).

‖**mama-san** (mamasan). Also **mamasan.** [Jap., f. *mama* mother + *san* honorific title.] In Japan and the Far East, a matron in a position of authority: *spec.* one in charge of a geisha-house; the mistress of a bar.

1949 L. H. CROCKETT *Popcorn on Ginza* xvi. 218 Mama-sans of some of the better Tokyo houses become well informed on all sorts of political intrigue. **1958** G. MIKES *East is East* 56 '*Mamasan*' is not surprised if someone wishes to linger late in one of those tiny little Japanese houses where the parties take place. **1962** A. CAMPBELL *Heart of Japan* iv. 113 The mama-san wanted us all to go home... A geisha party isn't supposed to go on more than three hours. **1968** *Manch. Guardian Weekly* 4 Jan. 10 We were visited by two enormous Sumo wrestlers, with their equally large Mama-San. **1971** *Nat. Geographic* Oct. 571/2 The representative bars have an institutional figure called 'mama-san', a matronly, amiable, garrulous, and straightforward woman who permits the sailors to fraternize with any of a covey of young ladies.

mamay, variant of MAMMEE.

mamba ('mæmbə). Also 9 **momba.** [ad. Zulu *imamba*.] A large venomous African snake of the genus *Dendroaspis* (family Elapidæ), esp. the ***green mamba*** (GREEN *a.* 13 b), *D. angusticeps*, and the ***black mamba***, *D. polylepis*. Also *attrib.*

1862 J. S. DOBIE in *S. Afr. Jrnl.* (1945) 44 He called it a green mamba and was about 9 feet long. **1878** P. GILLMORE *Great Thirst Land* xxix. 346 A black mamba—a description of snake common in Natal, and reported to be very deadly. **1897** J. BRYCE *Impressions S. Afr.* III. 23 The black *momba*, which is nearly as large as a rattlesnake, is a dangerous creature. **1910** J. BUCHAN *Prester John* iv. 80 A black mamba might appear out of the tangle. **1912** F. W. FITZSIMONS *Snakes S. Afr.* (new ed.) 194 There are two varieties of the Mamba. One is vivid leaf-green, the other is olive or brownish-black. **1921** *Chambers's Jrnl.* 26 Feb. 203/2 It was a mamba snake, eight feet long. **1939** S. CLOETE *Watch for Dawn* 62 With the bite of a mamba or a ringhals the heart sometimes beat even after life had gone. **1958** *Listener* 23 Jan. 154/1 Black mambas..have the unattractive habit of lurking in trees and dropping down on to the unwary. **1965** A. NICOL *Truly Married Woman* 96 A poisonous one, a mamba, its middle still rippling slowly. **1969** A. BELLAIRS *Life of Reptiles* I. v. 191 The deadly mambas (*Dendroaspis*) have fangs which are relatively a little shorter and thinner than those of the average cobra.

mambar, var. MIMBAR.

mamble ('mæmb(ə)l), *v. Obs.* exc. *dial.* Also 3–4 **mamel.** [ME. *mamelen*, possibly repr. an OE. **mamelian* = OHG. *mammalôn* to stammer, mutter, mod. Ger. dial. *memmeln* to mutter, also to chew slowly; an onomatopœic formation with frequentative suffix -LE: cf. MAMMER, MUMBLE *vbs.*]

1. *intr.* To mumble or mutter; to chatter.

c **1275** *Prov. Alfred* 492 in *O. E. Misc.* 132 þanne mud mamelit more þanne hit solde. **1377** LANGL. *P. Pl.* B. v. 21 Of þis matere I myȝte mamely ful longe. *Ibid.* XI. 408 Adam ..when he mameled aboute mete and entermeted to knowe þe wisdom and þe witte of god he was put fram blisse.

2. To eat lazily.

a **1825** FORBY *Voc. E. Anglia, Mamble v.*, to eat with seeming indifference, as if from want of appetite.

†'**mambler.** *Obs. rare*$^{-1}$. In 5 **mammlere.** [f. MAMBLE *v.* + -ER^{1}.] A voluble speaker.

a **1400–50** *Alexander* 4498 For marcure was manslaȝt a mammlere of wordis.

†'**mambling,** *vbl. sb. Obs.* [f. MAMBLE *v.* + -ING^{1}.] ? = MAMMERING 2.

1640 BP. HALL *Chr. Moder.* II. ii. 5 He could rather be content the Angell of the Church of Laodicea should be quite cold, then in such a mambling of profession. **1648** MANTON *Spir. Languish.* 16 We content ourselves with a lukewarmnesse and a mambling of profession midling it between Christ and the world.

mambo ('mæmbəʊ). [Amer. Sp., 'prob. fr. Haitian creole (voodoo priestess)' (Webster).]

1. A kind of rumba, a ball-room dance (and its music) of Latin-American origin.

1948 *Call-Bulletin* (San Francisco) 17 Sept. 11/1 Tony De Marco predicts the new dance fad will be 'The Mambo', which was introduced..last week. A zingier form of rhumba. **1950** *Newsweek* 4 Sept. 76 The difference between the rumba and the mambo is the difference between the regular foxtrot and the jitterbug. **1951** R. CHANDLER *Let.* 19 Apr. in *R. Chandler Speaking* (1966) 213, I doubt if he knows the new dance called a mambo, because it seems to be only recently discovered or developed. **1952** *Down Beat* 25 Jan. 2/2 Prado, who says he introduced the mambo in Mexico City in 1948, claims it is merely Afrocuban rhythm with a dash of American swing. **1955** *Caribbean Q.* IV. II. 102 Some St. Lucians..patronize the several clubs which have jukeboxes stocked largely with mambos of the Perez Prado school. **1957** J. KEROUAC *On Road* (1958) 93 Mambo blasted from jukeboxes. **1959** *Listener* 24 Sept. 473/1 Innumerable folk-dance sources, ranging from the square dance to Latin American mambos and the rest. **1964** W. G. RAFFÉ *Dict. Dance* 299/1 *Mambo* (Haiti), ritual dance of Voodoo; an initiation ceremonial which follows the ancient *Danse Shalame* (Salome) in its symbolic-realism. 'Mambo' is the official name for the chief priestess. **1966** *Crescendo* Dec. 27/1 Only bossa novas and mambos seem to be played with anything like enthusiasm by these bands. **1972** *Village Voice* (N.Y.) 1 June 4/3 Now the pop-music business, having scraped the hillbilly barrel and blown the froth off the mambo craze, has taken over R[hythm]-and-B[lues].

2. A voodoo priestess.

1964 R. SEVERN *Blood & Gold* x. 102 She must be a *Mambo*.., a *Voodoo* priestess. **1964** [see sense 1 above]. **1966** *Daily Tel.* 11 Aug. 18/6 The author and his herbalist friend became close companions with a girl who was often thus possessed, but had to be initiated and trained by an expert sorceress or *mambo*.

† **mambu.** *Obs.* Also 8 **mombu.** [a. OPg. *mambu* BAMBOO *sb.*] The bamboo.

1662 J. DAVIES tr. *Mandelslo's Trav.* 149 A sort of Canes, by the Iavians called Mambu. *Ibid.*, On the Coast of Malabar [etc.] this sort of Cane produces a drug called Sacar Mambus, that is, Sugar of Mambu. **1681** GREW *Musæum* II. 223 Part of a sort of Mambu, a great Indian Cane. *Ibid.* 225. **1797** *Encycl. Brit.* (ed. 3) II. 384/1 A substance called Tabaxir, or sugar of Mombu.

mame, obs. form of MAIM *sb.*, MALM, MAM^{1}.

mamea, -ee, -eia, obs. ff. MAMMEE.

mamel, variant of MAMBLE.

‖**mamelière.** *Hist.* Also 9 **mammelière, -illiere.** [Fr.: f. *mamelle* breast.] A piece of armour consisting of a circular plate of metal covering either breast.

1824 MEYRICK *Anc. Armour* III. *Gloss., Mamillaria, Mamillieres.* **1834** PLANCHÉ *Brit. Costume* 122 On the breast are fastened sometimes one, sometimes two round plates, called mamelières. **1885** FAIRHOLT *Costume in Eng.* (ed. 3) II. 277 The surcoat has openings or slits over the mamelières to allow of a chain passing through.

mamellated, variant of MAMILLATED *ppl. a.*

† **mamelle.** *Obs.* Also **mammill.** [a. F. *mamelle*:—L. *mamilla*, dim. of *mamma* breast.] A woman's breast. Also *fig.*

c **1430** *Hymns Virg.* (1867) 1 Thi mammillis, moder, ful weel y meene, Y had to my meete þat y myȝt not mys. **1483** CAXTON *Gold. Leg.* 135 b/2 Thenne Quyncianus.. comanded that her brestis and mamellis shold be drawen & cutte of. *Ibid.* 419/1 Nourysshed by the pappes and mamellys of the Scrypture of holy chyrche.

mamelon ('mæmələn). Also **mammillon, mammelon.** [a. F. *mamelon* nipple, f. *mamelle*: see prec.]

1. A rounded eminence or hummock.

1830 LYELL *Princ. Geol.* I. 206 This mammillon has been largely quarried for lime. **1848** D. BORRER *Campaign agst. Kabailes Algeria*, Upon the summit of two mammelons.. two French outposts were placed. **1893** E. H. BARKER *Wand. South. Waters* 289 An isolated hill or mamelon in the valley of the Lot.

2. A small hemispherical tubercle.

1872 NICHOLSON *Palæont.* 105 Ordinarily the tubercle consists of a rounded ball or hemisphere (the 'mamelon').

Hence **mamelonated** ('mæmələneɪtɪd) *a.*, covered with rounded protuberances.

1857 BULLOCK *Cazeaux' Midwif.* 47 Like the latter, its two surfaces are flattened, and it is besides slightly lobular and mamelonated. **1872** COHEN *Dis. Throat* 243 This gives the part a rough mamelonated appearance.

‖**Mameluco** (mæmə'l(j)uːkəʊ). Also 9 **mamalucco.** [Pg., lit. a mameluke: see next.] A cross-breed between a white and a Brazilian Indian.

1863 BATES *Nat. Amazons* i. 35 *note*, Mameluco denotes the offspring of White with Indian; Mulatto, that of White with Negro. **1874** BURTON *Captiv. Hans Stade* xv. (Hakl. Soc.) 45 Mamalucco, meaning the offspring of a white man by an Indian woman, is now obsolete in Sao Paulo, where Caboclo has taken its place. **1900** DENIKER *Races of Man* xiii. 545 The Mamelucos or Paulists of the province of Sao Paulo (Brazil), European and Indian half-breeds.

Mameluke ('mæməl(j)uːk). *Obs.* exc. *Hist.* Forms: 6 **mam(m)oluke, mam(m)eluc(k, mammaluke,** 6–8 **mamaluk,** 6–9 **-luke,** 7 **mammeluke, mamaluch, mameluch, mammaluck, mamuluke,** *pl.* after It. form **mamaluchi, mamaluc(c)hy,** 7–8 **mamaluc(k,** 8 **mamaluque, mameluc,** 6– **mameluke.** Also 9 **mamlouk, mamluk(e, memlo(o)k.** [Ultimately a. Arab. *mamlūk* slave, a subst. use of the pa. pple. of *malaka* to possess. The Turkish pronunciation is (mɛmluːk); cf. med.L. *mameluc, mameluchus* (12th c.), OF. *mameluz, mamelos* (mod.F. *mameluk, mamelouk*), Sp., Pg. *mameluco*, It. *mammaluco*.]

1. A member of the military body, originally composed of Caucasian slaves, which seized the throne of Egypt in 1254, and continued to form the ruling class in that country until the early part of the 19th century.

The Mameluke sultans reigned from 1254 to 1517, when the Ottoman Sultan Selim I assumed the sovereignty. Subsequently Egypt was governed, under the nominal rule of a Turkish viceroy, by 24 Mameluke beys. In 1811 the Mamelukes remaining after the French war were massacred by Mohammed Ali, pasha of Egypt.

1511 GUYLFORDE *Pilgr.* (Camden) 13 There was a grete Ambasset of the soldans towardes Venyce, that hadde in his companye many Mamolukes. **1529** MORE *Dyaloge* IV. Wks. 279/2 Mammolukes and Genisaries about yͤ Turk and Sowdan, haue vsed to christen their children of purpose. **1586** T. B. *La Primaud. Fr. Acad.* I. (1594) 598 Not long since the souldan of Cayre [was elected] out of the mammelucks. **1600** J. PORY tr. *Leo's Africa* VIII. 320 Certaine principall Mamalukes..euerie of whom was captaine of a thousand inferiour Mamaluks; and their office was to conduct the Soldans forces. **1648** C. WALKER *Hist. Independ.* I. 145 [The Egyptians lived] under vassalage to their own Mamaluchi or Mercenaries. **1658** EARL MONM. tr. *Paruta's Wars Cyprus* 46 It was taken by the aid of the mamalucchy, by James son to the same King illegitimate. **1704** *Collect. Voy.* (Churchill) III. 587/2 Most of the *Mamaluques*.. were slain. **1796** BP. WATSON *Apol. Bible* vi. 59 It [Egypt] became subject..to the Mamalucs, and now is a province of the Turkish empire. **1796** H. HUNTER tr. *St.-Pierre's Stud. Nat.* (1799) III. 463 The twelve Beys of Egypt, chosen from among the Mamelucs. **1801** WELLINGTON *Memorandum* in Gurw. *Desp.* I. 314 Supposing that the Mamelukes should be inclined to shake off the French yoke and to co-operate with us. **1813** BYRON *Br. Abydos* I. viii, With Maugrabee and Mamaluke, His way amid his Delis [he] took. **1845** ELIOT WARBURTON *Cresc. & Cross* vii. 57 The Mamelukes were young Georgian or Circassian slaves.

attrib. **1772** *Ann. Reg.* 18 The Mamaluck system. **1856** FREEMAN *Saracens* iv. (1870) 158 The Mameluke Sultans.

2. A slave (in Muslim countries).

1600 HAKLUYT *Voy.* III. 718, I shall presently banish all the Mamalukes and white men which dwell in any of those Indian townes. **1836** LANE *Mod. Egypt.* I. 163 Few of the Egyptians have memlooks, or male white slaves. **1844** *Mem. Babylonian P'cess* II. 179 His Mamelukes, both white and black. **1884** J. PAYNE *Tales fr. Arabic* I. 236 Now the Persian had a mameluke, as he were the full moon.

3. *fig.* A 'fighting slave' of the Pope, etc.

1531 TINDALE *Exp. 1 John* (1538) 41 Many..are be come the Antichristes of Romes mamelukes. **1679** 'TOM TICKLEFOOT' *Trials Wakeman*, etc. 9 When they were listed amongst the Pope's Mamalukes. **1680** BOLRON *Papist's Oath Secrecy* 7 That Oath which Blessed Ignatius Loyola imposed upon his Spiritual Mamaluks. **1833** COLERIDGE *Table-t.* 18 Apr., So long as the Bishop of Rome remains Pope, and has an army of Mamelukes all over the world, we shall do very little. **1902** *Contemp. Rev.* Dec. 788 The Assumptionists are mere mamelukes of the Vatican.

4. *attrib.*: **mameluke-bit**, the heavy iron bit used by the Mamelucos of Brazil (see MAMELUCO); **mameluke point**, the long double-edged cutting point of the Mameluke sabre; **mameluke sleeve**, a fashion of sleeve worn by women in Paris under the First Empire.

1826 SIR F. HEAD *Pampas* 177, I..took the iron *mameluke-bit out of his mouth. **1809** LD. VALENTIA *Voy.* III. 307 They [sabres] were all Persian, but some had been lengthened in Egypt at both ends, so as to give the *Mameluke point, which cuts both ways. **1898** LADY MARY LOYD tr. *Uzanne's Fashion in Paris* iii. 55 Towards the close of the [First] Empire, when..*mameluke sleeves, and hair dressed *à l'enfant*, struck a feudal and gothic note.

Hence '**Mamelukedom** *fig.*, the condition of being a Mameluke or fighting slave. '**Mamelukery** *fig.*, a body of 'Mamelukes', a party of enslaved depredators.

1824 LANDOR *Imag. Conv., Leopold & du Paty* Wks. 1853 I. 53/1 Our spiritual Mamelukery is as ambitious of power and riches as if it had children to inherit them. **1900** *Contemp. Rev.* Mar. 455 The reduction of an entire nation to intellectual serfdom and moral Mamelukedom.

mamente, mameny: see MAUMET, MALMENY.

mamere, variant of MAMMER *v.*

mameri, variant of MAHOMERY *Obs.*, mosque.

mamey: see MAMMEE.

mamie, variant of MAMMEE, MAMMY^{1}.

‖**mamilla** (mæ'mɪlə). Also 7–9 **mammilla.** [L., dim. of *mamma* breast, teat.]

1. The nipple of the female breast; also, the male 'mamma'.

1693 tr. *Blancard's Phys. Dict.* (ed. 2), *Mammilla.* **1706** PHILLIPS (ed. Kersey), *Mammilla*, a little Breast, Tet, or Dug. **1889** *Syd. Soc. Lex.*, *Mammilla*,..the nipple of the mammary gland. Also, the male breast, or mammary gland.

2. *transf.* (*Anat.*, *Bot.*, etc.) Any nipple-shaped organ or protuberance; a papilla.

1818 KIRBY & SP. *Entomol.* II. 279 In these apodous walkers the place of legs is supplied by fleshy and often retractile mamillæ or tubercles. **1828** R. KNOX tr. *Cloquet's Anat.* 454 There occurs on the surface of the brain..a sort of whitish mammilla, which seemed to be concealed in the interior of the nerve. **1843** J. G. WILKINSON tr. *Swedenborg's Anim. Kingd.* I. i. 21 Glandular mammillæ or papillæ. **1866** *Treas. Bot.* 714/2 (*Mamillaria*) The mamillæ..have little tufts of white hair between them. **1852** HENSLOW *Dict. Bot. Terms*, *Mamilla* (a little teat). Little granular prominences

on the surface of certain pollen. **1889** Baron in *Q. Jrnl. Geol. Soc.* XLV. 322 The crystals of others [*sc.* stones] assume a mamillated form, the mamillæ being covered with minute crystals. **1889** *Syd. Soc. Lex.*, *Mammillæ*,.. applied to the conical or cylindrical organs of the Arachnida,.. Also, the papillæ or apices of the Malpighian pyramids in the kidney.

mamillar (ˈmæmɪlə(r)), *a.* In quots. **mammillar.** [a. L. *mamillār-is*, f. *mamilla*: see MAMILLA.] = MAMILLARY 2.

1648 J. Beaumont *Psyche* IV. cxxi, [Osphresis loq.] By the Mammillar Processions, I Embrace those pleasures which my Sweets impart. **1832** Macgillivray tr. *Humboldt's Trav.* xviii. 251 Masses of rock.. emerge from its bosom, some of a mammillar form. **1897** *Allbutt's Syst. Med.* IV. 716 The surface is coarsely lobular or mammillar.

mamillariform (mæmɪˈlærɪfɔːm), *a. rare.* [f. L. *mamillāri-s* MAMILLAR + -FORM.] Mamilliform.

1869 *Eng. Mech.* 19 Nov. 225/1 A small mammillariform object.

mamillary (ˈmæmɪlərɪ), *a.* Also 7 **mammillarie, mammilary,** 7–9 **mammillary.** [f. L. *mamillāris*: see MAMILLA and -ARY[2].]

1. Of or pertaining to the breast; also, † having mammæ.

1669 W. Simpson *Hydrol. Chym.* 278 The.. milky juyce, passing.. through the mammilary conduits into the breasts. **1792** Belknap *Hist. New Hampsh.* III. 165 The only mamillary biped which we have, is the Bat. **1898** *Allbutt's Syst. Med.* V. 981 To the left of the mammillary or mid-thoracic line.

2. a. Of the form of a mamma; mammiform. ***mamillary body*** [prob. tr. mod.L. *corpus mamillare*], either of a pair of small white hemispherical structures lying side by side between the tuber cinereum and the posterior perforated substance in the interpeduncular fossa on the ventral surface of the brain. ***mamillary process***: (*a*) the mastoid process of the temporal bone; (*b*) *pl.* the metapophysis of the lumbar vertebræ; †(*c*) *pl.* the olfactory lobes.

1615 Crooke *Body of Man* 433 The mamillary processes which are the Organes of smelling. **1650** Bulwer *Anthropomet.* 16 The bottom of the Ear (in which place the Mammillary processe is). **1722** Quincy *Lex. Physico-Med.* (ed. 2) 126/1 It is the Entry to the Sinus in the Mammillary Process. **1741** Monro *Anat. Nerves* (ed. 3) 39 The Mammillary Processes of the Brain. **1797** M. Baillie *Morb. Anat.* (1807) 274 The mamillary portion of the kidney. **1832** J. Quain *Elem. Anat.* (ed. 2) viii. 642 A thin lamella of white substance,.. called *locus perforatus*,.. is triangular, the sides being formed by the crura cerebri, the base by the mammillary bodies. **1865** Lubbock *Preh. Times* 230 Small mammillary elevations which are known as Indian corn-hills. **1881** Mivart *Cat* 39 The anterior process.. is termed the mammillary process, or Metapophysis. **1921** Tilney & Riley *Form & Functions Cent. Nervous Syst.* xxxiv. 613 The mamillary body serves as a relay station in the olfactory tract. **1942** O. Larsell *Anat. Nervous Syst.* xviii. 249 The mammillary bodies are two elevations.. just rostral to the posterior perforated substance. **1967** G. M. Wyburn et al. *Conc. Anat.* vii. 190/2 The depressed area between the peduncles, the interpeduncular fossa, has the following structures from behind forwards: the posterior perforated substance, the paired mamillary bodies, the tuber cinereum and infundibulum.. and the optic chiasma.

b. Having mammiform protuberances.

1813 Bakewell *Introd. Geol.* 355 Mammillary, with a number of convex smooth surfaces. **1830** Lyell *Princ. Geol.* I. 202 Sometimes the travertin assumes precisely the botroidal and mammillary forms, common to similar deposits, in Auvergne. **1841** Trimmer *Pract. Geol.* 348 The sides of the cells are coated with mamillary concretions. **1846** Dana *Zooph.* (1848) 265 Gibbous and coarsely mammillary.

c. *mamillary brooch* (Antiq.): one consisting of two cup-shaped pieces connected by a handle.

1862 W. R. Wilde *Catal. Gold Antiq. R. Irish Acad.* 57 Mammillary Fibulæ—For the sake of distinction and arrangement, we have applied this term to a class of gold ornaments, of great diversity of size, found in abundance in Ireland. **1863** D. Wilson *Preh. Ann.* I. II. vi. 459 The dilated gold fibulæ styled.. Mamillary Brooches.

ˈmamillate, *a.* Also **mamm-.** [ad. L. *mamillāt-us*, f. *mamilla* MAMILLA + -ATE[1].] = next.

1826 Kirby & Sp. *Entomol.* IV. 311 Feelers (*Palpi*).. Mammillate.. when the last joint is very short, smaller than the preceding one, and retractile within it. **1847** W. Darlington *Amer. Weeds & Useful Pl.* (1860) Gloss., *Mamillate*, conical, with a rounded apex. **1875** Blake *Zool.* 38 The teeth in Mastodon mammillate, often numerous, and with every intermediate gradation.

mamillated (ˈmæmɪleɪtɪd), *ppl. a.* Also 8–9 **mammillated,** 9 **mammalated, mam(m)el(l)ated, mammilated.** [f. MAMILLATE *a.* + -ED[1].]

1. Having rounded protuberances or projections; covered with mammiform excrescences. *spec.* in *Path.* as a morbid condition of certain viscera; also *Geol.* and *Min.*

1741 Stack in *Phil. Trans.* XLI. 713 The inward Membrane had on its concave Surface a sort of Villosity wrinkled and mamillated. **1801** Bournon *ibid.* XCI. 172 This ore frequently assumes a mammillated form. **1823** W. Phillips *Introd. Mineral.* (ed. 3) p. lxxxv, A mineral presenting aggregations of large sections of numerous small globes is termed botryoidal; but when the globes are larger, and the portions are less, and separate, the appearance is expressed by the term mamillated. **1845** Darwin *Voy. Nat.* iii. (1879) 46 The mammillated country of Maldonado. **1865** Geikie *Scen. & Geol. Scot.* vii. 176 The rocks are worn into smooth mammillated outlines. **1898** *Allbutt's Syst. Med.* V. 920 This a merely mammillated or corrugated surface will not do.

2. Having a nipple-shaped process or part.

1839 Sowerby *Conch. Man.* 62 *Mammillated*, a term applied to the apex of a shell when it is rounded like a teat. **1851–6** Woodward *Mollusca* 119 Spire short, apex mammillated. **1861** Hulme tr. *Moquin-Tandon* II. III. v. 156 The cases from the pistacias are.. mammelated, light, with a turpentine flavour.

mamillation (mæmɪˈleɪʃən). In quots. **mammillation.** [f. MAMILLA + -ATION.]

1. The condition of being mamillated.

1856 Mayne *Expos. Lex.*, *Mammillation.* Term applied to the appearances of little prominences like granulations on a mucous surface, as of the stomach sometimes in *Phthisis*, etc. **1877** Roberts *Handbk. Med.* (ed. 3) I. 120 The stomach occasionally presents.. mammillation, softening [etc.].

2. *concr.* in *pl.* Rounded bosses.

1863 A. C. Ramsay *Phys. Geog.* xxiv. (1878) 382 Smoothing those large mammillations the Cumbraes. **1880** *19th Cent.* Nov. 850 The mammillations of the surface suggest that the rocks have been.. rounded by the passage of moving ice.

mamilliferous (mæmɪˈlɪfərəs), *a.* [f. MAMILLA + -(I)FEROUS.] Having or bearing mamillæ.

1856 in Mayne *Expos. Lex.* **1889** in *Syd. Soc. Lex.* **1891** *Athenæum* 30 May 703/1 The division of the mammalia into a mammilliferous and a non-mammilliferous series.

mamilliform (mæˈmɪlɪfɔːm), *a.* Also **mammilliform.** [f. MAMILLA + -(I)FORM.] Shaped like or resembling a mamilla; nipple-shaped.

1843 Forbes in *Proc. Berw. Nat. Club* II. No. 11. 79 Among which are.. interspersed numerous mammilliform tubercles. **1846** Dana *Zooph.* (1848) 423 With mammilliform prominences when contracted. **1888** A. S. Woodward in *Q. Jrnl. Geol. Soc.* XLIV. 147 The teeth upon this surface are quite mammilliform. **1880** Günther *Fishes* 162 The filaments.. are beset with mamilliform appendages.

mamilloid (ˈmæmɪlɔɪd), *a.* In quot. **mamm-.** [f. MAMILLA + -OID.] Resembling a mamilla.

1849–52 Todd *Cycl. Anat.* V. 925/2 The first and second plates [of the molar] have two mammilloid summits.

mamillose (ˈmæmɪˌləʊs), *a.* [f. MAMILLA + -OSE.] Having mamilliform organs or parts.

1856 in Mayne *Expos. Lex.* **1889** in *Syd. Soc. Lex.*

mamio, obs. form of MAMMEE.

†**ˈmamish,** *a. Obs. rare*$^{-1}$. [f. MAM *sb.*[1] + -ISH.] Uxorious.

?*a* **1641** Bp. Hall *Women's Veil* Rem. Wks. (1660) 240 If the Crown be set upon the head (as the husband may give honour to the weaker vessel) yet it is a pittyful head that is not better then the crown that adorns it... None but some mamish Monsters can question it.

Mamlouk, Mamluk(e, obs. ff. MAMELUKE.

mamma[1], **mama** (məˈmɑː). [A reduplicated syllable often uttered instinctively by young children, who are in many countries taught to use it as their word for 'mother' (esp. where the ordinary word in the language begins with *m*).

The Indogermanic type **mammā*, as a child's word for mother, is found as Gr. μάμμη, L. *mamma* (whence It. *mamma*), OSl., Russian *mama*, Lith. *mama*, Irish *mam* (O'Brien); also in Welsh *mam*, which is the only word for 'mother', though *modr-* survives in some compounds. The F. *maman* (Cotgr. 1611 *mammam*), like the earlier *mam-ma* (1584 in Hatz.-Darm.), appears to be an independent adoption of the instinctive infantine utterance; the Sp. *mamá*, Pg. *mamãe*, may perhaps be from French.

Apart from the two 16th c. quots. in which the word is used with reference to a child's first attempt to speak, the Eng. *mamma* has not been found earlier than near the end of the 17th c., after which time it rapidly became common. The Eng. word of the 17–18th c. (rimed by Shadwell with *awe*) prob. represents a spoken form adopted from the F. *maman*; the spelling may have been suggested by Latin or It., or it may possibly have been originally meant to express the native English form (ˈmamə, ˈmɒmə), which is still current in many dialects. In educated use, so far as is known, the stress has in England always been on the last syllable; in the United States, however, the stress ˈ*mamma* is the more usual; a prevailing U.S. pronunciation is represented by the spelling *momma*. The spelling *mama*, sometimes used in the 18th c., became somewhat common after 1800, and is especially frequent in the novels printed *c* 1830–50. It is now rare.]

a. A word employed as the equivalent of *mother*: chiefly used in the vocative, or preceded by a possess. pronoun (as 'my mamma'); also without article in the manner of a proper name (e.g. 'Mamma is well'); less usually with *a*, *the*, or in *plural*.

The status of the word has always been the same as that of PAPA[1]. In the 18th c., although ˈ*mamma* as used by young children was probably common, *ma'mma* seems to have been confined to the higher classes, and among them to have been freely used not only by children but by adults of both sexes. In the 19th c. its use was much extended, and among the lower middle class was a mark of 'gentility'. Latterly it has in England become unfashionable, even as used by children.

[**1555** Eden *Decades* 44 They were turned into frogges, and cryed toa, toa, that is, mama, mama, as chyldren are wont to crye for the mothers pappe.] **1579** Lyly *Euphues* (Arb.) 129 When the babe shall now begin to tattle and call hir Mamma, with what face can she heare it of his mouth, vnto whom she hath denyed Mamma? **1690** Locke *Hum. Und.* III. ii. §7. 191 The Ideas of the Nurse, and the Mother are well framed in their Minds... The names of Nurse and Mamma, the Child uses, determine themselves to those Persons. **1691** Shadwell *Scowrers* Epil., How can one stand in awe Of a vain Tawdry, Amorous Mamma? **1710** E. Ward *Brit. Hud.* III. 26 So the sweet Babe of Early Wit, To please Mamma does Daddy beat. **1727** Gay *Begg. Op.* I. viii. (1729) 11 My Mama drinks double the quantity. **1728** P. Walker *Life Alex. Peden* in *Biog. Presb.* (1827) I. 140 Our.. old Scots Names are gone out of Request; instead of Father and Mother, Mamma and Papa, training Children to speak Nonsense. **1748** Chesterf. *Lett.* (1792) II. clxxi. 132 At which I am uneasy not as a Mamma would be, but as a Father should be. **1758** Eliz. Rose in *Family Rose Kilravock* (Spald. Club) 431 Papa and mamma are well. **1773** Goldsm. *Stoops to Conq.* v. (ed. 2) 94 *Tony.* Alack, mama, it was all your own fault. **1811** L. M. Hawkins *C'tess & Gertr.* (1812) I. 52 Poor Tom must shift with his outgrown Coat, because Papa has just given Mama a row of pearls. *a* **1814** *Fam. Politics* III. iv. in *New Brit. Theatre* (1814) II. 224 *Edw.*.. One more trial, my delightful mama. *Lady Jez.* How often have I told you not to apply that vulgar appellation to me? **1819** Byron *Juan* I. xlviii, I can't but say that his mamma was right. **1838** Lytton *Alice* I. vi, You should make your mamma take you to town. **1848** Dickens *Dombey* xxxv, Florence is ready to receive her father and her new mama. **1887** Ruskin *Præterita* II. 241 [I read my] work to papa and mamma at breakfast next morning, as a girl shows her sampler.

b. Used as a prefixed title.

17.. Sir J. Marriot in Dodsley *Coll. Poems* (1755) IV. 289 The cruel Fates their rage relented, And mama Venus had consented.

c. *fig.* (jocular only).

1844 Thackeray *May Gambols* Wks. 1900 XIII. 443 The exhibition of the New Society.. has grown to be quite as handsome.. as that of its mamma, the old Society in Pall Mall East.

d. ***Mam(m)a mia!*** [It., lit. 'mother mine!']: an exclamation expressing surprise or astonishment.

1848 Mrs. Gaskell *Mary Barton* II. iii. 47 The little hopeless stranger.. spoke in some foreign tongue, with low cries for the far distant 'Mamma mia!' **1969** G. Greene *Trav. with my Aunt* I. vii. 72 There came a strange grating noise. '*Mamma mia*,' the nurse said, 'what's that?' **1971** R. Falkirk *Chill Factor* x. 94 'It rain every day?' asked the Italian. 'Every day,' I said. '*Mama mia*,' he said.

e. *Comb.*: ***mamma-in-law*** jocular = MOTHER-IN-LAW; ***mamma-pian*** [F. *maman pian*], a 'mother' tubercle of the disease known as 'yaws'; a 'yaw'; ***mamma's boy***, a boy who has been pampered and spoiled; one who is excessively timid; also applied to a man.

1850 C. M. Yonge *Henrietta's Wish* xiii. 183, I would not give a farthing for Fred if he was always to be the mamma's boy you would make him. **1855** Thackeray *Newcomes* II. 259 Recalling some of mamma-in-law's dreadful expressions which make me shudder when I hear them. **1861** C. M. Yonge *Young Step-Mother* xxiii. 336 It might be no great harm if Maurice were a tame mamma's boy. **1895** Clive Holland *Jap. Wife* (ed. 11) 36, I do not altogether like my mamma-in-law. **1889** *Syd. Soc. Lex.*, *Mama pian.* **1898** P. Manson *Trop. Diseases* xxvii. 428 *note*, A large persistent yaw is sometimes known as the 'mother', 'grandmother' or 'mama-pian'. **1929** W. Faulkner *Sound & Fury* 141 Yah.. go on then, mamma's boy. If he goes swimming he'll get his head wet and then he'll get a licking. **1967** A. M. Stein *Executioner's Rest* vi. 100 Who was this Erridge? He was mama's boy, and if you don't know the kind of trouble mama's boy tourists go looking for when they're loose on the shores of the Mediterranean, you just haven't travelled.

Hence **mamma** *v.*, to call by the name of 'mamma'.

1748 Richardson *Clarissa* (1811) III. 359 Pris. will Mamma-up Mrs. Sinclair.

‖**mamma**[2] (ˈmæmə). *Pl.* **-æ.** [L.] The milk-secreting organ of the female in man and the other mammalia. Also the corresponding but non-secreting structure in males.

c **1050** *Prudentius Gloss.* in *Germania* (1878) XI. 401 *In papillas*, an mamman. **1693** in tr. *Blancard's Phys. Dict.* **1706** Phillips (ed. Kersey), *Mamma*, a Breast, Pap, or Teat. **1727** Bailey vol. II, *Mamma* [with anatomists], a Breast, Pap or Teat; also a Dug in Cattle. **1795** [see MAMMARY 1]. **1804** Abernethy *Surg. Obs.* 21 In the mamma they [the vessels] seem to be rather large than numerous. **1845** Chambers *Vestiges* (ed. 4) 198 The mammæ of the human female.. also exist in the male. **1871** Darwin *Desc. Man* I. i. 17 The mammæ of male quadrupeds. **1887** Butlin in *Brit. Med. Jrnl.* I. 573/1 The very free removal of the mamma.. recommended by Mr. Banks [etc.]. **1887** *Athenæum* 8 Jan. 66/2 The pectoral position of the mammæ in the Sirenia.. gave rise to the legend of the mermaid.

†**ˈmammaday.** *Obs.* [Of obscure origin: cf. mod. dial. *mamady* (Linc.) 'a sweetmeat made of boiled sugar'.] ? Nurse's milk, 'pap' (*fig.*). Also *attrib.* **b.** As a term of contempt: A 'milksop'.

1589 G. Harvey *Pierce's Super.* (1593) 74 Nothing, but pure Mammaday, and a fewe morsels of fly-blowne Euphuisme, somewhat nicely minced for puling stomackes. *Ibid.* 136 This Mammaday hath excellently knocked himselfe on the sconse with his owne hatchet. **1603** Harsnet *Pop. Impost.* 29 If their Conies be Protestants.. then some holy Ceremonies.. must be solemnly used.. to bring them to lie betweene the sweete breasts of their holy mother the Romish Church that the Mammaday, which shall be given them, may doe them the more good. **1618** N. B. *Courtier & Countrym.* D 4 b, Thy meat tasts all of mammaday pudding,

which breaking at both ends, the stuffing runnes about the Pot.

mammæform: see MAMMIFORM.

mammal (ˈmæməl), *sb.* [First used in pl. as an anglicized form of MAMMALIA.] An animal of the class mammalia.

1826 GOOD *Bk. Nat.* II. ii. 52 As we have no fair synonym for it [Mammalia] in our own tongue, I shall beg leave now, as I have on various other occasions, to render it mammals. **1845** CHAMBERS *Vestiges* (ed. 4) 199 The ornithorhynchus is a mammal receding to near the grade of birds. **1859** DARWIN *Orig. Spec.* x. (1873) 283 True mammals have been discovered in the new red sandstone. **1859** GEO. ELIOT *A. Bede* vii, There is one order of beauty which seems made to turn the heads..of all intelligent mammals, even of women.

b. *attrib.*, as ***mammal fœtus, form, giant.***

1845 CHAMBERS *Vestiges* (ed. 4) 207 In the mammal fœtus, ..the organ has the form of a prolonged tube. *Ibid.*, It becomes a full mammal heart. **1879** tr. *Haeckel's Evol. of Man* I. i. 3 Amphibian and Mammal forms. **1902** T. GILL in *Pop. Sci. Monthly* Sept. 436 A whale may be alluded to as a gigantic mammal or a mammal giant.

† **mammal**, *a. Obs. rare.* [ad. late L. *mammāl-is.*] Pertaining to the mammæ or breasts.

1656 BLOUNT *Glossogr.* s.v. *Vein*, Mammal veine (*vena mammalis*) is double, an inward and an outward one, distributed among the parts of the brest. [From Cotgr., *Veine mammale.*]

mammalated, obs. form of MAMILLATED *a.*

‖**Mammalia** (mæˈmeɪlɪə), *pl.* [mod.L. *mammālia* (Linnæus), neut. pl. of late L. *mammālis* adj., f. *mamma*: see MAMMA².] A 'class' of the animal kingdom the members of which are characterized by the possession of mammæ in which milk is secreted for the nourishment of the young.

The *Mammalia* are divided into the *placental* and the *implacental* mammalia (see the adjs.), the latter comprising only the marsupials and monotremes. Except the monotremes, the mammalia are all viviparous.

1773 *Encycl. Brit.* III. 362/2 The First Class, Mammalia, is subdivided into 7 Orders. **1817** LAWRENCE *Lectures* (1823) 101 In the mammalia..we descend from man to the whale or seal. **1832** DE LA BECHE *Geol. Man.* (ed. 2) 297 The remains of mammalia have not yet been detected in the cretaceous group. **1881** MIVART in *Nature* No. 615.337 We and beasts constitute..the class *Mammalia*.

maˈmmalial, *a. nonce-wd.* = MAMMALIAN.

1835 T. HOOK *G. Gurney* in *New Monthly Mag.* XLIV. 167 Men, women, and children, not to speak of animals, ornithological and mammalial.

mammalian (mæˈmeɪlɪən), *a.* and *sb.* [f. MAMMALIA + -AN.]

A. *adj.* Of or belonging to the Mammalia.

1851 D. WILSON *Archæol. & Preh. Ann. Scotl.* I. i. 22 Extensive discoveries of mammalian remains. **1855** W. S. DALLAS in *Syst. Nat. Hist.* II. 375 Most of the bones in the Mammalian skeleton are solid. **1880** HAUGHTON *Phys. Geog.* iii. 81 The lower forms of Mammalian life.

B. *sb.* One of the Mammalia.

1835 KIRBY *Hab. & Inst. Animals* II. xxiv. 515 The bears, the foxes, and other Mammalians. **1865** FARRAR *Chapt. Lang.* 15 The action is as instinctive to them as sucking is to every infant mammalian.

mammaliferous (mæməˈlɪfərəs), *a. Geol.* [f. MAMMALI-A + -FEROUS.] Containing mammalian remains.

1851 *Richardson's Geol.* x. 356 The mammaliferous crag consists of shelly beds of sand [etc.]. **1857** H. MILLER *Test. Rocks* ii. 79 Not until the great mammaliferous period is fairly ushered in, do either the bats or the whales make their appearance in creation.

¶ Loosely used for MAMMALIAN.

1873 J. GEIKIE *Gt. Ice Age* xi. 150 The strata containing mammaliferous remains.

mammality (mæˈmælɪtɪ). *rare*⁻¹. [f. MAMMAL + -ITY.] The attribute of being mammalian.

1899 J. FISKE *Through Nature to God* II. xi. 125 The Australian duck-bill, a relic of the most ancient incipient mammality, is still oviparous.

mammalogical (mæməˈlɒdʒɪkəl), *a.* [f. MAMMALOGY + -ICAL; after F. *mammalogique.*] Pertaining to mammalogy.

1856 MAYNE *Expos. Lex.* **1859** OWEN *Classif. Mammalia* 34 Mammalogical systems which..have been proposed. **1879** tr. *De Quatrefages' Human Spec.* 163 Agassiz thus destroys the homogeneity of the mammalogical fauna.

mammalogist (mæˈmælədʒɪst). [f. MAMMALOGY + -IST; after F. *mammalogiste.*] One versed in mammalogy.

1839 *Penny Cycl.* XIV. 353/1 Aldrovandus, Jonston, and the rest of that class of mammalogists, seem to have followed Gesner. **1883** *Academy* 1 Dec. 365/3 [Cites the word as a 'neologism' from *Encycl. Americana*].

mammalogy (mæˈmælədʒɪ). [irreg. f. MAMMALIA + -LOGY; after F. *mammalogie.*] The science of mammals.

1835 *Penny Cycl.* III. 229/1 Fischer, the most recent writer upon mammalogy, enumerates eleven different species of baboons. **1854** OWEN *Skel. & Teeth* in *Circ. Sci., Organ. Nat.* I. 301 The Systematic Mammalogies.

Mammaluck, -luke, obs. ff. MAMELUKE.

mam-mam, reduplication of MAM¹.

mammaplasty (ˈmæməplæstɪ). *Surg.* Also **mammo-**. [f. MAMMA² + -PLASTY.] Alteration of the shape or size of a breast by plastic surgery. Hence **mammaˈplastic** *a.*

1938 *Revue de Chirurgie Structive* VIII. 39 *(heading)* Review of 80 cases of mammaplasty. **1947** H. MAY *Reconstructive & Reparative Surg.* xvii. 397 *(heading)* Mamma-plastic procedures in the female. **1968** *N.Y. Times* 4 Apr. 26 He said the mammoplasty in the first case involved the transplant of adipose (fatty) tissue. **1969** C. ALLEN *Textbk. Psychosexual Disorders* (ed. 2) xii. 296 The procedures included..construction of a pro-vagina and mammoplasty.

mammary (ˈmæmərɪ), *a.* [f. L. *mamma* (see MAMMA²) + -ARY¹.]

1. Of or belonging to the mamma or breast. Also *absol.* = mammary artery.

1682 T. GIBSON *Anat.* (1697) 21 It has Arteries and Veins from the Mammary, and Epigastrick, and from those of the Midriff, or the Phrenick. **1706** PHILLIPS (ed. Kersey), *Mammary Vessels*, the Arteries and Veins that pass thro' the Muscles and Glands, or Kernels of the Breasts. **1795** HOME in *Phil. Trans.* LXXXV. 230 The mammary branches run superficially under the false belly till they reach the mammæ. **1831** R. KNOX *Cloquet's Anat.* 831 The mammary gland. **1834** *Fraser's Mag.* X. 535 The women..are remarkable for the same mammary exuberance. **1862** H. W. FULLER *Dis. Lungs* 4 The mammary is bounded above by the third rib. **1901** *Brit. Med. Jrnl.* No. 2097 Epit. Med. Lit. 38 The third left rib was resected, the internal mammary ligatured.

2. Having the form of a mamma. † ***mammary sarcoma*** (see quot. 1889).

1804 *Med. Jrnl.* XII. 466 Below are small mammary projections about to be the outlets to the cysts beneath them. **1807–26** S. COOPER *First Lines Surg.* (ed. 5) 191 When the tumour is known..to be either a mammary, a tuberculated, or medullary sarcoma, care should be taken [etc.]. **1889** *Syd. Soc. Lex.*, *Mammary sarcoma*, an old name for one of the denser varieties of sarcoma..from its resemblance on section to a portion of mammary gland.

mammate (ˈmæmət), *a.* [ad. L. *mammāt-us*, f. *mamma* MAMMA² + -ATE².] Having mammæ.

1856 MAYNE *Expos. Lex.*, *Mammatus*,..having mammæ or breasts: mammate. [In mod. Dicts.]

mammato- (mæˈmeɪtəʊ), used as comb. form of L. *mammātus* (see prec.), in meteorological terms descriptive of clouds which have the form of rounded festoons, as ***mammato-cirrus, -cumulus.***

1880 LEY in *Nature* 1 Jan. 211/1 In the first sketch 'cumulus' is shown with 'fracto-cumulus';..in the third the characteristic base of 'mammato-cumulus'; and in the fourth that of 'mammato-cirrus'.

† **ˈmammeated**, *a. Obs.* ⁰. [f. L. *mammeāt-us* (irreg. f. *mamma* breast) + -ED¹.] = MAMMATE.

1656 BLOUNT *Glossogr.*, *Mammeated*, that hath Paps or Teats, or that hath great ones. [In mod. Dicts.]

mammee (mæˈmiː). Forms: 6 **mamea, mameia, mamio**, 7 **mamay(n, mamme, mammet, momin**, 8 **mamie, mammey**, 7–9 **mamey, mamee**, 9 **maumee, mammy**, 7– **mammee.** [In Sp. *mamey*, from Haitian; cf. F. *mamey, mammée* (the latter from mod.L. *Mammea*, introduced by Linnæus).]

1. A large tree (*Mammea americana*, N. O. *Guttiferæ*) of tropical America (now almost naturalized in parts of tropical Africa and Asia), which bears a large fruit with a yellow pulp of pleasant taste. Also, the fruit of this tree.

1572 HAWKS in *Hakluyt's Voy.* (1600) III. 464 Fruits of the countrey..as plantans, *sapotes*,..*mamios*, limons [etc.]. **1588** N. H. *Voy. T. Cavendish* in *Hakluyt* (1589) 811 Plantans, mameias, pineaples, oranges and limons. **1593** J. WHITE in *Hakluyt* (1600) III. 282 Yong plants of Orenges, Pines, Mameas, and Plantanos, to set at Virginia. **1604** E. G[RIMSTONE] *D'Acosta's Hist. Indies* IV. xxiv. 278 These Mamayes, Guayauos, and Paltos, be the Indians peaches, apples, and peares. **1666** J. DAVIES *Hist. Caribby Isles* 31 [*Momin*]. **1672** R. BLOME *Descr. Jamaica* 25 Pomegranates, Cocar-Nuts, Limes, Guavars, Mammes, Alumee-Supotas [etc.]. **1684** *Bucaniers of America* I. ii. 11 Some of the most ordinary [Fruits]..are..Mamayns, Ananaes. **1685** L. WAFER *Voy.* (1729) 301 The Samballoes are low, flat, sandy islands, covered with a variety of trees; especially with Mammees, Sapadilloes, and Manchineel. **1697** DAMPIER *Voy.* (1729) I. 187 The Mammet is a large, tall, and straight-bodied tree [etc.]. **1760–72** *Juan & Ulloa's Voy.* (ed. 3) I. 76 The Mameis are of the same colour as the sapotes. **1764** GRAINGER *Sugar Cane* IV. 502 Thee, verdant mammey, first her song shall praise. **1852** TH. ROSS *Humboldt's Trav.* I. iv. 153 The Delta..is a fertile plain covered with Mammees, Sapotas (achras),..and other plants. **1866** MARY B. CLARKE *Mosses fr. Rolling Stone* 120 And zapotas, rough and brown, With the mamey and the mango, Cast their luscious sweetness down.

2. = *mammee-sapota.*

1866 *Treas. Bot.* 715/1 Mammee, *Lucuma mammosum.*

3. *attrib.*, as ***mammee-stone, -tree***; **mammee-apple** (also ***mummy apple***) = sense 1; ***African mammee-a.*** (see quot. 1887); **mammee-sapota**, the marmalade tree, *Lucuma mammosa*, or its fruit.

1683 J. POYNTZ *Tobago* 9 The *Mamme Apple grows to the Magnitude of a Pound Pear... Then there's the Mamme Supporter, much of the same Nature with the former. **1796** STEDMAN *Surinam* II. xix. 73 Among many other excellent fruits, I observed one which is here called the Mammee apple. **1829** GEN. P. THOMPSON *Exerc.* (1842) I. 144 They will send a deputation..to give every honest woman a shaddock and a mamee-apple for her little boys. **1863** R. F. BURTON *Wand. W. Afr.* II. 34 Custard-apples, guavas,.. maumee-apples. **1887** MOLONEY *Forestry W. Afr.* 280 African Mammee apple (*Ochrocarpus africanus*), a tree 40 to 50 feet high. **1905** *Daily Graphic* 16 Jan. 4/4 The mummy-apple, a delicate tree-melon, springs up spontaneously wherever land is cleared. **1911** J. LONDON *Adventure* vii. 85 Mummy apples, which he had regarded as weeds, under her guidance appeared as appetizing breakfast fruit. **1683** *Mamme Supporter [see *mammee apple*]. **1697** DAMPIER *Voy.* (1729) I. 203 The Mammee-Sappota Tree is different from the Mammee described at the Island of Tobago. *a* **1726** H. BARHAM *Hortus Amer.* Index (1794), Mammee-sapota, *Achras sapota.* **1864** GRISEBACH *Flora W. Ind.* 785 Mammee-Sapota, *Lucuma mammosa.* **1681** GREW *Musæum* II. 190 A Great *Mammee-stone..A little Mammee-stone ..A round Mammee-stone. **1672** W. HUGHES *Amer. Physit.* 57 Of the *Momin-Tree, or Toddie-Tree. **1693** *Phil. Trans.* XVII. 620 The Mammee-Tree of the West-Indies. **1725** SLOANE *Jamaica* II. 123 The Mammee-tree..is above sixty Foot high [etc.]. **1871** TYLOR *Prim. Cult.* II. 56 The delicious fruit of the mamey trees.

mammelated, variant of MAMILLATED.

mammelière, variant of MAMELIÈRE.

mammellated, obs. form of MAMILLATED *a.*

mammelon, variant of MAMELON.

Mammeluck, -luke, obs. ff. MAMELUKE.

mammenye, variant of MALMENY *Obs.*

† **ˈmammer**, *v. Obs.* exc. *dial.* Forms: 5 **memere, mamere**, 6 **mamber, mam(m)or**, 6– **mammer.** [An imitative formation (with frequentative suffix -ER); cf. *mamble, mumble, stammer.*

It is doubtful whether this has any connexion with the OE. *mamrian* occurring in Ps. (Thorpe) lxiii. 5 (þær hi mamriað man & unriht = Vulg. *scrutantes scrutinio*), app. meaning 'to devise, think of', or with the *mamor* sb., found as a gloss on *sopor* sleep.]

intr. **a.** To stammer, mutter. **b.** To vacillate, waver, be undecided.

14.. *Anturs of Arth.* 110 (Douce MS.) Hit marred, hit memered, hit mused for madde. *c* **1425** *Voc.* in Wr.-Wülcker 668/26 *Mutulare*, to mamere [cf. *Ags. Glosses* ibid. 447/30 '*Mutulat*, stommeteð' i.e. stammers]. *a* **1555** BRADFORD in Coverdale *Lett. Mart.* (1564) 313 Tyl he [*sc.* Adam] forsoke god..began to mamber of the truth, & to frame hymselfe outwardly to doe that which his conscience reproued inwardly..til then, I say, god did not departe and leaue him to himselfe. **1566** DRANT *Horace, Sat.* II. iii. G v b, Yea when she daygnes to sende for hym, then mammeryng he dothe doute, What should I go? **1604** SHAKS. *Oth.* III. iii. 70, I wonder in my Soule What you would aske me, that I should deny, Or stand so mam'ring on? **1617** COLLINS *Def. Bp. Ely* II. vii. 254 Would you haue them to mammer, as Elias said merrily once of Baal, Perhaps he is gone to warre, ..so perhaps he is gone to Purgatory? **1842** AKERMAN *Wiltsh. Gloss.*, *Mammered*, perplexed. **1861** T. HUGHES *Tom Brown at Oxf.* III. vii. 127, I be that mad wi' myself, and mammered, and down, I be ready to hang myself. **1883** W. H. COPE *Gloss. Hampshire Words* 56 *Mammered*, perplexed. **1888** B. LOWSLEY *Gloss. Berks. Words* 108 *Mammered*, amazed, confused, puzzled.

ˈmammering, *vbl. sb.* Now *rare.* [+ -ING¹.]

1. A stammering, muttering.

c **1425** *Voc.* in Wr.-Wülcker 668/27 *Hec mutulatio*, mameryng. **1567** HARMAN *Caveat* (1869) 72 [He] drank to his wyfe and fell to his mammerings and mounched a pace. **1945** A. L. ROWSE *West-Country Stories* 17 The innumerable mammering of bats' voices.

2. A state of doubt, hesitation, or perplexity; chiefly in phr. ***in a mammering.***

1532 MORE *Confut. Tindale* Wks. 343/1 He was in a mamering whether he would retourne agayn ouer the sea. **1533** —— *Apol.* xlii. ibid. 911/2 Yᵉ matter was in a mammering before yᵉ change was made. **1537** *St. Papers Hen. VIII*, I. 527 The people in all partes..are very wylde,..at no stay, but in a mamoring, what they may do. **1579** W. WILKINSON *Confut. Familye of Love* 8 b, God..keepe us from falling away from the truth, or standing in mammering therof. **1609** [BP. W. BARLOW] *Answ. Nameless Cath.* 115 Hee..did protest euen while matters were in a mammering. **1612** R. CARPENTER *Soules Sent.* 72 The carnall man stands here at a mammering and maruelling how it can bee done. **1639** HORN & ROB *Gate Lang. Unl.* xc. §886 The one goes on forward..without respit, the other staggers (is in a mammering). **1941** E. R. EDDISON *Fish Dinner* (1972) vii. 108 Arquez, seeing..Clavius wounded and in a mammering whether to fly or fight: threw another chair. **1947** M. LOWRY *Let.* 13 Aug. (1967) 151, I am all of a doodah. I am in a mammering.

† **ˈmammering**, *ppl. a. Obs.* [f. MAMMER *v.* + -ING².] Hesitating.

1581 J. BELL *Haddon's Answ. Osor.* 358 This doctrine doth abolish quite the doctrine of the law, of repentaunce,.. and commaundeth a mammering doubtfulnesse.

† **ˈmammery.** *Obs. rare*⁻¹. In 6 mamorie. [f. MAMMER *v.* + -Y.] = MAMMERING *sb.*

1578 H. WOTTON *Courtlie Controv. Cupid's Cautels* To Rdr., My quill remayned long (as men say) in a mamorie, quiuering in my quaking fingers, before I durst presume to publishe these my fantasies.

mammet, obs. f. MAMMEE; variant of MAUMET.

mammetrous, -try, var. ff. MAUMETROUS, -TRY.

mammey, mammie, see MAMMEE, MAMMY[1].

mammifer (ˈmæmɪfə(r)). Now *rare.* [a. F. *mammifère*, orig. used in pl. as ad. mod.L. *mammifera*: see next.] = MAMMAL *sb.*

1832 LYELL *Princ. Geol.* II. 91 The terrestrial mammifers. **1877** DAWSON *Orig. World* 356 The carnivorous mammifer.

‖**Mammifera** (mæˈmɪfərə). *rare.* [mod.L. neut. pl. of **mammifer* adj., f. L. *mamma* (see MAMMA[2]) + *-fer* bearing. (Substituted by French naturalists *a* 1800 for Linnæus' *mammalia*).] = MAMMALIA.

1827 R. JAMESON tr. *Cuvier's Theory Earth* (ed. 5) 294 Among all these mammifera.. there has not been a single quadrumanous animal.

mammiferous (mæˈmɪfərəs), *a.* [f. as prec. + -OUS: see -FEROUS.]

1. = MAMMALIAN *a.*

1803 *Med. Jrnl.* IX. 495 The.. larger mammiferous animals. **1833** LYELL *Princ. Geol.* III. 59 None of the associated mammiferous remains belong to species which now exist. **1850** H. MILLER *Footpr. Creat.* viii. (1874) 148 A more exact resemblance to the mammiferous tail. **1859** DARWIN *Orig. Spec.* x. (1878) 271 Mammiferous remains.

2. Of a part of the body: Bearing the mammæ.

1878 BELL tr. *Gegenbaur's Comp. Anat.* 422 The marsupium.. encloses the mammiferous region of the abdomen.

mammiform (ˈmæmɪfɔːm), *a.* Also *incorrectly* **mammæform** (*Treas. Bot.* 1866). [f. L. *mamma* MAMMA[2] + -(I)FORM: cf. F. *mammiforme.*] Having the form of a mamma or breast.

1706 PHILLIPS (ed. Kersey), *Mastoidei*,.. the Mammiform, or Dug-like processes. **1843** FORBES in *Proc. Berw. Nat. Club* II. No. 11. 79 The upper series bear from one to four mammiform tubercles. **1878** *Ann. & Mag. Nat. Hist.* Nov. 393 Numerous large mammiform tubercles.

mammill, variant of MAMELLE *Obs.*

mammilla, -ar, -ate, etc.: see MAMILL-.

mammillon, variant of MAMELON.

mammitis (mæˈmaɪtɪs). *Path.* [f. MAMMA[2] + -ITIS.] Inflammation of the mammary gland.

1872 F. G. THOMAS *Dis. Women* (ed. 3) 103 At other times their proper tissue becomes inflamed, as we see that of the breast do in mammitis. **1889** in *Syd. Soc. Lex.*

mammlere, variant of MAMBLER *Obs.*

mammo- (ˈmæməʊ), comb. form of MAMMA[2], used in various medical and biological terms, as **mammoˈgenic** *a.* [-GENIC], stimulating the growth of the breasts, esp. at puberty; of or pertaining to this activity; so **ˈmammogen**, any substance which has or is supposed to have mammogenic activity; **mammoˈgenesis**, the stimulation of the growth of the breasts, esp. at puberty; **maˈmmography** *Med.* [-GRAPHY], a technique or procedure for diagnosing and locating abnormalities of the breasts by means of X-rays; an examination by this technique; hence **ˈmammogram, ˈmammograph**, a radiograph taken by this technique; **mammoˈgraphic** *a.*

1940 *Endocrinology* XXVII. 892 Only mammogen 1 (the duct growth factor) is present in ether-soluble extracts of the AP. Work is now progressing on the concentration of mammogen 2, the lobule-alveolar growth factor, and also on the perfection of a suitable technic for the assay of this hormone. **1958** *Proc. R. Soc.* B. CXLIX. 306 Oestrogen may resume its role as a mammogen. **1971** COWIE & TINDAL *Physiol. Lactation* iii. 115 Although the concept of *specific* mammogens of pituitary origin was never widely accepted .. the 'Mammogen' theory rightly centred attention on the role of the anterior pituitary in mammogenesis. **1958** *Proc. R. Soc.* B. CXLIX. 312 The placenta may contribute as much to mammogenesis as the pituitary and ovaries combined. **1971** COWIE & TINDAL *Physiol. Lactation* iii. 117 Only in the rat and mouse have such detailed analyses of the hormones concerned in mammogenesis been made. **1938** *Proc. Soc. Exper. Biol. & Med.* XXXVII. 608 This new pituitary principle will be called the 'mammogenic hormone'. **1940** *Endocrinology* XXVII. 888 (*heading*) Evidence for the presence of a second mammogenic (lobule-alveolar) factor in the anterior pituitary. **1958** *Proc. R. Soc.* B. CXLIX. 304 Mammogenic activities of the ovarian hormones. **1971** COWIE & TINDAL *Physiol. Lactation* iii. 122 There is.. a vast literature on the mammogenic potencies of ovarian steroids. **1937** N. F. HICKEN in *Surg., Gynecol. & Obstetr.* LXIV. 594/1 The procedure utilizes contrast fluids which are injected directly into the milk ducts, thus giving an accurate roentgenographic pattern of the ductal and secretory system of the mammary gland. The terms 'mammography' and 'mammograms' have been coined to describe these examinations. *Ibid.*, Gentleness, persistence, and patience are requisite in obtaining good mammograms. *Ibid.* 594/2 These mammographic visualizations afford an excellent method of studying both the physiological and pathological changes of the breast. **1969** *New Scientist* 13 Mar. 570/3 Preliminary designs for a commercial version of the system for producing mammograms. **1968** *N.Y. Times* 25 Mar. 25 This image Dr. Wolfe and many other radiologists agree is far clearer and more detailed than film mammographs. **1970** *Daily Tel.* 23 Oct. 17/4 The mammograph is another X-ray machine. Each breast is X-rayed individually, rather as though it were under a microscope. **1973** M. J. BRENNAN in Holland & Frei *Cancer Med.* xxvii. 1776/2 Combined clinical and mammographic screening detected breast cancer at a rate of 2·72 per 1,000 initial examinations. **1969** *New Scientist* 8 May 276/1 Thermography can detect presymptomatic breast cancers even when they are not palpable nor shown up by mammography. **1971** *Daily Colonist* (Victoria, B.C.) 26 Nov. 2/2 If you are still worried, you could have a mammography done—an X-ray technique commonly used in women with breast lumps that have to be identified.

mammock (ˈmæmək), *sb. arch.* and *dial.* (see E.D.D.). Also 6–7 **mammocke**, 7 **mamock**. [Of obscure origin: formed with the dim. suffix -OCK.] A scrap, shred, broken or torn piece. Also *fig.*

a **1529** SKELTON *Col. Cloute* 654 Whan mammockes was your meate, With moldy brede to eate. *c* **1600** DAY *Begg. Bednall Gr.* IV. i, Let me be torn into mammocks with wilde Bears if [etc.]. **1607** WALKINGTON *Opt. Glass* 62 Small mammocks of stone.. of the bignesse of dice. **1633** T. ADAMS *Exp. 2 Peter* i. 5. 100 God regardeth not the mammockes of our sacrifices. **1651** OGILBY *Æsop* (1665) 137 Their Masking Sutes are all in mamocks tore. *a* **1722** LISLE *Husb.* (1752) 247 Large cattle.. will make mammocks, that they will leave and not eat. **1828** SCOTT *F.M. Perth* xxxiii, I say, cut him to mammocks upon the spot! **1870** MORRIS *Earthly Par.* II. III. 40 This gangrel thief thought fit to tread The grass to mammocks by my head!

mammock (ˈmæmək), *v.* Now chiefly *dial.* (see E.D.D.). [f. MAMMOCK *sb.*] *trans.* To break, cut, or tear into fragments or shreds.

1607 SHAKS. *Cor.* I. iii. 71 Hee did so set his teeth, and teare it. Oh, I warrant how he mammockt it. **1641** MILTON *Reform.* I. Wks. 1851 III. 17 The obscene, and surfeted Priest scruples not to paw, and mammock the sacramentall bread. **1670** COVEL *Diary* (Hakl. Soc.) 262 This was ready mammockt and cut to our hands. **1764** *Francis Lett.* (1901) I. 65 After being all mammocked the fish were sent down to be boiled. **1852** *Fraser's Mag.* XLV. 523 The soft parts are cut.. and mammocked in every conceivable way. **1888** *Jrnl. Amer. Folk-lore* I. No. 2 A colored man.. frequently complains that the cows 'mammock the hay' so badly.

fig. **1806–7** J. BERESFORD *Miseries Hum. Life* (1826) VII. lxix, Hearing your favourite poem.. mammocked by the mouth of a forward Puppy. **1865** KNIGHT *Sch. Hist. Eng.* I. 660 He [Garrick] mangled Shakspere. And he patched the mammock'd plays with tawdry rags. **1890** *Athenæum* 29 Mar. 400/2 One or two lines have to be mammocked to fit them into the new arrangement.

mammoda, variant of MAHMUDI *Obs.*

mammodis, ? *pl.* ? *U.S.* ? *Obs.* [app. a. Urdū (Pers.) *maḥmūdī* a sort of fine muslin, f. *Maḥmūd*: see MAHMUDI.] (See quots.)

1828 WEBSTER, *Mammodis*, coarse, plain Indian muslins. **1889** *Century Dict.*, *Mammodis*, n. pl., Cotton cloths from India; commonly applied to the plain ones only.

mammoid (ˈmæmɔɪd), *a.* [f. MAMMA[2] + -OID.] Resembling a mamma.

1774 DARWIN in *Phil. Trans.* LXIV. 349 The mammoid process of the temporal bone.

mammole (ˈmæməʊl). The edible fruit of *Opuntia Tuna* (*Syd. Soc. Lex.* 1889).

Mammoluke, obs. form of MAMELUKE.

Mammon (ˈmæmən). Also 4, 6 **Mammona**, 6 **mammonde, mammony.** [a. late L. *ma(m)mōna* masc. (Vulg.), *ma(m)mon* (Diefenb.), a. Gr. (N.T.) μαμωνᾶς (late texts μαμμωνᾶς), a. Aramaic *māmōn, māmōnā* riches, gain (frequent in the Targums). Hence also Syriac *māmūnā*, Goth. *mammōna* wk. masc., mod.F. *mammon, mammone.*

The N. T. phrase μαμωνᾶς τῆς ἀδικίας (Eng. version 'mammon of unrighteousness'; earlier versions, 'mammon of iniquity', 'wicked mammon', etc.) represents exactly the Aramaic *māmōn di-rʾshaʿ*, 'riches or gain of wickedness' (Targ. Hab. ii. 9), and approximately the more common *māmōn di-sh'qar*, 'riches of falsehood'.]

1. The Aramaic word for 'riches', occurring in the Greek text of Matt. vi. 24 and Luke xvi. 9–13, and retained in the Vulgate. Owing to the quasi-personification in these passages, the word was taken by mediæval writers as the proper name of the devil of covetousness. This use appears in English in the 14–16th c., and was revived by Milton (*P.L.* I. 678, II. 228). The word does not occur in the N.T. translations of Wyclif and Purvey (who substitute *richessis*), but it was used by Tindale (1526–34) and subsequent translators, with the exception of those of the Geneva version. From the 16th c. onwards it has been current in English, usually with more or less of personification, as a term of opprobrium for wealth regarded as an idol or as an evil influence.

1362 LANGL. *P. Pl.* A. IX. 81 He.. with Mammonas moneye hath maked him frendes. **1502** *Ord. Crysten Men* (W. de W. 1506) II. xi. 117 A deuyll named Mammona made unto the couetous man .vi. commaundementes. **1526** *Pilgr. Perf.* (W. de W. 1531) 281 b, No persone may serue god eternal, & also yᵉ mammonde of iniquite, which is golde & syluer & other rychesse. **1530** LATIMER *Let. to Hen. VIII* in Foxe *A. & M.* (1563) 1346/1 Thys wycked Mammon, the goodes of thys worlde, whyche is their God. **1618** BP. HALL *Right. Mammon* 64 The foolish Siluer-smiths may shout out, Great is Mammon of the worldlings. **1620** T. GRANGER *Div. Logike* 102 He is the slaue of muddy Mammon. **1683** TRYON *Way to Health* xix. (1697) 418 Miserly Parents sacrificing their Children to Mammon is a wretched Idolatry. **1732** POPE *Ep. Bathurst* 171 Who sees pale Mammon pine amidst his store. **1773** *Observ. State Poor* 49 Eyes fascinated by Mammon the god of this world. **1781** COWPER *Charity* 45 Mammon makes the world his legatee Through fear, not love. **1836** KEBLE *Dissent* ii. in *Lyra Apost.*, A creed.. By Mammon's touch new moulded o'er and o'er.

b. Sometimes jocularly for 'money'.

1706 E. WARD *Wooden World Diss.* (1708) 101 While his Mammon lasts, he's a mad Fellow.

2. *attrib.* and *Comb.*, as ***mammon gospel, worship, worshipper***; ***mammon-blinded, worshipping*** adjs.

1826 E. IRVING *Babylon* II. 413 We.. are now a Mammon-worshipping people. **1843** CARLYLE *Past & Pr.* III. ii, We.. with our Mammon-Gospel, have come to strange conclusions. *Ibid.*, Verily Mammon-worship is a melancholy creed. *Ibid.* IV. viii, When Mammon-worshippers here and there begin to be God-worshippers. **1851** KINGSLEY *Yeast* vi. 108 However Mammon-blinded, he was kindly and upright. **1899** W. R. INGE *Chr. Mysticism* viii. 317 The sweet influences of the home deprive even mammon-worship of half its grossness.

mammon, obs. variant of MAMMOTH *sb.*

mammondom (ˈmæməndəm). [f. MAMMON + -DOM.] The realm or domain of Mammon.

1861 SALA in *Temple Bar* I. 304 All the gold of Mammondom could not.. bring cheerful warmth.

†**mammonet.** *Obs.* [ad. med.L. *mammonetus* (Promp. Parv. 327/1, Wr.-Wülcker 594/30), 'marmoset', f. *mammon* monkey.] A kind of monkey.

1607 TOPSELL *Four-f. Beasts* 7 Mammonets are lesse then an Ape,.. having a long and hairy taile.

mammoniacal (mæməˈnaɪəkəl), *a. nonce-wd.* [f. MAMMON: after *demoniacal.*] = next.

1848 THACKERAY *Bk. Snobs, Concl. Observ.*, All English society is cursed by this mammoniacal superstition.

mammonic (mæˈmɒnɪk), *a. nonce-wd.* [f. MAMMON + -IC.] Of or pertaining to Mammon.

1837 *Fraser's Mag.* XV. 362 The mammonic hydra.

mammonish (ˈmæmənɪʃ), *a.* [f. MAMMON + -ISH.] Influenced by or devoted to Mammon.

1837 SYD. SMITH *Let. to Archd. Singleton* Wks. 1859 II. 258/1 This, it will be said, is a Mammonish view of the subject. **1840** CARLYLE *Heroes* vi. (1858) 349 A great black devouring world not Christian, but Mammonish, Devilish. **1843** —— *Past & Pr.* III. ix. **1851** T. PARKER in Weiss *Life & Corr.* I. 381 Unitarian ministers have.. generally congregations more mammonish.. than the orthodox congregations.

mammonism (ˈmæmənɪz(ə)m). [f. MAMMON + -ISM. (Cf. G. *mammonismus.*)] Devotion to the pursuit of riches.

1843 CARLYLE *Past & Pr.* I. v, In whirlwinds of fire, you and your Mammonisms, Dilettantisms [etc.].. shall disappear! *Ibid.* II. xvi, If.. all except Mammonism be a vain grimace. **1897** PRICE HUGHES in *Daily News* 15 Nov. 2/4 It was necessary to protect the Lord's Day against Mammonism.

mammonist (ˈmæmənɪst). [f. MAMMON + -IST. Cf. obs. Da. *mammonist.*] A worshipper of Mammon; one who sets his heart on riches.

1550 CROWLEY *Inform. & Petit.* 13 b, Let them no more be named Christians,.. but Mammonistes after Mammon whose badge they beare. **1560** BECON *Catech.* IV. Wks. 1564 I. 415 They are all Mammonistes and worldlinges. **1667** *Causes Decay Chr. Piety* v. 105 Let him come to the converted Mammonist, and ask him which he finds the better Treasury, his own Coffer or the poor mans Bowels. **1702** C. MATHER *Magn. Chr.* III. 209 The Gains of Mammonists. **1817** COLERIDGE '*Blessed are ye that Sow*' 78 The.. world-honoured company of Christian Mammonists. **1886** W. GRAHAM *Soc. Probl.* 459 The mammonist money-maker.

mammonistic (mæməˈnɪstɪk), *a. rare.* [f. prec. + -IC.] After the manner of a mammonist.

1882 G. MACDONALD *Castle Warlock* III. xxiv. 333 The usual mammonistic feeling of the enormous importance of money. **1893** *Chicago Advance* 27 Apr., A mammonistic age.

mammonite (ˈmæmənaɪt). [f. MAMMON + -ITE.] = MAMMONIST.

1712 E. WARD *Misc. Writ.* III. II. 55 Your Hands are the Mammonites that convey unlawful Gain out of other Peoples Pockets into your own Till. **1841** HOR. SMITH *Moneyed Man* III. 263 The gold failed, and the mammonites vanished.

attrib. **1850** KINGSLEY *Alt. Locke* x. (1874) 84 It suits the venal Mammonite press.. to jumble them together. **1855** TENNYSON *Maud* I. i. 12 When a Mammonite mother kills her babe for a burial fee. **1861** *Macm. Mag.* V. 120 [They] are said to be invaded by the mammonite spirit.

mammonitish (ˈmæmənaɪtɪʃ), *a.* [f. MAMMONITE + -ISH.] Mammon-like.

1615 J. TAYLOR (Water P.) *Urania* lx. Wks. (1630) 6/2 Avarice.. makes his Mammonitish God his gaine. **1841** HOR. SMITH *Moneyed Man* II. 254 May the result of her nuptials be worthy.. the Mammonitish spirit in which they originate!

mammonization (ˌmæmənaɪˈzeɪʃən). *rare.* [f. next + -ATION.] The action of mammonizing.
18.. *Meth. Quart. Rev.* (Worcester 1860).

mammonize (ˈmæmənaɪz), *v. rare.* [f. MAMMON + -IZE.] *trans.* To influence through Mammon.
1819 'R. RABELAIS' *Abeillard & Heloisa* x. 314 One half too have been canoniz'd, Having Old Nick thus mammoniz'd, As to build structures unto God [etc.].

Mammo'nolatry. *nonce-wd.* [f. MAMMON + -(O)LATRY.] The worship of Mammon.
1820 COLERIDGE in *Lit. Rem.* (1839) IV. 98 [This] is impudence and Mammonolatry to boot.

mammontrie, variant of MAUMETRY *Obs.*

mammony, variant of MALMENY *Obs.*

mammooda, -dee, variants of MAHMUDI *Obs.*

mammoplasty, var. MAMMAPLASTY.

mammoring, variant of MAMMERING *vb. sb.*

mammose (ˈmæməʊs), *a.* [ad. L. *mammōs-us*: see MAMMA² and -OSE.] Having breast-like protuberances.
1856 MAYNE *Expos. Lex.* **1857** ASA GRAY *Less. Bot.* Gloss., *Mammose*: breast-shaped.

mammoth (ˈmæməθ), *sb.* and *a.* Also 8 **mammuth, mamant, maman, mamont, mammon, mammot, (mammoht)**, 8–9 **mammouth.** [a. Russian †*mammot*, whence *mammotovoi kost* mammoth's bones (Ludolf *Gram. Russ.* 1696, p. 92); now *mamant.* Hence also F. *mammouth*, †*mamant*, †*mammont.* The word is of obscure origin; the alleged Tartar word *mama* 'earth' (usually cited as the etymon) is not known to exist.] **A.** *sb.*

1. a. A large extinct species of elephant (*Elephas primigenius*) formerly native in Europe and northern Asia; its remains are frequently found in the alluvial deposits in Siberia.
[**1698** tr. Ludolf in *A. Brand's Emb. Muscovy into China* 122 The *Mammotovoy*, which is dug out of the Earth in Siberia.] **1706** tr. *Ides' Trav.* vi. 26 The old Siberian Russians affirm that the Mammuth is very like the Elephant. **1738** tr. *Strahlenberg's Descr. Russia* xiii. 403 The Russian Mammoth certainly came from the word Behemot. **1763** J. BELL *Trav. Asia* II. 148 Tartars.. have seen this creature, called mammon, at the dawn of day, near lakes and rivers. *Ibid.*, That kind of ivory called, in this country, mammon's horn. **1807** J. BARLOW *Columb.* I. 705 Where mammoth grazed the renovating groves. **1824** BYRON *Def. Transf.* III. i. 55 'Twas sport.. To go forth, with a pine For a spear, 'gainst the mammoth. **1863** A. C. RAMSAY *Phys. Geog.* xxviii. (1878) 463 Man, the Mammoth, and other extinct mammalia, were contemporaneous.

b. *attrib.* and *Comb.*, as *mammoth horn, ivory, tusk*; *mammoth-wise* adv.
1843 *Zoologist* I. 2 By the name of mammoth horns the Siberians designate the fossil tusks which are so numerous ..throughout the northern districts. **1868** SWINBURNE *Blake* 247 The spinal skeleton,..shaped mammoth-wise, in grovelling involution of limb. **1879** LUBBOCK *Sci. Lect.* v. 150 A fragment of mammoth-tusk. **1903** *Expositor* June 460 Wrought objects of mammoth ivory.

c. *U.S.* Often applied to the fossil mastodon.
1816 J. SCOTT *Vis. Paris* (ed. 5) 296 The Siberian Mammoth, or Elephant, and the American Mammoth, or Mastodonton. **1834** MCMURTRIE *Cuvier's Anim. Kingd.* 98 The Mammoth has been completely destroyed... Its remains are found..throughout all parts of North America. **1850** LYELL *2nd Visit U.S.* II. 197 The fossil remains of the mammoth (a name commonly applied in the United States to the mastodon).

2. *fig.* Something of huge size (cf. B).
1894 *Cornh. Mag.* Mar. 269 Bayle's 'Dictionnaire Historique', 5 vols. folio, or any kindred mammoth among books.

B. *adj.* **a.** Comparable to the mammoth in size; huge, gigantic.
Freq. in American usage before 1850. The reference in quots. 1802² and 1803 is to a large cheese presented to Jefferson.
1802 *Port Folio* (Philadelphia) II. 31 (Th.), A baker in this city offers Mammoth bread for sale. **1802** *Balance* (Hudson, N.Y.) 19 Oct. 331 (Th.), No more to do with the subject than the man in the moon has to do with the mammoth cheese. **1803** J. DAVIS *Trav. U.S.A.* ix. 329 Its extraordinary dimensions induced some wicked wag of a federalist to call it the Mammoth Cheese. **1813** *Niles' Reg.* IV. 32/2 The Mammoth bank bill passed the senate this day on a third reading. **1814** SIR R. WILSON *Priv. Diary* II. 309 The dancing very bad; the performers all had mammoth legs. **1820** KEATS *Hyperion* I. 164 But one of the whole mammoth-brood still kept His sovereignty. **1822** J. FLINT *Lett. Amer.* 309 *note*, The great cave in Kentucky is called the Mammoth Cave, although none of the remains of that animal have been found in it. **1850** SCORESBY *Cheever's Whalem. Adv.* iii. (1859) 36 The whale was thus got hold of, and the mammoth carcass secured to the ship. **1854** J. S. C. ABBOTT *Napoleon* (1855) I. xv. 262 All the streets of the mammoth metropolis. **1874** RAYMOND *Statist. Mines & Mining* 505 The Mammoth vein itself is about 23 feet thick. **1896** *Westm. Gaz.* 20 June 7/1 Yorkshire made another mammoth score. **1924** W. R. INGE *Lay Thoughts* (1926) III. ii. 192 The new journalism, with its 'mammoth combines', is good business, but bad democracy. **1956** *Hansard Commons* 10 May 1450/2 The coal industry today is having to undertake this mammoth reorganisation because of the failures of hon. Members opposite in the years between the wars. **1966** AUDEN *About House* 39 He offered Mammoth-marrow And, perhaps, Long Pig. **1974** *Economist* 21 Dec. 65/1 Britain's mammoth current account deficit.

b. *mammoth powder* (see quot. 1875); *mammoth-tree*, the *Sequoia* (*Wellingtonia*) *gigantea*, a large coniferous tree, native of California.
1866 *Treas. Bot.* 1051/1 The Wellingtonia of our gardens, and the Big or Mammoth-tree of the Americans. **1875** KNIGHT *Dict. Mech.* s.v. *Gunpowder*, For very heavy ordnance a much larger grained powder..called mammoth powder, was introduced by the late General T. J. Rodman.

mammothee, variant of MAHMUDI *Obs.*

†**mammothrept.** *Obs.* [ad. late L. *mammothrept-us* (Augustine), a. Gr. μαμμόθρεπτος brought up by one's grandmother, f. μάμμη grandmother + θρεπτός vbl. adj., f. τρέφειν to bring up.] A spoilt child; a nursling.
1599 B. JONSON *Cynthia's Rev.* IV. iii, *Amo...* How like you it, sir?—*Hed.* Verie well in troth.—*Amo.* But very well? O, You are a meere mammothrept in judgement. **1609** J. DAVIES *Holy Roode* (1878) 15 And for we are the Mammothrepts of Sinne, Crosse vs with Christ, to weane our joys therein. **1651** BIGGS *New Disp.* ¶55 If he be but an Academick, though a meer mammothrept, and perhaps a Midas.

¶ By Brathwait misused (from misunderstanding of quot. 1599 above) for: A severe critic.
1617 BRATHWAIT *Smoaking Age* O 2 b, Or what strict Mamothrept that man should bee, Who has done Chaucer such an injurie. **1635** —— *Arcad. Pr.* 217 These be the fruits of all severe mammothrepts who relish nothing but justice.

mammotrophic (mæməʊˈtrəʊfɪk), **-tropic** (-ˈtrəʊpɪk, -ˈtrɒpɪk), *a. Physiol.* [f. MAMMO- + -TROPHIC, -TROPIC.] Stimulating or having the ability to stimulate the breasts, *esp.* in relation to growth or milk secretion.
1935 *Proc. Soc. Exper. Biol. & Med.* XXXII. 1049 The hypophyseal mammotropic hormone. **1942** *Ibid.* LI. 308 (*heading*) The direct mammotrophic action of lactogenic hormone. **1970** *Sci. Jrnl.* June 47/1 All males normally produce small quantities of mammotrophic hormone, but to what end remains a mystery. **1973** *Nature* 8 June 349/2 To further define the relationship between the mammotrophic and sebotrophic hormones we have studied the effect of suckling on sebum secretion.

So **mammo'trophin, -'tropin** = PROLACTIN.
1935 *Proc. Soc. Exper. Biol. & Med.* XXXII. 1049 (*heading*) Detection of mammotropin in the urine of lactating women. **1952** [see *lactogen* s.v. LACTO-]. **1958** *Proc. R. Soc.* B. CXLIX. 309 By adding mammotrophin (*MH*) to these steroids, incomplete lobulo-alveolar growth was induced. **1961** *Lancet* 7 Oct. 792/1 The demonstration of mammotrophin activity.

mammotry, variant of MAUMETRY *Obs.*

‖**mammula** (ˈmæmjʊlə). Also (anglicized or after Fr.) **mammule.** [L. *mammula* a little teat, dim. of *mamma* MAMMA².] = MAMILLA.
1816 KIRBY & SP. *Entomol.* (1843) I. 344 Two additional spinners (or mammulæ) peculiar to this species. **1856** MAYNE *Expos. Lex.*, *Mammula*..a mammule.

Hence **'mammular, 'mammulose** *adjs.*, consisting of or having mammulæ.
1826 KIRBY & SP. *Entomol.* III. xxix. 155 The grub of a beetle..whose body is margined on each side by eight triangular fleshy mammular processes. **1889** *Syd. Soc. Lex.*, *Mammulose.*

mammy¹ (ˈmæmɪ). Also 7–9 -ie. [dim. of MAM¹: see -Y.]

1. a. A child's word for mother.
1523 SKELTON *Garl. Laurel* 974 Your mammy and your dady Brought forth a godely babi! **1560** *Nice Wanton* 452 (Manly), All this our Mammy would take in good worth. **1562** PHAER *Æneid* VIII. Z iij b, Their mammies teats they lap with hungry lipps. **1611** FLORIO, *Mamma*,..a breast. Also Mam, Mother-mine, or Mammie. **1719** D'URFEY *Pills* V. 18 She'll be a Mammy before it is long. **1773** MME. D'ARBLAY *Let. to Crisp* in *Early Diary*, I..proceed to be sorry and glad that you and your Mammy have been ill and are better. **1793** BURNS *Bonny Jean* 5 And ay she wrought her mammie's wark, And ay she sang sae merrilie. **1842** S. LOVER *Handy Andy* i, Andy grew up in mischief and the admiration of his mammy.

b. *Comb.*, as **mammy-sick** *a.* (*contemptuous*), distressed at being separated from (one's) mother.
1826 DISRAELI *Viv. Grey* I. I. iii. 14 'Mammy-sick!' growled Barlow *primus.* **1836–48** B. D. WALSH *Aristoph.*, *Clouds* III. iii, The town Will pronounce you a mammy-sick coddle. **1885** J. C. JEAFFRESON *Real Shelley* I. 51 A shy.. mammy-sick lad.

2. In the southern United States, esp. before the abolition of slavery: A coloured woman having the care of white children.
1837 *Southern Lit. Messenger* III. 744/1 [Aged Negro domestics] were greeted always by the kind appellatives of 'daddy and mammy'. **1859** BARTLETT *Dict. Amer.*, *Mammy*, the term of endearment used by white children to their negro nurses and to old family servants. **1887** T. N. PAGE *Ole Virginia* (1893) 164 The old mammies and uncles who were our companions and comrades. **1901** R. D. EVANS *Sailor's Log* i. 3 Like most Southern children, I was brought up and cared for by a 'black mammy'.

mammy². *W. Afr.* [Of obscure origin.] Used *attrib.*, as **mammy boat, mammy chair**, a (wicker) basket or chair used on ships for conveying persons to and from surf-boats on the West African coast; **mammy-cloth** (see quot. 1971¹); **mammy lorry, wagon**, a small open-sided vehicle in West Africa; **mammy trader**, a market woman in West Africa.
1904 *Chambers's Jrnl.* 3 Dec. 15/1 You may elect to travel over the side in the 'mammy-chair', a huge barrel with part of its side cut away slung in the air by the steam-winch. **1909** MOORE & GUGGISBERG *We Two in W. Afr.* 16 So I found myself sitting in the 'Mammy chair', an ordinary basket-chair with ropes slung to the arms and back,..and in a moment I was whisked off the deck, swung over the side at the end of a long derrick, [etc.]. **1920** *Blackw. Mag.* June 848/1 A mammy chair was lowered, and we made the usual undignified ascent to the main deck. **1928** *Daily Express* 27 Jan. 6/3 A 'mammy' boat, which is simply a wicker basket with seats, is slung over the ship's side by crane. **1935** L. G. GREEN *Great Afr. Mysteries* xv. 192 The 'mammy-chair' is like a swingboat at a fair; just a wooden box with two seats facing each other. **1957** *Times* 17 Dec. 9/6 As we drove on to the ferry a 'mammy-waggon' full of them [*sc.* Ghanaian students] was pushed on behind us. **1959** *Times* 9 Nov. (Ghana Suppl.) p. iv/7 Coordination of the activities of the vigorous 'mammy' traders. **1959** *Listener* 31 Dec. 1156/2 The car-park [in Ghana] with its taxis and mammy-lorries. **1961** G. GREENE *Burnt-Out Case* I. i. 7 When there were no European visitors there were always the old women,..their bodies wrapped in mammy-cloths. **1961** *Listener* 2 Nov. 697/1 The mammy-wagons are the friendly little open-sided buses which ply, always crowded, between towns and villages, and which have their names painted in bright colours. **1962** *Ibid.* 22 Feb. 335/1 A mammy-lorry had stopped just outside, and was disgorging its contents. **1965** W. SOYINKA *Road* 19 Goes into the mammy-waggon stall through hidden entrance up-stage. **1970** P. OLIVER *Savannah Syncopators* 59 (*caption*) Hausa women... One wears a 'mammy-cloth' printed with portraits of Queen Elizabeth the Second and Prince Philip. **1971** A. BAILEY *In Village* (1972) vii. 56 One man I knew used to dress in the evenings in a mammy cloth, the colorful cotton robe the Africans swaddled themselves in. **1971** *Reader's Digest* (U.S. ed.) Oct. 30/1 [In Jiddah] West African 'mammy traders' hawk cocoa beans, salves for arthritis and gaily colored cloth.

mamo (ˈmeɪməʊ). [Hawaiian.] The sickle-billed Sunbird, *Drepanis pacifica*, a native of the Sandwich Islands, having rich yellow feathers.
1891 S. B. WILSON & A. H. EVANS *Birds Sandwich Isl.* 11, *Drepanis pacifica.* Mamo... This wreath..is made entirely of Mamo feathers. **1893** NEWTON *Dict. Birds* 225 The Mamo (*Drepanis*), whose beautiful feathers..have led to its extirpation.

mamony, variant of MALMENY *Obs.*

mamooda, -dee, -do, variants of MAHMUDI *Obs.*

mamootie (ˈmæmətɪ). Also **mammotie, mamooty, mam(m)oty, mamuty, mometty.** [ad. Tamil *mammaṭṭi*, altered form of *maṇvetti*, f. *maṇ* earth + *veṭṭi* spade.] A digging tool used mainly in India, shaped like a hoe with the blade at an acute angle to the helve.
1782 C. SALMON in G. W. Forrest *Sel. Lett. Govt. India* (1890) III. 855 He marched..with two battalions of sepoys, leaving the cavalry..who were ordered to make a show of entrenching themselves by digging with mamuties. **1852** F. A. NEALE *Narr. Residence Siam* viii. 138 By means of a mometty or hatchet..this fellow dug..a reservoir. **1858** P. L. SIMMONDS *Dict. Trade Products* 238/1 *Mammotie*, a road hoe, used in Ceylon. **1881** W. W. GREENER *Gun* 587 For shooting on the plains nothing but a mamoty, a crowbar, a mallet, and a couple of axes are required, and these can all be had in India. **1920** *Blackw. Mag.* Oct. 467/2 A company of pioneers each man with pick or shovel or mamootie slung in leather slings on his back. **1934** 'G. ORWELL' *Burmese Days* (1935) vi. 83 He..swung his mamootie aloft again and hacked at the dry ground. **1940** *Nature* 20 July 91/2 The scraping is effected with an ordinary *mammoty* (like a pointed spade with a recurved handle), removing about ½ in. of soil.

mamoring, variant of MAMMERING *vbl. sb.*

mamoutrie, variant of MAUMETRY *Obs.*

‖**mampalon** (ˈmæmpəlɒn). [? Native name.
Mr. W. W. Skeat rejects the suggested connexion with Malay *tikus ambang-bulan*, the name of a Malaccan viverra (Raffles in *Linn. Soc. Trans.* XIII. 273).]

A small viverrine mammal, *Cynogale bennetti*, of semi-aquatic habits, native of Borneo.
1843 J. E. GRAY *List Specim. Mammalia Brit. Mus.* 53 The Mampalon, *Cynogale Bennettii* Gray. **1885** *Riverside Nat. Hist.* (1888) V. 440 The Mampalon..has webbed feet, a very short, cylindrical tail [etc.].

mampus (ˈmæmpəs). *dial.* [Of obscure origin.] A great number, a crowd.
c **1730** *Dorset Vocab.* in *N. & Q.* (1883) 21 July 45/1 A mampus, multitude. **1857** *Gloss. Provincial Words Dorset* 6 *Mampus*, a great number. **1880** HARDY *Trumpet-Major* I. ii. 32 The mampus of soldiers that have come upon the down. **1904** —— *Dynasts* I. II. iv. 46 What a mampus o' folk it is here to-day!

mamsell (mæmˈzɛl). *colloq.* [a. F. *mam'selle*, contraction of MADEMOISELLE.] = MADEMOISELLE 3.
1842 THACKERAY *Fitz-Boodle Papers* Pref., I shall take care, Mamsell, that you return to Switzerland.

mamudee, variant of MAHMUDI.

Mamuluke, obs. form of MAMELUKE.

mamunt, obs. variant of MOMENT.

† **ma'muque.** *Obs.* [a. F. *mamuque* (Du Bartas), ad. Sp. *mamuco* (Lopez de Gomara 1552–3), the source of which is the corrupt form *Mamuco Diata* occurring in the Cologne edition (Jan. 1523–4) of Max. Transylvanus *De Moluccis*, where the Rome edition of Nov. 1523 has the more correct *Manuccodiata*: see MANUCODIATA.] A fabulous bird, the description of which is founded on erroneous accounts of the Bird of Paradise.

1591 SYLVESTER *Du Bartas* I. v. 803 But note we now, towards the rich Moluques, Those passing strange and wondrous (birds) Mamuques... Food-less they live; for th' Aire alonely feeds them: Wing-less they fly. **1606** *Ibid.* II. iv. II. *Magnificence* 288 To th' ever-Bowrs her oft a-loft t'advance, The light Mamuques wingless wings she has.

‖**mamur** (ma'mu:r). [Arab. *ma'mūr.*] An Egyptian official governing a district.

1836 E. W. LANE *Account* I. iv. 152 The whole of Egypt is divided into several large provinces, each of which is governed by an 'Osma'nlee (or a Turk); and these provinces are subdivided into districts, which are governed by native officers, with the titles of *Ma-moo'r* and *Na'zir*. **1899** A. S. WHITE *From Sphinx to Oracle* 108 Shortly afterwards I received the Mamur, who was accompanied by the officer commanding the police. **1900** G. BELL *Let.* 2 May (1927) I. 86 The Mamur (the Sultan's land agent). **1901** F. W. FULLER *Egypt* 259 Each mamurieh is under the charge of a Mamur, or Sub-Governor, who has in most cases been selected from among the native officers of the Egyptian army. **1902** *Encycl. Brit.* XXVII. 691/1 The provincial police is under the direction of the local authorities, the *mudirs* or governors of provinces, and the *mamurs* or district officials. **1958** L. DURRELL *Mountolive* ii. 43 Today, with British rule, the Copt is debarred from holding the position of Governor or even of *Mamur*—the administrative magistrate of a province. **1962** E. E. EVANS-PRITCHARD *Ess. Social Anthropol.* vii. 145 A Zande Prince went through the ceremony of blood-brotherhood with a *mamur* (Egyptian or Sudanese official) to whom he was bitterly hostile.

mamzer. Also **momser, momza, momzer.** Pl. **mamze'rim.** [a. late L. *mamzēr*, a Heb. word (*mamzēr*) adopted by the Vulgate in Deut. xxiii. 2 (where it appears with the gloss 'id est de scorto natus'), and hence frequently used in the Middle Ages.] A bastard. Also in extended uses as a term of abuse or familiarity.

1562 WINZET *Cert. Tractates* Wks. 1888 I. 43 Thair suld nocht be sa mony..scabbit Moabites, Amonites, and sclanderous Mamzeres..maid preistis. **1612** BP. HALL *Serm.* v. 60 Whatever become of these Mamzers, which do thus exclude themselves from the congregation of God [etc.]. **1865** KINGSLEY *Herew.* II. iv. 73 The only power that is, whom I see in England..is William the Mamzer. **1955** H. KURNITZ *Let.* Dec. in G. Marx *Groucho Lett.* (1967) 250 When the momzerim in the aisle seats have finished clubbing me I will come to California. **1960** WENTWORTH & FLEXNER *Dict. Amer. Slang* 342/1 *Momzer, momser*, one who borrows frequently, or who expects much attention and many favors; a sponger... Any disliked person; a bastard. **1963** 'R. L. PIKE' *Mute Witness* (1965) ii. 23 Johnny Rossi? The west-coast hood?.. And we're keeping *momsers* like that alive, now? **1964** W. MARKFIELD *To Early Grave* (1965) iv. 86 That mass man, that totalitarian type, that *momza*. **1968** L. ROSTEN *Joys of Yiddish* 254 *Momzer*..is often used to describe a very bright child, a clever or ingenious person, a resourceful, gets-things-done, corner-cutting type. **1970** L. M. FEINSILVER *Taste of Yiddish* 47 *A Mamzer*..(a bastard, a thief; hence a dirty crook). **1972** *Guardian* 10 Oct. 4/2 The problem of Mamzerim, the Jewish bastard outcasts. **1973** *Jewish Chron.* 19 Jan. 1/4 Hanoch and Miriam Langer are a brother and sister declared by a rabbinical court in Petach Tikva more than seven years ago to be *mamzerim* (children of an adulterous union). *Ibid.* 2 Feb. 23/4 The husband could not be given permission to remarry in an Orthodox synagogue, so he married in a Reform synagogue. Incidentally, any child from this marriage is not a mamzer.

man (mæn), *sb.*[1] Forms: *Nom. (Acc.) Sing.* 1–4 **mann**, (1 **monn, manna**), 1–5, 8–9 *dial.* **mon**, 4–6 **manne**, *Sc.* **mane**, (5 **moon**), 1– **man**. *Nom. (Acc.) Plural.* 1–4 **menn**, 2 **mæn(n**, 3 **mannes, mannen**, 4–5 *Sc.* **mene**, (5 **menne**, 6 **men**), 1– **men**. *Genitive sing.* α. 1–5 **monnes**, 1–6 **mannes**, 4 **monnis, -ys, mannus, manes, mones**, 4–6 **manis, mannys**, 4–7 **mannis, mans**, 6– **man's**. β. uninflected (*north.*) 4–5 **man**, 5 **mane**. *Genitive plural.* α. 1–2 **manna, monna**, 2 **monnan**, 2–3 **manne(n, monne(n**. β. 3–6 **mennes**, 4 **menes, -ys**, 4–6 **mennis, -ys**, 6 **menis**, 4–8 **mens**, 8–9 **men's**. γ. 2 **mennen**, 4 **mennene, menne**. δ. uninflected (*north.*) 4 **men**. *Dative sing.* 1–3 **men**, (1 **menne**), 3–4 **manne, monne**. *Dative plural.* α. 1–2 **mannum, monnum**, 2 **mannan, monnan**, 2–3 **manne(n, monne(n**. β. 3 **mennen**, 3–4 **menne**. [Com. Teut.: OE. *man(n, mǫn(n* (pl. and dat. sing. *męn(n)*, also rarely *manna* wk. masc., corresponds to OFris. *man, mon*, OS. *man* (inflected *mann-*, pl. *man*), Du. *man* (pl. in MDu. *manne, man*, in mod.Du. *mannen*, rarely *mans*), OHG. *man* sing. and pl., (MHG. *mann* sing. and pl., mod.G. *mann*, pl. *männer*), ON. *maðr*, rarely *mann-r*, accus. *mann*, genitive *manns*, pl. *menn*, rarely *meðr*, *mæðr* (Sw. *man*, pl. *män*, Da. *mand*, pl. *mænd*), Goth. *manna*, accus. *mannans*, genit. *mans*, pl. *mans, mannans*. The forms in the various Teut. langs. belong to two declensional stems, the OTeut. forms of which would be **mann-* and **mannon-*. (The ON. *man* str. neut., slave, may possibly be related, but the connexion is doubtful). The OE. plural *męnn* is the regular descendant of OTeut. **manniz*, and the dative *męnn* of OTeut. **manni*, from the cons.-stem **mann-*.

It was formerly regarded as certain (on the ground of the supposed correspondence with Skr. *manu* man) that the *nn* of **mann-* was derived from an original *nw*. The now prevailing view is that the second *n* represents the zero-grade of the suffix of a stem of which the Gothic form would be **manan-*. This hypothesis accounts for the otherwise obscure form *mana-* which the word assumes in Gothic compounds; if it be correct, the Teut. word and the Skr. *manu* cannot have any nearer relation than that of independent derivatives of a common root. They have been usually referred to the Indogermanic **men-*, **mon-*, to think (see MIND *sb.*), so that the primary meaning of the sb. would refer to intelligence as the distinctive characteristic of human beings as contrasted with brutes. Many scholars, however, regard this as intrinsically unlikely to have been the original sense, though no plausible alternative explanation has been suggested.

In all the Teut. langs. the word had the twofold sense of 'human being' and 'adult male human being', though exc. in Eng. it has been mainly superseded in the former sense by a derivative (Ger., Du. *mensch*, Sw. *menniska*, Da. *menneske*: cf. MANNISH *sb.*).]

I. 1. A human being (irrespective of sex or age); = L. *homo*. In OE. the prevailing sense.

†**a.** In many OE. instances, and in a few of later date, used explicitly as a designation equally applicable to either sex. *Obs.*

In OE. the words distinctive of sex were *wer* and *wif*, *wǽpman* and *wifman*.

971 *Blickl. Hom.* 9 Heofonrices duru..belocen standeþ þurh þa ærestan men. *c* **1000** ÆLFRIC *Gram.* ix. (Z.) 36 *Hic et haec homo*..ægðer is man ʒe wer ʒe wif. *c* **1000** —— *Saints' Lives* viii. 185 [St. Agatha says:] Eala ðu min drihten þe me to menn ʒesceope. *c* **1000** *Sax. Leechd.* II. 332 ʒif wife to swiþe offlowe sio monað ʒecynd, ʒenim niwe horses tord [etc.]..þ se mon swæte swiþe. *c* **1121** *O.E. Chron.* an. 639 (Laud MS.), þæs dohter wæs ʒehaten Ercongota halifemne & wundorlic man. *c* **1325** *Metr. Hom.* 155 And yef thaie [the husband and wife] riht riche men ware. *Ibid.* 156 Wit tua men [Simeon and Anna], that him comly grette. **1597** J. KING *On Jonas* (1618) 480 The Lord had but one paire of men in Paradise. **1752** HUME *Pol. Disc.* x. 159 There is in all men, both male and female, a desire and power of generation more active than is ever universally exerted. **1793** BURKE *Lett., to Comte de Mercy* (1844) IV. 144 Such a deplorable havoc is made in the minds of men (both sexes) in France, ..that [etc.].

b. In the surviving use, the sense 'person' occurs only in general or indefinite applications (e.g. with adjs. like *every, any, no*, and often in the plural, esp. with *all, any, some, many, few*, etc.); in modern apprehension *man* as thus used primarily denotes the male sex, though by implication referring also to women.

The gradual development of the use of the unambiguous synonyms *body, person, one*, and (for the plural) *folk(s, people*, has greatly narrowed the currency of *man* in this sense; it is now literary and proverbial rather than colloquial.

c **825** *Vesp. Hymns* i. 8 in *O.E. Texts* 401 Ic uteode ongeʒn fremðes cynnes menn [L. *exivi obviam alienigenae*]. *c* **950** *Lindisf. Gosp.* Matt. xii. 19 Ne ʒeheres ænig mon [*c* **1000** *Ags. Gosp.* nan man] in worðum stefn his. *Ibid.* xvi. 13 Huelcne cueðas menn sie sunu monnes? *c* **1000** ÆLFRIC *Saints' Lives* x. 191 Hwæt eom ic manna þæt ic mihte god forbeodan? *c* **1175** *Lamb. Hom.* 3 ʒif oniman seid eawiht. *Ibid.* 39 We forʒeueð þan monne þe us to agulteð. *Ibid.* 127 He wes imacad to monne ilicnesse. *c* **1200** *Trin. Coll. Hom.* 139 He turnde ut of þe burh into wilderne and fro mennes wunienge to wilde deores. *c* **1290** *S. Eng. Leg.* I. 291/112 Ich habbe i-sunegut manne mest. *a* **1300** *Cursor M.* 108 Scho prais ai for sinful menn. **1377** LANGL. *P. Pl.* B. Prol. 197 For many mannus malt we mys wolde destruye. **1390** GOWER *Conf.* I. 2 That of the lasse or of the more Som man mai lyke of that I wryte. **1393** LANGL. *P. Pl.* C. xiv. 46 Ac yf þe marchaunt make hus way ouere menne corne. *c* **1450** *Merlin* 262 A companye of yonge Gentilmen that beth high mennes sones. *c* **1460** FORTESCUE *Abs. & Lim. Mon.* vii. (1885) 125 Off somme man is highnes shall haue more thanke ffor money then ffor lande. *c* **1475** *Rauf Coilʒear* 46 Men callis me Rauf Coilʒear. **1577** B. GOOGE *Heresbach's Husb.* I. (1586) 15 We must remember that seruantes be men. **1592** SHAKS. *Rom. & Jul.* III. i. 59. **1632** SANDERSON *Serm.* 14 Measuring other mens actions and consciences. **1634** BP. HALL *Contempl., N.T.* IV. iii, I regard not the body; the soul is the man. **1764** REID *Inquiry* vi. §7 Wks. I. 142/2 No man can be sure..that it has the same appearance to him as it has to another man. **1855** TENNYSON *Brook* 33 For men may come and men may go, But I go on for ever.

c. Used indefinitely without article.

Chiefly in negative contexts, also in proverbial collocations, as in the traditional inn sign 'Entertainment for man and beast'.

1382 WYCLIF *John* vii. 46 Neuere man spak so, as this spekith. [Similarly in all later versions.] *c* **1450** *Mirour Saluacioun* 1363 Out of a hille a stone with out mans hande was kytte. **1523** CROMWELL *Sp.* in Merriman *Life & Lett.* (1902) I. 31 Yf yt had bene possible by mannys industry. **1530** PALSGR. 710/1 He deserveth it as lytell as ever dyd man. **1596** DALRYMPLE tr. *Leslie's Hist. Scot.* I. 41 Be ony slauchtir, or ony scheding of manis blude. **1600** J. PORY tr. *Leo's Africa* 41 They haue shambles of mans-flesh as wee haue of beeues and muttons. **1754** RICHARDSON *Grandison* II. iv. 48, I never fear'd man, since I could write man. **1847** TENNYSON *Princess* III. 118, I was courteous, every phrase well-oil'd, As man's could be.

Prov. The wind that blows from the east Is neither good for man nor beast.

d. Used predicatively without article in phr. ***to be, become, be made man***: to have or assume human nature.

c **1357** *Lay Folks' Catech.* (T.) 26 Iesu crist..toke flesh and blode, and become man. **1377** LANGL. *P. Pl.* B. v. 493 Þi sone..bicam man of a mayde. **1413** *Pilgr. Sowle* II. xlii. (1859) 48 Thou man bycome thy selfe, for mannes nede. **1549** *Bk. Com. Prayer, Athan. Creed.* **1574** WHITGIFT *Serm. bef. Eliz.* (1714) 11 Whether the Pope be God or man or a meane betwixt both? **1605** SHAKS. *Lear* III. ii. 45 Since I was man,..Such groanes of roaring Winde, and Raine, I neuer Remember to haue heard. **1649** J. ECCLESTON tr. *Behmen's Epist.* ii. §57. 30 It was for the soules sake that God became man. **1898** A. G. MORTIMER *Cath. Faith & Practice* II. vii. 186 The theologians..have taught that our Lord as Man had three kinds of knowledge.

2. a. In abstract or generic sense, without article: The human creature regarded abstractly, and personified as an individual; human beings collectively; the human race or species; mankind. In *Zoology*: The human creature or race viewed as a genus (*Homo*: in the present classification consisting of only one species, *H. sapiens*) of animals.

In OE. a few examples occur with the definite article. The Eng. use of the word as a quasi-proper name, without article, differs from the practice of most of the modern European langs. (cf. F. *l'homme*, G. *der mensch*), and from the usage of Eng. itself with regard to other generic names of animals: cf. 'the anatomical structure of *man* and that of *the lion*'.

c **825** *Vesp. Psalter* viii. 5 Hwet is mon [*Thorpe* se mann] ðæt ʒemyndiʒ ðu sie his? *c* **1000** *Ags. Gosp.* Mark ii. 27 Reste-dæʒ wæs ʒeworht for þa men, næs se man for ðam reste-dæʒe. *c* **1175** *Lamb. Hom.* 59 Hit wes for mon alle þinge he makede. *c* **1250** *Gen. & Ex.* 753 For mannes sinne ðus it is went. *a* **1300** *Cursor M.* 552 Man es clepid þe lesse werld. *c* **1380** WYCLIF *Sel. Wks.* III. 376 Þo principal poynt and ende of Cristis dyinge..was to save monnis soule. *c* **1440** *York Myst.* xxi. 84 Kynde of man is freele. *c* **1450** tr. *De Imitatione* I. xix, For man purposiþ & god disposiþ. **1577** VAUTROUILLIER *Luther on Ep. Gal.* 2 Mans weakenes and miserie is so great, that [etc.]. **1619** PURCHAS *Microcosm.* viii. 90 This Centre is enuironed with a Circle, called *Iris*, of many colours in Man onely. **1732** POPE *Ess. Man* II. 2 The proper study of Mankind is Man. **1774** GOLDSM. *Nat. Hist.* (1776) II. 132 Man is said to live without food for seven days. **1797** *Encycl. Brit.* (ed. 3) X. 507/2 In the *Systema Naturæ*, Man (*Homo*) is ranked as a distinct genus of the *Primates*. **1829** CARLYLE *Misc.* (1857) I. 269 Man is not only a working but a talking animal. **1845** R. CHAMBERS *Vestiges* (ed. 4) 234 The brain of Man. **1859** LOWELL *Villa Franca* 14 Men are weak, but Man is strong.

b. With a qualifying word, applied to prehistoric types of man, as ***Cro-Magnon Man, Neanderthal Man, Peking Man***, etc. (see under the qualifying words).

3. a. In *Biblical* and *Theol.* use, with *inner, inward, outer,* †*utter, outward*, used to denote the spiritual and material parts (respectively) of a human person; also with *old, new*, to denote the spiritual condition of those who are unregenerate and those who are regenerate. **b.** Hence ***inner, outer, lower man*** are jocularly used to denote parts of the physical frame of a person.

c **1000**, etc. [see INNER *a.* 3]. **1382** WYCLIF *1 Pet.* iii. 4 The hid man of herte [**1535** COVERDALE yᵉ inwarde-man of yᵉ hert]. **1382**, etc. [see OLD MAN 2]. **1587** GOLDING *De Mornay* xiv. 214 In the inward man there are (as ye would say) three men, the liuing, the sensitiue, and the reasonable. **1840** DICKENS *Barn. Rudge* xli, Gabriel's lower man was clothed in military gear. **1843** LE FEVRE *Life Trav. Phys.* I. i. v. 83 The outer was forgotten in the inner man.

II. 4. An adult male person. **a.** With special reference to sex.

c **1000** ÆLFRIC *Saints' Lives* ii. 78 He..sæde hyre ʒewislice hwæt heo man ne wæs. *c* **1200** ORMIN 2389 Ʒho wass hanndfesst an god mann þatt Josæp wass ʒehatenn. *a* **1225** *Ancr. R.* 286 Ert tu so wroð wið mon oðer wið wummon þet [etc.]? *c* **1375** *Sc. Leg. Saints* x. (*Mathou*) 347 Mariage..to cople man & vemene. **1377** LANGL. *P. Pl.* B. XIV. 264 As a mayde for mannes loue her moder forsaketh. **1387** TREVISA *Higden* (Rolls) VI. 421 O mayde mennene drede [CAXTON mennes, L. *O terror virgo virorum*]. **1508** DUNBAR *Tua Mariit Wemen* 42 Sen ʒe war menis wyffis. **1603** *Philotus* lxxxi, Ʒour douchter..Ane mannis claithis hes on hir tane. **1605** SHAKS. *Lear* II. iv. 281 Let not womens weapons, water drops, Staine my mans cheekes. **1632** LITHGOW *Trav.* III. 116 They speake..here the Hebrew tongue, man, woman and child. **1671** LADY M. BERTIE in *12th Rep. Hist. MSS. Comm.* App. v. 23 The Dutchesse.. was very fine in..a short mans coat very richly laced. **1728–9** MRS. DELANY in *Life & Corr.* 191 Every man took the woman he liked best to dance country-dances. **1880** G. MEREDITH *Tragic Com.* (1881) 5 Men (the jury of householders empanelled to deliver verdicts upon the ways of women).

¶ *contextually* = 'man-child'. *Obs.*

1578 T. N. tr. *Conq. W. India* 155 Their Priests sacrificed ten children of three yeares of age,..fiue of these children were menne, and the other fiue wemen.

b. *generically* (without article: cf. 2). The male human being. Also *predicatively* (cf. 1 d).

1591 SHAKS. *Two Gent.* v. iv. 110 Were man But Constant, he were perfect. **1601** —— *All's Well* I. i. 123 Man is enemie to virginitie. **1832** COLERIDGE in *Life Sir W. Hamilton* (1882) I. 543 Man's heart must be in his head. Woman's head must be in her heart. **1847** TENNYSON *Princess* VII. 259 Woman is not undevelopt man, But diverse. **1859** —— *Vivien* 630 Man! is he man at all, who knows and winks? **1897** MARY KINGSLEY *W. Africa* 318 As for the men, well of

course they would marry any lady of any tribe, if she had a pretty face,..that's just man's way.

c. With special reference to adult age. Sometimes: A male who has attained his majority. ***man and boy*** (advb. phr.): from boyhood upwards. † ***to write man***: to be entitled by years to call oneself a man. †(***to grow up***, etc.). ***to man***: to man's estate, to adult age. Colloq. phr. ***to separate*** (or ***sort out***) ***the men from the boys***: to distinguish which persons in a group are mature, manly, expert, etc.

a **1200** *Moral Ode* 117 Al þet ech Mon haueð idon soððen he com to monne. *c* **1200** ORMIN 8053 Whil þatt I wass litell child Icc held o childess þæwess, & son summ icc wass wexenn mann, þa flæh I childess cosstess. **1390** GOWER *Conf.* I. 344 He began to clepe and calle, As he which come was to manne. **1500–20** DUNBAR *Poems* xix. 14 Thus will thay say, baith man and lad. **1530** PALSGR. 863/2 From mans state, *des aige parfaict.* **1545** ASCHAM *Toxoph.* (Arb.) 100 In shoting both man and boye is in one opinion, that [etc.]. **1600** J. LANE *Tom Tel-troth* (Shaks. Soc.) 43 When chast Adonis came to mans estate. **1601** SHAKS. *All's Well* II. iii. 208, I must tell thee sirrah, I write Man: to which title age cannot bring thee. **1602** —— *Ham.* v. i. 177 (1604 Qo.), I haue been Sexten heere man and boy thirty yeeres. **1622** MABBE tr. *Aleman's Guzman d'Alf.* I. 146 Albeit I did write man, yet I was but a young Lad to speake of. **1654** CROMWELL in *Whitelocke's Mem.* (1853) IV. 170 They thought it more noble to die by the hand of a man than of a stripling. **1712** ADDISON *Spect.* No. 453 '*When all thy Mercies*' vi, Thine Arm unseen convey'd me safe And led me up to Man. **1729** T. COOKE *Tales, Proposals*, etc. 18 Their Friendship early in their Youth began, Encreasing dayly as they rose to Man. **1754** [see 1 c]. **1798** SOUTHEY *Eng. Eclogues* i. Poet. Wks. 1838 III. 3 I've lived here, man and boy, In this same parish, well nigh the full age Of man. **1802** WORDSW. '*My heart leaps up*', The Child is father of the Man. **1837** DICKENS *Pickw.* xxiv, An elderly gentleman in top-boots, who had been..a peace officer, man and boy, for half a century. **1962** J. BRAINE *Life at Top* ii. 39 Every day one was tested, the men were separated from the boys. **1967** *Listener* 16 Feb. 239/1 It is always quite a pleasure to see some really professional jazz players and hear their sounds and one of the best examples is *Jazz Goes to College*..which certainly sorts out the men from the boys. **1968** *House & Garden* May 36/4 The Dry Martini..is a drink that will quickly separate the men from the boys and the girls from their principles. **1972** *Listener* 17 Aug. 201/3 The ability to memorise a whole [chess] game within a few minutes is..what separates the men from the boys.

d. without express contrast. (*The man* is occasionally used for 'he', with a slight implication of depreciation, sympathy, or other feeling; similarly ***the good man, the poor man***, etc. So also *colloq.* in expressions like 'the late man', 'the present man', etc., referring to the former or present holder of an office or position.)

c **1175** *Lamb. Hom.* 31 Bluðeliche þe mon wile gan to scrifte and segge þe preoste þet he haueð ireaueð and istolen. *c* **1200** *Vices & Virtues* 45 Priestes and munekes and þ ese hadede mannen. *c* **1290** *Beket* 302 in *S. Eng. Leg.* I. 115 þe guode Man seint thomas. *a* **1300** *Cursor M.* 4828 (Cott.) We ar all a man [*v. rr.* an monnes, a manes, oon monnes] barnteme. *c* **1375** *Sc. Leg. Saints* i. (*Petrus*) 114 To theophil sanct paule askyt þane, quhy þat he þat wrechit mane held swa in presone. *a* **1400** *Pistill of Susan* 227 He was borlich and bigge,..More miȝti mon þen we his Maistris to Make. **1449** *Rolls of Parlt.* V. 147/2 A man horsed, and armed in bryganders. *a* **1674** CLARENDON *Hist. Reb.* xv. §38 And there is no question the man [*sc.* Cromwell] was in great agony, and in his own mind he did heartily desire to be king. **1735** BOLINGBROKE *On Parties* Ded. 27 You may pass..for a Man of extreme good Parts, and for a Minister of much Experience. **1760–72** H. BROOKE *Fool of Qual.* (1809) I. 24 The man in gibbets who hung by the road. **1837** O. A. BROWNSON in Ht. Martineau *Soc. Amer.* III. 347 With the discerning it has already become more honourable to call one simply a man than a gentleman. **1851** THACKERAY *Eng. Hum.* vi. (1876) 357 [He] was hand and glove with some of the best men in town. **1871** DISRAELI *Viv. Grey* II. xvi, If the forty country gentlemen who follow..our friend Sir Berdmore..were to declare their opposition to any particular tax, the present men would be beaten. [Not in ed. 1, 1826.] **1879** MEREDITH *Egoist* xiii. (1889) 116 Sir Willoughby was flattered and satisfied... A steady look of hers had of late perplexed the man, and he was comforted by [etc.]. *Mod.* The late earl was not much liked; the new man seems to be more popular.

e. Used in the vocative by way of introducing a remark, or parenthetically, now usually implying contempt or impatience; dialectally (in stressless forms *mun, min*) it is in common use as a meaningless expletive, being used in addressing both males and females. Hence in more general use as a form of address to both men and women, as a meaningless expletive, or as an interjection expressing surprise, delight, deep emotion, etc.; esp.: (*a*) in *S. Afr.*; (*b*) among Blacks; (*c*) among jazz musicians and enthusiasts. Also, ***man alive!*** (see ALIVE 2 b).

a **1400** *Pistill of Susan* 315 Mon, bi þe muche god,.. Vndur a Cyne..my seluen I hir se. **1530** PALSGR. 661/2 Plucke up thy herte, man, for Goddes sake. **1589** *Hay any Work* 1 Heere be non but frends man. **1591** SHAKS. *Two Gent.* II. iii. 44 Tut, man. **1705** VANBRUGH *Country-ho.* II, *Char.* [to *Mariane*] You see I can keep a secret—I am no girl, mun. **1772** *Gentl. Mag.* XLII. 191 'Twas quite to'ther thing, mun twas all complaisance. **1773** GOLDSM. *Stoops to Conq.* v. Wks. (Globe) 672/2 *Tony.* Why, that's it, mon. **1826** DISRAELI *Viv. Grey* IV. iv, Hah! what—what's all this! Here, read it, read it, man. **1874** A. BATHGATE *Colonial Experiences* ix. 110 Man! they all looked as if they had been shot, and would hardly believe me. **1890** BESANT *Demoniac* vi. 69 Why, man, with such a vice as yours, you would love your life too well. **1896** H. A. BRYDEN *Tales S. Afr.* i. 29 'Man!' he said, 'if I had not not been *shamed* into following you, I would never have come across that place.' **1901** M. FRANKLIN *My Brilliant Career* (1966) ii. 7 Here,..with splendid roads, mail thrice weekly, and a railway platform only eight miles away, why, man, my fortune is made! **1933** *Metronome* Aug. 23 Trum's greeting was in the Negro dialect he usually employed: 'Man! How is you?' **1952** M. TRIPP *Faith is Windsock* i. 21 The Jamaican stood up and stretched himself. 'Glad you woke me, man,' he said. **1958** *Observer* 14 Dec. 7/7 The coloured boy..doesn't like the English. 'I'm nineteen, man, and when I go into a public house, they all look at me.' **1958** *Star* (Johannesburg) 17 Dec. 17/1 His second play captures a South African atmosphere in flashes—his policeman begins almost every sentence with 'Man!' and ends it with 'Hey!' **1960** *Monthly Rev.* May 27 Negroes habitually call each other 'man' in reaction to a lifetime of being addressed by white folk as 'boy'. **1961** 'B. WELLS' *Day Earth caught Fire* ix. 145 'Cut that out, man,' the beatnik said. **1966** *Evening Standard* 1 Feb. 8/1 'I like to speak the truth, man,' he said addressing me [*sc.* a woman] with the universal Jamaican appellation of 'man'. **1969** C. F. BURKE (*title*) God is beautiful, man. **1971** *Black Scholar* Jan. 43/2 Man, this would make these fighters so mad. **1971** *Black World* June 54/2 Hey, only the squares, man, only the squares have it to keep. **1972** *New Nation* (Singapore) 25 Nov. 8/5 Close-cropped Charlie continued: 'Oh, you live in Bukit Timah... I used to visit my uncle there, man.' **1973** *Caribbean Contact* Feb. 4/3 'No, man,' the St. Lucian replies.

f. ***little man***: a jocular expression for a young male child. Similarly ***young man*** (see YOUNG).

c **1380** WYCLIF *Serm.* Sel. Wks. I. 399 Jesus toke a litil child... Crist toke þis litil man, and putte him in myddil of apostlis. **1468** *Paston Lett.* II. 319, I beseche yow that ye wolbe good mastras to my lytyll man, and to se that he go to scole. **1598** SHAKS. *Merry W.* IV. i. 8 Ile but bring my yongman here to Schoole. **1772** JOHNSON *Let. to Langton* 14 Mar. in *Boswell*, I congratulate you and Lady Rothes on your little man, and hope you will all be many years happy together. **1854** THACKERAY *Newcomes* lxxx, Clive's black figure striding over the snow..the little man..perched on his father's shoulder.

g. ***a man***: used quasi-pronominally = 'one' (ME. MAN, MEN, ME *indef. prons.*) or 'any one', but implying a reference to the male sex only. So † ***a man's self, a man's own***: in 16–17th c. often = the modern 'oneself', 'one's own'.

c **1478** *Caxton's Bk. Curtesye* 283 Who that vsith a mannes tale to breke Letteth vncurteysly alle the audyence. *c* **1485** *Digby Myst.* I. 465 Her, virgynes, as many as a man wyll, shall holde tapers in ther handes. **1597** BACON *Ess., Honour & Reput.* (Arb.) 70 Enuie..is best extinguished by declaring a mans selfe in his ends, rather to seeke merite then fame. **1610** SHAKS. *Temp.* II. ii. 41 Misery acquaints a man with strange bed-fellowes. **1625** BACON *Ess., Praise* (Arb.) 357 To Praise a Mans selfe, cannot be Decent.. : But to Praise a Mans Office or Profession, he may doe it with Good Grace. **1637** HEYLIN *Answ. Burton* 53 A man would think that you had said enough against your soueraigne. **1705** ADDISON *Italy* 14 A Man would expect..to find some considerable Antiquities. **1842** TENNYSON *You ask me, why, tho' ill at ease* 8 The land, where..A man may speak the thing he will.

h. In the following phr. with the sense 'individual (male) person': ***man by man, between man and man, man for man, man to man, per man, as one man*** (app. orig. a Hebraism = unanimously, with one accord, †altogether), ***to a man*** (= without exception: see TO *prep.*). Also ***man to man*** as *adj.* or *adv. phr.* (freq. hyphenated), (*a*) straightforward(ly), frank(ly); hence (*nonce-wds.*) **man-to-man-ness, man-to-mannish** *a.*

1382 WYCLIF *1 Esdr.* ii 64 Al the multitude as o man [Vulg. *quasi unus*, **1535** COVERDALE as one man, *later versions* together, Heb. כאחד] two and fourti thousend thre hundrid and sixti. *Ibid.* iii. 2 Thanne is gedered the puple as oon [**1388** as o man, Vulg. *quasi vir unus*, **1535** COVERDALE and **1611** as one man, Heb. כאיש אחד] in to Jerusalem. **1517** TORKINGTON *Pilgr.* (1884) 23 Ther Screvener..wrytyng ower namys man by man. **1535** COVERDALE *Judg.* xx. 8 So all the people gat them vp as one man. **1577** *F. de L'isle's Leg.* C iij, The lord of Rochefort..was on a time chalenged man to man..by Francis Duke of Guise. **1611** BIBLE *Josh.* vii. 14 The housholdes which the Lord shall take, shal come man by man. **1615** BEDWELL *Arab. Trudg., Talby*, These..are authorized to draw writings betweene man and man. **1677** HUBBARD *Narrative* I. (1865) 161 [He] said they would fight it out to the last Man. **1708** *Lond. Gaz.* No. 4482/2 That the Prisoners taken on either side be exchanged Man for Man. **1712** STEELE *Spect.* No. 444 ¶1 The ordinary Quack-Doctors..are to a Man Impostors. **1809** MALKIN *Gil Blas* x. x. ¶39 The balance of justice, between man and man. **1827** SOUTHEY *Hist. Penins. War* II. 48 With no farther ammunition than ten rounds per man more. **1846** TENNYSON *Golden Year* 35 And light shall spread, and man be liker man. **1892** R. KIPLING *Barrack-r. Ballads* 11 Man for man the Fuzzy knocked us 'oller. **1901** E. A. ROSS *Social Control* 29 So long as the struggle is man to man..a conscience is a handicap. **1902** E. NESBIT *Five Children & It* ix. 239 The best 'man to man' tone at his command. **1908** *Daily Chron.* 11 Aug. 4/5 Another form of suasion is the 'man-to-man' talk. **1940** N. MARSH *Surfeit of Lampreys* (1941) x. 141 Mike gave Alleyn a man-to-mannish look. **1943** J. B. PRIESTLEY *Daylight on Saturday* xxi. 167 'e remembered..an' stood me a pint. Now that's what I call man-to-man style. **1948** *Dublin Rev.* II. 11 The [Chinese] character for 'jen' is made up of 'man' and 'two'... I translate it 'man-to-man-ness'. **1952** S. KAUFFMANN *Philanderer* (1953) ix. 146 Perry spread his palms wide. 'Why don't you ask her?' Confidentially, man-to-man. 'I'd like to do it just to show her our gratitude for that week-end.' **1955** *Times* 5 Aug. 7/3 Talks man to man can serve the great international peace settlement. **1958** E. HYAMS *Taking it Easy* 49 Bachelor had a brisk, man-to-man style [of writing] which was immensely popular. **1973** 'M. INNES' *Appleby's Answer* xv. 128 A confidential and man-to-man note will be in order. **1974** A. PRICE *Other Paths* I. iii. 30 We must talk man-to-man now—if you would leave us for a moment, Mrs. Mitchell.

(*b*) ***man-to-man*** (Sport, orig. U.S.), used chiefly *attrib.* to denote a type of defensive strategy in which each player is responsible for marking one member of the opposing team. Also ***man-for-*** (U.S. ***-on-***) ***man***. Contr. with ZONE *sb.* 2 d.

1923 J. W. WILCE *Football* ix. 163 Man-for-man defense in football is very much the same as the guarding of a man in basket-ball. **1927** G. S. WARNER *Football Coaches & Players* 191 There are three..systems of defense to forward passing. These are zone defense, the man-to-man defense, and a modified form of man-to-man defense. **1937** [see *zone-defence* s.v. ZONE *sb.* 10 a]. **1957** *Encycl. Brit.* III. 181B/2 There are several variations of the zone defense, and combinations of man-to-man and zone defense. **1963** *Maclean's Mag.* 14 Dec. 21/1 'He's always at the outer edge of the rulebook anyway,' says Eric Nesberenko of the Chicago Black Hawks, who has played frequently against Howe man-on-man. **1970** [see *zone defence* s.v. ZONE *sb.* 10 a]. **1981** J. LEHANE *Basketball Fund.* v. 186 Constant drilling on making the *transition* from offense to defense is a requirement for effective full-court man-for-man pressure.

i. ***as a man***: (considered) in respect of his personal character, as distinguished e.g. from his achievements, abilities or learning, rank or wealth, etc. Similarly ***the man***: what one is merely 'as a man'; the person in his human (as distinguished from his professional, etc.) capacity or character.

1674 WYCHERLEY *Plain-dealer* I. i, I weigh the man, not his Title. **1706** E. WARD *Wooden World Diss.* (1708) 45 There's as great a Difference betwixt the Man and the Priest, as betwixt the Duchess upon the Stage, and her behind the Scenes. **1709** POPE *Ess. Crit.* 523 Nor in the Critic let the Man be lost. **1742** YOUNG *Nt. Th.* VIII. 242 A Father's Heart Is tender, tho' the Man's is made of Stone. **1771** MACKENZIE *Man Feel.* xxxv. (1803) 73, I cannot throw off the man so much, as to rejoice at our conquests in India. **1812** *Antigallican Monitor* 17 May 558/3 The high estimation they entertained of the merits of that illustrious person, both as a Minister and a man. **1856** EMERSON *Eng. Traits* x, The incessant repetition of the same hand-work dwarfs the man, robs him of his strength, wit, and versatility, to make a pin-polisher, a buckle-maker, or any other specialty. **1879** B. TAYLOR *Stud. Germ. Lit.* 174 We feel that the man must have been greater than his works.

j. ***the (very) man*** (ellipt. in predicative use): the man intended by some previous allusion; the man most suitable *for* some office, work, or need; the kind of man qualified or likely *to do* something. †Also *jocularly* said of a thing (*obs.*). ***the man for me*** (colloq. ***for my money***: see MONEY): the man whom I should choose to employ or support; often as an emphatic expression of approval.

1535 COVERDALE *2 Sam.* xii. 7 Thou art euen the man. **1573** TUSSER *Husb.* (1878) 28 When Easter comes, who knowes not than, That Veale and Bakon is the man? **1588** SHAKS. *L.L.L.* IV. ii. 127 Ouiddius Naso was the man. **1599** —— *Much Ado* II. i. 123 You could neuer doe him so ill well, vnlesse you were the very man. **1678** LADY CHAWORTH in *12th Rep. Hist. MSS. Comm.* App. v. 49 The House met today and are violent upon chussing a new Speaker and Sir Sawyer is lyke to be the man. **1849** MACAULAY *Hist. Eng.* x. II. 549 Lauzun was in every respect the man for the present emergency.

k. With possessive, ***my, your***, etc. ***man***: the person who can fulfil one's requirements, or with whom one has to do. *spec.* one's representative or envoy *in* a specified place.

1611 BIBLE *1 Kings* xx. 20 And they slew euery one his man [*Heb.* 'a man his man']. **1679** DRYDEN *Troil. & Cress.* II. iii, If Hector be to fight with any Greek, He knows his man. **1787** 'G. GAMBADO' *Acad. Horsemen* (1809) 34 A horse has various methods of getting rid of his man. **1811** BYRON *Hints fr. Hor.* 53 For gallygaskins Slowshears is your man; But coats must claim another artisan. **1821** —— *Juan* IV. xlix, His man was floor'd, and helpless at his foot. **1830** *Chron.* in *Ann. Reg.* (1831) 165/1 He..did not fire for some seconds, until he had fairly covered his man. **1833** MARRYAT *P. Simple* x, Our sailors had every one seized his man. *a* **1845** HOOD *Agric. Distress* vi, 'Nine pund' says he, 'and I'm your man'. **1855** KINGSLEY *Westw. Ho!* i, And who don't agree, let him choose his weapons, and I'm his man. **1864** LEMON *Loved at last* II. 228 Mr. Rasper entered the room... Cecil knew his man,—he merely bowed to him. **1958** G. GREENE (*title*) Our man in Havana. **1961** I. FLEMING *Thunderball* xiv. 154 Seems to me your President is taking all this a bit more seriously than his Man in Nassau. **1963** L. DEIGHTON *Horse under Water* vi. 33 'Welcome to Gibraltar,' said Joe MacIntosh, our man in Iberia. *Ibid.* xxxix. 154 Through the twilight 'our man in Cardiff' lifted a finger at the crooked castle of Caerphilly.

l. ***to be one's own man***: (*a*) to have command or control of oneself; to be in full possession of one's senses, faculties, or powers.

1556 in Strype *Eccl. Mem.* (1721) III. II. App. lviii. 197 When you were lunatike and not your owne man. **1562** *Child-Marr.* 79 This respondent..fell into such sorowe that he was not his owne man. *a* **1635** NAUNTON *Fragm. Reg.* (Arb.) 14 The king ever called her his sweetest and dearest Sister, and was scarce his own man, She being absent. **1748** RICHARDSON *Clarissa* (1768) IV. 362 Faith, Jack, thou hadst half undone me with thy nonsense... But I think I am my own man again. **1859** THACKERAY *Virgin.* xxxvi, I ate a bit at six o'clock, and drunk a deal of small beer, and I am almost my own man again now. **1902** *Daily Graphic* 27 Oct. 3/1 To many hundreds of thousands..the Royal progress on Saturday will be as a sign..that the King is indeed his own man again.

(*b*) To be at one's own disposal, to be one's own master.

1608 WILLET *Hexapla Exod.* 461 So might the seruant be sold..being not his owne man, but to be disposed of at the will of his master. *a* **1610** HEALEY *Cebes* (1636) 138 Yet brought he al their fury under and now is become his owne man. **1773** GOLDSM. *Stoops to Conq.* v. iii, So Constance Neville may marry whom she pleases, and Tony Lumpkin is his own man again. **1839** LOCKHART *Scott* (1869) II. xiv. 263 After breakfast, a couple of hours more were given to his solitary tasks, and by noon he [Scott] was, as he used to say, 'his own man'. **1843** BORROW *Bible in Spain* xlii. (Pelh. Libr.) 287 Pardon me for not being quite frank towards you ..but I dare not; I am not now my own man.

m. Prefixed to a name. *the man (so-and so)*: the man previously known or mentioned as bearing the specified name (cf. F. *le nommé* in legal use); sometimes with contemptuous emphasis; so, still more emphatically, *that man (so-and-so)*. Also ***(every, not a) man Jack*** (written also ***man-Jack, man jack, man-jack, manjack***): see JACK *sb.*[1] 2c; and occas. ***man John, man Jonathan*** (in speaking of Americans).

1826 SCOTT *Woodst.* xvi, Know'st thou not..that I have followed the man Cromwell as close as a dog follows his master. **1832** MRS. F. TROLLOPE *Dom. Manners Amer.* (ed. 4) II. 65 Every man Jonathan of them sets off again full gallop. **1838** [see JOHN 1 b]. **1844** DICKENS *Chimes* ii. (1845) 64, I am very much indebted to you for your courtesy in the matter of the man William Fern. **1845** DISRAELI *Sybil* III. VI. vi. 214 My missus says that not a man John of them is to be seen. **1849** *Blackw. Mag.* 697 At length the men were all embarked—the sick, the wounded, every man John of them. **1864** LEMON *Loved at Last* III. 190 If that should be the man Kiddy, do not admit him.

n. With qualification denoting the nationality, birthplace, dwelling-place, or creed to which a man belongs or the person (etc.) in whose service he is.

c **950-** [see ENGLISHMAN]. *c* **1250** *Kent. Serm.* in *O.E. Misc.* 26 Herodes..was michel anud and alle his men. *c* **1275** *Passion Our Lord* 286 ibid. 45 Son her-after on oþer þer com gon And seyde siker þu ert myd him a galilewis mon. *a* **1300** *Cursor M.* 19385 Sua wex þe cristen mens tale, þat [etc.]. *a* **1400** *Pistill of Susan* 157 Whon kene men of hir court comen til hir cri. *c* **1450** HOLLAND *Howlat* 542 Reskewand it agane the hethin mennis harmes. **1530** PALSGR. 242/2 Man of Turkey, *Turc.* **1535** COVERDALE *Judg.* viii. 15 The men of Sucoth. **1693** *Humours Town* 92 He was an Iniskilling-Man, and had eat half an hundred Irish Men for a Breakfast. **1701** DE FOE *True-born Eng.* I. 152 He Canton'd out the Country to his Men. **1798** LANDOR *Gebir* II. 42 Ye men of Gades. **1878** TENNYSON *Revenge* i, For my ships are out of gear, And half my men are sick.

o. Qualified by *university*, *Oxford*, *Cambridge*, etc., applied to one who is or has been a member of a (particular) university, public school, etc.

1573 G. HARVEY *Lett.-Bk.* (Camd.) 54 He is a Pembrook Hal man, ergo a good schollar. **1580** SPENSER & HARVEY (*title*) Three proper, and wittie, familiar Letters passed between two Vniuersitie men. **1687** ALDWORTH in *Magd. Coll. & Jas. II* (O.H.S.) 42 Dr. Haddon was a Cambr. man. *c* **1720** PRIOR *Epil. to Phædra & Hippol.* 3 An Oxford man, extremely read in Greek. **1796** in Whibley *In Cap & Gown* (1889) 88 Ye Johnishe men, that have no other care, Save onelie [etc.]. **1853** C. BEDE *Verdant Green* I. iii, The thought that he was going to be an Oxford man. **1866** *John Bull* 24 Mar. 202/1 All old Westminster men..will regret to hear [etc.]. **1882** J. L. G. MOWAT *Sinon. Barthol.* (Anecd. Oxon.) 2 He gives the authority of Brian Twyne for stating that he was an Oxford man.

p. With prefixed noun (sometimes in the gen. case) *man* is used to denote: (*a*) one who is connected with a certain place, building, profession, business, society, etc., as ***assembly-man, Banbury man, barman, bondsman, clergyman, churchman, countryman, exciseman, harvestman, Inns of Court man, journeyman, linesman, Paul's man, postman, railway man, salesman, waterman***, etc.; (*b*) one who uses or is skilled in the use of an implement or the like, as ***axe-man, brake-man, canoe-man, hammer-man, lathe-man, penman, swordsman***, etc.; (*c*) a trader in or manufacturer of an article, as ***ale-man, coal-man, ice-man, lead-man, milk-man, oil-man, pork-man, rag-and-bone man, timber-man***, etc. These combs. are treated under the prefixed words, or in their alphabetical place as Main words. In those which have come to be apprehended as single words (whether written with or without a hyphen) the pronunciation is (-mən).

(*d*) *spec.* One who is a specialist in or is expert in a specified subject; a supporter or adherent of a specified person; one who favours a specified product. See also *cruelty man*.

1921 T. S. ELIOT *Let.* 26 Oct. in *Waste Land Drafts* (1971) p. xxii, I have wondered whether he is quite the best man for me as he is known as a nerve man and I want rather a specialist in psychological troubles. **1938** A. HUXLEY *Let.* 12 Apr. (1969) 435 The cancer-man..had hit on something very fundamental. **1958** *Listener* 25 Sept. 449/2, I am therefore wholeheartedly a Galbraith man... Professor Galbraith is the first writer to attempt a systematic economic analysis of such a society. **1960** *Ottawa Citizen* 25 Mar. 1/8 Pearkes 'Bomarc Man' Despite U.S. Cutbacks... Defence Minister Pearkes today denied the Bomarc-B missile is a 'dead pigeon' and affirmed he still retained full confidence in it as an air defence system. **1964** *College Composition & Communication* XV. iv, The program of English studies was in the hands, not of the wise dean who encouraged the variousness of my undergraduate program, but of several gentlemen called 'the Malory man', 'the Restoration drama man', and 'the *Paradise Lost* man'. **1969** *Listener* 24 July 102/1, I had been the *Daily Telegraph's* main German man for some time. **1973** J. WAINWRIGHT *Touch of Malice* 89, I wouldn't have thought..you were a beer man. **1974** *Country Life* 25 Apr. 1008/1 A wonderful cruising ground for the yachtsman, be he a power or sail man. **1974** P. LOVESEY *Invitation to Dynamite Party* ii. 25 'Is it the hard stuff that you've taken a fancy to?' 'Not me, Sarge. I never was a whisky man.'

q. For *best man, handy man, reading man, sick man*, etc., see the adjs.; also DEADMAN, FREEMAN, NEW MAN, OLD MAN, RED-MAN.

r. ***every*** (or ***each***) ***man for himself***: applied to a situation in which each person is preoccupied with his own safety or advancement.

c **1386** CHAUCER *Knight's Tale* (1894) 1182 At the kinges court, my brother, Ech man for him-self. *c* **1515** BARCLAY *Ecologues* (1928) I. 1009 Eche man for him selfe, and the frende for all. **1562** J. HEYWOOD *Dialogue of Proverbs* II. ix, in *Works* sig. k4 Every man for him selfe, and god for us all. **1629** T. ADAMS *Workes* 422 That by-word, Euery man for himselfe, and God for vs all, is vncharitable, vngodly; and impugneth directly the end of euery good calling, and honest kinde of life. **1825** J. NEAL *Bro. Jonathan* III. xxix. 90 'Forward! Forward!' were the cries, on every side of our hero. 'Forward! forward! every man for himself!' **1922** H. WALPOLE *Cathedral* I. i. 14 They had been troublous times. It had been every man for himself.

s. ***the man*** (also ***the Man***): a person in authority; such persons collectively; *spec.* (*a*) a prison governor; (*b*) a policeman or detective; the police; (*c*) one's employer, 'boss'; (*d*) (*Black slang*) a white man; white people collectively; (*e*) a drug-pusher (*U.S. slang*).

1918 G. M. BATTEY *70,000 Miles in Submarine Destroyer* (1919) 302 Any body in authority is 'the man'. **1928** R. FISHER *Walls of Jericho* 306 *The man*, designation of abstract authority. He who trespasses where a sign forbids is asked: 'Say, biggy, can't you read *the man's* sign?' **1933** *Amer. Speech* VIII. III. 29/2 Unuther goddam word out o' you-all, an' Ah'll send ev'ry goddam one of ye up t' the Man. **1953** W. BURROUGHS *Junkie* (1972) ix. 87 When I first hit New Orleans, the main pusher—or 'the Man', as they say there —was a character called Yellow. *Ibid.* 159 '*The Man*', junk seller. 'The Man' is a New Orleans expression, and can also refer to a Narcotics Agent. **1962** *Amer. Speech* XXXVII. 270 *Man*, a policeman. A word used by teen-age drivers. 'When I heard the siren, I knew it was the Man.' **1962** J. BALDWIN *Another Country* (1963) II. ii. 243 One of the musicians came to the doorway, and said, 'Ida, honey, the man says come on with it if you coming.' **1963** *N.Y. Times* 18 May 12/2 A well-educated Negro said today: 'The demonstrations, I think, suggested to "The Man" that tokenism won't make it and that he has to come to grips with the problem right now.' 'The Man', in Negro parlance, is the white man. **1965** *Times Lit. Suppl.* 25 Nov. 1035 *Man* is the title by which one Negro addresses another... *The Man* is the way in which he speaks of the enemy, of the white. **1968** *Blues Unlimited* Nov. 8 They were share-croppers but the last crop put them so deeply in debt with 'the man' that they plan to quit farming. **1970** *Guardian* 3 Nov. 10/1 'The Man is repressive. The Man is fascist...' To the bombers and kidnappers the Man is authority. He is every policeman. He is President Nixon. He is Prime Minister Trudeau. **1972** J. MILLS *Report to Commissioner* 106, I heard you were the man, and if I really believed you were the man, you'd be dead now. **1972** *Guardian* 12 Aug. 9 Rus is not Uncle Tomming it around Harlem with 'the Man'. He has brought a foreign visitor. **1973** *Black World* Nov. 92/2 Their writing mainly concerns the street life—the pimp, the junky, the forces of drug addiction, exploitation at the hands of 'the man'. **1974** R. THOMAS *Pork-choppers* xi. 98 They'll be on my back for telling them something that they don't think the man needs to know.

¶**5. a.** Applied to beings other than human, e.g. God, the Devil, Death. *Obs.*

c **1510** *Lytell Geste Robyn Hode* ccxl, For god is holde a ryghtwys man. *c* **1550** *Lusty Juventus* (*c* 1560) C ij, He wyl say that God is a good man. **1588** *1st Pt. Jeronimo* II. iii, Your the last man I thought on, saue the diuell. **1592** SHAKS. *Rom. & Jul.* III. iii. 42 (2nd Qo., 1599), Flies may do this, but I from this must flie: They are freemen, but I am banished. **1599** —— *Much Ado* III. v. 40. **1625** B. JONSON *Staple of N.* I. Intermean, *Expectation*. But was the Diuell a proper man, Gossip? *Mirth*. As fine a gentleman, of his inches, as euer I saw trusted to the Stage. **17..** POPE, etc. *Mem. of P.P.* in *Swift's Wks.* (1751) V. 241 Do all we can, Death is a Man, That never spareth none.

†**b.** In certain plays printed in the 17th c., to escape the penalties against profane language on the stage, *man* was substituted in oaths for *God*.

1633 B. JONSON *Tale of Tub* II. i, For the passion of man, hold. *Ibid.*, Breath of man!

6. a. In a pregnant sense: An adult male eminently endowed with manly qualities. Also phr. ***to play the man*** (also †***men***).

14.. *Prov. Gd. Counsel* 76 in *Q. Eliz. Acad.* (1869) 70 Grace and good maners makyþ A man. **1526** TINDALE *1 Cor.* xvi. 13. **1530** PALSGR. 435/1 Have I nat acquit me lyke a man? **1548** UDALL, etc. *Erasm. Par. Mark* i. 12–15 Thou haste here behaued thyselfe valiauntly, and played the manne a while. **1560** DAUS tr. *Sleidane's Comm.* 86 b, That they should play the men. **1598** MARSTON *Sco. Villanie* vii, A man, a man, a kingdome for a man! **1721** R. WODROW *Suff. Ch. Scot.* (1838) I. I. v. §2. 394/1 The boys endured their punishment like men and Christians. **1734** POPE *Ess. Man* IV. 203 Worth makes the man, and want of it, the fellow. **1864** TREVELYAN *Compet. Wallah* (1866) 299 How their sire played the man in the time of the great troubles. **1900** MORLEY *Cromwell* v. vii. 453 Of that pettish egotism which regards a step taken on advice as a humiliation, he [Cromwell] had not a trace; he was a man.

b. *man of men*: a man of supreme excellence.

1594 MARLOWE & NASHE *Dido* III. iii, That man of men. **1606** SHAKS. *Ant. & Cl.* I. v. 72. **1623** MASSINGER *Bondman* I. iii, Corinth..hath vouchsafed to lend vs Her man of men, Timoleon, to defend Our Country. **1671** MILTON *P.R.* I. 122 This man of men, attested Son of God. **1821** SCOTT *Kenilw.* I. iii. 47 Wilt thou suffer this guest of guests, this man of men..to fall into the meshes of thy nephew? **1887** BROWNING *Parleyings, Chas. Avison* xvi, Pym, the man of men!

†**c.** Put for: Manliness, courage. *Obs.*

1602 MARSTON *Ant. & Mel.* I. Wks. 1856 I. 15 Heape up thy powers, double all thy man. **1605** SHAKS. *Lear* II. iv. 42 Hauing more man then wit about me.

7. A person of position, importance, or note. In phr. ***a man or a mouse***: either 'made' or ruined. Also, ***to make*** (a person) ***a man***: to ensure his prosperity or success.

[With *a man or a mouse* cf. the Ger. *mann und maus*.]

1541 *Schole Ho. Women* 386 in Hazl. *E.P.P.* IV. 120 Fear not, she saith vnto her spouse, A man or a Mouse whether be ye. **1542** UDALL *Erasm. Apoph.* 267 b, He was vtterly mynded to put al in hasard to make or marre, & to bee manne or mous. **1584** R. SCOT *Discov. Witchcr.* xv. xvii. (1886) 357 Applie it, and thou shalt be made a man for ever. *c* **1622** FLETCHER *Love's Cure* II. ii, Your Father has committed you to my charge, and I will make a man, or a mouse on you. **1624** SANDERSON *Serm.* I. 251 [To] set him upon his legs, and make him a man for ever. **1671** TILLOTSON *Serm.* (vol. I.) 227 What poor man could not cheerfully carry a great burthen of Gold..thereby to be made a man for ever. **1859** LEVER *D. Dunn* xx, The game is made. Red, thirty-two. Now for it, Grog, man or a mouse, my boy. Mouse it is! **1869** TENNYSON *North. Farmer, N.S.* ii, Doesn't thou knaw that a man mun be either a man or a mouse?

8. a. A husband. Now only *Sc.* and *dial.*, exc. in phr. ***man and wife***. (Cf. GOODMAN 2 b.)

a **1300** *Cursor M.* 23335 If fader sagh his sun þare,..þe wijf hir man or man his wijf. **1382** WYCLIF *Gen.* iii. 16 Thow shalt be vndre power of thi man [1388 hosebonde]. **1471** RIPLEY *Comp. Alch.* Ep. i. in Ashm. (1652) 116 Our Man, our Wife. **1567** *Gude & Godlie B.* (S.T.S.) 188 God send euerie Priest ane wyfe, And euerie Nunne ane man. **1633** FORD '*Tis Pity* IV. i, Be not amaz'd; nor blush, young lovely bride, I come not to defraud you of your man. **1724** RAMSAY '*This is no my ain House*' iii, To make me still a prudent spouse And let my man command ay. **1749** FIELDING *Tom Jones* I. xii, In less than a month the captain and his lady were man and wife. **1821** CLARE *Vill. Minstr.* II. 21 The wary wife..Sits up in bed to strike her man a light. **1842** TENNYSON *Dora* 4 He..often thought 'I'll make them man and wife'. **1889** BARRIE *Window in Thrums* 108 Nor would Nancey take it kindly if I called her man names.

b. A lover, suitor. ? *dial.*

1874 T. HARDY *Far fr. Mad. Crowd* xxxi, Go and marry your man—go on! **1898** BESANT *Orange Girl* II. xiv, You've put my man in prison—the properest man in St. Giles's.

9. A LIEGEMAN or vassal. Now *Hist.* †In ME. poetry often used *fig.*, e.g. of a lover.

c **1122** *O.E. Chron.* an. 1072 (Laud MS.) Se cyng Melcolm ..griðede wið þone cyng Willelm..& his man wæs. *c* **1175** *Lamb. Hom.* 33 Gif þu me dest woh and wit beon anes lauerdes men. *c* **1205** LAY. 4300 þer fore his mon he bicom & hærdsumnesse him solde don. *a* **1310** in Wright *Lyric P.* 93 To the [seinte Marie] y crie ant calle, thou here me for thi man. **1423** JAS. I *Kingis Q.* lxiii, Quhen sall ȝowr merci rew vpon ȝowr man, Quhois seruice is ȝit vncouth vnto ȝow? *c* **1465** *Eng. Chron.* (Camden 1850) 44 The Erl Douglas of Scotland cam in to Englond, & was swore to the king for to be his trew manne. *a* **1533** LD. BERNERS *Huon* xlv. 150 To become my man, and to do me homage. **1609** SKENE *Reg. Maj.* 42 b, Homage suld be made in this maner, that is, the maker therof, sall become his over-lords man [etc.]. *c* **1670** HOBBES *Dial. Com. Laws* (1840) 93 The Tenant shall hold his Hands together between the Hands of his Landlord, and shall say thus; I become your Man from this day forth. **1871** FREEMAN *Norm. Conq.* (1876) IV. xviii. 129 By taking service in William's army he had become the man of the Duke of the Normans.

10. a. A manservant; a valet.

man Friday: a servile follower or attendant; a factotum or servant of all work. (The allusion is to Robinson Crusoe's servant, whom he usually refers to as 'my man Friday'.)

13.. *Guy Warw.* (A.) 393 þou þat art a garsoun, & art mi man, & man schalt be. **1377** LANGL. *P. Pl.* B. XIII. 40 Ac þis maister ne his man no manere flesshe eten. **1381** *Rolls of Parlt.* III. 113/1 Johannes Pope, Taverners-man. **1463** *Bury Wills* (Camden) 16 To Raffe Otle sumtyme my man a blak gownne. **1486** *Bk. St. Albans* E vj b, The mayster to his man makyth his Roys. **1500–20** DUNBAR *Poems* xv. 19 To serve and leif in beggartie To man and maistir is baith schame. **1617** MORYSON *Itin.* III. 151 A Gentleman and his Man shall spend as much, as if he were accompanied with another Gentleman and his Man. **1638** T. RANDOLPH *Amyntes* Dram.-Pers., Jocastus, a fantastic shepherd and a fairy knight, Bromius, his man, a blunt clown. **1639** J. ENDECOTT in *Massachusetts Hist. Coll.* Ser. IV. (1863) VI. 136 One Samuel Eale, a man of Mr. Nathan Rogers, which Nele hath caryed with him. **1728** SWIFT *My Lady's Lament.* 174 Find out..who's master, who's man. **1791** CHARLOTTE SMITH *Celestina* IV. 117 There was no possibility of his man giving Willoughby notice. **1870** RAMSAY *Remin.* vi. (ed. 18) 209 Another functionary of a country parish is usually called the minister's man. **1885** G. ALLEN *Babylon* xix, Awkward, when people mistake your man for your nephew. **1887** *Athenæum* 16 Apr. 504/3 Count von Rechberg,..was Prince Bismarck's man Friday.

b. ***man-of-all-work***: jocular formation after *maid-of-all-work* (see MAID *sb.* 4 b).

1830 MISS MITFORD *Village* Ser. IV. 278 Mrs. Villars's man-of-all-work, Joseph. **1836** F. MAHONEY *Rel. Father Prout* (1859) 73 A genius infinitely superior even to the man-of-all-work at Ravensworth Castle, the never-to-be-forgotten Caleb Balderstone. **1896** FURNIVALL *Eng. Conq.*

Irel. p. vii, But illness prevented him; and so I (as the Society's man-of-all-work) had to take the book up.

c. In wider sense, as the correlative of *master*. In recent use commonly applied (chiefly in *pl.*) to workmen in contradistinction to their employers.

c1375 Sc. Leg. Saints xii. (Mathias) 127 Iudas þane become his mane, & mad his dwelling with hym þane. [1486, 1500–20, 1728: see a.] 1860 Nat. Assoc. Soc. Sci., Rep. Comm. Trades' Soc. 109 The masters had locked out the men ..from seventeen factories. 1872 Brassey Work & Wages i. 6 The masters had found it necessary..to reduce the rate of wages; but the men.. refused to accept the reduction.

11. Applied (chiefly in *pl.*) to the members of a fighting force; now *esp.* to the common soldiers as distinguished from the officers.

c1205 Lay. 636 Þe king of his monnen monie þusend læs. c1450 Merlin 244 Ther were..moo than a thousande me[n] slayn. 1535 Coverdale Ps. xviii. 29 In the I can discomfit an hoost of men. 1536 Wriothesley Chron. (Camden) I. 57 The King sent the duke of Norfolke, with an armie of menn. 1622 Donne Serm. 15 Sept. 11 Should God haue stayd to leuie and arme..men enow to discomfit Sennacherib? 1630 R. Johnson's Kingd. & Commw. 111 Foure thousand men would have made a shrewd adventure to have taken his Indies from him. 1878 Tennyson Revenge 10 I've ninety men and more that are lying sick ashore. 1880 Wheeler Short Hist. India 604 The English had lost more than 2,400 officers and men.

12. In university and public-school language, an undergraduate or student (as contrasted with a graduate or a don). Cf. 4 p.

1803 Gradus ad Cantabr. 89 At Cambridge, and, eke, at Oxford, every stripling is accounted a Man from the moment of his putting on the gown and cap. 1811 Lex. Balatron., Man (Cambridge), any undergraduate from fifteen to thirty. As a man of Emanuel—a young member of Emanuel. 1874 Lays Mod. Oxford 43 Every bulldog when he spies a Man without a gown, Promptly chases him and tries a- Main to run him down. 1897 Barrère & Leland Dict. Slang II. 103/1 [At Winchester Coll.] When a master wishes a 'man' to taste the sweets of a flogging he tells him to order his name to.

III. Transferred uses.

13. Applied to any image or portrait of a man, or to anything bearing a resemblance to a human figure. ***man of straw*** (fig.): see straw *sb.*

1636 T. Randall in Ann. Dubrencia (1877) 17 They looke like yonder man of wood, that stands To bound the limits of the Parish lands.

14. With qualification used for: A ship. See also man-of-war, Indiaman, merchantman, etc.

1473 J. Paston in P. Lett. III. 81 A few Frenchmen be whyrlyng on the coasts, so that there no fishers go out. 1558 W. Towrson in Hakluyt Voy. (1589) 125 The Christopher being the headmost & the weathermost man, went roome with the Admirall. 1665 Lond. Gaz. No. 3/4 They chased a Barbadoes and a Jamaica man into Limrick. a1700 B. E. Dict. Cant. Crew, Tant,..Mast of a Ship or Man. 1709 [see East India]. 1712, 1844 [see Indiaman]. 1778 H. Walpole Last Jrnls. (1859) II. 284 The Brest fleet was sailed, twenty-eight men-of-the-line. 1788 J. May Jrnl. & Lett. (1873) 33 In order to put them on board the Kentucky-man.

15. One of the pieces used in chess, draughts, and backgammon. (Cf. chess-men and meinie.)

c1400 Beryn 1820 The Burgeyse seid: 'comyth nere! ye shul se þis man, How he shall be matid, with what man me list!' He drouȝe, & seyd 'chek mate!' c1440 Gesta Rom. xxi. 71 (Harl. MS.) The first man, þat goth afore hath not but oo poynt, but whenne he goth aside, he takith anoþer...The secund, scil. alphyn, renneth iij poyntes both vpward and douneward. 1562 Rowbotham Pleas. & Wittie Play of Cheests A ij, As if thei had the cheste-bourde and men in their handes. 1562 J. Heywood Prov. & Epigr. (1867) 110 Eche other caste thou bearest a man to many. 1611 Cotgr., Dame,..a man at Tables, or Draughts. 1668 Dryden Ess. Dram. Poesy (1889) 77 Like a skilful chess-player by little and little he draws out his men. 1735 Bertin Chess vi, Never croud your game by too many men in one place. 1806–7 J. Beresford Miseries Hum. Life vi. xxxi, On asking for a backgammon-board seeing one brought in in ruins, the men half lost and the dice quite. 1865 Dickens Mut. Fr. ii. iv, The huffing of Miss Bella, and the loss of three of her men at a swoop.

16. In Cumberland, Westmorland, and Lonsdale, a cairn or pile of stones marking a summit or prominent point of a mountain; cf. ***low man***, ***high man*** as local names for particular cairns, also applied to portions of the mountains themselves.

1800 Wordsw. Rural Archit. 6 And there they built up, without mortar or lime, A Man on the peak of the Crag. 1871 L. Stephen Playgr. Eur. (1894) vii. 166 A stone man or cairn. 1897 O. G. Jones Rock-climbing 68 They reached the Low Man, as the nearly horizontal crest of the first huge buttress is called. Ibid. 243 Then to the right comes the actual Pillar Rock, the 'High Man'. Ibid., The Low Man, the immense buttress that from below hides the true summit altogether.

17. The obverse of a coin used in tossing.

[Originally, the side of a penny which has the king's head, the 'woman' being the side with the figure of Britannia.]

1828 'Bee' Living Pict. London 241 The person calling for 'man' or 'woman'. 1858 Househ. Words 4 Dec. 1/2 Up goes the dollar... 'Heads or tails? Man or woman?'

IV. Phrases and combinations.

18. *Man* enters into an almost unlimited number of phraseological collocations in which it is connected by a preposition with another sb. denoting quality, character, occupation, or profession; e.g. †***m. of afterwits, m. of antipathies, m. of chaff, m. of character,*** †***m. of charge, m. of dignity, m. of feeling, m. of glee, m. of healing, m. of honour, m. of nothing to do, m. of office, m. of peace, m. of practice, m. of preferment, m. of property, m. of rank, m. of sense, m. of talent, m. of theory, m. of title, m. of weight, m. of wisdom, m. of years***; also **man of action**, a man whose life is characterized by physical activity or deeds rather than by thoughts and ideas; †**man with the beard**, a drinking mug on which a bearded man was represented; **man of Belial**, a worthless or wicked man (cf. 1 Samuel xxv. 25); †**man in black**, a clergyman; **man of blood** (a Hebraism), one who is laden with bloodguiltiness; **man in blue**, a policeman (Farmer *Slang* 1896); †**man of cabinets**, an antiquarian; **man-in-the-cars**, the U.S. equivalent of 'man-in-the-street'; †**man of the church**, an ecclesiastic = churchman 1; †**man of the long coat** = *gentleman of the* long robe; †**man of death** (a Hebraism), one worthy to be put to death; **man of destiny**, a man looked upon as an instrument of destiny; *spec.* Napoleon I; **man of distinction**, a person who is distinguished in his looks, manners, and bearing; **man of the earth** *U.S.*, the wild potato vine, *Ipomæa pandurata*; **man of God** (OE. and early ME. **godes man(n**, a Hebraism), a man devoted to the service of God, (*a*) a saint, (*b*) an ecclesiastic; **man of Kent** (see quot. 1787, and cf. Kentish *a.*); **man of the moment**: see moment *sb.* 1 c; †**man in the oak**, a spirit supposed to inhabit an oak; **man of the people**, a man who comes from or identifies himself with the common people; a working-class man; †**man of Rome**, the Pope. For *man of business, m. of clouts, m. of colour, m. of fashion, m. of figure, m. of (his) hands, m. of the house, m. of letters, m. of mark, m. of means, m. of motley, m. of numbers, m. of quality, m. of religion, m. of service, m. of sin, m. of sorrows, m. in the street, m. about town, m. of the town, m. of wax, m. of the wood(s, m. of one's word, m. of few* or *many words, m. of worship*, see these sbs. Also ***lady's*** or ***ladies' man*** (see lady *sb.* 18); †***world's man*** (see world); man-of-law, man of the world, etc.

1597 *Man of Action [see action 1 a]. 1828 Scott Fair Maid of Perth in Chron. Canongate 2nd Ser. I. vii. 140 Our neighbour Proudfute..is of course a man of action. 1853 C. Brontë Villette II. xxiv. 193 Dr. John could think, and think well, but he was rather a man of action than of thought. 1937 Discovery July 226/1 The outdoor man of action and the indoor man of thought. 1963 Auden Dyer's Hand vii. 435 It was inevitable that..a dramatist would ask himself if the artist-genius could be substituted for the traditional man-of-action as a dramatic hero. 1652–62 Heylin Cosmogr. iii. (1677) 13/1 The People of this Country were..said to be also the Inventors of Augury..And yet for the most part *men of after-wits. 1837 Hist. in Ann. Reg. (1838) 412/1 William the 4th was not a *man of antipathies. 1614 B. Jonson Barth. Fair iv. iii, He has wrashled so long with the bottle here, that the *man with the beard hash almosht streek up hish heelsh. 1692 Gentl. Jrnl. May 5 The *Man in black makes but one of two in less than half an Hour. 1382 Wyclif 2 Sam. xvi. 7 Go out, go out, thou *man of bloodis [1611 bloody man, marg. Hebr. man of blood]. 1605 Shaks. Macb. iii. iv. 126 The secret'st man of Blood. 1648 [see blood sb. 3]. 1698 M. Lister Journ. Paris (1699) 58 The Vulgar Name, by which those *Men of Cabinets distinguish them is..Des Lampes. 1888 Bryce Amer. Commw. III. iv. lxxvi. 7 That representative of public opinion whom Americans call 'the *man in the cars'. 1799 Wordsw. Poet's Epit. 14 Or art thou one of gallant pride, A Soldier and no *man of chaff? 1746 Rep. Cond. Sir J. Cope 115 General Keith..is a '*Man of Character'. 1590 Sir J. Smyth Disc. Weapons Ded. 9 All great Captaines, Chieftaines, and *men of charge. 1523 Ld. Berners Froiss. I. clxii. 199 *Men of the Churche that cometh and goeth for treaty of peace. 1530 Palsgr. 318/1 Man of the churche, ecclesiastique. 1579 Fenton Guicciard. i. (1599) 45 Certaine *men of the long coate (so are called in Fraunce Lawyers, Doctors, and men of Iustice). 1535 Coverdale 1 Kings ii. 26 Thou art a *man of deeth. 1642 Ess. of a King in Bacon's Wks. (1858) VI. 596 Not to suffer a man of death to live. 1827 Scott Life Napoleon Buonaparte IX. 329 The great plans which the *Man of Destiny had been called upon earth to perform. 1909 Westm. Gaz. 26 Aug. 5/1 His man-of-destiny characteristics made him an interesting study to the newspaper correspondents. 1921 G. B. Shaw Back to Methuselah iv. ii. 178 Napoleon (impressively). I am the Man of Destiny. a1300 Cursor M. 27170 *Man of office or dignite,..werlds man, or clerc, or closterer. 1699 M. Lister Journey to Paris 40 It is..much more pleasing to see..a dead Friend, or Relation, or..a *Man of Distinction, Painted as he was. 1954 'P. Quentin' Wife of R. Sheldon xix. 167 He'd never been so innocent, so the man of distinction. 1971 D. Lees Rainbow Conspiracy vii. 111 He had a nervous apprehensive look that contrasted strangely with his man-of-distinction appearance. 1846–50 A. Wood Class-bk. Bot. 442 Wild Potato. *Man-of-the-Earth. 1771 H. Mackenzie (title) The *Man of Feeling. 1799 Wordsw. Fountain 20 The dear old Man,..The grey-haired *man of glee. a900 tr. Bæda's Hist. iv. xxv[i]. (1890) 352 þa ȝesweare se *Godes mon semninga. c1200 Moral Ode 266 in Trin. Coll. Hom., He nolde ihere godes men þan he sat at his biede. 1382 Wyclif 2 Tim. iii. 17 [16] That the man of God be perfyt, lerud to al good werk. c1450 St. Cuthbert (Surtees) 3588 Spak to þaim þe goddis man. 1658 Sir T. Browne Hydriot. v. (1896) 180 The man of God lives longer without a tomb, than any by one. 1748 Thomson Cast. Indol. i. lxix, A little, round, fat, oily man of God. 1814 Cary Dante, Paradise xiii. 30 The wondrous life Of the meek man of God [St. Francis]. 1847 James Convict II. 195 As soon as the *man of healing was gone,..he sprang up in his bed, hurried on his clothes [etc.]. 1577 tr. Bullinger's Decades (1592) 193 *Men of honours letters, or some such like stuffe. 1641 S. D'Ewes in Lett. Lit. Men (Camden) 169 Like a brave gentleman and man of honour. 1711 Addison Spect. No. 99 ¶10 If every one that fought a Duel were to stand in the Pillory, it would quickly lessen the Number of these imaginary Men of Honour. 1787 Grose Prov. Gloss. s.v. Kent, All the inhabitants of Kent east of the river, Medway, are called *Men of Kent,..the rest of the inhabitants of the county are stiled Kentish-men. 1861 C. Bede New Rector x. 104 The 'Men of Kent', you know, were never conquered! 1719 De Foe Crusoe ii. x, Like a *man of nothing to do. 1584 R. Scot Discov. Witchcr. vii. xv. (1886) 122 Robin Goodfellow, the spoome, the mare, the *man in the oke. 1604 Middleton Witch i. ii, Dwarfes, Imps, the Spoone, the Mare, the Man i'th'oake; the Hell-waine, the Fire-drake, the Puckle. 1611 Bible Ps. cxx. 7, I am for peace [marg. Or, a *man of peace]. 1849 C. Brontë Shirley III. ii. 36 Mrs. Pryor..wondered how her daughter could be so much at ease with a '*man of the people'... She felt as if a great gulf lay between her caste and his. 1885 H. James Little Tour in France xxiii. 151 A man of the people,..extremely intelligent,..yet remaining essentially of the people. 1971 W. J. Burley Guilt Edged vii. 116 'You have the most revolting habits, Jimmy.' 'A man of the people, that's me!' 1973 P. Malloch Kickback vii. 47 He was a man of the people. He'd been born in the Gorbals and had left school at fourteen. 1843 Carlyle Past & Pr. iii. v, This..almost stupid *Man of Practice, pitted against some light adroit Man of Theory. 1698 Money Masters all Things, etc. 131 The ugly and crippled were the only *Men of Preferment. 1861 M. Pattison Ess. (1889) I. 45 When no *man of rank or property was safe. 1581 J. Walker in Confer. iv. (1584) Z iij b, He..hath..fled to the *man of Rome. 1680 Rochester Poems 12 Dares chide at Kings, and raile at *Men of sense. 1711 Steele Spect. No. 153 ¶4 It is thus in the life of a Man of Sense, a short Life is sufficient to manifest himself a Man of Honour and Virtue. 1843 Mozley Ess. (1878) I. 156 The acuteness, point, and clearness which his controversial writings show, give him.. an undoubted rank as a *man of talent. 1632 Massinger City Madam i. ii, A sin your *man of title Is seldom guiltie of. 1855 Macaulay Hist. Eng. xii. III. 153 If any *man of weight..would..explain the state of things. 1742 Young Nt. Th. v. 775 The *Man of Wisdom is the *Man of Years.

19. Obvious combinations: **a.** simple attrib. and appositive, as ***man-angel, -beast, -devil, -dinner, -dog, -eye, -excellence, -famine, -fiend, -fish, -flesh, -fly, -life, -management, -mark, -meat, -miracle, -monster, -nature, -plague, -satyr, -seed, -service, -sex, -shape, -smell, -soul.***

a1711 Ken Hymnotheo Poet. Wks. 1721 III. 315 A new extemporaneous Race Of those *Man-Angels peopled the whole place. 1633 Ford Love's Sacr. iv. i, Some strangely-shaped *man-beast. 1648 Hunting of Fox 38 That Man-beast, the Major of London. c1600 Timon i. iv. (Shaks. Soc.) 16 His name is Philargurus, a *man-devill. 1832 Miss Mitford Village Ser. v. 88 An odious *man-dinner at the Clarendon. 1884 Chamb. Jrnl. 10 May 304/2 The *Man dog came from Russia, and was for a long time exhibited in Paris. 1887 G. Meredith Ballads & P. 19 The man-dog for his mistress thinks, Not less her faithful dog. 1711 Shaftesb. Charac. (1737) II. 305 In such a tender frame, as is indeed wonderfully commodious to support that *man-excellence of thought and reason. 1932 W. Faulkner Light in August i. 23 She traverses the ranked battery of *maneyes and enters the store. 1876 T. Hardy Ethelberta (1890) 262, I..found a husband before the present *man-famine began. 1638 Ford Lady's Trial iii. i, There is no valour in tugging with a *man-fiend. 1892 C. R. B. Barrett Essex Highways, etc. 139 The catching..of a *man-fish, or sea-monster, in the reign of Henry II. 1812 Sporting Mag. XXXIX. 17 Crib having been known to be the best bit of *manflesh nature ever cast in her mould. 1833 Fonblanque Eng. under Seven Administ. (1837) II. 403 The injustice of depriving the planters of their property in man-flesh without compensation. 1923 R. Graves Whipperginny 25 And frozen music dulls their need Of drink and man-flesh greed. 1832 Miss Mitford Village Ser. v. 81 The sedan-chair—a much more dignified conveyance..than any of the race of flies, whether horse-fly or *man-fly. 1918 D. H. Lawrence New Poems 43 The *man-life north-imprisoned, shut in the hum of the purpled steel. 1967 A. Battersby Network Analysis (ed. 2) xv. 271 If the senior executives of a company really feel that the risk is great, they might do better to shelve network analysis and continue with existing methods until better *man-management relations have been forged. 1971 Mod. Law Rev. XXXIV. vi. 680 The principle of an employer's responsibility for the results of 'teamwork by his team' goes to the centre of all thinking upon the techniques of organisation of groups and 'man-management' in large organisations. 1971 C. Bonington Annapurna South Face i. 7 The smaller the party, the closer you can get to the mountains uncluttered by all the..complications of man-management caused by a larger expedition. 1888 G. M. Hopkins Poems (1967) 105 Squadroned masks and *manmarks treadmire toil there. 1962 W. Stegner Wolf Willow iii. ii. 148 'What's a windigo?' 'What the Crees used to call an Injun that made use of *man-meat.' 1971 B. Malamud Tenants 207 The sweaty youths, holding long spears, leaped and yelped as they danced, their man-meat swinging like grapes in bunches in their loincloths. 1898 G. Meredith Odes Fr. Hist. 34 Sure of the blade that served the great *man-miracle [Napoleon]. 1610 Shaks. Temp. iii. ii. 14 My *man-Monster hath drown'd his tongue in sacke. 1784 Cowper Task vi. 499. 1928 Blunden Jap. Garland 16 Claw-tendrils reach, *man-monsters glare. 1895 How to get Married 107 Her knowledge of *man-nature. a1649 Drumm. of Hawth. Poems Wks. (1711) 37/1 Who have no law to their ambitions will, But (*man-plagues!) born are humane blood to spill. 1780 Chron. in Ann. Reg. 196/2 A large fierce animal which Mr. Atkins affirmed to be a centaur ..it proved to be a *Man satyr. 1934 Dylan Thomas 18 Poems 27 The growing bones, the rumour of *manseed Within the hallowed gland. 1971 G. M. Brown Fishermen

with Ploughs 4 Hoof-fast Njal bore his manseed womb-furled waveward. **1862** ANSTED *Channel Isl.* IV. xxiv. (ed. 2) 552 Every male between the ages of seventeen and sixty-five in Jersey, .. is bound to render *man-service to the Crown. *c* **1879** G. M. HOPKINS *Poems* (1967) 82 Breathing bloom of a chastity in *mansex fine. **1888** *Ibid.* 105 *Manshape, that shone Sheer off, disseveral, a star, death blots black out. **1922** JOYCE *Ulysses* 368 Perhaps they get a *man smell off us. **1938** M. K. RAWLINGS *Yearling* xi. 113 I'm jest lonesome for boy-smell and man-smell. **1961** R. P. HOBSON *Rancher takes Wife* viii. 118 She [*sc.* a cow moose] would trot over to the timber, lick her calf to its feet, and lead it off—away from the contaminated area of man-smell. **1682** J. BUNYAN *Holy War* (1905) 190 For here lay the excellent wisdom of him that builded *Mansoul, that the Walls could never be broken down. **1929** R. BRIDGES *Testament of Beauty* IV. 1391 From this dilemma .. Man-soul made glad escape in the worship of Christ.

b. appositive, passing into adj. = 'male', as ***man cook, -friend***, MAN-CHILD, MANSERVANT; in comb. with a female designation, as ***man nurse***, MAN-MIDWIFE; occas. with names of animals, as ***man seal***. (Cf. 22 a.)

1530 PALSGR. 242/2 Man lover, *amant. Ibid.*, Man nourse, *novrricier*. **1596** DALRYMPLE tr. *Leslie's Hist. Scot.* VII. 8 The manbarnes following of him sall be heyires. **1624** HEYWOOD *Captives* I. i, The man-makarel and marchant of madens fleshe. **1640** BROME *Antipodes* IV. iv, Enter women and man-scold. **1734** BERKELEY *Let. to Prior* 30 Apr. in Fraser *Life* vi. (1871) 227 A man-cook would be a great convenience to us. **1736** LD. HERVEY *Mem.* (1952) 182 The King's letter to the Queen about this affair was an extraordinary one, asking her, as he would have done a man-friend, what she thought of all this business. **1746** H. WALPOLE *Lett.* (1846) II. 147 The principal man-dancer. **1754–64** SMELLIE *Midwif.* I. Introd. 55 The lives of many women and children were saved by the skill of the man-practitioner. **1886** EMMA MARSHALL *Tower on Cliff* v. 68 If ever there was a man-witch, it's Sir Thomas Cooke. **1889** BARRIE *Window in Thrums* 99 Every man-body and woman-body on the farm. **1893** *Ladies' Home Jrnl.* Apr. 39/1 There is no impropriety in a man friend writing to you without having asked your permission. **1901** *Munsey's Mag.* (U.S.) XXV. 355/2 Frequently a man seal will swim out to a lady seal [etc.]. **1922** D. H. LAWRENCE *Fantasia of Unconscious* xi. 204 The woman .. will have a new man-friend, if nothing more.

c. In phrasal comb. used attrib., as ***one-man show, two-man rule***, etc.

1597 SHAKS. *2 Hen. IV*, I. ii 255 If I do, fillop me with a three-man-Beetle. **1882** [see ONE 35]. **1891** *Times* 6 Oct. 7/5 'One-man' photographic exhibitions. **1900** SIR W. HARCOURT in *Westm. Gaz.* 24 Aug. 6/1 Their forefathers had renounced one-man rule, and they were not likely to go back to two-man rule. **1902** *Daily Chron.* 16 July 9/1 A couple of four-man teams.

d. objective and objective gen., as ***man-container, -destroyer, †-fisher, -maker, -marrer, -moulder, -murder(er, -picker, -planter, -pleaser, -stealer, -subduer, -tamer, -thief, -tracker, -trapper; man-abhorring, -baiting, -carrying, -catching, -compelling, -degrading, -destroying, -devouring, -fearing, -lifting, -loving, -maiming, -making, -mimicking, -pleasing, -selling, -stealing, -stopping, -supporting, -tracking***, vbl. sbs. and ppl. adjs.; ***man-idolatry, †-pleasance, †-stealth; man-shy, -worthy*** (hence ***-worthiness***) adjs. (Cf. 22 b.)

1846 PROWETT *Prometh. Bound* 33 The bands Of *man-abhorring Amazons. **1655** FULLER *Ch. Hist.* IV. i. §8 To see this *man-baiting, all people of all kindes flock'd together. **1909** *Westm. Gaz.* 25 Feb. 4/1 The latter .. achieved for the first time in history a *man-carrying machine propelled by its own motive power. **1961** *Times* 28 Apr. 3/6 The placing in orbit of a man-carrying satellite. **1876** T. HARDY *Ethelberta* (1890) 291 A harassing mistrust of her *man-compelling power. **1711** SHAFTESB. *Charac.* (1737) II. 373 This mansion-globe, this *man-container. **1788** COWPER *Negro's Compl.* 46 Our sufferings, since ye brought us To the *man-degrading mart. **1824** J. SYMMONS tr. *Æschylus' Agam.* 137 Nor turn thy wrath 'gainst Helen, that she was a *man-destroyer. **1743** BLAIR *Grave* 210 Th' oppressive, sturdy, *Man-destroying Villains. **1864** KINGSLEY *Rom. & Teut.* i. (1875) 14 A mighty *man-devouring ogre. **1881** BRIDGETT *Hist. Holy Eucharist Gt. Brit.* II. 297 Free from *man-fearing and man-pleasing. *c* **1305** *St. Andrew* 6 in *E.E.P.* (1862) 98 Come, he seide, after me: and ic wole ȝou make *Manfischers. **1647** H. MORE *Song of Soul* II. ii. III. iv, Nor forc'd conceit, nor *man-idolatry. **1846** *Pract. Mechanic* June 235/1 The *man-lifting engine erected at United Mines, Gwennap .. for lowering and raising the miners. **1899** *Rep. Brit. Assoc. Adv. Sci.* 948 Man-lifting kites might be used instead of a balloon. **1927** C. L. M. BROWN *Conquest of Air* 122 By 1905 Cody had attracted official attention to his man-lifting kites. **1895** W. JAMES in *Internat. Jrnl. Ethics* Oct. 8 The old warm notion of a *man-loving Deity. **1809** *Sporting Mag.* XXXIII. 63 The royal and martial games of cock-fighting, bull-baiting, and *man-maiming. **1649** G. DANIEL *Trinarch., Rich. II*, cclxviii, In his want Pittied, perhaps by Maiestie, who now Was a *Man-Maker. **1901** G. MEREDITH *Reading of Life*, etc. 7 Maid-preserver, man-maker. *a* **1600** B. JONSON *Case is Altered* v. i, Gold, gold, *man-making gold. **1675** COTTON *Scoffer Scoft* 25 Some say that Man-making was no treason. **1684** OTWAY *Atheist* v. i, What, Manslaying! when all my thoughts were upon Manmaking. **1902** *Edin. Rev.* Jan. 30 All the man-making pastimes of Eton boys. *a* **1500** *Colkelbie Sow* 149 And a *man merrour, An evill wyffis mirrour. **1711** SHAFTESB. *Charac.* (1737) II. 203 How the dangerous *man-moulder wou'd proceed; and what wou'd be the event of his tampering. *a* **1300** *Cursor M.* 17303 (Cott.) Ʒe *man mortherar[s] so crus. **1939** W. B. YEATS *Last Poems* 17 *Man-picker Niamh leant and sighed By Oisin on the grass. **1656** TRAPP *Comm. Gal.* i. 10 Dastardliness and *man-pleasance. **1564** *Brief Exam.* **** b, This is very sore judgement, to condemne all your brethren for *manpleasers. **1727** SWIFT *State Irel.* Wks. 1755 V. II. 169 A man-pleaser at the expence of all honour, conscience, and truth. **1669** BAXTER *Power Mag. & Ch. Past.* I. (1671) 16 No *man-pleasing, no worldly honour to invite them. **1860** GEN. P. THOMPSON *Audi Alt.* III. cxxxvii. 110 This is what you call your Crown; it can shake hands with *man-selling. **1931** F. D. DAVISON (*title*) *Man-shy. **1582** N. T. (Rhem.) *1 Tim.* i. 10 To *man-stealers, to liers, to periured persons. **1884** S. E. DAWSON *Handbk. Dom. Canada* 272 It was as man-stealers that Europeans made their debut upon this continent. **1577** tr. *Bullinger's Decades* (1592) 395 The offence called Plagium, that is *man-stealing. **1769** BLACKSTONE *Comm.* IV. Index, Manstealing. **1638** MAYNE *Lucian* (1664) 382 Are you not affraid he should accuse you of *Man-stealth, and summon you before the Areopagus? **1899** *Kynoch Jrnl.* Oct.–Nov. 15/2 The *manstopping powers of the .. bullets appear to be considerable at short ranges. **1905** *Ibid.* Apr.–June 96 Man-stopping bullets are not allowed. **1973** *Guardian* 17 Mar. 13/2 Both guns increase the 'man-stopping' effectiveness of police marksmen. **1899** R. WHITEING *5 John St.* 272 Woman, as the *man-subduer. **1856** KANE *Arct. Expl.* I. xxvi. 343 It had a bad look, this *man-supporting August ice. **1922** JOYCE *Ulysses* 526 Master! Mistress! *Mantamer! *c* **890** *Laws of Ælfred* c. 9 §2 Maniȝu witu maran ðonne oðru; nu sint ealle ȝelice butan *manþeofe, cxx scill. **1863** DICEY *Federal St.* II. 254 This nation .. has for two generations been the accomplice of man-thieves. **1931** D. RUNYON *Guys & Dolls* (1932) i. 32 Nip and Tuck go back to Georgia .. with a big reputation as *man-trackers. *Ibid.* i. 17 They is *man-tracking bloodhounds from Georgia. **1815** *Zeluca* III. 167, I hope I shall not be marked out as a *man-trapper for my friend as well as myself. **18..** COLERIDGE (Webster), A better and more *manworthy order of things. **1841** EMERSON *Method of Nat.* Wks. 1875 II. 233 How all that is called talents and success in our noisy capitals, becomes buzz and din before this *man-worthiness.

e. instrumental, as ***man-created, -devised, -enslaved, -filled, -girdled, -gripped, -measured, -named, -powered, -propelled, -taught*** ppl. adjs. Also MAN-MADE *a.*

1849 SAXE *Times* 149 Mitres and thrones are *man-created things. **1547** *Life Abp. Canterb.* To Rdr. F ij b, This Church off Englande allowinge no *mandeuised order off regular ministerie. **1871** E. F. BURR *Ad Fidem* xi. 207 Man-devised religion. *a* **1873** LYTTON *Pausanias* (1876) 67 In the city one is the god-born, the other the *man-enslaved. **1909** E. POUND *Personae* 30 A bustling *man-filled place. **1847** TENNYSON *Princess* v. 419 Almost our maids were better at their homes, Than thus *man-girdled here. **1921** D. H. LAWRENCE *Sea & Sardinia* vi. 215 How old the real Italy is, how *man-gripped, and how withered. **1943** D. GASCOYNE *Poems 1937–42* v. 60 In the pure ray shed by the loss Of all *man-measured value. **1836** MRS. BROWNING *Poet's Vow* II. xv, Stars—revealed to man, And *man-named. **1959** *Times* 27 July 7/6 A purely private effort .. to achieve a *man-powered 'ornithopter'. **1962** *Listener* 10 May 812/2 A man-powered flight. **1937** *Sunday Times* 10 Jan. 27/5 All *man-propelled or horse-drawn traffic would automatically be relegated to the service roads. **1884** J. TAIT *Mind in Matter* (1892) 304 The apostle Paul did not consider himself *man-taught.

f. parasynthetic, similative, originative, or predicative, as ***man-bodied, -born, -breasted, -centred, -faced, -grown, -headed, -high, -minded, -shaped, -smelling, -stale, -tall, †-turned, -visaged*** adjs.; ***man-fashion*** adv.

1880 S. LANIER *Sunrise* 19 Sweet burly-bark'd, *man-bodied Tree. **1839** BAILEY *Festus* xix. (1852) 301 All theosophic lore Of *man-born, or angelic mind. **1859** TENNYSON *Guinevere* 244 And strong *man-breasted things stood from the sea. **1959** D. COOKE *Lang. Mus.* ii. 54 A proud, *man-centred existence, in which the emphasis was on personal happiness. **1877** G. MACDONALD *Marquis of Lossie* II. x. 116 There's mair poetry in auld *man-faced Miss Horn nor in a dizzen like them. *a* **1930** D. H. LAWRENCE *Etruscan Places* (1932) iv. 123 Some acts .. the man-faced bull accepts calmly. **1890** L. C. D'OYLE *Notches* 32 She .. rode *man-fashion. [**1587** GOLDING *De Mornay* xvii. 320 Not being a babe or a yoong childe, but being come to yeeres of discretion and a *mangrowne.] *c* **1640** J. SMYTH *Lives Berkeleys* (1883) I. 168 His owne sonnes now man-growne. **1883** *Blackw. Mag.* June 800 He was man-grown and in the Scottish service in France between 1420 and 1430. **1855** J. GOTT *Lett.* (1918) 81 Rows of sphinxes *man-headed and god-headed. **1941** L. MACNEICE *Poetry of Yeats* v. 98 The hero of this poem .. is a man sailing through faerie seas haunted by man-headed birds. **1679** MOXON *Mech. Exerc.* 164 Part of the Battlement being Breast high .. the other part *Man-high, to secure Men from the shot of their enemies. **1837** LONGF. *Frithiof's Homestead* 4 Man-high was waving the rye-field. **1932** AUDEN *Orators* II. 44 After the death of their proud master, who Stood man-high in his socks and paid his debts. **1954** J. R. R. TOLKIEN *Two Towers* 171 Man-high, but with goblin-faces. **1973** C. BONINGTON *Next Horizon* xiv. 209 We .. had reached the grass-line—great tussocks of coarse, man-high grass. **1842** TENNYSON *Talking Oak* 51 When his [*sc.* Hen. VIII's] *man-minded offset rose To chase the deer at five. **1855** A. DE VERE *Poems* 120 That love, or none, is fit for one *Man-shaped like thee. **1871** DUNCAN in *Cassell's Nat. Hist.* I. 6 The man-shaped, or anthropomorphous apes. **1932** W. FAULKNER *Light in August* ii. 44 The house unpainted, small .. *mansmelling, manstale. **1938** S. SPENDER *Trial of Judge* I. 15 Electric advertisements In city squares—those *man-tall golden letters. **1615** CHAPMAN *Odyss.* I. 205 In a throne, he plac'd The *man-turnd Goddesse. **1920** R. GRAVES *Country Sentiment* 39 Sing then of ringstraked manticor, *Man-visaged tiger.

20. a. Special comb.: **man-ape**, an anthropoid ape; **†man-bane**, an opprobrious name for tobacco; **man-bound** *a.*, 'detained in port in consequence of being short of complement' (Smyth *Sailor's Word-bk.* 1867); **man-boy**, a youth, an immature man; **man-broker** = CRIMP *sb.*[1] 2 (*ibid.*); **man-car** *U.S.*, a kind of car used for carrying miners up and down the steeply inclined shafts of mines on Lake Superior (*Cent. Dict.* 1890); **†man-case**, *nonce-wd.* for 'body'; **†man-catch** *v.*, to trap (men); **man-catcher**, (*a*) one who catches or traps men; (*b*) an instrument used in New Guinea for catching men (see quot. 1898); so **man-catching** *vbl. sb.*; **man-crab** (see quot.); **man-crazy** *a.* = *man-mad* adj.; **man-dealer**, a slave-dealer; **†man-dream** [DREAM *sb.*[1]], human joy, loud mirth; **man-engine**, a kind of lift for lowering and raising miners in a shaft, consisting essentially of a reciprocating vertical rod with platforms at intervals; **†man-entered** *a.*, initiated into manhood; **†man-fish** *Her.* = MERMAN; **man-fungus**, a fungus of the genus *Geaster*; an earth-star (*Treas. Bot.* 1866); **man-hair**, a man's pubic hair; **†man-huckster** *nonce-wd.* (applied to a 'mistress of the male stews'); **man-hungry** *a.*, desirous of a man; **man-in-space** orig. *U.S.*, an astronaut; freq. *attrib.*; **man-keeper** *local*, the water newt, *Lissotriton punctatus*; **†man-leech**, a whore; **†man-litter**, a sedan chair; **man-load**, a load such as one man can carry; **man-machine**, (*a*) = *man-engine*; (*b*) a man who acts mechanically; an automaton (cf. quot. 1904 s.v. 22 a below); (*c*) used as *adj.* to denote a relationship or communication between a man and a machine; **man-mad** *a.*, madly desirous of a man or men (cf. *man-wood* adj.); **†man-mender**, a surgeon; **man-mercer**, one who deals in man's wear; **man-merchandise**, slave-dealing; **†man-miln** *Sc.*, a hand-mill for grinding; **†man-minister**, a chaplain; **man-monkey**, an anthropoid ape; **man-mountain**, the name given to Gulliver by the Lilliputians; hence *allusively*; now applied esp. to a wrestler; **man-mountainism**; **man orchis**, (*a*) also ***green man-orchis*** or ***greenman orchis***, the greenish-flowered orchid, *Aceras anthropophora*; (*b*) *Orchis mascula*; **man-pack, manpack**, a compact package containing equipment or supplies, designed to be carried easily by one man; also *attrib.*; **†man peach**, a variety of peach; **man-power**, (*a*) the power or agency of man in work; (*b*) used as a unit of power or rate of working; (*c*) the number of persons available for a purpose, esp. for military service; also *attrib.*; **man-rail** (see quot.); **man-riding** *Mining*, the vehicular transport of miners underground; freq. *attrib.*; so **man-rider**, a train of vehicles designed for this; **man-root**, the American *Ipomæa leptophylla* (*Cent. Dict.*); **man-rope** *Naut.*, one of the ropes on each side of a gangway or ladder, used in ascending and descending a ship's side, etc.; **man-rope (knot)** (see quot.); **manself** [after HIMSELF *pron.*] *nonce-wd.*, man's self; **man-shift**, (the amount of work done in) a single shift worked by one man; **man-size(d)** *a.*, of the size of a man; large, full-size; large enough to occupy, suit, or satisfy a man; **man-starved** *ppl. a.*, suffering from the lack of a man or men; desirous of a man; **†man-state**, the age at which a Roman youth assumed the *toga virilis*; **†man-steid** *a. Sc.*, supplied with men; **man-strength** = *man-power* (*c*); **man-sty** [after *pig-sty*], a dwelling-house or hut unfit for human habitation; **man-tailored** *a.*, of women's clothes: tailored after the fashion of men's clothes; **†man-thews**, human customs, manners; **man-trade**, the slave-trade (cf. *man-dealer*); **man-way** *U.S. Mining*, 'a small passage used by workmen, but not for transportation' (Raymond *Mining Gloss.* 1881); **manweed**, fuller's teazel, *Dipsacus fullonum*; **man-wise** *adv.* and *pred. a.*, in the fashion or way of men; in respect of a man; concerning individual men; **†man-wood** *a.*, 'man-mad' , madly desirous of a man; **†man-worth** (see quot. 1670).

1878 *N. Amer. Rev.* CXXVII. 44 The myriads of years which have elapsed since the *man-apes began to stand upright. *a* **1618** SYLVESTER *Tobacco Battered* 515 Th' Heat and Drought of th' Herb American Being intensive (fitter call'd *Man-bane). **1630** J. TAYLOR (Water P.) *Proclamation Wks.* II. 252/1 A foule contagious, stinking Manbane weede. **1927** W. DEEPING *Kitty* ix. 115 This husband of hers, this *man-boy, what was he? **1945** S. SPENDER *Citizens in War* iv. 35 Tolerance defeated the religious man-boy who expected at least to be persecuted. **1655** FULLER *Ch. Hist.* III. vii. §13 He had an handsome *man-case. **1682** HICKERINGILL *Black Non-Conf.* B, Bespatter them, Trepan them, Teague them, Taffee them, and *Man-catch them. **1702** C. MATHER *Magn. Chr.* vii. 63 Captain .. fell into the Hands of these desperate [Indian] *Man-catchers. **1898** *Dublin Rev.* July 170 Another instrument of capture is the 'man-catcher', a flexible rattan fastened at one end in a loop, into which a sharp spike protrudes. As it is slipped over the foe, a sudden jerk is given to it, which causes the latter to impale the base of the skull. **1681** E. HICKERINGILL (*title*) The Horrid Sin of *Man-catching: a Sermon on Jer. v. 25, 26. **1772** RUTTY *Nat. Hist. Dublin* I. 375 *Cancer latipes Rondeletti*, a small shell-fish about the bigness of a wall-nut,

which has something like the delineation of a human face upon it, whence it has been sometimes called the *Man-Crab. **1923** G. Atherton *Black Oxen* xlii. 262 The young women would say, in their nasty slang, that I was probably *man-crazy. **1967** H. Van Siller *Biltmore Call* 128 Never liked the woman... Man crazy and two-faced. **1972** A. Amin tr. *Ahmad's No Harvest but Thorn* xi. 115 Let them call her bold... That Jeha was man-crazy. **1860** Gen. P. Thompson *Audi Alt.* III. cxxxvii. 110 The Transatlantic *man-dealer. *Beowulf* 1264 He [Cain] þa fag ȝewat, morþre ȝemearcod *mandream fleon, westen warode. *c* **1205** Lay. 23945 þa aras þe mon-drem [*c* 1275 mannes drem] þat þe wolde dunede a-ȝen. **1865** *Morn. Star* 7 Jan., In a few mines the *man-engine, which hoists and lowers the men, has been introduced. **1881** Raymond *Mining Gloss.*, *Man-machine* or *Man-engine*, Corn. and Derb. **1607** Shaks. *Cor.* II. ii. 103 His Pupill age *Man-entred thus. **1688** R. Holme *Armoury* II. 360/1 A Mere-man, or a Man-marine, or a *Man-fish.. by others termed a Triton. **1928** *Man-hair [see maidenhair 5 b]. *a* **1625** Beaum. & Fl. *Custom Country* v. v, Be so, and no more, you *man-huckster. **1951** J. Cornish *Provincials* 220 Douglas fell..to a girl described by Bunty as twenty-eight and strictly *man-hungry. **1959** *Daily Tel.* 21 Nov. 1/2 Capsule recovery is a crisis point in our *man-in-space programme. **1962** *Amer. Speech* XXXVII. 43 Before April 12, 1961, the concept expressed by *cosmonaut*..was rendered..by such terms as..*man-in-space*. **1968** *Economist* 28 Dec. 11/2 The man-in-space programme has earned itself enemies in powerful reaches of the scientific establishment. **1824** Mactaggart *Gallovid. Encycl.* 392 He was fond of drinking filthy fluids, and his belly gave birth to some *asks* and **man-keepers*. **1825–80** Jamieson, *Man-keeper*, a name given to the newt..by the inhabitants of Dumfr. and Roxb., because they believe that it waits on the adder to warn man of his danger. **1687** Sedley *Bellamira* IV. i, Thou punk, thou cockatrice, thou *man-leech, that suck'st their marrow and their money. **1640** Brome *Sparagus Garden* II. ii, A couple of lusty able bodied men..carry mee in a *Man-litter into the great bed at Ware. **1878** H. M. Stanley *Through Dark Continent* I. xiv. 376 Suna commanded his Katekiro to make up 300 *man-loads of hoes and old iron. **1855** J. R. L[eifchild] *Cornwall Mines* 279 Where they descend by the *man-machines their journey is easy both down and up. **1951** M. McLuhan *Mech. Bride* (1967) 18/1 There is a wide range of mental states engendered in the same *man-machine relationship. **1953** R. Lehmann *Echoing Grove* 240 He was now an automaton, a man-machine. **1967** Cox & Grose *Organiz. Bibliogr. Rec. by Computer* IV. 99 This is what is meant by man-machine dialoguing. **1904** *Man-mad [def. of *man-wood* adj. see in *N.E.D.*]. **1928** R. Macaulay *Keeping up Appearances* vii. 62 If a woman went on that way about men you'd call her man-mad. **1959** *News Chron.* 28 Aug. 6/3 The man-mad duchess..picks up the young peasant painter. *a* **1641** Suckling *Goblins* I. (1648) 15 A *Man-mender,.. Has broacht me in so many places, All the Liquor in my body will run out. **1703** *Brit. Apollo* No. 3 Man-menders then had noble pay—Which we call surgeons to this day. **1837** Miss Mitford *Country Stories* (1850) 99 What business had he in a great shop? a *man-mercer's they call it. **1788** Cowper *Let. to Lady Hesketh* 16 Feb., It being impossible to alledge an argument on behalf of *man-merchandize that can deserve a hearing. **1566** *Inv. R. Wardr.* (1815) 173 Ane *mann-miln for making of poulder, with thre mortaris. **1580** *Ibid.* 302 Ane man myln with all hir ganging geir. **1715** M. Davies *Athen. Brit.* I. 52 Richard Paice..was at first but a *Mann-minister to Thomas Langton Bishop of Winchester. **1782** Miss Burney *Cecilia* VI. x, Why you won't pretend you did not hear Miss Beverley say you were the truest ourang outang, or *man-monkey, she ever knew? **1726** Swift *Gulliver* I. ii, In the Right Coat Pocket of the Great *Man-Mountain (for so I interpret the *Quinbus Flestrin*). **1942** Berrey & Van den Bark *Amer. Thes. Slang* §429/1 Corpulent person,..*man mountain*. *Ibid.* §707/2 *Man mountain*, a large wrestler. **1956** J. Symons *Paper Chase* xxx. 240 He was trying desperately to establish some kind of grip that would move this man mountain. **1960** E. W. Hildick *Jim Starling & Colonel* xii. 105 'Are you—er—Mr Thimble?'.. 'Well, I'm not Man-Mountain Dean.' **1972** J. Mosedale *Football* viii. 105 A man-mountain in his time, he played tackle for the Giants and Packers. *a* **1861** Mrs. Browning *Bk. Poets* Poems 1890 V. 204 While Gower may blame 'his fortune'..for the dry specimen crumbled off from his *manmountainism. **1776** Withering *Bot. Arrangem. Vegetables* II. 543 *Man Orchis. **1868** *Paxton's Bot. Dict.*, Green-man orchis. See *Aceras anthropophera*. **1882** *Garden* 27 May 365/3 The popular name of Man Orchis given to *Aceras anthropophora* is certainly well bestowed, as a resemblance to a hanging man in the singular flowers of this plant is very apparent. **1967** *Electronics* 6 Mar. 52/2 The jungle..absorbs and deflects transmissions from *man-pack radio sets. **1970** *Islander* (Victoria, B.C.) 8 Feb. 5/3 Transportation was all by man-pack, pack-horse, canoe and raft. **1664** Evelyn *Kal. Hort.*, *Aug.* (1679) 22 Roman Peach, *Man Peach, Quince Peach [etc.]. **1862** H. Spencer *First Princ.* II. xiv. §114 (1875) 325 When horse-power and *man-power were alone employed. **1893** *Eng. Mechanic* Dec. 332/2 Maxim's early trials gave.. about 1 lb. per man-power. **1898** *Century Mag.* July 346 Jinrikisha,—those most fascinating man-power carriages. **1917** W. S. Churchill in *World Crisis 1916–18* (1927) II. 378 It is not possible to settle the question of man-power without a clear idea of the plan of campaign. **1919** *Brit. Manufacturer* Nov. 25/1 One of these man-power ploughs, adapted for small holdings and for use on terraced land, is driven by a cable. **1926** A. Bennett *Lord Raingo* xii. 60 Biggest piece of political camouflage ever attempted, the Man-Power bill is. **1972** *Accountant* 28 Sept. 386/2 The popular vogue of 'man-power planning'..must be more competently compiled where new relevant facts and figures are fed back from the human resource accounting system. **1972** *Daily Tel.* 28 Nov. 16 A great deal of manpower was being wasted before the merger. **1871** *Routledge's Ev. Boy's Ann.* Dec. 24 Along each side of the boiler is fixed a hand-rail, called a *man-rail. **1967** *Gloss. Mining Terms* (*B.S.I.*) x. 11 **Manrider*, a manriding train. **1950** H. F. Banks in E. Mason *Pract. Coal Mining* II. xxxv. 530/2 Where locomotives and large mine cars are in use, they serve also as a means of *man riding. *Ibid.* 531/1 Fig. 78 illustrates one type of man-riding car. **1952** T. Bryson *Mining Machinery* (ed. 3) xiv. 381 The train..comprises six man-riding carriages with seating accomodation for 18 persons, two brake cars.., and one tool car. **1972** (*title*) Specification for cars for manriding in mines. (B.S.I.). **1973** *Times* 2 Mar. (Wales Suppl.) p. iii/3 The coal board is now concentrating on increasing 'manriding'—trains from pit bottom to coalface—wherever the geology makes it possible. **1769** Falconer *Dict. Marine* II. (1780) *Tire-veilles*, the *man-ropes, or entering-ropes of the side. **1851** H. Melville *Whale* viii. 42 With both hands grasping the ornamental knobs of the man-ropes. **1883** *Man. Seamanship for Boys' Training Ships R. Navy* (Admiralty) (1886) 121 A double-wall, double-crowned..is used for man-ropes, stopper-knots, &c., also called a man-rope knot. **1880** G. M. Hopkins *Note-bks. & Papers* (1937) 271 He..would raise man..infinitely above *man-self to the divine justice. **1930** *Engineering* 3 Jan. 23/3 Variations in the standard of living ..are reflected in the average output per *man-shift. **1946** *Nature* 17 Aug. 226/2 In 1938..the Ruhr coal miner produced 30·5 cwt. per man-shift; in the same year the British miner produced 23 cwt. per man-shift. **1913** R. W. Service *Rhymes of Rolling Stone* 103 The *man-size mountains palisade us round on every side. **1928** *Publishers' Weekly* 16 June 2441 Since writing is a man-size job, he would have his hands full. **1963** *House & Garden* Mar. 130/1 (Advt.), Fourpenn'orth of Phurnacite 'eggs' will heat enough water for a man-size bath. **1975** *Times* 13 Jan. 8/1 We would..drink whisky out of mansize glasses. **1920** J. Gregory *Man to Man* (1921) xvii. 209 He was trying to hide a pair of *man-sized feet behind his table. **1920** S. Lewis *Main St.* xxiii. 277 A regular man-sized pair of pants. **1954** 'N. Shute' *Slide Rule* vii. 167 These wood-workers, accustomed as they were to man-sized factories, regarded Airspeed Ltd as a joke. **1972** F. Durbridge *Bat out of Hell* v. 174 Thelma..blew her nose on a tiny handkerchief which seemed ridiculous in her man-sized hand. **1961** *Times* 24 Oct. 13/2 Beautiful, *man-starved women. **1558** Phaer *Æneid* Life Virgil (1573) A iij, When he was thirteene yeere of age, he receaued the garment of *manstate. **1610** Healey *St. Aug. Citie of God* 140 He tooke on his gowne of man-state. *a* **1578** Lindesay (Pitscottie) *Chron. Scot.* (S.T.S.) I. 228 Thrie greit scheipis weill *man steid, weill wittallit and artaillzeit. **1931** *Ann. Reg. 1930* I. 23 The United States was greatly adding to its *man-strength. **1799** Southey *Comm.-pl. Bk.* IV. 518 The most miserable and beastly collection of *man-sties I ever beheld. **1887** *Pall Mall G.* 4 May 5/1 The unutterable 'man-sties' which do duty for labourers' cottages. **1922** Joyce *Ulysses* 153 Molly had that elephantgrey dress with the braided frogs. *Mantailored with selfcovered buttons. **1970** *Women's Wear Daily* 23 Nov. 31 (Advt.), Man-tailored jeans by Anvil Brand are now available. *c* **1000** *Juliana* 410 þæt he *mon-þeawum minum lifȝe. *a* **1250** *Prov. Ælfred* 432 in *O. E. Misc.* 128 þe hwile hit is lutel ler him monþewes [*later text* monnis þewis]. **1760** J. Philmore (*title*) Two Dialogues on the *Man-Trade. **1828** *Burton's Diary* III. 258 *note*, This lettered barbarian,..in the genuine spirit of the man-trade, ' hoped never to see our negroes in America become Christians'. **1829** *Glover's Hist. Derby* I. 108 *Dipsacus fullonum*, *manweed or fuller's teasel. **1901** *Man-wise [see *group-wise* adv. s.v. group *sb.* 6]. **1930** D. H. Lawrence *A propos Lady Chatterley* 39 Men experience the great rhythm of emotion man-wise, women experience it women-wise. **1579–80** North *Plutarch Lycurgus & Numa* (1595) 84 Andromanes; to say, *manwood [*printed* manhood, *corrected* in ed. 1612]. *a* **1586** Sidney *Arcadia* II. (1598) 229 Women man-wood, & men effeminate. *c* **1000** *Laws Hloðhære & Eadric* c. 1 ȝif mannes esne eorlcundne mannan ofslæhþ..se aȝend þone banan aȝefe, and do þær þriо *man-wyrþ to. **1670–91** Blount *Law Dict.*, *Manworth*, the price or value of a Man's Life or Head; every Man, according to his degree, being rated at a certain price, according whereunto, satisfaction was, of old, made to his Lord, for the killing him.

b. With a period of time, as ***man-day***, ***-hour***, ***-minute***, ***-month***, ***-week***, ***-year***, a day, hour, etc., of one person's work (or life). Also in extended use. Cf. *man-load*, *-shift* (sense 20 a above).

1925 E. O. Shebbeare in E. F. Norton *Fight for Everest, 1924* III. vi. 364 Each case would contain a sufficient ration of all kinds of food for a given number of 'men-days'. **1957** M. Swan *Brit. Guiana* I. iv. 83 The doctor told me that before the conquest malaria accounted for about 55,000 hospital man-days a year. **1972** D. Haston *In High Places* vi. 74 As for food... Some dried meat, bacon, nuts, chocolate and a few hot drinks per man-day. **1972** M. D. Papagiannis *Space Physics & Space Astron.* 280 In less than 10 years from the first manned flight we have accumulated more than a year of man-days in space. **1917** *Anti-Submarine Rep.* (Admiralty, R. Naval Air Service) Dec., Many air stations have large complements, and a comparison of the number of 'man hour's' work carried out with the the hours of flying on anti-submarine service will be found of interest. **1924** H. H. Emsley *Factory Costing* 76 The number of productive 'man-hours' in each department during each 'cost period'. **1951** R. A. Knox *Stimuli* III. xxii. 131 Experts are uncomfortably reckoning out what chances ..we are throwing away in terms of man-hours. **1971** *Nature* 29 Oct. 625/1 Countless man-hours have been spent on 'measuring' such allegedly useful entities as 'IQ' and 'reading age'. **1973** D. Westheimer *Going Public* ix. 133 How many man-hours do you spend actually executing an assignment? **1934** Webster, Man-minute. **1947** Crowther & Whiddington *Science at War* ii. 111 The actual working-time was only 53 man-minutes. **1956** *Jrnl. Assoc. Computing Machinery* III. 65 At the cost of..two or three man-months of programming time. **1969** J. Argenti *Managem. Techniques* vii. 42 This package cuts out nearly all the hard, highly skilled man-months of programming. **1973** *Computers & Humanities* VII. 190 The preparation of the double transcription of the Vulgate text took seven man-months. **1945** *Times* 19 Jan. 2/4 About 1,300,000 man-weeks remained to be consumed by March 31 if the labour force remained the same. **1961** *Jrnl. Oil & Colour Chemists' Assoc.* XLIV. 296 With proper planning fifty paints can be fully investigated in approximately two man weeks. **1928** A. S. Eddington *Nature Physical World* ix. 180 We must describe the amount of humanity in it [*sc.* Great Britain] as 400 million man-years. **1956** J. Masters *Bugles & Tiger* ii. 71 All my family's hundreds of man-years of work now focused on me. **1969** J. Argenti *Managem. Techniques* vii. 41 Linear Programming..might take two man-years to develop an 'LP Model' of a company. **1973** *Times* 12 Feb. (Anchor Project Suppl.) p. i/5 This level is likely to be little more than half the output a man-year that will be expected from single, integrated works of more than seven million tonnes capacity.

21. Combinations with *man's*: † **man's age** = man-age; † **man's blood**, (*a*) a kind of thistle; (*b*) the Gr. ἀνδρόσαιμον, 'a kind of St. John's wort, with blood-red juice' (Liddell and Scott); † **man's-bond**, a slave, bondsman, in quot. *collect. sing.*; **man's enemy**, the Devil; † **man's kind** = mankind; **man's man**, a man whose qualities are appreciated by other men; a man who is popular with other men; so **man's woman** (see also quot. 1905); † **man's meat**, food for men; also *transf.* in indecent sense; **man's mercer** (see quot.); † **man's motherwort** = Palma Christi; † **man's queller**, an executioner (cf. manqueller).

1594 T. B. *La Primaud. Fr. Acad.* II. To Rdr., The bodie of man in the third part of his age, commonly called *mans-age [etc.]. **1601** Holland *Pliny* II. 98 Acorna, *marg.*, A kind of thistle: some call it *Mans bloud. *Ibid.* 275 Some cal this herbe Androsæmon, *marg.* Mans bloud. **1611** Florio, *Acorna*, a thistle called Mans blood. *c* **1330** R. Brunne *Chron.* (1810) 115 Now er þise bot *mansbond, rascaile of refous. *a* **1800** *Laird of Waristoun* v. in Child *Ballads* IV. 31/1 At her richt hand There stood *Man's Enemy. *a* **1300** *Cursor M.* 14909 For he þe time sais command nei, þar he for *mans kind wil dei. **1390** Gower *Conf.* II. 264 And what hir liste,..Sche dede..That passeth over manneskinde. **1897** G. Du Maurier *Martian* 214 He had been essentially a *man's man hitherto, in spite of his gay light love for lovely women; a good comrade par excellence, a frolicsome chum, a rollicking boon-companion, a jolly pal! **1902** J. Buchan *Watcher by Threshold* v. ii. 277, I know he's supposed to be a man's man..but I'm honest enough to own to detesting him. **1960** Man's man [see dig v. 6 c]. **1972** P. Newton *Sheep Thief* v. 39 He had had comparatively little to do with women. Essentially a man's man he had been wrapped up in his calling. **1475** *Bk. Noblesse* (Roxb.) 30 They finding bothe horsmete and *mannysmete to youre soudeours. **1586** J. Hooker *Hist. Irel.* in Holinshed II. 166/2 In dooing of his seruice, he shall take horsse-meat, and mans-meat where he list. **1629** Burton *Babel no Bethel* 46, I will not envy him, so long as I feed on that which is sound and mans meate (as we say). **1664** Falkland *Marriage Night* II. i. 13 But is she Mans meat? I..can scarcely digest one in her Teens. **1760** Foote *Minor* II. (1767) 53 Here she has brought a pretty piece of man's meat already; as sweet as a nosegay, and as ripe as a cherry. **1803** S. Pegge *Anecd. Eng. Lang.* 267 A *man's mercer—One who furnishes small articles to taylors', as twist, buckram, stay tape. **1597** Gerarde *Herbal* App., *Mans motherwort is *Palma Cristi*. *c* **1450** *Mirour Saluacioun* 3270 Qwene Thamare..Whilk Cirus..*mannes qwellere hevedid. **1905** A. Bennett *Sacred & Profane Love* II. vi. 191, I was at last a *man's woman. I had a protector. **1930** W. S. Maugham *Writer's Notebk.* (1949) 232 She is what is called a man's woman, and exchanges chaff across the dining-room with the other guests. **1968** E. McGirr *Lead-Lined Coffin* iii. 108 Jeanie's a man's woman, you know, not a woman's woman.

22. Combinations with *men*: **a.** appositive, serving as plurals of combs. with *man* (see 19 a, b, and main words, e.g. man-child). Also men-folk, men-kind.

[**1382** Wyclif *Joel* iii. 9 Alle Men-fiȝters [Vulg. *viri bellatores*] cum to, and stey vp.] **1611** Bible *Eccl.* ii. 8 Men singers and women singers. **1632** Lithgow *Trav.* x. 463 O strange inhumanity of Men-monster Manglers! **1646** M. Lluellin (*title*) Men-miracles with other Poemes. **1687** T. Brown *Saints in Uproar* Wks. 1730 I. 72 Both among the Men-Saints and Women-Saints. **1739** Cibber *Apol.* (1756) I. 105 Those other men actors who..were equally famous in the lower life of comedy. **1741** Richardson *Pamela* (1824) I. 179 Do you, Beck, help Pamela to 'tend us; we will have no men-fellows. *a* **1745** Swift *Direct. Serv.* ii. (1745) 36 The Custom began..to keep Men Cooks, and generally of the French Nation. **1814** Sir R. Wilson *Pr. Diary* II. 346 His holiness made his entrance yesterday, drawn by men cattle. **1864** Pusey *Lect. Daniel* vii. 442 Large colossi and very long men-sphinxes. **1892** E. Reeves *Homeward Bound* 141 We had a dispute which were men Cingalese and which women. **1904** *Westm. Gaz.* 22 Nov. 12/1 Nowadays the Kaiser's men-machines take the best part of the pavement from anyone whom they may safely elbow off. **1907** A. C. Benson *Diary* 31 Jan. (1926) 157 Yet I do not squabble with my men-friends. **1910** F. Barclay *Rosary* ii. 10 But of men friends she had many. **1923** D. H. Lawrence *Birds, Beasts & Flowers* 172 Men-peasants from jungle villages dancing and running with sweat and laughing. **1952** S. Spender *Shelley* ii. 9 Hogg..was the first in a series of rather earth-bound men-friends. **1973** J. Burrows *Like an Evening Gone* i. 12 How many attendant men friends?

b. objective, instrumental, etc., synonymous with the corresp. combs. with *man* (see 19 d, e and main words, e.g. man-eater).

1692 Bentley *Boyle Lect.* 125 Those mountainous kind of animals and *men-bearing trees. **1682** S. Pordage *Medal Rev.* 274 Rebels and Traytors they will still Create, And are *Men-Catchers of the highest rate. **1599** Hakluyt *Voy.* II. II. 104 Which made them beleeue that we were cruell people and *men-eaters. **1719** De Foe *Crusoe* I. xiii, They..being men-eaters. **1634** Sir T. Herbert *Trav.* (Table) 228 Anzigues, a *men-eating Nation. **1619** A. Newman *Pleas. Vis.* (1840) 42 They have such *men-inchanting features. *c* **1550** Cheke *Matt.* iv. 19 Come after me and J wil maak yow *menfischers. **1895** *Churchman* No. 185. 268 *Men-fishing is most difficult work, but He who bade us go has likewise said 'I am with you'. **1553** T. Wilson *Rhet.* 51 Such *menflesht vilaynes make small accompte for killynge anye one. **1834** *Tait's Mag.* I. 124 The *men-hunters found a Guahibi mother, with three children. **1832** Miss Mitford *Village* Ser. v. 337 The *men-like bathing women. **1753** Foote *Eng. in Paris* I. Wks. 1799 I. 33 All the fraternity of *men-makers..; taylors, peruquiers, hatters, hosiers. **1619** Fletcher *M. Thomas* II. iii, Whither goe all these *men-menders, these Physicians? **1526** Tindale *Eph.* vi. 6 Not with service in the eye sight, as *men pleasars. **1615** Hieron

Wks. I. 604 Such a time-seruing, *men-pleasing, forsaking of flockes. **1632** SANDERSON *Serm.* (1681) II. 19 S. Paul, who in one place professeth men-pleasing,.. taking it in the better sense. **1297** R. GLOUC. (Rolls) 9333 Robbeors.. & manquellars [*MS. B.* *menquellares]. **1422** tr. *Secreta Secret., Priv. Priv.* 164 Traytouris, and rebelle, and trew men quelleris. **1563–87** FOXE *A. & M.* (1596) 70/2 Which all were esteemed as men quellers. *a* **1300** *E.E. Psalter* lviii. 3 And *men-slaers, sauve me fra þa. **1380** *Lay Folks Catech.* 736 (Lamb. MS.) Bakbyters and sowers of fals lesynggys.. arn wykkyd men-sleers. *c* **1450** *St. Cuthbert* (Surtees) 810 Menslaers, robbours. **1526** TINDALE *1 Tim.* i. 10 To *menstealers: to lyars and to periured. *a* **1677** HALE *Hist. Placit. Cor.* (1736) I. 9 Men-stealers were punished with death. **1860** PUSEY *Min. Proph.* 134 The Tyrians.. were slave-dealers, and in the earliest time, men-stealers. **1796** MRS. M. ROBINSON *Angelina* I. 36 The *men-trappers rushed in, and they forced him away. **1865** J. H. INGRAHAM *Pillar of Fire* (1872) 164 We are still idolaters, that is, mere *men-worshippers.

c. men-only *a.*, designating a place, etc., restricted for the use of men.

[**1935** (*magazine-title*) Men only. **1955** H. W. ALLEN in *Stag Party with 'Men Only'* 12 *The Sporting Times*, affectionately known from the colour of its paper as the *Pink 'Un*, that spicy and diverting *Men Only* weekly of Victorian days.] **1965** 'S. RANSOME' *Alias his Wife* vi. 57 Without discouraging women as customers, it had become a men-only place. **1967** N. FITZGERALD *Affairs of Death* ii. 34 It's a men-only bathing place. **1972** G. BEARE *Bee Sting Deal* x. 123 There was one hotel.. rigidly dry and rigidly men-only.

23. Combinations with *men's*: †**mens-kind** = MEN-KIND, †**menskins**, of the male sex; **Men's Liberation, Men's Lib.** orig. *U.S.* [after *Women's Liberation, Women's Lib.*], a movement aimed at freeing men from traditional views of their character and role in society; **men's room** orig. *U.S.*, a lavatory for men; also (ellipt.) ***men's***; **men's wear, menswear**, clothes for men.

1534 *Will Sir W. Butler* (Somerset Ho.), Euerye of my seruauntes aswell menskynes as womenskynnes. **1592** KYD *Sp. Trag.* III. v. 3 Wee mens-kinde, in our minoritie, are like women in their vncertaintie. **1970** *New Yorker* 19 Dec. 101 We recently read in the *Times* about a group called Men's Liberation, Inc., whose aim is to free men from their traditional role of 'all-powerful provider' and embolden them to cry, complain, feel sorry for themselves, and change their minds. The members of Men's Lib say they are tired of 'having to prove our masculinity twenty-four hours a day' and believe that if their cause should prevail 'outmoded concepts would disappear in the face of reality'. **1971** *N.Y. Times* 17 June 41 To the Women's Liberation Movement the sex-role distinctions mean pressure to conform to separate and unequal rewards for being a woman. To the Men's Liberation Movement they mean pressure to conform to the 'ego ethic'—or conform to perform. **1972** 'J. MELVILLE' *Ironwood* ix. 154 Three months of Tessa and they [*sc.* her male assistants] must have been heading for freedom and Men's Lib. **1929** 'E. QUEEN' *Roman Hat Mystery* iii. 31 Search the lounge downstairs. The men's room, the ladies' room. **1947** AUDEN *Age of Anxiety* (1948) ii. 51 Malin excused himself and went to the men's room. **1957** S. BECKETT *All that Fall* 24 *Mrs. Rooney.* 'Where were you all this time?' *Mr. Rooney.* 'In the men's.' **1962** J. WAIN *Strike Father Dead* 138 He's in the men's room. He's been wanting to go all evening, but as long as you were playing he didn't want to miss a note. **1972** R. LOCKRIDGE *Preach No More* iii. 43 This friend of his had.. gone to the men's, or something. **1947** *Partisan Rev.* XIV. 364 Seymour's taste in clothes and men's wear was loud, practically spectacular. **1972** P. FLOWER *Cobweb* II. 58 Among the heaps of flowers a wreath from the Menswear Dept. **1973** D. ROBINSON *Rotten with Honour* 35 [He] looked at Hale as if Hale were modelling menswear. **1974** *Radio Times* 28 Feb. 4/3 The family textile and menswear business.

†**man**, *sb.*[2] *Obs.* [OE. *mán* str. neut. = OS. *mên*, OHG. *mein*, ON. *mein*:—OTeut. **mainom*, neut. of **maino-* adj.: see MAN *a.*] Wickedness. Also *Comb.*, †**man deed**, wicked act.

Beowulf 978 Ðær abidan sceal maȝa mane fah miclan domes. *c* **1000** *Ags. Ps.* (Th.) cxviii. 69 Ys nu mæniȝfeald ofer me man and unriht oferhydiȝra. *c* **1000** *Phœnix* 457 [He] leahtras dwæsceþ mirce mandæde. *c* **1175** *Lamb. Hom.* 99 Deofles gast wissað to sunnan and to mandeden. *c* **1200** ORMIN 4478 Þatt tu þe loke wel fra man Inn aþess & i witness.

†**man**, *sb.*[3] *Obs.* Also 5 **mane**. [a. late L. *man* (Vulgate), a. Heb. *mān.*] = MANNA.

a **1300–1400** *Cursor M.* 6384 (Gött.) Þai called it in þair langag man [*Cott.* manna]. **1382** WYCLIF *Exod.* xvi. 31 The hows of Yrael clepide the name of it man. *c* **1485** *E.E. Misc.* (Warton Cl. 1856) 14 O Crystes modyre, That feede ȝeure chyld with the heyvynly mane. **1604** HIERON *Wks.* I. 500 As soone as they came into the promised land, the man ceased. **1644** Z. BOYD *Gard. Zion* in *Zion's Flowers* (1855) App. 11/2 Th' Egyptian hotch potch which God's Israel Preferr'd to Man, their whilom—Angel's food.

†**man**, *a. Obs.* [OE. *mán* = MHG. *mein*, ON. *meinn*:—OTeut. **maino-*: according to some scholars a pa. pple. from the Indogermanic root **mei-*, **moi-* to change.] Wicked.

c **1000** *Ags. Ps.* (Th.) liv. 15 Forðam.. on hiora midle [is] man inwit-stæf. *a* **1300** *Cursor M.* 6848 Athes noiþer sothfast ne man [cf. MANATH].

†**man**, *indef. pron. Obs.* Also **mon**. See also the weakened forms MEN, ME *indef. prons.* [OE. *man, mon* = OS., OHG. (MHG., G.) *man*; an unstressed form of MAN *sb.*[1]] = ONE 21.

Beowulf 3176 Þæt mon his winedryhten wordum herȝe. *c* **1000** *Ags. Gosp.* Matt. xiv. 11 And man brohte þa his heafod on anum disce. *c* **1175** *Lamb. Hom.* 139 Muchel man ach to wurþen þis halie dei. *c* **1220** *Bestiary* 267 Ȝet is wunder of ðis wirm more ðanne man weneð. *c* **1250** *Gen. & Ex.* 1488 A mete ðat man callen lentil gete. **1340** *Ayenb.* 86 Yef man dede þet kuead to-yens wylle: hit nere non zenne. *a* **1375** *Treat. Mass* 2 in *Lay Folks Mass Bk.* App. iv. 128 Hou mon scholde here hys masse.

man (mæn), *v.* Forms: 1 **mannian**, 4–6 **manne**, 6–7 **mann**, 6– **man**. [OE. *mannian*, f. *mann* MAN *sb.*[1] Cf. MLG., MDu., Du., MHG., mod.G. *mannen*, ON., Sw. *manna*, Da. *mande.*]

1. a. *trans.* (orig. *Mil.* and *Naut.*) To furnish (a fort, ship, etc.) with a force or company of men to serve or defend it. Said also of the men.

c **1122** *O.E. Chron.* an. 1087 (MS. E.) Heora ælc ferde to his castele & þone mannoden. *c* **1450** *St. Cuthbert* (Surtees) 5876 With' halfe þair men þis schip þai mande. **1480** CAXTON *Chron. Eng.* ccxliii. 288 The thre carrikkes were lade with dyuerse marchaundyse and wel y manned. **1494** FABYAN *Chron.* VII. ccxix. 241 Kyng Wyllyam also made .iiii. Stronge Castelles,.. and manned theym with Normayns. **1592** *Nobody & Someb.* in Simpson *Sch. Shaks.* (1878) I. 328 Man the Court gates, barricade al the streets. **1596** DALRYMPLE tr. *Leslie's Hist. Scot.* IX. 155 Tha schot out the capitan Erskin, and manit the hous. **1600** HOLLAND *Livy* VI. 90 Every man cried Al'arm, ran up to the walls to man them. **1627** CAPT. SMITH *Seaman's Gram.* vi. 27 Man the Boat is to put a Gang of men.. into her. *c* **1645** T. TULLY *Siege of Carlisle* (1840) 3 He found the other side [of the river] manned wth regiments of hors and foot. **1694** MOTTEUX *Rabelais* IV. xxiv. (1737) 101 Man the Pinnace, and get her by the Ship's Side. **1781** GIBBON *Decl. & F.* xlv. (1869) II. 711 The ramparts were manned. **1795** NELSON 21 Mar. in Nicolas *Disp.* (1845) II. 20 A Fleet half manned, and in every respect inferior to the Enemy. **1833** MARRYAT *P. Simple* xi, At last the frigate was full manned. **1861** HUGHES *Tom Brown at Oxf.* xiv. (1889) 134 The Oriel boat was manned chiefly by old oars. **1865** CARLYLE *Fredk. Gt.* XIV. ii. (1872) V. 165 The garrison of Eger.. barely mans its own works. **1874** GREEN *Short Hist.* vii. §6. 410 The English ships.. were manned with 9000 hardy seamen. **1876** VOYLE & STEVENSON *Milit. Dict.*, *To man*, this term is commonly used in artillery to signify the arming of a battery with men, ready for action. **1885** U. S. GRANT *Pers. Mem.* I. xxi. 292 One hundred men left to man the guns in the fort.

absol. **1713** STEELE *Guard.* No. 170 ⁋21 It is very rare if the French ever make use of any other ships than their own; they victual and man cheaper than we.

b. *Naut.* To place men at or on (a particular part of a ship), as at the capstan to heave anchor, or on the yards to salute a distinguished person. Said also of the men.

1697 TUTCHIN *Search Honesty* v. 16 The Boatswain's whistle, and they Man the Side. **1706** PHILLIPS (ed. Kersey) s.v., *Man the Capstan... Man well the Top... Man the Ladder.* **1743** BULKELEY & CUMMINS *Voy. S. Seas* 174 He came close by our Vessel, we mann'd her, and gave him three Cheers. **1796** *Log 'Agamemnon'* 19 Jan. in Nicolas *Disp. Nelson* (1846) VII. p. xxxii, Manned Ship and cheered Sir John Jervis. **1817** BYRON *Beppo* xxvi, A better seaman never yet did man yard. **1840** R. H. DANA *Bef. Mast* xv. 41 We manned the windlass, and hove, and hove away. **1875** BEDFORD *Sailor's Pocket Bk.* vii. (ed. 2) 282 As soon as the signal is perceived by those on shore, the whip.. will be manned, and the hawser hauled off by it to the wreck.

†**c.** To equip and send (a boat, occas. an army) with its complement of men in a certain direction (*out, forth, after..*). *Obs.*

1494 FABYAN *Chron.* VI. clxxiii. 169 Ye Londoners.. manned out a certayne nombre of men of armys. **1556** W. TOWRSON in Hakluyt *Voy.* (1589) 99 We manned out our Skiffe in like case to laye him aboorde. **1611** SPEED *Hist. Gt. Brit.* IX. xiii. 599 The Townesmen of Portsmouth and Dart maund [*read* mannd] forth a few ships at their owne perill and charge. *a* **1659** OSBORN *Ess.* ii. Wks. (1673) 558 When God Mans out his Hosts, the Poor are found in the Forlorn Hope. **1698** FRYER *Acc. E. India & P.* 51 We had mann'd three Boats after them. **1719** DE FOE *Crusoe* II. xi, I.. manned out the pinnace. *a* **1774** GOLDSM. *Hist. Greece* I. 320 Lysander at first manned out a few ships.

†**2. a.** To supply with inhabitants; to people. *Obs.*

c **1400** MAUNDEV. (1839) xviii. 187 This Yle is fulle wel inhabyted, and fulle wel manned. **1433** *Rolls of Parlt.* IV. 445/1 Howe youre Toune.. is wele enhabited and manned. *a* **1548** HALL *Chron.*, *Hen. VI* 156b, The Englishemen wer not of puyssaunce, either to man the tounes.. or to inhabite the countrey. **1598** SYLVESTER *Du Bartas* II. i. IV. *Handie-crafts* 272 Man-kind with fruitfull Race began A little corner of the World to Man. *Ibid.* II. ii. II. *Babylon* 185.

†**b.** *nonce-use.* To fill up with men. *Obs.*

1596 SPENSER *F.Q.* VI. xi. 46 [He] slew the formost that came first to hand So long till all the entry was with bodies mand.

†**3. a.** To provide (a person) with followers or attendants. *Obs.*

14.. *Sir Beues* 3080 (MS. S.), [He] armed him foot hot And manned him welle in a bot. **1526** SKELTON *Magnyf.* 441 Counterfet capytaynes by me are mande. **1597** SHAKS. *2 Hen. IV*, I. ii. 18 Thou art fitter to be worne in my cap, then to wait at my heeles. I was never mann'd with an Agot till now. *Ibid.* 66. **1606** CHAPMAN *Mons. D'Olive* Plays 1873 I. 221 To be mand with one bare Page and a Pandare. **1621** BP. MOUNTAGU *Diatribæ* 446 Such roysters and rake-shames as Mars is manned with, Hercules is not sure to be attended withall. **1752** FIELDING *Amelia* IX. ix, Come along, Jack, I have seen her before; but she is too well manned already.

b. †To furnish (horses) with riders (*obs.*). Also (*Australian*), to catch hold of and restrain (a horse).

1535 COVERDALE *2 Kings* xviii. 23, I wil geue ye two thousande horses, let se yf thou be able to man them. **1655** E. TERRY *Voy. E. Ind.* 411 To have horses alwayes in readinesse well mann'd. **1890** 'R. BOLDREWOOD' *Col. Reformer* (1891) 193 Man the horses, Eachin!

4. To fill (a post, office, etc.) with a man or men. Also with *up*; *spec.* to supply with the full number of workers required.

1821 SOUTHEY in *Q. Rev.* XXV. 295 The pulpits were manned with seditious preachers. **1822** J. W. CROKER in *C. Papers* 25 Aug., No Government.. was ever better manned in the subordinate departments than ours. **1900** *Blackw. Mag.* Jan. 37/1 There are often twenty to thirty of these committees to be manned in a session. **1947** *Times* 6 Feb. 5/5 Must industries be fully 'manned up' rather than 'manned'? Must the strong, simple transitive verb.. become as obsolete in England as it appears to be in America? **1947** *Hansard Commons* 18 Dec. 1895/1 Mining and agriculture are the two most vital industries which we must man-up. **1951** E. A. G. ROBINSON in D. N. Chester *Lessons Brit. War Econ.* iii. 52 Their most urgent jobs were not in fact manned-up as they would have liked. **1955** *Times* 20 May 11/6 The need to 'man up' undermanned industries 'in the national interest' might justify higher wages. **1969** *Times* 6 Mar. 23/1 'We're manned up again,' came a voice of relief.. Superstitious members.. now have the satisfaction of seeing their numbers rise from 13 to 20.

†**5.** To escort (a person, *esp.* a woman). *Obs.*

1567 DRANT *Horace, Ep.* vi. D ij, A cut throte rutterkin.. Who will, and dare retche forthe his hande, and man the throughe the croude. **1580** LYLY *Euphues* (Arb.) 291 She saide: will you not manne vs Fidus, being so proper a man? **1599** PORTER *Angry Wom. Abingt.* (Percy Soc.) 61 Thou knowest that Barnses wife And I am foes: now, man me to her house. **1607** DEKKER & WEBSTER *Northw. Hoe* IV. F 1 b, Wife, on with your ryding suite, and.. let my Prentice get vp before thee, and man thee to Ware. **1688** R. HOLME *Armoury* III. 71/1 A Waiting Man.. goeth abroad with his.. Mistriss as a Companion, Manning or taking her by the hand in all dangerous places.

†**6. a.** *refl.* To play the man. *Obs.*

c **1330** R. BRUNNE *Chron.* (1810) 224 Þei manned þam so boldely, on þam had non entre.

†**b.** *to man it out*: to bear up manfully. *Obs.*

1668 DRYDEN *All for Love* II. i, Well, I must Man it out.

7. To make manly or courageous; to brace *up*; to fortify the spirits or strengthen the courage of. Chiefly *refl.*

1617 FLETCHER *Valentinian* II. iv, Good your Grace, Retire, and man your selfe. **1630** *R. Johnson's Kingd. & Commw.* 26 Courage, is able at a pinch to man up it selfe. *Ibid.* 31 The conscience is an active sparke, and can easily man up all the powers of soule and body. **1668** DRYDEN *All for Love* I. i, My Soul's up in Arms, And Mans each part about me. **1707** MRS. CENTLIVRE *Cruel Gift* III, I feel my spirits gather to my heart, And man it out with courage for the tryal. **1711** ADDISON *Spect.* No. 164 ⁋5 Theodosius having manned his Soul with proper Thoughts and Reflections. **1810** SCOTT *Lady of L.* V. x, He mann'd himself with dauntless air. **1813** BYRON *Corsair* II. iii, Submissive, yet with self-possession mann'd. **1883** J. HAWTHORNE *Dust* xxvii. 225 So he manned himself, and said, quietly and firmly: 'Though [etc.]'. **1875** EMERSON *Lett. & Soc. Aims* ix. 238 Only that is poetry which cleanses and mans me. **1881** MRS. C. PRAED *Policy & P.* II. 251 He had manned himself to the sacrifice of his dearest hopes.

8. a. To invest with manly qualities or aspect; to make man-like. *rare.*

1615 CHAPMAN *Odyss.* IX. 688 One Vlysses; who I thought was mand With great and goodly personage [Gr. φῶτα μέγαν καὶ καλὸν]. **1616–61** HOLYDAY *Persius* 289 The different seasons of his life, and so riper age, might easily more man his countenance. **1839** BAILEY *Festus* viii. (1848) 78, I am a man in love, I cried; My heart was early manned. **1883** E. PENNELL-ELMHIRST *Cream Leicestersh.* 152 We manned ourselves in breeches and gaiters.

†**b.** *to be manned*: to be made man. *Obs.*

1577 tr. *Bullinger's Decades* Introd., Who for vs men,.. was incarnate and manned [L. *humanatus*]. **1677** GILPIN *Demonol.* (1867) 167 Just like the ravings of H. Nicholas, David George, and others, who.. discourse of being 'godded with God',.. and of God's being 'manned with them'.

9. To be the master of; to manage, rule. *Obs.* exc. *dial.* (see E.D.D.).

c **1330** R. BRUNNE *Chron. Wace* (Rolls) 6436 To manne Armoriche [*v.r.* to haf a reume] þou were worthi. **1597–8** BP. HALL *Sat.* IV. vi. 18 Who like a cot-queene freezeth at the rocke, While his breach't dame doth man the forren stock. **1637** RUTHERFORD *Lett.* (1862) I. 337 Happy is your soul if Christ man the house.. and command all.

10. *Falconry.* To accustom (a hawk, occas. other birds) to the presence of men. Hence (*transf.* and *gen.*) to make tame or tractable.

[The spelling *mained* in quot. 1632, if not a mere misprint, seems intended to suggest derivation from F. *main* hand.]

1575 TURBERV. *Faulconrie* 79 To the ende your hawke may be the better manned and the sooner reclaimed. **1590** GREENE *Mourn. Garm.* (1616) 53 There are no Hawks sooner manned then they of India. **1590** —— *Orl. Fur.* (1599) 2 Those siluer Doues, That wanton Venus manth vpon her fist. **1596** SHAKS. *Tam. Shr.* IV. i. 196 Another way I haue to man my Haggard, To make her come, and know her Keepers call. **1607** MARKHAM *Caval.* II. (1617) 30 After your horse is thus mand, and made gentle to be drest, shod, and handled. **1621** BURTON *Anat. Mel.* II. ii. IV. (1651) 268 Some reclaime Ravens, Castrils, Pies &c. and man them for their pleasures. **1632** *Guillim's Heraldry* (ed. 2) 227 Birds or fowles of Prey that are throughly mained and brought to the fist. **1633** MASSINGER *Guardian* I. i, A cast of Haggard Falcons, by me man'd. **1668** SHADWELL *Sullen Lovers* V. Wks. 1720 I. 98 Must people then be tam'd into marriage, as they man Hawks with watching? **1881** *Macm. Mag.* Nov. 39 He [the young hawk] is 'carried' for some hours amongst men, children, dogs, and horses..; and by this means,.. is soon 'manned'.

Hence **manned** *ppl. a.* (now esp. relating to aviation and space travel).

1617 MORYSON *Itin.* III. 141 Shropshire.. was a fortified and manned frontyer against the Welsh. **1685** BOYLE *Enq. Notion Nat.* vii. 330 Like a manned boat, where,.. there is an intelligent being that.. steers it, or otherwise guides it.

1810 SCOTT *Lady of L.* II. xvi, Four manned and masted barges. **1906** *Nature* 8 Nov. 35/1 (*title*) The first 'manned' flying machine. **1907** *Ibid.* 4 Apr. 538/2 During the course of the last few years very rapid strides have been made in investigating the upper air by means of manned and unmanned balloons and kites. **1936** G. HEARD *Exploring Stratosphere* 18 As it was obviously impossible to obtain sufficient data by manned balloons, small sounding-balloons were released bearing a light cage containing self-recording instruments. **1946** H. HARPER *Dawn of Space Age* 4 It is intended to develop manned and instrument-carrying rockets capable of being projected in and beyond the earth's atmosphere. **1957** *Observer* 28 July 6/3 In the present phase of manned bombers, which will last into the mid-1960s, the United States Strategic Air Command has some 1,500 B47 medium bombers capable of attacking the Soviet Union from bases around its periphery. **1960** *John o' London's* 7 Apr. 395/1 Manned entry into interplanetary space is inevitable. **1968** *Times* 16 Oct. 8/7 The probe seemed to be a trial for an imminent manned flight to the moon. **1971** *Guardian* 3 July 1/3 The indication of a technical failure rather than a human failure..should be encouraging both to the Russian and the US manned space programmes.

man, var. MAUN *v.*, must; var. MAUND *sb.*[2], an Indian weight: obs. north. f. MOAN *v.*

mana ('mɑːnə). [Maori.] Power in general, authority, prestige; *spec.* in primitive religion, an impersonal supernatural power which can be associated with people or with objects and which can be transmitted or inherited.

1843 E. DIEFFENBACH *Trav. N.Z.* II. III. ix. 371/2 Mana —command, authority, power. **1855** R. TAYLOR *Te Ika a Maui* 279 The natives..feel..that with the land, their *mana*, or power, has gone likewise. **1858** *Richmond-Atkinson Papers* (1960) I. 367 The most loyal reverence for the Queen's name and 'mana'..[is] to be found in Ngapuhi. **1877** R. H. CODRINGTON *Let.* in Max Müller *Lect. Orig. & Growth Relig.* (1878) 54 There is a belief in a force altogether distinct from physical power, which acts in all kinds of ways for good and evil, and which it is of the greatest advantage to possess or control. This is Mana. *a* **1910** W. JAMES *Some Probl. Philos.* (1911) i. 17 What made things act was the mysterious energy in them, and the more awful they were, the more of this *mana* they possessed. **1920** *Times Lit. Suppl.* 29 Apr. 264/2 Notions of the type of mana or orenda are of 'a nascently philosophic order'. **1937** R. H. LOWIE *Hist. Ethnol. Theory* xii. 204 It is not merely spirits and deities that loom as sacred, but also the impersonal force Melanesians call 'mana'. **1951** R. FIRTH *Elem. Social Organiz.* vii. 215 The data accumulated on the character and functions of..principles of mana and taboo..have enabled large regions of human religious experience to be mapped out on a comparative basis. **1959** *Chambers's Encycl.* IX. 47/2 It is this rudimentary concept of a mystic, quasi-impersonal force connected with anything mysterious and arresting that finds expression in *mana*. **1965** *Listener* 2 Dec. 920/2 Warhol has always provided a good example of the kind of *mana* which emanates from certain chosen individuals in modern society. **1975** H. MCCLOY *Minotaur Country* v. 53 He has *mana*... The thing most people think they're talking about when they say charisma.

attrib. and *Comb.*

1924 W. B. SELBIE *Psychol. Relig.* 208 A fearful cringing before some mysterious mana-charged object. **1937** *Brit. Jrnl. Psychol.* Oct. 197 Their religious beliefs centre round a concept of magic of the 'mana' type i.e. vague, abstract, impersonal power. **1949** KOESTLER *Promise & Fulfilment* II. v. 274 He has a *mana*-circle in Tel Aviv.

manaass, obs. form of MENACE *v.*

†'**manable**, *a. Obs.* [f. MAN *v.* + -ABLE.] Of marriageable age.

1607 MIDDLETON *Fam. Love* IV. iv, Had you not been so manable, here are some would have saved you that labour. **1623** FLETCHER & ROWLEY *Maid in Mill* II. i, Shee's manable, is she not?

manablins, variant of MANAVILINS.

‖**manaca** ('mænəkə). [A Brazilian word, recorded in 1648 by Marcgrave *Hist. Nat. Brasil.* 69.] A Brazilian plant, *Franciscea uniflora*, the prepared root of which, known as 'vegetable mercury', is used in medicine.

1866 in *Treas. Bot.* **1889** in *Syd. Soc. Lex.*

manace, obs. form of MENACE *sb.* and *v.*

manachanite, obs. var. MENACCANITE *Min.*

Manachy, obs. form of MANICHEE.

manacle ('mænək(ə)l), *sb.* Forms: 4 **manykil**, **manykle**, 4–5 **manycle**, 4–7 **manicle**, 5 **manakelle**, 6 **manakle**, **mannicle**, *Sc.* **mannakill**, 7 **mannacle**, 4– **manacle**. [ME. *manicle*, a. OF. *manicle* handcuff (also, as in mod.F., gauntlet, handguard), ad. L. *manicula* little hand (also, handle of a plough, in med.L. gauntlet), dim. of *manus* hand. The late forms have the ending assimilated to that of words like *spectacle*, *oracle*, *miracle*.]

1. A fetter for the hand; usually *pl.*

a **1340** HAMPOLE *Psalter* cxlix. 8 For to bynde..þe nobils of þaim in manykils of yryn. *a* **1400** *Pistill of Susan* 176 While domus men were dempt þis dede to clare Marred in Manicles þat made wer newe. **1513** DOUGLAS *Æneis* II. iii. 147 And, first of all, the mannakillis and hard bandis Chargit he lows of this ilk mannis handis. **1590** WEBBE *Trav.* (Arb.) 20 Our handes fastned with a payre of manacles. **1607** SHAKS. *Cor.* I. ix. 57 Wee'le put you (Like one that meanes his proper harme) in Manacles, Then reason safely with you. **1734** tr. *Rollin's Anc. Hist.* (1827) I. 362 Twenty thousand pair of manacles were found. **1838** LYTTON *Leila* II. vii, Four soldiers..bearing with them one whose manacles proclaimed him a prisoner. **1897** A. BALFOUR *By Stroke of Sword* xii. 43/2 The men..fastened my wrists together with manacles.

¶**b.** *pl.* in wider sense: Fetters, shackles.

1838 PRESCOTT *Ferd. & Is.* I. xi. (1842) I. 459 Their limbs loaded with heavy manacles.

c. *fig.* Chiefly *pl.*, bonds, restraints.

1587 GOLDING *De Mornay* xvii. 271 That [the body] which was given it [the soul] for an instrument, is become Manicles and Stocks. **1603** SHAKS. *Meas. for M.* II. iv. 93 The Manacles Of the all-building-Law. **1611** —— *Cymb.* I. i. 122 For my sake weare this [*sc.* a bracelet], It is a Manacle of Loue. **1654** WHITLOCK *Zootomia* 27 No Poet durst have fetcht his Fancy so farr, as to call Prayer the Manicles of the Almighty, had not God himselfe..confessed it. **1670** *Moral State Eng.* 94 The Widow..is alwaies ready to hold out her hand for new manacles. **1677** *Govt. Venice* 3 They continued to elect a Prince, but with such manacles and restrictions, that they left him scarce any thing but the Title. **1852** M. ARNOLD *Morality* I [Nature] knew not yet the gauge of time, Nor wore the manacles of space.

†**2.** *transf.* A tether or shackle for a horse. *Obs.*

1556–68 WITHALS *Dict.* 38 b/2 The manakle for a horse nose, *postomis.* **1607** TOPSELL *Four-f. Beasts* 304 Bind with a manicle his [the horse's] fore-legge to the hinder-leg on the contrary side. *Ibid.* 321 There is a kind of Manicle for the pasternes of Horsses.

manacle ('mænək(ə)l), *v.* Also 4 **mankle**, 5 **manycle**, 6 **manakyll**, **mannacle**, 6–7 **manicle**, 7 **manakell**, **manackle**, 8 *Sc.* **mancle**. [f. prec. sb.]

1. *trans.* To fetter or confine (the hands); to fetter with handcuffs.

c **1306** *Song Exec. Sir S. Fraser* in *Pol. Songs* (Camden) 218 Y-fetered were ys legges under his horse wombe; Bothe with yrn ant with stel mankled were ys honde. **14..** *Voc.* in Wr.-Wülcker 594/39 *Maniculo*, to manycle. **1483** *Cath. Angl.* 227 To Manacle, *manicare.* **1530** PALSGR. 632/2, I manakyll a suspecte person to make hym to confesse thynges... And he will nat confesse it manakyll hym, for undouted he is gylty. **1534** BERNERS *Gold. Bk. M. Aurel.* Bb viij b, Anone thou manacleste oure handes. **1622** J. TAYLOR (Water P.) *Thief* Wks. (1630) II. 124/2 Thieues are manacled when they are found. **1630** WADSWORTH *Pilgr.* 41 Their masters manicling their hands before for feare they should make an insurrection. **1791** COWPER *Iliad* XXI. 38 Manacling their hands Behind them fast with their own tunic-strings. **1818** SCOTT *Hrt. Midl.* iii, Porteous..ordered him to be manacled. **1878** *Masque Poets* 27 Roman hands Can never manacle alive The daughter of the Ptolomies.

b. *loosely.* To fetter; to fasten, secure.

1582 STANYHURST *Æneis* I. (Arb.) 27 Thee gates of warfare wyl then bee mannacled hardly With steele bunch chayne knob. **1593** SHAKS. *2 Hen. VI*, v. i. 149 Wee'l bate thy Bears to death, And manacle the Berard in their Chaines. **1610** —— *Temp.* I. ii. 461 Ile manacle thy necke and feete together.

2. *fig.* (Very common in the 17th c.)

1577 *F. de L'isle's Legendarie* Pref. A iv b, I..being surprised, and as it were manicled with an ineuitable let. **1610** DONNE *Pseudo-martyr* 322 It seemes that the Pope.. when he would fetter and manacle them [*sc.* Princes] in perplexities..is content to send his Breues. **1625** CARPENTER *Geog. Del.* II. vii. (1635) 106 What should hinder the Red Sea to ouerflow all Egypt—vnlesse it were manicled with the Creatours power? **1649** LOVELACE *Poems* (1864) 99 Griefe too can manakell the minde. **1660** MILTON *Free Commw.* Wks. 1851 V. 440 A number of new Injunctions to manacle the native Liberty of Mankind. **1721** RAMSAY *Scribblers Lashed* 88 An ancle Or foot is seen, might monarchs mancle. **1858** BRIGHT *Sp., Reform* 21 Dec. (1876) 307 Men who seem to be manacled by the triumph of 1832.

Hence '**manacled** *ppl. a.*, '**manacling** *vbl. sb.*

1563–87 FOXE *A. & M.* (1596) 936/2 He remained so long manicled that his haire was folded togither. **1586** A. DAY *Eng. Secretary* I. (1625) 138 His manacled and benummed olde joynts. **1650** *Vind. Hammond's Addr.* 31 The infinite goodnesse of God..is a manicling, or restraining his Omnipotence. **1845** FORD *Handbk. Spain* I. 535 At the corner are figures of manacled Indians. **1861** *Sat. Rev.* 23 Nov. 523 A packed Assembly, reported by a manacled press.

manacy, obs. form of MANATEE.

manage ('mænɪdʒ), *sb.* Forms: α. 6–7 **mannage**, 7 **man(n)adge**, 6– **manage**. Also (in senses 1–3) MANÈGE. β. 7 **mennage**, 6– **menage**, (9 *erron.* **ménage**). [ad. It. *maneggio* (perh. through the F. *manege*, now *-ège*; but Fr. lexicographers have not found the word earlier than in Cotgr. 1611), vbl. sb. f. *maneggiare*: see MANAGE *v.* The earliest Eng. examples show assimilation of the ending to the frequent suffix -AGE; but in senses 1 3 the Fr. spelling was introduced in the 17th c., and is now usual: see MANÈGE. The β forms prob. arose from a confusion, on the part of Eng. writers, of this word with F. *menage* act of leading, f. *mener* to lead; there is also some evidence of confusion with F. *ménage* household: see MÉNAGE.]

1. The training, handling, and directing of a horse in its paces; a training to good paces. *the manage*: the art of training and managing horses. *Obs.* exc. *arch.* (Now usually MANÈGE.)

α. *a* **1586** SIDNEY *Astr. & Stella* Sonn. '*I on my horse*', He ..now hath made me to his hand so right, That in the Manage my selfe takes delight. **1596** SHAKS. *1 Hen. IV*, II. iii. 52 Speake tearmes of manage to thy bounding Steed. **1612** *Two Noble K.* v. iv, The hot horse..Forgets schoole dooing, being therein traind And of kind mannadge. **1667** DUCHESS NEWCASTLE *Life Dk. of N.* (1886) II. 99 His chief pastime and divertisement consisted in the manage of the two afore-mentioned horses. **1715–20** POPE *Iliad* XV. 823 A horseman..(Skill'd in the manage of the bounding steed). **1864** *Lond. Rev.* 28 May, It is the menage, the education of the animal, that gives him half his value. **1876** DOWDEN *Poems* 67, I know the careless grace My Perseus wears in manage of the steed.

β. **1760–72** H. BROOKE *Fool of Qual.* (1809) IV. 137 [He] rode out with him, and taught him the *menage.* **1833** J. HOLLAND *Manuf. Metal* II. 313 What in the language of the *ménage* is called the line of the banquet.

b. *transf.* and *fig.*

α. **1596** DRAYTON *Legends* iii. 507 And put Me forth upon my full Careere, On places slipperie, and my manage ill. **1608** SHAKS. *Per.* IV. vi. 69 My Lord, shees not pac'ste yet, you must take some paines to worke her to your mannage. **1691** J. WILSON *Belphegor* I. iii, Do but bring him to the right manage at first; humour him in every thing,..and the rest follows. **1739** WARBURTON *Comm. Pope's Ess. Man* in *Hist. Wks. Learned* I. 92 Till the Horse and the Ox come to know why they undergo such different Manage and Fortunes in the Hand of Man. **1755** YOUNG *Centaur* v. 227 Beasts of so gross a class as they [certain persons mentioned] choose to rank with, scarce deserve to be brought to the Manage.

β. **1590** SPENSER *F.Q.* III. xii. 22 The winged god him selfe Came riding on a Lion ravenous, Taught to obay the menage of that Elfe. **1742** YOUNG *Nt. Th.* II. 491 Rude thought runs wild in contemplation's field; Converse, the menage, breaks it to the bit Of due restraint. **1902** F. E. SCHELLING *Eng. Chron. Play* 240 The great horse of the Spenserian allegory had a pace beyond his [*sc.* Dekker's] menage.

2. The action and paces to which a horse is trained in the riding-school; any of the separate movements or evolutions characteristic of a horse so trained; *spec.* a short gallop at full speed. *Obs.* exc. *arch.*

α. **1577–87** HOLINSHED *Chron.* III. 1033/2 They were better practised to fetch in booties, than to make their manage or careire. **1589** *Pasquills Counterc.* A iij, It should seeme by the manages my beast made, that hee knewe his Maister had a speciall peece of seruice in hande. **1589** *Pasquills Ret.* C ij b, Howe souldier-like hee made an ende of his manage with a double rest. **1600** SHAKS. *A.Y.L.* I. i. 13 His horses..are taught their mannage. **1611** COTGR., *Air*,.. in horsemanship, a doing, or stirring manage, or manage raised aboue ground. *à demy air*, a certaine curuet, or manage, wherein the halfe of a horse is in the aire, the other on the ground. *Ibid.*, *Passade*,..the manage for combat, or souldiors manage. **1614** MARKHAM *Cheap Husb.* I. ii. (1668) 26 Manage with rest, and manage without rest, manage with single turns, and manage with double turns. **1659** DK. NEWCASTLE *Let.* in *Life* (1886) 361 One of my horses of manage which will be the quietest..he or any man can have. **1770** BARETTI *Journ. fr. Lond. to Genoa* (ed. 3) I. 175 By Bellém there is a noble structure.. where the King's horses are educated for the manage. **1805** WORDSW. *Prelude* x. 78 The horse is taught his manage.

β. **1617** BP. HALL *Quo Vadis?* §13 The horse is a noble creature... There is a double kinde of menage..—one for seruice, the other for pleasure. **1645** EVELYN *Diary* 3 Feb., One of his sons riding the menage with that address..as I had never seen any thing approach it. **1770** LANGHORNE *Plutarch* (1879) II. 640/1 She trained her youth as the colt is trained to the menage.

3. An enclosed space for the training of saddle-horses and for the practice of horsemanship; a riding-school.

α. **1655** STANLEY *Hist. Philos.* III. (1701) 103/1 How many courses will the manage hold? **1684** EVELYN *Diary* 18 Dec., To see the young gallants do their exercise, Mr. Faubert having newly rail'd in a manage. **1756** NUGENT *Gr. Tour Germany* II. 432 The bishop has built a manage or riding house. **1811** *Edw. Earl Clarendon's Relig. & Policy* Advt., Henry Viscount Cornbury..by a codicil to his will, dated Aug. 10. 1751. left divers MSS. of his great grandfather Edward Earl of Clarendon..with a direction that the money to arise from the..publication..should be employed 'as a beginning of a Fund for supporting a Manage or Academy for riding..in Oxford.

attrib. **1848** KINGSLEY *Saint's Trag.* I. i. 192 They are waiting For you in the manage-school, to give your judgment On that new Norman mare.

β. **1684** *Scanderbeg Rediv.* i. 7 He diligently applied himself to the best Exercises, as frequenting the Academies, Fencing, the Menage, &c.

4. The skilful handling *of* (a weapon, etc.).

α. *c* **1611** CHAPMAN *Iliad* II. 460 For the manage of his lance he generall praise did winne. **1633** FORD *Broken H.* IV. iii, The sonne of Venus hath bequeath'd his quiuer To Ithocles his manage. **1687** *Lond. Gaz.* No. 2276/5 The Satisfaction of seeing what..Address he had in the manage of his Horse and Arms. **1720** MRS. MANLEY *Power of Love* vi. (1741) 332 To learn his Exercises..and the Manage of the Sword.

β. **1670** *Moral State Eng.* 145 Each striving to go beyond the other..in the dextrous..menage of his Weapon.

†**5.** The action or manner of managing; management; conduct (of affairs); administration, direction, control. *Obs.*

α. **1581** SAVILE *Tacitus' Hist.* IV. v. (1612) 143 Mutianus.. drewe the whole manage of affaires into his owne handes. **1592** KYD *Sol. & Pers.* III. i. 119 Wilt thou be our Lieutenant there, And further vs in manage of these wars? **1596** SHAKS. *Merch. V.* III. iv. 25 Lorenso I commit into your hands, The husbandry and mannage of my house. **1612** BACON *Ess., Youth & Age* (Arb.) 258 Young men in the conduct and mannage of Actions, embrace more then they can hold. **1617** HALES *Serm.* 17 The greatnesse of the businesse, the manage of which they vndertake. **1642** —— *Gold. Rem., Tract on Schism* (1673) 1 Howsoever, in the common manage, Heresie and Schisme are but ridiculous terms. **1665** MANLEY *Grotius' Low C. Warres* 667 That they might..consult of the further manage of the War. **1683** KENNETT tr. *Erasm. on Folly* (1709) 104 St. Peter had the keys given to him, and that by our Saviour himself, who had never entrusted him, except he had known him capable of their manage and custody. **1697** COLLIER *Ess. Mor. Subj.* I.

(1709) 48 The Manage of his Employment is not prescribed by the Rector. **1756** TOLDERVY *Hist. 2 Orphans* I. 95 His opinion was not more against her humour, than his manage of it was to her mind.

β. **1665** WALTON *Life Hooker* 39 [Q. Elizabeth] having experimented his wisdom..in the menage of her affairs.. she made him archbishop of Canterbury. *Ibid.* 83 Revenge is so pleasing, that man is hardly persuaded to submit the menage of it to the..wisdom of his Creator. **1673** DRYDEN *Marr. à la Mode* I. i, For the mennage of a Family, I know it better than any Lady in Sicily. *a* **1683** OLDHAM *Poet. Wks.* (1686) 103 Fools..Who..justly forfeit all that praise.. Which we by our wise menage from a sin can raise. **1710** J. PALMER *Prov.* 7 Among all the errors..in our menage, nothing is more dangerous than entring into bonds.

†**b.** Power of management. *Obs.*

1639 N. N. tr. *Du Bosq's Compl. Woman* I. 40 The spirits which are without manage, in their enterprises, are also without courage in their afflictions.

†**c.** An administrative duty or office. *Obs.*

1651 *Life Father Sarpi* (1676) 21 [He] gave him employment in Congregations and other manages more frequently than was usual.

†**6.** Bearing, demeanour, conduct. *Obs.*

1593 G. HARVEY *New Let.* B 4 b, His talke was sweet, his Order fine; his whole menage braue.

†**7.** Treatment of persons or of material. *Obs.*

1608 CHAPMAN *Byrons Trag.* Plays 1873 II. 283 There is one sort of manadge for the Great, Another for inferiour. **1626** BACON *Sylva* §327 Quick-silver will not endure the Mannage of the Fire.

†**8.** A design. *Obs.*

1681 GLANVILL *Sadducismus* I. 30 The policy and menages of the Instruments of darkness. *Ibid.* 82 Our ignorance of the reasons and menages of Providence.

†**man-age.** *Obs.* [f. MAN *sb.*[1] + AGE *sb.*] The age at which one becomes a man; one's majority.

1611 W. SCLATER *Key* (1629) 172 Of youth they say, it must haue his swinge: when manage comes, mariage will bring staiednesse. *a* **1653** GOUGE *Comm. Heb.* i. 10 In his Infancy... In his Man-age... After his Resurrection... In the time of his Ascention. **1674** J. B[RIAN] *Harv.-Home* ii. 7 In Childhood, Youth, and Man-age.

manage (ˈmænɪdʒ), *v.* Forms: *α.* 6 **manege, mannadge,** 6–7 **mannage,** 6– **manage.** *β.* 6–8 **menage.** [Recorded earlier than the cognate MANAGE *sb.*, and prob. directly ad. It. *maneggiare* to handle, esp. to manage or train (horses) = Sp. *manejar*, F. *manier*:—vulgar L. type **manidiāre*, f. L. *man-us* (It., Sp. *mano*, F. *main*) hand.

Although the etymological form *manege* appears in our earliest example, the ending was, as in the sb., already in the 16th c. assimilated to the common suffix -AGE. The form *menage* in early examples is taken from the sb.; but in the late 17th and early 18th c. it was chiefly used where the sense closely approaches that of the F. *ménager* to use carefully, to husband, spare, f. *ménage* household. This Fr. vb. certainly influenced the sense-development of the Eng. word: indeed, in the writings of Dryden and his contemporaries, there are frequent instances of *manage* (as well as of *menage*) which can only be regarded as conscious gallicisms.]

1. a. *trans.* To handle, train, or direct (a horse) in his paces; to put through the exercises of the manège. Now merged in the wider senses 2 and 7.

α. **1561** T. HOBY tr. *Castiglione's Courtyer* I. (1577) D v b, It is the peculiar prayse of vs Italians..to manege wyth reason, especially rough horses. **1586** B. YOUNG *Guazzo's Civ. Conv.* IV. 226 Behold how..Lorde Frederike..rid on his horse..sometimes with curuettes..did so manage him, that it was a meruailous..spectacle to the beholders. **1632** J. HAYWARD tr. *Biondi's Eromena* 6 Having a while gently mannaged him [the horse] without finding him any way disobedient. **1645** G. DANIEL *Poems* Wks. II. 25 How shall we Spend the Day? Manage the lustie Steed? Or see the Eager Hounds pursue the pray? **1754** BERENGER tr. *Bourgelat's Hist. Horsem.* (1771) I. 169 They [the horses] all having been carefully handled, dressed, or managed as we call it.

β. **1590** SPENSER *F.Q.* I. vii. 37 A goodly person, and could menage faire His stubborne steed with curbed canon bitt. **1683** T. HOY *Agathocles* 8 An Hard-mouth'd Beast, for slacken'd Raines unfitt, And must be menag'd with the Spur and Bitt.

†**b.** *intr.* Of a horse: To perform the exercises of the manège. Also in narrower sense, to run a 'manage' (see MANAGE *sb.* 1). *Obs.*

1591 SYLVESTER *Du Bartas* I. v. 348 A large and mighty-limbed Steed Can never manage half so readily As Spanish Jennet. **1607** MARKHAM *Caval.* I. (1617) 16 Being able to passe a short carriere, to manage, beat a coruet and such like. **1614** —— *Cheap Husb.* I. ii. (1668) 25 You shall then teach him to manage which is the only posture for the use of the Sword on Horseback. **1614** SYLVESTER *Bethulia's Rescue* I. 41 The Horse Which standing still too-long..Forgets to manage. **1650** EARL MONM. tr. *Senault's Man become Guilty* 271 He [man] taught the horse to manage, and forced the noblest of creatures to endure the bit and spur. **1719** D'URFEY *Pills* IV. 10 [A horse speaks.] I could both Manage, Stop and Turn.

2. a. *trans.* To handle, wield, make use of (a weapon, tool, implement, etc.). Often in phr. †*to manage arms* = to fight. Now only, to regulate one's use of (a weapon, instrument, etc.) with greater or less success, to make (it) serve one's purpose (well or ill).

α. *c* **1586** C'TESS PEMBROKE *Ps.* CXLIV. i, Prais'd bee the Lord of might,..By whom my hands doe fight, My fingers manage armes. **1586** MARLOWE *1st Pt. Tamburl.* III. i, But if ..He be so mad to manage Armes with me, Then stay thou with him. **1591** SHAKS. *Two Gent.* III. i. 247 Hope is a louers staffe, walke hence with that And manage it, against despairing thoughts. **1592** —— *Rom. & Jul.* I. i. 76 Put vp thy Sword, Or manage it to part these men with me. **1603** KNOLLES *Hist. Turks* (1621) 1191 These soldiers.. mannaging their armes, whilest others hanged theirs by the wals. **1656** EARL MONM. tr. *Boccalini's Advts. fr. Parnass.* II. xiv. (1674) 153 [They] consume themselves in continual managing their Pen. **1659** PEARSON *Creed* (1839) 450 The scriptures to prove these attributes..are so many, that to manage them against the exceptions of the adversaries, would take up too much room. **1678** MOXON *Mech. Exerc.* 73 This way of handling may seem a preposterous posture to mannage an Iron Tool in. **1706** E. WARD *Wooden World Diss.* (1708) 104 He trusts most to his Head,..and does manage it with as much Skill and Force, as any Bull or Ram. **1872** TENNYSON *Gareth & Lynette* 1316 But Lancelot on him urged..How best to manage horse, lance, sword and shield. **1894** PARRY *Stud. Gt. Musicians, Schubert* 224 The German..however much he manages his language can never make it as purely beautiful in sound as an Italian.

β. **1590** SPENSER *F.Q.* II. ix. 27 A comely personage, That in his hand a white rod menaged. **1670** COVEL *Diary* (Hakluyt Soc.) 218, I..understand that these [stone balls].. have been in like manner menaged,..as particularly one of them over Adrianople gate..was menaged just before Mahomet 3d who..rewarded the man well.

†**b.** *intr.* To operate, manœuvre *with*. *Obs.*

1591 GREENE *Art Conny Catch.* II. Pref. 2 Though I cannot as he mannadge with my courtlax.

c. *trans.* To 'handle', work (a ship or boat).

1600 HAKLUYT *Voy.* III. 525 Our men..died continually, and..we were scantly able to manage [1589 manure] our shippe. **1801** STRUTT *Sports & Past.* II. ii. 81 The success of the champion depended upon the skilfulness of those who managed the boat. **1823** T. C. GRATTON *High-ways & By-ways* (ed. 2) I. 9 One solitary barge, managed by a single boatman, was working its way against the current.

3. a. To conduct or carry on (a war, a business, an undertaking, an operation). Now with more precise notion: To carry on successfully or the contrary; to control the course of (affairs) by one's own action.

α. **1579** FENTON *Guicciard.* (1618) 309 With great danger we managed warre many yeares against the most cruell Tyrant of the Turkes. **1600** FAIRFAX *Tasso* I. li. 29 But let vs manage war with blowes, like knights. **1611** SHAKS. *Wint. T.* IV. ii. 17 Thou hauing made me Businesses, (which none (without thee) can sufficiently manage). **1665** GLANVILL *Scepsis Sci.* iv. 19 As unconceivable..as that a blind man should manage a game at Chess, or Marshal an Army. *a* **1667** COWLEY *Mrs. K. Philips* iii, The Trade of Glory manag'd by the Pen..Does bring in but small Profit to us Men. **1678** WANLEY *Wond. Lit. World* v. ii §50. 471/1 Theodora..after the death of Constantine, managed for two years the affairs of the Empire. *Ibid.* §84. 472/2 He himself was a Prince unactive, managing the Wars by his principal Bassa's. **1720** DE FOE *Capt. Singleton* vi. (1840) 97 Our surgeon was very skilful in managing their cure. **1798** JANE AUSTEN *Lett.* (1884) I. 173 Mary does not manage matters in such a way as to make me want to lay in myself. **1818** LADY MORGAN *Autobiog.* (1859) 60 So you see, my dear Olivia, they manage these things better in France. **1841** MACAULAY *Ess., Warren Hastings* (The Trial), When Parliament met in the following winter, the Commons proceeded to elect a committee for managing the impeachment. **1861** M. PATTISON *Ess.* (1889) I. 47 By a committee of nine..all the affairs of the little world were managed.

β. **1597** HOOKER *Eccl. Pol.* v. lxxvii. §1. 227 Who should giue them their commission but he whose most inward affaires they menage? *Ibid.* lxxxi. §4. 259 They are able to dispose and menage their owne affaires.

†**b.** To fulfil the duties of (an office). *Obs.*

a **1627** HAYWARD *Four Y. Eliz.* (Camden) 54 About 140 passed under the sword and amonge them 12 of name, either for nobilitie of birth and state, or for honorable places they mannaged in the armie.

c. To work out (in literary treatment).

1697 DRYDEN *Ded. Æneis* Ess. (Ker) II. 162, I was loath to be informed..how a tragedy should be contrived and managed, in better verse..than I could teach others. **1714** POPE *Rape Lock* Ep. Ded., The character of Belinda, as it is now manag'd, resembles you in nothing but in Beauty. **1776** MICKLE *Diss. Lusiad* (1778) p. ccxviii, If the man of taste.. will be pleased to mark how the genius of a Virgil has managed a war after a Homer.

d. *absol.* To conduct affairs. Also, †to plot, scheme, intrigue.

1603 HOLLAND *Plutarch's Mor.* 229 He that enterteineth many friends, must of necessitie be conformable to them all: namely..with ambitious citizens, to sue and manage for offices [etc.]. **1693** DRYDEN *Juvenal's Sat.* x. 537 Intrust thy Fortune to the Pow'rs above. Leave them to manage for thee, and to grant What their unerring Wisdom sees thee want. **1791** MRS. RADCLIFFE *Rom. Forest* iv, If I had not managed very cleverly, they would have found me out. **1860–1** FLO. NIGHTINGALE *Nursing* 30 It is as impossible in a book to teach a person in charge of sick how to manage, as it is to teach her how to nurse. **1864** TENNYSON *Grandmother* ii, Her father..Hadn't a head to manage, and drank himself into his grave.

e. *intr.* (quasi-*pass.*) To admit of being managed.

1625 B. JONSON *Staple of News* IV. i, Is't a Cleare businesse? will it mannage well? My name must not be vs'd else.

4. *trans.* To control and direct the affairs of (a household, institution, state, etc.); to take charge of, attend to (cattle, etc.).

α. **1609** *Sir T. Smith's Commw. Eng.* I. xxiv. 34 To speake of the Commonwealth, or policy of England it is gouerned, administered, and mannaged [*edd.* 1583, 1584, 1589, 1594 manured] by three sorts of persons. **1709** in Picton *L'pool Munic. Rec.* (1886) II. 75 Trustees for manageing and takeing care of the said charity schoole. **1857** RUSKIN *Pol. Econ. Art* 15 If the household were rightly managed. **1865** DICKENS *Mut. Fr.* I. viii, There are no estates to manage. **1881** JOWETT *Thucyd.* I. 190, I have remarked again and again that a democracy cannot manage an empire.

β. **1670** *Moral State Eng.* 90 You must bid fair for her [an Heiress] to those who menage her. **1703** MAUNDRELL *Journ. Jerus.* (1732) 28 What Intervals of time they have..in menaging of their Flocks.

5. To administer, regulate the use or expenditure of (finances, provisions, etc.).

1649 BP. REYNOLDS *Hosea* i. 51 Mannage every one of his gifts to the closing of those miserable breaches which threaten an inundation of calamitie upon us all. **1683** *Brit. Spec.* 78 Besides these the Comes sacrarum largitionum, who managed the Emperors Finances. **1818** JAS. MILL *Brit. India* II. IV. iv. 155 The provisions..had been managed without economy.

absol. **1842** S. ATKINSON *Chancery Pract.* 270 In every order directing the appointment of a receiver of landed estate, there shall be inserted a direction that such receiver shall manage as well as let and set.

6. a. To deal with or treat carefully; to use sparingly or with judgement; to husband (one's health, life, money, etc.). [Cf. F. *ménager.*] ? *Obs.*

1649 BP. HALL *Cases Consc.* (1650) 72 Now the same God that hath ordained Soveraigne powers to judge of, and protect the life of others, hath given weighty charge to every man to tender and manage his owne. **1673** DRYDEN *Marr. à la Mode* Prol. 24 [She] manages her last half-crown with care, And trudges to the Mall on foot for air. **1697** —— *Æneid* XI. 1090 He spurs amidst the foes, Not managing the life he meant to lose. **1697** COLLIER *Ess. Mor. Subj.* II. (1703) 30 A man, as he manages himself, may die old at thirty, and a child at fourscore. **1701** SWIFT *Contests Nobles & Comm.* Wks. 1775 II. I. 43 Yet we may manage a sickly constitution; and preserve a strong one. **1726** —— *Gulliver* IV. vii, I began to..think the Honour of my own Kind not worth managing. **1733–4** BERKELEY *Let. to Prior* 17 Mar. Wks. 1871 IV. 218, I am obliged to manage my health, and I have many things to do.

†**b.** To treat (persons) with indulgence or consideration. Also *absol.*, to alter one's conduct from fear of giving offence. [= F. *ménager.*] *Obs.*

1714 SWIFT *Let. to Bolingbroke* 7 Aug., I do not find there is any intention of managing you in the least. **1727** OLDMIXON *Clarendon & Whitlock Comp.* 281 If the Parliament of England had manag'd them with the least Complacencey. **1796** BURKE *Regic. Peace* i. Wks. VIII. 147 He temporized; he managed.

7. To control, cause to submit to one's rule (persons, animals, etc.).

1594 MARLOWE & NASHE *Dido* I. i, And full three Sommers likewise shall he waste In mannaging those fierce barbarian mindes. **1657** JER. TAYLOR *Friendship* (ed. 2) 194 Our absolution does but..comfort and instruct your Conscience, direct and manage it. **1694** ADDISON *St. Cecilia's Day*, Musick..With unexpected eloquence can move And manage all the Man with secret art. **1834** MACAULAY *Ess., Pitt* (1887) 317 What probability was there that a mere drudge would be able to manage a large and stormy assembly? **1856** EMERSON *Eng. Traits, Race* Wks. (Bohn) II. 32 His attachment to the horse arises from the courage and address required to manage it. **1866** G. MACDONALD *Ann. Q. Neighb.* ix. (1878) 166 My mother.. was the only one that ever could manage him.

8. a. To bring (a person) to consent to one's wishes by artifice, flattery, or judicious suggestion of motives.

α. **1706–7** FARQUHAR *Beaux Strat.* II. i, London, dear London is the Place for managing and breaking a Husband. **1712** STEELE *Spect.* No. 444 ¶4 The Art of managing Mankind, is only to make them stare a little. **1777** A. HAMILTON *Wks.* (1886) VII. 483 He managed them with a good deal of address, and sent them away perfectly satisfied. **1826** DISRAELI *Viv. Grey* III. i, Managing mankind, by studying their tempers and humouring their weaknesses. **1840** LYTTON *Money* v. iii, I have managed even Sharp. **1849** MACAULAY *Hist. Eng.* vii. II. 223 The chief agent who was employed by the government to manage the Presbyterians was Vincent Alsop. **1866** GEO. ELIOT *F. Holt* (1868) 24 Managing one's husband is some pleasure.

β. **1673** WALKER *Educ.* (1683) 92 He embraceth the lies and flatteries of such as thereby gain and menage him.

†**b.** Const. *to* with inf., *towards*. *Obs.*

α. *a* **1715** BURNET *Own Time* (1724) I. 580 He..was so frighted, that he was easily managed to pretend to discover any thing that was suggested to him.

β. **1692** R. L'ESTRANGE *Josephus, Antiq.* VII. x. (1733) 187 With certain Hints how they were to menage the Heads of the Tribe of Judah towards his Restauration.

9. a. To operate upon, manipulate for a purpose (†const. *to* with inf.); to till (land).

1655 FULLER *Ch. Hist.* I. i. §11. 6 As much as one plow can handsomely manage. **1726** POPE *Odyss.* XXIV. 303 Who then thy master, say? and whose the land So dress'd and manag'd by thy skilful hand? **1765** A. DICKSON *Treat. Agric.* (ed. 2) 49 It may be increased by managing the soil in such a manner, as to enable it to attract this food in greater plenty.

b. To adulterate, sophisticate; to 'doctor'.

1820 *Blackw. Mag.* VI. 549 The art of managing or, according to the familiar phrase, doctoring wines.

†**10. a.** To convey by mechanism or contrivance. **b.** Naut. *to manage out*: to equip and send out (a boat). Cf. *to man out*. *Obs.*

a. **1650** FULLER *Pisgah* 423 How can we conceive that these solid stones..were managed hither..over a mountainous Country?

b. **1638** J. UNDERHILL *News fr. Amer.* in *3 Mass. Hist. Coll.* (1837) VI. 18 He had managed out a pinnace.

11. a. To bring to pass by contrivance; hence, to succeed in accomplishing. Also, with *inf.* as obj. (or ellipsis of this); often ironically, to be so unskilful or unlucky as *to do* something (cf. CONTRIVE *v.* 6).

1722 DE FOE *Relig. Courtsh.* I. i. (1840) 29 What, says he, child, is to be done in the affair while I am gone?..I know not how it will be managed, but I believe she will manage him no more. **1838** MACREADY *Diary* 3 Aug. *Remin.* (1875) II. 117, I find I managed to lose..£2,500. **1854** DICKENS *Hard T.* II.

vii, She is sharp enough; she could manage to coax it out of him, if she chose. **1879** McCarthy *Own Times* II. xxix. 400 His plays are among the very few modern productions which manage to keep the stage. **1883** Stevenson *Treas. Isl.* III. xiv. (1886) 112 My..obvious duty was to draw as close as I could manage. **1895** *Bookman* Oct. 33/1 After gaining any diplomatic success he managed to neutralise the effects of it by some act of fatuous folly.

b. *absol.* To succeed (under disadvantages) in accomplishing one's task; to 'make shift', contrive to get on *with* what is hardly adequate. *colloq.*

1854 M. L. Charlesworth *Ministering Children* iv. 47 Rose was..wondering how William would manage about getting some logs for Mercy's fire. **1873** 'S. Coolidge' *What Katy Did* xi. 195 I've been thinking how we are to manage about the housekeeping. **1895** 'G. Mortimer' *Like Stars that Fall* viii. 108 'How will you manage about your hair?' 'I shall cut it short, I think.' **1899** *Speaker* 29 July 107/1 'The press of work fairly bewilders me', he writes..but he managed almost without a hitch. *Mod.* I think I might manage with another yard of material.

12. With *can* or *be able*: to cope with the difficulties of; to succeed in using, dealing with, etc.; to 'tackle'.

[**1655**: see 9.] **1825** Lamb *Elia* Ser. II. *Superann. Man*, It seemed to me that I had more time on my hands than I could ever manage. **1903** *Blackwood's Mag.* Dec. 805/1 [I can] occasionally manage places which are too much for the average snipe-shooter.

manage, variant of MENAGE *Obs.*

manageability (mænɪdʒə'bɪlɪtɪ). [f. next: see -ITY.] The quality or condition of being manageable; manageableness.

1857 Buckle *Civiliz.* I. ii. 98 We have to look..at what may be called the manageability of Nature. **1879** W. H. White in *Cassell's Techn. Educ.* IV. 348/2 The limit will be determined by considerations of manageability.

manageable ('mænɪdʒəb(ə)l), *a.* Also 7 mannageable, maneggiable. [f. MANAGE *v.* + -ABLE. Cf. MANIABLE.] That can be managed; amenable to control or guidance, tractable; admitting of being wielded, manipulated, or administered, workable; capable of being accomplished by contrivance.

1598 Florio, *Maneggiéuole*, manageable, that may be handled. **1603** Florio tr. *Montaigne* II. xii. 280 To them [beasts] as their proper share we leave the essentiall, the maneagable [**1632** manageable: F. *maniables*], and palpable goods, as peace, rest,..and health. **1618** Bolton tr. *Florus* (1636) 73 Italy was now brought under, and made mannageable. **1625** Bacon *Ess., Viciss. Things* (Arb.) 576 The Conditions of Weapons..are..That the Carriage may be Light and Manageable; and the like. **1636** E. Dacres tr. *Machiavel's Disc. Livy* I. 32 If thou wouldst make a numerous and warlike people..thou mak'st them of such a temper, that they shall never be maneggiable at thy will. **1662** J. Davies tr. *Olearius' Voy. Ambass.* 253 The Chariot was drawn by two white Oxen, which..were as swift and manageable as our horses. *a* **1677** Hale *Prim. Orig. Man.* IV. vi. 346 The first Constitution and Order of things is not in Reason or Nature manageable by such a Law. **1712** Steele *Spect.* No. 479 ¶ 5 They who learn to keep a good Seat on horseback, mount the least managable they can get. **1740** J. Clarke *Educ. Youth* (ed. 3) 201 When the Number of Boys in a Class, arises above half a Dozen,..they become less manageable. **1748** *Anson's Voy.* II. x. 241 It is one convenience of their jars that they are much more manageable than casks. **1798** *Hull Advertiser* 4 Aug. 2/4 A gunboat..being very manageable in a strong tideway. **1856** Mrs. Browning *Aur. Leigh* I. 370 A meek and manageable child. **1866** Odling *Anim. Chem.* 14 Only a few of these metallic chlorides can be vaporised at manageable temperatures. **1884** *Manch. Exam.* 9 June 4/7 The right of the Chancellor of the Exchequer compulsorily to pay off two ..classes of Three per Cent. stocks in manageable amounts.

manageableness ('mænɪdʒəb(ə)lnɪs). [f. prec. + -NESS.] The attribute of being manageable.

1661 Boyle *Physiol. Ess.* (1669) 104 Which Disagreement ..may..be imputed to the greater or less exactness and manageableness of the Instruments employ'd. **1694** *Phil. Trans.* XVIII. 266 He thinks that the Excellency of the Greek Poetry might at first proceed from the manageableness of the Greek Language. **1768-74** Tucker *Lt. Nat.* (1834) II. 78 The ox, the horse, and the sheep have docility and manageableness given them for their characteristic. **1818** Cobbett *Pol. Reg.* XXXIII. 414 The manageableness of her means..will always keep England at the head of the nations of the world. **1903** *Contemp. Rev.* Sept. 393 The receptivity and the manageableness of the child are at their maximum within the first fifteen minutes of school hours.

manageably ('mænɪdʒəblɪ), *adv.* [f. MANAGEABLE + -LY².] In a manageable manner.

1830 Herschel *Stud. Nat. Phil.* 63 In the expansive force of gases, liberated slowly and manageably from chemical mixtures, we have a host of..powerful energies. **1890** *Universal Rev.* Sept. 159 The amount of really effective power which they can manageably wield at need.

managed ('mænɪdʒd), *ppl. a.* Also 7 mannaged, menaged, 9 (in sense 1) maneged. [f. MANAGE *v.* + -ED¹.]

1. Trained to the manège. *arch.*

1591 Greene *Maidens Dreame* xxi, Men might his stable full of coursers see, Trotters whose manag'd looks would som affright. **1644** Evelyn *Diary* 27 Feb., The Tennis Court, and Cavalerizzo for the menag'd horses, are also observable. **1687** Sedley *Bellamira* v. Wks. 1722 II. 163 He ..rides three manag'd Horses every Morning. **1722** *Lond. Gaz.* No. 6087/4 A bright dun manag'd Stone Horse..has been standing at John Hambrow's. **1773** Johnson in

Boswell 24 Sept., A Frenchman goes out upon a managed horse, and capers in the field. **1816** Scott *Old Mort.* xvi, Making his managed horse keep time by bounds and curvets to the tune which he whistled. **1835** Beckford *Recoll.* 148 Bestriding a maneged horse.

2. Controlled, conducted, administered. Chiefly with advs., as *well-*, *ill-managed.* **managed bond** (see quot. 1972); **managed currency,** a currency system which is not tied to the gold standard but is regulated by the government of the country concerned; **managed economy,** an economy in which the framework and general policies are regulated or controlled by the government.

1611 Cotgr., *Amesnagé*, Managed, gouerned, ordered, settled, as a household. **1923** J. M. Keynes *Tract on Monetary Reform* 166 This is what is meant by saying that gold has 'intrinsic value' and is free from the dangers of a 'managed' currency. *Ibid.* 167 Gold itself has become a 'managed' currency. **1924** W. F. Spalding *Eastern Exchange Currency & Finance* (ed. 4) p. v, India and one or two other Eastern nations have found defects in a 'managed' currency. **1929** G. D. H. Cole in *New Leader* 8 Nov. 16/3 A plea for a 'managed currency'..a currency that is regulated not automatically by the supply of gold, but deliberately. **1941** G. N. Clark *Holland & War* 9 In September 1936..France and Switzerland gave up the gold standard and Holland too went over to a managed currency. **1969** *Adv. Sci.* XXVI. 64/2 The first objective of a managed economy..was originally stability. *Ibid.* 66/2 In considering the problems of a managed economy it is well to begin by recognizing that management is by no means the same as control. [**1971** *Investors Chron.* 2 Apr. 22 (Advt.), It's called the Abbey Selective Investment Bond, and it's issued and managed by Abbey Life Assurance.] **1972** *Observer* 8 Oct. 18/2 In theory a managed bond is an ideal investment. The investor buys units in a special bond fund which the managers can invest in property, shares or fixed-interest stock according to their expert appraisal of the investment scene.

†**3.** Falsified, 'cooked'. *Obs.*

1810 *Sporting Mag.* XXXVI. 279 The mysterious and confused kind of evidence given by this paymaster and the production of those managed papers.

4. Of demeanour, expressions, etc.: Nicely restrained, measured. Now *rare.*

In Burke's use = F. *ménagé.*

1770 Burke *Pres. Discont.* Wks. 1842 I. 129 Throughout it was a satire, though in terms managed and decent enough, on the politicks of the former reign. **1771** —— *Corr.* (1844) I. 291 A behaviour, rather too reserved and managed for the purposes of opposition. **1819** Crabbe *T. of Hall* x, Well I can call to mind the managed air..That in a dubious balance held the mind. **1898** *Academy* 8 Oct. 23/1 A man of tireless energy, of managed affections.

managee (mænɪ'dʒiː). *nonce-wd.* [f. MANAGE *v.* + -EE.] The person who is managed.

1847 Helps *Friends in C.* Ser. I. I. vii, When the manager and the managee are both of the same mind.

management ('mænɪdʒmənt). Also 7 mannagement, menagement. [f. MANAGE *v.* + -MENT; in the 17-18th c. the development of meaning was influenced by association with the F. *ménagement,* f. *ménager* (see the etymological note to MANAGE *v.*).]

1. a. The action or manner of managing, in senses of the vb.; the application of skill or care in the manipulation, use, treatment, or control (of things or persons), or in the conduct (of an enterprise, operation, etc.). †In early use sometimes in *plural.*

1598 Florio, *Maneggio,*..management, businesse, handling, negotiation. **1601** R. Johnson *Kingd. & Commonw.* (1603) 256 Those..expences which are daiely laide out..for the mannagements of so many warres. **1603** Holland *Plutarch's Mor.* 230 In contracts and management of State affaires. **1657** R. Ligon *Barbadoes* (1673) 23, I had time enough to improve my self, in the knowledge of the management of a Plantation of this bulk. **1673** O. Walker *Educ.* (1677) 65 Over looked, not strictly watched unless there is reason to suspect some ill menagement. **1678** Moxon *Mech. Exerc.* 98 The Top-man observing to guide the Saw exactly in the line;..and the Pit-man drawing it.. down; but not so low that the upper and lower Handles of the Saw sink below both their managements. **1736** Butler *Anal.* I. iii. Wks. 1874 I. 52 Tranquillity, satisfaction,.. being the natural consequences of prudent management of ourselves, and our affairs. **1796** Horsley *Serm.* I. xi. (1812) 239 The holy angels are employed upon extraordinary occasions in the affairs of men, and the management of this sublunary world. **1828** Macaulay *Dryden in Edinb. Rev.* Jan. 26 In the management of the heroic couplet Dryden has never been equalled. **1832** Ht. Martineau *Life in Wilds* v. 66, I do not see why these skins should not make us caps and waistcoats, under Fulton's good management. **1834** J. Busby *Vineyards France & Sp.* 133 The same care has been extended to the making and subsequent management of their wine. **1865** D. G. Mitchell *Wet Days* 16 (Cent.) Management of the household, management of flocks, of servants, of land, and of property in general.

b. *spec.* The working or cultivation (of land); hence *dial.* the process of manuring; *concr.* manure. (See E.D.D. s.vv. *Management, Manishment.*)

†**c.** An instance of managing; an administrative act. *Obs.*

1609 Tourneur *Funerall Poeme Sir F. Vere* 34 His ways ..and intents In private and in publique managements. **1615** Brathwait *Strappado* (1878) 137 Thou Saint of Albion, Who had thy auncient consecration From thy religious mannagements, as farre Disperst, as Turke or Christian planted are. *a* **1618** Sylvester *Maiden's Blush* 658

His faithfull diligence And mature Wisdome in all managements. **1671** Evelyn *Diary* 14 Nov., Sir Cha. Wheeler, late Governor of the Leeward Islands, having ben complain'd of for many indiscreete managements, it was resolved..to advise his Majesty to remove him. **1676** Glanvill *Ess.* IV. 34 By inquiry into God's Works, we discover continually, how little we can comprehend of his Ways and Menagements.

†**d.** Manner of proceeding. *Obs.*

1649 Bp. Hall *Cases Consc.* (1650) 35 When some covetous extortioner..buys up the whole lading of the ship, that he may..sell..at pleasure..: The true judgment of which action, & the degrees of the malignity of it, must be fetcht..from the management of the buyer. *a* **1715** Burnet *Own Time* (1724) I. 217 By this management of his the thing grew publick.

e. *spec.* The administration of a commercial enterprise. Also in phrases designating specific methods of business administration, as *management by exception, by objectives.*

1906 Dicksee & Blain (*title*) Office organisation and management. **1962** A. Battersby *Guide to Stock Control* x. 95 They [*sc.* the junior staff] are the instruments of 'management by exception', filtering out the run-of-the-mill cases from the few unusual ones which call for the personal attention of the Materials Controller. **1962** H. O. Beecheno *Introd. Business Stud.* ii. 17 Trade union development and legislation on conditions of work, plus more enlightened management have eradicated most forms of unfair treatment of employees. **1965** H. I. Ansoff *Corporate Strategy* (1968) 9 Management of a business firm is a very large complex of activities which consists of analysis, decisions, communication, leadership, motivation, measurement, and control. *Ibid.* iii. 36 Their potential pervasiveness is such that objectives have been used as a basis for an integrated view on the entire management process which has become known as 'management by objectives'. **1968** Johannsen & Robertson *Managem. Gloss.* 81 *Management by Objectives*, setting targets within an organisation..as a basis for achieving greater efficiency and providing motivation and an incentive to managers. **1969** J. Argenti *Managem. Techniques* 146 Management by Exception..simply says, 'don't tell someone if everything is O.K.—only tell him if something has gone wrong'. **1970** *Lebende Sprachen* XV. 11/2 Operational research is an integral part of good management.

2. a. The use of contrivance, prudence, or ingenuity for effecting some purpose; often in unfavourable sense, implying deceit or trickery.

1666 Dryden *Ann. Mirab.* Acc. of Poem §4, I repose upon your management what is dearest to me, my fame and reputation. **1711** in Picton *L'pool Munic. Rec.* (1886) II. 4 Attempts have been..made.. to vacate and sett aside the present charter by the management of Mr. Henry Richmond. **1798** Washington *Let.* Writ. 1893 XIV. 63 If there has been any management in the business, it has been concealed from me. **1842** Borrow *Bible in Spain* xlviii. (Pelh. Libr.) 330 Through the management of Antonio, however, I procured one of the two chests. **1881** Jowett *Thucyd.* I. 118 We rely not upon management or trickery, but upon our own hearts and hands. **1888** Bryce *Amer. Commw.* II. xl. 102 Talent for intrigue or 'management' usually counts for more than debating power.

†**b.** A contrivance, device; in bad sense, a piece of trickery. *Obs.*

1736 Neve *Builder's Dict.* Pref. 8 The little Artifices, and low Managements, by which some Men in the Bookselling Trade..have..discredited their Business. **1748** *Anson's Voy.* II. viii. 220 By this management we never wanted turtle for the..four months..we continued at sea.

†**3.** A negotiation. *to be in a management*: to be engaged in negotiations *with. Obs.*

1705 Addison *Italy* 456 They say too that he [the Duke of Savoy] had great Managements with several Ecclesiasticks before he turn'd Hermite. *a* **1715** Burnet *Own Time* (1724) I. 346 Yet, while he made a base complying speech in favour of the Court, and of the war, he was in a secret management with another party.

4. Power of managing; administrative skill; also, †tact, ingenuity.

a **1715** Burnet *Own Time* (1724) I. 189 He was a very prudent man, and had such a management with it, that I never knew any Clergy-man so universally esteemed. **1760** *Ann. Reg.* 53 The argument was conducted with great management and address. **1809** Malkin *Gil Blas* III. iii. ¶ 4 If you have management enough to worm yourself into his confidence.

†**5.** Indulgence or consideration shown towards a person; politic moderation in the conduct of a case; an instance of this. [= F. *ménagement.*] *Obs.*

1727 Oldmixon *Clarendon & Whitlock comp.* 325-6 Decency seem'd to require a little more Management, considering he [Clarendon] was Cromwell's profess'd Enemy. *a* **1743** Ld. Hervey *Mem.* (1848) II. 257 He feared ..lest the King and Queen, who hated their son..might construe it to be a management for their son in Sir Robert Walpole, and never forgive it him. *Ibid.* 291 Sir Robert.. thought their suspicions of his having had any management or tenderness towards their son were most unjust. **1765** H. Walpole *Otranto* iii, The herald, who with so little management had questioned the title of Manfred. **1771** Burke *Lett., to C. Townshend* (1844) I. 268 When I have any thing to object to persons in power..I use no sort of managements towards them. **1773** *Ibid.* 432, I suppose this design of Lord Temple's is one cause of his management in opposition, in order to conciliate the Tories. **1790** *Ibid.* III. 135 You certainly do not always convey to me your opinions with the greatest tenderness and management. **1818** Jas. Mill *Brit. India* II. IV. iii. 110 Suraja Dowla..was too ignorant and headstrong to use management with his dislikes.

6. *collect.* A governing body, *e.g.* a committee, board of directors, board of control, board of governors, of any institution or business. *spec.*

that group of employees which administers and controls an industry in contradistinction to the labour force in that industry or in industry in general.

1739 CIBBER *Apol.* x. 273 Drury-Lane, under a particular Menagement. **1847** *Illustr. Lond. News* 10 July 27/2 Wherever they entered into engagements, the managements speak in high terms of their honourable conduct. **1864** *Morn. Star* 26 May 4 These 'authorised offices' do not profess to be 'authorised' by the management. **1902** ELIZ. L. BANKS *Newspaper Girl* 201 There are many necessary outlays which the management of the paper would not pay. **1912** F. W. RAFFETY *Modern Business Pract.* II. II. i. 197 Management..deals with the three sources of force or energy—capital, labor and land...The management should never lose sight of their important influence. **1940** W. TEMPLE *Hope of New World* i. 61 If there is to be tension at all, let it be between the financial interests of Shareholders and the productive interests of Management and Labour in co-operation. **1959** [see BOARD *sb.* 17]. **1965** H. I. ANSOFF *Corporate Strategy* (1968) i. 20 Management from top to bottom continually seeks to improve efficiency, to cut costs, to sell more, to advertise better. **1968** *Lebende Sprachen* XIII. 4/2 It has been part of management philosophy to encourage and support the self-development of its employees. **1969** J. ARGENTI *Managem. Techniques* 150 In every company there are two or three dozen absolutely vital ratios that must be watched and checked by the management.

7. *attrib.*, as (sense 1) ***management accounting, buy-out, committee, consultancy, consultant, expenses, game, science, share.***

1963 BROAD & CARMICHAEL (*title*) A guide to *management accounting. **1967** *Oxford Computer Explained* 32 *Management accounting*, the provision of a continuous and up-to-date check and control on income and expenditure. **1977** *Business Periodicals Index* XVIII. 294 (*heading*) Making two out of one (*management buyouts). **1980** *Financial Rev.* (Australia) 8 July 19/3 The British generally call it the 'management buy-out' but the meaning is the same—a company, very often the subsidiary of a large group, is bought 'out' by its senior directors. **1981** *Observer* 4 Oct. 21/1 Both are on probation as examples of a growing phenomenon in British business life: the hive-off, spin-off or demerger—the management buy-out, in fact. **1985–86** *Sight & Sound Q.* Winter 13/3 Chief Executive Gary Dartnall goes about trying to raise the cash for a management buy-out. **1903** *Westm. Gaz.* 12 Oct. 10/1 A member of the *Management Committee of the National Liberal Club. **1958, 1966** *Management consultancy [see CONSULTANCY]. **1972** *Accountant* 19 Oct. 487/1 The rapid development of management consultancy services has resulted in the profession extending its activities far beyond its traditional role of auditor. **1961** *Times* 14 July 2/2 *Management consultants..must also have..experience in personnel management. **1969** *Times* 6 Mar. 23/2 This brings the number of management consultants on the commission up to three. **1901** *Daily Chron.* 14 Aug. 4/3 The leaders of the men say this is due to heavy *management expenses. **1964** M. ARGYLE *Psychol. & Social Probl.* x. 133 There has been a swing away from traditional teaching methods towards group discussion, joint report-writing by syndicates, case-studies and the *management game. **1965** H. I. ANSOFF *Corporate Strategy* (1968) ix. 148 *Management science can offer only partial assistance to the decision maker. **1969** *Times* 2 May 34 (Advt.), Post-graduate studentships in management sciences. **1900** *Daily News* 20 Nov. 2/3 The existing 200 one pound *management shares would be divided into a thousand 4s. management shares.

Hence **manage'mental** *a.*, pertaining to the management.

1885 *19th Cent.* June 1061 Each manager reduces managemental expenses so far as lies in his power.

manager ('mænɪdʒə(r)). Also 7 **menager.** [f. MANAGE *v.* + -ER¹.]

1. One who manages (something specified); †the wielder (of a weapon), †the person who wages (a war); the conductor (of an affair). Now *rare* in general sense: see 2, 3.

1588 SHAKS. *L.L.L.* I. ii. 188 Adue Valour, rust Rapier, bee still Drum, for your manager is in loue. **1590** —— *Mids. N.* v. i. 35 Where is our vsuall manager of mirth? What Reuels are in hand? **1598** FLORIO, *Maneggiatóre*, a manager, a handler. **1612** BP. HALL *Imprese of God* II. Wks. (1625) 452 Warre..hath..two directors—Iustice and Charity: Iustice, that requires both authoritie in the menager, and innocence in menaging. **1711** HICKES *Two Treat. Christ. Priesth.* (1847) II. 16 The priest is the common manager..of sacred affairs betwixt God and the people.

2. Chiefly with qualifying adj.: One skilled in managing affairs, money, etc.

1670 COTTON *Espernon* I. II. 60 Her Estate therefore requir'd both a discreet manager to husband it, and a man well furnish'd with money, to disengage it. **1684** DK. YORK in Ellis *Orig. Lett.* Ser. I. III. 330, I must recommend to you both to be good managers, and to be sure to live within what you have. **1710** STEELE *Tatler* No. 248 ¶6 A Man of Business in good Company, who gives an Account of his Abilities..is hardly more insupportable than her they call a Notable Woman, and a Manager. **1728** YOUNG *Love Fame* VI. 181 Julia's a manager; she's born for rule; And knows her wiser husband is a fool. **1738** POPE *Epil. Sat.* I. 21 An artful Manager, that crept between His Friend and Shame, and was a kind of Screen. **1806** A. HUNTER *Culina* (ed. 2) 271 She is not what is called a good manager. **1871** C. GIBBON *Lack of Gold* ii, Everybody owned that she was a capital manager. **1884** *Leeds Mercury* 30 Apr. 4/6 The government Whips..seem incapable of contending with the astute managers on the other side.

3. One whose office it is to manage a business establishment or a public institution.

Chiefly in certain specific applications: One who conducts a theatre or other place of amusement; one employed to take charge of the working of a bank, factory, mine, or other mercantile or industrial establishment, or of some particular department of such an establishment; one who has charge of the financial arrangements and the mechanical production of a newspaper, as distinguished from the matters which come within the province of the editor; a person, or one of a body of persons, responsible for the general working of a public institution.

1705 ADDISON *Italy* 443 The Manager opens his Sluce every Night, and distributes the Water into what Quarters of the Town he pleases. **1741** RICHARDSON *Pamela* II. 341, I think, continued he, that little Kentish Purchase wants a Manager. **1764** *Oxf. Sausage* 38 Some who of old could Tastes and Fashions guide, Controul the Manager and awe the Play'r. **1779** SHERIDAN *Critic* I. i, Now that the manager has monopolized the Opera House, haven't we the signors and signoras calling here. **1809** *Med. Jrnl.* XXI. 173 Your physician has thought it his duty to propose to the [workhouse] managers, the vaccination of the whole number. **1840** CARLYLE *Heroes* iii. (1858) 269 This is our poor Warwickshire Peasant, who rose to be Manager of a Playhouse. **1863** FAWCETT *Pol. Econ.* I. vi. 77 In a joint-stock company, all depends upon the manager or agent. **1870** *Act 33 & 34 Vict.* c. 75 §3 The term 'managers' includes all persons who have the management of any elementary school. **1885** MABEL COLLINS *Prettiest Woman* viii, Then we can see the author, the manager.

4. One of several members of either house of parliament appointed for the performance of some specified duty connected with the functions of the two houses; *esp.* the arranging a conference between the two houses, and the presenting of articles of impeachment.

1666–7 MARVELL *Corr.* Wks. 1872–5 II. 209 We went up to the Lords to manage the impeachment against Lord Mordaunt. Our managers observed that he sat in the House. **1710** [ST. LEGER] *Managers Pro & Con* (ed. 3) 4 To Him and to Me, He and the Council seem'd to be the Managers for the Pretender; and the Commons Managers seem'd only to be of Council for the Queen and the Nation. **1791** BURKE *App. Whigs* Wks. VI. 157 Mr. Walpole (afterwards Sir Robert) was one of the managers on this occasion. **1817** *Parl. Deb.* 4 At the conference the managers for the Lords, ..communicated to those for the Commons the Address just agreed to. **1840** *Penny Cycl.* XVII. 277/2 The conference [between Lords and Commons] is conducted by 'Managers' for both houses. *Ibid.* 279/1 The managers should confine themselves to charges contained in the articles of impeachment. **1841** MACAULAY *Ess.*, *Warren Hastings* (The Trial), The House decided that Francis should not be a manager... The managers, with Burke at their head, appeared in full dress... Nor, though surrounded by such men, did the youngest manager pass unnoticed. **1855** —— *Hist. Eng.* xviii. IV. 124 Rochester, in the Painted Chamber, delivered to the managers of the Lower House a copy of the Treaty of Limerick. **1863** H. COX *Instit.* I. ix. 152 The number of members of the Commons named managers of a conference is double that of the Lords. *Ibid.* II. vi. 471 For the prosecution of the trial managers are appointed by the House of Commons.

5. *Law.* A person appointed, ordinarily by a court of chancery, to control, carry on and account for any business which may have fallen into the hands of the court for the benefit of creditors or others: usually ***receiver and manager.***

1793 F. VESEY jr. *Chancery Rep.* I. 139 Motion for an order, that the manager of an estate in one of the West India islands should give security faithfully to manage the estate [etc.]. **1821** *Jacob & Walker's Chancery Rep.* I. 299 Praying ..that in the meantime a receiver and manager might be appointed. **1827** F. VESEY jr. *Chancery Rep.* (ed. 2) XIX. 146 A Motion was made..for a reference to the Master to appoint a Manager and Receiver. **1880** *Law Rep.* 14 Ch. Div. 645 This was a petition..praying for the appointment by the Court of a manager of the undertaking of the Manchester and Milford Railway. **1880** *Ibid.* 655 When you come to give proper weight to..the ordinary course of the Court of Chancery in appointing a receiver as distinguished from a manager.

manageress ('mænɪdʒərɪs, mænɪdʒə'rɛs). [f. prec. + -ESS.] A woman manager, e.g. of a theatre or hotel.

1797 MRS. A. M. BENNETT *Beggar Girl* (1813) I. 20 The lady manageress's benefit had been stuck up at every door in the parish. **1819** SCOTT *Fam. Lett.* 23 Aug. (1894) II. 52 A play of Joanna Baillie's which she has sent to Mrs. Siddons (our manageress). **1885** MISS BRADDON *Wyllard's Weird* III. 81 Mdlle. Duprez..was known and welcomed with friendliest greeting by manageress and head waiter. **1902** ELIZ. L. BANKS *Newspaper Girl* 105, I had given a false name and false address to the manageress of the laundry.

managerial (mænɪ'dʒɪərɪəl), *a.* [f. as prec. + -(I)AL.] Of or pertaining to, or characteristic of, a manager, esp. the manager of a theatre. In more recent use esp. of a manager of a commercial enterprise.

1767 A. CAMPBELL *Lexiph.* 145 The latter were to be set off with all our inimitable Garrick's managerial art,..and judicious cast of parts. **1807** in *Spirit Pub. Jrnls.* XI. 370 They hail a scheme which promises them relief from managerial neglect and popular damnation. **1854** DICKENS *Hard T.* II. i, She usually embellished with her genteel presence a managerial board-room over the public office. **1895** *Times* (weekly ed.) 27 Sept. 778/1 To force the note of approbation at the close, by means of a managerial speech. **1895** *Tablet* 10 Aug. 230 The question of the managerial authority has attracted a great deal of public attention. **1912** F. W. RAFFETY *Modern Business Pract.* II. II. i. 204 Management..involves not only the forces of production but careful consideration of the results to be obtained... It is this latter purpose which distinguishes the man with managerial ability from the purely technical man. **1924** J. STAMP *Stud. Current Probl. Finance & Govt.* ii. 43 It [*sc.* the Excess Profits Duty Act] conferred quite a considerable number of discretions to the Commissioners of Inland Revenue, such as..the amount to be allowed as managerial remuneration. **1940** H. G. WELLS *Babes in Darkling Wood* IV. iii. 379 They would soon draw plenty of recruits and assistants from the managerial class in the big trade machines. **1941** J. BURNHAM *Managerial Revolution* vi. 70 The theory of the managerial revolution asserts..the following: Modern society has been organized through a.. set of major economic, social, and political institutions which we call capitalist... At the present time these institutions..are undergoing..transformation... Within the new social structure a different social group..—the managers—will be the dominant..class. **1955** P. F. DRUCKER *Pract. Managem.* xxii. 268 Opportunities for participation that will give him [*sc.* the worker] a managerial vision. **1958** *Listener* 30 Oct. 685/1 The salaried middle class of professional, technical, and managerial people. **1973** *Amer. Speech 1969* XLIV. 268 Managerial positions are unquestionably the highest occupational level of the three.

Hence **mana'gerialism**, belief in or the art of conducting or planning business or other enterprises by the use of managerial techniques; **mana'gerialist**, an adherent of managerialism; also *attrib.* or as *adj.*; **mana'gerially** *adv.*, in the manner or capacity of, or in relation to, a manager.

1882 *Daily News* 9 Mar. 2/3 The Croydon March Meeting, which finished as well as it commenced, managerially and financially speaking. **1902** *Westm. Gaz.* 15 Jan. 10/3 He was..managerially connected with a London theatre. **1946** 'G. ORWELL' *James Burnham* 5 According to Burnham..'managerialism' has reached its fullest development in the U.S.S.R. *Ibid.* 6 He describes the New Deal as 'primitive managerialism'. [Burnham did not use the word *managerialism* in *The Managerial Revolution.*—Ed.] **1952** K. R. POPPER *Open Society* (ed. 2) I. 4 A lapse into totalitarianism (or perhaps into 'managerialism'). **1965** H. I. ANSOFF *Corporate Strategy* (1968) iii. 40 A 'managerialist' point of view came into being which..subjected the microeconomic theory to thorough criticism. *Ibid.*, The managerialists have offered a number of substitute explanations of the behaviour of the firm. **1966** *Harper's Mag.* June 67 Many remained caught in the irrelevancies of such questions as whether the Soviet Union was a 'degenerate workers' state' or a 'managerialist bureaucracy'. **1970** *Guardian Weekly* 14 Feb. 8 No doubt some cynics and managerialists will deride them [*sc.* local city councils] as 'mere talking-shops'. **1973** *Human World* Feb. 7 The anxiety Mr Maddox senses in the environmentalists comes to no more than a yearning for a universal poeticized prosperity. This they find compatible with a beneficent world-wide managerialism.

managerie, obs. form of MENAGERIE.

managership ('mænɪdʒəʃɪp). [f. MANAGER + -SHIP.]

1. The office or position of a manager.

1883 *Jrnl. Educ.* XVIII. 151 A local managership of a life insurance company. **1892** *Daily News* 8 Mar. 6/1 Their chances are better than..before the qualifications for manager-ships became the subject of national law.

2. The control of a manager.

1864 *Reader* 24 Dec. 792/1 Under the most energetic and intelligent managership and stage-managership.

†**'managery.** *Obs.* Also 7–8 **menagery, -ie,** (7 **menagry**), **manadgery, mannagery,** 8 **man(n)agry.** [f. MANAGE *sb.* or *v.* + -ERY; but in many examples influenced in sense by F. *ménagerie* (†domestic administration): see MENAGERIE.]

1. Domestic or agricultural administration or economy.

1633 J. DONE tr. *Aristeas' Hist. Septuagint* 74 The Peasants therefore are very carefull..in their..Menagery.. by reason whereof..the region is all planted with Fruite trees. **1677** GREW *Anat. Seeds* iii. §1 The next step of Natures Managery, relates chiefly to the Growth of the Seed when it is sow'n. **1740** LADY POMFRET *Lett.* (1805) II. 214 The sacred cells, and all the managery Of holy nuns in their retreats, I see. **1720** STRYPE *Stow's Surv.* I. I. xxvi. 185/1 These Men that thus spake against the Managery of this Hospital. *a* **1734** NORTH *Life Ld. Keeper Guilford* (1742) 133 And with all this Menagery and Provision, no one..could observe any Thing more to do there, than in any other Nobleman's House.

b. Husbanding or judicious use of resources; economy.

1673 O. WALKER *Educ.* II. vii. 280 There is also required good menagery, or making your penny go further then another mans. **1705** STANHOPE *Paraphr.* II. 410 Managery is an Ornament and an Advantage to our Charity. **1705** TATE *Triumph* xii, They blest the Managry of those Supplies.

2. The art of managing (weapons, instruments).

1654 WHITLOCK *Zootomia* 55 Making Shirts and Smocks for the Poore, and such like Managery of their Needle or Wheele. **1667** *Decay Chr. Piety* v. 100 No expert General will bring a company of raw, untrain'd men into the Field, but will..teach them the ready managery of their Weapons. **1693** WALLIS in *Phil. Trans.* XVII. 846 This I thought fit to recommend to your Consideration, who do so well understand Telescopes, and the managery of them.

3. The function of managing or administering; managership; an administrative office.

1643 HEYLIN *Rebels Catech.* 14 Men who..ingrossed unto themselves the principal managery of the Common-wealth. **1650** R. STAPYLTON *Strada's Low C. Warres* v. 137 This Expedient was committed to the managerie of a Spanish Merchant. **1660** WATERHOUSE *Arms & Arm.* 152 In affaires of warre and peace, in Manadgery of Ecclesiastical, Civil, Naval and Land Trusts. *a* **1734** NORTH *Life Dudley North* (1744) 150 He thought that, in such a Managery, there was so much of Trust, that, of Necessity, they must be, more or less, cheated.

4. Cunning or adroit management; an instance of this.

1646 SIR T. BROWNE *Pseud. Ep.* VII. xvi. 371 However husbanded by Art, and the wisest menagery of that most subtile impostor. **1679** EVERARD *Prot. Princes Europe* 9 If France had not..been assured by his managery and tampering with some corrupt Ministers of that Crown, that [etc.]. **1689** *Bloody Assizes* 25 My Lords Threats and other Managery, so disposed the Jury, that..they brought the Lady in Guilty. *a* **1734** NORTH *Exam.* II. iv. §17 (1740) 241 Bedloe held him in Hand so craftily that, at last, he got him fast in the Trap. It was a nice Managery, and may be shewed for a Pattern.

5. a. Horsemanship: = MANAGE *sb.* 1. **b.** A place of exercise for horses: = MANAGE *sb.* 3.

1685 COTTON tr. *Montaigne* I. xxxviii. (1711) I. 347 In Menagery, Study, Hunting and all other Exercises, Men are to proceed to the utmost Limits of Pleasure. **1782** J. ADAMS *Diary* Wks. 1851 III. 298 The menagerie, where they exercise the horses, is near the end of the stables.

6. ? Management of health, hygienic treatment.

1697 R. PEIRCE *Bath Mem.* I. ix. 213 The Cautious and orderly Managery of Women..in bathing, and drinking these Waters, have such..successful Effects.

managery, obs. form of MENAGERIE.

managing ('mænɪdʒɪŋ), *vbl. sb.* [-ING[1].] The action of the vb. MANAGE.

1579 J. STUBBES *Gaping Gulf* D j b, Then will he..leaue thys poore prouence to the mannaging of a viceroy. **1590** SPENSER *F.Q.* II. iv. 8 The knight, that aye with foe In fayre defence and goodly menaging Of armes was wont to fight. **1593** NASHE *Christ's T.* 57 b, Wee kicke and winche, and will by no meanes endure his managing. **1596** DRAYTON *Legends* iii. 579 He Me notice gave, What the proud Barons had in managing. **1607** HIERON *Wks.* I. 407 The well ordring and managing of the wife is the glory of the husband. **1607** BP. HALL *Holy Observ.* I. (1609) 20 A charitable vntrueth, and an vncharitable truth, and an vnwise menaging of trueth or loue, are all to bee carefully auoyded. **1681-2** PRIDEAUX in Fox Bourne *Locke* (1876) I. viii. 470 Certainly there is some whig intrigue a-managing. **1682** BUNYAN *Holy War* 172 The handling of their arms, the managing of their weapons of war, were marvellous taking to Mansoul and me. **1707** MORTIMER *Husb.* (1721) I. A vij b, The Way of ordering and managing of Fowls. **1711** *Light to Blind* in *10th Rep. Hist. MSS. Comm.* App. v. 144 Their..officers signalized themselves in manageing of this last contention.

'managing, *ppl. a.* [-ING[2].] That manages.

1. Addicted to scheming or to assuming the direction of affairs.

a **1715** BURNET *Own Time* (1724) I. 475 She got him to be brought out of prison, and carried him to the Countess of Powis, a zealous managing Papist. **1848** THACKERAY *Van. Fair* xxxiii, That brisk, managing, lively, imperious woman.

2. Skilful and diligent in management; economical.

1754 RICHARDSON *Grandison* (1811) I. xiv. 89 Sir John spoke of him as a managing man, as to his fortune. **1797** T. WRIGHT *Autobiog.* (1864) 41 He was at this time as careful, sober, and managing a man as any in the neighbourhood. **1825** ESTHER HEWLETT *Cottage Comforts* v. 36 A managing young woman, when she goes to the shop..will take care to look about her. **1894** H. NISBET *Bush Girl's Rom.* 25 With the advent of the charming and managing Kathleen, he drew no more upon his sadly-diminished capital.

3. Having executive control. ***managing clerk*** (CLERK *sb.* 6 b); ***managing director*** (DIRECTOR 1 b).

1766 *Life of Quin* vi. (1887) 30 The general conditions were, two hundred pounds a year to each managing actor, and a clear benefit. **1799** *Times* 1 June 1/3 (Advt.), Wanted ..a managing clerk; he must understand well the Business of Conveyancing. **1847** DISRAELI *Tancred* II. ix, You want a firstrate managing man. **1861** MILL *Repr. Govt.* v. 91 Even a joint-stock company has always in practice, if not in theory, a managing director. **1865** A. D. RICHARDSON *Secret Service* 18, I found the Managing Editor in his office. **1866** MRS. H. WOOD *Elster's Folly* II. x. 230 The lawyer laughed. 'Hopkins did not know you; and strangers are generally introduced to..our managing clerk.' **1897** HAVELOCK-WILSON *Sp. Ho. Comm.* 25 Jan., He did not say that.. managing owners sent ships to sea for the purpose of gaining by insurance. **1902** ELIZ. L. BANKS *Newspaper Girl* 36 The managing-editor was an ex-Confederate colonel. *Mod.* The managing committee of the society. **1922** JOYCE *Ulysses* 484 They are immediately appointed to positions of high public trust..as managing directors of banks. **1940** W. TEMPLE *Hope of New World* i. 61 The great Managing Directors tend to rule the Boards of which they are at once both members and servants. **1972** M. GILBERT *Body of Girl* xiv. 128 She started here as my secretary. Then..she took on a number of jobs herself. I suppose you'd have called her a managing clerk by that time. **1972** J. MCCLURE *Caterpillar Cop* iv. 47, I would have you know that the managing director of your paper is a personal friend of mine. **1974** L. MEYNELL *Fairly Innocent Little Man* xiv. 180, I had a good job with a law firm. In time I daresay I would have become managing clerk.

‖**manaia** (ma'naia). [Maori.] A motif in Maori carving with a bird-like head and a human body.

1896 A. HAMILTON *Art Workmanship of Maori Race* 12 The thin board-like central piece with a human figure between two *pitau* spirals is called *Manaia* by the Arawas. **1910** J. COWAN *Maoris of N.Z.* xii. 165 Some of the wall slabs are carved into fantastic figures of fabulous water-monsters..others represent the mythical creatures known as the *manaia* and *wheku* with bird-like beaks and snaky tails all coiled in endless spirals. **1916** [see *bird-headed* (BIRD *sb.* 8)]. **1924** E. BEST *Maori* II. xxi. 574 A common design in the carved work of superior houses and elevated storehouses is that known as the *manaia*..a figure composed of a long, slim body, a birdlike head, and an indefinite number of legs. **1959** FREEMAN & GEDDES *Anthropol. in South Seas* 117 The important symbol in Maori carving termed the *manaia* I believe is basically avian in origin. **1963** T. BARROW *Life & Work Maori Carver* 23 The most fascinating [mystery] is the origin and nature of a small creature called a *manaia*. There are many explanations; that it represents a malignant spirit, that it is merely a human image seen in profile, that it is a bird that attacked man in ancient times, or that it represents the *mana* or spiritual power of the human figure it is with. **1966** *Encycl. N.Z.* II. 410/2 Apart from the naturalistic figure, every type of full-faced figure has a *manaia* to match. .. The head of the *manaia* can, in each case, be recognised as half of the head of the appropriate matching figure divided down the middle of the face.

†**'manakin.** *Antiq.* [Cf. F. *manicle*, *manique*, L. *manicula*: see MANACLE *sb.*] An alleged name for a kind of glove worn by soldiers in the twelfth century.

1824 MEYRICK *Anc. Armour* I. 25 The hauberk..is, with its hood, of the same piece but with sleeves fitting close to the arms, terminating with gloves, manakins, or mufflers, which cover the outsides of the hands and fingers.

manakin: see MANIKIN.

‖**mañana** (ma'ɲana, mə'njɑːnə), *adv.* and *sb.* [Sp., tomorrow, morrow, f. *cras mañana* lit. tomorrow early, f. pop.L. **maneana* early, f. L. *māne* in the morning.] **A.** *adv.* Tomorrow, on the day after today. **B.** *sb.* Tomorrow, the day next after the present. Often taken as a synonym of easy-going procrastination as said to be found in Spanish-speaking countries: the indefinite future. Phr. ***land*** (or ***kingdom***) ***of mañana***: sometimes applied *spec.* to Mexico.

1845 R. FORD *Hand-bk. for Travellers Spain* I. ii. 144 Andalucia... Nowhere will the stranger hear more frequently those talismanic words which mark national character..the Manaña [*sic*], [etc.]. **1879** J. W. BODDAM-WHETHAM *Roraima & Brit. Guiana* xviii. 208 With an Indian the morrow is as indefinite a period as 'mañana' with the Spaniards. **1885** *Harper's Mag.* Jan. 217/2 Is Cedar Keys just on the borderland of that vast region known as the kingdom of *Mañana*? **1889** E. RIPLEY *From Flag to Flag* 165 Their *mañana* never came, never was intended to come. **1903** A. ADAMS *Log of Cowboy* 138 Flood had had years of experience in dealing with Mexicans in the land of *mañana*, where all maxims regarding the value of time are religiously discarded. **1910** *Daily News* 27 Sept. 4 The 'manana' boys didn't work quick enough for him, so he put the crew on. **1927** D. H. LAWRENCE *Mornings in Mexico* 59 *Mañana*, to the native, may mean to-morrow, three days hence, six months hence, and never. **1938** 'G. ORWELL' *Homage to Catalonia* i. 12 A promise that there should be machine-gun instruction *mañana*. Needless to say *mañana* never came. **1961** *Guardian* 23 Jan. 6/7 'Mañana' is a concept that exists far outside the Spanish world. **1973** C. BONINGTON *Next Horizon* xiv. 201 The elaborate etiquette and principle of mañana (leave everything until tomorrow, in the absolute confidence that tomorrow will never arrive), which dominates all dealings in South America. **1973** *Nat. Geographic* May 658/1 With a dispatch that put the lie to those who claim this [*sc.* Mexico] is the land of *mañana*, the orders went out to build a subway.

manance, -anse, -anss, obs. ff. MENACE.

mananosay (mænə'nəʊseɪ). *U.S.* Also **mananose, maninose.** [prob. ad. Algonquian name.] The soft-shell clam, *Mya arenaria*.

[**1709** J. LAWSON *New Voy. Carolina* 162 Man of Noses are a Shell-Fish commonly found amongst us.] **1843** J. E. DEKAY *Zool. N.Y.* V. 240 *Mya arenaria*.. in some districts ..still retains its ancient aboriginal appellation of *Maninose*. **1859** BARTLETT *Dict. Amer.* (ed. 2) 84 The Soft Clam or Mananosay (*Mya arenaria*), obtained from the shores of tidal rivers by digging one or two feet in the loose sand. It has a long, extensible, cartilaginous snout, or proboscis, through which it ejects water; whence it is also called Stem-clam. **1870** *Putnam's Monthly Mag.* May 525/1 Even to the toothsome Manonosays that squirted water up through the sand what time the tides were out. **1895** *Sun* (N.Y.) 30 July 9/1 Mananosay, maninose (Maryland), man-of-noses (North Carolina), names for the round clam, from an Algonquian word meaning 'shellfish that one gathers by hand'. **1967** L. S. TAWES *Coasting Captain* xiii. 443, I used to take my launch and go fishing, sometimes digging mananoses.

†**manant**, *a.*[1] *Obs.* [a. OF. *manant* rich.] Opulent, powerful.

1422 tr. *Secreta Secret., Priv. Priv.* 155 The more ryche man be and manaunt, the more hym be-howyth that he be vmbethoght.

†**manant**, *a.*[2] *Obs.*—0 [ad. L. *mānant-em*, pres. pple. of *mānāre* to flow.]

1727 BAILEY vol. II, *Manant*, flowing or running.

†**manantie.** *Obs.* In 4 manauntie. [a. OF. *manantie*, f. *manant* inhabitant.] A dwelling.

c **1330** R. BRUNNE *Chron.* (1810) 325 And in his pes to lyue, and haf þer manauntie.

manaple, obs. form of MANIPLE.

manar, obs. form of MANOR, MANURE.

manarolins, variant of MANAVILINS.

manarvel (mə'nɑːvəl), *v. Naut. slang.* [Of obscure origin: related to MANAVILINS either as its source or as a back-formation from it.] (See quot.)

1867 SMYTH *Sailor's Word-bk.*, To Manarvel, to pilfer small stores.

manas(e, -ass(e, -as(s)h, obs. ff. MENACE.

manasseite (mə'næseɪaɪt). *Min.* [f. the name of E. *Manasse* (see quot. 1941) + -ITE[1].] A hydrated carbonate and hydroxide of magnesium and aluminium that is polymorphous with hydrotalcite and occurs as soft, foliated, whitish masses having a pearly lustre and a greasy feel.

1941 C. FRONDEL in *Amer. Mineralogist* XXVI. 310 These facts indicate with reasonable certainty that the mineral is identical in composition with hydrotalcite. The name manasseite is proposed for this mineral in honor of Ernesto Manasse (1875–1922), Italian chemist, mineralogist and petrographer,..who made important contributions to our knowledge of hydrotalcite and pyroaurite. **1962** W. A. DEER et al. *Rock-Forming Min.* V. 63 Spinel may alter to talc, mica, serpentine, or corundum: Struwe (1958) has also recorded its alteration to diaspore..and manasseite, $Mg_6Al_2CO_3(OH)_{16}.4H_2O$.

†**manat.** *Obs.* [Cf. *mennot*, *monnit*, the minnow (E.D.D.).] Some kind of fish.

1610 FOLKINGHAM *Art Surv.* IV. iii. 83 Fishing..in Fresh waters; as for Samon, Trout, Carpe, Pike, Manat, Breame, ..Minnowes, Crea-fish.

manat, obs. form of MANATEE.

man-at-arms. Orig. **man-of-arms.** [tr. OF. *homme d'armes*, *homme à armes*.] A soldier, warrior; *spec.* a heavy-armed soldier on horseback.

1390 GOWER *Conf.* III. 2 He is a noble man of armes. *c* **1430** *Syr Gener.* (Roxb.) 3425 Of men of armes thei broght x thousand,..And of othir men of fote also Thre thousand. **1439** *Rolls of Parlt.* V. 33/2 Noo Souldiours, Man' of Armes, nor Archer. **1500-20** DUNBAR *Poems* lxiii. 7 Men of armes, and vailȝeand knychtis. **1530** PALSGR. 242/2 Man of armes, a horse man, *lance. Ibid.* 244/2 Men of armes, *gens darmes*. **1581** PETTIE *Guazzo's Civ. Conv.* III. (1586) 161 Two brothers..both men at armes, and in pay with the King. **1598** BARRET *Theor. Warres* 141 The Man at Armes is armed complete, with his cuyrasses of proofe [etc.].., well mounted vpon a strong and couragious horse. **1630** *R. Johnson's Kingd. & Commw.* 109 They are able to bring to the field 2000. men at Armes, and infinite troopes of light Horsemen. **1795** SOUTHEY *Joan of Arc* VI. 300 A man-at-arms upon a barded steed. **1814** SCOTT *Ld. of Isles* VI. xii, His men-at-arms bear mace and lance. **1838** THIRLWALL *Greece* xvi. II. 334 Besides the 35,000 helots who attended the Spartans, each man of arms in the rest of the army was accompanied by one light armed. **1874** BOUTELL *Arms & Arm.* ii. 35.

fig. **1871** MORLEY *Voltaire* (1886) 9 Each controversial man-at-arms.

manatee (mænə'tiː). *Zool.* Forms: 6–7 **manat, manaty**, 6–9 **manati**, 7 **mannatee, manentine, manacy, mannaty, manitte**, 7–8 **manate, mannati**, 8 **mannasy, mannasi, manatea, manatae, minati, manatie, manattee**, 9 **mannittee, manatin**, 7– **manatee.** [a. Sp. *manati* (Oviedo 1535), a. Carib *manattoüi* (Raymond Breton *Dict. Caraïbe*, 1665). Cf. mod.L. *manātus* (Rondelet *De Pisc. Mar.* 1554, XVI. xviii), whence F. †*manat* (Cotgr.), *manate* (Littré), It. *manátto* (Florio). The word was commonly identified with the L. *manātus* 'furnished with hands', the animal having fins somewhat resembling hands.]

1. A large aquatic herbivorous cetacean of the genus *Manatus* (order *Sirenia*), esp. *M. americanus*; it inhabits the shallow waters of rivers and estuaries on the Atlantic shores within the tropics. Called also LAMANTIN.

1555 EDEN *Decades* 130 A yonge fyshe of the kynde of those huge monsters of the sea whiche thinhabitours caule Manati. **1568** HACKET *Thevet's New found World* lxxi. 115 Among the which [fish] there is one named Manaty. **1591** SYLVESTER *Du Bartas* I. ii. 1243 The Indian Manat and the Mullet float O'r Mountain tops, where erst the bearded Goat Did bound and brouz. **1634** SIR T. HERBERT *Trav.* 212 The Mannatee or Cow-fish for taste and shape can pose both feeders and beholders. **1684** *Bucaniers Amer.* III. vii. 82 A certain Animal, which the Spaniards call Manentines, and the Dutch, Sea-Cows. **1735** J. ATKINS *Voy. Guinea* 42 Fit haunts for the Manatea and Crocodile. **1799** W. TOOKE *View Russian Emp.* I. 204 Sea-bears, manatis and other sea-animals frequent these shores in herds. **1843** *Penny Cycl.* XXVII. 289/1 The American Manatee is of rounded form, and has been compared to a leathern bottle or wine-skin. **1883** MOLONEY *W. African Fisheries* 28 (Fish. Exh. Publ.) The flesh of the manatee is much appreciated by the natives, resembling a combination of veal and pork.

2. northern manatee, the edentulous animal *Rhytina Stelleri*, formerly existing in the Behring Straits. † **Saint Helena manatee**, app. some kind of seal.

1697 DAMPIER *Voy.* (1729) I. 547, I found the *Santa Hellena* Manatee to be, by their shapes..those Creatures called Sea-lyons. **1855** W. S. DALLAS in *Syst. Nat. Hist.* II. 413 The *Rhytina Stelleri*, or Northern Manatee, which like the Dodo, has become extinct.

3. *attrib.* and *Comb.*, as ***manatee-catching***; **manatee-grass**, a marine plant of the West Indies, *Thalassia testudinum*; **manatee-hide**, a whip made of the hide of the manatee; **manatee leather**, leather made from the hide of the manatee; **manatee strap**, a strap made of manatee leather; **manatee-trap**, a trap for harpooning manatees.

1843 *Penny Cycl.* XXVII. 289/2 The sport of *manatee-catching, thus conducted, is described as highly diverting. **1696** SLOANE *Catal. Plant. Jamaica* 5 *Alga Juncea*, ..*Manati Grasse. **1871** KINGSLEY *At Last* i, A bottom of white sand, bedded here and there with the short manati-grass. **1855** —— *Westw. Ho!* xxv, The driver applied the *manati-hide across his loins, once, twice, with fearful force. **1836** MACGILLIVRAY tr. *Humboldt's Trav.* xviii. 258 She was scourged with straps of *manatee leather. **1682** T. A. *Carolina* 32 With one of these Manaty Strapps I have seen a Bar of Iron cut and dented. **1883** MOLONEY *W. African Fisheries* 27 *Manatee-trap... Briefly described it is a harpoon of heavy wood tipped with iron, suspended by a string..from the cross-piece of a supporting wooden framework.

†**manath.** *Obs.* Forms: 1 *mán-áð*, 2–3 **manaþ**, **mon-oð**, 4 **mane-aþ**, **maineath**. [OE. *mán-áð*, f. *mán* MAN *sb.*[2] + *áð* OATH; cf. the equivalent OS. *mênêd* (MDu. *meineet*), OHG. (MHG., mod.G.) *meineid*, ON. *meineiðr* (Da. and Sw. *mened*). The normal mod. form would be **moan-oath*.] False oath, perjury.

a **1000** *Laws Æthelstan* I. c. 25 Seþe man-að [*v.r.* mænneað] swerige. *c* **1175** *Lamb. Hom.* 49 Alse þeos men doð þe liggeð inne eubruche and ine glutenerie and ine manaðas. *a* **1200** ORMIN 4480 þatt tu ne swere nan manaþ Forr lufe ne forr eȝȝe. *c* **1200** *Trin. Coll. Hom.* 215 On is leasing, oðer is mon-oð. *a* **1300** *Cursor M.* 27833 Fals foluing, fals wittnesing, Vnknaun lage, manath [*c* **1375** *Fairf.* mane-aþ, *a* **1400** *Cotton Galba* maineath], and lesing.

manati, manatin: see MANATEE.

manatine (ˈmænətaɪn), *a.* [ad. mod.L. type *manātīnus*, f. *manātus* MANATEE: see -INE.] Resembling, or related to, the manatee; manatoid.

In some recent Dicts.

†**ma'nation.** *Obs. rare.* [ad. L. *mānātiōn-em*, f. *mānāre* to flow.] The action of flowing out.

1656 BLOUNT *Glossogr.*, *Manation*, a flowing, or running, a trickling down. **1755** JOHNSON, *Manation*, the act of issuing from something else. **1814** BRACKENRIDGE *Views Louisiana* 288 Without speech, how could we ever communicate to each other, that we possess reasoning powers—a manation of the divine essence?

manatoid (ˈmænətɔɪd), *a.* and *sb.* [ad. mod.L. *manātoīdēs*, f. *manātus* MANATEE: see -OID.]

a. *adj.* Resembling the manatee. **b.** *sb.* One of the *Manatoidea*.

In some recent Dicts.

manattee, -atu, -aty: see MANATEE.

manauce, -aunce, -ze, -ause: see MENACE.

manavilins, manavlins (məˈnævɪlɪnz, məˈnævlɪnz), *sb. pl. slang.* Also **malhavelins** (*Whitby Gloss.*, 1876), **manablins**, **manarolins**, **menavelings**. [Of obscure origin: app. a vbl. sb. in -ING[1]. Cf. MANARVEL *v.*] Small matters, odds and ends; articles supplementary to the ordinary fare.

1865 *Hotten's Slang Dict.*, *Manablins*, broken victuals. *Menavelings*, odd money remaining after the daily accounts are made up at a railway booking-office,—usually divided among the clerks. **1887** G. B. GOODE *Fisheries of U.S.* Sect. v. II. 228 To the above-mentioned fare should be added,.. the 'manarolins [? *read* manarvlins] of the whale-men—that is, fresh meat, vegetables, milk, butter, eggs, and fruits. **1889** 'R. BOLDREWOOD' *Robbery under Arms* xxii, He'd a stool and table too..this Robinson Crusoe cove. No end of manavilins either. **1902** E. B. KENNEDY *Black Police Queensl.* viii. 101 Odds and ends..are described in the Colony by the one useful old naval word 'manavlins', a term which embraces every small thing.

manayr(e, obs. form of MANOR.

manbote (ˈmænbəʊt). *Obs.* exc. *Hist.* [OE. *mannbót*, f. *mann* MAN *sb.*[1] + *bót* BOOT *sb.*[1]] A fine paid to an overlord for the loss of a man.

a **1000** *Laws of Ine* c. 70 Æt twyhyndum were mon sceal sellan to monbote xxx. scill., æt vi. hyndum lxxx. scill., æt twelfhyndum cxx. *Ibid.* c. 76 Sie sio mæȝbot and sio manbot ȝelic. *a* **1201** HOVEDEN *Chronica* (Rolls) II. 224 Manbote in Denelaga, et de villano et de Scotman, duodecim horas; de liberis autem hominibus tres marcas. **1656** in BLOUNT *Glossogr.* **1872** E. W. ROBERTSON *Hist. Ess.* Introd. 35 A number of the more important members of the class had evidently been enrolled in the ranks of the feudal nobility and their manbote was 'reckoned in gold'.

manc, variant of MANK *Obs.*

mancala (mænˈkɑːlə). Also **mankalah**, **munckalah**. [ad. colloq. Arab. *manḳala*, f. *naḳala* to move.] A board game, originally Arabic but now common throughout Africa and Asia, played by two players on a special board (see quot. 1952) the object of which is the capture of the opponent's pieces. Also used as a generic term for regional variations of the basic game.

[**1813** J. GALT *Lett. from Levant* xxix. 242, I saw there today a game... The Idriots call it Mandoli, or the Almonds, and it is played at a board by two persons.] **1836** E. W. LANE *Acct. Manners & Customs Mod. Egyptians* II. iv. 46 One of the games most common among the Egyptians is that of the *munckalah*. **1877** *Encycl. Brit.* VII. 726/2 They [*sc.* the Egyptians] are acquainted with..other games, among which is one peculiar to themselves, called Mankalah, and played with cowries. **1952** H. J. R. MURRAY *Hist. Board-Games* vii. 158 Anthropologists use the term *mancala* for any similar game played on a board in which the pattern..usual for board-games is replaced by two, three, or four rows of holes deep enough to contain a number of pieces at the same time. **1969** R. C. BELL *Board & Table Games* II. iv. 72 Ba-awa played by the Twi people of Ghana, is one of the simpler forms of mancala and appears to be extremely ancient.

‖**mancando** (man'kando). *Mus.* [It. = lacking, failing.] A direction indicating a decrescendo, or lessening of tone, in an already soft passage (Grove *Dict. Mus.* 1880).

1811 in BUSBY *Dict. Mus.* (ed. 3).

†**man'cation.** *Obs.* [ad. med.L. *mancātiōn-em*, n. of action f. *mancāre* to mutilate, f. *mancus* one-handed, maimed.] Maiming, mutilation.

1727 EARBERY tr. *Burnet's St. Dead* 86 This brings me to the next Dispute, how far Mancation destroys this Identity; for as a River, by being divided into many Streams, may lose its Name. So would Man, if he could be supposed split into Halves.

mance, manch, obs. ff. MANSE, MUNCH.

manche[1], **maunche** (mɑːnʃ, -æ-). Forms: 5 *pl.* **mangys** (*Her.*), 7 **manch**, 6–7 **maunch**, 8–9 **maunche**, 4, 6–9 **manche**. [a. F. *manche*, fem. = Pr. *manga*, *mancha*, Sp., Pg. *manga*:—L. *manica*, f. *man-us* hand.]

1. A sleeve. *Obs.* exc. as applied by antiquaries to the form of sleeve imitated in the heraldic 'manche': see **2**.

1391 *Earl Derby's Exp.* (Camden) 90 Et per manus eiusdem a brawderere pro j manche, pro frenges et laces pro vsu domini, viij marc. pr. **1602** SEGAR *Hon. Mil. & Civ.* II. xi. 71/2 He shalbe apparelled in a blew gowne, with the Manches open in the maner of a Priest. **1688** R. HOLME *Armoury* III. 256 A Maunch or Sleeve of the newest Fashion, being now in use of the great Gallants of our times... It.. may fitly..be termed the Hounds Ear Maunch.

attrib. **1877** *Encycl. Brit.* VI. 465/2 Tunics..with long and loosely flowing skirts, and having the 'maunche' sleeves.

2. *Her.* A sleeve used as a charge, *esp.* the hanging sleeve of the 14th c.

[*c* **1250** *Roll* in *Planché's Pursuiv. Arms* (ed. 1873) 153 Reginald de Moun, de goules ou ung manche d'argent.] **1486** *Bk. St. Albans, Her.* b iij b, Mangys be called in armys a sleue. **1592** WYRLEY *Armorie, Ld. Chandos* 83 Sir Hue Hastings, armd gold, we do redeem, With gulie maunch and siluer labell on. **1610** GUILLIM *Heraldry* IV. vii. 205 Hee beareth Gules, a Dexter Arme habited with a Maunch, Ermine, the handle holding a Flowre de Lice, Or. **1640** YORKE *Union Hon., Names & Armes* 53 Thory. Argent on a bend sable, 3 manches of the first. **1648** HERRICK *Hesper.* 349 That Bar, this Bend; that Fess, this Cheveron; This Manch, that Moone [etc.]. **1688** R. HOLME *Armoury* III. 257/1 A Queens Maunch erected A. Pinked or Slashed G. with an hand out of it..is the Crest of Gollnitz of Swabish. **1780** EDMONDSON *Heraldry* II. Gloss., *Manche*, a sleeve... Some of our English Writers call it, though improperly, *Maunche*. **1864** BOUTELL *Her. Hist. & Pop.* xiv. (ed. 3) 151 Hastings or, a manche gu. **1868** CUSSANS *Her.* vii. (1893) 118 Manche, or Maunche: A hanging sleeve.

b. *manche maltale* [ad. F. *manche mal taillée*, lit. 'ill-cut sleeve'], an irregularly shaped manche.

a **1550** in Baring-Gould & Twigge *West. Armory* (1898) 1 *Achim*: Ar: a manch maltaile sab. **1562** LEIGH *Armorie* 176 He beareth Or, a Manche maltale Geules. **1572** BOSSEWELL *Armorie* II. 89.[**1610** GUILLIM *Heraldry* IV. vii. 205 Maunch ..of some Armorists, is termed Manche mal tailee, *Quasi manica malè talliata*, as an ill shapen Sleeue.]

Hence †**'manched** *a. Obs.*, having a (half) 'manche' or sleeve.

1688 R. HOLME *Armoury* III. 257/1 This is a Maunch half Maunched, being a close sleeve, with another open or wide sleeve coming over it, even to the bending of the Elbow. This was in fashion about the year 1620 and 1644.

‖**manche**[2] (mɑ̃ʃ). [F. *manche* masc., lit. 'handle' = Sp., Pg. *mango*, It. *manico*:—popular L. **manicum*, f. *man-us* hand.] (See quot.)

1876 STAINER & BARRETT *Dict. Mus. Terms*, *Manche*, the neck of a violin or guitar, &c.

manche[3]. [a. Malayālam *manji*.] A large flat-bottomed boat with one mast, used on the Malabar coast for landing cargoes. (Cf. MANCHUA.)

1855 in OGILVIE, Suppl. **1862** BEVERIDGE *Hist. India* I. I. x. 237 Manché of Calicut. A boat used on the Malabar coast, having a flat bottom, rendering it suitable for crossing the bars at the mouths of rivers.

manche: see MUNCH.

mancheat(e, obs. form of MANCHET.

Manchegan (mænˈtʃeɪgən), *a.* and *sb.* [ad. Sp. *manchego*, *-ga*: see -AN.] **A.** *adj.* Of or pertaining to La Mancha, a region (formerly a province) of central Spain. **B.** *sb.* A native or inhabitant of La Mancha.

[**1779** H. SWINBURNE *Trav. Spain* xxxvi. 319 The Manchegos have a pretty song about these eyes of the Guadiana.] **1841** BORROW *Zincali* I. II. ii. 245 Conde instantly unclasped one of those terrible Manchegan knives which are generally carried by contrabandistas. **1846** R. FORD *Gatherings from Spain* xxi. 296 The Manchegan bull, small, very powerful, and active, is considered to be the original stock of Spain. *Ibid.* xxiii. 326 Sancho, a true Manchegan,..maintained that for a *zapateo*, a knocking of shoes, none could beat him. **1897** A. F. JACCACI *On Trail of Don Quixote* iv. 96 It is arid, savage La Mancha which makes the Manchegan peasants shy, taciturn, and sombre. **1959** R. CROFT-COOKE *Quest for Quixote* i. 63 He was proud of being a Manchegan, a country-bred Spaniard. **1966** H. YOXALL *Fashion of Life* xxv. 239 Seven glasses were set in front of each of us, with a small piece of Manchegan cheese between each glass.

manchenille, obs. form of MANCHINEEL.

manche-present, var. MAUNCH-PRESENT.

‖**mancheron** (mɑ̃ʃrɔ̃). Also 8 **manceron**. [Fr., f. *manche* sleeve, MANCHE[1].] **a.** *Fr. Her.* A sleeve used as a bearing. **b.** Trimming on the upper part of the sleeve of a woman's dress.

1725 COATS *Dict. Her.*, *Mancheron* is a Sleeve, as us'd indifferently with Manche by French Heralds, and signifies any Sort of Sleeve, not to be confin'd to that in particular which we commonly call by the Name of Manche. **1727** BAILEY vol. II, *Manceron* (with *French Heral.*), a sleeve used indifferently with *Manche*, and signifies any sort of sleeve. **1835** *Court Mag.* VI. p. ix/1 Velvet mancherons of the shell form, edged with blond lace.

Manchester (ˈmæntʃɪstə(r)). The name of a large city in Lancashire, historically the chief centre of the cotton manufacture.

1. a. Used *attrib.* or as *adj.* chiefly in the names of various cotton goods produced there, as ***Manchester cottons***, etc. Also **Manchester-man** (see quot. 1851). **Manchester terrier**, a small, short-coated, black and tan terrier of the breed so called, once particularly popular in the Manchester area; also *absol.*; cf. *black and tan* (BLACK *a.* 14). **Manchester wares**, cotton goods manufactured at Manchester; hence ***Manchester warehouse***, ***warehouseman***.

1552 *Act 5 & 6 Edw. VI*, c. 6 §1 All and everie Cottonnes called Manchester Lancashire and Chesshire Cottonnes... And..all Clothes called Manchester Rugges otherwise named Frices. **1580** R. HITCHCOCK *Pol. Plat* F ij, At Rone in Fraunce..be solde our Englishe wares, as Welche and Manchester Cottons [etc.]. **1704** *Jrnl. Ho. Comm.* 27 Jan. 499/2 Linnen and Woollen cloth and other goods called Manchester Wares. **1762** *Lond. Chron.* 18–20 Mar. XI. 266/2 Blue Manchester velvets, with gold cords..are generally the uniform of Bum-bailiffs [etc.]. **1794** W. FELTON *Carriages* (1801) I. 24 A strong Manchester tape, called web. **1795** J. AIKIN *Descr. Manchester* 183 When the Manchester trade began to extend. **1851** MAYHEW *Lond. Labour* (1864) I. 419/1 The packmen are sometimes called Manchester-men. These are the men whom I have described as the sellers of shirtings, sheetings, &c. **1851** in *Illustr. Lond. News* (1854) 5 Aug. 119/1 [Occupations of People.] Manchester-warehouseman. **1858** SIMMONDS *Dict. Trade*, *Manchester and Glasgow Warehouse*, a sale depository for all kinds of cotton goods. **1894** R. B. LEE *Hist. & Descr. Mod. Dogs Gt. Brit. & Ireland*: *Terriers* iv. 75 The Kennel Club acknowledged it as the 'Manchester' terrier, as well as by its own name of the black and tan. **1899** *Daily News* 9 Jan. 2/4 Unlawfully applying a certain false trade description to 'Manchester linen'. **1943** 'C. DICKSON' *She died a Lady* v. 37 A so-called Manchester terrier sprang on the front of the chair. **1971** F. HAMILTON *World Encycl. Dogs* 461 The only acceptable color for a Manchester Terrier is black-and-tan. *Ibid.*, Manchesters are very attractive little dogs equally at home in town or country.

b. In the names of various colours, as ***Manchester black***, ***brown***, ***yellow***.

1862 O'NEILL *Dict. Calico Printing*, etc. 24 What was called Manchester black, was obtained by first steeping in galls or sumac, then [etc.]. **1870** J. W. SCLATER *Man. Colours* 113 Manchester Yellow (Jaune d'Or, Naphthylamine Yellow), the most splendid yellow colouring matter known, prepared from napthalin. *a* **1873** CRACE-CALVERT *Dyeing*, etc. (1876) 472 'Manchester yellow' or 'Martius' yellow',.. gives a very pure gold colour on silk and wool. **1885** [see BISMARCK 1]. **1957** *Encycl. Brit.* II. 828/2 Bismarck brown (Manchester brown), prepared by the action of nitrous acid on *m*-phenylene diamine, contains triaminoazobenzene.

2. ***Manchester school***: a name first applied by Disraeli to the body of politicians, led by Cobden and Bright, who, before the repeal of the Corn Laws, held their meetings at Manchester and advocated the principles of free trade. It was afterwards extended by their opponents to the party who supported those leaders on other questions of policy. Also, in ***Manchester policy***, etc., used derisively to designate a policy of laissez-faire and self-interest.

1848 DISRAELI *Sp. Ho. Comm.* 10 Mar., in Hansard 417 The great leaders of the school of Manchester..laid down this principle, that you were to buy in the cheapest and sell in the dearest market. **1849** —— *Sp.* 6 July ibid. 1495, I say the Manchester school. I have a right to use that phrase, for I gave them that name. I gave it them with all respect. **1851** BRIGHT in G. B. Smith *Life & Sp.* (1881) I. 345 [In an address to his constituents.] Now, we are called the 'Manchester Party', and our policy is the 'Manchester policy', and this building I suppose is the schoolroom of the 'Manchester School'. I do not repudiate that name at all. I think it is an honour [etc.]. **1881** MORLEY *Cobden* I. vi. 151 When we look back upon the affairs of that time [1854], we see that there were two policies open. Lord Palmerston's was one, the Manchester policy was the other. **1882** J. RAE in *Contemp. Rev.* Jan. 101 They repudiate the Manchester idolatry of self-interest. **1902** B. KIDD *West. Civiliz.* xi. 405 The inherent tendency of all economic evils to cure themselves if simply left alone—the characteristic doctrine of the Manchester school of thought in England.

3. *absol.* or *sb.* Some kind of cotton fabric.

1777 MME. D'ARBLAY *Early Diary* (1889) II. 169 Betsy.. had a very showy striped pink and white Manchester. **1799** W. TOOKE *View Russian Emp.* III. 509 Cotton-manufactories..make..coarse muslin, manchester,..&c.

4. *slang.* The tongue. ? *Obs.*

1812 in J. H. VAUX *Flash Dict.* **1820** *Lond. Mag.* I. 26/1 If, instead of bidding her hold her manchester, he had attended to her advice. **1823** *Grose's Dict. Vulgar Tongue.*

Hence ˈ**Manchesterdom** [formed after G. *Manchesterthum*, a word used by German socialists]; ˈ**Manchesterism**, the principles advocated by or attributed to the 'Manchester school'; ˈ**Manchesterist**, one who supports Manchesterism.

1882 J. RAE in *Contemp. Rev.* Jan. 101 Much of his [Todt's] work is devoted to show the..inner antagonism of Christianity and Manchesterdom... The merely nominal Christian..is always a spiritual Manchestrist, worshipping *laissez faire, laissez aller*, with his whole soul. **1883** SHUTTLEWORTH in *Pall Mall G.* 29 Nov. 10/1 Manchesterism, which enriched the few at the expense of the many. **1898** J. A. HOBSON *Ruskin* vi. 134 Manchesterism, which is sometimes taken as the type of commercial selfishness.

Manchesterian (mæntʃɪˈstɪərɪən), *a.* and *sb.* Also 8 **Manchestrian.** [f. MANCHESTER + -IAN.] **A.** *adj.* Of or pertaining to Manchester. **B.** *sb.* An inhabitant of Manchester; also, one of the Manchester School of politicians. Cf. MANCUNIAN *sb.* and *a.*

1778 J. WEDGWOOD *Let.* 3 Mar. (1965) 218 Nothing but half a score Highland, Manchestrian, and Liverpool regiments amongst us will raise their malignant spirits again. **1821** *Kaleidoscope* 3 July 423/3 Professing myself to be a plain Englishman and a Manchesterian. **1837** *Times* 5 Oct. 3/2 The engine went its way to Whitmore with the Liverpool passengers..and returned to fetch the unlucky Manchesterians. **1879** W. T. ARNOLD *Let.* 15 Aug. in D. Ayerst *Guardian* (1971) xxi. 206, I like the work very much, and strange to say like Manchester or at all events the Manchesterians. **1897** *Essays in Liberalism* 70 'Sordid inhuman wretch', 'brutal Manchesterian', are the terms applied to those who demonstrate the national loss of wealth which must result from the substitution of 'Fair' for Free Trade.

Hence **Mancheˈsterianism** = MANCHESTERISM.

1897 *Essays in Liberalism* 33 A sneer at Cobden, a contemptuous allusion to Manchesterianism and the 'dismal science'.

Manchesterize (ˈmæntʃɪstəraɪz), *v.* [f. MANCHESTER + -IZE.] *trans.* To make representative or typical of Manchester. Hence ˌ**Manchesteriˈzation.**

1925 E. T. SCOTT Let. 27 Dec. in D. Ayerst *Guardian* (1971) xxix. 452 The policy, both as to popularising and Manchesterising the paper..will be determined outside the Room. **1964** *Economist* 19 Dec. 1370/3 They do not want to see their [cotton] industries 'manchesterised'. **1965** *Ibid.* 23 Oct. 416/3 The [cotton] industry has argued..that the unrestricted entry of imported textiles from low-cost Commonwealth countries is largely to blame for the state of the industry. (The Continentals have a word for it: 'manchesterisation'.) **1971** D. AYERST *Guardian* xxix. 452 The policy of 'Manchesterisation' continued.

manchet (ˈmæntʃɪt). *Obs.* exc. *dial.* or *Hist.* Forms: 5–7 **manchett,** 6–7 **maunchet,** (5 **manchete, manged, mengyd, maynchett, maunchett,** 6 **mayngate, mancheat(e),** *Sc.* **manshote,** 7 **maincheat,** *Sc.* **mainschot, meaneschot,** 7, 9 *dial.* **manchent,** 8 *dial.* **manshut,** 9 **manchette,** *dial.* **manchun, manshun** (etc.: see E.D.D.), 5– **manchet.** [Of doubtful origin.

At Rouen, a ring-shaped cake of bread (in ordinary Fr. called *couronne*) is known as *manchette*, lit. 'cuff' (Robin *Patois normand*, and Littré *Suppl.*), but this name (which may be of recent origin) is obviously descriptive of shape, while the Eng. word in early use denotes a certain quality of bread. The identity of sense with PAINDEMAINE, DEMEINE, *maine-bread* (see MAINE *sb.*) suggests the possibility of etymological connexion with those words. The word might represent an AF. diminutive f. **demenche*:—L. *dominica*, or it might be an Eng. compound f. MAINE *sb.* + CHEAT *sb.*[2]; but either supposition involves some difficulties.]

†**1.** The finest kind of wheaten bread; = PAINDEMAINE. *Obs.*

c **1420** *Liber Cocorum* (1862) 53 Þou tost shyves of gode manchete,..Þenne Sawce hom with sugur. *c* **1450** [see CHEAT *sb.*[2]]. **1467** *Mann. & Househ. Exp.* (Roxb.) 409 Item, my mastyr paid at Douer for drynkenge pottes, glasses, and for manchett to haue to the schippe, v.s. **1540–1** ELYOT *Image Gov.* 84 He woulde eate a good quantitee of milke, sopped with fine manchet. **1567** GOLDING *Ovid's Met.* XI. (1593) 261 His officers..set downe sundrie sorts of meate and mancheat thereupon. **1577** HARRISON *England* III. i. in *Holinshed* M vij b, Of breade made of wheat we haue sundry sortes..wherof the first and most excellent is the manchet, which we commonlye call white bread, in latin *primarius panis.* **1620** VENNER *Via Recta* i. 20 Our manchet..is made of fine flower of wheat, hauing in it no leauen, but in steede thereof a little barme. **1698** FRYER *Acc. E. India & P.* 157 The finest Manchet it may be in the World is made here [Goa]. **1736** BAILEY *Housh. Dict.* 62 The best and principal bread is Manchet, which is order'd as follows. *a* **1791** GROSE *Olio* (1796) 304 They eat some manchet, and had five shillings worth of liquor.

†**b.** *transf. Obs. rare.*

1590 BARROUGH *Meth. Physick* III. vii. (1617) 110 Giue them [of a doglike appetite] manchet made of fat broths without hony.

c. *fig.* Used in Hanmer's translation of Eusebius and copied or used allusively by later historians.

1577 HANMER *Anc. Eccl. Hist.* III. xxxii. 55 [Ignatius said:] In so much that I am the wheate of God, I am to be grinded with the teeth of beastes, that I may be founde pure breade or fine manchet [L. *ut mundus panis inueniar.* Gr. ἵνα καθαρὸς ἄρτος εὑρεθῶ τοῦ Χριστοῦ]. **1610** BOYS *Wks.* (1622) 229. **1630** BRATHWAIT *Eng. Gentlem.* (1641) 230. **1642** FULLER *Holy & Prof. St.* III. xx. 206. **1650** S. CLARKE *Eccl. Hist.* (1654) I. 3. **1702** C. MATHER *Magn. Chr.* VII. 5.

2. A small loaf or roll of the finest wheaten bread. Now only *arch.* or *dial.*

The bread was moulded into small loaves, round and flattish, or into rolls, thicker in the middle than at the ends.

1481 CAXTON *Reynard* (Arb.) 68 Tho gaf I hym acopel of mayncheettis with swete butter. *a* **1483** *Liber Niger* in *Househ. Ord.* (1790) 22 The Kyng for his brekefast, two looves made into four maunchetts. **1562–3** in Swayne *Sarum Church-w. Acc.* (1896) 107 Mayngates and Cakes, vjs. **1629** *Burgh Recs. Stirling* (1887) I. 163 That na baxteris..sell ony meaneschottis..bott according to the paice and pryce of quhyt bread. **1655** MOUFET & BENNET *Health's Improv.* (1746) 340 Bread..of middle size between Gentlemens Rolls or little Manchets, and the great Loaves used in Yeomen's Houses. **1660** *Manch. Court Leet Rec.* (1887) IV. 277 Raph Burdsall for Makeing manchetts too light. **1688** R. HOLME *Armoury* III. 293/2 A Rowle, a Manchet, a Wigg, is White Bread moulded long ways, and thick in the middle. **1747** MRS. GLASSE *Cookery* ix. 109 A French Manchet does best; but there are little Loaves made on purpose for the Use. **1781** J. HUTTON *Tour to Caves* Gloss., *Manshut*, a load [*read* loaf] of bread. **1840** BARHAM *Ingol. Leg.* Ser. I. *St. Nicholas* xlii, And a manchette of bread..And a cup o' the best. **1870** MORRIS *Earthly Par.* I. I. 204 Ripe fruits and wheaten manchets fine.

fig. **1531** TINDALE *Exp. 1 John* (1537) 76 That mouthe haue they stopped with a leuended maunchet of theyr pharisaycall gloses.

b. A cake of the form of a manchet.

1562 BULLEYN *Bk. Simples* 2 b, The pouder thereof [anisseede], wyth the pouders of Fenell [etc.]..tempered with Wheate flower, water and red Wyne, and so baked in manchets or cakes. **1570** B. GOOGE *Pop. Kingd.* IV. 45 And after with the selfe same wine are little manchets [orig. *pastilli*] made, Agaynst the boystrous winter stormes.

c. *Her.* The representation of a manchet of bread used as a bearing.

1640 YORKE *Union Hon., Names & Armes* 43 Gentry of Lincolneshire. Pyster. argent, on a peele sable, 3 manchets proper. **1688** R. HOLME *Armoury* III. 293/2 He beareth Gules, a Rowl or Manchet, and a Loaf of Bread, Or. **1780** EDMONDSON *Heraldry* II. Gloss. **1847** in *Gloss. Her.*

3. *attrib.*, as ***manchet bread, cake, flour, loaf.***

c **1430** *Two Cookery Bks.* 43 Take mengyd [*MS. Douce* mayned] Flowre. *c* **1450** *Ibid.* 83 Then take manged brede [*MS. Douce* maynche brede] or paynman. **1542** BOORDE *Dyetary* xi. (1870) 258, I do loue manchet breade. **1551** BIBLE *1 Kings* iv. 22 And Salamons fode was in one day thyrtie quarters of manchet floure [Vulg. *similæ*]. **1595** DUNCAN *App. Etymol.* (E.D.S.) 74 *Simila*, manshote flour. **1620** VENNER *Via Recta* i. 20, I reiect not the vse of leauen, to the making either of manchet bread or of greater loaues. **1742** JARVIS *Quix.* I. IV. xxxi. (1885) 178 Winnowed by her hands it made the finest manchet bread. *a* **1847** *Johnnie Faa* iv. in Sheldon *Minstr. Eng. Border* 329 The Earl..Gied them red wine and manchet cake. **1859** TENNYSON *Geraint & Enid* 389 And Enid brought sweet cakes to make them cheer, And..manchet bread. **1881** *N. & Q.* 6th Ser. III. 430/1 The manchet loaf [in W. Cornwall] is in shape very much like an ordinary French roll, i.e. it is an oblong lump of dough which rises in the middle.

‖**manchette**[1] (mɑ̃ʃɛt). [Fr., dim. of *manche* sleeve, MANCHE[1].] A kind of trimming worn round the lower part of the sleeve of a woman's dress. Also *transf.*

1835 *Court Mag.* VI. p. xiv/1 A blond manchette of the antique form, looped in front by a bow of white satin riband terminates the sleeve. **1880** WEBSTER Suppl., *Manchette*, an ornamental ruffle or cuff. **1898** *Westm. Gaz.* 3 May 8/2 The hair..has to be fashioned out into bracelets or manchettes by the canine coiffeurs.

‖**manchette**[2]. *Obs.* [= F. *manchette* (Littré *Suppl.*), a Negro-Fr. corruption of Sp. *machete* MACHETE.] = MACHETE.

1761 *Char.* in *Ann. Reg.* 3/2 A kind of very short sabre called Manchette [by the Buccaneers of St. Domingo]. **1804** tr. *Piguenard's Zoflora* I. 89 Negroes..armed only with manchettes. *Note.* A kind of sabre with which the negroes trim the hedges in America.

man-child. Plural **men-children,** †**man-chylder(yn.** A male child.

a **1400** *Octouian* 101 Vppon Florence..He gette and wan Two man-chylderyn. *c* **1430** *Syr Tryam.* 1707 Man chylder had they twoo. **14..** *Sir Beues* 3640 (MS. C) Man chyldur [*A* knaue children, *M* men children] had sche two. **1471** CAXTON *Recuyell* (Sommer) I. 15 To espye..yf his wife broght forth men children. **1535** COVERDALE *Gen.* xvii. 10 Euery manchilde whan it is eight dayes olde, shalbe circumcyded. **1590** SPENSER *F.Q.* II. i. 53 Lucina came: a manchild forth I brought. **1605** SHAKS. *Macb.* I. vii. 72 Bring forth Men-Children onely: Fro thy vndaunted Mettle should compose Nothing but Males. **1700** CONGREVE *Way of World* IV. v, I denounce against all strait lacing, squeezing for a shape, till you mould my boy's head like a sugar-loaf, and instead of a man-child, make me father of a crooked billet. **1877** BLACK *Green Past.* iii. (1878) 23, I don't believe there is a man-child born in the town but you begin to wonder what the Government will do for him.

Hence † **manchildhood.**

a **1618** SYLVESTER *St. Lewis* 85 When Heav'ns assign'd him to his Father's Throne; And to the hands of his Man-Childehood left The glorious Burthen of this Scepter's heft.

manchineel (mæntʃɪˈniːl). Forms: 7 **mancinell, manchonele, -chioneel, -chionell, -tionell, -zanilla, manchinelo,** 7–8 **mançanilla,** 8 **mansanillo, mançanillo, -chinelo, mansaneel, manchaneel, mangeneel, manchenille, -eel, manchinelle, -ello, machinel,** 8–9 **machineel, manchineal,** 9 **machinelle, manchioneal, manzanillo,** 7– **manchineel.** [a. F. *mancenille*, a. Sp. *manzanilla*, dim. of *manzana* apple, altered form of OSp. *mazana* (= Pg. *mazãa*):—L. *matiāna* (neut. pl., sc. *poma, mala*) a kind of apple, named from the Roman gens *Matia.*]

1. A West Indian tree, *Hippomane Mancinella*, having a poisonous and caustic milky sap, and acrid fruit somewhat resembling an apple. Also *manchineel tree* (see 2).

1630 [see 2]. **1657** LIGON *Barbados* 68 And as this tree's poyson is in her sap, so the Mantionell's is in her fruit. **1672** BLOME *Descr. Jamaica* 27 Here is the Manchonele, which is a kind of a Crab, so common in all the Caribbee Isles. **1747** CATESBY in *Phil. Trans.* XLIV. 603 These Plants..grow on large Trees; particularly Mahogony, Sappadillo, Mançanilla, &c. **1777** ROBERTSON *Hist. Amer.* (1783) II. 101 In other parts of America, they employ the juice of the manchenille,..and it operates with no less fatal activity. **1793** W. MAVOR *Chr. Politics* 18 The Tree of Liberty, which has proved more baneful than the Manchineel to those who have sought its shade. **1801** SOUTHEY *Thalaba* IX. xxiii, With the mandrake and the manchineel She builds her pile accurst. **1871** KINGSLEY *At Last* i, We learnt to distinguish the poisonous Manchineel.

b. ***bastard manchineel***, a West Indian tree, *Cameraria latifolia.*

1838 LINDLEY *Flora Med.* 537 *Cameraria latifolia*... Bastard Manchineel tree. **1864** GRISEBACH *Flora W. Ind.* 785.

c. A poison obtained from the manchineel tree.

1891 'J. EVELYN' *Baffled Vengeance* iii. 35 Putting a pinch of manchineel or some other poison in his chocolate.

d. The wood of the machineel tree.

1683 J. POYNTZ *Tobago* 30 *Manchioneel*, is a sort of Timber for Plank, and Sheathing.

2. *attrib.*, as ***manchineel apple, bush, tree.***

1630 CAPT. SMITH *Trav. & Adv.* 55 The *Mancinell apple. **1750** G. HUGHES *Barbadoes* 123 The pulp of these Manchaneel apples. **1871** KINGSLEY *At Last* vi, To feel our way..cautiously..past the *Manchineel bush. **1696** PHILLIPS (ed. 5), **Manchinelo Tree*, a Tree that grows wild in the woods of Jamaica. **1707** SLOANE *Jamaica* I. p. cxx, In felling a mansanillo tree..some of the milk spurted into his eye. **1766** *Chron.* in *Ann. Reg.* 109/2 A very rich crimson die, from a preparation of the fruit of the manchineel tree. **1830** LINDLEY *Nat. Syst. Bot.* 105 The famous Manchineel tree ..is said to be so poisonous, that persons have died from merely sleeping beneath its shade.

manchip, obs. form of MANSHIP.

manch-present, var. MAUNCH-PRESENT.

Manchu (mænˈtʃuː), *sb.* and *a.* Also **Manchew, Manchoo, Manchow, Mantcheou, Mantchoo, Mantchu,** etc. [Manchu, 'pure', the name of a tribe descended from the Nü-chên Tartars.]

A. *sb.* **1.** A member of a Tungusic race inhabiting Manchuria, which conquered China in 1644 and was the ruling class until the Revolution in 1912.

[**1655** A. SEMEDO *Hist. China* III. 292 He used to cry out in their Language *Hoo Manzu.*] **1697** L. LE COMPTE *Mem. Journey through China* I. i. 17 One of the Petty Kings of the Eastern Tartary..whose subjects called Mouantchéou.. entered the Province of Leauton with a numerous Army. **1736** R. BROOKES tr. *Du Halde's Gen. Hist. China* IV. 86 The places belonging to the Mantcheoux have Mantcheou Names. **1759** *Universal Hist., Mod.* IV. 278 Here the present empire of the eastern Tatars, or Manchews..had its beginning. **1821** G. STAUNTON tr. *Narr. Chinese Embassy* 152 The Mantchoos and the Mongals bear a great resemblance to each other. **1883** S. W. WILLIAMS *Middle Kingdom* (new ed.) I. i. 44 The Manchus are an agricultural or a hunting people. **1940** E. POUND *Cantos* lviii. 77 Tai Tsong..Forbad manchus marry their sisters.

2. The language of the Manchus.

1822 G. STAUNTON *Misc. Notes China* 95 Table of Contents of a Chinese and Mantchoo-Tartar Dictionary. **1888** H. E. M. JAMES *Long White Mountain* 132 Yet, so wonderful are the ways of men, the Court and the people alike are now abandoning Manchu for the cumbrous and barbarous Chinese. **1920** *Contemp. Rev.* Apr. 526 Ferdinand Verbiest..to please Kang-hi had learnt Manchu.

B. *adj.* Of or pertaining to the Manchus, their country (Manchuria), or their language.

1736 R. BROOKES tr. *Du Halde's Gen. Hist. China* IV. 90 A great Number of Mantcheou Mandarins. **1770** W. GUTHRIE *New Geogr. Gram.* 472 The Chinese went to war with the Manchew Tartars. **1844** C. FOX *Jrnl.* 22 Aug. (1972) 153 They gave him a hymn to translate into the Manchow language. **1848** S. W. WILLIAMS *Middle Kingdom* II. 562 Out of a Manchu population of four thousand..not more than five hundred survived. **1882** *Encycl. Brit.* XIV. 96/1 Tobacco..grown in the province [*sc.* Manchuria] being greatly prized throughout the Chinese empire under the name of 'Manchu leaf'. **1898** *19th Cent.* Jan. 163 The Manchu dynasty is the cement that holds the heterogeneous components of the Chinese Empire together. **1948** N. WHYMANT *China Manual* i. 16 The Manchu leader.. mounted the throne and in 1644 the Ch'ing or Manchu dynasty began. **1972** T. SHABAD *China's Changing Map* ii. 45 The criteria used by the Chinese Communists in distinguishing a Manchu ethnic group are not entirely clear.

1972 *Mainichi Daily News* (Japan) 6 Nov. 17/6 The authors have no acquaintance with Korean or Manchu grammar.

manchun, dial. form of MANCHET.

Manchurian (mænˈtʃʊərɪən), *a.* [f. *Manchuria*, the country of the Manchus, now a dependency of China + -AN.] **1.** Of or pertaining to Manchuria.

1876 A. R. WALLACE *Geogr. Distribution Animals* I. 220 Japan and North China, or the Manchurian Sub-region. **1899** J. F. FRASER *Round World on Wheel* xxxi. 395 In five minutes down swooped several Manchurian officers. **1911** *Encycl. Brit.* XVII. 554/1 Eventually a Manchurian convention was arranged between China and Russia. **1937** *Discovery* Jan. 12/2 A candle copied from an old Manchurian pattern. **1972** W. B. LOCKWOOD *Panorama Indo-Europ. Lang.* 154 The Manchurian languages are dispersed over an immense tract of the Soviet Far East.

2. Manchurian crane, a crane found in eastern Asia, *Grus japonensis*; **Manchurian ermine** (see quot.); **Manchurian roe, sika, wapiti**, local races of deer, *Capreolus capreolus bedfordi, Cervus nippon mantchuricus*, and *C. canadensis xanthopygus*; **Manchurian tiger**, a subspecies of the tiger, *Panthera tigris longipilis*, found in Manchuria and Siberia, and distinguished by its large size and shaggy fur; also called Siberian tiger.

1869 *Proc. Zool. Soc.* 628 Mantchurian Crane. *Grus montignesia.* **1898** R. LYDEKKER *Deer of all Lands* 102 The Manchurian wapiti is said to be smaller than the (?typical) American race. *Ibid.* 115 (*caption*) Buck and Doe of Manchurian Sika in winter pelage. *Ibid.* 231 (*heading*) The Manchurian Roe—*Capreolus Manchuricus*. **1899** R. WARD *Rec. Big Game* (ed. 3) 458 Lastly, we have the Manchurian tiger (*F. tigris longipilis*), characterised by its large size, heavy build, short limbs, and the great length and thickness of the fur. **1931–4** J. D. D. LA TOUCHE *Handbk. Birds E. China* II. 298 The Manchurian Crane breeds in Manchuria, Corea, and Eastern Siberia, and passes through Japan on migration. **1957** M. B. PICKEN *Fashion Dict.* 219/1 *Manchurian ermine*, fur of Chinese weasel. **1964** A. L. THOMSON *New Dict. Birds* 162/1 Another species that has become alarmingly scarce is the Manchurian Crane *G[rus] japonensis*, a large white bird with black wings, a dark grey face, and a broad streak of the same colour running downwards at either side of the neck. **1964** R. PERRY *World of Tiger* i. 8 A Manchurian tiger does in fact tire quickly and rest often when traversing deep snow. **1972** G. K. WHITEHEAD *Deer of World* v. 74 The Manchurian Wapiti is similar to the North American animal. *Ibid.* 77 The principal distribution of the Manchurian Sika deer is in the central and southern parts of Manchuria. [*Ibid.* 84 Throughout the greater part of the Korean Peninsula the Roe is the Chinese or Manchurian race, *C[apreolus] c[apreolus] bedfordi*.]

Manchu-Tungus (mænˈtʃuːˈtʊŋgʊs). [f. MANCHU *sb.* and *a.* + TUNGUS.] Name given to a language family comprising Manchu and Tungus.

[**1933** L. BLOOMFIELD *Lang.* iv. 69 The Tunguse-Manchu family lies to the north of the Mongol, dividing Yakut from the rest of the Turco-Tartar area.] **1955** *Times* 15 Aug. 7/3 There are the peoples, often semi-nomad, who are in contact with civilization but only slightly affected by it: Indians and mestizos in Bolivia and Peru, the many groups, amounting in 1941 to nearly 25,000,000 souls, whom the Republic of India classifies as adivasis, the Paleoasiats and the Manchu-Tungus of the Soviet Far East. **1956** JAKOBSON & HALLE in Saporta & Bastian *Psycholinguistics* (1961) 349/2 In Manchu-Tungus and in Paleosiberian languages. **1964** *Language* XL. 301 Coordinate with Turkic, Mongolian, and Manchu-Tungus.

mancia (ˈmæntʃɪə). [It.] A gratuity, a tip.

1951 [see HAVE *v.* 15 d]. **1963** T. PYNCHON *V.* xiv. 409 Guides: there to do any bidding, to various degrees of efficiency, on receipt of the recommended baksheesh, pourboire, mancia, tip.

mancinism (ˈmænsɪnɪz(ə)m). *rare.* [ad. It. *mancinismo*, f. *mancino* left-handed: see -ISM.] The state or condition of being left-sided.

1890 H. ELLIS *Criminal* iii. 111 Anatomical mancinism is not necessarily related with motor mancinism.

mancio(u)n, obs. form of MANSION.

mancipable (ˈmænsɪpəb(ə)l), *a. Roman Law.* [ad. L. type **mancipābilis*, f. *mancipāre*: see MANCIPATE *v.* and -ABLE.] That may be conveyed or transferred by mancipation.

1875 POSTE *Gaius* II. (ed. 2) §22 Property in things mancipable..is conveyed by mancipation. **1876** ABDY & WALKER tr. *Ulpian* XIX. viii. 392 By usucapion we obtain the ownership of things both mancipable and non-mancipable.

mancipal, obs. form of MANCIPLE.

mancipant (ˈmænsɪpənt). *Roman Law.* [ad. L. *mancipant-em*, pr. pple. of *mancipāre*: see MANCIPATE *v.* and -ANT.] One who disposes of property by mancipation.

1880 MUIRHEAD *Gaius* I. §119 The coin..he then gives to the mancipant or party from whom the slave is being received.

†**ˈmancipate**, *pa. pple.* and *ppl. a. Obs.* [ad. L. *mancipāt-us*, pa. pple. of *mancipāre*: see next.] Made subject (*to*).

1502 ARNOLDE *Chron.* 60 b/2 The said gengemi was taken and to prison mancipate. **1577** HOLINSHED *Chron. Eng.* 192/1 As they whiche though they were partly free, yet in some poynt remayned styll as thrall and mancipate to the subiection of the English men. **1687** RENWICK *Serm.*, etc. (1776) 531 All are to be mancipate and enslaved to it.

mancipate (ˈmænsɪpeɪt), *v.* [f. L. *mancipāt-*, ppl. stem of *mancipāre*, f. *man-us* hand + root of *capĕre* to take.]

1. *Roman Law.* (*trans.*) To hand over by the formality of MANCIPATION.

1656 BLOUNT *Glossogr.*, *Mancipate*, to deliver possession, to give the right to another, to sell for money. **1870** ABDY & WALKER tr. *Gaius* I. cxx. 40 In this manner persons, both slaves and free, are mancipated. *Ibid.* cxxi, But estates can be mancipated when at a distance. **1880** MUIRHEAD *Gaius* I. §132 The father again mancipates him either to the same person..or to a different one—it is the usual practice to mancipate to the same.

†**2.** To make subject, enslave. Chiefly with *to*, *unto*. Often *transf.* and *fig. Obs.*

1574 NEWTON *Health Mag.* Pref., For their sakes..that live of themselves freely and are not enthralled or mancipated to the inconveniences abovesaide. **1621** BURTON *Anat. Mel.* I. ii. IV. vi. (1651) 160 They voluntarily mancipate, and sell themselves..to rich men to avoid hunger and beggery. **1633** W. STRUTHER *True Happiness* Ep., Aristotle..disputed much of Vertue; but proved miserable in his life, and with the rest mancipated vertue unto pleasure. **1644** H. PARKER *Jus Pop.* 23 When the election..of Judges, Commanders and Counsellors of State is requested, 'tis answered that this is to mancipate the Crowne. *a* **1677** HALE *Prim. Orig. Man.* I. ii. 47 Which cannot be done by Plants, who are mancipated and fixed to the place of their station or growth. *a* **1713** ELLWOOD *Autobiog.* (1855) 187 One to soft music mancipates his ear. **1755** JOHNSON, *Slave*, one mancipated to a master. **1756** *Monitor* No. 41 (1760) I. 397 What brought Gaveston to the block? but his mancipating the king.

¶**b.** (See quot.)

1623 COCKERAM, *Mancipate*, to tame.

†**3.** To devote or consecrate *to*. *Obs.*

1715 M. DAVIES *Athen. Brit.* I. 77 Monday is Mancipated to the Invocation of Saints. **1829** J. DONOVAN tr. *Catech. Council Trent* II. vii. Quest. 18 Know that thou art mancipated [ed. 2 (1839) altered to 'devoted': L. *mancipari*] to light the lights of the Church, in the Name of the Lord.

¶**4.** Misused for EMANCIPATE. *Obs. rare*$^{-1}$.

Cf. med.L. *mancipatio* (in Du Cange).

a **1677** BARROW *Serm.* Wks. 1686 II. 212 Such a dispensation is a pupillage, and a slavery, which he [man] earnestly must desire to be redeemed and mancipated from.

Hence **ˈmancipating** *ppl. a.*

1819 H. BUSK *Vestriad* III. 537 Coarcted by your mancipating spell.

mancipation (mænsɪˈpeɪʃən). [ad. L. *mancipātiōn-em*, n. of action f. *mancipāre* to MANCIPATE.]

1. The ceremonial process by which certain kinds of property (designated as *res mancipi*) were transferred (see quot. 1880).

1656 BLOUNT *Glossogr.*, *Mancipation*, a manner of selling before witnesses with sundry ceremonies, &c. **1774** HALLIFAX *Anal. Rom. Civ. Law* 24 By the old Roman laws Alienation of things Corporeal was of two kinds. 1. Mancipation. 2. Tradition. The former related to such things as were called *Res Mancipi*. **1849** COLQUHOUN *Rom. Civ. Law* §558 I. 474 The emption on the part of the husband was done in the same form as the usual quiritian mancipations. **1880** MUIRHEAD *Ulpian* xix. §3 Mancipation is a mode of alienation peculiar to *res mancipi*, and is performed by recital of certain words of style, in presence of a balance-holder and five witnesses.

2. *gen.* The action of enslaving; the state of being enslaved.

1577 tr. *Bullinger's Decades* III. vii. 395/1 If..any bondman were desirous to staye..his voluntarie bondage should be confirmed by the ceremonie of Mancipation. **1637** GILLESPIE *Eng. Pop. Cerem.* III. viii. 169 The consecration and mancipation of him to the holy Ministery. **1643** *Plain English* 9 The mancipation of themselves to the promiscuous service of the Queen. **1649** JER. TAYLOR *Gt. Exemp.* II. viii. 68 They who fall away..into a contradictory state of sinne and mancipation. **1663** WATERHOUSE *Comm. Fortescue* 187 They [the Romans]..prevailed against all mankinde to their Mancipation under them.

¶**3.** (See quot.)

1623 COCKERAM, *Mancipation*, a taming.

mancipative (ˈmænsɪpətɪv), *a. Roman Law.* [f. MANCIPATE *v.* + -IVE.] = next.

1875 POSTE *Gaius* II. 182 The mancipative will, or will by bronze and scale, probably began to supersede the older form as soon as the Twelve Tables had given legal force to the nuncupative part of mancipation.

mancipatory (ˈmænsɪpətərɪ), *a. Roman Law.* [f. MANCIPATE *v.* + -ORY.] Pertaining or involving mancipation.

1861 MAINE *Anc. Law* vi. (1876) 212 The Mancipatory Testament by which the *universitas juris* devolved at once and unimpaired. **1880** MUIRHEAD *Gaius* III. §167 Except when he [a slave] expressly stipulates or takes by mancipatory conveyance [etc.]. *Ibid.* IV. §131 An *actio ex empto* for mancipatory conveyance to us of lands we have bought.

mancipee (ˌmænsɪˈpiː). [irreg. f. MANCIP(ATE) *v.* + -EE.] The person to whom the property is transferred by mancipation.

1880 MUIRHEAD *Gaius* I. §123 Persons mancipated by parents..are appropriated by the mancipee with the very same words with which he would appropriate a slave.

manciple (ˈmænsɪp(ə)l). Forms: 4 **mauncipte**, (5 **mawnciple, -cypylle**, 6 **mansebyll**), 5–6 **mancyple**, (7 **mansiple**, 8 **mancipal**), 3– **manciple**. [a. OF. *manciple*, *mancipe* (for the ending cf. *principle*, *participle*), ad. L. *mancipium*, f. *manus* hand + root of *capĕre* to take.

In classical L. *mancipium* meant acquisition by purchase, absolute ownership, hence *concr.* a slave. In med.L. it meant also the office or function of a *manceps* or buyer in of stores (in late L. this word sometimes denoted the manager of a public bakery: so in late Gr. form μάγκιψ). It may be conjectured that in monastic use the word denoting the office was applied (like many similar terms) to the person charged with it, and that this application is the source of sense 1 below, which seems not to be known in OF.]

1. An officer or servant who purchases provisions for a college, an inn of court, a monastery, etc.

a **1225** *Ancr. R.* 214 Þe ȝiure glutun is þes feondes manciple. Uor he stikeð euer iðe celere, oðer iðe kuchene. His heorte is iðe disches. [Prob. a misunderstanding of a Lat. original which had *mancipium* in the sense of bondservant, slave.] *c* **1386** CHAUCER *Prol.* 567 A gentil maunciple was ther of a temple Of which Achatours myghte take exemple ffor to be wise in byynge of vitaille. **1401** *Pol. Poems* (Rolls) II. 98 Oones I was a manciple at Mertoun halle. **1482** *Monk of Evesham* (Arb.) 49 And thoo thyngys that were necessarye to the ornamentys of alle the chyrche, ..y wolde dylygently orden therfore, as y had be hys famylyar seruante and mawncypylle. **1530** in W. H. Turner *Select. Rec. Oxford* 78 The..Proctors requyrd the..xxv^{s} of the mansebyll. *Ibid.* 89 Gunter beyng a mancyple to scolers. **1641** MILTON *Reform.* II. 84 Furnish't with no more experience then they learnt betweene the Cook, and the manciple. **1660** WOOD *Life* (O.H.S.) I. 352 At Queen's Coll. Oxon is every year a bore's head provided by the manciple against Xtmasday. **1721–2** AMHERST *Terræ Fil.* No. 13 (1754) 63 Father William..made him manciple of his college, a sinecure worth twenty pounds a year. **1821** LAMB *Elia* Ser. I. *Old Benchers I.T.*, I remember..the cook applying to him [Jackson]..for instructions how to write down *edge* bone of beef... He decided the orthography ..[and]..dismissed the manciple (for the time) learned and happy. **1848** J. H. NEWMAN *Loss & Gain* (1853) 67 In came the manciple with the dinner paper, which Mr. Vincent had formally to run his eye over. **1891** *Daily News* 26 Dec. 2/5 The ancient ceremony of serving up a boar's head at Queen's College was duly observed yesterday... A splendid specimen, weighing upwards of sixty pounds, had been prepared by the College manciple. **1893** FOWLER *Hist. C. C. C.* (O.H.S.) 458 *note*, The offices of First Cook and Manciple were now [1868] combined. **1897** D. MACLEANE *Pembr. Coll.* iii. (O.H.S.) 32 He [the principal] did not cater for the aularians. This was done by an upper servant or manciple, 'wise in buying of vitaille', who was sometimes a scholar.

transf. **1744** M. BISHOP *Life & Adv.* 169 Finding that the Barrack I was to be in had four Beds, we..took it by turns to officiate as Manciple.

†**2.** A bondslave, servant. [= L. *mancipium*.]

1387 TREVISA *Higden* (Rolls) VII. 277 And anon he was made þe enemyes mauncíple [L. *ille mancipium hostis effectus*]. *c* **1440** HYLTON *Scala Perf.* (W. de W. 1494) II. vi, The same falleth to a Jewe or to a sarracyne the whyche or they ben crystened arne nought but mancyples of helle. **1537** CROMWELL in Merriman *Life & Lett.* (1902) II. 89 Euery man well perceyuethe the difference betwyxt a franke, a holy, a godly, a generall cownsaill, and an assemblie of ambicious manciples, of men sworne to pope's lustes and gaynes. **1563–87** FOXE *A. & M.* (1596) 294/2 For is not the king of England our [*sc.* the pope's] vassall? and to saie more, our manciple or page. [**1611** FLORIO, *Mancipio*, a manciple, a bondman, a thrall, a vassall.]

Hence **ˈmancipleship**, the office of a manciple.

1642 *B. N. C. Muniments* 28. 135 To perform his mancipleship faithfully.

mancipular (mænˈsɪpjʊlə(r)), *a. rare*$^{-1}$. [Badly f. MANCIPLE + -AR, after *manipular*.] Of a manciple.

1846 LANDOR *Imag. Conv.*, *Cromwell & Sir O. Cromwell* Wks. 1853 II. 230/1 Ye should leave unto them, in full propriety, the mancipular office of discharging the account.

manck, variant of MANK *Obs.*

manco (ˈmæŋkəʊ). *Sc.* Also 8–9 **mankie**, 8 **maunkie**, 9 **mank(e)y**. [Shortened form of CALAMANCO.] = CALAMANCO. In quots. *attrib.*

a **1779** [D. GRAHAM] *Hist. Buck-Haven* 5 [She] made coarse claiths, and callicoe mancoes [ed. 1782 mutches]. **1790** *J. Johnson's Scots Musical Mus.* III. 223 The lasses.. With mankie facings on their gown. **1824** MACTAGGART *Gallovid. Encycl.*, *Mankie*, an ancient kind of worsted stuff, much glazed, worn by females. **1828** MOIR *Mansie Wauch* xx. 297 Below which was a checked short gown of gingham stripe, and a green glazed manco petticoat. **1864** A. LEIGHTON *Myst. Leg. Edinb.* (1886) 261 [She] dressed herself in her mankey gown and red plaid.

mancorn, var. MONGCORN *Obs.* exc. *dial.*

mancoustan, obs. form of MANGOSTEEN.

†**mancowe.** *Obs.*$^{-0}$ A baboon. (The form is curiously suggestive of *monkey*, which, however, has not been found before the 16th c.)

14.. *Nom.* in Wr.-Wülcker 700/25 *Hic sinozephalus*, a mancowe.

Mancunian (mænˈkjuːnɪən), *sb.* and *a.* [f. L. *Mancunium* Manchester + -AN.] **A.** *sb.* A native or inhabitant of Manchester. **B.** *adj.* Of or pertaining to Manchester.

1904 H. BESWICK *Last Karkawbar* 134 'Th' Owd Rivvur' —as some old Mancunians dub the Irwell. **1908** *Westm. Gaz.* 22 Oct. 2/3 How strangely provincial—may we even say Mancunian?—is the very recent theory that Mr. Cobden invented Free Trade. **1926** *Glasgow Herald* 2 Oct. 8 In the

Manchester docks..lies the real secret or the industrial trick, as the Mancunians choose to phrase it, which is at the foundation of the city's greatness. **1931** *Daily Tel.* 6 Jan. 10/3 The Mancunians who wish to play bowls on Sunday might surely be allowed their simple pleasure. **1947** H. MILES tr. *Maurois's Disraeli* (ed. 2) II. iv. 124 A truly Mancunian rain had drowned the enthusiasm. **1963** *Times* 2 Feb. 9/3 Any middle-aged Mancunian..can remember posters drawing attention to celebrity concerts. **1973** P. GEDDES *Ottawa Allegation* ii. 18 Still the Mancunian accent, true, yet fading fast. **1973** *Guardian* 16 Mar. 13/2 Michael Croft, the beaming Mancunian who founded the National Youth Theatre.

mancus (ˈmæŋkəs). *Obs.* exc. *Hist.* Forms: 1 **mancus**, 7–9 **mancus**. *Pl.* 1 **mancses, mancsas, mancusas, mancos**, 2 **manke**, 7–8 **mancuses**, 7–9 **mancusses**. [OE. *mancus* masc., = OS. *mancus* (glossing *bazanticum, aureus*), OHG. **manchus*, acc. pl. *manchussa* (glossing *solidos, aureos, philippos*). The med.L. form *mancu(s)sus* occurs frequently in documents belonging to Germany, France, Italy, and Spain, and in one example in Du Cange it means some kind of ornament worn by a woman.] An Old English money of account of the value of thirty pence.

The statement sometimes made that *mancus* was also used to denote a unit of weight is based on misinterpretation of certain passages in which the word occurs.

811 in Haddan & Stubbs *Councils* III. 570 Pro ejus larga pecuniarum remuneratione hoc est centum et viginti VI. mancosas. *c* **1000** ÆLFRIC *Gram.* xlviii. (Z.) 296 Fif peneȝas ȝemaciað ænne scylling and þrittiȝ peneȝa ænne mancus. *c* **1000** —— *Saints' Lives* xxxiii. 132 Heo..nam mid hire fiftiȝ mancsas. *a* **1100** *Will of Wulfgat* in Birch *Cart. Sax.* (1893) III. 653, xx. mancses goldes. *a* **1200** *Moral Ode* 70 And þe ðe mare ne mai don do hit mid his gode þonke Alse wel se þe þe haueð golde fele manke. **1614** CAMDEN *Rem.* (ed. 2) 200 Thirty of these pence..made a Mancus, which some think to be all one with a Marke... They reckoned these Mancuse, or Mancus both in golde and siluer. **1655** FULLER *Ch. Hist.* II. iv. §1 He sent his Holinesse 120 Mancuses for a Present. **1761** HUME *Hist. Eng.* I. ii. 41 He made a perpetual grant of three hundred mancuses a year to that see. **1819** SCOTT *Ivanhoe* xv, 'These dog-Jews!' said he... 'They might have flung me a mancus or two'. **1848** LYTTON *Harold* I. iii, What in mancusses and pence Clapa lacked of the price. **1860** HOOK *Lives Abps.* (1869) I. v. 241 When a person of high rank was buried..a mancus of gold..was paid. **1875** JEVONS *Money* viii. 71. **1887** C. F. KEARY *Coins, Ags. Ser.* Introd. 34 The *Mancus* (pl. *Mancusas*) or *Mancos*... It was a coin of denomination in use upon the Continent quite as much as in England, and *may* have been imported into this country from abroad. **1899** GRUEBER *Handbk. Coins* Introd. 9.

-mancy, a terminal element, repr. OF. *-mancie*, late L. *-mantīa*, Gr. *μαντεία* divination, f. *μαντεύεσθαι* to prophesy, f. *μάντις* prophet, diviner. Some of the words with this ending go back to compounds recorded in classical or post-classical Greek, as *chiromancy, necromancy, ornithomancy, pyromancy*; others appear in late or med.Lat., and represent regularly formed compounds which prob. existed in late Gr., or were formed by persons familiar with that language, as *geomancy, hydromancy*; others have been formed after the revival of Greek learning on assumed Gr. types, as *crystallomancy, lithomancy*. No hybrid compound of *-mancy* seems to have been admitted into general Eng. use: for some suggested formations of this type see quot. 1709. The related adjs. end in -MANTIC.

c **1420** LYDG. *Assembly of Gods* 869 Adryomancy, Œnomancy, with Pyromancy, Fyaenancy also, and Pawmestry. **1709** J. STEVENS tr. *Quevedo's Com. Wks.* (ed. 2) 374 There are lines in the Neck, the Forehead, the Lips, the Hams, the Elbows, and the bottom of the Buttocks..and therefore..as there is Chiromancy, there ought to be Frontimancy, Collimancy, Pedimancy, Natimancy.

†**mand**, *sb.*[1] *Obs. rare*⁻¹. [? a. OF. *mand, mant*, vbl. noun f. *mander*: see MAND *v.*] A question.

14.. *Ipotis* (MS. Ashm. 61, lf. 87), The emperour.. Askyd a mand of þe chyld Why [etc.].

mand (mænd), *sb.*[2] [a. Hindī *mandūa*. Cf. MANGRASS.] An Indian grass of the genus *Eleusine*.

1862 *Chambers's Encycl.* IV. 6/2 *Eleusine corocana*, an Indian species, called Natchnee and Nagla Ragee, also Mand and Murwa.

mand (mænd), *sb.*[3] [Final element of *com)mand, de)mand*, etc.] B. F. Skinner's term for an utterance aimed at producing an effect or result, etc. Cf. TACT.

1957 B. F. SKINNER *Verbal Behavior* II. iii. 35 The term 'mand' has a certain mnemonic value derived from 'command', 'demand',..and so on... A 'mand', then, may be defined as a verbal operant in which the response is reinforced by a characteristic consequence and is therefore under the functional control of relevant conditions of deprivation or aversive stimulation. **1959** *Anthropol. Ling.* I. i. 41 It is interesting to speculate how far the program for the acquisition of mands and tacts will account for all verbal behavior. **1968** D. LAWTON *Social Class, Lang. & Educ.* iv. 56 For Skinner, language behaviour is an example of learning by operant conditions... Requests, demands or commands (mands) tend to be reinforced by satisfaction of needs. Another kind of utterance is termed a '*tact*', which is a response to a situation rather than a response to a need (e.g. 'this apple is red'). **1972** *Language* XLVIII. 482 Beneath the linguistically questionable trappings (cf. Chomsky 1959) of mands, tacts, and echoic responses—..is there a brilliance which linguists in general have been prevented from seeing? **1973** *Archivum Linguisticum* IV. 52 'The ethnography of communication'—contains the item ' mands'.

†**mand**, *v. Obs.* [a. OF. *mander*:—L. *mandāre*.] *trans.* **a.** To send forth. **b.** To send for. **c.** To command.

a **1310** in Wright *Lyric P.* 44 The mone mandeth hire lyht. **1483** CAXTON *Cato* C iv b, He maunded and sente for hyr parentes. *c* **1500** *Melusine* 18 [Thanne the Erle Emery] manded & desyred a moch fayre company. *Ibid.* 73 Alayn manded or sent for a grete foyson of hys frendes. **1589** WARNER *Alb. Eng.* VI. xxx. (1612) 147 Aske whatso else I haue to giue, thous maunde it for a kis.

mand: see MAUND.

Mandæan (ˈmændiːən), *a.* and *sb.* Also **Mandean, Mendæan**. [f. Mandæan Aramaic *mandayyā* (a rendering of Gr. *γνωστικοί* Gnostics: f. *mandā* knowledge, = late Heb. *maddāᵉ*, f. *yādaᵉ* to know) + -AN.] **A.** *adj.* The designation of a Gnostic sect still surviving in Mesopotamia, and of the Aramaic dialect in which their sacred books are written. **B.** *sb.* **a.** A member of the Mandæan sect. **b.** The Mandæan language.

1875 LIGHTFOOT *Comm. Col.* 165 *note*, These Mandeans are a rapidly diminishing sect living in the region about the Tigris. **1883** K. KESSLER in *Encycl. Brit.* XV. 467/2 Mandæans, also known as Sabians, Nasoræans, or St. John's Christians, an Oriental sect of great antiquity. *Ibid.* 468/1 *note*, Mandæan MSS. occur in the British Museum [etc.]. *Ibid.* 468/2 Primal Life, who is properly speaking the Mandæan god. **1886** *Ibid.* XXI. 649/1 There is a close resemblance between Mandæan and the language of the Babylonian Talmud. **1900** *Daily News* 15 Aug. 6/2 A large number of Hebrew and Mandæan vases..were discovered.

Mandaite (ˈmændeɪaɪt), *sb.* and *a.* Also **Mendaite**. [See prec. and -ITE.] = MANDÆAN.

1881 SAYCE in *Encycl. Brit.* XIII. 117/1 The Mendaite inscription of twenty lines discovered in a tomb at Abu-Shadr in south Babylonia. **1900** *Pilot* 23 June 515/2 Magic bowls with inscriptions in Syriac, Chaldæan, and Mandaite.

mandala (ˈmændələ). [Skr. *máṇḍala* disc, circle.] A symbolic representation of a magic circle usually with symmetrical divisions and figures of deities, etc., in the centre, used by Buddhists in meditation and found in many cultures as a religious symbol; *spec.* in *Jungian Psychol.*, an image of a similar magic circle visualized in dreams and symbolizing the dreamer's striving for unity of self and completeness. Also *attrib.*

1859 MAX MÜLLER *Hist. Anc. Sanskrit Lit.* i. 218 The division of the Sanhitâ which is adopted in the Brihaddevatâ, is that of Maṇḍalas, Anuvâkas, and Sûktas. **1882** *Encycl. Brit.* XIV. 228/1 Their practical belief.. busied itself almost wholly with obtaining magic powers (*Siddhi*), by means of..magic circles (*Maṇḍala*). **1927** W. Y. EVANS-WENTZ *Tibetan Bk. Dead* 136 (*caption*) The Great Mandala of the Knowledge-Holding and Wrathful Deities. **1931** C. F. BAYNES tr. *Wilhelm & Jung's Secret of Golden Flower* 97 For the most part, the *mandala* form is that of a flower, cross, or wheel, with a distinct tendency toward four. *Ibid.*, I have come across women who did not draw mandala symbols but who danced them. **1933** E. J. THOMAS *Hist. Buddhist Thought* xv. 193 The great spell..should be inscribed in a circle (maṇḍala) made of certain substances with appropriate divisions and figures. **1938** C. G. JUNG *Psychol. & Relig.* iii. 96 Historically..the mandala served as a symbol in order to clarify the nature of the deity philosophically. *Ibid.* iv. 109 Since modern mandalas have ..close parallels in ancient magic circles, in the centre of which we usually find the deity, it is evident that in the modern mandala man—the complete man—has replaced the deity. **1941** A. HUXLEY *Grey Eminence* iii. 66 An elaborate circular diagram, curiously like one of those symbolic *mandalas*, into which the Buddhists contrive to cram such a wealth of doctrinal significance. **1949** K. RAINE *Pythoness* 17, I piece the divine fragments into the mandala Whose centre is the lost creative power. **1966** P. WHITE (*title*) The solid mandala. **1973** *Jrnl. Genetic Psychol.* CXXII. 168 The complete, circular form of the Ufor is reminiscent of the mandala or 'magic circle': i.e., totality. **1974** *Time* (Canada) 18 Mar. 56/1 The appetite of the young for religious experience is leading along exotic paths these days—demons and gurus, mandalas and myths.

†ˈ**mandament.** *Obs. rare*⁻¹. [ad. L. *mandāment-um*, f. *mandā-re* to command: cf. MANDMENT.] Injunction, command.

1834 SIR H. TAYLOR *Artevelde* I. III. iii, But Virtue! where is that indissolute chain Which to thy anchor'd mandaments eterne The floating soul shall grapple!

‖**mandamus** (mænˈdeɪməs), *sb. Law.* [L. = 'we command', 1st pers. pl. pres. ind. of *mandāre* to command.] A term 'originally applied generically to a number of ancient writs, letters missive, or mandates, issued by the sovereign, directing the performance of certain acts', but afterwards restricted to the judicial writ (called 'the high prerogative writ of mandamus') issued in the King's name from the Court of King's Bench (now, from the Crown side of the King's Bench Division of the High Court of Justice) and directed to an inferior court, a corporation, an officer, etc., commanding some specified thing to be done. 'Its general object is to enforce the performance of some public duty in respect of which there is no other specific legal remedy' (G. H. B. Kenrick in *Encycl. Laws Eng.* s.v.).

[**1378** *Rolls of Parlt.* III. 51/2, Par force d'un mandamus a lui directe.] **1535** tr. *Natura Brevium* (1544) 171 b, There is fyue maners of enqueres ordeined after the death of the kynges tenaunte... The fyft is Mandamus, and that is after the yere. **1588** UDALL *Diotrephes* (Arb.) 27 Let no Colledge chuse his owne head, but let him haue a Mandamus, procured from the Queene. **1611** COTGR., *Mandat*, A Mandate, or *Mandamus* for the preferment of one to a Benefice. **1641** *Termes de la Ley* 199 Mandamus is a Writ that goes to the Escheator for the finding of an office after the death of one that died the Kings Tenant. **1664** J. WORTHINGTON *Mede's Wks.* Life (1672) 37 The Colledge had privy notice of a Stranger who had got a Mandamus for a Fellowship, either Fallen or Falling. **1672** MANLEY *Cowell's Interpr.*, *Mandamus* is also a Charge to the Sheriff, to take into the Kings hands all the Lands and Tenements of the Kings Widow, that against her Oath formerly given, marryeth without the Kings consent. **1736** F. DRAKE *Eboracum* 185 The royal authority has frequently interposed, and constituted a mayor by a mandamus. **1865** *Morn. Star* 3 Feb., You may find it necessary to apply to the Court of Queen's Bench for a mandamus against me. **1857** LONGF. *New Eng. Trag.*, *Endicott* IV. ii, Here is the King's Mandamus, taking from us..all power to punish Quakers.

fig. **1775** SHERIDAN *St. Patr. Day* II. iv, Death's a debt; his mandamus binds all alike.

†**b.** *attrib.* = Appointed by a mandamus.

1687 LUTTRELL *Brief Rel.* (1857) I. 421 The new mandamus fellowes [of Magdalen]. **1776** J. ADAMS in *Fam. Lett.* (1876) 216 A Mandamus Counsellor of New Jersey. **1876** BANCROFT *Hist. U.S.* IV. iv. 339 Councillors, called mandamus councillors from their appointment by the crown.

Hence **manˈdamus** *v. trans.*, to serve with a mandamus.

1823 *New Monthly Mag.* VIII. 496 If I do not ferk you out of all likelihood of ringing the beauty, why mandamus me! **1886** *Daily Tel.* 30 Mar. 5/3 Without waiting to be 'mandamused' the Vestry sent to the dust Contractor.

Mandan (ˈmændən), *a.* and *sb.* Also **Mandane, Mandano, Mandon.** [ad. Dakota *Matani*.]

A. *adj.* Of, pertaining to, or designating a Siouan Indian people of North Dakota. **B.** *sb.* This people; a member of this people; also, their language.

1794 in *Mass. Hist. Soc. Coll.* (1810) 1st Ser. III. 24 The tribes of Indians which he passed through, were called the Maskego Tribe..Mandon tribe, Paunees, and several others. **1806** M. LEWIS in *Deb. Congress U.S.* (1852) 9th Congress 2 Sess., App. 1065 The bridlebits and blankets I have seen in the possession of the Mandans. **1806** [see BERDACHE]. **1831** J. M. PECK *Guide for Emigrants* 21 At the Mandan villages, 1600 miles from the Mississippi, it [*sc.* the Missouri] is said to be nearly as wide..as at St. Charles. **1877** L. H. MORGAN *Anc. Society* II. vi. 158 In intelligence and in the arts of life the Mandans were in advance of all their kindred tribes. *Ibid.* III. iii. 440 In Mandan my brother's wife is my wife. **1911**, etc. [see HIDATSA]. **1933** L. BLOOMFIELD *Lang.* iv. 72 The Siouan family includes many languages, such as..Winnebago, Mandan, Crow. *Ibid.* xvii. 283 A Mandan Indian sent the..picture to a fur-trader. **1971** S. E. MORISON *European Discovery Amer.: Northern Voy.* iv. 86 Eventually the Mandan become the most favored tribe.

mandant (ˈmændənt), *a.* and *sb.* Also 7 **-ent**. [ad. L. *mandant-em*, pres. pple. of *mandāre* to command, to send forth: see MANDATE.]

†**A.** *adj. Phys.* Of an organ (chiefly in ***member mandant*** = mod.L. *membrum mandans*): That is the source of impulse; often said of the brain. *Obs.*

1543 TRAHERON *Vigo's Chirurg.* II. xvii. 63 b, The fourth intentyon which is to comforte the membre mandant [L. *membrum mandans*] that is to say, from which the mattier commeth by deriuation. **1544** PHAER *Regim. Life* (1553) I v b, They are all deriued from the member mandant, that is to saye, the brayne. **1650** BULWER *Anthropomet.* (1653) 190 There are many that drink without the moving of Transglutition; but that which they drink descends as if it were poured into a tankard. In this case they need no mandent member. **1670** MAYNWARING *Physician's Repos.* 32 Neither the nutritive juyces are..conveighed, nor excrementitious parts separated..but..regurgitate upon the mandant viscera. **1684** tr. *Bonet's Merc. Compit.* xv. 528 Care must be taken of the Head as the part Mandant.

B. *sb. Law.* = MANDATOR.

1681 VISCT. STAIR *Instit.* I. xii. (1693) 108 A Desire, Warrand, or Order, upon the part of the Mandant to the Mandatar. *a* **1768** ERSKINE *Instit.* III. iii. §31 (1773) II. 457 Mandate,..where it signifies a mutual contract, includes not only the act of the mandant who employs, but the acceptance of the mandatary. **1818** COLEBROOKE *Obligations* 120 If..a mandate be given for the benefit of the mandant himself or of a third party. **1842** MᶜGLASHAN *Sheriff Crts. Scotl.* §589. 154 A mandant may revoke his mandate at pleasure. **1875** POSTE *Gaius* III. Comm. (ed. 2) 430 Another case in which a guarantor and guarantee stand in the relation of mandant and mandatary is *delegatio*.

‖**mandarah** (ˈmændərə). [Arabic *mandaraʰ*, lit. 'place for seeing', f. *naḍara* to see.] In the East, a 'parlour' for receiving visitors.

1865 J. H. INGRAHAM *Pillar of Fire* (1872) 206 An open court, on the right side of which was the mandara for visitors. **1893** *Star* 4 Feb. 1/6 A Turkish mandarah or reception room.

mandarin[1] (ˈmændərɪn). Also 6 **mandeline, mandorijn,** 7 **mandarim,** 7–8 **mandorin,** 7–9 **mandarine,** 8 **mandareen.** [a. Pg. *mandarim*, a. Malay *mantrī*, a. Hindī *mantrī*:—Skr. *mantrin* counsellor, f. *mantra* counsel, f. root *man* to think.]

1. a. *Hist.* A generic name for all grades of Chinese officials; there were nine ranks, each of which was distinguished by a particular kind of 'button'. [Chinese *kwan*.] †Formerly extended to other Asiatic officials.

1589 PARKE tr. *Mendoza's Hist. China* II. II. iii. 252 The Mandelines of the sea, which be certaine iudges appointed to giue aduice of all such matters to the gouernor. **1598** W. PHILLIPS *Linschoten* I. xxiii. 39 Such are they that serue in euery Towne, and haue the gouernment of the same... They are called Loitias, and Mandorijns. **1604** E. G[RIMSTONE] *D'Acosta's Hist. Indies* V. xvi. 370 The Mandarins or ministers of Iustice [in China]. **1685** CROWNE *Sir C. Nice* III. Dram. Wks. 1874 III. 304 He will needs be attended like an Indian mandarine or lord. **1713** POPE *Let. to Gay* 23 Aug., In China; where it is ordinary for a Mandarine to fan himself cool after a debate. **1727** A. HAMILTON *New Acc. E. Ind.* II. 43 Every Province or City [Burma] has a Mandereen or Deputy residing at Court. **1813** *Examiner* 22 Mar. 187/2 A Mandarine of the first class. **1860** *All Year Round* No. 71. 504 The inferior 'one button' mandarins.

b. A toy representing a grotesque seated figure in Chinese costume, so contrived as to continue nodding for a long time after it is shaken.

1791 BOSWELL *Johnson* I. 5 From a man so still and so tame ..conversation worth recording could no more be expected, than from a Chinese mandarin on a chimney-piece. **1839** E. D. CLARKE *Trav. Russia* etc. 13/1 It reminds one of those Chinese mandarin images seen upon the chimney-pieces of old houses, which, when set a-going, continue nodding. **1845, 1855** [see NIDDLE-NODDLE *v.*].

c. *transf.* A person of much importance, a great man. Often used *colloq.* of Government officials, leading politicians or writers, etc.

1907 *National Rev.* Aug. 838 Our Parliamentary Mandarins are ineffably shocked at the impiety of an independent Radical. **1908** *New Age* 6 June 112/2 The chams, lamas, and mandarins of London letters are doubtless devising adjectives for it [*sc.* a book]. **1919** B. RUCK *Disturbing Charm* II. ix. 234 If you let it get known.. that you've got a view like that, you'll have some of the Mandarins snaffling that office of yours for themselves. **1925** FRASER & GIBBONS *Soldier & Sailor Words* 151 The Mandarins of the War Office. **1947** *Oxf. Univ. Handbk.* 261 If he is an athlete of any distinction, the mandarins of his particular game will know all about him long before he arrives. **1961** *Listener* 9 Nov. 782/3 Mr. Thody, who has written a book about Sartre no less brilliant than his two books on Camus, makes comparisons between the two *mandarins*. **1971** P. LORAINE *Photographs have been Sent* V. iii. 164 The Medical Mandarins maintained stony silence.

2. (With capital initial.) The language spoken in China by officials and educated people generally. Hence, any of the varieties of Kuan Hua or Mandarin spoken as a common language in China, *spec.* the Northern variety, which forms the basis of *putonghua*; = PUTONGHUA. Cf. KUO-YÜ. Also *transf.*

[**1604**: see *mandarin tongue* in 4.] **1727–41** CHAMBERS *Cycl.* s.v., Their publick officers, as notaries, lawyers, judges, and chief magistrates, write and speak the Mandarin. **1731** BAILEY vol. II, *Mandarin*, the language spoken by the Mandarins and in the court of China. **1910** *Encycl. Brit.* VI. 216/2 Farther north we come into the range of the great dialect popularly known as Mandarin (*Kuan hua* or 'official language'). **1917** S. COULING *Encycl. Sinica* 143/1 Mandarin or *Kuan hua* is the spoken language of about two-thirds of China. There are three forms of it, spoken typically in Peking, Nanking and Chêngtu... It would seem absurd to call mandarin a dialect, since it is the tongue of 250,000,000 people. **1959** V. CRONIN *Pearl to India* xiii. 188 Some philologists claimed Mandarin to be derived from Hebrew. **1963** *Listener* 17 Jan. 140/1 BBC Mandarin, or Announcers' English, was devised as a refined product, based on so-called 'southern educated' English. **1964** *Amer. Speech* XXXIX. 26 Home's own writings..are written in a kind of middle-class international Victorian Mandarin which defies analysis. **1966** *Chambers's Encycl.* III. 483/2 After the founding of the republic (1911), Mandarin, as *p'ut'unghua* (speech universally understood) or *Kuoyii* (the national language) was chosen as the standard language. **1968** [see KUAN, KWAN 1]. **1971** K. HOPKINS *Hong Kong* 235 Cantonese is very much the predominant language but there are minorities who speak..Mandarin. **1971** [see PUTONGHUA]. **1971** *Whitaker's Almanack 1972* 841/1 The Common Speech or *Putonghua* (often referred to as 'Mandarin')..is based on the northern dialect. **1975** *Language* LI. 875 The locative particle *yú* in the above sentences is no longer used; its replacement in Modern Mandarin is *zài*. **1984** *N.Y. Times* 24 Jan. C13/1 The lecture will be given in Mr. Tung's native Mandarin and will be translated by Margaret Yuen.

3. Short for *mandarin porcelain*.

1873 MRS. PALLISER tr. *Jacquemart's Ceram. Art* 96 The Red Mandarin of the third section.. The shagreened and gauffered Mandarins.

4. a. *attrib.*, as (sense 1) ***mandarin boat, dignity, governor, promotion, sepulchre***; (sense 2) ***mandarin Chinese, dialect, glossary, language, tongue***; **mandarin blue** (see quot. 1949); †**mandarin broth** (see quot.); **mandarin cap**, a child's cap resembling that worn by a mandarin; **mandarin cat**, ? a kind of Angora cat; **mandarin coat** (see quot. 1957); **mandarin collar**, a narrow collar standing up from a close-fitting neckline; **mandarin duck**, a duck of bright and variegated plumage, *Aix galericulata*, native to China; **mandarin hat**, one shaped like that worn by mandarins; **mandarin jar**, a jar of mandarin porcelain; **mandarin porcelain**, Japanese porcelain decorated with figures of mandarins; **mandarin sleeve**, a wide loose sleeve copied from the sleeves of the dress of mandarins (*Cent. Dict.* 1890); **mandarin vase**, a vase of mandarin porcelain.

1912 *Home Chat* 13 Apr. 112/2 In flamingo red, *Mandarin blue or wood-violet mauve linen. **1949** *Dict. Colours Interior Decoration* (Brit. Colour Council) 17/1 *Mandarin blue*, a descriptive name for one of the blues specially produced for China by British dyers at the beginning of the twentieth century. **1749** *Anson's Voy.* III. vii. 369 Two *Mandarine boats came on board from Macao. **1863** READE *Hard Cash* I. vii. 197 A gorgeous mandarin boat ..rowed with forty paddles by an armed crew. **1794** BARHAM *Hortus Amer.* 123 Sir H. Sloane saith, that Mr. James Cunningham wrote to him from China,..informing him that the bean, or *mandarin broth, so frequently mentioned in the Dutch Embassy..is only an emulsion made of the seeds of sesamum and hot water. **1860** THACKERAY *Round. Papers* (1863) 106, *De Juventute*, Children with..*mandarin caps. **1752** H. WALPOLE *Lett.* (1846) II. 425 *Mandarin cats fishing for gold fish. **1895** C. S. HORNE *Story of L.M.S.* 124 Certain Roman Catholic Chinamen are found willing to impart to him as much of the *Mandarin Chinese as they can. **1911** *Daily Colonist* (Victoria, B.C.) 22 Apr. 7/1 (Advt.), *Mandarin Coats. In exquisite hand-embroidered silks and silk lined. **1957** M. B. PICKEN *Fashion Dict.* 67/1 *Mandarin*, long, loose, richly embroidered silk coat with wide sleeves. **1972** *Vogue* June Special 94 Mandarin coat and slit dress of matching print. **1952** C. HOWARD *Compl. Dressmaking* 104 The collar is a *mandarin collar. [**1953** *News Chron.* 2 June 7/1 You can spot him [the Sultan of Selangor] by his yellow knee-length baju (jacket) with mandarin-type collar.] **1967** G. B. MAIR *Girl from Peking* vi. 69 I'll go Chinese. Gold and blue brocade with high mandarin collar and short sleeves. **1971** P. LORAINE *Photographs have been Sent* III. i. 91 A white silk suit with a mandarin collar. **1848** S. W. WILLIAMS *Middle Kingdom* I. x. 489 The court language, the *kwan hwa*, or *mandarin dialect. **1813** *Examiner* 26 Apr. 266/2 We think the Chammish Majesty, and the *Mandarin dignity were.. libelled. **1797** *Encycl. Brit.* (ed. 3) I. 664/1 (*Anas*), The galericulata, or Chinese teal of Edwards, has a hanging crest [etc.]... The English in China give it the name of *mandarin duck. **1861** JANE R. EDKINS *Chinese Scenes* (1863) 207 A *Mandarin Glossary. **1749** *Anson's Voy.* III. vii. 365 The *Mandarine Governor of Janson. **1882** *Harper's Mag.* III. 331 On the May gala day [of the Fish House at Schuylkill] the two *mandarin hats..are decorated with flowers. **1873** MRS. PALLISER tr. *Jacquemart's Ceram. Art* 97 *Mandarin jar. **1697** L. LE COMPTE *Mem. Journey through China* I. v. 134, I acquainted her that I spake the *Mandarin language ..which they constantly use at the Court. **1860** JANE R. EDKINS *Chinese Scenes* (1863) 165 My husband's knowledge of their language (the Mandarin). **1873** MRS. PALLISER tr. *Jacquemart's Ceram. Art* 95 The *Mandarin porcelain. **1874** R. TYRWHITT *Sketch Club* 6 Earnest expectation of firsts, fellowships, and *mandarin promotion. **1665** SIR T. HERBERT *Trav.* (1677) 375 Paquin..in which are..24000 *Mandarin [1638 Mandarins] Sepulchers. **1604** E. G[RIMSTONE] *D'Acosta's Hist. Indies* VI. v. 441 They call it the *Mandarin tongue, which requires a mans age to be conceived. **1727–41** CHAMBERS *Cycl.* s.v., The Mandarin tongue, or the language of the court. **1894** *Times* 22 Feb. 6/1 Four *mandarin vases and covers.

b. *attrib.* or quasi-*adj.*, in *transf.* sense of 'superior, esoteric, "highbrow"'; applied esp. to literary productions or style: 'ornate, refined; high-flown' (often in derogatory use).

1916 H. G. WELLS *Mr. Britling* I. i. 16 The conservative classes whose education has always had a mandarin quality —very, very little of it, and very old and choice. **1947** J. HAYWARD *Prose Lit. since 1939* vii. 47 If literature..is not to become the arcane cult of a mandarin class, it must impose its values. **1952** *Times Lit. Suppl.* 29 Aug. (Suppl.) p. xii/2 The influence that delivered the English novel from Mr. Bennett and Mrs. Brown turned out to be D. H. Lawrence and not his mandarin contemporaries. **1959** *Ibid.* 1 May 257/2 In reaction from Victorian pompousness, bureaucratic jargon, *fin de siècle* poetic prose, and 'mandarin English', a go-as-you-please attitude has crept into the language. **1962** *Listener* 13 Sept. 406/2 The conventionally acceptable accents and Mandarin prose we learn at school. **1973** *Times Lit. Suppl.* 6 July 787/2 M Bourdieu's style has, from the first paper onwards, been growing increasingly mandarin. *Ibid.* 787/3 The mandarin observer, 'freed from the constraints and urgencies of practice'.

Hence **ˈmandarindom**, mandarins collectively. **ˈmandariness**, a mandarin's wife. **mandaˈrinic** *a.*, pertaining to a mandarin (Webster 1864). **ˈmandarinism**, (*a*) the mandarin system, government by mandarins; (*b*) (an example of) pedantry, highbrow or esoteric study; cf. MANDARIN[1] 4 b. **ˈmandarinize** *v. trans.*, to make a mandarin of. **ˈmandarinship**, the position, office, or rank of a mandarin.

1897 *Blackw. Mag.* Dec. 837/1 The most decisive battle ever waged between British officials and *Mandarindom. **1809** LAMB *Lett.* ix. *to Manning* 87 How do you like the *Mandarinesses? **1853** LIEBER *Civ. Liberty* vii. 60 The whole Chinese code..under a systematic *mandarinism, is pervaded by the principle of [etc.]. **1891** *Critic* (U.S.) 5 Sept. 115/1 Is China always to be the land of..girl infanticide and sceptical mandarinism? **1976** *Amer. Speech* *1973* XLVIII. 269 It can never justify..the minute observance of the mandarinisms of edited written English. **1979** *Jrnl. R. Soc. Arts* CXXVII. 123/2 Another mandarinism thus took its place alongside the classics and mathematics. **1980** *Dædalus* Spring 63 He [*sc.* K. Mannheim] found in social science a replacement for the old mandarinism. **1879** BARING-GOULD *Germany* I. 35 In the Celestial Empire, the exaltation of a man to be a mandarin *mandarinises—excuse the expression—all his forefathers. **1697** L. LE COMPTE *Mem. Journey through China* I. i. 12 Executioners..ready to bind and cudgel whom his *Mandarineship should think fit. **1712** *Perquisite Monger* 20 He advanc'd him to a mandarinship of the first Rank. **1802** BENTHAM *Mem. & Corr.* Wks. 1843 X. 384 The appointment to a mandarinship. **1898** *Spectator* 9 Apr. 502/2 Mandarinship is not hereditary.

mandarin[2], **mandarine** (ˈmændərɪn, -iːn). [= F. *mandarine* (1878 in *Dict. Acad.*): perh. f. MANDARIN[1], the colour of the fruit being compared to that of the yellow silk robes of Chinese officials.]

1. A small flattened deep-coloured orange, with sweet-flavoured pulp and thin easily-separable rind. Also ***mandarin orange***.

1771 J. R. FORSTER tr. *Osbeck's Voy. China* I. 307 Here are two sorts of China oranges (*Citrus sinensis*). The first is that called the *Mandarin-orange*, whose peel is quite loose. **1816–20** T. GREEN *Univ. Herbal* I. 316/2 They [Chinese] have also the four-season or everlasting orange.. ; the large clove or mandarine; and the small clove or mandarine. **1834** G. BENNETT *Wand. New South Wales*, etc. II. 72 The *Citrus nobilis* or Mandarin orange. **1886** *New Zealand Herald* 8 Nov. 12/4 Oranges,..lemons,..mandarins. **1892** *Daily News* 16 Dec. 5/6 She accepted the gift of two mandarines from a peasant woman. **1926** H. H. HUME *Cultivation Citrus Fruits* xxix. 477 The other mandarin or kid-glove oranges are attacked [by citrus rust] but not often severely. **1969** *Oxf. Bk. Food Plants* 86/2 Tangerine (*Citrus reticulata*). The fruit is also known under several other names, one of which is 'mandarin', denoting its origin in the Far East.

attrib. **1892** *Daily News* 27 May 5/6 The orchards are full of orange and mandarine blossom. **1895** WORKMAN *Algerian Mem.* 46 Orange, mandarin, and lemon groves.

2. A colour (obtained from coal-tar) resembling that of the mandarin orange. Also ***mandarin-orange, -yellow***.

1883 *Cassell's Fam. Mag.* Nov. 755/1 There are three new dominant colours—Mandarin, a rich yellow like the rind of a Mandarin orange. **1890** THORPE *Dict. Applied Chem.* I. 239 Methyl Orange; Helianthin; Orange III; Gold Orange; Mandarin Orange. **1898** *Daily News* 4 Aug. 6/4 Teagown.. made of grass-lawn over mandarin yellow silk.

3. A liqueur.

1882 *Encycl. Brit.* XIV. 687/1 Noyeau,..trappistine.. bénédictine..peppermint liqueur,..mandarine, parfait amour [etc.]. **1903** *Smart Set* IX. 68/2 [He] ordered some mandarin liqueur, which Ferdinand presently produced in a flask of gold.

mandarin, obs. variant of MANDOLIN.

mandarinate (ˈmændərɪneɪt). [f. MANDARIN + -ATE[1].] **a.** The position or office of a mandarin. **b.** The body of mandarins; mandarins collectively. **c.** Government by mandarins.

1727–41 CHAMBERS *Cycl.* s.v. *Mandarin*, The Mandarinate is not hereditary, nor are any raised to it but men of letters. **1800** *Asiat. Ann. Reg., Chron.* 120/2 The sale of the mandarinates and public employs of the empire. **1889** *Times* 27 Sept. 13/4 The civil office controls the members of the mandarinate both as regards pay and promotion.

d. *transf.*

1884 J. RAE *Contemp. Socialism* 383 With the socialist mandarinate, the interest lies the other way, and the tendency of the head officials would be to multiply their subordinates.

ˈmandarining, *vbl. sb.* [f. MANDARIN[2] + -ING[1].] The process of giving an orange colour to silk or wool by the action of nitric acid.

1852–4 *Cycl. Usef. Arts* (ed. Tomlinson 1866) I. 531/2.

‖**mandat** (mɑ̃da). [a. F. *mandat* (see MANDATE *sb.*).] **1.** A paper money (in full ***mandat territorial***) issued by the French Revolutionary Government from 1796 to 1797, replacing the ASSIGNAT.

1858 P. L. SIMMONDS *Dict. Trade Products* 238/2 *Mandats*, a national paper-money, issued..in France to replace the assignats which had become wretchedly depreciated. **1902** J. R. MORETON-MACDONALD in Carlyle *French Revolution* (ed. C. R. L. Fletcher) III. 339 The Directory..destroyed the die of the *Assignats*, but immediately replaced them by *Mandats Territoriaux* which rapidly followed the same course. **1930** S. E. HARRIS *Assignats* ix. 225 The Assignats were to be exchanged for Mandats which were to be supported by a special security. **1955** E. POUND *Section: Rock-Drill* lxxxviii. 45 Willing to see a currency of hard money..as France since the time of mandats and assignats. **1974** *Encycl. Brit. Micropædia* I. 594/3 In early 1796 the assignats were replaced by the mandats territoriaux (land warrants) at the rate of one mandat for 30 assignats. The failure of the mandat to gain public confidence forced the Directory to return to a metallic currency (Feb. 4, 1797).

2. In France, a money-order.

1896 E. DOWSON *Let. c* 15 Mar. (1967) 345, I enclose a mandat for the price & postage, & shall be much obliged if you can get them [*sc.* newspapers] & post them here. **1939** E. AMBLER *Mask of Dimitrios* xii. 251, I received here a letter from him enclosing a *mandat* for the three thousand francs.

mandat, obs. form of MANDATE.

†**mandatar.** *Sc. Obs.* [ad. F. *mandataire* MANDATARY.] = next.

1681 VISCT. STAIR *Instit.* I. xii. (1693) 108 The management of the Mandant given to the Trust of the Mandatar. *Ibid.* 109 The singular and personal fitness of the Mandatar is chosen by the Mandator, and so cannot without his consent be altered.

mandatary (ˈmændətərɪ). [ad. L. *mandātāri-us*, f. *mandātum* MANDATE: see -ARY.]

† **1.** One who is appointed to a benefice by a papal mandate. *Obs.*

1611 Cotgr., *Mandataire*, a Mandatarie; one that comes to a Benefice by a *Mandamus*. **1726** Ayliffe *Parergon* 117 A Mandatary, to whom the Pope has.. given a Mandate for a Benefice.

2. One to whom a mandate is given. Chiefly in *Law*: see MANDATE 3.

1656 in Blount *Glossogr.* **1754** Erskine *Princ. Sc. Law* (1809) 315 The mandatary is at liberty not to accept of the mandate. *a* **1768** —— *Instit.* III. iii. §34 (1773) II. 458 Where a number of mandataries are named by a proprietor for the management of the same affair. **1793** Helen M. Williams *France* I. App. ii. 266 (Jod.) When the majesty of the people is violated by attempts committed against its mandataries. **1826** Kent *Comm.* (1873) II. xl. 571 If the mandatary undertakes to carry the article from one place to another. **1848** Shand *Pract. Crt. Sess.* I. 154 It never seems to have been disputed that a foreigner not in the country is bound to have a mandatary. **1861** *Sat. Rev.* 30 Mar. 307/2 For the consideration of a hundred pounds a year,.. the Ionian legislator views himself as the mandatary of the nation.

mandate (ˈmændət), *sb.* Also 6 **mandet**, 6–8 **mandat**. [ad. L. *mandāt-um*, neut. pa. pple. of *mandā-re* to command, enjoin, commit. Cf. F. *mandat*.]

1. *gen.* A command, order, injunction. Now *poet.* and *rhetorical*.

1576 Fleming tr. *Caius' Dogs* 12 The theeuishe Dogge,.. at the mandate and bydding of his master fleereth and leereth abroade in the night. **1604** Shaks. *Oth.* IV. i. 270 Sir I obey the Mandate, And will returne to Venice. **1625** Bacon *Ess.*, *Sedit. & Troub.* (Arb.) 395 Cauilling vpon Mandates and Directions, is a kinde of shaking off the yoake. **1681** Dryden *Abs. & Achit.* II. 917 The royal mandate issues forth, Dashing at once their treason, zeal, and mirth. **1760** Johnson *Idler* No. 99 ¶7 He speaks, and his mandate is obeyed. **1797** Mrs. Radcliffe *Italian* vi, She immediately obeyed the mandate of the abbess. **1814** Scott *Ld. of Isles* IV. xxx, Some friend shall bear Our mandate with despatch and care. **1843** Carlyle *Past & Pr.* IV. iv, The mandate of God to His creature man is: Work! **1859** Mill *Liberty* i. (1865) 3/1 Society can and does execute its own mandates. **1887** Bowen *Virg. Æneid* IV. 237 Let him to sea; my mandate is this; be the messenger thou.

2. *spec.* **a.** A judicial or legal command from a superior to an inferior; in early English law, a command of the king and his justices addressed to a court to control a suit; in *U.S. Law*, 'the document promulgated upon the decision of an appeal or writ of error, as by the Supreme Court of the United States, directing what shall be done in the court below' (*Cent. Dict.*).

1501 Douglas *Pal. Hon.* (*c* 1553) II. sig. F i Submyttand me.. ȝour plesour and mandate till obeysyng. **1552** *Forme of Makyng Bishoppes*, etc. B4, Then shall the Archbishop demaund the king's mandate for the consecration, and cause it to be read. **1588–9** *Act 31 Eliz.* c. 9 §1 Everye suche Bisshopp or Chauncelor.. shall by his or their Mandat directed to the Sherieff of the saide Countie Palantyne, cause Proclamacion to be made of the sames Writtes. **1597** Sir R. Cecil in Ellis *Orig. Lett.* Ser. I. III. 44 She [Q. Elizabeth] therfor tooke upon her, by mandat, to prohibite him and his Countreis. *a* **1623** Swinburne *Spousals* (1686) 172 A general Mandate to contract Marriage is not sufficient, unless his Ratification, which made the Mandate, do follow. **1656** Blount *Glossogr.*, *Mandate*.. In our Common Law it is a commandement judicial of the King or his Justices to have any thing done for the dispatch of Justice. **1669** J. Chamberlayne *Pres. St. Eng.* II. 49 Next goes forth a Mandate from the Archbishop to the Archdeacon of his Province, to instal the Bishop elected, confirmed and consecrated. **1798** Ferriar *Illustr. Sterne* v. 153 All that was now wanting, was a mandate from the Elector, to authorize the completion of the marriage. **1845** S. Austin *Ranke's Hist. Ref.* II. 129 [He] obtained.. a mandate wherein the princes were required to restore all his castles to him. **1849** Macaulay *Hist. Eng.* vi. II. 126 A similar change had recently been effected in England by judicial sentences: but in Scotland a simple mandate of the prince was thought sufficient. **1871** Dixon *Tower* III. xi. 109 He was recalled.. by a royal mandate to his place in the House of Lords. **1887** T. Roosevelt *T. H. Benton* v. 113 Towards the close of Adams's term, Georgia had bid defiance to the mandates of the Supreme Court.

b. A papal rescript, *esp.* with reference to preferment to a benefice (see quot. 1727–41).

1611 Cotgr., *Mandat*, A Mandate, or *Mandamus* for the preferment of one to a Benefice. **1727–41** Chambers *Cycl.*, *Mandate*, *Mandatum*, in the canon law, denotes a rescript of the pope, by which he commands some ordinary, collator, or presenter, to put the person there nominated in possession of the first benefice vacant in his collation. **1790** Burke *Fr. Rev.* Wks. V. 71 Mandates for deposing Sovereigns were sealed with the signet of 'the Fisherman'. **1848** Wharton *Law Lex.* **1871** Miss Yonge *Cameos* II. xxi. 235 A mandate came from Pope Innocent for the King's excommunication.

c. A command from the sovereign to elect a fellow of a college or to confer a degree. *Hist.*

1617 Moryson *Itin.* I. 1, I.. was chosen Fellow of the said College by Queene Elizabeths Mandat. *a* **1628** T. Grevil *Sidney* (1652) 223 Her [Q. Eliz.] Universities were troubled with few Mandates. **1665** J. Buck in Peacock *Stat. Cambridge* (1841) App. B. p. lxxxvii, If any Mandates are brought for Degrees in the Vacation time, then this or the like Grace is propounded to the Caput Senatus. **1761** J. Bennet *Ascham's Eng. Wks.* Life 15 The young man was made by the Queen's mandate fellow of a college in Cambridge.

d. *Roman Hist.* An imperial command sent to the governor of a province.

1883 S. Amos *Rom. Civ. Law* 83 Mandates, or instructions to public officials, usually the emperor's 'Legates'. *Ibid.*, Most of the mandates of which a record is preserved relate to criminal law or police matters.

† **e.** A pastoral letter. [= F. *mandement*.] *Obs.*

1763 *Ann. Reg.* 120 The archbishop of Paris.. lately published a mandate, or pastoral letter, to the people of his diocese. **1824** Watt *Bibl. Brit.* II. 767 *u*, Pompignan, John George le Franc.. Archbishop of Vienna.. Mandates prohibiting the reading of the Works of Rousseau and the Abbé Raynal.

3. a. *Roman Law.* A commission by which one person (called the MANDATOR) requested another (called the *mandatarius*: see MANDATARY) to act for him gratuitously, undertaking to indemnify him against loss. ***action of mandate*** = L. *actio mandati*, an action at law for the non-performance of a contract.

1756 G. Harris tr. *Justinian's Instit.* III. xxvii. §1. 87 A mandate is given solely for the benefit of the mandator, when he requires the mandatary to transact his business, to buy lands, or to become a surety for him. *Ibid.* §13. 91 If a man gives his cloaths to a fuller, that they may be cleaned, or to a taylor, that they may be mended, and there is no agreement or promise made, an action of mandate will lie. **1870** Abdy & Walker tr. *Gaius* III. clv. 222 A mandate arises, whether we give a commission for our own benefit or for another person's. **1883** S. Amos *Rom. Civ. Law* 236 By what has been called a qualified mandate (*mandatum qualificatum*) a person induced another to repose credit in a third person, and to that extent the principal became a sort of surety.

b. *Scots Law.* 'A contract by which one employs another to act for him in the management of his affairs, or in some particular department of them, of which employment the person accepts, and agrees to act' (W. Bell *Dict. Law Scot.* 1861).

1681 Visct. Stair *Instit.* I. xii. (1693) 108 The Terms in which Mandats or Commissions are expressed. **1753** *Stewart's Trial* 165 And deposes, that he gave no allowance or mandate to the pannel to make any application at Edinburgh against the removing. **1842** McGlashan *Sheriff Crts. Scot.* §575. 151 A mandate authorizing litigation or diligence to be carried on in name of a party who is out of the kingdom. **1870** *Bell's Comment. Law Scot.* (ed. 7) I. 516 The extent of a factor's authority and his powers are to be gathered from the mandate under which he acts.

c. A contract of bailment by which the mandatary undertakes to perform gratuitously some service in respect of a thing committed to his keeping by the mandator.

1781 Sir W. Jones *Law Bailments* 53 The great distinction then between a mandate and a deposit is, that the former lies in fesance, and the latter simply in custody. **1883** *Encycl. Brit.* (ed. 9) XV. 472 Mandate is retained by Story and others to signify the contract more generally known as gratuitous bailment.

4. *Politics.* [After F. *mandat*.] **a.** The instruction or commission as to policy supposed to be given by the electors to a parliament or one of its members. Also *transf.*

1796 Morse *Amer. Geog.* II. 375 [France] The members of the legislative body are not the representatives of the department which has chosen them, but of the whole nation, and no mandate instructions can be given them. **1880** McCarthy *Own Times* IV. 554 It would almost seem as if the present school of fiction is, to borrow a phrase from French politics, exhausting its mandate. **1886** *Hansard Commons* 9 Apr. 1244, I am perfectly aware that there exists in our constitution no principle of the mandate.. But.. I maintain that there are certain limits which Parliament is morally bound to observe, and beyond which Parliament has morally not the right to go in its relations with the constituents. **1901** *Daily News* 27 Mar. 4/4 Strictly speaking,.. there is no such thing in England as a mandate. Lord Salisbury was the first to introduce into English politics that essentially Jacobinical phrase. **1902** *Contemp. Rev.* Dec. 809 No practical politician can desire to lay too much stress upon the mandate theory of a general election. **1936** R. C. K. Ensor *England, 1870–1914* i. 25 Gladstone (who ten months earlier had been telling the queen that his work was done, his mandate exhausted, and he himself in need of a long rest) declared on 24 January [1874] his intention of dissolving parliament. **1968** *Daily Progress* (Charlottesville, Virginia) 11 July C14/4 We need to win only 36 [seats], which I am sure we can do, and that will be an overwhelming mandate for Scottish freedom.

b. *spec.* A commission issued by the League of Nations (1919–1946) authorizing a selected power to administer, control, and develop a territory for a specified purpose; the territory so allocated. Also *attrib.*

1919 *League of Nations Charter* Art. xxii, The character of the mandate must differ according to the stage of the development of the people, the geographical situation of the territory, its economic conditions, and other similar circumstances. **1920** *Glasgow Herald* 7 Aug. 9 It will still be necessary for the Council to set up a permanent Mandate Commission. **1921** *Spectator* 12 Feb. 189/2 The draft mandates for Palestine and Mesopotamia, which are to come before the Council of the League of Nations on February 21st, were published unofficially last week. *Ibid.* 2 Apr. 419/1 They apparently look upon mandate-making as a kind of old-fashioned diplomacy. **1924** *Brit. Weekly* 30 Oct. 98/4 The Mandate Section of the General Secretariat of the League of Nations. **1937** F. P. Crozier *Men I Killed* xii. 277 Are the British Mandates.. a success? **1946** *Ann. Reg. 1945* 166 The Trusteeship System, replacing the Mandate System of the League, will cover a wider range of backward territories. **1972** *Whitaker's Almanack 1973* 951/2 Syria, which had been under French mandate since the 1914–18 war, became an independent Republic during the 1939–45 war. **1974** *Encycl. Brit. Micropædia* VI. 557/3 Both the territories and the authority to administer them were called mandates. Among them were Britain's mandates in Palestine and Tanganyika. *Ibid.* 558/1 The Mandate System was replaced by the UN Trusteeship System in 1946.

c. ***doctor's mandate***: a mandate from the people empowering the government to take extreme measures in the national interest.

1931 *Times* 7 Oct. 14/1 Mr. MacDonald would issue a manifesto as the head of the National Government appealing for what is called a 'doctor's mandate'. **1961** I. Jennings *Party Politics* II. vii. 291 The Government appealed to the people on a 'doctor's mandate'. **1965** A. J. P. Taylor *Eng. Hist. 1914–45* x. 324 MacDonald asked for 'a doctor's mandate'—a blank authority for the National government to do whatever they could agree on. **1973** *Times* 17 Dec. 15/1 Some of the substantial voices that now call for a doctor's mandate from the people stand close enough to the Prime Minister for him to feel the full cogency of their persuasions. **1974** *Observer* 13 Jan. 1/3 The Prime Minister's main demand would be for a 'doctor's mandate' to enable him to take the measures he considers necessary to make the pay-and-prices policy effective.

5. *attrib.* = MAUNDY, in ***mandate bread***, ***mandate money***, ***Mandate Thursday***.

1546 *Mem. Ripon* (Surtees) III. 11 He payth' yerlie for breade wyne and waxe wt thexpencez of Mandet Thursday x li. **1657** Sparrow *Rationale Bk. Com. Pr.* 157 Hence it is called *Dies mandati*, Mandate or Maundy Thursday. **1797** *Encycl. Brit.* (ed. 3) X. 687/1 Maundy Thursday, is the Thursday in Passion week; which was called Maundy or Mandate Thursday. **1841** Hampson *Med. Ævi Kal.* I. 185 The bread given to the poor on Maunday Thursday was named mandate bread *mandati panes* in the monasteries; as the coin given was called maundate [*sic*] money.

mandate (mænˈdeɪt), *v.* [f. L. *mandāt-*, ppl. stem of *mandāre* to enjoin, command.]

1. *trans.* To command. *Obs. rare*$^{-0}$.

1623 Cockeram, *Mandate*, to command.

2. To commit (one's sermon) to memory. *Sc.*

1724 R. Wodrow *Life J. Wodrow* (1828) 32 After I have mandated my exercises. **1796** Simeon *Gospel Message* Pref. 3 He [Abp. Secker] then proceeds to express his disapprobation of what is called Mandating of Sermons, or repeating them from memory. This custom prevails much among foreign Divines, and throughout the whole Church of Scotland. **1860** J. Brown *Let. J. Cairns* in *Horæ Subs.* (1865) 97 His sermons being laboriously prepared, loudly mandated,.. and then delivered with the utmost vehemence and rapidity. **1893** Crockett *Stickit Minister* (1894) 135 He rose and walked his study, 'mandating' his opening sentences with appropriate gestures.

3. To assign (territory) under a mandate of the League of Nations. Cf. MANDATE *sb.* 4b. So **manˈdated** *ppl. a.*

1919 J. M. Keynes *Econ. Consequences Peace* 248 The Mandated States should be compelled to adhere to this Union for ten years. **1920** *Glasgow Herald* 7 July 11 The Island of Nauru in the Pacific (which is mandated to the British Empire). **1922** *Weekly Dispatch* 5 Nov. 8 We were authorised to raise local native forces to protect the mandated area. **1922** *Times Lit. Suppl.* 23 Nov. 756/3 The result of the late war has been to eliminate Germany from the map, her territories being mandated to the British and other nations. **1944** J. S. Huxley *On Living in Revolution* xii. 119 Crown colonies, protectorates, condominiums, mandated territories of various categories. **1958** A. R. Radcliffe-Brown *Method in Social Anthropol.* I. iii. 90 Cadets who are selected for the administration of the Mandated Territory are sent to the territory for one or two years to make acquaintance with the kind of life and work they will have. **1970** *Internat. & Compar. Law Q.* XIX. 218 When this section was enacted, New Guinea was a Mandated Territory of the League of Nations.

4. To give a mandate to, to delegate authority to (a representative, group, organization, etc.). Freq. as **manˈdated** *ppl. a.*, permitted to act on behalf of a group, etc., approved by means of a mandate.

1958 *Spectator* 20 June 191/1 A delegate conference was called, and garages invited to mandate their representatives to vote for or against continuance [of a strike]. **1967** *National Observer* (U.S.) 3 July 13 Mr. Reagan must raise the money to pay off that deficit and to pay for mandated new programs. **1968** Smith & Zurcher *Dict. Amer. Politics* (ed. 2) 231 *Mandated expenditure*, an expenditure which a State requires a municipal government to make, often from locally collected funds, and often without reimbursement from State funds. **1969** D. Widgery in Cockburn & Blackburn *Student Power* 126 Universities with a strong and democratic union came to Council with an elected delegation fully briefed and mandated on all issues by general meetings. **1972** *Daily Tel.* 29 Apr. 14 The [union] delegates are elected by, and frequently mandated by, those members who attend branch meetings. **1973** *Black World* May 35/2 The Committee mandated its current chairman.. to visit all O.A.U. member states. **1973** *Black Panther* 21 July p. B, Their annual salary increases exceed the nationally-mandated rate. **1974** *Daily Tel.* 25 May 6/5 Mr Thorne, a member of the national executive, said he was mandated to vote for industrial action.

mandaˈtee. *rare.* [f. MANDATE *sb.* + -EE.] = MANDATARY.

1774 Hallifax *Anal. Rom. Civ. Law* 64 A Commission might be constituted for the Benefit.. of the Mandator and Mandatee. *Ibid.* 86 A Proctor was 1. Extrajudicial, otherwise called a Mandatee.

manˈdation. *Sc.* [f. MANDATE *v.*: see -ATION.] The action of committing (a sermon) to memory.

1867 J. Macfarlane *Mem. T. Archer* i. 15 Some of the most acceptable ministers of the Gospel have been known to regard 'mandation' as a process of slow murder.

mandative (ˈmændətɪv), *a.* [ad. late L. *mandātīv-us*, f. *mandāre* to command: see

MANDATE *sb.* and -ATIVE.] Pertaining to command; occas. used in *Grammar* to render L. *modus mandativus*, denoting the imperative use of the future.

1651 J. ROCKET *Chr. Subject* x. §3 (1658) 114 Though servants have not a mandative power to lay their strict injunctions upon their Masters. **1845** STODDART *Gram.* in *Encycl. Metrop.* (1847) I. 51/1 [Kinds of Mood] imperative, mandative, conjunctive, subjunctive [etc.].

‖**mandator** (mæn'deɪtə(r)). *Law.* [L. agent-n. f. *mandāre* (see MANDATE).] One who gives a mandate (*esp.* in the legal senses).

1681 VISCT. STAIR *Instit.* I. xii. (1693) 110 As to the special kinds of Mandats, they are either express, or tacit, to one Mandatar,..for the Mandators behove, or in the Name of the Mandator. **1726** AYLIFFE *Parergon* 53 A Person is said to be a Client to his Advocate, but a Master and a Mandator to his Proctor. **1752** *Scots Mag.* (1753) Oct. 511/2 Himself the *mandator* and accomplice. **1793** J. WILLIAMS *Calm Exam.*, etc. 49 Every legal Mandator, should be a law expounder, not a law-maker. **1839** J. STORY *Law Bailments* 142 The mandator..contracts to reimburse the mandatary for all expenses and charges reasonably incurred in the execution of the trust. **1875** POSTE *Gaius* III. Comm. (ed. 2) 401 Solidary Intercession is exemplified by the Mandator in the contract called *mandatum qualificatum*.

mandatory ('mændətərɪ), *a.* and *sb.* [ad. late L. *mandātōrius*, f. *mandātor*: see prec.]

A. *adj.* **a.** Of the nature of, pertaining to, or conveying a command or mandate.

1576 FLEMING *Panopl. Epist.* B iv b, An epistle hortatorie, accusatorie,..mandatorie. *a* **1600** HOOKER *Eccl. Pol.* VII. iii. §1 A superiority of power mandatory, judicial, and coercive over other Ministers. **1611** SPEED *Hist. Gt. Brit.* IX. xv. §115. 801 Mandatory letters were sent by King Charles into Picardy, to put all places that held for him in those quarters into Henries possession. *a* **1680** CHARNOCK *Attrib. God* (1834) I. 727 We behold, in the life of Christ, a conformity to the Mandatory part of the law. **1726** AYLIFFE *Parergon* 358 Of a Mandatory Writ, in Latin stiled a *Mandamus*. *Ibid.*, Several Mandatory Writs have been granted. **1863** H. COX *Instit.* III. viii. 716 A mandatory writ was issued to a serjeant-at-arms. **1900** WYNDHAM *Sp. Ho. Comm.* 15 Feb., The proposals..were enabling and not mandatory. **1966** *Listener* 15 Dec. 880/1 Mr. George Brown..puts Britain's case for mandatory sanctions to Security Council. **1972** *Soviet Weekly* 26 Feb. 1 Each delegation has one vote, and only unanimous decisions are mandatory. **1972** *Incorporated Linguist* XI. 36 For further education, postgraduate training is not mandatory, but there is much to be said for it.

b. Of actions: Obligatory in consequence of a command. Const. *upon*.

1818 JAS. MILL *Brit. India* II. v. ix. 696 The regular communication to the councils of all correspondence was rendered mandatory upon the Governor-General. **1891** *Boston Daily Globe* 24 Mar. 5/6 The bill makes it mandatory upon the judge to impose a fine of $500.

c. *spec.* Designating a power or state in receipt of a mandate from the League of Nations, or the system of rule by mandate. Cf. MANDATE *sb.* 4 b.

1921 *First Assembly* (League of Nations Union) 260 The Commission shall examine the annual reports of the Mandatory States and advise the Council as to the execution of the terms of the Mandates. **1922** *Encycl. Brit.* XXX. 509/1 Under the Peace of Versailles a new form of colonial possession came into being... The 'mandatory' system was ..evolved. **1930** [see INCIDENT *sb.*[1] 1 b]. **1946** *Ann. Reg. 1945* 167 The compromise eventually adopted required the Mandatory Powers to express their willingness to place the territories for which they were responsible under the Trusteeship system. **1950** M. HAY *Foot of Pride* ix. 269 'It will be interesting,' wrote C. R. Ashbee, civil adviser of the mandatory administration, in 1922, 'to watch..the inevitable failure of the Rutenberg scheme.' **1958** *Listener* 21 Aug. 273/1 An underground organisation [in Palestine] ..directed against Britain, the mandatory power. **1974** *Encycl. Brit. Micropædia* VI. 558/1 Exercise of the mandates was supervised by the League's Permanent Mandates Commission, but the commission had no real way of enforcing its will on a mandatory power.

B. *sb.* **a.** One to whom a mandate is given; = MANDATARY.

1661 FELL in *Hammond's Wks.* (1674) I. Life 14 [The Visitors] sending their mandatory with a Musquetier to Dr. Hammond's lodging, commanded him to appear before them. **1711** HICKES *Two Treat. Chr. Priesth.* (1847) ii. 17 A priest..is an advocate, mediator, intercessor,..vicegerent, mandatory, interpellant. **1795** tr. *Mercier's Fragm. Pol. & Hist.* I. 432 The monarch with the mandatories of his Supreme, tutelar and beneficent, authority. **1833** ALISON *Hist. Europe* (1849–50) II. vii. §70. 182 If the people are violently alarmed, is it the part of their mandatories to refuse to hear them? **1842** MᶜGLASHAN *Sheriff Crts. Scot.* §582. 153 The mandatory to be sisted must be a responsible person. **1862** *Act 25 & 26 Vict.* c. 97 §20 To nominate..any person as the mandatory of such..proprietor, to attend, act, and vote at any meeting. **1898** BODLEY *France* I. I. ii. 141 Ecclesiastics regard themselves sometimes as the mandatories of a foreign potentate.

¶ **b.** Used for MANDATE. **c.** Something with the function of commanding.

1839 JAMES *Louis XIV*, II. 340 A Mandatory..was issued ..by Masaniello, requiring every citizen to take arms. **1865** BUSHNELL *Vicar. Sacr.* III. iv. (1866) 249 In itself, what we call law is impersonal, a cold mandatory of abstraction.

d. *spec.* A power or state in receipt of a mandate from the League of Nations to administer and develop a territory (in quot. 1927, the territory assigned in this way).

1919 *League of Nations Covenant* Art. xxii, The wishes of these communities must be a principal consideration in the selection of the Mandatory. **1927** *Daily Express* 24 May 3 A memorandum issued by the Arab Executive (Nationalists) ..accuses Great Britain of ignoring the covenant principle to assist mandatories to become self-governing. **1928** *Manch. Guardian Weekly* 8 June 443/3 He adopts quite frankly the very contestable position that sovereignty over the mandated territory belongs solely to the mandatory. **1936** V. MARGUERITTE *League Fiasco* ii. 83 The Mandates Commission, consisting of nine members, would have nothing to do but examine the annual reports submitted by the mandatories. **1937** H. F. ANGUS *Probl. Peaceful Change Pacific Area* iii. 155 It was assumed that whichever of these countries acted as mandatory would do more for the interests of native populations than had been done by their predecessor.

‖**mandatum** (mæn'deɪtəm). [L.] = MANDATE *sb.*

1586 J. HOOKER *Hist. Irel.* 87/1 in *Holinshed* II, Suddenlie commeth from the cardinall a mandatum to execute Kildare. **1587** FLEMING *Contn. Holinshed* III. 1306/1 Simon Mepham, then archbishop of Canturburie, sent his mandatum to this bishop, that he would visit his church. **1594** T. B. *La Primaud. Fr. Acad.* II. 652 They obtain so many letters of commaundement, so manie mandatums one in anothers necke, that [etc.].

M and B (ɛm ənd 'biː). Also **M & B**, and with points. A registered trade mark of the *May & Baker* Co. Ltd., applied to pharmaceutical preparations marketed by them, esp ***M & B 693***, sulphapyridine tablets.

A symbol incorporating the letters M and B was registered as a trade mark in 1935 (*Trade Marks Jrnl.* (1935) 30 Oct. 1349).

1938 *Lancet* 28 May 1210/2 For experimental infections in mice the effective dose of M. & B. 693 varies from 0·25 mg. per g. to 2 mg. per g. **1943** J. B. PRIESTLEY *Daylight on Saturday* i. 3 With ultra-violet rays and radiant heat and *M. & B. 693* to be had for the asking. **1951** W. S. CHURCHILL *Second World War* (1952) V. 373 The admirable M and B, from which I did not suffer any inconvenience, was used at the earliest moment, and after a week's fever the intruders were repulsed. **1953** *Trade Marks Jrnl.* 18 Feb. 139/1 M & B... Chemical products used in industry, science and photography; [etc.]... May & Baker Limited, Dagenham, Essex; manufacturing chemists. **1957** F. S. TAYLOR *Hist. Industr. Chem.* xvi. 250 Sulphapyridine (M & B 693) revolutionized the treatment of pneumonia. **1968** *Listener* 19 Dec. 815/3 One pocket stuffed with quinine and the other with M and B tablets.

Mande ('mɑːndeɪ), *sb.* and *a.* = MANDINGO *sb.* and *a.*

1883 R. N. CUST *Sk. Mod. Lang. Afr.* I. xi. 179 The Mande-nga occupy a mountainous Region... The final syllable is a Suffix, which conveys the meaning of the people themselves, while their language should properly be called Mande. *Ibid.* 186 The Mende are Pagans and turbulent. Care must be taken to distinguish the Mende from the Mande. *Ibid.* 186 They [*sc.* the Vei] belong to the Mande Cluster. **1911** *Encycl. Brit.* XVII. 564/2 Delafosse divides the Mandingo group linguistically into three main sections: (1) the *Mande-tamu*, (2) the *Mande-fu*, and (3) the *Mande-tã*, according as they use for the numeral 10 the root *tamu*, *tã* or *fu*. *Ibid.* 565/1 The manati was the totem of the Mande group. **1930** C. G. SELIGMAN *Races Afr.* iii. 59 The Mandingo—more correctly the Mendi or Mande—constitute one of the most important groups of French Senegal. **1952** WESTERMANN & BRYAN *Lang. W. Afr.* ii. 31 The Mande languages are spoken over a vast area extending from the Atlantic coast to the Black Volta. **1955** P. STREVENS *Papers in Lang.* (1965) ix. 114 Within the area..are spoken Temne and Mande languages in Sierra Leone, [etc.]. **1968** G. JACKSON *Let.* 6 Mar. in *Soledad Brother* (1971) 152 The oldest language is one spoken in Africa: Mande. **1970** P. OLIVER *Savannah Syncopators* 112 *Mandingo*. Mande-speaking peoples of which the Malinke are the largest.

mande, obs. form of MAUNDY.

mandelic (mæn'dɛlɪk), *a.* *Chem.* [f. G. *mandel* almond + -IC.] ***mandelic acid*** (G. *mandelsäure*): an acid formed by the action of hydrochloric acid upon amygdalin.

1844 FOWNES *Chem.* 430. **1885** REMSEN *Org. Chem.* (1888) 292.

mandell, variant of MANDILL *Obs.*

mandellion, variant of MANDILION.

‖**mandelstein** ('mandəlʃtaɪn). *Geol.* Also anglicized **mandelstone**. [G., f. *mandel* almond + *stein* stone.] = AMYGDALOID *sb.*

1799 KIRWAN *Geol. Ess.* 202 Mandelstein (or Amygdaloid). **1852** TH. ROSS *Humboldt's Trav.* I. i. 35 The porous basalt which passes into mandelstein.

mandement, variant of MANDMENT *Obs.*

manderelle, -il, obs. forms of MANDREL.

mandet, obs. variant of MANDATE.

[**mandevi(l)le**, corruption (in Planché, Fairholt, and recent Dicts.) of MANTEVIL *Obs.*]

† **mandglorye**. *Obs. rare.* Also **mond-**. [a. OF. *mandegloire* (cf. mod.F. *main de gloire* HAND OF GLORY), corruption of *mandregore* MANDRAGORA.] Mandragora.

1483 CAXTON *Cato* 3 b, An ensample of the pouldre of mondglorye and how hit maketh to slepe. **1489** —— *Faytes of A.* II. iv. 97 Certein herbe that is called mandglorye.

mandible ('mændɪb(ə)l), *sb.* Now only *Anat.* and *Zool.* Also 7 **-uble**, 7–8 **-able**. [ad. late L. *mandibula*, *-ulum*, f. *mandĕre* to masticate. Cf. OF. *mandible*, mod.F. *mandibule*.] A jaw or jaw-bone; *esp.* the lower jaw (in mammals and fishes).

1548–77 VICARY *Anat.* v. (1888) 41 The bones..of the Cheekes, be two:..of the vpper Mandibile, two. *c* **1560** *Misogonus* III. iii. 82 (Brandl) A neighboure of yours Which is payned in hir mandible with a wormetone toth. **1623** COCKERAM, *Manduble*, the iaw-bone wherein the teeth be set. **1674** JOSSELYN *Voy. New Eng.* 185 Rub the mandible with it. *c* **1675** R. CROMWELL *Let.* in *Eng. Hist. Rev.* (1898) XIII. 93 The nose of the skull, with an upper mandable. **1707** SLOANE *Jamaica* I. p. cxxxii, The swelling..being not so much in the throat, as mandibles and cheeks. **1770** G. WHITE *Selborne* xxvii. 76 With their upper mandible, which is much longer than their lower, they [hedgehogs] bore under the plant. **1854** EMERSON *Lett. & Soc. Aims, Comic* Wks. (Bohn) III. 210 To put something for mastication between the upper and lower mandibles. **1872** MIVART *Elem. Anat.* 86 The lower jawbone, or Mandible, consists of a curved osseous band.

b. In birds, (usually) either part, upper or lower, of the beak; but by some restricted to the lower jaw (see quot. 1893).

1686 PLOT *Staffordsh.* 234 The Mandibles [of a Raven] crossing one another, like those of the..Crossbill. **1766** PENNANT *Zool.* (1768) II. 477 A loose skin..reaches from the upper mandible round the eyes [of the cormorant]. **1845** DARWIN *Voy. Nat.* vii. (1879) 137 The lower mandible, differently from every other bird, is an inch and a half longer than the upper. **1865** LIVINGSTONE *Zambesi* iv. 100 Flocks of scissor-bills..ploughing the water with their lower mandibles. **1893** NEWTON *Dict. Birds* 534 *Mandible* (Lat. *Mandibula*), the lower jaw in Birds. *Ibid.* 539 *Maxilla*, a rather slender bone..forming part of the lateral margin of what is often called the Upper Mandible.

c. In insects, either half of the upper or anterior pair of jaws.

1826 KIRBY & SP. *Entomol.* III. 429 The mandibles close the mouth on each side under the *labrum* or upper-lip. **1859** DARWIN *Orig. Spec.* iv. (1873) 69 Male stag-beetles sometimes bear wounds from the huge mandibles of other males. **1874** LUBBOCK *Wild Flowers* i. 13 The mouth of an insect is composed of an upper lip, an under lip, a pair of anterior jaws or mandibles.

† **mandible** ('mændɪb(ə)l), *a.* *Obs. rare.* [ad. L. **mandibil-is*, f. *mandĕre* to chew: see -IBLE.] Capable of being chewed or eaten.

1656 BLOUNT *Glossogr.*, *Mandible*, eatable, or that may be eaten. **1671–80** R. HEAD *Eng. Rogue* I. iv. (1680) 39 Their Geese, Hens, Pigs, or any such mandible thing we met with.

‖**mandibula** (mæn'dɪbjʊlə). *Anat.* and *Zool.* [L.] = MANDIBLE *sb.*

1704 HARRIS *Lex. Techn.*, *Mandibula*,..the Jaw, is either Upper or Lower. **1798** AFZELIUS in *Trans. Linn. Soc.* IV. 255 The *Mandibulæ* are toothless and without sheaths. **1826** KIRBY & SP. *Entomol.* III. 417 Upper- and under-jaws (*mandibulæ* and *maxillæ*). **1855** GOSSE in *Phil. Trans.* CXLVI. 447 The dental organs in *Rotifera* are true *mandibulæ* and *maxillæ*.

mandibular (mæn'dɪbjʊlə(r)), *a.* [f. MANDIBULA + -AR.] Belonging to, connected with, or forming part of a mandible.

1654 GAYTON *Pleas. Notes* III. vi. 103 The many parts, joynts, sinews [etc.]..gutturall, dentall, mandibular, &c. **1706** PHILLIPS (ed. Kersey), *Mandibular Muscles*, the Muscles that belong to the Lower Jaw. **1816** KIRBY & SP. *Entomol.* (1818) II. 275 Besides their mandibular hooks, some of these grubs supply the want of legs by means of claws at their anus. **1875** BLAKE *Zool.* 2 In nearly all mammals teeth exist in a single row on the..mandibular bones. **1891** FLOWER & LYDEKKER *Introd. Mammals* 171 The mandibular symphysis is ankylosed.

mandibulary (mæn'dɪbjʊlərɪ), *a.* *rare.* [Formed as prec. + -ARY.] = prec.

1653 URQUHART *Rabelais* I. xxxviii, The mandibulary sinew or nerve of the jaw. **1880** GÜNTHER *Fishes* 563 Two pairs of mandibulary barbels. **1887** —— in *Encycl. Brit.* XXII. 189/1 The mandibulary symphysis is not by suture but by an elastic band.

mandibulate (mæn'dɪbjʊleɪt), *a.* and *sb.* *Ent.* [ad. mod.L. *mandibulātus*: see MANDIBULA and -ATE[2].]

A. *adj.*

1. Provided with mandibles: applied to a group of insects (the *Mandibulata*) which have the organs of the mouth adapted for mastication.

1826 KIRBY & SP. *Entomol.* III. 462 The *maxillæ* of the mandibulate hexapods. **1835** KIRBY *Hab. & Inst. Anim.* II. xx. 316 Metabolians..are considered..as constituting two Sections which are denominated Haustellate and Mandibulate Insects. **1874** LUBBOCK *Orig. & Met. Ins.* v. 92 The strongly mandibulate form which prevails among the larvae of Coleoptera.

2. Of organs: Adapted for mastication.

1835 KIRBY *Hab. & Inst. Anim.* II. xx. 316 The instrument of suction in a Haustellate mouth consists of pieces..analogous to those employed in mastication in a Mandibulate one. **1838** *Penny Cycl.* X. 494/2 *Hemiptera* ..with mandibulate mouths.

B. *sb.* A mandibulate insect.

In recent Dicts.

So **man'dibulated** *a.*, in the same sense.

1836–9 TODD *Cycl. Anat.* II. 855/2 Fabricius..divided Insects into..the Mandibulated..and the Haustellated. **1864** *Chambers's Encycl.* VI. 299 *Mandibulata*, mandibulated or masticating Insects.

mandibuliform (mænˈdɪbjʊlɪfɔːm), *a. Ent.* [ad. mod.L. *mandibuliformis*, f. *mandibula* MANDIBLE: see -FORM.] Shaped like a mandible.
1826 KIRBY & SP. *Entomol.* III. 127 They..catch the prey at which they aim by means of the mandibuliform plates. *Ibid.* IV. 310. **1856** in MAYNE *Expos. Lex.*

mandibulo- (mænˈdɪbjʊləʊ), irreg. combining form (see -O-) of L. *mandibula* MANDIBLE, used in compounds with the sense 'pertaining to the mandible (and some other part)', as ***mandibulo-hyoid, -maxillary, -suspensorial*** adjs.
1870 ROLLESTON *Anim. Life* 105 The mandibulo-maxillary apodema. **1875** HUXLEY in *Encycl. Brit.* I. 760/1 The hyosuspensorial and mandibulo-suspensorial ligaments.

mandibulous (mænˈdɪbjʊləs), *a. rare. Ent.* [f. MANDIBULA + -OUS.] Mandibular.
1835-6 TODD *Cycl. Anat.* I. 209/1 The mandibulous hook of spiders.

‖**mandil** (ˈmændɪl). Also 7 **mendil**, 9 **mundil**. [Arabic *mindīl*, *mandīl*, sash, turban-cloth, handkerchief, ad. L. *mantīle* (see MANTLE *sb.*).] A turban.
1662 J. DAVIES tr. *Olearius' Voy. Ambass.* v. (1669) 214 The Mendils and Mianbends, that is, the Turbant and Girdle, of Gold Brocado. **1665** SIR T. HERBERT *Trav.* (1677) 133 His Turbant or Mandil was of finest white silk interwoven with gold. **1731** BAILEY vol. II, *Mandil*, a sort of cap or turbant worn by the Persians. **1858** SIMMONDS *Dict. Trade*, Mundil. And in later Dicts.

mandilion (mænˈdɪlɪən). *Obs.* exc. *Hist.* Also 6 **mandilyon, maundilion**, 6-7 **mandilian, -illian**, 7 **-ellion, -ylian**, (? **madilion**). [a. F. *mandillon* (16th c.), ad. It. *mandiglione*, augmentative f. *mandiglia*: see MANDILL.] A loose coat or cassock, in later times sleeveless, formerly worn by soldiers and men-servants as a kind of overcoat.
1577 DEE *Relat. Spir.* I. (1659) 154 The men have things on their shoulders of beasts' skins, as instead of a Jerkin or a Mandillion. **1587** FLEMING *Contn. Holinshed* III. 1287/2 Their vniuersall liuerie was a mandilion of purple taffata, laid about with siluer lase. **1599** DALLAM *Trav.* (Hakl. Soc.) 74 Their coats were like a soldier's mandilyon. **1610** HOLLAND *Camden's Brit.* (1637) 249 He had a mandilian or cassocke, garnished with the bishops armes. **1615** G. SANDYS *Trav.* 230 In time of warre they [the Knights of Malta] weare crimson mandilions..over their armour. **1688** R. HOLME *Armoury* III. 18/2 He beareth Or, a Mandilion Azure. **1696**, **1706** PHILLIPS. **1860** [see MANTEVIL]. **1895** J. BROWN *Pilgrim Fathers* x. 280 Hooks and eyes for 'mandilions', these being garments large and full of folds, with which soldiers wrapped themselves against the cold.

†**mandill**. *Obs.* Also 7 **mandell, mandle**. [a. F. *mandil* (15-16th c., now *mandille*), a. Sp., Pg. *mandil* (cf. Pr. *mandil-s* table-cloth), a. Arab. *mandīl*: see MANDIL.] A loose coat or overcoat.
1579 *Inv. R. Wardr.* (1815) 281 Ane pair of breikis of blew velvott with ane mandill thairto broderit with gold. **1661** A. HAIG *Acc.* in J. Russell *Haigs* (1881) 471 A suett of cloeths, with a mandell. **1662** *Ibid.* 472 For making a mandle sute and furnertur.

Mandingo (mænˈdɪŋgəʊ), *sb.* and *a.* Also **Manding, Mundingo**. **A.** *sb.* **a.** A large group of Negro peoples of the upper Niger in West Africa; a member of these peoples. **b.** The language or languages of these peoples. **B.** *adj.* Of or pertaining to these peoples.
1623 R. JOBSON *Golden Trade* 27, I take my beginning from the mouth of the River, whereat our first entrance, we find the Black men called Mandingos. **1757** [see IBO *sb.* 1 a]. **1798** *Proc. Afr. Assoc.* 4 The inhabitants are chiefly Mandingoes, and seem to be a well disposed and peaceable race. *Ibid.* 9 Of the other wild animals in the Mandingo countries, the most common are the hyæna, the panther, and the elephant. *Ibid.* 13 By the Niger, is here undoubtedly meant, the river of Senegal; which in the Mandingo language is called *Bafing*, or the Black river. **1888** L. A. SMITH *Music of Waters* 329 Another very rhythmical air is the following Mandingo one. **1925** P. RADIN tr. *Vendryes' Lang.* II. ii. 112 A West African language, Mandingo, distinguishes *a fa* 'his father', from *a-ta kursi* 'his breeches'. **1930** C. G. SELIGMAN *Races Afr.* iii. 60 The typical Mandingo are described as tall and slender in build. **1936** G. GREENE *Journey without Maps* II. i. 99 Some Mandingo traders whom he caught smuggling goods over the border from French territory. **1948** *Caribbean Q.* I. i 11 Of these 101 were Mandingoes from Senegambia and the upper Niger. **1969** *Times* 19 July 9/5 Many of these slaves were..conversant with the two main languages of Senegambia: Wolof and Mandingo. **1972** *Times* 29 June 16/2 The term 'Manding' embraces a number of West African peoples who speak related forms of the same language and share a similar culture. The Manding language, in a variety of dialects.., is spoken by some 10 million people. *Ibid.* 16/5 The pious Manding who made a famous pilgrimage to Mecca in 1324. *Ibid.*, The Manding have always been natural travellers.

Mandinka (mənˈdɪŋkə), *sb.* and *a.* = MALINKE.
1957 M. BANTON *W. Afr. City* iv. 62 Tribes largely resident in Freetown or the Colony area, for example, Kru, Sherbro and Mandinka. *Ibid.* vii. 122 The Kissi..speak a separate language similar to that of the Bulom but now much influenced by Mandinka. *Ibid.* 127 There are about 125,000 Mandinka in West Africa, from Senegal to the Ivory Coast.

mandioc(a: see MANIOC.

†**manˈdition**. *Obs. rare*⁻¹. [irreg. f. L. *mandāre* to command + -ITION.] An injunction.
1597 *Pilgr. Parnass.* III. 344 My uncle..sent mee yesterday a letter and this mandition..'Studie not these vaine arts of Rhetorique, Poetrie and Philosophie'.

mandle, obs. f. MANDILL, MANTEL, MANTLE.

mandly, rare obs. form of MANLY.

†**mandment**. *Obs.* Forms: 3-6 **mandement, maundement**, 4-5 **mawndement**, 4-6 **mandment**, 5-6 **maundment**. [a. OF. *mandement*:—late L. *mandāmentum*, f. *mandāre* to command. The word is orig. trisyllabic (cf. COMMANDMENT); the disyllabic forms are characteristically northern.] A commandment, an order; that which is commanded. Also, the action of commanding, command, rule.
1297 R. GLOUC. (Rolls) 4011 Þis was a prout mandement & an heiuol dede. *c* **1357** *Lay Folks Catech.* 540 Who brekys þe fyrste maundement. Prowde men wordly men and fleschly men. **1375** BARBOUR *Bruce* IV. 332 His men his mandment has all done. *a* **1400-50** *Alexander* 4237 To þe modi kynge of Messedone þis maundment I write. *c* **1440** *Promp. Parv.* 330/2 Mawndement, *mandatum, preceptum*. *c* **1460** ASHBY *Active Policy* 654 Euery day he ware of that extremite Not to be hasty in mandement. **1467-8** *Rolls of Parlt.* V. 583/1 All Retornes of Writtes, Preceptes, Maundements and Billes. **1539** CROMWELL *Let.* 16 Apr., in Merriman *Life & Lett.* (1902) II. 211 Themperour hathe not consented to the popes desires nor that his Mandementes shuld be published. **1553** *Douglas' Æneis* x. Prol. 162 For quhay thy mandmentis [1513 mandat] kepis in accord, Bene ane with the, not in substance bot grace. **1567** *Reg. Privy Council Scot.* I. 567 Gevand..oure full plane power, speciall mandment..and charge, to compeir.

mandola (mænˈdəʊlə), **mandora** (mænˈdɔərə). Also 9 (*rare*) **mandura**. [a. It. *mandola, mandora*. Cf. F. *mandore, mandole*, and see BANDORE, PANDORA², MANDORE.] A larger variety of the mandolin.
1758 J. CLEPHANE in *Fam. Rose Kilr.* (Spald. Club) 461 If you have once made some progress on the spinet..the mandola will be an easy acquisition. **1825** L. HUNT *Bacchus in Tuscany* 850 Play to me too On the mandola. **1825** FOSBROOKE *Encycl. Antiq.* I. 628 The Pandura was of the lute kind, the Mandura a lesser lute. **1880** A. J. HIPKINS in Grove *Dict. Mus.* II. 204 It [the mandoline] is..less in size than the Mandóla or Mandóra, a much scarcer instrument. **1895** *Daily News* 22 May 7/3 Three mandolas (or mandoras), eighteen guitars..and a bass guitar.

mandolin, -ine (ˈmændəlɪn). Also 8 **mandarin**; and in It. form **mandolino**. [ad. F. *mandoline*, ad. It. *mandolino*, dim. of *mandola* (see prec.).] **1.** A musical instrument of the lute kind having from four to six metal strings stretched upon a deeply-rounded body.
1707 in Ashton *Soc. Life Q. Anne* (1882) II. 38 Signior Conti will play..on the Mandoline, an instrument not known yet. **1758** J. CLEPHAM in *Fam. Rose Kilr.* (Spald. Club) 461 The guitarre, or the mandolino, as it is called here by our London ladies. **1766** SMOLLETT *Trav.* 122 An excellent performer on the lute and mandolin. **1783** MME. D'ARBLAY *Diary* 1 Jan., A solo air, accompanied by the mandoline,..has a mighty pretty effect. **1796** PEGGE *Anonym.* (1809) 104 When the instrument now coming into use is called a Mandarin, we are led to think it to be something used by the Chinese Lords or Mandarins; but the truer pronunciation is Mandolin. **1856** MRS. C. CLARKE tr. *Berlioz' Instrument.* 70 The mandolin has almost fallen into desuetude at present. **1863** SALA *About Shrimpington* 102 A mandolin all covered with lacquer work.
2. *transf.* A kitchen utensil fitted with cutting blades and used for slicing vegetables. Usu. spelt *mandoline*.
1951 E. DAVID *French Country Cooking* 19 A vegetable slicer which goes by the charming name of *Mandoline*. **1959** *Times* 16 Nov. 15/4 Slice the peeled potatoes evenly and thinly (a slicing device known as a *mandoline* makes this task a matter of moments). **1961** *Spectator* 25 Aug. 270 With the aid of that blessed instrument called a mandoline the cucumber is thinly and evenly sliced. **1969** *Daily Tel.* 16 Jan. 17 Arrange a chopping board, sharp knife, grater and cucumber slice (or mandoline) around the colourful basket of raw vegetables. **1975** *Habitat Catal.* 68 Mandolin... Wood frame stainless steel slicer and crinkle cutter.
Hence **ˈmandolinist**, a performer on the mandolin.
1888 *Daily News* 14 May 3/3 A company of Neapolitan mandolinists and singers.

mandom (ˈmændəm). *rare*⁻¹. [f. MAN *sb.*¹ + -DOM.] The realm of man.
1844 MRS. BROWNING *Drama of Exile* Poems 1850 I. 72 Without this rule of mandom, ye would perish—beast by beast Devouring.

mandor (ˈmændɔə(r)). Also **mandore, mandur**. [Malay *mandor* (*mandur*), ad. Pg. *mandador* one who gives orders.] A foreman or overseer in Malaysia or Indonesia. Cf. KANGANY.
1889 S. J. HICKSON *Naturalist in North Celebes* 65 The coolies were under the supervision of two mandūrs or foremen. **1926** *Blackw. Mag.* Apr. 508/1 A Malay 'mandor' is told that at a certain time on that day he must bring so many men. **1928** *Ibid.* Apr. 473/1, I remember a Malay mandor of mine laughing aloud when he was told that another Malay and two children had died..from exposure. **1958** GINSBURG & ROBERTS *Malaya* ix. 333 In the managerial class the labor foremen, *kanganies* or *mandors*, are a combination of labor boss and patriarch depending on personality factors and on the strength of the trade-union organization. **1962** B. HARRISSON *Orang-Utan* iii. 119 We heard..through one of the road engineers..that one of his Malay mandors had been asked to look for a baby gibbon which somebody wanted to keep as a pet. **1965** C. SHUTTLEWORTH *Malayan Safari* iii. 41 An Indian *mandor* (foreman) was taken from the veranda of his house whilst sleeping. **1969** K. S. SANDHU *Indians in Malaya* iii. 114 *Mandurs* (overseers)..and railway porters were classified as skilled workers and allowed to return to Malaya [from India]. **1970** T. LILLEY *Projects Section* xv. 192 Raja Gopal's house..stands..about a hundred yards from the labour lines..of which Raja Gopal is..the Mandore in charge. **1972** *Sunday Times* (Kuala Lumpur) 30 Apr. 3/2 Tin mine mandore Yaacob bin Abdul Wahab had to master more than the course.

mandora: see MANDOLA.

mandore (mænˈdɔə(r)). [ad. F. *mandore*, ad. It. *mandora*.] = MANDOLA.
1823 ROSCOE *Sismondi's Lit. South Eur.* (1846) I. v. 128 A Jongleur..must..play on the citole and mandore. **1898** ZANGWILL *Dreamers Ghetto* i. 26 Amulets in the shape of miniature mandores or four-stringed lutes.

‖**mandorla** (mænˈdɔːlə). *Religious Art.* [It. = 'almond'.] An almond-shaped panel or decorative space.
1883 C. C. PERKINS *Ital. Sculpture* Introd. 20 Christ seated within a mandorla. **1895** M. R. JAMES *Abbey St. Edmund at Bury* 51 At top is Christ in a mandorla seated full-face with a book.

mandrag(e, -dragge, obs. forms of MANDRAKE.

†**mandragon**. *Obs.* [app. an altered form of *mandrag* MANDRAKE, after *dragon*.] = MANDRAKE.
1580 HOLLYBAND *Treas. Fr. Tong*, *De la mandragore*, an herbe called Mandragon. **1597** GERARDE *Herbal* II. lx. 281 In English we call it Mandrake, Mandrage, and Mandragon. **1611** COTGR., *Mandragore*, Mandrake, Mandrage, Mandragon.

mandragora (mænˈdrægərə). Forms: α. 1- **mandragora**, 3 **mandragores**, 6-7 **mandragoras**. β. (in anglicized form) 4 *pl.* **mandragoris**, 6 **mandragor, -er**, 8-9 **-ore**. [late L. *mandragora* (*mandragoras* Pliny), a. Gr. *μανδραγόρας*.]
1. a. The plant MANDRAKE. Now only *Hist.* **b.** *Bot.* The genus to which this plant belongs. **c.** Since Shakspere, taken as the type of a narcotic.
In Shaks. *Ant. & Cl.* I. v. 4 the First Folio has the misprint *mandragoru*, whence perh. *mandragorn* in Scott's *Kenilworth* (1821) I. xii. 311. Cf. however MANDRAGON.
c **1000** *Sax. Leechd.* I. 244 Ðeos wyrt þe man mandragoram nemneþ. *c* **1220** *Bestiary* 613 A gres, ðe name is mandragores. **1388** WYCLIF *Song Sol.* vii. 13 Mandrogoris han ȝoue her odour in oure ȝatis. **1398** TREVISA *Barth. De P. R.* XVII. civ. (Tollem. MS.), They þat diggen mandragora be besy to be war of contrarye wynde. **1535** COVERDALE *Gen.* xxx. 14 Ruben wente out..and founde Mandragoras in the felde. **1542** BOORDE *Dyetary* xx. (1870) 281 Mandragor doth helpe a woman to concepcion. **1578** LYTE *Dodoens* III. lxxxiv. 438 The greene and fresh leaues of Mandragoras. **1604** SHAKS. *Oth.* III. iii. 330 Not Poppy, nor Mandragora, Nor all the drowsie Syrrups of the world Shall euer [etc.]. **1605** CHAPMAN, etc. *Eastward Hoe* v. i, I haue..drunke Lethe and Mandragora to forget you. **1623** WEBSTER *Duchess of Malfi* IV. ii, Come violent death, Serue for Mandragora to make me sleepe. **1738** *Common Sense* II. 4 The Drug call'd Mandragore. **1830** GALT *Laurie T.* v. xi. (1849) 242 Earnest employment is the best mandragora for an aching heart. **1855** THACKERAY *Newcomes* II. 19 He dosed himself with poppy, and mandragora, and blue pill. **1876** FARRAR *Marlb. Serm.* vi. 56 The river of oblivion of sin repented of, the true mandragora for every guilty and sleepless soul.
attrib. **1398** TREVISA *Barth. De P. R.* XVII. cxii. (1495) 675 Oyle of Mandragora apples. **1826** W. AINSLIE *Materia Indica* I. 208 The anodyne and soporific qualities of the mandragore root. **1832** CARLYLE *Corn-law Rhymes* Misc. 1857 III. 161 Her Ariel Melodies, and mystic mandragora Moans.
d. = *mandrake wine*.
1844 MRS. BROWNING *Dead Pan* ii, Have the Pygmies made you drunken, Bathing in mandragora Your divine pale lips..?
†**2.** ***Chinese mandragoras***: ginseng.
1727-41 CHAMBERS *Cycl.* s.v.
Hence **manˈdragorite**, one who is habitually under the narcotic influence of mandragora.
1895 *Funk's Standard Dict.* **1902** WEBSTER *Suppl.*

mandrague (ˈmændreɪg). [Corruptly a. F. *madrague*.] A kind of large fishing-net.
1851 *Fraser's Mag.* XLIII. 252 The part of nets forming the modern mandrague. **1855** W. S. DALLAS in *Syst. Nat. Hist.* II. 49 The Tunny..is captured by means of a large net, called a mandrague.

mandrake (ˈmændreɪk). Forms: α. 4-6 **mandragge**, 4-7 **-drage**, 6-7 **-drag**, (6 **mendrage**). β. 5- **mandrake**, (4 **mondrake**, 5, 7 **mandrak**). [ME. *mandrag(g)e* (cf. MDu. *mandrage, mandragre*), a shortening of MANDRAGORA; the form *mandrake* (*mondrake*), though recorded earlier than *-drage*, is prob. due to association with *drake*.]
1. Any plant of the genus *Mandragora*, native to Southern Europe and the East, and characterized by very short stems, thick, fleshy,

often forked, roots, and fetid lance-shaped leaves.

The mandrake is poisonous, having emetic and narcotic properties, and was formerly used medicinally. The forked root is thought to resemble the human form, and was fabled to utter a deadly shriek when plucked up from the ground. The notion indicated in the narrative of Genesis xxx, that the fruit when eaten by women promotes conception, is said still to survive in Palestine.

α. **1382** WYCLIF *Gen.* xxx. 14 Ruben goon out in tyme of wheet heruest into the feeld, fonde mandraggis [**1388** mandragis]. *c* **1440** *Promp. Parv.* 324/2 Mandragge, herbe, ..*mandragora.* **1562** LEIGH *Armorie* (1597) 99 b, He beareth Argent, a mandrage proper. **1580** LYLY *Euphues* (Arb.) 473 They that feare theyr Vines will make too sharpe wine, must ..graft next to them Mandrage [ed. 1581 Mendrage], which causeth the grape to be more pleasaunt. **1594** —— *Moth. Bomb.* V. iii, Your sonne Memphis, had a moale vnder his eare:..you shall see it taken away with the iuyce of mandrage. **1601** HOLLAND *Pliny* II. 235 In the digging vp of the root of Mandrage, there are some ceremonies obserued. **1607** TOPSELL *Four-f. Beasts* (1658) 330 Oyl of Mandrag.. bindeth together..bones being either shivered or broken. **1656** BLOUNT *Glossogr.*, *Mandrake* or *Mandrage.*

β. *a* **1310** in Wright *Lyric P.* 26 Muge he is ant mondrake. *c* **1450** *ME. Med. Bk.* (Heinrich) 231 Leues of mandrake. *c* **1475** *Pict. Voc.* in Wr.-Wülcker 787/4 *Hec mandracora*, a mandrak. **1560** BIBLE (Geneva) *Gen.* xxx. 14 Reuben.. found mandrakes [*marg.* Which is a kinde of herbe, whose rote hath a certeine likenes of yͤ figure of a man] in the field. **1592** SHAKS. *Rom. & Jul.* IV. iii. 47 And shrikes like Mandrakes torne out of the earth. **1593** —— *2 Hen. VI*, III. ii. 310. **1600** HEYWOOD *2nd Pt. Edw. IV* Wks. 1874 I. 154 The mandrakes shrieks are music to their cries. **1610** DONNE *Pseudo-martyr* Pref. c iij, Annibal, to entrappe and surprise his enemies, mingled their wine with Mandrake, whose operation is betwixt sleepe and poyson. **1635** [GLAPTHORNE] *Lady Mother* V. ii. in Bullen *O. Pl.* II. 196 Horrid grots and mossie graves, Where the mandraks hideous howles Welcome bodies voide of soules. **1712** tr. *Pomet's Hist. Drugs* I. 80 The Mandrake is a Plant without a Stem. **1879** J. TIMBS in *Cassell's Techn. Educ.* IV. 106/1 The Greeks and the Romans used the root of the mandrake to cause insensibility to pain.

†**b.** in allusive and fig. uses: (*a*) as a term of abuse; (*b*) a narcotic; (*c*) a noisome growth.

1508 KENNEDIE *Flyting w. Dunbar* 29 Mandrag, mymmerkin, maid maister bot in mowis. *a* **1585** MONTGOMERIE *Flyting* 71 Trot, tyke, to a tow, mandrage but myance. **1593** G. HARVEY *Pierce's Super.* Wks. (Grosart) II. 293 Correct the Mandrake of scurrility with the myrrhe of curtesie. **1597** SHAKS. *2 Hen. IV*, I. ii. 67 Thou horson Mandrake. **1604** DEKKER *Honest Wh.* Wks. 1873 II. 9 Gods my life, hee's a very mandrake. **1610** J. MASON *Turk* II. i, Thou that amongst a hundred thousand dreames Crownd with a wreath of mandrakes sitst as Queene. **1636** DAVENANT *Wits* IV. i, He stands as if his Legs had taken root; A very Mandrake! **1649** JER. TAYLOR *Gt. Exemp.* I. iv. 132 When we lust after mandrakes and deliciousness of exteriour ministries. **1660** R. L'ESTRANGE *Plea for Limited Monarchy* 7 Our laws [*sc.* during the Commonwealth] have been Mandrakes of a Nights growth. **1676** MARVELL *Gen. Councils* Wks. 1875 IV. 101 If they have a mind to pull up that mandrake, it were advisable..to chuse out a dog for that imployment.

2. The root of White Bryony: see quots.

1585 LUPTON *Thous. Notable Th.* III. xliii. (1595) 61 The counterfeat Mandrag which hath bene sold by deceyuers for much money. **1597** GERARDE *Herbal* II. lx. 281 The idle drones that haue little or nothing to do but eate and drinke, haue bestowed some of their time in caruing the rootes of Brionie, forming them to the shape of men & women; which falsifying practise hath confirmed the errour amongst the simple..people, who haue taken them vpon their report to be the true Mandrakes. **1657** W. COLES *Adam in Eden* cxci. 300 The Root [of Briony] somtimes groweth to the bigness of a Childe of a yeare old, so that it hath been by some cut into the forme of a Man, and called a Mandrake, being set againe into the Earth. **1785** MARTYN *Rousseau's Bot.* xvi. (1794) 197 These pretended Mandrakes are said to be roots of Angelica or Bryony.

3. *U.S.* The May-apple, *Podophyllum peltatum.*

1836 *Backwoods of Canada* 248 There is a plant in our woods, known by the names of man-drake, may-apple, and duck's foot. **1845–50** MRS. LINCOLN *Lect. Bot.* App. 143/2 *Podophyllum peltatum* (wild mandrake, may-apple). **1887** *Family Physician* 872 Mandrake, may apple, or hog apple.

4. *attrib.*, as ***mandrake juice***, ***root***; **mandrake apple**, the fruit of the mandrake; †**mandrake shriek** (see sense 1, note); **mandrake wine** (see quot. 1753 for *mandrake root*).

1563 T. GALE *Antidot.* I. i. 1 b, Of simple medicines repercussiue these are some..*Mandrage apples, & iuse. **1603** SIR C. HEYDON *Jud. Astrol.* xx. 417 Rachel enuying her sister Leahs fertilitie importuned Mandrag apples, to supplie her barrennesse. *c* **1592** MARLOWE *Jew of Malta* V. (1633) I 2, I dranke of Poppy, and cold *mandrake juyce. **1753** CHAMBERS *Cycl. Supp.*, *Mandragorites Vinum, Mandrake Wine*, a sort of medicinal impregnation of wine with the virtues of *Mandrake root. **1824** HEN. PHILLIPS *Flora Hist.* I. 354 The Mandrake root is an anodyne and soporific. **1620** DEKKER *Dreame* Wks. (Grosart) III. 39 Being mounted on a Spirits back, which ran With *Mandrake-shrikes, and like a Lubrican. **1621** BURTON *Anat. Mel.* II. ii. VI. i. (1651) 293 A friends counsel is a charm, like *mandrake wine. **1753** [see *Mandrake root*].

mandram ('mændræm). *West Indian.* Also **mandrang.** (See quot. 1756.)

1756 P. BROWNE *Jamaica* 177 There is a mixture made and used in some of our colonies called Mandram,..which seldom fails to provoke an appetite in the most languid stomachs. The ingredients are sliced cucumbers, eschalots cut very small, a little lime juice, and Madeira wine with a few pods of bird pepper. **1814** LUNAN *Hortus Jamaicensis* I. 358 The mixture called man-dram is made from these peppers. **1841** ORDERSON *Creoleana* xiv. 148 The 'punch and mandram' had been handed round. **1845** MISS ACTON *Mod. Cookery* 312 Mandrang or Mandram. (West Indian Receipt.) Chop together, very small, two moderate-sized cucumbers [etc.].

Mandrax ('mændræks). *Pharm.* A proprietary name for tablets containing methaqualone and diphenhydramine hydrochloride, used as a sedative.

1963 *Trade Marks Jrnl.* 10 Apr. 485/1 Mandrax... Hypnotics, being pharmaceutical preparations and substances. Roussel-Uclaf,..Paris. **1967** *Scottish Med. Jrnl.* XII. 63/1 Mandrax..is a hypnotic preparation, which has been actively marketed in Great Britain since Autumn 1965... It has become commonly prescribed as a non-barbiturate hypnotic. **1970** L. LEECH in *Drug Dependence* (U.S. Nat. Inst. Mental Health) 22 Another factor of importance has been the increased use of non-barbiturate hypnotics, particularly methaqualone and diphenhydramine in the form of Mandrax, by young people within the 'pill scene'. **1972** *Police Rev.* 17 Nov. 1505/1 He admits taking Mandrax tablets obtained on prescription.

mandrel, mandril ('mændrəl, -ıl). Forms: 6 **manderelle**, 7–9 **maundril(l**, **mandrel**, **-il**, (8 **manderil**, **mandrell**, **maundrell**, 9 **mandrill**). [Usually believed to be an alteration of F. *mandrin*, which has the senses 3 and 4 below. The Fr. word, however, has not been traced earlier than 1690, and is of obscure origin.]

1. A miner's pick.

1516 *Test. Ebor.* (Surtees) V. 80 Item xlvj manderelles ij.*s.* viij.*d.* A gryndstone & cruke *xd.* Item ij spayddys & a shulle *vjd.* **1686** PLOT *Staffordsh.* 306 But he..by the help of his Maundrill, by degrees so wrought away the earth over head ..that [etc.]. **1747** HOOSON *Miner's Dict.* M iij, *Mandrel*, a Tool made after the manner of a Hack, but more Strong and Square, having both ends Sharp, Square Points. **1771** FLETCHER *Checks* Wks. 1795 II. 126 An ignorant collier, as great a stranger to your metaphysics as you are to his mandrell. **1860** *Eng. & For. Min. Gloss.* (*Derby Terms*), *Maundrill*, a pick for various purposes, but generally used to undermine. **1881** RAYMOND *Mining Gloss.*, *Mandril*,.. *Maundril*, Derb. and S. Wales, a prying pick with two prongs.

†**2.** Some instrument used by arrow-makers. *Obs.*

1659 HOWELL *Partic. Vocab.* §51 A maundrel, and bick-hornd, smoothing floates [etc.]... *Les outils de l'archer.*

3. In a lathe, an arbor or axis to which work is secured while it is being turned. Also applied to a similar part in a circular saw or cutter.

1665 *Phil. Trans.* I. 58 To give to the Axis or to the Mandril..that little Inclination. **1677** MOXON *Mech. Exerc.* (1703) 190 There is another sort of Mandrels called Hollow Mandrels. **1731** BAILEY vol. II, *Manderil*, a kind of wooden pulley, that is part of a turner's leath, of which there are several kinds, as flat, hollow, pin and skrew manderils. **1786** *Phil. Trans.* LXXVI. 25, I turned it..upon my great lathe in the air (that is, upon the end of the mandrel). **1796** MORSE *Amer. Geog.* I. 452 The manderil is moved by a band wheel. **1812–16** J. SMITH *Panorama Sci. & Art* I. 12 If the mandrel of a lathe were made of the best steel, sufficiently hard to wear well in the collar, it would be snapped by a sudden check. **1879** R. S. BALL in *Cassell's Techn. Educ.* VII. 62 By means of the band the pulley G, on what is called the 'mandril' of the lathe, is made to turn rapidly.

4. A cylindrical rod, core, or axis round which metal or other material is forged, cast, moulded, or shaped.

1790 in *Abridg. Specif. Patents, Metallic Pipes*, etc. (1874) 2, I cast the lead in lengths,..this is put upon a polished rod or round maundrell of iron or any other metal, such maundrells being made of different lengths and diameters. **1812–16** J. SMITH *Panorama Sci. & Art* I. 17 The hole may be finished..by hammering it at a low heat upon a smooth mandrel or pin. **1825** J. NICHOLSON *Operat. Mechanic* 364 When the pipe is cast, and the metal is set, this mandrel is drawn out of the mould, and another of smaller diameter is substituted. **1859** *Musketry Instr.* 49 Roll the stiff paper tightly about $2\frac{1}{4}$ times round the 'mandrel'. **1881** GREENER *Gun* 50 Their early barrels appear to have been made from one broad band of metal rolled over a mandril.

5. *attrib.*

1825 J. NICHOLSON *Operat. Mechanic* 325 This weight.. operates to keep the mandrel-band tight. **1875** KNIGHT *Dict. Mech.*, *Mandrel-lathe*, a lathe adapted for turning hollow work, which is clasped by a chuck on the end of the mandrel in the head-stock. **1888** HASLUCK *Model Engin. Handybk.* (1900) 58 The mandrel-cone centre point.

Hence '**mandrel** *v. trans.*, to operate upon with mandrels (*Cent. Dict.* 1890).

mandriarch ('mændrıɑːk). [ad. It. *mandriarcha*, a. late Gr. μανδριάρχης, f. μανδρία, Gr. μάνδρα fold, monastery. Cf. ARCHIMANDRITE.] A ruler or founder of a monastic order.

1871 MARIA F. ROSSETTI *Shadow of Dante* 205 The second dividing line, which consists of holy Mandriarchs; S. Francis, S. Benedict, S. Augustine being alone named.

mandrill ('mændrıl). Also -il. [app. f. MAN *sb.*[1] + DRILL *sb.*[3]] The largest, most hideous, and most ferocious of the baboons, *Cynocephalus maimon* or *mormon*, a native of Western Africa.

1744 W. SMITH *Voy. Guinea* 51 A strange sort of animal, called by the white men in this country [Sierra Leone] Mandrill, but why it is so called I know not,..except it be for their near resemblance to a human creature, though nothing at all like an Ape. **1774** GOLDSM. *Nat. Hist.* IV. vii. 214 The largest of the baboon kind is the Mandril; an ugly disgusting animal. **1840** *Cuvier's Anim. Kingd.* 59 The Mandrill Baboon (*Sim. maimon* and *mormon*).—Greyish brown, inclining to olive above;..cheeks blue and furrowed. **1863** HUXLEY *Man's Place Nat.* I. 10. **1898** *Daily News* 12 Dec. 9/1 The blue-faced Mandril.

'**mandrite.** *rare*[−1]. [ad. Gr. μανδρίτης (cf. ARCHIMANDRITE), f. μάνδρα fold.] (See quot.)

1844 W. KAY in J. H. Newman *Fleury's Eccles. Hist.* III. 81 *note*, A mandrite would at first be a person who lived in a solitary cave.

‖**mandritta** (mæn'drıtə). *Fencing. Obs.* [altered from It. *mandritto*, *manditto*, f. *mano dritta* right hand.] A cut from right to left.

1595 SAVIOLO *Practice* I. 10 b, Cannot euery one of himselfe without teaching giue a mandritta? **1603** DEKKER *Wonderfull Yeare* D 4, Hees the best Fencer in the world:.. He has his Mandrittaes, imbrocataes, stramazones and stoccataes at his fingers ends. **1855** KINGSLEY *Westw. Ho!* iii, Wiping maudritta [*sic*], closing embrocata, And all the cant of the honourable fencing mystery.

manducable ('mændjʊkəb(ə)l), *a. Obs.* or *arch.* [ad. L. type **mandūcābil-is*, f. *mandūcā-re*: see next and -ABLE.] Capable of being manducated; eatable.

1614 W. B. *Philosopher's Banquet* (ed. 2) 37 They are scarce manducable. **1634** SIR T. HERBERT *Trav.* 213 Tortoyses, (in which I haue seene aboue a thousand Egges, great and manducable). **1656** BLOUNT *Glossogr.* *c* **1810** COLERIDGE in *Lit. Rem.* (1838) III. 351 If tangible by Thomas's fingers, why not by his teeth, that is, manducable?

manducate ('mændjʊkeıt), *v.* [f. ppl. stem of L. *mandūcā-re* to chew: see -ATE[3].] *trans.* To chew, eat. Hence '**manducated** *ppl. a.*

1623 COCKERAM, *Manducate*, to eat. **1624** F. WHITE *Repl. Fisher* 490 To manducate, that is, to chew or swallow, and to let the Element receiued, passe into their stomach. **1654** JER. TAYLOR *Real Pres.* 147 Either we manducate the accidents only, or else the substance of bread, or the substance of Christs body. **1657** TOMLINSON *Renou's Disp.* 242 Being manducated, they confirm loose teeth. **1727** in BAILEY vol. II. **1822** *Blackw. Mag.* XI. 161 Whate'er front-tooth can bite, and grinders manducate. **1826** GOOD *Bk. Nat.* (1834) I. 276 The..manducated food. **1876** E. MELLOR *Priesth.* iv. 179 The literal interpreters..supposing that our Saviour referred to bread which could be manducated in the ordinary manner.

manducation (mændjuː'keıʃən). [ad. L. *mandūcātiōn-em*, n. of action of *mandūcā-re* to MANDUCATE. Cf. F. *manducation* (Theol.).]

1. The action of eating. Chiefly *Theol.* (following the patristic use of L. *manducatio*), the term applied (usually with qualification, as *carnal*, *corporal*, *literal*, *oral*, *real*, *sacramental*, *spiritual*) to the act of participation in the Eucharist.

1551 GARDINER *Explic. True Cath. Faith* 9 b, The mysterie of corporall manducation. **1553** KENNEDY *Compend. Tract.* in *Wodrow Soc. Misc.* (1844) 167 He makis mentioun baith of spirituale and reale manducatioun. **1597** HOOKER *Eccl. Pol.* v. lxvii. §9 A Literall, Corporall and Orall manducation of the very substance of his flesh and bloud. **1649** JER. TAYLOR *Gt. Exemp.* xv. §17 After the manducation of the Paschal lamb it was the custom of the nation to sit down to a second supper. **1660** —— *Duct. Dubit.* II. iii. rule 12 §11 Sacramental manducation. **1737** WATERLAND *Eucharist* (ed. 2) 453 None give so great advantage to the Figurists, as those that contend for oral manducation. **1821** LAMB *Elia* Ser. I. *Grace bef. meat*, The received ritual having prescribed these forms to the solitary ceremony of manducation. **1833** ROCK *Hierurg.* (1892) I. 197 A manducation of His real flesh and blood. **1850** E. H. BROWNE *Exp. 39 Articles* xxviii. §1 (1874) 679 Did they intend a spiritual manducation—an eating spiritually and a drinking in by the soul of the life-giving efficacy of the Body broken and the Blood shed?

2. The action of chewing.

1650 BULWER *Anthropomet.* 139 They who chaw not well, or..passe over the triple order of manducation, are ill nourished. **1746** R. JAMES *Introd. Moufet's Health's Improv.* 2 Manducation, or Chewing, is performed by means of the Biventer, or Digastric Muscles. **1826** KIRBY & SP. *Entomol.* III. 416 The *trophi* or organs of manducation. **1852** DANA *Crust.* II. 991 The mandible has a lateral process for manducation. **1877** HUXLEY *Anat. Inv. Anim.* i. 69 Powerful apparatus for the seizure and manducation of vegetable and animal prey.

manducatory ('mændjʊkətərı), *a.* Chiefly *Phys.* [f. L. *mandūcāt-* (see MANDUCATE) + -ORY.] Pertaining to or fitted for manducation.

1814 *Sch. Gd. Living* 40 Their noble perseverance, in fulfilling with so much courage their manducatory functions. **1850** H. MILLER *Footpr. Creat.* iv. (1874) 62 The framework through which an important class of functions, manducatory and respiratory, are performed. **1870** ROLLESTON *Anim. Life* 110 [It] consists of the manducatory ganglion fused with one thoracic ganglion. **1877** HUXLEY *Anat. Inv. Anim.* vi. 256 The..manducatory appendages (gnathites).

mandur, var. MANDOR.

mandura: see MANDOLA.

mandy, Mandy ('mændı). Colloq. abbrev. of MANDRAX (*tablet*).

1970 *Daily Tel.* 8 Sept. 2/3 Dr Tylden says that hypnotic tablets of methaqualone and antihistamine known as 'Mandies' to addicts, had been mentioned to her by youngsters from all parts of Britain... The favourite mixture was four 'Mandies' and half a pint of cider, which could lead to sudden unconsciousness. **1971** *Frendz* 21 May 11/2 Avoid dealing while tripping on Acid, Speed or Mandies—you'll goof on the action. **1973** *Daily Tel.* 11 July 2/8 Addicts, who call the white tablets [of methaqualone]

'mandies', 'mainline' by crushing the tablets and injecting themselves.

mandy, obs. form of MAUNDY.

mane (meɪn), *sb.* Forms: 1 manu, 4, 6 **maane**, 6 **mayn**, *Sc.* (**mone**), **meane**, 6–7 **mayne**, **maine**, 7 **maune**, 7, 8 **main**, 4– **mane**. [OE. *manu* str. fem. = MDu. *mane* (chiefly pl. *manen*; so in mod. Du.), OHG. *mana* fem. (MHG. *mane*, *man* fem. and masc., mod.G. *mähne* fem. with irregular umlaut), ON. *mǫn* fem. (gen. *manar*; Sw., Da. *man*):—OTeut. **manâ*. The Scandinavian langs. have also a dim. form prob. from LG.: Da. *manke* mane, Sw. *manke*, Icel. *makki* nape of the neck.

The primary sense of the OTeut. word must have been 'neck': cf. OE. *męne* masc., OS. *meni*, OHG. *menni* pl., ornament for the neck; L. *monīle* necklace; OIrish *muin*-neck (in *muin-torc* collar), *muince* (= Gaulish *μανιάκης*, Polybius) collar, *muinel* (= Welsh *mwnwgl*) neck, *mong* (= Welsh *mwng*) mane; Skr. *manyā* nape of the neck.]

1. a. A growth of long hair on the back of the neck and the shoulders, characteristic of various animals, esp. the horse and lion; a similar growth on other animals.

Formerly sometimes used (e.g. in quots. 1470–85, 1501, 1661) for the part on which the mane grows.

a **800** *Erfurt Gloss.* 1182 *Juba, setes porci et leonis cabalique*: manu, brystæ. **13..** *Gaw. & Gr. Knt.* 187 Þe mane of þat mayn hors much to hit lyke. *c* **1380** *Sir Ferumb.* 244 Þat gode hors blessede he þo, & louely strek ys mane. **1398** TREVISA *Barth. De P. R.* XVIII. xl. (1495) 801 The maare is prowde and hath joye of her maane. **1470–85** MALORY *Arthur* III. viii, The hole body of hyr lay before hym on his hors mane. **1501** DOUGLAS *Pal. Hon.* I. xii, Out throw the wod come rydand catiues twane, Ane on ane asse, a widdie about his mone, The vther raid ane hiddeous hors vpone. **1567** MAPLET *Gr. Forest* 74 b, There is also another kinde of wilde Oxe or Bull, called.. Bonasus, a little shorter than our Bull, but more thickly set, and hath his Mane like to our Horse. **1606** SHAKS. *Tr. & Cr.* III. iii. 224 And the weake wanton Cupid Shall.. like a dew drop from the Lyons mane, Be shooke to ayrie ayre. **1661** LOVELL *Hist. Anim. & Min.* Introd., Horses have most haire upon the mane, lions upon their shoulders. **1667** MILTON *P. L.* VII. 497 The Serpent.. with brazen Eyes And hairie Main terrific. *a* **1719** ADDISON tr. *Ovid* Wks. 1753 I. 157 Half dead with sudden fear he dropt the reins; The horses felt 'em loose upon their mains. **1774** GOLDSM. *Nat. Hist.* (1776) III. 387 It [the genett] has also along the back a kind of mane or longish hair, which forms a black streak from the head to the tail. **1828** STARK *Elem. Nat. Hist.* I. 45 Full Bottom Monkey. With a mane upon the neck, shoulders, and top of the back. **1863–5** J. THOMSON *Sunday at Hampstead* vii, One stroked with careless hand a lion's mane. **1883** G. STABLES *Our Friend the Dog* vii. 60 *Mane*, the feather on shoulders of Collie and Newfoundland, and that on the front of the chest of Blenheims.

fig. **1818** BYRON *Ch. Har.* IV. clxxxiv, And I have loved thee, Ocean!.. And laid my hand upon thy mane— as I do here. **1893** F. THOMPSON *Hound of Heaven* in *Poems* 49 To all swift things for swiftness did I sue; Clung to the whistling mane of every wind. **1927** JOYCE *Flood* in *Pomes Penyeach*, A waste of waters ruthlessly Sways and uplifts its weedy mane. **1936** R. CAMPBELL *Mithraic Emblems* 38 The World put down its lovely mane.

b. *transf.* Applied to a person's long hair.

c **1375** *Sc. Leg. Saints* xlix. (*Tecla*) 164 His mane in hir hand scho wan, & rawe of it a gret part done. **1647** WARD *Simp. Cobler* 32 Men use not to weare such manes. **1860** GEO. ELIOT *Mill on Fl.* I. iii, Maggie.. looked over the book, eagerly seizing one corner and tossing back her mane. **1881** *Scribner's Mag.* XXI. 71/2 Her.. red rippling mane falling about her. **1895** ZANGWILL *Master* II. ii. 135 Matt moved back towards his easel, passing a little dark man with a mane.

c. A tuft of hair attached to an artificial fly.

1867 F. FRANCIS *Angling* xi. (1880) 407 The Owenmore [Salmon Fly]... Manes of mohair from the back of each joint .. ; just under, as a support to each mane, is tied in a feather from the breast of the Indian crow.

2. The hackles on the neck of a game cock. ? *Obs.*

1614 MARKHAM *Cheap Husb.* II. i. 110 His mayne or necke-feathers would bee very long, bright, and shining, couering from his head to his shoulders. **1727** BRADLEY *Fam. Dict.* s.v. *Cock*, His eyes round and great, the colour answerable to the colour of his plume or Main.

3. *Agric.* A ridge or tuft of grass or stubble, left by the mowers.

1523 FITZHERB. *Husb.* §23 Take hede that thy mower mow clene and.. leaue not a mane bytwene. **1601** HOLLAND *Pliny* I. 595 Those tufts and manes which the mowiers passed over and left standing behind them. **1840** *Jrnl. R. Agric. Soc.* I. IV. 444 In using the scythe for barley and oats, the great art is to leave a short 'mane' or ridge of stubble, so that the ears of corn may rest thereon.

4. *attrib.*, as ***mane-flinging*** ppl. adj.; ***mane-like*** adj.; **mane-comb**, a comb for the horse's mane; † **mane-piece**, ? = CRINIÈRE; **mane-sheet** (see quot.).

1564 in Rogers *Agric. & Prices* III. 577/1 *Mane comb. **1573** TUSSER *Husb.* (1878) 35 A currie combe, mainecombe, and whip for a Jade. *a* **1613** OVERBURY *Characters, Ostler* Wks. (1856) 72 His mane-comb is a spinners card turned out of service. **1879** MRS. A. E. JAMES *Ind. Househ. Managem.* 67 Curry-combs, scrapers, mane-combs, and the rest of the usual stable paraphernalia. **1945** P. LARKIN *North Ship* 19 As some vast seven-piled wave, *Mane-flinging, manifold, Streams at an endless shore. **1864** TENNYSON *Aylmer's Field* 68 Eager eyes that.. beamed Beneath a *manelike mass of rolling gold. **1753** HANWAY *Trav.* (1762) I. III. xxxvii. 172 Bridles.. mounted with silver, with a *mane-piece of plate. **1727** BAILEY vol. II, **Mane-sheet* (with Grooms), is a covering for the Upper-part of a Horse's Head.

† **mane**, *a. Sc. Obs.* Also 6 **maine**, **magne**. [a. OF. *maine*, *maigne*, *magne*:—L. *magnum* great.] In ***Chairlis the mane***, Charles the Great, Charlemagne.

c **1475** *Rauf Coilȝear* 205 Thus said gentill Charlis the Mane To the Coilȝear. **1535** STEWART *Cron. Scot.* II. 344 Chairlis the Mane, the quhilk wes king of France,.. To king Achay ane herald he hes send. **1552** *Reg. Privy Council Scot.* I. 129 Sen the tyme of Achaus kyng of Scotland and Chairlis the Maine king of France. **1596** DALRYMPLE tr. *Leslie's Hist. Scot.* I. 264 The king, Charles the Magne.

mane, obs. f. MAIN, MAINE, MAN, MANY, MEAN *a.*; north. f. MOAN; variant of MAUN (= *must*).

-mane (meɪn), the ending of certain words adopted from Fr., as *Anglomane*, *bibliomane*, which have the general sense 'one who has a mania for (something)', and are formed on assumed Gr. types in *-μανής*: see MANIA. The words of this formation have never become entirely naturalized in Eng., the meaning being preferably expressed by formations in *-maniac*.

1832 tr. *Tour Germ. Prince* III. xi. 306 She is almost as great a 'parkomane' as myself. *Ibid.* IV. iii. 145.

‖**maneaba** (mæ'neɪəbə). [Native name.] In Kiribati and Tuvalu (formerly the Gilbert and Ellice Islands), a meeting-house.

1944 G. H. EASTMAN *Front Line Islands* 5 Landing at Nui Island we proceeded as our custom was to the public *maneaba* (meeting-house), where the Resident Commissioner spoke to the people. *Ibid.* 10 Our people at Hull Island.. have recently erected a large new *maneaba*, which is now used as school house and for women's meetings and various other community gatherings. **1952** A. GRIMBLE *Pattern of Islands* ii. 58 Every Gilbertese village of any size had its own maneaba, or speak-house, in those days. **1970** A. COATES *Western Pacific Islands* viii. 63 In the absence of any king, the wise men conducted affairs in their council house—*manéaba*—their jurisdiction extending just as far as was acceptable, which usually meant to the limits of the land occupied by the clans whose senior members had a reserved place in the *manéaba*, which is somewhat like a hereditary parliament, with the important—and very Pacific—exception that all decisions must be taken on the basis of unanimity. **1974** *Nat. Geographic* Dec. 753/2 Once ashore, I was escorted to the large meetinghouse, the *maneaba*, with thatched eaves that stood only four feet above the ground and a roof that soared upward to a crisscross of massive beams a full forty feet overhead.

maneall, obs. form of MENIAL *a.*

'man-ˌeater. [MAN *sb.*[1]] One who eats men.

1. A cannibal.

1600 J. PORY tr. *Leo's Africa* Introd. 31 They are man-eaters, and couragious in battaile. **1617** HIERON *Wks.* (1619–20) II. 103 How foule is the sinne of oppression, when the practisers of it are likened to man-eaters, that liue vpon flesh? **1681** T. FLATMAN *Heraclitus Ridens* No. 28 (1713) I. 180 They may talk of Jews, Turks, Pagans, Infidels, Canibals, Man-eaters, Killcraps. **1705** HICKERINGILL *Priestcr.* I. (1721) 33 There are Cannibals or Maneaters. **1837** M. DONOVAN *Dom. Econ.* II. 44 A stout ferocious-looking fellow.. was pointed out to me as a celebrated marksman and man-eater. **1854** *Old Story-Teller, Golden Roebuck* 61 The man-eater's mouth watered for human food.

2. a. An animal that eats or has a propensity for eating men; *colloq.* a horse given to biting.

1840 E. E. NAPIER *Scenes & Sports in For. Lands* I. v. 140 The larger horses.. are leggy, under-limbed, and, as far as vice goes, regular man-eaters. **1879** MRS. A. E. JAMES *Ind. Househ. Managem.* 68 Some horses in India are called 'man-eaters', and have to be blindfolded while you mount, or they would bite you. **1883** F. DAY *Indian Fish* 51 (Fish. Exh. Publ.) The common crocodile, *Crocodilus palustris* and *C. porosus*.. often termed man-eaters. **1922** BLUNDEN *Bonadventure* xvi. 95 To sleep there was to be slowly suffocated, let alone the folly of sleeping among man-eaters [*sc.* mosquitoes]. **1957** R. CAMPBELL *Portugal* iv. 61 Aulus Fedeus had another [moray].. a man-eater.

b. A man-eating shark; esp. *Carcharodon rondeleti*. Also ***man-eater shark***.

1837 HAWTHORNE *Twice-told T.* (1851) II. xviii. 259 To ascertain that the maneater [*sc.* a shark] had already met his own death. **1882** JORDAN & GILBERT *Fishes N. Amer.* 30 (*Bull. U.S. Nat. Mus.* No. 16) Man-eater Shark. **1884** G. B. GOODE, etc. *Nat. Hist. Usef. Aquatic Anim.* I. 671 A Shark closely related to our Man-eater.

c. In India, a man-eating tiger. Applied also to lions and hyenas.

1862 J. GREENWOOD *Wild Sports* 191 It marks the spot where.. fell one of the most terrible 'man-eaters' the world ever saw. **1881** J. GRANT *Cameronians* I. iv. 60 Sir Piers.. thought it very slow work compared with.. potting a man-eater from a howdah.

attrib. **1850** R. G. CUMMING *Hunter's Life S. Afr.* (1902) 134/1 A bloodthirsty man-eater lion.

3. *local U.S.* **a.** A large salamander. **b.** The dobson or hellgrammite (*Cent. Dict.* 1890).

1859 BARTLETT *Dict. Amer.*, s.v. *Water-Dogs*, In Pennsylvania and the Eastern States they [various species of salamanders] are called Spring-keepers and Man-eaters.

4. *fig.* Of a person (see quots.). *colloq.*

1906 E. DYSON *Fact'ry 'Ands* xi. 136 To Spats' Beauties she was always Porline or The Man-Eater. **1928** A. HUXLEY *Point Counter Point* xiv. 264 Marjorie isn't the only bore. Nor Lucy the only man-eater. **1929** F. C. BOWEN *Sea Slang* 88 *Man Eater*, a particularly tough officer under sail. **1944** T. RATTIGAN *While Sun Shines* II. 209 Aw, she's no man-eater. You don't get real man-eaters this side of the Atlantic. **1968** D. GRAY *Died in Red* xx. 122 'She's pretty, you said?' .. 'Very, sir.' 'And a man-eater?' 'I'd say so, yes, sir.' **1974** J. MONTGOMERIE *Implosion* xiii. 97 A womaniser, to use an old-fashioned term. Was a woman ever described as a maniser? No, but I'd heard the designation man-eater.

So **'man-ˌeating** *vbl. sb.* and *ppl. a.* (also *fig.*).

1607 HIERON *Wks.* I. 437 A raging, and (as I may terme it) a man-eating pestilence. **1612** BREREWOOD *Lang. & Relig.* x. 87 The Anzichi, being an idolatrous and man-eating nation. **1871** J. FORSYTH *Highl. India* 321 When a panther takes to man-eating, he is a far more terrible scourge than a tiger. **1880** *Chamb. Jrnl.* 15 May 316/2 Man-eating tigers.. are.. rare in British India. **1954** T. S. ELIOT *Confid. Clerk* II. 61 Between a couple of man-eating tigers like you and Lizzie, he's got to have protection. **1958** *Times Lit. Suppl.* 26 Dec. 749/4 He develops an obsession for a fearful man-eating television actress. **1959** *Times* 28 May 15/5 *The Affair in Arcady* has everything—a man-eating young heroine.. a sinister step-father, [etc.]. **1974** K. BENTON *Craig & Tunisian Tangle* xi. 158 That sadistic bitch... She's got her man-eating eye on you.

mane-ath, variant of MANATH *Obs.*

manece, obs. form of MENACE.

maned (meɪnd), *ppl. a.* Also 4 **imaned** (cf. OE. *ȝemǫn*), 6 **maaned**. [f. MANE *sb.* + -ED[2].]

a. Having a mane: also with prefixed word, as *long-maned*. In *Her.* = CRINED.

13.. *Sir Beues* (MS. A) 2667 He was boþe leiþ and grim; A was i-maned ase a stede. **1530** PALSGR. 318/1 Maaned as an horse, *creinu*. **1580** STOW *Chron.* 7 This forrest sometimes bred white Bulles, long maned like Lions. **1607** TOPSELL *Four-f. Beasts* (1658) 569 The Hyena is said to be rough and maned. **1780** EDMONDSON *Heraldry* II. Gloss., *Maned*, is said of a horse, unicorn, or other beast, whose mane is of a different tincture from its body. **1791** COWPER *Iliad* VIII. 49 Swift, brazen-hoofed, and maned with wavy gold. **1818** KEATS *Endym.* II. 644 Four maned lions hale The sluggish wheels. **1862** *Fraser's Mag.* July 59 The Feshtall is the maned moufflon of the Atlas. **1864** BOUTELL *Her. Hist. & Pop.* xvii. (ed. 3) 281 An unicorn arg., armed maned and unguled or. **1895** SCULLY *Kafir Stories* 91 A large, black-maned lion. **1903** *Q. Rev.* Jan. 45 The maned or red wolf of Brazil.

b. *transf.* of plants.

1578 LYTE *Dodoens* III. lxxii. 417 Passeflower.. hath rough hearie stemmes, all iagged,.. sometimes thicke maned.

c. *fig.*

1866 SYMONDS *Sk. Italy* i. (1874) 9 Huge waves crystalline in their transparency, and maned with fleecy spray. **1924** R. CAMPBELL *Flaming Terrapin* iv. 68 A fierce train, maned like a ramping lion With smoke and fire, thunders on rolling iron. **1925** E. SITWELL *Troy Park* 66 Whinnying, neighed the maned blue wind.

manede, variant of MANHEAD *Obs.*

maneer, obs. form of MANNER.

manefaire: see MAINFERRE.

‖**manège**, **manege** (manɛʒ). [Fr. form of the word earlier adopted as MANAGE *sb.*]

1. A riding school. (Cf. MANAGE *sb.*)

1644 EVELYN *Diary* 25 Oct., The Prince has a stable of the finest horses of all countries,.. which are continually exercised in the manège. **1705** ADDISON *Italy* 521, I saw here the largest Manege that I have met with any where else. **1756** H. WALPOLE *Lett., to Bentley* Aug. (1857) III. 32 The horseman Duke's manège is converted into a lofty stable. **1799** J. ADAMS (*title*) Analysis of Horsemanship, teaching the Whole Art of Riding in the Manege. **1833** *Regul. Instr. Cavalry* I. 40 It is.. desirable that all Cavalry should be often exercised in Open Manege. *Ibid.* 41 The Troops.. are to be drilled.. in the Open Manege.

2. a. The movements proper to a trained horse; the art or practice of training and managing horses; horsemanship. (Cf. MANAGE *sb.* 1.)

1776 GIBBON *Decl. & F.* ix. (1869) I. 182 Practised in the skilful evolutions of the Roman manege. **1791** BECKFORD *Pop. Tales Germans* I. 242 A knightly steed, well instructed in the manege. **1814** SCOTT *Wav.* (1816) I. vii. 94 Already a good horseman, he was now initiated into the arts of the manege. **1826** —— *Woodst.* III. i. 12 He seemed a champion of the menage, fit to have reined Bucephalus himself.

b. *transf.* and *fig.*

1825 T. MOORE *Mem. Life R. B. Sheridan* II. xxi. 493 Had his talents, even then, been subjected to the *manège* of a profession. **1955** E. POUND *Classic Anthol.* IV. 214 In the cars' manège war-skill appears. **1973** *Times* 12 Jan. 10/6 She has given up even attempting the fouettés in the ballroom scene; but if the manège she substituted was slightly tame, Nureyev made up by the electrifying speed of his pirouettes.

manege, obs. form of MANAGE *v.*

maneggiable, obs. form of MANAGEABLE.

‖**maneh** ('mɑːneɪ). *Heb. Antiq.* [Heb. *mānẹh* (the pl. is rendered 'pounds' in 1 Kings x. 17): see MINA.] A Hebrew coin and weight, equal to from sixty to one hundred shekels.

1611 BIBLE *Ezek.* xlv. 12 And the shekell shall be twentie Gerahs: twenty shekels, fiue and twentie shekels, fifteene shekels shall be your Maneh. **1899** SAYCE *Early Israel* vi. 260 The maneh was divided into sixty shekels.

maneir, obs. form of MANNER.

manekin, obs. form of MANIKIN.

mane-kynd, obs. Sc. form of MANKIND.

manel, obs. form of MANILLA[1].

maneless ('meɪnlɪs), *a.* [f. MANE *sb.* + -LESS.] Without or destitute of a mane.

maneless lion of Guzerat: see LION 1.
1828 STARK *Elem. Nat. Hist.* I. 106 Common Sea Bear. Fur brown; males maneless. **1833** SMEE in *Trans. Zool. Soc.* (1835) I. 165 The maneless Lion of Guzerat. **1870** ORTON *Andes & Amazons* vi. (1876) 105 The puma, or maneless American lion. **1893** *Roy. Nat. Hist.* (ed. Lydekker) I. 361 It may be that some adult specimens of the Indian lion are maneless; yet well-maned examples have been killed.

manellio, obs. form of MANILLA[1].

manentine, obs. form of MANATEE.

manequin(e, obs. form of MANIKIN.

maner(e, obs. ff. MANNER, MANOR, MANURE.

maneresse, obs. form of MINORESS.

manerial (mə'nɪərɪəl), *a.* ? *Obs.* [f. med.L. *manēri-um* MANOR + -AL[1].] = MANORIAL *a.*
1765 BLACKSTONE *Comm.* I. 106 The landed property of the Atholl family, their manerial rights and emoluments, and the patronage of the bishoprick. **1791** J. COLLINSON *Hist. Somerset* II. 47 The manerial province of this place is vested in J. F. Luttrell. **1818** HALLAM *Mid. Ages* ii. II. (1819) I. 244 The manerial court of every vavassor represented in miniature that of his sovereign. *Ibid.* ix. II. III. 420 Stones ..were employed in the construction of manerial houses. **1839** *Penny Cycl.* XIV. 388/1 The lord's fee, or manerial seigniory.

maneriall, obs. Sc. form of MINERAL.

manerlik, obs. form of MANNERLY.

† **manery**. *Obs. rare*[−1]. Also 6 **mannery**. [ad. med.L. *manēri-um* MANOR.] A mansion or manor.
14.. in Becon *Reliques of Rome* (1563) 254 Houses of holy church, graunges, personages, or vicaries, or any maneries of mens of holy church. **1598** HALL *Sat.* VII. 36 Get the fee-simple of fayre manneryes.

‖ **manes** ('meɪniːz, 'mɑːneɪz), *sb. pl.* [L. *mānēs* pl. By some scholars supposed to be the pl. of OLatin *mānis* good (cf. *im-mānis* cruel).]
1. The deified souls of departed ancestors (as beneficent spirits; opposed to *larvæ* and *lemures*, the malevolent shades of the Lower World). Also, the spirit, 'shade' of a departed person, considered as an object of homage or reverence, or as demanding to be propitiated by vengeance.
1390 GOWER *Conf.* II. 173 Thei hadden goddes,..And tho be name Manes hihten, To whom ful gret honour thei dihten. **1609** HOLLAND *Amm. Marcell.* XV. vii. 43 As if they meant with Romane bloud to sacrifice unto their wicked Manes. **1670** DRYDEN *1st Pt. Conq. Granada* IV. ii, The manes of my son shall smile this day, While I, in blood, my vows of vengeance pay. **1703** POPE *Thebais* 752 Let eternal fame Attend thy Manes, and preserve thy name. **1792** BURKE *Corr.* (1844) III. 381 The Chevalier may owe it to the manes of the fallen nobility..to put his name to his own defence and theirs. **1869** LECKY *Europ. Mor.* (1877) I. ii. 272 The games were..intended as human sacrifices to appease the Manes of the dead. **1880** HUXLEY *Sci. & Cult.* i. (1881) 1 We may hope that the manes of the burnt-out philosopher were then finally appeased.
fig. **1673** *Remarques Humours Town* 18 The delight, or the torment of reflections, being the Manes of past actions. **1726** C. D'ANVERS *Craftsm.* No. 2 (1727) 20 It is indeed only the manes of departed Liberty which makes the loss of the substance more grievous to us.
¶ **2.** Taken in the sense of 'mortal remains' (? by association with L. *mănēre* to remain); hence *transf.*
1707 *Curios. in Husb. & Gard.* 336 A certain Polander shut up the Manes of Plants in Glass Vessels.

manes(h, obs. form of MENACE.

maness ('mænɛs). *rare.* Also 6 **mannes**, 7 **manness**. [f. MAN *sb.*[1] + -ESS.] Woman as the feminine of man.
1594 T. B. *La Primaud. Fr. Acad.* II. 24 The man said, This nowe is bone of my bones, and flesh of my flesh: she shall be called mannes, or mannish, because she was taken out of man. **1643** TRAPP *Comm. Gen.* ii. 23 [She shall be called Woman] or Manness, of Man, as *Ishah* of *Ish*. **1855** BAILEY *Spir. Legend* in *Mystic*, etc. (ed. 2) 130 Taught the Ædenic mysteries of man And maness.

maness, obs. form of MENACE.

manesuere, manesweir, obs. ff. MANSWEAR *v.*

maneto, obs. form of MANITOU.

maneton (mantɔ̃). *Aeronaut.* [F. *maneton* crank-pin.] (See quot. 1949.)
1919 *Gloss. Aeronaut. Terms* (R. Aeronaut. Soc.) 44 *Maneton*, the small end of the crankshaft of a rotary engine. **1939** *Times* 30 Mar. 9/3 One simple device for assembling the maneton end of the crankshaft. **1949** *Gloss. Aeronaut. Terms* (*B.S.I.*) II. 11 *Maneton*, the detachable short end of a crankshaft in a rotary or radial engine.

Manetti (mæ'nɛtɪ). *Hort.* [Named after Xavier *Manetti* (1723–1784), a botanist of Monza.] A very vigorous dwarf variety of rose much used as a stock; also *Manetti rose*.
[**1843** T. RIVERS *Rose Amateur's Guide* (ed. 3) 113 *note*, The..Rosa Manettii..I received a few years ago from Italy. **1846** *Ibid.* (ed. 4) 150 It..seems to flourish on the Manettii stock better than on its own roots.] **1854** *Ibid.* (ed. 5) 182 The only method..is to employ the Manetti Rose as a stock. **1869** HOLE *Bk. Roses* 204 The Manetti will grow luxuriantly where the Brier will not grow at all.

maneuver, variant of MANŒUVRE.

'man-folk. *poet.* [MAN *sb.*[1]] People, human beings, men.
1875 W. MORRIS tr. *Virgil's Æneid* XII. 825 Let not that manfolk shift their tongue, or cast their garb aside. **1887** —— tr. *Homer's Odyssey* III. 252 Amid other dwellings of manfolk. *Ibid.* I. 393 Of all that befalleth manfolk dost thou deem it the evillest thing?

manful ('mænfʊl), *a.* Also 4 **monful**, 5 **man(n)fulle**, 5–7 **manfull**. [f. MAN *sb.*[1] + -FUL.]
1. Characterized by manly courage and resolution; brave, resolute.
a **1300–1400** *Cursor M.* 8306 (Gött.) Werrour art þu, manful wight, And many man slayn wid þi hand. **1399** LANGL. *Rich. Redeles* III. 103 They mornyd ffor the morthir of manffull knyȝtis. **1422** tr. *Secreta Secret., Priv. Priv.* 170 Sum men hym callyth a corageous man, or a manful man. **1513** BRADSHAW *St. Werburge* II. 412 The inhabitauntes of it manfull and liberall. **1576** FLEMING *Panopl. Epist.* 36 A stoute and manful minde. **1641** EARL MONM. tr. *Biondi's Civil Warres* IV. 76 They were inforced after twelve dayes manfull defence to surrender themselves upon discretion. **1865** CARLYLE *Fredk. Gt.* XVII. iii. (1872) VII. 27 Blakeney and Garrison stood to their guns in a manful manner. **1879** MORLEY *Burke* 189 A manful attempt was made to get the new constitution to work in the winter of 1791–92. **1891** SWINBURNE *Stud. Prose & Poetry* (1894) 18 The manful good sense which seems naturally to accompany a manly tenderness of nature.
† **2.** In occasional uses. **a.** Stately in appearance. **b.** Befitting a man, manly. *Obs.*
1493 *Festivall* (W. de W. 1515) 78 b, Thomas was as manfull in his araye, for he was clothed in yᵉ best and rychest clothe. **1655** FULLER *Ch. Hist.* VII. ii. §15 [He] being shooting at Butts, (a manfull, and healthfull Pastime..).
† **3.** *Comb.*: **manful-hardy** *a.*, brave (hence **-hardiness**). *Obs.*
c **1430** LYDG. *Compl. Bl. Knt.* 417 Sheding of blode, ne man-ful hardinesse. **1542** UDALL *Erasm. Apoph.* 15 Such as be manful hardye [orig. *fortes*]. *Ibid.* Pref. **ii, Concernyng mannefull hardynesse [orig. *fortitudinem*].

manfully ('mænfʊlɪ), *adv.* [f. MANFUL *a.* + -LY[2].] In a manful manner; with manly courage or resolution, bravely, valiantly.
c **1400** *Melayne* 1240 This day wirke þou Manfully With thi nobill Chevalry. *c* **1430** *Life St. Kath.* (1884) 57 Drede not..þou..welbeloued queene vn to god but do manfully. **1553** EDEN *Treat. Newe Ind.* (Arb.) 31 He manfullye defended him selfe in battayl. **1611** BIBLE *2 Macc.* ix. 10 Let vs die manfully for our brethren. **1782** COWPER *Gilpin* 76 Then over all..His long red cloak, well brush'd and neat, He manfully did throw. **1839** THIRLWALL *Greece* xlviii. VI. 141 The Greeks..continued to fight manfully. **1849** MACAULAY *Hist. Eng.* i. I. 50 Bishop Hooper, who died manfully at Gloucester for his religion. **1860** TYNDALL *Glac.* I. xxvii. 219 The labour was enormous, but it was manfully and cheerfully done.
† **b.** Honourably. *Obs.*
1591 SHAKS. *Two Gent.* IV. i. 27, I kil'd a man, whose death I much repent, But yet I slew him manfully, in fight.

manfulness ('mænfʊlnɪs). [f. MANFUL + -NESS.] The quality of being manful.
c **1400** *Beryn* 2693 But his grete wisdom, & his manfulness. **1546** BALE *Eng. Votaries* I. (1548) 49 b, Daniel than Byshop of Wynchestre sent thys wenefride to rome wyth hys letters of commendacyon for hys manfulnesse there shewed. **1681** R. KNOX *Hist. Ceylon* 134 The Metal and Manfulness of these men. **1833** HT. MARTINEAU *Loom & Lugger* I. v. 91 It took all my manfulness from me to see you so near the edge of the cliff. **1868** VISCT. STRANGFORD *Selections* (1869) II. 336 Sir Samuel, as good a type of manfulness and power in speech and action as one would ever wish to see.

† **mang**, *v.*[1] *Sc.* and *north. Obs.* **a.** *trans.* To bewilder, lead astray. **b.** *intr.* To be bewildered, go wrong; to go mad.
c **1440** *York Myst.* xlii. 132 What saie ȝe men? allas! for tene I trowe ȝe mang. *a* **1510** DOUGLAS *K. Hart* 104 And all that couth attene the castell neir, It made thame for to mer amiss, and mang. **1513** —— *Æneis* VIII. Prol. 16 Musing marris our myrth half mangit allmost. **1562** A. SCOTT *Poems* (S.T.S.) i. 79 To mend þat menȝe hes sa monye mangit God gif þe grace. *a* **1600** MONTGOMERIE *Misc. Poems* xlvii. 9 Resave, vhill than, a harte lyk for to mang. **1768** ROSS in Whitelaw *Bk. Sc. Song* (1875) 360/2 She chokit and boakit, and cried like to mang.

† **mang**, *v.*[2] *slang. Obs.* (See quot.)
1812 J. H. VAUX *Flash Dict.*, *Mang*, to speak or talk.

mang, variant of MONG *sb.*[1] and *v.*

‖ **manga** ('maŋga). [Sp. *manga* lit. 'sleeve':—L. *manica*: see MANCHE[1].]
1. A flowing robe, worn from the shoulders.
1824 W. BULLOCK *Six Months' Residence Mexico* xvii. 216 An elegant manga or cloak, of velvet, fine cloth, or fine figured cotton. **1851** MAYNE REID *Scalp Hunt.* vii. 55 It was purely a Mexican costume, and consisted of a purple manga. **1889** AMELIA E. BARR *Woven of Love & Glory* xiii. 301 It was a grand moving picture of handsome men in scarlet and gold —of graceful mangas and waving plumes.
2. The silk case used to cover a processional or other cross when not in use (Sp. *manga de cruz*).
1890 in *Century Dict.*

manga, obs. form of MANGO.

mangabey ('mæŋgəbeɪ). *Nat. Hist.* [The name of a region of Madagascar, erron. given by Buffon to a species of *Cercocebus* inhabiting the west coast of Africa.] A monkey of the African genus *Cercocebus*; esp. the Sooty Mangabey, *Cercocebus fuliginosus*.
1774 GOLDSM. *Nat. Hist.* IV. vii. 234 The fourth of this [the monkey] kind is the Mangabey... It is a native of Madagascar. **1879** W. LAUDER LINDSAY *Mind Lower Anim.* II. 83 A sooty mangabey (monkey) had acquired a good number of bad habits.

‖ **mangal** (maŋ'gal). Also 9 **manggall**, (in Dicts.) **mankal**. [Turkish *mangal* (also written *manqal*).] A kind of brazier.
a **1814** *Sorceress* II. ii. in *New Brit. Theatre* III. 13 Another room in the Palace; in the midst a Manggall with fire burning. **1851** *Offic. Catal. Gt. Exhib.* III. 1398 Brass mangal or brazier:—Manufactured by Mardiros Tombakdgi, Constantinople, exhibitor.

mangalin, variant of MANGELIN *Obs.*

mangal wurzel, obs. var. MANGEL-WURZEL.

mangan-, repr. MANGANESE (G. *mangan*) in many compound names of minerals, chiefly adopted from German (see A. H. Chester *Dict. Min.*, 1896), as **mangan-amphibole** = RHODONITE; **mangan-apatite**, a variety of apatite containing manganese; **manganblende** = ALABANDITE; **manganbrucite**, a variety of brucite containing much manganese; **manganchlorite**, a manganiferous variety of clinochlore; **mangancolumbite**, a variety of columbite in which the iron is largely replaced by manganese; **manganhedenbergite**, a manganiferous variety of hedenbergite; **manganpectolite**, a manganiferous variety of pectolite; **mangantantalite**, a variety of tantalite in which manganese largely replaces the iron. (Cf. MANGANO-.)
1861 BRISTOW *Gloss. Mineral.*, **Mangan-amphibole*. **1892** DANA *Syst. Mineral.* 764 *Manganapatite..contains manganese replacing calcium. **1836** T. THOMSON *Outl. Min., Geol.*, etc. I. 510 Sulphuret of Manganese. *Manganblende. Swartzerz. **1887** DANA *Man. Mineral. & Petrogr.* (ed. 4) 224 *Manganbrucite is a manganesian variety. **1892** —— *Syst. Min.* 648 *Manganchlorit. **1898** —— *Text-bk. Mineral.* 474 Manganchlorite, a chlorite from the Harstig mine near Pajsberg, Sweden. **1890** *Century Dict.*, **Mangancolumbite*. **1887** DANA *Man. Mineral. & Petrogr.* (ed. 4) 267 *Manganhedenbergite..contains 6 to 7 p.c. of manganese protoxide. **1892** —— *Syst. Min.* 373 *Manganpectolith. **1898** —— *Text-bk. Mineral.* 395 Manganpectolite. **1884** *Cassell's Encycl. Dict.*, **Manganosklerite*. **1887** DANA *Man. Mineral. & Petrogr.* (ed. 4) 202 *Mangantantalite contains more manganese than iron.

manganate ('mæŋgənət). *Chem.* [f. MANGAN-IC + -ATE.] A salt of manganic acid.
1839 *Penny Cycl.* XIV. 382/2 Manganate of potash is easily prepared. **1891** THORPE *Dict. Appl. Chem.* II. 500/1 All manganates..oxidise hydrochloric acid.

‖ **manganeisen** ('maŋganˌaɪzən). *Min.* [Ger., f. *mangan* manganese + *eisen* iron.] = FERRO-MANGANESE.
1881 [see FERRO-].

manganel(l, variant of MANGONEL.

manganeous: see MANGANOUS.

† **manga'nesane.** *Chem. Obs.* [f. MANGANESE + -ANE 2 a.] Chloride of manganese.
1818 HENRY *Elem. Chem.* (ed. 8) II. 65.

† **manga'nesate.** *Chem. Obs.* [f. MANGANESIC + -ATE.] = MANGANATE.
1819 BRANDE *Man. Chem.* 228 Manganesate of potassa.

manganese ('mæŋgəniːz). Also 7 **manganes**, 9 **manganeze**. [a. F. *manganèse* (16th c.), a. It. *manganese*, one of the many corrupt forms of L. *magnēsia*: see MAGNESIA 2. The word appears in Ger. as *mangan* (hence Du. *mangaan*, Sw. *mangan*). Cf. obs. F. *mangane*.]
1. A black mineral (now recognized as an oxide of a metal, to which its name has been transferred: see sense 2), used from ancient times in glass-making, and now in many industrial processes. Also called ***black manganese***, † ***glass-maker's manganese***. The name has been also applied with qualification to other ores of the metal: **grey m.**, = MANGANITE 1; **horn m.**, **corneous m.** [G. *hornmangan*, Jasche], an impure manganese silicate akin to photicite; **red m.**, = RHODOCHROSITE; **white m.**, manganese carbonate.
As the name is in chemical use now restricted to the metal (sense 2), its older application survives only in commercial and industrial use. The black manganese of commerce is usually a mixture of various oxides, but the term is considered to apply esp. to manganese dioxide, MnO_2, which is the valuable ingredient in the mixture.

1676 COLES, *Manganese* (in colour and weight like the loadstone), the most general ingredient of glass. *a* **1682** SIR T. BROWNE *Pseud. Ep.* II. iii. (1686) 52 In the making of glass it hath been an ancient practice to cast in pieces of magnet, or perhaps manganes. **1755** *Gentl. Mag.* XXV. 540 Our Manganese, supposed an iron ore, appears from some experiments to contain no iron. **1797** *Encycl. Brit.* (ed. 3) X. 528/1 This substance, commonly called black or glass-maker's manganese, is scarcely any other thing than the calx of a new semimetal. **1864** *Chambers's Encycl.* VI. 301/2 The *binoxide*, or *peroxide*, is the black manganese of commerce, and the *pyrolusite* of mineralogists. **1865** WATTS *Dict. Chem.* III. 808 *Grey Manganese*, a term sometimes applied to manganite and pyrolusite. **1883** *Encycl. Brit.* XVI. 398/1 *Dialogite* (Red Manganese). *Ibid.* 417/1 Allagite and Horn Manganese are mere mixtures.

2. *Chem.* The metallic element (symbol Mn) of which 'black manganese' is the oxide.

It is of a greyish white colour and a hard friable texture, somewhat resembling iron, but having no economic use in the metallic form.

1783 WITHERING tr. *Bergman's Outl. Mineral.* 114 Manganesium or Manganese... This new metal is soluble in all the acids. **1807** J. MURRAY *Syst. Chem.* III. 423 The name Manganese, which was formerly given to the native oxide, is now appropriated to the metal. **1812** SIR H. DAVY *Chem. Philos.* 49 The properties of manganese, which was announced as a peculiar metal by Kaim in 1770, were minutely investigated by Scheele and Bergman. **1816** P. CLEAVELAND *Mineral.* 544 Manganese, which is with great difficulty obtained in a metallic state, has a grayish white color with some lustre. **1879** C. A. CAMERON in *Cassell's Techn. Educ.* I. 15 Manganese is a metal somewhat allied to iron.

3. *attrib.* and *Comb.* **a.** as ***manganese metal, mine, ore, salt***; **manganese alum**, (*a*) *Chem.*: see ALUM *sb.* 3; (*b*) *Min.* = APJOHNITE; **manganese blende** = ALABANDITE; **manganese bronze**, (*a*) a bronze dye, (*b*) an alloy of copper and zinc with manganese; **manganese brown**, a brown dye, consisting of manganic hydrate obtained by various processes; **manganese copper** = *manganese bronze*; **manganese epidote** = PIEDMONTITE; **manganese garnet** = SPESSARTITE; **manganese glance** = ALABANDITE; **manganese glass**, glass in the manufacture of which manganese has been used; **manganese green**, an unstable green dye derived from manganate of barium; **manganese purple** = *manganese violet*; **manganese spar** = RHODONITE; also RHODOCHROSITE; **manganese steel**, a malleable mixture of iron and manganese; **manganese violet**, the purple colour derived from manganese, used in the decoration of pottery and porcelain; **manganese vitriol** = FAUSERITE, a sulphate of magnesium and manganese.

1842 T. GRAHAM *Elem. Chem.* 519 Iron alum, *manganese alum, and chrome alum. **1820** R. JAMESON *Syst. Mineral.* (ed. 3) III. 406 Prismatic *Manganese Blende. **1839** URE *Dict. Arts*, etc. 235 *Manganese bronze, buff and green. **1883** P. M. PARSONS in *Rep. Brit. Assoc.* 382 The manganese bronze has a great advantage over steel. *Ibid.* 383 That the manganese bronze propellers are incorrodible,..has now been proved. **1841** T. GRAHAM *Elem. Chem.* (1842) 533 *Manganese brown. **1902** *Encycl. Brit.* (ed. 10) XXVII. 564, art. *Dyeing*, Manganese brown is applied in wool, silk, and cotton dyeing. **1883** *Encycl. Brit.* XVI. 409/2 Piedmontite or *Manganese Epidote, brownish violet, from St. Marcel, has 20 per cent. of manganese peroxide. **1865** WATTS *Dict. Chem.* III. 817 **Manganese-glance*, syn. with *Manganese-blende*. **1875** tr. *Vogel's Chem. Light* xvii. 269 Explanation of the change of *manganese-glass. **1882** *Spon's Encycl. Arts, Manuf.* etc. V. 1549 [Recipe for making] *Manganese Green. **1883** *Encycl. Brit.* XV. 480/1 *Manganese metal is grey, like cast iron. **1839** *Penny Cycl.* XIV. 381/1 It occurs in Devonshire, Cornwall, in the Harz, and most *manganese mines. **1795** W. NICHOLSON *Dict. Chem.* II. 596 This new *manganese ore was found among the iron mines of Sem. **1821** R. JAMESON *Man. Mineral.* 255 Prismatic Manganese-Ore, or Black Manganese-Ore. *Ibid.* 256 Prismatoidal Manganese-Ore, or Grey Manganese-Ore. **1937** *Burlington Mag.* Dec. 277/2 A large jar of early Florentine maiolica..of the class painted in *manganese-purple and green, the only pigments at that time known to the maiolica painter. **1963** *Times* 25 May 11/5 An unpleasant manganese-purple tinge. **1802** T. THOMSON *Syst. Chem.* III. 88 The oxides of *manganese salts. **1821** R. JAMESON *Man. Mineral.* 325 *Manganese-Spar. (Baryte.) **1865** WATTS *Dict. Chem.* III. 817 *Manganese-spar*, syn. with Diallogite. Native carbonate of manganese. **1883** *Encycl. Brit.* XVI. 417/1 Rhodonite (Manganese Spar). **1895** *Daily News* 16 Sept. 2/7 *Manganese steel is being used..in the manufacture of shovels. **1902** *Encycl. Brit.* XXXI. 772 A metaphosphate of manganese which goes under the name of Nürnberg or *manganese violet. **1884** H. BAUERMAN *Descr. Mineral.* 298 The mineral described as *Fauserite* or **Manganese Vitriol*, from Herrengrund, in Hungary.

b. In names of salts.

1877 KINGZETT *Alkali Trade* 209 Manganese chloride. **1882** DANA *Man. Mineral. & Lithol.* (ed. 4) 188 Pyrolusite—Manganese Dioxide. *Ibid.* 191 Rhodochrosite—Manganese Carbonate.

manganeseous: see under MANGANESIC.

manganesian (mæŋgəˈniːz(ɪ)ən), *a.* [f. MANGANESE + -IAN.] Pertaining to manganese, or characterized by its presence.

1795 W. NICHOLSON *Dict. Chem.* II. 596 This powdery manganesian ore. **1837** J. T. SMITH tr. *Vicat's Mortars* 2 The argillaceous, magnesian,..manganesian [etc., varieties of limestone].

†**mangaˈnesic**, *a. Obs.* [f. MANGANESE + -IC.] ***manganesic acid*** = manganic acid. Similarly **mangaˈnesiate**, = MANGANATE; **mangaˈnes(e)ous** ***acid***, manganous acid; **mangaˈnesite**, manganite.

1819 BRANDE *Man. Chem.* 226 Manganesic acid. **1823** HENRY *Elem. Chem.* (ed. 9) II. 10 The proportions being 100 metal and 96·847 oxygen, constituting *manganeseous acid*; the green salt, therefore, is a *manganesite* of potassa. The red compound..contains an acid which may be called the *manganesic*, and its compounds *manganesiates*. **1828** WEBSTER, *Manganesious* (citing Henry).

‖**mangaˈnesum, -sium.** *Chem. Obs.* [mod.L., f. MANGANESE.] = MANGANESE 2.

1783 [see MANGANESE 2]. **1786** tr. *Scheele's Chem. Ess.* 67 On Manganese, Manganesium, or Magnesia Vitrariorum. **1774**. **1812** SIR H. DAVY *Chem. Philos.* 367 Manganesum was first procured in its pure form by Kaim and Gahn, between 1770 and 1775. **1876** HARLEY *Mat. Med.* (ed. 6) 195 Manganesium was discovered by Gahn in 1774.

manganetic (mæŋgəˈnɛtɪk), *a. rare*⁻⁰. [Badly f. MANGANESE, after *magnetic*.] = MANGANIFEROUS.

In mod. Dicts.

mangani- (ˈmæŋgənɪ), earlier **manganid-** [cf. FERRI-], used *Chem.* in names of certain cyanogen compounds, indicating the presence of manganese in its 'manganic' or highest degree of valency (cf. MANGANO-²). **ˌmanganicyanˈhydric** (or **-cyˈanic**) **acid**, H_3MnCy_6. **ˌmanganiˈcyanide**, a salt of this acid.

1852 WATTS tr. *Gmelin's Handbk. Chem.* VII. 426 Manganidcyanid of cadmium. **1876** [see MANGANO-².] **1889** MORLEY & MUIR *Watts' Dict. Chem.* II. 342.

manganic (mæŋˈgænɪk), *a. Chem.* [f. MANGAN-ESE + -IC.] Applied to compounds containing manganese in its highest valency. ***manganic acid***: an acid (H_2MnO_4) not known exc. in combination with alkalis, with which it forms *manganates*.

1836 BRANDE *Chem.* (ed. 4) 633 Manganic acid. **1877** KINGZETT *Alkali Trade* 209 Manganic chloride. **1878** ABNEY *Photogr.* (1881) 72 The permanganate is decomposed ..and insoluble manganic oxide is precipitated on the image.

manganiferous (mæŋgəˈnɪfərəs), *a. Min.* [f. MANGAN-ESE + -(I)FEROUS.] Containing or yielding manganese.

1851 WATTS tr. *Gmelin's Handbk. Chem.* V. 300 Manganiferous Magnetic Iron-ore. **1877** *Nature* XV. 57 The Deep-sea Manganiferous Muds.

manganin (ˈmæŋgənɪn). *Metallurgy.* [f. MANGAN-ESE + -IN¹.] An alloy of copper, manganese and nickel, much used in the construction of standard resistance coils.

1902 J. J. THOMSON in *Encycl. Brit.* XXVIII. 7.

manganite (ˈmæŋgənaɪt). [f. MANGAN-ESE + -ITE. Cf. F. *manganite*.]

1. *Min.* A hydrated sesquioxide of manganese, occurring massive and in pseudo-crystals; grey manganese ore.

1827 HAIDINGER in *Trans. Roy. Soc. Edinb.* (1831) XI. 122 Prismatoidal Manganese-ore. Manganite. *Ibid.* 125 The name of *Manganite*, proposed for this species, is formed in allusion to the metal which it contains. **1836** T. THOMSON *Outl. Min., Geol.*, etc. I. 502 Manganite. Hydrous sesquioxide of manganese. **1858** *Fownes' Man. Chem.* (ed. 7) 307 This compound occurs in nature as braunite, and in the state of hydrate as manganite.

2. *Chem.* A salt of manganous acid.

1865 WATTS *Dict. Chem.* III. 818 Salts which may be called manganites. **1877** KINGZETT *Alkali Trade* 209 This latter body..forms what Mr. Weldon has termed manganite of magnesium ($MgMnO_3$).

Hence **mangaˈnitic** *a.*, containing manganite.

1886 *Pall Mall G.* 6 Mar. 5/2 A very considerable formation of manganitic ore.

‖**manganium** (mæŋˈgeɪnɪəm). *Chem. rare*⁻⁰. [mod.L., f. MANGAN-ESE. So Fr.] = MANGANESE 2.

1850 in OGILVIE. **1856** MAYNE *Expos. Lex.*, *Manganium*, a term proposed by Berzelius for manganese.

manganize (ˈmæŋgənaɪz), *v. rare.* [f. MANGAN-ESE + -IZE.] *trans.* To treat or prepare with manganese. Hence **ˈmanganized** *ppl. a.*

1875 R. F. MARTIN tr. *Havrez' Winding Mach.* 13 Flat ropes, made of manganised steel.

ˈmangano-¹, used as combining form of MANGANESE in the construction of the names of certain minerals containing that element (see A. H. Chester *Dict. Min.* 1896): **manganocalcite**, a calciferous variety of rhodochrosite; also occas. = SPARTAITE; **manganocolumbite** = MANGANCOLUMBITE; **manganomagnetite** = JACOBSITE; **manganophyllite**, a manganiferous variety of biotite; **manganosiderite**, a ferriferous variety of rhodochrosite; **manganostibiite**, antimoniate of manganese occurring in small black grains; **manganotantalite** = *mangantantalite*; †**manganowolframite** = HÜBNERITE. (Cf. MANGAN-.)

1852 BROOKE & MILLER *Phillips' Mineral.* 678 Mangano-calcite. **1877** DANA *Text-bk. Mineral.* 290 Manganophyllite. **1887** —— *Man. Mineral. & Petrogr.* (ed. 4) 206 Manganostibiite contains both arsenic and antimony. **1892** —— *Syst. Mineral.* 731 Manganotantalite. **1898** —— *Text-bk. Mineral.* 491 Manganocolumbite.

ˈmangano-², used *Chem.* in names of compounds containing manganese with its lower or 'manganous' degree of valency (cf. MANGANI-).

1876 *Encycl. Brit.* V. 535/2 Chromi-cyanides and mangano- and mangani-cyanides, isomorphous with the corresponding iron compounds. **1889** MORLEY & MUIR *Watts' Dict. Chem.* II. 328 Manganocyanic acid (or manganocyanhydric acid) H_4MnCy_6.

manganoan (mæŋgəˈnəʊən), *a. Min.* [f. MANGAN(ESE + -OAN.] Of a mineral: having a (small) proportion of a constituent element replaced by bivalent manganese.

1930 W. T. SCHALLER in *Amer. Mineralogist* XV. 571/2 Manganese—manganoan. **1944** C. PALACHE et al. *Dana's Syst. Min.* (ed. 7) I. 777 Mossite is..reported also (manganoan) from Yinnietharra, Western Australia. **1968** I. KOSTOV *Mineral.* 11. ix. 498 Luckite is a manganoan melanterite.

†**ˈmanganolite.** *Min. Obs.* [f. MANGANO- + Gr. λίθος -LITE.] = RHODONITE.

1884 *Cassell's Encycl. Dict.* **1896** A. H. CHESTER *Dict. Min.*

manganosite (ˈmæŋgənəʊsaɪt). *Min.* [ad. G. *manganosit*, f. *mangan* MANGANESE.] Protoxide of manganese, occurring in small green octahedral crystals which turn black on exposure to the air.

1887 DANA *Man. Mineral. & Petrogr.* (ed. 4) 206.

†**mangaˌnoso-manˈganic**, *a. Chem. Obs.* [ad. mod.L. *manganōso-manganicus* (Berzelius): cf. MANGANOUS and MANGANIC.] Having a formula which is the sum of that of a 'manganous' and that of a 'manganic' compound. ***manganoso-manganic oxide***: red oxide of manganese, Mn_3O_4.

1845 PARNELL *Chem. Anal.* 331 Manganoso-manganic oxide. **1865** WATTS *Dict. Chem.* IV. 801 Manganese occurs ..as manganic and manganoso-manganic oxide.

manganous (ˈmæŋgənəs), *a.* Also 9 manganeous. [f. MANGAN-ESE + -OUS.] **a.** Of the nature of, or containing, manganese. **b.** *Chem.* Containing manganese with a valency of two.

1823 HENRY *Elem. Chem.* (ed 9) II. 11 The constitution of the manganeous acid. **1842** T. GRAHAM *Elem. Chem.* 530 Protoxide of manganese, Manganous oxide. **1884** H. BAUERMAN *Descr. Mineral.* 51 Manganous sulphide. **1884** *Health Exhib. Catal.* 49/2 Patent Manganous Carbon Filters of various kinds. **1891** THORPE *Dict. Appl. Chem.* II. 499/1 One-sixth of the weight of the manganous chloride employed.

mangas: see MANGO.

mangastan, -stene, obs. forms of MANGOSTEEN.

mange (meɪndʒ), *sb.*¹ Forms: α. 5 maniew(e, manyew, 6–7 mangie, 7 maungie, mangy. β. 6 maunge, 7 mainge, 6– mange. [Late ME. *manjewe*, a. OF. *manjue*, *mangeue* itch (also in the sense 'eating'), vbl. sb. f. *manjuer* = *mangier* (mod.F. *manger*) to eat. Cf. F. *démanger* to itch.]

1. A cutaneous disease analogous to the itch in man, occurring in many hairy and woolly animals, and caused by an arachnidan parasite. Also sometimes loosely, a dirty, scabby or scurfy condition of the skin. ***flying, quick, red, scabby mange***, varieties of this disease.

α. *c* **1400** *Master of Game* (MS. Digby 182) xii, þe houndes also hath an oþer sickenesse, þat is cleped þe Maniewe [*Bodl. MS.* manyew]. *Ibid.*, þat oþer manere of maniewe is cleped þe fleynge maniewe. *Ibid.*, þat one is cleped quyc maniewes, þe whiche pileth þe houndes. **1575** TURBERV. *Faulconrie* 363, I place the Mangie firste, as the capitall enemie to the quiete and beautie of a brave spanell. **1598** YONG *Diana* 306 The Iuniper oile may neuer helpe my flockes, With lothsome mangie being ouerrun. **1604** E. G[RIMSTONE] *D'Acosta's Hist. Indies* VI. xv. 465 If the mangie or the scurvie..take any beast, they were presently commaunded to bury it quicke. **1624** HEYWOOD *Captives* II. ii. in Bullen *O. Pl.* IV, Tis good phisick To cure thee of the mangy. **1647** R. STAPYLTON *Juvenal* 141 The dogs whose mangy eats away his haire.

β. **1540** *Act 32 Hen. VIII*, c. 13 §9 Anye horse, geldynge or mare infecte with scappe or mange. **1601** HOLLAND *Pliny* II. 450 The scurvie thicke roufe in the farcins or mange of horses. **1623** J. TAYLOR (Water P.) *Praise Hempseed* Wks. (1630) III. 66/1 Gangrenaes, Vlcers, wounds, and mortall stabs, Illiaca passioes, Megrims, Mumps, or Mange. **1663** BUTLER *Hud.* I. i. 612 And tell what Crisis does Divine The Rot in Sheep, the Mange in Swine. **1667** T. COXE in *Phil. Trans.* II. 451, I procured an old Mungrell Curr, all over-run with the Mainge. **1683** TRYON *Way to Health* 88 At last they [sheep] will break out with a Mainge or Scab. **1750** RUTTY in *Phil. Trans.* LI. 473 It cures the mange in horses, and the itch in men, by bathing. **1822** SCOTT *Fam. Lett.* 4 Sept. (1894) II. xviii. 149 As it was, I came off with a fit of

the mange, and it was a good escape. **1843** YOUATT *Horse* (1848) 379 Mange in cattle has been propagated to the horse. **1858** —— *Dog* 367 The Scabby Mange is a frequent form which this disease assumes. It assumes a pustular and scabby form in the red mange. **1868** *Regul. & Ord. Army* ¶567 The veterinary Surgeon will inspect all the horses of the detachments for the detection of Mange.

†**2.** *fig.* A restless desire. (Cf. ITCH 2.) *Obs.*

1648 HERRICK *Hesper., A Country Life* 22 Those that have the itch Of craving more are never rich. These things thou know'st to' th'height, and dost prevent That plague [*MS. Ashm.* 38. p. 90 Mange], because thou art content. *a* **1680** ROCHESTER *Sess. Poets* 56 Don Carlos his Pockets so amply had fill'd, That his Mange was quite cur'd. **1789** WOLCOT (P. Pindar) *Expost. Odes* x. 22 The Love of Flattery is the Soul's rank Mange. **1790** —— *Ep. to Sylv. Urban*, If yet thy head possess the Mange of Writing.

3. mange mite, a parasitic mite of the family Sarcoptidæ, causing mange in various mammals.

1873 A. S. PACKARD *Our Common Insects* xi. 125 (*caption*) Mange mite. **1911** *Encycl. Brit.* XXVIII. 13/1 The dermatozoa..are lice, fleas, ticks, acari or mange mites. **1950** *N.Z. Jrnl. Agric.* Jan. 68/1 Two types of mange mites affect pigs. **1962** METCALF & FLINT *Destructive & Useful Insects* (ed. 4) xx. 973 When hogs are scratching and rubbing vigorously and their hair is standing erect,..it is probable that the animals are infested with mange mites.

†**mange**, *sb.*² *Obs.* [? f. MANGE *v.*]

1. A meal.

a **1605** MONTGOMERIE *Cherrie & Slae* (revision) iii, I saw the hurcheon and the hare In hidlings hirpling heir and thair, To mak thair morning mange.

2. A food for animals.

1611 MARKHAM *Countr. Content.* I. i. (1668) 12 The best food is to give them Mange, made either of ground Oats, Barley Meale, Branne, or Mill-dust. *Ibid.* 13 Meat which if it be sweet is called the Mange, if otherwise Carrion or Garbage. **1615** —— *Eng. Housew.* (1660) 177 Nor is there any more..excellent meat for Swine in the time of sicknesse, then a mange made of ground Oates and sweet Whey.

†**mange**, *a.* *Obs. rare.* Also 5 **manyew**, 6 **maunge**. Cf. MANGED *a.* [f. MANGE *sb.*¹] Having the mange; = MANGY.

c **1410** *Master of Game* (MS. Digby 182) xii, Anoynt þe hounde þerwith as he is maniewed [*Bodl. MS.* manyew]. **1537** MATTHEW *Lev.* xxi. 20 Wether he be..gogeleyed, or maunge, or skaulde. *Ibid.* xxii. 22 Whether it..haue a wen, or be maunge, or scabbed. **1547** HOOPER *Answ. Bp. Winchesters Bk.* L 4 b, To saue hym [*sc.* a dog] he wax not mange.

†**mange**, *v.* *Obs.* Also 4, 6 **maunge**. [a. OF. *mangier*, *manjuer* (mod.F. *manger*) to eat:—L. *mandūcāre*: see MANDUCATE *v.*] *trans.* To eat. Hence †**manging** *vbl. sb.*

1362 LANGL. *P. Pl.* A. IX. 245 Þei han I-Maunget ouur muche þat makeþ hem grone ofte. *c* **1460** *Towneley Myst.* XII. 232 And two swyne gronys, All a hare bot the lonys, we myster no sponys here, at oure mangyng. **1582** STANYHURST *Æneis* III. (Arb.) 83 Feare not thee manging fortold of burdseat in hunger, Thee fats thee passage shal smooth. *Ibid.* IV. 117 Yea the lad Ascanius wel I might haue slaughtered, after At tabel of the father too set thee chield to be maunged.

mangeao (‖maŋge'aɔ, mæŋ'giːəʊ). Also 9 **mangi, mangiao,** 9- **mangeo.** [Maori.] A New Zealand tree, *Litsea calicaris*, of the family Lauraceæ, with tough, light brown wood.

1848 R. TAYLOR *Leaf from Nat. Hist. N.Z.* 20/2 Mangiao, a tree; the ash of this country. **1867** J. D. HOOKER *Handbk. N.Z. Flora* II. 766/1 Mangeao, *Tetranthera calicaris*. **1873** in E. E. Morris *Austral Eng.* (1898) 282/1 Mangi—remarkably tough and compact, used for ship-blocks and similar purposes. **1882** W. D. HAY *Brighter Britain!* II. 187 The perfumy mangiao. **1960** [see FIVE-FINGER 1 d]. **1963** POOLE & ADAMS *Trees & Shrubs N.Z.* 42 L[*itsea*] *calicaris*... Mangeao. Tree reaching 15m. Bark smooth, dark greyish brown... L[owland] Forest. North of North Island to lat. 38°.

†**manged**, *a.* *Obs.* [f. MANGE *sb.*¹ + -ED².] Suffering from mange.

c **1410** [see MANGE *a.*].

†**manged**, *ppl. a.* *Obs.* [f. MANG *v.* + -ED¹.] ? Rendered stupid or helpless.

1508 KENNEDIE *Flyting w. Dunbar* 546 Hangit, mangit, eddir-stangit, stryndie stultorum. **1508** DUNBAR *Tua mariit Wemen* 118 Than mak I nyne crocis, To keip me fra the cummerans of that carll mangit. **1513** DOUGLAS *Æneis* III. v. 52 To the ground half mangit fell sche doun. **1535** STEWART *Cron. Scot.* II. 632 Vther sum war of ane vther kynd, Richt mad & mangit, wod out of thair mynd. **1571** *Satir. Poems Reform.* xxv. 137 Aske at þe leving Lord, That hanged, or manged, Mot ilk man mak his end. *a* **1600** MONTGOMERIE *Misc. Poems* xxiv. 42, I sitt and sighis all soliter and sad, Half mangd in mynd, almost as I war mad.

manged, obs. form of MANCHET.

mangee, obs. form of MANJEE.

mangel ('mæŋg(ə)l), **mangold** ('mæŋgəʊld). Short for MANGEL-WURZEL. Also *attrib.* and *Comb.*, as ***mangel field, grower***; **mangel beetle**, a small blue-black beetle (*Silpha opaca*) whose larva feeds upon mangel-wurzel; **mangel-fly**, *Anthomyia betæ*.

α. **1877** *N.W. Linc. Gloss.*, *Mangles*, mangold wurzel. **1883** *Harper's Mag.* Apr. 652/1 A cow gets daily one bushel of sliced mangel. **1889** TENNYSON *Owd Roä* 14 All on it now Goan into mangles an' tonups. **1893** *Morn. Post* 8 Mar. 8/2 A pest mentioned..in these reports is the pigmy mangel beetle, and mangel growers are requested to keep a watchful eye upon the young roots.

β. **1856** *Farmer's Mag.* Jan. 62 Some swedes and yellow-globe mangolds grown by H.R.H. Prince Albert. **1882** *Garden* 14 Jan. 23/3 Mangold fly..the pest of our Mangold fields in the grub state. **1884** *Times* (weekly ed.) 19 Sept. 6/3 Nowhere in Ireland have I seen finer crops of hay and oats, of turnips and mangold.

‖**mangelin.** *Obs.* Also 6 **mangiar, mangelyn, mangiallin, mangalin.** [a. Telugu *manjāli* = Tamil *manjādi.*] A weight formerly used in Southern India and Ceylon for weighing precious stones, varying, apparently according to the district, from half a carat to two carats.

1555 EDEN *Decades* 234 A poyse or weight which they caule Mangiar, which wayeth two Tarre, and two thyrdes, which amount to two thyrdes or thirde partes of one caratte. **1584** W. BARRET in *Hakluyt's Voy.* (1599) II. I. 274 Another sort of weight called Mangiallins, which is 5 graines of *Venice* weight. **1598** W. PHILLIP *Linschoten* I. lxxxv. 133 Sometimes they find Diamonds of one hundred and two hundred Mangelyns, and more. **1615** tr. *De Monfart's Surv. E. Indies* 35 It waigheth 198. Mangelins, and each Mangelin waigheth fiue graines. **1678** J. PHILLIPS tr. *Tavernier's Trav.* II. II. xiv. 140 At the Mine of Raolconda they weigh by Mangelins, a Mangelin being one Carat and three quarters, that is seven Grains.

mangel-wurzel, mangold-wurzel ('mæŋg(ə)l-, 'mæŋgəld'wɜːz(ə)l). Forms: α. 8 **mangle wurzel, mangel wurtz, mangal wurzel,** 9 **mangel worsal, -wursel, mangol wurtzel, mangul wurzel,** 8–9 **mangel-wurzel** (*erron.* **-würzel**). β. 8–9 **mangold-wurzel,** (9 **-wurtzel**). [a. G. *mangold-wurzel* (corruptly *mangelwurzel*), f. *mangold* beet + *wurzel* root.

The corrupt form *mangelwurzel* (in Eng. now the prevailing form) suggested, or was suggested by, a pseudo-etymological association with G. *mangel* want, whence in the 18th and early 19th c. the name was often mistranslated 'root of scarcity' (and in Fr. *racine de disette*). The origin of G. *mangold* (MHG. *mangolt*) has not been determined: it may be an application of the OHG. personal name *Managolt*. The G. word has passed into other langs.: cf. Da. *mangold*, It. *manigoldo*.]

A variety of beet, with a root larger than that of the garden beet; cultivated as a food for cattle.

(Regarded by some botanists as a hybrid between the red and the white beet.)

α. **1779** [see b]. **1787** (*title*) tr. Abbé de Commerell's Account of the culture and use of the Mangel Wurzel. **1787** *Gentl. Mag.* Nov. 963/1 The Mangel Wurtz (*Wurzel*, you call it,) or Root of Scarcity. **1788** WOLCOT (P. Pindar) *Peter's Prophecy* Wks. (1823) 237/1 Beets, in whose just applauses we are hoarse all; Such are the wondrous powers of mangel worsal. **1844** H. STEPHENS *Bk. Farm* III. 762, I sowed the common long red or marbled mangel-würzel. **1881** H. TANNER *Sci. Agric. Pract.* lviii. 288 The Mangel wurzel.. obtained by the improvement of the Sea-Beet (*Beta Maritima*).

β. **1800** *Med. Jrnl.* III. 8 Mangold Wurzel, or Root of Scarcity. **1856** *Farmer's Mag.* Jan. 77 Mangold wurtzel.

b. *attrib.* and *Comb.*, as ***mangel-wurzel beet, leaf, plant***; **mangel-wurzel fly**, a small dipterous insect (*Anthomyia betæ*) the larva of which feeds on beet leaves; **mangel-wurzel potato**, a coarse variety of potato used as food for cattle.

1779 MAWE & ABERCROMBIE *Univ. Gardener* (1797) X b, The Mangel Wurzel Beet. **1851** H. STEPHENS *Bk. Farm* (ed. 2) II. 92/1 The mangold-wurzel plant..is attacked by the larva of a beetle,..*Silpha opaca*. *Ibid.*, The ultimate effect of these attacks on the mangold-wurzel leaves is not serious. **1862** *Q. Jrnl. Microscop. Sci.* II. 230 The Mangold-wurzel Fly. **1875** *Encycl. Brit.* I. 365/2 There are several varieties of the potato, such as 'yams', 'lumpers', 'mangel-wurzel potato', &c., which, although unfit for human food, are much relished by cattle.

mangeneel, obs. form of MANCHINEEL.

mangenel(e, obs. form of MANGONEL.

manger ('meɪndʒə(r)), *sb.*¹ Forms: 4 **manyour, maniore, mawnger, maungour,** 5 **maniure, maniowre, mangeour, mawngeur, mawnjowre,** 6 **mangeor, maungere, mangier,** 4- **manger.** [a. F. *mangeoire* (in 12th c. written *maingeure*) = Pr. *manjadoira*, Catal. *menjadora*, Pg. *manjadoura*, It. *mangiatoia*:—vulgar L. type **mandūcātōria*, f. *mandūcāre* (F. *manger*) to eat.]

1. A box or trough in a stable or cowhouse, from which horses and cattle eat. (Chiefly used for those kinds of food which cannot be placed, like hay and straw, in the rack above.)

c **1315** SHOREHAM *Poems* (E.E.T.S.) 120/145 þe oxe and asse in hare manyour. *c* **1330** R. BRUNNE *Chron. Wace* (Rolls) 11182 Bordes broughte, cordes & cables, & made mangers [*v.r.* maniores] to stande in stables. *a* **1400** *Sir Perc.* 441 A mawnger ther he fande Corne therin lyggande, Therto his mere he bande. *c* **1440** *Promp. Parv.* 325/1 Maniure (*S.*, *P.* maniowre), *mansorium, presepium, C., F., presepe*. **1465** *Paston Lett.* II. 254 An hows to ley inne hey and straw, and cost yow not but making of a rak and a mangeour. **1526** TINDALE *Luke* ii. 7 She..wrapped hym in swadlynge cloothes, and layed hym in a manger [so **1582** *Rheims* and **1611**; WYCLIF cracche, *Geneva* cretche: see CRATCH *sb.*¹ 1 b]. **1552** ABP. HAMILTON *Catech.* (1884) 24 The Asse has knawin the mangier of his maister. **1629** MILTON *Christ's Nativ.* 31 While the Heav'n-born-childe All meanly wrapt in the rude manger lies. **1791** MRS. RADCLIFFE *Rom. Forest* ii, My horse, I believe, smelt the corn in the manger by the rate he went at. **1868** *Regul. & Ord. Army* ¶570 To prevent infection..the rack and manger, are to be scoured with soft soap and hot water.

b. Used as the symbol of the Nativity.

1838 JACKSON tr. *Krummacher's Elisha* xiii. 294 The blissful mystery of the manger and the Cross.

c. Phr. ***in hack*** (***heck***) ***and manger***: see HACK *sb.*² 2, HECK *sb.*¹ 3; ***rack and manger***: see RACK *sb.*² 3 b, c, d. Also DOG-IN-THE-MANGER.

†**2.** *Astron.* (= L. *Præsæpe.*) The name of a nebulous tract in the constellation Cancer. *Obs.*

1551 RECORDE *Cast. Knowl.* (1556) 265 After Gemini foloweth Cancer containing 8 stars, beside a cloudy tract which is named yᵉ Manger or Crybbe.

3. *Naut.* A small berthing in the bows of a ship-of-war, intended to keep the water entering the hawse-holes from flooding the deck.

1627 CAPT. SMITH *Seaman's Gram.* ii. 10 A circle of planke either abaft or before the maine Mast called the Manger. *Ibid.*, The Bits..are..placed abaft the Manger in the ships loofe. **1836** E. HOWARD *R. Reefer* xliii, The manger, that part of the main-deck directly under the forecastle. **1867** in SMYTH *Sailor's Word-bk.* 466.

4. *attrib.* and *Comb.*, as ***manger-cradled*** *adj.*; **manger-board** (see quot.); **manger-doggishness** *nonce-wd.*, the character of a dog-in-the-manger; **manger-door**, the outlet from a ship's manger; **manger-food, -meat**, food which may properly be placed in the manger for cattle; **manger-scupper**, an aperture for carrying off water from a ship's manger.

1867 SMYTH *Sailor's Word-bk.*, *Manger*, a small berthing in the bows..separated on the after part from the rest of the deck by the *manger-board, a strong coaming rather higher than the hawse-holes. **1620** DEKKER *Dreame* 9 The *Manger-Cradled Babe, the Begger borne, The poorest Worme on the earth, the Heighth of Scorne. *a* **1631** DONNE *To C'tess Huntingdon* 14 Poems (1633) 91 As such a starre which Magi led to view The manger-cradled infant, God below. **1860** TROLLOPE *Framley P.* xxxi, Is not that *manger-doggishness one of the most common phases of the human heart? **1802** J. ANFREY in *Naval Chron.* VII. 48 A man was ..sentry at the *manger-door. **1805** R. W. DICKSON *Pract. Agric.* II. 599 A *manger food for the labouring teams. **1744–50** W. ELLIS *Mod. Husbandm.* I. II. 41 The best Sort of Pease for *Manger-meat. **1834** *Brit. Husb.* I. 141 The whole of this food is given as manger-meat, no part of it being put into the rack. *c* **1850** *Rudim. Navig.* (Weale) 131 The water is returned into the sea by the *manger-scuppers.

Hence '**mangerful**, a quantity that fills a manger.

1875 CHR. G. ROSSETTI *Goblin Market*, etc. 221 A breastful of milk And a mangerful of hay.

†**manger**, *sb.*² *Obs.* [a. OF. *mangier* to eat (the inf. used as sb.). Cf. GRAMAUNGERE.] A sumptuous meal; a banquet.

In the later quots. the word may be a jocular use of MANGER *sb.*¹

[**13..** *Minor Poems fr. Vernon MS.* xxx. 566 And þenne boþe bodi and soule i-fere Schal wende to þe graunt Mangere.] *c* **1420** *Laud Troy Bk.* 24 That gestoures often dos of hem gestes At mangeres and at grete ffestes. *c* **1460** *Towneley Myst.* xii. 201, I am worthy the wyne, me thynk it good skyll, My seruyse I tyne, I fare full yll, At youre mangere. **1548** LATIMER *Ploughers* (Arb.) 26 They are so troubeled wyth Lordelye lyuynge..mounchynge in their maungers..that they canne not attende it. **1605** CHAPMAN, etc. *Eastward Ho!* IV. i, Farewell thou horne of hunger that calst th' Innes a court to their Manger.

b. A prepared dish. ***manger blanc*** = BLANCMANGE(R.

1574 HELLOWES *Gueuara's Fam. Ep.* (1584) 98 They set before her..Manger blank, Pasties, Tarts, and other variable kinde of gluttonies. **1601** HOLLAND *Pliny* I. 246 A certain manger or broth made of their [barbels'] liuers. **1676** LADY FANSHAWE *Mem.* (1830) 209 Cakes, cheese, and excellent sweetmeats, especially manger blanc.

†**manger**, *v.*¹ *Obs. rare*⁻⁰. [a. F. *manger* (inf.).]

1613 R. CAWDREY *Table Alph.* (ed. 3), *Manger*, to eate.

manger ('meɪndʒə(r)), *v.*² *rare.* [f. MANGER *sb.*¹] *trans.* To fasten (an animal) to a manger.

1905 W. HOLMAN HUNT *Pre-Raphaelitism* II. 72 An old ram mangered by a halter.

[**mangering.** Error for *mamering*, MAMMERING in Parker Society ed. of Philpot's *Exam. & Writ.* 315, where there is a note, 'A mangering: perplexing, throwing their faith into confusion, is the probable meaning, from *mang*, a word of Celtic origin, meaning to *stupify* or *confound*.']

[**1559** PHILPOT *Jesus is God with us* C 3 b, Yᵉ simple people might be brought in a mamering of their faith, & stande in doubte whome they myght beleue.] Hence in some mod. Dicts.]

†'**mangery.** *Obs.* Forms: 4–5 **ma(u)ngeri, mangery,** 4–6 **mangerie,** 5 **maungery, mangere, mawngery, mangrie, maynerey,** 5–6 *Sc.* **maniory,** 6 *Sc.* **mangeory.** [a. OF. *mangerie*, f. *mangier* (mod.F. *manger*) to eat.]

1. A banquet; a ceremonial feast; a series of festivities.

a **1300** *Cursor M.* 15198 Til þe lauerd o þat hus Yee sai on mi parti, þat he yow wald len sum place, To mak vr mangeri. **13..** *E. E. Allit. P.* B. 1365 Such a mangerie to make þe man was auised. *c* **1375** *Sc. Leg. Saints* xxxvi. (*Baptista*) 501 [He] mad gret mangery þaim to, As afferit kyng to do. *c* **1400** *Laud Troy Bk.* 244 Til thre dayes were fulli paast, This

mangeri then so longe laast. c 1420 *Sir Amadace* (Camden) lv, Ther weddut he that lady briȝte, The maungery last a faurtenyȝte, With schaftes for to schake. 1422 tr. *Secreta Secret., Priv. Priv.* 153 Wher ben thay that helde the grete festes and grete mangries makid? c 1425 Wyntoun *Cron.* ii. xi. 1011 And ane vgsum maniory Off wlatsum corssis and vgly. ? c 1475 *Sqr. lowe Degre* 1098 That worthy wedding for to se, And come vnto that mangere. 1513 Douglas *Æneis* xiii. ix. 5 Onon the bankat and the mangeory For fest ryall according, by and by.

2. Banqueting, luxurious eating.

a 1470 Tiptoft *Orat. G. Flamineus* (Caxton 1481) F iv b/1, Supposest thou with thy sleep reste ydelnesse wyne mangerie lustes vnshamefastnes to get that worshipful fame which they gate. c 1470 Henryson *Mor. Fab.* ii. (*Town & C. Mouse*) xxvii, Thy mangerie is mingit all with cair, Thy guse is gude, thy gansell sour as gall.

3. Board; necessary food.

1596 Nashe *Saffron Walden* 119 The Minister then seruing at Saint Albanes in Wood-street..satisfied the House for his lodging and Mangerie.

mangestain, obs. form of MANGOSTEEN.

mange-tout (mɑ̃ʒtu). [Fr., lit. 'eat-all'.] In full, ***mange-tout pea***. A variety of pea producing pods which are eaten with the seeds they contain; = *sugar-pea* (SUGAR *sb.* 5 c).

1928 *Daily Express* 18 July 5/2 It [*sc.* a variety of pea] is largely grown in France, where it goes by the name of 'mange-tout'..and is eaten, shell and all. 1951 *Good Housek. Home Encycl.* 591/1 The seeds [*sc.* peas] are contained in a green pod, which is not usually eaten (except in the case of the sugar or mangetout variety). 1966 *Sunday Times* (Colour Suppl.) 27 Nov. 50/3 A bowl of *mangetout* peas. 1970 *Harrod's Summer Food News* 5/1 Whether you need..a pound of potatoes, or..mange tout peas, the quality is of the best at Harrods. 1972 *Country Life* 4 May 1121/3 From the French we are learning to enjoy the *Mangetout* or sugar pea. 1974 *Observer* (Colour Suppl.) 15 Sept. 12/3 Asked with impious briskness precisely when to sow mange-touts, divide artichokes or prune plums.

mangey, variant of MANGY.

manggall, manggo: see MANGAL, MANGO.

mangi, var. MANGEAO.

mangiallin, mangiar, vars. MANGELIN *Obs.*

mangie, obs. f. MANGE *sb.*[1], MANGY, MANJEE.

mangier, obs. form of MANGER *sb.*[1]

mangily ('meɪndʒɪlɪ), *adv.* In 7 mangely. [f. MANGE *sb.*[2] + -(I)LY[2].] In a mangy manner.

c 1620 Fletcher & Massinger *False One* ii. iii, Oh, this soundes mangely..and scurvely in a Souldiers mouth.

manginess ('meɪndʒɪnɪs). [f. MANGY *a.* + -NESS.] The condition of being mangy.

c 1400 *Master of Game* (MS. Digby 182) xii, Þer is IIII. maners of maniewenesse [*Bodl. MS.* manyewnesse]. 1535 Coverdale *Deut.* xxviii. 27 The Lorde shal smyte the..with scalle, and maungynesse. a 1571 Jewel *On 1 Thess.* (1611) 99 Who hath not heard of the patience of Iob?..his body stricken with a scurfe or mangines. 1579 Langham *Gard. Health* (1633) 279 For the white scurfe, leapry,.. manginesse..&c. 1611 Cotgr., *Mal de S. Roch*..an itching manginesse. 1725 Bradley *Fam. Dict.* s.v. *Rules for buying a Horse*, To have much Hair on the Mane, denotes intolerable Dulness;..and to be without none..shews the Worm in the Mane, the Itch, or else plain Manginess.

†**mangle**, *sb.*[1] *Obs.* [f. *mangle, MONGLE *v.*] *in mangle*: in a mêlée.

13.. *K. Alis.* 7412 While they weore so in mangle, Theo Yndiens gan gangle.

mangle ('mæŋg(ə)l), *sb.*[2] [a. Sp. *mangle* (Oviedo 1535): see MANGROVE.] = MANGROVE. Also *attrib.*, as ***mangle-bark, tree***.

[1597 Hartwell tr. *Pigafetta's Congo* iv. 24 The..barke of the tree which is called Manghi. (Orig. *di quell'albore nomato manghi.*)] 1613 Purchas *Pilgrimage* viii. ii. (1614) 733 Mangle is the name of a Tree, which multiplieth it selfe into a wood. [Cf. *ibid.* 698 *marg.*: Andrew Battell saith, That the tree which thus strangely multiplies itselfe is called the Manga tree.] 1693 *Phil. Trans.* XVII. 621 Two sorts of the Mangle-Tree, of the *Arbor de Raiz* kind, though no Figg. 1760–72 tr. *Juan & Ulloa's Voy.* (ed. 3) I. 171 In its neighbourhood [Guayaquil]..are great numbers of mangles, or mangrove trees. 1824 tr. *Spink & Martius' Trav. Brazil* I. 217 *note*, The mangle or mangrove tree. 1885 *U.S. Cons. Rep.* No. 59. 268 (Cent.) Mangle-bark is principally used in tanning leather.

mangle ('mæŋg(ə)l), *sb.*[3] [a. Du. *mangel* masc. (= G. *mangel* fem., recorded from the 18th c.), app. short for the synonymous *mangelstok*, f. stem of *mangelen* to mangle, f. MDu. *mange* (= MHG., mod.G. *mange*), a mangle, in early use also a mangonel. The Du. and G. word is ultimately from the Gr. μάγγανον (see MANGONEL), but its history has not been precisely traced: cf. the med.L. forms *mango, manga*. For the sense cf. It. *mangano*, 'a kind of presse to press buckrom, fustian, or died linnen cloth, to make it have a luster or glasse' (Florio 1598).] **a.** A machine for rolling and pressing linen and cotton clothing etc. after washing; in its older form, an oblong rectangular wooden chest filled with stones, worked backwards and forwards by a rack and pinion arrangement (or, earlier, by straps wound round a roller worked by a handle), and resting upon two cylinders, which were thus rolled with great pressure over the fabric spread upon a polished table beneath; now consisting of two or more cylinders working one upon another. Cf. CALENDER *sb.*[1] 2.

The possession of a mangle, for the use of which a small sum was charged, is, among the poorer class of English cottagers, a common means of earning money. The question 'Has your mother sold her mangle?' (quot. 1836–7) was at one time the commonest piece of 'chaff' used by London street-boys.

1774 in *Titles Patents* (1854) I. 193 A grant unto Hugh Oxenham,..carpenter and mangle maker, of his new invented mangle of an entirely new construction..to answer all the purposes of mangles without the incumbrance of weight. 1793 *Regal Rambler* 73, I might mention the mangle, also a curious machine, for pressing fine linen. 1836–7 Dickens *Sk. Boz, Scenes* xx, The only answer we obtained was a playful inquiry whether our maternal parent had disposed of her mangle. 1891 Hardy *Noble Dames* 186 While she, like a mangle, would start on a sudden in a contrary course, and end where she began.

b. *attrib.*, as ***mangle-keeper, -maker, -room, worker***; **mangle-board** [Da. *manglebræt*], a board with which linen and cotton may be pressed and smoothed; **mangle-wheel**, a wheel which, by an ingenious adjustment of rack and pinion, causes the movable part of a mangle to travel backwards and forwards, while the wheel itself rotates in only one direction; applied also to a similar wheel in textile machines; similarly **mangle pinion, rack**.

1774 Mangle maker [see above]. 1799 *Hull Advertiser* 12 Oct. 1/1 A very excellent Mansion House..with..mangle room. 1839 Ure *Dict. Arts*, etc. 798 The mangle wheel, has been introduced..into the machinery of the textile manufactures. 1858 Simmonds *Dict. Trade, Mangle-keeper*, the owner of a mangle; a smoother of linen. 1875 Knight *Dict. Mech.* 1383/2 *Mangle-rack*, a rack having teeth on opposite sides, engaged by a pinion which meshes with the opposite sides alternately. 1884 McLaren *Spinning* 141 By a series of wheels the mangle pinion shaft A A is worked, which drives the mangle pinion x, and this drives the mangle wheel. 1891 *Labour Commission Gloss., Mangle Workers*, the attendants at the mangles used for finishing jute and linen fabrics. 1892 E. Rowe *Hints on Chip-Carving* iii. 47 The border..may be seen on a mangle-board from Jutland, dated 1708. 1928 *Daily Express* 22 June 12/6 The exhibits include various examples from Denmark, Sweden, Norway and Holland... Dates on the mangleboards go back as far as 1590.

c. *fig.* A bicycle. *Austral. slang.*

1941 Baker *Dict. Austral. Slang* 45 *Mangle*, a bicycle. 1965 G. McInnes *Road to Gundagai* viii. 122 'Where's the grid?' 'My bike!' 'Yeah, the old mangle.'

mangle ('mæŋg(ə)l), *v.*[1] Also 5–6 mangel, 6 mangyll. [ad. AF. *mangler, mahangler* (cf. med.L. *mangulare* in a Fr. document of 1361), app. a frequentative form of *mahaignier*: see MAIM *v.* But cf. obs. F. *mangonner* 'to mangle or disfigure by mangling' (Cotgr.).]

1. *trans.* To hack, cut, or lacerate (a person or his members) by repeated blows; to reduce, by cutting, tearing, or crushing, to a more or less unrecognizable condition. †Formerly sometimes, to mutilate. †Also with *out*.

c 1400 *Destr. Troy* 5704 Who..Were..Martrid & murthrid, manglit in peses. c 1450 *Merlin* 445 The cristin neuer cessed to kille and to sle, and mangeled alle that thei myght take. 1526 *Pilgr. Perf.* (W. de W. 1531) 257 b, The.. blessed body thus mangled, torne & rent, lyenge in y[e] lappe of that gloryous virgyn his mother. 1574 Hellowes *Gueuara's Fam. Ep.* (1584) 339 But the Moores..mangled him and his men in peeces. 1600 Rowlands *Lett. Humours Blood* ii. 8 Or Mincepie-like Ile mangle out the slaue. 1611 Bible *2 Macc.* vii. 13 Now when this man was dead also, they tormented and mangled the fourth in like maner. 1632 J. Pory in Ellis *Orig. Lett.* Ser. ii. III. 272 It mist his eyes, yet it pitifully mangled his visage. 1678 Wanley *Wond. Lit. World* v. ii. §68. 471/2 His beautiful Empress, whom a young Burgundian..had most despitefully mangled, cutting off both her Nose and Ears. 1791 Gouv. Morris in Sparks *Life & Writ.* (1832) II. 138 Next morning two men were lanterned and mangled in the Parisian taste. 1829 Scott *Anne of G.* ii, I will see my Arthur once more, ere the wolf and the eagle mangle him. 1855 Macaulay *Hist. Eng.* xxii. IV. 737 A human head was found severed from the body..and so frightfully mangled that no feature could be recognised.

absol. 1818 Shelley *Rev. Islam* vi. iv, The red artillery's bolt mangling among them falls.

b. *transf.* and *fig.*

1579 Lyly *Euphues* (Arb.) 106 Both so mangled with repulse..and almost murthered by disdaine, that [etc.]. 1592 Shaks. *Rom. & Jul.* iii. iii. 51 How hast thou the hart ..To mangle me with that word, banished? 1713 Steele *Guard.* No. 17 ¶10 The Lock Hospital..is a receptacle for all sufferers mangled by this iniquity.

2. To cut or hack (a material thing) in a rough manner, so as to damage and disfigure; †to divide into rough or ragged parts.

1530 Palsgr. 632/2, I mangle a thyng, I disfygure it with cuttyng of it in peces or without order... You have mangylled this meate horrybly, it is nat to sette afore no honest man now. 1578 Lyte *Dodoens* iv. lxiv. 526 Cotton Thistel..beareth great large leaues al to mangled and cut by the edges. 1610 Holland tr. *Camden's Scot.* 37 The country runneth out in length and breadth, all mangled with fishfull pools: and in some places with rising mountaines. 1638 Junius *Paint. Ancients* 177 They did respect gemmes more than to mangle them with cutting. 1746 Smollett *Reproof* 124 But lo! a swarm of harpies intervene, To ravage, mangle, and pollute the scene! 1784 Cowper *Tiroc.* 303 The bench on which we sat while deep employed, Though mangled, hacked, and hewed, not yet destroyed.

3. *fig.* Now chiefly: To render (words) almost unrecognizable by mispronunciation; to spoil by gross blundering or falsification (a quotation, the text of an author). Formerly often (now rarely): To mutilate, deprive of essential parts, subject to cruel injury.

1533 Sir T. More *Confut. Tindale* ii. iv. Wks. 538/2 Tindal shal haue no cause to saye that I deface hys gaye goodlye tale, by mangling of his matter. 1559 Bp. Scot in Strype *Ann. Ref.* (1709) I. ii. App. x. 448 The reste of the Sacraments, which be eyther clearly taken awaye, or else mangled..by this newe booke. 1592 Shaks. *Rom. & Jul.* iii. ii. 99 Ah poore my Lord, what tongue shall smooth thy name, When I thy three houres wife haue mangled it. 1607 —— *Cor.* iii. i. 158 Your dishonor Mangles true judgement. 1641 Milton *Animadv.* i. Wks. 1851 III. 189 Remember how they mangle our Brittish names abroad. a 1683 Sidney *Disc. Govt.* iii. xlvi. (1704) 420 Queen Elizabeth..did not go about to mangle Acts of Parliament. 1700 Dryden *Fables* Pref., Wks. (Globe) 503 It was also necessary sometimes to restore the sense of Chaucer, which was lost or mangled in the errors of the press. 1738 Swift *Pol. Conversat.* Introd. 84 Such a Project..would intolerably mangle my Scheme. 1768–74 Tucker *Lt. Nat.* (1834) II. 443 Go to an Italian opera and you will hear the singers so clip and mangle their words, that..you will lose even the little sense they contain. 1873 Dixon *Two Queens* I. iv. iii. 191 To give up Rouen and Bordeaux would be to mangle France. 1901 *Athenæum* 27 July 121/1 Why mangle Virgil with a stupid 'hæc mortalia tangunt'?

absol. 1641 Milton *Ch. Govt.* i. vi. Wks. 1851 III. 122 If schisme parted the congregations before, now it rent and mangl'd, now it rag'd.

mangle ('mæŋg(ə)l), *v.*[2] [f. MANGLE *sb.*[3], or perh. a. Du. *mangelen* = G. *mangeln*.]

1. *trans.* To press smooth with a mangle.

1775 Ash *Suppl., Mangle*, to smooth linen by means of a mangle. 1790 in *Abridg. Specif. Patents, Bleaching*, etc. (1859) 51 A machine or machines for mangling and washing every article made of linen [etc.] that will bear washing. 1798 *Trans. Soc. Arts* XVI. 303 The Model of a machine for Mangling Linen. 1810 *Splendid Follies* I. 119 Mrs. Squasham desired her humble duty, and had had them [*sc.* clothes] mangled... Mangle the d—l!..exclaimed Sponge. .. I'll mangle every bone in her skin. 1837 Dickens *Pickw.* xv, Might have got up my linen as I came along..—queer thing to have it mangled when it's on one.

2. To beat (lead) flat on a roller.

1880 Lomas *Alkali Trade* 28 The process of mangling [lead]..consists in rolling the sheet tightly round a wooden mandril,..beating it meanwhile..with the plumber's mallet.

mangled ('mæŋg(ə)ld), *ppl. a.*[1] [f. MANGLE *v.*[1] + -ED[1].] In senses of the vb.

1561 T. Norton *Calvin's Inst.* i. 42 Yet are they not ashamed to picke out certaine mangled sentences. 1564 Becon *Wks.* I. Gen. Pref. B iv, He is a mangled minister, which eyther teacheth well & liueth euil, or liueth wel and teacheth euill. 1627 Drayton *Agincourt* 33 These [birds] came in deed On their owne mangled Carkases to feed. 1641 Milton *Animadv.* i. Wks. 1851 III. 194 The mangl'd pieces of a gash't Serpent. 1668 Culpepper & Cole *Barthol. Anat.* ii. xi. 124 According as the Voice comes to the Ear, intire or mangled. 1719 De Foe *Crusoe* ii. ix, Their poor mangled comrade. 1770 *Junius Lett.* Pref. 13 A multitude of spurious, mangled publications of the *Letters of Junius*. 1779 Forrest *Voy. N. Guinea* 64, I took him by the hand, and, pointing to the mangled anchor, laughed. 1841 D'Israeli *Amen. Lit.* (1867) 546 Most of our old plays come before us in a corrupt and mangled state. 1869 Freeman *Norm. Conq.* (1875) III. xi. 31 The mangled form of the martyr of Evesham.

Hence †'**mangledly** *adv.*, in a mangled manner.

1657 Sergeant *Schism Dispach't* 466 But why..do you go about to show that I put not down the Authors words aright, but mangledly and corruptly.

mangled ('mæŋg(ə)ld), *ppl. a.*[2] [f. MANGLE *v.*[2] + -ED[1]] Pressed in a mangle.

1775 in Ash *Suppl.* 1855 Thackeray *Newcomes* v, A.. freshly mangled surplice.

mangler ('mæŋglə(r)). [f. MANGLE *v.*[1] + -ER[1].]

1. One who mangles, in various senses of the vb.

In the first quot. the identity of the word is doubtful: cf. MONGER *sb.*

1561–2 *Reg. Privy Council Scot.* I. 201 Charge all and sindry flescheouris and manglaris of flesche. 1581 J. Bell *Haddon's Answ. Osor.* 194 They be nothyng els but.. manglers and spoylers of the best part and power of Gods Grace. 1583 Nowell & W. Day *Rep. Conference w. Campion* 14 Campion..hath charged vs as rasers, manglers, and spoylers of the holy Scriptures. 1624 Gataker *Transubst.* 61 Hee speaketh in these wordes..which this mangler of him omitteth. a 1723 Tickell *To Sir G. Kneller* 48 After thee may rise an impious line, Coarse manglers of the human face divine. 1800–24 Campbell *To Mem. of Span. Patriots* v, Manglers of the martyr's earthly frame!

2. ? *U.S.* A mincing-machine.

1875 Knight *Dict. Mech.* 1383/2 *Mangler*, a machine for grinding meat, to render it more easy to masticate or to stew.

mangler[2] ('mæŋglə(r)). [f. MANGLE *v.*[2] + -ER[1].]

1. One who smoothes fabric in a mangle.

a 1845 Hood *To Scotch Girl* 12 This industrious part Of washer, wearer, mangler, presser, stamper. 1885 R. L. & F. Stevenson *Dynamiter* ii. 9 A ticket announcing the business of the mangler.

2. An appliance for mangling clothes (forming part of a composite machine).

1882 *Echo* 17 May 7 (advt.) Unrivalled 'Villa' washer, wringer, and mangler.

mangling ('mæŋglɪŋ), *vbl. sb.*[1] [f. MANGLE *v.*[1] + -ING[1].] The action of MANGLE *v.*[1]

a **1652** J. SMITH *Sel. Disc.* ix. 407 Without any mincing or mangling of the words. **1727** SWIFT *Let. Eng. Tongue* Wks. 1755 II. I. 188 Most of the books we see now-a-days, are full of those manglings and abbreviations. **1807** *Med. Jrnl.* XVII. 245 He did not intend to declare positively, that the mangling of a vesicle..could not..produce so much mischief. **1902** *Daily Chron.* 29 Mar. 5/1 The mangling of British names by French newspapers is an old story.

mangling ('mæŋglɪŋ), *vbl. sb.*[2] [f. MANGLE *v.*[2] + -ING[1].] The pressing of linen, etc., in a mangle. Also *attrib.*

1775 in ASH *Suppl.* **1824** in *Spirit Pub. Jrnls.* (1825) 181 He has commenced business in Drury-Lane, in the Mangling Department. **1833** J. HOLLAND *Manuf. Metal* II. 254 By this machine the operation of mangling was well enough done.

mangling ('mæŋglɪŋ), *ppl. a. rare.* [f. MANGLE *v.*[1] + -ING[2].] That mangles, in the senses of the vb.

1592 SHAKS. *Ven. & Ad.* 1065 And then she reprehends her mangling eye, That makes more gashes, where no breach should be. **1794** SOUTHEY *Sonn. Slave Trade* iii, Gasping he lies..While that inhuman driver lifts on high The mangling scourge. **1813** SCOTT *Rokeby* VI. xxxiii, As mute as fox 'mongst mangling hounds.

Hence **'manglingly** *adv.*, in a mangling manner.

1608 T. MORTON *Preamb. Encounter* 13 Repeating the Latine, yet but manglingly.

mangnel(e, obs. form of MANGONEL.

mangnifyer, obs. form of MAGNIFIER.

mango ('mæŋgəʊ), *sb.*[1] Pl. **mangoes, -gos** ('mæŋgəʊz). Forms: 6–7 **manga(s**, 7 **mangue, manggo, mengue**, 7– **mango(e.** [a. Pg. *manga* (whence F. *mangue*, †*mengue*, mod.L. *mang(h)as*, the source of some Eng. forms), a. Malay *mangā*, a. Tamil *mān-kāy* (*mān* mango-tree + *kāy* = fruit).]

1. The fruit of *Mangifera indica* (N.O. *Anacardiaceæ*), a tree extensively cultivated in India and other tropical countries; it is a fleshy drupe, with more or less of a turpentine flavour; the best kinds are highly esteemed for eating ripe; the green fruit is used for pickles and conserves.

1582 N. LICHEFIELD tr. *Castanheda's Conq. E. Ind.* I. xvi. 42 The one sort of these [fruits] is called Lacas [*read* Iacas] and the other Mangas. **1598** W. PHILLIP *Linschoten* I. li. 94 The Mangas is inwardly yealowish, but in cutting it is waterish... The season when Mangas are ripe is in Lent. **1655** TERRY *Voy. E. India* 96 Another most excellent Fruit they have, called a Manggo. **1681** DRYDEN *Prol., 'Gallants, a bashful poet'* 28 Mangos and berries, whose nourishment is little, Though not for food, are yet preserved for pickle. **1727** ARBUTHNOT *John Bull* Postscr. ch. x, How he long'd for Mangos, Spices and Indian Birds-Nests. **1891** S. DICKINSON in *Boston* (Mass.) *Jrnl.* 21 Feb. 5/3 Bananas, pineapples, mangoes, and grenadillos are plentiful in Fiji.

2. The tree producing this fruit.

1678 J. PHILLIPS tr. *Tavernier's Trav.* II. I. iv. 34 All along the high-way, there grows a vast number of great Trees, which they call Mangues. **1693** *Phil. Trans.* XVII. 683 We have a compleat History of that Pruniferous Tree, called Mango by the English. *c* **1796** T. TWINING *Trav. Amer.* (1894) 172 It appears to me that the cajoor-tree of Bengal might be successfully introduced into the Southern States, as also possibly the mango. **1825** *Gentl. Mag.* XCV. I. 318 The mango, with the 'bread-fruit tree' was brought here [i.e. Jamaica] from Otaheite, about 30 years ago. **1871** KINGSLEY *At Last* ii, Handsome houses..embowered in mangos, tamarinds, and palmistes. **1903** *Pilot* 22 Aug. 173/1 Long groves of palm and mango and bamboo.

3. With prefixed word, applied to various other trees and their fruits, as **mountain mango**, *Clusia flava* (West Indies); †**water-mango** (*Barbados*), some West Indian fruit-tree (see quot. 1700); **West India mango**, the anchovy pear (*Grias cauliflora*); **wild mango (tree)**, (*a*) the bread-tree of Western Africa (*Irvingia barteri*); (*b*) = *mountain mango*; (*c*) *Spondias mangifera* of India.

1700 PLUKENET *Mantissa* (1769) 126 Manghas aquæ Americana, folio subrotundo, Barbadensibus Water Mangoes dicta. **1774** LONG *Hist. Jamaica* III. 810 Anchovy Pear or West India Mango. **1813** W. AINSLIE *Mat. Med. Hindostan* 222 Wild Mango. *Spondias Mangifera*. Lin... This fruit has got its name from its resemblance to a Mango. **1866** *Treas. Bot.* 628/1 The drupaceous fruits of two at least of the three species [of *Irvingia*] known are edible, and known under the name of Wild Mangoes. *Ibid.* 717/1 Mango ..Mountain or Wild, *Clusia flava*. **1878** H. M. STANLEY *Dark Cont.* II. xiii. 365 Wild mango-tree.

4. *Cookery.* A pickle, esp. of melons or cucumbers, resembling that made of green mangoes. (Cf. MANGO *v.*)

1699 EVELYN *Acetaria* App., Mango of Cucumbers. *Ibid.*, To make a Mango with them [i.e. walnuts]. **1728** E. S[MITH] *Compl. Housew.* (ed. 2) 59 To make Melon Mangoes. **1828–32** WEBSTER, *Mango*, a green muskmelon pickled. **1845** MISS ACTON *Mod. Cookery* (ed. 2) 503 The peaches may be converted into excellent mangoes by [etc.]. **1859** BARTLETT *Dict. Amer.*, *Mango*. We apply this name to a green musk-melon stuffed with horse-radish,..etc., and then pickled.

5. Short for *mango-bird, mango-fish*.

1819 REES *Cycl.*, *Mango*, in Ornithology, a species of *Trochilus*. **1879** ROSSITER *Dict. Sci. Terms*, *Mango*..2. A fish = *Polynemus risua*.

6. *attrib.* and *Comb.*, as ***mango blossom, bud, -chutney, -fruit, grove, pickle, -seed, -spray, -tree***; **mango-bird**, (*a*) an oriole (*Oriolus kundoo*), native of India; (*b*) a humming-bird (*Lampornis mango*), native of Jamaica; **mango-fish**, a golden-coloured fish, *Polynemus paradiseus* or *risua*, inhabiting the tropical seas between India and the Malay archipelago; the tupsee; **mango-fool**, a dish made of mangoes beaten to a pulp and mixed with cream or milk; **mango-ginger**, the pungent root of an East Indian plant (*Curcuma Amada*) nearly allied to turmeric; **mango-humming-bird**, *Lampornis mango*; **mango-showers**, 'used in Madras for showers which fall in March and April, when the mangoes begin to ripen' (Y.); **mango-tope**, a grove or plantation of mangoes; **mango (tree) trick**, an Indian juggling trick in which a mango-tree appears to spring up and bear fruit within an hour or two.

1738 ALBIN *Nat. Hist. Birds* III. 45 This Bird I had by the Name of the *Mango Bird, which I believe to be an imposed Name: It is one of the Humming Birds. **1839** JERDON in *Madras Jrnl.* X. 262 *Oriolus melanocephalus* L.—Black headed Mango bird or Oriole. **1841** ELPHINSTONE *Hist. Ind.* I. 289 The languid odour of the *mangoe blossoms. **1861** DORA GREENWELL *Poems* 104 The *Mango buds grow pale. **1751** G. EDWARDS *Nat. Hist. Birds*, etc. IV. 208, I believe it is call'd a *Mango-Fish, because it is of the Colour that Fruit bears when ripe. **1835** MACAULAY in Trevelyan *Life* (1876) I. 420 We support nature..by means of plenty of eggs, mango-fish, snipe-pies, and frequently a hot beef-steak. **1864** TREVELYAN *Compet. Wallah* (1866) 117 Roast kid and mint-sauce, and *mango-fool. **1681** R. KNOX *Hist. Ceylon* I A Tree the Natives call Ambo, (which bears the *Mango-fruit). **1840** PAXTON *Bot. Dict.*, *Mango ginger, see *Curcuma Amada*. **1800** *Asiat. Ann. Reg., Misc. Tr.* 256 A pretty thick *mangoe grove, on the south-west end of the town. **1782** LATHAM *Gen. Syn. Birds* II. 758 *Mango Humming-Bird. **1699** EVELYN *Acetaria* 22 The *Mango Pickle. **1903** *Blackw. Mag.* Apr. 467/2 A spearhead..shaped like a *mango-seed. **1879** E. ARNOLD *Lt. Asia* (1889) 37 In the *mango sprays The sun-birds flashed. **1800** *Asiat. Ann. Reg., Misc. Tr.* 200 The *mangoe tope in the middle of the village. **1687** A. LOVELL tr. *Thevenot's Trav.* II. 175 *Mango-Trees. **1698** FRYER *Acc. E. India & P.* 192 Others [Juglers] presented a Mock-Creation of a Mango-Tree. **1888** *Scientific American* 26 May 327/1 The celebrated *Mango tree trick. **1889** S. LAING *Probl. Future* vii. 182 The *mango and other tricks of Indian jugglers.

†**'mango**, *sb.*[2] *Obs. rare*[−1]. [a. L. *mango*.] A slave dealer.

1601 B. JONSON *Poetaster* III. i, And your fat Foole there, my Mango, bring him too [cf. *supra*, You mangonizing slave].

mango ('mæŋgəʊ), *sb.*[3] (See quot.)

1870 J. W. SLATER *Man. Colours* 114 *Mango*, a name given in the linen districts of Ireland to bleaching-powder and bleaching liquor.

†**'mango**, *v. Cookery. Obs.* [f. MANGO *sb.*[1]] *trans.* To pickle as green mangoes are pickled.

1728 E. SMITH *Compl. Housew.* (ed. 2) 63 To mango Cucumbers. Cut a little Slip out of the side of the Cucumber [etc.].

man-god.

1. One who is both man and God, or is both a man and a god. (Cf. GOD-MAN.)

When applied to Christ now written with capital initials.

1597 J. PAYNE *Royal Exch.* 45 Yt may be sayde that Marie was the Mother of God, in asmoche as he was Man-god. **1720** WELTON *Suffer. Son of God* II. xxix. 750 Can any one behold this Man-God, after He had given such infallible Proofs of His Divinity,..and not stand amaz'd at the Depths of the Divine Councils? **1839** BAILEY *Festus* xxii. (1852) 396 The Lord, Man-God, re-appears. **1864** KINGSLEY *Rom. & Teut.* 81 A Divus Cæsar, the man-god by whose head all nations swore. **1865** tr. *Strauss' New Life Jesus* II. II. xciii. 377 The Man-God of ecclesiastical doctrine. **1878** D. BOUCICAULT in *N. Amer. Rev.* CXXVI. 51 Prometheus, in the eyes of the Greek, was a man-god.

2. *occas.* **a.** A deified man. **b.** A god having the form of a man.

1826 GEN. P. THOMPSON *Exerc.* (1842) III. 381 The Christian world was sunk in the worship..of men-gods, and women-gods. **1878** *N. Amer. Rev.* CXXVII. 50 The old idolaters cut down a tree and made a man-god figure out of it.

mangold(-wurzel): see MANGEL(-WURZEL).

mangole, obs. form of MANGONEL.

‖**mangona** ('mæŋgənə). [med.L.: see next.] = MANGONEL.

1856 *Ecclesiologist* XVII. 116 The trébuchet..is another name for the mangona—an engine for discharging stones. [In some recent Dicts.]

mangonel ('mæŋgənɛl). *Obs.* exc. *Hist.* Forms: α. 3 **mangonele**, 3–4 **-genel**, 4 **-gunel, -genele, -gurnele**, 4–5 **mangnel**, 5 **maungenele, mangonelle**, 7 **-ell, manchonel**, 9 **manganel(l**, 4– **mangonel.** β. 3 **magnel**, 4 **-nale**, 4– 5 **-nelle**, 5 **maggenell, magonneaul, maygnelle**, 6–7 **magonel(l.** γ. 5 **mangole.** [a. OF. *mangonel*, also *mangonelle* fem. (mod.F. *mangonneau*; cf. Pr. *manganel*, It. *manganella*), dim. f. late L. *mangona, mangonum, mangōn-em*, ad. Gr. μάγγανον an engine of war, a pulley, etc.: see MANGLE *sb.*] A military engine used for casting stones and other missiles against an enemy's position.

[**1194** in J. HODGSON *Pipe Rolls Cumbld.*, etc. (1847) 173 Pro Maisremo ad Petrarium et Mangonell', vjs.] **1297** R. GLOUC. (Rolls) 8124 þat me ne miȝte noȝt ise bote arwen & flon, & stones out of liþeren & of magnels al so. *a* **1300** in *Pol. Songs* (Camden) 69 He saisede the mulne for a castel,..He wende that the sayles were mangonel. **13..** *K. Alis.* 1208 Alisaundre heom asailed fast, And with mangnelis to heom cast. *c* **1330** *Arth. & Merl.* 2430 (Kölbing), Our King Vterpendragon Him assailed..wiþ mangunels casteinge. *c* **1400** tr. *Secreta Secret., Gov. Lordsh.* 111 And if þou shall assayll castels, vse Instrumentz castyng stones, as Mangoles or Perrerers. *c* **1400** *Rom. Rose* 6279 Withouten stroke it mot be take Of trepeget or mangonel. **1489** CAXTON *Faytes of A.* II. xxxv. 154 The deffence aienst the said engyns were gode mangonnelles & grete bombardes. **1599** THYNNE *Animadv.* (1875) 41 The trepegett and magonell beinge all one. **1605** CAMDEN *Rem.* (1657) 205 Our nation had the practice..of mangonels..wherewith they used to cast mil-stones. **1795** SOUTHEY *Joan of Arc* VIII. 158 O'er the bayle..The assailants pass'd with all their mangonels. **1819** SCOTT *Ivanhoe* xxvii, You may win the wall in spite both of bow and mangonel. **1877** MISS YONGE *Cameos* III. viii. 68 He had only yielded it because his duchess was frightened by the mangonels of the besiegers.

†**'mangonism.** *Obs.* [a. F. *mangonisme*, f. L. *mangōn-*, *mango* broker, dealer in vamped goods: see -ISM.]

1. (See quot.)

1656 BLOUNT *Glossogr.* [copying Cotgr.], *Mangonism*, the craft of pampering, trimming or setting out saleable things.

2. A method of treating plants contrary to nature in order to produce changes in their growth.

1691 EVELYN *Kal. Hort., March* 41 Let Gentlemen and Ladies..trust little by Mangonisme, Insuccations, or Medicine to alter the Species, or indeed the Forms and Shapes of Flowers considerably. **1693** —— *De la Quint. Compl. Gard.* Dict. s.v. *a* **1722** LISLE *Husb.* (1752) 136 The flower or fruit, either in bulk or number, may not equally succeed by such mangonism.

†**'mangonist.** *Obs.* [f. L. *mangōn-* (see prec.) + -IST.] One who furbishes up inferior wares for sale.

1605 MARSTON *Dutch Courtesan* I. A4, The common bosome of a money Creature, One that sels humane flesh: a Mangonist. **1698** *Money masters all Things* 77 The Mangonist does feed and graith his Horse, In hopes that he thereby may fill his Purse.

†**,mangoni'zation.** *Obs.* [f. next + -ATION.] The action of 'mangonizing' or tricking out for sale.

1660 FISHER *Rusticks Alarm* Wks. (1679) 382 Was there ever the like piece of..meer Mangonization of matters made before by any Master in Israel as this. **1678** CUDWORTH *Intell. Syst.* I. iv. §15. 281 A kind of Mangonization of it [paganism] to render it more vendible and plausible.

†**'mangonize**, *v. Obs.* [ad. late L. *mangōnizāre*, f. L. *mangōn-, mango* (see MANGONISM).]

1. *trans.* To furbish up (inferior wares) for sale.

1623 COCKERAM, *Mangonize*, to polish for better sale. **1656** BLOUNT *Glossogr.*, *Mangonize*.

2. *intr.* To traffic in slaves.

1601 B. JONSON *Poetaster* III. i, No you mangonizing slaue, I will not part from 'hem.

†**mangony.** *Obs. rare*[−1]. [ad. L. *mangōnium*, f. *mangōn-* (see prec.).] = MANGONISM 1 and 2.

1623 COCKERAM, *Mangonie*, the Art to make things saleable. **1657** TOMLINSON *Renou's Disp.* 229 [Hortensian Mallows] which by culture and mangony will grow to a tree.

mangoost, mangor: see MONGOOSE, MANGOUR.

mangosteen ('mæŋgɒsti:n). Forms: 6 **mangestain**, 7 **mancoustan, mangosthan, mangustan**, 8 **mangastan, mangostane, mangoustan**, 8–9 **mangostan, mangusteen**, 9 **mangostin, mangoostan, mangastene, mangostein**, 8– **mangosteen.** [a. Malay *mangustan*.]

1. The fruit of the East Indian tree *Garcinia Mangostana* (N.O. *Guttiferæ*). It is about the size of an apple, with a thick reddish-brown rind, and a white juicy pulp of delicious flavour.

1598 W. PHILLIP tr. *Linschoten* I. liv. 96/2 There are yet other fruites, as Brindoijns, Durijndois, Iamboloens, Mangestains, and other such like fruites. **1660** F. BROOKE tr. *Le Blanc's Trav.* 87 Durions, Mancoustan, and Bananes. **1707** FUNNELL *Voy.* x. 286 The Mangastan is about the bigness of a Golden-Runnet. **1797** SIR G. STAUNTON *Macartney's Emb. China* I. 274 In March, among other fruits, the mangosteen was ripe. **1806** BARROW *Voy. Cochin China* 185 Mangoostan. **1845** DARWIN *Voy. Nat.* xx. 455 Mangostin. **1852** F. A. NEALE *Resid. Siam* xii. 194 That prince of all earthly fruits, the mangostein.

2. The tree producing this fruit.

1734 ZOLLMAN in *Phil. Trans.* XXXVIII. 232 The Mangostans is a kind of Pomiferous Tree, which grows in

the Molucca Islands. **1797** *Monthly Mag.* III. 208 Martin had introduced into the botanic garden there [Cayenne] the Ravengara, the Mangoustan, the Clove tree [etc.]. **1871** KINGSLEY *At Last* v, A group of young Mangosteens.

3. wild mangosteen (tree), *Embryopteris glutinifera*.

1753 CHAMBERS *Cycl. Supp.* s.v., There is a sort of wild Mangoustan, called by the Portuguese, *mato*, which grows in the woods both in the East Indies and in America. **1866** *Treas. Bot.* 717/1. **1885** G. S. FORBES *Wild Life in Canara* 42 Near at hand were two or three wild mangosteen trees.

4. A name used in Barbados for the jujube, *Zizyphus mauritiana*.

1750 G. HUGHES *Nat. Hist. Barbados* v. 134 The Dunktree, or Mangustine. This is a middle-sized Tree. **1859** BARTLETT *Dict. Amer.* (ed. 2) 263 *Mangosteen*, in Barbadoes this name is given to the Jujube (*Ziziphus jujube*). **1965** E. G. B. GOODING et al. *Flora Barbados* 272 (*heading*) *Zizyphus mauritiana*.. *Z. jujuba* (L.).. Mangustine.. Shrub or small tree, 2–4·5 m., young stems tomentose.

mangouay, obs. form of MAGUEY.

‖**mangour.** *Obs.* Also 6 **mangor,** 7 **mangur.** [Turkish *mangir* (Redhouse).] An obsolete Turkish copper coin.

1585 T. WASHINGTON tr. *Nicholay's Voy.* III. xxii. 112b, A Mangor, which is the 8. part of an Aspre. **1617** MORYSON *Itin.* I. 293 Sixteene brasse Mangouri made one silver Asper. **1683** T. SMITH *Acc. City Prusa* in *Misc. Cur.* (1708) III. 65 A Mangur is an ugly old Copper Piece. **1687** A. LOVELL tr. *Thevenot's Trav.* I. 67 They have also half Quadrins, which they call Mangours. *Ibid.* II. 158. **1696** tr. *Du Mont's Voy. Levant* xxiv. 329 He made a very considerable Addition to the usual Profits of that Office, by inventing..a certain Copper Coin, call'd Mangours.

mangoust(e, obs. form of MONGOOSE.

'man-grass. *W. Indies.* [Cf. MAND *sb.*[2]: but the currency of an East-Indian word in Barbados in 1672 would need explanation.] The name in Barbados for the gramineous plant *Eleusine indica*.

1672 R. BLOME *Descr. Jamaica*, etc. 77 (Barbados) The Mangrass-Tree, which is of an exceeding greatness. **1848** SCHOMBURGK *Hist. Barbados* 586 *Eleusina indica*,..Man Grass.

mangrel, mangrie: see MONGREL, MANGERY.

mangrove[1] ('mæŋgrəʊv). Also 7 **mangrowe, mangrave.** [Of obscure history. Synonymous words app. connected are Pg. *mangue* (16th c.), Sp. *mangle* (Oviedo 1535, who applies it to S. American species), whence F. *manglé* (16th c.), later *mangle* (now applied to the fruit only, the name of the tree being *manglier*). The Malay *maŋgi-maŋgi* mangrove (not now current in the Malay Peninsula, but recorded in early Dicts.) is usually regarded as the ultimate source, but it is difficult to account on this view for the early appearance of Sp. *mangle* referring to America. The Eng. forms *mangrowe, -grave* are unexplained (but cf. the word-play in quot. 1613); the mod. form is doubtless due to assimilation to GROVE *sb.*]

1. Any tree or shrub of the genus *Rhizophora*, or the allied genus *Bruguiera* (N. O. *Rhizophoraceæ*); esp. the ***common mangrove***, *R. Mangle*.

The genus *Rhizophora* is extensively represented in both hemispheres. The species are all tropical, growing in the mud on the sea-shore down to low-water-mark; they have large masses of interlacing roots above ground, which intercept mud and weeds, and thus cause the land to encroach on the sea. ***red mangrove*** (see also 2d): a name given to a West Indian variety of the Common Mangrove, formerly separated as *R. Candel*; also in Australia, to *Bruguiera rheedii*.

1613 W. C. *Plain Descr. Barmudas* F2b, Amongst all the rest there growes a kinde of tree called Mangrowes, they grow very strangely, & would make a man wonder to see the manner of their growing. **1657** R. LIGON *Barbadoes* 72 The mangrave is a tree of such note as she must not be forgotten. **1697** DAMPIER *Voy.* I. 151 Low swampy Land, overgrown with Red Mangroves. **1772–84** *Cook's Voy.* (1790) I. 193 A large lagoon, by the sides of which grows the true mangrove, such as is found in the West-Indies. **1845** DARWIN *Voy. Nat.* xxi. 498 The channel..was bordered on each side by mangroves, which sprang like a miniature forest out of the greasy mud-banks. **1889** MAIDEN *Usef. Native Plants* 316 *Bruguiera Rheedii*..Red Mangrove.

¶ Ligon's description of the 'mangrave' confuses it (as Sloane pointed out) with the Mahoe (see MAHOE[1] 1). Hence some later writers have applied the name mangrove-tree to the Mahoe.

2. Applied, on account of similarity of habit and appearance, to various other plants. **a.** Any tree or shrub of the genus *Avicennia* (N.O. *Verbenaceæ*), esp. the ***white mangrove*** (*A. officinalis*) found in Brazil and Australasia, and the ***black*** or ***olive mangrove*** (*A. nitida*) of tropical America and Africa. **b. button mangrove,** a small W. African tree, *Conocarpus erectus* (N.O. *Combretaceæ*). Also called ***Zaragoza mangrove*** (*Treas. Bot.* 1866). **c. white mangrove,** *Laguncularia racemosa* (N.O. *Combretaceæ*), found in the West Indies. **d.** In Australasia (see Morris *Austral Eng.* 1898) used with various qualifications in the names of certain plants indigenous or cultivated there, as **milky mangrove,** *Excœcaria Agallocha* (N.O. *Euphorbiaceæ*); **native mangrove** (in Tasmania), a leguminous tree, *Acacia longifolia*; **red mangrove** (see also 1), *Heritiera littoralis* (N.O. *Sterculiaceæ*); **river mangrove,** an East Indian tree, *Ægiceras majus* (N.O. *Myrsineæ*), naturalized in Australia; **rope mangrove,** *Hibiscus arboreus*.

1683 J. POYNTZ *Tobago* 29 White Mangrove is of little use, save only to make Ropes with. **1697** DAMPIER *Voy.* I. 54 The black Mangrove is the largest Tree. **1750** G. HUGHES *Barbados* 199 It is called the Rope-Mangrove, from the Use that is made of the Bark of it to make Ropes or Halters for Cattle. **1830** LINDLEY *Nat. Syst. Bot.* 238 Avicennia tomentosa, the White Mangrove of Brazil. **1887** MOLONEY *Forestry W. Afr.* 352 Button Mangrove (*Conocarpus erecta*, Jacq.). **1889** MAIDEN *Usef. Native Plants* 555 *Heritiera littoralis*..'Red Mangrove' of Queensland.

3. *attrib.*, as ***mangrove bark, bush, jungle, root, swamp, thicket, tree, wood***; **mangrove cascabel,** a South American rattlesnake; **mangrove crab,** some kind of crustacean of Jamaica; **mangrove cuckoo,** a North American cuckoo, *Coccyzus minor*; **mangrove family,** the *Rhizophoraceæ*; **mangrove fly,** a West African dipterous insect, *Chrysops dimidiatus*; **mangrove-grape (tree)** ?*Obs.*, ?*Coccoloba uvifera*; **mangrove-hen,** in Jamaica, a species of rail, probably *Rallus longirostris*; **mangrove-myrtle,** an Indian myrtaceous tree, *Barringtonia acutangula*; **mangrove oyster,** an edible oyster which grows upon the submerged roots of mangroves; **mangrove snapper,** a sparoid fish, *Lutjanus aurorubens*, native of the West Indies and the adjacent coast of America northward to South Carolina; **mangrove tannin,** a soluble extract of the bark of the mangrove.

1792 *Act 32 Geo. III*, c. 49 §2 Red *Mangrove Bark is subject to a Duty. **1897** *Allbutt's Syst. Med.* II. 1085, I have tried many other drugs..including..mangrove bark. **1796** MORSE *Amer. Geog.* I. 718 Low sandy islands and marshes, covered with *mangrove bushes. **1871** KINGSLEY *At Last* xiii, We found..two large snakes... They were, the Negros told us, 'Dormillons', or '*Mangrove Cascabel', a species as yet, I believe, undescribed. **1756** P. BROWNE *Jamaica* (1789) 422 The *Mangrove-Crab. This species is very common. **1782** LATHAM *Gen. Syn. Birds* I. II. 537 *Mangrove Cuckow. **1859** S. F. BAIRD *Catal. N. Amer. Birds* 71 (Smithsonian Misc. Collect. II) *Coccygus minor* Cab. Mangrove Cuckoo. **1883** MOLONEY *W. Afr. Fisheries* 42 (Fish. Exh. Publ.), The trees on which oysters are usually to be found in the tropics are of the *mangrove family. **1897** *Allbutt's Syst. Med.* II. 1067 A blood-sucking dipterous insect—*Chrysops dimidiatus* the '*mangrove fly'. **1696** SLOANE *Catal. Plant. Jamaica* 184 The *Mangrove Grape-tree. **1753** CHAMBERS *Cycl. Supp.* App., *Mangrove-grape* [identified with the *Guajabara* or 'seaside-grape']. **1760** J. LEE *Introd. Bot.* App. 313 Grape, Mangrove, *Polygonum*. **1842** HILL in Gosse *Birds Jamaica* (1847) 367, I..found that the *Mangrove-hens had been searching for small crabs. **1849** E. B. EASTWICK *Dry Leaves* 210 The North Point of the Richel mouth, which is covered with *mangrove jungle. **1847** LEICHHARDT *Jrnl. Overland Exped.* ix. 289 As its foliage and the manner of its growth resemble the mangrove, we called it the *mangrove-myrtle. **1683** J. POYNTZ *Tobago* 23 The *Mangrove Oyster. **1883** MOLONEY *W. Afr. Fisheries* 42 (Fish. Exh. Publ.), Mangrove oysters are not as much sought after as bed or rock oysters. **1699** DAMPIER *Voy.* II. II. 17 The *Mangrove-Roots that grow by the sides of the Creeks are loaden with them [*sc.* Oysters]. **1734** MORTIMER in *Phil. Trans.* XXXVIII. 316 The *Mangrove Snapper [*printed* Suapper]. It is esteemed pretty good Food. **1884** G. B. GOODE, etc. *Nat. Hist. Aquatic Anim.* I. 397 The 'Mangrove Snapper' of Charleston..is a much more slender..fish. **1851–6** WOODWARD *Mollusca* 298 In the mud of rivers, and in *mangrove swamps. **1894** *Nation* (N.Y.) 6 Sept. 176/3 *Mangrove-tannin comes principally from India. **1851** H. MELVILLE *Whale* xii. 61 A low tongue of land, covered with *mangrove thickets. **1672** W. HUGHES *Amer. Physician* 98 This tree is [in Jamaica] most familiarly called the *Mangrove-Tree, or by some the Oyster-Tree. **1697** DAMPIER *Voy.* I. 54 There are 3 sorts of Mangrove-Trees, black, red and white. **1855** KINGSLEY *Westw. Ho!* xx, A low line of *mangrove-wood, backed by primaeval forest.

mangrove[2]. An alleged name of a fish.

1828–32 in WEBSTER (citing Pennant).

manguay, obs. form of MAGUEY.

‖**mangue** (mæŋg). [a. F. *mangue*, perh. a colonial shortening of *Mangouste* MONGOOSE.] The KUSIMANSE (*Crossarchus obscurus*).

1840 *Cuvier's Anim. Kingd.* 93 The Mangue... Has the muzzle, teeth, pouch, and gait of the Surikate. **1843** *Penny Cycl.* XXVI. 409/1.

mangue, mangunel: see MANGO, MANGONEL.

mangur, -gurnele: see MANGOUR, MANGONEL.

mangustan, -een, vars. MANGOSTEEN.

mangy ('meɪndʒɪ), *a.* Also 6 **mangye,** 6–7 **maungy, mangie,** 7 **maingy,** 7, 9 **mangey.** [f. MANGE *sb.* + -Y.]

1. Having the mange; of the nature of or caused by the mange. †In 16–17th c. also of human beings or their ailments: Scabby (*obs.*).

1526 SKELTON *Magnyf.* (E.E.T.S.) 1123 *Fol.* In faythe, there is not a better dogge... *Fan.* Ye, but trowest thou that he be not maungey? *c* **1540** HEYWOOD *Four P. P.* 629 A goodly thynge for dogges that be mangy. **1571** in W. H. TURNER *Select. Rec. Oxford* (1880) 336 Any kynde of mangy cattle or horses infected wth the glaunders of the chyne. **1614** MARKHAM *Cheap Husb.* I. xl. 29 If the Mayne be mangie you shall annoynt it with Butter and Brimstone. **1647** TRAPP *Comm. Jas.* i. 25 So shalt thou see thy face..so shamefully sawcy, mangy, pocky and scabbed. **1683** TRYON *Way to Health* 68 Many Leperous and Mangy Diseases. **1688** *Persec. Piedmont* 40 By continual lying..these poor People were become so mangy, that their very skin..parted from their Flesh. *c* **1720** W. GIBSON *Farrier's Guide* II. xlix. (1738) 185 Rub the Mangy places gently with a woollen Cloth. **1743** BULKELEY & CUMMINS *Voy. S. Seas* 131 They had a mangey Dog. **1806** *Med. Jrnl.* XV. 157 In my last communication, I made a few remarks on Dr. Rowley's ox-faced boy; in my present I propose to give a short account of his mangey girl. **1889** J. K. JEROME *Three Men in Boat* 207 A French poodle,..mangy about the middle.

fig. **1606** DEKKER *Sev. Sinnes* VI. (Arb.) 39 And..being rubd with quicksiluer, which they loue because they haue mangy consciences.

Comb. **1609** DEKKER *Guls Horne-bk.* i. 8 To shew that you truly loath this polluted and mangy-fisted world.

2. Squalid, poverty-stricken, shabby, 'seedy'.

a **1529** SKELTON *Dk. Albany* 138 Euer to remayne In wretched beggary And maungy misery. **1546** BALE *Eng. Votaries* I. (1550) 32 He [hauynge] nothynge of them agayne but a mangye monkes cowle and hys buryall in Paules. **1594** NASHE *Unfort. Trav.* I Pantofles..mangie at the toes, lyke an Ape about the mouth. **1844** THACKERAY *Contrib. to Punch* Wks. (Biog. ed.) VI. 81 The Royal Palace..resembles Newgate whitewashed and standing on a sort of mangy desert. **1859** SALA *Twice round Clock* (1861) 172 It is full of bad smells, mangy little shops,..and bad characters. **1860** MAYHEW *Upp. Rhine* ii. §i. 62 The..gardens are little better than a mangey coppice. **1883** *Longm. Mag.* July 258 A mangy old cloth coat is preferred. **1886** H. F. LESTER *Under two Fig Trees* 177 A sprig or two of mangy grass.

3. Used as a general term of contempt: Beggarly, mean, 'lousy'.

1538 BALE *Thre Lawes* E vij b, The lorde doth not regarde Your mangy mutterynge. *a* **1625** FLETCHER *Woman's Prize* IV. i, You have abused me..such a way that shames the name of Husband, Such a malicious-mangy way. *a* **1653** G. DANIEL *Idylls* iii. 124 If some bolder wakes The Mangie Scribe tells what ye Pigeon speakes. **1694** MOTTEUX *Rabelais* IV. lxvi. (1737) 271 Thou mangy Noddy-peak! **1896** J. K. SNOWDEN *Web of Old Weaver* x. 127, I cannot see that it much benefits any man to tell him all these mangy quaverings. **1922** JOYCE *Ulysses* 735 We have to be thankful for our mangy cup of tea. *Ibid.*, The old mangy parcel he sent at Xmas. **1930** R. CAMPBELL *Poems* 10 The poet wags his mangy stump of rhyme. **1942** BERREY & VAN DEN BARK *Amer. Thes. Slang* § 30/4 Poor; mean; contemptible ..*mangy*.

mangy, obs. form of MANGE *sb.*[1]

mangys, obs. pl. of MANCHE.

mangzie, variant of MANYIE *Sc. Obs.*

manhad(d)en, variant of MENHADEN.

man-'handle, *v.* [f. MAN *sb.*[1] + HANDLE *v.*; in sense 3 cf. dial. *manangle* (Devon) to mangle, which may belong to MANGLE *v.* (AF. *mahangler*).]

†**1.** *trans.* To handle or wield a tool. *Obs.*

1457 R. FANNANDE *Mon. Christ's Hosp. Abingdon* xiii, The Mattok was man-handeled right wele a whyle.

2. *Naut.*, etc. 'To move by force of men, without levers or tackles' (Adm. Smyth).

1867 SMYTH *Sailor's Word-bk.* **1894** *Times* 27 Jan. 10/2 The larger weapons will be worked by electricity, but are also capable of being man-handled. **1902** *Blackw. Mag.* Mar. 331/2 I'm going to man-handle my gun down the slope. **1903** *Daily Chron.* 19 Feb. 3/3 Stalwart Punjabis.. hand out bags of stores,..or manhandle a fractious, restive animal.

3. *slang.* To handle roughly; to pull or hustle about.

1865 *Hotten's Slang Dict.*, *Man-handle*, to use a person roughly, as to take him prisoner, turn him out of a room, give him a beating. **1886** *Century Mag.* Apr. 905/1 Two of our roughs began to haze him: but they mistook their calling, and in two minutes were so mauled and manhandled that it was reported aft. **1888** CLARK RUSSELL *Death Ship* II. 253, I..was for..manhandling him, ghost or no ghost. **1891** KIPLING *Light that failed* iii, I'll catch you and man-handle you, and you'll die. **1894** R. H. DAVIS *Eng. Cousins* 24 The cry of 'Welsher',..which sometimes on an English race-course means death from man-handling.

'man-hater. A hater of mankind; a misanthrope. Also *occas.*, a hater of the male sex.

1579–80 NORTH *Plutarch*, *Alcib.* (1598) 218 Timon surnamed Misanthropus (as who would say, Loup-garou, or the manhater). **1641** MILTON *Ch. Govt.* II. Concl. 60 What will these man-haters yet with more despight and mischiefe do? **1678** SHADWELL (*title*) The History of Timon of Athens, the Man-hater. **1714** MANDEVILLE *Fab. Bees* (1725) I. 386, I would have no sagacious critick pronounce me a man-hater... I am a great lover of company. **1759** GOLDSM. *Pol. Learn.* vi, Rousseau, of Geneva, a professed man-hater. **1827** CARLYLE *Germ. Lit.* in *Misc. Ess.* (1872) I. 32 The grimmest manhaters..will be found in abundance. **1885** STEVENSON *Pr. Otto* II. ii. 85 Essentially he is to be numbered among the man-haters. **1896** *Westm. Gaz.* 5 Mar. 3/3 It is in no way true that we are man-haters and discontented women.

Manhattan (mæn'hætən). Also **manhattan**. [The name of the island on which the older part of New York is situated.] Used *ellipt.* for **Manhattan cocktail**, a cocktail made of vermouth and whisky with a dash of bitters.

1890 B. HALL *Turnover Club* 16 This order was as follows ..the Actor, 'A Manhattan cocktail'. **1895** C. D. WARNER *Golden House* v. 43 He and old Fairfax sipped their five-o'clock 'Manhattan'. **1906** *Mrs. Beeton's Bk. Househ. Managem.* xlix. 1511 *Manhattan.* Ingredients: ½ a wineglassful of vermouth, ½ a wineglassful of whisky, 30 drops of green syrup, 10 drops of Angostura bitters, 6 drops of Curaçoa, [etc.]. **1909** [see BRONX 1]. **1937** M. SHARP *Nutmeg Tree* viii. 84 If I could have one [a cocktail], I'd have a Manhattan. **1955** W. GADDIS *Recognitions* II. iv. 474 The dumpy woman was drinking a manhattan. **1963** C. D. SIMAK *They walked like Men* xii. 70 The bartender set my drink before me and began fixing her Manhattan. **1972** D. BLOODWORTH *Any Number can Play* x. 80 Larry returned with soda-water for Max and a manhattan for himself.

Man,hatta'nese, *sb.* and *a.* [f. prec. + -ESE.] **A.** *sb.* A native or inhabitant of New York or Manhattan Island; usu. *collect.*; also, the dialect of New York. **B.** *adj.* Of or pertaining to New York or Manhattan Island.

1828 J. F. COOPER *Notions Amer.* I. 200 The New Yorkers (how much better is the word Manhattanese!) cherish the clumsy inconvenient entrances. **1842** —— *Wing-and-Wing* I. 11 Hundreds collected on the spot, which, in Manhattanese parlance, would probably have been called a battery. *Ibid.* 193 This gentleman was an American, and a native Manhattanese; his near relatives, of the same name, still residing in New York. **1844** *Knickerbocker* XXIII. 586 The sound of India-crackers and the pleasant smell of lobsters is already perceptible to the senses of the awakening Manhattanese. **1875** W. WHITMAN in *Gentl. Mag.* Dec. 706, I was Manhattanese, friendly, and proud. **1904** *Forum* (N.Y.) Jan.–Mar. 410 'Her Own Way'..brings together a number of highly piquant Manhattanese types of to-day, sketched with captivating drollery. **1908** S. FORD *Side-Stepping with Shorty* vi. 91 He drops the imitation society talk that he likes to spout, and switches to straight Manhattanese. **1909** *Nation* (N.Y.) 9 Sept. 238/3 Perhaps the most amusing thing in the book is an interpolated story based on a difference of opinion between New Englanders and Manhattanese on the subject of doughnuts and crullers. **1942** BERREY & VAN DEN BARK *Amer. Thes. Slang* § 181/5 *Manhattanese*, language peculiar to New Yorkers.

†**'manhead.** *Obs.* Forms: 3 **manede, monheade**, 3–4 **manhede**, 3–6 **manhed**, 4 **manhiede**, *Sc.* **manheide**, 4–5 **monhede**, 4–6 *Sc.* **manheid**, 5 **monhedde**, 6 **manheed**, 6–7 **manhead**. [f. MAN *sb.*¹ + -HEAD. Cf. MANHOOD.]

1. The state of being human; the condition of belonging to humanity; human nature.

c **1220** *Bestiary* 690 He..drowing ðolede in ure manhede. **1340** HAMPOLE *Pr. Consc.* 5253 Þe gude men sal se hym in manhed þan, With þe godhed, als God and man. *c* **1350** *Will. Palerne* 4390 Sone schal þe puple se þi semli face, In manhede & in minde as it out to bene. **1390** GOWER *Conf.* I. 144 Forthi, my Sone, tak good hiede So forto lede thi manhiede, That thou ne be noght lich a beste. *c* **1440** HYLTON *Scala Perf.* (W. de W. 1494) II. xxx, For in oure lorde Jhesu are two kyndes, the manhede and the godhede. **1450–1530** *Myrr. our Ladye* 228 For anon the godhed was unyed to the manhed in the vyrgyns wombe. **1543** BECON *New Years Gift* Wks. 1564 I. 177 b, He only receaued his fleshe and manhed of Mary. **1588** A. KING tr. *Canisius' Catech., Cert. Prayers* 26 b, Luke, ô maist meike maker, on the manheid of thy weal beloued sone, and haue mercie vpon thy warkmanship.

b. Human shape or form.

c **1330** *King of Tars* 426 The blake hound,..To hire spac in monhede, In whit ermure as a kniht.

2. The quality of being manly; manhood; virility; courage, valour.

c **1275** LAY. 24671 Bote he were þries ifonded in fihte, and his manede icud and him seolf icnowe. *c* **1350** *Will. Palerne* 431 Me þinkes, bi his menskful maneres & his man-hede, þat he is kome of god kin. **1375** BARBOUR *Bruce* I. 402 Bot off manheid and mekill mycht, Till Ector dar I nane comper. *c* **1420** *Anturs of Arth.* 351 Here commes ane errant kniȝte; Do him resone and riȝte, For þi manhede. *c* **1475** *Partenay* 92 He wold preue his vertu and manhede With noble knightes and peple worthi. **1500–20** DUNBAR *Poems* xlvi. 82 Lufe is causs of honour ay, Luve makis cowardis manheid to purchass. **1567** *Satir. Poems Reform.* iv. 148 Samson also, for manheid and prudence, All Israell that had in gouernance, Dalila desauit in vnder couertoure.

b. Manly dignity; the dignity of manhood.

c **1290** *S. Eng. Leg.* I. 74/106 He was þo þe cuyndeste englische man þat was of enie manhede. *c* **1320** *Sir Tristr.* 1840 Lesen y mot mi manhed Or ȝeld ysonde me fro.

3. Homage.

1297 R. GLOUC. (Rolls) 5197 Hii dude him anon hor manhede, & ne contekede nammore. *Ibid.* 8716 Þeruore monie heyemen ne dude him none manhede.

4. Humanity, humaneness, kindness.

1382 WYCLIF *Titus* iii. 4 The benygnyte, and humanite, *or manhed*, of our sauyour God. **1387** TREVISA *Higden* (Rolls) III. 429 Alisaundre dede it nouȝt for love but for manhede [1432–50 manhode, L. *non amoris sed humanitatis causa*]. *c* **1450** *St. Cuthbert* (Surtees) 1415 Cuthbert welcomed him with manhede.

'man-hole. A hole or opening in a floor, pavement, boiler, sewer, etc., through which a person may pass to gain access to certain parts. Also, a recess in a wall, etc., used as a place of refuge, e.g. to avoid passing trains; a hole in a covered boat or canoe for the accommodation of a rower or paddler.

1793 SMEATON *Edystone L.* §274 The center stone was made large enough to admit of an opening, from floor to floor, or Man-Hole, to be made through it. **1839** R. S. ROBINSON *Naut. Steam Eng.* 120 In the crown of the boiler is a large circular opening, called a man hole. **1841** *Penny Cycl.* XXI. 318/1 To make apertures or man-holes..to enable persons..to enter and cleanse the sewers. **1853** KANE *Grinnell Exp.* (1856) 477 The pah, or man-hole, as we would term it, is very nearly in the centre [of the kayak]. *c* **1860** H. STUART *Seaman's Catech.* 61 They are sent down the main hatchway by a strop and toggle in the man-hole. **1881** RAYMOND *Mining Gloss.*, *Man-hole*, Corn. The hole in a sollar through which men pass upon the ladder or from one ladder to the next. **1892** E. REEVES *Homeward Bound* 119 Each rower sits in a manhole [of a 'decked' boat]. **1893** *Law Times* XCV. 204/2 His horse's foot struck the cover of a manhole in the middle of the road, and it fell.

attrib. **1844** H. STEPHENS *Bk. Farm* II. 316 The man-hole door. **1884** *Health Exhib. Catal.* 55/2 Patent Ventilating Man-hole Cover for Sewers. **1900** *Engineering Mag.* xix. 742/2 Manhole plates..in the shape of ovals.

manhood ('mænhʊd). Forms: see MAN *sb.*¹ and -HOOD.

1. a. The state or condition of being human; human nature.

a **1225** *Leg. Kath.* 986 Þe godcundnesse of godd, for mennesse of his monhad. **1340** *Ayenb.* 12 Þe pridde article ..belongeþ to þe zone as to þe manhode; þet is to zigge ase þet he is man dyadlich. *c* **1511** *1st Eng. Bk. Amer.* (Arb.) Introd. 30/2 They say that in christo is alone the godhed without the manhod. **1529** MORE *Dyaloge* I. Wks. 155/2 All yᵉ textes that seme to make him lesse, be nothynge to be vnderstanden of his godhedde, but of his manhode onely. **1548–9** (Mar.) *Bk. Com. Prayer* Athan. Creed, Equall to the father as touchyng his Godhead: and inferior to the father as touchyng his manhode. *Ibid.*, By takyng of the manhode into God. **1667** MILTON *P.L.* III. 314 Therefore thy Humiliation shall exalt With thee thy Manhood also to this Throne; Here shalt thou sit incarnate. **1703** ROWE *Fair Penit.* I. i. 222 Keep..A little Pity to distinguish Manhood Lest other Men..should..judge you to be number'd with the Brutes. **1848** R. I. WILBERFORCE *Doctr. Incarn.* xv. (1852) 440 That real manhood of Christ our Lord, which binds Him at this moment to collective humanity. **1865** LOWELL *Harvard Commem. Ode* ix, Yea, Manhood hath a wider span And larger privilege of life than man.

b. The dignity of man.

c **1400** *Arth. & Merl.* (Linc. Inn MS.) 1172 (Kölbing) Ȝef y telle þis folk by fore, How þat þow ware gete and bore, Þanne schal hit sprynge wide and brode, Þen hastow lore þy manhod.

2. The state of being a man: **a.** as opposed to childhood; **b.** as opposed to womanhood.

1390 GOWER *Conf.* I. 185 This Elda triste in special Upon a knyht, whom fro childhode He hadde updrawe into manhode. **1601** WEEVER *Mirr. Mart.* C j b, When riper yeares and manhoode made vs strong, Then we knew much, and more still would be showing. **1611** SHAKS. *Cymb.* III. iv. 195 *Pis.* [To Imogen, about to disguise herself.] To some shade, And fit you to your Manhood. **1667** MILTON *P.L.* x. 148 Was shee made thy guide, Superior, or but equal, that to her Thou did'st resigne thy Manhood. *Ibid.* XI. 246 His starrie Helme unbuckl'd shew'd him prime In Manhood where Youth ended. **1725** WATTS *Logic* I. vi. §6 Methuselah, when he was nine hundred and sixty Years old,..was the same Person as when he was in his full Vigour of Manhood, or when he was an Infant, newly born. **1856** FROUDE *Hist. Eng.* (1858) I. ii. 109 Children, as they grew to manhood, inherited the duty of revenging their fathers' deaths. **1882** A. W. WARD *Dickens* iv. 86 One likes to think of him in these years of vigorous manhood.

fig. **1630** *R. Johnson's Kingd. & Commw.* 138 The three ages of France: her child-hood, till Pepin: her man-hood, till Capet; her old age, till now. **1841** MYERS *Cath. Th.* III. §34. 123 Is it a disposition befitting spiritual manhood? Is it not characteristically childish?

3. The qualities eminently becoming a man; manliness, courage, valour. *arch.*

1377 LANGL. *P. Pl.* B. III. 184 Ȝit I may as I myȝte menske the with ȝiftes, And mayntene thi manhode more than thow knoweste. *c* **1392** CHAUCER *Compl. Venus* 4 Remembraunce Upon the manhod and the worthinesse,..Of him whos I am al, whyl I may dure. *c* **1402** LYDG. *Compl. Bl. Knt.* 333 Notwithstondyng his manhode and his myght, Love unto him did ful grete unright. **1530** PALSGR. 500/2 Whan he is well whyttelled, he wyll crake goodly of his manhode. **1577–87** HOLINSHED *Chron.* I. 50/1 The Britains aswell with constant manhood, as skilfull practise,..auoided and beat from them the arrowes and darts. **1590** SHAKS. *Mids. N.* III. ii. 412 Follow my voice, we'l try no manhood here. **1600** HOLLAND *Livy* xxv. Argt. 544 That province had beene quite lost, but for the singular manhood and industrie of L. Martius a knight of Rome. **1618** ROWLANDS *Night Raven* (1620) 29 Tom of his manhood boasts That he like butter-flies esteemes all Ghoasts. **1829** HOOD *Eug. Aram* xvi, There was a manhood in her look That murder could not kill. **1853** WHITTIER *Hero* 75 Peace hath higher tests of manhood Than battle ever knew.

†**4.** Humanity, humaneness. *Obs.*

1432–50 [see MANHEAD 4, quot. 1387]. **1470–85** MALORY *Arthur* v. x. 177 And so wyll I yf thou wylt socoure and ayde me that I maye be crystned and byleue on god. And therof I requyre the of thy manhode. **1555** WATREMAN *Fardle Facions* II. iii. 126 Suche tendrenes had been shewen to two, or three [children], as the mothers loked for, and manhode ..doth require. **1571** GOLDING *Calvin on Ps.* lxix. 27 Inasmuche as manhod willeth to succour the afflicted.

†**5.** Homage. *Obs.*

1340 *Ayenb.* 19 He ys wel renay þet þet land þet he halt of his lhorde deth in-to þe hond of his uyende, and deþ him manhode. *Ibid.*, He deþ manhode to the dyeule, and becomþ his þrel.

6. Men collectively; the adult male members of a population, nation, or the like.

1588 *Copy Let. sent to Mendoza* 27 The Lord Strange, the Earls sonne, and all the manhood of Lancashire and Cheshire, would goe ouer the Seas and fetch the Earle home. **1601** HOLLAND *Pliny* I. 15 The whole manhood of Greece fought the battell of Salamis. **1609** —— *Amm. Marcell.* 115 There followed a multitude of all sorts and degrees, picked and chosen out of the manhood of the nations adjoyning. **1640** YORKE *Union Hon.*, *Battells* 1 In the Rere-guard was the Duke himselfe, with his whole manhoode of Normans.

7. *attrib.*: **manhood suffrage**, that form of popular election in which the suffrage is granted to all male citizens of lawful age not disqualified by crime, insanity, etc.

1859 DISRAELI in *Hansard Commons* 31 Mar. 1245 Why, Sir, I have no apprehension myself that if you had manhood suffrage tomorrow the honest, brave, and good-natured people of England would resort to pillage, incendiarism, and massacre. **1864** *Q. Rev.* CXVI. 262 If Mr Gladstone is generally supposed to have taken up the battle-cry of manhood suffrage, he has only himself to thank for it. **1867** JOHN 1ST EARL RUSSELL *Let.* 27 Mar. in B. & P. Russell *Amberley Papers* (1937) II. 24 Dizzy must know that, & I believe means 'Manhood suffrage'. **1873** tr. *Strauss' Old Faith & New* lxxxi. 329. **1877** R. LOWE in *Fortn. Rev.* Dec. 728.

'man-,hunter. A hunter of men; usually a contemptuous term for cannibals, slave-dealers, brigands, or the like.

1555 EDEN *Decades* 142 *marg.*, Manhunters. **1819** *Metropolis* II. 219 All blood-suckers and man hunters, be they adders, blood-hounds, bailiffs, or even certain attornies. **1851** MAYNE REID *Scalp Hunt.* xxiv. 179 It was a picture such as may be seen only in a bivouac of guerilleros, of brigands, of man-hunters. **1892** ZANGWILL *Bow Mystery* 23 The hardened old man-hunter's voice was not free from a tremor.

So **'man-hunting** *sb.* and *a.*; also **'man-hunt** *sb.*

1555 EDEN *Decades* To Rdr., A pray to those manhuntynge woolues. *Ibid.* 142 All the whiche gyue them selues onely to manhuntynge. **1867** SMYTH *Sailor's Word-bk.*, *Man-hunting*, the impress service. **1881** BESANT & RICE *Chapl. of Fleet* I. 203 One time there was the mischievous practice of man-hunting. **1897** *Daily News* 9 Mar. 6/1 Those regions of man-hunts and hideous blood orgies. **1898** *Ibid.* 31 Dec. 2/3 The man-hunting trials promoted by the Association of Bloodhound Breeders.

mani¹ ('mɑːnɪ). Also 8 **many**, 9 **mannee**. [a. Sp. *mani* (Pineda); prob. from some S. American language.]

1. A South American earth-nut (see quot. 1866).

1717 tr. *Frezier's Voy.* 186 They have..a Sort of Fruit there [at Pisco], which grows in a Cod that does not rise out of the Earth..The Inhabitants call it Many. *Ibid.*, *marg.*, Many Fruit. **1760–72** tr. *Juan & Ulloa's Voy.* (ed. 3) I. 78 Another fruit, called mani, is produced by a small plant. It is of the size and shape of a pine cone. **1825** *Gentl. Mag.* XCV. I. 318 The Jack-fruit, sweet sops, sour sops, mannees [etc.]. **1866** *Treas. Bot.* 717/2 *Mani*,..a Spanish name of the Ground Nut, *Arachis hypogæa.*

2. A South American tree (see quot. 1866).

1866 *Treas. Bot.* 757/1 *M[oronobea] coccinea*, the Hog Gum tree... In Guiana and Brazil, where it is called Mani or Oanani, the natives make torches with it. **1800** *Asiat. Ann. Reg., Misc. Tr.* 75 *note*, The mani-tree, which yields a timber that is almost imperishable.

‖**mani**² ('mɑːnɪ). [Tibetan *máṇi*, f. Skr. *maṇí* precious stone (as in the jewel-lotus prayer *om maṇi padme hum* 'Oh the lotus-jewel, Amen').] In full, ***mani wall***. A Tibetan 'prayer wall', covered with stones piously inscribed (see also quots.)

1863 E. SCHLAGINTWEIT *Buddhism in Tibet* xiii. 196 Mani, originally a Sanskrit word meaning 'a precious stone',..is used to designate walls of about six feet in height and four to eight feet in breadth. **1882** *Encycl. Brit.* XIV. 197/2 It [*sc.* the palace at Lé] is surrounded by poplar plantations, with manis and ch'hordtens beyond. *Ibid.*, 'Mani', a long stone wall, several feet wide, running along the roadside, covered with loose stones deposited by the passers-by, inscribed with the prayer or ejaculation, 'Om mani padme hom'. **1925** B. BEETHAM in E. F. Norton *Fight for Everest, 1924* I. viii. 171 The mani-walls (prayer-stones) had once been of an unusually imposing nature. **1952** H. W. TILMAN *Nepal Himalaya* iv. 39 The longest mani wall I have ever seen—nearly three hundred yards of it... On each side are flat stones with carved Buddhas or religious texts for the benefit of passers-by. **1953** TSUNG-LIEN SHEN & SHEN-CHI LIU *Tibet* v. 118 The approach to a village or monastery is marked by a *Mani* wall or by a pagoda. **1959** *Times* 23 May 7/6 The people here are Buddhist and there is abundant evidence of their faith—*mani* (or prayer) walls.

mania ('meɪnɪə). [a. L. *mania*, a. Gr. μανία, related to μαίνεσθαι (:—*manye-) to be mad, f. wk.-grade of the Indogermanic root **men-*, represented in many words referring to mental states, emotions, etc. (cf. esp. Gr. μῆνις rage, μένος mood, passion): see MIND *sb.* In 14–17th c. rarely in the Fr. form MANIE.]

1. a. Mental derangement characterized by great excitement, extravagant delusions and hallucinations, and, in its acute stage, by great violence. Now a more general term for a condition of over-excitement and restless activity, usually denominated according to its severity (see quot. 1971). Cf. *hypermania*, HYPOMANIA.

c **1400** *Lanfranc's Cirurg.* 266, & wiþinne .iij. daies Mania come to hir and was oute of hir witt. **1547** BOORDE *Brev. Health* ccxx. (1557) 75 *Mania* is the greke. In latin it is named *Insania* or *Furor*. In Englishe it is named a madnes or wodnes lyke a wylde beaste. **1650** BULWER *Anthropomet.* 207 Some in Mania or Melancholy madnesse, have attempted the same. **1788** 'A. PASQUIN' *Childr. Thespis* (1792) 62 As the Magi their foul incantations prepare, And with seeds of the *mania* impregnate the air! **1853** CARPENTER *Princ. Hum. Physiol.* (ed. 4) §830 The state of Mania..is usually characterized by the combination of complete derangement of the intellectual powers, with passionate excitement upon every point which in the least degree affects the feelings. **1925** J. RIVIERE et al. tr. *Freud's Coll. Papers* IV. 164 The most remarkable peculiarity of melancholia, and one most in need of explanation, is the tendency it displays to turn into mania accompanied by a completely opposite symptomatology. **1969** ULLMANN & KRASNER *Psychol. Approach Abnormal Behavior* II. xxi. 417/1 A person may gradually progress from hypomania to delirious mania over time, or the delirious mania may, in rare instances, be emitted without a 'warm-up' period. **1971** T. ROBERTS *Handbk. Psychiatric Nurses* II. 62 *Mania.* There are four main types:—Hypomania... Acute mania, producing a wild frenzied aggressive attack of excitement and over activity. Chronic mania sometimes called Scott's mania. Hypermania: delirious or Bell's mania. **1973** *Sci. Amer.* Sept. 117/3 Mania is manifested by psychic elation, increased motor activity, rapid speech and the quick flight of ideas. The stigmata of depression are melancholia, the slowing of thought, unusual thought content (for example overwhelming guilt over imagined transgressions and delusions of rotting away), motor retardation, sleep disturbances and preoccupation with bodily complaints.

b. Applied *rarely* to a similar condition in lower animals.

1607 TOPSELL *Four-f. Beasts* (1658) 272, I judged him [a horse] to be vexed with a melancholy madness called of the Physitians Mania, or rather Melancholia. **1879** W. L. LINDSAY *Mind Lower Anim.* I. 97 They [bees] are..liable to ..temporary epidemic excitement, delirium, or mania.

c. Inspired frenzy or madness. *rare.*

1886 C. A. BRIGGS *Messianic Proph.* i. 12 The prophetic mania comes upon a man like Saul.

2. a. Great excitement or enthusiasm resembling madness. Chiefly with *a* or *the*: A vehement passion or desire; also, in weaker sense (after F. *manie*), a 'craze', 'rage'. Const. *for*, *of*. Also, a period of great excitement affecting a body of persons.

1689 EVELYN *Corr.* (1879) III. 443 So vaine a thing it is to set ones heart vpon any thing of this nature with that passion & mania, that unsatiable Earle..did, to the detriment of his estate and family. **1791–1823** D'ISRAELI *Cur. Lit.* (1858) III. 303 At the restoration of letters,..there prevailed a mania for burying spurious antiquities. **1807** C. W. JANSON *Stranger Amer.* 385 The mania of land speculation. **1815** W. H. IRELAND *Scribbleomania* 243 Catalogues, with a few annotations on the mania of portrait collectors. **1837** HT. MARTINEAU *Soc. Amer.* III. 199, I was told at Washington.. that 'the people of New England do good by mania'. **1855** MACAULAY *Hist. Eng.* xix. IV. 322 A mania of which the symptoms were essentially the same with those of the mania of 1720..seized the public mind. **1878** JEVONS *Prim. Pol. Econ.* 122 A prudent man would never invest in any new thing during a mania or bubble. **1879** MCCARTHY *Own Times* II. xxiii. 196 He had a detestation for democratic doctrines which almost amounted to a mania. **1884** GILMOUR *Mongols* 149 The mania which possesses the Mongols for making pilgrimages.

b. with qualifying word prefixed, indicating the kind of 'mania', as ***railway***, ***tulip mania***, etc.

1777 in *N. E. Hist. & Gen. Reg.* (1872) XXVI. 259 The rage for building in England..is somewhat similar to the tulip mania in Holland. **1796** MORSE *Amer. Geog.* I. 600 During the rage of the paper currency mania. **1896** *Godey's Mag.* (U.S.) Apr. 448/1 The heart mania has extended to the watch, a favorite design showing two linked hearts set with pearls. **1903** *Daily Chron.* 13 Oct. 5/1 In the last decade of that century a canal mania raged, in many ways resembling the railway mania of some sixty years ago.

-mania, a terminal element, repr. Gr. μανία MANIA in composition.

There were in Gr. a few compounds in -μανία (rare and chiefly post-classical), expressing the general sense 'a certain kind of madness', or 'the state of being mad after some object', and corresponding as nouns of quality or condition to the related adjs. (a much more frequent formation) in -μανής = '-mad'. Examples are γυναικομανία mad passion for women, ἐρωτομανία love-madness, ἱππομανία mad love for horses, ὑδρομανία 'water-madness', hydrophobia. In the 16th and 17th c. a number of quasi-Greek compounds, denoting species of mania, were invented and used in medical Latin, and some of these, as *nymphomania*, have been adopted in Eng. Other technical or quasi-technical words, formed in the 19th c., are *kleptomania*, *lypemania*, *megalomania*. In the 17–18th c. the currency of F. *manie* in the sense of a 'craze' or passion (e.g. for some pursuit, or the collection of some class of objects) suggested the formation of a number of quasi-Gr. compounds such as *bibliomanie* mania for books, *métromanie* mania for metre, *mélomanie* mania for song; and hybrid formations such as *Anglomanie* mania for things English, *tulipomanie* mania for tulips. Several of these words have been adopted in Eng. with the ending *-mania*, and in the 19th c. it became somewhat common to invent nonce-words with this ending. Examples are **bancomania**, a craze for establishing banks; **Graiomania** [L. *Grai-us* Greek], passion for things Greek; **Italomania**, wild enthusiasm for Italy; **Queenomania**, (applied by Southey to the popular devotion to the cause of Queen Caroline); **scribbleomania**, a craze for scribbling. The sbs. in *-mania* have, actually or potentially, correlative sbs. in **-maniac**; the words in -MANE are of rare occurrence, and are viewed as Gallicisms.

1788 *Trifler* No. 8. 104 'Till the wide Nugae-mania spread. **1792** COLERIDGE *Lett.* (1895) I. 35, I never had the scribble-mania stronger on me than for these last three or four days. **1815** [W. H. IRELAND] (*title*), Scribbleomania. **1820** SOUTHEY in *Life & Corr.* (1850) V. 53 The Queenomania will probably die away ere long. **1837** *Blackw. Mag.* XLI. 848 During all the late fury of land-jobbing schemes in the west, of building extravagances in the east, of banco-mania everywhere,..the cotton manufacture alone remains unscathed. **1855** MAURICE *Learn. & Work.* 254 This..would be a fair representation of the motives and arguments which created the Roman Graiophobia. And the Roman Graio-mania in the young men will have had as intelligible an explanation. **1860** LD. DERBY in *Ld. Malmesbury's Mem.* (1884) II. 213 His Italomania and his Free Trade policy.

†**'maniable**, *a. Obs.* Also 6–7 **manyable**, (7 **mannyable**, **maineable**). [a. OF. *maniable*, f. *manier* to handle (= It. *maneggiare*: see MANAGE *v.*), f. L. *manus* hand.]

1. Easy to handle; flexible, pliable, workable.

1484 CAXTON *Chivalry* 64 Gauntelots..to receyue the strokes yf it were so that his other armures manyable faylled to hym. **1520** *St. Papers Hen. VIII*, VI. 55 *note*, For the nymble handlyng wheroff [the sworde] He hathe or knowythe no feate, but thowght it not manyable, and callyd the Admirall, and cawsed hym to feell the weght theroff. **1590** SIR J. SMYTH *Disc. Weapons* 4 b, Short, strong, and light arming daggers are more maniable. **1610** DONNE *Pseudo-martyr* 140 Those instruments of battery..were left off..because they were not so maniable and tractable, and apt for transportation, as these are. *a* **1612** RALEIGH *To P. Henry* Rem. (1661) 251 If she [a ship] be bigger she will be of lesse use,..lesse nimble, lesse mannyable. **1633** R. ASHLEY *Barri's Cochin China* D iv b, It [the elephant's trunk] is so flexible and maniable that he extendeth and turneth it as he list. **1654** EARL MONM. tr. *Bentivoglio's Warrs Flanders* 183 The earth about it is everywhere manyable, so as Trenches may easily be made. **1727** BRADLEY *Fam. Dict.* s.v. *Gimbels*, Your Business only is to make the Paste firm, and to knead it well; if it be not maniable, and that if you cannot draw it with your Hands.. you must beat it in a Mortar.

b. Of a person or his attributes: Manageable, tractable.

c **1596–1604** BACON *Helps Intell. Powers* Wks. 1859 VII. 100 And as to the will of Man, it is that which is most maniable and obedient as that which admitteth most medicines to cure and alter it. **1605** —— *Adv. Learn.* I. ii. §8 Learning doth make the minds of men gentle, generous, maniable, and pliant to government. **1628** LE GRYS tr. *Barclay's Argenis* 275 This rage, which was..not maniable by any prudence or counsell. **1630** LENNARD *Charron's Wisd.* II. ix. §3. 334 To be supple and maniable, to know how to rise and fall, to bring himselfe into order, when there is need.

2. That may be handled or felt, palpable.

1483 CAXTON *Gold. Leg.* 27/1 He is not manyable ne may not be handled. *c* **1520** ANDREWE *Noble Lyfe* I. xlii. I iij, The Motte..is a maniable worm, and yet it hydeth him in yᵉ clothe that it can scantly be sene. **1665** J. SERGEANT *Sure Footing* 64 Actions, Sacraments, and all other outward shows which could be invented to make such mysteries maniable. **1686** COTTON tr. *Montaigne* II. II. xii. 261 We.. leave to them [Beasts] for their Divident, Essential, Maniable, and Palpable Goods, as Peace, Repose [etc.].

maniac ('meɪnɪæk), *a.* and *sb.* Forms: 7 **maniacque**, 7–8 **maniack**, 8– **maniac**. [ad. late L. *maniac-us* (as if a. Gr. *μανιακ-ός), f. μανία MANIA. Cf. F. *maniaque.*] **A.** *adj.*

1. Affected with mania; raving with madness.

1604 R. CAWDREY *Table Alph.*, *Maniacque*, mad, braine sick. **1817** SHELLEY *Rev. Islam* x. xlii, So, she scourged forth the maniac multitude To rear this pyramid. **1825** SCOTT *Talism.* xviii, My words shall be those of the maniac outcast which I am.

transf. **1856** BRYANT *Serenade* x, The maniac winds, divorcing The turtle from his mate.

2. Of, pertaining to, or characterized by mania; belonging to or characteristic of a maniac.

1727 KINNEIR in *Phil. Trans.* XXXV. 347, I..us'd Camphire in Maniac Disorders. **1817** BYRON *Lam. of Tasso* iii, The..maniac cry Of minds and bodies in captivity. **1850** ROBERTSON *Serm.* Ser. III. iii. (1872) 35 Like maniac ravings. **1879** GEO. ELIOT *Coll. Breakf. P.* 236 To gaze with maniac stare.

b. Characterized by wild excitement; frantic.

1809 JEFFERSON *Writ.* (1830) IV. 127 In the present maniac state of Europe. **1840** DICKENS *Old C. Shop* xxxiv, The performance of a maniac hornpipe. **1862** R. VAUGHAN *Nonconformity* 320 To the government this maniac proceeding was a godsend.

B. *sb.* One who is affected with mania.

a **1763** SHENSTONE *Eleg.* XVI. xxvi, Scornful she spoke, and, heedless of reply The lovely maniac bounded o'er the plain. **1775** H. FARMER *Demoniacs N.T.* I. viii. 143 All their [*sc.* demoniacs'] symptoms agree with those of epileptics and maniacs, who fancied they had evil spirits within them. **1784** COWPER *Task* II. 663 And 'tis a fearful spectacle to see So many maniacs dancing in their chains. **1828** SCOTT *F. M. Perth* xxix, His eye rolled like that of a maniac in his fever fit. **1877** BLACK *Green Past.* xxxvi, As though he half expected this maniac to turn and bite him.

b. *attrib.* and *Comb.*, as in ***maniac-like*** adv.; also appositively as in ***maniac-maiden***.

1821 SHELLEY *Prometh. Unb.* IV. 470, I, a most enamoured maiden..Maniac-like around thee move. **1845** G. MURRAY *Islaford* 149 The maniac-maiden singeth aye Of love.

-maniac: see -MANIA.

maniacal (mə'naɪəkəl), *a.* [f. MANIAC + -AL¹.]

1. Affected with mania. Also *absol.*

1678 CUDWORTH *Intell. Syst.* I. v. 704 When maniacal persons..speak in languages which they had never learnt. **1800** *Med. Jrnl.* IV. 106 Another patient..became decidedly and violently maniacal. **1865** W. H. O. SANKEY *Mental Dis.* iii. (1866) 71 Maniacal patients are not necessarily irascible... The maniacal will answer, but speedily ramble again from the point.

2. Of, belonging to or of the nature of mania; characteristic of a maniac.

1701 GREW *Cosm. Sacra* III. i. 89 Epilepsys, and Maniacal Lunacies, do usually conform..to the Age of the Moon. **1748** HARTLEY *Observ. Man* II. iv. §3. 384 Maniacal and other Disorders. **1842** DE QUINCEY *Cicero* Wks. VI. 196 The extravagant, almost maniacal, assertion. **1866** *Cornh. Mag.* Aug. 227 In maniacal frenzy. **1899** CROCKETT *Kit Kennedy* 405 With a quick access of maniacal strength, the prisoner cast his guards..from him.

Hence **ma'niacally** *adv.*

1846 E. B. BARRETT 10 July in *Lett. R. Browning & E. B. B.* (1899) II. 323 Poor Haydon! Think what an agony life was to him..—the man seeing maniacally in all men the assassins of his fame! **1860** W. COLLINS *Wom. White* xiii. 77 An expression of maniacally intense hatred and fear. **1894** SALA *Things Seen* II. 79 He usually came home..either boisterously, lyrically, pugilistically, or maniacally drunk.

maniack, -acque, obs. forms of MANIAC.

manic ('mænɪk), *a.* [f. MANIA: see -IC.] **1.** Of, pertaining to, affected with, or resembling mania. Also as *sb.*, a person affected with mania.

1902 *Buck's Handbk. Med. Sci.* (rev. ed.) V. 124/1 She showed a typical picture of a manic excitement with great exhilaration, flight of ideas, and distractability. **1921** R. M. BARCLAY *Kraepelin's Manic-Depressive Insanity & Paranoia* 54 The conspicuous contrasts between manic and depressive attacks. **1922** R. S. WOODWORTH *Psychol.* xi. 259 In the excited insane condition known as 'mania' or the 'manic state', the patient is excessively distractible. **1957** P. LAFITTE *Person in Psychol.* vi. 75 The manic hopelessly flees the devil wherever he goes. **1957** *Observer* 6 Oct. 18/7 That manic transatlantic zing which is part of the fascination of the Marx Brothers. **1964** *New Statesman* 6 Mar. 367/1 Entirely faithful as expositor, Dr. Segal brings to bear her own contributions, particularly in regard to what she calls manic reparation.

2. *Comb.* **manic depression**, the condition of manic-depressive illness; **manic-depressive** *a.*, characterized by or affected with alternating periods of elation and mental depression; also *fig.*; hence as *sb.*, a person so affected.

1958 M. ARGYLE *Relig. Behaviour* ix. 108 The upper and middle classes have higher rates for manic depression and neurosis. **1964** —— *Psychol. & Social Probl.* vi. 78 Schizophrenia is thought by some to be inherited by two or more recessive genes, manic depression via two or more dominant ones. **1973** *Nature* 16 Feb. 480/1 A disproportionate number of patients with schizophrenia or manic-depression were born in the early months of the year. **1902** A. R. DEFENDORF *Clin. Psychiatry* 282 Manic-Depressive Insanity. This term is applied to that mental disorder which recurs..throughout the life of the individual and in which a defective hereditary endowment seems to be the..prominent etiological factor. **1931** E. WILSON *Axel's Castle* iii. 92 The modern psychologists would probably diagnose him as introverted, narcissistic and manic depressive. **1934** P. BOTTOME *Private Worlds* xxi. 206 A gland experiment which would help them to get a certain physical reaction from manic depressives. **1943** J. S. HUXLEY *Evolutionary Ethics* ii. 13 Complete alternation of conflicting moods is exemplified in manic-depressives. **1959** R. GRAVES *Coll. Poems* 315 Have seen two parallel red-ink lines drawn Under their manic-depressive bank accounts. **1961** J. HELLER *Catch-22* (1962) xxvii. 298 Greed depresses you. Crime depresses you. Corruption depresses you. You know, it wouldn't surprise me if you're a manic-depressive! **1961** L. MUMFORD *City in Hist.* xv. 520 It was the manic-depressive rhythm of the market, with its spurts and stoppages, that made the large urban centre so important to industry. **1970** *Jrnl. Gen. Psychol.* LXXXIII. 76 A study of the neurotic tendencies shown in dementia praecox and manic depressive insanity. **1973** *Sci. Amer.* Sept. 117/3 Manic-depressive psychosis is marked by severe disturbances in mood that are self-limited in time but are recurrent and frequently cyclic.

‖**manica** ('mænɪkə). [L.; cf. MANCHE.] A sleeve (*obs. rare*⁻⁰). ***manica Hippocratis*** = Hippocrates' sleeve: see HIPPOCRAS 2, HIPPOCRATES. Hence †**'manicated** *a.*, sleeved (*obs. rare*⁻⁰).

1641 FRENCH *Distill.* ii. (1651) 46 Let the Liquor runne through a bagge called *Manica Hippocratis* made of white Cotten. **1671** GREW *Anat. Plants* I. ii. §23 The Sap.. through this, as through a *Manica Hippocratis*, is still more finely filtred. **1727** BAILEY vol. II, *Manica*, a Sleeve, Gantlet or Glove. L. *Ibid.*, *Manicated*, wearing a Sleeve, Glove or Gantlet.

manicate ('mænɪkeɪt), *a. Bot.* [ad. L. *manicāt-us* furnished with sleeves.] (See quot.)

1832 LINDLEY *Introd. Bot.* 39 Hairs also give the following names to the surface of any thing:—*Manicate*, when interwoven into a mass that can be easily separated from the surface. **1866** in *Treas. Bot.*

Manichæan, Manichean (mænɪ'kiːən), *a.* and *sb.* Also 6 **Manichian.** [f. L. *Manichæus* (see MANICHEE) + -AN.]

A. *adj.* Of or pertaining to the Manichees or their doctrine; characteristic of a Manichee.

1638 CHILLINGW. *Relig. Prot.* I. Pref. §1 If any thing more then ordinary might be said in defence of the Manichean Doctrine. **1710** BERKELEY *Princ. Hum. Knowl.* §154 Favourers of Atheism or the Manichean Heresy. **1784** COWPER *Task* v. 444 As dreadful as the Manichean God. Ador'd through fear, strong only to destroy. **1851** D. WILSON *Preh. Ann.* (1863) II. IV. ii. 230 Manichean symbols being introduced on such monuments. **1855** MILMAN *Lat. Chr.* IX. viii. (1864) V. 385 In another respect the followers

of Peter de Brueys rejected the usages of the Church, but in no rigid or ascetic, and therefore no Manichean spirit.

B. *sb.* = MANICHEE.

1556 CLEMENT in Strype *Eccl. Mem.* (1721) III. App. lxi. 214 Arians Eutichians Manichians..and all other heretikes. **1686** HORNECK *Crucif. Jesus* xi. 203 The Marcionites and Manichæans of old, who taught, that Christ had no real or substantial body. **1739** S. BOYSE *Deity* 98 Could the wild Manichæan own that guide, The good would triumph, and the ill subside! **1793** D. STEWART *Outl. Mor. Philos.* II. ii. §293 The Manicheans account for the mixture of good and evil in the universe, by the opposite agencies of two co-eternal and independent principles. **1869** LECKY *Europ. Mor.* (1877) I. iii. 426 St. Augustine relates that when he was a Manichaean, his mother for a time refused even to sit at the same table with her erring child.

b. *transf.*

1873 MORLEY *Rousseau* II. x. 39 Rousseau was never a manichaean towards nature. To him she was all good and bounteous. **1885** *Times* (weekly ed.) 29 May 12/3 As they are not Manicheans, it follows that nothing exists but what is good.

Manichæanize, Manicheanize (ˌmænɪˈkiːənaɪz), *v.* [f. prec. + -IZE.] **a.** *intr.* To incline to Manichæan opinions. **b.** *trans.* To introduce Manichæan principles into. Hence **ˌManiˈchæanized** *ppl. a.*, **ˌManiˈchæanizing** *vbl. sb.*

1838 G. S. FABER *Inquiry* 236 *note*, The articles wherein they were charged with manicheanising. **1865** *Pall Mall G.* 8 Sept. 10/2 The adherents of a Manichæanised Christianity.

Manichæism, Manicheism (ˈmænɪkiːɪz(ə)m). Also 7 **Manichisme**. [f. *Manichæus* (see MANICHEE) + -ISM.] The doctrine or principles of the Manichees. Also *transf.*

1626 [FEATLEY] tr. *Parallel* D b, This Doctrine bringeth into the Church Manichisme. **1679** T. PULLER *Moderat. Ch. Eng.* vi. 143 Which doctrine of J. S. is condemned..as the pith of Manicheism. **1756–82** J. WARTON *Ess. Pope* (ed. 4) II. ix. 100 The gloomy and uncomfortable scheme of Scepticism and Manicheism. **1853** MAURICE *Proph. & Kings* vi. 97 The Manichaeism which would lead us to think that evil may at last triumph, or hold a divided empire with God. **1861** PEARSON *Early & Mid. Ages* 143 The charge of Manicheism was brought against the promoters of celibacy. **1871** TYLOR *Prim. Cult.* II. 300 Manichæism..is based on the doctrine of two antagonistic principles of good and evil. **1894** W. ARCHER *Theatr. 'World' 1893* 224 The time is past for the elementary Manicheism on which *The Tempter* is based. **1959** B. & R. NORTH tr. *Duverger's Political Parties* (ed. 2) p. xv, The elementary Marxist opposition of middle class to working class will also often be used... There are many more shades of social stratification than this rough manicheism suggests.

Manichæist (ˈmænɪkiːɪst). *rare*⁻¹. [f. as prec. + -IST.] = MANICHEE.

1880 T. A. SPALDING *Eliz. Demonol.* 17 The second principle is that of the Manichæists: the division of spirits into hostile camps, good and evil.

Manichæistic (ˌmænɪkiːˈɪstɪk), *a.* Also **Manicheistic**. [f. as MANICHÆIST: see -ISTIC.] Of the nature of Manichæism.

1924 O. LODGE *Making of Man* ii. 49 A Manichæistic conception of existence can never have been really satisfying. **1932** *Times Lit. Suppl.* 3 Mar. 148/3 With something of Manicheistic fury Miss Leader tracks down the sense of physical abjection and inferiority.

Manichean, -ize: see MANICHÆAN, -IZE.

Manichee (mænɪˈkiː). Also 4 *pl.* **Manaches**, 6 **Manichey**, *pl.* **Mani-, Manycheis, Manacheis**, 7 **Manachy**. [ad. late L. *Manichæus*, late Gr. Μανιχαῖος, from the name of the founder of the sect (variously recorded as *Manes* and *Manichæus*) who lived in Persia in the 3rd century after Christ.] An adherent of a religious system widely accepted from the third to the fifth century, composed of Gnostic Christian, Mazdean, and pagan elements.

The special feature of the system which the name chiefly suggests to modern readers is the dualistic theology, according to which Satan was represented as co-eternal with God.

a **1380** *St. Augustine* 103 in Horstm. *Altengl. Leg.* (1878) 63 Þe Manichees þat heretykes weren. *Ibid.* 576 Austin.. Ouercom þe Manaches erryng. **1533** MORE *Debell. Salem* v. Wks. 939/2 For a certaine sorte there wer of the heretikes that wer the Manicheis. **1560** DAUS tr. *Sleidane's Comm.* 91 Whan the Arrians,..and the Manycheis, sowed abroade their opinions. **1594** HOOKER *Eccl. Pol.* IV. vii. §2 Faustus the Manichey. **1641** HINDE *J. Bruen* v. 15 Augustine confesseth of himselfe, he was first a Manachy before he was a Preacher. **1649** JER. TAYLOR *Gt. Exemp.* I. iv. 130 A Manichee (a hæretick, that denyed God to be the maker of things visible). **1702** ECHARD *Eccl. Hist.* (1710) 644 Pope Leo said that the Devil reigned in all other heresies, but had rais'd his very throne in that of the Manichees. **1833** J. H. NEWMAN *Arians* II. iv. (1876) 195 The Manichees considered the Son and Spirit as necessary emanations from the Father. **1842** BROWNING *Soli. Sp. Cloister* vii, If I trip him just a-dying..Spin him round and send him flying Off to hell, a Manichee?

Manichian, obs. form of MANICHÆAN.

manichord (ˈmænɪkɔːd). *Obs.* exc. *Hist.* Forms: 7–8 **manicordion**, 8 **-ium**, (7 **manycord**), 7–9 **manicord**, 8– **manichord**. [a. F. *manicorde*, *manichordion*, corruptly a. med.L. **monochordium*, *monocordum*, a. late Gr. μονοχόρδιον, Gr. μονόχορδον MONOCHORD; the word was perh. associated by popular etymology with L. *manus* hand. Cf. It. *mana-*, *manicordo* (Florio).] = CLAVICHORD.

1611 COTGR., *Monochordiser des doigts*, to quauer with the fingers, to wag or play with them, as if he touched a Manicordion. **1668** in *12th Rep. Hist. MSS. Comm.* App. VII. 378 Paid..for Ketty's Many-cords 01 06 00. **1670** *Ibid.* 381 For a moneths teaching of Katy and Alice on the harpsicalls and manicords 01 00 00. **1710** in E. W. Dunbar *Soc. Life* (1865) 15, I can play on the Treble and Gambo, Viol, Virginelles and Manichords. **1730–6** BAILEY (folio), *Manicordium*, a musical instrument in form of a spinet. **1823** ROSCOE tr. *Sismondi's Lit. Eur.* (1846) I. v. 128 The manicord, or claricorde, was a sort of spinet resembling the virginals. **1830** MRS. BRAY *Fitz of F.* xvii. (1884) 148 She has a curious hand at the lute, and the manichord.

manicle, obs. form of MANACLE.

†**ˈmanicon**. *Obs.* [a. L. *manicon*, Gr. μανικόν, f. root of μανία MANIA, μαίνεσθαι to be insane.] A kind of nightshade, supposed to cause madness.

1678 BUTLER *Hud.* III. i. 324 Bewitch Hermetick-men to run Stark staring mad with Manicon. **1727** BAILEY vol. II, *Manicon*, an Herb call'd also *Dorychnion*, a Kind of Nightshade.

manicord, -cordion, -ium: see MANICHORD.

‖**manicou** (maniku). [Fr.] An opossum of the genus *Marmosa*, found in Central and South America.

1953 P. L. FERMOR *Violins of St.-Jacques* 28 The most remarkable [pets] were a family of manicous, the mother of which carried her dozen young about by twisting her tail parallel to her spine in order that they might loop their own round it and secure their positions on the parent back. **1968** E. LOVELACE *Schoolmaster* xi. 171, I will go late and headlight in the forest for manicou.

manicure (ˈmænɪkjʊə(r)), *sb.* [a. F. *manicure* (1877 in Littré *Suppl.* Add.), f. L. *manus* hand + *cūra* care. Cf. the earlier *pédicure*.]

1. One who professionally undertakes the care and treatment of the hands and finger-nails.

1880 *Melbourne Bulletin* 12 Nov. 7/3 When one has not been endowed with a perfect hand at birth,..the skill of a manicure will improve it. **1887** FINCK *Rom. Love & Pers. Beauty* II. 230 Manicures use acids in their shops, but the lemon is quite as good. **1893** F. M. CRAWFORD *Marion Darche* I. 41 Hands..which neither ordinary scrubbing nor the care of the manicure can ever keep clean.

2. a. The treatment and care of the hands and finger-nails.

1887 FINCK *Rom. Love & Pers. Beauty* II. 230 There are not nearly as many secrets in manicure as people imagine. **1900** PINERO *Gay Ld. Quex* I. 2 The instruments and toilet necessaries employed in the process of manicure.

b. *attrib.* ***manicure case, department, girl, parlour, scissors, set, stick***, etc.

1895 *Montgomery Ward Catal.* 255/3 Combination Toilet and Manicure Case..contains complete set of 12 white Florence toilet and manicure fittings. **1967** 'K. O'HARA' *Unknown Man* ii. 10 There was a chip out of one nail, so that she would need the manicure case. **1887** *Mod. Society* 23 July 749/2 A young lady employed in the manicure department of one of our most popular establishments. **1900** PINERO *Gay Ld. Quex* I. 1 The scene represents a manicure establishment in New Bond Street. **1922** S. LEWIS *Babbitt* xviii. 219 Young women who had recently been manicure girls. **1946** *Vogue* June 35/1 The manicure-girls stare contemptuously. **1890** *Pall Mall G.* 6 Jan. 6/1 A set of manicure instruments. **1912** *Collier's* 9 Nov. 11/3 Jack Zelig was a daily patron of a manicure parlor. **1893** *T. Eaton & Co. Catal.* Spring & Summer 35/3 Scissors, manicure, 25 c. **1913** J. WEBSTER *Daddy-Long-Legs* 194 Sawing off picture wire with manicure scissors. **1952** M. NORTON *Borrowers* ii. 17 Homily..unhooked the blade and handle of half a pair of manicure scissors from a nail on the wall. **1973** H. NIELSEN *Severed Key* i. 14 Keith..located the cosmetic case... 'Women usually carry a manicure scissors in these things,' he said. **1897** *Sears, Roebuck Catal.* 435/2 Manicure and Button-hook set, fancy, Solid Sterling Silver handles. **1945** E. BOWEN *Demon Lover* 72 A manicure-set in a purple box; all the objects..lay in grooves on white velvet. **1962** *Guardian* 5 Dec. 6/4 A really complete manicure set..for 22s 6d. **1909** E. BANKS *Mystery F. Farrington* 162 Orange-wood manicure sticks.

manicure (ˈmænɪkjʊə(r)), *v.* [f. prec.] *trans.* To apply manicure treatment to. Also *absol.*, *transf.* and *fig.* Hence **ˈmanicured** *ppl. a.*, **ˈmanicuring** *vbl. sb.*

1889 *Century Mag.* Oct. 873/1 Where the mother's hands washed and cooked,..the daughter's shall..be soft and 'manicured' and daintily gloved. **1892** G. & W. GROSSMITH *Diary of Nobody* xviii. 230 I'm going in for manicuring. It's all the fashion now. **1893** *Black & White* 1 Apr. 384/2 [She] does her mistress's hair and manicures her. **1897** VIOLET HUNT *Unkist, Unkind!* xiii. (ed. 2) 246 Holding out a pretty manicured hand. **1900** PINERO *Gay Ld. Quex* IV. 176 The young gentleman, his manicuring being done, has risen. **1922** M. ARLEN *Piracy* III. vi. 192 Even her soul was manicured. *c* **1926** 'MIXER' *Transport Workers' Song Bk.* 97 You would make a good oil-painting if your face was manicured. **1936** F. CLUNE *Roaming round Darling* viii. 68 The only prisoner in sight was a 'lifer' manicuring the garden. **1957** J. BRAINE *Room at Top* i. 10 Big houses with drives and orchards and manicured hedges. **1964** M. MCLUHAN *Understanding Media* II. xxii. 217 This shift from the mobile open road to the manicured roots of suburbia may signify a real change in American orientation. **1972** *Times* (Jamaica Suppl.) 7 Aug. p. vi/3 Manicured and well-watered fairways of tourist golf courses. **1973** A. MACVICAR *Painted Doll Affair* xiv. 164 A tractor-powered gang-mower was manicuring the last of the fairways. **1975** *New Yorker* 19 May 115 (Advt.), Your day may be occupied..testing the exquisitely manicured golf course.

manicurist (ˈmænɪkjʊərɪst). [f. MANICURE + -IST.] = MANICURE *sb.* 1.

1889 *Columbus* (Ohio) *Disp.* 25 May, Ladies who patronize the manicurist. **1900** *Nature* LXII. 294/2 The surgeons, though they had ceased to rank with manicurists and barbers, were often little better than bone-setters.

manido, variant of MANITOU.

†**manie**. *Obs.* [a. F. *manie*, ad. L. *mania*. Cf. Pr., It., Pg. *mania*, Sp. *manía*.] = MANIA.

c **1386** CHAUCER *Knt.'s T.* 516 Manye Engendred of humour malencolik. **1598** SYLVESTER *Du Bartas* II. i. III. *Furies* 351 So this fell Fury, for forerunners, sends Manie and Phrenzie to suborne her friends. **1623** COCKERAM, *Manie*, a disease in the head cal'd madnesse.

manie, var. MEINIE, company, obs. f. MANY.

manier, obs. form of MANNER, MANURE.

‖**maniéré** (manjere), *a.* [Fr.] Affected or characterized by mannerism; = MANNERED *a.* 3.

1743 H. WALPOLE *Let.* 14 Aug. (1857) I. 263 The Sasso Ferrati you sent me..is not so *maniére* [*maniéré*, in *Corr.* (1955) XVIII] as the Dominichin. **1764** S. FOOTE *Patron* I. 2 But the figures are all finish'd alike. A maniere, a tiresome sameness throughout. **1813** A. ROMILLY in S. H. Romilly *Romilly-Edgeworth Lett.* (1936) 64 Her little maniéré airs are with difficulty supported for a few hours. **1839** THACKERAY in *Fraser's Mag.* June 749/1 You will see here a large drawing..which will shew at once how clever that young artist is, and how weak and maniéré. **1908** *Westm. Gaz.* 14 Nov. 19/1 The suit for outdoor wear delights in a daring *maniéré* simplicity.

‖**manière criblée** (manjɛr krible). [Fr., f. *manière* MANNER *sb.*¹ + *criblé* CRIBBLED *ppl. a.*] The cribbled style of engraving. Cf. CRIBBLED *ppl. a.* and CRIBLÉ *sb.* (and *a.*)

1903 *New Internat. Encycl.* XI. 834/2 Manière criblée. Probably the oldest process of engraving upon metal for the purpose of printing. It derives its name from the white dots with which the dark ground of the print is covered, resembling the holes of a sieve. **1960** H. HAYWARD *Antique Coll.* 174/1 *Manière criblée*, the name is derived from a group of dots made on the plate with a punch to break up otherwise black areas of background. Prints of this type were made in the late 15th and early 16th cent., especially in Florence. **1965** ZIGROSSER & GAEHDE *Guide to Collecting Orig. Prints* iv. 50 Those early prints known as dotted prints (*manière criblée, Schrotblatt*), made with various goldsmith's punches on metal.

maniew(e, obs. form of MANGE *sb.*¹

manifacture, obs. f. MANUFACTURE.

manifest (ˈmænɪfɛst), *sb.* [a. F. *manifeste* vbl. sb., f. *manifester* to MANIFEST. Cf. Sp. *manifiesto*, Pg., It. *manifesto*, of similar formation, though accidentally coinciding in form with the adj.]

1. *gen.* A manifestation, indication. Now *rare*.

1561 T. NORTON *Calvin's Inst.* II. viii. 119 He iudgeth that maner of swearing to be a manifest [L. *argumentum*] of manifest falling from his allegance. *c* **1640** J. SMYTH *Lives Berkeleys* (1883) I. 38 For restoring due honor to the dust of this Lord Robert, I present his posteritye with theis tuelue manifests thereof. **1650** H. BROOKE *Conserv. Health* 230 To give some manifest of a desire of good to the person we are angry withal. **1883** E. C. STEDMAN in *Century Mag.* XXV. 873 Such a writer must be judged by..his books;..the parol evidence of no associate can weigh against his written manifest for an instant.

2. A public proclamation or declaration; an open statement; a manifesto.

1618 *Decl. Demeanour Raleigh* 1 But for Actions, that are built vpon sure and solide grounds (such as his Maiesties are), it belongeth to them, to bee published by open manifests. **1641** CHAS. I, *Sp.* in Rushw. *Hist. Coll.* III. (1692) I. 308 My Nephew, the Prince Elector Palatine..hath desired me..to make a Manifest in my Name. **1667** WATERHOUSE *Fire Lond.* 126 His Proclamations and Manifests against Prophaneness. **1670** COTTON *Espernon* I. II. 75 There was printed a Manifest, subscrib'd by the Cardinal of Bourbon, as Head of the League. **1693** DRYDEN *Iliad* I. 473 But you, authentick Witnesses I bring, Of this my Manifest: That never more This Hand shall combate on the crooked Shore. **1739** *Col. Rec. Pennsylv.* IV. 382 After having laid the Queen's Manifest before the Assembly, declaring her Designs against Canada. **1752** CARTE *Hist. Eng.* III. App. 820 Murray and the others..publishing manifests to alarm the nation..were driven..out of the kingdom. **1915** A. HUXLEY *Let.* Dec. (1969) 87 Meanwhile all is forgiven and forgotten if you subscribe to the *Palatine* ..vide multicoloured manifest thus conceived, which you had better distribute. **1922** *Glasgow Herald* 12 Apr. 11 The annexation itself had been proclaimed by a personal manifest of the Emperor King.

3. The list of a ship's cargo, signed by the master, for the information and use of officers of Customs. Also, a similar list of freight or passengers carried by a train or aeroplane; hence a fast freight train (chiefly *U.S.*). Also *transf.*

1706 PHILLIPS (ed. Kersey), A *Manifest* (in *Traffick*), a Draught of a Master of a Ship's Cargo, shewing what is due to him for Freight from every Person, to whom the Goods in his Ship belong. *c* **1744** in Hanway *Trav.* (1762) I. v. lxxi. 327 The said commander..shall..make oath, that such.. goods..were..put on board..as in the said certificate or manifest is mentioned. **1800** COLQUHOUN *Comm. Thames* xiv. 399 No Goods shall be imported..unless the Master of the Vessel has on board a Manifest signed by himself, containing the names of all the Ports [etc.]. **1869** 'MARK

TWAIN' in *Buffalo Express* 21 Aug. 1/3 The doctor is not done taking inventory. He will make out my manifest this evening. **1872** in I. M. TARBELL *Hist. Standard Oil Co.* (1904) I. 286 The party..covenants and agrees..to make manifests or way-bills of all petroleum or its products, transported over any portion of the railroads. **1884** *Manch. Exam.* 21 Mar. 4/6 If the..quantities turned out differ from the manifest by one half package, the merchant is fined, the ship and its cargo confiscated. **1873** *Act 36 & 37 Vict.* c. 88 Sched. I, Such rice..not being entered on the manifest as part of the cargo. **1929** *Amer. Speech* IV. 342 *Manifest*, a fast merchandise freight train. **1931** G. IRWIN *Amer. Tramp & Underworld Slang* 127 *Manifest*, a fast freight train, from the 'manifest' of the goods carried. **1934** *Amer. Ballads & Folk Songs* 24 The manifest freight Pulled out on the stem behind the mail. **1936** MENCKEN *Amer. Lang.* (ed. 4) 582 A fast freight is a *manifest* or *red-ball*. **1956** W. A. HEFLIN *U.S. Air Force Dict.* 315/1 *Manifest*, a document that lists in detail the passengers or other items carried in one aircraft for a specific destination. **1959** R. COLLIER *City that wouldn't Die* ix. 143 Watching Schied initial the bomb manifest and hand it down to the chief armourer. **1969** *Jane's Freight Containers 1968–69* 128/1 Daily containers move in expedited Piggy-back trains and transcontinental manifest trains. **1971** *Sunday Australian* 8 Aug. 11/2 He came to my office with..samples of passenger manifests.

manifest ('mænɪfɛst), *a.* [ad. L. *manifestus*, earlier *manufestus*, believed to be f. *manu-s* hand + **festus* struck (cf. *infestus* dangerous), f. root found in *of-fendĕre*, *de-fendĕre*. The primary sense would thus be 'palpable'. Cf. F. *manifeste*, Sp. *manifiesto*, Pg., It. *manifesto*.]

1. a. Clearly revealed to the eye, mind, or judgement; open to view or comprehension; obvious.

c **1374** CHAUCER *Boeth.* III. pr. x. 72 (Camb. MS.) Thanne is it manyfest and opyn þat by the getynge of diuinite men ben maked blysful. *c* **1450** HOLLAND *Howlat* 255 It neidis nocht to renewe all myn vnhele, Sen it was menit to ȝour mynd, and maid manifest. **1535** COVERDALE *1 Esdras* ii. 18 Be it knowne and manifest to our lorde the kynge, that the Iewes..begynne to buylde it [the city] agayne. **1555** in Hakluyt *Voy.* I. 262 The better and also manifester testification of the trueth. **1581** J. BELL *Haddon's Answ. Osor.* 458 b, Three manyfest lyes about one poore platter. **1611** BIBLE *John* ix. 3 That the works of God should be made manifest in him. **1671** MILTON *Samson* 997 She's gone, a manifest Serpent by her sting. **1711** STEELE *Spect.* No. 71 ¶10 The contrary is so manifest, that I cannot think you in earnest. **1712** tr. *Pomet's Hist. Drugs* I. 179 A Gum that is..glewy in the Mouth, without manifest Taste. **1837** GORING & PRITCHARD *Microgr.* 181 It is a manifest and visible error. **1860** TYNDALL *Glac.* I. iii. 26 In many places..the mass showed manifest signs of lateral pressure. **1867** F. W. H. MYERS *St. Paul* 10 Rise and be manifest, o Morning Star!

b. *Pol.* **manifest destiny** (often written with capital initials). 'The doctrine of the inevitability of Anglo-Saxon supremacy. A phrase used by those who believed it was the destiny of the United States or of the Anglo-Saxon race to govern the entire Western Hemisphere' (*D.A.E.*). Also *transf. U.S.*

1845 J. O'SULLIVAN in *U.S. Mag. & Democratic Rev.* July & Aug. 5 Our manifest destiny to overspread the continent allotted by Providence for the free development of our yearly multiplying millions. **1856** *Spirit of Times* 13 Dec. 235/2 He was a 'manifest destiny' man. **1858** *Economist* 6 Feb. 139/2 What reasons can be shown for the manifest destiny to whip Africans which do not apply with equal force to prove the manifest destiny to subdue half-caste Spaniards into conformity with their will? **1867** J. R. LOWELL *Biglow Papers* 2nd Ser. p. vii, The incarnation of 'Manifest Destiny', in other words, of national recklessness as to right or wrong. **1927** J. W. PRATT in *Amer. Hist. Rev.* XXXII. 795 One can hardly read a work on the history of the United States in the two decades before the Civil War without meeting the phrase 'manifest destiny', widely used as a convenient statement of the philosophy of territorial expansion in that period. **1959** *Listener* 18 June 1048/2 The long and stern struggle by which Canada had maintained its separateness against American 'Manifest Destiny'.

c. *Sociol.* **manifest function.** (See quots.)

1949 R. K. MERTON *Social Theory* I. i. 51 *Manifest functions* are those objective consequences contributing to the adjustment or adaptation of the system which are intended and recognised by participants in the system; *Latent functions*, correlatively, being those which are neither intended nor recognised. **1957** M. BANTON *W. Afr. City* ix. 168, I shall describe..how the companies fulfil their explicit functions of providing mutual aid and entertainment—what R. K. Merton has termed the manifest functions.

†**2.** Having evident signs *of*; evidently possessed *of* or guilty *of*. [After the Latin construction with genitive.] *Obs.*

1681 DRYDEN *Abs. & Achit.* I. 204 Now, manifest of crimes contrived long since, He stood a bold defiance with his Prince. **1700** —— *Pal. & Arc.* II. 623 Calisto there stood manifest of shame. **1725** POPE *Odyss.* I. 277 Thus manifest of right, I build my claim Sure-founded on a fair Maternal fame.

†**3.** As *adv.* = MANIFESTLY. *Obs.*

c **1391** CHAUCER *Astrol.* II. §26 The excellence of the spere solide, amonges other noble conclusiouns, shewyth Manifeste the diuerse ascenciouns of signes in diuerse places.

manifest ('mænɪfɛst), *v.* Also 5 ma(g)nyfest. [ad. F. *manifest-er*, or L. *manifest-āre*, f. *manifest-us* (see prec.). Cf. Sp., Pg. *manifestar*, It. *manifestare*.]

1. *trans.* To make evident to the eye or to the understanding; to show plainly, disclose, reveal.

c **1374** CHAUCER *Boeth.* II. pr. viii. 44 (Camb. MS.), Thinken ye to manyfesten yowre renoun and don yowre name to ben born forth? **1483** CAXTON *Cato* E viij, The synnes ben ofte hydde for a tyme but afterward..they are knowen and manyfestyd. **1484** —— *Fables of Alfonce* xi. (1889) 281 The yonge man manyfested or descouered vnto her alle his courage and herte. **1508** DUNBAR *Tua Mariit Wemen* 73 To manifest my makdome to multitude of pepill. **1582** N. T. (Rhem.) *John* ii. 11 He manifested [**1611** manifested forth] his glorie. **1598** SHAKS. *Merry W.* IV. vi. 15 The mirth whereof so larded with my matter, That neither (singly) can be manifested Without the shew of both. **1602** MARSTON *Antonio's Rev.* IV. iii, Who riseth up to manifest her guilt? **1611** BIBLE *1 John* iv. 9 In this was manifested the loue of God towards vs. **1622** R. HAWKINS *Voy. S. Sea* (1847) 176 The sunnes rising manifested unto us our errour. **1654** BRAMHALL *Just Vind.* iii. (1661) 31 Whether the Act..were operative or declarative, creating new right, or manifesting or restoring old right. **1736** BUTLER *Anal.* I. iii. Wks. 1874 I. 49 He manifests himself to us under the character of a righteous governor. **1841** MYERS *Cath. Th.* IV. §3. 188 Nature manifests itself to us only through our senses. **1875** MANNING *Mission H. Ghost* viii. 210 He created our souls to manifest the light of His image.

b. Of things: To be evidence of, prove, attest.

1508 DUNBAR *Flyting* 82 Thy frawart phisnomy Dois manifest thy malice to all men. **1607** SHAKS. *Cor.* II. ii. 14 For Coriolanus neyther to care whether they loue, or hate him, manifests the true knowledge he ha's in their disposition. *a* **1674** CLARENDON *Surv. Leviath.* (1676) 125 The instance he makes of a Princes subduing an other people..should manifest to him the contrary. **1804** ABERNETHY *Surg. Obs.* 37 This remark is manifested by the present, as well as by many other cases in surgery.

c. with obj. a clause or accus. with inf., or †compl.

1597 SHAKS. *2 Hen. IV*, IV. v. 105 Thy Life did manifest, thou lou'dst me not. **1643** SIR T. BROWNE *Relig. Med.* I. §22 No man will be able to prove it, when, from the process of the Text, I can manifest it may be otherwise. **1659** PEARSON *Creed* (1839) 324 That it was actually so..the place itself will not manifest. **1667** in Picton *L'pool Munic. Rec.* (1883) I. 269 Neither..bowles or boxe had any inscripcion, manifesting them to be the gift of any p'ticular p'son. *c* **1680** BEVERIDGE *Serm.* (1729) I. 476 It is by this chiefly that we manifest ourselves to be christians. **1688** R. HOLME *Armoury* III. 326/2 The Triangle will presently manifest whether the place be higher or lower than your Eye. **1711** STEELE *Spect.* No. 153 ¶4 It is thus in the Life of a Man of Sense, a short Life is sufficient to manifest himself a Man of Honour and Virtue. **1756** P. BROWNE *Jamaica* 97, I have not yet seen the capsulæ of this plant, and place it here only from the habit, which seems to manifest it of this tribe.

†**2.** To expound, unfold, clear up (a matter).

1530 PALSGR. 632/2, I manyfest, I make a thyng clere or open... It is nat for all men to manyfest this mater. **1629** *S'hertogenbosh* 5 They..manifested their Cause also vnto the Burgers of the Brabandish head Towns. **1669** GALE *Crt. Gentiles* I. III. x. 108 An oration, if it does not manifest the mater, loseth its designe.

3. a. To display (a quality, condition, feeling, etc.) by one's action or behaviour; to give evidence of possessing, reveal the presence of, evince.

1567 *Satir. Poems Reform.* xiv. 67 He Abrahamis Faith, but feir, profest; He Dauidis mercy manifest. **1664** POWER *Exp. Philos.* II. 103 A large Bladder, full blown, will weigh more then itself emptied, and manifest this inequality upon a ticklish pair of scales. **1782** COWPER *Friendship* 112 They manifest their whole life through The needle's deviations too, Their love is so precarious. **1801** *Med. Jrnl.* V. 436 No influence, during that time, was manifested by the medicine. **1814** CARY *Dante, Par.* IX. 18 The eyes Of Beatrice..manifested forth Approval of my wish. **1825** LYTTON *Zicci* 8 Glyndon had also manifested a graceful faculty for verse. **1847** GROTE *Greece* II. xl. (1862) III. 434 The Medes..manifested great personal bravery. **1853** BRIGHT *Sp., India* 3 June (1876) 2 When the noble Lord made that announcement, considerable dissatisfaction was manifested on both sides of the House.

b. *refl.* Of a thing: To reveal itself as existing or operative. Similarly in *pass.*

1808 *Med. Jrnl.* XIX. 137 No tendency, in general, to dysentery, manifested itself at this time. **1871** B. STEWART *Heat* (ed. 2) §303 This heat..does not as a rule manifest itself by producing any increase of temperature. **1860** TYNDALL *Glac.* I. xx. 142 A strong polar action was manifested at many points of the surrounding rocks. **1876** BRISTOWE *Th. & Pract. Med.* (1878) 151 The first symptoms are said to have manifested themselves on the seventh or eighth day.

4. To record or enumerate in a ship's manifest.

1541 *Act 33 Hen. VIII*, c. 7 The double value of the saide mettall so declared and manifested. **1860** *Merc. Marine Mag.* VII. 120 Should a Captain manifest more packages than there are on board the ship,..he shall pay on each package so manifested. **1902** *Daily Chron.* 6 June 5/2 Every passenger is 'manifested' at the point of departure and various particulars about him set out.

5. *intr.* To make a 'manifestation' or public expression of opinion.

1898 *Daily News* 21 Feb. 5/6 In this astonishing country a gentleman of repute chooses his own time for going to prison, and is aided by the courtesy of the authorities in manifesting against the Court which condemned him. *Ibid.* 26 Sept. 4/4 Public opinion in France manifests entirely in the opposite direction. **1899** *Ibid.* 12 June 7/5 The object of the occupants being to manifest there for Loubet.

6. *Spiritualism.* Of a ghost or spirit (*refl.* and *intr.*): To reveal its presence, make an appearance.

1858 HAWTHORNE *Fr. & It. Note-Bks.* (1871) II. 171 Other séances were held in her bed-chamber, at which good and holy spirits manifested themselves. **1898** *Daily News* 29 Mar. 6/1 A certain 'Dr. Phinuit', who, however, for some time has not manifested at all. **1900** *Westm. Gaz.* 22 Dec. 2/2 She locks the skeleton up in the cupboard, and immediately the ghost manifests with renewed vigour.

7. *Hist.* In Spanish law, to protect (a person) by a 'manifestation'. (See MANIFESTATION 4.)

1818 HALLAM *Mid. Ages* iv. (1868) 279 'To manifest any one', says the writer so often quoted [*viz.* Zurita], 'is to wrest him from the hands of the royal officers that he may not suffer any illegal violence.' *Ibid.* 280 *note* [tr. Zurita], In such cases only the Justiciary of Aragon, when recourse is had to him, interposes by manifesting the person arrested.

manifestable (mænɪ'fɛstəb(ə)l), *a.* Also 7 *erron.* **manifestible.** [f. MANIFEST *v.* + -ABLE.] Capable of being manifested.

a **1512** FABYAN *Chron.* VII. 682 The forsaid storyes been manyfestable. **1646** SIR T. BROWNE *Pseud. Ep.* II. ii. 58 This is manifestible in long and thin plates of steel. **1713** NELSON *Life of Bull* 331 A difference in the divine nature of the Son from that of the Father, the one manifestable, the other not manifestable. **1809** COLERIDGE *Friend* (1866) 338 If a law of nature..be manifestable only in and to an intelligent spirit.

manifestant (mænɪ'fɛstənt). [ad. L. *manifestant-em*, pr. pple. of *manifestāre*: see -ANT.] One who manifests or demonstrates in public.

1880 *Daily News* 25 May 5/7 A manifestation with no manifestants, and but few spectators. **1894** *Daily Tel.* 28 June 8/2 The manifestants, however, were quickly dispersed by the police.

†**Manife'starian.** *Obs.* App. a religious sect.

1647 WARD *Simp. Cobler* 11 If there be roome in England for [among others] Arminians, Manifestarians [etc.]. **1689** R. WARE *Foxes & Firebrands* III. 198 These Sectaries..be as follows. 1. Independents..6. Manifestarians, or Arminians.

manifestation (mænɪfɛ'steɪʃən). [ad. late L. *manifestātiōn-em*, n. of action f. *manifestāre* to MANIFEST. Cf. F. *manifestation*, Sp. *manifestacion*, It. *manifestazione*.]

1. The action of manifesting or the fact of being manifested; the demonstration, revelation, or display of the existence, presence, qualities, or nature of some person or thing. †Also, exposition, explanation.

1432–50 tr. *Higden* (Rolls) V. 405 Tylle hit was made open by the manifestacion of a notable signe wheder parte awe to be folowede. **1526** *Pilgr. Perf.* (W. de W. 1531) 21 b, Of this manifestacyon or metynge of our lorde, speketh saynt Johan. **1532** MORE *Confut. Tindale* Wks. 371/2, I..haue spoken of this matter somwhat yᵉ more at large, for yᵉ manifestacion of their great blindnesse. **1570–6** LAMBARDE *Peramb. Kent* (1826) 297 The matter..requireth more wordes for the manifestation thereof than I may now affoorde. **1594** T. B. *La Primaud. Fr. Acad.* II. 201 The growing vp of mans body, and of the manifestation by little and little of the powers of the soule. **1685** BAXTER *Paraphr. N. T., Acts* i. 3 He shewed himself to them by unquestionable manifestation, at several times in the forty days space. **1864** BOWEN *Logic* ix. 288 What we mean by Personal Identity is sameness of substance under great differences of phenomenal manifestation. **1884** JENNINGS *Croker Papers* I. viii. 226 His friends dreaded that at his funeral there would be some manifestation of..ill-feeling.

b. An instance of this; hence, *concr.* or semi-*concr.* that by which something is manifested.

1785 PALEY *Mor. & Polit. Philos.* VI. x. (1786) 573 Certain credited manifestations of the divine will. **1794** SULLIVAN *View Nat.* II. 418 The universe is in the aggregate, a manifestation of the attributes of God. **1833** J. H. NEWMAN *Arians* II. ii. (1876) 153 The Jewish Scriptures introduce to our notice certain peculiar Attributes or Manifestations..of the Deity. **1838** DICKENS *Nich. Nick.* xv, Various odd manifestations of surprise and delight. **1858** GLADSTONE *Homer* II. iii. 180 Jupiter is..the supreme manifestation of Power and knowledge. **1861** STANLEY *East. Ch.* ix. (1869) 284 The third great historical manifestation of the Oriental Church is the formation of the Russian Church. **1867** MAX MÜLLER *Chips* (1880) I. Pref. 10 The first manifestation of thought is speech.

c. *Eccl.* Applied to the action of making known to another the state of one's conscience.

1657 *Penit. Conf.* vii. 134 Let that manifestation be granted to be confession. *c* **1826** DOYLE in W. J. Fitz-Patrick *Life* (1880) I. 523 A rule which requires that each of the sisters..should manifest on a certain day in each month to the female Superior the state of their conscience, which..you know would be carried to such a length that the manifestation would include secret temptations [etc.]; in a word, that the manifestation was in fact the same as the subsequent sacramental confession to the priest.

2. A public act on the part of a government intended as a display of its power and determination to enforce some demand; also, a collective action (e.g. a procession, public meeting, wearing of badges, etc.) adopted by a political party, etc., for the sake of calling attention to its views.

1844 H. H. WILSON *Brit. India* III. 55 The principal manifestation of the British power was directed against Rangoon. **1875** HELPS *Soc. Press.* iii. 57 Instead of discountenancing such political manifestations.

3. In the language of spiritualists, a phenomenon or number of phenomena by which the presence of a spirit is supposed to be rendered perceptible.

1853 H. SPICER *Sights & Sounds* 88 In..1850..Cincinnati first became the scene of manifestations through recognised *media*. **1860** *All Year Round* No. 66. 373 Some of the believers were quite overpowered with this 'manifestation'.

4. *Hist.* In Spanish law, a process by which an accused person might be protected from the

animus and precipitate action of judges and removed to a special prison out of their reach. Also, the prison provided for this purpose (= Sp. *carcel de los manifestados*).

1769 ROBERTSON *Chas. V* (1796) I. III. 140 He could remove the party accused to the Manifestation or prison of the State. **1818** HALLAM *Mid. Ages* iv. (1868) 280 *note*, This process [*sc.* jurisfirma], and that which is called manifestation have been the chief powers of the Justiciary [of Aragon], ever since the commencement of that magistracy.

Hence **manife'stational** *a.*, of or pertaining to (a) manifestation; **manife'stationist**, one who believes in manifestation.

1865 MASSON *Rec. Brit. Philos.* iv. 296 To these beliefs the manifestationists..have sought to add a doctrine. **1893** FAIRBAIRN *Christ in Mod. Theol.* II. II. I. iv. 398 No theory of manifestational forms and aspects can satisfy the conditions.

manifestative (mænɪˈfɛstətɪv), *a.* [ad. scholastic L. *manifestātīv-us*, f. L. *manifestāre*: see MANIFEST *v.* and -ATIVE. Cf. F. *manifestatif.*] Having the function or quality of manifesting or showing forth.

1642 T. GOODWIN *Heart Christ in Heaven* 132 The destruction of which enemies will add to the manifestative glory of his kingdome. **1654** JER. TAYLOR *Real Pres.* 167 The shape, the colour, the bignesse, the motion of a man, are manifestative, and declarative of a humane substance. **1738** JON. EDWARDS *Discourses Import. Subj.* 119 The Apostle James seems to use the word *justify* for *Manifestative Justification.* **1854** *Tait's Mag.* XXI. 663 Lotty's temperament was of the manifestative order. **1875** J. MORISON in *Expositor* I. 120 Our Lord is the manifestative eradiation of the Divine glory [Heb. i. 3].

Hence **mani'festatively** *adv.*, in a manifestative manner; in respect of manifestation.

1652 STERRY *Eng. Deliv. North. Presb.* 4 That Distinction of Glorifying God essentially, and manifestatively. *c* **1670** O. HEYWOOD *Diaries*, etc. (1881) II. 329 All the attributes of God are manifestatively glorifyed in this work. **1726** E. ERSKINE *Serm.* Wks. 1871 I. 274 This is not to be understood of God essentially but manifestatively. **1855** *Tait's Mag.* XXII. 422 Many women do love as eagerly, as manifestatively, as outspokenly, as pursuingly—as Caroline Helstone is said to have done.

†**manifestator.** *Obs.* [a. late L. *manifestātor*, agent-n. f. *manifestāre.*] = MANIFESTER.

1609 BP. W. BARLOW *Answ. Nameless Cath.* 23 We referre him againe to..the True Manifestator of their Æquiuocation.

manifested (ˈmænɪfɛstɪd), *ppl. a.* [f. MANIFEST *v.* + -ED¹.] Made manifest.

1603 SHAKS. *Meas. for M.* IV. ii. 169 To make you vnderstand this in a manifested effect, I craue but foure daies respit. *a* **1653** GOUGE *Comm. Heb.* xi. 35 It is against Gods Truth, against Gods manifested will. **1899** *Westm. Gaz.* 12 June 8/2 The vocal contributions of Miss M. B.. deserved the manifested appreciation of the audience.

Hence **'manifestedness** *rare*, the state of having been manifested.

In mod. Dicts.

manifester (ˈmænɪfɛstə(r)). [f. MANIFEST *v.* + -ER¹.] One who or that which manifests.

1612 WOODALL *Surg. Mate* Wks. (1653) 35 The Author or manifester of this Linament was [etc.]. **1613** MIDDLETON *Triumphs Truth* Wks. (Bullen) VII. 240 Zeal..as he is the manifester of Truth, he is likewise the chastiser of Ignorance. **1660** tr. *Paracelsus' Archidoxis* II. 83 The one is alwaies the sign and manifester of the other. **1862** F. HALL *Hindu Philos. Syst.* 91 Will and other like qualities are their own manifesters. **1863** J. G. MURPHY *Comm. Gen.* xv. 1, I, Jehovah..the Manifester of myself to man.

†**manifesteress.** *Obs. rare*⁻¹. [f. MANIFESTER + -ESS.] A female manifester.

1662 SPARROW tr. *Behme's Rem. Wks., Apol. conc. Perfection* 63 A Manifesteresse of the Power.

manifesting (ˈmænɪfɛstɪŋ), *vbl. sb.* [-ING¹.] The action of the vb. MANIFEST.

1603 KNOLLES *Hist. Turks* (1638) 132 It shall not be amisse..for the more manifesting of that..which.. followeth a little farther to fetch his race. **1685** BAXTER *Paraphr. N. T., Mark* iv. 22 Light is for the manifesting of all things.

'manifesting, *ppl. a.* [-ING².] That manifests.

1888 GLADSTONE in *19th Cent.* May 787 Those who.. desire to retain what was manifested, but to thrust aside the manifesting Person. **1902** FAIRBAIRN *Philos. Chr. Relig.* II. I. i. 326 This incarnate Word, this manifested and manifesting God, the evangelist identified with Jesus.

manifestive (ˈmænɪfɛstɪv), *a. rare.* [f. MANIFEST *v.* + -IVE.] = MANIFESTATIVE.

1846 SIR W. HAMILTON *Reid's Wks.* 771 *note*, On sense, experience, induction, it [this knowledge] is dependent, as on its exciting,..manifestive,..occasional cause. **1867** BAILEY *Univ. Hymn* 7 Hidden in Himself, self manifestive cause.

manifestly (ˈmænɪfɛstlɪ), *adv.* [f. MANIFEST *a.* + -LY².] **a.** In a manifest manner. (Now *rare.*) **b.** Used to qualify a statement: As is manifest, evidently, unmistakably.

1477 EARL RIVERS (Caxton) *Dictes* 11 By the whiche he hath manyfestely shewed vnto them the secretis of the lawe. **1484** CAXTON *Fables of Poge* v, The lymmes..were shewed manyfestly. **1509–10** *Act 1 Hen. VIII*, c. 6 *Preamble*, It is manefestely knowen that..forged informacions have ben pursued. **1612** BACON *Ess.*, *Great Place* (Arb.) 288 Whosoeuer..changeth manifestly, without manifest cause, giueth suspition of corruption. **1620** T. GRANGER *Div. Logike* 308 Sometimes the Proposition it selfe of an Oration, or Epistle is not manifestly expressed, but couertly insinuated. **1711** STEELE *Spect.* No. 43 ¶3 The Design and Transactions of too many Clubs are trifling, and manifestly of no Consequence to the Nation. **1759** ROBERTSON *Hist. Scot.* I. Wks. 1813 I. 76 The treaty was still so manifestly of advantage to England. **1860** TYNDALL *Glac.* I. xxii. 152 Fear was manifestly getting the better of him. **1878** LECKY *Eng. in 18th C.* I. iii. 422 Their cause was manifestly lost.

manifestness (ˈmænɪfɛstnɪs). [-NESS.] The quality or condition of being manifest.

1589 RIDER *Bibl. Schol.*, Manifestnesse, *evidentia.* **1727** BAILEY vol. II, *Manifestness*, plainness, &c. to be seen, &c. **1877** LEGGE *Confucius* 293 Such is the manifestness of what is minute!

manifesto (mænɪˈfɛstəʊ), *sb.* [a. It. *manifesto*: see MANIFEST *sb.*]

†**1.** A proof, a piece of evidence. *Obs.*

1644 BULWER *Chirol. & Chiron.* (title-p.), Consisting of the Naturall Expressions, digested by Art in the Hand,..by Historicall Manifesto's, exemplified out of the Authentique Registers of Common Life. **1646** SIR T. BROWNE *Pseud. Ep.* III. xvii. 148 Succeeding yeares produced the manifesto or evidence of their virilities. **1674** STAVELEY *Rom. Horseleech* (1769) Ep. Ded., Matters of fact drawn from the most authentic registers and manifestos of time. **1683** E. HOOKER *Pref. Pordage's Mystic Div.* 99 For here Hee maketh and giveth a Diaphanous Manifesto and perspicuous Demonstration. **1686** GOAD *Celest. Bodies* II. xii. 331, I reckon that discourse is so plain, it carryeth its Manifesto with it.

2. A public declaration or proclamation, usually issued by or with the sanction of a sovereign prince or state, or by an individual or body of individuals whose proceedings are of public importance, for the purpose of making known past actions, and explaining the reasons or motives for actions announced as forthcoming.

1647 WARD *Simp. Cobler* 50 It were good if States would let People know so much before hand, by some safe woven *manifesto.* **1651** tr. *Life Father Sarpi* 102 To the citation he made answer by a Manifesto. **1670** COTTON *Espernon* I. I. 38 At the same time a Manifesto was publish'd by the Cardinal of Bourbon. **1775** E. ALLEN in Sparks *Corr. Amer. Rev.* (1853) I. 463, I..delivered the General's written manifesto to the Chiefs. **1816** SINGER *Hist. Cards* 63 Manifestoes issued by several of the emperors. **1839** *Blackw. Mag.* XLV. 217 The manifestoes of modern agrarianism. **1855** MILMAN *Lat. Chr.* VII. ii. (1864) IV. 85 He addressed a spiritual manifesto to all Christendom. **1897** McCARTHY *Own Times fr.* 1880 x. 204 Mr. Gladstone issued a manifesto in the form of an address to the electors of Midlothian.

3. *Comb.*, as ***manifesto-like*** adj.

1819 *Metropolis* I. 13 His manifesto-like annunciation, that he should marry a very rich heiress.

manifesto (mænɪˈfɛstəʊ), *v. rare.* [f. prec.] *intr.* To issue a manifesto or manifestos.

1748 RICHARDSON *Clarissa* (1811) VIII. 261, I am to be manifestoed against, though no prince. **1837** CARLYLE *Fr. Rev.* II. VI. iii, Serene Highnesses who sit there protocolling, and manifestoing, and consoling mankind.

Hence **mani'festoing** *vbl. sb.*

1858 CARLYLE *Fredk. Gt.* III. xiv. (1872) I. 230 Treaties enough, and conferences, and pleadings, manifestoings. *Ibid.* xvi. 334 George Wilhelm followed his old scheme, peace at any price..and except complaining, petitioning, and manifestoing, studiously did nothing.

manifold (ˈmænɪfəʊld), *a.*, *adv.*, and *sb.* Now chiefly *literary.* Forms: α. 1 **maniȝ-, moniȝ-, mæniȝ-, meniȝf(e)ald, 1–2 mænifeald, 2 manifald, 2–3 -feald, 2–6 monifald,** (4 **monyfaulde**), 4–5 **many-, monyfald(e,** (6 **many-, mony-, moniefauld**). β. 1 **meni(ȝ)fæld, -feld, 3–4 manifeld.** γ. (2 **monifold, 3 maniuold, maniȝefold**), 3–7, 9 **manyfold,** (4 **manye-**), 4–6 **manyfolde** (5 **maniefoold, mony-, manye-, 6 manniefolde**), 6–7 **manifolde,** (7 **manyfould**), 3– **manifold.** [Common Teut.: OE. *maniȝfeald* = OFris. *manichfald*, OS. *managfald* (MLG. *mannichvolt*, MDu. *menichvout*), OHG. *manacfalt* (MHG. *manecvalt*, mod.G. *mannigfalt*), ON. *margfaldr* (OSw. *marghfalder, mangfalder*, Sw. *mångfalt*), Goth. *managfalþs*: see MANY *a.* and -FOLD. A form with adj. suffix (= -Y) occurs as MLG. *mannichvoldech*, MDu. *menichvoudich* (Du. *menigvuldig*), G. *mannichfaltig*, Sw. *mångfaldig*, Da. *mangfoldich.*]

A. *adj.*

1. a. Varied or diverse in appearance, form, or character; having various forms, features, relations, applications, etc.; †complex.

In OE. used *Gram.* for 'plural' (ÆLFRIC *Gram.* viii).

c **1000** ÆLFRIC *Hom.* I. 448 Þes pistol is swiðe meniȝ-feald us to ȝereccenne. *c* **1050** *Voc.* in Wr.-Wülcker 448/21 *Multimodam*, maniȝfealdne. *c* **1175** *Lamb. Hom.* 145 Alle we beoð in monifald wawe ine þisse wreche liue. *a* **1225** *Ancr. R.* 176 Vor þer beoð uttre & inre [uondunges]; & eiðer is moniuold. *a* **1240** *Ureisun* in *Cott. Hom.* 193 Mid ham is muruhðe moniuold wið-ute teone and treie. **1382** WYCLIF *1 Pet.* iv. 10 As goode dispenderes of the manyfolde grace of God. **1430** *Rolls of Parlt.* IV. 377/2 The horribilite of his so manyfolde Treson. **1535** COVERDALE *Wisd.* vii. 22 In hir is yᵉ sprete of vnderstandinge, which is holy, manifolde, one onely, sotyll. **1570** DEE *Math. Pref.* 17 Chorographie..is in practise manifolde, and in vse very ample. **1603** DANIEL *Panegyr. to King*, etc. *To Lady Margaret* 25 He sees the face of Right t'appeare as manyfold As are the passions of vncertaine man. **1667** MILTON *P. L.* x. 16 Which they not obeying, Incurr'd..the penaltie, And manifold in sin, deserv'd to fall. **1784** COWPER *Task* v. 769 This changeful life, So manifold in cares, whose every day Brings its own evil with it. **1832** LEWIS *Use & Ab. Pol. Terms* Introd. 12 The truth is one, error is manifold. **1849** MACAULAY *Hist. Eng.* iv. I. 497 He hated the Puritan sects with a manifold hatred, theological and political, hereditary and personal. **1865** W. G. PALGRAVE *Arabia* I. 424 Coffee though one in name is manifold in fact. **1865** SWINBURNE *Poems & Ballads, Hesperia* 21 Profound and manifold flower.

b. Qualifying a personal designation: That is such in many ways or in many relations; entitled to the name on many grounds. Also (*nonce-uses*) of persons: Many-minded, variable; having many diverse capacities.

c **1200** *Trin. Coll. Hom.* 187 Twifold oðer manifold is þe man þe nis stedefast ne on dade ne on speche ne on þonke. **1601** SHAKS. *All's Well* IV. iii. 265 The manifold Linguist, and the army-potent souldier. **1605** —— *Lear* v. iii. 114 If any man of qualitie..will maintaine vpon Edmund..that he is a manifold Traitor. **1694** CONGREVE *Double Dealer* v. xxiv, Secure that manifold villain. **1842** MOZLEY in *Brit. Critic* XXXI. 173 Like a man who is at once clear-headed and manifold, if we may be allowed the word, in his ideas. **1885** R. BRIDGES *Nero* II. iii, To sit upon their rare, successive thrones, A manifold Augusta!

c. In technical and commercial use.

1851 *Offic. Catal. Gt. Exhib.* II. 597 A manifold bell-pull constructed on an entirely new plan, by which one pull is made to ring bells in any number of rooms. **1857** TREGELLES tr. *Gesenius' Heb. Lex.* s.v. עוּגָב, *Ambubaja* (i.e. *tibicina* Hor.)..a double or manifold pipe, an instrument composed of many pipes. **1879** STAINER *Music of Bible* 95 Two classes of 'manifold-pipes' can exist, the one..a collection of *flauti traversi*, the other..of *flûtes à bec.* **1900** *Westm. Gaz.* 25 May 4/2 A model military balloon of the regulation-varnished manifold goldbeater's-skin variety.

2. Qualifying a plural sb. (†or collective noun): Numerous and varied; of many kinds or varieties. †Formerly simply: Numerous, many.

c **1000** ÆLFRIC *Gen.* xiii. 6 Heora æhta wæron meniȝfælde. *c* **1175** *Lamb. Hom.* 11 Muchel is us þenne neod..swiðe adreden ure monifolde sunne. *c* **1250** *Gen. & Ex.* 2502 And his kin wexen maniȝe-fold. *c* **1290** *S. Eng. Leg.* I. 293/179 Þat folk cam mani-folde A-boute Theofle in eche side. *? a* **1390** CHAUCER *Proverbes* i, What shul thise clothes many-fold, Lo! this hote somers day? *a* **1400** *Cursor M.* 27887 (Cott. Galba) Dronkinhede..And mase meschefes ful many falde. **1475** *Bk. Noblesse* (Roxb.) 41 Considering so many folde tymes we haue ben deceived. **1535** COVERDALE *Ps.* ciii. 24 O Lorde, how manifolde are thy workes. **1548–9** (Mar.) *Bk. Com. Prayer* Collect 4th Sund. Easter, The sondery and manifold chaunges of the worlde. **1586** A. DAY *Eng. Secretary* I. (1625) 114 You will runne into such vntimely sorrowes as with manifold teares will hardly be washed. **1588** A. KING tr. *Canisius' Catech* 86 b, Quhat fruict haue we of yis sacrament being deulie receauit? Verray gryt and monifald. **1597** HOOKER *Eccl. Pol.* v. lxviii. §6 Her manifolde varieties in rites and Ceremonies of Religion. **1605** in *10th Rep. Hist. MSS. Comm.* App. v. 372 The manyfould downefalles into synne. **1736** BUTLER *Anal.* I. iii. Wks. 1874 I. 47 The manifold appearances of design and of final causes, in the constitution of the world. **1784** COWPER *Task* III. 624 So manifold, all pleasing in their kind, All healthful, are the employs of rural life. **1844** STANLEY *Arnold* (1858) I. Pref. 1 The manifold kindnesses with which they have assisted me. **1849** MACAULAY *Hist. Eng.* vi. II. 146 Clarendon was overwhelmed by manifold vexations. **1880** GEIKIE *Phys. Geog.* ii. x. 67 It is from this circulation of water that all the manifold phenomena of clouds, rain, snow, rivers, glaciers, and lakes arise.

†**3.** *Math.* = MULTIPLE. ***manifold to*** = a multiple of. *Obs.*

1557 RECORDE *Whetst.* Bivb, There is one kinde of proportion, that is named *multiplex*, or manyfolde. **1660** BARROW *Euclid* VII. Post. 1 That numbers equal or manifold to any number may be taken at pleasure.

¶**4.** ***how manifold?*** (= *how many* + -FOLD): Of how many kinds? *Obs. rare*⁻¹.

1594 BLUNDEVIL *Exerc.* III. I. viii. (1636) 287 How manifold is the moving of this heaven? The moving of this heaven..is threefold.

B. *adv.*

†**1. a.** In many ways, modes, degrees, etc.; in first quot. = in many pieces. *Obs.*

13.. *Guy Warw.* (A.) 4024 Alle þai hadde to-broken his scheld, & his brini to-rent manifeld. **1340** HAMPOLE *Pr. Consc.* 3250 Þair payn es turned manyfalde, Now er þai in hete, and now in calde. *c* **1375** *Sc. Leg. Saints* xl. (*Ninian*) 413 God þai lowit mony-fald for þis merwale. *c* **1400** *Lanfranc's Cirurg.* 269 Þou muste make a plate of iren..þat mote be fooldid manie foold in þe forseid ligature. *c* **1450** LONELICH *Grail* xlii. 4 How that Nasciens þis writ gan beholde, and there-Onne loked ful Many folde. **1567** *Gude & Godlie B.* (S.T.S.) 122 Sinnand rycht mony fald. **1590** SPENSER *F.Q.* I. xii. 12 Then when his daughter deare he does behold, Her dearely doth imbrace, and kisseth manifold. **1593** *Tell-Troth's N. Y. Gift* (1876) 44 Thus shall loues followers be thrise happy, and thus Robin goodfellowes well-willers, in imitating his care, bee manifolde blessed.

†**b.** In the proportion of many to one. [The etymological sense.] *Obs.*

1611 BIBLE *Luke* xviii. 30 Who shall not receiue manifold more in this present time.

C. *absol.* and *sb.*¹

†**1.** Phr. ***by*** (rarely ***on***) ***manifold***: many times over; in the proportion of many to one. *Obs.*

1303 R. BRUNNE *Handl. Synne* 6900 He byeþ þyn almes on manyfolde. **1390** GOWER *Conf.* II. 186 Wherof the man.. Stant more worth..Than he stod erst be manyfold. *c* **1400** *Ywaine & Gaw.* 607 More Curtaysi Fand he..mar

conforth, by mony falde, Than Colgrevance had him of talde. **1415** HOCCLEVE *To Sir J. Oldcastle* 58 Thoffense.. Was nat so greet as thyn by many fold. **1567** *Gude & Godlie B.* (S.T.S.) 191 The theif Judas did greit trespas, That Christ for siluer sauld: Bot Preistis wil tak, and his price mak, For les be mony fauld. **1596** RALEIGH *Discov. Gviana* A iv, The countrey hath more quantity of Gold by manifolde, then the best partes of the Indies.

2. That which is manifold.

a. *spec.* In the Kantian philosophy, the sum of the particulars furnished by sense before they have been unified by the synthesis of the understanding.

This renders G. *mannigfaltiges, mannigfaltigkeit*. Some earlier English translations of Kant's works have MULTIFARIOUS, MULTIPLE, MULTIPLEX.

1855 MEIKLEJOHN tr. *Kant's Crit. Pure Reason* 63 By means of the synthetical unity of the manifold in intuition. **1877** E. CAIRD *Philos. Kant* II. i. 199 The activity of the mind must bring with it certain principles of relation, under which the manifold of sense must be brought.

b. *gen.*

1856 R. A. VAUGHAN *Mystics* (1860) I. 65 His aim should rather be.. instead of going out into the Manifold, to forsake it for the One. **1874** SAYCE *Compar. Philol.* vi. 243 Out of the manifold comes the simple, out of the multitudinous the single. **1889** SKRINE *Mem. E. Thring* 256 The chosen abstraction which gathers up into a focus the manifold of human duty, experience, and hope. **1902** *Q. Rev.* Oct. 496 The picturesque manifold of life.

3. *Math.* = MANIFOLDNESS 2.

1890 in *Century Dict.* **1902** B. A. W. RUSSELL in *Encycl. Brit.* XXVIII. 666/1 Riemann's Work contains two fundamental conceptions, that of a manifold, and that of the measure of curvature of a continuous manifold possessed of what he calls flatness in the smallest parts... Conceptions of magnitude, he explains, are only possible where we have a general conception capable of determination in various ways. The manifold consists of all these various determinations, each of which is an element of the manifold. **1902** G. B. MATHEWS *ibid.* XXXI. 281/2 A manifold may consist of a single element.

4. a. A copy made by a manifold-writer.

1884 in *Cassell's Encycl. Dict.*

b. Short for *manifold-paper*.

1897 B. STOKER *Dracula* xvii. 229, I began to type-write from the beginning of the seventh cylinder. I used manifold, and so took three copies of the diary. **1926** *Paper Terminol.* (Spalding & Hodge) ii. 16 *Manifold*, slightly waxed tissue or other thin interleaving paper made for employment with carbon paper. Also an extremely thin typewriting made for the multiplication to as many as ten or twelve carbon copies of typewritten letters. **1954** *Ibid.* 38 *Manifold*, papers similar in character to Bank, although thinner. They range in substance from $16\frac{1}{2} \times 21$ in. $4\frac{1}{2}$ lb. 500's to 8 lb. 500's and are used when a large number of carbon copies is required. **1967** KARCH & BUBER *Offset Processes* xi. 485 *Manifold*, thin, strong, [for] duplicate copies, sales books, etc.

5. *Mech.* Any pipe that splits into a number of branches; *spec.* the one running from the carburettor of an internal-combustion engine to the cylinders, and the one from the silencer to the cylinders.

a **1884** KNIGHT *Dict. Mech.* Suppl. 579/2 *Manifold*, the chambers with nozzles into and from which the pipes of a radiator lead. **1891** PATTERSON *Naut. Dict.* 332 *Manifold*, a pipe or chamber to which are connected several branch suction pipes with their valves and one or more main suctions to pump. **1919** [see *exhaust-manifold* s.v. EXHAUST *sb.* 3]. **1948** '*Motor*' *Manual* (ed. 33) v. 99 The induction manifold of a modern engine generally is heated by the exhaust. This.. can be easily and neatly arranged in most engines because the exhaust manifold usually is close to the inlet manifold. **1961** *Economist* 30 Dec. 1306/1 Ford provides only the carburettor, inlet manifold and camshaft for the Classic [motor car]. **1971** *Sci. Amer.* Sept. 222/3 All gases are admitted through needle valves to a manifold that connects to the laser.

D. *Comb.*: **manifold letter-book** (see quot. 1869); **manifold-paper**, carbonized paper used in making several copies of a writing at one time; **manifold writer**, an apparatus fitted with carbonized paper for making copies of a writing; so **manifold writing**.

1808 R. WEDGWOOD in *Abridg. Specif. Patents, Writ. Instr.* (1869) 14 A.. pen and stylographic manifold writer. **1851** in *Illustr. Lond. News* 5 Aug. (1854) 119/1 (Occupations of People) Manifold-paper-maker. **1862** W. CLARK in *Abr. Specif. Patents, Writ. Instr.* (1869) 319 An improved apparatus for manifold writing. **1869** *Ibid.* 275 Improvement in arranging manifold letter books. The patentee arranges leaves of copying and common writing paper alternately, and binds them together. **1872** *Routledge's Ev. Boy's Ann.* Dec. 12/1 The principle of the manifold writer, the great friend of newspaper reporters. **1876** PREECE & SIVEWRIGHT *Telegraphy* 289 The office copy is in pencil, the public copy in manifold writing.

ˈmanifold, *sb.*[2] *dial.* Also **manifolds**: for Forms see E.D.D. [f. MANY *a.* + FOLD *sb.*[3] Cf. G. *mannigfalt*.] The intestines or bowels; *spec.* the manyplies or third stomach of a ruminant.

c **1280** Monifauldes [see CHITTERLING 1]. **1774** GOLDSM. *Nat. Hist.* III. i. 4 The third stomach.. which is called the manyfold, from the number of its leaves. **1855** ROBINSON *Whitby Gloss.*, *Moneyfawd*,.. the countryman's term for a cow's stomach. **1864** WEBSTER, *Manifolds*, the third stomach of a ruminant animal. (*Local. U.S.*) **1869** *Lonsdale Gloss.*, *Manifolds*, the intestines. **1889** *N.W. Linc. Gloss.* (ed. 2), *Manifold*, the stomach; the bowels of man and the lower animals.

manifold (ˈmænɪfəʊld), *v.* Also 3 maniuolden, 4 *north.* many-, manifald. [OE. *maniȝfealdian* (Sweet), *mæniȝfealdian* (cf. *ȝemaniȝ-*, *ȝemæniȝ-*, *ȝemeniȝfealdian*, *fieldan*) = OHG. *managfaltôn*, *manacfaltan* (MHG. *manacvalten*, mod.G. *mannichfalten*), f. the adj.: see MANIFOLD *a.* The word became obs. in ME., and has recently been formed afresh from the adj.] *trans.* To make manifold, multiply. *rare* exc. as in b.

c **1000** in Napier *O. E. Glosses* 5215 *Amplificare*, mænifeal[dian]. *a* **1225** *Ancr. R.* 402 He wule.. moniuolden in ou his deorewurðe grace. *a* **1300** *E. E. Psalter* xxxvii. 20 And mani falded ere þai [L. *multiplicati sunt*] for-þi Whilk hated me wickeli. *a* **1340** HAMPOLE *Psalter* xv. 3 Many faldid ere thaire seknesis. **1767** [see *manifolded* below]. **1889** *Chicago Advance* 19 Sept., Manifolding its appliances, spiritual, educational, and social. **1903** AGNES M. CLERKE *Probl. Astrophysics* 45 The solitary success of 1896 was manifolded a year and a half later.

b. *spec.* To multiply impressions or copies of, as by a manifold-writer. Also *absol.*

1865 [see *manifolded* below]. **1879** tr. *Busch's Bismarck* II. 138 Afterwards I write, on the Chief's instructions, two articles, to be manifolded [orig. *die sich vervielfältigen sollen*]. **1879** *Print. Trades Jrnl.* No. 28. 25 Paper of velvet-like quality, impregnated so as to manifold with extreme ease. **1881** *Times* 27 July 10 The Home Secretary received such precise and timely information that he was enabled to have it manifolded. **1902** ELIZ. L. BANKS *Newspaper Girl* 122, I filled three sheets of paper with it; then I got carbon and manifolded it.

Hence **ˈmanifolded** *ppl.a.*, **ˈmanifolding** *vbl. sb.* (also *concr.*, = MANIFOLD *sb.*[1] 5).

1767 S. PATERSON *Another Trav.* II. 206 Has manifolded homebred mischief marred thy rest? **1865** KNIGHT *Passages Work. Life* III. viii. 162 The untiring Reuter appears.. with manifolded copies of his telegram. **1892** *Daily News* 20 June 11/4 Reporter wanted... Used to manifolding. **1901** *Blackw. Mag.* June 802/1 This manifolding process would augment in something like geometrical progression. **1938** *Times* 9 Aug. 8/7 To adjust the tappets it would be best to lift the manifolding. **1963** BIRD & HUTTON-STOTT *Veteran Motor Car* 52 Internal manifolding and clean-cut architectural appearance were all in marked contrast to most contemporary engines.

manifolder (ˈmænɪfəʊldə(r)). [f. MANIFOLD *v.* + -ER[1].] A machine for multiplying copies of a document, etc., or a person using this. Also used of a typeface (see quot. *c* 1961).

1903 in *Funk's Stand. Dict.* Suppl. **1911** WEBSTER (citing G. H. Putnam), He seems to have added to his employment that of a manifolder and seller of manuscripts. *c* **1961** *Imperial Type Faces* (Imperial Typewriter Co.), Pica Gothic type is an exceptionally good manifolder.

manifoldly (ˈmænɪfəʊldlɪ), *adv.* Now only *literary*. [OE. *maniȝfealdlíce*, f. *maniȝfeald* MANIFOLD: see -LY[2].] In manifold ways; †*occas.* in the proportion of many to one.

c **825** *Vesp. Psalter* lxii. 2 *Multipliciter*, moniȝfaldlice. *c* **950** *Lindisf. Gosp.* John x. 10 *Abundantius*, moniȝfal[d]-lice. *c* **1450** *Mirour Saluacioun* 3318 Mankynde.. cryed to goode manyfaldly. **1549** COVERDALE, etc. *Erasm. Par. 1 Tim.* 10 The deuilles snares (which he layeth manyfoldely). **1599** SANDYS *Europæ Spec.* (1632) 177 The proportion.. is manifoldly inferiour, not one to twenty. **1605** BACON *Adv. Learn.* II. ii. §13 So also is there another kind of history manifoldly mixed, and that is history of cosmography. **1669** WORLIDGE *Syst. Agric.* (1681) 38 Good Culture doth infinitely meliorate the Land,.. and manifoldly repay the expence and labour bestowed thereon. **1825** COLERIDGE *Aids Refl.* 83 The manifoldly intelligent ant tribes. **1855** PUSEY *Doctr. Real Presence* Note A. 27 These are divided manifoldly, in that some understand by conversion identity of place.. others.. an order of succession. **1873** A. W. WARD tr. *Curtius' Hist. Greece* I. I. i. 8 The country is so manifoldly broken up, that it becomes a succession of peninsulas.

manifoldness (ˈmænɪfəʊldnɪs). [OE. *maniȝfealdnis*, f. *maniȝfeald* MANIFOLD: see -NESS.]

1. The quality or condition of being manifold; varied character; multiplicity.

c **950** *Lindisf. Gosp.* Matt. xii. 34 *Ex abundantia cordis*, from moniȝfaldnisse hearta. *c* **1050** *Voc.* in Wr.-Wülcker 469/14 *Perplexitans* [read *perplexitas*], manifealdnes. **1611** COTGR., *Multicuple*, a manifoldnesse, great multiplication. *a* **1631** DONNE *Serm.* lxiii. 632 In the manifoldnesse, and in the weightinesse, and in the everlastingnesse thereof [*sc.* of Fire and Wormes]. **1809–10** COLERIDGE *Friend* (ed. 3) III. 145 The inordinate number and manifoldness of facts and phænomena. **1877** E. CAIRD *Philos. Kant* II. viii. 347 The consciousness of self.. as one in all the manifoldness and difference of its perceptions. **1894** T. H. WARD *Eng. Poets, Clough* IV. 590 Clough's poetry, marked as so much of it is by indecision and manifoldness of view.

2. *Math.* (See quots.) Cf. MANIFOLD C. 3.

(A transl. of Riemann's *mannigfaltigkeit*.)

1873 CLIFFORD tr. *Riemann's Bases of Geom.* in *Nature* VIII. 14–17. **1876** *Nature* (1877) XV. 515/1 We see.. that.. the conception of space is a particular variety of a wider and more general conception. This wider conception, of which time and space are particular varieties, it has been proposed to denote by the term *manifoldness*. **1883** CHRYSTAL in *Encycl. Brit.* XV. 629 One word has recently come into use which is very convenient, inasmuch as it draws attention.. to the prime object of mathematical contemplation, viz. 'manifoldness'... The assemblage of points on a surface is a twofold manifoldness; the assemblage of points in tridimensional space is a threefold manifoldness; the values of a continuous function of *n* arguments are *n*-fold manifoldness.

ˈmanifoldwise, *adv. Obs.* or *arch.* [See -WISE.] In various ways.

[*c* **1200** *Trin. Coll. Hom.* 207 He haueð ofte agilt.. and a manifeld wise.] *c* **1440** *Promp. Parv.* 325/1 Manyfolde wyse, *multipharie, multipliciter*. **1545** RAYNOLD *Byrth Mankynde* 18 [The] branches and armes.. manifold wise dispersid, spred, and commyxt. *Ibid.* 21 Small.. vaynes, reuoluing them self in & out a thousand fold and manifoldwise intricat together.

maniform (ˈmænɪfɔːm), *a.*[1] [ad. mod.L. *maniform-is*, f. L. *manus* hand: see -FORM.] Having the form of a hand; hand-shaped; *Ent.* chelate.

1826 KIRBY & SP. *Entomol.* IV. 310 Maniform. When they [palpi] are chelate or furnished with a finger and thumb. **1856** in MAYNE *Expos. Lex.*, and in mod. Dicts.

maniform (ˈmænɪfɔːm), *a.*[2] [Badly f. *mani-* (= MANY *a.*, as in MANIFOLD) + -FORM.] Multiform.

1835 *New Monthly Mag.* XLIII. 298 Their avenues of enjoyment are their maniform sympathies. **1863** READE *Hard Cash* III. 117 He favoured Julia and Edward with a full account of the maniform enormities he had detected them in.

manify (ˈmænɪfaɪ), *v. rare.* [f. MAN *sb.*[1] + -IFY.] *trans.* To make man-like.

1799 ANNA SEWARD *Lett.* (1811) V. 220, I have always seen genius manified, and imagination, or fancy, womanized. **1894** *Forum* (N.Y.) Sept. 101 Most women in America seem to be—what shall I call it?—manified.

maniȝ, obs. f. MANY.

†**maniglion.** *Obs.* [ad. It. *maniglione*, augmentative of *maniglio*, *maniglia* bracelet. Cf. MANILLA[1].] = DOLPHIN 6 a.

1704 HARRIS *Lex. Techn.* s.v. *Ordnance*.

manihot, var. MANIOC.

manikin (ˈmænɪkɪn). Forms: 6 **manneken**, 8 **manekin**, **manequine**, 9 **mannakin**, **man(n)equin**, 7– **manakin**, **man(n)ikin**. [a. Du. *manneken*, dim. of *man* MAN *sb.*[1]: see -KIN. App. first taken from Du. in sense 2 b; some of the forms represent the Fr. spelling *mannequin*.]

1. A little man (often *contemptuous*); a dwarf, pygmy. Also *fig.*

1601 SHAKS. *Twel. N.* III. ii. 57 This is a deere Manakin to you Sir Toby. **1609** B. JONSON *Sil. Wom.* I. iii, O, that's a precious Mannikin! **1653** *Dissert. de Pace* iv. 18 Shall we little manikins prescribe a law to his most free arbitrement? *a* **1700** B. E. *Dict. Cant. Crew*, *Mannikin*, a Dwarf. **1762** BEATTIE *Pigm. & Cranes* 97 Manikins with haughty step advance. **1840** W. H. AINSWORTH *Tower Lond.* II. xxxv, 'What is it?' replied the good-humoured giant, yawning as if he would have swallowed the teazing mannikin. **1843** LYTTON *Last Bar.* III. viii, Gloucester, the lynx-eyed mannikin, is there. **1894** *Q. Rev.* Jan. 213 Men become undignified and little-minded, local manikins.

2. †**a.** *gen.* A little figure of a man. *Obs.*

1601 HOLLAND *Pliny* II. 484 Prettie images or mannikins resembling cookes, which he termed Magiriscia. **1629** in *Archæologia* XLVIII. 212 One gilt shipp and cover with a manikin on the topp.

b. An artist's lay figure.

1570 DEE *Math. Pref.* 32 Thus, of a Manneken (as the Dutch painters terme it) in the same Symmetrie, may a Giant be made. **1730–6** BAILEY (folio), *Manequine* (with Painters, &c.), a little statue or model usually made of wax or wood, the junctures whereof are so contrived, that it may be put into any attitude at pleasure. **1762–71** H. WALPOLE *Vertue's Anecd. Paint.* (1786) V. 38 The use of the manekin or layman for disposing draperies. **1850** LEITCH tr. *C. O. Müller's Anc. Art* §69 (ed. 2) 38 These wooden figures.. had decidedly more resemblance to puppets (manequins) than to works of cultivated plastic art. **1858** SIMMONDS *Dict. Trade*, *Manequin*, an artist's model of wood or wax. **1900** DR. DILLON in *Gd. Words* July 451/2 'He [the Tsar] is as wiry as a mannequin', said an officer to me.

c. A model of the human body used for exhibiting the anatomical structure or for demonstrating surgical operations.

1831 E. BALDWIN *Ann. Yale Coll.* 263 The dry preparations, and particularly an apparatus called a manikin, are used for the demonstrations. This manikin is a very perfect and ingenious piece of mechanism, constructed in Paris, representing a male figure of the full size. **1895** *Arnold & Sons' Catal. Surg. Instr.* 523 Obstetric Manikin including a natural female pelvis, with leather foetus and placenta.

3. (Usually in the form **manakin**.) One of the small and usually gaily-coloured birds of the passerine family *Pipridæ*, inhabiting the tropical region of America.

Hence, or from the Du. source, the mod.L. *Manacus* designating one genus of this family.

crested, golden, Peruvian, rock manakin, species of the genus *Rupicola*. ***spotted manakin***, the Australian *Pardalotus punctatus* or diamond-bird.

1743 EDWARDS *Nat. Hist. Birds* I. 21 The Golden-headed Black Tit-mouse... I have seen Dutch Drawings of these Birds, entitled, Manakins, which is a name the Hollanders give to some European Birds also. **1774** GOLDSM. *Nat. Hist.* (1776) V. 354 The beauty of the little tribe of Manikin birds. **1781** PENNANT *Genera of Birds* 64 Crested Manakin.. Golden-headed Manakin. **1782** LATHAM *Gen. Syn. Birds* II. II. 519 Peruvian Manakin. *Ibid.* 534 Tuneful Manakin. **1825** WATERTON *Wand. S. Amer.* (1882) 26 When the fruit of the fig is ripe the manikin is on the tree from morn till eve. **1832** MACGILLIVRAY tr. *Humboldt's Trav.* xix. 282 The rocks, among which the Golden Manakin (*Pipra rupicola*), one of the most beautiful birds of the tropics, builds its nest. **1840** *Penny Cycl.* XVIII. 178/2 The spotted manakins of New Holland. **1855** KINGSLEY *Westw. Ho!* xxiii, The rock manakin, with its saffron plumage. **1896** NEWTON *Dict. Birds* 892 (Article *Song*), The whip-cracking of the Manakin.

4. *attrib.* or as *adj.* Dwarf, pygmy, diminutive, undersized; puny.

1840 Hood *Kilmansegg, Birth* i, One little manikin thing Survives to wear many a wrinkle. **1844** Disraeli *Coningsby* II. i, The manikin grasp of the English ministry. **1863** W. C. Baldwin *Afr. Hunting* 380, I have shot.. a splendid old manikin ostrich. *Ibid.* 410, I shot a very fine old manikin lion. **1884** D. G. Mitchell *Wet days & Lesser P., Theocritus* 22 Boors indeed; but they are live boors, and not manikin shepherds. **1898** J. Hollingshead *Gaiety Chron.* i. 2 Unlike Shakespeare, I have preserved the result of my mannikin efforts.

manikin, -kinnes, var. manykin, -kins. *Obs.*

manil(l, manilio: see next and manille.

manilla[1] (mə'nɪlə). Forms: α. 6 manillio, 6–7 -ellio, 7 -ilio, -illia, 6– manilla. β. 6 manil, -el, 8 me-, manille. [Sp., = Pg. *manilha*, It. *maniglia*; according to some a dim. of L. *manus* hand; others refer it to L. *monilia*, pl. of *monile* collar, necklace.] A ring of metal worn on the arm or wrist by some African peoples and used as a medium of exchange.

1556 W. Towrson in Hakluyt *Voy.* (1589) 101 We carried certain basons, manels, etc... We solde them both basons and manellios. **1558** *Ibid.* 130 Manils of brasse and some of lead. **1598** W. Phillip tr. *Linschoten* I. xlvi. 86/1 The women weare manillas, or arme bracelets theref, ten or twelue about each arme. **1625** Purchas *Pilgrims* I. iv. 418 About her wrists, tenne or twelue Manillias of Siluer. **1665** Sir T. Herbert *Trav.* (1677) 23 Of no small esteem are Bracelets, Copperchains, or Manellios. **1711** Lockyer *Acc. Trade India* 276 A Manilla is a solid Piece of Gold, of two or three Ounces Weight, worn in a Ring round the Wrist. **1731** Bailey vol. II, *Manille, Menille*, (in Africa) one of the principal commodities carried to those coasts by the Europeans to traffick with the Negroes in exchange for slaves. **1803** T. Winterbottom *Sierra Leone* I. vi. 100 Upon their arms they [the native women about Sierra Leone] wear large silver rings or bracelets, called manillas. **1851** D. Wilson *Archæol. Scotl.* 309 Manillas.. are regularly manufactured at Birmingham for the African traders.

Manilla[2], **Manila** (mə'nɪlə). Also (sense 2) with lower-case initial. [Native name: the form *Manila* is correct, but rare exc. in geographical use.]

1. The name of the capital of the Philippine Islands, used attrib. in the specific names of products of those islands, as ***Manilla copal, grass, tobacco, wood***; also **Manilla man**, a native of the Philippines.

1697 Dampier *Voy.* I. 304 The Frier sent us aboard.. 50l. of Manila Tobacco. **1745** P. Thomas *Jrnl. Anson's Voy.* 158 The celebrated Manila Wood, with which they build their Apaculpa Ships. **1849** *Blackw. Mag.* May 606 One was a fine, stout, middle-aged man, with immense whiskers and a cap of Manilla grass, a large blue jacket [etc.]. **1886** *Spectator* 6 Feb. 166/2 The two 'coolies' were palpably 'Manilla men', and not coolies,—that is, were half-caste sailors from Manilla.

2. a. (In full ***Manilla hemp.***) A fibrous material, obtained from the leaves of *Musa textilis* (see abaca), from which are made ropes, matting, textile fabrics, paper, etc. Hence ***Manilla cable, hat, paper, rope***, etc. Also, = *manilla paper* (now used of various papers of a light yellow-brown colour: see quots.).

1834 G. Bennett *Wand. N.S. Wales* I. xxi. 427 Manilla mat-bags. **1855** Royle *Fibrous Plants India* 48 He had some made into rope, which very much resembled Manilla rope. *Ibid.* 65 Manilla Hemp. **1862** *Catal. Internat. Exhib.* II. xix. 17 Manilla and coir mattings. *Ibid.* 18 Manilla and other cordage. **1870** Yeats *Nat. Hist. Comm.* 203 Manilla Hemp .. produces a woody fibre..; the elegant Manilla hats are manufactured from it. **1873** J. Richards *Wood-working Factories* 141 A layer of plain manilla paper. **1893** *Westm. Gaz.* 20 July 4/2 Her captain had her big 15in. manila cable paid out to the Olympia. **1897** *Daily News* 24 May 2/3 Tows, hemps, and flaxes meet with a ready market.. the finest Manillas making.. £16 per ton. **1926** *Paper Terminol.* (Spalding & Hodge) ii. 16 *Manilla*, a superfine tough quality of wrapping and label paper made from Manilla hemp. The term is now loosely applied to cheap imitations made from wood pulp. **1954** *Ibid.* 38 *Manil(l)a*, a coloured paper.. not necessarily containing Manila fibre. **1959** *Gloss. Packaging Terms* (*B.S.I.*) 67 *Manilla*, an imitation manila made in a wide variety of qualities. The term is now generally used to indicate the characteristic colour.

b. The light yellow-brown colour of manilla paper.

1934 in Webster. **1954** P. Highsmith *Blunderer* (1956) viii. 71 He put on old manila trousers.

3. (In full ***Manilla cheroot.***) A kind of cheroot manufactured in Manila.

1839 Marryat *Phant. Ship.* xxxii, On the evening of the third day, as they were smoking their Manilla cheroots. **1858** Simmonds *Dict. Trade, Manilas*, a name for a kind of cheroots made in the Philippines. **1881** Hedderwick *Villa by the Sea* 101, I will whiff a sad Manilla.

manille (mə'nɪl). *Cards.* Forms: 7 mal(l)illio, 9 malilla, 8 manil(l)io, manill, 8– manille. [Corruptly a. Sp. *malilla*, dim. of *mala* used in the same sense (prob. fem. of *malo* bad).] In quadrille and ombre, the second best trump or honour (being the deuce of a black suit or the seven of a red suit).

1674 Cotton *Compl. Gamester* (1680) 70 Of the Black there is first the *Spadillo*, or Ace of Spades; the *Mallillio* or black Deuce, the *Basto* or Ace of Clubs. **1710–11** Swift *Jrnl. to Stella* 25 Feb., I had.. often two black aces without a manilio. **1712–14** Pope *Rape Lock* III. 51 Spadillio first.. Led off two captive trumps, and swept the board. As many more Manillio forc'd to yield. **1794** *Sporting Mag.* IV. 201 The manille, or black deuce is the second [trump]. **1816** Singer *Hist. Cards* 266 The second Matador [at Ombre] is called Manilla, or Malilla;.. it is the seven in a red suit, and the deuce in black, the seven being the lowest card in red. **1851** Thackeray *Eng. Hum.* iv, About as much time as ladies of that age spent over spadille and manille. **1874** H. H. Gibbs *Ombre* ii. 11 In all Suits, when Trumps, the lowest card takes rank as Second Honour. It is called Manille.

manille, manillia, obs. forms of manilla[1].

manillio, obs. form of manilla[1], manille.

man in the moon.

1. The fancied semblance of a man (or a man's face) in the disk of the moon. Proverbial phr. ***no more than the man in the moon.***

a **1310** in Wright *Lyric P.* 112 Mon in the mone stond ant strit, on is bot forke is burthen he bereth. *a* **1548** Hall *Chron., Rich. III* 37 When the quene had heard this frendely mocion (which was as farre from her thought as the man that the rude people saie is in the moone). **1562** J. Heywood *Prov. & Epigr.* (1867) 205 Wee say (not the woman) the man in the moone. **1572** Abp. Parker *Corr.* (Parker Soc.) 404 He is no more my kinsman than the man in the moon. **1610** Shaks. *Temp.* II. ii. 141, I was the Man ith' Moone, when time was. **1676** Marvell *Mr. Smirke* 12 Which he knows no more then the Man in the Moon. **1722** De Foe *Col. Jack* (1840) 266, I thought no more of being serious.. than I thought of being a man in the moon. **1840** Marryat *Olla Podr.* (Rtldg.) 227 *Gum.* Then you don't know how things are settled? *Jel.* No more than the man in the moon.

allusively. **1695** Congreve *Love for L.* II. v, Thy Wife is a Constellation of Virtues; she's the Moon, and thou art the Man in the Moon.

2. Referred to as the type of an imaginary person.

In recent use, a jocular name for a pretendedly unknown person who supplies money for illicit expenditure at elections.

1596 Nashe *Saffron Walden* Wks. (Grosart) III. 175 *Non est inventus*: there's no such man to be found; let them that haue the Commission for the Concealments looke after it, or the Man in the Moone put for it. **1621** Laud *Serm.* 19 *June* 24 It is not now sufficient that the Iewes shall be.. conuerted... But these conuerted Iewes must meet out of all Nations: the ten Tribes, as well as the rest... Good God, what a fine people haue we here? Men in the Moone. **1866** *John Bull* 1 Sept. 584/1 [The witness] created some amusement by his description of Mr. Mum, the man in the moon, who, he said, was a necessary consequence of a Totnes election. **1881** *Rep. Oxf. Elect. Comm., Min. Evid.* 239 One of the first things Mr. M. said to me was, 'You know I am not a "man in the moon"'... I am simply come to see that the money is spent properly'. **1882** *Standard* 14 Jan. 5/2 Hundreds of highly respectable Parliamentary agents were ready to wink at the presence of the 'Man in the Moon'.

manioc ('mænɪɒk). Forms: α. 6–9 **manihot**, 7 **manyot, magniot.** β. 7– **mandioc, manioc**, (7 **manyoc, mandioque**, 8 **maniock**, 9 **magnoc**). γ. 7 **mandihoca**, 7, 9 **mandioca**, 9 **manioc(c)a.** [repr. Tupi *mandioca*, Guarani *mandio*, which denotes the root of the plant, the leaves being called in Tupi *manisoba*, the stalk *maniba* or *maniva*, and the juice *manipuera* (Burton *Highlands of Brazil*, 1869, II. 351).

The form *manihot*, adopted in botanical L. as the specific name, appears to be a Fr. spelling with silent *t*. The spelling *manioch* occurs in Fr. in 1614 (Claude d'Abbeville *Mission en Maragnan* 229).]

The plant cassava, q.v. (genus *Manihot*, formerly *Jatropha*). Also, the meal made from it.

α. **1568** Hacket tr. *Thevet's New found World* lviii. 93 The Americanes make meale of those rootes that are called Manihot [*Fr. orig.* (1558) Manihot]. **1611** E. Aston tr. *Boemus' Mann. & Cust.* 501 Rootes of Brasile called Aypi and Manyot. **1698** Froger *Voy.* 113 Their fields of Maes and Magniot. **1760** J. Lee *Introd. Bot.* App. 318 Manihot. *Jatropha.* **1802** [see β]. **1881** *Daily News* 12 Dec. 3/5 A species of manihot, from which the cearâ rubber was obtained.

β. **1660** F. Brooke tr. *Le Blanc's Trav.* 399 Mandioc a root is their chiefest diet, whereof they make flower. **1666** J. Davies tr. *Hist. Caribby Isl.* 50 A small tree called Manyoc, by some Manyot, and by others Mandioque. **1683** Lorrain *Muret's Funeral Rite* 132 Thou mightest have lived so well, ..thou didst want neither Manioc, nor Potato's. **1783** Justamond tr. *Raynal's Hist. Indies* V. 321 The manioc is a plant which is propagated by slips. **1802** *Naval Chron.* VIII. 149 *Manihot, magnoc*, or *manioc*, is a plant which grows in America and the West Indies. **1832** *Veg. Subst. Food* 157 The juice of Mandioc is.. fermented with.. molasses,.. into an intoxicating liquor. **1857** Livingstone *Trav.* xvii. 302 Manioc, which is looked upon here as the staff of life. **1871** Kingsley *At Last* xvi, The famous Cassava, or Manioc, the old food of the Indians, poisonous till its juice is squeezed out in a curious spiral grass basket.

γ. **1613** Purchas *Pilgrimage* (1614) 841 The roots of Mandioca had almost killed them all, but by a peece of Vnicornes horne they were preserved. **1663** Boyle *Usef. Exp. Nat. Philos.* I. v. 121 The root Mandihoca, that abounds with a very potent Poison. **1863** Bates *Nat. Amazons* x. (1864) 324 A superior kind of meal is manufactured at Ega of the sweet mandioca (*Manihot Aypi*). **1892** *Daily News* 20 Feb. 5/1 He found thousands of Saüba ants carrying off his store of mandioca.

b. *attrib.*, as ***manioc bread, bush, flour, meal, patch, plant, plantation, root, worm.***

1681 Grew *Musæum* II. 223 In Brasile, either eaten by themselves, or with their Mandioca-Flower. **1777** W. Robertson *Hist. Amer.* I. iv. 397 The art of extracting an intoxicating liquor from maize or the manioc root. **1792** Mar. Riddell *Voy. Madeira* 93 The jatropa manioc, or manioc plant. **1803** *Edin. Rev.* III. 89 A worm.. well known to [West Indian] planters as the Manioc or Indigo worm. **1816** Southey in *Q. Rev.* XVI. 370 A vessel laden with mandioc flour from the south. **1866** *Treas. Bot.* 718/1 Cassava or Mandiocca meal. **1897** Mary Kingsley *W. Africa* 209 This manioc meal is the staple food.

manion (= *many one*): see many.

maniorable, erron. form of manurable.

maniore, -owre, -ory: see manger, -ery.

maniple ('mænɪp(ə)l). Forms: (? 4), 7 manaple, 6 mainipul, manypule, manyple, *Sc.* manipil, 7 -pul, 7–8 -pule, (7, 9 manuple), 6– maniple. [a. OF. *maniple* (more commonly *manipule* as in mod.Fr.), ad. L. *manipul-us* handful, troop of soldiers, f. *manus* hand + **pl-*, weak form of root **plē-* to fill (as in *plēnus* full).

In med.L. *manipulus* was also used in sense 3 below. Henschel's Du Cange has several isolated instances in which *manipulus* and the related *manipula* seem to have meant 'something carried in the hand'; the latter is applied to a workman's tool (? a trowel), ? a staff, an apron; the former is applied to a bowl of some kind. There are also instances of *manipulus, manipula*, in the sense 'servant'.]

†**1.** A handful, *lit.* and *fig.* *Obs.*

1632 B. Jonson *Magn. Lady* I. 1, I ha' seen him waite at Court, there, with his Maniples Of papers, and petitions. **1651** Biggs *New Disp.* ⁋80 Why is not a manipule of Purselane equivalent to two grains of opium, when [etc.]. **1657** Tomlinson *Renou's Disp.* 136 A maniple with the medicks is as much as can be contained in a hand. **1658** Sir T. Browne *Hydriot.* Ep. Ded., With much excuse we bring these low delights, and poor maniples to your Treasure. **1688** R. Holme *Armoury* III. 442/1 A Manuple or great Handfull. **1694** Westmacott *Script. Herb.* (1695) 75 [Flax] when ripe, 'tis pulled and set up in maniples, or large handfuls, to dry them. **1752** Ainsworth *Lat. Dict.*, A maniple (handful) *Manipulus.* **1829** *Examiner* 371/2 Look at the mere maniples of people who say, speaking of themselves, *the* Church!

¶ **b.** Whimsically used for: The hand.

1833 *Fraser's Mag.* VIII. 658 His two unhallowed and incarnadine maniples of reeking digits. **1893** Gunter *Miss Dividends* 16 Ferdie finds his hand grasped warmly in a set of bronzed maniples.

2. *Roman Antiq.* A subdivision of the Roman legion, of which a cohort contained three, numbering 120 men each among the *hastati* and *principes*, and 60 each among the *triarii*.

1533 Bellenden *Livy* II. (S.T.S.) I. 148 The tothir consul .. Ischit furth.. with certane manipillis of armyt men. **1629** Maxwell tr. *Herodian* (1635) 271 The light armed souldiers had lanes made between the severall Maniples to sally forth as occasion served. **1658** Sir T. Browne *Gard. Cyrus* ii, Thus were the maniples and cohorts of the Hastiti, Principes and Triarii placed in their bodies. **1842** Arnold *Hist. Rome* III. 100 The Roman velites.. were soon driven back upon the hastati and principes, and passed through the intervals of the maniples to the rear. **1876** *Encycl. Brit.* IV. 750/2 Two 'maniples' or divisions of 60 men each.

attrib. **1891** Nettleship & Sandys *Seyffert's Dict. Class. Antiq.* 347/1 A further important novelty introduced by Marius was the use of the cohort-formation, instead of the maniple-formation.

†**b.** In modern warfare, a small band of soldiers of more or less definite number. *Obs.*

1574 H. G. *Briefe Tables* G ij, Thou, for to cause that the raye maye go with an euennesse, shalte cause this maniple to go by fiue in a ranke in breadth. **1598** Barret *Theor. Warres* III. ii. 46 A Maniple is here called so many rankes throughout the battell, as the battell is in length, at so many per ranke as they march in ordinance or array. *Ibid.*, Any part of shot or pikes, that be drawne a part, to be set to defend any straight, or to scarmush, may also bee called a Maniple. **1617** Moryson *Itin.* II. 66 Captaine Blany diuided his men into three Maniples. **1627** Capt. Smith *Seaman's Gram.* xiii. 62 They vse to martiall.. those squadrons in rankes like Manaples, which is foure square. **1641** Baker *Chron.* (1679) 232/2 The Rereward.. consisting of two thousand mingled Weapons, with two wings of Horsemen, .. all of them cast into square maniples. **1644** Milton *Areop.* (Arb.) 70 Untill hee see our small divided maniples cutting through at every angle of his ill united and unweildy brigade.

3. *Eccl.* In the Western Church, one of the Eucharistic vestments, consisting now of a strip of stuff from two to four feet in length and worn suspended from the left arm near the wrist by the celebrant, deacon, and subdeacon: said to have been orig. a napkin held in the left hand for the purpose of wiping the tears shed for the sins of the people; = fanon 1. (For a later interpretation of its symbolism see quot. *c* 1532.)

The words used on putting on the maniple, 'Merear, Domine, portare manipulum fletus et doloris', look like a reminiscence of Ps. cxxv[i]. 6 (Vulg.), and it seems possible that the term may have originated from this formula. (So, as one of several suggestions, in Durandus *Rationale* III. vi, *De Manipulo*; he explains 'manipulus' as = *præmium*.)

1346 in Heath *Grocers' Comp.* (1869) 49 *note*, Un vestement sainct, aube, manaple, stole et chesible. **1519** Horman *Vulg.* 16 b, Fyrst do on the amys, than the albe, than the gyrdell, than the manyple, than the stoole, than the chesybyll. *c* **1532** Du Wes *Introd. Fr.* in Palsgr. 1068 The manypule doth sygnifye the same [corde] wherof his precious handes were bounde. **1620** Melton *Astrolog.* 16 Albes, Copes, and Maniples. **1774** T. West *Antiq. Furness*

(1805) 361 With a stole about his neck, and a maniple on his left arm. **1849** ROCK *Ch. of Fathers* I. v. 424 The Anglo-Saxons..wore the maniple, as we do now, on the left wrist. **1853** HOOK *Ch. Dict.* (1871) 474 The maniple or manuple was originally a strip of linen suspended from the left arm of the priest, and used to wipe away the perspiration from the face. **1885** R. W. DIXON *Hist. Ch. Eng.* III. 190 According to the old offices, the deacons to be ordained were presented in amice, alb, girdle and maniple.

†**b.** App. used for: A wristlet or cuff. *Obs.*$^{-0}$

1611 COTGR., *Manchon d'hermines*, a Maniple charged, or powdered, with Ermines.

4. ***maniple of the curates*** [Eccl. L. *manipulus curatorum*]: a book containing a brief summary of certain ecclesiastical canons.

1706 tr. *Dupin's Eccl. Hist. 16th C.* II. IV. vii. 423 That Parish Priests shall..have a Bible with Commentaries and the Maniple of the Curates.

maniplies: see MANYPLIES.

manipulability (mə,nɪpjʊlə'bɪlɪtɪ). [f. MANIPULAB(LE *a.*: see -BILITY.] The quality of being manipulable.

1947 *Partisan Rev.* Sept.–Oct. 473 Every idea is judged in terms of its political manipulability. **1957** B. F. SKINNER *Verbal Behavior* v. 124 The increasing separability and manipulability of response elements in a minimal unit repertoire is a step toward ideal conditions. **1957** L. EISELEY *Immense Journey* (1958) 6 As I tapped and chiseled there in the foundations of the world, I had ample time to consider the cunning manipulability of the human fingers. **1967** *Punch* 11 Oct. 546/2 Doctors are no more gullible than the rest of us, but they are a captive audience, and the extent of their manipulability can be observed on a firm's local sales charts. **1971** J. B. CARROLL et al. *Word Frequency Bk.* p. vi, Only the Kučera-Francis work is of sufficient size and manipulability to yield a substantial word list and citation base for lexicography. **1974** *Time* 7 Jan. 60/3 His recommendations that society change its 'system of production, ownership and consumption' depend on faith in man's manipulability and desire to change.

manipulable (mə'nɪpjʊləb(ə)l), *a.* [f. late L. *manipulāre* to MANIPULATE: see -ABLE.] Capable of being manipulated.

1881 *Brit. Trade Jrnl.* XIX. 335 The substance..has to be rendered manipulable. **1957** B. F. SKINNER in Saporta & Bastian *Psycho-linguistics* (1961) 233/1 Suffixes such as *-ness* or *-hood* are usually readily manipulable as separate elements in composing new terms. **1963** *Punch* 2 Jan. 21/1 A swiftly manipulable key-board. **1965** J. FEINBERG in M. Black *Philos. in Amer.* 154 It would be an oversimplification ..to identify 'the cause' of an infelicitous condition with *any* manipulable necessary condition. **1971** *Nature* 12 Feb. 445/3 As well as being easy to learn and formally manipulable, [computer languages]..should be thought-provoking. **1971** *Human World* Nov. 14 Is sovereignty something that can be arranged like this? Is it so infinitely manipulable?

manipular (mə'nɪpjʊlə(r)), *a.* (*sb.*) [ad. L. *manipulār-is*, f. *manipul-us* MANIPLE.] **A.** *adj.*

1. Pertaining to the maniple in the ancient Roman army; characterized by formation in maniples.

1623 BINGHAM *Xenophon* etc., *Lipsius' Comp.* 6 The manipular Battalion insinuated it selfe into the void spaces, and so ouerthrew the Phalange. **1656** BLOUNT *Glossogr.*, *Manipular*, belonging to a band of men. **1833** in *Philol. Museum* II. 479 The earliest constitution of the manipular legion. **1886** PELHAM in *Encycl. Brit.* XX. 746/2 In the new manipular system, with its three lines, no regard was paid to civic distinctions.

2. Of the form of a sheaf. *rare.*

1805–17 R. JAMESON *Char. Min.* (ed. 3) 133 Manipular or sheaf-like. Consists of a number of crystals that diverge towards both ends, and are narrower in the middle, thus resembling a sheaf.

3. Of or pertaining to manipulation or handling.

The sense is not etymologically justifiable, being due to association with MANIPULATE *v.*

1831 *Fraser's Mag.* IV. 92 Such an unequivocal manipular token of resentment. **1841–4** EMERSON *Ess.* Ser. I. i. (1876) 16 What the former age has epitomized into a formula or rule for manipular convenience. **1849** LYTTON *Caxtons* II. XI. lviii, Denoting, symbolically, how he would like to do with Uncle Jack, could he once get him safe and snug under his manipular operations. **1852** J. MARTINEAU *Phases of Faith* Ess., etc. (1891) III. 7 Hence the invariable presence of some physical element in all that it [*sc.* Catholicism] looks upon as venerable. Its rites are a manipular invocation of God.

Hence **ma'nipularly** *adv.*, in a 'manipular' form (cf. sense 2 above).

1804 R. JAMESON *Syst. Min.* (1816) I. 305 The crystals are sometimes manipularly and scopiformly aggregated.

B. *sb.* A soldier of a maniple.

1862 MERIVALE *Rom. Emp.* (1865) VII. lvi. 91 The emperor himself,..regardless of the military indecorum, expostulated and reasoned with his manipulars.

ma'nipulary, *a. rare*$^{-1}$. [ad. L. *manipulāri-s*: see prec. and -ARY^2.] = MANIPULAR *a.* 1.

1780 COXE *Russ. Disc.* 222 Military ensigns representing hands... These hands resemble the manipulary standards of the Romans.

manipulatable (mə'nɪpjʊ,leɪtəb(ə)l), *a.* [f. MANIPULAT(E *v.* + -ABLE.] = MANIPULABLE *a.*

1934 in WEBSTER. **1964** E. A. NIDA *Toward Sci. Transl.* ix. 204 One must expect to find numerous and subtle distinctions, which cannot easily be reduced to readily manipulatable rules. **1970** *Computers & Humanities* IV. 327 These three considerations are separable and individually manipulatable.

manipulate (mə'nɪpjʊleɪt), *v.* [App. a back-formation from MANIPULATION: cf. F. *manipuler* (*a* 1814 in B. de St.-Pierre *Harmonies*), It. *manipolare*, *manipulare* 'to gripe or claspe with the hands; also to reduce into bottles or handfuls, to bundle vp' (Florio 1611); a med.L. *manipulare* is given in Henschel's Du Cange, with a single quot., in which it app. means 'to lead by the hand'.]

1. a. *trans.* To handle, esp. with dexterity; to manage, work, or treat by manual (and, by extension, any mechanical) means.

1831 CARLYLE *Sart. Res.* III. x, Or else, shut up in private Oratories, [they] meditate and manipulate the substances derived from her [the earth]. **1850** —— *Latter-d. Pamph.* ii. (1872) 44 Fraternity..has gone on, till it found itself unexpectedly manipulating guillotines by its chosen Robespierres. **1855** H. SPENCER *Princ. Psychol.* (1872) II. VII. iii. 335 The hand has been moulded into fitness for manipulating things. **1862** BURTON *Bk. Hunter* (1863) 154 A turner with a piece of wood in his lathe, which he can manipulate to his liking. **1870** *Echo* 11 Nov., The time.. when a photograph was admired simply because it was cleverly manipulated. **1876** C. M. DAVIES *Unorth. Lond.* (ed. 2) 179 He had promised..that he would refrain from manipulating contagious cases.

b. *absol.* or *intr.* in *Chem.* (cf. MANIPULATION 2).

1827 FARADAY *Chem. Manip.* Introd. 4 Of two persons having otherwise equal talents..the one who manipulates best will very soon be in advance of the other.

2. To operate upon with the mind or intelligence; to handle or treat (questions, artistic matter, resources, etc.) with skill.

1856 DOVE *Logic Chr. Faith* I. ii. 68 Philosophy (as hitherto manipulated) has been an attempt to do [etc.]. **1864** *Sat. Rev.* 31 Dec. 789/2 Nor are the questions..pleasant ones to manipulate. **1864** BOWEN *Logic* i. 22 Readily manipulated in thought. **1875** OUSELEY *Harmony* iii. 41 This [the third inversion of the added ninth] is perhaps.. the easiest to manipulate. **1879** FROUDE *Cæsar* xiii. 185 Crassus understood nothing beyond the art of manipulating money.

3. a. To manage by dexterous contrivance or influence; *esp.* to treat unfairly or insidiously for one's own advantage.

1864 CARLYLE *Fredk. Gt.* XII. xi. (1872) IV. 260 He had got his Electors manipulated, tickled to his purpose. **1866** *Totnes Elect. Comm., Min. Evid.* (1867) 73 Then who had manipulated Hill senior at the former elections? **1875** J. MORISON in *Expositor* I. 358 The hypothesis that the quotation has been..freely manipulated. **1893** CHAMBERLAIN *Sp. Ho. Comm.* 10 Apr., It will be possible for firms to manipulate their books. **1894** J. FISKE *Hist. Amer.* 399 Boards of canvassers were appointed for determining the results of disputed elections by manipulating the figures in counting the votes.

b. *Finance.* To cause (stocks) to rise or fall by affecting the market in other ways than those arising out of ordinary business; to influence (the market) in such ways.

1870 J. K. MEDBERY *Men & Mysteries Wall St.* 188 The stock..was most admirably manipulated, until it finally touched 152. **1903** S. S. PRATT *Work of Wall St.* 147 A market is rigged when it is manipulated.

4. To stimulate (the genitalia); also *refl.*, to masturbate.

1949 O. SCHWARZ *Psychology of Sex* ii. 31 The large majority of these children simply manipulate their genitals in a purely playful manner. **1953** A. C. KINSEY et al. *Sexual Behavior Human Female* v. 161 The female may stimulate them [*sc.* the breasts] with her hand..while she simultaneously manipulates her genitalia. **1965** MASTERS & JOHNSON in J. Money *Sex Research* iv. 107 It is a rare woman who directly manipulates the clitoris, or, if she does, maintains this type of stimulative activity for any significant length of time. **1971** 'V. X. SCOTT' *Surrogate Wife* 134 At one point he began manipulating himself.

Hence **ma'nipulated** *ppl. a.*, **ma'nipulating** *vbl. sb.*

1887 *Pall Mall G.* 3 Jan. 10/1 A Frenchman disposed of upwards of four thousand pounds' worth of manipulated diamonds in this country. **1892** *Athenæum* 4 June 722/1 This manipulating of a language. **1899** *Allbutt's Syst. Med.* VII. 749 This method is believed to produce temporary anæmia of the brain by causing a determination of blood to the manipulated parts. **1903** S. S. PRATT *Work of Wall St.* xi. 147 A deal is the operation resulting from a secret combination or agreement among Wall Street men to effect a certain purpose, generally of a manipulated character in the market.

manipulation (mə,nɪpjʊ'leɪʃən). [a. F. *manipulation* = Sp. *manipulacion*, Pg. *manipulação*, It. *manipolazione*, ad. mod.L. type **manipulātiōn-em*, f. **manipulāre* (= It. *manipolare*, F. *manipuler*: see MANIPULATE *v.*), f. L. *manipulus* handful.]

†**1.** The method of digging silver ore. *Obs.*

The sole sense recognized in Eng. Dicts. down to and including Todd, 1818.

1727–41 CHAMBERS *Cycl.*, *Manipulation*, a term used in the mines, to signify the manner of digging the silver, &c. out of the earth. **1731** in BAILEY vol. II.

2. *Chem.* The method of handling apparatus, etc. in experiments. In *Pharmacy*, 'the preparation of drugs' (Webster 1828–32).

1796 KIRWAN *Elem. Min.* (ed. 2) II. 482 It is only by an exact similarity in all the essential points of Manipulation, that results exactly similar can be expected. **1805** W. SAUNDERS *Min. Waters* 354 The various sources of inaccuracy to which chemical manipulations are liable. **1827** FARADAY in B. Jones' *Life* (1870) I. 396 The word manipulation,..though not usual in ordinary language, is so peculiarly expressive of the great object of these lectures, that I could not hesitate a moment to use it. **1854** RONALDS & RICHARDSON *Chem. Technol.* (ed. 2) I. 48 The average amount of ash obtained by laboratory manipulation.

3. *gen.* The handling of objects for a particular purpose; manual management; in *Surgery*, the manual examination of a part of the body. Also, making motions with the hand, manual action.

1826 KIRBY & SP. *Entomol.* IV. l. 536 However tedious some of the foregoing manipulations may seem, they are.. much less so than those required in several other branches of Natural History. **1846** GREENER *Sci. Gunnery* 403 The manipulation of this musket. **1852** MRS. STOWE *Uncle Tom's C.* xx. 207 In the zeal of her manipulations, the young disciple had contrived to snatch a pair of gloves and a ribbon, which she had adroitly slipped into her sleeves. **1853** FABER *All for Jesus* (1854) 246 A profound reverence for all the benedictions of the Church, for her sacraments, forms, and manipulations. **1872** F. G. THOMAS *Dis. Women* (ed. 3) 72 Conjoined manipulation is of great importance. **1878** A. H. MARKHAM *Gt. Frozen Sea* xv. 206 To handle delicate instruments, the manipulation of which, even in a temperate climate, requires the utmost care. **1879** J. J. YOUNG *Ceram. Art* 41 In Oriental work..we..find skill in manipulation, similitude in drawing, and beauty in color.

4. The act of operating upon or managing persons or things with dexterity; *esp.* with disparaging implication, unfair management or treatment (of documents, etc.).

1828 SIR W. NAPIER *Penins. War* I. 6 The organization of Napoleon's army was simple, the administration vigorous, the manipulations well contrived. **1843** RUSKIN *Mod. Paint.* II. III. ii. §10 The exquisite manipulation of the master gives to each atom of the multitude its own character and expression. **1864** BOWEN *Logic* xi. 364 No manipulation, no analysis, of these Truths previously demonstrated would enable him to evolve from them..the measure of this particular angle. **1875** STUBBS *Const. Hist.* II. xvii. 611 The third estate..was only too susceptible of royal manipulation. **1883** *Stubbs' Merc. Circular* 8 Nov. 982/2 The shirtings which are not susceptible of manipulation with clay and sizing. **1888** *Nation* (N.Y.) 9 Aug. 107/2 Manipulation signifies a common understanding and design on the part of a clique of operators to raise or depress values in order to get other people's money. **1908** *Westm. Gaz.* 26 Aug. 2/2 The opportunity for market manipulation is obvious.

manipulative (mə'nɪpjʊlətɪv), *a.* [f. MANIPULATE *v.*: see -ATIVE.] Of, pertaining to, concerning, or involving manipulation.

1836 I. TAYLOR *Phys. Theory Another Life* (1857) 154 A wonder of skill..as well as of manipulative execution. **1854** J. SCOFFERN in *Orr's Circ. Sci.*, *Chem.* 390 The manipulative details required..belong to the department of organic chemistry. **1862** SMILES *Engineers* II. 132 The workmen of that place [Birmingham] are still superior to most others in executing machinery requiring manipulative skill. **1881** ROSCOE in *Nature* XXIII. 599 Bunsen's untiring energy and wonderful manipulative power. **1890** *Spectator* 1 Nov. 615/2 One of those cunning feats of manipulative skill peculiar to the Oriental. **1909** *Westm. Gaz.* 8 Sept. 11/4 The powerful manipulative interests are watching events closely. **1947** M. M. LEWIS *Lang. in Society* i. 24 The manipulative and the declarative are the twin incentives by which the development of language is fostered in the child, and remain the essential functions of language in society. **1966** *New Statesman* 22 Apr. 581/2 The cause was won by the politicians' desire to appear manipulative about almost any issue, regardless of its suitability for manipulation. **1968** R. KYLE *Love Lab.* ix. 125 Lillian had just completed a manipulative session and was wearing only a wrapper. **1971** *Nature* 30 Apr. 578/2 For they are also clearly pre-adaptive to efficient use of the hands as manipulative organs, in such activities as food gathering and transport. **1972** *Maclean's Mag.* Mar. 61/1 Spicer is strong, attractive and manipulative. 'He's good at persuading people to do things they might not want to do.'

Hence **ma'nipulativeness.**

1949 M. MEAD *Male & Female* ii. 26 Greater awareness does not always mean greater manipulativeness. **1975** *N.Y. Times* 4 Mar. 31 You pity their failings—their determination to 'advance' their children as if life were a relay race,..their manipulativeness and insularity.

manipulator (mə'nɪpjʊleɪtə(r)). [a. mod.L. type **manipulātor*, f. **manipulāre* (see MANIPULATION). Cf. F. *manipulateur*.]

1. a. One who manipulates, in various senses.

1851 H. MAYO *Pop. Superstit.* (ed. 2) 90 The state into which mesmeric manipulators first plunge the patient. **1858** RUSKIN *Arrows of Chace* (1880) I. 140 As manipulators, none but the four men whom I have named.. were equal to Turner. **1864** *Soc. Sci. Rev.* 8 Science is nothing without experiment and a little practice will soon enable the teacher to become a successful manipulator. **1899** *Allbutt's Syst. Med.* VI. 69 An experienced surgical manipulator. **1902** J. S. PHILLIMORE *Sophocles* Introd. 79 As a manipulator of language we compare him [Sophocles] with Virgil.

b. With disparaging implication.

1864 *Morn. Star* 8 June 4 By the judicious application of patronage to an editorial staff a clever manipulator may gain for himself a character to which he has no title [etc.]. **1891** E. PEACOCK *N. Brendon* I. 285 A principal manipulator of the persecution company.

c. One who controls the price of stocks by specially contrived methods.

1888 *Economist* 17 Nov. 3/3 If the people are apathetic it is utterly useless for the manipulators to undertake to push prices up. **1903** S. S. PRATT *Work of Wall St.* 146 A professional may or may not be a manipulator, but a manipulator is always a professional. *Ibid.* 256 By false tips and matched orders or wash sales the manipulators endeavored to establish fictitious quotations for their stocks. **1904** *N.Y. Tribune* 15 May 4 Manipulators desperately

endeavoring to bring back recessions which will permit them to 'get even'.

2. An instrument used to facilitate manipulation.

spec. **a.** The transmitting instrument attached to the dial-telegraph (1875 Knight *Dict. Mech.*). **b.** In photography, a device for holding plates without handling them (ibid. Suppl.). **c.** An exercising machine for rubbing or pummelling the body (ibid.). **d.** A machine for manipulating blooms of iron or steel. **e.** An instrument used by those who instruct the deaf in the articulation of sounds.

1860 G. B. PRESCOTT *Electr. Telegr.* vi. 97 Fig. 48 is an instrument for bringing any number of batteries into circuit at pleasure,.. It is called a manipulator. **1886-7** MISS L. D. RICHARDS *Proc. Amer. Instruct. Deaf* 235, I use the manipulator very little. **1888** *Sci. Amer.* 15 Sept. 166/2 An Improved Ingot Manipulator.

f. A device for handling radioactive material, operated by remote control from behind a protective shield.

1952 *Nucleonics* Nov. 41/1 They have been named master-slave manipulators because all the seven degrees of freedom of the tongs are slaved to the single master handle. **1955** *Reactor Handbk.: Engin.* (U.S. Atomic Energy Comm.) 859 A general-purpose manipulator is considered to be a remotely-controlled mechanical arm capable of gripping diverse objects... All movements of the manipulator arm are controlled by a human operator... The manipulator may have a lower or higher load capacity than the human arm. **1958** *New Scientist* 24 Apr. 21/1 A manipulator believed to be the only one manufactured in Europe that is operated by electrical remote control will be displayed at next week's Hanover Fair... The power manipulator is equipped with interchangeable grasping units..and can lift and position objects weighing up to 750 lbs. **1962** *Newnes Conc. Encycl. Nucl. Energy* 488/2 These manipulators fall into three classes: 1. Handling tongs and sphere units... 2. Master-slave manipulators... 3. Rectilinear power manipulators. **1969** *IEEE Trans. Nucl. Sci.* XVI. 594/2 The geometry of the Brookhaven AGS and of other synchrotrons requires a larger degree of remoteness than is possible with mechanically-connected master-slave manipulators.

manipulatory (məˈnɪpjʊlətərɪ), *a.* [f. MANIPULATE *v.*: see -ORY.] Pertaining to or involving manipulation.

1827 FARADAY *Chem. Manip.* i. 24 A notion of the most necessary furniture of a small laboratory..may..be gathered from the manipulatory parts of the present work. **1838** MOORE *Mem.* (1856) VII. 225 To accompany him to the North London Hospital..to see Dr. Elliotson's manipulatory experiments. **1881** TYNDALL *Ess. Floating Matter of Air* 233 Even with considerable care and fairly disciplined manipulatory skill, success is not invariable. **1893** *Brit. Jrnl. Photogr.* 24 Nov. 748/2 In addition to photographic and manipulatory difficulties, the nausea of sea-sickness..has to be contended against.

manipule, manir, obs. ff. MANIPLE, MANNER.

Manipuri (mænɪˈpʊərɪ), *a.* and *sb.* [Native name.] **A.** *adj.* Of or pertaining to Manipur, a state in the region of Assam in north-east India; *spec.* used of a style of dancing (also *ellipt.*). **B.** *sb.* The people of Manipur; a member of this people; also, the Tibeto-Burman language of the Manipuri.

1906 E. A. GAIT *Hist. Assam* viii. 195 The Manipuri Raja was mindful of the services rendered him a few years previously. **1911** [see KHASI]. **1918** W. PETTIGREW *Tāngkhul Nāga Gram. & Dict.* 4 As in Manipuri, there are two noticeable changes in intonation in TN, a high and low tone to a great number of words which to the ignorant sound the same. **1927** *Blackw. Mag.* June 817/1 The Manipuris.. became such strict Hindus as even to 'out-Brahman' the Brahmans. **1948** D. DIRINGER *Alphabet* II vi. 365 The Oriya, Maithili and Early Manipuri characters seem also to be somewhat connected with the Bengali script. **1957** G. B. L. WILSON *Dict. Ballet* 178 *Manipuri*, in Hindu dancing, the style of north-east India. The dances are in the form of dance-drama (supported by dialogues and songs) and many dancers participate. It is mainly lyrical and lighter than the other Indian styles. **1968** *Encycl. Brit.* XIV. 790/2 About 60% of the population [of Manipur] speak Manipuri. *Ibid.* XV. 118/2 *Meithei*, also known as Manipuri, the dominant population of the valley of Manipur. **1969** *Femina* (Bombay) 26 Dec. 53/1 Kishori also left an imprint as a noted Manipuri dancer in the early dance dramas produced by the Indian National Theatre. Her rhythmic grace is still remembered. **1971** *Ceylon Observer* (Mag. Ed.) 19 Sept. 4/8 (Advt.), New silver motive white Manipuri saree.

‖**manis** (ˈmeɪnɪs). *Zool.* [mod.L. (Linnæus), said to be an assumed sing. of MANES.] The typical genus of the family *Manidæ* (scaly ant-eaters); any individual of this genus, a pangolin.

1770 *Phil. Trans.* LX. 36 A new Species of the Manis, or Scaly Lizard. **1802** BINGLEY *Anim. Biog.* (1813) I. 125 Of the manis tribe. **1850** R. G. CUMMING *Hunter's Life S. Afr.* (ed. 2) I. 247 The manis is met with throughout the interior of South Africa, but it is rare. **1872** MIVART *Elem. Anat.* ii. (1873) 58 The long tailed Pangolin or Manis.

manis, -isch, obs. Sc. forms of MENACE.

manish, Maniske, obs. ff. MANNISH, MANX.

‖**ma nishtana** (ma niʃˈtana). *Judaism.* Also **mah nishtan(n)ah.** [Heb., 'Why (is this night) different (from all other nights)?'] The opening words of the four questions in the Passover Haggadah, traditionally asked by the youngest member of a Jewish household on Seder Night; hence used to designate this part of the Passover celebrations.

1902 *Jewish Chron.* 18 Apr. 20/1 After the sanctification (*Kiddush*) with which our Haggadah begins..the four questions *Ma nishtana* are read. *Ibid.* 25 Apr. 20/2 In olden times the children were provided with small nuts and chestnuts to give more zest to the question, 'Ma nishtana'—'why is this night different from all other nights?' **1904** *Jewish Encycl.* VI. 141/2 Its initial words, 'Mah Nishtannah', are used as the name of the Haggadah, as in the question: 'What has Korah..to do in the Mah Nishtannah?' **1960** *Jewish Chron.* 8 Apr. 27/5 There was for me, the youngest boy, the important task of re-learning the Ma Nishtana. **1972** C. RAPHAEL *Feast of Hist.* iii. 90 The spirit of *ma nishtana*—the Four Questions in the Haggadah.

manism (ˈmeɪnɪz(ə)m). [f. MANES *sb. pl.* + -ISM.] The worship of the *manes* or shades of the dead; ancestor-worship. Hence **maˈnistic** *a.*

1904 G. S. HALL *Adolescence* II. xii. 179 Culture developed through the four stages of manism, when each [*sc.* the moon, sun, planets, etc.] was regarded as only the sensuous object it seemed, [etc.]. **1933** J. D. UNWIN *Sexual Regulations & Human Behaviour* i. 1 Uncivilised peoples.. Manistic—these do not erect temples but they pay some kind of post-funeral attention to their dead. **1937** A. HUXLEY *Ends & Means* xv. 311 All human societies are in one or another of four cultural conditions: zoistic, manistic, deistic, rationalistic. **1950** *Funk's Stand. Dict. Folklore* II. 673/1 Manism, the general term for the worship of the spirits of the dead, and, more specifically, for ancestor worship, is widespread in the world. **1956** E. E. EVANS-PRITCHARD *Nuer Relig.* xiii. 311 Many such origins have been propounded: magic, fetishism, manism, animism.

manitoka (mænɪˈtəʊkə). *S. Afr.* Also **manotoka.** [Perhaps a name fabricated by the botanist P. Macowan.] The South African name of a large shrub, *Myoporum insulare*, of the family Myoporaceæ, native to Australia and bearing small white flowers followed by edible blue berries.

1906 F. BLERSCH *Handbk. Agric. S. Afr.* xiii. 267 Hedge shrubs and trees... Manotoka (*Myoporum insulare*). **1948** H. V. MORTON *In Search of S. Afr.* ii. 48 The old buildings and houses of former occupants..were standing roofless and deserted in a jungle of manitoka trees. **1956** *Cape Times* 1 Mar. 8/6 The English myrtle hedge..is far more interesting, is greener and less likely to dry out. This can also be said of the manitoka and tecoma hedges. **1973** M. PHILIP *Caravan Caravel* 19 A tarred road circled the middle of the thickly grassed park, and the caravans were standing in rows on four different levels, with hedges of fleshy, narrow-leaved manitokkas [*sic*] bushing out between the caravan sites.

manitology (mænɪˈtɒlədʒɪ). [f. next + -(O)LOGY.] The branch of study that is concerned with the belief in manitous.

1851 SCHOOLCRAFT *Ind. Tribes U.S.* I. 34 The doctrine of Manitoes, or what may be denominated Manitology. **1881** DORMAN *Orig. Prim. Superst.* vi. 222 Totemism is explained by manitology, or the worship of manitous.

‖**Manitou** (ˈmænɪtuː). Also 7 **maneto,** 8 **menitto,** 8–9 **manitoo,** 9 **manito, manitu,** (**-ido**), **moneto.** [Algonquin *manito*, *manitu*.

According to Dr. Trumbull (*Trans. Amer. Philol. Assoc.* 1876, p. 167) *manit* is the active pple. of a vb. meaning to surpass, while *manitu* contains a predicative suffix, and so is equivalent to 'he or it is *manit*'. In 1587 Hariot says that the Indians of Virginia 'beleeue that there are many gods, which they call Mantoac' (Hakluyt III. 276).]

Among some American Indians, a spirit (of good or of evil) which is an object of religious awe or reverence; also, anything which is regarded as having supernatural power, as a fetish.

1698 G. THOMAS *Pensilvania* (1848) 2 They offer their first Fruits to a Maneto, or suppos'd Deity. **1701** C. WOLLEY *Jrnl. N. York* (1860) 37 They are of opinion that when they have ill success in their hunting, fishing, &c. their Menitto is the cause of it. **1804** C. B. BROWN tr. *Volney's View Soil U.S.* 416 First, they believe in a great Manito, or genius, who rules the world or universe. Under his supreme power are numberless Manitos, who traverse earth and air, and govern all things. **1817** J. BRADBURY *Trav. Amer.* 24 The Indians..often apply this term Manitou to uncommon or singular productions of nature which they highly venerate. **1856** BRYANT *Painted Cup* iii, The gentle Manitou of flowers. **1860** SCHOOLCRAFT *Ind. Tribes U.S.* V. 74 When a turtle, bird, quadruped, or other form of animated nature is adopted as the guardian spirit or moneto. **1895** W. J. HOFFMAN *Begin. Writing* 77 Fig. 31 represents the otter as a spirit or manido. **1899** *Jrnl. Anthropol. Inst.* I. 140 His Manitu or spirit, in trappers' jargon his medicine.

manitrunk (ˈmænɪtrʌŋk). *Ent.* [f. L. *manus* taken in the sense 'fore-leg' + *trunc-us* trunk.] The anterior segment of the thorax.

1826 KIRBY & SP. *Entomol.* III. 531 The first segment [of the trunk], because it bears the fore legs, I have named manitrunk (*manitruncus*).

manitu: see MANITOU.

maniure (= *manjure*), obs. form of MANGER.

manjack (ˈmændʒæk). A large West Indian tree, *Cordia macrophylla* or *C. elliptica.*

1864 GRISEBACH *Flora W. Ind.* 785 Manjack, *Cordia macrophylla.*

man-jack: see MAN *sb.*[1] 4 m, and JACK *sb.*[1] 2 c.

manjak (ˈmændʒæk). *West Indian.* Also 7 **mountjack,** 7–8 **munjack.** (See quot. 1902.)

1657 LIGON *Barbados* 101 Another gummy substance there is..called Mountjack. **1683** J. POYNTZ *Tobago* 37 This Munjack is nothing else than a Confirmation or Coagulation of the Tarr..into a more solid body, which Munjack [etc.]. **1902** *Encycl. Brit.* (ed. 10) XXVI. 145 (Barbados), The only mineral product is 'manjak', or glance-pitch, a form of asphalt, which occurs in the older rocks of the Scotland district.

‖**manjee** (ˈmændʒiː). Also 7 **mangee,** 8 **-gie,** 9 **manjy.** [Hindī *mānjhī.*] 'The master or steersman of a boat or any native river-craft' (Y.).

1683 SIR W. HEDGES *Diary* (Hakl. Soc.) I. 89 Which made our Mangee or Steerman advise us to fasten our boat in some Creeke. **1781** *India Gaz.* (Y.), The principal Gaut Mangies of Calcutta have entered into engagements at the Police office to supply all Persons that apply there with Boats. **1810** T. WILLIAMSON *E. Ind. Vade-Mecum* I. 283 The *Manjy*, *Goleeah*, and *Dandy*, are the steers-man, bow-man, and common rower in a boat, respectively. **1845** STOCQUELER *Hand-bk. Brit. India* (1854) 257 Few manjees, or steersmen of boats, leave the city without [etc.].

†**mank,** *sb.*[1] *Sc. Obs.* [app. a. F. *manque*, f. *manquer* to lack.] Want.

1500-20 DUNBAR *Poems* xxxi. 12 He that hes for his awin genȝie Ane plesand prop, but mank or menȝie, And schuttis syne [etc.]. **1718** RAMSAY *Christ's Kirk Gr.* III. xxiii, They drank, Till..in their maws there was nae mank. **1776** HERD *Scottish Songs* Gloss., *Mank*, a want.

†**mank,** *sb.*[2] *Obs.* (See quot.)

1683 TRYON *Way to Health* 284 Those fiery Steems [in food], which are of an hot griping windy Nature, and causing a Mank or Scurvey in the Blood.

†**mank,** *a. Obs.* Chiefly *Sc.* Also 6 **manke,** 7 **manc(k.** [a. OF. *manc*, *manque*:—L. *mancus* maimed.] Maimed, mutilated, defective.

1513 DOUGLAS *Æneis* v. Prol. 51 His febill prois bene mank and mutilait. **1559** BP. SCOT in Strype *Ann. Ref.* I. II. App. vii. 410 The church of Christe was not perfecte, but rather a manke bodye without a head. **1658** J. DURHAM *Exp. Rev.* xiii. v. (1660) 570 There is one thing yet to be cleared, without which all that is said seemeth to be manck. **1659** FULLER *App. Inj. Innoc.* III. 54 If the Bishops sit as a Third-estate, then Statutes made without them are manc and defective. **1722** *Wodrow Corr.* (1843) II. 622 When that mank volume comes over, I shall send one complete. **1723** MCWARD *Contendings* Pref. 12 Mr. Wodrow in his large, but mank and partial History [etc.].

mank (mæŋk), *v. Obs.* exc. *Sc.* [? f. MANK *a.*; cf. late (chiefly Frankish) L. *mancāre* to mutilate, f. *mancus*: see MANK *a.*] *trans.* To maim, mangle, mutilate.

a **1400-50** *Alexander* 4100 Bot alto-mankid hire with maces & mellis of Iren. *c* **1440** *Promp. Parv.* 325/1 Mankkyn, or maynyn, *mutilo.* *c* **1470** HENRY *Wallace* VII. 307 The myddyll off ane he mankit ner in twa. **1501** DOUGLAS *Pal. Hon.* III. xcii, Thay wretchis..That honour mankit and honestie mischeuit. **1573** *Satir. Poems Reform.* xl. 322 Let nouther lufe of friend, nor feir of fais, Mufe ȝow to mank ȝour Message. **1637-50** ROW *Hist. Kirk* (1842) 133 Ordour may be taken with them who hes mutilated and manked the Kirk's Registers. **1731** *Plain Reasons for Presbyterians dissenting* 116 It was past into an Act very quickly, lam'd and mank'd as it was. **1825-80** JAMIESON, *Mank*..2. To spoil or impair in any way.

Hence **manked** *ppl. a.* (whence **ˈmankedly** *adv.*, in a mutilated fashion; †**ˈmankedhead,** disabled condition), **ˈmanking** *vbl. sb.*

a **1300** *Cursor M.* 27884 Quen [man] es ouerlaid wit drunkenhede, þan in his mankidhed,..es turnd al into best state. *c* **1440** *Promp. Parv.* 325/1 Mankynge, or maymynge, *mutilacio.* **1513** DOUGLAS *Æneis* x. vi. 117 The rycht arm, from the schulder al to rent, Apon the mankyt sennonys hyngis by. **1553** KENNEDY *Compend. Tract.* in *Wodrow Soc. Misc.* (1844) 171 Thou sall understand, that thir wordis ar mankitlie allegit. *a* **1585** MONTGOMERIE *Flyting* 143 With mightie, manked, mangled meiter. **1671** *True Nonconf.* 288 Its mancking and confounding of Holy Scripture.

mankal, manke: see MANGAL, MANCUS.

mankalah, var. MANCALA.

ˈman-keen, *a.* [f. MAN *sb.*[1] + KEEN *a.*

Recorded later than the synonymous uses of *mankine*, MANKIND *a.*, but possibly its original form.]

1. Of animals (*rarely* of persons): Inclined to attack men; fierce, savage. (See KEEN *a.* 2 c.) Now *dial.*

1568 *Hist. Jacob & Esau* II. ii. Cjb, What? are you mankene now? I recken it best I, To bind your handes behind you euen as ye lye. *Esau.* Nay haue mercy on me, and let me not perishe. **1607** R. C[AREW] tr. *Estienne's World of Wonders* 263 He cured a man-keene wolfe..by making the signe of the crosse. **1625** JACKSON *Creed* v. vii. § 3 Boares and Bulls..grow often wilde, fierce, or mankene. **1632** SANDERSON *Serm.* 203 (If after all that they [dogs] still continue mankeen) knocke out their teeth. **1643** HERLE *Answ. Ferne* 6 How hard the Scripture is in yeelding any of its sincere milke for babes to these mankeene Gyants. **1737** BRACKEN *Farriery Impr.* (1757) II. 83 If we are over-kind to them [horses], it is more likely to make them Man-keen (as we say) than better conditioned. **1893** *Northumbld. Gloss.* s.v., Cattle are termed mankeen when they attack human beings.

†**b.** *absol.* or as *sb.* A savage animal. *Obs.*

1757 MRS. GRIFFITH *Lett. Henry & Frances* (1767) II. 281, I have got so far on my journey, having bought a horse for my servant... It is a mankeen in miniature.

2. Of women: Very fond of men. Now *dial.*

1683 G. Meriton *Yorkes. Dialogue* 17 Shees gane Eighteen And few but at that Age they are Man keen. **1876** *Whitby Gloss., Fellow-fond, Man-craz'd, Man-fond, Man-keen*, love smitten. 'She's desperate man-keen', very fond of the men. **1889** *N. W. Linc. Gloss.* (ed. 2).

Mankes, obs. form of Manx.

mankey, mankie, var. manco *Sc.*

mankey, var. manky *a.*

'man-killer. a. A killer of men; a homicide.

c **1440** *Gesta Rom.* xxvi. 141 (Harl. MS.), Whenne they [the knights] were putte oute of the palyse, some of hem.. bicome thevis, some man-killers. *a* **1533** Ld. Berners *Gold. Bk. M. Aurel.* (1546) G ij b, Such as accompanyeth with man kyllers and murtherers. **1660** R. Coke *Justice Vind.* 49 The Inhabitants of Switzerland.. who.. have.. continued Mercenary Man-killers to the interests of the Pope. **1895** *Pall Mall G.* 29 July 11/2 Even in those regions, where expert man-killers are by no means scarce, the style of shooting is altogether different from that of target shooting.

b. *transf.* and *fig.*

1899 *Daily News* 12 June 9/3 The new Mark IV. bullet, known among experts as 'The Man-killer'. **1929** F. C. Bowen *Sea Slang* 89 *Man-killer*, a hard-working sailing ship in which accidents were frequent. Some ships earned extraordinary reputations in that way. **1957** R. Campbell *Portugal* v. 86 They rechristened her [*sc.* a mare], Garota, or 'dear little girlie-wirlie', in order to.. give the impression that this man-killer was as sweet-tempered and innocent as she looked. Actually she had already killed two men. **1964** Mrs. L. B. Johnson *White House Diary* 24 July (1970) 183 This was a man-killer of a day for Lyndon.

So **'man-killing** *vbl. sb.* and *adj.*

1693 Dryden *Persius* iii. (1697) 446 A Spark, like thee, of the Man-killing Trade. **1880** *Chamb. Jrnl.* 15 May 316/2 These cattle-devouring tigers.. seldom take to man-killing. **1891** A. Forbes in *Daily News* 29 Dec. 2/1 The mankilling power of artillery. **1899** *Times* 27 Sept. 6/2 A new invention, either man-killing or labour-saving.

†**'mankin**[1]. *Obs.* Forms: see man *sb.*[1] and kin *sb.*[1] [OE. *mon-, mancyn(n*, f. *man* man *sb.*[1] + *cynn* kin *sb.*[1]] **a.** The human race, mankind. **b.** A race of men, a people. **c.** *rare.* Human nature.

Beowulf 110 Ac he hine feor forwræc.. mancynne fram. **971** *Blickl. Hom.* 129 For ealles mancynnes hæle. *c* **1000** Ælfric *Judg.* Proœm., Æfter þam þe Iosue.. þæt mankyn ʒebrohte.. to þam behatenan earde. *a* **1175** *Cott. Hom.* 225 Ic wille fordon al mancinn mid watere. *c* **1200** *Trin. Coll. Hom.* 19 Vre louerd he is cleped helende, for þat he mankin alesede. *c* **1275** *Passion our Lord* 11 in *O. E. Misc.* 37 Þrytty wyntre and more he wes among Monkunne. *a* **1300** *Cursor M.* 18433 Adam, fader of al man-kin. *c* **1330** *Florice & Bl.* (1857) 700 ȝif manken hit tholi might Twies I schold die with right. **13..** *E. E. Allit P.* A. 636 Inoȝe is knawen þat man-kyn grete, Fyrst was wroȝt to blysse parfyt. **13..** *Minor Poems fr. Vernon MS.* 37/4 And al soffrede swete Ihesu ffor monkunne sake þat sorwe.

mankin[2] ('mænkɪn). [f. man *sb.*[1] + -kin.] A diminutive or puny man; a manikin.

1820 Byron *Let. to Murray* 12 Oct. *Lett. & Jrnls.* (1901) V. 96 No more Keats, I entreat:.. there is no bearing the drivelling idiotism of the Mankin. **1831** Carlyle *Sart. Res.* ii. ii, The Mankin feels that he is a born Man.

mankind, *sb.* and *a.*[1] [f. man *sb.*[1] + kind *sb.* Cf. *man's kind* (man *sb.*[1] 21).] **A.** *sb.*

I. (Now mæn'kaɪnd.) **1.** The human species. Now only *collect.* Human beings in general. (First in *Cursor M.*; it superseded the older mankin[1].)

Formerly sometimes with sing. verb, or referred to with sing. masc. pronoun; now construed only as plural.

a **1300** *Cursor M.* 9372 Þe fader of heuen Dight his dere sun to send, Vntil erth, or flesche to ta for to bring man-kind o wa. *c* **1380** Wyclif *Sel. Wks.* III. 143 If monkynde in þo stat of innocense.. schulde not be ydel bot serve his God bisily. **1398** Trevisa *Barth. De P. R.* xvi. lxxi. (1495) 576 Onichius.. hath in itself colour medelyd lyke the naylle of mankinde. *c* **1420** Lydg. *Assembly of Gods* 1762 Thus was mankynde delyueryd from hys foon. **1480** Caxton *Descr. Brit.* 6 In Britayne ben hoot welles well arayed and adressyd to the vse of mankynde. **1541** R. Copland *Guydon's Quest. Chirurg.* D ij, Howe many in nombre are all the bones in a body of mankynde? **1560** Daus tr. *Sleidane's Comm.* 23 Sathan the ennemye of almankinde. **1587** Golding *De Mornay* xvi. 258 The great number of diseases wherwith mankinde is pained. **1610** Shaks. *Temp.* v. i. 183 How many goodly creatures are there here! How beauteous mankinde is! **1651** Hobbes *Leviath.* ii. xxvi. 139 A Law of Nature, equally obliging all man-kind. **1726** Butler *Serm. Hum. Nat.* iii. Wks. 1874 II. 33 Allowing that mankind hath the rule of right within himself. *a* **1774** Goldsm. *Hist. Greece* I. 202 Mankind never suffer any work to be lost which tends to make them more wise or happy. **1809** Syd. Smith *Serm.* I. 405 To study mankind aright, we must observe, no less the circumstances in which he is placed, than [etc.]. **1825** Lytton *Falkland* 14 Thrown early among mankind, I should early have imbibed their feelings. **1902** Greenough & Kittredge *Words* 158 The history of language is the history of mankind.

†**2.** The nature of man; human nature. Chiefly in phr. *to take* (or *fang*) *mankind*. *Obs.*

a **1300** *Cursor M.* 17288 + 43 Our lord ʒoght to tak mankynd and bring vus oute of woo. **1375** Barbour *Bruce* iv. 530 And mankynd biddis vs that we To procur vengeans besy be. *c* **1375** *Sc. Leg. Saints* xvi. (*Magdalena*) 242, & how mane-kynd þat he can fange. *c* **1449** Pecock *Repr.* ii. xvi. 245 God descended into mankinde, and.. couplid to him a singuler mankinde. **1493** *Festivall* (W. de W. 1515) 94 That our lorde had taken mankynde. **1567** *Gude & Godlie B.* (S.T.S.) 67 He come from heuin, and tuke mankynde.

†**b.** Human feeling, humanity. *Obs. rare*$^{-1}$.

1603 B. Jonson *Sejanus* v. x, O you, whose mindes are good, And have not forc'd all mankind, from your brests.

II. 3. (Now 'mænkaɪnd.) The male sex; persons of the male sex. (Cf. men-kind.)

1526 Tindale 1 *Cor.* vi. 9 Abusars of themselves with the mankynde. **1573** L. Lloyd *Marrow of Hist.* (1653) 141 If any mankind will enter therein.. he shall.. be bereft of his senses. And if any womankind.. go into that water, she [etc.]. *a* **1581** Bp. R. Cox *Injunctions*, Their chyldren and seruauntes both mankinde and womankinde. **1611** Shaks. *Wint. T.* i. ii. 199 Should all despaire That haue reuolted Wiues, the tenth of Mankind Would hang themselves. **1632** Lithgow *Trav.* iv. 155 Without admission of any man-kind in their company. **1874** Trollope *Lady Anna* ix. 67 The infinite simplicity and silliness of mankind and womankind at large.

B. *adj.*

†**1.** Human. *Obs.*

1584 R. Scot *Discov. Witchcr.* xv. xii. 412, I coniure you.. ye infernall kings.. to appeare.. in faire forme and shape of mankind kings.

†**2.** Male. *Obs.*

1633 Massinger *Guardian* i. ii, I keep no mankind servant in my house, In fear my chastity may be suspected. **1638** Ford *Lady's Trial* ii. ii, Sir, consider My sex; were I mankind, my sword should quit A wounded honour.

†**3.** Of women: Masculine, virago-like. *Obs.*

Sometimes indistinguishable from mankind *a.*[2]

1585 Higins *Junius' Nomenclator* 19 *Virago*, a manly woman, or a mankind woman. **1591** H. Smith *Prepar. Marr.* (Field) 61 A mankind woman is a monster, that is, halfe a woman and halfe a man. **1598** Florio, *Brifalda*, a bould, shamelesse, mankinde, virago woman. **1599** Porter *Angry Wom. Abingt.* (Percy Soc.) 62 Why, she is mankind; therefore thou mayest strike her. **1607** Shaks. *Cor.* iv. ii. 16 *Virg.* You shall stay too. I would I had the power To say so to my Husband. *Sicin.* Are you mankinde? *Volum.* I foole, is that a shame. **1607** Beaumont *Woman-Hater* iii. i, Are women growne so mankind? must they be wooing? **1619** Fletcher *M. Thomas* iv. vi, 'Twas a sound knock she gave me, A plaguy mankinde girle. **1635** *Life Long Meg of Westminster* (1816) 22 For that hee had heard shee was so mankind as to beat all she met withall, he would try her manhood.

†**'mankind**, *a.*[2] *Obs.* Also 6 **mankin(e.** [Of obscure origin: possibly a perversion of mankeen, though that form does not appear in our quots. till later.] Infuriated, furious, fierce, mad. = mankeen.

1519 Horman *Vulg.* 127 He set dogges, that were mankynde [L. *canibus efferatis*] vpon the man to be all to torne. *a* **1553** Udall *Royster D.* iv. viii. (Arb.) 77 Come away, by the matte she is mankine [*rime* minc]. I durst aduenture the losse of my right hande, If shee dyd not slee hir other husbande. **1598–9** Bp. Hall in *Marston's Sco. Villanie* iii. x. (1599) H i b, I ask'd Phisitions what theyr counsell was For a mad dogge or for a mankind Asse? **1605** Chapman *All Fooles* Wks. 1873 I. 167 Good Signor Cornelio be not too mankinde against your wife. **1632** Massinger *City Madam* iii. i, You brach, Are you turn'd mankind? **1672** Josselyn *New Eng. Rarities* 13 They [Bears].. are never mankind, i.e. fierce, but in rutting time.

Hence †**mankindly** *adv.*, cruelly, ferociously.

1606 *Sir G. Goosecappe* ii. i. in Bullen *O. Pl.* III. 30 You drive maids afore you,.. as mankindelie as if you had taken a surfet of our Sex lately.

mankle, manks, obs. ff. manacle *v.*, Manx.

manky ('mæŋkɪ), *a. local.* Also **mankey.** [f. mank *a.* + -y[1].] Bad, inferior, defective; dirty.

Possibly influenced by Fr. *manqué*.

1958 F. Norman *Bang to Rights* iii. 124 He would have to have all his teeth out as it seems that they were all mankey. **1971** B. W. Aldiss *Soldier Erect* 121 Have you chucked out that dirty manky beer you poisoned me with last time I came? **1973** A. Garner *Red Shift* 14 That's your manky palate, lad. The dressing and the wine have to balance. **1973** 'J. Patrick' *Glasgow Gang Observed* 231 Clatty, 'stourie', dirty, 'manky'. **1974** *Jrnl. Lancs. Dial. Soc.* XXIV. 28 [Westhoughton]. *Manky*, naughty.

manky, variant of manco *Sc.*

manless ('mænlɪs), *a.* [f. man *sb.*[1] + -less.]

1. a. Having no men (either in the sense of human beings or in that of adult male persons). Also (*nonce-use*), having no 'men' at chess.

c **1050** *Suppl. Ælfric's Gloss.* in Wr.-Wülcker 186/1 *Parietinae*, roflease and monlease ealde weallas. *a* **1400** *Sir Perc.* 1787 My modir alle manles Leved I thare! *a* **1626** Bacon *Consid. War with Spain* (1629) 31 It was no more but a stratagem of fireboats manlesse and sent vpon them by the fauour of the wind in the night time. **1640** R. Baillie *Lett. & Jrnls.* (1841) I. 270, I went forward with my companie manless. *c* **1640** *Game at Chasse* 22 in Maidment *Bk. Scot. Pasquils* (1868) 69 For still mismet and manles lousse the game. *a* **1670** Spalding *Troub. Chas. I* (1829) 112 His majesty's lieges should.. flee the covenant, and leave the cause manless. **1816** Byron *Darkness* 71 The world was void,.. Seasonless, herbless, treeless, manless, lifeless, A lump of death. **1834** Wrangham *Homerics* 22 When Amazonia's manless kind Their plains o'er-ran. **1863** W. Cory *Lett. & Jrnls.* (1897) 90 A humble, respectable, manless cottage. **1880** *Blackw. Mag.* Feb. 244 A melancholy expanse, treeless, dwellingless, manless.

b. Of a woman: lacking the company of men, *spec.* having no husband or suitor.

1924 [see manlessness]. **1942** E. Paul *Narrow St.* xix. 161 Like so many manless women, Thérèse was extraordinarily sensitive and hostile to the masculine touch. **1962** K. Orvis *Damned & Destroyed* xxv. 189 Fear of living out her life as a manless woman. **1970** O. Norton *Dead on Prediction* i. 5 I'd just been going through a pretty man-less period. **1972** *Guardian* 16 Feb. 13/2 The 24-year-old, man-less office worker.

†**2. a.** Unmanly, effeminate. *Obs.*

a **1529** Skelton *Sp. Parrot* 384 O causeles cowardes, O hartles hardynes! O manles manhod, enfayntyd all with fere! *c* **1611** Chapman *Iliad* iii. 30 O heauen, that thou hadst neare bene borne, Or (being so manlesse) neuer liu'd, to beare mans noblest state, The nuptiall honor. *Ibid.* xv. 319 The throtes of dogs shall graue His manlesse lims. **1621** Quarles *Div. Poems, Esther* (1717) 136 To yield The right and safe possession of the Shield, Was foul reproach, and manless cowardize. **1653** Waterhouse *Apol. Learn.* 82 That pusillanimity and manless subjugation, which by many in our Age scornfully is called Priest-riddenness.

†**b.** Inhuman. *Obs.*

c **1611** Chapman *Iliad* ix. 64 A hater of societie.. being stuft, with manlesse crueltie.

Hence †**'manlessly** *adv.*, in a manless manner; **'manlessness**, †(*a*) cowardice; (*b*) (of a woman) the state or condition of being manless.

1607 Chapman *Bussy D'Ambois* Plays 1873 II. 94 Let her wounds Manlesly digd in her, be easd and cur'd. **1667** Waterhouse *Fire Lond.* 92 That Dread and pavid manlessness, that seised the Inhabitants. **1924** *Public Opinion* 7 Nov. 460/2 We find girls robbed of wholesome excitements.. by the loneliness and manlessness of their lives.

manli, manlich, obs. forms of manly.

†**'manlihead.** *Obs.* Also 3 **manliched**, 5 **manlyhed(e**, 6 **manlihed.** [f. manly *a.* + -head.]

1. The condition of being human.

c **1250** *Gen. & Ex.* 23 Til god srid him in manliched. **1413** *Pilgr. Sowle* (Caxton) iv. xxix. (1859) 62 Ryght as an Image that nought hath of manlyhede, but only of lykenesse, by maner of shap withouten.

2. Virility, bravery, courage.

1422–83 *Pol. Poems* in *Archæologia* XXIX. 331 That saue alle Englond by his manly-hede. *c* **1475** *Partenay* 4352 And how this Geant bold Thens into a caue fled for fere and drede, Within the quike roche for all hys manlyhed. **1594** Carew *Tasso* (1881) 43 Fame hath through ech part of Egypt spred The tidings cleare of your great manlihed.

manlihood ('mænlɪhʊd). *rare.* [f. manly *a.* + -hood.] Manliness.

1641 Earl Monm. tr. *Biondi's Civil Warres* ii. 72 In such a case he would shew that manlihood which men.. void of judgement might now tax in him. **1819** Coleridge *Lett.* (1895) II. 699 Light, manlihood, simplicity, wholeness. These are the *entelechy* of Phidian Genius. **1887** D. C. Murray & Herman *Traveller Returns* iv. 56 The man-fool.. will not please the woman-fool out of his manlihood but by falling into her likeness. **1889** *Atalanta Mag.* Apr. 464/2 The earnestness and manlihood of the Elizabethan age.

manlike ('mænlaɪk), *a.* (*adv.*) Also 5–6 **-lyke.** [f. man *sb.*[1] + like *a.*]

1. Having the qualities or characteristics proper to a man as distinguished from a woman or child. Of women: Having masculine qualities; mannish.

c **1450** Holland *Howlat* 155 Thai apperit to the Pape and present thaim aye Fair farrand and fre,.. And manlyke. *c* **1470** Harding *Chron.* cxcii. iii, He then arest... The lorde Cobham full trewe and also manlyke. **1579** J. Stubbes *Gaping Gulf* D vij b, The smal reckoning which that manlike nation makes of Fraunce. **1605** Camden *Rem.* (1637) 95 Dido, A Phœnician name, signifying a manlike woman. **1715–20** Pope *Iliad* iii. 249 Against the manlike Amazons we stood. **1871** Smiles *Charac.* xi. 300 Men are sometimes womanlike, and women are sometimes manlike.

b. Belonging to or befitting a man; manly, masculine.

1561 T. Norton *Calvin's Inst.* iv. xx. (1634) 733 That among Christians may be a common shew of religion, and among men may be man-like civilitie. **1612** Drayton *Poly-olb.* xvii. 342 Elizabeth.. Digressing from her Sex, with Man-like gouernment This Iland kept in awe. **1624** Capt. Smith *Virginia* ii. 31 The men bestow their times in fishing, hunting, warres, and such man-like exercises. **1678** Cotterell *Davila's Hist. Fr.* 11 The Queen, a woman of a manlike [1647 p. 23 manly] spirit and subtil wit. **1728** Morgan *Algiers* I. iv. 108 Why then are the Africans alone to be called Savages and Barbarians for shewing a manlike Resentment. **1736** Shenstone *Verses to Lady* 7 Oct. 21 In glaring Chloe's man-like Taste and Mien, Are the gross splendors of the Tulip seen. **1839** Carlyle *Chartism* iii. (1858) 15 It is for a manlike place.. in this world.. that he struggles. **1895** H. S. Merriman *Grey Lady* ii. xiv. (1902) 335 From long association with men she had learnt a manlike reticence.

2. Resembling a man.

1590 T. Nelson in *Antiquary* XIII. 54/2 Whose form you see is monstrous, strange and rare, Before a manlike shape, behinde a fishes fell. **1604** Rowlands *Looke to it* 19 Man-like in shape, in manners but a beast. **1667** Milton *P.L.* viii. 471 Under his forming hands a Creature grew, Manlike, but different sex, so lovly faire. **1863** Huxley *Man's Place Nat.* 104 The structural differences between Man and the Manlike apes. **1899** W. H. Furness *Folk Lore Borneo* 21 When he stood upon the ground, he met a man-like being.

3. As *adv.* = manfully.

1577 Hellowes *Gueuara's Chron.* 34 Lucius Metellus.. fought so valiantly and manlike, that he left.. one only person. **1592** Stow *Annals* 459 Ioh. Ball.. biddeth them.. stand manlike together in trueth And helpe truth, and truth shall helpe you. **1837** Emerson *Misc.* (1884) 84 So is the danger a danger still; so is the fear worse. Manlike let him turn and face it. **1843** Carlyle *Past & Pr.* iv. iv, To have neither superior nor inferior, nor equal, united manlike to you.

Hence **'manlikely** *adv.*, **'manlikeness.**

1742 Willison *Balm of Gilead* viii. (1800) 82 The true motive of Christian love is a manlikeness and love to Christ more than to you. **1873** P. Brooks *New Starts in Life* xii. 209 Who does not rejoice that his divine Master could be

manlikely indignant? **1885** G. MEREDITH *Diana* I. xv. 322 She distinguished that he could only suppose, manlikely, one bad cause for the division. **1903** FAIRBAIRN in *Contemp. Rev.* Jan. 10 He saw . . into the godlikeness of man and the manlikeness of God.

manlily ('mænlɪlɪ), *adv.* Also 4–5 **-lyly, -lely, -lelie.** [f. MANLY *a.* + -LY².] In a manly manner.

1375 BARBOUR *Bruce* II. 486 Bot always, as a man off mayn, He mayntemyt him full manlyly. *c* **1440** *Alph. Tales* 114 His enmy come in manlelie agayns hym. **1896** ABP. BENSON *Jrnl.* 7 June in *Life* (1899) II. 715 [Holy Communion] unritually, but so solemnly and manlily administered by Whewell, Sedgwick, Martin, and their peers.

manliness ('mænlɪnɪs). [f. MANLY + -NESS.]

1. The state or quality of being manly; the possession of manly vigour, or of those virtues characteristic of a man.

1375 BARBOUR *Bruce* IX. 77 His vrechidnes so in thame gais, That thai thair manlynes sall tyne Throu vrechidnes of his covyne. *c* **1450** LYDG. & BURGH *Secrees* 2603 Colour reed Causyd of blood pure, Is signe of strengthe and greet manlynesse. **1569** GOLDING *Heminges Post.* 23 Stephan was . . full of grace and manlynesse [orig. *fortitudine*]. **1596** SPENSER *F. Q.* IV. vii. 45 Yet weend, by secret signes of manlinesse . . That he whilome some gentle swaine had beene. **1673** *Remarques Humours Town* A iv b, A person who . . should value the innocence and manliness of a Country one [*i.e.* life]. **1770** GOLDSM. *Des. Vill.* 384 Whilst her fond husband strove to lend relief In all the silent manliness of grief. **1880** TROLLOPE *Duke's Children* I. iii. 33 He was dark, with . . that expression of manliness . . which women love the best.

†**2.** Humanity; human kindness. *Obs.*

1382 WYCLIF *2 Macc.* xiv. 9 Thi manlynesse [Vulg. *humanitatem tuam*] shewid to alle men.

'**manling.** *rare.* [-LING¹.] A little man.

a **1637** B. JONSON *Discov.*, *Cens. Scal. in Lil. Germ.*, Augustus often called him his wittie Manling (for the littlenes of his stature). **17..** *Fashion* 65 in Dodsley *Coll. Poems* (1755) III. 276 'Tis meaner (cries the manling) to command A conquering host . . Than furl fair Flavia's fan, or lead a dance. **1895** KIPLING *Second Jungle Bk.* 184 A Manling with a knife threw stones at my head. **1922** A. S. M. HUTCHINSON *This Freedom* 276 Her baby boy, her tiny manling.

manly ('mænlɪ), *a.* For forms see MAN *sb.*¹ and -LY¹: also 5 *Sc.* **mandly.** *Superl.* 4 **manlokest.** [f. MAN *sb.*¹ + -LY¹.]

†**1.** Belonging to human beings; human. *Obs.*

c **1200** *Vices & Virtues* 43 For none winde of mannliche fandinge. *a* **1225** *Ancr. R.* 112 Swuc grure he hefde in his monliche vlesche aȝein þe stronge deorewurðe pinen þet he schulde drien. **1387–8** T. USK *Test. Love* II. iv. (Skeat) l. 46 The ilke three waies of liues . . whiche . . arne by names cleped, bestialliche, resonabliche, [and manlich. Resonablich] is vertuous. Manlich is worldlich. *c* **1422** HOCCLEVE *Jereslaus's Wife* 783 Be nat abassht it manly is to synne, But feendly is longe lye ther-ynne. **1491** CAXTON *Vitas Patr.* (W. de W. 1495) I. xcviii. 130 b/1 The ordenaunces that I haue yeue to them for to kepe, ben manly in asmoche as I that am a man haue enjoyed them to kepe them. **1554** KNOX *Fort for Afflicted* (1580) A 8 Wee haue another schoolemaister then manly reason. **1625** GILL *Sacr. Philos.* II. 134 Hee [Satan] thought that God should rather dwell in the being of the Angels . . then dwelling in the tabernacle of the manly being.

2. Possessing the virtues proper to a man as distinguished from a woman or child; chiefly, courageous, independent in spirit, frank, upright.

a **1225** *Ancr. R.* 272 Wummon is þe reisun, þet is, wittes skile hwon hit unstrencðeð, þet schulde been monlich & stalewarde & kene ine treowe bileaue. *c* **1350** *Will. Palerne* 3325 þei . . hadden gret ioye þa so manli a man wold mele in here side. *Ibid.* 3419 þe stiward had a newe but of ȝong age, on þe manlokest man þat men shold of heren. *c* **1450** *St. Cuthbert* (Surtees) 7507 He was honest and manly. *c* **1470** HENRY *Wallace* VI. 785 Lykly he was, rycht fair and weill farrand, Mandly and stout. **1535** COVERDALE *1 Sam.* iv. 9 Be stronge now and manly ye Philistynes. . . Be manly and fighte. **1606** SHAKS. *Tr. & Cr.* IV. v. 104 Manly as Hector, but more dangerous. **1632** LITHGOW *Trav.* IX. 421 A proud Nobility, a familiar and manly Gentry. **1791** MRS. RADCLIFFE *Rom. Forest* v, His person was manly, and his air military. **1800** FOSTER in *Life & Corr.* (1846) I. 124 It is more manly to confess than to extenuate. **1856** EMERSON *Eng. Traits, Race* Wks. (Bohn) II. 30 They [the English] are rather manly than warlike. **1879** L. STEPHEN *Hours in Library* III. 62 He [Fielding] was manly to the last.

b. Of a woman: Possessing qualities or attributes regarded as characteristic of a man.

c **1511** *1st Eng. Bk. Amer.* (Arb.) Introd. 33/1 These women be very manly in fytynge and hardy. *a* **1548** HALL *Chron., Hen. VI* 113 b, This wytch or manly woman . . the Frenchemen greatly glorified. *a* **1592** GREENE *Jas. IV*, IV. iv, *Dorot.* How looke I, Nano? like a man or no? *Nano.* If not a man, yet like a manlie shrowe. **1774** FOOTE *Cozeners* III. Wks. 1799 II. 186 As to fortune, she is totally careless in that. . . How manly that is in a woman! **1824** W. IRVING *T. Trav.* I. 42 My aunt was a lady of large frame . . she was . . a very manly woman.

c. *transf.* and *fig.*

1697 DRYDEN *Virg. Georg.* II. 70 The Vigour of the Native Earth Maintains the Plant, and makes a Manly Birth. **1799** J. ROBERTSON *Agric. Perth* 470 The house of Auchtertyre, with a manly front of cut granite. **1801** *Sk. Paris as it was* II. xliv. 86 The architecture has certainly lost that gloomy tint which gave to this building a manly and respectable character. **1864** LOWELL *Fireside Trav.* 185 It [iron] is a manly metal, with no sordid associations like gold or silver.

3. Of things, qualities, etc.: Befitting or belonging to a man; masculine.

c **1375** *Sc. Leg. Saints* xxxi. (*Eugenia*) 191 þo þu be a woman, manlyk ar þi dedis al. **1398** TREVISA *Barth. De P. R.* v. xlviii. (1495) 165 Yf the ballok stones be kut of manely strength passyth and male complexion changyth in to femall complexion. **1459** *Rolls of Parlt.* V. 348/2 Exortation . . made . . in so witty, so knyghtly, so manly, in so comfortable wise. **1592** SHAKS. *Mids. N.* III. ii. 157.—— *Rom. & Jul.* III. ii. 53, I saw the wound, . . here on his manly brest. **1617** MORYSON *Itin.* III. 48 The Germans speech is said to be manly, the Frenchmans sweet and fluent. **1671** MILTON *P. R.* II. 225 Therefore with manlier objects we must try His constancy. **1681** DRYDEN *Abs. & Achit.* I. 22 His conscious destiny made way, By manly beauty to imperial sway. *a* **1704** T. BROWN *Praise Drunkenness* Wks. 1730 I. 37 The drunkards voice is hoarse and manly, not like the squeaking trils of an Eunuch. **1851** MAYNE REID *Scalp Hunt.* liii. 401 In my earlier life I was addicted to what are termed 'manly sports'. **1894** GLADSTONE *Odes of Horace* III. xxiv. 54 Train we these minds effeminate With thoughts and ways of manlier state.

†**4.** Humane, charitable; generous. *Obs.*

1377 LANGL. *P. Pl.* B. v. 260 Artow manlyche amonge thi neiȝbores of thi mete and drynke?

†**5.** Having the attributes of a (liege) man; subservient. *Obs.*

c **1380** WYCLIF *Wks.* (1880) 65 And also ȝif þei ȝeuen a benefis for men ben of here kyn, . . or ellis for þe clerk is manly to þe lord in gay cloþinge, . . or ony oþere veyn iapis.

†**6.** 'Grown up'; adult, mature. *Obs.*

1579 W. WILKINSON *Confut. Familye of Loue, Heret. Affirm.* b j b, Not that they should alwayes remaine as subject thereunder [the ordinance of the Lord], but vntill the appoynted tyme, vntill the manly old age in the godly vnderstanding of the holy word. **1621** T. WILLIAMSON tr. *Goulart's Wise Vieillard* 14 Those men . . with the sinnes of their middle and manly age, doe fill vp the measure of their iniquities with the vices of a shamelesse old age. **1647** JER. TAYLOR *Lib. Proph.* xviii. 244 If the Infant vow be invalid till the Manly confirmation. **1691** WOOD *Ath. Oxon.* I. 6 William Galeon . . did in his Manly Years take upon him the Habit of the Friers of the Order of St. Austin.

7. *Comb.*, as ***manly-minded*** adj.

1818 MOORE *Mem.* (1853) II. 163 We . . walked home in the evening. Scully a good, honest, manly-minded fellow.

manly ('mænlɪ), *adv.* For forms see MAN *sb.*¹ and -LY². [f. MAN *sb.*¹ + -LY²; in OE. *mannlíce.*]

1. In a manly manner; like a man; manfully, courageously, with valour or energy. ? *Obs.* or *arch.*

In ME. alliterative poetry often used expletively.

Beowulf 1046 Swa man-lice mære þeoden, hord-weard hæleþa heaþo-ræsas ȝeald mearum ond madmum. *c* **1205** LAY. 26855 And hæhte heom amorȝen monliche arisen. *a* **1225** *Ancr. R.* 422 Holdeð ou ine swuche reste þet ȝe longe þerefter muwen ine Godes seruise þe monluker swinken. *a* **1300** *E. E. Ps.* xxx. 31 Dos manlike and your hert strenghþed be. *a* **1300** *Cursor M.* 21341 Man [he is] quils he manli him ledis. **1382** WYCLIF *1 Macc.* vi. 31 Thei maden engynys, and thei wenten out, . . and fouȝten manly. *c* **1400** *Destr. Troy* 7227 He met hom full monly with his mayn dynttes. *c* **1400** MAUNDEV. (Roxb.) xxi. 94 þe kyng hase all way agayne-standen him and putt him off mannely. **1586** MARLOWE *1st Pt. Tamburl.* III. ii, Faith, and, Techelles, it was manly done. **1607** ROWLANDS *Guy Warw.* 41 The ugly beast . . Comes at him manly, with most dreadful paws. **1632** LITHGOW *Trav.* v. 231 Our Souldiers . . stood manly to it, with their Bowes and Arrowes. **1755** JOHNSON, *Manly* adv., with courage like a man.

†**2.** Like a human being. **a.** Humanely, courteously; generously. **b.** After the fashion of fallen man; unregenerately. *Obs.*

1377 LANGL. *P. Pl.* B. x. 87 Who-so hath moche, spene manliche so meneth Thobie. **1382** WYCLIF *2 Macc.* ix. 27 Forsothe Y trist, hym to do myldly, and manly, or curteysly. —— *Acts* xxvii. 3 Iulius tretynge manly [*gloss.* or kurteysly] Poule suffride for to go to frendis. **1547** HOOPER *Declar. Christ* iv. D ij, Let hym tary style in the doctrine of man and lyue as manly and carnally as he list.

†**3.** Excellently, 'bravely'. *Obs.*

1605 SHAKS. *Macb.* IV. iii. 235 This time goes manly: Come go we to the King, our Power is ready, Our lacke is nothing but our leaue.

man-made ('mænmeɪd), *a.* Also (occas.) as two words and (more freq.) **manmade.** [f. MAN *sb.*¹ + MADE *ppl. a.*] Made by man; made or devised by human effort, i.e. not existing in nature; artificial: applied esp. to fibres and fabrics manufactured from chemicals of natural or synthetic origin. Also *ellipt.* and *fig.*

a **1718** PENN *Life* Wks. 1726 I. 170 What I meant by Clergy, viz. A Man-made and Mercenary Ministry. **1839** BAILEY *Festus* xxxiii. (1848) 356 Man-made gods. **1921** W. DE LA MARE *Mem. Midget* xxxiii. 237 There was nothing man-made in Fanny; and if there are women-shaped mermaids I know what looks will be seen in their faces. **1939** G. B. SHAW *In Good King Charles's Golden Days* I. 29, I tell you that from the moment you allow this manmade monster called a Church to enter your mind your inner light is like an extinguished candle. **1948** *Sci. News* VII. 86 When . . the country is small and the civilisation old, one finds that the landscape is eventually almost entirely man-made. **1955** *Times* 5 July 16/3 Man-made fibres, by which I mean those made by the viscose and acetate processes and the various synthetic fibres. *Ibid.* (Suppl.) p. ii/1 The first man-made forest of such a size to be used for large-scale paper-making will provide the raw material for the 300-acre combined pulp, newsprint and timber mill. **1960** *Farmer & Stockbreeder* 1 Mar. 62/1 Yet another Welsh valley is to be flooded. In time, another man-made lake. **1966** *McGraw-Hill Encycl. Sci. & Technol.* V. 242/1 Rayon is a man-made fibre but not a synthetic fiber. Nylon is a synthetic fiber. **1968** *Daily Tel.* 4 Nov. 2/1 Still no let-up is visible in the prodigious progress of man-made fibres. . . This year's man-made production at the ninth-month mark was more than 26 p.c. above last year's level at the same stage. *Ibid.*, Man-mades now have a quarter of the total world fibre output. **1969** D. C. HAGUE *Managerial Econ.* II. iv. 90 A large proportion of output in a modern economy is accounted for by . . large firms. In the United Kingdom, this happens in the . . manmade fibre industries. **1969** *New Yorker* 12 Apr. 85/1 In order to avoid capturing one of their own microflora or gathering any of the other manmade contaminants on the surface of the moon, the astronauts will have to take the sample for the exobiologists from underground. **1974** *Country Life* 3–10 Jan. 54/2 Coats and dresses in ultrasuede, a man-made, washable material.

'**man-'midwife.** Now *rare.* Pl. **men-midwives.** A man who assists women in childbirth; an accoucheur. Also *fig.*

1625 B. JONSON *Staple of N.* Induct., There are a set of gamesters within, in trauell of a thing call'd a Play, . . and they haue intreated me to be their Man-Midwife, the Prologue. **1638** SUCKLING *Aglaura* (1646) 5 That old doting man-mid-wife Time. **1727** BRADLEY *Fam. Dict.* s.v. *After-Birth*, That which Chirurgeons and Men-Midwives call Placenta. **1783** S. F. SIMMONS in *Med. Commun.* I. 176 Dr. Bland, physician man-midwife to the Westminster General Dispensary. **1797** *Directory Sheffield* 81 Hodgson, John, surgeon, and man-midwife. **1807** ROBINSON *Archæol. Græca* v. xiv. 476 The ancient Athenians used only men-midwives.

Hence **man-midwifery**, the practice or occupation of a man-midwife.

1681 T. FLATMAN *Heraclitus Ridens* No. 14 *Jest.* . . But you promised me I should see Mr. Character brought to bed. *Earn.* That you shall presently, of a Premunire at least, by the help of his own man-midwifery. **1684** EARL ROSCOM. *Ess. Transl. Verse* 244 A Quack (too scandalously Mean to Name) Had, by Man-Midwifery, got Wealth and Fame. **1790** P. THICKNESSE (*title*) Man-Midwifery Analyzed.

'**man-'milliner.** Pl. **men-, man-milliners.** A man who makes or vends millinery; 'hence, a man who is busied with trifling occupations or embellishments' (Webster).

1792 FLOYD in Southey *Life A. Bell* (1844) I. 439 Many unfortunate young gentlemen are put into the army by their barbarous friends, . . who have not constitutions for a man-milliner. **1796** SOUTHEY *Lett. fr. Spain* (1799) 223, I look upon a Man milliner not only as one of the most despicable members of society, but as one of the most injurious. **1807** *Sporting Mag.* XXIX. 185 The plaintiff is a Haberdasher and Man-milliner living in Piccadilly. **1813** *Examiner* 1 Feb. 76/2 Some men milliners deprecate the employment of women. **1814** HAZLITT *Pol. Ess.* (1819) 66 The *Morning Herald* sheds tears of joy over the fashionable virtues of the rising generation, and finds that we shall make better man-milliners, better lacqueys, and better courtiers than ever. **1839** T. HOOK *Birth, Deaths*, etc. I. ii. 53 He's an empty-pated fellow, and as conceited as a man-milliner. **1901** *Westm. Gaz.* 5 Feb. 5/2 One of the leading man-milliners hopes the strike [of ladies' tailors in Paris] will succeed.

attrib. **1850** THACKERAY *Contrib. to Punch* Wks. (Biogr. ed.) VI. 691 One of those twopenny-halfpenny men-milliner moralists.

'**man-'millinery.** A contemptuous term for clothing or apparel (e.g. uniforms, ecclesiastical vestments) to which men devote their attention trivially or unworthily (as is supposed).

1819 SCOTT *Let. to J. Richardson* 22 Aug. in *Lockhart*, There goes as much to the man-millinery of a young officer of hussars as to that of an heiress on her bridal day. **1846** *Ecclesiologist* Ser. II. V. 31 Those who . . call the ecclesiological movement 'manmillinery'.

manna¹ ('mænə). Also 1 **monna**, 2–3 **manne**, 4 **mana**. [a. late L. *manna* neut. indecl. (later also fem. *a* stem), a. Hellenistic Gr. *μάννα* neut. indecl. (LXX and N. T.), ad. (? through Aramaic *mannā*) Heb. *mān* (whence Gr. *μάν*, L. *man*, occurring more frequently than the longer form in the LXX and Vulgate O. T.: see MAN *sb.*³).

G. Ebers (*Durch Gosen zum Sinai*), gives plausible reasons for believing that the Ancient Egyptian *mannu* denoted the exudation of *Tamarix gallica*. As the Arab. *mann* has the same sense, it seems possible that the Heb. word may represent the name anciently current in the Sinaitic wilderness for this natural product, which in many respects agrees with the description of the miraculous manna, and which is still locally regarded as a dew falling from the sky.

The etymological tradition or conjecture preserved in Ex. xvi. 15 represents the word as having originated from the question *man hū?* 'what is it' (in Aramaic or supposed archaic Heb.), which grammatically admits of being interpreted 'It is *mān*'. (Cf. the Vulgate, l. c.: Dixerunt ad invicem: Manhu, quod interpretatur, 'quid est hoc?')

The word has been adopted in most versions of the Bible, and appears in figurative uses in the literature of most of the countries of Christendom. Cf. Goth., OHG. (MHG., mod.G.), Du., Sw., It. *manna*, F. *manne*, Sp. *maná*, Pg. *manná*.

Whether the Gr. *μάννα*, L. *manna*, fem., meaning a grain of frankincense (sense 9 below), is connected with this word is uncertain, though an oriental origin for it is probable.]

I. Biblical and allusive uses.

1. a. The substance miraculously supplied as food to the Children of Israel during their progress through the Wilderness. (See *Exodus* xvi.)

c **897** K. ÆLFRED *Gregory's Past. C.* xvii. 124 And eac sceal bion on ðæm breostum ðæs monnan swetnes. *c* **1000** ÆLFRIC *Exod.* xvi. 31 And nemdon þone mete Manna. *c* **1175** *Lamb. Hom.* 141 Sunnedei god sende manna from houene. *c* **1200** *Trin. Coll. Hom.* 99 He let hem reine manne to bilive and gef hem bred of heuene. *c* **1330** *Assump. Virg.* (B.M. MS.) 768–9 Thei ouerturned þat ilke stone; Bodi þei founde þer none; But þei sawe in þat stede þana Liand as it were a mana. That manna bitokned hure clene lyf. *c* **1400** MAUNDEV. (Roxb.) iv. 12 In þe toumbe of sayne Iohn men may fynd na thyng bot manna. *c* **1586** C'TESS PEMBROKE *Ps.* LXXVIII. x, He . . bade the cloudes ambrosian manna rain. **1651** C. CARTWRIGHT *Cert. Relig.* I. 124 The Apostle there calleth

Manna spirituall meat, yet was Manna a materiall thing. **1756-7** tr. *Keysler's Trav.* (1760) II. 183 And on the reverse the pot of manna, or, as others will have it, the censor. **1842** J. H. NEWMAN *Par. Serm.* VI. xi. 156 The manna in the wilderness was a real gift.

b. *transf.* and *fig.*

1593 G. HARVEY *Precursor Pierces Super.* Wks. (Grosart) II. 12 To make choice of..the most vertuous hearbes of Philosophie,..and the most heauenly manna of Diuinitie. **1596** SHAKS. *Merch. V.* v. i. 294 Faire Ladies you drop Manna in the way Of starued people. **1667** MILTON *P.L.* II. 113 His Tongue Dropt Manna, and could make the worse appear The better reason. **1684** OTWAY *Atheist* I. i, Do you dispise your own Manna indeed, and long after Quails? **1822** LAMB *Elia* Ser. I. *Roast Pig*, The lean, no lean, but a kind of animal manna. **1890** R. BRIDGES *Shorter Poems* III. *London Snow*, They gathered up the crystal manna to freeze Their tongues with tasting, their hands with snow-balling.

2. Spiritual nourishment; food divinely supplied, whether for mind or body, esp. the holy eucharist.

1382 WYCLIF *Rev.* ii. 17 To the ouercomynge I shal ȝiue manna hid, *or aungel mete.* [Similarly **1535** COVERDALE and **1611**.] *c* **1450** tr. *De Imitatione* III. xl. 110 To þe victour is yoven manna. **1654** JER. TAYLOR *Real Pres.* 58 The word of God, the most honourable and eldest of things is called Manna. **1843** NEALE *Hymns for Sick* (1863) 47 Let not Thy Manna fail me at the last. **1861** *Hymns A. & M.* No. 314 ('O food that weary pilgrims love'), O bread of Angel-hosts above, O Manna of the Saints.

†**3.** [After F. *manne.*] **a.** A valuable staple of food. *Obs.* (? *nonce-use.*)

1693 EVELYN *De la Quint. Compl. Gard.* I. 55 It is us'd in the Winter time to cover Fig-Trees, Artichokes, Succories, Selery, &c. Which are all Manna's of great Value in Gard'ning. *Ibid.* II. 194 Lettuces are Plants that are.. commonly seen in our Kitchen-Gardens, and are indeed the most useful Manna of them.

b. (See quots.)

1816 KIRBY & SP. *Entomol.* ix. (1818) I. 284 Between the 10th and 15th of August is the time when those [*sc.* Ephemeræ] of the Seine and Marne..are expected by the fishermen, who call them *manna.* **1864** *Intell. Observ.* No. 33. 151 Ephemeræ..commonly known by the name of Manna.

II. In *Pharmacy*, etc.

4. a. A sweet pale yellow or whitish concrete juice obtained from incisions in the bark of the Manna-ash, *Fraxinus Ornus*, chiefly in Calabria and Sicily; used in medicine as a gentle laxative. Also, a similar exudation obtained from other plants.

[*c* **1400** *Lanfranc's Cirurg.* 182 Cole hem, & resolue þeron cassia fistula ʒj., thamarindorum, manne ana ʒss., & boile hem a litil togidere.] **1533** ELYOT *Cast. Helthe* (1541) 58 Pourgers of Choler:..Manna vi drammes at the leaste, and soo to xxv, in the brothe of a henne or capon. **1543** TRAHERON *Vigo's Chirurg., Interpr. Strange Words*, Manna is a dewe thicked, and fallynge in certayne places vpon trees, ..and vsed for purgations. **1660** F. BROOKE tr. *Le Blanc's Trav.* 4 Upon the Mount Libanus..you may find the Manna, or Celestial dew, which I..took for snow. **1698** FRYER *Acc. E. India & P.* 241 This Manna is White and Granulated, and..I think not inferior to the Calabrian. **1764** CHESTERF. *Lett. to Godson* (1890) 354, I made him take a little manna, which has done him good. **1797** *Encycl. Brit.* (ed. 3) XIV. 764/2 Some manna was gathered from the green leaves [of a pine], but it could never be condensed. **1822-34** *Good's Study Med.* (ed. 4) IV. 344 It [juice of birch-tree] is easily obtained by wounding the trunk, and when fresh is a sweetish and limpid fluid in its concrete state affording a brownish manna. **1830** LINDLEY *Nat. Syst. Bot.* 92 The Manna of Arabia is produced by several species of Hedysarum. **1856** STANLEY *Sinai & Pal.* i II. 69 Feathery tamarisks..on whose leaves is found what the Arabs call manna.

b. with qualifying word, as ***cane, canulated, fat, flake, flaky, lachrymatory manna; Calabrian, Levant, Sicilian, Syrian, Tolfa manna***; **Australian manna**, a secretion of certain species of Eucalyptus, esp. *E. viminalis*; **Briançon manna**, a substance secreted by the common larch; **Hebrew, Jews', Mount Sinai, Persian manna**, the product of *Alhaga maurorum* or of *Tamarix gallica* var. *mannifera*; **lerp manna** = LERP; **Madagascar manna** = DULCITE.

1611 COTGR., *Manne de Calabre*, Calabrian Manna; the best and most lasting Manna... *Manne de Cotton*..the worse kind of Leuant Manna, and the worst of all others. **1727-41** CHAMBERS *Cycl.* s.v., Formerly the Syrian manna was in the most repute, but now it gives way to the Calabrian. **1753** *Ibid. Supp., Manna Mastichina*... This is what we usually know..under the name of *Manna Persicum*, or Persian Manna, which is at this time in use in medicine in the East. **1797** *Encycl. Brit.* (ed. 3) X. 537/2 The larger pieces, called *flake manna*, are usually preferred. *Ibid.* 538/2 This is the best kind, and by the people of [Sicily] is called *lachrymatory* or *cane* manna. *Ibid.*, The Sicilian manna is dearer and more esteemed than that of Calabria. **1811** A. T. THOMSON *Lond. Disp.* (1818) 179 It is collected in baskets, and known under the name of *manna grassa*, fat manna... A finer kind of manna is procured, which is called canulated or flaky manna, *manna in cannoli.* **1839** *Penny Cycl.* XIV. 386/1 The kind which is most abundant is by the Arabs called *toorunjbeen*, which is often translated 'Persian manna'. *Ibid.* 386/2 A sweetish exudation is produced on the larch (*Larix europea*), which forms the *Manna brigantiaca*, or Briançon Manna of some Pharmacopœias. **1864** *Chambers' Encycl.* VI. 307/2 The manna of the Israelites..appears probably.. to have been the saccharine substance called *Mount Sinai Manna.* **1883** *Encycl. Brit.* XV. 493/2 The Lerp manna of Australia is of animal origin.

c. manna in sorts [= F. *manne en sortes*, pharmaceutical L. *manna in sortibus*], **manna in tears** [= F. *manne en larmes*]: see quots.

1853 ROYLE *Man. Mat. Med.* (ed. 2) 542 *Manna in tears* is a pure kind, in bright and roundish white grains... Inferior kinds are in smaller pieces,..and often intermixed with impurities. These are called *Manna in sorts, Fat Manna, Tolfa Manna*, &c. **1866** *Treas. Bot.* 823/2 The inferior [kind], or 'manna in sorts' [is obtained] from cuts [in the stem of the Ash] near the ground.

†**5.** In early *Chemistry*: A white powder. *Obs.*

1694 SALMON *Bate's Dispens.* (1713) 209/1 This is the same Medicine which is call'd Manna of Lead by Schroder. **1706** PHILLIPS (ed. Kersey), s.v., *Chymical Manna*, a Substance distill'd from Precipitate, whiter than Snow.

6. (In full ***Poland*** or ***Polish manna*** = F. *manne de Pologne.*) = *manna seeds* (see 9).

1785 MARTYN *Rousseau's Bot.* xiii. (1794) 139 The seeds of this [*Festuca fluitans*].. appear there under the name of Manna. **1864** *Chambers' Encycl.* VI. 308/1 They [the seeds] ..are very palatable and nutritious, and are known in shops as *Polish Manna, Manna Seeds*, and *Manna Croup.* **1866** *Treas. Bot.* 718/2 *Manna*, Poland. *Glyceria fluitans.*

7. A species of grass, *Setaria* (*Panicum*) *italica*, better known as Italian or Hungarian millet, originally native of Asia, but now extensively cultivated for fodder in Europe and South Africa.

1897 *Agric. Jrnl. C. Good Hope* X. 108 You have done the sensible thing in sending a specimen of your so-called Manna for identification... Well, it is *Setaria italica*, Beauv., in one of its varieties.

†**8.** A grain (of frankincense); frankincense in grains. *Obs.*

[Strictly another word: a. Gr. μάννα, L. *manna*, fem. *a* stem: see etymological note above.]

1601 HOLLAND *Pliny* I. 367 As for the small crums or fragments [of incense] which fall off by shaking, we called Manna, (*i. Thuris*). **1753** CHAMBERS *Cycl. Supp., Manna Thuris*, the *Manna of Frankincense*, a term used by the ancient physicians to express such small pieces of frankincense..as broke off..in carriage.

9. *attrib.* and *Comb.*, as ***manna-dew, -meal; manna-bearing, -eating, -like, -yielding*** adjs.; **manna ash (tree)**, the tree *Fraxinus Ornus*; **manna-grass**, †(*a*) = DEW-GRASS; (*b*) the aquatic grass *Glyceria fluitans*; **manna-groats**: see MANNA-CROUP; **manna-gum**, a species of *Eucalyptus, E. viminalis*; **manna lichen**, either of the lichens *Lecanora esculenta* and *L. affinis*; **manna-mead**, a fermented beverage obtained from manna; **manna seeds**, the seeds of manna-grass, *Glyceria fluitans*; **manna sugar** = MANNITE; **manna tree** = *manna ash.* Also MANNA-CROUP.

1715 J. PETIVER in *Phil. Trans.* XXIX. 238 This..more resembles our *Manna Ash. **1892** *Pall Mall G.* 21 July 3/1 The slanting lights which played through manna-ash, acacia hedge, and tamarisk. **1864** *Chambers' Encycl.* VI. 307 There are several other manna-yielding plants besides the ash, especially the *manna-bearing Eucalyptus. **1819** KEATS *La Belle Dame* vii, She found me roots of relish sweet, And honey wild, and *manna-dew. **1875** E. WHITE *Life in Christ* III. xvii. (1878) 218 The physical death, died by the *manna-eating fathers. **1597** GERARDE *Herbal* I. xx. §1. 26 In English it may be called *Manna grasse, or Dew grasse. **1759** B. STILLINGFL. tr. *Gedner's Use Curiosity* in *Misc. Tracts* (1762) 182 The seed of the flote or manna grass, affords a very pleasing..nourishment to man. **1847** DARLINGTON *Amer. Weeds* (1860) 381 *Floating Glyceria.* Manna-grass. [**1834** G. BENNETT *Wanderings in N.S.W.* I. xvi. 319 The elegant drooping manna-trees..were numerous.] **1884** A. NILSON *Timber Trees New South Wales* 74 E[*ucalyptus*] *viminalis*—*Manna Gum;..Flooded Gum.— An elegant tree, attaining a height of 150 feet and a diameter of 8 feet. [**1887** Manna-drooping Gums: see GUM *sb.*^{2} 5]. **1937** *Discovery* Dec. 364/2 The Greater Gliding 'Possum..feeds also on several other eucalypts, particularly manna-gum and long-leafed box. **1940** H. ELLIS *My Life* iv. 102 The curious variety of manna gum I knew only there [*sc.* in Australia]. **1961** *Coast to Coast 1959–60* 60 Before me was a track running between walls of manna-gum casuarina, tea-tree in full blossom, and wedding-bush even whiter. **1864** *Reader* No. 85. 205/2 Authors who have described the *manna-lichen. **1874** LISLE CARR *Jud. Gwynne* I. vii. 235 As he listened to these *manna-like words. **1753** CHAMBERS *Cycl. Supp., Manna*,..the spirituous part of the *manna-mead. **1820** C. R. MATURIN *Melmoth* (1892) III. xxviii. 115 They partook of this *manna-meal,—this food that seemed to have dropped from heaven. **1764** *Mus. Rusticum* II. lxxxviii. 300 The seeds of this grass [flote fescue] are gathered yearly in Poland,..and sold under the name of *manna-seeds. **1836** BRANDE *Chem.* 906 Mannite; *Manna-Sugar. **1770** *Phil. Trans.* LX. 233 The *Manna tree..is a kind of ash tree. **1773** BRYDONE *Sicily* xxxvii. (1809) 353 The manna-tree is esteemed the most profitable. **1864** *Manna-yielding [see *manna-bearing* above].

Hence **'manna'd** *a.* (*nonce-wd.*) [-ED^{2}], sweetened as with manna; honeyed.

1776 MICKLE tr. *Camoens' Lusiad* IX. 377 Enraged, he sees ..each, for some base interest of his own, With Flattery's manna'd lips assail the throne.

‖**'manna**^{2}. *Obs. rare*$^{-1}$. [Hellenistic Gr. μάννα, *v.r.* μάναα (Vulg. *manna, manaa*), occurring freq. in the LXX as a transliteration of Heb. *minḥāʰ* offering, sacrifice. Cf. Syriac *mn*''.]

1382 WYCLIF *Baruch* i. 10 Makeþ manaa [**1388** Make ȝe sacrifice]. **1611** BIBLE *Ibid.*, Prepare yee manna [*margin*, Gr. corruptly for Mincha, a meat offering].

mannace, obs. form of MENACE.

manna-croup ('mænə'kru:p). [ad. Russian *mannaya krupa* (*mannaya* fem. adj. 'pertaining to manna', *krupa* groats), or the equivalent in some other Slavonic language. The Ger. synonym is *mannagrütze* (*grütze* = GRIT *sb.*^{2}).]

a. A coarse granular meal consisting of the large hard grains of wheat-flour retained in the bolting-machine, or in the grooves of the grinding-stones, after the fine flour has passed through, used for making puddings, soups, etc. **b.** A similar meal made from the seeds of the manna-grass, *Glyceria fluitans.*

1855 OGILVIE *Suppl., Manna Croup*, a granular preparation of wheat-flour deprived of bran. **1864** *Chambers' Encycl.* VI. 307/2 *Manna Croup*, or *Manna Groats*, a kind of semolina, prepared in Russia, usually from the hard wheats of Odessa and Taganrog... Another kind is made by husking the small grain of the aquatic grass, *Glyceria fluitans.* **1872** SOWERBY *Eng. Bot.* XI. 98 Floating Meadow-Grass... In several parts of Germany this grass is cultivated for its seeds, which form the manna croup of the shops.

mannadge, obs. form of MANAGE.

mannage, -ery, obs. forms of MANAGE, -ERY.

mannakin, variant of MANIKIN.

mannan ('mænæn). *Chem.* [f. MANN(OSE + *-an*, after GLUCOSAN.] Any of a group of polysaccharides that are composed chiefly of mannose residues and occur widely in plants, esp. as reserve foods.

1895 *Jrnl. Chem. Soc.* LXVIII. II. 128 (*heading*) Mannan as a reserve material in the seeds of Diospyros Kaki. **1931** [see FRUCTOSAN]. **1965** *New Scientist* 6 May 381/1 The cell-walls of the [coffee] bean consist of a mannan which is an insoluble polysaccharide..and protein.

mannance, mannas(s, obs. ff. MENACE.

mannasi, -asy, obs. forms of MANATEE.

mannatee, -ti, -ty, obs. forms of MANATEE.

mannee, variant of MANI^{1}.

mannequin ('mæni:kɪn, 'mænəkwɪn). [Fr.] A woman (or occas. a man) employed in the showrooms of dress-makers, costumiers, etc., to wear and show off garments. Also, a model of a human figure for the display of clothes, etc. Also *attrib.*

1902 *Pall Mall Mag.* XXVII. 119 Another salon.. ornamented with tall mirrors in which were reflected the slender elegant figures of several mannequins, most of them exceedingly pretty and all arrayed in magnificent dresses. **1919** BEERBOHM *Seven Men* 11 Then came 'Stark: *A Conte*', about a midinette who, as far as I could gather, murdered.. a mannequin. **1924** [see *film super* s.v. FILM *sb.* 7c]. **1927** *Sunday Express* 7 Aug. 3/6 Bogus mannequin schools.., of which there are several in London, promise to train girls to become expert mannequins. **1930** *Daily Express* 6 Oct. 13/5 Autumn Mannequin Parades will be held on Tuesday and Wednesday this week. **1939** M. B. PICKEN *Lang. Fashion* 97/2 *Mannequin*.., model of human figure for display of garments, hats, furs, etc. **1940** D. MCCARTHY *Drama* 217 The *mannequin* show illustrates the 'moral' and commercial exploitation of sex interest. **1951** M. MCLUHAN *Mech. Bride* (1967) 99/1 Her mannequin past is in the way. **1960** S. BECKER tr. *Schwarz-Bart's Last of Just* III. iii. 108 The mannequin and its one unscrewed foot. **1966** J. S. COX *Illustr. Dict. Hairdressing* 95/1 *Mannequin*.., an artificial head used to display a hair style, or on which to create a hair style, or work hair for a postiche.

Hence **'mannequining** *vbl. sb.*, **'mannequinism**, the business of mannequins.

1927 *Sunday Express* 15 May 5/3 'Mannequining is a serious business now,' said the head of a mannequin school to me. **1928** *Daily Express* 2 June 4/4 More and more.. distinguished women..have recently joined the ranks of teachers of mannequinism.

mannequin, variant of MANIKIN.

manner ('mænə(r)), *sb.*^{1} Forms: 2–6 **manere**, 3–7 **maner**, (4 **maneer, manyere**), 4–5 **manar**, 4–6 **maneir**, (5 **manur, moner(e**, 6 **manoure, manier**, *Sc.* **manir, manieir**, 6, 8 *Sc.* **mainer**, 7 **mannor**), 4– **manner**. [a. AF. *manere* (OF. *maniere*, mod.F. *manière*) = Pr. *maneira, manieira, maniera*, Sp. *manera*, Pg. *maneira*, It. *maniera*, repr. a popular L. type **man*(*u*)*āria*, app. an elliptical or absolute use of the fem. of L. *manuārius* belonging to the hand, f. *manus* hand (cf. OF., Pr. *manier*, Sp. *manero* carried in the hand, It. *maniero* manageable, tractable); the primary sense would thus be 'mode of handling'. The Fr. word has passed into most of the Teut. langs.: cf. OFris. *maniere*, MDu. *maniere*, *meniere* (Du. *manier*), MHG. *maniere* (G. *manier*), Sw. *manér*, Da. *maner*.

The word early became the recognized translation of the L. *modus* and *mōs*, and its sense-development has been affected by assimilation in meaning to both these words.]

1. a. The way in which something is done or takes place; method of action; mode of procedure. Chiefly in phr. formed with preps. ***in*** (†***on***, †***by, after***) ***this manner*** (= thus), ***in what manner*** (= how), ***in divers manners***, † ***in good manner***, etc. † ***in manner that***: so that.

c **1275** LAY. 18983 Þes þinges weren forþriht in þilke manere idiht [*c* 1205 þus weoren idihte]. **1297** R. GLOUC. (Rolls) 502 In þis manere iwis Corineus bi wan cornwaile to him. **1340** *Ayenb.* 51 Ine vif maneres me zenegeþ be mete and be drinke. **1390** GOWER *Conf.* III. 24 So as sche mai in good manere Hir honour and her name save. *c* **1420** LYDG. *Assembly of Gods* 5 Musyng on a maner how that I myght make Reason & Sensualyte in oon to acorde. *c* **1450** *Merlin* 2 We yede and assaied hym in alle the maners that we cowden. **1523** LD. BERNERS *Froiss.* I. lix. 80 *heading*, Howe therle of Heynault assayled the fortresse of Mortayne in Picardy by dyuers maners. **1530** PALSGR. 750/1, I have no joy to be taken up of you on this maner. **1557** N. T. (Geneva) *Heb.* i. 1 God spake at sondrie tymes & in diuers maners in the olde tyme to our fathers by the Prophetes. **1601** SHAKS. *Jul. C.* IV. iii. 189 For certaine she is dead, and by strange manner. **1611** BIBLE *Neh.* vi. 4 They sent vnto me foure times,..and I answered them after the same maner. **1646** (*title*) The True Mannor and Forme of the Proceeding to the Funerall of..the Earle of Essex. **1647-8** COTTERELL *Davila's Hist. Fr.* (1678) 21 They disposed the order of their Council in manner as followeth. **1766** GOLDSM. *Vic. W.* x, We should go there in as proper a manner as possible; not altogether like the scrubs about us. **1791** MRS. RADCLIFFE *Rom. Forest* iv, [He] sometimes thanked her in a manner more earnest than was usual with him. **1850** MRS. JAMESON *Leg. Monast. Ord.* (1863) 52 Chanting the divine services according to the Gregorian manner. **1875** JOWETT *Plato* (ed. 2) IV. 227 The mathematician..is not capable of giving a reason in the same manner as the dialectician.

b. ***in*** (†***on***) ***like manner***, also † ***like manner***: in a similar way, similarly. † ***in, by no manner***, also † ***no manner***: not in any way, not at all.

c **1325** *Spec. Gy Warw.* 628 He..þat nele be meke in none manere. **1382** WYCLIF *Matt.* xxi. 36 Eftsones he sente other seruauntis, mo than the firste, and liche maner [**1388** in lijk maner, Vulg. *similiter*] thei diden to hem. **14..** *Voc.* in Wr.-Wülcker 598/11 *Nullatenus*, no manere. **1470-85** MALORY *Arthur* I. xv. 56 Whan syr Arthur sawe the batail wold not be endyd by no maner. **1556** LAUDER *Tractate* 259 Than can ȝe be no maner want Gold. **1563** WIN3ET *Four Scoir Thre Quest.* Wks. 1888 I. 81 Baptim onlyke maner makis ws saif. **1611** BIBLE *Transl. Pref.* ¶8 In like maner, Vlpilas is reported..to haue translated the Scriptures into the Gothicke tongue. **1820** SHELLEY *Hymn to Mercury* lxi, He averred..that he did neither see Or even had in any manner heard Of my lost cows. **1863** LYELL *Antiq. Man* 25 Among other characters, the diminished thickness of the bones [etc.]..are relied on; and in like manner, the diminished size of the horns of the bull.

c. Const. *of* with gerund or noun of action (*arch.*). ***manner of speaking*** [perh. after. F. *manière de parler*]: form of expression. ***in a manner of speaking***: so to speak.

c **1391** CHAUCER *Astrol.* II. §3 Yif it be after the middel of the day, set the degree of thy sonne up-on the west side; tak this manere of setting for a general rewle. **1532** TINDALE *Exp. Matt.* v. 38-42 (? 1550) 42 To turne yᵉ other cheke is a maner of spekynge and not be vnderstand as the words sound. **1593** SHAKS. *Rich. II*, V. vi. 9 The manner of their taking may appeare At large discoursed in this paper heere. **1597** MORLEY *Introd. Mus.* 45 This is our vsual maner of pricking and setting downe of the Proportions. **1632** SANDERSON *Serm.* 47 Obserue secondly the Apostles maner of speech. **1729** BUTLER *Serm.* Pref., A manner of speaking not loose and undeterminate, but clear and distinct. **1763** GOLDSM. *Misc. Wks.* (1837) I. 549 A more just manner of thinking and expressing. **1809** ROLAND *Fencing* 118 The manner of executing it was [etc.]. **1890** 'R. BOLDREWOOD' *Col. Reformer* (1891) 219 The cattle..has been, in a manner of speaking, neglected.

d. *Gram.* ***adverb of manner***: one which answers, or which is equivalent to, the question *how?*

1727-41 CHAMBERS *Cycl.* s.v. *Adverb*, Adverbs..may be reduced under the general classes of Adverbs of time, of place, of order, of quantity, of quality, of manner [etc.]. **1872** R. MORRIS *Engl. Accid.* 193 Adverbs of..Manner or Quality, as *well, wisely* [etc.].

†**2. a.** ***the manner of***: the state of the case with respect to (a person, thing or event); the character, disposition, or nature of. (Also occas. without *of*.) *Obs.*

c **1330** R. BRUNNE *Chron. Wace* (Rolls) 15864 'Lo!' sche seide, 'wher he comeþ here!' & telde of Pellit al þe manere. *c* **1330** —— *Chron.* (1810) 275 A messengere þei sent, to telle alle þe manere, To þe Scottis he went, and said as ȝe may here. **1426** LYDG. *De Guil. Pilgr.* 6710 In that myrour dyde I se The maner hool off the cyte. **1470-85** MALORY *Arthur* X. lxiii. 522 Syre Palomydes told Hermynde alle the manere and how they slewe sir Lamorak. **1523** LD. BERNERS *Froiss.* I. xvii. 18 *heading*, Here the hystory spekeþ of the maner of the Scottis, and howe they can warre. **1530** PALSGR. 707/2, I scryve a thyng, I discrybe the maner of it. *a* **1557** MRS. M. BASSET tr. *More's Treat. Passion* M.'s Wks. 1383/2 As hys trespas was a great deale more heynous, so was the manoure of hys well deseruyd ende, muche more pyteous. **1653** H. COGAN tr. *Pinto's Trav.* v. i. 20 There was a..conflict between them, but..I am not able to deliver the manner of it. **1665** BUNYAN *Holy Citie* 59 These words..give us also to understand the manner of her strength.

b. ***in*** (***the***) ***manner of***: after the fashion of, in the guise of, in the same way as.

c **1386** CHAUCER *Pars. T.* ¶256 (Harl. MS.) Þay sowede of fige leues in maner of breches. **1486-1504** in W. Denton *Eng. in 15th Cent.* (1888) Note D 318 My lord byschope..dyd stand in maner of a wauereyng mynd. *a* **1533** LD. BERNERS *Gold. Bk. M. Aurel.* (1546) K v, There came a Centuryon in maner of a messager with great haste. **1585** T. WASHINGTON tr. *Nicholay's Voy.* II. xxi. 58 b, A purse..which hee holdeth in his hande in manner of a gloue. **1659** PEARSON *Creed* (1839) 358 The grave to him is in the manner of a womb to bring him forth. **1720** STRYPE *Stow's Lond.* VI. i. 8/1 To make a Dragon in Manner of a Standard or Ensign of certain red Samitt. **1907** G. B. SHAW *How he lied to her Husband* 142 Henry places himself on guard in the manner of a well taught boxer. **1967** E. SHORT *Embroidery & Fabric Collage* iii. 60 The coverlet tells the story of Tristan, in a series of scenes showing different incidents, in the manner of a strip cartoon.

3. a. Customary mode of acting or behaviour, whether of an individual or of a community; habitual practice; usage, custom, fashion. Now only *literary* or *arch.*

Phr. †***for the manner***: in accordance with the fashion.

a **1225** *Ancr. R.* 6 Vor þi mot þeos riwle chaungen hire misliche efter euch ones manere. *a* **1300** *Cursor M.* 4067 All luted him on þair maner. **13..** *Gaw. & Gr. Knt.* 90 Anoþer maner meued him eke, þat he þurȝ nobelay had nomen. *c* **1380** WYCLIF *Wks.* (1880) 156 Where goode prestis traueilen faste to lerne goddis lawe, þei gon for þe manere to cyuyle or canon. *c* **1420** *Anturs of Arth.* 498 Þe lordes by-lyue hom to list ledes With many seriant of mace, as was þe manere. *c* **1510** *Lyt. Geste Robyn Hode* viii, A good maner than had Robyn..Euery daye..Thre messes wolde he here. *a* **1533** LD. BERNERS *Gold. Bk. M. Aurel.* (1546) Ll vij, Them that be of a meke and still maner. **1598** W. PHILLIP tr. *Linschoten* I. xcii. 163/2 And now I will shew vnto you the manner that is vsed in the ships, when they sayle home againe. **1611** BIBLE *Jer.* xxii. 21 This hath bin thy maner from thy youth, that thou obeyedst not my voice. **1674** tr. *Scheffer's Lapland* 90, I shall add the figures of both Sexes habited after their manner. **1710** PRIDEAUX *Orig. Tithes* App. 3 The people..lay claim to customary manners of Tithing [etc.]. **1853** KINGSLEY *Hypatia* xiii. 155 She suddenly and silently, after the manner of mastiffs, sprang upon them. **1875** JOWETT *Plato* (ed. 2) I. 229 Here Ctesippus, as his manner was, burst into a roar of laughter.

b. ***to the manner born***: in Shaks., destined by one's birth to be subject to the (specified) custom. In later echoes often: Seeming to be congenitally fitted for some position or employment.

1602 SHAKS. *Ham.* I. iv. 15 (Qo. 1604) But to my minde, though I am natiue heere And to the manner borne, it is a custome More honourd in the breach, then the obseruance. **1893** *Times* 26 Apr. 9/5 Yankee experts to the manner born.

4. *collect. pl.* † **a.** A person's habitual behaviour or conduct, esp. in reference to its moral aspect; moral character, morals. *Obs.*

a **1225** *Ancr. R.* 218 Hwonne a mon haueð neoweliche wif iled hom, he nimeð ȝeme al softeliche of hire maneres. *c* **1369** CHAUCER *Dethe Blaunche* 1014 She vsed gladly to do wele These were hir maners euerydele. *c* **1410** *Sir Cleges* 21 The pore pepull he wold releve And no man wold he greve, Meke of maners was hee. **1509** BARCLAY *Shyp of Folys* 118 An olde prouerbe..Sayth that good lyfe and maners makyth man. **1535** COVERDALE *1 Cor.* xv. 33 Euell speakinges corruppe good maners. **1585** T. WASHINGTON tr. *Nicholay's Voy.* I. xviii. 21 [He] changed his good maners and vertues into most vitious tyrannies. **1596** SHAKS. *Merch. V.* II. iii. 19 Though I am a daughter to his blood, I am not to his manners. **1641** J. JACKSON *True Evang. T.* I. 6 The turning of fierce and brutall men..unto sweet..and sociable manners. **1757** JOHNSON *Rambler* No. 172 ¶1 Nothing has been longer observed, than that a change of fortune causes a change of manners. **1794** MRS. RADCLIFFE *Myst. Udolpho* i, In the few ornaments of the apartments that characterized the manners of its inhabitants.

†**b.** In a more abstract sense: Conduct in its moral aspect; also, morality as a subject of study; the moral code embodied in general custom or sentiment. *Obs.*

1589 NASHE *Anat. Absurd.* 42 Socrates who reduced all Philosophy vnto the manners, sayd, that this was the greatest wisedome, to distinguish good and euill thinges. **1597** BACON *Ess.* Ep. Ded. (Arb.) 4 Nothing..contrarie or infectious to the state of Religion, or manners. **1644** MILTON *Areop.* (Arb.) 76 That also which is impious or evil absolutely either against faith or maners no law can possibly permit. **1666** TILLOTSON *Rule of Faith* I. iii. Wks. 1742 IV. 571 Had they believed not the scriptures but something else to have been the rule of faith and manners. **1767** A. YOUNG *Farmer's Lett. to People* 184 It is manners alone which increase or decrease the number of people. **1776** GIBBON *Decl. & F.* ix. (1869) I. 179 Divorces were prohibited by manners rather than by laws.

c. The modes of life, customary rules of behaviour, conditions of society, prevailing in a people.

1340-70 *Alex. & Dind.* 199 We han, ludus, of ȝour lif listned ful ofte, Þat michil ben ȝour manerus fram oþur men varied. **1590** SHAKS. *Com. Err.* I. ii. 12 Ile view the manners of the towne, Peruse the traders, gaze vpon the buildings. **1605** CAMDEN *Rem.* 146 Many approoved customes, lawes, maners, fashions, and phrases have the English alwayes borrowed of their neighbours the French. **1718** LADY M. W. MONTAGU *Lett. to C'tess Mar* 10 Mar., Those..tales..are a real representation of the manners here. **1841** D'ISRAELI *Amen. Lit.* (1867) 582 Of all our dramatists, Jonson..alone professed to study the..manners of the age. **1870** ROGERS *Hist. Gleanings* Ser. II. 199 Contemporary novels are good evidence of manners.

d. Good 'manners', customs, or way of living.

1579 LYLY *Euphues* (Arb.) 148 We should not speake of manners or vertue to those whose mindes are infected with vice. **1596** SHAKS. *1 Hen. IV*, III. i. 184 Defect of Manners, want of Gouernment. **1802** WORDSW. *Sonn. Milton*, Oh! raise us up, return to us again; And give us manners, virtue, freedom, power.

†**e.** *Literary criticism.* Character, distinctive varieties of disposition and temperament, as portrayed in epic or dramatic poetry; the portraiture of character, viewed as one of the constituent elements of poetic art. (After Aristotle's use of ἤθη.)

1695 DRYDEN *Parallel Poetry & Paint.* Ess. (Ker) II. 132 The persons and action of a farce are all unnatural, and the manners false, that is, inconsisting with the characters of mankind. **1700** —— *Pref. Fables*, The Words are the Colouring of the Work, which..is last to be consider'd. The Design,..the Manners, and the Thoughts, are all before it. **1712** ADDISON *Spect.* No. 273 ¶1 This is Aristotle's Method of considering, first the Fable, and secondly the Manners; or, as we generally call them in English, the Fable and the Characters. **1727-41** CHAMBERS *Cycl.* **1780** HARRIS *Philol. Enq.* Wks. (1841) 434 When the principal persons of any drama preserve such a consistency of conduct,..that..we conjecture what they will do hereafter from what they have done already, such persons in poetry may be said to have manners, for by this, and this only, are poetic manners constituted.

†**f.** Habits (of animals). Cf. F. *mœurs*. *Obs.*

1576 FLEMING tr. *Cains' Dogges* A iv, The sundry sortes of Englishe dogges he discouereth so euidently,..their manners he openeth so manifestly. **1661** LOVELL *Hist. Anim. & Min.* Introd., As for their nature and manners, they [serpents] have their poyson in the taile. **1796** MORSE *Amer. Geog.* I. 202 In his manners he [the racoon] resembles the squirrel.

5. a. Outward bearing, deportment, or style of address. With reference to a speaker: Characteristic style of attitude, gesture, and utterance.

a **1300** *Cursor M.* 24078 Soth in speche, in maner mild. *c* **1374** CHAUCER *Anel. & Arc.* 249 Youre observaunce and so lowe manere. **1390** GOWER *Conf.* III. 64 Sche tok good hiede of his manere, And wondreth why he dede so. **1534** MORE *Comf. agst. Trib.* II. Wks. 1200/1 Arrogant maner, high solayn solemne port, ouerlooking the poore in woorde and countenance. **1557** *Tottel's Misc.* (Arb.) 234, I see well ..by thy lokes and thy manere,..That thou art stuffed full of wo. **1856** FROUDE *Hist. Eng.* (1858) II. vi. 109 Something in the boy's manner attracted the banker's interest. **1888** T. E. KEBBEL *Crabbe* v. 87 His manner to women seems to have been of the kind called philandering.

b. A distinguished or fashionable air.

1694 CONGREVE *Double Dealer* II. ii, *Cynt.* A Manner! what's that, Madam? *L. Froth.* Some distinguishing Quality, as for example, the Belle-air or Brillant of Mr. Brisk;..or something of his own, that should look a little *Jene-scay-quoysh.* **1773** GOLDSM. *Stoops to Conq.* II. Wks. (Globe) 656/2 We country persons can have no manner at all... But who can have a manner, who has never seen.. such places where the nobility chiefly resort? **1883** GRANT WHITE *W. Adams* 83 Her manners were quite as good as Lady Boreham's; and her manner was as superior as that of the so-called Venus of Milo might be to that of the Venus of a burlesque.

6. a. *pl.* (†formerly also *sing.*) External behaviour in social intercourse, estimated as good or bad according to its degree of politeness or of conformity to the accepted standard of propriety.

c **1385** CHAUCER *L. G. W.* 1504 *Hypsip.*, Sche..knew by hyre manyere..That it were gentil men of gret degre. **1530** PALSGR. 415/1 Thoughe thou do me good, it is not good maner to abrayde me therof. **1593** G. HARVEY *Precursor Pierces Super.* Wks. (Grosart) II. 9 Some of vs are not so deuoide of good manner, but we..will euer be prest to interteine Curtesie with curtesie. **1604** SHAKS. *Oth.* V. i. 94 These bloody accidents must excuse my Manners, That so neglected you. **1617** MORYSON *Itin.* I. 208 They hold it ill manners that one should touch the meat with his hand. **1711** STEELE *Spect.* No. 53 ¶5 The Women lost their Wit, and the Men their good Manners. **1791** *Gentl. Mag.* 20/2 The young minister would become a pattern to the manners as well as to the morals of his neighbourhood. **1855** MACAULAY *Hist. Eng.* xii. III. 168 His manners and conversation were those of a gentleman who had been bred in the most polite ..of all Courts. **1874** GREEN *Short Hist.* vii. §8. 443 Hugh.. was in manners and bearing an Englishman.

b. *transf.* Of a horse: Action.

1861 WHYTE MELVILLE *Mkt. Harb.* 20 There's some legs —there's some hocks and thighs!..Carries his own head, too; and if you could see his manners!

7. a. Polite behaviour or deportment; habits indicative of good breeding. In *pl.*; †rarely *sing.*

c **1374** CHAUCER *Compl. Mars* 294 Compleyneth her that euere hath had yow dere, Compleyneth beaute, fredom and manere. **1563-87** FOXE *A. & M.* (K. O.), It is no manners to [etc.]. **1588** KYD *Househ. Phil.* Wks. (1901) 254 That which for manner sake wee are wont to doe to others. **1605** SHAKS. *Lear* V. iii. 234 The time will not allow the complement Which very manners vrges. **1610** BIBLE (Douay) *Ecclus.* xxxi. 17 Leaue of first, for maners sake, and exceede not. *a* **1652** BROME *Queen & Concub.* III. vii. (1659) 61 *Cur.* Wilt thou be a Scholar? *Andr.* After you is manners. *Cur.* Now by mine intellect, discreetly spoken. **1663** DRYDEN *Wild Gallant* III. i, Have you no more manners than to overlook a man when he's a writing? **1760-72** H. BROOKE *Fool of Qual.* (1809) II. 117 He pressed us so earnestly to dinner, that we could not, in manners, refuse him. **1828** SCOTT *F. M. Perth* viii, Our manners would have taught us to tarry till your lordship had invited us. **1875** JOWETT *Plato, Gorgias* (ed. 2) II. 331 There is a great want of manners in bringing the argument to such a pass.

b. Forms of politeness or respect. *Obs.* exc. *arch.* or *dial.* in ***to do*** or ***make one's manners***.

1596 SHAKS. *Tam. Shr.* I. i. 247, I aduise you vse your manners discreetly in all kind of companies. **1601** —— *All's Well* IV. v. 93 Madam, I was thinking with what manners I might safely be admitted. **1701** DE FOE *True-born Eng.* II. 143 But like our Modern Quakers of the Town, Expect your Manners, and return you none. **1824** in *Spirit Pub. Jrnls.* (1825) 226 Having done their manners to his Worship, Mr. Dennis Macarthy proceeded to question his beloved. **1825** J. NEAL *Bro. Jonathan* I. 138 Declaring, with a bow, or a bob, that 'nobody needn't plague themselves..;' and— making their manners, once more—'and, whether or no'

[etc.]. **1863** Mrs. Gaskell *Sylvia's L.* ii. (ed. 2) I. 30, I humbly make my manners, missus.

8. a. Method or style of execution in art or literature. (In literary application often contrasted with ***matter***.)

1662 Evelyn *Chalcogr.* iii. 30 They..ruin'd all those..excellent Works, whereever they became Masters, introducing their lame, and wretched manner, in all those Arts which they pretended to restore. **1664** —— tr. *Fréart's Parallel Archit.* ii. 10 The heroick and gigantine manner of this Order [the Doric]..discovering a certain masculine and natural beauty, which is properly that the French call *la grand Maniere*. **1695** Dryden *Parallel Poetry & Paint.* Ess. (Ker) II. 123 Plato himself is accustomed to write loftily, imitating, as the critics tell us, the manner of Homer. **1708** Addison *Let.* in *Ann. Reg.* (1778) XXI. 176/2 The whole is concluded by a nightingale, that has a much better voice than Mrs. Tofts, and something of the Italian manner in her divisions. **1754** Gray *Let. to Wharton* 13 Aug., He [Kent] introduced a mix'd Style, which now goes by the name of the Battey-Langley-Manner. **1780** Cowper *Table T.* 542 Manner is all in all, whatever is writ, The substitute for genius, sense, and wit. **1824** Dibdin *Libr. Comp.* p. iv., Miniature engravings in the line manner. **1837** *Penny Cycl.* IX. 440/1 Goltzius..imparted a boldness to engraving which forms a striking contrast to the neat stiff manner of his predecessors. **1850** Blackie *Æschylus* I. Pref. 7 Poetry is distinguished from prose more by the manner than by the matter. **1878** R. W. Dale *Lect. Preach.* vi. 178 Lord Macaulay's manner is very contagious.

b. *spec.* The method or style characteristic of a particular artist, etc.; often in unfavourable sense = mannerism.

1706 *Art of Painting* (1744) 316 He at last degenerated into what we call manner, and very seldom consulted nature. **1797** *Encycl. Brit.* (ed. 3) X. 538/2 *Manner*, in painting..But the best painter is he who has no manner at all. **1813** *Examiner* 10 May 299/2 Most Artists have what is denominated a manner, unlike the unobtrusiveness of Nature. **1837** *Penny Cycl.* IX. 440/2 The great excellence of his works in other respects was enhanced by the absence of all *manner*, except such as belonged to the painter after whom he engraved. **1855** Bain *Senses & Int.* iii. ii. §19 (1864) 485 Let a composer vary his works as he may, there is a manner that usually sits upon every one of them.

c. One of the several distinct methods of an artist, which mark phases or periods in his career.

1727–52 Chambers *Cycl.* s.v., The curious in pictures..distinguish readily..between the antient and the new *manner* of the same painter. **1762–71** H. Walpole *Vertue's Anecd. Paint.* (1786) I. 85 A picture of Raphael in his first manner. **1867** Barry *Sir C. Barry* iv. 97 The building which most distinctly marks his 'second manner'. **1902** *Daily Chron.* 22 Apr. 3/1 Mr. Henderson's attempt to divide Wagner's works into four styles or manners is rather misleading.

9. a. Species, kind, sort. †Formerly often with ellipsis of *of*. Now only *arch.* in ***what manner of ...?*** (†corruptly, ***what manner a ...?***)

The origin of the ellipsis of *of* (which appears very early) is that *manner* was used in the place of the older kin *sb.*^{1}, and succeeded to its syntax: see kin *sb.*^{1} 6 b.

c **1175** *Lamb. Hom.* 51 Crabbe is an manere of fissce in þere sea. *c* **1290** *St. Brendan* 719 in *S. Eng. Leg.* I. 239 Ȝwane ore louerd eche-manere men to him haueth i-drawe. *a* **1300** *Cursor M.* 6765 Cow or shepe hors or oþer maner of aȝt. *c* **1374** Chaucer *Compl. Mars* 116 She ne founde ne saugh no maner wyght. *c* **1400** Maundev. (Roxb.) Pref. 3 Whare dwelles many diuerse maners of folke. *c* **1400** *Destr. Troy* 102 A maner of men, mermydons callid. **1456** Sir G. Haye *Law Arms* (S.T.S.) 13 He sett him in ane othir maner fassoun to procede. **1470–85** Malory *Arthur* xvii. iii. 692 His bones be of suche a maner of kynde that [etc.]. **1528** Tindale *Par. Wicked Mammon* 6 They fele no maner workynge of the spyryte. **1549** Latimer *1st Serm. bef. Edw. VI* (Arb.) 27 God prescrybid vnto them an order, howe the[y] shulde chose their kyng, and what manner a man he shoulde be. **1600** Fairfax *Tasso* xvii. iii. 296 Come say (my muse) what manner times these weare. **1611** Shaks. *Wint. T.* iv. iii. 89 What manner of Fellow was hee that robb'd you? **1651** Hobbes *Leviath.* i. x. 46 Kings..gave divers manners of Scutchions, to such as went forth to the War. **1674** Playford *Skill Mus.* ii. 101 There are three sorts of Bass-Viols, as there are three manners of ways in playing. **1690** W. Walker *Idiomat. Anglo-Lat.* 289, I believe you can tell what a manner of father I have. **1875** Jowett *Plato* (ed. 2) I. 234 What manner of man was he who came up to you and censured philosophy?

b. *sing.* with plural construction (cf. kind *sb.* 14 b), qualified by *all*, *many*, *these*, or a numeral. †In early use often with ellipsis of *of*. Now only in ***all manner of*** = all sorts of.

all manner was down to the 16th c. often written *almaner*; *thesemanner* also occurs as one word.

a **1225** *Ancr. R.* 10 þer beoð two dolen to two manere of men. *c* **1320** *Cast. Love* 1596 The threttenyth day all maner men Shull dyen. **1471** *Hist. Arriv. Edw. IV* (Camden) 34 Thes manar of writings. **1485** *Act 1 Hen. VII*, c. 10 §9 To have and enjoie almaner seisours forfaitures and penaltees. **1525** Ld. Berners *Froiss.* II. ccvi. [ccii.] 633 In many maner of wayes. **1526** Tindale *Matt.* x. 1 To heale all maner of sicknesses and all maner off deseases. **1542** Udall *Erasm. Apoph.* 142 These-maner monstres. **1556** *Chron. Gr. Friars* (Camden) 79 Dyschargyd from the crowne and from almaner of possessions of the kynge their fader. **1593** Shaks. *Rich. II*, iv. i. 296 These externall manner of Laments. **1609** Hieron *Wks.* (1614) I. 11 These maner speakings doe necessarily imply proceeding. *a* **1613** *Ibid.* 181 These manner of speeches the Scripture vseth. **1612** Bp. Andrewes *Serm. Nativity* vii. (1629) 54 Many manner waies. **1644** Heylin *Stumbling-block* Tracts (1681) 696, I shall endeavour to make [that] good by two manner of proofs. **1732** Law *Serious C.* iii. (ed. 2) 33 To practise all manner of righteousness. **1853–8** Hawthorne *Eng. Note-Bks.* (1879) II. 27 The English nose..disports itself in all manner of irregularity. **1875** Jowett *Plato* (ed. 2) I. 69 Hippothales changed into all manner of colours with delight.

†**c.** In adj. phrases used *predicatively*. *Obs.*

c **1475** *Pict. Voc.* in Wr.-Wülcker 767/9 *Hec musca*, a fflye, alle maner. **1534** Whitinton *Tullyes Offices* i. (1540) 4 Every questyon of Offyce is two maner [L. *duplex*.].

d. ***no*** (or ***any***) ***manner of...***: often used periphrastically for 'no, any (person or thing) whatever'. (†Formerly also with ellipsis of *of*.) ***by no*** (or ***any***) ***manner of means***: see means.

c **1420** Lydg. *Assembly of Gods* 600 No maner of thyng can hym hurt. **1426** *Paston Lett.* I. 25, I herde..no maner lykly ne credible evidence. **1523** Ld. Berners *Froiss.* I. lxxv. 96 Ther abode alyue no maner a person. **1533** Cranmer *Let. to Duchess Norfolk* in *Misc. Writ.* (Parker Soc.) II. 255 When it shall be by any manner way void. **1583** *Reg. Privy Council Scot.* Ser. i. III. 604 As pertening in na maner of way to the said George. **1606** G. W[oodcocke] *Hist. Ivstine* vii. 35 It had full scope and passage, without any manner interruption. *a* **1687** Petty *Pol. Arith.* viii. (1691) 107 Which I wish were true, but find no manner of reason to believe. **1704** Swift *Mech. Operat. Spirit* Misc. (1711) 275, I have had no manner of Time to digest it into Order. **1884** *Manch. Exam.* 13 May 5/2 There can be no manner of doubt as to the terms of his instructions.

†**e.** Phr. ***in, on, by this*** (or ***what, any, such,*** etc.) ***manner of wise*** = in this (etc.) way; also freq. with ellipsis of *of*, and occas. of the initial prep. *Obs.*

c **1340** Hampole *Prose Tr.* 14 One þis manerewyse þe more joy and blysse sall it hafe in heuene. **1390** Gower *Conf.* I. 78 Thurgh sleyhte of Calcas..It wan be such a maner wise. **1422** *Rolls of Parlt.* IV. 176/1 The paiements in eny maner wyse maad. **1499** in *Lett. Rich. III & Hen. VII* (Rolls) I. 132 Nor suffre hym in any maner of wise to abide. *c* **1510** More *Picus* Wks. 26 b, We wote not howe soone, nor in what manerwise. *c* **1530** Tindale *Pathw. Script.* Wks. (1573) 382/2 Christ standeth vs in double stede, and vs serueth two maner wise. **1588** Parke tr. *Mendoza's Hist. China* 81 By way of phisicke they do permit..to comfort themselues with some conserues..But wine in no maner of wise.

10. ***in a manner*** (formerly †***in manner***): in some way, in some degree, so to speak, as it were. Also, †to a considerable degree, almost entirely, very nearly (*obs.*). Similarly † ***in some good manner***.

c **1420** Lydg. *Assembly of Gods* 1075 The slepyr grasse made many of hem fall, And from thense in maner depart sodeynly. **1502** *Ord. Crysten Men* (W. de W. 1506) i. iii. 25 [They] ben uncrystened & made as in maner forsakynge theyr fayth. **1545** Ascham *Toxoph.* (Arb.) 34 The Persians which vnder Cyrus conquered in a maner all the worlde. **1560** Daus tr. *Sleidane's Comm.* 323 b, They..found in manner nothing. **1584** Cogan *Haven Health* ccxliii. (1636) 316 There dyed in the same disease in manner within sixe daies space..eight hundred persons. **1588** A. King tr. *Canisius' Catech.* 96 The worthy fruicts of pœnance, quhair be we recompense (at the least in a mainer) the..sinnes of our former lyf. **1606** Holland *Sueton.* 32 Of these murderers, there was not one in manner that either survived him aboue three yeares. **1615** W. Lawson *Country Housew. Gard.* (1623) 12 Fruits are..desired of so many (nay, in a manner of all) and yet few will..take paines to prouide them. **1619** Sir D. Carleton *Let.* in *Eng. & Germ.* (Camden) 44 His businés is in some good manner prepared for him. **1737** Whiston *Josephus, Hist.* Pref. §1 The war..hath been the greatest..in a manner of those that ever were heard of. **1790** Burke *Fr. Rev.* 148 Our education is in a manner wholly in the hands of ecclesiastics. **1838** Arnold *Hist. Rome* I. v. 74 The poorest citizens..were considered in a manner as supernumeraries. **1875** T. W. Higginson *Hist. U.S.* ix. 65 Massachusetts, being first settled, was in a manner the parent of these later colonies.

†**11. a.** Reason, cause. **b.** The condition upon which something is done. *Obs.*

1390 Gower *Conf.* III. 12 Why men pleigneth After the court,..I wol the tellen the manere. *c* **1425** *Eng. Conq. Irel.* 8 He was delyuered owt of preson on this manere, that he & Morice..shold..wend in-to Irland. *c* **1430** *Syr Gener.* (Roxb.) 2882 Sore he hated the prisonere, I can not tell for what maner.

†**12.** [= L. *modus*.] Measure, moderation. ***in manner***: in due measure. Cf. OF. *maniere* 'modération, mesure' (Godefroy). *Obs.*

In quot. 1382 a mere literalism.

1382 Wyclif *Prov.* xxiii. 4 But to thi prudence put maner [Vulg. *pone modum*]. **1390** Gower *Conf.* III. 157 By this ensample a king mai lere, That forto yive is in manere. **1399** —— *In Praise of Peace* 53 Bot yit it mot be tempred in manere. **1502** *Ord. Crysten Men* (W. de W. 1506) ii. viii. 106 Without maner & attemperaunce no vertue is perfyte.

†**13.** ***to find the manner***(***s to***: to find means to. ***to make no manner to*** [cf. OF. *faire manière de*]: to give no sign of (doing something). *Obs.*

c **1477** Caxton *Jason* 51 b, He sholde fynde the maners if he might to sende him in to the yle. **1523** Ld. Berners *Froiss.* I. cxix. 141 The erle of Derby made no maner to rescue theym. *a* **1533** —— *Huon* lii. 175 He wolde go &..fynde the maner to speake with her.

†**14.** A musical mode. [L. *modus*.] *Obs.* *rare*$^{-1}$.

1382 Wyclif *Ecclus.* xliv. 5 In ther wisdam sechende the musyk manerys [Vulg. *modos musicos*].

15. *Comb.* (objective), as ***manner-piercing*** adj.; **manners-bit** *dial.* (see quot.); **manners-like** *adv.*, in a mannerly way; †**manners-painting** *ppl. a.*, that depicts contemporary 'manners'; so †**manner-painter** (*nonce-wd.*).

1829 J. Hunter *Hallamsh. Gloss.*, **Manners-bit*, a portion of a dish left by the guests that the host may not feel himself reproached for insufficient preparation. *a* **1845** Hood *Last Man* viii, Full *manner's-like he tendered the dram. **1807** Coleridge *Lett.* (1895) 516 The character of the latter [Chaucer] as a *manner-painter. **1727–46** Thomson *Summer* 1577 Chaucer, whose native *manners-painting verse [etc.]. **1752** A. Murphy *Gray's Inn Jrnl.* No. 20 The Manners-painting Hand of Hogarth. **1786** Burns *Vision* ii. xix, I taught thy manners-painting strains, The loves, the ways of simple swains. **1776** Mickle tr. *Camoens' Lusiad* viii. (1778) 369 His fraudful art, though veil'd in deep disguise, Shone bright to Gama's *manner-piercing eyes.

manner, *sb.*^{2}: see mainour.

manner, obs. form of manor, manure.

'mannerable, *a.* *Obs.* exc. *dial.* [f. manner *sb.*^{1} + -able.] Well-mannered.

c **1460** J. Russell *Bk. Nurture* 1113 In a manerable mershalle þe connynge is moost commendable. *Ibid.* 1115 If þey haue gentille chere & gydynge manerable. **1886** Elworthy *W. Som. Word-Bk.*

mannerance, obs. form of manurance.

mannered ('mænəd), *a.* [f. manner *sb.*^{1} + -ed^2.]

1. Having manners of a specified kind (indicated by an advb. phr., or by a prefixed adj. or adv., as ***evil-***, ***gentle-***, ***rough-***, ***rude-***, ***simple-mannered***, ill-mannered, well-mannered).

1377 Langl. *P. Pl.* B. ii. 23 And Mede is manered after hym riȝte as kynde axeth. *c* **1489** Caxton *Sonnes of Aymon* xx. 448 He is not manered like a gentyll man. **1603** Owen *Pembrokeshire* v. (1891) 41, I finde..Pembrokshere to be worst manred and hardest to find personable. **1608** Shaks. *Per.* iii. iii. 17 Beseeching you to giue her Princely training, that she may be manere'd as she is borne. **1673** Temple *Observ. Netherl.* iv. 137 A people differently bred and manner'd from the Traders. **1821** Byron *Juan* iii. xli, He was the mildest manner'd man That ever scuttled ship or cut a throat. **1837** Ht. Martineau *Soc. Amer.* III. 103 The Americans are better mannered than others, in as far as they reverence intellect more than wealth and fashion. **1879** G. Macdonald *Sir Gibbie* III. ix. 145 He was well-dressed, and mannered like a gentleman. **1880** Disraeli *Endym.* III. iii. 25 The most sweetly mannered gentleman alive.

†**b.** Of a literary production: Exhibiting 'manners' or character. (Cf. Horace, *A. P.* 319 *morataque recte fabula*.) *Obs.*

1755 Grainger *Solitude* 215 Then know thyself, the human mind survey..Hence Inspiration plans his manner'd lays. **1789** T. Twining *Aristotle's Treat. Poetry* (1812) II. 232 The moral, or rather mannered Tragedy (for we seem to want a word here).

†**2.** Well-behaved, well-mannered. Also *transf.* (of a dwelling). *Obs.*

c **1450** Holland *Howlat* 240 Mansweit, but malice, manerit and meike. **1483** Caxton *Gold. Leg.* 150 b/1 Lerne of marye to be manerd and fere ful to all men. **1560** Rolland *Crt. Venus* ii. 121 Thair manerit Mans sa perfyit and preclair, Enuirond all aboit with hailsum air. **1568** T. Howell *Newe Sonets* (1879) 157 Who are more feate or trim traind vp, then manerd seruents are?

3. Characterized by manner or mannerism, *esp.* in art or literature.

1801 Fuseli in *Lect. Paint.* ii. (1848) 390 The mannered and feeble etchings of Theodore van Tulden. **1861** Thornbury *Turner* I. 157 The colour has a slightly greenish-blue tinge, which is mannered, but not unpleasing. **1884** Haweis *Musical Life* II. 633 That Spohr was too doctrinaire and mannered,..most musicians will allow. **1896** Mackail *Lat. Lit.* (ed. 2) 101 That passages in it [the Æneid] here and there are mannered, and even flat, is true.

†**4.** Moderate, within bounds. *Obs.* *rare*$^{-1}$.

1435 Misyn *Fire of Love* 94 Lufe..of kynsmen, if it be vn-manerd, fleschly affeccione it is cald..; And if it be manerd, kyndely it is calde.

†**'mannerhood.** *Obs.* *rare*$^{-1}$. [f. manner *sb.*^{1} + -hood.] ? Orderly condition, good order.

1622 Bacon *Hen. VII* 74 This did wonderfully concerne the Might and Manner-hood of the Kingdome.

†**'mannering.** *Obs.* [f. manner *sb.*^{1} + -ing^1.] Training in manners.

1581 Mulcaster *Positions* v. (1887) 28 But this mannering of them is not for teachers alone. *Ibid.* xi. 59 The manering and training vp of youth.

mannering, obs. form of manuring.

mannerism ('mænərɪz(ə)m). [f. manner *sb.*^{1} + -ism. Cf. F. *maniérisme* (Littré *Suppl.*).]

a. Excessive or affected addiction to a distinctive manner or method of treatment, *esp.* in art and literature. *spec.* (freq. with capital initial) applied to a style of art which originated in Italy *c* 1520 and preceded the Baroque, characterized by stylistic exaggeration in figure and composition, etc.

Apart from the generalized use illustrated below, the term has been used (*a*) of the followers of Michelangelo, Raphael, etc., as Bronzino, Pontormo, the Zuccari, etc. (mainly a 19th-c. use), (*b*) from *c* 1920 under the influence of M. Dvořak and W. Friedländer applied without pejorative associations to Italian art, in particular, from *c* 1520 to *c* 1590. Sense (*b*) is first found in English in the 1930s.

1803 *Edin. Rev.* II. 246 Mr. Stewart's style..has character without mannerism, or eccentricity. **1823** D'Israeli *Cur. Lit.* Ser. ii. I. 39 Art..sinks into mannerism, and wantons into affectation. **1845** A. Jameson *Mem. Early Italian Painters* II. vii. 203 Those faults which have rendered many of his [*sc.* Parmigiano's] works unpleasing, by giving the impression of effort, and of what in art is called mannerism. **1851** tr. *Kugler's Schools of Painting in Italy* (ed. 2) II. v. ix. 469 Many of the painters in question would, fifty years earlier, have done great things; now they fell into repulsive mannerism. **1873** Symonds *Grk. Poets* v. 152 At

the time of Pindar poetry was sinking into mannerism. **1891** tr. *J. Adeline's Art Dict.* 249 Mannerism may be defined as *manner* in a bad sense. Qualities of treatment which when moderately displayed mark individuality of style, when carried to excess and too often repeated degenerate into mannerism. **1937** E. K. WATERHOUSE *Baroque Painting in Rome* 1 From 1535 until 1590 the history of painting in Rome is the history of Mannerism. **1940** A. BLUNT *Artistic Theory in Italy 1450–1600* v. 76 Those, like Dolce and Aretino..unable to follow Michelangelo as he moved on into Mannerism. **1943** *Art Bulletin* Mar. 87/2 The word mannerism..is currently used either to designate the period between the High Renaissance and the Baroque or else as a name for the anti-classical movement in sixteenth-century art. **1947** D. MAHON *Stud. Seicento Art & Theory* 59 Though the relatively recent understanding of Mannerism as a quite different artistic language from Baroque has somewhat curtailed the original scope of the latter (involving the secession of such figures as Tintoretto and El Greco) the use of the expression Baroque as a general term in its widest sense (such as Gothic), seems to have come to stay. **1961** J. D. ROSENBERG *Darkening Glass* (1963) v. 88 What we study as Mannerism he [*sc.* Ruskin] dismissed as vapidity and affectation. **1962** *Listener* 12 July 54/1 It is to move out of the serene and classical harmony of High Renaissance portraiture into the contrivance of the style that is known as Mannerism. **1965** G. SHEPHERD in P. Sidney *Apology for Poetry* 66 In the history of the pictorial arts, Lommazo and Zuccaro are spoken of as theorists of a phase of late mannerism. **1972** F. GARVIE tr. *Wundram's Art of Renaissance* 42 Architecture in the age of Mannerism played a major part historically by overcoming the static in favor of the movemented.

b. An instance of this excessive or affected addiction; a habitual peculiarity of action, expression, artistic manipulation, etc., characteristic of a person; a 'trick of manner'.

1819 COLERIDGE in *Lit. Rem.* (1836) II. 378 Hints *obiter* are:—not..to permit beauties by repetition to become mannerisms. **1873** BLACK *Pr. Thule* xi. 178 Her harsh way of saying things..is only a mannerism. **1893** *Times* 29 Apr. 13/3 He has abandoned his mannerisms and been content to make a beautiful picture.

mannerist ('mænərɪst), *sb.* and *a.* Also 8 manierest. [f. MANNER *sb.*[1] + -IST. Cf. F. *maniériste.*] **1.** One who is addicted to mannerism. *spec.* an exponent or adherent of Mannerism in art (see prec.).

1695 DRYDEN *Dufresnoy's Art Paint.* 151 Those [Painters] whom we may call Mannerists, and who repeat five or six times over in the same Picture the same Hairs of a Head. **1716** R. GRAHAM *Short Acc. Painters* (ed. 2) 361 Pietro Berettini of Cortona... He is allow'd to have been the most agreeable Mannerist, that any Age has produc'd. **1751** WARBURTON *Notes on Pope's Imit. Hor.* Ep. II. i. 149 This excellent Colourist [Lely]..was an excessive Manierest. **1821** BYRON 6 Jan. in Moore *Lett. & Jrnls.* (1830) II. 399 The Italian comedian Vestris... Somewhat of a mannerist; but excellent in broad comedy. **1833** J. CONSTABLE in C. R. Leslie *Mem. Life J. Constable* (1843) xii. 135 A certain set of painters who, having substituted falsehood for truth, and formed a style mean and mechanical, are termed mannerists. **1845** A. JAMESON *Mem. Early Italian Painters* II. x. 250 In the middle of the sixteenth century Italy swarmed with painters: these go under the general name of the mannerists, because they all imitated the manner of some one of the great masters who had gone before them. **1864** R. N. WORNUM *Epochs of Painting* 303 Hosts of copyists and mannerists arose,..with a mania for representing the naked human figure, [who] sacrificed almost every beauty, quality, and motive, to the paramount desire of anatomical display. **1871** LOWELL *Pope* Pr. Wks. 1890 IV. 27 Wordsworth..came at a time when the school which Pope founded had degenerated into a mob of mannerists. **1880** DISRAELI *Endym.* xlix, Every one to a certain degree is a mannerist; every one has his ways. **1907** B. BERENSON *N. Italian Painters of Renaissance* 156 The Mannerists, Tibaldi, Zuccaro, Fontana, thus quickly give place to the Eclectics. **1926** [see ACADEMISM 2]. **1951** A. HAUSER *Social Hist. Art.* I. v. 388 The antitheses of 'Gothic' and 'Renaissance'..are still..irreconcilable in the outlook of the mannerists. **1956** A. HUXLEY *Adonis & Alphabet* 229 There is not the slightest reason to believe that Catholic fervour was less intense in the age of the Mannerists than it had been three generations earlier.

2. In appositive use, passing into *adj.*

1934 R. WITTKOWER in *Art Bulletin* XVI. 216 The Laurenziana belongs to a..group of buildings arranged on similar principles, common between 1520 and 1580/90 and to be called Mannerist. **1939** *Handbk. Drawings & Watercolours Dept. Prints & Drawings Brit. Mus.* 38 The leading figure of this mannerist movement, which is largely occupied in elaborate decorative schemes in palaces and churches, was Francesco Salviati. **1944** *Archit. Rev.* XCVI. 187 The author is, it seems, of the generation to which what we now define as Mannerist is nothing but a late phase of the Renaissance. **1964** *English Studies* XLV. 98 The transition from thc ambiguities of Mannerist expression to that of Baroque realism. **1972** *Guardian* 17 Nov. 12/3 It was the influence of Raphael that informed the Mannerist artists whose work clusters round that of the giants.

manneristic (mænə'rɪstɪk), *a.* [f. prec. + -IC.] Characterized by mannerism.

1837 J. H. NEWMAN *Lett.* (1891) II. 237 The danger which..at present besets the Apostolical movement of getting peculiar in externals, *i.e.* formal, manneristic, &c. **1869** LEVER *Boy of Norcotts* xiv. 107 Even with a first rate artist you need change, otherwise your dinners become manneristic.

So **manne'ristical** *a.*

1830 *Fraser's Mag.* II. 464 [Of an actress] Her general style is manneristical. **1864** *Daily Tel.* 27 Sept., Those curious and manneristical, but masculine, productions by which he [Landor] will be remembered.

'mannerize, *v. rare.* [f. MANNER *sb.*[1] + -IZE, after *mannerism.*] *trans.* To make manneristic.

1887 SAINTSBURY *Hist. Elizab. Lit.* ix. (1890) 328 A..mannerising of the verse. **1899** *Westm. Gaz.* 1 Feb. 4/1 Long runs tend to mannerize the actor—if I may use such a word. **1910** A. C. BENSON *Silent Isle* xv. 103 Tennyson..became solemn, mannerised, conscious of responsibility. **1956** *Archit. Rev.* CXIX. 161/2 The forms which have developed from the rationale and the initial ideology of the modern movement are being mannerized and changed into a conscious imperfectionism.

mannerless ('mænəlɪs), *a.* [f. MANNER *sb.*[1] + -LESS.] Without manners; unmannerly.

c **1460** ROS *Belle Dame sans Merci* 714 Iffe I medlyd with siche, or other mo Hit might be called pyte maner-les. **1581** PETTIE *Guazzo's Civ. Conv.* II. (1586) 113 They will become carelesse, mannerlesse, and lesse readie to commendable enterprises. **1682** SHADWELL *Lanc. Witches* I. Wks. 1720 III. 230 Thou fresh, insipid, witless, mannerless knight. **1864** *Daily Tel.* 4 Oct., [He] may not..necessarily be a morose and mannerless hog.

mannerliness ('mænəlɪnɪs). [f. next + -NESS.] The quality of being mannerly.

1625 PURCHAS *Pilgrims* II. 1657 They eate all greedily and in haste, holding it mannerlinesse not to be long in eating. *a* **1677** HALE *Prim. Orig. Man.* I. i. 34 Out of a piece of mannerliness and respect to God. **1874** T. HARDY *Far fr. Mad. Crowd* ix, Earnestness which consisted half of genuine feeling and half of mannerliness.

mannerly ('mænəlɪ), *a.* [f. MANNER *sb.*[1] + -LY[1].]

†**1.** Seemly, decent, respectable, modest. *Obs.*

13.. *Gaw. & Gr. Knt.* 1656 Mony aþel songez..& carolez newe, With alle þe manerly merþe þat mon may of telle. **1398** TREVISA *Barth. De P.R.* VI. xiii. (1495) 198 A good spouse and wyfe is..manerly [L. *modesta*] in clothynge. **1523** *Test. Ebor.* (Surtees) V. 171 As moche clothe as shall make them a manerly garmente. **1526** TINDALE *1 Tim.* ii. 9 That they arraye them selves in manerly [1534 comlye] aparell with shamfastnes. **1596** HARINGTON *Metam. Ajax* (1814) 4 A tale..more merry than mannerly. **1600** HOLLAND *Livy* III. xxvi. 106 But first he brushed off the dust, and wiped away his sweat, and made himselfe somewhat mannerly. **1647** N. BACON *Disc. Govt. Eng.* I. xliv. (1739) 72 [He] possessed himself of the long-desired prey; and yet he did it in a mannerly way. **1655** FULLER *Ch. Hist.* IX. vi. §19 A modest, and manerly, (*alias*) a crafty, and cunning begging of a contribution of the Catholick party. **1697** COLLIER *Immor. Stage* ii. (1698) 72 A very mannerly story!

†**2.** Moral, well-conducted. *Obs.*

c **1400** tr. *Secreta Secret., Govt. Lordsh.* 62 Techinges ful specyals and manerlys [L. *moralia*]. **1535** COVERDALE *1 Tim.* iii. 2 A Biszhoppe must be..sober discrete, manerly, harberous. **1549** COVERDALE, etc. *Erasm. Par. 1 Tim.* 2 This Timothee beyng an honest manierly towarde yonge man and well learned in holy scriptures.

3. Of persons, their actions, etc.: Characterized by good manners; well-mannered; polite.

a **1529** SKELTON *Wks.* (Dyce) I. 28 Manerly Margery Mylk and Ale. **1573** TUSSER *Husb.* (1878) 175 That pewter is neuer for manerly feastes, that daily doth serue so vnmanerly beastes. **1584** *1st Voy. Virginia* in *Hakluyt's Voy.* (1589) 729 In their behauiour as mannerly, and ciuill, as any of Europe. *a* **1639** W. WHATELEY *Prototypes* III. xxxix. (1640) 5 Learne how to carry yourselves to your Parents; if they call you, come, and give them dutifull and mannerly answers. **1676** WYCHERLEY *Pl. Dealer* II. (1735) 51 Be you mannerly to her, because you are to pretend only to be her squire. **1742** FIELDING *J. Andrews* IV. ix, The little boy..was chid by his mother for not being more mannerly. **1822** SCOTT *Nigel* i, Jin Vin, was so full of his gibes, and his jeers, ..and so mannerly all the while. **1887** *Spectator* 2 Apr. 458/2 Criticism must be truthful, but it may also be mannerly.

'mannerly, *adv.* [f. MANNER *sb.*[1] + -LY[2].]

†**1.** In a seemly manner, decently, becomingly, properly. *Obs.*

13.. *E.E. Allit. P.* B. 91 Ful manerly with marchal mad for to sitte. **1375** BARBOUR *Bruce* III. 72 He mycht, mar manerlik, Lyknyt hym to Gaudifer de Laryss. *c* **1460** J. RUSSELL *Bk. Nurture* 923 Kover with a keuerlyte clenly þat bed so manerly made. **1493** in *Somerset Medieval Wills* (1901) 306 Myn executours according to reason manerly for there labour rewarded. **1577** B. GOOGE *Heresbach's Husb.* (1586) 125 They [asses] be very apt to be taught, so as at this day in Alcayre you shall have them daunce very manerly. **1596** in *Harington's Metam. Ajax* Let. to Author A iij b, As you haue told in verse a baudy tale or two in Orland mannerly. **1615** CROOKE *Body of Man* 65 Aristotle calleth them ἴσχια,..we call it mannerly the *seate.* **1621–31** LAUD *Sev. Serm.* (1847) 9 Such a superior [as God] cannot be called into the Assembly mannerly, but by 'prayer'. **1647** TRAPP *Comm. Rom.* xiii. 13 *Let us walk honestly.* Handsomely, fashionably, mannerly, with an holy shamefacednes.

2. With good manners; politely, courteously.

1519 HORMAN *Vulg.* 62 Whether thou do a thynge in iape or in ernest do it manerlye. **1535** COVERDALE *Ecclus.* xxxi. 16 Eate the thinge that is set before the, manerly. **1611** SHAKS. *Cymb.* III. vi. 92 When we haue supp'd Wee'l mannerly demand thee of thy Story. **1677** HALE *Contempl.* II. 88 Lust must not be mannerly treated withall, but flatly denyed. **1704** NORRIS *Ideal World* II. xii. 471 We are afraid lest she should have too many [guests], and accordingly very mannerly withdraw. **1832** HT. MARTINEAU *Hill & Valley* vii. 110 It would be well if he behaved himself a little more mannerly.

†**3.** Morally. *Obs.*

1566 *Acts & Constit. Scotl.* To Rdr. ✠ iij, Gif thay will not onlie leif, bot als manerlie, weill, and godlie leif.

†**'mannerness.** *Obs. rare*[−1]. [f. MANNER *sb.*[1] + -NESS.] Moderation.

1382 WYCLIF *Prov.* xxii. 4 The ende of mannernesse [1388 temperaunce, Vulg. *modestiæ*] the drede of the Lord.

mannersome ('mænəsəm), *a. dial.* [f. MANNER *sb.*[1] + -SOME.] Mannerly.

1876 BLACKMORE *Cripps* xxviii, Mary was obliged to bite her tongue to keep it in any way mannersome. **1887** —— *Springhaven* (ed. 4) II. vii. 81 He had always known her to be kind and gentle, and what the old people called 'mannersome', to every living body. **1895** *Outing* (U. S.) XXVI. 65/1 Canady's a slick-spoken feller 'bout huntin', 'an a mannersome feller, too.

mannery: see MANERY *Obs.*

mannes, obs. form of MANESS.

†**'manness.** In 3 **mannesse, mennesse.** [app. f. MAN *sb.*[1] + -NESS; the umlaut form seems to be due to the analogy of *mennish,* MANNISH *a.*]

†**1.** Human nature. *Obs.*

a **1225** *Leg. Kath.* 1118 Þah he were dedlich, þurh þ he mon wes, onont his mennesse [*MS. C* mannesse], & deide.

2. = MALENESS.

1921 W. J. TURNER *Music & Life* p. ix, You are not concerned with their..brains..but with something which we may call their 'manness'. **1947** J. STEINBECK *Pearl* (1948) v. 64 The quality of woman..could cut through Kino's manness.

†**'mannet.** *Obs. nonce-wd.* [f. MAN *sb.*[1] + -ET[1], dim. suffix.] A little man.

1630 B. JONSON *New Inn* IV. i, A slight Man-net, to port her, vp, and downe.

mannicle, obs. form of MANACLE.

mannide ('mænaɪd). *Chem.* [f. MANNA[1] + -IDE.] A syrupy substance obtained by heating mannite with butyric acid.

1862 WATTS tr. *Gmelin's Handbk. Chem.* XV. 368 Mannide... Berthelot (1856). **1892** MORLEY & MUIR *Watts' Dict. Chem., Mannide* $C_6H_{10}O_4$. Second anhydride of mannite.

mannie ('mænɪ). orig. *Sc.* Also **manny.** [f. MAN *sb.* + -IE, dim. suffix.] A little man; also applied (as a term of endearment) to a little boy. In Jewish use: see quot. 1909.

The Jewish use is perhaps a contraction of *Emanuel.*

a **1689** W. CLELAND *Poems* (1697) 105 A puffie cheek'd red bearded mannie. **1823** LOCKHART *Reg. Dalton* I. II. i. 193 A decent, little auld manny, in..velveteen breeches. *a* **1828** in P. Buchan *Ball. N. Scot.* (1828) II. 103 Then spake the auld laird o' Kingcaussie, A canty auld mannie was he. **1886** STEVENSON *Kidnapped* 9 What'll like be your business, mannie? **1909** J. R. WARE *Passing Eng.* 173/2 *Manny* (Jewish E. London), term of endearment or admiration prefixed to Jewish name, as 'Manny Lyons'. **1914** JOYCE *Dubliners* 103 My little man! My little mannie! **1916** 'BOYD CABLE' *Action Front* 262 'My manny here was good enough,' said Macalister, 'to tell me he wouldna' bandage my eyes.' **1922** D. H. LAWRENCE *England, my England* 154 There's too much of the little mannie about him. **1971** M. WEST *Summer of Red Wolf* vi. 125 What do you want me to pack for the poor mannie?

manniferous (mæ'nɪfərəs), *a.* [f. mod.L. *mannifer* (+ *manna* MANNA + *-fer* bearing) + -OUS: see -FEROUS.] **a.** Yielding manna (Mayne *Expos. Lex.* 1856). **b.** Causing the production of manna. (Said of insects.)

In recent Dicts.

mannikin: see MANIKIN.

manning ('mænɪŋ), *vbl. sb.* [f. MAN *v.* + -ING[1].]

1. a. The action of furnishing (a ship, etc.) with men. Also *concr.*, the complement of men, crew. Also, in more recent use: the action of furnishing a factory, an industry, etc., with men.

1548 *Privy Council Acts* (1890) II. 172 To William Pures, for rigging of his ship,..and for mannyng of her. **1633** T. STAFFORD *Pac. Hib.* II. viii. (1810) 320 For the manning and making good of that Citie. **1651** HOBBES *Leviath.* II. xxii. 120 For..victualling and manning of ships. **1748** *Anson's Voy.* II. iv. 160 A number, greatly insufficient for the manning of the *Centurion.* **1765** BLACKSTONE *Comm.* I. vii. 255 The sole prerogative as well of erecting, as manning and governing of which, belongs to the king in his capacity of general of the kingdom. **1849** MACAULAY *Hist. Eng.* ii. I. 203 Money destined for the equipping and manning of the fleet. **1896** *Pall Mall Mag.* May 108, I reckon I've lost two days' coal for her [*sc.* coal-boat] and two days' wages and grub for her manning. **1955** *Times* 22 Aug. 7/4 He refers to the dockers' insistence on full manning, with the implication that this is a restrictive practice.

b. (See quot.)

1706 PHILLIPS (ed. Kersey), *Manning of the Ship,* (in Sea-Language) is when a Ship is to shew abroad all her Men.

2. The action of taming a hawk (see MAN *v.* 10).

1580 LYLY *Euphues* (Arb.) 372 Hawkes that waxe haggard by manning, are to be cast off. **1644** DIGBY *Nat. Bodies* xxxvii. (1658) 395 No whit more extraordinary, then a fawkners manning of a hawk.

3. *attrib.* and *Comb.*: **manning-piece** *jocular* (see quot. 1834); **manning-scale** (see quot. 1891).

1834 L. HUNT in *Lond. Jrnl.* I. 172/1, I am standing with my manning-piece by a hedge... You cannot say fowling-piece, when it is *men* that are to be brought down. **1891** *Labour Commission Gloss., Manning Scale,* a scale which fixes the minimum number of seamen to be employed on a

vessel. **1896** Sir C. Dilke in *Daily News* 6 Mar. 2/3 A very severe strain was put upon the manning powers of the Admiralty. **1953** *Britannica Bk. of Year* 638/2 Other compound nouns were *manning requirements* (the number of men required by an industry). **1962** *Listener* 1 Mar. 377/1 On the labour side there are..rules about manning-scales (that is, how many men to a job). **1975** *Times* 14 Apr. 12/2 We put them there, those too many men...Manning levels were never changed. **1975** *Times* 5 June 18/4 The stoppage is by 80 door hangers and welders, who are protesting about management plans to reduce manning scales.

manniparous (mæˈnɪpərəs), *a.* [f. mod.L. *mannipar-us* + -ous: see manna and -parous.] **a.** Of insects: Causing the flow of manna (Mayne *Expos. Lex.* 1856). **b.** Bearing or exuding manna (Webster *Suppl.* 1902).

†ˈ**mannish**, *sb. Obs.* In 1–2 mennisc, 2–3 **mannisshe, mannisse, mennisse.** [OE. *męnnisc*, properly neut. of *męnnisc* adj.: see next. In other Teut. langs. the wk. masc. form of the adj. is used subst. in the sense 'human being': cf. OFris. *manniska, menska*, OS. *mennisco* (MDu. *mensche*, Du. *mensch*), OHG. *mennisko* (mod.G. *mensch*).] People; a class of persons.

971 *Blickl. Hom.* 175 Þis is þæt mennisc þe ealle mine dæda mid heora wordum onwendan. *a* **1175** *Cott. Hom.* 225 Þa wearð þa redlice micel mennisc ȝewexon. *c* **1200** *Trin. Coll. Hom.* 39 Ðese fower mannisshe..beð þat erf þe þo herdes ouerwuakeden. *Ibid.* 163 Ðis lond þe ich nu of speke is þat mennisse þe nu liueð. *Ibid.* 165 Swo doð þis mannisse flieð fram iuele to werse.

mannish (ˈmænɪʃ), *a.* Forms: *α.* 1 mennisc, 2 mennesc, 3 mennish, *Orm.* mennisske; *β.* 4 **mannys(s)h,** (5 **mannisshe, monyssh**), 5–6 **mannishe, -ysshe,** (6 **manish,** 9 **man-ish**), 3, 5– **mannish.** [OE. *męnnisc* = OS. *mannisc, mennisc*, OHG. *mennisc* (MHG. *mennisch*), Goth. *mannisks*:—OTeut. **mannisko-*, f. **mann* man *sb.*[1] + *-isko-* -ish[1]. In the 13th c. the root vowel was already frequently assimilated to that of man *sb.*[1]

In many uses the existing word must be regarded as a new formation on man *sb.*[1] + -ish[1]; but it is hardly possible to separate the instances of this from those of the word inherited from OTeut.]

†**1.** Of or belonging to the human species; proper to or characteristic of mankind; human. *Obs.*

c **888** K. Ælfred *Boeth.* xxxiii. §1 Forðam þa fif eall nan mennisc man fullice habban ne mæȝ ða hwile [etc.]. *c* **897** —— *Gregory's Past. C.* xi. 70 Ne ȝegripe eow næfre nan costung buton mennescu. *c* **1175** *Lamb. Hom.* 91 God cweð ..þe he walde his gast asenden ofer mennesc flesc. *c* **1200** Ormin 218 He..let te posstless sen himm wel Inn hiss mennisske kinde. *c* **1386** Chaucer *Melib.* ¶298 The prouerbe seith that for to do synne is mannyssh. **1390** Gower *Conf.* III. 52 It was as in figure Most lich to mannyssh creature, Bot as of beaute hevenelich. **1567** Drant *Horace, Epist.* i. xiii. E iij, More meete to beare.. Then here in courte in mannishe shape The Asses part to plaie. **1674** N. Fairfax *Bulk & Selv.* 183 At the ending of the world there must be stuff enough left, unmade up into Manish bodies, wherewith to frame a new heaven and new earth.

2. Of a woman, her attributes, etc.: Resembling a man, man-like, masculine. Chiefly *contemptuous.*

c **1374** Chaucer *Troylus* i. 228 (284) But alle hir limes so wel answeringe Weren to womanhode, that creature Was neuer lasse mannissh in seminge. *c* **1430** Lydg. *Reas. & Sens.* 6183 God forbede That her sholde in womanhede Ben any monyssh tache at al. **1430–40** —— *Bochas* vi. i. (1494) t ij b, Nowe was she mannyssh nowe was she femynyne. *a* **1450** *Knt. de la Tour* (1868) 136 It is saide, a woman that is not humble and pitous she is mannishe and not womanly, whiche is a uice in womanhode to be rude or of hautinge courage. **1594** Carew *Huarte's Exam. Wits* xv. (1616) 269 She retaineth a mannish fashion..in her words, as in all her motions. **1606** Shaks. *Tr. & Cr.* iii. iii. 217 A woman impudent and mannish growne, Is not more loth'd, then an effeminate man. **1615** Crooke *Body of Man* 250 Her bodye grew mannish and hairie. **1653** Holcroft *Procopius, Goth. Wars* iv. 121 They..who think that there was neuer any such Mannish race of women. **1791** Mme. D'Arblay *Diary* Aug., Women..strolling along with wide mannish strides. **1824** Miss Mitford *Village* Ser. i. 239 She spoke in a loud deep mannish voice. **1886** Swinburne *Misc.* 235 The mannish woman was a nobler as well as a stronger creature than the womanish man.

3. Pertaining to or characteristic of a grown man (often opposed to *childish*); aping or simulating manhood or the characteristics of a man.

1530 Palsgr. 318/1 Mannysshe or manlyke, *viril.* **1600** Shaks. *A.Y.L.* i. iii. 123 *Ros[alind.]*..Weele haue a swashing and a marshall outside, As manie other mannish cowards haue, That doe outface it with their semblances. **1611** —— *Cymb.* iv. ii. 236 And let vs (Polidore) though now our voyces Haue got the mannish cracke, sing him to'th'ground As once to our Mother. **1647** S. Sheppard *2nd Pt. Committee-Man C.* i. ii, His chin has..a little downe, enough to give notice to the world, he now growes mannish. **1784** Cowper *Tiroc.* 208 Childish in mischief only and in noise, Else of a mannish growth. **1820** Lamb *Elia* Ser. I. *Old Benchers of Inner T.*, Why must every thing smack of man and mannish? Is the world all grown up? **1876** Farrar *Marlb. Serm.* xxxvi. 369 By manly I mean all that is eager, hearty, fearless, modest, pure; by mannish I mean that which apes the poorest externals of the lowest types of men.

4. Characteristic (chiefly in blameworthy or ludicrous respects) of a man as distinguished from a woman.

1748 Richardson *Clarissa* I. viii, With an air of mannish superiority, he seems rather to pity the bashful girl. **1836** Mrs. S. C. Hall in *New Monthly Mag.* XLVII. 427 True to his man-ish nature, there was a mingling of selfishness with his love. **1882** Hinsdale *Garfield & Educ.* ii. 407 The foremost students had no mannish pride that made them hesitate to ask her assistance. **1884** Lady Waterford in Hare *Two Noble Lives* (1893) III. 428 Oh! what a mannish room I waited in... Hats and caps of all sorts, fishing baskets, &c.

¶**5.** = mankind *a.*[2] *Obs. rare.*

1530 Palsgr. 427/2, I am mannysshe, as a beest is that is accoustumed to byte or devoure men. *Je suis humain.* It is a mannysshe beest: *cest une besté amorcée.*

†**6.** quasi-*adv.* Like a man. *Obs.*

c **1386** Chaucer *Merch. T.* 292 Men moste enquere.. Wher she be..Or riche, or poore, or elles mannyssh wood.

Hence †**mennisclezc** [see -laik], *rare*[−1], humanity; ˈ**mannishly** *adv.*, in a mannish manner.

c **1200** Ormin 85 He sennde uss..His Sune..To takenn ure mennissclezc..To lesenn mannkinn. **1867** Bushnell *Mor. Uses Dark Th.* 287 Some of the least of them march out mannishly in columns and fight pitched battles.

mannishness (ˈmænɪʃnɪs). [f. mannish *a.* + -ness.]

†**1.** The state of being in human form; humanity. (Said chiefly of Christ.) *Obs.*

a **900** tr. *Bæda's Hist.* iii. xv. [xxi.] (1890) 220 Ymb syx hund wintra & þreo & fiftig from Drihtnes menniscnesse. *a* **1175** *Cott. Hom.* 227 Næ worhte he þah nane wndre openlice er þan þe he was þritti wintre an þara mennisnisse. *c* **1200** Ormin 1373 Þær Cristess mennisscnesse Drannc dæþess drinnch o rodetreo Forr ure wozhe dedess. **1674** N. Fairfax *Bulk & Selv.* 11 Such a tang of manishness, or a mingle mangle of half man, half world.

2. The quality of being mannish, in various senses.

1612 Bp. Hall *Imprese of God* ii. Wks. (1625) 457 The painted faces, and mannishnesse..of the one sex, the factious hollownesse..in the other. **1882** *Pall Mall G.* 16 June 4/2 But now..all the exclusive mannishness of the colleges seems fast melting away before the new invasion [of women]. **1886** Miss Braddon *One Thing Needful* xi, The masculine woman is proud of her mannishness.

mannisse, variant of manness *Obs.*

mannitan (ˈmænɪtən). *Chem.* Also **-ane.** [f. next + -an.] A syrupy fluid, $C_6H_{12}O_5$, obtained by heating mannite.

1857 Miller *Elem. Chem.* III. 384 Mannitane. **1862** Watts tr. *Gmelin's Handbk. Chem.* XV. 369 Mannitan.

mannite (ˈmænaɪt). *Chem.* [f. mann-a[1] + -ite.] A substance, $C_6H_{14}O_6$, obtained chiefly from manna; = mannitol. Also called manna-*sugar*, and rarely ***mannite-sugar***.

1830 Lindley *Nat. Syst. Bot.* 224 The sweetness of this substance [Manna] is..due..to a distinct principle, called Mannite. **1880** Garrod & Baxter *Mat. Med.* (ed. 8) 222 It contains a resin..besides starch and mannite sugar. **1883** *Encycl. Brit.* XV. 493/2 In Italy mannite is prepared for sale in the shape of small cones.

mannitic (mæˈnɪtɪk), *a. Chem.* [f. mannite + -ic.] Derived from mannite. ***mannitic acid*** (see quot. 1865).

1862 Watts tr. *Gmelin's Handbk. Chem.* XV. 369 Mannitic ethers. **1865** —— *Dict. Chem.* III. 825 *Mannitic acid*, $C^6H^{12}O^7$, an acid produced, together with mannitose, by the oxidation of mannite under the influence of platinum-black. **1876** tr. *Schützenberger's Ferment.* 192 These gummy and mannitic ferments.

mannitie: see mannity.

mannitol (ˈmænɪtɒl). *Chem.* [f. mannite + -ol.] A sweet crystalline hexahydric alcohol, $CH_2OH(CHOH)_4CH_2OH$, known in three optically isomeric forms, which is found in many plants (such as sugar cane, celery, and larch) and is used in aqueous solution in kidney function tests. Now the usual name for mannite.

1879 *Jrnl. Chem. Soc.* XXXVI. 1034 Mannitylhexsulphuric acid is obtained as an uncrystallisable liquid by dissolving mannitol in sulphuric monochloride. **1902** *Encycl. Brit.* XXVI. 721/1 Mannitol is proved to be a hexhydric alcohol, $C_6H_8(OH)_6$, by its conversion into a hexanitrate. **1939** *Jrnl. Amer. Chem. Soc.* LXI. 761/2 To prepare the *l*-glyceraldehyde in an analogous way from *l*-mannitol was much more difficult, since the *l*-mannitol.. is not yet obtainable commercially. **1951** A. Grollman *Pharmacol. & Therapeutics* xxxii. 750 Mannitol, a hexahydric alcohol sugar is filtered through the glomeruli but is neither reabsorbed nor excreted by the tubules. **1957** *Technology* July 187/2 Mannitol, which also comes from seaweed, is used by the chemical, explosive, pharmaceutical and electrical industries. **1970** H. McLeave *Question of Negligence* (1973) xxvii. 208 'Intravenous saline and mannitol,' he murmured. His registrar injected the drug to shrink the brain and relieve the compression.

mannitose (ˈmænɪtəʊs). *Chem.* [f. mannite + -ose.] A substance, $C_6H_{12}O_6$, isomeric with glucose, obtained from mannite.

1862 Watts tr. *Gmelin's Handbk. Chem.* XV. 339 When mannite is oxidised under the influence of platinum-black [etc.], an unfermentable substance and a fermentable sugar (mannitose) are produced. **1865** [see mannitic *a.*].

mannittee, obs. form of manatee.

†ˈ**mannity.** *nonce-wd.* In 7 mannitie. [f. man *sb.*[1] + -ity.] The community of men.

1621 Molle *Camerar. Liv. Libr.* iii. v. 165 And therefore was it well said of a Pagan Philosopher..that he gaue not his almes to that man, or to this, but to all the masse of mankind..: not to a man, but to the mannitie, if it be lawfull to vse such a word.

Mannlicher (ˈmanlɪxər). [f. the name of *Mannlicher* (see below).] A firearm of a type invented by Ferdinand Ritter von Mannlicher (1848–1904), esp. a type of sporting rifle. Also *attrib.*

The umlauted *ä* in the Kipling example is erroneous.

1884 in H. Cholmondeley-Pennell *Smoke of Battle* (ed. 2) 16 (Advt.), The Mannlicher Rifle is the one of all the specimens of Repeating Arms..which seems to us the best arm for our soldiers. **1896** T. F. Fremantle *Notes on Rifle* xi. 175 The ·256 Mannlicher is capable of making very fair shooting at these long ranges. **1902** Kipling *Traffics & Discov.* (1904) 20 My gun was too good, too uniform—shot as close as a Männlicher [Mannlicher, 1902 magazine publ.] rifle. **1922** J. Buchan *Huntingtower* xiv. 267 McGuffog, who was a marksman, was also given a sporting Mannlicher. **1935** E. Hemingway *Green Hills Afr.* (1936) i. ii. 46 There was the short-barrelled explosion of the Mannlicher. **1970** I. V. Hogg *Military Pistols & Revolvers* 41/2 The Mannlicher uses a form of delayed blow-back action.

mannor, -our, -ure, obs. ff. manner, manor, manure.

mannose (ˈmænəʊs, -əʊz). *Chem.* [a. G. *mannose* (Fischer & Hirschberger 1888, in *Ber. d. Deut. Chem. Ges.* XXI. 1805), f. *mann(it)ose* mannitose.] A crystalline sugar, $C_6H_{12}O_6$, which is known in three optically isomeric forms which are epimers of those of glucose, and whose dextrorotatory form is obtained by the hydrolysis of mannans.

1888 *Jrnl. Chem. Soc.* LIV. 934 Mannose..is obtained by dissolving the above phenylhydrazone in four parts of hydrochloric acid..cooled with ice and salt. **1911** [see epimer]. **1949** M. A. Jennings in H. W. Florey et al. *Antibiotics* II. xxxi. 975 The series included strains known to vary in such properties as..fermentation of carbohydrates (mannite, trehalose and mannose). **1968** A. Sols in F. Dickens et al. *Carbohydrate Metabolism* I. iii. 71 Mannose can be efficiently metabolized by most tissues because it is a very good substitute for hexokinase.

†**manny,** *a. Falconry. Obs.* [f. man *v.* (sense 10) + -y.] Of a hawk: Manned, tame.

1773 J. Campbell *Mod. Falconry* 262 Managing, the making of a hawk manny or tame.

manny, obs. f. many; var. mannie *Sc.*

mannyable, variant of maniable *Obs.*

‖**mano** (ˈmɑːnəʊ). *Anthropol.* [Sp. *mano* hand.] A primitive stone implement, held in the hand and used for grinding cereals and other foodstuffs.

1901 *Ann. Rep. Board of Regents Smithsonian Inst. 1899* 37 The grinding-stone concordantly changes from a simple roller or crusher to a mano (or muller), and finally to a pestle, at first broad and short, but afterwards long and slender. **1911** W. K. Moorehead *Stone Age N. Amer.* II. xxvii. 103 The stones used on these [mortars] are flat, or oval water-worn stones and not finished, like mano stones common to the Cliff Dweller country. **1944** G. C. Vaillant *Aztecs Mexico* (1950) i. 35 The flat grinding-stones and mullers, still used in Mexico and called *metates* and *manos*, prove that the people relied on corn as their principal food. **1959** E. Tunis *Indians* 119/2 The grinding was done by rubbing the grains across it with another stone, the *mano*, held in the hands. **1960** C. Winick *Dict. Anthropol.* 342/2 *Mano*, a cylindrically shaped grindstone slightly tapered at both ends. It was held in the hand (whence its name handstone) and used as the upper stone in milling. **1964** A. D. Krieger in Jennings & Norbeck *Prehist. Man in New World* 32 The most important new trait, however, is that of food-grinding with stone implements: basin-shaped milling stones and manos. **1971** [see indigenization]. **1972** *Sci. Amer.* May 89/3 From the Maya Mountains came the metamorphic rock used to make not only axe heads of stone but also the *manos*, or stone rollers. **1974** *Encycl. Brit. Macropædia* XI. 936/2 They [*sc.* villagers of the Ocós and Cuadros phases of Meso-American civilization] were productive corn farmers as well, raising a small-eared race of maize called Nal-Tel, which their wives and daughters ground on *metates* and *manos* and cooked in globular jars.

‖**manoao** (ˈmanɔaɔ). Also monoao. [Maori.] A New Zealand evergreen tree, *Dacrydium kirkii*, of the family Podocarpaceæ; formerly applied to another species of *Dacrydium*, *D. colensoi*; also called *silver pine*.

1867 J. D. Hooker *Handbk. N.Z. Flora* II. 766/1 Manoao, *Dacrydium Colensoi.* **1889** T. Kirk *Forest Flora N.Z.* 191 (*heading*) The manoao. *Ibid.* 192 The wood of the manaoa [*sic*] is of a light-brown colour. **1950** *N.Z. Jrnl. Agric.* Feb. 115/2 The open pumice country, clothed in a tangled mass of manuka and manoao. **1951** *Post-Primary School Bulletin* (Wellington, N.Z.) V. xii. 274 The manoao (*Dacrydium kirkii*)—a tree related to the rimu but having its young leaves more than an inch long and its old leaves only an eighth of an inch long. **1963** Poole & Adams *Trees & Shrubs N.Z.* 26 Monoao. Tree reaching 25m. Bark light brown.

Manoeline, -lino, varr. MANUELINE *a.*

manœuvrability (məˌnuːvrəˈbɪlɪtɪ). Also (*U.S.*) **maneuverability.** [f. MANŒUVRABLE *a.*] Capacity for being manœuvred.

The spelling with medial *-e-* in quots. 1942 and 1954 is unusual.

1923 *Rep. & Mem. Aeronaut. Res. Comm.* No. 851. 1 (*heading*) The comparison of the manœuvrability of aeroplanes by the use of a cinematograph camera. **1927** *Daily Express* 24 Sept. 8 Much will depend on the skill of the pilots in taking the corner, and also on the manœuvrability of the machines. **1930** C. J. STEWART *Aircraft Instruments* p. xvii, The manœvrability and the adequacy of the various control surfaces of an aircraft. **1942** *Tee Emm* (Air Ministry) II. 85 A compromise between stability and manœuvreability would not be difficult. **1954** *Encounter* June 13/2 The European national economies..are peculiarly dependent upon world trade balances, and the area of manœuvreability is limited. **1968** *Encycl. Brit.* II. 874/1 Large steering gear ratios make high-speed maneuverability more difficult. **1972** *Drive* Summer 88/1 We were glad of the boat's manoeuvrability when the current increased under the bridge at Arundel.

manœuvrable (məˈnuːvrəb(ə)l), *a.* [f. MANŒUVRE *v.* + -ABLE.] Capable of being manœuvred, used esp. of aircraft and motor vehicles.

The spelling with medial *-e-* in quot. 1942 is unusual.

1921 *Aëronautical Jrnl.* XXV. 520 Getting off across wind ..is only attempted with relatively high-powered or manœuvrable aeroplanes. **1942** *Tee Emm* (Air Ministry) II. 86 The aircraft will become more stable, but it will be less manœuvreable. **1972** *Motor* 8 Apr. 21/1 (Advt.), There are other things that we've done to our cars which would make any size of car more manoeuvrable. **1973** J. DRUMMOND *Bang! Bang! You're Dead!* xxiv. 118 'What do you need?' 'A reasonable strike-force. Manoeuvrable.'

manœuvre (məˈnjuːvə(r), məˈnuːvə(r)), *sb.* Also 5 **maanovre**, 8–9 **maneuver**, 9 *U.S.* **manœuver.** [a. F. *manœuvre* (OF. also *manuevre, maneuvre*, 13th c.) = Pr. *manovra*, Sp. *maniobra*, Pg. *manobra*, It. *manovra*:—late L. *manopera*, vbl. sb. from *manoperāre*: see MANŒUVRE *v.*, which occurs in Fr. earlier than the sb. The OFr. word is represented in Eng. by MAINOUR and MANURE *sbs.*]

†**1.** Hand-labour. *Obs. rare*$^{-1}$.

1479 RICART *Calendar* (Camden) 28 This yere [24 H. III] was the Trenche y-made and y-caste of the ryvere,..by the maanovre of alle the Cominalte.

2. *Mil.* and *Naval.* The planned or regulated movement or evolution of troops or vessels of war; a strategic movement or change of position; a device in navigation; exercise or a movement in military or naval tactics.

1758 *Misc.* in *Ann. Reg.* 373/2 *Coup de main*, and *Manœuvre*, might be excusable in Marshal Saxe, as he was in the service of France..; but we cannot see what apology can be made for our officers lugging them in.., as a sudden stroke might have done for one, and a proper motion for the other. **1778** M. CUTLER in *Life*, etc. (1888) I. 66 The army was ordered..to embark and re-embark in the boats, that they might the better understand such a maneuver. **1793** J. TRAPP tr. *Rochon's Voy. Madagascar* Prelim. Disc. 54 All manœuvres became useless, and the ship was on the point of going down, when the Captain cast an anchor in such a manner as gave him hopes she would bear on some high flats. This manœuvre proved successful. **1795** NELSON 13 Mar. in Nicolas *Disp.* (1845) II. 13 The instant all were fired, braced up our after-yards, put the helm a-port, and stood after her again. This manœuvre we practised till one P.M. **1837** GURWOOD *Wellington Desp.* IV. 1 Major General Sir Arthur Wellesley was appointed to the command of a brigade..to the discipline, manœuvre and minute details of which he paid the most scrupulous attention. **1853** SIR H. DOUGLAS *Milit. Bridges* (ed. 3) 119 The manœuvre of withdrawing a bridge, by wheeling it, entire, alongside the bank. **1881** JOWETT *Thucyd.* I. 156 The manœuvres suited to fast-sailing vessels, such as breaking of the line or returning to the charge, cannot be practised in a narrow space. **1889** *Infantry Drill* 189 Manœuvre represents the application of the drill to the circumstances of supposed or actual conflict with an enemy.

b. Skilful management or working *of*; operation.

1834–47 J. S. MACAULAY *Field Fortif.* (1851) 129 The pieces of timber, laid across the sluice-gate for the manœuvre of the levers. **1867** SMYTH *Sailor's Word-bk.*, *Manœuvre*, a dexterous management of anything connected with the ship.

3. An agile or skilful movement made (by a person, animal, etc.) with intent to deceive or elude.

1774 J. BRYANT *Mythol.* II. 468 The whole was attended with shouts, and screams, and every frantic manœuvre. **1828** SCOTT *F. M. Perth* xxiii, At length, whether weary of these manœuvres, or [etc.]..Bonthron heaved up his axe for a down-right blow. **1845** DARWIN *Voy. Nat.* ii. (1879) 37 When still further disturbed, it practises a most curious manœuvre. **1883** *Century Mag.* July 379/2 And as he [the fish] fell back with a loud splash he dropped upon the line, by which maneuver he would have succeeded in tearing out the hook had the line still been taut.

4. *transf.* and *fig.* An artfully contrived plan; an adroit move; an ingenious expedient or artifice; also, management of affairs by scheming.

1774 J. ADAMS in *Fam. Lett.* (1876) 12 These Acts of Parliament and ministerial manœuvres will injure me. **1790** —— *Wks.* (1854) IX. 566 If the time should ever come when corruption shall be added to intrigue and manœuvre in elections. *a* **1797** BURKE *Sp. Durat. Parlts.* Wks. 1812 V. 377 The whole effect of the Bill is..here to fix their magazines and places of arms, and thus to make them the principal.. theatre of their manœuvres for securing a determined majority in Parliament. **1809** MAR. EDGEWORTH *Manœuvring* vii, In the midst of these multiplied manœuvres, Mrs. Beaumont sat with ease. **1832** LYTTON *Eugene A.* II. vii, He was capital, however, about the tricks he had played his creditors,—such manœuvres,—such escapes! **1850** *Bohn's Handbk. Games* 414 (Draughts) He who gives the draw shall not occasion any unnecessary delay by uselessly repeating the same manœuvres. **1864** *Standard* 18 Apr. 6 To this day they always speak of that Reform Bill as if it had been a dishonest manœuvre. **1886** RUSKIN *Præterita* I. 309 Watching the instrumental manœuvres of the [military] band.

†**5.** A method or manner of working. *Obs.*

1770 *Monthly Rev.* 537 The different tools and *manœuvres* of the joiner and turner. **1783** POTT *Chirurg. Wks.* II. 78 It is one of those manœuvres which can be learnt only by observation and practice. **1796** C. MARSHALL *Garden.* v. (1813) 65 Many manœuvres of intercropping are made by them as sowing or planting between rows. **1789** H. WALPOLE *Lett., to H. More* Sept. (1840) VI. 351, I do not understand the manœuvre of sugar.

6. *attrib.* and *Comb.*

1897 *Act 60–1 Vict.* c. 43 §4 Whenever an Order in Council is made under this Act a commission (in this Act called the Military Manœuvres Commission) shall be formed. *Ibid.* §10 This Act may be cited as the Military Manœuvres Act, 1897. **1897** *Daily News* 8 Nov. 4/7 Every torpedo, it seems, is sent out from the factory with two heads —a 'manœuvre head',..and another, intended for real warfare.

manœuvre (məˈnjuːvə(r), məˈnuːvə(r)), *v.* Forms: see prec. sb. [ad. F. *manœuvrer*, OF. *manuvrer* (11th cent.) = Sp. *maniobrar*, Pg. *manobrar*:—late L. *manoperāre* for L. *manū operārī* to work with the hand (*manū*, abl. of *manus* hand; *operārī*, see OPERATE *v.*).]

1. a. *intr. Mil.* and *Naval.* To perform manœuvres or evolutions; to make movements or changes of position in the disposition of troops, vessels, etc. Also ***to manœuvre it.***

1777 J. ADAMS in *Fam. Lett.* (1876) 303 Washington will manœuvre it with him a good deal to avoid it. **1795** NELSON 21 Mar. in Nicolas *Disp.* (1845) II. 21 Providence.. preserving my poor brave fellows, who worked the Ship in manœuvring about his [*sc.* the enemy's] stern and quarters. **1797** *Encycl. Brit.* (ed. 3) XVIII. 290/2 The two divisions might again manœuvre another way. **1803** WELLINGTON in Gurw. *Desp.* (1837) II. 331, I..determined to manœuvre by my left, and push the enemy upon the nullah. **1833** STRAITH *Fortif.* 81 A great extent of ground..upon which to manœuvre and fight to advantage. **1885** *Law Times Rep.* LIII. 12/1 There would be no culpability on the part of the officer in command of the other ship in not manœuvring for this porting.

b. *transf.* and *fig.*, esp.: To employ stratagem, to manage by artifice, to scheme. Also *occas.* with *adv.* or *prep.*: To contrive to get (*away from*).

1809 MAR. EDGEWORTH *Manœuvring* i, I remember her manœuvring to gain a husband, and then manœuvring to manage him. **1814** JANE AUSTEN *Lett.* (1884) II. 279, I had not to manœuvre away from her. **1837** W. IRVING *Capt. Bonneville* I. 177 After manœuvring so as to get within shot, they fired, but merely wounded him [a buffalo]. **1861** MAY *Const. Hist.* (1863) I. i. 13 When ministers, not of his own choice, were in office, he plotted and manœuvred until he overthrew them.

c. *trans.* with *prep.* To drive or entice *into* or *out of* by manœuvring; to make (one's way) *into* by manœuvring.

1886 MISS BRADDON *One Thing Needful* vi, I am not going to be manœuvred into a marriage with Clarice. **1888** *Century Mag.* Sept. 673/1 He had simply manœuvred the enemy out of position. **1899** *Daily News* 13 Dec. 7/6 If an enemy has elaborately fortified a particular position it is one of the most important duties of a General not..to attack him in it, but ..to manœuvre him out of it. **1903** *Blackw. Mag.* Oct. 497/2 He had manœuvred his way into the Painted Chamber.

2. a. *trans. Mil.* and *Naval.* To cause (troops or vessels) to perform evolutions or manœuvres; to alter the position or formation of for strategic purposes; to 'handle' (a boat).

1777 J. ADAMS in *Fam. Lett.* (1876) 282 Mr. Howe, by the last advices, was manœuvring his fleet and army in such a manner as to give us expectations of an expedition somewhere. **1797** *Encycl. Brit.* (ed. 3) XVIII. 276/2 To Manœuvre the Line of Battle... In this place it is intended to point out some of the various evolutions that are, or may be, performed by a fleet which is already formed in line of battle. **1811** WELLINGTON in Gurw. *Desp.* (1838) VII. 583 We do what we please now with the Portuguese troops: we manœuvre them under fire equally with our own. **1884** PAE *Eustace* 140 Crippled as they were by tattered sails and severed ropes, they could not manœuvre the vessel. **1886** *Graphic* 28 Aug. 210/1 The best method of manœuvring them [torpedo boats].

b. *transf.* and *fig.* To manipulate or conduct adroitly with a view to a purpose. Also *occas.* to effect by stratagem.

1801 [see MANŒUVRING *ppl. a.*]. **1815** *Zeluca* II. 142 Zeluca..manœuvred her praise, with a skilful eye to the feelings it was intended to create and invigorate. **1820** J. JEKYLL *Corr.* (1894) 97 The Mother Bankes affects not to have manœuvred her son's match with the Chancellor's daughter. **1823** *Examiner* 634/1 The stage is..said to afford great facilities for manœuvring the scenery. **1857** *Autobiog. Lutfullah* v, He frequently manœuvred his horse across my way and behind me, in such a manner as to show that he derided me. **1885** J. MARTINEAU *Types Eth. Th.* I. 150 A doctrine which so manœuvred the three substances, without relinquishing any of them. **1898** *Westm. Gaz.* 28 July 3/2 Thus manœuvred, a sailor hat can be worn minus the veil.

Hence **maˈnœuvred, maˈnœuvring** *ppl. adjs.*

1801 M. EDGEWORTH *Belinda* II. xvi. 122 This manœuvring lady represented this report as being universally known and believed, in hopes of frightening her niece into an immediate match with the baronet. **1822** J. JEKYLL *Let.* 9 Feb. (1971) 346 Mrs. Lock was one of the manoeuvring mothers who wanted to draw him in for her daughter. **1832** MARRYAT *N. Forster* xxxi, Their mother was a selfish,..manœuvring woman. **1889** *Harper's Mag.* June 79/1 The power to see a great deal through a very small opening in the skilfully manœuvred bandage. **1900** ST. BARBE *Mod. Spain* 41 The beast [*sc.* a bull] wheels round, and, charging, rips out the entrails of an ill-manœuvred horse.

manœuvrer (məˈnuːvrə(r)). Also **manœuverer.** [f. MANŒUVRE *v.* + -ER[1].]

1. One who manœuvres.

1800 A. CARLYLE *Autobiog.* 308 He had told him that Byng, though a much admired commander and manœuvrer of a fleet, would shun fighting. **1809** MAR. EDGEWORTH *Manœuvring* i, This charming widow Beaumont is a *manœuvrer*. We can't well make an English word of it. **1824** MISS MITFORD *Village* Ser. I. 98 Her sister was a match-making lady, a manœuvrer. **1884** C. L. PIRKIS *Jud. Wynne* I. xvii. 212 Your quiet, reserved girls are generally the sly, clever manœuvrers.

2. An implement for manœuvring.

18.. *Engineer* LXVII. 214 (Cent.) Different forms of simple, balanced, and divided rudders were then described, including..Thomson's stern-way manœuverer.

manœuvring (məˈnuːvrɪŋ), *vbl. sb.* [f. MANŒUVRE *v.* + -ING[1].] The action of MANŒUVRE *v.*

1787 I. LANDMANN tr. *Elem. Tacticks* III. 170 The advancing and manœuvring with a line, will never be well performed, if the battalions are not so perfectly well exercised. **1858** CARLYLE *Fredk. Gt.* IX. x. II. 520 The Campaign passed into a series of advancings, retreatings [etc.], painful manœuvrings, on both sides of the Rhine. **1883** R. BOSW. SMITH *Life Ld. Lawrence* I. 178 The reputation which John Lawrence acquired..by the masterly manœuvring of a small body of police.

attrib. **1814** JANE AUSTEN *Mansf. Park* I. v. 93 Speaking from my own observation, it [*sc.* marriage] is a manœuvring business. **1877** *Daily News* 5 Oct. 5/3 Their principal army is wanting in manœuvring power.

man-of-arms: see MAN-AT-ARMS.

man-of-law. *arch.* [Cf. F. *homme de loi* and LAWMAN.] A man skilled in law; a lawyer.

1340, *c* **1386** [see LAW *sb.*[1] 7]. *c* **1440** *Promp. Parv.* 325/2 Manne of lawe, *jurisperitus, scriba*. **1491** *Acta Dom. Concil.* (1839) 206/2 Dauid balfour of carraldstoune wes man of law for o[r] said Souerane lord in þe said mater. **1530** PALSGR. 500/1 Whan a man of lawe maketh a reason peremtorie, it can nat be contrepleted. **1582** BENTLEY *Mon. Matrones* II. 28 O Jesus Christ,..thou being my man of law, didst excuse and speake for me. **1636** MASSINGER *Bashf. Lover* I. i, He.. pays his fees as duly As ever Usurer did in a bad cause, To his man of law. **1841** R. P. WARD *De Clifford* II. xvi. 172 Another man of law..now came in, straight from the magistrates' chamber. **1899** CROCKETT *Kit Kennedy* 251 Ebenezer Fleming, W. S., was a wary man-of-law.

man of the world. †**a.** A secular person (*obs.*). **b.** In religious use (after Ps. xvii. 14), a worldly or irreligious person. **c.** A man who is instructed and experienced in the ways of the world and is prepared to accept its conventions.

c **1200** *Vices & Virtues* 7 ʒif menn of ðe world hes healdeð for hali menn. **1535** COVERDALE *Ps.* xvi[i]. 14 From the men off the worlde, which haue their portion in this life [so **1611**; the Prayer-book version differs]. **1749** FIELDING *Tom Jones* XIV. viii, This gentleman whom Mr Jones now visited, was what they call a man of the world; that is to say, a man who directs his conduct in this world as one, who being fully persuaded there is no other, is resolved to make the most of this. **1778** MME. D'ARBLAY *Early Diary* (1889) II. 244 A true, fashionable, unprincipled man of the world. **1876** LESLIE STEPHEN *Hrs. in Library* (Ser. II.) 209 Butler's sadness..is that of a recluse, and Johnson's that of a man of the world. **1891** *Spectator* 31 Jan. 164/1 Lord Hannen has always shown himself, in the best sense of the word, a man of the world.

attrib. in *pl.* *c* **1823** BYRON *To Mrs.* —— in Moore *Life & Lett.* (1860) 574 All my others are men-of-the-world friendships.

Hence **man-of-the-worldish** *a.*, **man-of-the-worldism, man-of-the-worldly** *a.* (whence **man-of-the-worldliness**).

1867 *Contemp. Rev.* VI. 394 A wide-awake, man-of-the-world-ish commonsense. **1868** *Ibid.* VII. 132 This bred in him a sort of cynical man-of-the-worldism. **1890** *Academy* 27 Sept. 268/2 The man-of-the-worldly sagacity of Teddy Rudall. **1891** SAINTSBURY tr. *Scherer's Ess.* 218 Beaconsfield ..has less substance, but more man-of-the-worldliness.

man-of-war (ˌmænəvˈwɔː(r)). Also **man-o'-war.** Pl. **men-of-war.** [In sense 1 app. after F. *homme de guerre*; for sense 2 cf. MAN *sb.*[1] 12.]

1. A fighting man; a soldier, warrior. *Obs.* exc. *arch.* or *jocular*.

1449 *Rolls of Parlt.* V. 148/1 They desired to have nombre of Men of werre made lesse. **1508** KENNEDIE *Flyting w. Dunbar* 466 Had thai bene prouuait sa of schote of gone By men of were but perile thay had past. **1535** COVERDALE *Exod.* xv. 3 The Lorde is the right man of warre [**1611** a man of warre (*lit. from Heb.*)]. **1577** B. GOOGE *Heresbach's Husb.* III. (1586) 114b, Souldiers and men of war, desire a fierse Horse. **1608** *Extracts Burgh Rec. Glasgow* (1876) I. 287 The saidis bailleis,..bieing convenit for outreiking of thair men of weir to thair Ilis..hes delyverit the armour following,..

to the said men of weir..viz. to Jhone Hammiltoun ane hagbit and flassis [etc.]. **1626** C. Potter tr. *Sarpi's Hist. Quarrels* 330 The Leuies of men of Warre within the State of Milan euery day increased. **1698** Farquhar *Love & Bottle* I. (1699) 3, I dread these blustring Men of War, the Officers. **1840** Thackeray *Catherine* vi, The men of war had clearly the best of it. **1869** Blackmore *Lorna D.* lxviii, The distinguished man of war..Master Bloxham.

2. a. A vessel equipped for warfare; an armed ship belonging to the recognized navy of a country.

1484 W. Cely in *C. Papers* (Camden) 144 As he cam to Callez wardd ij men of warre of Frensche mett wt hym and fawght wt hym. **1594** *Glenham's Newes fr. Levane Seas* in Collier *Illustr. Old Eng. Lit.* (1866) I. 4 In sight of the King of Spaynes men of warre, which were twenty two sayles. **1680** *Debates in Parlt.* (1681) 120 It [Tangier] will always be Serviceable, as well for our Men of War to resort to..as for the protection of our Merchant-men. **1759** *Ann. Reg.* 36 A fresh water harbour, capable of containing an hundred men of war of the line. **1887** Besant *The World went*, etc. iii. 28 If he who has commanded a man-of-war is not to have his own way in everything, who should?

attrib. **1748** *Anson's Voy.* III. x. 415 At Canton..we saw no more than four men of war junks. **1859** *All Year Round* No. 22. 519 The man-of-war brig. **1867** Smyth *Sailor's Word-bk.*, *Man-of-war fashion*, a state of order, tidiness, and good discipline.

b. *occas.* A man-of-war's man (see c).

1599 Nashe *Lenten Stuffe* 27 Hee is first broken to the Sea in the Herring mans Skiffe..once hartned thus, hee will needes be a man of warre..and weare a siluer Whistle. **1884** H. Collingwood *Under Meteor Flag* xxiv. 258 My father.. led the way to the library, with the skipper following... When the man-o'-war rejoined us, the first thing he did was [etc.].

c. ***man-of-war's-man***: a sailor serving on a man-of-war.

1774 J. Andrews *Let.* 30 Dec. (1866) 79 Partaking of the extreem ill qualities of a soldier as well as that of a man-of-war's man. **1840** R. H. Dana *Bef. Mast* xx. 60 [He] was a singular mixture of the man-of-war's-man and Puritan. **1875** Bedford *Sailor's Pocket Bk.* v. (ed. 2) 152 A man-of-war's man should lose no opportunity of volunteering to lay out targets. **1931** *Times Lit. Suppl.* 19 Feb. 124/4 'Matelot' is undoubtedly the French for sailor, but we are not told that it is the English man-of-war's-man's name for himself.

3. (In full ***man-of-war bird*** or † ***hawk***.) The frigate-bird, *Fregata aquila*. Also applied to the albatross and occas. to species of skua (Newton).

1657 Ligon *Barbados* 61 There is a Bird they call, a Man of war, and he is much bigger than a Heron. **1707** Sloane *Jamaica* I. 30 We saw here several Tropick-Birds, and Men of War Birds. **1789** P. Browne *Jamaica* 483 The Man-of-war Bird; or the dark-coloured Alcyon with a slender forked tail. **1862** Wood *Nat. Hist.* II. 762 The well-known Frigate Bird, Sea Hawk, or Man-of-War Bird. **1885** *Riverside Nat. Hist.* (1888) IV. 184 The 'man-of-war hawk', as they [frigate-birds] are often called. **1906** W. L. Sclater *Birds S. Afr.* IV. 495 The 'Cape Sheep', 'Great Albatros', 'Man of War Bird' and 'Goney' are all names which are sometimes applied to this bird [*sc.* the wandering albatross]. **1949** M. Lowry *Let.* May (1967) 178, I think he [*sc.* Melville] is confusing it with his man-of-war bird, the frigate bird. **1952** E. Hemingway *Old Man & Sea* 30 He saw a man-of-war bird with his long black wings circling in the sky. **1962** *Times* 6 Apr. 7/2 (Advt.), Some of the country's most spectacular birds live here [*sc.* in the Florida Everglades]. The snowy egrets, cranes, water turkeys, man-o-war birds, scarlet ibis, [etc.].

4. ***Portuguese man-of-war***: A marine hydrozoan of the genus *Physalia*; so called from the fact of its floating on the surface of the sea with a sail-like crest displayed.

1707 Sloane *Jamaica* I. 7 What the Seamen call a Caravel or Portuguese Man of War, which seems to be a Zoophytum, or of a middle Nature between a Plant and an Animal. **1883** *Harper's Mag.* Jan. 188/2 The Portuguese man-of-war (physalia) with its long azure tentacles.

5. *Mining.* (See quots.)

1860 *Eng. & For. Min. Gloss.* (S. Staffs.), *Man-o'-war*, a small pillar left in some critical situation in a side of work.

6. Used *attrib.* to designate a boy's garment resembling that worn by a sailor, a sailor suit. *Obs.* exc. *Hist.*

1883 in L. de Vries *Victorian Advts.* (1968) 49 Man-o'-war suit. Complete 10/9. **1911** *Daily Colonist* (Victoria, B.C.) 5 Apr. 2/5 (Advt.), Stylish summer hats for little boys and girls... Duck man-o-war hats tams. **1922** Joyce *Ulysses* 341 His little man-o'-war top and unmentionables were full of sand. **1965** Cunnington & Buck *Children's Costume in Eng.* 183 There was the man-o'-war suit..complete with lanyard, knife and good conduct stripes.

‖**manoir** (manwar). [a. F. *manoir* MANOR.] A French manor-house; a country house built in this style.

1853 C. Brontë *Villette* II. xviii. 136 This house..is rather a manoir than a chateau. **1885** A. Edwardes *Girton Girl* I. v. 107 The look of the old manoir was cheery. **1926** V. Hunt *Flurried Yrs.* I. 76 We would walk among high hedges..to this or that old ruined *manoir* that would not let. **1954** V. Sackville-West *Let.* 31 Aug. in H. Nicolson *Diaries & Lett.* (1968) 264 We can think back on that lovely country with the poplars..and the castles and the *manoirs*. **1968** F. White *Ways of Aquitaine* II. 32 The château of Meillant is a perfect example of the high Renaissance *manoir*.

manoir(e, obs. form of MANOR.

‖**manoletina** (manole'tina). [Sp., f. *Manolet(e*, the professional name of the Spanish bullfighter Manuel L. R. Sánchez (1917–47) + *-ina*.] In bullfighting, a decorative pass popularized by Manolete, in which the muleta is held behind the back in the left hand. Also known as the *orteguina*.

1952 J. Marks *To the Bullfight* v. 67 We may watch him [*sc.* the matador], at short range, ignoring it [*sc.* the bull] in imitation of *Manolete's* most imperious yet least estimable manner, as it rushes by under his right arm and the muleta that skims its back in a *manoletina*. **1957** A. MacNab *Bulls of Iberia* xv. 193 Three *manoletinas* (very exciting with such big horns, which come out under man's armpits each time). **1959** V. J.-R. Kehoe *Aficionado!* xvi. 201/2 This pass is called an *orteguina* or, more commonly today, a *manoletina*—after Domingo Ortega who revived it out of an old school, and Manolete who popularized and refined it to a high degree... it is another adorno. **1961** —— *Wine, Women & Toros!* x. 129/1 His faenas include..*manoletinas* looking at the crowd and then—surprise—he kills very well! **1971** J. Leibold *This is the Bullfight* xvii. 204 The manoletina is probably the most popular of all the decorative passes and is utilized by bullfighters of every degree of experience. The manoletina is always performed as a right-handed pass with the sword extending the cloth and while it is a very spectacular pass it is not nearly as dangerous as it appears. **1974** *Aiken* (S. Carolina) *Standard* 18 Apr. 4-c/4 Then the grandstand falls silent as Diaz prepares to execute a 'manoletina', a pass rarely seen in bullfighting. The matador must not turn his head as the bull comes pounding across the sand, but only feels the rush of wind as the animal charges by.

manometer (mə'nɒmɪtə(r)). [ad. F. *manomètre*, f. Gr. *μανό-ς* thin, rare + *μέτρον* measure.] An instrument for ascertaining the elastic force of gases or vapours. ***flame manometer***: = 'manometric capsule' (see MANOMETRIC).

[**1706** Varignon in *Mem. de l' Acad. Roy. des Sciences* 300 Manomètre, ou machine pour trouver la rapport des raretés ou raréfactions de l'air naturel d'un même lieu en différents tems ou [etc.].] **1730** Bailey (fol.) *Manometer, Manoscope*, an Instrument to measure or shew the Alterations in the Rarity and Density of the Air. **1774** Phipps *Voy. N. Pole* App. 128 Description of the Manometer, constructed by Mr. Ramsden. **1823** *Blackw. Mag.* XIV. 513 You see in it the indications of forthcoming storms..against Ministers, to whom it consequently acts as a manometer. **1867** W. W. Smyth *Coal & Coal-mining* 221 In order to test the different densities of the currents on opposite sides of a brattice,..a manometer or water-gauge is employed. **1875** D. Thomson *Acoustics* in *Encycl. Brit.* I. 115 The Flame Manometer. **1880** J. W. Legg *Bile* 203 If the aorta be connected with a manometer, the number and force of the pulsations of the heart can be easily registered. **1899** *Allbutt's Syst. Med.* VII. 239 This glass tube..is attached, by a T-tube, to a pressure-bottle and a mercury manometer.

Hence **ma'nometry**, the use of manometers.

1923 Glazebrook *Dict. Appl. Physics* III. 191/1 (*heading*) Medium-precision manometry. **1961** *Lancet* 12 Aug. 349/1 Articles on..manometry.., chromatography, and electrophoresis.

manometric (mænəʊ'mɛtrɪk), *a.* [f. prec. + -IC. Cf. F. *manométrique*.] Of, pertaining to, or made with the manometer. ***manometric capsule***: an apparatus devised by Koenig for analysing sounds by means of the alterations produced in the forms of flames by aerial vibrations; so ***manometric flame***.

1873 A. E. Dolbear in G. Prescott *Sp. Telephone* (1879) 262 While engaged in making a manometric flame capsule. **1898** *Allbutt's Syst. Med.* V. 464 Manometric observations reveal no increase of pressure in the auricle at the moment of closure of the auriculo-ventricular valves.

manometrical (mænəʊ'mɛtrɪkəl), *a.* [f. as prec. + -AL[1].] = prec.

1777 Roy in *Phil. Trans.* LXVII. 689 The manometrical experiments were made subsequently to the chief part of the barometrical observations. **1879** P. Smith *Glaucoma* 96 In the case of the living human eye the manometrical test is inapplicable.

manometrically (mænəʊ'mɛtrɪkəlɪ), *adv.* [f. MANOMETRIC, -METRICAL *adjs.*: see -LY[2].] In a manometric way; by means of a manometer.

1899 *Nature* 2 Feb. 321/1 The arc light cannot be used manometrically, nor..is it probable that the magnesium flame could be thus employed. **1936** *Biochem. Jrnl.* XXX. 2319 Acetoacetic acid was usually determined manometrically by the aniline citrate method. **1974** Passmore & Robson *Compan. Med. Stud.* III. xix. 97/1 Propulsive activity [of the colon] is more difficult to study manomtrically and detect radiographically.

manool (mæ'nəʊɒl). *Chem.* Also **manoöl**. [a. G. *manool* (Hosking & Brandt 1935, in *Ber. d. Deut. Chem. Ges.* LXVIII. 1311): see MANOAO and -OL.] A bicyclic diterpenoid alcohol, $C_{20}H_{34}O$, which occurs in the oil of *manoao* wood and is used as a base for perfumes.

1935 *Chem. Abstr.* XXIX. 6591 The red resin extd. with alc. from *D. biforme* yields..a neutral light yellow viscous oil .., giving on fractional distn. about 90% of a very viscous colorless liquid (II) solidifying to crystals of the compn. $C_{20}H_{34}O$... II is therefore a bicyclic diterpene alc. with 2 double bonds, for which the name *manoöl* is proposed. **1969** *N.Z. News* 23 July 4/3 Manool, an ambergris-like product which is extracted from trees that take hundreds of years to grow, may provide New Zealand with a new export market.

manor ('mænə(r)). Forms: 3–6 **maner**, 4 **manayre**, 4–5 **manere**, 5 **mano(i)re**, **manoyr(e**, **-ayr**, **manure**, 5–6 **manoir**, 6–7 **manner**, 6–8 **manour**, 6–9 **mannor**, 7–8 **mannour**, 6– **manor**. [a. OF. *manoir* dwelling, habitation, subst. use of *manoir* inf., to dwell:—L. *manēre* to remain.

Latinized as *manērium* in France and England as early as the 11th c.; subsequently *maneria* occurs in general continental use.]

†**1. a.** A mansion, habitation; a country residence; the principal house of an estate, 'capital messuage'.

A surviving trace of this use appears in the designations of certain ancient manor-houses, e.g. Wingfield Manor, Worksop Manor; the houses so named are of course locally known as 'the Manor'.

c **1290** *Beket* 524 in *S. Eng. Leg.* I. 121 Ich hote ov euerechone, þat ȝe beon þat ilke dai At mi maner at Clarindone. **1297** R. Glouc. (Rolls) 10231 Þe bissop of eli & þe king sone wende To a maner þer biside. **1375** Barbour *Bruce* XVI. 337 In the hawch of lyntoun-le He gert thame mak a fair maner. **1377** Langl. *P. Pl.* B. x. 308 Ac now is religioun a ryder, a rowmer bi stretes,..A priker on a palfray from manere to manere. *c* **1400** Maundev. (Roxb.) xxi. 95 Of þir redez þai make þare houses and maneres and schippez and þaire oþer necessaries. *c* **1450** *Bk. Curtasye* 601 in *Babees Bk.* 197 Of þe resayuer speke wylle I, þat..ouer-seys castels, maners a-boute. **1470–85** Malory *Arthur* VI. ix. 195 Whan that ye come within yonder manayr I am sure ye shal fynde ther many knyȝtes of the round table. **1530** Palsgr. 242/2 Manner a dwellyng place, *maison de plaisance*. **1549** Latimer *Ploughers* (Arb.) 26 They are so troubeled wyth Lordelye lyuynge,..and moylynge in their gaye manoures ..that they canne not attende it. **1556** *Chron. Gr. Friars* (Camden) 26 Thys yere the kynge byldyd new hys maner of Shene. **1561** J. Dolman (*title*) Those fyve Questiones, which..Cicero disputed in his Manor of Tusculanum. **1610** *Histrio-m.* v. 216 They have..ruin'd Churches, Townes, Burn't goodly Manours, and indeed lay'd wast All the whole Country.

†**b.** *fig.* An abode or resting place. *Obs.*

1362 Langl. *P. Pl.* A. VI. 76 Þe Mot is of Merci þe maner al abouten, And alle þe walles beþ of wit to holde wil þeroute. *c* **1369** Chaucer *Dethe Blaunche* 1004 Trouthe him selfe,.. Had chose his maner principal In her that was his restyng place. **1413** *Pilgr. Sowle* (Caxton 1483) III. x. 56 This pytte is the chyef and the manoyr of helle that is clepid Abissus. **1576** Fleming *Panopl. Epist.* 178, I shal be constrained, to entertaine some of them into the manour of my memorie.

†**2.** The mansion of a lord with the land belonging to it; hence, a landed possession. *Obs.*

[**1292** Britton II. xix. §4 Car en une vile porrount estre plusours paroches, et en une paroche plusours maners, et hameletz plusours porrount apendre a un maner.] *c* **1330** R. Brunne *Chron. Wace* (Rolls) 7431 Þe kyng gaf Hengist faire maners. **13..** *E.E. Allit. P.* A. 1028 Þenne helde vch sware of þis manayre, Twelue forlonge space er euer hit fon. **1382** Wyclif *John* iv. 5 Therfore Jhesu cam in to a citee of Samarie,..bisydis the manere [L. *prædium*],..that Jacob ȝaf to Joseph, his sone. *c* **1410** *Sir Cleges* 62 His maners he ded to wede sett. **1470–85** Malory *Arthur* IV. xii. 134, I wylle that ye gyue vnto your broder alle the hole manoir with the appertenaunce vnder thys forme, that sir Ontzelake hold the manoir of yow and yerely to gyue yow a palfrey to ryde vpon. **1600** Shaks. *All's Well* III. ii. 10, I know a man that had this tricke of melancholy hold [sold] a goodly Mannor for a song.

3. a. A unit of English territorial organization, originally of the nature of a feudal lordship.

The doctrine of the lawyers of the 17th c. is that a manor consists essentially of land held in demesne by the lord, to which is attached a seignory over freehold tenants sufficient in number (the minimum is variously stated as two or three) to constitute the court, called at a relatively late time the court-baron, which the lord is bound to hold and the tenants to attend. (The manor was often defined from the point of view of its relation to the lord, as an estate in land consisting of demesnes and services.) This restriction of the meaning of the word is destitute of early authority (though the kind of complex estate described probably existed from the 12th century), but is the basis of the present application. As the status of tenant in fee under a mesne lord is practically obsolete, a manor now consists of the lord's demesne (if any exists) and of lands from the holders of which he has the right to exact certain fees and fines, and within which he has certain privileges. A 'court customary' is held in all manors where there are copyhold or customary tenants of the demesne. A manor is usually named from the principal township, as 'the manor of Barnstaple'.

1538 tr. *Littleton's Tenures* (1544) 18b, In dyuers lordshyps & maners there is suche custome. **1601** Fulbecke *1st Pt. Parall.* 18 A manor is an inheritance of auncient continuance consisting of demesnes & seruices, perquisites, casualties, things appendant and regardant, customes, liberties, &c. **1605** Camden *Rem.* 221 A Mannor of a hundred tenements. **1608–28** Risdon *Note Bk.* (1897) 124 Unto him the king gave Constanc, his base daughter, with the mannor of South Tawton. **1620** J. Wilkinson *Court Leet* 141 If the Lord purchase their Lands, the Manor is destroyed. **1670** Cotton *Espernon* II. v. 235 This Ancient and Illustrious Family, are possessors of many goodly Mannors in Guienne. **1731** *Gentl. Mag.* I. 351 The Scholars, according to Custom, hunted a Ram, by which, the Provost and Fellows [of Eton] hold a Manor. **1797** *Encycl. Brit.* (ed. 3) X. 543/2 By an ancient custom of this manor [Mansfield], the heirs were declared of age as soon as born. **1812** Combe *Picturesque* XXII. (Chandos ed.) 86 You'll see what game my manor yields. **1818** Hallam *Mid. Ages* viii. (1868) 428 Few of English birth continued to enjoy entire manors, even by a mesne tenure. **1890** Sir F. Pollock *Oxford Lect.* 117 In the English manor the community is the oldest element, and the lordship a newer one.

fig. **1819** W. Lawrence *Comp. Anat.* ii. (1844) 28 The manor of living nature is so ample, that all may be allowed to sport on it freely. **1874** A. J. Munby *Diary* 20 Apr. in D. Hudson *Munby* (1972) 366, I was 'struck all of a heap' by seeing..a picture of Wigan wenches working at brow. What right had this artist to poach on my manor..?

b. With qualifications. **assessionable manor**, one of the manors into which the duchy of Cornwall is divided, to which commissioners are appointed periodically for the purpose of

assessing them, or letting them on the best terms; **customary manor** (see quot.); **reputed manor, manor by reputation**, a manor which has lost its manorial status by expiry of some necessary adjunct; **manor in ancient demesne**, a manor which at the time of the Conquest formed part of the royal domain; **manor in gross**, a manor from which the demesne has been separated, leaving only the incorporeal hereditaments to the lord.

1607 COWEL *Interpr.* s.v. *Maner*, A man may haue a maner in grosse (as the law termeth it) that is, the right and interest of a court Baron with the perquisites thereunto belonging: and another or others haue euery foote of the land thereunto belonging. **1839** *Penny Cycl.* XIV. 388/1 In the assessionable manors, parcel of the duchy of Cornwall, customary estates for years still subsist. *Ibid.* 389/1 Such an estate is however more frequently called 'a manor by reputation'. *Ibid.* 389/2 The estate of the grantor, which.. would consist of the mansion and the other ungranted portions of the villenage, with the services of the grantees appendant thereto, was called a customary manor. **1890** SIR F. POLLOCK *Oxford Lect.* 114 A 'reputed manor' will serve as well as a real manor for most purposes.

c. ***lord of the manor***, the person or corporation having the seignorial rights of a manor.

1605 *Order of keeping a Court Leet* 29 b, Note that all the vacant and wast land within the Manour, is to the Lord of the Manour. **1719** W. WOOD *Surv. Trade* 309 It is most strange and unaccountable Policy in many Lords of Mannors. **1765** BLACKSTONE *Comm.* I. xii. 387 All lords of manors, or barons, that held of the king *in capite*, had seats in the great council. **1817** W. SELWYN *Law Nisi Prius* (ed. 4) II. 834 Lords of manors are distinguished from other landowners with respect to the game. **1858** W. ARNOT *Laws fr. Heaven* Ser. II. xxix. 237 The lord of the manor passed by.

d. In some of the American colonies, authority was given by royal charter for the creation of 'manors' after the English model, with courts-baron and seignorial rights. The Dutch governors of what is now the State of New York also granted 'manors', with certain hereditary privileges now abolished. (See quot. 1870 and PATROON 4.) The term still continues to be applied to certain districts in the U.S. which were 'manors' in colonial times.

1639 *Act* in *Arch. Maryland* (1883) I. 71 Punishment of death shall be inflicted on a Lord of a Mannour by beheading. **1681** CHAS. II *Charter granted to Penn* §19 We give and grant Licence unto the said William Penn, and his Heirs, [etc.]..to erect any Parcels of Land within the Province aforesaid into Manors..; and in every of the said Manors to have and to hold a Court-Baron [etc.]. **1691** *Acts of Assembly New York* (1719) 2 The several Cities, Towns, Counties, Shires, Divisions, or Manors of this Province. *Ibid.* 69 Being a Free-holder in any Manor, Liberty, Jurisdiction, Precinct, or Out-Plantation. **1870** BURRILL *Law Dict.* s.v., In American Law, a manor is a tract held of a proprietor by a fee-farm rent in money or in kind, and descending to oldest son, who in New York is called a patroon. **1883** *Encycl. Amer.* I. 198 The manors, as the grants of the early Dutch rulers of New Netherland were called, have disappeared under the pressure of republican institutions.

e. *slang.* A police district; a local unit of police administration. Also *transf.*, one's home ground, one's own particular territory.

1924 S. SCOTT *Human Side Crook & Convict Life* vii. 107 There are straight crooks and crooked crooks on the 'Manor' of a detective, and he gets to know them apart. **1928** E. WALLACE *Gunner* xii. 93, I wouldn't advise you to break in on Gennett's 'manor'—he's rather touchy, and he's got charge of the case. **1945** M. ALLINGHAM *Coroner's Pidgin* xxiii. 202 Do you realize who the Coroner is for those parts? .. It's Montie Forster's manor. **1959** *Observer* 1 Mar. 10/1 This 'manor'—a tenement neighbourhood in North London—is theirs by right of birth and conquest. **1961** C. WITTING *Driven to Kill* 24 If anything's happened to Pearce, it's in my manor, so I'm interested. **1962** R. COOK *Crust on its Uppers* iv. 47 'Then they whipped him down to the nick on the hurry-up.' 'Which manor?' 'The local nick.' *Ibid.* 49 'Where to for the next one?' says he. 'Well off the manor, if you like.' **1970** P. LAURIE *Scotland Yard* 287 Every non-policeman knows that detectives call their working-area their 'manor' or ' patch'... What they actually said was 'ground'. **1974** *Times* 23 Nov. 2/6 Mr Buck is trying to alter that situation by appealing to everyone in his 'manor' (with a population one million higher than that of Northern Ireland) to dial 999 at the slightest sign of suspicious activity.

4. *attrib.*, as ***manor-court, -farm, -hall, law, lord, -pew, -yard.*** Also MANOR-HOUSE, MANOR-PLACE.

1786 W. GILPIN *Mount. & Lakes Cumbld.* (1788) II. 231 His *manor-courts are kept with great strictness. **1890** SIR F. POLLOCK *Oxford Lect.* 130 It will not do, therefore, to assume that the manor court was made out of an older township court. **1824** MISS MITFORD *Village* Ser. II. 51 It hath been anciently a great *manor-farm or court-house. **1856** EMERSON *Eng. Traits, Stonehenge* Wks. (Bohn) II. 126 It [Wilton Hall] is..esteemed a noble specimen of the English *manor-hall. **1887** *Athenæum* 20 Aug. 235/3 Books on *manor law became common. **1899** G. M. TREVELYAN *Engl. Age Wycliffe* 339 If Lollard preachers had attacked.. the rights of the *manor lords, they soon ceased to do so. **1892** J. C. BLOMFIELD *Hist. Heyford* 46 Pews of different sizes, with the *manor-pew overtopping the rest. **1667** DUCHESS OF NEWCASTLE *Life Dk. of N.* III. (1886) 158 The enemy..made a passage into the *manor-yard.

manor-house ('mænəhaʊs). [f. MANOR + HOUSE *sb.*[1]] The mansion of the lord of a manor.

1575 GASCOIGNE *Posies, Herbs* 147 Better Fermers fast, than Manour houses fall. **1588** SHAKS. *L.L.L.* I. i. 208. **1625** MASSINGER *New Way* IV. i, How far Sir Giles,..hold you it to be From your Mannor house to this of my Lady Alworths. **1762–71** H. WALPOLE *Vertue's Anecd. Paint.* (1786) III. 161 Salmon..mentions a Dr. Morecroft,..as architect of the manor-house of Fitzwalters. **1832** LYTTON *Eugene A.* I. vi, Several days elapsed before the family of the manor-house encountered Aram again.

manorial (mə'nɔərɪəl), *a.* [f. MANOR + -(I)AL.] Of or pertaining to a manor or manors; incidental to a manor. (Cf. MANERIAL.)

1785 PALEY *Mor. & Polit. Philos.* VI. xi. (1786) 634 This tenure [the right of common] is also usually embarrassed by the interference of manorial claims. **1794** SOUTHEY *Wat Tyler* III. i. Poet. Wks. II. 47 They have..demanded the abolition of personal slavery, vassalage and manorial rights. **1876** BANCROFT *Hist. U.S.* III. iii. 332 His tomb in the old manorial church. **1876** DIGBY *Real Prop.* i. §1. 8 These functions devolved in later times partly on the manorial court. **1890** SIR F. POLLOCK *Oxford Lect.* 129 The administration of a manorial domain.

Hence **ma'norialism**, the manorial system; **ma'norializing** *vbl. sb.*, making manorial (*attrib.* in quots.).

1897 MAITLAND *Domesday & Beyond* 138 We shall have the utmost difficulty if we would go behind manorialism. **1898** —— *Township & Borough* 45 A time when the feudalizing and manorializing processes are at work. **1918** *Eng. Hist. Rev.* Jan. 70 The king..must forestall the lord's manorializing tendency by adding these thegns and freemen to his own estates.

ma͵noriali'zation. [f. MANORIAL *a.* + -IZATION.] The process of making or becoming manorial. Also **ma'norialize** *v. trans.*, 'to conform or subject to the tenure of the manorial system' (Webster 1909).

1896 C. M. ANDREWS in R. H. I. Palgrave *Dict. Pol. Econ.* II. 684 Economic life had become manorialised but not feudalised. **1907** *Q. Rev.* July 147 Varieties occurred in the process of manorialisation. **1927** J. J. HOGAN *Eng. Lang. in Ireland* 15 Manorialization was in full progress at the beginning of the thirteenth century in Leinster. **1939** *Antiquity* XIII. 22 Villages which were but partially manorialized.

'manor-place. *arch.* = MANOR-HOUSE.

1426 *Act Jas. I Scot.* (1814) II. 13/2 In þe quhilk landis in auld tymes þare was castellis fortalycis & maner placis. *c* **1470** HENRYSON *Mor. Fab.* x. (*Fox & Wolf*) xxiii, Than to ane manure [*v. r.* manore] place thay hyit in haist. **1509** HAWES *Past. Pleas.* XXXIV. (Percy Soc.) 175 Tyll that we came unto a manour place, Moted about under a woode syde. **1578** TIMME *Caluine on Gen.* 241 Moses noteth here Nimrod's manour place. **1688** DALLAS *Syst. Stiles* (1697) 703 Letters for giving up and delivery of the said Castles,.. Mannor-places, and other houses pertaining to the said Bishoprick. **1791** NEWTE *Tour Eng. & Scot.* 171 It was the mansion, or manor-place of the Barony of Philorth. **1875** W. MCILWRAITH *Guide Wigtownshire* 90 The tower, fortalice, manor-place, yards, and orchards of Chappell.

'manor-seat. [f. MANOR + SEAT *sb.*[1]] = MANOR-HOUSE.

1828–32 in WEBSTER; and in later Dicts.

'manorship. [+ -SHIP.] = MANOR 3.

1778 *Eng. Gazetteer* (ed. 2), Market-Street..is a manorship in the parishes of Goldington, Studham, and Flamstead. **1920** *Public Opinion* 6 Aug. 127/3 Both names.. are..deeply associated with the neighbourhood of Old Jordans, its homesteads, and churches and manorships.

manoscope ('mænəskəʊp). *Physics.* [a. F. *manoscope*, f. Gr. μανό-ς (see MANOMETER) + -SCOPE.] = MANOMETER.

1730 [see MANOMETER]. **1823** J. MITCHELL *Dict. Math. & Phys. Sci.*, *Manometer*,.. It is sometimes called *manoscope*. **1875** KNIGHT *Dict. Mech.* 1384.

Hence **ma'noscopy** *rare*$^{-0}$, the science which is concerned with the determination of the density of vapours and gases.

1864 in WEBSTER; and in later Dicts.

manostat ('mænəʊstæt). [f. *mano-* (in MANOMETER) + -STAT.] Any device for automatically maintaining a constant pressure in an enclosed space. Hence **mano'static** *a.*

1900 *Jrnl. Physical Chem.* IV. 546 (*heading*) On a manostat. **1923** GLAZEBROOK *Dict. Appl. Physics* III. 191/2 The majority of manostats are designed on the broad principle that whenever the pressure departs from the desired constant value, the manometer itself, through the change in liquid level in one of its limbs, automatically actuates either a supply or removal of gas..or else some equivalent means of restoring the desired pressure. **1936** *Jrnl. Amer. Chem. Soc.* LVIII. 1703/1 The new manostatic technique. **1966** *Encycl. Industr. Chem. Analysis* I. 617 As a general rule, manostats controlling four fixed pressures of 10, 50, 100, and 200 Torr, and accurately adjusted to these pressures, provide a range of operating pressures quite adequate for every distillation situation. Below 50 Torr, pressure regulation is unsatisfactory when mercury is used as the manostatic fluid.

manotoka, var. MANITOKA.

manour(e, obs. ff. MANNER, MANOR, MANURE.

manoyr(e, obs. form of MANOR.

†**'manqualm.** *Obs.* [OE. *manncwealm*: see MAN *sb.*[1] and QUALM *sb.*[1]] Plague, pestilence.

a **900** *O. E. Chron.* an. 664 Þy ilcan geare wæs micel man cuealm. *c* **1205** LAY. 3908 Þær after com swulke mon-qualm þ lute hær cwike læfden. **1297** R. GLOUC. (Rolls) 8599 So gret manqualm þat monimon al vnbured lay. *a* **1340** HAMPOLE *Psalter* i. 1 Moryn or manqwalm..þat nerand corompis all men.

‖**manque** (mɑ̃k). [Fr., f. *manquer* to fail, lack: see quot. 1903.] In roulette, the name of one section of the cloth covering the numbers 1 to 18; a bet placed on this section.

1850 *Bohn's Handbk. Games* 348 The manque wins, when the ball enters a hole numbered eighteen, and all those under that number. **1885** CAPT. PALMER *Monte Carlo & Rouge et Noir* 8 The space for Manque is so marked on the table, and the ball stopping in any of the compartments containing any number up to 18 makes Manque win. **1903** 'L. HOFFMANN' *Card & Table Games* (ed. 3) 626 If he places his money on *Manque* (so called because in this event the ball 'fails'..to fall into a higher number than 18), he is considered to wager that the ball will fall into one of the numbers from 1 to 18 inclusive. **1923** L. H. DAWSON *Hoyle's Games Modernized* II. 279 To bet on both *Passe* and *Noir* or *Rouge* and *Manque* at the same time, two separate stakes would be required. **1953** T. KING *21 Games of Chance* 31 In addition to the central strip of numbers, there are outer spaces marked *Passe, Manque, Pair, Impair, Noir* and *Rouge*. **1969** J. BINSTOCK *Casino Administration* vi. 72 This [*sc.* roulette] is played on a table with 37 numbers from zero to 36, the so-called 'even chance' bets being *pair* and *impair*, *passe* and *manque*, *rouge* and *noir*.

‖**manqué** (mɑ̃ke), *a.* Fem. **manquée.** [Fr., pa. pple. of *manquer* to miss, be lacking.] After its noun: that might have been but is not, that has missed being. Also occas. *pred.*

1778 F. BURNEY *Diary* Aug. (1904) I. i. 54 Dr. Johnson's favourite is Mr. Smith. He declares the fine gentleman *manqué* was never better drawn. **1895** G. B. SHAW in W. Archer *Theatr. 'World' 1894* p. xxvi, A villain if you like.. a kicked, cuffed, duped pantaloon by all means; but a hero *manqué*, never. **1898** C. R. ASHBEE *Cellini's Treatises on Goldsmithing & Sculpture* p. xi, There is about his figures always something *manqué*. **1913** tr. *Gleizes & Metzinger's Cubism* i. 15 People have tried to present Cézanne as a sort of genius *manqué*. **1927** *Sat. Rev.* 17 Sept. 370/2 'The History of Anthony Waring' is a poem manqué. **1942** W. STEVENS *Let.* 29 July (1967) 4/4 That such a person [*sc.* a poet] is to be visualized as..an eccentric or a person somehow manqué is nonsense. **1948** F. R. LEAVIS *Great Tradition* ii. 61 Casaubon..is an intellectual *manqué*. **1960** V. BRITTAIN *Women at Oxf.* v. 86 Published memories of Miss Maitland..suggest that she was a hospital matron *manquée*. **1962** *Listener* 12 July 73/2 A clever, unhappy young writer *manqué*. **1974** *Listener* 26 Sept. 408/3 Was Lady O a courtesan manquée?

b. In other uses: defective, spoilt, missing, lacking, etc.

1773 H. WALPOLE *Let.* 27 Mar. (1904) VIII. 262 Dr. Goldsmith's *She Stoops to Conquer*... The author's wit is as much *manqué* as the lady's. **1793** F. BURNEY *Let.* 3 May (1972) II. 98 Our party was manqué in every way;—I came early, but with a head ache; your melancholy Note did not relieve it. **1841** THACKERAY in *Fraser's Mag.* June 724/1, I never yet had a good dinner in my life at Véfour's; *something* is always *manqué* at the place. **1876** C. M. YONGE *Womankind* i. 6 The single woman ceases to be *manquée*, and enjoys honour and happiness. **1881** H. JAMES *Notebks.* (1947) 31 He used to talk to me about Spain, about the East ..till it seemed to me that life would be *manquée* altogether if one shouldn't have some of that knowledge. **1894** R. FRY *Let.* 27 Mar. (1972) I. 158 Millais..is the most *gifted* man we ever had, but somehow he's *manqué*, never done what he might have done. **1940** W. STEVENS *Let.* 9 Aug. (1967) 362 Thus, one's chords remain *manqué*; still there they are.

†**'manquell,** *v. Obs. rare*$^{-1}$. [Back-formation from next.] *trans.* To murder.

a **1548** HALL *Chron., Edw. IV*, 221 b, Whom..they that stode about..murthered & pitiously manquelled.

†**'manquelle.** *Obs. rare*$^{-1}$. [:—OE. type **manncwella*, f. *mann* MAN *sb.*[1] + **cwella* (with agent-suffix *-a*).] A murderer.

c **1250** *Lutel soth Serm.* 28 in *O.E. Misc.* 186 Robberes and reueres and þe monquelle.

manqueller ('mænkwɛlə(r)). *Obs.* exc. *arch.* [f. MAN *sb.*[1] + QUELLER.] A manslayer, murderer.

c **1290** *Beket* 436 in *S. Eng. Leg.* I. 119 Þat a luþer þef, a manquellare hadde a so liȝt dom. *a* **1300** *Cursor M.* 2205 Nembrot..O babilon king..Reuer and man-queller. *c* **1380** WYCLIF *Sel. Wks.* III. 383 Þus Þei ben..manquellers of pore men, whose lyvelode Þei awey taken fro hom. *c* **1450** *Mirour Saluacioun* 2365 Semey [= Shimei] callid Dauid man of Belial and manqwhellere. **1529** MORE *Dyaloge* III. Wks. 244/1 No wise manne wer there that woulde put al weapons away because manquellers misuse them. **1597** SHAKS. *2 Hen. IV*, II. i. 58 Thou art a honyseed, a Man-queller, and a woman-queller. **1632** I. L. *Womens Rights* 343 If a man were slaine..and another man receiued the man-queller. **1681** W. ROBERTSON *Phraseol. Gen.* (1693) 863 A man-queller; *homicida*. **1870** BRYANT *Iliad* I. I. 14 While multitudes are perishing by the hand Of Hector, the man-queller.

b. An executioner. (Cf. MANSLAYER b.)

c **1300** *Seyn Julian* (MS. Ashmole) 185 Com uorþ he sede my manquellare..And smyt of hire heued. **1382** WYCLIF *Mark* vi. 27 A manquellere sent [Vulg. *misso spiculatore*].

† **manquelling,** *vbl. sb.* [f. MAN *sb.*[1] + QUELLING *vbl. sb.*] Manslaughter, homicide.

c **1380** WYCLIF *Wks.* (1880) 9 þis ilke fals religious is gilty of þefte and manquellyng also. *c* **1440** *Promp. Parv.* 325/2 Mann qwellynge, or man slawtur,.. *homicidium.* **1551** BIBLE (Hyll) *Deut.* xix. *note*, Here are shewed ii. maners of manquelling, one done wyllingly.. the other vnwyllingly. **1587** GOLDING *De Mornay* xx. 312 That which is Leachcraft in one Country, is not manquelling in another.

Manques, obs. form of MANX.

man-rate ('mænreɪt), *v.* [f. MAN *sb.*[1] + RATE *v.*[1]] *trans.* To make (a rocket, spaceship, etc.) suitable for manned flight; to certify as safe for manned flight. So **man-rated** *ppl. a.*; **'man-rating** *vbl. sb.*

1963 E. STUHLINGER et al. *Astronautical Engin. & Sci.* iv. 68 Manrating is a new term. To manrate a space vehicle means to make it suitable for carrying a manned payload. **1967** *Technology Week* XX. 23 Jan. 29/2 (Advt.), McDonnell testing and development facilities range from man-rated space chambers to Mach 28 wind tunnels. *Ibid.* 30/1 (Advt.), Their man-rated lunar descent engine is one of a family of small throttleable engines. **1968** *New Scientist* 21 Mar. 631 After it [*sc.* a new Soviet booster] has been man-rated, however, and used in orbital rendezvous and docking missions, the USSR will have achieved a major platform for further advance. **1971** *Sci. News Let.* 19 June 416 The general question of the reliability of unmanned spacecraft has always been a thorny problem for NASA. Manned spacecraft have redundant systems—back-up systems in case one fails. This method, called 'man-rating a spacecraft', is costly.

† **'manred.** *Obs.* Forms: α. 1 man(n)ræden(n, 3 monreden, -ræidene, -raddene, 3, 5 man-, monradene, 5 manredyn, 6–7 manratten, -rydden. Also *Sc.* 4–9 MANRENT. β. 2–6 manred; also 3–4 -rede, 4 -rade, 6 -ryd, -rode, 7 -roode. [OE. *mannrǣden*, f. *mann* MAN *sb.*[1] + *-rǣden* -RED.]

1. Homage. Phr. *to do* or *make, to take, fang,* or *nim manred.*

α. *c* **1000** ÆLFRIC *Josh.* ix. 11 þa cwædon ure frind, þæt we comon to eowre manrædene. *c* **1122** *O.E. Chron.* an. 1115 He dyde þæt ealle þa heafodmæn on Normandiȝ dydon manræden.. his sunu Willelme. *c* **1205** LAY. 6240 Ah eower monradene [*c* **1275** manradene] ich wulle fon. *a* **1300** *St. Gregory* 784 in *Archiv Stud. neu. Spr.* LVII. 784 Manredene, þat was to sayne To be boxum to his hond. *c* **1420** *Anturs of Arth.* 642 Here I make þe releyse,.. And siþene make the monradene.

β. *c* **1154** *O.E. Chron.* an. 1137 Hi hadden him manred maked & athes suoren. *c* **1290** *S. Eng. Leg.* I. 351/20 Heo wende a-boute ope al hire lond and nam hire manrede [*MS.* manrade]. *a* **1300** *Floriz & Bl.* 395 His manrede þu schalt fonge. *a* **1300** *Cursor M.* 20620 Suet moder.. al heuen court sal serue þe, To mak þe manred. *c* **1300** *Harrow. Hell* 88 Monrade dude y him me do. **1679** EARL SOMERVILLE *Mem. Somervilles* (1815) I. 75 To be obleidged and bound.. in mandred,.. to be with one another in all actiones.

2. Vassals collectively; the men whom a lord can call upon in time of war. Hence *gen.* a supply of men for purposes of warfare.

13.. *K. Alis.* 4665 Pays he dude anon grede To al Daries manrede. *c* **1400** *Laud Troy Bk.* 18596 He is ded and his kynred, And alle his frendis & his manred. **1543** WHARTON in *St. Papers Hen. VIII*, V. 311 In Northumbreland wher manryd of men er. **1549** CHEKE *Hurt Sedit.* (1641) 54 By destruction of Shieres, loosing of haruest,.. decaying of manrode. *c* **1550–1665** *Flodden Field* (Percy Folio) st. 95 [I geeve thee againe] The manrydden [*Harl.* 367 manratten] of Lancashire.. Att thy bidding euer to bee. **1559** ABP. PARKER *Corr.* (Parker Soc.) 99 Where the manred with the manors is withdrawn from us, that we be not.. charged with the setting forth of men of war. **1610** HOLLAND *Camden's Brit.*, *Scot.* II. 17 John Commin the mightiest man for manred and retinew in all Scotland. **1630** *R. Johnson's Kingd. & Commw.* 22 A good Manroode is an inexhaustible stocke. By populous armies did the Northerne Nations.. overrunne farre greater Nations than their owne.

3. The position of leader of fighting men; the 'conduct' (of an army).

1528 *St. Papers Hen. VIII*, I. 315 As schuld be seen moste expedient for the orderyng the men, and the manred theroff. **1570–6** LAMBARDE *Peramb. Kent* (1826) 453 That Gentleman, that had the manred (as some yet call it) or the office, to lead the men, of a Towne, or Parish. **1581** in Jeanes *Catal. Berkeley Chart.* (1892) 227 The manred, rule, government, leading and commandment of all his servauntes [etc.].

†**4.** Carnal intercourse. *Obs. rare*$^{-1}$.

c **1205** LAY. 25911 He wolde mon-radene [*c* **1275** manradene] habben wið þan maidene.

manredyn, variant of prec.

manrent ('mænrɛnt). *Sc.* Now *Hist.* [Sc. form of MANRED: see -RED.

It is doubtful whether the form goes back to the 14th c., as the MSS. of Barbour were written in 1487–9, and in one passage MS. E has the older form *manredyn*.]

1. Homage: = MANRED 1.

1375 BARBOUR *Bruce* XVI. 303 The kingis.. of the Eryschrye.. thair manrent [*MS. E* manredyn] till him can ma. **1457** *Sc. Acts Jas. II* (1814) II. 50 At na man duellande wᵗⁱⁿ burghe be fundyn in manrent. *c* **1470** *Golagros & Gaw.* 1218 Now wil I be obeyand, And make the manrent with hand. *c* **1560** A. SCOTT *Poems* (S.T.S.) xxxiii. 13 Quhat is thy manrent bot mischeif? **1681** VISCT. STAIR *Instit.* I. ii. (1693) 19 There was formerly a kind of Bondage in Scotland, called Man-rent, whereby free persons became the Bondmen or Followers of.. their Patrons and Defenders.

b. *band* (or *bond*) *of manrent* (see quot. 1597).

1528 in *St. Papers Hen. VIII*, IV. 499 He usit our autorite ..aganis our Baronis, and uyer our liegis yat wald nocht entir in band of manrent to him. **1538** in *Black Bk. Taymouth* etc. (Bannatyne Cl.) 181 Mutual Bond of Manrent and help between Johne Campbell of Glenurquhay and Archibald Campbell of Glenlyoune against all men. **1597** SKENE *De Verb. Sign.* s.v. *Homagium*, It is a bande of man-rent, quhen ony person promisis to serue ane vther, in sik sorte, that he sall be friend to all his friends, and foe to all his foes, against all deadly. *a* **1649** DRUMM. OF HAWTH. *Hist. Jas. V*, Wks. (1711) 82 How the great houses of Scotland were so joined and linked together, by kindred, alliances, bonds of service, or man-rent. **1759** ROBERTSON *Hist. Scot.* I. (1802) I. 231 Associations, which when made with their equals, were called 'leagues of mutual defence'; and when with their inferiors, 'bonds of manrent'. *a* **1862** BUCKLE *Civiliz.* (1869) III. ii. 65.

2. = MANRED 2, 3.

1536 BELLENDEN *Cron. Scot.* XIV. vii, Thair hicht and gret pissance, baith in manrent and landis, was sa suspect to the kingis.. that [etc.]. **1577–95** *Descr. Isles Scot.* in Skene *Celtic Scot.* (1880) III. App. 435 McCowle of Lorn hes the stewartship of the haill Ile and manrent thairof. **1583** *Reg. Privy Council Scot.* Ser. I. III. 614 Havand commandiment of the manrent of all and sindrie his Hienes lieges. **1586** FERNE *Blaz. Gentrie* 126 The greatnesse of his reuenewes and manrents.

manro(o)de, -ryd, variants of MANRED *Obs.*

-mans, an unexplained suffix frequent in the words of thieves' slang recorded in the 16th c. as *crackmans* hedge, *darkmans* night, *lightmans* day, *harmans* the stocks, *ruffmans* a hedge.

mansale, variant of MANZIL.

mansaneel, mansanillo, obs. ff. MANCHINEEL.

mansard ('mænsəd). *Arch.* [a. F. *mansarde* (*toit en mansarde*), f. name of François *Mansard*, French architect, 1598–1666.] **a.** A form of curb-roof, in which each face of the roof has two slopes, the lower one steeper than the upper. Usually *mansard roof*.

1734 *Builder's Dict.* II. s.v. *Roof*, This last is particularly called a Mansard, from M. Mansard, a famous French Architect, the Inventor. **1842** GWILT *Archit.* 547 The Mansard roof,.. with us called a Curb roof. **1873** MISS THACKERAY *Wks.* (1891) I. 18 They lived in a tall house, with a mansard roof. **1880** 'MARK TWAIN' *Tramp Abroad* I. 32 Foreign youth.. go to the University to put a mansard roof on their whole general education.

b. (See quot. and BOOBY *sb.*[1] 3.)

1882 KEMP *Yacht & Boat Sailing* (ed. 3) 552 *Mansard*, an American term for a booby hatch.

c. *Comb.*, as *mansard-roofed* adj.

1887 J. E. TAYLOR *Tourist's Guide Suffolk* 31 The Tower Ramparts, where the red-tiled, mansard-roofed cottages have been built on the very top. **1915** E. ATKINSON *Johnny Appleseed* 80 From there he saw the white mansard-roofed mansion.

Hence **'mansarded** *a.*

1903 *Westm. Gaz.* 11 Feb. 2/1 Handsome little hôtels, *mansarded* and *œil de bœuf'd*. **1951** W. SANSOM *Face of Innocence* viii. 100 Each pantiled or mansarded or beamed façade. **1962** *Listener* 5 Apr. 592/1 Why should we have to suffer tall mansarded roofs?

manscape ('mænskeɪp). [f. MAN *sb.*[1], formed in imitation of LANDSCAPE; see also SCAPE *sb.*[3]] A view or picture of a sea of faces in a crowd. (Fanciful.)

1927 *Sunday Express* 24 Apr. 1/1 A manscape of a hundred thousand souls is a moving spectacle. **1948** *Archit. Rev.* CIV. 11/1 But this is landscape. What of manscape?

mansclawth, variant of MANSLAUGHT *Obs.*

manse (mæns), *sb.* [ad. med.L. (Law and Eccl.) *mansus, mansum, mansa* dwelling, house; also, a quantity of land considered sufficient for the support of a family (cf. HIDE *sb.*[2]), f. L. *mans-*, ppl. stem of *manēre* to dwell, remain. Cf. mod.F. (Hist.) *manse*; the popular representatives of the Latin word in Rom. are OF. *mes*, Pr., Catal. *mas.*]

†**1.** A mansion house or 'capital messuage'. (Cf. MANOR 1.) *Obs.*

1490 *Acta Dom. Concil.* (1839) 149/1 þe auld mansioune þ at William Inglis has in tak & twa akeris liand besid þe said manss. **1513** DOUGLAS *Æneis* VIII. vi. 118 At thir ilk ȝettis heyr The conquerour entrit, douchty Hercules, This sobyr mans ressauit hym, but les. **1781** WARTON *Hist. Kiddington* (1783) 30 This lady died at her capital manse at Fencot near Bicester in 1111. [**1848** LYTTON *Harold* VI. i, And I shall be at his own favourite manse over the water at sunset.]

2. A measure of land regarded as sufficient for the support of a family. *Obs.* exc. *Hist.*

In this sense the Eng. form of the word appears to occur only with reference to ecclesiastical endowments.

1597 SKENE *De Verb. Sign.* s.v. *Mansus*, Carolus Magnus, to the effect that the Ministers of the worde of God suld not perish be hunger or povertie, gaue to ilke Kirke ane manse. **1625** in Cramond *Ann. Banff* (1893) II. 24 Anent the ministers mans being now desolat of building, and he excusing his inhabilitie to repair the samyn. **1794** W. TINDAL *Evesham* 4 The names of those Manses or farms next follow which the founder acquired for the first endowment of his monastery. **1844** LINGARD *Anglo-Sax. Ch.* I. iv. 162 Let an entire manse.. be assigned to each church. **1855** MILMAN *Lat. Chr.* IV. iii. (1864) II. 253 A monastery founded at Ripon and endowed with xxx manses of land. **1860** HOOK *Lives Abps.* (1869) I. v. 287 That there be given to the servants of God.. a certain hereditary portion of the lands possessed by persons of every degree, that is to say, the tenth manse.

3. An ecclesiastical residence, whether parochial or collegiate; now *esp.* the house allocated to or occupied by the minister of a parish in Scotland; sometimes applied to the residences provided for ministers of the congregational, presbyterian, and other denominations in Britain and the U. S. Also in phr. *son* (*bairn, child, daughter*) *of the manse*: the son (daughter) of a Protestant minister, *esp.* in the Church of Scotland.

1534 *Act 25 Hen. VIII* in *Stat. Irel.* (1621) 77 To have and to hold the same mance, glebe lands, altereges,.. and all other the premisses. **1583** in *Munim. Irvine* (1890) I. 222 To provyd ane sufficient manse and yard to the said minister. **1683** G. MARTIN *Reliq. Divi Andreæ* vii. §3 (1797) 104 The castle of St. Andrews.. had been the Bishop of St. Andrews his manse. **1710** CHAMBERLAYNE *Pres. St. Gt. Brit.* II. III. 435 They [Scottish Presbyterian ministers] are provided with convenient Manses (i.e. Parsonage Houses). **1754** ERSKINE *Princ. Sc. Law* I. (1809) 56 Under a manse are comprehended stable, barn, and byre, with a garden. **1791** BOSWELL *Johnson* 20 Aug. an. 1773, The manse, as the parsonage-house is called in Scotland, was close by. **1805** T. D. WHITAKER *Hist. Craven* 5, I would ask, whether.. it were possible to devise a method of supporting an incumbent equally wise and proper with that of a manse, glebe, and tithes. **1816** SCOTT *Old Mort.* xxvii, Poundtext bade adieu to his companions, and travelled forward alone to his own manse. **1855** MRS. OLIPHANT *Lilliesleaf* III. ix. 116 To think that this was our Mary, a bairn of the Manse. **1860** G. H. KINGSLEY *Vac. Tour* 121 If the Sutherland inn is full.. you can always get a bed somewhere, often at the manse. **1903** G. W. BALFOUR in M. C. Balfour *From Saranac to Marquesas* p. xix, One of the few survivors left of the happy company of 'children of the manse'. **1962** *Glasgow Herald* 8 Oct. 7 Dr McIntyre.. is a son of the manse, always a good step on the high road to fortune in Scotland. **1965** *Listener* 9 Sept. 372/2 Albert Schweitzer, a son of the manse, was born an Alsatian and brought up in the village of Günsbach. **1976** A. RICHARDS *Former Miss Merthyr Tydfil* 52 Dorothea was a daughter of the manse, a history graduate.

¶**4.** Confused with F. *mense* [ad. L. *mensa* table], sometimes written *manse* (Littré): The revenue of an abbey or of an ecclesiastic. *Obs.*

1710 T. GOODWIN *Life Bp. Stillingfl.* 101 He gives a learned account of the Manse and Maintenance settled upon each parish-priest. **1747** CARTE *Hist. Eng.* I. 245 The monasteries, whose abbatial manse, or the revenue of the abbot was annexed to the bishoprick.

† **manse,** *v. Obs.* Also 4 mance, monse. [Short for AMANSE *v.*] *trans.* To excommunicate, to curse. Hence **mansed** *ppl. a.*

c **1200** ORMIN 10522 Aȝȝ whannse preostess mannsenn her & shædenn þa fra Criste þat opennlike onnȝæness Crist All þeȝȝre þannkess wiþþrenn. *c* **1275** *XI Pains of Hell* 259 in *O.E. Misc.* 154 Oþer weren Mansed bi nome. **13..** *S.E. Leg.* (MS. Bodl. 779) in Herrig *Archiv* LXXXII. 347/75 To mancy him was swyþe loþ.. þerfore he tauȝt cristin to hate mansinge. **13..** *E.E. Allit.* P. B. 774 He syttez þer in Sodomis, þy seruaunt so pouere Among þo mansed men þat han þe much greued. **1377** LANGL. *P. Pl.* B. II. 39 And now worth þis Mede ymaried al to a mansed schrewe. **1399** —— *Rich. Redeles* III. 105 þe[y] monside þe marchall ffor his myssedede. **14..** *Sege Jerusalem* 154 For þat mansed man [*sc.* Judas] Mathie þey chossyn.

mansebyll, obs. form of MANCIPLE.

mansell: see MASUEL.

'man-,servant. Pl. **men-servants.** A male servant.

1551 BIBLE (Hyll) *2 Kings* v. 26 It is a tyme.. to receaue garments,.. oxen, shepe, menseruantes and maydeseruants? **1611** BIBLE *Gen.* xxiv. 35 Hee hath giuen him flocks, and heards,.. men seruants, and mayd seruants. **1632** SHERWOOD, A man-servant, *serviteur*. **1729** SWIFT *Direct. Serv.* viii, It is highly improper for Men Servants to know that fine Ladies have Occasion for such Utensils. **1784** JOHNSON *Will*, To the use of Francis Barber, my man-servant, a negro. **1902** T. M. LINDSAY *Ch. & Ministry in Early Cent.* viii. 355 The boy or man servant who followed his master when the latter went out of his house.

mansfield ('mænsfi:ld). *Min.* A magnesio-calciferous sandstone from near Mansfield in Nottinghamshire, used for building. Also *attrib.*

1842 GWILT *Archit.* 478 Mansfield, or C. Lindley's Red [Sandstone]. **1866** *Ecclesiologist* XXVII. 105 Good constructive colour by means of red Mansfield will be introduced externally.

manship ('mænʃɪp). Forms: 1 **manscipe,** 3 **mannshipe, monscipe, monschipe,** 4 **manschippe, manshupe, manscip, manschipe, manchip,** 5 **manschyp, manshyp, menschepe,** 5, 7, 9 **manship.** [OE. *manscipe*: see MAN *sb.*[1] and -SHIP. Cf. G. *mannschaft*.]

†**1.** Humanity, kindness; courtesy, civility. *Obs.*

a **1000** tr. *Pope Sergius' Let. to Aldhelm* in Birch *Cart. Sax.* I. 155 Manscipe ȝyfan be þearfendum & ælþeodiȝum [L. *humanitatem peregrinis et egentibus impendere*]. *c* **1330** *Arth. & Merl.* 7654 (Kölbing), 'Whider wostow, Ywain, for mi loue?' 'Dame, to seche min em Arthour, Of him to afong þe anour Of wiȝtschippe & cheualrie, & leren manschippe & curteisie!' **1393** LANGL. *P. Pl.* C. XIII. 105 For eche frend fedeþ oþer and fondeþ how he may quite Meles and manshupes eche a ryche man oþer.

†**2.** Homage, worship; honour, dignity. *Obs.*

a **1175** *Cott. Hom.* 235 Gif ic fader ham wer his mi manscipe [= Mal. i. 6 Vulg. *ubi est honor meus*?]. *c* **1200** ORMIN 19014 Forr þurrh þatt manness sawle iss lic Wiþþ

Godd inn onnlicnesse, þær þurrh maȝȝ itt ben nemmnedd mann, & wiþþ mannshipe wurrþedd. c 1205 LAY. 6234 We wulleð þine men beon þine mon-scipe herien. c 1275 *Ibid.* 13500 Ich ou wolle wel bi-wite mid mochelere mansipe. a 1300 *Cursor M.* 12565 And quen he suld to manscip ga,.. All þai felascip him bar. 13.. *Guy Warw.* (A.) 1688 He him underfeng with worthschipe And dede him miche manschipe [*Caius MS.* honour full manly]. c 1330 *Arth. & Merl.* 3634 (Kölbing), We beþ redi in al þing, Anon to go wiþ king Arthour, To his manschipe & his honour! *Ibid.* 6827 For leuer hem were be ded, sikerliche, In manschippe & in trewþe, þan euer more liue in rewþe. c 1450 *Cast. Perseverance* (E.E.T.S.) 74 We mustyr ȝou with menschepe, & Freyne ȝou of Frely frenchepe.

†3. Manly courage, valour; manliness. *Obs.*

c 1205 LAY. 3846 He fusede mid monschipe to ward Margane his mæie. 13.. *Coer de L.* 1848 Mariners arm your ships And do up your manships. c 1350 *Will. Palerne* 2676 Meyntenes ȝit ȝoure manchip manli a while, til god of his grete miȝt god tyding vs sende. *Ibid.* 3337 Men, for ȝoure manchipe na more þat suffreþ, but wendeþ ouȝt wiȝtli & wiþ ȝour fon meteþ. c 1400 *Sege Jerusalem* 777 More manschyp wer hit ȝit mercy [to] by-seche, þan metles marr þer no myȝt helpys. 1465 *Paston Lett.* II. 254 And how that ever ye do, hold up your manship.

4. The condition of being a man. *Obs.* exc. in *nonce-use*. †Also *concr.*, a man.

a 1300 *Cursor M.* 9849 Bot he war ferliful to call if þou it sagh, and sua moght fall, þat in a man all manscip war, Wit-vten less, wit-vten mare. 1600 *Look about you* C 4, Will you promise me to bring no maides To set vppon my litle manship there? 1899 *Westm. Gaz.* 27 June 1/3 He is too proud of his superior manship to allow it.

Hence †'**manshiply** *adv.*, faithfully as a liegeman.

13.. *Guy Warw.* (A.) 124 His lord he serued.. In al þing manschipeliche. c 1425 *Eng. Conq. Irel.* 92 The folke of þe londe, manshyply hym shold vptake, & worthly as lorde.

-manship, *suffix.* [f. MAN *sb.*[1] 4 p + -SHIP after CHURCHMANSHIP, CRAFTSMANSHIP, SPORTSMANSHIP, etc.] Used with prefixed sb. (occas. vb.) to denote skill in a subject or activity, esp. now so deployed as to disconcert a rival or opponent.

This traditional terminal element underwent a profound change of meaning after 1947 under the influence of GAMESMANSHIP. Cf. also *brinkmanship*, LIFEMANSHIP, *oneupmanship*.

1821 [see *bullmanship* s.v. BULL *sb.*[1] 11 a]. 1880 [see BUSHMANSHIP]. 1894 *Pall Mall Gaz.* 23 Oct. 4/3 Parisiennes continue to witch the world with noble bikemanship in their graceful kilted knickerbockers. 1909 M. B. SAUNDERS *Litany Lane* I. iii. 34 Otherwise the allegory—and the good-humoured clubmanship—sufficed. 1925 L. O'FLAHERTY *Informer* vi. 78 We can imagine him perfecting himself in the arts of gunmanship, deceit, [etc.]. 1939 *Amer. Speech* XIV. 80/1 Professor Kenneth B. Haas..inserted a short paragraph concerning 'Consumer Vocabulary' in an article entitled 'Buymanship as an Economic Prophylaxis'. 1950 *Sunday Times* 9 July, Many gamesmen find a specious field for the exercise of their knowledge in the allied craft of queuemanship. 1951 C. D. MILNER *Dolomites* 81 Many fine climbers who were..developing British cragmanship. 1959 *Evening Standard* 13 June 4/3 His hobbies..include farming, motoring..and general do-it-yourself-manship. 1962 *Economist* 28 July 338/2 Connoisseurs of conferencemanship will be happy to find resolutions calling for the abolition of indirect taxation, [etc.]. 1973 *Nature* 24 Aug. 526/1 He has some useful and pointed things to say on 'grantsmanship'.

manshun, -shut, dial. forms of MANCHET.

†'**mansing**, *vbl. sb. Obs.* Also 3 **mansingue, mansinge**, 4 **manzinge**, 5 **mansynge**. [f. MANSE *v.* + -ING.] Cursing.

c 1290 *S. Eng. Leg.* I. 28/50 Anon with þis mansingue al þat on half dachste a-doun. 1297 R. GLOUC. (Rolls) 9686 þe þridde was ȝuf eni man in mansinge were ibrouȝt & suþþe come to amendement ne aȝe riȝte nere noȝt. 1340 *Ayenb.* 148 þanne behoueþ come þet zuord hit uor to dele oþer be manzinge oþer be hotinge out of contraye. c 1425 *Eng. Conq. Irel.* 136 Thay..lytyl tel of othes & of mansynge.

mansion ('mænʃən), *sb.* Forms: 4–5 **mansioun**, 4–7 **mansyon**, (4 **mansyun**, 5 **mansyowne**, **manson**, 6 **mansyone**), 4–5 **mancioun**, (**moncion**), 4–6 **mancion**, **mancyon**, (5 **mencion**), 6 **mantioun**, **manchion**, 6, 8 **mantion**, 5–6 **mansione**, 4– **mansion**. [a. OF. *mansion* (13th c.), now only in certain technical senses (see 4 and 5 below), ad. L. *mansiōn-em*, n. of action f. *manēre* to remain, dwell. Cf. Sp. *mansion*, Pg. *mansão*, It. *mansione*.

The regular representative of the L. word in Fr. is *maison* house (= Pr. *maisó-s*); the It. *magione* and the OSp. *mayson* house, mod.Sp. *meson* inn, are adopted from Fr.]

†1. The action of remaining, abiding, dwelling, or staying in a place. Phr. ***to have, keep, make, take*** (one's) ***mansion*** = to dwell, abide. Also, permanence or continuance in a position or state.

a 1340 HAMPOLE *Psalter* v. 8 þai entire in till godis house of heuen, and takis þaire ioy and þaire mansyon eftire þaire perfeccioun. 1377 LANGL. *P. Pl.* B. XIV. 216 Pryde in ricchesse regneth rather þan in pouerte, Arst in þe Maister þan in þe man some mansioun he hath. c 1400 *Rom. Rose* 4908 If he there make his mansioun For to abyde professioun. c 1485 *Digby Myst.* (1882) III. 1461 In his name, lord, I beseche þe, with-In þi lond to have my mancyon. 1560 DAUS tr. *Sleidane's Commm.* 340 The other [chappell], and the fore-said Haulles, the Cardinals have theyr mansion. 1576 GASCOIGNE *Steele Glas* G iv, That malice make, no mansion in their minds. 1605 BACON *Adv. Learn.* II. vii. §7 That the solidness of the earth is for the station and mansion of living creatures. 1607 SHAKS. *Timon* v. i. 218 Timon hath made his euerlasting Mansion Vpon the Beached Verge of the salt Flood. c 1611 CHAPMAN *Iliad* III. Comm. 48 Who euer saw true learning, wisdome, or wit, vouchsafe mansion in any proud, vaineglorious, and braggartly spirit. 1637 H. SYDENHAM *Serm.* II. 35 Sitting presupposes stabilitie and mansion. 1667 DENHAM *On Cowley* 14 These poets near our Princes sleep, And in one grave their mansion keep. 1677 GALE *Crt. Gentiles* IV. 280 We have not a word which properly signifies the stable mansion of Eternitie. 1696 TATE & BRADY *Ps.* cxliii. 3 To Darkness chas'd and forc'd to seek A Mansion with the dead. 1710 STEELE *Tatler* No. 182 ¶ 1 The Visages of those in whom Love, Rage, Anger, Jealousy or Envy, have their frequent Mansions. 1722 WOLLASTON *Relig. Nat.* ix. 212 The soul..must be freed from the laws of bodies, and fall under some other, which will carry it to some proper mansion, or state.

2. a. A place where one stays or dwells; a place of abode, an abiding-place. Now *arch.*

c 1386 CHAUCER *Knt.'s T.* 1116 The grete temple of Mars in Trace Ther as Mars hath his souereyn mansion. c 1420 LYDG. *Assembly of Gods* 2089 The triumphall guerdoun That God reserueth to euery creature, aboue in hys celestiall mansioun. 1567 *Gude & Godlie B.* (S.T.S.) 96 Thow sall behald him, and his mantioun Be brocht to nocht. 1590 SPENSER *F.Q.* II. iii. 41. 1612 M. LOK *P. Martyr's Hist. W. Indies* in *Hakluyt* (1812) V. 167 Colonies or mansions of the Spaniardes. 1632 LITHGOW *Trav.* I. 41 This incomparable mansion [*sc.* Venice] is the only Paragon of all Cities in the World. 1667 MILTON *P.L.* VIII. 296 Thy Mansion wants thee, Adam, rise. 1725 POPE *Odyss.* v. 85 On whose high branches, waving with the storm, The birds of broadest wing their mansion form. 1764 GOLDSM. *Trav.* 167 Where the bleak Swiss their stormy mansion tread. 1774 —— *Nat. Hist.* (1776) IV. 30 It sometimes happens that its little mansion [*sc.* the squirrel's nest] is attacked by a deadly and powerful foe. 1777 HOWARD *Prisons Eng.* (1780) 25 That the penitent should..be driven again..to the practice which soon brings him back to his former mansion. 1871 R. ELLIS tr. *Catullus* lxviii. 34 Rome is alone my life's centre, a mansion of home.

†b. (Chiefly *pl.*) A separate dwelling-place, lodging, or apartment in a large house or enclosure.

c 1400 MAUNDEV. (1839) v. 41 And thoughe it be clept the Tour of Babiloyne, ȝit natheles there were ordeyned with inne many Mansiouns and many gret duellynge Places. 1432–50 tr. *Higden* (Rolls) I. 113 The kynges palice, with mansiones for his men. *Ibid.* II. 235 And also mansiones and other chambres [in Noah's Ark]. 1553 EDEN *Treat. Newe Ind.* (Arb.) 33 They came to a low cotage..hauing in it two mansions, in one of ye which were women and children and in the other only men. 1697 POTTER *Antiq. Greece* IV. xiii. (1715) 310 Grecian Houses were usually divided into two Parts, in which the Men and women had distinct Mansions assign'd.

c. *transf.* and *fig.*

c 1384 CHAUCER *H. Fame* II. 246 Thus euery thinge by thys reason Hath his propre mansyon To which [it] seketh to repaire. 1555 EDEN *Decades* 265 This sea at certeyne tymes of the yeare..dryueth furth his increase to seke newe mansions. 1687 DRYDEN *Hind & P.* II. 71 Suppose..The certain mansion were not yet assigned: The doubtful residence no proof can bring Against the plain existence of the thing. 1777 JOHNSON *Let. to Mrs. Thrale* 29 Oct., Oxford, the mansion of the liberal arts. 1798 WORDSW. *Tintern Abbey* 140 When thy mind Shall be a mansion for all lovely forms. 1821 LAMB *Elia* Ser. I. *Old & New Schoolm.*, My head has not many mansions, nor spacious.

d. Used in *pl.* to translate Gr. μοναί, Vulg. *mansiones*, in John xiv. 2. Hence *allusively*.

a 1340 HAMPOLE *Psalter* cxlix. 5 þai sall be fayn in þaire dennys, þat is, in sere mansyuns of heuen. 1526 TINDALE *John* xiv. 2 In my fathers housse are many mansions. a 1805 PALEY *Serm.* xxxv. (1810) 526 In the habitations of life are many mansions; rewards of various orders and degrees, proportioned to our various degrees of virtue and exertion here. 1845 FITZBALL *Maritana* II. 16 Oh! that angels now might waft him To the mansions of the blest!

e. Used in *pl.* for the abodes of Hell.

1629 MILTON *Nativ.* 140 Hell it self will pass away, And leave her dolorous mansions to the peering day. 1697 DRYDEN *Virg. Georg.* IV. 691 Th' Infernal Mansions nodding seem to dance [orig. *Quin ipsæ stupuere domus*, etc.].

3. A structure or edifice serving as a dwelling or lodging place. **†a.** *gen.* A house, tent, etc. *Obs.*

a 1340 HAMPOLE *Psalter* xiv. 1 Tabernakile propirly is þe mansyon of feghtand men and passand. 1412–20 LYDG. *Chron. Troy* II. xi, Euery paleys and euery mansyowne Of marbell were. 1444 HEN. VI in Willis & Clark *Cambridge* (1886) I. 340 A mansion or *hospicium*..called Saynt Johanes Hostel. 1495 *Act 11 Hen. VII*, c. 9 §2 Every mese and mancion or dwelling place within the lordship. 1509 *Brasenose Coll. Munim., Wycombe* M. 16 One Tenement or Mansion called the Lyon. a 1548 HALL *Chron., Rich. III* 28 b, With pitefull scriches she repleneshyd the hole mancion. a 1653 GOUGE *Comm. Heb.* III. (1655) 35 We usually call the Mansions which are here [Heb. xi. 9] stiled, 'Tabernacles', Tents. 1770 GOLDSM. *Des. Vill.* 140 The village preacher's modest mansion. 1781 COWPER *Let. to Unwin* 25 Aug., The building we inhabit consists of two mansions.

b. In early use: The chief residence of a lord; the 'capital messuage' of a manor, a manor-house. Hence, in later use, a large and stately residence.

a 1512 FABYAN *Will* in *Chron.* (1811) Pref. 3 If it happen me to decesse at my mansion called Halstedys. 1513 BRADSHAW *St. Werburge* I. 2614 Whiche place somtyme was the kynges mansyon, Translated to an abbay by her commaundyment. 1597 SHAKS. *2 Hen. IV*, III. ii. 351 The Case of a Treble Hoeboy was a Mansion for him: a Court. c 1630 RISDON *Surv. Devon* §41 (1810) 44 A fair dwelling house, which he maketh his mansion. 1641 *Termes de la Ley* 199 *Mansion* (*Mansio*) is in our law most commonly taken for the chief messuage..of the Lord of a Mannor, the Mannor house where he doth most remain. 1807 WORDSW. *Wh. Doe* VII. 25 The lordly Mansion of its pride Is stripped. 1841 W. SPALDING *Italy & It. Isl.* III. 159 The Quirinal Mount..contains on its summits and skirts several of the most magnificent Roman mansions. 1855 MACAULAY *Hist. Eng.* xiii. III. 364 At length the weary fugitives came in sight of Weems Castle. The proprietor of the mansion was a friend to the new government. 1865 *Dublin Univ. Mag.* I. 24 The fussy mistress of the 'mansion'..as in Brighton they call a lodging house. 1866 M. ARNOLD *Thyrsis* i, The village street its haunted mansion lacks. 1893 *Westm. Gaz.* 27 Oct. 1/1 What are called mansions—a mansion is a house with a back staircase—are a drug in the market.

c. The residence provided for an ecclesiastic.

1451 *Rolls of Parlt.* V. 221/2 Which Houses the Deans of the seide Chapell nave hadd for theire mansion. 1559 *Queen's Injunct.* B, All..Parsons, Vicars, & Clarkes, hauing Churches, chappels, or Mansions within this Deanrie.

d. *fig.* (e.g. of the body as enclosing the soul).

1526 TINDALE *2 Cor.* v. 1 Oure erthy mancion wherin we now dwell. *Ibid.* 2 Desyringe to be clothed with oure mansion which is from heven. 1596 *Edw. III*, II. ii, Shall the large limit of fair Britany By me be overthrown, and shall I not Master this little mansion of myself. 1611 SHAKS. *Cymb.* III. iv. 70 The innocent Mansion of my Loue (my Heart). 1617 MORYSON *Itin.* II. 296, I neuer saw a braue spirit part more mildly from the old mansion, then his did.

e. Used in *pl.* as the designation of the large buildings, divided into 'flats', which began to be erected in London about 1860.

1876 A. TROLLOPE *Prime Minister* II. iv. 67 He had been to look at a flat,—a set of rooms,—in the Belgrave Mansions, in Pimlico. 1892 A. W. PINERO *Magistrate* II. 105 *Messiter.* Where at, sir? *Vale.* Albert Mansions, Victoria Street. 1901 *Daily Chron.* 17 June 5/2 The inhabitants of Cornwall Mansions, finding that the word is now applied to less than ultra-select blocks of residences, have petitioned the Kensington Council to change the name to Cornwall-place. 1955 *Times* 15 July 10/3 The process happens more often in the case of a mews, a yard, or a court, and is almost frequent in the case of a 'mansions'. 1972 *Mainichi Daily News* (Japan) 7 Nov. 6/6 The earnings of the real estate division, including those obtained through sales of mansions (high class apartments) and lots for villas, will increase by 33 per cent.

†4. A halting-place in a journey; the distance between two halting-places; a stage. *Obs.*

1382 WYCLIF *Exod.* xvii. 1 Thanne goon forth al the multitude of the sones of Yrael fro the desert of Syn, bi her mansiouns [Vulg. *per mansiones suas*]. 1483 CAXTON *Gold. Leg.* 77/2 The fyrst mansion that they made was by the ryuer of tygre. 1613 PURCHAS *Pilgrimage* III. i. 191 Eight mansions from thence is the Region of Frankincense. 1614 RALEIGH *Hist. World* II. (1634) 222 From Marah he removed to Elim, the sixth Mansion, a march of eight miles. 1737 WHISTON *Josephus, Antiq.* XVI. ix. §2 Herod..in three days time marched seven mansions [Gr. σταθμούς].

5. *Astrol.* **a.** = HOUSE *sb.*[1] 8. **b.** Each of the twenty-eight divisions of the ecliptic, which are occupied by the moon on successive days.

c 1386 CHAUCER *Sqr.'s T.* 42 Phebus the sonne..was..in his mansion In Aries. —— *Frankl. T.* 402 The eighte and twenty mansions That longen to the moone. 1430–40 LYDG. *Bochas* VII. iv. (1494) B ij, Jupiter..within the fissh helde tho his mancion. 1509 HAWES *Past. Pleas.* XVIII. (Percy Soc.) 77 Dyane..Entred the Crab, her propre mancyon. 1552 LYNDESAY *Monarche* 6120 Als cleir As flammand Phebus in his Mantioun. 1690 LEYBOURN *Curs. Math.* 385 The dividing of the Heavens into XII. Mansions or Houses. 1879 PROCTOR in *Contemp. Rev.* June 419 The Chaldæan astronomy has not the twenty-eight lunar mansions.

†6. Formerly used *Hist.* to render med.L. *mansa*, *mansus* a hide of land: see MANSE *sb.* 2. *Obs.*

c 1450 *St. Cuthbert* (Surtees) 8329 Fyften mansyons in lyndesay He gaf to him and his for ay. 1513 BRADSHAW *St. Werburge* I. 564 He gaue a certayne mansyon To the prouynce of Lyndesy. 1647 N. BACON *Disc. Govt. Eng.* I. xi. (1739) 19 Yet could not the Tenth Hide, Tenth Mansion, or Tenth part of the Kingdom be granted. 1809 BAWDWEN *Domesday Bk.* 331 Three mansions, in which are situate eleven houses yielding four shillings and seven-pence.

7. *attrib.*, as †*mansion-globe*; †**mansion-seat**, a place of abode, dwelling-place; also, the chief residence of a landed proprietor. Also MANSION-HOUSE, MANSION-PLACE.

1618 BOLTON tr. *Florus* (1636) 41 The City which the Fates ordained to be the mansion Seat of men, and gods. 1711 SHAFTESB. *Charac.* (1737) II. 373 Yet is this mansion-globe, this man-container, of a much narrower compass even than other its fellow-wanderers of our system. 1751 CHESTERF. *Lett.* (1792) III. 224 A certain district of ground immediately contiguous to the mansion seat of a family. 1771 MRS. GRIFFITH *Hist. Lady Barton* III. 201 Castle W—..the mansion-seat where my father then resided.

†'**mansion**, *v. Obs. rare.* [f. prec. sb.] *intr.* To dwell, reside.

a 1638 MEDE *Par. Peter* (1642) 16 Visible as the clouds of heaven,..and other meteors; as also the rest of the creatures mansioning therein. a 1711 KEN *Christophil* Poet. Wks. 1721 I. 430 Love, when Faith sees my Jesus near, Will say, 'Tis good to mansion here.

mansional ('mænʃənəl), *a. rare*$^{-1}$. [f. MANSION *sb.* + -AL[1].] Of or pertaining to a mansion.

1813 'ÆDITUUS' *Metr. Remarks* 9 Our Mansional-house is the genuine descendant of the Castle. *Ibid.* 12 The Bowed Mansional Window.

mansionary ('mænʃənərɪ), *a.* and *sb.* [ad. med.L. *mansiōnārius*: see -ARY.]

A. *adj.* Staying or dwelling in a place, permanently abiding, resident. ? *Obs.*

1447 BOKENHAM *Seyntys* (Roxb.) 144 Phebus wych no wher is mansonarye Stedefastly but ych daye doth varye His

herberwe among the syngnys twelve. **1727–41** CHAMBERS *Cycl.* s.v. *Canon, Foreign Canons* were such as did not officiate in the Canonries to which they belonged.—To these were opposed *Mansionary Canons*, or *Canons Residentiary*.

B. *sb. Eccl.* **1.** A custodian of a church.

1708–22 BINGHAM *Orig. Eccl.* VIII. vii. §11 Wks. 1840 II. 476 The mansionaries, or keepers of the church. **1893** *Month* July 364 A mansionary of the church presented him [the Pope] with a reed on which was a lighted taper.

†**2.** An endowment for a chantry-priest. [med.L. *mansionaria*: see Du Cange.]

1651 HOWELL *Venice* 174 If the pains of Purgatory are sayed to be but temporary, wherefore shold the simplicity of peeple be perswaded to bequeath in the behalf of their souls perpetuall Legacies and Mansionaries?

mansioned (ˈmænʃənd), *ppl. a.* (*nonce-wd.*) [f. MANSION *sb.* + -ED².] Furnished with mansions.

1828 J. WILSON in *Blackw. Mag.* XXIII. 819 We surveyed ..county upon county, of rich, merry, sylvan England, mansioned, abbeyed, towered.

ˈ**mansion-house.** †**a.** A dwelling-house, a house in which a person resides. *Obs.*

1533 *Act 24 Hen. VIII*, c. 5 Any suche evill disposed persone..attempting..burgularly to breke Mansion houses. **1563** in *Vicary's Anat.* (1888) App. III. 164 Every mansion howse of this Cyty that..shalbe visited this Sommer season with the plage. **1577** HARRISON *England* II. xii. (1877) I. 237 The mansion houses of our countrie townes ..are builded in such sort generallie, as that they haue neither dairie, stable, nor bruehouse annexed vnto them vnder the same roofe. **1638** in T. Lechford *Note-Bk.* (1885) 54 All that parte of one new mansion house in Boston..wch lyes to the south end. **1672** *Cowell's Interpr.* s.v. *House*, Those that dig for Salt-peter, shall not dig in the Mansion-house of any Subject without his assent. **1712** STEELE *Spect.* No. 264 ¶2 He took his present Lodging in St. John Street, at the Mansion-House of a Taylor's Widow. **1718** in G. Sheldon *Hist. Deerfield, Mass.* (1895) I. 499 We propose that they..shall..Build each man a Mansion house upon their house lots. **1755** in F. Chase *Hist. Dartmouth Coll.* (1891) I. 11 A certain lott of Land..with a Mantion House thereon. *fig.* **1592** R. D. *Hypnerotomachia* 75 b, This place was the Mansion-house of Voluptuousnes. **1644** MILTON *Areop.* (Arb.) 69 A City of refuge, the mansion house of liberty.

b. The house of the lord of a manor, the chief residence of a landed proprietor; hence (now only U.S.), a large house of good appearance.

1641 EVELYN *Diary* (init.), Wotton, the mansion house of my father, left him by my grandfather. **1651** G. W. tr. *Cowel's Inst.* 149 The Wife also shall have..her lodging in her Husbands cheife Mansion house for 40. dayes. **1679** *Public Rec. Colony of Connecticut* (1859) III. 42 He shall build upon his sayd accomodations a good sufficient mansion house. **1711** *Lond. Gaz.* No. 4893/4 The Capital Messuage or Mansion-House, called Newborrough-Hall. **1725** DE FOE *Voy. round World* (1840) 290 Our good Chilian's mansion-house or palace. **1745** E. KIMBER *Itinerant Observations Amer.* (1878) 37 A Negro Quarter, is a number of Huts or Hovels, built at some distance from the Mansion-House. **1782** V. KNOX *Ess.* (1819) III. cxxi. 15 The landed gentry usually possess a share of pride fully proportionate to their estate and mansion house. **1812** *Niles' Reg.* III. 9/2 The majority then retired to the Mansion house. **1837** W. JENKINS *Ohio Gazetteer* 162 A large and elegant Mansion house has been erected on the ground with numerous smaller cottages and out buildings. **1844** in C. Cist *Cincinnati Misc.* (1845) I. 68/1 The mansion house of E. S. Haines..and various single buildings are observable for their fine appearance. **1848** SHAND *Pract. Crt. Sess.* II. 607 Where there is a proper mansion-house on a landed-estate, the eldest heir-portioner is entitled to that mansion-house. **1860** O. W. HOLMES *Elsie V.* v. (1861) 43 In this street were most of the great houses, or 'mansion-houses', as it was usual to call them... A New-England 'mansion-house' is naturally square, with dormer windows. **1899** CROCKETT *Kit Kennedy* iv. 32 The bunch of trees, under which nestled the mansion-house of Kirkoswald.

c. An official residence; †esp. that belonging to the benefice of an ecclesiastic. Now *spec.* the official residence of the Lord Mayor of London.

1546 *Mem. Ripon* (Surtees) III. 14 The Mansion house of the saide vicars. *a* **1600** HOOKER *Eccl. Pol.* VII. xxiv. §13 The Executors of Bishops are sued if their Mansion house be suffered to go to decay. **1609** *Mem. Ripon* (Surtees) III. 335 The Mansion House of the Prebendary which is situate in Rippon. **1738** KNOWLER *Strafforde's Lett.* Ded., Repairing of Churches and building Mansion-houses for Ministers. **1766** ENTICK *Hist. Lond.* etc. IV. 359 The lord-mayor's Mansion-house, a modern edifice begun in 1739 and finished in 1753. **1835** THIRLWALL *Greece* I. viii. 331 The Temple of Fear was erected near the mansion-house of the ephors. **1880** *Daily News* 18 Dec. 4/5 A conference..took place yesterday afternoon in the Egyptian Hall of the Mansion House, the Lord Mayor presiding.

†ˈ**mansion-place.** *Obs.* A dwelling-place, place of abode; a mansion-house; the chief seat of a landed proprietor. Also *fig.*

1473 *Rolls of Parlt.* VI. 91/2 An Inne, Mansion place or Beledying. **1523** FITZHERB. *Surv.* 31 b, Whan the tenaunt shall do homage to his chefe lorde of whome he holdeth his chefe maner or mancyon place. *c* **1540** BOORDE *The boke for to Lerne* A ij b, Who soeuer that wyl buylde a mansyon place or howse. **1548** GEST *Pr. Masse* A v, A christian & faithful hart..which..is the temple of the holy ghoste & the mansyon place of the blessed trynitie. *c* **1630** RISDON *Surv. Devon* §56 (1810) 59 [He] built there a fair house, and made it his mansion place. **1650** BULWER *Anthropomet.* 60 The imperial seat and mansion place of wisdome.

b. A halting-place: = MANSION 5.

1608 WILLET *Hexapla Exod.* 190 Kibroth hatauah, which was their next mansion place.

mansionry (ˈmænʃənrɪ). *rare.* Also 7 **mansonry.** [f. MANSION *sb.* + -RY.] ? Mansions collectively. In Shaks. perh. mispr. for *masonry.*

1605 SHAKS. *Macb.* I. vi. 5 This Guest of Summer, The Temple-haunting Barlet does approue, By his loued Mansonry, that the Heauens breath Smells wooingly here. **1876** BROWNING *St. Martin's Summer* x, Durable mansionry.

mansiple, obs. form of MANCIPLE.

mansitude, obs. variant of MANSUETUDE.

†ˈ**manslaught.** *Obs.* Forms: *α.* 1 **mannslyht, manslæht, -sleht(e, -sliht, mon(n)slieht, -slyht, monsliht,** 1–2 **manslyht,** 2 **monsleht,** 3 **man-, monslauȝt, -slæht, slecht, -sleiht,** 3–4 **-sleahte,** 3–5 **-slaȝt(e,** 4 **-slauȝte, -slauht, -slawhte,** 4–5 **-slaghte, -slaught(e, -slauȝt, -slaẃt(te.** *β.* (*Kentish* and *E. Anglian*) 4 **manslaȝþe, -sleȝþe,** 5 **mansclawth, -slauth.** [OE. (Anglian) *mann-, mǫnnslæht*, (WS.) *-slieht, -sliht*, f. *mann* MAN *sb.*¹ + *slæht, slieht*, masc., act of killing:—OTeut. **slahti-z*, f. **slah-* to strike, kill: see SLAY *v.* Cf. OS., OHG. *manslahta* str. fem.]

1. Manslaughter, homicide.

c **897** K. ÆLFRED *Gregory's Past. C.* xxi. 166 Se to anra ðara burȝa ȝefliho, ðonne mæȝ he beon orsorȝ ðæs monslihtes. *a* **1000** *Confess. Peccat.* (B.-T.), Manslæht. *c* **1175** *Lamb. Hom.* 103 Heo macað monslehtas. *c* **1205** LAY. 27826 Muchel mon-slæht wes þere. *a* **1225** *Ancr. R.* 210 Nis þis strong monsleiht, of golnesse awakened? *c* **1250** *Kent. Serm.* in *O. E. Misc.* 30 Lecherie spusbreche Roberie Manslechtes. **1297** R. GLOUC. (Rolls) 8125 Muche was þe manslaȝt þat þere was ido. *a* **1315** SHOREHAM *Poems* (E.E.T.S.) 94/249 Ȝef þer hys manslеȝþe pur. **1390** GOWER *Conf.* I. 364 Now mai men se moerdre and manslawhte. **1426** AUDELAY *Poems* 2 Monslaȝt with a rewful steven Hit askys vengans. *c* **1450** *Cov. Myst.* xxxii. (Shaks. Soc.) 312 Delyvere us the theff Barabas, That for mansclawth presonde was. **1469** in *10th Rep. Hist. MSS. Comm.* App. v. 307 If ony man..make ony affray, manslaught, other kyllyng, by his owne foly and not in defennce.

2. A murderer.

a **1300** *Ten Commandm.* in *E.E.P.* (1862) 16 Manslaȝt þou ne be. *c* **1315** SHOREHAM *Poems* (E.E.T.S.) 94/261 Manye suche manslеȝþen beþ. **1340** *Ayenb.* 171 Me ssel grede to god merci ase his þyef ase his manslaȝþe. *a* **1400–50** *Alexander* 4498 Marcure was manslaȝt.

manslaughter (ˈmænslɔːtə(r)), *sb.* Forms: see SLAUGHTER *sb.* Also 4 **mans-slaghter,** 4–5 **manes-slaghter.** [f. MAN *sb.*¹ + SLAUGHTER.]

1. †**a.** The killing of a human being by a human being; homicide; chiefly criminal homicide, *esp.* murder. *Obs.*

a **1300** *Cursor M.* 25457 O mans-slaghter had i na mak. *c* **1374** CHAUCER *Former Age* 64 In owre dayes nis but covetyse..Poyson and manslawhtre. *c* **1386** —— *Pars. T.* ¶491 Spiritueel manslaughtere is in vj. thynges. *a* **1400** *Relig. Pieces fr. Thornton MS.* 25 þer es manes-slaghter of hand, of tunge, of herte. **1462** *Paston Lett.* II. 83, I herd nevyr sey of so myche robry and manslawter in thys contre as is now within a lytyll tyme. **1581** LAMBARDE *Eiren.* II. vii. (1588) 223 Using Manslaughter, as a sort of Felonie that comprehendeth under it all maner of felonious Homicide whatsoeuer. **1601–2** FULBECKE *1st Pt. Parall.* 92 Manslaughter *se defendendo* is, where [etc.]. **1611** BIBLE *2 Esdras* i. 26 Your feete are swift to commit manslaughter.

b. The 'slaughtering' of human beings; destruction of human life.

c **1450** *Merlin* 244 Ther was a stronge bataile and grete man-slaughter on both sithes. **1532** MORE *Confut. Tindale* Wks. 352/2 What distruccion and man slaughter they haue caused. **1667** MILTON *P.L.* XI. 689 To overcome in Battel,.. and bring home spoils with infinite Man-slaughter. **1880** T. HODGKIN *Italy & Inv.* I. i. Introd. 14 It [*sc.* an army] soon ceases to be an efficient instrument even for its own purpose of scientific manslaughter. **1898** GERTRUDE TUCKWELL in *19th Cent.* Aug. 253 (art.) Commercial manslaughter.

2. *Law.* A species of criminal homicide of a lower degree of criminality than murder; now defined as criminal homicide without malice aforethought.

In etymological meaning there is no difference between *manslaughter* and *homicide* (L. *homicidium*, F. *homicide*, both used in early Eng. law-books). In its modern technical use, *manslaughter* corresponds generally to the 'simple homicide' of early Law French and Law Latin writers, which was used in contradistinction to 'murder' (though the distinction is not identical with the modern one), and ordinarily implied criminality.

According to the modern interpretation, *manslaughter* is committed when one person causes the death of another either intentionally in the heat of passion under certain kinds of provocation, or unintentionally by culpable negligence or as a consequence of some unlawful act.

In Scotland the term corresponding to *manslaughter* is 'culpable homicide'.

1447 *Rolls of Parlt.* V. 137/2 Robberies, Murthers, mayehemes and manslaut'. **1538** STARKEY *England* II. iii. 197 Robbery..wyth murdur and mansloughtur. **1601–2** FULBECKE *1st Pt. Parall.* 90 You seeme under your first member, which is the wilful killing of a man of malice forethought, to comprehend manslaughter, which is done in the heate and furie of anger and sodaine falling out. **1625** HART *Anat. Ur.* II. xi. 122, I cannot see any iust cause why it should not bee pronounced guiltie of man-slaughter at the least, if not of murther. *a* **1732** BOSTON *Crook in Lot* (1805) 21 Such as men-slaughter, purely casual, as when one hewing wood, kills his neighbour with the head of the ax slipping from the helve. **1769** BLACKSTONE *Comm.* IV. 190 In this there are also degrees of guilt, which divide the offence into man-slaughter, and murder. **1847** JAMES *Convict* xx, The foreman returned a verdict of 'Manslaughter' against Edward Dudley. **1898** *Daily News* 17 Jan. 6/6 The young man..who was convicted on Friday of manslaughter of a woman.

Hence **manslaughterous** *a.* [-OUS], of the nature of manslaughter, inclined for manslaughter.

1883 *Pall Mall G.* 6 Jan. 5 A murderous or even a manslaughterous part. **1898** *N. & Q.* 9th Ser. I. 183/1 A description which makes one feel almost manslaughterous.

manslaughter (ˈmænslɔːtə(r)), *v. colloq.* [f. the sb.] *trans.* To kill (a person) without malice aforethought.

1920 R. MACAULAY *Potterism* III. ii. 133, I had left the house morally certain that Arthur Gideon had murdered (or anyhow manslaughtered) Oliver Hobart. **1922** A. A. MILNE *Red House Mystery* ix. 81 'Murdered him?' 'Well, manslaughtered him, anyway.'

ˈ**manslaughterer.** [In sense a, f. MAN *sb.*¹ + SLAUGHTERER; in sense b, f. MANSLAUGHTER *sb.* + -ER.] **a.** One who slaughters men. **b.** One who commits manslaughter (sense 2).

1848 BUCKLEY *Iliad* 93 Mars, man-slaughterer. **1885** A. EDWARDES *Girton Girl* I. iii. 71 As a physician, I consider him a manslaughterer. **1912** E. A. PARRY *What Judge Saw* xvii. 297, I regarded the doctor as a manslaughterer at the time. **1965** *Lancet* 20 Nov. 1070/2 With cyclists, children, and old people safely tucked in bed, I do not have to feel a potential manslaughterer just because I sit behind the steering-wheel.

ˈ**man-slaughtering,** *ppl. a.* That slaughters human beings. So ˈ**manslaughtering** *vbl. sb.*

c **1705** BERKELEY *Cave of Dunmore* Wks. 1871 IV. 508 Ireland seems the freest country in the world from such manslaughtering animals. **1848** BUCKLEY *Iliad* 127 Battles and man-slaughterings. **1876** SWINBURNE *Erechtheus* (ed. 2) 475 Sickles of man-slaughtering edge.

manslauht, -auth, -awt(te: see MANSLAUGHT.

manslayer (ˈmænsleɪə(r)). Forms: see SLAYER; also 5 **monsle(e)r.** One who kills a man; a homicide; *occas.* one who commits manslaughter.

a **1300** *Cursor M.* 16441 þe man-slaer, he barabas. *c* **1375** *Sc. Leg. Saints* xxx. (*Theodera*) 258 Sa ma þu þe sauf fra hel quhare man-slaare sal ay duel. *c* **1425** AUDELAY *XI Pains of Hell* 37 in *O.E. Misc.* 211 þese were proud men,.. Extortioners, monslers, robbid mone one. **1526** *Pilgr. Perf.* (W. de W. 1531) 238 b, He that hateth his brother is a man-sleer. **1611** BIBLE *Num.* xxxv. 12. **1635** VISCT. WENTWORTH in Ellis *Orig. Lett.* Ser. II. III. 286 They that made me the manslayer of the E. of Sᵗ. Albans, will impute my Lo. Mountnorris unto me for willfull and plaine murther. **1741** RICHARDSON *Pamela* II. 281 All your Airs breathe as strongly of the Manslayer, as of the Libertine. **1835** THIRLWALL *Greece* I. vi. 171 That the manslayer withdrew into a foreign land and did not return to his country, till [etc.].

†**b.** An executioner. *Obs. rare*⁻¹.

c **1380** WYCLIF *Serm.* Sel. Wks. I. 388 þe kyng..sente for a man-sleere [Mark vi. 27].

So †ˈ**manslaȝe** *Early ME.* [*OE. slaȝa* slayer].

c **1000** ÆLFRIC *Deut.* v. 17 Ne beo þu manslaȝa. *c* **1175** *Lamb. Hom.* 53 Ah þah heo beoð..monslaȝen for heo slaȝeð heore aȝene saule. *a* **1225** *St Marher.* 11 Ichabbe isehen þene þurs of helle..ant te monslahe islein.

ˈ**man-slaying,** *vbl. sb.* Also 5 **manes-slaynge.** The action of killing a man; homicide. So ˈ**man-slaying** *ppl. a.*

c **1380** WYCLIF *Wks.* (1880) 238 Wrong oppressynge of pore men axiþ vengaunce of god, as doþ wrong mansleynge. *a* **1400** *Relig. Pieces fr. Thornton MS.* 25 Manes-slaynge of hande es when a mane slaes anoþer with his handes. **1526** *Pilgr. Perf.* (W. de W. 1531) 239 And so..in the other vyces of mansleynge and false testimony. **1625** F. HERING *Cert. Rules* a ij b, The rage of this manslaying Hydra [the Plague]. **1876** GLADSTONE *Homeric Synchr.* 55 Battles and man-slayings (androctasiai). **1880** FREEMAN in Stephens *Life* (1895) II. 198 He chose the man-slaying trade.

mansleahte, etc., var. ff. MANSLAUGHT *Obs.*

‖**manso** (ˈmanso). [Sp.] A meek, tame, or cowardly person or animal. Also *attrib.* or as *adj.* Cf. *Indio manso.*

Used esp. of 'cowardly' bulls in *Bullfighting.*

1836, 1860 [see INDIO]. **1912** A. CONAN DOYLE *Lost World* viii. 115 'Yes sir, war drums,' said Gomez, the half-breed. 'Wild Indians, bravos, not mansos; they watch us every mile of the way; kill us if they can.' **1932** E. HEMINGWAY *Death in Afternoon* 298 *Manso*, tame, mild and unwarlike; a bull which does not have the fighting blood is *manso*, as are also the steers called *cabestros* when they are trained. **1952** J. MARKS *To the Bullfight* v. 58 He [*sc.* the president] has also a green and a red one [*sc.* handkerchief], which he holds over the edge of the box:..the red to condemn a cowardly *manso* to the stigma of black banderillas. **1957** A. MACNAB *Bulls of Iberia* vii. 73 Since 1951, in Spain the 'firing' of *manso* bulls has been symbolical only;..the sticks have no fireworks. **1967** MCCORMICK & MASCAREÑAS *Compl. Aficionado* ii. 30 He could pick out the *mansos* with eighty per-cent accuracy, which is better than most toreros can do.

manson, obs. f. MANSION, MONSOON.

mansonia (mænˈsəʊnɪə). [mod.L. (J. R. Drummond 1905, in *Jrnl. Linn. Soc. Bot.* XXXVII. 260), f. the name of F. B. *Manson* (fl. 1905), a forester in Burma who collected the first specimens of *M. gagei.*] A large tree of the genus so called, belonging to the family Sterculiaceæ,

esp. the West African *Mansonia altissima* or the hardwood obtained from it. Also *attrib.*

[**1934** W. D. MacGregor *Silviculture Mixed Deciduous Forests Nigeria* iii. 29 *Mansonia* seedlings 4–9″ in height appear to be 1932 regeneration.] **1936** *Nature* 6 June 954/2 The Mansonia (*Mansonia altissima*)..occurs in the deciduous forests of west tropical Africa. **1958** *Archit. Rev.* CXXIV. 191/2 The floors are of mansonia wood blocks, the staircase and fittings of sapele and the ceilings gaboon plywood. **1969** B. J. Rendle *World Timbers* I. 134 Mansonia was introduced to the world market from Nigeria, as a substitute for walnut, in the 1930s.

†**man'sorious**, *a. Obs. rare.* [f. mod.L. *mansōri-us* pertaining to chewing (f. *mans-*, ppl. stem of *mandĕre* to chew, eat) + -ous.] The distinctive epithet of the masseter muscle.

1578 Banister *Hist. Man* I. 11 The mansorious, or eatyng Muscle.

mansound, obs. form of monsoon.

†'**mansuefy**, *v. Obs.*—⁰ [ad. L. *mansuēfacĕre*, f. *mansuē-*, *mansuēscĕre* (see mansuete) + *facĕre*: see -fy.] *trans.* To tame (Cockeram 1623). Hence **mansuefaction** [see -faction], 'a taming or making gentle' (Bailey vol. II, 1727).

mansuete (mæn'swiːt, 'mænswiːt), *a. Obs.* or *arch.* Forms: 4–8 **mansuete**, 5–6 **-swete**, 6 **-sweit**, 6–7 **-suet**. [ad. L. *mansuēt-us*, pa. pple. of *mansuēscĕre* to tame, become tame, f. *man-us* hand + *suēscĕre* to accustom, become accustomed (see custom). Cf. OF. *mansuet(e*, Sp., Pg., It. *mansueto*.] Gentle, mild; tame, not wild or fierce.

c **1374** Chaucer *Troylus* v. 194 She..stod forth mewet mylde and mansuete. *c* **1450** Holland *Howlat* 83 That is the plesant Pacok,..manswet and mure. **1535** Stewart *Cron. Scot.* III. 400 Ane fair ȝoung man..Mansweit and meik. **1621** S. Ward *Life of Faith* 66 Of Woluish and dogged makes the Will Lamb-like and Doue-like: of wild and haggard, morigerous and mansuete. **1660** F. Brooke tr. *Le Blanc's Trav.* 26 He kept this fish in a Pond..and delighted much to feed him with his own hand, the fish being very mansuete. **1691** Ray *Creation* (1701) 132 This holds not only in domestic and mansuete birds..but also in the wild. **1722** Wollaston *Relig. Nat.* ix. 176 It will oblige men..not to be proud..but candid, placable, mansuete. **1861** J. Brown *Horæ Subs.* Ser. I. 415 Our..clever, and not over-mansuete friend 'Fuge Medicos'.

Hence †**mansuetely** *adv.*, gently, mildly.

c **1460** J. Russell *Bk. Nurture* 887 Than pray youre souereyn with wordus mansuetely to com to a good fyre.

†**mansuetie.** *Obs. rare*⁻¹. = mansuetude.

1592 Wyrley *Armorie, Ld. Chandos* 105 More praisefull vertue in a conquerer Then mansuetie is none to be found.

mansuetude ('mænswɪtjuːd). *arch.* Also 6 **mansuetud, -swetude**, 7 **mansitude, -sutude**. [ad. L. *mansuētūdo*, f. *mansuētus*: see mansuete and -tude. Cf. F. *mansuétude* (from 13th c.; earlier *mansuetume*).] Gentleness, meekness.

c **1386** Chaucer *Pars. T.* ¶ 580 The remedye agayns Ire is a vertu that men clepen Mansuetude, that is Debonairetee. *c* **1460** Ashby *Active Policy* 880 Auoidyng al vengeance & displesance With al mansuetude conuenient. **1526** *Pilgr. Perf.* (W. de W. 1531) 97 b, Mansuetude or myldnes. **1681** Rycaut tr. *Gracian's Critick* 136 A Lion..whose fierceness had been lately turned to the Mansitude of a Lamb. **1799** W. Tooke *View Russian Emp.* II. 222 Their mansuetude and readiness to concur in all measures adopted by the government. **1869** Browning *Ring & Bk.* viii. 660 Our Lord Himself, made all of mansuetude.

†'**manswear**, *sb. Obs.* In 1 **mánswara, -swora**, 3 **manswore, monsware**. [OE. *mánswara* = ON. *meinsvare* wk. masc.; related to next.] A perjurer.

971 *Blickl. Hom.* 61 Myrþran, & manswaran. *c* **1205** Lay. 4149 Ne mai neuere mon sware mon-scipe longe aȝen. *c* **1275** *Ibid.* 22139 Bote he were so vuel bi-ȝete þat he were louerd-swike oþer to his louerd man-swore.

manswear ('mænswɛə(r)), *v. Obs.* exc. *arch.* and *dial.* Pa. t. **-swore**, pa. pple. **-sworn**. In 1 **mánswerian**, 5 **manesuere**, 5–6 **mensweare**, 6 **manesweir, mansweare, -swere, mannsuere, mensuer, -suir, -sweir**, 9 **mainswear**. [OE. *mánswęrian* (pa. t. *-swór*, pa. pple. *-sworen*), f. *mán* man *sb.*² + *swęrian* to swear. Cf. manath.]

1. *intr.* To swear falsely.

1... *Eccl. Inst.* c. 21 in Thorpe *Laws* II. 416 Ne swerige he þylæs þe he man-swerige. **1583** *Leg. Bp. St. Androis* 843 The man mensueris he saw sic thing. **1855** Robinson *Whitby Gloss.*, *Mainswear*, to swear falsely.

2. *refl.* To perjure oneself.

c **1375** *Sc. Leg. Saints* xxvi. (*Nycholas*) 839 þe quhilk, fra he mansuorn hym had, tuk his staf & mad na bad. **1456** Sir G. Haye *Law Arms* (S.T.S.) 248 What wit war it..that he suld brek his lautee to manesuere him for company. **1535** Coverdale *Wisd.* xiv. 28 Either they..prophecie lyes, or lyue vngodly, or els lightly mansweare them selues. **1567** *Satir. Poems Reform.* ii. 5 Willfullie yai man yame selves mensuir. *a* **1622** J. Welch in Burton *Scot Abr.* (1864) I. v. 286 He caused to take out of the grave the carcass of Formosus, who had mansworn himself. *c* **1817** Hogg *Tales & Sk.* V. 259, I made it clear..that Major Creighton and Mr. John Hay had both man-sworn themselves.

†**3.** *trans.* To swear falsely by (a god). *Obs.*

1533 Bellenden *Livy* iii. (1822) 237 The pepil war nocht sa necligent in thay dayis as thay ar now to manswere thare Goddis, or to fals thare wourdis. **1567** *Gude & Godlie B.* (S.T.S.) 74 Than man I outher reif or steill, Or than my Goddis name mansweir.

¶**4.** To renounce on oath, forswear. *Obs.*

1500–20 Dunbar *Poems* xxvii. 90 Thir new maid knychtis lay bayth in swoun, And did all armes mensweir. **1596** Dalrymple tr. *Leslie's Hist. Scot.* ix. 231 Normond Gourlai confirmet that al heresie he had mensworne afor ony man.

†'**manswearing**, *vbl. sb. Obs.* [f. manswear *v.* + -ing¹.] Perjury.

c **1440** *Alph. Tales* 329 Twa cetisens of Colayn confessid þaim of..manesweryng. **1574** *Reg. Privy Council Scot.* Ser. i. II. 368 Under the pane of infamy, repruif, mansweiring and tinsall of perpetuall traist and credite. **1605** in *Pitcairn's Crim. Trials* II. 454 Dilaitit of Periurie and mensweiring of thame selffis.

mansweit, -swete, etc.: see mansuete, etc.

mansworn ('mænswɔːn), *ppl. a.* and *sb.* [pa. pple. of manswear *v.*] **A.** *adj.* Forsworn, perjured. *Obs.* exc. *Sc.* and *north. dial.*

a **1300** *Cursor M.* 25794 Monsuorn man to petre loke, þat thris on a night crist for-soke. *c* **1400** *Ywaine & Gaw.* 3938 Tithandes tel i yow biforn, Other sal my lady be manesworn. **1456** Sir G. Haye *Law Arms* (S.T.S.) 87 For outhir, mon he be manesuorne or tyne his awin heretage. **1500–20** Dunbar *Poems* xxxiv. 100 The Deuill said then, 'Of commoun la All mensworne folk man cum to me'. *c* **1569** *Durham Depos.* (Surtees) 89 Such maynsworn harlotts as thou art kepes me from it. *c* **1610** in Row *Hist. Kirk* (1842) 305 Thou art a mensworn man. **1650** Hobart *Rep.* 126 Slater brought an action of the case against Franks for saying, Thou art a main-sworne Lad, and a bankrupt Lad... It stood upon the word Maine-sworne: against which it was said, that it was an unknowne word in these parts, and of an uncertaine sense, though in the North parts it was understood to be as much as perjured, as forsworne with his hand upon the book. **1725** Ramsay *Gent. Sheph.* ii. iv, Mony lads will swear, And be mansworn to twa in half a year. **1818** Scott *Hrt. Midl.* xv, I shall be man-sworn in the very thing in which my testimony is wanted. **1893** Stevenson *Catriona* xiii. 145 Prestongrange promised me my life; if he's to be mansworn, here I'll have to die.

absol. *a* **1300** *Cursor M.* 23112 Murthereres and monsuorn als.

†**B.** *sb.* Perjury. *Obs.*

1456 Sir G. Haye *Law Arms* (S.T.S) 273 [He] walde..accus him of the crime of manesuorne.

†**mant**, *sb.*¹ *Obs.* [a. F. *mante* fem., ad. Pr. *manta*, cogn. w. Sp., It., Pg. *manto*: see mantle *sb.* In the first quot. repr. Sp. *manto*. Cf. manta.] **a.** A mantilla. **b.** = manteau 1.

1651 tr. *De-las-Coveras' Don Fenise* 238 He..told him..to return to the Inne to fetch the three Ladies who were there, making them..put their Mants upon them (that is a great vail which the women have in Spain,.. which covereth all their bodies unto their heels). **1694** Echard *Plautus* 95 What a confounded Jargon o' names!.. There's your light Mant plated, your Stiff-bodied-Gown, &c. **1709** *Tatler* No. 32 ¶ 2 Her blue Mant and Petticoat is her Azure Dress. **1752** A. Murphy *Gray's Inn Jrnl.* No. 2 To recal a straggling Hair, to settle the Tucker, or compose the Mant.

mant (mænt), *sb.*² *Sc.* [f. mant *v.*] A stammer; an impediment in the speech.

1839 J. M. Wilson *Tales Border* V. 189 The former having what we call in Scotland a *mant*, a sullen visage, and a brawling temper. **1894** P. H. Hunter *James Inwick* ii. 19 That ane said he had a mant, an' the tither ane that he clippit his words.

mant (mænt), *v. Sc.* Also 6 **mante**, 8–9 **maunt**. [app. of Gaelic origin. Cf. Gaelic and Irish *manntach* toothless, stammering, f. MIrish *mant* gum.] *trans.* and *intr.* To stammer.

1562 A. Scott *Poems* (S.T.S.) i. 92 Thai tyrit God..With owklie abitis to augment þair rentalis, Mantand mort momlingis mixt wᵗ monye leis. **1629** Z. Boyd *Last Battell* 985 Hee who manteth or stammereth in his speach. **1716** Ramsay *On Wit* 12 There was a manting lad in Fife, Wha..never manted when he sang. **1873** *Guidman Inglismaill* 33 Noo an' than he mantit in his sang.

Hence '**manting** *vbl. sb.* and *ppl. a.* Also '**manter**, a stammerer.

1506 in *Ld. Treas. Acc. Scotl.* (1901) III. 199 Item, to mantand Adam to pas to Dunbertane with ane writing of the Kingis. *a* **1585** Polwart *Flyting w. Montgomerie* 775 Mad manter, vaine vaunter. *a* **1625** Sir J. Semple *Picktooth for Pope* in *Harp Renfrew* Ser. ii. (1873) 24 Its but the Matrons manting. **1716** [see mant *v.*]. **1789** D. Davidson *Seasons* 77 Auld mantin Michael's daughter.

‖**manta** ('mæntə). [Sp. *manta* blanket.]

1. a. A wrap or cloak worn by Spaniards.

1697 *C'tess D'Aunoy's Trav.* (1706) 112 When they opened their manta's, the light of the moon made the glory of their Gold and Precious Stones appear. **1845** Ford *Handbk. Spain* i. 31 Some substitute the 'mantas', which most Spaniards carry with them when on their travels. This is a gay-coloured Oriental-looking striped blanket, or rather plaid. **1902** E. L. Banks *Newspaper Girl* 24 It was at first suggested that I should don the manta, the national female garment of Peru.

b. A horse-cloth.

1828 W. Irving in *Life & Lett.* (1864) II. 306 They..lie on the mantas of their mules and horses.

2. [Amer. Sp. *manta*, adopted as a generic name by E. B. Bancroft in 1829.] In full, **manta ray.** A very large ray (ray *sb.*²) of the genus so called, found in tropical seas; also called devil-fish.

1760–72 *Juan & Ulloa's Voy.* (ed. 3) I. 130 The mantas or quilts... The name manta has not been improperly given to this fish..; for being broad and long like a quilt, it wraps its fins round a man, or any other animal,..and immediately squeezes it to death. **1783** Justamond tr. *Raynal's Hist. Indies* IV. 180 The manta fish. **1794** Morse *Amer. Geog.* 576 (Mexico.) The fish common to both oceans are, whales, dolphins,..manitis, mantas, porpoises [etc.]. **1829** E. N. Bancroft in *Zool. Jrnl.* IV. 454 The Manta has, I believe, been generally supposed to belong to the Ray family. **1905** D. S. Jordan *Guide to Study of Fishes* I. 448 The devil rays or mantas of the Tropical seas, *Manta* and *Mobula* being the most specialized genera. **1958** *Listener* 14 Aug. 247/2 The huge manta rays..opening their gills to let in the tiny cleaner-fish. **1972** *Islander* (Victoria, B.C.) 9 Apr. 7/1 A pair of manta rays making black silhouettes in the midday sun.

3. = mantelet 2.

1829 W. Irving *Conq. Granada* I. xxix. 264 Seizing their mantas, or portable bulwarks,..they made a gallant assault. **1843** Prescott *Mexico* v. ii. (1864) 280 It was called a manta, and was contrived somewhat on the principle of the mantelets used in the wars of the Middle Ages.

4. In *Mining*: **a.** A sackful or blanketful of mineral. **b.** A mineral placer.

1860 *Eng. & Foreign Mining Gloss.* Span. Terms 109 *Manta*, a blanket, or horse cloth, used to contain ores or tools. **1874** Raymond *Statist. Mines & Mining* 318 They pass through three rich streaks or *mantas*.

mantalet, obs. form of mantelet.

mantayne, obs. form of maintain.

mante, see mant *v.*, mantie; obs. pa. t. moan *v.*

manteane, obs. Sc. form of maintain.

manteau. *Obs.* exc. *Hist.* Forms: *α.* 7–8 **mantoe**, 7–9 **manto**; *β.* 7 **mantou, -ow**, 7–9 **manteau**. [a. F. *manteau*:—L. *mantellum*: see mantle *sb.*]

1. (See quot. 1706.)

α. **1678** Butler *Hud.* iii. i. 700 Jealous piques, Which th' Ancients wisely signify'd By th' yellow mantos of the bride. **1691** *Emilianne's Frauds Rom. Monks* (ed. 3) 408 Womens Cloaths; as Mantoe's, Stays and Petticoats. **1706** Phillips (ed. Kersey), *Mantoe* or *Mantua Gown*, (Fr.) a loose upper Garment, now generally worn by Women, instead of a straight-body'd Gown. *c* **1720** Dk. Montagu in *Buccleuch MSS.* (Hist. MSS. Comm.) I. 367 The women..with their mantoes stuck out behind. **1729–30** Lady Stanley in *Mrs. Delany's Life & Corr.* (1861) I. 235 Your sister Pendarvis sends you your manto and petticoat to be a bridesmaid.

β. **1671** Shadwell *Humorist* i. 2 A delicate white Mantou. **1687** Miege *Gt. Fr. Dict.* ii, Mantow, a sort of Women's Gown. **1690** Evelyn *Mundus Muliebris* 2 Three Manteaus, nor can Madam less Provision have for due undress. **1702** Addison *Dial. Medals* (1727) 17 An Antiquary will scorn to mention..a petticoat or a manteau. **1793** *Residence in France* (1797) I. 291 The ladies, equipped only in a short manteau and petticoat. **1816** Scott *Old Mort.* ix, Tell my gentlewoman to bring my black scarf and manteau.

b. *attrib.*, as ***manteau girdle, gown.***

1682 *True Protest. Mercury* No. 162. 2/2 Lost a Flowerd silk Manto Gown. **1690** Evelyn *Mundus Muliebris* 3 A Manteau Girdle.

‖**2.** *transf.* The plumage of a falcon.

1852 R. F. Burton *Falconry in Valley of Indus* vii. 74 Grease of all kinds injures the *manteau*. [*foot-note*] Coat or plumage.

Hence **manteau'd** *a.*, dressed in a manteau.

1788 'A. Pasquin' *Childr. Thespis* (1792) 43 Her vests mend her frame, as the harp tunes the wind; She is manteau'd fallacious before and behind.

†**manteau-maker.** *Obs.* (superseded by the incorrect mantua-maker). [See manteau.] One who makes women's robes; a dressmaker.

1699 Luttrell *Brief Rel.* (1857) IV. 551 Mrs. Potter, the manteau maker,..is still in custody of a messenger. **1702** Farquhar *Twin Rivals* iv. i. (1703) 45 One of 'em is a Manto-maker. **1795** *Gentl. Mag.* LXV. ii. 979 A man of distinguished abilities as a milliner and manteau-maker.

‖**manteca** (man'teka). *Obs.* Also 7 **manteque, mantegue**, 8 **mantecu**. [Sp. *manteca* (= Pg. *manteiga*, of obscure origin) butter, also applied to other fatty substances. Cf. F. *mantèque* (Buffon), also *mantègue* (corruptly *mantègne*).] A kind of butter or substitute for butter.

The Sp. *manteca de puerco* (hog's lard) occurs in R. Hawkins *Voy. S. Sea* (1593–1622).

1660 F. Brooke tr. *Le Blanc's Trav.* 8 They brought in..their melted butter called Manteque. **1687** A. Lovell tr. *Thevenot's Trav.* i. 165 A great deal of Mantegue or a kind of Butter comes running out at the holes. **1743** Pococke *Descr. East* I. 186 *note*, They carry in them [vases] the butter called Mantecu. **1748** *Earthquake of Peru* iii. 271 The Use of what they call Manteca, being Hogs-lard and Beef-suet, which they use instead of Butter.

†**man'teel.** *Obs.* Forms: 5 **manteill**, (7–8 *Dicts.* **mantile**), 8 **manteil, -teel(e.** [app. a. F. *mantille*, ad. Sp. *mantilla*: see mantilla.]

1. A soldier's cloak or mantle.

c **1470** Henry *Wallace* xi. 242 A gret manteill about his hand can ta, And his gud suerd. [**1656** Blount *Glossogr.*, *Mantile* or *Mantle*, a kind of cloak which Souldiers in times past used in Winter.]

2. Some kind of cape or mantle worn by ladies.

1733 Mrs. Delany in *Life & Corr.* (1861) I. 424, I am sick of manteils, and I have two by me. **1752** Fielding *Covent Gard. Jrnl.* 9 May, Ladies..covered their lovely necks with a cloak; this, being routed by the enemy [the vulgar], was exchanged for the manteel. **1786** Burns *Holy Fair* ii, Twa had manteeles o' dolefu' black, But ane wi' lyart lining.

†**mantegar.** *Obs.* Also 8 **manteger, -tyger, -tiger.** [Perh. a use of *mantegre, -tyger*, corrupt form of MANTICORE.] Some kind of baboon.

The descriptions suggest the mandrill, from which however the 18th c. naturalists considered it distinct.

1704 TYSON in *Phil. Trans.* XXV. 1571 The Mantegar is an Animal not described as I know of by any Author. *c* **1714** ARBUTHNOT, etc. *Mem. M. Scriblerus* I. xiv. (1741) 46 The glaring Cat-a-mountain..and the Man-mimicking Manteger. **1755** *Hist. Descr. Tower Lond.* 24 There is likewise a young Man Tyger, a curious Animal of astonishing Strength [etc.]. **1797** *Encycl. Brit.* (ed. 3) X. 544/2 Mantegar, or Man-tiger,..is the tufted ape.

mantegre: see MANTICORE.

mantegue, variant of MANTECA.

manteigne, mantein(e, obs. ff. MAINTAIN.

manteil(l, variant of MANTEEL *Obs.*

mantel (ˈmænt(ə)l), *sb.* Forms: 5 **mayntelle, mantelle,** 5-6 **mantell,** 6 **mantalle,** *Sc.* **mantil(l,** 6-9 **mantle,** 7 **mandle,** 6- **mantel.** [Variant of MANTLE *sb.*; the senses of both Eng. words are adopted from the F. *manteau.*]

†**1.** = MANTELET 2 a. *Obs.*

1489 CAXTON *Faytes of A.* II. xiv. 118 Mayntelles and barbakanes of tymbre shal be made fast to the batelmentes. *Ibid.* xxii. 135 Six grete mantelles for the said six grete gonnes. **1497** *Naval Acc. Hen. VII* (1896) 99 Barres of iren for the grete mantell. **1523** LD. BERNERS *Froiss.* I. cclxxxviii. 431 The Englysshmen ordayned mantels and other instrumentes of warr, wherby to aproche nere to the walles. *Ibid.* cccxxxii. 519 They of the hoost caused to be made dyuers mantels of assaute. **1549** *Compl. Scot.* vi. 41 Paueis veil the top vitht pauesis and mantillis. **1566** W. WREN *Voy. Fenner* in *Hakluyt's Voy.* (1599) II. II. 59 We sent to land a boate or skiffe wherein were eight persons,..and they caried with them two harquebusses, two targets and a mantell.

2. in *Comb.* †**mantel-wall** *Sc.*, a rampart, breastwork, or parapet.

1513 DOUGLAS *Æneis* IX. iii. 159 Quhat meyn thai be this myddill mantill wall? *Ibid.* XII. Prol. 24 The twinkling stremowris of the orient..Bet doun the skyis clowdy mantill wall. **1609** *Chron. Perth* (Maitland Club) 12 The great wind blew down the stanes of the mantil wall of the kirk.

3. a. The piece of timber or stone supporting the masonry above a fireplace; = MANTEL-TREE 1. ? *Obs.*

1519 *Churchw. Acc. St. Giles, Reading* (ed. Nash) 6 For ij° mantells for ij° chymneys ijs. viijd. **1561** in G. Roberts *Soc. Hist. South. Eng.* (1856) 359 It was commanded to John Somer to amend his mantalle, payne of v shillings. **1734** *Builder's Dict.* II, *Mantle*..is the lower Part of the Chimney, or that Part laid across the Jambs. **1774** *Act 14 Geo. III*, c. 78 §45 The Back of every Chimney to be built ..at least thirteen Inches thick from the Hearth, to the Height of twelve Inches above the Mantle. **1824** T. TREDGOLD *Warm. Publ. Build.* (ed. 2) 236 A high mantle has some advantage in producing a more effectual ventilation.

b. = MANTELPIECE 1.

1532 in J. Bayley *Tower Lond.* (1821) I. App. 31 Firste, a new worke wrought in the kynges dynyng chambre, a mantell of waynscot wrought wᵗ antyk sett over the chymney there. **1663** GERBIER *Counsel* 22 The Chimney-mantles ought to be all of Stone or Marble. **1890** H. FREDERIC *Lawton Girl* vi. 41 The massive carved side-board and the ponderous mantel.

c. = MANTELSHELF.

1742 *Phil. Trans.* XLII. 75 When it is in the Sun in Summer, and upon the Mantle of the Chimney in Winter.. it becomes perfect Soap in Four or Five Days. **1865** MRS. WHITNEY *Gayworthys* I. 275 Rebecca set the light upon the mantel, and took her to the bedside.

d. *attrib.*, as ***mantel-clock, -glass, -mirror***; **mantel-place** *southern U.S.* = MANTELPIECE; also MANTEL-BOARD, -PIECE, -SHELF, -TREE.

1870 W. M. BAKER *New Timothy* 25 The mantel-clock strikes six sharp insisting blows as she exclaims. **1884** F. J. BRITTEN *Watch & Clockm.* 193 It occasionally happens in mantel clocks that..the pendulum is just too long for the case. **1963** *Times* 18 May 6/5 Fabre paid £1,200 for a bronze and ormolu elephant mantel clock, also in the Caffieri manner. **1892** B. HINTON *Lord's Return* 190 Adjusting his necktie at the mantel-glass. **1865** MRS. STOWE *House & Home Papers* 86 Now come the great mantel mirrors for four hundred [dollars] more. **1842** W. G. SIMMS *Last Wager* in *Gift 1843* (Philadelphia) 286 You have a very singular ornament for your mantle-place.

†ˈ**mantel,** *v. Obs.* Also 5 **mantelle,** 7 **mantle.** [f. MANTEL *sb.* Cf. OF. *manteler.*] *trans.* To protect with or as with a mantel.

1475 *Bk. Noblesse* (Roxb.) 20 Mantelle, fortifie, and make yow strong ayenst the power of youre said adversaries of Fraunce. **1612** *Proc. Virginia* in *Capt. Smith's Wks.* (Arb.) 117 They conducted vs to their pallizadoed towne, mantelled with the barkes of trees. **1624** WOTTON *Archit.* II. 108 The Italians applie it [plastic] to the manteling of Chimneys, with great Figures. **1682** WHELER *Journ. Greece* I. 8 Its Bastions..are well..mantled with hewen stone.

mantel, obs. form of MANTLE.

ˈ**mantel-board.** A wide shelf of wood, usually draped, fixed upon the mantelshelf.

1885 *Instr. Census Clerks* 1881, 53 Mantel Board Maker. **1887** D. C. MURRAY *Old Blazer's Hero* viii. 127 Dropping his elbows noiselessly on the mantel-board.

mantelet, mantlet (ˈmæntlɪt). Forms: 5 **mauntolet, mantilett,** 5-6 **mantilet,** 6 **mantellet(t,** 8 **mantalet,** 9 **mantellette,** 6, 8-9 **mantlet,** 4- **mantelet.** [a. OF. *mantelet*, dim. of *mantel* (F. *manteau*) MANTLE, MANTEL *sbs.* Cf. It. *mantelletto.*]

1. A kind of short, loose, sleeveless cape, cloak, or mantle covering the shoulders.

c **1386** CHAUCER *Knt.'s T.* 1305 A Mantelet vp on his shulder hangynge Bretful of Rubies reede. **1440** *Test. Ebor.* (Surtees) II. 76 Item lego..Johannæ Hawnserd, sorori meæ, unam mantilet cum quatuos barbys et duobus forhedes. Katerinæ Thornyff unam mantilett. **1740** tr. *De Mouhy's Fort. Country Maid* (1741) I. 224 She had..a coarse red Mantelet over her Shoulders, adorned with Shells. **1772-84** *Cook's Voy.* (1790) IV. 1375 Mantalets composed of feathers, so..beautifully arranged, as even our English ladies would not disdain to wear. **1844** THACKERAY *Little Trav.* Wks. (Biogr. ed.) VI. 275 A lady in a little lace mantelet. **1887** *Daily News* 8 July 7/6 Coloured Velvet and Jet Mantelets.

†**b.** = MANTELLETTA. *Obs.*

1602 SEGAR *Hon. Mil. & Civ.* II. xvii. 89 The Soueraigne, Cardinals, Prelats, Commanders, and Officers, by Order.. wearing Mantels and Mantelets..goe to the Church to heare the Euensong. **1706** PHILLIPS (ed. Kersey), *Mantelet*, a short Purple Mantle which the Bishops of France wear over their Rochet upon some Occasions.

†**c.** A woollen covering for a horse. *Obs.*

a **1440** *Sir Degrev.* 1182 Greyth myn hors on hore gere And lok that thei be gay; That they be trapped a get In topteler and mauntolet. *a* **1548** HALL *Chron., Hen. VIII* 76 The whiche horse was Trapped in a Mantellet.

2. *Mil.* **a.** A movable shelter used to cover the approach of men-at-arms when besieging a fortified place. (Cf. MANTEL *sb.* 1.) *Obs.* exc. *Hist.*

1524 in Hakluyt *Voy.* (1599) II. I. 82 Beside the sayd mantellets that shot against the wall of England and Spaine with great bombards, were two mantellets in an hie place.. in the which were certaine double gunnes [etc.]. **1603** *North's Plutarch, Miltiades* (1612) 1230 Then hauing set vp his Gabions and Mantelets, he came neare the wals. **1731** J. GRAY *Gunnery* Pref. 10 The most considerable..answer nearly to our Penthouses, Mantlets, Galleries, and Blinds. **1819** SCOTT *Ivanhoe* xxvii, They bring forward mantelets and pavisses, and the archers muster on the skirts of the wood. **1885** BIBLE (R.V.) *Nahum* ii. 5 They make haste to the wall thereof and the mantelet is prepared. **1894** F. D. SWIFT *Jas. I of Aragon* 275 Another instrument common in siege operations of this period, was the Mantlet.

b. A screen or curtain, now usually of rope, to protect men working a gun from a enemy's bullets; with fortress guns mounted in casemates, serving also to prevent the smoke from the gun when fired from entering the casemate.

1859 *Gentl. Mag.* I. 123 The Russians returned to the use of the old cannon mantlet in the Crimean war. **1879** NUGENT in *Encycl. Brit.* IX. 453 'Mantlets'..are now invariably made of this material [*sc.* rope].

c. A bullet-proof shelter from which firing results can be observed and signalled.

1874 *Proc. Nat. Rifle Assoc.* 94 The markers..must retire into their mantelets as soon as the 1st gun..is discharged. **1880** *Daily Tel.* 9 Dec., Officers, in telegraphic communication with the firing-points, will be posted in mantlets before the targets.

‖ˈ**manteline.** *rare.* [F. *manteline* a mantle.] A short mantle or cape.

1843 LYTTON *Last Bar.* I. vi, In these times, the scholar must creep under the knight's manteline.

‖**mantelletta** (mæntɪˈlɛtə). Pl. **mantellette.** [It. *mantelletta*, dim. of *mantello* MANTLE *sb.* Cf. med.L. *mantelletum.*] (See quot. 1897.)

1853 DALE tr. *Baldeschi's Ceremonial* 6 These latter should wear stoles of the colour of the day; and if Prelates the mozetta, or mantelletta. **1897** *Cath. Dict.* (ed. 5), *Mantelletta*, a vestment made of silk or woollen stuff, open but fastened in front, reaching almost to the knees... It is worn by cardinals, bishops, abbots, and the 'prelati' of the Roman Court [etc.]... The mantellette of cardinals are of three colours.

ˈ**mantelpiece.** [f. MANTEL *sb.* + PIECE *sb.*]

1. The MANTEL (3 a) with its supports; the ornamental structure of wood, marble, etc., above and around a fireplace. Also *rarely* = MANTEL 3 a.

1686 *Lond. Gaz.* No. 2197/4 A New Art or Invention of Making, Marbling, Veining, and Finishing of Mantle-pieces for Chimneys. **1851** TURNER *Dom. Archit.* I. 14 At Coningsburgh castle the opening of the chimney is square, with shafts in the jambs, and what is called a straight arch, that is, the mantel-piece is formed of several stones joggled together.

2. = MANTELSHELF. Also *attrib.*

1827 G. BEAUCLERK *Journ. Marocco* viii. 92 A French mantle-piece clock. **1860** *All Year Round* 572 The looking-glass over the mantelpiece. **1892** ZANGWILL *Childr. Ghetto* I. 46 The mantelpiece mirror was bordered with yellow scalloped paper.

ˈ**mantelshelf.** [f. MANTEL *sb.* + SHELF.] That projecting part of a mantelpiece which serves as a shelf. Also *transf.* (esp. in *Mountaineering*).

1828-32 in WEBSTER. **1833** LOUDON *Encycl. Cottage Archit.* 1073. **1838** DICKENS *O. Twist* viii, A frying-pan.. which was secured to the mantelshelf by a string. **1888** 'BERNARD' *Fr. World to Cloister* i. 9 He stood up, leaning against the mantelshelf.

transf. **1897** O. G. JONES *Rock-climbing* 263 Close up against the wall that blocked the head of the gully, a long stride was to be taken across to a narrow 'mantelshelf' on the other side. **1941** C. F. KIRKUS *Let's Go Climbing!* iv. 60 Half-way up is a ledge..with no holds for some distance above... This is known as a mantelshelf. **1955** M. E. B. BANKS *Commando Climber* xii. 230 A little higher he was stopped by a rock wall capped by an icy mantelshelf. **1963** 'G. CARR' *Lewker in Norway* viii. 161 A firm right foothold, a smooth 'mantelshelf' movement, and he was up and standing on the rock bridge. **1968** P. CREW *Encycl. Dict. Mountaineering* 81 The mantelshelf technique has three main steps as follows: a pull up to raise the body as high as possible; changing one arm, and then the other, into a press-up position; cocking one leg up onto the ledge and slowly standing up.

ˈ**mantel-tree.** [f. MANTEL *sb.* + TREE.]

1. A beam across the opening of a fireplace, serving as a lintel to support the masonry above (Parker, 1850). In later use, a stone or arch serving the same purpose.

1482 *Nottingham Rec.* II. 332 Pro uno mantiltr', ad valentiam ijs. **1486** *Ibid.* III. 256 For enbowyng of a mantell' tree. **1583** FULKE *Defence* iii. 122 He might shewe vs the mantilltree of a chimney, and a brasse pot hanging ouer the fire. **1606** *Wily Beguiled* K 2, Old Grandsir Thickskin, you that sit there as melancholy as a mantletree. **1649** R. HODGES *Plain. Direct.* 14 Hee hang'd his mantle upon the mantil tree of the chimney. **1703** MOXON *Mech. Exerc.* 273 Semi-Oval Arches..are sometimes made..over Kitchin-Chimnies, instead of Mantle-trees. **1789** P. SMYTH tr. *Aldrich's Archit.* (1818) 121 The apertures are limited by two jambs, and the mantle-tree. **1811** *Self Instructor* 139 The chimney.. upright over the mantle tree.

2. = MANTELPIECE 1, 2.

1634 BRERETON *Trav.* (Chetham Soc.) 7 All the walls most richly gilded,..rich marble mantle-tree. **1641** HINDE *J. Bruen* 116, I comming once into his chamber and finding over the Mantletree a paire of new Cards. **1781** COWPER *Charity* 460 No charity but alms aught values she, Except in porcelain on her mantel-tree. **1902** E. PHILPOTTS *River* 13 For lack of mantel-tree Nicholas had nailed up a shelf to hold certain heirlooms.

manteme, mantene, obs. forms of MAINTAIN.

manteque, variant of MANTECA.

mantevil. *Obs.* exc. *Hist.* Also 9 corruptly **mandevil(l)e.** [Perh. a mistake for some form of MANTEEL.] A loose coat formerly worn by soldiers and menservants. (Cf. MANDILION.)

1688 R. HOLME *Armoury* III. 96/2 A Mandilion, or Madilion, or of old a Mantevil. **1834** PLANCHÉ *Brit. Costume* 267 Coats and jerkins,..some loose, which they called mandillians. [*Note*] Mandevilles, which Randal Holmes describes as a loose hanging garment. **1860** FAIRHOLT *Costume* Gloss. (ed. 2) 526 *Mandevile*, or *Mandilion.*

manteym(e, manteyn(e, obs. ff. MAINTAIN.

mantic (ˈmæntɪk), *sb. rare*⁻¹. [ad. Gr. μαντική (*sc.* τέχνη art), fem. of μαντικός: see next.] The art or science of divination.

[**1727** BAILEY vol. II, *Mantice*, divination or foretelling things to come.] **1891** MRS. COLYER FERGUSSON tr. *De La Saussaye's Man. Sci. Relig.* xvi. 137 The history of religion is full of mantic [rendering G. *die Mantik*].

mantic (ˈmæntɪk), *a.* [ad. Gr. μαντικός, f. μάντις prophet, diviner, lit. one affected by divine madness, f. root *man-*: see MANIA.] Pertaining to divination or prophecy.

1850 MRS. BROWNING *Prometh. Bound* 553, I fixed the various rules of mantic art. **1858** TRENCH *Synon. N.T.* vi. (1876) 21 Revelation knows nothing of this mantic fury.

So ˈ**mantical** *a.* = MANTIC; ˈ**mantically** *adv.*; ˈ**manticism,** the practice of divination.

1588 J. HARVEY *Disc. Probl.* 26 Any manticall, or magicall ..hypothesis whatsoeuer. **1652** GAULE *Magastrom.* To Astronomers, This disquisition..abhors..to end with any thing that is manticall. **1861** MCCAUL *Aids to Faith* iii. 81 It is useless..to go to the manticism of the heathen to get light as to the nature of Hebrew prophecy. **1903** SELWYN in *Expositor* Apr. 288 There is not a scrap of evidence to show that the bishops of Asia..accused the Montanists of being mantically inclined.

-mantic, repr. Gr. μαντικός (see prec.) in combination, is the ending of adjs. related to sbs. in -MANCY, as in *geomantic*, pertaining to geomancy, *hydromantic*, pertaining to hydromancy, etc.

manticore (ˈmæntɪkɔə(r)). *Obs.* exc. *Hist.* Also 4, 7-9 **mantichora,** 5 **mantissera,** 5, 7-9 **manticora,** 6 **mantycor(e,** 7 **martichore,** 7-8 **marticora;** β. (sense 2) 7 **mantegre,** 7-8 **mantyger,** 8-9 **montegre,** 9 **mantiger.** [ad. L. *manticora*, repr. Gr. μαντιχώρας, a corrupt reading in Aristotle *Hist. Anim.* (quoting Ctesias), where the better MSS. have μαρτιχόρας (another var. is μαρτιοχώρας), app. an OPersian word for 'man-eater', f. *martiya-* man (mod.Pers. *mard*) + root *xᵛar-* (Zend *xᵛaraiti*, mod.Pers. *xurden*) to eat.]

1. A fabulous monster having the body of a lion, the head of a man, porcupine's quills, and the tail or sting of a scorpion. (Cf. MANTEGAR, MANTIGER.)

13.. *K. Alis.* 7094 Ther he fond addren, and Monecores, And a feolle worm, Cales, and Manticores. **1398** TREVISA *Barth. De P.R.* XVIII. i. (1495) 740 Mantichora. **1481** CAXTON *Myrr.* e vij b, Another maner of bestes ther is in ynde that ben callyd manticora. **1494** *Will of Eburton* (Somerset Ho.), A standing cuppe of syluer with a couering with a straunge best called a mantissera enprinted in the

botome. *a* **1529** SKELTON *P. Sparowe* 294 The mantycors of the montaynes Myght fede them on thy braynes. **1601** HOLLAND *Pliny* I. 206. **1607** G. WILKINS *Miseries Enforced Marr.* I 2 b, Mantichoras, monstrous beastes, enemies to mankinde, that ha double rowes of teeth in their mouthes. **1646** HOWELL *Lewis XIII* 174 The Beast Marticora which is of a red colour, and hath the head of a man lancing out sharpe prickles from behind. **1656** BLOUNT *Glossogr.*, *Martichore.* **1863** KINGSLEY *Water Bab.* 166 Unicorns, fire-drakes, manticoras.

2. *Her.* A monster represented with the body of a beast of prey, the head of a man with spiral or curved horns, and sometimes the feet of a dragon.

c **1600** in Baring-Gould & Twigge *West. Armory* (1898) 89 *Radforde*: Sa: 3 mantygers arg. **1610** GUILLIM *Heraldry* III. xxv. (1611) 183 Mantegres, Satyrs, Monkfishes, . . and whatsoeuer other double shaped animall [etc.]. **1766** PORNY *Her.* (1777) 196 The Montegre. **1780** EDMONDSON *Heraldry* II. Gloss., *Man-tyger*, or *Manticora.* **1894** PARKER *Gloss. Her.* 519 The Mantiger or Lampago, called by writers Montegre and Manticora, also occurs.

† **man'ticulate**, *v. Obs. rare*⁻⁰. [f. ppl. stem of L. *manticulāri* to steal, act cunningly, f. *manticula* bag, purse.] (See quot.)

1656 BLOUNT *Glossogr.*, *Manticulate*, to do a thing closly, as to pick a purse. **1676** in COLES.

† **manticu'lation.** *Obs. rare*⁻⁰. [ad. L. *manticulātion-em*, f. *manticulārī*: see prec.] (See quot.)

1623 COCKERAM, *Manticulation*, deceitfull conueyance.

mantid ('mæntɪd). *Ent.* [f. MANTIS: see -ID³.] A mantis.

1895 *Athenæum* 30 Mar. 412/2 A species of a mantid, *Pseudocreobotra wahlbergi*, . . from . . Natal.

† **mantie, mante.** *Sc.* [? Shortened a. F. *démenti*, or perh. a. OF. *mente* lie.] = LIE *sb.*¹ 2 b.

a **1578** LINDESAY (Pitscottie) *Chron. Scot.* (S.T.S.) II. 48 The cardinall ansuerit furieouslie againe and gif the lie and mante [*MS. I.* mantie].

man-tiger. **a.** A man resembling a tiger in ferocity. **b.** A 'lycanthrope' who assumes the form of a tiger.

a **1652** BROME *Queene's Exchange* II. iii. Wks. 1873 III. 494 We have hitherto Pass'd by these man-Tygers, these wolvish Outlaws safely. **1871** TYLOR *Prim. Cult.* (1873) I. 102 The Lavas of Birma, supposed to be the broken-down remains of a cultured race, and dreaded as man-tigers. **1872** *Nature* 29 Feb. 343/1 The analogous belief in man-hyenas, man-tigers, &c. **1941** J. MASEFIELD *Gautama* 35 Man-tigers dragged the white form nearer As victim on that stone to lie.

mantiger: see MANTEGAR, MANTICORE.

mantil(l, obs. f. MANTEL, MANTLE, MANTEEL.

mantile, variant of MANTEEL *Obs.*

mantilet(t, obs. form of MANTELET.

mantilla (mæn'tɪlə). Also 9 **mantillo.** [a. Sp. *mantilla*, dim. of *manta*: see MANTLE *sb.*]

1. A large veil worn over a woman's head, and covering the shoulders.

1717 tr. *Frezier's Voy.* 259 They use that they call *Mantilla* for an Undress, to appear the more modest; and it is a Sort of Cloak, or Mantle, round at the Bottom, of a dark Colour, edg'd with Black Taffety. **1770** *Gentl. Mag.* XL. 530 A muslin or cambric veil called a *mantilla*, which hides the head and the upper part of their bodies. **1816** LADY MORGAN *F. Macarthy* (1819) III. iii. 126 Lady Clancare . . had exchanged her coarse unbecoming costume of the morning for a black Spanish dress and mantillo. **1882** DE WINDT *Equator* 129 The graceful mantilla is gradually but surely giving way to the Parisian bonnet.

attrib. **1884** CROSS *Life Geo. Eliot* III. 297 The abundant hair . . was draped with lace, arranged mantilla-fashion.

2. A small cape or mantle.

1859 *Edin. Rev.* CIX. 310 A smart bonnet, a silk dress, a mantilla, and a parasol for Sundays. **1860** MOTLEY *Netherl.* II. xvi. 263 Sir Francis Vere—conspicuous in the throng, in his red mantilla.

3. A deep draping of lace attached to the edge of a corsage.

1835 *Court Mag.* VI. p. ix/2 The *corsage* . . is trimmed with a mantilla, or else in the pelerine style, with blond lace.

Hence **mantilla'd** *a.*, clad in a mantilla.

1853 G. J. CAYLEY *Las Alforjas* I. 49 The stream of cloaked and mantilla'd figures passing through the Calle de Velasquez.

mantine, obs. Sc. form of MAINTAIN.

Mantinean (mæntɪ'ni:ən), *sb.* and *a.* Also 6 **Mantynyan**, 9 **Mantineian.** [f. Gr. *Μαντίνεια*, L. *Mantinea* Mantinea.] **A.** *sb.* A native or inhabitant of the ancient city of Mantinea in Arcadia. **B.** *adj.* Of or pertaining to Mantinea or its inhabitants.

1550 T. NICOLLS tr. *Thucydides' Hystory* [*Peloponnesian War*] v. fol. 145 That the Argiues shulde make allyance wyth the Lacedemonyans, forsakinge the same, whyche they had concluded wyth the Athenyans, the Mantynyans and the Elyans. **1629** HOBBES tr. *Thucydides' Peloponnesian War* v. 335 A thousand Athenians . . being come after the Battell to ayde the Mantineans. **1753** W. SMITH tr. *Thucydides Hist. Peloponnesian War* II. v. 180 Three thousand heavy-armed Eléans, as auxiliaries to the Mantinéans, came up. **1808** W. MITFORD *Hist. Greece* II. xvii. 263 The Tegeans, and all those other Arcadians who had not, with the Mantineians, renounced the Lacedæmonian alliance. **1846** G. GROTE *Hist. Greece* II. II. viii. 586 Sparta . . drove back the Mantineians within their own limits. **1877** L. H. MORGAN *Anc. Society* II. xiv. 349 Bachofen has collected and discussed the evidence of female authority . . among the . . Mantineans. **1951** J. B. BURY *Hist. Greece* (ed. 3) 327 The Mantineans . . were never ready to join hands with their Tegeate neighbours. *Ibid.*, The new synoecism of the Mantinean villages. **1968** V. EHRENBERG *From Solon to Socrates* vii. 284 Sparta . . made . . an expedition to free the Parrhasians in Arcadia from Mantinean rule. **1970** *Oxf. Classical Dict.* (ed. 2) 644/2 After the peace of 387 the Spartans obliged the Mantineans to dismantle their walls and live in villages.

† **mantiniment.** *Obs.* [ad. Sp. *mantenimiento* = MAINTAINMENT.] Maintenance.

1588 PARKE tr. *Mendoza's Hist. China* 7 They doo sowe rice, which is a common victuall or mantiniment vnto all people of the kingdome.

mantion, obs. form of MANSION.

mantionell, obs. form of MANCHINEEL.

‖ **mantis** ('mæntɪs). *Ent.* [mod.L., a. Gr. *μάντις* prophet, diviner (also, some insect): see MANTIC *a.*] An orthopterous insect of the genus *Mantis* or family *Mantidæ*; esp. the Praying Mantis, *M. religiosa*, which holds its forelegs in a position suggesting hands folded in prayer.

1658 J. R. tr. *Moffett's Theat. Insects* 982, I have seen only three kinds [of the lesser Locusts] . . they are called *Mantes*, foretellers. *Ibid.* 983 Of this Italian Mantis . . Rondeletius makes mention. **1703** DAMPIER *Voy.* (1729) III. 427 The green Mantiss . . like a Locust. **1706** PHILLIPS (ed. Kersey), *Mantis*, . . an Insect call'd The praying Locust. **1802** BINGLEY *Anim. Biog.* (1813) III. 156 The Orator Mantis. **1870** MATEER *Travancore* (1871) 90 Locusts, grass-hoppers, mantises, etc. abound. **1895** E. W. GOSSE *Crit. Kit-Kats* 290 That quaint insect, the praying mantis.

b. *attrib.*, as **mantis-crab**, **-shrimp**, a stomatopodous crustacean, *Squilla mantis* and other species.

1850 A. WHITE *List Crustacea Brit. Mus.* 46 *Squilla Desmarestii*, The Mantis Crab. **1871** T. R. JONES *Anim. Kingd.* (ed. 4) 449 The *Squilla mantis* or Mantis-Shrimp. **1884** G. B. GOODE, etc. *Nat. Hist. Usef. Aquatic Anim.* I. 823 The Mantis Shrimp, or Sea Mantis—*Squilla empusa*, Say.

mantissa (mæn'tɪsə). [a. L. *mantissa*, *mantīsa* makeweight; said to be of Etruscan origin.]

† **1.** An addition of comparatively small importance, esp. to a literary effort or discourse. *Obs.*

1641 MAISTERTON *Serm.* 20 Trifles, which . . should . . as a mantissa or an overplus be cast in at their bargain. **1642** CUDWORTH *Lord's Supper* i. (1676) 5 It will not be now amiss, if we add, as a Mantissa to that discourse, something of the Custom of the Heathens. **1671** *True Nonconf.* 5 Spurning at the righteousnes of Jesus Christ, and aspiring to adde a Mantissa, an addition of your own, to his sole purchase.

2. *Math.* The decimal part of a logarithm.

c **1865** *Circ. Sci.* I. 519/1 The decimal part of a logarithm is called the *mantissa*: the whole number is called the *characteristic*.

mantissera, obs. form of MANTICORE.

† **mantist.** *Obs.* [f. Gr. *μάντις* prophet + -IST.] A seer, prophet.

1588 J. HARVEY *Disc. Probl.* I. 84 Without which felicitie, neither Persian Magician . . nor Athenian Mantist . . shall euer passe with me for a prophet.

mantistic (mæn'tɪstɪk), *a.* [f. Gr. *μάντις* (cf. prec.) + -ISTIC.] Pertaining to divination or prophecy; prophetic, mantic.

1876 A. WILDER *Knight's Symbolical Lang. Anc. Art & Mythol.* 141 An idea of peculiar spiritual or mantistic qualities supposed to be peculiar to the female sex.

mantle ('mænt(ə)l), *sb.* Forms: 1-5 **mentel**, 2-7 **mantel**, 3-6 **mantil**, 4 **mantal**, **-tyle**, **mentil(e**, 4-5 **mantyl**, 4-6 **mantell**, **mantill**, 5 **mantyll(e**, **mauntil**, 5-6 **mantelle**, 6 **mauntelle**, **mantyll**, 7 **mandle**, 3, 5- **mantle.** See also MANTEAU, MANTUA. [Introduced from two sources. (1) OE. *męntel* masc.:—prehistoric *mantilo-z, ad. (after the native suffix *-ilo-*: see -EL) L. *mantellum*, *mantēlum* cloak, whence also OFris. *mentel*, OHG. *mantal*, *-dal* (MHG. *mantel*, *mandel*, mod.G. *mantel*), ON. *mǫttull* (OSw. *mantol*, *mantul*, mod.Sw., Da. *mantel*), MIrish *matal*. (2) In the 12th c. the word was taken up again in the OFr. form *mantel* (mod.F. *manteau*: see MANTEAU); cf. Pr. *mantel* cloak, It. *mantello* cloak. A special group of senses taken from the Fr. is now distinguished by the spelling MANTEL.

According to most philologists, the L. *mantellum* cloak is more correctly written *mantēlum*, and is etymologically identical with *mantēlum*, *mantēlium*, *mantīlium*, *mantēle*, *mantīle* table-cloth, towel. (Cf. Sp. *manteles* pl., table-linen; also MANTEEL.) On this supposition, the word must have been mistaken for a dim., and so have given rise by back-formation to the late L. *mantum* (7th c.), **manta*, whence Sp., Pg., It. *manto*, *manta*, F. *mante*, and the diminutives Sp. *mantilla* (see MANTILLA), Pg. *mantilha*, It. *mantiglia*.]

1. a. A loose sleeveless cloak of varying length.

The name was applied indifferently to the outer covering of men, women, and children, and at times acquired a specific application to one garment or another. Now its use is restricted to a cloak of silk or fine cloth worn by ladies; to the robe of state worn by kings, princes, and other persons of exalted and defined station; and to an infant's outer robe.

c **897** K. ÆLFRED *Gregory's Past. C.* xxviii. 197 He . . coerfarf his mentles ænne læppan. *a* **1000** *Ags. Voc.* in Wr.-Wülcker 210/26 *Colobium*, . . mentel. *c* **1200** *Trin. Coll. Hom.* 163 þe meshakele of medeme fustane and hire mentel grene oðer burnet. *c* **1200** *Vices & Virtues* 127 Se þe benimð ðe þine kiertel, ȝif him þine mantel. *c* **1205** LAY. 14755 He nom ænne spere-scæft . . & dude a þene ænde ænne mantel hende. *c* **1250** *Gen. & Ex.* 2033 Ðis mentel ic wið-held for-ði, To tawnen [ðe] ðe soðe her-bi. *a* **1300** *Cursor M.* 16619 þai clede him wit a mantel rede. *c* **1380** *Sir Ferumb.* 1242 Vnder hur mantel sche hidde þe staf. *c* **1420** LYDG. *Assembly of Gods* 267 And next vnto hym . . Sate the goddese Diana, in a mantell fyne. **1505** in *Ld. Treas. Acc. Scotl.* (1901) III. 168 Item, for ane mantill to Johne, fule, of Abirdene, ixs. **1590** SHAKS. *Mids. N.* v. i. 143 As she fled, her mantle she did fall. **1613** —— *Hen. VIII*, v. v. *Stage-direct.*, The Childe richly habited in a Mantle. **1700** DRYDEN *Flower & Leaf* 348 Attired in mantles all the knights were seen. **1735** DYCHE & PARDON *Dict.*, *Mantle*, . . also the upper-most Garment that Nurses wrap up young Infants in before they coat 'em. **1742** YOUNG *Nt. Th.* VI. 302 Fools, indeed, drop the man in their account, And vote the mantle into majesty. **1837** W. IRVING *Capt. Bonneville* II. 196 A mantle about four feet square, formed of strips of rabbit skins. **1904** *Home Notes* 28 July 181 The summer mantle is always a difficult garment to find.

b. Applied (often with qualification ***Irish mantle***) to a kind of blanket or plaid worn until the 17th c. by the rustic Irish, often as their only covering.

c **1470** HENRY *Wallace* I. 217 Ane Ersche mantill it war thi kynd to wer. **1582** *Rates Custome Ho.* F v b, Mantels called Irish mantles the pair. **1596** SPENSER *State Irel.* Wks. (Globe) 631 The out-lawe . . wandring in wast places . . maketh his mantell his howse. **1688** R. HOLME *Armoury* III. 232/2 A Brackin, or Irish Mantle.

c. Used allusively with reference to the descent of Elijah's mantle (2 Kings ii. 13).

1789 BELSHAM *Ess.* I. xii. 229 The sacred mantle which descended from Shakespeare to Milton. **1865** M. ARNOLD *Ess. Crit.* (1875) 183 On Heine . . incomparably the largest portion of Goethe's mantle fell.

† **d.** ***to take the mantle and the ring***: a symbolical act used to express the taking of a vow of chastity (properly, by a widow). *Obs.*

1424 in *E.E. Wills* (1882) 60 If she take þe mantel and þe rynge, and avowe chastite. *c* **1430** LYDG. *Min. Poems* (Percy Soc.) 34 She wol perhappous maken hir avowe, That she wol take the mantle and the ryng. **1574** J. STUDLEY tr. *Bale's Pageant Popes* To Rdr., How can that foundation stand which is made of Popes miters, Cardinals hats, . . rotchets, chrismes, mantel & the ringe [etc.].

† **e.** ***Apostle's mantle***: the kind of mantle which the Apostles were commonly depicted as wearing. *Obs.*

[**1496** *Dives & Paup.* 1st Comm. vii. (W. de W.) b j b, The apostles comonly . . ben paynted with manteles . . and a mantele is a louse clothynge not faste to the bodye but louse.] *a* **1586** SIDNEY *Arcadia* v. (1598) 447 A long cloake after the fashion of that which we call the Apostles mantle.

† **f.** ***white mantles*** (= *ordo alborum mantellorum*: see Du Cange): the Teutonic Order. *Obs.*

c **1500** *Melusine* 20 [He] toke on hym the ordre & Religion of the whit mantelles.

g. *Her.* = MANTLING *vbl. sb.* 2.

1577 HARRISON *England* II. v. (1877) I. 120 The crest with mantels to the helme belonging. **1815** SCOTT *Guy M.* xlii, The mantle upon the panels [of Mr. Glossin's coach] only bore a plain cipher of G. G. **1864** BOUTELL *Her. Hist. & Pop.* xiv. 170 Two or more shields may be grouped together by placing them upon a mantle of crimson velvet.

2. *transf.* and *fig.* Something that enfolds, enwraps or encloses; a covering.

a. of immaterial things.

c **1386** CHAUCER *Merch. T.* 554 Night with his Mantel þat is derk and rude Gan ouersprede the Hemysperie aboute. *c* **1430** LYDG. *Min. Poems* (Percy Soc.) 9 With a mantelle of prudens clad thou be. **1526** *Pilgr. Perf.* (W. de W. 1531) 78 To be hyd vnder yᵉ mantell of mekenes. **1593** SHAKS. *3 Hen. VI*, IV. ii. 22 Well couer'd with the Nights black Mantle. **1659** RUSHW. *Hist. Coll.* I. 607 We have cast a mantle on what was done last Parliament. **1667** MILTON *P.L.* IV. 609 The Moon . . unvaild her peerless light And o're the dark her Silver Mantle threw. **1742** YOUNG *Nt. Th.* IV. 386 How is night's sable mantle labour'd o'er. **1817** CHALMERS *Astron. Disc.* vi. (1852) 132 A mantle of deep obscurity rests on the government of God.

b. of material things. Cf. sense 11.

c **1470** HENRY *Wallace* IX. 23 Fresch Flora hir floury mantill spreid. **1593** DRAYTON *Eclogues* x. 5 The Groves . . In mossie Mantles sadly seem'd to mourne. **1829** SCOTT *Anne of G.* iii, Ruins, over which vegetation had thrown a wild mantle of ivy. **1839** MURCHISON *Silur. Syst.* I. xxxvi. 484 The elliptical shaped mass of the Wren's nest is . . composed of an exterior mantle of pure and impure limestone. **1859** TENNYSON *Merlin & V.* 105 [She] drew The vast and shaggy mantle of his beard Across her neck and bosom to her knee. **1878** HUXLEY *Physiogr.* 189 The ejected matter has fallen . . in conical layers, each forming a mantle thrown irregularly over the preceding layer. **1949** A. G. TANSLEY (*title*) Britain's green mantle. **1962** *Listener* 1 Mar. 376/1 Since . . the upper part of the atmospheric mantle is rich in carbon dioxide, advanced life-forms on the surface of Venus seem unlikely.

† **c.** *spec.* The foam that covers the surface of liquor; the green vegetable coating on standing water. (Cf. MANTLE *v.* 4.) *Obs.*

1601 HOLLAND *Pliny* I. 426 The flower or mantle which the wine casteth up to the top [L. *flos vini*]. **1605** SHAKS. *Lear* III. iv. 139 Poore Tom, that . . drinkes the green Mantle of the standing Poole.

†3. A kind of woollen cloth; a blanket of this material. Chiefly with qualification, e.g. ***Paris mantle***. *Obs.*

[**1410** *Rolls of Parlt.* III. 637/2 Les Worstedes appellez mantelles sengles, demy doubles, & doubles.] **1485** *Waterf. Arch.* in *10th Rep. Hist. MSS. Comm.* App. v. 318 [They] shal syll no manere fryse, nor mantill to no manere foreyne. **1538** ELYOT *Dict., Gausape*, a mantell to caste on a bedde. **1545** *Rates Custome Ho.* c ij b, Paris mantyls the pece. **1582** *Ibid.* A v, Blankets called Paris mantles, red or coloured the peece xiii.*s.* iiii*d.* Blankets called Paris Mantles, white the peece x.*s.*

†4. A measure of quantity of furs, containing from 30 to 100 skins according to size. *Obs.*

'In that work [Halyburton's Ledger] the words *Mantil* and *pane*, though not identical in meaning, are used to denote the same number of skins' (Jam. *Suppl.*).

1473 in *Ld. Treas. Acc. Scotl.* (1877) I. 15 Item coft fra Will Sinclare v mantill of banes to lyne a syde gowne to the King. **1490** *Ibid.* 190 Item..for iij mantillis of fwnȝeis. **1545** *Rates Custome Ho.* b ij b, Foxe skynnes the pane or mantel vi.*s.* viii.*d.*.. Fytcheues the pane or mantell v.*s.* *Ibid.* d j, White kydes the mantell ij.*s.* **1662** *Irish Act 14 & 15 Chas. II*, c. 8 (Rates Inwards), Furs vocat. Foxes the pain or mantle 15*s.*

5. *Mech.* A covering, envelope or shade employed in various mechanical contrivances.

a. A linen or other cloth employed in the swarming of bees. **b.** The leather hood of an open carriage. **c.** (See quot.) **d.** *Founding.* A porous clay matrix. **e.** *Building.* The outer covering of a wall, of a different material from its inner portion (Knight *Dict. Mech.* 1875). **f.** The outer wall and casing of an iron blast furnace, above the hearth (Raymond *Mining Gloss.*). **g.** A tubular wick or hood made by saturating cotton net or other fabric with various oxides, and then removing the fibre by burning, leaving a fragile lace-like tube which, fixed around a burning gas jet, becomes incandescent and emits a brilliant light.

a. 1609 C. BUTLER *Fem. Mon.* v. (1623) M j, Your Hiue being fitted and dressed..you must haue also in a readinesse a Mantle, a Rest, and a Brush. The Mantle may be a sheet, or halfe-sheet, or other linnen cloth, an ell square at the least. **1707** MORTIMER *Husb.* (1721) I. 274 Bring them [the swarms] together, shaking the Bees out of one Hive on the Mantle whereon the other Hive stands.

b. 1794 W. FELTON *Carriages* (1801) I. 197 The mantle, of which there are various shapes, is introduced only as an ornament. When mantles are much furled [etc.].

c. 1875 KNIGHT *Dict. Mech.* 1385/1 *Mantle*, an inclosed chute which leads the water from a fore-bay to a water-wheel.

d. 1875 KNIGHT *Dict. Mech.* 1385/1 The mantle and pattern are baked, the wax runs off [etc.].

g. 1887 *Pall Mall G.* 18 Mar. 12/1 His [Welsbach's] invention consists in fixing around the flame of a special form of gas burner a tubular wick or hood of open cotton fabric, termed the mantle.

6. *Zool.* The external fold of skin which in most molluscs encloses the viscera. Applied also to similar sacs or integuments, as the tunic of an ascidian. (Cf. PALLIUM 3 b and CLOAK 4.)

c **1460** J. RUSSELL *Bk. Nurture* 625 þe whelke looke þat.. his pyntill & gutt almond & mantille, awey þer fro ye pitt. **1828** STARK *Elem. Nat. Hist.* II. 7 Cephalopoda.—Lower part of the body contained in a bag-shaped mantle. **1855** W. S. DALLAS in *Syst. Nat. Hist.* 419 The animals forming one of these colonies [compound *Tunicata*] are usually united by their mantles. **1874** CARPENTER *Ment. Phys.* I. ii. §45 An Ascidian consists..of an external membranous bag or 'mantle', within which is a Muscular envelope.

7. *Anat.* (*a*) The name given by Reichert to the covering portion of the hemisphere-vesicle in the brain. (*b*) The *Panniculus carnosus*, a layer of fatty subcutaneous membrane connecting the true skin with the subjacent tissue.

1885 in *Cassell's Encycl. Dict.* **1889** in *Syd. Soc. Lex.*

8. *Bot.* †**a.** = OCREA (*obs.*). **b.** The growing cortical covering of the periblem, or primary cortex in a growing point.

1671–82 GREW *Anat. Plants* I. iv. §17 (1682) 32 Where none of all the Protections above-named are convenient, then the Membranes of the Leaves by continuation in their first forming..are drawn out into so many Mantles or Veils; as in Docks, Snakeweed, etc. **1884** BOWER & SCOTT *De Bary's Phaner.* 13 Each one of the inner layers..of this mantle has its initial group above the apex of the plerome.

9. *Ornith.* The plumage of the back and folded wings when distinct in colour, etc. from the rest. (So F. *manteau.*)

1840 *Cuvier's Anim. Kingd.* 263 The Barnacle Goose.. with a grey mantle. **1894** R. B. SHARPE *Handbk. Birds Gt. Brit.* I. 90 Sandy rufous, broadly streaked with black, except on the mantle.

10. = MANTLING *vbl. sb.* 5 b. *rare.*

1897 BLACKMORE *Dariel* xii. 111 'Young Earls!' exclaimed Grace, with an innocence so pure that it required a little mantle on her cheeks.

11. One of the three major layers composing the earth, extending from the bottom of the crust (at a depth of about 30 km.) for about 2,900 km. to the boundary with the region beneath (the core), and differing from the crust and the core in physical properties (esp. density) and in chemical composition.

Orig. not distinguished from the crust (see quots. 1940, 1955).

1940 R. A. DALY *Strength & Struct. Earth* i. 1 The earth contains a spheroidal core... The rest of the planet, beneath ocean and atmosphere,..may be distinguished as a whole by the name 'mantle'. *Ibid.* 21 At the depth of about 2,900 kilometers..there is..an interface or rapid transition between the earth's silicate mantle and its 'iron' core. **1955** *Sci. Amer.* Sept. 58/3 All the earth outside the core is called the mantle. The whole of the mantle (apart from the oceans and pockets of magma in volcanic regions) is now known to be essentially solid. **1958** *Nature* 13 Sept. 692/1 The Mohorovičić discontinuity is the boundary between the mantle and the assorted surface rocks of the earth, and it marks a very sharp change in the velocity with which earthquake waves travel. **1962** *Listener* 30 Aug. 304/1 Geophysicists are preparing to drill a hole six kilometres deep through the earth's crust to the mantle. **1969** *New Yorker* 12 Apr. 96/2 If the structure of the moon proves to be similar to the earth's—that is, to have a core, a mantle, and a crust—then geologists may be able to learn a good deal about the structure of the earth. **1973** *Sci. Amer.* Apr. 24/2 Outside the liquid outer core is a mantle of solid rock some 2,900 kilometers thick, which approaches to within 40 kilometers of the earth's surface under the continents and to within 10 kilometers under the oceans. The thin rocky skin surrounding the mantle is the earth's crust. No drill has penetrated the earth's crust deeper than a few kilometers.

12. *attrib.* and *Comb.*: **a.** (sense 1) as ***mantle-button, -cutter, -fold***, † ***lace***, † ***lap, maker, veil, worker***; also ***mantle-making*** sb. (whence by back-formation ***mantle-make*** vb.), ***mantle-like*** adj., ***mantle-wise*** adv.; **mantle-cavity**, the space between the mantle (sense 6) and the body of a mollusc or brachiopod; **mantle fibre** *Cytology*, any spindle fibre which is attached to a chromosome; **mantle-knot**, an ornament in the form of a clasp, composed of a number of precious stones [cf. F. *nœud de diamants*]; †**mantle-wind**, the wind produced by a winnowing-sheet.

1681 in *Thanes of Cawdor* (Spald. Club) 354, 7 duz. *mandle buttounis £2, 2*s.* **1853** *Phil. Trans. R. Soc.* CXLIII. 37 It [*sc.* the heart] lies parallel to the rectum, with the auricle forwards at the base of the *mantle-cavity. **1958** *New Biol.* XXV. 100 The visceral mass (of Cuttlefish) is closed all round by a muscular mantle in such a way that below and to the sides of it there is a cavity—the mantle cavity. **1884** *B'ham Daily Post* 23 Feb. 3/5 *Mantle-cutter. —Wanted a superior Cutter and Fitter. **1896** E. B. WILSON *Cell* ii. 74 The daughter-chromosomes are dragged apart solely by the contractile *mantle-fibres, the central spindle-fibres being non-contractile. **1920** L. DONCASTER *Introd. Study Cytol.* iii. 31 In some animals these fibres are said to be of different thickness, those attached to chromosomes being thicker and called 'mantle fibres' (from their appearance at a later stage). **1966** D. M. KRAMSCH tr. *Grundmann's Gen. Cytol.* iii. 149 We are dealing with a central spindle, on whose exterior aspect the chromosomal spindle fibres are attached as mantle fibres. **1814** SCOTT *Ld. of Isles* II. xi, Whence the brooch of burning gold, That clasps the Chieftain's *mantle-fold. **1896** *Star* 3 Oct. 2/4 A splendid collection of diamonds..is to be sold... The collection includes two *mantle-knots which belonged to the Empress Eugénie. **1480** *Wardr. Acc. Edw. IV* (1830) 136 *Mantell lace of blue silk. *c* **1350** *St. Mary Magd.* 573 in Horstm. *Altengl. Leg.* (1881) 87 It [a child] lurked vnder þe *mantill lapp. **1888** FAGGE & PYE-SMITH *Princ. Med.* (ed. 2) I. 81 An almost fibrous *mantle-like sheath. **1885** C. L. PIRKIS *Lady Lovelace* I. xviii. 268 The invitation of a large Paris firm to go across the Channel and *mantle-make for English customers. **1552** HULOET, *Mantle-maker, *braccarius.* **1903** *Daily Chron.* 24 Feb. 8/5 Girls wanted..to learn dress and *mantle making. **1879** E. WATERTON *Pietas mariana* 89 The *mantle-veil of our Ladye at Chartres. **1688** *Mantle Wind [see MANTLE *v.* 8]. *c* **1530** *Crt. of Love* 243 In sondry clothing, *mantil-wyse full wyde, They were arrayed. **1599** SANDYS *Europæ Spec.* (1632) 225 They weare certeine ornaments of embrodered linnen cast mantle-wise about their shoulders. **1862** G. P. SCROPE *Volcanos* (ed. 2) 170 The greater part..spread themselves mantlewise over its surface and slopes.

b. (sense 2 b) as **mantle-rock** *Geol.*, a superficial deposit.

1895 J. W. POWELL in *Physiogr. Processes* (Nat. Geogr. Monographs I. No. 1. 14) The materials may be called *mantle rocks or superficial deposits.

c. (sense 6) as ***mantle border, fin, flap, fold, fringe, lobe, margin, sac***; **mantle-breathers**, the *Palliobranchiata* or *Brachiopoda*; **mantle-breathing** *a.*, palliobranchiate.

1837 *Penny Cycl.* VII. 96/2 *Mantle-border smooth, but with tufts of hair at the lateral extremities of each plate. **1881** *Cassell's Nat. Hist.* V. 258 De Blainville's subsequently proposed title of '*mantle-breathers'. *Ibid.*, The Brachiopoda, or *mantle-breathing bivalves. **1835–6** TODD *Cycl. Anat.* I. 523/1 Octopods..characterized by the absence of *mantle-fins. **1878** BELL *Gegenbaur's Comp. Anat.* 322 As development goes on, the *mantle-fold becomes less intimately connected with the body. **1855** W. S. DALLAS in *Syst. Nat. Hist.* I. 430 The *mantle lobes are free all round. **1835–6** TODD *Cycl. Anat.* I. 533/1 The *mantle-sac is almost wholly filled with the viscera.

mantle ('mænt(ə)l), *v.* [f. MANTLE *sb.* Cf. OF. *manteler*; also MANTEL *v.*]

1. *trans.* To clothe or wrap in or as in a mantle. Also with *up, over.*

c **1450** *Mirour Saluacioun* 2312 Wharefore thay mantlid hym in swylk coloure for scorne. **1600** FAIRFAX *Tasso* XV. lxi, And her faire lockes..she gan at large vnfold; Which falling long and thicke, and spreading wide, The iuorie soft and white, mantled in gold. **1624** HEYWOOD *Gunaik.* I. 25 Canina lookes to them [infants] in their swathing bands, whilst they are bound up and mantled. **1685** BUNYAN *Pharisee & Publican* 18 He came into the Temple mantled up in his own good things. **1813** SCOTT *Rokeby* I. vi, The buff-coat, in ample fold Mantles his form's gigantic mould. **1881** M. ARNOLD *Westm. Abbey* x, The mourning-stole no more Mantled her form. **1883** *Cath. Dict.* 84/1 The priest, mantled with the veil, makes the sign of the cross.

b. By Milton used of wings. Also *absol.*

1667 MILTON *P. L.* v. 279 The pair [of wings] that clad Each shoulder broad, came mantling o're his brest With regal Ornament. *Ibid.* VII. 439 The Swan with Arched neck Between her white wings mantling proudly, Rowes Her state with Oarie feet.

2. *transf.* and *fig.* To cover or conceal; to obscure; to enfold, embrace, encircle or surround; to envelop; †to 'cloak', palliate (a fault).

c **1400** *Apol. Loll.* 104 þei lifen worldly, & hidun þer vicis wiþ a veyn hiȝt of better lif, & mantel it wiþ a name of ymaginid religioun. *c* **1430** *Pilgr. Lyf Manhode* II. cxxii. (1869) 121 It was maad..for to mantelle with my defautes and consele myne vnthriftes. **1589** GREENE *Menaphon* (Arb.) 68 A frown that was able to mantle the world with an eternall night. **1610** SHAKS. *Temp.* v. i. 67 Their rising sences Begin to chace the ignorant fumes that mantle Their clearer reason. **1650** T. VAUGHAN *Anthroposophia* 15 The Earth was so overcast, and Mantl'd with the Water, that no part thereof was to be seen. **1692** tr. *Sallust* 303 (*Orat. Lepidi*) Prosperity wonderfully obscures and mantles Vice. **1743** J. DAVIDSON *Æneid* VIII. 247 Night..with her dusky wings mantles the sky. **1830** J. G. STRUTT *Sylva Brit.* 60 Its venerable trunk is richly mantled with ivy. **1860** PUSEY *Min. Proph.* 275 A film comes over the eyes, and the brain is, as it were, mantled over. **1890** *Daily News* 31 Jan. 5/5 The mountains thus brilliantly mantled and capped with snow.

absol. **1586** WARNER *Alb. Eng.* II. xi. (1612) 49 The cloudes that mantling ride vpon the racking skie.

3. *Falconry. refl.* and *intr.* To spread first one wing and then the other over the corresponding outstretched leg for exercise, as a perched hawk does. *Obs.* exc. *Hist.*

1486 *Bk. St. Albans* a vj b, She mantellith and not stretchith whan she puttith her leges from hir oon after an other: and hir wynges folow after hier legges then she dooth mantill hir. *c* **1575** *Perf. Bk. Kepinge Sparhawkes* (Harting, 1886) 10 Let her styre, rouse, mantle, or warbile a while. **1596** SPENSER *F.Q.* VI. ii. 32 Ne is ther hauke which mantleth her on pearch,..But I the measure of her flight doe search. **1610** GUILLIM *Heraldry* III. xx. (1660) 223 She [a hawk] mantleth [etc.]. **1852** R. F. BURTON *Falconry Valley Indus* iii. 32 The Shikrah, who was quietly 'mantling' upon a clear branch in a nice sunny place.

fig. **1595** SPENSER *Sonn.* lxxii, There my fraile fancy, fed with full delight, Doth bath in blisse, and mantleth most at Ease.

¶**b.** *transf.* Of a horse: To bridle.

1664 COTTON *Scarron.* I. 79 Mantling like Mare in Martingale, She thus reply'd.

4. *intr.* Of liquids: To be or become covered with a coating or scum; to form a sparkling 'head' or froth; to cream.

1626 BACON *Sylva* §46 It drinketh fresh, flowreth and mantleth excedingly. **1669** WORLIDGE *Syst. Agric.* (1681) 53 The Bran of Wheat, a little thereof boiled in our ordinary Beer, maketh it Mantle, or Flower in the Cup when it is poured out. **1707** 12 MORTIMER *Husb.* (1721) II. 333 Your Cyder will acquire a fine briskness, and mantle in the Glass. **1725** POPE *Odyss.* x. 378 The poison mantled in the golden bowl. **1822** SHELLEY *Triumph Life* 359 In her right hand she bore a crystal glass, Mantling with bright Nepenthe. **1878** B. TAYLOR *Deukalion* II. iii. 73 As the remnant-wine in cup Fast shall fill and mantle up.

b. *transf.* and *fig.*

1596 SHAKS. *Merch. V.* I. i. 89 There are a sort of men, whose visages Do creame and mantle like a standing pond. **1809** CAMPBELL *O'Connor's Child* xiv, The green oblivious flood That mantles by your walls. **1813** SHELLEY *Q. Mab* VIII. 115 Health floats amid the gentle atmosphere, Glows in the fruits, and mantles on the stream. **1846** KEBLE *Lyra Innoc.* (1873) 55 A golden Chalice standing by,—What mantles there, is life or death.

†**c.** ? *fig.* To 'bubble' with desire. (Cf. MANTLING *ppl. a.* 3.) *Obs.*

1657 THORNLEY tr. *Longus' Daphnis & Chloe* 162 When Daphnis saw it, he mantled to be at it.

5. Of the blood: To suffuse the cheeks with a blush. Said also of a blush, etc. (rarely *trans.*). Of the face: To be suffused with glowing colour, to flush.

1707 [see MANTLING *ppl. a.* 4]. **1766** GOLDSM. *Hermit* xxii, Surpriz'd he sees new beauties rise, Swift mantling to the view. **1808** SCOTT *Marm.* III. xvii, The blood that mantles in her cheeks. **1809** W. IRVING *Knickerb.* II. iv. (1820) 118 The rosy blush of morn began to mantle in the east. **1813** SHELLEY *Q. Mab* VIII. 37 Such joy as when a lover..Sees her unfaded cheek Glow mantling in first luxury of health. **1870** DISRAELI *Lothair* ix, Her rich face mantling with emotion. **1884** *Punch* 16 Feb. 76/2 With downcast eyes and faint blush mantling his thoughtful brow.

6. *intr.* To form a mantle or covering; to spread or be extended over a surface.

1634–1770 [see MANTLING *ppl. a.* 2]. **1810** SCOTT *Lady of L.* I. xix, And seldom o'er a breast so fair, Mantled a plaid with modest care. **1812** COMBE *Picturesque* XIX. (Chandos) 71 The vine mantling on the thatch. **1830** LYELL *Princ. Geol.* I. 342 As countless beds of sand and scoriæ constitute the greater part of the whole mass, these may sometimes mantle continuously round the whole cone.

7. *dial.* (See quots.)

1674–91 RAY *N.C. Words* 46 *To Mantle*, kindly to embrace. **1869** *Lonsdale Gloss., Mantle*, to embrace kindly.

†**8.** (See quot.) *Obs.*

1688 R. HOLME *Armoury* III. 74/1 Mantling, or Mantle Wind, is to make Wind with a Winnow sheet, or course cloth held by two persons.

9. *trans.* In alum manufacture: To cover (an incandescent heap of alum ore) with a coating of ashes in order to shelter it from the weather.

1879 *Spon's Encycl. Arts, Manuf.*, etc. I. 327.

mantle: see MANTEL *sb.* and *v.*

mantled (ˈmænt(ə)ld), *ppl. a.* [f. MANTLE *sb.* and *v.* + -ED.]

1. Covered with or as with a mantle.
1552 HULOET, Mantled, or cladde in a mantle, *palliatus.* **1579** SPENSER *Sheph. Cal.* Nov. 128 The mantled medowes mourne, Theyr sondry colours tourne. **1610** SHAKS. *Temp.* IV. i. 182, I left them I'th' filthy mantled poole beyond your Cell. **1816** L. HUNT *Rimini* I. 177 The steeds also make a mantled show. **1896** H. O. FORBES *Handbk. Primates* I. 202 The Mantled Howler. *Alouatta palliata.*

2. *Her.* Adorned with a lambrequin or mantling.
1572 BOSSEWELL *Armorie* II. 86 Manteled Azure. **1678** *Lond. Gaz.* No. 1332/4 His crest an helmet mantled.

mantleless (ˈmænt(ə)llɪs), *a.* In 4 **mantal-les.** [f. MANTLE *sb.* + -LESS.] Without a mantle.
13.. *K. Alis.* 204 Dame Olimpias..rod, al mantal-les.

†**ˈmantleman.** *Obs.* = next.
1633 T. STAFFORD *Pac. Hib.* III. xiv. 351 Cormock.. creepeth in his shirt out of the window, where were divers mantlemen wayting of purpose to receive him.

†**ˈmantler.** *Obs.* [f. MANTLE *sb.* + -ER[1].] One of the poor Irish of the 15–17th c. whose clothing consisted of a single 'mantle' or 'plaid'.
1653 A. WILSON *Jas. I* 192 In Antwerp they pictured the Queen of Bohemia like a poor Irish Mantler.

mantlet, variant of MANTELET.

mantling (ˈmæntlɪŋ), *vbl. sb.* [f. MANTLE *v.* + -ING[1].]

†1. The action of making a mantle. *Obs.*
1507–8 in *Ld. Treas. Acc. Scotl.* (1902) IV. 30 Item, for mantilling of the said skinnis and lynyng of the goun, xxs.

2. *Her.* The ornamental accessory of drapery or scroll-work frequently depicted behind and around an achievement; a lambrequin; cf. MANTLE *sb.* 1 g.
1591 PERCIVALL *Sp. Dict., Follajes,* mantelling in armes, florishing, *Mangonizatio.* **1610** GUILLIM *Heraldry* VI. v. (1611) 267 Our now common received Mantelings vsed for the adorning of atchievements. *Ibid.*, These..may be more fitly termed flourishings than Mantelings. **1708** *New View Lond.* II. 553/1 One [monument]..composed of white Marble, adorned with a Mantling. **1893** CUSSANS *Handbk. Her.* (ed. 4) xv. 191 The Mantlings of Knights and Esquires are commonly depicted as depending from the helmet.

3. = MANTELPIECE 1.
1861 *Macm. Mag.* IV. 129/2 The mantlings or frames of fire-places.

4. What serves the purpose of a mantle; a protective or ornamental covering; a wrappage, envelope.
1652 LOVEDAY tr. *Calprenede's Cassandra* III. 182 His Mantling trayling to the ground, was also of a light Golden-Tissue. **1627–77** FELTHAM *Resolves* II. lxvi. 298 The troubles..which are as it were the Thorns and Mantlings wherewith a Crown is lined. **1671** GREW *Anat. Plants* iv. §16 The Stalk..giving the same Protection here, which in other Plants by the Leaves, or some particular Mantling, is contriv'd. *a* **1734** NORTH *Lives* (1826) III. 201 At home with us a private person divested of all his mantlings.

5. **a.** Of a liquor, etc.: The action of foaming or 'creaming'; also *fig.* **b.** A blush or suffusion of colour produced by emotion.
1697 JER. COLLIER *Ess. Mor. Subj.* (1703) II. 198 'Tis a Happiness without a Fund: 'Tis no more than a little mantling of the Spirits upon stirring. **1754** RICHARDSON *Grandison* (1781) I. xvi. 101 Such sensible, such good-natured mantlings. **1865** DICKENS *Mut. Fr.* I. viii, There had been a momentary mantling in the face of the man as he made the last answer.

6. The action of a hawk that mantles: see MANTLE *v.* 3.
1773 J. CAMPBELL *Mod. Falconry* 262 *Mantling*, the lowering of a hawk's wings down to her feet. **1832** J. P. KENNEDY *Swallow B.* xxvi. (1860) 230 He [the hawk] alternately stretched out first one wing, and then the other, along his leg,—in the action known by the name of mantling.

7. Material for making mantles.
1893 *Times* 10 July 4/3 Novelties in coatings, suitings, and mantlings.

8. *Alum-making.* (See MANTLE *v.* 9.)
1879 *Spon's Encycl. Arts, Manuf.*, etc. I. 327 When the process is complete, a thicker 'mantling' is laid on.

ˈmantling, *ppl. a.* [f. MANTLE *v.* + -ING[2].]

1. Of liquids: Gathering a scum or coating; sparkling to a 'head'. Also *transf.*
1633 P. FLETCHER *Purple Isl.* I. xxiii, The mantling stream Encounter'd by the tides..Of's way doth doubtfull seem. *a* **1718** PENN *Maxims* Wks. 1726 I. 829 'Tis not often, though it [wit] be lively and mantling, that it carries a great Body with it. **1732** POPE *Hor. Sat.* II. ii. 8 And the brain dances to the mantling bowl. **1822** LAMB *Elia* Ser. II. *Conf. Drunkard*, It were enough to make him dash the sparkling beverage to the earth in all the pride of its mantling temptation. **1851** HAWTHORNE *Twice-told T., Hollow of Three Hills*, They were said to stand around the mantling pool, disturbing its putrid waters.

2. That spreads and covers; enveloping.
1634 MILTON *Comus* 294, I saw them under a green mantling vine That crawls along the side of yon small hill. **1716** GAY *Trivia* II. 54 You'll sometimes meet a fop, of nicest tread, Whose mantling peruke veils his empty head. **1768** SIR W. JONES *Solima* Poems (1777) 4 Where mantling darkness spreads her dragon wing. **1770** GOLDSM. *Des. Vill.* 132 The brook with mantling cresses spread. **1862** G. P. SCROPE *Volcanos* (ed. 2) 164 The mantling beds or currents of lava that compose a large part of its substance. **1883** G. ALLEN in *Nature* 29 Mar. 514/1 The hop type belongs rather to mantling than to mere twining climbers.

†3. Eagerly desiring. (Cf. MANTLE *v.* 4 c.) *Obs.*
1657 THORNLEY tr. *Longus' Daphnis & Chloe* 42 The mantling Goats skipt and leapt.

4. Of the blood: Suffusing the face. Of the cheeks: Becoming suffused with heightened colour.
1707 E. SMITH *Phædra & Hipp.* II. (1709) 13 When mantling Blood Glow'd in his lovely Cheeks. **1812** CRABBE *Tales, The Confidant* (init.), And, at the distant hint or dark surmise, The blood into the mantling cheek would rise. **1872** BLACK *Adv. Phaeton* xxiii. 324 This girl with the mantling colour in her cheek.

‖**manto** (ˈmæntəʊ). [It. or Sp. *manto.*] A (Spanish, etc.) cloak or mantle. (See also MANTEAU.)
1679 RYCAUT *St. Grk. Ch.* 96 The G. Signor..presents him with a white Horse, a Manto or blacke Coole [etc.]. **1867** MISS YONGE *Six Cushions* xi. 90 A place that.. suggested Spanish cavaliers, with short manto, broad sombrero [etc.].

mantoa, mantoe: see MANTUA, MANTEAU.

†**manˈtology.** *Obs. rare.* [Badly f. Gr. μάντ-ις a diviner + -OLOGY.] The art or practice of divination.
1774 *Guthrie's Geog. Gram.* (ed. 4) 125 That remarkable mantology, or gift of prophecy, which distinguishes the inhabitants of the Hebrides under the name of second sight. **1783** W. F. MARTYN *Geog. Mag.* II. 423. **1828** in WEBSTER.

So **manˈtologist,** 'one skilled in mantology or divination; a diviner, prophet'.
1864 in WEBSTER; and in recent Dicts.

Manton (ˈmæntən). A fowling-piece made by Joseph Manton (?1766–1835), a noted gunsmith. Also ***Joe Manton.***
1816 SCOTT *Antiq.* xxxix, It's a capital piece; it's a Joe Manton, that cost forty guineas. **1859** LEVER *Dav. Dunn* xiii. 113 Every now and then you'll find a firelock in the hands that once held a double-barrelled Manton.

†**mantoon.** *Obs. rare*[−1]. [? ad. It. *mantone,* augmentative of *manto* cloak.] ? A large cloak.
1623 WEBSTER *Deuils Law-case* I. ii. B4b, I do heare there are Bawds abroad, That bring Cut-works, & Mantoons, & conuey Letters To such young Gentlewomen.

†**mantoplicee.** *Obs. rare*[−1]. [F. *manteau plissé* pleated cloak.]
1672 SHADWELL *Miser* I. 16.

mantou, -ow, variant ff. of MANTEAU *Obs.*

Mantoux (mɑ̃tuː, ˈmæntu). *Med.* The name of Charles *Mantoux* (1877–1947), French physician, used *attrib.* with reference to a method, introduced by him in 1908, of testing for past or present tuberculous infection by intradermal injection of diluted tuberculin.
1931 R. J. E. SCOTT *Gould's Med. Dict.* (ed. 3) 764/1 Mantoux test. **1932** *Observer* 28 Feb. 11/2 The Mantoux test has a definite though limited application in the diagnosis of tuberculous disease. **1956** *Nature* 25 Feb. 367/2 A study was made of the interrelationships of the Mantoux and Lepromin reactions. *Ibid.* 368/1 The Mantoux-negative individuals. **1971** D. LAMBERT in C. Bonington *Annapurna South Face* App. G. 290 Immunity [from tuberculosis] is tested first by the Mantoux Test, and this is examined after three days.

‖**mantra** (ˈmæntrə). *Indian.* Also 9 **mantram.** [Skr. *mantra*, lit. 'instrument of thought', f. *man* to think.] A sacred text or passage, esp. one from the Vedas used as a prayer or incantation. Also, a holy name, for inward meditation. Also *attrib.* and *fig.*
1808 COLEBROOKE *Vedas* in *Asiat. Res.* VIII. 391 The import of any mantra in the Indian scriptures, is generally found to be a prayer, containing either a petition to a deity, or else thanksgiving, praise, and adoration. **1817** tr. *Dubois' Mann. People India* xi. 77 The pretended virtues of the Mantra or Mantram. **1883** MONIER-WILLIAMS *Relig. Th. & Life India* i. 8 These Mantras or hymns were arranged in three principal collections. **1900** W. MAXWELL in W. W. Skeat *Malay Magic* v. 116 Numerous *mantra*, or charms.. are in use among the Pawangs. **1931** G. B. SANSOM *Japan* III. xii. 222 Recitation of the formulae known as *mantra.* **1956** E. WOOD *Yoga Dict.* 93 *Mantras*, forms of speech which carry a material effect upon the mind, emotions or body, or even on things... The scriptures contain many great *mantras*, of which the greatest is the word *Om. Ibid.*, If these [sounds] are arranged by some person competent in this matter, words..and sentences of power can be formed. Such a person was called a mantramaker (*mantrakāra*) in ancient India. **1962** BRAHMACHARINI USHA *Ramakrishna-Vedanta Wordbk.* 47 *Mantra*,..also mantram... The particular name of God... The mantra, regarded as one with God, represents the essence of the guru's instruction to his disciple, who is enjoined to keep it sacred and secret, and to meditate on the aspect of God which it symbolizes for the rest of his life. **1964** V. S. NAIPAUL *Area of Darkness* x. 249 The Tibetans..were suffering because they had forgotten the *mantras*, charms, which might have repelled their enemies. **1965** *New Statesman* 16 Apr. 616/3 He is less happy when defending the mantra, or holy names on which one must meditate. **1967** SINGHA & MASSEY *Indian Dances* iv. 56 The priest lit the sacred fire, recited the mantras (sacred texts), and tied the tali round the girl's neck. **1969** *Enactment* (Delhi) Nov. 18/1 You used to chant his name like a *mantra.* **1971** *Daily Tel.* 19 Aug. 10/4 People who ever have dinner in English country hotels know the *mantra*, or holy formula: 'Coffee will be served in the lounge.' **1972** *Language* XLVIII. 174 Secondly, the Brahmanas cannot be regarded far removed in time from the mantras, and therefore their authors might not render a particular mantra word..which..was not altogether unintelligible in their times. **1972** *Village Voice* (N.Y.) 1 June 76/3 The birds were placed in cardboard boxes..and rushed to a building where teams of hippies, chanting the Hare Krishna mantra, worked into the dawn of the next day to save their lives. **1973** *Times* 22 Jan. 20 The Maharishi uses a technique based on a mantra, a sound which each meditator is given to intone inwardly.

ˈman-trap, *sb.* A trap for catching men, *esp.* one for catching trespassers in private grounds.
1788 WOLCOT (P. Pindar) *Peter's Pension* Wks. 1812 II. 18 Your Man-traps, guards of goose and duck And cock and hens. **1791** BOSWELL *Johnson* 20 Mar. an. 1776, He should have warned us of our danger, before we entered his garden of flowery eloquence, by advertising, 'Spring-guns and men-traps set here'. **1880** BROWNING *Clive* 24 Did no writing on the wall Warn me 'Trespasser, 'ware man-traps!'
transf. and *fig.* **1773** GOLDSM. *Stoops to Conq.* III. Wks. (Globe) 663/2 There's Mrs. Mantrap, Lady Betty Blackleg [etc.]. **1840** DICKENS *Barn. Rudge* xiii, Mrs. Varden, regarding the Maypole as a sort of human man-trap, or decoy for husbands. **1846** GREENER *Sci. Gunnery* 197 Were you to bawl in the ears of those employed in the construction [of certain guns],..you would not affect nor abate one, in the number of these infernal man-traps. **1857** W. CHANDLESS *Visit to Salt Lake* II. xi. 330 The planks (of the streets) worn out and broken through, leaving large holes, popularly known as 'man-traps'. **1903** G. B. SHAW *Man & Superman* III. 121 You know better than any of us that marriage is a mantrap baited with simulated accomplishments. **1922** JOYCE *Ulysses* 425 You never seen me in the mantrap with a married highlander. **1929** W. FAULKNER *Sartoris* (1932) v. ii. 365 Some new kind of mantrap [*sc.* an aeroplane] that flies fine—on paper. **1965** H. SHEPPARD *Dict. Railway Slang* 7 *Man trap*, catch points to prevent unauthorised entry from siding. **1974** P. M. HUBBARD *Thirsty Evil* i. 9 She was no man-trap, but she did not miss much.

man-trap, *v.* [f. the sb.] *trans.* To beset with man-traps. Also *fig.* and as **ˈmantrapping** *ppl. a.*
1911 J. LONDON *Son of Sun* (1913) IV. iv. 159 Besides, the runs are all man-trapped—you know, staked pits, poisoned thorns, and the rest. **1952** DYLAN THOMAS *Let.* 8 Oct. (1966) 378 Every lane was mantrapped for me. *c* **1953** —— *Ibid.* 416 And eel up wheezily..from all the claws and bars and breasts of the mantrapping seabed. **1957** A. CLARKE *Later Poems* (1961) 61 Discharge, excrete, their centuries, Man-trapped in concrete.

‖**mantri** (ˈmæntrɪ). Also 8 **mantree.** [Hindi, f. Skr. *mantri*, f. *mantrín* wise, eloquent, skilled in sacred texts or spells, f. *man* to think; cf. MANTRA.] **a.** In India, etc.: a minister, counsellor. **b.** In Indonesia (including the former Netherlands East Indies): a minor official or subordinate functionary vested with some authority.
1783 W. MARSDEN *Hist. Sumatra* 287 The officers next in rank to the *Sultan* are called *Mantree*, which some apprehend to be a corruption of the word *Mandarin*, a title of distinction amongst the Chinese. **1814** T. S. RAFFLES *Substance of Minute on Land Rental on Island of Java* 218 In each division there shall be fixed a station of police, to which shall be appointed a competent officer, with such number of inferior *Mantris*, *Peons*, &c. as shall be deemed necessary. **1873** E. BALFOUR *Cycl. India* III. 146/2 *Mantra*, Sans. Counsel, hence mantri, Sans. a counsellor. **1896** CAREY & TUCK *Chin Hills* I. i. 3 The elders of the village, called..by the Lushai officers 'Kharbari' and 'Mantri', surround the person of the Chief. **1917** COOMARASWAMY & DUGGIRALA tr. *Mirror of Gesture* 15 *The Ministers* (mantri)—Those who shine as royal ministers are men of their word. **1965** I. SOUTHALL *Indonesia* xxiii. 227 If the villager ever does get to the hospital, he will find an outpatient clinic with a mantri in charge. It is the duty of this mantri to treat all simpler problems and refer the difficult to the doctor.

†**mantry.** *Obs. rare*[−0]. = MANTEL-TREE.
1530 PALSGR. 243/1 Mantry of a chimney, *manteav de cheminée.*

mantua (ˈmæntjuːə). Also 7 **mantoa.** [Corruption of MANTEAU, due to association with the place-name *Mantua.*

Perh. *mantua silk*, and the fabric referred to in 2 below, may have been called from the place-name, which seems to occur *attrib.* in the following: *a* **1618** *Bk. Rates* H 3 b, Hose of Cruell vocat. Mantua hose, the paire, iiijs.]

1. A loose gown, worn by women in 17–18th c. = MANTEAU 1.
1678 *Lond. Gaz.* No. 1287/4 One rich flowred Mantua lined with black, with a pair of very fine laced Sleeves. **1688** R. HOLME *Armoury* III. 95/2 A Mantua, is a kind of loose Coat without any stayes in it. **1693** SOUTHERNE *Maid's Last Prayer* III. i, He has not seen me in my new Mantoa yet. **1711** STEELE *Spect.* No. 80 ⁋3 Brunetta..came to a public Ball in a plain black Silk Mantua. **1722** DE FOE *Col. Jack* (1840) 278 A mantua of a better kind of calico. **1858** THACKERAY *Virgin.* xxxii, The girls went off straightway to get together their best calamancoes,..mantuas, clocked stockings, and high-heeled shoes.

†2. A material; ? = *mantua silk.*
1709 *Lond. Gaz.* No. 4540/6 The best broad Italian colour'd Mantua's at 6*s.* 9*d.* per Yard. **1766** W. GORDON *Gen. Counting-ho.* 426, 20 yards mantua. **1787** ANDERSON *Orig. Commerce* II. 569 The silks called alamodes and lustrings were entirely owing to them [Fr. refugees of *c* 1685]; also brocades, sattins, black and coloured mantuas.

3. *attrib.*, as ***mantua-cloth, gown, petticoat, silk.***
1706 PHILLIPS (ed. Kersey), *Mantoe*, or *Mantua-Gown*, a loose upper Garment, now generally worn by Women, instead of a straight-body'd Gown. **1731** in Planché *Cycl.*

Costume (1876) I. 363 A rose-coloured paduasoy mantua, lined with a rich Mantua silk of the same colour. **1755** STRYPE *Stow's Surv.* (ed. 6) II. v. xxx. 561/1 It must be a very poor Woman that has not a Suit of Mantua Silk..to appear abroad in on Holydays. **176.** in J. P. Malcom *Manners Lond.* (1810) II. 347 A scarlet-flowered damask Mantua Petticoat. **1882** CAULFEILD & SAWARD *Dict. Needlework*, *Mantua Cloths*, a term employed in trade to denote every description of cloth suitable for mantles, cloaks [etc.].

'mantua-ˌmaker. *Obs.* exc. *Hist.* or *arch.* One who makes mantuas; later, a dress-maker.

1694 MOTTEUX *Rabelais* v. 237 Mantuamaker. **1712** BUDGELL *Spect.* No. 277 ¶11 The most celebrated Tyre-women and Mantua-makers in Paris. **1841** in HODDER *Life Ld. Shaftesb.* (1886) I. 328 An enquiry into the state and treatment of the wretched milliners and mantua-makers. **1886** BYNNER *A. Surriage* xv. 165 Get on your hat and go with me to the mantua-maker.

So **mantua-making** *vbl. sb.* and *ppl. a.*

a **1704** T. BROWN *Walk round London* (1709) 41 That virtuous Profession Mantua-making. **1760–72** H. BROOKE *Fool of Qual.* (1809) III. 76, I must soon quit my mantuamaking business. **1824** MISS MITFORD *Village* Ser. I. 287 The young mantua-making school-mistresses.

Mantuan ('mæntjuːən), *a.* and *sb.* [ad. L. *Mantuān-us*, f. *Mantua*: see -AN.]

A. *adj.* Of or belonging to Mantua, a city in northern Italy near which Virgil was born; hence, of or pertaining to Virgil, Virgilian. ***the Mantuan Muse, Swan***, Virgil.

1538 KING HENRY VIII *Epistle* sig. B2 We moste hartely desyre you, that ye wol vouchesafe, to rede those thynges, that we wrote this laste yere, touchynge the Mantuan Councille. **1709** POPE *Ess. Crit.* 129 Still with itself compar'd, his [*sc.* Homer's] text peruse; And let your comment be the Mantuan Muse. **1780** COWPER *Table-t.* 557 Ages elapsed ere Homer's lamp appeared, And ages ere the Mantuan Swan was heard. **1940** G. F.-H. & J. BERKELEY *Italy in Making* III. viii. 141 The Mantuan volunteers.. gave a very creditable account of themselves.

B. *sb.* A native or inhabitant of Mantua. ***the Mantuan*** = Virgil.

1649 OGILBY *Virgil, Bucolicks* (1684) i. *note*, Virgil.. amongst other Mantuans, ejected out of his Inheritance, went to Rome for redress. **1827** G. DARLEY *Sylvia* (1892) 186 Who [*sc.* Milton] from the Mantuan's bleeding crown Tore the presumptuous laurel down. **1842** K. H. DIGBY *Mores Catholici* xi. i. 6 Mezentius is never named by the great Mantuan without the epithet 'contemtorque Deûm'. **1953** T. F. MURRAY tr. *Dal-Gal's Pius X* v. 91 He had not spent long among the Mantuans before his people..were charmed by his meekness and won by his charity.

mantyger, variant of MANTEGAR, MANTICORE.

†**manuable**, *a. Obs. rare.* [a. OF. *manuable*, f. L. *manu-* hand: see -ABLE. Cf. MANIABLE.]

1. That may be handled easily.

1594 BLUNDEVIL *Exerc.* VII. xii. (1636) 665 The yard thereof is of so great a length, as it is not manuable in a ship. *Ibid.* Most manuable, and therewith very light of carriage.

2. Of money: ? Of handy size.

1638 SIR R. COTTON *Abstr. Rec. Tower* 26 If wee marke but of the great quantities from the penny downward since H. 8. time stamped, how few remain. Whereas of all the Coynes from three pence upwards which are manuable (or manuall) plenty passe still in daily payment.

manual ('mænjuːəl), *a.* and *sb.* Forms: 5–8 **manuel**, (5 **manuele**), 5–7 **manuell**, 5–6 **manuelle**, **manwell**, **manuale**, 6–7 **manuall**, 6– **manual**. [ad. (the earlier form through F. *manuel*) L. *manuālis* pertaining to the hand; the neut. *manuāle* was used subst. in class. L. for 'a book-cover', in late L. for a handbook. Cf. Sp., Pg. *manual*, It. *manuale* adjs. and sbs.]

A. *adj.*

1. a. Of or pertaining to the hand or hands; done or performed with the hands. Now esp. of (physical) labour, an occupation, etc., as opposed to *mental*, *theoretical*. Also, as opposed to *automatic*, applied to hand-operated devices, systems, etc.

1406 HOCCLEVE *La Male Regle* 364 And of thy manuel labour, as I weene, Thy lucre is swich, þat it vnnethe is seene. **1532–3** *Act 24 Hen. VIII*, c. 4 Marchaundyse, made and broughte..into this realme, redye wroughte by manuall occupacion. **1593** FALE *Dialling* A iij, Beseeching the Lord (who hath endued you with extraordinary knoledge in all Manuall Sciences) to finish [etc.]. **1597** A. M. tr. *Guillemeau's Fr. Chirurg.* 19/1 Which eradication requireth a longe continued manuall operation. **1675** BAXTER *Cath. Theol.* I. 66 By manual Apprehension or Executive Election (As a man taketh a woman to wife). **1725** POPE *Odyss.* xv. 338 Patron of industry and manual arts. **1804** EARL LAUDERD. *Pub. Wealth* (1819) 346 The superior efficacy of the application of capital..over the most improved manual dexterity. **1857** RUSKIN *Pol. Econ. Art* Addenda 192 All youths of whatever rank, ought to learn some manual trade thoroughly. **1865** TYLOR *Early Hist. Man.* iv. 66, I expressed my ideas by manual signs. **1868** SIR R. PHILLIMORE in *Law Rep., Adm. & Eccl.* II. 199 The second prayer-book of Edward VI. omitted all reference to the manual acts, ordered in the first and last prayer-books, attending the consecration of the holy elements. **1921** *Conquest* Jan. 124/1 Consider what happens in an ordinary 'manual' telephone exchange when a subscriber makes a call. **1923** *Bell Syst. Techn. Jrnl.* Apr. 56 The system most commonly employed today for connecting [telephone] subscribers' lines together is the so-called 'manual' system; that is, a system in which operators..make the actual connections. **1959** *Gramophone* Sept. 82 (Advt.), The 'Conquest' Automatic Record Changer for stereophonic and monophonic play...Provision for manual operation. **1966** *McGraw-Hill Encycl. Sci. & Technol.* XIV. 43/2 There are two general types of transmission, manual shift and automatic. Manual-shift transmissions..are used in conjunction with a clutch.

b. Of a signature, etc.: Autograph. Chiefly in SIGN MANUAL; also in obsolete phrases formed after it, as ***seal m., subscription m., manual stamp***.

1522 *Extracts Aberd. Reg.* (1844) I. 101 In witnes of the quhilk, we haue causit our commond seill to be appensit to this present assedatioun, togidder with the subscriptioun manuel of our commissaris handis. **1563** *Reg. Privy Council Scot.* I. 254 Anent the Quenis Majesteis lettres past undir hir signet and subscriptioun manual. **1592** SHAKS. *Ven. & Ad.* 516 Which purchase if thou make, for feare of slips, Set thy seale manuell on my wax-red lips. **1632** LITHGOW *Trav.* I. 17 Their names, and manuall subscriptions. **1644** MILTON *Areop.* 23 Much lesse..that it should be uncurrant without their manuall stamp.

†**c.** ***compute manual*** (= L. *computus manualis*): a mediæval treatise on the art of reckoning on the hands the dates of Church feasts, etc., and containing many mnemonic nonsense-verses. *Obs.*

In the verse referred to, *Adam degebat ergo cifos adrifos* (sic), the 12 syllables stand for the 12 months.

1533 MORE *Answ. Nameless Heret.* IV. viii. (1534) 207 b, The commen verse of the compute manuell, *Ergo ciphos adrifex*.

d. Of a weapon, tool, etc.: That is used or worked with the hand or hands. Now rare except in ***manual (fire) engine*** as distinguished from *steam (fire) engine*.

1591 *Garrard's Art Warre* 184 Ye strength of their manual weapons. **1601** HOLLAND *Pliny* I. 481 Of this Smilax are made certain manuell writing-tables. **1632** LITHGOW *Trav.* x. 433 They delue, hollow, and turne ouer the ground, with manuall..instruments. **1888** MERRYWEATHER *Fire Brigade Handbk.* ix. 98 Manual Fire Engines... There is..no better manual engine..than that known as the London Brigade pattern.

e. *Mil.* ***manual exercise***, exercise or drill in handling a musket or rifle.

1760 (*title*) New Manual Exercise As Performed by His Majesty's Dragoons, Foot-guards, Foot, Artillery, Marines. **1802** C. JAMES *Milit. Dict.*, *Manual Exercise*, is the exercise of the musket, independent of powder and ball.

f. ***manual alphabet***: the finger alphabet. ***manual method***: 'a method of instructing the deaf which mainly employs the manual alphabet and signs for communicating ideas, as distinguished from the *oral method*' (Webster 1902).

2. *Law.* Of occupation, possession: Actual, in one's own hands, not merely prospective. †Hence of a thing possessed (see quot. 1607).

1538 tr. *Littleton's Tenures* (1544) 3 b, Of suche thynges as a man maye haue a manuel occupacyon [AF. *vn manuel occupacion*]: possession or resceyte, as of landes, tenementes, rentes and such other... But of suche thynges that lye nat in manuell occupacyon [AF. *en tiel manuell occupacion*] &c. as of auouson of a church..there he shal [etc.]. **1567** STAUNFORD *King's Prerog.* 54 But heruppon is there a distinction to be made, whether that y[t] the king is entitled vnto by office be a thinge manuell and whereof profit maye bee taken forthwith after the findinge of the office or not. **1581** LAMBARDE *Eiren.* II. vii. (1588) 274 If he [*sc.* the theefe] take the purse in his hand, and then cut the girdle, & afterward let them fal, that wil proue him a Felon, because he had a manuel possession of the purse remoued from the person. **1607** COWELL *Interpr.* s.v., *Manuel*, is a thing whereof present profit may be made... And a thing not manuell is that, whereof no present profit may be made, but hereafter, when it falleth. **1628** COKE *On Litt.* 17 Such things whereof a man may have manuell occupation or possession. **1766** BLACKSTONE *Comm.* II. 392 The law.. extends this possession farther than the mere manual occupation.

†**3.** Of money: = MANUABLE 2.

1638 [see MANUABLE 2].

4. That works with the hands. *arch.*

1658 SIR T. BROWNE *Gard. Cyrus* i. 93 Not only a Lord of Gardens, but a manuall planter thereof. **1687** *Connect. Col. Rec.* (1859) III. 407 Butchers, bakers,..barbers, millers and masons, with all other manual persons. **1851** CARLYLE *Sterling* III. iv. (1872) 204 He quite agreed with me as to the ..necessity and difficulty of doing something effectual for so satisfying the manual multitude as not to overthrow all legal security.

†**5.** Furnished with hands. *Obs.*

1646 SIR T. BROWNE *Pseud. Ep.* VII. ii. 343 Parts of the seed do seeme to containe the Idea and power of the whole; so parents deprived of hands, beget manuall issues.

6. Of a book, etc.: Of the nature of a manual; intended to be kept at hand for reference.

1881 WESTCOTT & HORT *Greek Test.* Introd. §20 We agreed to commence the formation of a manual text for our own use.

B. *sb.*

1. A small book for handy use. **a.** In the mediæval Church, a book containing the forms to be observed by priests in the administration of the sacraments, etc. (corresponding to the present *Rituale Romanum*).

1431 *Med. Rec. City Ch.* (E.E.T.S.) 29 Also ij legendes & a manwell & a Ordynall. *c* **1440** *Promp. Parv.* 325/2 Manuele, booke to minster wythe the sacramentys, *manuale*. **1549** *Act 3 & 4 Edw. VI*, c. 10 §1 That all Bookes called.. Processionalles, Manuelles,..shalbe..abollished. **1853** ROCK *Ch. of Fathers* IV. xii. 213 The Manual had in it all the services that a parish priest has to perform.

b. A concise treatise, an abridgement, a handbook. Often used as a title for books.

1533 (*title*) A booke called in latyn Enchiridion militis christiani, and in englysshe the manuell of the christen knyght..made by..Erasmus. **1565** GRAFTON (*title*) A Manuell of the Chronicles of Englande. **1663** GERBIER *Counsel* 3 b, If in your Building, you want instructions for your Clark; pray let him make use of this Manual. **1788** PRIESTLEY *Lect. Hist.* IV. xxv. 196 The..*Speculum Saxonicum*, which is an excellent manuel of the old laws of the ancient Saxons. **1879** FROUDE *Cæsar* iv. 36 A Greek manual of the art of war.

†**2.** Method of operating or working. *Obs.*

1597 A. M. tr. *Guillemeau's Fr. Chirurg.* 26/1 We must vse the manuall of Chyrurgerye thervnto, ether by cuttinge or inscisione. **1656** tr. *Valentine's Will* II. iii. 98 All these mixed impurities can be separated from it with artificial Manuals, and with little ado it may be brought into a perfect state.

3. Short for *manual exercise*: see MANUAL *a.* 1 e.

1762 STERNE *Tr. Shandy* V. xxxii, The corporal went through his *manual* with exactness. **1899** KIPLING *Stalky* 198, I know the drill—all except the manual.

4. †**a.** *pl.* 'Manual' tools (see A. 1 d) (*obs.*). **b.** Short for *manual fire-engine*.

1683 J. POYNTZ *Tobago* 38 Manuals with other things necessary for Planting. **1872** *Routledge's Ev. Boy's Ann.* 156/2 Manuals, steamers, and floating batteries. **1886** *Manch. Exam.* 8 Jan. 6/1 Steamers and manuals from all parts of the metropolis arrived at the fire.

5. a. A key-board of an organ played with the hands, as distinguished from the *pedals*.

1852 SEIDEL *Organ* 33 Every organ has two..key-boards; the one managed by the hands, and hence called 'the manual' [etc.]. **1880** E. J. HOPKINS in Grove *Dict. Mus.* II. 606/1 Thus an organ with one Manual and separate Pedal generally has at the least one coupler 'Manual to Pedal'.

b. 'In a musical instrument, a key or lever for the hands or fingers; a digital' (*Cent. Dict.* 1890).

c. *attrib.*

1852 SEIDEL *Organ* 49 These pedal-palates have much harder work to do than the manual-palates. *Ibid.* 67 A copula which connects two manuals with each other is called a manual-copula. **1881** C. A. EDWARDS *Organs* vi. 67 There may be..four, or even more, manual claviers to an organ, though there is usually only one pedal clavier. *Ibid.* 69 The pedal keys..are..much larger than the manual keys.

manualism ('mænjuːəlɪz(ə)m). *rare*$^{-1}$. [f. MANUAL + -ISM.] The action or process of teaching by means of the manual alphabet.

1883 *Amer. Ann. Deaf & Dumb* Apr. 93 Go utterly voiceless through all his life, with the mental education which manualism can at least give him.

manualist ('mænjuːəlɪst). [f. MANUAL + -IST.]

1. †**a.** One who works or labours with the hands (*obs.*). **b.** (See quot. 1861.)

1592 R. D. *Hypnerotomachia* 18 b, The chiefe inuention.. resteth in the..architect, but the labour and working therof to the vulgar and common sort of mannalists [*sic*] and seruants to the architect. **1706** PHILLIPS (ed. Kersey), *Manualist*, a Handicrafts-man, or Artificer. **1861** MAYHEW *Lond. Labour* III. 104 When I [a juggler] was in Ireland they called me a 'manualist'.

2. 'One who uses or advocates the use of the manual method of teaching the deaf' (Webster 1902).

1883 *Amer. Ann. Deaf & Dumb* Apr. 79 In the judgment of most manualists there can be no question that this fact alone, of prior speech, establishes such an important difference.

3. One who compiles a manual or handbook.

1897 *Dublin Rev.* July 227 It is apparently the fashion at the present time to despise manuals and manualists.

manualization (ˌmænjuːəlaɪ'zeɪʃən). *rare*$^{-1}$. The action of using the hands.

1887 *Sat. Rev.* 31 Dec. 890 A trick performed solely by means of personal skill and dexterity of manualization is, of course, conjuring *in excelsis*.

manually ('mænjuːəlɪ), *adv.* [f. MANUAL *a.* + -LY[2].]

1. With or by means of the hand or hands; by the operation of the hands; by manual labour.

1471 RIPLEY *Comp. Alch.* Ep. ii. in Ashm. (1652) 112 Which thyng is not wrought manually, But naturally. **1506** in *Mem. Hen. VII* (Rolls) 297 Both kings..went up to the high altar, and there sware upon the holy Evangelists, canon of the mass by them manually touched. **1874** FARRAR *Christ* vii. (1884) 40 And while they were occupied manually, we have positive evidence that these years were not neglected intellectually. **1877** J. D. CHAMBERS *Divine Worship* 199 The Presbyters manually should hand each Penitent to the Archdeacon.

2. *Law.* Personally, actually. (Cf. MANUAL *a.* 2.)

1628 COKE *On Litt.* 17 That which is manually occupied, manured and possessed.

3. With regard to the hands.

1882 SALA *Amer. Revis.* (1885) 185 An obliging waiter.. facially and manually as black as the Ace of Spades.

manuary ('mænjuːərɪ), *a.* and *sb.* [ad. L. *manuārius*, f. *manu-s* hand: see -ARY[1].]

A. *adj.*

1. Of or pertaining to the hand; performed by or with the hands; = MANUAL *a.* 1. Also, applied to the hands. *Obs.* exc. in affected use.

1576 WOOLTON *Chr. Manual* D vj, Artes both lyberall, and manuary. **1579** LYLY *Euphues* (Arb.) 158 Manuary

craftes. **1599** A. M. tr. *Gabelhouer's Bk. Physicke* 263/2 An excellent Handevngvente... An other Manvarye vnctione. **1609** Bp. Hall *Holy Observ.* I. 9 You shall rarely finde a man eminent in sundry faculties of minde, or sundry manuarie trades. **1612** Brinsley *Lud. Lit.* p. xv, The holy Ghost challengeth the faculty euen of manuary skill to his owne gifte. **1656** Blount *Glossogr.*, *Manuary*, gotten by handy labor, or that fils the hand. **1860** *Med. Times* 4 Feb. 118/2 Agitated mistresses institute manuary inspections among the Soyerinas of the basement.

†**2.** That works with the hands. *Obs.*

1652 C. B. Stapylton *Herodian* XIII. 111 Then Bridges built and Stones and Morter carry, As if he were a Workman Manuary. **1678** Cudworth *Intell. Syst.* I. i. §45. 54 A subordinate instrument of the divine wisdom, and the manuary opificer or executioner of it.

B. *sb.*

†**1.** One who works with his hands. *Obs.*

1581 Mulcaster *Positions* xxxix. (1887) 197 The common is deuided into marchauntes and manuaries generally. *a* **1656** Bp. Hall *Rem. Wks.* (1660) 151 Gifts of tongues.. and the like, which do no more argue a right to the son-ship of God, then the Manuaries infused skill of Bezaleel and Aholiab could prove them Saints.

†**2.** Manual work; handicraft trade. *Obs.*

1581 Mulcaster *Positions* v. (1887) 35 Whose vse [*sc.* of Drawing] all modelling, all mathematikes, all manuaries do finde and confesse to be to so notorious and so needefull. *Ibid.* 197 [After the words quoted under sense 1.] Marchandise containeth vnder it all those which liue.. by buying and selling: Manuarie those whose handywork is their ware. **1616** [see manubiary *sb.*].

†**3.** ? An amanuensis. *Obs.*

1613 Sir E. Hoby *Counter-snarle* 32 It seemeth.. my Manuaries haste, or the Printers misprision, hath turned *go* into (*sed*) as if the same had been continued.

†**4.** A factory. *Obs.*

1625 in *Reg. Privy Council Scot.* Ser. II. I. 159 By making of societies or manuaries in all the principall burrowis for making of stuffes and other wairis.

[¶. An alleged sense 'consecrated glove' given in recent Dicts., is evolved from misunderstanding of the following passage. (In the original Latin *manuarias* and the other words are adjs. agreeing with *indulgentias*.)

1537 tr. *Latimer's Serm. bef. Convoc.* D j b, Some brought forth.. pardons, & these of wonderfull varietie, some stationaries.. some Manuaries for handlers of reliques, some pedaries for pilgrimes.]

ma'nubalist(e. *Antiq.* [ad. late L. type *manuballista*, f. L. *manu-s* hand + ballista; after *arcuballista* arbalest.] A kind of cross-bow.

1867 in Smyth *Sailor's Word-bk.* 467. In some mod. Dicts.

†**manubial,** *a. Obs. rare*$^{-0}$. [ad. L. *manubiāl-is*, f. *manubi-æ* pl., spoils of war.] Belonging or having reference to the spoils of war.

1674 Blount *Glossogr.* (ed. 4) *Manubial*, belonging to a prey or booty. **1721** in Bailey. **1850** Ogilvie, *Manubial-column*, a column adorned with trophies and spoils.

†**manubiary,** *a.* and *sb. Obs. rare.* [ad. L. *manubiārius* adj., f. *manubi-æ* (see prec.).]

A. *adj.* Pertaining to the spoils of war.

1658 Phillips *Manubiary*, belonging to the spoil or prey. **1727-51** Chambers *Cycl.* s.v. *Column*, *Manubiary Column*, a column adorned with trophies, built in imitation of trees, whereon the spoils of enemies were antiently hung.

B. *sb.* **a.** The trade of plunder. **b.** One who lives by plunder.

1616 J. Deacon *Tobacco Tortured* 65 Tobacco fumes are able.. to transform nobilitie into gentrie, gentrie into yeomanrie,.. manuarie into manubiarie, manubiarie into [etc.]. **1623** Cockeram *Manubiarie*, one that hath part of the prey.

manubrial (mə'nju:brɪəl), *a. Anat.* [f. L. manubri-um + -al¹.] Of or pertaining to a manubrium (in various senses).

1835-6 Todd *Cycl. Anat.* I. 282/1 This mesial process [of the sternum in certain birds] we shall term the manubrial process. **1899** *Allbutt's Syst. Med.* VI. 389 If this [the percussion of the heart] be normal.. then any substernal or manubrial dulness which can be clearly defined as separate from this must be taken as of great significance.

manubriated (mə'nju:brɪeɪtɪd), *ppl. a.* [f. L. *manubriāt-us* (f. *manubrium*: see next) + -ed.] Having a manubrium.

1890 in *Century Dict.*

‖**manubrium** (mə'nju:brɪəm). Pl. **manubria, manubriums.** [L. *manubrium* a haft.]

†**1.** A handle or haft. *Obs.*

1660 Boyle *New Exp. Phys. Mech.* Proem. 14 The third piece of this Pump, namely, the handle or manubrium.

2. *Anat.* and *Zool.* **a.** The broad upper division of the sternum of mammals, with which the two first ribs articulate. **b.** A small tapering curved or twisted bony process of the malleus of the ear in man and many mammals. **c.** A small process, often bifurcate, at the root of the keel of the sternum in birds. **d.** The lower part of the malleus in rotifers. **e.** A peduncle which depends from the roof of the gonocalyx of hydroids or of the swimming-bell of medusæ.

1848 *Quain's Anat.* (ed. 5) I. 101 The first division of the sternum (manubrium or handle) is broader and thicker than the other. **1855** Gosse in *Phil. Trans.* CXLVI. 426 The inferior portion of the *malleus*, which I shall call the *manubrium*, is an irregularly-curved piece [etc.]. *Ibid.* 427 The *manubria* move also at the same time. **1885** Romanes *Jelly-Fish* 206 Unlike the manubriums of most of the other Medusæ [etc.]. **1890** Coues *Field & Gen. Ornithol.* 214 The sternum.. develops in the middle line in front a beak-like process called the *rostrum* or *manubrium*.

3. *Bot.* A process projecting from each of the shields forming the inner wall of the antheridium in characeous plants.

1875 Bennett & Dyer tr. *Sachs' Bot.* 285 *Fig.* 198.. *B* a manubrium with its head.

'**manucapt,** *v. nonce-wd.* [f. med.L. *manūcapt-us* taken by the hand: cf. next.] *trans.* To direct by a writ of manucaption.

1898 *Contemp. Rev.* Dec. 883 The burgess who was 'manucapted' to appear at Westminster.

manucaption (mænju:'kæpʃən). *Law. Obs.* exc. *Hist.* [ad. med.L. *manūcaptiōn-em*, noun of action f. *manū capĕre*, lit. to 'take by the hand'; cf. mainprise.] **a.** = mainprise. **b.** A writ directing the bringing in of a person charged with a felony, who was debarred from being admitted to bail by the sheriff or any inferior magistrate.

1588 Fraunce *Lawiers Log.* I. xii. 55 Bailement, maineprise or manucaption, and replevine.. they bee indifferently used to expresse that suretie which the prisoner is to finde. **1598** Manwood *Lawes Forest* xxiv. §5 (1615) 240 All pledges and Manucaptors which haue day by their Manucaption before the Iustice of the forest. **1875** Stubbs *Const. Hist.* II. xv. 235 The manucaption or production of two sureties.

manucaptor (mænju:'kæptə(r)). *Law. Obs.* exc. *Hist.* Also 7 **mani-**. [a. med.L. *manūcaptor*, agent-n. f. *manū capĕre*: see prec.] = mainpernor.

[**1523** in W. H. Turner *Select. Rec. Oxford* (1880) 34 As also the goods and cattall, surtus and manucaptores.] **1581** Lambarde *Eiren.* II. ii. (1588) 109 For some forme commaundeth him to take sufficient manucaptors.. so that hee will be answerable for it at his owne perill. **1620** J. Wilkinson *Coroners & Sherifes* 30 The principals, manicaptors or sureties shall make their fine. **1878** Stubbs *Const. Hist.* III. xx. 425 For each of them manucaptors or bailsmen were provided.

manucode ('mænjʊkəʊd). [a. F. *manucode* (Buffon), short f. mod.L. *manucodiāta*: see next.] †**a.** A bird of paradise (*obs.*). **b.** Any bird of either of the genera *Manucodia* and *Phonygama*, inhabiting the Papuan region, and formerly classed with the Birds of Paradise.

The F. *manucode* was originally applied to all the birds of the old genus *Manucodiata* (the genus *Paradisea* of Linnæus), and in this use was occas. employed by English writers. The generic name *Manucodia* (? a misprint for *Manucodiata*) was used by Boddaert 1783 in describing a species since discovered to belong to a distinct genus, for which English ornithologists adopted Boddaert's name. In English *manucode* was then restricted to the birds of this genus, which has since been divided into two.

1835 tr. *Lesson's Voy.* in *Penny Cycl.* IV. 422/1 The manucode presented itself twice in our shooting excursions, and we killed the male and female. **1881** *Daily News* 22 Apr. 2/3 The green manucode (*manucodia chalybeia*).

†**manucodiata.** *Obs.* Also 6 **manuccodiata,** 7 **manucadite.** [a. mod.L. *manucodiāta*, ad. Malay *mānuq dēwāta* 'bird of the gods'. Cf. mamuque.] A bird of paradise.

[**1523** Maximilianus Transylv. *Epist.* D iv b, Auiculam uero Manuccodiata appellauerunt.] **1555** Eden *Decades*, etc. 229 b, These Moores are of opinion that these byrdes coomme frome the heauenlye Paradyse, and therfore caule them *Manuccodiata*, that is the byrdes of god. **1613** Purchas *Pilgrimage* (1614) 538 The Moores.. call them Manucodiata, or holy birds. **1623** Cockeram III, *Manucadite*, the bird of Paradise. **1691** Ray *Creation* I. (1692) 147 The Manucodiata, or Bird of Paradise.

†**manuduce,** *v. Obs.* [ad. L. *manū dūcere* to lead by the hand.] *trans.* To lead, guide, direct.

1657 W. Morice *Coena quasi Κοινὴ* Def. xxviii. 275 There is nothing in the context that may incline and manuduce to such an interpretation. **1686** Goad *Celest. Bodies* To Rdr. 1 Contemplation of the Heavens conduced to the First, and therefore must manuduce to the Second.

†**manuducent,** *a.* and *sb. Obs.* [ad. L. *manū dūcent-em*, pres. pple. of *manū dūcĕre* (see prec.).] **A.** *adj.* Guiding, directing. *rare*$^{-1}$.

1677 Gale *Crt. Gentiles* IV. 494 The Greek Fathers, who terme medicinal efficacious grace, the spring of this supernatural infusion.. 'manuducent and assistent grace'.

B. *sb.* A guide, manuductor. *rare*$^{-1}$.

1615 J. Robinson *Manum. to Manuduction* To Rdr., in *Coll. Mass. Hist. Soc.* 4th Ser. I. 166 Needful it were in a matter of this.. weight, that the manuducent or handleader, should guide men by the plain.. way of the Scriptures.

†**manuduct,** *v. Obs. rare.* [f. L. *manū*, abl. of *manus* hand + *duct-*, ppl. stem of *dūcĕre* to lead.] *trans.* To lead or guide by the hand. Also *fig.*

1641 H. L'Estrange *God's Sabbath* 20 Adam and the succeeding Patriarchs (who.. were manuducted and guided by an inerring spirit) [etc.]. **1672** Sir C. Wyvill *Triple Crown* 164 At length, that Saint manuducts him into three or four sorts of Purgatories.

manuduction (mænju:'dʌkʃən). Also 6 manduccyon. [ad. med.L. *manūductiōn-em*, n. of action f. *manū dūcĕre* to lead by hand.]

1. The action of leading, guiding, or introducing; guidance, introduction, direction.

1502 *Ord. Crysten Men* (W. de W. 1506) IV. xxvii. 317 By the meane manduccyon of thynges corporalles & sensybles a man may come unto the contemplacyon of spyrytualles. **1624** F. White *Repl. Fisher* 514 Vertuous actions haue reference (not of desert, but of disposition, and instrumentall efficiencie or manuduction) to beatitude. **1642** Sir E. Dering *Sp. on Relig.* xvi. 85 Young Students.. wander for want of manuduction. **1723** *Pres. St. Russia* I. 18 Well stored with Money, but without any Instruction or Manuduction. **1872** Blackie *Lays Highl.* Introd. 54 Well satisfied if he has accomplished.. even one third of the ground over which he has accepted my hurried manuduction. **1896** Gladstone *Stud. Subsid. Butler* 88 The insight of anticipation which, without a manuduction (if the term may be allowed) by natural science, enabled him to forecast [etc.].

2. Means or instrument of guidance; a guide or introduction.

1624 F. White *Repl. Fisher* 586 He ascribeth no more vnto it, than to be a manuduction and guider to sauing veritie. **1625** T. James (*title*) A manuduction or introduction unto divinitie. **1713** Nelson *Life Bp. Bull* xvii. (1827) 84 He sent it [his book] abroad.. that it might serve as a manuduction to the candidates of divinity.

†**3.** A manual process or operation. *Obs. rare*$^{-1}$.

1778 Pryce *Min. Cornub.* Contents IV. ii, The various Manuductions used in dressing of Copper and Lead Ores.

†**manuductive** (mænju:'dʌktɪv), *a. Obs.* [ad. L. type **manūductīv-us*, f. *manū dūcĕre*: see manuduction.] That leads by the hand.

1626 W. Fenner *Hidden Manna* (1652) 2 There must be a special manu-ductive teaching. **1633** Ames *Agst. Cerem.* II. 151 If by accessorie worship he meaneth that which is appointed by man.. (which his manuductive interpretation beareth) then [etc.].

†**manuductor.** *Obs.* [ad. L. type **manūductōr-em*, agent-n. from *manū dūcĕre*: see manuduction.] A guide, director.

1657 Thornley tr. *Longus' Daphnis & Chloe* (1893) 98 But thou.. art kept alive and saved for us, in design to make us happy by more helps and manuductors to our Age. **1677** Gilpin *Demonol.* (1867) 378 The former opinion of Satan's taking of Christ, as a manuductor or guide, seems every way unreasonable.

b. *spec.* The conductor of a band or choir.

1785 Burney *Mus. Perform. Westm. Abb.* 15 This Commemoration is.. the first instance.. of any band, at all numerous, performing in a similar situation, without the assistance of a Manu-ductor, to regulate the measure. **1852** Hook *Ch. Dict.*, *Manuductor*.. was an officer who.. gave the signal to the choristers to sing,.. beat the time [etc.].

manuductory (mænju:'dʌktərɪ), *a.* [Formed as prec.: see -ory.] Leading by or as by the hand; that leads up to or towards.

1694 Westmacott *Script. Herb.* Ep. Ded. 5 These are the Manuductory Things, that Constitute an Expert and Real Artist. **1851** Chr. Wordsworth *Occas. Serm.* Ser. II. 34 They did not recognise this, its manuductory and provisional character.

manuel, -ell(e, obs. forms of manual.

Manueline ('mænjʊəlaɪn), *a.* Also **Manoeline, Manoelino, Manoellian, Manuelline.** [f. the name of *Manuel* I (b. 1469, reigned 1495–1521), King of Portugal.] Of or pertaining to a style of Portuguese architecture developed during the reign of Manuel I and characterized by its ornate elaborations of Gothic and Renaissance styles.

1908 W. C. Watson *Portuguese Archit.* x. 145 Nearly all these churches and palaces were built or added to in that peculiar style now called Manoelino. *Ibid.* 147 The Jesus College at Setubal.. is the best example in the country of a late Gothic church modified by the addition of certain Manoelino details. **1911** *Encycl. Brit.* XXII. 144/2 In architecture the name of King Emanuel was given to a new and composite style (the Manoeline or Manoellian), in which decorative forms.. were harmonized with Gothic and Renaissance designs. **1931** S. Sitwell *Spanish Baroque Art* ii. 50 There is always an imaginary Orient at the back of their ideas... In the Manoeline there are Moghul, Persian, Moroccan influences. **1937** *Archit. Rev.* LXXXII. 129/2 The Manoeline style of architecture is as distinct from what is termed Italian 'Renaissance' as Romanesque is from Gothic... In this respect by 'Manoeline' is meant Portuguese Renaissance. **1948** G. Kubler *Mexican Archit. 16th Cent.* II. viii. 382 In Portugal, the period before *ca.* 1525 was dominated by Manueline ornament. **1960** J. Lees-Milne *Baroque in Spain & Portugal* II. i. 144 The Manoeline style—if style it may be called—has a very positive bearing upon the last phase of Portuguese Baroque. **1968** *Encycl. Brit.* III. 271/2 The Capellas Imperfeitas ('unfinished chapels') are one of the most marvellous examples of Manuelline architecture.

†**manuensis.** *Obs.* = amanuensis.

1720 [A. Pennecuik] (*title*) Song of Songs.. Written.. by Solomon.. The inspired Manuensis of the Holy Ghost.

manuer, obs. form of manure *v.*

†**manufact,** *a.* and *sb. Obs.* [ad. late L. *manūfact-us* (*Vulg.* Acts vii. 48), f. *manū*, abl. of *manus* hand + *factus* made.]

A. *adj.* 'Made with hands'.

1539 *Man. Prayers* Y iv, We haue not the shewe bread of the Temple, for that manufact temple and the golden table are passed.

B. *sb.* The act of manufacturing, manufacture.
1690 D'Urfey *Collin's Walk* III. 105 And lay the Ensigns of their pride, Their Silken Ornaments aside; Which would have been a wholsome Act T'encourage Woolen Manufact. **1691** Maydman *Nav. Specul.* 312 The Decrease of our Wollen Manufacts... A great part of the Linen Manufact is done by Women and Children.

†**manu'faction.** *Obs.* [n. of action f. L. *manū facĕre* (*manū*, abl. of *manus* hand, *facĕre* to make) to make by hand.] Manufacture.
1602 *Proclam.* in *Moryson's Itin.* II. (1617) 263 We conceiue that there wanteth as yet for a time sufficient commodities of the growth or manufaction of this kingdome, wherewith to maintaine trafficke. **1730** *Phil. Trans.* XXXVI. 286 Thus from Castor, by a certain Manufaction, may be prepared an Oil sweeter than that of Cinnamon.

†**manufactor.** *Obs.* [agent-n. f. L. *manū facĕre* to make by hand: cf. MANUFACTURE.] A manufacturer or artificer.
a **1649** Drumm. of Hawth. *Jas. I* Wks. (1711) 8 The king ..drew unto him the best artisans and manufactors. ? **1667** Sir T. Browne *Brampton Urns* Miscell. (1712) 6 Inscriptions commonly signified..the Name of the Artificer, or Manufactor of such Vessels. **1812** J. J. Henry *Camp. agst. Quebec* 224 The vanilla of South America has been applied by the Spanish manufactors of tobacco in various ways.

manufactorage, var. MANUFACTURAGE.

manufactory (mænjuːˈfæktərɪ), *sb.* Also 7 -factry, 7–8 -factury. [ad. L. types **manūfactōria*, *-ōrium*, f. *manū facĕre*: see MANUFACTOR and -ORY[1].]
†**1.** Something that is produced by labour. = MANUFACTURE 2. *Obs.*
a **1618** Raleigh *Obs. Trade* in *Rem.* (1661) 186 Other Manufactories vendible to the number of about one thousand. **1685** *Lond. Gaz.* No. 2009/8 An Engine..for Beautifying of Cloth..Bays and all Woollen Manufactory. *a* **1734** North *Exam.* III. vi. §56 (1740) 464 The Manufactory and Product of England. **1776** Paine *Com. Sense* (1791) 55 We ought to view the building a fleet as an article of commerce, it being the natural manufactory of this country. **1786** Lady Jerningham in *J. Lett.* (1896) I. 37 A very fine silver gown. It is a new Norwich manufactory.
†**2.** The production of manufactured goods. *Obs.*
a **1618** Raleigh *Obs. Trade* Pref. in *Rem.* (1661) 164 Thereby to bring Manufactory into the Kingdome, and to set on work all sorts of people. **1657** R. Carpenter *Astrol.* 5 Mechanical, inferiour, and earthly Arts, pertaining to Manufactry, were invented by Cain and his Children. **1762** Sterne *Tr. Shandy* VI. xvii, To..work the machine to the improvement and better manufactory of the Arts and Sciences. **1812** J. J. Henry *Camp. agst. Quebec* 79 All neatly and warmly clothed in woolen, apparently of their own manufactory. **1828** Southey *Ess.* (1832) II. 332 The introduction of the linen manufactory is another instance. *fig.* **1846** G. S. Faber *Lett. Tractar. Secess.* 215 The deliberate manufactory of falsehood seems to be a regular part of the Popish system.
3. A factory or workshop. Also with prefixed word, as *cotton*, *milk manufactory*.
1692 Luttrell *Brief Rel.* (1857) II. 524 The queens manufactury in the Strand. **1827** Hone *Every-day Bk.* II. 591 Milk manufactories usurp the place Of..dairies. **1879** *Cassell's Techn. Educ.* III. 130/2 If the goods are fresh from the manufactory.

†**manu'factory**, *a.* *Obs.* [ad. L. type **manūfactōrius*, f. *manū facĕre*: cf. prec.] Pertaining to, or of the nature of, manufacture; engaged in manufacture.
1630 Lord *Banians* 70 Servile and manufactory men that should serve the uses of the world in the handicrafts. **1704** Swift *Tale Tub* §2 A Sort of Idol, who..did daily create Men by a Kind of Manufactory Operation. **1741** *New Hampsh. Prov. Papers* (1871) p. lxxvi, The manufactory notes of a Combination of Persons in the other Government.

manufacturable (mænjuːˈfæktjʊərəb(ə)l), *a.* [f. MANUFACTURE *v.* + -ABLE.] Capable of being manufactured. Also *fig.*
1784 Alchorne in *Phil. Trans.* LXXIV. 466 The bar obtained was no less manufacturable than at first. **1893** *Scribner's Mag.* Aug. 152/1 Talent is innate and not manufacturable.

†**manufacturage.** *Obs.* Also 7 -orage. [f. MANUFACTURE *sb.* + -AGE.] Manufacture.
1665 Dudley *Metallum Martis* (1854) 31 Lesse profitable to him that makes it into manufacturage, and lesse profitable to him that useth it. **1686** Plot *Staffordsh.* 162 More indeed to the Masters profit, but less to him that has the manufactorage of it. **1691** *Lond. Gaz.* No. 2670/4 For the Encouraging a Brandy Manufacturage in England.

manufactural (mænjuːˈfæktjʊərəl), *a.* [f. MANUFACTURE *sb.* + -AL[1].] Pertaining to manufacture.
1789 Morse *Amer. Geog.* 90 Some of our manufactural advantages and prospects. *Ibid.* 91 Pennsylvania has confessedly taken the lead..in manufactural improvements. **1852** S. Bailey *Disc.* 77. **1881** *Daily News* 30 Aug., The next process, and indeed the first in a manufactural sense, is that of converting the rough timber into a state for use.

manufacture (mænjuːˈfæktjʊə(r)), *sb.* Also 7 manifacture, mannifacture. [a. F. *manufacture* (16th c.), ad. med.L. **manufactūra*, f. *manū facĕre* (*manū*, abl. of *manus* hand; *facĕre* to make). Cf. Sp., Pg. *manufactura*, It. *manifattura*.]
1. †**a.** The action or process of making by hand.
1605 Bacon *Adv. Learn.* I. vi. §2 It is not set down that God said, Let there be heaven and earth, ..but actually, that God made heaven and earth: the one carrying the style of a manufacture, and the other of a..decree.
b. The action or process of making articles or material (in modern use, on a large scale) by the application of physical labour or mechanical power.
1622 Bacon *Hen. VII* 215 This Law pointed at a true Principle; That where forraine materials are but Superfluities, forraine Manufactures should bee prohibited. For that will either banish the Superfluitie, or gain the Manufacture. **1765** A. Dickson *Treat. Agric.* (ed. 2) 477 The custom of using sand in the manufacture of brick. **1835** Ure *Philos. Manuf.* 1 The most perfect manufacture is that which dispenses entirely with manual labour. **1892** Gardiner *Stud. Hist. Eng.* 8 The tin which they needed for the manufacture of bronze.
c. A particular branch or form of productive industry. Often with prefixed sb., as *linen*, *woollen*, *worsted manufacture*.
1683 J. Poyntz (*title*) The Present Prospect of the famous and fertile Island of Tobago. With a Description of the Situation, Growth, Fertility and Manufacture of the said Island. **1670** Sir S. Crowe in *12th Rep. Hist. MSS. Comm.* App. v. 15 If that manifacture [*sc.* of hangings] had beene under my charge. **1776** Adam Smith *W.N.* IV. ix. (1869) II. 262 By means of trade and manufactures, a greater quantity of subsistence can be annually imported. **1796** Morse *Amer. Geog.* II. 490 The late [Portuguese] minister of state,.. found it impracticable to raise a glass manufacture into consequence. **1835** Ure *Philos. Manuf.* 33 The capitalist has merely to state..the nature of his manufacture,..when he will be furnished with..estimates. **1843** *Penny Cycl.* XXVII. 555/2 The connection between employers and employed, buyers and sellers, in the woollen and worsted manufactures.
d. *fig.* Attributed to a quasi-personified natural agent.
1880 Haughton *Phys. Geog.* v. 204 The conditions to be fulfilled by a continent, for the successful manufacture of rivers, are [etc.].
e. Phrase. *of* (*home, foreign, English,* etc.) *manufacture*: manufactured at home, abroad, etc.
1669 Sturmy *Mariner's Mag., Penalties & Forfeit.* 1 Goods of the growth, production, and manufacture of Asia. **1844** *Mem. Babylonian P'cess* II. 168 Beschir sat on a handsome chair..of English manufacture. **1846** McCulloch *Acc. Brit. Empire* (1854) II. 35 A single article, either of domestic or foreign growth or manufacture. **1894** *Idler* Sept. 130 A small brass cannon of very antique pattern and manufacture.
f. Applied to the mechanical production or external 'getting up' of books.
1887 Gladstone in *Daily News* 10 Jan. 6/1 The most interesting of all manufactures, in my judgment, is the manufacture, apart from the production, of books. **1897** *Daily News* 30 June 6/3 A credit..to the fine art of what the publishers call the manufacture of books.
g. In depreciatory sense, applied to production involving mere mechanical labour, as contrasted with that which requires intellect. Also *fig.* applied, e.g., to literary work of a 'soulless' or mechanical kind, or to the deliberate fabrication of false statements on a large scale for the market.
1829 Carlyle *Misc., Germ. Playwr.* (1840) II. 92 Herein lies the difference between creation and manufacture. **1869** Ruskin *Q. of Air* §104 While manufacture is the work of hands only, art is the work of the whole spirit of man. **1872** —— *Eagle's N.* §88 Ignorance discontented, and dexterous, ..imitating what it cannot enjoy, produces the most loathsome forms of manufacture.
2. *concr.* †**a.** A product of hand-labour; a person's handiwork. Also *fig.* *Obs.*
1567 N. Sander *Treat. Images* viii. 72 Yet the image is rather a manufacture, to wit, a thing wrought vpon a creature by the artificers hand, then a seueral creature of it self. **1656** Earl Monm. tr. *Boccalini's Advts. fr. Parnass.* 78 Liberty may be rather said to be a Divine Manifacture, then any humane work. **1726** Pope *Odyss.* XX. 254 Thy manufacture, man.
attrib. **1700** Dryden *Fables, Baucis & Philemon* 14 Heav'ns Pow'r is Infinite: Earth, Air, and Sea, The Manufacture Mass, the making Pow'r obey.
b. An article or material produced by the application of physical labour or mechanical power. †Formerly also *collect. sing.*
1611 Donne *Paneg. Verses* in *Coryat's Crudities*, If they stoope lower yet and vent our wares Home-manufactures, to thicke popular faires. **1651** Hobbes *Leviath.* II. xxiv. 127 By selling the Manifactures, whereof the Materials [etc.]. *a* **1715** Burnet *Own Time* (1724) I. 229 The inhabitants.. brought with them a great deal of manufacture, which was lying on the hands of the clothiers and others. **1725** De Foe *Voy. round World* (1840) 276 Colchester baize, a coarse rug-like manufacture. **1809** Kendall *Trav.* II. xlvi. 132 The manufacture, of the process of which the following is the outline, is sea-salt. **1890** *Spectator* 26 Apr., The commercial proposals were at once rejected as giving them dear manufactures.
c. In depreciatory sense: Something produced by mere mechanical industry, or made to supply the demand of the market.
1871 Palgrave *Lyr. Poems* 135 The tale and the legend were gay Manufactures well wrought for the day.
†**3.** Working with the hands; a manual occupation, handicraft. *Obs.*
1625 Burges *Pers. Tithes* 7 Such as liue vpon Trade, or other Bargaining, or Manu-facture. **1638** Sir T. Herbert *Trav.* (ed. 2) 45 The other prophaner sort, the men of warre and manifactures, have [etc.]. **1647** Ward *Simp. Cobler* (1843) 57 Doth it become you..to..take up the Manufacture of cutting your Subjects throats? **1660** *Boston Rec.* (1877) II. 156 No person shall..occupy any manufacture or science, till hee hath compleated 21 years of age. **1699** Lister *Journ. Paris* 63 A private Anatomy Room is to one not accustomed to this kind of Manufacture, very irksome.
†**4.** A manufacturing establishment or business; a factory. *Obs.*
1653 H. Cogan tr. *Pinto's Trav.* xi. 35 Having seen..the Custom-house, the River, the Army, the Manufactures, stores of Powder, and other particulars..she was lodged in a fair house. **1704** De Foe in *15th Rep. Hist. MSS. Comm.* App. IV. 88 All my prospects were built on a manufacture I had erected in Essex. **1706** Phillips (ed. Kersey), *Manufacture*,..Also a Workhouse, or Place where such Works are carry'd on. **1783** Justamond tr. *Raynal's Hist. Indies* I. 370 The malversations that prevail in the manufactures, magazines, docks and arsenals at Batavia.

manufacture (mænjuːˈfæktjʊə(r)), *v.* [f. prec. Cf. F. *manufacturer*, It. *manifatturare*, med.L. *manifactūrāre*.]
1. *trans.* To work up (material) into forms suitable for use.
1683 Tryon *Way to Health* 81 Milk likewise altered and Manufactur'd (if I may call it so) by the good House-Wives Art and Industry, yields many other sorts of good Food. **1683** *Brit. Spec.* 13 Very fine Wooll..but being manufactured into Cloth and Stuffs, is dispersed all over the World. **1727** Swift *Pet. Colliers* Wks. 1755 III. I. 131 Totally prohibit the confining and manufacturing the sun-beams for any of the useful purposes of life. **1842** J. Aiton *Domest. Econ.* (1857) 217 The method of manufacturing milk just described—that is, of churning the whole into butter.
b. *transf.* To elaborate or work up (literary material).
1761 Gibbon *Jrnl.* 4 Aug. *Misc. Wks.* (1796) I. 107 It may afford such a fund of materials as I desire, which have not yet been properly manufactured.
2. To make or fabricate from material; to produce by labour (now esp. on a large scale).
1755 in Johnson. **1778** *Encycl. Brit.* (ed. 2) II. 1015/1 Of the bark..of a tree which they call *poerou* they manufacture excellent matting. **1878** Jevons *Prim. Pol. Econ.* 25 We cannot manufacture any goods unless we have some matter to work upon.
b. *transf.* Said of natural agencies.
1876 Bristowe *Th. & Pract. Med.* (1878) 876 The liver, besides manufacturing bile, is an organ for [etc.]. **1899** *Allbutt's Syst. Med.* VIII. 464 Poisons manufactured within the system can act in a similar manner.
3. *fig.* In disparaging sense: To 'fabricate', invent fictitiously; also, to produce (literary work, etc.) by mere mechanical industry.
1762 Gibbon *Misc. Wks.* (1814) IV. 110 The speech is evidently manufactured by the historian. **1771** *Junius Lett.* l. 259 He seems to manufacture his verses for the sole use of the hero. **1777** Hamilton *Wks.* (1886) VII. 512 Prisoners ..know very well how to manufacture stories calculated to serve the purposes of the side they belong to. **1876** Trevelyan *Macaulay* I. iii. 134 He was fond of setting himself to manufacture conceits resembling those on the heroes of the Trojan War. **1880** *Manch. Guard.* 15 Dec., The numerous outrages which have been reported, many of which he declared were 'manufactured'. **1902** B. L. Gildersleeve in *Amer. Jrnl. Philol.* XXIII. 449 The ancients manufactured a hostility between Homer and Hesiod, Pindar and Bakchylides, Aischylos and Sophocles.
4. *intr.* To permit of being manufactured.
1763 *Museum Rusticum* I. 12 The flax thus managed dresses and manufactures much better.

manufactured (mænjuːˈfæktjʊəd), *ppl. a.* [f. MANUFACTURE *v.* + -ED[1].]
1. Fabricated from raw material.
1680 W. Love in *Deb. Parlt.* (1681) 68 And it cannot be expected, that the Indians should grow weary, of exchanging their Manufactured Goods for our Gold and Silver. **1776** Adam Smith *W.N.* IV. ix. (1869) II. 263 A trading and manufacturing country naturally purchases with a small part of its manufactured produce, a great part of the rude produce of other countries. **1885** *Athenæum* 17 Oct. 500/2 [The] age..brings manufactured articles to every man's door.
2. Fraudulently invented or brought into existence.
1866 *Totnes Elect. Comm., Min. Evid.* (1867) 77 They were manufactured votes. **1903** *Daily Chron.* 24 Feb. 5/5 A more manufactured and baseless claim was never set up.

manufacturer (mænjuːˈfæktjʊərə(r)). [f. MANUFACTURE *v.* + -ER[1]. Cf. F. *manufacturier*.]
†**1.** An artificer, an operative in a manufactory.
1719 W. Wood *Surv. Trade* 312 Those who differ from the Established Church are generally of the lowest Rank, Mechanicks, Artificers and Manufacturers. **1776** Adam Smith *W.N.* I. x. I. (1869) I. 107 The wages of mechanics, artificers, and manufacturers should be somewhat higher than those of common labourers. **1812** *Gen. Hist.* in *Ann. Reg.* 38 The distresses which had driven the poor manufacturers [of Nottingham] to acts of outrage. **1849** Macaulay *Hist. Eng.* iii. (1858) I. 433 A shilling a day was the pay to which the English manufacturer then [in 1680] thought himself entitled.

2. One who employs workmen for manufacturing; the owner of a manufactory.

1752 HUME *Ess. & Treat.* (1777) II. 95 A manufacturer reckons upon the labour of his servants. **1832** BABBAGE *Econ. Manuf.* xiii. (ed. 3) 121 The magnitude of the order made it worth his while to turn manufacturer. **1901** *Daily News* 22 Mar. 3/2 It is the duty of a manufacturer to charge the highest price he can get.

b. With qualifying word, as *cloth, flannel manufacturer*.

1842 BISCHOFF *Woollen Manuf.* II. 120 John Nussey, cloth manufacturer, Birstal, Yorkshire... Jacob Tweedale, flannel manufacturer, Rochdale.

3. *transf.* and *fig.*

1802 J. RITSON *Anc. Eng. Metr. Rom.* I. p. cix, In what manner this ingenious editour conducted himself in this patch'd up publication wil be evident from the following parallel, which may be useful to future manufacturers in this line. **1847** EMERSON *Repr. Men, Napoleon* Wks. (Bohn) I. 378 The men of letters he slighted; 'they were manufacturers of phrases'.

Hence **manu'facturess**, a female manufacturer, or the wife of a manufacturer. Also *fig.*

1822 *Blackw. Mag.* XII. 657 'Buildresses of the lofty rhyme', or manufacturesses of fancy goods in verse. **1881** M. A. LEWIS *Two Pretty G.* III. 14 A good-humoured homely body, as far as possible removed from the typical rich manufacturess.

manufacturing (mænju:ˈfæktjʊərɪŋ), *vbl. sb.* [-ING¹.] The action of the vb. MANUFACTURE.

1690 CHILD *Disc. Trade* 178 Where there is little Manufacturing,..the profit of Plantations, viz. the greatest part thereof will not redound to the Mother-Kingdom. **1757** FOOTE *Author* I. Wks. 1799 I. 134, I have a larger cargo of my own manufacturing. **1865** *Morn. Star* 3 May, The roasting of ore and the manufacturing of arsenic. **1893** *Athenæum* 23 Sept. 412/2 The mere manufacturing of poetry.

attrib. **1834** PEEL in *Croker Papers* (1884) 24 Mar., Those gave the most reluctant votes whose Constituencies were most of a manufacturing character. **1896** *Daily News* 13 Jan. 7/5 Gas and manufacturing fuel and all kinds of coke are selling freely.

manufacturing (mænju:ˈfæktjʊərɪŋ), *ppl. a.* [-ING².] Engaged or concerned in manufacture.

1722 DEFOE *Jrnl. Plague Year* 257 The Manufacturing Trade in England suffer'd greatly. **1774** J. TUCKER *Four Tracts* Contents I, A rich manufacturing Country. **1776** [see MANUFACTURED I]. **1789** H. MORE *Lett.* (1925) 165, I have written to different manufacturing towns for a [school] mistress. **1825** MᶜCULLOCH *Pol. Econ.* II. i. 72 Labour..is said to be agricultural, manufacturing, or commercial. **1855** MACAULAY *Hist. Eng.* IV. 127 Throughout the country, but especially in the capital, in the seaports and in the manufacturing towns. **1892** *Rep. Vermont Board Agric.* XII. 140 As these manufacturing centers increase in size, so do the farm lands in like ratio increase in value. **1942** *Short Guide Gt. Brit.* (U.S. War Dept.) 7 The great 'midland' manufacturing cities of Birmingham, Sheffield and Coventry. **1959** *Chambers's Encycl.* IX. 51/1 The manufacturing industries of Manchester are much more varied than in a specialized manufacturing town.

‖**manuka** (məˈnu:kə; Maori ˈmɑ:nʊka). [Maori.] A name for several Australasian trees and shrubs of the genus *Leptospermum* (N.O. *Myrtaceæ*), which yield a very hard, dark, close-grained and heavy wood, and an aromatic leaf sometimes employed as a substitute for tea: **a.** Red manuka of New Zealand, *Leptospermum scoparium*. **b.** White manuka of New Zealand, *L. ericoides*. **c.** Manuka of Tasmania (Tea tree), *L. lanigerum*. Also *attrib.*

1832 G. BENNETT in *London Med. Gaz.* 18 Feb. 750/1 This tree..is probably a species of Leptospermum. It is found abundantly at New Zealand,..and is named Kaetatowa, or Manuka, by the natives. **1840** J. S. POLACK *Mann. N. Zealanders* II. 258 This wood, called by the southern tribes Mánuka, is remarkably hard and durable. **1851** MRS. WILSON *New Zealand* 46 Manuka, a very hard dark closegrained and heavy wood. **1882** W. D. HAY *Brighter Britain!* II. 195 The Manuka or Manukau..is the 'ti-tree' of settlers. **1959** *Tararua* XIII. 47 We may find on the topographical maps such New Zealand terms as..'teatree' in Auckland, 'manuka' further south. **1960** *New Scientist* 4 Aug. 330/1 Sheep farmers were beginning to get worried by manuka, which showed signs of investing large tracts of country. And then, suddenly the coccid appeared and started to destroy the weed.

attrib. **1875** WOOD & LAPHAM *Waiting for Mail* 38 A bit of deal board, fastened on a Manuka pole. **1920** *Nature* 22 July 667/1 The most abundant foods [for trout] were the green manuka-beetle,..the larvae of caddis-flies..and a small mollusc. **1936** 'R. HYDE' *Passport to Hell* ii. 47 The brown and white manuka blossoms. **1948** *Coast to Coast 1947* 76 Johnny put up a manuka shelter around the pool.

manul (ˈmɑ:nʊl). [Said by Pallas to be a Kirghiz word.] A cat, *Felis manul*, native of the steppes of Siberia and Tartary.

1871 *Cassell's Nat. Hist.* II. 59 The Manul seems to replace the common Wild Cat in Northern Asia.

manument, variant of MANYMENT *Sc. Obs.*

†**manumisable**, *a. Obs. rare*⁻¹. [f. MANUMISE *v.* + -ABLE.] Capable of being released from a burden or obligation.

1773 *Gentl. Mag.* XLIII. 76 Copyholds..may be annihilated by making them manumisable, upon paying a certain number of years rents.

†**manumise, manumiss**, *v. Obs.* Forms: 6–7 manumiss(e, manumyse, mannumise, 6–9 manumise, 7–9 manumize. [f. L. *manūmiss-*, ppl. stem of *manūmittĕre* to MANUMIT. The form *manumise* arises from assimilation to *commise, premise, promise*.] = MANUMIT *v.*

1523 FITZHERB. *Surv.* 26 b, It were a charytable dede..to manumise them that be bonde. **1581** J. BELL *Haddon's Answ. Osor.* 147 Mans Freewill..beyng manumysed..by Gods grace. **1628** COKE *On Litt.* I. 137 b, If a villeine be manumised. **1637** GILLESPIE *Eng. Pop. Cerem.* Ep. B b, They manumisse and set free the Simony,..of some of their owne side. **1708** COLLIER *Eccl. Hist.* I. II. 113/2 If a Slave is forc'd to work upon the Sunday by his Master's Order, let him be manumiz'd. **1769** *Boston News-Let.* 7 Sept. 2/2 A mulatto named Dick, formerly a slave to Mr. d'Harriette, but afterwards manumised,..has disappeared. **1812** SOUTHEY *Omniana* I. 321 Neither is it uncommon for the men slaves to purchase and manumize their wives. **1819** G. S. FABER *Dispensations* (1823) II. 111 The dead are no longer the object of God's..moral government, being manumised or set free from it as a slave was manumised or set free from the service of his master.

Hence †**manumised** *ppl. a.*, †**manumising** *vbl. sb.*

1541 PAYNEL *Catiline* xxxii. 51 b, P. Umbrenus, a man manumised. **1579–80** NORTH *Plutarch, Publicola* (1595) 111 The perfect manumissing and freeing of bondmen, is called *Vindicta*. **1624** [T. SCOTT] *Lawfuln. Netherl. Warre* 25 Exhort you them to proceed as they are best able..for the preservation and manumising of their owne lives and liberty. **1627** HAKEWILL *Apol.* (1630) 420 The daughter of a manumissed slave. **1796** STEDMAN *Surinam* I. i. 17 Two black soldiers, manumized slaves.

†**manumiss**, *sb. Obs.* [ad. L. *manūmiss-us*, pa. pple. of *manūmittĕre* to MANUMIT.] A freed slave.

1658 BROMHALL *Treat. Specters* I. 12 Trallianus a Manumisse of the Emperour Adrian.

manumission (mænju:ˈmɪʃən). *Obs.* exc. *Hist.* [a. F. *manumission*, ad. L. *manūmissiōn-em*, noun of action f. L. *manūmittĕre*: see MANUMIT *v.*]

1. The action of manumitting, or the fact of being manumitted; formal release from slavery or servitude; an act or instance of this.

charter, deed, letter, writ of manumission: a written grant of personal freedom by a feudal superior; also *fig.*

1432–50 tr. *Higden* (Rolls) I. 89 The peple of Parthia..amonge whom seruauntes be habundante, for thei haue not their manumission. **1523** FITZHERB. *Surv.* 26 Many noble men..haue made to dyuers of the sayd bonde men manumissions. **1591** LAMBARDE *Archeion* (1635) 108 That Great Charter of the Liberties of England, (which I may call the first Letters of Manumission of the people of this Realme [etc.]). **1610** WILLET *Hexapla Dan.* 178 The manumission and deliuerance of the Iewes. **1625** MASSINGER *New Way* Epil., Nor we, Nor he that wrote the Comedie, can be free Without your Mannumission. **1628** COKE *On Litt.* §204. 137 Manumission is properly when the Lord makes a deed to his villeine to enfranchise him by this word (*Manumittere*) which is the same as to put him out of the hands and power of another. **1658** CLEVELAND *Rustic Rampant* Wks. (1687) 480 Lister sends on Embassy..the Lord Morley..to obtain Charters of Manumission, and Pardon. **1737** J. CHAMBERLAYNE *St. Gt. Brit.* I. III. v. 182 Servants in the Saxon Times were properly Slaves, and very many Instances of their Manumissions are still extant. **1766** BLACKSTONE *Comm.* II. vi. 94 Villeins might be enfranchised by manumission, which is either express or implied: express, as where a man granted to the villein a deed of manumission. **1796** MORSE *Amer. Geog.* I. 231 Societies for the manumission of slaves. **1827** POLLOK *Course T.* VII, The writ of manumission, signed By God's own signature. **1862** TROLLOPE *Orley F.* x. (ed. 4) 69 He had been no Old Bailey lawyer, devoting himself to the manumission of murderers.

attrib. **1894** H. GARDENER *Unoff. Patriot* 97 When the manumission papers came, Katherine sent LeRoy..to tell the negroes to come to the 'big house'.

b. *transf.* and *fig.*

1549 COVERDALE, etc. *Erasm. Par. 1 Tim.* 16 They are set at lybertye by manumission from the bondeshyp of synne. *c* **1645** HOWELL *Lett.* (1655) IV. xix. 45 Languages by a regardless adoption of som new words, and manumission of old do often vary. **1779–81** JOHNSON *L.P., Addison* Wks. III. 82 It is not unlikely that Addison was first seduced to excess by the manumission he obtained from the servile timidity of his sober hours.

¶**c.** Misused for 'initiation.'

1596 NASHE *Saffron-walden* K 4 b Vpon his first manumission in the mysterie of Logique, because he obseru'd Ergo was the..driu'n home stab of the Syllogisme, hee [etc.].

†**2.** Graduation, laureation. *Sc. Obs.*

1604 in CRAUFURD *Hist. Univ. Edin.* 62 The Primar calling the candidates before him,..performeth the ceremony, by imposition of an bonnet (the badge of manumission) upon the head of every one of the candidats.

manu'missive, *a. Civil Law.* [f. L. *manūmiss-*, ppl. stem of *manūmittĕre* to MANUMIT + -IVE.] Concerned with manumitting.

1871 POSTE *Gaius* I. 82 Acquisition of manumissive capacity.

†**manumit**, *sb. Obs.* [f. MANUMIT *v.* (? as if pa. pple.).] A freed bondman.

1615 G. SANDYS *Trav.* 276 Effected by the labor of twenty thousand manumitts.

manumit (mænju:ˈmɪt), *v.* [ad. L. *manūmittĕre*, ante-class. *manū ēmittĕre*, lit. to send forth from one's 'hand', i.e. from one's control. Cf. OF. *manumetre, manumiter*, Sp. *manumitir*, It. *mano-, manimettere*.]

1. *trans.* To release from slavery; to release from bondage or servitude; to set free.

1432–50 tr. *Higden* (Rolls) VI. 283 But this Kenulphus..manumitte this kynge at the hie awter. ? **1538** LELAND *Itin.* II. 55 One of the Erles of Cornewalle hering them secretly to lament their state, manumittid them for Mony. **1590** SWINBURNE *Testaments* 196 If the testator do make his owne villeine executor, he doth manumit..his villeine from bondage. **1649** JER. TAYLOR *Gt. Exemp.* II. Disc. ix. 108 Christian masters were not bound to manumit their slaves. *a* **1671** LD. FAIRFAX *Mem.* in Arb. *Garner* VIII. 574, I thought fit to manumit the Lord Capel, the Lord Norwich, &c. over to the Parliament. **1757** BURKE *Abridgm. Eng. Hist.* II. ii. Wks. X. 267 The clergy..manumitted their new vassals. **1840** POE *Gold Bug* Wks. 1864 I. 93 An old negro, called Jupiter, who had been manumitted, before the reverses of the family.

b. *transf.* and *fig.*

1594 NASHE *Unfort. Trav.* I 2 b, My hand and my knife shall manumit mee out of the horrour of minde I endure. **1598** MARSTON *Pygmal.* etc. *Reactio* 66 Come, manumit thy plumie pinion, And scower the sword of Eluish champion. **1644** R. STAPYLTON *Juvenal* vi. 523 The Matron of the wheele in councell sits, Whose needle now her Lady manumits. **1653** GAUDEN *Hierasp.* 27 Striplings..which have but lately been manumitted from the rod and ferula. **1877** SPARROW *Serm.* iv. 43 A bondage to Satan, from which none can manumit us but the Son.

absol. **1742** YOUNG *Nt. Th.* IV. 667 Happy Day! that breaks our Chain; That manumits; that calls from Exile home. **1880** MUIRHEAD *Gaius* I. §36 It is not every man who pleases that can manumit.

†**2.** To graduate or confer a degree upon. *Sc. Obs.*

1607 in CRAUFURD *Hist. Univ. Edin.* 65 The 20th class..were manumitted with the magisteriall dignity, some 27 in number. **1635** *ibid.* 126 The 47th class..were solemnly manumitted in the lower hall of the Colledge.

Hence **manu'mitted, manu'mitting** *ppl. adjs.* Also **manu'mitter**, one who manumits.

1616 HOLYDAY *Persius* v. 214 Knowst thou no other Master, but he whom The Manumitting rod did free thee from? **1685** COTTON tr. *Montaigne* (1711) I. xxiii. 159 A mean manumitted slave. **1693** W. BOWLES in *Dryden's Juvenal* v. (1697) 108 At last thou wilt..receive the manumitting Blow On thy shav'd slavish Head. **1863** WHYTE MELVILLE *Gladiators* I. 55 These manumitted slaves were usually bound by the ties of interest. **1865** MOZLEY *Mirac.* vii. 145 The Church was the great manumitter and improver of the condition of the serf. **1875** POSTE *Gaius* I. (ed. 2) §39 The motives valid when the manumitting owner is under twenty, are admissible when the manumitted slave is under thirty.

manumotive (mænju:ˈməʊtɪv), *a.* [f. L. *manū*, abl. of *manus* hand + MOTIVE *a.*] Of a vehicle: Propelled by mechanism worked by hand.

1825 *Mech. Mag.* V. 97 (*heading*) Idea for a manumotive carriage. **1831** *Ibid.* XIV. 389 Some communications in the Magazine on manumotive carriages. **1889** *Spectator* 12 Oct., Steam-carriages,..and manumotive cars.

manumotor (mænju:ˈməʊtə(r)). [f. L. *manū*, abl. of *manus* hand + MOTOR.] A carriage propelled by mechanism worked by hand.

1844 [see PEDOMOTOR]. In recent Dicts.

manuple, obs. f. MANIPLE.

†**manuporter**. *Obs. rare*⁻⁰. [f. L. *manū* by hand + *portāre* to carry + -ER¹: cf. PORTER *sb.*] One who carries by strength of hand.

1688 R. HOLME *Armoury* III. 71/2 The Manuporter is him that bears or carries any thing by strength of hands; and such are Packing Porters.

†**manuprisor**. *Obs.* [Altered form of MAINPRISER, after L. *manū*, abl. of *manus* hand.] = MAINPERNOR.

1695 KENNETT *Par. Antiq.* ix. 419 The said Sir Eubulo..was Manuprisor or Security for Hugh Spencer. **1710** J. HARRIS *Lex. Techn.* II, *Manu-prisor*, one who was Bail-pledge or Security for another Person.

manurable (məˈnjʊərəb(ə)l), *a.* Also 7 **maynorable, maniorable** (corruptly for ***mainorable**), **manureable**. [f. MANURE *v.* + -ABLE.]

†**1.** *Law.* Admitting of being held in corporeal possession. *Obs.*

1628 COKE *On Litt.* 47 If a man demiseth the vesture or herbage of his land, he may reserue a rent, for that the thing is maynorable. *Ibid.* 142 A Rent seruice cannot be reserued out of any inheritance but such as is manurable, whereinto the Lord may enter and take a distresse, as in Lands and Tenements, Reuersions, Remainders, and as some haue said, out of the herbage of lands. **1767** COMYNS *Digest* s.v. *Pleader* C 35 If he alledges Seisin of Things manurable, as of Lands, Tenements,..&c. he shall say [etc.]. If of Things not manurable, as of an Advowson &c. he shall say [etc.].

†**2.** Of land: That can be worked or cultivated.

1630 *R. Johnson's Kingd. & Commw.* 544 The residue, except the sand, is made manurable, either for feeding of Cattell or Camels. *a* **1676** HALE *De Jure Maris* I. vi. in *Hargrave's Tracts* (1787) I. 26 For the most part the lands covered with these fluxes are dry and maniorable. **1756** P. BROWNE *Jamaica* 13 They laid a tax of five shillings per acre on all manurable lands that should not be forthwith opened and cultivated.

3. That can be manured or fertilized.

1828–32 in WEBSTER; and in later Dicts.

†**ma'nurage.** *Obs. rare.* [f. MANURE *v.* + -AGE. Cf. OF. *manouvrage.*] Occupation or cultivation of land.

1586 WARNER *Alb. Eng.* III. xiv. (1589) 56 Now, of the Conqueror this Isle had Brutaine vnto name, And with his Troianes Brute began manurage of the same. **1796** *Modern Gulliver* 107 No one..should be allowed to work on the farm, while under my course of manurage.

manurance (mə'njʊərəns). Also 5 **menurance, mannerance,** 6 **manuraunce.** [f. MANURE *v.* + -ANCE.]

1. Tenure, occupation (of land or other property); control, management. Now only in *Law.*

1468 *Paston Lett.* II. 331 Dischargyng hym utterly of the menurance, occupacion, and receyt of the revenuez. **1468** *Rolls of Parlt.* VI. 231/2 Accions for th' occupacion and mannerance of any of the seid premisses. **1538** FITZHERB. *Just. Peas* 116 b, Meses landes or tenementes in theyr owne manuraunce and occupacion. **1604** *Suppl. Masse Priests* i. B 3, How can they delight in peace and order and good manurance of the countrey? **1726** AYLIFFE *Parergon* 508 So long as the land continued in the Manurance of the Religious Persons themselves.

2. †Cultivation (of land), tillage (*obs.*); manuring.

1572 J. JONES *Bathes Buckstone* Ded. 2 Men liuing on the fruits of the Earth, without any manurance, as beasts. *c* **1630** RISDON *Surv. Devon* §1 (1810) 15 It is subject to thorns and briers, (if manurance did not prevent it). **1760** BURN *Eccles. Law* (1797) III. 210 [To] buy and sell corn and cattle for the only manurance, tillage, and pasturage of such farms. **1805** R. W. DICKSON *Pract. Agric.* App. v. 1240 The Prædial Tithes are such as arise from the land spontaneously or by manurance. **1854** THOREAU *Walden* vii. (1863) 177 See if they will not grow in this soil even with less toil and manurance.

†**b.** *fig.* Cultivation or training (of the character or faculties). *Obs.*

1594 CAREW *Huarte's Exam. Wits* xiv. 242 The Turks.. caused the Vniuersitie of Athens to passe vnto Paris... And (thus through want of manurance) so many gallant wits.. are vtterly perished. **1605** BACON *Adv. Learn.* II. xix. §2 The culture and manurance of minds in youth hath such a forcible..operacion, as [etc.]. **1615** J. DYKE *Myst. Self-deceit* 46 We should be loath to trust a Beare or Wolfe.. though by culture and manurance in their youth, their inborne fiercenesse be somewhat mitigated.

manure (mə'njʊə(r)), *sb.* Also 6 **menar, maner, -oure, maynor, -ure,** 6–7 **meano(u)r,** 7 **manier, manner.** [f. MANURE *v.*

Stressed '*manure* as late as 1784, though *ma'nure* occurs in Dryden. Some mod. dialects have ('mænə(r)).]

1. Dung or compost spread over or mixed with soil to fertilize it. Also, other substances, esp. various chemicals, used as fertilizers.

1549 in Willis & Clark *Cambridge* (1886) II. 410 The seyde College dothe..laye ther mucke and meanor..apon the foreseyde common grene. **1579** *Nottingham Rec.* IV. 190 Wee present Jhon Broune (ijd.) for layinge menar in they strett. **1598** BP. HALL *Sat.* v. i. 59 Tho many a lode of Marle and Manure led, Reuiu'd his barren leas, that earst lay dead. **1651** *Manch. Court Leet Rec.* (1887) IV. 53 Thomas Millington hath made a trespas vpon M[ris] Hallywell by laieinge manier..vnto her freehold in St. Mariegate. **1664** EVELYN *Sylva* (1679) 10 To barren ground with toyle large meanour add. **1697** DRYDEN *Virg. Georg.* II. 475 In depth of Earth secure Thy cover'd Plants, and dung with hot Manure. **1760** BROWN *Compl. Farmer* II. 3 The best manure for meadows is the bottom of hay-mows and hay-stacks. **1784** COWPER *Task* III. 517 The warm and genial earth that hides The smoking manure, and o'erspreads it all. **1794** R. KIRWAN in *Trans. R. Irish Acad.* V. i. 137 The substances principally used as manures, are chalk, lime..gypsum, [etc.]. **1824** J. C. LOUDON *Encycl. Gardening* (ed. 2) 243 Saline and calcareous substances form the principal fossil manures. **1858** GLENNY *Gard. Every-day Bk.* 56/2 The runners are to be planted out in beds of rich manure. **1904** T. W. SANDERS *Roses & their Cultivation* 70 It is of no use applying manure that has been allowed to decay naturally, because nearly all the essential salts have been washed out or evaporated. **1922** JOYCE *Ulysses* 698 James W. Mackey.. agent for chemical manures. **1951** *Dict. Gardening* (R. Hort. Soc.) III. 1248/2 Manures may be classified into Organic Manures which are substances of animal or vegetable origin, and Inorganic Manures which are of mineral origin. **1971** L. D. HILLS *Grow your own Fruit & Vegetables* ii. 27 There is a clear distinction between organic and inorganic manures and fertilizers.

†**2.** The action of 'manuring'; cultivation. *Obs.*

1677 PLOT *Oxfordsh.* 154 As to the manure of it, some sow but two bushels on the Statute Acre. **1696** WHISTON *Th. Earth* IV. (1722) 352 The Toil, Tillage and Manure of the Husbandman..must have been in the Primitive state very facile.

3. *attrib.* and *Comb.*, as ***manure-heap, -plough, -spreader,*** etc.

1766 *Museum Rusticum* VI. 32 The five-coultered, or.. manure-plough. **1832** *Scoreby Farm Rep.* 27 in *Libr. Usef. Knowl. Husb.* III, The manure-hill should be made in a compact form, and banked up square. **1844** H. STEPHENS *Bk. Farm* II. 648 The profits of the manure-dealer must be much greater than those of the farmer. **1865** *Florist's Jrnl.* 10 Water them freely with manure water, made with decayed sheep's dung. *a* **1884** KNIGHT *Dict. Mech.* Suppl. 580/2 *Manure Spreader*, a cart having a bed of traveling slats ..to distribute the load while the vehicle is moving over the surface of the ground. **1887** *Spectator* 8 Oct. 1342 The manure-heap [was] removed to a reasonable distance. **1915** J. LONDON *Let.* 26 Jan. (1966) 445 My plan still holds of using litter-carriers to dump manure..into..waiting manure-spreaders. **1943** J. S. HUXLEY *TVA* vi. 49 He insisted on buying a mechanical manure-spreader and using it with a tractor. **1969** K. M. WELLS *Owl Pen Reader* i. 46 The uphill clatter of Farmer Jim's manure-spreader as he drove it over the stubbles.

Hence **ma'nur(e)y** *a.*, splashed or littered with manure.

1890–3 E. M. TABER *Stowe Notes, Lett. & Verses* (1913) 29 The stable-yard repulsive, muddy and manury. **1932** *Sunday Express* 3 July 17/4 Many's the time I've seen him all mud and manurey.

manure (mə'njʊə(r)), *v.* Also 5 **maynoyre, manour, maynour(e, menure, mannor,** 6 **man(n)er, manar, -or,** 7 **mannure.** [a. AF. *maynoverer* to work with the hands = OF. *manouvrer*: see MANŒUVRE *v.*]

†**1.** *trans.* To hold, occupy (land, property); to have the tenure of; to administer, manage. *Obs.*

a **1400–50** *Alexander* 837* (Dubl. MS.) All þe marche of massydon he manours clene. **1430–31** *Rolls of Parlt.* IV. 385/2 The saide tenauntz and lond holders dar not inhabite, maynour nor occupye the saide Toun. **1457** *Peebles Charters*, etc. (1872) 119 The gud wif sal mannor thir thyngys qwil scho lefis. *a* **1577** SIR T. SMITH *Commw. Eng.* I. xxiv. (1589) 43 To speake of the Common wealth..of England, it is gouerned, administred and manured by three sortes of persons. **1581** PETTIE *Guazzo's Civ. Conv.* III. (1586) 148 b, They cannot manner their children well, vnlesse they haue a rod in their hand. **1596** DALRYMPLE tr. *Leslie's Hist. Scot.* I. IV. 208 To the Britanis delyuering it [the kingdome] to manure and inhabite [L. *Britannisque incolendum tradidit*]. **1628** COKE *On Litt.* 17 That which is manually occupied, manured and possessed. **1645** MILTON *Tetrach.* Wks. 1851 IV. 231 (Matt. xix. 8) Christ only told us that from the beginning it was not so; that is to say not so as the Pharises manur'd the busines.

†**b.** To inhabit (a place). Also *absol. Obs.*

c **1595** CAPT. WYATT *R. Dudley's Voy. W. Ind.* (Hakl. Soc.) 16 Not marveilinge that he founde noe inhabitante manuringe in that uninhabitable desarte. **1698** FRYER *Acc. E. India & P.* 67 Beyond it is Parell..to which appertains Siam, manured by Columbeens, Husbandmen.

†**2.** To till, cultivate (land). *Obs.*

?*a* **1400** *Morte Arth.* 2507 A mede..Mawene and unmade, maynoyrede bott lyttylle. **1513** DOUGLAS *Æneis* IV. v. 72 Ȝone woman..quham to we For to manure gave the strand of the sea [L. *cui litus arandum..dedimus*]. **1592** *Wills & Inv. N.C.* (Surtees) II. 214 To my mother..ij ackers of medow..and all her land to be mannered. **1601** R. JOHNSON *Kingd. & Commw.* (1603) 231 Hee manureth his owne fields with his owne slaves and cattle. **1671** tr. *Frejus' Voy. Mauritania* 28 We saw all the Countrey manured and green. **1700** ASTRY tr. *Saavedra-Faxardo* II. 148 A barren Sand, not capable of being manur'd by either Spade or Plow. **1741** C'TESS POMFRET *Corr.* (1805) III. 250 A beautiful vale, inhabited, manured, and planted. **1774** GOLDSM. *Nat. Hist.* (1776) III. 161 He is at the trouble neither of manuring his grounds, nor bringing in his harvests.

†**b.** To cultivate, train, rear (a plant). *Obs.*

1632 SIR T. HAWKINS tr. *Mathieu's Unhappy Prosperitie* 259 Omitting nothing in the sollicitous care of exact education, by manuring her as a plant. **1639** FULLER *Holy War* II. xi. (1840) 64 Who like a nut tree must be manured by beating. **1753** CHAMBERS *Cycl. Supp.* s.v. *Oost*, The people who manure hops.

†**c.** *fig.* with retention of the literal phraseology.

1561 T. NORTON *Calvin's Inst.* IV. xiv. (1634) 633 The worde of God..if it light upon a soul manured with the hand of the heavenly spirit, it will bee most fruitfull. **1645** Z. BOYD *Holy Songs* in *Zion's Flowers* (1855) App. 13/1 Manure your heart with diligence, and in it sow good seed.

†**d.** To cultivate, train (the body or mind, etc.).

c **1540** tr. *Pol. Verg. Eng. Hist.* (Camden No. 36) 10 Those Scotts which inhabit the southe, beinge farre the beste parte, are well manured. **1607** J. CARPENTER *Plaine Mans Plough* 9 O Father..manure our worke without, and prepare our mindes within. **1641** MILTON *Animadv.* xiii. Wks. 1851 III. 229 It is..his own painfull study..that manures and improves his ministeriall gifts. *a* **1781** R. CHALLONER *Medit.* (1843) I. 24 To manure you..with his word, his graces, and his sacraments.

†**e.** To practise, devote oneself to. *Obs.*

1596 DALRYMPLE tr. *Leslie's Hist. Scot.* I. 10 Thay manure Justice [L. *iustitiam colunt*].

3. To enrich (land) with manure; to apply manure to; to supply with fertilizing material.

1599 NASHE *Lent. Stuff* 63 Retailing theyr dung to manure landes. **1601** ? MARSTON *Pasquil & Kath.* I. 99 Onely to scrape A heape of muck: to fatten and manure The barren vertues of my progenie. *a* **1653** GOUGE *Comm. Heb.* xiii. 20 Sheep are in every thing profitable. Their wool and skin for clothing,..their dung for manuring ground. **1680** DODWELL *On Sanchoniathon* (1691) 109 The Slime it brought along with it, manured the Land for Corn. **1703** MOXON *Mech. Exerc.* 242 Lime also is useful..to Manure Land with. **1713** ADDISON *Cato* II. i, The Corps of half her Senate Manure the Fields of Thessaly. *a* **1862** BUCKLE *Misc. Wks.* (1872) I. 571 The land was inclosed, drained, and manured.

absol. (*fig.*) **1851** THACKERAY *Eng. Hum.* Wks. (Biogr. Ed.) II. 483 He had not worked crop after crop from his brain, manuring hastily, sub-soiling indifferently.

b. To spread or spill like manure. *nonce-use.*

1592 KYD *Sol. & Pers.* I. v. 36 So many valiant Bassowes slaine, Whose bloud hath bin manured to their earth.

†**4. a.** To work upon with the hand; to work up = MANŒUVRE *v. Obs.*

1431 in Madox *Formul. Anglic.* (1702) 331 John has selled ..alle the Underwodde..to hewe, kutte downe, occupie, brynne, and maynoure, and lede away..unto the ende of foure yere. **1575** LANEHAM *Let.* 50 Horn.. being neyther so churlish in weyght az iz mettall: nor so froward and brytl too manure, az stone.

†**b.** To manœuvre (a ship). *Obs.*

1569 SIR J. HAWKINS *Voy. Guynea* ad fin., We were scantlye able to manure oure ship.

manure, obs. form of MANOR.

manured (mə'njʊəd), *ppl. a.* [f. MANURE *v.* + -ED[1].] †**a.** Cultivated, tilled; (of plants) cultivated as opposed to 'wild' (*obs.*). **b.** Dressed with manure or other fertilizer.

1551 TURNER *Herbal* I. K i, It groweth in ranke and manored groundes. **1562** *Ibid.* II. 80 The gardin or sowen or manered carot. **1596** NASHE *Saffron Walden* 102 A dampe (like the smoake of a Cannon) from the fat manured earth ..(being the buriall place of fiue parishes). **1677** PLOT *Oxfordsh.* 155 Manured bastard Saffron. **1746–7** HERVEY *Medit.* (1818) 146 If God 'seal up the bottles of heaven'..the best manured plot becomes a barren desart. **1797** *Encycl. Brit.* (ed. 3) II. 384/1 *Arundo*... 1. The phragmitis, or common marsh reed... 2. The debax, or manured reed. **1896** *Allbutt's Syst. Med.* I. 763 It [the tetanus bacillus]..is especially associated with the stable and with manured fields.

†**manureless,** *a. Obs. rare*[−1]. [-LESS.] Without 'manure' or cultivation.

1595 T. WILLIAMS in Chapman *Ovid's Banq. Sense* To Author, Vngratefull Farmers of the Muses land, That..Let it manureles and unfenced stand.

†**manurement.** *Obs.* [f. MANURE *v.* + -MENT.] Cultivation (*lit.* and *fig.*).

a **1639** WOTTON *Surv. Educ.* in *Reliq.* (1651) 319 The manurement of Wits is like that of Soyles. **1707** J. ARCHDALE *Descr. Carolina* 9 Its natural Fertility and easy Manurement, is apt to make the People incline to Sloth.

manurer (mə'njʊərə(r)). [f. MANURE *v.* + -ER[1].] One who manures; † a cultivator, tiller; an occupier of land (*obs.*); a fertilizer of land. *lit.* and *fig.*

1560–1 *1st Bk. Discipl. Ch. Scot.* viii. (1836) 53 The labourers and manurers of the ground. **1569** *Act 11 Eliz.* in Bolton *Stat. Irel.* (1621) 301 That the inhabitants, manurers, or occupyers of the same doe beare..such charges [etc.]. **1607** HIERON *Wks.* I. 233 He is..the continuall dresser and manurer of His church. **1705** BOSMAN *Guinea* 16 A Land which yields its Manurers as plentiful a Crop as they can wish. **1829** E. JESSE *Jrnl. Nat.* 340 This animal [the earthworm] destined to be the natural manurer of the soil.

manurial (mə'njʊərɪəl), *a.* [irreg. f. MANURE *sb.* + -IAL.] Pertaining to, or of the nature of manure.

1861 *Chemical News* IV. 184 Sewage..retaining its manurial qualities. **1884** F. J. LLOYD *Sci. Agric.* 151 Sawdust itself possesses no manurial value.

manuring (mə'njʊərɪŋ), *vbl. sb.* Forms: see the vb. [f. MANURE *v.* + -ING[1].] †**a.** Occupation, tenure. †**b.** Cultivation, tillage. **c.** Fertilization by means of manure; †occas. *concr.* = manure.

1436 *Rolls of Parlt.* IV. 500/1 Fermours, and other men that usyn menuryng of lond. **1550** J. COKE *Eng. & Fr. Heralds* §204 (1877) 116 Parte of them may be put to tylth, manuring and habitacion. **1577** B. GOOGE *Heresbach's Husb.* II. (1586) 80 Couer it either with olde doung, or with the newest of any other kind of mannering. **1667** MILTON *P.L.* IV. 629 Yon flourie Arbors, yonder Allies green..That mock our scant manuring. **1726** SHELVOCKE *Voy. round World* 110 Almost every family have all the necessaries of life of their own manuring and feeding. **1872** YEATS *Techn. Hist. Comm.* 216 In every system of manuring, the chemical composition of the manure is that which constitutes its agricultural importance.

attrib. **1849** J. F. JOHNSTON *Exp. Agric.* 97 It may not be the same..with other manuring substances.

ma'nuring, *ppl. a.* [f. MANURE *v.* + -ING[2].] That manures, in various senses of the vb.

1635 SWAN *Spec. M.* vi. §2 (1643) 202 When their Nilus overflowed or when it first began to diffuse an ample portion of manuring bountie into the lap of the land. **1641** MILTON *Ch. Govt.* I. vi. Wks. 1851 III. 125 The manuring hand of the Tiller. *a* **1647** HABINGTON *Surv. Worcs.* in *Worcs. Hist. Soc. Proc.* II. 218 Chaunging..thys shyre from a wildernes of savage beastes to the freedome of manuryng husbandry.

‖**manus** ('meɪnəs). [L. *manus* hand.]

1. *Anat.* The terminal or distal segment of the fore limb of a vertebrate animal. Also, the claw or prehensile organ of a crustacean; *Ent.*, the tarsus of the anterior leg; *Ichth.*, the pectoral fin.

1826 KIRBY & SP. *Entomol.* xxxv. III. 681 *Tarsus* or *Manus*... The last portion of the leg. **1867** MIVART in *Phil. Trans.* CLVII. 299 *note*, I think it better, in a scientific treatise..[to adopt] for the anterior extremity (the carpus and all beyond it) the term *manus*, and for the homotypal posterior segment the term *pes*. **1878** BELL *Gegenbaur's Comp. Anat.* 481 In Birds..the reduction of the manus is still more marked. **1886** *Athenæum* 20 Feb. 268/1 The bones of the fore-arm and manus [in the chick] are longer than the corresponding segments of the leg and foot.

2. *Roman Law.* The power or authority of a husband over his wife.

1854 COLQUHOUN *Rom. Civ. Law* §2424 III. 664 The husband derived this jurisdiction from the *Manus*. **1871** POSTE *Gaius* 77 A filiusfamilias was capable of civil wedlock, but had no manus.

†**3. manus Christi** [L. = 'hand of Christ' (14th c. in Du Cange)], see quot. 1706. *Obs.*

1516 TH. ALEN *Let. to Earl Shrewsbury* in *Lett. & Pap. Hen. VIII*, II. 522, I have sent your lordship by this bearer one lb. of manus Christi. **1528** HENNEGE *Let. to Wolsey* 28 June, *ibid.* IV. 1938 Manws cresty. **1682** R. BURTON *Admir. Curios.* (1684) 30 He..administred *Manus Christi*, and the like Cordials. **1706** PHILLIPS (ed. Kersey), *Manus Christi*, refined Sugar boil'd with Rose-water, or that of Violets, or Cinamon; a sort of Cordial for very weak Persons.

†**manuscribe**, *v. Obs.* [f. L. *manū*, abl. of *manus* hand + *scrībere* to write: see MANUSCRIPT and cf. *transcribe*, etc.] *trans.* To write with one's (own) hand.
1649 *Faithf. Portr. Loyal Subj.* 4 Divers, who have seen the Original Copy, Manuscrib'd by the King himself.

manuscript ('mænju:skrɪpt), *a.* and *sb.* [ad. med.L. *manūscriptus*, f. L. *manū*, abl. of *manus* hand + *scriptus*, pa. pple. of *scrībere* to write. Cf. F. *manuscrit*, It. *manoscritto*, Sp. *manuscrito*, Pg. *manuscripto*.
Med.L. had only the neut. *manūscriptum* used sb. for a document written with a person's own hand (cf. CHIROGRAPH). In the sense of 'written' as opposed to 'printed', the adj. has been common in mod.L. from the 15th c., but has usually been written (more correctly) as two words, *manu scriptus*.]

A. *adj.* Written by hand, not printed. Abbreviated MS.
1597 *(title)* Certaine Worthye Manvscript Poems of great Antiquitie..now first published By J. S. **1601** R. JOHNSON *Kingd. & Commw.* (1603) 185 According to manuscript relations, and report of trauellers. **1625** BP. MOUNTAGU *App. Cæsar* 185 Origen in his Dialogue against the Marcionites, which I have manuscript. **1774** WARTON *Hist. Eng. Poetry* (1778) II. (Addit. to vol. I) d2, There is a manuscript copy of the poem, on vellum, in Trinity college library at Oxford. **1776** ADAM SMITH *W.N.* I. xi. III. (1869) I. 220 Several other very well authenticated, though manuscript, accounts. **1856** EMERSON *Eng. Traits, Univ.* Wks. (Bohn) II. 90 The manuscript Plato..brought by Dr. Clarke from Egypt. **1893** *Law Times* XCV. 10/2 Only the manuscript parts of the..proposal were read over to the assured, not the printed matter.

B. *sb.*

1. A book, document, or the like, written by hand; a writing of any kind, as distinguished from printed matter. Abbreviated MS., *pl.* MSS.

a. *esp.* A book, document, etc., written before the general adoption of printing in a country; a written copy of an ancient author or book.
1600 J. PORY tr. *Leo's Africa* VII. 288 Hither are brought diuers manuscripts or written bookes out of Barbarie. **1607** TOPSELL *Four-f. Beasts* (1658) 186 These lesser were found pictured in an old manuscript in Germany, which book did intreat of the Holy Land. **1615** G. SANDYS *Trav.* 82 In these Monasteries many excellent manu-scripts haue been preserued. **1774** WARTON *Hist. Eng. Poetry* (1778) II. 49 This translation..is now among the royal manuscripts in the British Museum. **1845** GRAVES *Rom. Law* in *Encycl. Metrop.* II. 765/1 The text of Tilius was taken from a Vatican manuscript..from which all other existing manuscripts of the work are copied. **1861** WRIGHT *Ess. Archæol.* II. xix. 130 The earlier illuminated manuscripts are chiefly copies of the Scriptures.

b. *gen.* A written composition which has not been printed. Often, an author's written (or typed) 'copy' as distinguished from the print of the same.
1607 BEAUM. & FL. *Woman-hater* IV. ii, *Mer.* I do knowe sufficiently, their shop-bookes cannot saue them; there is a further end—. *Pan.* Oh: Sir, much may be done by manescript [*sic*]. *Mer.* I do confesse it Sir, prouided still they be canonicoll. *a* **1631** DONNE *Valediction to his Bk.* 10 Study our manuscripts, those miriads Of letters which haue past 'twixt thee and me. **1651** BAXTER *Inf. Bapt.* 91, I took it out of his own Manuscript sent to me. **1692** *(title)* The Works Of..Mr. John Bunyan,..The First Volume, Containing Ten of his Excellent Manuscripts prepared for the Press before his Death, never before Printed. **1791** BOSWELL *Johnson* 30 Mar. an. 1778, The Life of Sir Robert Sibbald..in the original manuscript in his own hand writing. **1796** H. HUNTER tr. *St.-Pierre's Stud. Nat.* (1799) III. 611 After having received my manuscript they delayed putting it to the press under various pretexts. **1884** FROUDE *Carlyle's Life Lond.* (1890) I. 27 John Mill..borrowed the manuscript [of 'French Revolution'] as it was thrown off, that he might make notes and suggestions. **1967** R. A. WALDRON *Sense & Sense Devel.* vi. 116 *Manuscript* is no longer something necessarily 'written by hand' but is usually the author's original copy of the text of a printed book, etc. **1967** *Anglo-Amer. Catal. Rules: Brit. Text* 267 *Manuscript*, a writing made by hand. (Original typescripts are generally treated as manuscripts in libraries.) **1967** *Listener* 2 Mar. 282/3 Perhaps you are going to transcribe the tape-recording into typewritten manuscript.

c. *transf.* and *fig.*
1622 MASSINGER & DEKKER *Virg. Mart.* II. ii, Thou art the Manuscript Where Antoninus writes downe all his secrets. **1634** QUARLES *(title)* Mildreiados. To the Blessed Memory of that faire Manuscript of Vertue..Mildred, La. Lvckyn. **1859** FITZGERALD tr. *Omar* lxxii, Alas, that Spring should vanish with the Rose! That Youth's sweet-scented Manuscript should close!

d. *attrib.*
1770 PORTEUS *Life Secker* 47 (*S.'s Serm.* vol. I.) He expended upwards of £300 in arranging and improving the Manuscript Library at Lambeth. **18..** *Oxf. Univ. Cal.*, Bodleian Library... Special Assistant in the MS. Department.

2. a. Written characters or written documents in general; 'writing' as opposed to 'print'. ***in manuscript***: in written form, written (not printed).
1875 HELPS *Soc. Press.* iii. 35 If you look at the side-notes in manuscript of some book possessed by our book-loving ancestors. **1875** SCRIVENER *Lect. Text N. Test.* 7 All existing copies of Scripture whether in manuscript or printed.

b. (A person's) 'hand' or handwriting.
a **1849** POE *Purloined Letter* (end) Wks. 1865 I. 280 He is well acquainted with my MS. **1853** MRS. GORE *Dean's Dau.* III. 182 My friend Mordaunt's clerkly manuscript and lengthy style.

manuscriptal ('mænju:skrɪptəl), *a. rare.* [f. prec. sb. + -AL[1].] Of or pertaining to a manuscript or manuscripts; found or occurring in a manuscript.
1694 WESTMACOTT *Script. Herb.* 165 Ptolomy Philadelphus..hearing how Attalus King of Pergamus, by the benefit of this Ægyptian Paper, strived to excel him in Manuscriptal Magnificence, prohibited the carrying of it out of Ægypt. *a* **1763** BYROM *Crit. Rem., Epist. to Friend* 43 Having but one of all the Roman Lyrics To feed their Taste for slavish Panegyrics, The more absurd the Manuscriptal Letter, They paint, from thence, some fancy'd Beauty better. **1801** STRUTT *Sports & Past.* I. i. 4 The representation of a Saxon chieftain,..taken from a manuscriptal painting.

manuscription (mænju:'skrɪpʃən). *rare.* [f. L. *manū*, abl. of *manus* hand + *scriptiōn-em*, n. of action f. *scrībere* to write.] The action of writing by hand; that which is written by hand, a written inscription. *nonce-uses.*
1800 LAMB *Let. to Manning* in *Final Mem.* (1848) I. iv. 121 Manning's Algebra with a neat manuscription in the blank leaf, running thus 'From the Author'. **1835-8** S. R. MAITLAND *Dark Ages* (1844) 416 The press does a great deal, and might do a great deal more. It could easily as far outdo its present self, as it now outdoes manuscription.

†**manuscriptor.** *Obs. rare*$^{-1}$. [f. L. *manū* (see prec.) + *scriptor*, agent-n. f. *scrībere* to write.] The writer of a manuscript.
1698 *Christ Exalted* §113. 90 The Rebuker turns quick, and plays at sharp with the Manuscriptor, and accosts him for saying, What [etc.].

manu'scriptural, *a. rare.* [f. MANUSCRIPT (after *scriptural*).] = MANUSCRIPTAL.
1856 R. A. VAUGHAN *Mystics* (1860) I. VI. vii. 242 Don't you think Atherton has a very manuscriptural air to-night? **1874** RILEY *4th Rep. Hist. MSS. Comm.* 451/2 Minutiae of manuscriptural knowledge.

'**manusculpt.** *nonce-wd.* [f. L. *manū* (see MANUSCRIPT) + *sculpt-us*, pa. pple. of *sculpĕre* to carve.] An inscription carved or engraved by hand.
a **1859** DE QUINCEY *Mem. Chronol.* Posth. Wks. 1893 II. 115 Amongst a people so illiterate, how could manuscripts or manusculpts excite the interest which is necessary to their conservation?

†**manusculpture.** *Obs. rare*$^{-1}$. [f. L. *manū* (see MANUSCRIPT) + SCULPTURE.] Carving or engraving by hand; in quot. *fig.*
1704 NORRIS *Ideal World* II. vii. 365 These images described, as is supposed by the manusculpture or peinture of light in the fund of the eye.

manustu'pration. *rare.* Etymologizing alteration of MASTURBATION.
1832 JAS. COPLAND *Dict. Pract. Med.* (1858) III. 441/2, s.v. *Pollution*. **1889** in *Century Dict.*

†**manutenency.** *Obs.* [ad. med.L. *manūtenentia* (= F. *maintenance*), f. *manūtenent-em*, pr. pple. of *manū tenēre*: see MAINTAIN *v.* Cf. OF. *manutenence*.] The action of holding in the hand or upholding; support, maintenance.
1633 T. ADAMS *Exp. 2 Peter* iii. 17. 1484 Nothing can keepe a man from wandring but the manutenency of God. **1659** J. ARROWSMITH *Chain Princ.* 453 As when a man holds a staff in his hand, let him but take away his manutenencie, the staff falls immediately to the ground. **1699** J. BARRY *Reviving Cordial* Ded. (1802) 13, [I] who am to this very day kept alive and upheld by that divine manutenency.

manutention (mænju:'tɛnʃən). [In sense 1, ad. med.L. *manūtentiōn-em*, n. of action f. L. *manū tenēre* (see MAINTAIN *v.*); in sense 2, a new formation from the same L. phrase.]

†**1.** The action of upholding or maintaining, maintenance. *Obs.*
1603 FLORIO *Montaigne* I. xxii. (1632) 53 Christian religion hath all the markes of..justice.., but none more apparent than the exact commendation of obedience due unto magistrates, and manutention of policies. **1657** TRAPP *Comm. Job* xii. 16 All creatures subsist meerly by his manutention.

2. The action of holding by the hand. *rare.*
1854 BUCKNILL in *8th Rep. Comm. Lunacy* App. G 126 The plan of manutension [*sic*], or holding violent patients for a long time by the hands of attendants.

‖**manutergium** (mænju:'tɜ:dʒɪəm). *Eccl.* [L., f. *manus* hand + *tergēre* to wipe.] A towel.
1774 T. WEST *Antiq. Furness* (1805) 72 And over it hung the manutergium, on each side the cistern.

†**manu-tract.** *Obs.* [f. L. *manū*, abl. of *manus* hand + *tract-um*, neut. pa. pple. of *trahĕre* to draw.] What is traced by hand.
1660 N. C. *Ded. Verses* in T. Forde *Love's Labyrinth*, How far short comes the needle of the pen!.. Let spleen it self judge eithers manu-tract: Their female works can't speak, thy male-words Act.

‖**manvantara** (mæn'væntərə). Also **manw-**. [Skr., f. *Manu* + *antara* period.] In Hindu cosmology: One of the 14 periods, each presided over by a special 'Manu' or cosmic deity, which make up a KALPA.
1830 LYELL *Princ. Geol.* I. ii. 6 There has been a long succession of *manwantaras* or periods. **1834** *Nat. Philos.* III. *Astron.* App. 117 (Usef. Knowl. Soc.) The Kalpa was subdivided into 14 Manwantaras, each of 308448000 years with the addition of 1728000 years to make up the Kalpa.

manvell, obs. form of MANUAL.

manward ('mænwəd), *adv.* and *a.* [See -WARD.] **A.** *adv.* (In early use ***to manward***, also ***to menward***.) **a.** Towards man, in the direction of man. **b.** In relation to man.
c **1430** *Pilgr. Lyf Manhode* IV. iv. (1869) 176 Sithe þat man hath ouercome þee, þou shuldest not afterward be so boistous to manward. **1526** TINDALE *Titus* iii. 4 After that the kyndnes and love of oure saveoure to manwarde apered. **1594** HOOKER *Eccl. Pol.* I. viii. §7 It is the root out of which all lawes of duty to men-ward haue grown. **1642** J. EATON *Honey-c. Free Justif.* 38 Shee hath put on Christ himselfe, to God-ward by Justification; and to man-ward by Sanctification. **1816** SCOTT *Antiq.* xxxi, Mr. Blattergowl.. was nevertheless a good man, in the old Scottish presbyterian phrase, God-ward and man-ward. **1865** LOWELL *Thoreau* Pr. Wks. 1890 I. 368 Emerson..has drawn steadily manward and worldward.

B. *adj.* Tending or directed towards man.
1867 MONSELL *Our New Vicar* 84 'Priest' and 'Altar' speak of his God-ward office: 'Minister' and 'Lord's Table' refer to his man-ward ministrations. **1902** FAIRBAIRN *Philos. Chr. Relig.* II. III. ii. 543 His manward activities and relations.

manwell, obs. form of MANUAL.

man-woman. a. A hermaphrodite. **b.** *nonce-use.* One who combines the virtues of both sexes. **c.** A mannish woman.
1587 GOLDING *De Mornay* xxvi. 458 Concerning the creation of Man, the Ægyptians say hee was created both Male and female. Herevpon Plato gathereth that he was a Man-woman or Herkinalson [Fr. *Hermaphrodite*]. **1736** FIELDING *Pasquin* II. i, We shall see Fairbelly, the strange man-woman. **1889** TENNYSON *On one who affected an effeminate manner*, But, friend, man-woman is not woman-man. **1894** *Idler* Sept. 194 That stage of progress has been passed, and, as an outcome, we have the 'Emancipated Woman', or 'Man-Woman'. **1920** D. LINDSAY *Voy. Arcturus* xviii. 240 'What do you call men-women?' 'Persons of mixed sex, like yourself.' **1975** P. G. WINSLOW *Death of Angel* iv. 109 The new man-woman, emerging from the chaos that is matter.

Hence **man-womanly** *a.*, having the characteristics of both sexes.
1929 V. WOOLF *Room of one's Own* 148 It would be well to test what one meant by man-womanly.

Manx (mæŋks), *a.* and *sb.* Forms: 6 **maniske**, 7 **manques**, 7–9 **manks**, 9 **mankes**, **manx**. [Metathetic a. ON. **mansk-r* (whence directly the 16th c. form *maniske*), f. *Man-* (nom. *Mǫn*:—**Manu*, a. OIrish *Manu*), the Isle of Man.]

A. *adj.* **a.** Of or pertaining to the Isle of Man, its inhabitants, language, etc.
1572 *Act 14 Eliz.* c. 5 §34 Yf any suche Maniske or Iryshe Vacabounde or Beggar ben alredy or shall at any tyme hereafter be set on Land in any parte of England or of Wales. **1630** *R. Johnson's Kingd. & Commw.* 67 Scaliger never heard of the Manks language, spoken by ours of the Ile of Man. **1765** *Ann. Reg.* 61 Books of devotion in the Manks tongue. **1860** *All Year Round* No. 68. 420, I believe a Manx sermon is now seldom heard.

b. ***Manx cat***: a tailless variety of the domestic cat, indigenous to the Isle of Man. ***Manx codlin***: a kind of apple. ***Manx penny***: a coin stamped with the device of three legs arranged in a form suggestive of a Catherine wheel. ***Manx puffin*** or ***shearwater*** = *Puffinus anglorum*.
1678 *Ray's Willughby's Ornith.* Index, Puffin 325. Manks Puffin 333. **1818** in *Trans. Horticult. Soc.* (1826) III. 320 Manx Codlin. **1835** JENYNS *Man. Brit. Vertebr.* 285 *Procellaria Anglorum*, Temm. (Manks Shearwater). **1859** WOOD *Nat. Hist.* I. 202 The Manx Cat..possessing hardly a vestige of a tail. *a* **1881** CARLYLE in *Harper's Mag.* (1883) Nov. 877/1 [He] hadn't the heart to..watch a woman.. making a Manx penny of herself.

B. *sb.*

1. (As *pl.*) The people of the Isle of Man.
1688 R. HOLME *Armoury* III. 233/1 The Manks or Manings [are] a people that inhabit the Isle of Man. **1809** *Acc. Isle of Man* 74 The Manks pay a decent and feeling regard to the memory of their deceased friends. **1899** J. MACTAGGART *Mackinnon & Bards* 68 The Englishman, the Welsh, the Manx, The artless Irishman, the Scot.

2. The Celtic language spoken in the Isle of Man. (Now extinct).
1672 PETTY *Pol. Anat.* (1691) 106 The Language of Ireland is like that of the North of Scotland, in many things like the Welch and Manques. **1702** W. SACHEVERELL *Acc. Isle of Man* 8 In the Northern part of the Island they speak a deeper Manks, as they call it, than in the South. **1835** CREGEEN *Manks Dict.* Pref., The Manks is now seldom spoken or written in its original purity. **1859** W. GILL *Kelly's Manks Gram.* Introd. 9 In the schools throughout the Island the Manx has ceased to be taught. **1970** B. M. H. STRANG *Hist. Eng.* ix. 402 One IE language (Manx) has become extinct since the Second World War.

3. A Manx cat.
1889 *Daily News* 23 Oct. 7/1 A solitary couple of Manxes [at a cat-show].

Hence '**Manxman**, '**Manxwoman**, a native of the Isle of Man.

1702 W. SACHEVERELL *Acc. Isle of Man* 113 Michael, a Manksman, a Person of great Merit and Exemplary Life. **1823** SCOTT *Peveril* v, Born a Mankesman—bred and nursed in the island. **1894** HALL CAINE (*title*) The Manxman. **1904** [in *N.E.D.*]. **1974** J. MANN *Sticking Place* viii. 132 I'm a Manxwoman.

manxome ('mæŋksəm), *a. poet. nonce-wd.* [Invented word; cf. -SOME[1] (as in *fearsome*, *gruesome*, *loathsome*, etc.).] ? Fearsome.

1871 'L. CARROLL' *Through Looking-Glass* i. 22 Long time the manxome foe he sought.

many ('mɛnɪ), *a.* and *sb.* Forms: 1 **maniȝ, moniȝ, mæniȝ, maneȝ-, moni-,** 2–3 **maniȝ, moniȝ,** 2–5 **moni,** 3–4 **mani, meni,** 3–6 **manye, mony** (also 4–9 *Sc.*), 3–7 **manie,** (4 **meyne,** 4–5 **mane, mone,** 4–6 **meny, -ie,** 6 **monye, menny, meany(e, -ie, meyney, meinie,** 6–9 *Sc.* **monie,** 8 **manny),** 4– **many.** *Comp.* 5 **manyer.** *Superl.* (chiefly *Sc.*) 6 **moni-, monyest, -ast,** 6–7 **manyest,** 6–8 **maniest.** [Common Teut.: OE. *maniȝ*, *mǫniȝ* corresponds to OFris. *man(i)ch*, *monich*, *monech*, OS. *manag* (MDu. *menech*, Du. *menig*), OHG. *manag*, *menig* (MHG. *manec*, *maneg-*, mod.G. *manch*), OSw. *mangher* (Sw. *mången*, Da. *mange*; the ON. word is *marg-r*, the etymological identity of which is uncertain; but ON. has *mengi* sb., multitude, a derivative of the Com. Teut. adj.), Goth. *manag-s*:—OTeut. **manago-*:—Indogermanic **monogho-*, whence OSl. *mŭnogŭ* (Russian *mnogiĭ*); an ablaut variant exists in OIrish *menicc* abundant (mod.Irish *minic*, Gaelic *minig* frequent, Welsh *mynych* often).

OE. had a derivative sb., *mǫniȝeo*, *mǫniȝu* multitude = OS. *menigi* (MDu. *menige*, *menie*), OHG. *manegî*, *menegî* (MHG. *menege*, mod.G. *menge*, ON. *mengi*, Goth. *managei*:—OTeut. **managîn-* wk. fem., f. **manago-* (see above). The OE. sb., however, did not survive into ME., and the modern substantival use of *many*, though agreeing in sense with OE. *mǫniȝeo*, was a new development which has not been found earlier than the 16th c.]

A. *adj.* The adjectival designation of great indefinite number.

1. Used *distributively* with a *sing.* (Formerly sometimes combined with a plural verb.)

†**a.** with sb. in sing. without article. *Obs.*

many time adv. phr.: see TIME *sb.*

Beowulf 838 Ða wæs..ymb ða ȝifhealle guðrinc moniȝ. *c* **893** K. ÆLFRED *Oros.* I. i. §23 Þæt Estland is swyðe mycel, & þær bið swyðe maniȝ burh. *c* **1200** ORMIN 3076 Itt wass forr maniȝ daȝȝ Ær cwiddedd þurhh prophetess. *c* **1290** *S. Eng. Leg.* I. 16/512 Mani miracle þare feol a-day. *a* **1300** *Cursor M.* 2901 Mani man [*Fairf.* mony mon, *Gött.* Mani a man, *Trin.* Mony men], for ouer-wele, þam-self can noþer faand ne feil. **1375** BARBOUR *Bruce* I. 411 Thiddirwart went mony baroune. *c* **1402** LYDG. *Compl. Bl. Knt.* v, The floures, of many dyvers hewe. *c* **1470** HENRY *Wallace* II. 26 Til mony Scot thai did full gret suppris. **1583** BABINGTON *Commandm.* viii. (1590) 352 Countenance beares out many euill counseller, till [etc.].

b. with *an* or *a* prefixed to the sb. Sometimes reduplicated for emphasis, ***many and many a***, † ***many a many***.

this many a (*day*, *year*): see THIS. ***many a time*** (***and often***): see TIME *sb.*

c **1205** LAY. 5132 Al þa twa ferden of moni ane eærde. *c* **1275** *XI Pains of Hell* 244 in *O.E. Misc.* 154 Þar-inne is monyon hungri hund. *c* **1330** R. BRUNNE *Chron. Wace* (Rolls) 15442 Ost þey gadered of mania man. **1390** GOWER *Conf.* I. 5 Love, which doth many a wonder And many a wys man hath put under. *c* **1450** *Merlin* 56 Pendragon was ther deed, and many a-nother gode baron. ? *c* **1475** *Sqr. lowe Degre* 373 Many a page Have become men by mariage. **1595** SHAKS. *John* I. i. 183 A foot of Honor better than I was, But many a many foot of Land the worse. **1632** MILTON *L'Allegro* 95 To many a youth, and many a maid. **1692** L'ESTRANGE *Fables* xxxviii. 41 He's Beset with Enemies.. the Meanest of which is not without Many and Many a Way to the Wreaking of a Malice. **1719** DE FOE *Crusoe* I. xi, This wall I was many a weary month in finishing. **1809** MALKIN *Gil Blas* VI. ii. ¶3 Many a more unlikely thing has happened. **1853** M. ARNOLD *Scholar-Gipsy* x, When..many a scythe in sunshine flames. **1889** BROWNING *Let. to Tennyson* 5 Aug., In its hope that for many and many a year we may have your very self among us.

c. many one (in ME. written as one word, *maniȝon*, *manion*, *manyon*, etc.): serving instead of the absolute or elliptical use of the sing. adj. In poetical use, often placed after a plural sb. Now only *Sc.* (*mony ane*).

c **1250** *Gen. & Ex.* 630 Of hem [*sc.* kine] ben tudered maniȝon. *c* **1375** *Sc. Leg. Saints* iii. (*Andreas*) 295 [Þai] mad kirkis mony ane. **1390** GOWER *Conf.* I. 56 Thus ful manyon Deceived were. **1430–40** LYDG. *Bochas* (1558) 34 b, Bochas reherseth of wyves many one, Which..were ful contrarius. **1535** COVERDALE *Ps.* iii. 2 Many one there be that saye off my soule [etc.]. **1567** *Gude & Godlie B.* (S.T.S.) 43 With meruellis greit and mony one. **1622** S. WARD *Life of Faith in Death* (1627) 53 Many one hath acknowledged to my selfe the like. **1792** BURNS *Country Lassie* ii, It's ye hae wooers mony ane. *a* **1814** *Sulieman* II. iii. in *New Brit. Theatre* II. 24 As many one can show. **1818** SCOTT *Hrt. Midl.* v, There's mony ane wad hae thought themselves affronted, if [etc].

d. many a(n) one: = 'many a person'. Now chiefly *colloq.* †Also placed after a plural sb.

1509 BARCLAY *Ship of Fools* (1874) II. 297 Thy apparayle Aleyed gayly with perles many a one. **1542** UDALL *Erasm. Apoph.* 144 b, The selfe same woordes maye bee well spoken of many an one. **1548** UDALL, etc. *Erasm. Par. Mark* 88 This swete sauour..causeth many a one to desyer that they may be admitted. **1556** OLDE *Antichrist* 167 b, The cause of the greatest wickednesse that can be the undoing to many a one. **1869** FREEMAN *Norm. Conq.* (1876) III. xii. 156 Many an one carried off his two or three goodly steeds. *Mod.* I know many a one who would be glad of the chance.

e. *predicatively.* Only with inversion, in the phrase ***many is*** (or ***was***) ***the*** ——. Now *dial.*

1297 R. GLOUC. (Rolls) 209 Mani was þat gode bodi þat aslawe was þere. *c* **1300** *S. Nicholas* 431 in *S. Eng. Leg.* I. 252 Meni is þe faire miracle þat of seint Nicholas is. **13..** *Coer de L.* 4931 Manye was the hethene man, With Saladyn that come than. **1870** MRS. PHELPS *Hedged In* xviii. 269 An' mony's the time I've warned him o' the consequences.

2. With *pl. sb.* **a.** In ME. often coupled with FELE *a.*

many times, ***many ways***, (***on***) ***many wise***, advb. phr.: see the sbs. ***these*** or ***this many years*** (etc.): see THIS.

a **900** tr. *Bæda's Hist.* I. xiii. [xxiii.] (1890) 54 Ðæt he sende Agustinum & oðre moniȝe munecas mid hine. *c* **1175** *Lamb. Hom.* 97 Ealle þas þing and moniȝe oðre deð þe haliȝa gast. *a* **1225** *St. Marher.* 1 Weren monie martirs..to deaðes misliche idon. *c* **1305**, etc. [see FELE B. 1]. *c* **1375** *Cursor M.* 19515 (Fairf.) Miraclis dide he mani fele [*earlier texts* fele *only*]. **1386** *Rolls of Parlt.* III. 225/1 To the..Lordes.. compleynen..the folk of the Mercerye of London..of many wronges subtiles. *a* **1400–50** *Alexander* 1005 We hafe farne to þe fiȝt..mony fele wynter. *c* **1425** [see FELE B. 1]. *c* **1450** *Merlin* 56 Merlin wente to his maister Blase..and tolde hym many thinges. **1513** DOUGLAS *Æneis* VII. ii. 15 The birdis seir of mony diuers hewis. **1556** *Aurelio & Isab.* N 5 A litell courte, where the kinge helde menney Lions. **1582** LYLY *Let. to Burleigh* Wks. (ed. Bond) I. 28, I will not troble your honorable eares with so meinie idle wordes. **1602** SHAKS. *Ham.* III. iii. 9 To keepe those many many bodies safe. **1603** FLORIO *Montaigne* I. ix. 17 The opposite of Truth hath many-many shapes. **1644** EVELYN *Diary* 10 Nov., The famous statue of the Gladiator..so much follow'd by all the rare artists, as the many copies testifie. *c* **1710** BURNET *Autobiog.* in *Suppl. to Hist.* (1902) 474, I loved solitude..and so I avoided manny tentations. **1839** THIRLWALL *Lett.* (1881) I. 157 The translation which I made many years back. **1870** DICKENS *E. Drood* ii, We must drink many happy returns to her.

Proverbial phr. **1631** CAPT. SMITH *Advts. un-exp. Planters* 28 But we see many men many minds, and still new Lords, new lawes.

†**b.** Followed by a possessive or a superlative.

1606 G. W[OODCOCKE] *Hist. Ivstine* XVI. 66 Among manie their honorable actions, this one thing especiall, is woorthy to be recorded. **1606** SHAKS. *Ant. & Cl.* I. ii. 189 The Letters..Of many our contriuing Friends. **1607** —— *Timon* III. vi. 11. **1646** H. LAWRENCE *Comm. Angells* 61 Many the best and most things were lost to them.

c. Placed after the sb. (cf. 1 c, 1 d). *poet.* and *arch.*

c **1220** *Bestiary* 556 In ðe se senden selcuðes manie. **1526** TINDALE *1 Cor.* viii. 5 As there be goddes many and lordes many. [So **1611.**] **1871** R. ELLIS tr. *Catullus* lxii. 51 Many a wistful boy, and maidens many desire it.

d. *predicatively. arch.*

a **1425** *Cursor M.* (Trin.) 12577 Mony are his childehedes I of tolde Done ar he were tuelue yeer olde. **1508** DUNBAR *Tua mariit Wemen* 74 To..blaw my bewtie on breid, quhair bernis war mony. **1596** SPENSER *State Irel.* Wks. (Globe) 631/1 The inconveniences that therby doe arise are much more many. **1598** DRAYTON *Heroic. Ep.* xiv. 57 And if thou know'st, they many were before, By time increasing, they must needs be more. **1611** BIBLE *Ps.* xxxiv. 19 Many are the afflictions of the righteous. **1776** WITHERING *Brit. Plants* (1796) I. 314 Seeds many, roundish. **1846** TRENCH *Mirac.* Introd. (1862) 1 Where we have to do with aught which in many ways is significant, the names also will inevitably be many, since no one will exhaust all its meaning.

3. *ellipt.* and *absol.* in plural sense: **a.** Many individuals of the kind specified (often followed by *of*); also (as quasi-pronoun), many persons.

Beowulf 2091 He mec þær on innan unsynniȝne dior dædfruma ȝedon wolde maniȝra sumne. *c* **1000** *Ags. Ps.* (Th.) iii. 1 Moniȝe cweðað to minum mode, þæt hit næbbe nane hæle æt his Gode. *c* **1175** *Cott. Hom.* 225 And were swiðe maneȝe on yfele awende. **1297** R. GLOUC. (Rolls) 11392 Manie flowe in to þe water & some toward þe see. *c* **1400** *Destr. Troy* 12264 Þai keppit hom in company with knightes enarmit, And Vlixes also with angardly mone. **1567** MAPLET *Gr. Forest* 9 b, We be many of us cut off before we come to olde age. **1580** LUPTON *Sivqila* 120 Many with vs spends their goods, and leaues their lands scantly to such good vses. **1738** SWIFT *Pol. Conversat.* 39, I see, one Fool makes many. **1794** NELSON 8 July in Nicolas *Disp.* (1845) I. 429 They will from using as many again as is necessary be soon short of that article. **1845** M. PATTISON *Ess.* (1889) I. 22 He had but one voice amongst many. **1871** MORLEY *Voltaire* (1886) 6 Many of his ideas..did not belong to him peculiarly.

¶**b.** with *a* for *of*. *Obs.*

c **1400** MAUNDEV. (1839) xxvii. 278 There weren in that place many a dyverse thinges. **1523** LD. BERNERS *Froiss.* I. ccxv. 271 They..defoyled many a damoselles.

†**c.** in possessive form *many's*. *Obs.*

1598 GRENEWEY *Tacitus, Ann.* IV. xiii. (1622) 110 Which was cause of manies ouerthrow. *c* **1600** SHAKS. *Sonn.* xciii, In manies lookes the falce hearts history Is writ.

d. *the many* (= Gk. οἱ πολλοί): the great body of people; the multitude. Cf. *the few*.

1526 *Pilg. Perf.* (W. de W. 1531) 147 b, How ye many for lacke of mortifyenge tasteth not of this feest. **1688** NORRIS *Theory Love* II. i. 76 An old Rule, that we may talk with the Many, but must think with the Few. **1790** BURKE *Fr. Rev.* 75 The many are not capable of making this calculation. **1809–10** COLERIDGE *Friend* (1865) 75 The folly and foolish self-opinion of the half-instructed many. **1842** TENNYSON *Day-Dream, Arrival* ii, The many fail: the one succeeds. **1879** M. ARNOLD *Mixed Ess., Democr.* 39 It was the many who relished those arts [of ancient Athens].

†**4.** Phr. ***on*** (***in***) ***many***: into many parts, many times, manifold. *Obs.*

c **888** K. ÆLFRED *Boeth.* xxxiii. §1 God is anfeald & untodælendlic, þeah hine dysiȝe men on mæniȝ todælen. **1401** *Pol. Poems* (Rolls) II. 47 As the prophetes of Achab wer multiplied in many.

5. a. When qualified by AS, HOW, SO, TOO (q.v. for further treatment), the adj. has a weakened sense, expressing the notion of number in the abstract. With *pl. sb.*; also *ellipt.* and *absol.* = '(as, etc.) many persons'.

c **1000** ÆLFRIC *Interrog. Sigewulfi* (Maclean 1883) 66 On hu maneȝum wisum is Godes weorc? **1382** WYCLIF *Luke* xi. 8 He schal..ȝyue to hym, how manye [**1388** as many as] he hath nedeful. *a* **1400–50** *Alexander* 124 As many Besandis on his bake as he bere miȝt. **1471** *Paston Lett.* III. 5 Ye shall send me..asse mone of my men asse can com. **1638** JUNIUS *Paint. Ancients* 25 So did he then consider..how many armed men..might be required. **1714** SWIFT *Pres. State Affairs* Wks. 1755 II. I. 204, I have heard a physician pronounce..that he had cured so many patients of malignant fevers. **1807** CRABBE *Newspaper* 219 As many words as make an even line; As many lines, as fill a row complete; As many rows as furnish up a sheet.

†**b.** In compar. and superl. ***manier***, ***maniest*** (= *more*, *most* or *very many*). Frequent in Sc. *Obs.*

1422 tr. *Secreta Secret., Priv. Priv.* 214 Thou mayste vndyrstonde of manyer, othyr fewere. *c* **1440** *Jacob's Well* 111 Þe heremyte flytted his celle fyve myle ferthere fro þe welle, for to makyn þe manyere steppys, to haue þe more mede. **1500–20** DUNBAR *Poems* lviii. 2 Off benefice..Quha monyast hes makis maist requeist. **1548** TURNER *Names of Herbes* 56 The maniest that I have sene was in Kent. **1560** in Dunlop *Coll. Confess. Faith* (1722) II. 639 The maniest Votes, without Respect of Persone, hath the first Place in the Eldarschip. **1583** *Reg. Privy Council Scot.* III. 576 With sax horsmen at the monyast. **1597** MORLEY *Introd. Mus.* 119 Hee who could bring in maniest of them was counted the iollyest fellowe. **1676** W. ROW *Contn. Blair's Autobiog.* xii. (1848) 437 The Prelates are now busied to fill the places of outed ministers especially in the west where maniest were outed. **1728** P. WALKER *Life Peden* (ed. 3) Pref., This has had the maniest good Effects. **1794** *Hope's New Meth. Fencing* Law x. 232–3 Whoever..shall..have beat maniest, shall be declared..to have gain'd the Prize.

c. ***as many as***: used idiomatically for 'all who'.

Very common in the Bible translations beginning with Tindale, by whom it was app. introduced as a literal rendering of ὅσοι. (One earlier instance occurs in the second Wyclif version in Acts xiii. 48, where the Vulgate has the literalism *quotquot* instead of *quicumque*. The use in Luke xi. 8 is not to the point, because there ὅσοι, *quotquot*, *as many as*, have their literal sense.) Now *obs.* or *arch.*

1526 TINDALE *Rom.* ii. 12 And as many as haue synned vnder the lawe shalbe iudged by the lawe. **1667** MILTON *P.L.* III. 289 So in thee..shall be restor'd As many as are restor'd.

d. ***as many***: the same number of.

c **1400** [see AS *adv.* A. 5]. **1748** SMOLLETT *Rod. Rand.* viii, He found means to cut me [when shaving] in three places, in as many strokes. **1801** W. DUPRÉ *Neolog. Fr. Dict.* 131 [The hectolitre] contains an hundred and five pintes, equal to as many english quarts. *Mod.* He made twenty blunders in about as many lines.

e. ***one too many***: used predicatively of something not wanted or (also attributively) of something that is repeated to excess.

1590 SHAKS. *Com. Err.* III. i. 35 When one is one too many, goe get thee from the dore. **1592** —— *Rom. & Jul.* I. i. 135 Being one too many by my weary selfe. **1748** RICHARDSON *Clarissa* II. v. 26 He believes he has in me one sister too many for his interest. **1849** LYTTON *Caxtons* XII. vi. (heading), The confession of a youth who, in the Old World, finds himself one too many. **1865** WHYTE MELVILLE *Cerise* (1866) I. xv. 232 The Marquise was..left planted as one too many. **1941** H. L. MENCKEN *Newspaper Days* (1942) xii. 193 The poor old man..nursing a hangover from a Bar Association banquet, had thrown in one too many quick ones, and so got himself plastered. **1956** A. WILSON *Anglo-Saxon Attitudes* I. ii. 43 Some people have made one imaginative leap too many and show little sign of being able to return to the realm of reason.

f. ***too many for***: more than a match for. (Properly predicated of pl. subject, but in more or less jocular use said of a single person or thing.)

1692 R. L'ESTRANGE *Fables* xxxv. 35 They come to Vie Power and Expence with Those that are too High and too many for them. **1708** *Deplor. State New Eng.* 16 in *Sewall's Diary* (1879) II. 114* Your Governour..has been too many for you. **1722** DE FOE *Col. Jack* (1840) 319 We were too many for them, for we run out our guns..and..they retired. **1787** 'G. GAMBADO' *Acad. Horsemen* (1809) 29 Should your horse prove, what is properly termed too many for you, and make off. **1863** J. C. JEAFFRESON *Sir Everard's Dau.* 113 You can't rob me—I am too many for you!.. You're a clever one—but you're no match for me. **1872** HARDWICK *Trad. Lanc.* 189 On one occasion, however, the fiends were nearly 'too many' for the eternal toiler.

6. *Comb.* **a.** parasynthetic (unlimited in number), as ***many-acred***, ***-angled***, ***-antlered***, ***-belled***, ***-blossomed***, ***-branched***, ***-celled***, ***-centuried***, ***-chambered***, ***-cobwebbed***, ***-coloured***, ***-cornered***, ***-corridored***, ***-coultered***, ***-eared***, ***-eyed***, ***-faceted***, ***-fingered***, ***-flowered***, ***-folded***, ***-forked***, ***-formed***, ***-fountained***, ***-gifted***, ***-handed***, ***-hearted***, ***-horned***, ***-hued***, ***-knotted***, ***-languaged***, ***-layered***, ***-leaved***, ***-lived***, ***-lobed***, ***-minded***, ***-mooded***, ***-mouthed***, ***-nationed***, ***-parted***, ***-peopled***, ***-pillared***, ***-pleated***, ***-pointed***, ***-rowed***, ***-seated*** (hence ***many-seatedness***), ***-seeded***, ***-spangled***, ***-splendoured***, ***-steepled***, ***-stringed***, ***-syllabled***, ***-tailed***, ***-tinted***, ***-toned***, ***-tongued***, ***-towered***, ***-tribed***, ***-tubed***, ***-twined***, ***-valved***, ***-voiced***, ***-volumed***, ***-weathered***, ***-windowed***,

-wintered, -yeared adjs. Also ***many-dimensional*** adj.

1812 G. Colman *Two Parsons* xxvii, A *many-acred..ass, the squire. **1640** C. Harvey *Communion Table* iv, Square, oval, *many-angled, long, or round. **1892** W. B. Yeats *Countess Kathleen* iii. 57 Heaven's many-angled star reversed. **1930** Blunden *Poems* 48 Bronze noonlight domes the dim blue gloom Where *many-antlered oaks immure A hush. **1850** Thackeray *Pendennis* xlii, The doors are *many belled. **1840** Mrs. Norton *Dream*, etc. 238 The *many-blossom'd spring. **1861** Bentley *Man. Bot.* 424 *Many-celled spore-cases. **1848** J. R. Lowell *Columbus* in *Poems* 2nd Ser. 11 *Many-centuried shade Of some writhed oak. **1931** Blunden *To Themis* 53 Beneath the accustomed dome Of this chance-planted, many-centuried tree. **1868** E. P. Wright *Ocean World* iv. 83 They [Foraminifera] are generally *many-chambered. **1859** Tennyson *Geraint & Enid* 362 The dusky-rafterd *many-cobweb'd Hall. **1747** Johnson *Drury Lane Prol.* 3 Each change of *many-colour'd life he drew. **1821** Shelley *Adonais* lii, Like a dome of many-coloured glass. **1859** Tennyson *Vivien* in *Idylls of King* 132 The myriad-room'd And *many-corridor'd complexities Of Arthur's palace. **1665** Dryden *Indian Emp.* ii. i, Those *many cornered minds, Where women's crooked fancy turns and winds. **1731** Tull *Horse-Hoeing Husb.* xx. 299 The *many-coulter'd Plows. **1905** W. James in *Mind* XIV. 196 Satisfaction is a *many-dimensional term that can be realized in various ways. **1933** A. N. Whitehead *Adventures of Ideas* xi. 242 And space is many-dimensional. *a* **1963** C. S. Lewis *Poems* (1964) 102 The many-dimensional timeless rays. **1749** Fielding *Tom Jones* viii. ix, That many-eyed, many-tongued, many-mouthed, *many-eared Monster of Virgil. **1766** *Complete Farmer* s.v. *Seed* 6 S 1/2 Each plant of the many eared wheat. **1655** Moufet & Bennet *Health's Impr.* 3 *Many-eide Osiris. **1889** A. R. Wallace *Darwinism* (1890) 15 The potato..so well adapted to spread by means of its many-eyed tubers. **1909** *Daily Chron.* 7 Sept. 4/4 A *many-faceted diamond. **1947** *Mind* LVI. 291 The many-faceted problem of perception soon came to dominate the epistemological scene. **1909** E. Pound *Personae* 36 All tremulous beneath the *many-fingered breath. **1935** W. Empson *Poems* 19 Crossing and doubling, many-fingered, hounded. **1789** J. Pilkington *View Derbysh.* I. 386 *Erica multiflora*, *Many-flowered Heath. **1590** Spenser *F.Q.* ii. iii. 1 His..*many-folded shield he bound about his wrest. **1819** Shelley *Julian & Maddalo* 76 Where the swift sun yet paused in his descent Among the many-folded hills. **1697** C. Leslie *Snake in Grass* (ed. 2) 66 A *many-forked and involved Infallibility. *c* **1586** C'tess Pembroke *Ps.* lxxii. iii, While of sad night the *many-formed queene Decreas'd shall grow. **1832** Tennyson *Œnone* Poems (1833) 53 O mother Ida, *manyfountained Ida. **1868** J. H. Newman *Verses Var. Occas.* 108 The *many-gifted man. **1649** G. Daniel *Trinarch., Hen. IV* clii, This *Many-handed bodie moe hands lost Then [etc.]. **1852** Kingsley *Andromeda* 58 Twyformed, many-handed, terrible, shapeless. **1882** in *Eng. Dial. Dict.* (1903) IV. 33/1 (s. Dev.), He was always *many-hearted [= 'soft-hearted']. **1904** W. de la Mare *Henry Brocken* 193 Yonder fine many-hearted poplar. **1842** Bischoff *Woollen Manuf.* II. 290 The *many-horned sheep. **1812** Byron *Ch. Har.* ii. lvii, The Turk, the Greek, the Albanian and the Moor, Here mingled in their *many hued array. **1842** Tennyson *Morte d'Arthur* 63 The *many-knotted waterflags. **1655** Fuller *Hist. Camb.* 123 The *many Languaged-Bible. **1884** Bower & Scott *De Bary's Phaner.* 33 A much stronger *many-layered epidermis. **1605** Sylvester *Du Bartas* ii. iii. iii. *Law* 42 The *many-leaved locks Of thriving Charvel. **1876** Geo. Eliot *Dan. Der.* III. xlviii, The poor ship with its *many-lived anguish. **1830** Lindley *Nat. Syst. Bot.* 180 A plaited *many-lobed corolla. **1895** *Funk's Stand. Dict.*, **Many-minded*, showing changes of mind; changeable in opinion; fickle; versatile. **1932** W. B. Yeats *Words for Music* 37 Even Cicero And many-minded Homer were Mad as the mist and snow. **1920** *19th Cent.* Aug. 272 To know him [*sc.* Stephen Phillips] was to realise how *many-mooded and complex a man he was. **1935** C. Day Lewis *Time to Dance* 50 You shall recall one open as the day, Many-mooded as the light above English hills. **1749** *Many-mouthed [see *many-eared*]. **1917** D. H. Lawrence *Look! We have come Through!* 18 The spouse all full of increase Moiled over with the rearing of her many-mouthed young. **1598** Sylvester *Du Bartas* ii. i. iii. *Furies* 326 *Many-nam'd poyson, minister of Death. *c* **1611** Chapman *Iliad* ii. 497 These *many nation'd men. **1830** Lindley *Nat. Syst. Bot.* 176 Solitary flowers,..and *many-parted calyx. **1828** Landor *Imag. Conv., Xenoph. & Cyrus* III. 366 He waves his paternal blessing over the *many-peopled world. **1740** Dyer *Ruins of Rome* 10 The *many-pillar'd Portal. **1927** D. H. Lawrence *M. in Mex.* 81 The *many-pleated, noiseless mountains of Mexico. **1835–6** Todd *Cycl. Anat.* I. 472 The teeth [of Seals], sharp and *many-pointed. **1875** Bennett & Dyer tr. *Sachs' Bot.* 176 The *many-rowed flower-heads of the sunflower. **1808** Bentham *Sc. Reform* 36 The *many-seated has given place to single seated judicature. **1830** —— *Corr.* Wks. 1843 XI. 40 *Many-seatedness. **1776–96** Withering *Brit. Plants* (ed. 3) II. 246 *Lonicera*..*many-seeded. **1742** Blair *Grave* 135 Where hast thou hid thy *many-spangled head? *a* **1907** F. Thompson *Kingdom of God* in *Sel. Poems* (1908) 131 'Tis ye, 'tis your estrangèd faces, That miss the *many-splendoured thing. **1962** *Sunday Times* (Colour Suppl.) 25 Nov. 29 (*title*) The many-splendoured fisherman. **1971** *Nat. Geographic* Oct. 548/1 The Ocean Terminal and nearby Harbour Centre in Kowloon offer a dazzling promenade past 150 or more stores selling jewelry, watches, ginger jars, television sets.., pearls, and other many-splendored items. **1797** Coleridge *Lime-Tree Bower* 22 The *many-steepled tract magnificent Of hilly fields. **1852** H. Rogers *Ecl. Faith* (1853) 37 A *many-stringed lyre. **1635** Heywood *Hierarch.* vi. 355 Words *Many-syllabl'd, of obscure sence. **1766** Sharp in *Phil. Trans.* LVII. 85 The *many-tailed bandage. **1831** Carlyle *Sart. Res.* ii. v, A *many-tinted, radiant Aurora. **1812** Byron *Ch. Har.* ii. *Tambourgi* vii, Let her bring from her chamber her *many-toned lyre. **1749** *Many-tongued [see *many-eared*]. **1881** Henty *Cornet of Horse* xvii. (1888) 179 That many-tongued body the allied army. **1598** Sylvester *Du Bartas* ii. ii. iii. *Colonies* 77 And Ninevè..Above them [might] raise her *many-towred Crest. **1832** Tennyson *Lady of Shalott* i, To many-tower'd Camelot. **1768–74** Tucker *Lt. Nat.* (1834) I. 581 The *many-tribed weeds of the field. **1866** Geo. Eliot *F. Holt* i, The *many-tubed honeysuckle. **1909** E. Pound *Personae* 35 What should avail me the *many-twined bracelets? **1851** *Richardson's Geol.* viii. (1855) 259 The Balanidæ have a complicated, *many-valved shell. **1816** Shelley *Alastor* 669 A bright stream Once fed with *many-voiced waves. **1857** J. R. Lowell *Orig. Didactic Poetry* in *Atlantic Monthly* Nov. 112 *Many-volumed thunder. **1927** W. B. Yeats *Senate Speeches* (1961) 138 This many-volumed ancient history. **1794** Southey *Sonn., Even. Rainbow*, The day, Changeful and *many-weather'd. **1832** J. P. Kennedy *Swallow B.* (1860) 16 A plain, *many-windowed edifice of brick. **1842** Tennyson *Locksley Hall* 68 The *many-winter'd crow. *a* **1618** Sylvester *Job Triumph.* 771 So, Wisdome shall be to the *many-year'd.

b. (i) *poet.* with pres. pples. (and occas. pa. pples.) in quasi-advb. sense = 'in many ways, many times, much', as ***many-beaming, -bleating, -blossoming, -meaning, -mingled, -mingling, -sounding, -turning, -twinkling, -wandering, -winding*** adjs.

? **1818** Shelley *Homer's Hymn to Moon* 6 Where'er she spreads her *many-beaming wings. **1728–46** Thomson *Spring* 834 Around him feeds his *many-bleating flock. **1864** Tennyson *Boadicea* 43 *Many-blossoming Paradises. **1825** Coleridge *Aids Refl.* (1848) I. 24 That *many-meaning and too commonly misapplied expression. **1811** W. R. Spencer *Poems*, The *many-mingled cries. **1821** Shelley *Epipsych.* 358 Their many-mingled influence. **1861** Dora Greenwell *Poems* 129 Run in one the *many-mingling hues. **1745** Warton *Pleas. Melanch.* 198 The *many-sounding organ peals on high. **1728–46** Thomson *Spring* 157 The *many-twinkling leaves Of aspen tall. **1827** Keble *Chr. Y.* 2nd Sund. after Trin., The many-twinkling smile of Ocean. **1820** Shelley *Let. to Maria Gisb.* 262 Clouds..Piloted by the *many-wandering blast. **1812** Byron *Ch. Har.* i. xx, Then slowly climb the *many-winding way.

(ii) *attrib.* phrases consisting of *many* with a sb. in sense 'having, consisting of, many of the things named', as ***many-course, -electron, -interest, -particle, -volume, -word***.

1955 D. Chapman *Home & Social Status* xi. 172 The many-course dinner with wines. **1929** *Trans. Faraday Soc.* XXV. 672 We use this system of energy levels for the many-electron problem just as was done in atoms. **1970** G. K. Woodgate *Elem. Atomic Struct.* i. 5 In many-electron atoms the electrostatic interaction with the nucleus is summed over all the electrons. **1955** M. Gluckman *Custom & Conflict in Afr.* v. 135 They [*sc.* rituals] are inappropriate in the family, our single many-interest group. **1955** W. Pauli *Niels Bohr* 135 The states formed in the reaction are states of a many-particle system. **1941** *Mind* L. 141 That these naïve beliefs [*sc.* about ambiguity] are false is easy to realise in this age of many-volume dictionaries. **1924** R. M. Ogden tr. *Koffka's Growth of Mind* v. 329 Transference from a one-word to a many-word sentence is carried out. **1940** A. H. Gardiner *Theory of Proper Names* ix. 29 In some of my many-word names (e.g. Edgar Allan Poe) the coherence of the parts is much slighter than in others. **1973** A. Quinton *Nature of Things* v. 127 Many-word sentences have to be used to guard against the misunderstandings.

c. Special combinations: **many-berry**, a name for the American hackberry (*Cent. Dict.*); **many-body**, pertaining to or involving three or more bodies or particles; applied *spec.* to the problem of predicting their positions and motions at any future time given their present values and the way the bodies interact; †**many-feet (-foot)**, (*a*) = polype; (*b*) a general name for earwigs, woodlice, etc.; **many-many** *a.* (see quots.); **many-one** *a.*, applied to a correspondence or relation such that two or more members of one set are associated with or related to each member of a second set; hence **many-oneness; many-root(s**, the plant *Ruellia tuberosa*, native to Mexico and the West Indies; †**Many Saints' Day** ? *nonce-wd.*, a name for Pentecost; **many-seed**, a Barbados plant of the genus *Jussiæa*; **many-valued** *a.* [cf. G. *mehrwertig*] *Philos.*, 'possessing three or more truth-values in place of the customary two of truth and falsehood' (Webster 1961); **many-worded** *a.*, of a term or description involving the use of several words.

1847 W. Darlington *Amer. Weeds & Useful Pl.* (1860) 294 Hack-berry. *Many-berry. **1927** Fisher & Hartree tr. *Born's Mech. Atom* iv. 248 The analytical difficulties of the *many-body problem. **1962** W. B. Thompson *Introd. Plasma Physics* i. 2 The microscopic dynamics of a plasma must be understood as a study in many-body physics. **1964** L. Wilets *Theories Nucl. Fission* iv. 56 The first quantitative attempt to apply many-body techniques to finite nuclei was performed by Brueckner, Lockett, and Rotenberg... The results of the infinite many-body problem were used to obtain the K-matrix as a function of density. **1591** Sylvester *Du Bartas* i. v. 87 Th' inky Cuttles, and the *Many-feet. *Ibid.* 238 The..Many-foot, that fain A dainty feast of Oyster-flesh would gain. **1601** Holland *Pliny* I. 351 Some sea-fishes,..haue eight legs: namely, Manyfeet, Pourcuttles, Cuttles. **1658** Rowland *Moufet's Theat. Ins.* 1045 The Scolopendræ, and Juli, and Cheeselips..are called Many-feet. **1706** Phillips, *Ozæna*, a sort of the Fish Pourcontrel or Many-feet. **1922** W. E. Johnson *Logic* II. vii. 156 Here the denominating correlation is not one-one but *many-many, and yet the names and the things happen to be numerically equal. **1933** *Mind* XLII. 53 In this third use of 'term' the total situation located by 'Tom fears Francois' is not two-termed but many-termed, and the total situation located by 'England fears France' many-many-termed. **1965** *Language* XLI. 44 Transformational relations are one-one, but expansion relations are many-many. **1910** Whitehead & Russell *Principia Math.* I. ii. 438 Thus *many-one relations are the converses of one-many relations. *Ibid.* 575 The transition from series generated by one-one or many-one relations of consecutive terms to series generated by transitive relations of *before* and *after*. **1936** *Jrnl. Philos.* 17 Dec. 706 The relation of tokens to their type..is consistently many-one: a type can have many tokens, but a token only one type. But the relation of type to word is many-many. A word can be represented by many types; but so can a type represent many words. **1955** A. N. Prior *Formal Logic* 279 A 'many-one' relation, $Cls \rightarrow 1$, is an *R* such that if *x* is an *R* of any given thing then it is not an *R* of anything else... The null relation is many-one for the same sort of reason as it is one-many. **1959** E. M. Patterson *Topology* (ed. 2) iv. 82 A homomorphism between a group G_1 and a group G_2 is a many-one transformation. **1971** *Language* XLVII. 8 This overwhelming predominance of many-one mapping over one-many, as we move from semantics to phonetics, can then be seen as further evidence of language's directionality. **1966** S. Beer *Decision & Control* xvii. 441 The effect of that Act..was to provide a richer mapping, to reduce the *many-oneness of the homomorphic transformation. **1750** G. Hughes *Barbados* 210 The *Many-Roots. This Plant derives its Name from the great number of its Roots. **1858** Simmonds *Dict. Trade*, *Many-root*, a name for the Ruellia tuberosa. **1655** Fuller *Ch. Hist.* iii. Ded., Those three thousand gained (on *Many-Saints-day) by Saint Peter, at Jerusalem. **1750** G. Hughes *Barbados* 212 *Many-Seed. I have given this Plant a name from its many Seeds. **1848** Schomburgk *Hist. Barbados* 618. **1934** *Philos. of Sci.* I. 118 A *many-valued system of logic is a code of inference which endows propositions with truth values intermediate between true and false. **1936** *Mind* XLV. 273 His probability logic is a many-valued logic. **1963** R. Dickerson in H. W. Baade *Jurimetrics* 63 The potential usefulness of many-valued logic for building mathematical models helpful in dealing with problems of vagueness. **1965** *Philosophy* XL. 172 Languages based on a many-valued logic are artificial constructs. **1969** N. Rescher (*title*) Many-valued logic. *a* **1832** Bentham *Chrestomathia* App. 9. §2 in *Works* (1834) VIII. 188/1 In the *many-worded appellative, part of speech, the word *part* is instructive. **1843** Mill *Logic* I. i. ii. 30 A mixed term belongs to the class of what have been called many-worded names. **1901** A. Sidgwick *Use of Words in Reasoning* v. 143 Description..is more often than not many-worded. **1957** G. Ryle in M. Black *Importance of Lang.* (1962) 151, I am still not quite sure why..every possible grammatical subject of a sentence, one-worded or many-worded, stands to something.

B. quasi-*sb.* and *sb.*

1. quasi-*sb.* On the analogy of *a few* (see few 2), *a* has from the 16th c. been prefixed to *many* when followed by a pl. sb. or used *absol.* in plural sense. In such collocations *many* formally admits of being interpreted as a sb., meaning 'a great number'. This interpretation is somewhat strained when *a many* is immediately followed by a pl. sb., because the ellipsis of *of*, which must be assumed, is abnormal; but in the other cases it presents no difficulty, and it would often be impossible to determine whether in the consciousness of the speaker the word is an adj. used absol. in pl., or a genuine sb. Confusion with meinie, of which there are many traces in the 16th c., seems to have contributed to cause the word in this use to be apprehended as a sb. Often with prefixed adj. as in ***a †considerable, good, great, †pretty, †jolly many***; also ***† no small many***.

a. with pl. sb. (or *people*) immediately following.

In this use *a many* hardly differs in sense from *many*, and is now somewhat rare in literary use, though *a good many*, *a great many*, are common colloquially.

1590 Marlowe *Edw. II*, iv. ii, Though a many friends Are made a way. **1614** Day *Festivals* xi. (1615) 300 There are in this Israel, the Sacred Scriptures of God, a many, many Widowes. *a* **1643** J. Shute *Judgem. & Mercy* (1645) 180 Hee were a mad man that to Secure himselfe from the Fire, would pile a many Billets betweene him and the flame. **1653** H. More *Antid. Ath.* (1662) 97 A many such miracles. **1690** Luttrell *Brief Rel.* (1857) II. 126 And great many men were at work upon the fortifications. **1776** *Trial of Nundocomar* 23/2 A great many people have seen him besides. **1807** Crabbe *Par. Reg.* iii. 768 The rates are high; we have a-many poor. **1813** *Sk. Character* (ed. 2) I. 205 It is a good many years since I have seen him. **1832** Tennyson *Miller's Dau.* 219 They have not shed a many tears, Dear eyes. **1841** Catlin *N. Amer. Ind.* (1844) II. xlviii. 122 They use a vast many beads. **1884** *Manch. Exam.* 17 May 4/8 There are a great many schools..of technicology scattered over the Continent.

b. Const. *of*; now only followed by a definite sb. or pronoun. (Some early quots. may belong to meinie.)

1525 Ld. Berners *Froiss.* II. xxiv. 64 Beneth in the courte he sawe a great many of asses. **1530** Palsgr. 721/1 s.v. *Slyde*, A menye of brokes [*vng tas de ruisseaux*]. **1560** Whitehorne *Arte Warre* 60 Caius Sulpitius..set a greate many of Sackes vpon Mules. **1584** R. Scot *Discov. Witchcr.* xii. iii. (1886) 176 If Incubus could beget Merlins among us, we should have a jollie manie of cold prophets. **1652** Gaule *Magastrom.* 352 He..had invited a many of his kindred and friends. **1656** Earl Monm. tr. *Boccalini's Advts. fr. Parnass.* ii. xxiv. (1674) 173 An infinite many of men. **1711** Addison *Spect.* No. 37 ¶1, I had an Opportunity of turning over a great many of her Books. **1716** B. Church *Hist. Philip's War* (1865) I. 127 He pick'd up a considerable many of their Women and Children. **1840** *P. Parley's Ann.* 183 A many of them played the truant on purpose to see the soldiers go through their manœuvres. **1852** Thackeray *Esmond* i. iii, This was chiefly of the Catholic gentry, of whom there were a pretty many in the country.

c. *ellipt.* and *absol.* (Quots. 1556 and 1564 may belong to meinie.)

[1556 OLDE *Antichrist* 6 To the undoing of a great meanye. 1564 BECON *Display. Popish Mass* Wks. III. 47 b, Ye praye for Philippe and Chenye, mo than a good meany.] 1599 SHAKS. *Hen. V*, III. vii. 79 *Const.* And yet my Sky shall not want [*sc.* stars]. *Dolph.* That may be, for you beare a many superfluously. 1604 HIERON *Wks.* I. 507 These and the like are the thoughts and speeches of no small many. 1611 B. JONSON *Catiline* To Rdr., The commendation of good things may fall within a many, their approbation but in a few. 1788 T. TAYLOR *Proclus' Comm.* (1792) I. Diss. p. xcv, Plato is ignorantly accused by a many, for affirming that [etc.]. 1875 HIGGINSON *Hist. U.S.* viii. 64 A good many died of hardship and fatigue. 1888 BRYCE *Amer. Commw.* III. cii. 438 But even in the East a good many may come from straitened homes.

†2. *sb.* App. by confusion with MEINIE, used for: Company, host, flock; (one's) retinue or following. *Obs.*

1563-87 FOXE *A. & M.* (1596) 1609/2 We are.. murthered downe like a manie of sheep. 1579 SPENSER *Sheph. Cal.* May 23 Before them yode a lusty Tabrere, That to the many a Horne pype playd. 1586 WARNER *Alb. Eng.* I. v. (1589) 14 Those cruell Lions..which haue deuoured those Heards I had, and with my Manie's blood Imbrud their fierce deuouring chappes. 1596 SPENSER *F.Q.* v. xi. 3 And forth he far'd with all his many bad. 1609 C. BUTLER *Fem. Mon.* v. (1623) L ij, The manie begins to march along; thronging one another for haste. 1700 DRYDEN *Pal. & Arcite* III. 545 The chiefs divide And wheeling east and west before their many ride.

3. *Philos.* A multitude, plurality. Opposed to *one*.

a1619 FOTHERBY *Atheom.* II. x. §4 (1622) 309 All Ones, and all Manyes, all wholes, all parts. 1788 T. TAYLOR *Proclus' Comm.* (1792) I. Diss. p. xxiv, One idea, throughout all manys, wrapt up in one. 1864 BOWEN *Logic* i. 4 The Understanding has been called the *unifying* faculty, by which the many is reduced to unity.

many-: see MANI-.

manyatta (mæ'njætə). Also **manyat**. [Masai.] Among certain African peoples, particularly the Masai, a group of huts forming a unit within a common fence.

1905 A. C. HOLLIS *Masai* 292 Meat may not be eaten in the manyat, or warriors' kraals. 1921 *Blackw. Mag.* Jan. 118/1 The Manyatta, a rambling collection of dome-shaped huts surrounded by a straggling zeriba, seemed to have settled down for the day. 1964 *Listener* 30 July 163/2 He returned to the family *manyatta*—a thorn-fenced cluster of low mud hovels shared with the beasts. 1971 *E. Afr. Standard* (Nairobi) 13 Apr. 9/1 A gang of Borana tribesmen attacked a Samburu manyatta at Shaba Hills.

man-year: see MAN *sb.*[1] 20 b.

manyew, obs. form of MANGE.

manyfold ('mɛnɪfəʊld), *adv.* Also **many-fold**, **many fold**. [a mod. re-formation from MANY *a.* + -FOLD (after *three-*, *fourfold*, etc.), etymologically identical with MANIFOLD, though this was rarely used in this sense (MANIFOLD *adv.* 1 b).] In the proportion of many to one.

1879 [see -FOLD]. 1916 D. S. KIMBALL in *Mod. Business* (Alexander Hamilton Inst.) VII. II. vi. 293 If this difference is reflected many-fold in the product of a large and costly machine the difference in output might very well be marked. 1920 S. S. HUEBNER *Marine Insurance* p. v, The tonnage of vessels under the American Flag was, within a brief period, increased many fold. 1961 M. HYNES *Med. Bacteriol.* (ed. 7) x. 126 Urinary infections with resistant bacteria may respond to antibiotics that are concentrated many-fold by renal excretion. 1969 *Sci. Jrnl.* 36/1 If any nation can find.. all the major ingredients to produce unlimited supplies of energy, fertilizer, fresh water and other necessities, then the useful part of the Earth will be increased manyfold.

†'**manyfull**, *a.* *Obs.* [f. MANY + -FUL.] Abundant. (Also const. *of*.)

c1440 *Jacob's Well* 262 Many-full of woordys [*marg.* multiloquium]... He þat hath manye woordys faryth as a fool þat sellyth his chaffare wyth-outen wyȝte and mesure. 1526 in Ellis *Orig. Lett.* Ser. III. II. 80 All this mater I remytte unto your highe wisdome and manyfull goodnes.

†'**manygate(s**. *Obs.* [See GATE *sb.*[2] 9 b.] In many ways.

1375 BARBOUR *Bruce* I. 338 Knawlage off mony statis May quhile awailȝe full mony gatis. c1420 *Lay Folks Mass Bk.*, *York Hours* 35 Many fals witnes, þai wryed hym many gate.

many-headed, *a.* (Stress variable.) **a.** Having many heads. Often applied derisively to the people or populace (***the many-headed beast*** or ***monster***, after Hor. *Ep.* I. i. 76 *Belua multorum es capitum*).

a1586 SIDNEY *Arcadia* II. (1590) 220 O weak trust of the many-headed multitude. 1590 SPENSER *F.Q.* I. viii. 6 The proud Duessa..High mounted on her many headed beast. 1595 DANIEL *Civ. Wars* II. xii, This many-headed monster Multitude. c1611 CHAPMAN *Iliad* I. 478 That many-headed hill. 1680 G. HICKES *Spirit of Popery* 2 That Many-headed Pope the Presbyterian Government. 1737 POPE *Hor. Ep.* II. i. 305 The many-headed Monster of the Pit. 1819 LD. J. RUSSELL in *Hansard's Parl. Deb.* XLI. 1105 Are we then to conclude..that Somers [etc.] expelled a king in order to set up a many-headed tyranny? 1849 TENNYSON '*You might have won*' 20 Keep nothing sacred: 'tis but just The many-headed beast should know. 1852 HENSLOW *Dict. Bot. Terms*, *Many-headed*, when many distinct buds are seated on the crown of a root.

b. *absol.* (= 'the many-headed multitude'.)

1837 DICKENS *Pickw.* xix, The playful disposition of the many-headed. 1934 WODEHOUSE *Right Ho, Jeeves* xv. 181 We might have been a rather oversized greyhound and a somewhat slimmer electric hare doing their stuff on a circular track for the entertainment of the many-headed.

Hence **many'headedness**.

1827 HARE *Guesses* (1859) 96 A Review,—which, among diverse other qualities of Cerberus, has that of many-headedness. 1889 *Spectator* 5 Oct., The many-headedness of a Parliament.

†'**manyhede**. *Obs.* Also **mani-**. [f. MANY + *-hede*, -HEAD.] Multitude.

a1300 *E.E. Psalter* cl. 2 Loves him after mani-hede [Vulg. *secundum multitudinem*] of his mikelnesse. a1400 *Relig. Pieces fr. Thornton MS.* 45 For-þi þat anehede es gude and manyhede alswa, þare-fore it behouede nede þat anehede and manyhede bathe ware in Godd.

†'**manyie, 'menyie**, *sb.* *Sc.* *Obs.* Also 5 **manȝe**, ? **meniye**, 6 **menȝie, menze**, 6–7 **manzie**, 7 **menzie**, **mangzie**. [f. next vb.] = MAIM *sb.*

1456 SIR G. HAYE *Law Arms* (S.T.S.) 116 Quha ever strykis with wappin or othir villaynis manȝe. c1470 HENRYSON *Mor. Fab.* v. (*Parl. Beasts*) xxxv, This wretchit wolf weipand thus on he went, Of this meniye markand to get remeid. 1500-20 DUNBAR *Poems* xxi. 12 He that hes for his awin genȝie Ane plesand prop, but mank or menȝie. 1589 R. BRUCE *Serm.* (1591) Y 3 b, Without a notable inconvenient ather to body or soule, or to boath, without a notable menȝie, as we speak. 1597 SKENE *De Verb. Sign.*, *Machamivm*,..from the auld French worde Mehaigne, quhilk we call, Manzie, hurt, mutilation [etc.]. 1609 —— *Reg. Maj.* III. x. 51 b, Gif the seller did sell to the buyer ane thing, as without anie fault or menzie. *Ibid.* Table 86 b, Mangzie.

†'**manyie, 'menyie**, *v.* *Sc.* *Obs.* Also 4–5 **menȝe**, 6 **menȝie, mainzie**. [a. OF. *mahaignier*: see MAIM *v.*] = MAIM *v.*

a1400 *Trojan War* II. 2131 Woundand, menȝeand, and slaand. 1500-20 DUNBAR *Poems* lxxviii. 3 So sair the magryme dois me menȝie. 1597 SKENE *De Verb. Signif.* s.v. *Machamium*, He quha is mainzied, hes ane just cause to excuse himselfe fra singular battell.

†'**manykin, 'manykins**, *a.* *Obs.* Forms: 1 **maneȝra cynna**, 2–3 **monies cunnes, kunnes, kinnes**, 3 **mani cunnes, kinnes, -kine(s**, 4 **many kyn(nes, mani-, mony-kin**, 5 **manykins**, *erron.* **-kingis**. [Repr. early ME. *monies kinnes* (genit. sing. of MANY *a.* and KIN *sb.*[1]); in OE. the synonymous pl. genitive *maneȝra cynna* occurs.] Of many kinds.

a900 [see KIN *sb.*[1] 6 b]. c1000 *Ags. Ps.* (Th.) x. 7 Drihten onsent maneȝra cynna witu. c1175 *Lamb. Hom.* 103 Heo [*sc.* anger] macað monslehtas and monies cunnes ufel. c1220 *Bestiary* 460 Manikines ðing. c1275 LAY. 1292 þer bi-won Brutus mani kine þinges. c1375 *Cursor M.* 27412 (Fairf.) Manikin þing him mai be-tide [*Cotton* For nakin case þat mai tide]. a1400-50 *Alexander* 3864 Creuesses of manykins hewis. *Ibid.* 4530 Minerua was a maistres of many kingis [*sic*] werkis.

†'**manyment**. *Sc.* *Obs.* Also **manument**. [a. F. *maniement*, f. *manier* to handle.] Management.

1567 *Reg. Privy Council Scot.* Ser. I. I. 514 Sen hir Hienes arryvall..and taking of the manyment and governament of the effaris thairof on hir awin persoun. *Ibid.* II. 161 The maister of his Hienes awin Cunyiehouse or sic utheris as has the manyment thairof. 1600 *Sc. Acts Jas. VI* (1816) IV. 245/1 The saidis James and maister Johne had the governament and manument of his haill rentis, leving, and affairis.

manyness ('mɛnɪnɪs). *rare.* [f. MANY + -NESS.] Plurality, numerosity.

1609 SKENE *Reg. Maj.* 115 Be multiplication, or manynes of Hynes. 1886 HALL & JASTROW in *Mind* Jan. 60 The sense of manyness..acts as a stimulus to us to bend all available energy to tally as fast as possible.

manyogana (ma'njo:gana). Also **manyokana**. [Jap., f. *Manyō(shū* 'collection of a Myriad Leaves', name of an 8th-cent. anthology of Japanese poetry + *-gana* combining form of KANA (phonetic) letters, script.] A system of writing in use in Japan in the 8th century, found *spec.* in the Manyōshū, in which Chinese characters are used to represent Japanese sounds.

1868 J. J. HOFFMANN *Japanese Gram.* 6 The running-hand form was used in the old Japanese Bundle of Poems ..*Man-you-siu* or the Collection of the Ten Thousand Leaves, compiled about the middle of the eighth century. The first *Kâna*-form was, consequently, called *Yamáto-kâna*.., the other *Man-you-kâna*. 1909 tr. *S. Okuma's Fifty Yrs. of New Japan* II. i. 2 We also used these [Chinese] characters merely as symbols for our own sounds. This latter method..we find..generally used in our old works like the '*Kojiki*' and the '*Manyōshū*', whence these symbols came to be called the *Manyō-kana*. 1928 G. B. SANSOM *Hist. Gram. Japanese* i. 23 The name of this anthology was the *Manyōshū*, or 'collection of a Myriad Leaves', and the characters thus used were known as *Manyōgana*. 1934 S. YOSHITAKE *Phonetic System of Ancient Japanese* i. 7 It was that great philologist Motowori Norinaga who first discovered how strictly certain Man-yō-gana were differentiated. 1948 *Introd. Classic Japanese Lit.* (Kokusai Bunka Shinkokai) (1956) p. x, The choice of subject for ballads ranged much more widely..encouraged by the popularization of new methods of writing, by the introduction of the Japanese syllabary (*kana*) in the primitive form known as *man'yôgana* (*Man'yôshû* style *kana*) where the Chinese ideographs were used with their phonetic value. 1951 J. K. YAMAGIWA in Reischauer & Yamagiwa *Transl. Early Japanese Lit.* 277 In the eighth and ninth centuries, abbreviations and simplifications of the *Man'yōgana* resulted in the creation of the two syllabic scripts, the *katakana* and the *hiragana*. 1959 *Chambers's Encycl.* VIII. 58/2 Two [writing] systems gradually developed: one an elaborate distortion of Japanese into Chinese forms (*kambun*); the other a phonetic adaptation of Chinese characters for the reproduction of Japanese sounds (*manyōgana*). 1965 D. KEENE *Manyōshū* p. xviii, The so-called '*Manyō-gana*' are the Chinese characters which were commonly used as phonograms in the *Manyōshū*, from which the present system of *kana* was evolved. 1974 *Canad. Jrnl. Linguistics* XIX. 217 Taken together, the *ongana* and *kungana* comprise the *man'yōgana*, the eighth-century precursors of the later *kana* syllabaries.

manyot, manyour: obs. ff. MANIOC, MANGER.

manyplies ('mɛnɪplaɪz), *sb. pl.* Chiefly *dial.* Forms: 8 **monyple**, 8–9 **manyplus**, 9 **monny-, moni-, mani-, manyplies**. [f. MANY + *plies*, pl. of PLY, fold. Cf. MANIFOLD(s *sb.*[2]] The omasum or third stomach of a ruminant. Also, *jocularly* the stomach of a man.

1774 LAMBE *Hist. Battell Flodden* Notes 70 *Monyple*, a N.C. word. 1782 A. MONRO *Compar. Anat.* (ed. 3) 39 *Omasum, vulgo* the manyplus. 1803 *Prize Ess. Highl. Soc. Scotl.* II. 218 In the fold of the second [*sic*] stomach or monnyplies. 1833 M. SCOTT *Tom Cringle* xii. (1859) 268 As if he feared the very exertion of uttering a word or two might unsettle his moniplies. 1840 *Penny Cycl.* XVII. 82/1 The third stomach, the manyplus. 1861 HUME tr. *Moquin-Tandon* II. I. 43 In all the ruminating animals there are four stomachs: the ingluvies;..the reticulum;..the omasum or many-plies; and the abomasum.

manys(ch, obs. form of MENACE *v.*

many-sided, *a.* (Stress variable.)

1. Having many sides; multilateral.

1660 BARROW *Euclid* I. Def. xxii, Many-sided figures are such as are contained under more right lines than four. a1822 SHELLEY *Def. Poetry* Pr. Wks. 1888 II. 16 The drama ..is a prismatic and many-sided mirror. 1847 SMEATON *Builder's Man.* 172 To find the area of irregular polygons, or many-sided figures.

2. *fig.* Having many aspects, bearings, capacities, or possibilities. (Suggested by Ger. *vielseitig*.)

1843 GLADSTONE *Glean.* (1879) V. 37 Of many-sided aspect. 1868 —— *Juv. Mundi* x. (1870) 402 With many-sided intelligence. 1882 FARRAR *Early Chr.* II. 337 Since Christianity is manysided. 1892 GARDINER *Student's Hist. Eng.* 489 Raleigh was..a many-sided man; soldier, sailor, statesman, historian, and poet.

Hence **many'sidedness**.

1833 LYTTON *Eng. & English* (ed. 2) II. 97 Wordsworth.. has not, it is true, 'the many-sidedness' of Göthe. 1837 C. LOFFT *Self-formation* I. 275 It tends to give him the decantatum illud of the Germans,..manysidedness. 1866 *Sat. Rev.* 19 May 584/1 What men gain in manysidedness it is said they are losing in vigour. 1870 LOWELL *Among my Bks.* Ser. I. (1873) 345 The many-sidedness of truth.

manyssh, -yssyche, obs. ff. MENACE *v.*

manyways *adv.*: see WAY.

†**many-what**. *Obs.* Forms: 3 **maniȝwhatt**, **moniwhat**, 4 **mani-, mony-quat(t, -what**. [See WHAT and cf. *anywhat*, *somewhat*.] Many things.

c1200 ORMIN 1028 Enngless..wiþþ þe bisscopp spækenn O Godess hallfe off maniȝwhatt. a1225 *Ancr. R.* 352 Hore liflode is herre, uor pilegrim eileð moniwhat. a1300 *Cursor M.* 12598 (Cott.) Desputand tuix þaim he satt, And þai him asked mani-quat [*v. rr.* many quat, maniquatt, mony what].

'**many-where**. *rare.* Also 4 **maniquar(e**, 6–7 (with advb. *s*) **many wheres**. [f. MANY + WHERE.] In many places.

a1300 *Cursor M.* 21723 Bot has bitid oft mani quar, þat less folk ouercummen þe mar. 1565 JEWEL *Repl. Harding* (1611) 433 This kinde of Praier..was many wheres receiued. a1656 BP. HALL *Rem. Wks.* (1660) 289 It..can no more according to the natural being even of a body glorified be many wheres at once. 1902 LUBBOCK *Scenery Eng.* 52 Smoothed and polished rocks occur also 'many-where', if I may coin the word.

manywise *adv.*: see WISE *sb.*

‖**manzanilla** (mænzə'nɪlə, Sp. manθa'niʎa). [Sp., f. *manzanilla* camomile.] **1.** A kind of dry and light sherry with a somewhat bitter flavour.

1843 *Penny Cycl.* XXVII. 466/1 Manzanilla, which is the favourite wine of the Spaniards. 1872 THUDICHUM & DUPRÉ *Treat. Wine* 653 Some descriptions of Manzanilla wine.

2. A variety of olive, distinguished by small thin-skinned fruit.

1911 *Daily Colonist* (Victoria, B.C.) 13 Apr. 6/1 (Advt.), Your Easter Sunday menu will demand the luscious, healthful Olive. We carry a big stock, all kinds.. Manzanillas—Small Olives. 1964 *Economist* 8 Aug. 547/2 Special varieties [of olive]..like the Manzanilla and the Goodal in Spain. 1974 *Observer* (Colour Suppl.) 8 Sept. 66/3 The country around Seville in Spain is green olive country, both for the manzanillas and the huge queen olives.

manzanilla, -illo: see MANCHINEEL.

‖**manzanita** (mænzə'ni:tə, Sp. manθa'nita). Also **manzanito**. [Sp., dim. of *manzana* apple.] One of the berry-bearing shrubs of the genus *Arctostaphylos* found in the United States; the bearberry. Also *attrib.*

1848 E. BRYANT *California* xviii. 236 We have met occasionally with a reddish berry called by the Californians manzanita (little apple). 1869 C. L. BRACE *New West* xi. 138 Around her were..dishes of the manzanita seed. 1872 C.

KING *Mountain. Sierra Nev.* ii. 36 The reverence due to the Giver of manzanita berries. **1888** B. HARTE *Drift from Redwood Camp* in *Phyllis of Sierras* 227 A bent manzanito-bush..flew back against his breast. **1918** C. E. MULFORD *Man from Bar-20* xvii. 178 He pushed through matted thickets of oak brush and manzanito. **1928** A. BIERCE *Can Such Things Be?* i. 8 Unable in the darkness to penetrate the thickets of manzanita and other undergrowth. **1971** *Black Scholar* Apr.–May 47/2 Our job is to clear out 10 miles of oak trees, manzanita shrubs and sagebrush on both sides of the highway. **1972** *Village Voice* (N.Y.) 1 June 76/1 A sign next to a luxuriant manzanita plant welcomes you to God's land.

manzello (mæn'zɛləʊ). [Origin uncertain.] A musical instrument resembling a soprano saxophone.

1962 *Melody Maker* 7 July 7/3 The manzello, which he uses frequently in solos, sounds rather like a soprano while the stritch is somewhere in the tenor range. **1966** *New Statesman* 4 Nov. 677/1 On manzello he [*sc.* Roland Kirk] echoes some of Sidney Bechet's canary-yellow flights. **1969** *Daily Tel.* 15 Feb. 15/1 Kirk's solo ability on flute, tenor saxophone, manzello and stritch.

manzie: see MANYIE *Sc. Obs.*

‖**manzil** ('mʌnzɪl). Forms: 7 **manzeil, -eel, munsel, menzill,** 9 **mansale, munzil, -el, manzil.** [Arab. (hence Pers., Urdū) *manzil*, f. *nazala* to descend, alight.] **a.** A halting-place. **b.** The distance between two halting-places, a stage.

1634 SIR T. HERBERT *Trav.* 55 Our next nights Manzeil was at Gogoam. **1698** FRYER *Acc. E. India & P.* 231 In the middle of the Munsel (*i.e.* a whole Day's Journy) the Butler alights. **1840** J. B. FRASER *Koordistan* I. iv. 98 Fixing my first day's munzil..at a village..ten miles from Ooshnoo. **1880** L. WALLACE *Ben Hur* i. (1881) 8 On the desert, distance is.. measured..by the *saat*, or hour, and the *manzil*, or halt.

‖'**manzo.** *Obs. rare.* [It.] Bull-beef.

1594 CAREW *Huarte's Exam. Wits* (1616) 305 Cowes flesh, Manzo, bread of red graine,..the sonne engendred vpon these, shall haue strength like a bull, but withall, bee..of a beastly wit.

manzy, Sc. form of MEINIE.

Mao (maʊ). [f. *Mao* Tse-Tung; see MAOISM.] Used *attrib.* of a simple style of clothing based on dress in Communist China, as ***Mao cap, collar, jacket, trousers***, etc.

1967 *Guardian* 1 Aug. 5/5 A close-fitting standing collar to which Paris is now giving the name Mao. **1968** *N.Y. Times* 22 May 50 'Extravagances' such as the Mao jacket. **1968** *Punch* 24 July 107/2 Out, apparently, are Mao caps, Guevara beards, Maharishi gowns and Zapata moustaches. **1969** A. SINCLAIR *Last of Best* ix. 231 Silk Mao jackets. **1972** *Daily Tel.* 3 Mar. 14 The blue-clad men and women, all in Mao jackets and trousers. **1973** *Sunday Express* (Trinidad) 1 Apr. (Suppl.) 7/3 From the East was Madame Sung Chih-Kuang, 50, wife of the first Red Chinese Ambassador to Britain, who wore a grey cotton Mao suit. **1974** J. MITCHELL *Death & Bright Water* iii. 19 Mao boiler suit to show he was one of the righteous, but hand-sewn and made of silk.

b. Mao 'flu, Hong Kong influenza (see HONG KONG 2).

1968 *Guardian* 14 Dec. 1/1 Hongkong or Mao 'flu now sweeping the United States, is likely to reach Britain next month or in February. **1973** 'G. ASHE' *Life for Death* v. 49 He's had the damned Mao flu and it's put him right out.

Maoism ('maʊɪz(ə)m). [f. the name of *Mao* Tse-Tung (1893–1976), Chairman of the Central Committee of the Chinese Communist Party + -ISM.] The Marxist-Leninist theories of Mao Tse-Tung developed and practised in China. Hence '**Maoist** *sb.*, a follower of these theories; also *attrib.* or as *adj.*, of or pertaining to these theories.

1951 B. I. SCHWARTZ *Chinese Communism & Rise of Mao* xiii. 189 The essential features of Maoism. *Ibid.* 190 Another peculiar feature of the Maoist strategy..is the preference for 'border area' bases. **1961** *Listener* 23 Nov. 886/2 Maoist Marxism. **1962** *Ibid.* 18 Jan. 112/1 There are several kinds of communism in the world—Titoism, Khrushchevism, Maoism in China. **1964** *New Statesman* 17 Apr. 592/3 The Maoists are blind not to see this and to identify their cause with a nostalgia for the Stalin epoch. **1967** *Guardian* 15 May 6/1 The demonstrators have been conducting their affairs in Maoist style—little red books of quotations and all. **1968** *Listener* 28 Nov. 736/1 The awful children..are now revealed as a tiny Maoist cell at the heart of the family. **1969** *N.Y. Rev. Bks.* 16 Jan. 6/2 Many of the good facets of Maoism, such as participation in social and political life and the linking of practice and theory in education. **1970** G. GREER *Female Eunuch* 22 The most telling criticisms will come from my sisters of the left, the Maoists, the Trots. **1970** *New Scientist* 19 Mar. 539/2 Neither Tories nor Labourites can be blamed for sounding like Maoists, desperately looking for a Little Red Book. **1971** *Peace News* 5 Nov. 5/1 His blend of religious fervour and Maoist rhetoric does not endear him either to pacifists or to liberals. **1973** *Listener* 2 Aug. 147/2 This year Mao will be 80, so we may assume that the Maoist era is coming to its end.

Maoize ('maʊaɪz), *v.* [f. *Mao* (see MAOISM) + -IZE.] *trans.* To imbue with the doctrines of Maoism. So **Maoi'zation**.

1970 *Guardian* 18 Sept. 11/2 The guerillas' growing ideological dependence on China..could lead to the 'Maoisation' of the Middle East. **1971** *Time* 12 July 22 Mao demolished..others who did not share his own mystical concept of the revolution. He hoped to replace them with freshly radicalized, totally Maoized youth who would be prepared to spend their lives in permanent struggle.

maomao ('maʊmaʊ). *N.Z.* [Maori.] A blue-skinned marine food fish, *Scorpis violaceus* or *S. æquipinnis*, found in New Zealand and Australian waters.

1886 R. A. A. SHERRIN *Handbk. Fishes N.Z.* 67 The delicious little maomao may be caught at the Rurima Rocks in immense quantities. **1949** P. BUCK *Coming of Maori* (1950) II. viii. 215 The longest bag net..was used to catch *maomao* (*Scorpis violaceus*), a deep-sea fish which travelled in shoals. **1966** *Encycl. N.Z.* II. 408/2 The blue maomao also occurs in Australia, where it is known as the hardbelly.

maon: see MAHONE, MAUND[2].

Maori (‖'mɑːɔri, 'maʊərɪ), *sb.* (*a.*) Pl. **Maori, Maori(e)s.** [The native name: said to mean 'of the usual kind' (Morris *Austral Eng.*)]

1. a. A member of the Polynesian people inhabiting New Zealand. Also *attrib.* or *adj.* pertaining to this people or their language; *absol.* the language.

1843 *Penny Cycl.* XXVII. 752/1 The natives call themselves *maori* (aborigines), in contradistinction to the foreigners, or *pakea.* **1845** E. J. WAKEFIELD *Advent. N. Zealand* I. vi. 174 The Maori language..possesses..but few words which express abstract ideas... The Maori, as made a written language, is pronounced in the same way as German or Spanish. **1854** GOLDER *Pigeons Parlt.* 34 Through bush and clearing searching for ye Full of the thoughts of shooting Maori. **1884** *Century Mag.* XXVII. 919 Crowds of Maoris..thronged the streets.

b. *Comb.*, in names of plants and animals (see Morris *Austral Eng.* 1898): **Maori bug** (see quot. 1966); **Maori cabbage**, the wild cabbage of New Zealand; **Maori-chief**, a New Zealand Flathead fish, *Notothenia*; **Maori dog**, a type of dog, which is now extinct, first introduced to New Zealand by the Maoris; also in *fig.* use, ***cunning as a Maori dog***, a phrase of vulgar abuse; cf. KURI; **Maori-head**, a kind of sedge; **Maori-hen**, the Weka or Wood-hen of New Zealand, *Ocydromus*.

1944 *Mod. Jun. Dict.* (Whitcombe & Tombs) 251 *Maori bug*, a strong-smelling, dark-coloured beetle. **1959** *Numbers* IX. 8 We..shook Maori bugs out of the blankets. **1966** *Encycl. N.Z.* I. 269/1 *Bug, Maori* (*Platyzosteria novaezelandiae*). Maori bug is the commonly accepted name for the largest endemic cockroach of New Zealand... This species is capable of liberating a characteristic, unpleasant odour when disturbed. **1947** D. M. DAVIN *For Rest of our Lives* 103 Cunning as a Maori dog, you know him. **1950** *N.Z. Jrnl. Agric.* Feb. 136/1 Pastoralists..[in the early days] had their problems, too. Maori dogs were troublesome. **1953** M. SCOTT *Breakfast at Six* iii. 30 'The professional charmer,' jeered Larry... 'Cunning as a Maori dog,' supplemented Sam vulgarly. **1966** *Encycl. N.Z.* I. 491/2 The Maori dog (kuri)..was probably introduced during the period of the Great Migration (c. 1350 A.D.)... It became extinct some years after the arrival of the European settlers.

c. Special Comb. **Maori oven** = COPPER MAORI; **Maori P.T.** *N.Z. slang*, taking it easy and doing nothing.

1849 Maori oven [see *go-ashore* s.v. GO *v.* VIII]. **1905** [see COPPER MAORI]. **1961** PARTRIDGE *Dict. Slang* Suppl. 1179/1 *Maori P.T.*, 'taking it as easily as possible, i.e. resting when one should be undertaking physical training'.. : New Zealand soldiers': 1939–45. **1966** G. W. TURNER *Eng. Lang. Austral. & N.Z.* vi. 135 In New Zealand the word *Maori* sometimes enters into slang with contemptuous connotation, but there is a good-natured tolerance, even tinged with envy for an admirable adjustment to life's problems, in a term like *Maori P.T.*..to mean lying down and doing nothing. **1967** *Listener* 2 Mar. 299/3 *Maori P.T.* is New Zealand *dolce far niente.* **1969** *Pocket Oxf. Dict.* (ed. 5) 1035/2 *Maori P.T.*, (sl.) loafing, doing nothing.

2. A New South Wales fish, *Coris lineolatus.*

1882 TENISON-WOODS *Fish & Fisheries N. S. Wales* 74. **1883** E. P. RAMSAY *Food Fishes N.S. Wales* 25 (Fish. Exhib. Publ.) The 'Maori' (*Coris lineolatus*), a most varied and beautifully marked fish, of a rich vermilion.

3. ***black Maori, white Maori*** (N.Z.) (see quots.).

1883 *Illustr. Guide Dunedin* 169 (Morris), Tungstate of lime occurs plentifully in the Wakatipu district, where from its weight and colour it is called White Maori by the miners. **1965** G. J. WILLIAMS *Econ. Geol. N.Z.* xiii. 190/2 This hard ferro-manganese material forms the pebbles known to the early alluvial miners as 'black Maori' (as contrasted with 'white Maori'—scheelite).

Maoridom ('maʊərɪdəm). Also **Maori-dom.** [f. MAORI *sb.* + -DOM.] The Maori world; Maori culture.

1882 W. D. HAY *Brighter Britain!* I. 19 In the very heart of recent Maori-dom. *Ibid.* 278 Auckland city people know little or nothing of Maoridom. **1955** W. J. PHILLIPPS *Maori Carving Illustr.* 8 The tapu system of ancient Maoridom. **1974** *N.Z. Listener* 20 July 11/2, I told him the *Listener* should have an authentic Maori voice speaking in it, a voice that was recognisable throughout Maoridom.

Maoriland ('maʊərɪlænd). [f. MAORI *sb.* (*a.*) + LAND *sb.*] A name for New Zealand. '**Maorilander**, a white man born in New Zealand.

1863 F. E. MANING *Old N.Z.* i. 15, I prepared to make my *entrée* into Maori land in a proper and dignified manner. **1881** *Every Boy's Annual* 657/2 Our goose-wing pen bears us lightly down upon the Maori-land. Captain Abel Tasman, a Hollander, in 1642 discovered New Zealand. **1884** K. NICHOLLS (*title*) The King Country, or Explorations in New Zealand: a narrative of 600 miles of travel through Maoriland. **1896** *Melbourne Argus* 22 July 4/8 (Morris), Always something new from Maoriland! **1896** *Melbourne Punch* 9 Apr. 233/2 (Morris), Norman is a pushing young Maorilander. **1915** *Morning Post* 16 June 9/6 The Maorilanders gave 'Hakas' till their voices failed them. **1933** *Bulletin* (Sydney) 4 Jan. 11 A Maoriland youth.

Maoriness ('maʊərɪnɪs). [f. MAORI *sb.* + -NESS.] = MAORITANGA.

1963 *Times* 6 Feb. (Suppl.) p. ii/5 The failure of humanitarianism when confronted with Pakeha land hunger and Maori determination to hold fast to their *Maoritanga* (Maoriness) bred conflict. **1974** *N.Z. Listener* 20 July 10/3, I have a curious kind of status which derives from my work, from the fact of my Maoriness,—such as it is.

‖**Maoritanga** (maʊərɪ'tæŋə). [Maori.] The culture, traditions, and heritage of the Maori people; the individuality of the Maori; Maoriness.

1940 I. L. SUTHERLAND *Maori People Today* v. 176 What then..is meant by *Maoritanga*? It means an emphasis on the continuing individuality of the Maori people, the maintenance of such Maori characteristics and such features of Maori culture as present day circumstances will permit. **1948** N. SMITH *Maori People & Us* ii. 37 He [*sc.* the Maori] is very sensitive about the honour and standing of his tribe, his ancestry, and his *Maoritanga. Ibid.* xi. 218 An improved mode of living among the Maori people can be developed side by side with their *Maoritanga.* **1966** G. W. TURNER *Eng. Lang. Austral. & N.Z.* viii. 171 Should the Maori preserve his separate identity, his *maoritanga*, or should he become Europeanized as much as possible? **1968** B. BIGGS in E. Schwimmer *Maori People in Nineteen-Sixties* 76 Maori are remaining distinctively Maori without their language, often regarded as the *sine qua non* of Maoritanga. **1971** *N.Z. Listener* 8 Mar. 46 Pakehas who try to give Maoris a bad conscience about their knowledge of Maoritanga. **1974** *Ibid.* 20 July 10/4 The old man did the speaking and it gave me considerable pleasure to hear these men, these korouas, steeped in their Maoritanga, steeped in the tribal values and tradition of Tuhoe.

maormor: see MORMAOR.

Mao tai (maʊ taɪ). Also **Mao Tai, mao-tai, Mao-T'ai, Maotai.** [*Maotai*, name of a town in south-west China.] A mellow and strong pot-stilled spirit produced in Maotai.

1965 O. A. MENDELSOHN *Dict. Drink* 211 Maotai, Chinese strong pot-stilled..spirit as celebrated in the Far East as is cognac in the Western world. **1967** D. BLOODWORTH *Chinese Looking Glass* xxiii. 239 The famous Chinese white wines—Mao-T'ai, Mei-Kuei-Lu, Pai-kan..—have the mule-kick of a bath-tub gin. **1970** *Observer* 10 May 8/4 A glass of *mao-tai*, the potent Chinese equivalent of vodka. **1972** *Guardian* 22 Feb. 24/2 Mr Nixon..consumed little Mao Tai, a potent Chinese drink distilled from sorghum. **1973** *Times* 13 Sept. 16/6 Mao tai, the Chinese national spirit, had increased almost ten-fold in price on the Hongkong market since President Nixon set his lips to it.

map (mæp), *sb.*[1] Also 6–7 **mappe,** 6–8 **mapp.** [ad. L. *mappa*, in class.L. 'table-cloth, napkin', but in med.L. used *transf.* in the combination *mappa mundi* (see MAPPEMONDE).

Cf. the synonymous OF. *mappe* (rare; also in Rousseau *c*1770), Sp. *mapa*, Pg. *mappa*, G. *mappe* (obs.: the mod. sense 'portfolio' is not directly connected).]

1. a. A representation of the earth's surface or a part of it, its physical and political features, etc., or of the heavens, delineated on a flat surface of paper or other material, each point in the drawing corresponding to a geographical or celestial position according to a definite scale or projection.

A hydrographical map is now more usually called a *chart* (formerly †*card*).

1527 R. THORNE in Hakluyt *Voy.* (1589) 257 To make a bigger and a better mappe. **1589** G. HARVEY *Pierce's Super.* Wks. (Grosart) II. 130 The great Mapp of Mercator. **1601** SHAKS. *Twel. N.* III. ii. 84 He does smile his face into more lynes, then is in the new Mappe, with the augmentation of the Indies. **1625** N. CARPENTER *Geog. Del.* I. vii. (1635) 166 A Geographicall Mappe is a plaine Table, wherein the Lineaments of the Terrestriall Spheare are expressed. **1760** JOHNSON *Idler* No. 97 ⁋5 A rivulet not marked in the maps. **1867** W. W. SMYTH *Coal & Coalmining* 44 On examination of a geological map it will be seen that [etc.].

b. *transf.* †A table, chart (*obs.*). Also (*nonce-use*), applied to a mental conception of the arrangement of something.

1626 [FEATLEY] tr. *Parallel.* To Rdr. A iij, Errors..which, collected into a small map, they exhibite. **1855** BAIN *Senses & Int.* III. i. §43 (1864) 398 By a hurt on the ribs we come to connect feelings in the chest with the place on our map of the body.

c. A tract of country spread out like a map.

1784 COWPER *Task* I. 321 A spacious map Of hill and valley interpos'd between.

d. A figure resembling a map in form or outline.

1822 GOOD *Study Med.* IV. 571 Motley dandriff. Scaliness in diffuse maps of irregular outline, and diverse colours.

e. *fig.* In recent phrases: (*a*) ***off the map***: out of existence; into (or in) oblivion or an insignificant position; of no account; obsolete; also (with hyphens) as attrib. phr.; (*b*) ***on the map***: in an important or prominent position; of some account or importance; in existence (see also quots.); so ***to put on the map***: to establish the position or vogue (of someone or something).

MAP 349 MAP

(*a*) **1904** W. H. SMITH *Promoters* ii. 54 When she [*sc.* Carthage] wouldn't let up, the only thing left was to wipe her off the map. **1911** R. D. SAUNDERS *Col. Todhunter* vii. 99 A good set-to is the best way..to put a stop to quarrelin'. It just wipes the whole thing off the map. **1914** *Grand Mag.* Jan. 429/2 [He] had been so harried by the Federal officers that he had faded off the map. **1915** *War Illustr.* II. 328/1 One of the curious off-the-map incidents of the war was brought to notice the other day. **1922** *Tatler* 6 Sept. 386/I A man who owns a lot of coaches..said that the big stuff..was off the map as far as he was concerned. **1924** W. M. RAINE *Troubled Waters* xiii. 143 'Anything new, Matson?'.. 'Don't forget we've been off the map 'most three weeks.' **1928** *Weekly Dispatch* 13 May 2/6 Cochineal insects, except for making tinctures to colour jellies, are practically off the map today. **1938** E. BOWEN *Death of Heart* I. i. 19 An off-the-map, seedy old family friend. **1973** E. LEMARCHAND *Let or Hindrance* xi. 131 We're a bit off the map up here.

(*b*) **1913** C. E. MULFORD *Coming of Cassidy* viii. 122 Cowan had just put Buckskin on th' map by buildin' th' first shack. **1916** *Munsey's Mag.* June 146/2 'The Fortune Hunter', the play that put Winchell Smith on the dramatists' map. **1918** E. POUND *Let.* 4 June (1971) 138 He [*sc.* Henry James] certainly has put America on the map. Given her a local habitation and a name. **1919** WODEHOUSE *Damsel in Distress* vii. 93 What I mean to say is, you are on the map. You have a sporting chance. **1924** W. M. RAINE *Troubled Waters* xix. 205 Didn't know you knew I was on the map. You're sure honouring me. **1926** A. BENNETT *Lord Raingo* I. xii. 60 Some say if there's two members of the War Cabinet, it isn't Andrew Clyth and Tom Hogarth—it's Andrew Clyth and Andrew Clyth... But that isn't so. Tom's on the map all right. **1934** *B.B.C. Year-Bk.* 74 Weekly Chamber Concerts..further helped to put the Hall 'on the map'. **1944** F. CLUNE *Red Heart* 2 The war has put the Red Heart on the map. **1971** *Daily Tel.* 27 Nov. 12 Nepal is very much on the tourist map today, with many tours to the Far East including a few days there. **1973** *Times* 24 Apr. (São Paulo Suppl.) p. i/7 The exhibition was so successful that in one weekend São Paulo put Brazil firmly on to the export map.

f. A diagram representing the spatial distribution of anything or the relative positions of its components.

1833 *Rep. Brit. Assoc. Adv. Sci. 1831, 1832* 320 Fraunhofer counted about 590 of these lines; and in a fine map of the spectrum which he has published, he has inserted the strongest of them. **1881** *Phil. Trans. R. Soc.* CLXXI. 653 The research..on a method of photography by which the least refrangible end of the solar spectrum could be mapped has reached such a stage that it seems desirable that I should..present a map of the solar spectrum between wave lengths 7600 and 10,750. **1926** *Encycl. Brit.* III. 622/1 An excellent photographic map of this spectrum has been given by T. R. Merton. **1950** W. L. BRAGG *Rev. Recent Adv. X-Ray Analysis* ii. 41 (*caption*) Electron density map of the phthalocyanine molecule (left) and key to the structure (right). **1973** *Nature* 21–28 Dec. 509/1 The ability to record activity in many cells at once would allow the construction of a detailed map of the functional connections within a ganglion.

g. *Genetics.* A diagram which represents the linear order and relative distance apart of the known genes of (part of) a chromosome.

1915 T. H. MORGAN et al. *Mechanism Mendelian Heredity* iii. 64 In the construction of the chromosome maps shown in the frontispiece the distance taken as a unit is that within which 1 per cent. of crossing over will occur. **1935** *Genetics* XX. 317 (*heading*) Cytological and crossover maps. **1935** L. H. SNYDER *Princ. Heredity* xv. 160 (*caption*) Linkage map for *Drosophila melanogaster.* **1939** *Jrnl. Genetics* XXXIX. 335 There is now evidence for the existence of seven sex-linked genes, and for these he has furnished a tentative map. **1954** *Adv. Genetics* VI. 1 (*heading*) Map construction in *Neurospora Crassa.* **1970** AMBROSE & EASTY *Cell Biol.* x. 338 (*caption*) Linear genetic map of *Drosophila* showing the four linkage groups corresponding to the four chromosomes.

2. *fig.* **a.** A detailed representation in epitome; a circumstantial account of a state of things. Very common in the 17th c.; now *rare* or *Obs.*

c **1586** C'TESS PEMBROKE *Ps.* CXLII. i, My voice, [O Lord], ..Before thy face my cases mapp it laieth. **1607** ROWLANDS *Guy Warw.* 59 Who in her Face a Map of sorrow wears, A countenance compos'd all mournful, sad. **1647** SALTMARSH *Sparkles Glory* (1847) 2 So as man is all created excellency in the map or abridgment. **1782** COWPER *Hope* in *Poems* I. 171 He draws upon life's map a zig-zag line, That shows how far 'tis safe to follow sin. **1791** BURKE *Lett., to R. Burke* (1844) III. 227, I don't know the map of their situation. **1899** W. E. H. LECKY (*title*) The map of life.

†**b.** The embodiment or incarnation (*of* a virtue, vice, character, etc.); the very picture or image *of*. (So Sp. *mapa*.) *Obs.* (Common in the 17th c.)

a **1591** H. SMITH *Sinf. Man's Search* Six Serm. (1614) E, What were man if he were once left to himselfe? A map of misery. **1606** CHAPMAN *Mons. D'Olive* Plays 1873 I. 200 Farewell the true mappe of a gull. **1698** FRYER *Acc. E. India & P.* 83 They are the absolute map of sordidness, fareing hardly, and professing fairly.

†**c.** An aggregation, multitude. *Obs.*

a **1592** GREENE *Selimus* Wks. (Grosart) XIV. 199 In whose high thoughts A map of many values is enshrin'd. **1597** MIDDLETON *Wisd. Solomon* xv. 12 My soul, saith he, is but a map of shows, No substance, but a shadow for to please.

d. *slang.* A person's face.

1908 [see HANG *v.* 26 f]. **1922** WODEHOUSE *Clicking of Cuthbert* ix. 205 The portrait..was that of a man in the early thirties... 'What a map!' exclaimed the young man. **1935** —— *Luck of Bodkins* xv. 178 It's mostly a case of having a map that photographs well. **1936** J. CURTIS *Gilt Kid* xiv. 144 What d'you want to sit there staring at me for? I'm not a bloody oil-painting. You ought to know my map by now.

†**3.** [? After L. *mappa*; cf. G. *mappe* portfolio.] ? A wrapper. *Obs.*

1608 TOPSELL *Serpents* 220 But some then will demaund, where had Pope Alexander..that map or net at Rome wherin (it is said) the napkin of our Sauiour Christ is preserued.

4. *Math.* = MAPPING *vbl. sb.* 2.

1949 [see INCLUSION 3]. **1966** SZE-TSEN HU *Introd. Gen. Topology* ii. 27 Continuous functions will be called mappings or maps. *Ibid.* 28 A map $f: X \to Y$ from a space X into a space Y. **1971** G. GLAUBERMAN in Powell & Higman *Finite Simple Groups* i. 8 The main tool in investigating this property is the transfer homomorphism of G into S/S'. Unfortunately, we do not have time to define this map.

5. *attrib.* and *Comb.*, as ***map-board, -case, †-graver, -light, -maker, -monger, -mounter, paper, reference, -roller, -seller***; ***map-drawing, -making*** vbl. sbs.; ***map-like*** adj.; **map butterfly**, a butterfly with map-like markings; **map-fire**, artillery-fire in which maps are used for laying the guns; **map-flapping** *Mil.*, the process of transmitting by flag-signals the outline of a map (or other drawing); **map lichen**, a lichen, *Lecidea geographica*, the thallus of which has markings resembling a map; **map-measurer**, an instrument for measuring distances on maps (Knight *Dict. Mech.* 1875); **map-meter** = ***map-measurer***; **map-net** = GRATICULE 2; **map projection** = PROJECTION *sb.* 7; **map-reading** *vbl. sb.*, the inspection and interpretation of a map; so (as a back-formation) **map-read** *v.*, to consult and interpret a map; **map square**, one of several squares (sense 6) drawn on a map for ease of reference; **map-turtle**, an American turtle, *Malaclemmys geographicus*, so called from the markings of the shell (*Cent. Dict.*).

1947 D. M. DAVIN *Gorse blooms Pale* 192 The G.I. and the A.D.C. vaulted from their perch in the back of the jeep and then bent over it again to get their *map-boards. **1894** E. H. AITKEN *Naturalist on Prowl* 50 The delicately devised *Map Butterfly, *Cyrestis thyodamas.* **1916** H. G. WELLS *Mr. Britling* I. v. 181 He..turned over the map in the *map-case beside him, and tried to find his position. **1940** 'GUN BUSTER' *Return via Dunkirk* II. xx. 250 The A.C.P.O. and I had indulged ourselves in two expensive rain-proof map-cases. **1948** W. S. CHURCHILL *Second World War* I. II. xxii. 365 A few feet behind me, as I sat in my old chair, was the wooden map-case I had had fixed in 1911, and inside it still remained the chart of the North Sea. **1943** J. S. HUXLEY *Evolutionary Ethics* i. 6 This business of *map-drawing. **1971** *Guardian* 25 Feb. 2/4 Israel's formal reply to Cairo's offer is..likely to include the first tentative attempt at 'map drawing' since the six-day war. **1922** *Encycl. Brit.* XXX. 252/2 The precision with which '*map fire' could be carried out. **1886** *Longm. Mag.* Feb., (art.) *Map-flapping. **1662** EVELYN *Chalcogr.* Contents, Chart and *Map-gravers. **1796** NEMNICH *Polygl. Lex. Nat. Hist.*, *Map lichen. *Lichen geographicus.* **1963** *Times* 13 Mar. 10 Standard equipment includes two-speed screen wipers and washers—operated from the steering wheel—anti-dazzle mirror, reversing lights, *map light and a heating and ventilation system. **1966** L. COHEN *Beautiful Losers* (1970) I. 92 His cufflink gleamed in the maplight. **1904** *Map-like [in *N.E.D.*]. **1920** E. SITWELL *Wooden Pegasus* 60 Our map-like cheeks are painted red. **1935** AUDEN & ISHERWOOD *Dog beneath Skin* 11 Meadows where browse the Shorthorn and the maplike Frisian. **1775** ROMANS *Florida* App. 77 Our wise *map-makers..have corrupted it into Ponio bay. **1867** *Parkes' Catal. Instruments* 30 Opisometer or *Map Meter. **1639** FULLER *Holy War* v. xiv. (1840) 267 A great *mapmonger.. undertook to travel over England by help of his maps. **1858** SIMMONDS *Dict. Trade*, **Map-mounter*, a workman who backs maps with canvas, varnishes and fixes them on rollers [etc.]. **1932** J. W. CAMERON *Maps & Map-Work* iii. 30 A map projection is any definite system of drawing meridians and parallels, the network of lines thus formed being called a **map-net* or *graticule.* **1954** FISHER & LOCKLEY *Sea-Birds* p. xvi, One of these is on a mapnet invented by the late Professor C. B. Fawcett and is used with his permission and that of the Royal Geographical Society. **1942** H. A. MADDOX *Dict. Stationery* (ed. 2) 68 **Map paper*, a specially made smooth cartridge or strong printing paper—opaque, strong and free from atmospheric influence. **1963** R. R. A. HIGHAM *Handbk. Papermaking* vii. 202 Chart and map papers. The best grades are produced from rag pulps, although sulphite and sulphate mixtures are also used. **1890** *Map-projection [see TRAPEZIFORM *a.*]. **1905** [see PROJECTION *sb.* 7 b]. **1961** L. D. STAMP *Gloss. Geogr. Terms* 308/1 *Map-projection*, the representation of part or whole of the spheroidal surface of the earth on a plane-surface. **1960** *Lebende Sprachen* V. 166/2 The pilot is flying too high and too fast to *map-read his way across country. **1965** D. MACKENZIE *Lonely Side of River* 176 She map-read accurately, giving him plenty of time to respond to her directions. **1968** F. WHITE *Ways of Aquitaine* xii. 161 When one looks at a really fine map..it is easy for anyone who can map-read to see the whole shape of the landscape. **1919** H. SHAW *Text-bk. Aeronaut.* xviii. 208 **Map Reading.*—It is above all necessary for the pilot of a machine to be able to understand a map. **1937** *Discovery* June 192/1 Map-reading classes. *Ibid.*, More maps and yet more maps, is the author's demand..; and more map-reading, too, we must add. **1971** M. MCCARTHY *Birds of America* 10 At a very early age he became a whizz at map-reading. **1954** J. MASTERS *Bhowani Junction* I. vi. 53 This is the *map reference the Wimpy gave..where it spotted those men. **1955** E. WAUGH *Officers & Gentlemen* I. ix. 107 The assault of the island was rehearsed..scrambling inland to objectives which in Mugg were merely map-references, but, in the Mediterranean, were gun-emplacements. **1969** M. PUGH *Last Place Left* iii. 18, I..then gave him some of the facts and the map references. **1851** C. CIST *Sk. Cincinnati in 1851* 245 Shade and *map-rollers, turning in ivory, done in a superior style. **1710** *Lond. Gaz.* No. 4685/4 Sold by C. Browne, Print and *Map-seller. **1917** 'CONTACT' *Airman's Outings* 272, I looked overboard to make certain of the *map square.

Hence **'mapless** *a.*, without maps.

1659 FULLER *App. Inj. Innoc.* I. 5 Mr. Camden's Britania. His first Edition was a Babe in a little..Octavo;..the third, a Youth in a Quarto (but Map-less). **1889** T. HODGKIN *Dynasty of Theodosius* 151 Their deficiency of light cavalry prevented them from..obtaining, in those mapless days, the much-needed information.

map, *sb.*[2] *dial.* (*Sc.*) [Cf. *map* vb., to nibble (E.D.D.).] A rabbit. Hence **'mappie** (E.D.D.), †**mapkin** in the same sense.

1416 in *Rot. Pat. & Claus. Cancel. Hib. Cal.* (1828) I. 213/1 Rex assignavit Johannem Baxter..ad capiendum, emendum, & arrestandum quascunque pelles de martryns, mappekyns, cuniculorum [etc.]. **1825–80** JAMIESON, *Map*, lit., nibbler, a name sometimes given to a rabbit.

map (mæp), *v.*[1] Inflected **mapped** (mæpt), **mapping.** [f. MAP *sb.*[1] Cf. Sp. *mapar*, G. *mappieren*.]

1. a. *trans.* To make a map of; to represent or delineate on a map.

1602 WARNER *Alb. Eng.* XII. lxxi. (1612) 297 Not moop't at home, but mapping Lands. **1847** GROTE *Greece* II. xxvi. (1862) III. 19 Thrace, which is even now imperfectly known and badly mapped. **1849** MACAULAY *Hist. Eng.* iii. I. 411 While he, on the rock of Saint Helena, mapped the constellations of the southern hemisphere.

absol. **1901** R. KIPLING *Kim* xii. 321 They will plot and survey and map of course.

b. *transf.* and *fig.* *Obs.*

1586 WARNER *Alb. Eng.* VI. xxxii. (1589) 143 Of which letigious Famelies here mapped be the Lines. **1611** SHAKS. *Cymb.* IV. i. 1, I am neere to th' place where they should meet, if Pisanio haue mapp'd it truely. **1889** RIDER HAGGARD in *Illustr. Lond. News* 23 Feb. 237/1 The form of a man.. vaguely mapped upon the twilight.

c. *pass.* Of a landscape: To be extended to the eye as in a map.

1845 DARWIN *Voy. Nat.* xix. (1852) 449 To the south the broken land and water..was mapped with clearness before us. **1850** CLOUGH *Dipsychus* II. v.

d. *to map down*: to set down or delineate, as in a map.

1868 HELPS *Realmah* xiv. (1876) 379 He is just the sort of quiet, observant fellow to be mapping all our characters down.

e. *trans.* To establish the relative positions, or the spatial relations or distribution, of (the components of).

1881 [see MAP *sb.*[1] 1 f]. **1950** *Adv. Genetics* III. 117 With linked loci which are closely spaced the recombination value *y* may itself be used as a conventional measure of distance.. in which to map the chromosome. **1969** *Times* 13 Feb. 10/3 Professor Jacobson has inverted an eye from young toads.. and then mapped the connexions made between the retina and the brain. **1974** *Sci. Amer.* Mar. 122/3 Conformational analysis is the completion of the old program for mapping molecules in space. *Ibid.* 94/2 One laborious method for mapping wave forms consisted in noting a series of voltmeter readings and the corresponding angular positions of the alternator shaft.

f. *Math.* To associate with each element of (a set) one or more elements of another set in accordance with a mapping (sense 2); occas., to associate (an element) similarly. Const. *into*, *to*; also const. *onto* for a certain kind of mapping (see ON TO, ONTO *prep.*).

1939 M. H. A. NEWMAN *Elem. Topology of Plane Sets of Points* i. 12 A (1, 1)-correspondence is set up between the set of all positive integers, *I*, and the set of positive even integers, *E*, by mapping *n* of *I* on 2*n* of *E*. *Ibid.* iii. 57 A circle can be mapped continuously on a square region. **1941**, etc. [see HOMOMORPHICALLY *adv.*]. **1965** PATTERSON & RUTHERFORD *Elem. Abstr. Algebra* ii. 57 The correspondence is one-one and maps G_1/H onto Im *f*. **1971** *Sci. Amer.* Aug. 94/3 The symbolism $f: S \to \mathbf{R}$ expresses the fact that *f* causes each point of *S* to be assigned a value in **R**; the expression is usually read as '*f* maps *S* to **R**' or, more formally, as '*f* is a function from *S* to **R**'.

2. map out. a. To represent in detail on a map.

a **1656** BP. HALL *Rem. Wks.* (1660) 387 He..thinkes it not needfull to map out before the Traveller every Town and Village of all the Shires through which he should pass. **1910** *New Mag.* Nov. 204/2 A new country was mapped out by those two men.

b. *fig.* †(*a*) To record minutely (*obs.*). (*b*) To plan out (a course of conduct or behaviour), to divide up (a period of time) into sections allotted to different occupations.

1619 HALES *Lett. Synod Dort* 15 Jan. in *Gold. Rem.* (1673) II. 76 One amongst them there is who hath taken the paines to Mappe out your behaviour since your first footing in the Synod. **1853** MRS. GASKELL *Ruth* I. xii. 262 Don't let us perplex ourselves with endeavouring to map out how she should feel, or how she should show her feelings. **1883** F. M. CRAWFORD *Dr. Claudius* v, A woman of her position probably..mapped out her year among her friends. **1891** *Law Times* XCII. 130/1 These volumes..map out before us the whole law affecting the marriage contract. **1955** *Times* 9 May 10/1 The suggestion was made..to set the ball rolling and map out the times in which later discussion should proceed. **1972** *Daily Tel.* 15 Nov. 1/1 A political plan mapped out by President Lanusse.

c. To divide (a country) *into* districts, as by lines on a map.

1860 MOTLEY *Netherl.* (1868) I. i. 5 The territory of these countries was mapped out by no visible lines. **1870** E. PEACOCK *Ralf Skirl.* II. 248 The Continent was not then mapped out with tourists' routes.

3. *intr.* To fall into place on a map or plan.

1893 HARKNESS & MORLEY *Theory of Functions* 338 Show that..lines parallel to the axes map into unipartite Cartesians.

† **map**, *v.*² *Obs. rare*⁻¹. [? cogn. with MOPE *v.*] *trans.* To bewilder.

c **1425** *Festivals* 175 in *Leg. Rood* (1871) 216 Oure lady.. lay still doted and dased As a womman mapped and mased.

map: see also MOP.

Mapai (mæ'paɪ). [mod. Heb.] A Left-wing party in the State of Israel. Also *attrib.*

1949 KOESTLER *Promise & Fulfilment* II. v. 275 As he does not belong to the inner circle of Mapai, .. he can't get a job. **1950** THEIMER & CAMPBELL *Encycl. World Politics* 236 The largest party is the Labour Party known as Mapai.. similar in programme to West European labour parties. **1956** *Ann. Reg. 1955* 283 A State trial which had prejudicial consequences for Mapai. **1964** *Ann. Reg. 1963* 297 He had settled in Palestine in 1924 and become editor of a daily Hebrew newspaper of the Mapai Party. **1971** W. LAQUEUR *Dict. Politics* 268 The most powerful party in the *Knesset* is the Israel Labour Party made up of *Mapai*, [etc.].

Mapam (mæ'pɑːm). [mod. Heb.] A political party of the far Left in the State of Israel. Also *attrib.*

1950 THEIMER & CAMPBELL *Encycl. World Politics* 236 Mapam.. based on the communal agricultural settlements which are a feature of Israel. **1955** *Times* 9 May 9/3 The election should show the relative strength of the.. Mapam. **1956** *Ann. Reg. 1955* 284 The extreme Left, Mapam,.. increased their representation. **1972** *Guardian* 27 Mar. 4/2 A meeting between Mrs Meir and Mapam leaders.

mapamond(e, obs. form of MAPPEMONDE.

mapau ('mɑːpaʊ). *N.Z.* Also **mapou**. [Maori.] A name for several New Zealand trees, esp. *Myrsine* (or *Suttonia*) *australis*, of the family Myrsinaceæ, an evergreen bearing clusters of white flowers and black berries. Cf. MATIPO.

1868 *Trans. N.Z. Inst.* I. 37 White Mapau or Piripiriwhata (*Carpodetus serratus*)... Red Mapau (*Myrsine Urvillei*). **1882** W. D. HAY *Brighter Britain!* II. 198 The Mapau.. affords good material for fencing. **1889** T. KIRK *Forest Flora N.Z.* 75 By the settlers it is frequently called 'black mapou' on account of the colour of the bark. **1949** P. BUCK *Coming of Maori* (1950) I. iv. 57 The canoe also brought.. a *mapau* (*Myrsine urvillei*) named Ateateahenga to be used in planting ceremonies. **1951** *Dict. Gardening* (R. Hort. Soc.) IV. 2057/2 *S[uttonia] australis*. Mapou. Evergreen tree 10 to 20 ft., or a tall shrub. **1963** POOLE & ADAMS *Trees & Shrubs N.Z.* 166 *M[yrsine] australis*... Mapou.

maphrodite, aphetic f. HERMAPHRODITE *a.* 4 b.

1849 N. KINGSLEY *Diary* (1914) 33 She is to appearance a bark or maphrodite brig. *Ibid.* 35 Was rousted early this morning to see a ship close along side... she is a Maphrodite Brig.

mapkin: see MAP *sb.*²

maple ('meɪp(ə)l). Also 4-5 **mapil(l, -ul(le, -el, 7 mayple.** [OE. **mapel*, **mapul*, only in *mapeltréow* MAPLE TREE, and in *mapulder* of the same meaning: cf. OS. *mapulder* (Gallée), MLG. *mapeldorn*.

The late ON. *mǫpur-r* (rare⁻¹) seems to be an alteration of the Eng. word after the synonymous but unconnected ON. *mǫsurr*: see MAZER. Beside the OTeut. type **maplo-* represented in the Eng. and OS. word, there was a synonymous **matlo-* represented in OHG. *mazzaltra*, mod.G. *maszholder*; the relation between these two forms has not been explained.]

1. a. Any of the trees or shrubs of the genus *Acer*, flourishing in northern temperate regions, many of which are grown for shade or ornament, some valued for their wood, and some for a sugar product. The Common Maple is *Acer campestre*. The fruit of these trees is a double-winged samara or 'key'.

770 [see MAPLE TREE]. ? *a* **1366** CHAUCER *Rom. Rose* 1384 Maples, asshe, ook, asp, planes longe. *c* **1386** —— *Knt.'s T.* 2065 Mapul. **1590** SPENSER *F.Q.* I. i. 9 The Maple seeldom inward sound. **1632** T. MORTON *New Eng. Canaan* II. ii. (1637) 65 Mayple, .. very excellent, for bowles. **1732** *Gentl. Mag.* II. 673 The Maple blushing gratifies the Sight. **1856** WHITTIER *Ranger* v, Silver birches, golden-hooded, Set with maples, crimson-blooded.

b. With qualifying word, applied to various species of the genus *Acer*: e.g.

bird's-eye maple (cf. 2) = *sugar maple*; **black** or **black sugar maple**, *A. nigrum*; **Cretan maple**, *A. creticum*; **dwarf maple**, *A. glabrum* (Cent. Dict. 1890); **goose-foot maple** = *striped maple* (ibid.); **great** or **greater maple** = *sycamore maple*; **hairy maple**, *A. barbatum*; **hard maple** = *sugar maple*; **hedge maple**, *Acer campestre*; **Italian maple**, *A. Opalus*; **Montpellier maple**, *A. monspessulanum*, found in southern France; **mountain maple**, *A. spicatum*, found on mountains in North America; **Norway maple**, *A. platanoides*; **red** or **red-flowering**, **scarlet** or **scarlet-flowering maple**, *A. rubrum*; **rock maple** = *sugar maple*; **silver, silver-leaved**, or **white maple**, *A. dasycarpum*, of eastern North America; **soft maple**, 'either the red or the silver maple' (Cent. Dict.); **striped maple**, *A. pennsylvanicum* (or *striatum*), moosewood; **sugar maple**, *A. saccharinum* of North America, which yields maple-sugar; **swamp maple** = *red maple*; **sycamore maple**, *A. Pseudo-platanus* (see SYCAMORE); **vine maple**, *A. circinatum* (Cent. Dict.). Also **ash-leaved maple**, any tree of the genus *Negundo*; box-elder.

1597 GERARDE *Herbal* III. cxii. 1300 The great Maple, not rightly called the Sycomore tree.. is a stranger in England. **1797** *Encycl. Brit.* (ed. 3) s.v. *Acer*. **1800** *Med. Jrnl.* IV. 246 The sugar and silver maple, *Acer saccharinum*, and *A. dasycarpon*. **1866** *Treas. Bot.* **1876** BURROUGHS *Winter Sunshine* (1895) 93 Soft maple makes a very fine white sugar. **1906** *Westm. Gaz.* 13 Nov. 12/2 Every lane is aflame with hedge-maples. **1957** M. HADFIELD *Brit. Trees* 376 Common Maple. *Acer campestre* Linnaeus. Hedge maple, field maple. Usually a small tree.. but also seen in hedge-rows as a pollard or, owing to repeated cutting, a shrub.

2. a. The wood of any of these trees. ***bird's-eye maple*** (see BIRD'S-EYE 4). ***curled maple***: a wood in which the grain is much undulated or contorted, obtained from the broad-leaved, red, and sugar maples. ***mottled, Russian maple*** (see quot. 1875).

1396-7 *Durham Acc. Rolls* (Surtees) 214, ix sawsars de Mapill. **1663** COWLEY *Ess., Agric.* Wks. 1710 II. 714 He seats him in a Throne of Maple. **1664** EVELYN *Sylva* x. 28 The Maple.. was of old held in equal estimation almost with the Citron; especially the Bruscum, the French-Maple, and the Peacocks-tail-Maple. **1805** WORDSW. *Prel.* I. 515 The naked table, snow-white deal, Cherry or maple. **1847** W. DARLINGTON *Amer. Weeds*, etc. (1860) 92 The wood of the Red Maple—especially that variety or form of it, known as Curled Maple. **1875** *Ure's Dict. Arts* III. 216 The Russian maple is thought to be the wood of a birch tree... The bird's eye maple is the American variety... The mottled maple is a commoner variety.

b. The colour of maple.

1853 *Heal & Son Catal.* 60/1 Wardrobes, japanned maple, or any colour for gentlemen's use. **1926-7** *Army & Navy Stores Catal.* 297/2 Oil Varnish stains.. in the following colours.. Mahogany, Rosewood, Maple, Satinwood. **1967** [see DUCK'S EGG c].

3. *attrib.* and *Comb.*, as ***maple forest, grove, leaf, timber***; †***warr*** (= knot in tree), ***wood***; quasi-*adj.* with sense 'made of maple wood', as in ***maple chair, cup, dish***; ***maple-leaved, -timbered*** adjs. Also **maple beer**, a beverage made from maple sap; † **maple biscuit**, some kind of confectionery; † **maple block**, a block of maple wood on which tobacconists cut tobacco; **maple-borer**, an insect which bores the wood of maples (*Cent. Dict.* 1890); **maple bush**, the mountain maple, *Acer spicatum*; **maple candy**, a sweet made from maple sap; **maple disease**, a disease of certain maples caused by the fungus *Phyllosticta acericola* (*Cent. Dict.*); **maple eye**, in graining, an eye-shaped mark like those found in maple wood; † **maple face**, a spotted face; so **maple-faced** *a.*; **maple grey**, a kind of grey pea; **maple-honey** *U.S.*, the uncrystallized part of the sap of the sugar maple (Bartlett *Dict. Amer.* 1859); **maple key**, the fruit of a maple-tree (see KEY *sb.*¹ 14); **maple knob** (see quot.); **maple leaf**, a representation of the leaf of the maple tree (as an emblem of Canada); **maple molasses** *U.S.*, a syrup obtained by evaporating maple sap or dissolving maple sugar (*Cent. Dict.*); **maple pea**, a variety of garden pea with wrinkled seeds; = *maple rouncival*; also *absol.*; **maple rouncival**, a kind of rouncival pea (cf. *maple grey*); **maple sugar** *N. Amer.*, the sugar obtained by evaporation from the sap of certain maples; **maple sugary**, a maple sugar factory; **maple swamp**, a swamp in which maple is the prevailing tree; **maple syrup** = *maple-molasses*; hence **maple-syruping** *vbl. sb.*; **maple syrup (urine) disease**, a rare condition which is usu. fatal at a very early age or (if the infant survives) leads to mental deficiency, and is caused by the absence of an enzyme which decarboxylates various metabolites of the amino-acids leucine, isoleucine, and valine, so that these substances are present in high concentrations in the blood and urine and impart a characteristic smell of maple syrup to the latter. Also MAPLE-ROOT, TREE.

1788 *Amer. Museum* IV. 350/1 **Maple beer.*—To every 4 gallons of water (while boiling) add a quart of maple melasses. **1857** 'PORTE CRAYON' *Virginia Illustr.* I. 23 The table was spread with the best in the house—cold bread and meat.. maple beer. **1873** L. RUSSELL *Everyday Life Colonial Canada* viii. 103 Spruce beer, made from the tender twigs of that tree, and maple beer, from the late, weak sap fermented with hops. **1755** *Mem. Capt. P. Drake* II. iii. 45 A Flask of Pontack,.. with Cakes, *Maple Biscuits, and other Sweetmeats [at Allost, in Flanders]. **1610** B. JONSON *Alch.* I. iii, He has his *maple block, his siluer tongs. **1821** SCHOOLCRAFT *Trav.* 162 The small red twigs of the.. *maple bush. **1840** *N.Y. Mirror* 4 Apr. 37/2 Your great dealers in Newtown pippins and *maple candy. **1879** *Morning Chron.* (Halifax, Nova Scotia) 2 July 1/8 The average boy and a good sized lump of maple candy, form the materials from which we might deduct self-evident conclusion regarding the facility with which attachments are formed in early life. **1975** *Times* 22 Apr. 6 The Prince of Wales samples maple candy while visiting a sugar camp near Ottawa. **1649** OGILBY *Æneis* VIII. (1684) 292 A *Maple Chair, graced with a Lion's Skin. **1679** BLOUNT *Anc. Tenures* 7 The service of presenting the king with three *Maple-Cups on the day of his Coronation. **1634** MILTON *Comus* 391 Who would rob a Hermit of his Weeds, His few Books, or his Beads, or *Maple Dish? **1873** E. SPON *Workshop Receipts* Ser. I. 424/2 Put in the *maple eyes by hand. **1633** B. JONSON *Tale of Tub* II. i, What! Rowle-powle! *Maple-face! All fellowes! **1650** BULWER *Anthropomet.* 159 Ere long these adulterate Colours will moulder, and then the old maple-Face appeares. **1607** MIDDLETON *Five Gallants* IV. vii, Yon unlucky, *maple-faced rascal. **1840** *Knickerbocker* XVI. 267 A small and beautiful lake [with].. a rich tract of *maple forest on one side. **1910** KIPLING *Rewards & Fairies* 146 Still autumn sets the maple-forest blazing. **1805** R. W. DICKSON *Pract. Agric.* II. 583 The Marlborough gray, the horn gray, the *maple gray. **1876** *Encycl. Brit.* IV. 773/2 A *maple grove.. is.. regarded as a valuable feature on a Canadian farm. **1664** EVELYN *Kal. Hort., Oct.* (1679) 26 Ashen, Sycomor, and *Maple keys. **1858** HOMANS *Cycl. Comm.* 1316/1 In addition to the above-named varieties [curled and bird's-eye maples], two other kinds occur in the *wens*, or excrescences, which grow on the trunk or roots of this tree... The most valuable variety is known by the name of Variegated *Maple-knob. **1418** *E. E. Wills* (1882) 36 Wroght wit *mapil leues and fret of .iij. foill. **1860** *Trans. Lit. & Hist. Soc. Quebec* IV. 20 The Mayflower.. I am told is the emblem of Nova Scotia, as the Maple leaf is of Canada. **1900** *Daily News* 1 Jan. 3/2 The Canadians; the wearers of the maple leaf. **1964** *Globe & Mail* (Toronto) 29 Oct. 1/9 A single maple leaf on a white field flanked by red bars will be recommended to the House of Commons today as Canada's new flag. **1967** *Canadian Antiques Collector* Jan. 25/1 At least three different Maple leaf forms have been found in the pressed glass patterns of Canada. **1785** H. MARSHALL *Arbustrum Americanum* 77 *Maple-leaved Liquidamber Tree or Sweet Gum. **1813** H. MUHLENBERG *Catal. Plant.* 32 Maple-leaved Mealy Tree (*Viburnum acerifolium*). **1930** Maple-leaved [see *London plane*]. **1804** T. G. FESSENDEN *Orig. Poems* 29 The lips of my charmer are sweet, As a hogshead of *maple molasses. **1863** 'G. HAMILTON' *Gala-Days* 225 A land flowing with maple molasses and sugar. **1897** C. DURAND *Reminisc.* 83 We made our household sugar, and luscious maple molasses, not mixed as it is now too often with water and common Muscovado sugar. **1733** W. ELLIS *Chiltern & Vale Farming* xxxii. 219 The *Maple is a larger and sweeter Pea for the Hog. **1744** —— *Mod. Husbandman* Mar. vi. 53 (*heading*) The Nature and Culture of the common and rouncival Maple Pea. **1960** *Farmer & Stockbreeder* 23 Feb. 4/2 For maples interest is mostly restricted to seed lots. **1969** *Times* 14 Jan. 8/6 One pigeon, encouraged by occasional rewards of maple peas fed to it.. learnt to glide in a stationary position in a wind tunnel so that its performance could be measured. **1762** MILLS *Syst. Pract. Husb.* I. 466 The green and the *maple rouncivals require a stronger soil than the white. **1720** *Phil. Trans. R. Soc.* XXXI. 27 *Maple Sugar is made of the Juice of Upland Maple, or Maple Trees that grow upon the Highlands. **1784** J. BELKNAP in *B. Papers* (1877) II. 181 A sauce composed of raspberries, cream, and maple sugar. **1852** A. CARY *Clovernook* 74 Everyday in winter she used to feed them [*sc.* the bees] maple-sugar if she had it. **1885** 'MARK TWAIN' in *Century Mag.* XXXI. 195/2 We occupied an old maple-sugar camp. **1907** *Springfield* (Mass.) *Weekly Republ.* 9 May 16 The Holyoke canoe club opened the river year with a maple-sugar eat at their club-house. **1921** *Daily Colonist* (Victoria, B.C.) 30 Mar. 3/6 Up to the present the weather has not been favourable for the manufacture of maple sugar in the district of Quebec. **1931** W. CATHER *Shadows on Rock* V. i. 204 The country people had been coming.. bringing maple sugar, spruce beer. **1969** E. H. PINTO *Treen* 94/1 Maple Sugar Moulds... early 19th-century, carved wood moulds for maple sugar, from Quebec Province, Canada. **1974** *Country Life* 3-10 Jan. 28/3 Maple sugar was.. often the only source of sugar available to pioneers in the backwoods. **1890** E. W. GOSSE *P. H. Gosse* 95 A log-hut.. a young *maple-sugary, and four tons of hay. **1667** *Early Rec. Providence, Rhode Island* (1894) V. 317 Standing on the west Side of a *Maple Swampe. **1789** J. MORSE *Amer. Geogr.* 143 One species generally predominating in each soil has originated the descriptive names of.. maple, ash and cedar swamps. **1855** *Knickerbocker* XLVI. 225 Cutting hoop-poles in the maple swamps. **1849** in *Glimpses of Past* (Missouri Hist. Soc.) (1933) I. 5 At the different houses they received sugar, coffee, lard, candles, flour, *maple syrup, [etc.]. **1885** *Outing* Oct. VII. 77/1 A moment later, all smoking and puffy and swimming in maple sirup, it disappears. **1905** CALKINS & HOLDEN *Art of Mod. Advertising* 113 Maple-sirup is a product to which justice has never been done. [**1954** J. H. MENKES et al. in *Pediatrics* XIV. 462 (*heading*) A new syndrome: progressive familial infantile cerebral dysfunction associated with an unusual urinary substance... A characteristic feature of their illness was the passage of urine with an odor strikingly similar to that of maple syrup. **1957** *Amer. Jrnl. Dis. Children* XCIV. 571/2 (*heading*) Maple sugar urine disease.] **1959** *Brit. Med. Jrnl.* 10 Jan. 90/1 (*heading*) 'Maple syrup urine disease.' An inborn error of the metabolism of valine, leucine, and isoleucine associated with gross mental deficiency. *Ibid.* 92/2 A disease which may be related to 'maple syrup disease'. **1967** MRS. L. B. JOHNSON *White House Diary* 11 June (1970) 527 We went in to breakfast.., including blueberry pancakes, and, naturally, Vermont maple syrup. **1968** PASSMORE & ROBSON *Compan. Med. Stud.* I. xi. 23/1 Maple syrup disease, so rare as to be a clinical curiosity, is an inborn error of metabolism. **1969** *New Scientist* 3 July 10/1 Prevention of postnatal brain damage by dietary treatment has been reported in a number of other inborn errors of metabolism. Examples include galactosaemia, tyrosinosis, maple syrup urine disease and possibly homocystinuria. **1973** J. DRUMMOND *Bang! Bang! You're Dead!* xv. 39 A pretty girl, with a small cute body the colour of maple syrup. **1975** *Budget* (Sugarcreek, Ohio) 20 Mar. 3/8, March 17—Very damp on the outside again. Ideal weather for maple *syruping. **1845** C. M. KIRKLAND *Western Clearings* 3 He had purchased fine farming land and *maple timber. **1849** *Ex. Doc. 31st U.S. Congress 1 Sess. House* No. 5. II. 631 At 7½ a.m., went over good *maple-timbered land to corner. **1579** SPENSER *Sheph. Cal.* Aug. 26 A mazer ywrought of the *Maple Warre. **17..** MORTIMER *Husb.* (J.), Of the rottenest *maple wood burnt to ashes they make a strong lye. **1805** *Med. Jrnl.* XIV. 172 Maple wood is.. much used for the lathe.

Hence **mapled** ('meɪp(ə)ld) *a.*, grown with maples.

1851 WHITTIER *Chapel of Hermits* 371 This mapled ridge shall Horeb be.

maple, variant of MAPPLE *Obs.*, a mop.

maple-root. The root of the maple, formerly used medicinally.

1523 SKELTON *Garl. Laurel* 1377 [In the list of his own compositions.] The Murnyng of the mapely rote. **1609** *T. Ravenscroft's Pammelia* xxxi. C 3 b, My Ladie's gone to Canterbury, S. Thomas be her boote. Shee met with Kate

of Malmsbury, why weepst thou maple roote? **1640** PARKINSON *Theat. Bot.* XVI. xxvi. 1427 Or Maple roote in pouther made Take oft in Wine, a present med'cine knowne.

'maple tree. = MAPLE I.

770 in Birch *Cart. Sax.* (1885) I. 290 Of þam syrf treowe in þ ruʒ' mapel treow in forweard werdune. *c* **1425** *Voc.* in Wr.-Wülcker 646/19 *Hec ascer*, mapulletre. **1579** LYLY *Euphues* (Arb.) 100 Is not.. dunge [taken] out of the Maple tree by the Scorpion? **1660** *Early Rec. Warwick, Rhode Island* (1926) 322 Bounded by a mapell tree on the Northwest corner. **1700** *Early Rec. Providence, Rhode Island* (1893) IV. 139 The maple tree is the north east Corner bound. **1810** F. A. MICHAUX *Hist. Arbres Forestiers de l'Amérique Septentrionale* I. 28 Red flowering maple,.. Swamp maple,.. Soft maple..[ou] Maple tree.. dans Pensylvanie, la Virginia, et l'Ohio. **1859** GEO. ELIOT *A. Bede* ii, As Dinah walked.. towards the cart under the maple-tree. **1867** J. N. EDWARDS *Shelby* xx. 337 To send the blood coursing through his veins like the sap in the maple-trees. **1974** *Country Life* 3–10 Jan. 28/1 One of the earliest.. signs that the winter freeze is coming to an end is the sight of buckets hanging on the trunks of maple trees.

mapling ('meɪplɪŋ), *sb.* [f. MAPLE.] A ripple-like figure in wood, characteristic of maple.

1909 W. BATESON *Mendel's Princ. Heredity* 144 A damasked pattern showing where the mapling would have been if the plant had been a coloured one.

mapold, -olt: see MAPPLE *Obs.*

mappable ('mæpəb(ə)l), *a.* [f. MAP *v.*[1] + -ABLE.] That may be represented on or by a map.

1920 A. S. EDDINGTON *Space, Time & Gravitation* vi. 106 Hurdle-counts will no longer be accurately mappable on a plane sheet of paper, because they do not conform to Euclidean geometry. **1969** BENNISON & WRIGHT *Geol. Hist. Brit. Isles* i. 14 A bed of particular lithology, and mappable as a recognizable stratigraphic unit. **1974** *Nature* 8 Feb. 344/2 In area 105 a mappable disconformity has been recognised at a stratigraphic level just above the KBS Tuff.

Hence **mappa'bility**.

1969 *Proc. Geol. Soc.* Aug. 145 Vertical and lateral boundaries should be based on the lithological criteria that provide the greatest unity and practical utility (i.e. essentially, mappability).

mappel: see MAPPLE *Obs.*

mappemonde (mæp'məʊnd). Now only *Hist.* Forms: 4–5 **mappemounde, mapamond(e**, 6 **mappamo(u)nd**, 9 **mappemonde**. [a. F. *mappemonde*, ad. med.L. *mappa mundī* map of the world. Cf. mod.Pr. *mapomoundo*, Sp. *mapamundi*.] The map of the world; in early quots., the world itself.

138. CHAUCER *To Rosemounde* 2 Madame, ye ben of al beautè shryne As fer as cercled is the mappemounde [*MS.* mapamonde]. **1390** GOWER *Conf.* III. 102 And sette proprely the bounde Aftre the forme of Mappemounde. *c* **1450** HOLLAND *Howlat* 328 Marchonis in the mapamond.. nixt dukis in dignite. **1533** BELLENDEN *Livy* Prol. ii, The twynkland sternis about þe mappamound. **1560** ROLLAND *Crt. Venus* II. 125 Of all palice it was the luminair, That euer ȝit was maid on Mappamond. **1864** MAJOR in *Archæologia* XL. 1 Memoir on a Mappemonde by Leonardo da Vinci. **1891** J. WINSOR *Columbus* ii. 61 The mappemonde, which was drawn in 1500, by one of Columbus's pilots, Juan de la Cosa.

'mapper. [f. MAP *v.*[1] + -ER[1].] A map-maker.

1635 PERSON *Varieties* I. 44 Our moderne Navigators and Mappers. **1883** BURTON & CAMERON *Gold Coast* I. ii. 32 Columbus.. lived as a mapper with his father-in-law.

So **'mappery** (*contemptuous*), the making of maps.

1606 SHAKS. *Tr. & Cr.* I. iii. 205 They call this Bed-worke, Mapp'ry, Closset Warre. **1840** *Tait's Mag.* VII. 411 Protocols.. and what not, the mere mappery and paper projection of what has had, or may have, some relation to a deed.

mapping ('mæpɪŋ), *vbl. sb.* [f. MAP *v.*[1] + -ING[1].]

1. a. The action of MAP *v.*[1]; the drawing of maps, map-making; planning. Also with *out*, *down*.

1775 in ASH *Suppl.* **1849** MURCHISON *Siluria* v. 93 Corrections being made in the mapping of faults and strata. **1856** MRS. BROWNING *Aur. Leigh* IX. 838 Less mapping out of matter to be saved. **1860** GEO. ELIOT *Mill on Fl.* II. i, When the miller talked of 'mapping' and 'summing' in a vague and diffident manner. **1868** LOCKYER tr. *Guillemin's Heavens* (ed. 3) 390 The actual mapping down of the spectra of several of the brightest stars.

attrib. **1866** W. F. STANLEY *Math. Drawing Instr.* 12 A very fine kind of writing-pen, termed a mapping pen.

b. *Genetics.* The making of a genetic map (MAP *sb.*[1] 1 g); the process of determining the chromosomal position of a gene in relation to other genes.

1935 L. H. SNYDER *Princ. Heredity* xv. 153 (*heading*) The mapping of chromosomes. **1965** *Genetics* LI. 157 (*heading*) Mapping of temperature-sensitive mutants in bacteriophage T5. **1967** *Jrnl. Molecular Biol.* XXVII. 163 (*heading*) Genetic mapping in *Bacillus subtilis*. **1969** A. M. CAMPBELL *Episomes* i. 7 Of special interest was the mapping of the Hfr character itself. **1970** AMBROSE & EASTY *Cell Biol.* x. 334 (*heading*) Gene mapping with *Drosophila*.

2. *Math.* A correspondence by which each element of a given set has associated with it one element (occas., one or more elements) of a second set. (Some topologists use *transformation* in this sense and *mapping* in the narrower sense of a continuous transformation.)

1931 H. P. ROBERTSON tr. *Weyl's Theory of Groups & Quantum Mech.* iii. 110 A mapping or correspondence *S*.. is determined by a law which associates with each point *p* of the field a point *p'* as image. **1935** [see HOMOMORPHIC *a.* 2]. **1958** G. T. WHYBURN *Topological Analysis* ii. 24 A continuous transformation will be called a mapping. **1964** W. J. PERVIN *Found. Gen. Topology* i. 10 Other terms for mapping are 'function', 'transformation', and 'operator'. **1966** F. M. HALL *Introd. Abstr. Algebra* I. ix. 156 If the mapping θ is between the object space *A* and image space *B* we write $\theta{:}A\rightarrow B$ (a mapping θ of *A* into *B*). **1968** M. BRUCKHEIMER et al. *Math. for Technol.* ii. 17 An example of a one-many mapping is the mapping $a\rightarrow\pm\sqrt{a}$ of the set of non-negative real numbers to the set of all real numbers. **1971** *Nature* 17 Dec. 396/2 The ideal transducer.. neither stores nor dissipates energy; viewed as a mapping from input space, $(e_1 f_1)$, to output space $(e_2 f_2)$, $e_1 f_1 + e_2 f_2 = 0$.

'mappist. *rare.* [f. MAP *v.*[1] + -IST.] = MAPPER.

a **1618** SYLVESTER *Little Bartas* 311 Learned Mappists, on a Paper small, Draw (in Abbridgement) the whole Type of all. **1888** *Academy* 28 Jan. 63/3 The mappist Collins calls the river between Oxford and Wallingford the Isis.

†**mapple.** *Obs.* In 5 **mappel, mapolt, -old**, 6 **maple**. [app. ad. late L. *mappula* (? in monastic use), dim. of *mappa* napkin: see MAP *sb.*[1], MOP *sb.*] A mop.

c **1440** *Promp. Parv.* 325/2 Mappel, *idem quod* Malkyn. **1466** *Mann. & Househ. Exp.* (Roxb.) 346 Thrommes for pyche mapoltes. **1486** *Naval Acc. Hen. VII* (1896) 16 Shepe skynnes for mapoldes. **1599** NASHE *Lenten Stuffe* Ded. A 2, With Cales beards, as broade as scullers maples, that they make cleane their boates with.

'mappy, *a.* [f. MAP *sb.*[1] + -Y.] Like a map.

1861 THORNBURY *Turner* (1862) I. 230 He had a horror of what he said Wilson called 'being too mappy'. **1873** MISS BROUGHTON *Nancy* III. 152 A dead colourless flat, dotted with little round trees,.. one of those mappy views, that lack even the beauties of a map.

mapul(le, obs. form of MAPLE.

maquaroon, obs. form of MACAROON.

‖**maquereau** (makəro). Pl. **-eaux**. [Fr.] = MACKEREL[2].

In quot. 1920 the form with final *-o* is idiosyncratic.

1898 A. M. BINSTEAD *Pink 'Un & Pelican* xi. 256 His head was pounded like a Hamburg steak, and sixty-five dollars rolled into the basket, principally contributed by the females who had been accustomed to support the maquereau during his life. **1919** C. MACKENZIE *Sylvia & Michael* i. 21 The officer.. called him a *maquereau*. **1920** E. POUND *Hugh Selwyn Mauberley* 14 Bewildered that a world Shows no surprise At her last maquero's Adulteries. **1922** F. M. FORD *Let.* 15 Aug. (1965) 144 It is really too much to expect the very mildest of men to aid in sharpening a pen whose sole occupation is the describing of himself as, let us say, maquereau. **1933** 'G. ORWELL' *Down & Out* x. 78, I counted the number of times I was called *maquereau* during the day. **1939** E. AMBLER *Mask of Dimitrios* xi. 214 The clientèle began to change... We had.. more *maquereaux* and fewer gentlemen, more *poules* and fewer *chic* ladies. **1971** D. WALLIS *Bad Luck Girl* I. iii. 30 No girl.. goes on ship these days. They.. lead you to some place where her *maquer[e]au* can slug you.

maquerel, -el(l)a: see MACKEREL[1] and [2].

maquette (mæ'kɛt). [Fr. (1752), ad. It. *macchietta* speck, little spot, dim. of *macchia* spot, f. *macchiare* to spot, stain, f. L. *maculāre*; cf. MACULATE *v.*] A small preliminary model, in wax or clay, etc., or a preliminary painted sketch, from which a work in sculpture is elaborated. Also *transf.* and *fig.*

1903 *Athenæum* 24 Jan. 122/3 M. J. B. E. Detaille has, after a long delay, executed four *maquettes*, each comprehending three large panels. **1926** W. J. LOCKE *Stories Near & Far* 78 The maquette or model in clay. **1951** H. READ *Meaning of Art* (ed. 3) II. 240 The sculptor's maquette, or model, was reproduced, generally by other hands, either by being cast in bronze, or by being reproduced to scale by mechanical methods in marble. **1958** *Times* 8 Oct. 6/4 One might describe his art as a prolonged *maquette* for some ultimate synthesis or other. **1965** ZIGROSSER & GAEDHE *Guide to Collecting Orig. Prints* ii. 16 In some instances, the artist has actively collaborated in the adaptation of his own *maquette*, or sketch, by working on the plates or stones, and by 'proving' and approving the color separations. **1970** *Country Life* 31 Dec. 1280/3 This was the noble terra-cotta of a mourning woman.. the maquette for the figure of the wife on the Westminster Abbey monument to the poet Nicholas Rowe. **1972** P. MARKS *Collector's Choice* iii. 181, I don't know why you had to go out and buy those Carpeaux maquettes last week. **1973** *Times* 11 Apr. 6/4 (*caption*) A maquette of Henry Moore's 'Family Group'.

‖**maqui** (ma'ki). Also 8 **mague**. [Chilean Sp.] The Chilean shrub *Aristotelia Maqui* (N.O. *Tiliaceæ*), yielding a valuable fibre, and producing berries often used in the adulteration of wine.

1704 *Ovalle's Chili* in *Churchill's Voyages* III. 48 There are also trees call'd Magues. **1809** tr. *Molina's Nat. Hist. Chili* I. 37 The maqui, a species of cornel. **1860** *Treas. Bot.* 719/2 Maqui (Fr.), *Aristotelia*. **1890** *Daily News* 5 Feb. 5/4 The Chilian Consul-General expresses his opinion that the attention of our farmers will soon be called to the cultivation of the plant known in Chili as the Maqui... The sudden demand for the dried Maqui berry in France is.. not without significance.

‖**maquillage** (makijaʒ). [Fr., f. *maquiller* to make up one's face, f. OF. *masquiller* to stain, alt. of OF. *mascurer* to darken.] The action of applying make-up to one's face; also, make-up, cosmetics; also *transf.* Hence **maqui'llaged** *a.* made up.

1892 *Ladies' Home Jrnl.* Dec. 8/2 All this is.. thrown away upon the devotees of maquillage. **1921** M. SADLEIR *Privilege* vi. 82 It was a relief to find Anthony innocent, at least, of maquillage. **1929** D. H. LAWRENCE *Pansies* 55 The caged mind.. leaves a rind Of maquillage and pose and malice to shame the brutes. **1938** E. AMBLER *Cause for Alarm* iii. 47 The edge of a heavy and clumsily applied *maquillage*. **1941** 'R. WEST' *Black Lamb* (1942) II. 417 Doubly dazzling with the radiance of a Slav blonde and the maquillage of her profession. **1957** S. GAINHAM *Cold Dark Night* iv. 49 Her voice did not rise and there seemed no change in the beautifully maquillaged face. **1959** R. GRAVES *Coll. Poems* 304 Confirming hazardous relationships By kindly maquillage of Truth's pale lips. **1972** *Daily Tel.* 25 Sept. 7/3 Plastering the players all over with visual and aural *maquillage* in the form of endlessly changing lights and phonic effects.

maquis ('mɑːkiː). Also **macquis**, (erron.) **maqui**. [Fr., 'brushwood, scrub', ad. Corsican It. *macchia* thicket, MACCHIA, f. L. *macula* spot.]

1. The dense scrub characteristic of certain Mediterranean coastal regions, esp. in Corsica, often used as a refuge by fugitives. Also applied to similar areas of scrub or brushwood elsewhere.

1858 T. FORESTER *Rambles Corsica & Sardinia* viii. 65 There are also.. several lagoons on the coast, of which the Stagna di Biguglia, near which we turned off into the *maquis*, is the largest. **1900** 'H. S. MERRIMAN' *Isle of Unrest* xxii. 246 It is.. usual for a man to take to the macquis the moment that he finds himself involved in some trouble. **1906** CONRAD *Mirror of Sea* xlii. 259 Dominic's brother had to go into the *maquis*, into the bush on the wild mountain-side. **1913** A. HUXLEY *Let.* 30 July (1969) 52 The maquis.. is thicker than anything I've ever seen before, oak, hazel, maple, wild cherry and a pine or two in the more open spaces. **1923** *Nature* 24 Feb. 268/2 These types of vegetation, like the Mediterranean 'maqui', develop in regions of winter rains and long dry summers. **1932** *Forestry* VI. 173 The nature of the undergrowth—dense shrubby maquis. **1945** G. MILLAR *Maquis* xi. 226 Boulaya met us with a long face in the Maquis. **1957** J. BRAINE *Room at Top* xv. 136 The village ends abruptly.. beyond it is nothing but the moors.. and a solitary farm-house a mile west. That too has a military air; the moors are Gilden's maquis and behind its walls are planned the sudden raid.. the ambush. **1966** J. BERRISFORD *Wild Garden* 167 The Jerusalem Sage.. may be used to form a ground-smothering *maquis* in conjunction with cistuses, lavenders, rosemary and other sun-loving shrubs. **1973** *Daily Tel.* 13 Oct. 9/6 We were.. standing in a hillside garden in the Alpes Maritimes. Around us spread the maquis for unending miles. **1975** *Islander* (Victoria, B.C.) 9 Feb. 5/2 Most of the vegetation [in Corsica] is not forest as we know it.. but a tangled growth called maquis.

2. *transf.* A secret army of patriots in France during the German occupation in the war of 1939–45, so named from their being conceived as hiding in country of this kind; also, a member of this army. Also in extended use (applied to similar groups) and *attrib.*

1944 *Ann. Reg. 1943* 230 The patriots of the 'maquis' fought with admirable courage. **1944** *New Statesman* 27 May 346/2 The Italian *Maquis*, whose guerrilla operations.. are now being co-ordinated and encouraged by the Allied Command. **1944** *Hutchinson's Pict. Hist. War* 12 Apr.–26 Sept. 523 (*caption*) Field-Marshal Montgomery stops his car to have a word with a Maquis guard. **1945** W. S. CHURCHILL *Victory* (1946) 7 The tributes which are paid to the heroic French or Belgian Maquis. **1951** N. ANNAN *Leslie Stephen* iv. 160 Victorian thinkers.. appeared to be unaware of the spiritual maquis burrowing underground in Europe. **1965** B. SWEET-ESCOTT *Baker St. Irreg.* vii. 205 If it had still been considered important to raise a maquis in Hungary, it might well have been worth exploring. **1966** M. R. D. FOOT *SOE in France* xi. 365 A large group of maquis known to exist in the Auvergne mountains.

3. *attrib.* and *Comb.*

1937 *Brit. Birds* Sept. 98 Small parties were seen.. flying about the maquis-covered slopes. **1944** *Times* 24 Apr. 5/6 The *maquis* country is usually thought of as confined to Haute-Savoie. It is in fact much more extensive. **1971** *Homes & Gardens* Sept. 89/1 Panoramic vistas of maquis-covered foothills merging into the stark blue inland peaks of over 2,500 feet. **1974** J. THOMSON *Long Revenge* ii. 22 The Maquis radio operator.. contacted us.

Hence **maquisard** (mɑːkiː'zɑː(r)), a member of the maquis. Also *transf.* and *attrib.*

1944 *Times* 24 Apr. 5/7 Often enough the *maquisards* have had to fight against heavy odds... Today.. the situation is better. Arms are reaching the *maquis* in growing volume. **1945** G. MILLAR *Maquis* v. 85 The grey-headed Maquisard, a local railway worker in peace-time. **1959** *Economist* 3 Jan. 23/2 He has always insisted that, except for a tiresome band of *maquisards* in the eastern extremity of the island [Cuba], everything was under control. **1963** N. FREELING *Gun before Butter* II. 103 During the war presumably, he had got acquainted with the border. Maquisard formation, doubtless. **1967** 'E. PETERS' *Black is Colour* viii. 152 The moustache that would have done credit to a Corsican *maquisard*. **1973** *Times* 18 Jan. 19/6 The German onslaught.. was disastrous to the maquisards who stayed and fought.

mar (mɑː(r)), *sb.*[1] Also 3 **mer(e**, 6 **marr**, 7 **marre**. [f. MAR *v.*]

†**1.** A hindrance, obstruction; an impediment in speech. *Obs.*

a **1300** *Cursor M.* 67 For þan sal mede witouten mere, be mette for dede or bettur or were. *Ibid.* 24802 A gret resun wel sceu he cuth, wit-vten ani mer in muth. **1653** R. BAILLIE *Dissuas. Vind.* (1655) 43 The main marre of their labour was the common error of Independency. **1824** MACTAGGART *Gallovid. Encycl.*, *Maunt*, to speak thick and fast; to have a marr in the speech.

2. Something that mars or impairs; a drawback *to*. In early use, †a fault. *rare.*

1551 ASCHAM *Let. to E. Raven* 18 May *Eng. Wks.* (1761) 384, I trust my will to write shall match the marrs I make in it. **1876** DK. EDINBURGH in *Daily News* 1 May 2/6 The only mar to the pleasure I feel in again hoisting the pennant. **1901** *Pall Mall Mag.* Sept. 70/1 It was no mar to the day for Roderic to share Miss Allan thus.

3. *Comb.*: **mar resistance**, resistance to loss of gloss by abrasion; so ***mar-resistant*** adj.

1942 L. BOOR in *Mod. Plastics* Sept. 80/2 Depending on the type of plastic under consideration, various methods of evaluating the optical degradation of the test areas may be used... The particular aspect of hardness of which this test is a measure has been given the tentative designation 'mar resistance'. **1969** C. O. RASPOR in W. R. R. Park *Plastics Film Technol.* iv. 87 The gloss of the marred area is measured and compared to the unabraded film to determine the mar resistance. **1973** *Washington Post* 13 Jan. C3/4 (Advt.), Seven-drawer kneehole desk..with mar-resistant top.

Mar (mɑː(r)), *sb.*[2] [Aramaic.] An honorific title for saints and higher clergy, chiefly in the Nestorian and Jacobite churches.

1694 M. GEDDES tr. *Hist. Church of Malabar* 11 Their Bishop at that time..was one Mar Joseph, who..had been sent thither by Mar Audixa, Patriarch of Babylon. **1864** G. B. HOWARD *Christians of St. Thomas* iv. 154 In the year 1856 a certain Mar Athanasius Stephanos made his appearance, ..claiming to be the rightful Metropolitan of the Christians of St. Thomas. **1892** G. M. RAE *Syrian Church in India* xix. 304 The first native of Malabar that ever received consecration..was Mar Athanasius Matthew. *Ibid.* 309 The pretensions of Mar Koorilos were finally disposed of; Mar Dionysius resigned his dignity..; Mar Athanasius was by royal proclamation declared metropolitan. **1933** *Downside Rev.* LI. 399 Fr Hugh Conolly was editing a number of Texts and Studies consisting of a translation of certain Syriac liturgical homilies of Mar Narsai, a fifth century Nestorian writer. **1956** N. ZERNOV *Christian East* ix. 103 In 1665 a Monophysite bishop, Mar Gregorius, arrived in South India from Palestine. *Ibid.* 105 The Bishops Mar Mathew Athanasius and Mar Thomas Athanasius formed a separate Church, now known under the name of the Mar Thoma Church. **1964** P. F. ANSON *Bishops at Large* 27 They have given themselves impressive ecclesiastical titles,.. Hierarch, Mar, Metropolitan..and so on.

mar (mɑː(r)), *v.* Forms: 1 **merran, mierran, mirran, myrran,** 3 **mære,** 3–5 **merre,** 3–6 **mer(e,** 3–7 **marre,** 3–8 **marr,** 4 **mire,** 5–7 **mare,** 4– **mar.** [Com. Teut. OE. *merran* corresponds to OFris. *meria* to hinder (only once, in 3rd pers. sing. pres. ind. *meert*), OS. *merrian* to cause to stumble or err, to hinder (MLG., MDu. *merren* to hinder, also intr. to loiter, mod.Du. *marren* to fasten, tie up, to loiter), OHG. *marren, merren* to hinder, disturb (MHG. *merren* to hinder, also intr. to linger, delay), ON. *merja* to bruise, crush, Goth. *marzjan* to cause to stumble, offend. A parallel formation from the same Teut. root **marz-* appears in OE. *mearrian* to go astray, err, MHG. *marren* to linger, loiter. The Teut. word was adopted in Romanic as OF. *marrir* to lose (one's way), to lead astray, perplex, afflict, distress (mod.F. only in pa. pple *marri* grieved), It. *smarrire* to bewilder, Sp. *marrido* adj., grieved.

According to some philologists, the OTeut. *marzjan* is formally equivalent to Skr. *marṣaya-*, causative stem of *mṛṣ* to forget (Indogermanic root **mers-*, whence Lith. *mirszti* to forget); the root may have had a wider sense than that preserved in Skr. and Lith.]

†**1.** *trans.* To hamper, hinder, interfere with, interrupt or stop (a person, event or thing). *Obs.*

c **1000** ÆLFRIC *Exod.* v. 4 Hwi mirrað ȝit þis folc fram heora weorcum? *a* **1300** *Cursor M.* 2254 Now we haue vs sped sa ferr Vr wil may he noght vs merr. *c* **1375** *Sc. Leg. Saints* xiii. (*Marcus*) 75 Sathanas sal nocht mare me. *c* **1440** *York Myst.* xli. 100 Bot thowe, myghty Lorde, my mornyng mar! Mar ye, for it shulde me well pay, So happy to se hyme yf I warr. **1513** DOUGLAS *Æneis* x. vii. 173 So thyk in stayll all marryt wolx the rout, Oneys mycht ony turn hys hand about To weyld his wappin. **1530** PALSGR. 705/2 If these bordes shrinke, all my purpose is marred. **1578** BANISTER *Hist. Man* VIII. 109 Mouyng is marred, when..solution of continuitie is made. **1590** SIR J. SMYTH *Disc. Weapons* 3 In case anie horseman..should bee wounded..his fighting for that day were marred. **1727** A. HAMILTON *New Acc. E. Ind.* I. xxv. 308 [He] had certainly dispatched him, if a large Brass Lamp which was burning over his Head, had not marred the Blow. **1827** CARLYLE tr. *Tieck's Elves, Germ. Rom.* II. 121 'Then we shall see which of us is swifter'. 'Done', said Mary, and began to run; 'for we shall not mar one another by the way' [orig. *so hindern wir uns auch nicht auf demselben Wege*]. **1849** *Chambers's Inform.* II. 653/2 [Glasgow regulations for Bowls.] If a bowl is accidentally marred by an opponent, it shall be in the option of the party playing to let it rest, or play it over again.

2. To spoil, impair. **a.** With obj. a material thing: To damage so as to render useless; to destroy or impair the quality of. Now *rare.* Also in OE. †to waste, squander (property).

c **897** K. ÆLFRED *Gregory's Past. C.* xliv. 325 Ðylæs mon unnytlice mierre ðæt ðæt he hæbbe. **13..** *E.E. Allit. P.* C. 474 Þen wakened þe wyse of his wyl dremes, & bluschedto his wodbynde þat broþely was marred. *c* **1400** *Destr. Troy* 5700 But his shippes..rut on a Rocke, & rent all to peses, þat mony was mard & the men drownet. **1483** CAXTON *G. de la Tour* H iij b, Wyn taken ouer mesure..marreth and corrupteth the good blood. **1530** PALSGR. 458/2 You have blotted this shete of paper so sore that it is marred. ? **1538** LELAND *Itin.* VII. 47 Fische Garthes marre the Haven. **1562** TURNER *Baths* 1 The bathes of brimstone hurte the stomack and mar it. **1611** BIBLE *Mark* ii. 22 The wine is spilled, and the bottles will bee marred. **1612** BRINSLEY *Lud. Lit.* 252 Making markes vnder euery hard word in each page, without marring our bookes. *a* **1677** BARROW *Serm.* Wks. 1716 I. 22 There is ever some dead fly in our box, which marreth our ointment. **1728** YOUNG *Love Fame* iv. 52 Thunder mars small beer, and weak discourse. *a* **1848** R. W. HAMILTON *Rew. & Punishm.* vii. (1853) 336 The vessel is so marred that it cannot be repaired. **1878** BROWNING *La Saisiaz* 36 The breath is not the flute, Both together make the music; either marred and all is mute.

b. With immaterial obj.: To impair fatally, ruin. Often in proverbial antithesis with *make* (see MAKE *v.*[1] 46 b) or MEND *v.* In mod. use with somewhat lighter sense: To detract from the perfection or completeness of. Also *absol.*

c **1230** *Hali Meid.* 9 Adam & eue..merden ure cunde. *Ibid.* 43 Sone so þu telles te betere þen an oðer..þu marres ti meidenhad [*MS. Bodley* merrest þin meiðhad]. *a* **1300** *Cursor M.* 17988 Harde hap he werred me aȝayn, And myche marred of my mayn. *c* **1420, 1542** [see MAKE *v.*[1] 46 b]. *c* **1440** *York Myst.* xxiii. 87 It marres my myght. *a* **1568** ASCHAM *Scholem.* I. (Arb.) 34 Some wittes, moderate enough by nature, be many tymes marde by ouer moch studie. *Ibid.*, Galene saith, moch Musick marreth mens maners. **1579** W. WILKINSON *Confut. Familye of Loue* 4 An euill exposition marreth the text. **1605** SHAKS. *Lear* I. iv. 369 Striuing to better, oft we marre what's well. **1616** SURFL. & MARKH. *Country Farm* 9 It marreth the voice, bringing Hoarsenesse, and a little Cough. **1624** WOTTON *Archit.* I. 23 It will marre all the mirth in the House. **1719** YOUNG *Revenge* IV. i, There they'll revel, and exult to find Him sleep so fast, who else would marr their joys. *a* **1732** BOSTON *Crook in Lot* (1805) 4 What God sees meet to mar, one will not be able to mend in his lot. **1744** HARRIS *Three Treat.* I. iii. (1765) 172 The Dread of them may marr the Rectitude of our Purposes. **1833** HT. MARTINEAU *Briery Creek* v. 99, I cannot mar my satisfaction by groundless doubts. **1853** MRS. GASKELL *Ruth* III. i. 43 For the present she would neither meddle nor mar in Ruth's course of life. *c* **1865** G. M. HOPKINS *Poems* (1967) 121 So be it; I must maim and mar. **1867** LADY HERBERT *Cradle L.* viii. 212 The pleasure of shopping was marred by the surliness of the inhabitants. **1889** [see MAKE *v.*[1] 46 b]. **1896** *N. & Q.* 8th Ser. IX. 160/1 Though marred by eccentricities and extravagances of language, the play has genuine dramatic fibre.

†**c.** Phrases. ***to mar all***: to act so as to prevent a project or operation from being carried to a successful issue; to 'spoil everything', to act badly. ***to mar (one's) market***: see MARKET *sb.* 4 c. *Obs.*

c **1420** *Liber Cocorum* (1862) 57 Ȝif þou cast salt þer to, iwys þou marres alle, so have I blis. **1535** COVERDALE *Judg.* ii. 19 Whan the iudge dyed, they turned backe, and marred all more then their fathers. **1624** CAPT. SMITH *Virginia* 90 As they had beene troublesome at Sea, began againe to marre all ashore.

†**d.** *intr.* for *refl.* To become deteriorated; to spoil; to perish. *Obs.*

c **1230** *Hali Meid.* 13 Þat ha [*sc.* hire limen & hire wittes] ne merren ne formealten þurh licomliche lustes i flesche fulðe. **13..** *E.E. Allit. P.* C. 172 Lo al synkes in his synne & for his sake marres! *c* **1440** *York Myst.* i. 93 My mighte and my mayne es all marrande, Helpe, felawes, in faythe I am fallande. **1530** PALSGR. 638/1 The beste thyng in the worlde, if it be myskept, will marre in processe of tyme. **1609** C. BUTLER *Fem. Mon.* i. (1623) C iv, The Host..could not choose in that space but melt and marre.

3. *trans.* To harm, injure (a person, etc.). **a.** To inflict destructive bodily harm upon. In later use, to mangle, disfigure (now *arch.*).

c **1205** LAY. 1903 Vfele he [a wrestler] hine mærde ah na wiht he hit ne mende. *Ibid.* 22345 Arðures men letten fleon vnimete flan and merden Irisc folc, & hit swiðe ualden. *c* **1400** *Destr. Troy* 5553 What mighty were marrit, & martrid to dethe. *c* **1470** *Gol. & Gaw.* 96 Quhy has thow marrit my man, with maistri to mene? *c* **1489** CAXTON *Sonnes of Aymon* vi. 140 Goo backe agen, & marre not your horse about noughte. **1530** PALSGR. 598/2 And you heale his legge up afore you kyll the deed flesshe quyte you marre hym for ever. **1535** COVERDALE *Isa.* iii. 15 Wherfore do ye oppresse my people, and marre yᵉ faces of the innocentes? **1575** TURBERV. *Venerie* 21 You may kepe them from going out, and that other dogs do not byte them, or that they be troden upon or marred with mens feete. **1656** CULPEPER *Eng. Physic. enlarged* 59, I am confident..That if you mar the very Apple of their [young swallows'] Eyes with a Needle, she shal recover them again. **1692** RAY *Disc.* I. iv. (1713) 57 Those..Embryos may, by a violent cause, be marred or deformed in the womb. **1812** SCOTT *Let. to Miss J. Baillie* 17 Jan., in *Lockhart*, The watchword of these young heroes..was—Mar him. **1845–6** TRENCH *Huls. Lect.* Ser. II. vi. 233 Some limbs of his body broken off and some marred and battered by the..waves. **1887** BOWEN *Virg. Æneid* VI. 495 Noble Deiphobus here he beholds, all mangled and marred.

†**b.** To ruin, damage seriously (a person, his fortunes, etc.). Often in antithesis with *mend. Obs.*

c **1350** *Will. Palerne* 1171 Heiȝh king of heuene..ne fauore nouȝt my fo [*MS.* so my] þat falsly me so marres. *c* **1394** *P. Pl. Crede* 66 Þe foles foundeden hem-self freres of the Pye, And maken hem mendynauns & marre þe puple. *c* **1400** *Destr. Troy* 720 Soche a maiden to mar þat þe most louet! *c* **1440** *York Myst.* xxvii. 119 The fende is wrothe with ȝou and me, And will ȝou marre if þat he may. **1560** BECON *Sick Man's Salve* Wks. II. 220 b, Thys sycknesse hath vtterly marred me. **1607** SHAKS. *Lear* I. i. 97 Mend your speach..lest it mar your fortunes. **1611** BIBLE *Jer.* xiii. 9 After this maner will I marre the pride of Iudah. **1614** CHAMBERLAIN *Let.* in *Court & Times Jas. I*, I. 320 The parliament will mend him or quite mar him. **1616** R. C. *Times' Whistle* III. 1151 But now this boy..doth all his fortunes marre. **1622** R. HAWKINS *Voy. S. Sea* (1847) 104 Pittie marreth the whole cittie.

c. To ruin or damage morally. *Obs.* exc. *dial.* to 'spoil' a child by indulgence: cf. MARRED *ppl. a.*

1530 PALSGR. 483/1 You cherysshe this chylde so moche that you shal marre him. **1605** BACON *Adv. Learn.* I. ii. §1 That it [learning] doth marre and peruert mens dispositions for matter of gouernment and policie. *a* **1639** W. WHATELEY *Prototypes* II. (1640) 153 Those that have these good abilities, must take heede of marrying [*sic*] themselves, and defiling them by being proud of them. **1684** WOOD *Life* 9 Oct. (O.H.S.) III. 114 Digby Lord Gerard..was utterly mar'd by keeping company with base lewd fellowes.

†**4.** To confuse, bewilder; to perplex, trouble; to grieve, distress. [Cf. OF. *marrir.*] *Obs.*

13.. *Cursor M.* 15725 Ful merred war þai in þair mode. *a* **1310** in Wright *Lyric P.* vii. 29 On molde y waxe mad, a maide marreth me. *c* **1350** *Will. Palerne* 884 He ferd as a mased man an marred neiȝ honde. *c* **1375** *Sc. Leg. Saints* vi. (*Thomas*) 354 He..Is lyk a man þat merknes merryse. *c* **1485** *Digby Myst.* IV. 1054 To blame ye are, With this dedly sorow your-self to marre. **1535** STEWART *Cron. Scot.* II. 523 O mad monstour! marrit out of thi mynd. **1590** SPENSER *F.Q.* III. x. 31 But minds of mortall men are muchell mard And mov'd amisse with massy mucks unmeet regard. **1603** *Philotus* cxlviii, As ane out of his mynde or marrit, He hes mee of his hous debarrit.

†**5.** *intr.* To err; to go astray; to be or become bewildered or confused. *Obs.*

c **950** *Lindisf. Gosp.* Matt. xxii. 29 ȝie merras *vel* ȝe duellas [Vulg. *erratis*]. *c* **1420** *Anturs of Arth.* 110 (Douce MS.) Hit marred, hit memered, hit mused for madde. *c* **1440** *York Myst.* xliv. 166, i *Doct.* Þai are drounken, all þes menȝe, Of muste or wyne, I wolle warande. ii *Doct.* Nowe certis þis was wele saide, Þat makis þer mynde to marre. *c* **1475** *Rauf Coilȝear* 22 Amang thay myrk Montanis sa madlie thay mer. *a* **1510** DOUGLAS *K. Hart* I. 104 All that couth attene the castell neir, It made thame for to mer amiss, and mang.

mar, obs. f. MAYOR, MERE *sbs.*; MORE *sb.* and *a.*

mar-, *vbl. stem,* **a.** prefixed to sbs., forming sbs. (chiefly 17th cent. nonce-wds.), with sense 'one who or something which mars', and *adjs.*, with sense 'that mars'; as ***mar-all*** sb. and adj., ***mar-feast*** (*arch.*), ***-good, -hawk, -joy; mar-right*** adj.; †**mar-tail,** a derisive term for a prostitute. Also MARPLOT.

1611 FLORIO, *Ser sparecchia*, a *mar-all, a spoile-all, a busie-headed fellow. *a* **1625** FLETCHER *Chances* I. i, And what now Meane they to study, Anthony, Morall Philosophy, After their mar-all women? **1821** SCOTT *Kenilw.* i, I will drink a round..rather than be termed a *mar-feast. **1887** W. MORRIS tr. *Homer's Odyssey* XVII. 446 What God this plague, this mar-feast, hath hither sent to us? **1922** JOYCE *Ulysses* 710 Superannuated bailiff's man, marfeast, lickplate, spoilsport, [etc.]. **1647** TRAPP *Comm. Rev.* iii. 2 Hypocrisie, that pernicious *mar-good. **1575** TURBERV. *Faulconrie* 142 Such a man..shall seldome prove a perfecte falconer but a *marrehawke. *a* **1628** F. GREVIL *Alaham* IV. i, He hath no good: you have no ill but he: This *Marre-right yielding's honors Tyranny. *c* **1620** FLETCHER *Chances* IV. ii, Well, my sweet mistress, well, good madam *martaile!

b. *esp.* in **mar-prelate,** first used in the pseudonym 'Martin Marprelate', adopted by the writer or writers of certain tracts issued in 1588–9, which gave rise to a fierce controversy; hence *attrib.*, as ***marprelate controversy, tracts***; also **marprelate** *v.*, to inveigh in the style of 'Marprelate'; **marprelatist,** *attrib.* belonging to the Marprelate party. Also in many nonce-words occurring in the Marprelate tracts or in later works referring to them.

1588 *Marprel. Epist.* (Arb.) 20 You are called Elmar, but you may be better called marelme..hauing cut them all downe. **1589** *Mar Martine* 6 Hee might have cald himselfe Mar-preest. **1589** *Hay any Work* (1844) 32 As for Mar-church, and Mar-religion, they haue [etc.]. *Ibid.* 44 You Mar-prince, Mar-law, Mar-magestrate. **1636** H. SYDENHAM *Serm. Sol. Occ.* (1637) 270 Those tongues which..Mar-Prelated..of old against the Ecclesiasticke Hierarchy. **1862** R. VAUGHAN *Nonconformity* 56 The notorious Marprelate tracts. **1879** *Sat. Rev.* 6 Sept. 298 The series of marprelatist characterizations of the contemporary Anglican episcopate.

mara[1] (ˈmɑːrə). A large hare-like cavy, *Dolichotis patachonica*, native of Patagonia.

1833 *Penny Cycl.* I. 214/2 The Mara or Patagonian Cavy. **1859** WOOD *Nat. Hist.* I. 578.

‖**Mara**[2] (ˈmɑːrə). [Skr. *Māra*, f. *mṛ* to die.] The 'Satan' of Buddhist mythology.

1871 ALABASTER *Wheel of Law* p. xliii, The army of Mara, the evil one. **1879** SIR E. ARNOLD *Lt. Asia* VI. xix. 159 The ten chief Sins came—Mara's mighty ones, Angels of evil.

†**marabas.** *Sc. Obs.* [After F. *bonnet à la marrabaise* (Rabelais), from OF. *marrabais* 'crypto-Judæus', MARRANO.] *attrib.*, in ***marabas bonnet*** 'a large flat cap' (Jam.).

1538 *Burgh. Rec. Edin.* (1871) II. 91 To ilk ane of the said 7 officeris ane marabas bonet with ane quhyte fedder. **1539** *Ld. Treas. Acc.* in Pitcairn *Crim. Trials* I. 297* Ane Marrabas Bonett.

marabbot(h, -abbutt, -abot(e: see MARABOUT.

marablane, obs. form of MYROBALAN.

marabou[1] ('mærəbuː). Also **marabout, marabu.** [a. F. *marabou(t*, app. repr. a vulgar Arabic use of *murābiṭ* hermit, MARABOUT. 'The stork is said to be *Mrabt*, i.e. holy' (Pagni in Dozy *Suppl. aux Dictt. arabes*, s.v. *murābiṭ*).]

1. A large stork or heron, *Leptoptilus marabou* or *crumenifer*, a native of Western Africa. Now applied also to the adjutant-bird of India, *Leptoptilus dubius* or *argala*. Also ***marabou stork.***

1826 *Denham & Clapperton's Trav. N. & Central Africa* App. 203 M. Temminck..has given it [*sc.* this African species] the name of *Argala*, while for the Indian bird,..he proposes the name of *Marabou*. We have ventured to reverse the order of these names;..we have assigned the African species the title of *Marabou*, which..is a word peculiar to Africa. **1861** DU CHAILLU *Equat. Afr.* xiv. 223 The ugly marabouts, from whose tails our ladies get the.. feathers for their bonnets. **1872** BAKER *Nile Tribut.* xi. 175, I shot a crocodile, and a marabou stork.

2. A tuft or plume of the soft white downy feathers found under the wings and tail of these birds, used for trimming hats and dresses. Also ***marabou feather, plume.*** Also *collect. sing.*, trimming made of these feathers.

1823 *Repos. Arts*, etc. Ser. III. I. 57 A good many [hats] are trimmed with marabouts only. *Ibid.* 184 Marabout plumes. **1828** LADY GRANVILLE *Lett.* (1894) II. 15 Lady George in a *toque* with marabouts. **1839** THACKERAY *Second Lect. Fine Arts* ii. Wks. 1900 XIII. 276 A marabou feather which she wears in her turban. **1884** *Illustr. Lond. News* 11 Oct. 338/3 Ladies who rejoice in the soft fluffy white feather trimming called marabout.

transf. **1862** H. MARRYAT *Year in Sweden* II. 444 Birch varies the scene with its drooping marabouts.

3. An exceptionally white kind of raw silk which can be dyed without first removing the natural gum.

1835 URE *Philos. Manuf.* 248 It is only a finishing degree of twist which marabout receives after dyeing. **1879** *Cassell's Techn. Educ.* IX. 155 Marabout is silk thrown twice. **1929** *Times* 31 Oct. 11/6 An attractive bridge coat..in artificial silk velvet finished with a marabout collar. **1975** *Lady* 1 May 801/1 Marabou cap and muff.

‖**Marabou**[2]. [Louisiana Fr.] (See quot.)

1859 BARTLETT *Dict. Amer.*, *Marabou*, the variety of negro which springs from a mulatto and a griffe.

‖**marabout** ('mærəbuːt). Forms: 7 **maribot(t, marybot, -buck, morabit, marabot, morabot, marabou,** 8 **marabbot(h, marabbutt, marahbut, marabote, marbut,** 9 **marabut,** 7– **marabout.** [repr. Arab. *murābiṭ* hermit, monk. The mod. Eng. form is from Fr. Cf. Pg. *marabute*, Sp. *morabito*.]

1. A Muslim hermit or monk, particularly amongst the Arabs and Berbers of North Africa.

a **1623** R. JOBSON in Purchas *Pilgrims* (1625) II. ix. 1572 Their Marybucks or Bassareas, are their Priests or Religious persons. *c* **1645** HOWELL *Lett.* (1650) II. xi. 11 Their Hoggies, Magitians and Maribotts, were tampring with the ill Spirit of the Air. **1660** F. BROOKE tr. *Le Blanc's Trav.* 15 In a certain place there, the Marabouts immolate at this time. **1704** J. PITTS *Acc. Mohammetans* 12 The Marabbot or Saint. **1863** R. F. BURTON *Wand. W. Afr.* I. 172 The Marabut, who does not drink, and the Soninki, or Sonalki, who does. **1903** E. J. DILLON in *Contemp. Rev.* Feb. 281 Marabouts foretold the coming of divine wrath.

2. A shrine marking the burial-place of a marabout.

1859 J. W. BLAKESLEY *4 Months Alg.* ii. 25 Besides the mosques, there are several marabouts in Algiers and the neighbourhood. **1867** SMYTH *Sailor's Word-bk.*, *Marabout*. .. Small edifices on Barbary headlands, occupied by a priest. **1881** *Times* 10 May 5 The French troops took yesterday the Sidi-Adallah-Ben-Djemel, which is the most venerated marabout in all Tunis.

marabout, marabu: see MARABOU[1].

marabunta (mærə'bʌntə). [Native name.] In Guyana, a name used for several social wasps. Also *attrib.*

1883 E. F. IM THURN *Among Indians Guiana* v. 150 The wasps vary much more in general appearance and size, some of them being large and beautifully coloured insects. The forest-dwelling social species are indiscriminately called by the colonists marabuntas. **1898** H. KIRKE *25 Yrs. Brit. Guiana* iii. 76 A large brown wasp, called a marabunta, builds his pretty paper combs under the eaves and galleries of our houses; his sting is severe. **1918** C. W. BEEBE *Jungle Peace* (1919) iv. 81, I listened to the buzzing of a *marabunta* wasp. **1934** E. WAUGH *Handful of Dust* v. 267 A marabunta had left a painful swelling on his left hand. **1958** J. CAREW *Black Midas* i. 12 Marabuntas built clay nests in the thatch. *Ibid.* vi. 141 Tonic and Woody Sam removed spiders, cobwebs, marabunta nests..from the roof.

†**marabuto.** *Naut. Obs.* Also **marabut.** [a. Sp. *marabuto*, also *maraguto*.] A jib-sail.

1622 MABBE tr. *Aleman's Guzman d'Alf.* II. II. x. 191 They tooke out another lesser one [*sc.* sail] which they call Marabuto..which is a kinde of triangulary sayle. **1659** HOWELL *Lex.*, *Vocab.* vi, The marabut, a triangular kind of sayl belonging to a Carvel, *il marabuto*. **1867** SMYTH *Sailor's Word-bk.*, *Marabut*, a sail which galleys hoisted in bad weather.

maraca (mə'rækə). Also **maracca.** [Pg. *maracá*, prob. from Tupi (Webster).] Usu. *pl.* A Latin-American percussion instrument made from the dried shell of a gourd or other material with beans or beads, etc., inside to produce a rattling sound; a gourd rattle. Also *attrib.*

1824 H. E. LLOYD tr. *Spix & Martius's Travels in Brazil* II. IV. ii. 226 The *Maracá*, a longish gourd shell, filled with maize, fastened to a handle, with which in their dancing, they make a rattling as with castanets. **1928** *Vanity Fair* (N.Y.) Nov. 72 A fashionable evening event along the Havana water-front is a concert by black boys with their primitive African instruments, the bongo, timbales, guiro, maracas, and claves. **1933** *Punch* 4 Jan. 6/3 It [*sc.* the rumba] may be recognised by a number of taps produced in rapid succession... They are made by a couple of maraccas in the orchestra... Maraccas..are the dried husks of the calabash fruit. **1952** [see ELLINGTONIAN *a.* and *sb.*]. **1954** J. STEINBECK *Sweet Thursday* ii. 16 An orchestra took shape—two guitars, a guitarón, rhythm and maraca men. **1966** *Melody Maker* 23 July 10/5 Alan Haven mentioned maracca sticks and jingle-sticks. **1971** 'E. ANTHONY' *Tamarind Seed* i. 13 A coal-black barman..rattling a shaker as if he were playing the maraccas. **1972** *Jazz & Blues* Sept. 5/1 The almost African rhythms with much maracca shaking.

Maracaibo (mærə'kaɪbəʊ). Name of the northern province of Venezuela, used attributively in **Maracaibo-balsam**, a copaiba obtained from *Copaifera officinalis*; **Maracaibo-bark**, the bark of *Cinchona tucujensis*.

1843 HOLTZAPFFEL *Turning* I. 94 Maracaybo is a furniture wood of moderate size, as hard as good mahogany, and in appearance between it and tulip-wood. **1889** in *Syd. Soc. Lex.*

‖**maracan** (mærə'kæn). Also 8 **maracana.** [a. Tupi *maracanä*.] A Brazilian macaw.

1753 CHAMBERS *Cycl. Supp.*, *Maracana*. **1828–32** WEBSTER, *Maracan*. In mod. Dicts.

marace, obs. form of MARISH.

‖**maracock** ('mærəkɒk). *Obs.* exc. *Hist.* Forms: 7 **maricock, maracoco, -coko, amaracoc,** 7–8 **maracoc,** 8 **maracot, marococ, marcor,** 7– **maracock.** [From the Virginian dialect of Algonquin.] The fruit of certain American passion-flowers, esp. the 'may-pop', *Passiflora incarnata*, native of Virginia, and the granadilla, *Passiflora quadrangularis*, of Brazil and the West Indies. Also the plant itself.

1612 STRACHEY *Virginia* (Hakl. Soc.) 60 The maricock apple. **1612** CAPT. SMITH *Virginia* 17 They plant also Maracocks a wild fruit like a lemmon. **1649** *Perf. Descr. Virginia* (1837) 18 Fruits they have, Strawberries.. Maracokos [etc.]. **1660** SHARROCK *Vegetables* 34 The Amaracoc or Passion flower. **1704** *Dict. Rust. et Urb.* s.v. *March*, Toward the end [of March] sow..Marcors or Passion-Flower. **1707** *Curios. in Husb. & Gard.* 285 The Maracot is a Plant that creeps like Ivy. **1753** CHAMBERS *Cycl. Supp.* s.v. *Granadilla*, The common granadilla, called the maracot and passion flower. **1896** P. A. BRUCE *Econ. Hist. Virginia* I. 98 In addition, there were..maracocks or mayapples, beans and pumpkins.

‖**marae** (mə'raɪ, formerly ma'rae). Also 9 **marai.** [Polynesian.] An altar or sacred enclosure at which human sacrifices are offered amongst the Tahitians and other Polynesians (now only *Hist.*) Now, among Polynesian peoples, a space in front of a meeting-house or among the houses of a village, set apart for social functions. Also *fig.*

1814 W. BROWN *Hist. Propag. Chr.* II. 350 Many were the marais and altars reared at his command. **1865** TYLOR *Early Hist. Man.* iii. 46 A large white cloth, spread on the pavement of a marae. **1877** RANKEN in *Jrnl. R. Anthrop. Inst.* VI. 236 The *marais*, or terraced enclosures for sacred purposes, are exactly like those of Mexico and Peru. **1905** W. B. *Where White Man Treads* 276 Every order and tribal regulation had to be decided in meeting-house convened, and proclaimed in the marae (village green) to the whole people. **1910** J. COWAN *Maoris N.Z.* xxxi. 338 We fall in on the river bank for the parade up to the village *marae*. **1910** C. G. SELIGMANN *Melanesians Brit. New Guinea* xx. 223 Each local group of each clan has..at least one *marea* [*sic*], which serves as the meeting place for the men of the local group, and is their clubhouse in the fullest sense of the term. **1924** R. W. WILLIAMSON *Social & Pol. Syst. Cent. Polynesia* I. x. 350 This *male* was, I presume, a *malae* or open space where meetings..were held, as in Samoa and Tonga. *Ibid.* II. xv. 60 In some islands the *marae* or *malae* was merely an open space..along with a special wooden house erected in it. **1934** *Nature* 10 Nov. 740/2 The turtle..was the food of the gods [in Tahiti], eaten only by chiefs and keepers of the marae. **1943** N. MARSH *Colour Scheme* ix. 166 They were hangin' about the Marae in groups. **1949** P. H. BUCK *Coming of Maori* (1950) IV. iii. 480 Turning to New Zealand, it is a curious fact that the two fundamental features of the central Polynesian temples were not combined but remained as distinct entities. Thus the open court, distinguished by the term *marae*, is retained as a secular feature in front of the tribal or family meeting houses. **1959** A. MCLINTOCK *Descr. Atlas N.Z.* 72 In the country proper [i.e. rural districts] the Maori has retained his traditional mode of life which is symbolised in the *marae*. In a literal sense the term means the open courtyard in front of the communal meeting house; today, however, it embraces all aspects of community life—community buildings, tribal gatherings, church activities, and recreation. **1959** TINDALE & LINDSAY *Rangatira* iii. 32 The open-air marae temple, floored with slabs of basalt. *Ibid.* x. 93 They entertained their guests on the open marae ground among the houses. **1963** *Weekly News* (Auckland) 1 May 6/6 Dominating the marae was a cross 40 feet high illuminated with coloured lights. **1969** *Islander* (Victoria, B.C.) 6 July 5/2 The design [of a hotel in Tahiti] is reminiscent of ancient Tahitian outdoor worshipping temples (marae). **1974** *N.Z. Listener* 20 July 10/3 There was a group being welcomed on to the marae as I arrived.

marag, obs. form of MARRIAGE.

marage ('mɑːreɪdʒ), *v. Metallurgy.* [f. MAR(TENSITE + AGE *v.*] *trans.* To allow (a maraging alloy) to cool slowly in the air so that it develops great strength without significant changes in dimensions as a result of the transformation of austenite to martensite and subsequent age-hardening of the martensite.

1962 *Trans. Amer. Soc. Metals* LV. 524/2 Specimens were initially maraged at one temperature, and then maraged for various times at a second temperature. **1963** *Engineering* 24 May 715 When homogenized and maraged it [*sc.* steel] is claimed not to be notch sensitive despite its exceptional strength.

So **'maraged** *ppl. a.*, **'maraging** *vbl. sb.*, esp. in ***marag(e)ing alloy, steel***, steel that has been or may be hardened by maraging, generally containing up to 25 per cent nickel and smaller amounts of titanium, cobalt, molybdenum, or other elements.

1961 *Engineering* 24 Mar. 407/3 The original American release says that the steel develops its high strength by means of a remarkably easy heat treatment involving age-hardening of martensite. For this they have invented a term 'mar-aging'. **1962** *Trans. Amer. Soc. Metals* LV. 61/2 Maraged hardness increased linerly [*sic*] as the product, cobalt times molybdenum, increased. *Ibid.* 529/2 In annealing of 18% Ni maraging steel, temperatures in the range 1100 to 1300 F should be avoided to prevent retained austenite. **1968** R. KUMAR *Physical Metall. Iron & Steel* xi. 292 In marageing alloys, the role of interstitial carbon in raising the strength of steel is taken over by substantial amounts of nickel, cobalt, and molybdenum. *Ibid.*, Maraged steel is hardened without as much sacrifice of ductility. **1969** *Times* 2 May (Suppl.) p. iv/8 The Deep Quest, which has reached 8,350 ft., the deepest point yet attained by a submersible, has a hull of maraging steel of high strength allied to exceptional toughness and weldability. **1970** *McGraw-Hill Yearbk. Sci. & Technol.* 348/2 Hardening by maraging does not produce distortion or surface softening.. so that no machining is necessary after hardening. **1972** T. H. G. MEGSON *Aircraft Struct.* vii. 204 Maraging steels have been used as: aircraft arrester hooks, rocket motor cases, in helicopter undercarriages, gears, ejector seats and various structural forgings.

‖**marah** ('mɑːrə). Also 4–5 **marath,** 4 **mara,** 5 **marra.** [Heb. *mārāʰ*, fem. of *mar* bitter.] The Heb. word for 'bitter' or 'bitterness', used as a proper name in two different applications (Exod. xv and Ruth i: see below); hence used in allusions to the Scripture passages.

[**1382** WYCLIF *Exod.* xv. 23 Thei myȝten not drynk the watris of Marath, forthi that thei weren bitter; wherfor and a couenable name he putte to the place, clepynge it Mara, that is, bitternes. —— *Ruth* i. 20 Ne clepe ȝe me Noemy, that is to sey, fayr, but clepith me Mara, that is, bittir.] **14..** HOCCLEVE *Wks.* (E.E.T.S.) III. p. xlii, Wel my men call or name me 'marra' Fro hen[ne]s forth. **1678** *Yng. Man's Call.* 13 The young man by mistake fondly calls it Naomi, and says it is pleasant. The elder by dear-bought experience finds it Marah, and cries out 'Oh! it is bitter!' **1831** MACAULAY *Ess.*, *Byron* (1887) 168 Never had any writer so vast a command of the whole eloquence of scorn, misanthropy, and despair. That Marah was never dry. **1852** LONGF. *Jew. Cemetery at Newport* 40 The wasting famine of the heart they fed, And slaked its thirst with marah of their tears.

marahbut, obs. form of MARABOUT.

marahuana, marajuana, varr. MARIJUANA, MARIHUANA.

marai, marais: see MARAE, MARISH.

marakina, variant of MARIKINA.

marakle, obs. form of MIRACLE.

‖**maral** ('mɑːrəl). [A Tartar word.] The Caspian or Persian red deer, *Cervus maral*.

1863 MRS. ATKINSON *Tartar Steppes* viii. 181, I must now tell you of a maral we had. **1894** *Roy. Nat. Hist.* (ed. Lydekker) II. 348 In the Caspian provinces of Persia,..the red deer group is represented by the maral (*Cervus maral*).

maram, variant of MARRAM, reed-grass.

maramotto, obs. form of MARMOT *sb.*

maramuffe: see MARRY-MUFF *Obs.*

Maranao ('mærənaʊ). Also **Maranaw.** [ad. Maranao *Maranáw*, f. *ranaw* lake.] **a.** A Moro people inhabiting the province of Lanao del Sur and parts of central Cotabato province in the island of Mindanao (in the Republic of the Philippines), and some areas of northern Borneo. **b.** The Austronesian language of these people.

1957 [see ILLANO]. **1962** H. C. CONKLIN in J. A. Fishman *Readings Sociol. of Lang.* (1968) 429 Pronoun systems in Tagalog, Ilocano.., Maranao.., and some other Philippine languages. **1963** H. OSTELIUS *Islands of Pleasure* xiii. 78 There are also the inland Moros. The Maranao and Magindanaw are farmers... Because their main home is located around Lake Lanao on the island of Mindanao the

Maranaos are commonly called the Lake Moros. **1968** J. Kirkup *Filipinescas* viii. 154 The noble movements.. portrayed a Maranaw warrior. **1969** J. Cockcroft *Philippines* 55 About 87 different languages and dialects are spoken in the Philippines... Tagalog, spoken in Manila,.. Maranao, in Lanao. **1974** *Encycl. Brit. Micropædia* VI. 595/1 Like other Filipino Muslims, the Maranao differ markedly from the Christians. **1975** *Language* LI. 365 At the opposite extreme is a language like Maranao, in which there seems to be a specific Voice morpheme for each possible realization of a verb's subcategorization feature.

‖**Maranatha** (mærəˈnæθə). [In Gr. form μαραναθά; the Aramaic form is variously conjectured to be *mārǎn ǎthā* 'Our Lord has come', or *marǎnā 'thā* 'O our Lord, come thou'.] An Aramaic phrase occurring in 1 Cor. xvi. 22; often erroneously regarded as composing with the word that precedes it in the text a formula of imprecation, ANATHEMA MARANATHA. Hence (as an abbreviation of this formula) used *subst.* for: A terrible curse.

Coverdale's spelling (see below) is a corruption of Luther's *maharam motha*, which represents the fictitious Heb. *mohŏrām māvthāʰ* 'devoted to death'.

1382 Wyclif *1 Cor.* xvi. 22 If ony man loued not oure Lord Jhesu Crist, be he cursid, Maranatha, that is, in the comynge of the Lord. **1526** Tindale *ibid.*, Anathema maranatha. **1535** Coverdale *ibid.*, Anathema Maharan Matha. **1604** R. Cawdrey *Table Alph.*, *Maranatha*, accursed. **1640** Bp. Hall *Chr. Moder.* II. iv. 20 Those who ..shall invent..pernicious doctrines,..are worthy of a *Maran-atha*, and the lowest hell. **1721** Bailey, *Maranatha*, the highest Degree of Excommunication. **1846** W. F. Hook *Church Dict.* (ed. 5) 598 *Maranatha* could not be any part of the form of excommunication, but only a reason for pronouncing *Anathema* against those who express their hatred against Christ, by denying His coming. **1882** Farrar *Early Chr.* I. ix. 193 How does the writer meet their objections? Not by thundering forth with yet deeper conviction *Maran-atha*, but [etc.]. **1913** F. B. Macnutt *Advent Certainties* vi. 97 To the Corinthian Christian and to St. Paul alike 'Maran atha' was the expression of a supreme reality..which is the keynote of the New Testament. **1926** A. Chambers tr. *Arseniew's Mysticism & Eastern Church* II. vi. 123 And, finally, the closing cry quivering with joyous awe: *Maranatha* ('Come, our Lord!'). This appeal in Aramaic takes us back to the earliest period of the primitive Church in Jerusalem. **1961** New Eng. Bible *1 Cor.* xvi. 22 *Marana tha*—Come, O Lord! **1964** E. A. Nida *Toward Sci. Transl.* viii. 170 Such expressions as 'Abba Father', *Maranatha*, and 'baptized into Christ' could be used with reasonable expectation that they would be understood.

marane, marang: see Marrano, Meringue[1].

maranism, -ismus, obs. ff. Marranism, -ismus.

†**maranite.** *Min. Obs.* [ad. G. *maranit* (Link 1801), f. name of the Sierra de *Marão* (Portugal): see -ite.] = chiastolite.

1884 in *Cassell's Encycl. Dict.* **1896** in Chester *Dict. Min.* 167.

†**marant.** *Bot. Obs.* [Anglicized form of next.] Lindley's name for any plant of the old N.O. *Marantaceæ*.

1846 Lindley *Veg. Kingd.* 168.

‖**Maranta** (məˈræntə). *Bot.* [mod.L. (Plumier 1703), f. the name of Bartolommeo *Maranta* of Venosa, a 16th c. writer on medicinal plants.] A genus of herbaceous plants native of tropical America; a plant of this genus.

1812 J. Smyth *Pract. of Customs* (1821) 29 Arrow Root, produced from a Plant called Maranta, is a farinaceous alimentary root. **1882** *Garden* 14 Jan. 20/1 Fine foliaged plants, such as Marantas, Crotons [etc.]. **1899** Rodway *Guiana Wilds* 32 She made a cup of a maranta leaf.

†**maranˈtaceous**, *a. Bot. Obs.* [f. mod.L. *Marantāceæ*, f. Maranta: see -aceous.] Pertaining to the (obsolete) N.O. *Marantaceæ* of which Maranta was the typical genus.

1863 Bates *Nat. Amazons* iv. (1864) 84 A long, flexible cylinder made of the peel of a marantaceous plant, plaited into the proper form.

marantic (məˈræntɪk), *a. Path.* [ad. Gr. μαραντικός, f. μαραίνειν to wither, waste away.] Pertaining to, or of the nature of, marasmus.

1866 A. Flint *Princ. Med.* (1880) 28 Marantic thrombi. **1899** *Allbutt's Syst. Med.* VII. 594 Marantic thrombosis.

maras, variant of marish.

‖**marasca** (məˈræskə). Also 9 **marazque**, **marasque**. [It. *marasca*, aphetic f. *amarasca*, f. *amaro* bitter.] A small black cherry, *Prunus avium*, grown in Dalmatia, and esp. about Zara, for the distilling of maraschino.

1864 *Chambers's Encycl.* VI. 146/2 *Maraschino* is distilled from cherries..a very firm delicately-flavoured variety, called *Marazques*,..is used. **1889** *Syd. Soc. Lex.*, *Marasca cherry*, a cultivated variety of the cherry.

maraschal, obs. form of marshal.

maraschino (mærəˈskiːnəʊ). Also 8 **marischini**, mareschini, 8–9 **mareschino**, **marasquin**, 9 maresquino. [It. f. *marasca*: see prec. Cf. F. *marasquin*, whence some of the Eng. forms.]

a. A liqueur distilled from the marasca cherry.

1791–3 in *Spirit Pub. Jrnls.* (1799) I. 321 Hob-a-nobbed in some right marasquin. **1793** *Europ. Mag.* XXIII. 466 Such fine liqueurs with nectar may compare, From Marischini to the Vin Musca. **1796** Mrs. M. Robinson *Angelina* I. 297 After they had drank their mareschino, Lady Selina ordered tea. **1797** Southey *Lett. Resid. Spain* 394 He..regularly after dinner drank a bottle of mareschini, and lived in peace with all men. **1818** Moore *Fudge Fam. Paris* (ed. 8) 88 Divine *maresquino*, which —— Lord, how one swallows! **1831** *Society* I. 104, I recommend this Mareschino. **1842** Barham *Ingol. Leg.* Ser. II. *Blasphemer's Warn.*, Marasquin, Curaçoa, Kirschen Wasser, Noyeau. **1875** Jas. Grant *One of the 600* I. vii. 98 The mocha and maraschino.

b. *attrib.*, as *maraschino jelly*, *punch*. Also, **maraschino cherry**, a cherry preserved in real or imitation maraschino.

1820 Shelley *Œdipus* II. ii. 31 Give me a glass of Maraschino punch. **1850** Thackeray *Pendennis* II. i. 6 Did you taste the plombière, ma'am, and the maraschino jelly? **1905** 'O. Henry' in *N.Y. World Mag.* 22 Jan. 2/1 The world seemed no larger than the seed of a Maraschino cherry in a table d'hote grapefruit. **1918–19** *T. Eaton & Co. Catal.* Fall & Winter 385/1 Luscious Whole Red Maraschino Cherries in a semi-liquid cream, coated with fine chocolate. **1961** [see crème 1 b]. **1964** J. Drummond *Welcome, Proud Lady* xxi. 96 Maraschino cherries, olives, sliced lemon, salted nuts were arranged in small crystal bowls.

†**marasme.** *Obs.* [a. F. *marasme.*] = marasmus.

1625 Hart *Anat. Ur.* II. vii. 95 It is againe sometimes an Hecticke, which endeth in a Marasme. **1714** *Phil. Trans.* XXIX. 76 About the 40th day he dy'd of his Marasme.

marasmic (məˈræzmɪk), *a.* [f. marasm-us + -ic.] Pertaining to or arising from marasmus; suffering from marasmus.

1876 tr. *Wagner's Gen. Pathol.* (ed. 6) 582 Emaciation and a series of marasmic conditions set in. **1899** *Allbutt's Syst. Med.* VI. 587 She became progressively marasmic.

marasmoid (məˈræzmɔɪd), *a. Med.* [f. marasm-us + -oid.] Resembling marasmus.

1895 in *Funk's Stand. Dict.* **1902** in Cassell *Suppl.*

marasmolite (məˈræzməlaɪt). *Min.* [f. Gr. μαρασμός decay: see -lite.] A 'rotten' sphalerite or zinc blende, containing free sulphur.

1851 C. U. Shepard in *Proc. Amer. Assoc. Adv. Sci.* IV. 315 Marasmolite. Primary form, cube [etc.].

marasmous (məˈræzməs), *a.* [f. marasm-us + -ous.] Resembling or of the nature of marasmus.

1856 in Mayne *Expos. Lex.* **1889** in *Syd. Soc. Lex.*

marasmus (məˈræzməs). [mod.L., a. Gr. μαρασμός, f. μαραίνειν to wither, waste.]

a. Wasting away of the body, esp. in undernourished children.

1656 Trapp *Comm. Job* xix. 20 (1657) 171 Now, alas, I lie under a miserable *Marasmus*. **1661** Lovell *Hist. Anim. & Min.* 29 Diverse having kept them in their beds, have got an hectick feaver or marasmus thereby. **1753** N. Torriano *Gangr. Sore Throat* 76 How often was I apprehensive, Miss Blossac would fall into a Marasmus or a Languor? **1837** Syd. Smith *Let. Archd. Singleton* Wks. 1859 II. 268/2 Everybody has their favourite death: some delight in apoplexy, and others prefer marasmus. **1856** *Athenæum* 26 Apr. 515 The milk itself has been yielded by stalled cows dying of marasmus. **1902** W. G. Thompson *Pract. Dietetics* (ed. 2) VIII. 564 Marasmus is a form of starvation occurring chiefly in artificially fed infants, but also in those at the breast, in whom there is great wasting of the muscular and other soft tissues. **1951** R. W. B. Ellis *Dis. in Infancy & Childhood* vii. 254 Marasmus (Infantile atrophy). This is a condition of extreme and chronic malnutrition, and whilst it often arises simply from underfeeding, it may also be due to a variety of other causes, e.g. congenital syphilis..or parasitic infection. It is not therefore a disease *sui generis* but a clinical picture of which it is first necessary to determine the etiology. **1968** Meneghello & Rizzardini in A. Dorfman *Child Care in Health & Dis.* iii. 42 Almost all children in Chile suffer from so-called caloric-protein malnutrition, or marasmus, and this form of malnutrition is the major problem in Chile... The other form, protein malnutrition or kwashiorkor, is the most common type in other countries of the region. **1971** *Sci. Amer.* Oct. 14/3 They have advanced the understanding of the starvation disease called marasmus, which is increasing in many developing countries because mothers are giving up prolonged breast-feeding and their infants are not receiving an adequate substitute diet during a critical time in development.

b. *transf.* and *fig.*

1681 Nevile *Plato Rediv.* 24, I am one of those Unskilful Persons, that cannot discern a State *Marasmus*, when the danger is so far off. **1885** tr. *Hehn's Wand. Pl. & Anim.* 23 The notion that there is any such thing as a senile marasmus of nature.

marasque, variant of marasca (cherry).

marasquin, variant of maraschino.

marasse, variant of marish.

Maratha, var. Mahratta.

Marathi, var. Mahratti.

marathon (ˈmærəθən). Also **Marathon**. [The place-name *Marathon* (Gr. Μαραθών) on the north-east coast of Attica: see Marathonian *a.*]

a. The name first given on the occasion of the revived Olympic Games held in Athens in 1896 to a long-distance foot-race (now usu. of 26 miles 385 yards), with allusion to the run of Pheidippides at the time of the battle at Marathon in 490 B.C., as recorded in Herodotus and later sources. Also *attrib.*

Herodotus records that Pheidippides ran from Athens to Sparta to secure aid before the battle, but the race instituted in 1896 was based on a later less sound tradition that Pheidippides ran from Marathon to Athens with news of the Persian defeat.

1896 *Fortn. Rev.* June 950 We now come to the great glory of the Greeks—the victory in the Marathon Race. **1905** *Programme of Olympic Games Athens 1906* 3 Flat Races..e. Marathon Race, 42 kilometres. From Marathon to Athens on the road. **1908** T. A. Cook *Olympic Games* 82 The whole of Hellas seemed concentrated at Athens to see the result of the great Marathon Race in the stadium. **1908** *Westm. Gaz.* 22 July 1/3 There are two things which no one who wishes to win the Marathon can ever afford to forget. **1936** *Discovery* Feb. 48/2 Never speak to me again about a snail's pace except with reference to a Marathon runner or a racing car. **1955** J. H. Peters *In Long Run* viii. 71 On July 21st.. the A.A.A. Marathon Championship was due to be run at Birmingham on a roughly circular out-and-home course. **1964** M. Watman *Encycl. Athletics* 108/1 Owing to the disparity in the nature, if not distance, of various courses, marathon times should not be taken too seriously. *Ibid.*, The only woman on record as having completed a full marathon is Dale Greig. **1966** J. Hopkins *Marathon* 11 British runners are to be found among the leaders in almost every international Marathon.

b. In extended uses, applied to other long-distance races or competitions calling for endurance. Also *attrib.* (and as quasi-*adj.*).

1908 *Daily Chron.* 5 Nov. 1/2 A competition..under a title of 'The Murphy Marathon' was decided last night... It was intended that the contestants should..peel a quarter of a hundredweight of potatoes. **1928** *Daily Express* 2 July 11/5 The dance marathon here ended at midnight, nine couples left in the competition stopping together after twenty days of continuous dancing. **1932** G. Morton *Mystery of Hermit's End* ii. 19 The latter was taking intensive training for marathon swimming. That form of sport had caught on of late. **1932** *Times Lit. Suppl.* 26 May 393/1 His friend Cap Bridges, the marathon swimmer. **1968** *Radio Times* 28 Nov. 8/3 The London-Sydney Motor Marathon. Progress Reports. **1969** *New Yorker* 20 Dec. 64/2 One of the phenomena of America's Depression days was the marathon dance. **1975** *Ibid.* 10 Mar. 100/2 It's an album of pictures: line dancing, marathon dancing, the Lindy.

c. Other *transf.* and *fig.* uses. Esp. an event or activity of long duration.

1915 'Bartimeus' *Tall Ship* x. 185 'That was a bit of a Marathon, wasn't it?' He measured the distance across the lawn with a humorous eye. **1951** *N.Y. Herald-Tribune* 29 Nov. 3 The House of Commons finally went home..after sitting through a marathon session of 20 hours and 20 minutes. **1953** C. Day Lewis *Italian Visit* iii. 39 After a marathon walk through the Vatican galleries. **1955** W. Gaddis *Recognitions* II. vii. 613 There's been somebody tagging around after me all day, this marathon walker, I met him in a bar. **1971** *Britannica Bk. of Year 1970* 779/2 *Marathon, specif.*, a group session in which members remain together for an extended period (as 24 hours) and interact openly and responsively so as to increase self-understanding. **1972** *Daily Tel.* 2 June 2/3 The question whether a judge and special assessors should replace the conventional jury in complicated and marathon criminal cases.

Hence **ˈmarathon** *v. intr.*, to run as in a marathon race (*rare*); **ˈmarathoning** *ppl. a.* (*rare*).

1920 *Chambers's Jrnl.* Aug. 519/2 Do I have to marathon ten miles and back? **1964** M. Watman *Encycl. Athletics* 107/2 He [*sc.* Kolehmainen] won by less than 13 sec... the closest result in Olympic marathoning history.

Marathonian (mærəˈθəʊnɪən), *a.* [f. L. *Marathōni-us* (f. *Marathōn*) + -an.] Of or pertaining to Marathon, or to the battle of Marathon (490 B.C.) in which Athens defeated the Persians. Also *sb.*, a native of Marathon.

1767 [W. L. Lewis] *Statius' Thebaid* XII. 1082 But as the Son of Ægeus high display'd The Spear of Marathonian Oak, whose Shade O'erhangs the Foe. **1797** *Encycl. Brit.* (ed. 3) X. 552 The Marathonians worship those who were slain in the battle. **1871** Swinburne *Songs bef. Sunrise, Eve of Revol.* 106 Sea, have thy ports not heard Some Marathonian word? **1875** Browning *Aristoph. Apol.* 136 The Marathonian muscle, nerved of old To maul the Mede.

†**Maratism.** *Obs.* [f. name of Jean Paul *Marat*, a leader in the French Revolution, assassinated by Charlotte Corday in 1793: see -ism.] The anarchic doctrines advocated by Marat. Also †**Maratist**, one who supports these doctrines. †**Maratize** *v. trans.* (*nonce-wd.*), to assassinate as Marat was assassinated.

1793 A. Young *Examp. France* (ed. 3) 157 The red hot Maratism of the miscreant Society. **1794** *Sporting Mag.* IV. 106 In pursuit of Robespierre, whom she vowed to Maratise in due time. **1795** Barruel *Hist. Clergy during French Rev.* 323 One must have spent four years in France amidst the Constitutionalists, the Girondins, the Maratists, and the Jacobins of every description, to conceive [etc.]. **1798** Jefferson *Writ.* (1859) IV. 254, I have contemplated every event which the Maratists of the day perpetrate.

maraud (məˈrɔːd), *sb. rare.* [a. F. *maraude*, f. *marauder*: see maraud *v.*] The action of raiding or plundering. Also in phr. *on the maraud*: intent on plundering.

1837 W. Irving *Capt. Bonneville* II. 151 It was the hour for Indian maraud. **1839–40** —— *Wolfert's R.* (1855) 9 He had an Indian's sagacity in discovering when the enemy was

on the maraud. **1884** *St. Nicholas* XI. 534 Certain neighboring tribes that made maraud upon them.

maraud (mə'rɔːd), *v.* Also 8 **marode.** [a. F. *maraud-er*, f. *maraud* rogue, vagabond.

Cf. Sp. *merodear* to maraud, *merode* masc., act of marauding; also G. *marodiren* to maraud, *marode* adj., worn out with marching (said orig. of stragglers belonging to an army), *marode* fem., act of marauding, *marodebruder*, *marodereiter* straggler, deserter. The Fr. words were adopted in German in the 17th c., and were punningly associated with the name of Count Mérode, an imperialist general in the Thirty Years' War, whose troops were notorious for want of discipline.]

1. *intr.* To make a raid for the purpose of plundering. Const. *on*, *upon*.

1711 ADDISON *Spect.* No. 165 ⁋5 They met with a Party of French that had been Marauding. **1711** MRS. CENTLIVRE *Marplot* I. i, Ask your Brother, Don Lopez, who will have it that you send your eyes a maroding for English forage. **1813** SCOTT *Trierm.* II. i, The Saxon stern, the pagan Dane, Maraud on Britain's shores again. **1856** DOVE *Logic Chr. Faith* IV. ii. §5. 229 He [the Arab] will no longer maraud, because..he is placing himself in danger of being marauded upon.

b. *transf.* To go about pilfering.

1770 *Monthly Rev.* 132 A flea..Upon a taylor's neck was taken Marauding for a dinner. **1816** SCOTT *Antiq.* xxxiv, Juno—who, though formally banished from the parlour, failed not to maraud about the out-settlements. **1844** LD. BROUGHAM *A. Lunel* I. v. 138 He was an old offender, probably come from Marseilles to maraud at the Candlemas fair of Nismes.

2. *trans.* To plunder; to harry.

1829 W. IRVING *Chron. Granada* I. xii. 112 The tract of country they intended to maraud was far in the Moorish territories. **1894** G. MOORE *Esther Waters* 321 One is always marauding the other's territory.

marauder (mə'rɔːdə(r)). Also 7–8 **maroder.** [f. MARAUD *v.* + -ER[1]; after F. *maraudeur.*] One who roves in quest of plunder; a freebooter, plunderer.

1698 [R. FERGUSON] *View Eccles.* 89 To be a Maroder and Pillager upon the street and Field of Humane Credit and Reputation is worse..than to turn common Padders. **1712** *Lond. Gaz.* No. 5031/5 A Band of Maroders, consisting of Men of several Nations. **1782** VALLANCEY *Collect. De Rebus Hibernicis* No. 10. 72 *note*, To keep the cattle safe by night from moroders [*sic*]. **1808** SIR J. MOORE in Jas. Moore *Camp. in Spain* (1809) 19 He is determined to shew no mercy to plunderers and marauders. **1870** BURTON *Hist. Scot.* (1873) VI. lxx. 212 The marauders hovered round them like vultures round a wounded man.

b. *transf.* (e.g. of animals).

1764 GRAINGER *Sugar Cane* II. 79 Some place decoys, nor will they not avail, Replete with roasted crabs; in every grove These fell marauders gnaw. **1847** H. MILLER *First Impr.* v. (1861) 65 Exposed to every hungry marauder of the deep. **1862** TROLLOPE *Orley F.* xxii, The raisins shall become the prey of those audacious marauders only who dare to face the presence of the ghost.

marauding (mə'rɔːdɪŋ), *vbl. sb.* [f. MARAUD *v.* + -ING[1].] The action of the vb. MARAUD.

1755 *Connoisseur* No. 58 ⁋3 They might also be of great use in maroding, or getting in forage. **1839** W. IRVING *Wolfert's R.* (1855) 7 The yeomanry who had suffered from these maraudings. **1858** FROUDE *Hist. Eng.* IV. xviii. 4 A population who were trained from their cradles in licensed marauding.

attrib. **1764** GOLDSM. *Hist. Eng. in Lett.* I. 128 The history of a maroding party in one of our modern gazettes. **1879** FROUDE *Cæsar* x. 118 His campaign was not a marauding raid.

ma'rauding, *ppl. a.* [-ING[2].] That marauds.

1798 MALTHUS *Popul.* (1817) I. 184 Surrounded by marauding neighbours. **1874** L. STEPHEN *Hours in Library* (1892) II. vii. 227 He watches the marauding sparrows.

maravedi (mærə'veɪdɪ). *Obs.* exc. *Hist.* Forms: 5, 7 **maravedis,** 6 **marivade, marvedie, marvadie,** 7 **marvedi, marvedee, myravid, merviade, maravidi,** 8 **marevedi,** 7 *erron.* **malvady,** 7– **maravedi.** [a. Sp. *maravedí* (= Pg. *maravedim*), a derivative of Arab. *Murābiṭīn* (pl. of *murābiṭ*: see MARABOUT), the name of a Moorish dynasty (usually designated the *Almoravides*, this being the same word preceded by the Arabic article) which reigned at Cordova 1087–1147.]

1. An old Spanish gold coin, weighing about 60 grains and of the value of fourteen shillings.

1643 PRYNNE *Sov. Power Parl.* App. 64 Imposing 5. Maravidis of gold for every person. **1700** ASTRY tr. *Saavedra-Faxardo* II. 138 Henry III. who tax'd 'em at five Marvedees of Gold apiece.

2. A former Spanish copper coin and money of account, valued at about $\frac{1}{6}$ of a penny sterling.

?**1430** in Purchas *Pilgrims* (1625) II. VIII. 1230 And then into Spayne fear ye schon, Iakkes ben ther of little prise: For there beginneth the Maruedisez. **1540** *Act 32 Hen. VIII*, c. 14, lxx. maruadies, which is .xi. d. and the third parte of a peny starlyng. **1606** HEYWOOD *Chall. for Beauty* II. i. (1636) C 3 If you distrust his word, take mine, which will passe in Spaine for more Myravids, then the best Squiers in England for Farthing-tokens. **1690** DRYDEN *Don Sebastian* I. (1692) 14, I ask for him [a slave] a thousand Crowns. *1st Mer.* Thou mean'st a thousand Marvedis. **1706** PHILLIPS, *Malvady*, a Spanish coin, of which about 13 make one Farthing. [Some error: *Maravedis* is also given, with the correct value.] **1728** MORGAN *Algiers* II. v. 313 He never parted with a maravedi but with the view of pocketing a Ducat, if not a Doblon. **1819** SCOTT *Ivanhoe* xxxiii, I will strip thee of every maravedi thou hast in the world. *a* **1839** PRAED *Poems* (1864) II. 408 He flung the Slave who moved the lid A purse of maravedis. **1891** J. WINSOR *Columbus* ix. 209 He promised a silken jacket, beside the income of ten thousand maravedis.

maray (mə'reɪ). [? Native Australian.] An Australian food-fish, *Clupea sagax*, closely resembling the pilchard.

1882 TENISON-WOODS *Fish & Fisheries N.S. Wales* 147 The 'maray' (*Clupea sagax*) is a very rich, oily, well tasted fish of the herring family.

marazque, variant of MARASCA (cherry).

marber, marbir: see next.

marble ('mɑːb(ə)l), *sb.* Forms: α. 3–7 **marbre,** 4 **maubre,** 5 **marbir,** 6 **marber, marbyr.** β. 3–5 **marbel,** 4 **merbel, -ul,** 4–5 **marbil,** 4–6 **marbyl, -ul,** 5 **marboll, -ole, -elle, -ylle, -ulle, -ille, merbyl,** 5–6 **marbill, -yll, -ull,** 6 **marbell,** 4– **marble.** [ME. *marbre*, *marble*, a. F. *marbre*, (OF. rarely *marble*, *malbre* by dissimilation) = Pr. *marme-s*, Sp. *mármol*, Pg. *marmore*, It. *marmo*, Romanian *marmure*:—L. *marmor*, ad. or cogn. w. Gr. μάρμαρος shining stone, marble (prob. orig. an adj. 'sparkling', whence μαρμαίρειν to sparkle).

The L. word was adopted early into the Teut. langs.: OE. *marma* (in comb. *marm-*), OHG. *marmul* (MHG., mod.G. *marmel*, also *marmor*), MDu. *marmer*, *marmel*, more commonly *marber*, *marbel* from Fr. (mod.Du. *marmer* marble, *marmel* 'marble' to play with), ON. *marmari.*]

I. The simple word.

1. a. Limestone in a crystalline (or, less strictly, also a granular) state and capable of taking a polish. There are many varieties of this stone (see b), which is much used in sculpture and architecture.

When used without qualification, the word suggests either the pure white varieties commonly employed in sculpture (hence often referred to as a type of whiteness), or those with mottled or variegated surface (cf. senses 5, 7 e).

α. *c* **1290** *S. Eng. Leg.* I. 249/315 In one toumbe of Marbre he was i-leid. **1390** GOWER *Conf.* II. 124 A tumbe riche..Of marbre and ek of jaspre stones. **1585** T. WASHINGTON tr. *Nicholay's Voy.* IV. xxv, A great bridge of stone of Marbre. *a* **1693** *Urquhart's Rabelais* III. xxviii. 227 The most durable Marbre or Porphyr.

β. [*c* **1200**: see MARBLE-STONE.] *c* **1320** *Sir Beues* 4609 A faire chapel of marbel fin. *c* **1330** R. BRUNNE *Chron.* (1810) 341 Of marble is þe stone, & purtreied þer he lies. *c* **1400** MAUNDEV. (Roxb.) iii. 9 All þe pilers er of marbill. **1474** CAXTON *Chesse* 92 Also colde and harde as marbyll. **1553** EDEN *Treat. Newe Ind.* (Arb.) 25 Ouer this ryuer is a very fayre bridge of marble. **1617** MORYSON *Itin.* I. 162 All the pauement is most beautifull of ingrauen Marble. **1794** MRS. RADCLIFFE *Myst. Udolpho* xv, From the portico they passed a noble hall to a staircase of marble. **1857** RUSKIN *Pol. Econ. Art* i. 46 Marble..lasts quite as long as granite, and is much softer to work.

Proverb. **1593** SHAKS. *3 Hen. VI*, III. ii. 50 Hee plyes her hard, and much Raine weares the Marble.

b. With qualifying word: (*a*) an adj. denoting colour or appearance, e.g. ***black***, ***fibrous***, GREEN (12 d), ***grey***, RED (17 e), ***variegated***, ***white marble***; (*b*) a proper name denoting the locality in which it is found, e.g. ***African***, ***Carrara***, ***Derby***(*shire*), ***Egyptian***, ***English***, ***Genoese***, ***Italian***, ***Kilkenny***, PARIAN, ***Pentelican***, ***Portsoy***, ***Purbeck marble***; (*c*) applied to substances resembling or made to imitate marble, as †**brimstone marble**, a preparation of brimstone in imitation of marble; **metallic marble**, native sulphate of barium (*Syd. Soc. Lex.* 1889). See also BRECCIA, BROCATELLO, CIPOLIN, FIRE (B. 5), FOREST (*sb.* 5), LANDSCAPE *sb.* (5), LUMACHELLA, MADREPORE (4), ONYX (4), RUIN, SERPENTINE, SHELL, VERD ANTIQUE *marble.*

(*a*) *a* **1300** *Cursor M.* 8288 Vnder þis tre..A stapul was o marbul grai. *c* **1386** CHAUCER *Knt.'s T.* 1035 A gate of Marbul whit. **1585** T. WASHINGTON tr. *Nicholay's Voy.* II. i, A harde slipperie rocke of black marber. **1624** CAPT. SMITH *Virginia* IV. 126 No place hath more white and blew Marble than here. **1659** HOWELL *Lex.*, *Vocab.* xxvi, The Marble gentle, viz. the whitest hard marble..Serpentine or streaked Marble [etc.]. *a* **1728** WOODWARD *Fossils* (1729) I. I. 21 Black Marble.

(*b*) **1681** GREW *Musæum* III. vi. 316 Two pieces of Ægyptian Marble. *Ibid.*, A Piece of the worst sort of Cornish Marble, used for Lime. **1727–41** CHAMBERS *Cycl.* s.v., Derbyshire Marble is variously clouded and diversified with brown. *a* **1728** WOODWARD *Fossils* (1729) I. 20 The white Genoese Marble. *Ibid.* 25 The common white Carara marble. **1891** T. HARDY *Tess* (1900) 8/1 With your effigies under Purbeck-marble canopies.

(*c*) **1753** CHAMBERS *Cycl. Supp.* s.v. *Brimstone*, Brimstone Marble, a preparation of brimstone in imitation of marble.

c. A kind or variety of marble.

1640 WILKINS *New Planet* II. (1672) 119 That this rocky Substance is a Loadstone, rather than a Jaspis, Adamant, Marble, or any other. **1813** BAKEWELL *Introd. Geol.* (1815) 87 Very beautiful marbles occur [in England] which will receive a high polish. **1879** RUTLEY *Study Rocks* iii. 20 Limestones..capable of receiving a polish are called marbles.

d. Taken as a type of something hard, inflexible, durable, or smooth.

1586 WHITNEY *Choice of Emblems* 183 In marble harde our harmes wee alwayes graue. **1588** SHAKS. *Tit. A.* II. iii. 144 The milke thou suck'st from her did turne to Marble. **1613** PURCHAS *Pilgrimage* (1614) 638 Writing all injuries in marble. **1620** *Swetnam arraigned* G 4 b, Can you behold this sacred Cabinet,..And not let fall a teare: you are vnkind. Not Marble but would wet at such a sight. **1812** MISS MITFORD in L'Estrange *Life* (1870) I. vi. 219 Sir Charles Grandison..is a man of marble, or rather a man of snow. **1818** SHELLEY *Rosal. & Helen* 1252 The liquid marble of the windless lake. **1886** MISS BRADDON *One Thing Needful* ix, She had done all in her power to deter Clarice;..but Clarice had made up her mind to be a marchioness, and she was marble.

e. The stone as being the material of which a tomb or tombstone is made. *poet.* (Cf. 2 b.)

1613 SHAKS. *Hen. VIII*, III. ii. 434 When I am forgotten ..And sleepe in dull cold Marble. **1757** GRAY *Epit. on Mrs. Jane Clerke* 1 Lo! where the silent marble weeps, A friend, a wife, a mother sleeps. **1850** TENNYSON *In Mem.* lxvi[i], Thy marble bright in dark appears.

2. a. A piece, block, or slab of marble; a marble monument; †a marble vessel. Also *fig.*

c **1290** *Becket* 2118 in *S. Eng. Leg.* I. 167 Þe point of is swerd brak In þe Marbre ato. *c* **1380** *Sir Ferumb.* 5701 To a gret holw marbre was he broȝt,..Whych was wonyd beo fillid wyþ wyn. **1590** SPENSER *F.Q.* III. v. 33 The soveraine weede betwixt two marbles plaine Shee pownded small. **1644** EVELYN *Dairy* 22 Oct., The vacant stayrecase, marbles, statues [etc.]. **1715** LEONI *Palladio's Archit.* (1742) II. 62 An Inscription on a Marble. **1865** KINGSLEY *Herew.* x, The blood stained marbles of the Amphitheatre.

†**b.** A marble tomb or tombstone. *Obs.*

c **1330** R. BRUNNE *Chron.* (1810) 230 At Westmynstere he lis toumbed richely, In a marble bis of him is mad story. *a* **1533** LD. BERNERS *Gold. Bk. M. Aurel.* (1546) Ii ij b, In the felde of Elinos, vnder a marble, is the pouders of Sysifo Seteno. **1640** GLAPTHORNE *Ladies Priviledge* IV. Plays 1874 II. 141 My Ancestors, whose dust Would 'a broke through the Marbles, to revenge To me this fatall infamy. **1730** POPE *Epit. Fenton* 1 This modest Stone, what few vain Marbles can, May truly say, here lies an honest Man.

c. *Antiq.* (*pl.*) Applied, with specific qualification, to certain collections of sculptures, etc.; e.g.

Arundel, ***Arundelian***, or ***Oxford marbles***, a collection of sculptures and inscribed stones made by the Earl of Arundel (died 1646) and presented to the University of Oxford. ***Elgin marbles***, a collection (now in the British Museum) of ancient sculptures from the Parthenon, which was brought to England by Lord Elgin and sold by him to the nation in 1816.

[**1624** J. SELDEN (*title*) *Marmora Arundeliana.*] **1667** EVELYN *Diary* 19 Sept., To London with Mr. Hen. Howard of Norfolk, of whom I obtain'd the gift of his Arundelian Marbles. **1727–41** CHAMBERS *Cycl.* s.v., Arundel Marbles, ..or the Oxford Marbles. **1817** KEATS (*title*) On the Elgin Marbles. **1833** *Penny Cycl.* I. 142/1 The Æginetan, added to the Athenian, and Phigaleian marbles which we possess in the British Museum, would have formed a complete specimen of Grecian sculpture, as applied to the decoration of temples.

3. *techn.* [= F. *marbre.*] **a.** A slab of marble used for grinding paints on; **b.** A printer's imposing-stone (Knight *Dict. Mech.* 1875); **c.** = MARVER.

1671 SALMON *Syn. Med.* III. 474 The reducing of any thing into a fine powder, by grynding it on a Marble. **1698** *Phil. Trans.* XX. 466 Which they grind upon a Marble, such as Painters use. **1745** DE COETLOGON *Univ. Hist. Arts & Sci.* II. 3 To give it [the glass] a Polish, we roll it to and fro on a Stone, or Marble.

4. a. [= G., Du. *marmel.*] A little ball (varying from about $\frac{1}{2}$ inch to an inch in diameter), originally made of marble, now usually of baked clay, porcelain, glass, or composition, used in a children's game; hence in *pl.* the game itself. Also a similar ball (e.g. of glass) used in other games.

In playing the game, a number of marbles are arranged in a ring (or sometimes in a row), from which the players attempt to dislodge them by 'shooting' a marble at them with the finger and thumb.

1694–5 J. HOUGHTON *Collect. Husb. & Trade* No. 189 (1727) II. 29 The next are marbles for boys to play with. **1709** STEELE *Tatler* No. 112 ⁋3 A Game of Marbles, not unlike our modern Taw. **1792** S. ROGERS *Pleas. Mem.* I. 142 On yon gray stone..we shot the marble thro' the ring. **1866** R. CHAMBERS *Ess.* Ser. II. 3 There was the floor on which.. I had played at marbles, a pattern in the carpet serving as the ring. **1885** *New Bk. Sports* 301 Marbles is not the popular game it once was.

b. Phr. *to pass in one's marble* and varr., to die, to give up. *Austral. slang.*

1908 *Austral. Mag.* 1 Nov. 1250 Instead of dying you can 'chuck a seven', 'pass in your marble', or 'peg out'. **1918** A. WRIGHT *Over Odds* 102 'I suppose the old pot knew y'old man before he passed in his marble,' ventured Dick. **1924** *Truth* 27 Apr. 6 *Throw in the marble*, to relinquish. **1951** D. STIVENS *Jimmy Brockett* 304 I'm not going to pass in my marble just yet.

c. Phr. ***to make one's marble good***: to make a good impression (on a person), to ingratiate oneself, to improve one's position. *N.Z.* and *Austral. slang.*

Quot. 1938 illustrates a similiar *S. Afr.* use.

c **1926** '*MIXER*' *Transport Workers' Song Bk.* 31 Some tap the boss before they join,..By this they make their marble good. **1938** A. M. BROWN *Let.* 15 Apr. in Partridge *Dict. Slang* (1961) Suppl. 1179/1 A word I have heard used in the Cape [Province], mostly from people attending Rhodes University College, Grahamstown, is *marble*. Examples are: 'His marble is high'—he is 'well-in' (with such-and-such a person). 'He is polishing his marble with so-and-so' = he is trying to ingratiate himself. **1944** J. H. FULLARTON *Troop Target* iii. 26, I was making my marble good. **1947** D. M. DAVIN *Gorse blooms Pale* 206 The crowd..wanted to see if he could make his marble good with us. **1963** D. CRICK *Martin Place* 223 Take my tip, if you wanter make your marble good: say nothing.

†**5. a.** A mottled or dappled colour resembling that of variegated marble; hence, a cloth of such a colour. (Cf. 7e.) *Obs.*

1520 *Mem. Ripon* (Surtees) III. 274 Pro xiij virg. panni lanei coloris marble. **1541–2** *Act 33 Hen. VIII*, c. 18 Kerseies..of the colours of black, marble, russet, and white. **1549** *Act. 3 & 4 Edw. VI*, c. 2 §1 Russets, Musters, Marbles, Grayes, Royes, and suche lyke colors. **1555** *Richmond Wills* (Surtees) 86 A yard of marble xx^d^. **1720** STRYPE *Stow's Surv. Lond.* (1754) I. I. xxix. 297/1 In a livery of grey Marble.

b. *Bookbinding.* The marbled pattern or paper used in ornamenting books.

1699 WANLEY in *Lett. Lit. Men* (Camden) 277 In knowing what sort of Paper is in use,..or to please myself..with looking on the fine colors, marbles, &c. **1817** DIBDIN *Bibliogr. Decameron* II. 532 In lieu of gilt, you may..order marble coloured edges: but gilt upon the marble—oh! 'tis the very luxury—the 'ne plus ultra' of the bibliopegistic art! **1823** *Bookbinder's Compl. Instructor* 28 Common Marble. *Ibid.* 29 Transparent Marble. *Ibid.* 30 Egyptian Marble.. Purple Marble..Stone Marble. *Ibid.* 31 Rice Marble.. Chinese Marble..Red Marble. *Ibid.* 32 Wainscoat Marble.

c. (See quots.) Also ***marble crust***.

1924 *Tourist* Winter Sports No. 12/2 *Marble*, a snow-crust formed by alternate freezing and thawing. Found on Southern slopes. **1948** P. LUNN *Ski-ing Primer* xviii. 90 Marble crust is so slippery that it is almost impossible to obtain a purchase on it with the skis. **1969** M. HELLER *Ski* xiv. 185 *Marble crust* looks like its name and is formed by the wind. The snow is dull and extremely hard... It is very common at high altitude in early winter.

6. *pl.* †**a.** ***French marbles***: syphilis. *Obs.*

[? Corruption of F. *morbilles* 'the small pockes' (Cotgr.).] *a* **1592** GREENE *Thieves falling out* (1615) C 3, Looke into the Spittles, and Hospitalles, there you shall see men diseased of the French Marbles.

†**b.** As transl. of L. *marmor*: A stony concretion in the joints of a horse. *Obs.*

1748 tr. *Renatus' Distemp. Horses* 190 Oftentimes in the knees or joints there arises either a Phlegmon, or Marbles, or Puffs or Wind-galls.

c. As (false) transl. of F. *meubles*: furniture, movables, personal effects; 'the goods'. *slang.*

1864 HOTTEN *Slang Dict.* 176 *Marbles*, furniture, movables; 'money and marbles', cash and personal effects. **1867** TROLLOPE *Claverings* II. vi. 67 She won't get any money from me, unless I get the marbles for it. **1896** FARMER & HENLEY *Slang* IV. 280/1 *Marbles*,..furniture; moveables. *Money and marbles* = cash and effects. [From Fr. *meubles*]. Hence, any substantial *quid pro quó*. English synonyms. Belongings; household gods; lares and penates; moveables; sticks; sprats, slows; traps. **1923** J. MANCHON *Le Slang* 190 *Marbles*,..des meubles (corrupt. du français). **1937** PARTRIDGE *Dict. Slang* 509 *Marbles*, furniture; moveables: somewhat low..; ob[solescent].

d. *pl.* Mental faculties; brains; common sense. *slang.* (orig. *N. Amer.*).

1927 *Amer. Speech* II. 360 *Marbles, doesn't have all his* (verb phrase), mentally deficient. 'There goes a man who doesn't have all his marbles.' **1935** A. J. POLLOCK *Underworld Speaks* 75/1 *Marbles*, the brain. **1957** M. MILLAR *Soft Talkers* i. 7 She's a fattish little *hausfrau* with some of her marbles missing. **1958** WODEHOUSE *Cocktail Time* xvii. 148 Do men who have got all their marbles go swimming in lakes with their clothes on? **1967** M. L. ROBY *Cat & Mouse* i. 19 He ain't right in the head. Got a few marbles missing. **1969** J. WAINWRIGHT *Take-Over Men* i. 8 You lost your goddam' marbles? You gone completely crazy, you nutty slob? **1973** *Ottawa Jrnl.* 6 Feb. 9/4 'I still have most of my marbles,' he said cheerfully. **1973** R. PARKES *Guardians* xi. 204 Crazy bastard... I think he's blown his marbles.

II. Attrib. and Comb.

7. *attrib.* passing into *adj.* **a.** Made or consisting of marble. (For the corresp. parasynthetic adjs. see 8c.) Also, like that of marble.

13.. *Coer de L.* 6182 He leet make a marbyl ymage. **1382** WYCLIF *Esther* i. 6 Thei weren vnderset with marbil pileeris. **1577** B. GOOGE *Heresbach's Husb.* I. (1586) 8 Suche stately dwellinges and marble floores. **1646** EVELYN *Diary* (? Apr.), A marble Madona like a Colosse. **1747** MRS. GLASSE *Cookery* ix. 78 Take a Quart of Almonds..and beat them in a Marble Mortar. **1852** M. ARNOLD *Empedocles* II. 88 Her flush'd feet glow on the marble floor.

b. White, hard, cold, or rigid like marble. (Rarely used *predicatively*.) Hence in parasynthetic adjs. ***marble-breasted, -hearted, -minded***.

1591 FLORIO *2nd Fruites* 43 *P.* Oh filthie..fashion of some Englishmen, to ride with these hard, straight, and little saddles. *T.* They are English toyes, to vse..such marble pinching sadles [Ital. *queste selle marmoree*]. **1593** SHAKS. *3 Hen. VI*, III. i. 38 Her teares will pierce into a Marble heart. **1601** —— *Twel. N.* v. i. 127 The Marble-brested Tirant. **1605** —— *Lear* I. iv. 283 Ingratitude! thou Marble-hearted Fiend. **1611** —— *Wint. T.* v. ii. 98 Who was most Marble, there changed colour. **1612** DRAYTON *Poly-olb.* ii. 94 Her Marble-minded breast. *a* **1618** SYLVESTER *Wood-mans Bear* lxxv. (Grosart) II. 312 Moan I must for never was Marble-hearted Mermidon But would moan [etc.]. **1675** SOUTH *12 Serm.* (1692) 570 His Marble, obdurate Heart. **1784** *Unfortunate Sensibility* I. 175 What is virtue? is it a certain marble-mindedness, the elder brother of insensibility. **1812** BYRON *Ch. Har.* II. xxxiii, That seeming marble-heart. **1817** SHELLEY *Rev. Islam* VI. xxxiii, Her marble brow, and eager lips. **1818** —— *Rosal. & Helen* 186 His fancy on that spring would float, If some invisible breeze might stir Its marble calm. **1875** JOWETT *Plato* (ed. 2) II. 102 Under the marble exterior of Greek literature was concealed a soul thrilling with spiritual emotion. **1927** R. GRAVES *Poems (1914–26)* 203 Not marble-hearted but your own true love.

c. Enduring as marble, or as if carved in marble.

1596 FITZ-GEFFRAY *Sir F. Drake* (1881) 27 Cease to eternize in your marble verse The fals of fortune-tossed Venerists. **1682** SIR T. BROWNE *Chr. Mor.* III. §17 They write not their obligations in sandy but marble memories.

d. *poet.* Smooth as marble. (Cf. L. *marmoreum æquor.*) Hence ***marble-faced*** adj.

1557–8 PHAER *Æneid* VI. R iij b, All what marblefacyd seas conteines of monstrous fries. **1667** MILTON *P.L.* III. 564 Through the pure marble Air.

e. Of a variegated or mottled colour (†occas. used *predicatively*); marbled. †Also, made of cloth or stuff of such a colour (see 5). Hence ***marble-coloured, -covered, -edged*** adjs.

c **1430** *Two Cookery-bks.* 29 Caste þer-to Saunderys & Safroun, & loke it be marbylle [*Ashmole MS.* marbely]. *Ibid.* 34 Take a lytyl Saunderys & a lytyl Safroun, & make it a marbyl coloure. **1539** *Test. Ebor.* (Surtees) VI. 91 To William Cay my marbill jacket. **1545** *Ibid.* 230 My marbell colered cote. **1591** *Lanc. Wills* III. 54, I geve Willm Cooke my marble hose. **1703** *Lond. Gaz.* No. 3930/4 An Almanack ..with a Marble Vellum Cover. **1705** *Ibid.* No. 4108/3, 77 half Chests of Marble-Soap. **1808** HAN. MORE *Cœlebs* II. 74 Countless marble-covered octavos. **1811** *Self Instructor* 120, 3-thread fine marble stockings. **1817** DIBDIN *Bibliogr. Decameron* II. 533 The *peau de veau* of the French, with gilt upon marble edges! **1876** ROCK *Text. Fabr.* vii. 76 Marble silk had a weft of several colours so woven as to make the whole web look like marble.

†**f.** ***marble colours***: used *fig.* by Drummond to express ostentatious splendour. *Obs.*

1613 DRUMM. OF HAWTH. *Cypress Grove* Wks. (1711) 118 The marble colours of..funeral pomp. *a* **1649** —— *Hist. Jas. III*, ibid. 41 The marble colours of false greatness.

8. Obvious combinations. **a.** attributive (of, pertaining to, or concerned with marble), as ***marble chips, †grit, mart, -mason, -mill, -quarry, saw***; (used in the game of marbles) as ***marble-ring***; **b.** objective, as ***marble-cutter, -polisher, -worker***; **c.** parasynthetic and instrumental, as ***marble-arched, -built, -chequered, -flagged, -imaged, -paved, -piled, -pillared, -ribbed, -sculptured, -slabbed, -stoppered*** adjs.; **d.** similative, as ***marble-constant, -hard, -like, -looking, -still, -tall, -white*** adjs.; ***marble-wise*** adv.

1636 G. SANDYS *Paraphr. Ps.* viii. 9 The *marble-arched Skie. **1791** W. BLAKE *French Revolution* I, in *Compl. Writings* (1972) 138 Shall this *marble built heaven become a clay cottage..? **1879** F. W. ROBINSON *Coward Consc.* I. iv, Across the *marble-chequered hall. **1926** H. CRANE *Let.* 19 Aug. (1965) 273 Examining pebbles and cinders and *marble chips through the telescope. **1946** *Happy Landings* (Air Ministry) July 1/2 White stone or marble chips spread out and rolled into the macadam surface form an excellent substitute. **1606** SHAKS. *Ant. & Cl.* v. ii. 240 Now from head to foote I am *Marble constant. **1611** COTGR., *Marbrier. A *marble-cutter.* **1889** W. B. YEATS *Wanderings of Oisin* 53 A *marble-flagged, pillared room. *c* **1420** *Pallad. on Husb.* I. 405 With *marbul greet ygrounde & mixt with lyme. *a* **1618** SYLVESTER *Elegy H. Parvis* (Grosart) II. 328 In his stone-breast no pitie moves relenting, Rough and remorselesse, more then *marble-hard. **1832** [R. CATTERMOLE] *Beckett*, etc. 179 With all thy high and *marble-imaged line. **1530** PALSGR. 318/1 *Marbylyke, of the coloure of marbyll. **1854** J. S. C. ABBOTT *Napoleon* (1855) I. ix. 163 He could impress a marble-like immovableness upon his features. **1846** DE QUINCEY *Antigone* Wks. 1863 VIII. 221 The unchanging expression in the *marble-looking mask. **1818** BYRON *Ch. Har.* IV. l, The paltry jargon of the *marble mart. **1816** J. SMITH *Panorama Sci. & Art* II. 808 The plasterers, *marble-masons, and other artisans who use this article. **1835** URE *Philos. Manuf.* 58 Sawing comprehends every species of mill..such as..*marble-mills. **1812** BYRON *Ch. Har.* II. lxii, In *marble-paved pavilion. **1777** WARTON *Poems* 45 What though no *marble-piled bust Adorn his desolated dust. **1754** ARMSTRONG *Forced Marr.* v. iv. *Misc.* (1770) II. 110 This *marble-pillar'd castle. **1756** BURKE *Subl. & B.* Introd., Wks. I. 113 In the question about the tables, the *marble-polisher will unquestionably determine the most accurately. **1887** J. C. HARRIS *Free Joe*, etc. (1888) 127 To invest money in Georgia *marble-quarries. **1820** SHELLEY *Tower of Famine* 11 Each *marble-ribbed roof. **1821** CLARE *Vill. Minstr.* I. 5 The 'I spy', 'halloo', and the *marble-ring. **1839** URE *Dict. Arts* 801 The *marble saw is a thin plate of soft iron, continually supplied..with water and the sharpest sand. **1875** KNIGHT *Dict. Mech.* 1393/1 Marble-Saw. **1890** *Cent. Dict.*, *Marble-saw*,..a machine for cutting marble... Such machines will cut a block of marble into several slabs simultaneously, or can be arranged to cut out pyramidal blocks, or to shape a cylinder or a frustum of a cone. **1844** MRS. BROWNING *Brown Rosary* III. xii, He knelt like a child *marble-sculptured and white. **1864** *Harper's Mag.* Dec. 40/1, I..had a snug *marble-slabbed brick house. **1933** 'R. CROMPTON' *William—the Rebel* viii. 162 Lay his catch upon the marble-slabbed hat-stand in the hall of the inn. **1904** W. DE LA MARE *Henry Brocken* xiii. 168 He stood, thus, *marble-still. **1972** *Country Life* 30 Nov. 1481/3 The screw-topped or *marble-stoppered lemonade bottles of long ago. **1938** BELLOC *Sonnets & Verse* 196 The Islands have received it, *marble-tall. **1877** A. B. EDWARDS *Up Nile* xxii. 720 The quarried cliffs of Toora, *marble-white. **1687** MIEGE *Fr. Eng. Dict.* s.v., To marble Paper, to paint it *marble-wise with several Colours. **1875** KNIGHT *Dict. Mech.* 1393/2 *Marble-worker's Files.

9. Special comb.: **marble bone** *Path.* [tr. G. *marmorknochen*], (*a*) (also *pl.*) = OSTEOPETROSIS; also called ***marble bone(s) disease***; (*b*) an affected bone in a person with osteopetrosis; †**marble butterfly**, ? = *marbled white*; **marble cake** orig. *U.S.*, a cake made of light and dark sponge, having a mottled appearance suggestive of marble; †**marble-crab**, a crab having a marbled or mottled shell; †**marble dew**, some imaginary antaphrodisiac; †**marble-flint**, ? flint having a mottled appearance; **marble gall**, a gall made by the insect *Cynips Kollari*; **marble leg**, 'the pale shining leg of *Phlegmasia dolens*' (Syd. Soc. Lex.); **marble orchard** *U.S. slang*, a cemetery; **marble-paper**, paper coloured in imitation of marble; **marble paste**, a white porcelain paste used for casts of statues (in recent Dicts.: a transl. of F. *pâte de marbre*); **marble-player, marbles-player**, one who plays the game of marbles; **marble seal**, *Phoca fetida*; **marble-top** usu. *attrib.*, designating a piece of furniture the top of which is covered with marble; also ***marble-topped*** adj.; **marble town** *U.S. slang* = *marble orchard*; **marble veal** (*Cookery*), potted veal interspersed with lumps of tongue, having a mottled surface when cut; **marble-wood**, (*a*) see quot. 1753; (*b*) a large East Indian tree, *Diospyros Kurzii*, having a variegated wood (*Cent. Dict.*); (*c*) an Australian tree, *Olea paniculata*, having mottled timber (Morris *Austral Eng.*).

1922 *Arch. Surg.* V. 462 In 1921, Schultz discussed the nature of the disease of *marble bones (Albers-Schönberg). **1922** *Jrnl. Amer. Med. Assoc.* 2 Dec. 1955/2 A patient..was found, on roentgen-ray examination, to have a pathologic fracture as the result of a rather obscure bone condition which has been termed osteosclerosis fragilis generalisata, Marmorknochen (marble bone), or Albers-Schönberg disease. **1947** *Arch. Path.* XLIII. 75 Marble bone disease is due to..an unknown agent which damages the bone-forming blastema at the beginning of the second period of development of each individual bone. *Ibid.* 73 Fractures in marble bones, for the most part, do not splinter. **1961** R. D. BAKER *Essent. Path.* xxi. 560 In osteopetrosis (Albers-Schönberg's disease; marble bones) the bones are abnormally hard and thick, but also easily fractured. **1973** FORFAR & ARNEIL *Textbk. Paediatrics* xxiii. 1525/1 (*heading*) Albers-Schonberg disease (osteopetrosis, marble bones disease). **1749** B. WILKES *Eng. Moths & Butterflies* 52 The Marmoris, or *Marble-Butterfly. **1796** NEMNICH *Polygl. Lex. Nat. Hist.*, Marble-butterfly. *Pap. Galathea.* The black-eyed Marble butterfly. *Papilio Semele.* **1871** MRS. T. J. V. OWEN *Illinois Cook Bk.* 202 *Marble Cake... White part... Three teacupsful white sugar,..Dark part... Three teacupsful brown sugar, One teacupful molasses, [etc.]. **1878** N. A. DONNELLEY *Lakeside Cook Bk.* 29/1 Marble Cake. **1903** K. D. WIGGIN *Rebecca* xxvi. 290 She began to stir the marble cake. **1971** M. MCCARTHY *Birds of America* 74 My husband used to like a marble cake. **1668** CHARLETON *Onomast. Zoicon* 176 *Cancer..Marmoratus* sive *Varius* (quod testa tegitur..maculis viridibus, cæruleis, albis, nigris, cinereis..), the *Marble Crab. *a* **1621** BEAUM. & FL. *Thierry & Theod.* III. i, The teares of mandrake and the *marble dew, Mixt in my draught, haue quencht my natural heate. **1633** MASSINGER *Guardian* III. i, I would..bathe my self, night by night, in marble dew. **1686** *Phil. Trans.* XVI. 27 Burnt *Marble-flint quench'd in Vinegar. **1882** *Garden* 14 Oct. 334/2 The *Marble and Artichoke galls are formed from buds. **1929** M. A. GILL *Underworld Slang* 8/1 **Marble orchard*, cemetery. **1941** J. M. CAIN *Mildred Pierce* 155 You'll get your names in this marble orchard soon enough. **1973** B. BROADFOOT *Ten Lost Years* x. 110 A couple more punches and it would have been the marble orchard for him. **1680** *Lond. Gaz.* No. 1566/4 Two Books..covered with *Marble Paper. **1737** BERKELEY *Letter* Wks. 1871 IV. 247, I would have these pamphlets covered with marble paper pasted on white paper. **1862** *Catal. Internat. Exhib.* II. xxviii. 5 Marble papers. **1910** A. BENNETT *Clayhanger* I. i. 9 Six men playing the noble game of rinkers... They were celebrated *marble-players. **1955** *Publ. Amer. Dial. Soc.* XXIII. 7 Marble players are not imaginative as far as their terminology is concerned. **1959** I. & P. OPIE *Lore & Lang. Schoolch.* xi. 228 Young marbles players..easily become prey to strange thoughts. *Ibid.*, In some places marble players are addicted to charms. **1896** J. W. KIRKALDY & E. C. POLLARD tr. *Boas' Text Bk. Zool.* 519 The Ringed or *Marble Seal (*Ph. fœtida*). **1883** *Heal & Son Catal.* Sept. 200/2 Hall Table,..St. Ann's *Marble Top. **1891** 'O. THANET' *Otto the Knight* 60 [She was] a woman of property, ..owning two marble-top bureaus and a sewing-machine. **1963** *House & Garden* Feb. 1 Marble top coffee table, 36" × 15", £38.10.0. **1849** *Marble-topped [see LONGFULLY *adv.*]. **1864** MRS. GASKELL *French Life* i, in *Fraser's Mag.* Apr. 435/2 The 'guéridon' (round, marble-topped table)..the one indispensable article in a French drawing-room. **1886** 'MARK TWAIN' *Let.* 7 Aug. (1920) 257 They never used a stove, but cooked their meals on a marble-topped table. *a* **1941** V. WOOLF *Captain's Death-bed* (1950) 181 There are marble-topped tables at the corner. **1959** W. GOLDING *Free Fall* iv. 85 When we were sitting at the marble-topped table my plans began to come apart. **1971** M. LEE *Dying for Fun* xlii. 203 Would he have to change the décor of his flat.., those marble-topped café tables? **1975** *Times* 6 Sept. 1/4 The bomb..was thought to have been placed under one of the marble-topped tables in..the [hotel] lobby. **1945** L. SHELLY *Jive Talk Dict.* 29 **Marble town*, a graveyard. **1970** C. MAJOR *Dict. Afro-Amer. Slang* 80 *Marble town*, (1940's) a cemetery. **1789** FARLEY *Lond. Art Cookery* II. iii. (ed. 6) 274 *Marble veal. **1753** CHAMBERS *Cycl. Supp.*, **Marble Wood*, a name given by the people of some parts of America to the *lignum rhodium*, or rose-wood, from the heart of the tree being sometimes variegated like Marble.

marble ('mɑːb(ə)l), *v.* [f. MARBLE *sb.* Cf. F. *marbrer*.]

1. *trans.* To stain or colour (paper, edges of books, soap, etc.) so as to give the appearance of variegated marble.

1683 *Lond. Gaz.* No. 1874/4 A..strong leather Pad-saddle marbled. **1686** PLOT *Staffordsh.* 123 Which two colours they break with a wire brush, much after the manner they doe when they marble paper. **1714** GAY *Sheph. Week* II. 13 Marbled with Sage the hard'ning Cheese she press'd. **1725** BRADLEY *Fam. Dict.* s.v. *Potage*, Marbling it with very brown Veal-Gravy. **1846** RUSKIN *Mod. Paint.* I. II. VI. i. §19

With about as much intelligence or feeling of art as a house-painter has in marbling a wainscot. **1885** J. PAYN *Talk of Town* II. 228 Liquids used by bookbinders in marbling covers.

b. To make (a design) by the process of marbling.

1885 C. G. W. LOCK *Workshop Receipts* Ser. IV. 267/1 Take..a green calf and marble a tree upon it.

2. To make white like marble. *rare.*

1791 H. WALPOLE *Let. to Han. More* 29 Sept., Mrs. Porteus's accident..may have marbled her complexion, but I am persuaded has not altered her..good-humoured countenance. **1878** B. TAYLOR *Deukalion* II. iii. 67 Thy features, marbled by the moon.

†**3.** To pickle (fish). *Obs.*

[**1598**, **1611**: see MARL *v.*^{3}] **1661** RABISHA *Cookery Dissected* 14 To Marble Sowls, Plaice, Flounders, Smelts.

marbled (ˈmɑːb(ə)ld), *ppl. a.* [f. MARBLE *sb.* and *v.* + -ED.]

1. In various occasional uses: Portrayed in marble; having buildings or sculptures of marble; turned into marble (*fig.*); decorated or covered with marble.

1599 STORER *Wolsey* C4b, Looke how the God of Wisdome marbled stands, Bestowing Laurel wreathes. **1760–72** H. BROOKE *Fool of Qual.* (1809) III. 143 Marbled effigies and monumental deposits of the renowned. **1821** BYRON *Juan* III. lxxxvi. xvi, Place me on Sunium's marbled steep. **1844** LD. HOUGHTON *Mem. Many Scenes, Scott at Tomb of Stuarts* 132 His marbled form will meet the attentive eye. **1851** G. MEREDITH *Sleeping City* 109 A marbled City planted there With all its pageants and despair. **1885** H. O. FORBES *Nat. Wand. E. Archip.* 6 Fine residences..conspicuous by the blaze of light that lit up their pillared and marbled fronts.

2. Variegated in colour like certain marbles.

a. Coloured or stained by a technical process with variegated patterns.

1671 BOYLE *Usef. Nat. Philos.* II. IV. 14 Those fine Covers of Books that, for their resemblance to speckld Marble, are wont to be call'd Marbled. **1699** WANLEY in *Lett. Lit. Men* (Camden) 276 Common marbled paper. *a* **1769** S. DAVIES *Whalley* in Dodsley *Coll. Poems* (1782) V. 106 Variety of troops..In marbled regimentals. **1885** C. G. W. LOCK *Workshop Receipts* Ser. IV. 242/1 The edge of marbled books should correspond with their marbled ends.

b. Veined, mottled, or dappled (*with* markings of various colours). Chiefly *Nat. Hist.* and *Path.*

1694 *Acc. Sev. Late Voy.* II. 18 The snow was marbel'd, and look'd as if it were boughs and branches of Trees. **1719** D'URFEY *Pills* (1872) VI. 557 At the break of morning light, When the marbled Sky looks gay. **1818** *Art Preserv. Feet* 154 If the chilblain is merely neglected, the skin..becomes livid and of a marbled appearance. **1890** WOODBURY *Encycl. Photogr.*, *Marbled Prints*, a defect in printing... The prints appear..unevenly marked, somewhat resembling the appearance of marble. **1899** *Allbutt's Syst. Med.* VIII. 462 It [i.e. an eruption on the skin] may be uniform, or figured, or marbled.

c. Of meat: Having the lean streaked with thin layers of fat. (A sign of the best quality.)

1770–4 A. HUNTER *Georg. Ess.* (1803) IV. 355 There is no better sign of good flesh, than when it is marbled. **1834** YOUATT *Cattle* 270 The meat is finely marbled and well-flavoured.

3. Used as the specific designation of various animals and plants which have mottled or dappled markings (freq. = L. specific name *marmoratus, -a*).

marbled beauty, the moth *Bryophila perla*; **marbled green**, the moth *Bryophila glandifera*; **marbled white (butterfly)**, *Arge galathea*; **marbled rose** (see ROSE *sb.*).

1699 PETIVER *Musei Petiver.* 33 The white marbled female Butterfly. **1707** MORTIMER *Husb.* (1721) II. 164 The Marbled Rose,..its Leaves are larger, of a light red Colour marbled and veined. **1840** *Cuvier's Anim. Kingd.* 95 The..Marbled Cat (*F[elis] marmorata*). **1844** H. STEPHENS *Bk. Farm* III. 762 The common long red or marbled mangel-würzel. **1867** H. T. STAINTON *Brit. Butterflies & Moths* iii. 31 The Marbled White Butterfly. *Ibid.* vi. 66 The Marbled Beauty. **1870** *Eng. Mech.* 25 Feb. 571/2 The Marbled Green (*Bryophila glandifera*). **1876** *Encycl. Brit.* IV. 595/2 The Marbled White (*Arge galathea*) is the species often met with in Britain.

marbleize (ˈmɑːb(ə)laɪz), *v.* orig. *U.S.* [f. MARBLE *sb.* + -IZE.] *trans.* To colour in imitation of marble; = MARBLE *v.*

1875 KNIGHT *Dict. Mech.* 1391/2 *Marbleizing Slate*, coloring its surface in imitation of variegated marble. **1884** *Advt.*, All white and marbleized..wrought-iron hollow ware. **1888** HOWELLS *Annie Kilburn* xi. 114 The marbleised iron shelf..supported two glass vases. **1892** *Harper's Mag.* 936/2 Soap of a marbleized reddish color. **1909** GALSWORTHY *Fraternity* vii. 60 She had before her..two little books. One of these was bound in marbleized paper. **1974** *State* (Columbia, S. Carolina) 3 & 4 Mar. G 13/6 She was more than happy to pay the extra baggage fees on two dozen heavy gold-and-white marbleized candles.

marbleness (ˈmɑːb(ə)lnɪs). *rare*$^{-1}$. [f. MARBLE *sb.* + -NESS.] Hardness like that of marble.

1629 DONNE *26 Serm.* (1661) 65 My holy sighs..have worn out my Marble Heart, that is, the Marbleness of my heart.

marbler (ˈmɑːblə(r)). Also 5 **marbyler, merbler**, 6 **marbular, merbeler**, 5–6, 8 **marbeler**. [f. MARBLE *sb.* and *v.* + -ER^{1}. Cf. F. *marbrier* (= senses 1, 2), *marbreur* (sense 3).]

1. A quarryman or hewer of marble. ? *Obs.*

1457 in Dugdale *Warwicksh.* (1656) 355 Iohn Bourde of Corff Castle, in the County of Dorset, Marbler. **1478** *Church-w. Acc. St. Andrew's East Cheap* in *Brit. Mag.* XXXII. 37 Item to a Marbeler for hauyng oute of a Marbyll Ston iiij^{d}. **1538** LELAND *Itin.* I. 94 (1768) I. 88 Marble, wont to be taken up..by Marbelers of Barnardes Castelle and of Egleston. **1885** *Harper's Mag.* Jan. 243/1 The quarriers, or 'marblers', as they are called in the old papers relating to the body [at Purbeck].

†**2.** One who carves, or works in, marble; a sculptor. *Obs.*

1469–70 *Fabric Rolls York Minster* (Surtees) 73 Robert Spillesby..equitanti pro les merblers..37*s.* 4*d.* *a* **1470** TIPTOFT *Orat. G. Flammeus* (Caxton 1481) He [Socrates] had to his moder a mydwyf and to his fader a marbyler. **1538** LELAND *Itin.* VII. 25 Many Marbelers working in Alabaster. **1649** FULLER *Just Man's Funeral* 23 Let..the most accurate Marbler erect the Monument. **1720** STRYPE *Stow's Surv. Lond.* (1754) II. v. xiv. 312/1 The Company called by the name of Marblers for their excellent knowledge..in the art of insculpting Personages for tombs. **1868** STANLEY *Westm. Abb.* iii. 153 [Preparation for Henry VI's tomb, an. 1472] The 'marbler' (or, as we should now say, the statuary).

3. One who marbles paper, etc. Also, an instrument used for marbling paper.

1835 J. HANNETT *Bibliopegia* 206. **1885** CRANE *Bookbind. for Amateurs* 97 Of all the varieties of gum, there is but one that is of any use to the marbler..gum tragacanth. **1890** ZAEHNSDORF *Bookbinding* 75 Leo's Mechanical Marblers.

ˈmarble-stone. *Obs.* exc. *dial.* Forms: see MARBLE *sb*; also MARM-STONE. [Cf. *chalkstone, limestone.*] = MARBLE; a marble floor, monument, tomb, etc.

c **1200** *Trin. Coll. Hom.* 145 Hie [marie magdalene]..nam ane box ȝemaked of marbelstone. *a* **1225** *Leg. Kath.* 1489 Þu schalt habben..of marbrestan a temple. **1297** R. GLOUC. (Rolls) 9787 Þe point of is suerd brec in þe marbreston a tuo. *c* **1386** CHAUCER *Prioress' T.* 229 In a temple of Marbul stones cleere Enclosen they his litel body sweete. *c* **1430** LYDG. *Minor Poems* (Percy Soc.) 50 Harde to lyke hony out of a marble stone. **1530** PALSGR. 530/1 Water by often droppyng may make a hole in a marbyll stone. **1585** T. WASHINGTON tr. *Nicholay's Voy.* I. vi, In the middest of the pauement which was of Marber stone. **1682** CREECH *Lucretius* (1683) 94 If that's an Ill, why not as great an one To be opprest with Earth, or Marble-stone? **1896** A. E. HOUSMAN *Shropshire Lad* li, I met a statue standing still. Still in marble stone stood he, And stedfastly he looked at me.

marblet (ˈmɑːblɪt). [f. MARBLE *sb.* + -ET^{1}, after the F. *marbré.*] A South American lizard, *Polychrus marmoratus.*

1840 *Cuvier's Anim. Kingd.* 276 The Marblets..have palatal teeth, and femoral pores, like the Iguanas. **1890** in *Cent. Dict.*

marbling (ˈmɑːblɪŋ), *vbl. sb.* [f. MARBLE *v.* + -ING^{1}.] The action of the vb. MARBLE.

1. The process, practice, or art of staining paper, etc. with variegated colours in imitation or conventional imitation of marble.

1686 *Lond. Gaz.* No. 2197/4 A New Art..of Making, Marbling, Veining, and Finishing of Mantle-pieces. **1731** BAILEY vol. II, *Marbling* of Books (in Book-binding) the sprinkling them with colours on the outside. **1753** in *Patents Specif., Skins* etc. (1872) 3 For the making, marbling, veining [etc.] any linen, silks, canvas, paper, and leather. **1901** *Daily Chron.* 3 Dec. 9/6 Graining and Marbling wanted.

2. *concr.* **a.** Colouring or marking resembling that of marble, or some conventional imitation of it.

1727–52 CHAMBERS *Cycl.* s.v. *Porcelain*, There is..a kind of marbled porcelain, which is not made by applying the marblings with the pencil. **1774** GOLDSM. *Nat. Hist.* VII. 7 The only marblings, which appear in its body, are the colour of the food, which is seen through its transparent intestines. **1883** SOLON *Art Old Eng. Potter* 93 Agate-ware was a complicated process; the marbling, instead of being produced on the surface, went through the body. **1894** R. B. SHARPE *Handbk. Birds Gt. Brit.* (1896) I. 97 Marblings and spots of light brown or reddish-brown. **1897** *Allbutt's Syst. Med.* II. 103 In children infested by fleas or lice the general tint of the rash may be deepened by very numerous petechiæ or by 'marbling'.

b. In meat: the quality or state of having the lean streaked with thin layers of fat. Cf. MARBLED *ppl. a.* 2c.

1925 W. H. TOMHAVE *Meats & Meat Products* xvii. 203 Marbling is always present in ribs, loins, and chucks. **1929** *Daily Express* 7 Nov. 3/4 There are certain indications by which the official graders can detect clearly whether or not there is 'marbling' in the beef while it is in the side. **1963** *New Yorker* 22 June 21 Marbling is the most important thing in a steak. **1972** T. MCHUGH *Time of Buffalo* xxiii. 311 Despite the greater cost, buffalo meat is not overpriced, for its marked leanness entails less fatty marbling and less trimming.

3. A marble-like incrustation. *rare.*

1872 C. KING *Mountain. Sierra Nev.* i. 21 The summit piercing through a marbling of perpetual snow up to the height of ten thousand feet.

4. *Comb.*: **marbling-rod**, the rod or pole used in the apparatus for glazing marbled paper; **marbling trough**, the trough into which the paper is dipped in the process of marbling.

1835 HANNETT *Bibliopegia* 82 After this they [the books] must be glaired equally over, and when dry placed upon the marbling rods, the sides of the books extending over, and the leaves hanging between. *Ibid.* 184 The marbling trough is generally made of oak.

marbling (ˈmɑːblɪŋ), *ppl. a.* [-ING^{2}.] = MARBLED *ppl. a.* 2c.

1958 *Times* 8 Dec. (Suppl.) p. viii/3 Tender beef can be produced..from older animals that are well-finished, i.e., in which there has been considerable deposition of 'marbling' fat between the muscle bundles. **1971** *Country Life* 9 Sept. 643/3 The older mature animal that is well finished can still provide meat of a high quality, due in part to the intimate penetration of 'marbling fat' into the deep muscle tissue.

marblish (ˈmɑːblɪʃ), *a. rare*$^{-1}$. [f. MARBLE *sb.* + -ISH^{1}.] Resembling marble.

1826 MOORE *Mem.* (1854) V. 80 The smooth, marblish, effeminate colouring.

marbly (ˈmɑːblɪ), *a.* Also 5 **marbely**, 7 **marblie**. [f. MARBLE *sb.* + -Y.] Resembling, or having the appearance of, marble. Hence, rigid, cold, or calm like marble.

1439 [see MARBLE *sb.* 7e, quot. *c* 1430]. *a* **1619** FOTHERBY *Atheom.* II. i. §4 (1622) 179 Whatsoeuer Monsters strange, in marbly Seas doe breed. **1635** SWAN *Spec. M.* vi. (1643) 299 Salt-gem..is also called stonie, marblie Salt. *a* **1814** *Mermaid* II. i. in *New Brit. Theatre* II. 486 The marbly lustre of her skin. **1845** BROWNING *Bishop orders his tomb* 75 And have I not..mistresses with great smooth marbly limbs? **1856** STANLEY *Sinai & Pal.* i. (1858) 69 Above the blue sea rose the white marbly terraces. **1858** G. MACDONALD *Phantastes* (1878) II. xiv. 33 The marbly stillness of thousands of years.

marbole, -boll, marbre, obs. ff. MARBLE.

†**marbryn(e**, *a. Obs.* [a. OF. *marbrin*, f. *marbre* MARBLE *sb.*] Of marble.

1319 in Riley *Mem.* (1868) 131. *a* **1400–50** *Alexander* 4353 Ne mote ne marbryn werkis. **1490** CAXTON *Eneydos* xxi. 74 Her wymmen..bare her in-to her chambre marbryne.

marbul(l, marbular: see MARBLE, MARBLER.

marbut, obs. form of MARABOUT.

marbyl(l, -yr, -yler: see MARBLE, MARBLER.

marc (mɑːk). Also 7 **marre, mare**: and see MURK. [a. F. *marc*; explained by Hatz.-Darm. as a vbl. noun f. *marcher* in the sense 'to crush'. The *c* in the Fr. word is mute, even before a vowel; hence prob. the 17th c. Eng. forms *marre, mare.*]

a. The refuse which remains after the pressure of grapes or other fruits; *spec.* = *marc brandy.*

1601 HOLLAND *Pliny* II. 530 The marre [ed. **1634** mare] or refuse of grapes after they be pressed. **1670** EVELYN *Sylva* viii. (ed. 2) 56 The Lees, or Marc of the Pressing [oil from walnuts] is excellent to fatten Hogs with. **1707** SLOANE *Jamaica* I. p. xlv, The Marc or remainder of the Sugar Canes after the juice is squeezed out. **1707** *Curios. in Husb. & Gard.* 138 Marc of Olives after they are press'd. **1852** MORFIT *Tanning & Currying* (1853) 45 The marc, or pressed cake, which still retains some tannin, is made to yield it. **1883** R. HALDANE *Workshop Receipts* Ser. II. 10/2 The juice and the refuse ('marc') are fermented. **1934** O. SITWELL *Let.* 15 Aug. in Mrs. Belloc Lowndes *Diaries & Lett.* (1971) 126 We settled them with a glass each of the strongest Marc-de-Bourgoyne. **1946** G. MILLAR *Horned Pigeon* xvi. 252 Ramon and Alban sat inside, drinking marc. *Ibid.* 253 Ramon ordered three more marcs. **1956** J. BALDWIN *Giovanni's Room* ii. 44, I ordered black coffee and a cognac, a large one. Giovanni was far from me, drinking *marc.*

b. *attrib.*: **marc brandy**, brandy distilled from marc.

1852 FOWNES *Man. Elem. Chem.* (1863) 512 The fusel-oil of the *marc-brandy* of the South of France.

marc, obs. form of MARK, MARQUE^{1}.

marcal, variant of MERCAL.

Marcan (ˈmɑːkən), *a.* Also **Markan**. [f. L. *Marc-us* or f. *Mark* + -AN.] Pertaining to the Gospel of St. Mark.

1902 J. A. ROBINSON *Study of Gospels* iv. *heading*, The use of the non-Marcan Document by St. Matthew and St. Luke. **1903** H. B. SWETE in *Expositor* June 415 The Marcan tradition. **1909** B. W. BACON *Beginnings Gospel Story* p. xxviii, Let the reader simply subtract mentally the Markan element from Luke. **1926** V. TAYLOR *Behind Third Gospel* v. 130 Again the Markan stripe is characterized by unity of subject-matter. **1930** A. G. HEBERT tr. *Brilioth's Eucharistic Faith & Pract.* i. 5 An energetic analysis of the texts leads him to the conclusions that the Markan narrative is alone authentic and original, [etc.]. **1971** *Novum Testamentum* XIII. 187 In general the changes made by Matthew and Luke to their Markan source reveal primarily a Matthean and Lukan redaction history and not a Markan one.

†**marcantant.** *Obs. rare*$^{-1}$. [Corruption of It. *mercatante.*] A merchant.

1596 SHAKS. *Tam. Shr.* IV. ii. 63 *Tra.* What is he..? *Bio.* Master, a Marcantant [*so Folios and Qo.*; *Pope reads* mercantant, *Capell* mercatantè], or a pedant.

†**marcasin(e**. *Obs. rare.* Also **marcassin**. [= F. *marcassin* (Cotgr.).] = next.

1601 HOLLAND *Pliny* II. 509 These two Marcassins. *Ibid.* 588 There is another fire stone going under the name of Pyrites or Marcasin. *Ibid.*, These Marcasines.

marcasite (ˈmɑːkəsaɪt). *Min.* Also 5 **markasit**, 5–8 **marchasite**, 6 **-it, marcazite**, 6–7 **-quesit(e**, 7 **-quisat(e, merquisate, marchesit(e, -gasite**, 7–8 **-casit, -c(h)assite**, 8 **-kasite**. Also in mod.L. form 7–8 **marcasites**, (7 **margasites**). [ad. med.L. *marcasīta* (whence F. *marcassite*, Sp. *marquesita*,

It. *marcassita, marchesita*), app. formed with suffix L. *-īta*, Gr. *-ίτης*, -ITE[1].

The etymology is obscure, as the Arabic *marqashīthā* or *marqashīṭā*, often cited as the source, is probably adopted from some European language.]

1. Pyrites, *esp.* the crystallized forms of iron pyrites used in the 18th c. for ornaments; by some restricted to the arsenical varieties of pyrites; in recent use, white iron pyrites (iron disulphide).

For the vague notion attached to the word in pre-scientific chemistry, see quots. 1616 and 1727–52. The 'marcasites' of gold and silver seem to have been specimens of copper and iron pyrites with the lustre of gold and silver, and hence wrongly supposed to contain traces of those metals.

1471 RIPLEY *Comp. Alch.* Ep. i. in Ashm. (1652) 116 Our Marchasite, our Magnete, and our Lead. **1572** J. JONES *Bathes of Bath* II. 20 Copper, Iron, and Marquesite. **1610** B. JONSON *Alch.* II. iii, Your marchesite, your tutie, your magnesia. **1616** BULLOKAR *Eng. Expos.*, *Marchasite*, a stone participating with the nature of some mettall, yet in so small quantity, that the mettall cannot be melted from it, but will vapour away in smoake, the stone turning to ashes. **1684** tr. *Bonet's Merc. Compit.* XIX. 852 Glass of Antimony..is nothing but the meer Marchasite of Lead. **1695** WOODWARD *Nat. Hist. Earth* IV. 172 A common Marcasite or Pyrites shall have the Colour of Gold most exactly;..and yet..yield nothing of worth, but Vitriol, and a little Sulphur. **1727–52** CHAMBERS *Cycl.*, *Marcasite, Marcasita*, a sort of metallic mineral, supposed by many to be the seed or first matter of metals. On this principle, there should be as many different marcasites as metals... There are only three kinds in the shops, which are called, marcasite of gold, of silver, and of copper: though some repute the loadstone to be a marcasite of iron; bismuth, marcasite of tin; and zink, or spelter, marcasite of lead. *a* **1728** WOODWARD *Fossils* I. (1729) I. 172, I could never perceive any Arsenic in the Pyritæ; in which they differ from the Marcasits, most of which contain more or less of that Mineral. **1778** WOULFE in *Phil. Trans.* LXIX. 15 The Derbyshire and Eckton Cauk, which is commonly covered with copper marcassite. **1796** KIRWAN *Elem. Min.* (ed. 2) II. 256 Arsenical Pyrites or Marcassite. **1836–41** BRANDE *Chem.* (ed. 5) 861 Bismuth was sometimes called Marcasite. **1844** BROWNING *Colombe's Birthday* I. 344 Yon gray urn's veritable marcasite, The Pope's gift. **1865** WATTS *Dict. Chem.* III. 851 *Marcasite*, white Iron Pyrites. **1879** RUTLEY *Study Rocks* x. 157 Marcasite resembles pyrites, except that it crystallises in the rhombic system.

attrib. **1588** LUCAR *Colloq. Arte Shooting* App. 17 The marchasite stone. **1601** HOLLAND *Pliny* II. 558 It commeth of a certaine marquesit stone, wherupon also they call it Chalcitis. *a* **1728** WOODWARD *Fossils* I. (1729) I. 181 The Marcasite Grains are of a bright Yellow.

2. A piece or specimen of marcasite; an ornament made of crystallized iron pyrites.

Formerly used for striking a light: cf. FIRESTONE I.

1555 EDEN *Decades* 115 *margin*, Marchasites are flowers of metals by the colours wherof the kyndes of metals are knowen. **1682** N. O. *Boileau's Lutrin* III. 54 From his Pocket He takes his Marchasite, begins to knock it With hardned Steel, out springs an Active spark. **1773** GOLDSM. *Stoops to Conq.* III. i, Half the ladies of our acquaintance,..carry their jewels to town, and bring nothing but paste and marcasites back. **1877** W. JONES *Finger-ring* 307 Two hearts surmounted by a crown..set with marcasites.

Hence **marca'sital** (*rare*—[0]), **marca'sitical** *adjs.*, pertaining to or containing marcasite.

1670 BOYLE *Tracts Cosm. Qual.* etc. IV. 21 A great quantity of marchasiticall Earth, if I may so call it. **1731** BAILEY vol. II., *Marcasital* [ed. 1737 *Marcasitical*], of or pertaining to marcasites. **1779** *Phil. Trans.* LXIX. 30 On one side there was a slight marcasitical coating.

‖**marcassin** (mɑːˈkæsɪn). *Her.* [Fr.] A young wild boar, used as a charge.

1727 in BAILEY vol. II. **1847** *Gloss. Heraldry*, *Marcassin*, a young wild boar, distinguished from an old one by having its tail hanging down instead of twisted.

marcassin, variant of MARCASIN(E.

marcassite, obs. form of MARCASITE.

marcato (mɑːˈkɑːtəʊ), *adv.* and *a. Mus.* [It., pa. pple. of *marcare*, to mark, accent, of Gmc. origin: cf. MARK *v.*] (With each note) emphasized. Also *transf.*

1840 BUSBY & HAMILTON *Dict. 3,000 Mus. Terms* (ed. 3) 109 *Marcato*, a term implying a strong and marked style of performance. **1842** J. F. WARNER *Universal Dict. Mus. Terms* 56/1 *Marcato*, marked, distinguished, rendered prominent, as e.g. Ben marcato, well marked, in a clearly marked, distinct manner... This term is sometimes used over such passages or individual notes, as the composer may wish particularly to have heard. **1922** JOYCE *Ulysses* 214 He read, *marcato*. **1961** *Times* 6 Dec. 17/7 Mr. Spaić got exciting results with tense 'marcato' arrangements.

marcatt(e, Marce, obs. ff. MARKET, MARS.

Marcel (mɑːˈsɛl), *sb.* Also with lower-case initial. [f. the name of François *Marcel* Grateau (1852–1936), French hairdresser who invented the method.] In full, ***Marcel wave***. A kind of artificial wave of the hair produced by using heated curling-tongs. Also *fig.*

1895 in *N. & Q.* (1941) 6 Sept. 129/1 (Advt.), Experts in the Marcel and Last Vienna Wave. **1908** *Smart Set* Sept. 86/1 And when she 'comes to', her Marcelle wave is straight as a shad. **1909** 'O. HENRY' *Roads of Destiny* 62 Man, what do you suppose she did? Loosened up like a Marcel wave in the surf at Coney. **1926** *Glasgow Herald* 25 Sept. 9 It began to rain... Many a beautiful marcel was sacrificed to save a masterpiece of millinery. **1930** R. MACAULAY *Staying with Relations* xvi. 226 Little marcel waves lapped at the Eugenia's white sides as she lay at anchor in the San José harbour. **1934** E. SITWELL *Aspects Mod. Poetry* i. 11 Mr. Austin Dobson, and his Marcel Waves, the wriggling, giggling horrors of his Triolets and other imitations of French forms. **1964** L. HAIRSTON in J. H. Clarke *Harlem* 285 The waves in my hair done unstrung... I..called Sonny for an appointment; I *had* to have a marcel!

b. *Comb.*, as ***Marcel-waved, -waver, -waving***.

1908 'O. HENRY' *Gentle Grafter* ii. 71 A combination steak beater, shoe horn, marcel waver. **1923** *Chambers's Jrnl.* Sept. 568/1 She could lie without turning one of her exquisitely marcel-waved hairs. **1925** *Daily Tel.* 13 May 20/5 (Advt.), Expert Marcel Waver and Manicurist. *Ibid.*, Marcel and water waving. **1927** *Daily Express* 30 Nov. 13 Miss Aylwin has been earning her living..doing shingling and marcel waving. **1932** [see *finger-waving* vbl. sb.]. **1968** *Times* 30 Jan. 9/7 Your head is frizzed or Marcel-waved. **1974** *Daily Tel.* 7 Aug. 11/2 This drawing-room comedy of 1931 has been carefully resuscitated..with wind-up gramophone, a marcel-waved heroine and snip-snap jokes. **1974** *Observer* 24 Nov. 29/6 There's a lady in Wellington, New Zealand, who was still doing marcel waving from the first time round when it came back again.

marcel (mɑːˈsɛl), *v.* [f. prec. sb.] *trans.* To wave (hair) in the 'Marcel' fashion. Also *fig.*

1906 B. VON HUTTEN *What became of Pam* I. x. 71 A gentleman who *marcelled* heads in an Oxford Street shop. **1926** KIPLING *Debits & Credits* 155 The wind marcelling the grasses. **1928** *Daily Express* 28 Dec. 11/1 Her unbobbed hair is marcelled in broad waves from a high forehead. **1951** E. PAUL *Springtime in Paris* iv. 81 Word and figures may be dyed, marcelled or manoeuvred like veils around a dancer. Behind them, the nakedness is there.

Hence **mar'celled** *ppl. a.*; **mar'celling** *vbl. sb.* Also *fig.*

1909 'O. HENRY' *Options* 103 A stone house with an engraving of an idol with marcelled hair, playing a flute, over the door. **1922** F. COURTENAY *Physical Beauty* 42 If you want that 'marcelled' look, there are comb sets (mounted on springs) which will give it. **1926** *Daily Colonist* (Victoria, B.C.) 17 Jan. 6/2 (Advt.), Swan-Marinello perfect marcelling. Home appointments made. **1927** *Daily Express* 14 Oct. 6 Women's heads in the late Roman period..are represented not only with distinct marcelling, but also with elaborate jewellery to emphasise the waves. **1930** R. MACAULAY *Staying with Relations* xvi. 228 The rippling, marcelled sea. **1932** L. C. DOUGLAS *Forgive us our Trespasses* (1937) xi. 219 Victor..calmly continued his monologue in a marcelled, affected baritone. **1936** [see BOBBY PIN]. **1938** D. BAKER *Young Man with Horn* (1939) i. 20 Even marcelling hadn't gained any real ground. **1971** K. WHEELER *Epitaph for Mister Wynn* (1972) xxvii. 350 The halo of silver hair.. was in marcelled good order.

‖**marceline**[1] (ˈmɑːsəlɪn). Also **marcelline** (*Dicts.*). [Fr.] A silk fabric used for linings.

1835 *Court Mag.* VI. p. ii/1 The breakfast dress is lined with coloured marceline.

marceline[2] (ˈmɑːsəlɪn). *Min.* [a. F. *marceline* (Beudant), f. name of St. Marcel, Piedmont.] A siliceous oxide of manganese.

1849 J. NICOL *Man. Min.* **1883** *Encycl. Brit.* XVI. 387/2 Marceline has violet tarnish.

marcella, marsella (mɑːˈsɛlə). [Anglicized pronunciation of MARSEILLES.] A kind of twilled cotton or linen cloth used for waistcoats, etc.

1812 *Chron.* in *Ann. Reg.* 81/2 In black silk stockings, black small clothes, Marcella waistcoat, and dressing gown. **1861** *Eng. Wom. Dom. Mag.* III. 263/1 The waistcoat may be made either in white silk or marcella. **1882** CAULFEILD & SAWARD *Dict. Needlework*, *Marcella* or *Marsella*, a description of cotton Quilting or coarse Piqué,..for making toilet covers, dressing table mats, and other articles.

Marcellian (mɑːˈsɛlɪən). *Eccl.* [ad. med.L. *Marcelliān-us*, f. *Marcellus*.] A follower of Marcellus, bishop of Ancyra in the fourth century, who is said to have held heretical views resembling Sabellianism.

Hence **Mar'cellianism**.

1607 T. ROGERS *39 Art.* (1625) 6 Some denyed the Trinity ..: so did..the Marcellians. **1727–41** CHAMBERS *Cycl.*, *Marcellianism*, the doctrine and opinions of the Marcellians.

marcerye, obs. form of MERCERY.

marces, obs. pl. of MARCH *sb.*[3]

marcescent (mɑːˈsɛsənt), *a.* (*sb.*) *Bot.* [ad. L. *marcēscent-em*, pr. pple. of *marcēscĕre*, inceptive f. *marcēre* to be faint or languid.]

A. *adj.* Of parts of a plant: Withering but not falling off.

1727 BAILEY vol. II. **1777** ROBSON *Brit. Flora* 29, 32. **1870** BENTLEY *Man. Bot.* (ed. 2) 222 When it is persistent and assumes a shrivelled or withered appearance, it is marcescent. **1904** J. C. WILLIS *Man. Flowering Plants* (ed. 2) 77 If it [*sc.* the perianth] remains unwithered round the fruit, persistent, withered, marcescent, enlarged as in Physalis, accrescent. **1964** *Acta Phytogeographica Suecica* XLIX. 51 (*caption*) Around the stem..there is a dense insulating mantle of marcescent dry leaves. **1974** *Kew Bull.* XXIX. 536 The stems of forest species of Giant Lobelia are usually bare of marcescent foliage.

B. *sb.* A plant having marcescent parts.

1859 TODD *Cycl. Anat.* V. 254/2 A single cell of the leaf of a marcescent..is seen still to contain a primordial vesicle.

Hence **mar'cescence** [see -ENCE], marcescent condition.

1857 TODD *Cycl. Anat.* V. 232/2 Cessation of vegetation and marcescence. **1890** *Temple Bar* Nov. 443 They are ugly in their marcescence and scent incipient putrefaction. **1974** *New Phytologist* LXXIII. 981 Mature pachycauls..exhibit several characteristics often associated with the 'juvenile' stages of trees, e.g. wide pith, presence of starch-sheath, unbranched axis and marcescence.

†**mar'cescible**, *a. Obs.*—[0] In early Dicts. spelt **marcessible**. [a. F. *marcescible* (in 16th c. written *marcessible*), f. *marcēscĕre*: see MARCESCENT and -BLE.] Liable to wither or fade. Hence **mar'cescibleness, marcesci'bility**.

1656 BLOUNT *Glossogr.*, *Marcessible*, apt or easie to rot or putrifie. **1727** BAILEY vol. II, *Marcessibility*, a pining away, a Consumption. **1731** *Ibid.*, *Marcessibleness*, withering or fading nature.

marcgrave: see MARGRAVE.

†**march**, *sb.*[1] *Obs.* Forms: 1 merici, merice, (*Northumb.* meric), merece, merce, mearce, 4–7 merche, 6 march(e. [OE. *merece* str. masc. = OS. (glosses) *merk*, *merka* (MLG. *merk* masc.), G. *merk* masc., MSw. *märke*, *merkie* fem., Da. *merke*.] Smallage or wild celery, *Apium graveolens*.

a **700** *Epinal Gloss.* 24 *Apio*, merici. *a* **800** *Corpus Gloss.* 182 *Apio*, merice. *c* **1000** *Sax. Leechd.* II. 134 Genim merce nioþoweardne. *c* **1000** ÆLFRIC *Gram.* (Z.) 27 *Apiaster*, merce. **1398** TREVISA *Barth. De P.R.* XVII. xiii. (Helmingham MS.), Merche is calde Apium. **1545** ELYOT *Dict.*, *Hipposelinon*, some suppose it to bee the herbe called smallache, or marche. **1562** TURNER *Herbal* II. 68 b, Hipposelinon hath leues lyke vnto march or smalache, but roughe. **1572** BOSSEWELL *Armorie* II. 76 b, A Pyle in poyncte betwene two slippes of Merche, verte. **1578** LYTE *Dodoens* V. xlii. 606 Of Marish Parsley, March, or Smallache. **1632** *Guillim's Heraldry* IV. xvi. (ed. 2) 353 Apium..is called in English Merche.

March (mɑːtʃ), *sb.*[2] Forms: 3–4 **Marz**, 4 **Mars**, 3 **Marrch, Mearch**, 4–7 **Marche**, (6 *Sc.* **Merche**), 4– **March**. [Early ME. *march*, a. AF. *marche* (Gaimar), OF. *march(e* (Godefr. *Compl.*), a north-eastern var. of the more usual *marz*, *mars* (mod.F. *mars*):—L. *Martium* (nom. *Martius* sc. *mēnsis*, lit. month of Mars), whence also Pr. *martz*, *mars*, Sp. *marzo*, Pg. *março*, It. *marzo*, OHG. *Merzo* (MHG. *Merze*, mod.G. *März*), MDu. *maerte*, *merte* (modDu. *Maart*), Sw. *Mars*, Da. *Marts*, late Gr. *Μάρτιος*.]

1. a. The third month of the year in the Julian and Gregorian calendars. Abbreviated Mar.

In the Roman pre-Julian calendar it was the first month, and originally began at the vernal equinox.

[*c* **1050** *Menologium* 36 Hrime ȝehyrsted, haȝolscurum færð ȝeond middanȝeard Martius reðe, Hlyda healic.] *c* **1200** ORMIN 1891 þatt wass i Marrch, acc Marrch wass þa Neh all gan ut till ende. *a* **1225** *Juliana* 79 þe fowrtuðe Kalende of mearch þat is seoððen. *a* **1300** *Cursor M.* 10926 þe dai þat hir was send þis saand O marz [*c* **1375** *Fairf.* march] þe fiue and tuentiand. *c* **1386** CHAUCER *Nun's Pr. T.* 368 The Monthe in which the world bigan That highte Marche. **1390** GOWER *Conf.* III. 371 And afterward the time is schape, To frost, to Snow,.. Til eft that Mars be com ayein. *c* **1440** *Promp. Parv.* 326/1 Marche, monythe, *marcius*. **1500–20** DUNBAR *Poems* lxiv. 11 Merche, with his cauld blastis keyne, Hes slane this gentill herbe. **1601** SHAKS. *Jul. C.* III. i. 1 *Cæs.* The Ides of March are come. *Sooth.* I Cæsar, but not gone. **1712** SWIFT *Jrnl. to Stella* 26 Mar., I forgot to wish you yesterday a happy New Year. You know the twenty-fifth of March is the first day of the year. **1870** MORRIS *Earthly Par.* I. I. 103 Welcome, O March! whose kindly days and dry Make April ready for the throstle's song.

Personified. **1398** TREVISA *Barth. De P.R.* IX. xi. (1495) 355 Marche is paynted as it were a gardyner. **1821** SHELLEY *Dirge for Year* iv, March with grief doth howl and rave. **1842** TENNYSON *Gardener's Dau.* 28 Love..made..that hair More black than ashbuds in the front of March.

b. Proverbs. (See also 2 a, 2 b.)

1598 B. JONSON *Case is Altered* V. iv. (1609) K, Marche faire al, for a faire March is worth a kings ransome. **1624** FLETCHER *Wife for Month* II. i, *Me.* I would chuse March, for I would come in like a Lion. *To.* But you'ld go out like a Lamb, when you went to hanging. *a* **1632** G. HERBERT *Jacula Prudent.* 739 February makes a bridge and March breakes it. **1678** RAY *Prov.* (ed. 2) 44 March many weathers.

2. *attrib.* and *Comb.*: **a.** *simple attrib.*, as ***March air, -bloom, dust, morning, wind***; ***March-hatched*** adj.

1863 TENNYSON *Welcome Alexandra* 16 Clash, ye bells, in the merry *March air! **1877** G. M. HOPKINS *Poems* (1967) 67 Look! *March-bloom, like on mealed-with-yellow sallows! *c* **1530** HEYWOOD *Play of Wether* 622 (Brandl) One bushell of *march dust is worth a kynges raunsome. **1557** TUSSER *100 Points Husb.* cii, A bushel of Marche dust, worth raunsomes of gold. **1685** BOYLE *Salubr. Air* iii. (1690) 55 It is proverbially said in England, that a Peck of March Dust is worth a King's Ransom: So unfrequent is dry Weather during that Month, in our Climate. **1921** F. M. FORD *Let.* 15 July (1965) 135 *March hatched cockerels. **1960** *Farmer & Stockbreeder* 5 Jan. 103/1 My February- and March-hatched pullets started to lay. **1833** TENNYSON *May Queen* Concl. vii, All in the wild *March-morning I heard the angels call. **1530** PALSGR. 484/1, I chyppe, as ones handes do,..with the *Marche-wynde. **1846** *Denham's Coll. Prov.* (Percy Soc.) 36 March winds and April showers Bring forth May flowers.

b. Special comb.: **March ale, beer**, a strong ale or beer brewed in March; also *attrib.*; **March brown**, a fly used in angling; †**March chick** *transf.*, applied to a precocious youth; **March fly**, (*a*) *U.S.*, a dark-coloured, hairy fly of the family Bibionidæ; (*b*) *Austral.*, a blood-sucking horse-fly of the family Tabanidæ; **March hare**, a proverbial type of madness (see HARE *sb.* 1 b);

†**March mad** = mad as a March hare; **March moth**, the moth of a caterpillar infesting plum trees (see quot.); **March violet** [cf. OF. *violette de Mars*], the common garden violet, *Viola odorata*; also *attrib.*

1632 LITHGOW *Trav.* III. 106 Strong *March-Ale, surpassing fine Aqua-vitæ. **1576–7** *Acts Privy Council* 298 Beare..commonly called *March beere. *a* **1704** T. BROWN *Last Observator* in *Collect. Poems* (1705) 101 Hast with thee brought some..Protestant March-Beer, to raise my Fancy? **1856** 'STONEHENGE' *Brit. Rural Sports* 245 The *March-Brown. **1863** OUIDA *Held in Bondage* (1870) 8 Flinging his March brown into the stream. **1599** SHAKS. *Much Ado* I. iii. 58 A very forward *March-chicke. **1895** J. H. & A. B. COMSTOCK *Man. Study of Insects* xix. 450 They [*sc.* Bibionidae] are most common in early spring, which has suggested the name *March-flies; but some occur later in the season. **1907** W. W. FROGGATT *Austral. Insects* 294 They [*sc.* Tabanidæ] are popularly known in Australia as 'March Flies'; in England and America they usually go under the name of 'Horse or Gad Flies'. **1908** E. J. BANFIELD *Confessions of Beachcomber* I. vii. 221 The sluggish 'march' fly..goes about the business of blood-sucking in a lazy..style. **1947** I. L. IDRIESS *Isles of Despair* viii. 58 A vicious March fly with threatening buzz dived at her. **1970** COLLESS & MCALPINE in *Insects of Australia* (Commonwealth Sci. & Industr. Res. Organization) xxiv. 701/2 Tabanidae (March flies, horse flies;..). In Europe and North America, the term 'March fly' is applied to the Bibionidae. **1972** SWAN & PAPP *Common Insects N. Amer.* 603 March flies appear in large numbers early in the spring. **1973** *Islander* (Victoria, B.C.) 12 Aug. 2/1 Many a March-fly-bitten mango packer..longs to pick peaches where there are no March flies to worry about, only wasps. **14..** *Blowbol's Test.* (MS. Rawl. C 86 lf. 111 b), Thanne þey begynne to swere and to stare, And be as braynles as a *Marshe hare. **1526** SKELTON *Magnyf.* 930 As mery as a Marche hare. *a* **1529** —— *Replycacion* 35, I saye, thou madde Marche hare. *a* **1619** FLETCHER *Mad Lover* I. i, Keep him darke, He will run *March mad else. *a* **1625** —— *Noble Gent.* I. i, He is March mad: Farewell Monsieur. **1890** MISS E. A. ORMEROD *Injur. Insects* (ed. 2) 335 *March Moth. *Anisopteryx æscularia*, Schiff. **1578** LYTE *Dodoens* II. i. 148 The sweete Violet is called..in English Violets, the garden Violet, the sweete Violet, and the *Marche Violet. **1601** HOLLAND *Pliny* II. 621 It turneth into a March Violet colour.

march (mɑːtʃ), *sb.*[3] Forms: 3–7 marche, 6–7 *Sc.* merch(e, 3– march. Pl. 1, 4–6 marchis, 5 marchez, -ys, 6 marces, marchesse, marchies, *Sc.* marchis, merche(i)s, mer(s)chis, mairches, 4– marches. [a. F. *marche* fem., a Com. Rom. word = Pr., Sp., Pg., It. *marca*, ad. Teut. **markâ* (OHG., OS. *marka*, OE. *mearc*): see MARK *sb.*[1]]

1. Boundary, frontier, border. **a.** The border or frontier of a country. Hence, a tract of land on the border of a country, or a tract of debatable land separating one country from another. Often *collect. plural*, esp. with reference to the portions of England bordering respectively on Scotland and on Wales. Now *Hist.* and *arch.*

In early examples *the March* (*of Wales*) is an etymological rendering of *Mercia*. *Court of* (*the*) *Marches*: see quot. 1848.

c **1290** *S. Eng. Leg.* I. 345/2 He was kyng in Engelonde: of þe Marche of Walis. **1297** R. GLOUC. (Rolls) 60 þe king of westsex and of kent & of norþhomber..& þe kyng of þe march þat was here amidde. **1375** BARBOUR *Bruce* XVI. 357 Of the marchis than had he The gouernale and the pouste. **1387** TREVISA *Higden* (Rolls) II. 61 Schroysbury is a citee vppon Seuarn in þe marche of Engelond and of Wales. *a* **1400–50** *Alexander* 913 þan was a man in Messadone in þe marche duellid, A proued prince. **1425** *Rolls of Parlt.* IV. 276/2 Wardeyns of oure Est and West Marches. **1523** LD. BERNERS *Froiss.* I. cxxxvii. 165 The quene of Englande..was as thanne in the marchesse of the Northe, about Yorke. **1532–3** *Act 24 Hen. VIII*, c. 12 §2 Any personne..resiaunte..within any the Kinges saide Dominions or Marches of the same. **1560** DAUS tr. *Sleidane's Comm.* 50 Henry Zutphan was put to death..by them of Dietmary, which is in the marces of Germany. **1577–87** HOLINSHED *Chron.* III. 1213/1 The lord Hunsdon lord warden of the east marches, and gouernor of Berwike. **1584** WHITGIFT *Let. to Burleigh* in Fuller *Ch. Hist.* IX. (1655) 157 Sure I am it is most usuall in the Court of the Marches (Archers rather) whereof I have the best experience. **1602** WARNER *Alb. Eng.* Epit. (1612) 355 The Pictes..then occupying those parts which we now call the middle Marches, betwixt the English and Scots. **1612** DRAYTON *Poly-olb.* vii. 8 The Herefordian floods..with their superfluous waste Manure the batfull March. *c* **1630** RISDON *Surv. Devon* §225 (1810) 238 And 'twas 'twixt Britts and Saxons made the march. **1655** FULLER *Ch. Hist.* IX. vi. §51 This Oath..is usually tendered in Chancery, Court of Requests, Councel of Marches, and Councel in the North. **1848** WHARTON *Law Lex.* s.v., Court of Marches, an abolished tribunal in Wales, where pleas of debt or damages, not above the value of 50*l.*, were tried and determined. **1859** TENNYSON *Geraint & Enid* 41 He craved a fair permission to depart And there defend his marches. **1867** FREEMAN *Norm. Conq.* (1876) I. iv. 157 Granted in fief..as a march or border territory. **1875** STUBBS *Const. Hist.* II. xvi. 345 Hugh came into collision with..the rest of the rival lords of the marches.

b. The boundary of an estate; the boundary dividing one estate from another. Chiefly *Sc.*

1540 in *5th Rep. Hist. MSS. Comm.* 609/1 The rycht meithis and merchis is and salbe..betuix the saidis landis. **1637–50** ROW *Hist. Kirk* (Wodrow Soc.) 196 No man shall ever let me see where any of the apostles sat as judges to other men, or to sett in marches, or to divyde men's lands. **1818** HOGG *Brownie of B.* vii, It was..in the march between two lairds' lands, that he preached that day. **1839** DE QUINCEY *Recoll. Lakes* Wks. 1862 II. 2 Woodlands..intervening the different estates with natural sylvan marches. **1886** *Act 49 & 50 Vict.* c. 29 §21 Any questions relating to the boundaries or marches between crofters' holdings.

†**c.** A boundary mark, landmark. *Obs.*

1513 DOUGLAS *Æneis* XII. xiv. 30 Ane ald crag stane..Quhilk..was liggand neyr, A marche set in that grund..Of twa feildis. **1577** HOLINSHED *Chron., Hist. Scot.* 255/2 In the middest of Stanemoore there shall be a Crosse set vp, with the king of Englandes image on the one side, and the king of Scotlands on the other, to signifie that the one is marche to England, and the other to Scotland.

d. *fig.*

1637 RUTHERFORD *Lett.* lxxxii. (1862) I. 207 When..ye are in the utmost..border of time and shall put your foot within the march of eternity. **1786** A. GIB *Sacred Contempl.* 269 A march ought to be fixed between his private and his public obedience. **1879** G. MACDONALD *P. Faber* III. xvi. 265 Over the march of two worlds, that of the imagination, and that of fact, her soul hovered fluttering.

e. ***to redd, rid, ride the marches***: see REDD *v.*[2] 2 c, RID, *v.*, RIDE *v.*

†**2.** Used for: Country, territory. [Cf. L. *fines.*]

13.. *K. Alis.* 3019 He hath y-wonne..Theo marche of Fraunse, and of Spayne, And Tolouse, and eke Almayne. **1377** LANGL. *P. Pl.* B. xv. 438 And þorw myracles..al þat marche he [Austyn] torned to cryst. **1470–85** MALORY *Arthur* I. x, Vlfius & Brastias..shold haue suche chere as myghte be made them in tho marchys. *c* **1489** CAXTON *Sonnes of Aymon* vi. 138 Blessed be the hour that ye were borne, and cam in to thyse marches.

3. In renderings of continental names of territories. †**a.** Applied to the MARK of Brandenburg (*obs.*). **b.** = It. *Marca* (see quot. 1875).

1726 LEONI *Alberti's Archit.* I. 30/2 In the March of Ancona,..they find a white Stone, which [etc.]. **1758** *Ann. Reg.* 20 Richlieu..made his way into..the old marche of Brandenburg. **1875** *Encycl. Brit.* II. 9/2 Ancona..forms part of the old district of the Marches, which passed from the dominion of the Pope to that of Victor Emmanuel in 1860. The Marches comprise the March of Ancona on the north and the March of Fermo on the south.

4. *attrib.* and *Comb.*, as (sense 1 b) ***march-balk***, ***-dike***, ***-ditch***, ***-fence***, ***-line***; (sense 1 a) ***march*** †***captain***, †***cause***, †***garrison***, ***law***, ***shire***, ***-treason*** (arch.); †**march-day**, ? a court held to try cases of infraction of border laws; †**march-gat** (? GATE *sb.*[2]), ? a way across a frontier; †**march parts, -party**, the marches; †**march-ward**, 'a warden of the marches' (Webster 1864). Also MARCH-LAND, MARCH-MAN, MARCH-STONE.

1683 *Fountainhall's Decis. Lds. Counc. Session* (1759) I. 224 In regard the witness had deponed upon her tilling and riveing out the *march-balk. **1537** *St. Papers Hen. VIII*, II. 452 Every of His Gracis subjectis, having landes in like places of daungier, bee orderid to departe therwith to *marche capitayns. **1538** *Ibid.* III. 37 Marches capitaynes. **1537** *Ibid.* 489 That ther were, in every marche, wardens..whiche shulde have auctorytye..to here and redresse all robberyes, *marche causeis [etc.]. **1900** A. LANG *Hist. Scot.* I. x. 293 In ruling the Borders, making raids and holding *March-days. **1794** R. HERON *Gen. View Hebudæ* 90 Let the landlords take upon themselves the expence of building every where sufficient *march-dykes. **1830** W. CARLETON *Traits Peas.* (1843) I. 118 This river..was the *march ditch, or *merin* between our farms. **1882** *Bell's Dict. Law Scot.* 619/2 A tenant..is bound..to maintain *march-fences erected by the landlord during the lease. **1537** *St. Papers Hen. VIII*, II. 429 Distrusting to commytt the custodie of dyvers of the *marche garrisons to any of this landes birthe. *a* **1400–50** *Alexander* 5076 He leuys all þe *march gats I neuend ȝow before. **1612** DAVIES *Why Ireland*, etc. 123 That no Englishman be ruled in the definition of their debates by the *March-Law or the Brehon Law. **1886** G. MACDONALD *What's Mine's Mine* III. ix. 158 If he did not everywhere know where the *march-line fell, at least he knew perfectly where it ought to fall. **14..** *Chevy Chase* 120 (Skeat) For towe such captayns as slayne wear thear on the *march parti shall neuer be non. *Ibid.* 138 Ther was neuer a tym on the *marche partes [etc.]. **1917** *Eng. Hist. Rev.* Oct. 483 The Warden..had simply taken over certain duties hitherto discharged by the sheriff in the *March shires. **1805** SCOTT *Last Minstr.* IV. xxiv, We claim from thee William of Deloraine, That he may suffer *march-treason pain.

march (mɑːtʃ), *sb.*[4] Also 6 martch. [a. F. *marche*, vbl. noun from *marcher*: see MARCH *v.*[2]]

I. Action of marching.

1. a. The action of marching; the regular forward movement together and in time of a body of troops. Also, the orderly forward movement of a company, an exploring party, a procession, etc.; also, a procession organised as an expression of (esp. political) dissent, or to draw attention to a particular problem, etc.; cf. *hunger-march*.

1590 SIR J. SMYTH *Disc. Weapons* Ded. 8 Also, whereas it hath been the vse of all great Captaines and Chieftaines, vpon anie long march and enterprise intended. **1591** SHAKS. *1 Hen. VI*, IV. iii. 8 Two mightier Troopes..Which ioyn'd with him, and made their march for Burdeaux. **1667** MILTON *P.L.* v. 775 For whom all this haste Of midnight march. **1672** SIR W. TALBOT (*title*) The Discoveries of John Lederer, in three several Marches from Virginia to the West of Carolina. **1781** SIMES *Mil. Guide* (ed. 3) 12 They [pioneers] are to..make preparations for the march of the army. **1837** W. IRVING *Capt. Bonneville* I. 159 A march of three or four days..brought Captain Bonneville to..Jackson's Hole. **1850** GROTE *Greece* II. lxx. (1888) VII. 270 Three days of additional march brought them to the Euphrates. **1908**, etc. [see *hunger-march* s.v. HUNGER *sb.* 4 e]. **1952** *Ann. Reg. 1951* 105 In May the Commando arranged a symbolic 'march' to Capetown to present a formal petition to Parliament. **1962** [see ALDERMASTON]. **1970** K. GILES *Death in Church* ii. 29 He's a crank and a fire-brand... Not a 'march' goes by without him carrying a banner. **1973** *Black World* Nov. 42/2 Perhaps the most arresting result of the thousands of 'sit-ins' and 'marches' by Afro-Americans in the early Sixties..has been the obligation and opportunity of the entire world to re-evaluate the contributions of the Black American to world society.

b. Phrases. ***column of march*** (see quot. 1876). ***line of march***: direction or route of marching; *transf.*, course of travelling, way. ***in*** (†***a full***) ***march***, ***on*** or ***upon*** (***a*** or ***their***) ***march***: marching.

1639 *Articles Mil. Discipl.* 11 Every man is to keep his own rank and file upon the march. **1667** MILTON *P.L.* I. 413 When he entic'd Israel in Sittim on their march from Nile. **1707** *Lond. Gaz.* No. 4353/1 The Duke of Savoy's Army are in a full March for this Place. **1734** tr. *Rollin's Anc. Hist.* (1827) II. II. ii. 2 They attacked the Carthaginians, who were upon their march. **1780** A. HAMILTON *Wks.* (1886) VIII. 11 All the army is in march toward you. **1781** SIMES *Milit. Guide* (ed. 3) 12 The routes must be so formed, that no column cross another on the march. **1835** W. IRVING *Tour Prairies* xviii, They crossed the line of our march without..perceiving us. **1844** H. H. WILSON *Brit. India* II. 236 Detachments of the 65th regiment,..on their march to join the 4th division. **1860** TYNDALL *Glac.* I. xxvii. 202 The snow above us, broke across, forming a fissure parallel to our line of march. **1875** JOWETT *Plato* (ed. 2) III. 414 Whether in actual battle or on a march. **1876** VOYLE & STEVENSON *Milit. Dict.*, *Column of March*, a formation assumed by troops on the line of march.

c. Applied to steady progression of animals on a long journey. Also, with reference to persons, a long and toilsome walk.

1691 RAY *Creation* II. (1692) 124 The swiftness and continuance of the march, for which this Animal [the camel] is almost indefatigable. **1697** DRYDEN *Virg. Georg.* IV. 86 The Motions of their hasty Flight attend; And know to Floods, or Woods, their airy March they [Bees] bend. **1705** ADDISON *Italy* 238 We came to the Roots of the Mountain, and had a very troublesome March to gain the Top of it. **1832** LYTTON *Eugene A.* I. ii, I have had a long march of it. **1888** *Harper's Mag.* July 198/2, I knew they [*sc.* elephants] would be on the march again before daylight.

d. In comb. with following adv., forming nouns of action to phrases of the verb, as ***march out***, a sortie; ***march past*** (*spec.* see quot. 1876).

1863 *Illustr. Lond. News* 27 June 706/1 During the march past the band played. **1869** A. W. WARD tr. *Curtius' Hist. Greece* II. III. i. 273 Themistocles insisted upon a second march-out against the enemy. **1876** VOYLE & STEVENSON *Milit. Dict.*, *March Past*, an expression made use of when a regiment or any larger body of men pass in review order before the sovereign or reviewing officer. **1924** O. W. CAMPBELL *Shelley & Unromantics* II. 10 Telling them [*sc.* Shelley's friends] over is like calling for a march past of the Seven Deadly Sins. **1928** *Manch. Guardian Wkly.* 10 Aug. 101/1 The march past of the pilgrims in the Grand Place of Ypres. **1961** *Times* 5 June 3/5 The teams [of swimmers] risked a premature ducking by a carefully routed march-past.

2. *transf.* and *fig.* Advance, forward movement, progress. Also, course or direction of advance.

a. With reference to the 'journey' of life.

a **1625** FLETCHER *Hum. Lieut.* III. v, Our lives are but our martches to our graves. **1804** CAMPBELL *Soldier's Dream* iv, I flew to the pleasant fields travers'd so oft In life's morning march, when my bosom was young. **1816** BYRON *Ch. Har.* III. xcviii, We may resume The march of our existence. **1871** MORLEY *Voltaire* (1886) 6 Voltaire's march was prepared for him, before he was born.

b. Of physical things.

1683 A. SNAPE *Anat. Horse* I. xxviii. 63 [The Veins] continue their march through the Allantoides to the Chorion... Their [*sc.* Arteries] march and insertions are the same with those of the Vein. **1794** COWPER *Needless Alarm* 29 The sun, accomplishing his early march. **1899** *Allbutt's Syst. Med.* VI. 108 Mediastinal cancer..makes its onward march involving whatever may come in its path. *Ibid.* VII. 260 Then followed a march of a sensation of pins and needles down the opposite side of the body. *Ibid.* 290 No exact description is given of the march of the spasms.

c. Of time, events, population, etc.

a **1797** H. WALPOLE *Mem. Geo. III* (1845) I. i. 3 The regular march of history. **1798** MALTHUS *Popul.* (1817) II. 40 The march of the population in both periods seems to have been nearly the same. **1833** LAMB *Elia* Ser. II. Pref., He did not conform to the march of time. **1833** *Fraser's Mag.* VIII. 343 The common person [is] sadly puzzled to understand the ordonnance and march of the plot. **1852** GROTE *Greece* II. lxxii. (1856) IX. 259 Doubtless each [Lysandrian Dekarchy] had its own peculiar march: some were less tyrannical; but perhaps some even more tyrannical [than the Thirty at Athens]. **1871** FREEMAN *Norm. Conq.* (1876) IV. xviii. 108 These Northumbrian disturbances had little bearing on the general march of events.

d. Of knowledge, etc., esp. in the phrase ***march of intellect*** or ***mind***. Also *attrib.*

Very common (esp. in ironical allusion) between 1827 (the date of the foundation of the Society for the Diffusion of Useful Knowledge) and 1850.

[**1775** BURKE *Speech moving Conciliation with Colonies* 51 The march of the human mind is slow.] **1818** KEATS *Let.* 3 May (1931) I. 157 It proves there is really a grand march of intellect. **1821** LADY MORGAN *Italy* I. viii. 170 Impediments are now thrown in the march of mind... To retrograde, not to advance, is the order of the times. **1827** *Gentl. Mag.* XCVII. II. p. ii, What is 'the march of intellect'—The mighty march of mind? **1833** R. H. FROUDE *Rem.* (1838) I. 309, I tried hard to get up the march-of-mind phraseology about pictures and statues. **1844** S. R. MAITLAND *Dark Ages* 185 He was quite a march-of-intellect man. **1852** TENNYSON *Ode Wellington* 167 And drill the raw world for the march of mind, Till crowds at length be sane and crowns be just.

3. a. *Mil.* The portion of marching done continuously; the distance covered by troops in one day. ***forced march***: see FORCED *ppl. a.* 3.

1594 SHAKS. *Rich. III*, v. ii. 13 From Tamworth thither, is but one dayes march. **1650** R. STAPYLTON *Strada's Low C. Warres* VII. 77 He by long Marches passing the Rhine came to Delph in Holland. **1724** DE FOE *Mem. Cavalier* (1840) 171 It gave the king a full day's march of him. **1813** WELLINGTON in Gurw. *Desp.* (1838) X. 431 The army are.. within two or three marches of the Ebro. **1895** *United Service Mag.* July 430 The precautions for the night march to prevent a light from being seen.

fig. **1845** LONGF. *Belfry of Bruges, Carillon*, Still I heard those magic numbers, As they loud proclaimed the flight And stolen marches of the night.

b. Phrases. ***to* (*gain, get*) *a march on*** or ***upon***: to get ahead of to the extent of a march. ***to steal a march* (*on*** or ***upon*)**: to gain a march by stealth; often *fig.*

1707 *Lond. Gaz.* No 4353/3 His Royal Highness hath gain'd a March upon Monsieur de Guebriant. **1745** H. WALPOLE *Lett.* (1846) II. 59 The young Pretender.. has got a march on General Cope. **1771** SMOLLETT *Humph. Cl.* I. 127 She yesterday wanted to steal a march of poor Liddy. **1833** MARRYAT *P. Simple* xxiii, We must be off early,.. and steal a long march upon them. **1844** POE *Oblong Box* in *Godey's Lady's Bk.* Sept. 133/1 He evidently intended to steal a march upon me, and smuggle a fine picture to New York, under my very nose. **1950** T. S. ELIOT *Cocktail Party* II. 93 He's quite triumphant Because he thinks he's stolen a march on her.

4. a. The regular and uniform step of a body of men, esp. of troops. Also with qualifying adj., as ***double, quick, slow march***. See also QUICK MARCH 1.

1773–83 HOOLE *Orl. Fur.* XVI. 566 So loud their march, the Scots suspended hear, They leave their ranks and stain their fame with fear. **1820** SHELLEY *Ode to Naples* 127 Hear ye the march as of the Earth-born Forms Arrayed against the everliving Gods? **1889** *Infantry Drill* 25 The length of which [plummet-string].. must be as follows for the different degrees of march. *Ibid.* 29 The Slow March. *Ibid.* 31 The Quick March. *Ibid.* 32 The Double March.

b. *fig.* Of verse: Rhythmic movement.

1635–56 COWLEY *Davideis* I. 450 Till all the Parts and Words their Places take And with just Marches Verse and Musick make. **1737** POPE *Hor. Epist.* II. i. 269 But Dryden taught to join The varying verse, the full-resounding line, The long majestic march, and Energy divine.

5. *Mil.* A beating of the drum in a particular rhythm as an accompaniment to the marching of troops.

c **1572** GASCOIGNE *Fruites Warre*, L'enuoié, If drummes once sounde a lustie martch in deede, Then farewell bookes, for he will trudge with speede. **1617** MORYSON *Itin.* III. 267 A man can hardly distinguish betweene the beating of the drums of the Sweitzers, and Germans, saue that the former march is more graue and slow. **1727–41** CHAMBERS *Cycl.* s.v. *Drum*, There are divers beats of the Drum: as the march, double march, assembly, charge [etc.]. **1781** SIMES *Milit. Guide* (ed. 3) 12 The general beats at 2; the assemblé at 3; and the march in 20 minutes after. *Ibid.*, The drummers are to beat a march, and fifers play at the head of the line.

6. *Mus.* **a.** A tune or composition of marked rhythm (of which the rhythmical drum-beats, sense 5, originally formed the essential, and still often form a subsidiary, part), designed to accompany the marching of troops, etc.; also any composition of similar character and form; usually in common time, and with a subsidiary intermediate section or 'trio'. So also ***march past. dead march***: see DEAD D. 2; also ***funeral march. rogue's march, wedding march*** (see ROGUE, WEDDING).

1603 DEKKER *King's Entert.* (1604) E 2, Nine Trumpets, and a Kettle Drum, did very sprightly & actiuely sound the Danish March. **1706** ADDISON *Rosamond* I. iv, 'Tis Henry's March! the tune I know. **1719** *Dancing-Master* II. 29 Duke of Marlborough's March. *Ibid.* 221 The Foot-guards march: Or, Boatswain William's Delight. **1784** COWPER *Task* IV. 647 He hates the field, in which no fife or drum Attends him, drives his cattle to a march [etc.]. **1822** BYRON *Werner* IV. i. 272 I'll play you King Gustavus' march. **1839** LONGF. *Psalm of Life* iv, Our hearts.. Still, like muffled drums, are beating Funeral marches to the grave. **1876** VOYLE & STEVENSON *Milit. Dict.* 244/1 Each regiment in the British service has its special march for marching past. **1896** NEWNHAM-DAVIS *Three Men & a God* 77, I could hear Kelley.. whistling the regimental march-past.

b. *attrib.*, as in ***march-movement, -time***.

1864 BROWNING *Dîs aliter visum* viii, Schumann's our music-maker now; Has his march-movement youth and mouth?

7. *Euchre.* (See quot.) [Cf. It. *marcio* 'a lurch or maiden set at any game' (Florio).]

1886 *Euchre: how to play it* 108 *March*, where all the tricks are made by one side. **1895** in *Funk's Stand. Dict.* (with phrase *to make a march*).

II. Various senses adopted from F. *marche*.

†**8.** Foot-print (of an otter). *Obs. rare*$^{-1}$. (Cf. MARK *sb.*^{1} 13 c.)

c **1410** *Master of Game* (MS. Digby 182) x, Men clepeth þat þe stepes or þe marches of þe Otyr, as men clepeth þe traces of þe herte.

9. *Chess*, etc. The move of a 'man'.

1672 BARBIER *Saul's Fam. Game Chesse* iv, What is the draught or marche of each peece. **1850** *Bohn's Handbk. Games* 503 (Polish Draughts) The march of the Pawn.. is the same as in the English game.

fig. **1587** GREENE *Carde of Fancie* (1593) E, Houering betweene feare and hope, hee began the assault with this march. Madame (quoth he) for that [etc.].

10. *Weaving.* (See quot.)

1875 KNIGHT *Dict. Mech.* 1393/2 *March* (Weaving), one of the short laths laid across the treadles under the shafts.

march (mɑːtʃ), *v.*^{1} Forms: 4 **marchen**, 4–6 **marche**, 6 *Sc.* **mairch**, **mearch**, 6–7 **merch**, 5– **march**. [In sense 1, a. OF. *marchir*, f. *marche* MARCH *sb.*^{3} In sense 2, f. MARCH *sb.*^{3}; cf. obs. F. *marcher* to bound (Rabelais).]

1. *intr.* To border *upon*; to have a common frontier *with*. Formerly also †const. *to, unto*. Said of countries, estates, etc., and hence of their rulers, owners, or inhabitants.

c **1330** R. BRUNNE *Chron. Wace* (Rolls) 7929 He graunted þem þanne to haue Southsex, Oxenfordschire, & Middelsex, ffor þey marchen vpon Kent. **1375** BARBOUR *Bruce* I. 99 Till occupy Landis, that war till him marcheand. ? *a* **1412** LYDG. *Two Merch.* 16 This riche lond.. With Surry marchith toward thorient. **1481** CAXTON *Myrr.* II. ii. 66 Europe.. endureth fro the weste unto the north, & marcheth vnto Asie. **1515** *St. Papers Hen. VIII*, II. 19 Orayly is the strongeyst Iryshe rebell that marcheyth with the countye of Meathe. *c* **1530** LD. BERNERS *Arth. Lyt. Bryt.* (1814) 100 Ioynynge to thys erledome there marched a duchy. **1598** HAKLUYT *Voy.* I. 65 The.. Don, vpon the banke whereof marcheth a certain prince. **1818** SCOTT *Hrt. Midl.* xxviii, She displayed so much kindness to Jeanie Deans, (because she herself, being a Merse woman, *marched* with Mid-Lothian, in which Jeanie was born) [etc.]. **1822** GALT *Provost* xl. (1868) 117 A piece of ground that marched with the spot whereon it was intended to construct the new building. **1883** ARNOLD-FORSTER in *19th Cent.* Sept. 399 Nor do they refrain from fighting because they march on each other and do a good business across the frontier. **1889** *Times* 25 Feb. 9/4 The frontiers of Dakota, Montana, and Washington march with the Canadian Dominion.

†**b.** ? To join. *Obs.*

The quots. may possibly belong to MARCH *v.*^{2}

1377 LANGL. *P. Pl.* B. Prol. 63 Many of þis maistres Freris mowe clothen hem at lykyng, For here money and marchandise marchen [**1362** meeten ofte] togideres. *a* **1578** LINDESAY (Pitscottie) *Chron. Scot.* (S.T.S.) I. 270 The Inglischemen war all come ower the brige and the wangaird was neir mearchant togither. Then the trumpitis blew.. and the wangairdis ioynitt togither.

†**2.** ? To serve for the defence of a frontier. *Obs.*

1577–87 HARRISON *England* I. xii. in *Holinshed*, At this Poulruan is a tower of force, marching against the tower on Fawy side.

†**3.** *trans.* To fix the bounds of; to mark the boundaries of with landmarks. *Sc. Obs.*

1541 *Aberdeen Reg.* XVII. (Jam.), The Baillie ordanit the lynaris to pass to the ground of the said tenement, and lyne and marche the same. **1588** *Burgh Rec. Glasgow* (1876) I. 121 And to stob and merche the samyn [landis] that the quantitie may be knawin. **1659** A. HAY *Diary* (S.H.S.) 42, [I] did set fut-stons and merch and meith all the propertie of Locarthill wher it is contiguous wt Symontoun.

march (mɑːtʃ), *v.*^{2} Also 6 **mersh**, **merch**, 6–7 **martch**. [a. F. *marcher*, orig. to tread, trample (12th c.), hence, to walk. In the specific military application the word has been adopted not only in Eng. but in other European langs., as Sp., Pg. *marchar*, It. *marciare*, G. *marschiren*, Du. *marcheren*, Da. *marschere*, Sw. *marschera*.

The etymology of F. *marcher* is obscure; the prevailing view is that the oldest recorded sense 'to trample' was developed from a sense 'to hammer', and that the word represents a Gaulish Latin **marcāre*, f. L. *marcus* hammer.]

1. a. *intr.* To walk in a military manner with regular and measured tread; of a body of men or troops, to walk in step, to go forward with a regular and uniform movement. Also, to begin to walk in step; to start on a march, to set out from quarters. Also with advbs., as *away, forth, forward, off, on, out, past*.

? **1515** *Scotish Field* 146 in *Percy Fol.* I. 219 Then he bowneth him boldlye ouer the broad waters, & manlye him Marcheth [Lyme MS. (Chetham Misc. 1856 II) *reads* marketh] to the Mill feelde. *a* **1548** HALL *Chron., Rich. III* 39 The duke with all his power mershed through the forest of deane. **1591** *Garrard's Art Warre* 54 They.. which march in the formost ranckes. **1617** MORYSON *Itin.* III. 267 When they are to march, the law commands them to lay aside all priuate quarrels. **1710** *Lond. Gaz.* No. 4710/1 The Garrison marched out.. in the Forenoon. **1742** POPE *Dunc.* IV. 101 There march'd the bard and blockhead, side by side. **1781** SIMES *Milit. Guide* (ed. 3) 12 The army marches to-morrow. *Ibid.*, The field-pieces march with the columns. **1828** SCOTT *F.M. Perth* xxxiv, The champions were now ordered to march in their turns around the lists. **1844** H. H. WILSON *Brit. India* II. 453 The troops marched against the Arabs. **1855** TENNYSON *Maud* I. v. 10 Singing of men that in battle array,.. March with banner and bugle and fife, To the death. **1860** *Illustr. Lond. News* 23 June 598/3 When her Majesty returns to the Royal standard the volunteers will march past in quick time.

†**b.** Conjugated with *be*. *Obs.*

1597 SHAKS. *2 Hen. IV*, II. i. 187 Fifteene hundred Foot, fiue hundred Horse Are march'd vp to my Lord of Lancaster. **1648** *Hamilton Papers* (Camden) 206 His tertia, consisting of 5 regiments, is alreadie marcht. **1707** FREIND *Peterborow's Cond. Sp.* (ed. 2, corrected) 220, I hope Collonel Wills is March'd.

c. *fig.*

1684 T. HOCKIN *God's Decrees* 352 In the camp, where sin and vice did march uncontroul'd. **1697** DRYDEN *Virg. Georg.* III. 370 The spumy Waves proclaim the watry War; And mounting upwards, with a mighty Roar, March onwards, and insult the rocky Shoar. **1711** ADDISON *Spect.* No. 34 ⁋11 Having thus taken my Resolutions to march on boldly in the Cause of Virtue and good Sense.

d. quasi-*trans.* To go upon (a warfare); to traverse (a distance) in marching. Also rarely *trans.* by ellipsis of *prep.*

1619 SIR J. SEMPILL *Sacrilege Handled* App. 38 Whether we march a Warfare in our Conquering Word, *Dieu et mon droit*; If [etc.]. **1813** T. BUSBY *Lucretius* I. III. 1240 He.. bade his legion march the briny main. **1884** J. COLBORNE *Hicks Pasha* 27 Forty-five miles have to be traversed; this will be marched in three days.

e. *Mil.* Used in the imperative as a word of command. Also ***march on***.

1593 SHAKS. *Rich. II*, III. iii. 61 March on, and marke King Richard how he lookes. **1760** *New Manual Exerc.* (ed. 3) 4 On the Word *March*, the Officers stepping off with their Left-feet [etc.]. **1832** *Regul. Instr. Cavalry* III. 116 Walk, Trot, or Gallop, March. **1833** *Ibid.* I. 21 The word *March*, given singly, at all times denotes that 'slow time' is to be taken.

f. To engage in a protest, etc., march (see MARCH *sb.*^{4} 1 a).

1967 *Freedomways* VII. 102 Where is the Federal Government today as civil rights workers in Louisville face screaming mobs, throwing rocks and bottles at them as they peacefully march to end housing discrimination? **1969** *New Yorker* 14 June 76/3 He has repeatedly been asked to march and picket. **1972** *Times* 19 Oct. 5/7 (*heading*) Doctors march in Vienna.

2. To walk in a steady or deliberate manner; to go, proceed, travel. Also with advbs., as *off, on, out*.

1572 *Lament. Lady Scotland* 332 in *Satir. Poems Reform.* xxxiii, 'Becaus', quod thay, 'that ȝe alone tuik Pryde, And thocht that we suld not marche ȝow besyde'. **1585** T. WASHINGTON tr. *Nicholay's Voy.* II. xxv. 66 If a man did see them [Græcian women] as they do march, he woulde take them to be Nymphes. **1594** T. B. *La Primaud. Fr. Acad.* II. 409 That God hath made them men, and not beastes ramping on the earth, or marching vpon all foure. **1604** E. G[RIMSTONE] *D'Acosta's Hist. Indies* I. iii. 13 In my trauell passing the great gulfes of the Ocean, and marching by other regions of so strange lands. **1634** W. TIRWHYT tr. *Balzac's Lett.* (vol. I.) 77 From thence I march into a meddow. **1735** POPE *Donne Sat.* iv. 249 Thus finish'd,.. They march, to prate their hour before the Fair. **1770** MME. D'ARBLAY *Early Diary* 7 Feb., Tea being over, we marched into a larger room, and minuets were begun. **1810** *Splendid Follies* I. 156 Do march on and shew the village lions. **1852** MRS. STOWE *Uncle Tom's C.* xxv, Miss Ophelia marched straight to her own chamber. **1896** A. E. HOUSMAN *Shropshire Lad* xvii, Now in Maytime to the wicket Out I march with bat and pad.

fig. *c* **1586** C'TESS PEMBROKE *Ps.* L. vii, Loe, thou see'st I march another pace And come with truth thy falshood to disclose.

3. In various transf. and fig. senses. **a.** Of inanimate things: To travel, go with a steady and regular movement.

1604 E. G[RIMSTONE] *D'Acosta's Hist. Indies* I. ii. 7 This space and region by which they faine that stars do continually march and rowle. **1632** LITHGOW *Trav.* IX. 392, I haue seene in an euening march along for Recreation aboue 60 coaches. **1852** CLOUGH *Songs in Absence* i. 6 Without a strain the great ship marches by.

b. To advance, make progress. Also ***to march on***.

1648 J. BEAUMONT *Psyche* III. lxiii, So wrought this nimble Artist, and admir'd Her self to see the Work march on so fast. **1856** KANE *Arct. Expl.* I. xvii. 200 His symptoms marched rapidly to their result. **1868** J. H. BLUNT *Ref. Ch. Eng.* I. 250 After this events marched quickly. **1882** SERJT. BALLANTINE *Exper.* ii. 14 Bricks and mortar, marching in all directions, have eaten up many a green field. **1884** *Pall Mall G.* 12 Aug. 3/1 The Congress at Versailles is at last beginning to march. **1889** SKRINE *Mem. E. Thring* 203 It was the president who made the enterprise march.

†**c.** To be assigned to a specified rank or position in a series; to 'rank' *with, after*, etc. *Obs.*

1600 E. BLOUNT tr. *Conestaggio* 69 Making them march in one degree of equall iustice with their inferiours. **1625** HART *Anat. Ur.* I. iv. 37 My purpose is, first to propound some reasons against the same: and in the next place shall march some authorities of the learned. **1630** *R. Johnson's Kingd. & Commw.* 96 Nor are our Cities of sufficiencie to march in the first ranke of magnificence. **1640** BP. HALL *Episc.* III. i. 208 These [Elders] sometimes marched with the highest offices; so we have Elders and Iudges,.. Princes and Elders.

†**d.** ***to march off***: (*a*) to become a bankrupt; (*b*) to die. *Obs.*

1683 LUTTRELL *Brief Rel.* (1857) I. 251 Mr. Temple, an eminent banker.., is lately broke for £150,000, and tis thought severall of that calling will march off also. **1693–4** WOOD *Life* Jan. (O.H.S.) III. 441 Lord Sidney.. was taken also with a fit, and would have marched off, had it not been for.. Dr. Radcliff his physitian.

4. a. *trans.* (causatively). To cause to march or move in military order.

1595 SHAKS. *John* III. i. 246 [Shall we] Vn-sweare faith sworne, and on the marriage bed Of smiling peace to march a bloody hoast? **1642** in *Buccleuch MSS.* (Hist. MSS. Comm.) I. 527 There are great numbers both of horse and foot raised and marched into divers parts of this our Kingdom. **1701** LUTTRELL *Brief Rel.* (1857) V. 9 That they may be ready to march them on any occasion. **1724** DE FOE *Mem. Cavalier* (1840) 66 As they were wheeled, or marched, or retreated by their officers.

b. To cause (a person) to walk or go, to force to go, to conduct. Also ***to march off***.

1884 *Manch. Exam.* 4 June 4/7 Many a Persian peasant.. has been marched off captive by Turcoman slave-raiders. **1896** 'M. FIELD' *Attila* II. 45, I should be glad to march you to the gate.

march, obs. or dial. form of MARSH *sb.*^{1}

marchal(e, -all, obs. forms of MARSHAL.

marchalsey, -sy(e, etc., vars. MARSHALCY, -SEA.

marchand, -ant, etc.: see MERCHANT, etc.

‖**marchantia** (mɑːˈkæntɪə). [mod.L.: f. the name of a French botanist N. Marchant (*a*1678).] A genus of plants including the liverwort (*M. polymorpha*); a plant of this genus.
1861 H. MACMILLAN *Footn. Nature* 51 The most interesting of all the scale-mosses is the common marchantia or liverwort (*Marchantia polymorpha*).

marchas(s)ite, obs. forms of MARCASITE.

marchasye, obs. form of MARSHALSEA.

marchaulcy, -ausy: see MARSHALCY, -SEA.

marchaund, -aunt, etc.: see MERCHANT, etc.

marche: see MARCH *sb.*[1], wild celery.

marcheis, obs. pl. MARCH *sb.*[2], obs. f. MARQUIS.

marchell, obs. form of MARSHAL.

‖**märchen** (ˈmɛːrçən). Also **Märchen**. [G., fairy-tale, f. MHG. *merechyn* short verse narrative, f. OHG. *mārī*, MHG. *mære* news, tale (f. OHG. *mārī*, MHG. *mære* famous, MERE *a.*[1]) + the dim. suffix OHG. *-chīn* -KIN.] A folk-tale or story. Usu. const. as *pl.* Also *attrib.*
1871 L. M. ALCOTT *Good Wives* x. 130 You and I will read these pleasant little Märchen together. **1885** *Athenæum* 22 Aug. 230/2 The Punjaub tales..are, naturally, rather modern and civilized..more so than Servian and Romaic *Märchen.* **1902** A. LANG in *Folk-Lore* XIII. 359 Mr. J. G. Frazer..starts from the idea so common in *Märchen*, of the person whose 'soul', 'life', or 'strength', is secretly hidden in an animal, plant, or other object. **1908** *Mod. Philol.* V. 402 There is no doubt..that the story of the shadowy Anglian king Offa, blended with *märchen* elements, was well known in England in the time of Cynewulf. **1928** W. W. LAWRENCE *Beowulf & Epic Trad.* 166 Study of *märchen*, both for their own sake and for the light that they throw upon sophisticated literature. **1950** H. L. LORIMER *Homer & Monuments* viii. 515 Outside the apologoi the poet of the *Odyssey* prefers to eliminate elements of the *märchen* type. **1963** BROWN & FOOTE *Early Eng. & Norse Stud.* 189 The French märchen-material. *Ibid.*, Oriental märchen-motives. **1964** C. S. LEWIS *Discarded Image* vi. 135 The Gnomes are closer to the Dwarfs of *märchen.*

marcher[1] (ˈmɑːtʃə(r)). *Obs.* exc. *Hist.* Also 5 **marchere, marcheyre, marchowr**, 5–6 **marchier**, 5, 7 **marchour**, 7 **murcheour, -iour**. [f. MARCH *sb.*[3] + -ER; there may have been an AF. **marchier.*]
†**1.** One whose territory adjoins that of another. Const. *to.* [Cf. med.L. *marchio.*] *Obs.*
c **1440** *Partonope* 5044, 5047 Ther ys no lord that now ys heere But he ys in lond A marchere To som of lords afore sayd. Eche of hem therfore wold be wyll payde To haue hym a kyng to whom he ys marcheyre.
2. An inhabitant of a march or border district.
1470 in *10th Rep. Hist. MSS. Comm.* App. v. 308 Who that ever marchour, be he Irishe or Inglish..if such marchours take ony chalaunge or action agaynste ony man duellyng within the saide citie. **1607** COWELL *Interpr.*, *Marchers*, be the noble men dwelling on the Marches of Wales or Scotland: who in times past..had their priuate lawes, much like as if they had beene Kings. **1612** DAVIES *Why Ireland*, etc. (1787) 132 And euery lord of a country, and euery marcher, made war and peace at his pleasure. **1621** BOLTON *Stat. Irel.* Ep. Ded. a 4 b, Many of those Stat. ..concerning Marchiors..are..repealed. *Ibid.* 14 The said Marcheours..doe guide the said Irish enemies and their theeues into the English countrey. *a* **1648** LD. HERBERT *Hen. VIII* (1683) 492 That Marchers should dwell upon their March Lands. **1752** CARTE *Hist. Eng.* III. 166 Sir Thomas Wharton and Sir W. Musgrave advancing against them with a body of marchers they fell into confusion. **1856** FROUDE *Hist. Eng.* II. 269 The robber chief instantly rose and attacked the pale. The Marchers opened their lines to give his banditti free passage.
b. *Lord Marcher* (pl. *Lords Marchers*), a lord who enjoyed royal liberties and had exclusive jurisdiction over territory in the marches which he obtained by border warfare. Hence *Lordship Marcher*, territory so obtained and held.
1449 *Rolls of Parlt.* V. 151/1 The Lordes Marchiers, of the whiche such misdoers..holden ther Londes. **1535–6** *Act 27 Hen. VIII*, c. 26 §19 The Lordes Marchers..have used to putt their tenauntes within their Lordshippes Marchers under suche common maynprise [etc.]. **1614** SELDEN *Titles Hon.* 216 The ancient Lords Marchers of Wales... Of these Marchers mention is in the Statute of Prerogative: *Exceptis Feodis Comitum & Baronum de Marchia.* *a* **1648** LD. HERBERT *Hen. VIII* (1683) 435 Insomuch, that in about some 141 Lordships Marchers..many strange and discrepant Customs were practised. **1700** TYRRELL *Hist. Eng.* II. 913 A day..was assigned for..the Lords Marchers to appoint Arbitrators. **1863** *Sat. Rev.* 384 While the Lords Marchers did the border this good service, they grew apace in powers of combined action.
†**c.** *Earl Marcher*: used for MARGRAVE.
1630 *R. Johnson's Kingd. & Commw.* 402 Saros Patak, where the Palatine or Earle-marcher of that part of Hungaria..usually keeps his residence.
†**3.** A border-territory or march. *Obs.*
1475 *Bk. Noblesse* (Roxb.) 45 Carenten, and Valoigney, withe alle othir forteressis and villages in that marcher.
4. *attrib.*, as *marcher-baron, -lord, -town.*
1570–6 LAMBARDE *Peramb. Kent* (1826) 187 It is a frontier, and Marchier Towne of this Shyre. **1841** HARTSHORNE *Salop. Antiq.* 497 Marcher Lords. *Ibid.* 498 This policy led to the erection of the Marcher Lordships. **1877** GREEN *Hist. Eng. People* I. 305 Indignities which the Marcher-lords had offered to the body of the great Earl. **1887** *Dict. Nat. Biog.* XI. 72/2 Representing the marcher barons.
Hence ˈ**marchership**, the office of Lord Marcher.
1859 PARKER *Turner's Dom. Archit.* III. II. vii. 372 All this area was parcelled out into marcherships, holding from the English crown 'by the sword' only. **1875** STUBBS *Const. Hist.* II. xvi. 341 Wales, where the chief marcherships were in the hands of the great English earls.

marcher[2] (ˈmɑːtʃə(r)). [f. MARCH *v.*[2] + -ER[1].]
1. a. One who marches or walks. Chiefly with adjs. of qualification.
c **1611** CHAPMAN *Iliad* XIX. 162 Thirst, hunger,..take away a marcher's knees. *a* **1661** HOLYDAY *Juvenal* (1673) 23 What nettle thus, great marcher [L. *Gradive*], does inflame Thy nephews? **1809** SIR J. MOORE 10 Jan. in Jas. Moore *Camp. Spain* 199 Soldiers who pretend to be bad marchers. **1869** E. A. PARKES *Pract. Hygiene* (ed. 3) 394 The best marchers are men of middle size.
b. *spec.* A person who takes part in a protest, etc., march (see MARCH *sb.*[4] 1 a).
1908, 1922 [see *hunger-marcher* s.v. HUNGER *sb.* 4 e]. **1939** C. DAY LEWIS *Child of Misfortune* III. ii. 334 He had hoped, perhaps, for..a feeling of community with his fellow marchers. **1960** *Times Lit. Suppl.* 10 June 362/4 We observe its [*sc.* war's] direct and unquestioned influence on 'marchers' and others whom most people consider wrong-headed. **1960** *Guardian* 28 Oct. 7/4 Many bright remarks about French politics, anti-bomb marchers..and the like. **1961** *Ibid.* 7 Mar. 8/6 Marchers of all kinds protested beside the Holy Loch. **1969** *New Yorker* 14 June 78/2 I'm not a marcher. I'm not a sign carrier.
†**2.** Some part of a draw-net. *Obs.*
1727 BRADLEY *Fam. Dict.* s.v. *Draw Net*, Fasten it, by putting some of the Ends of the Marcher *H.* against the Stick *H.*

marches, obs. form of MARQUIS.

‖**marchesa** (marˈkeza). [It.: fem. of MARCHESE.] In Italy: A marchioness.
1797 MRS. RADCLIFFE *Italian* i, The *Marchesa* had observed his absence. **1878** L. W. M. LOCKHART *Mine is Thine* I. iv. 75 The favourite maid of an Italian *marchesa.*

marchesal: see MARQUISAL.

‖**marchese** (marˈkeze), *sb.* [It.: see MARQUIS.] In Italy: A marquis.
1517 TORKINGTON *Pilgr.* (1884) 11 All these thyngs I sawe whanne they war shewyd to the Marchose [? *read* Marchese] of Mantua. **1754** RICHARDSON *Grandison* (ed. 8vo) III. ii. 14 The Marchese della Porretta..is a nobleman of great merit. **1797** MRS. RADCLIFFE *Italian* i, But the *Marchese* did not return home till after Vincentio. **1806** CHARLOTTE DACRE *Zofloya* I. 2 At this time the Marchese di Loredani had been married seventeen years.

†**marchese**, *v.* *Obs.* [ad. obs. F. *marchiser* (Cotgr.), f. *marche*, MARCH *sb.*[3]] *intr.* = MARCH *v.*[1]
1525 LD. BERNERS *Froiss.* II. xxii. 48 Which countie.. marchesed on the countre of Tholousin.

marchese, obs. form of MARSHALSEA.

marchesit(e, obs. forms of MARCASITE.

marchesse, obs. pl. of MARCH *sb.*[3]

marchet, obs. form of MARKET, MERCHET.

marchier, obs. form of MARCHER[1].

marchies, obs. pl. of MARCH *sb.*[3]

marching (ˈmɑːtʃɪŋ), *vbl. sb.* [f. MARCH *v.*[2] + -ING[1].] **a.** The action of MARCH *v.*[2]; an instance of this.
1560 BIBLE (Genev.) *1 Macc.* vi. 41 All they that heard the noyce of their multitude, and the marching of the companie, ..were astonished. **1617** MORYSON *Itin.* IV. IV. iii. (1903) 379 No people..vseth lesse Ceremonyes and Pompous shewes or marchings, in festiuall solemnityes than those of the Vnited Provinces. **1724** DE FOE *Mem. Cavalier* (1840) 53 The discipline and order of their marchings, camping, and exercise was excellent. **1855** BROWNING *An Epistle* 27 The country-side is all on fire With rumours of a marching hitherward. **1861** W. H. RUSSELL in *Times* 24 Sept., The drills..are still of the most elementary character, but their marching is very good indeed.
†**b.** The move of a chess-man. *Obs. rare*[−1].
1562 ROWBOTHAM *Play of Cheasts* A vij, Beholde here his marchinges, and his libertie prouided that he haue had no checke.
c. *marching-past.* The action of performing the 'march past' (MARCH *sb.*[4] 1 d). Also *attrib.*
1833 *Regul. Instr. Cavalry* I. 37 In marching past, the Lieutenant-Colonel is to be in front of the leading Troop. **1860** *Illustr. Lond. News* 23 June 598/3 During the marching past the Staff..will be drawn up opposite the Royal standard. **1896** NEWNHAM-DAVIS *Three Men & a God* 120 On marching-past parade.
d. *attrib.* and *Comb.*: *marching day, front, music, parade*; †**marching malady**, ? (of a horse) illness caused by travelling; **marching money** (see quot.); **marching order**, equipment for marching; *pl.*, orders to march (also *fig.*).
1781 SIMES *Milit. Guide* (ed. 3) 8 On *marching days, he follows the Major-general of the day with the encampment. **1888** *Encycl. Brit.* XXIV. 362/2 The men marched eight abreast... This unusually wide *marching front was taken up by the infantry. **1621** J. TAYLOR (Water P.) *Taylors Motto* A 4 b *marg.*, I will turne Farrier. I doe not thinke that any Horse-leech can blazon such a pedigree of *marching maladies. **1837** *Coll. Warrants & Regul. Army* (1844) 7 A daily Allowance in South Britain of *Marching Money..as the payment to the Innkeeper for the hot meal which he is required to furnish to the Soldier. **1853** STOCQUELER *Mil. Encycl.*, *Marching Money*, the additional pay which officers and soldiers receive for the purpose of covering the expenses necessarily incurred when marching from one place to another. **1941** BAKER *Dict. Austral. Slang* 46 *Marching money*, money to travel. **1962** R. COOK *Crust on its Uppers* (1964) ii. 18 There were no wages—hardly marching money, even. **1866** CARLYLE *Inaug. Addr.* 197 A kind of road-melody or *marching-music of mankind. **1780** W. HEATH *Let.* 31 July in *Mass. Hist. Soc. Coll.* (1905) 7th Ser. V. 93 George Washington has put the main army under *marching orders. **1837** *King's Regulations Army* 32 General Officers are to cause the Troops..to be frequently paraded, and exercised at least once a week in Heavy Marching Order. **1848** A. H. CLOUGH *Let.* 26 Feb. in T. Arnold *N.Z. Lett.* (1966) 78, I anticipate considerable trouble in getting any Constitution into Marching Order. **1848** THACKERAY *Van. Fair* xx, The Duke's in Belgium already, and we expect marching orders every day. **1850** J. J. HORT *Horse Guards* 24 In many garrisons the greater part of his time thus employed is in heavy marching order. **1867** SMYTH *Sailor's Word-bk.*, *Marching order.* A soldier fully equipped..carries from 30 to 35 lbs. In *service marching* order..he carries nearly 50 lbs. But *heavy marching* order..was yet heavier. **1918** L. E. RUGGLES *Navy Explained* 127 If the stew is covered over with a crust..they call it stew in heavy marching order. **1937** B. DE HOLTHOIR tr. *Duhamel's Pasquier Chron.* 88 The barometer, too, nearly had its marching orders, but mother said: 'Oh, for what it will fetch it might as well stay where it is.' **1961** S. CHAPLIN *Day of Sardine* vi. 132 He was never any good to you. It makes no difference to me if you give him his marching orders...and hitch up with the Lodger. **1974** 'M. INNES' *Appleby's Other Story* x. 79 An eye should be kept on him, to my mind. Given his marching orders, he ought to be. **1791** BENTHAM *Panopt.* Postcr. 168 Even the roof of the building, might..be made to answer the purpose of a [prisoner's] *marching parade.

†**marching**, *ppl. a.*[1] *Obs.* [f. MARCH *v.*[1] + -ING[2].] That marches or adjoins; that serves as a march.
1444 *Rolls of Parlt.* V. 108/1 The seide Shire of Northumberland, is marchyng to the Scottes the Kynges Enemyes. **1548** UDALL *Erasm. Par. Luke* v. 33 He was as a marchyng bordre betwene the lawe yᵗ should afterward ceasse, & the libertee of the ghospell shortely after to arise. **1577** HARRISON *England* III. iv. in *Holinshed* 103/2 In old tyme he onelie was called Marquise, *Qui habuit terram limitaneum*, a marching prouince vpon the enimies countreis.

marching (ˈmɑːtʃɪŋ), *ppl. a.*[2] [f. MARCH *v.*[2] + -ING[2].] That marches.
1. a. *Mil.* That marches or is used in marching. ***marching regiment*** (see quot. 1802).
1667 in *10th Rep. Hist. MSS. Comm.* App. v. 31 Your petitioners were directed by the Lieutenant of his Majestie's Ordinance to make a marching barricade, to carry six small gunns. **1690** LUTTRELL *Brief Rel.* (1857) II. 2 He should provide two hospitalls.., a fixt one and a marching one. **1775** SHERIDAN *Rivals* III. i, This is my return..for putting him, at twelve years old, into a marching regiment. **1802** C. JAMES *Milit. Dict.*, *Marching Regiments*, a term given to those corps who had not any permanent quarters, but were liable to be sent not only from one end of Great Britain to the other, but to the most distant of her possessions abroad. **1883** *Pall Mall G.* 7 Dec. 3/1 All this does not mean that the Mahdi will have an effective marching army wherewith to advance on Egypt. **1885** *Athenæum* 18 Apr. 502/1 From the point of view of the marching soldier the physical aspect of the country..is far from attractive.
b. ***marching band***, a band that marches; ***marching girl*** (*Austral.* and *N.Z.*), a girl trained to march in formation, a drum-majorette.
1952 *Here & Now* (N.Z.) July 9 Not for a long time have I observed such a symptom of our *malaise* as the business of 'marching girls'. **1954** *N.Z. Listener* 10 Dec., Preceded, of course, by marching girls to provide just that touch of military pageantry so dear to us all. **1955** KEEPNEWS & GRAUER *Pict. Hist. Jazz* ii. 19 Laine's music was distinctively that of the marching bands and of ragtime. **1956** M. STEARNS *Story of Jazz* (1957) vii. 72 The New Orleans jazzbands, with their marching-band tradition, did not use a piano in the early days. **1961** *N.Z. Listener* 24 Nov. 36/4 Visitors from America say that as a major attraction, our marching girls are much superior to their Drum Majorettes. **1963** *Sunday Mirror* (Sydney) 27 Jan. 2 (*caption*) In gay, colorful uniforms marching girls were cheered by city crowds as they strode through city streets during the Australia Day celebrations. **1974** *Fiji Times* 3 July (*caption*) Marching girls parade through Lautoka during the Salusalu Festival at the weekend. **1974** P. DE VRIES *Glory of Hummingbird* i. 4 The sousaphone tuba he played in the local marching band.
2. Progressive.
1842 J. AITON *Domest. Econ.* (1857) 56 These pushing, marching, money-making times.

†**marchion.** *Obs.* In 4 marchiun, 5 *Sc.* marchon, merschion. [ad. med.L. *marchiōn-em*, f. *marca* MARK, MARCH *sb.*[3] (The med.L. equivalent of MARQUIS.)] A captain of the marches.
a **1380** *St. Augustine* 1609 in Horstm. *Altengl. Leg.* (1878) 89 Men of Papye Weren itake..Of þe marchiun of Malaspyn And in a prison put. *c* **1450** HOLLAND *Howlat* 328 Goiss Halkis war..Marchonis in the mapamond. *Ibid.* 685 Merschionis of mychtis.

†**marchionat.** *Obs. rare*⁻¹. [ad. med.L. *marchiōnāt-us*, f. *marchiōn-em*: see prec.] Marquisate or 'march' (of Ancona).

c **1449** Pecock *Repr.* III. xiii. 359 Matilde a greet ladi which ȝaf the greet..marchionat of Anchon to the pope.

marchioness ('mɑːʃənɪs). Also 7 **-esse, -isse, marquionesse.** [ad. med.L. *marchiōnissa*, f. *marchiōn-em*: see MARCHION and -ESS.]

1. The wife or widow of a marquis, or a lady holding in her own right the position equal to that of marquis.

[**1533** in *Rymer's Fœdera* XIV. 477/1 Cum..Domina Anna, tunc Marchionissa Penbrochiæ, nunc vero Regina]. **15..** *Bk. Precedence* in *Q. Eliz. Acad.* (1869) 14 Item, a dukes daughter is borne a Marchionesse. *Ibid.* 15 A Marquesse must goe after his Creation.., and the Marchionesse his wife according to the same. **1611** Cotgr., *Marquise*, a Marchionesse. **1613** Shaks., etc. *Hen. VIII*, II. iii. 63 The Kings Maiesty..Doe's purpose honour to you no lesse flowing, Then Marchionesse of Pembrooke. **1615** Thomas *Lat. Dict.*, *Præses limitaneus*, a marques, or marquionesse. *c* **1630** Risdon *Surv. Devon* §312 (1810) 324 The lady marchioness of Winton. **1631** B. Jonson *Underwoods* c. *Elegy on Lady Jane Pawlet*, Shee was the Lady Jane, and Marchionisse Of Winchester; the Heralds can tell this. **1829** Lytton *Disowned* xl, His day with the beautiful marchioness was over. **1883** *Encycl. Brit.* XV. 565/1 His [a marquis'] wife, who also is 'most honourable', is a marchioness, and is styled 'my lady marchioness'.

b. *allusive.* A maid-of-all-work.

[**1840** Dickens *Old C. Shop* lvii, 'To make it seem more real and pleasant, I shall call you the Marchioness, do you hear?' The small servant nodded.] **1883** Sala in *Illustr. Lond. N.* 24 Nov. 499/1 A little bit of a maid-of-all-work... This 'Marchioness'..has..been the object of the most astounding 'manifestations'. **1885** 'J. S. Winter' *Bootles' Baby* ii. 36 To develop into the unnaturally widened and unkempt hand of a 'Marchioness'.

2. A kind of pear. (Cf. MARQUIS 5, MARQUISE 2.)

1706 London & Wise *Retir'd Gard.* I. 32 The Marchioness... 'Tis very butterish, and of a sweet Muskish Juice. **1875** Hogg *Fruit Man.* (ed. 4) 479.

3. A size of slate measuring 22 inches by 11, or 20 by 12.

1878 D. C. Davies *Slate & Slate Quarrying* 136 Princesses..Duchesses..Marchionesses..Countesses.

marchiour, obs. form of MARCHER¹.

marchis, obs. pl. MARCH *sb.*³, obs. f. MARQUIS.

marchiun, variant of MARCHION *Obs.*

'march-land. [f. MARCH *sb.*³ + LAND *sb.*¹ (OE. had *mearc-land* in the same sense.)] Land comprising the marches of a country; a border territory; border-land, frontier-land.

1536 *St. Papers Hen. VIII*, II. 369 Litle ynough..for the surveiyng of the Kinges marche landes. **1611** Speed *Hist. Gt. Brit.* IX. viii. §36. 552 Some march-lands betwixt two neighbour-Nations. **1869** Freeman *Norm. Conq.* (1876) III. xiii. 315 A warrior from the marchland of Tours and Blois. **1893** T. F. Tout *Edward I*, xi. 186 In the great marchland of Glamorgan one Morgan broke out in rebellion.

'march-man. *Obs.* exc. *Hist.* Also 5 **marches-man.** [f. MARCH *sb.*³ + MAN *sb.*]

1. An inhabitant of the marches or borders.

a **1400-50** *Alexander* 2540 A watere..þat with þa marches-men [*Dublin MS.* marche-men] Mocian was hatten. **1494** Fabyan *Chron.* VII. 634 They..gatheryd to them a stronge hoost of men, as of Marchemen and other. **1586** Ferne *Blaz. Gentrie* 136 In the old Teutch or Dutch speach he was called a Marquier, that is to saye the marcheman or frontier man. **1627** Drayton *Agincourt*, etc. 9 Of March-men mustring a rebellious Band, Henry againe his Southerne people prest. **1805** Scott *Last Minstr.* I. xxx, Now Bowden Moor the march-man won, And sternly shook his plumed head. **1889** Ruskin *Præterita* III. 172 The march-men..of Cheviot.

2. = MARKSMAN 4 (see quot. 1813 there).

marchon, variant of MARCHION *Obs.*

marchour, obs. form of MARCHER¹.

marchpane: see MARZIPAN.

march stone. Chiefly *Sc.* and *north. dial.* [f. MARCH *sb.*³ + STONE *sb.* Cf. MARKSTONE.] A stone set up to mark the boundary of an estate.

1536 *Laing Charters* (1899) 108 To the merch steane with ane croce on the heid theiron. **1587** in A. Peterkin *Notes Ork. & Zetl.* (1822) 127 They to set down march-stanes thereafter to stand for ever. **1639** *Declar. Chas. I Tumults Scot.* 164 What is the use of merch-stones upon borders of Lands, the like use hath Confessions of Faith in the Kirk. **1789** Brand *Hist. Newcastle* I. 461 Round the moor the march-stones, i.e. the boundary-stones, are placed a little within the hedge. **1899** *Shetland News* 29 Apr. (E.D.D.), I sat me doon apon a mairch stane.

marchys, obs. pl. of MARCH *sb.*³

marciable, variant of MERCIABLE *a. Obs.*

marcial, -ian: see MARSHAL, MARTIAL, -IAN.

‖**marciaton.** *Med. Obs.* Also 6 **mart-**. [med.L. *marciātōn* (Du Cange).] Some kind of unguent.

c **1550** Lloyd *Treas. Health* K ij b, Washe thy handes, or anoynte them wyth Martiaton. *Ibid.* O iij, Take of marciaton, waxe, pitche, ship rosen [etc.]. **1856** in Mayne *Expos. Lex.*

†**'marcid**, *a. Obs.* [ad. L. *marcid-us*, withered, f. *marcē-re* to wither.]

1. a. Withered, wasted, decayed, rotten. **b.** Weak, feeble, exhausted.

1656 Blount *Glossogr.*, *Marcid*, withered, rotten, feeble, lither. **1657** Tomlinson *Renou's Disp.* 503 Poppies heads.. must be cocted till they be flaccid and marcid. **1693** Bowles in *Dryden's Juvenal* v. (1697) 101 He on his own Fish pours the noblest Oil..That to your marcid dying Herbs assign'd, By the rank smell and taste betrays its Kind. **1822** T. Taylor *Apuleius* 85 She dismissed her marcid eyes [L. *marcentes oculos*] to sleep. *Ibid.* 260 Sleep surrounding me, again oppressed my marcid mind [L. *marcentem animum*].

2. *marcid fever*: a fever that causes wasting.

1666 Harvey *Morb. Angl.* ii. (1672) 6 The softer and moister parts being thus melted away, the Febril heat continuing its adustion upon the dryer fleshy parts, changes into a Marcid Feaver. **1684** tr. *Bonet's Merc. Compit.* XIX. 814 In Hectick and other marcid..Fevers, Venesection is to be rejected.

†**marcidious**, *a. Obs. rare*⁻⁰. [f. MARCID + -IOUS.] (See quots.)

1656 Blount *Glossogr.*, *Marcidious*, very rotten, feeble, &c. **1775** Ash, *Marcidious*, lean, withered.

†**marcidity.** *Obs. rare*⁻⁰. [f. MARCID + -ITY.] Wasted or withered condition.

1658 Phillips, *Marcidity*, a withering away, rottennesse. **1775** Ash, *Marcidity*, leanness, the want of flesh.

marcie, marcill, obs. ff. MERCY, MARTIAL.

Marcionism ('mɑːʃ(ɪ)ənɪsm). *Eccl.* [f. *Marcion* + -ISM.] The doctrine of the Marcionites.

1882 Salmon in *Smith's Dict. Chr. Biogr.* III. 821/2 If we accept this as the original form of Marcionism, Marcion owed more to the older Gnostics than we should otherwise have supposed.

Marcionist ('mɑːʃ(ɪ)ənɪst). *Eccl.* Also 6 *erron.* **Martionist.** [ad. late L. *Marciōnist-a*, late Gr. *Μαρκιωνιστής*: see next and -IST.] = MARCIONITE.

1546 Gardiner *Declar. Art. Joye* 50 And then the Arryane maye be saued by his faythe, and..the Marcyoniste by hys faythe. **1584** R. Scot *Discov. Witchcr.* I. i. (1886) 2 The Martionists acknowledged one God the authour of good things, and another the ordeiner of evill. **1882-3** Schaff *Encycl. Relig. Knowl.* II. 1402 Theodoret tells us, that..he had converted more than one thousand Marcionists.

attrib. **1875** *Expositor* 434 The Marcionist party.

Marcionite ('mɑːʃ(ɪ)ənaɪt). *Eccl.* Also 6 *erron.* **Marcianite.** [ad. late L. *Marciōnīt-a*, f. *Marcion*: see -ITE.] An adherent of the sect founded at Rome in the 2nd century by Marcion of Sinope.

Marcion accepted as sacred books ten of St. Paul's epistles and a garbled form of the gospel of Luke, and regarded the creation of the material world and the revelation of the Old Testament as the work of a finite and imperfect God, whose authority is abrogated by the manifestation of the supreme God in Jesus Christ. He discouraged marriage, and inculcated the most rigorous asceticism.

a **1540** Barnes *Wks.* (1573) 315/2 The Marcianites, they receiue no man to bee a Christen man, excepte hee forsweare maryage. **1594** Hooker *Eccl. Pol.* IV. xi. §9 Slanderers of the Law and Prophets, such as Marcionites & Manichees were. **1660** Jer. Taylor *Ductor Dubit.* II. iii. rule 14. 8 (1676) 363. **1883** *Ch. Q. Rev.* XV. 394 By Encratites and Marcionites intoxicating liquors would have been denounced.

attrib. **1885** R. W. Dixon *Hist. Ch. Eng.* III. 288 It is not unlike the Marcionite heretics.

Hence **Marcio'nitic, Marcio'nitish** *a.*, of or pertaining to the Marcionites; **'Marcioni,tism**, the doctrines of the Marcionites.

1874 *Supernat. Relig.* II. II. vii. 86 Much of the Marcionitish text was more original than the Canonical. **1875** W. Sanday in *Fortn. Rev.* June 859 The Marcionitic Gospel. **1894** *Thinker Mag.* VI. 355 This is a modern Marcionitism.

marcipan: see MARZIPAN.

marck, obs. form of MARK.

'Marco,brunner. Also **Marcobrunn, Markbrunner, Markobrunn, Markobrunner.** [G., f. the name of a vineyard in the Rheingau.] A Rhenish white wine.

1825 T. Hook *Sayings & Doings* 2nd Ser. I. 48 Ruydersheimer and Markbrunner. **1851** C. Redding *Hist. Mod. Wines* (ed. 3) viii. 224 Marcobrunner is an excellent wine, of a fine flavour. **1862** C. Tovey *Wine & Wine Countries* 201 The landlord, pitying his condition, pressed upon him a bottle of his Marcobrunner. **1884** *Encycl. Brit.* XVII. 238/2 s.v. *Nassau*, By far the most valuable product of the soil is its wine, which includes several of the choicest Rhenish varieties (Johannisberger, Marcobrunner, Assmannshauser, &c.). **1918** H. A. Vachell *Some Happenings* xvi. 280 Let us drink your health in some Marcobrunner. **1924** 'Sapper' *Third Round* i. 33 An excellent bottle of Marcobrunner followed by a glass of his own particular old brandy. **1967** A. Lichine *Encycl. Wines* 432/2 The alternative [name] Marcobrunner will be found on the labels of two estates,..which own the best parts of the district. *Ibid.* 434/2 *Markobrunn*, sometimes written Marcobrunn.

Marconi (mɑː'kəʊnɪ), *sb.* [The name of the inventor, Guglielmo, Marchese *Marconi* (1874–1937), of a system of wireless telegraphy.]

1. Used *attrib.* in designations of this system, and things connected therewith.

1897 *Daily News* 10 June 5/2 The new Marconi system of signalling... Marconi messages have been sent between Penarth and Brean Down. **1898** R. Kerr *Wireless Telegr.* 97 [The box] contains a small Marconi receiver. *Ibid.* 104 The filings in the Marconi coherer.

2. *transf.* Used *attrib.* to designate a type of rig used on sailing vessels, or the various parts of such a rig (see quot. 1961).

1912 *Yachting Monthly* XIII. 256/2 Istria, Mr. Allom's 'Marconi' boat, promptly installed herself as the yacht of the year. **1915** *Ibid.* XIX. 151/1 Mr. Charles Nicholson, whose 'Marconi' topsail, first used on Istria in 1912, created such a sensation. **1916** *Rudder* 421/1 In the coming races for the Manhasset Bay Challenge Cup, Nahma will use a Marconi rig. **1921** *Ibid.* 28 [They] will carry 125 square feet of canvas in one sail on a so-called Marconi mast. **1940** W. Martyr *Wandering Years* 14 That eighty-foot Marconi mast was held in place by a network of steel wire shrouds. **1956** A. F. Loomis *'Hotspur' Story* ii. 14, I expressed to Rigg my preference for a fast, marconi-rigged, windward-working cutter. **1961** F. H. Burgess *Dict. Sailing* 142 *Marconi rig*, a sailing rig with a jib-headed mainsail set to a tall curved mast with an elaborate staying system; so named because it resembles a wireless mast. **1975** *Motor Boating & Sailing* Jan. 136/1 This little cruiser has a very attractive appearance in either Marconi or gaff configuration.

Hence **mar'conigram**, a wireless telegram; **mar'conigraph** *sb.*, the apparatus used for transmitting these messages; also as *v. trans.* and *intr.*, to send a message by marconigraphy (to); **mar'conigraphing** *vbl. sb.*; **marco'nigraphy**, Marconi's system of radiotelegraphy; radio; **Mar'conism**, the theory or practice of Marconi's telegraphy. (All now *disused.*)

1902 *Daily Chron.* 30 Jan. 6/4 When do you expect to start sending Marconigrams at commercial rates across the Atlantic? **1903** *Westm. Gaz.* 7 Feb. 9/1 Installations of Marconism on the sea-coasts. *Ibid.*, A monopoly of Marconism and cable-methods. **1903** *Daily Chron.* 21 Mar. 5/2 A school for Marconigraph operators. **1903** *Nature* 23 Apr. 583/1 The history of the series of inventions and discoveries which have culminated in Transatlantic Marconigraphy. **1907** *Daily Chron.* 27 Sept. 5/2 The Lusitania was marconigraphed at 5.30 p.m. yesterday 200 miles west of Fastnet. **1909** G. Stratton-Porter *Girl of Limberlost* xxiv. 453 If..I want you..I'll cable, marconigraph, anything. **1911** R. Brooke *Let.* Mar. (1968) 284 It is..cleverer and queerer than the telephone, though not so clever as Marconigraphing.

marconi (mɑː'kəʊnɪ), *v. Disused.* [f. the sb.]

1. *trans.* and *intr.* To send a message by radio (to).

1912 C. N. & A. M. Williamson *Heather Moon* I. iv. 47, I marconied her an hour after he'd said that he would come. **1919** *Times* 25 June 13/6 Messages were signalled to the coastguards requesting them to marconi to the Fleet.

2. *trans.* To transmit by radio. Also *fig.*

1908 *Isle of Man Weekly Times* 12 Sept. 9/4 An author sometimes dreams of the ideal actress who shall 'Marconi' across the footlights the puppet he has given birth to. **1922** *Glasgow Herald* 2 Nov. 6/2 These figures represent a code which can be wired, cabled, or marconied anywhere. **1926** P. Bottome *Old Wine* xi. 104 Marconiing the news..across space.

Marconist (mɑː'kəʊnɪst). *Disused.* [f. MARCON(I + -IST.] The operator of a Marconi radiotelegraphy system.

1900 in *Encycl. Dict.* (*c* 1904) Suppl. s.v., Then the Marconists began to pull the enemy's leg by sending what our Marconist calls 'Rot'. **1933** *Jrnl. R. Aeronaut. Soc.* XXXVII. 628 On board of the machine, an increase of the crew to probably three pilots, two Marconists and one mechanic.

marcor ('mɑːkɔː(r)). Also 7 **-our.** [a. L. *marcor*, f. *marcēre*: see MARCID.] †**a.** *gen.* Decay (*obs.*). **b.** *Path.* Emaciation or wasting of the body.

1646 Sir T. Browne *Pseud. Ep.* III. ix. 124 The resolution and languor ensuing that act in some, the extenuation and marcour in others. **1657** Tomlinson *Renou's Disp.* 160 That they may be long conserved without putretude and marcour. **1666** Harvey *Morb. Angl.* ii. 11 The said Marcor may likewise be caused by famine. **1741** A. Monro *Anat.* (ed. 3) 61 *Marcor* and *Atrophia* of the whole Body. [**1876** tr. *Wagner's Gen. Pathol.* 287 Simple emaciation, *macies, emaciatio, marcor*,..is distinguished from..*tabes*.]

Marcosian (mɑː'kəʊzɪən), *sb.* and *a. Hist.* [f. Eccl. Gr. *Μαρκώσι-ος* (Epiphanius; app. f. Syriac *Marqūs* Marcus) + -AN.] **a.** *sb.* An adherent of a Gnostic religious system founded by a certain Marcus in the 2nd century; known mainly from the account by Irenæus. **b.** *adj.* Belonging to this sect.

1587 T. Rogers *39 Art.* II. 29 Some, as the Marcosians, at the ministration of Baptisme haue vsed certaine Hebrue wordes. **1708** Bingham *Orig. Eccl.* XI. ii. §1 Those who were called Marcosian heretics. **1875** Lightfoot *Comm. Col.* 209/1 The baptismal formula of the Marcosians.

marcottage (mɑːkɒ'tɑːʒ, mɑː'kɒtɪdʒ). *Hort.* Also **marcotting.** [Fr. *marcottage* layering.] A method of propagating trees or shrubs in which a ring of bark is removed from a branch, and the wound covered with a thick layer of soil, moss, etc., into which new roots grow, before the plant is cut from its parent. Hence (as a back-formation) **marcot**, the wound from which new

roots grow, or the new plant is formed. Also as *v. intr.*, to use this method of propagation.

1926 F. M. Esguerra in *Philippine Agriculturist* XV. 63 Marcottage is the term applied to the process of reproduction by which a branch of a plant is 'girdled' and wrapped with soil or other media in order to induce rooting while still attached to the mother plant. A marcot is the branch so treated.. Planting marcots instead of seeds has several advantages. *Ibid.* 64 Time for marcotting. It is preferable to marcot during the rainy season. 1934 [see *air-layering* (air *sb.*¹ B. II)]. 1955 R. C. M. Wright *Plant Propagation* xv. 99 'Air layering', 'Chinese layering' or 'marcotting' is believed to have been used by gardeners for thousands of years. 1958 R. J. Garner *Grafter's Handbk.* (rev. ed.) iii. 60 Marcotting..is variously known as air layering, Chinese layering, circumposition, or, in India and elsewhere, as gootee. *Ibid.*, An ingenious method of securing a continuous supply is to suspend a vessel containing water above the marcot. 1959 Hartmann & Kester *Plant Propagation* xiv. 406 The ancient Chinese gootee or marcottage method consists of plastering a ball of clay or other soil mixture about the ring or girdle, which is then covered with moss or fiber. 1969 *Gloss. for Landscape Work* (*B.S.I.*) v. 12 Marcotting. A form of air layering in which a soil-based rooting medium is used.

marcour, Marcs, obs. forms of Marcor, Mars.

Marcure, -ry, obs. forms of Mercury.

Marcusian (mɑː'kuːzɪən), *a.* and *sb.* [f. the name of Herbert *Marcuse* (1898–1979), American philosopher and writer.] **A.** *adj.* Of, pertaining to, or connected with Marcuse or his political views. **B.** *sb.* One who holds the political views of Marcuse.

1968 *Economist* 20 July 25/3 In Italy, as elsewhere, it has brought to the surface a number of groups who are more articulate than the mass and can variously and very approximately be classified as maoist, trotskyist, castroist, marcusian and so forth. 1968 *Listener* 31 Oct. 594/2 (*heading*) Marcusians. *Ibid.*, The boring old proletariat is unrepresented in this Marcusian world. 1969 *Guardian* 2 Sept. 9/6 Marcuse, and the hippie generation who represent Marcusian premature antifascists, herald a radical shift towards the sensory, the imaginative and the quietist. 1969 *Pacifist* Oct. 5/2 A Marcusian analysis of the developed world shows the system beginning to transcend itself where it is most successful. 1970 G. Greer *Female Eunuch* 309 The Red Stockings..concentrate on consciousness-raising in the Marcusian sense. 1970 A. MacIntyre *Marcuse* iv. 53 The whole recapitulation thesis in its Marcusean form [is] untenable. 1971 *Guardian* 19 Jan. 10/1 It will be asked whether the Guevarist or Marcusian infection is beginning to take effect in this country.

marcussotte, var. Marquisotte *Obs.*

marcyable, -al(l: see Martiable, Martial.

marcylite ('mɑːsɪlaɪt). [f. the name of Gen. R. B. *Marcy*, its discoverer (1854) + -lite.] An impure or decomposed form of copper pyrites from the Red River district of Louisiana.

1884 in Cassell. 1896 in Chester *Dict. Names Min.*

Marcz, obs. form of Mars.

mard (mɑːd), *a.* = marred *ppl. a.* b. *dial.*

1903 in *Eng. Dial. Dict.* 1911 D. H. Lawrence *White Peacock* vii. 493 The little devils are soft, mard-soft. 1913 —— *Love Poems* 53 Eh, tha'rt a mard-'arsed kid. 1959 I. & P. Opie *Lore & Lang. Schoolch.* x. 187 Elsewhere the weak one may carry the label..mard 'un.

mard (mɑːd), *v. dial.* [Cf. prec. and mar *v.* 3 c.] To 'spoil' (a child).

1874 in *Eng. Dial. Dict.* (1903). 1911 D. H. Lawrence *White Peacock* vii. 493 She marded 'em till they were soft.

mard, -er: see Merd, Marter.

Mardi gras (‖mardi gra, ˌmɑːdɪ 'grɑː). [Fr., lit. 'fat Tuesday'.] Shrove Tuesday; the last day of carnival, esp. in France. In U.S. esp. as celebrated in New Orleans. Also *attrib.*

1699 M. Lister *Journey to Paris* (ed. 3) 177 My Lord Ambassador was at a Ball at Monsieur de Montargis mardy Gras. 1780 T. Blaikie *Diary Scotch Gardener* (1931) 161 Went to Versailles..this being Mardi gras saw the people masked. 1832 *Boston Even. Transcript* 13 June 1/3 Yesterday was '*Mardi Gras*'—the last day of the reign of Folly. 1848 H. Greville *Diary* 8 Mar. (1883) I. 236 This motley crew..dressed more ludicrously than any masks on a *Mardi-gras*. 1883 'Mark Twain' *Life on Mississippi* xlvi. 416 The largest annual event in New Orleans is..the Mardi-Gras festivities. 1900 Ade *Fables in Slang* 148 His Father was too Serious a Man to get out in Mardi Gras Clothes. 1909 'O. Henry' *Options* 184 The reception they were going to put up would make the Mardi Gras in New Orleans look like an afternoon tea in Bury St Edmunds with a curate's aunt. 1924 *Blackw. Mag.* Nov. 709/2 There are those to whom Mardi-Gras is yet a religious festival. 1931 *Times Lit. Suppl.* 9 Apr. 285/3 The Mardi Gras irresponsibility..excuses the daring prank of a naughty youth. 1931 H. Crane *Let.* 12 Dec. (1965) 392 It isn't any sort of Mardi-Gras mood at all that the Indians express, despite the flamboyant colors of their costumes. 1941 *Sat. Even. Post* 15 Mar. 14 Mardi Gras at Coney. 1972 *Guardian* 29 Dec. 12/1 Russell Harty took an 'Aquarius' [TV] team to Mardi Gras, the great New Orleans Shrove Tuesday freak-out.

mardy ('mɑːdɪ), *a. dial.* [f. mard *a.* + -y¹.] 'Spoilt', sulky, whining. Also as *sb.*, a spoilt child.

1903 *Eng. Dial. Dict.* IV. 34/1 A boy who cries with pain is called by his fellows a 'mardy baby'. 1913 D. H. Lawrence *Sons & Lovers* vi. 127 'Now, Miriam,' said Maurice, 'you come an' 'ave a go.' 'No,' she cried, shrinking back. 'Ha! baby. The mardy-kid!' said her brothers. 1915 —— *Rainbow* i. 12 Young Tom, whom he called a mardy baby. *a* 1930 —— *Phoenix II* (1968) 170 As for Harold, he was all right. He was very respectable and a bit of a mardy, perhaps..but he was all right. 1959 J. Braine *Vodi* i. 22 'Don't be so bloody soft, man,' Tom said. 'I don't want to go.' 'You're mardy. You're dead mardy.' 1961 J. I. M. Stewart *Man who won Pools* 35 'E were a mardy one as a nipper, our Phil. 1975 D. Clark *Premedicated Murder* v. 83 'You can get all mardy about it if you like,' said Green, unabashed.

mare¹ (mɛə(r)). Forms: 1 myre, mire, 1, 3–6 mere, 4 mure, maare, 4–5 mer, meer(e, 6 *Sc.* meir, meyr, 6–7 meare, 7 *Sc.* meire, 8 mear, 2– mare. [OE. *mere* (WS. *miere, myre*) wk. fem. = OFris., MLG., MDu. *mer(r)ie* (mod.Du. *merrie*), OHG. *meriha* (MHG. *meriche, merhe*, mod.G. with altered sense *mähre* jade), ON. *merr* str. fem. (Sw. *märr*, Da. *mær*):—OTeut. **marhjô(n)*-, f. **marho-z* horse (OE. *mearh*, OHG. *marah*, MHG. *marc*, ON. *marr*):—pre-Teut. **marko-s* (= Gaulish μάρκαν acc. sing., Pausanias x. xix; Irish, Gael. *marc*, Welsh *march*).]

1. a. The female of any equine animal (as the horse, ass, or zebra), but esp. applied to the female of the domestic horse (*Equus caballus*).

a 900 tr. *Bæda's Hist.* iii. xii. [xiv.] (1890) 196 Cwist ðu þæt þe sy leofre þære myran sunu þonne þæt Godes bearn? *c* 1000 Ælfric *Gloss.* in Wr.-Wülcker 119/36 *Equa*, mere. *c* 1175 *Lamb. Hom.* 85 He brohte hine uppen his werue [= *jumentum* Luke x. 34] þet is unorne mare. *c* 1290 *Becket* 1161 in *S. Eng. Leg.* I. 139 Þo wende forth a man, þat with him eode: and huyrde him a mere, For an Englichs peni. *c* 1386 Chaucer *Reeve's T.* 161 Youre hors goth to the fen With wilde mares. 1398 Trevisa *Barth. De P.R.* xvii. xl. (1495) 801 A maare foolyth stondynge and louyth her coltes passynge other beestys. *a* 1400–50 *Alexander* 2853 Meeris & mulis & all maner of bestis. 14.. *Nom.* in Wr.-Wülcker 697/34 *Hec equa*, a mer. *Ibid.* 698/7 *Hec equifera*, a wyld mer. 1467 in *Eng. Gilds* (1870) 371 No horsez ner marys stande in the markett. 1549 *Compl. Scot.* vi. 39 Baytht horse & meyris did fast nee, & the folis nechyr. 1576 in *Ripon Ch. Acts* (Surtees) 377 An old meare. 1594 in *Black Bk. Taymouth* (Bannatyne Cl.) 298 Off greit meirris xlvi; off twa yeir auld hors, v... Off greit mearis xxxviii..off yeir auld meiris, iiii. 1615 Crooke *Body of Man* 334 A Bitch whelps at foure moneths; a Mare Foales the ninth. *a* 1774 Goldsm. tr. *Scarron's Com. Romance* (1775) I. 295 A park, where he kept mares for breed. 1855 Thackeray *Newcomes* II. 152 He comes to me with another letter and a face as long as my mare's.

¶ Used for: The mother, dam (of a horse).

a 1400 *Octouian* 1416 Thys ys a stede of Arabye..An vnycorn..Begat hyt thare: A rabyte..Therto was mare.

b. In various proverbial phrases.

grey mare: see grey *a.* 4 b.

1546 J. Heywood *Prov.* (1867) 43 Of auncient fathers she tooke no cure nor care, She was to them, as koy as a croker's mare. *Ibid.* 62 This biteth the mare by the thumbe, as they sey. 1562 A. Scott *Poems* (S.T.S.) i. 142 The heidismen hes 'cor mundum' in þair mouth, Bot nevir wᵗ mynd to gif þe man his meir. 1590 Shaks. *Mids. N.* iii. ii. 463. 1597 —— *2 Hen. IV*, ii. i. 47 How now? whose Mare's dead? what's the matter? 1606 *Choice, Chance*, etc. (Grosart) 68 Can seeme as sober as a Millers Mare, And cannot blush at any villany. 1607 *Acc. Christmas Prince* (1816) 40 Now Night growes old, yet walkes here in his trappinge Till Daye come catch him, as Mosse his graymare, nappinge. 1611 Cotgr., *A desprouveu*, at vnawares..vnlooked for; napping, as Mosse tooke his Mare. 1659 Howell *Lex., Prov.* 6/2 Money makes the grey Mare to go. 1698 *Money Masters All Things* 3 [Money] Makes the old Wife trot, and makes the Mare to go. 1827 T. Creevey in *C. Papers* (1904) II. 123 No tidings of the Beau yet! but he must have his mare again.

c. Applied, orig. contemptuously, to a woman.

1303 R. Brunne *Handl. Synne* 7980 And shame hyt ys euer aywhare To be kalled 'a prestēs mare'. 1508 Kennedie *Flyting w. Dunbar* 261 This Dewlbeir, generit of a meir of Mar, Wes Corspatrik, Erle of Merche. 1590 Shakes. *Mids. N.* iii. ii. 463 The man shall have his mare again. 1922 Joyce *Ulysses* 231 She's a gamey mare and no mistake. 1953 C. W. Ogle in *Caribbean Anthol. Short Stories* 43 Forgot her keys! Bah! These mares give me the creeps.

2. *transf.* in various applications, chiefly with implication of a metaphorical 'riding.'

a. The gallows. ? *Obs.*

1568 Fulwell *Like will to like* C iv, This peece of land wherto you inheritours are: Is called the land of the two legged mare. 1685 *Roxb. Ball.* V. 600 Should it..be his Fate (as needs he must fear) To leap from low Pillory up the Mare, She'll swear she had never such rider before. 1694 Motteux *Rabelais* v. iv. (1737) 14 The two or three-legg'd Mare that groans for them. 1834 H. Ainsworth *Rookwood* iii. v, Here's to the three leg'd mare. *Ibid.*, For the Mare-with-three-legs, boys, I care not a rap.

† **b.** *the wild mare*: (*a*) a see-saw; (*b*) a wooden frame on which soldiers were made to 'ride' for punishment; = horse *sb.* 6 b (also ***wooden, timber mare***). ***shoeing the wild mare***: some childish Christmas game. *Obs.*

a 1586 Sidney *Arcadia* ii. (1590) 211 b, Bestriding the mast, I gat..towards him, after such manner as boies are wont, (if euer you saw that sport) when they ride the wild mare. 1609 Armin *Maids of More-Cl.* (1880) 92 Christmas gambuls, father, shooing the wilde mare. *a* 1625 Fletcher *Woman's Prize* ii. v., She should ride the wild Mare once a week, she should. *a* 1670 Spalding *Troub. Chas. I* (Spalding Club 1850) I. 290 Ane tymber meir, quhairvpone runnaget knaves and runaway soldiouris sould ryde. *Ibid.* 295 He..syne rode the meir, to his gryte hurt and pane. 1680 [J. Speed] *Batt upon Batt* 5 Our Batt can..play..At..Shooing the wild Mare. 1819 Scott *Leg. Montr.* xiv, He had an hour's ride on the wooden mare for his pains.

† **c.** ***Hick's mare*** (see quot.). *Obs.*

1585 Higins *Junius' Nomenclator, Oscillatio*..a kind of gambol called the haltering of Hix mare.

¶ For *Shanks's mare* (i.e. one's own legs as a means of conveyance) see shank.

3. *dial.* (See quots.)

1670 Blount *Glossogr.* (ed. 3) s.v., *To cry the mare* is an ancient custom in Herefordshire, viz. when each husbandman is reaping the last of his Corn, the Work-men leave a few blades standing, and tye the tops of them together, which is the *Mare*, and then stand at a distance, and throw their Siccles at it, and he that cuts the knot has the prize [etc.]. 1883 Burne & Jackson *Shropsh. Folk-lore* 373 Crying, calling, or shouting the mare, is a ceremony performed by the men of that farm which is the first in any parish or district to finish the harvest.

4. *Sc.* **a.** A kind of trestle used by masons. **b.** A bricklayer's hod.

a. 1651 *Burgh Recs. Stirling* (1889) 306 For half a hunder nailles to mak the meare. 1821 Galt *Ann. Parish* xxxvi. 295 The three were seated aloft, on a high stage, prepared on purpose, with two mares and scaffold-deals, borrowed from Mr. Trowel the mason.

b. 1823 Tennant *Card. Beaton* v. iv. 155, I think I set my apron and my mare as weel as you your apparel.

5. A particular throw in wrestling. Also ***flying mare*** (cf. *flying horse* s.v. flying, *ppl. a.* 1 d).

1602 Carew *Cornwall* 76 Many sleights and tricks appertaine hereunto ['wrastling']..Such are the Trip, fore-Trip,..the Mare and diuers other like. 1612 Drayton *Poly-olb.* i. 245 Or by the girdles graspt they practise with the hip, The forward, backward, falx, the mare, the turne, the trip. 1754 [see flying *ppl. a.* 1 d]. 1863 Thornbury *True as Steel* III. 40 An old wrestling trick, well known as 'the flying mare'.

6. *attrib.* and *Comb.* **a.** appositive, as ***mare colt, foal, mule***.

1523 Fitzherb. *Husb.* §68 At the foolynge tyme I haue vpon one daye a horse fole, and on the nexte day, or seconde, a mare fole. 1532 J. Catvoord in Weaver *Wells Wills* (1890) 74 A bullock of one yere hold, and a mare colte. 1600 Surflet *Countrie Farme* i. xxx. 200 The mare-mules are..longer liuers then the horse-mules. 1886 Burton *Arab. Nts.* (Lady B.'s ed.) I. 232 He came up, riding a mare-mule.

b. simple attrib., as ***mare-head***; objective, ***mare-milker, mare-stealing***; similative, ***mare-faced, -headed***, adjs. Also **mareful** *Sc.*, as much as a hod will hold (cf. 4 b); **mare grass**, grazing-grass sufficient to feed one mare; † **mare roiling**, the condition of rutting in a stallion; † **mare-wood** *a.*, **mare-mad** (of a stallion).

1685 *Lond. Gaz.* No. 2036/8 A light dapple Gray Gelding, ..long pasternd,..and a little *Mare-fac'd. 1823 Tennant *Card. Beaton* v. iv. 155 I've a *marefu' o' as good lime here as ever cam out o' a lime-kill. 1523 Fitzherb. *Surv.* 3 A horse grasse or a *mare grasse maye be dere ynoughe twelfe pens or twentie pens by yᵉ yere. 1709 *Lond. Gaz.* No. 4603/4 A..Gelding,..with a thickish *Mare Head. 1684 *Ibid.* No. 1950/4 A Black Nag, about 14 hands high,..*Mareheaded, and Rat tailed. 1847 Grote *Greece* ii. xvii. III. 317 Other tribes..whom the poet knows as milk-eaters and *mare-milkers. 1589 Fleming *Virg. Georg.* iii. 41 Th' horsmasters earnest be Before the time (of *mareroiling). 1664 Evelyn *Sylva* (1776) 564 The severity of our laws against *Mare-stealing. 1613 Purchas *Pilgrimage* vi. i. 464 In the Spring they are *mare-wood.

c. Combinations with *mare's*, as ***mare's milk***; † **mare's evil**, a disease; **mare's fat** *dial.*, = fleabane; **mare's son**, a horse.

c 1400 Maundev. (1839) xxiii. 253 A Cuppe fulle of Mares mylk. 1649 *Eng. Farrier* G ij, The *Mares Evill. *a* 1825 Forby *Voc. E. Anglia*, *Mare's-fat, *Inula dysenterica* Lin. 1598 *Mare's milk [see cosmos²]. 1607–1876 [see koumiss]. 1470–85 Malory *Arthur* ix. iii. 342, I calle my self neuer the wers knyght whan a *marys sone fayleth me. *Ibid.* xx. xxii. 837 Yf thys marys sone hath faylled me, wyt thou wel a kynges sone and a quenes sone shal not faylle the.

† **mare**². *Obs.* Also 1 mære, mere, 6 meare, maare, 6–7 *Sc.* mair. [OE. *mare* wk. fem. = MLG. *mar* masc. and fem., MDu. *mare, maer* masc., OHG. *mara* fem. (MHG. *mar, mare* masc. and fem., mod.G. dial. *mahr* masc.), ON. *mara* fem. (Sw. *mara*, Da. *mare*):—OTeut. **maron-, -ôn-*; cogn. w. the synonymous Polish *mora*, Czech *můra*. The Teut. word is the source of OF. *mare*, appearing also in the compound *cauchemar* nightmare, f. *caucher*, to trample.]

1. A kind of goblin supposed to produce nightmare by sitting on the chest of the sleeper; the nightmare itself.

a 700 *Epinal Gloss.* 558 *Incuba*, maere. *c* 1000 *Sax. Leechd.* II. 140 Gif mon mare ride; ʒenim elehtran. 14.. *Voc.* in Wr.-Wülcker 597/37 The mare *i. Epialtes. c* 1440 *Promp. Parv.* 326/1 Mare, or ny3hte mare, *epialtes. c* 1500 *Rowlis Cursing* 65 in Laing *Anc. Poet. Scot.*, The mowlis, and in thair sleip the mair. 1562 Bulleyn *Def. agst. Sickness, Sicke men* 70 The verie cause is, liyng or slepyng on their backe. And not through the mare, or night spirit, as thei term it. 1565 Cooper *Thesaurus* s.v., *Ephialtes*, the disease called the maare. *a* 1585 Montgomerie *Flyting* 319 The mair and the migrame, with the meathes in the melt. 1626 Bacon *Sylva* §966 The Incubus, which we call the Mare. 1627 Drayton *Nymphidia* vii, And Mab..by night Bestrids young Folkes that lye vpright, (In elder Times the Mare that hight). 1755 in Johnson.

b. *transf.* The 'blues', melancholy.

a 1529 Skelton *E. Rummyng* 110 Now away the mare And let vs sley care. *a* 1536 *Interl. Beauty & Gd. Prop. Wom.* A ij, Tush, syr, be mery, let pas awey the mare. 1611

T. Ravenscroft's Melismata vi, Eigh ho, away the Mare, let vs set aside all care.

2. A spectre, hag.

c **1440** *Promp. Parv.* 326/1 Mare, or wyche, *magus, maga, sagana.* *a* **1529** SKELTON *P. Sparrow* 76 From Medusa, that mare, That lyke a fende doth stare.

3. *Comb.* in ***mare-hag***: see HAG *sb.*[1]

1638 FORD *Fancies* IV. i, Out mare-hag mule! avaunt!

† **mare**[3]. *Obs.* (See quot.)

1688 R. HOLME *Armoury* III. 288/2 If in the Reeling of the Yarn upon the Reel, they chance to lay a thred cross or contrary to the true way of Reeling: it is in our Countrey termed a Mare.

mare[4] (ˈmɑːreɪ, ˈmɑːriː, ˈmæriː). *Astr.* Pl. **maria** (ˈmɑːrɪə), occas. **mares.** [L., = 'sea': used in 17th-c. L. works (e.g. J. Hevelius *Selenographia* (1647) vi. 133); the proper names (which are still current) given to the various regions were taken into Eng. often without translation.] Any of the extensive areas of flat land ('seas') on the surface of the moon, which appear dark and were once thought to be seas; also, any of the dark areas visible on Mars.

[**1765** R. TURNER *View of Heavens* 11 The Oceans, Seas, and Lakes are, *a* Mare Hyperboreum, [etc.].] **1860** *Monthly Notices R. Astron. Soc.* XX. 69 Whatever force might have broken down the portion of the wall towards the mare. **1876** E. NELSON *Moon* iii. 25 Although water is absent from the lunar surface, the Mares present in many places the appearance of alluvial deposits. **1895** T. G. ELGER *Moon* 6 The Maria are only level in the sense that many districts in the English Midland counties are level, and not that their surface is absolutely flat. **1901** G. P. SERVISS *Pleasures of Telescope* ix. 167 The precipitous Mount Hadley..rises more than 15,000 feet above the level of the Mare. **1938** *Ann. Reg. 1937* 356 The 'maria' are regarded as lava fields from fissure eruptions. **1962** F. I. ORDWAY et al. *Basic Astronautics* iii. 74 Other conspicuous features on Mars are the so-called maria, dark areas easily distinguished from the surrounding, desert-colored, lighter expanses. **1964** D. H. MENZEL *Field Guide Stars & Planets* vii. 251 Mares are rolling plains, generally somewhat darker than the surrounding territory. **1967** *Punch* 28 June 936/1 The maria are plains with low hills and scattered craters. Nearly half of the moon's surface which we see is covered with these maria. **1970** *Sci. Jrnl.* Mar. 83/3 A catastrophic event hit both the Earth and the Moon, melting the lunar surface—or at least surfaces of the mares. **1970** *Nature* 6 June 925/1 The form and magnitude of the mascon anomalies can be accounted for by sheets of mare volcanic rock denser than the rock of the adjacent highlands.

mare: see MAR, MARC, MAYOR, MERE, MORE.

mareag(e, -agh, obs. forms of MARRIAGE.

mareblob (ˈmɛəblɒb). *Obs.* exc. *dial.* Also 7 -blab, 9 mere-blob. [? f. *mare* MERE *sb.* + BLOB.] The marsh-marigold.

1649 BLITHE *Eng. Improv. Impr.* (1653) 19 That corrupt feeding, or springy moisture, that breeds and feeds the Rush, Flag, and Mareblab. **1866** *Treas. Bot.* 721/2 Mare-blobs, *Caltha palustris.*

† **marechal.** *Obs.* In 7 **marshal,** 8 **marechelle, mareschal,** 8–9 **marechale, -chall, -châle.** [App. some kind of application of F. *maréchal* marshal, or *maréchale* marshal's wife. But cf. Sp. *marcial* an aromatic powder.] **a.** A scent or perfume. **b.** A hair powder scented with this. Also *attrib.*

1676 SHADWELL *Virtuoso* III. 55, I have..Frangipand, Neroly, Tuberose, Jessimine, and Marshal. **1687** SEDLEY *Bellamira* I. 2, I gave her but a dozen pair of Marshal Gloves. *Ibid.* 6 Her Gloves right Marshal. **1778** SHERIDAN *Camp* II. iii, Battle-powder mixed with marechelle. **1782** [T. VAUGHAN] *Fashionable Follies* I. lxxxix. 136 She could not bear the smell of marechale powder. **1788** ANNA SEWARD *Lett.* (1811) II. 91 [A wig] powdered with marechall. **1790** *Trans. Soc. Arts* VIII. 218 Powdered, they [the leaves of Cinnamon] are a good aromatic species, or mareschal perfume. **1820** *Hermit in London* V. 35 Marechale powder, pomatum and perfume. **1852** MUNDY *Our Antipodes* (1857) 129 White, brown, and whity-brown subjects, in..silks and satins, mats and blankets, shark's oil and marechâle. **1863** MRS. GASKELL *How First Floor went to Crowley Castle* in *All Year Round* Extra Christmas No., 3 Dec. 16/2 Her hair delicately powdered and scented with maréchale. **1905** *Smart Set* Sept. 113/1 Liszt was interpreted as ylang-ylang, myrrh, and maréchale.

‖ **maréchal** (mareʃal). Also 7 **Marishal,** 8 **Mareschall,** *Sc.* **Marichal.** [Fr.] The French word for 'marshal' or 'field-marshal' used occas. in English.

1699 M. LISTER *Journey to Paris* (ed. 3) 207 The Marishal his Father..embraced me, and saluted me. **1745** M. W. MONTAGU *Let.* 27 Jan. (1966) II. 349 It is reported here that the takeing of Mareschall Bell lisle will make the residence of France very unsafe to all the English. **1783** T. BLAIKIE *Diary Scotch Gardener* (1931) 187 At St Germains the Marichal de Noel..has a very curiouss gardin. **1919** J. BUCHAN *Mr. Standfast* xx. 355 They will not pass. Your Maréchal will hold them. **1921** W. J. LOCKE *Mountebank* xiv. 170 Were British Generals real, like French Generals, Lyautey and..Foch before he became *maréchal*?

Maréchal Niel (mareʃal nil). Also anglicized **Marshal Niel.** [Fr., f. the name of Adolphe *Niel* (1802–69), Marshal of France: see prec.] A climbing Noisette rose of the variety so called, introduced in 1864, and bearing large, well-formed, fragrant, yellow flowers.

1864 *Gardeners' Chron.* 17 Dec. 1202/2 First-class Certificates have been given to a Tea Rose called Maréchal Niel, produced by M. Eugène Verdier, of Paris...This variety appears to be one of the noblest of the yellows. **1867** T. RIVERS *Rose Amateur's Guide* (ed. 9) 136 The rose to which I allude is Marshal Niel. **1898** H. KIRKE *25 Yrs. Brit. Guiana* iv. 81 Gardens in British Guiana are as a rule, disappointing... Roses, except the strong tea-scented ones like Maréchal Niel, will not flower successfully. **1899** O. WILDE *Importance of being Earnest* II. 67 *Algernon.* Might I have a button-hole first?.. *Cecily.* A Maréchale [*sic*] Niel? **1905** *Smart Set* Sept. 157/2 You had a great bowl of Maréchal Niels on the piano. **1928** [see GLOIRE DE DIJON]. **1955** G. S. THOMAS *Old Shrub Roses* I. ix. 82 'Cloth of Gold' was the parent of the famous 'Maréchal Niel'. **1971** N. YOUNG *Compl. Rosarian* v. 76 Chromatella (also known as Cloth of Gold) became the parent in 1864 of Maréchal Niel which was the most esteemed of all yellow roses until well into this century.

marechȝeuen, var. MORYEVE, 'morning-gift'.

‖ **mare clausum** (ˈmɑːriː ˈklɔːzəm). [L., closed sea, from the title of a Latin work (1635) by John Selden (1584–1654), English jurist, written in answer to *Mare liberum* (1609) by Grotius.] A sea under the jurisdiction of a particular country.

This term and *mare liberum* originated during the struggle between England and the Netherlands in the 17th century.

1652 M. NEDHAM tr. *Selden's Of Dominion of Sea* sig. gI Mare Clausum is the Sea possessed in a private manner, or so secluded both by Right and Occupation, that it ceaseth to bee common. **1849** J. ALLEN *Navigation Laws Gt. Brit.* iv. 34 Although at one time the professed admirers of Mare Liberum, the Dutch began to consider that Mare Clausum possessed more substantial charms. **1856** *Newsp. & Gen. Reader's Compan.* I. §1013 The Yellow Sea, which for ages has been, with few exceptions, a *mare clausum*, is now a *mare liberum* to all the world. **1911** *Encycl. Brit.* XVII. 698/2 *Mare clausum* and *mare liberum*..in international law, terms associated with the historic controversy which arose out of demands on the part of different states to assert exclusive dominion over areas of the open or high sea. **1949** *Canad. Jrnl. Pol. & Social Sci.* XV. 344 The old theory of mare clausum, under which coastal waters were sometimes fixed at sixty miles, one hundred miles, two days' journey, etc., from the shore, and under which claims were also made by agreement between two or more countries over an ocean common to them. **1973** [see MARE LIBERUM].

maree, marees: see MARROW *sb.*[1], MARISH.

Maree, var. MARIA *sb.* and *a.*

mareȝeuen, var. MORYEVE, 'morning-gift'.

maregolde, -grave: see MARIGOLD, MARGRAVE.

mareing, obs. form of MARRYING *vbl. sb.*

mareis, variant of MARIS *Obs.*, womb.

mareis(h, obs. forms of MARISH.

mareit, obs. pa. t. and pa. pple. of MARRY *v.*

Marek (ˈmærɛk). The name of Dr. Josef *Marek*, Hungarian veterinary surgeon, used in the possessive in **Marek's disease** to designate *fowl paralysis* (FOWL *sb.* 5 c), first described by him in 1907.

1961 *Brit. Vet. Jrnl.* CXVII. 332 It is suggested that this complex be termed Marek's disease, a term which has some precedence and which implies a disease and not a pathological entity. **1964** *Black's Vet. Dict.* (ed. 7) 353/1 Fowl paralysis itself (Marek's disease) has of recent years become more common. **1970** *Q. Poultry Bull.* Dec. 12 The control of Marek's Disease by vaccination is at present very topical. **1972** *Country Life* 3 Feb. 284/1 No sooner had a vaccine for Marek's Disease been found than Fowl Pest swept through our poultry flocks.

marekanite (ˈmærɪkənaɪt). *Min.* [Named by Pallas 1793, from the Siberian river *Marekanka*: see -ITE.] Pearl-stone.

1821 J. MAWE *New Catal. Min.* (ed. 4) 91.

marekin, -kyn(e, variants of MAROQUIN *Obs.*

Marelady, ? misprint: see MAY-LADY.

mareleyne, variant of MARGELINE *Obs.*

‖ **mare liberum** (ˈmɑːriː ˈlaɪbərəm). [L., free sea, from the title of a Latin treatise (1609) by Hugo Grotius (1583–1645), Dutch jurist.] A sea open to all nations. Cf. MARE CLAUSUM.

1652 M. NEDHAM tr. *Selden's Of Dominion of Sea* sig. a2 This People [the Netherlanders]..carried out their design ..by..a daily intrusion upon the Territorie by Sea, that in time they durst plead and print *Mare Liberum*..to defie the Dominion of England over the Sea. **1806** J. RANDOLPH in *Abridgm. Deb. Congress U.S. 1789–1856* (1857) III. 428/2 Again: Is the *mare liberum* any where asserted in this unnamed book, that free ships make free goods? No, sir; the right of search is acknowledged; that enemy's property is lawful prize, is sealed and delivered. **1849**, etc. [see MARE CLAUSUM]. **1973** *Times* 9 May 16/2 Should we discover that we too might benefit from wider zones of national jurisdiction, we should after all only be returning to the philosophy prevailing before Grotius' idea of *Mare Liberum* took hold, to John Selden's equally respectable *Mare Clausum.*

maremaid, -man, obs. ff. MERMAID, -MAN.

‖ **maremma** (məˈrɛmə). Pl. **maremme.** [a. It. *maremma*, 'a country by the sea shore' (Baretti).]

1. a. Low marshy insalubrious country by the sea shore.

1832 tr. *Sismondi's Ital. Rep.* vii. 170 Telamone, a port in the maremma of Sienna. **1866** RUSKIN *Eth. Dust* 227 The steady increase of deadly maremma round Pisa and Venice.

b. *transf.* The malarial exhalations of a maremma.

In mod. Dicts.

2. *attrib.*, as ***maremma sheep-dog.***

1945 C. L. B. HUBBARD *Observer's Bk. Dogs* 102 Maremma Sheepdog. **1948** —— *Dogs in Brit.* III. xviii. 202 Common in central Italy from Tuscany to the Abruzzes, the Maremma Sheepdog is also called the Cani da Pastor Maremmani, Abruzzi Sheepdog and Maremmes Sheepdog. The breed is centuries old and has been bred pure by Tuscan farmers for herding sheep and cattle; lately the race has been in more general use, particularly as a guard dog. **1972** *Country Life* 2 Nov. 1186/3 Maremma (Italian) Sheep Dog.

Hence **mareˈmmatic, mareˈmmese** *adjs.*, belonging to a maremma; **maˈremman** *a.*, as in ***maremann dog.***

a **1905** Maremmatic, Maremmese: in recent Dicts. (*N.E.D.*) **1924** A. HUXLEY *Little Mexican* 283 The old gentleman..taking his big maremman dog for a walk [in Tuscany].

maremusset, obs. form of MARMOSET.

marenell, marener: see MARINAL, -ER.

marenga, variant of MORINGA.

Marengo (mæˈrɛŋgəʊ). [See def.] The name of a village in northern Italy, the scene of Napoleon's victory over the Austrians in 1800, used in the name of the dish ***chicken, fowl, poulet à la Marengo***, said to have been served to Napoleon after the battle of Marengo.

1861 MRS. BEETON *Bk. Househ. Managem.* 464 (*heading*) Poulet à la Marengo... Fowl à la Marengo. **1877** E. S. DALLAS *Kettner's Bk. of Table* 121 (*heading*) *Chicken à la Marengo*,—the chicken..is fried in oil. **1959** *Good Food Guide* 169 Chicken Marengo and tournedos.

Marennin (məˈrɛnɪn). [f. *Marenn-es*, the name of a district in France: see -IN.] A peculiar pigment which gives to the Marennes oysters their characteristic green colour.

1885 E. RAY LANKESTER in *Q. Jrnl. Microsc. Sci.* XXVI. 87, I propose henceforward to speak of the blue pigment of Navicula ostrearia as Marennin. **1898** *Nat. Science* Nov. 294 Other forms of greenness..have no connection with copper, but depend upon the presence of a special pigment, Marennin.

mareogram (ˈmæriːəʊgræm). [f. L. *mare* sea + -O + -GRAM.] A graphical record of variations in sea level.

1904 *Publ. Earthquake Investigation Comm. Foreign Lang.* (Japan) XVIII. 24 The following table..gives the mean monthly values of the distance between the sea surface and the datum line in the mareogram at each of the two places. **1931** C. DAVISON *Japanese Earthquake of 1923* xii. 104 The mareogram at Toba is reproduced in Fig. 25. Here, the first movement occurred at 0.57 p.m., the maximum amplitude (of 4 ft. 1½ in.) being reached with the fifth wave at 3.37 p.m. **1949** GUTENBERG & RICHTER *Seismicity of Earth* 95/1 Tsunamis are frequently recorded on mareograms written by tide gages.

Hence **mareoˈgraphic** *a.*

1939 *Jap. Jrnl. Astron. & Geophysics* XVII. 121 The tunamis that were associated with earthquakes..left conspicuous records on some of our mareographic stations. **1956** *Jrnl. Earth Sci. Nagoya Univ.* IV. 5 Some of these after-shocks were strong,..but no tunamis were observed, even on the mareographic records.

mares, obs. form of MARISH.

mareschal, -cy, -sy, obs. ff. MARSHAL, -CY.

mareschini, -no, obs. ff. MARASCHINO.

mareshall, -elsey: see MARSHAL, -ALSEA.

mare's-nest. [MARE[1]. Cf. †*horse-nest*, which is recorded earlier (HORSE *sb.* 28).] Originally in the fig. phrase ***to have found a mare's nest***: to imagine that one has discovered something wonderful, which in fact has no existence. Hence, an illusory discovery, esp. one that is much vaunted and displays foolish credulity.

a **1619** FLETCHER *Bonduca* V. ii, Why dost thou laugh? What Mares nest hast thou found? **1738** SWIFT *Pol. Conversat.* 51 You have found a Mare's Nest. **1840** HOOD *Up the Rhine* Pref. 1 Such Critics as are fond of climbing up a Mât de Cocagne for a Mare's Nest at the top. **1892** *Times* (weekly ed.) 21 Oct. 18/2 Colonel S.'s discovery is a mere mare's nest.

¶ *Confused use.* **1857** J. W. CROKER in *C. Papers* 1 Feb. (1884) I. iii. 83 Tierney was ashamed of himself to be taken in such a mare's nest.

Hence **mare's-nest** *v.* to go after mare's-nests.

1859 LEVER *Dav. Dunn* xv. 134 He's always mare's nesting.

marespike, variant of MORRISPIKE.

maresquino, obs. form of MARASCHINO.

maress(e, marest, obs. forms of MARISH.

maresshall, obs. form of MARSHAL.

mare's tail, mares-tail (ˈmɛəzteɪl).
1. A common book-name for aquatic or marsh plants of the N.O. *Halorageæ*, esp. *Hippuris vulgaris*, formerly called Female Horsetail (see HORSETAIL 2b); often wrongly applied to the cryptogamous genus *Equisetum* (HORSETAIL 2). Also *attrib.*

1762 HUDSON *Fl. Anglica* 2 *Hippuris..Anglis* Mare's-tail. **1864** TENNYSON *Aylmer's F.* 92 The petty marestail forest, fairy pines. **1868** SIR J. HOOKER *Addr.* in *Rep. Brit. Assoc.* p. lxv, The existing family of Equisetaceæ..contained previously but one genus, that of the common mare's tails of our river-banks and woods. **1879** JEFFERIES *Wild Life in S. Co.* 374 On the shore, where it is marshy, the mares-tail flourishes.

2. *pl.* Long straight streaks of cirrus, supposed to foretoken stormy weather.

1775 DALRYMPLE in *Phil. Trans.* LXVIII. 408, A.M. sky mare's tails. **1853** KANE *Grinnell Exp.* xxix. (1856) 246 It resembled the mackerel fleeces and mare's tails of our summer skies at home. **1895** *Edin. Rev.* Apr. 531 It is the cloud known to seamen..as 'goats' hair' or 'mares' tails'. *attrib.* **1886** HUXLEY in *19th Cent.* XIX. 202 The wildest streaks of marestail clouds in the sky.

3. *Anat.* Rendering mod.L. *cauda equina*, the name given to a bundle of nerves at the lower extremity of the spine.

In some recent Dicts.

maretine, obs. form of MARITIME.

marevedi, obs. form of MARAVEDI.

marew, obs. form of MARROW *sb.*[1]

mareye, mareys(e, obs. ff. MARRY, MARISH.

Marezine (ˈmærəziːn). *Pharm.* Also **marezine**. [f. *mare-* + PIPER)AZINE.] 1-Methyl-4-α-phenylpiperazine hydrochloride, $C_{18}H_{22}N_2$.HCl, used in the form of tablets as an anti-emetic, esp. for the prevention and treatment of motion sickness. In the *British Pharmacopœia* called *cyclizine hydrochloride*.

Marezine is registered as a proprietary name in the U.S.

1952 *Official Gaz.* (U.S. Patent Office) 23 Dec. 1007/1 Burroughs Wellcome & Co... *Marezine* for medicinal preparations intended for use in the prevention or treatment of allergies, motion sickness, nausea and vomiting in pregnancy, or nausea due to other causes. **1954** *Jrnl. Pharmacol. & Exper. Therap.* CXII. 297 (*heading*) Pharmacologic properties of cyclizine hydrochloride (marezine). **1965** *Economist* 6 Nov. 615/2 The Food and Drug Administration announced last week that three anti-histamines—Bonine, Marezine and Cyclizine—which are used to combat nausea, including morning sickness, must carry a warning on their labels that, if taken by a pregnant woman, they may harm her unborn child. **1969** *Guardian* 21 July 9/2 Each [astronaut]..carries..45 milligrams of marezine for motion sickness.

marezzo (mæˈrɛtsəʊ). [It., f. *marezzare* to water (silk), marble.] A kind of artificial marble (see quots.). More fully ***marezzo marble***.

1876 *Encycl. Brit.* IV. 508/1 Marezzo marble is made of cement mixed with fibre for strength and to resist a blow. **1901** *Notes on Building Construction* (ed. 5) III. iii. 250 The basis of Marezzo marble, as well as of Scagliola, being plaster of Paris, neither of them is capable of bearing exposure to the weather. *Ibid.*, The Artificial Marble now manufactured in London is made on the same principle as the Marezzo, but differs from it in the character of the cement used. **1958** F. S. MERRITT *Building Construction Handbk.* XII. 9 *Marezzo*, an imitation marble formed with Keene's cement to which colors have been added. **1964** J. S. SCOTT *Dict. Building* 201 *Marezzo marble*, an artificial marble like *scagliola*, which differs from it mainly in having no chips of added coloured material. When precast, it is cast on a smooth sheet of plate glass or slate to give a polished surface.

marfaylle, obs. form of MARVEL.

mar-fire (ˈmɑːfaɪə(r)). *dial.* Also **mer-**. [app. a half-translated adoption of ON. *mauru-eldr*, *mǫru-eldr* (Da. *morild*) phosphorescence, esp. in the sea (according to Vigf. = **maura-eldr*, 'ants' fire', but form and sense are both difficult; Torp and Falk connect the first element with words denoting putrescence). The Eng. forms might however represent an OE. type **mere-fýr*, 'sea-fire'.] Phosphorescence on the sea.

1887 HALL CAINE *Deemster* xi. 74 When we're lying at anchor,..and the stars just makin' a peep, and the moon, and the mar-fire. **1892** *Northumbld. Gloss.*, *Mer-fire*, the luminous appearance of the sea at night. **1894** R. LEIGHTON *Wreck Golden Fleece* 31 There bean't much mar-fire moving.

marfounder: see MORFOUNDER.

marg (mɑːg). Now *dial.* Also **murg**. [? Short for MARGARET. Cf. the synonymous *margan*, *morgan* (E.D.D.).] Stinking Camomile, *Anthemis Cotula*. (Also pl.: cf. *maythes*.)

1609 C. BUTLER *Fem. Mon.* vi. H 2, The most stinking and poysonful weeds, as redweed, marges [*marg.* Mathers or May-weed], henbane. **1883** *Hampsh. Gloss.*, *Marg*,..*Murg*, *Anthemis fœtida*.

marg, var. MARGE[2].

margaceous (mɑːˈgeɪʃəs), *a.* *rare*[−1]. [f. L. *marga* marl: see -ACEOUS.] Marly.

1804 J. PARKINSON *Organ. Rem.* I. 423 The soft margaceous..matter, on the borders of lakes.

margant, obs. form of MARGENT.

margarate (ˈmɑːgərət). *Chem.* [f. MARGAR-IC + -ATE.] A salt of margaric acid.

1819 BRANDE *Chem.* vii. §9. 455 [Margaritic acid] unites with potassa in two proportions... These compounds have been termed margarates of potassa. **1897** *Allbutt's Syst. Med.* IV. 235 Margarate, stearate, and palmitate of lime.

margareit, obs. form of MARGARITE[1].

Margaret (ˈmɑːgərɪt). Also 3 **Marherete, Maregrete**, 4 **[Magote], margret, Mergrete**, 4–6 **margarete**, 5 **-ette**, 6 **-ite**. [a. OF. *Margarete*, *-ite* (mod.F. *Marguerite*), ad. late L. *Margarīta*, a female name, an application of L. *margarita* pearl: see MARGARITE[1].]

1. A female name.

[*a* **1300** *Cursor M.* 25456 (Cott.) Wit magote and wit mariori.] **1362** LANGL. *P. Pl.* A. IV. 37 Hou he Rauischede ..Mergrete of hire Maydenhod. *c* **1380** WYCLIF *Wks.* (1880) 205 Sussanne, katerine, margare [*v.r.* margarete], anneys. *a* **1649** DRUMM. OF HAWTH. *Poems*, An Epitaph of one named Margaret. In shells and gold pearls are not kept alone, A Margaret here lies beneath a stone. **1696** PHILLIPS (ed. 5), *Margaret*, (Greek) Pearl; the Christian Name of divers Women, contracted Marget.

†**2.** A daisy; esp. *Bellis perennis*: called also ***herb Margaret*** (see HERB *sb.* 7b), ***Margaret's herb***, ***brave Margaret***. (Cf. MARGUERITE.) *Obs.*

[According to French etymologists, this use of F. *marguerite* is not from the personal name, but comes directly from the sense 'pearl' (see MARGARITE[1]), having reference to the appearance of the flower (? or bud). It has, however, commonly been associated with the proper name: hence in recent times *Daisy* has been current in England as a pet-name for Margaret.]

a **1500** *Assemb. Ladies* 57 With margarettes growing in ordinaunce. **1503** HAWES *Examp. Virt.* XII. xxii, Bryngynge me a floure called the margarete. **1597** GERARDE *Herbal* II. cxciii. 512 The Daisie is called..of some *Herba Margarita*: or Margarites herbe. *a* **1607** LYTE *MS. notes in Dodoens* (Bibl. Mus. Brit. 442, h. 9) p. 126 (Britten & Holl.), Brave Margaret. **1640** PARKINSON *Theat. Bot.* Table, Margarites herbe or Daysies.

3. A variety of apple, and also of pear.

1664 EVELYN *Kal. Hort.* July (1679) 20 The Margaret-apple. **1707** MORTIMER *Husb.* (1721) II. 294 The Margaret, the Maudlin, the Cluster Pear. **1834** *Penny Cycl.* II. 190/1 (*Apple*) Early red Margaret.

4. A magpie; = MADGE[1] 2.

1854 MISS BAKER *Northampt. Gloss.* II. 2. **1890** *Cent. Dict.*

5. *U.S.* = MARGATE-FISH. Also ***margaret-grunt*** (Cent. Dict.). ***bastard margaret*** (see quot.).

1903 J. A. HENSHALL *Bass*, etc. 330 The Sailor's Choice (*Hæmulon parra*). This grunt is sometimes called bastard margaret by the Key West fisherman.

margaret(e, -ette, obs. ff. MARGARITE[1].

†**margaretton**. *Obs.* (See *diamargariton* in DIA- *pref.*[2])

1485 *Digby Myst.* III. 339 Dya, galonga, ambra, and also margaretton.

margari, variant of MARGERY *Obs.*, a pearl.

margaric (mɑːˈgærɪk), *a.* *Chem.* [mod. f. Gr. μάργαρ-ον = μαργαρίτης pearl + -IC, in reference to the pearly lustre of the crystals or scales.] In **margaric acid**: †**a.** orig. the name (*acide margarique*) given by Chevreul to one of the three fatty acids (*oleic*, *margaric*, *stearic*), the glyceryl derivatives of which (olein, margarin, stearin) were thought by him to form the chief constituents of animal fats. The composition assigned to margaric acid was (reduced to the new notation) $C_{17}H_{34}O_2$. So ***margaric ether***. *Obs.*

It was shown by Heintz in 1852 (*Journ. Prakt. Chem.* LXVI. 1) that the three fatty acids of animal fat are the oleic, palmitic, and stearic, and that the 'margaric' of Chevreul was really a mixture of palmitic ($C_{16}H_{32}O_2$) and stearic acid ($C_{18}H_{36}O_2$); and in this use the name is now obs., though it remained long in popular manuals, and its former prevalence is commemorated in the names MARGARINE and OLEO-MARGARINE.

1819 J. G. CHILDREN *Chem. Anal.* 314 Margaric acid was obtained from hog's lard by Chevreul in 1813. **1836** BRANDE *Chem.* III. vii. §12 (ed. 4) 962 Margaric Acid, so named from its pearly lustre,..bears a striking resemblance to stearic acid. It is obtained by decomposing the margarate of potassa. **1863** FOWNES *Chem.* (ed. 9) 533 Margaric ether is prepared by a similar mode of proceeding. *c* **1865** LETHEBY in *Circ. Sci.* I. 95/2 Margaric,..and other..Fatty Acids, are obtained from the oils.

b. By recent chemists, applied to an acid of composition $C_{17}H_{34}O_2$, artificially prepared.

1865–8 WATTS *Dict. Chem.* III. 852 Margaric acid forms white crystals, melting at 59·9°, and solidifying in crystalline scales on cooling. **1891** THORPE *Dict. Appl. Chem.* II. 101/2 Margaric acid $C_{16}H_{33}COOH$ may be formed by boiling margonitrile with alcoholic potash. **1892** MORLEY & MUIR *Watts' Dict. Chem.* III. 194. **1899** E. F. SMITH *Richter's Organ. Chem.* I. 250 Margaric Acid, $C_{17}H_{34}O_2$, does not apparently exist naturally in the fats. It is made in an artificial way by boiling cetyl cyanide with caustic potash.

margarin (ˈmɑːgərɪn). *Chem.* Also **-ine**. [ad. F. *margarine* (Chevreul), f. *margarique* MARGARIC: see -IN.] The margarate of glyceryl or glyceride of margaric acid. †**a.** Originally applied to a fatty substance contained in certain animal and vegetable oils, supposed to be the glyceride of the 'margaric acid' of Chevreul, really a mixture of stearin and palmitin. *Obs.* **b.** Now, the glyceride of margaric acid in its later application (see prec. b). Also *attrib.*

1836 BRANDE *Chem.* III. vii. §12 (ed. 4) 963 Margarine. This substance forms a part of mutton-suet, hogs'-lard, and some other animal fats. **1852** WATTS tr. *Gmelin's Handbk. Chem.* VII. 237 Human fat (a mixture of margarin and olein). *c* **1865** LETHEBY in *Circ. Sci.* I. 93/1 We have..tallow and its derivatives stearine and stearic acid, margarine and margaric acid. **1878** *Encycl. Brit.* VI. 104/2 The oil [cod-liver oil] contains olein and margarin. **1899** CAGNEY tr. *Jaksch's Clin. Diagn.* iv. (ed. 4) 136 Fatty Crystals (Margarine needles).—These are seen chiefly in putrid bronchitis and pulmonary gangrene.

margarine (ˈmɑːgəriːn, mɑːdʒəˈriːn). [a. F. *margarine*, a misapplication of the chemical term: see prec.] **a.** A substance made from edible oils and meat fats with water or skimmed milk, used as a spread on bread, etc., and as a cooking fat. Cf. BUTTERINE.

1873 *U.S. Patent Specif.* No. 146012. **1876** *World* V. No. 111. 12 Margarine is no novelty; it was brought out two or three years ago in Paris. **1887** EARL WEMYSS in *Times* 4 Aug. 8/3 On Friday next the great fight 'Butterine versus Margarine' will come off in the Lords. **1888** *Times* 3 Jan. 4/5 After adopting successively the names 'oleomargarine', 'butterine', and 'margarine', Parliament finally, after several struggles, resolved on the last. *Ibid.* 9/4 Margarine, as we formally record this morning, has begun its actual legislative existence. **1888** *Lancet* 14 Jan. 83/1 The word 'margarine' is, from a scientific point of view, inappropriate. **1890** [see FILLED *ppl. a.* 1 b]. **1907** *Act 7 Edw. VII* c. 21 §13 For the purposes of the Sale of Food and Drugs Act and this Act the expression 'margarine' shall mean any article of food, whether mixed with butter or not, which resembles butter and is not milk-blended butter. **1960** A. E. BENDER *Dict. Nutrition* 79/1 Margarine... Compulsorily fortified in many countries (and voluntarily in most) with vitamins A and D, so that it is nutritionally equal to butter. **1963** *Which?* July 211/1 Margarine is made from a selection of vegetable oils, sometimes whale or fish oil, and often lard, usually with skimmed milk, and water. **1975** *Listener* 16 Jan. 80/3 Sheep's head..mixed..with minced onion and margarine.

b. *attrib.*, as ***margarine factory***, ***works***; **margarine Act**, Act 50 & 51 Vict. (1887) c. 29, by which the name margarine is given to butter imitations; **margarine-cheese** (see quots.).

1887 *Act 50 & 51 Vict.* c. 29 §1 This Act may be cited as the Margarine Act, 1887. **1895** *Westm. Gaz.* 11 Sept. 3/2 Other particulars about the margarine factories. **1899** *Act 62 & 63 Vict.* c. 51 §25 The expression 'margarine-cheese' means any substance, whether compound or otherwise, which is prepared in imitation of cheese, and which contains fat not derived from milk. **1902** *Encycl. Brit.* XXV. 93/2 From America cheese has come into the English market, made from skim-milk which has again been provided with fatty matter, generally emulsified margarine—hence the term 'margarine cheese' or 'filled cheese'. **1909** *Chambers's Jrnl.* Jan. 24/1 Margarine works are equipped with cooling machinery.

c. *attrib.* = sham, 'bogus'.

1891 F. S. HADEN in *19th Cent.* May 780 One of those things which I fear I must call a 'margarine' substitute for an etching. **1897** SIR W. HARCOURT in *Daily News* 26 Nov. 3/3 Take care you do not get margarine Liberalism.

Hence **margaˈrine** *v. trans.*, to smear or spread (bread) with margarine; **margarined** *ppl. a.*

1918 *Punch* 15 May 315 She knows which side her bread's margarined. **1924** GALSWORTHY *White Monkey* III. iv. 243 'Well,' he said, over their cocoa and margarined bread: 'I must see Mr. Mont, that's certain.' **1960** D. STOREY *This Sporting Life* II. i. 159 She..began to margarine the bread.

Margarita (mɑːgəˈriːtə). Also **margarita**. [f. a woman's name.] **1.** A Spanish wine.

1920 G. SAINTSBURY *Notes on Cellar-Bk.* ii. 21 My cellars ..have seldom for fifty years been without a certain 'Margarita'. **1924** *Trade Marks Jrnl.* 17 Dec. 2876 Very superior very pale dry sherry. Margarita... Sherry wine, the produce of Spain. John Harvey & Sons, Limited,.. Bristol; wine and spirit merchants.

2. A cocktail made with tequila and citrus fruit juice.

1965 O. A. MENDELSOHN *Dict. Drink* 212 *Margarita*, mixed drink made from tequila and citrus juice, drunk from vessel whose rim has been dipped in salt. **1969** *Sat. Rev.* (U.S.) 8 Feb. 32/3 You'll learn how to make..mixed drinks, ranging from Margaritas and Mai-Tais to Irish Coffee and Moscow Mules. **1969** *Guardian* 4 July 7/4 Serve as an appetizer with..if you happen to have both limes and *tequila* —margaritas. **1969** A. GLYN *Dragon Variation* ix. 288 She handed the telephone back to the bartender and sipped her margarita. **1971** C. FICK *Danziger Transcript* (1973) 44 Her husband moved past us into..the bar... 'I'm dying for a margarita.'

margaritacean (mɑːgərɪˈteɪʃ(ɪ)ən), *a.* and *sb.* *Conch.* [f. mod.L. *Margaritāce-a*, f. L. *margarīta* pearl + -AN.] **a.** *adj.* Belonging to the *Margaritacea*, De Blainville's third family of lamellibranchiates. **b.** *sb.* A bivalve of this family.

In recent Dicts.

margaritaceous (mɑːgərɪˈteɪʃəs), *a. Nat. Hist.* [f. mod.L. *margarītāceus*, f. *margarīta*: see -ACEOUS.] Pearly.
1826 KIRBY & SP. *Entomol.* IV. 282 Margaritaceous.. Glossy white with changeable tints of purple, green, and blue. **1842** JOHNSTON in *Proc. Berw. Nat. Club* II. No. 10. 35 Shell cinereous,..interior magaritaceous.

margaritate (ˈmɑːgərɪteɪt). *Chem.* [f. MARGARITIC: see -ATE[1].] A salt of margaritic acid.
1839 *Penny Cycl.* XIV. 414/1.

margarite[1] (ˈmɑːgəraɪt). *Obs.* exc. *arch.* Also 4–6 **margaret, -it, -yte,** 5 **margrite, marguarite, -garette,** 6 **margareit, -garete, -grete, mergreit.** [a. OF. *margarite* (mod.F. *marguerite*), ad. L. *margarīta* (whence OF. *margerie* MARGERY, Sp. *margarita*, It. *margarita, margherita*), ad. Gr. μαργαρίτης (also μαργαρῖτις or μαργαρὶς λίθος, and simply μαργαρίς), f. μάργαρ-ον pearl, μάργαρ-ος pearl-oyster + -ίτης: see -ITE. In the early Teut. langs. the word was adopted with etymologizing perversion: the Goth. *marikreitus* (from the Greek), is influenced by *mari-, marei* sea, while the WGer. forms, OE. *meregrot, -grota,* OS. *merigri(o)ta,* OHG. *merigreoz, marigreoz,* MHG. *mergriez(e,* are altered so as to express the sense 'sea-pebble'.
The word is prob. adopted from some oriental lang. (Pliny refers to it as 'barbarous'): cf. Skr. *manjarī* cluster of flowers, also (according to the Indian lexicographers) pearl, cogn. w. *manju* beautiful. The Pahlavī *marvārīt* (:—**mary-*), Pers. *mervārīd*, Syriac *marganīthā* (whence Arab. *marjān*) are prob. from Greek.]
1. A pearl. Now only *arch.*
[*c* **1000** *Ags. Gosp.* Matt. xiii. 46 Þa he funde þæt an deorwyrðe meregrot.] **1310** in Wright *Lyric P.* v. 26 The myht of the margarite haveth this may mere. **1382** WYCLIF *Matt.* vii. 6 Nether sende ȝe ȝour margaritis [*gloss* or preciouse stoonys] before swyne. *a* **1450** *Knt. de la Tour* (1868) 163 A precious margarite, the whiche is a bright thinge, rounde, white, and clene. **1535** STEWART *Cron. Scot.* II. 367 The relict of Sanct Andro..Adornit wes..With diamontis ding, and margretis mony one. **1567** MAPLET *Gr. Forest* 14 The Margaret of all Gemmes, those which be in their kindes white, is esteemed the chiefest. **1698** FRYER *Acc. E. India & P.* 321, I have taken out of these Shell-fish many Margarites. **1772** NUGENT tr. *Hist. Friar Gerund* I. 207 That margarite or pearl..in a dissolution of which.. Cleopatra drank Anthony's health. **1885** R. F. BURTON *Arab. Nts.* (1887) III. 327 A collar set with margarites and rubies.
attrib. **1387–8** T. USK *Test. Love* III. i. (Skeat) l. 35 A Margarit perle, that is so precious a geme with clere and litell. **1598** TOFTE *Alba* (1880) 20 Rich Margarite Pearle.
¶ **b.** Taken to mean 'precious stone'.
c **1430** LYDG. *Min. Poems* (Percy Soc.) 188 Men shuld not put a precious margarite, As rubies, saphires,..Emeraudes ner rounde perles whight, To-fore rude swyne.
c. As the type of something precious: cf. *pearl.*
a **1450** *Knt. de la Tour* (1868) 157 The sowle is the precious marguarite vnto God. **1549** *Compl. Scot.* 1 Marie queen of Scotlande, the margareit and perle of princessis. **1635** BRATHWAIT *Five Senses*, etc. in *Archaica* (1815) II. 37 Meantime, that precious margarite, incased in this art-affected cabinet, may lose her lustre.
†**2.** (See MARGARET 2.) *Obs.*
Hence †**margaˈrital** *a.*, pearl-like.
a **1618** SYLVESTER *Sonn.* xii. Wks. (Grosart) II. 323/2 The margaritall-gem For praise deserves thy name.

margarite[2] (ˈmɑːgəraɪt). *Min.* [f. Gr. μάργαρον pearl + -ITE.] 'Pearl mica', a hydrous silicate found in scales having a pearly lustre.
1823 W. PHILLIPS *Introd. Min.* (ed. 3) 208 Margarite. This mineral is in the mass of a greyish white colour... It has lately been brought into this country from the Tyrol.

margaritic (mɑːgəˈrɪtɪk), *a. Chem.* [f. L. *margarita* pearl + -IC.] ***margaritic acid***: †**a.** used for Chevreul's *acide margarique* (MARGARIC a) (*obs.*); **b.** the name (*a. margaritique*) given by Bussy to one of the fatty acids resulting from the saponification of castor oil.
1819 BRANDE *Chem.* vii. §9. 455 A peculiar acid, called by Chevreul, from its pearly appearance, margaritic acid.

margaritiferous (ˌmɑːgərɪˈtɪfərəs), *a.* [f. L. *margarītifer* (Pliny), f. *margarīta* MARGARITE: see -FEROUS.] Producing pearls. Also (*nonce-use*), wearing pearls.
1656 BLOUNT *Glossogr.*, *Margaritiferous.* **1682** T. A. *Carolina* 26 Some of which [oysters] are margiriteferous [*sic*]. **1838** *New Monthly Mag.* LIII. 554 The margaritiferous reader. **1839** SOWERBY *Conch. Man.* 62. **1887** *Standard* 30 Apr. 5/2 But it is only within comparatively recent times that Western Australia has been known to be margaritiferous.

margaritite (ˈmɑːgərɪtaɪt). [f. MARGARITE + -ITE.] A fossil pearl-producing shell.
In recent Dicts.

margarodite (ˈmɑːgərədaɪt). *Min.* [ad. G. *margarodit* (Schafhäutl, 1843), f. late Gr. μαργαρώδης pearly, f. μάργαρον pearl: see -ITE[1] 2 b.] A variety of potash mica having a pearly lustre.
1849 WATTS tr. *Gmelin's Handbk. Chem.* III. 451 Margarodite forms the matrix of the black tourmaline from the Zillerthal. **1854** DANA *Syst. Min.* (ed. 4) II. 223.

margaron, -one (ˈmɑːgərɒn, -əʊn). *Chem.* [ad. F. *margarone* (Bussy 1832), f. *margarique* MARGARIC: see -ONE.] A solid fatty substance crystallizing in pearly scales, formed by the distillation of margaric acid with lime.
1834 *Lond. & Edinb. Philos. Mag.* V. 153 On Margaron, Stearon, and Oleon. **1836** BRANDE *Chem.* III. vii. §12 (ed. 4) 963 Margarone. **1863** FOWNES *Chem.* (ed. 9) 533 A fatty body, incapable of saponification, termed *margarone.*

margary, variant of MARGERY *Obs.*, a pearl.

margasite, obs. form of MARCASITE.

ˈmargate-fish, ˈmargate-grunt. [Of obscure origin: variants given in Dicts. are *market-, maggot-fish* and *margaret-grunt.* Cf. MARGARET 5.] A pearly-white fish, *Hæmulon album*, found in the Gulf of Mexico.
1734 MORTIMER in *Phil. Trans.* XXXVIII. 315 *Perca marina Gibbosa cinerea.* The Margate-Fish. This is esteem'd very good Meat. **1775** ROMANS *Florida* App. 19 Margate-fish, rock-fish [etc.]. **1903** J. A. HENSHALL *Bass,* etc. 328 The Margate-fish (*Hæmulon album*). The margate-fish, or margate grunt, is the largest of the family.

‖**Margaux** (ˈmɑːgəʊ, Fr. margo). Also 8 **margose, margou.** Claret manufactured in the commune of Margaux, department of Gironde, France.
1705 *Lond. Gaz.* No. 4128/4, 230 Hogsheads of new Pontac and Margose Wine. **1725** WELSTED *Oikographia* 12 Nor Margou, stor'd in Priestly Cells, That on the Palate grateful dwells. **1734** SHERIDAN *Let. to Swift* 16 Aug. S.'s Wks. 1841 II. 724, I drink right French margose. **1858** HOMANS *Dict. Comm.* 192 (Bordeaux) The third-rate wines comprise those called *Pauillac, Margaux, St. Jullien, St. Estèphe, St. Emilion,* etc.

margay (ˈmɑːgeɪ). [a. F. *margay* (Buffon), altered from *margaia* (Claude d'Abbeville 1614), an inexact representation of Tupi *mbaracaïa.*] A South American tiger cat, *Felis tigrina.*
1781 SMELLIE tr. *Buffon* (1791) VII. 249 The Margay, or Cayenne Cat. **1838** HUNTER tr. *Azara's Quadrup. Paraguay* 239 Buffon describes a margay, which name, after Abbeville, he derives from..*maragaya*, the appellation he supposes to be given to it in Brazil. **1859** WOOD *Nat. Hist.* I. 185 The Margay is a very handsome example of the Tiger Cats.

marge[1] (mɑːdʒ). Now *poet.* or *rhet.* [ad. F. *marge*:—L. *margin-em* MARGIN.]
1. = MARGIN *sb.* 1.
1551 RECORDE *Pathw. Knowl.* II. lxxvi, The marge or edge of the circumference of the circle. **1596** SPENSER *F.Q.* IV. viii. 61 As by the flowrie marge On a fresh streame I with that Elfe did play. **1612** DRAYTON *Poly-olb.* ii. 25 So Pleasantlie in-il'd on mighty Neptune's marge. **1753** WARTON *Approach of Summer* 92 Near the rush'd marge of Cherwell's flood. **1805** WORDSW. *Prelude* VIII. 459 The western marge of Thurston-mere. **1849** M. ARNOLD *Strayed Reveller* 16 The ivy-wreath'd marge Of thy cup. **1898** W. K. JOHNSON *Terra Tenebr.* 72 By the marble marge of unstirred wells.
b. of immaterial things.
1876 FARRAR *Marlb. Serm.* vi. 59 That great future which blooms.. beyond the marge of death. **1878** BROWNING *La Saisiaz* 70 Mind to-morrow's early meeting! We must have our journey marge Ample for the wayside wonders.
2. = MARGIN 2. *rare.*
1577 HANMER *Anc. Eccl. Hist.* VI. xii. 370 (marg.) In the marge of the Greeke copie there was written as followeth. **1657** J. SERGEANT *Schism Dispach't* 74 As cited in the marge by himself. **1859** TENNYSON *Vivien* 519 Every page having an ample marge.
Hence **marge** *v. trans.*, to fringe, edge.
1852 *Fraser's Mag.* XLVI. 166 Little bays, marged with printless yellow sands.

marge[2] (mɑːdʒ), **marg** (mɑːg, mɑːdʒ). Colloq. abbrevs. of MARGARINE, as pronounced (mɑːdʒəˈriːn) or (ˈmɑːgəriːn).
1922 JOYCE *Ulysses* 150 Potatoes and marge, marge and potatoes. **1933** 'G. ORWELL' *Down & Out* xxiv. 179 'No butter, only marg,' she said, surprised. **1937** E. GARNETT *Family from One End Street* iv. 82 Fetch me a bit of marg. Lily Rose—I can't waste butter on him. **1939** N. MONSARRAT *This is Schoolroom* viii. 197 Living on the dole ..bread-and-marge, and meat once a month. **1960** J. BETJEMAN *Summoned by Bells* vii. 70 In quieter tones we asked in Hall that night Neighbours to pass the marge. **1974** W. FOLEY *Child in Forest* II. 161 The remembered slice of marge-spread toast.

margeant, obs. form of MARGENT.

margelene, obs. form of MARJORAM.

†**margeline.** *Obs.* Also 7 **margellane, mareleyne, morgeline.** [Corruption of F. *morgeline* 'ivie Chickweed, Henne-bit; also, the small, or fine Chickweed; also, Pimpernel' (Cotgr.).
Cooper 1565 (s.v. *Anagallis*) gives *margelina* as Latin. F. *morgeline* is:—L. *morsus gallinæ*, lit. 'hen's bite' (cf. HENBIT).]
The Scarlet Pimpernel, *Anagallis arvensis.*
1572 HULOET (ed. Higins), Margeline an herbe, *asyla.* **1601** HOLLAND *Pliny* II. 234 They haue recourse..to an herbe for remedy called in Greeke Asyla, and by vs in Latine Ferus oculus (*i.* the wild and cruell eie, or Margellane). **1611** COTGR., *Mauvais œil*, Ivie Chickweed, Morgeline, Henbit. **1648** HEXHAM, *Roodt Guychelheyl*, Red Mareleyne, an herbe. **1783** AINSWORTH *Lat. Dict.* (ed. Morell) v, *Asyla,* ..an herb wherewith cattle cure themselves, when they have eaten of pimpernel, or margeline.

margent (ˈmɑːdʒənt), *sb.* Now *arch.* and *poet.* Also 5 **mariante,** 5–6 **margente,** 6 **mergent(e,** 7 **marg(e)ant, -gint.** [Altered form of MARGIN *sb.*; cf. *ancient, pageant, peasant, pheasant, tyrant.*]
1. = MARGIN *sb.* 1.
1538 ELYOT *Dict.*, *Margo*, the brymme or edge of euery thynge, the margent. **1553** EDEN *Treat. Newe Ind.* (Arb.) 25 Grauen Lions on euery syde adourning the rayles or highest margentes of the same. **1596** SPENSER *F.Q.* V. x. 3 From th' utmost brinke of the Armericke shore Unto the margent of the Molucas. **1634** MILTON *Comus* 232 By slow Meander's margent green. **1649** JER. TAYLOR *Gt. Exemp.* II. §12. 39 Jesus sate himself down upon the margent of Jacob's well. **1742** GRAY *Ode Eton* 23 Say father Thames, for thou hast seen Full many a sprightly race Disporting on thy margent green. **1837** MISS MITFORD *Country Stories* (1850) 107 Coppices with wide turfy margents on either side. **1853** G. JOHNSTON *Nat. Hist. E. Bord.* I. 157 It..often hides midst brushwood on the margent of a burn. **1901** HENLEY *Hawthorn & Lavender* 6 From reluctant woods..And sering margents, forced To be lean and bare.
fig. **1679** PULLER *Moder. Ch. Eng.* (1843) 329 By catching at some little scattered parts, of the skirts and margent of the cause.
2. = MARGIN *sb.* 2.
1432–50 tr. *Higden* (Rolls) I. 41 Y schalle purpulle the mariantes [TREVISA margyns]..with a dowble ordre of yeres. *c* **1485** *Digby Myst.* IV. 273 Looke How many bludy letters beyn writen in þis buke, Small margente her is. **1532** MORE *Confut. Barnes* VIII. Wks. 776/1 And thys himselfe confesseth in the mergent of his booke. **1555** EDEN *Decades* 188 Whiche the lymmers of bookes are accustomed to paynte on the margentes of churche bookes. **1588** SHAKS. *L.L.L.* v. ii. 8 A sheet of paper Writ on both sides the leafe, margent and all. **1612** BRINSLEY *Lud. Lit.* 71 Let them learne euery rule..and the summes of the rules which are set in the margents. **1645** MILTON *Colast.* Wks. 1851 IV. 345 A big margent, litter'd and overlaid with crude and huddl'd quotations. **1722** SEWEL *Hist. Quakers* (1795) I. IV. 364 We have seen some of your laws, that have many Scriptures in the margent. **1834** LANDOR *Exam. Shaks.* Wks. 1853 II. 282/2 Such were the very words; I wrote them down with two signs in the margent.
b. The margin of a book as being the place for a commentary upon or summary of the text; hence, the commentary or summary itself.
1579 W. WILKINSON *Confut. Familye of Loue* 48 These his vayne payntyngs of his margent, shall hereafter make his cause more odious. **1589** LYLY *Pappe w. Hatchet* Wks. 1902 III. 413 Beware my Comment, tis odds the margent shall bee as full as the text. **1592** SHAKS. *Rom. & Jul.* I. iii. 86 And what obscur'd in this faire volume lies, Find written in the Margent of his eyes. **1602** —— *Ham.* v. ii. 162. **1657** AUSTEN *Fruit Trees* I. 18 As the Margint renders it. **1733** SWIFT *Brother Protest.* Wks. 1755 IV. I. 182 That blockhead.. Who knows in law nor text, nor margent.
3. = MARGIN *sb.* 4 a.
1678 MOXON *Mech. Exerc.* 106 The Middle Rail hath commonly two breadths of the Margent of the Stile. *Ibid.* 110. **1823** [see MARGIN *sb.* 3 a].
4. *attrib.* (or quasi-*adj.* = marginal).
1555 EDEN *Decades* Contents *ad fin.*, Reade the margente notes of the same. **1643** R. SALTONSTALL *To Winthrop* (Cent.), Margent notes upon a French text. **1811** W. R. SPENCER *Poems* 113 The margent thistles of the Tweed.
Hence †**margent** *v. trans.*, to insert as a marginal note, to add marginal notes to.
1610 R. NICCOLS *Eng. Eliza* To Rdr., I present it in one whole entire Hymne, distinguishing it only by succession of yeares, which I haue margented through the whole storie. **1662–3** PEPYS *Diary* 23 Jan., Finishing the margenting of my Navy-Manuscript.

margerain, -ome, -yn, obs. ff. MARJORAM.

†**ˈmargery.** *Obs.* Also 4 **margari, -ary, -yrye, mariari, -iori,** 4–5 **margerie, -ye.** [a. OF. *margerie*:—L. *margarītam*: see MARGARITE[1].] A pearl. Chiefly *attrib.* in ***margery pearl, stone.***
13.. *Propr. Sanct.* (Vernon MS.) in Herrig *Archiv* LXXXI. 113/16 He fond a precious Margari-ston. **1362** LANGL. *P. Pl.* A. XI. 9 *Noli mittere* margeri-perles Among hogges. **13..** *E.E. Allit. P.* A. 1036 Þe portalez pyked of rych platez & vch ȝate of a margyrye, A parfyt perle þat neuer fatez. *c* **1430** *Pilgr. Lyf Manhode* I. ci. (1869) 55 It is thing michel more worth than a margerye, and more precious. **1530** PALSGR. 243/1 Margery perle, *nacle.*

†**ˈmargery-ˈprater.** *Cant. Obs.* Also 7 **mergery-.** A hen.
1567 HARMAN *Caveat* 83. **1622** FLETCHER *Beggar's Bush* V. i, Or mergery-praters, Rogers, And Tibs o' th' buttry. **1641** BROME *Jov. Crew* II. F 3, Here's Grunter and Bleater, with Tib of the Buttry, And Margery Prater, all drest without sluttry. *a* **1700** B. E. *Dict. Cant. Crew.*

margh(e, marghty, obs. ff. MARROW *sb.*[1], -Y.

marȝen, obs. form of MORN.

margin (ˈmɑːdʒɪn), *sb.* Also 4–6 **mar-, mergyn(e,** 4–7 **margine,** (6 **mergin,** *Sc.* **mairgeane**); and see MARGENT. [ad. L. *margin-em* (nom. *margo*), cogn. w. MARK *sb.*[1] A single instance of OF. *margine* (15th c.) is cited by

Godefr. Cf. F. *marge* (see MARGE), Sp. *márgen*, Pg. *margem*, It. *margine*.
The word was little used in the 17th c., its place being taken by MARGENT.]

1. a. That part of a surface which lies immediately within its boundary, esp. when in some way marked off or distinguished from the rest of the surface; also, the space immediately adjacent to a well, a river, or piece of water; an edge, border, or brink.

1382 WYCLIF *Exod.* xxviii. 24 The rynges that ben in the mergyns of it [Vulg. *marginibus*; 1388 brynkis]. *c* **1391** CHAUCER *Astrol.* I. §21 The names of the sterres ben writen in the Margyn of the riet. **1463–4** *Rolls of Parlt.* V. 501/2 In the utter partie of the mergyne of the same cloth. **1530** PALSGR. 243/1 Margyn or brinke of any thyng, *bort*; *riue*. **1739** S. SHARP *Surg.* Introd. 4 All the Advantage to be gathered from it is only from the Evenness of its Margin. **1774** M. MACKENZIE *Maritime Surv.* iv. 41 On the Margin of a Lake, close to the Edge of the Water. **1805** SOUTHEY *Madoc in W.* vii, Between the mountain-base And the green margin of the waters. **1860** TYNDALL *Glac.* I. v. 40 The chasms at the margin of the glacier. **1870** F. R. WILSON *Ch. Lindisf.* 34 Tweedmouth Church stands upon the margin of the Tweed. **1887** MOLONEY *Forestry W. Afr.* 426 Limited to swampy lowlands or margins of lagoons.

b. *Nat. Hist.* Applied either to the contour or boundary line of a body, or to a distinct border differing in texture, etc. from the main body.

1760 J. LEE *Introd. Bot.* I. xi. (1765) 24 The Variations of the Calyx in respect to..its Equality, Margin and Apex, or Top. **1807–26** S. COOPER *First Lines Surg.* (ed. 5) 467 At the very point where the spermatic cord emerges from under the lower margin of the transverse muscle. **1861** BENTLEY *Man. Bot.* 133 The lines connecting the base and apex of the leaf are called the *edges* or *margins*, or collectively the *circumscription*. **1872** L. P. MEREDITH *Teeth* (1878) 240 One of his upper incisors broken entirely off at the margin of the gum.

†**c.** A boundary. *Obs.*

c **1586** C'TESS PEMBROKE *Ps.* XCVIII. ii, [God's promise] ev'ry margine of this earthy spheare Now sees performed.

2. *fig.* **a.** A condition which closely approximates to the limit below or beyond which something ceases to be possible or desirable.

1863 FAWCETT *Pol. Econ.* II. iii. 141 In any given condition of a country there is some land which will just pay for cultivation if it is let at a nominal rent. Thus, as it were, a margin of cultivation is marked, below which the cultivation of land cannot descend, unless some circumstances should occur which should either induce men to be satisfied with smaller profits, or should increase the productiveness of land. **1869** ROGERS *Adam Smith's W.N.* I. II. iii. 335 *note*, No tax can be levied from those who are on the margin of bare subsistence.

b. An amount (of space, time, money, material, etc.) allowed or available in addition to what is estimated to be strictly necessary for a certain purpose, and serving as a provision for unforeseen contingencies, or admitting of being applied to other purposes; *spec.* profit(s), profit margin.

1851 C. CIST *Sh. Cincinnati in 1851* 319 We are in the enjoyment of a clear margin, of at least, half a cent per pound, over our eastern neighbors. **1852** E. WARBURTON *Darien* Introd. I. 5 The purchase of an annuity..secured to him an ample supply for his simple wants, and left him besides a wide margin for the charities in which his brave old heart delighted. **1858** FROUDE *Hist. Eng.* III. xiii. 145 The King, in his instructions, left a wide margin of discretion to the generals. **1865** MILL *Pol. Econ.* (ed. 6) IV. iv. §5 The fall of profits would be retarded if money wages did not rise, or rose in a less degree; but the margin which can be gained by a deterioration of the labourer's condition is a very narrow one. **1865** DICKENS *Mut. Fr.* III. vi, Within a certain margin of hours. **1866** ROGERS *Agric. & Prices* I. iv. 81 The narrow margin of profit had been reduced to a minimum. **1873** HAMERTON *Intell. Life* v. iii. (1875) 190 The shortening of the hours of labour may afford some margin of leisure. **1890** *Congress. Rec.* 25 June 6499/2 When an employer feels that his margin is slipping away from him, the first thing done is to scale down the price of wages. **1940** *Economist* 31 Aug. 291/1 Fixed margins, which were established..to check an incipient boom, are now..the subject of some controversy. **1971** *Daily Tel.* 21 Oct. 23 (*heading*) Doubled margins work wonders for Spillers. **1972** W. A. PANTIN *Oxf. Life* iv. 48 The estates allotted to the support of chairs were in some cases left in the hands of the university, which paid out of them the appropriate salary to the professor, and sometimes made a profit out of the margin. **1972** *Times* 16 Oct. 4/6 Wheat..is grown as much for the straw as for its £57 an acre gross margin. *Ibid.* 4/7 Bulbs..give easily the biggest margin to the acre.

c. *Stockbroking* and *Comm.* (*a*) A certain sum deposited by a speculative seller or buyer with his broker to cover the risk of loss on a transaction on account. (*b*) *U.S.* 'A deposit made by each of two brokers, parties to a contract, when one is called up (as it is termed) by the other' (*Cent. Dict.* 1890).

1848 W. ARMSTRONG *Stocks* 10 The purchaser then hands over this margin to the person with whom he hypothecates the Stock. **1870** J. K. MEDBERY *Men & Mysteries Wall St.* 62 Seven per cent a year is generally allowed on all margins advanced by customers. **1880** *Harper's Mag.* Oct. 782/2 All speculated, but they did not speculate on margins. **1882** *Pall Mall G.* 15 July 5/1 Egyptian Unified bonds went crawling down to below 48, and alarmed bankers were sending after their 'margins'. **1883** *St. James's Gaz.* 1 Nov., In Liverpool sales of cotton for future delivery are made without any deposit of 'margins'. **1885** *Harper's Mag.* Mar. 611/1 The speculators were..caught without any margin. **1888** BRYCE *Amer. Commw.* III. xcii. 288 Ohio punishes by fine and imprisonment the offering to sell 'options' or exhibiting any quotations of the prices of 'margins', 'futures' or 'options'. **1902** *Westm. Gaz.* 11 Nov. 11/3 The bulk of the shares in what are called the speculative lines are held by speculators on margin. **1934** S. S. HUEBNER *Stock Market* xxiii. 434 If the customer purchases stock worth $100 and deposits $20 as margin,..he has a margin of 20 per cent. **1971** *Investors Chronicle's Beginners, Please* (ed. 5) 310 The latter [*sc.* the broker] makes an interest charge..and receives from his client..sufficient to maintain an adequate 'margin' to protect the broker against fluctuations in the value of the collateral.

d. *Life-insurance.* = LOADING *vbl. sb.* 3.

1881 [see LOADING *vbl. sb.* 3].

e. ***margin of safety***: an allowance made for safety, *spec.* a number equal to the factor of safety (FACTOR *sb.* 8) minus one.

1888 R. S. BALL *Exper. Mech.* (ed. 2) ii. 33 So great a margin of safety is necessary on account of the jerks and other occasional great strains that arise in the raising and the lowering of heavy weights. **1905** *Trans. Inst. Naval Archit.* XLVII. II. 203 One hears, both in the lecture theatre and drawing office, much talk of 'margins of safety'. **1941** N. H. ANDERSON *Aircraft Layout* vii. 179 If the margin of safety comes out a negative quantity, the design is not satisfactory; in all cases a positive margin of safety is required. **1968** F. K. TEICHMANN *Fund. Aircraft Structural Analysis* 78 In general, the designer of aircraft structures selects structural elements with a margin of safety of zero. This does not mean that safety is not built into the craft..since the loads, or load factors actually imposed on the craft are determined rather precisely.

3. a. The space on a page between the extreme edge and the main body of written or printed matter, often partly taken up with notes, references, illuminations, or the like. Often in narrower sense, applied to the margins at the sides of the page ('inner' and 'outer' margins) as distinguished from the 'head' and 'foot.'

1362 LANGL. *P. Pl.* A. VIII. 20 Marchauns in þis Margin [of a bull] hedden mony ȝeres [of pardon]. **1398** TREVISA *Barth. De P.R.* XV. xxiv. (1495) 497 Loke in the nexte pagyn in thende of the mergyn. **1532** MORE *Confut. Barnes* VIII. Wks. 756/2, I lette passe that he noteth in the margine these woordes how a manne maye knowe the church. **1589** *Reg. Privy Council Scot.* IV. 442 Thay wer nocht contenit in the body of the said principall letter..bot interlynnit on the mairgeane thairof. **1611** BIBLE *Transl. Pref.* ¶15 Some peraduenture would haue no varietie of sences to be set in the margine. **1621** BP. MOUNTAGU *Diatribæ* 219 For this we haue Scripture and Fathers in the margine. **1783** JOHNSON in *Boswell* 1 May, I know when I have been writing verses, I have run my finger down the margin, to see how many I had made, and how few I had to make. **1817** DIBDIN *Bibliogr. Decam.* II. 471 Books with larger margins are no where to be found. **1851** LONGF. *Gold. Leg.* IV. *Scriptorium*, I..will sketch her thus, in her quiet nook, For the margin of my Gospel book.

b. The annotations placed in the margin of a work (cf. MARGENT 2 b); in quot. *transf.*, an explanatory indication.

1824 HOGG *Conf. Sinner* 88 She viewed Mrs. Logan with a stern, steady gaze, as if reading her features as a margin to her intellect.

4. a. *Joinery.* The flat part of the stiles and rails of framed work. **b.** *Building.* 'That part of the upper side of a course of slates which appears uncovered by the next superior course' (Gwilt).

[**1678**: see MARGENT *sb.* 3.] **1823** P. NICHOLSON *Pract. Build.* 226 Margins or Margents.—The flat part of the stiles and rails of framed work. **1855** F. REINNEL *Masons*, etc. *Assist.* 70 The part of the back of every course which is exposed to the eye is called the margin of that course.

5. *attrib.*, as ***margin-cell, light, sand***; **margin call**, a demand by a broker that an investor deposit further cash or securities to guarantee the margin (sense 2 c) on his investment; **margin clerk**, one who records dealings in margins (sense 2 c); **margin draft, draught** = DRAFT *sb.* 6 a (Ogilvie 1850); **margin line** *Naut.* (see quot.); **margin release, marginal release**, the mechanism on a typewriter which enables the typewriting to run into the set margin; hence **margin release key**, the key on the machine which operates this mechanism; **margin-tailed** *a.*, having a marginate tail (*Cent. Dict.*).

1961 R. E. BADGER et al. *Investment Princ. & Pract.* (ed. 5) iv. 84 If the market value of the securities in an account declines, the broker issues a '*margin call' to the customer, requesting the deposit of additional cash or securities to protect against loss on the loan. **1963** PHILLIPS & LANE *Personal Finance* vii. 180 If a stock declines in market price, a margin call may be issued by the broker who must require the required margin coverage at current market prices, else he must sell the stock to protect the interests of the creditors who have supplied the previously borrowed funds. **1972** *N.Y. Law Jrnl.* 14 Nov. 2/2 The deficit arose after defendant was unable to meet margin calls. **1882** VINES *Sachs' Bot.* 142 This wall intersects the dividing wall of the *margin-cell previously formed. **1886** *Harper's Mag.* July 213/2 Speculative sales of land..are also made in the Call Room..the caller of provisions and *margin clerk presiding. **1973** *N.Y. Law Jrnl.* 30 July 4/6 The regulation should be ..in the language of the brokers and margin clerks who must work under it. **1858** *Skyring's Builders' Prices* (ed. 48) 34 Deal cased frames..with *margin lights or rail *c* **1850** *Rudim. Navig.* (Weale) 131 **Margin line*, a line or edge parallel to the upper side of the wing transom, and about five inches below it, at which place terminate all the butts of the bottom planks abaft. **1913** *Pitman's Commercial Encycl. & Dict. Business* IV. 1620/2 Note what a wonderful improvement there is..in all the minor parts, such as ..*margin release keys. **1914** *Pitman's Commercial Self-Educator* I. 163/1 Closely connected with these Marginal Stops is the Margin Release, which in the latest models takes the form of a key marked 'Marginal Release' or 'M.R.' **1939** F. A. FAUNCE *Secretarial Efficiency* II. vi. 87 Notice the location of..the backspacer, the margin release, and the ribbon shift. **1962** J. B. PRIESTLEY *Margin Released* p. viii, Typewriters..have a key labelled 'Margin Release', frequently needed by hasty and careless typists like myself. **1967** J. HARRISON *Secretarial Duties* (ed. 3) viii. 106 When erasing, move the carriage fully to the left or right, using the margin-release key. **1820** KEATS *Hyperion* I. 15 Along the *margin-sand large foot-marks went.

Hence **'marginless** *a.*, having no margin.

1839 D. MACMILLAN *Mem.* (1882) 89, I have had to cut away all the margin... This marginless volume..will be [etc.].

margin ('mɑːdʒɪn), *v.* [f. prec. sb. Cf. late L. *margināre*, F. *marginer*.]

1. *trans.* To furnish with marginal notes; to annotate or summarize in the margin.

1607 HIERON *Defence* I. 78 Though it be his use, to margin his English, with greek or latin or both. **1616** SIR T. ROE *Jrnl.* 4 Sept. (1899) 260, I receiued my Articles back from Asaph chan, who tooke now att last many exceptions, and margined them with his Pen in most Insolent sort. **1651** C. CARTWRIGHT *Cert. Relig.* I. 52 If any man may be permitted to appeale to Scriptures: margind with his own notes. *a* **1734** NORTH *Exam.* I. i. § 7 (1740) 18 These he deals forth..as the notable Matters, margined for better Notice. **1885** E. S. FFOULKES *Prim. Consecr.* iv. 73 Of the four prayers margined by Mr. Hammond as 'Recital of the work of Redemption, Words of Institution, Confession of Faith, and the Great Oblation', not a trace occurs in S. Cyril.

2. To specify in the margin of a page.

c **1640** J. SMYTH *Lives Berkeleys* (1883) I. 294 Whereto add these records here margined. **1868** *Voice of Truth* May 117 There are no fewer than 2283 articles, all numbered, named, and the places they came from carefully margined.

3. a. To provide with a margin, edge, or border. Freq. in *pass.*

1715 tr. *Pancirollus' Rerum Mem.* I. IV. ii. 158 Hats..were margin'd with Brims, as a commodious Shelter. **1725** H. BOURNE *Antiq. Vulgares* 65 If its water was..margin'd with the tender grass. **1797** MRS. RADCLIFFE *Italian* xix. 102/1 Entering the little bay, where the hamlet margined the beach. **1860** GOSSE *Rom. Nat. Hist.* 35 The broad belt of reeds which margined the river. **1865** *Pall Mall G.* 16 Sept., A vellum pamphlet..each leaf of which was numbered and neatly margined with red ink. **1883** F. M. CRAWFORD *Dr. Claudius* i, A variety of mathematical figures, margined all round with odd-looking equations.

b. *Nat. Hist.* and *Path.* (Cf. MARGIN *sb.* 1 b.)

1840 *Cuvier's Anim. Kingd.* 244 The feathers margined with greyish during the winter. *Ibid.* 249 The membranes margining the toes. **1849** J. E. GRAY *Catal. Specim. Snakes Brit. Mus.* 113 The upper band-like, transverse, like a frontal, margining the rostral. **1881** J. S. GARDNER in *Nature* XXIII. 251 The leaves are smaller..the parenchyma reduced to a narrow expansion margining each vein. **1898** J. HUTCHINSON *Arch. Surg.* IX. 125 [The eruption] consisted of patches which were not abruptly margined.

4. *Stockbroking.* To deposit a 'margin' upon (stock). Also *intr.* in ***to margin up*** (U.S.): to provide additional 'margin' when what has been paid is insufficient.

18.. *Amer. Economist* III. 176 (Cent.) The concern then had $42,500,000 locked up on Bourse, having trebled its liabilities in the vain attempt to margin up after a fall begun in September, 1881. **1896** *Westm. Gaz.* 4 Aug. 7/3 The banks are indifferent, as the stocks held are securely margined. **1902** H. L. WILSON *Spenders* xxxiv. 408 As the stock fell, the banks requested the brokers to margin up their loans, and the brokers, in turn, requested Percival to margin up his trades. **1973** *N.Y. Law Jrnl.* 30 July 4/2 Once a margin account has been properly margined, the regulation imposes no further requirements respecting the status of the account in the absence of a subsequent transaction.

marginal ('mɑːdʒɪnəl), *a.* and *sb.* [ad. mod.L. *marginālis*, f. *margin-*, *margo*, MARGIN *sb.* Cf. F. *marginal*.] **A.** *adj.*

1. a. Written or printed in the margin of a page, as ***marginal note, reference***. Hence ***marginal bible***, one with marginal notes.

1576 FLEMING *Panopl. Epist.* 34 *margin*, Thes words are.. made plaine, in the first Epistle, Li. 6. in a marginall note. **1611** COTGR. s.v. *Marc*, Looke the next marginall word. **1641** MILTON *Ch. Govt.* II. 41 To club quotations with men whose learning and beleif lies in marginal stuffings. *a* **1656** HALES *Gold. Rem.* (1673) 288 That so you may bring them [*sc.* scattered notes] together by marginal references. **1683** MOXON *Mech. Exerc.*, *Printing* xxii. ¶5 Marginal Notes come down the side (or sides, If the Page have two Columns). *a* **1732** T. BOSTON *Crook in Lot* (1805) 78 Here there is a line reading, and a marginal. **1733** NEAL *Hist. Purit.* II. 48 Mr. Canne, author of the Marginal References to the Bible. **1860** DICKENS *Lett.* (1880) II. 113, I thought the marginal references overdone. **1885** *Act 48 Vict.* c. 15 Sched. ii. *Precept* §35 You are..to publish..the register with your marginal additions. **1903** *Expositor* July 1 Fuller lists..in what are called 'marginal bibles'.

†**b.** ***marginal finger***: a 'finger' or hand set in the margin to call attention to something; hence *fig.*

1604 DEKKER *Honest Wh.* Wks. 1873 II. 6 Let it stand Within the Wizards booke (the kalendar) Markt with a marginall finger. **1632** MASSINGER & FIELD *Fatal Dowry* III. i, To haue mens marginall fingers point At Charaloys, as a lamented story!

2. a. Pertaining to an edge, border, or boundary; situated at the extreme edge (of an area, mass, etc.).

1658 PHILLIPS, *Marginal*, belonging to the margin or margent, *i.* the brink or brim of any thing. **1831** BREWSTER *Optics* vi. 54 The central parts of the lens..refract the rays

too little, and the marginal parts too much. **1872** Black *Adv. Phaeton* vii. 100 A marginal growth of willow and flag. **1882** *Garden* 25 Mar. 202/2 Lobelias..are most useful, as marginal plants for flower beds and borders. **1892** *Photogr. Ann.* 229 The lenses are of special optical glass, constructed with the nicest precision of curvature, so maintaining good marginal definition. **1893** Lane-Poole *Aurengzib* xii. 190 The extreme point south of Trichinopoly, and the marginal possessions of the Portuguese. **1925** J. Laird *Our Minds & their Bodies* ii. 31 For scientific purposes the marginal or borderline cases are usually the most instructive. **1934** H. C. Warren *Dict. Psychol.* 159/1 *Marginal contrast*, an accentuated type of simultaneous contrast, which occurs in regions close to the boundary between two contrasting areas. **1950** tr. *Mountaineering Handbk.* (Assoc. Brit. Members Swiss Alpine Club) ix. 88 Marginal crevasses.. run diagonally upwards and towards the centre of the glacier. **1957** R. G. Collomb *Dict. Mountaineering* 52 The changing course of a glacier causes marginal crevasses (i.e. splits at the edges)..; the changing angle of slope over which it flows causes marginal crevasses and transverse crevasses in mid-stream. **1962** Blake & Trott *Periodontology* v. 49 Marginal gingivitis involves only the free gingiva. **1962** M. L. Haselgrove *Photographers' Dict.* 141 (*caption*) A beam parallel to the principal axis will not be brought to a focus at the principal focus; marginal rays will converge to *M* while axial rays converge to *A*. **1965** G. Y. Shevelov *Prehist. of Slavic* 74 As in many other cases this columnal final stress was replaced by the marginal final stress.

b. *Nat. Hist.* (Cf. margin *sb.* 1 b.)

1776–96 Withering *Brit. Plants* (ed. 3) IV. 97, I never observed the seeds exposed in the marginal sinusses. **1800** *Phil Trans.* XC. 436 When the marginal lips are brought together, the animal will have a considerable power of suction. **1859** J. R. Greene *Man. Anim. Kingd., Protozoa* 20 To send forth pseudopodia through the marginal pores. **1875** Bennett & Dyer tr. *Sachs' Bot.* 298 Adventitious shoots, arising in the thalloid forms from cells of the older marginal parts.

c. *Psychol.* Of, on, or pertaining to the edge of the field of consciousness.

1894 C. L. Morgan *Introd. Compar. Psychol.* i. 17 We.. pay attention solely to focal consciousness, omitting all reference to the great body of marginal subconsciousness. **1899** W. James *Talks to Teachers* ii. 18 The expressions 'focal object' and 'marginal object', which we owe to Mr. Lloyd Morgan, require, I think, no further explanation. **1903** F. W. H. Myers *Hum. Personality* I. Introd. 14 They speak of 'fringes' of ordinary consciousness; of 'marginal' associations. **1927** W. E. Collinson *Contemp. Eng.* 108 The field of consciousness with its focal and marginal presentations.

3. a. That is on the 'margin', or close to the limit, below or beyond which something ceases to be possible or desirable. Freq. in *Econ.*; esp. of or pertaining to goods produced and marketed at a small margin of profit; *spec.* in phrases ***marginal cost, man, utility.***

1887 *Daily News* 23 May 2/8 Competition is as keen as ever and prices as marginal as they can be. **1890** Marshall *Princ. Econ.* III. iii. (1898) 168 That part of the thing which he is only just induced to purchase may be called his *marginal purchase*, because he is on the margin of doubt whether it is worth his while to incur the outlay required to obtain it. And the utility of his marginal purchase may be called the *marginal utility* of the thing to him. *Ibid.* I. p. x, The term 'marginal' increment I borrowed from von Thünen, and it is now commonly used by German economists. **1909** J. A. Hobson *Industr. Syst.* v. 109 So with the case of the 'marginal shepherd', the tenth man whom a farmer calculates it is just worth his while to employ because he can get him for the price of twenty sheep a year, and he will just save that number by his work. *Ibid.*, Marginal productivity of labour..the productivity of any single man, 'marginal' or other. **1920** A. Marshall *Princ. Econ.* (ed. 8) VI. i. 517 The farmer's interests are equally served by hiring 10 or 11 men; but..the eleventh man (supposed to be of *normal* efficiency) is the marginal man, when the markets for labour and sheep are such that one man can be hired..for the price of 20 sheep. **1925** J. M. Keynes in A. C. Pigou *Memorials A. Marshall* 22 It undoubtedly gave Jevons priority of publication as regards the group of ideas connected with 'marginal' (or, as Jevons called it, 'final') utility. **1930** *Economist* 28 June 1441/1 The proposals were based upon marginal cost on full-time running. **1931** *Encycl. Social Sci.* V. 366/1 In 1871..W. Stanley Jevons coined the phrase final utility, Carl Menger spoke of marginal utility and Léon Walras used the term rarity. **1934** *Punch* 17 Oct. 424/1 People babble cheerfully about the Marginal Man, the law of Diminishing Returns and so on. **1957** *Times* 21 Dec. 5/2 The weather at Idlewild international airport was reported to be 'marginal', and the captain had to ensure that sufficient fuel remained to divert to an alternative base. **1958** *Listener* 25 Sept. 447/1 The ordinary American citizen enjoys amenities which not even the rich enjoyed a century ago, and marginal output consists of goods that by any standards are patently inessential. *Ibid.* 448/1 Marginal production in affluent America today..is in general much less urgent..than was marginal production 100 years ago. **1963** *Times* 16 Apr. 13/1 At any point of time there are some who would buy less coal if the price went up, either economizing in fuel or switching to some alternative. We economists call these the 'marginal' users. **1969** J. Argenti *Managem. Techniques* 155 Marginal cost calculations can be extremely complex in a large multi-product company... Unless marginal costing is used, the answer given to the question 'will it pay us to meet this order or should we turn it down?' will be wrong. **1973** *Black Panther* 8 Sept. 12/3 In Southern Appalachia, Black Appalachians are 'marginal' (just above the poverty level).

b. Applied to land, ore, etc., barely worth developing. Also applied to a person working such land, etc. (Cf. margin *sb.* 2 a, quot. 1863.)

1910 P. H. Wicksteed *Common Sense of Pol. Econ.* II. vi. 571 'Marginal land'..is not land..considered with reference to the volume of supply. **1935** *Economist* 30 Nov. 1095/2 Huge quantities of marginal ore which, unattractive at the old price of gold, are attractive at the new. **1943** J. S. Huxley *TVA* i. 7 Reafforestation and the proper use of marginal lands. **1944** *Ann. Reg. 1943* 283 Policy..of aiding the thousands of inefficient marginal farmers to raise their standards of farming. **1954** M. Beresford *Lost Villages* x. 346 Derbyshire... There seems to have been surprisingly little retreat of settlement from marginal lands in the Peak. **1975** *Times Lit. Suppl.* 2 May 471/3 The bringing back into production of marginal agricultural land..formed part of his [*sc.* Keynes's] vision.

c. *Sociol.* Of an individual or social group: partly belonging to two differing societies or cultures but not fully integrated into either.

1928 R. E. Park in *Amer. Jrnl. Sociol.* May 881 (*heading*) Human migration and the marginal man. *Ibid.*, One of the consequences of migration is to create a situation in which the same individual..finds himself striving to live in two diverse cultural groups. The effect is to produce an unstable character... This is the 'marginal man'. *Ibid.* 893 It is in the mind of the marginal man—where the changes and fusions of culture are going on—that we can best study the processes of civilization. **1937** E. V. Stonequist (*title*) The marginal man. **1957** V. W. Turner *Schism & Continuity in Afr. Society* iv. 108 Sandombu was from many points of view.. an atypical, marginal man in Mukanza Village. **1963** *Rev. Eng. Stud.* XIV. 258 A homosexual, he regarded himself as a marginal man, out of step with society, yet contemptuous of its hypocritical standards. **1964** Gould & Kolb *Dict. Social Sci.* 407/1 Sociologists wrote of the second generation immigrants as the most distinctively marginal group, measured by their relatively high index of crime. **1964** R. D. Hopper in I. L. Horowitz *New Sociol.* 324 The Creole marginal group constituted about 10 per cent of the population at the time of the revolution. **1964** L. A. Costa Pinto in *Ibid.* 471 In a marginal society it is possible to find strong support..for quite opposite decisions.

d. Of minor importance, small, having little effect; usu. const. *to*.

1929 *New Statesman* 1 June 232/1 For the 'marginal' voter—he who is at the point of indifference whether he comes to the poll or not—is unlikely..to be induced to do so by any really important consideration. **1954** M. Beresford *Lost Villages* vii. 261 The lands marginal to medieval corn-growing. **1955** *Times* 11 June 9/6 Most of the changes are.. shifts of emphasis rather than reversals of previous policy; they are important but they are marginal. **1959** *Times* 14 Jan. 3/6 There is no major writer who uses the stage as his preferred medium of creation... Mr. Graham Greene and Mr. Angus Wilson, for example, still seem marginal to the drama. **1959** *Times Lit. Suppl.* 29 May 321/3 Twenty-six changes of punctuation, of which four or five seem..to be improvements, fourteen almost certainly wrong, and seven or eight marginal. **1964** [see marginality]. **1969** *Listener* 16 Jan. 92/3 The lack of a character with which we can identify —..the soldiers..remain uncharacterised and marginal— soon stills our wish to be emotionally involved.

e. *Pol.* Pertaining to a constituency, etc., in which an election or issue is likely to be closely contested and the majority very small. Also *ellipt.* as *sb.*

1951 *Times* 25 Oct. 6/3 (*heading*) Marginal seats... A significant feature of today's General Election polling is the substantial number of constituencies which may be described as marginal, and where the result of the voting is problematical. **1955** *Times* 7 June 7/4 A marginal constituency is one where the retiring member, having won the last election by a small majority, stands a sporting chance of being defeated at the next one. **1960** Butler & Rose *Brit. Gen. Election 1959* xi. 135 Despite the concentration on marginal seats, the Conservatives managed to put on a full-scale campaign almost everywhere. **1965** *Listener* 24 June 921/1 It was difficult for him to give a lead on this particular topic directly after such a marginal vote in his favour. **1966** *New Statesman* 25 Feb. 246/1 For Labour MPs in 'marginals'..it means that their perilous positions could be secured. **1970** *Guardian* 16 June 10/4 Three of the four Labour-held marginals theoretically at risk would be lost only on a swing against Labour of between 4 and 5 per cent. **1974** *Times* 13 Feb. 4/6 Redistribution can make a safe seat marginal.

4. *Stock-broking.* Pertaining to, of the nature of, margins (sense 2 c).

1870 J. K. Medbery *Men & Mysteries Wall St.* 59 Nor is there any dissimilarity between the conditions of purchase in complete and in marginal transactions. *Ibid.* 62 The broker..demands of his customer either solid deposit of money or stocks, or marginal deposit of money. **1930** *Economist* 22 Mar. 653/1 Dominion and colonial stocks.. attracted only the 'marginal' business of the market. **1936** *Ibid.* 15 Feb. 368/2 The Great Western, whose 'marginal' security is an ordinary stock. **1938** J. B. Williams *Theory Investment Value* iii. 21 To the marginal investor, it will be indifferent whether he invests in stock or in promissory notes. **1954** B. Graham *Intelligent Investor* ii. 34 Marginal trading—a potent cause of financial ruin to many—has been held within strict limits and at times suspended entirely.

B. *sb.* **1.** A marginal note, reference, or decoration. Now *rare.*

1602 *2nd Pt. Return fr. Parnass.* I. ii. 248 For Lodge and Watson, men of some desert, Yet subiect to a Critticks marginall. **1618** J. Smyth *Lives Berkeleys* (1883) II. 205 What great services hee often did against the French,..the marginall will informe his posterity. **1641** 'Smectymnuus' *Vind. Answ.* §4. 59 Doth not the Marginall tell you..that the holy Church was founded in the state of Prelacie? **1743** Emerson *Fluxions* 34 The Values of the Marginals on the left. **1884** *Times* (weekly ed.) 10 Oct. 7/4 The text is printed in old black letter type, with pictorial headings and marginals.

2. *Zool.* A feather on the edge of a bird's wing.

1887 *Proc. Zool. Soc.* 347 They [*sc.* feathers along the posterior border of the wing] are best termed marginals (*tectrices marginales*). **1898** F. E. Beddard *Struct. & Classification Birds* 9 The patagium is mainly filled up with several rows of feathers, which are collectively termed the marginals.

Hence **'marginal** *v. trans.*, to enter in the margin of a book; to add marginal notes to.

1618 J. Smyth *Lives Berkeleys* (1883) I. 212 The records here marginald. **1787** Bentham *Wks.* (1843) X. 170, I am marginaling *Essai sur les Recompenses.* All I have to say..is marginaled and ready for reading.

‖**marginalia** (mɑːdʒɪˈneɪlɪə), *sb. pl.* [L. neut. pl. of *margināls* marginal.] Marginal notes.

1832 Coleridge *Let.* 22 Apr. (1895) II. 761 A facsimile of John Asgill's tracts with a life and copious notes, to which I would affix Postilla et Marginalia. *a* **1849** Poe (*title*) Marginalia. **1853** Lockhart in *Croker Papers* (1884) III. xxviii. 294, I have read some slips of Moore, and when I get a larger portion will send you a set with marginalia. **1891** J. Winsor *Columbus* i. 7 Some manuscript marginalia found in three different books..are also remnants of the autographs of Columbus.

marginalic (mɑːdʒɪˈnælɪk), *a.* *nonce-wd.* Suggestive of 'marginalia'.

a **1849** Poe *Marginalia* Wks. 1864 III. 484 A model of manners, with a richly marginalic air.

marginalism (ˈmɑːdʒɪnəlɪz(ə)m). *Econ.* [f. marginal *a.* + -ism.] An economic analysis which gives prominence to marginal factors in the economy. Hence **'marginalist** *a.*, of or pertaining to marginalism; also *sb.*, an adherent of marginalism.

1926 J. A. Hobson *Free-Thought in Social Sci.* iii. 118 The recent extension of Marginalism treats 'doses' as infinitesimal quantities, applies them to the demand as well as the supply side of the economic equation..and to all economic activities. *Ibid.* 119 Our modern Marginalists commit a..mistake in affecting to treat economic material in general as being..other than it actually is. **1929** —— *Wealth & Life* II. iii. 119 The development of a marginalist doctrine, representing the movements of minutely divisible units of capital and labor into businesses and trades. **1951** J. O. Kamm *Econ. Investment* ii. 33 (*heading*) Marginalism and investment policy. **1956** R. F. Harrod in A. Pryce-Jones *New Outl. Mod. Knowl.* 470 Such were the Austrian school of marginalists and their counterpart in England, Jevons. **1969** P. Anderson in Cockburn & Blackburn *Student Power* 220 Alfred Marshall, father of marginalist economics. **1973** K. Menger in Hicks & Weber *Carl Menger* iii. 38 Austrian marginalism and mathematical economics. *Ibid.*, The Austrian marginalists and the mathematical economists agree in most of their fundamental economic views.

marginality (mɑːdʒɪˈnælɪtɪ). [f. marginal *a.* + -ity.] The quality or state of being marginal (in various senses of the adj.).

1929 *Pitman's Econ. Educator* III. 1352/1 The exchange value of commodities determines their marginal utility and itself expresses their marginal cost. The notion of marginality in this way sheds light upon the economic conflict. **1951** M. S. Rix *Investment Arithmetic* xii. 117 Priority percentages are also sometimes used to compare the gearing, or marginality, of one company's equity with another. **1955** *Times* 21 June 11/7 The region now has 28 Conservative to 15 Labour marginal seats. Conservatives also have the larger share of 'marginality' in the South and West. **1961** S. R. Herman in J. A. Fishman *Readings Sociol. of Lang.* (1968) 508 The choice of language at the various stages in the above case history reflects the passage from a position of marginality..to a position of adjustment as a member of Israel society retaining the elements of identity derived from socialization in another culture. **1963** L. Trilling in N. Frye *Romanticism Reconsidered* 96 And the converse of what explains Nietzsche's relative marginality explains Dostoevsky's position at the very heart of the modern spiritual life. **1964** R. D. Hopper in I. L. Horowitz *New Sociol.* 19 Marginality here means that, in pre-revolutionary societies, there is formed a group that is marginal to the structure of political power and social prestige. **1971** *World Archaeol.* III. 146 All of these facts combine to form a general picture of marginality in resources. **1974** R. Jessop *Traditionalism, Conservatism & Brit. Polit. Culture* ii. 42 A marginal [social] class..is more likely to become class-conscious than one that is relatively secure and unexploited. Marginality in turn can be due to adverse market conditions, to technological change, to political action, to bad luck, or some other factor.

marginalize (ˈmɑːdʒɪnəlaɪz), *v.* *rare.* [f. marginal + -ize.] *trans.* and *intr.* To make marginal notes (upon).

a **1832** Bentham *Mem. & Corr.* Wks. 1843 X. 68, I used ..to marginalize and make notes on cards. **1872** F. Jacox *Aspects of Authorship* 102 Augustine's *Confessions*..he [Abp. Leighton] similarly marginalized. *Ibid.* 112 *note*, Byron could marginalize with similar fertility and facility.

marginally (ˈmɑːdʒɪnəlɪ), *adv.* [f. marginal + -ly[2].] **a.** In the margin of a page; as a marginal note; *Bot.* towards the margin.

1601 Bp. W. Barlow *Defence* 218 That text of S. Paul marginally misalleaged. *a* **1682** Sir T. Browne *Tracts* 7 Still retained at least marginally in some translations. **1882** Wolseley in *Standard* 9 Sept. 2/1, I advanced with the troops marginally noted. **1884** Bower & Scott *De Bary's Phaner.* 301 In Ginkgo the two bundles which pass from the petiole into the lamina, branch repeatedly into marginally directed forks. **1970** M. Jones *Ducal Brittany* ii. 47 The Breton version of the homage, transcribed..at the back of the *Livre des Ostz*, is marginally glossed as simple homage.

b. Round or about the margin or edge of anything; in a way that is close to the limit or margin; by a small margin, slightly.

1909 H. G. Wells *Tono-Bungay* III. ii. 250 Wandering marginally through distinguished gatherings, I would catch the whispers: 'That's Mr. Ponderevo!' **1931** *Brit. Jrnl. Psychol.* Jan. 226 Attention is directed to locating the proper box for response rather than to picking up a card (because this is such a very common process and everyone can do it 'sub-consciously' or 'marginally'). **1965** *New Statesman* 30 Apr. 672/1 The situation in Britain is only marginally less alarming. **1972** *Accountant* 17 Aug. 191/1 The law will be applied strictly..where schemes differ marginally from the prescribed conditions. **1974** 'A. Garve' *File on Lester* xxxvi.

128 The papers are terrible this morning—the *Star* marginally the worst, but only marginally.

marginant (ˈmɑːdʒɪnənt), *a. Bot.* [ad. L. *marginant-em*, pr. pple. of *margināre* to MARGIN.] Becoming a marginate.
In recent Dicts.

marginate (ˈmɑːdʒɪnət), *a. Nat. Hist.* and *Path.* [ad. L. *margināt-us*, pa. pple. of *margināre*, f. *margin-* MARGIN *sb.*] Having a distinct margin, marginated.
1777 ROBSON *Brit. Flora* 35 *Marginate*, having a leafy border. **1822** J. MAWE *Wodarch's Conchol.* (ed. 2) p. xiii, *Marginate* (in Univalves), having the sides of the shell thickened; (in Bivalves), surrounded with an elevated margin. **1826** KIRBY & SP. *Entomol.* IV. 327 Marginate... When an impressed line or channel separates the edge of the prothorax from the rest of its surface, and so forms a margin. **1874** COOKE *Fungi* 57 The marginate species. **1897** *Allbutt's Syst. Med.* III. 50 The erythemas occur chiefly in children, in marginate, papular, or urticarious forms.

marginate (ˈmɑːdʒɪneɪt), *v.* [f. L. *margināt-*, ppl. stem of *margināre*, f. *margin-* MARGIN *sb.*]
†**1.** *trans.* To annotate with marginal notes.
1609 BP. W. BARLOW *Answ. Nameless Cath.* 335 That speech is vsed but onely in one of those places, marginated by his Maiestie.
2. To furnish with a margin or border.
1623 COCKERAM, *Marginate*, to make brimmes or margents. **1880** R. B. WATSON in *Jrnl. Linn. Soc.* XV. 100 Suture sharply impressed..being marginated on its upper side by a minute flat surface. **1881** *Ibid.* 440 Marginating the suture below is a fine thread.

marginated (ˈmɑːdʒɪneɪtɪd), *ppl. a.* [f. L. *margināt-us*. pa. pple. of *margināre* (see prec.) + -ED².] = MARGINATE *a.*
1727 BAILEY vol. II. **1753** CHAMBERS *Cycl. Supp.* s.v. *Lycoperdon*, The smooth, oblong and inwardly marginated lycoperdon. **1802** BINGLEY *Anim. Biog.* (1813) III. 145 The marginated water-beetle. **1839** SOWERBY *Conch. Man.* 62 *Marginated*, having an edge or border thicker than the rest of the shell. **1849** D. J. BROWNE *Amer. Poultry Yd.* (1858) 53 Golden Hamburgh fowls..of barred or marginated markings.

margination (mɑːdʒɪˈneɪʃən). [f. MARGINATE *v.*: see -ATION.] **1.** A marginated appearance or marking.
1896 *Allbutt's Syst. Med.* I. 69 The so-called 'margination' of leucocytes. *Ibid.* 71 A commencing margination of the white corpuscles was discernable. **1898** SIR H. HOWORTH in *Archæol. Jrnl.* LV. 128 Obvious either from the nature of the print or from distinctly-marked margination.
2. Annotation with marginal notes. *rare.*
1874 SWINBURNE *Let.* 13 July (1959) II. 308, I quite agree with you that the Homeric margination ought to be most carefully preserved.

†**marginean**, *a. Obs.*$^{-0}$ [f. late L. *margine-us* (f. *margin-* MARGIN *sb.*) + -AN.] Marginal.
1656 BLOUNT *Glossogr.*

margined (ˈmɑːdʒɪnd), *a.* and *ppl. a.* [f. MARGIN *sb.* or *v.* + -ED.] Having a margin, *esp.* one of a specified kind; chiefly *Nat. Hist.* (often as pple. followed by 'with'); *Bot.* applied to seeds having a distinct projecting edge.
In spec. names of animals it represents L. *marginatus*.
1826 KIRBY & SP. *Entomol.* III. xxix. 97 The margined egg just mentioned. **1828** STARK *Elem. Nat. Hist.* I. 212 Wings and tail black, margined with gray. **1832** *Pop. Zool.* 390 The Margined Tortoise (*Testudo Marginata*). **1844** J. E. GRAY *Catal. Tortoises*, etc. *Brit. Mus.* 61 The Margined Crocodile, *Crocodilus marginatus*. **1882** M. ARNOLD *Irish Ess.* 245 Books shapely, well printed, well margined. **1897** *Allbutt's Syst. Med.* II. 280 If it be erythema the redness will shew itself in abruptly margined patches.

marginellacean (mɑːdʒɪnɪˈleɪʃən), *a. Conch.* [f. mod.L. *Marginellacea*, f. *Marginella* (see below), f. *margin-*, *margo* MARGIN *sb.*] Pertaining to the *Marginellacea* or *Marginellidæ*, a family of gasteropods. So **margiˈnellid**, a gasteropod of the family *Marginellidæ*; **margiˈnelliform** *a.*, having the form of a gasteropod of the genus *Marginella*; **margiˈnelloid** *a.*, resembling the genus *Marginella*.
In recent Dicts.

marginicidal (ˈmɑːdʒɪnɪˌsaɪdəl), *a. Bot.* [f. L. *margin(i)-*, *margo* (see MARGIN *sb.*) + *-cīd-*, weakened root of *cædĕre* to cut + -AL¹.] (See quot.)
1889 *Syd. Soc. Lex.* **1900** B. D. JACKSON *Gloss. Bot. Terms*, *Marginicidal*, dehiscent by the disjunction of the united margins of the carpels, a form of septicidal dehiscence.

marginiform (mɑːˈdʒɪnɪfɔːm), *a.* [ad. mod.L. *marginiform-is*: see MARGIN *sb.* and -FORM.] Resembling or forming a margin.
1856 MAYNE *Expos. Lex.*, *Marginiformis*... Applied by H. Cassini to the appendices of the periclinium of the *Synanthereæ*, when they resemble a border: marginiform. **1890** *Century Dict.* (citing COUES).

margining (ˈmɑːdʒɪnɪŋ). [f. MARGIN *sb.* or *v.* + -ING¹.] Margins collectively; edging of a distinct colour or texture from the main body.
In recent Dicts.

ˌ**marginiˈrostral**, *a. Ornith.* [f. L. *margin(i)-* MARGIN *sb.* + *rostr-um* beak + -AL¹.] Of feathers: Growing round the basal margin of the bill.
1837 MACGILLIVRAY *Hist. Brit. Birds* I. 80.

margint, obs. form of MARGENT.

margon, obs. f. MURGEON *sb.*¹, dirt, earth.

margorie, margorum, obs. ff. MARJORAM.

‖**margosa** (mɑːˈgəʊsə). [Short for Pg. *amargosa*, fem. of *amargoso* bitter] An East Indian tree, *Azadirachta indica* (*Melia Azadirachta*), yielding a bitter oil; also called *neem.*
1813 AINSLIE *Mat. Med. Hindostan* 127 A certain portion of Margosa oil. **1846** LINDLEY *Veg. Kingd.* 464 It is supposed that the Melia Azedarachta, or neem-tree of India, possesses febrifugal properties;..it is also called the Margosa-tree. **1871** MATEER *Travancore* 98.

margose, margou, obs. forms of MARGAUX.

margravate (ˈmɑːgrəvət). [f. next + -ATE¹.] = MARGRAVIATE.
1802 *Brookes' Gazetteer* (ed. 12), Lusatia, a margravate of Germany. **1864** BURTON *Scot Abr.* I. v. 260 Inexhaustible varieties of palatinates, margravates [etc.].

margrave (ˈmɑːgreɪv). *Hist.* Also 6 **mergrave**, 6–8 **marc-**, 7–9 **markgrave**, 9 **mar(k)graf**. [a. MDu. *markgrave* (mod.Du. *markgraaf*), = OHG. *marcgrâvo* (MHG. *markgrâve*, mod.G. *markgraf*), lit. 'count of a mark or border territory': see MARK *sb.*¹ and GRAVE *sb.*⁴ Cf. med.L. *margrāvius*, F. *margrave*.] A German title, orig. given to the military governor of a border province; subsequently the hereditary title of the princes of certain states of the Holy Roman Empire.
Rendered in Latin by *marchio*; in Fr. and Eng. formerly sometimes by *marquis*.
1551 ROBINSON tr. *More's Utop.* I. (1895) 23 The chiefe and the head of them was the Marcgraue (as they cal him). **1568** GRAFTON *Chron.* II. 84 All such Rulers of townes or Countries as are nere the sea, are called Mergraue, as at this day in Andwarpe. **1577–87** HOLINSHED *Chron.* III. 1208/2 Christopher prince and margrave of Baden. **1614** SELDEN *Titles Hon.* 209, 213, 221. **1617** MORYSON *Itin.* III. 236 The Margraue (or Marquis) of Brandeburg is..the last of the Electors, but more powerfull then any of them in the number of Vassals. **1695** *Lond. Gaz.* No. 3130/2 The Margrave of Bareith is still at Amsterdam. **1790** WOLCOT (P. Pindar) *Adv. to Fut. Laureat* Wks. 1812 II. 335 Emperors, Electors, dead to hospitality, Margraves and miserable Dukes. **1855** MOTLEY *Dutch Rep.* (1861) I. 472 John van Immerzeel, Margrave of Antwerp.
Hence **ˈmargravely**, **marˈgravial** *adjs.*, pertaining to a margrave.
1762 tr. *Busching's Syst. Geog.* V. 378 The marggravial territory of Onolzbach. **1865** J. SKELTON ('Shirley') *Campaigner at home* vii. 136 Many royal, margravely, princely crimes. **1876** *Tinsley's Mag.* XIX. 61 In the grand duchy of Baden, in the fair margravial land.

margraviate (mɑːˈgreɪvɪət). [ad. med.L. type **margrāviātus*, f. *margrāvius* MARGRAVE.] The territory ruled by a margrave.
1702 *Lond. Gaz.* No. 3870/2 They proceeded to the Margraviate of Anspach. **1870** BURTON *Hist. Scot.* (1873) VI. lxx. 206 German grand-duchies and margraviates.

margravine (ˈmɑːgrəvɪn). Also 7 **-inne**. [a. Du. *markgravin* (= G. *markgräfin*) fem. of *markgraaf* MARGRAVE. Cf. F. *margravine*.] The wife of a margrave.
1692 *Lond. Gaz.* No. 2738/3 There is a Discourse of a Marriage being proposed between his Electoral Highness and the Margravinne of Anspach. **1753** HANWAY *Trav.* (1762) I. VII. xcii. 423 He placed the margravine of Bareith at his right hand.

margrete, -rite, obs. forms of MARGARITE¹.

margthe, obs. form of MARROW *sb.*¹

marguarite, obs. form of MARGARITE¹.

marguerite (ˈmɑːgəriːt). [a. F. *marguerite* (see MARGARET 2), originally the name of the daisy (*Bellis perennis*) and hence applied to larger flowers of similar shape.]
1. The common Daisy (*Bellis perennis*). *rare*$^{-0}$.
1866 in *Treas. Bot.* **1878–86** BRITTEN & HOLLAND *Plant-n.*, Margaret's Herb, or Marguerite. In recent Dicts.
2. The Ox-eye Daisy, *Chrysanthemum Leucanthemum*; also *C. frutescens* or Paris Daisy. **blue marguerite**, *Agathæa* (*Detris*) *cœlestis*.
1866 MISS THACKERAY *Village on Cliff* xiv. (1867) 218 A drawer in the bureau where she had already thrown some dead marguerites. **1882** *Garden* 18 Feb. 122/1 Flowers of the blue Marguerite (*Agathæa cœlestis*). *Ibid.* 16 Dec. 526/1 Paris Daisies, or white Marguerites, constitute just now one of the chief features in the gardens at Chiswick.

margullie, *v. Sc.* Also **murgullie**. [a. OF. *margul(l)ier*, *-goillier* to roll in the mud, soil, pollute, bruise, mutilate.] *trans.* 'To spoil, to destroy, to mangle; to mar any business' (Jam.).
1721 RAMSAY *Address to Town Council* i, They spoil'd my sense, and staw my cash, My muse's pride murgully'd. **1774** C. KEITH *Farmer's Ha'* lvii, Nature, unhurt by thrawart man, And nae margullied by chicane. **1836** J. STRUTHERS *Dychmont* III. 142 Wasting time murgullying Greek.

margyrye, variant of MARGERY *Obs.* (pearl).

Marhatta, obs. variant of MAHRATTA.

marhenȝiue, variant of MORYEVE *Obs.*

mari, obs. f. MARROW *sb.*¹, MARRY, MARY.

Maria (ˈmærɪə), *sb.* and *a.* Also **Maree**.
A. *sb.* A member of a jungle-dwelling Dravidian people of central India; also, the native (Dravidian) language of this people. **B.** *adj.* Of or pertaining to this people or their language.
1827 R. JENKINS *Rep. Territories Rajah of Nagpore* ii. 33 The wildest of these Gonds are the Marees. They generally go in a state of complete nudity, and even their women have no covering, but aprons of leaves. *a* **1863** S. HISLOP in G. Smith *Stephen Hislop* (1888) 22 Moria Gonds..are more civilized than the Márias. **1863** *Sel. Rec. Govt. India Foreign Dept.* No. 39. 14 The language in this talook is Teloogoo and Maria. The population is composed mainly of Marias and Telingas. **1882** H. B. ROWNEY *Wild Tribes India* I. i. 5 The Máree Gonds..live in the wildest parts of the province of Nágpore. **1938** W. V. GRIGSON *Maria Gonds of Bastar* iii. 49, I divide the so-called Marias into two divisions, the Hill Marias of the Abujhmar mountains, and the Bison-horn Marias. **1944** I. SINGH *Gondwana & Gonds* ii. 22 The Marias formerly roamed about in a state of nature and then ..adopted leaves and barks as their garments. **1962** *Listener* 29 Nov. 893/1 Every young member of Indian jungle tribes like the Maria. **1971** [see GOND *sb.* and *a.*].

maria, *pl.* of MARE⁴.

mariable, mariage etc.: see MARRIABLE, etc.

‖**mariachi** (mærɪˈɑːtʃɪ). [Mexican Sp. *mariache*, *mariachi*.] A group of itinerant Mexican folk musicians; also, a member of such a group. Also *attrib.*
1941 *Time* 19 May 97 There are stacks of records by the omnipresent Mexican street bands, the *mariachis*. **1948** 'P. QUENTIN' *Run to Death* xiii. 106 The *mariachis* had started to play. Over the frenzied twang of guitars a deep, chesty baritone was extolling Guadalajara. **1964** *Listener* 16 July 90/3 The *mariachis* personify all the robust colour of Mexico... They have the looks and the swagger of brigands and the dress-sense of toreadors, and they make jarring, irresistible music in the convulsive patterns of Latin-American rhythms. **1966** [see CHARRO]. **1967** S. BLANC *Rose Window* (1968) viii. 79 The breeze carried snatches of *mariachi* music from the terrace where the guests were dining. **1970** W. APEL *Harvard Dict. Mus.* (ed. 2) 526/2 Characteristically Mexican is the *mariachi*, the typical band that serves to entertain people in cafés and at village and country dances and celebrations. **1971** *Islander* (Victoria, B.C.) 19 Dec. 2/2 A mariachi band was ordered and two bottles of tequila to make their evening's work more pleasurable.

‖**mariage blanc** (marjaʒ blɑ̃). [Fr., lit. 'white marriage'.] An unconsummated marriage.
1926 *Irish Statesman* 13 Nov. 234 It is improbable, and yet quite possible, this story of a *mariage blanc*. **1931** *Times Lit. Suppl.* 17 Sept. 702/2 One must admire the tact with which Mr. Church handles the painful theme of the full-blooded Norah's revolt against the frustration of a *mariage blanc*. **1958** *Observer* 23 Feb. 14/2 We get a hint that Evan's and Cherry's is really a *mariage blanc*. **1958** G. MITCHELL *Spotted Hemlock* xi. 214 'The autopsy revealed that the girl was a virgin.'..'*Un mariage blanc*? Good Lord!' **1975** *Listener* 21 Aug. 253/3 Opal..suggested a *mariage blanc* between Natalie and Bosie that would have enabled Opal and Bosie to have a lasting liaison.

‖**mariage de convenance** (marjaʒ də kɔ̃vənɑ̃s). [Fr., lit. 'marriage of convenience'; cf. CONVENIENCE *sb.* 6.] A marriage arranged or contracted from motives of convenience (sense 6) or expediency. Also *fig.* Cf. *marriage of convenience* (MARRIAGE 8).
1854 THACKERAY *Newcomes* I. xxviii. 275 What the deuce does a *mariage de convenance* mean but all this. **1864** TROLLOPE *Small House at Allington* I. ix. 83 I'm only a half sort of lover, meditating a mariage de convenance to oblige an uncle. **1912** I. NITOBÉ *Jap. Nation* vi. 163 The sorrows of *mariage de convenance* in Europe. **1923** J. S. HUXLEY *Ess. Biologist* vii. 295 Some men are pragmatic and utilitarian in regard to Truth; by others she is worshipped as fanatically as any goddess. So some men deliberately make *mariages de convenance*. **1955** *Bull. Atomic Sci.* Mar. 97/3 History suggests that the evil partnership between Communist China and the Soviet Union may yet develop the brittle quality of a mariage de convenance. **1957** L. DURRELL *Justine* IV. 235 Someone trapped into a *mariage de convenance*. **1974** M. CECIL *Heroines in Love* iv. 91 The fashionable world, with its ill-bred ideas about money and *mariages de convenance*.

maria-glass. *Min.* Anglicized form of MARIENGLAS (Chester *Dict. Names Min.* 1896).

†**maria-groschen.** *Obs.* In 7 -grosh(en. [ad. G. *Mariengroschen*, f. *Marien-* Mary + GROSCHEN.] A German coin equivalent to eight pfennigs.
1617 MORYSON *Itin.* I. 35 Here each man paid..seuen maria-groshen for meat. *Ibid.* 286 At Brunswicke a Doller was worth six and thirty Maria Grosh, which are of equall value with foure and twenty siluer Misen Grosh.

mariahuana, var. MARIJUANA, MARIHUANA.

†**marial**[1]. *Obs. rare*$^{-1}$. Some herb.
1486 *Bk. St. Albans* C vj b, Take Fenell Maryall and Kersis ilich moch.

†**marial**[2]. *Obs.* [ad. med.L. *marīāle*, neut. of *marīālis*, f. *Marīa* Mary: see -AL[1]. Cf. Sp. *marial*.] Something written in praise of the Virgin Mary.
1622 S. WARD *Christ All in All* (1627) 12 They giue it [= ascribe honour] to the blessed Virgin, in the Closes of their riming Marials.

Marial (ˈmɛərɪəl), *a.* [F. *marial* = MARIAN *a.*[1] 1; cf. MARIAL[2].] = MARIAN *a.*[1] 1.
1904 *Catholic Herald* 23 Dec. 8/4 On the initiative of the Archbishop of Leopol [*sic*], a grand Marial Congress was organised and held in his Cathedral city. **1952** D. M. J. LANGDON *Our Lady of La Salette* v. 30 Montserrat in the mountains of Spain, and hundreds of other centres of Marial devotion. **1966** *Approaches* Nov. 123 The Marial Congregations for men, which are now actively organising their lay apostolate in all fields of public life.

marialite (ˈmɛərɪəlaɪt). *Min.* [ad. G. *marialit*, perh. f. *Maria* Mary, on account of its whiteness: see -LITE.] A silicate of aluminium, calcium and sodium, found near Naples; also = HAÜYNITE.
1854 DANA *Syst. Min.* (ed. 4) II. 230 Hauyne..Marialite, Ryllo. **1879** RUTLEY *Study of Rocks* x. 112 The species meionite and marialite are closely related to scapolite. **1896** CHESTER *Dict. Names Min.*

Marian (ˈmɛərɪən), *sb.*[1]
1. A female name; in quot. applied to a light woman. See also MAID MARIAN.
1567 HARMAN *Caveat* 62 Hee..offeres the same closely to this manerly marian.
2. ***Marian's*** (occas. ***Marian***) ***Violet*** [repr. med.L. *Viola Mariana*], ***Coventry Marian***, rarely simply *Marian*: Canterbury Bells, *Campanula Medium*.
1578 LYTE *Dodoens* II. xx. 171 Whan they be close, they haue fyue crestes or playtes like the Belfloures, or Couentrie Marians. *Ibid.* xxii. 173 Of Marians violet, or Couentrie Belles. **1629** PARKINSON *Parad. in Sole* (1656) 357 We call it generally..Coventry Bels. Some call it Marian, and some Mercuries Violets. **1658** PHILLIPS, *Mariets*, a sort of violets, called also Marian Violets.

Marian (ˈmɛərɪən), *a.*[1] and *sb.*[2] [f. L. *Marīa* Mary + -AN.] **A.** *adj.*
1. Pertaining to the Virgin Mary, or characterized by special devotion to her.
1701 (*title*) An Account of Livonia with a Relation of the Rise, Progress, and Decay of the Marian Teutonick Order. **1829** SOUTHEY *Sir T. More* II. 106 The propagandists of the Monkish and Marian religion. **1865** PUSEY *Truth Eng. Ch.* 120 In Spain and Portugal devotion to the Blessed Virgin is in its natural home. They are familiarly called Marian Kingdoms.
2. Pertaining to Mary Queen of England or her time (1553–58).
1608 WILLET *Hexapla Exod.* 61 The late daies of the Marian persecution in England. **1655** FULLER *Ch. Hist.* VII. i. §29 Of all the Marian-Martyrs, Hooper, and Ridley suffered with most torture. **1849** MACAULAY *Hist. Eng.* v. I. 647 In this way, with the help of some invention and exaggeration, was formed a copious supplement to the Marian martyrology.
3. Relating to Mary Queen of Scots (1542–87).
1902 A. LANG *Hist. Scot.* II. x. 267 A Marian conspiracy worked by Lennox.
B. *sb.*
1. A worshipper, or devotee of the Virgin Mary.
1635 A. STAFFORD *Fem. Glory* 223 Till they are good Marians, they shall never be good Christians; while they derogate from the dignity of the Mother, they cannot truely honour the Sonne. **1693** *Emilianne's Hist. Monast. Ord.* III. 287 [The Teutonic knights] built there..a Church in honour of the Virgin Mary, from whence they were called Marianes. **1699** T. DORRINGTON *Pres. St. Relig.* 58 It would ..be no hard and unjust Appellation, if one should call the People of that Communion rather Marians than Christians.
2. An adherent of Mary Queen of Scots; also, one who takes her side in historical discussion.
1893 *Athenæum* 11 Nov. 653/2 For twenty years Mr. Skelton has been known as a prominent Marian. **1902** A. LANG *Hist. Scot.* II. xii. 293 Sir Robert Melville, a strong Marian, had organised the business. **1969** A. FRASER *Mary Queen of Scots* II. xxii. 433 The castle of Edinburgh, so long held by Kirkcaldy and Maitland on behalf of the Marians.. was at last effectively besieged. *Ibid.*, Maitland..had died a loyal Marian. **1974** G. DONALDSON *Mary Queen of Scots* v. 122 Kirkcaldy and Maitland did not emerge as open Marians until much later and were at first numbered among 'secret favourers of the Queen'. *Ibid.* 134 Balfour of Pittendreich became a Marian, though he was not at Langside.
3. An English Catholic of Queen Mary's reign (1553–8).
1868 H. H. MILMAN *Ann. S. Paul's Cathedral* xi. 256 The Primate Pole was in his grave, Heath of York a strong Marian. **1899** F. W. MAITLAND *Coll. Papers* (1911) III. 130 Canon MacColl laboured under the misfortune of knowing something about the votes that these Marians gave in Parliament. **1904** W. H. FRERE *Eng. Church 1558–1625* ii. 23 The champions of the Marians..were to dispute with the champions of the exiles. **1955** C. READ *Mr. Secretary Cecil* iv. 101 He abandoned flight and decided to throw in his lot with the Marians.
Also **Mariˈanic** *a.* = MARIAN *a.* 1.
1845 G. B. CHEEVER *Wand. Pilgrim* lix. (1848) 311 The artful mixture of the Gospel scheme of redemption..in this Marianic system.

Marian (ˈmɛərɪən), *a.*[2] (and *sb.*[3]) [ad. L. *Mariān-us*, f. *Marī-us* (see below).] **a.** *adj.* Of or pertaining to Gaius Marius, a famous Roman general (died 86 B.C.), or his party. **b.** *sb.* A follower of Marius. (In the first quot. the pl. is used instead of *Mariuses*.)
1579–80 NORTH *Plutarch, Cæsar* (1896) V. 1 Sylla told them againe, that..there were many Marians in that young boy [Julius Cæsar]. **1797** *Encycl. Brit.* (ed. 3) XVI. 375/2 Sertorius, one of the generals of the Marian faction. **1842** *Penny Cycl.* XXIII. 253/2 After this defeat of the Marian party, Sulla repealed the laws of Sulpicius.

Marian (ˈmɛərɪən), *a.*[3] [f. *Mariānus*: see below.] Used to designate a method of lithotomy, introduced by Marianus Sanctus in 1524.
1839 *Penny Cycl.* XIV. 52/1 Apparatus Major, or Marian Method. *Ibid.*, The Marian section. **1889** *Syd. Soc. Lex.* s.v. *Lithotomy*, *Marian L.*, the older form of median lithotomy.

Marianism (ˈmɛərɪənɪz(ə)m). *rare*$^{-1}$. [f. MARIAN *a.*[1] + -ISM.] = next.
1845 G. B. CHEEVER *Wand. Pilgrim* xxiv. (1848) 159 Our Mother who art in heaven (says this great system of Marianism, instead of Christianity).

†**Mariˈanity.** *Obs. rare*$^{-1}$. [f. MARIAN *a.*[1] after *Christianity*.] A religious system based upon the cultus of the Virgin Mary.
1677 W. HUGHES *Man of Sin* II. iii. 50, I think the World hath much nicknam'd both the Romanists, and their Religion likewise. This, at the best ought to be called Marianity, and not Christianity.

Marianne (mærɪˈæn). Also in anglicized form (*rare*) **Mary Anne.** [Fr.] The name of a Republican Secret Society formed in France after the coup of 1851 to restore a Republican Government; hence a familiar name for the Republican form of Government and, by extension, a personification of the French Republic.
1870 DISRAELI *Lothair* I. xi. 100 Our refreshment at council is very spare..but we always drink one toast... It is to one whom you love and whom you have served well. Fill glasses, brethren, and now 'To *Mary-Anne*'. **1890** BARRÈRE & LELAND *Dict. Slang* II. 45/2 'La Marianne'..was the name of a secret Republican Society in France. **1933** KIPLING *Souvenirs of France* ii. 53, I asked a friend, an Alsatian General, whence the flood of material had come. 'From Marianne,' was the reply. 'She has all sorts of things like these in her stocking— when she needs them.' **1934** H. G. WELLS *Exper. Autobiogr.* II. ix. 747 (*caption*) Marianne asks Dadda to tell her all about it. **1940** —— *Babes in Darkling Wood* IV. iii. 374 Nor will Marianne be in a position to act the vindictive hostess this time... France and Britain had their chance of making a world peace in 1918, and they muffed it. **1958** H. J. GREENWALL *When France Fell* II. i. 66, I went to the *Marianne* office in the Avenue des Champs Elysées. **1962** *Listener* 12 July 57/2 Had Daumier wished to treat a similar theme we can be almost certain he would have selected Marianne or the Gallic cock as an impersonal national emblem. **1971** *Guardian* 3 Apr. 3/5 There is no official model for the bust of Marianne, the incarnation of the Republic, found in every Mairie in France.

†**Mariaˈnolatry.** *Obs. rare.* [f. MARIAN *a.*[1] + -(O)LATRY.] = MARIOLATRY. So **Mariaˈnolatrist** = MARIOLATER.
1736 BAILEY (folio) Pref., *Marianalatrists* [*sic*]. **1755** AMORY *Mem.* (1766) II. 188 If they had not blended with this religion a marianolatory [*sic*]. *Ibid.* 193 A marianolatry, a demonolatry [etc.].

mariari, variant of MARGERY *Obs.*

†**maria-tree.** *Obs.* [= Sp. *árbol de María* 'tree of Mary'.] The tolu tree.
1745 P. THOMAS *Jrnl. Anson's Voy.* 168 The Maria-Tree is lofty, and its Leaves not quite unlike the Bay, but larger and thicker. **1760–72** tr. *Juan & Ulloa's Voy.* (ed. 3) I. 48 The cedar, the maria, and the balsam tree.

Mariavite (ˈmɛərɪəvaɪt). [Pol. *Mariawita*, f. L. phr. *qui Mariæ vitam imitantur*.] A member of a Polish Christian sect which flourished in the early 20th century; also *attrib.*
[**1906** *Daily Chron.* 23 Apr. 5/5 The church at Leschno.. had been occupied by the sect of Marianites. **1906** *Times* 28 May 5/3 The *Osservatore Romano* publishes to-day an Encyclical..condemning the doctrine of the so-called Marianisti, and definitely suppresses the Marianisti congregation.] **1906** *Tablet* 9 June 897/2 Some priests..had founded, without permission from their lawful superiors, a kind of pseudo-monastic society, known as the *Mariavites* or *Mystic Priests*. *Ibid.* 898/2 The so-called Mariavite priests who are in good faith may no longer be led astray. **1949** D. ATTWATER *Catholic Encycl. Dict.* 306 *Mariavites*, a sect in Poland originating in 1906 with a number of apostate clergy. **1957** *Oxf. Dict. Chr. Ch.* 857/2 *Mariavites*, a Polish sect, founded in 1906 by J. Kowalski, a priest of Warsaw, and Felicia Kozlowska, a Tertiary sister,..on their excommunication from the RC Church.

maribone, obs. form of MARROWBONE.

maribot(t, obs. forms of MARABOUT.

marice, mariche, var. ff. MARIS, MARISH.

‖**mariche.** *Obs. rare*$^{-1}$. [It. *mariche* pl., in G. Botero Benese *Relationi* (1605) I. i. 123, whence the passage is taken.] A beast alleged to exist in Cambodia (see quot.).
1613 PURCHAS *Pilgrimage* (1614) 459 In these parts [*sc.* Camboia, Siam, etc.] are huge woods, harbours of Lions, Tigers, Ownces, and Mariches, which haue Maidens faces and Scorpions tailes.

maricock, obs. form of MARACOCK.

maricolous (məˈrɪkələs), *a.* [f. L. *mari-*, *mare* sea + *-colus* inhabiting, *colĕre* to inhabit.] Inhabiting the sea.
In recent Dicts.

‖**mari complaisant** (mari kõplɛzɑ̃). [Fr.] A husband who tolerates his wife's adultery.
1898 W. J. LOCKE *Idols* xv. 211 You are three outstanding people... Hang it all—the *mari complaisant*—and Merriam is the last man in the world—it beats me altogether. **1933** *Times Lit. Suppl.* 5 Oct. 673/1 Without being the *mari complaisant* he has hitherto stood aside, probably seeing much more than he could admit. **1937** MRS. BELLOC LOWNDES *Diary* 20 Jan. (1971) 145 The unfortunate Mr Simpson was..regarded as *un mari complaisant*. **1950** D. AMES *Corpse Diplomatique* ix. 72, I don't understand English women. In France there is such a thing as a *mari complaisant*, but I've never heard of an *amant complaisant*! **1958** L. DURRELL *Justine* I. 29 She was reputed to have had many lovers, and Nessim was regarded as a *mari complaisant*. **1972** P. M. HUBBARD *Whisper in Glen* xii. 115 If you see him as the *mari complaisant*, you'd better think again... If he knew I was carrying on with you..he'd fling me out.

mariculture (ˈmærɪkʌltjʊə(r), -tʃə(r)). [f. L. *mari-*, *mare* sea + CULTURE *sb.*] The cultivation of the resources of the sea, esp. of fish for food. So **mariˈcultural** *a.*, of or pertaining to mariculture; **mariˈculturist**, one who engages in or specializes in mariculture.
1903 *Science* 9 Oct. 461 Such maps would be purely agricultural and maricultural, dependent upon the harvests of the land and sea. **1909** *Cent. Dict.* Suppl., *Mariculture*, the development of the resources of the sea, especially with respect to food-fish; coined in distinction from *agriculture*. **1969** *Sci. Jrnl.* Dec. 30 The man who studies agriculture stands in a different place from the man who studies mariculture. There are other differences between the two fields but not so basic as the need for the mariculturist to swim. **1970** *New Scientist* 20 Aug. 378/1 The first step in an effort to use the deep ocean water for mariculture, the generation of electrical power and the production of fresh water. **1971** *McGraw-Hill Yearbk. Sci. & Technol.* 23 If we are very optimistic and assume for a moment that the yield of the traditional fishery will not change, mariculture could perhaps lead to an increment in the crop produced from the sea from the present 1% to 1.1%. **1973** *Daily Colonist* (Victoria, B.C.) 12 Apr. 12/4 Some areas should be left wild; others should be utilized for recreation; others might be developed and employed for mariculture; and still other areas might be exploited or used as dumping grounds. **1974** *Victorian* (Victoria, B.C.) 5 Apr. 2/1 The federal-provincial governments have allotted $38,000 to two companies involved in oyster mariculture in a cost-sharing program to improve and develop the oyster industry in British Columbia.

‖**Marid** (ˈmærɪd). [repr. two Arabic forms: *'mārid* pr. pple. of *marada* to rebel, and *ma'rīd*, f. the same root.] In Muslim demonology, a jinn of the most powerful class.
1839 LANE *Arab. Nts.* (1859) I. 72 When the Márid heard these words of the fisherman, he said, There is no deity but God! **1889** J. PAYNE *Alaeddin* 92 Alaeddin looked and saw a Marid.

Marie (ˈmɑːrɪ). Also **marie.** A female Christian name used *attrib.* of a type of plain sweet biscuit.
1878 *Official Guide & Album Cunard Steamship Co.* 186/3 (List of Biscuits) Marie. **1888** *Mrs. Beeton's Bk. Househ. Managem.* ii. 31/2 Biscuits..Marie..1*s.* 9*d.* per tin. **1906** E. NESBIT *Railway Children* ii. 27 There were biscuits, the Marie and the plain kind. **1919** D. ASHFORD *Young Visiters* vi. 50 He swollowed his tea and eat a Marie biscuit hastilly. **1947** E. TAYLOR *View of Harbour* xii. 203 A jug of cocoa and a plate of Marie biscuits. **1966** B. KIMENYE *Kalasanda Revisited* 43 Though they sipped their tea, they simply could not bring themselves to touch a marie biscuit. **1972** C. DRUMMOND *Death at Bar* i. 10 The old tea lady..slopped the fluid over on to the marie biscuits in the saucer.

marie, obs. f. MARROW *sb.*[1], MARRY, MARY.

Marie Antoinette (ˈmɑːrɪ æntwɑːˈnɛt). The name of the Austrian queen consort (1755–1793) of Louis XVI of France, used *attrib.* to designate various styles of dress, decorative art, etc., characteristic of her or her reign (see quots.).
1925 F. SCOTT FITZGERALD *Great Gatsby* v. 110 We wandered through Marie Antoinette music-rooms. **1950** '*Mercury*' *Dict. Textile Terms* 337 *Marie Antoinette*, a

curtain, having appliqué sprays, flowers and leaves of cord and tape. **1960** CUNNINGTON & BEARD *Dict. English Costume* 133/1 *Marie Antoinette skirt*, . . a day skirt with 7 gores, 1 in front, 2 on each side, and 2 behind, box-pleated. **1966** J. S. COX *Illustr. Dict. Hairdressing* 96/1 *Marie Antoinette chignon*, a full globular low dressed chignon. *Marie Antoinette coiffure*, hair styles similar to those worn by Marie Antoinette.

mariege, obs. form of MARRIAGE.

Marie Louise (ˈmɑːrɪ luːˈiːz). The name of *Marie Louise* (1791–1847), second wife of Napoleon I, used to designate a variety of yellow-skinned pear. Also *attrib.*

1817 *Trans. Hort. Soc.* II. 406 A box of Pears, sent to the Society by Dr. Van Mons, of Brussells, was examined... They are stated, by Dr. Van Mons, to be seedlings raised by himself: 1, Napoleon..; 2, Marie Louise: in shape and size resembling a small Bon Chrétien; yellow, with bright red next the sun; very rich, and ripe about the middle of October. **1820** *Ibid.* IV. 519 Specimens of the Marie Louise Pear were received. **1860** R. HOGG *Fruit Manual* 200 Marie Louise... One of our very best pears. Ripe in October and November. **1894** 'MRS. ALEXANDER' *Choice of Evils* I. ii. 34 Not even the Mervyn gardens could produce finer pears than the solitary 'Marie Louise' tree. **1929** E. A. BUNYARD *Anat. Dessert* 104 Marie Louise, cannot be overlooked, .. being named after that most acquiescent of Empresses, Napoleon's second wife, and, like her, it needs the support of a strong arm to stay its languishing growth. **1958** [see DOYENNE[1]].

‖**marienglas.** Also 8 **-glass.** [Ger., f. *Marien*, comb. f. *Marie* Mary + *glas* GLASS.] A name applied to mica and selenite.

1762 tr. *Busching's Syst. Geog.* I. 380 The famous Marienglass, called by some Muscovy glass, or ising-glass. *Ibid.* 474 Marienglas. **1799** W. TOOKE *View Russian Emp.* I. 358 A window of glass or marienglass.

marierim, -om(e, -um, obs. ff. MARJORAM.

†**mariet.** *Obs.* In 6 **mariette.** [a. F. *mariette*, f. *Marie* Mary.] The Canterbury Bell, *Campanula Medium*.

1597 GERARDE *Herbal* II. cix. 363 Couentrie bels are called in Latin *Viola Mariana*, or Mercuries violets, .. and of some Mariettes. **1611** COTGR., *Mariets*, Mariets, Marians Violets, Couentrie bells. **1658** [see MARIAN *sb.*[1] 2].

marigenous (məˈrɪdʒɪnəs), *a.* [f. L. *mare* sea + -GEN + -OUS.] Produced in or by the sea.

1599 R. LINCHE *Fount. Anc. Fiction* N iv b, One of those Tritons..(or as wee may tearm them) marigenous men. **1799** KIRWAN *Geol. Ess.* v. 224 Secondary or epizootic mountains. These are either marigenous or alluvial. **1843** HUMBLE *Dict. Geol.*, etc.

marigh, obs. form of MARROW *sb.*[1]

marigold (ˈmærɪgəʊld). Forms: 4, 6–7 **mary-gould**, 4–6 **marigolde**, 5–9 **marygold**, 6 **mary-, maregolde, marigoulde, mary gowles**, *Sc.* **mariguild**, 7 **marry-gold**, 6– **marigold.** [f. the proper name MARY (presumably with references to the Virgin Mary) + GOLD *sb.*[2] Cf. MDu. *marienbloemkijn*, MLG. *marienblome*, 'Mary's flower', rendering *solsequium* in glossaries.]

1. The name of several plants having golden or bright yellow flowers. **a.** A plant of the genus *Calendula* (N.O. *Compositæ*), esp. *C. officinalis*, common in country gardens; it has some medicinal properties; its flowers were formerly made into a conserve, and are still sometimes used as a flavouring for soup, and to give a yellow colour to cheese.

The property possessed by the flower of opening when the sun shines (whence the L. name *solsequium*, F. *souci*) was often referred to by writers of the 16–17th c.

13.. in *Med. Wks. 14th C.* (ed. Henslow) 81 Take..i quatron of mary-goulden. *a* **1400** in *Reliq. Ant.* I. 55 Another drynk to wounde: tak confery, marigolde, matfelon [etc.]. **14..** *Sloane MS.* 5 in *Promp. Parv.* 361 *note*, *Solsequium*, Rodewort, oper marygoldys. ? **1516** *Grete Herball* cxxxi, Calendula. Mary gowles, or ruddes. **1578** LYTE *Dodoens* II. xiii. 164 The conserue that is made of the floures of Mary-goldes..cureth the trembling..of the harte. **1594** NASHE *Unfort. Trav.* 9 The Marigold, which opens and shuts with the Sunne. **1597** GERARDE *Herbal* II. ccxliii. 600 *Calendula multiflora orbiculata*. Double Globe Marigolde. *Ibid.* 603 *Calendula alpina*. Mountaine Marigold. *a* **1613** OVERBURY *A Wife*, etc. (1638) 70 His wit, like the Marigold, openeth with the sun. **1714** GAY *Sheph. Week* I. 46 Fair is the Mary-gold, for Pottage meet. **1848** DICKENS *Dombey* viii, The small front-gardens had the unaccountable property of producing nothing but Marigolds. **1849** MACAULAY *Hist. Eng.* iii. I. 321 They.. brewed gooseberry wine, cured marigolds, and made the crust for the venison pasty.

fig. (*allusive.*) **1558** [HALES] *Orat. Q. Eliz.* in Foxe *A. & M.* (1631) III. xii. 977/1 Men..who were Marigoldes, that followed Maries mad affections.

b. Any plant of the genus *Tagetes*, native to South America and Mexico, also grown in India and China, and much cultivated in gardens. **African marigold**, *T. erecta*; **French marigold**, *T. patula*.

1548, 1578 [see FRENCH A. 5 a]. **1597** GERARDE *Herbal* II. ccxlvi. 609 There be extant at this day fiue sorts of Turkie Gilliflowers or African Marigolds. **1611** COTGR., *Oeillet d'Inde*, the Turkie, or Affrican Marigold, or Gilliflower; also, the French Marigold, or Gingioline flower (which is the single kind of the Affrican). **1785** MARTYN *Rousseau's Bot.* xxvi. (1794) 395 French and African Marigolds, two of the gaudy annuals of the flower-garden. **1895** MRS. B. M. CROKER *Village Tales* (1896) 150 Wreaths of evil-smelling marigolds (that noxious flower so insanely dear to the native of India).

c. *Chrysanthemum segetum*; usually CORN-MARIGOLD, also ***field, wild, yellow marigold.***

1578 LYTE *Dodoens* II. xxxiii 190 Of Goldenfloure, or the wild Marygolde. **1597**, etc. [see CORN MARIGOLD]. **1818** KEATS *Endym.* II. 397 Ripe October's faded marigolds. **1838** MARY HOWITT *Birds & Fl., Harvest-Field Fl.* ii, The poppy red, the marigold, The buglos brightly blue.

d. Applied with qualification to plants of other genera. †**marigold of Peru**, the sunflower, *Helianthus*; **Cape m.**, any plant of the genus *Dimorphotheca* (Cent. Dict. 1890); **fetid m.**, *Dysodia chrysanthemoides* (ibid.); †**Spanish m.**, *Anemone coronaria*; **water m.**, *Bidens Beckii* (Treas. Bot. 1866); **West Indian m.**, *Wedelia carnosa* (*ibid.*). For *bur, fig marigold* see the first words. Also MARSH MARIGOLD.

1597 GERARDE *Herbal* II. ccxlvii. 612 Of the flower of the Sunne, or the Marigolde of Peru. **1629** PARKINSON *Parad. in Sole* xxv. (1656) 207 The great double Windflower of Constantinople... Some gentlewomen call this Anemone, The Spanish Marigold.

2. An ornamental representation of the flower.

1634 in *Anc. Invent.* (Halliw. 1854) 24 One other linnen sweete-bagge imbroydered with marygolds.

3. A variety of apple (in full ***marigold apple***): see quot. 1676. ? *Obs.*

1577 B. GOOGE *Heresbach's Husb.* 87 We haue at this day that are cheefe in price the Pippin, the Romet, the Pomeroyal, the Marligold [*sic*]. **1664** EVELYN *Kal. Hort.*, *Jan.* (1679) 8 Winter-Queening, Marigold, Harvey-apple. **1676** WORLIDGE *Vinetum Brit.* 40 The Marigold-apple (sometimes called Johns Pearmain, the Kate-apple, and the Onion-apple). *Ibid.* 159 The Marigold-Apple (so called from its being marked in even stripes in the form of a Marigold).

†**4.** *slang.* A gold coin; a sovereign. *Obs.*

1663 COWLEY *Cutter of Coleman-st.* II. iii, *Aur.* Give but a Bill under your Hand to pay me five hundred Pounds when [etc.]... *Pun.*.. I'll..presently go put five hundred Marygolds in a Purse for you.

†**5.** ? Some yellow enamel. *Obs.*

1529 in *Wills Doctors' Comm.* (Camden) 19 A mullett of dyamountes set in maregolde.

6. A small cake garnished with almonds and currant jelly, made to resemble the flower.

1896 *Sun* 11 Dec. 1/7 Those dainty little cakes called 'marigolds'.

7. The colour of the marigold flower; hence *attrib.* passing into *adj.*, of this colour, bright yellow.

1774 Marigold colour [see sense 8]. **1839** [see *café au lait* (CAFÉ 3)]. **1872** G. M. HOPKINS *Let.* 22 Mar. (1956) 55, I am jaundiced all marigold under the eyes. **1916** D. H. LAWRENCE *Amores* 49 Cluck, my marigold bird, and again Cluck for your yellow darlings. **1923** *Daily Mail* 28 Feb. 1/3 (Advt.), Shades of .. Jade, Silver Grey or Marigold. **1975** *Country Life* 20 Mar. 744/2 Their clothes are matched to a limited number of colours... there are cornflower/cool cornflower, mint/cool mint, and marigold/cool marigold.

8. *attrib.* and *Comb.*, as ***marigold arrangement, colour, flower, leaf***; **marigold apple** (see 3); **marigold bird, finch**, the golden-crested wren or kinglet, *Regulus cristatus*; †**marigold sunflower**, Gerarde's name for the 'female' sunflower; †**marigold (flower) water**, a decoction of marigold flowers; **marigold window** *Arch.*, a rose window.

1899 CAGNEY tr. *Jaksch's Clin. Diagn.* i. (ed. 4) 65 Where the segments are fewer..and result in the characteristic *marigold arrangement, the diagnosis of quartan fever may be made. **1772** RUTTY *Nat. Hist. Dublin* I. 313 Nettle creeper or *Marigold Bird, from the fine crown on its head, of the colour of a Marigold flower. **1774** GOLDSM. *Nat. Hist.* (1776) VIII. 56 A gummy fluid, of a *marigold colour. **1828** FLEMING *Brit. Anim.* 72 Golden-crested Wren..*Mary-gold Finch. **1566** PAINTER *Pal. Pleas.* I. 32 The flaring *marigold floure, which in the moste feruent heate of the sommers day, doth appeare most glorious. **1747** WESLEY *Prim. Physic* (1762) 89 Eat Marigold Flowers daily as a Sallad. *c* **1450** *ME. Med. Bk.* (Heinrich) 169 Tak *marigolde leues..& do per to a good quantyte of hony. **1597** GERARDE *Herbal* II. ccxlvii. 614 The female or *Marigolde Sunne flower hath a thicke and wooddie roote. **1652** T. CADEMAN *Distiller of Lond.* 12 *Aq. Calendulæ*, *Marigold-water. **1692** Y-WORTH *Art Distill.* 78 *Aqua Calendularum*, or, Marigold Water. **1696** SALMON *Fam.-Dict.* (ed. 2), Marigold-Water, ..This is an excellent Water for Inflamed Eyes... Marigold-flower-Water. **1736** F. DRAKE *Eboracum* II. ii. 529 A fine piece of masonry [in York Minster] in form of a wheel, or as Mr. Torre writes a marygold, from whence it is called the *marygold window. **1837** R. B. WINKLES *French Cathedrals* 7 A rose or marigold window is placed over the central opening.

‖**marigot** (ˈmærɪgɒt). [F. *marigot* (Littré).] In Western Africa, a side channel of a river.

1759 tr. *Adanson's Voy. Senegal* in *Pinkerton's Collect.* (1814) XVI. 610 Before I could get thither, I was obliged to cross two *marigots*; these are rivulets with which the whole country is intersected. **1864** R. F. BURTON *Dahome* I. 35 Passing up a *marigot* or branch channel, worn down by porters' feet to a deep wet ditch. **1894** *Q. Rev.* July 273 The French troops..crossed 172 'marigots', with steep banks and full of water.

marigraph (ˈmærɪgrɑːf, -æ-). [f. L. *mari-*, *mare* sea + -GRAPH.] An instrument for automatically recording the rise and fall of the tide; a tide-gauge. Hence **mariˈgraphic** *a.*, pertaining to or obtained by a marigraph. Also **ˈmarigram** [see -GRAM], a record made by the marigraph. (In recent Dicts.)

1858 SIMMONDS *Dict. Trade*, *Marigraph*. **1884** *Sci. Amer. Suppl.* 28 June 7067/3 For registering the height of the tide at every instant, hydrographic services generally adopt quite a simple marigraph.

mariguild, obs. Sc. form of MARIGOLD.

mariit, obs. form of MARRIED.

marijuana, marihuana (mærɪˈhwɑːnə). Also **mara-, maria-; mariguan(a.** [Amer. Sp.]

1. a. A preparation of the hemp plant, *Cannabis sativa* (see CANNABIS), for use as an intoxicating and hallucinogenic drug; usu. applied to a crude preparation of the dried leaves, flowering tops, and stem of the plant that is generally smoked.

1894 *Scribner's Mag.* May 596/2 [The] 'toloachi', [and] the 'mariguan', .. are used by discarded women for the purpose of wreaking a terrible revenge upon recreant lovers. **1918** *Jrnl. Amer. Med. Assoc.* 21 Dec. 2094/1 The symptoms mentioned..as being produced by smoking Mara Huiwane or marajuana are similar to those produced by the mescal plant. **1923** W. SMITH *Little Tigress* 102 The cockroach is unable to stagger around any more because he has no more marijuana to smoke. *Marijuana* is a form of drug that brings false heart to the user. **1927** *Amer. Speech* III. 37 The tobacco of the Turkish coffee-houses has been replaced in Mexico by marihuana, the native variety of hashish. **1928** *Daily Express* 11 Oct. 3 What is Marijuana? A deadly Mexican drug, more familiarly known as 'Mary Jane', which produces wild hilarity when either smoked or eaten. **1935** J. STEINBECK *Tortilla Flat* xiv. 246 His eyes were as wide and pained as the eyes of one who smokes marihuana. **1939** [see DAGGA[1]]. **1944** R. A. MOORE *Textbk. Path.* lix. 657 After long-continued use of marihuana there is mental deterioration. **1952** M. MCCARTHY *Groves of Academe* (1953) ii. 19 On one occasion, even, marijuana had been smoked on the steps of the gymnasium. **1960** N. POLUNIN *Introd. Plant Geogr.* ix. 267 Cannabis consumption as hashish, marijuana, etc., causes states of ecstasy and stupefaction. **1968** P. OLIVER *Screening Blues* ii. 83 The song *Weed Smoker's Dream* referred to the hallucinations induced by marijuana. **1968** *Times* 19 Dec. 4/6 Basic findings are that ..subjects who have not smoked marihuana before do not have strong subjective experiences, even after strong doses.

b. *fig.*

1948 *Sat. Rev.* (U.S.) 19 June 24/3 One of the most cogent reasons for the success of the comics, is namely, that they are the marijuana of parents as well as of their offspring. **1965** *New Statesman* 10 Dec. 916/2 The politician who gave the Beatles the MBE..knows that if he suddenly cut off about 20 million young addicts from their supply of aural marijuana the withdrawal effects could produce unpleasant political side-effects.

2. The hemp plant; = CANNABIS 1.

1907 A. B. LYONS *Plant Names* (ed. 2) 511 (Cannabis) a. Add Syn[onym] Marihuana (Mex.). **1934** R. E. CARRADINI *Narcotics & Youth Today* 1 In this classification [of narcotic drugs] should be included..*Cannabis Indica*, popularly known as Indian hemp or hashish, and the native plant, *mariahuana*. **1934** *Jrnl. Amer. Med. Assoc.* 21 July 212 On appeal to the Supreme Court of Utah, Navaro contended that the term 'mariguana', as used in the statute, signified a plant, not a drug. **1959** *Encounter* Oct. 56/2 The land where the marihuana grows. **1973** *Daily Tel.* 4 July 4 Nepal is to ban the growing of marijuana and poppies and the production of cannabis and opium.

3. *attrib.* and *Comb.*, as ***marijuana addict, cigarette, habit, -smoker, -smoking*** vbl. sb. and ppl. adj., ***weed***.

1936 *Amer. Speech* XI. 12 Argot of narcotic addicts... *Twister*, ..one who rolls his own twists, or marajuana cigarettes or, by extension, a marijuana addict. **1938** *Manch. Guardian Weekly* 2 Sept. 188/3 Some [swing players] are 'mugglers' (Marijuana addicts). **1933** *Jrnl. Amer. Med. Assoc.* 28 Oct. 1398/1 The first person to be convicted in Hillsborough County [in Florida] of selling marajuana cigarets..was sentenced..to a year in the county jail. **1966** T. PYNCHON *Crying of Lot* 49 iii. 64 Leonard the drummer..produced a fistful of marijuana cigarettes. **1953** W. BURROUGHS *Junkie* (1972) x. 107, I told them you were sick and that you needed a shot of morphine, and they said, 'Oh, we thought it was just a question of a marijuana habit.' **1951** E. PAUL *Springtime in Paris* xi. 202 Narcotics addicts and marihuana smokers are infiltrating the cafés. **1935** *Amer. Mercury* Aug. 426/1 Such practices as adultery, marihuana smoking, gambling, ..and rowdyism seldom worry the investigator. **1957** P. FRANK *Seven Days to Never* iii. 102 She married..a marijuana-smoking drugstore cowboy. **1958** *Times* 3 Dec. 6/6 Unauthorised clubs..were a great moral danger to young people. The marihuana weed was smoked.

mariken, -kin, variants of MAROQUIN *Obs.*

‖**marikin** = next. (In recent Dicts.)

‖**marikina** (mærɪˈkiːnə). Also 8 **marikini**, 9 **marakina.** [repr. Tupi *miriquiná*; the form *marikina* comes (through Buffon) from Claude d'Abbeville *Mission en Maregnan* 1614.] A small South American monkey, the silky tamarin, *Midas rosalia*, having silky golden-yellow hair.

1774 GOLDSM. *Nat. Hist.* IV. 237 The fourth is the Marikina; with a mane round the neck, and a bunch of hair at the end of the tail, like a lion. **1854** H. G. DALTON *Brit. Guiana* (1855) II. 452 The Marakina or Silky Tamarin. **1893** MIVART *Types Anim. Life* (1894) 32 The marikina or silky marmoset is clothed with fur of a golden yellow.

†**marill**, *v. Obs.* ? = MARINATE *v.* 1. (Cf. MARL *v.*[3])

1651 T. BARKER *Art of Angling* (1653) 14 Baked Trouts, Trouts marilled.

‖**marimba** (mə'rɪmbə). [Congo.] A kind of deep-toned xylophone, originating in Africa and consisting of wooden keys on a frame with a tuned resonator beneath each key. Hence, a modern orchestral instrument evolved from this. Also *attrib.*

1704 tr. *Merolla's Voy. Congo* I. in *Churchill's Voy.* I. 695 The Instrument most in request us'd by the Abundi..is the Marimba; it consists of sixteen Calabashes orderly plac'd along the middle between two side-boards join'd together, or a long frame, hanging about a Man's Neck with a Thong. **1866** LIVINGSTONE *Last Jrnls.* (1873) I. xii. 305 Marimbas and square drums formed the bands. **1875** MONTEIRO *Angola* II. 138 The Marimba is the musical instrument par excellence of the natives of Angola. **1923** A. H. NEWBOLD *Bamboo Curtains* 27 You and I on a polished floor, And a big marimba band. **1924** S. SITWELL *13th Cæsar* 58 Loud is the marimba's note Above these half-salt waves. **1927** *Melody Maker* Aug. 732/3 (Advt.), The Rage To-Day.—'Foote' Xylophones and Marimbas. **1934** A. HUXLEY *Beyond Mexique Bay* 119 The visitor of 1933 may think himself lucky if he hears a *marimba* orchestra discoursing tangos. **1957** WODEHOUSE *Over Seventy* iii. 42 You can dance nightly to the strains of somebody's marimba band. **1958** A. JACOBS *New Dict. Mus.* 226 Milhaud wrote a concerto (1947) for marimba and vibraphone. **1961** *Guardian* 22 May 5/5 Her company of 75 dancers, singers, and marimba players presented us with authentic reconstructions of the Aztec ritual dances. **1970** J. BLADES *Percussion Instruments* xvi. 425 In *Vision of St. Augustine* Tippett writes for marimba.

marimbaphone (mə'rɪmbəfəʊn). [f. prec. + Gr. φωνή sound, voice.] = prec.

1921 *Daily Colonist* (Victoria, B.C.) 9 Oct. 23/2 The instrumentation will be as follows: 25 Violins, 6 Pianists.., 4 Marimbaphones, [etc.]. **1923** *Weekly Dispatch* 11 Mar. 5 The marimbaphone or Mexican xylophone..depends for its depth of tone on a number of tubes of varying lengths filled with liquid. **1926** A. HUXLEY *Jesting Pilate* IV. 263 Organ chimes, giant marimbaphone, vibraphone. **1962** *Listener* 22 Nov. 885/3 A marimbaphone and six chimes.

‖**marimonda** (mærɪ'mɒndə). [American Sp., prob. from some native lang.] A spider-monkey of tropical America, *Ateles belzebuth.*

1758 J. ADAMS tr. *Juan & Ulloa's Voy.* v. i, These forests [near Caracol] are..infested with snakes and monkeys, particularly a kind called Marimondas. **1871** KINGSLEY *At Last* xvii, The very fine Marimondas..now dying, I fear, in the Zoological Gardens at Bristol.

‖**marina**[1] (mə'riːnə). Also erron. **marino**. [It. and Sp.: fem. of *marino* MARINE *a.*]

1. A promenade or esplanade by the sea.

1805 W. IRVING in *Life & Lett.* (1864) I. 106 The whole town was immediately in an uproar; the Marino was crowded with spectators. **1869** LONGF. in *Life* (1891) III. 130 Then we landed at the Marina [at Capri] amid a noisy crowd of men, women, and donkeys. **1901** *Scribner's Mag.* XXIX. 441/1 We were gently wafted over the bar in a lighter and deposited,..on the marina of Rabat.

2. A dock or basin with moorings for yachts and other small craft. Also *attrib.* orig. *U.S.*

1935 *Yachting Monthly* LIX. 223/2 Fees for keeping a yacht in a municipal 'marina' (trick name for basin) are modest. Yachts are tied up in slips in these marinas. **1959** *Manch. Guardian* 15 Aug. 5/2 Everywhere in the United States the outboard motor, the cabin cruiser, the 'marina' (a little dock for pleasure craft) are to be seen. **1960** *Sunday Times* 3 Apr. 37/5 But what about entering and leaving this well-dammed basin, or marina—the American word? **1961** *Times* 28 Apr. 6/3 (*heading*) Hayling Island marina plan to be pressed. **1963** R. I. MCDAVID *Mencken's Amer. Lang.* 264 Spanish may share with Italian the credit for the current vogue of *marina*, as a de luxe designation for a yacht basin. **1969** *Daily Tel.* 11 Jan. 19/3 It will include two hotels, flats, 'boatels', yacht clubs, restaurants, two public houses and a 'marina drome'. **1971** *N.Z. Listener* 25 Oct. 7/1 In 1928 boat-owners added another word to their vocabulary, 'marina'. Coined in the United States to describe a new kind of luxury boating facility..it has altered the style and living of an increasing number of New Zealanders.

marina[2] (mə'riːnə). *Dyeing.* (See quot.)

1874 CROOKES *Handbk. Dyeing* 232 The madder..is next dried in the sun, and after this treatment is known as Marina.

Marina[3] (mə'riːnə). [f. the name of H.R.H. Princess *Marina*, Duchess of Kent (1906–68).] Used *attrib.* in ***Marina green***, a shade of green.

[**1934** *Times* 29 Nov. (Suppl.) p. iii/2 The going away *ensemble* [of Princess Marina] will be in almond-green tweed.] **1935** *Discovery* Aug. 231/1 There is a popular shade of green at present in vogue, termed 'Marina green'. **1935** *Times* 18 Nov. 21/4 Cleverly designed dinner gowns in satin and lace in rust, Marina green, and royal blue. **1958** M. DICKENS *Man Overboard* iii. 46 That sickly colour which was once foisted on to a loyal public as Marina green when the Duchess of Kent was married.

marinade (mærɪ'neɪd), *sb.* [a. F. *marinade*, ad. Sp. *marinada*, f. *marinar* (= It. *marinare*, F. *mariner*) to pickle in brine, f. *marino* MARINE *a.*]

1. A pickle, generally composed of wine and vinegar, with herbs and spices, in which fish or meat is steeped; also, the fish or meat thus pickled.

1704 *Dict. Rust.* (1726) H h iij b, *Marinade*, a pickled Meat either of Flesh or Fish. **1725** BRADLEY *Fam. Dict.* s.v., A Marinade of Veal serves to garnish farced Breasts of Veal. *Ibid.*, To the End that the Marinade may penetrate into the Flesh. **1859** F. E. PAGET *Curate Cumberworth*, etc. 243 In making the marinade in which it is to be stewed, she had fallen into the heresy of using red wine only. **1863** 'OUIDA' *Held in Bondage* II. ii. 40 'Of course they will', said De Vigne, eating his marinade leisurely. **1877** *Cassell's Dict. Cookery* 408 Prepare a marinade [for fish] by boiling together..vinegar..an onion in rings, and some cayenne and salt.

2. A cake made of the edible core of the cabbage-palm in the West Indies.

1888 *Harper's Mag.* Aug. 327/2 Those delicious little cakes called *marinades*, which you hear the colored peddlers calling out for sale.

marinade ('mærɪneɪd), *v.* [f. MARINADE *sb.*] *trans.* To steep in marinade; to marinate. Hence '**marinaded** *ppl. a.*, '**marinading** *vbl. sb.*

c **1682** J. COLLINS *Salt & Fishery* 120 To Marine or preserve Fish..after the Italian manner, called Marinading. **1727** BRADLEY *Fam. Dict.* s.v. *Breast*, To Marinade a Breast of Veal; cut it into great Slices, marinade them in Vinegar [etc.]. **1807** SIR H. DAVY *Rem.* (1858) 68, I am much obliged to you for the marinaded pilchards. **1901** *Daily News* 15 June 6/2 Should a close, stifling day arrive,..any meat that cannot at once be cooked should be marinaded.

†**mari'nado**, *v. Obs.* [f. **marinado* sb., corruption of Sp. *marinada* MARINADE *sb.*] = prec.

c **1682** J. COLLINS *Salt & Fishery* 108 Signior Dominico is noted for the many sorts of Fish, which he Marines, or renders Marinado'd.

†**marinage.** *Obs.*[−1] [f. MARINE *sb.* + -AGE; = Sp. *marinage.* (OF. had *marinage* adj., maritime, and sb., seaman.)] Seamanship.

1511 GUYLFORDE *Pilgr.* (Camden) 63 The wynde fell somwhat mete to put vs, with helpe and crafte of marynage, from the shore.

†**ma'rinal**, *a.* and *sb. Obs.* Forms: 4–6 **marinel**, 6 **marinell, -enell, marynal, -el**, 6–7 **marinall**, 7 **-al.** [a. OF. *marinal, -el*, adj. and sb., ad. med.L. *marīnālis* f. L. *marīn-us* MARINE *a.*: see -AL[1].]

A. *adj.* = MARINE.

1. Of or pertaining to the sea; saline.

1614 T. ADAMS *Divells Banket* 21 These, here, are Festiuall, not Marinall Waters. **1640** J. GOWER *Ovids Fest.* IV. 76 The same instinct [of love] doth guide marinall things, Which fills with thousand fish the water-springs.

2. Nautical.

1620 tr. *Boccaccio's Decam.* 52 Being no way able to comprehend..what course they tooke, neither by marinal judgement, or any apprehension whatsoever. *a* **1644** QUARLES *Sol. Recant.*, Sol. ix. 21 The prudent Pilot whose marinall skill Makes the proud windes obedient to his will.

B. *sb.* A mariner, sailor. *Sc.* and *north.*

a **1300–1400** *Cursor M.* 24850 (Gött.) þe marinelis [*Cott.* mariners] war selcuth radd. **1540** *Aberdeen Reg.* (1844) I. 173 To deliuer the marenellis thair feis. **1549** *Compl. Scot.* vi. 42 The master gart al his marynalis & men of veyr hald them quiet. **1565** *Durham Depos.* (Surtees) 83 William Loye, of Newcastle upon Tyne, marinell. **1596** DALRYMPLE tr. *Leslie's Hist. Scot.* x. 378 The craig, quhilk the marinelis cal S. Ebbis heid.

†**marinaller.** *Obs.* In 5 **maryneller.** [f. prec. + -ER[1].] A mariner.

1470 in Rye *Cromer* (1889) 156 [Will of Nichs. Kaye of Croumer], maryneller.

marinar, obs. form of MARINER.

†**marinary.** *Obs. rare.* [ad. med.L. *(*ars*) *marīnāria* the art of navigation.] Seamanship; knowledge of navigation.

1684 *Bucaniers Amer.* III. (ed. 2) 45 Through their ignorance in Marinary, they stranded their Vessel.

†'**marinate**, *ppl. a. Obs.* Also 7 **marrionate.** [ad. It. *marinato*, pa. pple. of *marinare*: see MARINADE *sb.*] Marinated.

1651–7 T. BARKER *Art of Angling* (1820) 18 The marrionate Trout..wil keep. **1789** FARLEY *Lond. Art Cookery* I. xii. (ed. 6) 146 Marinate Soles. **1886** R. F. BURTON *Arab. Nts.* (abr. ed.) I. 115 Stews well marinate.

marinate ('mærɪneɪt), *v.* Also 7 **marinat, mar(r)ionate, marrinate.** [ad. It. *marinare* or F. *mariner*: see MARINADE *sb.* and -ATE.]

1. a. *trans.* To pickle (fish, etc.) with marinade. Also *absol.*

c **1645** HOWELL *Lett.* I. v. xxxviii, He can marinat fish. **1651** T. BARKER *Art of Angling* (1653) 15 The way to marrionate a Trout or other fish. **1725** BRADLEY *Fam. Dict.* s.v. *Frogs*, These [frogs] being marinated with Verjuice, Pepper, Salt,..must be fry'd till they assume a fine Colour. **1863** H. C. PENNELL *Angler-nat.* 170 A few dozen Bleak marinated form an excellent breakfast dish. **1960** *Times* 18 Jan. 15/5 Fillet [steak] is exceptionally tender and should not need to be marinated or beaten. **1970** *Daily Tel.* (Colour Suppl.) 30 Oct. 62 It is..absolutely in order to make the 'gamey' flavour less pungent by marinating.

†**b.** To prepare (poultry) by a certain method of stuffing. *Obs.*

1747 MRS. GLASSE *Cookery* ii. 38 To marinate Fowls. **1805** ELIZ. RAFFALD *Eng. Housekeeper* (new ed.) 126 To marinate a Goose.

†**2.** *slang.* To transport over sea. *Obs.*

1673 R. HEAD *Canting Acad.* 16 The other was (nub'd) hang'd, and the last (marrinated) transported. *a* **1700** B. E. *Dict. Cant. Crew, Marinated*, transported into some foreign Plantation.

marinated ('mærɪneɪtɪd), *ppl. a.* [f. prec. + -ED[1].]

†**1.** Impregnated with salt; saline. *Obs.*

1658 EVELYN *Fr. Gard.* (1675) 286 This [Brine] we call Marinated water. **1674** BLOUNT *Glossogr.* (ed. 4), *Marinated*, pertaining to the Sea, that tastes of salt water.

2. Pickled with marinade. †Of fowls (see MARINATE *v.* 1 b).

1659 HOWELL *Lex.*, *Vocab.* xliii, Marinated or pickled fish, *pesce marinato.* **1696** PHILLIPS (ed. 5), *Marinated Fish*, ..Fish fryed in Oyl, and then put up in Pickle. **1725** BRADLEY *Fam. Dict.* s.v. *Roach*, A Side-dish of marinated Roaches. **1789** FARLEY *Lond. Art Cookery* I. xi. (ed. 6) 134 Fowls marinated. **1875** M. G. PEARSE *Dan. Quorm* 122 Marinated pilchards. **1969** *Daily Tel.* 14 Jan. 15 Spicy marinated pork.

marine (mə'riːn) *a.* and *sb.* Also 4 **-yn**, 5–6 **-yne**, 7 **marrine.** [a. F. *marin* (fem. *marine*) = Sp., It. *marino* (fem. *-a*), Pg. *marinho*:—L. *marīn-us*, f. *mari-*, *mare* sea.

The present pronunciation with (-iːn) instead of (-aɪn) is due to the influence of the Fr. fem. *marine.* Owing to the non-occurrence of the word in rimes, it is not possible to say when this pronunciation arose.]

A. *adj.*

1. a. Of or belonging to the sea; existing or found in the sea; produced by the sea; *Zool.* inhabiting the high seas, pelagic.

marine band: a geological horizon containing fossils of marine origin situated between horizons of freshwater origin. ***marine rainbow***: a rainbow formed on sea-spray. ***marine sauce***: a name for the common laver, *Porphyra vulgaris* (*Treas. Bot.* 1866).

c **1420** *Pallad. on Husb.* XI. 291 Of see quyete vptaketh they maryne Water purest. **1484** CAXTON *Fables of Poge* v, Ther was fond within a grete Ryuer a monstre maryn or of the see. **1592** KYD *Sol. & Pers.* I. iii. 80 The earth is my Countrey, As the aire to the fowle, or the marine moisture To the red guild fish. **1637** HEYWOOD *Royal Ship* 28 Then, O you marine Gods, who with amaze On this stupendious worke (emergent) gaze. **1727–41** CHAMBERS *Cycl.* s.v. *Rainbow*, The marine or sea-bow is a phænomenon sometimes observed in a much agitated sea. **1832** DE LA BECHE *Geol. Man.* (ed. 2) 219 Several marine shells are discovered in these strata. **1833** LYELL *Princ. Geol.* III. 145 The term 'marine alluvium' is, perhaps, admissible if confined to banks of shingle thrown up like the Chesil bank, or to materials cast up by a wave of the sea upon the land, or those which a submarine current has left in its track. **1855** W. S. DALLAS *Syst. Nat. Hist.* II. 176 The Bernicle Geese..are marine in their habits, and feed..upon Algæ [etc.]. **1878** HUXLEY *Physiogr.* 181 Marine denudation is not equally active at all depths of the sea. **1920** W. GIBSON *Coal in Gt. Brit.* xxii. 277 With the exception of the marine fauna of Skipsey's Marine Band and of that above the Slaty Band Ironstone, the invertebrate fauna is not of much variety. **1939** RAISTRICH & MARSHALL *Nature & Orig. Coal Seams* ii. 33 The remains of fresh-water or marine shells are less common, forming when they occur in quantity 'mussel bands' and 'marine bands'. **1969** BENNISON & WRIGHT *Geol. Hist. Brit. Isles* ix. 224 The marine horizons (called marine bands) are sometimes of great lateral extent.

†**b.** *Old Chem.* Applied to substances obtainable from the sea. ***marine alkali***: soda. ***marine salt***: common salt, sodium chloride; later, any salt of 'marine acid', a chloride. ***marine acid***: the acid obtained from 'marine salt', hydrochloric acid. ***dephlogisticated*** or ***oxygenated marine acid*** or ***gas***: chlorine. ***marine ether***: chloric ether. ***marine epsom***: magnesium chloride. ***marine selenite***: calcium chloride. *Obs.*

1605 TIMME *Quersit.* I. v. D 2 b, Three kindes of Salts: namely, the marine and fixed..the Niterus..and the Armoniac. **1758** REID tr. *Macquer's Chym.* I. 306 The affinity which Mercury hath with the Marine Acid. **1790** WEDGWOOD in *Phil. Trans.* LXXX. 313 Crystals of marine alkali, melted and dried. **1791** HAMILTON *Berthollet's Dyeing* I. I. I. iii. 46 The properties of oxygenated marine acid. **1796** KIRWAN *Elem. Min.* I. 6 Nitrous selenite, heated to redness, easily parts with its acid..but marine selenite obstinately retains it. *Ibid.* II. 33 It [fibrous salt] usually contains Marine Epsom, which renders it deliquescent. **1797** *Encycl. Brit.* (ed. 3) IV. 579/1 The dephlogisticated marine acid..does not dissolve ice nor camphor; in which respects it differs from the common marine acid gas. *Ibid.*, Marine ether. *Ibid.* 579/2 Dephlogisticated marine gas. **1800** tr. *Lagrange's Chem.* I. 273 The muriatic acid drawn from marine salt by the sulphuric acid. **1825** J. NICHOLSON *Operat. Mechanic* 761 Digest the ore in marine acid.

†**c.** Of sculptured figures, etc.: Representing sea gods, fishes, sea-shells, or the like. *Obs.*

1703 MAUNDRELL *Journ. Jerus.* (1732) 137 Sea-gods,..and other Marine Figures. **1727–41** CHAMBERS *Cycl.* s.v. *Fountain*, *Marine Fountain*, that composed of aquatic figures, as sea divinities, naiads, tritons, rivers, dolphins, and other fishes, and shells. *Ibid.* s.v. *Freeze*, Marine Freezes are those representing sea-horses [etc.].

d. Of a painter, etc.: That depicts sea subjects.

1883 G. H. BOUGHTON in *Harper's Mag.* Jan. 176/1 The river Maas..is most sketchable to a marine painter. **1889** BRYDALL *Art in Scot.* xiv. 311 He was employed as a marine-draughtsman.

†**2.** Belonging to, or situated at, the sea-side; bounded by the sea; maritime. *Obs.*

1610 R. NICCOLS *Eng. Eliza* in *Mirr. Mag.* 819 With loud clamour to the marine shore, The armed people clustred in thicke swarmes. **1632** LITHGOW *Trav.* v. 189 Tripoly..standing a mile from the marine side. *Ibid.* VII. 353 The marine Bourge of Molino. *Ibid.* VIII. 362 The marine Prouinces which lye betweene Ægypt and Sewty. **1728** ELIZA HEYWOOD *Mme. de Gomez's Belle A.* (1732) II. 59 Happening in this marine Ramble, to pass by this Coast.

3. Connected with the sea in operation, scope, etc.; pertaining to shipping, a navy, or naval force; relating to naval matters.

marine board (see quot. 1867). ***marine insurance***, insurance against perils at sea. Also occas. in collocations where *maritime* is more usual, as ***marine interest, marine law***.

1566 *Act 8 Eliz.* c. 13 §1 Men..browght upp to Water Crafte, most meete for her Maties Marine Service. **1579** FENTON *Guicciard.* XVI. (1599) 738 Her marine enterprises. **1630** *R. Johnson's Kingd. & Commw.* 16 The Grecians they deemed it no discredit to borrow..from the Carthaginians and Sicilians, the Art Marine. **1683** *J. Houghton's Lett. Husb. & Trade* IV. No. 5. 107 His Merchants are everywhere respected, and he is now one of the great Marine Princes of the World. **1765** BLACKSTONE *Comm.* I. xiii. 405 The laws of Oleron..are received by all nations in Europe as the ground and substruction of all their marine constitutions. **1772** *Act 12 Geo. III*, c. 67 An Act for Incorporating the Members of a Society, commonly called The Marine Society [founded in 1756]. **1839** *Penny Cycl.* XIV. 418/2 Marine insurances differ..from fire and life insurances in the mode of conducting the business. **1848**, **1872** [see INSURANCE 4]. **1858** HOMANS *Dict. Comm.* 1693/2 Wages in such cases would be contrary to the principle of marine law—that freight is the mother of wages [etc.]. **1860** (*title*) Reed's New Guide Book to the Local Marine Board Examinations of Masters and Mates. **1867** SMYTH *Sailor's Word-bk., Marine Boards*, establishments at our different ports for carrying into effect the provisions of the Merchant Shipping Act.

4. a. Of soldiers: Serving on board ship, as ***marine force***. †***marine regiment*** (= *maritime regiment*: see MARITIME *a.* 3): the marines. †***marine soldier***: a marine; so ***marine captain***, etc. (but cf. B. 6 b).

1690 LUTTRELL *Brief Rel.* (1857) II. 1 The earls of Pembroke and Torrington have each a commission to raise a marine regiment. **1699** *Lett. conc. Mariners* 6 The Marine Soldiers on board receive the Wages of Sailors. **1708** *Royal Proclam.* 20 May in *Lond. Gaz.* No. 4440/1 To the Marine-Captains, Sea-Lieutenants and Master, shall be allowed one Eighth Part..The Marine-Lieutenants, Boatswain, Gunner, Purser,..one Eighth Part. **1713** *Lond. Gaz.* No. 5176/3 That several of the Marine Soldiers..have obtain'd their Pensions by forged..Certificates. **1769** FALCONER *Dict. Marine* (1780), *Marine*, or *Marine-Forces*, a body of troops employed in the sea-service, under the direction of the lords of the admiralty. **1802** JAMES *Milit. Dict.* s.v., The marine forces have of late years been considerably augmented.

b. *slang.* (See quot. and B. 4 d.)

1785 GROSE *Dict. Vulg. Tongue, Marine Officer*, an empty bottle, (*sea wit*) marine officers being held useless by the seamen.

5. Used or adapted for use at sea; chiefly in technical names of instruments, as ***marine barometer, chronometer, galvanometer, watch***.

marine alarm, an alarm used at sea and operated by water or wind (Knight *Dict. Mech.* (1875) 55/2); †**marine belt** (see quot. 1765); **marine boiler**, a boiler adapted for use in steam vessels (Knight); **marine chair**, a contrivance from which the celestial bodies may be steadily observed at sea; †**marine collar**, a life-preserving appliance to be placed on the neck to keep the head out of water; **marine engine**, a form of steam engine used in seagoing vessels; **marine glue**, an adhesive composition used in ship carpentry (Young *Naut. Dict.* 1846); **marine governor**, the governor of a marine engine (Knight); **marine metal** (see quot.); **marine railway**, 'a slip for hauling vessels on to repair' (Smyth *Sailor's Wordbk.* 1867); **marine soap** (see quot.); †**marine surveyor**, a machine designed for measuring the way of a ship.

1704 J. HARRIS *Lex. Techn.* I, **Marine Barometer*, is an Instrument contrived by Dr. Hook, for the use of those that would make a Philosophical Experiment at Sea. **1765** H. WALPOLE *Let.* 27 Aug., There is a man who has just invented what he calls a *marine belt; you buckle it on, and walk upon the sea as you would upon a grassplot. **1891** 'TRIPLEX' (*title*) *Marine Boilers. **1765** *Chron.* in *Ann. Reg.* 86/2 Christopher Irwin, esq.; inventor of the *marine chair. **1862** *Catal. Internat. Exhib.* II. xv. 66 *Marine chronometers. **1764** in *Titles Patents* (1854) 148 A grant unto William Walker..& John Carass..of their new invented *marine collar & belt. **1822** *Specif. of Brunel's Patent* No. 4683. 2 The *marine engine represented with its parts. **1873** F. JENKIN *Electr. & Magn.* xiii. §12 (1881) 199 The *Marine galvanometer is a galvanometer adapted for use at sea. **1866** BRANDE & COX *Dict. Arts*, etc., **Marine Metal*, an alloy of lead and antimony with about two per cent. of mercury, introduced in 1833 by Wetterstedt for sheathing ships. **1873** E. SPON *Workshop Receipts* Ser. I. 381/2 This soap [cocoanut-oil soap] is sometimes called *marine soap, as it will lather well with sea-water. **1767** *Ann. Reg.* 103 A new *marine surveyor: the machine consists of an open tube..on the outside is fixed an oblique plane like a screw, upon which the water acts so as to turn it round swifter or slower. **1854** W. K. KELLY & TOMLINSON tr. *Arago's Astron.* (ed. 5) 161 *Marine watches, or chronometers, are of great assistance in determining longitude.

6. marine biology, the study of plants and animals living in the sea; hence **marine-biological** *a.*; **marine biologist**, one engaged in this study; **marine iguana**, a large lizard, *Amblyrhynchus cristatus*, found on the Galapagos Islands; **marineland**, a type of zoological garden, designed to exhibit and preserve marine animals; **marine science** orig. *U.S.*, the interdisciplinary study of the sea and the life, minerals, etc., contained in it; any of the individual disciplines involved in this; hence **marine scientific** *a.*; **marine scientist**, a person engaged in marine science.

1884 in *Jrnl. Marine Biol. Assoc.* (1887) I. 22 Report of the Foundation Meeting of the *Marine Biological Association. **1959** D. A. BANNERMAN *Birds Brit. Is.* VIII. 119 The expedition..was mainly to investigate some of the marine-biological and agricultural problems of the Tristan da Cunha group. **1963** T. A. SEBEOK in J. A. Fishman *Readings Sociol. of Lang.* (1968) 30 Aristotle was also the first marine biologist who accurately classed the dolphin with the mammals. **1887** *Jrnl. Marine Biol. Assoc.* I. 1 It is not proposed to limit the contents of this journal to formal reports..but to include within its pages..brief records of observations relating to the *marine biology and fisheries of the coasts of the United Kingdom. **1936** *Discovery* June 166/2 M. Paul Lemoine..referred to his [*sc.* Sir Robert Mond's] work on behalf of marine biology. **1967** *Oceanogr. & Marine Biol.* V. 111 Of all the different facets of marine science, marine biology is perhaps the oldest in India. [**1839** DARWIN *Jrnl.* in Fitzroy & Darwin *Narr. Voy. H.M.S. Adventure & Beagle* III. xix. 453 (*heading*) Marine lizard feeds on sea-weed.] **1924** C. W. BEEBE *Galapagos* v. 111 The sea or *marine iguana is as good a name as could be desired. **1962** C. J. & O. B. GOIN *Introd. Herpetology* viii. 136 *Amblyrhynchus cristatus*, the Marine Iguana of the Galápagos Islands, feeds on marine algae at low tide. **1972** *Country Life* 6 Apr. 842/3 In addition to the giant tortoises ..there are the marine iguanas. **1963** *Times* 17 Apr. 12/5 Southsea Castle committee agreed today to open negotiations with Billy Smart's Circus for the proposed establishment of a *marineland in the castle grounds. **1968** *N.Z. News* 16 Oct. 6/2 Complete plans and specifications have been drawn up and a tender accepted for a marineland on Windsor Reserve at Devonport, Auckland. **1945** *Inst. Marine Sci. Publ.* (Univ. of Texas) No. 1. 5 In conjunction with the establishment of the Institute of *Marine Science ..it was planned to provide for appropriate publication of results of investigations on..oceanography of the Gulf of Mexico. **1967** [see *marine biology* above]. **1969** [see OCEANOLOGY]. **1984** A. C. & A. DUXBURY *Introd. World's Oceans* p. xxiv, Students were attracted to the marine sciences in record numbers. **1960** *U.S. Congr. Sen. Hearings Marine Sci.* 10 Witnesses will tell us the relation between *marine scientific research and development and submarine operation. **1974** *Marine Technol. Soc. Jrnl.* Dec. 17/1 This article reviews briefly the present status of the law of the sea negotiations that concern marine scientific research. **1957** *Science* 27 Dec. 1322/1 A broadly based international organization..can thereby assist *marine scientists in different countries to obtain support for their work. **1984** A. C. & A. DUXBURY *Introd. World's Oceans* p. xxiv, In these projects marine scientists shared their knowledge.

B. *sb.*

†**1.** [= F. *marine*; cf. MARINA[1].] The sea coast or shore; a promenade by the sea; also, the country or district in immediate proximity to the coast. *Obs.*

13.. *Coer de L.* 4881 That they scholden hye Ones more forth by the maryn To the cyte off Palestyn. *a* **1400** *Octouian* 1361 Maryners hym broghte to the maryn Of Gene cost. *c* **1450** *Merlin* 230 That..hadde robbed..all the maryne and the portes toward Dover. **1615** G. SANDYS *Trav.* 245 Every evening they solace themselves along the Marine (a place left throughout betweene the Citie wall and the hauen). **1687** B. RANDOLPH *Archipelago* 46 In the summer time every evening the marine is full with all sorts of people with musick, singing, and dancing. **1698** FRYER *Acc. E. India & P.* 118 They supply the Marine with Carts drawn by Oxen, the Ships with Wood and Water. **1703** MAUNDRELL *Journ. Jerus.* (1810) 41 We rid out after dinner to view the marine. It is about half an hour distant from the city.

2. [= F. *marine.*] The collective shipping, fleet, navy, or naval service of a country; maritime interest as represented by ships; sea-going vessels collectively, esp. with reference to nationality or class, as ***mercantile marine*** (now the chief use).

1669 R. MONTAGU in *Buccleuch MSS.* (Hist. MSS. Comm.) I. 455 The well-regulating of all things belonging to the marine. **1706** PHILLIPS (ed. Kersey), The *Marine*, the whole Body of a Navy or Fleet; as The Officers of the Marine. **1757** J. H. GROSE *Voy. E. Indies* 67 All these vessels that formed the military marine of Bombay were chiefly manned with English. **1769** BURKE *Late St. Nation* Wks. 1842 I. 98 What naval force, what naval works, and what naval stores..are necessary to keep our marine in a condition commensurate to its great ends. **1842** BORROW *Bible in Spain* xxxi, To this inconsiderable number of vessels is the present war marine of Spain reduced. **1849** COBDEN *Speeches* 18 France knew that America had the largest mercantile marine. **1894** C. N. ROBINSON *Brit. Fleet* 6 The Navy..has always been based..upon the existence of a merchant marine.

‖**3.** That department in the French and other continental governments which deals with naval matters, corresponding to the English *Admiralty*.

1784 *Life Paul Jones* (ed. 4) 24 Count D'Orvilliers transmitted an account of his expedition to the Minister of the Marine. **1835** URE *Philos. Manuf.* 112 The French Minister of Marine. **1848** W. H. KELLY tr. *L. Blanc's Hist. Ten Y.* II. 501 It left the ministry of public works to M. Martin (du Nord), that of marine to M. de Rosamel. **1886** LD. BRASSEY *Nav. Annual* 503 The Council of the [Russian] Empire..ordered the Ministry of Marine to present a plan of construction.

4. One who serves on board ship. †**a.** A sailor, mariner (*obs.*). [= F. *marin.*]

c **1575** J. HOOKER *Life Sir P. Carew* (1857) 33 He had in his ship a hundred marines, the worst of them being able to be a master in the best ship within the realm. **1634** BRERETON *Trav.* (Chetham Soc.) 14 If any soldier, marine, or tradesman die.

b. A soldier who serves on board a man-of-war; one of a body of troops enlisted to do military service on board ship, also at dockyards or on shore under certain circumstances; also in *pl.* used collectively. [See A. 4.]

Royal Marines, troops who serve on British men-of-war. See also HORSE-MARINE[2].

1672 CAPT. S. TAYLOR *Let.* 30 May in L. Edye *Hist. R. Marines* (1893) I. 148 Those marines of whom I soe oft have wrote to you behaved themselves stoutly. **1703** *Lond. Gaz.* No. 3912/1 A Detachment of 400 Men, and the Regiment of Marines. **1709** STEELE *Tatler* No. 79 ¶2 An honest rough Relation of ours..who is a Lieutenant of Marines. **1740** *Lond. Mag.* 413 Sir, a Soldier and a Marine are, I may say, quite different creatures. **1818** CRUISE *Digest* (ed. 2) III. 142 A commission in the marines. **1876** VOYLE & STEVENSON *Mil. Dict.* s.v., The royal marines are a non-purchase Corps, and the officers..rise by seniority. **1894** C. N. ROBINSON *Brit. Fleet* 478 The red-coated marine may be seen all over the world sharing the work..of his blue-frocked brother.

c. Phr. ***tell that to the marines***: a colloquial expression of incredulity. Cf. quot. 1892 s.v. HORSE-MARINE[2].

1806 J. DAVIS *Post Captain* v. 29 He may tell that to the marines, but the sailors will not believe him. **1823** BYRON *Island* II. xxi, 'Right', quoth Ben, 'that will do for the marines'. [*Note*] 'That will do for the marines, but the sailors won't believe it', is an old saying. **1824** SCOTT *Redgauntlet* ch. xiii, Tell that to the marines—the sailors won't believe it. *c* **1829** D. JERROLD in M. R. Booth *Eng. Plays of 19th Cent.* (1969) I. 179 No palaver; tell it to the marines. What, tacking and double tacking! Come to what you want to say at once. **1864** TROLLOPE *Small Ho. at Allington* xli, Is that a story to tell to such a man as me! You may tell it to the marines! **1902** J. CONRAD in *Blackw. Mag.* Dec. 802/2 'You shall get nothing from me, because I have nothing of mine to give away now.' 'Tell that to the marines!' **1928** *Times* 21 July 17/5 He said that I should.. most likely be shot. I ventured to suggest that he should tell that to the Marines. **1933** E. O'NEILL *Ah, Wilderness!* (1934) IV. ii. 145 And I suppose you just sat and let yourself be kissed! Tell that to the Marines! **1944** W. S. MAUGHAM *Razor's Edge* vii. 279 '*A d'autres, ma vieille*,' I replied, which I think can best be translated by: 'Tell that to the marines, old girl.' **1967** D. FRANCIS *Blood Sport* xiv. 172 'When this is over you can sleep for a fortnight.' 'Yeah?' he said sarcastically. 'Tell it to the marines.'

d. (***dead***) ***marine***: an empty bottle. *slang.* (Cf. A. 4 b.)

1831 TRELAWNY *Adv. Younger Son* I. 48 To see their case-bottles properly filled,—no marines among them,—with plenty of grog in their lockers. **1880** J. B. STEPHEN *Austral. Ball., Drought & Doctr.*, We filled a dead marine, Sir, at the family watering-hole.

e. *Naut. slang.* (See quot.)

1840 R. H. DANA *Bef. Mast* xvii. (1854) 86 *note*, 'Marine' is the term applied..to a man who is ignorant and clumsy about seaman's work—a green-horn—a land-lubber.

5. *Painting.* A sea piece.

1846 RUSKIN *Mod. Painters* (ed. 3) I. II. v. i. 340 One of the marines of Salvator. **1884** E. MASON in *Harper's Mag.* Feb. 416/1 Ruysdael's marines are easily distinguished.

6. *attrib.* and *Comb.* **a.** †**marine-set** *a.*, placed on the sea-coast.

1632 LITHGOW *Trav.* VII. 333, I hastned to the next Watch-tower, marine set.

b. = belonging to the marines, as in ***marine barracks, boat, coat, officer, provost***; **marine blue**, a dark blue, the colour of the uniform worn by the Royal Marines; freq. *ellipt.* as *marine*.

1727–41 CHAMBERS *Cycl.* s.v. *Provost*, The French have a provost-general of the marines..besides a marine provost in every vessel. **1797** NELSON 17 July in Nicolas *Disp.* (1845) II. 417 To put as many Marine coats or jackets on the seamen as can be procured. **1801** *Med. Jrnl.* V. 204 The prodigious numbers received from the ships of war and marine barracks, labouring under Phthisis Pulmonalis. **1867** SMYTH *Sailor's Word-bk., Marine Clothing-room*, a compartment of the after-platform, to receive the clothes and stores of the royal marines. *Ibid., Marine Officer*, an officer of the Royal Marines. Jocularly and witlessly applied to an empty bottle. **1873** *Young Englishwoman* IV. 78/1, I should suggest..one polonaise of black cashmere..and one of deep marine blue vigogne. **1895** *Montgomery Ward Catal.* 3/1 Cashmere... All the fashionable colors..black, marine blue, light blue. *Ibid.* 12/3 Plain China silk..navy, marine, gray. **1899** F. T. BULLEN *Way Navy* 55 A Marine boat's crew from the 'Hannibal'. **1910** *Encycl. Brit.* VIII. 746/2 The following is a list of the more important basic colours derived from coal-tar..marine blue, indoïne blue, [etc.]. **1925** E. SITWELL *Poor Young People* 2 The colours most in favour are marine Blue,..myrtle green. **1930** MAERZ & PAUL *Dict. Color* 168/1 In the early nineteenth century there became popular in the general textile field a color adapted from the uniforms of sailors. This color seems first to have been called *Marine Blue*, followed shortly by the name *Navy Blue*. The color was long dyed with indigo. **1934** *Times* 30 Nov. 20/2 The Queen of Denmark's dress and..coat were both of deep marine-blue velvet. **1961** H. E. BATES *Now sleeps Crimson Petal* 43 The marine blue thorns of sea-thistle were touched with sepia rose.

†**marine** (mə'riːn), *v. Obs.* [ad. F. *mariner*: see MARINADE *sb.*] *trans.* = MARINATE *v.*

c **1682** J. COLLINS *Salt & Fishery* 108 Fish, which he Marines, or renders Marinado'd. *Ibid.* 120 To Marine or preserve Fish..after the Italian manner, called Marinading.

marined (mə'riːnd), *a. Her.* [f. MARINE *a.* + -ED.] (See quot. 1823.)

1823 CRABB *Technol. Dict., Marined*, an epithet for an animal in coat armour that has the lower part of the body like a fish. **1847** *Gloss. Heraldry* s.v., *Lion marined*: see *Lion poisson*.

marinel(l, var. forms of MARINAL *Obs.*

mariner ('mærɪnə(r)). Forms: 4 marineer(e, marynare, 4–5 maroner, marynere, marener, 4, 6 marynar, 4–7 maryner, 4, (8–9) marinere, 5 maryneer, marouner, maronner, 6 merriner, maryoner, marryner, marinar, marinour, 6–7

marriner, 3- **mariner**. [a. AF. *mariner* = F. *marinier*, Sp. *marinero*, Pg. *marinheiro*, It. *marinajo*, med.L. *marinārius*, f. L. *marīnus* MARINE *a.*]

1. One who navigates or assists in navigating a ship; a sailor, seaman; in law the term includes all persons employed on ships.

c **1290** *S. Eng. Leg.* I. 329/220 Marineres us token into heore schipe. **13..** *Metr. Hom.* (Vernon MS.) in Herrig *Archiv.* LVII. 313 A pore schip broken marinere. **13..** *Sir Beues* (MS. A.) 2556 A dromond hii fonde þer stonde,.. Boute þai nadde no maroner. *c* **1386** CHAUCER *Prioress' T.* Prol. 3 Now longe moote thou saille by the cost,..gentil Maryneer! *c* **1430** LYDG. *Min. Poems* (Percy Soc.) 152 A blynd maryneer that doth no sterre knowe. *c* **1450** *Merlin* 379 Thei..entred in to the shippes..and hadde..goode maroners hem for to gide. **1481** CAXTON *Myrr.* II. i. 63 Another sterre that ledeth the maronners by the see. **1517** TORKINGTON *Pilgr.* (1884) 60 The Maryoners made a grett Showte. **1585** T. WASHINGTON tr. *Nicholay's Voy.* I. xi. 13 If our marriners had not nimbly bestirred them selues in taking in of their sailes. **1598** STOW *Surv.* xxvii. (1603) 233 Sir Francis Drake, that famous Mariner. **1610** SHAKS. *Temp.* V. i. 98 There shalt thou finde the Marriners asleepe Vnder the Hatches. **1677** W. HUBBARD *Narrative* II. 75 An Ancient Marriner yet living in these parts, a person of good Credit. **1774** GOLDSM. *Nat. Hist.* (1776) I. 348 The mariner takes one part of the year to go from Java to the Moluccas [etc.]. **1798** COLERIDGE (*title*) The Rime of the Ancyent Marinere. **1817** W. SELWYN *Law Nisi Prius* (ed. 4) II. 1144 No mariner shall fail in any action, &c. for the recovery of wages, for want of such agreement being produced. **1836** W. IRVING *Astoria* I. 40 They were to take with them fifty or sixty men, artificers and mariners. **1858** HOMANS *Dict. Comm.* 1693/2 Mariners are bound to contribute out of their wages for embezzlements of the cargo, or injuries produced by the misconduct of any of the crew. **1871** MORLEY *Voltaire* (1886) 10 Whole generations that might have produced their share of skilful and intrepid mariners.

b. ***master mariner***: a 'shipmaster or captain of a merchant vessel' (Adm. Smyth). See also MASTER *sb.*[1] 30.

1838 D. JERROLD *Men Char.* II. 322 Edward Seabright, master-mariner. **1886** *Daily Tel.* 23 Apr. 4/8 Most of them [officers] the possessors of master-mariner certificates.

†**c.** *Cant.* (See quot.) *Obs.*

1567 HARMAN *Caveat* 48 These Freshwater Mariners, their shipes were drowned in the playne of Salisbery. These kynde of Caterpillers counterfet great losses on the sea.

†**2.** *spec.* A fighting man on board ship; a marine.

a **1642** SIR W. MONSON *Naval Tracts* I. (1704) 214, 500 Men at Sea, whereof 340 Mariners, 40 Gunners, 120 Sailors. **1699** (*title*) A Letter to a Member of Parliament concerning The four Regiments commonly called Mariners.

3. *Tasmania.* A bronze-coloured shell.

[Said to be a corruption of a native name *merrina.*]

1898 in MORRIS *Austral Eng.*

4. *attrib.* and *Comb.*, as ***mariner-like*** adj.; †**mariner portage**: see PORTAGE *sb.*[1]; **mariner's card, compass, needle** (see those words); †**mariner's ring**, the astrolabe.

1548–67 THOMAS *Ital. Dict.*, *Marinaresco*, *marinerlike. **1522** in *10th Rep. Hist. MSS. Comm.* App. v. 327 The bying of *mariner portages. **1627** HAKEWILL *Apol.* III. x. §4. 263 Among other rare Inventions, that of the *Marriners compasse is most worthy of admiration. **1605** BACON *Adv. Learn.* II. xiii. §1 Like as the West Indies had never been discovered if the use of the *mariner's needle had not been first discovered. **1574** BOURNE *Regiment for Sea* vi. (1577) 26 b, The *Mariners Ring, called by them the Astralaby.

Hence †**'marinership**, the mariner's art.

1542 UDALL *Erasm. Apoph.* 6 To sitte and holde the stierne in a shyppe, hauyng none experience in ye feats of marinershyp. **1613** PURCHAS *Pilgrimage* (1614) 90 The Phœnicians, famous for Merchandise and Marrinership.

‖**marinera** (mari'nera). [f. Sp. *marinero, -a* marine, seafaring.] = CUECA.

1926 D. L. JOSEPH in J. F. Dobie *Rainbow in Morning* (1965) 54 Play for him a *Marinera* While they whip him. **1964** W. G. RAFFÉ *Dict. Dance* 305/1 Of Spanish extraction, the *Marinera* came to Peru from Chile and was originally called *Cueca Chilena*, or *Chilena*, the name being changed to *Marinera* during the 19th century when Peru and Chile were at war (1879–1883). The new name honoured the Peruvian Navy. **1973** K. BENTON *Craig & Jaguar* v. 53 They even succeeded in making me dance a *marinera* with one of the—er—very nubile young women. **1974** *Encycl. Brit. Macropædia* I. 669/1 This uncertain major–minor tonality pervades the Andean music. It appears in the *chinguinada* for church festivals, with a bass ostinato (repeated melodic-rhythmic pattern); in the mestizo *yaraví* serenade and in the mestizo *marinera* couple dance, with its metre alternating $\frac{3}{4}$ and $\frac{6}{8}$ patterns.

marinescape (mə'riːnskeɪp). [f. MARINE *a.* and *sb.* + SCAPE *sb.*[3], after LANDSCAPE.] A picturesque view or prospect of maritime scenery. Cf. SEA-SCAPE.

1928 *Daily Express* 13 Jan. 11 The Mediterranean was like a sheet of sapphire... Everywhere the marinescape was dotted with rowing boats and other vessels. **1969** J. W. MAVOR *Voy. Atlantis* v. 112 It was the most awesome marinescape that I had ever seen.

marine store(s.

1. *pl.* **a.** (See quot. 1867.) **b.** Old ships' materials as an object of merchandise.

c **1829** D. JERROLD in M. R. Booth *Eng. Plays of 19th Cent.* (1969) I. 184 Go into the mercantile line—take a shop for marine-stores. **1831** J. HOLLAND *Manuf. Metal* I. 144 Old iron..is collected..by a class of persons calling themselves 'dealers in marine stores'. **1852** DICKENS *Bleak Ho.* v, A shop, over which was written..Krook, Dealer in Marine Stores. **1867** SMYTH *Sailor's Word-bk.*, *Marine Stores*, a general term for the ironwork, cordage, sails, provisions, and other outfit, with which a vessel is supplied.

fig. **1858** CARLYLE *Fredk. Gt.* VIII. i. II. 295 These confused Prussian History-Books, opulent in nugatory pedantisms and learned marine-stores.

2. *sing.* A shop where marine stores are sold.

1837 BARHAM *Legend H. Tighe* in *Ingol. Leg.* (1840) 1st Ser. 158 In Ratcliffe Highway there's an old marine store. **1840** MARRYAT *Poor Jack* xii, Old Nanny..kept a marine store.

3. *attrib.* and *Comb.*, as ***marine-store dealer, shop.***

1836–9 DICKENS *Sk. Boz, Scenes* xxi, There is not a marine-store shop in the neighbourhood, which does not exhibit for sale some faded articles of dramatic finery. **1836** DICKENS *Sk. Boz* 1st Ser. I. 91 The marine-store dealer at the corner of the street. **1844** *Ainsworth's Mag.* VI. 112 A marine-store keeper of the pilfered orts and ends of literature. **1869** *Punch* 17 July 22/1 They were marine-store dealers.

Marinism (mə'riːnɪz(ə)m). [f. *Marini* + -ISM.] The affected style of writing characteristic of the Italian poet Giovanni Battista Marini (*d.* 1625).

1867 *Pall Mall G.* No. 813. 1007/2 Euphuism and Marinism. **1886** SYMONDS *Renaiss. It.*, *Cath. React.* I. ii. 71 The Renaissance riots itself away in Marinism, Gongorism, Euphuism, and the affectations of the Hôtel Rambouillet.

Marinist (mə'riːnɪst). [Formed as prec. + -IST.] An imitator of Marini. Also *attrib.*

1838 *Penny Cycl.* XI. 297/1 The extravagant notions of the Italian Marinists. **1864** *Chambers's Encycl.* VI. 328/2 The Marinist school of poetry. **1885** E. W. GOSSE *Shaks. to Pope* 15 Chiabrera..disdaining the folly of the Marinists,..attained a position somewhat analogous to that of Cowley.

marino: see MARINA.

marinorama (mə,riːnə'rɑːmə). *rare*[–0]. [f. MARINE after *panorama.*] A panoramic representation of sea views.

1847 in WEBSTER. In mod. Dicts.

‖**mariola** (mə'raɪələ). [eccl. L., dim. of *Marīa* MARY. Cf. MARIOLE.] An image of the Virgin Mary.

[**1299–1300** *Liber Quotid. Contrarot. Garderobæ* (1787) 352 Quatuor mariole beate Marie.] **1876** W. BAYLISS *Witness of Art* 74 Fresco and canvas, mariola and shrine.

Mariolater (mɛərɪ'ɒlətə(r)). [f. Gr. *Μαρία* Mary + *-λατρης* worshipper.] One who practises Mariolatry.

1861 STANLEY *East. Ch.* iii. 109 The grand gathering of all the Heretics of the world, Sabellians, Mariolaters, Arians.

Mariolatrous (mɛərɪ'ɒlətrəs), *a.* [f. as prec. + -OUS.] Characterized by Mariolatry.

1844 *Ecclesiologist* III. 181 Mr. Close charges us with 'Mariolatrous' doctrine. **1889** *Whitehall Rev.* 24 Aug. 9 One of them preached a sermon which was considered Mariolatrous by the Father Superior.

Mariolatry (mɛərɪ'ɒlətrɪ). [f. Gr. *Μαρία* Mary + *λατρεία* (see LATRIA, -LATRY), after IDOLATRY.] The idolatrous worship of the Virgin Mary attributed by opponents to Roman Catholics.

1612 T. JAMES *Corrupt. Scripture* II. 85 The reading, *ipsa* [in Gen. iii. 15] (the best ground of their Mariolatrie). **1844** CLOSE *Reply to Arnold* 36 Whether this exhibition of Mariolatry had destroyed many souls..none can tell. **1874** GREEN *Short Hist.* v. §1. 214 The religious enthusiasm had developed into the pretty conceits of Mariolatry.

†**mariole.** *Obs.* [OF.] = MARIOLA.

c **1330** R. BRUNNE *Chron.* (1810) 94 Þe Mariole [AF. *La Marye*] þer scho sat.

Mariological (mɛərɪəʊ'lɒdʒɪkəl), *a.* Also with small initial. [f. MARIOLOG(Y + -ICAL.] Of or pertaining to Mariology. So **mario'logically** *adv.*

1954 *Theology* LVII. 90 A mariological interpretation. *Ibid.*, Interpret the text mariologically. **1967–8** H. R. MCADOO in Clark & Davey *Anglican/R.C. Dialogue* (1974) vi. 93 There are..similarly differences as between Roman Catholics and Anglicans, and Anglicans would add Mariological definitions. **1969** E. L. MASCALL in A. Richardson *Dict. Christian Theol.* 208/1 By a small majority it was decided by the [Second Vatican] Council not to issue a separate Mariological document. **1971** *Catholic Dict. Theol.* III. 264/1 The most notable event in the Mariological deliberations of the Vatican Council was the vote taken on 29 October 1963 to decide whether the schema *de Maria matre ecclesiae* should be taken as a final chapter of the decree on the Church or as a decree by itself. **1974** *Encycl. Brit. Macropædia* XI. 563/1 The extravagances of Marian cult and Mariological thought that have sometimes tended to go beyond the limits both of biblical foundation and of ecclesiastical regulations.

Mariology (mɛərɪ'ɒlədʒɪ). Also **Maryology.** [f. Gr. *Μαρί-α* MARY + -OLOGY. Cf. *Christology.*] The body of dogma and pious opinion relating to Mary as Virgin mother of the Son of God.

1857 J. S. HARFORD *Michael Angelo* I. 295 In the cycles of the third, and of the earlier part of the fourth century, and even later, we find nothing that can be resolved into Maryology. **1903** *Dublin Rev.* Jan. 211 Mariology is exhaustively treated in the four hundred and fifty pages which are here devoted to it.

mariolyne, obs. form of MARJORAM.

marionate, obs. form of MARINATE.

marionette (mærɪə'nɛt). Also 7 -onet, 9 -onnette, marrionette. [a. F. *marionnette*, f. *Marion*, dim. of *Marie* MARY: see -ETTE. Cf. OF. *mariotte* in the same sense.]

1. A puppet actuated by strings and used to represent persons (or animals) in action.

c **1620** W. BROWNE *Brit. Past.* III. i, A little spruce elfe then (just of the sett Of the French dancer or such marionett). **1664** ETHEREDGE *Com. Rev.* III. iv, Me did look to see De Marioneté and de Jack-puddingé. **1789** MRS. PIOZZI *Journ. France* I. 115 One word of solid instruction to the ear conveys more knowledge to the mind at last than all these marionettes presented to the eye. **1839** LONGF. *Hyperion* IV. iii, Quick, nervous, hinge-like motions, much resembling those of a marionette.

fig. **1863** 'OUIDA' *Held in Bondage* I. 258 Men and women are marionettes. **1868** HANNAY *Stud. Thackeray* (1869) 15 He did not invent a complicated intrigue and then a set of marionettes to carry it out.

2. The buffle-headed duck, *Bucephala albeola.*

1838 AUDUBON *Ornith. Biog.* IV. 217 Buffel-headed Duck ..being known in these different districts [of the U.S.] by the names of..Marrionette, Dipper, and Die-dipper.

3. A mechanism at the end of the batten in a ribbon-loom, for actuating the racks of the shuttles, the movements of which suggest those of a marionette.

1890 in *Century Dict.*

4. *attrib.*, as ***marionette figure, play, player, show.***

1856 R. A. VAUGHAN *Mystics* (1860) I. 34 The countless marionette figures in the brain of the theosophist. **1868** LIGHTFOOT *Ep. Philippians* (1869) 268 In the marionette plays of his native Spain St. Seneca takes his place by the side of St. Peter and St. Paul. **1875** JOWETT *Plato* (ed. 2) V. 41 The marionette-players will please the children. **1885** 'E. GARRETT' (Mrs. Mayo) *At Any Cost* ix. 152 No drama at all, but only a very cleverly managed marionette show.

marionettish (mærɪə'nɛtɪʃ), *a.* Also **marionetish.** [f. MARIONETT(E + -ISH[1].] Suggestive of a marionette in appearance or movement.

1921 E. O'NEILL *Emperor Jones* v. 184 There is something stiff, rigid, unreal, marionettish about their movements. **1930** *Observer* 18 May 26/2 'Intimate Snapshots' was fresher and rounder in conception than in execution... I thought the liftman unclear in his explanation, and the journalists marionetish. **1963** A. ROSS *Australia 63* x. 196 If fast, short-pitched bowling induces an initial, marionettish jerkiness he soon settles down to more convincing methods. **1969** E. WILKINS *Rose-Garden Game* viii. 192 Their marionettish aspect encourages the impression that at any moment the gilded mandorla might begin to turn on its axis and spin.

mario'nettist. Also **marionnettist.** [f. MARIONETT(E + -IST.] One who operates marionettes.

1918 *Marionnette* (Florence) Jan. 98 The Marionnettist has put his dolls in their box...his wife is counting the pennies. **1924** *Glasgow Herald* 10 May 8 It was here the man of so many quarrels..fought the mock duel with..the marionettist's monkey. **1936** R. S. SIBBALD *Marionettes in North of France* I. 44 M. Delannoy..gives a list of the marionettists who applied to the city of Lille..for permission to show their dolls.

marionite ('mærɪənaɪt). *Min.* [f. the name of *Marion* County in Arkansas + -ITE.] Hydrous carbonate of zinc.

1858 W. ELDERHORST in *Geol. Rep. Arkansas* 153 (Chester *Dict. Min.*).

marioram, -um, obs. forms of MARJORAM.

mariori, variant of MARGERY *Obs.*

Mariotte ('mærɪɒt). Also erron. **Marriotte.** The name of Edme *Mariotte* (*c* 1620–84), French physicist, used in the possessive and *attrib.* to designate apparatus he devised and a principle he enunciated: **Mariotte('s) bottle** or **flask,** a bottle with an outlet near the bottom and an adjustable glass tube passing through a cork in the neck, which if filled to above the bottom of the tube gives a flow of constant head equal to the height of the bottom of the tube above the outlet; **Mariotte's law,** Boyle's law (see LAW *sb.*[1] 17 c (*b*)); **Mariotte's tube,** a U-tube having one arm short and sealed at the end and the other elongated and open to the air.

1845 E. WEST tr. *Peschel's Elem. Physics* I. v. iii. 220 On the same principle Mariotte's flask acts. *Ibid.* iv. 228 In such a case it is more convenient..to use..a Mariotte's tube.., which being graduated according to Marriotte's [*sic*] law, will show the amount of pressure. **1898** J. C. P. ALDOUS *Elem. Course Physics* 171 (*heading*) Boyle's (or Marriotte's [*sic*]) law. *Ibid.* 172 (*heading*) Boyle's (or Mariotte's) tube. **1930** DOUGALL & DEANS tr. *P. P. Ewald's Physics Solids & Fluids* v. 217 The experiment is conveniently carried out by using the so-called Mariotte's bottle. **1966** *McGraw-Hill Encycl. Sci. & Technol.* II. 313/1 The phenomenon was discovered independently by Edme Mariotte about 1650 and is known in Europe as Mariotte's law. **1974** *Nature* 26 Apr. 798/1 Continuous flow of fluid..was maintained relatively constant by means of gravity flow from a Mariotte flask. **1975** WILLIAMS & WILSON *Biologist's Guide to Princ. & Techniques Pract. Biochem.* iii. 93 This can be overcome

by the use of a Mariotte flask which will keep the operating pressure constant.

‖**mariposa** (mari'posa). [Sp., lit. 'butterfly'.] In *Bullfighting*, a movement in which the bullfighter draws the bull by flapping the cape behind his own back. Also *fig.*

1932 [see FAROL]. **1936** R. CAMPBELL *Mithraic Emblems* 143 If you would lepidopterize These mariposas that I fling. **1957** A. MACNAB *Bulls of Iberia* xv. 169 The bull..is attacking what looks like a giant butterfly... The butterfly is Estudiante himself, and he is doing the famous *quite* of the *mariposa*... The matador holds the cape behind him,..as he holds out his arms sideways to form the 'wings' with the cape... As the bull turns and goes for one wing, he drops his arm and that wing folds up. **1967** MCCORMICK & MASCAREÑAS *Compl. Aficionado* iii. 92 Like all beginning novilleros, Domingo longs to learn the adornos first, the *revolera*, the *serpentina*, the *mariposa* with the cape.

mariposa lily (mærɪ'pəʊsə,lɪlɪ). [f. Sp. *mariposa* butterfly + LILY.] A bulbous plant of the genus *Calochortus*, belonging to the family Liliaceæ, and native to the Pacific coast of North America and Mexico. Also **mariposa tulip** and *absol.*

1868 A. WOOD in *Proc. Acad. Nat. Sci. Philadelphia* 169 This splendid flower [sc. *Calochortus venustus*]..has long been known to the native Californians by the name of *Mariposa* (Spanish for butterfly). **1869** J. MUIR *Jrnl.* 9 June in *My First Summer in Sierra* (1911) 43 The grasses and flowers in glorious array,..monardella, Mariposa tulips, lupines. **1882** *Garden* 30 Sept. 291/1 The Mariposa Lily. **1920** B. M. & R. RICE *Pop. Stud. Calif. Wild Flowers* 27 It would probably be more correct to say Mariposa Tulip than Mariposa Lily, for botanists place them in the tulip family. **1925** J. L. COTTER *Culture of Bulbs* 108 The name Calochortus now embraces the Mariposa Lily proper, and the Star Tulip. **1934** S. E. WHITE *Folded Hills* 198 Here also were..mariposas. **1971** P. M. SYNGE *Collins Guide to Bulbs* (ed. 2) 71 It is in..the Mariposa lilies or Mariposa tulips that we chiefly find the most outstanding horticultural plants [of the genus *Calochortus*]. *Ibid.* 73 The leaves of this section are..more conspicuous than those of the Mariposas.

mariposite (mærɪ'pəʊzaɪt, -saɪt). *Min.* [f. *Maripos-a*, the name of the county in California, U.S.A., where it was first found + -ITE[1].]

A variety of muscovite that contains a relatively high proportion of silica and up to one per cent. chromic oxide and is found as green or greenish-yellow crystals.

1868 B. SILLIMAN in *Proc. Calif. Acad. Sci.* III. 381 The mineral is probably new, and must be referred to the mica section of an hydrous silicate. Should it..prove to be new, I would suggest the name *Mariposite* as an appropriate name for it, as it was on the Mariposa estate that it first attracted my attention, and where it exists in great abundance. **1916** *Bull. U.S. Geol. Survey* No. 610. 139 A comparison of the two analyses of mariposite made by Hildebrand with Penfield's analysis of alurgite shows that the two minerals are probably identical. **1946** *Amer. Mineralogist* XXXI. 1 Chrome micas, classed variously as fuchsite, mariposite, and chromiferous muscovite are of wide distribution throughout gold-bearing districts of the Canadian Shield. **1965** G. J. WILLIAMS *Econ. Geol. N.Z.* x. 149/2 The majority of overseas occurrences of fuchsite (and mariposite) seem to have a direct ultramafic association.

‖**mariput** ('mærɪpʌt). [Native name.] The African zoril, *Zorilla capensis*, a small animal of the weasel family with black and white stripes.

Formerly named *Viverra zorilla* in accordance with the erroneous notion that it was a kind of civet.

1828–32 in WEBSTER; and in later Dicts.

†**maris.** *Obs.* Forms: 4–5 marice, marys, marrys, maris, mareis. [a. OF. *marris*:—L. *mātrice-m* (see MATRIX *sb.*).] The womb.

a **1340** HAMPOLE *Psalter* lvii[i]. 3 Aliend ere synful fra maghe [*MS. S* marice]. *c* **1400** *Lanfranc's Cirurg.* 94 If þat he be growen..in þe mareis [*MS. Add.* marys]..it is bettere nouȝt to cure þe cankre þan to cure. *Ibid.* 209 If þe enpostym ..be in a wommans maris, þan [etc.]. **1422** tr. *Secreta Secret., Priv. Priv.* 232 The seede wythyn the marice is defiet. ?**14..** *MS. Addit.* 12195 lf. 158 (Halliw.) Marrys.

maris, obs. form of MARISH.

‖**marisca** (mə'rɪskə). *Path.* [L.; lit. a coarse fig. (For the application cf. FICUS.)] Hæmorrhoids, piles; also, 'an excrescence of a fleshy nature from the eyes or eyelids' (*Syd. Soc. Lex.*). Hence **ma'riscal, ma'riscous** *adjs.* of the nature of mariscæ; affected with mariscæ.

1693 *Blancard's Phys. Dict.* (ed. 2), *Marisca*, the same that [*sic*] *Ficus*. **1706** PHILLIPS (ed. Kersey), *Marisca*, the Hemorrhoids or Piles. **1822** GOOD *Study Med.* I. 347 Mariscal tumours..are most common in persons who possess a very strong action of the sphincter ani. *Ibid.*, 348 Mariscal excrescences. **1856** MAYNE *Expos. Lex.*, *Marisca*, ..applied to a hemorrhoidal tumour, like a large fig. *Ibid.*, *Mariscosus*, Having, or full of Mariscæ: mariscous.

mariscall, -ischal(e, obs. ff. MARSHAL *sb.*

marischini, obs. form of MARASCHINO.

marish ('mærɪʃ), *sb.* and *a.*[1] *Obs.* exc. *poet.* and *dial.* Forms: α. 4–5 **mar(r)ais(s, marys(e, mares,** 4–6 **mar(r)eis, -eys,** 5 **maryce, -ysse, -ise, -eyse, -eyes,** 5–6 **maress(e, marres(s(e, -ys,** 5–7 **marisse,** 6 **-ice, -is, -ese, -ees, marryce,** 6–7 **marris(e, marrice,** 7 **marraies;** 4–5 **marace, maras,** 4–6 **marras(s,** 5 **marasse,** 6 **marrase.** β. 6 **marysh, marys(s)he, marris(c)he, -ysh, merish,** 6–7, 9 **marrish,** 7 **mareish, (marest),** 6– **marish.** [ME. *mareis*, *mares*, a. OF. *marais*, *mareis* (mod.F. *marais*):—med.L. *mariscus* a. OTeut. **marisko-* MARSH *sb.*[1] The origin of the β forms is somewhat obscure; they may represent the occasional OF. *maresche* (:—med.L. **marisca* fem.), or may possibly stand for a dialectal variant of the native English MARSH (cf. the disyllabic OE. *męrisc* beside *męrsc*).

The It. *marese* is ad. F. *marais*; if independent, it would represent a popular L. type **marēnsis* adj., the Fr. form of which would coincide with that of *mariscus*.]

A. *sb.*

1. = MARSH[1].

α. *c* **1330** R. BRUNNE *Chron.* (1810) 325 William Waleis,.. In mores & mareis with robberie him fedes. **13..** *Coer de L.* 6038 Kyng Richard garte al the Ynglys Schere rysches in the marys. **1375** BARBOUR *Bruce* VI. 55 He..vent hym doune till a marrass. *c* **1400** MAUNDEV. (Roxb.) xiv. 65 men may noȝt wele ga þat way..for waters and maracez þat er þare. **1432–50** tr. *Higden* (Rolls) II. 357 A marras callede Lerna. *a* **1450** *Knt. de la Tour* (1868) 63 They yode over a mareys for the next waye, but thei felle in the myre. *c* **1450** *Merlin* 604 Above this marasse was a chauchie. **1480** CAXTON *Chron. Eng.* clxx. 155 As his hors ran it stert into a myre of mareys vp to the bely. **1501** DOUGLAS *Pal. Hon.* I. iv, The soyl was nocht but marres, slike, and sand. **1535** STEWART *Cron. Scot.* II. 97 In mos, in marres, and in mony myre. **1545** ASCHAM *Toxoph.* I. (Arb.) 74 Lurkyng in fennes and marisses lyke frogges. **1601** HOLLAND *Pliny* II. 431 Tortoises found in muddie waters and marraies. **1609** BIBLE (Douay) *1 Macc.* ix. 45 Bankes, and marrises, and forests.

β. **1523** LD. BERNERS *Froiss.* I. lviii. 32 b, Sir Vauflart de la Croyse, who was in the marysshe, trustyng..to haue scaped, was spyed by some that rode a longe by the marese. **1596** SPENSER *F.Q.* V. x. 23 These marishes and myrie bogs, In which the fearefull ewftes do build their bowres. **1611** BIBLE *Ezek.* xlvii. 11 The myrie places thereof, and the marishes thereof, shall not be healed. **1623** LISLE *Ælfric on O. & N. Test.* Ded. 12 Your Forests breed you Deere, Your Marests Fowle. **1667** MILTON *P.L.* XII. 630 As Ev'ning Mist Ris'n from a River o're the marish glides. **1726** SWIFT *On Poetry* Misc. 1735 V. 166 Like a Bridge that joins a Marish To Moorlands of a diff'rent Parish. **1765** A. DICKSON *Treat. Agric.* xx. (ed. 2) 149 There are many marishes in Scotland. Some have been drained. **1830** TENNYSON *Dying Swan* ii, Far thro' the marish green and still The tangled water-courses slept. **1858** MORRIS *Sir P. Harpdon's End* 74 We struggled in a marish half the day. **1880** *Times* 17 Sept. 8/5 [Yorkshire] In the carrs and marishes both corn and turnips are under water.

2. *attrib.*

1398 TREVISA *Barth. De P.R.* XIX. lxxix. (1495) 910 Egges of marreys foule ben yelowe. **1489** CAXTON *Faytes of A.* I. xiv. 38 Fer from eny palusche or mares grounde. **1625** K. LONG tr. *Barclay's Argenis* II. ii. 71 The King's horses.. chafed with the stinging of the marish gnats. **1658** OSBORN *Adv. Son* Wks. (1673) 234 Making a like use of Scripture and Reason of State, as Marishmen do of their Sluces, by which they keep out the Sea. **1830** TENNYSON *Mariana* 40 The cluster'd marish-mosses.

†**b.** In spec. names of plants, as ***marish dog-stones*** (see DOGSTONES), ***marish mallow*** = MARSHMALLOW, ***marish parsley*** (see PARSLEY), ***marish whorts*** (tr. Bot.L. *Vaccinia palustria*), cranberries.

1548 TURNER *Names of Herbes* (1881) 11 Althea..is named..in Englishe marish mallowe. **1578** LYTE *Dodoens* V. xlii. 607 Smallache is called..in English,..Marrishe Parsley. *Ibid.* VI. xi. 671 We..do cal them in Latine, Vaccinia palustria, that is to say, Marrish Whorts, and Fen berries. **1597** GERARDE *Herbal* I. xcviii. 157 Marish Dogs stones hath many thicke blunt leaues next the roote.

B. *adj.*

1. Of the nature of a marsh, marshy; such as is produced in a marsh.

The ending *-ish* has given to the sb. used attrib. the aspect of an adj., and has thus favoured the development of the genuine adjectival use.

1543 TRAHERON *Vigo's Chirurg.* II. ix. 42 He must abstaine ..from marryshe fyshes and fennie. **1578** LYTE *Dodoens* VI. lxviii. 633 This herbe groweth also in moyst marrishe places. **1600** SURFLET *Country Farm* IV. v. 637 If there be any marrish or dead water in..your medow: you must cause it to ..draine out. **1601** HOLLAND *Pliny* II. 142 A kind of marish or moorie Lentils. **1685** BOYLE *Salubr. Air* 3 Marrish Grounds, and wet Soils are wont to be unhealthfull. **1859** WHITTIER *Proph. Sam. Sewall* 160 Hillside berries and marish seeds. **1883** STEVENSON *Silverado Sq.* 7 A wooden footway, bridging one marish spot after another.

†**b.** Used predicatively. *Obs.*

1549 in *Cal. Scot. Papers* (1898) I. 145 Cutters of mosses for makinge of mean landes of thos that be but marresse. **1616** SURFL. & MARKH. *Country Farm* 13 That [earth].. which is watrie and marish. **1707** SLOANE *Jamaica* I. p. lxxix, The country thereabout is marish and wet. **1775** CHANDLER *Trav. Greece* (1825) II. 368 The other wells are not easily to be..examined the spot being marish.

c. *fig.*

1599 HARSNET *Agst. Darell* 235 He would neuer haue set the frame of all his cosening practises vpon that moist and marish conceit that Somers in his fits was altogether sencelesse. **1602** MARSTON *Antonio's Rev.* II. iii, What danke marrish spirit But would be fyred with impatience? **1869** LOWELL *Dara* 24 The frank sun of natures clear and rare Breeds poisonous fogs in low and marish minds.

†**2.** Salt, saline. (? A misapprehension.) *Obs.*

1609 *Ev. Woman in Hum.* I. i. in Bullen *O. Pl.* IV, That mooving marish element, that swels and swages as it please the Moone. **1621** QUARLES *Q. Ester* K 4 b, Her cheekes o'reflowne With marish teares.

Hence †'**marishness**, marshiness.

1652–62 HEYLIN *Cosmogr.* II. (1682) 107 The Marishness of the Ground. **1678** WANLEY *Wond. Lit. World* IV. xxvii. §1. 409/1 Work was hindred by..the Marishness of the Grounds.

marish ('mɛərɪʃ), *a.*[2] *rare.* In 7 mareish. [f. MARE *sb.* + -ISH.] Like, or like that of, a mare.

1679 *Lond. Gaz.* No. 1452/4 A bay..a little white on his two hind fetlocks, and a Mareish head.

marishal, obs. form of MARSHAL.

†'**marishy**, *a.* *Obs.* [f. MARISH *sb.* + -Y[1].] Marshy.

1607 TOPSELL *Four-f. Beasts* 207 The Palustrians or Marishye Elephantes. **1690** J. MACKENZIE *Siege London-Derry* 24/2 Boggs, and Marishy places. **1727** A. HAMILTON *New Acc. E. Ind.* II. xlv. 148 The inland Country is.. towards the Sea very low and marishy.

‖**marisma** (ma'risma). [Sp.: cf. MAREMMA.] The waste lands near the Guadalquivir.

1884 A. CHAPMAN in *Ibis* Ser. v. II. 70 My next expedition was to the 'marismas' of the Guadalquivir. *Ibid.* 71 In winter the marisma abounds with wildfowl. **1889** H. SAUNDERS *Man. Brit. Birds* 548 The Black-winged Stilt.. breeds..abundantly in the marismas of Southern Spain.

†**marisse**, *v.* *Obs.* Also 4 **marissch, marissi.** [irreg. ad. F. *marier* MARRY *v.*] *trans.* To marry.

c **1315** SHOREHAM i. 1476 Ryȝt y-marissched schelle hy be In heuene-ryche blysse. **1340** *Ayenb.* 48 Þe vifte [kind of adultery] is mid wyfman ymarissed. *Ibid.* 220 Wyþoute þet þet he him moȝe marissi yef he wyle.

marisse, obs. form of MARISH.

Marist ('mɛərɪst). [a. F. *Mariste*, f. *Marie* Mary: see -IST.] A member of the Roman Catholic Society of Mary, founded by a French priest early in the 19th century and devoted to the work of foreign missions and to teaching. Also *attrib.*

1877 W. MCDOWALL in *Encycl. Brit.* VII. 528/1 A commercial academy connected with the Marist Brotherhood, and dedicated to St. Joseph. **1880** *Daily News* 11 Nov. 5/8 A sympathiser with the Marists. **1894** *Ibid.* 3 July 4/5 The chapel of the Marist Fathers near Leicester square.

marit, obs. form of MARRIED.

maritage ('mærɪtɪdʒ). *Law.* [ad. med.L. *marītāgium*, a latinization of F. *mariage* MARRIAGE.]

†**1.** = DOWER, DOWRY 1, 2. *Obs.*

1502 ARNOLDE *Chron.* 82 A wydou after yͤ deth of her husbond..must haue maritage & her herytage whiche that her husbond and she helde yͭ day of the obyt of him her husbond. **1574** tr. *Littleton's Tenures* 137 If yͤ husbande of the wife alien the heritage or maritage of his wife. **1609** SKENE *Reg. Maj.* 29 b, Lands given as Maritage, or Tocher.

2. *Hist.* The right possessed by a feudal superior (in England only by the king) of exacting a fine for the marriage of a vassal; also, the profits accruing to the crown or lord from this source. Also in L. form *maritagium.*

The *maritagia* within a certain district were sometimes granted to a particular person or corporation.

1563–87 FOXE *A. & M.* (1596) 251/1 Maritages which K. John committed to his keeping at the daie of his death. **1851** *Orig. Paroch. Scotiæ* I. 283 King Robert Bruce..in 1326 granted to the monks all wards, reliefs, maritages [etc.].. belonging to himself and heirs within the sheriffdom of Roxburgh.

marital ('mærɪtəl), *a.* Also 7 **-all.** [ad. L. *marītālis*, f. *marīt-us* husband: see -AL[1]. Cf. F., Sp., Pg. *marital*, It. *maritale.*]

1. Pertaining or relating to a husband; husbandly.

1616 BULLOKAR *Eng. Expos.*, *Maritall*, husbandlike. **1644** MAXWELL *Prerog. Chr. Kings* 23 A woman by her choice and consent designeth her husband, but the maritall power and dominion is onely from God. **1726** AYLIFFE *Parergon* 49 Christian Charity as well as Marital Affection. **1861** THACKERAY *Philip* VII, The two poor sisters had had to regulate their affections by the marital orders, and to be warm, cool, moderate, freezing, according to their husbands' state for the time being.

2. Of or pertaining to marriage; matrimonial, connubial.

1603 FLORIO *Montaigne* III. v. (1632) 476 He depainteth her some what stirring for a maritall Venus. **1660** JER. TAYLOR *Duct. Dubit.* II. ii. rule III. §27 The Dearnesses of Brother and Sister..if they were not made holy and separate by a law would easily change into Marital loves. **1840** THACKERAY *Paris Sk.-bk.* (1872) 81 What a deal of marital discomfort might have been avoided. **1858** LD. ST. LEONARDS *Handy-Bk. Prop. Law* xii. 79 The restitution of marital rights would be enforced if sought for. **1902** A. THOMSON *Lauder & Lauderdale* xiii. 131 Although the two Houses were in marital relationship, they were almost always at daggers drawn.

3. Special collocation. **marital rape** *Law* (orig. *U.S.*), sexual intercourse forced on a woman by her husband, knowingly against her will.

1975 S. BROWNMILLER *Against our Will* xii. 381 The most famous *marital rape in literature..is that of Irene by Soames in *The Forsyte Saga.* **1986** *Economist* 15 Mar. 40/3 The country which outlaws marital rape in half its states.. also allows television cameras into many of its courts.

Hence **mari'tality**, excessive affection of a wife for her husband (correlative to *uxoriousness*);

ˈmaritally *adv.*, as if married, as a married person.
1812 W. Taylor in *Monthly Mag.* XXXIII. 42 The uxoriousness of the husband was in neither case requited by the maritality of the wife. *a* **1832** Bentham *Deont.* Wks. 1843 I. 235 Maritality, uxoriality, paternity, maternity, filiality. **1869** *Daily News* 13 Feb., The illegitimate children are the offspring of people living maritally and as quietly as married people. **1880** *Daily Tel.* 13 Nov., Another of the prisoners, Kviatkoffsky, with whom she had been living maritally, according to Nihilist notions of ethics.

maritan(e, obs. forms of maritime.

†**maritated**, *pa. pple. Obs.*—⁰ [f. L. *marītāt-us* pa. pple. of *marītāre* to marry: see -ed¹.] Having a husband; married.
1727 in Bailey vol. II.

maritayne, obs. form of maritime.

†**marite.** *Obs.* [a. OF. *marit* (mod.F. *mari*) or its source L. *marītus*.] A husband.
c **1330** R. Brunne *Chron.* (1810) 210 William he þouht to greue, for þat grete despite, þat he withouten leue, his douhter gaf marite. **1398** Trevisa *Barth. De P.R.* xv. xii. (Tollem. MS.) Þey [the Amazons] wolde compelle here marites to wende from hem.

maˈritiˌcidal, *a. rare.* [f. L. *marītus* husband + -cide¹ + -al¹.] Husband-slaying.
1819 H. Busk *Vestriad* iv. 500 Near each the steel mariticidal bleeds. **1821** *New Monthly Mag.* II. 392 The mariticidal mother.

†**maˈritimal**, *a. Obs.* Also -all. [f. L. *maritim-us* maritime + -al¹.] = maritime *a.*
1586 J. Hooker *Hist. Irel.* in Holinshed II. 161/1 An excellent maritimall man, and verie expert in all seruices at the seas. *c* **1611** Chapman *Iliad* xxiii. 50 The friend, the shores maritimall Sought for his bed. **1627** Speed *England* xxviii. §2 Minerall and Maritimall reuenew.

†**maˈritimate**, *a. Obs.* [f. L. *maritim-us* (see next) + -ate (? after *legitimate, ultimate*).] = maritime. (Freq. in Sir W. Raleigh.)
1601 R. Johnson *Kingd. & Commw.* 37 Peru..containeth by the maritimate coast 12000 and 600 miles. **1614** Raleigh *Hist. World* i. (1634) 183 This City being maritimate used all their devotions to Neptune. **1638** Sir. T. Herbert *Trav.* (ed. 2) 323 Ports and Villages marittimat. **1665** —— *Trav.* (1677) 352 Upon which consideration it is (as I suppose) that Mercator stretches Aurea Chersonesus from Sumatra to Japan, both in reference to the Isles and Coast Maritimate.

maritime (ˈmærɪtaɪm), *a.* and *sb.* Forms: α. 6 **myrytayne, maritayne,** 7 **maritan(e, maritin, marratine, maretine,** 7–8 **maritine;** β. 7 **marittime,** 7–8 **maritim,** 6– **maritime.** [ad. L. *maritim-us*, f. *mari-*, *mare* sea + suffix *-timus* (occurring in *fīnitimus* neighbouring, *lēgitimus* lawful; also forming superlatives as *intimus* inmost, *ultimus* last).
The β forms are from the L. directly or through mod.F. *maritime* (cf. Sp. *marítimo*, Pg. *maritimo*, It. *marittimo*). An OF. form, *maritim*, was corrupted, partly owing to confusion of suffixes, into *maritin*, *maritaim*, *maritain* (latinized *maritānus*), whence the α forms above.]

A. *adj.*

1. a. Of countries and peoples: Bordering on the sea; living near the sea-coast. †*occas.* predicative.
α. **1623** Cockeram. *Maritan*, bordering on the sea. **1627** Hakewill *Apol.* ii. vi. §3 (1630) 115 And in them specially their maritine parts. **1632** Lithgow *Trav.* viii. 365 Tents, filled with maritine people, that were fled hither from the Sea coast. **1652** Earl Monm. *Hist. Rel. Flanders* i. vii. 12 Of their Maretine Forces. **1652** —— tr. *Bentivoglio's Hist. Relat.* 12 The Marratine parts of Friesland. **1654** —— tr. *Bentivoglio's Wars Flanders* i. iv. 56 The City of Embden,.. one of the most considerable Towns of all the Maretine part. **1667** Milton *P.L.* xi. 398 Ercoco and the less Maritine Kings Mombaza [etc.].
β. **1598** Barret *Theor. Warres* v. i. 122 If the confines of the Kingdome bee Maritime or sea coast. **1603** Holland *Plutarch's Mor.* 489 To inhabit the maritime cities and townes, neere unto the sea side. **1634** Sir T. Herbert *Trav.* 225 Brittany (a marittime part of France). **1654** Flecknoe *Ten Years Trav.* 19 Comparing them with the Maritime Women of other Seas (for the most part fowl, ugly, and weather-beaten). **1673** Temple *Observ. United Prov.* Wks. 1731 I. 44 The opening and cleansing of the old Channel of the Rhine..by which the Town of Leyden would grow Maritime. **1692** Luttrell *Brief Rel.* (1857) II. 359 The king, before he leaves England, intends to visit all the maritime yards. **1726** Swift *Gulliver* i. v, Seamen, who dwell in the maritime parts. **1813** Vancouver *Agric. Devon* 1 Devonshire is a maritime county. **1854** Milman *Lat. Chr.* iv. iv. (1864) II. 265 Though a maritime people, on a line of seacoast, they were ignorant of the art of fishing.

b. Of animals, plants, etc.: Living or found near the sea.
1608 Topsell *Serpents* (1658) 798 There are Maritine Rocks called *Scelestæ*. **1763** Mills *Syst. Pract. Husb.* IV. 409 The antients looked upon the olive as a maritime-tree. **1807** J. E. Smith *Phys. Bot.* 418 *Statice*,..a beautiful maritime genus. **1856** Grindon *Life* xxv. (1875) 319 Broccoli and the cauliflower are modifications of the coarse maritime cabbage. **1881** Greener *Gun* 525 Undrained and marshy land is..best suited to this bird [the lapwing], whose habits are partly maritime.

2. Connected with the sea in relation to navigation, commerce, etc.; relating to or dealing with matters of commerce or navigation on the sea.
maritime insurance = *marine insurance*. **maritime interest**, premium or interest on a bottomry bond. **maritime positions**, 'the intersection of the geographical coordinates of the latitudes and longitudes of places on the globe' (Smyth *Sailor's Word-bk.* 1867). **maritime state**, that department of the state which consists of the officers and mariners of the navy.
α. *c* **1615** *God & the King* (1663) 25 In this maritane passage he submitteth himself unto the conduct and direction of the pilot.. **1632** Lithgow *Trav.* viii. 362 Two thousand and three hundred Maritine miles. **1675** Ogilby *Brit.* Ded., You have laid open to us all those Maritin Itineraries. **1686** J. S[ergeant] *Hist. Monast. Convent.* 150 The Chamberlain..exerciseth his Jurisdiction amongst Marriners; and what relates to Maritine affairs.
β. **1591** Horsey *Trav.* (Hakl. Soc.) 159 Novogorode and Plœsco, two greatest mart maritime or traide towns..of all the easteren parts. **1601** R. Johnson *Kingd. & Commw.* (1603) 24 The English people are maruellous expert in maritime actions. **1654** Earl Monm. tr. *Bentivoglio's Warrs Flanders* 113 His want of skill in maritime affairs. **1765** Blackstone *Comm.* I. Introd. §1. 14 The spiritual and maritime courts of this kingdom. *Ibid.* xiii. 405 The maritime state is nearly related to the former [*viz.* the military]: though much more agreeable to the principles of our free constitution. *Ibid.*, In the maritime reign of queen Elizabeth. **1774** M. Mackenzie *Maritime Surv.* ii. i. 69. **1776** Gibbon *Decl. & F.* xiii. I. 364 Britain,..already assumed its natural and respectable station of a maritime power. **1813** Wellington in Gurw. *Desp.* (1838) X. 361 To prevent the enemy's maritime communication between Bayonne and Santoña. **1841** *Penny Cycl.* XXI. 406/2 A maritime insurance is a contract [etc.]. **1846** Young *Naut. Dict.* 43 A high rate of interest, termed Maritime Interest, or Bottomry Premium, being charged. **1861** Bright *Sp., America* 4 Dec. (1876) 96 Maritime law..consists of opinions and precedents for the most part.

3. Of a fighting force: Intended for service at sea. †*maritime regiment*: earlier name of the marines.
α. **1550** J. Coke *Eng. & Fr. Heralds* §105 (1877) 90 Th' erle of Arundell..with a puissaunt army myrytayne dystroyed..all the navy of Flanders. **1653** *Nissena* 49 Without much weakening the Maritin forces. **1707** Freind *Peterborow's Cond. Sp.* 180 We hope for a Maritine Force betimes in these seas.
β. **1668** in L. Edye *Hist. Marines* (1893) I. 102, 2 Maritim Regim^ts consisting of 26 Compa^nyes. **1684** *List Military* 15 His Royal Highness the Duke of York and Albany's Marittime Regiment of Foot. **1839** *Penny Cycl.* XIV. 419/2 In the beginning of Queen Anne's reign (1702), six regiments of maritime soldiers were raised.

4. Of, pertaining to, arising from, or existing in, the sea. Now *rare* or *Obs.*
1624 B. Jonson *Neptune's Triumph* Stage Direct., A maritime Palace, or the house of Oceanus. **1663** Boyle *Usef. Exp. Nat. Philos.* ii. xiv. 252 The Maritime Air and steames. **1784** Cowper *Task* ii. 258 That no rude savour maritime invade The nose of nice nobility! **1796** H. Hunter tr. *St.-Pierre's Stud. Nat.* (1799) II. 139 The maritime winds unite their efforts toward the autumnal equinox. **1835** Sir J. Ross *Narr. 2nd Voy.* v. 67 An interesting maritime landscape.

5. Characteristic of a seaman; nautical.
1743 Bulkeley & Cummins *Voy. S. Seas* Ded. 5 The following Pages..are written in a plain maritime Stile. **1848** Dickens *Dombey* iv, He was far from having a maritime appearance. **1889** D. Hannay *Capt. Marryat* viii. 122 This sailor had an altogether maritime ignorance of women.

6. maritime pine, the cluster pine, *Pinus pinaster*, a southern European tree distinguished by cones in clusters, often planted in coastal areas to bind sandy soil.
1894 H. M. Ward *Laslett's Timber & Timber Trees* (ed. 2) xxxi. 349 The Cluster Pine..much used in the south and west of France, where it is known as the Maritime Pine from the extensive planting on the coasts, yields a highly resinous reddish wood. **1914** W. J. Bean *Trees & Shrubs Hardy in Brit. Is.* II. 187 Cluster Pine, Maritime Pine..is, as its common name implies, admirably adapted for maritime localities. **1969** T. H. Everett *Living Trees of World* 54/1 Of all two-needled pines, the species with the longest leaves,.. is the cluster pine or maritime pine..a southern European tree that thrives in coastal areas.

B. *sb.*

1. †**a.** The sea-coast; a country or region adjoining the sea. *Obs.*
1591 *Decl. Gt. Troubles* 5 Certayne skroles or beadrolles of names of men dwelling in sundry partes of our Countries,.. but specially in the maritimes. **1598** Barret *Theor. Warres* Gloss. 251 Maritime is sea coast countrie, or countries adioyning vnto the sea. **1635** Pagitt *Christianogr.* i. ii. (1636) 83 In the south Maritime and in Ethiopia. **1657** Thornley tr. *Longus' Daphnis & Chloe* 75 The General.. comes up to the maritims of Mitylene, and hostilely invades them.

b. In *pl.*, with capital initial. The eastern provinces of Canada adjoining the Atlantic Ocean (Nova Scotia, New Brunswick, and Prince Edward Island).
1926 *Daily Colonist* (Victoria, B.C.) 24 July 1/2 Continuing his Maritime tour, Premier Meighan in an address here tonight again stressed his policy for the Maritimes. **1934** W. M. Whitelaw (*title*) The Maritimes and Canada before Confederation. **1938** L. M. Montgomery *Anne of Ingleside* viii. 58 The July night was unreasonably cold as even a summer night in the Maritimes sometimes is. **1947** G. Taylor *Canada* xvi. 385 The three small provinces linked as the Maritimes..together only amount to 1.5 per cent of the area of the Dominion. **1956** C. R. Fay *Life & Labour in Newfoundland* viii. 134 Schooners come from the Maritimes with much needed provisions and lumber. **1960** *Times* 21 Nov. (Canada Suppl.) p. v/6 The salty Maritimes or the wide-open Prairies. **1970** M. M. Orkin *Speaking Canad. Eng.* vii. 186 Nova Scotia is *The Mayflower Province*, and New Brunswick *The Loyalist Province*. Together with Prince Edward Island, they are collectively known as the *Maritime Provinces* or, more familiarly, the *Maritimes*.

†**2.** A person living near the sea. *Obs. rare*—¹.
1655 Stanley *Hist. Philos.* i. (1687) 27/1 Lycurgus was head of the Country-men, Megacles of the Maritimes.

ˌmaritoˈnucleus. *Biol. rare.* [f. *marito-*, used as comb. f. of L. *marītus* married + nucleus.] (See quot.)
1884 Hyatt in *Proc. Boston Soc. Nat. Hist.* XXIII. 54 Reserving..the name of maritonucleus or married nucleus for the renovated nucleus of the egg after its union with the male pronucleus.

†**mariˈtorious**, *a. nonce-wd.* [Humorously f. L. *marītus* husband.] Fond of one's husband.
1607 Chapman *Bussy D'Ambois* ii. 22 Dames maritorious ne're were meritorious.

mariˈturient, *a. nonce-wd.* [Formed (in jocular imitation of L. desideratives) on L. *marītāre* to marry.] Eager to marry.
1765 Gray *Let. to T. Wharton* 29 Apr., Our friend, the Precentor, who has so long been in a mariturient way, is not yet married.

marivade, obs. form of maravedi.

‖**Marivaudage** (marivodaʒ). [Fr., f. the name of P. C. de *Marivaux* (1688–1763), novelist and dramatist.] The expression of affected language and exaggerated sentiment in the style of Marivaux; an overdone attempt at refinement, affectation.
1765 H. Walpole *Let.* 19 Nov. in *Corr.* (1948) XIII. 144 Crébillon is entirely out of fashion, and Marivaux a proverb: *marivauder*, and *marivaudage* are established terms for being prolix and tiresome. **1882** G. Saintsbury *Short Hist. French Lit.* iv. ii. 410 All the work of Marivaux, dramatic and non-dramatic, is pervaded more or less by a peculiarity which at the time received the name of Marivaudage. This peculiarity exists partly in the sentiment, and partly in the phraseology. The former is characteristic of the eighteenth century, disguising a considerable affectation under a mask of simplicity, and the latter (sparkling with abundant, if somewhat precious wit) is ingeniously constructed to suit it and carry it off. **1894** Beerbohm in *Yellow Bk.* II. 284 The qualities that I tried.. to travesty—paradox and marivaudage. **1930** *Mod. Lang. Rev.* XXV. 71 *Marivaudage* ..to quote Faguet..'consists much more in analysing to excess a just thought than in decking out to excess an empty one'. **1959** *Oxf. Compan. French Lit.* 455/2 The term *marivaudage*, coined from his name, is used to signify the analysis of the delicate sentiments of the heart and the subtle, affected style used by Marivaux to this end in his comedies. **1969** *Observer* 12 Jan. 26/5 It [*sc.* Lesbianism] is a tricky subject, poised on the brink of either tiresome *marivaudage* or tasteless titillation.

marjoram (ˈmɑːdʒərəm). Forms: α. 4–6 **maiorane,** 5 **mageron, -am, maioron, -um,** 6 **maioram, -om, magerym,** 6–7 **majoram,** 7 **-an.** β. (chiefly *Sc.*) 6 **mar-, meriolyne, maryolayn, margelene,** 7 **majorlame.** γ. 6. **margerain, -am, -om(e, -um, -yn, marierum, -ierom, -ioram, -om, merierum, -gerum,** 6–7 **marierome,** 7 **-jerim, -jerom(e, -jorom, -gorum,** *Sc.* **margorie,** 7–9 **marjorum,** 7– **marjoram.** (In the earlier forms *i* = *j*.) [a. OF. *majorane* (13th c.), **marjoraine*, whence F. (from 14th c.) by dissimilation *marjolaine*, = Pr. *majorana*, Sp. *majorana*, *mayorana*, now usually *mejorana*, Pg. *mariorana*, *mangerona*, It. *majorana*, *maggiorana*, Rumanian *măgheran*, med.L. *majorāna* (once *majoraca* or *-us*). The Rom. word has passed into the Teut. and other langs., as MDu. *mayoleine*, *margelleine*, *meieraen* (mod.Du. *marjolein*), MHG. *margram*, *meigramme*, *meyeron*, *maigaron*, *maioran*, etc. (mod.G. *majoran*, dial. *meigram*), Sw. *mejram*, Da. *merian*, Russian (? from G.) *maeran*, mod.Gr. *ματζουράνα*.
The ultimate etymology is obscure. Many of the Rom. forms appear to have been perverted by assimilation to L. *mājor* (It. *maggiore*, Sp. *mayor*) greater. There seems to be no adequate ground for the current assumption that the ultimate source is the L. *amāracus* (a. Gr. ἀμάρακος, -ον), which was in the Middle Ages identified, perh. correctly, with marjoram.]

Any plant of the genus *Origanum* (N.O. *Labiatæ*); esp. *O. vulgare*, ***wild marjoram*** (***common, field,*** † ***grove m.***), a common plant in limestone or chalky districts, and *O. Majorana*, ***sweet marjoram*** († ***marjoram gentle,*** † ***English,*** † ***fine, knotted m.***), an aromatic herb used in cookery. *O. Onites* is ***pot*** or ***winter marjoram***, *O. heracleoticum*, ***winter sweet marjoram.***
α. **1390** Gower *Conf.* III. 133 Of Majorane his herbe is grounded. *c* **1440** *Promp. Parv.* 319/2 Mageram [*K.* maiorum, *S.* mageron, *P.*, *W.* magerym, *J.* margeryn]. **1481** Botoner *Tulle of Old Age* f 5 Rosemarynes, maiorons, gylofres. **1573** Tusser *Husb.* (1878) 95 Maierom knotted, sowe or set at the spring. **1597** Gerarde *Herbal* ii. ccvii. 539 Marierome is called..in English Sweete Marierome, Fine Marierome, and Marierome gentle; of the best sort Maiorane. **1601** Holland *Pliny* I. 382 Maioran,..in Cyprus & at Mitylene, where great store of sweet Majoran grows.
β. **1513** Douglas *Æneis* i. x. 69 Tendir mariolyne [L. *mollis amaracus*] and sweit flouris. **1527** Andrew *Brunswyke's Distyll. Waters* L vi b. **1570** *Satir. Poems*

Reform. xv. 10 Thow Lauand, lurk; thow time, be tint; Thow Margelene, swaif. **1689** in *Thanes of Cawdor* (Spald. Club) 353, 1 unce Majorlame, 10s.

γ. **1523** SKELTON *Garl. Laurel* 906 With margerain ientyll, The flowre of goodlyhede. *c* **1550** LLOYD *Treas. Health* xv. E v b, Let thy teeth be washed with the decoction of wilde Margerum [**1585** Margeram]. **1578** LYTE *Dodoens* II. lxix. 236 *Origanum Heracleoticum.* Spanish Origan. Bastard Margerom. *Origanum syluestre.* Wilde Origan. Groue Margerom. *Ibid.* 237 *Marum quibusdam.* English Margerom. **1597** GERARDE *Herbal* II. ccvii. 539 The pot Marierome is also called Winter Marierome. *Ibid.* ccix. 543 *Tragoriganum.* Goates Marierome. **1640** PARKINSON *Theat. Bot.* 12 The wilde or field Marjerome. **1656** MARNETTÉ *Perf. Cook* II. 1 Take the tops of Time and Margerum and Winter Savoury, a handfull of each. **1689** in *Thanes of Cawdor* (Spald. Club) 352 Sweit Margorie thrie drap, 6s. **1760** J. LEE *Introd. Bot.* App. 318 Marjoram, winter sweet. **1856** MISS MULOCK *J. Halifax* xxi. (1859) 220 A plant of wild marjoram. **1882** *Garden* 25 Feb. 137/1 Knotted Marjoram, sweet Savory, and Sweet Basil are much sought after in early spring.

b. *attrib.* and *Comb.*, as ***marjoram bed, leaf; marjoram-leaved*** adj.; **marjoram camphor**, a camphor obtained from oil of marjoram (Watts tr. *Gmelin's Handbk. Chem.* 1860, XIV. 379).

1821 CLARE *Vill. Minstr.* I. 115 Thy Marjoram-beds so doubly sweet. **1811** A. T. THOMSON *Lond. Disp.* (1818) 277 Common Marjoram leaves. **1882** *Garden* 4 Feb. 82/3 The Marjoram-leaved Toadflax.

mark (mɑːk), *sb.*[1] Forms 1 mearc, *Anglian* merc, (also ȝemierce, ȝemęrce, *Northumb.* merce, merca), 2 marc, 3–5 merk(e, (Orm. merrke), merc(k, marck(e, 4, 7 marque, 4– **mark.** [OE. *mearc*, Anglian *merc*, str. fem., boundary, landmark, sign = OFris. *merik(e, merke*, boundary, sign, OS. *marka* boundary (MDu. *marke*, mod.Du. *mark*), OHG. *marcha* boundary (MHG., mod.G. *mark* fem.), ON. *mǫrk* (known only in the derived sense 'forest'; Sw., Da. *mark* field, ground), Goth. *marka* boundary, landmark:—OTeut. **markâ*. A neuter form (:—OTeut. type **marko*ᵐ) exists in several Teut. langs. with the senses 'sign', 'landmark', 'standard', etc.: MDu. *mark* (mod.Du. *merk*), MHG. *mark* (mod.G. has *marke* fem., prob. influenced by F. *marque*), ON., MSw. *mark*. The ME. form *merke* (disyllable), while normally representing the OAnglian pronunciation *merc*, may in part descend from ONorthumb. *męrce* (also written *męrca*), token, sign, and in part also from an adoption of the equivalent ON. *merki* neut., landmark, standard, sign (Sw. *märke*, Da. *merke*):—OTeut. type **markjo*ᵐ, f. **markâ* (see above); it may also, in northern dialects, represent partly the ONorthumb. *ȝemęrce* sign, token (= WS. *ȝemierce*, OHG. *gimerchi* boundary:—OTeut. **ga-markjo*ᵐ), as the prefix *ȝe-* of sbs. did not survive into ME., and the palatalized *c* in final syllables became *k* in northern Eng. According to phonetic law the ME. *merke* regularly became *mark* in mod.Eng., thus coalescing with the descendant of WS. *mearc*.

The Teut. word and its derivative vb. were early adopted into Romanic; the sb. appears as OF. *merc, marc* masc., F. *marque* fem., mark, sign, etc., *marche* (ONF. *marque*) boundary (see MARCH *sb.*[3]), Pr., Sp., Pg., It. *marca* mark, sign, boundary. Some of the senses developed in F. *marque* have coloured the application of the Eng. word.

The OTeut. **markâ* appears to be cogn. w. L. *margo* MARGIN, OCeltic **mrogi-* country (Gaulish *brogi-* in place-names, Welsh *brô*, OIrish *mruig, bruig*), Persian *marz* boundary. The extra-Teut. relations confirm the view which is suggested by the evidence of Teut. itself, that the primitive sense is 'boundary'. The order of development of senses which appears most probable, and is assumed as the basis of the arrangement below, is 'boundary', 'sign of a boundary', 'sign in general', 'impression, trace or device used as a sign', 'impression, trace, etc. in general'. Some scholars, however, have considered the sense 'visible trace' as primitive (comparing Lith. *margas* parti-coloured), and have supposed the sense 'boundary' to be either derived from this or to belong to an independent word.]

I. Boundary.

1. a. A boundary, frontier, limit; rarely in *pl.* †territories. *Obs.* exc. *Hist.* and *arch.*

701 in Birch *Cart. Sax.* (1885) I. 148 Swa be mearce to grenmenes stiȝele . . ponon suð andlang mearce to þes gores suð ende. *c* **1250** *Gen. & Ex.* 3490 He ledde hem to ðe muntes fot, Non but non [? *read* he] forðere ne mot, And on is broðer aaron; God bad hem ðat merke ouer-gon. **1340–70** *Alisaunder* 173 The marques of Molosor menskliche hee aught. **1387** TREVISA *Higden* (Rolls) II. 45 But afterward, for þe weyes were not so sette wiþ certeyn markes [orig. *certis limitibus distinctæ*], þe weies were vncerteyn and stryf was bygonne. *Ibid.* 103 þe merkes and þe meres þerof [Mercia] were in þe west side þeryuer Dee . . ; in þe est þe est see, in the souþ Temse. *c* **1400** MAUNDEV. (1839) xiii. 144 In þat contre of libye is the see more high þan the lond, and it semeth þat it wolde couere the erthe, and natheles ȝit it passeþ not his markes. **1447** BOKENHAM *Seyntys* (Roxb.) 36 In a wode of the markeys of that cuntre Two hermytys dwellyd. **1494** FABYAN *Chron.* v. cix. 82 The meris or markis of this Kyngdome of North humberlande were [etc.]. **1530** PALSGR. 243/1 Marke bytwene two places, *limite.* **1535** COVERDALE *Prov.* viii. 29 He shutt the see within certayne bowndes, that yᵉ waters shulde not go ouer their marckes. ? **1832** 'B. CORNWALL' (B. W. Proctor) *Sea* i, The Sea! the Sea! the open Sea! . . Without a mark, without a bound. **1883** *Chamb. Jrnl.* 36 When the Marquis of Leominster was a Marquis indeed, with a mark to guard. **1892** HENLEY *Song of Sword*, etc., *Lond. Volunt.* iii. 22 The afflicted city, prone from mark to mark In shameful occultation.

†**b.** Of immaterial things: A limit or precise boundary line or point. *Obs.*

a **1000** *Cædmon's Gen.* 1719 (Gr.) þa þæs mæles wæs mearc agongen. *a* **1225** *Ancr. R.* 228 Auh iðe temptaciun he haueð iset to þe ueonde a merke, ase þauh he seide—tempte hire so ueor [etc.]. **1340** *Ayenb.* 223 Liȝtliche huanne þe lost ne paseþ naȝt þe markes ne þe zetnesses of spousbrod. *c* **1400** *Destr. Troy* 7696 The Sun in his Sercle set was o loft, At the merke of þe mydday. **1435** MISYN *Fire of Love* 38 þou art þe end of heuynes, þe mark of labirs, beginyng of fruyts. *c* **1449** PECOCK *Repr.* I. x. 50 These craftis kepten not to hem silf her propre and seuerel to hem silf boundis and markis.

2. *Hist.* The name applied in mediæval Germany to the tract of land held in common by a village community. Hence used by many modern scholars to denote the tract of land similarly held by one of the village communities of primitive Teutonic times. Also *attrib.*, as in ***mark-community, -family, -system; markmoot*** (pseudo-*arch.*), a (supposed) assembly of the inhabitants of the 'mark'.

Kemble's fancy that OE. *mearc* was the name of a unit of territorial organization next below the shire (*scír* or *gá*) has no foundation. The alleged OE. **mearcmót* 'mark-moot', has no existence: the *mercemot* occurring in a schedule of boundaries of land at Barrow-on-Humber in 971 (Birch *C.S.* No. 1270) may perh. mean 'parsley-bed', and in any case does not admit of Kemble's interpretation.

1848 KEMBLE *Saxons in Eng.* (1876) I. iii. 76 As then the word Mark is used to denote two distinct things,—a territorial division and a corporate body,—so does the word Gá or Scír denote both [etc.]. **1867** FREEMAN *Norm. Conq.* (1876) I. iii. 84 Such a community occupies its own territory, its mark. *Ibid.* 98 The unit is the Mark, roughly represented by the modern parish or manor. **1874** STUBBS *Const. Hist.* (1875) I. ii. 34 We have not the mark system. *Ibid.* v. 84 *note*, That the markmoot was a court of justice . . seems altogether improbable. *Ibid.* 85 It is as an owner of land, not as a member of the mark-community, that the freeman has rights. **1876** DIGBY *Real Prop.* i. §1. 5 Each community occupied a territory or mark, which was divided into three, or rather four portions. **1887** *Edin. Rev.* Jan. 10 In all Teutonic countries the same conflict was waged between the manor and the mark.

3. Used to represent G. *Mark* as the proper name of certain principalities, esp. the **Mark of Brandenburg**. †Also repr. It. *Marca* in ***the Mark of Ancona.*** (Cf. MARCH *sb.*[3] 3.)

1726 LEONI *Alberti's Archit.* I. 65/1 The Town of Cingoli . . in the Mark of Ancona. **1797** *Encycl. Brit.* (ed. 3) III. 514/2 They reckon in the whole Mark [of Brandenburg] 120 towns [etc.]. **1884** *Harper's Mag.* Apr. 690/2 The two Frederics . . were to have the Mark.

II. An object indicating a boundary, position, etc.

†**4.** A pillar, post, stone, fence, etc., placed to indicate the position of a boundary; = LANDMARK *sb.* 1.

c **1250** *Gen. & Ex.* 440 Met of corn, and wiȝte of fe, And merke of felde, first fond he. *c* **1320** *Sir Tristr.* 2710 Her fader . . ȝaf hem londes wide . . Markes were set bi side. *c* **1330** R. BRUNNE *Chron.* (1810) 77 Saynt Cutberte's clerkes . . At Geruans set þer merkes, a hous þe gan vpspede. *c* **1440** *Promp. Parv.* 333/2 Meer, marke be-twene ij. londys, *meta, meris.* **1535** COVERDALE *Deut.* xxvii. 17 Cursed be he, yᵗ remoueth his neghbours mark. **1697** DRYDEN *Virg. Georg.* I. 193 No Fences parted Fields, nor Marks nor Bounds Distinguish'd Acres of litigious Grounds.

†**5.** A stone or other monument set up or standing as a memorial, or as a guide. *Obs.*

c **1000** ÆLFRIC *Exod.* xxiv. 4 Moyses . . ȝetimbrode twelf mearca. *c* **1250** *Gen. & Ex.* 1887 Iacob dalf hire and merke dede, ðat is ȝet sene on ðat stede. **1340–70** *Alex. & Dind.* 1139 Whan graue was þe graie ston þe grime king rydus & alle meven his men fro þe marke euene. **1565** COOPER *Thesaurus, Cippus*, a littell hill or marke called a barrow. **1582** N. LICHEFIELD tr. *Castanheda's Conq. E. Ind.* I. ix. 9 b, A certaine marke or Piller, with the King of Portingales Armes, and a Crosse. *a* **1591** H. SMITH *Serm.* (1594) 237 Being now recouered to his right way, [he] stands like a marke of knowledge in the turnings . . to direct al those that passe by.

fig. **1511** COLET *Serm. Convoc.* B v b, Vnto you we loke as vnto markes of our direction.

†**6.** A standard or banner. *Obs.*

c **1000** ÆLFRIC *Gram.* lxiv. (Z.) 71 *Victricia tollite signa*, nymað þa siȝefæstan mearca. *c* **1205** LAY. 18869 Beornes scullen rusien reosen heoren mærken [*c* **1275** marke]. *Ibid.* 19099 Cador þe kene scal beren þas kinges marke.

7. a. A target, butt, or other object set up to be aimed at with a missile or projectile. Hence *transf.*, the thing that is or may be aimed at in shooting or throwing.

c **1205** LAY. 4229 Heoræ sceaftes weoren strake of his flæsces heo makeden here marce [*c* **1275** marke]. *c* **1305** *St. Edm. King* 44 in *E.E.P.* (1862) 88 Hi stode afur & bende here bowes, & here arewes riȝte And as to a merke schote to him. **1526** *Pilgr. Perf.* (W. de W. 1531) 160 The sayd arowe is caryed to the marke. **1535** COVERDALE *Lam.* iii. 12 He hath bent his bowe, and made me as it were a marck to shute at. **1617** HIERON *Wks.* II. 400 A shooter, who afarre off aymeth at a marke in the midst of a white; hee seeth the white, but not the marke; hee cannot hit the marke, which he seeth not, except hee hit the white, which hee seeth. **1660** F. BROOKE tr. *Le Blanc's Trav.* 167 Then the hunters all choose their marke, taking pleasure in darting their lances. **1780** COWPER *Progr. Err.* 570 None sends his arrow to the mark in view, Whose hand is feeble, or his aim untrue. **1856** 'STONEHENGE' *Brit. Rur. Sports* 508/2 Do not look from the mark to the arrow and back again. **1859** *Musketry Instr.* 23 To fire with accuracy it is necessary the sights should be carefully aligned between the eye and the mark.

†**b.** The quarry of a hawk, etc. *Obs.*

1577 B. GOOGE *Heresbach's Husb.* IV. (1586) 157 b, They . . are alwaies the fairest marke in a Hawke, or a Bussardes eie. **1589** GREENE *Menaphon* (Arb.) 42 The Hobbie catcheth no pray, vnlesse she mount beyonde her marke. **1672** DRYDEN *Marr. à la Mode* v. i, It vexes me to the heart . . to have flown her so often to a mark, and still to be bobbed at retrieve. **1686** BLOME *Gentl. Recr.*, *Hawking* v. 30 After she hath flowen to mark, she will sit or fly according to her mettle and nature. **1691** DRYDEN *K. Arthur* III. ii, Oh, still thou think'st to fly a fool to mark.

c. The object at which a blow or thrust is aimed; *spec.* in *Pugilistic slang*, the pit of the stomach, the 'wind'. Also † ***Broughton's mark.***

1747 J. GODFREY *Sci. Defence* 6 The smaller his [a fencer's] mark is, the harder it is for him to hit. *Ibid.* 57 Gretting had the nearest Way of going to the Stomach (which is what they [pugilists] call the Mark) of any Man I knew. **1823** 'J. BEE' *Dict. Turf*, *Mark (ring)*, the pit of the stomach is termed 'the mark', and 'Broughton's mark'. **1851** BORROW *Lavengro* lxxxviii, I happened to hit Tom, of Hopton, in the mark, as he was coming in, so that he lost his wind.

d. *fig.* or in fig. context. Also *slang* (see quot. 1897); ***a soft*** or ***easy mark*** (cf. EASY *a.* 13 b), a person who is easily persuaded or deceived (*slang*, orig. *U.S.*); (*Austral. slang*), ***a good*** (or ***bad***) ***mark*** (see quot. 1941).

1549 *Compl. Scot.* xv. 123, I am the merk of the but, contrar the quhilk euere man schutis arrous of tribulatione. *c* **1586** C'TESS PEMBROKE *Ps.* LV. i, [I am] A mark to wrath, and hate, and wrong assign'd. **1608** D. T[UVIL] *Ess. Pol. & Mor.* 114 b, Must needes discouer the marke of his disordinate Ambition. **1742** YOUNG *Nt. Th.* v. 1011 Death loves a shining Mark, a signal Blow. **1753** *Discov. J. Poulter* (ed. 2) 4 At Night the Horses came by, and he shew'd us all one particular Pack, and said that's your Mark. **1842** TENNYSON *Walk. Mail* 65 He thought himself A mark for all, and shudder'd lest a cry Should break his sleep by night. **1845** R. HOWITT *Impressions Australia Felix* 233, I heard it casually from the lips of apparently respectable settlers as they rode on the highway, 'Such and such a one is a good mark!'—simply a person who pays his men their wages, without delays or drawbacks; a man to whom you may sell anything safely. **1860** F. & J. GREENWOOD *Under a Cloud* II. xiv. 332 'There's a mark!' exclaimed one to the other, looking towards the spot where Hatcher was standing. **1871** BLACKIE *Four Phases* i. 10 There was something . . that could not fail to make him the mark of general observation. **1871** R. ELLIS tr. *Catullus* lxviii. 2 Thy sad tear-scrawl'd letter, a mark to the storm. **1883** J. GREENWOOD *Tag, Rag & Co.* iii. 24 Publicans . . are usually the unfortunate tradesmen fixed on as a mark. **1896** ADE *Artie* xvi. 150 He was the wise guy and I was the soft mark. *Ibid.* xviii. 173 When that kind of a mark comes in they . . get ready to do business. **1897** BARRÈRE & LELAND, *Mark* (Swindlers), one marked by thieves or swindlers as easy to dupe or rob. **1904** G. H. LORIMER *Old Gorgon Graham* 288 He was too easy a mark to succeed in Wall Street. **1922** JOYCE *Ulysses* 75 Didn't catch me napping that wheeze. The quick touch. Soft mark. **1929** 'E. QUEEN' *Roman Hat Mystery* xiii. 187 For a shrewd man, he certainly was an easy-mark for the wiseacres. **1941** BAKER *Dict. Austral. Slang* 46 *Mark, good (or bad)*, a general term of approval (or disapproval) for a person. **1956** H. GOLD *Man who was not with It* (1965) i. 6, I floated down . . to kick the smaller mark where it would tell on him. **1962** J. LUDWIG in R. Weaver *Canad. Short Stories* (1968) 2nd Ser. 255 He was repulsive, old, a mark, a fool—his nerve went. **1966** 'J. HACKSTON' *Father clears Out* 93, I was a bit nervous and an easy mark to bamboozle. **1968** B. TURNER *Sex Trap* xv. 148 You thought I might like to turn myself into an ugly mark! A square with a loud voice and a shopping-bag! Marriage! **1971** *Frendz* 21 May 11/2 In 90% of all rip-offs the naive mark hands over his capital to some virtual stranger who never returns. **1973** E. MCGIRR *Bardel's Murder* ii. 31 In the twenties it was the Yanks who was the suckers, but now . . it's us who are the marks.

e. In phrases, ***beside, †besides, far from, near, short of, wide of*** (or ***†from***) ***the mark; to hit, miss the mark***, to attain or miss some desired object or end.

c **1350** *St. Andrew* 290 in Horstm. *Altengl. Leg.* (1881) 8 In saint Andrew he had swilk trist; And of þat merk nothing he myst. *a* **1352** MINOT *Poems* ix. 13 Bot now has sir Dauid missed of his merkes. **1633** T. STAFFORD *Pac. Hib.* I. v. (1821) 71 Both one and the other were besides the marke. **1655** FULLER *Ch. Hist.* II. iii. §17 Venerable was found out as an Expedient to accommodate the Difference, luckily hitting the Mark, as a Title neither too high nor too low. **1666** PEPYS *Diary* 23 Sept., It cannot, I believe, be far wide from the mark. **1749** FIELDING *Tom Jones* VI. ix, As when two doves, . . or as when Strephon and Phyllis (for that comes nearest to the mark) are retired into some pleasant solitary grove [etc.]. **1845** MᶜCULLOCH *Taxation* I. iii. (1852) 92 It may, however, be . . very wide of the mark when applied to the case of out-of-door labourers. **1889** J. STALKER *Imago Christi* ix. §5 (1891) 178 Many a preacher misses the mark because, though he knows books, he does not know men. **1861** WHYTE MELVILLE *Good for Nothing* I. 146 Gilbert's efforts to amuse her often fell short of the mark. **1883** [see BESIDE B. 5 b]. **1885** J. K. JEROME *On the Stage* 6 Five or six pounds per week would be near the mark.

f. *Bowls.* The JACK. Also, a position which is allowed for the jack; 'a fair bowling distance' (see quot. 1753).

1630 J. TAYLOR (Water P.) *Wit & Mirth* Wks. II. 193/2 The marke which they ayme at hath sundry names and Epithites, as a Blocke, a Jacke, and a Mistris. **1753** CHAMBERS *Cycl. Supp.* s.v. *Bowling*, *Mark* is a proper bowling distance, not under so many yards; and being at least a yard and a half from the edge of the green. **1875**

'STONEHENGE' *Brit. Sports* III. I. iii. §3. 683 If the leader in two trials shall fail to deliver the jack a mark, his opponent is then entitled to set the mark. **1876** *Encycl. Brit.* IV. 180/2 A game termed *carreau*..somewhat similar to bowls, the jack or mark being set up on a square stone at the end of an alley. *Ibid.*, 'Mark', or 'set a mark', means the delivery of the jack at the commencement of a game.

8. A post or other object placed to indicate the terminal point of a race; a goal. Often *fig.*, an object desired or striven for (cf. 7 d).

c **1330** R. BRUNNE *Chron.* (1810) 271 Sir Roberd Roos of Werk with þe Scottis fled, He set so ille his merk, þat neuer eft he ne sped. **1535** COVERDALE *Phil.* iii. 14, I forget that which is behynde..& preace vnto yᵉ marck apoynted. **1555** LATIMER *Let.* in Strype *Eccl. Mem.* (1822) III. II. 305 He that runnythe at the merk doth not loke on other that stands by..but lokyth altogether on the glove or merk, and on them that ronne with him. **1561** T. NORTON *Calvin's Inst.* II. viii. (1634) 187 Let this be our perpetual marke, to aide all men faithfully. **1642** ROGERS *Naaman* Ep. Ded. 3, I know your Honour hath long made this your marke. **1789** COWPER *Let. to Mrs. King* 1 Aug., The end is in view; I seem almost to have reached the mark. **1850** TENNYSON *In Mem.* liii, For fear divine Philosophy Should push beyond her mark, and be Procuress to the Lords of Hell.

9. An object on shore or at sea, which, by its ascertained and known position, serves to guide a traveller proceeding in a given direction, *esp.* a LANDMARK *sb.*, *leading-mark* (see LEADING 1 b), SEA-MARK. Also *fig.*

[**1398** TREVISA *Barth. De P.R.* XVII. cxlii. (1495) 699 Ofte knottes ben made on trees and in busshes: in token and marke of the highe waye: to shewe the certen and sure waye to waye farynge men.] **14..** *Sailing Direct.* (Hakl. Soc.) 12 Yif ye go oute of Orwell waynys to the Naisse ye must go south west fro the Nasse to the merkis of the spetis your cours is west south-west. *Ibid.*, Bring your markis to gidre that the parissh steple be owte by est. the abbey of Seint Hosies. **1577** STANYHURST *Descr. Irel.* iii. in *Holinshed*, Hulke tower, which is a notable marke for pilots, in directing them which waie to sterne their ships [etc.]. **1598** MANWOOD *Lawes Forest* i. 4 They seeme to vnderstand this word *Meta*, a marke, for any thing that hath an ascending from the ground vpward in height, that they call a marke, as, a hill, a Church, a Tree, or such like. **1650** HOBBES *Hum. Nat.* v. §1. 44 Men that have past by a Rock at Sea, set up some mark, thereby to remember their former danger, and avoid it. *a* **1676** HALE *Narr. Customes* iii. in S. A. Moore *Foreshore* (1888) 338 As fixing of piles, or layinge in of anchors without buoyes or markes. **1708** PENN in *Pa. Hist. Soc. Mem.* X. 290, I have shewn my regard to him, and a fair mark I gave him to direct his steps. **1781** JUSTAMOND *Priv. Life Lewis XV*, II. 120 *note*, This is a mark, sometimes made by a floating tun, sometimes by a mast raised upon a bank. **1834** *Nat. Philos.* III. *Navig.* I. iii. 9 (Useful Knowl. Soc.) The marks themselves are called the leading marks.

III. A sign, token, indication.

10. a. An appearance, action, or event that indicates something; a sign, token, symptom.

c **950** *Lindisf. Gosp.* Mark xvi. 17 ȝemerca [Vulg. *signa*] ðonne ða ðaðe ȝelefdon ða ȝefylȝeð. *c* **1200** ORMIN 17982 & wha sitt iss þatt takeþþ wiþþ Hiss wittness tunnderrfanngenn, He setteþþ merrke off þatt he wiss Iss Godd soþfasst i spæche. *a* **1225** *Ancr. R.* 250 Lokeð nu ȝeorne, uor his deoruwurðe luue, hwuch one merke he leide uppen his icorene, þoa he steih into heouene. *a* **1300** *Cursor M.* 18330 'Lauerd', þai said, al wit a steuen, 'Als þou has sett þi merck in heuen O þi blis lauerd godd [etc.]. *c* **1386** CHAUCER *Pars. T.* ¶819 That hooly ordre is chief of al the tresorie of god, and his especial signe and mark of chastitee. **1599** SHAKS. *Much Ado* II. iii. 255 Shee's a faire Lady, I doe spie some markes of loue in her. **1604** E. G[RIMSTONE] *D'Acosta's Hist. Indies* III. xiii. 160 They found peeces of blew cloth, and other markes and signes that some men of Europe had passed there. **1669** GALE *Crt. Gentiles* I. Introd. 6 Is it not a great Marque of Honor. **1711** ADDISON *Spect.* No. 73 ¶10 She bestows a Mark of her Favour upon every one of them. **1725** WATTS *Logic* II. v. §4 In some Reports there are more Marks of Falshood than of Truth, and in others there are more Marks of Truth than of Falsehood. **1748** *Anson's Voy.* II. vi. 192 Our people soon observed several lights..in the fort, and other marks of the inhabitants being in great motion. **1842** BORROW *Bible in Spain* lvii, His body..exhibited every mark of strength and vigour. *a* **1862** BUCKLE *Civiliz.* (1873) III. v. 463 How unusual it is to meet with any one..whose writings bear marks of..original thought. **1884** SKEAT *Gamelyn* Introd. 11 The 'master outlaw' in the tale of Gamelyn is left unnamed. This is a mark of a somewhat early date.

b. A characteristic property; a distinctive feature, criterion; *spec.* in *Logic* (see quot. 1860).

1522 MORE *De quat. Noviss.* Wks. 73/2 He that by good vse and experyence, hathe in his eye the ryghte marke and very trewe lustre of the Dyamonte. **1561** T. NORTON tr. *Calvin's Inst.* I. xv. 53 Neither is their opinion to be approued, which sett the Image of God in the power of dominion geuen vnto him, as if he resembled God onely in this mark, that he is [etc.]. **1612** BACON *Ess., Wisd. for Man's Self* (Arb.) 184 Therefore let Princes..chuse such seruants, as haue not this marke. *a* **1625** FLETCHER *Noble Gent.* IV. iv, Yet from this pitch can I behold my own, (From millions of those men that have no mark). **1774** GOLDSM. *Nat. Hist.* (1776) IV. 232 By these marks the monkies of either continent, may be readily distinguished from each other. **1860** ABP. THOMSON *Laws Th.* §51. 78 Those properties by which we recognise any object, and assign it a place under some appropriate conception, are called marks. **1884** tr. *Lotze's Logic* I. iii. 89 Life without intelligence is a possible mark of an animal, but not intelligence without life. **1885** R. L. & F. STEVENSON *Dynamiter* 194, I recognise in you the marks of an accomplished anarch.

c. *spec.* A depression caused by a fold in the enamel of a horse's incisor tooth, which by its appearance and gradual disappearance gives some indication of the age of the animal. (Cf. COUNTER-MARK, *sb.* 3.) Also ***mark of mouth***.

c **1420** *Pallad. on Husb.* IV. 886 Their [horses'] myddel teeth aboue at too yeer age They cause, at yeeris iiij another gage;..At vij yeer are alle ylike longe, The markis of their age ar lost at seuen. **1626** BACON *Sylva* §754 At eight yeares old, the Tooth is smooth, and the Hole gone, And then they say; That the Marke is out of the Horses Mouth. **1680** *Lond. Gaz.* No. 1562/4 A Bright Bay Gelding, near 15 hands high, ..the mark out of his mouth. **1707** *Curios. in Husb. & Gard.* 41 We may..say..as the Jockeys do of a Horse of eight or nine Years old, who has no longer certain Teeth in his Mouth; that his Mark is out. **1852** R. S. SURTEES *Sponge's Sp. Tour* xliv, 'He's past mark of mouth; but I think a hunter's age has very little to do with his worth.' **1897** *Encycl. Sport* I. 537 (Horse) *Mark*, the hollow upon the top of a young horse's teeth which wears down with years.

fig. and *allusive.* **1589** R. HARVEY *Pl. Perc.* (1590) 4 The marke is not out of thy mouth, for thou hast a Colts tooth in thine head still. *a* **1616** BEAUM. & FL. *Wit without Money* IV. v, Biscuit That bawds have rubb'd their gums upon, like corals, To bring the mark again. **1824** MACTAGGART *Gallovid. Encycl.* s.v., Old maidens are said sometimes to have lost the mark o' mouth. **1857** G. A. LAWRENCE *Guy Liv.* viii. 77 Two ancient virgins, long past 'mark of mouth'.

†**d.** A vestige, trace. *Obs.*

c **1325** *Metr. Hom.* 61 Bot of thair not yet standes merk, In Babilony the tour yet stands. **1585** T. WASHINGTON tr. *Nicholay's Voy.* IV. xxv. 141 In whiche place are the markes of the ruines of Lacedemonia.

11. A sign affixed or impressed for distinction.

a. A device, stamp, seal, label, brand, inscription, written character, or the like, placed upon an article as an indication of ownership or origin, as an attestation of quality, as a means of identification, etc. †In early use often, the stamp or impress of a coin.

c **1250** *Gen. & Ex.* 457 He was hirde wittere and wal; Of merke, and kinde, and helde, & ble, sundring and sameni[n]g taȝte he. **1377** LANGL. *P. Pl.* B. xv. 343 þe merke of þat mone [*sc.* the lushburg] is good, ac þe metal is fieble. *c* **1394** *P. Pl. Crede* 177 Wyde wyndowes..Schynen wiþ schapen scheldes..Wiþ merkes of marchauntes y-medled bytwene. **1420** in *E.E. Wills* (1882) 46 A tastour of siluer with myn owne merke ymade in þe bottom. *c* **1440** *Promp. Parv.* 334/1 Merke, tokyne, ***signum***, ***caracter***. *c* **1450** in *Rel. Ant.* II. 280 Thay salle be brynte on the hippe, chapmans merke. **1477** *Rolls of Parlt.* VI. 185/1 The merke or signe of every Goldsmyth, shuld be knowen to the Wardeyns of the same craft. **1524** *Act 14 & 15 Hen. VIII*, c. 3. §9 This present act..for limittyng of markes to the maker of worsteds, saies, and stamins. **1567** HARMAN *Caveat* 33 The markes shalbe pycked out cleane, and [the clothes] conuayed craftely fare of, to sell. **1594** T. B. *La Primaud. Fr. Acad.* II. 543 Hee will appoynt to haue a stone layde vpon his graue, in which his name shall bee ingrauen, & his marke, or some such like thing. **1607** HEYWOOD *Wom. Kild w. Kindn.* Wks. 1874 II. 142 Take with thee every thing that hath thy marke. **1617** MORYSON *Itin.* I. 38, I set a marke vpon these peeces, lest I should spend them. **1687** A. LOVELL tr. *Thevenot's Trav.* I. 201 We spent all Tuesday..in getting Marks put upon our Arms, as commonly all Pilgrims do. **1696** PHILLIPS (ed. 5), *Mark*,..Also a particular Character imprinted by Public Authority upon several things, either for the payment of Duties, or to prevent Adulteration. **1698** FRYER *Acc. E. India & P.* 207 The Company's Mark upon all their Goods, Bales, and Parcels. **1704** NORRIS *Ideal World* II. v. 293 A mark of the artificer impressed upon his work. **1797** *Directory Sheffield* 137 Directory of the Manufacturers, with their marks. **1838** DICKENS *O. Twist* ix, I'll show you how to take the marks out of the handkerchiefs. *c* **1850** *Arab. Nts.* (Rtldg.) 640 The robber quickly made a mark on the door with some chalk he had for the purpose. **1885** *Encycl. Brit.* XIX. 186 The first of these [Hall-marks] was the *King's mark*—a leopard's or lion's head crowned.

b. With prefixed defining sb., as ***age***, ***cattle***, ***flock***, ***gunpowder***, ***pedigree***, ***pitch***, ***raddle***, ***sheep***, ***wool mark***. Also EAR-, HALL-, TRADE-MARK.

1523 FITZHERB. *Husb.* §52 And se that they [sheep] be well marked, both eare marke, pitche marke, and radel marke. **1573** TUSSER *Husb.* (1878) 38 A sheepe marke, a tar kettle [etc.]. **1603** OWEN *Pembrokeshire* (1892) 56–7 As many as they can finde by the eare marke, for woolle markes is vsed but of few. **1607** COWELL *Interpr.* s.v. *Clack*, To clack wooll is to cut off the sheepes marke which maketh it to waigh less. **1802** JAMES *Mil. Dict.*, *Mark*..Gunpowder Marks. The different sorts of gunpowder are distinguished by the following marks. **1833** HT. MARTINEAU *Briery Creek* ii. 34 What about the cattle-marks? **1886** C. SCOTT *Sheep-Farming* 147 Sheep Marking—The flock mark, the age mark, and the pedigree mark, are all put on the ears of the stock lambs.

c. A visible sign, as a badge, brand, etc., assumed by or imposed on a person; *occas.* in *pl.* †insignia.

†***Christ's***, ***God's mark***, ***mark of clergy***, ***of holy church***: the tonsure. ***mark of the Beast***: see Rev. xvi. 2 and BEAST *sb.* 7.

c **1200** *Vices & Virtues* 57 Sume oðre nimeð godes marc on hem, wandeþ here claðes and naht here þeawes. *c* **1205** LAY. 29855 Biscopes and clærckes and preostes mid godes mærkes. *c* **1250** *Gen. & Ex.* 1003 Quuo ne bar ðanne is merk [*sc.* circumcision] him on fro godes folc sulde he be don. *a* **1300** *Cursor M.* 27252 Quar he..clething beres þat feris to clerc, or cron þat es o clergi merc. *Ibid.* 29283 Qua smites preist or clerk or ani berand cristes merk, als munk, or frer, nun, or chanun,..he is cursd. *c* **1330** R. BRUNNE *Chron.* (1810) 130 þorgh God I þe forbede to chalange any clerke In lay courte for non nede, of holy kirke has merke. **1340** HAMPOLE *Pr. Consc.* 4402 Bot with þas þat had Criste forsaken And the merk of anticrist had taken [etc.]. **1382** WYCLIF *Rev.* xvi. 2 The carecte or marke of the beast. **1399** LANGL. *Rich. Redeles* II. 78 Me thynketh, That no manere meyntenour shulde merkis bere, Ne haue lordis leuere þe lawe to apeire. **1535** COVERDALE *Gen.* iv. 15 And the Lorde put a marck vpon Cain. **1560** DAUS tr. *Sleidane's Comm.* 118 b, Neyther maye any others, than suche as have the greate beastes charact, or Balles marke, be permitted to occupie that trade of marchaundyse. **1592** *Newes fr. Scotld.*, *Life & D. Dr. Fian* B, They suspecting that she had beene marked by the Diuell (as commonly witches are)..found the enemies marke to be in her fore crag. **1604** E. G[RIMSTONE] *D'Acosta's Hist. Indies* V. viii. 350 The priest..was decked with the markes of the idoll. **1680** *True Protest. Intelligence* No. 3. 1/2 One of them, as it is said, had the Thieves mark in her hand. **1706** tr. *Dupin's Eccl. Hist. 16th C.* II. v. 4 He [Catharinus] believes the Marks of St. Francis. **1727–51** CHAMBERS *Cycl.* s.v. *Herald*, Their persons are under the protection of the law of nations, when they bear the marks of their offices publicly, i.e. the trumpeter his trumpet, and the drummer his drum; as the herald his coat. **1874** GLADSTONE *Ritualism* in *Contemp. Rev.* Oct. 672 [The undivided clerical waistcoat] was deemed so distinctly Popish, that it acquired the nickname of 'The Mark of the Beast'; and..among the tailors..was familiarly known as 'the M.B. waistcoat'. **1881** SANDS *Sk. Tranent* 39 It was believed that Satan put a mark upon all who had enlisted into his service.

†**d.** ***God's marks***: an appearance betokening impending death. (See GOD *sb.* 16 c.) *Obs.*

e. A character made with a pen, usually a cross, used by illiterate persons in place of a signature.

c **1020** *Rule St. Benet* (Logeman) lviii. 98 Oððe soðes ȝif he na can stafas, oðer fram him ȝebeden write & se nicumena mearce do. **1434** in *E.E. Wills* (1882) 102 And y pray yowe loki thys marke and thys Seell, acorde as y Roger wyl answere afore god. **1588** in Arber *Marprel. Controv.* 82 William × Stanghtons marke. **1593** SHAKS. *2 Hen. VI*, IV. ii. 110. **1627** in *Barnfield's Poems* (Arb.) Introd. 17 Peter Serieantes his × mark. **1766** BLACKSTONE *Comm.* II. xx. 305 Which custom our illiterate vulgar do..keep up; by signing a cross for their mark when unable to write their names. **1851** H. MELVILLE *Whale* xviii. 100 Dost thou sign thy name or make thy mark?

f. A written symbol.

1737 J. CHAMBERLAYNE *St. Gt. Brit.* II. III. 150 (List Councilmen Lond.) This * Mark denotes the New Members. **1862** ANSTED *Channel Isl.* II. ix. (ed. 2) 200 A mark of interrogation (?) [will denote] doubtful species. **1890** H. SWEET *Prim. Spoken Eng.* 2 The stress-marks are put before the element on which the stress begins. *Ibid.* 3 The tone-marks are put before the word they modify.

g. (*a*) ***good***, ***bad mark***: a written character used by teachers, jailers, etc., in their registers as a symbol of an instance of good or bad conduct respectively; hence *fig.* a point noted or remembered to a person's credit or discredit. (*b*) Originally, in schools, a vertical line placed opposite to a pupil's name as a record or a correct answer in class of some other point of merit, his place in the class being determined by the number of 'marks' which he obtains. Hence, the unit of the numerical award given by a teacher or examiner to the person whose comparative merit is to be ascertained. Also *fig.* in phr. ***full marks*** used as an expression of considerable praise or commendation; also ***top marks***.

1829 LYTTON *Devereux* I. iii, I was one hundred marks before my brother. **1837** *Orders & Regul. Harvard Univ.* 8 The average of the marks given by the members of the [examining] Committee. **1887** D. A. LOW *Machine Draw.* (1892) 124 Inking-in,..and shading,..are not required in the examination, and receive no marks. **1891** H. MATTHEWS in *Law Times* XCII. 96/1 A convict who gains by steady industry the maximum number of marks during each day of his sentence. **1893** LELAND *Mem.* I. 73 The punishments were bad marks, and for every mark the boy was obliged to go to bed an hour earlier than the others. **1934** D. L. SAYERS *Nine Tailors* II. v. 175 That is well observed. Yes, Bunter, you may have full marks for that. **1941** H. NICOLSON *Let.* 27 Mar. (1967) 154 It is a fine show and I give Ronnie Campbell full marks. **1945** W. DE LA MARE *Scarecrow* 22 'Full marks, my dear,' said Mr. Bolsover, squeezing her hand. **1966** *Listener* 29 Sept. 472/3 Full marks for the deadly opening sentence. **1973** *Times* 2 June 9/4 Full marks as always, to this hard-up, persevering, resourceful and imaginative museum. **1973** J. THOMSON *Death Cap* xiii. 177 He gave Holbrook top marks for finding such a delightfully sharp and acid old lady.

†**h.** In schools, a badge worn by the pupil who had last committed some particular fault. ***to pass the mark***: to get rid of the badge on detecting a schoolfellow in the same fault; also *fig. Obs.*

1832 MISS MITFORD *Village* Ser. v. 198 French was the universal language of the house, and an English mark was passed among the young ladies, transferred from culprit to culprit as they were detected in the fact, and called for three times a day, when the unlucky damsel who happened to be in possession of the badge was amerced in the sum of three-pence;..this order of demerit [was] an oval piece of wood, with ENGLISH, in large capitals engraven on its front, suspended by a riband from the neck. **1849** THACKERAY *Pendennis* xxxi, Bacon liked to be treated with rudeness by a gentleman, and used to pass it on to his inferiors as boys pass the mark. *c* **1855** MRS. GASKELL *Traits & Stories Huguenots* ad fin., I have now told all I know about the Huguenots. I pass the mark to some one else.

i. *Her.* A small charge added to a coat of arms as a sign of distinction; esp. in ***mark of*** CADENCY.

1625 B. JOHNSON *Staple of News* IV. iv, Were he a learned Herald, I would tell him He can giue Armes, and markes. **1702** [see CADENCY]. **1718** PRIOR *Henry & Emma* 49 This lord..Had brought back his paternal coat enlarg'd With a new mark. **1797** *Encycl. Brit.* (ed. 3) VIII. 445 Of all the forementioned marks of distinction, none but the label is affixed on the coats of arms belonging to any of the royal family.

j. *Freemasonry.* Used *attrib.* (with reference to sense 11 a) to designate a degree, grade, or rank immediately superior to that of the free and accepted mason (see 23).

12. a. Something (e.g. a line, dot, notch, or an object fixed or attached) intended to record or indicate position.

Plimsoll's mark: a load-line required by the Merchant Shipping Act, 1876 (the bill for which was introduced by S. Plimsoll, M.P. for Derby) to be placed upon the hull of a British vessel to indicate how far she may be loaded.

c **1460** *Towneley Myst.* xxiii. 146 *Quartus tortor.* That was well drawen that that; ffare fall hym that so puld! ffor to haue getten it to the marke, I trow lewde man ne clerk Nothyng better shuld. **1530** Palsgr. 529/1 You have dronke to me, but you muste drinke agayne, for you tolde me nat whether you dranke to a marke or els al out. **1635–56** Cowley *Davideis* iv. Note 29 Almost all great changes in the world are used as Marks for separation of Times. **1725** J. Bradley in *Penny Cycl.* (1836) V. 320/1 Adjusted y^{e} mark to the Plumb Line and then y^{e} Index stood at 8. *Ibid.*, By this observation y^{e} mark is about 3″ $\frac{3}{4}$ too much south, but adjusting y^{e} mark and plumbline I found y^{e} Index at 8$\frac{1}{2}$. **1807** Hutton *Course Math.* II. 59 Having set up marks at the corners, which is to be done in all cases where there are not marks naturally; measure [etc.]. **1870** Miss Bridgman *Rob. Lynne* I. xiii. 216 She slips the letter in her novel for a mark. **1881** *Daily Tel.* 28 Jan., I see Plimsoll's mark there—pretty high up, isn't it, skipper? **1903** *Daily Chron.* 8 Jan. 5/2 The floods..call attention to the little interest that is taken by local authorities as regards erecting flood-marks.

b. *Naut.* A measured notification on a hand lead-line, indicated by a piece of white, blue, or red bunting, a piece of leather or a knot.

marks and deeps: the method of indicating the depths on the hand lead-line, the marks being indicated fathoms and the deeps estimated fathoms between the marks (Smyth *Sailor's Word-Bk.* 1867).

1769 Falconer *Dict. Marine* (1780) s.v. *Sounding*, If the mark of 5 fathoms is close to the surface of the water he calls 'By the mark five!' *c* **1860** H. Stuart *Seaman's Catech.* 43 Suppose you had five fathoms of water, what soundings would you call? By the mark five.

c. *fig.*, esp. in certain phrases, as ***to be above, beneath, near, under, up to, within the mark***: to be above (etc.) a fixed or recognized standard. Also with prefixed figure representing a limit or total, or an approximation of this.

1765 Foote *Commissary* iii. (1782) 75 He is rather under your mark, I am afraid; not above twenty at most. **1821** Jefferson *Autobiog.* Writ. 1892 I. 15 He feared that Mr. Nicholas, whose mind was not yet up to the mark of the times, would undertake the answer. **1822** Cobbett *Weekly Reg.* 2 Feb. 286 If prices fall a great deal lower than their present mark. **1842** Borrow *Bible in Spain* xliii. (Pelh. Libr.) 298, I..have a horse that will just suit him; one that is..eight inches above the mark. **1845** McCulloch *Taxation* ii. vi. (1852) 270 It is, if anything, rather below than above the mark. **1851** Mayhew *Lond. Labour* I. 336/2 Say half a million turned over in a year, Sir,..and you're within the mark. [**1860** Thackeray *Roundabout Papers* vi, in *Cornh. Mag.* Aug. 256 The *Cornhill Magazine*..having sold nearly a hundred thousand copies, he (the correspondent) 'should think forty thousand was now about the mark'.] **1861** Goschen *For. Exch.* 14 The indebtedness under the present hypothesis is not excessive but under the mark. **1861** F. W. Robinson *No Church* I. 309 He made the sum come pretty near the mark—just a five pound note out. **1878** Geo. Eliot *Coll. Breakf. P.* 629 A vanity Which finds the universe beneath its mark. **1887** Rider Haggard *Jess* viii, John..guessed that he could not weigh less than seventeen stone, and he was well within the mark at that. **1888** W. E. Norris *Rogue* ix, There wouldn't be much excuse for me if I weren't up to the mark. **1890** Stockton in *Century Mag.* Feb. 543/1 The story don't step up to the mark. **1929** *Star* 21 Aug. 18/2 Dennis Brothers' 1s. shares can usually be regarded as a reasonable purchase under the £3 mark. **1946** *R.A.F. Jrnl.* May 170 The membership already exceeds the twenty-five hundred mark. **1948** D. Ballantyne *Cunninghams* iii. 15 Around the forty mark. **1965** N. Paul *Cine-Photogr.* ii. 19 There is a tremendous range of models on the market today, especially in the 8 mm. gauge, where they can..soar up to the £300 mark. **1973** *Times* 14 Apr. (Nepal Suppl.) p. ii/9 If the present trend continues, the 25 million mark may be reached before the end of the century.

d. *Rugby Football.* The heel-mark on the ground, made by a player who has obtained a 'fair catch'. Also *Austral. Rules Football* (see quots. 1968). Cf. mark *v.* 15 d.

1867 *Rugby School Football Laws* 2 A Fair Catch is a catch from a kick, or a knock on from the hand..of the opposite side, or a throw on, when the catcher makes a mark with his heel. **1896** *Field* 1 Feb. 172/2 A mark by a Devon man gained much relief. *Ibid.* 173/1 A goal had also been kicked by Finlay from a mark. *Ibid.* 8 Feb. 207/1 Hughes made his mark without success. **1965** *Sun-Herald* (Sydney) 4 July 51 Geelong Rover, Terry Farman, won a trophy for the best mark taken by his team. **1967** *Ibid.* 16 Apr. 67 Ryan's first kick struck the back of the Collingwood man on the mark, but Perkins ruled he had moved back over the mark. **1968** Eagleson & McKie *Terminol. Austral. Nat. Football* ii. 22 *Mark*,..the catching of the ball on the full directly from the kick of another player. *Ibid.* 23 *Mark*,..the spot at which a player caught the ball ('took a mark'), and behind or over which he must make his kick. **1969** *Sun-Herald* (Sydney) 13 July 48/1 Close took a beautiful one-handed mark, his tenth for the game,..but kicked only a point.

e. *Athletics.* A line drawn to indicate the starting-point. Also in phrases (lit. and fig.), as ***on your mark(s)***, ***(get set, go)***, the instructions given to competitors at the start of a race; ***to be first off the mark***: to gain an initial lead over one's opponents; ***to be quick off*** (or ***on***) ***the mark***: to lose no time in starting, to waste no initial advantage; ***to be slow off the mark***: to start slowly or sluggishly; to waste time in starting; ***to get*** (or ***be***) ***off the mark***: to start (well); ***to overstep the mark***: to infringe the rules by placing one's foot over or beyond the mark; so *fig.*, to go beyond a fixed limit or standard, to 'go too far'; cf. the phr. ***overshoot the mark*** (overshoot *v.* 2 b, and mark *sb.*^{1} 7 a, e); ***to toe the mark*** (see toe *v.* 2).

1887 M. Shearman *Athletics & Football* 65 It requires, however, much skill and practice not to 'take off' before the mark [in jumping]. *Ibid.* 198 Nothing was said until the men got upon their marks. **1905** *Pearson's Mag.* Sept. 290/2 He ..beat his field by a yard or two off the mark. **1912** E. H. Ryle *Athletics* 91 This method..assists a runner to keep steady on the mark while awaiting the report of the pistol. **1917** E. Pound *Let.* 12 Aug. (1971) 114, I have been a bit slow getting the *Little Review* off the mark. **1919** E. P. Oppenheim *Strange Case J. Thew* i. xiii. 112 'Did he make any trouble?' 'He had no chance..I was first off the mark.' **1921** *Daily Colonist* (Victoria, B.C.) 24 Mar. 13/3 It was felt that the Parent-Teachers' Associations were in some cases overstepping the mark in regard to requests. **1928** *Observer* 5 Feb. 23/5 When you really wish to get going you have a second, a third and a top speed change which will get the car off the mark, in the old phrase, in an inspiriting manner. **1929** F. N. Hart *Hide in Dark* i. 25 All set? On your mark! **1930** L. W. Olds *Track Athletics* iv. 26 On Your Marks... Get Set... Go or Gun. **1931** *Oxford Mail* 29 Aug. 8/3 G. Fisher and L. Rogers were quickly off the mark, 20 runs being scored in the first ten minutes. **1934** Wodehouse *Right Ho, Jeeves* i. 9 Get off the mark..like a scalded cat, and your public is at a loss. **1938** R. Warner *Professor* x. 227 Now he appeared like a person who fears that he has in some way overstepped the mark, has involuntarily wounded another's feelings, or alluded to some subject that were better left unmentioned. **1943** *Endeavour* Apr. 74/2 The dog-breeder and poultry farmer were comparatively quick off the mark in using the new therapy. **1946** B. Marshall *George Brown's Schooldays* v. 22 On your marks, go. The thing was to lob them [*sc.* rissoles] out like fives pills. **1947** 'G. Orwell' *Eng. People* 24 With all their political ignorance the English people will often show surprising sensitiveness when some small incident seems to show that 'They' are overstepping the mark. **1954** G. Mitchell *On your Marks* xv. 172 'On your marks,' said the starter. The swimmers were poised and ready. 'Go!' **1958** J. Wain *Contenders* v. 102 Ned was off the mark at once... Blue Seal Pottery seemed to become a vogue overnight. **1970** Marlow & Watts *Track Athletics* ii. 18 It is recommended that the shoulders should be forward when the athlete settles into the blocks on the command 'On your marks'. **1971** *Morning Star* 19 Oct. 2 The Institute of Teachers and the Association of Science Teachers were quick off the mark, followed by the more orthodox national trust. **1972** R. Adams *Watership Down* xxvii. 208 The pursuit was a bit slow off the mark..because poor old Bugloss wasn't there to give the orders. **1972** W. A. Pantin *Oxf. Life* iv. 50 Dr. William Buckland..was very quick on the mark with putting in plans for the future use of the building. **1973** *South Wales Echo* 30 June (Suppl.) 1/2 Then the whole Burke Special team can get off their mark. **1973** *Guardian* 8 Oct. 10/2 Beatrix Potter..wrote about Tommy Brock (the badger) and Mr. Todd (the fox) living on terms of toleration—until Tommy badly overstepped the mark.

13. a. A visible trace or impression diversifying a surface, whether produced by nature, accident, or design, as a line, dot, written character, spot, stain, discolouration, scar, or the like. Also with prefixed sb., as ***birth-***, ***bullet-***, ***file-mark***.

c **1325** *Metr. Hom.* 57 Thar his throt was scorn wit knif, A red merk was al his lyf. **1388** Wyclif *Lev.* xix. 28 Nether ȝe schulen make to ȝou ony fyguris, ether markis in ȝoure fleisch. **1413** *Pilgr. Sowle* (Caxton 1483) iv. xxxvi. 84 The honoure of suche persones ben many markes of woundes. **1500–20** Dunbar *Poems* xiv. 19 Sic losin sarkis, so mony glengoir markis Within this land was nevir hard nor sene. **1530** Palsgr. 699/1 It was scaulded whan I was yonge, but I shall beare the marke so longe as I lyve. **1590** Shaks. *Com. Err.* i. ii. 82, I haue some markes of yours vpon my pate: Some of my Mistris markes vpon my shoulders. **1593** —— *Lucr.* 538 For markes discried in mens natiuitie, Are natures faultes, not their owne infamie. **1613** Purchas *Pilgrimage* vii. x. (1614) 702 Their blacke skinnes, white eyes, and cauterised markes seeme to conspire a dreadfull and gastly deformitie in their faces. **1687** A. Lovell tr. *Thevenot's Trav.* i. 9 The Arms of the Great Masters, who have been wounded in Action, are to be seen there, with marks upon them. **1805** Ring in *Med. Jrnl.* XIV. 405 The marks he bore, were deemed a sufficient security against..the small-pox. **1828** Fleming *Hist. Brit. Anim.* 96 Some feathers have a dark mark in the middle. **1831** *Ann. Reg., Chron.* 112 The mark of a bunch of currants on his breast, with which the boy was born. **1848** W. H. Bartlett *Egypt to Pal.* x. (1879) 220 The long marks of ancient cutting-tools were still seen overhead and around. **1849** Dickens *Dav. Copp.* xx, She has borne the mark ever since, as you see;..and she'll bear it to her grave. **1858** O. W. Holmes *Aut. Breakf.-t.* (1883) 86 A bullet-mark on his right cheek. **1868** Darwin *Anim. & Pl.* II. xiii. 42 A Spanish mule with strong zebra-like marks on its legs. **1888** Hasluck *Model Engin. Handybk.* (1900) 131 File-marks running in straight parallel lines.

b. ***to leave, make a mark***: to leave or make a permanent, important, or obvious impression. ***to make one's mark***: to attain distinction.

a **1847** T. Chalmers in Bartlett *Dict. Amer.* (1860) 262 Men..called out to make and leave their mark upon the world. **1854** *Harper's Mag.* Sept. 561/2 There was a time when Jacob made his mark upon the stock-brokers and money-changers of that monetary locality. **1857** Buckle *Civiliz.* I. xiii. 707 The movement was now becoming sufficiently active to leave its marks on the writings of far inferior men. **1867** O. W. Holmes *Guard. Angel* II. v. 95 Not one promised to make such a mark in society if she found an opening. **1868** Miss Braddon *Dead Sea Fruit* ii. ix. 211 Those little verses..have made their mark. **1893** F. F. Moore *I Forbid Banns* (1899) 7 It may safely be predicted that they will make their mark in the world. **1898** *Daily News* 11 Jan. 6/7 Politicians who have left their mark upon the first sixty years of New Zealand's existence. **1905** L. Strachey *Characters & Commentaries* (1933) i. iv. 34 Whether he himself [*sc.* Walpole] might not have made his mark in politics is perhaps a futile speculation. **1921** R. Macaulay *Dangerous Ages* xi. 208 Why dream wistfully of doing one's bit, making one's mark, in a world already as full of bits..as a kaleidoscope? **1927** C. Bell *Landmarks 19th Cent. Painting* 147 They have not failed to leave a mark on history. **1952** A. J. Cronin *Adventures in Two Worlds* i. 15 In medicine, or some other field, I believe that you will make your mark. **1973** *Observer* (Colour Suppl.) 5 Aug. 18/2 Woolton..making his mark as Civilian Boot and Shoe Controller in World War I. **1974** *Radio Times* 3 Jan. 49/4 Pop music has produced many trendsetters—we pick three who've made their mark in the 70s.

c. *Hunting.* Applied *spec.* to the footprints of certain animals. (Cf. march *sb.*^{3} 9.)

a **1700** B. E. *Dict. Cant. Crew, Marks*, the Footing of an Otter. **1727–51** Chambers *Cycl.* (s.v. *Hunting*).

d. *Cards.* (See quot.)

1876 Capt. Crawley *Card Players' Man.* (*Quadrille*) 196 *Mark* means the fish put down by the dealer.

e. *Telecommunications.* Each of a succession of marks on paper whose relative duration and separation are used to convey information in telegraphy; hence, any kind of signal that conveys information by its presence or absence (rather than by its magnitude). Opp. *space*: hence **mark-space** *attrib.*

1837 *Amer. Jrnl. Sci. & Arts* XXXIII. 187 [*Describing Morse's telegraph.*] To read the marks; count the points at the bottom of each line. **1859** T. P. Shaffner *Telegr. Manual* xxxiv. 469 The length of the mark or of the space upon the ribbon paper will be precisely the same as the length of the contact made with the key. **1891** C. L. Buckingham in C. F. Brackett et al. *Electr. in Daily Life* 143 In 1846 Bain proposed to employ perforated strips of paper to effect automatic transmission in connection with an electro-chemical process for recording, in which marks upon a moving band of paper are made by discoloration attending the passage through it of signalling currents. **1938** *Admiralty Handbk. Wireless Telegr.* II. K. 59 When the key is pressed, the valve oscillates and we have the mark period. *Ibid.*, During mark, the oscillating circuit constitutes the load. **1953** *Electronics* July 183/2 Mark-Space Phototubes. As the perforated tape passes through the keying head, pulses of light from the exciter lamps pass through the holes and alternately strike the tone-on (mark) and tone-off (space) phototubes. The phototubes conduct and produce alternate pulses of current. **1958** P. E. K. Donaldson et al. *Electronic Apparatus for Biol. Res.* xv. 234 The circuit performs oscillations with a mark-space ratio of approximately unity, the waveforms having the form of Figure 15.14. **1969** J. J. Sparkes *Transistor Switching* iii. 52 A circuit capable of producing rectangular waves with very sharp rising and falling edges, at mark-space ratios of between 1:1 and 500:1,..is shown. **1972** *Sci. Amer.* Dec. 16/3 The computer's input element is a photoelectric paper-tape reader that handles 1,000 'marks' (punched holes) per second.

†**14.** *Sc.* A stone or cluster of stones of larger size, placed at intervals in a jewelled chain. *Obs.*

1573 *Reg. Privy Council Scot.* II. 247 Ane chayn of rubeis with twelf markes of dyamontis and rubeis, and ane mark with twa rubeis.

15. That which is signified by a mark.

†**a.** Those who bear a particular mark or stamp (*fig.*); a person's race, sect, etc. *Obs.*

c **1386** Chaucer *Wife's Prol.* 696 They [wommen] wolde han writen of men moore wikkednesse Than all the mark of Adam may redresse. **1542–5** Brinklow *Lament.* 11 Not the Bisshope of Rome alone, but he and all his marke with hym. **1555** in Strype *Eccl. Mem.* (1721) III. App. xliv. 124 The Magistrates and Gentlemen may have like cause against them [Popish clergy], and al the Company of that Mark, which..was Cause of their Perjury.

b. A particular 'brand', make, quality, or size of an article. Also, freq. followed by a numeral, a designation of the stage of development in design and construction of a manufactured product or piece of equipment, as a weapon, an aeroplane, etc. Abbrev. Mk. Also *transf.* and *fig.* ***Mark I***: first class (*slang*).

1669 Sturmy *Mariner's Mag.* v. xii. 68 In regard of the several differences of the length and marks, or Diameter of her Base and Muzzle-ring, no certain proportion can be generally assigned. **1758** *Monthly Rev.* 204 The prices of Grinding..and Diamond-cutting the several Marks or Sizes [of plate-glass]. **1888** *Treat. Mil. Small Arms & Ammunition* 52 Enfield Revolver Pistol, Mark II. **1899** *Kynoch Jrnl.* Oct.–Nov. 12/1 Despite the unfortunate failures at Edinburgh and Bisley of the bullet known as Mark iv. **1904** *Speaker* 11 June 240/2 The same mark varies so much from year to year that no one would dare to purchase without examining a sample bale [of wool]. **1914** *Times Bk. Navy* vii. 99 The gun has progressed through successive stages, or 'marks' as they are technically known. Marks 3, 4, 5, and 5w were 'built' guns. **1916** T. E. Lawrence *Let.* 22 Dec. (1938) 214 Will you please wire for 4 locks complete for Gun Maxim Converted Mark II to be sent to Yenbo? **1926** L. Nason *Chevrons* 120 This is going to be a real, old issue, Mark I scrap. **1942** W. S. Churchill in *Second World War* (1951) IV. 768 There should be no difficulty in sparing 1,000 tanks and 1,000 anti-tank and A.A. guns. No doubt older marks might form the bulk. **1946** *R.A.F. Jrnl.* May 180 No fewer than 26 different 'Marks' were built and put into service... In accordance with Service custom they merited and received the bestowal of a special Mark number. **1948** 'N. Shute' *No Highway* i. 7 The Mark I model [*sc.* an aeroplane] which went into production first had radial engines. **1959** *Listener* 19 Mar. 514/1, I trust the Ministry of Supply is making sure that all senior naval, military, and air force officers are supplied with Mark II* crystal balls. **1973** P. Johnson in Johnson & Gale *Highland Jaunt* i. i. 13 Time's winged chariot is hurrying near, powered by the latest mark of internal combustion engine. **1973** J. Wainwright *Devil you Don't* 5 It was a great car—a Jag Mark II. **1974** *Economist* 21 Dec. 29/3 They are calling him [*sc.* Helmut Schmidt] Kissinger Mark II. **1975** J. Symons *Three Pipe Problem* xv. 129 For his white clients

Riverboat often played the role of American Negro, Mark One.

c. *vulgar*. (One's) 'style of thing', what will suit one's needs or tastes.

1760 FOOTE *Minor* II. (1767) 53 Hark'e, knight, did I not tell you, old Moll was your mark. Here she hath brought you a pretty piece of man's meat already. **1887** HENLEY *Culture in Slums* iii, My mark's a tidy little feed, And 'Enery Irving's gallery.

†**16.** A flock or 'game' of swans marked with the same identifying brand. Also ***swan-mark***. *Obs.*

1482 *Rolls of Parlt.* VI. 224 Markes and Games of Swannes, in divers Countres. **1489** *Will of N. Hardy*, Unum marke de signis. **1500** *Will of R. Tyllisworth*, All that my marke and game of Swannys swymmyng within the Kinges ryver of the Thamyse. **1550** *Will of L. Bawdrey*, lx^s. the price of a swan marke.

†**17.** ? A bundle or packet of definite size. *Obs.*

1583 *Rates Custom Ho.* E iij b, Sheres for Sempsters the mark contayning two dosen.

18. ***(God) bless*** (or ***save***) ***the mark*** (or †***sample***): an exclamatory phrase, prob. originally serving as a formula to avert an evil omen (cf. quot. 1833) and hence used by way of apology when something horrible, disgusting, indecent or profane has been mentioned. In mod. literary use (after some of the examples in Shaks.), an expression of impatient scorn appended to a quoted expression or to a statement of fact.

[It has been affirmed (see W. A. Henderson in *N. & Q.* 8th ser. VII. 373) that the phrase was used by midwives at the birth of a child bearing a 'mark'. This may possibly be its original use: cf. quot. *a* 1625 below. The meaning of 'mark' in the expression may, however, have been 'sign' or 'omen' (see 11). There is no foundation for the statement copied in recent Dicts. from Dr. Brewer, that the phrase was originally used by archers.]

1591 SHAKS. *Two Gent.* IV. iv. 21 Hee had not bin there (blesse the marke) a pissing while, but all the chamber smelt him. **1592** —— *Rom. & Jul.* III. ii. 53 (Qo. 2, 1599), I saw the wound, I saw it with mine eyes, God saue the marke, here on [Qo. 1, 1597 the sample, on] his manly brest. **1593** CHURCHYARD *Challenge* 240 Browne and blacke I was, God blesse the marke: Who calls me faire dooth scarce know Cheese from chalke. **1596** SHAKS. *1 Hen. IV*, I. iii. 56 (Qo. 1, 1598) To see him..talke so like a waiting-gentlewoman, Of guns, and drums, and wounds..God saue the mark. **1604** —— *Oth.* I. i. 33 (Qo. 1, 1622) He in good time, must his Leiutenant be, And I, God blesse the marke, his Worships Ancient. *a***1625** FLETCHER *Noble Gent.* IV. iv, Indeed he was just such another coxcomb as your husband, God blesse the mark, and every good mans childe. **1761** STERNE *Tr. Shandy* III. xxxiii, My father..had no more nose, my dear, saving the mark, than there is upon the back of my hand. **1820** W. IRVING *Sketch Bk., Sleepy Hollow* (1865) 440 The motherly tea-pot sending up its cloud of vapor from the midst—Heaven bless the mark! **1824** CARLYLE in Froude *Life* (1882) I. 261 The best of my talents (bless the mark) shut up even from my own poor view. **1833** *Dublin Penny Jrnl.* II. 23/2 'An' they say', remarked a third, 'that if a body swears in the wrong wid that [the garvarry] about his neck, his face'll be turned to the back of his head, God bless the mark!' **1849** JAMES *Woodman* ii, God save the mark, that I should give the name of king to one of his kindred. **1902** W. JAMES *Varieties Relig. Exp.* 204 *note*, The crisis of apathetic melancholy..from which he emerged by the reading of Marmontel's Memoirs (Heaven save the mark!) and Wordsworth's poetry.

19. A die or stamp for impressing a manufacturer's mark on goods. (Cf. *mark-maker* in 23.)

IV. Remark, notice (= senses of NOTE *sb.*).

†**20.** Attention, notice. *Obs.*

1377 LANGL. *P. Pl.* B. XVII. 103 And may vch man se and gode merke take, Who is bihynde and who bifore, and who ben on hors. *c***1440** *York Myst.* viii. 68 Of shippe-craft can I right noght, Of ther makyng haue I no merke. **1600** HOLLAND *Livy* VII. xxxiv. 273 All this went hee to espie.. clad in a common souldiours jacket..; to the end, that the enemies might not take marke of the Generall himselfe. **1671** SIR C. LYTTELTON in *Hatton Corr.* (Camden) 70 One marke they take of it is employing Sr George Downing embassador thither. **1823** SCOTT *Peveril* ix, Little matter worthy of mark occurred.

21. ***of mark***; noteworthy, important, conspicuous. Chiefly following a sb.; rarely *predicative*. Also ***of great, little,*** etc. ***mark***.

Cf. F. *homme de marque* (Cotgr.). The etymological allusion is probably to the mark placed on goods to indicate quality (see sense 11).

1590 NASHE *Pasquil's Apol.* I. Wks. (Grosart) I. 220 The wisedome of the land..compared our Nobilitie and men of marke, to the flowers that stand about the Princes Crowne. **1596** SHAKS. *1 Hen. IV*, III. ii. 45 A fellow of no marke, nor likelyhood. **1600** HOLLAND *Livy* XXVI. xxxiii. 609 They were of greater marke and calling than the rest. *a***1614** D. DYKE *Myst. Self-deceiving* (ed. 8) 355 They grieue at those good works of others, if of any marke, wherein they haue had no hand themselues. **1622** S. WARD *Christ All in All* (1627) 8 This whole Vniverse,..and all the things of mark and vse in it,..but for him should not have been. **1647** MAY *Hist. Parl.* Pref. 4 Sufferings of..so high a mark. **1791** BURKE *App. Whigs* Wks. VI. 200 These are the notions which..several persons, and among them persons of no mean mark, have associated themselves to propagate. **1860** LONGF. *Wayside Inn, K. Olaf* IX. ii, A learned clerk, A man of mark. **1861** THACKERAY *Four Georges* i, A rascal of more than ordinary mark. **1879** MCCARTHY *Own Times* II. xxix. 399 He still held a place of great mark in literature. **1885** *Mag. Art* Sept. 450/1 Granada was a place of little mark as compared with Cordova.

22. (*dial.* and *slang.*) ***a mark on*** (something): one with an astonishing appetite for. ***a mark at***, a good hand at.

1881 *Punch* 3 Dec. 263/2 Till my chummy Scholard Mike, who's a mark at A.B.C., Read me Littler's little tale. **1883** MISS BRADDON *Golden Calf* xxv. 274 Vernon was what Rogers the butler called 'a mark on' strawberries and cream. **1895** DOWNE *Ballads* 31 (E.D.D.) A mark on swearin? Ah, sir, that he be.

V. 23. *attrib.* and *Comb.*: (sense 11 g) ***mark-sheet, system***; †**mark-arrow**, an arrow used only for target practice; **mark-boat**, a boat moored at a particular spot as a seamark; **mark-book**, a book for recording conduct marks; †**mark-feast**, a school feast provided at the end of the half-year from the scholars' fines for holding the mark (sense 11 h); **mark-getter**, a student who obtains marks; **mark-lodge**, a lodge of mark masons; **mark-maker**, a maker of stamp marks; **mark man, mark mason, mark master (mason)**, a freemason holding a certain rank in mark masonry; **mark masonry** (see 11 j); †**mark-mear**, a boundary; **marks paper**, a paper for recording students' or other merit marks; †**mark's point**, the bull's-eye of a target (*fig.*); **mark sensing**, the process by which a machine 'senses' or reads data in the form of electrically conducting marks made by hand on cards with a lead pencil; so **mark-sense(d** *a.*, marked in this way and for this purpose; †**mark-shot**, the distance between the butts in archery; **mark tooth**, the tooth of a horse containing the mark (cf. 11 e); **mark-vessel**, = *mark-boat*; †**mark-white**, the bull's-eye of a target (*fig.*).

1527 *Lanc. Wills* (Chetham Soc. 1854) 31, I will that the said Percyvall..have..the half of my *mark aroys. **1879** *Daily News* 7 Apr. 3/2 They paddled below the *mark-boats, and drifted up with the tide. **1894** *Outing* (U.S.) XXIV. 36/1 We were still fully two miles from the mark-boat. **1900** *Westm. Gaz.* 28 June 2/1 My *mark-book with its blank column for disorder-marks against her name was a striking contrast to those of the other mistresses. **1832** MISS MITFORD *Village* Ser. v. 200 Readily would the whole company have foregone all the luxuries of the *mark-feast. ?*c***1860** W. CORY *Lett. & Jrnls.* (1897) 571 A good 'examination boy', or *mark-getter. **1869** *Edin. Rev.* Oct. 554 The highest mark-getters generally turn out well. **1898** *Mark lodge [see *mark master*]. **1797** *Directory Sheffield* 56 Cartwright, George, *mark-maker, and penknife cutler. **1883** *Kelly's Sheffield Directory* 194 Ashmore, Cornelius, mark maker and letter cutter. **1853** OLIVER *Dict. Symbol. Masonry* s.v. *Mason Marks*, Those brethren who have been initiated into the degrees of *Mark-Man and *Mark-Master. *Ibid.*, **Mark Masons*. The degree of Mark-Master Mason may be considered as appendant to that of Fellow Craft, although entirely distinct..from it. **1862** *Builder* 1 Nov. 784/3 Gunn, who had cut out the cup, was a good mark-mason... Referring to *mark-masonry, Mr. Gowans said [etc.]. **1898** *Daily News* 25 Oct. 2/1 There was a distinguished gathering of Mark Master Masons at Windsor yesterday, when the Grand Mark Master of England, the Prince of Wales, having issued a warrant for a new *Mark Lodge to be established at Windsor, the consecration took place at the Masonic Hall. **1582** STANYHURST *Æneis* I. (Arb.) 28 Thow seest large Affrick, thee Moores, and Towne of Agenor, Thee Libye land *marckmears. **1880** *Plain Hints Needlework* 13 This should always have a special column in the *marks-paper. **1553** KENNEDY *Compend. Tract.* in *Wodrow Soc. Misc.* (1844) 102 In the understanding of this consistis the heale purpose, and *markis poynt quhilk we schute at. **1965** *Math. in Biol. & Med.* (Med. Res. Council) I. 10 They used '*mark-sense' cards for the details of the investigation and for the results of calculations. **1971** *Computers & Humanities* VI. 16 A newer approach employs mark-sense cards upon which musical symbols have been printed. This allows the person doing the encoding to accomplish it in a single step, quietly, and without the need for cumbersome equipment. **1964** T. W. MCRAE *Impact of Computers on Accounting* i. 14 Figure 1.8 illustrates a *mark sensed card. The mark sensed positions are in columns 70–78 and the holes punched from these..are in columns 31–33. **1959** E. M. GRABBE et al. *Handbk. Automation, Computation, & Control* II. v. 19 *Mark sensing uses special electrical conducting marks placed in various positions on punched cards. **1970** O. DOPPING *Computers & Data Processing* iii. 55 Information can also be recorded in a card with a pencil, and in a subsequent operation, 'mark sensing', the markings are translated to punched holes in the cards. **1961** *Oxf. Local Exam.* (*Latin, Paper 1*) p. 3 The total mark ..is to be halved before it is entered on the *marksheet. **1964** *Oxf. Mag.* 12 Mar. 254/1 Now that the dust has settled on the marksheets of the January Part II examination. **1375** BARBOUR *Bruce* XII. 33 Schir Henry of Bowme..Com on a steid, a *merk-schot neir Befor all othir that thair wer. *c***1450** *Merlin* 287 Thei were putte bakke the space of a mark shote. **1885** *Encycl. Brit.* XIX. 754/2 He devised an ingenious system of recording the convicts' daily industry by marks... The *mark system had already been tried with good results in Ireland. **1626** BACON *Sylva* §754 At foure yeares old there commeth the *Mark-Tooth,..at eight yeares old, the Tooth is smooth,..and then they say; That the Marke is out of the Horses Mouth. **1884** *World* 20 Aug. 22/2 The Royal London Yacht Club had..a *mark-vessel off Lymington. **1596** SPENSER *F.Q.* V. v. 35 At the *marke-white of his hart she roved.

mark (mɑːk), *sb.*² Forms: 1–5 (also from Fr. 8–9) **marc**; 4–7 **marke**, 5 **marcke**, 5–6 *Sc.* **merke**, 5–9 *Sc.* **merk**, 3– **mark**. [Found in all the Teut. and Rom. langs.; Late OE. *marc* neut. (9th c.), OFris. *merk* fem., MDu. *marc* fem., neut., masc. (Du. *mark* neut.), MHG. *mark, marke* fem. (mod.G. *mark* fem.), ON. *mǫrk* fem. (Sw., Da. *mark*); med.L. *marca* (? 9th century), *marcus* (12th c.), F. *marc* masc. (11th c.), Pr. *marc* masc., Sp., Pg., It. *marco* masc., It. *marca* fem.

The form of the OE. word (with *a* not 'broken' before *rc*) shows that it is not a native word; some scholars have supposed it to be from ON., but the gender perhaps points rather to popular Latin as the source. The proximate origin appears to be Romanic; whether the word is ultimately Teutonic (connected with MARK *sb.*¹) is doubtful.]

1. A denomination of weight formerly employed (chiefly for gold and silver) throughout western Europe; its actual weight varied considerably, but it was usually regarded as equivalent to 8 ounces (= either $\frac{2}{3}$ or $\frac{1}{2}$ of a pound, according to the meaning given to the latter term).

a. As an English or Scottish weight, or without reference to locality. *Obs.* exc. *Hist.*

886 *Ælfred & Guthrum's Peace* §2 Ealle we lætað efen dyrne Engliscne & Deniscne, to viii. healfmearcum [*v.r.* marcum] asodenes goldes. *c***1205** LAY. 22392 ȝet ich wulle mære..ælche ȝere of mine londe seouen þusand punde [thee send] & senden heom to þine londe & sixti mark of golde. *c***1400** *Destr. Troy* 11724 To the grekes bus vs gyffe, to graunt vs for pes, Twenty thowsaund thristy, þrungyn togedur, Markes full mighty, all of mayn gold. **1438** in *E. E. Wills* (1882) 111 Euery cuppe weynge a mark & a half of Troye. **1483** CAXTON *Gold. Leg.* 189b/1 He departed emonge them a marcke of golde. **1505** *Ld. Treas. Acc. Scot.* (1900) II. 244 Quhilk weyit lv mark, and ilk mark contenand viij unce of gold. **1530** PALSGR. 243/1 Marke of golde or silver, *marc*. **1568** GRAFTON *Chron.* II. 735 A hundreth Markes of siluer made in Plate, whereof euery Marke is .viii. ounces sterlyng.

b. Used to represent its etymological equivalent in various continental langs., as the name of a foreign weight.

1731 *Gentl. Mag.* I. 112 Fine silver at 24 [Dutch] Guilders 2 Stivers Banco *per* Mark fine. **1811** P. KELLY *Univ. Cambist* I. 96, 480 Marks Cologne weight = 451 Ounces English Troy. **1902** *Encycl. Brit.* XXVII. 11/1 In silver and copper mining the marc (8 ounces) is commonly used to express the richness of the metal [in Chile].

†**c.** In the Orkneys: see quot. 1859. *Obs.*

1576 in *Oppress. Orkney & Zetland* (Abbotsf. Cl.) 41 Lykwyiss the merk of copper of auld was sauld for twa schillingis of wairis, and now thai tak four schillingis thairfor. **1859** *Ibid.* Gloss. 127 *Mark*,..a weight = 8 ounces or $\frac{1}{24}$ of a Lispund or Setteen, gradually raised to 20 ounces.

2. A money of account, originally representing the value of a mark weight of pure silver.

a. In England, after the Conquest, the ratio of 20 sterling pennies to an ounce was the basis of computation; hence the value of the mark became fixed at 160 pence = 13*s.* 4*d.* or $\frac{2}{3}$ of the £ sterling. *Obs.* exc. *Hist.*

In legal use (in stating the amount of a fine) as late as 1770. Sir Roger de Coverley's use of the mode of reckoning by marks (quot. 1712) is prob. intended as an example of an old-fashioned habit of speech.

*c***1050** *O.E. Chron.* an. 1040 (MS. C), Swiðe strang ȝyld, þ man hit uneaðe acom, þ wæs viii marc æt ha. *a***1200** *Moral Ode* 296 Ȝut hi bud a wurse stede on þere helle grunde ne sculle hi neure comen vp for marke ne for punde. **1297** R. GLOUC. (Rolls) 8084 He..borewede þer uppe of him an hondred þousend marc. *c***1386** CHAUCER *Pard. T.* 62 By this gaude have I wonne, yeer by yeer, An hundred mark sith I was Pardoner. *a***1400** *Octouian* 889 That wyf hym taught markes and poundes; He purueyde haukes and houndys. *c***1412** HOCCLEVE *De Reg. Princ.* 1224, Vj marc yeerly, to scars is to sustene The charges þat I haue. **1526** SKELTON *Magnyf.* 1121 In my purse was twenty marke. *a***1529** —— *Col. Cloute* 729 His benefyce worthe ten pounde, Or skante worth twenty marke. **1542** RECORDE *Gr. Artes* (1575) 198 Poundes, Markes, and shillings, whiche though they haue no coynes, yet is there no name more in vse than they. **1607** NORDEN *Surv. Dial.* IV. 173 Thirteene shillings and foure pence, or a Marke of money. **1652** *Plymouth Col. Rec.* (1855) III. 12 Leiftenant Samuell Nash..is to haue for his wages 20 marke p. annum. **1712** ADDISON *Spect.* No. 269 ¶5, I.. have deposited with him thirty Marks, to be distributed among his poor Parishioners. **1771** *Gentl. Mag.* XLI. 82 On the 28th of November 1770, the defendant was brought up for judgment... The judgment of the Court was, to pay ten marks (*i.e.* 6*l.* 13*s.* 4*d.*) to the King.

b. In Scotland, the value of the mark was lowered proportionately with that of the shilling and penny, so that it represented 13*s.* 4*d.* Scots, reckoned as = 13$\frac{1}{3}$*d.* English. †***mark mark like*** Sc. [after MDu. *mark markgelike*]: mark for mark, in the same proportion.

1480 *Acta Dom. Concil.* (1839) 72/2 þat the saides Macolme & Arthure sall pay in like proporcioune of þe said annuel, efferand to þe part of þe land þat ather of þaim has, mark mark lyke, comptand be þe eld extent. **1482** *Bond* in *Thanes Cawdor* (Spalding Cl.) 66 Fyw hundreth merkis of the usualle money of Scotlande. **1639** DRUMM. OF HAWTH. *Consid. to Parlt.* Wks. (1711) 187 Under the pain of ten merks. **1710** *Agreement in Family of Rose of Kilravock* (Spalding Cl.) 401 Ane contract of wodseate..seting and resing the tenents at tuo thusand merk per chalder of free rent. **1858** M. PORTEOUS *Souter Johnny, To Burns* 33 'Twill cost some fowks twal hunner merk, Or aiblins near.

c. Representing the various continental forms of the same word, as a name of foreign moneys of account. ***mark banco*** (Hamburg): see BANCO. ***mark Lubish, Lubs***: see LUBISH *a.*

1475 *Bk. Noblesse* (Roxb.) 32 Lifelode of londes and tenementis yoven in the counte of Mayne to the yerely valeu of .x.M^l. marcs yerely, whiche was .lx.M^l.li. Turneis. **1523** LD. BERNERS *Froiss.* I. xiv. 14 The kyng..dyd gyue hym cccc. markis. *Ibid.*, The kyng..dyd gyue to Philip of

Chastaulxe, his chef esquyer,..C. marke of rent yerely. **1753** Hanway *Trav.* (1762) II. I. iii. 17 They [Hamburg traders] keep their accounts in marks and schillings, sixteen schillings to a mark. **1902** *Encycl. Brit.* XXXI. 289/2 The first reform in the coinage of the German Empire occurred in 1871, when the new gold money was introduced, which had for its unit the silver mark (a money of account) of 100 pfennigs.

3. *Shetland.* A denomination of land, from the feu duty formerly paid to the superior.

1774 G. Gifford in G. Low *Orkney* (1879) 145 The term Pennyland..in Schetland..marks the quality, and according to the value of the land, every Mark contains more or fewer Pennies. **1793** *Statist. Acc. Scotl.* V. 195 *note*, In some instances, a merk may be less than an acre; in others, perhaps, equal to two acres. **1884** *Scotsman* 26 July 3/1 (Shetland Advt.) Three Merks, One Ure and One-Third of an Ure of Land.

4. As the name of a coin. (Never so used with reference to English coinage.)

a. In Scotland, a coin of the value of 13*s.* 4*d.* Scots (see 2 b). ***half-mark***: a coin of the value of 6*s.* 8*d.* Scots. *Obs.* exc. *Hist.*

1480 *Acta Dom. Concil.* (1839) 74/1, v marcis scotis for ilk pund grete. **1570–1** *Reg. Privy Council Scotl.* XIV. 89 Ane silver penny to have course and passage for xiijs. iiijd. of this realme, to be callit the merk peice, and the half of the same for vjs. viiid., to be callit the halff merk peice.

b. Used to represent its etymological equivalents in various foreign languages, as the name of various copper and silver coins current at various times on the Continent, esp. a silver coin of the German Empire first issued in 1875, containing 77·16 grains troy, and worth slightly less than the English shilling. Now the name of the unit of German currency.

1727–52 Chambers *Cycl.* s.v., Mark is a copper-coin in Sweden, equal to two-pence farthing sterling. **1839** *Penny Cycl.* XV. 324/2 *Mark*, a silver coin in Hamburg... The mark is worth 1s. 2¾d. **1883** *Encycl. Brit.* XVI. 732 *note*, The substitution of the mark for the older thaler came into force [in Germany] 1st January 1875. **1911** E. Sykes *Banking & Currency* (ed. 3) viii. 61 The Imperial Bank of Germany can issue notes to the value of 550,000,000 marks against the deposit of securities. **1932** J. W. Angell *Recovery of Germany* (rev. ed.) ii. 19 Mark prices fell... In..1921..two things happened which definitely sealed the fate of the old mark currency. *Ibid.* 21 Everyone who was unfortunate enough to possess mark currency was in danger of having it lose half its value in his pocket overnight. *Ibid.* 56 The mark notes, bank deposits, and securities became practically worthless. **1933** E. Roll *Spotlight on Germany* i. 39 The function of the mark as a medium of exchange had disappeared almost as completely as its ability to form a standard of value. *Ibid.* 41 The mark was finally stabilized at one million-millionth of its pre-war value. **1964** M. McLuhan *Understanding Media* (1967) II. xiv. 156 The depreciation of the citizen went along with that of the German mark.

†**5.** *attrib.*: **mark pound, weight** (see quots.).

1576–77 *Reg. Privy Council Scotl.* II. 601 Deduceing onelie for his panis sex schillingis for the merk wecht. **1706** Phillips (ed. Kersey), *Mark-weight*, a foreign weight commonly of 8 Ounces; and *Mark-Pound* is two such Marks, or 16 Ounces. **1902** D. Macleane *Coronation* 123 [The oblation of] A 'Purse of Gold' was, until Victoria, 'a Mark weight of gold'—i.e. 8 ounces troy.

mark (mɑːk), *v.* Forms: 1 (**mærcian, mearcian,** *Northumb.* **merciȝa**), 2 **merki, markian,** 3 **mærcen,** 3–5 **merke,** 3–7 **marke,** 4 **merkke,** 4–6 **merk,** 5 **marc, mirk, mork,** 6 **merck,** 6–7 **marck(e,** 4– **mark.** [OE. *mearcian* = OFris. *merkia*, OS. *markon*, *gimarkon* to destine, appoint, observe, remark (MDu. *marken, merken* to set a mark on, to observe, Du. *merken* to set a mark on), OHG. *marchôn* to limit, plan out, destine (mod.G. as new-formation *marken* to set a mark in, stamp), ON. *marka* to draw the outline of, put a mark on, observe:—OTeut. **markôjan*, f. **markâ* Mark *sb.*[1] A parallel formation from the sb. (OTeut. **markjôn*) appears in OHG., MHG. *merchen, merken* (mod.G. *merken*), ON. *merkja* (Sw. *märka*, Da. *merke*). The Rom. langs. have a corresponding formation from the adopted sb.: F. *marquer* (which is the source of some of the uses of the Eng. vb.), Pr., Sp., Pg. *marcar*, It. *marcare*.]

I. To put a mark upon.

1. *trans.* To trace out boundaries for; to plot out (ground); to set out the ground plan of (a building); *fig.* to plan out, design. **a.** *simply.* (Now only *fig.* in poetic use.)

c **888** K. Ælfred *Boeth.* xxxix. §6 Ælc cræfteȝa ðencð & mearcað his weorc on his mode ær ær he hit wyrce. *c* **1000** Ælfric *Deut.* i. 33 Se mearcode þa stowa þe [Vulg. *metatus est locum, in quo*] ȝe eowre ȝeteld on slean sceoldon. *a* **1225** *St. Marher.* 20 þu wisest wruhte of alle, markedest eorðe, þu stores mon of sea stream, þu wissent ant weldent of alle wihtes. **1297** R. Glouc. (Rolls) 2500 In an harde rochi stede is þuong aboute he drow & þer wiþinne al to is wille Markede place inou & rerde þer an castel. *c* **1384** Chaucer *H. Fame* III. 13 If..thou Wilt helpe me to schewe now That in myn hede y-marked is [etc.]. **1604** E. G[rimstone] *D'Acosta's Hist. Indies* IV. vi. 222 To note and marke the mine, and so much ground in circuite for him, which the Lawe graunts.. those that discover any mine. **1747** P. Francis *Hor. Sat.* I. i. 140 Some certain mean in all things may be found, To mark our virtues, and our vices bound. **1844** [see Idea *sb.* 2].

b. with *out.*

1611 Bible *Isa.* xliv. 13 The carpenter stretcheth out his rule:..he marketh it out with the compasse, and maketh it after the figure of a man. **1769** Goldsm. *Hist. Rome* (1786) I. 411 This extraordinary man [J. Cæsar]..had, from the beginning of his life, marked out a way to universal empire. **1842** Borrow *Bible in Spain* xxx. (Pelh. Libr.) 218 To ascend the mountain, where, no doubt, he has been marking out a camp. **1879** Browning *Martin Relph* 78 And all that time stood Rosamund Page..Bandaged about, on the turf marked out for the party's firing-place. **1890** 'R. Boldrewood' *Miner's Right* v. 52 The Major and I..are on our way to mark out that very claim.

†**c.** *poet.* in alliterative phrases: To fashion, frame. *Obs.*

c **1400** *Destr. Troy* 4286 For hom wit lacket Of þe Godhed giffen, þat grew from the sun, þat all mightyle made & merket of noght. **14..** *Siege Jerus.* 112 þe þridde in heuen myd hem is þe holy goste, Neþer merked ne made bot mene fram hem passyþ. *c* **1420** *Sir Amadace* (Camden) lvii, The fayrist knyȝte, That euyr ȝette I see with syȝte, Sethen I was market mon. *c* **1460** *Towneley Myst.* xix. 3 God, that mayde both more and les,..And merkyd man to his lyknes.

†**d.** To fix the position of; to set or place (in a particular situation). *Obs.*

13.. *E. E. Allit. P.* A. 142 By-ȝonde þe broke..I hope[de] þat mote merked wore. *Ibid.* B. 637 Messez of mylke he merkkez bytwene.

2. a. To make a mark or marks on (anything) as by drawing, stamping, impressing, applying, cutting, or the like.

a **1035** *Laws of Canute* II. c. 32 (Schmid) Gif þeowman æt þam ordale ful weorðe, mearcie man hine æt þam forman cyrre. *c* **1175** *Lamb. Hom.* 87 God het Moyses.. þet heo sculden..merki mid þan blode hore duren. *a* **1300** *Cursor M.* 21698 To tuelue men taght þai wandes tuelue, Ilkan merked his him-self. *c* **1420** *Pallad. on Husb.* II. 401 Nowe is tyme..The lambis and the beestis more & lesse To marke. ? **1466** Sir J. Paston in *P. Lett.* II. 293 Ther is on potte that is morkyn ondre the bottome ij tymes with thyes letteris M.P. **1483** Caxton *Gold. Leg.* 431 b/1 He was marked or tokened on the lyppes of hym with an hote and brennyng yron. *c* **1490** —— *Rule St. Benet* (E.E.T.S.) 136 Yf that he can not write & marke it with his owne sygne. **1523** Fitzherb. *Husb.* §52 Se that they [the sheep] be well marked. **1560** Daus tr. *Sleidane's Comm.* 80 b, The byshoppes ministers are wont to marke mens foreheades with Asshes. **1611** Shaks. *Cymb.* III. iii. 56 My bodie's mark'd With Roman Swords. **1682** *True Protest. Mercury* No. 105. 2/2 He stole a Silver Tankard, marked I. F. **1712–13** Swift *Jrnl. to Stella* 22 Feb., Miss is recovering [from the small-pox]. I know not how much she will be marked. **1844** Halliwell *Octavian* (Percy Soc.) Pref. 11 In the Cambridge manuscript, now marked Ff. ii. 38, his name is spelt Octavyan. **1868** Dickens *Uncomm. Trav.* xvii, The Guard comes clambering round to mark the tickets.

absol. **14..** *Debate Carpenter's Tools* in Halliw. *Nugæ Poet.* 15 'ȝe, ȝe', seyd the lyne and the chalke..'I schall merke upone the wode And kepe his mesures trew and gode'. *Mod.* This pencil won't mark.

b. *spec.* †(*a*) To embroider (*obs.*); (*b*) To place an identifying mark on linen or other household furniture by means of embroidery or stitching, or with marking-ink.

c **1400** *Emare* 386 She tawghte hem to sewe and marke all maner of sylkyn werke. **1530** Palsgr. 633/1 All my thynges be marked with this marke. **1704** *Lond. Gaz.* No. 3981/4 Handkerchiefs, marked with W. **1713** *Rules Lambeth Girls' Sch.* v. in *N. & Q.* (1902) 9th Ser. X. 256/2 They are to be taught to Read, Write, Spin, Knit and Sew and Mark. **1888** J. Payn *Myst. Mirbridge* xvii. II. 17 We are marking the house linen. **1890** Sarah Tytler *Jean Keir* 42 She marked their handkerchiefs.

c. *Comm.* To attach to (an article) figures or signs indicating the price. ***to mark down***: to label (goods) with a lower figure; to reduce the indicated price of (anything); hence ***marked-down*** ppl. adj., also *ellipt.* as *sb.*; cf. Mark-down *sb.*; ***to mark up***: to label (goods) with a higher price; to raise in price.

1859 *N.Y. Herald* 5 Jan. (Advt.), Mark every article Way Way Way down To some price which will make it..Sell and go quick. **1870** *Amer. Naturalist* III. 3 The prices of venison and other game was so far 'marked up' that gold..was charged for salmon. **1894** *Daily Tel.* 16 Jan. 5/7 All seaborne qualities [of coal] were marked down 3*s.* per ton. **1896** Howells *Impressions & Exp.* 53 She was dressed in a.. ready-made suit, which somehow suggested itself as having been 'marked down'. *Mod. Advt.* All goods are marked in plain figures. **1902** G. H. Lorimer *Lett. Merchant* iv. 52 The clerks all knocked off their regular work and started in to mark up prices. **1908** *Sat. Even. Post* 24 Oct. 13/1 At another store there is a marked-down sale of parasols. **1910** 'Saki' *Reginald in Russia* 43 They have turned instead to the muddy lanes and cheap villas and the marked-down ills of life. **1913** F. H. Burnett *T. Tembarom* vi. 67 A remnant of crimson stuff secured from a miscellaneous heap at a marked-down sale at a department store. **1923** E. O'Neill *Moon of Caribbees* 18 Don't you boys forget to mark down cigarettes or tobacco or fruit, remember! Three shillin's is the price. **1942** M. Schlauch *Gift of Tongues* (1943) vi. 135 'Marked-downs' (overheard in a department store for 'reduced dresses'). **1962** E. Godfrey *Retail Selling & Organization* xvi. 164 A minority of firms..have abandoned them [*sc.* fixed profit margins] in favour of marking-up each item on its merits. **1965** A. Christie *At Bertram's Hotel* xii. 113 She also availed herself of some marked down lines in furnishing fabrics. **1974** *Times* 22 Oct. 12/6 Exclusive goods can be marked up to carry a full, and I suspect..very high, profit margin.

d. *pass.* To have or bear natural marks. Also *fig.*

c **1400** *Destr. Troy* 5477 His kyngdom was clene clustrit with hilles, All merkyd with mounteyns, & with mayn hylles. **1600** *Maydes Metamorph.* v. i. 127 Is not this hard luck to wander so long, And in the end to finde his wife markt wrong. [She has been transformed into a man.] **1697** Dryden *Virg. Georg.* IV. 150 The better Brood, unlike the Bastard Crew, Are mark'd with Royal Streaks of shining Hue. **1855** W. S. Dallas in *Syst. Nat. Hist.* I. 387 The species of the genus *Argynnis*..are elegantly marked with silvery spots.

e. ***to mark off*** (Engin. and Shipbuilding): to mark (an object) with lines to serve as a guide for subsequent cutting, machining, alignment, etc.; to represent (a dimension or detail) on an object in this way.

1894 W. J. Lineham *Text-bk. Mech. Engin.* vi. 185 If the work is too large to mark-off on a table it should be levelled, and all lines be drawn by reference to an ideal horizontal or vertical plane. **1895** J. Donaldson *Drawing & Rough Sketching for Marine Engineers* (ed. 6) 87 When the forging of a crank shaft, or other part of an engine, is delivered..it is essential..that it be accurately marked off for machining. *Ibid.*, The throw of the vertical crank is marked off from the horizontal line. **1925** F. J. Drover *Marine Engin. Repairs* xix. 120 The cheeks are marked off for thickness. **1966** J. H. Dixon tr. *Dormidontov's Shipbuilding Technol.* i. 15 Hull details are marked off from the full-size or scaled down lofting data and from working drawings. *Ibid.* vi. 127 When the metal is being marked off, the outlines of the components are drawn full size, with an indication of the allowances and tolerances for machining.

f. To mark the ears of (a lamb, or less commonly a calf); also, to dock and geld. Cf. Marking *vbl. sb.* 1 c. *Austral.* and *N.Z.*

1933 *Press* (Christchurch, N.Z.) 4 Nov. 15/7 *Mark*, to ear-mark. Now a frequent euphemism for *cut and tail.* **1941** Baker *Dict. Austral. Slang* 46 *Mark*,..to geld lambs. **1950** *N.Z. Jrnl. Agric.* Sept. 197/1 Lambs are usually marked at between 1 to 6 weeks of age; 3 weeks is probably the ideal age.

3. To form or portray by making marks.

1390 Gower *Conf.* III. 123 The nynthe Signe..Is cleped Sagittarius, The whos figure is marked thus, A Monstre with a bowe on honde. *c* **1391** Chaucer *Astrol.* I. §12 Next the forseide Cercle of the Abc., under the cros-lyne, is marked the scale. *a* **1400–50** *Alexander* 2636 He cled him all in clene stele a conyschaunce ouire, þat made was & merkid on þe messedone armes. **1687** A. Lovell tr. *Thevenot's Trav.* I. 201 They'll have this to be the Figure of St. Jerome, which God was pleased should be marked upon that Stone, because of the great love he had for that place.

†**4.** Used to render L. *signāre* 'to seal'. *Obs.*

c **950** *Lindisf. Gosp.* Matt. xxvii. 66 *Signantes lapidem*, mercande ðone stan. **1382** Wyclif *John* iii. 33 He that hath takun his witnessing, hath markid that God is sothfast.

†**5.** To make with the hand (the sign of the cross); to make the sign of the cross upon (one's breast, etc.), to 'cross' (oneself). Also, to invest (a person) with the sign of the cross in token of his joining a crusade. *Obs.*

c **1175** *Lamb. Hom.* 127 Vppon heom alswa we er seiden we sculen markian þet tacne of þere halie rode. **1303** R. Brunne *Handl. Synne* 7848 þe bedde, ne hym, ne durst þey touche, So had he marked hym with þe crouche. *a* **1330** *Otuel* 891 þei markeden hem alle þre, To him þat þolede dep on tre. *c* **1440** *Alph. Tales* 80 þan þis holie man sayd vnto hym; 'Bruther, Cros & mark þi harte! what is þat att þou spekis vnto þi selfe?' **1460** Capgrave *Chron.* (Rolls) 155 Herry [III] was merkyd with the tokne of the Holy Crosse, for to go to Jerusalem. *c* **1550** *Battle of Otterburn* xliv. in Child *Ballads* III. 297 Euery man thynke on hys trewe-love, And marke hym to the Trenite. **1577** in Picton *L'pool Munic. Rec.* (1883) I. 49 First of all he did mark himself unto God.

6. *fig.* **a.** To designate as if by placing a mark upon; to destine. Const. *for*, †*to, down, to* and inf. †Also with complement, to designate as being (so and so). (*Obs.*)

a **1000** *Cædmon's Gen.* 459 (Gr.) þa him to ȝingran self metod mancynnes mearcode selfa. **1362** Langl. *P. Pl.* A. xi. 253, I was markid withoute mercy & myn name entrid In þe legende of lif longe er I were. *c* **1400** *Destr. Troy* 12136 My maydynhed I merk to myghtifull goddis. *c* **1440** *York Myst.* xvii. 257 Hayll! þou marc us þi men and make vs in mynde. **1566** Clough in Burgon *Life Gresham* (1839) II. 168 Some that were his friends bade hym gett hym awaye for that he was markyd: wheruppon he went home, and went to his bed. **1590** Marlowe *Edw. II*, III. ii, A boy..Thou art not markt to manie daies on earth. **1596** Shaks. *1 Hen. IV*, III. i. 41 These signes haue markt me extraordinarie. **1599** —— *Hen. V*, IV. iii. 20 If we are markt to die, we are enow To doe our Countrey losse. **1638** Quarles *Hieroglyph.* i. 46 Ere he had life, estated in his Vrne, And markt for death. **1750** Gray *Elegy* Epit. 4 Melancholy mark'd him for her own. **1856** Froude *Hist. Eng.* (1858) I. iii. 265 The persons whom he named..became marked at once for persecution. **1871** Freeman *Norm. Conq.* (1876) IV. xviii. 154 The high ground..which William's keen eye would at the first glance mark as the site of the future castle. **1892** Kipling *Barrack-r. Ballads, Cleared* vi, They never marked a man for death.. They only said 'intimidate'. **1894** 'R. Andom' *We Three & Troddles* xxii. 210 The demon dyspepsia had marked him down.

b. with *out.*

c **1400** *York Myst.* xxx. 519 And þerfore, to go with yone gest, Yhe marke vs out of þe manliest men. **1706** E. Ward *Wooden World Diss.* (1708) 20 That lucky Youth is certainly mark'd out for a Commission. **1818** Cruise *Digest* (ed. 2) III. 345 The law will not pass him over, and marks him out, *in rei exemplum et infamiam.* **1853** Lytton *My Novel* III. xxiv, Suspected persons were naturally marked out by Mr. Stirn, and reported to his employer. **1862** Stanley *Jew. Ch.* (1877) I. xviii. 338 The little mantle..had from his earliest years marked him out as an almost royal personage. **1871** Freeman *Norm. Conq.* (1876) IV. xviii. 241 The men of Durham, who had been marked out for the slaughter. **1893** Traill *Social Eng.* Introd. 48 The country..which had been marked out by destiny to become the greatest manufacturer in the world.

†**c.** To mete out, allot, apportion. (Chiefly in alliteration with *meed.*) Const. *dat. Obs. poet.*

1340–70 *Alisaunder* 284 Hee . . swore swiftliche his othe . . too merken hem care. *Ibid.* 497 With menne of Mesopotame to mark þe teene. *c* **1375** *Cursor M.* 272 (Fairf.) Mirþ he merkis mon to mede. **1377** LANGL. *P. Pl.* B. XII. 186 Wo was hym marked that wade mote with the lewed! *c* **1400** *Rule St. Benet* 66/678 He til vs merkes slik mede. *c* **1460** *Towneley Myst.* xx. 630 He shall no more hym godys son call. We shall marke hym truly his mede. *c* **1470** *Gol. & Gaw.* 807 Yone berne in the battale wil ye noght forbere, For al the mobil on the mold, merkit to meid.

d. To separate *from* something else as by drawing a boundary line or imposing a distinctive mark. Now chiefly with *off*. Also with *out from*.

1703 ROWE *Ulyss.* IV. i. 1532 This Night . . Mark'd from the rest of the Revolving Year, And set apart. **1792** CHARLOTTE SMITH *Desmond* I. 63 Amiable people of rank . . who are no longer marked by their titles from that canaille with which [etc.]. **1869** TOZER *Highl. Turkey* II. 264 The Popular Tale is thus marked off by features of its own from ordinary stories. **1871** G. MEREDITH *H. Richmond* lvi, I know that this possession of hers [her courage], which identifies her and marks her from the rest of us, would bear the ordeal of fire. **1877** tr. *Tiele's Hist. Relig.* 16 He marks off the Semites from them very decidedly. **1888** MRS. H. WARD *R. Elsmere* I. viii. 222 The even gentleness which always marked her out from others. *Ibid.* III. xxxii. 34 The reasoning faculty . . which marks us out from the animal. **1905** T. E. HARVEY *Rise of Quakers* ii. 10 Her son's serious ways, by which he was marked out from his other brothers and sisters.

7. To express or indicate by marks or signs.

a. † To indicate in writing, note. *Obs.* Also, to indicate or represent by symbolic marks.

a **1000** *Phœnix* 333 Weras . . mearciað on marm-stane hwonne se dæᵹ and seo tid dryhtum ᵹeeawe frætwe flyht-hwates. *a* **1225** *Ancr. R.* 42 þeo ureisuns þet ich nabbe bute imerked beoð iwriten oueral. *c* **1374** CHAUCER *Boeth.* II. met. vii. 47 (Camb. MS.) What is now brutus or stierne catoun? The thynne fame yit lastinge of hir ydel names is marked with a fewe letterys. *c* **1380** WYCLIF *Wks.* (1880) 387 þai wer not constrenyd be nede for to begge; as grete clerkis merken vp-on þis worde of þe gospelle where criste saiþ þus: 'When þu makist þine feeste, þat is', of almes, 'calle pore, feble, lame & blynde'. **1387** TREVISA *Higden* (Rolls) I. 41 Wherfore in þis book I schal marke as I may how and in what ȝeres such defautes fille. *a* **1794** GIBBON *Autobiog.* (1896) 257 After marking the date . . the manuscript was deposited in my bureau. **1879** PEROWNE in *Expositor* IX. 411 He draws the chart and marks the sunken reefs. **1890** H. SWEET *Prim. Spoken Eng.* 3 If a word has two strong stresses . . both must be marked.

b. In games: To record (the points gained by the players). Chiefly *absol.* and in phr. ***to mark the game***.

1816 SINGER *Playing Cards* 239 If he cannot answer him by shewing the third of them, he who asks the question marks five points. **1861** WHYTE MELVILLE *Good for N.* I. 154 John Gordon good-naturedly proposed a [billiard] match with the young lady, if Miss Jones would come and 'mark'. **1870** 'CAVENDISH' *Game of Bézique* 21 Eleven counters are required by each player—one large round one that marks 500 [etc.]. **1886** *Euchre: how to play it* 108 *Marking the Game*, counting.

c. *colloq.* ***to mark up***: to add (an item) to a tavern score; hence, to give credit for; = CHALK *v.* 3 b.

1899 *Tit-Bits* 22 July 322/1, I shaved a gentleman who asked me to mark it up.

d. *absol.* Of a horse: To indicate its age by 'mark of mouth'.

1842 C. W. JOHNSON *Farmer's Encycl.* s.v., A horse . . is said to *mark* when he shows his age by a black spot . . which appears at about five and a half years old, in the cavities of the corner-teeth, and is gone when he is eight years old.

e. Of a graduated instrument: To show, 'register' (so many degrees, etc.).

1882 FLOYER *Unexpl. Baluchistan* 179 The barometer marked 27·265, being about 3,540 feet.

f. ***to mark down***: to make a note of; to set down in writing; ***to mark up***, to correct or annotate (copy or proofs) for typesetting, printing, etc., esp. by making copy-preparation or proof-reading marks; also, to gloss.

1881 J. FOTHERGILL *Kith & Kin* II. ix. 241 More than one matron then present had silently marked him down . . in her book of 'eligibles'. **1936** *Discovery* May 145/1 An exhaustive search was not feasible, but 51 nightingales were marked down in Devon. **1973** A. DAVIS *Graphics* iii. 74 When he is marking-up an article for a publication of established format, its title, followed by the words 'Usual style', may give all the guidance the printer needs. **1973** S. JENNET *Making of Books* (ed. 5) v. 92 Hard copy may be read as a proof by the printer's reader . ., and marked up in the usual way. **1978** *Hart's Rules for Compositors & Readers* (ed. 38) 34 The marks should also be used by copy-editors in marking up copy. **1984** *N.Y. Times* 14 Feb. C13/3 Miss Whitelaw marks up her copy of a Beckett manuscript with brief, sometimes cryptic remarks.

g. In phr. ***to mark (someone's) card*** [CARD *sb.*² 6 e]: (from the practice in horse-racing) to provide (someone) with information; to tip (someone) off; to 'put (someone) right'. *slang.*

1961 PARTRIDGE *Dict. Slang* Suppl. 1179/2 *Mark (someone's) card*, to give him the information he needs; to put him right: barrow-boys': since ca. 1945. Ex the race-course. **1962** R. COOK *Crust on its Uppers* ii. 34 They'd marked my card there was a new dance-hall been opened over at Peckham. **1970** P. LAURIE *Scotland Yard* 291 *Mark X's cards, to*, to brief X discreetly. **1970** G. F. NEWMAN *Sir, You Bastard* 282 The third was to phone the insurance assessor and mark his card.

8. In immaterial sense:

a. To make perceptible or recognizable, by some sign or indication. **b.** To manifest, 'testify' (one's approval, displeasure, etc.) by some significant act, or by reward or punishment. (Now only with obj. qualified by possessive.) †Also, with clause as obj.: To indicate by action.

a. 1904 *Grove's Dict. Mus.* I. 18/1 The famous instrumentalists of the classical school . . were accustomed to mark the natural accent . . by a hardly perceptible prolongation of the first note of the bar.

b. 1791 *Duchess of York* II. 91 The King continued to mark the same degree of favor to him as ever. **1807** C. SIMEON in Carus *Mem. & Life* (1847) ix. 227 Unless God, by a special interposition of his Providence, . . mark his own will respecting it. **1808** SCOTT *Marm.* VI. xxvii, Eustace . . A look and sign to Clara cast, To mark he would return. **1863** MRS. GASKELL *Sylvia's Lovers* xliii, She dusted a chair . . for Sylvia, sitting down herself on a three-legged stool to mark her sense of the difference in their conditions.

9. To be a mark of or upon. **a.** To be an indication of the position or course of.

1687 A. LOVELL tr. *Thevenot's Trav.* I. 265 Pillars . . are put there to mark the way, because it is a Desart. **1697** DRYDEN *Virg. Georg.* I. 486 The Sov'reign of the Heav'ns has set on high The Moon, to mark the Changes of the Sky. **1762** FALCONER *Shipwreck* (1796) I. 164 Eternal powers! What ruins from afar Mark the fell track of desolating war. **1770** ? LOGAN *Cuckoo* ii, Hast thou a star to guide thy path Or mark the rolling year? **1823** F. CLISSOLD *Ascent Mt. Blanc* 23 A circle of thin haze . . marked dimly the limits between heaven and earth. **1860** TYNDALL *Glac.* I. xxvii. 209 A withered pine on the opposite mountain marking the other terminus. **1868** M. ARNOLD *Sch. & Univ. Cont.* 154 Wolf's coming to Halle in 1783 . . marks an era [etc.]. **1869** TOZER *Highl. Turkey* I. 36 The Bunarbashi river, which is marked at first by the plantation at its source, and afterwards by the green marshes which fringe its sides. **1878** BROWNING *La Saisiaz* 17 Where the blue lake's wrinkle marks the river's inrush pale.

b. *pass.* Of lines, features, etc.: To be (more or less) strikingly noticeable. Chiefly with adverbs. (Cf. MARKED *ppl. a.*)

1824 MACAULAY *Mitford's Hist. Greece* Misc. Writ. 1860 I. 156 The line of demarcation between good and bad men is so faintly marked as often to elude the most careful investigation. **1850** LEITCH tr. *C. O. Müller's Anc. Art* §204 (ed. 2) 193 The wrinkles about the eyes and mouth [are] strongly marked. **1860** TYNDALL *Glac.* II. x. 280 The junction between it and its neighbours is plainly marked.

c. To be a distinguishing mark or character of (a person, etc.); to be a noteworthy feature or attendant circumstance of (an action, incident). Often *pass.*, to be characterized, distinguished, or made remarkable (now only const. *by*).

a **1661** FULLER *Worthies* (1662) I. *Essex* 334 They being mark'd alike in their poeticall parts [etc.]. **1791** BOSWELL *Johnson* an. 1744 His [Savage's] character was marked by profligacy, insolence, and ingratitude. **1863** FR. A. KEMBLE *Resid. in Georgia* (N.Y. ed.) 246 To-day . . my visit to the Infirmary was marked by an event which has not occurred before—the death of one of the poor slaves while I was there. **1863** COWDEN CLARKE *Shaks. Char.* x. 253 No triumph—no exultation . . marks her manner. **1874** GREEN *Short Hist.* ii. §1. 62 The long internal tranquillity which marked the rule of our foreign masters. **1878** MACLEAR *Celts* ii. (1879) 20 Solemn ceremonies marked the gathering of the plant.

d. To diversify, be a landmark upon.

1830 TENNYSON *Mariana* 43 For leagues no other tree did mark The level waste, the rounding gray.

10. *Mil.* **a.** To indicate the pivots, formations, etc. in military evolutions.

1796 *Instr. & Reg. Cavalry* (1813) 160 Its adjutant and those of the regiments standing to its left . . will mark each his own left, the adjutants of the regiments to its right . . will mark each its own right [etc.]. **1889** *Infantry Drill* 88 If the horses are unsteady, they [the officers] must dismount and mark the points on foot. *Ibid.* 186 The assistant adjutants-general of the base division will mark the point of appui, and assistant adjutants-general will mark the distant points for their respective divisions.

b. ***to mark time***: to move the feet as in marching but without advancing. Also *transf.* and *fig.*

1833 *Regul. Instr. Cavalry* I. 17 On the word *Mark Time*, the foot then advancing completes its pace, after which the cadence is continued, without gaining any ground. **1837** MACAULAY *Ess.*, *Bacon* (ed. Montague) II. 200 The human mind accordingly, instead of marching, merely marked time. **1903** F. W. H. MYERS *Hum. Personality* II. 296 The Agnostic's appeal to us to halt and mark time.

II. To direct one's course or aim.

†**11.** To direct (one's way). Also *refl.* and *intr.*, to proceed, advance. *Obs.*

c **1205** LAY. 5642 þa cnihtes weoren wise . . and heom markede forð, touward Munt-giu heo ferden. *Ibid.* 26309 Forð þa eorles wenden . . and mærcoden enne wæi þe ouer anne munte læi. *c* **1375** *Sc. Leg. Saints* xvi. (*Magdalena*) 784 Scho til wildirnes has socht, . . & yddir ewinely can hyr mark. ? *a* **1400** *Morte Arth.* 3595 Nowe bownes the bolde kynge with [his] beste knyghtes, . . Merkes ouer the mowntaynes fulle mervaylous wayes. **14..** *Henryson's Twa Myss* 195 in *Bannatyne MS.* (1881) 965 Quhen scho was furth and fre, scho . . mirrely mirkit vnto the mvre. **1500–20** DUNBAR *Poems* lxxi. 20 Oft thow hes refusit Till cum ws till, or ȝit till merk ws neir. **1513** DOUGLAS *Æneis* Exclamacioun 1 Now throw the deip fast to the port I mark. **1596** DALRYMPLE tr. *Leslie's Hist. Scot.* x. 406 The Quene hard this ansuer, quhilk quhen scho hard, she markes to Dunbar.

†**12. a.** To aim a blow or missile at; to strike, hit.

13.. *Gaw. & Gr. Knt.* 1592 þe mon merkkez hym wel, as þay mette fyrst, . . Hit hym vp to þe hult. **1399** LANGL. *Rich. Redeles* III. 268 Rewlers of rewmes . . Were not yffoundid . . To leue al at likynge . . But to laboure on þe lawe . . And to merke meyntenourz with maces. ? *a* **1400** *Morte Arth.* 2206 He merkes thurghe the maylez the myddes in sondyre. *a* **1400** *Pistill of Susan* 320 He [an Angel] haþ brandist his brond brennynde so briȝt. To Marke þi middel at a Mase in more þen in þre, No lese. *c* **1400** *Destr. Troy* 7327 He merkit hym in mydward the mydell in two, þat he felle to þe flat erthe. *c* **1402** LYDG. *Compl. Bl. Knt.* 462 Who that is an archer, and ys blend, Marketh nothing, but sheteth as he wend. **1513** DOUGLAS *Æneis* XII. v. 132 Of quham this dart hit ane . . at the myddill markyt hym full rycht. **1529** RASTELL *Pastyme* (1811) 172 One marked hym with a quarell and smote hym in the hede.

b. *intr.* To aim a blow. Const. *to*. Also *Sc.* to aim, intend *to do* something. *Obs.*

a **1400** *Sir Perc.* 2067 By then hys swerde owt he get, Strykes the geant withowttene lett, Merkes evene to his nekk. *c* **1400** *Destr. Troy* 7034 He merkit to Menestaus with a mayn dynt, þat he hurlit fro his horse to þe hard erthe. *c* **1470** HENRYSON *Mor. Fab.* v. *Parl. Beasts* xxxv, Of this meniye markand to get remeid. **1570** *Satir. Poems Reform.* xii. 76 Sen double murther markis to reule the rout. **1596** DALRYMPLE tr. *Leslie's Hist. Scot.* x. 399 Prepareng with al . . thair harte, the destructione of the Catholik and Romane Kirk, quhilk vttirlie tha mark to ouirthraw.

III. To notice or observe.

13. To notice or keep the eye upon (a person or material object); to observe; to watch.

1377 LANGL. *P. Pl.* B. XII. 132 Lyueres to-forn vs vseden to marke The selkouthes that thei seighen her sones for to teche. **1462** J. PASTON in *P. Lett.* II. 122 They ar morkyn well inowe, and so is John Bylyngforthe. **1530** PALSGR. 730/2 Mark hym whan he daunseth, you shall se hym springe lyke a yonckher. **1596** SPENSER *F.Q.* VI. ii. 5 Him stedfastly he markt, and saw to bee A goodly youth of amiable grace. **1667** MILTON *P.L.* XII. 50 God who oft descends to visit men Unseen, and through their habitations walks To mark their doings. **1711** BUDGELL *Spect.* No. 116 ¶5, I saw a Hare pop out . . I marked the Way she took. **1725** POPE *Odyss.* XVII. 448 Full well I mark'd the features of his face. **1757** FOOTE *Author* I. 12 He has not mark'd me yet. **1805** WORDSW. *Prelude* IV. 390 So near that . . I could mark him well, Myself unseen. **1810** SCOTT *Lady of L.* II. vi, While yet he loiter'd on the spot, It seemed as Ellen mark'd him not. **1832** DISRAELI *Contarini Fleming* II. III. v. 241, I looked up, I marked the tumultuous waving of many torches. **1849** C. BRONTË *Shirley* II. xii. 278 She smiled, well pleased to mark the delight of her pupil. **1860** THACKERAY *Four Georges* i, in *Cornh. Mag.* July 5 Lift up your glances respectfully, and mark him eyeing Madame de Fontanges. **1893** KIPLING *Many Inventions* p. viii, The children wise of outer skies Look hitherward and mark A light that shifts. **1901** G. B. SHAW *Caesar & Cleopatra* v. 199 Rufio, satisfied, nods at Cleopatra, mutely inviting her to mark that. **1922** C. BELL *Since Cézanne* 11 They babble in the Burlington Fine Arts Club—where nobody marks them. **1972** 'M. INNES' *Open House* II. xi. 99 He paused to mark this [*sc.* a compliment] going home.

14. To consider; to observe mentally, give heed or attention to. Often with *well*.

c **1430** LYDG. *Min. Poems* (Percy Soc.) 119 Marke this in yowre mynde. **1481** CAXTON *Reynard* (Arb.) 4 He muste . . ernestly and diligently marke wel that he redeth. **1529** *Supplic. to King* (E.E.T.S.) 36 Marke well what they purpose by this estatute. **1535** COVERDALE *Isa.* xxviii. 23 Take hede and heare my voyce, pondre and merck my wordes wel. **1591** SHAKS. *1 Hen. VI*, III. i. 153 And if your Grace marke every circumstance, You haue great reason to do Richard right. **1611** BIBLE *Ps.* xxxvii. 37 Marke the perfect man, and behold the vpright: for the end of that man is peace. **1788** MRS. HUGHES *Henry & Isabella* III. 30 They had marked a more than ordinary regard in his Lordship's behaviour to her. **1790** *Norman & Bertha* II. 166 She recollected the husband of her former attendant, . . and having marked him framed for villainies [etc.]. **1814** CARY *Dante, Paradise* II. 123 Mark me well. **1842** MIALL in *Nonconf.* II. 8 Another feature of the times is worth marking. **1865** KINGSLEY *Herew.* xxii, Mark my words, Sir Hereward, that cunning Frenchman will treat with them one by one.

15. *Sport.* **a.** *trans.* To note and keep in mind the spot to which (the game) has retired after having been 'put up'. Also ***to mark down***.

When pheasants or partridges are driven from cover, and are flying towards the guns, the beaters cry 'Mark—Over!'

c **1450** *Treat. Hawking* in *Rel. Ant.* I. 297 If she neme oon rewarde her apon here foule, then merke the covey and goo afore them somwhat. **1486** *Bk. St. Albans* b ij b, And go after yᵗ by laysour to the partrich that be marked and doo as I shall tell yow here folowyng. **1749** FIELDING *Tom Jones* III. ii, The birds flew into it, and were marked, (as it is called) by the two sportsmen. **1803** COL. HAWKER *Diary* (1893) I. 1 We marked the former [ducks] down. **1849** E. E. NAPIER *Excurs. S. Africa* II. 331 He now dashed . . up the opposite bank, having marked a second flock of oxen. **1864** *Cornh. Mag.* X. 840 It is no good to talk of having marked birds down, unless you have distinctly seen a certain toss up of the wings as they pitch. **1874** J. W. LONG *Amer. Wild-fowl Shooting* 154 Mark! Let them go over. I'll call them down. **1898** *Encycl. Sport* II. 92 *Mark down*, to keep in view or memory the spot at which the boar went to cover.

b. Of a hound: also *absol.*

1880 CARNEGIE *Pract. Trap.* 16 The dog marked when it tried the hole again. *Ibid.*, The dog still remained marking, so I went back. **1899** *Westm. Gaz.* 17 Nov. 2/2 A fox was then roused . . and hounds ran him . . finally marking to ground after a gallop lasting nearly half an hour.

c. *Football.* (See quot. 1897.)

1887 SHEARMAN *Athletics & Football* 317 When practicable he should mark the same man throughout the game, and when the ball is thrown he should always be on the alert. **1897** *Encycl. Sport* I. 429 (Football) *Marking a man*, keeping close to an opponent in order to hamper him if he should receive the ball. **1901** *Scotsman* 11 Mar. 4/8 The Scottish players . . marked the opposition too carefully to permit of their being very troublesome.

d. *Austral. Rules Football* (see quot. 1968). Cf. MARK *sb.*¹ 12 d.

1968 EAGLESON & MCKIE *Terminol. Austral. Nat. Football* II. 23 *Mark*, catch the ball on the full directly from

the kick of another player. **1969** *Sun-Herald* (Sydney) 13 July 48/1 Hudson marked 35 yards out, but a bad kick fell well short of the goal.

16. *absol.* or *intr.* To take notice; to keep watch; to fix (one's) attention; to consider. Sometimes followed by indirect question: To ascertain by observation (*what*, *whether*, etc.). Also, ***mark you*** (or ***me***, etc.); cf. *look you* s.v. LOOK *v.* 4 a.

1526 TINDALE *Luke* i. 36 And marke, thy cosen Elizabeth, hath also conceaved a sonne in her olde age. **1563** T. WILSON *Logike* (1580) 61 The aunswerer muste at the firste hearing of hys [opponent's] argument, marke whether it bee made accordyng to rules of Logique, or otherwise. *a* **1591** H. SMITH *Serm.* (1637) 309 You marked when your Master taught you your trade. **1596** SHAKS. *Merch. V.* IV. i. 313 O vpright Iudge, Marke Iew, o learned Iudge. **1611** BIBLE *1 Kings* xx. 7 Marke, I pray you, and see how this man seeketh mischiefe. **1669** STURMY *Mariner's Mag.* v. xii. 72 Mark diligently until the Plumb-Line..cut these assigned degrees ..that you are to Mount the Gun by. **1781** COWPER *Truth* 59 The self-applauding bird, the peacock see,—Mark what a sumptuous Pharisee is he! **1837** E. HOWARD *Old Commodore* I. v. [*sc.* vi] 210 Mark you me, Mr. Alsop, mark you me. We have done our duty, sir. **1862** MRS. H. WOOD *Channings* II. ix. 137 'Impudence,' shortly answered Yorke. 'Mark you, Miss Channing! I have not done with you.' **1867** A. J. EVANS *St. Elmo* xvii. 232 It remains to be seen whether a grand success is not destined to crown it. Mark you! The grapple is not quite over. **1875** BRYCE *Holy Rom. Emp.* i. (ed. 5) 3 We shall mark how the new religion, rising in the midst of a hostile power ends by embracing and transforming it. **1875** JOWETT *Plato* (ed. 2) I. 282 What they say is—mark, now, and see whether their words are true—they say that the soul of man is immortal. **1903** G. B. SHAW *Man & Superman* I. 23 For mark you, Tavy, the artist's work is to shew us ourselves as we really are. **1922** JOYCE *Ulysses* 139 It was the speech, mark you, the professor said, of a finished orator. *a* **1953** E. O'NEILL *Touch of Poet* (1957) III. 94 Provided, mark you, that you and your daughter sign an agreement I have drawn up. **1966** *Listener* 17 Feb. 240/1 Well, mark you, I wouldn't be the inveterate optimist I am, if I didn't live in the belief that the year of my life is yet to come.

mark, obs. form of MARQUE[1], MIRK.

markable ('mɑːkəb(ə)l), *a.* Also 7 **marckable, markeable.** [f. MARK *v.* + -ABLE.]

†**1.** Worthy or capable of being marked or noted; remarkable. *Obs.* [Cf. obs. F. *marquable* (16th c.).]

c **1449** PECOCK *Repr.* IV. iv. 447 Tho othere now seid bischopis, which thei made aftirward out of the noumbre of xij., as therto sowneth miche the processe, Acts ie. c̃., bi manie therto markable wordis. **1584** *Leycesters Commonw.* (1641) 11 Such a one..so markeable to the simplest subiect of this Land by the publique insignes of his tyrannous purpose. **1608** HIERON *Defence* II. xii. 162 Some speciall & markeable defectes in his plea. *a* **1645** HABINGTON *Surv. Worc.* in *Worc. Hist. Soc. Proc.* II. 155 And thease which maie seeme to some scarce worth the wrytynge, to a curious eye maye perhaps be marckable. **1651** *Raleigh's Ghost* 260 Men..illustrious and markable..for sanctity of life.

2. Capable of receiving a mark or imprint. *rare.*

1862 MRS. CROSLAND *Mrs. Blake* III. 288 He thought Emily Neville a beautiful name, and now all 'markable' gifts were so inscribed.

Hence †'**markably** *adv.*, remarkably.

1650 BULWER *Anthropomet.* 262 So markably uncertain and giddy-headed herein are we.

markal, variant of MERCAL *Sc. dial.*

Markan, var. MARCAN *a.*

markasit(e, obs. forms of MARCASITE.

mark-down ('mɑːkdaʊn), *sb.* [f. *to mark down* s.v. MARK *v.* 2 c.] A reduction in price; an article the selling price of which has been reduced. Also *attrib.*

1880 in *Dict. Amer. Eng.* (1942) III. 1486/2 The success of our mark-down sales. **1962** *Economist* 2 June 891/1 Specialists found it difficult to absorb shares without drastic markdowns in price. **1962** E. GODFREY *Retail Selling & Organization* ii. 16 Goods are bought in specially or are mark-downs from other sections of the store. **1972** *Oxford Times* 27 Oct. 9 To show a false mark-down price in a sale is a definite offence. **1974** *Oxford Mail* 10 Jan. 2/1 (Advt.), Gigantic genuine mark-down Fashion Sale..Headington.

marke, obs. form of MARQUE[1], MIRK.

marked (mɑːkt), *ppl. a.* [f. MARK *v.* and *sb.*[1] + -ED.]

1. a. Having a visible mark. Also, impressed or affixed as a mark; expressed by a mark.

931 in Birch *Cartul. Sax.* (1887) II. 358 Ðære ʒemearcodan æc æt aleburnan. **1609** DOULAND *Ornith. Microl.* 9 Of Keyes some are..marked Keyes, others are called vnmarked Keyes. Of the marked, there are fiue principall..which the Ambrosians..did mark with colours. **1617** MORYSON *Itin.* I. 227 A marked stone in the pavement. **1753** CHAMBERS *Cycl. Supp.* s.v. *Card*, Among sharpers divers sorts of false or fraudulent cards have been contrived; as marked cards. **1768** *N. Car. Col. Rec.* VII. 853 From the top of Tryon Mountain beginning at the marked Trees thereon [etc.]. **1875** *Chamb. Jrnl.* 16 Jan. 45 A number of prettily marked ones [*sc.* snails]. **1892** F. ANSTEY *Voces Populi* Ser. II. 5 Herr Von K. is preparing to fire a marked half-crown from a blunderbuss.

absol. **1623** WODROEPHE *Marrow Fr. Tongue* 319/2 From the Marcked of the Hand of God, and from Traytors Hands, the Lord keepe vs.

b. Special collocations: **marked bar**, a particular form of pig-iron; **marked cheque** (see quots. 1907 and 1951); **marked file**, a file of newspapers or journals upon the articles in which the names of the writers have been recorded; **marked iron** = *marked bar*; **marked price**, the price indicated by written signs placed on goods offered for sale; **marked proof**, an impression of an engraving in which some detail is left unfinished as a mark of an early state of the plate; **marked transfer** (see quots.).

1888 *Daily News* 24 Sept. 2/7 Marked bars are almost the only class of iron that have not been advanced... Most marked bar houses are in a better position than they have been for a year or two past. **1896** R. H. I. PALGRAVE *Dict. Pol. Econ.* II. 695/2 Marked cheques are payable in the first clearing of the next day, and cannot be refused for any reason. **1907** W. G. CORDINGLEY *London Commercial Dict.* 115 *Marked cheque*, a cheque marked by the banker on whom it is drawn, stating that it is 'good' for the amount named upon it. **1930** HUTCHINSON & LOVELL *Short Dict. Legal, Commercial & Econ. Terms* 77 *Marked cheques*,.. cheques initialled by a banker as an indication that he holds sufficient balance to meet such cheque when presented. **1951** R. W. JONES *Thomson's Dict. Banking* (ed. 10) 395 *Marked Cheque*. Marking cheques takes one of two forms —marking for clearing purposes and marking at the request of the drawer. **1902** *Daily Chron.* 1 May 5/2 There are many 'marked files' in the British Museum. *Daily News* 10 Dec. 2/8 Marked iron is unchanged. **1887** *Ibid.* 19 Oct. 2/6 In many instances the marked prices are clearly prohibitive. **1901** W. G. CORDINGLEY *Dict. Stock Exchange Terms* 59 *Marked Transfers*. The company..then issue a fresh Certificate to him for the part unsold, and endorse the Transfer that they hold Certificates to cover the number of shares sold, when the Transfer is said to be 'Marked' or 'Certified'. **1961** WEBSTER, *Marked transfer*, an instrument for transferring a portion of the shares of a stockholder's certificate after being certified as good by a proper official on the London stock exchange.

c. Of a linguistic construction, form, etc.: distinguished or determined by a particular feature; distinguished as intrinsically unnatural (see also MARKER 7; opp. *unmarked*).

The corresponding Russian word was used by Trubetzkoy before Bloomfield: see R. Jakobson *Selected Writings* (ed. 2, 1971) I. 734 ff.

1933 L. BLOOMFIELD *Lang.* xvi. 268 A phrase consisting of the preposition *to* and an infinitive expression belongs to the special form-class of *marked infinitive phrases*, whose function differs from that of unmarked infinitive expressions. **1953** C. E. BAZELL *Ling. Form* ii. 19 The Latin marked construction here can be uniquely derived from the unmarked in every case. **1959** R. QUIRK in Quirk & Smith *Teaching of English* i. 44 It seems likely that this structural notion of marked and unmarked members of opposing pairs can be applied cautiously but with profit to many of the binary choices in usage at more complex linguistic levels than the lexical. **1963** *Canad. Jrnl. Ling.* VIII. 92 Whenever a demonstrative system is reduced to a binary one, the first member which can be correlated with the first person always remains and thus becomes the marked member. **1965** *Amer. Speech* XL. 175 There are certain marked forms [of the verb] which are past and future respectively. **1968** CHOMSKY & HALLE *Sound Pattern Eng.* 402 Certain aspects of this general problem can be dealt with if we incorporate the Praguian notion of 'marked' and 'unmarked' values of features into our account in some systematic way, and if we then revise the evaluation measure so that unmarked values do not contribute to complexity. *Ibid.* 404 A major difference between the Praguian conception of markedness and our own is that in the former the marked coefficient of a feature was assumed always to be + and the unmarked coefficient always −. **1972** M. SHAPIRO in *Language* XLVIII. 345 In my concept and utilization of the terms marked and unmarked, the former is to be understood as denoting relative complexity and differentiatedness, the latter as denoting the absence of these relative attributes.

2. ***marked man***: one whose conduct is watched with hostile intent; one who is kept in mind as an object for suspicion or vengeance.

1833 HT. MARTINEAU *Manch. Strike* xi. 125 You are a marked man in Manchester,..no master in any trade will take you in among his men. **1855** MACAULAY *Hist. Eng.* xviii. IV. 235 If they had fancied that they were marked men, they might..have become traitors. **1882** J. H. BLUNT *Ref. Ch. Eng.* II. 285 On the accession of Queen Mary he naturally became a marked man.

3. a. Emphasized, rendered evident; clearly defined, easy to distinguish or recognize. Also with prefixed adv., as ***well-***, ***strongly-marked***.

1795 LD. AUCKLAND *Corr.* (1862) III. 281, I do not think the rule applicable to this case; it was too marked and too official. **1797** M. BAILLIE *Morb. Anat.* (1807) 72 Any well marked example of this disease. **1802** MAR. EDGEWORTH *Moral T.* (1816) I. vii. 42 He looked at the flower-pot with marked disdain. **1836** J. M. GULLY *Magendie's Formul.* (ed. 2) 9 A quarter of a grain has generally a marked action on a healthy man. **1841** BREWSTER *Mart. Sci.* II. iii. (1856) 134 We slightly resented a piece of marked incivility. **1853** LYTTON *My Novel* x. xiv, Of those qualities enumerated above,..Audley Egerton only exhibited to a marked degree —the common sense and the readiness. **1875** W. S. HAYWARD *Love agst. World* i, The third with more marked features. **1888** *Poor Nellie* 82 George avoided you in the most marked manner. **1899** *Allbutt's Syst. Med.* VIII. 933 The antipyrine-rash..is not accompanied by marked fever.

b. Of rhythm, accent, etc.

1818 HALLAM *Mid. Ages* IX. i. (1868) 599 Their hymns depended, for metrical effect, on the marked accents and powerful rhymes which the Latin language affords.

markedly ('mɑːkɪdlɪ), *adv.* [f. MARKED *a.* + -LY[2].] In a marked manner or degree.

A favourite 19th c. adverb.

1811 in Southey *Life A. Bell* (1844) II. 389 The Bishop.. was markedly civil, both to myself and Davis. **1842** J. STERLING *Ess.* etc. (1848) I. 442 The collection includes poems of four markedly different kinds. **1899** *Allbutt's Syst. Med.* VIII. 838 As a rule epithelioma of the muco-cutaneous functions affects the glands early and markedly.

markedness ('mɑːkɪdnɪs). [f. MARKED *a.* + -NESS.] The condition, quality, or state of being marked; *spec.* in *Linguistics* (f. MARKED *ppl. a.* 1 c).

1846 POE *L. G. Clark* Wks. 1864 III. 110 The markedness by which he is noticeable for nothing. **1865** J. GROTE *Moral Ideals* xix. 451 Individuality of character is markedness. **1968** [see MARKED *ppl. a.* 1 c]. **1968** *Language* XLIV. 714 The notion of markedness as developed within Praguean phonology..allows phonological segments to be differentiated. **1972** *Sci. Amer.* Sept. 78/3 Any syntactic structure is a member of a transformational chain and any two partially synonymous constructions display an interrelation of markedness and unmarkedness. **1973** A. H. SOMMERSTEIN *Sound Pattern Anc. Greek* iii. 82 The Markedness theory holds that phonological features are not in general symmetrical: that for each feature in each environment, one of its possible values is more normal, more 'unmarked', than the other.

markee, markenes, obs. ff. MARQUEE, MURKNESS.

marker ('mɑːkə(r)). [f. MARK *v.* + -ER[1]. OE. had *mearcere* as a gloss on L. *notārius*.]

1. One who marks. **a.** One whose duty it is to mark game (see MARK *v.* 15).

1486 *Bk. St. Albans* B iij b, Let yowre spanyellis fynde a Couy of partrichys and when thay be put vpp..ye most haue markeris to marke som of thaym, and then cowple vp yowre houndys. **1898** *Encycl. Sport* II. 75 When either of the markers has marked birds, he should blow his whistle once.

b. One who records the score in competitive games (e.g. tennis, billiards, etc.), or at target practice; †in *Cricket* = scorer. Also, one who records prices on the stock exchange.

1532 MORE *Confut. Tindale* Wks. 403/2 It is pitie yt the man wer not made a marker of chases in some tenis play. **1679–88** *Secr. Serv. Money Chas. & Jas.* (Camden) 177 John Webb, John and Charles Dimion, markers in the tennis courts at Whitehall and Windsor. **1754** J. LOVE *Cricket* (1770) 5 Save when the [billiard] Marker bellows out, *Six love.* **1774** *Covent-Garden Mag.* Aug. 283/2 [Cricket] If one of these gentry should be appointed marker, he will favour the side that he wishes to win. **1859** LEVER *Davenport Dunn* 27 Sam Crozier was a marker at a billiard-table in Tralee. **1861** *Times* 23 Aug., A private of the Royal Marines..was acting as a marker at the targets during the firing of the Volunteers. **1870** J. K. MEDBERY *Men & Mysteries Wall St.* 21 The 'marker' or black-board clerk writes off the prices upon the tablet. **1898** *Encycl. Sport* II. 242 Most games [of rackets] at clubs, and all matches, are played under the eye and voice of a marker who is placed in the gallery.

c. One employed to keep a record of attendances, in a class, school, or college.

At Cambridge, a person appointed to prick off the names of those present at the service in a college chapel.

1798 COLERIDGE *Let.* 19 Feb., Every ward [in Christ's Hospital] was governed by four Monitors,..and by four Markers. **1820** LAMB *Elia* Ser. I. *Christ's Hosp. 35 Yrs. ago*, The markers (those who were appointed to hear the Bible read in the wards on Sunday morning and evening). **1849** *Blackw. Mag.* May 601 His name prick'd off upon the marker's roll, No twinge of conscience racks his easy soul. **1893** *Month* Aug. 490 There are [in a Manchester industrial school] two non-commissioned officers, or monitors, who are termed the *striper* and *marker* respectively.

d. In Welsh slate quarries: An official employed to check the quantity of work done by the men.

1901 *Daily Chron.* 15 May 8/6 One man..who occupied the position of marker in the quarries..turned back.

e. *Mil.* One who is placed as a pivot or formation mark in military evolutions.

1796 *Instr. & Reg. Cavalry* (1813) 100 Markers will always be placed, to give the precise ground on which the counter-march is to be made. **1832** *Prop. Regul. Instr. Cavalry* III. 53 The Markers to be employed for Regimental Movements are the Adjutant, the Regimental Serjeant Major, and one non-commissioned Officer for each Squadron.

f. One who puts a mark, stamp, brand, etc. upon something. ***marker-off***: a workman who performs certain processes in pianoforte scale making.

1553 *Act 7 Edw. VI*, c. 7 §1 The penaltie..dependeth.. not upon the seller, ne maker, marker or fellor of the same [Fuell]. **1737** *Chamberlayne's St. Gt. Brit.* II. III. (ed. 33) 94 Marker of Dice, John Rollos. **1889** *Work* 23 Nov. I. 564/3 The business of the marker-off is..to plane the bridges to their proper height, mark the scale [etc.]. **1901** *Daily Chron.* 3 Dec. 10/6 Piano Markers-off and Assistant Markers-off wanted. **1907** S. E. WHITE *Arizona Nights* I. viii. 149 In the meantime the marker was engaged in his work. First, with a sharp knife he cut off slanting the upper quarter of one ear [of a calf]. **1928** *Collier's* 29 Dec. 6/2 There was a lull in the stream of lumber. The marker turned for a look at the order board.

†**g.** One who notes or observes. *Obs.*

c **1550** CHEKE *Matt.* xvi. *note*, As in ye beginning of Orestes of Euripides it mai appear, and els whear communli to a marker hearof.

†**h.** *slang.* (See quot.) *Obs.*

1591 GREENE *2nd Pt. Conny catching* Wks. (Grosart) X. 86 In Lifting Law, He that first stealeth [is] the Lift. He that receiues it the Markar.

i. *nonce-use.* A marksman.

1820 Scott *Monast.* xviii, The best marker may shoot a bow's length beside.

j. *U.S.* In surveying: a person who makes the marks on trees to indicate boundaries or lines of survey.

1743 *New Jersey Archives* (1883) 1st Ser. VI. 154 You are to employ..an assistant surveyor..& also proper chainbearers & markers. **1843** *Amer. Pioneer* II. 379 In running the back line of the survey..I was about one hundred yards in advance of the chainmen and marker.

2. An implement or tool for marking.

In many specific applications, e.g. an implement for tracing lines on the ground in laying out garden beds, preparing for planting rows of trees, etc.; an appliance in a sewing machine for making a crease on the cloth to serve as a guide for stitching or folding; a pointed tool or stylus for marking wood to be cut.

1725 W. Halfpenny *Sound Building* 52 With a Marker describe the Cross-Joints. **1870** *Advt.*, Bézique Playing Cards..with Markers. **1884** Knight *Dict. Mech.* Suppl. 584/2 *Marker*... An implement for marking off rows on the ground, as a guide for planting or dropping.

b. = *marker pen*, sense 8 below. *U.S.*

1951 *Sears, Roebuck Catal.* Fall-Winter 10002B/2 'Magic Marker' waterproof, instant drying black ink Marker, write on any surface, ideal for packages or cartons. Has built-in felt brush. **1967** *Ibid.* Fall-Winter 902/1 Set of 8 Felt-tip Markers. Write on almost anything. Instant drying ink. Waterproof, won't rub off. Use for drawings, labeling, addressing pkgs, etc.

3. a. = *book-marker* (book *sb.* 19).

1852 Miss Mitford *Recoll.* II. 184, I had no marker, and the richly bound volume closed as if instinctively. **1853** Dale tr. *Baldeschi's Ceremonial* 293 When carrying the Missal, he will take care not to displace the markers.

b. A monument, memorial stone, etc., marking a place of special interest.

1906 *Springfield* (Mass.) *Weekly Republ.* 15 Feb. 16 The committee appointed to investigate the matter of a marker for the Washington elm reported in favor of a granite marker. **1959** A. G. Woodhead *Study of Greek Inscriptions* iv. 45 The commonest types of monument were the small cylindrical marker (*columella*), seldom more than two feet high, [etc.].

c. A flare, distinctive sign, or object of any kind used as a guide to a pilot of an aircraft seeking a particular area, obstruction, etc.; *spec.* a flare dropped from an aeroplane to illuminate or mark a target. Also with defining word, as ***ground marker, sky-marker***, etc. (see these sbs.).

1936 M. B. Garber *Mod. Mil. Dict.* 195 *Marker*, a symbol, letter, or figure on the ground, visible from aircraft, by means of which the operators are able to determine their position. **1944** *Times* 22 Mar. 4/5 The leading aircraft then dropped markers right across the middle of the target. **1944** R. C. K. Ensor *Miniature Hist. War* iv. 53 Accuracy was also greatly improved by the system of 'pathfinders' dropping 'markers' to guide the rest. **1951** *Gloss. Aeronaut. Terms* (*B.S.I.*) 111. 24 *Markers*, objects of approved shape or colour indicating specific areas and obstructions.

4. *slang.* Something worthy to be compared.

1888 *Congress. Rec.* 12 Dec. 202/2 The waving of the bloody shirt would not have been a marker. **1895** H. P. Robinson *Men Born Equal* 145 It ain't a marker to what's ahead. **1904** W. H. Smith *Promoters* xxv. 366 What little I've told you isn't a marker to other things he said.

5. a. In various games such as bridge or whist, a scoreboard or card, or other implement used to record the score. (See also *bridge-marker*, bridge *sb.*[2] c.)

1907 *Army & Navy Stores Catal.* 198/2 Whist marker, inlaid, pair 2/7. *Ibid.* 375/2 Playing card table..with drawer divided to take cards and bridge scoring blocks, whist cards and markers. **1960** R. C. Bell *Board & Table Games* I. vi. 157 Little bone sticks marked with..dots are used to keep the score... Usually each player [at Mah Jong] starts with.. 2 markers with 10 red dots [etc.].

b. *U.S. slang.* A promissory note; an I.O.U.

1887 F. Francis *Saddle & Mocassin* xii. 225 Before half the deal was over, the whole bank of checks was gone, and Cuff was giving markers for hundreds as hard as he could go it. **1931** D. Runyon *Guys & Dolls* (1932) vii. 147 Now I am going to pay my landlady, and take up a few markers here and there, and feed myself up good. *Ibid.* xiii. 279 He is willing to take Charley's marker for a million if necessary to get Charley out.

6. *Genetics.* Any allele (usu. one which is easily recognized phenotypically and whose gene has been located on a specific chromosome) which is used in genetic experiments to identify a chromosome or to locate less well-known genes on a genetic map.

1930 *Genetics* XV. 219 There is a certain expected amount of crossing over between the two mutant genes treated as markers of a given point. **1938** *Ibid.* XXIII. 291 In order to obtain Notch deficiencies, normal males carrying yellow (*y* —0·0) as a marker..were mated with females homozygous for cherry (w^{ch}—1·5) and wavy (*wy*—40·7). **1940** *Nature* 10 Aug. 199/2 It is..possible to recognise, by means of the markers used, what combination of chromosomes is present in the pseudo-backcross progeny. **1961** *Proc. Nat. Acad. Sci.* XLVII. 378 (*heading*) Transformation studies on the linkage of markers in the tryptophan pathway in *Bacillus subtilis*. **1969** A. M. Campbell *Episomes* ii. 22 Phage resulting from DNA infection is distinguished from progeny of the helper phage itself by genetic markers.

7. *Linguistics.* A word, affix, etc., which distinguishes or determines the class or function of the form, construction, etc., with which it is used. Also *attrib.*

1933 L. Bloomfield *Lang.* xvi. 269 Our determining adjectives, our prepositions, our co-ordinating conjunctions, and our subordinating conjunctions, may be viewed as markers. **1953** C. E. Bazell *Ling. Form* v. 67 *And* [in 'hot and cold'] may be described as a 'marker', after which no question of constituents arises. **1960** E. Delavenay *Introd. Machine Transl.* vii. 110 Those strictly linguistic markers sought in the sentence by the programmers of automatic translations. **1961** R. B. Long *Sentence & its Parts* iii. 65 The marker pronouns and adverbs are not themselves usable in declaratives ordinarily, but the marker verb forms are. **1964** *Amer. Speech* XXXIX. 53 The German plural marker *-er* is historically a derivational suffix. **1968** P. M. Postal *Aspects Phonol. Theory* i. 13 By the 'markers' of a linguistic level I refer to the formal structures which the rules of that level assign to sentences as part of their total structural description. **1972** Hartmann & Stork *Dict. Lang. & Ling.* 137/1 Markers may indicate the category of a linguistic unit at any level of analysis. **1973** *Archivum Linguisticum* IV. 32 The remaining forms are sufficiently distinguished for person, i.e. in the absence of specific person markers, by differing marks of gender-cum-number.

8. *attrib.* and *Comb.*, as (sense 3c) ***marker burner; marker flag, light;*** **marker beacon** (see beacon *sb.* 6d); **marker bomb**, a bomb emitting a coloured light, dropped in an air-raid to serve as a point of direction; **marker pen** orig. *U.S.*, a felt-tipped or similar pen used esp. for highlighting words or passages in a text, or for marking indelibly.

1929 Marker beacon [see beacon *sb.* 6d]. **1934** *Jrnl. R. Aeronaut. Soc.* XXXVIII. 828 When a pilot had to maintain height, to observe instruments to ensure that he did not get into difficulties, and had also to listen for the marker beacon. **1935** *Times* 19 Oct. 9/5 The installation will consist of a main beacon at one corner of the aerodrome and two marker beacons 300 yards and 3,000 yards away respectively. **1971** *Gloss. Electrotechnical, Power Terms* (*B.S.I.*) iii. vi. 24 *Marker beacon*, in aviation, radio beacon which radiates a signal to define an area above the beacon. **1944** *Hutchinson's Pict. Hist. War Oct. 1943–Apr. 1944* 84 (*caption*) Different stages in the lighting up of a target by a marker bomb. **1947** *Shell Aviation News* No. 113. 7/3 These marker burners would give a clear patch in bad weather that would provide the pilot with actual visual contact with the ground. **1945** *Penguin New Writing* XXIII. 9 Dan buoys appeared..their marker flags drowned and bedraggled. **1959** *Listener* 12 Feb. 278/2 Among the maze of wheel tracks and hoof marks, I noticed a red marker flag. **1943** *Chambers's Techn. Dict.* Suppl. 964/1 *Marker light* (Signalling), an indicating light on a signal post, to indicate the position or aspect of the main signal should its light have failed. **1960** O. Skilbeck *ABC of Film & T.V.* 82 *Marker light*, device giving synch. between picture and sound film by simultaneous photographic exposure instead of the Clapper board. Outmoded by the use of Magnetic film for Direct recording. **1971** M. Tak *Truck Talk* 104 *Marker lights*, the small lights that serve to outline a truck's length and width at night and in bad weather. **1980** *N.Y. Times* 8 June iii. 19/3 For ages there was just the quill. Then came the fountain pen, the pencil,..the ball point pen,..the marker pen, the felt-tip pen, [etc.]. **1984** *Which?* Jan. 4/2 You can do the marking by engraving, punching, etching or painting, or by using a marker pen. **1985** *New Age* Spring 2/2 A new marker pen is being used by Luton police in a bid to stop thefts from elderly people... The identification mark [on valuables] can be read under an ultra violet lamp at the police station. **1986** *Daily Tel.* 15 Oct. 15/5 (Advt.), A special Property Marker Pen is *free* with every Sun Alliance Home Insurance policy issued with this offer. Use it to mark your precious objects invisibly with your house number and postcode.

market ('mɑːkɪt), *sb.* Forms: α. 2 (*dat.*), 4–6 **markete**, 3 (*dat.*), **marcatte**, 4 **markatte**, 4–6 **markette**, 4–6 **markat**, 4–7 **marcat**, **-kett**, 6 **marcatt**, (4 **marked**, 5 **markyth(e**, **marget**, 5–6 **markit**, 6 **-yt**, **-yd**, **-eth**, **marchet**, 7 **marquet**), 2– **market**. β. (chiefly *Sc.*) 4–6 **merkat**, 5–8 **mercat**, 5–7 **mercate**, (4 **merkete**, 5 **-et**, 6 **-ett**, **-it**, **-yte**, 7 **merkate**). [Late OE. *market*, a. ONF. *market* (Central OF. *marchiet*, *marchié*, mod.F. *marché*) = Pr. *marcat-z*, Sp., Pg. *mercado*, It. *mercato*:—L. *mercātu-s*, f. *mercārī* to trade: see mercantile. The Romanic word was early adopted into the Teut. langs.: cf. OHG. *markât*, *merkât*, *merchât* (MHG. *market*, *merket*, mod.G. *markt*), OFris. *merked*, Du. *markt* (see mart *sb.*), ON. *markaðr*, *marknaðr* (Sw. *marknad*, Da. *marked*).

It is not certain that the word was introduced into England before the 12th c., though it occurs in documents ostensibly of the 11th and 10th centuries; even if these be in substance genuine, they are modernized in language.]

1. a. The meeting or congregating together of people for the purchase and sale of provisions or livestock, publicly exposed, at a fixed time and place; the occasion, or time during which such goods are exposed for sale; also, the company of people at such a meeting. † ***high market***: the time when the market is busiest.

After *to* or *from* the article is very often omitted.

c **1154** *O. E. Chron.* an. 1125 (Laud MS.) He ne mihte cysten ænne peni at anne market. *c* **1220** *Bestiary* 491 Ðe man ðat oðer biswikeð..in mot er in market. *c* **1380** Wyclif *Wks.* (1880) 172 Prestis also ben ma[r]chauntis..& beten marketis [etc.]. **1413** *Pilgr. Sowle* (Caxton 1483) iii. vii. 54 Vsurers wyllen nought be hyghely renomed of theyr craft ne cryen it in the markett. **1480** Caxton *Chron. Eng.* ccvi. 187 He lete crye thurgh his patent in euery faire and in euery markete of Englond. **1563** in W. H. Turner *Select. Rec. Oxford* 306 Everye Satterdaye..there shalbe a commen markett for..cattell. **1564** *Reg. Privy Council Scot.* I. 280 To by or sell any maner of tymmer, greit or small, bot in oppin and plane marcattis. *a* **1649** Winthrop *New Eng.* (1853) I. 148 By order of court a mercate was erected at Boston, to be kept upon Thursday. **1775** S. J. Pratt *Liberal Opin.* xlviii. (1783) II. 67 There [at Smithfield] it is high market. **1839** *Penny Cycl.* XIV. 424 When the whole bulk of the articles to be sold is brought into the market.., the market is called a *pitched* market; when only a small portion is brought..it is called a *sample* market. **1849** Lytton *Caxtons* 39 My mother had coaxed Caxton to walk with her to market. **1899** *Blackw. Mag.* Jan. 45/2 A rendezvous.. where a market was opened for the Indians in the vicinity. **1905** *Delineator* Mar. 498/3, I patronize a small market.. kept by an old Frenchman and his son. They are experts on cutting and trimming meat.

fig. **1340** *Ayenb.* 23 Þet is þe dyeules peni huermide he bayþ alle þe uayre pane-worþes ine the markatte of þise wordle. **1600** Shaks. *A.Y.L.* iii. v. 60 Thanke heauen, fasting, for a good mans loue;..Sell when you can, you are not for all markets.

b. Phrases, more or less metaphorical. † ***to be at market***: to be for sale (*lit.* and *fig.*). ***to bring to market***: to offer for sale (*lit.* and *fig.*). ***to bring one's eggs*** (or ***one's hogs***) ***to a bad market***: to suffer the failure of one's schemes. ***to feed*** (cattle) ***to market***: to feed for sale. ***to go to market***: (*colloq.*) to make an attempt at something; also *fig.* (*Austral.* and *N.Z.*), to behave in an angry manner, to become angry. ***to go*** (***badly***, etc.) ***to market***: to make a (bad, etc.) bargain. ***to put into market***: to make a matter of bargain and sale. † ***to run before one's horse to market***: to count the gain before the bargain is made.

1594 Shaks. *Rich. III*, i. i. 160 But yet I run before my horse to Market. **1613** Beaum. & Fl. *Cupid's Rev.* i. i, We haue brought Our eggs and muskadine to a faire market. *a* **1616** —— *Bonduca* v. ii, You have brought your hogs to a fine market. **1639** G. Daniel *Ecclus.* x. 25 Such a Man would bring His Soule to Mercate. **1776** Adam Smith *W.N.* i. vii. I. 68 When the quantity of any commodity which is brought to market falls short of the effectual demand. **1800** Jefferson *Let. to J. Madison* 4 Mar., Writ. 1854 IV. 324 H. Marshal voting of course with them, as did, and frequently does***, of****, who is perfectly at market. **1801** —— *Let. to Monroe* 24 Nov. *Ibid.* IV. 420 A very great extent of country, north of the Ohio,..is now at market. **1809** Malkin *Gil Blas* ii. ix. ¶7 The schoolmaster..brought his eggs to a bad market. **1812** *Sporting Mag.* XXXIX. 23 When..they found they had been badly to market, they declared themselves off. **1821** Lamb *Elia* Ser. i. *Imperf. Symp.*, They seldom wait to mature a proposition, but e'en bring it to market in the green ear. **1844** Emerson *Lect., Yng. Amer.* Wks. (Bohn) II. 300 This is the good and this the evil of trade, that it would put everything into market. **1890** 'R. Boldrewood' *Col. Reformer* I. xi. 168 If you hadn't come forward..the first time he propped, he mightn't have gone to market at all. **1893** Stevenson *Catriona* 156 These [sheep] being specially fed to market. *a* **1925** F. S. Anthony *Follow Call* (1936) 17 Peter came home drunk once every week, and made his poor wife milk the herd of twenty-four cows by herself; and then about 8 p.m. he'd arise from the sofa and go to market because the poor woman hadn't cooked a hot tea for him. **1945** Baker *Austral. Lang.* 121 A man in a temper is said..*to go to market*.

c. ***market overt*** (in *Law*): open market; the exposal of vendible goods in an open place so that any one who passes by may see them.

1602 Fulbecke *1st Pt. Parall.* 7 If a felon sell a Horse without couin in a Market ouert, this doth alter the property. **1766** Blackstone *Comm.* II. xxx. 449 Market overt in the country is only held on..special days..; but in London every day, except Sunday, is market day. **1880** *Sat. Rev.* 28 Feb. 281 A certain article was submitted for analysis by its proprietors to a distinguished analyst, who thoughtfully provided himself with another sample of it bought in market overt.

d. *Stock Exchange.* (See quot. 1887.)

1880 *Guide to Stock Exch.* 35 The distinctions between classes of business on the Stock Exchange are known as 'markets', and each jobber is supposed to operate in his own market. **1887** *Encycl. Brit.* XXII. 557/1 What are known as the 'markets' in the stock exchange are simply groups of jobbers distributed here and there on the floor of the house.

2. *Law.* The privilege granted to the lord of a manor, a municipality or other body, to establish a meeting of persons to buy and sell.

a **1150** *Charter of Eadweard* in Kemble *Cod. Dipl.* IV. 209 Þæt..se abbod and ða ȝebroðra into Ramesege habben ða socne on eallen þingen ofer heom and ðat market æt Dunham. **1464** *Rolls of Parlt.* V. 521/1 Courtes, Warennes, Mercates, Rentes..to the seid Priory..belongyng. **1607** Cowell *Interpr.*, *Market*,..signifieth..also the liberty or priuiledge whereby a towne is enabled to keepe a market. **1818** Cruise *Digest* (ed. 2) III. 276 So where a man has a market to hold on the Saturday, and he holds it on another day, the market shall be forfeited.

3. a. A public place, whether an open space or covered building, in which cattle, provisions, etc. are exposed for sale; a market-place, market-house. Also, now, = supermarket.

c **1250** *Kent. Serm.* in *O.E. Misc.* 33 So ha kam into þe Marcatte so he fond werkmen þet were idel. **13..** *K. Alis.* 1515 A temple ther was, amydde the market. *c* **1477** Caxton *Jason* 79 They began a bataile upon the market. **1521** *Test. Ebor.* (Surtees) VI. 4 A howse in the markett. **1549** *Compl. Scot.* xvii. 149 The comont pepil..conuoyit them to the plane mercat befor the capitol. **1718** Lady M. W. Montagu *Let. to C'tess Bristol* 10 Apr., The markets are most of them handsome squares. **1872** *All Year Round* 13 Apr. 470/1 This charitable lady decided on building a market. **1888** *Ladies' Home Jrnl.* June 2/2 Cherries..should be avoided when.. sold in city markets. **1895** *Funk's Stand. Dict.*, *Market*,..a private store for the sale of provisions; as, a meat-*market*. **1911** *Woman's Home Compan.* Apr. 4/2, I have used inadequately filtered water, uninspected milk and shopped in markets where inspection of sanitary conditions was

never dreamed of. **1967** 'D. SHANNON' *Rain with Violence* (1969) i. 19 She's pretty sure Mrs. Gerner usually shopped at the nearest market up on Marengo. **1972** *Jrnl. Social Psychol.* LXXXVII. 78 Markets were chosen which served a relatively large number of black customers.

b. With prefixed word, indicating the chief commodity sold, as ***cattle, corn, fish, meat-market***, etc., for which see those words.

4. a. The action or business of buying and selling; an instance of this, a commercial transaction, a purchase or sale; a (good or bad) bargain, *lit.* and *fig. Obs.* exc. in certain phrases: see c.

1525 LD. BERNERS *Froiss.* II. xxxviii. 116 Lytell and lytell we shall wynne the castells that these pyllers holde, though they departe nowe with a good market. *Ibid.* xci. [lxxxvii.] 272 He hadde so good a markette as to escape alyue. *a* **1548** HALL *Chron., Hen. VI* 130b, The remmaunt not likyng their market, departed. **1548** UDALL *Erasm. Par. Luke* xiv. 126b, I must..goe to proue them, whether I haue made a good mercate in bying of them or not. *c* **1550** CHEKE *Matt.* xxii. 4 Y^ei^..went yeer wais, sum to his own ground, sum to his mercat. **1599** *Warn. Faire Wom.* I. 525 She must defer her market till to-morrow. **1620** MIDDLETON *Chaste Maid* II. ii, *Second Pro.* I prithee look what market she hath made. *First Pro.* Imprimis, sir, a good fat loin of mutton. **1625** B. JONSON *Staple of N.* II. iv, What Lickfinger? mine old host of Ram-Alley? You ha' some mercat here. **1660** T. M. *Hist. Independ.* IV. 12 The Juncto..willing to make the best of a bad market, prepare for war. **1689–90** TEMPLE *Ess. Pop. Discont.* Wks. 1731 I. 257 Every Man speaks of the Fair as his own Market goes in it. **1693** DRYDEN *Persius* v. 201 And with Post-haste thy running Markets make, Be sure to turn the Penny. **1699** KIRKTON *Ch. Hist.* (1817) 373 She hade two daughters,..and for these she thought she might make a better mercat in Scotland than in England.

†**b.** The marketing or selling *of* (a commodity). Also *fig. Obs.*

1604 SHAKS. *Ham.* IV. iv. 34 (Qo. 2) What is a man, If his chiefe good and market of his time Be but to sleepe and feede, a beast, no more. **1680** MORDEN *Geog. Rect., Tartary* (1685) 80 Some of them now grown Wealthy, by the Market of their Slaves,..wear Sables.

c. Phrases. † ***to make market***: to trade, buy and sell; *fig.* to have dealings or intercourse *with*. ***to make a*** or ***one's market of*** (a possession, an occasion): to make (it) an object or occasion of bargaining or profit, to barter away; also, rarely, to victimize, make illicit profit out of (a person). ***to make one's market***: to do one's bargaining or dealing (*lit.* and *fig.*). ***to mar another's*** or ***one's market***: to spoil his or one's own trade (*lit.* and *fig.*). ***to mend one's market***: to improve one's bargain.

1340 *Ayenb.* 36 And huanne hy hise yzeþ poure and nyeduol: þanne makeþ hy mid ham marcat to do hire niedes. *a* **1400–50** *Alexander* 421 He saȝe, as him thoȝt, Amon his awen god in armes with his qwene, And make with hire market as [he] a man were. **1529** FRITH *Antithesis* Wks. (1573) 103/2 He that saith it is better to giue our charity to the poor..goeth aboute to marre the Popes market. **1577** *Reg. Privy Council Scot.* II. 658 He..ressavit ane coip bill as ane marchand, gevand him licence to mak marcat in the cuntre. **1597** SPENSER *Sheph. Cal.* Sept. 37 They..maken a market [1579–91 mart] of their good name. **1601** DENT *Pathw. Heaven* 94 So far off are you from mending your market any whit thereby. **1605** in *Burgh Rec. Glasgow* (1876) I. 230 It is..ordainit..that it salbe leasum to owttintownis fleschouris ilk day in the oulk to mak marcat of flesche in this towne. **1611** BIBLE *Transl. Pref.* ⁋17 It is a grieuous thing to neglect a great faire, and to seeke to make markets afterwards. *a* **1635** NAUNTON *Fragm. Reg.* (Arb.) 58 There was in him..a humour of travelling: which had not some wise men about him laboured to remove..he would (out of his naturall propension) have marred his own market. **1681** DRYDEN *Abs. & Achit.* I. 503 The next for interest sought to ..make their Jewish markets of the throne. **1709** S. SEWALL *Diary* 17 Feb., Mr. Gerrish courted Mr. Coney's daughter: and if she should have Mr. Stoddard, she would mend her market. **1713** STEELE *Guardian* No. 6 ⁋3 With his ready Mony the Builder, Mason and Carpenter are enabled to make their Market of Gentlemen..who inconsiderately employ them. **1714** GAY *Sheph. Week* Thur. 121, I made my market long before 'twas night, My purse grew heavy, and my basket light. **1793** BURKE *Policy Allies* Wks. VII. 171 Prussia..thinks of nothing but making a market of the present confusions. **1861** HEYWOOD *Pref. to J. Seaton's Let.* (Chetham Soc.) 3 Houses hereditarily accustomed to make a market of their swords.

5. a. Sale as controlled by supply and demand; hence, demand (for a commodity).

1689 EVELYN *Diary* (1827) IV. 315 They expect a quicker mercate. **1781** COWPER *Charity* 522 'Tis called a Satire... Strange! how the frequent interjected dash Quickens a market, and helps off the trash. **1848** MILL *Pol. Econ.* I. III. ii. §4. 529 The extra quantity can only find a market, by calling forth an additional demand equal to itself. *Ibid.* §5. 531 Had they persisted in selling all that they produced, they must have forced a market by reducing the price. **1861** M. PATTISON *Ess.* (1889) I. 47 Such commodities, however,.. found little market as yet. **1896** EDITH THOMPSON in *Monthly Packet* Christm. No. 83 Stredza..has lived long enough to know that there is a market for treason.

b. *to make a market* (Stock Exchange): to induce active dealing in any particular stock or shares, by being both a buyer and a seller at about the same price; to bring an enterprise to the notice of the public by interesting dealers in it (by means of options or otherwise).

1899 *Westm. Gaz.* 6 Mar. 8/1 Amongst the points in company law reform..the next [question] will relate to the old abuse of making a market.

6. Opportunity for buying or selling. ***to lose one's market***: to miss one's chance of doing business. ***to overstand one's market***: to stand out about terms till the opportunity is lost.

1684 DRYDEN tr. *Theocritus' Idyll.* iii. 85 What Madman would o'erstand his Market twice? **1691** LOCKE *Money* Wks. 1727 II. 6 He that wants a Vessel, rather than lose his Market, will not stick to have it at the Market-Rate. **1822** LAMB *Elia* Ser. I. *Mod. Gallantry*, When the phrases 'antiquated virginity', and such a one has 'overstood her market'..shall raise immediate offence.

7. a. ***the market***: the particular trade or traffic in the commodity specified in the context. Chiefly in ***in*** or ***on the market***. ***to be in the market***: (of a person) to be a buyer; also (of a possession) to be offered for sale (so ***to come into the market***). *fig.* ***to engross the market***: see quot. 1872.

1678 R. FILMER *Disc. Use for Money* 38 The borrowers do trade by buying and selling in the Mercat at the same prices that the owners of money do. **1776** ADAM SMITH *W.N.* I. xi. I. 265 There are commonly in the market only fourteen or fifteen ounces of silver for one ounce of gold. **1791** WASHINGTON *Lett.* Writ. 1892 XII. 66 A great quantity of bonds, thrown suddenly into the market,..could not but have effects the most injurious to the credit of the U.S. **1841** LEVER *C. O'Malley* vi, Every imaginable species of property coming into the market. **1864** TENNYSON *En. Ard.* 535 Enoch..bought Quaint monsters for the market of those times. **1866** *Standard* 7 May 2/3 A backwardation of $\frac{1}{2}$ per cent. was freely paid for the delivery of shares, such was the scarcity of them in the market. **1872** YEATS *Growth Comm.* 379 Edicts..against engrossing the market, i.e., buying up the stock of any commodity in order to sell it again at an enhanced price. **1883** BLACK *Yolande* I. v. 89 If ever Monaglen comes into the market, she'll snap it up. **1890** 'R. BOLDREWOOD' *Col. Reformer* II. xx. 169 You'd have had your money in your pocket now, and might have been in the market for some of these..store cattle. **1891** *Cycl. Tour. Club Monthly Gaz.* Nov. 320 The only type of air tyre on the market. **1908** M. DIVER *Great Amulet* x. 115, I don't feel called upon..to advertise the fact that I am not..'on the market'. **1929** *Amer. Speech* V. 123 A widow who was ready for another husband was said to be..'in the market'. **1936** L. C. DOUGLAS *White Banners* x. 212 She was in the market for diversion. **1955** 'A. GILBERT' *Is she Dead Too?* vii. 136 When I'm in the market for trouble of that kind I'll tip you the wink. **1955** *Times* 30 Aug. 3/1 This..is an important match with third place in the County table still in the market.

b. With specifying word prefixed. For ***copper-***, ***ore-***, ***wage-market***, etc., see those words. Also MONEY-MARKET. ***black market*** (see as main entry), ***buyer's market*** (see BUYER 3), ***common market*** (see COMMON *a.* 21), ***seller's market*** (see SELLER).

1832 *Fraser's Mag.* IV. 720 Even the home market was thrown open to the goods of the stranger. **1840** DICKENS *Old C. Shop* xxxii, In this depressed state of the classical market, Mrs. Jarley made extraordinary efforts to stimulate the popular taste. **1886** C. SCOTT *Sheep-Farming* 137 Sheep intended for the fat market.

c. In Horse Racing, the kind or amount of business done in bets, the state of betting.

1886 EARL OF SUFFOLK & BERKS. et al. *Racing & Steeple-Chasing* v. 85 On arriving at the rails, which separate the private stands' enclosure from the ring, he finds the market well set. **1897** E. H. COOPER *Mr. Blake of Newmarket* xxvi. 255 'I've missed the market!' My friend..explained..that he had not got the best bet against the horse which he might have got. **1972** J. MITCHELL *Betting* ii. 34 Because of..the shortness of the period..for which the betting market on a race is active, racecourse bookmakers keep their betting as simple as possible.

8. The rate of purchase and sale; price in the market, market value.

1546 J. HEYWOOD *Prov.* (1867) 31 The market goth by the market men. **1586** A. DAY *Eng. Secretary* II. (1625) 71, I hope you will haue regard to the selling of these commodities to my best aduantage, wherein I pray you doe your best endeuour as the Market serueth. **1647** WARD *Simp. Cobler* (1843) 7 They deal wisely that will stay till the Market is fallen. **1780** BURKE *Sp. Econ. Reform* Wks. III. 272 These lands at present would sell at a low market. **1800** PITT in *G. Rose's Diaries* (1860) I. 280 The market..has.. fallen 7*s.* per quarter. **1886** T. HARDY *Mayor of Casterbr.* xxiii, Just when I sold the markets went lower, and I bought up the corn of those who had been holding back. **1890** 'R. BOLDREWOOD' *Col. Reformer* (1891) 246 The cattle having 'topped the market', and sold extremely well.

fig. **1535** LYNDESAY *Satyre* 3186 The markit raisit bene sa hie, That Prelats dochtours..Ar maryit with sic superfluities [etc.]. **1614** RALEIGH *Hist. World* Pref. A4b, For those Kings, which haue sold the blood of others at a low rate; haue but made the Market for their owne enemies, to buy of theirs at the same price. **1650** TRAPP *Comm. Deut.* ix. 4 We are all apt to..set a price upon ourselves above the market. **1751** R. PALTOCK *P. Wilkins* (1884) II. xxiii. 279 For 'tis all one to her with whom she [*sc.* a mistress] engages, so she can raise but the market by a change.

9. A place or seat of trade; a country, district, town, etc. in which there is a demand for articles of trade; hence, the trade of such a country, etc.

1615 E. S. *Britain's Buss* in Arb. *Garner* III. 651 Surely it were too great poverty for English minds..to fear to speed worse in any market or place than they. **1752** HUME *Ess. & Treat.* (1777) I. 334 We lost the French market for our woollen manufactures. **1821** SHELLEY *Œdipus* II. i. 18 The failure of a foreign market for Sausages, bristles, and blood puddings,..is but partial. **1891** S. C. SCRIVENER *Our Fields & Cities* 90 Professor Seely tells us that all the wars since 1700 have been wars for a market... A blustering Yankee captain, who was fighting for a market for goods manufactured in the Northern States.

10. *attrib.* and *Comb.*: **a.** simple attrib., as ***market-boat, -boy, -cart, -due, -girl, -hall, -keeper, -maid, -net, -people, -sloop, survey, -talk, -time, -toll, -wagon***; (with reference to the money-market) as ***market-money, -operator, -quotation***; also ***market-made*** adj.

1780 *New Jersey Archives* (1914) 2nd Ser. IV. 401 Mrs. Roker, and one other woman, were going in a *market boat from Philadelphia. **1853** 'P. PAXTON' *Stray Yankee in Texas* 278 [He] bought a market-boat, and tried trading upon the bayou. **1863** *Cornh. Mag.* Feb. 180 The market-boats bring alongside his ship the grapes and figs with which [etc.]. **1863** A. D. WHITNEY *Faith Gartney's Girlhood* v. 44 The *market-boys, and the waiters, and the confectioners' parcels. **1833** HT. MARTINEAU *Briery Creek* iii. 49 Her employer was driving his *market-cart. **1875** JOWETT *Plato* (ed. 2) III. 303 *Market and harbour dues. **1832** TENNYSON *Lady of Shalott* II. ii, The red cloaks of *market girls. **1732** LEDIARD *Sethos* II. VIII. 207 They saw before them the greatest *market-hall in Lixa. **1835** *1st Munic. Corp. Comm. Rep.* App. III. 1686 [Preston] Other Officers of the Corporation are..Market Looker, *Market Keeper. **1947** AUDEN *Age of Anxiety* (1948) ii. 44 You will soon Not bother but acknowledge yourself As *market-made, a commodity Whose value varies. **1578** WHETSTONE *1st Pt. Promos & Cass.* IV. vi, Other *market maydes pay downe for their meate, But that I haue bought, on my score is set. **1606** SHAKS. *Ant. & Cl.* III. vi. 51 But you are come A Market-maid to Rome. **1891** G. CLARE *Money Market Primer* xii. 127 *Market-money, roughly speaking, is other people's money. **1922** JOYCE *Ulysses* 219 She passed out with her basket and a *market net. **1895** A. J. WILSON *Gloss. Stock Exch.* 62 *Market operators are tempted by a drop in the price to sell for the fall. **1696** *Mass. Bay Acts & Laws* 162 Hucksters and Traders of the Town, shall not..Buy of any of the *Market People there. **1830** J. F. COOPER *Water Witch* I. xi. 259 The rogues will pass the pennant like innocent market people. **1891** G. CLARE *Money-Market Primer* ix. 105 Immediately it becomes known that gold has actually arrived, the *market-quotation gives way. **1873** 'VIEUX MOUSTACHE' *Boarding-School Days* 36 He had been a hand on a New York *market-sloop. **1885** *Outing* VII. 206/2 A big market-sloop came along bound west. **1967** C. BERNERS-LEE in Wills & Yearsley *Handbk. Managem. Technol.* 4 Do the conclusions of this *market survey stand up? *Ibid.* 13 Useful programs for planning advertising campaigns have been written, based partly on market survey data. **1973** J. GOODFIELD *Courier to Peking* vii. 92, I don't think any market surveys have been done. **1670** EACHARD *Cont. Clergy* 44 Such things as are ridiculous, that serve for chimney and *market-talk. **1503** *Act 19 Hen. VII*, c. 6 It shall be lawful..to put them in the Pillory all the *Market-time. **1832** *Boston Herald* 6 Mar. 4 Acts of parliament to establish the right of *market tolls. **1802** *Deb. Congress U.S.* (1851) 18 Mar. 1027 In the state of New Jersey five hundred and forty two [of the carriages taxed] are..principally *market-wagons. **1895** C. D. WARNER *Golden House* i. 9 Here and there [was] a lumbering market-wagon from Jersey.

b. Special comb.: **market basket**, a large basket used to carry provisions, etc. purchased in the market; *spec.* see quot. 1884; ‖ **market-beater**, one who idles or lounges about a market; **market bell**, a bell rung to announce the commencement of a market; **market-clerk** = *clerk of the market* (see CLERK *sb.* 6c); **market-coin**, coin current in the market; in quot. *fig.*; **market-crier** ? *U.S.* (see quot.); **market-custom**, the dues levied on goods brought to market; † **market dame**, 'a strumpet' (Farmer); † **market-dasher** = *market-beater*; **market economy**, a system of economy which is subject to free competition; **market fair** *dial.*, a fairing or present from the market; **market-fish** *U.S.*, (*a*) fish, esp. cod-fish, of a marketable size (see quot.); (*b*) 'a corruption of *margate-fish*' (*Cent. Dict.* 1890); **market-fresh** *a. dial.* (see quot. 1841); † **market-friendship**, a friendship in business affairs; **market-fuddled** *a. dial.* = *market-fresh*; **market-garden**, a piece of land on which vegetables are grown for the market; hence ***market-gardener***; **market gardening**, keeping a market garden; † **market geld**, † **ȝeld** (see quots.); **market-horse** (*slang*), 'a horse simply kept in the betting-lists for the purpose of being betted against' (*Hotten's Slang Dict.* 1874); **market-house**, a building in which a market is held; a small house erected in a market-place for the use of market-folk; **market hunter**, one who hunts game for the market; so **market-hunting** *vbl. sb.*; † **market lash**, public flogging; in quot. *fig.*; **market-lead**, in *Silver-refining*, that portion of the metal which is sufficiently desilverized to be sold as lead; **market looker** (see quot. 1821); **market-maker**, †(*a*) a bargain-maker (*obs.*); (*b*) in the Stock Exchange (see 5b); so ***market-making***; **market mammy** *colloq.*, an African woman stallholder; **market master** (Pennsylv.), an officer having supervision of markets (*Cent. Dict.*); † **market-match**, a match made for pecuniary gain; **market-merry** *a. dial.* = *market-fresh*; hence ***market-merriness***; **market money**, money for buying things in a market (see also quot. 1891 in sense 10a); † **market-monger**, one who engrosses the market; **market-mongering**,

discreditable dealing in the share-market; **market-ordinary**, the ordinary provided for market people; **market-peace** *Hist.* [= G. *marktfriede*], the peace or truce which prevailed in a market on market-days; **market-penny**, a perquisite made by one who buys for another; †**market-plenty**, plentifulness of the market; **market-pot**, in *Silver-refining*, the last of a series of crystallizing pots, containing the market-lead; **market potential** (see quots.); **market-price**, the current price which a commodity fetches in the market; †**market-quality**, the quality of being a market town; **market-rate**, the current value of a commodity; **market reporter**, one who records the market rates of goods or stocks; **market research**, the systematic investigation of the demand for particular goods, a branch of marketing research; also *attrib.* and as vb. (to carry out market research); so ***market-researched*** ppl. adj., **market researcher**, a person engaged in this activity; **market-rigger**, one who 'rigs the market' (see RIG *v.*); hence ***market rigging*** vbl. sb.; †**market runner** = *market beater*; †**market-set** = MARKET-PLACE; **market shooter**, one who shoots game for the market; †**market-sieve**, ? one for sifting rice for the market; **market socialism**, an economic system in which a country's resources are publicly owned but production is geared to the private customer; hence **market-socialist** *attrib.*; **market square**, an open square in which a town market is held; also *fig.*; **market stall**, a standing-place or booth in a market; **market stallage**, the right of erecting or the rent paid for a market-stall; **market stance** *Sc.* = MARKET-PLACE; **market-table**, one frequented by marketers; **market-trot**, a steady trot like that of a person going to market; **market value**, current value in the market, saleable value; **market-woman**, (*a*) a woman who sells in the market; (*b*) with adj., one (more or less) skilled in marketing; **market-work**, the growing of produce for the market; also, the work connected with selling goods in a market. Also MARKET CROSS, DAY, MAN, -PLACE, -STEAD, TOWN.

1807 *Salmagundi* 27 June 247 Particular description of *market-baskets, butchers' blocks and wheel-barrows. **1853** DICKENS *Bleak Ho.* xxxiv. 333 Her market-basket..is a sort of wicker well with two flapping lids. **1884** *Cassell's Encycl. Dict.*, *Market-basket*, a basket used by dealers in the London fruit and vegetable markets. It contains 56 lbs. of potatoes. *c* **1380** WYCLIF *Wks.* (1880) 242 ȝe, þouȝ he be a *market betere. *c* **1386** CHAUCER *Reeve's T.* 16 He was a market-beter atte fulle. **1483** *Cath. Angl.* 236/1 Merketbeter, *circumforanus.* **1591** SHAKS. I *Hen. VI*, III. ii. 16 *Watch.* Enter, goe in, the *Market Bell is rung. **1616–61** HOLYDAY *Persius* 298 Being *market-clark..He break their earthen vessels less then measure. **1817** COLERIDGE *Biog. Lit.* 212 Words used as the arbitrary marks of thought, our smooth *market-coin of intercourse. **1846** WORCESTER (citing LEE), **Market-crier*, a crier of the market. **1844** H. STEPHENS *Bk. Farm* II. 89 The..dues incidental to the road and markets, such as tolls, forage, ferries, and *market-custom. **1705–7** E. WARD *Hud. Rediv.* (1715) II. II. ii. 25 Punks, Strolers, *Market Dames. *c* **1440** *Promp. Parv.* 326/2 *Market daschare, *circumforanus.* **1951** R. FIRTH *Elem. Social Organiz.* iii. 117 The other frame of organization consists of a *market economy where a man lives largely by selling his produce or his labour in competition with others. **1966** *Listener* 24 Nov. 755/2 A market economy is an arrangement by which people, by their purchases, make clear what they want or do not want. Their market behaviour, in turn, is an instruction to producers as to what they should produce or not produce. **1968** *Ibid.* 4 July 7/2 In the market economy of classical capitalism the interests of the working class ran clean counter to those interests which relied upon the smooth working of the economic system. **1972** *Accountant* 5 Oct. 409/1 In a market economy, in which prices of goods and services are ultimately determined by the forces of supply and demand, any intervention by government in the form of fixing or holding prices and incomes cannot for long be effective. **1821** *Blackw. Mag.* VIII. 433 The rogues escaped from task, Here take their stand, the '*market fair' to ask. **1894** *Outing* (U.S.) XXIII. 404/1 *Market fish are those [cod] measuring less [than 22 in.], but weighing 3 lbs. or more. **1841** HARTSHORNE *Salop. Ant.* 498 **Market-Fresh*, that dubious degree of sobriety with which farmers too commonly return home from market. **1651** HOBBES *Govt. & Soc.* i. §2. 4 If they meet for Traffique,..a certain *Market-friendship is begotten. **1895** 'M. E. FRANCIS' *Frieze & Fustian* 142 Jem..was not by any means '*market-fuddled'. **1840** *Penny Cycl.* XVII. 96/1 [The land] would make excellent *market-gardens. **1865** DICKENS *Mut. Fr.* II. i, Where the railways still bestride the market-gardens that will soon die under them. **1826** *Westm. Rev.* V. 20 The fruit and vegetables of a *market gardener, on which his subsistence depends. **1832** *Chambers's Edin. Jrnl.* 7 Apr. 76/2 An industrious but rather unsuccessful market-gardener..from Kirkcaldy. **1839** *Penny Cycl.* XIII. 188/1 Market-gardeners, who raise vegetables..for the supply of the London markets. **1963** *Times* 22 Feb. 10/3 Sir Thomas Playford, orchardist and market gardener, has all the assurance even in the uncertain world of politics of a man who knows that he will reap what he sows. **1875** *Encycl. Brit.* I. 384/1 **Market Gardening*... The growth of fruits and of culinary vegetables is in various parts of Great Britain an important department of farming. **1958** HAYWARD & HARARI tr. *Pasternak's Dr. Zhivago* I. vii. 218 It is not for the sake of market gardening that we are going all this enormous distance. ? *a* **1500** in Blount *Law Dict.* (1670) s.v., Et valent per an. le Streteward & le *Marketzeld xviiis. **1684** MANLEY *Cowell's Interpr.* (ed. 2), *Marketzeld*, more truly *Marketgeld*, It signifies Toll of the Market. **1561** STOW *Eng. Chron.* (1565) 136 This yeare the *market house called the Stockes in London was begon to be buylded. **1840** *Penny Cycl.* XVII. 102/1 A town-hall [at Witney]..with a piazza underneath for a market-house. **1874** J. W. LONG *Amer. Wild-Fowl Shooting* 185 Blue-winged teal..are much sought for by *market-hunters. **1940** M. B. TRAUTMAN *Birds Buckeye Lake, Ohio* 170 According to former market hunters and old sportsmen, the Eastern Least Bittern was the most numerous transient and summering species between 1860 and 1900. **1897** *Outing* XXX. 293/1, I had little dreamed that Michigan would ever so far forget herself as to encourage *market-hunting in preference to sportsman like methods. **1627–77** FELTHAM *Resolves* I. lviii. 91 Every offence meets not with a *Market lash. Private punishments sometimes gripe a man within. **1877** RAYMOND *Statist. Mines & Mining* 181 Rich lead on the one hand and *market-lead on the other. **1591** *Manch. Court Leet Rec.* (1885) II. 57 To delyuer..them [the weights] to the *marketlokers. **1821** DE QUINCEY *Richter* Wks. 1863 XIII. 143 *note*, 'Market-lookers' is a provincial term..for the public officers who examine the quality of the provisions exposed for sale. **1647** WARD *Simp. Cobler* 36 When Christ whips *Market-makers out of his Temple. **1340** *Ayenb.* 42 The vifte [twig of Simony] is ine ham þet be *markat makinde leteþ hare benefices oþer chongeþ. **1902** *Westm. Gaz.* 14 Jan. 5/1 He put down contracts of this kind as 'advertising' and 'market making'. **1962** A. LEJEUNE *Duel in Shadows* vii. 91 There were two Africans, a small man..and his wife, fat as a *Market Mammy. **1966** *Punch* 21 Sept. 457/1, I stared at..this old market-mammy who had lost her 'touch' and was clinging so stubbornly to the last shreds of her trading reputation. **1972** *Daily Tel.* 21 Jan. 4/3 About 7,000 white-clad market mammies—women stallholders—with drummers and horn blowers yesterday demonstrated through Accra in support of last week's military coup against the Busia regime. **1851** C. CIST *Sk. Cincinnati in 1851* 87 A city treasurer, a marshal, a wharf and three *market masters are elected. **1913** J. W. SULLIVAN *Markets for People* 104 The Pennsylvania markets usually get along with a single market-master. **1605** BRETON *Old Man's Lesson* B iij b, *Market-matches where Marriages are made without affections. **1898** WATTS-DUNTON *Aylwin* (1900) 143/1 The moment that he had passed into '*market-merriness'. **1847** HALLIWELL *Provinc.*, **Market-merry*, tipsy. **1633** G. HERBERT *Church Porch* in *Temple* 13 Think heav'n a better bargain, then to give Onely thy single *market-money for it. **1868** *Putnam's Mag.* Jan. 40/2 Strawberries are down to ten cents a box..but you didn't leave a cent of market-money. **1629** GAULE *Holy Madn.* 389 A *Market-monger, Corne-hoorder. **1901** *Westm. Gaz.* 10 Jan. 9/1 The evils of such a system of *market mongering. **1769** BURKE *Lett., to Marq. Rockingham* (1844) I. 193 The freeholders dined..at a *market-ordinary. **1872** YEATS *Growth Comm.* 379 The *market-peace afforded security to the multitudes who congregated together. **1735** *Poor Robin* Observ. Oct., They can go to Market, buy Victuals, and spend the *Market penny in the Morning. **1815** *Paris Chit-Chat* (1816) I. 53 Your cook..never considers her market penny an unfair advantage. **1643** TRAPP *Comm. Gen.* xxvi. 28 The Church of Rome borrows her mark from the *market-plenty, or cheapness. **1860** *Ure's Dict. Arts* (ed. 5) II. 664 The '*market pot'. **1962** S. STRAND *Marketing Dict.* 436 **Market potentials*, determining the marketability of a product. **1969** J. M. RATHMELL *Managing the Marketing Function* v. 200 *Market potential* is an expression of a market's absorption of a total industry's production in units or dollar sales... The major operational value of market potential is its usefulness in determining spatial rather than temporal objectives. *c* **1440** *Jacob's Well* 212 ȝif þou sell hym derere þan þe *markett prise, þou owyst to restore it. **1601** SHAKS. *All's Well* v. iii. 219. **1880** C. R. MARKHAM *Peruv. Bark* 434 The quinine will be sold at market prices. **1745** H. WALPOLE *Let. G. Montagu* 25 June, On the right and left..lie two towns; the one of *market quality, and the other with a wharf where ships come up. **1700** *Prior Robe's Geogr.* 22 To Those, who at the *Market-Rate Can barter Honour for Estate. **1825** MCCULLOCH *Pol. Econ.* III. vii. 336 The market rate of wages. **1854** B. J. TAYLOR *Jan. & June* 83 And so, as *Market Reporters have it, 'we have movements to note'. **1926** *Market Res. Agencies Guide to Publ.* (U.S. Dept. Commerce) p. iii, With large sums of money being spent for *market research..the necessity of having an inventory of accomplishments becomes obvious. **1927** *Ibid.* p. iv, Market research is the study of all problems relating to the transfer of goods from producer to consumer, involving relationships and adjustments between production and consumption, preparation of commodities for sale, their physical handling, wholesale and retail merchandising, and financial problems concerned. **1931** R. SIMMAT *Market Res.* i. 7 Reputable agencies will not accept the advertising for a product which market research has revealed to be unsuitable. **1937** *Discovery* Feb. 47/2 Another field for psychological investigation in many parts of the Special Areas is in market research, where methods of sale and customers' psychology need to be examined side by side. **1951** M. MCLUHAN *Mech. Bride* (1967) 31/2 As market-research tyranny has developed, the object and ends of human consumption have been blurred. **1956** *Planning* XXII. 19 Individual publishers and individual booksellers continue to do what they can for themselves in the way of market research and sales promotion. **1964** M. ARGYLE *Psychol. & Social Probl.* xiii. 162 One of the earliest pieces of market research discovered that coffee had an unfavourable image of being connected with tiredness and strain. **1965** *Spectator* 1 Jan. 3/1 The *Sunday Times* ..claimed that £100,000 was to be spent on market research. **1969** P. DICKINSON *Pride of Heroes* 58, I commissioned a little firm in Chicago to market-research the American idea of what English beer ought to taste like. **1970** *New Scientist* 1 Jan. 4/2 A 'hard sell' is necessary and this must be preceded by market research. **1973** *Times* 1 Feb. 8/2 (Advt.), Some market research experience would be an advantage. **1964** *Economist* 17 Oct. 276/3 The 1800 is as much a challenge to orthodox *market-researched motoring as the Mini was five years ago. **1951** M. MCLUHAN *Mech. Bride* (1967) p. vi/2 Today the tyrant rules not by club or fist, but, disguised as a *market researcher, he shepherds his flocks in the ways of utility and comfort. **1969** J. ARGENTI *Managem. Techniques* 157 Market Researchers rely heavily on the analysis of statistics—a notoriously difficult subject—and on answers to questionnaires—also notoriously unreliable. **1975** *Country Life* 2 Jan. 51/2 Editors have been convinced by accountants, market-researchers and computers that stories don't help to sell their products. **1881** GOLDW. SMITH *Lect. & Ess.* 179 A mere *market-rigger and money-grubber. **1897** *Westm. Gaz.* 23 Aug. 5/1 The rise..is largely attributed to *market rigging. **1486** *Cath. Angl.* 236/1 A *Merkett rynner, *circumforarius.* **1552** LATIMER *Serm., St. John Evang. Day* (1584) 284 It was a common stable in the *Market set. **1880** *Golden Days for Boys & Girls* 6 Mar. 3/2 He knew very well that the ambitious and high-spirited Oscar was not a *market-shooter from choice. **1897** *Outing* XXX. 293/2 The market-shooter, with no dogs to take care of, can sneak through the known haunts of the quail. **1761** *Descr. S. Carolina* 8 Afterwards, by a Wire-Sieve called a *Market-Sieve, it is separated from the broken and small Rice. **1965** *Listener* 15 Apr. 547/2 The new methods involve a form of *market socialism, on the Yugoslav model... Production would be largely guided by the market. **1969** *Guardian* 3 July 12/5 The effect of the Czechoslovak events has been to discredit, in the eyes of the official [Russian] Establishment, the idea of 'market socialism'. **1972** D. COLLARD *Prices, Markets & Welfare* iv. 41 Where preferences are private but the ownership of resources public we have a market-socialist system. *Ibid.* xiii. 119 In the early 'thirties..Lange, Lerner and Dickinson..suggested a series of devices known as 'market socialism'. **1794** *Mass. Hist. Soc. Coll.* 1st Ser. III. 254 Besides the lower floor of Faneuil hall being used as a flesh market, a number of stalls are erected on *Market square..and let to the market men. **1836** D. B. EDWARD *Hist. Texas* 148 A block shall be designated for a market square. **1963** *Times* 14 Feb. 8/5 The scientist who refuses contact with the people and opts for the Ivory Tower rather than the Market Square is a traitor to himself and to humanity. **1827** DRAKE & MANSFIELD *Cincinnati in 1826* vi. 55 The Revenue of the Corporation is derived; From..Rent of *Market-stalls. **1859** LD. LYTTON *Wanderer* (ed. 2) 276 Those windows with the market-stalls before. **1832** *Boston Herald* 6 Mar. 4 *Market Stallage. **1899** *Blackw. Mag.* Jan. 46/1 The *market-stance in the wilderness was free to all comers. **1850** W. P. SCARGILL *Eng. Sketch-Bk.* 3 Such agricultural bucks..are generally..the oracles of the *market-table. **1856** *Househ. Wds.* XIII. 497/1 The ex-groom..walked his pony on in silence..breaking occasionally into a *market-trot. **1691** LOCKE *Money* in *Wks.* (1824) IV. 99 According to the *market value. **1791** *Deb. Congress U.S.* (1834) 1st Congr. App. 1993 The rapid increase that has taken place in the market value of the public securities. **1848** MILL *Pol. Econ.* I. III. ii. §4. 528 There are persons ready to buy, at the market value, a greater quantity than is offered for sale. **1880** C. R. MARKHAM *Peruv. Bark* 109 Bark from that district is of no market value. **1552** HULOET, *Market woman, *foratia.* **1624** MASSINGER *Parl. Love* II. i, Of such as trade in the streets,..Of progress laundresses, and marketwomen. **1755** *Connoisseur* No. 91 ¶2 My wife is particularly proud of being an excellent Market-woman. **1863** MISS BRADDON *Eleanor's Vict.* i, To buy peaches..of the noisy market women. **1887** H. H. JACKSON *Between Whiles* iv. 226 Donald liked slow cruising and the *market-work best.

market (ˈmɑːkɪt), *v.* [f. MARKET *sb.*]

1. *intr.* To deal in a market, buy and sell; to go to market with produce; to purchase provisions.

1635 HEYLIN *Sabbath* II. (1636) 214 That no man should presume to Market on the Lords day. **1747** MRS. GLASSE *Cookery* xxi. 160 How to market. **1776** ADAM SMITH *W.N.* I. xi. I. 246 A contract of this kind saves the farmer the expence and trouble of marketing. **1821** MOORE *Mem.* (1853) III. 207 Went into town..in order to market for to-morrow's dinner.

2. *trans.* To dispose of in a market, to sell; also, to bring or send to market.

1649 G. DANIEL *Trinarch., Hen. V*, xcviii, The Treasurer ..for a Price Mercates his Maister, to extend his Purse. **1657** BP. H. KING *Poems* III. (1843) 90 The Captiv'd Welch, in Couples led, Were Marketted, like Cattell, by the Head. **1791** COWPER *Iliad* XVIII. 358 Our wealth Is marketted. **1865** *Daily Tel.* 11 Aug., The Seven-thirty Loan has now been all marketed. **1892** *Times* 24 Sept. 12/2 Foreign farmers are obliged to market their corn immense distances by rail, canal, and sea.

3. To 'trade *on*', to take advantage of.

1906 HARDY *Dynasts* II. I. i. 10 These cloaked visitors of every clime That market on your magnanimity To gain an audience.

marketable (ˈmɑːkɪtəb(ə)l), *a.* Also 7 **markettable, mercatable.** [f. MARKET *v.* + -ABLE.]

1. Capable of being marketed; that may or can be bought or sold; suitable for the market; that finds a ready market; that is in demand; saleable.

1600 SHAKS. *A.Y.L.* I. ii. 103 *Ros.* Then shal we be newes-cram'd. *Cel.* All the better: we shalbe the more Marketable. **1610** —— *Temp.* v. i. 266 *Seb.* Will money buy em? *Ant.* Very like: one of them Is a plaine Fish, and no doubt marketable. **1652–62** HEYLIN *Cosmogr.* IV. (1682) 7 They do transport their Marketable Commodities from one place to another. **1677** PLOT *Oxfordsh.* 151 This Corn..proving Mercatable, is now become one of the commonest grains of this County. **1745** *De Foe's Eng. Tradesman* ii. (1841) I. 16 The goods are not of a marketable goodness. **1812** BYRON *Waltz* Ep., Our girls being come to a marriageable (or, as they call it, marketable) age. **1851** BRIMLEY *Ess., Wordsworth* 162 Unpossessed of any marketable talent. **1890** 'R. BOLDREWOOD' *Col. Reformer* (1891) 241 Such fat cattle as were up to the marketable standard.

2. Of or pertaining to buying or selling; concerned with trade. Of price, value: That may be obtained in buying or selling.

1602 FULBECKE *1st Pt. Parall.* 3 If hee sende him to Fayres or Markets, to buy, to sell, or to doe other things markettable. **1690** LUTTRELL *Brief Rel.* (1857) II. 91 Their goods unladen, and they are sent home with assurance of a marketable price for the same. **1837** HAWTHORNE *Twice-told T.* (1851) I. xi. 186 Being calculated to reduce the

marketable value of the true gem. **1872** YEATS *Growth Comm.* 298 To enlarge the marketable area by enfranchising other ports would violate the Marketable Act.

Hence ˌ**marketaˈbility**, ˈ**marketableness**, the condition or fact of being marketable.

1809–10 COLERIDGE *Friend* (1818) II. 65 The marketableness of our manufactures in foreign marts. **1877** R. GIFFEN *Stock Exch. Securities* 89 The difference of marketability arising..from the greater mass of some securities than others. **1884** *Macm. Mag.* Oct. 415/1 The marketability of land.

marketably (ˈmɑːkɪtəblɪ), *adv.* [f. MARKETABLE + -LY^2.] So as to be marketable.

1842 *Jrnl. R. Agric. Soc.* III. II. 337 A sufficient judge of beasts to know whether they are marketably fat or not. **1873** *Contemp. Rev.* XXII. 700 Meagre or turgid attempts at being..marketably graphic.

market cross. A cross erected in a market-place (see also quot. 1850).

1448 *Aberdeen Reg.* (1844) I. 17 John Voket..yheide to the merkate corss, and opynly proclamyt the land..to be sald. **1535** STEWART *Cron. Scot.* III. 457 Content he wes.. In Lundoun toun evin at the mercat corce, On fit to fecht. **1702** *Lond. Gaz.* No. 3806/7 The Mayor..caused an Ox to be roasted whole at the Market Cross. **1850** PARKER *Gloss. Archit.* s.v. *Cross*, Market crosses were usually polygonal buildings with an open archway on each of the sides, and vaulted within, large enough to afford shelter to a considerable number of persons.

market day. The fixed day on which a market is held.

1436 *Rolls of Parlt.* IV. 497/2 At every market day within two wekes. **1593** SHAKS. *2 Hen. VI*, IV. ii. 62, I haue seene him whipt three Market dayes together. **1672** PETTY *Pol. Anat.* (1691) 63 The number of People living within a Market-days Journey. **1871** CARLYLE in *Mrs. C.'s Lett.* I. 141 It must have been Saturday,.. Carlisle market-day.

Proverb. **1695** J. SAGE *Article* Wks. 1844 I. 235 Behold the difference in Market-days, as we say.

marketeer (mɑːkɪˈtɪə(r)). [See -EER^1.]

1. One who sells in a market; a market-dealer.

1832 *Boston Herald* 6 Mar. 4 Placing the permanent taxed shopkeepers more on a level with the weekly untaxed marketeers. **1847** ROBB *Squatter Life* 116 The sucker marketeer drew off a few paces, to be ready to run. **1859** SALA *Tw. round Clock* (1861) 10 A genuine Billingsgate marketeer.

2. *Racing slang.* (See quot.)

1874 *Hotten's Slang Dict.*, *Marketeer*, a betting man who devotes himself, by means of special information, to the study of favourites, and the diseases incident to that condition of equine life. The Marketeer is the principal agent in all milking and knocking-out arrangements.

3. A supporter of Britain's entry into the Common Market (cf. COMMON *a.* 21).

1962 *Listener* 15 Nov. 799/2 The Marketeers within the Labour Party. **1969** *Guardian* 29 Aug. 16/8 The TUC General Council is trying to avoid an embarrassing public debate on the Common Market... Pro- and anti-Marketeers united in angry condemnation of Mr. Jenkins's attempts to force the issue on to the agenda. **1970** *Times* 4 May 8/2 Mr. Douglas Jay..leads his all-party group of anti-Marketeers, under the banner of the new Common Market Safeguards Campaign. **1971** *New Scientist* 27 May 522/1 The Paris summit has made the marketeers a little bolder. **1975** *Times* 25 Feb. 14/2 A keynote of the marketeers' case is..that Britain is in Europe and that the decision is.. whether to come out.

marketer (ˈmɑːkɪtə(r)). ? *U.S.* [f. MARKET *v.* + -ER^1.] One who goes to market; one who buys or sells in a market.

1787 M. CUTLER in *Life*, etc. (1888) I. 271 The marketers seemed to be all in and every thing arranged. **18..** *Pop. Sci. Monthly* XIII. 430 (Cent.) A superficial sameness in the appearance of meat which it is the business of a good marketer to see through. **1900** H. JAMES *Little Tour* xxiv. 166, I sat down with a hundred hungry marketers, fat, brown, greasy men.

marketh, obs. form of MARKET.

marketing (ˈmɑːkɪtɪŋ), *vbl. sb.* [f. MARKET *v.* + -ING^1.]

1. a. The action of the vb. MARKET; buying or selling; an instance of this. Also *fig.*

1561 T. NORTON *Calvin's Inst.* IV. xviii. 148 How filthy markettinges they vse, how vnhonest gaines they make wᵗ their massinges. **1636** HEYLIN *Sabbath* I. v. 108 All other marketting was unlawfull on the Sabbath dayes. **1833** LYTTON *Eng. & Engl.* (ed. 2) I. 124 A notorious characteristic of English society is the universal marketing of our unmarried women. **1885** MABEL COLLINS *Prettiest Woman* ix, He did certain necessary marketings, and returned for her.

b. The action or business of bringing or sending (a commodity) to market.

1884 *Harper's Mag.* Mar. 506/1 This marketing of supplies was the beginning..of its prosperity. **1894** *Daily News* 26 Jan. 5/4 Facilities for the marketing of labour in country districts.

2. a. Something bought in the market; a purchase.

1701 PEPYS *Let.* 4 Dec., Sorting and binding together my nephew's Roman marketings. **1755** *Connoisseur* No. 91 ¶2 Above half her marketings stink and grow musty, before we can use them.

b. Produce to be sold in the market; also, a consignment of such produce.

1886 P. FITZGERALD *Fatal Zero* li. (1888) 290 The honest creatures..who till the soil here and bring in marketing. **1893** *Times* 10 July 4/6 The marketings of dairy butter have been smaller than of late.

3. *attrib.* and *Comb.*, as (sense 1) ***marketing advantage, agent, conference, day, director, policy, problem, revolution, strategy, survey***; (sense 2 a) ***marketing bag, basket***; **marketing mix** (see quot. 1969); **marketing research**, the systematic study of all the factors involved in marketing a product (see quot. 1963); so **marketing researcher**.

1919 A. MARSHALL *Industry & Trade* App. J. 800 The low grade industries which congregate in London owe comparatively little to the marketing advantages which are to be found there. **1951** M. MCLUHAN *Mech. Bride* (1967) 92/1 The marketing agents reciprocate by using still more applied science. **1934** T. S. ELIOT *Rock* ii. 65 Enter Mrs. Ethelbert with marketing bag, hilariously. **1925** W. DE LA MARE *Two Tales* 20 A small, old, spectacled lady with a large marketing-basket, was..issuing out from behind the shop. **1970** *Brit. Printer* June 57 The BFMP's fourth marketing conference in London served to emphasise the urgent need for printers to understand the term 'marketing' let alone employ its principles. **1619** J. DYKE *Counterpoison* 24 A marketting and a iunketting, a selling and a swilling day both. **1961** *Times* 14 July 2/2 Marketing Director to organize and direct the Sales Organization. **1969** D. C. HAGUE *Managerial Econ.* III. xiv. 293 One of the major issues in all business is how to arrive at the correct 'marketing mix'—the correct balance of product design, price, advertising and other promotional expenditure, spending on the sales force, and so on. **1972** *Lebende Sprachen* XVII. 46/1 *Marketing mix.* **1930** G. R. COLLINS *Marketing* v. 78 The process of formulating marketing policies should recognise the fact that consumers' demands are the origins of economic impulses. **1920** P. T. CHERINGTON *Elem. Marketing* 3 Increase of the scale of production alone introduces maladjustments between producing and consuming conditions with regard to quantity, quality, time, and place, which it becomes part of the marketing problem to correct. **1951** E. S. BRADFORD *Marketing Res.* p. xi, Marketing research is coming to be recognized as essential to a successful development of marketing. **1956** G. R. COLLINS *Marketing* (rev. ed.) v. 78 Marketing research..must..have for its major objective the minimizing of errors in marketing judgment. **1963** *Gloss. Managem. Terms* (Brit. Inst. Managem.) (Typescript), The distinction between market research and marketing research is important but is not yet as widely used and understood in the U.K. as in the U.S.A. One is a study of the market for the product and the other is a study of the marketing of the product. **1967** G. WILLS in Wills & Yearsley *Handbk. Managem. Technol.* 175 Marketing research began in the second decade of the century as a commercial tool for the collection of facts for a better direction of sales effort. *Ibid.* 178 The analysis of territorial sales potential..is within the marketing research function of the business. *Ibid.* 179 Any marketing problem has three certain dimensions which marketing manager and researcher ignore at their peril—time, cost, and resources. **1963** *Times* 5 June 17/4 Today we [*sc.* the British] are lagging behind in a..transition that might be described as the Marketing Revolution. **1969** D. C. HAGUE *Managerial Econ.* III. xiii. 288 Dr Rothschild was impressed by the ease with which military terminology insinuates itself into discussions of oligopoly. We talk of price wars, sales campaigns, marketing strategies, industrial espionage and so on. **1974** *Times* 18 Feb. 12 Many hoteliers now regard conferences as an integral part of the marketing strategy for their establishments. **1941** 'BALBUS' *Reconstruction & Peace* 58 Marketing surveys and campaigns for increasing consumption.

marketing (ˈmɑːkɪtɪŋ), *ppl. a.* [f. MARKET *v.* + -ING^2.] That markets, in the senses of the verb.

1851 D. JERROLD *St. Giles* xi. 105 Money in this marketing world of ours may buy much. **1872** HOWELLS *Wedd. Journ.* (1892) 28 A marketing mother of a family.

market man. One who deals in a market; one who goes to market to buy or sell.

1542 UDALL *Erasm. Apoph.* 336 b, As the mercatemenne ..dooe bryng out a litle modicum of wheate..in a treen dishe for a saumple. **1591** SHAKS. *1 Hen. VI*, v. v. 54 So worthlesse Pezants bargaine for their Wiues, As market men for Oxen. **1654** GATAKER *Disc. Apol.* 18 The Market-man counteth that but an evil Market-day, that he hath not gained somewhat on. **1762** *Ann. Reg.* 127 He being always the market-man for cheese, as he knew how to buy it good better than any other of the family. **1868** BROWNING *Ring & Bk.* I. 98 Thick-ankled girls..made place For marketmen glad to pitch basket down.

b. *Stock exchange.* (See MARKET *sb.* 1 d.)

1895 *Westm. Gaz.* 19 Jan. 7/1 Market men who attended ..reckoned that the natural course of the shares was to fall.

ˈ**market-place.** The place where a market is held, usually a square or wide open space in a town. Also *fig.*

c **1386** CHAUCER *Merch. T.* 339 As who-so toke a mirour.. And sette it in a commune market-place. **1503** *Act 19 Hen. VII*, c. 6 It shall be lawful..in the Market-place to put them in the Pillory all the Market-time. **1607** SHAKS. *Cor.* I. v. 27 Go sound thy Trumpet in the Market place. **1756–7** tr. *Keysler's Trav.* (1760) III. 3 In the market-place..is a superb bronze statue of Urban VIII. **1847** *Act 10 & 11 Vict.* c. 14 §14 After the Market Place or Place for Fairs is opened for public Use. **1958** J. BARZUN in Caplow & McGee *Academic Marketplace* p. v, The observers' point of departure was the current problem of mobility within the academic marketplace. **1975** *Times* 10 Apr. 16/1 Pension schemes..tied to the earnings-related inequalities of the market-place.

marketstead (ˈmɑːkɪtstɛd). *arch.* [f. MARKET *sb.* + STEAD.] = MARKET-PLACE.

1386 *Mem. Ripon* (Surtees) I. 134 De uno burgagio in Ripon in le Marketstede. *c* **1425** *St. Mary of Oignies* II. ii. in *Anglia* VIII. 152/17 A place in þe comun marketstede. **1577** *Burgh Rec. Glasgow* (1876) I. 63 It is..ordanit that the marcatt sted of gers, stray, and hay be in the New Kirk yarde. **1650** FULLER *Pisgah* II. ix. 189 The greatest place of receipt in Samaria (which might serve them for a market-stead). **1870** MORRIS *Earthly Par.* I. I. 118 Through the marketstead Swiftly he passed.

market town. A town which has the privilege of holding a market; also, †a trading town.

1449 *Rolls of Parlt.* V. 150/2 In..markettownes. **1553** EDEN *Treat. Newe Ind.* (Arb.) 12 Of Calicut, the moste famous markette towne of India. **1632** MASSINGER *City Madam* III. iii, Here lay..a sure deed of gift for a market town. **1715** GAY *What d'ye call it?* I. 3 They would have burnt him at our Market Town. **1809–10** COLERIDGE *Friend* (1865) 148 A small market town in the south-west of England.

markgraf, -grave: see MARGRAVE.

‖**markhor(e** (ˈmɑːkɔː(r)). *Nat. Hist.* Also 9 **markhoor.** [Pers. *mārkhōr*, lit. 'serpent-eater'.] A large wild goat (*Capra falconeri*), of a slaty gray colour, with long spiral horns, native of the mountainous country between Persia and Tibet.

1867 A. L. ADAMS *Wand. Nat. in Ind.* 213 The markhore ..is found on the mountains of Persia, Afghanistan, and.. is plentiful on the ranges round the Khyber Pass. **1868** DARWIN *Anim. & Pl.* I. 101 *note*, The Asiatic markhor. **1889** *Spectator* 9 Nov. 637/1 A herd of markhor.

marking (ˈmɑːkɪŋ), *vbl. sb.* [f. MARK *v.* + -ING^1.]

1. a. The action of the verb MARK.

c **1315** SHOREHAM *Poems* 15/415 Þe signe his of þis sacrement Mid creyme þe markinge. **1588** SHAKS. *L.L.L.* I. i. 288, I doe confesse much of the hearing of it, but little of the marking of it. **1672** C. BEALE in H. Walpole *Vertue's Anecd. Paint.* (1786) III. 130 Much more..then my heart cou'd with her most carefull marking learn from his painting either this, or Dr. Cradock's picture. **1840** DICKENS *Old C. Shop* viii, The art of needle-work, marking, and samplery, [taught] by Miss Jane Wackles. **1891** R. WALLACE *Rural Econ. Austral. & N.Z.* ii. 43 Lamb-tailing and marking were on at this time—the end of June. **1904** *Grove's Dict. Mus.* I. 14/1 The strong marking of the accent seems to have been only usual in dance music. **1946** F. DAVISON *Dusty* iv. 45 He handled lambs at marking time..as gently as if he owned them. **1950** *N.Z. Jrnl. Agric.* Sept. 197/1 Lamb marking consists of three different operations: the placing of a distinguishing mark in one or both ears, the amputation of tails, and the castration of male lambs.

†**b.** Manner of marking: notation. *Obs.*

1597 MORLEY *Introd. Mus.* 90 For when they marke tripla of three minimes for a stroke, they doe most vsuallie set these numbers before it $\frac{3}{2}$: which is the true marking of sesqui altera.

c. With advs., freq. in *attrib.* uses.

1726 LEONI *Alberti's Archit.* I. 37/1 The very marking out of the Platform ought to be done under proper Auspices. **1894** W. J. LINEHAM *Text-bk. Mech. Engin.* vi. 183 (*heading*) Marking-off, machining, fitting and erecting. **1909** *Westm. Gaz.* 24 Mar. 10/3 A marking-down process was also indulged in in anticipation of selling by speculators and profit-taking. **1917** [see ASSEMBLY 1 b]. **1948** R. DE KERCHOVE *Internat. Maritime Dict.* 451/2 Marking-off platers work to drawings supplied from the drawing office and information given from the mold loft. **1964** S. CRAWFORD *Basic Engin. Processes* i. 36 A typical marking-out table is shown. *Ibid.* 39 This mild-steel clamp is machined to length, width, and thickness prior to marking-out. **1966** J. H. DIXON tr. *Dormidontov's Shipbuilding Technol.* v. 115 A template work-shop..fitted with optical marking apparatus and a marking-off table.

d. *Stock Exchange.* The recording of prices at which bargains are made.

1903 *Pitman's Business Man's Guide* 305/1 *Marking*,..on the Stock Exchange this signifies the recording of the prices at which actual business has been done in any security between the hours of eleven and three. **1930** *Economist* 22 Mar. 653/1 Dealings begin, the marking of bargains is effected in one or other of the Stock Exchange Daily Lists, [etc.]. **1934** F. E. ARMSTRONG *Bk. Stock Exchange* iii. 52 The marking of bargains in the *Official* and *Supplementary Lists* is..the record of business actually transacted, and provides an index to an established price level. **1959** *Times* 7 Apr. 10/6, 20,451 separate bargains were recorded. This is the highest total reached since the 'marking' of bargains was inaugurated. **1971** T. G. GOFF *Theory & Pract. Investment* v. 53 A symbol beside a marking may indicate that there is some unusual feature about the underlying deal.

†**2.** Notice, consideration. *Obs.*

1585 T. WASHINGTON tr. *Nicholay's Voy.* Ep. Ded., Doth it not deserue diligent marking and remembring? **1603** KNOLLES *Hist. Turks* (1638) 171 But it is worth the marking, how things appointed to befall us are by no means to be auoided.

3. *concr.* A mark or pattern of marks, natural or artificial.

1382 WYCLIF *Kings* Prol. p. 2 The Lamentaciouns of Jeremye..with the same abicees or markyngis ben noumbrid [L. *iisaem alphabetis vel incisionibus supputantur*]. **1641** [see MARL *v.*^{1} 3]. **1803** MONTAGUE *Ornith. Dict.* (1831) 326 These birds are subject to some variety in markings. **1837** GORING & PRITCHARD *Microgr.* 162 No one who..did not know there actually were lines or markings upon it, would suspect their existence. **1894** R. B. SHARPE *Handbk. Birds Gt. Brit.* (1896) I. 42 Eggs..exactly like those of the Goldfinch in size and markings.

4. *attrib.* and *Comb.*, as ***marking brush, pencil***; † **marking axe**, an axe used by foresters for marking trees; **marking board**, (*a*) a board constructed to register the score in certain games; (*b*) a board in the Stock Exchange upon which transactions are posted; **marking cotton** (see quot. 1882); **marking flag**, a flag used by soldiers for marking a position; † **marking fruit** = *marking nut*; **marking-gauge** = GAUGE *sb.* 11;

marking ink, (*a*) an indelible ink used for marking linen, etc.; (*b*) a mixture used for marking packing-cases and the like with a stencil or otherwise; †**marking instrument** = next; **marking iron**, (*a*) a branding iron; (*b*) see quot. 1747; **marking-nut**, the fruit of the tree *Semecarpus Anacardium*, the juice of which makes an indelible black stain on linen, etc.; **marking-nut tree**, an Indian tree which bears the marking-nut; **marking-plough** (see quot. 1805); **marking-pot**, a vessel containing paint for stencilling packages; **marking stitch**, a stitch used in marking linen, etc.; †**marking-stone**, an earthy stone used for marking cattle, etc.; **marking wheels**, two wheels attached to a sowing drill to regulate the distance between the rows; †**marking-yarn** (see quot. 1744).

1384–5 *Durham Acc. Rolls* (Surtees) 390 Pro j *m'kyngax, xvj*d*. **1856** 'CRAWLEY' *Billiards* (1859) 4 A..Thurston table, cues, balls, and *marking board, all complete. **1900** *Westm. Gaz.* 26 Sept. 9/1 [Stock Exchange.]The marking board should be above suspicion. **1855** 'Q. K. P. DOESTICKS' *Doesticks, what he Says* xxii. 198 A dry-goods box with a *marking brush sticking out of the top of it. **1882** M. H. FOOTE *Led-Horse Claim* xvii. 228 He..swept, with one stroke of his marking-brush, a black circle around the figures. **1805** E. S. BOWNE in *Scribner's Mag.* II. 180/2, I enclose the *marking cotton. **1882** CAULFEILD & SAWARD *Dict. Needlework*, *Marking Cotton*, an ingrain coloured sewing cotton, to be had in Turkey-red and blue, and sold in small balls and reels. **1901** KIPLING *Kim* xiii. 343 The Babu, the slack of his thin gear snapping like a *marking-flag in the chill breeze, stood by. **1866** *Treas. Bot.* 722/2 *Marking fruit, *Semecarpus Anacardium*. **1875** KNIGHT *Dict. Mech.*, **Marking-gage*. **1710** *Lond. Gaz.* No. 4719/4 Shopkeepers common Writing or *Marking Ink. **1819** BRANDE *Chem.* 315 Nitrate of silver..is employed for writing upon linen, under the name of *indelible* or *marking ink*. **1888** J. PAYN *Myst. Mirbridge* xvii. II. 21 It won't wash out any more than that marking-ink. **1398** TREVISA *Barth. De P. R.* XVI. vii. (1495) 557 A *merkynge instrument [L. *cauterium*] of syluer kepyth from synkynge: and comfortyth feble membres. *c* **1420** *Pallad. on Husb.* I. 1163 Here most be *markyng yrons for oure beestis, And toolis forto gelde, and clippe, and shere. **1538** in *10th Rep. Hist. MSS. Comm.* App. IV. 425 A markyng irne to brene a convyct clerke. **1682** *2nd Plea for Nonconf.* 51 Let them receive from us some Tokens of Affection, and not be burnt with the Marking-irons of Anger. **1747** MRS. GLASSE *Cookery* viii. 75 Shape your Upper-crust..and mark it with a Marking-iron for that purpose, in what Shape you please, to be hollow and open to see the Fruit through. **1756** ELLIS in *Phil. Trans.* XLIX. 873 They are known all over India by the name of *Marking-nuts. **1830** LINDLEY *Nat. Syst. Bot.* 128 Semecarpus anacardium, the *marking nut-tree of commerce. **1886** *Marking pencil [see *B*, *BB*, *BBB* (B III)]. **1961** *Lebende Sprachen* VI. 70/1 Marking pencil. **1805** R. W. DICKSON *Pract. Agric.* I. 13 The *Marking-Plough is an useful instrument for the purpose of straightening, as well as regulating the distance of ridges, where the practice of drilling is in use. **1868** M. H. SMITH *Sunshine & Shadow in N. York* 252 They did the hard work, swept out the stores, made the fires, used the *marking-pot. **1861** MRS. STOWE *Pearl of Orr's Island* I. xvii. 152, I was going to begin and teach her some *marking stitches. **1880** *Plain Hints Needlework* 22 The real marking stitch, called in old times 'Brave Bred' stitch,..lasts longer. **1545** *Rates Custome Ho.* b vij b, *Markynge stone the pounde iiii.*d.* **1676** WORLIDGE *Cyder* 51 It is good with a Marking-Stone or piece of Chalk ..to mark one coast of every Tree. **1793** TULL *Horse-Hoeing Husb.* xxiii. 381 To a Drill that plants upon the Level, *Marking Wheels are necessary. **1744** *Rigging & Seamanship* 55 **Marking-yarn*, a white thread, untarred, laid in rope for the king's or East-India Company's mark.

marking ('mɑːkɪŋ), *ppl. a.* [f. MARK *v.* + -ING².]

†**1.** Observing, observant. *Obs.*

1577–87 HOLINSHED *Chron.* I. 178/2 It would make a diligent and marking reader both muse and moorne. *c* **1580** SIDNEY *Ps.* I. i, Night and day he calls [Gods law] to marking mind. **1605** CAMDEN *Rem.* 213 Whosoever will with a marking eie consider [etc.].

†**2.** Expressive. *Obs.* (Quot. 1766 may belong to sense 1.)

1766 *Life of Quin* i. 5 He had..an expressive countenance; a marking eye; a clear voice. **1778** MME. D'ARBLAY *Diary* Sept., He has repeatedly asked me to read a tragedy to him, ..and when I ask him why, he says I have such a marking face.

3. *Mil.* That marks (see MARK *v.* 10).

1796 *Instr. & Reg. Cavalry* (1813) 32 The horses heads of the line, and of the marking persons will then touch. *Ibid.*, When divisions come up..successively into line, they come up to the horses heads of the marking persons.

4. That characterizes or accentuates.

1795 BURKE *Corr.* (1844) IV. 319 What you are to say of the character..of a man, must..consist rather of a few light marking touches than of a long discussion. **1797** MRS. RADCLIFFE *Italian* ii. (1824) 541 A full sense of the value of birth is a marking feature in the characters of the Marchese and Marchesa di Vivaldi. **1884** *Athenæum* 30 Aug. 271/1 The tragic story of Saigo Kichinosuke's despair and death.. for all time must be the marking incident of its history.

Hence †'**markingly** *adv.*, attentively.

a **1586** SIDNEY *Arcadia* IV. (1598) 404 Pyrocles markingly hearkened to all that Dametas said.

markis, markiseese: see MARQUIS, -QUISESS.

markka ('mɑːkɑː). Also **marka**. [Finn.] **a.** The principal monetary unit of Finland, equal to 100 penniä. **b.** The name of the coin equal to this amount. (Cf. MARK *sb.*² 4 b.)

1903 *Finland by the 'Nord' Steamers* 11 The standard coin is the Marka, equal to 10d. of our money, divided into 100 Penni. **1911** G. RENWICK *Finland Today* 336 Finnish coinage presents no difficulties, the Finnish markka (plural, markkaa) being equal to the French franc. **1963** *Economist* 1 June 925/3 Some forest owners are speculating on a rise in prices, possibly via a devaluation of the [Finnish] markka. **1972** *Daily Tel.* 3 Aug. 19/4 Your pound's worth in London. ..Finland..9·95 markkas.

markland ('mɑːklənd). *Sc.* [f. MARK *sb.*² + LAND.] A division of land, originally of the annual value of a mark; = MARK *sb.*²

As 'a markland' and 'a mark (of) land' were equivalent, it is often difficult to determine whether in the early examples the combination is a compound or a syntactical collocation.

1550 in *Black Bk. Taymouth* (Bannatyne Cl.) 407 The markland of Drimleyort, the half markland of Glenkinglas [etc.]. **1774** PENNANT *Tour Scot. in 1772*, 197 The island is divided into marklands, each of which ought to maintain fourteen cows and four horses. **1793** *Statist. Acc. Scot.* VII. 393 The lands are reckoned by a peculiar measurement, by what are called merks-land. Each merk-land ought to contain 1600 square fathoms. **1884** CAMPBELL *Rec. Argyll* 61 This parish, divided into 116 marklands, is [etc.].

markless ('mɑːklɪs), *a.* [f. MARK *sb.*¹ + -LESS.] Without mark or a mark.

1834 LD. HOUGHTON *Mem. Many Scenes*, *Vis. Argonauts*, A..plain..Trackless and markless as fresh-fallen snow.

Hence '**marklessly** *adv.*, unnoticed.

1844 THOM *Rhymes Weaver* 39 Unkent, uncared its ruin, Sae marklessly it grew.

marklet ('mɑːklɪt). *rare*⁻¹. [f. MARK *sb.*¹ + -LET.] A little mark; in quot. †a badge.

1647 WARD *Simp. Cobler* (1843) 32 Souldiers use to weare other marklets or notadoes in time of battell.

†**markly**, *a. Sc. Obs.* [f. MARK *sb.*¹ + -LY². Cf. ON. *merkiliga*.] Definitely.

1533 GAU *Richt Vay* (1888) 69 Sanct Paul vritis..Plane and marklie of our lordis resurrectione.

marklynis, obs. form of MURKLINS *adv.*

markman ('mɑːkmən). [f. MARK *sb.*¹ + MAN *sb.*¹]

†**1.** = MARKSMAN 1. Also *fig. Obs.*

1577 STANYHURST *Descr. Irel.* viii. 28 in *Holinshed*, The kerne, who is an ordinary souldior, vsing..sometimes hys peece, beyng commonly so good markemen as they will come within a score of a great castle. **1592** SHAKS. *Rom. & Jul.* I. i. 212 A right good marke man. **1654** FLECKNOE *Ten Years Trav.* 78 Arrows (with which they are the best mark men in the world).

2. *Antiq.* A dweller in a mark (MARK *sb.*¹ 2).

1874 STUBBS *Const. Hist.* I. iii. 49 Each of the mark-men has there his homestead.

markois, obs. form of MARQUIS.

markoke, obs. form of MOORCOCK.

Markov ('mɑːkɒf). *Math.* Also **Markoff**. [The name of Andrei Andreevich *Markov* (1856–1922), Russian mathematician, who investigated such processes.] ***Markov process***: any stochastic process for which the probabilities, at any one time, of the different future states depend only on the existing state and not on how that state was arrived at. ***Markov chain***: a Markov process in which there are a finite or countably infinite number of possible states or in which transitions between states occur at discrete intervals of time; also, one for which in addition the transition probabilities are constant (independent of time). Also ***Markov property***, the characteristic property of Markov processes.

1939 *Jap. Jrnl. Math.* XVI. 47 (*heading*) Markoff process with an enumerable infinite number of possible states. **1942** *Trans. Amer. Math. Soc.* LII. 37 Then $p_{ij}(t)$ can be considered a transition probability of a Markoff chain: A system is supposed which can assume various numbered states, and $p_{ij}(t)$ is the probability that the system is in the *j*th state at the end of a time interval of length *t*, if it was in the *i*th state at the beginning of the interval. **1950** W. FELLER *Introd. Probability Theory* I. xv. 337 A Markov process is the probabilistic analogue of the processes of classical mechanics, where the future development is completely determined by the present state and is independent of the way in which the present state has developed. *Ibid.* 337 A definition of the Markov property. **1953** J. L. DOOB *Stochastic Processes* v. 170 A Markov chain is defined as a Markov process..whose random variables can (with probability 1) only assume values in a certain finite or denumerably infinite set. The set is usually taken, for convenience, to be the integers 1,..., *N* (finite case) or the integers 1, 2,...(infinite case). *Ibid.* 186 The problem of card mixing is a good example of the application of Markov chains. **1953** J. B. CARROLL *Study of Lang.* iii. 85 A Markoff process has to do with the different 'states' into which a phenomenon can get, and the statistical probabilities which govern the transition of the phenomenon from one state to another. **1956** *Nature* 4 Feb. 207/1 The most simple case is when all the atoms of the assembly are supposed to have no volume and no interactions (such as in an ideal gas). In that case it can be treated as a Markov process. **1960** KEMENY & SNELL *Finite Markov Chains* ii. 25 A finite Markov chain is a finite Markov process such that the transition probabilities $p_{ij}(n)$ do not depend on *n*. **1962** J. RIORDAN *Stochastic Service Syst.* iii. 28 The simplest infinite-server system is unique among its fellows in the possession of the Markov property that future changes are independent of the past. **1966** S. KARLIN *First Course in Stochastic Processes* ii. 27 A discrete time Markov chain $\{X_n\}$ is a Markov stochastic process whose state space is a countable or finite set, and for which $T = (0, 1, 2, \ldots)$. *Ibid.*, The vast majority of Markov chains that we shall encounter have stationary transition probabilities. **1968** P. A. P. MORAN *Introd. Probability Theory* iii. 140 Thus a Markov chain observed in the reverse direction of time will be a Markov process. However, it will not in general be a Markov chain because the observed transition probabilities will not be independent of *t*. **1973** *Manch. Sch. Econ. & Social Stud.* XLI. 401 (*heading*) A Markov chain model of the benefits of participating in government training schemes.

Markovian (mɑːˈkəʊvɪən), *a.* [f. prec. + -IAN.] Having the Markov property.

1950 W. FELLER *Introd. Probability Theory* I. xv. 338 Examples of non-Markovian processes... Let $X^{(n)}$ equal 1 or 0 according to whether the *n*th drawing [from the urn] results in a black or a red ball. The sequence $\{X^{(n)}\}$ *is not* a Markov process. **1965** N. CHOMSKY *Aspects of Theory of Syntax* ii. 89 A derivation involving only phrase structure rules (rewriting rules) has a strict 'Markovian' character. That is, in a derivation consisting of the successive lines $\sigma_1, \ldots, \sigma_n$.., the rules that can be applied to form the next line σ_{n+1} are independent of $\sigma_1, \ldots, \sigma_{n-1}$, and depend completely on the string σ_n. **1972** *Nature* 3 Mar. 20/2 To render the process Markovian, we have assumed exponential distributions of division times for both normal and abnormal cells.

markque, obs. form of MARQUE¹.

markry, obs. form of MERCURY.

Marks and Sparks (mɑːks ænd spɑːks). Also **Marks**. Colloq. name for the merchandising company of Marks and Spencer plc or any of the stores owned by this firm. Freq. *attrib.* of clothes bearing the firm's trademark.

1951 PARTRIDGE *Dict. Slang* (ed. 4) Add. 1106/2 *Marks*, a Marks & Spencer store. **1964** *Sunday Times* 5 Apr. 41/5 In their Marks and Sparks' woollies and living in what looks like a remarkably nice housing estate, Topsy and Tim clearly stand in for classless society. **1966** A. PRIOR *Operators* i. 8 His Marks and Sparks shirt. **1971** 'D. HALLIDAY' *Dolly & Doctor Bird* xi. 141, I sat there in my Marks and Sparks knickers and brassière. **1972** R. QUILTY *Tenth Session* 104 The girls get just about all their odds and ends in Marks and Sparks or the bargain basement at C & A.

marksman ('mɑːksmən). [f. *mark's*, genitive of MARK *sb.*¹ + MAN *sb.*¹]

1. a. One skilled or practised in shooting or aiming at a mark. (Cf. the earlier MARKMAN.)

1660 F. BROOKE tr. *Le Blanc's Trav.* 110 Often, the King gives rewards to the best marks-men. **1709** STEELE *Tatler* No. 39 ¶ 36 A good Marks-man will be sure to hit his Man at 20 Yards Distance. **1816** SCOTT *Antiq.* xx, M'Intyre is said to be a marksman. **1885** *Manch. Exam.* 14 July 4/6 The rather low records made by old marksmen on the Common.

b. A title of merit awarded for a certain recognized degree of proficiency in rifle practice.

1859 *Musketry Instr.* 72 Certain of the first-class shots to be styled 'marksmen'.

2. One who marks out land.

1654 in Sir W. Petty *Down Surv.* iii. (1851) 16 The admeasurers..paid little for their diet and lodging, bounders, marksmen, spademen, &c.

3. One who makes a mark in place of a signature.

1777 NICHOLSON & BURN *Hist. Westmoreld. & Cumberl.* II. 324 *note*, In the Original Solemn League and Covenant ..there are abundance of marksmen, all of whom, from their abhorrence of popery..leave the cross unfinished. **1813** COL. BAGWELL *Sp. Ho. Comm.* 24 Feb., Of these 3000 names, none were marksmen. **1885** T. HUGHES in *Law Times* LXXX. 45/1 The..drover who signed the contract was a marksman.

4. A grade or degree amongst Orangemen.

1800 in *Orange Syst. Exposed* (1823) 81, I will keep this part of a Marksman from an Orangeman, as well as from the ignorant... I will be aiding and assisting to all true honest Orange Marksmen. **1813** *Gen. Hist.* in *Ann. Reg.* 93/2 The oath of a Marchman or Marksman, the name of one further initiated in their secrets.

5. One who ranges competitors in a race.

1887 M. SHEARMAN *Athletics & Football* 57 The starter is helped by a 'marksman', who places the men on the scratch. **1897** *Encycl. Sport* I. 62 s.v. *Athletics*.

6. (See quot.)

1901 *Blackw. Mag.* Nov. 660/1 The 'Marksman'..whose function it is to superintend the marking of the Forest Ponies.

'**marksmanship**. [f. prec. + -SHIP.] The function, quality or art of a marksman.

1859 TENNENT *Ceylon* II. VIII. iii. 324 There is little opportunity for the display of marksmanship in an elephant battue. **1899** *Daily Tel.* 23 Oct. 19/2 The Cape Police.. deride the Boer marksmanship.

markstone ('mɑːkstəʊn). *Obs.* exc. *dial.* [f. MARK *sb.*¹ + STONE *sb.* Cf. G. *markstein*.]

A boundary stone.

1364 *Durham Halmote Rolls* (Surtees) 31 Promisit quod ipse venire faciet le merkstans. **1535** COVERDALE *Gen.* xxxi. 45 Then toke Iacob a stone and set it up for a piler or markestone. **1587** HARRISON *England* I. v. 12/1 in *Holinshed*, The marke stone [1577 stone] which Turnus threw at Æneas. **1610** HEALEY *St. Aug. Citie of God* 841 They are wont to lay coales vnder bounders and marke-stones for lands. **1824** MACTAGGART *Gallovid. Encycl.* 338 *Markstanes*, stones set up on end for marks in the days of yore, that farmers might know the marches of their farms.

'markswoman. [Cf. MARKSMAN.] A woman practised in shooting at a mark.

1802 *Sporting Mag.* XX. 300 She is an excellent markswoman. **1824** SCOTT *St. Ronan's* xviii, There might then be room for less exalted but perhaps not less skilful markswomen to try their chance.

'mark-up. [f. the vbl. phr. *to mark up*: see MARK *v.* 2 c, 7 f.] **1.** The amount added by a retailer to the cost price of goods to cover overhead charges and provide profits.

1920 P. I. CARTHAGE *Retail Organization & Accounting Control* ii. 44 The mark up of merchandise refers to the percentage or the amount of money added to the cost in order to obtain the selling price. **1931** J. F. PYLE *Marketing Princ.* xx. 518 *Mark-up* is..the difference between the marked price of the merchandise, at retail, and the cost of merchandise bought. Thus the mark-up represents the gross margin that is *hoped for*. **1936** *Economist* 22 Feb. 422/1 The 'mark up' (retailers' margin) is evidently adequate to provide relatively stable earnings on a stabilised capital investment. **1957** *Times* 19 Aug. 9/2 Shops often add to the price which they pay for their merchandise to manufacturers and wholesalers a percentage 'mark up' of 30 or 40 per cent. **1965** *Spectator* 22 Jan. 116/3 A big, new market for poor-quality materials and an even larger mark-up where the garments are supplied ready-made. **1972** M. WOODHOUSE *Mama Doll* xiii. 175 The estimated value of the items on the inventory is somewhere around fifty-five million pounds... Allowing a hundred per cent markup on sale, that would make their wholesale value some twenty-seven million pounds. **1974** *Times* 7 Feb. 20/8 The exorbitant mark-up imposed by European booksellers.

2. a. In the preparation of text for printing, typesetting, etc.: the process or result of writing instructions on lay-out, style, and other matters, in a code convertible by the compositor or typesetter.

1973 A. DAVIS *Graphics* iii. 74 The type mark-up by which the designer conveys his instructions to the compositor is one of the essential tools of the trade. **1986** *Bookseller* 7 June 2275/1 Traditionally, copy preparation and typographical markup have involved the use of a large, rather ill-defined set of words, abbreviations and signs.

b. *Computing* The process of assigning tags to the various elements of a text, indicating the nature of each in relation to the structure of the text; the tags so assigned.

1980 *IBM Tech. Disclosure Bull.* 5130 A program which generates a report from machine-readable data does not insert format-related information directly into its output, but instead inserts GML (Generalized Markup Language) tags into the output file to describe significant data items. **1985** *New OED System Design* (Oxf. Univ. Press) 2 Since structural information is only partially contained in the text captured by the keyboarding contractor, structural mark-up will be generated and inserted by the system. **1986** P. R. KING in G. Coray et al. *Text Processing & Document Manipulation* 189 Mark-up in W consists in specifying a document as a hierarchy of nested components. **1986** *Computer Jrnl.* XXIX. 193/2 The basic principle is that of the generic markup of the structural elements of a document, their manner of presentation being a separate matter.

'markworthy, *a.* [f. MARK *sb.*[1] + WORTHY *a.*; after G. *merkwürdig*.] Worthy of note.

1827 SCOTT *Napoleon* i, And—mark-worthy circumstance! in La Vendée alone was any stand made. **1865** G. MEREDITH *Rhoda Fleming* xxviii. (1889) 236 A rather mark-worthy young man.

markyd, markys, obs. ff. MARKET, MARQUIS.

markyt, -yth(e, obs. forms of MARKET.

marl (mɑːl), *sb.*[1] Also (4 marll, 6 merle), 4–9 marle. [a. OF. *marle* (still in dialects; replaced in mod.Fr. by the variant *marne*):—late L. *margila* (whence OHG. *mergil*, MHG., mod.G., Du. *mergel* (MDu. also *marl* from Fr.), Da. *mergel*, Sw. *märgel*), dim. of L. *marga* (whence It., Sp. *marga*), said by Pliny to be a Gaulish word.

It does not, however, occur in the mod. Celtic langs.: the alleged Breton *marg* does not correspond phonetically; the Breton *merl* is from Fr., and the Welsh *marl* and Irish and Gaelic *marla* are from English.]

1. A kind of soil consisting principally of clay mixed with carbonate of lime, forming a loose unconsolidated mass, valuable as a fertilizer.

The *marl* of lakes is 'a white, chalky deposit consisting of the mouldering remains of *Mollusca*, *Entomostraca*, and partly of fresh-water algæ' (Geikie in *Encycl. Brit.* X. 290/2).

1372 *Durham Halmote Rolls* (Surtees) 115 Quod nullus eorum permittat aliquibus capere marll. **1387** TREVISA *Higden* (Rolls) II. 15 In þis ilond vnder þe torf of þe lond is good marl i-founde. **1393** LANGL. *P. Pl.* C. XIII. 231 Lond ouere-layde with marle and with donge. *c* **1420** *Pallad. on Husb.* x. 25 For laak of donge in sondy lond be spronge Good marl. *c* **1440** *Promp. Parv.* 327/1 Marl, or chalke, *creta*. **1523** FITZHERB. *Husb.* §2 Some meane erthe, some medled with marle. **1530** PALSGR. 244/2 Merle ground, *marle*. **1669** W. SIMPSON *Hydrol. Chym.* 296 A more stiff clay or marle. **1774** GOLDSM. *Nat. Hist.* IV. 10 Chalks, marles, and all such earths as ferment with vinegar, are nothing more than a composition of shells. **1846** MCCULLOCH *Acc. Brit. Empire* (1854) I. 183 Turnips form the basis of the Norfolk husbandry; and, in conjunction with marl, may be said 'to have made the county'. **1879** *Cassell's Techn. Educ.* II. 67/2 Amber..occurs..in the Cretaceous marls of France and Germany.

b. With qualifying word, e.g. an adj. of colour or a word denoting the composition, preponderant element, source, etc., as *argillaceous, blue, calcareous, chalky, chloritic, clay, earth, gravel, green-sand, sand, sandy, sea, shell, white, yellow marl.*

†**cushat marl** (see quot. 1682); **dice** or **steel marl** (see quots. 1682, 1766); **delving** or **peat marl, flag, shale, slate,** or **stone marl** (see quots. 1682, 1707, 1762). For *chalk, lime,* and *paper marl* see the prefixed words.

1603 OWEN *Pembrokeshire* (1892) 11 Claye marle, stone marle, lyme, sande, or gravell marle. *Ibid.* 71 Claye Marle soe called for difference betweene it and the sea marle. **1682** A. MARTINDALE in J. Houghton *Coll. Lett. Husb. & Trade* I. 121 Cowshut-Marle (so called, as I suppose, for its resemblance in colour to Stock-doves, or Queoca, which the Vulgar in this Country call Cowshuts) being of a brownish colour, bespangled with blew veins... 2. Stone-Marle, or Shale-Marle... 3. Peat-Marle, or Delving-Marle, which is ..very fat or unctuous... 4. Clay Marle, resembling it in colour, and in my Opinion, being of great affinity to Clay... 5. Steel-Marle in the bottom of some Pits, which of it self is apt to break into little Bodies almost Cubical. **1686** PLOT *Staffordsh.* iii. 120 Harder, stony, slatty sorts of Marles, at some places called Slat, at others Dice-Marle. **1707** MORTIMER *Husb.* (1721) I. 87 Stone, Slate, or Flag-marle, which is a kind of a soft Stone..of a blue or bluish Colour. **1762** MILLS *Syst. Pract. Husb.* I. 38 The marle which is usually found at the depth of about two feet..in wet boggy grounds..is commonly called peat-marle, or delving-marle. **1766** *Complete Farmer* 5 M 2/2 Dice Marle, a name given by the people of Staffordshire to a reddish marle, that breaks into small square pieces like dice. **1799** J. ROBERTSON *Agric. Perth* 293 Shell marle is found for the most part in small lakes. **1832** DE LA BECHE *Geol.* 223 That the blue marls were deposited in a sea, perhaps somewhat similar to the Mediterranean. **1834** *Brit. Husb.* (L.U.K.) I. 309 For all practical purposes, it may be sufficient to divide it [shelly marl] into *earth-marl* and *shell-marl*. **1877** *Encycl. Brit.* VI. 353/2 The Chloritic Marl in the Wealden district.

c. red marl: (*a*) marl of a red colour; (*b*) reddle; (*c*) *Geol.* the New Red Sandstone.

c **1630** RISDON *Surv. Devon* (1810) 4 It consists of a red and blue marle. **1748** J. HILL *Hist. Fossils* 46 The Red Marles. *Ibid.* 47 Soft, heavy, red Marle, call'd Common Reddle. **1833** LYELL *Princ. Geol.* III. 333 A group of red marl and sandstone..is found in England interposed between the lias and the carboniferous strata. **1867** W. W. SMYTH *Coal & Coal-mining* 62 On the south-east of Tamworth, the clearing away of the red marls reveals a coalfield.

d. *burning marl*: used symbolically, after Milton, for the torments of Hell.

1667 MILTON *P.L.* I. 296. **1814** CARY *Dante's Inf.* XVII. 30. **1876** GEO. ELIOT *Dan. Der.* VIII. lxvi, It seems the unjoyous dissipation of demons, seeking diversion on the burning marl of perdition.

2. *poet.* Used generically (like *clay*) for: Earth.

1590 SPENSER *F.Q.* II. xi. 33 To seize upon his foe flatt lying on the marle. **1599** SHAKS. *Much Ado* II. i. 66 To make account of her life to a clod of waiward marle? *a* **1770** AKENSIDE *Poems* (1789) II. 56 Now, Hesper, guide my feet Down the red marle with moss o'ergrown. **1898** HALL CAINE in *Daily News* 30 May 5 His feet laid hold of the marl and earth, his head was in the sky.

3. Short for *marl-brick*.

1815 J. SMITH *Panorama Sci. & Art* I. 187 The marls are made in the neighbourhood of London. **1855** F. REINNEL *Masons*, etc. *Assist.* 33 Marles, stocks, and place-bricks.

4. *attrib.*, as *marl-bed, -brick, clay, -lake, soil, -stock*; also *marl-like* adj.; **marl-grass,** Zigzag Clover, *Trifolium medium*; also Red Clover, *T. pratense*; **marl slate** *Geol.* (see quot. 1877); **marl-stone** *Geol.*, argillaceous and ferruginous limestone, which lies between the upper and lower Lias of England. Also MARL-PIT.

1828 FLEMING *Hist. Anim. Kingd.* 28 Bones of individuals [pigs] are occasionally found in *marl-beds. *a* **1670** SPALDING *Troub. Chas. I* (1829) 45 A..great bed of sand.. mixed with *marle-clay and stones. **1876** PAGE *Adv. Text-bk. Geol.* xx. 411 Marl-clay..occurs as a whitish friable clay with an admixture of lime. **1778** W. HUDSON *Flora Angl.* 326 *Trifolium alpestre*..perennial Trefoil, Clover, or *Marle-grass. **1875** *Lyell's Princ. Geol.* II. III. xlviii. 573 A *marl-lake in Forfarshire. **1796** MORSE *Amer. Geog.* I. 171 *note*, A sediment of one inch of impalpable *marle-like substance. **1877** A. H. GREEN *Phys. Geol.* ii. §6. 72 If the rock [marl] splits into plates it is called *marl-slate. ? **1842** LANCE *Cottage Farmer* 6 Marsh, alluvial and *marl soils. **1836** *Penny Cycl.* V. 409/1 *Marl stocks..differ from the bricks just described. **1839** *Ibid.* XIV. 429/1 **Marlstone*, sandy, calcareous, and irony strata, which divide the upper from the lower lias clays.

†**marl,** *sb.*[2] *Obs.* exc. *dial.* Contraction of MARVEL *sb.*[1]

1609 B. JONSON *Sil. Wom.* III. i, Your band, and cuffes, ..'Tis mar'l you ha 'hem on now. **1616** R. C. *Times' Whistle* Sat. v. 2132 Noe marle though he with drunkennesse dispence. **1746** *Exmoor Scolding* (E.D.S.) 130 Es marl who's more vor Rigging or Rumping..than thee art thyzel. **1886** ELWORTHY *W. Som. Word-bk.* s.v., 'Tis a marl, however 'twas, they had'n all bin a killed.

marl (mɑːl), *sb.*[3] *dial.* Contraction of MARBLE.

1860 GEO. ELIOT *Mill on Fl.* v, How stodgy they [a boy's pockets] look, Tom! Is it marls (marbles) or cobnuts?

marl (mɑːl), *sb.*[4] [Reduced form of MARBLED *ppl. a.* 2.] A yarn made from two different coloured threads twisted together so as to produce a mottled effect; the fabric produced from this yarn. Usu. *attrib.*

1892 *Queen* 5 Mar. p. xi (Advt.), Ladies write for Patterns of the entirely new designs in..Marls, Tweeds,..and Beiges. **1922** *Daily Mail* 18 Dec. 1 (Advt.), Knitted sports suit in rich Marl mixtures and plain colours. **1926** *Illustr. Official Jrnl.* (Patent Office) 20 Oct. 1668 Spinning marl or multi-ply yarns. **1968** E. GALE *From Fibres to Fabrics* iv. 45 Two marl threads are sometimes twisted together to form one yarn. **1970** A. M. COLLIER *Handbk. Textiles* iv. 88 A marl yarn is produced by combining two yarns of uneven thickness, with uneven rates of delivery so that there is excess material at intervals.

marl (mɑːl), *v.*[1] Also (5 marly, 6 merl), 5–8 marle. [f. MARL *sb.*[1] Cf. F. *marner*, MDu. *marlen*, med.L. *marlāre*.]

1. *trans.* To apply marl to (ground); to fertilize or manure with marl.

1387 TREVISA *Higden* (Rolls) II. 15 Euere þe þickere þe felde is i-marled, þe better corn it wil bere. **14..** *Voc.* in Wr.-Wülcker 576/23 *Cretifico*, to marly. **1538** LELAND *Itin.* V. 90 The Sandy Grounde of sum Partes of Shropshire.. wille not bere Corne plentifully but it be merlyd. **1625** B. JONSON *Staple of N.* II. iv, Who would hold any Land To haue the trouble to marle it? **1882** JESSOPP in *19th Cent.* 748 It was a general practice to marl the land periodically.

†**b.** To spread (marl) as manure. *Obs.*

1791 *Trans. Soc. Arts* IX. 82 If any good marl can be had ..it should then be well marled upon the clover root.

2. To enrich as with marl; to manure, fertilize.

1544 tr. *Littleton's Tenures* 16 Yf I delyuer to a man my shepe to dunge or marle his lande. *a* **1555** BRADFORD in Coverdale *Lett. Martyrs* (1564) 462 Yf god..beginne to mucke and marle you: to pour hys showers vpon you [etc.]. **1651** OGILBY *Æsop* (1665) 135 Realms, marl'd and water'd with the fertile Nile. **1833** H. COLERIDGE *Fields of Fame*, Marl'd with bleaching bones.

†**3.** *intr.* To crumble *away* like marl. *Obs.*

1641 BEST *Farm. Bks.* (Surtees) 70 Some advised to putte eight pownde of pitch to a gallon of tarre, but that is thought to make the markinge over brittle, and to breake sooner and marle away.

marl (mɑːl), *v.*[2] Also 5 marlyn, 8–9 marle. [a. Du. and LG. *marlen* (whence Sw. *märla*, Da. *merle*), app. a frequentative f. MDu. *merren* to tie.]

†**1.** *trans.* To tie, noose. *Obs.*—⁰

c **1440** *Promp. Parv.* 327/1 Marlyn, or snarlyn, *illaqueo*.

2. *Naut.* To fasten with marline or small line; to secure *together* by a succession of half-hitches; to wind marline or other small stuff round (a rope), securing it with a hitch at each turn.

1704 J. HARRIS *Lex. Techn.* I. s.v. *Marline, Marling a sail*; is, when being so rip'd out of the Bolt Rope, that it cannot be sewed in again, the Sail is fasten'd by Marline..unto the Bolt Rope. **1769** FALCONER *Dict. Marine* II. (1780), *Merliner une voile*, to marle a sail to it's foot-rope. **1820** SCORESBY *Acc. Arctic Reg.* II. 482 The two edges were marled to two pieces of a hawser. *c* **1825** CHOYCE *Log of Jack Tar* (1891) 87 The catamarans were made of bundles of dry bulrushes well marled together. *c* **1860** H. STUART *Seaman's Catech.* 30 Marl them well down.

†**marl,** *v.*[3] *Obs.*—⁰ [Of obscure origin; cf. MARILL *v.*] (See quots.)

1598 FLORIO, *Carpionato pesce*, fish that is marlde, as they vse at Hampton. **1611** *Ibid.*, *Accarpionare*, to souse..fish with vinegre to bee eaten cold, to marle fish.

marl, *v.*[4] *Obs.* exc. *dial.* Also 7 mar'le, 7–9 marle. Contraction of MARVEL *v.*

1598 B. JONSON *Ev. Man in Hum.* (Qo.) I. ii. 35, I marle, sir, you weare such ill-fauourd course stockings, hauing so good a legge as you haue. *a* **1627** MIDDLETON *Wom. beware Wom.* I. ii, I mar'l my Guardianer do's not seek a wife for me. **1648** MAINE *Amorous Warre* v. vii. 79, I mar'le, my Lord, Our Amazons appeare not. **1795** WOLCOT (P. Pindar) *Royal Tour* Wks. 1812 III. 339 [They] marle that children talk as well as kings. **1822** SCOTT *Nigel* iii, 'I marle the skipper took us on board', said Richie. **1886** ELWORTHY *W. Som. Word-bk.*, *Marl*.

marl *dial.*: see MERELLES.

marlaceous (mɑː'leɪʃəs), *a.* [f. MARL *sb.*[1] + -ACEOUS.] Of the nature of or resembling marl.

1794 KIRWAN *Elem. Min.* (ed. 2) I. 373 This marlaceous loam may be either sandy or clayey.

marlberry ('mɑːlˌberɪ). *U.S.* A small, evergreen tree, *Ardisia paniculata*, of the family Myrsinaceæ, bearing clusters of pink flowers and dark red berries, and found in the West Indies and tropical America.

1884 C. S. SARGENT *Rep. Forests N. Amer.* 100 *Ardisia Pickeringia* Marlberry-Cherry. **1897** G. B. SUDWORTH *Nomencl. Arborescent Flora U.S.* 316 *Icacorea paniculata*. Marlberry. **1917** *Rep. Board of Regents Smithsonian Inst.* 384 In addition to these are the paradise tree or bitterwood; soapberry tree;..marlberry; [etc.]. **1924** J. A. THOMSON *Sci. Old & New* v. 27 Even the names transport us into a land of pure delight—the paradise tree, the myrtle-of-the-river, the marlberry, and the bois-fidèle.

Marlborough ('mɑːlbərə; often 'mɔːlbrə). The name of a town in Wiltshire; used *attrib.* in **Marlborough chalk,** ? chalk for writing with; **Marlborough dog** [from the title of the Duke of Marlborough, owner of Blenheim Palace], a Blenheim spaniel (see BLENHEIM); **Marlborough wheel** *Mech.*, a thick 'idle wheel' (see IDLE *a.* 5 b).

1764 *Low Life* (ed. 3) 94 Publicans taking the Advantage of their Companies being either in a deep Discourse, half Drunk, or at Supper, to vse Marlborough-Chalk. **1841** R. WILLIS *Princ. Mechanism* 205 Such a thick idle wheel is termed a Marlborough wheel, in some districts. It is employed in the roller frames of spinning machinery. **1861**

Chambers's Encycl. II. 153 *Blenheim Dog*, or *Marlborough Dog*, a small and very beautiful variety of spaniel.

Marlburian (mɑːlˈbjʊərɪən). [f. *Marlborough* (as if in form **Marlbury*) + -AN.] One educated at Marlborough College.

1881 HUGHES *Rugby, Tennessee* III. iii. 130 A nephew of mine, aged twenty-one, a Marlburian.

†**marle** (mɑːl). *dial. Obs.* Also 7–8 **marrel**, 9 **marl**, ? erron. **male**. (See quots.)

a **1700** B. E. *Dict. Cant. Crew, Marrel*, a Bird about the bigness of a Knot. **1747** MRS GLASSE *Cookery* 162 How to choose.. Goodwets, Marle, Knots, Ruffs, Gull, Dotterels, and Wheat Ears. [In ed. 1767 indexed as 'Marle, a fish, how to chuse'.] **1864** ATKINSON *Prov. Names Birds*, Marl, Prov. name for Knot, *Tringa Canutus*. **1885** SWAINSON *Prov. Names Birds* 105 Knot.. various names.. Male (Essex).

marle, variant of MEDLE *Obs.*, medlar.

marled (mɑːld), *ppl. a.*^{1} [f. MARL *sb.*^{1} or *v.*^{1} + -ED.] Manured or fertilized with marl.

1610 W. FOLKINGHAM *Art of Survey* I. x. 32 They let and set such Marled grounds, vnder twenty yeeres at an incredible rate of monies in hand. **1707** MORTIMER *Husb.* (1721) I. 139 All sorts of Pease love limed or marled Lands.

marled (mɑːld), *ppl. a.*^{2} Chiefly *Sc.* Also 9 **merled**. [Cf. OF. *merellé*.] Marbled, mottled, spotted, variegated, streaked.

1603 MONIPENNIE *Cert. Matters Scot.* K, They delight in marled clothes, specially, that haue long stripes of sundrie colours. **1698** FRYER *Acc. E. India & P.* 216 Agats for Hafts of Knives, white and well marled are good. **1703** M. MARTIN *W. Isl. Scot.* 58 Marled Salmon,.. being lesser then the ordinary Salmon, and full of strong Large Scales. **1787** BURNS *Answ. Verses fr. Guidwife of Wauchope-House* v, The marled plaid ye kindly spare. **1793** YOUNG *Ann. Agric., Kent* XX. 266 (E.D.S.), The fine eating meat being that which is marled flesh and spread well. **1820** *Blackw. Mag.* VI. 568 The merled neck and smooth breast of the Maivis. **1871** C. GIBBON *Lack of Gold* i, Its pale yellow marled sheepskin binding.

marler^1 (ˈmɑːlə(r)). *dial.* [f. MARL *v.*^{1} + -ER^1.] One who digs marl. Also, one who spreads marl on land (see E.D.D.)

1808 *Athenæum* IV. 291 The men who are employed in getting the marl out of these pits are termed marlers. **1810** *Ann. Reg.* 672 The most prevalent custom of this county [Cheshire] is the shouting of the marlers, when any money has been given to them.

marler^2 (ˈmɑːlə(r)). [f. MARL *v.*^{2} + -ER^1.] A marline-spike.

1929 J. MASEFIELD *Hawbucks* 15 A strong sheath knife with a marler at the back.

†**marlet.** *Obs.* Also 6 -ett(e, 7 -ot. [a. OF. *merlette* the heraldic martlet, app. a dim. of *merle* blackbird.] A martin or martlet.

1556 WITHALS *Dict.* (1568) 5 a/1 A marlette, whiche is of the quantitee of a swalow, hauying no feete to go, but onely stumpes, *cypsellus*. **1578** COOPER *Thesaurus*, *Cypselus*,.. a byrde called a marlett [*ed.* 1565 martlette]. **1605** SHAKS. *Macb.* I. vi. 5 The Temple haunting Barlet [*read* Marlet]. ? **1645** C. MORTON *Enquiry* in *Harl. Misc.* (1810) V. 499 The summer birds that breed here, as the nightingale, the cuckow, marlot, &c. *Ibid.* 505 The swallow swift and marlet are almost always flying.

marleyon, obs. form of MERLIN.

‖**marli** (ˈmɑːlɪ). Also **marly**. [Fr.]

1. A kind of lawn or gauze used for embroidering; embroidery on this material. (Cf. QUINTIN.)

1821 H. WILSON *Wonderful Char.* II. 213 She sews and hems perfectly well, and is no less skilful in making *marly*.

2. The raised rim of a dish or plate.

In recent Dicts.

marlian, -in, obs. forms of MERLIN.

marlin, *sb.*^{1} [? Cf. MARLE.] 'Applied in the east coast of North America with qualification to any species of curlew or godwit' (Newton).

1893–6 NEWTON *Dict. Birds* 367 America possesses two species of the genus [*Limosa*], the very large Marbled Godwit or Marlin, *L. fedoa*,.. and the smaller Hudsonian Godwit, *L. hudsonica*.

marlin (ˈmɑːlɪn), *sb.*^{2} [App. abbrev. of MARLINSPIKE, from the shape of the beak.]

A large, marine, game fish belonging to the genera *Makaira* or *Tetrapterus* of the family Istiophoridæ, having the upper jaw elongated to form a beak.

1917 *Vanity Fair* (N.Y.) July 62/1 The marlin—*Tetrapterus mitsukurii*—is sometimes called the Japanese swordfish. **1923** D. K. TRESSLER *Marine Products of Commerce* 737/1 The marlin (*Tetrapterus mitsukurii*).. is also called spikefish. **1926** *Glasgow Herald* 24 June 4/5 The extract concerning the loss of a black marlin swordfish, estimated to weigh 600 lb., is one of the most dramatic passages. **1931** *Times Lit. Suppl.* 16 Apr. 301/1 Since then marlin have been taken, on heavy tackle, of 372 lb. **1937** *Discovery* Nov. 357/1 One [swordfish], a black marlin, has been recorded in New Zealand weighing 976 lbs. **1940** *Nature* 6 Apr. 555/2 The black marlin differs from the striped and the blue marlin in the fact that the pectoral fin, when adducted, remains in the horizontal position, whilst in the others it can be brought up flat against the side of the body. **1959** *Angling Times* 13 Mar. 6/3 Madeira has them: the white marlin and the blue marlin. **1970** M. SLATER *Caribbean Cooking* 11 *Marlin*, one of the most sought-after game fish, found in rocks and reefs.

marline (ˈmɑːlɪn), *sb. Naut.* Forms: 5 **marlyne**, 6 **marlyn**, 6–8 **marlin**, 7 **merlin**, (**martling**), 7–8 **merline**, 7– **marling**, **marline**. [Perh. two synonymous words have been confused: *marline* a. Du. *marlijn* (f. *marren* to bind + *lijn* LINE *sb.*) and *marling* ? a. Du. *marling* vbl. sb. f. MARL *v.*^{2} (= Du. *marlen*) + -ING^1. The two words seem to have been confused already in Du. Cf. MLG. *merlink*, *marlink* (mod.LG. *marlink*); the word has passed into other langs. as Sw., Da. *merling* (also Sw. *merla*, Da. *merle*), Fr., Sp. *merlin*, Pg. *merlim*.] Small line of two strands, used for seizings.

1485 *Naval Acc. Hen. VII* (1896) 70 Canuas.. j bolte, Saile twyne.. vi lb, Marlyne.. vi lb. **1558** in *Wills & Inv. N.C.* (Surtees No. 2) 167, xij^{lb} of marlyn iiij^{s}. **1627** CAPT. SMITH *Seaman's Gram.* v. 25 Marling is a small line of vntwisted hemp, very pliant and well tarred, to sease the ends of Ropes from raueling out,.. if the Saile rent out of the Boltrope, they will make it fast with marlin till they haue leisure to mend it. **1666** DRYDEN *Ann. Mirab.* cxlviii, Some the galled ropes with dawby marling bind. **1723** *Trial Pyrates taken by Capt. Ogle* 31 He.. was down seeing and ordering her Sails out on board the Pyrate, in particular some Marling and Housling. **1769** FALCONER *Dict. Marine* II. (1780), *Merlin*, marline, or merline. **1886** *Encycl. Brit.* XXI. 604/1 *Marling*, soft-laid white line for securing sails to the bolt-rope.

ˈ**marline**, *v. rare*$^{-0}$. [f. prec.: perh. a mere error.] *trans.* = MARL *v.*^{2} 2.

1706 PHILLIPS (ed. Kersey), *To Marling a Sail*. [A misapprehension of quot. 1704 under MARL *v.*^{2} 2.] **1721** BAILEY, *To Marline a Sail*. **1828** in WEBSTER; and in later Dicts.

marline-spike, marlinspike (ˈmɑːlɪnspaɪk), *sb.* Also 7 **marlin-speek**, 7–9 **marling-**, 8– **marlin(e)spike**. [orig. app. *marling-spike*, f. MARLING *vbl. sb.*^{2} + SPIKE *sb.*, the first element being subseq. interpreted as MARLINE *sb.*]

1. *Naut.* An iron tool tapering to a point, used to separate the strands of rope in splicing, as a lever in marling, etc.

1626 CAPT. SMITH *Accid. Yng. Seamen* 3 The Boteswaine is to haue the charge of all the Cordage.. sailes.. and marling spikes. **1693** R. LYDE *True Acc. retaking 'Friend's Adventure'* 14, I look't about the Beams for a Marlin-speek, or any thing else to strike them withal. **1757** SMOLLETT *Reprisal* II. xv, As brisk a seaman as ever greased a marlin spike. **1863** P. BARRY *Dockyard Econ.* 178 The British seaman who can only fight with his fists or with a marlinspike.

b. *attrib.*: **marline-spike hitch**, a certain hitch used in marling (see quots.); **marline-spike seamanship** *U.S.*, skill in handling the marline-spike.

1867 SMYTH *Sailor's Word-bk., Marline-spike hitch*, a peculiar hitch in marling, made by laying the marline-spike upon the seizing stuff, and then bringing the end of that seizing over the standing part, so as to form a jamming bight. **1882** NARES *Seamanship* (ed. 6) 21 Marling-spike, or Midshipman hitch. **1888** *Harper's Mag.* July 170/1 Before this is ended he has learned a great deal of marline-spike seamanship. **1896** *United Service Mag.* 187 There is not nearly so much marlin-spike seamanship as in the days of our forefathers.

2. A sailor's name for a tropic-bird (*Phaethon*) and a jäger or skua-gull (*Stercorarius*), in allusion to the two long pointed median tail-feathers.

1867 SMYTH *Sailor's Word-bk.*, Boatswain-bird, *Phaeton æthereus*... It is distinguished by two long feathers in the tail, called the marling-spike. **1890** *Century Dict.*

marling (ˈmɑːlɪŋ), *vbl. sb.*^{1} [f. MARL *v.*^{1} + -ING^1.] The action of MARL *v.*^{1}; manuring with marl.

a **1400** *Parlt. 3 Ages* 142 His rentes and his reches rekened he full ofte Of mukkyng of marlelyng and mendynge of howses. **14..** *Voc.* in Wr.-Wülcker 576/25 *Certificatio* [sic], marlynge. **1603** OWEN *Pembrokeshire* (1892) 74 This kynde of Marlinge is neclected. **1707** MORTIMER *Husb.* (1721) I. 38 The marling of St. Foin, when 'tis almost worn out, makes a great Improvement of it for three or four Years. **1875** *Act 38 & 39 Vict.* c. 92 §5 Where.. a tenant executes on his holding an improvement comprised in.. claying of land, liming of land, marling of land.

attrib. **1556** *Richmond Wills* (Surtees) 93 On marlyng wembell. **1577** *Inv.* in Hall *Eliz. Soc.* (1887) 153 Marling wains.

ˈ**marling**, *vbl. sb.*^{2} *Naut.* [f. MARL *v.*^{2} + -ING^1.] The action of MARL *v.*^{2} Chiefly *attrib.*: **marling-cord, -line, -twine** = MARLINE; **marling-hitch** = *marling-spike hitch*; †**marling iron** = MARLINE-SPIKE.

1485 *Naval Acc. Hen. VII* (1896) 51 Merlyng Irenes. **1496** *Ibid.* 167, x lb weight marlyng Twyne. **1548** *Privy Council Acts* (1890) II. 174 Marlin lyne, lx lb. **1668** J. WHITE *Rich Cab.* (ed. 4) 113 Strong canvas being.. tyed hard on a pike with marlin cord. **1769** FALCONER *Dict. Marine* (1780), *Marling*, the act of winding any small-line, as marline, spun-yarn, packthread, &c. about a rope. **1867** SMYTH *Sailor's Word-bk.* s.v. *Marle*, To attach the foot of a sail to its bolt-rope, &c., with marling hitches. *Ibid.*, *Marline-holes*, holes made for marling, or lacing the foot-rope and clues in courses and topsails.

†ˈ**marling**, *vbl. sb.*^{3} *Obs.*$^{-0}$ [f. MARL *v.*^{3} + -ING^1.] The action of MARL *v.*^{3}

1598 FLORIO, *Accarpionare*, to dresse any maner of fish with vineger to be eaten colde, which at Southampton they call marling of fish.

marlin(g)spike: see MARLINE-SPIKE.

marlion, obs. form of MERLIN.

marlite (ˈmɑːlaɪt). *Min.* Also **-yte**. [f. MARL *sb.*^{1} + -ITE^2.] A variety of marl which resists the action of the air.

1794 KIRWAN *Elem. Min.* (ed. 2) I. 82 So mixed with argill as rather to pass for marlytes. **1850** LYELL *2nd Visit U.S.* 42 The common name for the marlite, of which this treeless soil is composed, is 'rotten limestone'. **1879** DANA *Man. Geol.* (ed. 3) 233 Calcareous marlytes.

Hence **marlitic** (mɑːˈlɪtɪk) *a. rare*$^{-1}$, partaking of the qualities of marlite.

1794 KIRWAN *Elem. Min.* (ed. 2) I. 361 This earth may be pure,.. or marly, or marlitic.

marlock (ˈmɑːlək), *sb. dial.* A frolic, gambol; a piece of fun; a sportive gesture. (See E.D.D.) Also ˈ**marlock** *v. intr.*, to frolic, gambol.

c **1746** J. COLLIER (Tim Bobbin) *View Lancs. Dial.* (1862) 70 He blest an he pray'd, an mede sitch Marlocks that [etc.]. **1860** MRS. GASKELL *Sylvia's L.* xi, Dost ta mean to say as my Sylvie went and demeaned hersel' to dance and marlock wi' a th' fair-folk at th' 'Admiral's Head'? *Ibid.* xxvii, As if thou'd send thy eyes after him, and he making marlocks back at thee. **1885** E. F. BYRRNE *Entangled* I. I. xii. 231 There's a deal less harm in the Fiend when he's marlocking in the air than when he's harboured in the heart.

marloes (ˈmɑːləʊz), *sb. pl. local.* Also **marleys** (see E.D.D.). [? f. MARL *sb.*^{3}] Marbles.

1827 *Sporting Mag.* XX. 92 Boys.. who would play at marbles (or marloes) with you. **1842** G. DANIEL *Merrie Eng.* I. ix. 191 Oh yes! I pass my time at dumps and marloes.

Marlovian (mɑːˈləʊvɪən), *a.* (*sb.*) [f. the name of the dramatist Christopher *Marlowe* (1564–1593) + -IAN.] **a.** *adj.* Pertaining to or characteristic of Marlowe. **b.** *sb.* An admirer or student of Marlowe. So **Marlowˈesque**, ˈ**Marlowish** *adjs.* Also ˈ**Marlowism**, the style, opinions, etc. of Marlowe.

1593 G. HARVEY *Pierce's Super.* Wks. (Grosart) II. 234 No honesty, but pure Scogginisme; no Religion, but precise Marlowisme. **1798** LAMB *Lett.* (1888) II. 97 Your recipe for a Turk's poison is invaluable, and truly Marlowish. **1885** J. M. HART in *Nation* (N.Y.) 26 Mar. 264/3 Which of the Marlovians, past or present, has bethought him of the simple device of reprinting verbatim, side by side, the editions of 1604, 1609, and 1616? **1887** *Pall Mall Budget* 28 July 30/2 This.. is Marlovian. **1896** A. W. VERITY *Marlowe's Edw. II*, Gloss. 124/2 The phrase 'quenchless fire' is Marlowesque.

marl-pit (ˈmɑːlpɪt). [f. MARL *sb.*^{1} Cf. MDu. *marleput*.] A pit from which marl is dug.

c **1386** CHAUCER *Miller's T.* 274 He walked in the feeldes for to prye Vp on the sterres.. Til he was in a Marleput yfalle. *c* **1440** *Promp. Parv.* 327/1 Marlpytte, or chalkepytte, *cretarium*. **1538** LELAND *Itin.* V. 81 Sum [Pooles] be likelyhod have begon of Marle Pittes. **1625** FLETCHER & SHIRLEY *Nt. Walker* III. i. (1640) E 4 Or shall I drive her.. over some rotton bridge, Or by a Marle pit side? **1707** MORTIMER *Husb.* (1721) I. 294 Carps delight in Marlpits. **1868** PEARD *Water-Farm.* xv. 158 Old marl or gravel-pits.

marly (ˈmɑːlɪ), *a.*^{1} Also 6, 8 **-ey**, 7–8 **-ie**. [f. MARL *sb.*^{1} + -Y.] Resembling, or partaking of the qualities of, marl; composed of marl; abounding with marl.

c **1420** *Pallad. on Husb.* I. 252 Lond is best for whete If hit be marly, thicke, and sumdel weete. **1572** J. JONES *Bathes Buckstone* 1 b, It should not onely bee of another collour marly yellow, or swarty greene; but also [etc.]. **1616** SURFL. & MARKH. *Country Farm* 13 All Clayes which are blacke, gray, or marlie. **1791** W. BARTRAM *Carolina* 183 A loose.. sandy loam, on a clay or marley foundation. **1866** GEO. ELIOT *F. Holt* 3 The land around was rich and marly.

marly (ˈmɑːlɪ), *a.*^{2} *Sc.* and *dial.* Also *Sc.* **mirl(e)y**. [See MARLED *ppl. a.*^{2}] Spotted, streaked, marbled.

1721 RAMSAY *Tartana* 161 But if behind some marly cloud he [the sun] steal. **1790** A. WILSON *Wren* Poems 188 What woe Gars thee sit mourning.. And rive thy mirley breast? **1807** TANNAHILL *Poems* (1815) 191 The mirly-breasted birds.

marly, variant of MARLI.

marlyn, obs. form of MARLINE, MERLIN.

marlyng, variant of MERLING *Obs.*, whiting.

marlyon, obs. form of MERLIN.

marm (mɑːm, mæm). [Var. of MA'AM, freq. in U.S. writers.]

1. = MA'AM 1.

1837 R. M. BIRD *Nick of Woods* I. 120 Say the word, marm. **1845** C. M. KIRKLAND *Western Clearings* 17 'Massy no, marm!' said Jane, with a giggle. *Ibid.* 18 No, Marm; but —this 'ere is something about the team, I guess. **1850**, **1885** [see MA'AM].

2. = MA'AM 2.

1837 HALIBURTON *Clockm.* Ser. I. x, Marm Pugwash is as onsartin in her temper as a mornin in April. **1887** M. E. WILKINS *Humble Romance* 107 Marm Lawson was not a

duchess; but she was Marm Lawson. The 'Marm' itself was a title. *a* **1922** T. S. ELIOT *Waste Land Drafts* (1971) 59 line 50 The pleasant violin At Marm Brown's joint, and the girls and gin.

3. = MA'AM 3.

1865 S. HALE *Lett.* (1919) 16 The silk is seven dollars a yard, and the marm that makes it asks a great deal. **1872** *Congress. Globe* 42nd Congress 2 Sess. App. 632/3 It will be seen that in the great race thus far the English and American marms are about 'nip and tuck'.

b. Used for 'mother'. (Also in address.)

1835 J. F. COOPER *Monikins* II. i. 35 He could scare one by threatening to tell his *marm* how he behaved. **1838** —— *Eve Effingham* II. xvi. 168 Who taught you to call me marm!.. Say 'ma' this instant. **1845** S. JUDD *Margaret* I. 37 'Has your marm got that done?' asked Martha Madeline. **1890** S. O. JEWETT *Strangers & Wayfarers* 9 You've got real nice features, like your marm's folk.

marmaduc, -ady, ? misprints for MARAVEDI.

1571 Q. ELIZ. *Let.* in Digges *Compl. Ambass.* (1655) 41 He hath not the value of a Marmaduc in land or livelihood. **1605** *Play of Stucley* I 2 b, Why should there want a Marmady? a mite?

marmadyn(e, -maide(n, obs. ff. MERMAID(EN.

marmalade ('mɑːməleɪd), *sb.* Forms: 6 marmylate, -elad, -ilat, -ilade, mormelade, marmlet, mermelado, 6–7 marmelet(t, -alad, -alate, 6–8 marmalet, -elade, 7 marmilad, -ilitt, -alit, -alett, -ulade, -ulate, -ulet, -aled, -eleta, -elate, mermalade, 8 marmolet, mermelade, 6– marmalade. [a. F. *marmelade*, in Cotgr. *mermelade*, a. Pg. *marmelada*, f. *marmelo* quince, repr. (with dissimilation of consonants) L. *melimēlum*, a. Gr. μελίμηλον ('honey-apple', f. μέλι honey + μῆλον apple) the name of some kind of apple which was grafted on a quince. From the Pg. word are also Sp. *marmelada*, It. *marmellata*, and (through Fr.) G., Du., Da. *marmelade*, Sw. *marmelad*.]

1. a. A preserve or confection made by boiling fruits (orig. quinces, now usually Seville oranges) with sugar, so as to form a consistent mass.

Often with prefixed word, as ***apricot, lemon, orange, quince marmalade***; when there is no word prefixed, orange marmalade is now commonly meant.

[**1524** in *Lett. & Papers Hen. VIII* (1870) IV. I. 339 Presented by Hull of Exeter one box of marmalade.] **1533** ELYOT *Cast. Helthe* (1541) 44 b, A piece of a quynce rosted or in marmelade. *Ibid.* 79 b, Marmalade of quynces. **1580** LYLY *Euphues* (Arb.) 266 Therfore you must giue him leaue after euery meale to cloase his stomacke with Loue, as with Marmalade. **1621** BURTON *Anat. Mel.* II. ii. I. i, Marmalet of plummes, quinces &c. **1634** SIR T. HERBERT *Trav.* 168 A healing powder of Gall and Marmalate of Dates. **1767** MRS. GLASSE *Cookery* App. 353 Marmalade of cherries. Put the cherries into the sugar, and boil them pretty fast till it be a marmalade. **1769** MRS. RAFFALD *Eng. Housekpr.* (1778) 223 To make Orange Marmalade. Take the clearest Seville oranges you can get [etc.]. *Ibid.* 225 To make Apricot Marmalade. **1845** ELIZA ACTON *Mod. Cookery* 457 Marmalade for the [Apple] Charlotte. Weigh three pounds of good boiling apples.. let these stew over a gentle fire, until they form a perfectly smooth and dry marmalade. *Ibid.* 489 Very fine imperatrice-plum marmalade. **1862** ANSTED *Channel Isl.* IV. xxi. (ed. 2) 487 The fruit is without much flavour,.. though it is well adapted for marmalade.

b. *Proverbial* and *fig.*

1592 G. HARVEY *New Letter* Wks. (Grosart) I. 280 Euery Periode of her stile carrieth marmalad and sucket in the mouth. **1607** WALKINGTON *Opt. Glass* 53 The marmalade and sucket of the Muses.

2. The fruit of *Lucuma mammosa*; also, the tree itself. Also called ***natural marmalade***.

1797 *Encycl. Brit.* (ed. 3) I. 69/1 [*Achras mammosa*.] Fruit .. inclosing a thick pulp called *natural marmalade*. **1821–2** LINDLEY in *Trans. Horticult. Soc.* (1824) IV. 97 The Mammee Sapota.. is called Natural Marmalade. **1846** —— *Veg. Kingd.* 591 The Marmalade (*Achras mammosa*). **1866** *Treas. Bot.* 698/1 *Lucuma mammosum*.. is cultivated for the sake of its fruit, which is called Marmalade, or Natural Marmalade.

3. a. *attrib.*: **marmalade box,** (*a*) a box for marmalade; (*b*) the fruit of *Genipa americana* = GENIPAP; †**marmalade-eater,** ? one daintily brought up; **marmalade fruit,** the fruit of the marmalade-tree; †**marmalade-madam,** a strumpet; **marmalade-plum,** the fruit of the marmalade-tree or the tree itself (J. Smith *Dict. Pop. Names Plants*, 1882); **marmalade-tree,** the mammee-sapota (see sense 2).

1624 *Althorp MS.* in Simpkinson *Washingtons* (1860) App. p. lviii, 6 galley potts and 12 *marmalett boxes for Mrs. Segrave. **1796** STEDMAN *Surinam* II. xxviii. 318 A singular kind of fruit, called here the marmalade box,.. the husk.. opens in halves like a walnut, when the pulp appears like that of a medlar. **1614** R. TAILOR *Hog hath lost Pearl* II. D, Th'art as witty a *marmaled eater as euer I conuerst with. **1840** SCHOMBURGK *Brit. Guiana* 100 The Pine-apple, the Guava, the *Marmalade fruit. **1674** JOSSELYN *Voy. New Eng.* 162 The Gallants a little before Sun-set walk with their *Marmalet-Madams, as we do in Morefields. **1717** E. WARD *Wks.* II. 351 More Marmulet Madams will be met strolling in the Fields, than Honest Women in the Streets. **1866** *Treas. Bot.* 722/2 *Marmalade-Tree, *Lucuma mammosum.*

†**b.** quasi-adj. = 'sweet'. *Obs.*

1629 MASSINGER *Picture* I. i, I cannot blame my ladies Vnwillingnesse to part with such marmulade lips.

c. quasi-*adj.*: of the colour of marmalade (so ***marmalade-coloured*** adj.).

1926 S. T. WARNER *Lolly Willowes* III. 184 Jim was.. a mottled marmalade cat. **1938** K. HALE (*title*) Orlando, the marmalade cat. **1951** 'C. CARNAC' *It's her own Funeral* iv. 38 James, the marmalade cat, was sitting disapprovingly outside. **1957** *Times Lit. Suppl.* 15 Nov. p. xvii/2 Miss White's account of how a fierce little Siamese and an unsnubbable marmalade kitten learnt to live amicably together. **1961** *Guardian* 20 Jan. 9/7 A magnificent dark marmalade-coloured Persian cat. **1965** G. MCINNES *Road to Gundagai* ii. 29, I faced a crowd of blonde giants with marmalade fuzz on their chests. **1972** J. AIKEN *Butterfly Picnic* iii. 55 The local marmalade-coloured rock. **1973** 'E. PETERS' *City of Gold & Shadows* iii. 47 A very austere dress in a dark russet-orange shade that touched off the marmalade lights in her eyes.

Hence **'marmalady** *a.*, resembling marmalade in sweetness, etc.; also *fig.*

1602 MIDDLETON *Blurt* III. i, The Frenchman you see has a soft mermaladie heart. **1920** JOYCE *Let.* 3 Jan. (1957) I. 135 *Nausikaa* is written in a namby-pamby jammy marmalady .. style. **1960** P. COLERIDGE *Running Footsteps* 59 A clipped marmaladey moustache.

'marmalade, *v.* [f. the sb.] *trans.* To spread with marmalade. Hence **'marmaladed** *ppl. a.*

1967 D. PINNER *Ritual* x. 107 David.. selected a piece of toast, marmaladed it, and munched it. **1968** C. NICOLE *Self Lovers* i. 18 Brice marmaladed toast. **1975** J. WOOD *North Kill* vii. 106 Eating steamed haddock along with marmaladed toast.

marmala-water ('mɑːmələ'wɔːtə(r)). [f. **marmala* corruption of Pg. *marmelo*: see MARMELOS.] A liquid distilled from the flowers of the marmelos, used in Ceylon as a perfume for sprinkling.

1857 in BALFOUR *Cycl. India.*

marmaled, -et(t, obs. forms of MARMALADE *sb.*

marmalite, variant of MARMOLITE.

Marmaric (mɑː'mærɪk), *a.* Also 5 -merike, -morike, 7 -maricke. [ad. L. *Marmaric-us*, adj. of *Marmarica* (see below).] Of or belonging to the ancient Marmarica (now Benghazi) on the north coast of Africa. So **Mar'marican** *a.*, in the same sense; *sb.*, an inhabitant of Marmarica.

c **1470** HARDING *Chron.* XLIX. i, As prounde and bryme as lyon Marmerike. *Ibid.* CLXXXVII. iii, In all the world was then no prince hym like.. in the felde a lyon marmorike. **1593** Q. ELIZ. *Boeth.* IV. met. iii. 11 Another the Marm[ar]ican lion [orig. *Marmaricus leo*; CHAUCER *has* a lyoun of þe contre of marmorike] With Tuske and paw indueth. **1607** TOPSELL *Four-f. Beasts* (1658) 359 These also are the epithets of lions:—wrathful,.. violent, Marmarican. **1627** MAY tr. *Lucan* III. E 2 b, Marmaricke troops the horned Ammon prest. *Ibid.* IV. G 5 b, Swift Marmaricans.

†**marmaritin.** *Obs.* *rare*$^{-1}$. [app. f. L. *marmarītis* a plant that grows in marble quarries, a. Gr. μαρμαρῖτις (not recorded in this sense), f. μάρμαρος marble.] Some drug.

1604 MIDDLETON *Witch* (1778) 70 *Firestone.* I have some Mar-martin, and Mandragon. *Heccaty.* Marmaritin, and Mandragora, thou wouldst say.

marmarize ('mɑːməraɪz), *v.* [f. Gr. μάρμαρ-ος marble + -IZE.] *trans.* To subject to marmarosis. (Cf. MARMORIZE *v.*)

1893 GEIKIE *Text-bk. Geol.* IV. VIII. ii. (ed. 3) 603 On the east side of the great intrusive mass of Fair Head the chalk is likewise marmarised.

marmarosis (mɑːmə'rəʊsɪs). *Geol.* [f. Gr. μάρμαρ-ος marble + -OSIS.] The conversion of limestone into marble by metamorphism.

1882 GEIKIE *Text-bk. Geol.* IV. VIII. ii. 577 Marmarosis.

marmaset(t, -it, -assed, obs. ff. MARMOSET.

marmatite ('mɑːmətaɪt). *Min.* [a. G. *marmatit*, f. *Marmato* (S. Amer.).] A ferriferous variety of sphalerite.

1843 *Penny Cycl.* XXVII. 781/2.

marmayd(en, obs. forms of MERMAID(EN.

marmazat, -et, obs. forms of MARMOSET.

marmelade, -ate, -et(t, obs. ff. MARMALADE *sb.*

‖**marmelos** ('mɑːmɪlɒs). [mod.L., f. Pg. *marmelo* quince.] The Bengal quince, *Ægle Marmelos.*

1823 CRABB *Technol. Dict.* **1866** *Treas. Bot.* 722/2 Marmelos, *Ægle Marmelos.* **1887** *Standard* 16 Sept. 5/3 On how many tables does the marmelos make its appearance?

‖**marmennill** (mɑː'mɛnɪl). [Icelandic; dim. f. *mar-r* sea + *mann-, mað-r* man.] A merman.

1805 *Naval Chron.* XIV. 303 It was the body of a Marmennill, and not that of a human being. **1863** BARING-GOULD *Iceland* 352 The verses sung by a marmennill, when he was carried back to his favourite element.

Marmerike, obs. form of MARMARIC.

marmeset(te, -ot, obs. forms of MARMOSET.

marmilad(e, -at, -itt, obs. ff. MARMALADE *sb.*

marmissed, -isset, obs. forms of MARMOSET.

marmit ('mɑːmɪt). *dial.* and *Naut.* ? *Obs.* [ad. F. *marmite* pot or kettle.] (See quots.)

c **1758** *Inv.* in Miss Jackson *Shropsh. Word-bk.* 2 Potts—1 Marmitt. **1841** HARTSHORNE *Salopia Antiq.* 500 *Marmit*, a pot with hooks at each side. **1867** SMYTH *Sailor's Word-bk.*, *Marmit*, a pot fitted with a hook for hanging it to the bars of the galley-range. **1879** MISS JACKSON *Shropsh. Word-bk.*, *Marmint, Marmot*, a three-legged iron pot—holding about four quarts—to be hung over the fire.

marmite ('mɑːmaɪt, ‖marmit). [a. F. *marmite* pot or kettle: see MARMIT.] **1. a.** An earthenware cooking-vessel; a stockpot.

1805 C. JAMES *New Mil. Dict.* (ed. 2), *Marmite*,.. porridge-pot, kettle; a machine in which soldiers boil their victuals. **1882** C. M. YONGE *Unknown to Hist.* II. xxi. 294 The French suite, every one of whom liked to have his own little arrangements of cookery, and to look after his own *marmite* in his own way. **1919** B. RUCK *Disturbing Charm* I. xi. 107 The door into the huge French kitchen stood open, giving a glimpse of marmites, burnished copper pans, crocks, and five-decker cookers. **1955** L. WOOLLEY *Alalakh* vi. 218 'Marmite', Type 154, of normal cooking-pot ware, black clay reddened on surface. **1960** *Home & Garden* Oct. 150/2 A range of ovenware.. 5s. 6d for a marmite.

b. *slang.* A bomb or shell resembling a pot.

1915 G. ADAM *Behind Scenes at Front* 48 The graves in the churchyard have been torn open by 'marmites'. **1919** [see BLACK MARIA 2].

2. ('mɑːmaɪt.) (Properly with capital initial.) The proprietary term for an extract made from fresh brewer's yeast.

1907 *Yesterday's Shopping* (1969) 18/1 Marmite (Vegetable Ext.)... Marmite Bouillon, in tubes. **1920** *Trade Marks Jrnl.* 25 Aug. 1588 *Marmite...* A Concentrated Culinary Preparation, being an Article of Food. The Marmite Food Extract Co., Limited. **1923** *Nature* 12 May 626/2 In the prevention of beri-beri the addition of oat-meal and dhall to the British ration, the addition of marmite, and later, the issue of bread containing 25 per cent. of atta, were found valuable. **1925** D. H. LAWRENCE *Let.* 17 Dec. (1962) II. 871 So Sonya will never cook us another goose, only marmite pie and nut-cutlet. **1928** R. MACAULAY *Keeping up Appearances* i. 5 Doctors.. prefer that one should breakfast .. on marmite, Ry-Vita biscuits, and an apple. **1934** *Nature* 20 Oct. 623/2 The yeast extract 'Marmite' has long been recognised as a source of the vitamin B complex. **1947** T. H. WHITE *Mistress Masham's Repose* i. 7 She had.. brown eyes the colour of marmite, but more shiny. **1966** A. E. LINDOP *I start Counting* xviii. 208 He knocked me up a Marmite sandwich.

‖**marmiton** (marmitɔ̃). [Fr., f. *marmite* pot, kettle.] A kitchen scullion.

1754 CHESTERF. *Let. to Dayrolles* 2 Apr., I wish.. that you could find me at Brussels an humble *marmiton, tournebroche*, or other animal, who could roast and boil decently. **1847** DISRAELI *Tancred* I. i, One of my marmitons has disappointed me.

marmlet, obs. form of MARMALADE *sb.*

marmol(e, variant forms of MORMAL *Obs.*

marmolet, obs. form of MARMALADE *sb.*

marmolite ('mɑːməlaɪt). *Min.* Also **marmalite.** [Formed by Nuttall, who refers to Gr. μαρμαίρειν to shine: see -LITE.] A laminated serpentine, of a pearly lustre and pale green colour.

1822 T. NUTTALL in *Amer. Jrnl. Sci.* IV. 17 A contiguous substance which as a peculiar mineral I shall distinguish by the name of marmalite. *Ibid.* 19 Marmolite. **1848** C. A. JOHNS *Week at Lizard* 107 Rare minerals, such as marmolite. **1849** WATTS tr. *Gmelin's Handbk. Chem.* III. 395 Noble Serpentine or Ophite (together with Marmalite [etc.]).

†**marmor.** *Sc. Obs.* Also 4, 6 -our, -ore. [a. L. *marmor* MARBLE.] Marble. Also *attrib.*

c **1375** *Sc. Leg. Saints* xxi. (*Clement*) 888 þai.. fand a kyrk .. of marmore mad. **1596** DALRYMPLE tr. *Leslie's Hist. Scot.* I. 79 This marmore stane in forme of a chyre. *Ibid.* 129 The marmour chyre of Destinie. *Ibid.* 132 The sentences in Marmor war hewin.

marmoraceous (mɑːmə'reɪʃəs), *a. rare.* [f. L. type **marmorāce-us*, f. *marmor* MARBLE: see -ACEOUS.] Pertaining to, or like, marble.

1688 R. HOLME *Armoury* II. 313/1 Marmo[ra]ceous, a Marble colour, a black blue. **1822** T. NUTTALL in *Amer. Jrnl. Sci.* IV. 18 This marmoraceous mineral. **1848** MAUNDER *Treas. Nat. Hist.*

marmorate ('mɑːməreɪt), *a.* [ad. L. *marmorāt-us*, pa. pple. of *marmorāre* to overlay with marble, f. *marmor* MARBLE.]

†**1.** Overlaid with or enclosed in marble. *Obs.*

1537 *Epitaph* in Fuller *Worthies, Lond.* II. (1662) 205 Under this Stone closyd and marmorate Lyeth Iohn Kite.

2. *Nat. Hist.* Variegated or veined like marble.

1826 KIRBY & SP. *Entomol.* IV. 289. **1866** *Treas. Bot.* 722/2.

So †**'marmorated** *a.*

1731 BAILEY vol. II, *Marmorated*, made of, wrought in, covered with marble.

marmoration (mɑːmə'reɪʃən). *rare*$^{-0}$. [ad. late L. *marmorātiōn-em*, n. of action f. *marmorāre* (see prec.).] (See quots.)

1661 BLOUNT *Glossogr.* (ed. 2), *Marmoration*, a building with marble. **1730–6** BAILEY (fol.), *Marmoration*, a covering or laying with marble.

marmoreal (mɑːˈmɔərɪəl), *a. poet.* and *rhet.* [f. L. *marmore-us* (f. *marmor* MARBLE) + -AL[1].]

1. Resembling marble or a marble statue; cold, smooth, white, etc., like marble.

1798 LANDOR *Gebir* Wks. 1846 II. 494 Looking recumbent how Love's column rose Marmoreal. **1817** SHELLEY *Rev. Islam* I. xlix, Paving with fire the sky and the marmoreal floods. **1868** BROWNING *Ring & Bk.* IX. 53 Marmoreal neck and bosom uberous. **1892** *Sat. Rev.* 15 Oct. 443/1 Blank-verse studies of merit, but somewhat cold and marmoreal in their severity.

2. Made or composed of marble.

1825 *New Monthly Mag.* XIII. 181 Spurs of marble, and marmoreal limbs. **1880** W. WATSON *Prince's Quest, Sunset* (1892) 134 Minaret And terrace and marmoreal spire.

Hence **marˈmoreally** *adv.*

1847 SIR A. DE VERE *1st Pt. Mary Tudor* v. iii, Cold, but composed, marmoreally rigid! **1887** SAINTSBURY *Eliz. Lit.* 455 The marmoreally-finished minor poems of Ben [Jonson].

marmorean (mɑːˈmɔərɪən), *a.* [f. L. *marmore-us* (f. *marmor* MARBLE) + -AN.] Composed, or made, of marble; resembling marble.

1656 BLOUNT *Glossogr.*, *Marmorean*.., of marble, or that is like it in colour, hardness, &c. **1836** *Fraser's Mag.* XIV. 24 Her neck's marmorean whiteness. **1902** *Speaker* 1 Mar. 608/1 The marmorean Leconte de Lisle.

†**marmoreous**, *a. Obs.*—[0] [Formed as prec. + -OUS.] = prec.

1727 BAILEY vol. II.

marmoric (mɑːˈmɒrɪk), *a. rare*—[1]. [f. L. *marmor* marble + -IC.] Of marble.

1811 PINKERTON *Petralogy* I. 130 Hardness, between marmoric and basaltic.

marmorize (ˈmɑːməraɪz), *v.* [f. L. *marmor* + -IZE. Cf. F. *marmoriser* and mod.L. *marmorisatio*.] = MARMARIZE *v.*

1897 GEIKIE *Anc. Volcanoes* I. 32 Marmorised limestone.

‖**marmortinto** (mɑːməˈtɪntəʊ). [? A mistake for It. *marmo tinto* (*marmo* marble, *tinto* dyed, coloured).] An Italian process (used in the 18th c.) of decorating walls, etc. in imitation of marble.

1844 *Mech. Mag.* XL. 31 The inventor of marmortinto was born in 1762. **1854** FAIRHOLT *Dict. Art*, *Marmortinto*.

marmose (ˈmɑːməʊs). [a. F. *marmose* (Buffon), possibly from colonial Du.: cf. MDu. *marmoyse*, *mermoyse* (see MERMOYSE), marmoset, believed to be a shortening of F. *marmouset*.] One of several species of small South American opossums (as *Didelphys dorsigera* and *D. murina*) which have only a rudimentary pouch and carry their young on their back.

1774 GOLDSM. *Nat. Hist.* (1824) II. 162 An animal greatly resembling the former [*i.e.* the opossum], is the Marmose.

marmoset (ˈmɑːməˌzɛt). Forms: 4–5 **marmusette, marmesette,** 5, (9) **marmozette, -usete, -isset, maremusset,** 5–6 **marmesette, -osette,** 5–7 **marmeset,** 6 **mermoset, -osite, marmosete, -azat, -asit, -issed, -esot, mormosett, marmsat,** 6–7 **marmeset(t,** 6, 8 **marmouset,** 6–9 **marmozet,** (9 **marmozette**), 7 **marmosit(e, -azet, -osat, -uset, -ousite, -osett, mormaset, malmaset,** 5– **marmoset.** [a. OF. *marmouset* grotesque image, in 1280 latinized *marmosetum* (not *marmoretum* as given by Littré); in mod.F. the word means also 'little man'; the sense 'ape', though not found in Fr. dicts., is in provincial use (see Honnorat *Dict. Prov.*). Hence MDu. *marmoset* in all three senses.

The origin of the Fr. word is obscure; it has been conjectured to be a derivative of L. *marmor* marble, but the form is not easy to account for. It can hardly be unconnected with F. *marmot* little child (whence prob. It. *marmocchio*), in early use also 'monkey', 'grotesque statuette'; forms app. cognate are med.L. *marmōnetus*, *mammōnetus* (Promp. Parv.), *mammōn-em* monkey. Some have supposed the source to be OF. *merme* small (:—L. *minimus*); others have suggested that the word in the sense 'grotesque figure' was an architectural term derived in some way from Gr. μορμώ bugbear.]

†**1.** A grotesque figure. **a.** Applied in scorn to an idol. *Obs.*

1426 LYDG. *De Guil. Pilgr.* 20954 To worshepe A Marmoset, Wych to helpe..Hath no puissaunce. **1563–83** FOXE *A. & M.* II. 882/2 Get thee away from me thou naughty person: with thy marmoset of wood.

attrib. *a* **1572** KNOX *Hist. Ref.* Wks. 1846 I. 259 A marmouset idole was borrowed fra the Gray Freiris.

†**b.** (See quot. 1706.) *Obs.*—[0]

1687 MIEGE *Gt. Fr. Dict.* II, *Marmoset*, a kind of Grotesk, *Marmouset*. **1706** PHILLIPS (ed. Kersey), *Marmoset*,..an odd kind of Grotesk figure in a Building. **1736** NEVE *Builder's Dict.*

2. †**a.** In early use: Any small monkey (*obs.*). **b.** Now restricted to the tropical American monkeys of the family *Hapalidæ* (or *Midïdæ*), comprising two genera, *Hapale* (the true marmosets) and *Midas* (the tamarins).

The *Hapalidæ* are of the size of a small squirrel, have non-prehensile bushy tails, and (in many species) long eartufts or a mane of whitish hair. They have often been kept as pets, on account of their gentle, playful nature.

1398 TREVISA *Barth. De P.R.* XVIII. i. (1495) 748 Some beestes seruyth for..mannys myrth: as apys and marmusettes [*MS. Bodl.* marmesettes] and popyngayes. *c* **1400** MAUNDEV. (1839) xix. 210 Apes, Marmozettes [*Roxb.* marmusetes, Fr. orig. *marmoz*], Babewynes, and many other dyverse Bestes. *c* **1425** *Voc.* in Wr.-Wülcker 639/32 *Hic zenozephalus*, maremusset. **1519** HORMAN *Vulg.* 109b, The marmeset hath a very longe tayle. **1551** ROBINSON tr. *More's Utopia* II. vi. (ed. Lupton) 215 A mormosett chaunced vpon the booke..whyche..plucked owte certeyne leaues, and toore them in pieces. **1559** W. CUNNINGHAM *Cosmogr. Glasse* 191 Mermosites. **1610** SHAKS. *Temp.* II. ii. 174 The nimble Marmazet. **1625** PURCHAS *Pilgrims* II. 1771 There are many Monkies or Marmosets, that doe great hurt to the Palme trees. **1679** T. TRAPHAM *Disc. Jamaica* 115 The Malmaset, as among the Indians of the more Southern Main of America. **1706** PHILLIPS (ed. Kersey), *Marmoset*, a sort of black Monkey, having a shaggy Neck. **1715** tr. *Pancirollus' Rerum Mem.* I. II. xvi. 104 An Egyptian Cat, which we call a Marmoset, or Monkey. **1822** SCOTT *Nigel* viii, I have seen her..as changeful as a marmozet. **1840** *Cuvier's Anim. Kingd.* 62 Marmosets (*Hapale*, as restricted). **1863** BATES *Nat. Amazons* II. 55 The monkeys belonged to a very pretty and rare species, a kind of marmoset. **1893** [see MARIKINA].

attrib. **1851** P. H. GOSSE *Nat. in Jamaica* 327 *note*, I have heard the Marmozette Monkey (*Jacchus*) produce the very same sound. **1876** 'OUIDA' *Winter City* vii. 224 The quick marmoset eyes of little Mme. Mila.

†**3.** Applied to a person: **a.** to a woman or child, as a term of endearment or playful reproach: cf. *monkey*. *Obs.*

1526 SKELTON *Magnyf.* 462 What, wanton, wanton, nowe well ymet! What, Margery Mylke Ducke, mermoset! **1604** DEKKER *1st Pt. Honest Wh.* vi. C4b, Saue thee little Marmoset: how doest thou good pretty roague? **1614** BEAUM. & FL. *Wit at sev. Weap.* III. i, *Sir Greg.* [To his niece.] O dissembling Marmaset! **1754** RICHARDSON *Grandison* (1781) VII. xliii. 211 How shall I hold the little marmouset, if you devour first one of my hands, then the other?

b. to a man, as a term of abuse or contempt: cf. *ape*. Sometimes (as in OF.) a favourite, 'ingle'.

? *a* **1500** *Chester Pl.* x, I will..mar that misbegotten marmoset. **1523** LD. BERNERS *Froiss.* I. ccclxxxvii. 661 Alwayes the Erle hath these marmosettes about him, as Gylbert Mahewe and his bretherne. *a* **1529** SKELTON *Agst. Garnesche* ii. 39 Thow mantycore, ye marmoset, garnyshte like a Greke. *a* **1585** POLWART *Flyting w. Montgomerie* 795 Beld bisset! marmissed! lansprezed to the lownes! **1615** BRATHWAIT *Strappado* (1878) 48 See, see her cerus cheeke, made to delight Her apple-squire, or wanton Marmosite. **1825** SCOTT *Talism.* xxiv, A king's son..is at least a match for this marmozet of a Marquis.

Hence †**marmoˈsetical** *a.*, characteristic of a marmoset; apishly foolish.

1630 J. TAYLOR (Water P.) *Wit & Mirth* Wks. II. 187/2 A Mercers seruant espying his marmositicall Apishnesse.

marmot (ˈmɑːmət). Also 8 **mar(a)motto, marmotta,** ? *erron.* **marmout,** 8–9 **marmotte.** [ad. F. *marmotte* fem. (whence prob. Sp., Pg. *marmota*, It. *marmotta*, also †*marmotto* masc.), prob. an altered form, due to assimilation to OF. *marmotte*, *marmot* monkey (see MARMOSET), of Rumonsch *murmont*:—L. type *mūrem montis* 'mountain mouse', whence OHG. *muremunto*, *murmainti*, *murmenti*, MHG. *mürmendîn*, mod.G. dialects *murmentel*, *murmeten*, *murmetli*, mod.G. *murmeltier*, whence Du. *mormeldier*, Da. *murmeldyr*, Sw. *murmeldjur*.]

1. A rodent of the genus *Arctomys* or subfamily *Arctomyinæ* of the squirrel family, esp. *A. marmotta*, which inhabits the Alps and the Pyrenees, sometimes called the Alpine marmot.

With qualification applied to other animals of the same and allied genera: †**American** or **Maryland m.**, the woodchuck, *A. monax*; **bobac** or **Polish m.**, *A. bobac* (see BOBAC); †**Canadian** or **Quebec m.**, *Spermophilus empetra*; **earless** or **pouched m.**, the suslik, *S. citillus*; **hoary m.**, the whistler, *A. pruinosus*; †**Lapland m.**, the lemming; **prairie m.**, the prairie dog (genus *Cynomys*).

1607 TOPSELL *Hist. Four-f. Beasts* (1658) 405 Scaliger describeth them in this manner, a Marmot (saith he, for so he tearmeth an Alpine Mouse in French) is a Beast about the bigness of a Badger. **1704** RAY *Creation* II. (ed. 4) 337 The Marmotto or *Mus Alpinus*, a Creature as big or bigger than a Rabbet, which absconds all Winter. **1753** CHAMBERS *Cycl. Supp.*, *Marmotte*, *Marmotta*, the mountain rat, a creature very common in many parts of Europe. **1762** tr. *Busching's Syst. Geog.* I. 495 Mice, maramottos, and wild-fowl are their favourite dishes. **1774** GOLDSM. *Nat. Hist.* (1776) IV. 38 The Marmot is..almost as big as an hare, but it is more corpulent than a cat, and has shorter legs. **1781** PENNANT *Quadrup.* II. 396 Alpine Marmot. *Ibid.* 397 Quebec Marmot. *Ibid.* 398 Maryland Marmot. *Ibid.*, Hoary Marmot. *Ibid.* 399 Bobuk Marmot. **1796** [see EARLESS]. **1797** *Encycl. Brit.* (ed. 3) XII. 463/1 The monax, or American marmot... The bobac, or Polish marmot... The empetra, or Canadian marmot. **1861** G. F. BERKELEY *Sportsm. W. Prairies* xv. 259 The prairie dog or marmot. **1896** KIRKALDY & POLLARD tr. *Boas' Text Bk. Zool.* 529 The Pouched Marmot (*Spermophilus citillus*) of East Europe.

¶ **b.** In full ***Cape marmot, marmot of the Cape***: the Cape cony or daman, *Hyrax capensis*.

1861 HULME tr. *Moquin-Tandon* II. III. ii. 122 The Daman of the Cape (*Hyrax Capensis*),..commonly called..Marmot of the Cape.

2. A kind of bathing cap. [After F. *marmotte*.]

1897 *Westm. Gaz.* 22 July 3/3 The newest bathing cap is 'the marmotte'..fastening in a knot on the forehead. **1902** *Ibid.* 31 July 3/2 The silk caps are a little more varied in shape; one sees the tammie and the marmot.

†**marmot(t)ane.** *Obs. rare.* [a. OF. *marmottaine*, corruptly repr. L. *mūrem montānam* mountain mouse.] = MARMOT 1.

1601 HOLLAND *Pliny* I. 216 The Rats..of the Alpes, *i.* Marmottanes, which are as bigge as Brockes or Badgers. *Ibid.* 217 Such like Marmotanes there be in Ægypt.

marmour, variant of MARMOR *Sc. Obs.*

marmouset, -ousite, -ozet(te, marmsat, obs. ff. MARMOSET.

†**marm-stone.** *Obs.* [OE. *marmstán*, also *marmanstán*, f. *marm* marble + *stán* STONE.] Marble; a block, slab, etc. of marble.

971 *Blickl. Hom.* 203 Beforan ðære norðdura þære ciricean on þæm marmanstane. *c* **1000** ÆLFRIC *Saints' Lives* xxxi. 1128 þa afylde sum cnapa þæt fæt unwærlice uppon þone marm-stan. *c* **1205** LAY. 1138 [A temple] imaked of marme stæne [*later text* marbre stone]. *Ibid.* 1317, 32097.

marmulade, -ate, -et, obs. ff. MARMALADE *sb.*

marmuset(e, -ette, obs. forms of MARMOSET.

‖**maro** (ˈmarɔ). [Polynesian.] A loin-cloth used by certain South Sea Islanders.

1772–84 *Cook's Voy.* (1790) VI. 2047 A piece of thick cloth, called the maro, about a foot in breadth, which passes between the legs, and is fastened round the waist. **1833** A. SMITH in M. D. Frear *Lowell & Abigail* (1934) 63 Many others wear nothing but a narrow strip of tapa about their loins, called a *maro*. **1860** MAYNE REID *Odd People* 213 A coarser and scantier pareu is to be seen among the poorer people,..and not unfrequently this is only a mere strip wrapped around the loins; in other words, a 'malo', 'maro', or 'maso'—as it is indifferently written in the varied orthography of the voyagers. **1898** [see TAPA[1]]. **1969** R. T. WILCOX *Dict. Costume* (1970) 201 *Malo*, the Hawaiian man's girdle or loincloth. Originally of tapa cloth which was made from tree bark, but now of cotton dyed in brilliant colors.

maro, obs. form of MARROW *sb.*[1]

marocain (mærəˈkeɪn). [f. F. *maroquin*: see MAROQUIN *a.* and *sb.*] A dress fabric of ribbed crêpe. Also, a garment made from marocain.

1922 *Glasgow Herald* 28 June 8/6 For her going away dress the bride had a three-piece suit of grey wool marocain. **1922** *Tatler* 30 Aug. 354/2 An evening frock of black crêpe marocain. **1923** *Weekly Dispatch* 14 Jan. 15 A new evening model..had a trailing skirt with narrow draperies of black panne, while the upper part..was in white marocain. **1926** C. SIDGWICK *Sack & Sugar* xi. 126, I wore an embroidered marocain. **1957** M. B. PICKEN *Fashion Dict.* 88/1 *Marocain*.., ribbed crepe of silk or wool or combination.

marocchine, -okin(e, obs. ff. MAROQUIN.

marode, obs. form of MARAUD.

†**maron.** *Obs.* [a. obs. F. *marron* (Rabelais); in med.L. *mar(r)ōn-em*.] A mountain guide.

1506 GUYLFORDE *Pilgr.* (Camden) 80 We tok moyles to stey vs vp the mountayne, and toke also marones to kepe vs frome fallynge. **1611** CORYAT *Crudities* 80 My authour of this tale or figment is our Maron of Turin [*marg.* That is guide or conductor]. **1670–98** LASSELS *Voy. Italy* I. 49 Marons, or men with little open chairs to carry you up and down the hill for a crown. *Ibid.* 51 After two hours tugging of our chairmen or Marons we came to the top of the hill.

marone, maroner: see MAROON, MARINER.

†**Maˈronian,** *a. Obs.* [f. L. *Marōn-em* the cognomen of Virgil + -IAN.] Virgilian.

1648 HERRICK *Hesper.*, *To M. Denham*, Thy brave, bold, and sweet Maronian Muse. *a* **1693** *Urquhart's Rabelais* III. x. 84 The Maronian Lottery [orig. *sors Virgilianes*].

†**ˈMaronist**[1]. *Obs.* [f. L. *Marōn-em* + -IST.] A disciple of the poet Virgil (Publius Vergilius Maro); a Virgilian student or scholar.

1597–8 BP. HALL *Sat.* I. iv. 7 He, like some imperious Maronist, Conjures the Muses that they him assist. **1599** *Preserv. Hen. VII* (1866) 10, I would I were but as Ennius to a fine Maronist.

†**Maronist**[2]. *Obs.*—[0] Variant of MARONITE.

1737 in BAILEY vol. II.

Maronite (ˈmærənaɪt), *sb.* (and *a.*) Also 6 **Moronite.** [ad. late L. *Marōnīta*, f. *Marōn* name of the founder of the sect: see -ITE.

There was a Syrian of this name in the 4th c., and another in the 7th c.; the sect was probably named from one of these; recent authorities favour the earlier date.]

One of a sect of Syrian Christians, dwelling in the Lebanon and Anti-Lebanon; they were originally Monothelites, but subsequently became united with the Roman Church. Also *attrib.* (quasi-*adj.*).

c **1511** *1st Eng. Bk. Amer.* (Arb.) Introd. 31/1 The syxte [cristened] nacyon... They be named Moroniten. **1617** MORYSON *Itin.* I. 215 A Maronite Christian. **1703** MAUNDRELL *Journ. Jerus.* (1721) 35 The Maronite Bishop of Aleppo. **1885** *Cath. Dict.* (ed. 3) s.v., A schism was caused through Greek influence, and a Maronite Patriarch fell away... Ever since [1216] the Maronites have been steadfast Catholics.

maronner, obs. form of MARINER.

maroo, obs. form of MARROW *sb.*[2]

maroodi (mə'ruːdɪ). Also **maroudi.** [ad. Arawak *marodi.*] In Guyana, any of several birds included in species of guan belonging to the genera *Penelope* or *Pipile*.

1825 C. WATERTON *Wanderings S. Amer.* 23 The forest contains an abundance of..maams, maroudis and waracabas. **1876** C. B. BROWN *Canoe & Camp Life Brit. Guiana* 345 Maroodies of two kinds (the common and white-headed)..were also numerous. **1883** E. F. IM THURN *Among Indians Guiana* 62 Now and then a maroodi (*Penelope*) cried shrilly from among the trees. **1922** *Blackw. Mag.* Apr. 535/1 A quail and a maroodi rewarded their zeal.

maroon (mə'ruːn), *sb.*[1] and *a.*[1] Forms: 6–9 **marron,** 7–9 **marone,** 8–9 **marrone,** 9 **marroon,** 7, 9 **maroon.** [a. F. *marron*, ad. It. *marrone.*]

A. *sb.*

†**1.** A large kind of sweet chestnut native to Southern Europe; also, the tree bearing this nut. Also ***marron chestnut***. *Obs.*

1594 R. ASHLEY tr. *Loys le Roy* 28 Dates, chestnuts, and marrons. **1601** HOLLAND *Pliny* I. 525 Such plots of ground as do affoord coppises of Chest-nut trees, are stored with plants comming of marrons or nut-kernels. **1699** EVELYN *Acetaria* App. P viij, Roasted Maroons, Pistachios, Pine-Kernels [etc.]. [**1877** SCUDDER *Recoll. S. Breck* iii. 66 The fine large marron chestnuts were brought to us..for a cent a hundred.]

2. a. [= F. *marron*, from the quasi-adj. use as in *couleur marron.*] A particular kind of brownish-crimson or claret colour.

1791 HAMILTON *Berthollet's Dyeing* I. I. II. i. 144 Darker colours such as browns and marones. *Ibid.* II. II. III. vii. 216 This gives it a cinnamon colour, or light marrone. **1835** *Court Mag.* VI. p. ii/1 Some velvet [mantles] of maroon and other rich winter colours. **1844** HAY *Law Harm. Colouring* (ed. 5) 17 A series of other colours, such as brown, marone, slate. **1882** *Garden* 14 Oct. 347/1 A rather small flower..of a deep rich maroon.

b. A coal-tar dye obtained from the resinous matters formed in the manufacture of magenta.

a **1873** CRACE-CALVERT *Dyeing*, etc. (1876) 432 Aniline Maroons and Browns.

3. a. A firework composed of a small cubical box of pasteboard, wrapped round with twine and filled with gunpowder; it is intended to imitate in exploding the report of a cannon. (Used as an air-raid warning, etc., in the war of 1914–18.)

1749 *Machine for the Fireworks* 15 Marrons, 5000. **1818** *Handbill* July in *Pall Mall G.* (1885) 5 Nov. 4/2 A battery of maroons, or imitation cannon. **1840–1** HOOD *Kilmansegg, Birth* xviii, To have seen the maroons, And the whirling moons. **1875** KNIGHT *Dict. Mech.* 1401/2 *Marron.* **1884** *St. James's Gaz.* 13 June 10/2 The display last night included signal maroons..rockets, and shells. **1918** *Flying* 6 Feb. 90/1 Clearly, the authorities ought to have posted notices.. explaining that the maroons are warnings to take cover. **1918** *Daily Mirror* 12 Nov. 2/1 London went wild with delight when the great news came through yesterday... Bells burst into joyful chimes, maroons were exploded, bands paraded the streets, and London gave itself up wholeheartedly to rejoicing. **1934** E. WHARTON *Backward Glance* xiii. 358 Four years of war had inured Parisians to every kind of noise connected with air-raids, from the boom of warning maroons to the smashing roar of the bombs.

b. *Artillery.* (See quot. 1876.)

1859 F. A. GRIFFITHS *Artil. Man.* (1862) 282 Marroons are boxes containing from 1 to 6 ounces of powder. **1859** MCCLINTOCK *Voy. 'Fox' in Arctic Sea* i. 9 Powder for ice-blasting, rockets, maroons, and signal-mortar were furnished by the Board of Ordnance. **1876** VOYLE & STEVENSON *Milit. Dict.* (ed. 3), *Marroons*, decorations for rockets. They are cubes filled with grained powder, and enveloped with two or three layers of strong twine or marline.

c. 'A bright white light used for signals in the East Indies' (Ogilvie *Suppl.* 1855).

B. *adj.* Of the colour described in A. 2.

1843 JAMES *Forest Days* ii, He was dressed in close-fitting garments of a dark marone tint. **1871** KINGSLEY *At Last* ii, A most lovely Convolvulus..with purple maroon flowers. **1876** OUIDA *Winter City* vi. 114 They had put out her marron velvet with the ostrich feathers. **1878** FOSTER *Phys.* II. ii. §3. 267 Venous blood of a dark purple or maroon colour.

Comb. **1840** BARHAM *Ingol. Leg.* Ser. I. *St. Gengulphus*, Good, stout maroon-colour'd leather. **1876** HARLEY *Mat. Med.* 233 A maroon-red precipitate.

maroon (mə'ruːn), *sb.*[2] and *a.*[2] Forms: 7–8 **maron,** 8 **marone, meroon,** 8– **maroon.** [a. F. *marron* (*maron* in *Hist. Antilles* 1658, p. 322), said to be a corruption of Sp. *cimarron* wild, untamed.]

A. *sb.*

1. One of a class of Blacks, originally fugitive slaves, living in the mountains and forests of Surinam and the West Indies.

[**1626** NICHOLS *Sir F. Drake revived* (1628) 7 The Symerons (a blacke people, which about eightie yeeres past, fled from the Spaniards their Masters).] **1666** J. DAVIES *Hist. Caribby Isles* 202 They will run away and get into the Mountains and Forests, where they live like so many Beasts; then they are call'd Marons, that is to say Savages. **1795** *Hist. Eur.* in *Ann. Reg.* (1796) 60/1 The hostilities against the free negroes in the Island of Jamaica known by the denomination of Maroons had been carried on a long time without effect. **1797** *Encycl. Brit.* (ed. 3) X. 694/2 (Mauritius) The Marones, or wild negroes. **1843** MARRYAT *M. Violet* xl, A gang of negro maroons was hanging about. **1895** *Nation* (N.Y.) 8 Aug. 98/2 The savage Maroons were called in and let loose upon the peasantry.

attrib. **1796** (*title*) The Proceedings of the Governor and Assembly of Jamaica, in regard to the Maroon Negroes. **1828** G. W. BRIDGES *Ann. Jamaica* II. xv. 221 Many who distinguished themselves in the Maroon war of Jamaica.

b. *fig.* (Also *attrib.*)

1823 MACAULAY *Misc. Writ., R. Soc. Lit.* (1860) I. 22 It will furnish a secure ambuscade behind which the Maroons of literature may take a certain and deadly aim. *a* **1859** —— *Hist. Eng.* xxiii. (1861) V. 113 A warrant of the Lord Chief Justice broke up the Maroon village [of thieves in Epping Forest] for a short time.

2. *Southern U.S.* In full ***maroon*** †***frolic, party***: A pleasure party, esp. a hunting or fishing excursion of the nature of a picnic but of longer duration.

1779 I. ANGELL *Diary* (1899) 59 Lt. Cook..Come from the Meroon frolick last night. [*Editor's note*: A hunting or fishing trip, or excursion, in Southern United States, to camp out after the manner of the West Indian Maroons.] **1785** in *South Carolina Hist. & Geneal. Mag.* (1912) XIII. 188 On Monday we form a maroon party to visit some saw mills. **1838** C. GILMAN *Recoll. Southern Matron* xxxii. 223 Feeling the necessity of refreshment, we alighted for a while beneath a tree by the roadside, for a *maroon*.

3. A person who is marooned.

1883 STEVENSON *Treas. Isl.* xi, Well, what would you think? Put 'em ashore like maroons?

B. *adj.* Run wild, having reverted to a state of nature (*Cent. Dict.*). [So F. *marron.*]

maroon (mə'ruːn), *v.* Also 7–8 **mo-.** [f. prec.]

†**1. a.** *passive* or *intr.* To be lost in the wilds. **b.** *intr.* (? *fig.*) ? To miss one's object. *Obs.*

1699 DAMPIER *Voy.* II. II. 84, I began to find that I was (as we call it, I suppose from the Spaniards) Morooned, or Lost, and quite out of the Hearing of my Comrades Guns. **1716–17** S. SEWALL *Letter-Bk.* 15 Jan. II. 63, I had rather myself bear part of the charge, then that the poor young man moroon'd and return home with shame and disappointment.

2. *trans.* To put (a person) ashore and leave him on a desolate island or coast (as was done by the buccaneers and pirates) by way of punishment.

1726 *Brice's Weekly Jrnl.* 1 July 2 He farther says, that Lowe and Spriggs were both maroon'd, and were got among the Musketoo Indians. **1822** SCOTT *Pirate* xxii, I was.. condemned..to be marooned, as the phrase goes, on one of those little sandy, bushy islets, which are called, in the West Indies, keys. **1891** *Athenæum* 17 Jan. 82/2 Magellan 'marooned' a mutinous priest on the coast of Patagonia.

b. *transf.* To place or leave in a position from which one cannot escape. Also *fig.*

1910 *N.Y. Even. Post* 6 Jan. (Th.), Train No. 4.. , due here from Los Angeles on January 1, is marooned in the desert. **1912** *Ibid.* 15 July 1/7 Rescue parties found dazed families..marooned on roofs. *Ibid.*, The torrent rushed.. through the [station] yard, marooning several hundred passengers. **1916** W. OWEN *Let.* 19 June (1967) 395, I am marooned on a Crag of Superiority in an ocean of Soldiers. **1946** *Sun* (Baltimore) 10 Aug. 4/1 It comes out for..direct assistance and encouragement to farmers marooned in declining or unproductive lines. **1973** *Jewish Chron.* 29 June 16/2 Marooned in the decaying house, she hears voices and sees the ghosts of the family. **1974** *Sunday Tel.* 7 July 26/2 Living a few miles out [of a city] is all very well in itself, but it often involves two cars—one for an otherwise marooned wife and family.

3. *intr.* Of slaves: To escape from service and take to the woods and mountains.

1831 TYERMAN & BENNET *Voy. & Trav.* II. lii. 496 The slaves [in Mauritius] sometimes maroon, as it is called, that is, they run away from their bondage.

4. *Southern U.S.* To camp out for several days on a pleasure party. (Cf. MAROON *sb.*[2] 2.)

[**1777**: Implied in MAROONING *vbl. sb.* 2.] **1855** HALIBURTON *Nat. & Hum. Nat.* II. 283 He used to delight to go marooning. [*Footnote.*] Marooning differs from picnicing in this—the former continues several days, the other lasts but one. **1871** KINGSLEY *At Last* vi, A bathing party of pleasant French people, 'marooning' (as picnic-ing is called here) on the island.

5. To idle, 'hang about'.

1808 SOUTHEY *Lett.* (1856) II. 59 To juniperise within doors, to maroon without. **1865** *Pall Mall G.* 13 Nov. 2 To purchase for these 300,000 blacks the liberty to squat and maroon or to hang about the towns of the island.

Hence **ma'rooned** *ppl. a.*

1883 STEVENSON *Treas. Isl.* xv, The marooned man in his goatskins. **1889** CLARK RUSSELL *Marooned* xxv, As decent a lodging as marooned people have a right to expect.

marooner (mə'ruːnə(r)). Also 7 ? **marownar.** [f. MAROON *v.*]

1. A buccaneer, pirate.

1661 HICKERINGILL *Jamaica* 67 A few French Buckaneers, or Hunting Marownaes [? *read* Marownars]. **1728–36** BYRD *Westover Papers* (1841) 13 On the south shore dwelt a marooner, that modestly called himself a hermit. **1887** H. PYLE in *Harper's Mag.* Aug. 357 (art.) Buccaneers and Marooners of the Spanish Main.

2. a. One who maroons persons on a desolate coast.

1881 *Sat. Rev.* 3 Sept. 293 The original marooners of Ariadne were soon out of hail.

b. A person left on a desolate island as a punishment; = MAROON *sb.*[2] 2.

In Dicts.

3. *Southern U.S.* One who goes marooning (see MAROON *sb.*[2] 3).

In Dicts.

†**4.** = MAROON *sb.*[2] 1. *Obs. U.S.*

a **1738** W. BYRD *Hist. Dividing Line* in *Writings* (1901) 37 We were told that on the South Shore, not far from the Inlet, dwelt a Marooner that Modestly call'd himself a Hermit.

ma'rooning, *vbl. sb.* [f. MAROON *v.* + -ING[1].]

1. The action of MAROON *v.* 2.

1724 C. JOHNSON *Hist. Pyrates* 170 Marooning. This was a barbarous Custom of putting the Offender on Shore, on some desolate or uninhabited Cape or Island. **1896** *Spectator* 2 May 639 Cabot..was apparently the inventor of the ruthless practice called marooning.

2. The action or practice of going on a maroon-party. Chiefly *attrib.* in ***marooning party, season.***

1777 G. FORSTER *Voy. round World* I. 165 It may be curious to know the nature of our marooning parties, as the seamen called them. **1824** SOUTHEY *Lett.* (1856) III. 425 She is very much missed here at all times, and will be still more so when the marooning season begins. **1856** OLMSTED *Slave States* 411 Two lads..had returned..from a 'marooning party', with a boat-load of venison [etc.].

†**maroquin,** *a.* and *sb. Obs.* Forms: 6 **marykyne, marekyn(e, maryskyn, marokin(e, -ockin,** 7 **marekin, marocchine, mariken, -kin,** 7–9 **mar(r)oquin,** 8 **meroquin.** [a. F. *maroquin*, orig. an adj. 'pertaining to Morocco', f. *Maroc* Morocco.] **a.** *adj.* (in ***maroquin skins, leather***; also with the sense 'made of morocco') = MOROCCO *a.* **b.** *sb.* Morocco leather.

1511 *Ld. Treas. Acc. Scot.* (1902) IV. 196, v marykyne skynnis to ane sadill and harnesing of the Kingis mule. **1546** *Aberdeen Reg.* (1844) I. 236 Tua Marekyne cotis, ane reid.. ane wther blak. **1548** *Ibid.* XX. (Jam.), iiij dosoun of maryskyn skynnes. **1585** T. WASHINGTON *Nicholay's Voy.* IV. xxv. 141 Faire maroquins and skins of al sorts. **1613** PURCHAS *Pilgrimage* VI. xi. 518 That lether which..is called Marocchine. **1644** EVELYN *Diary* 1 Apr., Bookes, all bound in maroquin and gilded. **1661** *Sc. Acts Chas. II* (1820) VII. 253/2 Mariken skinnes made in Scotland. **1712** W. ROGERS *Voy.* (1718) 33 The fine Marroquin leather. **1731** BAILEY vol. II, *Marroquin*, commonly called *Morocco.* **1748** SMOLLETT *Rod. Rand.* xxxiv, Shoes of blue meroquin. **1819** SCOTT *Ivanhoe* vii, His maroquin boots and golden spurs. **1823** CRABB *Technol. Dict.*, *Marocco* or marroquin.

‖**maror** (mɑː'rɔə(r)). Also **moror.** [Heb. *mārōr.*] A dish of bitter herbs eaten as part of the Jewish Passover *seder*.

1893 [see CHAROSET(H)]. **1903** W. ROSENAU *Jewish Ceremonial Institutions* viii. 122 A dish is placed, on which are put three unleavened cakes... On the top of them are put ..the 'Charoseth' (a mixture of scraped apples and almonds), 'Moror' (bitter herbs), parsley and salt water... The bitter herbs, usually consisting of horseradish, stand, on account of their pungent taste, for the hard work of the Israelites in Egypt. **1905** *Jewish Encycl.* XI. 146/1 None has done his duty on that night [*sc.* Passover] until he has given voice to the three words 'pesah' (pascal lamb), 'mazzah' (unleavened bread), and 'maror' (bitter herb). **1959** [see CHAROSET(H)]. **1968** A. MATTS tr. *Sperling's Reasons for Jewish Customs* 188 The best choice for *maror* is a piece of horseradish, because horseradish has a particularly sharp and bitter taste. **1972** C. RAPHAEL *Feast of Hist.* ii. 37 Passover..was instituted with three binding ceremonies: (1) *Pesach*—a special sacrifice at the Temple... (2) *Matzah* (unleavened bread)... (3) *Maror* (bitter herbs)—eaten at the Seder to remind us of the bitterness of the Egyptian slavery.

‖**marotte** (marɔt). Also 7 **marrot.** [Fr.]

1. A fool's bauble. †***to crown with a marotte*** = F. *coiffer d'une marotte*, to make a fool of.

In the first quot. the explanation is meant derisively.

1611 R. PHILIPS *Panegyr. Verses* in *Coryat's Crudities* c 7 b, Thee of the Marrot worthy doe we deeme. [*Marg.* i.e. Lawrell from *Marrot* a French Poet.] **1630** J. TAYLOR (Water P.) *Laugh & be fat* Wks. II. 72/2 They crowne thee with a Marrot or a Mard. **1840** H. AINSWORTH *Tower Lond.* II. xiv, This last shaft likewise hit its mark, though Jane [the Fool] endeavoured to ward it off with her marotte.

2. A pet notion, craze.

1852 LD. MALMESBURY *Mem.* (1884) I. 324 To be Emperor has been his [*sc.* Louis Napoleon's] *marotte* since he was twenty years old.

marou, -ough(e, -ouȝ, -ouh, obs. ff. MARROW.

maroudi, var. MAROODI.

‖**marouflage** (maruflaʒ), *sb. Art.* [f. F. *maroufler* to attach (a painted canvas to a wall) with *maroufle*, a strong adhesive (also, a lining or layer of such adhesive): see -AGE.] **1.** The act or process of pasting a painted canvas to a wall, traditionally using an adhesive made of white lead ground in oil. Hence **marouflage** *v.*, **marouflaging** *vbl. sb.*

1883 J. W. MOLLETT *Illustr. Dict. Art & Archæol.* 205/2 *Marouflage*, a method of house-painting in France, upon a lining of prepared canvas fixed upon the surface to be decorated. **1909** *Cent. Dict.* Suppl., *Marouflage*, this device allows mural paintings to be in oil colors, and also allows the work to be done at a distance from the building for which it is intended. **1934** H. HILER *Notes Technique Painting* iv. 265 *Marouflage* as the different methods of gluing the canvas to the wall are called, was very popular throughout the nineteenth century, and most modern European wall decorations were executed by this method. *Ibid.*, A paste of rye flour, to which two or three heads of garlic were added, was the commonest way of marouflaging on the Continent. **1969** R. MAYER *Dict. Art Terms & Techniques* 235/1 Traditionally, the adhesive used in marouflage is commercial white lead in oil.

2. [Transf. sense of *marouflе* a lining, layer (of glue): see prec. sense.] In ironwork, a piece of leather or other material used as a backing to show off decoration.

1957 R. LISTER *Decorative Wrought Ironwork* 55 This decoration was called *Marouflage*. Examples of door plates backed with leather are to be seen in King's College Chapel, Cambridge. **1960** H. HAYWARD *Antique Coll.* 175/2 *Marouflage*, a scarlet cloth backing to pierced lock plates.

marouner, marow(e: see MARINER, MARROW.

marower, obs. Sc. form of MOREOVER.

marowna, ? obs. form of MAROONER.

marplot ('mɑːplɒt), *sb.* and *a.* [See MAR-.]

A. *sb.* One who mars or defeats a plot or design by officious interference, or hinders the success of any undertaking. Said also of things.

1708 MRS. CENTLIVRE *Busie Body* Dram. Pers., *Marplot.* **1824** LADY GRANVILLE *Lett.* May (1894) I. 295 What a marplot anxiety is. **1876** GEO. ELIOT *Dan. Der.* xxxii, But what is the use of my taking the vows and settling everything as it should be, if that marplot Hans comes and upsets it all?

B. *adj.* That mars or defeats a plot or design.

1850 KINGLAKE *Crimea* VI. ix. 230 There were some of his fellow-countrymen..whose marplot disclosures seemed likely to bring down..a new onslaught of Russian masses.

marprelate: see MAR-.

marque[1] (mɑːk). Forms: 5, 8 **mark, marc, margue** (? *error for* **marque**), 6 **markque, merk,** 6–7 **marke,** 7– **marque.** [a. F. *marque* (OF. also *merke*), ad. Pr. *marca*, vbl. sb. f. *marcar* (med.L. *marcāre*) to seize as a pledge.

It is uncertain whether this is connected with MARK *sb.*[1]]

†**1.** Reprisals; occas. = *letter of marque* (see 2).

[**1354** *Act 27 Edw. III*, Stat. 2 c. 17 Purveu..que..nous eions la lei de Mark & de represailles. **1417** *Act 4 Hen. V*, Stat. 2 c. 7 Que de toutz attemptatz faitz par ses ennemys.. encountre le tenure daucunes Trieuves..en les quelles nest pas fait expresse mencion que toutz marques & reprisailles cesseront..nostre Signior le Roi a toutz qi lour sentiront en tiel cas grevez, voet grauntier marque en due forme.] **1456** SIR G. HAYE *Law Arms* (S.T.S.) 205 Be way of mark..; that is to say..a lettre of leve to tak ony man of that contree. *Ibid.* 220 The king aw to geve letter of powar to tak mark apon thame. **1473** *Rolls of Parlt.* VI. 65/2 Any Sentence, Jugement, Margue or Reprisale yeven. **1614** SELDEN *Titles Hon.* 210 The lawes of Marque, or Reprisales.

2. letter of marque. a. Usually pl., *letters of marque (and reprisal)*. Originally, a licence granted by a sovereign to a subject, authorizing him to make reprisals on the subjects of a hostile state for injuries alleged to have been done to him by the enemy's army. In later times this became practically a licence to fit out an armed vessel and employ it in the capture of the merchant shipping belonging to the enemy's subjects, the holder of letters of marque being called a privateer or corsair, and entitled by international law to commit against the hostile nation acts which would otherwise have been condemned as piracy. Also † *letters of mart*: see MART *sb.*[5]

So far as European nations are concerned the issue of letters of marque was abolished by the Congress of Paris in 1856.

1447 *Rolls of Parlt.* V. 135 To graunte to youre saide Besechers, letters of Marc and Reprisail. **1545** *Reg. Privy Council Scot.* I. 10 Ane letter of mark gevin and grantit be the maist cristin king of France. *a* **1548** HALL *Chron., Hen. VIII* 145 b, Shewyng hym how their goodes were taken, by letters of Marke, their shippes restrained [etc.]. **1702** *Royal Declar.* June in *Lond. Gaz.* No. 3815/3 Her Majesty having Impowered the Lord High Admiral of England to grant Letters of Marque, or Commissions for Privateers. **1789** *Constit. U.S.* Art. i. §8 Congress shall have power..to grant letters of marque and reprisal. **1855** MOTLEY *Dutch Rep.* (1861) II. 299 To make war upon Alva was the leading object of all these freebooters, and they were usually furnished by the Prince of Orange..with letters of marque for that purpose.

b. A ship carrying letters of marque; a privateer.

c **1800** MISS KNIGHT *Autobiog.* I. 106 A Ragusan commanding a letter-of-mark. **1836** MARRYAT *Midsh. Easy* xxxviii, As letter of marque, I shall have the right of capture.

c. *attrib.* in *letter of marque man, ship.*

1703 *Lond. Gaz.* No. 3910/4 A French Letter of Marque Man. **1708** *Ibid.* No. 4440/2 Any such Privateer or Letter of Marque Ship.

marque[2] (mɑːk). [Fr., = mark, sign.] = MARK *sb.*[1] 15 b. A model or brand esp. of motor vehicle.

1906 C. JARROTT *Ten Yrs. Motors & Motor Racing* x. 174 Half-way to Bordeaux, and out of the first four cars two were Dietrich—this seemed a good record for the *marque.* **1956** *Road & Track* Oct. 5 (Advt.), The marque of Mercedes-Benz. *Ibid.* 14 The firm and marque has not actively participated in competition. **1958** *N. & Q.* Feb. 86/1 'Marque' is surely a recent borrowing from the French language where it is in general use to denote a particular type of variety of a product, e.g. Frigidaire, Hoover, etc... The channel whereby the word has passed from French to English is doubtless international motor-racing. **1960** *Times* 4 July (Suppl.) 1/1 Sixty years is long..also in the reign of a branded product—particularly in the reign of a *marque* of cigarette. **1972** *Daily Tel.* 28 Jan. 6/8 The Renault 5 has all the comfort associated with the marque, despite its lack of size. **1973** *Times* 5 Oct. (Safety Suppl.) p. iv, But it should be emphasized that both marques are in the executive/luxury category and that to make a small family saloon as safe as a Mercedes or a Volvo would involve problems of weight and cost that are probably insuperable.

marquee (mɑːˈkiː). Also 8 **marquée, marki,** 8–9 **markee.** [An assumed sing. f. MARQUISE apprehended as pl.] A large tent, as an officer's field-tent, or one used at a public entertainment, exhibition, or the like.

1690 *Lond. Gaz.* No. 2542/4 A good Marquee, two French Tents. **1758** *Lond. Chron.* 19–22 Aug. 173/3 General Abercrombie would not suffer any of the officers to carry any chests, beds, or markees, with them. **1744** M. MACKENZIE *Maritime Surv.* 106 A Captain's Tent and Marki. **1812** *Chron.* in *Ann. Reg.* 99 The..band was stationed in a marquee on the lawn. **1831** TRELAWNY *Adv. Younger Son* II. 118 A summer-room, exactly of the form and colour of a markee. **1884** *Times* (weekly ed.) 7 Nov. 3/2 The meeting was held in a marquee erected behind the Fountain Hotel.

b. *attrib.*, as in ***marquee manufacture, tent; marquee coop*** *U.S.*, a tent-shaped hen-coop.

1775 *Connect. Col. Rec.* (1890) XV. 15 Ninety marquee or officers tents. **1834** *Tait's Mag.* I. 218/2 Benjamin Edgington, Marquee and Tent Manufacturer. **1849** D. J. BROWNE *Amer. Poultry Yd.* (1855) 122 The marquee coop.

marques, marquesate, etc.: see MARQUIS, etc.

‖**marquesa** (marˈkeza, mɑːˈkeɪzə). [Sp.; cf. MARCHESA.] In Spain: a marchioness.

1846 R. FORD *Gatherings from Spain* xviii. 249 We well remember the death of a kind and venerable Marquesa at Seville. **1966** H. YOXALL *Fashion of Life* vii. 63 The *marquesa* of the great neighbouring house was interested. **1968** A. BROWN *Slay me Suddenly* ix. 131 A *marquesa* may have dignity because she belongs to one of the oldest lineages in Spain.

Marquesan (mɑːˈkeɪsən, -z-), *a.* and *sb.* [f. *Marquesas* Islands in the Pacific + -AN.]

A. *sb.* One of the Polynesian aborigines of the Marquesas Islands; also, the language spoken by them. **B.** *adj.* Of or pertaining to the Marquesas Islands.

1799 J. WILSON *Missionary Voy. S. Pacific* 138 Several of the Marquesans were continually plaguing the captain to take them to Otaheite. **1837** *Evangelical Mag.* Aug. 395 The spiritual enemies, which the Marquesan islanders have to encounter. **1845** J. COULTER *Adventures Pacific* xii. 155 Any liability to capsize is counteracted by the out-rigger that all the Marquesan canoes have attached to them. *Ibid.* xiv. 211 Eight or ten nuts (commonly known as the candle-nut, from their emitting a bright flame, and being used by Marquesans as a substitute for candles) are strung on a piece of reed. **1896** R. L. STEVENSON *In South Seas* I. ii. 13 The alarms and sudden councils of Marquesan chiefs. **1919** F. O'BRIEN *White Shadows South Seas* iii. 28 Hence descended the Marquesans, vikings of the Pacific, in giant canoes, and sprang upon the fighting men of the Tahitians. *Ibid.* ix. 96 The Catholic chants sung thus in Marquesan took on a wild barbaric rhythm that thrilled the blood. **1936** V. A. DEMANT *Christian Polity* xi. 192 In regard to..Oceania.. mention need only be made of..the effigies of chiefs among the Marquesans. **1969** J. H. VANCE *Deadly Isles* (1970) xvi. 118 A massive white-haired Marquesan with a face carved from teak. **1974** *Listener* 21 Nov. 679/2 The pathetic dependence of the Marquesans on imported foodstuffs. *Ibid.*, Curiosity about ancient Marquesan culture.

marquesit(e: see MARCASITE.

marquet, obs. form of MARKET.

marquetry, marqueterie ('mɑːkɪtrɪ). Forms: 6 **marketrey, merquetry,** 7 **marquettrie, (marhutery),** 6– **marqueterie,** 7– **marquetry, (-ie).** [a. F. *marqueterie* (1416 in Hatz.-Darm.), f. *marqueter* (1386) to variegate, f. *marque* MARK *sb.*[1]] Inlaid work, esp. as used for the decoration of furniture.

1563 SHUTE *Archit.* F j b, Fine woodes in marketrey. **1589** PUTTENHAM *Eng. Poesie* II. xi[i]. (Arb.) 108 All set in merquetry with letters of blew Saphire and Topas artificially cut and entermingled. **1596** DANETT tr. *Comines* (1614) 279 The curious worke called Musaique, or Marqueterie. **1601** HOLLAND *Pliny* I. 49 Marquetry and other inlaid works. **1665** SIR T. HERBERT *Trav.* (1677) 138 Of that kind the Arabs called Marhutery, but the Jews Mosaick. **1817** MOORE *Lalla R., Veiled Proph.* (ed. 2) 89 The flashing of their swords' rich marquetry. **1847** DISRAELI *Tancred* II. xiii, A large table of ivory marquetry. **1881** YOUNG *Every man his own Mechanic* §39 Hungarian Ash.. suitable as a groundwork for marquetry.

b. *attrib.* and *Comb.*

1849 THACKERAY *Pendennis* xxxvii, Marqueterie tables. **1851** in *Illustr. Lond. News* (1854) 5 Aug. 119/2 *Occupations of People*..marqueterie-inlayer. **1872** OLIVER *Elem. Bot.* II. 159 Tunbridge marquetry ware. **1879** KNIGHT *Dict. Mech.* 2803 Yacca-wood [used for] Cabinet and marquetry work.

Hence †**'marquetrize** *v.* (*nonce-wd.*) *intr.*, to make inlaid work: in quot. *fig.*

1610 W. FOLKINGHAM *Art of Survey* To Rdr. 3 What curious-quaint Em[b]ellishments diffuse? Musaick-Mazes-Marquetrizing Muse?

marquionesse, obs. form of MARCHIONESS.

marquis, marquess ('mɑːkwɪs). Forms: 4 **marchis,** 6 **marches;** 4–5 **markis, markys,** 5 **markesse, markeys, markois,** 5–6 **markyse, markes,** 6 **markas, marcas, -cus, marks;** 5 **marquoys, marquyus,** 5–6 **marques,** 5–7 **merques,** 6–7 **marquesse,** 6– **marquess;** 5 **marquys,** 6 **marquisse, marquise,** 6–9 **marquiss,** 7– **marquis.** [a. OF. *marchis*, later altered to *marquis* (whence Du. *markies*); corresponding to Pr. *marques, -is*, Sp. *marqués*, Pg. *marquez*, It. *marchese*; f. Com. Rom. *marca* (see MARCH *sb.*[3], MARK *sb.*[1]) frontier, frontier territory + *-ese*:—L. *-ēnsem* suffix forming adjs. from place-names (see -ESE). The word is thus etymologically an adj., the sb. understood being that represented in Eng. by COUNT, so that the title was equivalent to MARGRAVE. The med.L. representative was *marchiŏnem* (*marchio*), still preserved in heraldic Latin: cf. *marchioness*.

The prevailing spelling in literary use appears to be *marquis*. Some newspapers, however, use *marquess*, and several English nobles bearing the title always write it in this way.]

1. In various European countries, the title of the ruler of certain territories (originally 'marches' or frontier districts). This gradually passed, in Romanic-speaking countries, into a mere title indicating a certain grade of noble rank, immediately below that of duke and above that of count. In English it is commonly used to designate a person of this titular rank in the modern nobility of foreign countries (though the foreign forms, It. *marchese*, Sp. *marqués*, etc. are sometimes retained), and also *Hist.* as the appellation of those territorial lords to whom it was applied in earlier times. Formerly it was often employed (now rarely) as the English equivalent of MARGRAVE.

13.. *Guy Warw.* (A.) 5171 Herhaud of Ardern, þe gode marchis. *c* **1330** R. BRUNNE *Chron.* (1810) 177 Þe marchis of Mounfraunt. *c* **1386** CHAUCER *Clerk's T.* 8 A Markys whilom lord was of that londe. **1387** TREVISA *Higden* (Rolls) VI. 417 Albericus the markys [**1432–50** markesse] expulsede Saracenys from Ytaly. *c* **1475** *Partenay* 6342 For discended is fro so hy A place, Off kynges, Dukes, Markois full of grace. **1503** in *Lett. Rich. III & Hen. VII* (Rolls) I. 200 The marques of Brandenburg[he]. **1529** RASTELL *Pastyme* (1811) 71 The markes Brandenburgh. **1535** HARVEL in Ellis *Orig. Lett.* Ser. II. II. 75 The Marks of Guaste hath in Sicile 150 sailis. **1552** ASCHAM *Affairs of Germany* (1570) 15 b, There be at this day fiue Marchesses of Bradenburge. *Ibid.* 16 Marches Albert is now at this day xxxi. yeares old. **1596** SHAKS. *Merch. V.* I. i. 125 A Venecian..that came hither in companie of the Marquesse of Mountferrat. **1636** BRATHWAIT *Rom. Emp.* 121 Neare the suburbane Orchards of the Marquesse Castelli. **1756–7** tr. *Keysler's Trav.* (1760) III. 39 Many a spot of land not worth above fifty dollars a year gives the title of marquis to the owners. **1867** FREEMAN *Norm. Conq.* (1876) I. iv. 248 The Dukes, Counts and Marquesses had in this way grown into sovereigns. **1871** E. C. G. MURRAY *Member for Paris* II. 282 Our ex-contributor M. Horace Gerold (the Marquis of Clairefontaine).

2. At the end of the 14th c. the title was introduced into England to designate a specific degree of the peerage, between those of duke and earl. Late in the 15th c. this degree was adopted in the peerage of Scotland. The title still continues, indicating the same relative rank, in the peerage of the United Kingdom and in those of Scotland and Ireland. When a duke is also a marquis, his second title is given 'by courtesy' to his eldest son: thus the eldest son of the Duke of Devonshire is called 'the Marquis of Hartington'.

The title of a marquis is usually territorial in form, as 'the Marquis of Salisbury', but in some instances 'Marquis' is prefixed to a surname, as 'the Marquis Cornwallis'.

1399 *Rolls of Parlt.* III. 452/1 The Dukes..and the markys here present. **1445** *Ibid.* V. 394 William de la Pole, than Marquoys and Erle of Suffolk. **1451** *Ibid.* 226/1 The Name or Estate of Duke, Marquys or Erle. **1473** WARKW. *Chron.* (Camden) 4 The Kynge made Lorde Montagu, Marquyus Montagu. *Ibid.* 10 Of late tyme hade he made hym Markes of Montagu. **15..** *Bk. Precedence* in *Q. Eliz. Acad.* (1869) 13 Item. a Dukes Eldest sonn is Borne a Marquesse, and shall goe as a Marquisse. **1509** FISHER *Funeral Serm. C'tess Richmond* Wks. (1876) 293 Erles, markyses, dukes, and princes. **1513** MORE *Rich. III*, Wks. 38/2 The Lorde Marques Dorsette the Quenes sonne by her fyrste housebande. **1594** SHAKS. *Rich. III*, I. iii. 255 Peace Master Marquesse, you are malapert, Your fire-new stampe of Honor is scarce currant. **1646** WHITELOCKE *Mem.* (1853) II. 26 The king sent orders to the marquis of Montrose to disband his forces. **1702** ROWE *Tamerl.* Ded., To the Right Honourable William Lord Marquiss of Hartington. **1844** H. H. WILSON *Brit. India* I. 147 Information of the death of Marquis Cornwallis arrived in England at the end of January, 1806. **1901** *Empire Rev.* I. 466 First in rank come the dukes,..then follow in order of precedence, marquises, first created by Richard II.

†**3.** In the 16–17th c. often employed as a female title, equivalent to the later MARCHIONESS. *Obs.*

It is not easy to see how far this was regarded as an application of the masculine title, and how far it was taken as an anglicization of MARQUISE. The spelling *marquess* was commonly preferred in this use, prob. through association with the suffix -ESS. *Lady* was often prefixed.

1503 *Will of Katherine Lady Hastings* (Prerog. Crt. Canterbury), Marquesse Dorset. *Ibid.*, My lady marquisse. **1527–8** *Will of Lady Dorset* (ibid.), I lady Cecill' marques Harrington and Bonvill late the wife of the right honorable Thomas marques Dorset. **1529** *Act 21 Hen. VIII*, c. 13 §28 Any Chaplain of any Duchess, Marquess, Countess, Viscountess, or Baroness. **1538** WARNER in Ellis *Orig. Lett.* Ser. I. II. 97 My lady Marques ys in the tower. **1539**

CROMWELL in Merriman *Life & Lett.* (1902) II. 214 The marquise hath bene examyned, and.. albeit she pretendeth Ignorance [etc.]. **1623** in *Archæologia* XLVIII. 211 Given.. by the kinge's owne hands to the Ladie Marquesse of Buckingham a cupp of gold and cover. **1626** PORY in Ellis *Orig. Lett.* Ser. I. III. 243 The Foure Englishe ladies sworne of her Bed-chamber are the Duchesse of Buckingham, the Marques Hamiltoun, and the Countesses of Carlile and Denbigh. **1669** PEPYS *Diary* 30 Apr., My Lady Marquess of Winchester, Bellassis, and other great ladies. **1691** *D'Emilianne's Frauds Rom. Monks* (ed. 3) 223 Two Ladies of Quality, the one a Lady Marquess, and the other a Countess.

4. A North American variety of spring wheat. Also *attrib.*

1906 C. SAUNDERS in *Bull. Canad. Dept. Agric.* No. 57. 29 *Chelsea* and *Marquis* are new cross-bred sorts produced at the Central Experimental Farm. **1924** J. A. THOMSON *Sci. Old & New* xliii. 253 Marquis is a hard, red spring wheat with excellent milling and baking qualities; it is now the dominant spring wheat in Canada and the United States. **1936** DENTON & LORD *World Geogr. for Canad. Schools* 85 Dr. Charles E. Saunders, the Dominion cerealist, had been experimenting for several years, trying to produce a new wheat which would ripen earlier than Red Fife. In 1903 his efforts were crowned with success. The new wheat was named 'Marquis'. **1960** D. E. BUBLITZ *Life on Dotted Line* 51 Marquis wheat was chosen as their crop that first year. **1965** I. REEKIE *Along Old Melita Trail* x. 150 Marquis wheat, developed from a cross of Red Fife, was released in 1911.

5. *attrib.*: **marquis hat**, a particular shape of ladies' headgear; **marquis pear** = MARQUISE 2, MARCHIONESS 2 (Hogg *Fruit Man.*, ed. 4, 1875, p. 479).

Marquiss as the name of a pear occurs in London & Wise *Retired Gard'ner* (1706) I. 48.

1901 *Westm. Gaz.* 6 June 3/2 The Marquis, or three-cornered hat, is more popular than ever.

marquisado, variant of MARQUISOTTE *Obs.*

marquisal (ˈmɑːkwɪsəl), *a. nonce wd.* In quots. **marchesal** (after the Italian form), **marquesal**. [See -AL[1].] Pertaining to a marquis.

1832 MAGINN in *Blackw. Mag.* XXXII. 426 *note*, The promises of ducal and marchesal head-pieces, so copiously and judiciously employed by the present Ministry. **1857** TROLLOPE *Barchester T.* (1861) 309 The countess, who.. had been accustomed to see all eyes, not royal, ducal, or marquesal, fall before her own, paused.

marquisat(e, obs. forms of MARCASITE.

marquisate (ˈmɑːkwɪsət). Also 6, 9 **marquessate**, 7 **marquesad(e, -at, -quisat, -quizat, marchasate, -esate, -isat(e**. [f. MARQUIS + -ATE[1], after F. *marquisat*, It. *marchesato*, Sp. *marquesado*.]

1. The dignity or status of a marquis. Also, †a place from which a marquis takes his title.

15.. *Bk. Precedence* in *Q. Eliz. Acad.* (1869) 15 A Marquesse must goe after his Creation, and not after his marquisate. **1675** OGILBY *Brit.* 4 Worcester.. a city honoured with the title of Marquisate in the Right Noble Henry Marquess and Earl of Worcester. **1762–71** H. WALPOLE *Vertue's Anecd. Paint.* (1786) I. 218 She restored him too to the Marquisate of Exeter. **1844** DISRAELI *Coningsby* I. ii, The very day he was raised to his Marquisate, he commenced sapping fresh corporations. **1902** *Athenæum* 26 Apr. 521/2 On the duke's death the marquessate of Douglas.. passed to the Duke of Hamilton, as male heir.

2. In various countries of Europe: The territorial lordship or possessions of a marquis or margrave.

1591 PERCIVALL *Sp. Dict.*, *Marquesado*, a Marquessate. **1612** BREREWOOD *Lang. & Relig.* To Rdr., The marchasates of Silesia and Brandeburge. *Ibid.*, The marchesates of Lusatia, Moravia [etc.]. **1630** *R. Johnson's Kingd. & Commw.* 300 In Germany (you are to understand) a Dukedome may be contained within a Marquisate. **1711** *Lond. Gaz.* No. 4803/1 An Earthquake has been felt in the Marquisate of Ancona. **1842** MACAULAY *Ess., Fredk. Gt.*, Rheinsberg is a fertile and smiling spot, in the midst of the sandy waste of the Marquisate.

†**marquisdom.** ? *Obs.* [f. MARQUIS + -DOM.] = MARQUISATE.

1530 PALSGR. 243/2 Marquesdom, *marquisat*. **1586** HOLINSHED *Chron. Scot.* 284/1 Francis Scotia lord of Pine and Mondone, and other nobles of the marquesdome of Saluce, are descended from the Scots. **1643** TRAPP *Comm. Gen.* xlvi. 32 Galeacius Caracciolus.. returned to his Marquesdom in Italy. **1706** PHILLIPS (ed. Kersey), *Marquisate* or *Marquisedom*, the Territory or Jurisdiction of a Marquess.

‖**marquise** (mɑːˈkiːz, Fr. markiz). In sense 3 also 8 *erron.* **marquis**. [F. *marquise*, fem. of *marquis*, in senses 1, 2, 3.]

1. = MARCHIONESS. Only as a title of foreign nobility. (But cf. MARQUIS 3.)

1894 *Nation* (N.Y.) 30 Aug. 160/1 She anticipates not only the French marquise of the last century, but even more our American great ladies.

2. A kind of pear. (Cf. MARCHIONESS 2.)

1706 LONDON & WISE *Retired Gard'ner* I. 63 Dwarf Pears... The Marquise. **1741** *Compl. Fam.-Piece* II. iii. 406 These Pears; [Nov.] Martin Sec,.. Sucrevert, la Marquise. **1875** HOGG *Fruit. Man.* (ed. 4) 479.

3. a. A kind of tent (see quot. 1788); = MARQUEE.

1783 in Conway *Life T. Paine* (1892) I. 197 The tables were spread under a marquise or tent. **1788** GROSE *Milit. Antiq.* II. Descr. Plates 2 A field-officer's tent or marquis. The word marquis and tent are promiscuously used, though strictly speaking they are different things; the internal part commonly made of ticking, the marquis; the external covering, canvas. **1792** FENNELL *Narr. Proc. Paris* 187 A great marquise was erected on the east side of the altar.

b. *Archit.* (See quot. 1891.)

1891 tr. *J. Adeline's Art Dict.* 251/2 The term *marquise* is applied to a light roof which projects from the façade of a building. It is generally placed over a flight of steps. On the outside of theatres marquises of considerable length are not infrequently to be seen. Almost invariably they have a glass roof. **1904** B. VON HUTTEN *Pam* v. i. 237 A moment later, she stood in the door, under the little 'marquise'. **1924** 'L. MALET' *Dogs of Want* i. 7 [She] stood under the glass marquise, at the top of the flight of steps. **1930** A. BENNETT *Imperial Palace* vii. 28 On the steps under the marquise she took off her cloak.

4. In full, ***marquise ring***: A finger-ring set with a pointed oval cluster of gems.

1885 *Cassell's Encycl. Dict.*, Marquise-ring. **1896** *Westm. Gaz.* 30 Jan. 5/3 Other witnesses deposed to as to the promise of a marquise ring. **1903** *Ibid.* 10 Dec. 4/2 A marquise formed of a single diamond, or a single sapphire, or a single ruby, is, of course,.. not very usual.

†**marquisess.** *Obs.* [f. MARQUIS + -ESS.] = MARCHIONESS.

c **1386** CHAUCER *Clerk's T.* 227, I wole with othere maydens stonde.. and se The Markysesse. **1491** *Act 7 Hen. VII*, c. 16 §13 Anne Marquisses Berkeley. *a* **1548** HALL *Chron., Hen. VIII* 216 Euery Marquesses put on a demy Coronal of golde.

marquisette (mɑːkiːˈzɛt). [Fr., dim. of *marquise* MARQUISE.] (See quots. 1968.)

1908 *Tatler* 6 May (Suppl.) p. iv, A simple house gown of black marquisette. **1909** *Daily Chron.* 12 Apr. 7/1 The soft marquisettes and satin-faced foulards. **1913** [see FOURREAU]. **1928** *Times* 9 May 11/3 A picture gown of fine gold embroidered marquisette, over peach georgette. **1930** *Times* 13 Mar. 11/6 Lovely ankle-length frocks in flowered and plain chiffons, lace, satins, and marquisettes. **1957** *New Yorker* 5 Oct. 110/1 Its dazzling décolletage veiled in black marquisette. **1968** E. GALE *From Fibres to Fabrics* xii. 132 Some marquisettes are not woven, but are produced on a simple type of lace machine. **1968** J. IRONSIDE *Fashion Alphabet* 240 *Marquisette*, a lenoweave gauze fabric made of cotton, rayon, silk or synthetic fibres.

†**marquisina.** *Obs. rare*[−1]. [? ad. It. *marchesina* young marchioness, dim. of *marchesa*; but Sterne was prob. thinking of *marchesana* = *marchesa*.] An Italian marchioness.

1768 STERNE *Sent. Journ.* (Rtldg.) 321 (*Translation*), I was.. just entering the door of the hall, when the Marquisina de F*** was coming out.

†**marquisotte**, *v. Obs.* Also 6 **marquesotte, -ezate, marcussotte, marquisado**, 7 **merquizotte**. [f. F. *marquisotte* ('*Barbe faitte à la marquisotte*, cut after the Turkish fashion, all being shauen away but the mustachoes,' Cotgr.).] *trans.* To cut (the beard) in the fashion described above. Also *pass.* of the person, to have the beard so cut.

1567 GOLDING *Ovid's Met.* XIII. 169b, His sturre stiffe heare he kembeth.. And with a sythe dooth marcussotte his bristled berd. *c* **1580** JEFFERIE *Bugbears* I. iii. 81 in *Archiv Stud. neu. Spr.* (1897) 313 He is coombed and slicked and frizeled and marquisotted. **1588** *Losses Span. Navy* in *Harl. Misc.* (1753) I. 135 A very little Beard, marquesotted. **1592** GREENE *Def. Conny-catching* Wks. (Grosart) XI. 72 Then hee must be Marquisadod, with a side peake pendent. **1619** *North's Gueuara's Diall Pr.* 625/1 To see a foolish Courtier.. have his beard merquizotted.

†**marquisship.** *Obs.* [f. MARQUIS + -SHIP.] = MARQUISATE.

1464 *Rolls of Parlt.* V. 565/1 The markeship of the holy Empere. **1586** Stanihurst *Chron. Irel.* 118/2 in *Holinshed*, As for the marqueship of Corke being a matter of great weight [etc.]. **1587** HOLINSHED *Chron.* III. 1336/1 An offer of the marqueesship of the sacred empire made to the monsieur. **1676** LADY FANSHAWE *Mem.* (1830) 184 We took our leave of Cordova, lodging that night at Carpio, the Marquisship of Don Lewis de Haro.

†**marquisy.** *Obs. rare*[−1]. In quot. **marquesy**. [f. MARQUIS + -Y.] = MARQUISATE.

1586 T. B. *La Primaud. Fr. Acad.* I. (1594) 561 One.. politicall communion compounded of manie villages, townes,.. baronries, counties, marquesies, dukedomes.

marquois (ˈmɑːkwɔɪz). *Surveying.* [app. a blunder for F. *marquoir* marking instrument, 'a sort of ruler used by tailors' (Hatz.-Darm.).] Used *attrib.* in ***marquois scale*** (***and triangle***), an apparatus devised for the purpose of drawing equidistant parallel lines with speed and accuracy.

Sometimes written *Marquoi's*, *Marquois's*, as if the genitive of a proper name.

1834 *Catalogue Instr. Troughton & Simms* 2 Plotting, Marquois and Gunter's Scales. **1849** HEATHER *Math. Instr.* 45 The pair of Marquois's scales now before us. **1878** MARKS in *Jrnl. Franklin Inst.* CV. 418 An improved form of Marquoi's scale. **1883** W. H. RICHARDS *Text Bk. Milit. Topogr.* 153 A large rolling ruler, or the marquois scale and triangle, is available for carrying a parallel line. **1886** *Athenæum* 4 Sept. 307/2 There is one.. instrument, namely, the marquois scales, which it is rather surprising to see omitted in this list.

†**marquot.** *Obs.* [a. F. *marquotte* (Cotgr.), now *marcotte*.] 'A Sucker, or young plant, that spurts vp from the root of a vine, &c.; or is of it selfe rooted' (Cotgr. 1611).

1600 SURFLET *Country Farm* VI. vi. 737 Howsoeuer the plant set of a crosset may make the better foote and roote, yet for certaine it is harder to take then the marquot [orig. *la marquotte*].

marr, dial. form of MERE *sb.*

marrais(s, obs. forms of MARISH.

marram (ˈmærəm). Also 8 **marem, marran, morrane**, 9 **maram, mar(r)um, murram**. [a. ON. *maralm-r*, f. *mar-r* sea + *halm-r* HAULM.]

1. A local name (chiefly *E. Angl.*) for the Sea Reed or Bent Grass, *Psamma arenaria*, the roots of which bind together and keep stable the sands of the sea-shore in Northern Europe. Also ***marram-grass***, ***sea-marram***.

1640 PARKINSON *Theat. Bot.* 1200 We in English [call *Spartum*] Helme and Matweede, but the people all along the Coasts of Norfolke and Suffolke call it Marram. **1726** THRELKELD *Syn. Stirp. Hibern.* K 5, Our Country Women in Fingall call these Morranes. **1787** W. MARSHALL *Norfolk* (1795) II. 383 Gloss., *Marram* or *Marem*, *Arundo arenaria*, sea-reed-grass. **1830** LYELL *Princ. Geol.* I. 268 Dry sand, bound in a compact mass by the long creeping roots of the plant called Marram. **1834** *Penny Cycl.* II. 427/2 *Arundo arenaria*, the sea-reed or marrum-grass. **1872** OLIVER *Elem. Bot.* II. 274 The Sea Maram.

2. A sand-hill grown over with this grass.

1834 PAGET *Nat. Hist. Yarmouth* Introd. 22 The hills of drifted sand which form the marrams. **1867** LYELL *Princ. Geol.* II. xx. (ed. 10) I. 513 Hills of blown sand, called 'Marrams',.. now occupy the site.

attrib. **1879** R. LUBBOCK *Fauna of Norfolk* 112 The marum banks on the coast.

marrangle, erron. form of MERINGUE[1].

1826 MISS MITFORD *Vill.* Ser. II. 211 My good cousin.. left it to my own senses to discover the merits of brioche and marrangles.

‖**Marrano** (maˈrrano). *Obs.* exc. *Hist.* In 6 **marrane, maranne**, *pl.* **marrany**, 6–7 **maran(e, marano**. [Sp. *marrano*, of unknown origin.]

A name applied in mediæval Spain to a christianized Jew or Moor, esp. to one who merely professed conversion in order to avoid persecution. Also *attrib.*

1583 STOCKER *Civ. Warres Lowe C.* IV. 50 The women, chose rather to drowne them selues.. then to be dishonored with so Barbarous a Maran. **1585** T. WASHINGTON tr. *Nicholay's Voy.* II. xiii. 49 An infinite multitude of Iewes and Marannes driuen out of Spain. *Ibid.* IV. xvi. 130b, The Maranes of late banished and driuen out of Spaine and Portugale. **1599** SANDYS *Europæ Spec.* (1632) 164 A sort of people of the Marrany as they terme them, who are baptized Jews and Moores. **1600** O. E. *Repl. Libel* I. ii. 55 Those that will not suffer Christians to liue.. dispense with apostataes, maranoes, and rinegued Turkes. *Ibid.* II. iii. 58 They absolue.. most wicked rebels, yea Marans and apostataes. **1645** PAGITT *Heresiogr.* (1662) 205 A very christened Jew, a Maran. **1901** *Westm. Gaz.* 12 Aug. 3/1 Two years later the Crypto-Jews or Marranos of London had acquired 'untrammelled trading rights'. **1941** G. G. SCHOLEM *Major Trends Jewish Mysticism* vii. 240 The beginning of the persecution of the Jews in Spain and the appearance of Marrano Judaism after 1391. **1942** L. B. NAMIER *Conflicts* 133 More logical were those who attempted amalgamation: but even this, as a mass movement, merely produces Marranos. **1960** L. P. GARTNER *Jewish Immigrant* i. 16 The mid-seventeenth century, when the earlier flight of Marranos from Spain and Portugal was no longer important. **1973** *Jewish Chron.* 2 Feb. 3/5 The 90 members of the tribe near the town of Pachuca.. claim that some of their ancestors were Marranos (baptised Jews suspected of secret adherence to Judaism) who were burnt at the stake in Mexico during the 16th century. **1973** *Publishers Weekly* 3 Sept. 44/1 The term 'Marranos' originally denoted those Spanish Jews who, during the Inquisition, or long before it, converted to Catholicism but continued secretly to practice their Jewish faith; loosely it denotes all secret Jews.

Hence **Maˈrranic** *a.*, **ˈMarranism**, †**ˈMarranized** *ppl. a.*, **Maˈrranoism**.

[**1563–83** FOXE *A. & M.* II. 905/1 All these thinges were a meere *Maranismus*, that is, sauoured of the law of *Maranorum*.] **1611** COTGR., *Marranisé*,.. Marranized, renegaded. **1694** MOTTEUX *Rabelais* v. (1737) 216 Apostates and marraniz'd Miscreants. **1737** OZELL *Rabelais* III. 232 *note*, There were several Sons and Grandsons of the Family, which Jos. Scaliger suspected of Maranism (Judaism). **1924** *Glasgow Herald* 25 Sept. 6 In most Latin American countries, the arrivals find no organized Jewish life—only Marranoism. **1941** G. G. SCHOLEM *Major Trends Jewish Mysticism* vii. 254 The descendant of a Marranic family. *Ibid.* viii. 311 The conception of a voluntary Marranism.

marras, variant of MARISH.

marratine, obs. form of MARITIME.

Marrch, obs. form of MARCH *sb.*[2] (the month).

marre: see MAR, MARC, MERE, a lake.

marred (mɑːd), *ppl. a.* [f. MAR *v.* + -ED[1].]

†**a.** Perplexed, distracted. **b.** Spoilt, injured. Now *rare* exc. *dial.* of a child: 'Spoilt', peevish. See also MARD *a.* **c.** Disfigured, mutilated.

c **1350** *Will. Palerne* 664, I am Meliors, neiȝh marred, man, for þi sake. **1447** BOKENHAM *Seyntys* (Horstm.) i. (*Margarete*) 291 Euere musynge in his marryd mood How.. He myht bereuyn hyre hyr virginyte. **1552** LYNDESAY *Monarche* Prol. 220 Sick marde Musis may mak me no supplee. **1611** BIBLE *Isa.* lii. 14 His visage was so marred

more then any man. **1611** COTGR., *Mauvais*..depraued, corrupt, mard. **1790** PENNANT *London* (1813) 358 A marble groupe..with London and Commerce whimpering like two marred children. **1856** GERALDINE E. JEWSBURY *Sorrows of Gentility* II. i. 2 The grandfather gave it [a baby] impatiently back to the nurse with the observation that 'It was very marred'. **1870** *Pall Mall G.* 10 Dec. 12 The shadow of their marred journey rests upon the souls of all the English members of the party. **1898** W. K. JOHNSON *Terra Tenebr.* 92 Let the marred earth tremble and pass. **1903** *Blackw. Mag.* June 632/2 With his marred face [said of a man whose nose had been cut off].

Hence **'marredness**.

1587 GOLDING *De Mornay* xvii. 275 Notwithstanding all this marrednesse, yet the Soule liueth..pure and clean in God.

marree, variant of MERE *sb.*⁶, Maori war-axe.

marreis, obs. form of MARISH.

†**marrement.** *Obs. rare*⁻¹. [f. MAR *v.* + -MENT.] Trouble, affliction.

1390 GOWER *Conf.* III. 196 And thus upon his marrement This paien hath made his preiere.

marrer ('mɑːrə(r)). [f. MAR *v.* + -ER¹.] One who mars; a destroyer, injurer, spoiler.

c **1420** LYDG. *Assembly of Gods* 690 Marrers of maters, and money makers. **1529** MORE *Suppl. Soulys* Wks. 295/1 They be yᵉ marrars & distroyers of the realme. **1581** MULCASTER *Positions* xxxix. (1887) 218 The deuill himself..our most suttle, and despitefull marrer. *a* **1619** FOTHERBY *Atheom.* II. x. §4 (1622) 307 *One* is the maker, and *One* is the marrer of euery number. **1639** FULLER *Holy War* IV. xviii. (1640) 199 His friends, the Pisans and Genoans, reviled him as the marrer of their mart. **1830** SOUTHEY *Lett.* (1856) IV. 180 As for the Fitz-Romilly law-menders, makers, or marrers, I think of these as you do. **1877** *Tinsley's Mag.* XXI. 203 She was no match-maker, but she was no match-marrer.

marret, variant of MARROT, a guillemot.

marre(y)s(se, obs. forms of MARISH.

marri ('mærɪ). [Aboriginal name.] A Western Australian red gum tree, *Eucalyptus calophylla*, or its timber.

1920 R. GRIMWADE *Anthography of Eucalypts* plate 75 *E[ucalyptus] calophylla.* Marri. Western Australian Red Gum... A tall, sturdy tree, well distributed over the coastal regions of Western Australia. **1934** W. F. BLAKELY *Key to Eucalypts* 84 *E. calophylla*, R.Br. 'Marri' or 'Red Gum'... A medium-sized to large tree. Bark rough, flaky, persistent on trunk and branches. **1938** A. W. D'OMBRAIN *Gallery of Gum Trees* 48 In Western Australia..there are two distinctive and beautiful red flowering gums, the Scarlet Flowered Gum,..and..the much larger Pink Flowered Marri. **1963** *Times* 12 Mar. (Austral. Suppl.) p. v/7 Marri and gimlet and grey-barked tuart, and..other valuable timbers. **1969** T. H. EVERETT *Living Trees of World* 269/1 The marri or red gum (*E. calophylla*) has its home in southwestern Australia. It becomes 150 feet tall with a trunk 5 feet in diameter... Its flowers, in large decorative terminal clusters, are cream-colored or pink; they produce abundant nectar. This is a good ornamental and shade tree. Its lumber is used for boxes and light construction.

marriable ('mærɪəb(ə)l), *a.* Now *rare.* Also 5–6 **mari-**, **maryable**, 6 **marryable**. [a. OF. *mariable*, f. *mari-er* to MARRY.] That may be married; in early use = MARRIAGEABLE.

c **1440** *Promp. Parv.* 326/1 Maryable,..*nubilis.* **1543** GRAFTON *Contin. Harding* 540 The lorde Harbarte had a syster maryable. *c* **1555** HARPSFIELD *Divorce Hen. VIII* (Camden) 154 Until that Sela came of marriable years. **1569** ABP. PARKER *Corr.* (Parker Soc.) 352 The parties marriable must be so allowed by two justices of the peace or by the Ordinary. **1587** HOLINSHED *Chron.* III. 38/1 The kings daughter..being now viripotent or mariable. **1820** COLERIDGE in *Lit. Rem.* (1839) IV. 150 The Reformed Church of England with its marriable and married clergy.

marriage ('mærɪdʒ). Forms: 3–7 **mariage**, 4–6 **maryage**, 4 **mariag**, 5 **mareagh**, **maryag**, **-ache**, 6 **marrage**, **marag**, **mar(r)yge**, **marie(a)ge**, 7 **mareag(e**, **mariadge**, 6- **marriage**. [a. F. *mariage* (from 12th c.) = Pr. *maridatge*, Sp. *maridaje* (Pg. has a different formation, *maridança*), It. *maritaggio*:—popular L. type **marītāticum* f. *marīt-us* husband: see MARITAL *a.* and -AGE.

In Eng., as also in Fr., the word tends to be apprehended (in accordance with a frequent function of the suffix *-age*) as if it were a derivative of the related verb.]

1. a. The condition of being a husband or wife; the relation between married persons; spousehood, wedlock.

1297 R. GLOUC. (Rolls) 1499, & [he] sede þat it was to him gret prou & honour To be in such mariage alied to þe emperour. *c* **1400** MAUNDEV. (Roxb.) xx. 89 In þat cuntree es na mariage betwene man and womman. **1456** SIR G. HAYE *Law Arms* (S.T.S.) 21 *marg.*, The mareagh of kyrk men. **1513** BRADSHAW *St. Werburge* I. 1754 Many dyuers persones ..Refused this worlde..Renounsynge vayne pleasures ryches and maryage. **1567** *Gude & Godlie B.* (S.T.S.) 202 Mariage is ane blissit band. **1606** B. JONSON *Hymenæi, Barriers* 39 Marriage Loves obiect is. **1624** DONNE *Serm.* ii. 17 Nor does he dishonour Marriage that praises Virginity. **1647** COWLEY *Mistr., Constant* ii, All Love is Marriage on thy Lovers side, For only Death can them divide. **1767** A. YOUNG *Farmer's Lett. to People* 189 Marriage will ever flourish, when there is no danger of children proving an incumbrance. **1873** MERIVALE in *Summary Proc. St. Etheldreda Fest.* 17 The two pillars upon which God has founded the edifice of civilized society are, after all, property and marriage.

†**b.** In certain phrases used for: The marriage vow. *Obs.*

c **1386** CHAUCER *Wife's Prol.* 710 He..writ in his dotage That wommen kan nat kepe hir mariage! *a* **1450** *Knt. de la Tour* (1868) 60 No man nor woman shulde..breke her mariage. **1530** PALSGR. 464/1 Thou haste broken thy marryage, *tu as faulcé ton mariage.*

c. Phr. with preps. ***in marriage*** (now arch.): in the matrimonial state, in wedlock. ***to give, take in*** (†*to*, †*into*) ***marriage***: to give, take as husband or wife. †***but marriage*** (Sc.): unmarried.

a **1300** *Cursor M.* 12667 A man in mariage hir tok. *c* **1375** *Sc. Leg. Saints* xli. (*Agnes*) 107 My spouse..has giffine me in mariage, þat neuir sal fal3e, his herytage. *c* **1470** HENRY *Wallace* IV. 723 Thai..said scho suld be weddyt with ane knycht..that was but mariage. **1535** COVERDALE *Ps.* lxxvii[i]. 63 Their maydes were not geuen to mariage. **1594** MARLOWE & NASHE *Dido* III. ii, Why should not they then ioyne in marriage? **1700** DRYDEN *Pal. & Arc.* III. 1120 Then I propose that Palamon shall be In marriage joined with beauteous Emily. **1877** [see GIVE *v.* 5].

d. *Anthropol.* with defining word. ***communal marriage***: the system prevailing amongst some uncivilized peoples, by which within a small community all the men are regarded as married to all the women, and vice versa; sometimes called ***group marriage***. ***plural marriage***: polygamy.

1870 LUBBOCK *Orig. Civiliz.* 67 Communal marriage, where every man and woman in a small community were regarded as equally married to one another. **1880** FISON & HOWITT *Kamil. & Kurnai* 146 Considering how easy it is to mistake instances of group marriage for polyandry.

2. a. Entrance into wedlock; the action, or an act, of marrying; the ceremony or procedure by which two persons are made husband and wife.

civil marriage: a marriage performed by an officer of the state, as distinguished from one that is of the nature of a religious ceremony. ***fleet marriage***: see FLEET *sb.*² 2. ***Scotch marriage***: a marriage according to the Scots law, effected by a mutual declaration before witnesses, without other formality; chiefly applied to the runaway marriages (formerly frequent) of couples who crossed from England into Scotland in order to escape the restrictions imposed by English law on the marriage of minors without the consent of their guardians.

a **1300** *Cursor M.* 3337 Þe mariage þen did he mak Bituix rebecca and ysaac. *c* **1386** CHAUCER *Merch. T.* 75 Mariage is a ful greet sacrement. **1490** CAXTON *Eneydos* xiv. 52 Yf I wyst that thou, venus, were not of accorde for the maryag of eneas to dydo, I shulde make hym fyrst to departe wythout eny respyte. *c* **1555** HARPSFIELD *Divorce Hen. VIII* (Camden) 245 St. Hierome and St. Gregorie that will not call our ladie's marriage nuptialls. **1699** T. BROWN in *R. L'Estrange's Erasm. Colloq.* (1725) 341 For when Marriage is once legally contracted, no human Power you know can disannul it. **1766** BLACKSTONE *Comm.* II. 334 As, when lands are conveyed to the use of A and B, after a marriage shall be had between them. **1832** MARRYAT *N. Forster* xxxiv, A marriage on board of a king's ship, by the captain, duly entered in the log-book, is considered..valid. **1879** MISS BRADDON *Cloven Foot* xix, A good many years ago..I got myself entrapped into a Scotch marriage.

b. The nuptial ceremony together with the accompanying festivities; a wedding. ? *Obs.* or *arch.*

c **1386** CHAUCER *Wife's Prol.* 558, I made my visitacions.. To pleyes of myracles and to mariages. **1526** TINDALE *John* ii. 2 Iesus was called also and his disciples vnto the mariage. *c* **1610** *Women Saints* 17 He reproueth Virgins that were present at mariages.

3. a. A particular matrimonial alliance or union.

cross marriage: applied to the marriage of a man to the sister of his sister's husband.

1473 WARKW. *Chron.* (Camden) 3 The Erle of Warwyke was sent into Fraunce for a maryage for the Kynge. **1539** CROMWELL in Merriman *Life & Lett.* (1902) II. 175 To induce and persuade the kinges hieghnes..to make a crosse maryage bitwen the yong duke of Cleves and my lady Mary. **1559** *Mirr. Mag., Dk. Suffolk* xi, I sought a mariage for my soveraine Lorde. **1580** LYLY *Euphues* (Arb.) 471 Mariages are made in heauen. *a* **1586** SIDNEY *Arcadia* II. (1590) 129 Euarchus made a crosse mariage also with Dorilaus his sister. **1586** A. DAY *Eng. Secretary* II. (1625) 50 You haue deliuered forth..that..I..led him..into a deceitfull marriage. **1663** DRYDEN *Rival Ladies* I. i, For hapning both to Love each others Sisters, They have concluded it in a cross Marriage. **1860** FROUDE *Hist. Eng.* xxxi. (1893) V. 304 The fears of Renard..were occasioned by the unanimity of Catholics and heretics in the opposition to the marriage. *Mod.* They disapproved of his marriage.

†**b.** *concr.* A person viewed as a prospective husband or wife; a (good or bad) match. *Obs.*

1523 LD. BERNERS *Froiss.* I. ccliii. 375 The erle of Flaunders..thought that the yonge duke of Bourgoyn was a mete mariage for her [his daughter]. **1621** LADY M. WROTH *Urania* 357 He was perswaded..to go see a Lady, a great marriage, and to wooe her. *Ibid.* 438 A great marryage she was likely to be.

4. *transf.* and *fig.* (from the preceding senses). Intimate union.

c **1420** *Pallad. on Husb.* IV. 27 Into the lond let synke A reed right by, and bynde in mariage Hem to, lest wynde offende her tender age. *c* **1570** (*title*) A new and Pleasaunt enterlude intituled the mariage of Witte and Science. *a* **1586** SIDNEY *Arcadia* III. (1590) 331 The cruel villayne forced the sworde with another blowe to diuorce the faire marriage of the head and body. **1613** PURCHAS *Pilgrimage* IV. i. (1614) 342 They plant their Vines at the foote of great Trees, which marriage proueth very fruitfull. *a* **1693** AUBREY *Lives* (1898) I. *Briggs* 123 He considered..the convenience of making a mariage between those rivers. **1876** T. HARDY *Ethelberta* (1890) 68 In which of the cases do you consider the marriage of verse and tune to have been most successful?

5. = MARITAGE 2. *Obs.* exc. *Hist.*

1459 *Rolls of Parlt.* V. 371/1 The Warde and Maryage of Thomas..belonged unto the Kyng. *c* **1460** FORTESCUE *Abs. & Lim. Mon.* ix. (1885) 130 The grete lordis off þe lande by reason..off mariages, purchasses, and oþer titles, shall often tymes growe to be gretter than thai be now. *a* **1578** LINDESAY (Pitscottie) *Chron. Scot.* (S.T.S.) I. 62 The Earle of Douglas..obtenit fre the King the ward and marieage of [Annas] Dunbar. **1885** PLUMMER *Fortescue's Abs. & Lim. Mon.* 270 *marg.*, Lord's right of *marriage* under the feudal system.

†**6.** A dowry. *Obs.* (Cf. MARITAGE 1.)

c **1330** R. BRUNNE *Chron. Wace* (Rolls) 2328 Þerfore y schal myn heritage Gyue þy sistres in mariage [Wace: *en mariage*]. **1362** LANGL. *P. Pl.* A. II. 50 To witnesse..In what manere that Meede in mariage was i-feffed. **1577–87** HOLINSHED *Chron.* III. 1131/2 He [John Gresham] gaue also to maids mariages.

7. *Cards.* In certain games, e.g. bezique, the 'declaration' of a king and queen of the same suit.

1861 *Macm. Mag.* Dec. 138/2 [Bazique.]..King and queen of the same suit are called 'marriage', and score two; but the marriage of trumps scores four. **1870** 'CAVENDISH' *Game of Bézique* 16 King and queen of any suit not trumps (called marriage). King and queen of the trump suit (called marriage in trumps or royal marriage).

8. *attrib.* and *Comb.*, as ***marriage-blessing, bond, -bower, -ceremony, chain, chamber, choice, contract, covenant, -day, -dinner, dowry, -dues, duty, faith, feast, fruition, -hall, -hater, -hindering*** adj., ***hour, joy, -knell, -knot, life, -maker, manual, market, mart, -monger, -morn, -morning, night, -register, -rites, state, supper, table, -tie, -treaty, -vow.*** Also **Marriage Act**, any of the Acts of Parliament regulating marriages (see quot.); **marriage articles**, an antenuptial agreement embodying the terms agreed on by the parties with respect to rights of property and succession; †**marriage bawd**, an opprobrious term for a match-maker; **marriage bell**, a church bell rung on the occasion of a marriage in token of joy; **marriage brokage, brokerage**, consideration given for bringing about a marriage (contracts for which are void by English law); **marriage broker**, (*a*) an opprobrious term for a match-maker; (*b*) in cultures in which arranged marriages are the norm, one who arranges marriages for a fee; **marriage bureau**, an agency which arranges introductions with a view to marriage; also *fig.*; **marriage certificate**, a copy of the record of a legal marriage which is given to the contracting parties; **marriage counselling, guidance**, the giving of advice on problems connected with marriage, usu. as a form of social service; also **marriage counsellor, marriage guidance counsellor**; †**marriage deed** = *marriage articles*; **marriage favours**, 'knots of white ribbons or bunches of white flowers, worn at weddings' (Ogilvie *Suppl.* 1855); †**marriage finger**, the finger on which the wedding-ring is placed; †**marriage gear** (*Sc.*), †**marriage good**, marriage portion, dowry; **marriage lay** = *marriage-song*; **marriage licence**, an official permission to marry (in England, a document granted by the ordinary or his surrogate, authorizing a couple to be married by a clergyman of the Church of England without the proclamation of banns); **marriage lines**, a certificate of marriage; **marriage of convenience** = MARIAGE DE CONVENANCE; **marriage payment** *Anthropol.*, payment of a traditional kind made in many tribal societies to a bride or her parents by the bridegroom or his parents; cf. BRIDE *sb.*¹ 5; **marriage portion**, a portion or dowry, etc., given to a bride at her marriage; **marriage rate**, the ratio of the number of marriages per year to the population (usually expressed per thousand); **marriage-ring**, a wedding-ring; **marriage service**, the form of words prescribed for the religious ceremony of marriage; **marriage settlement**, an arrangement made by deed in consideration of an intended marriage, whereby certain property is secured for the wife, and sometimes also for the children; **marriage-song**, an epithalamium. See also MARRIAGE BED.

marriage life, marriage state, formerly common expressions, are now almost superseded by *married life, married state.*

1753 *Gentl. Mag.* Sept., Contents, Accounts of the new *mariage act. **1841** STEPHEN *Comm.* (1874) II. 246 The principal marriage Acts now in force, are 4 Geo. IV. c. 76, and 6 & 7 Will. IV. c. 85. **1711** STEELE *Spect.* No. 2 ¶2 The Father sends up every Post Questions relating to *Marriage-Articles, Leases, and Tenures. **1698** VANBRUGH *Prov. Wife* v. iii, My innocent lady..turns *marriage-bawd to her niece. **1816** BYRON *Ch. Har.* III. xxi, And all went merry as a *marriage-bell. **1610** SHAKS. *Temp.* IV. i. 106 Honor, riches, *marriage blessing..be still vpon you. **1644**

MILTON *Judgm. Bucer* xxvii, That under pretence of the *marriage bond they be not sold to perpetual vexations. **1831** CARLYLE *Sart. Res.* III. iii, The fair clustering flowers that over-wreathe..the *Marriage-bower. *a* **1721** VERNON *Chancery Cases* (1726) I. 412 The Bill was to be relieved against a *Marriage Brocage Bond. **1787** W. P. WILLIAMS *Chancery Cases* III. 75 *note*, Cares of direct marriage brocage. **1681** OTWAY *Soldier's Fort.* IV. i, Make me a Match-maker? a filthy *Marriage-Broker! **1892** I. ZANGWILL *Childr. Ghetto* I. 18 The same mould covers them all—..the *marriage-brokers repose with those they mated. **1932** L. GOLDING *Magnolia Street* I. ii. 32 She didn't marry again, though she was only in the middle thirties when he died and the marriage-brokers got busy. **1968** L. ROSTEN *Joys of Yiddish* 325 A wisecrack defines a *shadchen* as 'a marriage broker who knows the perfect girl for you—and married the wrong girl himself'. **1847** ADDISON *Law of Contracts* 568 *Marriage brokerage contracts. **1942** OLIVER & BENEDETTA *Marriage Bureau* 19 How much better it would be if there were an organization that could arrange the actual match-making and see that suitable people met each other. And this way my idea for the *Marriage Bureau. **1953** 'H. JENNER' *Marriage is my Business* i. 19 The story has often been told of the two ex-debs and how they coped with opening a marriage bureau. **1960** N. EPTON *Love & English* VI. v. 355 The marriage bureau..lists *all* your assets for the calm perusal of registered clients. *Ibid.* 356 This modern matchmaker, the marriage bureau, is middle-class and eminently respectable. **1972** *Accountant* 5 Oct. 411/3 Its aim would be the establishment of a 'marriage bureau' for the smaller businesses of Europe. **1766** *Chron.* in *Ann. Reg.* 106 Thus was she led..to the altar, where the *marriage-ceremony was performed. **1848** MRS. GASKELL *Let.* 11 Nov. (1966) 62, I wish I had five sisters, who were bound to love me by their parents' *marriage certificate. **1860** E. EDEN *Semi-Attached Couple* II. xviii. 225 He had seen too much of life, to believe in these sudden discoveries of marriage certificates. **1911** G. B. SHAW *Doctor's Dilemma* III. 61 She carried her marriage certificate in her face and in her character. **1945** MENCKEN *Amer. Lang.* Suppl. I. 475/1 *Marriage lines* is confined to the vulgar. On higher levels *marriage certificate* is used. **1967** 'G. NORTH' *Sgt. Cluff & Day of Reckoning* xi. 101 Brittle where it had been folded, the marriage certificate held his gaze. **1703** ROWE *Fair Penit.* I. i, Never to load it with the *Marriage Chain. **1611** BIBLE *Tobit* vi. 16 When thou shalt come into the *mariage chamber. *c* **1586** C'TESS PEMBROKE *Ps.* LXXVIII. xxv, The virgins live despair'd of *mariage choise. **1824** MILL in *Westm. Rev.* I. 537 Plato is represented as exceedingly wicked, for having expounded, in his Republic, the footing upon which he thought that the *marriage contract could most advantageously be placed. **1961** NEW ENG. BIBLE *Matt.* i. 19 Joseph desired to have the marriage contract set aside quietly. **1945** *Marriage counselling [see COUNSELLING *vbl. sb.*]. **1959** HERBERT & JARVIS (*title*) A modern approach to marriage counselling. **1970** *Guardian* 31 July 18/6 In the 30 years the marriage counselling movement has been in existence the lack of specific privileges for marriage counsellors has never come to a showdown. **1946** *Marriage counsellor [see COUNSELLOR 1 b]. **1970** G. GREER *Female Eunuch* 19 The revolutionary woman must know her enemies, the doctors, psychiatrists,..marriage counsellors. **1644** MILTON *Judgm. Bucer* xxvi, That all holiness and faith of *marriage covenant should be observed. **1594** MARLOWE & NASHE *Dido* I. i, These linkèd gems, My Iuno ware vpon her *marriage day. *a* **1640** MASSINGER et al. *Old Law* (1656) v. 69 As I am Lord of the day (being my marriage day the second) I doe advance bonnet. **1852** M. ARNOLD *Tristram* I, in *Empedocles on Etna* 115 That her lord and she Might drink it on their marriage day. **1907** W. B. YEATS *Deirdre* 36 Although her marriage-day had all but come. **1678** BUTLER *Hud.* III. i. 834 For what can we pretend t'inherit, Unless the *marriage-deed will bear it? **1552** LATIMER *Serm.*, *Parable Kings Son* (1584) 183 b, This banket or *mariage dinner. **1603** SHAKS. *Meas. for M.* III. i. 230 The portion and sinew of her fortune, her *marriage dowry. **1767** *Chron.* in *Ann. Reg.* 64 A young nobleman..gave five guineas..in order to ..pay the *marriage-dues. **1645** MILTON *Colast.* Wks. (1847) 222/2 Diversity of religion breeds a greater dislike to *marriage duties than natural disagreement. **1671** —— *Samson* 1115 Breaking her *Marriage Faith to circumvent me. **1588** SHAKS. *L.L.L.* II. i. 40 At a *marriage feast..saw I this Longauill. **1711** ADDISON *Spect.* No. 58 ¶13 To get the Measure of his Mistress's *Marriage-Finger. **1645** MILTON *Tetrach.* Wks. (1847) 207/1 (Matt. xix. 9) That a person so hatefully expelled should..be turned..out of all *marriage fruition. **1515** in *Fam. Rose of Kilravock* (Spalding) 185 For the quhilk marriage the said Huchon Ros sall giff sex scor of Merkis of *mariage geyr. **1600** HOLLAND *Livy* XLII. xxxiv. 1134 [My wife] brought nothing with her for *marriage-good, but freedome of birth [etc.]. **1935** *Time* 13 May 28/2 Old Stone Church is one of an increasing number whose pastors run '*marriage guidance bureaus'. **1945** *Times* 25 July 5/5 Groups of people in the provinces have recently been setting up their own local marriage guidance councils. **1948** D. R. MACE *Marriage Counselling* iii. 18 Marriage guidance..falls into three natural divisions. The first is education for marriage... The second is marriage preparation..intensive preparation of engaged couples... The third is marriage counselling..offering help to married people who are confronted with difficulties. **1965** HALL & HOWES *Church in Social Work* iii. 63 Started in 1938 and revived and reconstituted on a national basis in 1943, the National Marriage Guidance Council..quickly became established. **1967** O. WYND *Walk Softly, Men Praying* xii. 186 About all that was available to me was the kind of noise that might have come from a junior apprentice marriage-guidance counsellor. **1970** G. GREER *Female Eunuch* 17 Women are not happy even when they do follow the blue-print set out by sentimental and marriage guidance counsellors and the system that they represent. **1924** W. J. LOCKE *Coming of Amos* xvi. 204 Of the marriage in the bleak *marriage-hall of the Mairie, she remembered little. **1692** D'URFEY (*title*) The *Marriage-Hater Matched. **1864** TENNYSON *Aylmer's F.* 374 This filthy *marriage-hindering Mammon. **1591** SHAKS. *Two Gent.* II. iv. 179 We are betroathd: nay more, our *mariage howre Determin'd of. **1594** —— *Rich. III*, IV. iv. 330 The sweet silent houres of *Marriage ioyes. **1693** CONGREVE *Old Bach.* v. xiii, I thought the chimes of verse were passed, when once the doleful *marriage-knell was rung. **1627** SANDERSON *Serm.* I. 262 In the *marriage-knot there is some expression and representation of the love-covenant betwixt Christ and His church. **1850** TENNYSON *In Mem.* Concl., Demand not thou a *marriage lay. **1797** *Encycl. Brit.* (ed. 3) X. 584/1 To forge ..a *marriage licence. **1836–7** DICKENS *Sk. Boz, Scenes* viii, Doctors' Commons being..the place where they grant marriage-licences to love-sick couples. **1711** STEELE *Spect.* No. 149 ¶5 The *Marriage-Life is always an insipid, a vexatious, or an happy Condition. **1829**, **1840** *Marriage lines [see LINE *sb.*[2] 23 f]. **1591** PERCIVALL *Sp. Dict.*, *Casamentero*, a *marriage maker. **1855** TENNYSON *Maud* I. xx. iii, A dinner and then a dance For the maids and marriage-makers. **1936** H. M. & A. STONE (*title*) A *marriage manual. **1965** MASTERS & JOHNSON in J. Money *Sex Research* iv. 109 If the suggestions of the marriage manuals are followed, the male develops the concept that he is to find the clitoris and stay with it. **1969** 'J' *Sensuous Woman* (1970) xix. 121 Don't let any marriage manual talk you into missing that moment when he explodes in you. **1973** I. SINGER *Goals of Human Sexuality* vi. 149 The fifteen popular marriage manuals..all treat sexual response as if it were work. **1850** *Punch* 3 Aug. 54/2 If..the Duke of Cambridge were permitted to take his coronet into the home *marriage-market. **1875** *Chamb. Jrnl.* No. 133. 54 Lord Hardwicke's Act caused quite a flutter in the marriage-market. **1942** E. BOWEN *Seven Winters* 46 The ulterior designs of the marriage market. **1971** R. RUSSELL tr. *Ahmad's Shore & Wave* iv. 45 The oldest, it was true, was married to a prosperous consultant engineer, but the other two were still in the marriage market. **1823** BYRON *Don Juan* XII. xlvi. 7 The Smithfield Show Of vestals brought into the *marriage mart. **1972** *Village Voice* (N.Y.) 1 June 70/3 For all our talk about being liberated, most of my friends are too shy, or perhaps just too snobby, to show up at marriage marts. **1854** THACKERAY *Newcomes* I. 305 There are articles which the *marriage-monger cannot make to convene at all. **1842** TENNYSON '*Move Eastward*', Ah, bear me with thee.. And move me to my *marriage-morn. **1821** BYRON *Juan.* v. lxxvi, The finest lace Which e'er set off a *marriage-morning face. **1664** LD. FALKLAND (*title*) The *Marriage Night. **1711** *Marriage of convenience [see CONVENIENCE *sb.* 6]. **1949** G. B. SHAW *Buoyant Billions* IV. 53 The proportion of happy love marriages to happy marriages of convenience has never been counted. **1972** C. DRUMMOND *Death at Bar* ii. 64 Reg and June are a bit peculiar in that it was simply a marriage of convenience... They went their own way. **1975** *Listener* 16 Jan. 84/3 The co-ordinators had..paired each of the piano sonatas with each of the string quartets. Was this just a marriage of convenience..for numerical rather than musical reasons? **1924** W. H. RIVERS *Social Organisation* iii. 46 Marriage by exchange..may co-exist with marriage by purchase, and..in some cases, it is only a means of avoiding ..the *marriage payments. **1951** *N. & Q. Anthropol.* (ed. 6) II iv. 111 In either case the settlement of a marriage-payment..may be the custom. **1957** V. W. TURNER *Schism & Continuity in Afr. Society* ix. 265 He..affected to take umbrage because the marriage-payment..he had made for her in cloth was not returned. **1963** W. J. GOODE *World Revolution & Family Patterns* iv. 167 The marriage payment or groom service points to the great concern with the legal possession of children. **1766** *Chron.* in *Ann. Reg.* 106 The girl was advised to do this, that he might be intitled to no other *marriage-portion than her smock. **1859** *Marriage rate [see *birth-rate* (BIRTH *sb.*[1] 13)]. **1891** G. B. LONGSTAFF *Stud. in Statistics* iii. 14 Speaking generally, the birth-rate corresponds to the marriage-rate, but with marked exceptions. **1970** W. D. BORRIE *Growth & Control World Population* iv. 62 There was a suggestion of a considerable degree of rationality in the reactions of these populations to the food situation, with marriage rates rising in good times and falling in bad times. **1797** *Encycl. Brit.* (ed. 3) X. 584/1 To make a false entry into a *marriage-register. *a* **1631** DONNE *Jeat Ring Sent* in *Poems* (1633) 292 *Marriage rings are not of this stuffe. **1825** J. NEAL *Bro. Jonathan* II. 154 She never had sich a cold in all her life, as when she left her marriage ring off. **1878** O. WILDE *Ravenna* 5 A moon of fire Round-girdled with a purple marriage-ring. **1913** J. MASEFIELD *Daffodil Fields* 82 She dropped her marriage-ring upon the table. [According to modern editors *marriage rite* or *rites* should be read in SHAKS. *Pericles* IV. Gower 17, where the first Quarto (1608) has 'Euen right for marriage sight'.] **1621** BRATHWAIT *Natures Embass.*, *Sheph. Tales* Egl. ii. 198 For I your patience might wrong, To stand vpon these *marriage rites too long. *a* **1661** HOLYDAY *Juvenal* vi. (1673) 91 He Acts no new sinne, Posthumus, that sleights The Genius of another's Marriage-Rites. **1833** *Tracts for Times* No. 3. p. 1 There are persons who wish the *Marriage-Service emended. **1712** STEELE *Spect.* No. 272 ¶1, I have a young Kinsman..who shall shew you the rough Draught of the *Marriage Settlement. **1597** DRAYTON *Heroic Ep.*, *Dk. Suffolk to Mary the Fr. Queen* 122 And in precession as they came along, with Himeneus sang thy *marriage song. **1714** *Spectator* No. 607 ¶5 Good-Nature is a third necessary Ingredient in the *Marriage-State. **1611** BIBLE *Rev.* xix. 9 Blessed are they which are called vnto the *marriage supper of the Lambe. **1602** SHAKS. *Ham.* I. ii. 181 The Funeral Baktmeats Did coldly furnish forth the *Marriage Tables. **1693** DRYDEN tr. *Ovid's Met.* I. 653 Give me..to live and die A spotless maid, without the *marriage-tie. **1865** G. M. HOPKINS *Note-bks. & Papers* (1937) 54 The Frenchman said the marriage-tie was in every case a bad thing. **1951** R. FIRTH *Elem. Social Organiz.* ii. 59 The marriage-tie is made the basis of service as a cook. **1710** PALMER *Proverbs* 127 He that loves at first sight..finishes a *marriage-treaty without taking so much time as [etc.]. **1598** SHAKS. *Merry W.* II. ii. 258 The ward of her purity, her reputation, her *marriage-vow. **1935** B. MALINOWSKI *Coral Gardens* II. VI. v. 234 Whether the marriage vows are treated as a sacrament or as a mere legal contract. **1965** A. CHRISTIE *At Bertram's Hotel* vii. 79 The walls of Jericho seemed to be a symbolical way of referring to a certain lady's marriage vows... They tumbled down.

marriageable (ˈmærɪdʒəb(ə)l), *a.* (*sb.*) Also 6–7 **mariageable**. [f. MARRIAGE + -ABLE.]

1. Of persons: Fit for marriage, of an age to marry.

c **1555** HARPSFIELD *Divorce Hen. VIII* (Camden) 174 If you would tarry until they should be marriageable, you should be old women ere you married. **1625** K. LONG tr. *Barclay's Argenis* IV. iv. 252 There were no neighbour-princes which were marriageable. **1712** ADDISON *Spect.* No. 311 ¶1, I am the Father of a young Heiress, whom I begin to look upon as Marriageable. **1841** LYTTON *Nt. & Morn.* I. i, He boasted two very pretty marriageable daughters. **1885** J. PAYN *Talk of Town* II. 56 Your united ages scarcely make up that of a marriageable man.

b. *transf.* Of plants, *esp.* the vine: Fit to be joined to other plants.

1663 COWLEY *Verses & Ess.*, '*Happy the Man*' 9 Sometimes the beaut'ous Marriageable Vine He to the lusty Bridegroom Elm does joyn. **1667** MILTON *P.L.* v. 217. **1824** *Blackw. Mag.* XVI. 2 The ruby clusters of Bacchus himself, glowing amidst the foliage of some tall marriageable elm.

c. Of age (†formerly also of qualities, etc.): Befitting marriage or the married state.

1597 T. PAYNE *Royal Exch.* 43 Wch mariageable tearmes ..teacheth..husbands and wyves to be so lyncked in love as to lyve and love togethers most affectionatly. **1643** MILTON *Divorce* I. xii, It is most sure that some..are destitute of all other mariageable gifts. **1725** DE FOE *Voy. round World* (1840) 246 Twelve years old, which the Spaniards count marriageable. **1889** JESSOPP *Coming of Friars* v. 228 A.. damsel..very near the marriageable age.

2. *sb.* A marriageable person.

1826 MOORE *Mem.* (1854) V. 49 Dined at Mrs. Branigan's: a children's party in the evening, with the intermixture of two or three rather pretty young marriageables.

Hence **ˈmarriageableness** (*rare*$^{-0}$); **marriageaˈbility**.

1687 MIEGE *Gt. Fr. Dict.* II, Marriageableness, *âge d'être marié*. **1727** in BAILEY vol. II. **1895** in *Funk's Stand. Dict.* **1910** *Encycl. Relig. & Ethics* III. 345/2 The karöh (lit. 'seclusion'), or declaration of marriageability of girls, is celebrated with great solemnity. **1944** G. B. SHAW *Everybody's Pol. What's What?* viii. 61 Equality of income and complete touchability and marriageability exist at present at different levels in the trades, the professions, the ranks, and the classes. **1974** *Sci. Amer.* Sept. 113/1 According to Oriental astrology, girls born that year may murder their husbands, which tends to reduce their marriageability.

marriage-bed. The bed used by a married couple; hence *transf.* marital intercourse, with its rights and duties. ***to defile, violate the marriage-bed***: to commit adultery.

1590 SHAKS. *Com. Err.* II. i. 27 *Adri.* This seruitude makes you to keepe vnwed. *Luci.* Not this, but troubles of the marriage bed. **1675** TRAHERNE *Chr. Ethics* 414 The great felicity which lovers promise to themselves, and taste also when they meet together in the marriage-bed. **1712** ADDISON *Spect.* No. 446 ¶6 We do not find any Comedy.. raised upon the Violations of the Marriage-Bed. **1776** ADAM SMITH *W.N.* II. iii. (1869) I. 351 The marriage-bed of James the First of Great Britain was, a few years ago, the ornament of an alehouse at Dunfermline. **1869** LECKY *Europ. Mor.* (1877) II. iv. 7 During the period of penance, the penitent was compelled to abstain from the marriage-bed. **1896** A. E. HOUSMAN *Shropshire Lad* xxviii, Ages since the vanquished bled Round my mother's marriage-bed. **1913** D. H. LAWRENCE *Love Poems* 5 The low-built shed Where hangs the swallow's marriage bed. **1922** JOYCE *Ulysses* 458 He felt it his mission in life to urge me, to defile the marriage bed, to commit adultery at the earliest possible opportunity.

married (ˈmærɪd), *ppl. a.* and *sb.* [f. MARRY *v.* + -ED[1].]

A. *ppl. a.* **1. a.** United to another in wedlock; living in the matrimonial state. ***married couple***, a husband and wife; often in contexts where they are acting jointly as domestic servants.

1362 LANGL. *P. Pl.* A. x. 109 Ʒif þou beo Mon I-Mariet.. Hold þe stable. **1456** SIR G. HAYE *Law Arms* (S.T.S.) 241 The knychtis wyf beris the privilege of hyr maryt husband. **1526** *Pilgr. Perf.* (W. de W. 1531) 252 Kynges, prynces,.. and maryed persones, and all christen people [etc.]. **1606** SHAKS. *Ant. & Cl.* I. iii. 20 What says the married woman? **1752** HUME *Pol. Disc.* x. 174 Marry'd slaves..were esteem'd very inconvenient. *a* **1817** JANE AUSTEN *Persuasion* (1818) III. viii. 147 Admiral and Mrs. Croft..among the married couples. **1871** *Monthly Packet* Oct. 388 The grandmother had at that time as lodgers a married couple and a single man. **1890** W. BOOTH *In Darkest Eng.* II. vi. 209 We shall be confronted with married couples who..demand that we should provide for them lodgings. **1897** MARY KINGSLEY *W. Africa* 648 Your Kruboy is very much a married man. **1962** *Times* 22 Oct. 1/3 Mr. and Mrs. G. K. require a married couple—chauffeur house-parlourman and cook-housekeeper. **1965** J. S. GUNN *Terminol. Shearing Indust.* II. 35 s.v. *Twins*. Two shearers who travel and work together, neither being prepared to 'take a pen' unless his mate gets one too. These inseparable mates are sometimes referred to as a 'married couple'. **1971** C. WHITMAN *Death Suspended* iv. 80 The staff..consisted of..a married couple employed as manager and housekeeper. **1972** *Listener* 21 Dec. 861/2 Up-and-coming young married couples who..are the people on whom the future of society depends. **1973** *Times* 7 Apr. 26/3 (Advt.), Young married couple needed. See domestic situations.

b. *fig.*

1592 SHAKS. *Rom. & Jul.* I. iii. 83 (2nd Qo. 1599) Examine euery married liniament And see how one an other lends content. **1703** POPE *Vertumnus* 66 And this fair vine, but that her arms surround Her marry'd elm, had crept along the ground. **1856** BRYANT *After a Tempest* v, The noise of war shall cease from sea to sea, And married nations dwell in harmony. **1973** *Times* 23 May 19/1 The..happily married Paternoster pedestrian precinct and the extended churchyard to the north-east.

2. Pertaining to or characteristic of married persons or matrimony.

1588 SHAKS. *L.L.L.* v. ii. 912 Cuckow, Cuckow: O word of feare, Vnpleasing to a married eare. **1608** —— *Per.* II. v. 4 That for this twelue-month shee'le not vndertake A married life. **1712** STEELE *Spect.* No. 278 ¶2 When I enter into a married State. **1834** BUCKSTONE (*title*) Married Life; a comedy. **1873** MISS BROUGHTON *Nancy* II. 57, I put on a silk gown..as looking more married than the cobweb muslins. **1894** 'J. S. WINTER' *Red-Coats* 47 He..turned to the orderly

officer and growled out, 'I wonder why the devil the other married quarters can't be kept like this?'

3. Special collocation: ***married print*** *Cinemat.*, a positive film carrying both pictures and a sound track.

1953 K. REISZ *Technique Film Editing* 276 From this cut negative and the negative of the re-recorded composite sound-track, a married print is prepared which is ready for projection to cinema audiences. **1959** F. CHAGRIN in Halas & Manvell *Technique Film Animation* xix. 238 Sound and vision have equal importance; they are equal partners, aiming at an ideal married-print status and preparing for it scrupulously by synchronizing their moods and their movements. **1965** P. WAYRE *Wind in Reeds* ix. 135 From this original the first 'married' print was produced with an optical sound track down one side of the film.

B. *sb.* A married person; also *collect.* Freq. in phr. ***young marrieds***.

1890 A. JAMES *Diary* 30 Nov. (1964) 159 The married, however, thro' their ignoble state are doomed to shatter all the ideals of the soaring spinster. **1934** J. O'HARA *Appointment in Samarra* i. 8 The kids home from boarding-school and college, and the younger marrieds, most of whom she knew by their first names, and then the older crowd. **1938** *Time* 5 Dec. 8/3 No representative letter can be chosen from such heterogeneous applications—from men and women, from youngsters, young marrieds, middleaged, and oldsters. **1939** [see CUT-IN *sb.* 1]. **1958** *Times* 22 Nov. 7/7 These teeming 'young marrieds' are very different from those less numerous in the Depression, a generation ago. **1959** *House & Garden* June 8 Smart young marrieds go 'natural' with Irish Linen. **1963** A. HERON *Towards Quaker View of Sex* i. 11 Among the married, faithfulness may be achieved by 'working to rule'. *Ibid.* 57 Free heterosexual relations between the young unmarried or between the married. **1965** *New Statesman* 30 Apr. 672/2 Wealthy parents, who are subsidised by the bachelors and the childless married. **1970** K. GILES *Murder Pluperfect* ii. 14 Victorian marrieds, of a certain class, used to sleep around. **1972** J. CASSON *Lewis & Sybil* ix. 192 Our life together as young naval marrieds was to begin in Alexandria.

marrier (ˈmærɪə(r)). Also 7 **maryer**. [f. MARRY *v.* + -ER^1.] One who marries (in various senses).

1589 *Rare Tri. Love & Fort.* v. in *Five Old Plays* (Roxb. Cl.) 146 Youle have us marry her, heere be them come of the marriers. **1629** *Reg. Privy Council Scot.* N.S. III. 258 Persouns suspect..of the crymes particularly underwrittin, viz.,..maryers of twa wyffes..stealers of beeskaips. **1830** MISS MITFORD *Village* Ser. IV. 91 The Rector of Ashley,.. the favourite marrier of the county, was wanted to tie the hymeneal knot. **1883** *Harper's Mag.* June 100/2 The determined marrier who..chooses a Jewess.

marrinate, -ine, etc., obs. ff. MARINATE, etc.

marring (ˈmɑːrɪŋ), *vbl. sb.* Forms: see MAR *v.* [OE. *mierring*, *męrrung*, f. *mierran*, *męrran*: see MAR *v.* and -ING^1.] The action of the verb MAR (in various senses); †squandering, waste; †hindrance; injury, impairment.

c **897** K. ÆLFRED *Gregory's Past. C.* xx. 149 Ðylæs..se ȝitsa for his goda mierringe ȝielpe. *c* **950** *Lindisf. Gosp.* Mark, Argt. (1871) 5 Merrunga, *seductiones*. *a* **1300** *Cursor M.* 8779 Þai fand gret merring in þair merck, Þe wrightes þat suld rais þe werck. **1357** *Lay Folks Catech.* 124 Withouten ony merryng of hir modirhede. **1561** DAUS tr. *Bullinger on Apoc.* 94 b, Of the traditions of men, and their marring of the Scripture, ariseth darkenes. **1649** MILTON *Eikon.* vi, The making or the marring of any Law. **1860** PUSEY *Min. Proph.* 65 Man shrinks from the violent marring of his outward form.

marring (ˈmɑːrɪŋ), *ppl. a.* [-ING^2.] That mars. Hence ˈ**marringly** *adv.*

1831 *Blackw. Mag.* XXIX. 677 This open expression.. brings out marringly the lesson. **1836** GLADSTONE in Morley *Life* (1903) I. II. iii. 36 [Wordsworth] named the discrepancy between his [Shelley's] creed and his imagination as the marring idea of his works. **1891** R. DOWLING *Isle of Surrey* 256 Mottled with marring blotches of scorbutic red.

marrionate, obs. form of MARINATE.

marrionette, variant of MARIONETTE.

Marriotte, erron. var. MARIOTTE.

marris(e, -ische, -ish(e, obs. ff. MARISH.

Marrism (ˈmɑːrɪz(ə)m). [f. the name of N. Ya. *Marr* (1865–1934), Russian linguist and archæologist + -ISM.] The linguistic theories advocated by Nikolai Yakovlevich Marr, in which language is regarded as a phenomenon of social class rather than of nationality; the advocacy of such theories. Hence ˈ**Marrist** *a.*

1950 *Archivum Linguisticum* II. 116 The quintessence of Marrism, he [*sc.* B. Serebrennikov] tells us, resides in four fundamental theses, viz. the four elements as the source of the world's vocabularies, linguistic growth by hybridisation, stadial evolution, and the semantic transformation of primitive totem-names. *Ibid.* 118 It is he [*sc.* V. Vinogradov] who summarises the three existing attitudes to Marr among Soviet scholars, viz. (1) that Marrism is Marxism in linguistics, [etc.]. *Ibid.* 8 Her [*sc.* R. Šor's] articles are perhaps the first reasoned statement of the Marxist standpoint that is not at the same time Marrist. **1960** [see HYBRIDIZATION 2]. **1963** V. KIPARSKY in *Current Trends in Ling.* I. 94 From 1925 to World War II, when the only officially accepted linguistic school in Soviet Russia was Nikolaj Marr's 'Japhetology', later simply called 'Marrism', there was no interest..in Slavic languages. **1965** H. KUČERA in *Language* XLI. 118 The rehabilitation of comparativist techniques—another by-product of the 1950 renunciation of Marrism. *Ibid.* 125 The reader will find many brief references to the Marrist controversy of 1950. **1966** B. COLLINDER in Birnbaum & Puhvel *Anc. Indo-European Dial.* 199 Marrism, which was officially encouraged in Russia for political reasons, has raged as a kind of Asiatic flu in some European universities west of the Iron Curtain.

marrite (ˈmɑːraɪt). *Min.* [f. the name of John Edward *Marr* (1857–1933), British geologist + -ITE^1.] A sulphide and arsenide of lead and silver, $PbAgAsS_3$, which is found as grey monoclinic crystals in dolomite at Lengenbach, Switzerland.

1904 [see LENGENBACHITE]. **1905** R. H. SOLLY in *Mineral. Mag.* XIV. 76 The colour of marrite is lead-grey to steel-grey, but the crystals are usually tarnished with iridescent colours... The name marrite is proposed in honour of Dr. John Edward Marr, F.R.S., of Cambridge. **1967** *Zeitschr. für Kristallogr.* CXXV. 459 Marrite, a rare sulfosalt from the Binnatal, Switzerland, has been shown to have composition $PbAgAsS_3$. The phase is monoclinic, space group $P2_1/a$.

marrock, variant of MARROT.

marroe, marron(e: see MARROW *sb.*^{2}, MAROON.

†**marroneer.** *Obs.* [a. F. *marronier*, f. *marron*: see MAROON *sb.*^{1}] A kind of chestnut-tree.

1693 EVELYN *De la Quint. Compl. Gard.*, *Refl. Agric.* 47 A Wallnut, a Marroneer, an Orange, or Cherry-Tree.

‖**marron glacé** (marɔ̃ glase). [F. *marron* chestnut + GLACÉ *a.*] A sweetmeat consisting of a chestnut preserved in syrup.

1871 *Leisure Hour* 23 Sept. 600/1 'Marrons glacées' appeared at the confectioners'. **1875** *All Year Round* 2 Jan. 279/2 Old women are..preparing chestnuts for their.. destinies as 'marrons glacés', &c. **1880** G. A. SALA *Amer. Revisited* (1882) I. 57 Did my stock-in-trade comprise a few *marrons glacés*, so much the better for my youthful patroness. **1904** A. BENNETT *Great Man* v. 45 'A pound of marrons glacés.'..'What are they?'..'Taste.'..'It's like chestnuts,' Harry mumbled through the delicious brown frosted morsel. **1906** KIPLING *Actions & Reactions* (1909) 210 Oranges, bits of banana, and *marron*[*s*] *glacés*. **1925** C. SIDGWICK *Humming-Bird* xviii. 188 Behind the loaded counter the proprietor and his assistants were weighing chocolates and marrons glacés. **1967** 'L. BLACK' *Two Ladies in Verona* ii. 18 A low table garnished with..an enormous box of marrons glacés. **1973** *Times* 1 Dec. 14/1 Marrons glacés. 14 oz. tins. 2 for £5.20... Marrons in syrup. Large whole chestnuts in extra heavy syrup..18 oz. tins. 3 for £5.25.

marroquin, obs. form of MAROQUIN.

marrot (ˈmærət). Also **marrock, marrott, morrot, murot.** [Origin obscure; cf. MURRE.] A local name for the guillemot, razor-bill, and puffin.

1710 SIBBALD *Hist. Fife* 48 *Alka Hoieri*: Our People call it the Marrot, the Auk or Razor-Bill. **1863** KINGSLEY *Water-Bab.* 259 The very marrocks and dovekies have got wings. **1880** *Act 43 & 44 Vict.* c. 35 (*Wild Birds Protect. Act*) Sched. Marrot.

marrou, marrouh, obs. ff. MARROW *sb.*^{2} and *sb.*^{1}

marrow (ˈmærəʊ), *sb.*^{1} Forms: α. 1 **maerȝ, merȝ, mearh, mærh**, 4 **merȝ, marȝ**, 4–5 **margh(e,** (5 **margthe**, 6 **marthe**), 4–5 *northern* **merghe**, 4–6 *northern*, 6–9 *Sc.* **mergh**, 4–9 *Sc.* **merch**, (6 *Sc.* **mairch**). β. 4 **maruȝ, mar(r)ouh, merouȝ, -owȝ,** 4–5 **marouȝ**, 5– 6 **marughe**, 6 **marough(e**, 4 **merewe**, 4–5 **merow(e**, 5 **maro**, 4–5 **marw(e**, (5 **marwhe**), 5–6 **merwe**, 5 **marew**, 4–7 **marowe**, 6–7 **marrowe**, 6– **marrow**. γ. 3 **meari**, 4–6 **mary(e**, (5 **marigh, merryghe**), 5–6 **maree, marie**, 6 **marry**. [Com. Teut.: OE. *mearȝ*, *mearh* (Anglian *merȝ*, *mærh*) neut. (once masc.), corresponds to OFris. *merg*, *merch* neut. and masc., OS. *marg* (MDu. *march*, *marg-*, mod.Du. *merg* neut.), OHG. *marg*, *marag* neut. (MHG. *marc*, *marg-*, mod.G. *mark* neut.), ON. *merg-r* masc. (Sw. *merg*, *märg*, Da. *marv*):—OTeut. **mazgo-*:—pre-Teut. **mozgho-*, corresponding to OSl., Russian *mozg*, Avestic *mazga*; the Skr. *majjan* is anomalous, as it would point to an OAryan type with *g* instead of *gh*.]

1. a. The soft vascular fatty substance usually contained in the cavities of bones. (The marrow of animals used for food is regarded as a dainty.)

In OE. the word occurs as a gloss on *lucanica*, which means a sort of sausage; but this was prob. a mistranslation.

a **700** *Epinal Gloss.*, *Lucanica*, maerh. *c* **725** *Corpus Gloss.* (Hessels) L 294 *Lucanica*, mærh. *Ibid.* M 195 *Medulla*, merȝ. *c* **1000** *Sax. Leechd.* I. 366 Wið..leoða sarum nim leon ȝelynde & heortes mearȝ. **10..** *Ags. Voc.* in Wr.-Wülcker 292/10 *Medulla*, mearh. *a* **1225** *Juliana* 58 þat meari weol ut imenget wið blode. *c* **1375** *Sc. Leg. Saints* xlviii (*Juliana*) 161 Syne hir banys sa to-quassyt, þat þe self merch out passyt. **1382** WYCLIF *Job* xxi. 24 The bones of hym ben moistid with marȝ [**1388** merowis]. **1382** —— *Ps.* lxv[i]. 15 Brent sacrifises ful of merȝ [**1388** merowȝ] I shal offre to thee. *c* **1386** CHAUCER *Pard. T.* 214 Out of the harde bones knokke they The mary. *c* **1400** *Lanfranc's Cirurg.* 47 Þe schuldre to þe elbowe be kutt al atwo, so þat þe marie go out. **14..** *Nom.* in Wr.-Wülcker 678/36 *Hec medulla*, margthe. **1426** LYDG. *De Guil. Pilgr.* 24216 First I souke vp (for the nones) The mary closed in the bones. *c* **1440** *Anc. Cookery* in *Househ. Ord.* (1790) 453 Take..pouder of pepur, and maree, and tempur hit togedur. *c* **1430** *Two Cookery-bks.* 44 Þen take merow, & putte it on a straynourys ende. *Ibid.* 51 Take fayre Marwe, & Datys y-cutte in ij or iij & Prunez. **1513** DOUGLAS *Æneis* IV. ii. 38 The subtell quent fyre Waistis and consumis merch, banis, and lyre. **1528** PAYNELL *Salerne's Regim.* G iij, The mary of veale..is moste holsome. **1533** ELYOT *Cast. Helthe* (1539) 31 Marowe is more dilectable than the brayne. **1541** R. COPLAND *Guydon's Quest. Chirurg.* C j b, The membres colde and moyste are the flewme, fat or the grece, and the maroughes. **1562** BULLEYN *Bk. Simples* 86 b, What saie you of Mary, whiche in some place is called Marthe; contained within the bone of beastes? **1567** GOLDING *Ovid's Met.* IX. (1593) 215 The poyson even in his bones the maree melts at length. **1575** TURBERV. *Faulconrie* 297 That done, take suger clarified, and the Maree of a Beefe. **1717** PRIOR *Alma* III. 214 He din'd on Lion's marrow, spread On toasts of ammunition-bread. **1769** MRS. RAFFALD *Eng. Housekpr.* (1778) 179 Shred half a pound of marrow very fine. **1823** BYRON *Juan* VII. viii, By Souvaroff, or Anglicè Suwarrow, Who loved blood as an alderman loves marrow. **1896** CLELAND & MACKAY *Anat.* 30 Marrow is of two kinds, the yellow..and the red.

b. Proverbial and hyperbolical uses. (In 16th–17th c. love was often said to 'burn' or 'melt the marrow'.)

1520 WHITINTON *Vulg.* (1527) 27 b, A man myghte as soone pyke mary out of a mattock, as [etc.]. **1592** SHAKS. *Ven. & Ad.* 142 My flesh is soft, and plumpe, my marrow burning. **1594** NASHE *Unfort. Trav.* Wks. (Grosart) V. 168 They basted him with a mixture of Aqua fortis, allam water, and Mercury sublimatum, which..searcht him to the marrowe. **1697** DRYDEN *Virg. Georg.* III. 428 When at the Spring's Approach their Marrow burns..The Mares to cliffs of rugged Rocks repair. **1763** CHURCHILL *Duellist* I, O for a noble curse Which might his very marrow pierce. **1798** SOUTHEY *Bp. Bruno* 62 His marrow grew cold at the touch of Death. **1840** DICKENS *Barn. Rudge* xvii, The very marrow in my bones is cold. **1886** KIPLING *Depart. Ditties* (1888) 22 For twenty reeking minutes, Sir, my very marrow froze.

c. The substance forming the spinal cord. Now always ***spinal marrow***.

1398 TREVISA *Barth. De P.R.* v. lviii. (1495) 174 The marowe..of the rydge bones..is callyd Mycha amonge physicyens. **1533** ELYOT *Cast. Helthe* I. i. (1541) 13 The mary of the backbone. **1615** CROOKE *Body of Man* 871 Of these Nerues..others are deriued from the Brayne and the spinall Marrow. **1626** BACON *Sylva* §750 The Skull hath Braines, as a kinde of Marrow, within it. The Back-Bone hath one Kinde of Marrow, which hath an Affinity with the Braine. **1874** CARPENTER *Ment. Phys.* I. ii. §61 (1879) 62 The spinal cord (commonly termed the spinal marrow).

†**d.** Used (chiefly after L. *medulla*) for: The pith (of a plant); the pulp (of a fruit). Also ***marrow of wheat***: a literal rendering of *medulla tritici* (Vulgate), the finest flour. *Obs.*

c **1000** *Sax. Leechd.* II. 358 Wiþ maȝan wærce wudu þistles þone grenan mearh þe biþ on þam heafde sele him etan mid hatan ele. *c* **1340** HAMPOLE tr. *Deut.* xxxii. 14 (¶21) in *Psalter* (1884) 516 And gayte with merghe of whete. [Similarly **1382**, **1388** WYCLIF and **1609** (Douay).] *c* **1374** CHAUCER *Boeth.* III. pr. xi. 84 (Camb. MS.), [Herbes and trees] shedyn by hyr maryes hyr wode and hyr bark. **1398** TREVISA *Barth. De P.R.* XI. vi. (Tollem. MS.), He [*sc.* dew] ..makeþ floure, piþþe and marghe encrese in corne and graynes. *c* **1420** *Pallad. on Husb.* IV. 477 Thay seyn their bitter margh wol chaunge swete. *Ibid.* XI. 236 Yf a tender tree Me kitte at footis tweyne, and thenne hit cleue Vnto the roote, and with an yron se The mary rased out. **1562** TURNER *Herbal* II. A j b, It that is within, whiche they cal the marye, the pythe, and the harte. **1567** MAPLET *Gr. Forest* 30 The Alder tree..is in his Wood and inwarde Marie very soft. **1623** BINGHAM *Xenophon* 31 This was the place, where the Souldiers first fed vpon the Marrow of the Nuts of Palme. **1727** BRADLEY *Fam. Dict.* s.v. *Cive*, Take some sweet Almonds.., pound 'em with some Vinegar, and strain 'em thro' a Linnen-cloth.., that you may have the Marrow or Milk of them. **1793** MARTYN *Lang. Bot.*, Marrow, *Medulla.* The pith of a vegetable.

2. In various figurative applications.

a. Taken as the type of rich and nutritious food. Chiefly in the Bible phrase ***marrow and fatness***.

1382 WYCLIF *Gen.* xlv. 18 And I shal ȝyue to ȝow al the goodis of Egipte, that ȝe eeten the mary of the loond [Vulg. *medullam terræ*]. **1535** COVERDALE *Ps.* lxii[i]. 5 My soule is satisfied euen as it were with marry & fatnesse. **1818** HAZLITT *Eng. Poets* vi. (1870) 151 His words are of marrow —unctuous, dropping fatness. **1845** JAMES *A. Neil* iv, He left that paper with me, which he said must be marrow and fatness to all well-disposed noblemen like yourself.

b. Viewed as the seat of animal vitality and strength.

c **1425** *Seven Sag.* (P.) 1685 My lordys merryghe hys welne gone. **1576** FLEMING *Panopl. Epist.* 154 If I were in the pearle of my youth, and had in my bones marrowe..I wold not [etc.]. **1601** SHAKS. *All's Well* II. iii. 298 Spending his manlie marrow in her armes. **1602** *2nd Pt. Return fr. Parnass.* IV. iii. 1935 Spending the marrow of their flowring age In fruitelesse poring on some worme eate leafe. **1793** HOLCROFT tr. *Lavater's Physiogn.* xvii. 87 All English women..appear to be composed of marrow and nerve. *a* **1823** G. BEATTIE *John o' Arnha'* (1826) 40 Alack-a-day! waesucks for John! His mergh an' mettle now are gone. **1847** DISRAELI *Sybil* (Rtldg.) 315, I always was against washing; it takes the marrow out of a man. **1848** LYTTON *Harold* v. iii, The pith and marrow of manhood.

c. The inmost or central part.

c **1400** *Apol. Loll.* 91 Wene we not þe gospel to be in wordis of writingis, but in wit; not in ouer face, but in þe merowe. **1434** MISYN *Mend. Life* 118 Þe inhirliest mergh of our hartis. **1549** COVERDALE, etc. *Erasm. Par. Jas.* 28 Expressing by godly workes, that which he sticked fast in the marye of the soule. **1821** LAMB *Elia* Ser. I. *My Relations*, He never pierces the marrow of your habits.

d. The vital or essential part; the essence; the 'goodness'. Formerly often in titles of books. Often ***pith and marrow***.

1530 TINDALE *Answ. More* Pref. *Wks.* (1573) 247/2 He neuer leaueth searchyng till he come at the bottome, the pith, the quicke, the lyfe, the spirit, the marow, & very cause why. ?*c* **1560** ROLLAND *Seuin Seages* 261 This was the Mairch of the mater in deid. **1570** BILLINGSLEY *Euclid* x. def. 11. 232 Wherein standeth the pith and mary of the hole science. **1599** *Broughton's Let.* vii. 20 You set vpon him with this..Libell, wherein is contained the marrow of your wisedome. **1614** T. GENTLEMAN *Eng. Way to Wealth* 12 They haue sucked out all the marrow of the Mault and good Scotsh-ale. **1640** T. B[RUGIS] (*title*) The Marrow of Physicke. **1647** TRAPP (*title*) Mellificium Theologicum or the Marrow of Many good Authours. **1650** S. CLARK (*title*) The Marrow of Ecclesiastical Historie. **1653** MILTON *Hirelings* Wks. 1851 V. 383 To how little purpose are all those piles of Sermons,..Bodies and Marrows of Divinity, besides all other Sciences, in our English Tongue. **1665** BUNYAN *Holy Citie* (1669) 169 Christ in all his Benefits is the very Marrow, Life and Sum of all their Teaching. *a* **1680** CHARNOCK *Delight in Prayer* Wks. (1849) 231 Delight is the marrow of religion. **1763** COLMAN *Deuce is in him* Prol., Thus gave at once the bards of Greece, The cream and marrow of the piece. **1862** MERIVALE *Rom. Emp.* lv. (1865) VII. 12 The clients and retainers of the old nobility..still formed the pith and marrow of the commonwealth.

e. Short for 'The Marrow of Modern Divinity', the title of a book (advocating strongly Calvinistic views) written by E. F. in 1645, the condemnation of which by the General Assembly of the Church of Scotland in 1720 led to a prolonged controversy. Used attrib. as in ***Marrow controversy***; also **Marrow-men**, the designation of those members of the Assembly who defended the book.

1720 T. BOSTON *Mem.* (1899) 351 The assembly's act condemning the Marrow. **1725** WODROW in *W. Corresp.* (1843) III. 204 The Marrow people. *Ibid.* 205 The Marrow affair was ended. **1853** BURTON *Hist. Scot.* II. 319 Those who adhered to this document, received the party-title of the Marrow-men. *Ibid.*, The Marrow controversy. **1894** CROCKETT *Lilac Sunbonnet* i. 12 Allan Welsh, minister of the Marrow Kirk in the parish of Dullarg.

3. vegetable marrow: a. A kind of gourd, the fruit of *Cucurbita ovifera*, used as a table vegetable.

1816 J. SABINE in *Trans. Hort. Soc.* (1822) II. 255 (*title of paper*) A Description and Account of the Cultivation of a Variety of Gourd called Vegetable Marrow. **1882** *Garden* 25 Mar. 191/3 In no other country does one see so many Vegetable Marrows as in this.

b. The fruit of the avocado, *Persea gratissima*.

1763 [see AVOCADO]. **1866** *Treas. Bot.* 867/1.

4. A marrowfat pea.

1882 *Garden* 15 July 58/3 A dwarf round blue Marrow.

5. *attrib.* and *Comb.*, as ***marrow-eater***; ***marrow-boiling***, ***-burning***, ***-chilling***, ***-eating***, ***-freezing***, ***-like***, ***-melting***, ***-piercing***, ***-searching***, ***-thrilling*** adjs.; **marrow cell** *Histology*, one of a particular class of cells (resembling enlarged white blood corpuscles) occurring in marrow; **marrow kale** = *marrow-stem (kale)*; **marrow oil**, a dressing for the hair (cf. MARROWFAT 2); **marrow pasty**, = *marrow pie*; **marrow pea**, = *marrowfat pea*; **marrow pie**, a pie containing beef marrow; **marrow pudding**, (*a*) a pudding made with (beef or vegetable) marrow; (*b*) *West Indian*, a kind of worm; **marrow scoop** = *marrow-spoon*; **marrow sheath**, the white matter of Schwann surrounding the cylinder axis of a medullated nerve fibre (*Syd. Soc. Lex.* 1889); **marrow-spoon**, a spoon for extracting the marrow from bones; **marrow-squash**, an American name for the vegetable marrow (Webster 1864); **marrow-stem (kale)** = CHOU MOELLIER (see quot. 1925); also ***marrow-stemmed kale***.

1598 SYLVESTER *Du Bartas* II. i. I. *Eden* 537 Their *marrow-boyling loves. **1592** KYD *Sol. & Pers.* v. ii. 14 Such is the force of *marrow burning loue. **1877** SCHÄFER *Histol.* 92 The so-called proper *marrow-cells. **1612** W. PARKES *Curtaine-Dr.* (1876) 16 Lust, the *marrow-eater of the world, the canker of health. **1592** SHAKS. *Ven. & Ad.* 741 The *marrow-eating sicknesse, whose attaint Disorder breeds by heating of the blood. **1847** C. BRONTË *Jane Eyre* I. xv. 295 A *marrow-freezing incident enough. This was a demoniac laugh. **1900** *Sketch* 21 Feb. 191/2 A play..of a rather marrow-freezing kind. **1872** R. HOGG in *Jrnl. Roy. Hort. Soc.* III. 174 *Marrow Kale..is the *Chou moellier* of the French, a form of the Jersey kale which produces a long, thickly swollen stem like a gigantic cigar, the swollen part being filled with a mass of tender pith. **1894** H. NISBET *Bush Girl's Rom.* 184 The large succulent grubs..which the natives enjoy either roasted or raw, delicate *marrow-like pupæ. **1897** *Allbutt's Syst. Med.* IV. 756 A gumma which looks yellowish and marrow-like just before breaking down. *a* **1618** SYLVESTER *Tetrastica* xlvi. (Grosart) II. 27 That heart-swelting, *Marrow-melting Fire. **1855** F. DUBERLY *Let.* 29 Jan. in E. E. P. Tisdall *Mrs. Duberly's Campaigns* (1963) iv. 124, I want you to write to Savory & Moore, Bond St. for 2 Large Bottles *Marrow Oil, 4 Bottles of Bandoline. **1864** TROLLOPE *Can You forgive Her?* I. xl. 310 All his apparatus for dressing,—his marrow oil for his hair, [etc.]. **1696** SALMON *Fam. Dict.* (ed. 2), **Marrow-Pasty*: Take six Marrow-Bones [etc.]. **1733** TULL *Horse-Hoeing Husb.* xxii. 349 Sufficient for all sorts of Corn and Seeds which we commonly sow, from *Marrow Pease to Turnep-seed. **1598** MARSTON *Sco. Villanie* iii. 71 Hence Holy-thistle, come sweet *marrow pie, Inflame our backs to itching luxurie. **1674** T. P. etc. *Eng. & Fr. Cook* 157 Marrow Pyes. Take Veal, mince it [etc.]. **1616** B. JONSON *Devil is an Ass* II. i, No youths, disguis'd Like country-wiues, with creame, and *marrow-puddings. **1664** BUTLER *Hud.* II. ii. 794 Pamper'd and edifi'd their Zeal With Marrow-puddings many a Meal. **1789** P. BROWNE *Jamaica* 383 Fasciola 4. Marina major verucosa. The warted Marrow-Pudding. Fasciola 5. Marina maxima glabra. The large smooth Marrow-Pudding. **1846** D. JERROLD *Mrs. Caudle* xi, And then you recollect her marrow puddings? **1969** E. H. PINTO *Treen* 79 The *marrow scoop and toothpick are missing. **1970** *Canad. Antiques Collector* Mar. 23/1 There were numerous objects ..such as soup ladles..marrow scoops. **1972** *Collector's Guide* Aug. 10/2 (Advt.), Fine Marrow Scoop (crested), by Wm. Chawner, 1763, £40. **1627–47** FELTHAM *Resolves* 405 Wishing..that he had such wings as could procure his escape from death and *marrow-searching Judgment. **1693** *Lond. Gaz.* No. 2853/4, 1 Sweat-meat Spoon, 1 *Marrow Spoon, 1 Ladle and Skillet. **1795** WALKER in *Phil. Trans.* LXXXV. 273, I use a marrow-spoon. **1920** *Conquest* Apr. 256/3 In place of grass it is possible to grow crops such as cabbage, vetches, rape, *marrowstem kale, [etc.]. **1925** MALDEN & NISBET in W. G. R. Paterson *Farm Crops* II. 191 The Marrow-stem Kale is what is known as a 'variety-hybrid'. That is, it is the result of crossing two distinct varieties—the kohl-rabi and the Thousandhead Kale, each a variety of *Brassica oleracea*. *Ibid.* 194 Mildews and moulds do less damage to the marrow stem than to turnips. **1960** *Farmer & Stockbreeder* 8 Mar. 131/2 Marrow-stem kale goes fibrous and woody very quickly after Christmas, and loses most of its feeding value. **1961** I. MOLNAR *Man. Austral. Agric.* 214 The Marrow Stemmed Kale (chou mollier) is a kale with a swollen axis. **1972** D. H. ROBINSON *Fream's Elem. Agric.* (ed. 15) x. 281 Marrowstem Kale is capable of producing very large quantities of greenstuff greatly relished by stock. **1888** FENN *Dick o' the Fens* 281 A strange *marrow-thrilling cry.

marrow ('mærəʊ), *sb.*[2] *Obs.* exc. *dial.* Also 5 **maroo, marwe,** 5–7 **marow(e,** 6 **mar(r)ou, marrowe, marroll,** 7 **marroe.** [Of obscure origin.

The localities would seem to point to a Scandinavian etymology, but no possible Scandinavian source is known, unless indeed the sense of the Eng. sb. can have been developed from that of ON. *marg-r* (lit. 'many') friendly, communicative. Phonologically this etymon would be admissible, as the word occurs so late that the absence of recorded forms with guttural causes no difficulty.]

1. a. A companion, fellow-worker, partner, mate.

c **1440** *Promp. Parv.* 327/2 Marwe, or felawe yn trauayle, *socius, compar.* *c* **1460** *Towneley Myst.* xiii. 436 Com coll and his maroo, Thay will nyp vs full naroo. *c* **1470** HENRYSON *Mor. Fab.* XIII. (*Frog & Mouse*) xxii, Better but stryfe allane to leif in le, Than to be matchit with ane wickit marrow. **1513** DOUGLAS *Æneis* VI. ix. 9 Bot sone hym warnis Sibilla.. His trew marrow [L. *comes*]. **1561** *Reg. Privy Council Scot.* I. 159 That nane of thame speik nor commoun of ony mater nor round with his marrow. **1573** TUSSER *Husb.* (1878) 134 Yet chopping and changing I cannot commend, with theefe and his marrow, for feare of ill end. **1577** GRANGE *Gold. Aphrod.* F iii b, Forsakyng his marroll [*i.e.* his partner in a dance]. *a* **1578** LINDESAY (Pitscottie) *Chron. Scot.* (S.T.S.) I. 193 Quhair he was lyand with his marrow and companioun Sir Edward braikinberrie. **1578** WHETSTONE *1st Pt. Promos & Cassand.* II. iv, Marrowes adew: God send you fayre wether. **1621** B. JONSON *Metam. Gipsies* Wks. 1640 II. 68 Oh, my deare marrowes! **1645** RUTHERFORD *Tryal & Tri. Faith* (1845) 325 Faith with love cannot endure a marrow. **1822** GALT *Sir A. Wylie* I. v. 37 It was nae a richt thing o' us to be marrows in ony sic trade wi' cripple Janet. **1843** HARDY in *Proc. Berw. Nat. Club* II. No. 11. 54 Only two individuals play, but they can have an indefinite number of marrows or sidesmen. **1860** *Eng. & For. Min. Gloss.* (Newcastle Terms), *Marrow*, a partner. **1935** A. J. CRONIN *Stars look Down* I. ii. 20 His dad had gone with the marrows in his set. *Ibid.* xxii. 205 Jack Reedy..and his marrow, Cha Leeming, worked their shift in the Scupper Flats.

¶**b.** Apparently misunderstood by Blount.

1656 BLOUNT *Glossogr.*, *Marrow* (Fr. *marauld*), a fellow, a knave, or Rascal.

2. A husband or wife. (Cf. HALF-MARROW 1.)

a **1578** LINDESAY (Pitscottie) *Chron. Scot.* (S.T.S.) II. 132, I maryed ane puire woman to be marrow to me. **1632** RUTHERFORD *Lett.* (1862) I. 97 Christ's fair Bride, a marrow dear to Him. **1721** RAMSAY *Mary Scot* iii, When Mary Scot's become my marrow, We'll make a paradise on Yarrow. **1724** W. HAMILTON *Braes of Yarrow* i, Busk ye, busk ye, my bony bony bride, Busk ye, busk ye, my winsome marrow. **1816** SCOTT *Rob Roy* xxxv, I hae been misdoubting your cousin Rashleigh since ever he saw that he wasna to get Die Vernon for his marrow.

3. a. One's equal or like; one's match in a contest.

1548 *Compl. Scot.* xx. 173 Iulius vald nocht hef ane marrou in rome, and pompeus vald nocht hef ane superior. *a* **1572** KNOX *Hist. Ref.* Wks. (1846) I. 89 Thare did everie man reaconter his marrow. *a* **1578** LINDESAY (Pitscottie) *Chron. Scot.* (S.T.S.) I. 174 He contit no lord to be marrow to him. **1637** RUTHERFORD *Lett.* (1862) I. 300 You have many marrows. **1896** 'IAN MACLAREN' *Kate Carnegie* 212 Ay, ye may traivel the warld ower or ye see his marrow.

b. Used of things.

1596 DALRYMPLE tr. *Leslie's Hist. Scot.* I. 46 The toune.. standes in sa pleisand a place, that it hes na marrow. *c* **1690** N. BURN *Leader-haughs* 15 in *Roxb. Ball.* VI. 607 One house there stands on Leader side..Men passing by do often say in [th'] South it has no marrow. **1891** BARRIE *Little Minister* xv, Sam'l Fairweather has the marrows o't on his top coat.

4. A thing which makes a pair with another.

1674 RAY *N.C. Words* 31 A pair of gloves or shoes are not marrows, i.e. fellows. **1681** COLVIL *Whigs Supplic.* (1751) 18 Some had bows, but wanted arrows; Some had pistols without marrows. **1737** RAMSAY *Sc. Prov.* (1797) 101 Your een's no marrows. **1787** J. BEATTIE *Scoticisms* 16 My buckles are not marrows. **1855** ROBINSON *Whitby Gloss.*, *Marrows*, pairs to match; fellows or equals. **1889** BARRIE *Thrums* xv. 138 Wearin' a pair o' boots 'at wisna marrows!

†**marrow**, *a. Obs.* exc. *dial.* [From the appositive use of MARROW *sb.*[2]] Resembling something of the same kind.

1585 *Inv. R. Wardr.* (1815) 320, I ressavit of the marrow garnissing of thir fourtene pece thre chattonis, quhilk makis xvii in the haill. **1861** E. WAUGH *Birtle Carter's T.* 21 Aw never sprad my e'en upo' th' marrow trick to this!

marrow ('mærəʊ), *v. Sc.* and *north.* [f. MARROW *sb.*[2]]

†**1.** *trans.* To join, associate; to match, pair. Also *refl. Obs.*

1488 *Burgh Recs. Edinb.* (1869) I. 55 Sic a burges bot na vther persoun marrow him with ane maister of substance [etc.]. **1542** *Sc. Acts Mary* (1814) II. 414/2 Ane to be put and marrowit to paim by my lord gouernour at his plesoure. **1823** GALT *Entail* I. xvii. 132 Charlie Walkinshaw and Bell Fatherlans were a couple marrowed by their Maker.

b. *intr.* To be a partner or fellow-worker (*with*).

1538 *Aberdeen Reg.* XVI. (Jam.), To marrow and nychtbour with wtheris. **1842** J. AITON *Domestic Econ.* (1857) 152 Saunders Heavyside, with whom he marrows. **1844** THOM *Rhymes* 53 Hae ye fausely strayed 'mang misty groves, Wi' ice-wreathed maidens to marrow. **1851** A. MACLAGAN *Poems* 280 He's wise wha marrows wi' content, Though in a rustic biel'.

2. *trans.* To be a companion to; to marry.

1721 RAMSAY *Mary Scot* i, Did you there see me mark'd to marrow Mary Scot the flow'r of Yarrow? **17..** *Song by a Buchan Ploughman* in *Burns' Wks.* (1800) II. 152 Thou shalt not sit single, but by a clear ingle I'll marrow thee, Nancy, when thou art my ain.

3. To resemble, to be equal to; also, to produce something equal to; to match.

a **1586** MONTGOMERIE *Misc. Poems* l. 38 Venus..Wald have preferrit this paragon, As marrowit, but matche, most meit The goldin ball to bruik alone. **1785** W. HUTTON *Bran New Wark* l. 14 (E.D.S.) On the sabbath we say aur prayers, and the rest of the week ya day marrows another. **1877** P. BURN *Poems* (1885) 294 A beild I hae that marrows thy ain.

marrowbone ('mærəʊbəʊn). [f. MARROW *sb.*[1]]

1. A bone containing edible marrow.

c **1386** CHAUCER *Prol.* 380 A Cook they hadde with hem for the nones, To boille the chiknes with the Marybones. *c* **1430** *Two Cookery-bks.* 5 Take beeff and merybonys, and boyle yt in fayre water. **1555** W. WATREMAN *Fardle Facions* II. vii. 158 The bridegrome eateth to his supper..a litle of the maribone of a Chamel. **1632** T. MORTON *New Eng. Canaan* II. vii. (1838) 59 For daintinesse of diet they [Basse] excell the Marybones of Beefe. **1768–74** TUCKER *Lt. Nat.* (1834) II. 655 There is no more reason..why the sight of a human skull and bones in a charnel-house should shock us more than the sight of a calve's head or a pair of marrow-bones in a dish. **1846** G. WARBURTON *Hochelaga* I. 155 The wretch sucked a couple more marrow bones, and became torpid.

b. *fig.* in various applications.

1554 LATIMER *Wks.* (Parker Soc.) II. 483 Ye said upon Saturday last, that ye could not find the mass nor the marrow-bones thereof in your book. **1634** S. R. *Noble Soldier* I. ii. in Bullen *O. Pl.* (1882) I. 268 What I knocke out now is the very Maribone of mirth. **1681** W. ROBERTSON *Phraseol. Gen.* (1693) 471 This is the marrow bone of the difference or matter. **1878** *N. Amer. Rev.* CXXVII. 13 The scraps and marrow-bones of office.

2. ***marrowbones and cleavers***: see CLEAVER[1] 2 b.

3. *pl.* Jocularly: The knees. (Rarely *sing.*)

1532 MORE *Confut. Tindale* Wks. 727/2 Down he fel vpon his maribones. **1667** DRYDEN & DK. NEWCASTLE *Sir M. Mar-all* II. ii, Down on your marrowbones, and confess the truth. **1791** WOLCOT (P. Pindar) *Remonstrance* i, Bring on his marrowbones th' apostate down. **1870** KINGSLEY *Legend La Brea* 95 Magic brings some positivists Humbly on their marrowbone. **1888** G. MACDONALD *Elect Lady* 108, I only want to bring them to their marrow-bones.

b. ***to ride in the marrow-bone coach*** or ***stage***, to go on foot. [? With allusion to *Marybone* = *Marylebone*.]

1838 *Monthly Mag.* (Flügel), Marrow-bone stage.

4. *pl.* = CROSS-BONES.

1832 SCOTT *Redgauntlet* ch. xiv. [xv.], I..sailed under the black flag and marrow-bones. **1875** W. MCILWRAITH *Guide Wigtownshire* 40 Here are the typical marrow-bones, skull, and sandglass.

5. *pl.* (*slang*). Fists as weapons; ? pugilists.

a **1625** FLETCHER *Noble Gent.* III. i. (1st fol.) 35/1 The great Band Of Maribones that people call the Switzers. **1812** *Sporting Mag.* XL. 249 He was alike a stranger to fear in the field of either bayonets or marrowbones. **1818** *Ibid.* N.S. II. 165 The distance of twenty-four miles from Lunnun rather damped the ardour of the Marrow-bone fraternity.

†**6.** A child's game. *Obs.*

1532 MORE *Confut. Tindale* Wks. 574/2 Suche..playes.. as chyldren be woont to playe, as cheristone, mary bone [etc.].

7. *attrib.*, as †***marrowbone-man*** (? sense 2 ? or 5), ***music***, ***pie***, ***pudding*** (cf. *marrow pie*, *pudding*).

1614 B. JONSON *Barth. Fair* I. i, None but a scatterd couey of Fidlers, or one of these Rag-rakers in dung-hills, or some *Marrow-bone man at most, would haue beene vp, when thou wert gone abroad. **1884** *Graphic* 13 Sept. 270/3 Making the most unearthly '*marrow-bone' music on frying pans, tin kettles and empty pails. **1595** W. W. *Menæcmi* I. ii. in *Six Old Plays* (1779) 118 Some oysters, a *mary-bone pie or two, some artichockes, and potato rootes. **1608** MIDDLETON *Mad World* I. ii. B 1 b, All her wanton Pamphlets, as Hero and Leander, Venus and Adonis, oh two lushious mary-bone pies for a yong married wife. **1623** WEBSTER *Deuils Law-case* I. ii. B 4 b, Let none of these come at her..Nor the woman with *Maribone puddings.

marrowed ('mærəʊd), *ppl. a.* Also 4 **merghed, meryhed.** [f. MARROW *sb.*[1] + -ED[2].]

1. Full of marrow. *lit.* and *fig.*

a **1300** *E.E. Psalter* lxv[i]. 15 Offrandes merghed [Vulg. *holocausta medullata*] bede I sal To þe. *a* **1340** HAMPOLE *Psalter* ibid. **1612** AINSWORTH *Annot. Ps.* lxvi. 15 Marrowed rammes: that is, fat and lusty. **1644** QUARLES *Barnabas & B.* I. (1651) 19 They can..devour and gurmundize..and wipe the guilt from off their marrowed mouths. **1654** GATAKER *Disc. Apol.* 84 Some called Separatists..are better marowed, and more Evangelical, then these Pulpit *Ignesfatui.* **1840** BROWNING *Sordello* v. 500 He was fresh-sinewed every joint, Each bone new-marrowed.

†**2.** Cooked in marrow. *Obs.*

1633 MASSINGER *Guardian* II. iii, Fride Frogs, Potato's Marrow'd, Cavear [etc.].

marrowfat ('mærəʊfæt). [f. MARROW *sb.*¹ + FAT *sb.*] **1.** (More fully ***marrowfat pea.***) A kind of large rich pea. (Cf. *marrow pea*, MARROW *sb.*¹ 5.)

1733 MILLER *Gard. Dict.* (ed. 2) s.v. *Pisum*, The Marrowfat or Dutch Admiral Pea. *Ibid.*, Observing to allow the Marrow-fats..at least three Feet between Row and Row. **1766** *Complete Farmer* s.v. *Pease*, The marrowfat is the best tasted of all the large kinds of peas. **1840** BARHAM *Ingol. Leg.* Ser. I. *Tragedy*, The Duchess shed tears large as marrow-fat peas. **1864** *Reader* 13 Aug. 191 In Jersey..peas attain nearly double the size of the British marrow-fat.

2. *N. Amer.* A tallow-like substance prepared by boiling down marrow.

1717 J. KNIGHT *Jrnl.* 16 Aug. (1932) 164 These Indians gave me..2 pretty bigg bladders of Marrow fatt. **1791** in *Publ. Champlain Soc.* (1934) XXI. 528 They broke the Bones of the Buffalo & made marrowfatt. **1841** G. CATLIN *Lett. on N. Amer. Indians* I. 116 'Marrow-fat' is collected by the Indians from the buffalo bones which they break to pieces, yielding a prodigious quantity of marrow, which is boiled out and put into buffalo bladders. **1846** R. B. SAGE *Scenes Rocky Mts.* viii. 79 Marrow-fat, an article in many respects superior to butter. **1888** *Century Mag.* XXXVI. 898/1 Then he slicked his hair with marrow-fat from a horn. **1947** *Beaver* Dec. 21 Clean Marrow fat rendered down like white butter.

†**3.** *U.S. slang.* (See quot.) *Obs.*

1903 A. B. HART *Actual Govt. Amer. Conditions* 75 The 'marrow-fat' fraud consists in a voter's putting in more than one ballot, while the clerk puts down fictitious names to cover the extra ballots.

marrowish ('mærəʊɪʃ), *a.* [f. MARROW *sb.*¹ + -ISH.] Of the nature of, or resembling, marrow.

1597 LOWE *Chirurg.* (1634) 143 The nerue which is soft, and marrowish. **1621** BURTON *Anat. Mel.* I. i. II. iv, The Braine, which is a soft marrowish and white substance.

marrowless ('mærəʊlɪs), *a.*¹ [f. MARROW *sb.*¹ + -LESS.] Having no marrow. *lit.* and *fig.*

1605 SHAKS. *Macb.* III. iv. 94 Thy bones are marrowlesse, thy blood is cold. **1607** TOURNEUR *Rev. Trag.* I. i, O, that marrow-lesse age Should stuffe the hollow Bones with dambd desires. **1707** tr. *Wks. C'tess D'Anois* (1715) 451 Break off this ungodly Match between this Marrowless Curmudgeon and your young Daughter. *a* **1823** G. BEATTIE *John o' Arnha'* (1826) 58 They..lent each other ruthless paiks Athort the bare and merghless spaiks. **1877** ROSENTHAL *Muscles & Nerves* 104 These marrowless fibres are grey.

'marrowless, *a.*² *dial.* [f. MARROW *sb.*² + -LESS.] Without a 'marrow'; companionless; unmarried; unequalled, unmatched; not matching, wanting the other member of the pair, 'odd'.

1637 RUTHERFORD *Lett.* (1862) I. 433 My matchless, and my most marrowless and marvellous Wellbeloved. **1660** DICKSON *Sel. Writ.* (1845) I. 58 Know thou art not marrowless in thy exercise. **1844** CROSS *Disruption* xxiii. (E.D.D.), A marrowless glove.

†**'marrowship.** *Sc. Obs.* [f. MARROW *sb.*² + -SHIP.] Association, companionship.

15.. *Aberd. Reg.* (Jam.), Throucht falt of marrowschip or insufficient nychtbourschip.

marrowsky (mə'raʊskɪ). Also **marouski, Marowsky, morowski, mowrowsky.** [Asserted to have been derived from the name of a Polish count, doubtfully identified with Count Joseph Boruwlaski. See *N. & Q.* 13th Ser. I. 331, 437, 467.] **a.** A variety of slang, or a slip in speaking, characterized by transposition of initial letters, syllables, or parts of two words. Also ***marrowsky language.***

1863 R. NICHOLSON *Autobiogr. Fast Man* xviii. 200 Fanny King, or as Bill Leach, in the interesting language called *Marouski*, termed her, Kanny Fing. **1883** G. A. SALA *Living London* 491 The vocabulary of Tim Bobbin, Josh Billings,..and the 'Marowsky' language.

b. An instance of this.

1923 in *N. & Q.* 27 Oct. 331/2 In my childhood..an old cousin used to entertain me with what we now call *spoonerisms*, but which she termed *morowskis.* **1962** V. NABOKOV *Pale Fire* 185, I remember one perfect evening when my friend sparkled with quips, and marrowskies, and anecdotes.

Hence **ma'rrowskyer**, one who uses marrowsky language or makes marrowskies in his speech; **ma'rrowskying** *vbl. sb.*, the intentional or accidental transposition of initial letters, etc.

1860 HOTTEN *Dict. Slang* (ed. 2) 173 s.v. *Medical Greek*, At the London University they have a way of disguising English..which consists in transposing the initials of words.. This disagreeable nonsense is often termed *marrowskying.* **1912** *Brit. Med. Jrnl.* 22 June 1443 It would be interesting if 'marrowskyers' ' blunders could also be classified. *Ibid.*, All actors live in dread of 'marrowskying', that curious transposition of syllables. **1922** O. JESPERSEN *Lang.* viii. 150 'Marrowskying' or 'Hospital Greek' transfers the initial letters of words, as *renty of plain.*

marrowy ('mærəʊɪ), *a.* Also 4 **merewi**, 5 **marghty**, 6 **marowy**, 8 *Sc.* **merchy.** [f. MARROW *sb.*¹ + -Y¹.]

1. Full of marrow. Also *fig.*

1382 WYCLIF *Isa.* xxxiv. 6 The blod of merewi wetheres [Vulg. *medullatorum arietum*]. **1435** MISYN *Fire of Love* 75 A marghty offerynge [L. *holocausta medullata*; cf. MARROWED 1, *a* 1300]. **1709** BRUCE *Soul Confirm.* 18 (Jam.) The Lord is reserving a merchy piece of the word of his promise to be made out to many of his friends and people. **1820** HAZLITT *Lect. Dram. Lit.* 79 In his *Women beware Women* there is a rich marrowy vein of internal sentiment. **1882** HOLMES in *Atlantic Monthly* LI. 66 The period..of marrowy and vigorous manhood.

2. Of the nature of marrow.

1541 R. COPLAND *Guydon's Quest. Chirurg.* C ij b, It is colde and moyste, bycause it hath a marowy substaunce. **1662** J. CHANDLER *Van Helmont's Oriat.* 185 The Brain being wholly a marrowie part. **1764** GRAINGER *Sugar Cane* I. 45 *note*, When ripe, the skin peels easily off, and discovers a butyraceous, or rather a marrowy-like substance. **1872** J. G. MURPHY *Comm. Lev.* iii. 9 The tail of the broad-tailed sheep..consists almost wholly of marrowy fat.

Hence †**'marrowiness** (in 8 Sc. *merchiness*).

1709 BRUCE *Soul Confirm.* 18 (Jam.) The Israelites had never known the merchiness of that promise, if a Red Sea had not made it out.

†**ma'rrube.** *Obs.* Also 4 in Latin form **marrubium**, 5 **marube.** [ad. L. *marrubium*, perh. connected with the name of the Latin city *Marrubium* or *Marruvium.* Cf OF. *marubre.*] The plant horehound, *Marrubium vulgare.*

1390 GOWER *Conf.* III. 130 The Saphir is his propre Ston, Marrubium his herbe also. *a* **1400–50** *Stockh. Med. MS.* 205 Marube or horrowne: *marubina.* **1607** TOPSELL *Four-f. Beasts* (1658) 69 The fat of a Calf and Marrube with the juyce of Leeks.

marrubiin (mæ'ruːbɪɪn). *Chem.* [f. L. *marrubium* (see prec.) + -IN. Cf. F. *marubine.*] A bitter principle obtained from *Marrubium vulgare.*

1871 WATTS tr. *Gmelin's Handbk. Chem.* XVIII. 234 Marrubiin. The bitter principle of *Marubium vulgare.*

Marrucinian (mæruː'sɪnɪən), *sb.* and *a.* Also **Mar(r)ucine, Marucian, Marusian.** [f. L. *Marrucini* + -AN.] **A.** *sb.* **a.** A member of an Oscan-Umbrian people living near Teate in ancient Eastern Italy. **b.** The language of this people. **B.** *adj.* Of or pertaining to this people or their language.

1578 tr. *Appian's Auncient Historie of Romanes Warres* I. 25 The Marsians, the Malinians, the Vestinians, the Marucians,..and the Samnites, whiche people before had euer bin enimies, and hurtfull to the Romaines. *Ibid.* 31 A little Marusian aunswered hym, and kylled hym. **1600** P. HOLLAND tr. *Livy's Rom. Hist.* VIII. 302 Every one of them, namely, the Marsians, the Pelignians and Marucines, were in feats of armes comparable and egall to the Samnites every way. *Ibid.* XXVII. 660 Hee dispatched likewise messengers before, through the territories of the Larinates, Marrucines, Ferentines, and Pretutians. **1601** —— tr. *Pliny's Nat. Hist.* II. lxxxiii. 39 Medowes and olive rowes..in the Marrucine territorie. **1863** W. P. DICKSON tr. *Mommsen's Hist. Rome* III. IV. vii. 235 The small but hardy confederacies in the Abruzzi—the Pælignians, Marrucinians, Frentanians, and Vestinians. *Ibid.* 237 The territory of the Pælignians, situated in the centre of the Marsian, Samnite, Marrucinian, and Vestinian cantons. **1888** J. WRIGHT tr. *Brugmann's Elem. Compar. Gram. Indo-Germanic Lang.* I. 9 Of the Volscian, Picentine, Sabine, Aequiculan, Vestinian, Marsian, Pelignian and Marrucinian dialects we have only very scanty remains. **1933, 1939** [see MARSIAN *sb.* and *a.*]. **1966** M. S. BEELER in Birnbaum & Puhvel *Anc. Indo-European Dial.* 51 The so-called minor dialects such as Paelignian, Volscian, and Marrucinian. **1974** R. A. HALL *External Hist. Romance Lang.* 48 The Sabellic dialects..: Sabine..; Paelignian, Marrucinian, Vestine, and Marsic in the central Apennines east of Rome; and Volscian.

marrum, variant of MARRAM.

marry ('mærɪ), *v.* Inflected **marrying, married.** Forms: 3–4 (6 *Sc.*) **mari**, 3–7 **marie**, 4 **mariȝe(n**, 4–5 **marie(n**, 4–6 **marye**, 4–8 **mary**, 5 **marye(n**, **(maryyn)**, 6 **mareye, marrye, (mariy)**, 6–7 **marrie**, 6– **marry.** [a. F. *marier* = Pr., Sp., Pg. *maridar*, It. *maritare*:—L. *marītāre*, f. *marītus* ppl. adj., married (also as sb. masc., husband, whence F. *mari*, Pr. *marit-z*, Sp., Pg. *marido*, It. *marito*; and as sb. fem. *marīta* married woman), f. *mari-* (nom. *mās*) man, male; the L. ppl. a. must have been originally used of women, and acquired its wider sense by a later extension.]

I. *trans.*

1. To join in wedlock or matrimony; to join for life as husband and wife; to constitute as man and wife according to the laws and customs of a nation. Const. *to* (*unto*, Sc. *on*, *upon*); also *together.*

a. in *passive* (with ref. either to the act and ceremony, or to the wedded state as a result).

1297 R. GLOUC. (Rolls) 709 þe fader..bad ire vnderstonde To ȝwan sse wolde imaried be. **13..** *E.E. Allit. P.* B. 815 His two dere doȝterez..þat wer maydenez ful meke, maryed not ȝet. *c* **1375** *Sc. Leg. Saints* xli. (*Agnes*) 102 þane agnes sad hym schortly: 'certis, gud sir, maryt ame I'. *c* **1400** MAUNDEV. (1839) xviii. 193 ȝif a man, that is maryed, dye in that Contrie, men buryen his Wif with him alle quyk. **1533** BELLENDEN *Livy* I. (S.T.S.) 100 ȝoung tullia,..was maryit on Aruns terquyne. **1536** —— *Cron. Scot.* (1821) I. 127 The eldest of hir dochteris wes married upon.. Marius. **1536** WRIOTHESLEY *Chron.* (1875) I. 43 The King was maried secreetlie at Chelsey..to one Jane Seymor. **1603** SHAKS. *Meas. for M.* IV. iii. 183 They would..haue married me to the rotten Medlar. **1722** DE FOE *Relig. Courtsh.* I. I. (1840) 4 Well, girls, you little think now, which of you all is like to be first married. **1888** HOWELLS *Annie Kilburn* xi. 133, I presume she isn't very happily married; he's too old.

b. Said of the priest or other functionary who performs the rite. Also *absol.*

1530 PALSGR. 633/1 What preest was it that maryed them togyther: *quel prestre fut ce qui les marya ensemble?* **1559** in Strype *Ann. Ref.* (1709) I. xiv. 183 As to minister the Holy Communion to them that shall be thereto disposed, as to mary and baptize. **1600** SHAKS. *A.Y.L.* IV. i. 125 Come sister, you shall be the Priest, and marrie vs. **1714** GAY *What d'ye Call it* II. viii, Tell him..that he [the Curate] shall marry the Couple himself. **1891** *Century Mag.* Nov. 64 He asked if I could marry people.

c. ***marry up***: to tie up or preoccupy in matrimony. *colloq.* Also *fig.* (const. *with*).

1698 J. COLLIER *Short View Immorality Eng. Stage* iv. 154 This Spark..makes a lucky Hand on't at last, and marries up a rich Lady. **1822** J. FLINT *Lett. Amer.* 225, I believe that the girls there are all married up. **1857** KINGSLEY *Two Y. Ago* II. 8 Married up, when a girl, to a man for whom she did not care. **1865** —— *Herew.* xvi, I would have married her up to my poor boy, if he had but lived. **1865** MRS. CARLYLE *Lett.* III. 274 My only fear about her is that she will be married-up away from me. **1942** *Tee Emm* (Air Ministry) II. 97 They already have had the idea of taking photos of the countryside and marrying them up with similar areas on a map. **1958** *Times* 15 Feb. 7/3 Now that poverty-stricken Jordan is married up with a rich relation. **1970** BAKEWELL & GARNHAM *New Priesthood* iv. 44 If a writer..is not ripe for TV drama, then we would certainly sit down with him, pull his script to bits, send it away, come back, try again, try it on an editor, marry them [*sic*] up with an editor if possible.

2. a. To give in marriage, cause to be married. Said esp. of a parent or guardian.

1297 R. GLOUC. (Rolls) 700 Ich þe wole marie [*v. rr.* mariȝen, marien] wel..To þe nobloste bacheler þat þin herte wile to stonde. *c* **1330** R. BRUNNE *Chron. Wace* (Rolls) 2338 In þys tyme..He mariede þe oþere doughtres boþe. *c* **1386** CHAUCER *Clerk's T.* 1074 And richely his doghter maryed he Vn-to a lord. *c* **1400** MAUNDEV. (1839) v. 35 He wolde have maryed me fulle highely, to a gret Princes Daughtre, ȝif I wolde han forsaken my Lawe and my Beleve. *a* **1450** *Knt. de la Tour* 18 She knew welle that folke were aboute to marie us togedre. **1526** TINDALE *Matt.* xxii. 2 The kyngdome of heven is lyke unto a certayne kinge, which maryed his sonne. **1598** SHAKS. *Merry W.* III. iv. 87 Good mother, do not marry me to yond foole. *a* **1633** G. HERBERT *Jacula Prudentum* 149 Marry your sonne when you will; your daughter when you can. *c* **1710** CELIA FIENNES *Diary* (1888) 141 Yᵉ Earle having just marry'd his Eldest daughter ..there was Company to wishe her joy. **1861** M. PATTISON *Ess.* (1889) I. 33 The same influence led him..to marry his daughter to Henry the Lion. **1894** BARING-GOULD *Deserts S. France* II. 248 Napoleon married him..to his youngest sister.

b. With *off.*

1860 QUEEN VICTORIA *Let.* 18 Dec. in R. Fulford *Dearest Child* (1964) 292, I do wish somebody would go and marry her off—at once. **1865** M. C. HARRIS *St. Philip's* viii. 59 If the young girls did not mind being..finally married off to some of her *protégés*, it was all very well. **1894** V. HUNT *Maiden's Progress* i. 2, I sincerely hope you will be married off before *I* come on, or I shall have no peace. **1908** *Smart Set* June 14/1 Mr. Hardcastle was insisting upon marrying off Aunt Ella to Señor Dominguez y Aguirra. **1973** 'E. FERRARS' *Foot in Grave* viii. 150 I've worked quite hard at trying to get you married off.

3. a. Said of either of the contracting parties: To take in marriage; to accept as husband and wife.

Now the most familiar use.

1432–50 tr. *Higden* (Rolls) III. 439 He [Alexander].. suffrede his knyȝhtes and men to mary [1387 TREVISA wedde] women whom he had taken in captivite. **1456** SIR G. HAYE *Law Arms* (S.T.S.) 40 [He] had maryte king Latynis sister. **1577** tr. *Bullinger's Decades* (1592) 228 That vsuall Prouerbe: Marrie a wife of thine owne degree. **1611** BIBLE *Mal.* ii. 11 Iudah..hath maried the daughter of a strange God. **1711** ADDISON *Spect.* No. 94 ¶8 He married a Woman of great Beauty and Fortune. **1830** TENNYSON *Mermaid* 46 The king of them all would carry me, Woo me, and win me, and marry me. **1888** F. HUME *Mme. Midas* I. i, He had added to his crime by marrying a pretty girl.

b. To obtain (something) by getting married. Esp. in phr. ***to marry money***: to marry a rich spouse.

1858 TROLLOPE *Doctor Thorne* I. xiv. 297 He must marry money, or he will be a ruined man. **1911** L. J. VANCE (*title*) Marrying money. **1914** JOYCE *Dubliners* 98 There'll be no mooning and spooning about it. I mean to marry money. **1934** *Harrap's Stand. French & Eng. Dict.* I. 329/1 *Épouser ..une grosse dot*, to marry money. **1936** HERZOG & BLOOAH *Jabo Proverbs from Liberia* 180 If you marry a beautiful woman, you marry trouble.

†**4.** *refl.* and *reciprocal. Obs.*

a **1300** *Cursor M.* 10698 Here-of in consail suld þai spek, And depeli..þai suld lok hu Sco moght hir mari and hald hir vou. **1393** LANGL. *P. Pl.* C. xi. 281 Maydenes and maydenes marieþ ȝow to-gederes. *c* **1412** HOCCLEVE *De Reg. Princ.* 1632 þey þat marien hem for muk & good Only, & noght for loue of þe persone. **1535** COVERDALE *Wisd.* viii. 2, I dyd my diligence to mary my self with her, soch loue had I vnto hir beutye. **1621** LADY M. WROTH *Urania* 454 The young Princesse soone after tooke her minde and former resolution, marrying her selfe with her chosen loue. **1697** POTTER *Antiq. Greece* (1715) I. I. xxvi. 170 No Athenian Woman shall marry herself to an exotick Family. *a* **1774**

GOLDSM. *Song Intended for 'Stoops to Conq.'*, Ah me! when shall I marry me? Lovers are plenty; but fail to relieve me. **1818** SCOTT *'Proud Maisie'*, Tell me, thou bonny bird, When shall I marry me?

5. *transf.* and *fig.* **a.** To unite intimately, join closely or permanently.

1526 *Pilgr. Perf.* (W. de W. 1531) 293 b, This conformyte of loue maryeth the soule to god. **1576** FLEMING tr. *Caius' Dogs* in Arb. *Garner* III. 261 The natures of men are so moved, nay rather married to novelties. **1610** B. JONSON *Alch.* II. iii, *Svb.* Are you sure, you loos'd 'hem, I' their owne menstrue? *Fac.* Yes, sir, and then married 'hem. **1632** MILTON *L'Allegro* 137 Lap me in soft Lydian Aires, Married to immortal verse. **1649** OGILBY *Virg. Georg.* I. *init.*, In what Cœlestial Signs 'Tis good to Plow, and marry Elms with Vines. **1673** GREW *Acc. Veget. Roots* §30 It is then the Oyl, chiefly, by which these Vessels are Tough: for being of a tenacious Nature, by taking hold of other Principles, it marries them together. **1693** EVELYN *De la Quint. Compl. Gard.* II. 115 They must be joyn'd together neatly, plaining and proportioning the Extremities that are to be Marry'd together exactly. **1796** BURKE *Let. Noble Ld.* Wks. 1842 II. 273 Revolutions which consolidated and married the liberties and the interests of the two nations for ever. **1835** THIRLWALL *Greece* I. 360 The unequal lines of the couplets to which he married his fiery thoughts. **1890** SAINTSBURY *Hist. Elizab. Lit.* ix. 342 This hybrid and bizarre vocabulary is.. admirably married to the substance of the writing. **1908** *Daily Chron.* 19 Aug. 4/7 By 'marrying' or blending the wine from different vineyards he discovered that there resulted an effervescing wine. **1919** KIPLING *Years Between* 63 With a thin third finger marrying Drop to wine-drop domed on the table. **1925** BELLOC *Mr. Petre* vi. 150 A genius who could marry the commonest tricks to unheard rapidity and daring. **1942** L. BENNETT *Jamaica Dial. Verses* 44 Pumpkin? yuh wi Haffe buy cho-cho wid i, Dem married, same like 'ow cassada Married to yampi. **1952** M. KERR *Personality & Conflict in Jamaica* 59 Soap and rice are popular gifts, as the shopkeepers in the country tend to 'marry them'. **1958** *Times Lit. Suppl.* 3 Oct. 567/4 It is always something of a problem with a heavily illustrated book to know how best to marry a long text with the illustrations relating to it. **1960** O. SKILBECK *ABC of Film & TV* 82 *Marry*, to combine related mute and sound negatives in printing, or different picture negatives in optical work. **1963** *Times* 24 Apr. 12/7 Rolls-Royce believe that their success with a combination of silica and aluminium opens up the possibility of 'marrying' different types of ceramics and metals. **1967** CASSIDY & LE PAGE *Dict. Jamaican Eng.* 294/1 *Marry*, to couple something in short supply (and much in demand) with something not much wanted, so that one must purchase the latter in order to have the former. **1969** *Daily Tel.* 11 Nov. 6/7 Scientists are 'marrying' strains, such as the Hongkong virus, to other influenza viruses that are known to reproduce and spread faster.

b. *Naut.* To fasten (two ropes) end to end, in such a way that the joining may not prevent their being drawn through a block. (See also 1867.)

1815 *Falconer's Dict. Marine* (ed. Burney), To *Marry*, in splicing ropes, is to join one rope to another, for the purpose of reeving it, which is performed by placing the end of each close together, and then attaching them by worming. *Ibid.*, To *Marry* two Ropes, is to knot the yarns together in a kind of splice, so as not to be thicker at the juncture than at any other part. *c* **1860** H. STUART *Seaman's Catech.* 29 Marry both ends together. **1867** SMYTH *Sailor's Word-bk.*, *To Marry the Ropes, Braces, or Falls*, to hold both together, and by pressure haul in both equally. Also so to join the ends of two ropes that they will pass through a block.

c. In certain card games. Of the king or queen, *to be married*: to be declared as held in the same hand with the queen or king of the same suit. Cf. MARRIAGE 7.

1870 'CAVENDISH' *Game of Bezique* 20 The bézique queen .. having been once married .. cannot be married again.

d. *Stockbrokers' slang.* To set (one transaction against another).

1931 *Economist* 10 Oct. 675/1 The shareholders .. can do nothing, for the Trust only agrees to 'marry' buying orders for clients against selling orders. **1959** *Ibid.* 21 Mar. 1099/1 The brokers in these shares then find it convenient to 'marry' the buying and selling orders.

II. 6. *intr.* **a.** To enter into the conjugal or matrimonial state; to wed, contract matrimony; to take a husband or wife. Const. *with* (formerly very common); occas. *to*, also (*Sc.*) *upon*. Also ***to marry into***: to enter (a family, etc.) by marrying; to obtain by getting married; ***to marry well***: to have a successful marriage (in terms of harmony, material gain, or social standing).

a **1300** *Cursor M.* 10653 Þan did þe biscop command þar, þat all þe maidens .. Be send all to þair frendes dere, For to mari and forto spus. *c* **1511** *1st Eng. Bk. Amer.* (Arb.) Introd. 31/2 They mareye but ones in theyr lyfe. **1526** TINDALE *1 Cor.* vii. 39 Yf her husbande slepe, she is at her liberte to mary with whom she woll, only in the lorde. **1530** —— *Answ. More* III. xiii. Wks. (1573) 313/2 For, when the husband is dead, the wife is free to mary to whom she will. **1590** GREENE *Never too late* I. (1600) C 3, Such as marry but to a faire face tie themselues oft to a foule bargaine. **1602** SHAKS. *Ham.* III. iv. 29. **1604** [see WELL *adv.* 6 c]. **1614** DAY *Festivals* (1615) 282 Marrying in hast, and Repenting at leisure. **1639** DRUMM. OF HAWTH. *Consid. to Parlt.* Wks. (1711) 187 That the church-race marry only among themselves, ministers sons upon ministers daughters. **1602** STILLINGFL. *Orig. Sacræ* II. ii. §9 Especially when he.. married into that branch of the family that was remaining there. **1755** J. SHEBBEARE *Lydia* (1769) I. 319 Beseeching him .. never to permit his daughter to marry with any man beneath noble. **1819** BYRON *Juan* I. lvii, She married .. With an Hidalgo. **1845** *Punch's Almanack* Jan., Advice to persons about to marry.—Don't. **1849** THACKERAY *Pendennis* viii, Gentlemen .. occasionally marry out of their kitchens. **1871** GEO. ELIOT *Middlem.* (1872) I. I. iv. 61, I wish you to marry well; and I have good reason to believe that Chettam wishes to marry you. **1876** C. M. YONGE *Womankind* xxxi. 281 Mothers .. cherish wishes that their girls may 'marry well'; *i.e.* richly. **1899** O. WILDE *Importance of Being Earnest* I. 39 You can hardly imagine that I and Lord Bracknell would dream of allowing our only daughter .. to marry into a cloak-room, and form an alliance with a parcel. **1904** H. O. STURGIS *Belchamber* i. 10 They both married, and married what is called 'well', while many of their fairer .. sisters were left ungathered on the stem. **1905** A. BURVENICH *Eng. Idioms* 224 *Marry*... To—into a fortune; *épouser une fortune, een rijk huwelijk doen.* **1923** R. MACAULAY *Told by Idiot* I. xiii. 50 What chances does a girl want, except to marry well? **1931** *Daily Express* 21 Sept. 19/1 He married into money, so that I find it difficult to credit that his contemplated return is for the purpose of restoring his balance at the bank. **1933** R. H. LOWIE in *Encycl. Social Sci.* X. 146/2 No Masai of good standing marries into a blacksmith's family. **1946** [see BROUHAHA]. **1963** *Listener* 14 Feb. 274/1 A socialist politician who has married into a farm. **1974** 'J. MELVILLE' *Nun's Castle* i. 19 Among the other luxuries life provided for Lady Dorothy were kindred on the eastern seaboard of the United States... Probably she had someone married 'well' into the Kremlin if the truth were told.

†**b.** To contract a matrimonial alliance *with*. *Obs.*

1476–7 *Paston Lett.* III. 168 My husbonde .. wold that ȝe schuld go un to my maistresse yowr modur, and asaye if ȝe myght gete the hole xx *li.* in to ȝowr handes, and then he wolde be more gladd to marye with ȝowe, and will gyffe ȝowe an C *li.*

c. *transf.* and *fig.* To enter into intimate union; to join, so as to form one. Also, (of wine, etc.) to mature. Now esp. ***to marry up with***, to link with.

1508 KENNEDIE *Flyting w. Dunbar* 296 Syne merreit with the Diuill for dignite. **1654** WHITLOCK *Zootomia* 138 And since he first divorced knowledge and practice in our first Parents, he is loath they should ever marry againe. **1850** TENNYSON *In Mem.* lxxxv, First love, first friendship, equal powers, That marry with the virgin heart. **1855** —— *Brook* 81, I .. crost By that old bridge .. where the waters marry. **1960** T. MCLEAN *Kings of Rugby* xi. 170 Risman began to bear to the left to marry up with the outside backs. **1963** *Harper's Bazaar* Aug. 26 Blended .. the whisky must now 'marry' another year before bottling. **1969** *New Yorker* 27 Sept. 120/2 The juices are the foundation for a generous gravy, in which blanched vegetables like carrots, onions .. are heated and then allowed to marry for an hour or more. **1969** [see GAZPACHO]. **1971** C. BONINGTON *Annapurna South Face* App. C. 257 Even though there were indications that the British mask used on Kanchenjunga and the American mask used on Everest were superior in design, I preferred to keep things as simple as possible, eliminating any risk of parts failing to marry up.

d. ***to marry above, below*** or ***beneath***, (oneself): to marry a person of higher or lower social position.

1721 J. KELLY *Compl. Coll. Scottish Proverbs* 252 Marry above your Match, and you get a Master. **1741** RICHARDSON *Pamela* (1742) III. 4 For who will offer to reproach me for marrying, as the World thinks, below me. *Ibid.* IV. 246 A Man, who .. marry'd beneath him. **1860** A. J. MUNBY *Diary* 21 Feb. in D. Hudson *Munby* (1972) 51 Saw Mrs Lock (herself considerably reduced in the world, being in fact a *lady* who married beneath her). **1876** TROLLOPE *Prime Minister* III. xx. 336 He had married much above himself in every way. **1895** A. W. PINERO *Second Mrs. Tanqueray* IV. 160 All my family have chucked me over... Jus' because I've married beneath me.

e. ***to marry out***: to marry a person of a different clan, group, religion, etc.

1842 *Southern Lit. Messenger* VIII. 331/2 'Marrying out', as the Friends call one of a different faith, is regarded by them with especial horror. **1923** C. ROTH *Hist. Marranos* xii. 316 His son, Jacob Israel Bernal, married out of the faith and left the community. **1954** E. E. EVANS-PRITCHARD *Inst. Primitive Society* vi. 68 The rule of exogamy—the rule of marrying-out—which required that a man must not marry inside a defined set of his own kin. **1957** V. W. TURNER *Schism & Continuity in Afr. Society* ix. 287 Most women marry out at least once. **1959** F. M. WILSON *They came as Strangers* III. iv. 212 When his daughter married a Gentile .. he never reproached her for marrying 'out'. **1964** E. HUXLEY *Back Street New Worlds* ii. 20 Jewish women stick much closer to their own kind, with only between one-tenth and one-fifth marrying 'out'. **1973** *Jewish Chron.* 19 Jan. 23/4 The smugness .. may be one of the reasons for the apathy among Orthodox Jews which leads to marrying out.

marry ('mærɪ), *int. Obs.* exc. *arch.* or *dial.* Forms: 4–6 **marie**, 4–7 **mary**, 5–7 **marye**, 6 **marrye**, 6–7 **marrie**, (9 *dial.* **marrey**), 5– **marry**. [Originally, the name of the Virgin MARY used as an oath or an ejaculatory invocation. In the 16th c., when *marry* had prob. ceased to be commonly apprehended as anything more than a mere interjection, the sound of the oath *by Mary Gipcy* (i.e. 'by St. Mary of Egypt') seems to have suggested the addition to it of the interjections GIP, GUP; and, as these were commonly used in driving horses, the equivalent *come up* (COME *v.* 74 k) was afterwards substituted.] An exclamation of asseveration, surprise, indignation, etc.

a. Simply. (Often used in answering a question, and implying surprise that it should be asked: = 'why, to be sure'.)

c **1350** *Will. Palerne* 4840 'Marie, sire', sede þe messageres 'ȝe mowe vs wel trowe, þe milde mayde meliors in palerne now dwelles.' *c* **1386** CHAUCER *Can. Yeom. Prol. & T.* 509 Ye sire, and wol ye so? Marie ther-of I pray yow hertely! *c* **1450** *Dial. Husb. & Gent.* in Roy *Rede me* (Arb.) 136 *Husbondman.* Howe dyd they youre auncesteres compell? *Gentillman.* Mary in threatnynge the paynes of hell. **1550** LEVER *Serm.* (Arb.) 128 Yea marrye, why should we not kepe oure corne in oure owne barnes? **1552** LATIMER *Serm.* (1584) 227 b, What is that? Marry fayth: and beliefe. **1598** SHAKS. *Merry W.* I. i. 170, I will say marry trap with you [? = 'be off with you'], if you runne the nut-hooks humor on me. **1605** WILLET *Hexapla Gen.* 405 Many suddenlie will say (marye) hauing no intent to sweare. **1693** CONGREVE *Old Bach.* I. iv, Marry, quotha! I hope, in heaven, I have a greater portion of grace. **1766** GOLDSM. *Vic. W.* xii, Marry, hang the idiot .. to bring me such stuff. **1816** SCOTT *Antiq.* xxxv, Marry, my lord, the *phoca* had the better. **1855** ROBINSON *Whitby Gloss.* s.v., One person says, 'It is coming on rain,' the other will add, 'Ay Marrey! it is, sure enough'.

†**b.** with asseverative words: ***marry (a) God, marry (and) amen.*** Also ***marry of God, God's marry, marry a me, marry of me*** (all in *Look about you*, 1600). *Obs.*

c **1574–5** G. HARVEY *Story M. Harvey* Wks. (Grosart) III. 94 By yᵉ Marie-god. **1592** SHAKS. *Rom. & Jul.* IV. v. 8 God forgiue me: Marrie and Amen: how sound is she a sleepe? **1600** *Look about you* E 3 b, Mary a god my wife would chide me dead. **1601** SHAKS. *Twel. N.* IV. ii. 109 God buy you good sir Topas: Marry Amen. I will sir, I will. **1606** HEYWOOD *2nd Pt. Know not me* Wks. 1874 I. 267 Shake hands; by the marry-god, Sir Thomas, what else? **1695** CONGREVE *Love for L.* III. i, Miss! miss! miss Prue!—mercy on me, marry and amen!—Why, what's become of the child?

c. with interjection or exclamatory phrase: ***marry gip, marry (and) gup (gap, gep, guep***, in Scott erron. ***quep***): see GIP, GUP, QUEP *ints.* Also ***marry faugh, marry-go-look*** (in quot. used as sb.).

[**1523** SKELTON *Garl. Laurel* 1455 Thynke what ye wyll Of this wanton byll; By Mary Gipcy, *Quod scripsi, scripsi.*] **1590** GREENE *Never too late* II. (1600) K 3 Marry gep giglet, thy loue sits on thy tongs end. **1592** LYLY *Midas* V. ii, Melancholy? marie gup, is melancholy a word for a barbars mouth? **1598** E. GUILPIN *Skial.* (1878) 44 Mary and gup! haue I then lost my cap? **1600** DEKKER *Shoemaker's Hol.* ii. (1862) 12, I .. looked at him, he at me, indeed spake to him, but he to me not a word, Marry gip, thought I, with a wanion! He past by me as proud—Marry foh! are you grown humorous, thought I? **1601** MUNDAY *Downfall Earl Huntington* I. i. (1828) 15 He thinketh all lost In tumbling of books Of marry go looks. **1604** DEKKER *Honest Wh.* vi. D, Marry fah, hang-em. **1605** CHAPMAN etc. *Eastw. Hoe* I. i, *Quick.* Mary fough goodman flat-cap. **1607** HEYWOOD *Fayre Mayde Exch.* Wks. 1874 II. 43 Mary gip Minx. **1621** J. TAYLOR (Water P.) *Taylors Motto* Wks. (1630) II. 44/1 Marry gep With a horse night-cap doth your Iadeship skip? **1631** *Celestina* XVIII. 179 Imbrace him? Mary gup with a murraine! I had rather see him under the power and rigour of the law. **1663** BUTLER *Hud.* I. iii. 202, I thought th' hadst scorn'd to budge a step, For fear. (Quoth Echo) Marry guep. Am not I here to take thy part? **1676** WYCHERLEY *Pl. Dealer* III. i, Marry-gep! if it had not been for me, thou hadst been yet but a hearing-counsel at the bar. **1699** 'MISAURUS' *Honour of Gout* (1720) 34 Marry Gap, quoth she.

d. ***marry come up***: used to express indignant or amused surprise or contempt: = 'hoity-toity'.

1592 SHAKS. *Rom. & Jul.* II. v. 64 Marrie come vp I trow, Is this the Poultis for my aking bones? **1608** —— *Per.* IV. vi. 159. **1662** J. EATON *Honey-c. Free Justif.* 14 Taunting and reproachfull termes, as, *Marry come up.* **1663** COWLEY *Cutter of Coleman St.* Wks. 1710 II. 804 Marry come up; won't one of my chusing serve your turn as well as one of your own. **1742** FIELDING *J. Andrews* IV. i, Slipslop .. departed tossing her Nose, and crying, 'Marry come up! there are some People more jealous than I, I believe'. —— *Tom Jones* x. iv, Her tongue .. muttered many 'marry-come-ups' .. with other such indignant phrases. **1862** BORROW *Wild Wales* I. xxiv. 276 Unworthy? marry come up! I won't hear such an expression.

marry, marryce, obs. ff. MARROW *sb.*[1], MARISH.

marry-gold, obs. form of MARIGOLD.

marrying ('mærɪɪŋ), *vbl. sb.* [f. MARRY *v.* + -ING[1].] **a.** The action of the verb MARRY. Also **marrying-in, -out.** Also *transf.* and *fig.*

a **1300** *Cursor M.* 10657 Bot maria wald na mariing, Bot maiden liue til hir ending. **1549** SIR T. HOBY *Trav.* (1902) 17 Venice .. they have a wonderous great ceremonie abowt the maryinge of the see. **1579** E. K. *Gloss. Spenser's Sheph. Cal.* Mar. 97 He was busie aboute the marying of *Polyxena*. **1667** MILTON *P.L.* XI. 716 All now was turn'd to jollitie .. Marrying or prostituting, as befell. **1891** *Athenæum* 17 Jan. 86/3 There is plenty of love and some marrying. **1917** B. GRIMSHAW *Nobody's Island* v. 61 Such greens, such blues, such marryings of both, not brush and colour, nor pen and ink, could paint. **1940** *Chambers's Techn. Dict.* 528/1 *Marrying*, the process of lashing poles together in scaffold erection. *Ibid.*, *Marrying* (*Cinema*), the printing of the mute negative and the negative sound-track on the release print. **1952** *Economist* 8 Nov. 401/1 The marrying of reactors with power generators. **1964** GOULD & KOLB *Dict. Social Sci.* 239/2 Endogamy and exogamy are processes of marrying-in and marrying-out. **1973** *Times Lit. Suppl.* 6 July 775/2 A drama of 'marrying out' (a painful process which one does not have to be Jewish to experience).

b. *attrib.* as in ***marrying age, day***; † **marrying ring**, a wedding-ring.

1504 in *Bury Wills* (Camden) 98 Item I bequeth to ouʳ Lady of Walsyngʰam .. my maryeng ryng. **1546** J. HEYWOOD *Prov.* (1867) 15 Sens our one mariyng or marryng daie. *a* **1548** HALL *Chron., Hen. VIII.* 240 b, Aboute her mariyng ryng was written: God sende me wel to kepe. **1869** TOZER *Highl. Turkey* II. 120 Daughters .. when they reach nineteen .. are looked upon as almost past the marrying age.

marrying ('mærɪɪŋ), *ppl. a.* [f. MARRY *v.* + -ING[2].] **a.** Inclined or likely to marry. **b.** That performs the marriage ceremony.

1778 MISS BURNEY *Evelina* lxxv, I think Miss Anville the loveliest of her sex; and, were I a *marrying man*, she, of all the women I have seen, I would fix upon for a wife. **1855**

DICKENS *Dorrit* II. xv, She had not thought Edmund a marrying man. **1861** THACKERAY *Four Georges* i, Duke George, the marrying duke. **1891** E. KINGLAKE *Australian at H.* 62 If a minister knowingly marries a minor without consent of guardians he is liable to a fine of £300... These marrying gentry are not much given to inquiring into the circumstances under which their clients come to them.

† **marry-muff**, *sb.* and *int. Obs.* Also 7 **mary-, maramuffe.**

A. *sb.* Some kind of cheap textile fabric; a garment made of this.

1604 *Meeting of Gallants* B 2 b, He that would haue braude it.. might haue made a Sute of Sattin cheaper in the Plague-time, then a Sute of Marry-muffe in the Tearme-time. **1604** MIDDLETON *Ant & Night.* F 3, She drewe her white Bountifull hand out of her Mary-muffe, and quoited a single Halfe-peny. **1640** in Entick *London* (1766) II. 178 Piramides or Maramuffe, the piece, narrow, 1*d.*

B. *int.* Used as a derisive exclamation. (Cf. MARRY *int.*)

1602 MIDDLETON *Blurt* II. ii, Wearied Sir? mary muffe. **1605** *Tryall Chevalr.* in Bullen *O. Pl.* (1884) III. 288 Mary muffe!.. I scorne to humble the least part about me to giue answere to such a trothing question. **1613** WITHER *Abuses Stript* i. in *Juvenilia* (1633) 13 His Poetry is such as he can cull From Plaies.. And yet his fine coy Mistresse, Mary-Muffe, The soonest taken with such broken stuffe.

marryner, obs. form of MARINER.

marrys, variant of MARIS *Obs.*, womb.

marrys(h, obs. forms of MARISH.

Mars (mɑːz). Also 4–5 **Marcz, Marcs, Marce.** [a. L. *Mārs* (stem *Mart-*), app. a reduced form of the archaic *Māvors* (*Māvort-*). The Oscan name of the god, *Māmers* (*Māmert-*) is prob. cognate, at least so far as the first element is concerned.]

1. a. The Roman god of war; identified from an early period with the Greek Ares. Often, after Roman practice, used for: Warfare, warlike prowess, fortune in war.

camp or ***field of Mars, Mars' field***, the Campus Martius at Rome. ***Mars' hill, hill of Mars***, the Areopagus at Athens.

c **1374** CHAUCER *Compl. Mars* 75 (Harl.) Venus kyssith Mars [*Camb. MS.* Marcs] þe god of armes. **1387–8** T. USK *Test. Love* I. vii. 11 (Skeat), I profered my body.. that Mars shulde have juged the ende. *c* **1412** HOCCLEVE *De Reg. Princ.* 3905 Mars haþ euer ben frend to ȝour worþi lyne. **1590** C'TESS PEMBROKE *Antonie* 1061 A man.. In Marses schole who neuer lesson learn'd. **1602** SHAKS. *Ham.* III. iv. 57 An eye like Mars, to threaten or command. **1611** BIBLE *Acts* xvii. 22 Then Paul stood in the mids of Mars-hill. **1616** HOLYDAY *Persius* Sat. v. (ed. 2) D 3, A third doth Mars-field wrastlings duely keepe [L. *Hic campo indulget*]. **1638** SIR T. HERBERT *Trav.* (ed. 2) 94 Bengala is a Province.. peopled with Mahometans and Idolaters, addict to Mars and Merchandize. *a* **1700** B. E. *Dict. Cant. Crew, Son of Mars*, Soldier. **1715** POPE *Iliad* II. 139 Ye sons of Mars! partake your leaders care. **1785** BURNS *Jolly Beggars*, I am a son of Mars, who have been in many wars.

b. *allusively.* A great warrior.

1569 PRESTON *Cambyses* 10 A manly Marsis heart he bare. **1593** SHAKS. *Rich. II*, II. iii. 101 The Black Prince, that yong Mars of men. *c* **1630** RISDON *Surv. Devon* §134 (1810) 149 This Mars vanquished the Arragonois.

2. a. *Astr.* The fourth planet in the order of distance from the sun, revolving in an orbit lying between that of the Earth and Jupiter.

the hill or ***plain of Mars***: in Palmistry, the fleshy part of the thumb.

c **1385** CHAUCER *L.G.W.* 2589 *Hypermn.*, A rede Mars was that tyme of the ȝere So feble that his maleyce is hym beraft. **1578** BANISTER *Hist. Man* IV. 62 b, That fleshy part of the thombe, which Palmesters do terme the hill of Mars. **1601** SHAKS. *All's Well* I. i. 206 *Hel.* You were borne vnder a charitable starre. *Par.* Vnder Mars I. **1630** *R. Johnson's Kingd. & Commw.* 15 Those who have Mars Lord in their Nativities, become either Souldiers or Trades-men. **1653** R. SANDERS *Physiogn.* 56 Wee allow to Mars all that space within the Triangle, which is made by the line of the Liver, that of the Head, and that of Saturn; and we call that place the Plain of Mars,.. the strongest place of the Hand. **1855** TENNYSON *Maud* III. vi. 13 [She] pointed to Mars As he glow'd like a ruddy shield on the Lion's breast.

†**b.** *Old Chem.* The name of the metal iron. *Obs.*

crystals, salt, or ***vitriol of Mars***: green vitriol, (ferrous sulphate). ***extract of Mars***: 'a tincture of a salt of iron' (*Syd. Soc. Lex.* 1889). ***saffron of Mars, Mars' saffron***: = 'crocus of iron' (see CROCUS 3).

c **1386** CHAUCER *Can. Yeom. Prol. & T.* 274 Sol gold is,.. Mars Iren Mercurie quyk siluer we clepe. **1676** BOYLE *New Exper. Fluids* II. in *Phil. Trans.* XI. 807 A Mass of Regulus made of Antimony without Mars. **1678** SALMON *Lond. Disp.* 836/2 Filings of Steel are digested in Spirit of Vitriol, to make Vitriol of Mars. *Ibid.*, The Salt of Mars. **1727–41** CHAMBERS *Cycl.* s.v. *Crocus, Crocus martis aperiens*, opening saffron of mars. **1758** [see JUPITER 2 b].

†**c.** *Her.* The name for the tincture red in blazoning by the names of the heavenly bodies. *Obs.*

1572 BOSSEWELL *Armorie* II. 67 The fielde is partie per Fesse, Saturne, and Mars.

d. = *Mars yellow*: see 4.

1899 B. W. WARHURST *Colour Dict.* 47 *Mars*, dull deep yellow, also an orange.

3. The proprietary name of a chocolate-covered bar with a toffee-like filling. Usu. in form ***Mars bar.***

1932 *Trade Marks Jrnl.* 5 Oct. 1273 *Mars*,.. a sweetmeat. Mars Confections Limited. **1943** *Penguin New Writing* XVI. (verso front cover, Advt.), Mars are made from the finest available materials—including chocolate.., glucose.., separated milk. **1948** C. DAY LEWIS *Otterbury Incident* ix. 112 Toppy gave the errand boy half a Mars bar he had in his pocket. **1963** L. DEIGHTON *Horse under Water* xi. 45 He did that twenty years ago when you were wearing a Micky Mouse gas-mask and saving your coupons for a Mars bar. **1973** J. WHITE *Norfolk Child* 176 But there were peppermints,.. and, of course, Mars. We.. cut them into slices to make them last longer; first we bit the toffee off the top of the slice, then we nibbled the chocolate round the edges, and last of all.. the delicious honey-sweet centre. **1973** C. BONINGTON *Next Horizon* iii. 57 'I've got a can of sardines and two Mars Bars,' I said. **1973** *Times* 20 Sept. 18/8 Getting an overweight patient to regulate his eating habit (using a knife and fork to eat a Mars Bar).

4. *attrib.* and *Comb.*, as ***Mars-adoring, -beloved, -daunting, -like*** adjs.; **Mars colours**, as ***Mars brown, red, violet, yellow***, pigments prepared from earths, and coloured with iron oxide; † **Mars-starred** *a.*, born under the planet Mars.

a **1649** DRUMM. OF HAWTH. *Poems* Wks. (1711) 39/1 A *Mars-adoring brood is here. **1598** SYLVESTER *Du Bartas* II. ii. II. *Babylon* 688 *Mars-daunting Martialist. *Ibid.* II. i. II. *Imposture* 628 The valiant Heav'n-assisted sword Of *Mars-like Essex. **1894** *Athenæum* 5 May 584/2 Her *mars-red gown over a yellow petticoat. **1635** HEYWOOD *Hierarch.* VI. 395 The Scythians (souldiers not to be despis'd) A *Mars-starr'd people.

Mars, obs. form of MARCH *sb.*[2] (the month).

Marsa, Mars(e, varr. MASSA, MAS.

‖**Marsala** (mɑːˈsɑːlə). Also **Marsalla.** [The name of a town on the west coast of Sicily.] (More fully ***Marsala wine.***) A class of white wines resembling a light sherry, exported from Marsala.

1806 JEFFERSON in *Harper's Mag.* (1885) Mar. 541 Two Pipes Marsalla wine. **1848** THACKERAY *Bk. Snobs* xxv, I prefer sherry to marsala when I can get it.

marscal, -schal, -schel, etc.: see MARSHAL.

mars(e)banker, -bunker, var. ff. MOSSBUNKER.

‖**Marseillais** (marsejɛ), *a.* (*sb.*) Also 7 **Marsillies**, 8 **Marsellois**, 9 **Marseillois** (anglicized **Marseillese**). [Fr., f. *Marseille* Marseilles: cf. -ESE.]

1. *adj.* Belonging or pertaining to Marseilles.

1686 tr. *Chardin's Trav. Persia* i. 7 [The Turks call Spanish money] Marsillies, by reason that the Merchants of Marseilles first brought it in great Quantities into Turkie. **1864** in WEBSTER; and in later Dicts. **1896** C. M. YONGE *Release* II. xxi. 294 Rumours reached us of the arrival of the Marseillais tigers. **1966** M. R. D. FOOT *SOE in France* xi. 377 He.. sank himself without effort into the marseillais underworld.

2. *absol.* as *sb. pl.* **a.** Inhabitants of Marseilles. Also in *sing.*, an inhabitant of Marseilles.

1837 CARLYLE *Fr. Rev.* VI. iv, Those black-browed Marseillese marching, dusty, unwearied. **1839** *Penny Cycl.* XIV. 446/2 The Marseillois appear to have been actively engaged in the Crusades. **1939** E. AMBLER *Mask of Dimitrios* i. 12 The other guests were a very noisy pair of Marseillais. **1951** E. PAUL *Springtime in Paris* ix. 159 Auvergnats, Catalans, Basques, Normans, Bretons, Marseillais. **1966** M. R. D. FOOT *SOE in France* ix. 248 The marseillais Basset and his Burgundian mate, Jarrot.

b. *Hist.* The members of the Cordeliers Club in the French Revolution.

1795 tr. *Barruel's Hist. Clergy during Fr. Rev.* 211 [The section] of Cordeliers had taken the name of Marsellois.

‖**Marseillaise** (marsɛjɛz, mɑːsəˈleɪz). Also **Marseillois(e, Marseillais.** [Fr., fem. of prec.] (Also ***Marseillaise hymn.***) The national song of the French Republic, written and composed by Rouget de l'Isle in 1792; so named from having been first sung in Paris by a band of 'patriots' from Marseilles.

1826 MOORE *Copy Intercep. Desp.* viii, If the Marseillois Hymn could command Such audience, though yell'd by a Sans-culotte crew. **1827** SCOTT *Napoleon* V. 66 Chenier, author of the hymn of the Marseilloise. [**1831** CARLYLE *Sart. Res.* III. iii, Your.. Marseillese Hymns, and Reigns of Terror.] **1842** BORROW *Bible in Spain* vii, The drunkard then commenced singing, or rather yelling, the Marseillaise hymn. **1848** [see LABIAL *a.* A. 1].

b. *Comb.* **Marseillaise-wise** *adv.*, in the manner customary when singing the Marseillaise.

1870 DICKENS *E. Drood* ii, As the boy.. lays a hand on Jasper's shoulder, Jasper cordially and gaily lays a hand on *his* shoulder, and so Marseillaise-wise they go in to dinner.

Marseilles (mɑːˈseɪlz). Also 8 **Marsailles.** [The Eng. name of a seaport (in Fr. *Marseille*) in southern France; used *attrib.* and *ellipt.*]

1. A stiff cotton fabric, similar to piqué. Also ***Marseilles quilting.***

1762 BICKERSTAFFE *Love in Village* III. iv. (1765) 60 Four counterpanes in Marsailles quilting. **1824** MISS MITFORD *Village* Ser. I. 223 Her exterior garment was always quilted, varying.. from simple stuff, or fine white dimity, or an obsolete manufacture called Marseilles, up to silk and satin. **1893** GEORGIANA HILL *Hist. Eng. Dress* II. 234 White waistcoats of Marseilles quilting were generally worn.

2. Marseilles hartwort, French hartwort, *Seseli tortuosum* (formerly *massiliense*). **Marseilles vinegar**, *Acetum prophylacticum* or thieves' vinegar.

1822 PARIS *Pharmacologia* (ed. 5) II. 15 *note*, Thieves Vinegar, or Marseilles Vinegar. **1856** in MAYNE *Expos. Lex.*

3. Applied *attrib.* to a type of pottery produced in Marseilles during the seventeenth and eighteenth centuries.

1870 C. SCHREIBER *Jrnl.* (1911) I. 101 Bought.. cover of Marseilles ware,.. two Marseilles plates with Chinese figures. **1960** R. G. HAGGAR *Conc. Encycl. Cont. Pott. & Porc.* 302/2 The subsequent history of Marseilles faience is one of great trade expansion and the multiplication of factories... The death blow was given to the industry by the increased demand for earthenware of English type, and the French Revolution. **1974** *Times* 29 Oct. 19/4 A fine Marseilles *Veuve Perrin* soup tureen.

marsella: see MARCELLA.

marsement, obs. variant of MERCEMENT.

marsh[1] (mɑːʃ). Forms: α. 1 mersc, mærsc, merisc, 3 mersche, 3–6 mershe, 4 merss, 4, (7) mersh, 5 mersch, merche, merssh(e; β. 6 mars(s)he, marche, 7–9 *dial.* march, 7–9 *Eng.* and *U.S. dial.* mash, 5– marsh. [OE. *mersc, merisc* masc. = M.Du. *mersch(e* masc., fem., MLG. *mersch, marsch, masch* fem., neut., whence G. *marsch* fem., Da. *marsk* neut.; repr. W.Ger. **marisk-* (whence med.L. *mariscus* and its Rom. forms: see MARISH *sb.*) f. OTeut. **mari-* sea, lake, MERE *sb.*: see -ISH.]

I. 1. a. A tract of low lying land, flooded in winter and usually more or less watery throughout the year.

c **725** *Corpus Gloss.* (Hessels) C 140 *Calmetum*, mersc. **971** *Blickl. Gloss.* 261/1 On s[a]ltne mersc, *in salsilaginem.* *a* **1250** *Owl & Night.* 304 Wenestu that haveck bo the worse, Thoȝ crowe bi-grede him bi the mershe? **1382** WYCLIF *Gen.* xli. 18 Seuen oxen.. the which in the pasture of mershe [1388 marreis] the grene leswis cheseden. *c* **1475** *Pict. Voc.* in Wr.-Wülcker 796/17 *Hoc marescum*, a merche. **1523** LD. BERNERS *Froiss.* I. xviii, There were meruaylouse great marshes and daungerous passages. **1594** SHAKS. *Rich. III*, V. iii. 345 My Lord, the Enemy is past the Marsh. **1673** TEMPLE *Obs. United Prov.* Wks. 1731 I. 8 By.. the Course of Waters from the higher into lower Grounds.. the flat Land grows to be a Mixture of Earth and Water,.. which is call'd a Marsh. **1770** N. NICHOLLS in *Corr. w. Gray* (1843) 118 The marshes which I see from my bed-chamber window are become an ocean. **1835** THIRLWALL *Greece* i. I. 11 The lake is little more than a marsh, containing some deep pools. **1875** JOWETT *Plato* (ed. 2) I. 490 Like ants or frogs about a marsh.

β. **1671** *Coll. S. Carolina Hist. Soc.* (1897) V. 336 About ye rivers mouth & up the river beyond ye mashes. **1840** *Knickerbocker* XVI. 210, I reckon you won't get nothing for him without you turn him out on the mash. **1876** W. WHITMAN *Specimen Days* (1882–3) 94 The sedgy perfume.. reminded me of 'the mash' and south bay of my native island.

b. *local.* A meadow; a stretch of grassland near a river or the sea.

1787 W. MARSHALL *Rural Econ. Norfolk* I. 320 The upper sides [of the fens] being frequently out of the water's way, afford a proportion of grazable land: hence, probably, they are provincially termed marshes. **1852** L. A. MEREDITH *My Home in Tasmania* I. 163 (Morris), A marsh here is what would in England be called a meadow, with this difference, that in our marshes, until partially drained, a growth of tea-trees.. and rushes in some measure encumbers them; but, after a short time, these die off.. and a thick sward of verdant grass covers the whole extent. **1892** J. E. TAYLOR *Tourist's Guide Suffolk* (ed. 2) 23 Some of the larger river-valleys, such as the Stour, Orwell, Deben, Alde, Blyth, and Waveney, have these soils laid down in grass, forming rich and well-known grazing land, or 'marshes' as they are locally termed. **1892** P. H. EMERSON *Son of Fens* iii. 23, I went back to the sheep... I used to drive 'em down to mash along with the cows.

II. *attrib.* and *Comb.*

2. a. Simple attrib. sometimes passing into adj. (cf. MARISH): Consisting of a marsh or marshes; existing, found, or constructed in marshes; arising from or caused by marshes or their exhalations.

11.., etc. [see MARSHLAND]. *c* **1386** CHAUCER *Sompn. T.* (Ellesm. MS.) Ther is in yorkshire.. A merssh [*other texts* mersshy] contree called Holdernesse. **1523** FITZHERB. *Husb.* §54 Peny grasse.. groweth lowe by the erthe in a marsshe grounde. **1634** W. WOOD *New Eng. Prosp.* (1865) 44 On the other side of the River lieth all their Medow and Marsh-ground for Hay. **1726** LEONI *Alberti's Archit.* II. 110/1 Of all Marsh-water that is accounted the very worst which breeds horse-leeches. **1799** *Med. Jrnl.* II. 181 Not far dissimilar from marsh-miasmata. **1813** VANCOUVER *Agric. Devon* 302 Should the marsh-ooze be required for ploughed ground. *a* **1817** T. DWIGHT *Trav. New Eng.*, etc. (1821) I. 183 The substance which here so rapidly accumulates is what in this country is called marsh-mud; the material, of which its salt marshes are composed. **1852** WIGGINS *Embanking* 75 In Essex.. the soil is particularly favourable, both to sustain embankments, and as a material for making them, and is called Marsh clay. **1869** E. A. PARKES *Pract. Hygiene* (ed. 3) 71 Villages placed under the same conditions as to marsh air.

b. Applied to persons, animals, and plants living in marshes.

1607 TOPSELL *Four-f. Beasts* (1658) 165 The same.. driveth Gnats or marsh-flies out of a house. **1626** BACON *Sylva* §526 To take Marsh-Herbs, and Plant them upon Tops of Hills, and Champaignes. *a* **1861** WOOLNER *My Beautiful Lady* (1863) 109 Lone marsh-birds winged their misty flight. **1870** SWINBURNE *Ess. & Stud.* (1875) 326 A tuft of marshlilies midway on a steep and bare hill-side.

1890 'R. BOLDREWOOD' *Miner's Right* (1899) 122/2 Dismal waterlogged flats, where only the marsh-frogs made chorus.

3. Objective, instrumental, locative, etc., as ***marsh-dweller***; ***marsh-dwelling***, ***-girt***, ***-like*** adjs.

1891 J. A. OWEN etc. *Fishing Village* 287 The slow thinking and acting graziers and old *marsh dwellers. **1889** C. C. R. *Up for the Season* 259 Sad, *marsh-dwelling, porter-drinkers. **1889** DOYLE *Micah Clarke* 327 Its damp, *marsh-girt position. **1839** BAILEY *Festus* xix. (1852) 219 Doth not nature—All light in life, shine *marsh-like too, in death? **1888** RIDER HAGGARD *Maiwa's Revenge* iv. (1891) 40 We..took up the spoor..and followed it into the marsh-like land beyond.

4. a. Special combinations: †**marsh butter**, ? = *bog-butter* (see BOG *sb.*[1] 4); **marsh fever**, malaria fever; **marsh-fire, -light**, a will-o'-the-wisp; **marsh hay**, hay made from marsh grasses; †**marsh mutton**, mutton reared on Tilbury Marshes in Essex, from September to Christmas; **marsh-poisoning**, poisoning caused by the inhalation of vapours rising from marshes; **marsh rod**, a measure of length used for embanking work (see quots.); **marsh spot**, a deficiency disease of garden peas, caused by a lack of manganese; †**marsh wall**, a dike; **marsh-work**, work done on marshes; also †an establishment for making salt by evaporation of sea-water. See also MARSH-GAS, MARSHLAND, MARSHMAN.

c **1450** *ME. Med. Bk.* (Heinrich) 217 Tak anote schale, & ful hyt wyþ *mersch butter. **1752** PRINGLE *Obs. Dis. Army* (1765) 173 These *marsh-fevers are..apt..after intermitting for some days, to change again into continual fevers of a putrid and malignant nature. **1801** HAMILTON (*title*) On Marsh Remittent Fever. **1882** OUIDA *Maremma* I. 38 Her sons had died of the marsh fever. **1865** BARING-GOULD *Werewolves* 3 Its tongue out, and its eyes glaring like *marsh-fires. **1742** W. ELLIS *Mod. Husbandman* (1750) IV. 101 Curing coarse *Marsh-Hay. **1839** *Cultivator* VII. 33 The common marsh hay is no better than the 'bog meadow hay' of the east. **1852** *Trans. Mich. Agric. Soc.* III. 132 They feed well at the straw stack and thrive on marsh hay. **1895** A. PATTERSON *Man & Nature on Broads* 50 A sack of sweet 'mesh' hay an' a blanket or tew to tuck yerself in. **1924** *Beaver* Sept. 460/2 There is every indication of a poor [hay] crop... The Indians who depend upon the marsh hay have the same cry. **1961** J. W. ANDERSON *Fur Trader's Story* iii. 24 Marsh hay was used at these posts to feed the cattle. **1870** MORRIS *Earthly Par.* III. iv. 213 With gleaming, sand-choked, reed-clad pools, And *marsh-lights for the mock of fools. **1770** H. CHAMBERLAIN *Surv. Lond.* 649/2 This is what the butchers call, by way of excellence 'right *marsh mutton'. **1885–8** FAGGE & PYE-SMITH *Princ. Med.* (ed. 2) I. 186 The remittent forms of *marsh-poisoning. **1790** *Trans. Soc. Arts* VIII. 94 At the rate of thirty shillings the *marsh rod of twenty-one feet. **1852** WIGGINS *Embanking* 111 At 5s. per marsh rod of 18 feet forward. **1931** J. BRYCE in *Essex Farmers' Jrnl.* X. 71/1 *Marsh-Spot disease of peas..is carried in the seed. *Ibid.*, Marsh Spot is usually brought on to a farm in the seed peas. **1934** *Jrnl. Ministry of Agric.* Dec. 833 From time to time complaints are raised concerning a defect in pea seeds to which the name Marsh Spot has been given. The term appears to have originated from the fact that the trouble is most common in seeds from crops grown in low-lying marsh land... The defect..shows itself mainly in the form of a dark, often slightly sunken spot..on the face of each seed-leaf. **1959** *New Biol.* XXX. 91 Diseases such as ..'marsh spot' of peas are caused by the low availability of manganese in the soil. **1577** B. GOOGE *Heresbach's Husb.* I. (1586) 9 Some building vpon Riuers, some without or within the *Marshe walles. **1708** *Lond. Gaz.* No. 4453/3 A Dwelling-house and a *Marsh-work..with large Store-ponds, and Sun-ponds, for making of Brine. **1869** BLACKMORE *Lorna D.* lix, Seeing thus no track of men, nor anything but marshwork, and stormwork. **1897** *Jrnl. R. Agric. Soc.* Dec. 614 The boots..are similar to those used for marsh-work.

b. In names of animals inhabiting marshes, as **marsh blackbird**, the American red-winged blackbird or starling, *Agelæus phœniceus*; **marsh cow** *Palæont.*, a breed of cattle of which the remains are found in the Swiss lake-villages; **marsh deer**, a South American deer, *Cariacus paludosus*; **marsh-diver**, some kind of marsh-bird, ? the Water Rail, *Rallus aquaticus*; **marsh-fish**, the mudfish, *Amia calva*; **marsh fritillary**, a tawny butterfly, *Euphydryas aurinia*, formerly called the *greasy fritillary* (GREASY *a.* 9); **marsh-goose**, the greylag goose, *Anser cinereus*; **marsh harrier**, the moor buzzard, *Circus æruginosus*; **marsh hawk**, the American marsh harrier, *C. hudsonius*; **marsh hen**, the moorhen, *Gallinula chloropus*; *U.S.* applied to other rails, esp. *Rallus elegans* and *R. crepitans*; **marsh hog** *Palæont.*, a variety of the domestic swine of which the remains are found in the Swiss lake-villages; **marsh quail** *U.S.*, the meadow lark, *Sturnella magna*; **marsh ringlet**, the butterfly *Cœnonympha Davus* (Stainton *Brit. Butterflies* 1867); **marsh shrew**, a North American aquatic shrew, *Neosorex palustris*; **marsh tacky** *U.S.*, a small pony bred in marshy districts; **marsh tern**, the gull-billed tern, *Sterna anglica*, or the genus *Hydrochelidon*; **marsh tit** or **titmouse**, *Parus palustris*; **marsh treader** *U.S.*, a water bug of the family Hydrometridæ; **marsh worm**, a worm used as a bait in angling (see quot. 1856); **marsh wren** *U.S.*, a wren of the genus *Cistothorus*.

1831 A. WILSON & BONAPARTE *Amer. Ornith.* I. 199 They [red-winged starlings] are known by various names in the different States of the Union; such as..*marsh blackbird [etc.]. **1863** LYELL *Antiq. Man* 24 There were two races of cattle, the most common being of small size, and called by Rutimeyer..the *marsh cow. **1893** R. LYDEKKER *Horns & Hoofs* 343 The *marsh-deer (C. paludosus). **1847** TENNYSON *Princess* IV. 105 *Marsh-divers, rather, maid, Shall croak thee sister. **1836** J. RICHARDSON *Fauna Bor. Amer.* III. 236 *Amia ocellicauda*, *Marsh-fish. **1890** C. W. DALE *Hist. Brit. Butterflies* 202 The *Marsh Fritillary varies more generally than any other British butterfly. **1958** *Listener* 24 July 125/2 A series of observations on the Marsh Fritillary butterfly. **1768** PENNANT *Brit. Zool.* II. 448 The *marsh-goose, or grey-leg. **1802** G. MONTAGU *Ornith. Dict.* (1831) 315 *Marsh Harrier.—A name for the Moor Buzzard. **1831** A. WILSON & BONAPARTE *Amer. Ornith.* I. 90 Formerly the *marsh hawk used to be numerous along the Schuylkill and Delaware. **1802** G. MONTAGU *Ornith. Dict.* (1831) 188 Gallinule..Provincial.—Moor-hen. *Marsh-hen. *a* **1849** POE *Gold Bug*, Jupiter..bustled about to prepare some marsh-hens for supper. **1863** LYELL *Antiq. Man* 25 There were two tame races of the pig.., one large..the other smaller, called the *'marsh-hog', or *Sus scrofa palustris*. **1750** J. BIRKET *Some Remarks Voy. N. Amer.* (1916) 32 Killd some Squirrels and some very pretty birds called *Marsh quails something bigger than a field fare. **1883** *Century Mag.* 653 The meadow lark or marsh quail. **1935** J. C. LINCOLN *Cape Cod Yesterdays* 137 The Cape Cod market gunner of yesterday also shot upland birds for the market—quail, partridge, snipe,..'marsh quail' and an occasional pheasant. **1829** J. RICHARDSON *Fauna Bor. Amer.* I. 5 *Sorex Palustris*, American *Marsh-Shrew. **1838** C. GILMAN *Recoll. Southern Matron* xix. 131 An accident happening to my horse, I was obliged to hire one of the little animals called '*marsh tackies' to carry me over a creek. **1937** D. C. HEYWARD *Seed from Madagascar* 118 He could..gallop his 'marsh tackey' through thickets so dense that a rabbit could scarcely get through them. **1831** A. WILSON & BONAPARTE *Amer. Ornith.* III. 152 The *marsh tern is fourteen inches in length [etc.]. **1852** MACGILLIVRAY *Hist. Brit. Birds* V. 658 *Hydrochelidon nigra*, the Black Marsh-tern. **1802** G. MONTAGU *Ornith. Dict.*, *Marsh Tit. **1676** *Willughby's Ornithol.* 175 The *Marsh Titmouse or Black-cap. **1895** J. H. & A. COMSTOCK *Man. Study of Insects* xiv. 124 The *Marsh-treaders, family Limnobatidæ. **1902** L. O. HOWARD *Insect Bk.* 282 The Marsh Treaders (*Hydrometridæ*). **1972** SWAN & PAPP *Common Insects N. Amer.* 115 Marsh treader; *Hydrometra martini*. **1653** WALTON *Angler* iv. 94–5 The *marsh-worm. **1856** 'STONEHENGE' *Brit. Rural Sports* 236/1 The Marsh-Worm, or Blue-Head, is found in moist and undrained localities..In colour they are of a light dirty or brownish-purple. **1831** A. WILSON & BONAPARTE *Amer. Ornith.* II. 194 The *marsh wren arrives in Pennsylvania about the middle of May.

c. In the names of many plants that grow in marshes, as **marsh asphodel**, *Narthecium ossifragum*; †**marsh beetle** (BEETLE *sb.*[1]), the reed-mace, *Typha latifolia*; **marsh bent (grass)**, *Agrostis vulgaris*; **marsh centaury**, *Cicendia filiformis*; **marsh fern**, *Nephrodium Thelypteris*; **marsh flower**, any species of *Limnanthemum*, esp. *L. nymphæoides*; **marsh gentian**, *Gentiana Pneumonanthe*; **marsh gilliflower**, ragged robin, *Lychnis Flos-cuculi*; **marsh grass**, any grass that grows in marshy land, *spec.* one of the genus *Spartina*; **marsh-locks**, *Comarum palustre*; **marsh nut**, the marking-nut, *Semecarpus Anacardium*; **marsh orchis**, *Orchis latifolia*; **marsh penny-wort**, *Hydrocotyle vulgaris*; †**marsh pestle** = *marsh beetle*; **marsh reed**, *Phragmites communis*; †**marsh rocket**, a kind of watercress; **marsh rosemary**, *Ledum palustre*, *Andromeda polifolia*, *Statice Limonium*, or *S. caroliniana* (Treas. Bot.); **marsh samphire**, glasswort, *Salicornia herbacea*; **marsh tea**, *Ledum palustre* (Cent. Dict.); **marsh trefoil** [tr. L. *Trifolium palustre*], the buckbean, *Menyanthes trifoliata*. Also MARSHMALLOW, MARSH MARIGOLD, MARSHWORT.

For *marsh arrow-grass*, *m. bog-bean*, *m. cinquefoil*, *m. clover*, *m. daisy*, *m. elder*, *m. felwort*, *m. fleawort*, *m. hawk(s)-weed*, *m. helleborine*, *m. hog's fennel*, *m. horse-tail*, *m. lousewort*, *m. parsley*, etc., see these words.

1863 PRIOR *Plant-n.* 145 *Marsh Asphodel. **1578** LYTE *Dodoens* IV. liii. 513 Turner calleth it..in Englishe, Reede Mace, and Cattes tayle: to the which we may ioyne others, as Water Torche, *Marche Betill, or Pestill. **1764** *Museum Rusticum* II. lxxxviii. 300 The grass..proved to be the flote fescue, with a mixture of the *marshbent. **1857** MISS PRATT *Flower Pl.* V. 70 *Marsh Bent-grass. **1796** WITHERING *Brit. Plants* (ed. 3) II. 194 *Exacum filiforme*..Least Gentian, *Marsh Centory. **1857** MISS PRATT *Flower. Pl.* VI. 173 *Marsh Fern. **1866** *Treas. Bot.*, *Marsh-flower, *Limnanthemum*. **1722** QUINCY *Lex. Physico-Med.* (ed. 2) 349 **Marsh-Gentian*. **1578** LYTE *Dodoens* II. vii. 157 The fourth ..is called *Vetonica sylvestris*: in English wilde Williams, *Marshe gillofers, or Cockow gillofers. **1796** MORSE *Amer. Geog.* I. 180 Every appearance of a salt marsh, that is, *marsh grass, marsh mud, and brackish water. **1868** *Putnam's Mag.* May 592/1 Clumps..begin to make their appearance above the reeds and tall marsh-grass. **1936** D. MCCOWAN *Animals Canad. Rockies* xix. 169 His supper was often of coarse marsh grass. **1972** *Islander* (Victoria, B.C.) 23 Jan. 6/1 Acres of marsh grass where animals and birds feed. **1776** WITHERING *Bot. Arrangem. Vegetables* I. 310 *Comarum*..*Palustre*, *Marshlocks. **1866** *Treas. Bot.* 1047/2 Malacca-beans or *Marsh-nuts. **1857** MISS PRATT *Flower. Pl.* V. 210 *Marsh Orchis. **1578** *Marche Pestill [see *marsh beetle*]. **1761** STILLINGFLEET *Cal. Flora* 27 June, *Marsh pennywort, *Hydrocotule vulgaris*. **1885** *Outing* VII. 179/1 All the ground about is carpeted with the light-green leaves of the marsh-pennywort. **1960** *Oxf. Bk. Wild Flowers* 46/2 Marsh Pennywort or White-rot (*Hydrocotyle vulgaris*). This small, creeping or floating plant..differs from other Umbellifers in having undivided round leaves, with the leaf stalk attached at the centre of the leaf blade. **1797** *Encycl. Brit.* (ed. 3) II. 384/1 The phragmitis, or common *marsh-reed, grows by the sides of rivers and in standing waters. **1739** MILLER *Gard. Dict.* II. *Sisymbrium palustre minus* ..the lesser *Marsh-rocket. **1787** tr. *Linnæus' Fam. Plants* I. 294 *Ledum*. *Marsh Rosemary. **1845–50** MRS. LINCOLN *Lect. Bot.* v. App. 173 *Statice limonium* (marsh-rosemary, sea-lavender). **1861** MRS. STOWE *Pearl Orr's Island* I. x. 82 'Marsh rosemary is a very excellent gargle.' Said Mr. Sewell. [**1960** *Oxf. Bk. Wild Flowers* 118/2 Bog Rosemary or Marsh Andromeda (*Andromeda polifolia*). This small evergreen shrub up to 1 foot high has leaves which are shiny above and covered with a white bloom below.] **1727** THRELKELD *Synopsis Stirpium Hibern.* F 2 b, The English use the pickled shoots like Sampire to stir up an Appetite, and call it *Marsh-sampire. **1597** GERARDE *Herbal* II. ccccIxxxi. 1025 Marish Trefoile is called..in English marsh Clauer, *marsh Trefoile, and Buckes Beanes. **1764** *Museum Rusticum* I. 435 That the marsh-trefoil will cure the rot, I cannot, from experience, corroborate.

Marsh[2]. The name of James *Marsh* (1794–1846), British chemist, used in the possessive and *attrib.* to designate a sensitive test for the presence of arsenic in a substance (published by him in 1836), in which the substance is subjected to the action of nascent hydrogen so that any arsenic in it forms the gas arsine, which may be detected by decomposing it (e.g. by passing it through a heated glass tube) and looking for a dark stain of arsenic (distinguishable from a similar stain given by antimony by its solubility in sodium hypochlorite solution).

1855 J. SCOFFERN *Elem. Chem.* 479 Arseniuretted hydrogen thus employed, as a means of removing and discovering arsenic, is called Marsh's test, from its inventor, Mr. Marsh. **1930** D. L. SAYERS *Strong Poison* xx. 265 In a small apartment usually devoted to Bunter's photographic work..stood the apparatus necessary for making a Marsh's test of arsenic. **1968** *Materials & Technol.* I. ix. 399 Very minute quantities of arsenic can be detected by means of the Marsh test.

marsh, obs. form of MASH *v.*[1], MESH.

marshal ('mɑːʃəl), *sb.* Forms: α. 3 **marescal**, 3–9 **mareschal**, 5 **maresshall**, **mareschaul**, 5–7 **mareshall**, 6 **mareschall(e**, **marischale**, 7 **mariscall**, 7–8 **marishal**, 8 **marischal**, **maraschal**; β. 3–4 **marschal**, 3–5 **marchal**, **marschalle**, 4 **marscal**, 4–5 **marschale**, **marchall**, 4–6 **marschall**, 4–9 **marshall**, 5 **marschael**, **-schail**, **marchale**, **-chell**, **marshalle**, **-schel(l**, **-sshall**, **merschale**, **-sshall**, 5–6 **mershall**, 6 **merchal**, **marchaele**, 4–**marshal**; γ. 4 **marcial**, 5 **marchiale**, 5 6 **marciall**, **marcheall**, 6–7 **martiall**, 7 **marshial**, 7, 9 **martial**. [a. OF. *mareschal*, *marescal* (mod.F. *maréchal*) = Pr. *manescalc-s*, It. *mariscalco*, *maliscalco*, *maniscalco* farrier, marshal (Sp., Pg. *mariscal*, It. *maresciallo*, marshal, are from OFr. or Fr.):—Frankish Latin *mariscalcus*, ad. OHG. *marahscalh* or OS. **marhscalc* (MHG. *marschalch*, *-schalc*, early mod.G. *marschalk*, later *marschall*; MLG. *marschalk*, MDu. *maerschalc*, mod.Du *maarschalk*; Sw. *marskalk*, Da. *marskal* are from LG.):—OTeut. type **marhoskalko-z* lit. 'horse-servant', f. **marho-z* horse (whence fem. **marhjâ* MARE) + **skalko-z* servant (OE. *scealc* servant, G. *schalk* rogue). Compounds of equivalent meaning are OS. *ehuscalc*, OE. *horspegn*.

For the development by which a word originally meaning a groom or stable-man came to be a title of various high offices in royal households and in the army, cf. the parallel history of CONSTABLE. In Fr. and It. the sense 'farrier' has subsisted alongside the use as a title of dignity; in the Teut. langs. only the titular use has survived.]

†**1. a.** One who tends horses; *esp.* one who treats their diseases, a farrier. (Cf. *horse-marshal* s.v. HORSE *sb.* 28.) **b.** A shoeing smith. [F. *maréchal vétérinaire*, *maréchal ferrant*.] *Obs.*

c **1330** R. BRUNNE *Chron. Wace* (Rolls) 11179 þer maistres mareschals ferde aboute, Deliuered innes [*v.r.* stedes] wyþynne & wyþoute; Bordes broughte, cordes & cables, & made mangers to stande in stables. **1428** in *Surtees Misc.* (1888) 1 Burn, smyth in Bouthum and John Holgate, marsshall in the suburbe of Walmegate. **1474** CAXTON *Chesse* III. ii. E vj, Alle maner of werkmen; as goldsmythes, marchallis, smythes of alle forges. **1588** *Richmond Wills* (Surtees) 256 *note*, I have made an estatt unto Robert Selbye,..of my tenement..now in the tenure of Mr. Wedrington, mershall, and of the housses, stables, and grownde ower agaynst yt. **1618** SIR W. HOPE (*title*), The Parfait Mareschal, or, Compleat Farrier. **1639** T. DE GREY *Compl. Horsem.* 45 Skilfull ferrier or marshall he shall never be. *c* **1720** W. GIBSON *Farrier's Guide* II. xxii. (1738) 71 Such remedies as the Practise of the best Marishals has warranted.

2. One of the chief functionaries of a royal household or court; in the middle ages usually entrusted with the military affairs of his sovereign.

a. A high officer of state in England; now EARL MARSHAL, q.v. Formerly also ***Marshal of England***, ***High***, ***King's***, ***Lord Marshal***.

1258 *Eng. Proclam. Hen. III* Rog' Bigod eorl on Northfolk' and Marescal on Engleneloand'. **1297** R. GLOUC. (Rolls) 10081 þo þe king adde normandie in god stat ibrouȝt al þut lond he tok to loke william þe mareschal þat was erl of penbroc. *c* **1330** R. BRUNNE *Chron.* (1810) 292 After þe ersbisshop þe erle Marschalle Rogere Bifor þe kyng ros vp. **1480** CAXTON *Chron. Eng.* ccxiv. n 5 b, Thomas of Brothertone the Erle marchall. **1548** HALL *Chron., Hen. IV* 13 The erle of Westmerland his high Marshal. **1596** SHAKS. *1 Hen. IV*, IV. iv. 2 Beare this sealed Briefe With winged haste to the Lord Marshall. **1596** DALRYMPLE tr. *Leslie's Hist. Scot.* VIII. 142 The Duke of Norfolkis sone, cheif Tresurer and Merchall in Jngland. **1598** SYLVESTER *Du Bartas* II. i. II. *Imposture* 628 Mars-like Essex, England's Marshall-Earle. **1839** *Penny Cycl.* XIV. 447/2 One of the principal officers of state is the king's marshal, which office is now held hereditarily by the duke of Norfolk.

b. (Usually with spelling *marischal.*) A similar high officer of state in Scotland.

The office was hereditary in the family of Keith, and from 1458 the holder had the peerage title of Earl Marischal. The office became extinct by the attainder of George 10th Earl Marischal in 1716.

c **1375** BARBOUR *Bruce* XI. 456 Schir Robert of Keth, that wes Marshall of all the host of fee. **1461** *Liber Pluscardensis* x. x, Comes Eril Marschael [*v.r.* Marschail, Marchiale] nominatus. **1596** DALRYMPLE tr. *Leslie's Hist. Scot.* v. 302 That in perpetuall ane of that surname [Keith] sal be Mareschall in the kingis hous. **1715** EARL OF MAR *Procl.* in *Thanes Cawdor* (Spalding Club) 411 Some of his faithful subjects and servants met here, viz. the Lord Huntley, the Lord Tullybardine, the Earl Marischal [etc.].

c. ***Earl Marshal of Ireland***: a title conferred in 1574 upon Walter Devereux, Earl of Essex.

3. As a title of military rank.

†a. In early use employed vaguely: A commander, general. Subsequently (esp. in the forms ***marshal of the field*** or ***camp***, FIELD-MARSHAL), an officer of a definite rank, which varied according to period and country. *Obs.*

a **1300** *Cursor M.* 7630 Of a thusand men o wal, He made him ledder and marscal. **1362** LANGL. *P. Pl.* A. III. 194 Hedde I be Marchal of his Men. **1456** SIR G. HAYE *Law Arms* (S.T.S.) 112 The ledare of the bataille, that men callis now constable, or marschall in his absence. *a* **1450** *Knt. de la Tour* (1868) 16 The king of Hungry, that is of right marschalle of cristendom in the werres ayenst the hethen. **1548** UDALL, etc. *Erasm. Par. Acts* xxiii. 9–10 The marciall [L. *tribunus*] fearyng lest that Paul [etc.]. **1571** DIGGES *Pantom.* Pref. A ij b, The Marshall of the fielde shall.. appoynt place conuenient for his Campe. *a* **1587** GARRARD *Art War* (1591) 234 The high Marshall of the fielde, or maister of the Campe. **1593** NASHE *Unfort. Trav.* Wks. (Grosart) V. 33 The Marshall generall of the field. **1611** BIBLE *Jer.* lii. 12 Nebuzaradan the captaine of the guard [*marg.* chief marshal]. *a* **1628** F. GREVILLE *Sidney* (1652) 143 Meeting the Marshall of the Camp lightly armed. **1696** PHILLIPS (ed. 5), *Marshals* are also Military Officers, as the Camp-Marshal, who is the next Officer to the Lieutenant General.

fig. **1612** BACON *Ess., Atheism* (Arb.) 332 That an Army of infinite small portions or seeds vnplaced should haue produced this order, and beauty without a diuine Marshall.

b. A general officer of the highest rank in certain foreign armies. Often as prefixed title. (In 18th c. usually with semi-Fr. spelling *mareschal.*)

In the French army the full designation is *Maréchal de France* (Englished ***Marshal of France***).

1560 DAUS tr. *Sleidane's Comm.* 422 b, There were manye of the Nobilitie taken, amonges whome was the hyghe Mareshall of Fraunce. **1630** *R. Johnson's Kingd. & Commw.* 157 For the Marshals of France, 18000 [crownes] apeece, when they were but foure; for now it is a Title only, without either pension or command, save only in the foure chiefe. **1710** STEELE *Tatler* No. 174 ⁋1 He and the Duke of Berwick are to command the French Army, the rest of the Mareschals being only to assist in Council. **1752** HUME *Ess. & Treat.* (1777) II. 285 Such is the excellence which St. Evremond ascribes to mareschal Turenne. **1816** J. SCOTT *Vis. Paris* (ed. 5) p. lxi, Some of our Marshals have been invited to visit the Allied lines. **1878** BROWNING *La Saisiaz* 80 What might be the Marshal's next move, what Gambetta's counter-play.

†c. An officer in some military orders. *Obs.*

1615 G. SANDYS *Trav.* 230 The Martiall, the Maister of the Hospitall, the Admirall, the Chancelor, &c. [of the Knights of Malta].

d. Designating an officer of high rank in the Royal Air Force, as ***Marshal of the Royal Air Force***, ***Air Chief Marshal***, ***Air Marshal***, ***Air Vice-Marshal***; also **†** ***Marshal of the Air*** (obs.).

1919 *Times* 4 Aug. 12/6 His Majesty..has approved of new titles for the commissioned ranks of the Royal Air Force. These are..Marshal of the Air, Air Chief-Marshal, Air Marshal, Air Vice-Marshal... It will probably be some time before we have a Marshal of the Air, as at present there is no officer of the rank of either Air Chief-Marshal or Air Marshal. *Ibid.* 7 Aug. 14/6 Air Vice-Marshal Trenchard.. made the Air Force become the powerful and formidable fighting machine that it was. *Ibid.* 19 Aug. 10/4 The King has been pleased to approve the promotion of Air Vice-Marshal Sir H. Trenchard, K.C.B., to Air-Marshal. **1922** *Man. Seamanship* (Admiralty) I. 11 Marks of Rank... R.A.F. Marshal of the Air. R.N. Admiral of the Fleet. **1943** W. S. CHURCHILL *End of Beginning* 141 Most of the air-marshals, the leading men in the Air Force, think little of dive bombers. **1947** *Whitaker's Almanack* 461 (*heading*) Marshals of the Royal Air Force. **1968** *Who's Who* 1331/2 (*heading*) Harris, Marshal of the Royal Air Force Sir Arthur Travers.

4. †a. An officer of a court of law answerable for the charge and custody of prisoners and for the keeping of order, and frequently entrusted with the keeping of a prison. Also ***Marshal of the Exchequer***, ***of the King's*** (or ***Queen's***) ***Bench***. *Obs.*

These officers obtained the title as being deputies of the Marshal of England (see 2 a).

1290 *Becket* 802 in *S. Eng. Leg.* I. 129 Oþur is Marschales scholden swiþe anon is bodi to prisone take. *Ibid.* 805 þe Marchales i-redie weren to prisone him lede a-non. **1437** *Rolls of Parlt.* IV. 509/2 Was committed to the Marchall, in prison to abide. **1485** *Ibid.* VI. 291/2 The same William, was late Marshall of the Marshallsie of the Kings Bench. **1530** TINDALE *Gen.* Table Exp. Words s.v., And therfore I call him cheffe marshall an officer as is the lefetenaunte of the toure, or master of the marshalsye. **1674** *Ch. & Court of Rome* 9 He that..goes at large on his Parole.., is..no less a Prisoner, than when under Guard, and in the Marshals custody. **1690** *Lond. Gaz.* No. 2541/2 William Lenthall Esq; now Marshal of the King's Bench. **1768** BLACKSTONE *Comm.* III. 285 When once the defendant is taken into custody of the marshall, or prison-keeper of this court [of king's bench]. **1855** [see MARSHALSEA 1].

b. ***marshal of the admiralty***: an officer of the Court of Admiralty.

1769 *Ann. Reg.* 102 From the marshal of the admiralty in Holderness. **1802** *Naval Chron.* VIII. 423 The Deputy Marshal of the Admiralty.., with his silver oar. **1875** *Encycl. Brit.* I. 162 s.v. *Admiralty*, The marshal is now paid by a salary of £500, in addition to his travelling expenses.

c. ***judge's marshal***: an official (now usually a barrister) who accompanies a judge on circuit, and is charged with certain duties chiefly secretarial.

1861 M. ARNOLD *Lett.* 20 Mar., My brother-marshal, young Thesiger,..is a very good fellow.

5. a. An officer charged with the arrangement of ceremonies, *esp.* with the ordering of guests at a banquet, etc. (in this use often **†** ***marshal of the hall***).

In the English royal household the 'Marshal of the ceremonies' is now an official of the Lord Chamberlain's department, ranking below the 'Master of the ceremonies'.

13.. *Coer de L.* 1543 Hys mareschal swythe com hym too: 'Sere, he sayde, hou schal we doo? Swylk fowayle as we bought yistyrday, For no catel gete I may'. *c* **1386** CHAUCER *Prol.* 752 A semely man oure hoost was with alle For to been a Marchal in an halle. *c* **1460** J. RUSSELL *Bk. Nurture* 1002 The office of a connynge vschere or marshalle with-owt fable must know alle estates of the church goodly and greable. **1495** *Act. 11 Hen. VII*, c. 33. §14 John Hanley Squyer, oon of the Marshallis of oure Hall. **1520** WHITINTON *Vulg.* (1527) 4 After that the marshall [A.V. *John* ii. 9 ruler of the feast] dyd taste of the water tourned in to wyne. **1631** FULLER *David's Sinne* xxxvi, Others strive Like sturdy martialls, far away to drive The drowsy droanes that harbour in the hive. **1636** FEATLY *Clavis Myst.* iii. 31 They..send their Harbingers before to take up lodgings, and Martials to make way. **1706** PHILLIPS (ed. Kersey), *Marshal of the Ceremonies*, an Officer whose Business it is in all things, to receive Commands from the Master of the Ceremonies..for the Queen's Service. **1813** SCOTT *Trierm.* II. xiv, A shrilly trumpet shook the ground, And marshals clear'd the ring.

fig. **1590** SHAKS. *Mids. N.* II. ii. 120 Reason becomes the Marshall to my will, And leades me to your eyes.

†b. ***marshal of the King's*** (or ***Queen's***) ***house***; = ***knight marshal*** (see 6 b). *Obs.*

1433 *Rolls of Parlt.* IV. 447/1 The Steward and Marshall of his [the King's] houshold. **1543** tr. *Act 2 Hen. IV*, c. 23 The mareschal of the mareschalsye of the court of our soueraygne lord the kinges house. **1641** *Termes de la Ley* 200 b, The Marshall of the K. house. **1706** PHILLIPS (ed. Kersey), *Marshal of the Queen's House*, whose Office is to hear and determine Pleas of the Crown within the Queen's Palace... *Clerk Marshal of the Queen's House*, an Officer that attends the Marshal [of the Queen's House] in his Court.

c. (More fully ***City marshal.***) An officer of the corporation of the City of London. (See quot.)

1632, **1714** [see CITY 9]. **1761** *Lond. & Environs* IV. 265 *City Marshal*... His business is to see the laws of the city put in execution, and in solemn processions he rides before the Lord Mayor. **1905** *Whitaker's Almanack* 356 Officers of the City of London..Marshal, Capt. E. J. T. Kearns.

6. knight marshal. †a. A military officer, with functions corresponding to those of quartermaster; often used to render L. *tribunus militum. Obs.* **b.** *Hist.* An officer of the English royal household, who had judicial cognizance of transgressions 'within the king's house and verge', i.e. within a radius of twelve miles from the king's palace. The office was abolished in 1846.

[**1548**: cf. 3 a.] **1556** *Chron. Gr. Friars* (Camden) 65 Edmund Boner beynge prisoner in the Marchelse..the knyght marchalle takynge away hys bedde..because he wolde not geve the knyght marchall x li. **1592** NASHE *P. Penilesse* (ed. 2) 18 b, The Knight Marshals men, that naile vp Mandates at the Court gat. **1601** HOLLAND *Pliny* II. 116 Being a colonell and knight marshal of the campe [orig. *tribunus militum ab exercitu*]. **1617** MINSHEU *Ductor* s.v. *Knight*, Knight Martiall..*Tribunus militum, mariscallus*. **1623** COCKERAM I. s.v. *Tribune*, The other was called Tribune of the Souldiers, who had charge to see them well armed and ordered, being as the Knight Marshall is with vs. **1713** *Lond. Gaz.* No. 5135/3 His Excellency was receiv'd at the Palace Gate by Sir Phillip Meadows, Knight-Marshal.

fig. *a* **1591** H. SMITH *Serm.* (1594) 518 That God would make him [Satan] Knight Marshall ouer the world, to slay and kill as many as he hated.

7. The title of various functionaries charged with certain police duties, or with the office of superintending the infliction of punishment.

†a. = PROVOST-MARSHAL. *Obs.*

1596 SPENSER *State Irel.* Wks. (Globe) 644/1 That were a harde course, Eudoxus, to redresse every abuse by a Marshall. **1633** T. STAFFORD *Pac. Hib.* I. vii. (1821) 97 Moroghe Mac Shihy, Marshall to James Fits Thomas, and the Marshall of Dermond. *Ibid.* II. xxi. 416 The President, and the Marshall advanced forwards towards the Scout.

†b. *Naut.* An official on board ship who superintends the carrying out of punishments. *Obs.*

1627 CAPT. SMITH *Seaman's Gram.* viii. 35 The Marshall is to punish offenders, and to see iustice executed according to directions; as ducking at the yards arme [etc.]. *Ibid.* xv. 73 In English ships they seldome vse any Marshall.

8. In English university use. **a.** *Oxford.* The chief of the proctors' attendants or 'bulldogs'. **b.** *Cambridge.* Each of two officials appointed by the Vice-chancellor to act as his messengers, to summon meetings, etc.

1810 *Oxford Univ. Cal.* p. xvii, University Officers, &c... Belman...Marshal. **1853** 'C. BEDE' (E. Bradley) *Verdant Green* xi, The proctor with his marshal and bull-dogs.

9. *U.S.* **a.** 'In America, a civil officer, appointed by the President and Senate of the United States, in each judicial district, answering to the sheriff of a county. His duty is to execute all precepts directed to him, issued under the authority of the United States' (Webster 1828–32).

1793 JEFFERSON *Writ.* (1859) IV. 52 Rescuing a vessel out of the hands of the marshal who had arrested her by process from a court of justice. **1800** J. ADAMS *Wks.* (1854) IX. 76, I have agreed to the appointment of Major David Hopkins to be marshal of Maryland. **1856** OLMSTED *Slave States* 513 By the returns of the South Carolina marshals, the cash value of land, in the State, appears to be $5.08 an acre. **1872** RAYMOND *Statist. Mines & Mining* 107 The aggregate production [of bullion] was reported by the assistant marshal as follows.

b. ***marshal-at-arms***: an official in the House of Representatives corresponding to the English sergeant-at-arms.

1792 M. CUTLER in *Life* (1888) I. 483 The Speaker..sent the Marshall-at-Arms to summon them to attend the House.

c. An officer of a body of men or a society appointed to regulate its ceremonies, etc.; e.g. ***fire-marshall***, the chief officer of a fire brigade.

1903 *Daily Chron.* 31 Dec. 5/5 The fire marshal himself went up to the balcony.

¶**10.** For *marshal court*, *law*, see MARTIAL *a.*, COURT-MARTIAL.

marshal ('mɑːʃəl), *v.* Forms: 5 **mar(s)chal, mer(s)chal, marschel, marchell,** 6 **merschel,** 6–7 **marshall,** 6–9 **martial,** 7 **marshial,** 5– **marshal.** [f. MARSHAL *sb.*]

I. † 1. *trans.* To tend (horses) as a farrier. Also, to 'doctor' or 'fake up' for sale. *Obs.*

c **1430** *Pilgr. Lyf Manhode* III. xxviii. (1869) 150 Manye harmes dooth this hand; O time she marchaleth [orig. F. *cossonne*] hors, and maketh þe badde seeme good to hem þat wolen bigge hem. *c* **1470** HENRY *Wallace* v. 762 With his gud suerd the captayn has he tayn, Quhill hors agayne he marscheld neuir nayn. **1506** *Ld. Treas. Acc. Scot.* (1901) III. 202 Item, to deif Andro that marshalit foure hors to the King xiiijs.

II. Senses relating to MARSHAL *sb.* 3 and 5.

2. *trans.* To arrange, place, or rank in order at a feast, table, etc.

c **1450** HOLLAND *Howlat* 693 All war merschallit to meit meikly and myth. *c* **1470** *Gaw. & Gol.* 1160 The meryest on mold marschalit at mete. *a* **1548** HALL *Chron., Hen. VIII* 6 b, The Kyng caused the Quene to kepe the estate, and then satte the Ambassadours and Ladies, as they were Marshalled by the kyng, who would not sit, but walked from place to place. **1709** STEELE *Tatler* No. 96 ⁋1 It has cost me very much Care..to marshal and fix the People under their proper Denominations. **1814** SCOTT *Ld. of Isles* II. vi, And there he marshall'd them their place, First of that company. **1825** LYTTON *Zicci* 76 The guests were marshalled to the board. **1843** MACAULAY *Ess., Mme. D'Arblay* (ed. Montague) III. 299 In order that we may..marshal her to the exact seat to which she is entitled, we must carry our examination somewhat further.

†b. To put in a certain company, *among* or *with* certain people. *Obs.*

1530 LYNDESAY *Test. Papyngo* 587 The Erle of Marche wes merschellit yam amang. **1583** in Strype *Ann. Ref.* (1728) III. 183 The painful Pastors and Ministers of the Word.. are marshalled with the worst Malefactors.

†c. To arrange (a banquet). Also with *up*. *Obs.*

1587 FLEMING *Contn. Holinshed* III. 1490/1 The vshers marshalled the feast. **1613** DEKKER *Strange Horse-Race, Bankrouts Banq.* F 3 b, These Bankrouts..Martiald vp a Banquet, rellishing likewise of their name, carriage, and condition.

3. *Her.* To combine (two or more coats of arms) in one escutcheon, so as to form a single composition; also, to associate (accessories) with a coat of arms, so as to form a complete heraldic composition.

1572 BOSSEWELL *Armorie* II. 121 b, I haue omitted to marshal the same [coat] either with helme, wreathe, or mantle. **1610** GUILLIM *Heraldry* VI. ii. (1611) 256 If a bordured Coat be to be Marshalled amongst other Coats quarterly. **1864** BOUTELL *Her. Hist. & Pop.* xiv. 139 The arms of a Husband and Wife are marshalled in a single Shield.

4. To arrange or draw up (soldiers) in order for fighting, exercise, or review; to arrange in a body or procession; to arrange (competitors) for a race, etc.

1587 GREENE *Euphues Censure* Wks. (Grosart) VI. 254 A day of battell was set, wherein when both the armies were martialed..in their seuerall ranckes. **1598** BARRET *Theor. Warres* III. i. 49 To commaund the men to be marshalled into the order that shall bee appointed. **1601** DANIEL *Civ. Wars* v. xvii. (1609) 117 Those..troops so marshalled,.. That euen his soule seem'd onely to direct So great a body, such exployts t'effect. **1611** BIBLE *Josh.* i. 14 Ye shall pass before your brethren armed [*marg.* marshalled by five]. **1785** SARAH FIELDING *Ophelia* I. xxvi, A new way of martialing his army. **1791** COWPER *Iliad* IV. 271 Marshalling his numerous host. **1838** PRESCOTT *Ferd. & Is.* (1846) III. xii. 71 The duke..had marshalled his forces in a very different order. **1853** C. BRONTE *Villette* xxxiii, We were marshalled in order and soon started. **1868** FREEMAN *Norm. Conq.* (1876) II. viii. 260 Henry and William..were now marshalling their troops.

b. *transf.* and *fig.*

1698 [R. FERGUSON] *View Eccles.* Pref., Yet being otherwise Regimented and Marshal'd into sentences. **1852** M. ARNOLD *Empedocles* II. 276 Ye stars, Who slowly begin to marshal..Your distant, melancholy lines! **1878** BOSW. SMITH *Carthage* 226 The hostile Senate..had even then marshalled against him a long array of omens and portents.

†**c.** To marshal soldiers along (streets). *Obs.*

1587 FLEMING *Contn. Holinshed* III. 1332/1 Ten others [ensigns] had marshalled the streets unto the market place.

d. *refl.* and *intr.* To take up positions in or as in a military array or a procession.

1687 *Death's Vis.* vii, See, How they Marshall! How their Forces Join! **1691** RAY *Creation* I. (1692) 49 These new diminutive Particles should again assemble and marshal themselves into Corpuscles. **1806** A. DUNCAN *Nelson* 37 The procession was marshalling. **1854** S. DOBELL *Balder* xxviii. 190 Her serving men..marshal mutely round, and look from each to each with eye-lids red. **1903** F. C. MONTAGUE *Macaulay's Ess.* III. 1 His ideas marshal themselves in an unbroken rhetorical order.

5. *trans.* To dispose, arrange or set (things, material or immaterial) in methodical order.

Now chiefly with some metaphorical notion of an armed force or a procession; in the 17th c. used much more freely.

a **1550** *Vox pop., vox Dei* 335 in *Skelton's Wks.* (1843) II. 405/2 Then showld ye se the trade That marchantmen frist mayde, Whyche wysse men dyd marshall For a welth vnyversall. **1579** J. STUBBES *Gaping Gulf* D 3 Noble men and other great landed ones..in their vsuall conveighances do marshall the fal of theyr inheritances by limitation vpon limitation euen to the tenth son of theyr body begotten. **1586** I. ROSSE *Verses pref. to Ferne's Blaz. Gentrie*, In like sort shall you see How states of men are martialed, and placed in degree. **1614** RALEIGH *Hist. World* II. (1634) 542 These narrations of Herodotus may every one of them be true; tho' not in such order of time as he hath marshalled them. **1624** WOTTON *Archit.* (1672) 21 There are five Orders of Pillars..thus marshalled. **1639** FULLER *Holy War* III. xxx. (1640) 161 Provident Nature in marshalling the elements, assigned fire a place in the verge and border of this lower world. **1666** PEPYS *Diary* 21 Dec., So to the office in the evening to marshall my papers. **1725** POPE *Odyss.* I. 249 With feeble steps from marshalling his Vines Returning. **1765** BLACKSTONE *Comm.* I. 472 Having thus marshalled the several species of corporations, let us [etc.]. **1859** SMILES *Self-Help* iii. (1860) 59 With his books of reference marshalled round him on the floor. **1891** *Law Times* XC. 463/2 Clients..need to be represented by those who are adepts in marshalling facts and handling witnesses.

b. *Comm.* To arrange (assets or securities) according as they are available to meet various kinds of claims.

1773 VESEY *Chancery Rep.* II. 5 Though the court will help her by marshalling assets. **1818** CRUISE *Digest* (ed. 2) II. 178 [The court's] rules for marshalling assets. **1902** H. G. NEWTON in *Encycl. Brit.* XXVI. 136/1 s.v. *Bankruptcy in U.S.*, In partnership cases the creditors of the partnership elect the trustee... The assets are marshalled, partnership assets being applied first to partnership claims and individual assets to individual claims.

c. *U.S.* 'To arrange (the cars of a freight-train) in proper station order' (*Cent. Dict.*).

1880 *Car-Builder's Dict.* (Cent.).

6. To usher, guide (a person) on his way; to lead as harbinger; to conduct ceremoniously; also (*nonce-use*) to point *out* (the way).

1586 MARLOWE *1st Pt. Tamburl.* III. iii, Our conquering swords shall marshal vs the way We use to march upon the slaughter'd foe. **1605** SHAKS. *Macb.* II. i. 42 Thou marshall'st me the way that I was going. **1606** DEKKER *Sev. Sinnes* VI. (Arb.) 39 Mark in what triumphant and proud manner, he is marshalled through Newgate. *a* **1764** LLOYD *Prol.* 10 Himself shall marshal out the way to taste. **1821** BYRON *Two Fosc.* IV. i, Each night I see them Stalk frowning round my couch, and, pointing towards The ducal palace, marshal me to vengeance. **1831** SCOTT *Cast. Dang.* x, The abbot marshalled him to the door of Augustine's chamber. **1867** TROLLOPE *Chron. Barset* II. lxiii. 211 Mr. Crawley had marshalled him into the room.

Hence 'marshalling *ppl. a.*

1873 BLACK *Pr. Thule* xxvii, The first scouts of the marshalling forces of the clouds came up in flying shreds.

marshal, obs. form of MARTIAL.

'Marshalate. [f. MARSHAL *sb.* + -ATE^1.] **1.** The period of the rule of Marshal MacMahon as President of the French Republic (1873–79).

1874 *Daily News* 12 Jan. 5/2 What if we are to have a second Marshalate in Europe? **1889** W. S. LILLY *Cent. Revolut.* 2 This is the movement..which, thwarted for eighteen years by the Second Empire, and for five years more by the Marshalate, has since [etc.].

b. The order of Marshal in the French army.

1945 R. HARGREAVES *Enemy at Gate* 80 Commanders.. ear-marked..for ultimate promotion to the Marshalate of France. **1973** *Times Lit. Suppl.* 16 Nov. 1390/4 A slighter but handsomely produced and welcome book on the marshalate. *Napoleon's Marshals* is partly [etc.].

2. (With lower-case initial.) *U.S.* The office of a marshal (cf. MARSHAL *sb.* 9 a).

1954 W. FAULKNER *Fable* 159 After some months under the threat of the full marshalate, he compromised with his father on the simple deputyship.

marshalcy ('mɑːʃəlsɪ). Forms: α. 4 **marschalcie**, 4–5 **marchalsy(e, -sie**, 6 **marshalcye**, 6–8 **-sy**, 7 **-sie, mar-, merchaulcy, mareschalcy**, 8 **-sy**, 7– **marshalcy**. β. 4–5 **marchalsey, -se**, 5–6 **marshalse**, 6–8 **marshalsey**, 7 **marchalce**; and see MARSHALSEA. [ME. *marschalcie*, a. AF. *mareschalcie* (OF. *mareschaucie*):—Frankish L. *mariscalcīa*, f. *mariscalcus* MARSHAL *sb.* The β forms represent the OF. *mareschaucíee* (mod.F. *maréchaussée*), an extended form corresponding to med.L. *mariscalciāta* (1232 in Du Cange). As now used, the word is prob. a new formation on MARSHAL *sb.* + -CY, parallel with *generalcy*, *captaincy*, etc.]

†**1.** The art or occupation of a farrier; farriery.

a **1400** *Octouian* 1389 [He] seyde he hadde lerned marchalsye..And all maner of hors he knew. *c* **1720** W. GIBSON *Farrier's Guide* II. v. (1738) 17 Times and seasons.. which we find so much observ'd in Books of Marshalsy.

2. The office, rank, or position of a marshal.

c **1330** R. BRUNNE *Chron.* (1810) 292 Þe kyng for on sent, Sir Geffrey Geneuile, & of þe marschalcie presented him þe ȝerde. *c* **1330** —— *Chron. Wace* (Rolls) 7102 Fortyger hadde alle þe maystrie, Þe kyng at wille, & þe marchalsye [*v. r.* marchaucie; WACE *senescaucie*]. **1599** THYNNE *Animadv.* (1875) 72 Y^ou shall here some what of the marshalls office sett downe..in the Customes whiche Thomas of Brothertonne..challenged to his office of marshalcye. **1614** SELDEN *Titles Hon.* 232 Edward ii. afterward reciting this Surrender of Bigod grants the Honor and Marshalsie to his Brother Thomas of Brotherton in Taile.

b. *Hist.* The department of the marshal of the king's house. Also *attrib.*

1601 F. TATE *Househ. Ord. Edw. II* (1876) 38 A chief clarke of the marshalsy. *Ibid.* 39 He shal take iiij^d ob a day for his bouche in the marshalsy rolle.

†**3.** The military force under the command of a marshal. *Obs.* Chiefly as tr. F. *maréchaussée*.

1480 CAXTON *Chron. Eng.* clxxxix. 167 The children that were put in hostage..folowed the kynges marchalsye many dayes fetered in strong yrens. **1691** *Emilianne's Frauds Rom. Monks* (ed. 3) 386 The Archbishop..sent away all his Marshalsey, composed of the Barigel or Provost, and Threescore Sbirries or Serjeants. **1726** CAVALLIER *Mem.* IV. 317 Fifty Archers of the Mareschalsy of Diion. **1748** *St. James's Even. Post*, M. de Beauvais, Grand Provost of the Army..with all his Marshalsy and 80 Grenadiers.

'marshaless. [f. MARSHAL *sb.* + -ESS.] The wife of a marshal.

1787 CHARLOTTE SMITH *Romance Real Life.* I. 205 The Marshaless her mother, Madame Saligni, sister of the deceased Marshal. **1882** *Standard* 26 Dec. 3/1 The adventurous little Marshaleoooo..of the Third Empire. **1888** *Univ. Rev.* Oct. 227 The Marshaless struggled to keep in society.

marshalist, obs. form of MARTIALIST.

Marshall ('mɑːʃəl). The name of George C. *Marshall* (1880–1959), Secretary of State in the U.S.A. from 1947 to 1949, used *attrib.* to designate a plan initiated by him in 1947 to supply financial assistance to certain Western European countries to further their recovery after the 1939–45 war. Also applied to the aid so given or the nations receiving it.

1947 *N.Y. Times* 28 Dec. VI. 24/3 If at the end of the first year of the Marshall plan, Europe is not showing dividends, you will see what a collapse there will be. **1948** *Observer* 18 Apr. 4/6 The Paris conference of the 16—now, with the accession of the Western zones of Germany, 17—Marshall nations has made history. **1950** *Times* 6 July 5/2 Marshall aid authorizations for Britain during the month were..the second largest sum earmarked in May. **1952** R. KNOX *Hidden Stream* vi. 54 Almighty God never goes in for Marshall plans, he always gives us more than we ask for. **1958** *Listener* 24 July 117/2 It looks..as though the United States are now beginning a new sort of Marshall Aid policy towards their southern neighbours. **1958** *Spectator* 15 Aug. 233/3 The Marshall-planned reconstruction of Europe. **1959** *Political Sci. Q.* LXXIV. 240 The principal object of the Marshall plan was to assist Europe to rehabilitate its factories and workshops so that its citizens would once again find employment and make their contributions to the channels of trade. **1975** *Sat. Rev.* 25 Jan. 16/3 The United States is back in the business of propping up Europe, although by more sophisticated mechanisms than the straight-aid programs of the Marshall Plan. **1975** *Times* 9 May 16/7 In the postwar period most West Germans regarded America as the great good place, the magnanimous victor whose Marshall Aid raised them from the ruins.

marshalled ('mɑːʃəld), *ppl. a.* [f. MARSHAL *v.* + -ED^1.] In senses of the verb: Drawn up in ranks, arranged in order, etc.

1667 MILTON *P.L.* IX. 37 Marshal'd Feast Serv'd up in Hall with Sewers, and Seneshals. **1693** DRYDEN *Juvenal* x. (1697) 246 Unwieldy Sums of Wealth, which higher mount Than Files of Marshall'd Figures can account. **1726** POPE *Odyss.* xx. 342 By Heralds rank'd, in marshal'd order move The city-tribes. **1853** M. ARNOLD *Sohrab & Rustum* 140 Marshall'd battalions bright in burnish'd steel.

'marshaller ('mɑːʃələ(r)). [f. MARSHAL *v.* + -ER^1.] One who marshals; a marshal.

1616 J. LANE *Contn. Sqr.'s T.* XI. 247 Within a while more trumpettes gann resound, that more knightes binn arivd.. for whome large space was made by th' marshallers. **1718** J. TRAPP tr. *Virgil's Aeneid* I. p. xlix, He [*sc.* Dryden] was the great Refiner of our English Poetry, and the best Marshaller of words. **1910** *Westm. Gaz.* 11 Apr. 8/3 The marshallers were everywhere, watching and directing. **1960** *Times* 6 Aug. 4/2 Manchester airport marshallers, who are responsible for manoeuvring airliners on the tarmac.

Marshallese (mɑːʃə'liːz), *sb.* and *a.* [f. the *Marshall* Islands in the Pacific Ocean + -ESE.] **A.** *sb.* **a.** The language of the inhabitants of the Marshall Islands. **b.** The inhabitants themselves. **B.** *adj.* Of or pertaining to this language.

1945 *Language* XXI. 267 (*heading*) Notes on Marshallese consonant phonemes. *Ibid.*, The orthography of Marshallese was devised by American Protestant missionaries in the middle of the last century. **1964** E. A. NIDA *Toward Sci. Transl.* iii. 54 In Marshallese, a language of Micronesia, a number of psychological states are described in terms of the throat. **1970** *Language* XLVI. 672 He [*sc.* Bender] claims that the mid-high vowels of the surface representations of Marshallese are not present in the underlying representations. **1971** *Ibid.* XLVII. 734 The glossary..differentiates between some Marshallese words which are semantically and phonemically distinct but tend to be spelled alike by previous European students of the language—and by most Marshallese. **1972** J. L. DILLARD *Black English* iv. 161 In the case of Melanesian Pidgin,..he also recognizes the influence of a similar structure in Marshallese.

marshalling ('mɑːʃəlɪŋ), *vbl. sb.* [f. MARSHAL *v.* + -ING^1.] The action of the verb MARSHAL. Also *attrib.*, esp. in ***marshalling yard***, a railway yard in which goods trains are assembled and distributed.

c **1460** J. RUSSELL *Bk. Nurture* 1165 Thus may ye devise youre marshallynge,..to þe honoure and worshippe of youre souereyn euery where. **1591** PERCIVAL *Sp. Dict.* F iv, The marshalling of the letters in the alphabet. *a* **1635** NAUNTON *Fragm. Reg.* (Arb.) 39 (*Knowls*) If I be not a little mistaken in their names and martialling. **1768** BLACKSTONE *Comm.* III. 105 The marshalling of coat-armour..is now greatly disregarded. **1816** BYRON *Ch. Har.* III. xxviii, The midnight brought the signal-sound of strife, The morn the marshalling in arms! **1877** BLACK *Green Past.* xxvi, The marshalling of the innumerable hosts of heaven. **1889** G. FINDLAY *Working & Managem. Eng. Railway* xi. 172 At certain important places throughout the country..schemes of marshalling sidings of elaborate construction and great extent have been laid down. **1906** *Railway Mag.* XVIII. 180/1 On one side of the line is seen the recently constructed sorting and marshalling yard. **1940** *Times* 25 Sept. 4/1 One of the aircraft which bombed a marshalling yard only a few miles from the heart of Berlin. **1955** *Times* 12 July 3/4 He had just heard from the commission that they had approved new works at Perth, including the construction of a fully mechanized hump marshalling yard. **1967** G. F. FIENNES *I tried to run a Railway* v. 56, I started to draw a double direction marshalling yard.

marshallist, obs. form of MARTIALIST.

marshal-man. Orig. marshal's man. The designation of various officers. **a.** (More fully †***knight-marshal's man*** (obs.), ***king's marshal-man.***) One of a number of men (formerly under the orders of the knight marshal) belonging to the royal household, and going before the king in processions to clear the way. **b.** A similar officer under the orders of the marshal of the City of London.

1638 RANDOLPH *Muses Looking-gl.* I. i. 3 Bailies, Promooters, Iaylors, and Apparitours, Beadles, and Martialls men, the needfull instruments Of the Republique. **1697** *Lond. Gaz.* No. 3341/2 The Messengers of the Chamber and Knight-Mareschalls Men attending the Proceeding in their proper Stations. **1707** J. CHAMBERLAYNE *Pres. St. Eng.* II. III. 541 (*List Househ. Off. below Stairs*) Sir Philip Meadows Knight-Marshal. John Lester [etc.], Marshal's Men. **1763** *Brit. Mag.* IV. 219, 1st, the king's marshalmen, two and two. **1778** *Ann. Reg.* 175 The court then proceeded to the election of a marshalman. **1879** *Daily Chron.* 26 June, William Willshire, formerly marshalman at Hampton Court Palace. **1902** *Westm. Gaz.* 11 Aug. 9/1 His Majesty's Marshalmen, in scarlet.

marshalment ('mɑːʃəlmənt). *Law.* [f. MARSHAL *v.* + -MENT.] The act of 'marshalling' assets.

1818 CRUISE *Digest* (ed. 2) I. 214 That the whole annuity, by an equitable marshalment, shall be thrown upon the two remaining thirds.

marshalsea ('mɑːʃəlsiː). *Hist.* Forms: see MARSHALCY; also 4 **marchasye**, 5 **marschalse**, 6 **marshialshy, mareshelsey, marchese, marshashey**, 7 **marshall sea, (martial sea)**, 6– **marshalsea.** [The same word which in other senses is spelt MARSHALCY. In the 16–17th c. the word was imagined to be f. MARSHAL + SEE, seat.]

1. A court (abolished in 1849) formerly held before the steward and the knight-marshal of the royal household of England (latterly before a barrister appointed by the knight-marshal), originally for the purpose of hearing cases between the king's servants, but afterwards with wider jurisdiction. Also, a prison in Southwark

under the control of the knight-marshal (abolished in 1842).

1389 in *Eng. Gilds* (1870) 354 He sholde make whitbred, and wel y-bake, after þe sale of corn, and vp-on þe a-syse of þe marchasye. **1428** in *E. E. Wills* (1882) 78 The prisons of Ludgate, Marchalsie, Kyngesbenche. **1436** *Ibid.* 106 To the Prisoners of the Marchalse. *c* **1500** *God speed the Plough* 77 Then commeth the tipped-staves for the Marshalse, And saye they haue prisoners mo than Inough. **1501** in *Bury Wills* (Camden) 89 The prisoners in Newgate, Ludgate, to the Kyngs Benche, and to the Marshalsy. *c* **1550** *Manifest Detect. Diceplay* (Vele) C iij b, Your fine chets..made both in yᵉ kings bench & in yᵉ marshalsea. **1545** Brinklow *Compl.* xi. C vj, The court of the marshalse. **1549** Latimer *4th Serm. bef. Edw. VI* (Arb.) 120 Thre wekes sessions at newgate, and fourthnyghte sessions at the Marshialsy. **1556** *Chron. Gr. Friars* (Camden) 63 He was send unto the Marchese. **1591** Lambarde *Archeion* (1635) 21 The Marshalsey for matters within the Verge or limits assigned to the Kings House or Palace. **1613** Shaks. *Hen. VIII*, v. iv. 90 Ile finde A Marshallsey, shall hold ye play these two Monthes. **1639** in *Verney Papers* (1853) 215, I praye lett mee heare how businesses goes att the marshall seas, boat[h] in the prison and in the courte. **1641** Prynne *Antip.* 239 He was committed to the Marshashey among Rogues and murtherers. **1654** Warren *Unbelievers* 236 We..must commit his Minor to the Marshalsie as a Rebel against reason. **1660** *Trial Regic.* 146 In the Case of Martial sea, and in the Common Pleas. **1768** Blackstone *Comm.* III. 76 The court of the marshalsea, and the palace court at Westminster, though two distinct courts, are frequently confounded together. **1855** Dickens *Dorrit* i. xxxii, The Marshal of the Marshalsea..had got him hard and fast.

attrib. **1764** Burn *Poor Laws* 48 A reasonable allowance to the constable..to be paid out of the gaol and marshalsea money. **1813** *Gentl. Mag.* i. 480 The Southern boundary wall of the Marshalsea Prison. *a* **1825** Forby *Voc. E. Anglia*, *Marshalsea-money*, the county rate.

2. Used as the name of certain prisons elsewhere than in London.

1657 *Pittington* etc. *Vestry Bks.* (Surtees) 309 For payment of the arreares for the jaole and marshalsey [Houghton-le-Spring].

¶ **3.** Used *Hist.* for marshalcy 2 b.

1904 Mary Bateson *Miscell. Scot. Hist. Soc.* II. Introd. 10 [A record of 28 Ed. I] shows that a number of persons were not 'at the king's wage in the roll of his marshalsea' [orig. *in rotulo Marescalcie sue*].

marshalship (ˈmɑːʃəlʃɪp). [f. marshal *sb.* + -ship.] The office or position of marshal.

1530 Palsgr. 243/1 Marshalshyppe, *marchalcee.* **1549** Edw. VI *Jrnl.* Lit. Rem. (Roxb.) II. 244 The lord Protectour..lost his protectourship, treasourirship, marschalshipe [etc.],..by acte of parliement. **1592** Kyd *Sp. Trag.* iii. vi. 28 To your marshallship First I confesse..I am the man. **1606** G. W[oodcocke] *Hist. Ivstine* xiii. 58 The Marshallship of the campe fortuned to Seleuchus, the sonne of Antiochus. **1670** G. H. *Hist. Cardinals* ii. iii. 187 To that Marshalship [Marisciallo di Santa Chiesa], belongs the keeping of the Conclave. **1815** Southey in *Q. Rev.* XIII. 493 The more ambitious spirits who aspired to Marshalships [etc.]. **1881** *Nation* (N.Y.) XXXII. 362 When they find the Administration giving marshalships..to persons [etc.].

marshashey, obs. form of marshalsea.

marshbanker, -bunker: see mossbunker.

marsh gas. Light carburetted hydrogen, CH_4, found in coal-mines and about stagnant pools. (Cf. fire-damp.)

1848 Fownes *Elem. Chem.* 189 Marsh-gas. **1881** *19th Cent.* No. 48. 245 Light carburetted hydrogen, or marsh gas, ..is the cause of explosions in collieries.

marshial(e, -iall, obs. ff. marshal, martial.

marshialshy, obs. form of marshalsea.

marshiness (ˈmɑːʃɪnɪs). [f. marshy + -ness.] Marshy nature or condition of ground.

1710 *Lond. Gaz.* No. 4757/1 The wet Weather and the Marshyness of the Ground make our Approaches very difficult. **1763** W. Roberts *Florida* 64 The worst circumstance..was the marshiness of the soil, where they were sometimes obliged to sleep in the water. **1876** *Daily News* 27 Oct. 5/5 The marshiness of the alluvial soil about the river.

marshing (ˈmɑːʃɪŋ), *vbl. sb. local.* [f. marsh *sb.*¹ + -ing².] **a.** The keeping of cattle for a period on salt marshes. **b.** Work done on a marsh.

1778 [W. Marshall] *Minutes Agric.* 7 Nov. 1776 [To] give them [*sc.* cattle] three weeks or a month's marshing, during the summer-vacation. **1892** P. H. Emerson *Son of Fens* 78 Mashing includes marsh-mowing, dyke-cutting, bottom-fying, dike-drawing, &c.

marshite (ˈmɑːʃaɪt). *Min.* [f. the name of its discoverer, C. W. *Marsh*, 19th-cent. Australian mineralogist + -ite¹.] Native cuprous iodide, CuI, found as colourless to pale yellow isometric crystals that redden when exposed.

1893 A. Liversidge in *Jrnl. & Proc. R. Soc. New South Wales* XXVI. 328 Mr. Marsh forwarded to me a small specimen of the copper iodide, and I have verified the principal characteristics as given in his description; as the mineral appears to be a new one, I suggest that it be named Marshite. **1939** *Amer. Mineralogist* XXIV. 629 Marshite, the natural cuprous iodide, was discovered by C. W. Marsh (1893) in the oxidized zone of the lead, zinc, and silver deposit at Broken Hill...In 1937, some crystals intimately associated with atacamite were found at the south end of the oxidized ore body at Chuquicamata [in Chile]. **1964** *Mineral. Abstr.* XVI. 491/2 The fluorescence of the halides sylvine, halite, marshite, and calomel is described.

marshland (ˈmɑːʃlænd). [OE. *mersclond*: see marsh *sb.*¹ and land *sb.*¹] Land consisting of marsh; marshy country.

c **1122** *O. E. Chron.* an. 1098 For neah ælc tilð on mersc lande for ferde. [*a* **1300** *E. E. Psalter* cvi. 34 In saltmersche land fruitberande.] **1426** Lydg. *De Guil. Pilgr.* 21044 A Maryssh, or elles a mersshe lond, That peryllous was, and ful profounde. **1651** N. Bacon *Disc. Govt. Eng.* ii. xxxiii. (1739) 150 Malicious breakings of the Dikes and Banks in Marshlands. **1700** Tyrrell *Hist. Eng.* II. 803 The Marshland of Norfolk. **1834** *Good's Study Med.* (ed. 4) I. 602 The febrile miasma issuing from marsh lands. **1843** 'R. Carlton' *New Purchase* I. ix. 58 They had been sufficiently fortunate as to..learn the nature of 'mash land'. **1901** *Spectator* 17 Aug. 215/2 On the other side of the creek a flat expanse of marshland extends for a mile or two.

b. *attrib.* or as *adj.*

1870 Morris *Earthly Par.* III. iv. 220 The marshland haze. **1889** Hissey *Tour in Phaeton* 182 Rich marshland pasturage. **1893** J. A. Owen, etc. *Forest Tithes* 195 One marshland farm I often visited.

Hence **ˈmarshlander**, (*a*) (see quot.); (*b*) an inhabitant of marshland.

1787 W. Marshall *Norf.* (1795) II. 383 *Marshlanders*, cattle of the marshland or short-horned breed. **1896** W. A. Dutt *George Borrow in E. Anglia* v. 46 Farther away the marshlanders have seized upon any slight piece of rising ground.

marshlock, obs. form of mashloch *Sc.*

† **ˈmarshly**, *a. Obs. rare*⁻¹. In 4–5 mersschly. [f. marsh *sb.*¹ + -ly¹.] Marshy.

c **1386** Chaucer *Sompn. T.* 2 (Harl.) Þere is in Engelond, I gesse, A mersschly lond, called Holdernesse.

marshmallow. Forms: see marsh *sb.*¹ and mallow. [OE. *merscmealwe.*] **a.** (Also *pl.*, const. as *sing.*) A shrubby herb, *Althea officinalis* (NO. *Malvaceæ*), which grows near salt marshes, having ovate leaves, pale rose-coloured flowers, and a mucilaginous root.

For various local applications of the name see *E.D.D.*

c **1000** *Sax. Leechd.* I. 140 Ðeos wyrt þe man hibiscum & oðrum namen mersc mealwe nemnaþ. *a* **1100** *Ags. Voc.* in Wr.-Wülcker 296/21 *Arthea*, merscmealewe. *c* **1450** *Alphita* (Anecd. Oxon.) 22/2 Bismalua, alta malua, altea idem,.. wymalue uel marshmalue. **1543** Traheron *Vigo's Chirurg.* ii. ii. 14 b/1 Take..of the rootes of Altea called Holyhocke, or marche mallowes.., a pounde. **1597** Gerarde *Herbal* ii. cccliii. (1633) 935 The leaves of Marsh Mallow are of the power to digest. **1683** Tryon *Way to Health* 576 Mallows and Marsh-Mallows..will cure near Fifty Diseases. **1718** Quincy *Compl. Disp.* 112 *Althææ.* Marshmallows. It flowers in July and August. **1876** tr. *von Ziemssen's Cycl. Med.* IV. 210 For the relief of the irritable cough,..an infusion of marsh mallow or expectorant herbs.

attrib. **1612** Woodall *Surg. Mate* Wks. (1653) 205 Decoction of March Mallow roots in water. **1753** Bartlet *Farriery* 96–7 The marshmallow ointment. **1755** *New & Compl. Dict. Arts & Sci.* IV. 3023/2 Sydenham recommends..a posset drink, in which two ounces of marsh-mallow roots have been boiled. **1836** J. M. Gully *Magendie's Formul.* (ed. 2) 105 Marshmallow syrup.

b. A confection made from the root of this plant. Also *fig.*, esp. something or someone that is soft at the centre, 'gooey', sentimental.

1884 *Chamb. Jrnl.* 4 Oct. 640/2 Gum-arabic..makes about thirty per cent. of the best quality of gum-drops, marsh-mallow, and jujube paste. **1902** *Westm. Gaz.* 11 Aug. 12/1 Chocolates, 'marsh-mallows', and other toothsome delicacies. **1935** A. Woollcott *Let.* 19 Dec. (1946) 126 It is the substance of this editorial that as a recommender of books over the radio, I take advantage of a nation-wide network to further the sale of soft, sentimental works. 'Marshmallows' was the term employed. **1962** *Listener* 20 Sept. 452/1 The result was a marshmallow. The production [of a radio play], the music, and the story pulled apart. **1966** *Punch* 1 June 817/3 The situations are witty, the songs as true, her eyes as mistily, romantically happy as I remembered. Perhaps it is just that I am more of a marshmallow than I was as a teenager. **1971** *Guardian* 10 May 10/5 Nine tenths of what actually goes on in schools is emotional marshmallow. **1973** M. Yorke *Grave Matters* i. ii. 14 So tough, you'd like us all to think, but inside you're a veritable marshmallow. **1974** *Times* 30 Apr. 9/3 Andy Williams might seem like marshmallow on television but.. has a superb flair.

c. *attrib.* and *Comb.* (also in *fig.* sense of 'soft, delicate; sticky, cloying, excessively sweet'); **marshmallow roast**, a party at which marshmallows are served.

1906 *Amer. Illustr. Mag.* Mar. 562/1 Girls assemble shreds and patches, buttons and marshmallow boxes. **1914** *Nation* 27 Aug. 242 A lady of the very highest fashion had been that evening entertaining at a 'marshmallow roast'. **1918** in C. B. de Mille *Autobiogr.* (1959) x. 209 The photoplay is breaking away from the marshmallow school of drama. **1926** *Hutchinson's Best Story Mag.* Nov. 109/1 Chocolate marshmallow ice cream. **1930** E. Pound *XXX Cantos* xxix. 137 Languor has cried unto languor about the marshmallow-roast. **1934** T. Wilder *Heaven's my Destination* 43 A campfire sing and marshmallow roast. **1936** M. H. Bradley *Five-Minute Girl* 235 It was to be a marshmallow roast, with coffee. **1959** *Times* 14 Feb. 9/7 His [*sc.* a pianist's] exquisite, marshmallow-fingered touch. **1973** *Washington Post* 13 Jan. A. 18/3 (Advt.), Refined, traditional sleep sofa..84" with deep tufted back and marshmallow front loose seat cushions. **1973** L. Hellman *Pentimento* (1974) 188, I never heard his name through the marshmallow English syllables. **1973** *N.Y. Law Jrnl.* 4 Sept. 4/7 A prosecutor in his summation is not required to hit the defendant with marshmallow blows, but his attack must be fair and within recognized limits of law.

ˈmarshman. A dweller in marshy country; an inhabitant of a particular stretch of marshland, e.g. Romney Marsh.

1573 Tusser *Husb.* (1878) 38 Sharpe cutting spade, for the deuiding of mow, with skuppat and skauel, that marsh men alow. **1587** Fleming *Contn. Holinshed* III. 1540/2 That sir Thomas Scot would throughlie informe himselfe by conference with the marshmen. **1610** Holland *Camden's Brit.* i. 350 In the Saxons time the inhabitants heereof [Rumney] were called Mersc-ware, that is Marshmen. **1827** *Sporting Mag.* XX. 39 These birds (*colymbus minutus*) are.. called by the Marshmen *Spider Divers.* **1889** Doyle *Micah Clarke* 294 The riot had now changed into open mutiny among these marshmen and miners.

marsh marigold. Also 7 March-. A ranunculaceous plant, *Caltha palustris*, growing in moist meadows and bearing showy golden flowers.

1578 Lyte *Dodoens* i. xx. 31 The small Celandyne, and the Braue Bassinet, or Marsh Marigold, do grow in moyst medowes. **1597** Gerarde *Herbal* ii. cclxxx. 670 Marsh Marigold hath great broad leaues somewhat round, of a gallant greene colour,..among which rise vp thicke fat stalkes..whereupon do growe goodly yellow flowers. **1657** S. Purchas *Pol. Flying-Ins.* i. xv. 94 Bees gather of these flowers following..In April..March-marigold. **1756** C. Lucas *Ess. Waters* II. 131 All over it [grow] rushes, red rattle, marsh-marygold [etc.]. **1833** Tennyson *May Queen* i. 31 The wild marsh-marigold shines like fire in swamps and hollows gray. **1882** *Garden* 15 Apr. 261/2 Wild Marsh Marigolds fill a large bowl on a hall table.

marshwort (ˈmɑːʃwɜːt). [See marsh *sb.*¹ and wort.] The umbelliferous plant *Helosciadium* (*Sium*) *nodiflorum*.

1776 Withering *Bot. Arrangem. Vegetables* I. 127 Marshwort, *Samolus.* **1897** *Jrnl. R. Agric. Soc.* Dec. 617 Procumbent marsh-wort, *Helosciadium nodiflorum*, is a plant with the habit of watercress.

¶ An error for *marsh* or *marish whort* (see marish 2 b).

1864 Prior *Plant-n.* 146.

marshy (ˈmɑːʃɪ), *a.* Also 4 mershi. [f. marsh *sb.*¹ + -y.] Pertaining to or of the nature of a marsh; consisting of or containing marshes or marshland.

1382 Wyclif *Gen.* xli. 2 Thei weren fed in mershi places. **1580** Hollyband *Treas. Fr. Tong*, *Lieu marescageux*, marshy ground. **1697** Dryden *Virg. Georg.* iii. 605 And from the marshy Land Salt Herbage for the fodd'ring Rack provide. **1703** Maundrell *Journ. Jerus.* (1732) 21 A restless night, in a marshy and unwholsome ground. **1876** Bancroft *Hist. U.S.* VI. liv. 425 Over a marshy ravine in front of the right, a large redoubt was placed.

b. Produced in or characteristic of marshland.

1697 Dryden *Virg. Georg.* iii. 277 Their wanton Appetites not only feed With Delicates of Leaves, and marshy Weed, But [etc.]. **1870** A. R. Wallace *Nat. Sel.* (1871) 53 The prevalent forms and colours of marshy vegetation.

Marsi (ˈmɑːsiː). *Hist.* [L.] A Sabine people who lived near the Fucine Lake in ancient Central Italy.

1578 tr. *Appian's Auncient Hist. Romanes Warres* i. 29 (*marginal note*) Marsi a valiant people in Latio. **1764** N. Hooke *Roman Hist.* III. vii. viii. 110 The Marsi, a people renowned for bravery,..gave their name to this war, because they were the first in the revolt. **1949** [see next].

Marsian (ˈmɑːsɪən), *sb.* and *a.* [f. prec. + -an.] **A.** *sb.* **a.** One of the Marsi. **b.** The language of the Marsi. **B.** *adj.* Of or pertaining to the Marsi or their language. Also **ˈMarsic** *a.*

1578 tr. *Appian's Auncient Hist. Romanes Warres* i. 29 C. Marius did followe valiantly the Marsians that lay against them. **1632** J. Vicars tr. *Virgil's Aeneid* vii. 972 Herbs that grow on Marsian mountains high. **1697** Dryden tr. *Virgil's Georgics* ii. 230 Hence rose the Marsian and Sabellian Race. **1764** N. Hooke *Roman Hist.* III. vii. viii. 108 (*heading*) The war called the Marsic, the Social, the Italic war. **1882** *Encycl. Brit.* XIV. 327/1 Oscan or Samnite..the language of the Sabines, the Marsians, and the Volscians, of which but scanty traces remain. **1883** C. C. Perkins *Hist. Handbk. Italian Sculpture* i. i. 21 The ruins of the old Marsian city of Alba. **1890** *Cent. Dict.*, Marsic. **1897** R. S. Conway *Italic Dial.* I. 288 The Marsian, Aequian and Faliscan inscc... vary from the normal urban Latin of their time. **1933** C. D. Buck *Compar. Gram. Greek & Latin* 24 The Oscan-Umbrian group..includes also the minor dialects of central Italy, as Paelignian, Marrucinian, Vestinian, Volscian, Marsian, Sabine, [etc.]. **1939** L. H. Gray *Foundations of Lang.* 334 The third group, conventionally termed *Sabellian*, occupies a position midway between Oscan and Umbrian, but its remains are lamentably scanty. Here belong Paelignian, Marrucinian, Vestinian, Volscian, Marsian, Aequian, and Sabine. **1940** E. H. Warmington *Remains Old Latin* IV. 59 Dialect-Latin or mixed Marsian and Latin. *Ibid.*, A sacred gift to Angitia on behalf of Marsian legions. **1949** *Oxf. Classical Dict.* 541/2 The Marsi ..took the initiative in demanding Roman citizenship in the Social War (hence often called Marsic War). *Ibid.*, Marsic magicians were famous for miraculous snake-bite cures. **1974** [see Marrucinian *sb.* and *a.*].

‖ **Marsilea** (mɑːˈsɪlɪə). *Bot.* Also marsilia. [mod.L. (Linnæus 1742), f. name of L. F. Marsigli (*Marsilius*), an Italian naturalist (died 1730).] The typical genus of the N.O. *Marsileaceæ* of cryptogamous plants; a plant of this genus.

1887 *Athenæum* 7 May 610/3 The ferns with the salvinias and marsilias are united into one group.

marsileaceous (mɑːsɪlɪ'eɪʃəs), *a. Bot.* [f. mod.L. *Marsileāce-æ* (f. *Marsilea*: see prec.): see -ACEOUS.] Belonging to the N.O. *Marsileaceæ*.

1856 in MAYNE *Expos. Lex.* **1862** ANSTED *Channel Isl.* II. viii. (ed. 2) 184 A little marsiliaceous plant (*Isoetes hystrix*).

† **mar'silian.** *Obs.* Also **marsiliane, marsiliana.** [ad. It. *marsigliana*, f. *Marsiglia* Marseilles.] (See quot. 1769.)

1687 *Lond. Gaz.* No. 2246/3 Being embarqued, the Foot on 8 Ships and the Horse on 6 Marsilians. **1769** FALCONER *Dict. Marine* II. (1780), *Marsiliane*, a square-sterned ship, navigated on the Gulph of Venice..the largest carrying about 700 tons. **1867** SMYTH *Sailor's Word-bk.*, *Marsiliana*, a Venetian ship of burden, square-sterned.

Marsilid ('mɑːsɪlɪd). *Pharm.* Also **marsilid.** A proprietary name for iproniazid phosphate.

1952 *Trade Marks Jrnl.* 7 May 393/2 Marsilid... All goods included in class 5...Roche Products Limited. **1953** *Internat. Jrnl. Leprosy* XXI. 64 The actions of Nydrazid and Marsilid on mouse leprosy were studied. **1965** J. POLLITT *Depression & its Treatment* iv. 56 The monoamine oxidase inhibitors include several members, among them phenelzine (Nardil), iproniazid (Marsilid), [etc.]. **1972** *Acta Histochem.* XLII. 246 After application of marsilid a strong decline of the neurosecretion..can be watched.

marsipobranch ('mɑːsɪpəʊbræŋk), *sb.* and *a. Zool.* [Anglicized form of mod.L. *Marsipobranchiī*, f. Gr. μάρσιπο-ς pouch (see MARSUPIUM) + βράγχια gills.] **a.** *sb.* One of the *Marsipobranchii*, a class of vertebrates having gills in the form of pouches, and comprising the lampreys and hags. **b.** *attrib.* or *adj.* Pertaining to animals of this class.

1872 MIVART *Elem. Anat.* 42 All Vertebrates, save those.. like the Lancelet and Marsipobranchs. **1875** HUXLEY in *Encycl. Brit.* I. 770/2 The skull of the lowest *Urodela* has.. advanced but little beyond the Marsipobranch stage.

Hence **,marsipo'branchiate** *sb.* and *a.* = MARSIPOBRANCH.

1872 T. GILL *Arrangem. Fam. Fishes* p. xx, The Marsipobranchiates (Lampreys, etc.). **1889** *Syd. Soc. Lex.*, *Marsipobranchiate*, having gills in the form of small pouches.

marsokhod ('mɑːzəkɒd, -xɒd). Also **Marsokhod.** [a. Russ. *marsokhód*, f. *Mars* MARS (after LUNOKHOD).] A type of Russian self-propelled vehicle for transmitting information about the planet Mars as it travels over its surface.

1970 *Sci. News Let.* 21 Nov. 397/3 In addition to discussing future Lunokhod explorations of the moon, the Soviets also described similar automated stations and robots for Venus, Mars and Mercury. These they call 'planetokhods' or 'marsokhods'. **1973** *Nature* 23 Mar. 219/2 The possibility of a 'Marsokhod' seems to have reached the stage of constructive planning...The lunokhods are controlled from Earth—a Mars vehicle would have to be self-controlling at least as far as such vital commands relating to its motion as 'start' and 'stop' are concerned.

† **marsoline.** *Obs.* [ad. It. *marzolino.*] A kind of cheese made near Florence.

1636 DAVENANT *Wits* IV. i, Your Marsoline and Parmesan of Lodi.

‖ **marsouin** (marswɛ̃). Also 7–9 **marsuin,** 9 *Canadian* **marsoon** (mɑː'suːn). [Fr.: see MERESWINE.] A name applied to various cetaceans of the family *Delphinidæ*.

In early quots., after European Fr., the porpoise. In recent examples, after Canadian Fr., = BELUGA 2.

1666 J. DAVIES *Hist. Caribby Isles* 101 The Marsouins are the Sea-hogs or Porposes. [*a* **1672** WILLUGHBY *Hist. Pisc.* (1686) 31 Cimbris Marsuin vel Porcus marinus: Angl. A Porpesse.] **1753** CHAMBERS *Cycl. Supp.*, *Marsuin*, a name by which many have called the *phocæna* or *porpesse*. **1854** EMERSON *Lett. & Soc. Aims* Wks. (Bohn) III. 208 Everybody now appears to me narwhale, porpoise, or marsouins. **1884** GOODE, etc. *Nat. Hist. Aquatic Anim.* I. 18 The names [of the White Whale] in use are..Marsuin or Marsoon in Canada.

marsupial (mɑː'sjuːpɪəl), *a.* and *sb.* Also 7– -eal. [ad. mod.L. *marsūpiālis*, f. L. *marsūpi-um* pouch, purse (see MARSUPIUM). The zoological use of the L. word was introduced by Tyson, who in 1698 uses the neuter *marsupiale* as a generic name for the opossum; he also has *ossa marsupialia* marsupial bones (see A. 2 b).]

A. *adj.* **1.** Pertaining to or resembling a 'marsupium' or pouch. ***marsupial muscle*** (in mod.L. *musculus marsupialis*): see quot. 1696. ***marsupial capsule***: in a colony of Polyzoa, an individual serving only for the reception of ova.

1696 PHILLIPS (ed. 5), *Marsupeal Muscle*, the ninth Muscle in order whereby the Thigh is mov'd. **1843** OWEN *Lect. Comp. Anat. Invertebr.* 109 In this state they are transferred from the ovarium to the marsupial vesicles... In the ova of the marsupial sacs, Siebold could no longer discern the germinal vesicle... The marsupial ova next assume an increase of size. **1878** BELL *Gegenbaur's Comp. Anat.* 132 Some persons may serve only for the reception of ova, and form the so-called marsupial capsules.

2. Used as a designation of mammals (including the kangaroos, opossums, etc.) of the family *Marsupialia*, characterized by having a pouch (covering the mamillæ) in which to carry their young, which are born imperfectly developed; of or pertaining to this family.

1825 *Zool. Jrnl.* I. 405 These three states of genital products require three distinct situations, which in the normal mammifera, are found within the sexual canal; but in the marsupial they are very differently distributed. **1832** LYELL *Princ. Geol.* II. 89 More than forty species of the marsupial family. **1870** ROLLESTON *Anim. Life* 64 From the reproductive gland to the marsupial pouch. **1898** MORRIS *Austral Eng.* 288 *Marsupial Mole*, the only species of the genus *Notoryctes*, *N. typhlops*.

b. Connected with the pouch in marsupial animals.

1819 REES *Cycl.* s.v. *Didelphis*, The abdominal pouch is sustained by means of two bones of a peculiar structure, and which in allusion to their functions have been called the marsupial bones. **1834** OWEN in *Phil. Trans.* CXXIV. 334 These bones..defend the abdominal viscera from the pressure of the young as these increase in size during their mammary or marsupial existence. *Ibid.*, The subject of marsupial generation. **1896** KIRKALDY & POLLARD tr. *Boas' Text Bk. Zool.* 496 The Marsupials have marsupial bones.

B. *sb.* A marsupial animal.

1835 *Penny Cycl.* III. 127. **1839** *Ibid.* XIV. 450 The leading peculiarity in these Marsupials is, so to speak, the premature birth of their young. **1896** [see A. 2 b].

attrib. **1885** H. FINCH-HATTON *Advance Australia* 106 An Act known as the Marsupial Act was accordingly passed to encourage their destruction... Some of the squatters have gone to a vast expense in fencing in their runs with marsupial fencing.

marsupialian (mɑːsjuːpɪ'eɪlɪən), *a.* and *sb.* [f. mod.L. *marsūpiāl-is* (see prec.) + -IAN.] = prec.

1848 MAUNDER *Treas. Nat. Hist.* 793 *Marsupialian*, belonging to the class *Marsupialia*.

marsupialization (mɑː,sjuːpɪəlaɪ'zeɪʃən). [f. next + -ATION.] The formation of a pouch, or of a pouch-like cavity (*Syd. Soc. Lex.* 1889).

marsupialize (mɑː'sjuːpɪəlaɪz), *v.* [f. MARSUPIAL + -IZE.] *trans.* To convert into something resembling the pouch of a marsupial.

1899 *Brit. Med. Jrnl.* 23 Dec. 102 The operator managed to marsupialise the edges of the pouch, which was drained through the abdominal wall with gauze.

mar'supialoid, *a.* and *sb.* [f. MARSUPIAL + -OID.] Resembling the marsupials.

1860 WORCESTER (citing HITCHCOCK). **1895** *Pop. Sci. Monthly* Sept. 693 A few marsupialoids.

marsupian (mɑː'sjuːpɪən), *a.* and *sb.* [f. MARSUPIUM + -AN.] = MARSUPIAL.

1835 KIRBY *Hab. & Inst. Anim.* II. xvii. 175 A marsupian animal like the Kanguroo. **1854** BAKEWELL *Geol.* 50 The lower jaw bones of animals, which Prof. Owen has determined belong to the genus of marsupians, or opossums.

marsupiate (mɑː'sjuːpɪeɪt), *a.* and *sb.* [f. MARSUPI-UM + -ATE.] = MARSUPIAL.

1834 OWEN in *Phil. Trans.* CXXIV. 361 The impregnated uteri of the Edentate and Marsupiate genera. **1849** *Fraser's Mag.* XXXIX. 297 A marsupiate sea-monster is horribly unorthodox. **1858** W. CLARK tr. *Van der Hoeven's Zool.* II. 594 The placenta..occurs in the mammals alone; but it is, however, wanting in the Marsupiates and Monotremes.

Hence **mar'supiated** *ppl. a.* in the same sense.

1890 in *Century Dict.*

marsupite ('mɑːsjʊpaɪt). *Geol.* [mod.L. *marsūpītes*, f. MARSUPIUM: see -ITE.] A fossil crinoid, the shell of which resembles a purse.

1835 KIRBY *Hab. & Inst. Anim.* II. xiii. 11 The Marsupites..form the link which connects the proper or pedunculated Crinoïdeans with the Stelleridans. **1885** GEIKIE *Text-bk. Geol.* (ed. 2) 828 The middle division, or Margate Chalk, has been named the Marsupite zone by Dr. Barrois.

‖ **marsupium** (mɑː'sjuːpɪəm). Also 9 (after Gr.) **marsupion, marsypion.** [L. *marsūpium*, *marsuppium*, ad. Gr. μαρσύπιον, -σίπιον, dim. of μάρσιπος purse, bag.] In various scientific uses: A bag or pouch, or something resembling a pouch.

1. *Zool.* **a.** The bag or pouch of a marsupial.

1698 TYSON *Anat. Opossum* 11 Herein all agree, that the use of this Bag, Pouch, or Marsupium, is for the Preservation of the Young Ones, and securing them upon any Occasion of Danger. **1825** *Zool. Jrnl.* I. 406 The difference..is solely in the fœtal domicile; we call it matrix in the one, and pouch, or marsupium in the others. **1839** *Penny Cycl.* XIV. 450 Their young..attach themselves by the mouth to the teats, which are situated in the marsupium, or pouch, of the mother. **1891** FLOWER & LYDEKKER *Introd. Mammals* 160 All the species have a marsupium or pouch formed by a fold of the skin of the abdomen.

b. A pouch for similar use in other animals, e.g. a receptacle for eggs in certain crustaceans, marsipobranchiate fishes, etc.

1843 OWEN *Lect. Comp. Anat. Invertebr.* 289 The development of the ovum takes place in this temporary marsupium. **1851–6** WOODWARD *Mollusca* 245 In *Cyclas* the inner gills form the marsupium, and only from 10 to 20 of the fry are found in them at one time. **1896** KIRKALDY & POLLARD tr. *Boas' Text Bk. Zool.* 214 The Isopoda possess a marsupium under the thorax, formed of the lamellate appendages of the basal joints of the thoracic limbs.

c. A folded or corrugated vascular membrane in the eye of a bird; = PECTEN 3 a.

1795 HOME in *Phil. Trans.* LXXXVI. 16 In the eyes of birds there is a substance which is peculiar to that class of animals, called the marsupium. **1841–71** T. R. JONES *Anim. Kingd.* (ed. 4) 779 A vascular organ, called the marsupium or pecten, which is lodged in the posterior part of the vitreous humour.

2. *Anat.* **a.** The large sac of the peritoneum (*Syd. Soc. Lex.* 1889). **b.** A term for the scrotum (*Ibid.*). **c.** The alar ligaments of the knee-joint (*Cent. Dict.*).

3. *Surg.* (See quot.)

1855 DUNGLISON *Dict. Med.* (ed. 12), *Marsupion*, a sac or bag, with which any part is fomented.

mart (mɑːt), *sb.*[1] *dial.* Forms: [1 **mearð, mærth, merð,** 2 ? **merthe**], 8– **mart.** [App. evolved in the mod.Eng. period by analysis of *foulmart* (FOUMART), where *-mart* is an altered form, due to absence of stress, of OE. *mearð* masc.: see MARTEN, MARTER. Exc. in this compound, the OE. word did not survive beyond the 12th c., being superseded by MARTER.] The marten.

a **700** *Epinal Gloss.* 425 *Furuncus*, mearth. *c* **893** K. ÆLFRED *Oros.* I. i. §18 Se byrdesta sceall ȝyldan fiftyne mearðes fell. *c* **1200** *Moral Ode* (Trin. MS.) 366 Ne aquerne ne me[r]theschele [*Egerton MS.* martres cheole] ne beuer ne sabeline. **1713** RICHARDSON in *Phil. Trans.* XXVIII. 170 *Foumart, quasi* foul Mart, or stinking Mart, in opposition to the Martes which emit a musky Smell. **1801** W. SEWARD *Yordes Cave* 9 The Otter fierce, the badger and the mart. **1830** *Blackw. Mag.* XXVIII. 1 Wolves, hyenas, foxes, marts, and hares. **1885** *Bazaar* 30 Mar. 1249/3 Wanted, fresh caught badger,..sweet mart, foumart, and otter. **1895** *Westm. Gaz.* 3 Oct. 2/3 A Mart Hunt [in Westmorland].

mart (mɑːt), *sb.*[2] *Sc.* and *north.* Forms: 4–6 **marte,** 6 **merte,** (9 **mert**), 6–9 **mairt,** 4– **mart.** [a. Gael. *mart* = Irish *mart* cow, ox.]

1. An ox or cow fattened for slaughter.

As 'marts' were usually killed about Martinmas as provision for the winter, the word popularly acquired an etymological association with *Martinmas*; cf. *Martinmas beef*.

1307–8 *Durh. Acc. Rolls* (Surtees) 2 In ccxxviij martis emptis..non deductis coriis [etc.]. *c* **1320** *Sir Tristr.* 454 Martirs [? *read* martis] as it ware þat husbond men had bouȝt. **1368** *Priory of Finchale* (Surtees) p. lxxx, Et de viij li. v s. receptis de xv marts de eodem manerio venditis. **1489** *Sc. Acts Jas. IV* (1814) II. 219/1 þat all..martis mutounes poultre..may cum in to oure souerane lorde. **1520** *Extracts Burgh Rec. Stirling* (1887) 7 In byin of mertis, mutton, talk and skennis. **1573** in *Reg. Privy Counc. Scot.* II. 269, xxx martis of salt beif. *a* **1670** SPALDING *Troub. Chas. I* (1829) 25 They..caused to kill altogether threescore marts. **1798** D. CRAWFORD *Poems* 16 (E.D.D.) He may next year get for his mart a highland cow. **1820** SCOTT *Monast.* i, Each family killed a mart, or fat bullock, in November. **1872** E. W. ROBERTSON *Hist. Ess.* 135 In a pastoral state of society he [the ox] was of comparatively little use except as a mart—to be eaten. **1881** GREGOR *Folk-Lore N.E. Scot.* 151 The 'mairt' or the pig, that was to be salted, must be killed when the moon was on the increase.

b. *fig.*

1589 R. BRUCE *Serm.* (1843) 166 As for the fed-marts of this world the Lord..has appointed them for slaughter. **1722** RAMSAY *Three Bonnets* III. 41 Get up, get up, ye lazy mart.

† **c.** *transf.* A carcase, slain animal. *Obs.*

c **1375** *Sc. Leg. Saints* ii. (*Paulus*) 842 [He] fand a tre..and syne on It slewit hym-self rycht to þe hart, and offerit to þe fend þat mart. *a* **1400** *Sir Perc.* 207 His modir hase gyffene hym that darte, Therwith made he many marte.

† **2.** (See quot.) *Obs.*

1689 R. COX *Hist. Irel.* I. Expl. Index, *Mart*, a yearly Rent in Beef.

† **Mart,** *sb.*[3] *Obs.* [ad. L. *Mart-em*: see MARS.]

1. Mars, the Roman god of war.

c **1384** CHAUCER *H. Fame* III. 356 For yren Martes metal ys, Which that god is of bataylle. **1515** DUNBAR *Poems* xxxiii. 67 Sum held he had bene Dedalus,..Sum the Martis smyth Wlcanus. **1590** SPENSER *F.Q.* I. Introd. iii, Triumphant Mart, In loves and gentle jollities arraid.

2. War, battle. (***in equal mart*** = L. *æquo Marte.*)

1432–50 tr. *Higden* (Rolls) II. 149 The Scottes..wente furthe and toke to theyme seetes, what thro marte [*L. ferro*] other fauor, nye to the Pictes. **1513** DOUGLAS *Æneis* I. Prol. 516 The horrible sterne dedis of Mart. **1567** TURBERV. *Ovid's Ep.* vii. G iij b, But if thou long for warre, or young Iulus seeke By manly Mart to purchase prayse, and giue his foes the gleeke. **1600** FAIRFAX *Tasso* VI. xxxvi, These fooles thus vnderfoot I tread, That dare contend with me in equall mart. **1636** MASSINGER *Bashf. Lover* II. vii, My father (on whose face he durst not look In equal mart).

3. The planet Mars. (Frequent in Gower.)

1390 GOWER *Conf.* III. 130 Complexion he takth of Marte.

mart (mɑːt), *sb.*[4] Also 5–7 **marte.** [a. Du. *markt* (formerly also written *mart*, and still commonly so pronounced): see MARKET *sb.*]

1. A periodical gathering of people for the purpose of buying and selling (in early use chiefly with reference to the Low Countries); a fair. *Obs.* or *arch.*

1437 *Libel Eng. Policy* in *Pol. Songs* (Rolls) II. 179 And wee to martis of Braban charged bene Wyth Englyssh clothe. **1483** CAXTON *Dialogues* 19/1, I thinke to goo..To the feste of bruges, To the marte of andwarp, To the marte of berow. **1502** ARNOLDE *Chron.* (1811) 231 At yͤ free passe marte of this said towne of Barowe last passed. **1530** TINDALE *Pract. Prelates* H iv b, The Cardinall..lefte nothing vnprouided to bring the marte from Antwarpe to

Cales. **1541** *Act. 33 Hen. VIII*, c. 34 They..shall..hold within the said borough two faires or martes euery yere. **1590** SHAKS. *Com. Err.* I. i. 18 Siracusian Marts and Fayres. **1631** T. POWELL *Tom All Trades* (1876) 163 To benefit betweene the Mart and the Market. **1719** DE FOE *Crusoe* II. (Globe) 540 The Fair or Mart, usually kept in this Place, had been over some Time. **1748** *Anson's Voy.* II. x. 245 At the time of the mart, whilst the Manila galeon is in the port. **1788** COWPER *Negro's Compl.* 46 By our sufferings, since ye brought us To the man-degrading mart. **1839** STONEHOUSE *Axholme* 309 After Gainsbrough mart in October, until the next mart at Easter, the people in these villages seldom thought of going anywhere.

†**b.** *spec.* The German booksellers' fair, held at Easter, originally at Frankfurt, and afterwards at Leipzig. (Sometimes app. used *transf.* for the 'publishing season' in England.) *Obs.*

1613 PURCHAS *Pilgrimage* (1614) 177 Let him reade *Buxdorfius* and his *Bibliotheca Rabbinica*, printed this last Mart. **1620** E. BLOUNT *Horæ Subs.* 42 Copied out of some absurd booke, printed the last Mart. *c* **1620** WOTTON in *Reliq.* (1651) 472 We may expect some Pamphlet the next Mart from Ingolstat, or Collen. **1655** DIGGES *Compl. Ambass.* 273 By certain that returned from Frankfort Mart, I understand that one of the Gentlemen..died.

2. A public place for buying and selling; a market-place, market hall, etc. Now *poet.* or *rhetorical*, exc. in the sense of 'auction room' (more fully ***auction-mart***), and as applied by tradesmen to designate their shops, as in ***boot and shoe mart.***

1590 SHAKS. *Com. Err.* I. ii. 74 My charge was but to fetch you from the Mart Home to your house. *Ibid.* III. i. 12 You beat me at the Mart. **1616** R. C. *Times' Whistle* iv. 1235 Our lawes for Mammons cursed golde Like as at open mart are bought and solde. **1764** GOLDSM. *Trav.* 295 The crowded mart, the cultivated plain. **1815** SCOTT *Ld. of Isles* VI. i, When breathless in the mart the couriers met. **1844** LONGF. *Nuremburg* 14 Fountains..standing in the common mart. **1863** BURTON *Bk. Hunter* 60 The fashionable mart where all the thorough libraries in perfect condition went to be hammered off. **1882** P. FITZGERALD *Recreat. Lit. Man* (1883) 189 This [goblet] I had seen in the window of a mart.

3. In wider sense: A city, region, or locality where things are bought or sold; an emporium.

1611 BIBLE *Isa.* xxiii. 3 She is a mart of nations. **1719** W. WOOD *Surv. Trade* 283 Cadiz, Port St. Mary's, &c., which Places were the Mart of our Manufactures for the Indies. **1850** MERIVALE *Rom. Emp.* (1865) I. v. 228 They possessed no great cities, no great marts of industry and commerce. **1874** STUBBS *Const. Hist.* (1875) I. iv. 61 London, the mart of the merchants. **1874** GREEN *Short Hist.* vii. §5. 386 Antwerp and Bruges were..the general marts of the world.

b. *transf.* and *fig.*

1602 MARSTON *Antonio's Rev.* IV. iii, O world,..Ile leave thee; farewell, mart of woe. **1762** GOLDSM. *Nash* 21 To this great mart of every folly, sharpers from every country daily arrived.

†**4.** Buying and selling; traffic; bargaining. Also, a bargain. Phr. ***to make a*** (or ***one's***) ***mart.*** *Obs.*

1568 GRAFTON *Chron.* II. 716 The lowe Countries, where the Englishe men for the most part, made their martes. **1575** GASCOIGNE *Dan Barthol.*, Posies *Flowers* 69 Then mighte you see howe fansie fedde his minde, Then all alone he mused on his marte. **1579** SPENSER *Sheph. Cal.* Sept. 37 They..maken a Mart of their good name. **1596** SHAKS. *Tam. Shr.* II. i. 329 Now I play a marchants part, And venture madly on a desperate Mart. **1597** HOOKER *Eccl. Pol.* v. xii. §5 Christ could not suffer that the temple should serue for a place of Mart. **1599** MARSTON *Sco. Villanie* I. ii, Vengeance pricks me on, When mart is made of faire Religion. *a* **1618** SYLVESTER *Maidens Blush* 464 Therefore forthwith one to them let us send, The mart to offer, and the price to make, As of a Slave. **1637** R. HUMPHREY tr. *St. Ambrose* I. 118 Places of mart where hee may best vent them.

†**5.** *attrib.*, as in ***mart-day, -time, -town.***

1641 HINDE *J. Bruen* xxxii. 102 That he might..buy Wine and Milk without money,..upon such of the Lords *Mart and Market dayes. **1624** MASSINGER *Renegado* I. i, This *Mart time Wee are allowde free trading. **1549** COVERDALE, etc. *Erasm. Par. Corinthians* I Corinthe..was..the moste famous, and richest *marte towne of all Asia. **1647** TRAPP *Comm. 1 Cor.* v. 9 It [i.e. Corinth] was..a most filthy Mart-town of abominable lusts. **1736** DRAKE *Eboracum* I. vii. 227 That York was formerly the chief emporium, place of trade, or mart-town in the north of England is certain. **1761** *London & Environs* IV. 6 During the Saxon heptarchy, London was..as we are told by Bede, a princely mart-town.

†**mart**, *sb.*[5] *Obs.* [Alteration of MARQUE[1] app. by association with MART *sb.*[4] Cf. CONTRA-, CONTRE-, COUNTERMART.] = MARQUE[1]; in phr. ***letters*** (***scripts, writ***) ***of mart.***

1587 GREENE *Penelopes Web* Wks. (Grosart) V. 197 Abradus the great Macedonian Pirat thought euery one had a letter of mart that bare sayles in yᵉ Ocean. **1602** WARNER *Alb. Eng.* XI. lxiv. (1612) 277 With letters then of credence for himselfe, and marte for them, He puts to Sea for England. *a* **1612** HARINGTON *Epigr.* II. xxx. (1618) E7, You'le spoile the Spaniards, by your writ of Mart. **1627** DRAYTON *Batt. Agincourt* 10 All men of Warre with scripts of Mart that went. **1726** J. KER *Mem.* 153 Letters of Mart were issued to Sundry People, who all went to the East-Indies.

b. *attrib.*, as in ***letter(s of mart man, ship.***

1695 LUTTRELL *Brief Rel.* (1857) III. 543 Three letters of mart ships are ordered for the West Indies. **1704** *Lond. Gaz.* No. 4071/3 The Good Alliance,..being taken by a Letter of Mart-Man belonging to this Port. **1753** N. TORRIANO *Gangr. Sore Throat* p. xv, Thus much by way of Preface to this Translation; after which I shall send it into the World as a Letter of Mart Ship,..hoping that it may meet with some Prize of Approbation.

†**mart** (mɑːt), *v. Obs.* [f. MART *sb.*[4]; cf. Du., G. *markten* (G. dial. *marten*).]

1. *intr.* To do business at a mart; hence, to chaffer, bargain.

1553 *Req. True-hearted Eng.* 5 Our marchauntes do by martyng in Antwerp spende yerely [etc.]. **1598** SYLVESTER *Du Bartas* II. i. II. *Imposture* 349 She would, she should not; glad, sad; coms and goes: And long she marts about a Match of Woes. **1602** FULBECKE *Pandectes* 72 The Athenians, who had vtterlie secluded them from their Hauens, and from marting with them. **1628** GAULE *Pract. Theory* (1629) 181 Judas is busie marting and chaffering among them.

2. *trans.* To make merchandise of, to traffic in. Also with *out.*

1589 WARNER *Alb. Eng.* VI. xxix, Let Pesantes marte their marriages, and thriue at peraduenture. **1598** B. JONSON *Ev. Man in Hum.* (Q.) I. i. 172, I had thought my son could not have straied, So farre from iudgement, as to mart himselfe Thus cheapely, (in the open trade of scorne). **1601** SHAKS. *Jul. C.* IV. iii. 11 To sell, and Mart your Offices for Gold To Vndeseruers. **1652** GAULE *Magastrom.* xxvi, Hereupon the astrologers doe mart or vent the effects of the heavens and the stars, &c. **1788** ANNA SEWARD *Lett.* (1811) II. 6 Reviewers may be venal without directly marting out their decisions for money.

Hence †'**marting** *vbl. sb.*

1553 [see 1]. **1608** BP. HALL *Epist.* I. i, Marting of pardons.

‖**Martaban** ('mɑːtəbæn). Also 7 **mortaban**, 7–8 **mortivan**. The name of a town in Pegu, used *attrib.* (esp. in ***Martaban jar***) as the designation of a kind of glazed pottery made there. Hence as *sb.*, Martaban ware, a Martaban jar.

[The ware has been called in Arabic *martabānī* from the 14th c.]

1698 FRYER *Acc. E. India & P.* 180 An huge Heap of long Jars like Mortivans. **1699** DAMPIER *Voy.* II. i. 98 These they call Mortaban Jars, from a Town of that name in Pegu. **1711** C. LOCKYER *Acc. Trade India* 35 Mortivan and small Jars. **1903** *Blackw. Mag.* Feb. 229/1 Large glazed earthen jars called by Europeans 'Pegu jars' and known all over the East by the name of 'Martaban'.

martagon ('mɑːtəgən). Also 6 **mortegon**, 7 **martagan, -igon**. [a. F. *martagon* = Sp., Pg. *martagon*, It. *martagone*, a. Turk. *martagān* 'a special form of turban adopted by Sultan Muhammed I; hence the martagon lily' (Redhouse).] The Turk's-cap lily, *Lilium Martagon*. Also ***scarlet martagon***: the Scarlet Turk's-cap, *L. chalcedonicum*.

1477 NORTON *Ord. Alch.* iii. in Ashm. (1652) 39 Herbes..as..Vervaine, Lunara, and Martagon. ? **1540** tr. *Vigo's Lyt. Pract.* xxxviii. Biij b, The powdre of Mortegon. **1548** TURNER *Names of Herbes* (E.D.S.) 85. **1597** GERARDE *Herbal* I. xciv. §4. 152 The Lillie of Constantinople is called likewise in England Martagon of Constantinople. **1629** PARKINSON *Parad. in Sole* iv. 9 The Martagons, both white and red, both blush and yellow, that require to be set by them-selues apart. **1637** B. JONSON *Sad Sheph.* II. vii, The Stupifying Hemlock! Adders tongue! And Martagan! **1737** P. COLLINSON in Darlington *Mem. J. Bartram & H. Marshall* (1849) 97 The Marsh Martagon is going to flower very strongly. **1866** LIVINGSTONE *Last Jrnls.* (1873) I. vii. 171 Here and there the scarlet martagon.

attrib. **1773** H. WALPOLE *Let.* 29 May, I send you two martagon roots. **1892** DOBSON *18th Cent. Vignettes* 146 Scarlet martagon-lilies.

martail: see MAR-.

martar, variant of MARTER *Obs.*

marteir, obs. form of MARTYR.

martel ('mɑːtəl), *sb.*[1] Also 4 **martell**; 5 *pl.* **martews, marteaulx**, 9 **marteaux**. [a. OF. *martel* (mod.F. *marteau*) = Pr. *martel-s*, Sp. *martillo*, Pg., It. *martello*:—pop.L. **martellum*; a synon. L. *martulus* occurs in Pliny, and other post-Augustan writers have *marcellus, marculus, marcus*, but the relation between these forms has not been determined.]

1. A hammer; after the 15th c. esp. one used in war. Also ‖**martel-de-fer** [Fr. = 'iron hammer'] (see quot. 1824). *Obs.* exc. *Antiq.*

1474 CAXTON *Chesse* 70 Al maner of smythes ben signefyed by the martel or hamer. **1481** —— *Myrr.* II. xxviii. 122 Smytynge of marteaulx or hamers. **1525** BERNERS *Froiss.* (1812) II. cxciv. 595 The lorde Olyuer of Clysson had not..delyuered vp the Martell, whiche is the token of the Constable of Fraunce. **1824** MEYRICK *Anc. Armour* III. Gloss., *Martellus*, the martel de fer, a weapon which had at one end a pick and at the other a hammer, axe-blade, half moon, mace head or other fancy termination. **1857** *Archæol. Jrnl.* XIV. 280 A Turkish martel, the head inlaid with brass, ornamented with punched markings. **1868** *Ibid.* XXV. 141 A large number of marteaux or horsemen's hammers of a peculiar type. **1890** A. PRINCE *Palomide* 93 The storm Of thunder-hoofs, of martel, spear and sword.

†**2.** *pl.* The game of 'five-stones' or 'snobs'. [So in OFr.; Rabelais has the form *martre*, Ronsard *martres.*]

1426 LYDG. *De Guil. Pilgr.* 8433 At the martews, the gentyl play Vsyd in fraunce many day.

†**martel**, *sb.*[2] *Obs.* [? Corrupt form of MARTER or MARTEN.] = MARTEN.

1607 TOPSELL *Four-f. Beasts* 495 Of the Marder, Martell, or Marten.

†'**martel**, *sb.*[3] *Sc. Obs.* Shortened form of *Martilmas*, MARTINMAS.

17.. in *Scots Songs* (1790) I. 60 Oh, Martel's wind, when wilt thou blaw And shake the sear leaves aff the tree?

†'**martel**, *v. Obs. rare*$^{-1}$. [f. MARTEL *sb.*[1] Cf. F. *marteler*, Sp. *martillar*, It. *martellare.*] *intr.* To hammer, deal blows as with a hammer (*on*).

1590 SPENSER *F.Q.* III. vii. 42 Her dreadfull weapon..Which on his helmet martelled so hard That [etc.].

†'**martelaise**. *Obs.* In 5 **marteleise, martileys**. [a. OF. *martelais* (:—med.L. type **martellāticium*), f. *marteler*: see prec.] A fighting with martels; a hammering.

c **1450** *Merlin* 211 Ther was soche marteleise and soche noise as so many Carpenteres in a wode. *Ibid.* 334 Thei..haue all day..endured the medle and the martileys.

martelé ('mɑːtəleɪ), *a. Mus.* [Fr., pa. pple. of *marteler* to hammer.] = MARTELLATO *a.*

1876 in STAINER & BARRETT *Dict. Mus. Terms* 281/1. **1961** D. D. BOYDEN in A. Baines *Mus. Instruments* vi. 124 The new bow..was more powerful, and its strength and the quicker take-up of the hair permitted *sforzando* effects such as *martelé*, which had been rare previously. **1962** *Punch* 28 Nov. 804/3 The martelé string chords of the first subject.

martelege, variant of MARTILOGE *Obs.*

martelet(t(e, obs. forms of MARTLET.

marteline ('mɑːtəlɪn). [a. F. *marteline*, f. OF. *martel*: see MARTEL *sb.*[1]] A small hammer, pointed at one end, used by sculptors and marble-workers. ***marteline chisel***, a sculptor's chisel, driven by a mallet or hammer.

1875 in KNIGHT *Dict. Mech.*

martellate ('mɑːtɪleɪt), *v. nonce-wd.* [f. It. *martell-are* + -ATE[2].] *trans.* To hammer (*fig.*).

1829 LANDOR *Imag. Conv., Albani & Pict.-Dealers* Wks. 1853 II. 9/1 They belabor and martellate my ears worse than the terza rima of Dante.

‖**martellato** (mɑːtɪ'lɑːtəʊ), *a. Mus.* [It., pa. pple. of *martellare* to hammer.] Lit. 'hammered'; said of notes which are heavily accented and left before their full time has expired. Also *transf.* Hence as *adv.* and *sb.*

1876 in STAINER & BARRETT *Dict. Mus. Terms* 281/1. **1928** G. B. SHAW *Let.* 6 Feb. in *B. Shaw & Mrs. Campbell* (1952) 267 Such music as your [dramatic] pupils may have must come from within them; all you can teach them is the value of your..*martellato molto*. **1928** *Daily Express* 27 Aug. 3/2 The notes in small type preceding the long B. flat..must be played *martellato* and with clearness. **1931** G. JACOB *Orchestral Technique* v. 50 The martellato in the left-hand part of the original. **1959** *Listener* 8 Oct. 596/2 One was put instantly in mind of William Walton's *martellato* style. **1969** *Times* 7 Nov. 13/1 His *martellato* octaves sounding like sharp cracks of a gun. **1973** *Times* 28 Mar. 11/8 Verne Reynolds's Sonata, composed last year and proving to be no more than an impersonal essay in virtuoso keyboard devices, all sound and no real fury, despite an excess of *martellato* in the outer movements.

Martello (mɑː'tɛləʊ). [Corruption (through association with It. *martello* hammer) of the name of Cape *Mortella* in Corsica (from It. *mortella* wild myrtle), where there was a tower of this kind which the English fleet captured with some difficulty on 8 Feb. 1794; it had been captured by the English and again abandoned in Sept. 1793.

The tower was of a type common in the Mediterranean; the stout resistance which it was able to make with a small force led to a belief among English military experts that the construction had great defensive value, and the erection of 'martello' towers was therefore strongly urged on the British government, but it was not until 1804 that any were actually erected. Windham's account of the events of 1793–4 is grossly inaccurate, but there appears to be no reason for doubt that he refers to these.]

Martello tower (also, rarely, ***martello***): a small circular fort with massive walls, containing vaulted rooms for the garrison, and having on the top a platform for one or two guns; usually erected on a coast to prevent the landing of enemies.

[**1794** LT.-GEN. DUNDAS *Disp.* 21 Feb. in *Ann. Reg.* App. to Chron. 101*/1 Expecting little opposition from Mortella tower. *Ibid.*, The same day we began to batter the tower of Mortella.] **1803** WINDHAM *Sp.* 9 Dec. (1812) II. 140 What were known to our officers under the name of Martello Towers, a species of edifice so called from a memorable instance of one at Martello, in Corsica; where, by a tower of this sort, garrisoned by some ten or a dozen men, and mounted with about two guns, a ship of the line of ours, and a frigate, were, during the last war, completely foiled and driven off. **1867** SMYTH *Sailor's Word-bk.* 470 A martello is built circular, and thus difficult to hit. **1883** BLACK *Shandon Bells* xxvii, The wide water, the Martello tower.

fig. **1828** J. W. CROKER *Diary* 11 Jan. in *C. Papers* (1884) I. xiii. 405, I..told him [Herries] that in quitting his finance he had surrendered his Martello-tower. **1848** LOWELL *Biglow P.* Poems 1890 II. 88, I esteem my ignorance of other languages as a kind of Martello-tower, in which I am safe from the furious bombardments of foreign garrulity.

martemper ('mɑːtɛmpə(r)), *v. Metallurgy.* [f. MAR(TENSITE + TEMPER *v.*] *trans.* To treat (steel) so as to reduce its tendency to crack or distort by quenching rapidly to a temperature just above that at which martensite begins to

form, allowing the temperature to equalize throughout, and then cooling slowly. So **'martempered** *ppl. a.*, **'martempering** *vbl. sb.*

1943 B. F. SHEPHERD in *Iron Age* 28 Jan. 50/1 Martempering is a term used to describe a heat treating operation whereby martensite is produced with a minimum of residual hardening strains. **1943** —— in *Metal Progress* July 105/2, I have coined the term 'martempering' to describe this operation of hardening by cooling quickly. **1947** *Steel Processing* XXXIII. 103/2 Steel was more susceptible to cracking when martempered than when treated by the more conventional method. **1953** AITCHISON & PUMPHREY *Engin. Steels* iii. 115 The properties of a martempered steel are in no way inferior to those of the same steel quenched and tempered in the traditional manner. *Ibid.* 116 Martempering is unlikely to supplant the direct quenching of normal, commercial steels. **1956** *Jrnl. Iron & Steel Inst.* CLXXXIII. 447/1 Warpage was least on martempered specimens. **1968** E. R. PETTY *Physical Metall. Engin. Materials* xi. 206 Quench stresses and attendant distortion or cracking may be reduced by.. an interrupted quench (martempering).

marten ('mɑːtən). Forms: α. 5 martiron, martren, martroun, -tryn, marterount, 5–7 martron(e, 6 marteron, -tyron, 5–8 martern(e. β. 6 matron, materne, 7 mattern(e. γ. 6–9 martin, 7 martyn, marton, 6– marten. [Late ME. *martren*, a. (perh. through MDu. *martren*) OF. *martrine* marten fur, subst. use (with ellipsis of *peau* skin) of *martrin* adj., pertaining to the marten, f. *martre*: see MARTER[1].

The word, originally denoting the fur, came to be used as the name of the animal itself, instead of MARTER *sb.*[1], which it finally displaced. The dropping of the *r* in the last syllable may have been partly due to association with MARTIN.]

† **1.** The skins or fur of the animal now called marten: see sense 2. Often in *plural*. *Obs.*

14.. LYDG. *Life Our Lady* (*MS. Soc. Antiq.* 134 lf. 25) (Halliw.), Ne martryn, ne sabil, y trowe, in god fay, Was none founden in hire garnement. **1422** in *E.E. Wills* (1882) 50 Myn eche daies gowne of marterount. **1436** *Libel Eng. Policy* in *Pol. Poems* (Rolls) II. 186 Irish wollen, lynyn cloth, faldynge, And marternus gode. *c* **1489** CAXTON *Blanchardyn* xv. 50 A longe gowne furred wyth fyn martrons. **1555** *Lanc. Wills* II. 192 My newe clothe gowene furred wt Marterons. **1575** *Inv.* in *Archæol.* XXX. 17 An old tawny damaske cassock, edged with matrons. **1596** DANETT tr. *Comines* (1614) 85 A goodly gown furred with martins. *a* **1612** HARINGTON *Sch. Salerne* in *Babees Bk.* (1868) 255 Garments of.. Martyn or Wolfe-skinnes. **1653** H. COGAN tr. *Pinto's Trav.* xl. 160 Crimson sattin cassocks lined with marterns. **1696** PHILLIPS (ed. 5), *Marternes*, or *Sables*, a kind of rich Fur.

2. An animal belonging to any one of certain species of *Mustela*, yielding a valuable fur. Often with distinguishing word, as **beech-marten, stone marten,** *M. foina*; **pine** (or †**fir**) **marten,** *M. martes*; **American pine marten,** *M. americana*.

14.. *Voc.* in Wr.-Wülcker 595/8 *Martrix*, a martron. **1463–4** *Rolls of Parlt.* V. 505/1 Furres of Martirons, Furres, Letyce. **1486** *Bk. St. Albans* e j, The Fox and the Martron, and the wilde Roo. **1580** HOLLYBAND *Treas. Fr. Tong*, *Vne Marte*, a beaste that is called the Marten. **1587** HARRISON *England* II. xix. (1877) I. 310 The beasts of the chase were commonlie the bucke, the roe, the foxe, and the marterne. **1589** ? LYLY *Pappe w. Hatchet* Wks. 1902 III. 402 Be thou Martin the bird or Martin the beast. **1594** in Crompton *Jurisd.* 195 b, One claimed a free chase within the forest, for Hare, foxe, wild cat, and martrons. **1602** CAREW *Cornwall* 22 Beastes of Venery persecuted for their case, or dammage feasance, are Marternes, Squirrels. **1643** HORN & ROB. *Gate Lang. Unl.* xvii. §209 The.. matterne (poll-cat), sable, and ermine are good for furres. **1675** DUGDALE *Baronage* I. 467/1 Certain Dogs for the destruction of Wolves, Foxes, Martrons, Cats, and other Vermine. **1741** *Compl. Fam.-Piece* II. i. 307 A Martern is about the Bigness of a Cat, having a long Body and short Legs, with a Head and Tail like a Fox. **1768** PENNANT *Brit. Zool.* (1776) I. 78 Pine Martin. **1827** J. F. COOPER *Prairie* I. i. 17 The martin's fur of his cap was of a fineness.. that a queen might covet. **1859** WOOD *Nat. Hist.* I. 345 The chief distinction between the Pine and the Beech Martens.

b. *Zool.* By some writers used as a vernacular name for the genus *Mustela*, including the ferret, weasel, etc., together with the species ordinarily known as martens.

1896 KIRKALDY & POLLARD tr. *Boas' Zool.* 516.

3. ***spotted marten***: a name for an Australian marsupial of the genus *Phascologale*. (Not in Morris *Austral Engl.*)

1890 in *Century Dict.*

4. *attrib.*, as ***marten-skin, -tails***; **marten-cat, -weasel,** = sense 2; **marten-cub,** a marten of the first year (Phillips 1696); **marten family** *Zool.*, the *Mustelidæ* (see quot.).

1798 CHARLOTTE SMITH *Yng. Philos.* II. 170 The wood.. was infested by Wild or *Martin cats. **1845** *Zoologist* III. 1018 A specimen of the marten-cat (*Martes Foina*) was taken in a trap. **1884** *Pall Mall G.* 9 Sept. 2/2 The martin-cat is nearly extinct. **1896** KIRKALDY & POLLARD tr. *Boas' Zool.* 516 The *Marten family (*Mustelidæ*) [comprises] (*a*) Martens (*Mustela*)..(*b*) The Otters (*Lutra*)..(*c*) Badgers (*Meles taxus*). **1823** J. F. COOPER *Pioneers* i. (1869) 4/2 A cap of *martin skins. **1691** *Lond. Gaz.* No. 2711/4 A large Muff of *Martin-Tails. **1607** TOPSELL *Four-f. Beasts* 497 So may this *Martin-weasel render a sweet excrement.

marten, -enet, -enist: see MARTIN, -ET, -IST.

Martenot, shortened form of ONDES MARTENOT.

1931 *Electronics* July 18/1 As an example of a very fully developed [electronic musical] instrument.. the 'Martenot' may be cited, named after its inventor. **1932** *19th Cent.* May 606 The Martenot instrument.. looks like a small portable harmonium, from which connexions run to one or more loud-speakers. *Ibid.* 607 Anyone already able to play the piano can make a fair showing on a Martenot after a few hours' practice. **1936** *Discovery* July 222/1 The Martenot instrument... Honegger, Milhaud, Ibert are among the composers who have scored for it, and Stokowski has made use of it in his orchestra. **1938** *Oxf. Compan. Mus.* 287/2 The instrument known as Ondes Musicales.. or the Ondium Martenot, or the Martenot.. is purely melodic.

martensite ('mɑːtɛnzaɪt). *Metallurgy.* [f. name of Prof. A. *Martens*, a German metallurgist + -ITE.] See quot. 1902. (Cf. PEARLITE 2.)

1898 ROBERTS-AUSTEN *Introd. Metallurgy* (ed. 4) 147 Martensite is the very hard substance of which hardened steel consists. **1902** H. M. HOWE in *Encycl. Brit.* XXIX. 572 *Martensite*, the characteristic and chief constituent of hardened steel, is a hard brittle mass, with a needle-like structure, consisting of iron containing carbon in proportions which vary from nothing up to about 2 per cent.

martensitic (mɑːtɛn'zɪtɪk), *a. Metallurgy.* [f. MARTENSIT(E + -IC.] Pertaining to or containing martensite; resembling the structure or mode of formation of martensite.

1909 in *Cent. Dict.* Suppl. **1915** *Chem. Abstr.* IX. 437 A martensitic structure is produced in 0·28% C steel without increase in hardness by heating to white heat and then cooling slowly. **1937** *Discovery* May 153/2 Carbon is mainly responsible for the characteristic martensitic mode of hardening. **1950** J. OSBORNE *Dental Mech.* (ed. 3) xii. 222 Two types of stainless steel find application in dentistry, Martensitic and Austenitic steels. **1967** A. H. COTTRELL *Introd. Metall.* xvii. 265 An important example of a shear transformation occurs when steel is quench-hardened. The F.C.C. austenitic structure then transforms by shear, with some dilatation, into martensite, the distorted form of B.C.C. iron... In recognition of this, shear transformations are often referred to as martensitic transformations.

Hence **marten'sitically** *adv.*, in a martensitic manner.

1972 *Physics Bull.* Dec. 712/1 The difficult areas of x ray crystallography, such as in the study of martensitically transformed materials,.. can be opened up by an electron microscope technique.

†**'marter**[1]. *Obs.* Also 3–5 martre, martir, 6 marter, martyr, 7, 9 (from Ger. originals) marder. [ME. *martre*, a. F. *martre* (recorded from 11th c.) = It. *martora*, ad. W.Ger. **marþr-* in OS. **marthar* (whence *marthrîn* adj.; Du. has *marter* from Fr.), OHG. *mardar* (MHG., mod.G. *murder*) masc.; app. an extended form of OTeut. **marþu-z* (OE. *mearð*, MHG. *mart*, ON. *mǫrð-r*, Sw. *mård*, Da. *maar*), whence the Rom. forms F. *marte* fem., Pr. *mart-z* masc., Sp., Pg. *marta*.] The marten.

12.. *Moral Ode* 182 (Egerton MS.) Ne ocquerne ne martres cheole [*Trin. Coll. MS.* metheschele, see MART *sb.*[1]] ne beuer ne sabeline. **1481** CAXTON *Reynard* (Arb.) 112 The ostrole, the Martre.. and the squyrel. **1588** PARKE tr. *Mendoza's Hist. China* 20 *marg.*, Great abundance of Marters furres. [**1607** TOPSELL *Four-f. Beasts* 495 It is called a house, and rocke-marder. **1805** *Med. Jrnl.* XIV. 334 The owl, the marder.]

b. *pl.* The fur of the marten.

1420 in *E.E. Wills* (1882) 53 Also I will þat Gerard my brothir haue a newe fure of martirs. **1466** in *Somerset Med. Wills* (1901) 210 A gowne of cremesyn, furrid with martees [? *read* marteres]. **1530** PALSGR. 559 Martyrs and sabyls be for great estates.

†**'marter**[2]. *Obs.* Also 6 martar. [f. MART *v.* + -ER[1].] One who bargains; *esp.* in thieves' slang, a dealer in stolen goods.

1591 GREENE *Disc. Coosnage* II. (1592) 3 The Priggar is he that steales the horse, and the Martar is he that receiues him, and chops and changeth him away in any Faire, Mart, or other place. **1598** FLORIO, *Barattiere*, a barterer, a trucker, a marter,.. a fripper.

marter, -erisse, obs. ff. MARTYR, MARTYRIZE.

martern(e, marteron, -ount, obs. ff. MARTEN.

martews: see MARTEL *sb.*[1]

Martha ('mɑːθə). The name of the sister of Mary and Lazarus in Bethany; hence used with allusion to Luke x. 40, 41 for one much concerned with domestic affairs. In Christian allegory a symbol of the active life, opp. MARY 4.

a **1225** *Ancrene Wisse* (1962) f. 112a/8 Husewifschipe is marthe dale. Marie dale is stilnesse & reste of alle worldes noise. **1907** [see MARY 4]. **1907** M. HALL *Woman's Trek from Cape to Cairo* ix. 133 My host was equally busy.. while his wife, 'Martha like', busied herself in seeing a chicken cooked. **1909** *Westm. Gaz.* 30 July 2/1 The domestic servant problem.. could never have become just what it is had this generation of mistresses followed in the steps of that ancestry which accorded the Marthas of the homes a certain amount of appreciation for services rendered. **1910** S. R. CROCKETT *Dew of their Youth* II. xviii. 140 You are of the tribe of Marthas, Jen, and you certainly work hard enough for everybody. **1938** E. GOUDGE *Towers in Mist* x. 277 She belonged to that noble army of Marthas who cook the dinners that the Marys gobble up to keep them going between their visions and their dreams. Grace was the best kind of Martha. **1953** G. GREENE *Living Room* I. i. 8 In this household she is obviously the anxious Martha; the weaker character intent on carrying out orders. **1962** J. D. SALINGER *Franny & Zooey* 158 For all I know, I may be a little jealous. .. It may very well be that I hate like hell to play Martha to someone else's Mary. **1962** *Friend* 3 Aug. 951/1 The Marthas and Marys are both essential. There is no division between the Mystical and the Practical. **1967** MRS. L. B. JOHNSON *White House Diary* 10 Aug. (1970) 553 The 'Mary' and the 'Martha' in my life have an eternal war.

b. Martha-coloured *a.*, used *transf.* (see quot. 1936) by the poet Edith Sitwell.

1924 E. SITWELL *Sleeping Beauty* xiv. 50 The Martha-coloured scabious Grew among dust as dry as old Eusebius. **1936** —— *Sel. Poems* Pref. 25 'The Martha-coloured scabious'.. is the result of a personal memory... As a child, I had a nursery maid called Martha, who always wore a.. gown.. exactly the colour of a scabious. **1937** —— *I live under Black Sun* II. x. 296 The Martha-coloured scabious waved aimlessly.

Martha Gunn ('mɑːθə gʌn). *Pottery.* (See quot. 1957.) Also *attrib.*

1922 R. K. PRICE *Astbury, Whieldon & R. Wood Figures & Toby Jugs* 86 Another rare Ralph Wood Toby jug in the collection is Martha Gunn. **1957** MANKOWITZ & HAGGAR *Conc. Encycl. Eng. Pott. & Porc.* 141/2 *Martha Gunn*, a female Toby jug, modelled in the likeness of Martha Gunn (1727–1815) the celebrated Brighton bathing-woman who is alleged to have dipped the Prince of Wales in the sea. **1960** R. G. HAGGAR *Conc. Encycl. Cont. Pott. & Porc.* 135/2 A large number of jugs called *Jacquelines*.. are comparable to the English 'Martha Gunn' toby jugs made by Ralph Wood and others.

marthe, marther, obs. ff. MARROW, MARTYR.

marthy, obs. variant of METHY, burbot.

marthyr, obs. form of MARTYR *v.*

†**'martiable,** *a. Obs.* In 5 marciable. [? Altered form of MARTIAL *a.*, after -ABLE.] = MARTIAL.

1470 HARDING *Chron.* LXXIII. xv, For many were, through actes marcyable [*rime* honourable] Dispended then by warres violence.

martial ('mɑːʃəl), *a.* and *sb.* Forms: 4–6 marcial, 5 marcyal(l, martialle, (5 marcill, 6 mershal), 5–6 marciall, mercial(l, mercyall, 5–7 martiall, 6 martyall, 6–8 marshal(l, (7 marshiall), 6– martial. [a. F. *martial* (= Sp., Pg. *marcial*, It. *marziale*), ad. L. *martiālis* of or belonging to Mars, f. *Mart(i)-* MARS.] **A.** *adj.*

1. a. Of or pertaining to war or battle.

c **1374** CHAUCER *Troylus* IV. 1641 (1669) Ne veyn delit,.. or torney Marcial,.. Ne made me to Rewe on youre distresse. **1430–40** LYDG. *Bochas* VIII. i. (1494) C iij b, His victorious marcyall hye prowesse Done in almayne. *c* **1430** —— *Min. Poems* (Percy Soc.) 5 Alle assautis that were martialle For his sake he proudly wold endure. **1529** LYNDESAY *Complaynt* 457 Thow.. hes thy honour done awance, In Scotland, Ingland, and in France, Be Merciall dedis honourabyll. **1532–3** *Act 24 Hen. VIII*, c. 13 Iustes, tourneis,.. or other marciall feates or disguisings. **1586** MARLOWE *1st Pt. Tamburl.* I. ii, My martiall prises.. Wun on the fiftie headed Vuolgas waues. *a* **1625** FLETCHER & MASSINGER *Laws of Candy* I. ii, That yong-man, who was not.. skil'd In Martiall play. **1671** MILTON *P.R.* III. 304 See .. in what martial equipage They issue forth. **1676** HOBBES *Iliad* II. 180 In counsel or in Martial Array. **1760** JOHNSON *Idler* No. 96 ¶ 1 His martial achievements remain engraved on a pillar of flint. **1773–83** HOOLE *Orl. Fur.* XVI. 307 Rinaldo flies, with martial ardor prest. **1791** COWPER *Iliad* IV. 515 With martial order terrible. **1872** BAGEHOT *Physics & Pol.* (1876) 81 So long as there was continual fighting there was a likelihood of improvement in martial virtues.

b. Of sports, exercises, etc.; Serving as training for warfare. ***martial art*** (usu. *pl.*), any of various fighting sports or skills mainly of Japanese origin, such as judo, karate, and kendo.

1412–20 LYDG. *Chron. Troy* Prol., Yt longeth to manhode .. To haunte his bodye in playes marciall. **1568** GRAFTON *Chron.* II. 670 The king entendyng to see this martiall sport, ..caused listes royall for the Champions.. to be newly erected in West Smithfield in London. *a* **1586** SIDNEY *Apol. Poetrie* (Arb.) 51 Before Poets did soften vs, we were full of courage, giuen to martiall exercises. **1632** PARKER *True Tale of Robin Hood* 39 in Child *Ballads* III. 229 And shewd to them such martiall sport, With his long bow and arrow. **1776** GIBBON *Decl. & F.* xvii. (1869) I. 458 They soon became careless of their martial exercises. **1815** WORDSW. *Laodamia* 118 While my youthful peers before my eyes.. Prepared themselves for glorious enterprise By martial sports. **1869** FREEMAN *Norm. Conq.* (1876) III. xii. 227 There he was entertained with martial exercises. **1933** *Official Guide to Japan* (Japanese Government Railways) p. clxxxvi, Contests [of kendo] take place nowadays at the annual meetings of the Butoku-kai, or Association for Preserving the Martial Arts, in Kyōto. **1955** E. J. HARRISON *Fighting Spirit of Japan* (ed. 2) x. 97 Of that branch of Japanese esoterics which belongs to what may generically be styled *bujutsu*, literally 'martial arts', though the Japanese terminology has a far wider and more comprehensive scope than its English equivalent, I may justly claim to know something. **1966** [see KENDO]. **1968** [see KUNG-FU]. **1974** *Isle of Wight County Press* 23 Nov. 31 Mr. Singleton, who holds a Kendo black belt, a brown belt in Karate, and has just taken up Ju-Jitsu, said he had no intention of 'cashing in' on the current martial arts boom.

c. Of music: Appropriate to warfare.

1662 DRYDEN *Astræa Redux* 198 The incensed powers beheld.. An heaven.. Which durst with.. martial brass, belie the thunder's sound. **1667** MILTON *P.L.* I. 540 All the while Sonorous mettal blowing Martial sounds. *a* **1704** T. BROWN *Praise of Drunkenness* Wks. 1730 I. 37 The martial

kettle-drum. **1708** POPE *Ode St. Cecilia* 37 When our Country's cause provokes to Arms, How martial musick ev'ry bosom warms! **1784** COWPER *Task* VI. 3 The ear is pleased With melting airs or martial. **1869** RAWLINSON *Anc. Hist.* 36 They had a lively and martial music.

2. Of or pertaining to 'the Army', or the military profession. *Obs.* exc. in COURT MARTIAL, 'military' as opposed to 'civil' or 'civilian'. † ***martial name***: a fictitious name adopted by a soldier (= F. *nom de guerre*).

1470 HARDING *Chron.* CLXXVIII. xx, Without rule of marcill gouernaunce. *a* **1548** HALL *Chron., Hen. IV* 7 b, He ..caused dyvers lustie men to appele divers olde men upon matters determinable as the common lawe in the court marcial. **1590** R. WILLIAMS (*title*) A Briefe Discourse of Warre: with his opinion concerning some parts of the Martiall Discipline. **1625** BACON *Ess., Love* (Arb.) 447, I know not how, but Martiall Men, are giuen to Loue. **1631** WEEVER *Anc. Funeral Mon.* 546 Dauid de Argenton, a Norman, and a martiall knight. **1715** *Lond. Gaz.* No. 5322/3 To be Advocate-General, or Judge Martial of all His Majesty's Forces in England. **1757** CHESTERF. *Lett.* (1792) IV. cccxxiv. 102 Some are for a Parliamentary inquiry, others for a Martial one. **1761** *Ann. Reg.* II. 3 They laid aside their surnames, and assumed nick-names, or martial names.

3. martial law. a. That kind of military government of a country or district, by which the ordinary law is suspended, and the military authorities are empowered to arrest all suspected persons at their discretion, and to punish offenders without formal trial. †**b.** Formerly sometimes applied to what is now called 'military law', viz. the body of enactments and rules for the government of the army; an enactment or rule forming part of this.

Originally these two senses (in which the adj. has respectively senses 1 and 2) would not always be distinguishable, as military law existed only in war-time, and consisted mainly of temporary and occasional ordinances; our earliest quots., however, distinctly exhibit the same use as is now current. In early examples the adj. is often assimilated in spelling to MARSHAL *sb.*, and it was a common opinion that 'marshal law' was so called as being the law emanating from the lord marshal. Mod. Fr. has *loi martiale*, but perh. from English.

1533 MORE *Debell. Salem* II. xv. 61 Yf the lawe were so that the iudges myght procede and put felons to answere without endyghtementes, as in treason is vsed in thys realme by the lawe marshall vppon warre rered. **1537** HEN. VIII *Let. Dk. Norf.* in *State Papers* (1830) II. 537 We doo ryght well approve and allowe your proceedings in the displayng of our Baner. And forasmoche as the same is now.. displayed..the cours of our lawes must geve place to thordenaunces and estatutes marciall; our pleasure is that.. you shal..cause such dredfull execution to be done upon a good nombre of thinhabitauntes of euery towne, village and hamlet that have offended in this rebellion..as they may be a ferefull spectacle to all other herafter, that wold practise any like mater. *a* **1548** HALL *Chron., Hen. VIII* 231 According to the law mershal thei wer adiudged to die. **1568** in J. Hooker *Life Sir P. Carew* (1857) 207 Not by martyall lawe, but by veredicte of twelve men, orderly. **1599** SHAKS. *Hen. V*, IV. viii. 46 Please your Maiestie, let his Neck answere for it, if there is any Marshall Law in the World. **1617** MORYSON *Itin.* II. 27 His Lordship had power..to make Martiall Lawes (he being Lord Martiall of England), and to punish the transgressors. **1633** T. STAFFORD *Pac. Hib.* II. xxiv. (1821) 449 Wee doe hereby giue, and commit unto you full power and authority to execute by Marshall Law, all notable and apparent Offenders. *c* **1645** HOWELL *Letters* II. lix. (1650) 86 The Lawes themselves, civil as well as martiall, were publish'd and executed in Latine. *a* **1676** HALE *Common Law* (1713) 40 Touching..Martial Law, these Things are to be observed... First, That in Truth and Reality it is not a Law, but something indulged rather than allowed as a Law; the Necessity of..Order and Discipline in an Army, is that only which can give those Laws a Countenance... Secondly, This indulged Law was only to extend to Members of the Army, or to those of the opposite Army. **1751** *Affect. Narr. Wager* 40 [He] protested that he would go as far in punishing the Criminals as the Martial Law would permit. **1827** HALLAM *Const. Hist.* (1876) I. v. 241 For this ordinary crime the queen could hardly be prevented from directing him to be tried instantly by martial law. **1844** H. H. WILSON *Brit. India* II. 143 Martial law was proclaimed. **1851** WELLINGTON in *Hansard's Parl. Deb.* Ser. III. CXV. 880 Martial law was neither more nor less than the will of the general who commands the army. In fact, martial law meant no law at all.

attrib. **1900** *Daily News* 12 Mar. 5/3 Newspapers.. published outside the Martial Law districts.

4. Warlike; brave; valiant; given to fighting. Formerly often with some notion of sense 7 a.

1430–40 LYDG. *Bochas* VIII. vi. (1494) C v b, A werre began Geyne romaynes this marciall [1554 ed. mercial] woman. **1591** SHAKS. *1 Hen. VI*, II. i. 21 *Bur.* But what's that Puzell... *Tal.* A Maid, they say. *Bed.* A Maid? And be so martiall? **1625** BACON *Ess., Viciss. Things* (Arb.) 573 The Northern Tract of the World, is in Nature the more Martiall Region. **1642** FULLER *Holy & Prof. St.* II. xix. 120 Women have often been the nets to catch and ensnare the souls of many Martiall men. **1736** S. WESLEY *Battle of Sexes* 56 Sounding trumpets' breath Kindles in martial breasts stern love of war. **1744** HARRIS *Three Treat.* (1841) 40 There are sounds to make us cheerful, or sad; martial, or tender. **1821** BYRON *Mar. Fal.* III. ii, My nephew and the clients of our house Many and martial. **1870** BRYANT *Homer* I. II. 56 Wake the martial spirit in their breasts.

Comb. **1603** KNOLLES *Hist. Turks* (1638) 296 The poore Prince..as a martiall minded man..said [etc.]. **1629** H. BURTON *Babel no Bethel* 97 Who seeing the Martiallike Prelate accompanied with armmed men, begun to laugh.

5. Characteristic of or befitting a warrior.

1592 SHAKS. *Rom. & Jul.* III. i. 166 He Tilts With Peircing steele at bold Mercutio's breast, Who..with a Martiall scorne, with one hand beates Cold death aside, and with the other sends It back to Tybalt. **1602** —— *Twel. N.* III. ii. 45 *An.* Will either of you beare me a challenge to him? *To.* Go, write it in a martial hand, be curst and briefe. **1608** D. T[UVIL] *Ess. Pol. & Mor.* 37 b, By reason of his Martiall carriage and aspect. **1784** COWPER *Task* IV. 640 He steps right onward, martial in his air, His form, and movement. **1816** L. HUNT *Rimini* III. 20 Some tastes there were indeed that would prefer Giovanni's countenance as the martialler. **1817** WOLFE *Burial Sir J. Moore* iii, But he lay like a warrior taking his rest, With his martial cloak around him. **1866** G. MACDONALD *Ann. Q. Neighb.* xxvii. (1878) 474 With almost a martial stride the little creature walked up to the speaker.

6. Resembling what pertains to the god Mars.

1611 SHAKS. *Cymb.* IV. ii. 310 His Foote Mercuriall: his martiall Thigh: The brawnes of Hercules.

7. Of, or belonging to, the planet Mars.

a. *Astrol.* (often, subject to the influence of Mars; hence applied to venomous animals and to plants with violently active properties). **b.** *Astron.* (= MARTIAN). Now with capital initial.

1621 BURTON *Anat. Mel.* I. II. i. ii. (1676) 27/1 Gregorius Tholosanus makes seven kinds of ætherial Spirits or Angels, according to the number of the seven Planets Saturnine, Jovial, Martial. **1646** SIR T. BROWNE *Pseud. Ep.* VI. xiv. (1658) 417 The fixed Stars..are esteemed Martial or Jovial, according to the colours whereby they answer these Planets. **1647** LILLY *Chr. Astrol.* xv. 84 A Martiall Man, is many times full faced with a lively high colour. **1652** CULPEPPER *Eng. Physic.* (1656) 377 Suppose a Man be bitten or stung by a Martial Creature, Wormwood an herb of Mars, giveth you present cure. *Ibid.* 42 They are furious Martial Plants. **1784** HERSCHEL in *Phil. Trans.* LXXIV. 273 The point Aries on the martial ecliptic answers to our 19° 28′ of Sagittarius. **1868** LOCKYER *Guillemin's Heavens* (ed. 3) 210 The Terrestrial and Martial seasons. **1878** NEWCOMB *Pop. Astron.* III. iii. 321 Clouds in a Martial atmosphere.

8. In early *Chemistry*: Of or pertaining to iron; containing iron. *Obs.* exc. in certain names (now little used) of chemical compounds and pharmaceutical preparations.

1684–5 BOYLE *Min. Waters* ad fin., I found..that more than one of our English Martial Springs..were too much weakened by the Water that Rained into them. **1704** J. HARRIS *Lex. Techn.* I, *Martial Regulus* of *Antimony*. **1708** J. PHILIPS *Cyder* I. 36 Our Mines produce As perfect Martial Ore. **1741** HANKEWITZ in *Phil. Trans.* XLI. 828 All Martial Waters will, with Galls, turn blackish or inky. **1756** C. LUCAS *Ess. Waters* I. 14 This volatile acid..flies off, leaving the iron to precipitate in the form of a martial earth. **1776** J. CLEGG in T. Percival *Ess.* (1776) III. App. 333 Lime-water tends to deepen the colour produced by some astringents and martial vitriol. **1789** A. CRAWFORD in *Med. Commun.* II. 311, I had..made trial of the tincture of martial flowers. **1796** KIRWAN *Elem. Min.* (ed. 2) II. 82 It was a compleat Martial Liver of sulphur. **1822** IMISON *Sci. & Art* II. 105 Black oxide of iron formerly martial ethiops. **1823** P. NICHOLSON *Pract. Build.* 330 The smallest quantity of clay, gypsum, or martial matter. **1825** J. NICHOLSON *Operat. Mechanic* 765 Humid Assay of Gold mixed with Martial Pyrites. **1889** *Syd. Soc. Lex.*, *Martial preparations*, medicaments containing iron or a salt of iron.

†**9.** Of the month of March. *Obs. rare*$^{-1}$.

1423 JAS. I *Kingis Q.* cxci, Thankit mot be the sanctis marciall, That me first causit hath this accident.

B. *sb.*

†**1.** *pl.* Poems about wars. *nonce-use.*

1589 FLEMING *Virg.* Argt. 3 His Bucoliks, or Pastoralls.. his Georgiks or ruralls..his Æneids or Martialls.

†**2.** ? One born under the influence of Mars. *Obs.*

1605 TIMME *Quersitanus* I. xi. 47 There are starres which haue their most cold & moyste spirites..others most hote & drie, as the Solarie & Martialls.

†**3.** A martial person, a soldier. *Obs.*

c **1611** CHAPMAN *Iliad* XVIII. 469 The Queene of martials And Mars him selfe conducted them.

4. A Martian. *rare.*

1880 P. GREG *Across Zodiac* I. v. 115 Every Martial can write at least as quickly as he can speak.

martial, obs. form of MARSHAL.

martialism ('mɑːʃəlɪz(ə)m). [f. MARTIAL *a.* + -ISM.] Warlike qualities.

1608 D. PRICE *Chr. Warre* 8 Wrestling, running, fighting, and other feats of Martialisme. **1784** *Europ. Mag.* VI. 113 A due portion of martialism elevates the soul in a remarkable degree. **1885** A. FORBES *Souvenirs some Cont.* 38 A rugged, motley crowd of staunch fighting men, of whose martialism he had had experience in his Asiatic warfare.

martialist ('mɑːʃəlɪst). Also 6 **martialiste**, 6–7 **marshallist**, **martiallist(e**, 7 **marshalist**. [f. MARTIAL *a.* + -IST.]

†**1.** *Astrol.* A person born under the influence of the planet Mars. *Obs.*

1569 J. SANFORD tr. *Agrippa's Van. Arts* 50 b, She pronounceth..that man a Martialiste or Solist. **1647** LILLY *Chr. Astrol.* x. 67 Generally Martialists have this forme. **1686** GOAD *Celest. Bodies* III. iii. 449 He not dreaming of such Martialists, hath recourse to the Nature of the Month.

2. A military man; one skilled in warfare; a warrior. Also *transf.* and *fig.* Now *rare.*

1576 FLEMING *Panopl. Epist.* 296 Your sonne died in the quarel of his countrie, like a valiant Martialist. **1595** LYLY *Wom. in Moone* II. i, Ile worke such warre within Pandoraes brest,..That..She shall become a vixen Martialist. **1603** H. CROSSE *Vertues Commw.* (1878) 49 A true Martialist he is indeed, that by strong hand labours to suppresse his rebellious lusts. **1611** SPEED *Hist. Gt. Brit.* IX. xxii. 61 The French sought to trie fortune for their Iles in the Seas..their preparations were great, and their Marshallists many. **1658** W. BURTON *Itin. Anton.* 67 Septimius Severus..deservedly equalled with the greatest Martialists of any age. **1749** J. POTE *Hist. of Windsor* 130 The stoutest and most famous Martialists of that age. **1830** MISS MITFORD *Village* Ser. IV. 123 Their wives..were as complete martialists [etc.]. **1882** SWINBURNE *Child's Battles* in *Tristr. Lyonesse* 270 Howe'er he look demurely, Our martialist will surely Have his way. **1884** *Daily News* 11 Feb. 5/4 These martialists of the smug pattern.

3. A Martian. *rare.*

1870 PROCTOR *Other Worlds* 101 Then it must be a fine day for the Martialists, for clouds over Mars..must produce quite as bad an effect..as similar phenomena on earth.

martiality (mɑːʃɪ'ælɪtɪ). [f. MARTIAL *a.* + -ITY.] The quality or state of being martial.

1632 LITHGOW *Trav.* IV. 134 This Emperour..was more giuen to venery, then martialitie. **1823** *Blackw. Mag.* XIV. 529 He..acquires a superior fierceness or martiality of aspect.

martialize ('mɑːʃəlaɪz), *v. rare.* Also 6 **martiallize**. [f. MARTIAL *a.* + -IZE.] *trans.* To make martial. Hence **martiali'zation**.

1600 TOURNEUR *Transf. Met.* lxxviii, Only the muses deare to Martialize. **1685** F. SPENCE tr. *Varilla's Ho. Medici* 57 They could not conceive, why, his army being the strongest and best martialliz'd, he [etc.]. **1823** *New Monthly Mag.* VII. 126 The Rebellion broke out, and the genius of loyalty martialized the various classes of the community. **1848** L. HUNT *Town* (1858) 439 [The march in 'Figaro'] has ever since been played there to the martialisation of hundreds of little boys.

martiall(e, obs. forms of MARSHAL, MARTIAL.

martiallist(e, obs. forms of MARTIALIST.

martially ('mɑːʃəlɪ), *adv.* [f. MARTIAL *a.* + -LY[2].] In a martial manner.

1586 WARNER *Alb. Eng.* IV. xxi. (1592) 95 Whil'st either king thus Martially defends. **1596** DALRYMPLE tr. *Leslie's Hist. Scot.* I. 167 Galdie..obteines na les triumphe..than gif he martiallie and valȝeantlie had ouircum thame. **1670–98** LASSELS *Voy. Italy* I. 158 It did not become Rome built by the son of Mars to take towns otherwise than martially. **1709** STEELE *Tatler* No. 46 ⁋ 11 Who could be the Author of a Piece so martially written.

†**b.** In accordance with martial law. *Obs.*

1583 *Exec. for Treason* (1675) 33 Shall she forbear..to put his Souldiers..to the Sword martially, or to execute her Laws..civilly.

†**c.** ? With regard to military matters. *Obs.*

a **1658** CLEVELAND *Gen. Poems*, etc. (1677) 94 Look upon him Martially, and he is a Justice of War.

martialness ('mɑːʃəlnɪs). [f. MARTIAL *a.* + -NESS.] The quality or state of being martial.

1727 in BAILEY vol. II. **1844** L. HUNT *Imag. & Fancy* (1846) 22 In some far island which its foes besiege, Who all day long with dreadful martialness [*Iliad* XVIII. 209 στυγερῷ Ἄρηϊ] Have pour'd from their own town.

martial sea, obs. form of MARSHALSEA.

Martian ('mɑːʃən), *a.* and *sb.* Also 4 **Marcien**. [f. L. *Marti-us* pertaining to Mars (f. *Mart-em* MARS) + -AN.] **A.** *adj.*

1. †**a.** Having the temperament due to the influence of the planet Mars (*obs.*). **b.** Of or pertaining to Mars or its supposed inhabitants. Also *transf.*

c **1386** CHAUCER *Wife's Prol.* 610, I am a Venerien In felinge, and myn herte is Marcien. **1880** A. R WALLACE *Isl. Life* 160 The duration of such phenomena on Mars being reckoned in Martian months equivalent to one-twelfth of a Martian year. **1892** *Pall Mall G.* 6 Aug. 1/3 We may therefore perhaps be excused for taking a more immediate interest in Martian matters than in the affairs of worlds so infinitely more distant. **1898** H. G. WELLS *War of Worlds* II. ii. 210 Long before the Martian invasion. **1950** A. HUXLEY *Themes & Variations* 256 Man's Martian aggression against himself. *Ibid.*, The Martian forces of overpopulation and erosion. **1953** *News Chron.* 2 June 1/1 Step by step, in Martian clothing, the two figures move forward, pursuing their race against time and the mountain in the slowest of slow motion.

†**2.** Of or pertaining to war or battle. *Obs.*

1591 SYLVESTER *Du Bartas* I. vi. 398 The Beasts that fill'd the Martian Field With blood and slaughter. **1596** SPENSER *F.Q.* IV. v. 6 The judges..Into the Martian field adowne descended.

3. Of or pertaining to the month of March.

1623 COCKERAM, *Marcian-moneth*, the moneth of March. **1842** MACAULAY *Lays, Lake Regillus* 17 Gay are the Martian Kalends.

B. *sb.* An inhabitant of the planet Mars.

1883 W. S. LACH-SZYRMA *Aleriel* III. iii. 109 He..brought with him another Martian, differently attired. **1892** *Pall Mall G.* 6 Aug. 2/1 Can it be..that the Martians..are endeavouring to signal to some other planet? **1898** H. G. WELLS *War of Worlds* I. v. 31 The glimpse I had had of the Martians emerging from the cylinder in which they had come to the earth from their planet. **1901** G. B. SHAW *Three Plays for Puritans* Pref. p. xvii, He feels concerned about the ..destruction of the human race by the Martians. **1949** [see EARTHLING *sb.*[2] 1]. **1951** R. BRADBURY *Silver Locusts* 108 From the back of the machine a Martian with melted gold for eyes looked down at Tomás. **1967** MRS. L. B. JOHNSON *White House Diary* 13 May (1970) 519 What will I remember about Camp David? The two 'Martians' in their silver suits..fire-fighters on hand for any emergency.

†**'martiated**, *ppl. a. Chem. Obs.* [f. **martiate* vb. (f. L. *Marti-us* pertaining to Mars) + -ED[1].] Impregnated with iron.

1694 SALMON *Bate's Dispens.* (1713) 195/1 The martiated Salt, sublim'd from Gads of Iron. *Ibid.* 369/1.

martiaton, variant of MARCIATON.

martichore, variant of MANTICORE.

†**Mar'ticolist.** *Obs. rare*$^{-0}$. [f. L. *Marticola* (f. *Mart(i)-* MARS + *col-ĕre* to worship) + -IST.] A worshipper of Mars.

1727 in BAILEY vol. II.

marticora, variant of MANTICORE.

†**mar'tigenous**, *a. Obs.* [f. L. *Martigen-a* (f. *Mart(i)-* MARS + *gen-*, *gignĕre* to beget) + -OUS.] Mars-born, begotten by Mars.

1727 BAILEY vol. II.

martilage, -ildge, -ilege, var. ff. MARTILOGE.

martilet, obs. form of MARTLET.

martileys, variant of MARTELAISE.

Martilmas: see MARTINMAS.

†**'martiloge.** *Eccl. Obs.* Forms: 4–5 **martilage, martilogie, -ye, martirlogi,** 4–6 **martiloge,** 5 **martelege, martilege, -logge, martloge, martylogye, mertelage, mertilloge,** 6 **martylage.** [ad. med.L. *martilogium*, *-legium*, corrupt forms of *martyrologium* MARTYROLOGY.] A list or register of martyred saints; a martyrology.

[*c* 1000 *De Consuet. Monach.* in *Anglia* XIII. 400 þeah þe on martirloȝian (L. *in martyrlogio*) na si hæfþ.] **13..** *S. Erkenwolde* 154 in Horstm. *Altengl. Leg.* (1881) 269 Merkid is in oure martilage his mynde for euer. **1387** TREVISA *Higden* (Rolls) V. 81 By þe martiloge it semeth þat he regnede sixtene ȝere. *c* **1425** *St. Mary of Oignies* II. viii. in *Anglia* VIII. 173/30 She halowed festful dayes writen in hir mynde and impressed in hir herte as in a martiloge. **1432–50** tr. *Higden* (Rolls) I. 331 Wherefore hit is redde in the martilogge: 'Suche a day at Scotlande Seynte Brigida'. **1483** CAXTON *Gold. Leg.* 164/2 Of whome the martiloge of holy chirche speketh not. **1524** in Nichols *Mann. Anc. Times* (1797) 272 A boke called a Pye, and a boke called a Martylage. **1548** UDALL *Erasm. Par., Luke* Pref. 4 b, The holye Bible, legenda Sanctorum, .. & martiloges.

martin[1] ('mɑːtɪn). Also 5 **martoune,** 6, 9 **marten,** 7 **martyn.** [Presumably a use of *Martin* (a. F. *Martin*, ad. L. *Martīnus*), a male Christian name common in Western Europe after St. Martin bishop of Tours (4th c.), whose festival is 11th Nov. (MARTINMAS). The name is applied in Fr. to various birds, as in *martin-chasseur*, the hen-harrier, *martin-pêcheur*, the kingfisher; the dim. *martinet* (see MARTINET) denotes the house-martin and the swift.

The application of the Christian name to birds has no obvious reason, and may have been purely arbitrary. Many writers of the 17th c. say that the martin is so called because it comes in March and departs about Martinmas.]

1. A well-known bird of the swallow family, *Chelidon urbica*. It builds a mud-nest on the walls of houses, etc.; hence called **house-martin**. The **sand-martin** or **bank-martin** is *Cotileriparia*; the **purple martin** of N. America is *Progne subis* or *purpurea*. For Australian use see quot. 1883.

bee-martin, the American king-bird, *Tyrannus carolinensis*. **black martin, screech-martin**, local names for the swift, *Cypselus apus*.

c **1450** HOLLAND *Howlat* 213 The Martoune, the Murcoke, the Myresnype in ane, Lichtit, as lerit men, law by that laike. **1589** ? LYLY *Pappe w. Hatchet* C b, There is small difference between Swallowes and Martins, either in shape or nature. **1591** PERCIVALL *Sp. Dict.*, *Arrexaque*, a bird called a marten. **1678** RAY *Willughby's Ornithol.* 213 The Sand Martin, or Shore-bird. *Ibid.* 214 The black Martin or Swift. *a* **1682** SIR T. BROWNE *Tracts* 107 Building in holes of pits, like some martins. **1773** G. WHITE *Selborne*, To Barrington xvi, The house-martin, or martlet. **1774** *Ibid.* xx, The sand-martin, or bank-martin, is by much the least of any of the British *hirundines*. *Ibid.* xxi, The swift or black-martin. **1808–14** A. WILSON *Amer. Ornith.* (1831) II. 37 The purple martin, like his half-cousin the king bird, is the terror of crows, hawks, and eagles. **1842** *Penny Cycl.* XXIII. 363/1 The Common Swift.. is the.. Screech Martin.. and Black Martin of the country-people. **1865** Fairy Martin [see FAIRY C. 2]. **1883** NEWTON in *Encycl. Brit.* XV. 581/2 The ordinary Martin of Australia is the *Hirundo* or *Hylochelidon nigricans* of most ornithologists, and another and more beautiful form is the Ariel or Fairy-Martin of the same country, *Hirundo* or *Lagenoplastes ariel*. **1887** J. C. HARRIS *Free Joe*, etc. (1888) 141 In the upper air a bee-martin was fiercely pursuing a sparrow-hawk.

†**2.** A dupe. *Obs.* [Perh. a different word.]

1591 GREENE *Discov. Coosnage* Wks. (Grosart) X. 37 In High Lawe, The Theefe is called a High lawier... He that is robd the Martin When he yeeldeth, stouping. **1610** ROWLANDS *Martin Mark-all* G, I haue heard.. a high-way lawyer rob a man in the morning, and hath dined with the martin or honest man so robbed the same day at an Inne. **1621** FLETCHER *Isl. Princess* II. i, We are all meere Martins.

3. *attrib.* and *Comb.*, as *martin-haunted* adj.; **martin-box, -coop** *U.S.*, a box or coop used in America for martins to build in; **martin bug**, a blood-sucking bug, *Oeciacus hirundinis*, whose principal host is the house-martin; **martin-cage**, a cage for holding martins; **martin-house** = *martin-box*; **martin-snipe**, a provincial name for the green sandpiper, *Totanus ochropus*.

1828 *Farmer's Almanac 1829* (Wendell, Mass.) sig. F3^{v} Whose house is that with white capped chimnies, black sashed windows, and a nice little *marten [*sic*] box just an epitome of the State House? **1854** B. F. TAYLOR *Jan. & June* 60 A martin-box of a cottage scuds round the corner of the Meeting House. **1858** HAWTHORNE *Fr. & It. Note-Bks.* II. 47 Its lofty, machicolated and battlemented tower.. looking exceedingly like a martin-box, on a pole. **1871** MRS. STOWE *Oldtown Fireside Stories* 108 Your questions tumbles over each other thick as martins out o' a martin-box. **1946** J. STUART *Tales Plum Grove Hills* 85, I know what Mom is thinking when she looks at the martin boxes. **1923** E. A. BUTLER *Biol. Brit. Hemiptera-Heteroptera* 322 By most authors the *martin bug is considered to be generically distinct from the rest of our British Cimicina, and is referred to the genus *Oeciacus*. **1935** *Brit. Birds* XXVIII. 278 The martin bug is rarer and resembles the much-disliked bed-bug which infests human habitations. **1959** SOUTHWOOD & LESTON *Land & Water Bugs Brit. Isles* vii. 187 The martin bug is recorded from most English counties south of a line from the Wash to the Bristol Channel. **1844** *Knickerbocker* XXIII. 442 Like a superannuated old man with a *martin-cage upon his crooked back. **1807** W. IRVING *Salmag.* (1824) 264 Knocking down a mouldering *martin-coop, with his tennis-ball. **1864** TENNYSON *Aylmer's F.* 163 Almost to the *martin-haunted eaves A summer burial deep in hollyhocks. **1826** 'A. SINGLETON' *Lett.* 74 The tasteful slave makes, perchance a *martin-house, by erecting a high pole having a number of hollow calabashes hung around the top of it. **1835** R. M. BIRD *Hawks of Hawk-Hollow* I. iii. 44 Here's.. the identical old Folly, with.. the pot in the chimney, and the martin-house on a pole. **1854** B. P. SHILLABER *Life & Sayings Mrs. Partington* 101 He heard Gruff scolding Ike for throwing snowballs at his new Martin-house. **1884** 'C. E. CRADDOCK' *In Tennessee Mts.* I. 40 There was a lofty martin-house whence the birds whirled fitfully. **1870** H. STEVENSON *Birds Norfolk* II. 224 Provincially, this bird [the Green Sandpiper] is known as the.. '*Martin Snipe'.

†**'martin**[2]. *Obs.* [The name *Martin* (see prec.) given to the monkey in *Reynard the Fox*.] A kind of monkey. Also ***martin-ape, -monkey.***

13.. *K. Alis.* 6464 Visage after martyn apen: Folke heo buth ful eovel y-schapen! **1388** WYCLIF *Isa.* xxxiv. 14 (*gloss*) Martynapis ben liyk apis, and ben tailid. **1589** ? LYLY *Whip for an Ape* 7 Who knoweth not, that Apes men Martins call. **1607** TOPSELL *Four-f. Beasts* 7 The *Cepus*, or Martine Munkey. The Martin called *cepus* of the Greeke word, *Kepos*. *a* **1697** J. AUBREY *Lives* (1898) II. 48 Their [the Martins'] crest is an ape; men use to say 'a Martin ape'.

b. Comb.: ***martin-drunk*** (cf. *ape-drunk*, *lion-drunk*, etc., in the same list).

1592 NASHE *P. Penilesse* 24 The sixt [kind of drunkard] is Martin drunke, when a man is drunke and drinkes himselfe sober ere he stirre.

Martin[3] ('mɑːtɪn). Also 6 **Marten, -yn, Merteryn.** The name of St. Martin (see MARTIN[1]) used *attrib.* and in *Comb.*

†**1. Martin chain**, a sham gold chain. (Cf. 3 b.)

a **1560** BECON *Jewel of Joy* Wks. II. 19 b, Certayne lyght braynes.. wyll rather weare a Marten chayne, the pryce of .viii.d. then they woulde be vnchayned.

2. More fully †**Martin dry**, also [Fr.] ‖**Martin sec**: a kind of pear, so called from being ripe at Martinmas. [Cf. G. *Martinsbirne*.]

1664 EVELYN *Kal. Hort.* (1679) 34 Pears... November... Martin sec. **1672** —— tr. *Fr. Gard.* (1675) 118 (Pears) The dry Martins. **1708** KERSEY, *Martin-dry*, a kind of Pear, that ripens at the middle of November. **1860** HOGG *Fruit Man.* 200 Martin Sec (Dry Martin). **1875** *Ibid.* (ed. 4) 479 The Martins are perhaps the earliest varieties [of pears] grown amongst us.

3. †**a. St. Martin**: St. Martin's day, Martinmas.

1533 *Presentm. Juries* in *Surtees Misc.* (1888) 34 That every man make his fens.. before Seynt Merteryn.

†**b. St. Martin's**: the parish of St. Martin-le-Grand, London, formerly celebrated as the resort of dealers in imitation jewellery.

1572 in *Extracts Acc. Revels at Court* (Shaks. Soc.) 24 John Wever of Saint Martins for Copper silver frenge, xvij oz^{ce} at [blank] the ounce. **1607** DEKKER *Westw. Ho* II. i, You must to the pawne to buy Lawne: to Saint Martins for Lace. **1618** MYNSHULL *Ess Prison* 23 They are like the rings and chaines bought at S. Martines, that weare faire for a little time, but shortly after will proue Alchimy or rather pure Copper.

c. (St.) Martin's, in composition. **St. Martin's bird**, the hen-harrier [= F. *oiseau de S. Martin*, Cotgr.]; **St. Martin's day**, the 11th of November, Martinmas; **(St.) Martin's eve**, the eve of St. Martin's day, 10th November; **St. Martin's evil**, drunkenness (Cent. Dict.); **St. Martin's flower** (see quot.); †**St. Martin's fowl**, = *St. Martin's bird*; **St. Martin's herb**, = *herb of St. Martin* (see HERB 7 b); **St. Martin's Lent**, the forty days between Martinmas and Christmas Eve (see LENT *sb.*[1] 3 b); †**St. Martin's rings**, imitation gold rings (see 3 b, and cf. *St. Martin's ware*); †**St. Martin's stuff, ware**, counterfeit goods (cf. 3 b); **St. Martin's Summer**, a season of fine mild weather occurring about Martinmas; also *fig.*

1897 F. S. ELLIS *Reynard* 38 And straightway hove within his sight Saint *Martin's bird. **1517** in Nichols *Mann. Anc. Times* (1797) 272 Payd on Seynt *Marten's day, for bred and drynke for the syngers, vs. **1592** STOW *Ann.* an. 1280. 300 On S. *Martins euen a great thunder ouerthrew many houses and trees in England. **1598** BP. HALL *Sat.* IV. iv. 30 Dried Fliches of some smoked Beeue; Hang'd on a writhen with since Martins eue. **1866** *Treas. Bot.* 46/1 *Alströmeria Flos Martini*, the St. *Martin's Flower of Chili. **1500–20** DUNBAR *Poems* xxxiii. 73 The myttane, and Sanct *Martynis fowle, Wend he had bene the hornit howle. **1866** *Treas. Bot.*, St. *Martin's herb, *Sauvagesia erecta*. **1589** R. HARVEY *Pl. Perc.* 4, I doubt whether all be gold that glistereth, sith Saint *Martins rings be but Copper within. **1617** FENNOR *Compter's Commonw.* 28 This kindnesse is but like Alchimy or Saint Martins rings, that are faire to the eye, and haue a rich outside, but if a man breake them a sunder and looke into them [etc.]. **1598** GUILPIN *Skial.* (1878) 41, I had thought the last mask.. Had.. Taught thee S. *Martins stuffe from true gold lace. **1591** SHAKS. *1 Hen. VI*, I. ii. 131 This night the Siege assuredly Ile rayse: Expect Saint *Martins Summer, Halcyons dayes. **1864** TENNYSON *Aylmer's F.* 560 Then ensued A Martin's summer of his faded love. **1884** *St. James's Gaz.* 7 Nov. 14/2 The arrival of November has only varied matters by bringing in a St. Martin's summer. **1648** C. WALKER *Hist. Independ.* I. 122 These letters may be St. *Martins ware, counterfeit stuffe.

martin[4] ('mɑːtɪn). [Perh. called from the surname of inventors or makers.]

1. A grinding-tool consisting of a brass plate with a flat stone facing (Knight *Dict. Mech.*).

†**2.** ***martin panel.***

1760 FOOTE *Minor* I. Wks. 1799 I. 241 Let the Martin pannels for the vis-a-vis be carried to Long-Acre, and the pye-balls sent to Hall's to be bitted.

3. ***martin bit***: see quot.

1884 KNIGHT *Dict. Mech.* Suppl., *Martin Bit* (*Manège*), a stiff-bar bit, having a spoon-shaped port [etc.].

4. (with capital initial) ***Martin ware***, ***Martinware***, a type of brown, salt-glazed, freq. elaborately modelled pottery, made by the Martin brothers in the late 19th and early 20th centuries. (See quot. 1897.)

1897 F. LITCHFIELD *Chaffers's Marks Pott. & Porc.* (ed. 8) 870 *Martin Ware.* The four brothers Martin carry on a small pottery at Southall. The initiator of the business was Robert Wallace Martin... He was joined by his three brothers.. to produce the ware which now bears their name. .. A great point with the Martins is that the decoration of a specimen is never repeated. **1918** E. CLARKE *Story of My Life* xxxi. 411 On the top of the low book-shelves stand a few choice bronzes.. and some fine specimens of my favourite Martin-ware. **1922** J. F. BLACKER *ABC Eng. Salt-Glaze Stoneware* xxv. 219 The best period of Martin ware. **1937** *Times Lit. Suppl.* 25 Sept. 696/3 The four brothers Martin responsible for the production of the nineteenth and early twentieth century pottery known as Martinware. **1957** MANKOWITZ & HAGGAR *Conc. Encycl. Eng. Pott. & Porc.* 142/1 A large collection of Martinware is exhibited at the Public Library and Museum, Southall, Middlesex. **1966** G. A. GODDEN *Illustr. Encycl. Brit. Pott. & Porc.* 214 (*caption*) A selection of Martinware birds with loose heads. **1973** *Times* 16 Feb. 21/5 A Martinware bird of exceptional size was sold at Sotheby's.. for £1,250.

'martin[5]. *dial.* (from Yorks. southward: see E.D.D.) = FREEMARTIN. Also ***martin-calf, -heifer.***

The sense 'spayed heifer', quoted in E.D.D. from Kennett *Par. Antiq.* (1695) and Peacock *Lonsdale Gloss.* (1869), if genuine, is now obsolete.

1856 P. THOMPSON *Hist. Boston* 714 A twin-heifer is called a martin, and is said to be incapable of bearing young. **1903** *Rep. Kansas State Board Agric.* 1901–2 II. 211 Pure-bred steer, spayed or martin heifer, two years old and under three.

martin, variant of MARTEN.

†**'martinet**[1]. *Obs.* Forms: 5 **mart(e)net, mertenet(te, mertinet,** 5–6 **martynet, martnette,** 7–9 **martinet.** [a. F. *martinet*, dim. of the proper name *Martin*: see MARTIN[1].]

1. A name for the martin and the swift. (Cf. MARTLET[2] 1.) ***bank martinet***, the sand martin.

c **1460** J. RUSSELL *Bk. Nurture* 437 Quayle sparow larke & litelle mertinet. **1513** *Bk. Keruynge* in *Babees Bk.* 159 Quayle, sparow, larke, martynet. **1530** PALSGR. 243/2 Martynet a byrde, *martinet*. **1544** TURNER *Avium Præcip. Hist.* F 2, Minores [apodes] Angli uocant rok martinettes or chirche martenettes... Tertium genus, quod in ripis nidulatur, Angli a bank martnet.. nominant. **1565** COOPER *Thesaurus*, *Apus*.. a martnette, the seconde kind of swallowes. **1601** HOLLAND *Pliny* I. 288 A third sort there is of these Swallows and Martinets. **1610** [see MARTLET[2] 2]. **1678** RAY *Willughby's Ornithol.* 213 The Martin, or Martinet, or Martlet. **1691** RAY *Creation* I. (1692) 147 Those Birds which have but short Feet, as the Swift and Martinet. **1736** AINSWORTH *Lat. Dict.* II, *Apiastra*,.. a bird that eateth bees, called midwal, or martinet. **1833** RENNIE *G. Montagu's Ornith. Dict.* 316 Martinet. A name for the Window Swallow.

‖**2.** *Hist.* (See quot.)

1831 SIR W. HAMILTON *Discuss.* (1852) 405 The *martinets* or scholars of the University [of Paris] not belonging to Colleges at all. **1885** *Durh. Univ. Jrnl.* VI. 104 'Day-students' were well-known in medieval days in the University of Paris; and they were called 'Martinets' because they had their dwellings, so to speak, beneath the eaves.

†**'martinet**[2]. *Obs.* [ad. mod.L. *martīnettus*, *martīnellus* (Grillandus), dim. of *Martīnus* Martin.] The demon who had the office of summoning witches to their assemblies. (Cf. MARTINIST 4.)

1609 B. JONSON *Masque Queens* B 2, Their litle Martin is he that calls them to their Conuenticles. *Ibid.* B 4 b, Which makes that their little Masters or Martinets, of whom I haue mention'd before, vse this forme in dismissing their conuentions.

martinet[3] ('mɑːtɪnɪt). Also 5 **martymette,** 6 **martynette,** 6–9 (sense 4) **martnet.** [a. F. *martinet* in various unconnected senses, possibly belonging to etymologically distinct words.]

1. A military engine for throwing large stones. *Obs.* exc. *Hist.*

1523 LD. BERNERS *Froiss.* I. cxx. 144 These four martynettes dyd cast out..great stones. **1795** SOUTHEY *Joan of Arc* VIII. 259 Him passing on, A ponderous stone from some huge martinet, Struck.

†**2.** A water-mill for an iron forge (Cotgr.). *Obs.*

1483 *Cath. Angl.* 229/2 A Martinett, *irristiticus, & dicitur de Irriguo.*

†**3.** (See quot.) *Obs.*

1489 CAXTON *Faytes of A.* II. xxiii. 137 Litel cartes called martymettes for to carye the mantelles & the tymbre that serueth for yᵉ engins from the shippes vnto the place where as thei shal be dressed.

4. *Naut.* One of the leech-lines of a sail.

1582 N. LICHEFIELD tr. *Castanheda's Conq. E. Ind.* I. xxviii. 71 The Mariners and ship boyes, some in the fore-castell haling bollings, braces, and Martnets. **1627** CAPT. SMITH *Seaman's Gram.* v. 24 The top-saile martnets are made fast to the head of the top gallant mast. **1706** PHILLIPS (ed. Kersey) s.v., *To Top the Martnets*, is to hale them up. **1867** in SMYTH *Sailor's Word-bk.* 471.

‖**5.** A kind of cat-o'-nine-tails formerly used in French schools.

1881 DU CHAILLU *Land Midnight Sun* II. 262, I saw.. what resembled a policeman's club, at the end of which was a thick piece of leather, the whole reminding one of a martinet.

martinet[4] (ˈmɑːtɪˌnɛt). [From the name of General *Martinet*, a French drill-master of the reign of Louis XIV.]

†**1.** The system of drill invented by Martinet. *Obs.*

1676 WYCHERLEY *Pl. Dealer* III. i, What, d'ye find fault with Martinet?..'tis the best exercise in the World.

2. A military or naval officer who is a stickler for strictness of discipline; hence in wider sense, a rigid disciplinarian.

1779 J. MOORE *View Soc. Fr.* (1789) I. xxxix. 339 Let our Martinets say what they please. **1816** 'QUIZ' *Grand Master* VII. 24 If a tyrannic low-bred Colonel Would be a martinet infernal. **1847** DISRAELI *Tancred* II. vii, She knew that the fine ladies..were moral martinets with respect to any one not born among themselves. **1868** LD. BLOOMFIELD in Lady G. Bloomfield *Remin.* (1883) II. xix. 320 He is considerate, strict but not a martinet. **1888** *Poor Nellie* 300 A true-born martinet never thinks he is at all severe.

¶**b.** One who drills with precision.

1853 KANE *Grinnell Exp.* xxix. (1856) 254 We had drilled with knapsack and sledge, till we were almost martinets in our evolutions on the ice.

3. *attrib.* passing into *adj.*

1814 SCOTT *Wav.* lii, A sort of martinet attention to the minutiæ and technicalities of discipline. **1821–30** LD. COCKBURN *Mem.* i. (1874) 26 Martinet dowagers and venerable beaux acted as masters and mistresses of ceremonies. **1873** H. SPENCER *Stud. Sociol.* vii. 163 Protests like those made against martinet riding regulations..and against our 'ridiculous drill-book'. **1903** A. AINGER *Crabbe* viii. 145 The martinet father and his poor crushed wife.

Hence **ˈmartinet** *v.*, to act the martinet; **ˈmartinetdom**, **ˈmartinetship**, the system of government by martinets; **ˈmartiˌnetism**, the spirit or action characteristic of a martinet; **ˈmartiˌnet(t)ish** *a.*, having the characteristics of a martinet; whence **martinet(t)ishness.**

1827 *Sporting Mag.* XX. 107 Betwixt the system of martinetting too much and too little, the pro's and con's are nearly equal. **1827** HOR. SMITH *Tor Hill* (1838) II. 236 No garrison had ever been governed with so rancorous and unrelenting a martinetship. **1835** *Blackw. Mag.* XXXVIII. 322 He called them 'discipline'—his boast being martinetism. **1852** JERDAN *Autobiog.* I. vii. 53 The martinettish General had..enough ado to keep his Aides under military discipline. **1866** *Cornh. Mag.* Nov. 554 Educated in the traditions of military martinetdom which Frederick the Great had handed down to his successors as the basis of Prussia's greatness. **1878** R. H. HUTTON *Scott* i. 4 Sir Walter's father reminds one, in not a few of the formal and rather martinetish traits which are related of him, of the father of Goethe. **1882** *Pall Mall G.* 13 Sept. 3 Disgust at the martinettishness of their commanding officer. **1887** *Standard* 16 May 5/3 A martinetism..repugnant to the English character.

martineta (mɑːtɪˈneɪtə). [Amer. Sp., prob. f. Sp. *martinete* night heron.] A species of tinamou, *Eudromia elegans*, found in southern Argentina. Also *attrib.*

1872 W. H. HUDSON in *Proc. Zool. Soc.* 546 The Martineta frequents the elevated tablelands. **1892** W. R. KENNEDY *Sporting Sk. S. Amer.* 7 The 'Martinetas', or large Partridge (*Rhynchotus rufescens*), are generally found in pairs, and if one rises the other is probably not far off. **1925** L. E. ELLIOTT in J. A. Hammerton *Countries of World* VI. 4140/2 On the great undulating plains [of Uruguay] are thousands of..the double quail or martineta. **1961** G. DURRELL *Whispering Land* iv. 94 The commonest bird we saw was undoubtedly the martineta, a species of tinamu. It is plump, a partridge-shaped little bird, about the size of a bantam. Its plumage is a rich array of autumn browns, speckled and streaked with golds, yellows and creams... On its head there is an elongated crest of dark feathers, which curves like a half-moon over its head. **1964** A. L. THOMSON *New Dict. Birds* 822/2 The Martineta Tinamou *Eudromia elegans* is earth-coloured and adorned with a long slender crest which the bird when excited carries directed forwards.

martingale (ˈmɑːtɪŋgeɪl), *sb.* Also 6–7 **martingall**, 7–9 **martingal.** [a. F. *martingale* (Cotgr. 1611 in sense 1), of obscure etymology.

First found in Rabelais in *chausses a la martingale* hose that fastened at the back (hence Sp., It. *martingala* a sort of hose, in Sp. also cuishes). This is commonly supposed to mean literally 'hose after the fashion of Martigues' (in Provence), and the 'martingale' for a horse is assumed to have been so named from its similarity to hose of this kind. It is, however, doubtful whether Rabelais's *a la martingale* is anything but a jocular application of the term of the manege, though the mod. Prov. dicts. give *martegalo* as one of the Pr. forms of the word.]

1. A strap or arrangement of straps fastened at one end to the noseband, bit, or reins and at the other to the girth to prevent a horse from rearing or throwing back his head.

1589 ? LYLY *Pappe w. Hatchet* Wks. 1902 III. 410 Thou shalt be broken as Prosper broke his horses, with a muzroule, portmouth, and a martingall. *a* **1616** BEAUM. & FL. *Scornf. Lady* II. i, Lord what a hunting head shee carries, sure she has been ridden with a Martingale. **1661** HOWELL *Twelve Treat.* 237 Some people are to be rid with strong bitts and curbs, and martingalls. **1727** BRADLEY *Fam. Dict.* s.v. *Colt*, Then put on a Martingal. **1826** DISRAELI *Viv. Grey* III. iv, If you found a martingale for the mother, Vivian, it had been well if you had found a curb for the daughter. **1903** *Blackw. Mag.* July 83/1 Where is the saddle, the martingale?

2. *Naut.* A rope for guying down the jib-boom to the dolphin-striker; also called ***martingale-guy, -stay.*** ***flying martingale***, a similar supporting rope for the flying jib-boom. ***martingale backrope***, a guy-rope for the dolphin-striker.

1794 *Rigging & Seamanship* I. 233 Martingal-stay, to support the jib-boom. **1815** *Falconer's Dict. Marine* (ed. Burney), Martingale in a ship is a name given to the rope extending downwards from the jib-boom end to a kind of bumkin. **1840** R. H. DANA *Bef. Mast* xxxv. 132 Tackle [was] got upon the martingale backrope. **1882** NARES *Seamanship* (ed. 6) 13 The flying jib-boom is supported downwards by a flying martingale.

b. A dolphin-striker (see DOLPHIN 9).

1794 *Rigging & Seamanship* I. 170 Martingal, an ash bar, fixed downwards from the fore-side of the bowsprit-cap, and by which the martingal-stay supports the jib-boom. **1853** KANE *Grinnell Exp.* iii. (1856) 27 We ran into an iceberg.., and carried away our jib-boom and martingale. **1899** F. T. BULLEN *Log Sea-waif* 17 Seated far out ahead of the ship by the martingale.

3. A system in gambling which consists in doubling the stake when losing in the hope of eventually recouping oneself.

1815 *Paris Chit-chat* (1816) III. 52, I found him and his Mentor..calculating the infallible chances of a martingale. **1854** THACKERAY *Newcomes* I. 266 You have not played as yet? Do not do so; above all avoid a martingale if you do. **1878** *Daily News* 9 Mar., She was to pay him £20 per annum at the end of 1875, £40 at the end of 1876, £80 in 1877, and so on, in a sort of martingale. **1894** MASKELYNE *Sharps & Flats* xiv. 325 Sometimes, of course, the martingale will answer its purpose splendidly for a while.

martingale (ˈmɑːtɪŋgeɪl), *v.* [f. MARTINGALE *sb.* Cf. F. *martingaler* in sense 1.]

1. *intr.* (See quot.)

1823 'JON BEE' *Dict. Turf*, *Martingale*, at play, to double stakes constantly, until luck taking one turn only, repays the adventurer all.

2. *trans. Naut.* To secure with a guy-rope.

1882 NARES *Seamanship* (ed. 6) 211 If the wind is likely to freshen, martingale the..studding-sail boom.

‖**martingana** (martiŋˈgana). Also anglicized **-gane.** [Sicilian It.] A kind of boat used in Sicily.

1886 *List of Ships Reported* Dec., Abbrev., *Ma.* Martingana. **1893** F. M. CRAWFORD *Children of King* I. 6 A couple of clumsy 'martinganes'.

Martini[1] (mɑːˈtiːniː). In full, ***Martini-Henry*** (***rifle***). A rifle used in the British army from 1871 to 1891, combining a breech-mechanism invented by Friedrich von Martini with a ·45-calibre barrel devised by Benjamin Tyler Henry (see HENRY[1]). So ***Martini-Henry carbine.***

1870 *Colburn's United Service Mag.* I. 361 The rapid improvements which have taken place..since the introduction of..Brown Bess in 1842, to that of the Martini-Henry in the present year. *Ibid.* 367 The only thing then remaining to be done was to fit the Martini breech to the Henry barrel, and thus we have the Martini-Henry rifle complete. **1876** *Rifle Shot's Man.* 21 With the Martini..a considerably increased allowance can be made. **1890** KIPLING *Soldiers Three* (1891) 65 The good and virtuous people who hardly know a Martini from a Snider. **1890** KIPLING *Barrack-Room Ballads* (1892) 11 We sloshed you with Martinis. *Ibid.* 48 When 'arf of your bullets fly wide in the ditch, Don't call your Martini a cross-eyed old bitch. **1892** R. CHURCHILL *Men, Mines & Animals S. Afr.* viii. 115 A good magazine is probably a better weapon than a Martini-Henry. **1900** [see DANE GUN]. **1915** OMMUNDSEN & ROBINSON *Rifles & Ammunition* iii. 59 Another arrangement ..was to make the grooves deeper at the breech than at the muzzle. The principle was adopted for the Enfield and retained in the Martini-Henry. **1962** H. L. PETERSON *Bk. Gun* 182/1 From 1871 until after the adoption of smokeless powder, the Martini served as the principal British single-shot weapon. **1967** ROBERTS & WATERS *Breech-Loading Single-Shot Match Rifle* i. 28 Martini-Henry rifles chambered for the various large British hunting cartridges were..popular in Africa and India.

Martini[2] (mɑːˈtiːnɪ). [f. the name of *Martini* and Rossi, Italian wine-makers.] The proprietary name of a type of vermouth; a cocktail consisting of gin and vermouth; ***dry Martini***, such a cocktail containing more gin than vermouth, sometimes with the addition of orange bitters. Also *attrib.*

1894 *Puck* (U.S.) 28 Nov. 238/2 (Advt.), The Club Cocktails Manhattan, Martini, Whisky, [etc.]. **1896** *Crescent* (Brooklyn, N.Y.) 1 Aug. 11/2 As he sipped his martini and inhaled its seductive bouquet, a far-away look came into his baby-blue eyes. **1903** ADE *People you Know* 20 It was an actual mystery to him that any one could dally with a Dry Martini while there was a Hydrant on every Corner. **1906** *Mrs. Beeton's Bk. Househ. Managem.* xlix. 1511 Martini cocktail. **1909** [see BRONX 1]. **1919** C. MACKENZIE *Sylvia & Michael* v. 203 What are you going to have? Ordered a Martini here the other day. **1930** WODEHOUSE *Very Good, Jeeves!* ii. 57 A nicely-balanced meal, preceded by a couple of dry Martinis, washed down with half a bot. **1953** D. A. EMBURY *Fine Art of Mixing Drinks* 36 Martinis, Manhattans, and other cocktails containing wine can be stirred with a rod or long spoon. *Ibid.* 106, I have already referred to the Martini as the most perfect of apéritif cocktails. **1958** *Times Lit. Suppl.* 19 Dec. 733/4 The sham, artificial life of all-night martini parties. **1962** 'E. MCBAIN' *Like Love* (1964) vii. 100 A tray with a Martini shaker and two iced Martini glasses. **1967** A. LICHINE *Encycl. Wines* 542/1 The Italian Cinzano may be red or white, sweet or fairly dry—as also may Martini and Gancia. **1968** [see GIBSON[2]]. **1972** J. MOSEDALE *Football* vii. 100 People tend to think of us professionals as guys who spend all their time around the swimming pool with a blonde in one hand and a martini in the other... A lot of us don't like martinis.

martinia, variant of MARTYNIA.

Martiniquan (mɑːtɪˈniːkən), *a.* and *sb.* Also **Martinican, Martiniquian, Martiniquien.** [f. *Martinique* (see below) + -AN.] **A.** *adj.* Of or pertaining to Martinique, an island of the West Indies. **B.** *sb.* A native or inhabitant of Martinique. So **Martiniquais** *a.* and *sb.* [Fr.].

1890 L. HEARN *Two Yrs. French W. Indies* 358 In Louisiana an almost similar dish is called *jimbalaya*: chicken cooked with rice. The Martiniquais think it..a delicacy. **1891** W. F. HUTCHINSON *Under Southern Cross* vi. 58 The Cuban becomes twice a Spaniard, a Barbadian three times an Englishman, and a Martiniquien four times a Frenchman. *Ibid.* 69 (*caption*) A fair Martiniquienne. **1907** A. E. ASPINALL *Pocket Guide W. Indies* xiv. 255 St. Pierre.. was for all the world like a small French provincial city, with its cabarets and cafés, at the tables of which the Martinicans passed their leisure hours. **1926** A. BELL *Spell of Caribbean Islands* xvi. 256 The outstanding features of Martinican life. **1942** N. SMITH *Black Martinique* (1943) iii. 26 A wild-eyed youth.., brown-skinned, a true Martiniquais, came bursting toward us through the crowd. **1953** *Caribbean Q.* III. I. 28 Trinidadian patois has more faithfully retained truly Creole words which the Martiniquan has lost. *Ibid.* 29 The Martiniquan humour of M. Gratiant. **1955** *Ibid.* IV. I. 13 Another example of this poem of solidarity with Africans is the Martiniquais Paul Niger's *Je n'aime pas l'Afrique.* **1964** *Sat. Rev.* (U.S.) 10 Oct. 75/1 Lafcadio Hearn..wrote so poignantly of the 'little' Martiniquans. **1967** D. LOWENTHAL in R. D. Abrahams *Positively Black* (1970) iii. 75 A black or colored man from Jamaica or Martinique is simply a Jamaican or Martiniquian. **1970** J. BROWN *Unmelting Pot* vii. 99 '*Peau noir, masque blanc.*' The old Martiniquan saying sums up as well as any the central predicament of West Indian man. **1972** F. WARD *Golden Islands Caribbean* ii. 47 (*caption*) The Creole costume remained in vogue with Martinican women. *Ibid.* 48 A Martinican is unequivocably [*sic*] and irrevocably a Frenchman. **1973** *Nation* (Barbados) 23 Dec. 32/4 The Barbadians..will be allowed to fish freely in Martiniquan waters. *Ibid.* 32/5 Martiniquans do not eat flying fish. **1975** *New Yorker* 31 Mar. 54/3 We're all here by accident, and a Haitian and a black American could just as easily have been a Martinican or a Jamaican.

†ˈ**Martinish**, *a. Obs.* [f. *Martin* + -ISH.] Of or pertaining to the Martinists.

1592 G. HARVEY *Four Lett.* ii. Wks. (Grosart) I. 203 This Martinish and Counter-martinish age.

ˈ**Martinism.** [f. *Martin* + -ISM.]

1. The tenets of 'Martin Marprelate' (see MAR-b).

1589 *Pasquil's Ret.* A iv, It is a common reporte that the faction of Martinisme hath mightie freends. **1597** HOOKER *Eccl. Pol.* v. Ded. §7 The scurrilous and more then Satyricall immodestie of Martinisme.

2. The system of L. C. de Saint-Martin (see next 3).

1879 *Encycl. Brit.* IX. 751 (art. *Freemasonry*), The rivalry of such romantic systems as Martinism was still..keenly felt.

Martinist (ˈmɑːtɪnɪst). Also 7 **martenist.** [f. the proper name *Martin* + -IST.]

1. A partisan of 'Martin Marprelate'.

1589 ? LYLY *Pappe w. Hatchet* Wks. 1902 III. 405 Twas a mad knaue and a Martinist, that diuided his sermon into parts for memorie sake. *a* **1600** HOOKER *Eccl. Pol.* VII. vi. §7 Tell the Martinist of the High-Priests great authority.. what other thing doth serve his turn but the self-same shift. **1659** GAUDEN *Tears Ch.* I. v. 61 After such..Satyrick Pasquils (worthy of such *Martenists*) came open menacings of Princes and Parlaments, Priests and People too.

2. A follower of Martin Luther (as described by Swift in *The Tale of a Tub*).

1751 EARL ORRERY *Remarks Swift* (1752) 194 The criticisms of the Martinists (whom we may suppose the members of the church of England).

3. [F. *Martiniste*.] A member of a mystical school of religionists founded by L. C. de Saint-Martin (1743–1803), a disciple of Martinez Pasqualis (died 1779).

1871 MORLEY *Crit. Misc.* Ser. I. 183 Peradventure the twelve apostles might please you better than the philanthropists and Martinists.

†**4.** ? Used erron. for MARTINET². *Obs.*

1652 GAULE *Magastrom.* 179 How many magicians, astrologers, [etc.]..have had their..martinists, maisterels, and ministrels, their imps and familiars, as well as other witches?

martinite (ˈmɑːtɪnaɪt). *Min.* [Named by J. H. Kloos 1887–9 after Prof. K. *Martin*, who collected it.] Hydrous phosphate of calcium found at Curaçao (Chester *Dict. Min.* 1896).

†ˈ**Martinize**, *v. Obs.* [f. *Martin* + -IZE.] *intr.* To discourse in the strain of 'Martin Marprelate'.

1591 GREENE *Farew. Folly* Ded., Wks. (Grosart) IX. 228, I cannot Martinize, sweare by my faie in a pulpit, and rap out gogs wounds in a tauerne.

Martinmas (ˈmɑːtɪnməs). Forms: 3, 5 **martinmasse**, 4 **martynmesse**, 4–7 **martimes, martymes**, 5 **martymasse, martynmese, myrtynmes**, 6 **martil-, martylmas, -messe, mertymas, -mes**, 6–7 **martlemas**, 7 **martinmass, martynmasse**, 8 **martilmasse**, 9 **martinmas**. [f. *Martin* + MASS.]

1. The feast of St. Martin, 11 Nov. Formerly sometimes †***Martinmas in Winter***, for distinction from the feast of the translation of St. Martin, 4 July.

In Scotland one of the two term-days recognized by common law. In many parts of England it was the usual time for hiring servants, and fairs were often held on this day. It was also common to slaughter cattle at Martinmas to be salted for winter provision.

[*c***918** *OE. Chron.* an. 918 Foran to Martines mæssan.] **1297** R. GLOUC. (Rolls) 10579 A conseil hii made at martinmasse at bristowe ich vnderstonde. *c***1330** R. BRUNNE *Chron.* (1810) 230 After þe Martynmesse þat he died here. **1375** BARBOUR *Bruce* IX. 127 This wes eftir the Martymes, Quhen snaw had helit all the land. **14..** *Plumpton Corr.* (Camden) 148, iiij mark & xx^d. now dew unto him at this Martymasse last. *c***1450** *Merlin* vi. 96 The kynge is now deed sithe Martinmasse. **1472** *Presentm. Juries* in *Surtees Misc.* (1888) 26 We desyer þ^t he be wodyd be Myrtynmes next comyng. **1523** FITZHERB. *Surv.* viii. (1539) 12 From Myghelmas to Martylmas. **1557** TUSSER *100 Points Husb.* xxxiii, For Easter, at Martilmas hange vp a biefe. **1609** SKENE *Reg. Maj.*, *Quon. Attach.* 91 b, The ane half at the feast of Whit-sunday, and the other halfe at the feast of Martymes. **1641** BEST *Farm. Bks.* (Surtees) 120 Att Martynmasse,..wee sette our foreman to cuttinge of white-wilfes [etc.]. **1666–88** DALLAS *Stiles* (1697) 536 At two Terms in the year, Whitsunday and Martinmass in Winter. **1848** BELL *Dict. Law Scot.* 986 The crop is understood to be fully sown at the term of Whitsunday, and to be reaped at the term of Martinmas. **1867** FREEMAN *Norm. Conq.* (1876) I. v. 345 After Martinmas they took up their winter quarters. **1889** JOHNSTON *Chron. Glenbuckie* 81 Ye ken it [money lent] should have been paid at Martinmas.

†**2.** Used as a derisive appellation. *Obs.*

1597 SHAKS. *2 Hen. IV*, II. ii. 110 And how doth the Martlemas, your Master? [*sc.* Falstaff: cf. III. iii. 199, O my sweet Beefe.]

3. *Comb.*, as ***Martinmas term***; †**Martinmas beef, flesh, meat**, the meat of an ox salted at Martinmas; **Martinmas summer**, = St. Martin's summer (in quot. *fig.*); **Martinmas Sunday** *Sc.*, the Sunday nearest to Martinmas.

1530 PALSGR. 243/2 *Martylmas befe, *brezil*. **1542** BORDE *Dyetary* xxix. (1870) 292 Refrayne from eatynge of red heryng, martylmas beef and baken. **1620** VENNER *Via Recta* (1650) 72 Beefe Salted, and after dried, which we commonly call Martimas-Beef is of very hard concoction. **1849** MACAULAY *Hist. Eng.* iii. I. 315 Under Charles the Second it was not till the beginning of November that families laid in their stock of salt provisions, then called Martinmas beef. **1656** RIDGLEY *Pract. Physick* 329 *Martlemas flesh a year old, tosted and dried. **1352** *Wynnere & Wastoure* 345 For alle es *Martynmesse mete þat I with moste dele Noghte bot worttes with the flesche withowt wilde fowle. **1885** R. BUCHANAN *Annan Water* i, It was *Martinmas Sunday. **1895** G. ALLEN *Woman who did* 178, I almost feel tempted to give way to this *Martinmas summer of love. **1592** *Extracts Aberd. Reg.* (1848) II. 79 The *Martomes terme last bypast and Witsonday terme to cum.

Martionist, obs. form of MARCIONIST.

martir, variant of MARTER, a marten.

martir(e, obs. forms of MARTYR *sb.* and *v.*

martirlogi, variant of MARTILOGE *Obs.*

martiron, obs. form of MARTEN.

martite (ˈmɑːtaɪt). *Min.* [f. L. *Mart-em* (see MARS) + -ITE.] 'A pseudomorph of hematite after magnetite' (Chester *Dict. Min.*).

1851 WATTS tr. *Gmelin's Handbk. Chem.* V. 194 Sesquioxide of Iron... Occurs in the forms of..Iron-glance, Red Hæmatite..and Martite. **1879** RUTLEY *Stud. Rocks* xi. 200 The magnetite probably being converted into martite.

martlemas, obs. form of MARTINMAS.

†ˈ**martlet**¹. *Obs.* Also 5 **mertlete**. [Altered form of MARTRET. Cf. MDu. *martel*, var. of *marter* marten; also med.L. *martalus* marten (once in Du Cange from a document written in Germany).] A marten; also, the fur of the marten.

1440 in Peacock *Eng. Ch. Furniture* (1866) 182 A vestment of white fustiane with black mertletes. **1693** RAY *Syn. Quadr.* 200 *Martes aliis Foyna*, a Martin or Martlet. **1753** CHAMBERS *Cycl. Supp.*, *Martes*, the Martin, or Martlet..the name of a creature of the weasel kind. **1802** SIBBALD *Chron. Scot. Poetry* IV. Gloss., *Martlet*, more commonly Mertrick, a kind of large weesel, which bears a rich fur.

martlet² (ˈmɑːtlɪt). Also 6 **mart(e)lette**, 7 **martilet**, 8 **mart(e)lett**. [a. F. *martelet*, app. an altered form of *martinet* (see MARTINET²), perh. assimilated to *roitelet* wren.]

1. The swift, *Cypselus apus*, formerly often confused with the swallow and the house-martin, to which some of the examples refer.

1538 ELYOT *Dict.*, *Apedes*, a byrde whose fete be so lytle, that they seeme to haue none. I suppose they be martlettes. **1575** TURBERV. *Faulconrie* 134 Yong sparrowes martelettes and other small byrdes. **1596** SHAKS. *Merch. V.* II. ix. 28 Which..like the Martlet Builds in the weather on the outward wall. **1666** DRYDEN *Ann. Mirab.* cx, First the martlet meets it in the sky. **1678** [see MARTINET¹ 1]. **1771** SMOLLETT *Humph. Cl.* 8 June, The sweet twitter of the martlet at my window. **1773** [see MARTIN¹ 1]. **1821** *Blackw. Mag.* X. 443 I'll stay here till the woodcock comes, and the martlet takes her wing. **1854** SYD. DOBELL *Balder* xxiii. 109 When airy martlet, sipping of the pool, Touches it to a ripple that stirs not The lilies.

2. *Her.* An imaginary bird without feet, borne as a charge. Used as a mark of cadency for a fourth son.

In French heraldry the corresponding bird (described as having neither feet nor beak) is called *merlette* (OF. *merlete, meslete*; AF. heraldry had *merelot, merlot*, with differing dim. suffix). This word is app. a dim. of *merle* blackbird; according to Littré it has the sense 'female blackbird', but only the heraldic sense appears in Hatz.-Darm. It seems possible that the heraldic bird may originally have been intended for a 'little blackbird', represented without feet by accident or caprice, or with symbolical intention, and that the English heralds of the 16th c. or earlier identified the bird so depicted with the 'martlet' or swift, which has short legs, whence its mod. specific name *apus* = Gr. ἄπους footless. It is noteworthy that the 'martlets' (so called in the 16th c.) in the pretended arms of Edward the Confessor were at an early period portrayed with feet. The anglicized form of *merlete*, MARLET, does not occur in heraldic use, but appears in several 16th c. instances with the sense of *martlet*, i.e. a swift or a martin. According to English heraldic writers, the use of the footless bird as a mark of cadency for younger sons was meant to symbolize their position as having no footing in the ancestral lands.

*a***1550** in *Baring-Gould & Twigge's West. Armory* (1898) 5 Bodleigh: Arg: 5 martlets 3, 2, on a cheife sab: 3 coronets or. **1610** GUILLIM *Heraldry* III. xvii. (1611) 163 He beareth Azure, a Bend Argent, Cottized Or, betweene six Martlets of the same... The Martlet or Martinet (saith Bekenhawb) hath legges so exceeding short, that they can by no meanes goe. **1642** FULLER *Holy & Prof. St.* I. xv. 48 The fourth Brother gives a Martlet for the difference of his Armes. **1664** BUTLER *Hud.* II. iii. 417 The strangest long-wing'd Hawk that flies, That, like a Bird of Paradise, Or Herauld's Martlet has no legs. **1704** J. HARRIS *Lex. Techn.* I, *Martlet*, the Term in Heraldry for a Pidgeon, with its Feet erased or torn off; 'tis also the Difference, or mark of Distinction in an Escutcheon for the fourth Brother or Family. **1880** G. T. CLARK in *Encycl. Brit.* XI. 690/2 The imputed arms of the Confessor, 'gules, a cross patonce between 5 martlets or'.

†ˈ**martlit**. *Obs.*⁻¹ *Naut.* ? = MARTINET³ 4.

1626 CAPT. SMITH *Accid. Yng. Seamen* 15 The Robins, garnit, Clew garnits, tyes, martlits.

martloge, variant of MARTILOGE *Obs.*

†ˈ**martly**, *a. Obs.* [f. MART *sb.*⁴ + -LY¹.] Appointed every 'mart' or periodical fair-time.

1655 in Thurloe *St. Papers* (1742) III. 119 It is in the breast of the company orderly assembled..to make choice of a martly deputy or for what other term or continuance they shall find convenient.

†ˈ**martly**, *adv. Obs.* [f. MART *sb.*⁴ + -LY².] Every 'mart' or fair-time (the period when accounts were made up in Germany).

*c***1600** in *Trans. Roy. Hist. Soc.* (1902) XVI. 45 Foure and twentye Assystents..to bee chosen martly or as occasion shall serve from tyme to tyme. **1721** STRYPE *Eccl. Mem.* II. II. x. 327 The Emperor..ran..martely great and excessive interest for large sums already had.

martnet(te, variant forms of MARTINET.

marton, martoune, obs. ff. MARTEN, MARTIN.

martre, variant of MARTER *Obs.*, MARTYR.

martren, obs. form of MARTEN.

†ˈ**martret**. *Obs.* [f. *martre* MARTER + -ET¹.] A pole-cat.

14.. *Voc.* in Wr.-Wülcker 582/28 Fecontria, a martret.

†ˈ**martrix, martrick**. *Sc. Obs.* Also 5–6 **mar-, mertrik**, 6 **matrik**, 5–8 **mertrick**. [a. and ad. med.L. *martrix* (Wr.-Wülcker 595), a fem. coined to correspond to *martor* MARTER, the suffix being apprehended as if that of an agent-noun.] A marten; also, the fur of the marten.

1423 JAS. I *Kingis Q.* clvii, The bugill, draware by his hornis grete; The martrik, sable, the foynȝee, and mony mo. *c***1470** HENRYSON *Mor. Fab.* v. (*Parl. Beasts*) xvii, The mertrik with the cuning and the con. **1536** BELLENDEN *Cron. Scot.* (1821) I. 21 Mony hidis and skinnis of oxin, scheip, gait and martrikis. **1564** *Reg. Privy Council Scot.* I. 308 Ane goun of drogat, lynit with martrikis, begareit with velvot. **1596** DALRYMPLE tr. *Leslie's Hist. Scot.* I. 21 He dryues the foxis, the martrix, the brok and the wilkatt. **1630–56** SIR R. GORDON *Hist. Earls Sutherland* 3 Martrixes, hares, and fumarts. **1703** M. MARTIN *Descr. West. Isl.* 36 The Mertrick ..about the size of a big Cat, is pretty numerous in this Isle. **1707** MIEGE *St. Gt. Brit.* ii. 30 Deer-skins, Foxes,.. Mertricks. **1802** [see MARTLET¹].

attrib. **1424** *Sc. Acts Jas. I* (1814) II. 6/1 þ^t na man haif mertrik skynnis out of the realme. **1535** STEWART *Cron. Scot.* (1858) I. 151 For fox and fulmart and of mertrik skin, Anew thair wes tha landis than within.

martron(e, martroun, obs. ff. MARTEN.

martspaine, obs. form of MARZIPAN.

martyall, obs. form of MARTIAL.

martylage, -logye, var. ff. MARTILOGE *Obs.*

Martylmas, -messe, obs. ff. MARTINMAS.

Martymasse, -mes, obs. ff. MARTINMAS.

martymette: see MARTINET.

martyn, obs. form of MARTEN, MARTIN.

‖**martynia** (mɑːˈtɪnɪə). *Bot.* Also 8 **martinia**. [mod.L. (Linnæus), f. name of Prof. J. *Martyn*, died 1768.] A genus of American plants of the N.O. *Pedalineæ*; a plant of this genus.

1753 in CHAMBERS *Cycl. Supp.* **1796** H. HUNTER tr. *St.-Pierre's Stud. Nat.* (1799) II. 220, I did not know of what country the martinia was a native. **1860** DARLINGTON *Amer. Weeds* 222 Long-beaked Martynia, Unicorn Plant... This plant..is cultivated for its singular fruit—which, in its young state..is used for making pickles.

martyr (ˈmɑːtə(r)), *sb.* Also 1–6 **martir**, 3–6 **-ter**, 4 **-tire**, 4–5 **-tyre, -tre**, 5 **-tier**, 6 *Sc.* **-teir, -ther**. [OE. *martyr*, ad. Eccl.L. *martyr*, a. Gr. *μάρτυρ*, Æolic and late Gr. form of *μάρτυς* (stem *μαρτυρ-*) witness (in Christian use, martyr), f. Aryan root **smer-* (whence Skr. *smar*) to remember.

The Gr. word was adopted in Goth. as *martyr*. The Lat. word passed into all the Rom. langs. (OF. *martir*, Pr., mod.F., Pg. *martyr*, Sp. *martir*, It. *martire*) and some of the Teut. langs. (OFris., OS. *martir*, MLG. *marter*, Sw., Da. *martyr*); in Ger. and Du. the sense was expressed by a derivative (OHG. *martirâri*, MHG. *merterer*, mod.G. *märtyrer*; MHG. *martelære*, MLG. *martelere*, MDu. *martelare*, mod.Du. *martelaar*), f. OHG. *martira, martela* (MHG. *martere, martel*, mod.G. *marter*, MDu., MHG. *martele*, mod.Du. *martel-* in Combs.) fem., ad. L. *martyrium* martyrdom. In ON. *píslarváttr* ('torture-witness') was substituted.]

1. *Eccl.* **a.** The specific designation of honour (connoting the highest degree of saintship) for: One who voluntarily undergoes the penalty of death for refusing to renounce the Christian faith or any article of it, for perseverance in any Christian virtue, or for obedience to any law or command of the Church.

A sect which regarded its distinctive principles as part of the Christian faith could apply the title, in this strict sense, to its own members who died under persecution, while by others the application would be repudiated, or only conceded ironically. Popularly, however, this sense has long tended to be apprehended as a specific use of sense 2.

*a***900** tr. *Bæda's Hist.* I. vii, Ðær wæs þa heafde beslaȝen se strengesta martyr Sancts Albanus. *c***1000** *Menologium* 69 Sculan we hwæðere ȝyt martira ȝemynd ma areccan. **1154** *O.E. Chron.* an. 1137 (Laud MS.) Ne uuæren næure nan martyrs swa pined alse hi wæron. *a***1225** *Ancr R.* 50 þe reade [creoice] limpeð to þeo þat beoð, uor Godes luue, mid hore blodshedunge irudded & ireaded, ase þe martirs weren. *c***1330** R. BRUNNE *Chron.* (1810) 35 He gate of hir S. Edward, þat is þe martere. *c***1388** in *Wyclif's Sel. Wks.* III. 489 Of Seint Steven men bene certayne by holy writte þat he is a gloriouse martire. *c***1400** *Destr. Troy* 3488 Dyssmembrit as marters, & murtheret to dethe. **1474** CAXTON *Chesse* 61 Abel was the fyrst martir in the olde testament. **1529** MORE *Dyaloge* I. Wks. 134/2, I thanke god & his holy marter, I can se nowe as well as any man. **1586** B. YOUNG *Guazzo's Civ. Conv.* IV. 218 b, If I had not giuen credence to that Prouerbe, That it is better to bee a Martyr than a Confessour. **1611** BIBLE *Acts* xxii. 20 When ye blood of thy martyr [*other versions* witness (Vulgate *testis*)] Steuen was shed. **1653** A. ROSS *View of all Relig.* xii. 403 Barrowists, so called from Barrow, their first Martyr. **1672** EVELYN *Diary* 20 Feb., K. Charles our Martyr. **1704** NELSON *Fest. & Fasts* xxviii. (1739) 361 It was necessary to resist unto blood, to acquire the glorious Privilege of a Martyr. **1850** MRS. JAMESON *Leg. Monast. Ord.* (1863) 97, I am not sure that the title of martyr properly belongs to St. Edward, for his death was not voluntary, nor from any religious cause.

¶ The events of the Reformation period caused the word to be popularly associated esp. with death by fire. Hence sometimes *transf.*

1666 DRYDEN *Ann. Mirab.* cii, And burning ships, the martyrs of the fight, With paler fires beheld the eastern sky.

†**b.** Used with sarcastic emphasis for: One who suffers death in an evil cause. *Obs.*

*c***1380** WYCLIF *Sel. Wks.* III. 171 But Lord! what mede were it to feden and norischen þus Anticrist martres! —— *Wks.* (1880) 211 Sathanas children & marteris of glotonye. **1577** VAUTROUILLIER *Luther on Ep. Gal.* 234 The doers of the lawe..are rightly called the Deuils martyrs. They take more paynes..in purchasing hell..then the Martyrs of

Christ doe in obtaining heauen. **1653** H. Cogan tr. *Pinto's Trav.* xxxvii. 247 This action of theirs brought these Martyrs of the Divell into the Number of the Saints. **1841** Ld. Houghton *One Tract More* 10 Melancthon mentions that the German Lutherans named those that had suffered for the reformed cause in England, *the Devil's Martyrs*.

c. Used in the etymological sense of: Witness.

1642 Milton *Apol. Smect.* Wks. 1851 III. 301 These opening the prisons and dungeons cal'd out of darknesse and bonds, the elect Martyrs and witnesses of their Redeemer. *a* **1677** Barrow *Serm.* (1686) III. 95 Having such a cloud of Martyrs [*Heb.* xii. 1].

2. a. One who undergoes death (more loosely, one who undergoes great suffering) on behalf of any religious or other belief or cause, or as a consequence of his devotion to some object. Const. *to*.

1597 Shaks. *2 Hen. IV*, iv. i. 193 Were our Royall faiths Martyrs in Loue. **1652** Bp. Hall *Invis. World* ii. i, That heathen martyr Socrates. **1695** Congreve *Love for L.* i. ii, Who would die a martyr to sense in a country where the religion is folly? **1715** De Foe *Fam. Instruct.* i. iv. (1841) I. 92 You are like to be a Martyr in the worst cause that ever saint suffered in. **1737** Pope *Hor. Ep.* i. i. 151 The Fool, whose Wife elopes some thrice a quarter, For matrimonial solace dies a martyr. **1777** Watson *Philip II* (1839) 325 His father had died a martyr for that cause, which he now wanted so basely to betray. **1793** Burke *Corr.* (1844) IV. 185 That patience and fortitude..which distinguished the martyrs of your family in their last calamitous struggle. **1863** *Chem. News* 14 Feb. 84/1 (*heading*) A Martyr to Science.

b. One who dies a victim (*to..*).

1792 S. Rogers *Pleas. Mem.* i. 286 [He] sinks a martyr to repentant sighs. **1800** Mar. Edgeworth *Murad* iii, Murad ..died a martyr to the immoderate use of opium.

3. *hyperbolically*. **a.** One who suffers tortures comparable to those described in the legends of martyrs; a constant sufferer. Const. *to* (an ailment, etc.).

A common use in mod. Fr. (In the first quot. the word may be a verb intr., 'to suffer as a martyr': Godef. cites a very similar passage as example of the OF. *martirer*.)

c **1560** A. Scott *Poems* (S.T.S.) xvi. 12 To lufe & serf his lady bricht, And want hir syne, As I do, martir day and nyt. **1847** Fr. A. Kemble in *Rec. Later Life* (1882) III. 186 She is a martyr to dyspepsia and bad cooking. **1892** *Law Times* XCII. 160/1 The deceased..had been a martyr for years to rheumatic gout.

b. *to make a martyr of*: to subject to hardship or inconvenience. Now often jocularly, ***to make a martyr of oneself***: to make a real or pretended sacrifice of one's inclinations for the sake of gaining credit for it.

1599 Peele *Sir Clyom.* Wks. (Bullen) II. 168 He even means to make a martris [*sic*: ? meant as an illiterate blunder] of poor Shift his man. **1882** Miss Braddon *Mt. Royal* iv, You shall not make a martyr of yourself for my sake.

4. *attrib.* and *Comb.* **a.** appositive (quasi-*adj.*).

1651–3 Jer. Taylor *Serm. for Year* II. iv. 43 The monuments of the Martyr Prophets. **1710** Pope *Windsor For.* 313 Here o'er the martyr-king the marble weeps. **1833** Marsden *Early Purit.* 9 The martyr-bishop Hooper. *c* **1862** E. Dickinson *Poems* (1955) II. 417 The Martyr Poets—did not tell—But wrought their Pang in syllable—..The Martyr Painters—never spoke. **1863** I. Williams *Baptistery* ii. xxii. (1874) 67 That fam'd Antioch's martyr-maid. **1870** *Brewer's Dict. Phr. & Fable* 558/2 *The Martyr King*, Charles I. of England, beheaded January 30th, 1649. **1876** G. M. Hopkins *Wreck of Deutschland* xxi, in *Poems* (1967) 58 Thy unchancelling poising palms were weighing the worth, Thou martyr-master. **1883** *Century Mag.* July 328/1 One [town] called Garfield, in honour of the martyr president. **1908** L. Dawson *Nicknames & Pseudonyms* 194 *Martyr King*.., Charles i..King of England. *Ibid.* 195 *Martyr President*.., Abraham Lincoln. **1939** R. Campbell *Flowering Rifle* iv. 117 The Press then bills him as a martyr-hero. **1942** Berrey & Van den Bark *Amer. Thes. Slang* §184/14 The Martyr President,..Uncle Abe, *Abraham Lincoln*.

b. simple attrib., as ***martyr-cell, -conduct, -death, -fire, -flame, -habit, -legend, -spasm, -spirit, -stake, -task, -train, -zeal***; ***martyr-like*** adv. **c.** objective, as ***martyr †-queller, -slaying***. Also **martyr complex**, an exaggerated desire to sacrifice oneself for others and to have the sacrifice recognized; **martyr-maker, -man**, contemptuous names for the martyrologist John Foxe (1517–1587); **martyr-vase** *Antiq.*, a vessel in which relics of a martyr were preserved.

1860 W. H. Ainsworth *Ovingdean Grange* 242 Dulcia may be..placed..in the *martyr-cells beneath the White-Hart. **1931** *Times Lit. Suppl.* 22 Jan. 58/4 In Rachel, we are asked to believe they fix a '*martyr-complex', or give her a taste for unnecessary self-sacrifice. **1831** Carlyle *Charact.* Misc. 1857 III. 17 Heroic *martyr Conduct. **1798** Sotheby tr. *Wieland's Oberon* (1826) II. 129 Huon with lingering *martyr-death decays. **1849** Stovel *Introd. Canne's Necess.* 50 Meeting..round the *martyr-fires which consumed their brethren. **1830** Tennyson *To* —— ii, Nor *martyr-flames, nor trenchant swords Can do away that ancient lie. **1902** W. James *Varieties Relig. Experience* iv. 98 The 'misery-habit', the '*martyr-habit', engendered by the prevalent 'fearthought'. **1902** W. M. Ramsay in *Expositor* Oct. 284 A good example of the way in which *martyr-legends grew round a really historical name. **1580** Hollyband *Treas. Fr. Tong.*, *Martyrement*, *Martyr like. **1826** W. E. Andrews *Exam. Fox's Cal. Prot. Saints* 413 The *martyr-maker appears to have been unacquainted with their christian names. **1826** Cobbett *Hist. Prot. Reform.* xvi. §471 The 'pious young Saint Edward', as Fox, the *martyrman, most impiously calls him. **1532** More *Confut. Tindale* Wks. 352/1 Murtherers & *martyr quellers. **1826** E. Irving *Babylon* I. iii. 189 This new *martyr-slaying power. **1916** Blunden *Harbingers* 66 Marble writhed to *martyr-spasm. **1817** Mrs. Hemans *Mod. Greece* xlii, The *martyr-spirit of resolve was fled. **1798** Sotheby tr. *Wieland's Oberon* (1826) II. 210 Already stand before the *martyr-stake The pair that perish for each others sake. **1827** Mrs. Hemans *Last Constantine* xix, Some high *martyr-task. **1827** Keble *Chr. Y.*, *Holy Innocents*, Their palms and garlands telling plain That they are of the glorious *martyr-train. **1846** C. Maitland *Ch. in Catacombs* 147 Between the heathen lacrymatory and the so-called *martyr-vase there exists no well defined difference. **1805** Southey *Madoc in Azt.* xv, Her Priests..fought with *martyr zeal.

martyr ('mɑːtə(r)), *v.* Forms: 1 (ȝe)martyrian, (ȝe)martrian, 3–4 martri, 3–5 martre(n, 3–7 -tir(e, 4 -trye, -tiry, 4–6 -ter, -tyre, 5 -tur, mertre, 6 *Sc.* marthyr, 4– martyr. [f. martyr *sb.*; cf. OF. *martirer*.]

1. *trans.* To put to death as a martyr; to make a martyr of. (†occas. *refl.*)

c **893** K. Ælfred *Oros.* vi. vi. (Sweet) 262 Þæt hie Petrus & Paulus ȝemartredon. *a* **900** tr. *Bæda's Hist.* i. vii, Ða wæs eac swylce heafde besleȝen & ȝemartyrad se mon, se ðe.. wiðsoc þæt he ðone Godes andettere sloȝe. *c* **1205** Lay. 10901 Þus ferde Maximien: he martrede seint Alban. **1297** R. Glouc. (Rolls) 1601 He worrede cristendom..& let martri seint denis. *a* **1300** *Cursor M.* 8924 Þis womman [Maximilla] was þe first men wist þat martird was for ihesu crist. **1377** Langl. *P. Pl.* B. xv. 551 In sauacion of the fayth seynt Thomas was ymartired. **1450–1530** *Myrr. our Ladye* 124 In greate desyre to be martyrde for the loue of oure lorde Iesu cryste. **1480** Caxton *Chron. Eng.* xl. 28 Seynt peter.. wente to Rome and was made pope til that Nero the emperour lete hym martren. **1641** J. Jackson *True Evang. T.* ii. 120 Matthias..was..Martyred by the Axe or Hatchet. **1709** Hearne *Collect.* 5 Jan. (O.H.S.) II. 162 Tyndale was martyr'd at Fylford. **1853** J. H. Newman *Hist. Sk.* (1873) II. i. iii. 104 The German tribes..martyred St. Boniface and other..missionaries who came to them.

†2. To kill, slay, esp. by a cruel death. Also with *down* (cf. *cut down*). *Obs.*

c **1305** *St. Kenelm* 101 in *E.E.P.* (1862) 50 Oure louerd nold noȝt þat he scholde so liȝtliche ymartred beo. *c* **1400** *Destr. Troy* 5553 What mighty were marrit, & martrid to dethe. *a* **1400–50** *Alexander* 3644 Þare was þe Medis martird. *c* **1470** Henry *Wallace* iv. 377 Our kingis men he haldis at gret wnrest, Martyris thaim doun. **1530** Palsgr. 633/1, I martyr a person, I put him to dethe by turmentynge... They have martyred hym amongest them. **1579** Lyly *Euphues* (Arb.) 81 My father shall sooner martir mee in the fire than marye me to Philautus. **1794** J. Williams *Shrove Tuesday* 11 When Strathmore's Countess martyrs all her Cats.

3. To inflict grievous suffering or pain upon; to torment, torture.

c **1240** *Wohunge* in *Cott. Hom.* 283 Lauedi moder and meiden þu..was wiðinne martird iþi moderliche herte. *c* **1386** Chaucer *Knt.'s T.* 704 Wrecched Palamoun, That Theseus martireth in prisoun. **1491** Caxton *Vitas Patr.* (W. de W. 1495) i. li. 104 b/2 Soo moche as they martred him, soo moche more he louyd theym. *a* **1533** Ld. Berners *Huon* xxvi. 81, I shall so marter thee that thy body shall not endure it. **1596** Spenser *F.Q.* iv. vii. 2 The lovely Amoret, whose gentle hart Thou martyrest with sorow and with smart. **1621** Lady M. Wroth *Urania* 4 If you be..some furie of purpose sent to vex me, vse your force to the vttermost in martyring me. **1737** Pope *Hor. Ep.* i. vi. 54 Rack'd with Sciatics, martyr'd with the Stone. **1860** Hawthorne *Marb. Faun* (1879) II. xxiv. 237 They must..pelt him and absolutely martyr him with jests. **1893** R. T. Jeffrey *Visits to Calvary* 116 His blessed body martyred and quivering in its every nerve with aching torture.

†4. To inflict wounds or disfiguring blows upon; to mutilate; also, to disfigure (the face) with weeping. *Obs.*

1590 C'tess Pembroke *Antonie* 734 Hir faire discouer'd brest..she still martireth with blowes. **1621** Lady M. Wroth *Urania* 53 With the flowing of teares, her face was martyred so much, as [etc.]. *a* **1656** Ussher *Ann.* (1658) 316 Theodotus himself..sorely martyred with wounds.

†b. *transf.* To mutilate, spoil (a thing). *Obs.*

c **1450** *Erle Tolous* 1110 They hewe thorow helme and basenet, And martyrd many a mayle. **1600** Surflet *Countrie Farme* iii. xxviii. 485 Apples must be gathered..by hand..otherwise the fruite would be much martred. **1655** Fuller *Ch. Hist.* i. iv. §11 Of such Monuments as were transmitted to Posterity, it is probable most were martyred by the Tyranny of the Pagans. **1658** Sir T. Browne *Hydriot.* Ep. Ded., Time hath so martyred the Records, that [etc.].

5. To represent as a martyr. *nonce-use.*

1649 Milton *Eikon.* Pref., Though the Picture sett in front would Martyr him and Saint him to befoole the people.

martyr, variant of marter, a marten.

†martyrago. *Obs. nonce-wd.* [After *virago*.] A female martyr having the courage of a man.

1654 Whitlock *Zootomia* 562 That one speech of a cheerfull Martyrago, when she said, farewell Faith.. farewell Hope..but welcome Love.

martyrdom ('mɑːtədəm). Forms: see martyr *sb.*[1]; also 4–5 -dam, 4–7 -dome. [OE. *martyrdóm*: see martyr *sb.* and -dom. Cf. mod.G. *märtyrerthum* (in Goethe also *martyrthum*), Sw., Da. *martyrdom*.]

1. The sufferings and death of a martyr. Also, the act of becoming or condition of being a martyr.

a **900** tr. *Bæda's Hist.* i. vii, Ðær wæs cyrice ȝeworht..his þrowunge & martyrdome wyrþe. *c* **1200** *Vices & Virtues* 129 Maniȝe þusend..here clannesse ihelden and manieskennes martirdom ðar fore ðolede. **1297** R. Glouc. (Rolls) 9830 He huld it al wreche of god vor sein tomas martirdom. *c* **1386** Chaucer *Sec. Nun's T.* 274 The palm of martirdom for to receyue. **1456** Sir G. Haye *Law Arms* (S.T.S.) 32 The faith has tane..strenth throu the tribulaciouns and persecuciouns, and marterdome of haly marteris. **1590** Spenser *F.Q.* iii. iii. 39 An huge host..With which he godly Oswald shall subdew, And crowne with martiredome his sacred head. **1634** Brereton *Trav.* (Chetham Soc.) 58 We saw..another show, representing the martyrdom of all the Apostles. **1704** Nelson *Fest. & Fasts* viii. (1739) 101 The Martyrdome of the Holy Innocents..is..commanded to be for ever celebrated in the Church. **1856** Froude *Hist. Eng.* (1858) II. ix. 374 He had spent his time in encouraging catholics to persevere to martyrdom for their faith.

attrib. **1688** Evelyn *Diary* 30 Jan., The Martyrdome day of K. Charles the First.

b. *transf.*

a **1703** Burkitt *On N.T.*, *Matt.* xiv. 11 It is as true a martyrdom to suffer for duty, as for faith. **1847–9** Helps *Friends in C.* (1851) I. 107 Social martyrdoms place no saints upon the calendar. **1849** Macaulay *Hist. Eng.* vii. II. 215 To suffer martyrdom for the property and liberty of his plunderers and oppressors.

c. The name given to the N.W. transept of Canterbury cathedral, where Becket was murdered.

1631 Weever *Anc. Funeral Mon.* 228 Here lies interred in the Martyrdome an Archbishop. **1691** Wood *Ath. Oxon.* I. 551. **1855** A. P. Stanley *Mem. Canterb.* 65.

†2. Slaughter, *esp.* in ***to make martyrdom***. *Obs.*

1375 Barbour *Bruce* vi. 289 He sic martirdome thair maid, That he the furde all stoppit had. *c* **1450** *Merlin* x. 163 As soone as the kynge Ban com in-to the medlee he be-gan to do so grete martirdom of peple, and so grete occision, that [etc.]. **1485** Caxton *Chas. Gt.* 188, I shold make grete marterdom on these Paynyms.

3. Torment, torture; extreme pain or suffering.

c **1386** Chaucer *Knt.'s T.* 602 Who koude ryme in englyssh proprely His martirdom [*sc.* in prison]? *c* **1489** Caxton *Sonnes of Aymon* iv. 117 Yf we were suche as I trowed we sholde not suffre the martyrdome that we endure. **1550** Coverdale *Death* ii. i. 177 Chryste hangynge in great Martyrdome vpon the crosse. **1658** Sir T. Browne *Hydriot.* iii. (1736) 36 Were the Happiness of the next World as closely apprehended as the Felicities of this, it were a Martyrdom to live. **1811** Miss Mitford in L'Estrange *Life* (1870) I. v. 139 Only think what martyrdom I underwent in entertaining..this prim damsel from one o'clock to seven.

†martyre. *Obs.* Also 4–6 martir(e, 5 -ter. [a. OF *martire*, earlier *martirie* (mod.F. *martyre*):—eccl. L. *martyrium*, a. Gr. *μαρτύριον*, f. *μάρτυρ-* (see martyr *sb.*).] Torment, torture; extreme suffering; also, slaughter (in phr. ***to make martyre***).

c **1330** R. Brunne *Chron. Wace* (Rolls) 15382 Ouer mykel was þeir ire, Of so fele to make martire. **1399** Gower *Praise of Peace* 341 Whan him was levere his oghne deth desire Than do the yonge children to martire. *c* **1400** *Rom. Rose* 2547 Than thou shalt brenne in greet martyr. *c* **1450** *Merlin* xiii. 193 It was merveile to se the martire that Gawein made. *c* **1477** Caxton *Jason* 45 O what payne is to a true louar unfortunat for to be in contynuel martire. *c* **1489** —— *Sonnes of Aymon* iii. 93 The whiche kyll and slea your folke, And put them to a grete marter. **1597** Tofte *Laura* in *Alba* (1880) Introd. 33 My griefes and martires, which I still sustaine.

martyred ('mɑːtəd), *ppl. a.* [f. martyr *v.* + -ed[1].] Made to suffer martyrdom; made a martyr of; †tormented, mutilated (*obs.*).

1580 in Stanyhurst *Æneis*, etc. (Arb.) 152 Martyred Alban. **1632** Lithgow *Trav.* x. 483 What a martyrd anatomy I was. **1636** Brathwait *Rom. Emp.* 289 Seeing such a strange spectacle of martir'd faces. **1685** Evelyn *Diary* 2 Oct., His [K. James II] martyr'd and blessed father. **1711** Pope *Temp. Fame* 174 Here his abode the martyr'd Phocion claims. **1855** Browning *Before*, Who's the martyred man? **1897** H. S. Merriman *In Kedar's Tents* xiv. 154 'You are always kinder to her than you are to me', went on the lady in her most martyred manner. **1904** *Edin. Rev.* Jan. 140 The martyred legionaries of Sebaste.

†martyrement. *Obs.* [a. OF. *martirement*, f. *martirer* to martyr.] Intense suffering.

1340 *Ayenb.* 77 Efterward wayes of pouerté, of zorȝe, and of martirement.

†martyrer. *Obs.* [f. martyr *v.* + -er[1].] One who martyrs.

1471 Caxton *Recuyell* (ed. Sommer) I. 29 Shall thy moder be thy marterar. [A mistranslation: Fr. has *marrastre* stepmother.] **1552** Lyndesay *Monarche* 5807 Those creuell bludy bowchouris, Martyreris of Prophetis and Prechouris. **1627** W. Sclater *Exp. 2 Thess.* (1629) 29 To Martyrers of Saints [belongs] the depth of hellish torments.

†'martyress. *Obs.* [f. martyr *sb.* + -ess.] A female martyr.

1471 Caxton *Recuyell* (ed. Sommer) I. 107 Alas my fader am I born vnder so vnhappy constellacion for to be a marteresse and prisonner. **1678** *Festa Anglo-Romana* 125 St. Lucia..Unspotted Virgin, and Resolute Martyress.

†mar'tyrial, *a.* *Obs.* *rare*[−1]. [f. L. *martyrem* martyr *sb.* + -ial. Cf. med.L. *martyriālis* (f. *martyrium*).] Befitting a martyr.

1678 J. J[ones] *Brit. Ch.* 592 A martyrial breast, and a fixed resolution.

'martyring, *vbl. sb.* [f. martyr *v.* + -ing[1].] The action of the verb martyr.

c **893** K. Ælfred *Oros.* (Sweet) 254 Ymbe Cristes tacnunga, & ymbe his martyrunga [L. *passione*]. *a* **1300** *Cursor M.* 9103 Þat sare, þat scam, þat martiring, Was neuer sene on suilk a king! **1607** Markham *Caval.* i. (1617) 85 This tyrannicall martyring of poore horses. **1692** Locke

Toleration III. ix. Wks. 1727 II. 398 'Tis well if Dragooning and Martyring can do it.

'martyring, *ppl. a.* [-ING².] That martyrs.

1674 J. B[RIAN] *Harv. Home* vii. 45 To bear so many a martyring misery. **1830** W. MACKRAY *Church of Rome* 26 She lighted up the martyring fires of Smithfield.

†**martyriologer.** *Obs. rare*⁻¹. [f. assumed Gr. *μαρτυριολόγος (f. μαρτύριον testimony, martyrdom + -λόγος) + -ER¹.] A martyrologist.

1643 PRYNNE *Sov. Power Parl.* III. 143 As an ancient Martyriologer saith.

martyrion (mɑːˈtɪrɪən). Also in L. form **martyrium.** Pl. **martyria.** [Gr. μαρτύριον, L. *martyrium* martyr's tomb or shrine.] = MARTYRY 2.

1711 J. BINGHAM *Origines Ecclesiasticæ* (ed. 2) III. VIII. i. 110 (*heading*) Why some Churches called *Martyria. Ibid.*, Such [Churches] as were built over the Grave of any Martyr, or called by his Name to preserve the Memory of him, had usually the distinguishing title of *Martyrium*, or *Confessio*, or *Memoria* given them. **1884** ADDIS & ARNOLD *Cath. Dict.* 553/1 The name 'martyrium' (μαρτύριον)..at first meant the church built over a martyr's remains. **1931** D. ATTWATER *Catholic Encycl. Dict.* 328/1 *Martyrion*, a primitive name for the place of burial of a martyr, for a church built over a martyr's tomb, and then for any church. **1931** *Times Lit. Suppl.* 23 July 584/1 The second is the largest church at Korykos and perhaps a 'martyrion'. **1960** *Antiquity* XXIV. 131 In the course of the 4th century a Christian cemetery grew up round this martyrion. **1965** *Virtue's Catholic Encycl.* II. 659/2 The original name for a church was a *martyrium*, since it was often built upon the actual site of martyrdom. **1974** *Times Lit. Suppl.* 8 Nov. 1267/1 Those of Syria and Mesopotamia were largely intended as cathedrals (rather than 'martyria').

martyrish (ˈmɑːtərɪʃ), *a. nonce-wd.* [f. MARTYR *sb.* + -ISH.] Having the air of a martyr.

1888 F. BARRETT *Recoiling Vengeance* II. vi. 83 Awdrey's quiet, long-suffering, martyrish manner.

†**martyrizate,** *v.* In pa.t. and pa.pple. **martirizate.** [f. L. *martyrizāt-*, ppl. stem of *martyrizāre* to MARTYRIZE.] = MARTYR *v.* 1.

1432-50 tr. *Higden* (Rolls) V. 11 Sixtus, the pope succeeded Alexander, whiche was martirizate. *Ibid.* 95 This emperour..martirizate mony trewe peple of Criste.

martyrization (ˌmɑːtɪraɪˈzeɪʃən). [ad. med.L. *martyrizātio*, f. *martyrizāre*: see next and -ATION.] The action of subjecting to martyrdom.

1432-50 tr. *Higden* (Rolls) I. 381 The matirizacion of Seynte Thomas of Canterbery. **1789** MRS. PIOZZI *Journ. France* II. 115 Three fountains..which were said to have burst from the ground at the moment of his martyrization.

†**b.** *Alch.* Applied to the various processes to which metals were subjected in the laboratory.

1610 B. JONSON *Alch.* II. v, Name the vexations, and the martyrizations of mettalls, in the worke.

martyrize (ˈmɑːtɪraɪz), *v.* Also 5-7 **martirize,** 6 **marterisse, -ize,** 7 **-yze, martarize.** [ad. med.L. *martyrizāre*, f. *martyr*: see MARTYR *sb.*¹ and -IZE. Cf. F. *martyriser*, Sp. *martirizar*, Pg. *martyrisar*, It. *martirizzare.*]

1. *trans.* To make a martyr of, cause to suffer martyrdom; = MARTYR *v.* 1. Now *rare*.

c **1450** *Mirour Saluacioun* 2832 When Abel of wikked kayme was slayne and martirizid. **1588** A. KING tr. *Canisius' Catech.* in *Cath. Tractates* (S.T.S.) 185 S. Dympna virgin dochter to the king of Irland marterissed be hir awin father vnder Leo the 3. **1657-83** EVELYN *Hist. Relig.* (1850) II. 124 Thousands of Christians..were all martyrized so soon as they had finished the work. **1834** BECKFORD *Italy* II. 207 St. Vincent..was martyrized near the Cape.

transf. **1595** SPENSER *Col. Clout* 475 To her my heart I nightly martyrize.

2. To cause suffering or misery to; = MARTYR *v.* 3.

1656 EARL MONM. tr. *Boccalini's Advts. fr. Parnass.* I. i. (1674) 2 Many loathsome things present themselves..to the sight..; and to behold them is to martyrize ones self. **1797** W. TOOKE *Cath. II* (1798) III. xiii. 347 *note*, He martyrized them [*sc.* Jews] by stripping them naked in the depth of the winter, and pouring cold water on their heads. **1803** MARY CHARLTON *Wife & Mistress* IV. 150, I must still martyrize the curiosity of Caroline. **1885** SULLY in *19th Cent.* June 963 How thought can crucify and martyrise any one.

†**3.** To disfigure or mutilate by the infliction of wounds or blows: = MARTYR *v.* 4. *Obs.*

1635 J. HAYWARD tr. *Biondi's Banish'd Virg.* 106 Martyrizing her with so many wounds, that her body was seene all over pierced through with stabbes. **1637** MONRO *Exped.* II. 151 Now men are marteryzed and cut downe..by those furious and thund'ring Engines of great Cannon. **1718** BP. HUTCHINSON *Witchcraft* xiii. 210 Thousands martyrizing their own Bodies, by tearing the Flesh.

4. To cause to suffer hardship on behalf of a cause.

1844 THACKERAY *Box of Novels* Wks. (Biogr. ed.) XIII. 402 The Irish press is at present martyrising the most successful member of its body. **1879** L. WINGFIELD *Lords of Strogue* III. i. 12 It would be impolitic to martyrise them too openly.

b. *refl.* To make a 'martyr' of oneself.

1887 MISS BRADDON *Like & Unlike* xxviii, She is martyrising herself—and for what? **1896** A. MORRISON *Child of the Jago* 86 She proceeded to martyrise herself by a show of 'setting to rights' in the room.

5. *intr.* To be or become a martyr. *rare*.

1524 WILL. MALVERN in *R. Glouc. Chron.* (1724) 582 Arilde that blessed Virgin, Which martyrized at Kinton. **1846** LANDOR *Albani & Picture-d.* Wks. II. 14 We must bleed and martyrise: no end or remission of our sufferings.

Hence **'martyrized** *ppl. a.*, **'martyrizing** *vbl. sb.* Also **'martyrizer,** one who martyrizes.

1635 J. HAYWARD tr. *Biondi's Banish'd Virg.* 84 An exquisite (though martyrized) beauty. **1636** BRATHWAIT *Rom. Emp.* 141 The martyrizing and bannishing of the Christians. **1810** BENTHAM *Packing* (1821) 83 This noble army, not of martyrs but of martyrizers. **1843** THACKERAY *Mr. & Mrs. Frank Berry* ii, She only gave a martyrised look, and left the room. **1900** A. LANG *Hist. Scot.* I. xvi. 436 Henry quotes the deeds of the murderer Jehu as warrant for his own martyrising of a bishop.

martyrly (ˈmɑːtəlɪ), *a. rare.* [f. MARTYR *sb.* + -LY¹.] Resembling or characteristic of a martyr; martyr-like.

1659 GAUDEN *Tears of Ch.* Embl. Trees **4 Without any respect to their..Martyrly Constancy. **1891** G. MEREDITH *One of our Conq.* III. iii. 47 [He] mused on London's East, and martyrly service there.

So **'martyrly** *adv.*, in a manner befitting a martyr.

1818 BYRON *Juan* I. ccxi, The Edinburgh Review and Quarterly Treat a dissenting author very martyrly. **1823** in *Spirit Pub. Jrnls.* 419 Enduring the scorn of all England most martyrly.

martyrolatry (mɑːtɪˈrɒlətrɪ). [f. MARTYR *sb.* + -OLATRY.] The worship of martyrs.

1889 FARRAR *Lives of Fathers* I. xii. 702 The Christianity which he despised..was mainly associated with a superstitious martyrolatry and a grovelling relic-worship. **1894** *Westm. Gaz.* 20 Aug. 3/2 This Anarchist martyrolatry began with the famous execution at Chicago in 1887.

†**martyrologe.** *Obs.* Also 6 **marteralage,** 7 **martiologe,** 8 *erron.* **martyrologue.** [a. F. *martyrologe*, ad. med.L. *martyrologium*: see MARTYROLOGY.] = MARTYROLOGY 1.

1500 *Inv. Ch. Goods* in *Gentl. Mag.* (Dec. 1837) 569/2 A marteralage and a sawter. **1563-87** FOXE *A. & M.* (1596) 41/1 The martyrologe of Isuardus. **1622** DRAYTON *Polyolb.* xxiv. 26 She..Of her deare Countries Saints, the Martyrologe would sing.

Comb. **1716** M. DAVIES *Athen. Brit.* I. 223 There were in the same dark ninth Century two Martyrologue-makers.

b. *transf.* = MARTYROLOGY 1 b.

1631 WEEVER *Anc. Funeral Mon.* 752 Registred in the Martirologe of this house.

martyrological (ˌmɑːtɪrəʊˈlɒdʒɪkəl), *a.* [f. MARTYROLOGY + -IC + -AL¹.] Pertaining to martyrology or a martyrologist; concerning the history or sufferings of martyrs. Also *rarely* **martyro'logic** *a.*

1656 OSBORN *Adv. Son* I. ii. 60 To be registred in one of his [*sc.* Love's] Martyrological Ballads, & sung by dairy-maids to a pityfull Tune. **1658** SIR T. BROWNE *Gard. Cyrus* i. Hydriot. etc. 37 Some Martyrological Histories. **1849** *Fraser's Mag.* XXXIX. 288 The meaning of Christian and martyrologic symbols. **1868** J. H. BLUNT *Ref. Ch. Eng.* I. 392 Stripped of its martyrological sensationalism, that story offers a good illustration of the state of feeling in 1514-1515.

martyrologist (mɑːtɪˈrɒlədʒɪst). [f. MARTYROLOGY + -IST.] A writer of martyrology; one versed in the history of martyrs.

1676 I. MATHER *K. Philip's War* (1862) 100 That famous Martyrologist Mr. Fox. **1762-71** H. WALPOLE *Vertue's Anecd. Paint.* (1786) V. 133 Samuel Clarke, martyrologist. **1841** W. SPALDING *Italy & It. Isl.* II. 34 The legends of the martyrologists.

martyrologue. *rare*⁻². [f. MARTYR *sb.*: see -LOGUE.] A martyrologist.

1647 TRAPP *Comm. Philemon* i. 10 The Roman Martyrologue saith, that he was stoned to death at Rome. **1657** —— *Comm. Job* xvi. 8 Mr. John Fox the Martyrologue.

martyrology (mɑːtɪˈrɒlədʒɪ). See also MARTILOGE, MARTYROLOGE. [ad. med.L. *martyrologium*, a. late Gr. μαρτυρολόγιον, f. μάρτυρ MARTYR *sb.*¹ + λόγος account: see LOGOS.]

1. A list or register of martyrs; *spec.* a book containing a list of Christian martyrs and other saints in the order of their commemoration, with some account of their lives and sufferings.

1599 SANDYS *Europæ Spec.* (1632) 95 The Martyrologies of such as rendred by their deaths a testimonie to that truth which [etc.]. **1681-6** J. SCOTT *Chr. Life* (1747) III. 335 In the ancient Martyrologies of the Church, we meet with sundry Relations of the Appearances of Angels. **1846** MASKELL *Mon. Rit.* I. p. cxliii, It was at length ordered that nothing should be read in the Martyrology, but the name and date of the martyrdom of the Saint.

b. *Antiq.* The necrology of a religious house.

1710 J. HARRIS *Lex. Techn.* II.

c. *transf.* An account of those who have suffered death in a cause.

1659 *Gentl. Calling* Pref., I fear if the martyrologie even of these suffering times were scanned, Venus and Bacchus would be found to have had many more martyrs, than God and Loyalty. **1732-8** NEAL *Hist. Purit.* (1822) I. 87 It is not within the compass of my design to write a martyrology of these times; nor to follow bishop Bonner and his brethren through the rivers of Protestant blood which they spilt.

2. The histories of martyrs collectively; that department of ecclesiastical history or literature which deals with the lives of martyrs.

[Properly a distinct word, as if f. a Gr. type in -λογία: see -LOGY.]

1801 FUSELI in *Lect. Paint.* xxi. (1848) 377 Monastic legend and the rubric of martyrology. **1849** MACAULAY *Hist. Eng.* iv. I. 501 The courage of the survivor was sustained by an enthusiasm as lofty as any that is recorded in martyrology. **1867** FREEMAN *Norm. Conq.* (1876) I. vi. 493 We are here on the dangerous ground of martyrology.

'martyrship. *rare*⁻¹. [f. MARTYR *sb.* + -SHIP.] The status of a martyr.

a **1661** FULLER *Worthies* iii. (1662) I. 13 [They] now will willingly allow Martyrship to those from whom they wholly with-held (or grudgingly gave) it before.

martyry (ˈmɑːtɪrɪ). See also MARTYRE. [ad. med.L. *martyrium*, a. Gr. μαρτύριον witness, martyrdom, f. μάρτυρ MARTYR *sb.* Cf. F. *martyre*, Sp. *martirio*, Pg. *martyrio*, It. *martirio*, *martiro*, *martorio*. A derivative of the med.L. word appears in OHG. *martara*, *martira* (G. *marter* torture).]

†**1. a.** Martyrdom. **b.** Suffering, torment. *Obs.*

c **1325** *Metr. Hom.* 158 For than pin we our bodye, With torfir and with martyrye. **1677** GALE *Crt. Gentiles* II. III. 131 Clemens Alexandrinus cals martyrie the purgation of sin.

2. A shrine, oratory, or church erected in memory of a martyr; an erection marking the place of a martyrdom or the spot where a martyr's relics lie.

1708-22 BINGHAM *Orig. Eccl.* VIII. i. §8 Wks. 1840 II. 349 Constantine..adorned..Constantinople with many..ample martyries. *a* **1727** NEWTON *Observ. Proph. Daniel* I. xiv. (1733) 206 Those of the Church are not allowed to go into the Cœmeteries or Martyries, as they are called, of hereticks. **1842** J. H. NEWMAN *Miracles* (1843) 146 The proposed Martyry or Church of the Resurrection. **1889** FARRAR *Lives of Fathers* I. 86 They met year by year at his martyry to celebrate the day of death. **1901** T. R. GLOVER *Life & Lett. 4th Cent.* vi. 136 On her way back she made a deviation to see St. Thecla's martyry.

marughe, maruȝ, obs. forms of MARROW *sb.*¹

marula (məˈruːlə). Also **maroela** (Afrikaans), **maroola, meroola, merula, -ley, -li, morala, morula.** [Afrikaans, ad. Tswana and North Sotho *morula.*] A tree, *Sclerocarya caffra*, of the family Anacardiaceæ, found in central and southern Africa, and bearing an oval yellow fruit about two inches long that is used locally for making an intoxicating drink; also, the fruit of this tree. Also *attrib.*

1857 D. LIVINGSTONE *Missionary Travels & Researches in S. Afr.* viii. 165 Another tree, the 'Morala'..has never been known to be touched by lightning. **1868** D. OLIVER *Flora Trop. Afr.* I. 449 *S[clerocarya] Caffra*,..Mozamb. Distr. Lake Nyassa and other localities in Zambesi-land. Native name 'Morula'. **1877** T. BAINES *Gold Regions S.E. Afr.* i. 9 The Marula, as large as a peach and with a kernel almost like one, has a pleasant flavour. **1881** E. E. FREWER tr. *Holub's Seven Yrs. S. Afr.* II. 391 We passed some more of the morula-trees. **1888** P. GILLMORE *Days & Nights by Desert* vii. 47 A ridge..here and there studded with meruli and mimosa trees. **1890** —— *Through Gasa Land* 296 The meruley tree..seems to be a cross between a green plum and a walnut or hickory. **1907** *Transvaal Agric. Jrnl.* Jan. 411 The Meroola or Marula..a few specimens of the whole fruit of this tree were obtained. **1910** J. BUCHAN *Prester John* ix. 168 Tied up to a merula tree, were two of the finest beasts I had seen in Africa. **1920** *Nature* 6 May 298/2 The palms and morula-trees yield wine. **1932** C. FULLER *Louis Trigardt's Trek* x. 124 With him came three Indunas who brought a calabash of 'appel bier' (Morula wine). **1939** S. CLOETE *Watch for Dawn* xxix. 430 The wagon was jacked up by a big marula tree. **1950** *Cape Argus* 17 July 7/7 The maroela, a plant found in the Transvaal. **1955** T. V. BULPIN *Ivory Trail* (ed. 2) ii. 27 Native-made maroela beer. *Ibid.* xi. 116 September..when the maroela trees show their first flowers. **1972** *Daily Colonist* (Victoria, B.C.) 4 Apr. 21/1 Johannesburgh—The tempting marula fruit is ripe once more in South Africa's Kruger National Park and thousands of happy elephants are on their annual spree... The berry is green and about the size of a plum... The fruit ferments in the big beast's belly and the elephant acts as a ponderous four-legged still.

marum (ˈmɛərəm). *Obs.* exc. *arch.* [a. L. *marum*, ad. Gr. μάρον.] A name for two aromatic labiate plants (natives of Spain, etc.), *Thymus Mastichina* or herb mastic, and *Teucrium Marum* or cat-thyme, formerly used *Med.* as errhines.

1664 EVELYN *Kal. Hort.* Apr. (1679) 15 Slip and set Marums. **1693** tr. *Blancard's Phys. Dict.* (ed. 2), *Marum*, an Exotic Plant, like in Figure and Vertue to Marjoram. **1707** MORTIMER *Husb.* (1721) II. 151 Mastick Tyme or Marum is increased by slips. **1753** CHAMBERS *Cycl. Supp.*, *Mastichina*, ..the herb mastic, or garden marum. **1774** GOLDSM. *Nat. Hist.* (1862) I. IV. i. 357 The cat is excessively fond of some plants, such as valerian, marum, and cat-mint. **1834** LANDOR *Exam. Shaks.* Wks. 1853 II. 268/1 No kitten upon a bed of marum ever played such antics.

marum, variant of MARRAM, beach grass.

Marut, var. MURUT.

marvadie, -vedee, -vedi(e: see MARAVEDI.

marvel (ˈmɑːvəl), *sb.*¹ Forms: *α.* 3, 5-7 **mervel,** 4 **merwayle, -wal(e, -waal,** 4-5 **merveille, -vaille, -veyle, -vayl,** 4-6 **mervell, -veile, -vayle,** 4-7 **mervaile,** 5 **merveil(l, -velle, -vale, -veylle, -vayll,**

5–6 **mervaill, -val, -vaylle, -well,** *Sc.* **-waill(e,** 5–7 **mervail,** 6 **merveyll;** *β.* 4 **marveil,** 4–7 **marveile, -vaile,** 4–8 **marvail,** 5 **marvile, -velle (marfaylle),** 5–6 **marveyle, -vayle,** 4–7 **marvaylle, -veyl, -veille,** 6–7 **marvell,** 6– **marvel.** See also MARL *sb.*[2] [a. OF. *merveille* fem. (mod.F. *merveille*), a Com. Rom. word = Pr. *meravelha*, Sp. *maravilla*, Pg. *maravilha*, It. *maraviglia*, *meraviglia*, a fem. sing. sb. repr. (with some irregularities of form not fully explained) L. *mīrābilia*, neut. pl. of *mīrābilis* adj., wonderful, f. *mīrārī* to wonder at.]

†**1.** = MIRACLE 1. *Obs.*

a **1300** *Cursor M.* 16762 + 147 (Cott.) Mony þat stode & saȝe þoo mervels doyn in dede, Torned & wore baptized. *c* **1375** *Sc. Leg. Saints* Prol. 67 How til hel he vent in hy, & of þe merwalis he vrocht þare. *c* **1400** MAUNDEV. (1839) v. 61 Lord, thi Merveyles ben thi Witnesse. **1483** CAXTON *Gold. Leg.* 55 b/2, I shal stratche out my hand and shal smyte egypte in all my meruaylles that I shal doo amyd emong them. *a* **1600** MONTGOMERIE *Sonn.* ii. 13 Prais him, O man! His mervels that remarks.

2. A wonderful or astonishing thing; a cause of surprise, admiration or wonder; a wonder.

c **1330** R. BRUNNE *Chron.* (1810) 178 Oft tille our Inglis men was schewed a mervaile grete, A darte was schot to þem, bot non wist who it schete. *c* **1386** CHAUCER *Sqr.'s T.* 652 Neuere yet was herd so grete merueilles. **1387** TREVISA *Higden* (Rolls) I. 361 In þe vttermeste endes of þe world falleþ ofte newe meruailles and wondres. **1390** GOWER *Conf.* II. 70 The worthi Hercules, Whos name schal ben endeles For the marveilles whiche he wroghte. *c* **1420** *Anturs of Arth.* 73 Þis mekel mervaile þat I shal of mene. *c* **1450** *Merlin* i. 3 Thei..tolde their maister the marvelle of the moreyn, that was fallen a-monge the bestes. **1485** CAXTON *Malory's Arthur* Pref. 3 Wherfor it is a meruayl why he is nomore renomed in his owne contreye. **1526** *Pilgr. Perf.* (W. de W. 1531) 39 b, Therfore theyr werkes were meruayles, but no myracles. **1555** EDEN *Decades* To Rdr., It was accompted for one of the marueyls of the worlde. **1674** BREVINT *Saul at Endor* 313 Sprinkle a little of this holy water upon yourself ..; it will do Marvails. **1798** FERRIAR *Illustr. Sterne* vi. 168 All these curiosities are..great marvels for fools. **1808** SCOTT *Marm.* III. xviii, Marvels still the vulgar love. **1818** BYRON *Ch. Har.* IV. xviii, [Venice] Perchance even dearer in her day of woe, Than when she was a boast, a marvel, and a show. **1866** G. MACDONALD *Ann. Q. Neighb.* vii. (1878) 113 It was a marvel to me afterwards that nobody came near me. **1875** JOWETT *Plato* (ed. 2) III. 229 Among other marvels he beheld a hollow brazen horse.

†**b.** A subject for surprise. *Obs.*

1456 SIR G. HAYE *Law Arms* (S.T.S.) 7 It suld nocht be grete mervaillis to se grete weris and bataillis in this warld here. *c* **1540** J. HEYWOOD *Four P.P.* 701 And whiche of you telleth most meruell, And most vnlyke to be true, Shall most preuayle. *a* **1568** ASCHAM *Scholem.* I (Arb.) 58, I will tell yow the most meruell of all, and yet soche a trothe, as no man shall denie it.

c. Wonderfulness.

1866 M. ARNOLD *Thyrsis* xix, And all the marvel of the golden skies.

d. A wonderful example *of* (some quality).

1873 BLACK *Pr. Thule* xxv. 418 The house was a marvel of neatness and comfort.

†**3.** A wonderful story or legend. *Obs.*

13.. *K. Alis.* 6755 Wite ye eghwar by my weyes, Any merveilles by this wayes, That Y myghte do in storye. **1303** R. BRUNNE *Handl. Synne* 3910 Þe porter ȝede vp to þe halle, And þys merueylë told hem alle. *c* **1400** *Destr. Troy* 13776 (*heading*) Here Ye A Meruayle Of A Lady By Nygramansy. **1483** CAXTON *G. de la Tour* E j b, I shalle reherce yow merueil which a good lady dyde recount to me. **1484** —— *Fables of Poge* v, The whiche merueylle was announced or sayd to the sayd Pope.

4. Astonishment, surprise, admiration or wonder. *Obs.* or *arch.* Phrase, † *to have marvel*: to be struck with astonishment or wonder.

1303 R. BRUNNE *Handl. Synne* 3927 Þe lorde and þe gestes alle..Had merueyle þat hyt was so, Þat he myȝte swych myracle do. **13..** *E.E. Allit. P.* A. 1129 Delit þe lombe for to deuise, With much meruayle in mynde went. *c* **1386** CHAUCER *Sqr.'s T.* 79 In al the halle ne was ther spoken a word, For merueille of this knyght. *c* **1400** *Destr. Troy* 4954 Þai..hade maruell full mekull of þat mayne place. *c* **1450** *Merlin* I Whan the fendes sien that, they hadden right grete feer and gret merveile. **1493** *N. Riding Rec.* (1894) 125 To our great marvile and displeasure. **1535** COVERDALE *Rev.* xvii. 6 When I sawe her I wondred with greate mervayle. **1586** A. DAY *Eng. Secretary* II. (1625) 26, I haue great marueile that..we can by no possibility heare of your being. **1587** *Mirr. Mag.*, *Brennus* xlv, Our peace did all to ioy and maruaile move. **1601** W. T. *Ld. Remy's Civ. Consid.* 8 To the great meruaile of the French themselues, [he] consented that his sonnes should compound with the French. **1618** ROWLANDS *Sacred Mem.* 31 They said with maruell and great admiration, How strange and sodainc is this alteration? **1805** SCOTT *Last Minstr.* II. xxxii, Use lessens marvel, it is said. **1884** *W. Morn. News* 11 Sept. 4/3 Sir Richard Cross ..is..to nobody, if the look of marvel in his eyes may be trusted, a greater marvel than to himself.

†**b.** Phr. *to marvel* (= F. *à merveille*): wonderfully. *Obs.*

c **1500** *Melusine* 348 Wherof they were al joyfull & glad to meruayll.

5. Phrases. † *it is marvel*: it is a wonder (*obs.*). ***what marvel, no marvel***: = what wonder, no wonder (*arch.* or *rhetorical*).

c **1380** WYCLIF *Wks.* (1880) 265 It is grett meruaile þat god ..distroieþ not alle þis cursed peple. *c* **1420** LYDG. *Assembly of Gods* 103 Hit was gret merueyle how I myght endure. *c* **1450** *Cursor M.* 17406 (Laud) No maruayle though ye vs not trow. **1470–85** MALORY *Arthur* VII. ix. 225 Merueylle me thynketh said the grene knyght to the damoysel why ye rebuke this noble knyghte as ye doo. **1526** *Pilgr. Perf.* (W. de W. 1531) 2 b, And no meruayle, For in the syght of the deite resteth all. **1529** S. FISH *Supplic. Beggers* (1871) 3 Is it any merueile that youre people so compleine of pouertie? **1545** BRINKLOW *Compl.* xi. (1874) 26 It is meruel..that fyre descend not down from heauen. **1607** HIERON *Wks.* I. 204 It is no meruaile though there be euery where so many empty soules. **1611** BIBLE *Transl. Pref.* ¶4 And what maruaile? —— *Ecclus.* xvi. 11 It is merueile, if he escape vnpunished. **1615** W. LAWSON *Country Housew. Gard.* (1626) 31 No maruell then, if Trees make their shoots, and put their spraies disorderly. **1647** CLARENDON *Hist. Reb.* I. §10, I say, it is no Marvail..that he could think of no better way [etc.]. **1815** SCOTT *Ld. of Isles* III. xxvii, No marvel, 'mid such musings high, Sleep shunn'd the monarch's thoughtful eye. **1857** BUCKLE *Civiliz.* I. x. 609 What marvel if..the most insignificant trifles should swell into matters of the highest importance?

†**b.** with *inf.*

c **1400** *Destr. Troy* 1985 A myst and a merkenes was meruell to se. *a* **1400–50** *Alexander* 318 How he is merkid & made is mervaile to neuyn. *Ibid.* 1245 Slik a mynd vn-to me ware meruaill [*Dubl. MS.* mervell] to reken. **1470–85** MALORY *Arthur* XVI. i. 664 And eyther made grete Ioye of other, that it were merueyle to telle.

6. marvel of Peru, of the world. The plant *Mirabilis Jalapa*, native of tropical America, with handsome funnel-shaped flowers of various colours which expand towards night: = FOUR O'CLOCK 1.

1597 GERARDE *Herbal* II. liii. 272 The maruell of Peru, or the maruel of the world. **1660** SHARROCK *Vegetables* 28 In the seed of Mervayle-of-the-world..you must chuse out such flowers as be variable while they blow. **1721** MORTIMER *Husb.* (ed. 5) II. 230 Marvel of Peru, so termed from its wonderful Variety of Flowers on the same Root. **1882** *Garden* 6 May 317/3 Marvel of Peru..will look well at the back part of the borders.

7. *Comb.*, as ***marvel-monger***; ***marvel-loving*** adj.

1648 J. BEAUMONT *Psyche* XVIII. xcii, The Marveilmongers grant that He Was moulded up but of a mortal metal. **1903** *Edin. Rev.* Apr. 326 The marvel-loving chronicler.

marvel ('mɑːvəl), *sb.*[2] Also **marvil.** Common Eng. and U.S. dial. var. of MARBLE *sb.*

a **1734** J. COMER in *Rhode Island Hist. Soc. Coll.* (1893) VIII. 17 A little lad..was playing marvils..near the Old North Meeting House, Boston, and a cart laden passing by, a marvil rolling under the cart he stept to get it. **1743** W. ELLIS *Mod. Husbandman* July 27 A Worm,..bred in them, which raised a Wart as big as a Marvel on them. **1823** E. MOOR *Suffolk Words & Phr.* 221 *Marvels*, boys' marbles. **1845** J. J. HOOPER *Some Adventures Simon Suggs* xi. 136 Sometimes..I play marvels. **1867** P. KENNEDY *Banks of Boro* i. 5 In the season we shot marvels on the road. **1876** 'MARK TWAIN' *Tom Sawyer* ii. 13 Jim, I'll give you a marvel. **1929** *Amer. Speech* V. 19 *Marvels*,..marbles. 'Th' young-uns has got some o' these hyar store-boughten marvels.' **1942** BERREY & VAN DEN BARK *Amer. Thes. Slang* §665/2 *Marble*, ivory, marb, marvel, man, mig, miggle.

†**marvel,** *a. Obs.* [a. OF. *merveil* adj., evolved from *merveille* sb.: see MARVEL *sb.*[1]] Marvellous, wonderful.

13.. *E.E. Allit. P.* C. 81 Þis is a meruayl message a man for to preche. *c* **1420** *Pallad. on Husb.* v. 87 Eke meruel thinge affermeth Marcyal. *c* **1420** *Chron. Vilod.* 889 And vnder a tre he doune hym leyde, A meruayle sweuene þo con he mete. *Ibid.* 1429 Bot when þey seyn þis merfeyle syȝt ..þey cryede god mercy alle þat nyȝt. *c* **1460** *Towneley Myst.* xiv. 422 And also, sir, to you I tell The meruellest thyng that euer fell. **1470–85** MALORY *Arthur* II. xiv. 92 He is the merueyllest knyȝt that is now lyuyng. **1523** LD. BERNERS *Froiss.* I. 384 They..dyd ther feates of armes mervaile to recorde. **1525** *Ibid.* II. liii. [lii.] 188 They were the falsest people and of the merueyllest condycyons yᵗ were in all the royalme. **1530** RASTELL *Bk. Purgat.* I. xvii, Thys is now one of the mervelest conclusyons that ever I herd.

marvel ('mɑːvəl), *v.* Now only *literary.* Forms: see the sb. [a. OF. *merveillier*, f. *merveille*: see prec. sb. Cf. Sp. *maravillar*, Pg. *maravilhar*, It. *maravigliare*, *meravigliare*.]

1. *intr.* To be filled with wonder or astonishment; to be struck with surprise. (In mod. use a stronger word than *wonder*.)

a. without construction.

13.. *K. Alis.* 5314 Also the kyng was meruelynde, A cry he hereth gret behynde. *c* **1374** [see MARVELLING *ppl. a.*]. *c* **1450** *Merlin* i. 3 When the heirdes sye their bestes so deyen in the feldes, thei merveyled gretly. **1563** *Homilies* II. *Receiv. Sacrament* I. I iii iij, Take then this lesson..that when thou goest vp to the reuerent Communion..thou maruell with reuerence. **1632** SANDERSON *Serm.* 481 Let vs not mervaile if he begin to deale something strangely. **1782** WOLCOT in J. J. Rogers *Opie & Wks.* (1872) 22 The Queen turned up the whites of her eyes, marvelling. **1839** J. H. NEWMAN *Par. Serm.* IV. xix. 333 A religious mind is ever marvelling, and irreligious men..scarcely at it because it does.

b. const. *at*, formerly †*of*, †*on*, †*upon*.

c **1374** CHAUCER *Boeth.* II. pr. v. 32 (Camb. MS.), I wondre gretely þat men meruaylen on swyche thynges. *c* **1375** *Cursor M.* 11271 (Fairf.) What they had herd & sene thei told Alle marvailid on. *c* **1375** *Sc. Leg. Saints* l. (*Katerine*) 111 Bot þu suld movse here & merwall, of hewine & erth. *a* **1425** *Cursor M.* 18774 (Trin.) Gode men of galile wher vpon merueile ȝee? **1535** JOYE *Apol. Tindale* (Arb.) 37 Meruel not at this thyng. **1590** SPENSER *F.Q.* II. ix. 43 Guyon mervayld at her uncouth cace. **1605** in *10th Rep. Hist. MSS. Comm.* App. v. 372 Let not any man mervaylle of the manyfould downefalles into synne. **1666** BUNYAN *Grace Ab.* ¶41 Presently I found two things within me at which I did sometimes marvel. **1667** MILTON *P.L.* IX. 551 Into the Heart of Eve his words made way, Though at the voice much marveling. **1841** W. SPALDING *Italy & It. Isl.* III. 250 Their annual liquefaction of the blood of Saint Januarius, over which they never tire of marvelling. **1865** TROLLOPE *Belton Est.* xiii. 142 She was one of those whose lot in life drives us to marvel at the inequalities of human destiny.

indirect passive. **1583** R. TANNER *Prob. Conject.* B iij b, It is a thing greatly to bee meruayled at. **1585** T. WASHINGTON tr. *Nicholay's Voy.* I viii. 7 b, It is not to be marueiled at thogh they haue great plentie of such pullen.

c. with clause, expressing the object of wonder.

1390 GOWER *Conf.* I. 117 Now schalt thou noght forthi mervaile That I doun fro my Charr alihte. **1465** *Paston Lett.* II. 220, I merveyll that I here no tidynggеs from yow hough ye have do at the assises. **1538** STARKEY *England* I. iii. 88, I can not agre wyth you, but rather I maruayle that you can say so. **1611** BIBLE *Gal.* i. 6. **1784** COWPER *Task* IV. 713, I marvelled much that..his beauties had then first Engaged my wonder. **1820** SCOTT *Abbot* ii, I marvel your ladyship could bear so long with her insolence.

d. const. *inf.*

1535 COVERDALE *Ps.* xlvii. 3 They marveled, to se soch thinges. **1535** CROMWELL in Merriman *Life & Lett.* (1902) I. 437, I cannot a little marvayle to understand that..ye have [etc.]. **1582** N. LICHEFIELD *Castanheda's Conq. E. Ind.* I. ix. 23 He shoulde not meruaile to see them bring theyr weapons.

2. To feel astonished curiosity: to ask oneself wonderingly. Const. interrogative clause.

c **1380** WYCLIF *Wks.* (1880) 366, I merueyle wher þe pryuelegis commen alonde wherby [etc.]. **1390** GOWER *Conf.* III. 7 Everich be himself merveilleth What thing it is that me so eilleth. *c* **1400** *Melayne* 529 Thay mervelde why the bellis so range. *c* **1470** HENRY *Wallace* VIII. 497 Sotheroun marueld giff it suld be Wallace. **1530** PALSGR. 581/1, I marvayle what you meane. **1606** SHAKS. *Tr. & Cr.* I. ii. 238, I maruell where Troylus is. **1643** SIR T. BROWNE *Relig. Med.* I. §45, I cannot but marvaile from what Sibyl or Oracle they stole the Prophesie of the worlds destruction by fire. **1875** MRS. RANDOLPH *Wild Hyacinth* I. 44 Christian was marvelling more and more what her father could possibly want with her.

†**3. a.** *refl.* = senses 1 and 2. *Obs.*

c **1330** R. BRUNNE *Chron. Wace* (Rolls) 963 Merueille þe nought ȝyf þey haue grace, ffraunchise & fredom to purchace. ? *a* **1400** *Morte Arth.* 1314 My lorde meruailles hym mekylle..Why thow morthires his mene. *c* **1400** MAUNDEV. (Roxb.) xv. 70, I meruailed me gretely. *c* **1489** CAXTON *Blanchardyn* ii. 15 Blanchardyn..coude not merueylle hym self to moche..of the dyuerse and strange werkes that he perceyued. **1548** GESTE *Pr. Masse* B iv b, I maruel me muche that many of them..haue in earnest meyntenaunce transubstanciation.

†**b.** *impers.* ***me marvels***: = I marvel. (occas. with direct obj.) *Obs.*

c **1325** *Song of Yesterday* 97 in *E.E.P.* (1862) 135 Me meruayles ouer al þat god let monymon croke and elde. *c* **1330** R. BRUNNE *Chron.* (1810) 65 Me meruailes of my boke. **1390** GOWER *Conf.* II. 277 So that the more me merveilleth, What thing it is mi ladi eilleth. ? **1401** *Pol. Poems* (Rolls) II. 75 Me merveilith moche of thin lewidheed! *a* **1425** *Cursor M.* 11671 (Trin.) Marye he seide me merueileþ þe þat seest þe heȝenes of þis tre. **1496** *Dives & Paup.* (W. de W.) Int. x. a v b, Me meruayleth moche why Cryste taught more that yonge riche man the commaundementes of the seconde table than of the fyrste.

†**c.** *pass.* = senses 1 and 2. (Chiefly const. *of*.)

1390 GOWER *Conf.* II. 196 Wherof the world is yit merveiled Of the maistries that he wroghte. *a* **1400–50** *Alexander* 3218 He..Was on þe make of þat mote noȝt mervalled a lytyll. **1523** LD. BERNERS *Froiss.* I. 324, I am greatly marveled of the letters ye have sent me. *Ibid.* cclxxiii. 409 They are all greatly marueyled..that..ye wolde nat yssue out of your strayte to fight with them.

†**4.** *trans.* To wonder or be astonished at. (Often in *pass.* with clause attached.) *Obs.*

1382 WYCLIF *Judith* x. 7 [Thei]..stoneȝende merueileden [Vulg. *mirati sunt*] ful miche the fairnesse of hir. *c* **1400** *Rom. Rose* 2062, I merveile thee asking this demande. **1432–50** tr. *Higden* (Rolls) I. 233 Hit is to be mervaylede how that so hevy a thynge myghte be soe erecte. **1513** DOUGLAS *Æneis* I. xi. 31 Thai mervailit the riche giftis of Eneas. **1523** LD. BERNERS *Froiss.* I. 441 It myght well be marveyled howe they endured so long. **1565** T. STAPLETON *Fortr. Faith* 46 That were, surely, worth the lerning, and much to be marvailed, if [etc.]. **1625** BACON *Ess.*, *Deformity* (Arb.) 255 Let it not be Maruelled, if sometimes they proue Excellent Persons. **1819** W. TENNANT *Papistry Storm'd* i. (1827) 33 Sir Knicht did hing a while on wing, Marvellin' the meanin' o' that thing.

†**5.** To cause to wonder; to astonish. *Obs.*

a **1400** *Berlam & Josaphat* 260 (Harl. MS.) Þis meteyng meruaild all his mode. **1432–50** tr. *Higden* (Rolls) II. 369 There were iij. sustyrs as of oon pulcritude, whiche meruaylede theire beholders. **1470–85** MALORY *Arthur* XVI. i. 665 One thynge merueilled me. **1560** ROLLAND *Crt. Venus* I. 505 This mater maruellis me [etc.]. **1567** *Satir. Poems Reform.* vii. 15 It dois merueil me Quhat causit hes the Lordis of Scotland Tak on ane enterpryse of sic folie.

†**marvellable,** *a. Obs.* [a. OF. *merveillable*: see MARVEL *v.* and -ABLE.] = MARVELLOUS.

1483 CAXTON *Gold. Leg.* 430 b/2 God..wyllyng hym self shewed wonderful and meruaylable. *c* **1500** *Melusine* 177 Theire meruayllable shottyng with gonnes & arowes.

†**marve'llation.** *Obs.* (Meant as a vulgarism.) [f. MARVEL *v.* + -ATION.] Cause of wonder.

1599 PEELE *Sir Clyom.* Wks. (Rtldg.) 518/1 Why, it is marvellation to see.

marvelling ('mɑːvəlɪŋ), *vbl. sb.* [f. MARVEL *v.* + -ING[1].] The action of the verb MARVEL.

c **1430** *Life St. Kath.* (1884) 40 Whiche hath turned vs alle in suche stonyynge and merueylyng. **1552** LATIMER *Serm. 3rd Sund. Epiph.* (1584) 305 Which word [of God], if it light vpon a good ground..it turneth with his strength the same, and bringeth a meruaylyng. **1592** STOW *Ann.* an. 1280, 300 On S. Martins euen a great thunder ouerthrew many houses and trees in England, to the maruailing of many.

marvelling (ˈmɑːvəlɪŋ), *ppl. a.* [f. MARVEL *v.* + -ING².] That marvels.

c **1374** CHAUCER *Boeth.* I. Met. iii. 5 (Camb. MS.) Thanne ..phebus..smyteth with his beemes in marveylynge Eyen. **1839** BAILEY *Festus* vi. (1852) 78 These same marvelling eyes of mine. **1841** D'ISRAELI *Amen. Lit.* (1867) 212 They.. impressed on the marvelling reader that [etc.].

Hence **ˈmarvellingly** *adv.*, in a marvelling manner.

1891 G. MEREDITH *One of our Conq.* III. viii. 155 Nataly marvellingly named Mrs. John Corwyn.

marvellous (ˈmɑːvələs), *a.*, (*sb.*) and *adv.* Forms: α. 4–7 **merveil(l)ous**, 4 **mervilous, mervelis, merva(i)lous(e, mervellos, merveilows,** 4–6 **mervel(l)ous(e,** 5 **mervel(l)us, merveyllous, mervelo(i)se, merveyleux, -l(i)ouse, mervelious, mervelyows(e, merwalus,** 6 **mervaylous(e,** 7 **mervailous**; β. 4 **marvelliows,** 5 **marvelus,** 5–6 **marveylous,** 6 **marvaylus, marvayl(l)ous,** (*Sc.*) **marwolus,** 7 **marveilous,** 6–9 **marvelous,** 6– **marvellous.** *Superl.* 4–5 **merveillousest, -oust (-ous), mervelyouste(ste, merviloste, merveiluste,** 6 **marvelloussest.** [a. OF. *merveillos* (mod.F. *merveilleux*), f. *merveille*: see MARVEL *sb.*¹ and -OUS. Cf. Sp. *maravilloso*, It. *meraviglioso*.]

A. *adj.* **a.** Such as to excite wonder or astonishment; wonderful, astonishing, surprising.

13.. *K. Alis.* 6445 Another folk bysyde ther is, Swithe merveillous folke, y-wis. *c* **1330** R. BRUNNE *Chron.* (1810) 228 Men norise childre þer inne, on merveilous wise. **1362** LANGL. *P. Pl.* A. IX. 59 þe Meruiloste Meetynge Mette I me þenne þat euere dremede driht In drecchynge. *a* **1400** *Stockh. Med. MS.* 141 A maruelliows drink. ? *a* **1400** *Morte Arth.* 129 Sir Lucius.. That es þe meruelyousteste mane þat on molde lengez. *c* **1400** *Destr. Troy* 1572 And all of marbill was made with meruellus bestes. *c* **1410** *Master of Game* (MS. Digby 182) xxxiv, For certeyne it is þe merueiluste beeste þat is. *c* **1420** LYDG. *Assembly of Gods* 1513 Where I behelde the meruelous story That euer I yet saw in any pycture. *c* **1450** *Merlin* iii. 56 Ther Pendragon dide merveloise knyghthode a-monge his enmyes. **1471** RIPLEY *Comp. Alch.* v. x. in Ashm. (1652) 150 Lyke to the Raynbow mervelose unto syght. **1470–85** MALORY *Arthur* II. xix. 99 Balyn and Balan foughte to gyders the merueillous batail that euer was herd of. **1502** ATKYNSON tr. *De Imitatione* III. v. 199 The marueylous warkes of god. **1533** GAU *Richt Vay* (1888) 39 The marwolus conceptione and birth of Iesus Christ. **1548** LATIMER *Ploughers* (Arb.) 29 Moyses was a meruelous man, a good man. **1612** T. TAYLOR *Comm. Titus* ii. 13 Finally, he shall be glorious, yea merueilous in his Saints. **1651** HOBBES *Leviath.* II. xxvi. 148 Miracles are Marvellous workes: but that which is marvellous to one, may not be so to another. **1742** YOUNG *Nt. Th.* VII. 1423 We nothing know, but what is Marvellous; Yet what is Marvellous, we can't believe. **1802** WORDSW. *Resol. & Independ.* vii, I thought of Chatterton, the marvellous Boy. **1894** H. DRUMMOND *Ascent Man* 352 Nature always makes her changes with a marvellous economy.

b. *spec.* Of poetic material: Concerned with the supernatural.

1715 POPE *Iliad* Pref., Fable may be divided into the probable, the allegorical, and the marvellous... The marvellous fable includes whatever is supernatural, and especially the machines of the gods. **1869** TOZER *Highl. Turkey* II. 259 The marvellous element is introduced with such perfect simplicity..as to appear perfectly natural.

c. *the marvellous*: that which is prodigious or extravagantly improbable.

1749 FIELDING *Tom Jones* Contents VIII. i, A wonderful long chapter, concerning the marvellous. **1755** JOHNSON s.v., *The marvellous* is used, in works of criticism, to express any thing exceeding natural power, opposed to *the probable*. **1761** GIBBON *Misc. Wks.* (1814) V. 488 The history of Richard I of England..is alluring by the marvellous. **1825** WATERTON *Wand. S. Amer.* I. ii. (1879) 127 The first have erred by lending a too willing ear to the marvellous. **1873** M. ARNOLD *Lit. & Dogma* (1876) 53 The prodigies and the marvellous of Bible-religion are common to it with all religions.

d. **marvellous apple** = *balsam apple*: see BALSAM 10.

1578 LYTE *Dodoens* III. lxxxviii. 442 *Charantia*, Balsam apple, the male, Maruelous apples..the Marvelous apples are named Charantia. *Ibid.* 443 The Oyle of Momordica, or Maruelous Apples..putteth away al scarres and blemishes, if it be applyed thereto. **1866** HOGG *Fruit Man.* (ed. 3) 31 (Apples) Marvellous. Fruit small and oblate.

e. Weakened use of sense a; also in affected use; also as *Comb.*

1924 E. O'NEILL *Welded* I. 94 You're going to be marvelous!.. It's going to be the finest thing we've ever done! *Ibid.* 97 The play was such a marvelous success! **1927** L. MAYER *Just between Us Girls* ii. 13, I had no iDEA you were going, my dear—how SIMply MARvelous! **1931** *Amer. Speech* VI. 181 No reviewer is fluent without adjectives.. ; 'marvelous power'; 'quiet beauty'. **1933** M. LINCOLN *Oh! Definitely* v. 57 'You write, don't you.'.. 'Yes.'.. 'Marvellous!' she said with enormous sincerity, whilst her blue eyes shouted, 'What piffle!' *Ibid.* 58 'You must let me get you seats,' I said. 'Marvellous of you,' said Ursula. **1950** M. LOWRY *Let.* 1 Mar. (1967) 190, I feel another million thanks are in order to..the Book Club for the marvelous-looking book.

†**B.** *sb.* [= F. *merveilleux*.] An exquisite, dandy. *Obs. rare.*

1819 *Metropolis* (ed. 2) II. 57, I did not stay very late at the party; and our marvellous promised to give us a list of the company..the ensuing day. [Cf. p. 59 Our military Exquisite.]

†**C.** *adv.* = MARVELLOUSLY. *Obs.*

c **1330** R. BRUNNE *Chron.* (1810) 174 Sir, ouer meruailouse our duellyng here is hard. *c* **1400** MAUNDEV. (1839) v. 52 Merveyllouse grete & hye. **1530** RASTELL *Bk. Purgat.* Prol., Sayd yᵗ he woldbe mervelous glad. **1535** COVERDALE *Ps.* cxliv. [cxlv.] 3 Greate is the Lorde, & maruelous worthy to be praysed. **1590** SHAKS. *Mids. N.* IV. i. 26, I am maruellous hairy about the face. **1621** BURTON *Anat. Mel.* II. ii. III. (1651) 264 The country..hath a marveilous fair prospect. **1664** H. MORE *Myst. Iniq.* 408 Τὸ δέκατον τῆς πόλεως will have a sense marvellous coincident therewith. **1777** SHERIDAN *Sch. Scandal* IV. i, Here's my great uncle, Sir Richard Ravelin, a marvellous good general in his day.

marvellously (ˈmɑːvələslɪ), *adv.* [-LY².] **a.** In a marvellous manner or degree.

c **1330** R. BRUNNE *Chron.* (1810) 93 His dede com him suythe meruellosly. **1377** LANGL. *P. Pl.* B. VII. 159 And Ioseph mette merueillously how the mone and the sonne, And the elleuene sterres hailsed hym alle. *c* **1470** HENRY *Wallace* IV. 151 He with power partyt merwalusly. **1530** PALSGR. 425/1 He his mervayloușly come up within a yere or two. **1585** T. WASHINGTON tr. *Nicholay's Voy.* IV. ix. 121 b, The children of Israel..had maruellously passed dry foote through the redde sea. **1640** HOWELL *Dodona's Gr.* (1645) 127 His tutelar Angel stil mervailously garded him. **1710** *Tatler* No. 190 ¶2 The People of this Land be marvelously given to Change. **1874** MOTLEY *Barneveld* I. ii. 137 The King was marvellously out of humour. **1881** LADY HERBERT *Edith* 7 Her hands and feet were marvellously small.

b. In affected use; see MARVELLOUS *a.* e.

1926 E. O'NEILL *Great God Brown* 16 He can paint beautifully and write poetry and he plays and sings and dances so marvellously.

marvellousness (ˈmɑːvələsnɪs). [-NESS.] The quality of being marvellous.

1557 *Sarum Primer* L vij, Open myne iyes, and I shall consider the merveilousnesse of thy lawe. **1614** RALEIGH *Hist. World* I. xi. §2. 204 The maruelousnesse of some workes..hath beene the cause of this slaunder. **1794** KIRWAN *Elem. Min.* (ed. 2) I. 452 The sublimity and marvellousness of these stupendous operations. **1862** H. SPENCER *First Princ.* I. iii. §17 (1875) 56 Habit blinds us to the marvellousness of this phenomenon.

†**ˈmarvelly,** *a.* and *adv.* *Obs.* Forms: 4–5 **mervelly,** 5 *compar.* **marfeyllogur.** [f. MARVEL *sb.*¹ + -LY.] = MARVELLOUS, MARVELLOUSLY.

c **1330** R. BRUNNE *Chron. Wace* (Rolls) 1691 Merueyloslike [*v.r.* Meruelly] was he hardy. *c* **1420** *Chron. Vilod.* 1370 þis miracle was do þus as ychaue sayde, & more marfeyllogur þen y telle cone. *c* **1450** *Cov. Myst.* (Shaks. Soc.) 156 ȝit saw I nevyr so mervelly a syne Shapyn upon the skyes.

ˈmarvelment. *rare.* [f. MARVEL *sb.*¹ + -MENT.] The condition of marvelling.

1823 T. G. WAINEWRIGHT *Ess. & Crit.* (1880) 311 The sample which genuine travellers occasionally expose to the marvelment of the commons.

†**ˈmarvelness.** *Obs.* [f. MARVEL *a.* + -NESS.] = MARVELLOUSNESS.

1434 MISYN *Mending Life* 110 Of wylfull pouert on þis wyse takyn procedis vertues & meruilnes vntrowed.

marvelry (ˈmɑːvəlrɪ). *poet.* [f. MARVEL *sb.* + -RY.] A marvellous thing.

1874 A. O'SHAUGHNESSY *Mus. & Moonlight* 12 And the moon's pallid taper fingers played With all the scarce-seen marvelries that stayed In the strange fitful glimmer.

marver (ˈmɑːvə(r)), *sb.* [Corruptly a. F. *marbre*: see MARBLE *sb.* 3.] A polished slab of marble or iron upon which glass-blowers roll and shape the plastic glass while still on the blow-pipe.

1832 G. R. PORTER *Porcelain & Gl.* 169 The next operation is to roll the glass on..a smooth horizontal iron plate called the marver, a name corrupted from the French word '*marbre*'. **1890** W. J. GORDON *Foundry* 132 [One of the men] rolls the lump of glass on a flat slab of stone called a 'marver'.

Hence **ˈmarver** *v.*, to roll (glass) upon a marver.

1852–4 *Cycl. Usef. Arts* (ed. Tomlinson 1866) I. 768/1 He then marvers it,..and placing the hot glass in a brass mould [etc.].

marvyl(e, marvile, obs. forms of MARVEL.

Marwari (ˈmɑːwɑːriː), *sb.* and *a.* Also **Marvari, Marwaree, Marwarry.** [Hindi, f. Skr. *maru* desert, wilderness.] **A.** *sb.* **a.** A native or inhabitant of Marwar, a region in the state of Rajasthan in India. **b.** The dialect of Hindi used in Marwar. **B.** *adj.* Of or pertaining to the Marwar region.

1815 J. R. CARNAC *Let.* Feb. in *Trans. Lit. Soc. Bombay* (1819) I. 297 The failure of rain in Marwar, and the ruin by the locusts of the products of the land..drove the inhabitants of that unfortunate country into..Guzerat... Miseries seemed to follow the footsteps of the Marwarees. **1826** W. B. HOCKLEY *Pandurang Hari* II. iii. 70, I.. implicated by name..Sewchund the Marwarry, and many others. **1832** J. TOD *Ann. Rajast'han* II. III. ii. 234 The wealthy bankers and merchants of these regions scattered throughout India, are all known under one denomination, *Marwari*, which is erroneously supposed to apply to the Jodpoor territory. **1855** H. H. WILSON *Gloss. Judicial & Revenue Terms* 332/2 *Márwárí* bankers are mostly of the Jain religion. **1880** [see BUNNIA]. **1885** G. C. WHITWORTH *Anglo-Indian Dict.* 199/2 Márwári is also the name of the language of Márwár. **1899** KIPLING *From Sea to Sea* I. xiv. 129 A black, flamboyant Marwari stallion. **1908** G. A. GRIERSON *Ling. Survey India* IX. II. 16 Standard Mārwāṛī varies but little from Jaipuri. **1926** A. HUXLEY *Jesting Pilate* I. 72 These houses..are the palaces of the Marwari merchants, the Jews of India. **1960** 'S. HARVESTER' *Chinese Hammer* xxv. 202 A cluster of Marwari women was achingly brilliant in rainbow-coloured saris. **1964** S. K. CHATTERJI in D. Abercrombie et al. *Daniel Jones* 412 In Rajasthani,..the passage will be as follows (in the Marwari dialect). **1971** R. RUSSELL tr. *Ahmad's Shore & Wave* viii. 92 Money-lenders ..in their Marwari turbans.

marwe, -whe, obs. forms of MARROW.

Marxian (ˈmɑːksɪən), *a.*¹ and *sb.*¹ [f. the name of Karl *Marx* (1818–83), German-born socialist writer + -IAN.] **A.** *adj.* Of or pertaining to the socialist doctrines or theories of Karl Marx. Also ***Marxian-Soviet*** adj., of or pertaining to the type of socialism found in the U.S.S.R.

1887 G. B. SHAW *Let.* 17 May (1965) 169 Your notion that he is getting the best is a Marxian illusion. **1896** B. RUSSELL *German Social Democracy* 71 The 'honourable' Social Democrats, as they called themselves, the party of thorough-going Marxian Communism. **1902** B. KIDD *Princ. Western Civilisation* 87 [Spencer] really has in view, like the Marxian socialists, a state of society in which [etc.]. **1919** J. SPARGO *Psychol. Bolshevism* iii. 12 Only an infinitesimal minority of those who call themselves Marxian Socialists have ever studied Marx at first hand. **1920** M. BEER *Hist. Brit. Socialism* II. III. i. 21 He [*sc.* Harney] stood much nearer to O'Brien and Louis Blanc than to the Marxian policy. **1930** T. OKEY *Basketful of Memories* vii. 61 The Marxian revolutionary social teaching was slow in penetrating this country. *Ibid.*, Indications were obvious.. that the Marxian bible..had begun to leaven English democratic thought. **1948** J. TOWSTER *Political Power in U.S.S.R.* i. 4 (*heading*) The Marxian-Soviet view of state and law. **1949** KOESTLER *Promise & Fulfilment* II. v. 281 The marxian dictum that man is a product of his environment. **1959** C. MACKENZIE *Lunatic Republic* xi. 190 We also regard revisionism as treachery to Marxian ideology. **1966** E. A. CARLSON *Gene* ix. 95 'Morganism', to this rival school, represented 'reactionary' and 'idealistic' tendencies which ran counter to the 'materialist' attitudes expressed by Marxian and Leninist (later Stalinist) outlooks on science. **1966** P. HEATH tr. *Wetter's Soviet Ideology Today* III. x. 294 The Marxian theory of value and surplus value has encountered its most serious troubles over the question of the average rate of profit. **1971** Z. A. JORDAN *Karl Marx* 20 Recent contributions concerning the concept of alienation.. follow the Hegelian rather than the Marxian path.

B. *sb.* One who holds or supports Marxian views; a follower of Marx. Cf. MARXIST *sb.*¹

1896 B. RUSSELL *German Social Democracy* 89 Although this programme showed, on the whole, a victory of the Marxians, Marx protested against it. **1918** E. B. BAX *Reminisc.* 138 The question of Internationalism was indeed one of the great bones of contention between them and the Marxians. **1923** E. A. ROSS *Russ. Soviet Republic* 394 Even though it fell in partly with the program of the extreme Marxians, the expropriation of the landlords and capitalists was not really a thing planned. **1935** D. FAHEY *Mystical Body Christ* ix. 199 Marxians will take account of circumstances, in order to get their programme accepted.

Hence **ˈMarxianism**, adherence to Marxian doctrines or theories. Cf. MARXISM¹.

1896 B. RUSSELL *German Social Democracy* 93 The new philosophy of life which Marxianism had introduced. **1905** J. R. MACDONALD *Socialism & Society* iv. 99 Marxianism, however, is a product of German thought during the second and third decades of the nineteenth century. **1912** *Eng. Rev.* June 413 The British workman will never take up the theoretics of orthodox Marxianism. **1926** *Spectator* 22 May 871/2 It was Western Europe which gave Marxianism to Russia.

Marxian (ˈmɑːksɪən), *a.*² and *sb.*² [f. the name of the *Marx* Brothers (Chico, Harpo, Groucho and Zeppo), American comedians + -IAN.] **A.** *adj.* Of or pertaining to the Marx Brothers. **B.** *sb.* An admirer of the Marx Brothers. So **ˈMarxism²**, (*a*) the type of comedy performed by the Marx Brothers; (*b*) a witticism typical of the Marx Brothers. Also **ˈMarxist** *a.*² and *sb.*²

1933 *Cherwell* 25 Feb. 131/2 No one who disliked *Monkey Business* will be converted to Marxism by *Horse Feathers*. **1940** G. MARX *Groucho Lett.* (1967) 47 Don't come out bluntly and say, 'How much dough have you got?' That wouldn't be the Marxian way. **1946** *Times* 6 July 5/4 There will be something like mourning among Marxists in London next week. **1951** K. CRICHTON *Marx Brothers* xv. 196 They opened on Thursday night and closed on Saturday. The post-mortem was short and typically Marxian. They had gambled, they had lost, and there would be no lamentations. **1962** *Sunday Times* 1 Apr. 32/8 Dr McCabe asked Groucho for a few words. The resultant Marxism is very much to the point. **1962** *Oxford Mail* 21 July 6/2 There are only one or two Marx Brothers comedies left in circulation now, so I recommend this..to Marxians. **1965** *Oxf. Mag.* 29 Apr. 303/2 We might not have been so much amused if there had not been a grain of zany probability—almost Marxist, in the Bros. sense—in it. **1966** A. EYLES *Marx Brothers* xvii. 156 'It made sages out of screwballs and accused wise men of being fools.' A perfect description of comedy's Marxism. We could be in *Duck Soup*, but this was American politics. **1969** *New Yorker* 25 Jan. 104/3 *The Marx Brothers at the Movies*. ..The book is the work of dedicated Marx fans, and its ideal readers are the nation's equally dedicated Marxists.

‖**Marxisant, marxisant** (marksizɑ̃), *a.* Also (*erron.*) **marxisan.** [Fr., f. *Marxis(te* + *-ant* pr. pple. ending.] With Marxist leanings.

1961 *New Left Rev.* May–June 31/2 The Marxist and *marxisan* tradition. **1966** G. LICHTHEIM *Marxism in Mod. France* iii. 89 It took the full-scale assimilation of contemporary German philosophy after 1945 to render Existentialism popular, even fashionable, among *Marxisants* intellectuals. **1967** *Philosophy* XLII. 287 The Dialectical Laws..are seen as some *Marxisant* positivists saw them in the thirties. **1968** *Listener* 18 July 81/2 Malcolm

X's abandonment of black racism, his conversion to Islam, his *Marxisant* tendencies.., all meant a move in a direction incompatible with that taken by the present-day Black Power movement. **1969** J. MANDER *Static Society* iv. 118 Almost the entire Latin American intelligentsia is *marxisant.* **1970** *New Society* 5 Mar. 406/3 Marxists, marxisant or radical, the New Past men exemplify the ambiguities of Plumb's inevitably conditioned 'rationality'.

Marxism[1] ('mɑːksɪz(ə)m). [f. *Marx* (see MARXIAN *a.*[1] and *sb.*[1]) + -ISM, or ad. F. *Marxisme*, G. *Marxismus.*] The political and economic theories of Marx, esp. that, as labour is basic to wealth, historical development, following scientific laws determined by dialectical materialism, must lead to the violent overthrow of the capitalist class and the taking over of the means of production by the proletariat. Cf. DIALECTICAL *a.* 1 b.

1897 *Social-Democrat* Dec. 365 Marxism, as generally conceived, is a catastrophic theory rather than a theory of development. **1903** *Social Democrat* Feb. 88 Both ultra-revolutionaryism and opportunism .. rest in contradistinction to Marxism on an ideological or quasi-ideological basis. **1908** H. G. WELLS *New Worlds for Old* xi. 251 It seemed to me, that fatalistic Marxism crumbled down to dust. **1920** *Q. Rev.* Apr. 477 M. Millerand..was throwing sops to the Cerberus of unchained Marxism. **1935** F. A. VON HAYEK *Collectivist Econ. Planning* I. 18 It is essentially in this form that Marxism has been interpreted by the social-democratic parties on the Continent. **1959** OVERSTREET & WINDMILLER *Communism in India* II. xx. 488 But according to Marxism, the prime movers of history were not nations but classes. **1968** J. H. KAUTSKY *Communism & Politics of Devel.* iv. 76 Leninism is an adaptation of Marxism, a product of the industrialized West, to the conditions of an underdeveloped country.

So **'Marxism-'Leninism**, the doctrines of Marx as interpreted and put into effect by Lenin; Leninism; official communist interpretation of the doctrines of Marx as implemented by Lenin developed as a set of principles to guide policy and behaviour. Cf. LENINISM.

1932 (*title*) The Marxist Library: works of Marxism-Leninism. **1934** [see DIALECTICAL *a.* 1 b]. **1936** J. STRACHEY *Theory & Pract. Socialism* IV. xxviii. 356 The science [*sc.* Marxism] is now sometimes referred to as 'Marxism-Leninism'. **1946** tr. *Lenin's Sel. Works* Pref. 13 The revolutionary theory of Marxism-Leninism 'gives practical workers the power of orientation,..faith in the victory of our cause' (*Stalin*). **1948** [see LENINISM]. **1966** P. HEATH tr. *Wetter's Soviet Ideology Today* 328 The struggle against the various revisionist tendencies gave birth to Marxism-Leninism. **1970** D. JAMES *Ché Guevara* xv. 312 But it is revolutionary thought *outside* Marxism-Leninism with which Ché Guevara appears to have most in common. **1973** *Listener* 26 July 118/2 The Chinese leadership..still has this notion of China as the homeland of Marxism-Leninism.

Marxism[2]: see MARXIAN *a.*[2] and *sb.*[2]

Marxist ('mɑːksɪst), *sb.*[1] and *a.*[1] [f. as MARXISM[1] + -IST or ad. F. *Marxiste*, G. *Marxist.*] **A.** *sb.* A follower of Marx's theories or doctrines; a member of a political organization with international affiliations which is based on Marxism.

1886 [see GUESDIST]. **1889** E. SIMCOX *Diary* 18 Sept. in K. A. McKenzie *Edith Simcox & George Eliot* (1961) 56 The Anarchists [were] bestowing most of their attention on the Marxists. **1908** H. G. WELLS *New Worlds for Old* xv. 350 Those 'class war' ideas of the Marxist that have been superseded in English socialism. **1918** B. MIALL tr. *Hamon's Lessons of World-War* vii. 206 They [*sc.* German Social Democrats] professed to be Marxists..and they were acting as supporters of the capitalist class in the war which was then commencing. **1928** E. & C. PAUL tr. *Stalin's Leninism* 210 Comrade Trotsky is apparently unmindful of the fact that Lenin (who was surely a Marxist!)..was writing of 'the need for an immediate transfer of all power into the hands of the revolutionary democracy'. **1938** J. F. SCANLAN tr. *Mauriac's Communism & Christians* 209 Marx himself was a person in revolt against the world, but Marxists can no longer be such. **1947** HENDERSON & PARSONS tr. *Weber's Theory Social & Econ. Organization* ii. 199 There is the type, which includes especially the Marxists, which is evolutionary. **1964** D. CAUTE *Communism & French Intellectuals* IV. i. 263 The first generation of communist intellectuals in France were conspicuously immature Marxists.

B. *adj.* Of or pertaining to Marxism. Freq. in *Comb.*

1897 *Social-Democrat* Dec. 367 It [*sc.* the Italian Socialist party] is gradually losing the catastrophic character with which the Marxist teachings have stamped it. **1928** E. & C. PAUL tr. *Stalin's Leninism* 349 In other words, Leninism includes all that Marx taught, with the addition of Lenin's contribution to the Marxist treasury. **1938** J. F. SCANLAN tr. *Mauriac's Communism & Christians* 209 In such a case judgements and condemnations of the moral kind take the place of psychological theses, and this is the defect of the whole Marxist theory of man. **1949** J. LINDSAY *Marxism & Contemporary Sci.* ix. 223 One brief example will serve to show how essential Marxist method has beaten against the Hegelian dualism. **1957** J. S. HUXLEY *Relig. without Revelation* (rev. ed.) iii. 63 Marxist Communism is much better organised and more competent [than Nazism], but its purely materialist basis has limited its efficacy. **1957** *Times Lit. Suppl.* 25 Oct. 645/3 What had been the house of the local Marxist-Socialist party, who had left it filthy. **1959** *Encounter* Jan. 20/1 In the West, where thought tends to be either Marxist-materialistic or Christian-supernatural..it is difficult to envisage a religion not based on transcendental hopes and promises. **1964** *Daily Tel.* 15 Jan. 14/2 It is not sufficient to make Marxist-sounding speeches,..or even to embrace Mr. Khruschev. All these things Dr. Castro has done before. **1969** R. C. TUCKER *Marxian Revolutionary Idea* vi. 213 The history of radical movements, Marxist ones included, suggests that Mao's fear of the coming deradicalization of Chinese communism is well founded. **1973** *Times* 28 June 16/7 A Labour Party led by Mr Wilson and controlled, to the extent that it already is, by its Marxist wing.

So **'Marxist-'Leninism**, = *Marxism-Leninism*; **'Marxist-'Leninist** *a.*, of, pertaining to, or characteristic of Marxism-Leninism; cf. *Leninist-Marxist.* Also **Mar'xistically** *adv.*

1933 in K. Marx *Critique Gotha Programme* Introd. 8 The successes of socialist construction are the result of a revolutionary Marxist-Leninist policy. **1937** J. M. MURRY *Necessity of Pacifism* iii. 49 Those Socialists who imagine that Marxism, or Marxist-Leninism will either supply, or stiffen it, imagine a vain thing. **1938** *New Statesman* 15 Jan. 87/1 The wretched Mensheviks were Marxistically correct in supporting the Provisional Government.., but they found their attitude difficult to explain to hungry workers and mutinous sailors. **1940** tr. *Stalin's Leninism* 653 There is hardly need to dwell on the cardinal importance of Party propaganda, of the Marxist-Leninist training of our people. **1945** KOESTLER *Yogi & Commissar* III. ii. 173 A question which automatically cropped up in every marxistically trained mind. **1948** J. TOWSTER *Political Power in U.S.S.R.* 9 Interests of the Soviet Union cannot be deduced only from a study of the..Marxist-Leninist Ideology. **1957** *Times Lit. Suppl.* 6 Dec. 731/2 The Titoists regard Stalinism as the negation of Marxist-Leninist principles. **1963** Z. A. JORDAN *Philos. & Ideology* III. xi. 228 By denying that knowledge is relative to the mind, Marxist-Leninist thinkers put reality beyond the reach of the mind. **1966** *Listener* 20 Oct. 559/3 Marxist-Leninist philosophy is a dark room in which you're looking for a black cat, and there is no cat, but every so often you shout: 'I've got it! I've got it!' **1970** *New Society* 5 Mar. 408/1 Marxist-leninist theory has tended to play down the specific nature of agricultural production, which limits its applicability to developing countries. **1973** *Denver Q.* VIII. ii. 94 The long-term goal is the elimination of the capitalist bourgeois society, and within the universities, the gradual replacement of conservative professors with Marxistically trained and oriented scholars. **1975** *New Yorker* 21 Apr. 141/1 The Hanoi Communists are not, as far as is known, dogmatic Marxist-Leninists.

Marxist, *a.*[2] and *sb.*[2]: see MARXIAN *a.*[2] and *sb.*[2]

Marxite ('mɑːksaɪt), *a.* and *sb.* [f. as MARXIAN *a.*[1] and *sb.*[1] + -ITE[1].] = MARXIST *sb.*[1] and *a.*[1]

1895 *New Age* 12 Sept. 377/3 Mutual concessions on the part of Catholic Socialists on the one hand and revolutionary Marxite Socialists on the other, would..result in a great and victorious movement for the regeneration of society. **1902** *Amer. Jrnl. Sociol.* July 68 This idea is implicit in the position of the 'orthodox' Marxite. **1914** A. CLUTTON-BROCK *William Morris* viii. 153 Mr. Hyndman..was, and still is, a Marxite. *Ibid.* 154 His aim was to make and keep the Federation a Marxite body.

Marxize ('mɑːksaɪz), *v.* [f. as MARXIAN *a.*[1] and *sb.*[1] + -IZE.] To form, adapt, etc., in accordance with the doctrines of Karl Marx; to follow or advocate Marxism. Hence **Marxi'zation**; **'Marxizing** *vbl. sb.* and *ppl. a.*

1940 'G. ORWELL' *Inside Whale* 163 By being Marxised literature has moved no nearer to the masses. **1951** *Scrutiny* XVIII. 49 The days of Public School Marxising and Fellow-travelling had begun. **1972** J. WAIN in Cox & Dyson *20th-Cent. Mind* II. x. 346 During the Marxizing decade, poets whose imaginative world was subjective rather than objective..had tended to be crowded out of the centre of the stage. **1975** *Times* 15 Apr. 15/5 The 'Socialist' fixation that the Marxization of the West will be hindered with Britain in the EEC.

Mary ('mɛəri). Forms: 1 **Maria**, 1–6 **Marie**, 3 *Orm.* **Marȝe**, 5–7 **Marye**, 5– **Mary**. [OE. *Maria*, *Marie*, a. L. *Maria*, a. Gr. *Μαρία*, *Μαριάμ*, a. Heb. *Miryām*, Miriam (the name of the sister of Moses, Exod. xv.).] A female Christian name.

1. a. The mother of Jesus Christ, commonly called the (Blessed) Virgin Mary, or Saint Mary.

herb Mary: see HERB *sb.* 7 b.

c **1000** *Ags. Gosp.* Matt. i. 16 Iacob ȝestrynde ioseph marian wer. [*Lindisf.* maries, *Rushw.* maria, *Hatton* marie.] *a* **1175** *Cott. Hom.* 237 Acenned of þam unwemmede mede sante Marie. *c* **1200** ORMIN 2335 Þe laffdiȝ Sannte Marȝe. *c* **1394** *P. Pl. Crede* 48 Þei [the Carmelites] makeþ hem Maries men..And lieþ on our Ladie many a longe tale. *c* **1460** J. RUSSELL *Bk. Nurture* 691 Maydon mary þat holy virgyne. **1850** ROSSETTI *Blessed Damozel* ii, A white rose of Mary's gift For service meetly worn.

b. In asseverations (cf. MARRY *int.*).

c **1350** *Will. Palerne* 838 Be Marie in heuene. *Ibid.* 955 For Marie loue of heuene. *c* **1410** *Sir Cleges* 259 Be God and Seint Mari. **1423** JAS. I *Kingis Q.* xvii, Help, Calyope, and wynd, in Marye name! **1530** *Proper Dyaloge* in Roy *Rede me* (Arb.) 149 By seynt mary syr that is a starcke lye. **1542** UDALL *Erasm. Apoph.* 147 By saint Marie, I begynne to doubte whether [etc.]. **1613** SHAKS. *Hen. VIII*, v. ii. 33 By Holy Mary (Butts) there's knauery. *a* **1650** *Sir Lambewell* 500 in Furniv. *Percy Folio* I. 160 He bad his barons giue iudgment, 'or I will my-selfe, by mary gent'.

c. Combinations and phrases: **Mary-ale**, a merry-making held on a festival of the Virgin Mary; **Mary Ann** *Taxi-drivers' slang*, a taximeter; **Mary-bud** (*obs.* exc. in echoes of Shaks.), the bud of a marigold; † **Saint Mary day**, one of the festivals of the Virgin Mary (cf. LADY-DAY); † **Saint Mary garlic**, some unidentified plant; **Mary-lily**, the white or Madonna lily; † **Saint Mary maythe** (see MAYTHE); † **Saint Mary priest**, a chaplain employed to say mass in honour of the Virgin Mary; **Mary Queen of Scots cap**, a Mary Stuart cap (MARY STUART); † **(Saint) Mary's bath** [tr. L. *balneum Mariæ*], see BATH *sb.*[1] 14; **(Saint) Mary's flower**, (*a*) the Rose of Jericho, *Anastatica hierochuntina*; (*b*) the Western Australian genus *Marianthus* (Treas. Bot. 1866); **Mary-sole**, local name for the whiff, *Rhombus megastoma*, or the smear-dab, *Pleuronectes microcephalus*; † **Mary's seal**, Black Bryony, LADY'S SEAL 2; † **Saint Mary's seed**, *Sonchus oleraceus*; **Saint Mary thistle** = LADY'S THISTLE, *Carduus Marianus*.

1857 *Mary-ale [see ALE A. 3]. **1939** H. HODGE *Cab, Sir?* 218 It [*sc.* the taximeter] has other names... '*Mary Ann'. **1611** SHAKS. *Cymb.* II. iii. 25 And winking *Mary-buds begin to ope their Golden eyes. *c* **1310** *MS. Ashmol.* 43 in *S. Eng. Leg.* p. xiv, 25 *St. Marie dai in leynte. *c* **1450** *ME. Med. Bk.* (Heinrich) 232 Tak talow of an hert, such as he pyssep by twene two seynt mary dayes. **1623** MARKHAM *Eng. Housew.* I. i. (ed. 2), Take the stalke of Saint *Mary Garlycke, and burne it. **1893** *Westm. Gaz.* 24 Feb. 5/1 The white flower of the Italian painters is the *Mary-Lily. **1446** *Bury Wills* (Camden) 231 Capellano vulgariter nuncupato *seyntmarypriest. **1813** M. EDGEWORTH *Let.* 1 May (1971) 44, I may venture to praise Angelica..with a lace *Mary Queen of Scots cap. **1966** J. S. COX *Illustr. Dict. Hairdressing* 96 Mary Queen of Scots cap. **1600** SURFLET *Country Farm* I. xii. 76 For them that are more dainty and delicate, you shall distill the said snailes in *Maries bath [orig. *au bain de Marie*]. **1839** *Penny Cycl.* XIII. 105 Rose of Jericho..The Jews call it Kaf Maryam, or St. *Mary's Flower. **1822** *Mary sole [see *lantern-fish*, LANTERN *sb.* 9]. **1836** YARRELL *Brit. Fishes* II. 221 Lemon Dab. Smooth Dab... Mary-sole, Devonshire. **1600** SURFLET *Country Farm* II. ii. 204 Iesamin, *Maries seale [orig. *seau nostre dame*], muske roses. **1597** GERARDE *Herbal* App., S. *Maries seede is Southistle seede. **1579** LANGHAM *Gard. Health* (1633) 635 Make broth of S. *Mary Thistle.

d. In various names, as ***Mary Ann***, ***Mary Warner***, etc., used as slang substitutes for MARIJUANA. Cf. also MARY JANE 2.

1925 *Writer's Monthly* June 487/1 Laughing-weed, Mary Ann—A Mexican 'dope' rag-weed. **1935** A. J. POLLOCK *Underworld Speaks* 75/2 *Mary and Johnny*, marihuana. **1938** *New Yorker* 12 Mar. 36/2 Marijuana cigarettes..are sticks, reefers, Mary Anns. **1938** *Detective Fiction Weekly* 8 Jan. 47/2 He found plenty of marijuana. As always it came in cigarettes, called 'reefers', 'muggles',..or sometimes, playfully, 'Mary Warners'. **1949** PARTRIDGE *Dict. Underworld* 433 *Mary Ann*, a Mexican drug—the 'loco weed'... An alteration of *Mary Jane*, the English of the folk-lore interpretation of marijuana... *Mary Warner*, a marijuana cigarette. **1971** E. E. LANDY *Underground Dict.* 129 *Mary Ann*,..marijuana... *Mary Warner*,..marijuana.

2. *Australian slang.* A native woman. Also ***white Mary***, in Pidgin, a white woman.

1817 J. L. NICHOLAS *Narr. Voyage to N.Z.* I. vii. 201 The sister of one of our New Zealand sailors, a damsel who dispensed unlimited favours among our people, to whom she was well known by the name of Mary. **1882** A. J. BOYD *Old Colonials* 234 They [*sc.* the 'Australian black-fellows'] also fail to comprehend how it is that a Chinaman who is 'baal white fellow' can get a white woman for a wife. They say, 'Chinaman got 'im white Mary; black fellow get 'im white Mary.' **1884** *Pall Mall G.* 16 Aug. 2/1 The vessels generally average a little over 100 tons, 130 to 150 'boys' and Marys may be regarded as an average full cargo. **1898** DAVITT *Life & Progr. Australasia* l. 273 If a Kanaka has a 'Mary' on 'enlisting' the woman comes too and works like a man. **1931** V. PALMER *Separate Lives* 68 White mary no walk about all day. She belonga one boss, sit down longa one house. **1956** T. RONAN *Moleskin Midas* v. 326 Harness up the buggy and take this Mary back to town. **1962** *Coast to Coast 1961–2* 54 Some of the older marys did not remove frayed or dirty skirts. They put new ones on over the old.

† **3. Mary royal** (Sc.): see quot. *Obs.*

1565 *Reg. Privy Council Scot.* I. 413 That thair be cunyeit ane penny of silver callit the Marie ryall.

4. The sister of Martha and Lazarus in Bethany; hence used with allusion to Luke x. 39, 42, for a contemplative or intellectual person, opp. Martha (see MARTHA a).

a **1225** [see MARTHA *a*]. **1907** KIPLING *Twenty Poems* (1918) 1 The Sons of Mary seldom bother, for they have inherited that good part; But the Sons of Martha favour their Mother of the careful soul and the troubled heart. **1929** C. MACKENZIE *Gallipoli Memories* xv. 272 She was the Mary of the household, sitting back and entertaining the guest with tales of a cosmopolitan life. **1938**, etc. [see MARTHA a].

5. *Little Mary*: see LITTLE *a.* 13.

mary, obs. f. MARROW *sb.*[1], MARRY; var. MERI[1].

maryall, variant of MARIAL[1].

marybot, -buck, obs. forms of MARABOUT.

maryce, obs. form of MARISH.

marye, obs. form of MARROW *sb.*[1], MARRY.

maryes, obs. form of MARISH.

marygo(u)ld(e, mary gowles: see MARIGOLD.

† **maryhinchc(h)o.** *Obs.* (See quots.)

1610 MARKHAM *Masterp.* II. cxvi. 415 The string-halt, of some called the mary-hinchcho, is a sodaine twitching vp of the horses hinder legges. **1614** B. JONSON *Barth. Fair* III. ii, Poore soule, shee has had a Stringhalt, the Maryhinchco.

Mary Jane ('mɛəri dʒeɪn). The female Christian names *Mary* and *Jane* used in *transf.* senses:

1. [Proprietary name.] A type of low-heeled shoe with a strap round the ankle or across the instep, worn chiefly by young girls. Also *attrib.*

1921 *Amer. Wholesale Corporation (Baltimore) Catal.* 341 Infants' first step Mary Janes. *Ibid.*, Infants' soft sole 'Mary Jane' slippers. **1938** D. BAKER *Young Man with Horn* II. iii. 115 The little girl..was wearing pink cotton half socks and black patent leather Mary-Janes. **1967** J. J. PARETI *How to sell Footwear Profitably* xi. 130 Bell bottom trousers and mini skirts..are complemented by low-heeled barebacks, Mary Janes, T-strap sandals and boots. *Ibid.* xv. 159 *Mary Jane.* The classic party shoe previously for little girls, now for adults as well. Black leather patent pump with instep strap and bow. **1968** *Guardian* 26 July 1/5 Soft-soled Mary Jane shoes or supple white boots. **1969** R. JAFFE *Fame Game* (1970) i. 21 She had on white stockings and black patent Mary Janes. **1973** *Washington Post/Potomac* 30 Dec. 4/1 Massey's shoe store..had the low-heeled Mary Janes made for her.

2. Also **Mary J, maryjane.** = MARIJUANA. *slang.* Cf. MARY 1 d.

1928 *Daily Express* 11 Oct. 2/7 What is Marijuana?.. A deadly Mexican drug, more familiarly known as 'Mary Jane', which produces wild hilarity when either smoked or eaten. **1940** *Amer. Speech* XV. 336 The cigarettes are usually called reefers, but other names are:..Mary Anns, Mary Janes. **1959** N. MAILER *Advts. for Myself* (1961) 245, I had marijuana. Mary-Jane..was the door back to sex. **1965** F. SARGESON *Mem. of Peon* vii. 254 He..returned with the news that the backyard was all overgrown with a harvest of Mary Jane. **1967** *Boston Sunday Herald* 26 Mar. IV. 1/1 Marijuana..is better known..as 'pot', 'grass' and 'Mary J'. **1967** *Punch* 26 July 123/2 He probably wouldn't even need the pot, grass, boo or maryjane. **1970** 'D. SHANNON' *Unexpected Death* (1971) x. 146 'What did they buy?' asked Mendoza. 'Oh, Mary Jane. Twenty reefers,' said Callaghan. **1971** D. HEFFRON *Nice Fire & Some Moonpennies* i. 11 'You Indians were onto this kinda stuff long before *we* were.' 'Onto *what?*' 'Mary Jane, Maizie, Mary *Jane*!' **1972** *Sunday Sun* (Brisbane) 2 July 14/3 Detectives from the CIB Drug Squad in Brisbane are becoming quite familiar now with words like..mezz, Mary Jane.

Maryland (ˈmɛərɪlænd). The name of one of the eastern states of North America (named in 1632 after Queen Henrietta *Maria*) used *attrib.* in **Maryland chicken**, a piece of chicken covered in breadcrumbs and fried, and served with sweet corn and bacon; also **chicken (à la) Maryland; Maryland end, parson** (see quots.); **Maryland yellow-throat**, a ground warbler, *Geothlypis trichas*, found in the eastern United States.

1906 A. FILIPPINI *Internat. Cook Bk.* 125 *Chicken Maryland*... Arrange six thin slices fresh broiled bacon on top of the chicken and, lastly, place six freshly prepared crisp corn fritters..around the dish and serve. **1929** *Amer. Speech* IV. 499 Can any reader of *American Speech* give me any information concerning the origin of the expression 'chicken à la Maryland', or the dish? **1935** M. MORPHY *Recipes of all Nations* 610 Maryland chicken... Young chickens are jointed.., coated with..egg and fine bread-crumbs, and sauté in clarified butter. **1941** F. M. FARMER *Boston Cooking-School Cook Bk.* (ed. 7) 376 Maryland Chicken... Season chicken with salt and pepper, dip in flour, then in 1 egg, beaten slightly with 2 tablespoons cold water, then in soft bread crumbs. **1959** *Good Food Guide* 76 Occasionally Maryland chicken and veal escalop appear. **1969** B. SIAS *Chicken Cookbk.* 48 Chicken à la Maryland..is said to have originated in St. Clement Island and was later introduced into Maryland by Lord Baltimore. **1975** *Times* 26 Sept. 16/6 Maryland chicken with corn fritters. **1859** BARTLETT *Dict. Amer.* (ed. 2) 265 *Maryland end*, said of the hock of the ham. The other is the Virginia end. **1903** S. CLAPIN *New Dict. Amer.* 270 *Maryland end*, in Maryland and Virginia, the curious name given to the hock end of a ham. **1811** A. GRAYDON *Mem.* 292 Mr. L—seemed in all respects to be what was then called in Pennsylvania a Maryland parson; that is, one who could accommodate himself to his company. **1702** PETIVER *Gazophyl.* I. 10 *Avis Mary-Landica gutture luteo.* The Mary-Land Yellow-Throat. **1839** J. J. AUDUBON *Ornith. Biogr.* V. 75 The Maryland Yellow-throat..keeps near the ground in low bushes. **1948** *N. & S. Dakota Horticulture* July–Aug. 106/1 From a nearby coulee came the odd but musical notes of a Maryland Yellow Throat.

b. Used *attrib.* or *ellipt.* of tobacco from Maryland.

1867 P. L. SIMMONDS *Dict. Trade* (rev. ed.) Suppl. 445/1 *Maryland*, a mild kind of tobacco. **1930** KIPLING *Limits & Renewals* (1932) 324 He exhaled the smoke through his finely-cut nostrils. 'Yes, it *is* Smyrna.... Good! And Monsieur appreciates our "Marylands" also? Hmm. *I* remember the time when our Government tobaccos were a national infamy.' **1933** *Discovery* Mar. 74/1 Experiments were carried out..by Garner and Allard as a result of difficulties they experienced in making a variety of tobacco (Maryland Mammoth) produce flowers. **1953** J. E. BROOKS *Mighty Leaf* ix. 207 By the early thirties the culture of the Maryland Broadleaf began in the Valley and this type, of fine texture and subtle odor, soon supplanted other local kinds.

ˈ**Marylander.** Also **Marilander.** [f. prec. + -ER¹.] A native or inhabitant of the state of Maryland in the United States; also, something characteristic of Maryland.

1665 in *Mass. Hist. Soc. Coll.* (1849) 3rd Ser. X. 55 A forbearance of such hostility..may prevent the destruction of divers dutch or English of the hither parts, or Marilanders. **1678** *Rec. Court of New Castle on Delaware* (1904) 234 They had gott out of Maryland for old debts due for Cattle sold to the Marylanders. **1755** L. EVANS *Geogr. Ess.* 14 The Sasquehannocks, after the great Defeat by the Marilanders, were easily exterminated by the Confederates. **1838** J. F. COOPER *Homeward Bound* I. xii. 298 This beef is not indigestible, and here is a real Marylander, in the way of a ham. **1860** O. W. HOLMES *Prof. at Breakfast-Table* ii. 57, I am a Marylander. **1931** *Times Lit. Suppl.* 7 May 359/2 Naturally, a book dealing with Maryland houses is of the greatest interest to the owners of the houses, and next to other Marylanders. **1948** *Chicago Tribune* 9 May 3/2 Marylanders, used to disappointments, are keeping their fingers crossed. **1949** B. A. BOTKIN *Treas. S. Folklore* IV. i. 552 Marylanders grow lyrical over Brunswick stew, diamond-back terrapin. **1967** *National Observer* (U.S.) 3 July 12/2 Captain Kusel admits that the Marylanders look and sound better in drill. **1974** *Times* 6 Nov. (Maryland Suppl.) p. i/3 He spoke for a lot of Marylanders when he added: 'I like our provincialism.'

Marymass (ˈmɛərɪmæs). Also 6–7 *Sc.* **Marymess.** [f. MARY + MASS *sb.*¹]

1. A festival of the Virgin Mary, esp. †(*a*) in OE., Candlemas, 2 Feb.; (*b*) the Assumption, 15 Aug. (now only *local Sc.*); †(*c*) *latter Marymass*, the Nativity of the Virgin, 8 Sept. Also *attrib.* in †***Marymas fast, Marymass holidays.***

c **1000** *Menologium* 20 (February) And þæs embe ane niht þæt we Marian mæssan healdað..for þan heo Crist on þam dæȝe..brohte to temple. **1052** in Kemble *Cod. Dipl.* IV. 290 Ehta daȝas to ðære ærre sanctæ Marian mæssan and ehta daȝas to ðære æftran sancta Marian mæssan. **1492** *Acta Dom. Conc.* (1839) 265/2 Þe somme of jᶜ merkis..at þe fest of Sanct Iohne þe baptist callit midsommer nixt tocum, & ane vther jᶜ merkis at þe latter marymess nixt þareftir. **1546** *Reg. Privy Council Scot.* I. 34 This letter marymess. **1578** WHETSTONE *1st Pt. Promos & Cass.* II. v, Tenne to one I read his fortune by the Marymas fast. **1823** GALT *R. Gilhaize* xiv, Was na it my Lord himsel', at last Marymas, when he sent for me to make a hoop to mend her leg. **1903** *Glasgow Herald* 20 Aug., Irvine Harbour. Marymass Holidays. [Work suspended between Friday 21 Aug. and Tuesday 25 Aug.]

†**2.** A mass in honour of the Virgin Mary; in 16th c. used in the asseveration ***by the Mary mass.***

1532 MORE *Confut. Tindale* Wks. 715/2 She..sayde he wer worthy by the mary masse to be hanged by the necke. **1553** *Respublica* II. ii. 11 (Brandl) 301 Yea, by the Marye Masse. **1852** ROCK *Ch. of Fathers* III. i. 264 The gilds in the parish often helped to keep up the Mary-Mass.

mary-muffe, variant of MARRY-MUFF *Obs.*

marynal, variant of MARINAL.

marynar(e, -neer, obs. forms of MARINER.

marynel, -eller: see MARINAL, MARINALLER.

maryner(e, -nes: see MARINER, MERRINESS.

Maryology, variant of MARIOLOGY.

maryoner, obs. form of MARINER.

marys, variant of MARIS *Obs.*, womb.

marys(e, -ysh(e, obs. forms of MARISH.

maryskyn, variant of MAROQUIN *Obs.*

marysse, -yssh(e, obs. forms of MARISH.

Mary Stuart (ˈmɛərɪ ˈstjuːət). Also **Marie Stuart.** The name of Mary, Queen of Scots (1542–87), used *attrib.* and *ellipt.* to designate styles of clothes, hair, etc., similar to those she wore, *spec.* headwear with a central dip or peak over the forehead.

1852 E. RUSKIN *Let.* 26 Jan. in M. Lutyens *Effie in Venice* (1965) II. 254 A coiffure I have made for myself... It is a piece of scarlet velvet with a fringe of large and small pearls all round; a point à la Marie Stuart comes in front. **1873** *Young Englishwoman* Mar. 130/1 A Marie Stuart bonnet of rice straw lined with blue silk. **1880** in *American Mail Order Fashions* (1961) 18 *The Mary Stuart.* Jetted lace bonnet ..$6.50. *a* **1913** F. ROLFE *Desire & Pursuit of Whole* (1934) x. 93 The kind of female liable to wear Mary Stuart caps by night. **1965** *Listener* 20 May 743/3 Then came the Mary Stuart cap, worn both with and without a veil. **1965** J. LAVER *Contini's Fashion* 231/1 The return of the Royal family to Paris brought the first signs of romanticism... Then the first Mary Stuart belts appeared, which tended to lower the waist. **1966** J. S. COX *Illustr. Dict. Hairdressing* 96/1 *Marie Stuart Coiffure*, (1) a coiffure similar to that worn by Mary, Queen of Scots.. ; (2) a woman's hair style of *circa* 1865 based on that worn by Mary Queen of Scots.

Marz, obs. form of MARCH *sb.*² (the month).

marzacotto (ˌmɑːtsəˈkɒtəʊ, -z-). *Ceramics.* [It. (Florio, 1598, 'an instrument or toole that potters use').] A transparent glaze used by Italian majolica workers (see quots.).

1873 C. D. E. FORTNUM *Descr. Catal. Maiolica* 152 Glazing it with 'marzacotto', a mixture of oxide of lead, sand and potash. **1885** *Encycl. Brit.* XIX. 625/1 The white enamel, 'bianco', was composed of thirty parts of 'marzacotto' to twelve of oxide of tin. **1960** R. G. HAGGAR *Conc. Encycl. Cont. Pott. & Porc.* 304/1 *Marzacotto*, a silicate of potash..used as the basis of the tin-enamel or tin-glaze of the maiolica potter. **1972** J. SCOTT-TAGGART *Italian Maiolica* 56 *Marzacotto*..is a potassium silicate made by fusing a mixture of sand and calcined wine-lees. *Ibid.*, This *marzacotto* provides the 'glassy' element.

marzhaunt, obs. form of MERCHANT.

Marzine (ˈmɑːziːn). A trade name in the U.K. for MAREZINE.

1954 *Trade Marks Jrnl.* 24 Mar. 297/1 Marzine... All goods included in class 5 [pharmaceutical, veterinary, and sanitary substances, etc.]. The Wellcome Foundation Limited,..London,..manufacturing chemists. **1956** *Approved Names* (Brit. Pharmacopœia Commission) Suppl. Aug., Cyclizine, 1-Methyl-4-α-phenylbenzylpiperazine. Marzine is the hydrochloride. **1958** *Martindale's Extra Pharmacopœia* (ed. 24) I. 1112 Marzine (known in U.S.A. as Marezine Hydrochloride) (Burroughs Wellcome). Cyclizine hydrochloride. **1959** *Lancet* 25 Apr. 853/1 Cyclizine hydrochloride ('Marezine', 'Marzine') in doses of 50 mg. daily was also found effective [in motion sickness].

marzipan (ˌmɑːzɪˈpæn), **marchpane** (ˈmɑːtʃpeɪn). Forms: α. 5, 8 **marchpayne**, 6 **marche payne, -pane, (martspaine, martchpane), march pain, (-payine, -pine)**, 7 **marchpayn, (6, 9 marchpan)**, 6–7 **marchpaine**, 6– **marchpane.** β. 6–7 **mazapane.** γ. 6 **marzepaine**, 9 **marzipan, (marzapane, marcipan).** [Occurs as F. *massepain* (in 16th c. *marcepain*), It. *marzapane*, Sp. *mazapan*, Pg. *maçapão*, Ger. *marzipan* (*martzepan* 1521, glossing *panis marcius*), Du. *marsepein* (*marcepain* in 1486), Da., Sw. *marsipan*; the Eng. forms come from various continental sources. In recent times the sweetmeat has been known chiefly as imported from Germany; hence the Ger. form *marzipan* has greater currency than the traditional Eng. form *marchpane*.

The word is believed to have come into the other Rom. langs. from Italian. Its etymology is obscure. What seems to be the same word occurs in various Rom. forms and in med.L. with the senses 'small box', 'a certain mediæval weight', and 'a mediæval coin'. Kluyver, in *Zeitschr. f. deutsche Wortforschung* July 1904, ingeniously tries to prove that the last-mentioned sense is the source of all the others. He identifies the word with med.L. *matapanus*, a Venetian coin bearing a figure of Christ on a throne (Du Cange), and suggests that it represents Arab. *mauthabān* 'a king that sits still' (Lane), which he conjectures to have been used by Saracens as a derisive name for this coin.]

1. a. A kind of confectionery composed of a paste of pounded almonds, sugar, etc., made up into small cakes or moulded into ornamental forms.

α. **1556** WITHALS *Dict.* (1568) 49 b/2 Deyntie dysshes as marche payne, tartes, &c., *Bellaria.* **1587** HARRISON *England* II. vi. (1877) I. 148 Marchpaine wrought with no small curiositie. **1592** SHAKS. *Rom. & Jul.* I. v. 9. ? **1606** DRAYTON *Poems Lyr. & Past., Ecl.* iv. E 1 b, The silke well couth she twist and twine, And make the fine Marchpine. **1615** MARKHAM *Eng. Housew.* (1660) 93 To make the best March-pane, take the best Jordan Almonds. **1725** BRADLEY *Fam. Dict.* s.v., The Paste in that which they call the Royal March-Pane. **1848** OXENFORD tr. *Goethe's Autobiog.* (Bohn) I. 64 The tarts, biscuits, marchpane and sweet wine. **1884** *Health Exhib. Catal.* 151/2 Marchpane and other cakes and confectionery made with honey. **1901** *Board of Trade Jrnl.* 11 July 84 The edible article known variously as 'march-pane', 'marzipan', or 'marcipan', which consists of..flour, sugar, almonds, &c., made in fancy forms..is..dutiable.

β. **1598** FLORIO, *Pasta*,..marchpane, or mazapane.

γ. **1866** HOWELLS *Venet. Life* xviii. 278 A cake called *marzapane.* **1897** *Daily News* 23 Nov. 2/1 The stuff..smelt very much like the sweetmeat called marzipan.

b. A cake or shaped piece of this composition.

α. **1494** FABYAN *Chron.* VII. 587 A march payne garnysshed with dyuerse fygures of aungellys. **1517** TORKINGTON *Pilgr.* (1884) 13 The Duke sent to the Pilgryms gret basons full of Marchepanys. **1548** UDALL *Erasm. Par. Luke* vii. 25 Wylde honey and locustes hathe he preferred before the martspaines and other swete delycates of kynges. **1616** SURFL. & MARKH. *Country Farm* 585 Marchpanes are made of verie little flower, but with addition of greater quantitie of Filberds, Pine Nuts, Pistaces, Almonds, and rosed Sugar. **1725** BRADLEY *Fam. Dict.* s.v. *Tourte*, For a Sugar'd Pan-pie..take five or six Biskets, Marchpanes, or Macaroons [etc.]. **1853** SOYER *Pantroph.* 288 Begin by covering the whole of the base with a layer of marchpans. **1882** MISS YONGE *Unknown to Hist.* I. 254 All the ladies and serving women were called on to concoct pasties.., cakes and march-panes. **1884** *Health Exhib. Catal.* 151/2 Polish Honey Cakes, Marchpanes, and Chocolate.

β. **1657** TOMLINSON *Renou's Disp.* 106 A certain kinde of condite which is called Pasta Regia or a Mazapane.

γ. **1542** UDALL *Erasm. Apoph.* 128 To feede of tartes and marzepaines, the meates of denty mouthed persones.

†**c.** *fig.* Chiefly as the type of something delicious or exquisite. *Obs.*

1592 G. HARVEY *Four Lett.* 5 Rayling was the Ypocras of the drunken rimester: and Quipping the Marche-pane of the madde libeller. **1599** B. JONSON *Cynthia's Rev.* IV. i, *Mor.* I was then esteemd——. *Phi.* The very March-pane of the Court, I warrant? **1613** BEAUM. & FL. *Coxcomb* IV. iii, You are very curious of your hand... Let me see it?—Ay marry, here's a hand of march-pane. *a* **1652** BROME *City Wit* IV. ii, You have your Kickshaws, your Players Marchpaines; all shew and no meat.

2. *attrib.*

1587 FLEMING *Contn. Holinshed* III. 1355/1 A verie statelie tragedie named *Dido*, wherein the quænes banket.. was liuelie described in a marchpaine patterne. **1602** SIR H. PLATT *Delights for Ladies* (1611) B 4 b, To make an excellent Marchpane paste to print off in molds for banqueting dishes. **1616** R. C. *Times' Whistle* vi. 2771 Candid eringoes, and rich marchpaine stuffe. **1891** 'J. S. WINTER' *Lumley* iv. 31 Marzipan *bon-bons.*

†**b.** quasi-*adj.* with the sense: Dainty, superfine.

1598–9 B. JONSON *Case is Altered* IV. iv, A march paine wench. **1640** GLAPTHORNE *Wit in Constable* v, What would you've done With two such March-pane husbands? **1649** G.

DANIEL *Trinarch., Hen. V*, ccclxvi, Let not these Marchpane follies Dull your Sence To better rellish.

Hence †**march panado** *v.* [see PANADA], *trans.* to mould, after the manner of marchpane.

1650 B. *Discolliminium* 46 The constitution of my body was a cleare transparent Marmulate.. March Panado'd into the shape of a strait Gentleman.

Mas, *sb.*[1] Also 6–7 masse, 7–9 mass, 7 mes, 8–9 mess. *β. U.S.* 9– mars(e. Cf. also MAST *sb.*[4] [Shortened f. MASTER *sb.*]

1. A vulgar or jocular shortening of *master*, usually followed by a proper name or official title.

1575 *Gamm. Gurton* Prol. 12 Mas Doctor was sent for, these gossyps to staye, Because he was Curate, and estemed full wyse. **1578** WHETSTONE *1st Pt. Promos & Cass.* v. v, Well, masse Grimball. **1588** *Marprel. Epist.* (Arb.) 4 An Archb. is very weakely defended by masse Dean. *a* **1592** GREENE *Jas. IV*, v. iv, What sees Mas Lawyer in this state amiss? **1605** B. JONSON *Volpone* II. i, Is Mass' Stone dead! **1625** —— *Staple of N.* II. iv, Sir, by both Your worshipfull Titles, and your name Mas Broker, Good morrow. **1678** BUTLER *Hud.* III. ii. 1239 The Isle of Wight.. Where Hinderson, and th' other Masses, Were sent to Cap Texts, and put Cases. *a* **1722** MRS. CENTLIVRE *Platonick Lady* I. i, Is there any thing so disagreable on earth as the sayings of Miss and Mass repeated? **1837** *Southern Lit. Messenger* III. 174 Mass Phil been very uneasy about you.

β. mars(e.

Freq. in Black English contexts.

1874 'H. CHURTON' *Toinette* xxviii. 301 He gave Toinette to young Marse Geoffrey. **1880** A. W. TOURGÉE *Bricks without Straw* 408 The old time 'Marse' was now almost universally used, and few 'niggers' presumed to speak to a white man.. without removing their hats. **1884** 'MARK TWAIN' *Huck. Finn* xxxviii. 391 Why, Mars Tom, I doan' *want* no rats. **1901** B. T. WASHINGTON *Up from Slavery* 12, I recall the feeling of sorrow among the slaves when they heard of the death of 'Mars' Billy'. **1909** 'O. HENRY' *Roads of Destiny* ii. 39 Marse Robert robbing the bank! *Ibid.* xxi. 350 I'm not going back on Mars' Jeff. **1949** [see LINE *sb.*[2] 17 b]. **1950** R. AMES in A. Dundes *Mother Wit* (1973) 488/1 The old time darky's.. love for 'ole marse' and 'ole mist'ess'. **1955** E. POUND *Classic Anthol.* I. 8 Thaar's where ole Marse Shao used to sit.

2. Mas John, applied jocularly or contemptuously to a Scottish Presbyterian minister, in contradistinction to an Anglican or Roman clergyman. *arch.*

? **1661** JER. TAYLOR *Serm.* Wks. 1850 VIII. 533 To prefer the private minister before the public, the presbyter before a bishop,.. and Mas John before the patriarch of Jerusalem. **1672** MARVELL *Reh. Transp.* I. 136 In.. Scotland there were I know not how many Mas Johns restored in one day to the work of their Ministry. **1682** H. MORE *Contin. Remark. Stories* 27 The Narration.. being rather a Collectation of Mes John and the Presbytery on one side, and the foul Fiend ..on the other side. **1695** SAGE *Fund. Charter Presbyt.* (1697) 395 But Mas John takes the Chair without Election; and would not be a little grated if the best Laird in the Parish should be his Competitor. **1790** BURKE *Fr. Rev.* Wks. V. 44 These new Mess-Johns in robes and coronets. **1821** GALT *Ann. Parish* i. 14 The bairns, when they saw me coming, ran crying to their mothers, 'Here's the feckless Mess-John.' **1826** SCOTT *Woodst.* xxviii, You are not, I apprehend, either a Catholic priest or a Scotch Mass-John to claim devoted obedience from your hearers.

‖**mas** (mɑs), *sb.*[2] [Pr.] A farm or cottage in the South of France; a house.

1921 *English* May 495 We see the flocks returning to the 'mas' after having spent the long summer in the mountains. **1924** R. FRY *Let.* 2 July (1972) II. 555 Two peasant proprietors who live in a little Mas. **1932** R. CAMPBELL *Taurine Provence* 48 The 'Mas' is a mixture between a manor and a huge farm-house. **1942** 'A. BRIDGE' *Frontier Passage* xii. 221 The peasant's rough-and-ready method of defending his *mas*. **1964** F. WHITE *West of Rhone* iv. 51 The *mas*, the farms, were devoted to stock-raising. **1966** 'R. STANDISH' *Widow Hack* vi. 69 The villa was a well-faked *mas provençal*, but instead of the conventional rounded Roman [roof] tiles, they were flat.

mas, obs. f. MASS *sb.*[1], and *makes*, MAKE *v.*

masage, -aker, obs. ff. MESSAGE, MASSACRE.

Masai ('mɑːsaɪ, mə'saɪ). [Bantu.] **A.** *sb.* **a.** A pastoral people of mixed Hamitic stock inhabiting parts of Kenya and Tanzania; a member of this people. **b.** The Nilotic language of this people. **B.** *adj.* Of or pertaining to this people or their language.

1857 ERHARDT & KRAPF (*title*) Vocabulary of the Enguduk Iloigob, as spoken by the Masai-tribes in East Africa, in two parts (Masai-English, and English-Kimasai, with a song of the Masai). **1873** [see KAVIRONDO]. **1894** [see KIKUYU]. **1898** E. CLODD in R. M. Dorson *Peasant Customs* (1968) I. 384 Among the Masai.. while it is bad form to kiss a lady, it is *comme il faut* to spit on her. **1902** *Encycl. Brit.* XXV. 140/1 The Masai east of Lake Victoria.. are undoubtedly Hamites, mixed.. with negro elements. **1933** L. BLOOMFIELD *Lang.* iv. 67 Among the languages of this region.. we may mention.. Nuba,.. Dinka, and.. Masai. **1947** *E. Afr. Ann.* 1946–7 41/2 The Samburu.. are closely associated with the Masai and are called from the Masai word 'Samburer' which means 'butterfly'. **1955** *Times* 12 July 9/7 The Mau Mau gangs must be leading a life not altogether unlike that which their grandfathers led in the struggles with the Masai over 60 years ago. **1962** *Listener* 6 Sept. 343/2 No one lived there and even Masai cattle seldom came. **1967** M. J. COE *Ecol. Alpine Zone Mt. Kenya* 1 The retention in the Masai language of many words that refer to Mt. Kenya. **1969** *Reporter* (Nairobi) 13 June 36/4 This new spirit of the Masai is exemplified by 700 Masai families who migrated from their motherland some years ago. **1973** *Sunday Express* 11 Mar. 23/2 She has just come back from Kenya.., where she has been photographing the Masai.

masalyne, masar, obs. ff. MASLIN[1], MAZER.

Masarwa (mə'sɑːwə). *S. Afr.* [Native name.] **A.** *sb.* The name given to the Bushmen distributed over the Northern Kalahari desert. **B.** *adj.* Of or pertaining to this group.

1871 J. MACKENZIE *Ten Yrs. North of Orange River* viii. 128 The other subject race is that of the Bushmen, called Barwa by the Bechuanas in the south, and Masarwa by those in the north of the country. **1896** H. A. BRYDEN *Tales S. Afr.* ii. 42 You may never.. see a Masarwa Bushman.. who does not show marks of fireburn upon the nether limbs. **1905** G. W. STOW *Native Races S. Afr.* xiv. 265 Bushman speaking peoples as the Masarwa. **1928** E. H. L. SCHWARZ *Kalahari & its Native Races* viii. 172 The term Masarwa.. is used for all Bushmen in the Northern Kalahari. *Ibid.* 174 There were several Masarwa women about the palace precincts. **1931** [see *game-land* (GAME *sb.* 16 a)]. **1971** *Sunday Times* (Johannesburg) (Mag. Section) 28 Mar. 3/3 The people of Dilepe.. are not prepared to receive a Masarwa in their midst.

mascabado, variant of MUSCOVADO.

mascagnine (mæ'skænjaɪn). *Min.* Also -in. [Named by Karsten 1800, after the discoverer, Prof. *Mascagni*: see -INE.] = next.

1836 T. THOMSON *Min., Geol.*, etc. I. 95 Sulphate of Ammonia, Mascagnine. **1846** *Penny Cycl.* Suppl. II. 308/1 *Mascagnin.* **1849** WATTS tr. *Gmelin's Handbk. Chem.* II. 462.

mascagnite ('mæskənjaɪt). *Min.* [See prec. and -ITE.] 'Sulphate of ammonium, occurring in crusts and stalactitic forms near volcanoes'.

1896 CHESTER *Dict. Min.*

mascal, var. MASCLE *sb.*[1], MESCAL.

mascall, var. MASCUE *v.*

mascalonge, variant of MUSKELLUNGE.

mascara (mæ'skɑːrə). Also (*rare*) mascaro. [It. *mascara, maschera*, Sp. *máscara* MASKER *sb.*[1]] A preparation for colouring the eyelashes and eyebrows.

1890 *Cent. Dict.*, *Mascaro*, a kind of paint used for the eyebrows and eyelashes by actors. **1922** I. & H. KLUMPH *Screen Acting* 59 You will have your own make-up.. cold cream, mascara for the eyelashes. **1927** N. MARTIN *Constant Simp* (1928) vi. 101 No black globules of mascara hung from the tips of her long lashes. **1930** H. RUBINSTEIN *Art Feminine Beauty* xvi. 250 My mother had brought us up to use a little powder on our faces but would have been horrified at the thought of rouge or lipstick, or mascara for the eyes. **1938** M. ALLINGHAM *Fashion in Shrouds* xvi. 267 Her long eyelashes thick with mascara. **1958** E. DUNDY *Dud Avocado* I. vii. 121 My eyes, which stung and swam from the running mascara. **1966** T. PYNCHON *Crying of Lot 49* v. 125 She knew she looked terrible—knuckles black with eye-liner and mascara from where she'd rubbed.

Hence **ma'scara** *v. trans.*, to treat with mascara. So **ma'scaraed** *ppl. a.*

1935 S. LEWIS *It can't happen Here* xxxviii. 407 A lady with mascaraed eyelashes. **1938** N. MARSH *Death in White Tie* iii. 36 Our hostess's mascaraed eyes. **1944** W. S. MAUGHAM *Razor's Edge* ii. 68 They had the same heavily mascaraed eyelashes, the same brightly painted lips, the same rouged cheeks. **1961** M. HOWARD *Surgeon's Dilemma* viii. 247 Adelia, frantically mascaraing her eyelashes.

mascarade, -ado, obs. ff. MASQUERADE.

‖**mascaret** (maskarɛ). [Fr. (16th c.), f. Gascon *mascaret* spotted cow, f. *mascara* (cf. Pr. *mascarar*, OF. *mascurer*, F. *mâchurer*) to daub, to black the face: app. arising from the resemblance of the tidal bore to the movement of running cattle.] A tidal bore in an estuary in France.

1841 W. A. BROOKS *Treat. Improvement Navigation of Rivers* xi. 127 The mascaret of the Dordogne consists of two, three, and sometimes four lofty waves, which follow each other rapidly, damming back the whole breadth of the river. **1900** P. DEARMER *Highways & Byways in Normandy* xii. 315 At high tides there is the spectacle of the famous *mascaret* or bore. **1902** *Encycl. Brit.* XXXII. 508 The tide begins to make itself felt at Poses, 11 miles above Elbeuf, and between Caudebec and Villequier the *mascaret*, or bore, has its greatest development. **1959** *Listener* 5 Feb. 248/1 The *mascaret* is to the Seine what the bore is to the Severn. **1971** S. E. MORISON *European Discovery Amer.: Northern Voy.* viii. 256 The navigation of the Seine is more hazardous.. and even dangerous when a tidal bore, the *mascaret*, sweeps up the river unexpectedly.

‖**mascaron** (maskarɔ̃, 'mæskərən). [Fr., = grotesque mask (1603 in Robert), ad. It. *mascherone*, f. *maschera* MASK *sb.*[3]]. In decorative art: a grotesque face or mask (cf. MASK *sb.*[3] 4 a).

1664 EVELYN tr. *Fréart's Parallel Antient Archit. with Mod.* Pref. 3 They produce nothing save Mascarons, wretched Cartouches, and the like idle and impertinent Grotesks. **1883** J. W. MOLLETT *Illustr. Dict. Art & Archaeol.* 207/1 *Mascaron*,.. the face of a man or animal employed as an ornamentation for decorating the key-stones of arches or vaults, or the stones of an arch, &c. **1926** R. GLAZIER *Man. Hist. Ornament* (ed. 4) II. 169 The Italians from about 1480 favoured elaborate borders [in MSS.].. composed of classical columns,.. mascarons, etc.

mascellez, variant of MASCLELESS.

mascellin(e, -celyn(e, obs. ff. MASLIN.

mascerate, obs. form of MACERATE.

maschel: see MASHEL *Obs.*

mascherade, -ate, obs. ff. MASQUERADE.

masches, maschets, variants of MACHES *Obs.*

†**maschevalent**, ? error for MACHIAVELLIAN.

1600 R. LOGAN *Let.* in *Pitcairn's Crim. Trials* (1833) II. I. 285 The Maschevalent massakering of owr deirest frendis.

maschscherel: see *mash-roll*, MASH *sb.*[1] 5.

mascle ('mɑːsk(ə)l, -æ-), *sb.*[1] Also 4 maskle, 5 maskill, mascule, 7 mascal. [Of somewhat obscure etymology.

Senses 1 and 2 coincide with senses of L. *macula*; senses 2 and 3 with senses of F. *macle*, first quoted from 1584, and regarded by French lexicographers as ad. L. *macula*; OF. *mascle* (= sense 3 below) occurs in the Roll of Caerlaverock *c* 1300, and with date 1397 in Nicholls *Roy. Wills* (1780) 155; cf. further med.L. *mascula* mesh (early 15th c. in Diefenbach, perh. an alteration of L. *macula* after OHG. *masca* mesh), and OE. *mæscre*, glossing L. *macula*, whether in the sense of mesh or in that of spot is doubtful. With sense 1 cf. the 16th c. Du. *maschel* spot, stain (Kilian).]

†**1.** A spot, speck. *Obs.*

13.. *E.E. Allit. P.* A. 725 With-outen mote oþer mascle of sulpande synne. *Ibid.* B. 556 With-outen maskle oþer mote. *a* **1400–50** *Alexander* 4989 All þe body.. Was finely florischt .. Of gold graynes & of goules full of gray mascles.

†**2.** = MESH of a net. *Obs.*

1329 in Riley *Mem. Lond.* (1868) 172 [The meshes of which nets which are called] mascles [ought to be 1½ inch in size]. *c* **1410** *Master of Game* (MS. Digby) fol. 21 Men taketh hem [*sc.* foxes].. with heyes, and with pursnettes. But he kutteth with his teth þe mascles. **1688** R. HOLME *Armoury* I. 108/2 Mascle, a Mash of a Net. **1696** PHILLIPS, *Mascle*,.. the mash or hole of a net.

†**b.** *attrib.* in *mascle lace*. *Obs.*

a **1500** *MS. Harl.* 2320 f. 62 in *Catalogue*, [Kinds of lace in fashion under Hen. VI. and Edw. IV.] Lace Maskel.

3. *Her.* A charge in the form of a lozenge with a lozenge-shaped opening through which the 'field' appears. (Cf. MESH.) Also *attrib.*

1486 *Bk. St. Albans, Her.* F iij b, Here ye shall knaw the differans be twix fusillis, masculys and losyngys. **1572** BOSSEWELL *Armorie* II. 126 Whensoeuer ye shall see eyther Losenge, Mascle, or other thynge voyded of the fielde, Fesse, bende &c. whereon theye stande, it is sufficient to saye, voyded, onelye. **1610** GUILLIM *Heraldry* IV. xix. (1632) 359 A Mascle differeth from both the Fusill and Lozenge; first, because [etc.]. **1680** *Lond. Gaz.* No. 1503/4 Several pieces of Plate engraven with a Leopards head.. and five Mascals. **1688** R. HOLME *Armoury* III. 322/2 A Mascle Buckle Bottony.. is generally termed by the name of a Losenge or Mascle Shooe Buckle. **1797** *Encycl. Brit.* (ed. 3) VIII. 455/1 Opinions have varied very much about the original of the mascles or mashes. **1893** CUSSANS *Her.* (ed. 4) 71 The Mascle is a Lozenge voided.

transf. **1863** KINGLAKE *Crimea* II. 204 The outline of the ground covered by their troops took the shape of a lozenge. Within the mascle or hollow lozenge thus formed, there marched the Turkish battalions.

4. *Antiq.* One of the perforated lozenge-shaped plates of metal fastened to the outer surface of the military tunic of the 13th century. (Cf. MACLE 4.)

1822 *Gentl. Mag.* XCII. I. 308 But two different kinds of mail, the mascled and flat ringed, are all that can be found in them, the mascles being sometimes lozenge-shaped and sometimes square. **1824** MEYRICK *Anc. Armour* I. Introd. 69 A tunic,.. coated with perforated lozenges of steel, called.. macles, or mascles. **1846** FAIRHOLT *Costume in Eng.* 88 These mascles were lozenge-shaped plates of metal.

†**mascle**, *a.* and *sb.*[2] *Obs.* Also 5 mascul. [a. early OF. *mascle*: see MALE *a.*] = MALE *a.* and *sb.* *mascul thure*: 'male incense' (see MALE *a.* 6).

c **1410** *Master of Game* (MS. Digby 182) i, An hare shall dure well IIII. myle or more or lasse, and she be an olde hare mascle. *Ibid.* iv, For alle þe sesoun a mascle and a femell abydith togyders. *c* **1420** *Pallad. on Husb.* XI. 412 A vnce of mascul thure Wel smellynge, and an vnce of pipur dure. **1455** *Rolls of Parlt.* V. 329/2 Thaim and thaire heires mascles. **1587** STANYHURST *Descr. Irel.* ii. 19 in *Holinshed*, Without the coupling of mascle or female.

masclechon, obs. form of MASLIN[2].

mascled ('mɑːsk(ə)ld, -æ-), *a.* [f. MASCLE *sb.*[1] + -ED[2].] Covered with mascles.

1818 MEYRICK in *Archæologia* (1821) XIX. 126 The earliest specimen I have found of the mascled hauberk. **1828–40** TYTLER *Hist. Scot.* (1864) I. 321 He [Alexander II] appears clothed in a complete coat of mascled mail. **1846** FAIRHOLT *Costume in Eng.* 88 The mascled armour of this era [13th c.].

†'**mascleless**, *a.* *Obs.* In 4 mascellez, maskel(l)ez, -es. [f. MASCLE *sb.*[1] + -LESS.] Spotless.

13.. *E.E. Allit. P.* A. 731 To bye hym a perle was mascellez. *Ibid.* 780 A makelez may & maskellez.

masclin(e, -yne, obs. forms of MASLIN.

mascobado, variant of MUSCOVADO.

mascon ('mæskɒn). *Astr.* [f. *mass con*centration.] One of the concentrations of denser material thought to exist under some lunar maria, discovered as a result of the

variations they produce in the speed of an orbiting satellite; also, a similar region on another planet.

1968 MULLER & SJOGREN in *Science* 16 Aug. 680/1 The Urey-Gilbert theory of lunar history has predicted such large-scale high-density mass concentrations below these maria, which, for convenience, we shall call mascons. **1969** *Times* 22 Feb. 7/7 Exactly what the mascons are has puzzled selenologists since the discovery last year, and one explanation is that they are the remnants of enormous meteorites. **1969** *Sci. Jrnl.* May 61/1 The so-called mascons extend laterally for 50 to 200 km, are about 5 km thick and lie at a depth of between about 50 and 100 km. **1971** *Nature* 26 Nov. 168/2 The following findings were announced... Gravitational anomalies which may be caused by martian mascons. **1973** J. STRONG *Search the Solar Syst.* x. 104 Density anomalies, or 'mascons' on the Moon were located by their disturbance of the lunar orbiters.

mascot ('mæskɒt). Also 9 **mascotte**. [ad. provincial F. *mascotte*, perh. cogn. with mod.Pr. *masco* witch. The word was brought into notice by E. Audran's opera 'La Mascotte', played 29 Dec. 1880.] A person, or a thing, animate or inanimate, supposed to bring luck.

1881 FARNIE & REECE *Mascotte* I. 4 Ah! blest their lot whom fate shall send A true Mascotte, a fairy friend!.. Luck's his for ever! **1884** *Lisbon* (Dakota) *Clipper* 11 Dec. 7 This dining room girl..lays claim to being a mascot. **1899** E. PHILLPOTTS *Human Boy* 118 That rat's a sort of 'mascotte' to me. A 'mascotte' 's a thing that brings luck. **1918** E. M. ROBERTS *Flying Fighter* 328 Each man had his own little fetish. It was known as the pocket-piece or mascot. In some cases it might be a dice or a playing-card. .. In other cases it might be a locket, then again a medal, while many of us carried little wooden dolls. **1921** R. HICHENS *Spirit of Time* vi. 106 'She says you brought her luck.'.. 'I didn't know I was a mascot,' he remarked. **1955** *Halsbury's Statutory Instruments* II. 2276 No mascot shall be carried by a motor vehicle..where it is likely to strike any person with whom the vehicle may collide. **1975** *Times* 6 June 17/4 Christie's..launched a new collecting field yesterday with a sale of motoring mascots, the figurines mounted on car bonnets.

attrib. **1898** *Speaker* 31 Dec. 783/2 His mascot snakes that were kept, buried in flannel, in an oblong glass-topped box.

'mascotism. [-ISM.] = next.

1924 W. J. LOCKE *Coming of Amos* viii. 94 If there is anything in luck, in mascotism or anti-mascotism, one might have reason to believe that Amos..had the most maleficent of influences.

mascotry ('mæskɒtrɪ). [f. MASCOT + -RY.] Attachment to or belief in mascots; the use of mascots.

1916 *Church Times* 7 Apr. 332/4 Mascotry,..the growing superstition with regard to mascots. **1923** *Sunday at Home* May 504/3 There is a worse aspect of mascotry than mere folly,..for mascotry is, in its essence, simply idolatry.

†**mascue**, *v. Obs.* Also 5 **maskowe, maskewe, mascall**. [Variant of MACHECOLE *v.*] *trans.* To machicolate.

1412-20 LYDG. *Chron. Troy* II. xx. (1513) M iv, Theyr wall mascued and agayne our skalys Truste[t]h theron made great ordynaunce. **1421** —— *Thebes* (E.E.T.S.) 2757 [Ethiocles] maskowed his walles and his heghe tours. **1461** *Rolls of Parlt.* V. 493/2 To enbatell, carnell, mascall, or to make eny Toure, Castell or Forteresse.

mascul: see MASCLE *a. Obs.*

mascularity (mæskju:'lærɪtɪ). *rare.* [f. L. *mascul-us* + -AR + -ITY.] = MASCULINITY.

1817 N. DRAKE *Shaks.* II. 67 The subsequent sonnets.. bear the strongest..testimony to the mascularity of the person addressed. **1853** KANE *Grinnell Exp.* xlvi. (1856) 425 To some the unmentionables might savor of mascularity.

'masculate, *v. rare.* [f. L. *mascul-us* (see MALE *a.*) + -ATE.] *trans.* To make masculine.

1623 COCKERAM, *Masculate*, to make strong. **1812** SOUTHEY *Omniana* II. 56, I am not sure (he adds) whether in time it may not perfectly masculate the sex.

†**'masculated**, *a. Her. Obs.* [f. Anglo-L. *mascul-a* MASCLE + -ATE + -ED[1].] = MASCULY.

1486 *Bk. St. Albans, Her.* c v, This cros is called a cros masculatit for he is made of masculys.

masculation (mæskju:'leɪʃən). [f. L. *mascul-us* male + -ATION.] Artificial fertilization (of plants).

1855-6 R. F. BURTON *El Medinah* (1861) II. 202 January and February are the months for the masculation of the palm. **1859** —— *Centr. Afr.* in *Jrnl. Geog. Soc.* XXIX. 368 Bees also swarm in the jungles, performing an important part in the vegetable economy by masculation or caprification, and the conveyance of pollen.

mascule, masculée: see MASCLE, MASCULY.

masculine ('mæskjʊlɪn), *a.* and *sb.* Also 4, 6 **masculin**, 6 **masculyne**, 7 **masculen**. [a. F. *masculin, -ine*, ad. L. *masculīn-us* f. *mascul-us*: see MALE *a.* and -INE.] **A.** *adj.*

1. Of persons or animals: Belonging to the male sex; male. Now *rare.*

c **1374** CHAUCER *Boeth.* II. Pr. iii. 28 (Camb. MS.) The oportunite and noblesse of thi masculyn chyldren þat is to seyn thi sones. **1398** TREVISA *Barth. De P.R.* IV. vii. (1495) 91 Yf a woman that is with a chylde masculyn be sodenly callyd, she meuyth first the ryght fote. **1545** RAYNOLD *Byrth Mankynde* 90 Yf the ryghte breste slake or flagge, the masculyne or male byrth is in parell: yf the lefte, the female byrthe. **1604** in *Eng. Gilds* (1870) 432 The lord shall haue his best oxe or cowe and all his masculen horses. **1606** SHAKS. *Tr. & Cr.* v. i. 20 *Patro.* Male Varlot you Rogue? What's that? *Ther.* Why his masculine Whore. **1614** TAILOR *Hog hath lost* II. D, Could any Masculine flatterer on earth So far bewitch thee, to forget thy selfe, As now to leaue me? **1661** LOVELL *Hist. Anim. & Min.* 55 The Masculine, or male Goat. **1667** MILTON *P.L.* x. 890 O why did God..that peopl'd highest Heav'n With Spirits Masculine, create at last..this fair defect Of Nature. **1688** *Lond. Gaz.* No. 2348/1 God Almighty, as we hope and pray, will grant You an Heir Masculine of your Body.

b. With reference to the vegetable kingdom: = MALE *a.* 2.

1691 RAY *Creation* I. (1692) 97 The Flowers serve to cherish..the masculine or prolifick Seed contained in the Chives or Apices of the Stamina.

†**2.** Said of inanimate objects to which the male sex was attributed on the ground of some quality, e.g. relative superiority, strength, activity, etc. ***masculine hour*** (*Astrol.*): one ruled by a masculine planet. *Obs.*

1590 SPENSER *F.Q.* II. ix. 22 The one [*sc.* the triangle] imperfect, mortall, fœminine, Th' other [*sc.* the circle] immortall, perfect, masculine. **1601** HOLLAND *Pliny* I. 44 Wee haue been taught, that this Planet [the Sun] is Masculine, frying and sucking vp the humidity of all things. **1613** M. RIDLEY *Magn. Bodies* 82 The Adamant is Masculine unto his beloved the Iron and Steele, and these are Feminine. **1621** BURTON *Anat. Mel.* I. ii. IV. vii. (1651) 167 The Emperor would not touch his new Bride, till an Astrologer had told him a masculine hour. **1696** PHILLIPS, *Masculine Planets or Signs*, are those which excel in active Qualities, that is, Heat and Coldness. **1819** J. WILSON *Dict. Astrol.* 285 Fortunately all the masculine planets are diurnal. *Ibid.* 286 Masculine signs.

†**b.** ***masculine frankincense, gum*** = *male incense* (see MALE *a.* 9). *Obs.*

1555 EDEN *Decades* 79 A greate barell of woodde full of moste excellente masculine frankensence. **1603** B. JONSON *K. Jas.'s Entertainm.* (1604) D 2 Heere no wight To sacrifice, saue my deuotion comes, That brings, insteed of those thy Masculine gummes. My Cities heart.

c. The designation of a choice kind of apricot.

1629 PARKINSON *Parad. in Sole* (1656) 579 The Mascoline Apricock. **1718** J. LAWRENCE *Fruit-g. Kalendar* 78 The latter end of this Month [June] the Masculine Aprecot is ripe. **1860** HOGG *Fruit Man.* 41 Red Masculine [Apricot].

3. *Gram.* Of or pertaining to the gender to which appellations of males normally belong.

a **1380** *St. Theodora* 110 in Horstm. *Altengl. Leg.* (1878) 36 Hire name, þat was femynyn Of gendre, heo turned in to masculyn. **1387-8** T. USK *Test. Love* II. iii. (Skeat) I. 14 No mo genders ben there but masculyn and femenyne. **1530** PALSGR. Introd. 24 A substantive of the masculyne gender. **1612** I. BRINSLEY *Lud. Lit.* 128 Hee can shew it, to bee the Masculine Gender, because in wordes of three terminations, the first is the Masculine, the second the Feminine, the third is the Neuter. **1875** *Expositor* 171 Sun and sea and streams had, in the infancy of the world, masculine and feminine names.

b. *Prosody.* ***masculine rime***: in French versification, a rime between lines ending in stressed syllables, as opposed to the 'feminine rime' ending in a mute *e*. Hence *gen.* a 'single' rime on a stressed syllable. (Cf. MALE *a.* 7.)

1581 SIDNEY *Apol. Poetrie* (Arb.) 71 Euen the very ryme it selfe, the Italian cannot put in the last silable, by the French named the Masculine ryme. **1727-41** CHAMBERS *Cycl.* s.v. *Rhyme*, Masculine Rhymes are those of all other words [than such as end with an *e* mute]. **1844** [see FEMININE 6 b]. **1870** LOWELL *Study Wind.* (1871) 201 The verses of the first [stanza] have all of them masculine rhymes. **1891** J. C. PARSONS *Eng. Versif.* 44 Rhyme between final syllables is called single or masculine rhyme.

4. Pertaining to the male sex; peculiar to or assigned to males; consisting of males.

1601 SHAKS. *Twel. N.* v. i. 257 If nothing lets to make vs happie both, But this my masculine vsurp'd attyre: [etc.]. **1616** H. GOSNOLD in *Lismore Papers* Ser. II. (1887) II. 20 We ioyne in our thankfull commendaccons to ye all, congratulating of your masculin increase. *a* **1618** RALEIGH *Prerog. Parl.* (1628) 10 Hee was soone after slaine in Ireland, and his whole Masculine race, ten yeres extinguished. **1655** FULLER *Ch. Hist.* II. i. §4 The People of the same Place.. erected a Masculine Church (Women being interdicted the Entrance thereof). **1781** COWPER *Hope* 686 Whether at the toilet of the fair He laughed and trifled..Or if in masculine debate he shared. **1790** GIBBON *Misc. Wks.* (1814) III. 360 The genuine masculine descent of the Princes of Brunswick must be explored beyond the Alps. **1801** CHARLOTTE SMITH *Lett. Solit. Wand.* II. 317 She assumed masculine attire. **1880** H. C. COOTE *Eng. Gild Knights* 17 That peculiar fashion of devolution which the Normans had introduced —masculine primogeniture.

5. Having the appropriate excellences of the male sex; manly, virile; vigorous, powerful. Rarely of persons; usually of attributes, actions, or productions.

1629 H. BURTON (*title*) Babel no Bethel... In answer to.. two masculine Champions for the Synagogue of Rome. **1639** N. N. tr. *Du Bosq's Compl. Woman* I. 35 Masculine spirits very easily resist this tyrannie. **1647** CLARENDON *Contempl. on Ps.* Tracts (1727) 433 The argumentation of Manoah's wife..might very well have become the more masculine understanding. **1678** WANLEY *Wond. Lit. World* v. ii. §89. 473/1 He proved a stout and masculine Prince. *a* **1704** T. BROWN *Eng. Sat.* Wks. 1730 I. 28 His heat was masculine and always pointed against vice. **1712** ADDISON *Spect.* No. 363 ¶ 10 Adam's Speech abounds with Thoughts ..of a more masculine and elevated Turn. **1756-82** J. WARTON *Ess. Pope* (ed. 4) I. vii. 401 *note*, The forcible and masculine images with which the ancients strengthened their compositions. **1829** LYTTON *Devereux* I. iv, I grew more gentle, and he more masculine. **1850** BLACKIE *Æschylus* I. Pref. 6 Aeschylus..was famous..for the fearless, masculine licence with which he handled the most flexible of all languages. **1856** EMERSON *Eng. Traits, Lit.* Wks. (Bohn) II. 105, I find..the whole writing of the time charged with a masculine force and freedom.

†**b.** Of material things or physical qualities: Powerful in action, strong. (Cf. 2.) *Obs.*

1637 T. MORTON *New Eng. Canaan* (1883) 188 [Herbes] of a more maskuline vertue than any of the same species in England. **1664** BEALE *Aphor. Cider* §57 in Evelyn *Pomona* 29 Let the Cider be..Masculine and in full body, yet..well tasted of the Apple. **1675** EVELYN *Earth* (1676) 66 Let this pulveriz'd Earth..be expos'd for a Summer and a Winter to the vicissitudes and changes of the seasons..you will find it will have obtain'd such a generous and masculine pregnancy,..as [etc.]. **1728** EARBERY tr. *Burnet's St. Dead* II. 45 The true Fertility that brings Corn to a Masculine Perfection, is in Countries far from the Equinox.

6. Of a woman, her qualities or attributes: Having the capacities, manners, appearance, or tastes appropriate to the male sex. †***masculine-feminine***: a 'mannish' woman. *Obs.*

1617 MORYSON *Itin.* III. 1 The masculine women of the Low Countries vse to make voyages for trafficke. **1620** (*title*) Hic Mulier: or, The Man-Woman: Being a Medicine to cure the Coltish Disease of the Staggers in the Masculine-Feminines of our Times. **1766** FORDYCE *Serm. Yng. Wom.* (1767) I. iii. 104 A masculine woman must be naturally an unamiable creature. **1801** STRUTT *Sp. & Past.* Introd. §43. 48 Some of these masculine females have occasionally made their appearance. **1808** *Spirit Pub. Jrnls.* XI. 86 That masculine feminine, the late Princess Dashkoff. **1838** THIRLWALL *Greece* V. 279 She was a woman of masculine spirit.

Comb. **1683** TRYON *Way to Health* xi. (1697) 192 Neither are any [Women] so..Masculine Spirited. **1899** CROCKETT *Kit Kennedy* 207 A..masculine-looking woman.

B. *sb.*

1. That which is of the male sex.

c **1550** *Schole-House Women* 342 in Hazl. *E.P.P.* IV. 118 And all that euer they may imagine, Is to alure the masculine. **1621** LADY M. WROTH *Urania* 16 They stept back in wonder to see that beautie, which yet in the masculine they came neere to. **1650** BULWER *Anthropomet.* 87 Nature makes the Masculine perfect.

2. A person of the male sex.

1652 GAULE *Magastrom.* 265 If he had abused himselfe with a masculine..he was forced..to kill himselfe. **1739** G. OGLE *Gualtherus & Griselda* 107 You, the Masculine, to Labour bred. **1886** BYNNER *A. Surriage* xxvii. 306, I shall be ill at ease among such an array of masculines. **1890** F. W. ROBINSON *Very Strange Family* 63 She flounced out of the room and left the masculines to themselves.

b. *transf.* of the signs of the zodiac. (Cf. A. 2.)

1653 R. SANDERS *Physiogn.* 7 Of these Signs, the masculines are fiery and aiery, the Feminines earthly and watery.

3. *Gram.* The masculine gender; a word or form of the masculine gender.

1530 PALSGR. 67 As *consile, miracle* be masculynes. *Ibid.* 70 All adjectives whose masculyn gendre endith in *e*, have their masculynes and femynines all one. **1607** TOPSELL *Four-f. Beasts* (1658) 90 The plurall of the Masculine is Zebaim, and of the feminine Zebaoth. **1612** [see FEMININE B. 2]. **1872** MORRIS *Eng. Accid.* 83 There are three ways of distinguishing the masculine and feminine in English.

masculinely ('mæskjʊlɪnlɪ), *adv.* [f. MASCULINE *a.* + -LY[2].] In a masculine manner. Also, in the masculine gender.

1611 B. JONSON *Catiline* III. iii. H b, You haue done most masculinely within, And plaid the Orator. **1627** W. SCLATER *Exp. 2 Thess.* (1629) 230 Whither hee meanes masculinely, *that euill one*, the diuell..or rather *euill worke* ..is no matter of curious inquiry. **1732** J. WHALEY *Poems* 48 The Face was masculinely hard. **1865** *Sat. Rev.* 29 Apr. 514/1 A man..who can admit that an author's style is.. masculinely vigorous and sublime, and yet cannot admire it!

†**b.** In the male line. *Obs.*

1658 WALTON *Life of Donne* (ed. 2) 5 His Father was masculinely..descended from a very ancient Family.

c. Of riming: cf. MASCULINE *a.* 3 b.

1837-9 HALLAM *Hist. Lit.* I. I. i §30. 26 All the lines in each stanza rhyming masculinely with each other.

masculineness ('mæskjʊlɪnnɪs). [f. MASCULINE *a.* + -NESS.] The quality of being masculine.

1662 J. SPARROW tr. *Behme's Rem. Wks., Consid. upon Stiefel* 16 His Sprout groweth in Gods Kingdome;..Not in Adams Masculinenesse. **1806** W. TAYLOR in *Ann. Rev.* IV. 250 All the excesses of masculineness broke loose and overspread the country. **1901** *Daily News* 9 Mar. 6/1 She affects a masculineness of diction which [etc.].

masculinism ('mæskjʊlɪnɪz(ə)m). *rare.* [f. MASCULINE *a.* + -ISM.] **a.** Tendency to masculine physical traits in a woman. **b.** Advocacy of the rights of men.

1895 [see INFANTILISM]. **1916** H. ELLIS *Essays in War-Time* viii. 88 The advocates of Woman's Rights have seldom been met by the charge that they were unjustly encroaching on the Rights of Man. Feminism has never encountered an aggressive and self-conscious Masculinism.

masculinist ('mæskjʊlɪnɪst). [f. MASCULINE *a.* + -IST.] **1.** An advocate of men's rights, opp. FEMINIST *sb.* Cf. HOMINIST.

1918 V. WOOLF *Writer's Diary* (1953) 6 He [*sc.* Milton] was the first of the masculinists. **1967** *Times* 13 Oct. 8 No militant masculinists stooped to conquer; indeed almost the only men to be seen on the premises, apart from the staff, were male journalists invited to help celebrate the occasion.

2. A person of the female sex who adopts or affects characteristics or qualities usually thought of as masculine.

1928 *Daily Express* 11 July 5/3 The suffragists modelled their appearance, their manners, and their education on that of boys and men... They were, in short, thorough-going masculinists.

3. *attrib.*

1951 R. Campbell *Light on Dark Horse* xvii. 257 Bloomsbury still awaits its 'masculinist' Messiah.

masculinity (mæskjuːˈlɪnɪtɪ). [ad. F. *masculinité*, f. *masculin*: see MASCULINE and -ITY.]

1. The quality or condition of being masculine.

1748 T. Ruddiman *Dissertation* 42 Besides the Prerogative of his Sex, or Masculinity (as the French call it). 1865 *Sat. Rev.* 21 Oct. 527/1 The obnoxious airs of masculinity affected by some of his countrywomen. 1882 *Athenæum* No. 2867. 462 It is not easy to see why *courbe, tangente, parallèle*, are given as exceptions to the masculinity of 'parts of speech when taken substantively'. 1898 Bodley *France* II. IV. ii. 354 Some.. inheriting, too, the masculinity of that illustrious princess.

b. *pl.* Things characteristic of the male sex.

1877 Mrs. Oliphant *Carita* II. xxiv. 144 That furtive cigars and other precocious masculinities were not criminal.

2. That which is masculine.

1860 Geo. Eliot *Mill on Fl.* I. v, This pink-and-white bit of masculinity with the indeterminate features.

masculinization (ˌmæskjʊlɪnaɪˈzeɪʃən). [f. next: see -IZATION.] The action of MASCULINIZE *v.* (in either sense); the process of becoming masculine; also, a masculine state or condition.

1895 H. James *Notebks.* (1947) iv. 196 There is a big comprehensive subject in the *avènement*, or rather in the masculinization of women. 1922 F. H. A. Marshall *Physiology of Reproduction* (ed. 2) xv. 696 (*caption*) Masculinisation of guinea pig. 1924 *Glasgow Herald* 24 Dec. 4 The masculinisation of woman deprives society of a 'precious asset'. 1927 *19th Cent.* Aug. 266 We find him throwing all his authority against the masculinisation prevalent in our schools. 1952 Srb & Owen *Gen. Genetics* xiv. 287 Freemartins are sterile, and show considerable masculinization in a number of traits. 1970 *Sci. Jrnl.* June 50/2 They are of course normal genetic and anatomical females on whom the male sex hormones from their adrenals have imposed a false masculinization. 1971 *Daily Tel.* (Colour Suppl.) 10 Dec. 18/2 In the production of millions of children a year, it is not surprising that occasionally nature's complex technology should break down to produce an imbalance of hormones with masculinisation of the female foetus or feminisation of the male.

masculinize (ˈmæskjʊlɪnaɪz), *v.* [f. MASCULIN(E *a.* + -IZE.] *trans.* **a.** To render masculine or more masculine in nature, form, or character.

1912 Mme Moret tr. *A. Moret's Kings & Gods Egypt* i. 29 She even tried to change the very name she had received at her birth and to masculinise it by omitting the feminine ending. 1927 C. C. Martindale *Relig. of World* 19 The first way in which Brahmā could be '*thought*', was, as sufficiently 'masculinised' (Brahmā) to be a god, supreme, yet to that extent specified.

b. *Biol.* To induce male sexual characteristics in.

1924, 1962 [see FEMINIZE *v.* 2]. 1971 *Daily Tel.* (Colour Suppl.) 10 Dec. 21/3 The amount of androgen required for normal masculinizing of the brain is greater than that required to masculinize the genitalia.

Hence **ˈmasculinized** *ppl. a.*, **ˈmasculinizing** *ppl. a.* and *vbl. sb.*

1927 *Daily Express* 28 Sept. 8/7 The second type of masculinised female is the politically-minded woman. 1928 *Sunday Express* 19 Aug. 5 'The Cinderella Man'.. was a masculinised version of the old story. 1936, 1939 [see ANDROGEN]. 1961 M. F. A. Montagu *Genetic Mechanisms in Human Dis.* xii. 113 Completely masculinised genetic females are almost common, forming something like 1 in 40 of the masculine population. 1970 *Nature* 3 Oct. 94/2 In the glow-worm *Lampyris* the apical cells of the testis produce a masculinizing hormone.

masculinoid (ˈmæskjʊlɪnɔɪd), *a.* [f. MASCULIN(E *a.* + -OID.] Masculine (but not male); of male form or appearance.

1921 [see ADRENAL *a.* and *sb.* A]. 1923 J. S. Huxley *Ess. Biologist* iv. 145 The 'masculinoid' woman (to use the current jargon) tends physically also to be less feminine.., while the 'feminoid' man shows the reverse tendency.

†**mascull**, *a. Obs.* Also 5 maskyll. [Of obscure origin: ? identical with MASCLE *a.*] ***tun mascull***: some variety of the tun (liquid measure).

1432 *Rolls Parlt.* IV. 405/2 ['The wynes of Gascoigne and Guyen' had only 4 or 5 inches of lees] in a tonne maskyll. 1531 in *Sel. Pleas Admiralty* (Selden Soc.) I. 36 Accounting always a ton mascull for a ton, ij pipes for a ton, [etc.].

masculo- (ˈmæskjʊləʊ), used as combining form of L. *mascul-us* male. **ˈmasculo-ˈfeminine** *a.*, partly masculine and partly feminine. **ˈmasculo-ˈnucleus** *Embryology* (see quot. 1884); hence **ˈmasculo-ˈnuclear** *a.*, pertaining to a masculo-nucleus.

1646 Sir T. Browne *Pseud. Ep.* III. xvii. 149 Hermaphroditicall and masculo-feminine generations. 1830 Lyell *Princ. Geol.* I. 11 One.. fiction of the Egyptian mythology was the supposed intervention of a masculo-feminine principle. 1884 Hyatt in *Proc. Boston Soc. Nat. Hist* XXIII. 54 We propose.. to call the original undifferentiated generative body the nucleus, and its products respectively the male or masculonucleus, and the female or feminonucleus.

masculonge: see MUSKELLUNGE.

†**ˈmasculous**, *a. Obs. rare.* [f. L. *mascul-us* male + -OUS.] = MASCULINE *a.*

1619 Balcanqual *Lett.* in *Hales' Gold. Rem.* II. (1673) 117 It was learned, devout, and the stile masculous. 1633 W. Struther *True Happines* 101 This is not only the language of Canaan, but also the masculous Schiboleth.

masculy (ˈmæskjʊlɪ), *a. Her.* Also 9 masculée, mascally. [f. **mascule*, MASCLE + -Y.] Covered with mascle-shaped figures.

a 1550 in *Baring-Gould & Twigge's West. Armory* (1898) 4 *Belmarsh*.. Gul: masculy arg: 4, 3, 2, 1. 1562 Leigh *Armorie* (1597) 35 b, Vert a crosse Masculy Argent. 1610 Guillim *Heraldry* v. iv. (1632) 377 Masculy, that is.. Mascle-waies. 1864 Boutell *Her. Hist. & Pop.* xv. 196 Shields *masculée*.. may have been intended by early Heralds to indicate Difference. 1869 W. S. Ellis *Antiq. of Her.* viii. 163 *note*, We see on the wings.. the mascally pattern. 1878 Burke *Gen. Armory* 819/2 *Powges*, Ar. masculy sa.

mascun, obs. form of MASON.

mascurado, obs. variant of MASQUERADE.

mascy tinter, obs. form of MEZZOTINTO.

Masdeu (masdø). [See quot. 1851.] A sweet firm-bodied wine of a dark colour and mellow flavour produced at a vineyard in the South of France.

1851 C. Redding *Hist. Mod. Wines* (ed. 3) vi. 154 This wine is not a factitious French port from the harbour of Cette... It is a genuine production called Masdeu, from the vineyard which produces it, between Perpignan and Collioure. 1903 *Whitaker's Almanack* 453 Of wines imported in casks the following are the usual measurements: Pipe of Port or Masdeu = 115 gallons, [etc.]. 1958 A. L. Simon *Dict. Wines* 108/1 *Masdeu*, red, fortified wines of Roussillon, very popular in England in early Victorian days. Also written *Masdu* and *Masdieu*. 1965 O. A. Mendelsohn *Dict. Drink* 214 *Masdeu*, French (Roussillon) red dessert wine.

masdevallia (mæsdɪˈvælɪə). [mod.L. (H. Ruiz Lopez & J. Pavon *Floræ Peruvianæ et Chilensis Prodromus* (1794) 122), f. the name of Jose *Masdevall* (d. 1801), Spanish physician and botanist + -IA[1].] An epiphytic orchid of the large genus so called, belonging to the family Orchidaceæ and native to the cool, mountainous regions of South America.

1845 *Curtis's Bot. Mag.* LXXI. 4164 Windowed Masdevallia... is one of the very curious productions of nature. 1896 F. H. Woolward *Genus Masdevallia* 1 The first *Masdevallia* known to science was.. discovered by the Spanish botanists, Ruiz and Pavon, in the Andes of Peru, during their residence in that country from 1777 to 1794. 1911 *Encycl. Brit.* XX. 172/1 *Masdevallia* is common in cultivation and has often brilliant scarlet, crimson or orange flowers. 1970 B. & W. Rittershausen *Pop. Orchids* ix. 211 The flower [of *Masdevallia muscosa*] is of a translucent yellow colour, the lip being somewhat large for Masdevallias.

†**mase**, *sb. Obs. rare.* Also masse. [a. G. *mase* (now *dial.*); cf. MASERS.] A spot, freckle.

1527 Andrew *Brunswyke's Distyll. Waters* F iv b, The same water.. withdryveth the spottys and masses oute of the face. *Ibid.* L ij b, Mases.

mase (meɪz), *v.* [Back-formation from MASER, the ending *-er* being treated as the suffix -ER[1] of agent nouns.] *intr.* To LASE, esp. in the microwave part of the spectrum. Hence **ˈmasing** *vbl. sb.*

1962 *Engineering* 2 Feb. 191 The device 'mases' 30 per cent of the time. 1962 *New Scientist* 1 Mar. 486 One knows when the alignment is good enough only by the fact that the device starts to 'mase'. 1964 *Encycl. Sci. Suppl.* (Grolier) 308/1 Many substances have been made to 'mase' and 'lase'—that is, to behave like masers or lasers. 1966 Smith & Sorokin *Laser* vii. 369 At this point the stage was nearly set for the actual achievement of an injection maser. The main remaining question was: in what sort of a structure could masing action be achieved? 1973 *Nature* 21/28 Dec. 468/1 Since none of the CH lines have so far been seen in absorption, irrespective of the nature of the source where they have been found, one is led to believe that all transitions are masing weakly.

mase, obs. form of MACE, MAZE, MEASE, MESS.

masedliche, obs. form of MAZEDLY.

maseer, obs. form of MAZER; var. MAHSEER.

masel, masele(y)n(e: see MEASLE, MASLIN[1].

maseliche, obs. form of MAZILY.

†**maselin.** *Obs.* [a. OF. *maselin*, also *mazerin*, *maderin*, f. *mazre*, *madre*, bowl of maple-wood.] A bowl of maple-wood; = MAZER.

a 1290 *S. Eustace* 395 in Horstm. *Altengl. Leg.* (1881) 219 Men beden him sittan and drinken vin Wiþ coupe and eke wiþ maselin. *c* 1330 *Arth. & Merl.* (Kölbing) 6944 Plater, disse, cop & maseline. *c* 1386 Chaucer *Sir Thopas* 141 They sette hym first sweete wyn And Mede eek in a Mazelyn.

maselinges, obs. form of MEASLINGS.

maseljohn, obs. form of MASLIN[2].

maselyd, obs. form of MEASLED.

maselyn, -yn(n)e, obs. forms of MASLIN[1].

masement, variant of MAZEMENT.

masendewe, -due: see MEASONDUE, hospital.

maser (ˈmeɪzə(r)). [An acronym: see quot. 1955[2].] A laser, esp. one that emits microwaves.

The first masers emitted microwaves. Later ones emitted in other parts of the spectrum, and these were also called masers for a time until *laser* came to be adopted as the general name for all such devices.

1955 *Sci. News Let.* 5 Feb. 83/1 Scientists can, for the first time, generate microwaves of extremely high frequency by tapping directly the energy of molecules, Dr. Charles H. Townes of Columbia University's physics department reported in New York. His device for doing so is known as the 'maser'. *Ibid.*, Work on the maser began three years ago. 1955 Gordon, Zeiger, & Townes in *Physical Rev.* 15 Aug. 1264/1 The device utilizes a molecular beam in which molecules in the excited state of a microwave transition are selected. Interaction between these excited molecules and a microwave field produces additional radiation and hence amplification by stimulated emission. We call an apparatus utilizing this technique a 'maser', which is an acronym for 'microwave amplification by stimulated emission of radiation'. 1958 Schawlow & Townes in *Ibid.* 15 Dec. 1940 (*heading*) Infrared and optical masers. 1960 *Times* 17 Oct. 2/2 (Advt.), Development work on existing long range programmes in: solid-state millimetre and optical masers, parametric amplifiers, [etc.]. 1960, 1962 [see LASER[2]]. 1962 *Engineering* 2 Feb. 190/2 The basic type of maser, from which the principle of *optical* masers is derived, is a quite recent electron device... Research later extended the upper frequency range of this technique of low-noise signal amplification, until it eventually reached the visible region—giving rise to the optical maser, otherwise known as the laser. 1967 T. P. Melia *Introd. Masers & Lasers* iv. 34 The power output of the ammonia maser is very small (about 10^{-10} watt) but the frequency stability is of the order of 1 in 10^{12} over a 1 minute period and 1 part in 10^{10} over very much longer periods. 1968 *Nature* 30 Mar. 1237/2 (*heading*) Is interstellar hydrogen capable of maser action at 21 centimetres? 1969 S. G. & H. Lipson *Optical Physics* xi. 369 A maser is, of course, a very-narrow-band amplifier; it is because of its narrow band that the noise-level achieved is very low, since there is a theoretical minimum noise-level per unit band-width. 1972 *Sci. Amer.* Sept. 136/3 The greatest contributor.. to the receiver's ability to handle Telstar's faint signals (about 10^{-12} watt) was a maser amplifier that combined very high gain with extremely low noise.

maser, variant of MAZER.

†**masers.** *Obs.* [a. G. *masern*.] = MEASLES.

1561 Hollybush *Hom. Apoth.* 41 b, Variole is a disease that noyeth children greatly called Pockes and Masers.

mash (mæʃ), *sb.*[1] Forms: 1 másc-, máx- (in Comb. *máscwyrt*, *máxwyrt*), 5 **masche**, 6–7 **mashe**, 6–9 **mesh**, 6– **mash**. See also MASH-FAT. [OE. *másc-*, *máx-*, corresponds to late MHG., mod.G. *meisch* masc., crushed grapes for wine-making, infused malt for beer (also, in 15th c. coupled with *met* mead, in a gloss for L. *mulsum*), and to Sw. *mäsk*, Da. *mask*, grains for pigs. It has been variously regarded as related by ablaut to OE. *miscian* to MIX, and as cogn. w. OSl. *mězga* sap.]

1. a. *Brewing.* Malt mixed with hot water to form wort.

[*c* 1000: see *mash-wort* in 5 below. 1335, etc.: see MASH-FAT.] 1587 Harrison *England* II. vi. 169/2 in *Holinshed*, She letteth her mash run till the malt be left without liquor. 1729 G. Smith *Fermentation* 28 Some farther sprinkle the top of the Mash over with dry Malt ground. 1742 *Lond. & Country Brew.* I. (ed. 4) 23 The Malt.. is worked by several Men with Oars.. and is called the first and stiff Mash. 1830 M. Donovan *Dom. Econ.* I. 151 The first mash is agitated and allowed to rest during a longer period than the second. 1889 Barnard *Noted Breweries* I. 241 The grist is covered with water a second and sometimes even a third time, the extract being always called a 'mash'.

†**b.** *transf.* The substance upon which the liquor is poured in lixiviation. (Cf. MASH *v.*[1] 1 c.) *Obs.*

1775 *New Hampsh. Prov. Papers* (1873) VII. 653 The Liquor may then be.. put on another mash [in the making of salt petre].

2. A mixture of boiled grain, bran or meal, etc., given as a warm food to horses and cattle. Also with qualifying word, as ***bran-mash***: see BRAN.

1577 B. Googe *Heresbach's Husb.* III. (1586) 131 Graines .. mingled with Floure, fried Beanes, and meale of Lentyls all stirred together, and giuen him in a mash. 1614 B. Jonson *Barth. Fair* IV. iii, How now! my Galloway Nag, the staggers? ha!.. I'le gi' him a mash, presently, shall take away this dizzinesse. 1669 Worlidge *Syst. Agric.* (1681) 328 A Mash, or Mesh; Ground-Corn, or such like, boiled in Water for Cattle to eat. 1726 Swift *Gulliver* IV. ii, So that each Horse and Mare eat.. their own Mash of Oats and Milk. 1844 Stephens *Bk. of Farm* §1558 The mash [for farm-horses] consists of either steamed potatoes, boiled barley or oats, mixed sometimes with bran. 1881 Besant & Rice *Chapl. of Fleet* II. xix, [He] was.. superintending the preparation of a warm mash for his hack.

3. a. *gen.* Something reduced to a soft pulpy consistence, by beating or crushing, by mixing with or steeping in water, etc.

1598 Florio, *Mescola*,.. a medlie, a mixture, a blending, a mesh, a hochpoch. 1658 A. Fox *Wurtz' Surg.* III. xxiii. 291 Boil it [flesh] again to a mash... Then spread that mash on a thick cloth, apply it like a Cataplasm. 1690 N. Lee

Massacre of Paris v. ii. 45 With this mangled flesh held to Heav'n, This horrid mash of Blood, and Bone, and Marrow.. I beg the Power Divine [etc.]. **1701** Penn in *Pa. Hist. Soc. Mem.* IX. 50 An empty pipe or two to put the mash of the apples in. **1771** Smollett *Humph. Cl.* 8 June, The pallid, contaminated mash, which they call strawberries; soiled and tossed by greasy paws through twenty baskets crusted with dirt; and then presented with the worst milk. *Ibid.* 13 July, One of his great toes was crushed into a mash. **1816** L. Towne *Farmer & Grazier's Guide* 13 After the Grass has been chewed over again, it is reduced to a kind of Mash, not unlike boiled Spinach. **1880** J. Payn *Confid. Agent* II. 107 The streets are one mash of snow.

transf. **1852** Surtees *Sponge's Sp. Tour* viii. 33 He [a huntsman who had had many injuries from falls] was a complete mash of a man.

b. *fig.* A confused mixture; also, a muddle, 'hash'. (Cf. mish-mash.)

1598 B. Jonson *Ev. Man in Hum.* iv. xi, *Bray.* I haue made a faire mash on't. **1851** Helps *Comp. Solit.* vi. (1874) 85 Our charity is so mixed up in a mash of sentiment and sickly feeling. **1861** Thornbury *Turner* (1862) II. 163 His will is an extraordinary mash of grammar.

c. (without article.) The state of being mashed or reduced to a soft mass. *lit.* and *fig.* Chiefly in ***to beat, boil,*** etc. ***to mash, in mash.***

1630 Lord *Banians* 88 Some [of the earth's inhabitants] blowne from the tops of high mountains, other bruised to mash. **16..** *Ballad of Robin Hood & Tanner* xxi. in Child *Ballads* III. 138/2 For here we may thresh our bones all to mesh, And get no coyn at all. **1691** J. Wilson *Belphegor* iii. iv, She 'as beaten me to mash. **1693** Dryden *Let.* Wks. 1893 XVIII. 111 Buy me a sieve-full [of damsons] to preserve whole, and not in mash. **1751** Lady Luxborough *Let. to Shenstone* 5 Sept., The paper is boiled to mash. **1760–72** H. Brooke *Fool of Qual.* (1809) II. 115 [He] dashed all the eggs into mash. **1839** J. Rayson *Poems* (1858) 34 But we've a gipsy creature here In vice will bang them aw to mash.

d. *slang.* Mashed potatoes; esp. in the phr. ***sausage(s) and mash.***

1904 A. E. W. Mason *Truants* xxii. 213, I..go into a public-house..and have a sausage and mash and a pot of beer. **1939** W. S. Maugham *Christmas Holiday* i. 7 They could drop in..and eat kedgeree and sausages and mash. **1973** 'H. Carmichael' *Too late for Tears* vi. 85 He..ordered sausage and mash with peas. **1974** *Woman* 4 May 18/1 Sizzling sausages and tasty mash.

4. = *mash-staff* (Heraldry).

1688 R. Holme *Armoury* iii. 296/2 He beareth Azure, a Brewers Mash in Bend sinister.

5. *attrib.* and *Comb.*: ***mash †bowl, †coomb, keeve***; **†mash-back**, a receptacle into which the mash is drawn off from the mash-tub; **mash-cooler** (see quot.); **mash copper**, a copper in which wort is made; **mash-liquor**, the water put to the malt in the process of mashing; **mash-machine** (see quot.); **mashman**, an operative in a brewery or distillery who has charge of the mashing of malt; **mash-pulper** = *mash-machine* (Knight *Dict. Mech.* Suppl. 1884); **mash-roll** (*dial.* **-rule**), **-rudder**, **-staff**, the instrument used to stir the malt in the mash tub; **mash-tub**, **tun**, **vat**, a tub in which malt is mashed; **†mash-wise** *adv.*, after the manner of a mash; **mash-wort** (OE. *máscwyrt*), wort, infused malt. Also mash-fat.

1729 G. Smith *Fermentation* 28 Put 'em into the *Mash-backs to ferment. *a* **1529** Skelton *E. Rummyng* 196 Than Elynour taketh The *mashe bolle. **1875** Knight *Dict. Mech.*, **Mash-cooler*, a stirring-trough in which mash or wort are stirred to expedite cooling. **1588** *Lanc. Wills* III. 137 In the..brewe house..one *mashe combe. **1864** *Auld Ayr* 93 The measurement of the *mesh copper. **1815** J. Smith *Panorama Sci. & Art* II. 580 The worts..were run through the *mash-kieve. **1830** M. Donovan *Dom. Econ.* I. 155 If a *mash-liquor be of such heat as is [etc.]. **1839** Ure *Dict. Arts* 111 The malt is agitated..by a mechanism contained within the mash-tun... The *mash machine is shown.. in fig. 106. **1889** Barnard *Noted Breweries* I. 191 Two or three of the *mash-men..had been in the same occupation..over forty years. **1388–9** in *1st Rep. Hist. MSS. Comm.* 80/1 De xviiid. solutis pro ii. *masshe rolles in pistrina. *c* **1440** *Promp. Parv.* 328/1 Maschel, or rothyr, or maschscherel, *remulus, palmula, mixtorium.* **179.** Pegge *Derbicisms* (E.D.S.) 111 *Mash-roll*, the staff with which they stir the malt in the mash-tub. **1854** Miss Baker *Northampt. Gloss.*, *Mash-rule*, the instrument used for stirring up the malt and hops in brewing. **1454** in Rogers *Agric. & Prices* III. 555/1, 2 *mash rothers. **1727** Bradley *Fam. Dict.* s.v. *Baking*, Let one put in the Water, and another with the Mash-Rudder stir some of the Flower therewith. **1688** R. Holme *Armoury* iii. 296/2 The Pole is termed a *Mash-Staff. **1841** Hartshorne *Salop. Antiq.*, s.v. *Mash fat*, The grain is stirred round with a wooden implement, termed a mash-staff. **1543** in *Trevelyan Papers* (Camd.) 185 The bruyng howse... Item ij. new malte sackes... Item a *maxstobe. **1683** Tryon *Way to Health* 154 Put it into your Mash-Tub. **1837** Whittock, etc. *Bk. Trades* (1842) 69 The 'mash-tub'..is a large vessel which has a false bottom.. pierced with small holes. **1713** J. Ward *Yng. Math. Guide* (ed. 2) 450, I have omitted the Business of gauging *Mash-Tuns. **1741** *Compl. Fam.-Piece* i. vi. 277 Your Mesh Tun must be..big enough to contain 6 Bushels of Malt. **1880** *Act 43 & 44 Vict.* c. 24 §23 (3) The distiller must convey the specified sugar..to the mash tun. **1729** G. Smith *Fermentation* 28 The Malt being first put into your *Mash-vat or Tub. **1610** Markham *Masterp.* i. lvii. 121 Let his drinke be warme water and branne made *mash-wise. *c* **1000** *Sax. Leechd.* II. 216 Drince wermod on *max-wyrte awyllede. *Ibid.* III. 74 ȝenim mascwyrt. **1875** *Ure's Dict. Arts* I. 316 The whole of the drainage, when mixed with the first mash-wort, constitutes [etc.].

mash (mæʃ). *sb.*² [Hindī *māsh.*] A common Indian pulse, *Phaseolus radiatus.*

1800 *Asiat. Ann. Reg., Misc. Tracts* 44/1 The principal crop of this country [Assam] consists of rice and mash.

mash (mæʃ), *sb.*³ *slang.* [f. mash *v.*²]

1. A person on whom one of the opposite sex is 'mashed' (see mash *v.*² 2). Also, a dandy, 'swell'.

1882 *Punch* 11 Feb. 69/1 At his fav'rite burlesque theatre he's known as 'such a Mash'. **1888** Kipling *Phantom Rickshaw* 25 She's a hot-headed little virago, your mash.

2. The action of the vb. mash², in ***on the mash.*** Also, ***to make*** (or ***have***) ***a mash*** (***on***).

1884 E. W. Nye *Baled Hay* 135 Two Laramie girls on horseback yanking a fly drummer along the street..because he tried to make a mash on them. **1888** *Daily Tel.* 15 Nov. (Farmer), An impecunious fellow who was always on the mash. **1909** 'O. Henry' *Roads of Destiny* iv. 61, I certainly seemed to have a mash on her. **1912** D. Canfield *Squirrel-Cage* iii. xxix. 319, I thought it would be fun to tease Paul about the mash you made on old What's-his-name.

Comb. **mash note**, a love-letter.

1890 B. Hall *Turnover Club* 134 He is greatly afflicted by that dreadful bane of fine-looking actors, yclept the 'mash note' in the profession. **1899** *Chicago Record* 7 Jan. 4/6, I was writin' mash notes to myself. **1913** R. W. Chambers *Gay Rebellion* i. 6 That poem seemed to deal a direct blow at this suffragette strike. Several women subscribers sent in mash notes. **1930** W. R. Burnett *Iron Man* 85 He gets mash notes by the ton. **1970** *New Yorker* 14 Nov. 87/2 (Advt.), A pen that roared through the Twenties and Thirties writing checks, letters, autographs..jazz and mash notes.

mash (mæʃ), *sb.*⁴ [? f. mash *v.*¹ (sense 2); cf., however, F. *masse* sledge-hammer, mace *sb.*¹] A hammer for breaking stones. Also ***mash-hammer.***

1825–80 Jamieson, *Mash-hammer*, a large weighty hammer for breaking stones, &c., Aberd. **1886** J. Barrowman *Gloss. Sc. Mining Terms* in *N. & Q.* Ser. vii. (1888) VI. 264 *Mash*, a double-headed hammer for breaking coals. **1893** *Northumbld. Gloss.*, *Mash*, a mason's large iron hammer. **1902** *Cassell's Cycl. Mech.* II. 205/1 [Granite] mouldings..are cut..with a small hand hammer, called a mash hammer. *Ibid.* 238/1 Tools for dressing Granite... A hand hammer (sometimes termed a mash or maul).

mash, *sb.*⁵ Eng. and U.S. dial. variant of marsh.

mash (mæʃ), *v.*¹ Forms: 3 **meshe**, **meysse**, 5 **masche**, 6 **mas(s)he**, **mes(s)he**, 6–7 **meash(e**, 6, 8 **mesh**, 7 **messh**, 8 **marsh**, 6– **mash**. [f. mash *sb.*¹; the earliest forms appear to point to an OE. **mæscan* (:—**maiskjan*) f. *másc-* (see the sb.). Cf. G. *meischen*, Sw. *mäska*, Da. *mæske.*]

1. *Brewing. trans.* To mix (malt) with hot water to form wort. (Also with *up.*)

13.. [implied in mashing *vbl. sb.*]. *c* **1440** *Promp. Parv.* 328/1 Maschyn, yn brewynge, *misceo.* **1577** Harrison *England* i. iii. i. 96/1 in *Holinshed*, They seeth theyr woort ..before they mashe, or mixe it with the mault. **1598** Hakluyt *Voy.* I. 496 Quasse, which is nothing else (as we say) but water turned out of his wits, with a litle branne meashed with it. **1616** Surfl. & Markh. *Country Farm* 589 You must boile it [the malt] well, then mash it. **1688** R. Holme *Armoury* iii. 104/2 Terms used by Beer-Brewers... *Mash it up*, blend or mixt [*sic*] the Malt and warm Water together in the Comb. **1745** Dodsley *Agric.* i. 131 Some expert..To mash the malted barley, and extract Its flavour'd strength. **1880** *Act 43 & 44 Vict.* c. 24 §24 A distiller must not mash any materials..between eleven o'clock [etc.]. **1889** Barnard *Noted Breweries* I. 22 Each tun mashes 800 bushels at one time.

absol. or *intr.* **1692** Y-worth *Art Distill.* 10 The stiffer you Mash, the better it is. **1743** *Lond. & Country Brewer* iv. (ed. 2) 272 Stir the Malt very well in, and let it stand two Hours, and let that run, and mash again. **1830** M. Donovan *Dom. Econ.* I. 223 The practice of some distillers is to mash four times.

†b. To brew (ale, beer, etc.). Also with *out.*

1530 Palsgr. 633/2 Come and drinke with us, we mashe to morowe. *Ibid.* 759/1, I tonne, I masshe ale, *je brasse.* **1592** Greene *Upst. Courtier* Wks. (Grosart) XI. 274 And you masse Brewer, that..mash out a tunning of smale beare. **1633** P. Fletcher *Purple Isl.* ix. xxviii, Yet was it Angels wine, which in her eyes was masht.

†c. To lixiviate (ashes). *Obs. rare*⁻¹.

1605 Timme *Quersit.* ii. iii. 115 The lye-wash which is made of ashes and water; the which being oftentimes messhed and drawen away, the ashes leave all their life and strength.

d. *dial.* To infuse (tea). Also *intr.* of the tea: To draw. (Cf. mask *v.*³ 2.)

1845 *Round Preacher* v. 83, I suppose as you..put the tea in the oven to mash, before you went to chapel. **1876** Miss Braddon *J. Haggard's Dau.* I. 304 'The tea's mashed', she said. **1891** Cotes *2 Girls on Barge* 36 Mrs. Bargee 'mashed' our tea... To mash your tea is colloquial canal.

2. To beat into a soft mass; to crush, pound, or smash to a pulp. Also with *up.*

a **1250** *Owl & Night.* 84 Ac þu þretest to mine fleshe, Mid þine cliures woldest me meshe. **1642** H. More *Song of Soul* iii. App. lxxxvii, Let him..persist Th' intentionall species to mash and bray In marble morter. **1679** C. Nesse *Antid. agst. Popery* Ded. 3 A sharp threshing instrument..to mash in pieces those mighty mountains. **1715–20** Pope *Iliad* xxiii. 778 This hand shall..Mash all his bones, and all his body pound. **1719** Baynard *Health* (1731) 28 It's [*sc.* the heart's] office is to mesh and beat, And make the Chyle consimulate with balmy Blood and nitrous Air. **1780** *Phil. Trans.* LXXII. 44 The foot..looked as if two had been squeezed or rather mashed together. **1781** *Encycl. Brit.* (ed. 2) VII. 4892 The room..fell down, killed all the persons in it, and so mashed their bodies, that..they could not be known one from another. **1844** Browning *Laboratory* 9 Grind away, moisten and mash up thy paste. **1865** Dickens *Mut. Fr.* iii. ii, She [a steam-boat] mashed up Thames lightermen with her paddles. **1893** *Scribner's Mag.* June 713/2 A falling limb [of a tree] mashes some poor fellow's shoulder.

b. To pound or stamp *one's way.*

1859 Dickens *T. Two Cities* i ii, With drooping heads and tremulous tails, they mashed their way through the thick mud.

†c. To make a 'hash' of. *Obs.*

1642 H. More *Song of Soul* Notes 162/1 Greek writers have strangely mash'd this word יהוה, some calling it ἰωβᾶ, others ἰαῶ.

d. *intr.* To admit of being crushed or pounded.

1877 Le Conte *Elem. Geol.* (1879) 183 The lower one [lamination line]..consists of coarse sand which could not mash, and therefore has been thrown into folds.

3. *esp.* in the preparation of food: To reduce (fruit, vegetables, etc.) to a homogeneous mass by crushing, beating, or stirring.

1615 Markham *Eng. Housew.* (1660) 83 Open the pye, and put the Cream therein, and mash the Codlins all about. **1699** Evelyn *Acetaria* 105 Yolks of..Eggs..to be mingl'd and mash'd with the Mustard, Oyl, and Vinegar. **1747** Mrs. Glasse *Cookery* i. 11 Put them [*sc.* turnips] in a Pan and mash them with Butter and a little Salt. **1759** tr. *Duhamel's Husb.* iii. xii. §6. 417 [The grapes] are thrown into large tubs, and there mashed or bruised to pieces. *a* **1845** Hood *Drop of Gin* iii, No cold mutton to hash,..not even potatoes to mash. **1861** Calverley *'There stands a City'* 45 At my side she mashed the fragrant Strawberry.

b. *fig.*

1827 Scott *Jrnl.* 28 Mar., I can clear the ground better now by mashing up my old work..with new matter. **1858** E. FitzGerald *Lett.* (1889) I. 266 Many Quatrains are mashed together. **1865** *Lond. Rev.* 9 Sept. 271/1 There is no tendency whatever on the part of womandom to mash up their 'rights' and 'wrongs' into a 'patent treacle'.

†4. To mix, mingle. *Obs.*

a **1591** H. Smith *Serm.* (1594) 467 The Lord will not haue the wine of his word to be mingled and mashed with the water of humane inuentions. **1607** [cf. mashing b]. **1611** Cotgr., *Mistionner*, to mix, mingle, mash, mell, blend, or temper with. **1722** Sewel *Hist. Quakers* vii. 383 Ye are so forward to mash the Innocent and Guilty together.

5. To feed with a mash. *rare.*

1859 *Times* 28 Mar. 8/4 How say you, Lord Derby?.. Will you be stalled and stabled, and mashed..in Lord Palmerston's stables?

mash (mæʃ), *v.*² *slang* (? orig. *U.S.*).

1. *trans.* To fascinate or excite sentimental admiration in (one of the opposite sex). Also *absol.*

1882 Leland *Gypsies* 108 These black-eyed beauties by mashing men for many generations, with shafts shot sideways and most wantonly, at last sealed their souls into the corner of their eyes. **1883** *Masher* 4 July 3/1 When a fellow is married, he can't go on mashing, don't you know. **1885** F. Anstey *Tinted Venus* v. 59, I saw directly that I'd mashed her. **1897** Barrère & Leland *Slang, Jargon & Cant* s.v., About the year 1860 *mash* was a word found only in theatrical parlance in the United States. When an actress.. smiled at..a friend in the audience, she was said to *mash* him.

2. pass. ***to be mashed on***: to have a sentimental admiration for, to be 'gone' on. Also *intr.*

1883 *Pall Mall G.* 11 Oct. 11/1 The participle 'mashed' was in use in America before the substantive. A person who was 'very spooney on' another was said to be 'mashed'. **1893** Milliken *'Arry' Ballads* 66 Bell Bonsor is mashed on me proper. **1893** McCarthy *Dictator* II. 22 He is fond of mashing on to young and pretty women.

Hence **ˈmashing** *vbl. sb.* and *ppl. a.*

1883 *Illustr. Lond. News* 9 June 563/3 Cornet Masham, whose name may..be intended by the author to cover his involuntary 'mashing' capacity. **1884** *Pall Mall G.* 11 Aug. 6/2 The ex-Parisian gallant and mashing gay deceiver.

†mash, *v.*³ *Sc. Obs.* [f. mash *sb.*⁴] *intr.* To use a 'mash' hammer.

1762 Bp. Forbes *Jrnl.* (1886) 228 The General made his way..with blowing and mashing, most of the Road being altogether forced on the Declivity of..Mountains.

mash, obs. form of mesh *sb.* and *v.*

‖**masha** (ˈmæʃə). [Hindi *māshā.*] An Indian weight, equivalent to about fifteen grains troy or eight rattis, originally based on the weight of a seed of the bean *Phaseolus mungo* var. *radiatus.*

1848 J. H. Stocqueler *Oriental Interpreter* 148/2 Masha, a weight of fifteen grains troy. Used by native goldsmiths and jewellers, and in the native evaluation by assay of the precious metals. **1855** E. Acton *Mod. Cookery* (rev. ed.) xxxii. 612 Five eggs, two tolahs of milk, one masha of salt, two mashas of cayenne pepper. **1969** *Daily Tel.* 1 Oct. 19/8 Customers had their purchases weighed in tolas, mashas and ruttees by a Pakistani shopkeeper.

mashallah (mæˈʃælə), *int.* [Arab. phrase *mā shā'llāh*, what God wills (must come to pass).] An exclamation used by Muslims.

1855 in Ogilvie Suppl. **1857** Dufferin *Lett. High Lat.* (ed. 3) 148, I..dismissed the disconsolate culprits, with the Asiatic form of condonation: 'Mashallah, you have made your faces white! Go in peace!'

Masham (ˈmæʃəm). The name of a small town in the northern part of Yorkshire, used to designate a breed of sheep produced by crossing Wensleydale or Teeswater rams with Blackface or Swaledale ewes.

1951 A. Fraser *Sheep Husbandry* (ed. 2) ii. 68 The Wensleydale..is pre-eminently a crossing breed... It provides sires to cross with the hill breeds of sheep indigenous to the North of England... The cross lambs thus produced are variously known as 'Mashams'—Half-breds

—or Greyfaces, and are very useful lambs for feeding on low ground. **1971** *Farmers' Weekly* 19 Mar. 43/3 Certain wool types such as Blackface..have met a better market demand than..Masham.

mashed (mæʃt), *ppl. a.* (and *sb.*) [f. MASH *v.*[1] + -ED[1].]

1. Beaten or crushed to a mash.

1635 *Voy. Foxe & James to N.W.* (Hakl. Soc.) II. 281 Wee had great store of masht Ice. **1693** DRYDEN *Juvenal* iii. (1697) 65 Nor Limbs, nor Bones, nor Carcass wou'd remain: But a mash'd heap, a Hotchpotch of the Slain. **1727** GAY *Fables* I. xxxvii. 126 Her mash'd eggs bestrow'd the way. **1747** MRS. GLASSE *Cookery* ix. 99 Mashed Potatoes. **1841** THACKERAY *Men & Pictures* Wks. 1900 XIII. 328 The cool clear shadows are mashed-down masses of sienna and indigo. **1844** J. T. HEWLETT *Parsons & W.* ii, Bacon and a few mashed turnips. **1856** KANE *Arct. Expl.* I. xxiii. 289 [We] set forward over the worst sort of mashed ice.

b. Hence as *sb.*, mashed potatoes (esp. in the phr. ***sausage and mashed***). *slang.*

1923 in J. MANCHON *Le Slang.* **1926** G. B. SHAW *Translations & Tomfooleries* 225 One [*sc.* a public-house] had a placard up 'Sausage and Mashed'. **1934** T. S. ELIOT *Rock* I. 40 Restaurants where you can get..sausage and mashed or toad-in-the-'ole for twopence. **1963** H. GARNER in R. Weaver *Canad. Short Stories* (1968) 2nd Ser. 52, I ate a lunch of meat pie, mashed and gravy.

2. *Brewing.* Of 'liquor': Treated with mash.

1839 URE *Dict. Arts* 99 The mashed liquor is let off into a large back.

†**mashel.** *Obs. rare.* In 5 **maschel.** [f. MASH *v.*[1] + -EL.] = *mash-rudder* (see MASH *sb.*[1] 5).

c **1440** *Promp. Parv.* 328/1 Maschel, or rothyr, or maschscherel, *remulus, palmula, mixtorium.*

mashelton, dial. form of MASLIN[2].

masher[1] ('mæʃə(r)). [f. MASH *v.*[1] + -ER[1].]

†**1.** One who mashes (malt) or mixes (wine). *Obs.*

?*a* **1500** *Chester Pl., Harrowing of Hell* II. 82 With all mashers minglers of wyne in the nighte. *a* **1603** T. CARTWRIGHT *Confut. Rhem. N.T.* (1618) 449 The difference onely between these minglers and your mashers, is, that they put not so much water into the wine, that it ceased to be wine still. **1611** FLORIO, *Mescitore*, a mesher, a mingler, a blender.

2. A machine, vessel, or instrument for mashing malt, fruit, vegetables, etc.

1878 *Ure's Dict. Arts* IV, *Masher*..[for use in] a new system of preparing the mash for the distillation of potato spirit. **1889** BARNARD *Noted Breweries* II. 337 A spray of hot liquor issuing from the top of the masher. **1893** K. SANBORN *S. California* 155 The ponderous rollers and keen knives of the masher mash the fruit.

masher[2] ('mæʃə(r)). *slang.* A name applied to a fop of affected manners and exaggerated style of dress who frequented music-halls and fashionable promenades and who posed as a 'lady-killer'.

The word was common in 1882 and for a few years after. It is said to have been introduced from the U.S.

1882 *Theatre* Nov. 316 The 'Masher', that poor debilitated sickly creature of 1882. **1883** *Globe* 16 May 1/5 Moths of fashion who have come to be generally known by the generic title of 'mashers'. **1889** BESANT *Bell of St. Paul's* I. 7 The once brilliant masher of the music-hall.

b. *attrib.* passing into *adj.* Pertaining to or characteristic of a masher.

1884 *Girl's Own Paper* Nov. 58/1 A very feeble looking blue, with tiny white dots, is called a 'masher blue'; because it was affected by those weak boys for their waistcoats. **1890** J. HATTON *By Order of Czar* (1891) 195, I hate those horrid comic..bragging masher songs.

†**mash-fat.** *Obs.* Forms: 4 **massh-**, **masche-**, 5 **mach-**, **maysh-**, **masshe-**, **mesch-**, 5–6 **mas-**, 5–7 **mesh-**, 6 **mashe-**, **messhe**, 8 **mesch-**, 5– **mash-**, and see FAT *sb.*[1] A mashing-vat.

1335 in Riley *Mem. Lond.* (1868) 194 [One] masshfat [value 18*d.*]. **1465** *Paston Lett.* III. 435 A grete lede to brew v. comb malte with..a mayshsate [*read* mayshfate]. *a* **1529** SKELTON *E. Rummyng* 190 The hennes ron in the mashfat. **1577** B. GOOGE *Heresbach's Husb.* I. (1586) 28 b, I..put the meale into a Mash Fatte. **1677** PLOT *Oxfordsh.* 76 Mesh-fats for Brewing. **1727** BRADLEY *Fam. Dict.* s.v. *Brewing*, Many put their Malt first into the Mesch-Fat, and then pour in their Liquor for the first Wort.

mashie, mashy ('mæʃɪ). *Golf.* [? Corrupt a. F. *massue* club.] An iron club (see quot. 1881).

1881 FORGAN *Golfer's Handbk.* ii. 15 The 'Mashy' is used for the same purposes as the Niblick proper, and only differs from it in its sole and face being straight instead of rounded. **1891** *Daily News* 23 May 5/2 All the forms of the golfing iron, from the driver to the cleek and mashie.

mashie-niblick. *Golf.* [f. MASHIE, MASHY + NIBLICK.] An iron club combining the features of the mashie and the niblick, now called the number 7 iron.

1907 W. M. BUTLER *Golfer's Manual* 5 The marriage of different pairs of clubs has produced such implements as mashie-niblicks and putting-cleeks. **1912** H. VARDON *How to play Golf* vii. 146 Nowadays tools called mashie-niblicks are popular. **1929** WODEHOUSE *Mr. Mulliner Speaking* vi. 196 How bitterly he regretted now those raking drives, those crisp flicks of the mashie-niblick of which he had been so proud ten minutes ago. **1931** *Times* 28 Feb. 4/6 A little bullet-headed mashie niblick..was also highly efficient. **1964** J. STOBBS *A.B.C. of Golf* 61 Out have gone..the tried and proved regular favourites... Among these..the mashie niblick, a large round-shaped-faced lofted mashie (modern equivalent the 7-iron). **1972** T. SCOTT *Club Golfers' Handbk.* 127 *Mashie-niblick*, another name which has been replaced by a number.

mashing ('mæʃɪŋ), *vbl. sb.* [f. MASH *v.*[1] + -ING[1].] The action of MASH *v.*[1]

a. *Brewing.* The action or process of mixing malt with warm water to form wort.

13.., **1532**, **1573** [see *mashing-fat, -tub* in c below]. **1692** Y-WORTH *Art Distill.* 9 Pouring on as much warm Liquor as you intend to make use of in that Mashing. **1707** MORTIMER *Husb.* (1721) II. 318 In all the Mashings..before you let it run out, you draw out some of the Liquor first, and see if it run clear. **1822** IMISON *Sci. & Art* II. 156 When the mashing is completed the tun is covered in. **1887** BARNARD *Whisky Distill.* 10 The mashing with hot water on the same grains was then repeated.

b. In other senses of the verb.

c **1440** *Promp. Parv.* 328/2 Maschynge, *mixtura, mixtio.* **1607** *Schol. Disc. agst. Antichr.* I. i. 31 This iustifieth..the Adiaphorist in all his mixtures and meshings with poperie. **1818** COBBETT *Pol. Reg.* XXXIII. 472 A mashing up of proceedings at police-offices along with scraps of plays, gambling-house news and boxers' slang. **1877** LE CONTE *Elem. Geol.* iii. (1879) 253 A mashing together horizontally.

c. *attrib.* (cf. MASH *sb.*[1] 5), as ***mashing-back, -gear, machine, machinery, oar, rake, staff, stage, -stick, -tub, -tun, -vat*** (†***-fat***), ***water.***

1889 BARNARD *Noted Breweries* I. 23 *Mashing backs for the reception of weak worts. *Ibid.* 22 They [*sc.* tuns] all possess double-acting *mashing-gear. **1839** URE *Dict. Arts* 113 Fig. 106 is the *mashing-machine. **1830** M. DONOVAN *Dom. Econ.* I. 224 The *mashing machinery should be kept in motion for two or three hours. **1826** MISS MITFORD *Village* Ser. II. 233 He has..lost a finger in a *mashing-mill. **1836** *Penny Cycl.* V. 403/2 [The malt in the mash-tub] is worked up by means of instruments termed *mashing oars. **1688** R. HOLME *Armoury* III. 296/2 The Pole is termed..a *Mashing Staff. **1889** BARNARD *Noted Breweries* II. 299 Leaving the *mashing stage we descended to the underback room below the tuns. **1830** 'B. MOUBRAY' *Dom. Poultry*, etc. 317 A Funnel, *Mashing-stick, Casks. **1573** *Lanc. Wills* (Chetham Soc.) III. 60 One *mashtowinbe [*read* mashintowbe]. **1707** MORTIMER *Husb.* 565 Put one third part of it into the Meshing-tub. **1865** *Pall Mall G.* 17 May 7 One of the supervisors..found in the mashing tub five quarters, two bushels, and seven gallons of malt. **13..** *Gloss. W. de Bibbesw.* (Camb. MS.) in *Rel. Ant.* II. 81/1 *Mahssingfate [*sic*], *keuerel.* **1532** MORE *Confut. Tindale* Wks. 679/2 He maye happe ere aught long, to fal into the messhing fatte. **1741** *Compl. Fam.-Piece* I. vi. 285 Be sure you cover your Meshing-fat very well. **1743** *Lond. & Country Brew.* IV. (ed. 2) 272 *Mashing-Vat. **1830** M. DONOVAN *Dom. Econ.* I. 89 Well-mellowed malt will permit the use of a hotter *mashing water.

†'**maship.** *Obs.* Forms: 6 **mas(s)hyp(pe, mas(s)hip(pe.** [An abbreviation of *mastership*: cf. MAS *sb.*[1] Common in 16th c.] = MASTERSHIP. Only with poss. pron., as ***his, your maship***, etc.

Apparently the abbreviated form (at least when used in writing) implied disrespect: cf. quot. 1567–9.

1526 *Hundred Mery Talys* (1866) 16, I shall gyue your mashyp a good reward. **1546** BP. GARDINER *Declar. Art. Joye* 51 b, And so your masshyppe hathe sayde truelye. **1567–9** JEWEL *Def. Apol.* (1611) 412 How vainely you snap ..now at our Masterships: now at our Maships: (for this is the sobriety and grauitie of your speech). **1579** GOSSON *Sch. Abuse, Apol.* (Arb.) 74 And because his mashippe would seeme learned, he heyred him seruauntes with great stipendes. **1600** W. WATSON *Decacordon* (1602) 132 He must (if out of credit with their maships) do som desperate act.

mashlam, -lin, dial. forms of MASLIN[2].

mashloch ('maʃləx). *Sc.* Also 6 **masleach, -loch, mashlowe, marshlock,** 7 **maischloch.** [? Alteration of MASLIN.] = MASLIN[2].

1575 *Rec. Elgin* (New Spalding Cl. 1903) I. 150 Katherein Ros..wes decernit to keip neborat in schawing masleach in the Schanehery hill. **1584** *Burgh Rec. Edinb.* (1882) IV. 340 Na baxteris..sall grynd..any masloch bot sic as cumis furth of vther cuntreis. **1595** DUNCAN *App. Etymol.* (E.D.S.), *Farrago*, a mixture of sundrie stuffs; mashlowe. **1609** SKENE *Reg. Maj., Stat. Gild* 143 b, Na man sall presume to grind quheit, maischloch, or rye, with hand mylnes; except [etc.]. **1780** ARNOT *Hist. Edin.* ii. (1816) 45 In the Mescelin or Mashloch, the flour was almost entirely sifted from it, a portion of rye was mixed with the bran. **1884** ROGERS *Soc. Life Scot.* I. vii. 236 The mashloch was of sifted flour conjoined with rye.

mashlum, Sc. form of MASLIN[2].

Mashona (mə'ʃəʊnə), *sb.* and *a.* Pl. **Mashona, Mashonas.** [Native name.] **A.** *sb.* **a.** A group of Bantu peoples inhabiting parts of Zimbabwe and Mozambique; a member of one of these peoples. **b.** Any of the languages of these peoples. **B.** *adj.* Of or pertaining to these peoples.

1835 A. SMITH *Diary* (1940) II. 222 The Bakalaka and the Mashoona speak a different language to the Bechuanas. **1846** H. H. METHUEN *Life in Wilderness* vi. 143 To the north-east the land becomes mountainous, and the Mashona, a tribe possessing guns, inhabit it. **1893** A. M. HARTMANN (*title*) A grammar of the Mashona language. **1894** —— (*title*) English-Mashona dictionary. **1895** G. W. H. KNIGHT-BRUCE *Memories Mashonaland* ii. 41 The Mashona..are very fond of meat, but they hardly ever get it. To give him meat is the one way that will nearly always ensure a wild Mashona working well. **1896** *Scientific African* 78 (Pettman), The careful workmanship displayed in the crude musical instrument known as the Mashona piano. **1900** A. H. KEANE *Boer States* vii. 101 Mashonas..and several other smaller groups for whom there is no collective national or racial designation, except the all-comprehensive 'Kaffre'. **1911** *Encycl. Brit.* XVII. 837/2 The name Mashona has been derived from the contemptuous term *Amashuina* applied by the Matabele to the aborigines owing to the habit of the latter of taking refuge in the rocky hills with which the country abounds... The Mashona..are in general a peaceful, mild-mannered people. **1911** J. G. FRAZER *Golden Bough: Magic Art* (ed. 3) I. vi. 352 The king of the Matabeles..prays..: 'O great spirits.., I thank you for having granted last year to my people more wheat than to our enemies the Mashonas.' **1928** C. BULLOCK *Mashona* iii. 12 The word Mashona is used *faute de mieux*; nor need we look for its etymological derivation, because it has none. It is simply one of those British bowdlerisations..a race name to cover numerous clans. **1936** J. BUCHAN *Island of Sheep* iv. 68 They are Mashonas and are timid as rabbits. **1959** *Chambers's Encycl.* II. 107/2 In the Shona (Mashona) group [*sc.* of Bantu languages] there are about 40 dialectal forms. **1972** *Police Rev.* 24 Nov. 1521/1 Cecil John Rhodes..began negotiating..for rights to explore the mineral wealth of the regions east of the royal kraal at Bulawayo, at that time inhabited by the Mashona tribe.

mashwa ('mæʃwə). Also **machwa, mashua, mashuwa.** [Marathi, 'fishing-boat', f. Skr. *matsya* fish.] A kind of small open boat (see quots.).

1885 G. C. WHITWORTH *Anglo-Indian Dict.* 184/1 The machwás of different ports vary slightly in build. They are considered to be amongst the swiftest sailing-vessels known; they are very sharp in the bows, with hollow keel, well rounded in the stern, and the mast slopes a little forward; these vessels are chiefly made of teak, and cost from Rs. 300 to Rs. 400; they last about forty years. **1906** H. W. SMYTH *Mast & Sail in Europe & Asia* ix. 310 A smaller class of Zanzibar vessel is the *mashuwa*, or open fishing-boat worked by the Arab of the neighbourhood. They are generally dilapidated little crafts with the usual long bow and transom-stern. **1929** *Ibid.* (ed. 2) x. 359 The term Mashwa, or Mashuwa on the African coast, is applied apparently to any small round-stern vessel, meaning originally a fishing-boat. The larger seagoing craft all carry a small 'mashwa' on deck. **1942** *Mariner's Mirror* XXVIII. 21 The *Mashwa* or *Machwa.* The larger Arab fishing boats, the *mashwas*, are built after the design of the *sambuk* and the *jehazi* in their respective home ports. At Zanzibar they are employed also for the transport of coral rag and firewood. All are fitted with a single mast and are undecked save at the ends; the stern is of the square transom type; the tack of the sail is extended by means of a bowsprit as in the *jehazi.* **1948** R. DE KERCHOVE *Internat. Maritime Dict.* 453/1 *Mashuwa, mashwa*, generic name in the Persian Gulf and in Southern Arabia for an open ship's boat with straight or curved stem and transom stern, usually propelled by oars, but also rigged with one mast on occasion... This name also refers to a small open boat with raking stem and rounded stern of Deccan used for fishing and local trading on the Gujarat coast between Bombay and Cam-Bay.

mashy ('mæʃɪ), *a.* [f. MASH *sb.*[1] + -Y[1].] Of the nature of a mash.

1730–46 THOMSON *Autumn* 700 Then comes the crushing swain; the country floats And foams unbounded with the mashy flood.

mashy, masicot: see MASHIE, MASSICOT.

masin, obs. form of MASON.

‖**masjid** ('mʌsdʒɪd). Also **musjid.** [a. Arab. *masjid*: see MOSQUE.] A mosque.

1845 STOCQUELER *Handbk. Brit. India* (1854) 204 There are many mosques or musjids in Patna. **1849** E. B. EASTWICK *Dry Leaves* 38 In the small island of Khwája Khizr..is a masjid, or mosque. **1882** FLOYER *Unexpl. Baluchistan* 96 A ground plan of a house marked in white stones and evidently intended for a masjid.

Mas John: see MAS *sb.*[1]

mask, *sb.*[1] *Obs.* exc. *dial.* Also 1 **max,** 5– **maske.** [It is uncertain whether the mod. word represents OE. **masc* (by metathesis *max*) str. neut., or is adopted from the cognate ON. *mǫskve*; in the former case the phonology may be compared with that of ASK *v.* (For the further etymology see MESH *sb.*)] A mesh. (In OE. a net.)

c **1000** ÆLFRIC *Colloq.* in Wr.-Wülcker 92 Ic brede me max, *Plecto mihi retia. Ibid.* 93 Ic astiȝie min scyp and wyrpe max mine on ea. **1343** in Riley *Mem. Lond.* (1868) 215 [Seeing that the] masks [of the same nets, according to the custom of the City, ought to be 2 inches wide at least]. *c* **1440** *Jacob's Well* 239 Smale lytell fyssches skyppyn thruȝ the maskys of a nett into the watyr. *c* **1575** [see HECK *sb.*[1] 2]. **1584–5** *Act 27 Eliz.* c. 21 Greate destruction of the Frye of Fisshe there enseweth, by reason of the smallnes of the Maskes of suche Nettes as they use. **1607** *Lingua* II. vi, The maskes [of a net] are made so strong, That I my selfe vpon them scal'd the heauens. **1669** in *North Riding Rec.* VI. 134 Two men presented for fishing with a net of which every maske was not 2 in. broad and 1 in. long. **1886** *Chester Gloss.*, *Maske*, a mesh of a net.

†**mask,** *sb.*[2] Chiefly *Sc. Obs.* [Northern var. MASH *sb.*[1]] = MASH *sb.*[1] Also *Comb.*, as ***mask ruther*** (= rudder), ***wort.*** Also MASK-FAT.

1508 in *Ld. Treas. Acc. Scot.* IV. 111 Item,..for maskis of malt to the said hors. **1567** *Satir. Poems Reform.* viii. 35 Ane mask of malt. **1588–9** *Extracts Rec. Glasgow* (1876) I. 129 Ane mask ruther.

mask (mɑːsk, -æ-), *sb.*[3] Forms: (6 **measque**), 6–7 **maske,** 6–9 **masque,** 7– **mask.** [a. F. *masque* masc. (in 16th c. also fem.) of disputed origin, whence also G., Du. *maske* fem., Da. *maske* com., Sw. *mask* fem. MASQUE *sb.* was orig. a sense of the same word, now differentiated in spelling.

The Fr. word (first recorded in 16th c.) is usually believed to be ad. the synonymous Sp. *máscara*, It. *maschera* (see MASKER *sb.*[1], MASQUERADE). But it is difficult to believe that the word has no connexion with med.L. *mascus*, *masca*, which render OE. *grima* mask, spectre, in the Corpus Glossary *c* 725. *Mascha* is used *c* 680 by Aldhelm in association with *larva*, which had the senses 'mask' and 'spectre', and *masca* occurs in the Lombard Laws *c* 800 with the sense 'witch'; cf. Pr. *masco* witch (see MASCOT). On the whole the most plausible view seems to be that the representative of med.L. *mascus*, *masca* survived in some Fr. dialect, and was thence taken into literary use as an equivalent of the like-sounding Sp. *máscara*. The origin of med.L. *mascus*, *masca*, is undetermined; some scholars think the original sense was 'mask', and that the word was from Teut. **maskwo-* net (see MESH *sb.*).]

1. A covering for the face, worn either as a disguise or for protection.

a. A covering, usually made of velvet or silk (with apertures for seeing), concealing the face or the upper part of it, worn for disguise at balls, masquerades, etc. ***in mask*** = masked.

1534 LD. BERNERS *Gold. Bk. M. Aurel.* (1535) 102 b, The vices that they brought [from Asia] to Rome..The patritiens bearyng Measques, the Plebeyens usynge smelles, and the emperours to weare purple. **1581** PETTIE tr. *Guazzo's Civ. Conv.* (1586) I. 28 There are certaine glorious fellowes, who at shrouetide goe with Maskes on their face, and yet woulde faine be knowne what they are. **1617** MORYSON *Itin.* III. 177 Gentlemen and Citizens wiues when they goe out of dores, weare vpon their faces little Maskes of silk, lined with fine leather. **1666–7** PEPYS *Diary* 18 Feb., One of the ladies would, and did sit with her mask on. **1691** *Lond. Gaz.* 2651/3 To march out with their Arms and Baggage, Colours Flying,..30 Covered Wagons, and 50 Persons in Masks, &c. **1722** DE FOE *Moll Flanders* 341, I had no Mask but I ruffled my Hoods so about my face that [etc.]. **1727** —— *Eng. Tradesm.* x. (1732) I. 117 A Ball, where people appear in Masque, and act a part to make sport. **1833** HT. MARTINEAU *Three Ages* I. 1 A troop of gentlemen.. whose country could not be divined from their complexions, since each wore a mask.

b. A covering worn on the face for protection; now esp. a screen of wire, gauze, etc. to protect the face from injury in dangerous games or manufactures. Also = *gas mask*.

1591 SHAKS. *Two Gent.* IV. iv. 158 Since she did neglect her looking-glasse, And threw her Sun-expelling Masque away. **1601** HOLLAND *Pliny* I. 367 He..hath a thicke coife or maske [L. *persona densusque reticulus*] about his head, for doubt that hee should bestow any [frankincense] in mouth or eares. **1688** R. HOLME *Armoury* III. 13/1 A Mask.. This is a thing..Gentlewomen used to put over their Faces..to keep them from Sun burning. **1823** ROLAND *Fencing* 25 *note*, Each fencer wears a closely wrought wire mask for the security of his face. **1831** BREWSTER *Nat. Magic* xii. (1833) 306 A casque or cap, with a mask large enough to leave a proper space between it and the asbestos cap. **1844** BROWNING *Laboratory* i, Now that I, tying thy glass mask tightly, May gaze thro' these faint smokes curling whitely. **1875** KNIGHT *Dict. Mech.*, *Mask*,..a wire cage to protect the face from a stray cut or thrust with a foil in fencing... A face protection to be worn in glass-works or foundries, to protect against radiant heat. **1901** H. MCHUGH *John Henry* 68 Baseball masks. **1915** H. W. WILSON *Great War* IV. 331 A Highlander wearing a mask. **1918** *Ibid.* XI. 454 French soldiers wearing the masks, fitted with goggles and respirators, that rendered them immune to noxious gases. *Ibid.* 455 Special masks were devised for the horses.

c. *Antiq.* The hollow figure of a human head worn by ancient Greek and Roman actors, intended both to identify the character represented and to increase the volume of the voice.

1705 ADDISON *Italy* 103 (Venice), Could we suppose that a Mask represented never so naturally the general Humour of a Character, it can never suit with the Variety of Passions that are incident to every single Person in the whole Course of a Play. **1732** LEDIARD *Sethos* II. x. 435 The actor whose mask represented Cheres..went off from the stage. *a* **1862** BUCKLE *Misc. Wks.* I. 487 The Romans sometimes played without masks: the Greeks never.

d. A grotesque representation of a face, made of pasteboard moulded and painted; worn at merrymakings, carnivals, etc.

1837 D. JERROLD in *New Monthly Mag.* LI. 317 The mask fixed upon the effigy [of Guy Fawkes].

e. A likeness of a person's face in clay, wax, etc.; esp. one made by taking a mould from the face itself. Also ***death-mask*** (see DEATH *sb.* 19).

1780 ROGERS in *Archæologia* (1782) VI. 107 An account of certain earthen Masks from the Musquito Shore... Masques..which, his Indian conductors told him, were the likenesses of chiefs..who had been formerly buried there. **1846** *Penny Cycl.* Supp. II. 705/2 They [the wax *imagines* of the Romans] were probably cast from moulds taken from models, though such masks [taken after death] may have been used in the formation of the models. **1877** CLARA BELL tr. *Ebers' Uarda* I. 311 *note*, Such a mask of the dead is not unfrequently found at the head of mummy cases.

2. *fig.* **a.** A 'cloak', disguise, pretence; esp. in phr. ***under the mask of, to put on, assume, throw off, pull off***, or ***drop the mask (of)***, etc.

1577 *F. de L'isle's Legendarie* F iv b, That their nephue Francis serued but as a maske and cloke to their fellonie. **1605** *His Maiesties Speach*, etc. H b, And the Racke onely offred and shewed vnto him [Guido Fawkes], when the maske of his Romaine fortitude did visibly begin to weare & slide off his face. **1647** CLARENDON *Hist. Reb.* III. §31 No man had ever a greater power over himself, or was less the man that he seemed to be, which shortly after appeared to every body when he cared less to keep on the mask. **1701** DE FOE *True-born Eng.* 8 The Mask thrown off, Plain Devil his Title stands. **1748** RICHARDSON *Clarissa* (1768) IV. 350 If I write not in time, but that thou hast actually pulled off the mask; let [etc.]. **1766** GOLDSM. *Vic. W.* xxx, A base, ungenerous wretch who under the mask of friendship has undone me. **1812** CRABBE *Tales* xvi. Wks. 1834 V. 138 She veiled her troubles in a mask of ease. **1832–4** DE QUINCEY *Caesars* Wks. 1862 IX. 31 He himself by way of masque attended a public spectacle. **1849** MACAULAY *Hist. Eng.* I. 400 He had covered his failings with the mask of devotion. **1876** FREEMAN *Norm. Conq.* IV. xvii. 37 The way in which ..wrong contrived to assume the mask of right.

b. Something which covers or hides from view.

1752 MASON *Elfrida* 25 To..be led Veil'd in the mask of night, to Edgar's chamber, A counterfeit Matilda. *a* **1821** KEATS *Sonn.*, *Lover's Compl.*, The new soft-fallen mask Of snow upon the mountains. **1886** WILLIS & CLARK *Cambridge* III. 540 The series of melancholy attempts..to convert the medieval style of our colleges into Italian by a mere mask of ashlar.

3. a. A masked person; a person wearing a mask or in masquerading dress; a masker.

1580 LYLY *Euphues* (Arb.) 335 By this time entered an other Masque. **1676** ETHEREDGE *Man of Mode* I. i. (1684) 3, I remember there was a Mask observed me indeed. **1712** ADDISON *Spect.* No. 383 ¶6 A Masque, who came behind him, gave him a gentle Tap upon the Shoulder. **1749** FIELDING *Tom Jones* XIII. vii, This Mask was one of those ladies, who go to a masquerade only to vent ill-nature. **1794** MRS. RADCLIFFE *Myst. Udolpho* xvi, Groups of masks were seen dancing on the moonlight terraces. **1832** DE QUINCEY *Klosterheim* ix, A Masque, armed cap-a-pie. **1834** *L. Hunt's Lond. Jrnl.* No. 25. 198 Amongst the ambulating masks..I must not omit the most interesting.

†**b.** ? A masquerade dress, domino. *Obs.*

1577 in Cunningham *Revels Accts.* 114 A large Maske of murrey satten..with sleeves of gold tyncell.

4. Various technical uses.

a. *Arch.*, etc. A representation (often grotesque) in stone of a face or face and neck, used in panels, keystones of arches, etc.; a similar representation in metal on a shield. Also, a kind of corbel the shadow of which is like a man's profile; = BUCKLE *sb.* 4.

1731 BAILEY vol. II, *Masque* (with Architects), certain pieces of sculpture, representing some hideous form; grotesque or satyrs faces, used to fill up or adorn some vacant places. **1784** H. WALPOLE *Let.* 7 Sept. (1858) VIII. 502 Mrs. Damer herself is modelling two masks for the key-stones of the new bridge at Henley. **1848** T. RICKMAN *Styles Archit.* (ed. 5) Introd. xxx, A good bold corbel-table.. carried on masks, a name given to a peculiar corbel because the shadow of it is the same as that from a head. **1870** F. R. WILSON *Ch. Lindisfarne* 111 The labels terminate in grotesque masks. **1874** BOUTELL *Arms & Armour* ii. 19 The shield..in either case was adorned by having the head of an animal nailed in the centre..or a mask executed with the hammer (*repoussé*) in bronze, was fixed in a similar position.

b. *Hunting.* The face or head of a fox (occas. of an otter); phr. ***to set his mask for*** (said of a fox) to head *for*, make *for*. Also, the head-skin of any 'game'; the face or muzzle of a dog.

1828 *Sporting Mag.* XXII. 244 The masks of a bitch fox and five of her cubs were nailed against the door of his keeper's kennel. **1853** 'C. BEDE' *Verdant Green* vii, Over the mirror was displayed a fox's mask. **1891** *County Gentl.* XXIX. 1684 A second fox..set his mask for Vowes's Gorse. **1894** C. PHILLIPPS-WOLLEY et al. *Big Game Shooting* II. xv. 417 Peel off the whole mask from the antlers downwards to the muzzle. **1904** *Westmorld. Gaz.* 2 July 5/5 Captain Thompson presented..the pads [of the otter] to the Misses Cheetham..and the mask..to Isaac Fletcher, the huntsman. **1928** C. S. STOCKLEY *Big Game Shooting* 88 Skins..should..be..hung on a frame to dry, the mask being filled with dry grass or paper. **1945** C. L. B. HUBBARD *Observer's Bk. Dogs* 214 A light Cairn may have a dark mask. **1972** *Daily Tel.* 8 Apr. 17/4 Six more dog pelts, all complete with masks—the head of the dog—have been found..at Nuneaton... Mr. Horner, whose firm exports between 40,000 and 50,000 dog skins a year, commented: 'I am baffled as to why someone should prepare pelts with masks.'

c. *Fortif.* A screen to protect men engaged in constructing a work, to conceal a battery, etc.; also, a casemated redoubt serving as a counter-guard to the caponier (Voyle & Stevenson *Mil. Dict.* 1876).

1802 JAMES *Mil. Dict.* s.v., Several masks must be hastily thrown up, whilst the men are employed behind one. *Ibid.*, The engineer, or artillery officer, places himself behind this mask and draws his plan. **1884** *Mil. Engin.* I. 86 A floating mask, may be necessary for the protection of the men forming the head of the bridge. The mask should be of planks covered with iron or steel plate if possible. *Ibid.*, As the work proceeds, a parapet must be erected on the causeway under cover of the mask to protect the men from the flank-fire of the enemy.

d. *Ent.* The enlarged labium of the larval and pupal dragon-fly. Also *Zool.* a formation or coloration of the head resembling a mask.

1797 *Encycl. Brit.* (ed. 3) X. 20/1 (*Libella*) This mask, fastened to the insect's neck,..serves to hold its prey while it devours it. **1840** *Cuvier's Anim. Kingd.* 174 The mask, formed by the fringed feathers that surround the eyes, is greatly extended [in the barn owl]. **1896** tr. *Boas' Text-bk. Zool.* 255 The larvæ [of dragon-flies]..are characterised by the modification of the labium into a long eversible prehensile organ (the mask).

e. *Photogr.* A piece of opaque paper used to cover any part of a negative, lantern-slide, or print which it is desired to obscure or shade; *esp.* the margin of a piece from which a disk has been cut.

1876 ABNEY *Photogr.* (ed. 3) 118 [Sunning down a bright spot on a print] may be secured by making a brown paper mask, cutting out the shape of the object to be toned down. **1889** T. C. HEPWORTH *Bk. Lantern* (ed. 2) 141 Now take a slide, duly fitted with its black mask, and a cover glass.

f. *Surg.* A piece of linen, with apertures for the eyes, nose, and mouth, used for applications to the face (*Syd. Soc. Lex.* 1890).

g. A cosmetic preparation, a face-pack.

1931 H. G. WELLS *Work, Wealth & Happiness of Mankind* I. v. 221 She has her face put under a 'mask', an affair of beaten-up eggs and other ingredients which tightens on the face. **1934** M. VERNI *Mod. Beauty Culture* I. v. 28/2 The foundation for a general type of mask is fuller's earth made into a paste with liquid. *Ibid.*, If the operator has neither given nor received a mask treatment before, she should give herself one. **1955** C. HART *Handbk. Beauty* 29 Masks serve the purpose of stimulating the circulation, thus improving your complexion color... You can buy a mask ready-made or concoct one at home. Buttermilk all by itself is a good mask; so is oatmeal..so is an egg. *Ibid.*, Cover your hair.. , because the mask stuff is sticky.

h. *Electronics.* In the manufacture of microcircuits, a thin surface layer that is removed in parts so as to permit selective modification of the underlying material.

1956 *Bell Syst. Techn. Jrnl.* XXXV. 25 For the emitter, a film of aluminium approximately 1,000 Å thick was evaporated onto the surface through a mask which defined an emitter arc of 1 × 2 mils. **1957** *Jrnl. Electrochem. Soc.* CIV. 549/1 A SiO_2 surface layer provides a selective mask at high temperatures against the diffusion of some donors and acceptors into Si. **1967** *Electronics* 6 Mar. 60/2 Faster IC's can be built with the dimensional resolutions possible in present diffusion masks. **1973** *Sci. Amer.* Apr. 65/2 Masks can be made from various types of material, for example insulators such as silicon dioxide,..or metals such as aluminum, molybdenum and gold. To expose the regions in which ion implantation is desired the mask is removed by chemical etching.

5. *attrib.* and *Comb.*, as ***mask-maker***; ***mask-like*** adj.; **mask-ball**, a masked ball, masquerade; **mask-crab**, a crab of the family *Corystidæ*, with mask-like markings on the carapace, as *Corystes cassivelaunus*; **mask-flower** [tr. of the Peruvian name *ricaco*, or *ricarco*], any one of several Peruvian plants of the genus *Alonsoa*; **mask jug**, a jug with a lip or front shaped like a face; also ***masked jug***; **mask-man**, a masker; **mask-shell**, 'any spiral marine-shell of the genus *Persona*, having a curiously twisted aperture' (*Funk's Stand. Dict.*); **mask-wall** *Fortif.*, 'the scarp-wall of a casemate' (*Cent. Dict.*).

1818 LADY MORGAN *Autobiog.* (1859) 286 This fashion in France of profiting by the custom *d'intriguer* at *masque balls. **1895** G. A. SALA *Life & Adv.* II. xxxviii. 78 In the evening we went to a grand mask ball at the Opera. **1863** WOOD *Nat. Hist.* III. 596 The *Mask-crab buries itself in the sand or muddy bed of the sea. **1857** E. BALFOUR *Cycl. India*, *Mask flower, *Alonsoa.* **1910** DOWNMAN & GUNN *Eng. Pott. & Porc.* (ed. 5) 58 (*caption*) *Masked jug in Fulham brown stoneware of the 18th century. **1963** *Times* 1 May 15/5 A Worcester yellow-ground mask jug fell to Tilley at £700. **1970** *Canad. Antiques Collector* Jan. 30/1 Mask jugs, in which a face, or even a figure, formed the shape of the front of the jug, opposite the handle, had been made for centuries in most European countries. **1899** BULLEN *Way Navy* 42 His face was *mask-like. **1836–48** B. D. WALSH *Aristoph.*, *Knights* I. ii, The *maskmakers were so afraid of him, They would not copy them. **1652** KIRKMAN *Clerio & Losia* 87 For this hour hath this same *Maskman talked to me in Italian.

mask, *v.*[1] *Obs.* exc. *dial.* [f. MASK *sb.*[1]] *trans.* To mesh, enmesh: *lit.* and *fig.*

c **1374** CHAUCER *Tr. & Cr.* III. 1734 He was so narwe y-masked and y-knet, That [etc.]. **1556** J. HEYWOOD *Sp. & Flie* xv. 20 Neuer was there flie in this net, thus masked, That euer scapte. **1628** FELTHAM *Resolves* I. ii. 4 Like a Partridge in the net, he maskes himselfe the more, by the anger of his fluttering wing. **1825–80** JAMIESON, To *Mask*, to catch in a net. In this sense, a fish is said to be maskit, Ayrs[hire]. **1882** BUCKLAND *Notes & Jottings* 69 We quickly perceived from the bobbing of the corks that the fish..were 'masked' in the trammel.

absol. **1557** in *Tottel's Misc.* (Arb.) 133 Thus in the net of my conceit I masked styll among the sort Of such as fed vpon the bayt, That Cupide laide for his disport.

†**mask**, *v.*[2] *Obs.* [app. a shortened form of MASKER *v.*] *intr.* To be bewildered, lose one's way. Also quasi-*trans.* (quot. 1599).

c **1290** *S. Brandan* 118 in *S. Eng. Leg.* 223 Hi wende alond as maskede [*v.r.* masid] men, hi nuste whar hi were. **1387** TREVISA *Higden* (Rolls) II. 67 Elidurus..fonde his broþer Archgalon maskynge [L. *aberrantem*] in a wode [FABYAN *Chron.* II. xl. (1811) 28 *has* maskelyng or wandryng in the thykest of yᵉ wood]. *a* **1550** *Image Hypocr.* in *Skelton's Wks.* (1843) II. 433/2 Lest it be to late To trust on hadd I wist, Imasked in a myst. **1581** J. BELL *Haddon's Answ. Osorius* 119 Followyng herein (as it seemeth) his forerunner Hosius, who maskyng in the like maze, doth affirme [etc.]. **1599** BP. HALL *Sat.* IV. iii. 59 Or whiles thou seest some of thy Stallion-race, Their eyes boar'd out, masking the miller's-maze. **1639** FULLER *Holy War* III. xii. 129 He doeth the benighted traveller a discourtesie..who lendeth him a lantern to take it away, leaving him more masked then he was before.

mask (mɑːsk, -æ-), *v.*[3] *Sc.* [Northern var. MASH *v.*[1]]

1. *trans.* = MASH *v.*[1] (occas. *absol.*). Also, to brew.

1480 *Cath. Angl.* 230/1 To Maske, *ceruidare*. **15..** *Chalmerlan Ayr c.* 26 §6 (in *Sc. Acts* I.) Item þat þai grynd jt [malt] our small þat jt will nocht ryn quhen jt is maskit. **1639** RUTHERFORD *Lett.* 1 Oct. (1881) 409, I hope, for His sake, who brewed and masked this cup [of affliction] in

heaven, ye will gladly drink. *c* **1650** in W. Ross *Aberdour & Inchcolme* x. (1885) 284 [To impose a fine..on 'browsters' who 'masked' on Sabbath night]. **1743** R. MAXWELL *Trans. Soc. Improv. Agric.* 352 A Brewing-keeve, wherein Brewers mask their Drink. **1871** W. ALEXANDER *Johnny Gibb* xxx. 214 There's naething like a starn gweed maut, maskit i' yer nain bowie.

2. To infuse (tea); = MASH *v.*[1] 1 d.

1814 SCOTT *Wav.* xlii, I hope your honours wil tak tea.. and I maun gang and mask it for you. **1883** ANNIE S. SWAN *Aldersyde* II. i. 78 Marget will mask anither cup o' tea for ye. *transf.* **1846** JOHNSTON in *Proc. Berw. Nat. Club* II. 176 One dozen stalks are 'masked' in a pint of boiling water.

3. *to be masking*: (*a*) of a storm, to be 'brewing'; (*b*) of a person, to be sickening *for* a disease.

183. ALEX. RODGERS in *Whistle-Binkie* Ser. I. 108, I saw the storm was masking fast, That soon wad fa' on me. **1866** W. GREGOR *Banff. Gloss.*, *Mask*, to gather..; as, 'It's maskin', or maskin' up for anither shoor'. **1876** *Whitby Gloss.* s.v., It's masking for thunder. **1887** SERVICE *Dr. Duguid* xviii. 116, I could see that he was maskin' for the pocks.

mask (mɑːsk, -æ-), *v.*[4] Also 6–7 **maske**, 7–9 **masque**. [f. MASK *sb.*[3] Cf. F. *masquer*.]

1. a. *trans.* To cover (the face or head) with a mask. Chiefly *pass.* To wear, be disguised with, a mask.

1588 SHAKS. *L.L.L.* v. ii. 157 The Trompet sounds, be maskt, the maskers come. **1593** —— *Lucr.* 794 Where now I haue no one to blush with me,..To maske their browes and hide their infamie. **1611** DEKKER & MIDDLETON *Roaring Girl* 204 Good faces maskt are Iewels kept by spirits. Hide none but bad ones. **1617** MORYSON *Itin.* III. 173 The Women no lesse then Men..goe masked. **1711** STEELE *Spect.* No. 8 ¶4 All the Persons who compose this lawless Assembly are masked. **1825** LYTTON *Zicci* 15 A tall figure, masked and mantled, appeared. **1839** LANE *Arab. Nts.* I. 73 At the fair of Okaz, the heroes were masked.

b. *gen.* To disguise.

1847 TENNYSON *Princess* v. 386 A rout of saucy boys Brake on us..Mask'd like our maids. **1903** *Edin. Rev.* Apr. 411 His ghost masks himself in no futile disguises.

c. To provide with a gas mask.

1916 *War Illustr.* IV. 607 Machine-gun section masked, ready for the enemy. **1918** H. W. WILSON *Great War* XI. 455 French soldier with one of the French army dogs, both masked against enemy gas attack.

2. *transf.* **a.** To hide or conceal from view, by interposing something.

1583 STANYHURST *Æneis* III. (Arb.) 86 Whilste thee sunbeams are maskt, hyls darcklye be muffled. *c* **1600** SHAKS. *Sonn.* xxxiii, The region cloude hath mask'd him from me now. **1605** —— *Macb.* II. i. 125 Masking the Businesse from the common Eye. **1634** CRASHAW in T.S. tr. *Lessius' Hygiasticon* To Rdr., A soul, whose intellectuall beams No mists do mask, no lazie steams. **1833** LYELL *Princ. Geol.* III. 210 The talus *d*, *e*, which masked the inland cliff until it was artificially laid open to view. **1871** L. STEPHEN *Playgr. Eur.* iv. (1894) 102 Rocky fragments..frequently masked by cushions of fresh fallen snow.

b. *Mil.* and *Fortif.* (*a*) To conceal (a battery, a force, etc.) from the view of the enemy. (*b*) To hinder (a fortress, army, fleet) from acting on the offensive by watching it with a sufficient force. (*c*) To hinder the efficiency of a friendly force by standing in the line of its fire.

1706 *Lond. Gaz.* No. 4256/2 Many Persons might march out with the Garison masked as the Governor should think fit. **1763** *British Mag.* IV. 204 The seamen..mounted all the guns in the battery, which we masked. **1802** JAMES *Mil. Dict.* s.v., One toise and a half of epaulement will require two chandeliers, and 60 fascines, to mask it. **1811** WELLINGTON in Gurw. *Desp.* VII. 338 The other fleche was masked. **1868** KIRK *Charles the Bold* III. v. iii. 411 The idea of leaving Morat unassailed, masking it with a portion of his army while prosecuting operations with the rest. **1870** *Pall Mall G.* 3 Sept. 2 Bazaine..has succeeded in convincing the Prussians that it requires a large force to mask him. **1875** BEDFORD *Sailor's Pocket Bk.* vii. (ed. 2) 268 Such boats must be cautioned not to mask the fire of any boats employed for the same purpose. **1884** *Pall Mall G.* 29 Oct. 2/2 To command the sea we must be prepared at a moment's notice to mask the enemies' fleets by forces..equal to his.

c. *Arch.*

1828 STEUART *Planter's Guide* 518 It appeared extremely desirable to that artist to mask or conceal the Approach from the House and adjoining grounds. **1867** BARRY *Life Sir C. Barry* viii. 291 A cloister with one story above it, or an open arcade, might mask the building from the high ground of Bridge Street. **1879** SIR G. SCOTT *Lect. Archit.* II. 100 The roofs, internally, may be proved to have been masked by level ceilings.

d. *Zool.* and *Bot.*

1843 OWEN *Invert. Anim.* (1855) 436 That stage of the Orthopterous..insects, in which they are masked by the vermiform or true larval condition. **1857** A. GRAY *1st Less. in Bot.* xv. (1866) 106 In Catalpa this number is masked in the calyx by irregular union, and in the stamens by abortion.

e. *Cookery.* (See quot.)

1877 *Cassell's Dict. Cookery* 1177/2 *Mask*, to cover meat with any rich sauce, ragoût, &c.

f. *Photogr.* To cover, shade or mount with a mask.

1881, **1884** [see MASKING *vbl. sb.*[2] 2].

g. To disguise the real character of or diminish the effect of.

1922 W. G. KENDREW *Climates of Continents* 18 The south-east trades..are now at their greatest strength, but sea breezes mask them on the immediate littoral. **1931** *Times* 18 Feb. 6/5 It was this late stroke, masked, into the left corner which defeated the game of Joshua Crane.

h. Of a sound or other object of perception: to diminish or prevent the perception of (another stimulus, usu. one affecting the same sense).

1923 *Physical Rev.* XXI. 706 When the masking tone is loud it masks tones of higher frequency better than those of frequency lower than itself. **1949** MCCORD & WITHERIDGE *Odors* xvii. 190 The opportunity for masking objectionable textile odors by..impregnating the goods with a definitely noticeable perfume seems to be negligible. **1960** *Lang. & Speech* III. 160 The low-frequency noise masks the voicing of a consonant. **1966** *Jrnl. Exper. Psychol.* LXXII. 233/1 Backward masking refers to the power of certain stimuli, the masking stimuli, to disrupt or mask the processing of other stimuli, the target stimuli, which have been presented *earlier*. **1973** D. L. RICHARDS *Telecommunication by Speech* iii. 113 Room noise that masks speech from the other station will make conversation more difficult. **1974** *Encycl. Brit. Macropædia* XVI. 555/1 The substantially greater intensity of one odour may mask another.

i. *Chem.* To prevent (a substance or ion) from taking part in a certain reaction by causing it to undergo another preliminary reaction.

1934 in WEBSTER. **1936** *Industr. & Engin. Chem. (Analytical Ed.)* 15 Nov. 409/1 A characteristic example in the analysis of anions is that..in which sulfite is masked by the addition of formaldehyde. **1970** D. D. PERRIN *Masking & Demasking Chem. Reactions* i. 2 Silver is masked by ammonia against precipitation as the hydroxide or chloride.

3. *fig.* To disguise (feelings, etc.) under an assumed outward show; to conceal the real nature, intent, or meaning of.

1588 SHAKS. *L.L.L.* I. ii. 98 Most immaculate thoughts Master, are mask'd vnder such colours. **1594** PLAT *Jewell-ho.* I. 55 Howsoeuer the same was masked, or disguised in shew. **1656** BRAMHALL *Replic.* iii. 153 Sedition masked under the Visard of Religion. **1777** SHERIDAN *Sch. Scand.* I. i, He has been obliged to mask his pretensions. **1841** D'ISRAELI *Amen. Lit.* (1867) 683 Polemical studies become political when the heads of parties mask themselves under some particular doctrine. **1865** DICKENS *Mut. Fr.* III. v, Its old simplicity of expression got masked by a certain craftiness. **1870** MORRIS *Earthly Par.* I. I. 215 Masking with a smile The vain regrets that in their hearts arose.

†**4. a.** *intr.* To take part in a masque or masquerade; to be a masquer, to masquerade. Also *to mask it*. Also *fig. Obs.*

a **1562** G. CAVENDISH *Wolsey* (1893) 108 An other maske ..of noble gentilmen, who daunced & masked with these fayer ladyes. **1589** NASHE *Pasquill & Marforius* 1, I wonder how I missed you? *Pasquill.* Neuer maruaile at that, I haue learned to maske it. **1591** SPENSER *Tears of Muses* 180 Where be the sweete delights of learnings treasure..In which I late was wont to raine as Queene, And maske in mirth with Graces well beseene? **1597** BEARD *Theatre God's Judgem.* (1612) 435 Six [masquers] that masked it to a marriage at the hostell of St. Paules in Paris. **1606** *Choice, Chance & Change* (1881) 50 After they had masked and mummed, away they went. **1731** BAILEY vol. II, *Mask*,..to go to masks or masquerades.

b. *trans.* To perform after the fashion of a masque. *Obs.*

1560 PILKINGTON *Expos. Aggeus* (1562) 58 These be the dueties of good shepeheardes..and not maskynge masses, and mumming mattyns.

†**5.** *intr.* To be or go in disguise; to hide one's real form or character under an outward show. Often *fig. Obs.*

1579 SPENSER *Shep. Cal.* Jan. 24 Now is come thy wynter's stormy state, Thy mantle mard, wherein thou maskedst late. *c* **1585** *Faire Em.* I. 86 Thus must we mask to save our wretched lives. *a* **1591** H. SMITH *Six Serm.* (1618) A 4, Like Æsops Asse, masking in the Lions skinne. **1619** HIERON *Wks.* I. 21 The spirituall venome that masketh vnder these deceitfull shadowes, is either not beleeued or not thought vpon. **1632** LITHGOW *Trav.* IX. 394 The French men..were cruelly massacred..; which exploit masketh vnder the name of Vesperi Siculi. **1649** DRUMM. OF HAWTH. *Irene* Wks. (1711) 170 How bravely soever ye mask and flowrish in words.

mask(e, var. ff. MASQUE; corrupt var. MAST *sb.*[2]

maskalonge: see MUSKELLUNGE.

maskarado, obs. form of MASQUERADE.

†**masked**, *ppl. a.*[1] [f. MASK *v.*[2] + -ED[1].] Amazed, bewildered.

c **1290** [see MASK *v.*[2]].

masked (mɑːskt, -æ-), *ppl. a.*[2] Also 7–9 **masqued**. [f. MASK *sb.*[3] or *v.*[4] + -ED.]

1. a. Having, wearing, or provided with a mask.

a **1637** B. JONSON *Underwoods, Death Sir H. Morison* 23 For, what is..masked man, if valu'd by his face, Above his fact? **1681** WYNDHAM *King's Concealm.* 75 Thus entred these masqued Travellers, to enquire where they were. **1751** H. WALPOLE *Lett.* (1846) II. 397 Where there are a few good pictures, and many masked statues. **1841** SPALDING *Italy* II. 371 These characters were represented by masked actors.

b. *masked ball* [F. *bal masqué*]: a ball at which those taking part wear masks; = MASQUERADE I.

1813 *Sk. Character* (ed. 2) I. 201 She's going to give a masqued ball in February. **1825** *Greenhouse Comp.* I. 250 At masqued routs. **1873** OUIDA *Pascarel* I. 151 It was the masked ball of the Carnival.

c. Used (often repr. L. *larvatus*, *personatus*) as the specific name of animals having some conformation or marking resembling a mask.

1840 *Cuvier's Anim. Kingd.* 130 The Masked Boar (*Sus larvatus*). **1859** WOOD *Nat. Hist.* I. 245 *Paguma larvata*, ..Masked Glutton. **187.** *Cassell's Nat. Hist.* II. 343 The Japan, or Masked Pig (*Sus pliciceps*, Gray). *Ibid.* IV. 162 The Masked Finfoot (*Podica personata*). **1882** *Ibid.* VI. 200 The Masked Crab [= *mask-crab*, MASK *sb.*[3] 5]. **1896** H. O. FORBES *Handbk. Primates* I. 163 The Masked Titi. *Callithrix personata*.

d. *Bot.* Of a corolla: = PERSONATE.

1793 MARTYN *Lang. Bot.*, *Personata corolla*, a personate or masked corolla. **1839** LINDLEY *Introd. Bot.* (ed. 3) I. ii. 167 If the upper and lower sides of the orifice are pressed together, as in Antirrhinum, it [the corolla] is personate or masked, resembling the face of some grinning animal.

e. *masked jug*: see MASK *sb.*[3]

2. *transf.* and *fig.* **a.** Having the real features or character concealed or disguised. Also *occas.* Concealed from view.

1585 T. WASHINGTON tr. *Nicholay's Voy.* III. xviii. 105 The masked hypocrisie of this olde foxe. *a* **1586** SIDNEY *Arcadia* II. (1590) 223 b, [He] was not the sharpest pearcer into masked minds. *c* **1600** SHAKS. *Sonn.* liv, When sommers breath their masked buds discloses. *a* **1628** LD. BROOKE *Poems, Of Humane Learn.* lxxxi. 38 Nothing new But masked euill which still addeth terror. **1815** W. H. IRELAND *Scribbleomania* 270 *note*, Others..pursue it..with invidious sarcasms and masqued sneers. **1904** HEWLETT *Queen's Quair* I. viii. 113 None could under-read her masked words.

b. *Nosology.* Of diseases, esp. intermittent fevers: presenting anomalous symptoms; not recognizable by the usual criteria.

1833 *Cycl. Pract. Med.* II. 234/1 (Fever). Masked intermittents. *Ibid.* 235/1 Masked ague. **1843–71** WATSON *Lect. Princ. & Pract. Physic* (ed. 5) I. 821 Sometimes the patient is said to have *lurking* gout or *masked* gout. **1897** *Allbutt's Syst. Med.* II. 317 Masked malarial fever. **1899** *Ibid.* VIII. 558 The psoriasis may remain masked.

c. Of a sound or other stimulus (see MASK *v.*[4] 2 h, MASKING *vbl. sb.*[2] 2 b).

1924 *Physical Rev.* XXIII. 270 The frequency of the masked tone is indicated on each curve. **1965** T. S. LITTLER *Physics Ear* vii. 134 We usually determine the level at which a sound has to be maintained in order to be just audible in the presence of another. This is known as the masked threshold of the masked or maskee sound in the presence of the masking or masker sound.

d. *Chem.* Of a substance or molecular group: prevented from taking part in a certain reaction by being in a bound form, esp. as a result of another preliminary reaction.

1932 *Discovery* Mar. 96/2 The first traces of the masked iron indicative of haemoglobin appear in the nuclei of certain cells. **1940** R. E. OESPER tr. *Feigl's Specific & Special Reactions for Qualitative Analysis* iv. 49 This fact was used ..to release the cationically masked sulfate groups in the green complex chronic sulfate solutions. **1974** *Angewandte Makromolekulare Chemie* XXXIV. 111 Tertiary aliphatic amines containing masked methylol groups, e.g. methylolalkylether.. , prove efficient catalysts in the production of polyurethane foams.

3. *Mil.* and *Fortif.* Chiefly in ***masked battery***: see MASK *v.*[4] 2 b. Also *fig.*

1759 DILWORTH *Life Pope* 52 Mr. Addison, to vent his spleen against Mr. Pope by the means of a masked battery. **1768** GOLDSM. *Good-n. Man* IV. (near end), You shall.. burst out upon the miscreant like a masqued battery. **1783** JUSTAMOND tr. *Raynal's Hist. Indies* V. 462 A masked battery, intended to cover the harbour and town of Paramabiro. **1800** *Asiat. Ann. Reg.* II. 145/2 The attempt which was made to annihilate an inquiry of such importance, by the masked battery of an amendment.

†**'maskeler.** *Obs.* Also **masculer.** [? alteration of MASKER *sb.*[1]] ? A mask. ? Hence (by substitution of suffix) **'maskeling** (in quot. *-yn*), a masquerade.

1511 in Collier *Hist. Dram. Poetry* (1879) I. 79 To Richard Gybson opon a warraunt for the revells, called a maskelyn at New-hall in Essex, 20*l.* 5*s.* 1½*d.* **1512** *Ibid.*, Also for masculers and other diverse things. *a* **1548** HALL *Chron., Hen. VIII* 80 b, Euery one visered himselfe, so that they were unknowen..and so in maskeler passed the toune of Arde.

maskeles, -ez, var. ff. MASCLELESS *Obs.*

maskeline, obs. form of MASLIN[2].

maskelles, -ez, variant ff. MASCLELESS *Obs.*

maskelonge, -enozha, var. ff. MUSKELLUNGE.

maskelynite ('mæskəlɪnaɪt). *Min.* [ad. G. *maskelynit* (G. Tschermak 1872, in *Sitzungsber. d. K. Akad. d. Wissensch. (Math.-Natur. Cl.)* LXV. 131), f. the name of Nevil Story-*Maskelyne* (1823–1911), English mineralogist): see -ITE[1].] A colourless aluminosilicate of calcium and sodium which has a composition near to that of andesine and is found in some kinds of meteorite.

1875 E. S. DANA in J. D. Dana *Syst. Min.* (ed. 5) App. II. 37 Maskelynite. **1921** *Bull. Geol. Soc. Amer.* XXXII. 402 The name maskelynite..was first given by Tschermak to an isotropic constituent of the habit and composition of a labradorite feldspar occurring in the stone of Shergotty. The name has since been extended to cover a colorless interstitial substance, sometimes quite isotropic and sometimes faintly doubly refracting, of like appearance and habit, and a common if not universal constituent of the chondritic meteorites. **1971** *Physics Bull.* Oct. 578/2 It appears that intense shock disorders the lattice to produce the isotropic mineral maskelynite.

masken: see MASQUIN *Obs.*

†**masker**, *sb.*[1] *Obs.* Also 6 maskyr. [ad. It. *maschera*: see MASQUERADE *sb.*] A mask. Phr. *in masker*: disguised with a mask, in masquerade.

1519 in Ellis *Orig. Lett.* Ser. I. I. 143 The King..woll come..and see your Grace in Calais in maskyr. **1532** MORE *Confut. Barnes* VIII. Wks. 758/1 Their maskers [to be] taken of and their hipocrisie to be dyscouered. **1548** THOMAS *Ital. Gram.* (1567), *Maschera*, a masker, or a visour.

masker, *sb.*², **masquer** (ˈmɑːskə(r), -æ-). [f. MASK *v.*⁴ + -ER¹. Cf. F. *masqueur.*] One who takes part in a masquerade or masque; a person in masquerade, a masquerader.

α. *a* **1548** HALL *Chron., Hen. VIII* 16 After the banket doen, these Maskers came in. **1590** SPENSER *F.Q.* III. xii. 6 The whiles the maskers marched forth in trim aray. **1613** CHAPMAN *Maske Inns Court* A 1 b, Then rode the chiefe maskers, in Indian habits, all of a resemblance. **1722** STEELE *Conscious Lovers* I. i. (1755) 12 You know I was last Thursday at the Masquerade:..the Maskers you know followed us. **1828** SCOTT *F.M. Perth* xiii, They show themselves in the streets as the companions of maskers. **1867** PARKMAN *Jesuits in N. Amer.* iii. (1875) 15 A party of maskers at the Carnival.

β. **1580** LYLY *Euphues* (Arb.) 332 Masquers do therefore couer their faces that they may open their affections. **1625** BACON *Ess., Of Masques* (Arb.) 540 Let the Sutes of the Masquers, be Gracefull, and such as become the Person, when the Vizars are off. *a* **1777** GOLDSM. *Epil. to 'Sisters'* 12 The world's a masquerade! the masquers, you, you, you. **1814** SCOTT *Lord of Isles* v. xxiv, In masquers quaint attire She sought his skiff. **1849** DICKENS *Barn. Rudge* iv, Your blockhead father..slips him on a mask and domino, and mixes with the masquers. **1873** OUIDA *Pascarel* I. 23 The masquers reeled on out of sight.

Comb. **1593** NASHE *Christ's T.* 71 b, Your mornelike christall countenaunces shall be netted ouer, and (Masker-like) cawle-visarded, with crawling venomous wormes.

†**b.** *transf.* and *fig.*

1593 NASHE *Christ's T.* 73 b, England,..the continuall Masquer in out-landish habilements. **1647** CLARENDON *Contempl. Ps.* Tracts (1727) 406 Those maskers in religion and honesty.

masker (ˈmɑːskə(r), -æ-), *v. Obs.* exc. *dial.* Forms: α. 4 **malscre, malskre**; β. 5–9 **masker**, (7 **maskar, maskre**). [OE. **malscrian*, implied in *malscrung* vbl. sb.; app. cogn. w. Goth. **malsks* (? foolish) in *untila-malsks* precipitate (tr. Gr. προπετής 'heady' A.V., 'headstrong' R.V., 2 Tim. iii. 4), OS. *malsc* proud. Cf. MASK *v.*²]

a. *trans.* To bewilder, confuse. **b.** *pass.* and *intr.* To be bewildered. Hence ˈ**maskering** *vbl. sb.* and *ppl. a.*

c **725** *Corpus Gloss.* F 55 (Hessels) *Festinatio* [i.e. *fascinatio*], malscrung. *c* **1000** *Sax. Leechd.* III. 36 Wið malscrunge minra [? *read* manra] wihta. *c* **1350** *Will. Palerne* 416 How he hade missed is mayne & malskrid a-boute. **13..** *E.E. Allit. P.* B. 991 Þe ledez of þat lyttel toun wern lopen out for drede, In-to þat malscrande mere. *a* **1400–50** *Alexander* 1270 And þat left ware on lyfe bot a litill meȝne, Ware als malscrid [*miswritten* malstrid: *Dubl. MS.* maistrett] & mased. *c* **1450** *Cast. Persev.* (E.E.T.S.) 76/75 Mankynd is maskeryd with mekyl varyaunce. **1577–87** HOLINSHED *Chron.* II. 716 They..so maskered his understanding, that..they brought him to tract the steps of lewd demeanour. **1600** HOLLAND *Livy* III. lx. 129 To masker their troubled heads the more, hee assaileth them with a great shout and maine violence. **1601** DEACON & WALKER *Answ. to Darel* To Rdr. 4 An intricate Labyrinth, or maskaring maze. **1681** H. MORE *Expos. Dan.* Pref. 7 Why might not the wise men..be so maskard that they could not read the handwriting on the wall? *a* **1800** PEGGE *Suppl. Grose* (1814), *Masker'd*, stunned; also nearly choaked. North. **1841** HARTSHORNE *Salop. Antiq.* 503 Sich a dark neet I was masker'd like. **1879** MISS JACKSON *Shropsh. Word-bk.*, *Maskered*, confused, bewildered.

maskerade, -at, obs. forms of MASQUERADE.

†ˈ**maskery**, ˈ**masquery**. *Obs.* Also 6 **maskarye, mascarie**. [a. F. *masquerie*, f. *masque* MASK *sb.*³: see -ERY.] Masking, wearing of masks; a masquerade. Also, masquerader's attire.

a **1548** HALL *Chron., Hen. VIII* 80 b, Another compaignie of .x. lordes in whiche maskery the kyng was himselfe. **1554** in Maitland *Ess. Reform.* (1849) 303 Such as have most wickedly called the Mass a Maskarye. **1554** YAXLEY in Ellis *Orig. Lett.* Ser. III. III. 313 A brave maskery of cloth of gold and syluer, apparailed in maryners garments. **1561** T. HOBY tr. *Castiglione's Courtyer* II. (1577) M vj b, I being in maskerie passed by. **1585** T. WASHINGTON tr. *Nicholay's Voy.* III. xiii. 95 b, Disguysing themselues with certaine masquerie, as with heades and Cranes neckes. **1640** NABBES *Unfort. Mother* E 4 b, *Mac.* Wee'l first thanke Heaven, And then wee'l see some maskery.

fig. **1569** J. SANFORD *Agrippa* 170 b, They attire him [*sc.* Christ] in diuers maskeries of sophismes. **1598** MARSTON *Sco. Villany* III. viii. G 3, Me thinks I heare swart Martius cry, Souping along in warrs fain'd maskerie. **1655** GURNALL *Chr. in Arm.* I. 306 The masquery and cheating glory of the great ones of this world.

masket, masquet (ˈmɑːskɪt, -æ-). *dial.* [The phr. *a masket* perh. represents OE. **ȝemalscrod*, pa. pple. of **malscrian* MASKER *v.*] *to go, run a masket*: to lose one's way.

1570 JEWEL *Holy Script.* (1582) 158 The Professours thereof oftentimes runne a masket; they leese them selues. **1697** *Let. in MS. Lansd.* No. 1033. 2 (Halliw.) To go a masked. **1897** THORNTON *Remin.* vi. (E.D.D.), O sir, do'ee please come down, the gentleman has gone a masquet.

maskett, obs. form of MASSICOT.

maskette (mɑːskˈɛt, -æ-). [f. MASK *sb.*² + -ETTE.] (See quot. and cf. MASKOID.)

1881–2 W. H. DALL in *3rd Rep. Bureau Ethnol.* (1884) 93 The *Maskette*, an object resembling a mask, but intended to be worn above or below the face. *Ibid.* 105 A number of maskettes and head dresses from New Mexico and Arizona.

maskewe, var. MASCUE *v. Obs.*

†**mask-fat.** *Sc.* and *north. dial. Obs.* Forms: 3 **mascfat**, 4–6 **mask fat**, (4 **maxfate**), 5–6 **mask-fatt**, (6 **maskefatt, -fate**). [Northern var. MASH-FAT: see MASK *sb.*² and FAT *sb.*¹] A mashing vat.

1263 *Excheq. Rolls Scotl.* (1878) I. 14 Item, in ij cunys, scilicet, mascfats, emptis, ij s. **1367** *Finchale Priory Acc.* (1837) p. lxxviii, j maskfat, j gylfat. **1378** in *Test. Karleol.* (1893) 127 Unum plumbum cum uno maxfate. **1430** *Test. Ebor.* (Surtees) II. 12 Unum maskfatt. **1567** *Wills & Inv. N.C.* (Surtees) I. 267 A maskfatt and a swett wort fatt. **1600** *Acc. Bk. W. Wray* in *Antiquary* XXXII. 279 Item one maskefate. **1753** CHAMBERS *Cycl. Supp.* s.v. *Brewer*, The..utensils of a brewer..are a furnace..a copper..a mask-fat.

†ˈ**maskful**, *a. Obs. rare*⁻¹. [f. MASK *sb.*³ + -FUL.] Of the nature of masquerade.

1655 tr. *Com. Hist. Francion* v. 11 There is a great Feast within, full of all maskfull Recreations.

maskill, obs. form of MASCLE *sb.*¹

masking (ˈmɑːskɪŋ, -æ-), *vbl. sb.*¹ *Obs.* exc. *Sc.* or *dial.* [f. MASK *v.*³ + -ING¹.] = MASHING *vbl. sb.*

1654 *Extracts Burgh Recs. Stirling* (1887) 211 They sall pay for ilk maskene lost in thair default fourtie shilling. **1797** *Encycl. Brit.* (ed. 3) III. 544/1 (*Brewing*), This part of the operation is called masking.

b. A sufficient quantity (of tea, etc.) for an infusion.

1825–80 JAMIESON. **1893** *Northumbld. Gloss.*, *Maskin.*

c. *Comb.* (cf. MASH, MASHING), as ***masking-fat***, ***lead*** (see LEAD *sb.*¹ 5 a), ***-loom*** (see LOOM *sb.*¹ 2), ***rudder***, ***tub***; **masking pot (pat)** *Sc.*, a tea-pot.

? *a* **1400** *Chalmerlan Ayr* c. 26 (in *Sc. Acts* I. 337/1) Et ea est causa quod cum coquitur in lie *masking fat non currit. **1659** A. HAY *Diary* (1901) 94, I payed him for the great masking fat 4 merks. **1822** SCOTT *Pirate* xxiv, She found him drowned in his own masking-fat. **1465** *Finchale Priory Acc.* (1837) p. ccxcix, In primis j *maskyng leyd. **1711** RAMSAY *Maggy Johnstoun* xii, The pith of broom That she stow'd in her *masking-loom. **1786** BURNS *When Guilford good* i, Then up they gat the *maskin-pat. **1648** *Invent.* in *Spottiswoode Misc.* (1844–5) I. 372 Ther is in the brewhous ..and ane *maskine rudder. **1457** *Peebles Charters*, etc. (1872) 119 A *maskyn tub with the laf that langis it.

masking, masquing (ˈmɑːskɪŋ, -æ-), *vbl. sb.*² [f. MASK *v.*⁴ + -ING¹.]

1. a. The action of performing or taking part in a masquerade or masque.

α. **1546** BALE *Eng. Votaries* I. (1548) 50 b, Theyr maskynges in yᵉ night after yᵉ paganes maner. *c* **1560** in *T. Warton's Life Sir T. Pope* (1772) 85 In Shrovetide, 1556, sir Thomas Pope made for the ladie Elisabeth all at his owne costes, a greate and rich maskinge in the greate halle at Hatfelde. *c* **1640** C'TESS LINDSEY in *Buccleuch MSS.* (Hist. MSS. Comm.) I. 285 There will be masking at Quort at Twelfth-night. **1711** *Lond. Gaz.* No. 4836/1 There was a publick Masking permitted for three Days and Nights. **1864** BURTON *Scot Abr.* I. v. 309 Those who thus go a-masking on New Year's eve,..are called guisards or guizers.

β. *a* **1616** B. JONSON *Love Restored* ad init., I tell thee, I will haue no more masquing. **1716–8** LADY M. W. MONTAGUE *Lett.* I. xxi. 64 The carnival is begun, and all sorts of diversions..except that of masquing. **1742** H. WALPOLE *Lett.* (1903) I. 175 The Duchess..makes a grand masqueing next week.

b. Used with contemptuous reference to the Mass.

[**1546, 1550**: see 3.] **1555** PHILPOT in Foxe *A. & M.* (1583) II. 1828 Ye haue deceiued the people with that your sacrifice of the Masse, which ye make a masking. **1563–83** FOXE *A. & M.* II. 1203 Playne, seeing a Priest go to Masse, said, Now you shall see one in masking.

2. a. The action or process of using a mask; obscuring or covering (wholly or in part) by the interposition or overlaying of something. Also ***masking-out***.

1881 ABNEY *Photogr.* 242 In the printing of the picture..by a judicious masking of parts he can cause pictures which would be inartistic to become merely inoffensive. **1884** *Ibid.* (ed. 6) 212 Masking the Negative. **1933** E. MOLLOY *Mod. Motor Repair* III. 980/1 Where a line is required or a clear finished edge, this is obtained by masking. *Ibid.*, Any upholstery will require masking..if the whole car is going to be sprayed. **1949** C. E. CHAPEL et al. *Aircraft Maintenance & Repair* xxi. 361/1 Figure 6 illustrates the masking of an airplane wing in order that the wing may be finished in two colors. **1951** *Electronics* Feb. 109/1 In color photography a technique known as 'masking' has been developed in which a negative image is combined with a positive image in printing, thus effectively introducing negative light in the final result. **1956** *Bell Syst. Techn. Jrnl.* XXXV. 334 If part of the work is coated with an insulating varnish, electrolytic etching will take place only on the uncoated surfaces. This technique, often called 'masking', has the limitation that the etching undercuts the masking if any considerable amount of material is removed. **1967** E. CHAMBERS *Photolitho-Offset* iv. 39 Additional equipment should include an airbrush, for use in connection with continuous tone negatives and positives complete with frisket-paper for masking-out and vignetting. **1972** L. LAMB *Picture Frame* i. 16 Adhesive tape was used for temporary masking-out so that a colour could be given a straight, hard-edge.

b. The action of one stimulus in diminishing the sensitivity of a subject to another (cf. MASK *v.*⁴ 2 h).

1923 *Physical Rev.* XXI. 706 For tones introduced into the same ear, except when the frequencies are so close as to produce beats, the masking is greatest for tones nearly alike. **1949** MCCORD & WITHERIDGE *Odors* xvii. 186 Masking is an effect produced at the point of sense perception in the respiratory passages together with the final interpretation in the brain and does not constitute an aromatic correction of the aerial components. **1962** A. NISBETT *Technique Sound Studio* x. 170 A second reason for holding effects back..is the masking that is caused by even moderately quiet background sound. **1967** *Science* 15 Sept. 1335/3 Visual backward masking consists in the retroactive interference with the perception of one visual stimulus, the target, by another visual stimulus, the mask, closely following the target in time. **1974** *Encycl. Brit. Macropædia* IX. 243/2 Some dentists use auditory analgesia (a 'masking' of pain by sound).

c. *Chem.* The prevention of a substance or ion from taking part in a certain reaction by causing it to undergo another preliminary reaction.

1936 F. FEIGL in *Industr. & Engin. Chem.* (*Analytical Ed.*) 15 Nov. 409/1 The masking of certain reactions of mercury, copper, nickel, and cobalt by cyanide and thiocyanate has been known for a long time. **1963** P. W. WEST in E. W. Berg *Physical & Chem. Methods of Separation* xviii. 343 The term *masking* was introduced many years ago by Prof. Fritz Feigl, who utilized this technique in making specific or highly selective spot tests when the available reagents were general. **1971** *Nature* 19 Mar. 194/1 Generally speaking 'masking' has come to mean the prevention of the normal reaction of an ion upon addition of a reagent with which it reacts.

3. *attrib.* passing into *adj.* Used in, appropriate to, or consisting of a 'masking' or masquerade; masquerading.

1542 *Nottingham Rec.* III. 220 One maskynge garment of sarcenet. **1546** BALE *1st Exam. A. Askew* 34 b, Their popish portyfolyoms and maskynge bokes. *c* **1550** BECON *Jewel of Joy* Wks. 1560 II. 30 The papists affirme yᵗ theyr massekyng Masse is a perfecte sacrifyce for the quycke and the deade. *Ibid.* The papistes put on masking apparel Albes, girdels [etc.]. **1581** G. PETTIE tr. *Guazzo's Civ. Conv.* III. 137 To maintaine their wiues in suche pompeous and masking sorte. *a* **1586** SIDNEY *Apol. Poetrie* (Arb.) 41 Therefore [they] made Mistres Philosophy very often borrow the masking rayment of Poesie. **1612** in *Buccleuch MSS.* (Hist. MSS. Comm.) I. 243 Now the masking sports shall follow. **1649** MILTON *Eikon.* Pref., The conceited portraiture before his Book, drawn out to the full measure of a Masking Scene. *c* **1670** A. WOOD in *Life* (1848) 77 *note*, He hath compositions in courtly masquing ayres. **1673** DRYDEN *Marr. à la Mode* Prol., We shall show to-day A masking ball, to recommend our play. **1812** BYRON *Ch. Har.* II. lxxviii, In motley robe to dance at masking ball. **1821** SCOTT *Kenilw.* xl, Men, still habited in their masquing suits.

4. *Comb.* **masking board** *Photogr.*, the board on which the printing paper is fixed in an enlarger; **masking frame** *Photogr.* (see quot. 1940); **masking tape**, adhesive tape used for masking, esp. to protect certain areas of a surface before applying paint.

1958 *Newnes Compl. Amat. Photogr.* 319 The paper is removed from the masking board, and the next negative lined up in position. **1972** G. L. WAKEFIELD *Exposure Control in Enlarging* viii. 110 As a good masking board for the enlarger easel is expensive..it is worth making one. **1940** F. J. MORTIMER *Wall's Dict. Photogr.* (ed. 15) 441 *Masking frame*, an accessory used with vertical enlargers to hold the paper flat and provide a white border. **1958** *Newnes Compl. Amat. Photogr.* 318 The sheet of bromide paper is then placed in the masking frame. **1972** G. L. WAKEFIELD *Exposure Control in Enlarging* viii. 107 It had been intended to build the microammeter and associated electronics into a masking frame. **1936** BRIMM & BOGGESS *Airplane & Engine Maintenance* 282 After the numbers or letters have been outlined by pencil, they should be blocked in with masking tape. **1962** *Which? Car Suppl.* Oct. 138/1 Marks had been left by masking tape on the right rear body panel. **1971** D. E. WESTLAKE *I gave at the Office* (1972) 53 Someone had fairly recently put strips of masking tape over some sort of company name on the doors [of the trucks].

†ˈ**masking**, *ppl. a.*¹ *Obs.* [f. MASK *v.*² + -ING².] Bewildering.

1387 TREVISA *Higden* (Rolls) II. 219 Man..fel..out of hous in to maskynge and wayles contray [L. *de domo ad devium*].

†**masking**, *ppl. a.*² *Obs.* [f. MASK *v.*¹ + -ING².] Ensnaring, trammelling.

1578 TIMME *Calvin on Gen.* 170 When we are so carried away with the maskingnettes of beauty, that [etc.]. **1601** DEACON & WALKER *Spirits & Divels* 287 You are almost quite ferreted foorth from all your starting holes, and are now brought in a manner before the very mouth of that masking net, which will so entangle your toong, as [etc.].

masking (ˈmɑːskɪŋ, -æ-), *ppl. a.*³ [f. MASK *v.*⁴ + -ING².] That masks, in various senses of the vb. In early use, †hypocritical.

1577–87 HOLINSHED *Chron.* III. 1143/1 She should both to Christ shew hir selfe a false christian, and vnto hir prince a masking subiect. **1596** GOSSON *Pleas. Quips Gentlew.* (Percy Soc.) 7 Our masking dames can sport, you knowe, sometime by night, sometime by day. *a* **1652** J. SMITH *Sel. Disc.* vi. 237 That which was acted upon it..every one will grant to have been a masking or imaginary business. **1725** RAMSAY *Gentle Sheph.* III. iv. Prol., Sir William draps his masking beard. **1863** W. THORNBURY *True as Steel* II. 133 No one ever confesses that he has committed an injury; he calls it retaliation, or justice, or conceals it by some masking name. **1900** *Westm. Gaz.* 2 May 5/2 The masking force will have to be a strong one. **1923** [see MASK *v.*⁴ 2 h]. **1969** T. C. THORSTENSEN *Pract. Leather Technol.* viii. 115 In the study of masking agents it was established very early in chrome tanning research that the anions could be listed in order of increasing affinity for the chromium tanning complex. **1970** D. D. PERRIN *Masking & Demasking Chem. Reactions* i. 1 A masking reagent..is one that lowers the concentration of a free metal ion or a free ligand to such a level that certain of its chemical reactions are prevented. **1970** *Jrnl. Gen. Psychol.* LXXXII. 37 An exhaust fan provided masking noise.

maskins ('mæskɪnz). *Obs.* exc. *dial.* Also meskin(s. [f. MASS *sb.*[1] + *-kins*, as in *bodikins*, *pittikins* (cf. -KIN).] ***by the maskins***: by the mass; an asseverative exclamation.

1611 CHAPMAN *May-day* IV. I 2b, By the meskin me thought they were so indeede. **1647** BARON *Cyprian Acad.* I. 53 By the Maskins I would give the best cow in my yard, to find out this raskall. **1664** COTTON *Scarron.* IV. (1741) 85 And now this Swabber, by the Maskins, Thunders up Dido's Galligaskins. **1721** in BAILEY. [For 19th c. examples (Yorks., Lancs. & Derbysh.) see *Eng. Dial. Dict.*]

maskle, obs. form of MASCLE *sb.*[1]

maskoid ('mɑːskɔɪd, -æ-). [f. MASK *sb.*[2] + -OID.] (See quot. and cf. MASKETTE.)

1881-2 W. H. DALL in *3rd Rep. Bureau Ethnol.* (1884) 93 The *Maskoid*, an object resembling a mask or face, but not intended to be worn at all. *Ibid.* 105 Maskoids of stone,.. jasper, and jadeite. *Ibid.* 166 Wooden mortuary maskoid.

maskowe, variant of MASCUE *v. Obs.*

maskre, variant of MASKER *v.*

masleach, variant of MASHLOCH *Sc.*

maslin[1] ('mæzlɪn). Now *dial.* Forms: 1 mæstlin(g)c, -ling, *Northumb.* mæslen(n, 3 me(a)stling, 3-4 mastling, 4 masalyne, messelinge, -lyng, 4-6 maselyn, 5 mastelyn, mascelyne, masselen, messlyng, messelyne, 5-6 maslyn, 6 mastlyn(e, -line, masclyne, mystiltyne, maslyne, -leyn, -lenn, -lyn(n, maseleyn(e, -lyn(n)e, -len, massellen, measelen, meslyn, messilling, messelyng, 6-7 maslen, 7 mastlin, masline, mascellin, 4- maslin. [OE. *mæs(t)ling*, *mæslen* neut., app. formed (? with suffix -LING[2]) on an unrecorded **mæs* (the *t* being possibly a euphonic insertion) cogn. w. MHG. *mess(e* neut., brass (early mod.G. *mess*, *möss*, *mesch*, *mösch*; still *dial.*), whence (with suffix = -ING[3]) the synon. MHG., MDu. *messinc*, *missinc* masc., neut. (G., Du. *messing* neut.); adoptions from this or an equivalent LG. form were ON. *messing*, *mersing* fem. (OSw. *mäsinger*, Sw. *messing* masc., Da. *messing* com.); LG. has a parallel formation *mesken* (see -KIN).

Most scholars have regarded the OHG. *mess(e* neut., brass, as identical with MHG. *mässe*, *messe* fem., lump (of metal), usually believed to be a derivative of L. *massa* MASS *sb.*[2] The supposition involves serious difficulties, and has latterly been questioned (Kluge, Franck), but no plausible alternative has been found. It does not seem possible to connect the words with L. (*æs*) *miscellum* mixed brass, or with the popular Lat. word represented in MASLIN[2]. The MHG. *messinc* passed into Slavonic (Czech, Upper Serb. *mosaz*, Lower Serb. *mjesnik*, Little Russian *mošaž*, White Russian *mosenz*:—**mosengjŭ*) and Lith. (*masadis*). The view of Schrader that the Slav. word is the source of the MHG. is improbable, and leaves the OE. forms and the MHG. *messe* unexplained. On the other hand, Schrader's comparison of certain oriental words for brass (Kirghiz *moes*, Kurdish *mys*, Persian *mis*, Mazendoran *mers*, *mis*) seems worthy of consideration.]

1. A kind of brass. Now only *attrib.* (see 3).

c **950** *Lindisf. Gosp.* Mark vi. 8, *æs*, mæslen. *a* **1000** *Colloq. Ælfric* in Wr.-Wülcker 96/20 Mæstlingc ær and tin, *auricalcum, æs, et stagnum.* *a* **1225** *Ancr. R.* 284 *note*, Golt, seluer, stel, irn, copper, mestling, breas: al is icleopet or. *c* **1230** *Hali Meid.* 9 And is þat tu wendest gold iwurðen to meastling. *c* **1320** *Sir Beues* 3998 (Kölbing) Foure hondred copes of gold fyn And ase fele of maslin. **1398** TREVISA *Barth. De P.R.* XVI. v. (1495) 554 Laton.. though it be bras of Messelyng: yet it shyneth as golde wythout. **1403** *Nottingham Rec.* II. 20, ij. patellarum de maslyn. **1509** *Test. Ebor.* (Surtees) V. 4 A fore basyn of mystiltyne. **1530** PALSGR. 243/2 Masclyne brasse. **1601** HOLLAND *Pliny* II. 487 This precious Mascellin, this compound mettall I mean of gold, siluer, and brasse. **1607** *Lingua* IV. i. G4b, It must not be.. Brasse, nor Copper, nor Mastlin. **1688** R. HOLME *Armoury* III. 29/2 An Atchison, is a Mettle peece, neither Silver, Copper, Brass, Lead, or Tin, it is like Masline.

2. A vessel made of 'maslin'; now (*dial.*) = *maslin kettle* (see 3).

c **1000** *Ags. Gosp.* Mark vii. 4 Calicea frymða & ceaca & arfata & mæstlinga. **1854** *N. & Q.* 1st Ser. X. 393 An old brazier informs me that three-legged pots made of the same metal as tops, generally called bell-metal, were formerly known as maslin pots, or maslins. **1882** [see 3].

3. *attrib.* or *adj.* = Made of 'maslin'. Now chiefly in **maslin kettle**, a large pan used mostly for boiling fruit for preserve.

c **1450** *ME. Med. Bk.* (Heinrich) 99 Take a quart of good whit wyn, and do hit in a clene masselen panne. **1492** *Nottingham Rec.* III. 22 Unum maslyn basyn. **1553** *Inv. Ch. Goods, Staffs.* in *Ann. Lichfield* (1863) IV. 76, ij maselen candelstykes. **1555** *Richmond Wills* (Surtees) 86, ij messilling bassens. **1870** in Miss Jackson *Shropsh. Word-bk.*, Maslin kettle. **1882** *N. & Q.* 6th Ser. VI. 158 Brass vessels for boiling fruits, &c., are called *maslin pans* in the Birmingham trade; and from this cast iron enamelled goods for the same purpose are also called *maslins*. **1896** *Warwickshire Gloss.*, *Maslin-kettle*, a brass preserving-kettle.

maslin[2] ('mæzlɪn). Now *dial.* Forms: α. 4 mastlyoun, 5 mestylyon, -ilione, mystelon, mystlyone, mastilȝon, 5-6 mestlyon(e, mestelyn. β. 5 mastcleyne, 5-6 mestlyn, 6 mastlin (also 9), -linge, mestlen, -lin. γ. 6 masclyne, maskeline, myskelen, 7 mesclin. δ. 6 mascelyn, miscelin, -yne, mescelline, masseling, misseling, miscelling, 6-8 mescelin(e, 7 mascelline, masolin, mis(s)elin(e, miscel(l)an(e, -el(l)ine, misciline, messeline, -ling, missellan(e, misceling, 8 measeline, massellin. ε. 6 masclechon, masseljon, -jen, maseljohn, misleden, 7 massledine, masslegen, 8 mesledine, 9 machelson, maslegin, masselgem, mashelton. ζ. 6 mislin, myslen, 6-7 meslen, mesline, -lyne, 7 maslen, -land, -lyne, mislane, -leyne, mesling, -lyn, -lon, 7, 9 mashlin, 8 masling, mislen, (*Sc.* 8-9 mashlum, 9 -lam), 7- meslin, 6- maslin. (See also E.D.D. s.vv. *Mashelton*, *Maslin*[1].) [a. OF. *mesteillon* (for the many varieties of form see Godefr.):—late L. *mistiliōnem*, extended form of **mistilium* (whence OF. *mesteil*, mod.F. *méteil*), f. L. *mistus*, pa. pple. of *miscēre* to mix. Cf. MDu. *masteluun* (Du. *masteluin*).

Of the many Eng. forms, some represent dialectal varieties in OF.; others are due to popular etymology (the word having esp. been often associated with Eng. *mash* sb. or vb.); others again to learned pseudo-etymology, the spelling being assimilated to that of L. *miscellānea* 'hodge-podge', neut. pl. of *miscellāneus* (see MISCELLANEOUS, MISCELLANE).]

Mixed grain, *esp.* rye mixed with wheat. Also, bread made of mixed corn.

α. **1303** R. BRUNNE *Handl. Synne* 10125 Þe paste.. Shal nat be of no medel corne,.. Þe mastlyoun shul men lete. *c* **1440** *Promp. Parv.* 334/2 Mestlyone, or monge corne (.. *K.* mestilione). **1466** *Mann. & Househ. Exp.* (Roxb.) 211 A combe mystelon for the kervelle. **1482** MARG. PASTON in *P. Lett.* III. 295 [They] lodyn bothe cartes with mestlyon and whete. **1483** *Cath. Angl.* 230/1 Mastilȝon, *bigermen, mixtilio.* **1530** PALSGR. 244/2 Mestlyon corne.

β. **14..** *Harl. MS.* 1587 in *Promp. Parv.* 335 *note*, Mastcleyne, *mixtilio.* **1466** *Paston Lett.* II. 269, ii bushel of mestlyn, xvd. **1573** TUSSER *Husb.* xxxvii. (1878) 90 If worke for the thresher ye mind for to haue, Of wheat and of mestlen vnthreshed go saue. **1616** SURFL. & MARKH. *Country Farm* 501 Sow it.. with mastling and wheat. **1815** *Pocklington Canal Act* 52 Rye, Mastlin, Pease.

γ. **1530** PALSGR. 244/1 Masclyne corne. **1538** *Inv. Merevale Abbey* in *Promp. Parv.* 335 *note*, Grayne at the monastery, myskelen, xij strykes. **1558** *Will of Wylde* (Somerset Ho.), A quarter of maskeline. **1635** Mesclin [see c].

δ. **1534** in W. H. Turner *Select. Rec. Oxford* (1880) 121 Mascelyn, benes, and pesen. **1577** B. GOOGE *Heresbach's Husb.* (1586) 32b, Amongst the sommer seedes is miscelin to be reckoned. **1619** W. SCLATER *Exp. 1 Thess.* (1630) 426 The Lord to Israel permitted no medleyes:.. his people might not.. sow their field with Miscellane. **1631** *Celestina* Ep. Ded., It is good plaine houshold-bread, honest messeline. **1654** WHITLOCK *Zootomia* 459 You may know.. who eateth Masolin, who pure Wheat. **1665** *Phil. Trans.* I. 93 The Kinds of Grain or Seed usual in England, being supposed to be either Wheat, Miscelane, Rye, Barley. **1677** PLOT *Oxfordsh.* 244 Its most agreeable grains are.. miscellan, i.e. wheat and rye together. **1741** *Compl. Fam.-Piece* III. 422 Rye is a Grain used next to Wheat for Bread, and sometimes both are mixed together in the sowing, which is called Measeline. **1745** tr. *Columella's Husb.* XI. ii, One modius of ..mescelin. **1789** MADAN tr. *Persius* (1795) 133 *note*, Farrago is a mixture of several grains—mesceline.

ε. **1572** *Wills & Inv. N.C.* (Surtees) I. 387 One pecke of wheat and one pecke of masclechon. **1599** A. M. tr. *Gabelhouer's Bk. Physicke* 360/2 Take vnpeeled Barlye, M.iiij. & Misleden. **1631** in J. J. Cartwright *Chapters Hist. Yorks.* (1872) 316 Masslegen under 19tene shillings the load. **1727** *Beverley Beck Act 2* Every quarter of wheat, rye, mesledine. **1819** *Rees' Cycl.* XXII, *Mashelson*, a term used to signify a mixture of wheat and rye, or what is sometimes called meslin. **1829** J. HUNTER *Hallamsh. Gloss.* App., *Maslegin*, bread made of wheat and rye mixed. **1829** BROCKETT *N.C. Words*, *Masselgem.* **1855** [see b].

ζ. **1561** [see c]. **1577** B. GOOGE *Heresbach's Husb.* I. (1586) 35b, Tares and Oates make a good meslyne sowed together. **1594** HOOKER *Eccl. Pol.* IV. vi. §3 Charging them withall not to sow their fields with mesline [cf. Lev. xix. 19]. **1600** SURFLET *Countrie Farme* V. xvii. 684 Maslin.. is not one kind of corne but a mixture of wheate and rie. **1652** *Inv.* in *Gentl. Mag.* (1861) II. 506, 2 quart^rs of mashlin. **1653** GAUDEN *Hierasp.* 30 When they sow that forbidden mislane, the Tares and Cockle of passionate novelties. **1765** *Museum Rusticum* IV. 225 They who like meslin.. may mix them to their mind when carried to the mill. **1811** W. AITON *Agric. Ayrshire* 270 The late pease were frequently sown with oats which in Ayrshire was denominated mashlum. **1864** *Sat. Rev.* 478/2 Maslin.. is.. used [in the Northern counties] as a somewhat cheaper food than wheaten flour.

†**b.** *fig.* A mixture, medley. (See also MISCELLANE *sb.* and *a.*)

1574 WHITGIFT *Def. Aunsw.* ii, You haue made very euill meslyn, and you haue put in one, things which are not payres nor matches. **1668** KIRKMAN *Eng. Rogue* II. xviii. (1671) 162 Having his pockets well lined with Maslin of Gold and Silver. **1674** N. FAIRFAX *Bulk & Selv.* 102 They were neither Hogs nor Devils.. but a mesling of two. **1855** ROBINSON *Whitby Gloss.*, *Mashelton* or *Machelson*, a mixture of wheat and rye in a mash. A person is said to make mashelton of his discourse, who puts fine and coarse words together with an affected pronunciation.

c. *attrib.*, as ***maslin bread, corn, seed***; also as *adj.* (*fig.*), mixed, mingled.

1544 *Will Dando of Littleton* (MS.), j bushell of mastlinge corne. **1561** in *Leland's Itin.* (1769) VI. Pref. 17, 3 Loves Mislin Bread. **1575** *Durham Depos.* (Surtees) 305 Masseljon corne, being most part benes. **1584** COGAN *Haven Health* iv. (1636) 29 A kind of bread named misseling or masseling bread. **1590** BARROW & GREENWOOD in *Confer.* 45 This prophane miscelyne people. **1597** J. KING *On Jonas* (1618) 59 Such meslen seed [cf. Lev. xix. 19] light vpon that ground which I wish no prosperity vnto. **1607** B. JONSON *Volpone* Ded., The present trade of the Stage, in all their misc'line Enterludes. **1626** BP. HALL *Contempl. O.T.* XXI. i, These mesline Jewes. **1635** J. TAYLOR (Water P.) *Old Parr* C2b, Course Mesclin bread. **1649** BLITHE *Eng. Improv. Impr.* (1653) 109 Wheat, Rye, or Meslin Stubble. *a* **1659** BP. BROWNRIG *Serm.* (1674) I. iv. 61 God abhors a misceling Religion. **1725** BRADLEY *Fam. Dict.*, *Masling-far*, Food made of Wheat and Rye by putting them to steep in Water. **1786** BURNS *Earnest Cry* xx, I'll be his debt twa mashlum bonnocks. **1844** *Ayrshire Wreath* 154 There was a big bing o' mashlam scones.

masloch, variant of MASHLOCH *Sc.*

masly: see MASSILY *Obs.*

masnel: erron. form of MASUEL.

masochism ('mæsəkɪz(ə)m, 'mæzəkɪz(ə)m). [f. the name of Leopold von Sacher-Masoch, an Austrian novelist, who described the thing + -ISM.] A form of sexual perversion in which a person finds pleasure in abuse and cruelty from his or her associate (cf. SADISM). Recently applied more generally to a form of perversion in which a sufferer derives or is believed to derive pleasure from pain or humiliation.

1893 *Dunglison's Med. Dict.* (ed. 21), *Masochism*, sexual perversion, in which a member of one sex takes delight in being dominated, even to the extent of violence or cruelty, by one of the other sex. **1899** *Allbutt's Syst. Med.* VIII. 196 [Group iii] with predominant perversion of moral and sexual nature (for example, moral insanity, uranism, masochism, etc.). **1930** W. R. INGE *Christian Ethics & Mod. Probl.* iii. 109 Modern psychology has invented the word masochism for that perversion of the sex-instinct which takes the form of self-torture. **1943** H. READ *Politics of Unpolitical* ii. 18 Masochism is the unconscious impulse to dissolve oneself in the power of another person and to participate in his annihilating power. **1963** A. HERON *Towards Quaker View of Sex* 71 *Masochism*, obtaining pleasure (usually sexual) through suffering pain, subjugation or humiliation. **1974** *Listener* 21 Nov. 679 That Johnson had masochistic fantasies.. was first mooted 20 years ago... That Johnson's masochism did not stop at fantasy seems to be indicated by.. entries in Mrs Thrale's diary.

masochist ('mæsəkɪst). [f. as MASOCHISM + -IST.] One who is given to masochism.

1895 tr. *M. Nordau's Degeneration* V. i. 538 Masochists or passivists.. clothe themselves in a costume which recalls, by colour and cut, feminine apparel. **1917** C. R. PAYNE tr. *Pfister's Psychoanal. Method* 78 Very many tormentors of animals are.. sadists, consequently also, more or less masochists. **1957** *London Mag.* Jan. 75 Psychologically her affinities were with the more heroic type of masochist, such as Saint-Exupéry, T. E. Lawrence, and Orwell. **1974** 'J. MELVILLE' *Nun's Castle* iv. 88 'Are you telling me Lynnet was some sort of masochist?'.. 'I think she associated love and pain.'

masochistic (mæsə'kɪstɪk), *a.* Also (*erron.*) masso-. [f. prec. + -IC.] Of, pertaining to, resembling or characterized by masochism.

1904 G. S. HALL *Adolescence* II. 112 Women may acquire a Massochistic love of violence and pain for the ideal of pleasure. **1928** *Music & Lett.* July 125 The almost masochistic melancholy of the average fox-trot. **1958** *Essays & Stud.* XI. 65 The very energy of the style is masochistic —a tormenting awareness of its own impotence to do, or change, anything. **1959** *Times* 30 Sept. 13/5 Eighteenth-century patrons seemed to take a masochistic delight in seeing themselves lampooned on the stage. **1974** [see MASOCHISM].

Hence ˌ**maso'chistically** *adv.*, in a masochistic manner.

1936 *Times Lit. Suppl.* 18 July 597/2 Minor Canons speak of themselves masochistically as 'mere' minor canons. **1947** S. J. PERELMAN *Westward Ha!* (1949) vii. 87 Masochistically allowing chickens to peck at our bare tootsies.

masolin, obs. form of MASLIN[2].

mason ('meɪs(ə)n), *sb.*[1] Forms: α. 3 **machun, machoun, mascun.** β. 4 **mazoun,** 4-5 **macon, masown(e,** 4-6 **masoun,** 6 **masin, masson, maison, meson,** *Sc.* **maissoun,** 7 *Sc.* **meason,** 5-6 **masone,** 4- **mason.** [The α and β forms are respectively a. ONF. *machun* and Central OF. *masson*, *maçon* (mod.F. *maçon*) = Pr. *masso*:—popular Latin type either **măciōn-em* (*măcio*) or **mattiōn-em* (*mattio*). The recorded forms in med.L. are *machio* (7th c. in Isidore, who explains the word as a derivative of *māchina* machine), *matio* (8th c. in the Reichenau Glosses, *c*1000 in Ælfric), *macio*, *mattio*, *mactio*, and (latinized from the Fr.) *macho*, *maco*.

The ulterior etymology is obscure. The evidence of Isidore tends to show that the form with *c* is original, and some scholars have suggested that the word is from the root of L. *māceria*. wall. On the other hand, the stem *mattiōn-* agrees with the OHG. *mezzo* (also in comb. *steinmezzo*, mod.G. *steinmetz*, stonemason):—prehistoric **mattjon-*. This is commonly regarded as the source of the Rom. word, but it has no affinities in Teut. (unless it be cogn. w. OE. *mattuc* MATTOCK), and may be adopted from late Latin.]

1. A builder and worker in stone; a workman who dresses and lays stone in building.

c **1205** LAY. 15465 Machunnes heowen. *Ibid.* 15478 Machunes [*c* **1275** machuns]. *c* **1290** *S. Eng. Leg.* I. 71/33 Machouns.. Bi laddren cloumben up and doun. *a* **1300** *Floris & Bl.* (Cambr. MS.) 326 Ber wiþ þe squire and schauntillun, Also þu were a gud Mascun. **13..** *K. Alis.* 2370 On either half they laiden on So the mason on the ston. *c* **1400** *Rom. Rose* 4148 Aboute him lefte he no masoun, That stoon coude leye, ne querrour. *c* **1489** CAXTON *Sonnes of*

Aymon xxviii. 577 Ye are more like a Kyng than a mason or laborer. **1535** COVERDALE *1 Chron.* xxiii. 15 Mesons and carpenters in stone and tymber. **1599** SHAKS. *Hen. V*, I. ii. 198 The singing Masons building roofes of Gold. **1697** E. LHWYD in *Phil. Trans.* XXVII. 503 The Masons Marks on the Stones. **1703** MOXON *Mech. Exerc.* 237 The White Mason, which is the Hewer of Stone. **1874** PARKER *Goth. Archit.* I. iii. 34 The Normans being far better masons than the Saxons. **1878** JEVONS *Prim. Pol. Econ.* 71 Masons totally declined to set stones shaped and dressed by machinery.

2. = FREEMASON 1, 2.

[**1425** *Rolls of Parlt.* IV. 292 Les annuelx congregaions & confederacies faitz par Masons en lour generall Chapiters & Assembles.] **1483** *Aberdeen Reg.* (1844) I. 39 The masownys of the luge. **1672** MARVEL *Rehearsal Transp.* I. Wks. (Grosart) III. 55 As those that have the Mason's word, secretly discern one another. **1731** *Gentl. Mag.* I. 431 The Author tells us, that a Mason is obliged by his Tenure, to obey the Moral Law. **1772** WESLEY *Jrnl.* 22 Apr. (1827) III. 446, I preached..in the Masons' Lodge. **1776** ABIGAIL ADAMS in *J. Adams' Fam. Lett.* (1876) 151 The Dr. was buried on Monday; the Masons walking in procession from the State House. **1845** D. JERROLD *Mrs. Caudle* viii, Do you suppose I'd ever suffered you to go and be made a mason, if I didn't suppose I was to know the secret, too?

3. *attrib.* and *Comb.* as ***mason-craft***; ***mason-like*** adv.; **mason-work**, stone-work, masonry; also in a number of obs. compounds where the attrib. use takes the place of the possessive *mason's*, as ***mason-axe***, ***-chip***, ***-device***, ***-line***, ***-lodge***, ***-rule***.

1412–13 *Durham Acc. Rolls* (Surtees) 610 Factura de *Mason axes, pickes [etc.]. [*c* **1440** *Promp. Parv.* 329/1 Masonys ex, *lathomega*.] **1497–8** *Fabric Rolls York Minster* (Surtees) 90 Pro vj mason axis. **14..** *Nom.* in Wr.-Wülcker 687/32 *Hic petro*, a *mason schype. **1509–10** *Fabric Rolls York Minster* (Surtees) 95 Pro cariagio lyme,..mason chippes and fier erth. **1412** *Catterick Ch. Contract* (Raine 1834) 8 He sall make the Kirke..newe als werkemanschippe and *mason craft will. **1418** *Twenty-six Polit. P.* (E.E.T.S.) 62/42 þe wyseman his sone forbed Masoun-craft and all clymbyng. **1831** CARLYLE *Sart. Res.* (1858) 59 Bright, nimble creatures [swallows], who taught you the mason-craft? *c* **1400** *Destr. Troy* 1645 Toures..Made all of marbyll with *mason deuyse. [*Ibid.* 10584 A toure..Meruelously made with masons deuyse.] **1387** in *Registr. Cart. Eccl. S. Egidii* (Bann. Cl.) 25 Tha ylk men sal mak..a wyndow with thre lychtys in fourme *masonnelyke. **14..** *Nom.* in Wr.-Wülcker 687/35 *Hec amussis*, a *mason lyne. **1797** *Monthly Mag.* III. 215/1 In some *Mason Lodges in his neighbourhood, Burns had soon the fortune..to gain the notice of several gentlemen [etc.]. **14..** *Nom.* in Wr.-Wülcker 687/33 *Hec regula*, a *mason rewlle. **1629** *Burgh Rec. Glasgow* (1876) I. 370 For working of the *mearson work..of the liberarie hous. **1859** TENNYSON *Vivien* 4 It look'd a tower of ruin'd masonwork. **1896** *Archæol. Jrnl.* LIII. 39 Detached blocks of stone, presenting well-marked indications of mason-work.

b. in the names of animals, esp. certain insects, which build a nest of sand, mud, or the like; as ***mason-ant*** (= F. *fourmi maçonne*), ***-fly***; **mason-bee** (= F. *abeille maçonne*), an insect of the genera *Osmia*, *Chalicodoma* and *Anthophora*; **mason spider**, a trap-door spider (*Mygale*); **(free) mason-wasp**, a solitary wasp, *Odynerus murarius*. Also **mason-shell**, a genus of molluscs (*Phorus* or *Xenophora*) which carry pieces of coral, stone, etc. fixed to the shell; a carrier-shell.

1816 KIRBY & SP. *Entomol.* xvii. (1818) II. 97 M. Huber ..speaking of a *mason-ant, not found with us. **1774** GOLDSM. *Nat. Hist.* (1776) VIII. 93 *Mason Bees make their cells with a sort of mortar, made of earth. **1867** *Intell. Observ.* No. 60. 415 Mason-bees of the genus Anthophora. **1750** G. HUGHES *Barbadoes* 83 It is called a *Mason-fly from the great quantity of mire and mortar which it carries into houses and elsewhere, wherewith to build its nests. **1884** *Riverside Nat. Hist.* (1888) I. 326 The..genus..*Phorus*, which embraces the carrier or *mason-shells of the eastern seas. **1826** KIRBY & SP. *Entomol.* III. xxxiv. 492 The trapdoor or *mason spider (*Mygale cœmentaria*). **1861** HULME tr. *Moquin-Tandon* II. v. ii. 260 The Mygales (Crab Spiders and Mason Spiders). **1792** M. RIDDELL *Voy. Madeira* 73 The free *mason wasp is so domestic as to build its nest, which is made of mud or clay, in the inhabited chambers of houses. **1815** KIRBY & SP. *Entomol.* (1818) I. 449 One species called by Reaumur the mason-wasp (*Odynerus muraria*, Latr.).

Hence **'masonship**.

1833 CARLYLE *Ct. Cagliostro* ii. *Misc.* (1857) III. 270 Cagliostro, then, determines on Masonship. **1881** *Daily News* 17 Feb. 5/2 His [Herr Pietsch's] elaborate investigation of Goethe's fifty years of Masonship.

†**'mason**, *sb.*² *slang. Obs.* One who acquires goods fraudulently by giving a bill which he does not intend to honour. Also †**'masoner** (in the same sense); †**'masoning** *vbl. sb.* and *ppl. a.*

1753 *Discov. J. Poulter* (ed. 2) 6, 24, 27, 29.

Mason ('meɪs(ə)n), *sb.*³ orig. *U.S.* [f. the name of John *Mason*, who was granted the patent for such jars in 1858.] ***Mason jar***: a wide-mouthed glass jar with an airtight screw top widely used in home bottling; also ***Mason fruit-jar***.

1885 *N.Y. Weekly Tribune* 6 Aug. 13/2 The Illinois Agricultural Society calls attention to the fact that Mason fruit-jars have been sent to that State packed in straw foul with Canada thistle. **1888** L. HARGIS *Graded Cook Bk.* 472 Quince and apple butter... Put a little of the mixture in a plate and invert, if it adheres the butter is done. Fill Mason jars and seal. **1947** *Nat. Geogr. Mag.* June 822/1 His annual cherry crop amounted to one forlorn little cherry which he covered with a mason jar. **1950** *N.Z. Jrnl. Agric.* Jan. 51/3, 2-pint mason jar feeders..were placed in the group of hives. **1972** H. C. RAE *Shooting Gallery* ii. 80 Landscapes evolved in his mind, like smoke in a Mason jar. **1973** J. JONES *Touch of Danger* xxvii. 162, I began to swish the martini mixture in the big Mason jar.

mason ('meɪs(ə)n), *v.* Also 5 **masown**, **masson**. [ad. F. *maçon-ner* (12th c.), f. *maçon* MASON *sb.*¹] *trans.* To build of stone (or brick, etc.); to construct of masonry; to build up or strengthen with masonry. Also with *together*, *out*.

c **1430** *Pilgr. Lyf Manhode* I. x. (1869) 7 She hadde founded thilke house and masowned it..xiij c. yer and xxx bifore that time. **1489** CAXTON *Faytes of A.* II. xiv. 117 With certain yssues and steppes welle massonned. **1523** LD. BERNERS *Froiss.* I. i. 1 Al buyldynges are masoned and wroughte of dyuerse stones. **1682** WHELER *Journ. Greece* IV. 295 A round Temple of Brick, masoned together with a very hard cement. **1703** *Chatsworth Building Accts.* in *Jrnl. Derbysh. Archæol. Soc.* (1881) III. 31 For masoning, raising and setting upp 4 other urnes. **1862** LATHAM *Channel Isl.* III. xviii. (ed. 2) 412 About fifty yards south from the temple were five tumuli, masoned on every side. **1881** *Contemp. Rev.* Apr. 510 The watercourse beneath it is masoned out with solid stone.

absol. *c* **1483** CAXTON *Dialogues* 40/9 Laurence the masone Hath take to masone.

†**b.** To build *in* or *into* (a wall). *Obs.*

1527 ANDREW *Brunswyke's Distyll. Waters* b iv, A trevet in the middest of the fornys with the iii fete masoned in the wall of it. **1596** DANETT tr. *Comines* (1614) 217 He caused also to bee masoned into the wall a great number of iron speares.

Hence **'masoning** *vbl. sb.*

1711 C. LOCKYER *Trade in India* ii. 44 Masoning is what they understand least of.

Mason and Dixon. *U.S.* = *Mason's and Dixon's line*: see LINE *sb.*² 17 b. Now usu. **Mason-Dixon.**

1779 in W. B. Reed *Life & Corr. J. Reed* (1847) II. 134 The Virginia gentlemen offer to divide exactly the 40th degree with us... Perhaps we [of Penna.] would be as well off with Mason and Dixon's line continued. **1834** C. A. DAVIS *Lett. J. Downing* 36 And he tell'd me Georgia would go for me, arter the Gineral, as soon as any north of mason and dickson. **1843** *Knickerbocker* XXII. 185 The writer, who dwelleth near Mason and Dixon, descants upon the awful climate. **1948** *Downers Grove* (Illinois) *Reporter* 21 Oct. 3/2 Two Dixiecrats, out of their element north of the Mason-Dixon, nevertheless registered their convictions on the States' Rights issue. **1969** I. KEMP *Brit. G.I. in Vietnam* vii. 155 You're crazy, Limey! You couldn't keep me here for all the girls south of the Mason-Dixon Line. **1975** *Times* 20 Aug. 12/3 The tortured condition of the Jewish middle-class intellectual seems..the dominant subject of novels written north of the Mason-Dixon line.

Also *transf.*

1948 *Sat. Even. Post* 30 Oct. 124/4 This same little band has long since adopted three war-ruined families in the old country—two in Bizonia, one on the other side of Europe's bitter Mason and Dixon's line. **1970** *New Yorker* 22 July 4/3 Sub-Mason-Dixon dining.

mason-dewe, -due, obs. forms of MEASONDUE.

masondre, obs. form of MASONRY.

masoned ('meɪs(ə)nd), *ppl. a.* [f. MASON *v.* + -ED¹.] Formed of or strengthened with masonry.

1612 *Two Noble K.* v. i, The masond Turrets. **1869** LD. LYTTON *Orval* 93 Moss-mason'd haunts where hermit violets hide. **1892** —— *King Poppy* iv. 422 The gallery ended in the mason'd base Of a deep well-shaft.

b. *Her.* (Also 7–8 **massoné**(e = F. *maçonné*.) Marked with lines representing the joints or divisions between blocks of stone. Also *gen.*

1688 R. HOLME *Armoury* I. 69/1 He beareth Argent, Masoned into seven divisions Sable. *Ibid.* I. 94/2 The French Blazon it, A. Massonee of seven pieces S. **1718** NISBET *Ess. Armories, Terms Her.*, *Massone*, is said of Castles, Towers, and other Buildings, when the Cement is of a different Tincture from the Stones, as in the Arms of Castile. **1722** —— *Syst. Heraldry* I. 418 A Castle Triple Towered Or, Masoned Sable, Windows and Ports shut Azure. **1727** BAILEY vol. II, *Massoné, Massonéd.* **1864** BOUTELL *Her. Hist. & Pop.* xxix. (ed. 3) 446 A low pillar, the base and capital masoned. **1868** CUSSANS *Her.* xiv. 167 The Mural Crown..has the circle masoned. **1900** HOPE in *Yorks. Archæol. Jrnl.* XV. 282 The whole wall surface was 'masoned' with broad red or white lines.

masone dew, obs. form of MEASONDUE.

masoner. *Obs.* exc. *dial.* (See E.D.D.) [f. MASON *v.* + -ER¹.] A mason or bricklayer.

1605 *MS. Indenture*, Francis Hooll..of Brough, co. York, masoner. **1847** HALLIWELL, *Masoner*, a bricklayer.

masoness ('meɪs(ə)nɪs). *nonce-wd.* [f. MASON *sb.*¹ + -ESS¹.] A female freemason.

1833 CARLYLE *Ct. Cagliostro* ii. Misc. (1857) III. 270.

masonic (mə'sɒnɪk), *a.* [f. MASON *sb.*¹ + -IC.]
1. Of or pertaining to masons or masonry. *rare.*

1810 SIR A. BOSWELL *Edinburgh* Poet. Wks. (1871) 55 The City grows and spreads on every side, In all the honour of masonic pride. **1821** BYRON *Juan* v. lxiii, The masonic folly Of those..Who give themselves to architecture wholly. **1895** S. R. HOLE *Little Tour Amer.* 308 The Washington Obelisk, said to be the highest masonic structure in the world.

2. Relating to, or characteristic of, freemasons or freemasonry. Also *transf.*

1797 *Encycl. Brit.* (ed. 3) X. 625/1 Some scrupulous brethren, who were alarmed at the publication of the masonic constitutions. **1810** WELLINGTON *Let.* 4 Jan. in Gurw. *Desp.* V. 410, I beg..that the meeting of the masonic lodges in their corps, and the wearing of all masonic emblems and all masonic processions may be discontinued during the time they may be in Portugal. **1831–57** DE QUINCEY *Whiggism* Wks. VI. 125 This sublime masonic tie of brotherhood we ourselves possess, we members of Christendom. **1836–9** DICKENS *Sk. Boz, Scenes* xxiii, Cheap silver pen-holders and snuff-boxes, with a masonic star. **1879** STEVENSON *Trav. Cevennes* (1886) 18 [He] finally taught me the true cry or masonic word of donkey-drivers.

Masonite¹ ('meɪs(ə)naɪt). [f. *Mason* + -ITE.] An adherent of the fanatical (millenarian) doctrines of John Mason of Water Stratford (*died* 1694).

1710 STEELE & ADDISON *Tatler* No. 257 ¶12 Brownists, Independents, Masonites, Camisars, and the like.

masonite² ('meɪs(ə)naɪt). *Min.* [Named by C. T. Jackson, 1840, after Owen *Mason*: see -ITE.] A variety of chloritoid found in Rhode Island.

1840 C. T. JACKSON *Geol. Rhode Isl.* 88 (A. H. Chester).

Masonite³ ('meɪsənaɪt). Also **masonite**. The proprietary name of a type of fibreboard made from wood-fibre pulped under high-pressure steam.

1926 *Official Gaz.* (U.S. Patent Office) 23 Nov. 802/1 Mason Fibre Company, Laurel, Miss. Filed July 24, 1926. *Masonite. Particular description of goods.*—Fiber Board, Insulating Board, Composite Construction Board, Synthetic Lumber, or Artificial Lumber. **1933** *Sci. Amer.* Jan. 39/1 Floors will be of Masonite cushioned flooring. **1948** *Archit. Rev.* CIII. 270 (*caption*) The walls are covered with masonite sheeting fixed with broken recessed joints and slightly rounded corners, and painted grey-white. **1950** in W. Schack *Man. Plastics & Resins* 279 *Masonite* (trade name) refers to a series of headboards having considerable structural strength and resistance to abrasion and moisture. **1970** *Jrnl. Gen. Psychol.* LXXXII. 58 A five-digit counter, a speaker, two lights, and two standard Gerbrands rat levers were mounted on the lower panel (the unused lever was concealed by a masonite mask). **1970** *Southerly* XXX. 186 His blunted thumb jerked over the hump of his shoulder, pierced the masonite lining, pierced the weatherboards, rode the thirty odd miles of train-tracks and arrived in Sydney. **1973** *Jrnl. Genetic Psychol.* CXXII. 19 The stimuli used for pretraining and oddity training were multidimensional common household items and toys mounted on 4 × 4 inch brown-masonite squares.

masonry ('meɪs(ə)nrɪ), *sb.* Forms: 4 **masonerie**, 4–5 **masonrye**, 5 **masonri**, **masynry**, **masounrye**, **masondre**, 5–7 **masonrie**, 6 **massonnery**, 5– **masonry**. [a. F. *maçonnerie* (14th c.), f. *maçon* MASON *sb.*¹: see -ERY, -RY. Cf. med.L. *massoneria* (Du Cange).]

1. The art, skill, or occupation of a mason; the art or work of building in stone. Now *rare.*

a **1400** *Constit. Masonry* (Halliw. 1844) 13 At these lordys prayers they cownterfetyd gemetry, And ȝaf hyt the name of masonry. *c* **1420** *S. Etheldred* 789 in Horstm. *Altengl. Leg.* (1881) 300 Of no masonry to deyȝt þat ston, þey nadde no nede. *c* **1449** PECOCK *Repr.* I. x. 50 Lijk as he schulde vnresonabili and repreuabili aske, if he askid of a treuthe in masonry, where it is groundid in carpentrie. **1530** PALSGR. 429/1, I am skylled or connynge in physicke or palmestrye or massonnery. *c* **1600** SHAKS. *Sonn.* lv, When wastefull warre shall Statues ouer-turne, And broiles roote out the worke of masonry. **1632** LITHGOW *Trav.* VI. 261 [It] hath beene hewen out of the Rocke, by..men, experimented in Masonry. **1748** HUME *Ess., Understanding* xi. (1777) II. 152 Brick and stone and mortar, and all the instruments of masonry.

2. *concr.* That which is built or constructed by a mason; work executed by a mason; stonework.

? *a* **1366** CHAUCER *Rom. Rose* 302 Sorowe was peynted next Envye Upon that walle of masonrye. *c* **1384** —— *H. Fame* III. 213 Hit nedith nought you more to tell..how they hate yn masoneryes, As corbettz fulle of ymageryes. **1426** LYDG. *De Guil. Pilgr.* 335 The masounry wrought ful clene, Off quyke stonys bryht & schene. **1586** J. HOOKER *Hist. Irel.* in *Holinshed* II. 151/2 The faire bridge of Athlon..he builded with masonrie and free stone. **1601** SHAKS. *All's Well* II. i. 31, I shal stay here..Creeking my shooes on the plaine Masonry. **1752** MASON *Elfrida* Poems 1830 II. 33 From its base..All is of choicest masonry. **1843** BORROW *Bible in Spain* xv, Several gates had been blocked up with masonry. **1865** CARLYLE *Fredk. Gt.* XXI. ii. (1872) IX. 276 It shows excellent sound masonries. **1876** ROUTLEDGE *Discov.* 29 The exterior is formed of a casing of solid masonry strengthened with iron hoops.

transf. **1774** PENNANT *Tour Scotl. in 1772*, 120 The strata narrow and regular, forming a stupendous natural masonry. **1860** TYNDALL *Glac.* I. i. 3 The particles..arrange themselves in layers, like courses of atomic masonry.

3. a. The craft, principles, and mysteries of freemasons; = FREEMASONRY 1, 2. Also *transf.*

1686 PLOT *Staffordsh.* 316 A large parchment volum they have amongst them, containing the History and Rules of the craft of Masonry. **1753** *Scots Mag.* Sept. 427/2 In Masonry let me be blest. **1826** *Mem. Margravine of Anspach* II. i. 14 He was ignorant of the machinations of modern Masonry. **1839** *Penny Cycl.* XIV. 482/2 An act was passed against Masonry in the third year of Henry VI. **1926** J. BLACK *You can't Win* xv. 202 George..took no pains to hide himself, feeling sure that the masonry of the road..would protect him against the common enemy—the law.

b. (See quot. 1896). *slang.*

1841 LYTTON *Night & Morning* (ed. 2) II. III. viii. 178, I was one of them, and know the masonry. **1896** FARMER & HENLEY *Slang* IV. 289/1 *Masonry*, secret signs & pass-words.

4. *attrib.* Composed or built of masonry.

1875 R. F. MARTIN tr. *Havrez' Winding Mach.* 96 M. Kraft has carried his drum shaft upon a group of cast-iron columns, without any masonry walls whatever. **1880** *Responsib. Opium Trade* 5 It is exposed for a considerable time in large masonry tanks. **1899** *Westm. Gaz.* 4 Dec. 2/1

Girder bridges can obviously be destroyed much more easily than masonry arches.

Hence **'masonry** *v. trans.*, to build or strengthen with masonry. Also **'masonried** *ppl. a.*

1842 *Mechanics' Mag.* XXXVI. 480 If they [certain tunnels] were not masonried throughout..a serious fall of earth and rock will take place. **1864** C. P. SMYTH *Our Inheritance* v. xxii, It..can be explained in a much easier manner, than by going up, in the teeth of masonried facts, to the primeval antiquity of the world. **1883** *Siderial Messenger* II. 177 Marked by masonried station signals.

masooka, mazuca (mə'zuːkə). *U.S.* [? Corruption of Sp. *besugo* sea-bream.] (See quot.)

1884 G. B. GOODE, etc. *Nat. Hist. Aquat. Anim.* I. 370 The Lafayette or 'Spot' *Liostomus xanthurus*,..is known..in the Saint John's River, Florida, as the 'Masooka'. **1902** WEBSTER Suppl., *Mazuca*.

masoola, masor: see MASSOOLA, MAZER.

‖**Masora(h, Massora(h** (mə'sɔərə). Also **Mas(s)oreth** (mə'sɔərɛθ). [More correctly *Masoreth*, repr. Heb. *māsōreth*, a word occurring in Ezek. xx. 37, where (by those scholars who do not regard the text as corrupt) it is interpreted 'bond (of the covenant)', and referred to the root *'sr* to bind. In post-biblical Heb. the word became common in the sense of 'tradition', being apprehended as from the root *msr* to deliver, hand down; on this view of its etymology the normal punctuation would be *massōreth*, which many modern scholars have adopted, though without ancient authority. The mod.Heb. *māsōrāh* (whence mod. Latin *Masora*, F. *Massora*, *Massore*, G. *Masora*, Eng. *Masora*, *Masorah*), is said to date only from the 16th c., and (with this vocalization) is an abnormal formation from the root *msr*.] The body of traditional information relating to the text of the Hebrew Bible, compiled by Jewish scholars in the tenth and preceding centuries; the collection of critical notes in which this information is preserved. Also occas. used as a collective name for the scholars whose opinions are embodied in the Masorah, and to whom is ascribed the constitution of the present Hebrew text and the addition of the vowel-points, etc.

1613 PURCHAS *Pilgrimage* (1614) 179 That most profitable Treasure, which is called Masoreth. **1632** B. JONSON *Magn. Lady* I. (1640) 15 She could the Bible in the holy tongue: And reade it without pricks: had all her Masoreth. **1659** BP. WALTON *Consid. Considered* 263 The Masora..was not written all at one time, nor the work of one man, or perfected in one age. **1723** S. MATHER *Vind. Bible* 60 These sections of the law are quoted by the Masorah, instead of chapters. **1870** F. J. SMITH *Ewald's Heb. Gram.* (ed. 3) 37 Since..the Massôra, or the grammatical doctrine of the schools, could not venture to alter the letters of the text. **1904** *Athenæum* 13 Aug. 205/2 This rather abstruse little treatise will be studied eagerly by specialists in Hebrew grammar and Masorah.

¶ Milton seems (misled by the rendering 'tradition') to have supposed the word to be applicable to the exegetical traditions of the Rabbis, by which the severity of the Law was increased.

1643 MILTON *Divorce* Introd., Wks. 1851 IV. 11 He who hedg'd in from abolishing, every smallest jot and tittle of precious equity contain'd in that Law, with a more accurate and lasting Masoreth, then either the Synagogue of Ezra, or the Galilean School at Tiberias hath left us.

Masorete, Massorete ('mæsəriːt). Forms: 6 **Massoreth, Mazaroth,** 7 **Masoreth, Massorat,** (9 *erron.* **Mazorete**), 7–9 **Massoret,** 9 **Masoret,** 8– **Massorete, Masorete.** [Originally a misapplication of *Masoreth*, better form of MASORAH. So F. *Massoretz* pl. (Rabelais); the later F. *Massorètes*, G. *Mas(s)oret(h)en*, mod.L. *Mas(s)orētæ*, Eng. *Mas(s)oretes*, are due to association of the ending with that of words of Gr. origin like *exegete*, *athlete*.

The apparently abnormal formation led to the invention of MASORITE as a more correct substitute, but the older word is still the more frequently used.]

One of the Jewish scholars who contributed to the formation of the Masorah.

1587 GOLDING *De Mornay* xxx. 486 In stead of *Caru*..the Jewes will neede reade *Ca ari*..: their Massoreths (who haue made a Register of all the Letters of the Scriptures) doe witness that in al good Copies it is written *Caru*. *Ibid.*, The Jewes..are warned by their Mazaroths, that that sence is vnperfect. **1642** MILTON *Apol. Smect.* Wks. 1851 III. 282 Which the Masoreths and Rabbinicall Scholiasts not well attending, have often us'd to blurre the margent with *Keri* instead of *Ketiv*. *a* **1693** *Urquhart's Rabelais* III. xiv. 123 The *Cabalists* and *Massorats*, Interpreters of the Sacred Scriptures. **1778** LOWTH *Transl. Isaiah* xxxviii. 13 *note*, The Masoretes divide the sentence, as I have done. **1866** J. G. MURPHY *Comm., Exod.* xxiii. 13 It is remarkable that the Masoretes have no division whatever at this point of the text. **1875** FARRAR in *Expositor* I. 106 The long labours of the Jewish Masorets. **1882** *Athenæum* 7 Oct. 456/3 These causes [of errors in Hebrew MSS.] are..admitted..by some even of the Massorets. **1886** C. A. BRIGGS *Messianic Prophecy* x. 301 *note*, An example of introverted parallelism, which has escaped the notice of the Massoretes.

Masoretic, Massoretic (mæsə'rɛtɪk), *a.* [f. prec. + -IC. Cf. F. *massorétique*, G. *massoretisch*.] Pertaining to, or proceeding from, the Masoretes.

1701 GREW *Cosm. Sacra* IV. i. 140 The Jerusalem Talmud..is observed to mention some of the Masoretick Notes. **1778** LOWTH *Transl. Isaiah* Prelim. Diss. (1822) I. p. lxxi, The Masoretic punctuation..is in effect an interpretation of the Hebrew text made by the Jews of late ages, probably not earlier than the eighth century. **1870** F. J. SMITH *Ewald's Heb. Gram.* (ed. 3) 37 In the Massoretic schools of learning. **1882–3** SCHAFF *Encycl. Relig. Knowl.* II. 1430 The so-called Massoretic text.

Maso'retical, *a.* Now *rare.* Also 8 **Mazoretical,** 9 **Masorethical.** [See -AL[1].] = prec.

a **1693** *Urquhart's Rabelais* III. xxxviii. 317 Masoretical fool. **1723** S. MATHER *Vind. Bible* 258 This Masoretical note is mentioned in the Talmud. *Ibid.* 306 Later paraphrasts, who wrote since the Masoretical age. **1755** *Gentl. Mag.* XXV. 9 In a place where the *dagesh forte* is used by Mazoretical writers. **1835** *Penny Cycl.* IV. 372/1 The general correctness of the Masorethical text.

Masorite ('mæsəraɪt). Also 7 **Mazorite,** 9 **Mazorete.** [f. MASORA(H + -ITE.] = MASORETE.

1613 PURCHAS *Pilgrimage* (1614) 179 Martinius affirmeth, That these Masorites inuented the prickes wherewith the Hebrew is now read. **1645** MILTON *Tetrach.* Wks. 1851 IV. 234 Why..should they be such crabbed masorites of the Letter, as not to mollifie a transcendence of literal rigidity? **1827** TOWNLEY *Reasons Laws Moses* 35 The Masorites or Mazoretes..were the first who distinguished the books and sections of the books of Scripture into verses.

attrib. *a* **1682** SIR T. BROWNE *Tracts* viii. (1683) 132 Whereas by the Mazorite Points and Chaldee Character the old Letter stands so transformed, that [etc.].

masoun de Dieu, obs. form of MEASONDUE.

masowyr, obs. form of MAZER.

masque (mɑːsk, -æ-). Also 6–7 **maske,** 7–9 **mask.** [Orig. the same word as MASK *sb.*[2]; the Fr. spelling *masque*, formerly used indifferently with *mask(e* in all senses, is now retained to distinguish the senses explained below.]

1. A masquerade, masked ball. [So in Fr.] Now *rare*.

1514 *Liber Numer. Scacc. Hen. VIII* in Collier *Hist. Dram. Poetry* (1831) I. 78 *note*, Johi. Farlyon Custod... apparatuum omnium singulorum jocorum, larvatorum, vocat. Maskes, Revelles, and Disguysings. **1533** MORE *Answ. Poysoned Bk.* Pref., Wks. 1039/2 Some..full boldlye come daunce in a maske. *a* **1548** HALL *Chron., Hen. VIII* 16 The kyng with a .xi. other were disguised, after the maner of Italie, called a maske, a thyng not seen afore in Englande. **1601** SHAKS. *Twel. N.* I. iii. 121, I delight in Maskes and Reuels. **1667** MILTON *P.L.* IV. 768 Mixt Dance, or wanton Mask, or Midnight Bal. **1719** D'URFEY *Pills* (1872) IV. 146 Lately I went to a Masque at Court Where I see Dances of every sort. **1735** POPE *Ep. Lady* 26 Sappho fragrant at an ev'ning Masque. **1903** *Smart Set* IX. 58/2, I should have liked to go to a ball—a masque would have suited me best.

2. A form of amateur histrionic entertainment, popular at Court and amongst the nobility in England during the latter part of the 16th c. and the first half of the 17th c.; originally consisting of dancing and acting in dumb show, the performers being masked and habited in character; afterwards including dialogue (usually poetical) and song.

1562 *MS. Lansdowne* 5 in Collier *Hist. Dram. Poetry* (1879) I. 179 The Seconde Night. First a Castell to be made in the haule, called the Courte of Plentye; then the maske after this sorte. **1599** B. JONSON *Cynthia's Rev.* Ind., All the courtiers must prouide for reuels; they conclude vpon a Masque, the deuice of which is [etc.]. **1604** (*title*) The true description of a royal masque presented at Hampton Court upon Sunday-night, being the eighth of January 1603–4. **1621** in Ellis *Orig. Lett.* Ser. I. III. 122 At the practising of a Maske that is intendid by the Queene to be presented to the Kinge. *a* **1674** CLARENDON *Hist. Reb.* XIV. §67 There being a Masque at the Court that the King liked very well, he perswaded the Chancellor to see it. **1791–1823** D'ISRAELI *Cur. Lit.* (1858) III. 8 The essence of the Masque was pomp and glory. **1827** HALLAM *Const. Hist.* (1876) II. viii. 38 The queen..had performed a part in a mask at court. **1879** M. PATTISON *Milton* ii. (1880) 21 A Mask was an exhibition in which pageantry and music predominated, but in which dialogue was introduced as accompaniment or explanation. **1898** H. A. EVANS *Eng. Masques* Introd. 34.

b. *transf.* and *fig.*

1642 FULLER *Holy & Prof. St.* v. xvii. 427 His phansie presents him with strange masques, wherein onely Fiends and Furies are actours. *a* **1822** SHELLEY (*title*) The Masque of Anarchy. **1838** *Brit. Cycl. Biog.* II. 905/1 s.v. *Scott, Sir Walter*, The splendid masque, 'Ivanhoe'. **1860** HAWTHORNE *Marb. Faun* (1879) II. xviii. 185 And now, after a mask in which love and death had performed their several parts, she had resumed her proper character.

3. A dramatic composition intended for the kind of representation described under sense 2.

1605 B. JONSON (*title*) The Qveenes Masqves. The first, Of Blacknesse. **1637** MILTON (*title of Comus*) A Maske presented at Ludlow Castle, 1634. **1709** STEELE *Tatler* No. 98 ⁋7 A Passage in a Mask writ by Milton. **1865** LECKY *Ration.* (1878) II. 315 The musical dramas known under the name of masques elicited some of the noblest poetry of Ben Jonson and of Milton.

†**4.** A set of masquers. *Obs.*

1599 B. JONSON *Cynthia's Rev.* v. iii. Stage direct., The Masques ioyne, and they dance. **1625** BACON *Ess., Of Masques* (Arb.) 540 Double Masques, one of Men, another of Ladies, addeth State, and Variety.

5. *attrib.* and *Comb.*

1634 BP. HALL *Contempl. N.T.* IV. 167 If it were but some mask-house,..neither white staves nor halberts could keepe you out. **1645** *Jrnl. Ho. Comm.* 16 July IV. 210/1 Ordered that the boarded Masque House at Whitehall..be forthwith pulled down and sold away. **1647** TRAPP *Comm. Matt.* xxiii. 23 Capistranus..got a great deal of respect to his doctrine by putting down..mask-interludes, &c. **1768** BARETTI *Mann. & Cust. Italy* II. 21 She..had found means in mask-time to get out of the convent. **1903** ANDERS *Shakespeare's Bks.* 153 Puck and the other fairies give a very masklike performance at the close of Midsummer Night's Dream.

masque, obs. form of MASK *sb.*[2] and *v.*[2]

masque alonge, masquenonger, var. forms of MUSKELLUNGE.

masquer: see MASKER *sb.*

masquerade (mɑːskə'reɪd, -æ-), *sb.* Forms: *α.* 6 **masquerada,** 6–7 **mascarado, masquerado,** 7 **mascurado, maskarado.** *β.* 7– **masquerade;** also 7 **mascarad, maskerade, -at, mascherade,** 7–8 **mascarade.** [ad. Sp. *mascarada* (whence F. *mascarade*), f. *máscara* mask, MASKER *sb.*[1] (= It. *maschera*, whence *mascherata* masquerade).

The Sp. *máscara*, It. *maschera*, are regarded by most recent etymologists as a. Arab. *maskharah* laughing-stock, buffoon (the sense 'man in masquerade', given by Richardson and Bocthor, is said by Dozy to be a modern importation from Romanic), f. root *sakhira* to ridicule. Some scholars, however, reject this view, and connect the word with Pr. *mascarar*, Catal. *mascarar*, Pg. *mascarrar*, OF. *mascurer*, *mascherer* (mod.F. *mâchurer*) to black (the face), of Teut. origin: cf. OE. *mæscre* 'macula' (? spot, or ? mesh), MDu. *maschel*, *mascher* spot. For the possible relation to MASK *sb.*[2], see that word.]

1. An assembly of people wearing masks and other disguises (often of a rich or fantastic kind) and diverting themselves with dancing and other amusements; a masked ball.

α. **1597** MORLEY *Introd. Mus.* 181 The Italians make their galliardes..plaine, and frame ditties to them, which in their mascaradoes they sing and daunce. **1612** J. MORE in *Buccleuch MSS.* (Hist. MSS. Comm.) I. 126 The masqueradoes on Monday and Tuesday. **1653** A. WILSON *Jas. I* 104 He loved such Representations, and Disguises in their Maskaradoes, as were witty, and sudden. **1660** F. BROOKE tr. *Le Blanc's Trav.* 365 They have sometimes their Mascurados called *Quacones*, disguising themselves like Devils.

β. **1613** DRUMM. OF HAWTH. *Tears Death Moeliades* (1614) To Rdr., The Name which..he Himselfe in the Challenges of his Martiall Sports, and Mascarads, was wont to vse. **1632** LITHGOW *Trav.* VIII. 369 They haue Bull-beating, Maskerats, singing of rimes, and processions of Priests. **1671** LADY M. BERTIE in *12th Rep. Hist. MSS. Comm.* App. v. 23 They say the King hath put out a Proclamation to forbid maskerades. *c* **1720** PRIOR *Venus's Adv. Muses* 8 The loose dance, and wanton masquerade. **1742** H. WALPOLE *Lett. to Mann* (1834) I. 106, I was last week at the masquerade dressed like an old woman and passed for a good mask. **1877** MAR. M. GRANT *Sun-Maid* vii, You would do for a masquerade in that costume.

b. *transf.* and *fig.* usually with reference to the fantastic or motley character of a masquerade.

1587 HARMER tr. *Beza's Serm. Cant.* 134 The Masquerada of a high masse. **1608** TOPSELL *Serpents* (1658) 668 Although they pretend a matchlesse understanding in these mysteries of Philosophy, they have caused others..to be blinded with the mascarados of absurdities. **1612** *Proc. Virginia* 45 in *Capt. Smith's Wks.* (Arb.) 124 These feindes..cast themselues in a ring about the fire, singing and dancing with excellent ill varietie;..Hauing spent neere an houre, in this maskarado [etc.]. **1614** DRUMM. OF HAWTH. *Urania* ii, A Nought, a Thought, a Mascarade of Dreames. **1702** POPE *Wife of Bath* 284 Visits to ev'ry Church we daily paid, And march'd in ev'ry holy Masquerade. **1750** JOHNSON *Rambler* No. 75 ⁋16 The rich and powerful live in a perpetual masquerade, in which all about them wear borrowed characters. **1841–4** EMERSON *Ess., Poet* Wks. (Bohn) I. 167 Æsop reports the whole catalogue of common daily relations through the masquerade of birds and beasts.

2. Disguise such as is worn at a masquerade; masquerade dress. †**a.** *lit. Obs.*

1668 DRYDEN *Even. Love* III. i, There are some women without in masquerade. **1691** *Emilianne's Frauds Rom. Monks* (ed. 3) 399 As he was going one Evening to the Play-House he met with a Lady of Quality in Masquerade. **1774** H. WALPOLE *Let. to Mann* 8 June, Everybody is to go in masquerade, but not in mask.

b. *transf.* (contemptuously). Also, the action of 'masquerading'.

1868 MISS BRADDON *Run to Earth* I. xi. 260 'What, in heaven's name, is the meaning of this masquerade?' The surgeon removed his broad-brimmed hat [etc.]... Nothing could have been more perfect than his disguise. **1902** ELIZ. BANKS *Newspaper Girl* 268 During my masquerade as an American heiress.

c. *fig.* Disguise; false outward show; pretence.

1674 *Ch. & Court of Rome* 23 This convention..was nothing but a Scene dressed up in Masquerade. **1680** *Hon. Cavalier* 16, I openly declare, without any Masquerade, That [etc.]. **1691** WOOD *Ath. Oxon.* II. 21 The Presbyterians said..that he [Chillingworth] was always a Papist in his heart, or, as we now say, in masquerade. **1726** DE FOE *Hist. Devil* II. iii. (1840) 204 The Devil in masquerade, Satan in full disguise. **1781** CRABBE *Library* 25 The smooth tongue's habitual masquerade. **1823** BYRON *Juan* XI. xxxvii, And, after all, what is a lie? 'Tis but The truth in masquerade. **1863** WOOLNER *My Beautiful Lady* Introd. 7 For none can strip this complex masquerade And know who languishes with secret wounds.

d. *concr.* A travesty, counterfeit. *rare.*

1847 DISRAELI *Tancred* III. v, 'Thou son of a slave!' exclaimed the lady, 'thou masquerade of humanity!'

†**3.** One who takes part in a masquerade. *Obs.*
1651 tr. *De-las-Coveras' Don Fenise* 244 All the company were mute, considering for what cause this troope of unknown people were come into this assembly. Some thought that they were some Mascarads. **1667** *Lond. Gaz.* No. 130/3 Several Citizens.., going disguised as Mascarades. **1670** LASSELS *Voy. Italy* II. 187 Here also it is that the Mascarades march in Carneval time. **1727** BOYER *Fr. Dict.*, *Masque*, (*Personne masquée*) a masker, a mascarade.

†**4.** A Spanish cavalry exercise. *Obs.*
a **1674** CLARENDON *Life* (1761) I. 223 The Masquerade is an Exercise They learned from the Moors, performed by Squadrons of Horse, seeming to charge each other with great Fierceness; with Bucklers in their left Hands and a Kind of Cane in their right.

†**5.** Used as a name for one or more textile fabrics. *Obs.*
1711 *Countrey-Man's Let. to Curate* 95 He goes Generally in Winter in good thick Rug, and in Summer most part in a Highland Plaid, masquerade being at any time too Limber for him. **1714** A. JAFFRAY *Let.* in *Scott. N. & Q.* June 12 If you want any women's cloth or mascarads for your ladie. **1846–60** FAIRHOLT *Costume in Eng.* (ed. 2) Gloss., *Masquerade*, a shot silk of various tints.

6. *attrib.*, sometimes passing into *adj.* = befitting a masquerade; also *fig.*
1720 WELTON *Suffer. Son of God* II. xvi. 430 This very same Temptation oftentimes attacks the Servants of God, in a more Masquerade Address. **1749** FIELDING *Tom Jones* XIII. vii, The female still speaking in her masquerade voice. **1766** GOLDSM. *Vic. W.* (1767) I. xviii. 84 [He] demanded whether I was the real chaplain of the company, or whether it was only to be my masquerade character in the play. **1766** PORNY *Heraldry* vi. §3 (1787) 222 This Ornament [*sc.* the mitre], with other Masquerade Garments. **1772** FOOTE *Nabob* II. Wks. 1799 II. 304 A masquerade ticket, is more negotiable there than a note from the bank. **1772** *Songs Costume* (Percy Soc.) 249 An ass may look fierce in a masquerade dress. **1824** MISS MITFORD *Village* Ser. I. 236 A Spanish masquerade-dress. **1841** MARRYAT *Poacher* xliii, The first masquerade-night at Vauxhall.

masquerade (mɑːskəˈreɪd, -æ-), *v.* Also 7 mascherate. [f. prec. sb.]
†**1.** *trans.* To disguise as at a masquerade. *Obs. rare.*
1654 COKAINE *Dianea* II. 131 Wicked man,..how skilfull thou art to mascherate thy excuses! **1681** T. FLATMAN *Heraclitus Ridens* No. 34 (1713) I. 218 Torying, Tantivying and Masquerading his Majesty's most loyal and dutiful Subjects. **1717** KILLINGBECK *Serm.* xi. 229 To masquerade Vice, and to make it wear the Habit and Shape of that Virtue it most resembles.

†**2.** To make like a masquerade, as by variety of costume. *Obs. rare*$^{-1}$.
1757 MRS. GRIFFITH *Lett. Henry & Frances* (1767) IV. 239, I am just come up from the Shore, which I left masqueraded with People, I believe, from every Nation of the Earth.

3. *intr.* To appear or go about in disguise; to pass oneself off under a false character; to have or assume a deceptive appearance.
1692 R. L'ESTRANGE *Fables* ccxxiv. 196 An Ass.. Masquerading up and down in a Lyon's Skin. **1809–10** COLERIDGE *Friend* (1865) 215 He..masqueraded on the bloody stage of revolution, a Caligula with the cap of liberty on his head. **1850** H. ROGERS *Ess.* (1874) II. ii. 123 Some may probably deem that..philosophy is here masquerading it a little too freely for her character. **1863** W. PHILLIPS *Speeches* xxiv. 533 Virginia has a government, and is not a horde of pirates masquerading as a state.

†**masqueˈraded,** *ppl. a. Obs. rare.* [f. MASQUERADE *sb.* or *v.* + -ED.]
1. ? Coloured like 'masquerade'.
1678 *Lond. Gaz.* No. 1348/4 Eight pieces of..taffaty Ribon, all cloth-colour, one ashe, one maskeraded.
2. Disguised.
1752 A. MURPHY *Gray's Inn Jrnl.* (1756) I. 142 A very Considerable Number of masqueraded Shillings..so well disguised, that they passed among the Company for Guineas.

masqueˈrader. [f. MASQUERADE *v.* + -ER^1.]
a. One who takes part in a masquerade. **b.** One who 'masquerades' or assumes disguise. *lit.* and *fig.*
1677 LADY CHAWORTH in *12th Rep. Hist. MSS. Comm.* App. v. 36 Lord Purbecke hath hired..Sir John Benett's house..for to make a ball to the Mascaraders in next week. **1718** HICKES & NELSON *J. Kettlewell* III. xv. 221 He strenuously Opposed such Religious Masqueraders. **1775** SHERIDAN *Rivals* I. i, Love..has been a masquerader ever since the days of Jupiter. **1836** HOR. SMITH *Tin Trump.* (1876) 206 Many masqueraders on the stage of real life betray themselves by overacting their part. **1879** O. W. HOLMES *Motley* xv. 94 Diplomatic masqueraders of the 16th century.

masqueˈrading, *vbl. sb.* [f. MASQUERADE *v.* + -ING^1.] The action of MASQUERADE *v.*; participation in masquerades; assumption of disguise.
1672 DRYDEN *Marr. à la Mode* IV. ii, This masquerading is a most glorious invention. *a* **1715** BURNET *Own Time* (1724) I. 262 At this time the Court fell into much extravagance in masquerading. **1886** *Athenæum* 20 Feb. 257/3 How much of dramatic masquerading there is in any poem no critic can ever say.
attrib. **1723–4** DK. WHARTON *True Briton* No. 71 II. 609 An Intrigue that began last Masquerading Time. **1840** DICKENS *Barn. Rudge* ii, 'No masquerading tricks', said the locksmith. **1850** KINGSLEY *Alt. Locke* i, They were to me God's angels shining in..fairy masquerading dresses.

masqueˈrading, *ppl. a.* [f. MASQUERADE *v.* + -ING^2.] That masquerades; addicted to masquerading.
1682 *Roxb. Ballads* (1884) 193 From all the Masquerading French,..*Libera nos, Domine!* **1717** CROXALL *Ovid's Met.* x, Down with his masquerading wings he flies. **1856** R. A. VAUGHAN *Mystics* (1860) II. 232 In this masquerading world of ours. **1876** T. HARDY *Ethelberta* (1890) 89 You don't escape me, masquerading madam.

masqueˈradish, *a. rare.* [f. MASQUERADE *sb.* + -ISH.] Befitting a masquerade.
1681 T. FLATMAN *Heraclitus Ridens* No. 6 (1713) I. 36 It makes him look so Masqueradish, that all the Women and Children..take him for a Devil Incarnate. **1819** *Hermit in London* III. 170 Her very masqueradish figure.

†**masquin.** *Obs.* Also 6 **masken,** 7 **masquine.** [? for MASKING *vbl. sb.*] A masquerade or masquerading costume.
1578 *Inv. R. Wardr.* (1815) 237 Fyve masking garmentis of crammosie satin,..Sex maskenis of the same. **1653** J. HALL *Paradoxes* 67 They must put off their Masquine habits. **1658** R. FRANCK *North. Mem.* (1821) 23 The Church of Rome..where mattins are metamorphosed into masquins, collects translated into collations [etc.].

mass (mæs; *in the use of Roman Catholics freq.* mɑːs), *sb.*^{1} Forms: 1–3 **mæsse** (Northumb. **measse**), 1–7 **messe,** 2–7 **masse,** 3 (in comb.), 4–6 chiefly *Sc.* and *north.* **mes,** 4–6 *Sc.* and *north.*, 7–9 (sense 6) **mess,** 4– 7 **mas,** (4 **misse,** 5 **mase, mese,** 6 **miss**), 6– **mass.** [OE. *mæsse* (Kentish and Mercian *messe*) wk. fem., a. vulgar L. *messa* (whence F. *messe*, Pr., It. *messa*; Sp. *misa*, Pg. *missa*, are from written Latin):—Eccl. L. *missa*. The Teut. forms, partly from vulgar Lat. and partly from written Latin, are: OFris., OS. *missa* (MDu. *misse*, *messe*, mod.Du. *mis*), MHG. *misse*, *messe* (mod.G. *messe*), ON. *messa* (Sw. *messa*, Da. *messe*).

It is now generally agreed that the L. *missa* is a verbal sb. (formed like *repulsa*, *collecta*, *offensa*) from L. *mittĕre* (pa. pple. *missus*) to send, send away, dismiss. The earliest known examples of the word belong to the last quarter of the 4th century, occurring in the Epistles of St. Ambrose and the Itinerary of Silvia of Aquitania. In the early centuries it had the general sense of 'religious service', being applicable, e.g., to matins and vespers, though in an eminent sense it always denoted the Eucharist. In secular application it occurs, though rarely, in the 5th and 6th centuries with the sense 'dismissal'. The origin of the liturgical application has been much disputed. Isidore (*a* 636) conjectured that the original reference was to the dismissal of the catechumens which was the preliminary to the eucharistic service. This explanation is not favoured by modern scholars, who consider that the wider sense 'religious service' is more likely than the narrower sense to have been the original. Some think that *missa* at first denoted the solemn dismissory formula at the conclusion of a service, *Ite, missa est*, and hence came to be applied to the service itself. Others (as Kattenbusch in Herzog's *Encycl.*) have suggested, on confessedly slender and doubtful evidence, that *missa* in secular use had some such sense as 'commission', 'official duty', and was therefore adopted as the rendering of Gr. λειτουργία (see LITURGY), which had primarily a similar meaning, but in ecclesiastical language was used for 'religious service' and specifically for the Eucharist. Several other theories have been proposed, but none of them has gained wide acceptance among scholars.]

1. The Eucharistic service; in post-Reformation use, chiefly that of the Roman Catholic Church.

In the 16th c. the Protestants generally objected to the term as being unscriptural, and as associated with the 'popish' view of the nature of the sacrament. (In Sweden and Denmark, however, the equivalent words are applied to the Lutheran communion service.) In the first Prayer-book of Edward VI (1548–9) the heading of the service reads 'The Holy Communion, commonly called the Masse', but in the subsequent Prayer-books the word was not used. In recent years some of the Anglican clergy have applied the term to their own rite.

a. The celebration of the Eucharist. Freq. without article, e.g. ***at mass***, (*to go*) ***to mass***; *to say, sing, hear, attend* ***mass***.
a **900** tr. *Bæda's Hist.* IV. xxii. (Schipper) 460/1 Fram underntide, þonne mon mæssan oftust singeð. *c* **1175** *Lamb. Hom.* 9 Ic eou segge..þet nis hit nan þerf þet me..for his saule bidde pater noster ne messe singe. *a* **1225** *Ancr. R.* 32, I þe messe..siggeð þeos uers stondinde. *c* **1330** R. BRUNNE *Chron. Wace* (Rolls) 7620 Of prest was þer no benisoun, Ne messe songen, ne orysoun. **13..** *E.E. Allit. P.* A. 1114 Mylde as maydenez seme at mas. **1375** BARBOUR *Bruce* XI. 376 Thai herd the mess full reuerently. **1457** *Test. Ebor.* (Surtees) II. 207 The stall quer I sit at mese. **1538** STARKEY *England* I. iv. 132 They can no thyng dow but pattur vp theyr matyns and mas. **1646** SIR J. TEMPLE *Irish Rebell.* (1746) 177 Fitz-Patrick..did endeavour all he could to turn them to mass. **1686** EVELYN *Diary* 19 Jan., Dryden..and his two sonns..were said to go to masse. **1759** ROBERTSON *Hist. Scot.* III. Wks. 1813 I. 263 The earls of Lennox, Athol and Cassils openly attended mass. **1885** MABEL COLLINS *Prettiest Woman* ix, She goes to early mass each morning. **1893** *Ch. Times* 6 Oct. 997/4, I commenced having Mass on all Holy Days at 9 a.m.

b. A particular celebration of the Eucharist, esp. one having a special object or intention. Often *pl.*
a **831** *Charter Oswulf* in Sweet *O.E. Texts* 444 Ðætæghwilc messepriost ʒesinge fore Osuulfes sawle twa messan. *c* **1200** *Vices & Virtues* 65 Ðurh masses and bienes and ælmesses ðe me doð for ðe. **1297** R. GLOUC. (Rolls) 11321 Hii massen & orisons uaste uor him bede. *a* **1300** *Cursor M.* 21189 þe first mess þat sent petre sang Was þar þan na canon lang. *c* **1380** WYCLIF *Wks.* (1880) 212 To make solempnyte whanne riche men ben dede wiþ dirige & messis. **1420** *E.E. Wills* (1882) 48, xx trentalez off messez for my soule. **1562** *Articles of Religion* xxxi. (1571) 19 The sacrifices of Masses, in the which it was commonly said that the Priestes did offer Christe for the quicke and the dead. **1648** GAGE *West Ind.* xv. (1655) 102 They are not able to continue in the Church while a Masse is briefly hudled over. **1797** MRS. RADCLIFFE *Italian* xi, [This] announced that the first Mass was begun. **1828** SCOTT *F.M. Perth* xx, Suitable masses said for the benefit of his soul. **1845** FORD *Handbk. Spain* I. 55 The Spaniards always, whenever they can, hear a mass.

2. a. In pre-Reformation use, the sacrament of the Eucharist; subsequently, the Eucharist as administered and doctrinally viewed by Roman Catholics.
c **1000** *Ælfric's Past. Ep.* xxi. in Thorpe *Laws* II. 376 Nu is seo mæsse..ʒemynd his [Drihtnes] mæran þrowunge. **13..** *Minor Poems fr. Vernon MS.* xlvi. 69 þou leuest not in þe Mes, þat euer God þer in Is. *c* **1375** *Lay Folks Mass Bk.* (MS. B.) 2 þo worthyest þing..In al þis world, hit is þo messe. **1560** DAUS tr. *Sleidane's Comm.* 34 These men.. admonishing..to put downe the Masse. **1563** WINȜET *Four Scoir Thre Quest.* To Rdr., Wks. 1888 I. 56 The mayst blissit, feirfull, and haly sacrifice of the mes. **1635** PAGITT *Christianogr.* I. iii. (1636) 96 A true, Reall, Propitiatorie and unbloudie Sacrifice, under the name of the Masse. **1853** MARSDEN *Early Purit.* 28 Admitting a real presence in the mass.

b. The rite or form of liturgy used in the (pre-Reformation or Roman) celebration of the Eucharist.
c **1375** *Sc. Leg. Saints* xxxix. (*Cosme & Damyane*) 1 Of haly messe in þe secre Syndry sanctis set we se. **1548–9** (Mar.) *Bk. Com. Prayer, Communion* (heading), The Svpper of the Lorde, and the holy Communion, commonly called the Masse. **1628** P. SMART *Van. Superst. Popish Cerem.* *ij b, The Author of this sermon telling him [Cosens] upon occasion the Masse is disallowed: hee replyed roundly: Will you deny that our Service is a Masse? **1634** CANNE *Necess. Separ.* (1849) 85 The papists like well of the English mass (for so King James used to call it). **1879** T. F. SIMMONS *Lay Folks Mass Bk.* 352 The York use..was in the main the ancient Gregorian mass, according to the Roman rite of the eighth century. **1883** J. S. BLACK in *Encycl. Brit.* XVI. 509/2 The Statio ad S. Mariam Majorem [etc.] prefixed to most of the masses in the Gregorian Sacramentary.

¶ **c.** Shakspere's mention of ***evening mass*** is prob. due to ignorance or forgetfulness of the fact that mass was not (normally) celebrated in the evening. In ecclesiastical antiquities, however, the expression is a literal rendering of L. *missa vespertina*, where the sb. has the wider sense mentioned in the etymological note above.
1592 SHAKS. *Rom. & Jul.* IV. i. 38 Are you at leisure, Holy Father now, Or shall I come to you at evening Masse? **1903** W. H. HUTTON *Eng. Saints* iii. 122 It was Saturday night, and he [Columba] went to the chapel for the evening mass (as Adamnan still calls the night office).

d. Phr. †***neither mass nor matins***: nothing of very serious import.
1528 SIR T. MORE *Dial. conc. Heresyes* I. xx. Wks. 145/2 Men say sometyme when they would saye or doo a thyng and cannot well come thereon..it maketh no matter they saye, ye maye beginne agayne and mende it, for it is nother masse nor mattyns.

3. With qualification denoting the ritual form or the intention of the service.
a. high (or **solemn** or †**great**) **mass,** mass celebrated with the assistance of deacon and subdeacon, with incense and music. (Also attrib. in ***high mass time***.) **low** (or †**little**) **mass,** mass said without note and with the minimum of ceremony. (Also ME. *swimesse* = silent mass.) **mass of the day,** †(*a*) the first mass of the day (or 'morrow-mass'); (*b*) the mass which has its variable parts corresponding with the choir office of the day on which it is celebrated (opposed to ***votive mass***). **private mass,** (*a*) as rendering of *missa privata*, a term sometimes applied to a mass celebrated otherwise than in presence of a congregation, e.g., in a private oratory (also sometimes explained as = *low mass*); (*b*) by the Protestant controversialists of the 16th c. applied to a celebration at which the congregation, though present, were not allowed to communicate. **dry mass** (L. *missa sicca*), a celebration without either consecration or communion.
b. In the titles of occasional masses, as ***mass of the Trinity, of the Holy Ghost, of our Lady***, MARYMASS, JESUS *mass*, †***Apostle's mass*** (at St. Paul's Cathedral).
c. See also *mass of the* PRESANCTIFIED, *of* REQUIEM, MORROW-MASS, HUNTER'S, HUNTING *mass*, *red mass* (RED *a.* 19), †SOUL-*mass*, VOTIVE *mass*.
1154 *O.E. Chron.* an. 1125 He sang ðone heh messe on Eastren dæi. *c* **1200** *Trin. Coll. Hom.* 97 Prest hem seið atte swimesse turneð þe bred to fleis and þe win to blod. *c* **1386** CHAUCER *Merch. T.* 650 Whan þat the heighe masse was ydoon. ? **14..** in *Q. Eliz. Acad.* (1879) 34 Masse of our Lady. *Ibid.*, The second masse of the trynite. *Ibid.*, The third masse must bee of Requiem. *c* **1450** *Merlin* 97 Thei rounge to messe of the day. **1490** *Aberdeen Reg.* (1844) I. 46 At hie mestim. *c* **1550** BALE *K. Johan* (Camden) 41 Masse of the v wondes. **1556** *Chron. Gr. Friars* in *Monum. Franciscana* (Rolls) II. 220 A commandement from the councelle vn-to Powlles that they shulde haue no more the Apostylle masse in the mornynge. **1560** DAUS tr. *Sleidane's Comm.* 15 After y^t all be comen together, they shal haue a messe of the holy Ghost. **1560** BECON *Catech.* v. Wks. 1564 I. 453 In times paste, before this deuelishe priuate masse brast in, the minister and the people together dyd receive the holy misteries of the body and bloud of Christ, and not the priest alone, as the manner is now. **1568** GRAFTON *Chron.* II. 309 After the thirde Agnus was sayde in time of a low Masse. **1770** BARETTI *Journ. London to Genoa* II. 199 The Priest who celebrated the Great Mass this morning. **1898** C. WORDSWORTH *Mediæval Services* 22 The Mass of the day at the high altar. *Ibid.* 33 When the Bishop was performing a solemn Mass.

4. Qualified by the name of a saint, etc.: A feast-day or festival. Survives as *-mas* in CANDLEMAS, CHILDERMAS, CHRISTMAS, LAMMAS, MARTINMAS, MICHAELMAS; also *Allhallowmas(s, Ladymass*, MARYMASS.

c **950** *Lindisf. Gosp.* John vii. 2 Temples mæssa, *scenopegia*. *c* **1000** ÆLFRIC *Gram.* (Z.) 43 *December*: se monoð onginð anum dæge æfter andreasmæssan. *c* **1330** *Arth. & Merl.* 3391 (Kölbing) Sone after seyn Jones misse [*rime* lesse]. **1452** *Paston Lett.* I. 236 Be twixt this and Seynt Margretys messe. **1584** in Littlejohn *Aberd. Sheriff Court* (1904) Introd. 44 To Andirsmes Evin nixtocum.

5. A musical setting of those parts of the mass which are usually sung, viz. the Kyrie, Gloria, Credo, Benedictus, and Agnus.

1597 MORLEY *Introd. Mus.* 21 In the Tenor part of the Gloria of his Masse *Aue Maris stella.* **1667** SIMPSON *Compend. Pract. Mus.* 137 Masses, Hymns, Psalmes, Anthems..&c. **1782** BURNEY *Hist. Mus.* II. 494 In every movement of Josquin's Mass, some part or other, but generally the Tenor, is singing the tune in different notes and measures. **1846** *Penny Cycl.* Suppl. s.v. *Palestrina*, His first work, consisting of four masses for four voices.

6. Used in oaths and asseverations: ***by the mass***, mod. dial. *amess*, and simply *mass* (often *mess*).

c **1369** CHAUCER *Dethe Blaunche* 928 By the masse I durste swere..That [etc.]. **1526** SKELTON *Magnyf.* 2201 By the messe, I shall cleue thy heed to the waste. **1592** KYD *Sol. & Pers.* II. i. 220 Mas, the foole sayes true. **1599** SHAKS. *Hen. V*, III. ii. 122 By the Mes, ere theise eyes of mine take themselues to slomber, ayle de gud seruice. **1695** CONGREVE *Love for L.* III. vi, So, so, enough Father—Mess, I'd rather kiss these Gentlewomen. **1754** RICHARDSON *Grandison* (1811) II. xxviii. 276 Pray, sir, do you withdraw, if you please. *Mr. Gr.* Not I, by the mass! **1756** FOOTE *Eng. fr. Paris* I. Wks. 1799 I. 98 Oh, a British child, by the mess. **1816** W. IRVING in *Life & Lett.* (1864) I. 350 By the mass, I look back with..much longing to her bounteous establishment. **1848** KINGSLEY *Saint's Trag.* I. ii, Mass! I had forgot.

7. *attrib.* and *Comb.*, as ***mass-bread***, ***church***, ***-goer***, ***music***, ***-rite***, ***-time***, ***-vestment***, ***-work***; objective, etc., as ***mass-hearing***, ***-hunter***, ***-mumbler***, ***-sayer***, ***-saying***, ***-seer***, ***-singing***; ***mass-borrowed***, ***-like***, ***-mumbling*** adjs. Special combs.: **mass-bell**, (*a*) a bell that calls people to mass; (*b*) a bell that is rung during mass, a sacring-bell; †**mass-cake**, an opprobrious term for a wafer used in the mass; †**mass-closet**, a Roman Catholic chapel; †**mass clothes**, mass vestments; †**mass-cope**, a chasuble; †**mass-gear**, the instruments, etc. used in celebrating mass; †**mass-gospeller**, a protestant who (hypocritically) attends mass; †**mass-groat** = MASS-PENNY; **mass-hackle** (now *arch.*), a chasuble; †**mass-kiss** (ME. *messecos*), the kiss of peace at the mass; **mass-money**, (*a*) offerings of money made at mass; (*b*) money paid to a priest for saying mass; †**mass-reaf**, mass-vestments; **mass rock** *Hist.*, a rock at which persecuted Irish Catholics would gather to celebrate the mass in secret; †**mass-song**, the singing or celebration of mass; †**mass-while**, the hour for celebrating mass. Also MASS-BOOK to MASS-PRIEST.

14.. in *Rel. Ant.* I. 61 Quhan I rynge the *messe belle. **1863** LONGF. *Wayside Inn, Saga K. Olaf* XI. viii, The mass-bells tinkled. **1642** MILTON *Apol. Smect.* Wks. 1851 III. 290 Scandalous ceremonies and *masse-borrow'd Liturgies. **1473** *Acc. Ld. Treas. Scotl.* (1877) I. 64 Item for *mess bred for the hale ȝere. **1579** FULKE *Heskins's Parl.* 78 Their whole *Masse cakes. *a* **1555** BRADFORD *Hurt of hearing Mass* (Copland) C vj, As though the *masse church were yᵉ catholyke churche. **1656** HEYLIN *Surv. France* 92 Little Chappels, or *Masse-closets. *c* **1440** *Alph. Tales* 144 He..did on his *mes clothis & stude att þe altar befor þe bisshopp. **13..** *Minor Poems fr. Vernon MS.* xxxvii. 773 Cum whon he [þe prest] doþ of his *masse-cope. *c* **1300** *Havelok* 188 The caliz, and the pateyn ok, The corporaus, the *messe-gere. **1843** BORROW *Bible in Spain* xlvi, Antonio, though by no means a *mass-goer [etc.]. *a* **1555** BRADFORD *Hurt of hearing Mass* (Copland) C vij, Suche be popyshe protestauntes, *masse gospellers, or, as they woulde be called, bodelye massemongers and spirytuall gospellers. **1550** BALE *Eng. Votaries* II. I iij, Of them that gaue aultre clothes..*masse grotes and trentals. *c* **1122** *O.E. Chron.* an. 963 (Laud MS.) Min *messe hacel, & min stol, & min ræf. *c* **1200** *Trin. Coll. Hom.* 163 Ðe meshakele is of medeme fustane. **1842** SIR H. TAYLOR *Edwin the Fair* I. viii, This shaveling's meagre face, With his mass-hackle and his reef and stole. *c* **1425** AUDELAY *XI Pains of Hell* 86 in *O.E. Misc.* 213 [þai] let oþer men of *mas hereng. *a* **1555** BRADFORD *Hurt of hearing Mass* (Copland) C vj, They that are *masse hunters. *c* **1200** *Trin. Coll. Hom.* 91 Tocne of sehtnesse, þat is *messe cos. *c* **1300** *Beket* 1779 He nolde cusse massecos to cusse Seint Thomas. **1637–50** ROW *Hist. Kirk* (Wodrow Soc.) 394 The Communion is discharged to be before the pulpit..(for that were not so *Masse-lyke). **1664** H. MORE *Myst. Iniq.* 431 *Mass-money, Oblations to Saints and their Images, and the like. **1897** *Daily News* 18 Nov. 6/1 For the purpose of earning mass money men are ordained at the earliest possible age. **1543** BALE *Yet a Course*, etc. 88 b, *Masse momblers, holye water swyngers [etc.]. **1566** *Pasquine in a Traunce* 106 b, So many thousand of *Masse mombling priestes. **1835** *Court Mag.* VI. 24/2 The accompaniments to the songs and the *mass music. *a* **1000** *Canons of Edgar* c. 33 in Thorpe *Laws* II. 250 Ðæt ælc preost hæbbe..eal *mæssereaf wurðlice behworfen. *c* **1200** *Trin. Coll. Hom.* 215 Boc oðer belle, calch oðer messe-ref. **1803** SCOTT *Eve of St. John* 91 He who says the *mass-rite for the soul of that knight. **1914** W. P. BURKE *Irish Priests in Penal Times* p. vii, The '*Mass Rock'.., the 'Priests' Hollow',..and many a similar name..are witnesses..to a hunted priesthood. **1932** H. CONCANNON *Blessed Eucharist in Irish Hist.* xix. 389 He was often placed on the summit of a high rock, to signal the approach of the 'priest hunters', while around a great stone, 'a Mass rock',..the parishioners were assembled for Mass. **1933** FATHER AUGUSTINE *Ireland's Loyalty to Mass* x. 166 Carraig an Aifrinn, (the Mass Rock). **1959** D. D. C. P. MOULD *Peter's Boat* vi. 79 There are, in fact, an enormous number of known Mass rocks in this country, and that is to be expected, for they were in use whenever persecution was hot, and in fact, come almost into living memory. **1554** BRADFORD *Let.* Wks. (Parker Soc.) I. 393 Then these *mass-sayers and seers shall shake. *c* **1440** *Alph. Tales* 442 And so þe bisshopp was trublid herewith, & lefte his *mes-saying. **1546** BALE *Eng. Votaries* I. (1548) 31 For the fyrst .iii [considerations] a prest ought not, he sayth, to abstayne from his masse sayenge. **1554** *Mass seer [see quot. for mass-sayer]. **1340** HAMPOLE *Pr. Consc.* 3702 Þat *mes syngyng May titest þe saul out of payn bryng. **1553** BECON *Reliques of Rome* (1563) 198 b, In Masse singyng, in almosse geuing. *a* **900** tr. *Bæda's Hist.* I. xxvi. (Schipper) 58 On þysse cyricean ærest þa halȝan lareowas ongunnan..*mæssesong don. *c* **1250** *Gen. & Ex.* 2466 Elmesse-gifte, and messe-song. **1483** in *N. & Q.* (1973) Apr. 125/1 His Highnes wyth a sword in his hand berying yt upright all the *masse tyme. **1530** PALSGR. 804/2 At masse tyme. **1845** 'C. MALONE' in S. J. Brown *Poetry of Irish Hist.* (1927) 258 At Mass-time once I went to play. **1922** JOYCE *Ulysses* 279 And once at masstime he had gone to play... A boy. A croppy boy. **1879** T. F. SIMMONS *Lay Folks Mass Bk.* 335 *note*, The full *mass-vestment of the priest. **13..** *Gaw. & Gr. Knt.* 1097 Ȝe schal lenge in your lofte..To morn quyle þe *messe-quyle. **1840** CARLYLE *Heroes* (1858) 282 Fasts, vigils, formalities and *mass-work.

mass (mæs), *sb.*² Also 5, 7 **mase**, 5–8 **masse**. [a. F. *masse* (recorded from 11th c.), ad. L. *massa*, prob. (as ancient grammarians believed) a. Gr. μᾶζα barley-cake, perh. cogn. w. Gr. μάσσειν to knead:—**maky-*:—pre-Hellenic **mn̥qy-*, f. root **mn̥q-*, *menq-*; cf. Lith. *minkyti* to knead.]

1. a. A coherent body of plastic or fusible matter (as dough, clay, metal), not yet moulded or fashioned into objects of definite shape; a lump of raw material for moulding, casting, sculpture, etc. Now merged in sense 2. *in* (*the*) *mass*: said of metal in the form of masses or lumps.

c **1400** MAUNDEV. (1839) xiv. 158 Men fynden..hard Dyamandes in a Masse, that cometh out of Gold, whan men puren it..out of the Myne. **1582** N. LICHEFIELD tr. *Castanheda's Conq. E. Ind.* I. xxxiii. 80 Two Masses of siluer. **1611** BIBLE *Ecclus.* xxii. 15 Sand, and salt, and a masse of yron is easier to beare then a man without vnderstanding. **1630** PRYNNE *Anti-Armin.* 166 Out of the same masse are made vessels of mercy. *a* **1729** CONGREVE tr. *Ovid's Art of Love* III. Wks. 1730 III. 307 Myro's Statues, which for Art surpass All others, once were but a shapeless Mass.

†**b.** Metal, esp. gold or silver, in the lump.

1477 *Rolls of Parlt.* VI. 184/2 Nor Plate, Vessell, Masse, Bullion, nor Juelx of Gold. **1555** W. WATREMAN *Fardle Facions* II. i. 115 Limall of golde in greate plentie, Whiche they..do neuer fine into masse. **1597** HOOKER *Eccl. Pol.* v. lxxix. §5 Of Gold in Masse eight thousand..Cichars. **1601** HOLLAND *Pliny* I. 46 Brasse and lead in the masse or lumpe, sinke downe,..but if they be driuen out into thin plates, they flote.

c. An amorphous quantity of material used in or remaining after a chemical or other operation; in *Pharmacy*, the compound or other substance from which pills are made.

1562 EDEN *Let.* in *1st Eng. Bks. Amer.* (Arb.) Introd. 44/1, I stilled of the water from the masse or Chaos lefte of them bothe. **1643** J. STEER tr. *Exp. Chyrurg.* xiii. 51 With *Syrup. Rosar. lenit.*, make a Masse of Pill. **1666** BOYLE *Orig. Formes & Qual.* 329 The remaining Masse would be..of an Alkalizate nature. **1756** C. LUCAS *Ess. Waters* I. 122 The best method is to wash the whole mass carefully. **1809** *Med. Jrnl.* XXI. 351 A compact mass produced in an operation, which weighs nearly 100 grains. **1880** GARROD & BAXTER *Mat. Med.* 196 One grain of opium is contained in five grains of the pill-mass.

†**d.** A kind of matter capable of being fashioned; a plastic substance. *Obs.*

1471 RIPLEY *Comp. Alch.* Pref. in Ashm. (1652) 123 As of one Mase was made all thyng. **1596** SPENSER *F.Q.* IV. x. 39 The Goddesse selfe did stand Upon an altar of some costly masse. **1700** DRYDEN *Sig. & Guis.* 502 When the world began, One common mass composed the mould of man.

2. a. In wider sense: A body of coherent and (really or apparently) ponderous matter of relatively large bulk; a solid physical object filling a great amount of space. In modern *Physics*, often contrasted with *molecule* or *atom*.

c **1440** *Promp. Parv.* 328/2 Masse, or gobet of mete, or other lyke, *massa*. *a* **1547** SURREY *Æneid* II. (1557) A iv, Wherto was wrought the masse of this huge hors? **1581** SAVILE *Tacitus' Agricola* (1604) 188 A deepe masse of continuall sea is slower sturred to rage. **1692** BENTLEY *Boyle Lect.* vii. 247 Those Atoms would there form one huge sphærical Mass. **1810** SCOTT *Lady of L.* I. xi, Round many an insulated mass, The native bulwarks of the pass. **1842–3** GROVE *Corr. Phys. Forces* 73 When the magnet as a mass is in motion. **1849** JAMES *Woodman* i, A large gray, indistinct mass stretched all along from east to west. **1860** TYNDALL *Glac.* I. ii. 21 Adjacent to us rose the mighty mass of the Finsteraarhorn. *Ibid.* II. xix. 329 What is true for masses is also true for atoms.

†**b.** applied to the created universe or the earth.

1587 GOLDING *De Mornay* iii. (1617) 33 When hee had layd the foundations of this goodly Masse. **1602** SHAKS. *Ham.* III. iv. 49 Yea this solidity and compound masse,..Is thought-sicke at the act. **1697** DRYDEN *Virg. Georg.* IV. 324 God the whole created Mass inspires.

†**c.** *Phys.* The whole quantity of blood or fluid dispersed through an animal body. *Obs.*

1693 tr. *Blancard's Phys. Dict.* (ed. 2), *Massa*, all the Blood is commonly called the Mass of Blood. **1698** FRYER *Acc. E. India & P.* 16 That the Misty Vapours might not hinder the kind operation begun on their tainted Mass of Blood. **1731** ARBUTHNOT *Nat. Aliments* (1735) 175 If there is not a sufficient Quantity of Blood..to subdue it, it [acid] may infect the whole Mass of the Fluids. **1732** LAW *Serious C.* xi. 178 Poison..corrupts the whole mass of blood.

d. *Mining.* (See quots.)

1855 J. R. LEIFCHILD *Cornwall Mines* 83 *Masses* are sometimes termed *pipe-veins* by miners... The best conception that can be formed of them is, that of an irregular branching cavity, descending either vertically or obliquely into the rock, and filled up with metalliferous matter. **1883** C. LE N. FOSTER in *Encycl. Brit.* XVI. 441/2 Masses. These are deposits of mineral, often of irregular shapes, which cannot be distinctly recognized as beds or veins.

3. A dense aggregation of objects apparently forming a continuous body.

1609 BIBLE (Douay) *1 Sam.* xxv. 18 Two hundred mases [Vulg. *massas*] of drie figges. **1660** F. BROOKE tr. *Le Blanc's Trav.* 15 The Mosca or Temple of Meka is a masse of stones built round. **1716** ADDISON *Freeholder* No. 26 ¶4 Such a beautiful mass of colours. **1776** WITHERING *Brit. Plants* (1796) II. 503 The whole mass of seeds upon the fruitstalk. **1866** *Treas. Bot.*, *Masses*. Collections of anything in unusual quantity; as, for example, pollen-masses, which are unusual collections of pollen. **1875** BUCKLAND *Log-bk.* 90 One solid mass of living cod. **1880** OUIDA *Moths* II. 32 There were masses of camellias and azaleas. **1884** BOWER & SCOTT *De Bary's Phaner.* 361 A many-layered mass of sclerenchymatous fibres.

4. *transf.* and *fig.* (from senses 2 and 3).

a. A large quantity, amount, or number (either of material or immaterial things); often with the notion of oppressive or bewildering abundance. Freq. in *pl.*

1585 T. WASHINGTON tr. *Nicholay's Voy.* II. vi. 36 b, The whole masse..may amount too about 150. caces. **1604** SHAKS. *Oth.* II. iii. 289, I remember a masse of things, but nothing distinctly. **1626** T. H[AWKINS] *Caussin's Holy Crt.* 71 The children of rich men become drouthy amongst a masse of fountaynes. **1630** *R. Johnson's Kingd. & Commw.* 227 In the Silver-Mines, which were discovered in Potosie ..hath beene found so huge a masse of Bullion, that [etc.]. **1647** CLARENDON *Hist. Reb.* I. §4 Like so many atoms contributing jointly to this mass of confusion now before us. **1650** FULLER *Pisgah* 396 Of this last [*viz.* salt] a mass was spent in the Temple. **1772** *Junius Lett.* lxviii. (1820) 353 Taking the whole of it together..it constitutes a mass of demonstration..complete..to the human mind. **1849** MACAULAY *Hist. Eng.* vi. II. 110 A mass of near twenty thousand pages. **1855** *Ibid.* xi. III. 87 They removed a vast mass of evil without shocking a vast mass of prejudice. **1865** TYLOR *Early Hist. Man.* i. 13 Any one who collects and groups a mass of evidence. **1879** RUSKIN *Arrows of Chace* (1880) II. 206 There is a mass of letters on my table this morning. **1958** *Observer* 18 May 16/4 If you weren't a poor little rich girl, or very pretty or exciting socially, there were still masses of fun to be had. **1974** A. MORICE *Killing with Kindness* viii. 56 I'm sure you've got masses to do.

†**b.** *spec.* of money, treasure, etc. Also *absol.*, a sum of money, a stock or fund. In *Gaming* (*rare*⁻⁰, after F. *masse*), the amount of a person's stake. *Obs.*

1568 GRAFTON *Chron.* II. 37 By reason whereof he gathered a great masse of money. **1577** HELLOWES *Gueuara's Chron.* 89 The officers of the treasurie, that is to saye, suche as had the collection and keeping of the masse of Rome. **1592** WARNER *Alb. Eng.* VII. xxxiv. (1612) 166 And he for Masses great was brib'de Earle Henry to betray. **1593** SHAKS. *2 Hen. VI*, I. iii. 134 Thy sumptuous Buildings,.. Haue cost a masse of publique Treasurie. **1622** BACON *Hen. VII* 159 Hauing alreadie made our great Masses of the Treasure of our Crowne. **1650** FULLER *Pisgah* IV. iv. 65 Carefully keeping their money for them, till it amounted to a mass. **1727** BOYER *Fr. Dict.*, *Masse* (fonds d'une Hérédité ou d'une Société), Mass, or Stock. *Ibid.*, *Masse*, (en Termes de jeu de hazard) the Mass, at Play.

c. used *hyperbolically*, esp. in phrase ***to be a*** (or ***one***) ***mass of*** (e.g. bruises, faults, mistakes, etc.).

1616 B. JONSON *Devil an Ass* IV. iii, I am a woman.. match'd to a mass of folly. **1623** GOUGE *Serm. Extent God's Provid.* §15 Papists..whose doctrine is a masse of ancient heresies. **1845** MARRYAT 5 Apr. *Life & Lett.* (1872) II. 197 The country is really, without exaggeration, one mass of violets. **1867** SMILES *Huguenot's Eng.* i. (1880) 2 The Church itself was seen to be a mass of abuses.

d. applied to an extensive unbroken expanse (of colour, light, shadow, etc.). Also, in *Fine Art*, one of the several main portions which the eye distinguishes in a composition, each characterized by a certain degree of unity in colour or lighting throughout its parts.

1662 EVELYN *Chalcogr.* v. 120 There are some parts in them commonly to be distinguished from the Mass in gross; for example, the hairs in men, eyes, teeth, nails, &c., that as one would conceive such lines, or hatches on those masses, others may likewise be as well fanci'd upon those lesser, and more delicate members. **1695** DRYDEN *Dufresnoy's Art Paint.* 141 This he did..by making the Masses of the Lights and Shadows, greater and more disentangl'd. **1710** J. HARRIS *Lex. Techn.* II, *Masses*, in Painting, are the large parts of a Picture containing the great Lights and Shadows. **1797** *Encycl. Brit.* (ed. 3) XIII. 609/1 Some technical knowledge of the effect producible by *masses* of light and shade. **1843** RUSKIN *Mod. Paint.* I. II. II. v. §10 The *masses* which result from right concords and relations of details are sublime and impressive; but the *masses* which result from the eclipse of details are contemptible and painful. **1875** MCLAREN *Serm.* Ser. II. x. 173 All striped with solid masses of blackness. **1895** ZANGWILL *Master* II. i. 121 The

occasional fineness of line, the masterly distribution of masses.

e. A volume or body of sound; in *Music* used esp. of the effect of a large number of instruments or voices of the same character.

1873 E. ATKINSON tr. *Helmholtz's Pop. Lect. Sci. Subjects* 1st Ser. 101 Although we are not usually clearly conscious of these beating upper partials, the ear feels their effect as a want of uniformity or a roughness in the mass of tone. **1879** STAINER *Music of Bible* 174 The grand musical results of harps.. and other simple instruments, when used in large numbers simultaneously or in alternating masses.

†f. ? Something burdensome; a grief. *Obs. rare.*

1592 WYRLEY *Armorie* 144 It is a world to marke the iollitie Of seamen floting in the liquid sea... A masse it is to note his miserie When raging tempests bustle on the flood.

g. *Psychol.* (See *apperceiving mass, apperception mass.*)

1907 W. JAMES in *Jrnl. Philos.* 18 July 397 My statements may seem less obscure if surrounded by something more of a 'mass' whereby to apperceive them.

5. a. Of human beings: A large number collected in a narrow space; a compact body. Also, a multitude of persons mentally viewed as forming an aggregate in which their individuality is lost.

1713 BERKELEY *Guardian* No. 83 ¶1 The whole mass of mankind. **1814** SCOTT *Wav.* xlvii, Their extended files were pierced.. in many places by the close masses of the clans. **1848** W. H. KELLY tr. *L. Blanc's Hist. Ten Y.* I. 134 The king.. sent him orders.. to concentrate the troops round the Tuileries, and to act with masses. **1860** EMERSON *Cond. Life* vii. (1861) 145 Away with this hurrah of masses, and let us have the considerate vote of single men. **1874** GREEN *Short Hist.* iv. §1. 155 The unconquered Britons had sunk into a mass of savage herdsmen.

b. *Mil.* A formation of troops in which the battalions, etc. are arranged one behind another. Opposed to *line*.

1889 *Infantry Drill* 165 A Mass wheeling into Line of Quarter Columns... A Line of Quarter Columns wheeling into Mass.

6. a. ***the* (*great*) *mass of***: the greater part or majority of.

1625 BACON *Ess., Vicissitude of Things* (Arb.) 571 Comets.. haue.. Power.. ouer the Gross and Masse of Things. **1711** SWIFT *Contests Athens & Rome* v. Wks. 1751 IV. 61 The mass of the people have opened their Eyes. **1806** JEFFERSON *6th Ann. Message* Writ. 1854 VIII. 68 The great mass of the articles on which impost is paid is foreign luxuries. **1863** H. COX *Instit.* I. viii. 107 The great mass of the people had no part in the election of representatives. **1875** JOWETT *Plato* (ed. 2) III. 158 We cannot expect the mass of mankind to become disinterested.

b. ***the mass***: the generality of mankind; the main body of a race or nation.

1675 BAXTER *Cath. Theol.* I. I. 65 The Corrupted Mass simply considered was the object of no one of all these graces. **1855** BROWNING *Luria* v, Those who live as models for the mass. **1848** LOWELL *Biglow Papers* Ser. I. v, The mass ough' to labour an' we lay on soffies. **1875** WHITNEY *Life Lang.* ix. 159 The language of the mass goes on changing unchecked.

c. ***the masses***: the populace or 'lower orders'.

The antithesis with 'the classes' seems to have been first used by Gladstone in 1886.

1837 MOORE *Mem.* (1856) VII. 174 One of the few proofs of good Taste that 'the masses', as they are called, have yet given. **1863** W. PHILLIPS *Speeches* vi. 139 The masses are governed more by impulse than conviction. **1887** M. ARNOLD *Kaiser Dead* vii, Since 'gainst the classes, He heard, of late, the Grand Old Man Incite the masses.

7. †a. ***in mass*** = EN MASSE, bodily, all at once.

1798 ANNA SEWARD *Lett.* (1811) V. 133 Our nation has almost risen in mass. **1807** SOUTHEY *Espriella's Lett.* I. 179 The levy in mass, the telegraph, and the income-tax are all from France. **1869** F. W. NEWMAN *Misc.* 78 To adopt their superstitions in mass.

b. ***in the mass***: without distinction of component parts or individuals; in the aggregate.

c **1820** S. ROGERS *Italy, Nat. Prej.* (1834) 149 We condemn millions in the mass as vindictive. **1832** HT. MARTINEAU *Hill & Valley* v. 75 We speak of society as one thing, and regard men in the mass.

c. ***in a mass***: in a lump sum.

1845 MARRYAT *Let. to Forster* in *Life & Lett.* (1872) II. 196 They have.. become a little income to me; which I infinitely prefer to receiving any sum in a mass.

8. *abstr.* **a.** Solid bulk, massiveness.

1602 SHAKS. *Ham.* IV. iv. 47 This army of such mass and charge Led by a delicate and tender prince. **1606** —— *Tr. & Cr.* I. iii. 29 But in the Winde and Tempest of her frowne, Distinction.. winnowes the light away; And what hath masse, or matter by it selfe, Lies rich in Vertue, and vnmingled. **1757** J. H. GROSE *Voy. E. Indies* 245 When exasperated by wounds, to which their mass makes them [*sc.* elephants in war] a mark hard to miss. **1856** KANE *Arct. Expl.* II. xxiii. 225 Gathering mass as it travelled.

b. *Physics.* The quantity of matter which a body contains; in strict use distinguished from *weight*, though the two terms are often used indiscriminately. ***centre of mass***: see CENTRE *sb.* 16.

1704 J. HARRIS *Lex. Techn.* I, *Masse*, this Word is used by the Natural Philosophers to express the Quantity of Matter in any Body. **1812–16** PLAYFAIR *Nat. Phil.* (1819) II. 283 The mass of the Comet.. cannot have been $\frac{1}{500}$th of the mass of the Earth. **1868** LOCKYER *Guillemin's Heavens* (ed. 3) 25 The mass of the Sun alone however is equal to 750 times the united masses of all the bodies which it maintains in its sphere of attraction. **1876** TAIT *Rec. Adv. Phys. Sci.* (1885) 357 When you buy a pound of tea you buy a quantity of the matter called tea equal in mass to the standard pound of platinum. **1893** SIR R. BALL *Story of Sun* 97 What the periodic time of the Moon would have been if our satellite had been devoid of mass.

¶9. Used for med.L. *massa*, a holding of land.

1854 MILMAN *Lat. Chr.* I. 443 *note*, One mass or farm had been compelled.. to pay double rent.

10. *attrib.* and *Comb.*, passing into *adj.* Examples, of which a selection is listed below, are very numerous in the 20th century. Used to mean: of, involving, composed of masses of people (or things) or the majority of people (or a society, group, etc.); done, made, etc., on a large scale. ***mass-appeal, art, audience, behaviour, circulation, communication*** (hence ***mass communicator***), ***consciousness, consumer*** (hence ***-consuming, consumption***), ***cult, culture, deportation, education, emotion*** (hence ***emotional*** adj.), ***entertainment, fear, grave, hypnosis*** (hence ***-hypnotized*** adj.), ***hysteria, immigration, literacy, migration, mind*** (hence ***-minded*** adj., ***-mindedness***), ***movement, murder*** (hence ***mass murderer***), ***party, persuasion, propaganda, psychology, public, society, suggestion, suicide, unemployment***; ***mass-made*** ppl. a.; ***mass-advertising, -buying, -merchandising*** (also ***-merchandised*** ppl. a., ***-merchandiser***), ***-selling, -thinking*** vbl. sbs. **a.** Also *Arch.* 'Arranged in large masses', as ***mass-pier***. **b.** *Mil.*, etc. 'Involving masses of people', as ***mass attack*** (also as vb.), ***-bombing*** vbl. sb., ***drill, formation, raid, vote***. **c.** *Physics*, as ***mass-attraction, -brightness, -flow, -moment, transport***.

1958 *New Statesman* 20 Dec. 881/2 Not all the spice goes into the thick wedges of Christmas pudding; and surely, as we sink deeper and deeper in the treacle of *mass-advertising, we deserve this one tiny life-saver? **1944** L. MACNEICE *Christopher Columbus* 14 To assert.. that all art should have *mass-appeal is like asserting that all mathematics should be 'for the million'. **1962** *Rep. Comm. Broadcasting 1960* 16 in *Parl. Papers 1961–2* (Cmnd. 1753) IX. 259 It has been said that in fact people watch these items; that the justification lies precisely in the fact that they are mass-appeal items. **1962** S. STRAND *Marketing Dict.* 441 In marketing, a product is said to have *mass appeal* when it is desired by the multitudes in all income levels. **1938** *Current Hist.* Feb. 54 (*caption*) A *Mass Art. **1959** M. MCCARTHY *Sights & Spectacles* p. xiv, Some of the editors felt that the theatre was not worth bothering with, because it was neither a high art, like Art, nor a mass art, like the movies! **1964** HALL & WHANNEL *Pop. Arts* iii. 68 Mass art often destroys all trace of individuality and idiosyncrasy which makes a work compelling and living. **1970** I. C. JARVIE *Towards Sociol. of Cinema* vii. 99 Cinema is in a real sense a mass art, not only in that it appeals to the mass audience, but also in that the individual is lost in the darkness of the continuous performance. **1947** CROWTHER & WHIDDINGTON *Science at War* 101 When convoys of merchant ships were *mass-attacked by U-boats in 1942, they were liable to suffer heavy losses. **1959** *Chambers's Encycl.* XIV. 733/1 On 8 August a mass attack was launched on a convoy near the Isle of Wight. **1960** L. L. SNYDER *The War 1939–45* vi. 117 August 6, 1940. From his country home.. Goering issued orders for the first great mass attack on England. **1903** AGNES CLERKE *Problems in Astrophysics* 3 The universality of an apparent *mass-attraction was a great fact. **1938** *Time* 21 Nov. 53/1 Hitchcock pictures.. are often too intricately built and written to appeal to *mass audiences. **1957** R. HOGGART *Uses of Literacy* vi. 147 Genuine controversy.. alienates, divides and separates, the mass-audience. **1957** P. MARTINEAU *Motivation in Advertising* xiv. 169 The 'mass-audience' housewife. **1967** M. MCLUHAN *Medium is Massage* 22 The mass audience.. successor to the 'public'. **1974** *B.B.C. Handbk.* 261/2 Opera, so obviously appropriate to television but with a limited appeal to the mass audience. **1940** HARRISSON & MADGE *War begins at Home* i. 21 When hundreds of those replies show similar attitudes, we know we are on to something really important in terms of *mass behaviour. **1941** E. C. SHEPHERD *Mil. Aeroplane* 4 Anti-aircraft fire can.. break up the formations so that *mass bombing or pattern bombing becomes impossible. **1890** AGNES CLERKE *Syst. Stars* 209 The '*mass-brightness' of these objects is twelve times that of the sun. **1929** *Mass buying [see *mass selling* below]. **1950** B. SCHULBERG *Disenchanted* (1951) v. 61 Occasionally appearing in *mass circulation magazines with stories increasingly ordinary. **1957** F. WILLIAMS *Dangerous Estate*: *Anat. Newspapers* xviii. 284 The tabloids and mass-circulation Sunday newspapers. *Ibid.* 291 The great mass-circulation newspapers.. command their millions. **1963** *Times Lit. Suppl.* 26 Apr. 298/4 The mass-circulation magazines. **1941** BEALS & BRODY *Lit. Adult Educ.* v. 139 Concentration of power in the agencies of *mass communication is vicious. **1946** J. S. HUXLEY *Unesco* ii. 25 The spread of information through all media of Mass Communication—in other words, the press, the cinema, the radio and television. **1954** J. B. PRIESTLEY *Magicians* ii. 47 Mass communications become stronger in their effects every year. **1968** P. OLIVER *Screening Blues* 9 Mass communication through recording, and later through radio, spread the culture of the blues beyond the local definition until the whole Negro world was its habitat. **1971** B. MAFENI in J. Spencer *Eng. Lang. W. Afr.* 100 The great potentialities of the language [*sc.* Nigerian Pidgin] as a medium of mass communication. **1965** *Punch* 9 June 858/1 One way and another Lord Thomson is quite a *mass communicator. **1967** *Ibid.* 4 Jan. 23/2 The delusion you are suffering from usually attacks columnists, commentators and other mass communicators. **1922** D. H. LAWRENCE *Aaron's Rod* x. 139, I want to get myself awake, out of it all—all that *mass-consciousness. **1947** KOESTLER in *Partisan Rev.* XIV. 141 Structural changes in economy without functional changes in mass-consciousness, must always lead to a dead end. **1931** A. HUXLEY *Music at Night* IV. 208 A man who has no interest in the things of the mind.. is the ideal consumer, the *mass consumer. **1971** G. STEINER *In Bluebeard's Castle* iv. 87 The informational energy required by a mass-consumer society is being transmitted pictorially. **1954** *Encounter* Mar. 5/2 Those who accept conformity do not challenge the existence of a mass-producing, *mass-consuming society, even though they refuse its values. **1969** R. B. FULLER *Operating Man. Spaceship Earth* viii. 117 As we study industrialization, we see that we cannot have mass production unless we have mass consumption. **1963** *Spectator* 14 June 783 Mr. Macdonald's target is 'mass culture' and its nauseating child 'Midcult', which, if anything, is worse than '*Masscult'. **1971** M. W. YOUNG *Fighting with Food in Massim Society* i. 11 Cargo beliefs are still held by many individuals, however, and a fresh catalyst could well provoke another mass cult. **1939** *Life* 24 July 65/2 The State of Texas.. has never been properly recognized for its contributions to U.S. *mass culture. **1957** R. HOGGART *Uses of Literacy* i. 23 We are moving towards the creation of a mass culture. **1957** *Economist* 5 Oct. 45/1 Whether the reader turns to Shakespeare or to Mr Erle Stanley Gardner for solace may depend less on his psyche and the state of 'mass culture' than on the thorny economics of the book business. **1975** *Listener* 9 Jan. 40/2 The mass culture which is everyone's hope.. depends upon everyone sharing what has previously been the preserve of a privileged few. **1952** C. P. BLACKER *Eugenics* 146 Since these words were written, we have witnessed the inhumanities of concentration and extermination camps, of labour camps and *mass deportations, which have scarcely been surpassed by previous tyrannies. **1955** KOESTLER *Trail of Dinosaur* 160 The mass-deportations in the 'thirties produced new waves of the plague. **1896** *Daily News* 25 Nov. 3/7 All these smart little children were doing a *mass drill. **1927** A. HUXLEY *Proper Stud.* 113 The ordinary system of *mass education. **1940** GRAVES & HODGE *Long Week-End* iv. 50 The terms 'thriller' and 'shocker'.. had been in use since the Eighties—an early by-product of mass-education. **1964** C. BARBER *Ling. Change Present-Day Eng.* ii. 20 The influence of mass-media and of mass-education. **1927** A. HUXLEY *Proper Stud.* 183 Periodic revivalism and the evoking of great *mass-emotions on such occasions as pilgrimages provide the necessary emotional excitement. **1961** A. O. J. COCKSHUT *Imagination of Charles Dickens* v. 78 Mingling with the crowd he is untouched by mass emotions. **1963** *Economist* 3 Aug. 445/2 Everyone interested in political, *mass emotional, historical causes should read it. **1933** *Radio Times* 14 Apr. 71/1 A music-hall or other large centre of *mass-entertainment. **1960** *20th Cent.* Dec. 557 The hugh metropolitan machines of mass entertainment. **1932** H. NICOLSON *Public Faces* xii. 324 There is only one human emotion stronger than mass-hatred, and that is *mass-fear. **1952** PANKHURST & HOLDER *Wind-Tunnel Technique* i. 31 The rate of *mass flow per unit cross-sectional area (the mass velocity) is given by [etc.]. **1957** *Times* 4 Oct. 11/7 In the by-pass engine a given thrust is obtained by a greater mass-flow of air at reduced velocity, the engine being both bigger and heavier than the 'straight jet'. **1917** A. G. EMPEY *Over Top* 299 **Mass formation*, a close order formation in which the Germans attack. **1948** E. POUND *Pisan Cantos* (1949) lxxvii. 49 By getting me onto the commission To inspect the *mass graves at Katin. **1972** *New Statesman* 28 Jan. 109/3 The communists.. murdered several thousand political prisoners, whose bodies were later discovered.. in three separate mass graves. **1974** *Times* 4 Sept. 8/1 Turkish troops today uncovered more bodies from the mass grave at the Turkish Cypriot village of Maratha. **1951** M. MCLUHAN *Mech. Bride* (1967) 10/2 Power, glitter and *mass hypnosis engendered by regular ranks. **1967** G. PLAYFAIR *Prodigy* iii. 82 There was.. an element of mass-hypnosis in Bettymania, as there is in all such manifestations of idolatry. **1946** R. CAMPBELL *Talking Bronco* 61 *Mass-hypnotized, dinned drunken by the tireless Mechanic repetition of the wireless. **1934** A. HUXLEY *Beyond Mexique Bay* 276 The mindless *mass hysteria of howling mobs. **1954** *Economist* 22 May 611/1 Yet Mr Graham does not produce mass hysteria, although he is certainly dramatic. **1969** MILGRAM & TOCH in Lindzey & Aronson *Handbk. Social Psychol.* (ed. 2) IV. xxxv. 507 Such diverse phenomena as 'collective excitement, social unrest.., riots.., mass hysteria, [etc.]'. **1973** *Times* 7 Dec. 19/4 There is an argument for introducing rationing in London where some form of mass hysteria seems to have occurred. **1949** KOESTLER *Promise & Fulfilment* vii. 69 The next transformation came after the First World War when *mass immigration started in earnest. **1973** *Times* 5 Dec. 18/2 Israel was founded on.. mass immigration as the dynamic of growth. **1937** C. MADGE in C. Day Lewis *Mind in Chains* 147 A fact of to-day which is so near to us that it is hard for us to see it is *mass-literacy. **1967** *Economist* 15 Apr. p. i/3 The Franklin Book Programs Inc.. uses all kinds of techniques from mass-literacy and mass-distribution schemes to training programmes. **1934** T. S. ELIOT *Rock* I. 46 Those whose souls are choked and swaddled In the.. new winding sheets of *mass-made thought. **1959** V. PACKARD *Status Seekers* (1960) i. 3 They can dine on *mass-merchandised vichyssoise. *Ibid.* 4 Everybody could enjoy the good things of life—as defined by mass merchandisers. **1962** S. STRAND *Marketing Dict.* 442 *Mass merchandising*, a large-scale selling method, appealing to the population as a whole with convincing advertising. **1972** R. H. BUSKIRK et al. *Concepts of Business* xii. 169 The mass-merchandising specialty store.. frequently calls itself a discount house. **1901** E. A. ROSS *Social Control* xxix. 396 The common perils of war or *mass migration may call for stricter corporate discipline. **1935** HUXLEY & HADDON *We Europeans* ix. 273 Mass-migration and military conquest. **1932** H. J. MASSINGHAM *World without End* x. 264 A man or woman who deserts his or her distinctive colour of being and joins the *mass-mind. **1936** G. M. YOUNG *Victorian Eng.* xxviii. 158 The propagandist, the advertiser and all other agents of the mass-mind. **1955** KOESTLER *Trail of Dinosaur* III. 242 An unexpected mutation of the mass-mind may occur. **1964** M. MCLUHAN *Understanding Media* xi. 107 Creating the paradox of the 'mass mind' and the mass militarism of citizen armies. **1934** WEBSTER, *Mass-minded. **1942** D. POWELL *Time to be Born* (1943) xii. 280 The masses of women.. too mass-minded in their ambitions to be even faintly understood by her. **1939** H. J. MASSINGHAM *Countryman's Jrnl.* xxxiii. 143 It is good for a man.. to converse with his own spirit or what *mass-

mindedness has left of it. **1961** *Ann. Reg. 1960* 430 The first of these was Eugene Ionesco's *Rhinoceros*, a savage satire on mass-mindedness. **1882** MINCHIN *Unipl. Kinemat.* 108 The theorem of *mass-moments, which expresses the distance of the centre of mass of any body..from a plane, in terms of the masses of the constituent particles and their several distances from the plane. **1897** *Amer. Jrnl. Sociol.* Nov. 344 They are cultivating mass sympathies and drilling themselves in *mass movements. **1927** D. H. LAWRENCE *Let.* 11 July (1932) 684 They [*sc.* the Germans] are capable of mass-movement. **1935** *Discovery* Oct. 292/1 Occasional mass-movements, like those of the lemmings of Scandinavia, were not to be confused with true migration. **1939** *Encycl. Brit. Bk. of Year* 19/2 In the United States there is taking place what may roughly be termed a mass movement towards Adult Education. **1967** H. ARENDT *Orig. Totalitarianism* (new ed.) x. 313 The decisive differences between nineteenth-century mob organizations and twentieth-century mass movements are difficult to perceive. **1931** S. NEARING (*title*) War: organized destruction and *mass murder by civilized nations. **1945** R. A. KNOX *God & Atom* vi. 79 Democracy labours for breath, when the power of mass-murder is concentrated..in the hands of a few. **1958** *Times Lit. Suppl.* 13 June 334/3 His solution for the whole problem of mass-murders is 'family-love'. **1967** H. ARENDT *Orig. Totalitarianism* (new ed.) xii. 421 The bulk of the armed SS served at the Eastern front where they were used for 'special assignments'—usually mass murder. **1952** B. WOLFE *Limbo* (1953) vii. 80 Look at this baby-faced *mass murderer. **1960** *Sunday Express* 25 Dec. 10/2 A reprieved mass-murderer in Dartmoor. **1947** 'G. ORWELL' *Eng. People* 22 The Communist Party [in Britain]..has never shown signs of growing into a *mass party of the kind that exists in France. **1954** B. & R. NORTH tr. *Duverger's Pol. Parties* I. ii. 63 The mass-party technique in effect replaces the capitalist financing of electioneering by democratic financing. **1848** B. WEBB *Continent. Ecclesiol.* 253 There are *mass-piers below those of the upper church. **1956** C. W. MILLS *Power Elite* xiii. 310 The increased means of *mass persuasion that are available. **1960** J. B. PRIESTLEY *Lit. & Western Man* ii. 16 The time of vast urban masses and all our techniques of mass persuasion. **1950** KOESTLER et al. *God that Failed* 65 Independent of the *mass-propaganda methods of the Münzenberg enterprises. **1967** H. ARENDT *Orig. Totalitarianism* (new ed.) viii. 264 Entirely new and complicated forms of mass propaganda were adopted by all parties. **1900** *Amer. Jrnl. Sociol.* Jan. 521 This is the reason why ethnology is finding its most promising developments today in the line of ethnic or folk-psychology, which is only a cross-section of *mass-psychology. **1916** B. RUSSELL *Princ. Social Reconstruction* ii. 60 Even the few questions which are left to the popular vote are decided by a diffused mass-psychology. **1929** CHESTERTON *Thing* xxii. 166 The abandonment of individual reason, in favour of press stunts and suggestion and mass psychology. **1937** KOESTLER *Spanish Testament* II. 308, I could wish that everyone who talks of mass psychology should experience a year of prison. **1960** H. READ *Forms of Things Unknown* IV. xi. 179 A resort to mass psychology is evasive. **1938** *Times Lit. Suppl.* 17 Sept. 598/1 The *mass-public does not want opinion, it wants news. **1960** *New Left Rev.* May-June 65/2 Personalities..with an existence quite different in tone from the mass public. **1939** *War Weekly* 25 Oct. 1313/1 First night *mass raid on London... On the Tuesday night, a night mass air attack was tried for the first time. **1929** *Publishers' Weekly* 19 Oct. 1928/1 Our shop, like other small shops, is not geared for *mass selling or mass buying. **1968** *Listener* 29 Aug. 285/3 There is now hardly a significant publication, from the weekly reviews to the mass-selling dailies, which does not have equity in one or other of the programme-contracting companies. **1948** T. S. ELIOT *Notes Def. Culture* ii. 40 This gives it [*sc.* 'bourgeois' society] a difference in kind from the aristocratic society which preceded it, and from the *mass-society which is expected to follow it. **1950** *Antioch Rev.* X. 382 Mass society is no more stable under dictatorship than it is under democracy. **1957** F. WILLIAMS *Dangerous Estate: Anat. Newspapers* xviii. 285 The straits to which an industrial mass-society has brought millions of its members. **1967** G. STEINER *Lang. & Silence* 69 The possibility that..certain elements in the technological mass-society..have done injury to language is the underlying theme of this book. **1901** E. ROSS *Social Control* 148 In public opinion there is something which is not praise or blame, and this residuum is *mass suggestion. **1920** W. MCDOUGALL *Group Mind* ii. 42 A proposition which voices the mind of the crowd..and so comes with the power of a mass-suggestion. **1924** W. B. SELBIE *Psychol. Relig.* 116 We have here to reckon with the influence of mass suggestion. **1947** *Mind* LVI. 60 There can be mass suggestion, there are methods of group persuasion, but reasoning is carried on by each of us not only for himself but by himself. **1937** M. COVARRUBIAS *Island of Bali* (1972) vii. 199 The famous krisses of the kings of South Bali taken by the Dutch as war booty at the time of the great *mass-suicide of Den Pasar in 1906. **1959** *Manch. Guardian* 9 July 6/6 A ..policy of mass suicide masquerading as a policy of defence. **1924** *Public Opinion* 30 May 528/3 Our modern saints of co-operative *mass-thinking. **1958** R. WILLIAMS *Culture & Society* III. 298 Mass-thinking, mass-suggestion, mass-prejudice would threaten to swamp considered individual thinking and feeling. **1953** *Phil. Trans. R. Soc.* A. CCXLV. 535 The *mass-transport velocity can be very different from that predicted by Stokes on the assumption of a perfect, non-viscous fluid. **1957** G. E. HUTCHINSON *Treat. Limnol.* I. v. 347 The small deepwater waves of negligible amplitude..produce virtually no mass transport of water. **1974** *A.I.Ch.E. Jrnl.* XX. 84/1 One of the potential advantages of slurry reactors is reduction of intraparticle mass transport resistances. **1937** 'G. ORWELL' *Road to Wigan Pier* viii. 153, I wanted to see what *mass-unemployment is like at its worst. **1965** J. L. HANSON *Dict. Econ.* 387 Mass unemployment is the most serious type since it is due to a general deficiency of demand. **1974** *Times* 5 Nov. 15/3 The monetarists fear that some unemployment may be the necessary price of avoiding mass unemployment. **1887** *Spectator* 24 Sept. 1265 A *mass vote of the people.

d. Special comb.: **mass action,** (*a*) *Chem.*, the effect which the concentration of a reactant has on the rate of a chemical reaction; (*b*) the action of a mass of people; **mass-area** *Physics* (see quot.); **mass balance** *Aeronaut.*, a state in which inertial coupling between the angular movement of a control surface and other degrees of freedom of the aircraft is eliminated, so avoiding flutter of the surface; also, a mass attached to a control surface to bring about such a state; also as *v. trans.*; so **mass-balanced** *ppl. a.*, **mass-balancing** *vbl. sb.*; **mass concrete**, concrete which is not reinforced; **mass-copper**, 'native copper, occurring in large masses' (Raymond *Mining Gloss.* 1881); **mass defect**, a deficiency of mass; *spec.* in *Nuclear Physics*, the sum of the masses of the constituent particles of a nucleus, as free individuals, less the mass of the nucleus (a quantity which effectively represents the binding energy needed to disperse the particles of the nucleus); **mass distribution**, the distribution of goods in bulk; **mass-effect**, (*a*) (see quot. 1902); (*b*) *Metallurgy*, the effect of size and shape in causing different rates of cooling, and so different hardnesses, in different parts of an object following heat treatment; (*c*) (usu. in *pl.*) a total or 'grand' effect; (*d*) an effect due to or dependent on mass; **mass-energy**, (*a*) the property of which mass and energy are regarded as different but interconvertible manifestations, being related by the equation $E = mc^2$ (propounded by Einstein in *Ann. d. Physik* (1905) XVIII. 641), where E is the energy equivalent of a mass m and c is the speed of light; (*b*) *attrib.*, relating to (the equivalence of) mass and energy; **mass man**, a hypothetical average man; one typical of mass society, characterized by a lack of individuality and a tendency to be manipulated by stereotyped ideas from the mass media; **mass market**, the market for mass-produced goods; also (with hyphen) as *vb.*; hence **mass-marketed** *ppl. a.*, **mass-marketing** *vbl. sb.*; **mass meeting** (see quot. 1847–54; orig. *U.S.*); also *transf.* and *fig.*; **mass noun**, a noun which in common usage lacks a plural form (opp. *count-noun*); **mass number** *Nuclear Physics*, the total number of protons and neutrons in an atomic nucleus; **mass phenomenon** (see quot. 1968); **mass-point** *Physics*, an entity conceived as having mass and (like a geometrical point) occupying a position but lacking spatial extension; **mass radiography**, radiography of the chests of large numbers of people by a quick routine method; **mass-ratio**, the ratio of the masses of two things; *spec.* in *Aeronaut.*, the ratio of the mass of a rocket with full fuel tanks to that of the same rocket with empty fuel tanks; **mass-reflex** *Physiol.*, (in patients who have suffered gross injury to the spinal cord) a reflex which may involve all parts of the body innervated from the part of the spinal cord below the lesion; **mass-resistivity**, *Physics* (see quot.); **mass spectrograph**, a type of mass spectrometer (in the broader sense) in which deflected ions are made to strike a photographic plate so as to produce a photographic mass spectrum; hence ***mass-spectrographic*** adj.; **mass spectrometer**, any instrument in which material in a vacuum is ionized and the resulting ions are formed into a beam, separated according to the ratios of their mass to their net electric charge (e.g. by deflecting them in a magnetic field or accelerating them in an electric field), and then detected; *esp.* one in which the detection is done electrically rather than photographically; so **mass spectrometry**; also ***mass-spectrometric*** adj., ***-spectrometrically*** adv.; **mass spectroscope** (*rare*), an instrument for producing a mass spectrum; a mass spectrometer (in the broader sense); **mass spectroscopy**, the art of using the mass spectrometer or mass spectrograph; that branch of science which involves the use of these instruments; so ***mass-spectroscopic*** adj.; **mass spectrum**, a record obtained with a mass spectrometer or mass spectrograph, in which ions from a sample material are represented as dispersed according to their mass-to-charge ratio; **mass transfer** *Chemical Engin.*, movement of one substance through or into another on a molecular scale; **mass unit** = *atomic mass unit* (s.v. ATOMIC *a.* and *sb.* A. 1); **mass-vector** *Physics* (see quot.); **mass wasting** *Geomorphol.*, movement of rock, soil, fallen snow, or the like under the influence of gravity; **mass-word** = *mass noun*. See also MASS MEDIUM, MASS OBSERVATION, MASS PRODUCTION.

1891 G. M'GOWAN tr. *E. von Meyer's Hist. Chem.* 461 Berthollet..deduced precisely the opposite from his own assumption—that mass-action comes into play in chemical processes. **1903** H. C. JONES *Princ. Inorg. Chem.* xxviii. 346 If these crystals are redissolved in more water, and the solution evaporated to crystallization, the neutral salt will separate, showing a further splitting off of sulphuric acid due to the mass action of the water. **1924** W. B. SELBIE *Psychol. Relig.* 73 It is not only that mass action has a marked effect upon the will, but that [etc.]. **1958** R. WILLIAMS *Culture & Society* III. 298 The derived ideas have arisen from urbanization..from the working class, mass-action. **1970** PASSMORE & ROBSON *Compan. Med. Stud.* II. iii. 1/2 Whatever the nature of a receptor, its reaction with a drug is presumably chemical and can be described by the Law of Mass Action. **1974** *Daily Tel.* 17 Sept. 6/3 He went on to justify the disruption of academic life during student campaigns, and said that mass action in support of student policies would go ahead. **1876** MAXWELL *Matter & Motion* lxviii. 56 When a material particle moves from one point to another, twice the area swept out by the vector of the particle multiplied by the mass of the particle is called the mass-area of the displacement of the particle with respect to the origin from which the vector is drawn. **1931** *Flight* 11 Sept. 906/1 The control surfaces have been mass-balanced in order to reduce the risk of flutter. **1935** PIPPARD & PRITCHARD *Aeroplane Struct.* (ed. 2) xii. 238 A bob weight used to give mass balance to an aileron should be placed as far outboard of any point of wing support as possible. **1959** J. L. NAYLER *Dict. Aeronaut. Engin.* 168 The mass balance may be a single lump of metal or be distributed along the span of the control surface and connected to it by a series of links. **1966** F. G. IRVING *Introd. Longitudinal Static Stability Low-Speed Aircraft* viii. 82 Full mass-balance..may not be required as an anti-flutter measure on slow-speed aircraft. **1934** *Jrnl. R. Aeronaut. Soc.* XXXVIII. 76 Aeroplanes employing mass-balanced ailerons. *Ibid.*, Those [aeroplanes] in which the anti-flutter device of mass-balancing is incorporated. **1947** C. F. TOMS *Introd. Aeronaut.* v. 195 There can arise cases in which dynamic mass-balancing with a single mass is not possible and two masses are required. **1972** T. H. G. MEGSON *Aircraft Struct.* xiii. 468 The position of the inertia axis may be adjusted by a redistribution of wing weight, a process known as mass-balancing. **1930** *Engineering* 25 July 101/2 After the completion of the mass concrete foundation, the reinforcement was erected for the columns. **1924** J. G. A. SKERL tr. *Wegener's Orig. Continents & Oceans* xi. 160 Subterranean mass-defect and mass-excess above the sea-level..mutually counterbalance, isostasy thus prevailing in mountain masses. **1927** F. W. ASTON in *Proc. R. Soc.* A. CXV. 510 There would have been no loss of energy, that is mass defect, in the latter [*sc.* alpha particles] to represent the binding forces holding the four particles together. **1962** H. D. BUSH *Atomic & Nucl. Physics* iii. 69 According to the principle of the equivalence of mass and energy, the mass defect is equivalent to the energy necessary to separate the constituent particles: $\Delta E = c^2.\Delta M$. This relation shows that a mass defect of one a.m.u. is equivalent to a binding energy of 931 × 10^6 eV (931 MeV). **1936** J. F. PYLE *Marketing Princ.* (ed. 2) xviii. 575 Mass distribution, the corollary of mass production, is made possible through the effective use of sales-promotional methods and devices. **1951** C. W. MILLS *White Collar* I. ii. 26 What good would your mass production be without our mass distribution? **1967** *Economist* 15 Apr. p. i/3 One of the most effective spearheads of American book publishing..uses all kinds of techniques from mass-literacy and mass-distribution schemes to training programmes. **1902** HILLEBRAND & PENFIELD in *Amer. Jrnl. Sci.* CLXIV. 217 The alkalies and lead play so small a rôle, and the remaining constituents so prominent a part in the complex chemical molecules, that the latter control or dominate the crystallization by virtue of what may be called their mass-effect. **1925** *Jrnl. Iron & Steel Inst.* CXII. 473 (*heading*) Initial temperature and mass effects in quenching. **1934** WEBSTER II. 1510/2 Arranged in or involving masses, as a mass effect. **1936** *Mind* XLV. 226 It may be true that macroscopic phenomena involve—or, if we like to say so, are mass-effects of—large quantum numbers. **1939** CARPENTER & ROBERTSON *Metals* II. xvi. 1362 To discover whether duralinium was subject to mass-effect in the same way as steel, Teed quenched 5 in. diam. and 0·564 in. diam. bars of the same material from 490°C. into water. **1945** H. D. SMYTH *Gen. Acct. Devel. Atomic Energy Mil. Purposes* iv. 35 It was found that the total absorption of neutrons by such spheres could be expressed in terms of a 'surface' effect and a 'mass' effect. **1947** A. EINSTEIN *Mus. Romantic Era* xvi. 248 The rhythmic piquancy and the mass-effects of Auber. **1968** D. R. CLIFFE *Technical Metall.* v. 112 The actual cooling rate depends upon several factors, including the diameter of the bar or thickness of section (i.e. mass effect). **1970** G. K. WOODGATE *Elem. Atomic Struct.* ii. 28 This is an example of isotope shift arising from the normal mass effect. **1935** *Proc. R. Soc.* A. CXLIX. 415 The data..afford strong evidence of the validity of the laws of conservation of mass-energy, and of momentum, in some atomic transmutations. **1938** EINSTEIN & INFELD *Evolution of Physics* 208 According to the theory of relativity, there is no distinction between mass and energy... Instead of two conservation laws we have only one, that of mass-energy. **1942** J. D. STRANATHAN *'Particles' of Mod. Physics* ix. 374 According to the mass-energy equivalence concept, the rest mass of an electron represents an energy $V = ..0{\cdot}511 \times 10^6$ EV. **1968** M. S. LIVINGSTON *Particle Physics* i. 6 The released energy [in fission and fusion] comes from the excess mass which is transformed into energy... We can compute the energy release through the Einstein equivalence relation $E = mc^2$. This mass energy was stored in the heavy nuclei and in the very light nuclei in the form of excess mass at the time our galaxy was formed. **1928** A. HUXLEY *Point Counter Point* v. 76 They were armed to protect individuality from the mass man, the mob. **1945** H. READ *Coat Many Colours* lxxi. 348 Screwed-up tissue papers, cigar butts, all the characteristic droppings of Mass-man. **1966** D. JENKINS *Educated Society* ii. 70 They will become increasingly dependent on the public media..on the way to becoming mass-men. **1973** *Black World* May 8/1 Black community newspapers and talk shows on Black radio stations are other avenues for reaching our mass man. **1959** *Times* 9 Mar. (Britain's Food Suppl.) p. vii/7 The housewife who has an outside job now forms an important factor in the mass-market. **1959** *Time* 16 Mar. 61/1 An ultrasonic dishwasher for the home is already technically feasible but too expensive to mass-market. **1962** *Guardian* 7 Feb. 8/1 The mass-

market furniture designers. **1971** *Engineering* Apr. 41/3 For which their whole mass-market philosophy had prepared them. **1960** *New Left Rev.* Sept.-Oct. 3/2 Mass-marketed commodities. **1945** B. NASH *Developing Marketable Products* ii. 23 This relationship between the large-volume manufacturer, the many different users, and the mechanisms of mass marketing is typified by the activities of every manufacturer using mass-marketing methods. **1733** B. LYNDE *Diary* (1880) 39 Our mass meeting at which the village intend to urge their being a township. **1847–54** WEBSTER, *Mass-meeting*, a large assembly of the people to be addressed on some public occasion, usually political. *U. States.* **1851** A. O. HALL *Manhattaner* 4 We steamed..by mass meetings of democratic looking logs and snags. **1855** MOTLEY *Dutch Rep.* (1861) I. 23 Those tumultuous mass-meetings. **1880** A. E. HOUSMAN *Let.* 10 May (1971) 20 They were chairing Harcourt from the station to a mass-meeting at the Martyrs' Memorial. **1904** WODEHOUSE *Gold Bat* viii. 90 They would never run the risk involved in holding mass-meetings in one another's studies. **1960** R. CAMPBELL *Coll. Poems* III. 73 In the mass-meeting of the waves. **1970** *Daily Tel.* 17 Apr. 2 Their 10-man executive committee would be calling a mass meeting of the 2,000-strong student body. **1933** L. BLOOMFIELD *Lang.* xii. 205 Mass nouns never take *a* and have no plural. **1963** *Language* XXXIX. 209 The mass noun *blood* in the singular takes *the* and *some* but not numerical quantifiers. **1965** [see COUNT *sb.*[1] 9]. **1970** *Archivum Linguisticum* I. 24 There is no special class of mass-nouns in Portuguese marked by the absence of metaphony. **1923** F. W. ASTON in *Phil. Mag.* XLV. 945 These integers are provisionally called 'mass-numbers'. The mass-number may be taken to represent the number of protons in the atom. **1946** *Electronic Engin.* XVIII. 153/2 The separation of the uranium isotope of mass number 235 ..from that of mass number 238..constituted one of the major investigations in the development of the atomic bomb. **1962** H. D. BUSH *Atomic & Nucl. Physics* iii. 63 A nuclide is indicated by the chemical symbol with the mass number as a superscript and atomic number as a subscript, the latter often being omitted. For example, $_7N^{14}$ or N^{14} refers to one of the isotopes of nitrogen (Z = 7), namely the one which has mass number 14. **1936** J. R. KANTOR *Objective Psychol. Gram.* iii. 32 Comparative grammar deals with auditory-vocal mass phenomena. **1954** R. W. BROWN in G. Lindzey *Handbk. Social Psychol.* II. xxiii. 833/2 Social scientists have not been content to define mass phenomena as collective misbehavior. **1967** H. ARENDT *Orig. Totalitarianism* (new ed.) ix. 277 Statelessness, the newest mass phenomenon in contemporary history. **1968** A. F. C. WALLACE in *Internat. Encycl. Social Sci.* X. 55/2 'Mass phenomenon' signifies that class of social event in which a large number of people at the same time behave in a way which constitutes a notable interruption of their routine, socially sanctioned role behavior. **1911** J. WARD *Realm of Ends* xii. 255 The mass-points of the modern physicist.. Leibniz held to be only phenomenal. **1956** E. H. HUTTEN *Lang. Mod. Physics* vi. 243 Newtonian mechanics..treats only of such phenomena as can be described in terms of a few concepts, e.g. masspoint, force, etc. **1971** *Amer. Jrnl. Physics* XXXIX. 484/2 Consider a finite one-dimensional mass-point lattice in which nearest neighbors are joined by massless ideal springs. **1943** *Electronic Engin.* XVI. 108 Equipment for mass radiography installed in a large industrial concern for examination of the workers. **1954** E. JENKINS *Tortoise & Hare* x. 114 These mobile X-ray units for mass radiography. **1971** *Brit. Med. Bull.* XXVII. 93/2 Of the people screened by mass radiography..a large number have disabilities that warrant referral to a medical practitioner. **1946** A. S. EDDINGTON *Fund. Theory* ii. 32 (*heading*) Mass-ratio of the proton and electron. **1949** W. LEY *Conquest of Space* (1950) i. 26 The mass-ratio is 2·7:1 —that is,..the rocket at take-off weighs 2·7 times as much as its empty hull, machinery and payload. **1958** *New Scientist* 9 Jan. 19 To obtain an intercontinental range of 2,500 miles requires a mass ratio of 12:1, to achieve a satellite orbit requires a ratio of 25:1, and to escape to the Moon needs a ratio of 100:1... The German V2 had a mass ratio of only 3·2:1. **1968** R. A. LYTTLETON *Mysteries Solar Syst.* i. 42 The Earth and Mars can be paired together satisfactorily as components resulting from a single rotationally unstable planet since their mass-ratio is as high as 9:1. **1917** HEAD & RIDDOCH in *Brain* XL. 233 It is evident, therefore, that under certain conditions the spinal cord below the level of the lesion may show signs of diffuse reflex activity. Scratching the sole of the foot may not only evoke a flexor spasm, but may cause premature evacuation of the bladder and an outburst of excessive sweating. This we have spoken of as a 'mass-reflex'. **1970** M. HOLLANDER tr. *Monnier's Functions Nervous Syst.* II. xii. 242 A mass reflex is an irradiation phenomenon consisting of flexion of the legs with visceromotor reflexes: sweating, micturition and defecation. **1902** J. J. THOMSON in *Encycl. Brit.* XXVIII. 5/1 We may express the resistivity [of a metal] by stating the resistance in ohms offered by a wire of the material in uniform cross-section, one metre in length, and one gramme in weight. This numerical measure of the resistivity is called the *Mass-Resistivity.* **1920** F. W. ASTON in *Phil. Mag.* XXXIX. 611 The Positive Ray Spectrograph or, as it may be more conveniently termed, Mass-Spectrograph. **1945** H. D. SMYTH *Gen. Acct. Devel. Atomic Energy Mil. Purposes* x. 109 Kellex, whose mass spectrograph methods of isotope analysis were sufficiently advanced as to become of great value to the project, as in analyzing samples of enriched uranium. **1963** J. B. FARMER in C. A. McDowell *Mass Spectrometry* ii. 8 The primary, although not the exclusive, task of mass spectrographs is..mass comparison... Mass spectrometers are primarily useful for work involving abundance determination. **1935** *Proc. R. Soc.* A. CL. 253 The masses which we have suggested give a much closer fit with the observed transmutation data than do the mass-spectrographic values. **1957** G. E. HUTCHINSON *Treat. Limnol.* I. iii. 215 The more modern mass spectrographic determinations..indicate very clearly that..the D and O^{18} contents [of water] vary concomitantly. **1932** *Physical Rev.* XL. 429 A new type of mass spectrometer..in which no magnetic fields are used. **1955** *New Biol.* XVIII. 66 It is possible by using a mass-spectrometer to determine the proportions of heavy nitrogen, N^{15}, and the normally more abundant isotope, N^{14}, in a given sample. **1963** Mass spectrometer [see *mass spectrograph* above]. **1966** A. J. AHEARN *Mass Spectrometric Analysis of Solids* i. 2 In the past, the term mass spectrometer was reserved for electrical detection. However, the term mass spectrometry is now the generally accepted designation for this mass analysis technique regardless of the type of detection employed. **1969** PRICE & WILLIAMS *Time-of-Flight Mass Spectrometry* p. ix, There are now about 300 time-of-flight mass spectrometers in use throughout the world. **1966** D. G. BRANDON *Mod. Techniques Metallogr.* iii. 124 We shall also consider the possibility of ion-bombarding a specimen to sputter a thin layer from the surface, followed by a mass-spectrometric analysis of the atoms in this layer. *Ibid.* 172 The surface of the sample is bombarded by positive ions, and the sputtered ions are collected and analysed mass-spectrometrically. **1952** (*title*) Mass spectrometry (Inst. Petroleum, London). **1974** *Nature* 29 Mar. 458/1 The first fraction..was evaporated to dryness and subjected to mass spectrometry... Molecular ions at m/e 420 and m/e 448 are consistent with the product being a mixture of palmitic and stearic aldehyde 2,4-dinitrophenylhydrazones. **1958** H. E. DUCKWORTH *Mass Spectroscopy* 204 Mass spectroscopes. **1963** J. B. FARMER in C. A. McDowell *Mass Spectrometry* ii. 7 The term mass spectroscope is applied to any device which has the ability to separate gaseous ions according to mass-charge ratio. **1938** R. W. LAWSON tr. *Hevesy & Paneth's Man. Radioactivity* (ed. 2) xix. 178 Mass-spectroscopic investigations. **1968** M. S. LIVINGSTON *Particle Physics* vi. 120 The results of mass-spectroscopic measurements have been summarized from time to time to deduce by least-squares analysis the best values of atomic masses. **1926** R. W. LAWSON tr. *Hevesy & Paneth's Man. Radioactivity* xviii. 135 Not until the method of mass-spectroscopy had been devised and developed was it possible to establish that many of the ordinary elements are..mixed elements. **1958** H. E. DUCKWORTH *Mass Spectroscopy* i. 10 For many years photographic plates had served as the standard ion detectors in mass spectroscopy, but in the early 1930's these began to be supplanted by systems of electrical detection. **1920** F. W. ASTON in *Phil. Mag.* XXXIX. 611 (*heading*) The mass-spectra of chemical elements. *Ibid.* 625 A positive ray spectrograph capable of giving a focussed mass-spectrum is ..described. **1966** *Encycl. Industr. Chem. Analysis* II. 465 Mass spectra are related in a direct and simple way to molecular structure, thereby providing a unique and characteristic spectrum for each molecule which can be vaporized in the ion source. **1937** W. H. WALKER et al. *Princ. Chem. Engin.* (ed. 3) xiv. 447 The mass transfer from the main body of the gas to the interface can be visualized as meeting two resistances in series, that of the turbulent main body of gas and that of the gas film. **1962** J. C. WRIGHT *Metall. in Nucl. Power Technol.* ix. 169 Mass transfer between ferrous constructional materials and a sodium coolant circuit is accelerated if the oxygen content exceeds 30 p.p.m. by weight. **1971** R. HARDBOTTLE tr. *Grassman's Physical Princ. Chem. Engin.* ix. 553 A typical feature of mass transfer is the slowing down of transfer of the migrating components by components not participating in mass transfer. **1942** POLLARD & DAVIDSON *Appl. Nucl. Physics* v. 74 If a positron is emitted it must be treated as costing 0·0011 mass unit or 1 Mev extra. **1953** BARNETT & WILSON *Inorg. Chem.* iv. 28 There has been a loss of 0·0184 mass units. **1966** GUCKER & SEIFERT *Physical Chem.* (1967) ii. 25 Prior to 1961 two different mass units were used: the physical mass unit..and the chemical mass unit. **1876** MAXWELL *Matter & Motion* lix. 50 Let us define a mass-vector as the operation of carrying a given mass from the origin to the given point. The direction of the *mass*-vector is the same as that of the vector of the mass, but its magnitude is the product of the mass into the vector of the mass. **1951** *Ohio Jrnl. Sci.* LI. 299 (*heading*) Mass wasting, classification and damage in Ohio. **1968** R. W. FAIRBRIDGE *Encycl. Geomorphol.* 697/2 Frequently the immediate cause of mass wasting can be related directly to changes in shearing stress brought about by (1) increase in the weight of materials, (2) withdrawal of support, or (3) earth tremors. **1914** O. JESPERSEN *Mod. Eng. Gram.* II. v. 115 Words which represent 'uncountables'..are here called mass-words; they may be either material..such as *silver, quicksilver, water, butter*,..or else immaterial, such as *leisure, music, traffic, progress*, [etc.]. **1935** *Jrnl. Eng. & Germ. Philol.* XXXIV. 429 Masswords (like *gold, embers, knowledge*). **1954** PEI & GAYNOR *Dict. Ling.* 133 *Mass-word*, Jespersen's term for words denoting concepts, properties or things which ordinarily cannot be separated into distinct component units.

† **mass**, *sb.*[3] *Obs.* [a. Du. *maas*.] A mesh.

1641 S. SMITH *Herring Buss Trade* 3 Four Deepings of 70 Masses apiece, makes a Net.

Mass, *sb.*[4] Var. MAS *sb.*[1]

mass (mæs), *v.*[1] Now *rare* or *Obs.* Forms: 1 **mæssian**, 3 **messe**, **massi**, 5 **massy**, 6–7 **masse**, 6– **mass**. [OE. *mæssian*, f. *mæsse* MASS *sb.*[1]]

1. *intr.* To celebrate mass; to say or sing mass. (From 16th c. used derisively.) †Also *to mass it* and with cognate obj.

c **1000** ÆLFRIC *Saint's Lives* (1900) II. 276 He..eode to cyrcan and sona mæssode. *a* **1225** *Ancr. R.* 268 Ase ofte ase þe preost messeð & sacreð þet meidenes bearn, Jesu. *c* **1290** *St. Mihhel* 129 in *S. Eng. Leg.* I. 303 ȝwane huy a-rereth anie churche, to massi Inne. **1453** in *Trevelyan P.* (Camden) 84 Item, the chaplan, and all his successours, shall attend.. unto ten of the clocke, and then massy. **1546** BALE *Eng. Votaries* I. (1550) 60 b, He massed without consecracion, he gaue holye orders in hys stable [etc.]. **1562** *Answ. Apol. Priv. Mass* iii. 19 In one churche ye shal haue at one time .vii. or .viii. massing in sundry corners. **1570** *Durham Depos.* (Surtees) 157 He..came to Robert Peirson..being redy to go to masse, and said to hym 'Do you masse this?' And he ..said, 'Ye'. **1624** BP. MOUNTAGU *Gagg* 57 Your morrow Massmungers when they masse it alone. **1677** W. HUGHES *Man of Sin* II. ii. 219 He [Silvester II.] perceived his death whilst he was Massing. **1851** S. WILBERFORCE *Let.* in R. S. Wilberforce *Life* (1881) II. iv. 124 What blind belief in a priest massing for them!

†**2.** To hear mass. *Obs. rare.*

c **1770** J. GRANGER *Lett.* (1805) II. 70 Chapel so contrived that men and women may mass, and not see one another.

3. *trans.* in occasional uses: To subject to the operation of the mass; to pass *away* (time) at mass.

1546 BALE *Eng. Votaries* I. (1560) 92 b, They are.. Mattensed, Massed, Candeled, Lighted, Processioned,.. Perfumed and worshypped. **1784** R. BAGE *Barham Downs* II. 89 And I find the ancient might sacrifice, and the modern Mass away a dozen hours per diem in all holiness.

mass (mæs), *v.*[2] Also (? 4 mace), 7 masse. [a. F. *masser* (from 13th c.), f. *masse* MASS *sb.*[2]]

1. *trans.* To form or gather into a mass; to collect, arrange, or bring together in masses. †Also with *up*, to heap up, to amass.

The first quot. is doubtful: the word may be miswritten for *y-maked*.

c **1380** *Sir Ferumb.* 3326 Her with-inne ys gold y-maced faste to cast out day & nyȝt. **1604** T. WRIGHT *Passions* VI. 343 When the rich man hath massed vp his treasures. **1622** MABBE tr. *Aleman's Guzman d'Alf.* I. 206 If thou aske these men, why they masse vp money. **1820** SHELLEY *Sensit. Pl.* III. 33 Indian plants..Leaf after leaf, day after day Were massed into the common clay. **1827** STEUART *Planter's G.* (1828) 513 The style, in which the removed are mixed and massed up with the older Trees. **1849** M. ARNOLD *To Gipsy Child* 4 Who mass'd, round that slight brow, these clouds of doom? **1898** *Rev. Brit. Pharm.* 27 The whole being mixed and massed with kaolin 115 gr.

b. *Painting.*

1753 HOGARTH *Anal. Beauty* xiii. 112 Painters..divide theirs [*sc.* compositions] into fore-ground, middle-ground, and distance or back-ground; which simple and distinct quantities *mass* together that variety which entertains the eye. **1843** RUSKIN *Mod. Paint.* I. II. II. v. §18 It is impossible to go too finely, or think too much about details in landscape, so that they be rightly arranged and rightly massed.

c. *Mil.*; also, to 'concentrate' (troops) in a particular place.

1861 MUSGRAVE *By-roads* 305 Instead of dispersing their force in brigades..they massed them in phalanx form. **1878** BOSW. SMITH *Carthage* 116 His infantry he masses much more closely together and in much deeper formations than was common among the Romans. **1885** *Manch. Examiner* 10 Nov. 4/6 Austria is massing troops in Herzegovina.

d. *Law. to mass an estate*: see quot.

1896 H. H. JUTA *Selection of Leading Cases* II. 111 The language of the Privy Council in clause (a) [viz. the mutual will disposes of the joint property on the death of the survivor, or, as it is sometimes expressed, where the property is consolidated into one mass for the purpose of a joint disposition of it] has given rise to the expression 'massing of an estate'. *Ibid.*, By the mutual will in that case only part of the joint estate was 'massed'.

†**2.** ? To occupy with a mass of soldiers. *Obs.*

a **1627** HAYWARD *Edw. VI* (1630) 108 They feared least.. the French might..either with filling or massing the house, or else by fortifying make such a piece as might annoy the haven.

3. *refl.* and *intr.* To collect, assemble, or come together in masses.

1563 *Reg. Privy Council Scot.* I. 248 The Clangregour.. hes massit thame selfis in greit cumpanyis bot als [etc.]. **1861** TULLOCH *Eng. Purit.* ii. 282 His reasonings run in great lines, or mass in blocks of system. **1869** RUSKIN *Q. of Air* §16 But all these virtues mass themselves in the Greek mind into the two main ones. **1879** STEVENSON *Trav. Cevennes* 74 The weather had somewhat lightened, and the clouds massed in squadron. **1892** W. PIKE *North. Canada* 45 The great bands of caribou..mass up on the edge of the woods.

†**4.** *Gaming.* To set the 'mass' or stake. $Obs.^{-0}$

1727 BOYER *Fr. Dict.*, Masser, (Terme de jeu de Hazard) to mass, lay, or set.

mass, *v.*[3] *rare.* [ad. F. *masser*: see MASSAGE.] *trans.* To massage. (Cf. MASSING *vbl. sb.*[3])

1786 *Misc.* in *Ann. Reg.* 119/1 A servant..then *masses*, and seems to knead the body without giving the slightest sensation of pain. **1888** D. MAGUIRE *Art of Massage* (ed. 4) 42 In going from one extremity to the other of the part to be massed. *Ibid.* 56, I will commence my description of general massage by that of massing the superior members.

mass, obs. form of MACE *sb.*[1]

Massa. Also **massa**, **marsa**. Also written **Mas'r**. Representing *master* in the written form of Black speech.

1774 FOOTE *Cozeners* III. Wks. 1799 II. 190 Who opened the window?.. Little massa. **1821** P. EGAN *Life in London* II. v. 289 But the black *slavey*, who is entering the room, is singing out, '*Massa*, you ought to be shamed.' **1852** MRS. STOWE *Uncle Tom's C.* vi, 'Lord bless us, Mas'r', said Sam. **1881** R. M. BALLANTYNE *Giant of North* v, What am it, massa? Why, it am a bit o' salt pork. **1890** *Century Mag.* Nov. 65 Suit you, marsa? **1935** in Z. N. Hurston *Mules & Men* (1970) I. i. 25 It was night and Ole Massa sent John, his favorite slave, down to the spring to get him a cool drink of water. **1953** *Caribbean Q.* III. III. 157 As one writer put it: ..It has ever been their practice, to prevent the extension of useful practical knowledge, other than the hewing of cane fields, and feeding the mill, to the Negro lest he may one day rise to the rank of an Overseer, and supersede Massa Busher (Overseer). **1973** *Sunday Express* (Trinidad & Tobago) 8 Apr. 13/3 Day after day he sat glued to the t.v. and behaved generally as though he didn't know 'massa day is done'. **1973** J. RYDER *Trevayne* (1974) xi. 94 'I'll set up interviews.' Bonner looked at Andrew and laughed. '*Your* interviews, massa.'

massa-bowl. [app. f. G. *masse* (= MASS *sb.*[2]) in the sense of 'paste' for porcelain, pottery, etc.] A pipe-bowl made from the waste parings of meerschaum.

1858 HOMANS *Cycl. Comm.* 1533/1 The kind of meerschaum bowls called *massa-bowls*.

massache, obs. form of MESSAGE *sb.*

†**massacote.** *Obs.* [a. Sp. *mazacote*: see MASSICOT.] = BARILLA 2 a.

1622 MALYNES *Anc. Law-Merch.* 275 The stuffe called Soda Bariglia, or Massacote whereof Glasses are made.

massacre (ˈmæsəkə(r)), *sb.* Also 6 **massachre, -aquer,** 7 **mas(s)aker, massacker, -cher, massacry,** 8 (9 *illiterate*) **massacree.** [a. F. *massacre* masc., in OF. *maçacre, machacre, macecle, mececle* shambles, slaughter-house (whence *maceclier*, AF. *macegrier* butcher: see MACEGRIEFS), also, butchery, slaughter; in the latter sense latinized in the 13th c. *mazacrium, masacrium.*

Spenser stresses *maˈssacre*, Shaks. and Marlowe ˈ*massacre*. The origin of the OF. word is unknown; Diez suggested derivation from a Teut. source, comparing LG. *matsken* (18th c.) to hack to pieces, but this word is itself of Rom. etymology. The forms *macecle* synon. with L. *macellum*, and *maceclier* with *macellarius*, suggest the possibility of these being corrupted adoptions from monastic Latin.]

1. The unnecessary indiscriminate killing of human beings; a general slaughter, carnage, butchery; also occas. the wholesale killing of wild animals.

1586 T. B. *La Primaud. Fr. Acad.* I. 718 There is no corner of this kingdome where the people..have not committed infinite and cruell massacres. **1588** SHAKS. *Tit. A.* V. i. 63, I must talke of Murthers, Rapes, and Massacres. **1590** WEBBE *Trav.* (Arb.) 23 How the women of ye towne did plie themselues with their weapons, making a great massacre vpon our men. **1611** BIBLE *1 Macc.* i. 24 Hauing made a great massacre. **1624** CAPT. SMITH *Virginia* 143 They made a massacre of Deere and Hogges. **1655** MILTON (*title of Sonnet*) On the late Massacher in Piemont. **1688** R. HOLME *Armoury* III. 271/1 She went down into Egypt from Herods Bloody Massacry. **1774** FLETCHER *Hist. Ess.* Wks. 1795 IV. 15 The horrible massacres of Catholics. **1843** BORROW *Bible in Spain* xxxvi, Plunder and massacre had been expected. **1897** GLADSTONE *E. Crisis* 4 They are treading on the burning cinders of the Armenian massacres.

b. In appellations of certain historic massacres.

Massacre of St. Bartholomew (earlier often †***M. of Paris***): the massacre of the Huguenots of France on the 24th of August 1572. ***M. of Glencoe***: the massacre of the Macdonalds of Glencoe on February 13th 1692 by their enemies the Campbells, acting under an authority obtained from William III. ***M. of the Innocents***: see INNOCENT B. 2.

[*c* **1592** MARLOWE (*title*) The Massacre at Paris.] **1617** MORYSON *Itin.* I. 131, I wondred to see the Massacre of Paris painted vpon the wall. *a* **1715** BURNET *Own Time* (1734) II. 156 The Massacre in Glencoe made still a great noise. *Ibid.* 157 The Report of the Massacre of Glencoe was made in full Parliament. **1756–7** tr. *Keysler's Trav.* (1760) II. 394 A Venus, by Titian; the massacre of the Innocents, Susanna, and Galatea, by Lanfranchi. **1833** L. RITCHIE *Wand. by Loire* 187 The massacre of Saint Bartholomew did not take place here [at Nantes].

c. *fig.*

1595 SPENSER *Amoretti* x, See how the Tyrannesse doth ioy to see The huge massacres which her eyes do make. **1608** ARMIN *Nest Ninn.* (1842) 29 The maydes..finding such a masaker of their dairie,..thought a yeere's wages could not make amends. **1748** JOHNSON *Van. Hum. Wishes* 22 The knowing and the bold Fell in the gen'ral massacre of gold.

†**2.** A cruel or peculiarly atrocious murder. *Obs.*

1589 GREENE *Sp. Masquerado* E 1 b, He..caused..some to be torne with horses, some to haue their handes cut off, and so many sundry Massaquers as greeueth any good minde to report. **1594** SHAKS. *Rich. III*, IV. iii. 2 Tyr. The tyrannous and bloodie Act is done, The most arch deed of pittious massacre That euer yet this land was guilty of. **1608** D. T[UVIL] *Ess. Pol. & Mor.* 43 b, Nor was the massacre of this his warlike sonne the period of his furie.

3. *Her.* 'A pair of antlers or attires attached to a piece of the skull, used as a bearing' (*Cent. Dict.* 1890). [Fr. *massacre.*]

[**1722** NISBET *Syst. Heraldry* I. 338 The French use the Word Massacree, for a Head Caboched.]

massacre (ˈmæsəkə(r)), *v.* Also 7 **masakre, massacar, massacher,** 8 (9 *illiterate*) **massacree,** 9 *Sc.* **mashacker.** [a. F. *massacrer*, f. *massacre*: see prec.]

1. *trans.* To kill indiscriminately (a number of human beings, or occas. animals); to make a general slaughter or carnage of. Also occas. *absol.*

1581 SAVILE *Tacitus' Hist.* (1612) 180 The cohort was massacred by the fraude of the Agrippinenses. **1588** SHAKS. *Tit. A.* I. i. 450. *c* **1592** MARLOWE *Massacre Paris* I. v, These are the Guisians, That seeke to massacre our guiltles liues. **1606** G. W[OODCOCKE] *Hist. Ivstine* VIII. 39 When men of warre run massacaring vp and down in euery corner of a city. **1670** MILTON *Hist. Eng.* VI. Wks. 1851 V. 245 He caus'd the Danes all over England..in one day perfidiously to be massacherd, both Men, Women, and Childern. *a* **1715** BURNET *Own Time* (1724) I. 502 To bring over a French army and to massacre all the English. **1727** C. COLDEN *Hist. Five Ind. Nations* 83 Your Warriors..have Massacreed Men, Women and Children. **1809** SCOTT *Poacher* 102 Grouse or partridge massacred in March. **1855** MACAULAY *Hist. Eng.* xvi. III. 650 They were..always forming plans for massacring their tyrants.

fig. **1601** DENT *Pathw. Heaven* 330 Satan doth continually ..massacre innumerable soules.

2. To murder cruelly or violently. †Also *refl.* to lay violent hands upon oneself.

1601 HOLLAND *Pliny* II. 500 Harmodius and Aristogiton, massacring the tyrant Pisistratus. **1606** —— *Sueton.* Annot. 8 Caesar..was masakred with 23. wounds. **1621** BURTON *Anat. Mel.* I. ii. IV. vi. (1651) 160 Two brothers of Lovain.. in a discontented humour massacred themselves. **1661** *Virginia Stat.* (1823) II. 24 That execrable power that soe bloodyly massacred the late king Charles the first. **1834** JAMES *J. Marston Hall* viii, That he would be massacred the moment he showed his face amongst the infuriated mob. **1881** SHORTHOUSE *J. Inglesant* II. xviii, But that his coach was resolutely defended..he would have been massacred by the furious mob.

fig. **1880** RUSKIN *Arrows of Chace* (1880) II. 280, I heard *William Tell* entirely massacred at the great opera house.

†**3.** To mutilate, mangle. *Obs.*

1589 *Hay any Work* 19 That the magistrate may lawfully cut off the members of Christ from his body, and so may lawfully massacre the body. **1651** tr. *De-las-Coveras' Don Fenise* 303 The shame of seeing my face massacred by his rash hands. [**1818** SCOTT *Hrt. Midl.* xvii, Her throat's sair misguggled and mashackered.]

Hence **ˈmassacred, ˈmassacring** *ppl. adjs.*

1590 SPENSER *F.Q.* III. iii. 35 And Bangor with massacred Martyrs fill. **1597** A.M. tr. *Guillemeau's Fr. Chirurg.* 10/2 The fracture is soe greate, with such a huge quantitye of massacred and crushed bones. **1738** NEAL *Hist. Purit.* IV. 561 Imagining the massacring knife to be at their throats.

massacrer (ˈmæsəkrə(r)). [f. MASSACRE *v.* + -ER^1.] One who massacres.

1581 MULCASTER *Positions* iv. (1887) 20 To[o] much moisture,..the most vile, and violent massacrer, of the most, and best studentes. **1600** W. WATSON *Decacordon* (1602) 58 Cursed be these bloudie massacrers. **1796** BURKE *Regic. Peace* i. Wks. VIII. 132 Assassins, Massacrers, and Septembrizers. **1892** *Nation* (N.Y.) 17 Nov. 371/2 Coconas was one of the most active massacrers in that fatal night of Saint Bartholomew.

ˈmassacring, *vbl. sb.* [f. MASSACRE *v.* + -ING^1.] The action of the verb MASSACRE.

1602 F. HERRING *Anat.* 20 Such torturing and massacring of Men. **1680** H. MORE *Apocal. Apoc.* 216 There shall be.. no more bloody massacrings of the Faithful Witnesses of Christ. **1840** CARLYLE *Heroes* (1858) 293 A poor barren country, full of continual broils, dissensions, massacrings. **1863** J. C. MORISON *St. Bernard* I. vii. 93 The perpetual.. plundering and massacring, caused by the baronial wars.

†**ˈmassacrous,** *a. Obs.* [f. MASSACRE *sb.* + -OUS.] Of or pertaining to massacre; murderous.

1593 G. HARVEY *Pierce's Super.* 155 In his impetuous and massacrous sallyes. **1593** NASHE *Christ's T.* (1613) 63 The massacrous monstrousnesse of this quicke Marshal-law. **1608** D. T[UVIL] *Ess. Pol. & Mor.* 114 b, What massacrous, and impious thoughts, had..anchred in his bosom.

massacry, obs. variant of MASSACRE *sb.*

massage (ˈmæsɑːʒ, mæˈsɑːʒ), *sb.* [a. F. *massage*, f. *masser* to apply massage to (the body).

The Fr. verb (*macer, masser*) is given by Le Gentil (*Voy. dans les mers de l'Inde* I. 128) as the word used by the French colonists in India in 1779. It is perh. a. Pg. *amassar* to knead, f. *massa* dough (= MASS *sb.*^{2}).]

a. *Therapeutics.* The application with the hands of pressure and strain upon the muscles and joints of the body, by friction, kneading, etc., in order to stimulate their action and increase their suppleness. Also *attrib.* and *fig.*

1876 BARTHOLOW *Mat. Med.* (1879) 73 Massage by friction consists in rubbing, rolling under the fingers, and gently pinching the skin, and rubbing, tapping, kneading, and exercising the muscles and joints. **1888** D. MAGUIRE *Art of Massage* (ed. 4) 14 She could not bear it longer, especially if she attempted several massages per day. **1892** F. M. CRAWFORD *Three Fates* II. 4 'There's nothing for you, Tom', she said, 'but a milk cure and massage'. **1896** *Allbutt's Syst. Med.* I. 375 Most massage procedures, to be of use, should be repeated at least once daily. **1907** *Yesterday's Shopping* (1969) 538/3 Massage Rollers, for the face..13/0. **1929** H. WALPOLE *Hans Frost* II. iii. 143 Then with that by now practised and customary spiritual massage she set to work on herself. **1963** E. H. EDWARDS *Saddlery* xxii. 168 A convenient and efficient massage pad..can be made from leather stuffed with hay. **1966** J. S. COX *Illustr. Dict. Hairdressing* 97/1 *Massage oil*, an oil which is applied to the scalp to aid the process of massage and increase its beneficial effect. **1969** E. H. PINTO *Treen* 17 The massage roulette.. is English, of mahogany, and was advertised for sale between 1880 and 1890. The three rollers revolve independently. **1973** *Times* 8 Aug. 7/1 At present £52m is spent annually on pills and low calorie foods, then there are health hydros, sauna baths, massage parlours, exercising machines, gymnasiums and slimming clubs.

b. Used *euphem.* for: sexual activity.

The expressions ***massage establishment, parlour***, etc., used as signs outside a building, are frequently alleged to mean 'brothel' (see quots.).

1913 *Collier's* 25 Jan. 7/1 Along with them go the announcements of 'massage parlors' (an all-too-obvious euphemism), free whiskies, and other agencies of public injury. **1921** E. WEEKLEY *Etym. Dict. Mod. Eng.* 1416 *Stew*^{1} ..Brothel... The public hot-air baths acquired a reputation like that of our massage establishments some time ago. **1966** *Economist* 3 Sept. 894/2 The American authorities..allow their free-spending men to attract the usual proliferation of bars, night-clubs and 'massage parlours'. **1971** *Sunday Tel.* (Brisbane) 16 May 42/5 A sheriff's deputy herds a group of women arrested in raids last month on 22 'massage parlors' in Los Angeles. **1972** D. BLOODWORTH *Any Number can Play* ix. 66 The imitation opium den and the model massage parlour. **1972** *Screw* 12 June 33/3 (Advt.), A totally dominant English massage by a lovely female, in your home or office. **1972** *Times* 4 Nov. 9/1, I noticed a few discreet establishments that looked as unauthentic, or as authentic according to your viewpoint, as New York's massage parlours. **1973** *Publishers Weekly* 8 Jan. 66/2 There is a difference between what a massage used to be, and what it has come to be a euphemism for lately. **1973** *Listener* 5 Apr. 439/2 The bars and massage parlours are..to re-open. But where are the clients now?.. The Americans have gone. **1974** *Publishers Weekly* 29 Apr. 45/1 The 'massage parlors' which have mushroomed in America's big cities. *Ibid.*, Massage parlor prostitutes in New York. *Ibid.*, 'Massage parlor' prostitution is considered by many to be 'glamorous' therapy.

massage (ˈmæsɑːʒ, mæˈsɑːʒ), *v.* [f. prec.] *trans.* To apply massage to; to treat by means of massage. Also *transf.* and *fig.*; *spec.* (*colloq.*) to manipulate (data, figures, etc., or their presentation), esp. in order to give a more acceptable result. Cf. DOCTOR *v.* 3. Hence **maˈssaging** *vbl. sb.*

1887 TIBBITS *Massage* 14 In Massaging joints. **1889** *Lancet* 2 Mar. 423/1 Although abdominal massage will effect a great deal of good, it will not be productive of lasting benefit if we omit to massage the spine. **1897** *Allbutt's Syst. Med.* III. 187 The stiffened and swollen joints should be cautiously massaged. **1924** R. HICHENS *After Verdict* III. §1. 314 Arabs were washing sacks below the dam and massaging them with persistently stamping bare brown feet. **1931** *Times Lit. Suppl.* 30 Apr. 340/2 'Shellacking', 'massaging' .., euphemisms which cover the long ordeal of beating, pounding..by which the detective learns the truth. **1936** F. CLUNE *Roaming round Darling* viii. 68 In the outer courtyard were several straw-hatted inmates in cover-alls massaging the lawns. **1966** *Aviation Week & Space Technol.* 5 Dec. 23/2 The interim has permitted an overall massaging of the initial reports, which resulted..in the revision that last week amounted to a major change in design philosophy for post-Apollo. **1974** *Globe & Mail* (Toronto) 23 Sept. 7/5 The Japanese government's efforts to massage the press coverage of the visit have been substantial. It offered to pay the fares of Canadian journalists to go to Tokyo for the interview and is bringing 30 Japanese journalists with the Prime Minister. **1976** *Guardian* 25 Nov. 1 The most frequent kind of cheating detected was 'data massage'—a splendidly bland phrase which means that findings are eased and stretched to fit a desired result. Seventy-four per cent of the total apparently massaged their data. **1981** *Times* 11 June 14/6 The money was massaged by managements and distributed on their behalf to staff..or paid into an independent tronc fund. **1982** *Daily Tel.* 11 Dec. 14 The Labour administration massaged the basis of the calculation of the exchange rate against a basket of currencies in 1975 so as to make the situation appear better. **1985** *Globe & Mail* (Toronto) 10 Oct. B25/6 To encourage traders to 'massage' the numbers..the bank subsidizes the purchase of personal computers by traders for their homes.

massage, obs. form of MESSAGE.

massageer, -ger, obs. forms of MESSENGER.

massager (ˈmæsɑːʒə(r)). [f. MASSAGE *v.* or *sb.* + -ER^1.] **a.** One who practises massage, = MASSEUR, MASSEUSE.

1921 E. G. LOWRY *Washington Close-Ups* 85 He is..a politician to his finger tips and a strong josher; a real handshaker and an elbow massager.

b. A massaging machine.

1940 *Life* 4 Nov. 54 Wooden barrel massager with rollers like clothes wringers is designed for action on the hips and buttocks. **1969** E. M. BRECHER *Sex Researchers* (1970) x. 291 Dr. Dickinson was responsible..for the introduction into American gynecological practice of the electrical vibrator or massager. This device, applied to the mons area near the clitoris, produces intense erotic stimulation. **1969** 'J' *Sensuous Woman* (1970) iii. 29 Since the machine is advertised as a facial massager, you can purchase it without embarrassment.

Massagetæ (mæsəˈgiːtaɪ). Also **Massagetes.** [L. *Massagetæ*, Gr. Μασσαγέται, perh. f. native name *Masakata* Great Sakas.] An ancient Scythian people that lived to the east of the Caspian Sea.

1601 HOLLAND tr. *Pliny's Nat. Hist.* VI. xvii. 123 The principall nations of Scythia, bee the Saræ, Massagetæ, [etc.]. **1709** I. LITTLEBURY tr. *Herodotus' Hist.* I. I. 134 The Massagetes resemble the Scythians in their Habit and Way of Living. **1874** G. GROTE *Hist. Greece* III. II. xvii. 329 The Scythians, originally occupants of Asia, or the regions East of the Caspian, had been driven across the Araxês, in consequence of an unsuccessful war with the Massagetæ. **1911** J. G. FRAZER *Golden Bough: Magic Art* (ed. 3) I. i. 15 The Spartans, Persians, and Massagetae sacrificed horses to him [*sc.* the sun]. **1926** *Cambr. Anc. Hist.* IV. i. 15 Cyrus died fighting... His opponents were the Massagetae, a savage race who occupied the great plain to the East of the Caspian. **1967** C. A. ROBINSON *Anc. Hist.* (ed. 2) xxi. 410 The first business of the Greek king of Bactria was to protect this land, the gateway of Iran, from the semibarbarism of the north, and in particular to guard against the strong confederacy of the Massagetae, who were massed across the Oxus and Jaxartes rivers. **1969** J. CONWAY tr. *Bengtson's Greeks & Persians* xv. 318 Alexander was unable to capture him [*sc.* Spitamenes], but the Scythians beyond the Jaxartes, the Massagetae, to whom Spitamenes had fled, cut off his head and sent it to Alexander as a gift. **1973** G. WIDENGREN in D. J. Wiseman *Peoples Old Testament Times* xiii. 320 When Cyrus..again turned to the east, he ultimately suffered a defeat in a battle against some nomadic northern people of Iranian origin, either..the Massagetae.. or the Danae.

massagist (mæˈsɑːʒɪst). [f. MASSAGE *v.* + -IST.] One who practises massage; a masseur or masseuse.

1889 *N. York Tribune* 30 May (Cent.), A slashing criticism by one massagist of another's book. **1899** KELSEY tr. *Mau's Pompeii* 195, The sound varying according as the massagist strikes with flat or hollow palm.

Massalian, variant of MESSALIAN.

Massaliot(e: see MASSILIOT *sb.* and *a.*

massaly, variant of MASSILY *Obs.*

massanger(e, obs. forms of MESSENGER.

massard, obs. f. MAZARD *sb.*, kind of cherry.

massasauga (mæsəˈsɔːgə). Also **-saugua.** [Presumably American Indian.] A small, very venomous, dark-coloured, North American rattlesnake of the genus *Sistrurus*, esp. *S. catenatus.* Also *attrib.*

1835 C. BRADLEY in *Ohio Archaeol. & Hist. Soc. Publ.* (1906) XV. 257, I learned that my conquered enemy was the massassagua, the Michigan rattlesnake. **1842** HOLBROOK *N. Amer. Herpetol.* III. 32 Dr. Kirtland..observes that this animal [*Crotalophorus Kirtlandi*] is commonly known under the name Massasaugua, a word of Indian origin. **1853** BAIRD & GIRARD *Catal. N. Amer. Reptiles* I. 14 *Crotalophorus tergeminus*..Prairie Rattlesnake, Massasauga. *Ibid.* 16 *Crotalophorus Kirtlandii*..Black Massasauga. **1884–5** *Riverside Nat. Hist.* (1888) III. 397 *Caudisona tergemina*, the black rattlesnake or massasauga, is found in Ohio and Michigan [etc.]. **1941** *Amer. Midland Naturalist* XXV. 659 (*title*) Habit and habitat studies of the massasauga rattlesnake. **1954** R. C. STEBBINS *Amphibians & Reptiles Western N. Amer.* 464/1 The massasauga is usually unaggressive, but the venom is dangerous.

massay, obs. form of MASSOY.

massbanker: see MOSSBUNKER.

ˈmass-book. [f. MASS *sb.*[1] + BOOK *sb.*] = MISSAL. (Occas. used erron. for other service books.)

c **1000** *Canons of Ælfric* c. 21 in Thorpe *Laws* II. 350 Saltere and pistolboc, godspellboc and mæsseboc..ðas bec sceal mæssepreost nede habban. *c* **1200** ORMIN *Ded.* 31 þa Goddspelless..þatt sinndenn o þe messeboc Inn all þe ȝer att messe. *c* **1300** *Havelok* 186 A wol fair cloth bringen he dede, And ther on leyde the messebok. *c* **1380** WYCLIF *Wks.* (1880) 290 Blessed be god, þat in euery chirche haþ ordeyned masse bookis to witnesse his gospel. *c* **1440** *Promp. Parv.* 334/2 Messboke, *missale.* **1511** *Ld. Treas. Acc. Scot.* IV. 322 Ane miss buik bocht be him to the chapele. **1642** MILTON *Apol. Smect.* Wks. 1851 III. 315 We then using a Liturgy farre more like to the Masse-book then to any Protestant set forme. *c* **1714** *MS. Catal. Bks. bequeathed to Corp. Chr. Coll. Oxf. by Dr. T. Turner*, A Primer (or Masse Book) in English and Latin. **1873** LONGF. *Wayside Inn* III. *Monk of Casal-Maggiore* 23 A..monk..Who..to the mass-book gave but little heed.

†**mass-creed.** *Obs.* [MASS *sb.*[1]] The Nicene Creed, as occurring in the service of the Mass.

c **1000** *Canons of Ælfric* iv. in Thorpe *Laws* II. 344 On þam sinoþe [on þære ceastre Nicea] wæron ȝesette þa halȝan cyricþenunga, & se mæsse-creda. *c* **1225** *Ancr. R.* 20 Et te messe crede. **13..** *Minor Poems fr. Vernon MS.* xxxvii. 771 Atome maiȝt þou do good nede And come to þe masse-crede. *c* **1440** *Cast. Persev.* 2371 Take it sothe as mes crede. **1563–83** FOXE *A. & M.* II. 1670, I beleeue all the Articles conteyned..in the Creede called the Masse Creede.

ˈmass-day. *arch.* [OE. *mæssedæȝ*: see MASS *sb.*[1] and DAY *sb.*] A feast-day.

971 *Blickl. Hom.* 47 þæt hi Sunnandaȝum & mæssedaȝum Godes cyrican ȝeorne secan. **1154** *O.E. Chron.* an. 1132 He com on S' Petres messe dei..into þe minstre. *a* **1300** *E. E. Psalter* lxxiii. 8 To reste make we mes-daies alle Of God fra erthe for oght mai falle. *c* **1315** SHOREHAM *Poems* (E.E.T.S.) i. 2031 Ne hy ne wondeþ messeday, Ne none holy tyde. **1867** FREEMAN *Norm. Conq.* (1876) I. v. 313 The observance of Eadward's mass-day was ordered in 1008.

‖**massé** (ˈmæseɪ, mase), *a.* and *sb. Billiards.* Also **masse.** [Fr., pa. pple. of *masser* to make a stroke of this kind, f. *masse* MACE *sb.*] Applied to a stroke made with the cue held perpendicular.

1873 BENNETT & 'CAVENDISH' *Billiards* 351 The hazard may be made by a masse stroke. **1897** *Westm. Gaz.* 27 Feb. 2/3 The technicalities of nursery cannons, masse cannons, and winning and losing hazards. **1901** *Q. Rev.* Apr. 484 [He] played the *massé* well for an Englishman.

massé (ˈmæseɪ), *v. rare.* [ad. F. *masser*: see MASSAGE *sb.*] *trans.* To massage.

1887 *Buck's Handbk. Med. Sci.* IV. 660 In masséing the face of a fat patient, the tissues can only be rolled and stretched under the fingers and palm. **1888** D. MAGUIRE *Art of Massage* (ed. 4) 55 We are no longer in those days when four, or six, or eight persons were employed at one time to massé you. [In ed. 1 (1886) the writer uses *masser* (in roman) as an imperative.]

masse, obs. f. MACE, MASS, MAZE; var. MAS *Obs.*

masseager, obs. form of MESSENGER.

massecuite (mæsˈkwiːt). Also **masse cuite.** [Fr., lit. = cooked mass.] In sugar-making, the juice of the sugar-cane after concentration by boiling.

1882 *Spons' Encycl. Industr. Arts* v. 1927 The *massecuite* is quickly let out of the pan into a tank. **1886** *Harper's Mag.* June 88/2 After the *masse-cuite* has left the pan, the crystallization is completed by cooling. **1921** [see *box-hand* (BOX *sb.*[2] 24)]. **1925** *Chambers's Jrnl.* June 368/2 This dark-looking mass of semi-liquid substance is called masse-cuite. **1968** *Encycl. Brit.* XXI. 379/2 The cycle..varies from 2 minutes for very high-test massecuites to 15 minutes or more for low grades.

massed (mæst), *ppl. a.* [f. MASS *v.*[2] + -ED[1].]

1. Gathered into a mass. Also with *up.* ***massed entry***: see quot. 1964.

1881 'MARK TWAIN' *Prince & Pauper* ix. 84 The massed world on the river burst into a mighty roar of welcome. **1884** J. PARKER *Apost. Life* III. 315 Do not ask for proofs in words and paragraphs and massed-up sentences. **1885** W. C. SMITH *Kildrostan* I. i. 259 The breeze Rustles their higher leaves over a tower Green with massed ivy. **1896** *Daily News* 21 May 5/1 Thirty massed regimental orchestras. **1955** W. W. GREG *Shakes. First Folio* v. 157 In *The Winter's Tale*..there are massed entries in all but two scenes, but some individual entries are repeated later on. **1964** F. BOWERS *Bibliogr. & Textual Crit.* v. i. 137 A massed entry is the notation at the start of a scene of the entrance in a group of all the characters, although some will make their entrances later at different points in the scene.

2. In reference to carved or written inscriptions, having the words arranged to form a solid column of lettering.

1906 A. E. R. GILL in E. Johnston *Writing & Illuminating* xvii. 392 In that space set out the Inscription, either 'Massed' or 'Symmetrical'. **1940** G. HEWITT *Lettering* xvi. 163 Italics..are not often successful when massed.

3. massed practice, training, trials *Psychol.*, a method of conditioning or training in which practice is concentrated with hardly any rest between repetitions.

1938 *Jrnl. Exper. Psychol.* XX. 201 The method of distributed practice should, therefore, yield relatively less accumulated inhibition than the method of massed practice. **1940** HILGARD & MARQUIS *Conditioning & Learning* vi. 148 Spaced practice favors conditioning over massed practice. **1949** B. J. UNDERWOOD *Exper. Psychol.* xi. 366 Several studies have shown that conditioning takes place more rapidly by distributed than by massed trials. *Ibid.* 631 *Massed training*, training in which trials are given in rapid succession with little if any time intervening between successive units of work. **1953** C. E. OSGOOD *Method & Theory Exper. Psychol.* III. xii. 504 The empirical law that 'distributed practice is superior to massed practice' has been found to hold under nearly all conditions. **1960** H. J. EYSENCK *Behaviour Therapy & Neuroses* i. 17 The extinction of 4 tics in a female patient by..repeated voluntary repetition of the tic by massed practice. **1969** W. MAYER-GROSS et al. *Clin. Psychiatry* (ed. 3) 186 The optimal technique was massed practice..followed by prolonged rest to permit the dissipation of reactive inhibition.

†**massedness.** *Obs.* In 4 **massydnes.** [f. MASS *sb.*[2] + -ED[2] + -NESS.] Massiveness.

1398 TREVISA *Barth. De P.R.* v. xxvii. (1495) 136 The bones of the armes ben holow that they ben not to heuy bi massydnes.

massee, masselen, obs. ff. MASSY, MASLIN[1].

masselgem, -ing, -jen, -jon, -lin: see MASLIN[2].

massels, massely: see MEASLES, MASSILY.

†**massenger.** *Obs.* [Possibly repr. an AF. form (cf. *balinger*) of OF. *massonyer, maisonier*:—late L. *mansiōnārius*: see MANSIONARY. Cf. the surname *Massinger* (which, however, may be for *messenger*).] ? An inmate of a religious house. (But perh. for *mass-singer* or *messenger*.)

1553 BECON *Reliques of Rome* (1563) 190 The brethren or massengers of the said order. *a* **1564** —— *Acts of Christ & Antichr.* Wks. III. 401 To Minstrels, to Massengers, to Friers, to Flatterers.

masse(n)ger(e, -inger(e, obs. forms of MESSENGER.

†**ˈmasser**[1]. [OE. *mæssere*, f. *mæssian*, MASS *v.*[1]: see -ER[1].] One who celebrates mass; a mass-priest; also, one who attends mass. (After OE. only as a Protestant term of derision.)

a **1000** *Azarias* 149 Bletsien þe þine sacerdos, soðfæst cyning, milde mæsseras mærne dryhten. **1543** BALE *Yet a Course*, etc. 38 A good mattenser, masser, and so forth: but no true gospell preacher. **1579** J. STUBBES *Gaping Gulf* A viij, The Spanish massers had theyr customers more then ynough.

†**masser**[2]. *Obs. rare*$^{-1}$. *attrib.* **masser-scourer**, said to mean 'gong-farmer' or scavenger.

c **1515** *Cocke Lorell's B.* 3 Than came a gonge fermourer, Other wyse called a masser scourer.

masser[3], **-or** (ˈmæsə(r)). [f. F. *mass-er* (see MASSAGE *sb.*) + -ER[1], -OR.] One who practises massage; a masseur or masseuse.

1888 D. MAGUIRE *Art of Massage* (ed. 4) 32 The masser. [Perh. a misprint for *masseur*, which occurs twice on the same page.] **1899** *Allbutt's Syst. Med.* VIII. 158 A successful massor (if I may coin a word we stand in need of) of either sex must have gentle manners, and a delicate touch. **1902** *Encycl. Brit.* XXX. 573 A single masser should have strength enough to do the work without too obvious exhaustion.

masser, obs. form of MACER[1], MAZER.

masserate, obs. form of MACERATE.

massereen, obs. form of MAZARINE *sb.*[1]

masseter (mæˈsiːtə(r)). *Anat.* [a. mod.L. *massētēr* (whence F. *masséter*), a. Gr. μασητήρ (formerly miswritten μασσ-), agent-n. from μασᾶσθαι to chew. (The Gr. sb. occurs in apposition with μῦς muscle.)] (Usually ***masseter muscle.***) One of the principal masticatory muscles, passing from the malar bone and zygomatic arch to the ramus of the lower jaw.

1666 J. SMITH *Old Age* (1676) 77 It [the upper jaw] hath ..one wonderful pair of Muscles, called, the Masseters. **1694** *Phil. Trans.* XVIII. 24 A Child..who had just then received a large Wound upon the Masseter Muscle. **1849** *St. George's Hosp. Rep.* IX. 685 The masseters were rigid. **1881** DAVEY in *Jrnl. Psychol. Med.* VII. 1, A tetanic rigidity of the temporal and masseter muscles.

†**masseteral**, *a. Obs. rare.* In 6 **-all.** [ad. mod.L. *massētērālis*: see MASSETER and -AL[1].] = MASSETERIC.

1578 BANISTER *Hist. Man* I. 15 Towards the sides where the temporall Muscle is, as also the originall of the Masseterall.

masseteric (mæsɪˈtɛrɪk), *a.* and *sb.* [f. MASSETER + -IC.]

A. *adj.* Of or pertaining to the masseter muscle.

1831 R. KNOX *Cloquet's Anat.* 463 The..masseteric, buccal and pterygoid twigs. **1891** FLOWER & LYDEKKER *Introd. Mammals* 171 The masseteric fossa of the mandible.

B. *sb.* A masseteric nerve, muscle, artery, etc.

1840 E. WILSON *Anat. Vade M.* 386 The masseteric, which crosses the sigmoid notch with the masseteric artery to the masseter muscle. **1875** SIR W. TURNER in *Encycl. Brit.* I. 836/1 The lower jaw..is elevated by the temporal muscles ..and by the massetericS.

masseterine (mæˈsiːtərɪn), *a.* [a. F. *massétérin*: see MASSETER and -INE.] = prec. A.

1855 DUNGLISON *Med. Lex.* (ed. 12), *Masseterine Artery.* .. *Masseterine Nerve*... *Masseterine Vein.*

‖**masseur** (masœr). [Fr.; agent-n. f. *masser*: see MASSAGE *sb.*] A man who practises massage.

1876 BARTHOLOW *Mat. Med.* (1879) 73 *Masseur* is a male rubber, and *masseuse* a female rubber. **1899** *Allbutt's Syst. Med.* VIII. 22 It is very important that the masseur should be gentle in the exercise of his craft.

‖**masseuse** (masøz). [Fr.; fem. formation corresp. to prec.] A woman who practices massage.

1876 [see MASSEUR]. **1897** *Allbutt's Syst. Med.* IV. 342 Treves has seen a normal kidney worked out of its place by a vigorous masseuse who mistook it for a fæcal mass.

massey, obs. form of MASSY *a.*

ˈmass-house. *Obs.* exc. *Hist.* [MASS *sb.*[1]] In 17–18th c. a common designation used by Protestants for a Roman Catholic place of worship.

1644 in Wallington *Notices of Reign of Chas. I* (1869) II. 205 They build their Mass houses in every street. **1688** EVELYN *Diary* 7 Oct., A Jesuite, who in the Masse-house.. had disparag'd the Scripture. **1780** JOHNSON *Lett. to Mrs. Thrale* 9 June, At night the outrages began by the demolition of the mass-house by Lincoln's Inn. **1809** KENDALL *Trav.* III. lxvii. 54 On the farm are small remains of the missionary church, called by the protestant colonists the mass-house. **1849** MACAULAY *Hist. Eng.* vi. II. 101 Great crowds assembled in Cheapside to attack the new mass house.

massi, obs. form of MASS *v.*[1], MASSY *a.*

Massic (ˈmæsɪk), *a. Obs.* exc. *Hist.* [ad. L. *Massic-us* the name of a mountain in Campania.] Designating an ancient wine produced in Campania, Italy. Also *ellipt.*

1638 T. HAWKINS tr. *Horace's Odes* I. i. 19 Some others use Old Massique wines to ply. **1653** B. HOLYDAY tr. *Horace's Odes* I. i. 19 In Massic Wines some bouze their time away. **1751** J. STIRLING tr. *Horace's Odes* I. i, in *Horace's Works* I. II. 2 Cups of old Massic. **1833** C. REDDING *Hist. Mod. Wines* 8 The Falernian..grew upon the volcanic Campania near Naples, where also the Massic was produced. **1920** *Punch* 15 Sept. 209, I raise my cup of massic Not to the earlier but the later 'classic'. **1961** H. W. ALLEN *Hist. Wine* v. 10 Massic appears to mean, not an individual wine, but any really fine Campanian wine. Virgil, Horace and Martial all use it in this rather general sense. **1965** O. A. MENDELSOHN *Dict. Drink* 214 *Massic*, a wine from Campania, Italy, mentioned in classical writings.

massicot (ˈmæsɪkɒt). Forms: α. 5–8 **masticote**, 6 **mastecott**, 7 **masticoate, -cut**, 8 **-coat**, 6– **masticot.** β. 6 **maskett**, 8 **masicot**, 7– **massicot.** [a. F. *massicot* (1480 in Hatz.-Darm.), in 16th c. once *masticot* (Godefr., who explains it as 'mastic', app. erroneously). Of obscure origin: cf. the synonymous It. *marzacotto*; also Sp. *mazacote* kali, mortar.] Yellow protoxide of lead, used as a pigment.

α. **1472** *Fabric Rolls York Minster* (Surtees) 79 Pro ij lb. masticote pro pictura supradictorum candelabrorum. **1546** *Inv. Ch. Surrey* (1869) 106 Item for a li. of mastecott ij[d]. **1573** *Art of Limning* 2 The like sise may you make with..red or yellow okir, orpiment or masticot. **1658** W. SANDERSON *Graphice* 84 Yellow. The best is Masticoate. **1695** DRYDEN *Du Fresnoy's Art Paint.* 172 The Masticot is very Light, because it is a very clear yellow, and very near to white. **1735** *Dict. Polygraph.* s.v. *Face*, For the faintest and weakest colour..[use] a very small quantity of pink or masticote. **1823** P. NICHOLSON *Pract. Build.* 415 Masticot, as a pigment is flake-white, or white-lead gently calcined, by which it is changed to a yellow.

β. 1532 in E. Law *Hampton Crt. Pal.* (1885) I. 363, 12 lb. of white lead..1 lb. of maskett. 1658 Phillips, *Massicot*, a kinde of Oaker, made of Ceruse, or white Lead. 1776 *Phil. Trans.* LXVI. 620 The massicot had a pale greenish cast, owing to iron. 1796 Kirwan *Elem. Min.* (ed. 2) II. 488 Masicot or yellow Calx. 1873 *Fownes' Chem.* (ed. 11) 450 Litharge or massicot.

massie, obs. form of massy.

‖**massif** ('mæsɪf). Also 6 -ife. [Fr.: subst. use (in various applications) of *massif* massive *a.*] **a.** A block of building. **b.** ? A mass of stone. **c.** A mass or clump of plants or shrubs. **d.** A large mountain-mass; the central mass of a mountain; a compact and more or less independent portion of a range.

1524 in *Hakluyt's Voy.* (1599) II. i. 86 The sayd trauerses and repaires..beganne at the massife of Spaine made by the reuerend lord great master Mery d'Amboise, & ended at the church of S. Saluador. 1862 Ansted *Channel Isl.* ii. xi. 282 The massif of the north pier at St. Peter's Port. 1885 Geikie *Text-bk. Geol.* (ed. 2) 40 A large block of mountain ground, rising into one or more dominant summits, and more or less distinctly defined by longitudinal and traverse valleys, is termed in French a *massif*—a word for which there is no good English equivalent. 1888 *Blackw. Mag.* Aug. 219 Those monsters of horticulture known as *massifs*. 1899 *Nature* 15 June 152/2 The central part of the *massif*..of Mont Blanc consists of a granitoid rock called protogine. 1899 *Ibid.* 2 Nov. 20/2 The formation of a dune tract or dune massif appears to be chiefly determined by the presence of ground moisture. 1966 *New Statesman* 13 May 701/2 Martin proposes to remove everything in favour of his uniform *massif* of offices. 1973 *Times* 9 Jan. 12/7 There must, dear God, be something between slums and concrete massifs.

massif(f)e, obs. forms of massive.

massiform ('mæsɪfɔːm), *a.* [f. L. *mass-a* mass *sb.*² + -(i)form.] 'In the form of a mass' (*Syd. Soc. Lex.* 1890).

massify ('mæsɪfaɪ), *v.* [f. mass *sb.*² + -ify.] *trans.* To form into a mass, *spec.* a mass society. Also **massifi'cation**; **'massified** *ppl. a.*

1954 W. G. Peck *Christian Econ.* i. 20 We shall further massify and denature our people. *Ibid.* x. 162 He has been calling for security through the further 'massification' of his society. 1961 R. Williams *Long Revolution* iii. 350 What the Americans call the 'massification' of society can only happen..if a majority of the people whom they regard as 'the masses' accept this version of themselves. 1966 D. Jenkins *Educated Society* ii. 59 The Nazis carried to its ruthlessly logical conclusion the attitude of those who wish to massify society for their own ends. *Ibid.* iv. 176[A] society suffering from a dull uniformity..is because people have become massified or because those in positions of privilege have become listless. 1967 D. Cooper *Psychiatry & Anti-Psychiatry* ii. 45 Human motivation in courts of law and also in massified political judgements. 1969 G. S. Jones in Cockburn & Blackburn *Student Power* 42 Although there has been a substantial increase in the number of students, there has been nothing like the same process of massification that has occurred in the USA or Japan.

‖**mässig** ('mɛːsɪç). *Mus.* [Ger.] = moderato *adv.*

1884 F. Niecks *Conc. Dict. Mus. Terms* 171 *Mässig* (Ger.), Moderate. 1938 *Oxf. Compan. Mus.* 545/2 *Mässig* (Ger.), (a) 'Moderate', 'moderately'; (b) 'in the style of' (e.g. *Marschmässig*, 'in march style').

Massilian, variant of Messalian.

Massiliot (mæ'sɪlɪət), *sb.* and *a.* Also **Massaliot, Massaliote, Massilian.** [f. L. *Massilia*, Gr. *Μασσαλία* Massalia.] **A.** *sb.* A native or inhabitant of Massalia (or Massilia, mod. Marseilles), a Greek colony founded *c* 600 b.c. to the east of the mouth of the Rhône on the Mediterranean coast of southern France. **B.** *adj.* Of or pertaining to Massalia or its inhabitants.

1601 P. Holland tr. *Pliny's Nat. Hist.* iii. iv. 55 Townes in the other parts..namely, Agatha, in times past belonging to the Massilians. 1856 Grote *Hist. Greece* XII. ii. xcviii. 614 In an age when piracy was common, the Massaliot ships and seamen were effective in attack and defence. *Ibid.* 615 Except the Phenicians and Carthaginians, these Massaliots were the only enterprising mariners in the Western Mediterranean. 1873 G. W. Kitchin *Hist. France to 1453* i. ii. 23 The whole seaboard from Var to Rhone was given to the Massiliots. 1898 A. Hassal *Jervis's Hist. France* (rev. ed.) i. 7 Pompey was beaten, and Cæsar's hand fell heavily on the Massiliots. 1932 *Times Lit. Suppl.* 8 Sept. 617/2 The voyage of the Massilian Pytheas. 1945 *Proc. Prehist. Soc.* XI. 56 Massilian coins have been obtained from the archaeological strata. 1949 *Oxf. Classical Dict.* 543/2 Massiliot seamen played an important part in the Second Punic War. 1957 *Encycl. Brit.* XIV. 965/1 The Massaliots made their way by prudence and by vigilant administration of their oligarchical government. *Ibid.*, In the 4th century b.c. the Massaliot Pytheas visited the coasts of Gaul. 1963 Cary & Warmington *Anc. Explorers* (rev. ed.) ii. 36 Syracusan and Massilian traders could join hands in the ports of Rome. 1964 J. Boardman *Greeks Overseas* v. 227 In the sixth century the Marseilles route is vouched for by the Massaliot and Phocaean pottery found at Mt Lassois. 1970 *Oxf. Classical Dict.* (ed. 2) 654/1 Massaliote ships helped Rome in the Second Punic War.

massily ('mæsɪlɪ), *adv.* Also 5 masly, 5–6 massely, 6 -alie. [f. massy + -ly².] Massively.

c 1400 *Destr. Troy* 3923 Troilus þe tru was..Full massely made, & of mayn strenght. *Ibid.* 3975 Ecuba, the onest & onerable qwene, Was..Massily made as a man lyke. *c* 1420 *Avow. Arth.* iii, He [the boar] is masly made. 1513 Douglas *Æneis* x. xiii. 38 The tother..Abydis stowtly, fermyt in his fors, And massely [*v. r.* (1710) massalie] vpstude with bustuus cors. *a* 1668 Sir W. Waller *Div. Medit.* (1839) 86 Let our houses be never so strongly and massily built, if.. we lean upon them, they shall not stand. 1922 E. R. Eddison *Worm Ouroboros* vii. 75 Benches of green jasper massily built and laden with velvet cushions.

Massim ('mæsɪm). Also **Misima**. The eastern Papuo-Melanesian people of Papua New Guinea; also, a member of this people; the language of this people. Also as *adj.*

[1889 E. T. Hamy in *Revue d'Ethnogr.* VII. 504 La plupart des Mélanésiens de la mer d'Entrecasteaux sont aujourd'hui appelés collectivement *Massims*.] 1893 S. H. Ray in *9th Internat. Congr. Orientalists* II. 760 Of these, the Misima is the same as the New Guinea Melanesian, whilst the Nada forms..show the pronouns usual as possessive suffixes. 1894 A. C. Haddon *Decorative Art Brit. New Guinea* 184 Following Dr. E. T. Hamy, I adopt the term Massims as a collective name for the mixed people inhabiting the archipelagoes off the south-east of New Guinea... The term Massim..originally arose from an imperfect knowledge of the island of Misima, but I employ it solely as a convenient conventional name. 1910 C. G. Seligmann *Melanesians Brit. New Guinea* 9 The most characteristic cultural feature of the Massim is the existence of a peculiar form of totemism with matrilineal descent. 1936 R. Firth *Art & Life New Guinea* 22 The Massim area, in the south-east, is particularly famous for the wealth of carving with which its spatulæ are embellished. 1961 B. A. L. Cranstone *Melanesia* 42 The prow-boards of Massim canoes..are always carved by specialists. 1971 M. W. Young *Fighting with Food in Massim Society* iii. 54 Unlike in many areas of the Massim, men do not attribute malevolent supernatural powers to women.

massindewe, obs. form of measondue.

massiness ('mæsɪnɪs). [f. massy + -ness.] The quality of being massy; massiveness.

1570 Dee *Math. Pref.* bij, The Solidity, Massines and Body of the Sonne. 1587 Golding *De Mornay* 47 The massinesse of things is that..that maketh them vnable to do things. Contrariwise the more spirituale a thing is, the more actiue it is. 1625 Laud *Wks.* (1847) I. 110 It is not the great massiness of a pillar, but [etc.]. 1712 J. James tr. *Le Blond's Gardening* 33 Avoiding too great a Slenderness, as well as too great a Massyness of Ornaments. 1773 Johnson *Let. to Mrs. Thrale* 12 Aug., The cathedral has a massyness and solidity such as I have seen in no other place. 1810 Shelley *Zastrozzi* xv, A lamp, whose rays..showed..the extreme massiness of the passages.

massing ('mæsɪŋ), *vbl. sb.*¹ Also 3 mesing-, 4 mesin-, 4, 6 messyng, 5 mesyng. [f. mass *v.*¹ + -ing¹.] The action or practice of celebrating mass.

1340 Hampole *Pr. Consc.* 3589 Four maners of helpes.. prayer and fastyng, And almus dede and messyng. 1542–5 Brinklow *Lament.* (1874) 105, I will exhorte all prestes..to fle and geue ouer that abhominable massynge, which is a blasphemy to Christes bloude. 1546 Bale *Eng. Votaries* i. (1548) 19 b, Pranked vp with tabernacles & lyghtes, sensynges & massinges. 1661 J. Stephens *Procurations* 111, I cannot fix the original of this due, forasmuch as the act of Massing *quolibet die dominico* being too generall..doth not fitly denominate the pay. 1850 *Elder's House* 166 These Catholics are always for praying and massing.

†**b.** *attrib.* and *Comb.*, as ***massing apparel, cope, furniture, matter, robe, room, sacrifice, vestment, wine***; **massing closet** = *mass-closet*; **massing-mate** (? *nonce-wd.*), the celebrant at mass; **massing penny** = mass-penny; **massing-priest** = mass-priest.

1566 *Answ. Exam. pretending to mayntayne Apparell* 132 Being required of papisticall persecutours to do on all their *massing apparell. 1656 Heylin *Surv. France* 180 In this *Massing Closet over the Altar there was hanged a tablet. 1610 Bp. Hall *Apol. Brownists* §46 What meane you to charge our churches with 'carued and painted images'?.. What more? '*Massing copes and surplices'. 1594 Hooker *Eccl. Pol.* iv. xi. §2 All their *Massing furniture almost they tooke from the law. 1607 R. C[arew] tr. *Estienne's World of Wonders* 294 The *Massing-mate [Fr. *messatizant*] hath the Deacon and Subdeacon to assist him. 1549 Latimer *5th Serm. bef. Edw. VI* (Arb.) 139 *Scala cœli*, is a preachynge matter I tell you, and not a *massyng matter. 1292 *Durham Acc. Rolls* (Surtees) 490 Et de ixs. iiijd. ob. de *Mesingpenis de e[odem] t[ermino]. 1536–7 *Ibid.* 667 De messyngpennys nichil, quia dimittuntur cum tota villa. 1560 Becon *Catech.* v. Wks. 1564 I. 457 But if ther bee none other remedy but that the *massinge priestes will sacrifice Christe in their masses. 1574 *Life 70th Abp. Canterb.* To Rdr. F ij, It had some reason to call the Massinge Prieste, a priste secular. 1656 Jeanes *Fuln. Christ* 63 Their massing priests, and masse sacrifice. 1625 *Gonsalvio's Sp. Inquis.* 140 They despoiled him of those vile and wicked *Massing robes. 1623 Goad *Dolef. Euen-Song* 12 A Chamber..being the vsuall *Massing roome for the English resorting thither. *c* 1571 Northbrooke *Poore Mans Garden* Ep. Ded. 1 More diligent to mooue them to believe in..the *Massing Sacrifice, then Christes Oblation. 1612 T. James *Corrupt. Scripture* i. 5 *marg.*, *Massing vestiments. 1647 Trapp *Comm. Rom.* x. 2 He thought he had never sufficiently mingled his *massing wine with water.

massing ('mæsɪŋ), *vbl. sb.*² [f. mass *v.*² + -ing¹.] The action of mass *v.*²

1804 K. White *Let. R. A.* 7 May, What the painters call the massing, or getting the effect of the more prominent lights and shades by broad dashes of the pencil. 1870 *Daily News* 9 Dec., To-day there has been a massing of German troops, but no fighting.

massing ('mæsɪŋ), *vbl. sb.*³ The action of mass *v.*³; the practice of massage.

1855 Dunglison *Med. Lex.* (ed. 12), *Massing*, shampooing. 1902 *Encycl. Brit.* XXX. 573 Without going so far as to make massing a closed profession.

massive ('mæsɪv), *a.* Forms: 5 massiffe, massyve, 5–6 massife, 6– massive. [ad. F. *massif*, f. *masse* mass *sb.*²: see -ive.]

1. a. Forming or consisting of a large mass; having great size and weight or solidity. †Of a person: Bulky, large-bodied (*obs.*).

c 1410 Lydg. *Reas. & Sens.* 2730 Ful of trees..Massiffe and grete and evene vpryght. 1481 Caxton *Myrr.* ii. xxi. h 4 b The erthe meueth so strongly, that it behoueth to falle all that whiche is theron thaugh it were a massyue tour. 1485 —— *Chas. Gt.* 165 The portyer..is a paynym hydous and grete, massyf, stronge and felonnous. *a* 1806 Bp. Horsley *Serm.* (1816) I. vii. 124 The common military sword is a heavy massive weapon, for close engagement. 1840 Dickens *Barn. Rudge* i, Its ceilings..heavy with massive beams. 1868 J. H. Blunt *Ref. Ch. Eng.* I. 342 The buildings were too massive to be destroyed.

b. Of articles of gold or silver: Solid, not hollow or plated.

1582 Stanyhurst *Æneis* ii. (Arb.) 68 Theare massiue gould cups bee layd. 1662 Evelyn *Diary* 9 June, The greate looking-glasse..of beaten and massive gold. 1851 D. Wilson *Preh. Ann.* (1863) II. iii. v. 133 A massive silver chain.

†**c.** Solid, having three dimensions. = massy 1 c.

1589 Puttenham *Eng. Poesie* (Arb.) 310 Painting and keruing, whereof one represents the naturall..in the superficiall or flat, the other in a body massife.

†**d.** Of textile fabrics: Thick, substantial. *Obs.*

1670–98 Lassels *Voy. Italy* I. 87 The silk-stockings..are twice as strong as ours, and very massive.

e. Of architectural or artistic style: Presenting great masses, solid.

1841 W. Spalding *Italy & It. Isl.* I. 162 That broad, massive, severe classicism which marked the newly emancipated age of Phidias. 1861 M. Pattison *Ess.* (1889) I. 44 When the Company proceeded to rebuild, they no longer did so in the massive and imposing style of the fourteenth century.

f. Of the features, head, forehead, etc.: Largely moulded or modelled.

1843 Lytton *Last Bar.* i. iv, His forehead was singularly high and massive. 1885 Miss Braddon *Wyllard's Weird* I. i. 14 The features are firmly modelled, bold, and massive.

2. *transf.* and *fig.* **a.** Of immaterial things: Solid, substantial; great or imposing in scale. Now freq. used in weakened senses, 'large, great, far-reaching'.

1581 Mulcaster *Positions* xxxix. (1887) 221 Religious skill is farre more massiue. 1833 Herschel *Astron.* iii. 154 One result of maritime discovery on the great scale is, so to speak, massive enough to call for mention as an astronomical feature. 1858 Hawthorne *Fr. & It. Note-Bks.* (1871) I. 262 Mighty figures..looking as if they were necessarily so gigantic because the thought within them was so massive. 1874 L. Stephen *Hours in Library* (1892) I. iv. 151 Scott was a man of more massive and less impulsive character. 1958 [see air-lift 2]. 1958 G. Kennan *Russia, Atom & West* v. 77 The Marxists claim, of course, that colonialism invariably represented a massive and cruel exploitation of the colonial peoples. 1958 *New Statesman* 6 Sept. 306/2 The tendency to make *massive* a substitute not merely for *enormous, immense* and *huge* but even for *large* and *extensive* as applying to all sorts of phenomena, social, financial, political and psychological. 1963 *Daily Mail* 25 Feb. 16/6 Cowdrey again showed massive good form to make 86 in 163 minutes. 1965 R. & D. Morris *Men & Snakes* ix. 201 We required a massive sample of the population. 1973 *Word 1970* XXVI. 119 He died suddenly of a massive heart attack.

b. *Psych.* Of a sensation, a state of consciousness: Having large volume or extensive magnitude.

1855 Bain *Senses & Int.* 92 A massive or voluminous feeling of comparatively little acuteness or intensity. *Ibid.* 132 The..sensation of chillness..is..not acute but massive and powerful. 1872 Spencer *Princ. Psychol.* §513 II. 579 As this aggregate [of pleasurable recollections] grows by accumulation, it becomes vague in proportion as it becomes massive. 1892 Stevenson *Across the Plains* 4 All the activities of my nature had become tributary to one massive sensation of discomfort.

c. *Path.* Of a disease, etc.: Affecting a large continuous portion of tissue.

1897 *Allbutt's Syst. Med.* II. 767 Massive gangrene sometimes occurs. 1899 *Ibid.* VIII. 496 In massive swellings of the tongue and throat relief has been given by [etc.].

d. *Mus.* Presenting a large volume of sound.

1861 Calverley *Verses, 'There stands a City'* 28 Still I.. Hear you humming of 'the gal you'd Left behind' in massive bass. 1885 *Athenæum* 7 Feb. 192 Some numbers were splendidly given, notably the massive chorus,..and the whole of the processional choruses.

e. massive retaliation, name given to a military strategy, inaugurated in the U.S.A. by J. F. Dulles in the 1950s, which uses the threat of a punitive response with thermonuclear weapons to deter aggression.

[1954 *N.Y. Times* 13 Jan. 2/3 [Speech of J. F. Dulles] Local defense must be reinforced by the further deterrent of massive retaliatory power.] 1954 *Times* 29 Mar. 5/5 The plan of 'meeting any aggression with massive retaliation in places of our choosing'. 1955 *Bull. Atomic Sci.* Jan. 29/1 We believe that the announced concept of massive retaliation contains the elements of adequate military support to arrest the expansive aims of communism. 1959 *Times Lit. Suppl.* 25 Sept. 542/2 Mr. Dulles's 'massive retaliation' speech of

January 1954..could hardly be read in the Soviet Union otherwise than as a threat. **1971** E. LUTTWAK *Dict. Mod. War* 128/1 Massive retaliation was never central US policy, and was in any case associated with the diplomatic technique of brinkmanship.

3. Forming a solid or continuous mass; compact, dense, or (sometimes, merely) uniform in internal structure; existing in compact continuous masses. Now *rare* exc. *Min.* as the epithet of minerals not definitely crystalline; *Geol.* as applied to rocks or formations presenting no structural divisions; *Zool.*, applied to organisms which are compact in structure.

1558–68 WARDE tr. *Alexis' Secr.* 64 If it should boile but a little more than it ought to boile, it would be thicke and massife. *Ibid.* 64 b, Seeth them in a kettle untill they be neither to much nor to litle boiled, but even hole and massive not broken. **1573** *Art of Limning* 7 The galles must be smal curled, and massive within. **1796** KIRWAN *Elem. Min.* (ed. 2) II. 226 Mercury..Second family. Slaty... Found Massive. **1860** RUSKIN *Mod. Paint.* V. VII. ii. 112 Clouds may be broadly considered as of two species only, massive and striated. I cannot find a better word than massive, though it is not a good one, for I mean it only to signify a fleecy arrangement in which no lines are visible. **1871** *Jukes' Man. Geol.* (ed. 3) 99 The leading differences of structure among igneous rocks are the *bedded*..; *amorphous*..; *massive*, occurring in large masses which can be broken or quarried in any direction [etc.]. **1888** ROLLESTON & JACKSON *Forms Animal Life* (ed. 2) 250 There appear to be two fresh-water Sponges in Great Britain... The former is branched, the latter massive and lobate.

fig. **1600** TOURNEUR *Transf. Metam.* lvii, (Had he beene a man of massive hart) He would haue melted at her mermaide's part.

4. Pertaining to masses as distinguished from molecules; molar.

1877 E. R. CONDER *Bas. Faith* iii. 122 The control of mind over the material world..is limited to the power of producing motion, massive or molecular.

massively (ˈmæsɪvlɪ), *adv.* [f. MASSIVE + -LY[2].]
a. In a massive manner or form.

1550 SIR R. BOWES in Hodgson *Hist. Northumb.* III. (1828) II. 200 That side to be massively rampiered with earth. **1844** MRS. BROWNING *Vision of Poets* 747 And so..Rose the full notes; now parted off In pauses massively aloof, Like measured thunders. **1858** HAWTHORNE *Fr. & It. Note-Bks.* I. 259 Houses built so massively..that [etc.]. **1959** *Times Lit. Suppl.* 20 Feb. 97/2 The road of elaborate verbal analysis of a poem which the trained reader immediately and massively *feels* to be wrong. *Ibid.* 27 Feb. 113/3 We must have massively responded..to a poem..before we can usefully talk about it. **1962** *Listener* 29 Mar. 540/1 The Administration was never crystal-clear on exactly how we would massively retaliate with nuclear weapons. **1974** *Physics Bull.* Apr. 132/3 Past CEGB technological choices and commercial practices have resulted in massively unproductive investments.

b. *nonce-use.* By masses of persons.

1876 GEO. ELIOT *Dan. Der.* lix, An assumption which.. was massively acted on at that date of the world's history.

massiveness (ˈmæsɪvnɪs). [f. MASSIVE + -NESS.] The state or quality of being massive.

1530 PALSGR. 243/2 Massyfnesse, *solidité*. **1603** *North's Plutarch, Life Plutarch* (1612) 1204 Doest thou think it is by reason of the massiuenes or weight, or by the swiftnesse, or strength of the eyes? **1620** VENNER *Via Recta* i. 19 Bread made of Rie..is cold, heauy, and hard to digest, and by reason of the massiuenesse thereof, very burdensome to the stomacke. **1855** BAIN *Senses & Int.* 92 The peculiarity of it [*sc.* the feeling of fatigue] as a pleasure is not intensity or acuteness, but quantity, massiveness, or volume. **1870** F. R. WILSON *Ch. Lindisf.* 93 The sombre massiveness of the tower.

massivity (mæˈsɪvɪtɪ). [f. MASSIVE *a.* + -ITY.] The fact or condition of being massive.

1908 W. H. DAWSON *Evolution Mod. Germany* 13 Everywhere one sees the worship of massivity, the striving after crude, imposing effects—in the modern monuments, the public buildings, the bridges. **1921** S. GRAHAM *Europe* xiv. 186 A mighty stone structure, of great height and massivity. **1953** E. BARKER *Age & Youth* iv. 72 But New College had a massivity, if I may coin that word—an invisible massivity which matched the visible physical massivity of its chapel and hall and cloisters and tower—that captured my spirit and stretched my powers.

Mass-John: see MAS *sb.*[1] 2.

massledine, -legen, obs. ff. MASLIN[2].

massless (ˈmæslɪs), *a.* [f. MASS *sb.*[2] + -LESS.] Having no mass. Also **ˈmasslessness**.

1879 THOMSON & TAIT *Nat. Phil.* I. I. §345 A material particle supported by massless springs. **1947** *Mind* LVI. 50 Consider a weight of mass *m* hanging downwards under gravity on a (massless) elastic strand. **1963** K. W. FORD *World of Elementary Particles* 115 One necessary condition for masslessness seems to be the absence of charge. Every charged particle has mass, although not every neutral particle is massless. **1971** *Guinness Bk. Records* (ed. 18) v. 70/1 Of all sub-atomic concepts only the neutrino calls for masslessness. **1972** *Sci. Amer.* June 53/1 Massless uncharged particles that interact so little with other particles that the outer layers of the sun and solid bodies such as the earth are virtually transparent to them.

mass medium (ˌmæs ˈmiːdɪəm). [f. MASS *sb.*[2] + MEDIUM *sb.*] A medium of communication (such as radio, television, newspapers, etc.) that reaches a large number of people; usu. in pl. *mass media*.

The *pl.* form *mass media* is sometimes erroneously construed as *sing.*

1923 S. M. FECHHEIMER in N. T. Praigg *Advertising & Selling* v. 238 (*title*) Class appeal in mass media. *Ibid.*, The several million readers of a big mass medium. G. SNOW in *Ibid.* 240 Mass media represents the most economical way of getting the story over the new and wider market in the least time. **1942** D. WAPLES *Print, Radio & Film* 19 Radio (which, according to German propaganda theory, is the 'real' mass medium). **1946** J. S. HUXLEY *Unesco* ii. 58 The media of mass communication—the somewhat cumbrous title (commonly abbreviated to 'Mass Media') proposed for agencies, such as the radio, the cinema and the popular press, which are capable of the mass dissemination of word or image. *Ibid.* 60 The use of the mass media to foster education, science and culture... Regarded from this angle, the mass media fall into the same general category as the libraries and museums—that of servicing agencies for man's higher activities. **1957** R. HOGGART *Uses of Literacy* ii. 27 A great deal has been written about the effect on the working-classes of the modern 'mass media of communication'. **1964** M. ARGYLE *Psychol. & Social Probl.* vii. 101 Propaganda over the mass media may be intended to change behaviour, beliefs or feelings, or all three. *Ibid.* xiii. 157 Mass media such as TV, radio, newspapers and posters. **1966** N. TUCKER (*title*) Understanding the mass media. **1968** P. OLIVER *Screening Blues* 3 For the Negro in Tuscaloosa, Alabama.., the blues record afforded the first real opportunity of contact through a mass medium with others of his social status. **1971** *New Scientist* 18 Mar. 610/1 The department's trendy, mass-media sounding title is a historical accident. **1974** *Black World* Dec. 5/1 Nevertheless, the mass media continues to emphasize the attitudes, beliefs and rhetoric of a minority of the Black community.

ˈmass-ˌmonger. *arch.* [MASS *sb.*[1]] A contemptuous term for a Roman Catholic.

Common in the 16th c.

1550 BALE *Eng. Votaries* II. 27 Callynge both hym & hys masmongers..fleshe makers. *a* **1649** DRUMM. OF HAWTH. *Skiamachia* Wks. (1711) 199 Ye are mass-mongers, adorers of angels, [etc.]. **1826** SOUTHEY *Vind. Eccl. Angl.* 211 This scheme for bringing custom to the mass-mongers at Tunnacester.

So †**ˈmass-ˌmonging** *vbl. sb.* and *ppl. a.*

1552 LATIMER *Serm. 23rd Sund. Trin.* (1584) 209 An other denying of Christ is this Massemongyng. **1607** R. C[AREW] tr. *Estienne's World of Wonders* 204 Another Masse-monging gentleman of Lorraine. **1612** W. SCLATER *Minister's Portion* 8 Things giuen to superstitious vses, suppose to maintain masmonging.

mass observation (ˌmæs ɒbzəˈveɪʃən). [f. MASS *sb.*[2] + OBSERVATION.] The study and record of the social habits of people (taken in the mass); also (with capital initials) the name of an organization established for this purpose. Also *attrib.* So **mass-observationist, -observer; mass-observe** *v. trans.*

1933 L. BLOOMFIELD *Lang.* ii. 38 The observer..by this mass-observation, gives us a statement of the speech-habits of a community. **1937** MADGE & HARRISSON *Mass-Observation* 8 If after reading the pamphlet you should wish to co-operate by becoming a Mass-Observer, send a card. *Ibid.* i. 10 A group of people started *Mass Observation*, which aims to be a scientific study of human social behaviour, beginning at home. **1937** JENNINGS & MADGE (*title*) May the twelfth: Mass-Observation day-surveys 1937. **1938** *Times* 10 Mar. 15/4 Nor are they mass-observationists..testing the movements of public opinion with cold curiosity. **1939** 'N. BLAKE' *Smiler with Knife* xvi. 233 'I thought..you wur one of them Mass Observers...' 'No. I'm just one of the mass-observed.' **1948** J. BETJEMAN *Coll. Poems* (1958) 229 The Mass-Observer with the Hillman Minx. **1951** 'A. GARVE' *Murder in Moscow* ii. 34 He's supposed to have an assignment..but he spends all his time doing his own private mass observation. **1967** G. WILLS in Wills & Yearsley *Handbk. Managem. Technol.* 184 The two other major quantification techniques are the consumer survey..and the mass-observation study. **1970** *Guardian* 10 Dec. 8/4 The Mass Observers..mass observed blind drinkers. **1974** *Daily Tel.* (Colour Suppl.) 19 Apr. 23/3 The Mass-Observation method..is the absolute opposite of interviewing.

masson, -nery, obs. ff. MASON, MASONRY.

massondew: see MEASONDUE.

massoné(e, *Her.*: see MASONED *ppl. a.* 2.

‖**massoola(h** (mæˈsuːlə). Forms: 7 **musoola**, 7, 9 **mussoola**, 8 **(mausolo)**, 9 **(masuli)**, **muss-, mas(s)ulah, mussoolah**, 8–9 **mas(s)oola, massoolah**. [Of obscure origin: see conjectures in Yule.] A large surf-boat used for conveying passengers and goods between ships and the shore on the Coromandel coast. Often ***massoolah-boat***.

1685 W. HEDGES *Diary* 3 Feb., This morning two Musoolas & two Cattamarans came off to yᵉ Shippe... [We] got into yᵉ Mussoola. **1760–1879** [see quots. in Yule s.v. *Mussoola*]. **1793** HODGES *Trav. India* 4 A boat of the country, called a Massoolah boat. **1899** F. T. BULLEN *Log Sea-waif* 203 The crazy 'massulah' boats..so often described by visitors to Madras.

massor: see MASSER *sb.*[3], MAZER.

Massora(h: see MASORA(H.

Massorat, -ete, -ite: see MASORETE, -ITE.

massoy (ˈmæsɔɪ). Also 8 **massay**, 9 **massoi, mussoey, mussoi**, *Dicts.* **missoy**. [a. Malay *masūi.*] The bark of an East Indian tree, *Cinnamomum Kiamis.* Also ***massoy-bark, massoy-camphor, oil***: products obtained from this bark.

1800 *Asiat. Ann. Reg., Chron.* 35/2 Bird's nests, tripangs, massay, agamgar..shall pay 5 per cent. *Ibid., Misc. Tracts* 74 *note*, It is much more esteemed than the massoy bark. **1859** *Times* 29 June 9/2 A fragrant aromatic bark, called mussoey. **1860** WATTS tr. *Gmelin's Handbk. Chem.* XIV. 380 Oil of Massoy. *Ibid.* 381 Massoy-camphor. White powder, heavier than water. **1884** *Encycl. Brit.* XVII. 389/2 Massoi bark.

ˈmass-penny. *arch.* [MASS *sb.*[1]] An offering of money made at mass.

1362 LANGL. *P. Pl.* A. III. 217 Prestes..Askeþ Meede and Masse-pons and heore Mete eke. *c* **1386** CHAUCER *Sompn. T.* 41 A goddes halfpeny or a masse peny. **1470–85** MALORY *Arthur* XVIII. xx. 761 Praye for my soule & bery me atte leest & offre ye my masse peny. **1528** TINDALE *Obed. Chr. Man* Pref. xv, He..fetteth here a masse peny, there a trentall, yonder dirige money. **1849** ROCK *Ch. of Fathers* II. vii. 504. **1877** MISS YONGE *Cameos* III. xvii. 156 He had been at the chapel..and offered his mass-penny.

attrib. **1579** E. K. *Gloss. Spenser's Sheph. Cal.* June 25 Theyr packed pelfe and Masse-penie religion.

ˈmass-priest. *arch.* [MASS *sb.*[1]] A priest whose function it is to celebrate mass.

In OE. applied *gen.* to any priest (Christian or Jewish); in ME. app. used *spec.* for a secular priest as opposed to a monk, or for one employed to say masses for the souls of the dead. From the 16th c. chiefly a contemptuous designation for a Roman Catholic priest.

c **893** K. ÆLFRED *Oros.* (Sweet) 282 Arrius se masse-preost. *c* **1000** ÆLFRIC *Hom.* Pref., Ic Ælfric, munuc and mæssepreost. *c* **1200** *Trin. Coll. Hom.* 23 þanne he his muchele synnes..bimurneð, and sheweð hem his messe preste. *c* **1205** LAY. 29872 Vt wenden munekes & þa masse-preostes. **13..** *Gaw. & Gr. Knt.* 2108 Monk, oþer masse-prest, oþer any mon elles. **1554** BRADFORD *Let.* Wks. (Parker Soc.) I. 391 God is no merchant, as our mass-priests be. **1632** LITHGOW *Trav.* III. 92 Among the foure Friars, there was but one Masse-Priest. **1686** EVELYN *Diary* 11 July, The late King's glorious chapell [at Windsor] now seiz'd on by the masse priests. **1902** J. BUCHAN *Watcher by Threshold* II. 109 The family changed its faith, and an Episcopal chaplain took the place of the old mass-priest in the tutoring of the sons. **1922** JOYCE *Ulysses* 379 She said that he had a fair sweet death through God His goodness with masspriest to be shriven, holy housel and sick men's oil to his limbs.

mass production. [f. MASS *sb.*[2] + PRODUCTION.] The production of manufactured articles in large quantities by a standardized process. Also *transf.* and *attrib.*

1920 *Teacher's World* 19 May 283/2 (Advt.), Mass production. High class..chairs. **1922** TURNER & WOOD *Man. Up-to-Date Organisation* 110 Mass Production is a continuous replica of a standardised master-pattern or design. **1923** J. M. SCOTT-MAXWELL *Costing & Price-Fixing* 31 Factories on a mass production basis will have all material most carefully specified, examined, and tested. **1929** W. DEEPING *Roper's Row* xxxii. 353 The new world of smudged faces, mass-production man in the making. **1930** G. B. SHAW *Apple Cart* I. 25 Don't forget our racing motor boats and cars, sir: the finest on earth, and all individually designed. No cheap mass production stuff there. **1944** W. TEMPLE *Church looks Forward* x. 82 The problems due to mass-production press upon us. **1946** J. S. HUXLEY *Unesco* i. 18 A mass-production system can indirectly destroy creative initiative and aesthetic appreciation. **1947** J. HAYWARD *Prose Lit. Since 1939* 26 Literary and historical biography was already a flourishing industry. What particular..forces were concerned in its mass-production cannot be investigated here. **1948** [see *conveyor belt* s.v. CONVEYOR 4 c]. **1962** H. O. BEECHENO *Introd. Business Stud.* x. 86 Mass-production methods have called for mass-selling methods. **1967** M. MCLUHAN *Medium is Massage* 50 Printing..provided the first uniformly repeatable 'commodity', the first assembly line—mass production.

Hence **ˌmass-proˈduce** *v. trans.* and *intr.*, to manufacture (articles) by mass production; also **ˌmass-proˈduced** *ppl. a.*; **ˌmass-proˈducer; ˌmass-proˈducing** *ppl. a.*; **ˌmass-ˈproduct.**

1922 JOYCE *Ulysses* 661 They drank..Epps's mass-product, the creature cocoa. **1923** *Daily Mail* 22 Jan. 5 All cars made in the United States are not necessarily mass-produced. **1929** E. GILL *Art-Nonsense* 318 The ordinary person..says, what is to hinder him from having..mass-produced pots and pans designed by artists to look artistic? **1929** A. HUXLEY *Do what you Will* 90 The mass-producers will do their best to make everybody more and more prosperous. **1930** —— *Vulgarity in Lit.* vii. 45 Asceticism is not popular in this mass-producing age. **1938** *New Statesman* 23 July 143/2 Trades which mass-produce luxury or semi-luxury goods. **1940** *Life* 9 Dec. 84/2 U.S. now mass-produces. **1950** M. HAY *Foot of Pride* iii. 74 St. Vincent Ferrer and other preachers sent thousands of panic-stricken people to the font where a priest mechanically turned them into Christians. Theologians..decided that these mass-produced Christians had been validly baptized. **1954** *Encounter* Mar. 5/2 A mass-producing, mass-consuming society. **1958** Mass-produce [see BATTERY 13 c]. **1967** E. SHORT *Embroidery & Fabric Collage* iii. 68 There is no way of mass-producing patchwork. **1973** *Country Life* 15 Mar. 718/1 This is our 18th Century style bedroom suite. Not for everyone because it is not mass-produced.

massula (ˈmæsjʊlə). *Bot.* [mod.L., dim. of L. *massa*: see MASS *sb.*[2]] (*a*) In heterosporous ferns of the genera *Azolla* and *Salvinia*, the tissue surrounding the maturing microspores; (*b*) in certain orchids, a cluster of pollen grains developed from a single cell.

1856 J. S. HENSLOW *Dict. Bot. Terms* (ed. 2) 105 Massula (a little lump). One of the smaller fragments which.. compose the pollen mass in Orchidaceæ. **1882** S. H. VINES tr. *F. G. J. von Sachs's Text-bk. Bot.* II. 454 In the microsporangia [of *Azolla*] the mucilage looks like a large-

celled tissue, and forms from two to eight separate clumps (*Massulæ*), each of which encloses a number of microspores. In some species.. these massulæ have their surfaces covered with hair-like appendages. **1894** S. H. VINES *Students' Text-bk. Bot.* I. III. 410 In *Azolla* the microspores are likewise embedded in this substance, but in more than one group or massula according to the species. **1895** — — *Ibid.* II. III. 564 The pollinium may consist..of larger groups of cells, termed *massulæ* (e.g. Orchis). **1938** G. M. SMITH *Cryptogamic Bot.* II. ix. 358 The functional macrospore lies in the large massula at the base of a sporangium. *Ibid.* 360 A microspore remains embedded within a massula during the entire course of its development into a gametophyte. **1959** WIRTH & WITHNER in C. L. Withner *Orchids* v. 157 In some genera, such as *Peristylus*, there is a variation on the normal mode of development. All the cells resulting from the divisions of an archesporial cell remain attached to each other, eventually forming a small cluster of tetrads known as a massula. **1965** BELL & COOMBE tr. *Strasburger's Textbk. Bot.* 582 *Azolla* is of interest for the arrangements which ensure fertilization. After liberation from the microsporangium the sixty-four microspores are aggregated into 5–8 roundish floating balls (massulae) formed of the frothy periplasmodium. Arising from the surface of each massula are a number of stalked, barbed hooks.

massy ('mæsɪ), *a.* Also 4 **massee**, 4, 6 **massye**, 5 **massi**, 6–8 **massie**, **-ey**. [f. MASS *sb.*² + -Y. In early instances perh. a. OF. *massi*, *massis*, *masseïs*, f. *masse* with suffix repr. L. *-itus*, *-īcius*, *-ātīcius*.

Formerly in common use; now rhetorical or *arch.*; in ordinary prose use superseded by MASSIVE.]

1. Full of substance or 'mass'.

a. Solid and weighty; heavy as consisting of compact matter. Said esp. of the precious metals: Occurring in mass; wrought in solid pieces, without hollow or alloy.

1382 WYCLIF *Ecclus.* l. 10 As a massee vessel of gold. **1398** TREVISA *Barth. De P.R.* XVI. vii. (1495) 555 The syluer compownyd is massy & sad. *c* **1470** HENRYSON *Fab.* (*Son of Fox*) in *Anglia* IX. 368 The leopardis come with croun of massie gold. **1553** BRENDE *Q. Curtius* L v, He founde in that citie an incredible treasure .L.M. talentes of massy silver uncoyned. **1598** DRAYTON *Heroic. Ep.* ii 80, I can march all day in massie Steele. **1638** BAKER tr. *Balzac's Lett.* (vol. III) 175 There are none now but poor Gentlemen that will offer to weare the Massiest silver lace. **1777** SHERIDAN *Sch. Scand.* III. iii, A great quantity of massy old plate. **1805** SCOTT *Last Minstrel* Introd. 33 Whose ponderous grate and massy bar Had oft [etc.]. **1853** MACAULAY *Biog.*, *Atterbury* (1867) 10 An inestimable treasure of massy bullion. **1877** A. B. EDWARDS *Up Nile* i. 20 Seen in certain lights, the Pyramids look like piles of massy gold.

†**b.** *gen.* Solid, not hollow. *Obs.*

1382 WYCLIF *Exod.* xxxviii. 7 And thilk auter was not massye [Vulg. *solidum*], but holwȝ of tabled thingis, and with ynne voyde. *c* **1440** *Promp. Parv.* 328/2 Massy, noȝt hole, *solidus.* **1673** *Phil. Trans.* VIII. 6004 By cramming into them many Crystal-bullets, both hollow and massy ones.

†**c.** Solid, having three dimensions. Applied to sculptures, as opposed to paintings on the flat.

1551 RECORDE *Pathw. Knowl.* I. Def., By Depenesse..I meane the massie thicknesse of any bodie, as in exaumple of a potte. **1571** DIGGES *Pantom.*, *Math. Disc.* Hh ij, A Transformed Dodecaedron is a massie or solide figure. **1612** BREREWOOD *Lang. & Relig.* xviii. 167 Rejecting carved or massie images, but admitting the painted. *c* **1645** HOWELL *Lett.* (1650) I. 331 Abhorring the use of massy statues.

d. Close, compact, dense (in texture or consistency). ? *Obs.*

1519 HORMAN *Vulg.* 37 b, They that haue massye bonys neuer swete or thristethe. **1567** MAPLET *Gr. Forest* 33 It is nothing solid or massie, but much porouse. **1579–80** NORTH *Plutarch*, *Romulus* (1595) 39 A grosse vapour, darke & massie. **1805** R. W. DICKSON *Pract. Agric* I. 428 The more massy sorts of manure. **1814** CARY *Dante*, *Paradise* XIII. 6 Stars,..that, with lively ray serene, O'ercome the massiest air.

2. Consisting of a large mass or masses of heavy material; having great size and weight. Of buildings: Consisting of great blocks or piles of masonry.

1587 GOLDING *De Mornay* i. 2 Yee see..the Earth altogether heavie and massie, and yet notwithstanding.. hanged in yᵉ Aire. **1660** PEPYS *Diary* 26 Apr., It was very pleasant to observe the massy timbers that the ship is made of. **1775** A. M. TOPLADY *Let.* Wks. 1828 VI. 270 He hurled the massy folio at the poor bookseller's head. **1821** SCOTT *Kenilw.* vi, A massy oaken table. **1855** MACAULAY *Hist. Eng.* xiv. III. 422 The massy remains of the old Norman castle. **1871** R. ELLIS tr. *Catullus* lxiii. 40 The rude seas, earth's massy solidity.

b. Of architecture: Presenting great masses.

1819 SHELLEY *Let.* Pr. Wks. 1880 IV. 85 The proportions are extremely massy. **1846** GROTE *Greece* I. xx. (1862) I. 498 The massy and Cyclopian style of architecture employed in those early days.

3. Spreading in a mass or in masses; having considerable bulk or volume.

1672 MARVELL *Reh. Transp.* I. 68 Stragling by Temple-bar, in a massy Cassock and Surcingle. **1727–46** THOMSON *Summer* 669 Deep in the night the massy locust sheds Quench my hot limbs. **1812** BRACKENRIDGE *Views Louisiana* (1814) 112 The foliage of the corn is so rich and massy, that it shades the earth. *a* **1834** LAMB *Reynolds Gallery* Misc. Wks. (1871) 367 The long, graceful, massy fingers. **1839** ALISON *Hist. Europe* liv. §53 (1850) VIII. 610 Their infantry in four massy columns was observed to be descending.

b. Of persons and animals: Bulky, large-bodied.

c **1400** *Destr. Troy* 3885 He was massy & mekull, made for þe nonest. **1607** WALKINGTON *Opt. Glass* 11 The massier and more gyantly body must be maintained with large.. diet. *a* **1667** COWLEY *Ess.*, *Greatness*, He would have no Servants, but huge, massy Fellows. **1824** BYRON *Juan* XVI. lxxx, There were some massy members of the Church. **1849** H. MILLER *Footpr. Creat.* vi. (1874) 119 One of the massier fishes disporting amid the same four or five small ones. **1866** CARLYLE *Remin.* I. 255 A..massy, earnest, forcible-looking man.

4. *transf.* and *fig.* (of immaterial things).

1588 GREENE *Perimedes* G 2 b, She sits shrind in a Cannapie of Clouds, Whose massie darkenesse mazeth euery sense. **1645** MILTON *Tetrach.* Wks. 1851 IV. 215 The most grosse and massy paradox that ever did violence to reason and religion. **1663** BP. PATRICK *Parab. Pilgr.* ix. (1668) 46 How solid and massy those future enjoyments are. **1794** MRS. RADCLIFFE *Myst. Udolpho* viii, She turned her eyes from the massy darkness of the woods. **1822–56** DE QUINCEY *Confess.* (1862) 155 It cost eight-and-twenty massy hours for us..to reach the General Post-office. **1840** —— *Th. Grk. Trag.* Wks. IX. 72 The dialogue [of Greek tragedy] is always..severe, massy, simple.

5. *Comb.*, as ***massy proof*** adj.

1632 MILTON *Penseroso* 158 With antick Pillars massy proof. **1788** WARTON *Ode for New Year* 1 Rude was the pile, and massy proof.

massy, Eng. and U.S. dial. var. of MERCY *sb.* 4.

1817 A. ROYALL *Lett. from Alabama* (1830) ix. 22 Massy upon me! **1867** W. F. ROCK *Jim an' Nell* 31 Law! massy, Jim. **1884** J. C. EGERTON *Sussex Folk & Ways* 41 'Massy!' she said, 'the girls nowadays don't know naun about work!' **1905** *Dialect Notes* III. 17 *Massy sakes! sakes alive!* interj. All feminine exclamations. **1944** H. WENTWORTH *Amer. Dial. Dict.* 380/1 Massy = mercy.

massymore (mæsɪ'mɔə(r)). *Sc.* Also 8 **masmore**. [? ad. Sp. *mazmorra* dungeon: cf. MATTAMORE.] An alleged local term for a castle dungeon.

1789 GROSE *Antiq. Scotl.* I. *53 [Crighton Castle, Edinburghshire.] The dungeon called the Mas-More is a deep hole, with a narrow mouth. **1802** SCOTT *Minstr. Scott. Bord.* I. Introd. 79 *note*, One of the ancient lairds had imprisoned, in the Massy More, or dungeon of the castle, a person named Porteous. **1808** —— *Marm.* IV. xi, Crichtoun! ..still may we explore..The darkness of thy Massy More.

mast (mɑːst, -æ-), *sb.*¹ Forms: 1 **mæst**, 4–6 **maste**, 3– **mast**. [Com. Teut.: OE. *mæst* masc. = MDu., Du., OHG., MHG., mod.G. *mast*, Icel. *mastr*, Sw., Da. *mast*:—OTeut. **masto-z*:—W. Indo-germanic type **mazdo-s*, whence L. *mālus* (with the change of *d* to *l* frequent in L.).

The Teut. word appears in popular L. of the 8th c. as *mastus*, whence OF. *mast* (Fr. *mât*), Pr. *mast*, *mat*, Pg. *masto*, *mastro*.]

1. a. A long pole or spar of timber, iron or steel set up more or less perpendicularly upon the keel of a ship, to support the sails.

A ***pole-mast*** is made of one piece (see POLE), a ***made-mast*** of several pieces (see MADE 2 b). The larger masts are composed of several lengths, called ***lower mast***, TOP-MAST, TOPGALLANT-*mast* and ROYAL-*mast*. See also FOREMAST, MAINMAST, MIZZENMAST, *jigger-mast* (JIGGER *sb.*¹ 8); JURY-MAST, SPANKER-*mast*, etc.

Beowulf 1905 (Gr.) þa wæs be mæste merehræȝla sum, seȝl sale fæst. *c* **1205** LAY. 1100 Heo ræрden heora mastes, heo wunden up seiles. *c* **1300** *Havelok* 709 Hise ship he greyþede..an..þer-inne dide a ful god mast. *c* **1374** CHAUCER *Anel. & Arc.* 314 She that hem trustith shall hem fynde als faste As in a tempest is þe roton maste. *a* **1440** *Sir Eglam.* 1262 Sche askyth be what chesone he bare A schyp of golde, bothe maste and ore. **1590** SHAKS. *Com. Err.* I. i. 80 A small spare Mast, Such as sea-faring men prouide for stormes. **1642** HOWELL *For. Trav.* (Arb.) 71 To see..The New Towne of Amsterdam, and the Forrest of Masts, which lye perpetually before her. **1667** MILTON *P.L.* I. 293 The tallest Pine Hewn on Norwegian hills, to be the Mast Of some great Ammiral. **1834** LYTTON *Pompeii* I. ii, Afar off you saw the tall masts of the fleet.

transf. **1868** RUSKIN *Pol. Econ. Art* Add. 194 To look well at the beautiful circlet of the white nettle blossom, and work out..the way it is set on its central mast.

b. A piece of timber suitable for a mast. Now *spec.* (see quot. 1847). ***hand mast***: see HAND *sb.* 65.

1496 *Naval Acc. Hen. VII* (1896) 183, ij mastes to make a newe Mayne yarde for the seyd Ship. **1842** GWILT *Archit.* §1706 From Riga a great deal of timber is received under the name of masts and spars: the former are usually 70 or 80 feet in length, and from 18 to 25 inches in diameter; when of less diameter they take the latter name.

2. Phrases. ***afore*** or ***before the mast***: see AFORE B. 1, BEFORE 2 d. ***at the mast***: on deck by the mainmast (the usual place of assembly for public sale, conference, etc. on board ship). ***dolphin of the mast***: see DOLPHIN 6 b (*a*). ***to nail one's colours to the mast***: see COLOUR *sb.* 7 d. ***to spring, step a mast***: see SPRING, STEP *vbs.*

[**1626** CAPT. SMITH *Accid. Yng. Seamen* 6 The Lyer..is so proclaimed at the maine Mast by a generall cry, A lyer, a lyer, a lyer.] **1745** P THOMAS *Jrnl. Anson's Voy.* 273 We sold some of the Prize Goods..at the Mast, as it is called, or publick Auction.

3. A pole resembling the mast of a ship; *e.g.* the tall upright pole of a derrick or similar machine; a climbing pole in a gymnasium. Also used in various special senses (see quots.).

1646 EVELYN *Diary* (1879) I. 282 We passe by severall tall masts set up to guide travellers [in the Alps]. **1762** FRANKLIN *Lett.* Wks. 1840 V. 407 To secure a powder magazine from lightning I think they cannot do better than to erect a mast not far from it. **1880** *Encycl. Brit.* XI. 350/2 The horizontal bar, the bridge ladder..and the mast.. permit of a great variety of exercises. **1886** *Fortn. Rev.* Feb. 222 The vistas of lamp-posts, electric-light masts, and telegraph poles. **1910** *Flying in Bournemouth* (Souvenir Wallisdown Flying Whit-Week) 13 (*caption*) Mast with supporting wires. **1914** R. STANLEY *Text-bk. Wireless Telegr.* xiv. 189 The aerial to be supported by ten tubular steel masts each 300 feet high. **1918** E. S. FARROW *Dict. Mil. Terms* 371 *Mast*, in aëronautics, the upright part, usually extending upward from the center of a monoplane for support of controls and guy or truss wires; a vertical upright in the main or supplementary planes. **1920** [see HORN *sb.* 22 h]. **1924** *Harmsworth's Wireless Encycl.* II. 1409 *Mast*, term used in wireless work to describe generally any structure used to raise and support the aerial wires. **1931** D. ROSE *J. de la Cierva's Wings of Tomorrow* 110 A sort of whipping action of the rotor blades [of a helicopter] which jerked at the mast as they turned in their circle. **1956** W. A. HEFLIN *U.S. Air Force Dict.* 317/1 *Mast* n., 1. A spar for the support of an antenna. 2. A rotor mast... 3. In certain early airplanes, any of various vertical members used to hold guy wires or struts. **1966** *Listener* 1 Dec. 799/2 The German pavilion..is made of a semi-transparent plasticized fabric supported on a network of cables slung between a very few slender steel masts.

4. a. *attrib.* and *Comb.*, as ***mast-pole***, ***-top***; objective, as ***mast-maker***, ***-making***; instrumental, as ***mast-thronged*** adj.; similative, as ***mast-great***, ***-high***, ***-like*** adjs. and advs.

1600 FAIRFAX *Tasso* III. xvii, *Mast great the speare was which the gallant bore. **1798** COLERIDGE *Anc. Mar.* I. xiii, Ice *mast-high came floating by. **1855** KINGSLEY *Heroes* IV. ii. (1868) 124 He saw a heron come flying mast-high. **1807** J. BARLOW *Columb.* I. 787 Their cluster'd dates the *mast-like palms unfold. **1666** PEPYS *Diary* 10 Aug., Mr. Wood's son the *mast-maker. **1794** *Rigging & Seamanship* I. 13 The practice of *mastmaking. **1601** HOLLAND *Pliny* II. 511 That *Mast-poles comming thereof should be able to beare saile in wind and weather. **1647** TRAPP *Comm. Matt.* xxvi. 45 Will ye, with Solomon's drunkard, sleep upon a mast-pole? **1833** TENNYSON *Œnone* 116 Tax and toll, From many an inland town and haven large, *Mast-throng'd. **1871** R. ELLIS tr. *Catullus* Frag. v, Where yon lucent *mast-top [L. *carchesia*], a cup of silver, arises.

b. Special comb.: **mast-buoy**, one which carries a mast; **mast-cloth**, †(*a*) a piece of bunting placed for decoration on a mast (*obs.*); (*b*) see quot. 1794; **mast-coat** (see quot.); **mast-dock**, a dock in which vessels are fitted with masts; **mast-hole**, **-hoop** (see quots.); **mast-house**, a building in a dockyard in which masts are made and stored; **mast-leech**, the border or edge of a sail next the mast; **mast-lining** = *mast-cloth*; **mast-partner** (see quot.); **mast-pocket**, a socket for the mast of a derrick-crane; **mast-pond**, **-prop**, **-room** (see quots.); **mast-rope**, one for raising and lowering a mast; **mast-ship**, a ship which carries a store of masts; **mast-step**, a block fixed to the keelson into which the mast is set; **mast-tree**, a name given to certain tall erect trees (see quots.); †**mast-yard**¹, a yard of a mast; **mast-yard**², a yard in which masts are made.

1675 *Lond. Gaz.* No. 1005/4 A *Mast-Buoy to be laid on the West-side of a dangerous Rock. **1642** CHAS. I *Declar.* 12 *Aug.* 21 Lighters, and Long-boats..dressed up with *Mastclothes and Streamers. **1794** *Rigging & Seamanship* I. 88 *Mast-cloth*, the lining in the middle on the aft side of the topsails, to prevent the sail being chafed by the mast. *Ibid.* 170 **Mast-coats*, coverings made of well tarred canvas to prevent the water going down the mast-hole. **1689** *Lond. Gaz.* No. 2162/4 The *Crown* and the *St. Anthony*,..each lying in the *Mast-Dock at Deptford. **1867** SMYTH *Sailor's Word-bk.*, **Mast-holes*, the apertures in the deck-partners for stepping the masts. *Ibid.*, **Mast-hoops*, the iron hoops on made or built masts. **1770** *Ann. Reg.* 132 A fire..in the dock-yard..communicated itself..to the little *mast-house. **1794** *Rigging & Seamanship* I. 88 The curve on the *mast-leech of some fore and aft sails. **1886** *Encycl. Brit.* XXI. 154/2 Such pieces as *mast-lining clew and head, tack, and corner pieces. **1846–63** YOUNG *Naut. Dict.*, **Mast-partners*, pieces of timber let in between two of the beams to form a framing for the support of a vessel's masts. **1890** *Cent. Dict.* (citing *Car-Builder's Dict.*), **Mast-pocket.* **1769** FALCONER *Dict. Marine* II. (1780), *Fosse aux mâts*, a *mast-pond, or place where the masts are kept afloat in salt-water, in a dockyard. **1840** MARRYAT *Poor Jack* xxxviii, Our ship laid at the wharf, off the mast pond. **1805** *Shipwright's Vade-m.* 117 Large carlings which are placed at the sides of the *mast-rooms. *c* **1850** *Rudim. Navig.* (Weale) 131 *Mast-rooms*, the spaces between those beams where the masts are to be fixed. *a* **1000** *Cædmon's Exod.* 82 (Gr.) Swa þa *mæst-rapas men ne cuðon ne ða seȝlrode ȝeseon meahton. **1841** R. H. DANA *Seaman's Man.* 21 To send up a Topmast... Lash a top-block to the head of the lower-mast; reeve a mast-rope through it [etc.]. **1666** PEPYS *Diary* 29 Nov., Some..do fright us with the king of Sweden's seizing our *mast-ships at Gottenburgh. **1760** W. DOUGLASS *Brit. N. Amer.* II. 54 The mast ships built peculiarly for that use..carry from forty-five to fifty good masts per voyage. **1863** YOUNG *Naut. Dict.*, **Mast-step.* **1597** GERARDE *Herbal* III. xl. 1182 Abies: ..in English Firre tree, *Mast tree, and Deale tree. **1862** BALFOUR *Timber Trees India* (ed. 2) 127 *Guatteria longifolia* ..Mast tree. **1879** *Encycl. Brit.* IX. 405/1 The extensive forests [of Borneo]..produce..sago palm, and the mast (*Calophyllum*) and camphor trees (*Drabalonops*). *c* **1530** *Battle of Aginc.* A ij, These goodly shyppes lay there at rode, With *mast-yardes a crosse. **1765** *Ann. Reg.* 97 A *mast-yard adjoining to the river.

c. with prefixed numeral forming an adjectival compound with the sense 'having two (etc.) masts'.

1804 *Naval Chron.* XI. 456 A *Petiàugua*, a two-mast boat used by the Caribs.

mast (mɑːst, -æ-), *sb.*² Forms: 1, 3 **mæst**, 5–8 **maste**, 3– **mast**. *β.* 7 **maske**, 9 **mask**. [Com. WGer.: OE. *mæst* masc., MDu., MLG., OHG., MHG. *mast* masc., fem., neut. (mod.G. *mast*

fem.):—OTeut. type *masto-, -â; believed to represent a pre-Teut. *mazdo-:—maddo- (cf. Skr. *mēda* fat), f. OAryan root *mĕd-* 'to be fat, to flow', whence L. *madēre* to be wet, Goth. *mat-s* food (see MEAT).]

1. A collective name for the fruit of the beech, oak, chestnut, and other forest trees, esp. as food for swine. Rare in *pl.*

825 in Birch *Cart. Sax.* I. 536 Ðrim hunde swina mæst. *c* **1205** LAY. 21263 Al wæs þe king abolȝen swa bið þe wilde bar þenne he i þan mæste [*c* **1275** maste] monie swyn imeteþ. *c* **1374** CHAUCER *Former Age* 7 They eten mast hawes and swych pownage. **1523** FITZHERB. *Surv.* 8 Whanne there is any mast growyng in yᵉ lordes wodes. **1607** SHAKS. *Timon* IV. iii. 422 The Oakes beare Mast, the Briars Scarlet Heps. **1697** DRYDEN *Virg. Georg.* I. 10 Bacchus and fost'ring Ceres, Pow'rs Divine, Who gave us Corn for Mast, for Water Wine. **1726** SWIFT *Gulliver* III. v. 66 Acorns, Dates, Chesnuts, and other Maste..whereof these Animals are fondest. **1822** LAMB *Elia* Ser. I. *Roast Pig*, The swineherd, Ho-ti, having gone out into the woods..to collect mast for his hogs. **1824** LOUDON *Encycl. Gardening* (ed. 2) 977 Trees and Shrubs bearing Nuts, Acorns, Masts, Keys, etc. **1870** YEATS *Nat. Hist. Comm.* 87 Oak, beech, and chestnut fatten with their mast immense numbers of hogs.

β. **1640** FULLER *Joseph's Coat* 147 Like Hogs, eating up the Maske, not looking up to the hand that shaketh it downe. **1879** MISS JACKSON *Shropsh. Word-bk.*, *Mask..Mass*, acorns; mast. **1882** H. FRIEND *Devonsh. Plant-n.*, *Masks*, *Masts*, acorns. Also applied to the fruit of the Beech.

fig. *a* **1617** DONNE *Let.* Wks. 1839 VI. 369, I stand like a tree, which once a-year bears, though no fruit, yet this mast of children.

†**2.** The state or condition of feeding on mast. Only in phrases ***to lie at mast, to put to mast.*** *Obs.*

1620 MARKHAM *Farew. Husb.* xvii. 158 Now put your swine to mast. **1664** COTTON *Scarron.* 51 We were..sent.. To fetch a Sow that lies at Mast.

†**3.** *fig.* Luxurious or fattening food. *Obs.*

1575–85 ABP. SANDYS *Serm.* x. 157 He..feedeth still vpon his mast, and blesseth himselfe when hee waxeth fat. **1592** NASHE *P. Penilesse* 20 b, There is no mast like a Marchaunts table.

4. *attrib.* and *Comb.*: **a.** simple attrib, as ***mast hog, time***; **b.** objective, as ***mast-bearer***; ***mast-bearing*** adj.; **c.** instrumental, as ***mast-fed*** adj. Also **mast cell** [after G. *mastzelle*], one of the cells filled with basophile granules, found in the connective tissue and in foci of chronic inflammation (Gould *Dict. Med.* 1900); **mast-tree**, a tree producing mast (recent Dicts. explain it as 'cork-tree', app. after the OE. gloss '*suberies*, mæstentriow', Wr.-Wülck. 137/23); **mastwood** (see quot.); **mastworts** *pl.*, Lindley's name for the *Corylaceæ*; **mast year**, a year in which forest trees produce a good crop of fruit. Also MAST-HOLM.

1664 EVELYN *Sylva* 109 Where a single Tree is observ'd to be..a constant, and plentiful *Mast-bearer. **1610** HOLLAND *Camden's Brit.* II. 92 Woods of *Mast-bearing trees. **1898** *Allbutt's Syst. Med.* V. 638 Leucocytes with '*mast-cell' granules. **1899** *Ibid.* VIII. 472 Mast-cells are in no great abundance. **1566** DRANT *Horace, Sat.* iv. G viij b, *Mastefedde bores. **1843** 'R. CARLTON' *New Purchase* II. lvi. 246 It was *mast* fed, i.e. fed on acorns and beech nuts. **1851** C. CIST *Sk. Cincinnati in 1851* 284 Much the larger share of this, is..made of mast-fed and still-fed hogs. *c* **1440** *Promp. Parv.* 329/1 *Mast hog, ..*maialis.* **1682** S. WILSON *Acc. Carolina* 14 In the *Mast time they are very fat. **1577** B. GOOGE *Heresbach's Husb.* II. (1586) 101 The *mast trees [L. *glandiferas*], and such as serue for tymber. **1652** BLITH *Eng. Improv. Impr.* (ed. 3) 166 The Beech is also a mast-tree. **1864** GRISEBACH *Flora W. Ind.* 785 *Mast-wood, yellow, *Tobinia coriacea.* **1846** LINDLEY *Veg. Kingd.* 290 *Corylaceæ* —*Mastworts. **1744** W. ELLIS *Mod. Husbandman* (1750) VI. II. 89 Under these Trees, the Hogs generally get Pork in a *Maste-Year. **1760** W. DOUGLASS *Brit. N. Amer.* II. 375 Anno 1733, a good mast year, one man..salted up three thousand barrels of pork. **1927** *Forestry* I. 28 The rarity of full mast years and heavy weed growth are often held responsible for the failure of most attempts at natural regeneration of oak. **1953** H. L. EDLIN *Forester's Handbk.* ii. 30 But with many kinds [of trees] full seed crops are only found at intervals of three or four years—the *mast* years.

†**mast**, *sb.*[3] *Obs.* [? Corrupt form of MASS *sb.*[2] In quots. *c* 1420 and 1502 that word may be intended; in quot. 1502 the weight differs from that assigned in quot. 1674 to the 'mast'.] A weight (for certain articles of commerce) = 2½ lbs. Troy.

[*c* **1420** *Chron. Vilod.* 3493 He..come to Wiltone..And brouȝt wᵗ hym of wax a mast. **1502** *Will of Somer* (Somerset Ho.), A mast of corall weyng vjˡⁱ skant.] **1545** *Rates Custom-ho.*, Ambre the maste x.*ss.* Corall the mast xx.*ss.* **1674** JEAKE *Arith.* (1696) 73 Troy Weight hath seldom any greater denomination than the pound, yet sometime 2½ lb. thereof is called a Mast allowed for Amber and Gold and Silver Thread. **1706** PHILLIPS (ed. Kersey), *Mast of Amber*, the quantity of Two Pounds and a half Weight.

†**mast**, *sb.*[4], shortened form of MASTER.

Possibly merely a graphic abbreviation. But cf. MAS *sb.*[1] *c* **1460** *How Marchande dyd hys Wyfe betray* 59 in Hazl. *E.P.P.* I. 199 The marchandys man to hys mast dyd speke. *c* **1550** *John Bon & Mast Person* ibid. IV. 5 Nowe good morowe, mast Parson.

†**mast**, *sb.*[5] *Billiards. Obs.* [Corruption (by confusion with MAST *sb.*[1]) of F. *masse* MACE *sb.*[1]] A kind of heavy cue, of which the broad end was used for striking.

1731 *Gentl. Mag.* I. 268 The Capt. gave the Boy a blow on the head with his Billiard Mast. **1734** SEYMOUR *Compl. Gamester* III. (ed. 5) 73 Of Billiards. There is belonging to the Table an Ivory Port,..two small Ivory Balls and two Sticks (called Masts)... The Masts are made of..weighty Wood, which at the broad End are tipped with Ivory. **1784** COWPER *Task* IV. 221 A billiard mast Well does the work of his [*sc.* Time's] destructive scythe. [**1873**: see MACE *sb.*[1] 3.]

‖**mast** (mɑst), *sb.*[6] [Pers.] (See quots.)

1819 W. OUSELEY *Trav. East* I. vi. 268 Here also was abundance of *mâst*,..coagulated milk or clotted cream, slightly sour, which when diluted with water forms *âb i dûgh* ..a beverage in warm weather equally grateful and salubrious. **1933** *Discovery* Sept. 284/1, I was given *mast* or sour milk [in Persia]. **1963** *Times* 6 Feb. 12/6 Quantities of tea served in glasses and drunk, at any rate by the Iranians, with lots and lots of sugar and the local yoghourt, known as *mast.* **1968** C. RODEN *Bk. Middle Eastern Food* 60 Yoghourt is an essential part of the Middle Eastern diet... In Iran today it is known as *mâst.*

mast (mɑːst, -æ-), *v.*[1] [f. MAST *sb.*[1] Cf. OF. *master* (F. *mâter*).] *trans.* To furnish with masts.

1627 CAPT. SMITH *Seaman's Gram.* iii. 15 When a ship is built, she should be masted. **1682** S. WILSON *Acc. Carolina* 12 Pynes big enough to Mast the greatest Ships. **1705** *Lond. Gaz.* No. 4117/4 Directions to Build, Rigg, Yard, and Mast any Ship. **1813** HOBHOUSE *Journey* (ed. 2) 903 Engines for masting ships. **1856** T. GUTHRIE *Ezek.* 319 Here is a noble ship... The forests have masted her.

†**mast**, *v.*[2] *Obs.* Also 5 meyste. [OE. *mæstan* = OHG. *masten*, *mesten* (mod.G. *mästen*) Du. (*vet*)*mesten*:—WG. **mastjan*, f. **masto-* MAST *sb.*[2]]

1. *trans.* To feed (animals) on mast; to fatten.

c **974** in Birch *Cart. Sax.* III. 629 Ic wylle þæt man mæste minum wiue twa hund swyna. *c* **1440** *Promp. Parv.* 329/2 Mastyn beestys, *sagino.* *Ibid.* 334/2 Meysten, *idem quod* mastyn.

2. *transf.* To feed (oneself) gluttonously.

a **1560** BECON *Jewel of Joy* Wks. 1560 II. 9 b, The benefyced men..mastyng them selues lyke hogges of Epycurus flock. **1647** TRAPP *Marrow Gd. Auth.* in *Comm. Ep.* 613 Those greedy gully-guts, that..mast themselves like hogs.

mast, obs. form of MOST, MUST *v.*

‖**mastaba(h** (ˈmæstəbə). Also 7 mastabe. [Arab. *miç-*, *maçṭabaʰ* (of Pers. origin).]

1. A bench, seat.

1603 KNOLLES *Hist. Turks* (1621) 834 Sitting vpon a pallet, which the Turks call Mastabe. **1665** SIR T. HERBERT *Trav.* (1677) 175 At the upper end (surmounting the rest so much onely as two or three Mastaba's or white silken shags would elevate) sat the Pot-Shaw. **1687** A. LOVELL tr. *Thevenot's Trav.* II. 29 A Mastabe is a kind of a half pace, that's to say, that the Floor is raised two or three foot from the ground, and there the Travellers lodge.

2. An ancient Egyptian tomb, rectangular or square in plan, flat-topped, with sides sloping outward to the base. Also *attrib.* and *Comb.*

1882 *Nature* XXVI. 57 The mastabas were the mausolea of the richer and more important personages. **1883** V. STUART *Egypt* 469 Stone mastabahs with inscriptions. **1883** *Encycl. Brit.* XX. 122/2 They have been extended upwards and around into a great stepped mass of masonry.., the successive faces of which rise at the characteristic mastaba angle of 75°. **1931** G. A. REISNER *Mycerinus* i. 3 Some of the mastaba tombs also belonged to members of the royal family. **1932** *Times Lit. Suppl.* 26 May 389/1 The concession of the area of that pyramid and of large areas in the vast mastaba-field of Giza. **1936** *Ibid.* 13 June 501/1 Around the three great pyramids..are grouped..the *mastaba*-tombs of the nobles. **1952** E. B. GARSIDE tr. *Ceram's Gods, Graves, & Scholars* II. x. 120 A mastaba is an oblong structure with sloping sides containing cult rooms and connected by a shaft with a burial chamber in the rock beneath. **1964** W. L. GOODMAN *Hist. Woodworking Tools* IV. i. 160 The only tool shown in use on mastaba reliefs. *Ibid.*, This method of constructing the cabin or house with overlapping vertical boards may explain why the walls of the early mastaba tombs..show the deep recesses.

mastage (ˈmɑːstɪdʒ, -æ-). *Obs.* exc. *Hist.* [f. MAST *sb.*[2] or *v.*[2] + -AGE.] The fruit of forest-trees collectively: = MAST *sb.*[2] 1. Also, the right of feeding animals on mast.

1610 W. FOLKINGHAM *Art of Survey* I. vi. 13 What Trees, Plants, Shrubs: what Fruitage, Mastage, Gummage. **1762** tr. *Busching's Syst. Geog.* VI. 287 The mastage..from the oaks and beech. **1794** PRINGLE *Agric. Surv. Westmorland* 51 Regulations..full of the mention of forests, and chaces,.. and mastage, and pannage, and vert. **1881** *Cornh. Mag.* XLIV. 342 The English..divided out the land..with.. right of..mastage for so many swine in the woodlands.

‖**mastalgia** (mæˈstældʒɪə). *Path.* [mod.L., f. Gr. μαστός breast + -αλγία, ἄλγος pain.] Neuralgia of the breast.

1856 in MAYNE *Expos Lex.* In some recent Dicts.

†**mastard.** *Obs.* A stallion.

1598 *Ripon Corporation Rec.* 10 June, Whosoever hath any stoned horse or mastard uppon the Comons afforesaid.

‖**mastax** (ˈmæstæks). [mod.L. *mastax*, f. Gr. μάσταξ mouth.] (See quot. 1855.)

1855 GOSSE in *Phil. Trans.* CXLVI. 425, I propose then to appropriate to the sub-globose muscular bulb, which contains the manducatory organs in most Rotifera, the term *mastax.* **1877** HUXLEY *Anat. Inv. Anim.* iv. 187 At the bottom is a muscular pharynx, or mastax.

maste, mastecott, obs. ff. MOST, MASSICOT.

mastectomy (mæˈstɛktəmɪ). *Surg.* [f. Gr. μαστός breast + -ECTOMY.] Excision or amputation of a breast.

1923 in STEDMAN *Med. Dict.* (ed. 7). **1935** *Jrnl. Med. Assoc. Georgia* XXIV. 119 (*heading*) The seasponge as a postoperative dressing following radical mastectomy. **1973** M. J. BRENNAN in Holland & Frei *Cancer Med.* xxvii. 1777/1 Since skillful biopsy followed by a short wait before definitive treatment does not penalize results, there is no reason for immediate mastectomy when the frozen section does not give certain diagnosis.

masted (ˈmɑːstɪd, -æ-), *ppl. a.*[1] [f. MAST *v.*[1] or *sb.*[1] + -ED.]

1. Furnished with a mast or masts.

1627 CAPT. SMITH *Seaman's Gram.* ii. 15 If either too small or too short, she is vnder masted or low masted. **1725** DE FOE *Voy. round World* (1840) 100 A great heavy boat.. but ill masted. **1753** CHAMBERS *Cycl. Supp.* s.v., A ship is said to be *masted* when she has all her masts compleat. **1810** SCOTT *Lady of L.* II. xvi, Slow enlarging on the view Four manned and masted barges grew. **1836** MARRYAT *Midsh. Easy* xiii, A one-masted xebeque. **1877** *Daily News* 19 Oct. 5/3 There will not be another masted ironclad forthcoming for years.

2. Of a harbour, etc.: Thronged with masts.

1757 DYER *Fleece* III. 591 Our various hills and vales, Nowhere far distant from the masted wharf. **1882** J. HAWTHORNE *Fort. Fool* I. xviii, Away to the right might be discerned the..masted harbour of a town.

†**masted**, *ppl. a.*[2] *Obs.* In 5 mestyde, mastid, 7 mested. [f. MAST *v.*[2] + -ED[1].] Fed with mast, fatted.

c **1440** *Promp. Parv.* 151/2 Fat fowle, or beste, mestyde to be slayne, *altile.* *c* **1490** *Ibid.* 329/1 Mast hog (*MS. K.* mastid swyne), *maialis.* *a* **1622** AINSWORTH *Annot. Pentat.* Deut. xxxii. 24 *Burnt*..others translate it, filled or mested.

mastelyn(e, obs. forms of MASLIN.

master (ˈmɑːstə(r)), *sb.*[1] Forms: 1 **mægister, mæȝester, maȝister**, 2–3 **meistre**, 2–5 **meister**, 3 *Ormin* **maȝȝstre**, 3–5 **maystre**, 3–6 **maistre, mayster**, 3–7, 9 (*dial.*) **maister**, 4 **maystir, meyster, mesteir, maistere**, 4–5 **mastir, maystur**, 4–6 **maistir**, 5 **meistir, maistur, mastre, ma(y)styr, mastur**, 6 **muster, maiester**, 3 **master**. [ME. *meister*, *-tre*, *maister*, *-tre*, partly:—OE. *mæȝester*, *maȝister*, a. L. *magister*, *magistrum*, in vulgar Latin pronunciation (ˈmajɛstɛr, -tro), whence also OFris. *mâster*, *mêster*, OS. *mêster* (Du., LG. *meester*), OHG. (MHG., mod.G.) *meister*, ON. *meistare* (Sw. *mästare*, Da. *mester*); partly a. OF. *maistre* (mod.F. *maître*) = Pr. *magestre-s*, *maestre-s*, OSp. *mestro*, *-tre* (mod.Sp. *maestro*, *-tre*), Pg. *mestre*, It. *maestro*, *mastro*:—L. *magistr-um*, *magister* (in OLatin *magester*), related to *magis* adv., more, as the correlative *minister* (see MINISTER *sb.*) to *minus* less.]

I. A man having control or authority.

†**1. a.** *gen.* One having direction or control over the action of another or others; a director, leader, chief, commander; a ruler, governor. *Obs.*

c **1000** ÆLFRIC *Exod.* i. 11 Witudlice he sette him weorka mæȝestras [Vulg. *magistros operum*], þæt hiȝ ȝehyndon mid hefeȝum byrðenum. *c* **1175** *Lamb. Hom.* 43 And heore [the 12 'master devils'] aȝene pine neure nere þe lesse þah heo meistres weren. *a* **1240** *Wohunge* in *Cott. Hom.* 281 Hwen þu wes henged bituhhe twa þeofes, As hwa se seie, He þis is mare þen þeof, And for þi as hare meister he henges ham bituhhen. *c* **1250** *Gen. & Ex.* 4072 Ðe mestres of ðise hore-men. *a* **1300** *Cursor M.* 6408 Moyses þan cald sir iosue And mad him maister o þat semble. **13..** *Sir Beues* (MS. A) 1643 And, for is meisters [*i.e.* the two jailers] wer boþe ded, þre daies after he ne et no bred. *c* **1330** R. BRUNNE *Chron. Wace* (Rolls) 13084 þe Bretons..toke Preton, þe maister Romayn. *c* **1450** *Merlin* xxvii. 549 These foure hit herden that were maistris of the hoste and conditoures. **1596** DALRYMPLE tr. *Leslie's Hist. Scot.* I. 104 Quhen thay sett vpon the ennimie ..thay pas in ordour, following thair maistiris.

b. *transf.* (Chiefly of animals.)

1390 GOWER *Conf.* I. 197 The vessell..Which Maister was of al the Flete. **1588** SHAKS. *Tit. A.* v. i. 15 Like stinging Bees..Led by their Maister to the flowred fields. **1710** ROWE tr. *Lucan* IX. 1237 Some Master of the Herd, some mighty Bull. **1748** *Anson's Voy.* II. i. 121 The Master of the herd posted himself fronting the enemy, the rest of the goats being all behind him.

2. *spec.* (*Naut.*) **a.** The captain of a merchant vessel, called also *master mariner* (see MARINER 1 b); †in early use also *pl.*, ? the officers or the crew. **b.** The officer (ranking next below a lieutenant) entrusted with the navigation of a ship of war as distinguished from the commander of a ship during warlike operations. Subsequently styled *navigating officer* (Robinson *Brit. Fleet*, 1894, p. 406). †**c.** ***master and commander***: until 1814 the title of the officer in the navy since called COMMANDER. *Obs.*

c **1330** R. BRUNNE *Chron. Wace* (Rolls) 12085 þo maistres [*v.r.* mariners] þat were slie. *c* **1350** *Will. Palerne* 2744 þe maistres..manli in come, & faire at þe fulle flod þei ferden

to sayle. **1450** *Paston Lett.* I. 124 The maister of the Nicolas. **1553** CABOT *Ordinances* in *Hakluyt's Voy.* (1589) 259 The master and pilot of euery ship. *a* **1568** ASCHAM *Scholem.* I. (Arb.) 61 An vnhappie Master he is, that is made cunning by manie shippe wrakes. **1594** *1st Pt Content.* F 1 b, And then enter the Captaine of the ship and the Maister, and the Maisters Mate. **1610** SHAKS. *Temp.* II. ii. 48 The Master, the Swabber, the Boate-swaine & I. **1626** CAPT. SMITH *Accid. Yng. Seamen* 1 The Maister is to see to the cunning the Ship, and trimming the sailes. **1725** DE FOE *Voy. round World* (1840) 18 Our pilot, or master, as we called him. **1748** LIND *Lett. Navy* ii. (1757) 76 The master, and some other gentlemen of the Essex. **1801** NELSON in A. Duncan *Life* (1806) 198 Captain Bedford,..with Captain Gore,..offered their services to serve under a master and commander. **1849** MACAULAY *Hist. Eng.* iii. I. 303 The captain..treated the master with lordly contempt. **1860** *Reed's Guide Bk. Local Marine Bd. Exams.* 11 A Master must be twenty-one years of age. **1902** *Encycl. Brit.* XXXI. 775/1 Pilotage certificates may also be granted..to masters and mates of ships.

d. master's mate, an officer subordinate to but working with the master of a ship of war. Also *fig.*

1496 *Naval Acc. Hen. VII* (1896) 166 The Maisters mate & iiij quartermaisters. **1598** W. PHILLIP *Linschoten* I. iii. 4 The *Seto Piloto*, which is the Masters mate, hath 1200 reyes. **1642** FULLER *Holy & Prof. St.* IV. xvi. 322 It often hapning in Commonwealths, that the Masters mate steers the ship thereof, more then the Master himself. **1724** R. FALCONER *Voy.* (1769) 6 There's an excellent Master's Mate. **1836** MARRYAT *Midsh. Easy* xviii. 59 The worthy master's mate.

3. a. One who employs another in his service: correlative with *servant*, *man*; also with *apprentice*, where the original sense is that of branch II.

1362 LANGL. *P. Pl.* A. III. 211 Seruaunts..Takeþ Meede of heore Maystres. *c* **1386** CHAUCER *Cook's T.* 35 This ioly prentys with his maistir bood. *c* **1450** *Merlin* i. 3 The heirdes ..tolde their maister the mervelle. **1526** *Hundred Mery Tales* (1866) 146 Here is nother mayster nor man. **1596** SHAKS *Merch. V.* v. i. 47 My Master will be here ere morning. **1623** JAS. I in Rushw. *Hist. Coll.* (1659) I. 127 He is a happy man that serves a good Master. **1711** STEELE *Spect.* No. 107 ¶1 The general Corruption of Manners in Servants is owing to the conduct of Masters. **1728** SWIFT *My Lady's Lament.* 174 Who's master, who's man. **1765** BLACKSTONE *Comm.* I. xiv. 416 A Master may by law correct his apprentice. **1835** URE *Philos. Manuf.* 319 List of Prices ..as agreed to by Masters and Men. **1843** CARLYLE *Past & Pr.* II. x, Continued vigilance, rigorous method, what we call 'the eye of the master', work wonders. **1843** BORROW *Bible in Spain* xxxiv, I have lived in many houses and served many masters. **1880** MCCARTHY *Own Time* IV. liv. 171 The masters and the workmen.

b. *Proverbs.*

1548 [see LIKE *a.* 2 d]. **1554** in Strype *Eccl. Mem.* (1721) III. xxiii. 190 The old proverbe is true..'such a master, such a servant'. **1655** FULLER *Ch. Hist.* IX. vi. §34 He crossed the Proverb, *like Master, like Man*, the Patron being Cruel, the Chaplain Kinde. **1665** BOYLE *Occas. Refl.* IV. viii. (1848) 218 Fire and Water, they cannot be so good Servants, but that they are worse Masters. **1692** R. L'ESTRANGE *Fables* xxxviii. 38 Fire and Water,..are Good Servants, but Bad Masters.

c. Applied to a sovereign in relation to his ministers or officers. Now chiefly *Hist.*

1470–85 MALORY *Arthur* IV. xxiii. 151 The woful knyghte told her how his mayster and lorde was bitrayed. **1596** DALRYMPLE tr. *Leslie's Hist. Scot.* I. 96 Thay ar bent mair willinglie..gif thair maistir commande thame, to seditione. **1601** SHAKS. *All's Well* IV. v. 75 The King my master. **1611** BIBLE *1 Sam.* xxiv. 6 The Lord forbid that I should doe this thing vnto my master the Lords Anoynted. **1612** BACON *Ess., Fortune* (Arb.) 379 Extreme Louers of their Country, or Masters, were neuer fortunate. **1712** SWIFT *Jrnl. to Stella* 21 Dec., The Spanish Ambassador desired him to tell me that his master, and the King of France..were more obliged to me than any man in Europe. **1885** LOWE *Bismarck* I. 396 M. le Comte Benedetti, French Ambassador at Berlin.. sped to Vienna with the latest proposal of his master.

d. In public school use: The boy whom another serves as a fag.

1833 LYTTON *Eng. & Engl.* (ed. 2) II. 108 The fag loathed his master. **1863** [HEMYNG] *Eton School Days* iv. (1864) 42 College rolls..were never so tempting to me when I had been to get them for my 'master'.

4. a. The owner of a living creature, as a dog, horse, slave; also, the man whom an animal is accustomed to obey. Also in *fig.* context.

14.. *Sir Beues* (MS. M.) 3758 Stedis..With oute maisters. *c* **1440** *Alphabet of Tales* 188 þe hunde..gruchid not to be burnyd with his maister bodie. **1535** COVERDALE *Isa.* i. 3 An oxe knoweth his lorde and an Asse his masters stall. **1611** SHAKS. *Wint. T.* I. ii. 157 My Dagger muzzel'd, Lest it should bite its Master. **1718** PRIOR *Solomon* II. 424 Till the lov'd dog [should] declare his master near. **1788** COWPER *Negro's Complaint* iii, Think, ye masters iron-hearted. **1833** WHITTIER *Abolitionists* Pr. Wks. 1889 III. 64 A majority of the masters..are disposed to treat their.. slaves with kindness. **1863** WOOLNER *My Beautiful Lady* 64 An unruly horse Checked by a master's hand. **1884** 'RITA' *My Lord Conceit* I. III. iii. 297 The little dog..sat..looking as if he were holding a court-martial upon the proceedings of his two little masters.

Proverb. **1605** CAMDEN *Rem., Prov.* (1614) 313 The Maisters eye maketh the horse fat.

b. *his* (or *her*, *my*, etc.) *master's voice*, a catch-phrase, originating from the trade name of a gramophone record company, denoting, freq. ironically, the voice of authority.

[**1910** *Trade Marks Jrnl.* 5 Oct. 1604 His Master's Voice.... Talking machines, talking machine needles, talking machine records and other talking machine accessories,..The Gramophone Company, Limited,.. London,..manufacturers.] **1922** M. A. VON ARNIM *Enchanted April* xviii. 297 'Francesca!' shouted Briggs. She came running... 'Her Master's Voice,' remarked Mr. Wilkins. **1922** JOYCE *Ulysses* 465 My master's voice. **1969** 'H. PENTECOST' *Girl with Six Fingers* (1970) I. iv. 68 'He —he'd hesitate to do anything that would displease Angela.' 'Not when he hears his master's voice,' said Jericho. **1972** R. QUILTY *Tenth Session* 42 Bank's personal secretary.. announced..that the doctor would like to see Angus in his office... 'His master's voice,' he informed Norman.

5. a. The male head of a house or household.

1536 in Ellis *Orig. Lett.* Ser. II. II. 80 Mr. Shelton saythe he es Master of thys Hows. **1577–87** HOLINSHED *Hist. Scot.* 278/1 The people generallie lamenting his death with no lesse sorow..than as is seene in a priuat house for the deceasse of the welbeloued maister and owner thereof. **1611** BIBLE *Exod.* xxii. 8 The master of the house shall be brought vnto the Iudges. **1651** BAXTER *Saints' R.* (ed. 2) III. xiii. §11 The last whom I would perswade to this great Work..is Parents, and Masters of Families. **1709** STEELE *Tatler* No. 82 ¶4 The Master of a Family that wholly depended upon his Life. **1797** *Encycl. Brit.* (ed. 3) X. 309/1 As a husband, a father, or the master of a family, he was as nearly faultless as the imperfections of humanity will easily permit. **1798** *Monthly Mag.* V. 395 Mr. Munday, late master of the Falstaff inn. **1841** LANE *Arab. Nts.* I. 123 The master of the house begins first.

b. With possessive adj.: (One's) husband. *dial.*

c **1400** *Destr. Troy* 8430 A fuerse dreme, That she met of hir maister. **1459** *Paston Lett.* I. 435 As for my mayster, my best beloved that ye call. **1852** DICKENS *Bleak Ho.* viii, I'm a-watching for my master. **1879** J. FOTHERGILL *Probation* I. xix, A rough 'measter' to make and mend and 'do' for.

6. A possessor, owner. Now *rare*, exc. in the phrase *to be master of*: to possess, have at one's disposal (now usually, some immaterial thing); often, with approach to sense 15, to have a 'mastery' or thorough knowledge of (a subject).

c **1400** *Apol. Loll.* 55 Wen..þei are opunly maistris of alle iuelis, how are þey not heretyks? *a* **1450** *Knt. de la Tour* (1868) 58 Whanne that two vices be sette one euelle delite, gladly they bringe her maister into temptacion. **1456** SIR G. HAYE *Law Arms* (S.T.S.) 178 How suld thai be callit sauf condytis, bot gif thai condyte thair maisteris saufly? **1484** CAXTON *Fables of Æsop* III. vi, Synne retorneth euer vpon his mayster. **1563** B. GOOGE *Sonn.* (Arb.) 97 Eche Torment ..Lyght here vpon this cursed hand..And plague the part that durst presume his Mayster to disgrace. **1604** E. G[RIMSTONE] *D'Acosta's Hist. Indies* IV. viii. 229 Divers mines which are..divided betwixt divers Masters. **1607** DEKKER & WEBSTER *Northw. Hoe* IV. i. Wks. 1873 III. 45 Clothes sometimes are better Gentlemen than their Masters. **1608** *Merry Devil of Edmonton* (1631) 9 To see if he could finde the Maister of the tongue that called him. *a* **1715** BURNET *Own Time* (1724) II. 353 Some houses fell and crushed their Masters to death. **1726** SWIFT *Gulliver* II. vi, Those..qualities of mind that he was master of. **1785** TRUSLER *Mod. Times* III. 29, I was master of more than twenty pounds. **1787** 'G. GAMBADO' *Acad. Horsemen* (1809) 21 Scarce one of them [dray-horses] but is master of thirty stone or upwards. **1818** CRUISE *Digest* (ed. 2) III. 19 Judgement and discretion, which an infant was not master of. **1853** 'C. BEDE' *Verdant Green* I. iv, Mr. Filcher was laden with coats and boots that had just been brushed and blacked for their respective masters.

7. a. One who has the power to control, use, or dispose of something at will. Chiefly *predicative.*

a **1340** HAMPOLE *Psalter* xvii. 47 God makis vs maysters of vices. *c* **1400** *Gamelyn* 314 We wiln be maistres heer. *c* **1470** HENRY *Wallace* I. 131 Quhar that stayne is, Scottis suld mastir be. **1500–20** DUNBAR *Poems* xli. 13 Be now and ay the maistir of 3our will. *c* **1510** MORE *Picus* Wks. 5/2 He was his owne maister. **1542** UDALL *Erasm. Apoph.* 290 b, To be myne owne maister. **1600** HOLLAND *Livy* 444 They saw the enemies maisters of the land. **1601** R. JOHNSON *Kingd. & Commw.* (1603) 48 No man is maister of himselfe. **1606** SHAKS *Tr. & Cr.* V. x. 1 Yet are we maisters of the field. **1670** COTTON *Espernon* I. I. 43 To make themselves Maisters of Affairs. **1693** *Humours Town* A v, The Master of my own Time. *Ibid.* 39 Ev'ry Woman that will make a Man Master of her Person..makes him Master of her Purse. **1697** DRYDEN *Virg. Georg.* IV. 709 Th' unwary Lover cast his Eyes behind, Forgetful of the Law, nor Master of his Mind. **1706** E. WARD *Wooden World Diss.* (1708) 102 It would be a..scandal to him to go off Master of his Legs. **1768** *Ann. Reg., Char.* (1786) 29/1 Master of the Queen's soul, which he guided as he pleased; [etc.]. **1782** PRIESTLEY *Corrupt. Chr.* II. x. 262 The bishops were almost masters..of France and Germany. **1790** BURKE *Fr. Rev.* 318 The person who really commands the army is your master; the master (that is little) of your king, the master of your Assembly, the master of your whole republick. **1872** YEATS *Growth Comm.* 100 You will become masters of all the gold in Christendom. **1874** GREEN *Short Hist.* vii. §6. 410 To secure a landing at all, the Spaniards had to be masters of the Channel. **1891** *Law Rep., Weekly Notes* 200/1 The tenant for life was master of the situation. **1904** *People* 4 Dec. 17/7 Two..cart horses; suitable for coal or timber merchants; master of two tons.

b. *transf.* of things more or less personified.

1362 LANGL. *P. Pl.* A. III. 162 Such a Mayster is Meede A-Mong Men of goode. **1390** GOWER *Conf.* I. 42 Love is maister wher he wile. **1591** SHAKS. *Two Gent.* I. i. 39 Loue is your master. **1633** BP. HALL *Occas. Medit.* (1851) 114 An honest man's word must be his master. **1678–9** DRYDEN & LEE *Œdipus* I. i, But it's a hard world, neighbours, If a man's oath must be his master. **1797** GODWIN *Enquirer* I. vi. 44 Language is not his master, but he is the master of language. **1873** BRIDGES *Poems, Triolet*, When first we met we did not guess That Love would prove so hard a master.

¶ **c.** *to be master*: to be free to do as one pleases (in a specified matter). [A Gallicism.]

1752 CHESTERF. *Lett.* (1792) III. cclxxxv. 304 Would you saunter at some of the small courts, as Brunswick..? You are master.

8. One who overcomes another, a victor.

c **1290** *S. Eng. Leg.* I. 11/342 With þis signe þou schalt maister beo. *a* **1400** *Octavian* 923 The people to the wallys can go To see the batelle betwene them two..hys fadur, wo was he Tylle he wyste whych schulde maystyr be. **15..** *Smyth & Dame* 159 in Hazl. *E.P.P.* III. 207 Than our Lorde gan say,..Smyth,..Thy mayster thov me call. **1557** BARCLAY tr. *Sallust* 84 b, Him which is strongest and is maister hauynge the vpper hand. **1864** TENNYSON *En. Ard.* 31 If they quarrell'd, Enoch stronger-made Was master.

9. *Bowls.* [Short for *master bowl.*] A small bowl placed as a mark for the players to aim at; = JACK *sb.*[1] 18. (Cf. MISTRESS.)

1530 PALSGR. 478/1 Who shall caste the mayster boule? **1579** GOSSON *Sch. Abuse* (Arb.) 60 At Bowles euery one craues to kisse the maister. **1600** HEYWOOD *2nd Pt. Edw. IV*, IV. iii, This cheese shall be the maister.

10. a. An original disc (†or cylinder) with grooves cut by a stylus during recording. **b.** (Also *master matrix.*) A disc with ridges in place of grooves that is made from the plating of an electroplated original and is used as a stamper or (more usually) to make a 'mother'.

1904 S. R. BOTTONE *Talking Machines & Records* 69 With the master running in the phonograph, the trained ears of the specialists enable them to detect the most minute imperfections. **1908** *Daily Chron.* 29 Oct. 7/1 A special room is devoted to recording, or making the master from which copies are to be taken. **1918** H. SEYMOUR *Reproduction of Sound* 68 The original master is recorded by means of a feed thread... This is thereupon electro-typed—that is, a metallic negative is grown upon it, and this is called the master matrix. A small number of casts in wax are made from this... These are similarly electro-typed, and become the working matrices. **1935** H. C. BRYSON *Gramophone Record* vi. 130 (*caption*) Stripping copper masters from the wax. *Ibid.* 142 The wax is positive, the copper master is negative, the mother is positive, the stamper is negative, and the record produced from it is therefore positive and will play on a gramophone. **1952** GODFREY & AMOS *Sound Recording & Reproduction* v. 139 Only one master can be prepared from a wax original.., but more than one master can sometimes be made from a lacquer-coated disk. **1962** A. NISBETT *Technique Sound Studio* 259 The master has ridges instead of grooves. In half processing (when only a small run is required) the master is also used as a stamper. **1972** *Jazz & Blues* Oct. 29/2 The final batch of King Jazz recordings were done in 12" masters.

c. (See quot. 1958.)

1930 W. DESBOROUGH *Duplicating & Copying Processes* iii. 21 The master is produced in negative or mirror form by placing the face of a special hekto carbon at the back of the sheet of paper on which the master is to be made. **1957** G. W. W. STEVENS *Microphotogr.* xi. 213 The time and care expended on a master negative give it considerable value.. therefore..it is advisable to make at least two masters, once the camera has been set up. **1958** T. LANDAU *Encycl. Librarianship* 204/2 *Master*, the original plate or stencil in duplicating processes from which copies are made. In photocopying, the negative from which a positive print is made. **1971** R. BUSBY *Deadlock* iv. 39 Could you make that four copies?.. You'll need two for the index apart from this master.

II. A teacher; one qualified to teach.

11. A man to whose care a child or children are committed for purposes of instruction; a tutor, preceptor; in later use chiefly a teacher in a school, a schoolmaster; also, a professional teacher of some special subject, as an art or a language.

c **888** K. ÆLFRED *Boeth.* xxix. §2 Se unrihtwisa Neron wolde hatan his agenne magister [orig. *præceptoremque suum*] ..acwellan. *a* **1225** *Ancr. R.* 64 Sum is so wel ilered..þet heo wolde þet he wuste hit; þe sit & spekeð..& bicumeð meister, þe schulde beon ancre. **13..** *K. Alis.* 665 The sevethen maister taught his pars. **1387** TREVISA *Higden* (Rolls) VI. 435 þe childes maister siʒ þat, and slow þe sewere anon. *c* **1430** LYDG. *Min. Poems* (Percy Soc.) 185 It sittethe a maister..at large to teche his lesson. **1596** DALRYMPLE tr. *Leslie's Hist. Scot.* VIII. 126 He..was elected maister to the prince. **1599** SHAKS., etc. *Pass. Pilgr.* xv, It was a Lording's daughter..That liked of her maister as well as well might be. **1694** BOYER (*title*) The compleat French-master. A short grammar, [etc.]. **1711** STEELE *Spect.* No. 168 ¶3, I was bred myself, Sir, in a very great School, of which the Master was a Welchman. **1770** GOLDSM. *Des. Vill.* 196 The village master taught his little school. **1856** (*title*) French in a fortnight without a Master. **1867** C. S. PARKER in *Quest. Reformed Parl.* 164 Without consulting the vicar, he dismisses the certificated master.

12. He whose disciple one is; the teacher (in religion, philosophy, art, science, or scholarship) from whom one has chiefly learned, or whose doctrines one accepts. *the* (*our*, *my*, *his*, etc.) *Master*: often applied to Christ, with mixture of sense 3.

c **1200** ORMIN 12898 Þatt ta twa Lerninngcnihhtess Herrdenn whatt teʒʒre maʒʒstre spacc Off Christ [etc.]. *a* **1300** *Cursor M.* 20915 His maister..And he aght noght haf al a dome, For he was noght worþi þer-till. **1382** WYCLIF *John* iii. 10 Art thou a maistir in Israel, and knowist not thes thingis? **1412–20** LYDG. *Troy-bk.* end (Schick), My maister Chaucer. **1529** MORE *Dyaloge* II. Wks. 179/2 Yet bee there not onely as many sectes almoste as men, but also the maisters them selfe chaunge theyr mindes and theyr oppynions euery daye. **1533** GAU *Richt Vay* (1888) 25 We neid noder to seik or leir of oder vane maisters quhat guid warkis we suld dw. **1629** MURE *True Crucifix* 3125 With hearts right set, their Maister's will to know. **1748** THOMSON *Cast. Indol.* II. lii, Ne had my master Spenser charmed his Mulla's plains. **1771** BURKE *Corr.* (1844) I. 284 The advice of one of our great masters in the science of life and morals. **1827** WILLIS *Healing Daughter Jairus* 57 Closer drew The twelve disciples to their Master's side. **1843** BORROW *Bible in Spain* xxxviii, Why should I be ashamed of their company when my Master mingled with publicans and thieves? **1904** SAINTSBURY *Hist. Crit.* III. 427 John Keats..and his master Leigh Hunt.

†**13. a.** A man of approved learning, a scholar of authority. *Obs.*

a **1225** *Leg. Kath.* 120 Modi meistres & fele fondeden hire ofte o swiðe fele halue, for to undernimen hire. *a* **1300** *Cursor M.* 11462 And did he suith to samen call þe maisters

of his kingrik all, And fraind at þaim if þai wist, Quar suld he be born, þat crist. **1377** LANGL. *P. Pl.* B. x. 384 Maistres þat of goddis mercy techen men and prechen. **1456** SIR G. HAYE *Law Arms* (S.T.S.) 179 And as for me and othir maisteris and doctouris, me think this the rycht oppin. **1597** HOOKER *Eccl. Pol.* v. lxxviii. §1 Terming..Scribes and interpreters of the law, Masters.

b. ***Master of the Sentences*** (*magister sententiarum*), the name given to Peter Lombard, Bishop of Paris in the 12th c., from his book *Sententiarum libri quatuor*, a collection of patristic comments on passages of Holy Scripture. ***Master of Stories*** (*magister in historiis*), a name given to Petrus Comestor, from his work called *Historia Scholastica*.

c **1380** WYCLIF *Wks.* (1880) 2 [Of the Essenes] spekeþ þe maister of stories. **1387** TREVISA *Higden* (Rolls) VIII. 43 He wroot aȝenst þe maister of þe sentence [**1432–50** sentencez]. **1398** —— *Barth. De P.R.* XIII. xii, As yᵉ mayster sayth in Historiis. **1594** HOOKER *Eccl. Pol.* VI. vi. 8. **1605** BACON *Adv. Learn.* II. xxv. §11 The first writings of the fathers, whence the Master of the Sentences made his sum.

14. In academic sense, = med.L. *magister*: One who has received a specific degree, originally conveying authority to teach in the university. In English use before the 19th c. confined to the Faculty of Arts (the corresponding title in the other faculties being *doctor*): the full designation of the graduate is in L. *artium magister*, in Eng. ***Master of Arts*** (formerly †*of Art*), denoted by the abbreviation M.A. or (now rarely, exc. in the U.S.) A.M. In more recent times the degrees of ***Master of Science*** (M.Sc.), ***Master in*** or ***of Surgery*** (*Magister Chirurgiæ*, M.Ch.), etc. have also been awarded.

Master of Divinity, Theology (*obs.* exc. *Hist.*), titles belonging to graduates of certain continental universities.

138. WYCLIF *Sel. Wks.* III. 376 Capped freris, þat ben calde maystres of dyvynite. *c* **1400** *Rom. Rose* 6553 The maistres of divinitee Somtyme in Paris. *c* **1425** [see ART *sb.* 7]. **1484** CAXTON *Fables of Poge* ad fin., There were duellynge in Oxenford two prestes bothe maystres of arte. **1494**, **1604** [see REGENT *sb.* 3a]. **1573** G. HARVEY *Letter-bk.* (Camden) 2 This is mi year to commens master in. *a* **1661** FULLER *Worthies* I. (1662) 150 A Boisten horse and a Cambridge Master of Art, are a couple of Creatures that will give way to nobody. **1709** STEELE *Tatler* No. 39 ¶4 Being a Master of Arts of Oxford. **1847** PRESCOTT *Peru* (1855) II. v. i. 215 He [Pedro de la Gasca] received the degree of Master of Theology. **1853** 'C. BEDE' *Verdant Green* I. iv, Please not to walk on the grass, sir; there's a fine agen it, unless you're a Master. **1888** *Encycl. Brit.* XXIII. 835/1 It is in this licence [*licentia docendi*] that the whole significance of the master of arts degree is contained. *Ibid.* 835/2 'Regents', that is, masters actively engaged in teaching. **1900** *Oxford Univ. Calend.* 71 Fees... Before the Examination for the Degree of Master of Surgery, £5.

15. a. Originally, a workman who is qualified by training and experience to teach apprentices and to carry on his trade on his own account. (Chiefly in appositional combs., as *master carpenter* etc., for which see 25d.) Hence, (*a*) a workman who is in business on his own account, as distinguished from a journeyman; in modern use merged in sense 3; (*b*) a workman of approved skill, one who thoroughly knows his trade; also *transf.* and *fig.*

c **1400** *Destr. Troy* 8733 Þo maisturs gert make a meruelous toumbe. *c* **1489** CAXTON *Sonnes of Aymon* x. 265, I sholde goo gyve you suche a stroke..that ye sholde saye it is a stroke of a maister. **1585** T. WASHINGTON tr. *Nicholay's Voy.* IV. xxiv. 140 An ingenious maister..proposed vnto him [Alexander] that..he would make to be cut in humain figure, the mount of Athos. **1693** *Humours Town* 35 Masters in their Profession. **1706** E. WARD *Wooden World Diss.* (1708) 27 In this kind of Billingsgate Clashing he's a much greater Master, than [etc.]. **1759** JOHNSON *Rasselas* vi. (1893) 50 He..found the master busy in building a sailing chariot. **1829** SOUTHEY *Sir T. More* II. 174 A craft in which any one may commence master, without having served an apprenticeship.

†**b.** Used predicatively without article (quasi-*adj.*) with the sense 'highly skilled'. Const. *inf.*

1297 R. GLOUC. (Rolls) 9325 Mayster he is to bitraye, is word is al falshede. *c* **1375** *Sc. Leg. Saints* xix. (*Cristofore*) 84 Þe dewil is mare master þan þu. *c* **1489** CAXTON *Sonnes of Aymon* xxiv. 499, I am mayster for to begge brede. **1642** FULLER *Holy & Prof. St.* v. vii. 387 He was a man master in the art of dissembling. **1722** RAMSAY *Monk & Miller's Wife* 137 Think ye..his gentle stamock's master To worry up a pint of plaister.

16. a. An artist of distinguished skill, one of those who are regarded as models of excellence in their art. ***old master***: a 'master' who lived before the period accounted 'modern'; chiefly applied to painters from the 13th to the 16th or 17th century.

1533, **1651** [see FENCE *sb.* 2]. **1598** R. HAYDOCKE tr. *Lomazzo's Art Paint.* I. 23 Raphaell, Perino del Vaga,..and all other famous Maisters. **1622** PEACHAM *Compl. Gent.* xi. 102 Peter Phillips,..now one of the greatest Masters of Musicke in Europe. **1662** EVELYN *Chalcogr.* 36 Albert Durer [at the age of 10–14] performing such things as might shame most of the best Masters. **1703** ROWE *Fair Penit.* II. i. 530 Let the Master touch The sprightly String. **1711** ADDISON *Spect.* No. 129 ¶1 Great Masters in Painting never care for drawing People in the Fashion. **1747** J. GODFREY *Sci. Defence* 18, I have now done with the Small-Sword, and shall only do Justice to the Merits of two or three Masters. **1757** GRAY *Bard* 21 With a Master's hand, and Prophet's fire. **1797** *Encycl. Brit.* (ed. 3) XIII. 609/1 The observations of ancient authors on the best paintings of the ancient masters. *Ibid.* 615/2 A painter ought attentively to consider ..all the different styles of the great masters. **1840** *Penny Cycl.* XVII. 145/2 As a painter of animals, Edwin Landseer far surpasses any of the old masters. **1841–4** EMERSON *Ess.*, *Art* Wks. (Bohn) I. 149 The pictures of the Tuscan and Venetian masters. **1869** 'MARK TWAIN' *Innoc. Abr.* 260 Who painted these things? Why, Titian..Raphael—none other than the world's idols, the 'old masters'. **1870** B. HARTE *Dickens in Camp* iv, He read aloud the book wherein the Master Had writ of 'Little Nell'. **1889** G. B. SHAW in *Hawk* 13 Aug. 172/2 Behind the Master's house is the Master's grave; for Wagner..is 'buried in the back garden, sir, like a Newfoundland dog'. **1897** MRS. LYNN LINTON *Geo. Eliot* in *Women Novelists* 101 A task beyond the power of any but the few Masters of our literature. **1908** *Pop. Mechanics* Nov. 741/2 A Munich artist and inventor has devised an electric machine by which the famous paintings of the 'old masters' can be renewed. **1937** H. G. WELLS *Camford Visitation* v. 58 All his fancied novelties of criticism were fully foreseen by the Master [*sc.* Karl Marx]. **1959** *Times* 20 Aug. 9/5 In calling the anonymous hero of *The Aspern Papers* 'H. J.' I may have misled a few people into thinking that I have attempted to make 'the publishing scoundrel' into a portrait of 'The Master'. **1962** *Listener* 14 June 1043/3 The style, a pastiche of Nabokov's..is a style less functional, more baroque, than the Master's.

b. Used for: A work (of painting or sculpture) by a master. Now only with qualification, as ***old master***, and occasionally ***modern master***. ***The Old Masters***: the name given to the annual Winter Exhibition of the Royal Academy from the name of the first exhibition (1870), 'Exhibition of the Works of the Old Masters'.

[**1694** DRYDEN *Sir G. Kneller* 141 Those masters, then but seen, not understood, With generous emulation fired thy blood.] **1752** FOOTE *Taste* II. Wks. 1799 I. 18 'Tis a thousand pities that any of these masters should quit England. **1824** J. FISHER *Let.* 18 Jan. in C. R. Leslie *Mem. Life J. Constable* (1845) viii. 130, I am shut up in lodgings here,—the walls covered with *old masters*. **1851** D. JERROLD *St. Giles* xxviii. 287 As a picture-dealer stares at an alleged old master. **1861** G. MEREDITH *Let.* 19 Nov. (1970) I. 111 He is in new chambers full of pictures, Old Masters, we hear. **1870** *Times* 3 Jan. 5/1 Exhibition of old masters at the Royal Academy. The noble new rooms of the Royal Academy..the place of exhibition of a selection from the finest works of the old masters in English private galleries, opened..for the public today. **1880** GEO. ELIOT *Let.* 5 Feb. (1956) VII. 248 If you had come to town you would have liked to see..the Old Masters at the Academy but perhaps you may yet come before they are removed. **1890** G. B. SHAW *London Music in 1888–89* (1937) 284 My ticket for the Press view at the Old Masters on Friday! **1908** *Outlook* 19 Dec. 848/2 The disappointment at the prospect of no Old Masters exhibition this winter is barely mitigated by the *menu* of the banquet provided by the McCulloch collection. **1968** S. C. HUTCHISON *Hist. R. Acad.* xiii. 141 The Old Masters Exhibition of 1879 was conceived on a much larger scale than its forerunners and occupied nine galleries. **1975** *Times* 23 June 12 The value of Old Masters is perhaps more subjectively determined than in any other field... The Old Master market has been very strong in the 1970s.

c. *spec.* in *Chess.* Cf. *chess-master*, GRAND MASTER 4.

1852 H. STAUNTON *Chess Tournament* p. l, To reward the ability of first-rate masters throughout the world, they offered..prizes. **1910** *Encycl. Brit.* VI. 104/1 The terms *master* and *amateur* are not used in any invidious sense, but simply as designating, in the former case, first-class players, and in the latter, those just on the borderland of highest excellence. **1969** *Times* 25 Jan. 17/7 There are three types of F.I.D.E. master title: international grand-master, international master, and international woman master. **1973** *Daily Tel.* 25 Apr. 16/3 After six of the 11 rounds of the Birmingham International Chess Tournament, Tony J. Miles, 18, the Birmingham schoolboy, still leads the mixed concourse (one grand master, several international masters, candidate masters and others). **1973** *Sci. Amer.* June 93/2 Kalme is a senior master with a rating of 2,455 on the International Chess Federation scale, on which 2,200 denotes a master and Fischer's rating is 2,785.

III. As a specific title of office.

17. The head or presiding officer of many societies or institutions: e.g. of certain colleges (in Oxford, Cambridge, and elsewhere), guilds, corporations, livery companies, etc. (in some of which, however, the title is given not to the head but to the members of an administrative body subordinate to him), hospitals, etc. Formerly also used for GRAND-MASTER, *great master* (see 20), the title of the head of a military order. Also with postfixed adj. (after med.L.) in the titles of dignitaries of monastic and other religious organizations, as ***master-general***, ***master provincial***.

†***Master of Prussia*** (***Pruse, Pruseland***): the grand-master of the Teutonic Order. ***Master of the Temple***: (*a*) *Hist.* the grand-master of the Knights Templar; (*b*) the principal clergyman of the Temple Church, London, appointed by royal letters patent.

1389 in *Eng. Gilds* (1870) 4 Þe maistres & bretheren tofore said. **1427** in Heath *Grocers' Comp.* (1869) 4 John Melborne, John Olyve, Maistres. **1430–1** *Rolls of Parlt.* IV. 370/2 Master and Prestes of the Chapell. **1442** *Ibid.* V. 65/2 The Kyng wille and is disposed, to sende his Letters to the Maistr' of Pruce. **1463–4** *Ibid.* 502/2 Every Mayer, where Mayer is; every Maister, where Maister is, where noo Mayer is. **1550** CROWLEY *Way to Wealth* Bj, A Maister of an house in Oxforde or Cambridge. **1560** DAUS tr. *Sleidane's Comm.* 48b, Albert of Brandenburge, master of Pruselande [orig. 95 *Prussiæ Magister*]. **1568** ASCHAM *Scholem.* II. (Arb.) 143 Pelting matters, soch as in London commonlie cum to the hearing of the Masters of Bridewell. **1586** *Reg. Privy Council Scot.* IV. 74 Maisteris Andro and James Melvillis, maisteris of the New College. **1642–6** in Quincy *Hist. Harvard Univ.* (1840) I. 517 The Overseers and Master of the College. **1648** GAGE *West Ind.* 210 Fryer Nicholus Rodulfius of the same whole Order [of Preachers] Master Generall... Fryer Nicholas Master of the Order... Fryer Ignatius Ciantes Master Provinciall of England. **1654** GATAKER *Disc. Apol.* 36 Mr. Masters Master of the Temple. **1691** WOOD *Ath. Oxon.* I. 101 He was made Master of Balliol Coll. **1706** PHILLIPS (ed. Kersey), *Templars*, a Religious Order, which ..had a Governour..in England, who was styled *Master of the Temple*..: Whence the chief Minister of the Temple-Church in London..is still dignify'd with that Title. **1722** in Cox *Old Constit. Masons* (1871) 23 A Lodge of five Free-Masons, at the least, whereof one to be a Master or Warden of that Limit or Division where such Lodge shall be kept. **1762** tr. *Busching's Syst. Geog.* V. 450 Master of the Teutonick order in Germany. **1825** SCOTT *Talism.* ix, The celebrated Master of the Templars. **1829** HEATH *Grocers' Comp.* (1869) p. vii, The Master, Wardens, and Court of Assistants of the Worshipful Company of Grocers. **1853** 'C. BEDE' *Verdant Green* I. iv, Mr. Verdant Green..proceeded with his father to Brazenface College to call upon the Master. **1876** FIRTH *Munic. Lond.* 50 The name of 'Livery Company' has remained... The control by Master or Wardens of the dress of members has ceased.

18. In the designations of certain legal functionaries, as ***Master of the*** (or ***in***) ***Chancery***, (*a*) until 1852, one of the twelve assistants to the Lord Chancellor, the chief of whom was Master of the Rolls; (*b*) since 1897 any one of four chief clerks of the Chancery Division of the Supreme Court; ***Master of the Court*** (***of Common Pleas, of the King's Bench, of the Exchequer***), any one of five officers in each of those courts (now, in the corresponding division of the Supreme Court) charged with the duty of recording the proceedings.

Also ***Master of the Faculties***, see FACULTY *sb.* 11b; ***Master in Lunacy***, see LUNACY *sb.* 1; ***Master of the Requests*** (†***M. of Request***), see REQUEST; ***Master of the Wards*** (***and Liveries***), see WARD.

1425 *Rolls of Parlt.* IV. 306/1 Maistres of ye Chauncerie beyng occupied in ye Chauncerie. **1797** *Encycl. Brit.* (ed. 3) XIII. 763/1 On the other wool-sacks are seated the judges, masters in chancery, and king's council. **1818** CRUISE *Digest* (ed. 2) IV. 260 The usual order was obtained, referring it to the Master to inquire whether a good title could be made. **1837** *Act 7 Will. IV & 1 Vict.* c. 30 §3 There shall be in each of the said Courts..Five Principal Officers, and no more, to be called respectively the Masters of each of the said Courts. **1846** *Act 9 & 10 Vict.* c. 95 §62 A Master Extraordinary in Chancery. **1853** DICKENS *Bleak Ho.* i, Every master in Chancery has had a reference out of it [Jarndyce and Jarndyce]. **1886** *Encycl. Brit.* XX. 342/1 In the Queen's Bench Division..the duty of registrars is performed by the masters. **1891** *Law Times* XCII. 107/1 Application was made by the plaintiff [in the Court of Q.B.], to a master at chambers, for leave to issue execution. **1897** *Westm. Gaz.* 4 Mar. 10/1 The Chancery chief clerks are henceforth to be styled 'Masters'.

19. a. In many designations of officials having duties of the nature of control, superintendence, or safe-keeping, as †***Master of Assay*** = ASSAY-MASTER; †***M. of the Coin*** = M. of the Mint; ***M. of the*** (***King's, Queen's***) ***Household*** (also Sc. †***Master Household***), an officer under the Steward of the Royal Household; ***M. of the Jewel-house***, the keeper of the Crown Jewels in the Tower of London; ***M. of the*** (***King's***) ***Music***, an officer of the Royal Household, the conductor of the King's band; †***M. of the Posts*** (see quot. 1706); ***M. of the Robes***, ***of the Wardrobe***, the keeper of the 'great' wardrobe of the King, Queen, or other exalted personage; ***Master of*** (***the***) ***Works*** or (now dial.) ***Work***, an official who superintends building operations.

For *Master of Ceremonies*, *M. of the Mint*, *M. of Misrule*, *M. of the Revels*, *M. of the Rolls*, see the second sbs.

1423 *Rolls of Parlt.* IV. 256/2 The forsaid Maistre of the koyne. *Ibid.*, The Maister of the mynte aforeseid. **1454** *Ibid.* V. 273/2 Bi th' oversight of the Maistir of the Werks there. **1528** *St. Papers Hen. VIII*, VII. 61 The Maister of the Postes shall gyve horses to noo man, oonles [etc.]. **1529** in *Proc. Soc. Ant. Scot.* XXX. (1896) 53 Ane lettre..makand hym maister of wark within the castell of Striveling. **1548** in Ellis *Orig. Lett.* Ser. III. III. 297 The Mʳ housholde to the Quene. *a* **1578** LINDESAY (Pitscottie) *Chron. Scot.* (S.T.S.) I 334 Maister houshald witht mony wther offeceris. **1597–8** *Act 39 Eliz.* c 7 §12 Maister of the Juell House. *Ibid.*, Master of the Warderobe. **1677** in *12th Rep. Hist. MSS. Comm.* App. v. 42 Master of the Robes to the Duke. **1696** PHILLIPS, *Master of the King's Houshold.* **1703** *Lond. Gaz.* No. 3914/4 His Grace..was served at Table by..the Duke of Argyle, as Master Houshold. **1704** in *Buccleuch MSS.* (Hist. MSS Comm) I. 352 Your son shall have the reversion of the Master of the Great Wardrobe for life. **1706** PHILLIPS (ed. Kersey), *Master of Assay. Ibid.*, *Master of the Posts*, was an Officer of the King's Court, who had the appointing of all such throughout England as provided Post-horses for the speedy passing of the King's Messages, &c. **1901** *Lond. Gaz.* 8 Oct. 6569 Sir Walter Parratt, M.V.O., to be Master of The King's Music in Ordinary to His Majesty.

b. *Mil.* in various titles of command, as †***Master of the Armoury***, †***M. of the Artillery***; ***Master*** (***General***) ***of the Ordnance***, the controller of the Ordnance and Artillery (subsequently, the head of the Board of Ordnance). Also (in translations from Latin of Fr.) †***master of chivalry***.

1382 WYCLIF *Gen.* xxxvii. 36 Putiphar, the geldyng of Pharao, the mayster of chyualrye. **1485** *Rolls of Parlt.* VI.

354/2 The Offices of Maister of oure Ordinaunces and Maister of oure Armery. **1489** CAXTON *Faytes of A.* I. vii, The souerayn maystre of the chyualrye of the prynce. **1512** *Aberdeen Reg.* (1844) I. 83 Maisteris of the said artailȝerie. **1533** BELLENDEN *Livy* II. xviii. (S.T.S.) 159 Spurius cassius [was] þe first maister of cheuelrie. **1548** PATTEN *Exp. Scot.* A i b, Syr Fraunces Flemmynge knight, master of the ordinaunce. **1597–8** *Act 39 Eliz.* c. 7 §12 The Maister and Leiftenaunte of the Ordynance,.. Maister of the Armory, [and others]. **1695** *Lond. Gaz.* No. 3131/3 The Earl of Romney Master-General of the Ordnance. **1863** H. COX *Instit.* III. viii. 708 The Master-General of the Ordnance.

c. ***master of the horse***: (*a*) the officer who has the management of the horses belonging to a sovereign or other exalted personage; in England, the title of the third official of the royal household (formerly sometimes †***m. of horses***); also rarely *transf.* in jocular use, a head groom or stableman; (*b*) *Antiq.* used as transl. of L. *magister equitum*, master of the 'knights' or horsemen (cf. HORSE *sb.* 3 b), under the Roman republic the title of the commander of the cavalry appointed by a dictator.

(*a*) **1449** *Rolls of Parlt.* V. 154/1 By the avys of the Maister of the Kyngs Hors for the tyme beyng. *c* **1450** *Bk. Curtasye* 611 in *Babees Bk.*, A maystur of horsys a squyer þer is. **1568** GRAFTON *Chron.* II. 735 Sir John Cheiney, maister of the Kinges horses. **1570–81** in Digges *Compl. Ambass.* (1655) 303 The Emperors Ambassador, who is Master of the horse. **1754** RICHARDSON *Grandison* (1811) I. xxxv. 258, I was to be this gentleman's master of the horse abroad. **1886** *Encycl. Brit.* XXI. 37/2 The master of the horse is the third dignitary of the court.

(*b*) **1781** GIBBON *Decl. & F.* xvii. II. 33 *note*, The masters of the horse of the ancient dictators.

d. The official custodian of certain animals kept for sport or pleasure. Formerly in many titles of office in the English court, as ***Master of the Bears***, ***of the Hawks***, ***of the Swans***; now chiefly in ***Master of the Buckhounds***, the fourth great officer of the household. Also ***Master of the Game***: the officer entrusted with the preservation of game in certain royal forests; occas. *jocularly* a gamekeeper.

c **1410** *Master of Game* (MS. Digby) fol. 3 The whiche booke shall.. be named.. maistre of game. **1449** *Rolls of Parlt.* V. 167/2 William Brocas Squyer, Maister of your Bukhounds. **1485** *Ibid.* VI. 354/1 The Office of Maister of the Herthunds. *Ibid.* 360/2 The Office of Maister of oure Swannes. *Ibid.* 365/2 Maister and Rueler of the Kings Beres. **1530** PALSGR. 916/1 The master of hawkes, *le grant faulconner*. **1671** F. PHILLIPS *Reg. Necess.* 132 Mr. Pitcarnes (the Master of the Hawkes) Man. **1711** STEELE *Spect.* No. 118 ¶2 Sir Roger's Master of the Game. **1860** FORSTER *Gr. Remonstr.* 104 The fee of the Master of the Cocks [under James I] exceeded the united salaries of two Secretaries of State. **1886** *Encycl. Brit.* XXI. 38/1 The master of the buckhounds, who is also one of the ministry, ranks next to him [*sc.* the master of the horse].

e. ***master of hounds***: one who owns, or has the control of, a pack of hounds; usually, the member of a hunt who is elected to have the control of the kennels and of the hunting arrangements generally; chiefly equivalent to ***master of foxhounds*** (abbreviated M.F.H.). Also in ***m. of beagles***, ***harriers***, ***staghounds***, etc., and with the designation of a particular pack of hounds.

1781 COWPER *Progr. Error* 114 He takes the field, the master of the pack Cries—'Well done, saint!' and claps him on the back. **1852** R. S. SURTEES *Sponge's Sp. Tour* (1893) 130 Masters of hounds are always jealous of each other... No man in the master-of-hound world is too insignificant for censure. **1856** 'STONEHENGE' *Brit. Sports* 101 The master of a pack of foxhounds, staghounds, or even of harriers, ought [etc.]. **1868** HOLME LEE *B. Godfrey* xxviii. 147 Sir Ralph has the hounds, and is a very good master. **1881** *Encycl. Brit.* XII. 394/2 It is the master's duty to say what covers are to be drawn. **1899** T. M. ELLIS *Three Cats-eye Rings* 29 The master of the Storr-hinton beagles.

†**20. great master.** = GRAND-MASTER 1 and 2.

1524 in *Hakluyt's Voy.* II. I. 86 The massife of Spaine made by the reuerend lord great master Mery d'Amboise. **1531** CROMWELL in Merriman *Life & Lett.* (1902) I. 341 His Highnes also woll that ye shall moue the gret maister [of France] in that behalf. **1547** EARL SUSSEX in Ellis *Orig. Lett.* Ser. I. II. 137 The Lord St. John lord president of the Counsaile and Gret Master. **1577** *F. de L'isle's Legendarie* A viij b, The Constable at that time great master and Marshal of France entreated for him. **1685** *Lond. Gaz.* No. 2114/1 The great Master [of the Knights of Malta] has given Orders [etc.].

IV. As a title of rank or compliment.

21. Used vocatively as a term of respect or politeness. **a.** *sing.* = Sir. Now only in uneducated use. **b.** *pl.* (in later times always ***my masters***) = Sirs, gentlemen. Now *arch.* or *rhetorical*, chiefly in ironical or derisive context.

In the first quot. rendering L. *magister*, prob. applied to Nectanabus as being a man of learning.

1340–70 *Alisaunder* 587 þe Queene.. quikly saide, 'Maister, welcome, ywis; will[e] yee sitte?' **1536** in Wriothesley *Chron.* (Camden) I. 39 The Lord of Rochford .. sayde these wordes.. on the scaffolde.. Maisters all, I am come hither not to preach and make a sermon. **1563** *Reg. Privy Council Scot.* I. 244 Sa hes it plesit the Quenis Majestie, my maisters, to grant the lik commissioun. **1591** SHAKS. *1 Hen. VI*, I. i. 152 Farwell my Masters, to my Taske will I. **1602** —— *Ham.* II. ii. 440 Y'are welcome Masters, welcome all. **1608** MIDDLETON (*title*) A mad World, my Masters. **1653** WALTON *Compl. Angler* 85 Come on my masters, who begins? **1798** WORDSW. '*We are Seven*' 64 'O Master! we are seven'. **1837** MARRYAT *Dog Fiend* xxix, 'Put up your fiddle, master'. **1843** BORROW *Bible in Spain* xxxi, Many is the wetting that you will get, my masters, before you reach Oviedo. **1903** *Eng. Dial. Dict.*, *Master*, a term of address to a superior or stranger; Sir.

22. A title prefixed to the name or designation of a man. Originally used only in speaking of or to a man either of high social rank or of learning (sometimes, esp. in Scotland, applied *spec.* to a Master of Arts), but gradually extended in application. In ordinary use now only *dial.*, but in literature sometimes *arch.* or *Hist.*; otherwise superseded by MR. (pronounced 'mɪstə(r)).

The obscured pronunciation resulting from proclitic use doubtless began while the written form *master* was still commonly employed. Before the end of the 17th c. the abbreviation *Mr.* (originally only one among many others used for the word in all applications) had come to be restricted to the use in which the pronunciation was obscured, and to be the only permitted mode of writing the word in that use. Thenceforward *master* and *Mr.* were practically two words, distinct both in function and in form. In this Dictionary the abbreviation MR., in all its historical varieties of use, is treated in its alphabetical place.

a. Prefixed to a surname or a Christian name.

Down to the 16th c. or a little later, *master* could be prefixed to the name of a knight or a bishop; at an earlier period it was freely used with the names of personages of ancient history and ancient writers. Some modern dialects have only one form for *Master* and *Mr.* as prefixed titles; others have both prefixes with a difference of function, *Mr.* being the superior title. (See E.D.D.)

1297 R. GLOUC. (Rolls) 8722 Maister willam gyffard he ȝef þe bissopriche Of winchestere & maister anselin þe erche-bissopriche. *a* **1300** *Cursor M.* 6936 Fosterd he was And lered wit maister moyses. *c* **1330** R. BRUNNE *Chron. Wace* (Rolls) 57 One Mayster Wace þe Frankes telles, þe Brute, all þat þe Latyn spelles. **1425** W. PASTON in *P. Lett.* I. 19 Maister John Ixworthe told me that he hadde lettres fro a frende of yowres. **1459** *Aberdeen Reg.* (1844) I. 22 Maister John of Levington, vicar of Inuerugy. **1532** in Ellis *Orig. Lett.* Ser. III. II. 252, I have harde hym soo often breke Master Precyens hede. **1563–83** FOXE *A. & M.* (ed. 4) 1770 Maister Latymer encouraged Maister Ridley when both were at the stake. **1570** *Ane Trag.* 8 in *Satir. Poems Reform.* x. 82 Schir Morpheus.. led me captiue vnto Maister Slumber. **1579** SPENSER (*title*) The Shepheardes Calender. .. Entitled to.. M. Philip Sidney. **1612** WEBSTER *White Devil* To Rdr., The right happy and copious industry of Master Shakespeare, Master Dekker, and Master Heywood. **1650** B. *Discolliminium* 33, I could wish we might be allow'd to call him Master Charles, for most men thinke He is a Gentleman borne. **1861** M. PATTISON *Ess.* (1889) I. 45 Two allegorical pieces by Master Hans Holbein.

†**b.** Prefixed to a title of office or profession, or occas. to a personal designation of some other kind.

1470–85 MALORY *Arthur* x. lix. 514 Maister maronners said sire Tristram what meaneth that letter. **1523** *St. Papers Hen. VIII*, VI. 122 The Popis Holynes, informed by Maister Doctor Hanibal of my commyng, sent word that I shulde tary a day. *a* **1548** HALL *Chron.*, *Hen. VIII* 54 The master of the rolles & master Subdeane with other doctours unknowen. **1548** PATTEN *Exped. Scot.* A ij, My lorde Lieuetenaunt and Master Treasurer [of the Army]. **1550** BALE *Apol.* 42 But tell me maistre person, who hath taught yow to playe so wycked partes as these are. *a* **1555** LATIMER *Let.* in Foxe *A. & M.* (1583) 1741 They.. craftely defeated mayster Maiors appoyntment. **1588** SHAKS. *L.L.L.* IV. ii. 87 Marry M. Schoolmaster, hee that is likest to a hogshead. **1599** —— *Much Ado* III. iii. 17 Master Constable. **1607** —— *Timon* IV. ii. 1 Here you M. Steward, where's our Master? **1609** B. JONSON *Sil. Wom.* v. i, *Cut.* By your fauour Master Parson— *Ott.* You shall giue me leaue, Master Doctor. **1625** HART *Anat. Ur.* II. ix. 116 And yet master Parson must not be called couetous. **1640** in Rushw. *Hist. Coll.* III. (1692) I. 125 Master Speaker, the first Writs that were sent out.. I.. was as ignorant of, as any one Member of this House.

23. a. In early use (***my***) ***young master***, ***little master***, occur as designations applied by servants and inferiors generally to the boys and young men of the families of their superiors. App. as a development from this mode of expression, the word *master* (after the phonetic separation of *Mr.*) came to be the usual prefix to the name of a young gentleman not considered old enough to be entitled to be called 'Mr.'. Hence occas. ***masters and misses*** = young people. Also †***master-miss***: an effeminate youth.

1563–83 FOXE *A. & M.* (ed. 4) 1596 The time was thought to be nie, that this young Maister [Queen Mary's expected child] should come into the world. **1596** SHAKS. *Merch. V.* II. ii. 52 Talke you of yong Maister Launcelet? **1601** B. JONSON *Poetaster* I. i, Young master, master Ovid, doe you heare? **1693** DRYDEN Jr. *Juvenal* xiv. 6 If Gaming does an Aged Sire entice, Then my Young Master swiftly learns the Vice. **1710** SWIFT *Jrnl. to Stella* 13 Dec., Maids, misses, and little master.. in a third [coach]. **1720** —— *Mod. Educ.* Wks. 1755 II. II. 35 These wretched pedagogues are enjoyned.. that master must not walk till he is hot. **1754** FOOTE *Knights* II (? 1778) 5 The master-misses of the present age. **1754** RICHARDSON *Grandison* (1811) II. xxxix. 304 Miss Cantillon, Miss Barnevelt, and half a dozen more misses and masters. **1760** H. BROOKE *Fool of Qual.* I. 18 Lord Richard and some other masters of quality about his age. **1775** in J. L. Chester *Westm. Abbey Reg.* (1876) 419 May 12, Master Frederick Gell; aged 12 days. **1776** *Ibid.* 241 Mar. 20, Master Albany-Charles Wallis, a Westminster scholar; in his 14th year. **1824** MISS FERRIER *Inher.* xxxii, Well-dressed, talking, smiling, flirting masters and misses. **1849** DICKENS *Dav. Copp.* iii, Wait a bit, Master Davy, and I'll—I'll tell you something. *c* **1874** D. BOUCICAULT in M. R. Booth *Eng. Plays of 19th Cent.* (1969) II. 201 Did you see the young master? **1898** G. B. SHAW *Plays, You never can tell* II. 242, I presume, sir, you are Master Philip. *Philip.* I was Master Philip..; just as you were once Master Finch. **1923** WODEHOUSE *Inimitable Jeeves* i. 9 He had been clearing away the breakfast things, but at the sound of the young master's voice cheesed it courteously.

b. Prefixed, with disparaging implication, to the name of an adult.

1885 C. M. YONGE *Nuttie's Father* II. ix. 105 I'm not going to have a *tête-à-tête* with Master Mark. **1959** *Listener* 22 Jan. 155/2, I never liked Jinnah... I thought a great deal of his ambition was for Master Jinnah rather than anything else. **1975** T. HEALD *Deadline* vii. 151, I think you'll find Master Wimbledon will do very well at anything if he thinks it will further his career. He's an exceedingly ruthless and ambitious young man.

24. The heir-apparent to a Scottish peerage (below the rank of earl; formerly, below that of marquis) is in many instances known as ***The Master of——***; the specific designation being usually identical with the baronial title of the family.

1489 *Ld. Treas. Acc. Scotl.* (1877) I. 107 The Maister of Crafurde. **1530** *Aberdeen Reg.* (1844) I. 139, I Johne Lord Forbes.. becummiss souerte.. for myself, Johne Maister of Forbes, my sone [etc.]. **1548** PATTEN *Exped. Scot.* B vii, Anderwyke pertained to the lorde of Hambleton, and was kept by hys sonne & heyre (whom, of custume they call the Master of Hambleton). **1569** *Reg. Privy Council Scot.* II. 2 Johnne Maister of Grahame nepote and heyre to the Erll of Montroise. *Ibid.*, William Maister Marschell sone to the Erll Marschell. *Ibid.* 37 Quhilk Andro.. presentit to him ane writting of the Maister of Marschellis. **1584** *Ibid.* III. 644 Mr. Thomas Lyoun, Master of Glammis. **1641** R. BAILLIE *Lett. & Jrnls.* (1841) I. 379 Before King James went to England, noblemens eldest sonnes were bot Masters, and their younger brethren pretended not to take place of Barrons. **1798** *Monthly Mag.* VI. 437 The Viscount of Arbuthnott's eldest son is stiled Master of Arbuthnott. **1818** SCOTT *Br. Lamm.* ix, The Master of Ravenswood led the way.

V. Attributive uses and Combinations.

25. Used appositively or as *adj.* in the sense 'that is a master'. **a.** Formerly prefixed freely to all kinds of designations of persons, with the sense 'chief', 'leading', 'commanding'. Now *rhetorical*, with implication of imposing greatness or power, esp. in ***master spirit*** (after Shaks.).

c **1175** *Lamb. Hom.* 41 And þa welle bi-wisten .xii. meister deoflen swilc ha weren kinges. *c* **1200** ORMIN 7454 Wass maȝȝstredwale, an defless þeww, þatt Arriuss wass nemmned. *c* **1250** *Gen. & Ex.* 3756 Meistres princes he wolden hem maken. *a* **1300** *Cursor M.* 13594 þe maisters Iuus þan bigan To mistru o þis sinful seli man. *a* **1300** *K. Horn* 659 þe meyster kinges heued He haddit him by reued. *c* **1375** *Sc. Leg. Saints* xxviii. (*Margaret*) 502 Scho ourcumyne had þe maister feynd. **1382** WYCLIF *Jer.* li. 23, I shall hurtle in thee dukes and the maister ȝugis [Vulg. *magistratus*]. *a* **1400** *Octavian* 559 þe maysterowtlawe spake thene. *c* **1449** PECOCK *Repr.* v. i. 478 In ȝou schulen be maistris liers, that schulen bringe yn sectis of perdicioun. *c* **1450** *Merlin* xxiii. 436 Merlin is maister Counseller to kynge Arthur. **1575** *Gamm. Gurton* IV. ii, The master-deuil, Belsabub. **1590** STOCKWOOD *Rules Construct.* A iij b, My master schollers of the higher forms. **1601** SHAKS. *Jul. C.* III i. 163 The Choice and Master Spirits of this Age. **1607** B. JONSON *Volpone* Ded., The great and Maister Spirits of our World. **1609** —— *Sil. Wom.* III. ii, That falls out often, madam, that hee that thinkes himselfe the Master-wit, is the Master-foole. **1617** *Janua Ling.* To Prince, Whose but yours, that are a maister-prince. **1643** 'F. GREVILLE' 5 *Yrs. Jas. I* 44 One Simon, master servant unto Sir Tho. [Monson]. **1701** ROWE *Amb. Step-moth.* III. iii, See where the Master Villain stands! **1725** POPE *Odyss.* XXIV. 26 Yet still a master ghost, the rest he awed. **1759** MASON *Caractacus* 84 The master-mover in this business. **1837** ALISON *Hist. Europe* (1849–50) VIII. xlix. §96. 101 The master-spirit had fled from the helm when Lord Wellesley embarked for England. **1849** AYTOUN *Execution Mrq. Montrose* vii, The master-fiend Argyle! **1865** KINGSLEY *Herew.* xxv, One of those unfathomable master-personages.

b. Prefixed to names of animals, to denote the leader of a herd, or one superior in fighting strength to the rest. (Cf. 1 b.)

1589 FLEMING *Virg. Bucol.* ix. 27 Take heed to meet the maistergote. **1672** TEMPLE *Ess. Orig. Nat. Govt.* Miscell. I. (1680) 56 This makes the Authority.. of a Master-Buck in a numerous herd. **1692** R. L'ESTRANGE *Fables* cccxxxiv. 292 A Master-Pike, that for his Bulk, Beauty, and Strength, was look'd upon to be the Prince of the River. **1725** POPE *Odyss.* IX. 523 The master Ram at last approach'd the gate. **1764** *Museum Rust.* III. xxxix. 175 A master hog deters a weaker from approaching. **1812** SIR J. SINCLAIR *Syst. Husb. Scot.* I. 21 The cattle must often be injured.. by master cattle preventing the others from feeding. **1850** R. G. CUMMING *Hunter's Life S. Afr.* (1902) 7/1 A princely master-stag. **1856** KANE *Arct. Expl.* II. xxii. 222 Toodla, our master-dog, was seized with a violent fit. **1860** G. H. K. in *Vac. Tour* 174 The antlers of the master-hart.

c. In titles of office or employment, to distinguish the official who has the command over the others similarly designated. Now chiefly *Hist.* (see also 30). Hence also in derivatives denoting the offices, as ***master forestership***, ***sergeantship***, ***ushery***.

c **1250** *Gen. & Ex.* 3412 Al bi ðhusenz ðis folc was told, Ilc ðhusent adde a meister wold. *Ibid.* 3886 Eleazar.. Was mad bissop and meister prest. *a* **1300** *Cursor M.* 4434 Son was ioseph halden dere wit þe maister jailere. **1423** JAS. I *Kingis Q.* cxxv, The maister portare, callit pacience, That frely lete vs in. *c* **1440** *Alphabet of Tales* 514/2 Som tyme þer was a kyng þat had a wardrop[er] þat was maister-shaper [cf. quot. 1658 in d] of his clothyng; and he had many servandis vnder-nethe hym. **1450** *Rolls of Parlt.* V. 192/1 Oure Maister Foster of the said Forest. **1455** *Ibid.* 312/2 The Maister Fostershipps of the Forestes of Macclesfeld, Mare and

Moundreme. **1464** *Ibid.* 545/1 Th' Offices of Maister Carpenter of oure Castell of Lancastre. **1485** *Ibid.* VI. 369/1 The Office of Maister Sergeauntship of the Vale of Monmouth. **1508** Kennedie *Flyting w. Dunbar* 437 In Parise wyth the maister buriawe Abyde, and be his prentice. **1553-4** *Reg. Privy Council Scot.* I. 152 Ordanis my Lord Thesaurar to deliver furth the prenting irnis..to the Maister Cunyear. **1565** *Ibid.* 347 The offices of Chalmerlanerie and Maistir Ischearie. **1604** E. G[rimstone] *D'Acosta's Hist. Indies* III. x. 154 The report which the master Pilot that passed it made, seemeth notable vnto me. **1676** *Lond. Gaz.* No. 1127/4 Mr. Chiffinch Master Falconer to His Majesty. **1682** G. Rose (*title*) A perfect School of Instructions For the Officers of the Mouth: shewing The Whole Art of..a Master Carver, a Master Butler, a Master Confectioner, a Master Cook, a Master Pastryman. **1702** *Lond. Gaz.* No. 3822/4 Her Majesty has been pleased to constitute..William Bridges Esq.; Master Surveyor..of the Ordnance. **1769** Falconer *Dict. Marine* (1780) Y y iij b, To observe that the master-shipwrights do in no ways depart from the draught. **1862** J. Grant *Capt. Guard* i, The king's master butcher.

d. In designations of trade, to denote one who is a 'master' as distinguished from an apprentice or journeyman, or one who has others in his employ.

a **1300** *Cursor M.* 1666 Þi self sal be þe maister wright. **1444** *Rolls of Parlt.* V. 112/2 Ye wages of eny free Mason or maister Carpenter, excede not by the day iiiid. *Ibid.*, A maister Tyler or Sclatter. **1483** Caxton *G. de la Tour* A vj b, It cam from the handes of the mayster goldsmythe. **1496** *Naval Acc. Hen. VII* (1896) 180, iiij Smythes..iij of theym takyng..xv^{d} by the weke... And the iiijth as Maister Smyth viij^{s} vj^{d}. **1647** R. Stapylton *Juvenal* 81 The master-barber now Trimms thee. **1658** R. Franck *North. Mem.* (1821) 146 Here [Perth] they call a taylor master-fashioner forsooth. **1683** Moxon *Mech. Exerc., Printing* ii. ¶1, I shall begin with the Office of a Master-Printer. **1707** Fleetwood *Chron. Prec.* (1745) 133 A Master Calker. **1739** Labelye *Short Acc. Piers Westm. Br.* Pref. 4, I consulted the respective Master-Artificers. **1776** Adam Smith *W.N.* v. ii. (1869) II. 461 The rise which such a tax might occasion in the wages of manufacturing labour would be advanced by the master manufacturer. **1800** Mar. Edgeworth *Murad* i, In these disturbances the master bakers frequently lose their lives. **1823** P. Nicholson *Pract. Build.* 423 The master-glazier takes upon himself the risk of windows being broken. **1824** R. Humphreys *Mem. J. Decastro* 76 He calls for his scene-painter, composer, master-carpenter, property-man. **1834** *1st Rep. Poor Law Comm.* (1885) 199 Master barbers who might have saved enough money to keep them from the parish. **1837** Lockhart *Scott* lxiv, The master printer is entitled to an equal sum. **1863** Kingsley *Water-Bab.* i, He would be a man and a master-sweep. **1897** *Daily News* 8 Mar. 3/1 Mr. George Holder, master sinker, who had charge of the pit. **1933** *Burlington Mag.* Nov. 239/2 A master-clockmaker of the class of Thomas Tompion. **1936** *Ibid.* Aug. 54/1 At nineteen he was..a master-carpenter and a painter. **1964** W. L. Goodman *Hist. Woodworking Tools* II. vii. 78 The wide-ranging migrations of the master-masons and master-carpenters of the Middle-Ages.

e. With the sense 'supremely or consummately skilled'. Also, in ME. occas. = 'consummately wicked', 'accomplished', as in †*master gaveller*.

1340 *Ayenb.* 35 Þise byeþ þe mayster gaueleres. *c* **1440** *Jacob's Well* 123 3if þou be wel plesyd þerwyth, þou art mayster vsurere. *c* **1440** *Alphabet of Tales* 6 Þis Abbott said vnto þis maister thieff [etc.]. **1565** Cooper *Thesaurus, Autolicus*, a maister thiefe. **1601** Holland *Pliny* II. 515 That great architect and master deuiser, of Alexandria.. Dinocrates. **1677** Gilpin *Demonol.* III. ii. 11 We may rely upon the great Master-contriver, for relief..or deliverance; as there is need. **1736** Ainsworth *Lat.-Eng. Dict., Athleta*, a master-wrestler, a champion. **1751** J. Harris *Hermes* I. vii. (1765) 111 The character of a Master-Artist, or Man of practical Wisdom. **1850** Tennyson *In Mem.* lxxxvii, And last the master-bowman, he, Would cleave the mark. **1900** *Westm. Gaz.* 4 Jan. 1/3 The French consider the English the master-colonists of the world. **1930** *English Jrnl.* XIX. 628 The Minnesota *Quarterly* is at present running a series of tales about a master criminal. **1932** Wodehouse *Louder & Funnier* 72 The psychology of the Master Criminal is a thing I have never been able to understand. **1939** T. S. Eliot *Old Possum's Pract. Cats* 33 He's the master criminal who can defy the Law. **1968** D. M. Smith *Mod. Sicily* lv. 505 That notorious character Don Calogero Vizzini,..master criminal and boss of Villalba,..made a fortune out of wartime shortages. **1975** L. Deighton *Yesterday's Spy* vi. 54 Champion was some kind of master spy.

f. *Chess.* Designating play or players of the highest class at national or international level. (Cf. 16 c.)

1894 J. Mason *Princ. Chess* 186 In the case of master players, a slight initial error..will permeate the remainder of the game. **1938** P. W. Sergeant *Championship Chess* 191 The *Benoni Counter-Gambit* had for years been out of favour in master-play. **1958** *Listener* 13 Nov. 803/1 It is really only in master chess..that knowledge of the latest variations and finesses becomes important. **1959** *Ibid.* 5 Nov. 794/1 You need not go as slow as the sixteen moves an hour customary in master practice.

26. Applied *transf.* as a qualification of things, with the sense 'main', 'principal', 'controlling'.

In some of the combinations so formed, *master* is apprehended as a separate adj.; the majority, however, are always felt as compounds, while in many the grammatical character is uncertain or fluctuating.

a. Of material things (after the similar use of F. *maître*; esp. frequent in terms relating to building, machinery, and popular anatomy), as ***master-altar, bathroom, -beam, bedroom,*** †***-bone,*** †***-borough, -bough, branch, -chord,*** †***city, current, dish, -drain, -feeder, fortress, furrow, -gate,*** †***gonfanon, -line, list, lode, -metal, -moulding, pattern*** (also *fig.*), ***pillar,*** †***-pock, river, sail, -screw, -shoot, star, stem, street, -string, switch, tape, temple, -tissue, tooth, tower,*** †***town,*** †***-turnip, wave, way, -wheel, wire.***

1833 L. Ritchie *Wand. by Loire* 116 The *master-altar. **1959** *Sunday Times* 3 May 19/4 The kitchen and *master bathroom. **1632** Sherwood, A summer (or great *master-beame in building), *sommier*. **1638** Drumm. of Hawth. *Irene* Wks. (1711) 170 The props, stays, master-beams of religion, being faith, hope, and charity. **1926** *New Republic* 7 Apr. p. iii (Advt.), Large living-room and dining-room opening on court, four *master bedrooms. **1937** M. Hillis *Orchids on your Budget* ii. 35 Crisp white argentine curtains in the master bedroom. **1945** Nelson & Wright *Tomorrow's House* ii. 12/2 The discussion continued in the privacy of the master bedroom. **1972** *Country Life* 5 Oct. (Suppl.) 32d/2 Master bedroom suite with dressing room, bath and shower rooms. **1677** W. Vincent in *Harl. Misc.* (1809) II. 328 One hand being rotted from the wrist, that you may not only see through the *master-bones, but also [etc.]. **1800** C. Winter in W. Jay *Mem.* J.'s Wks. 1843 V. 157 The master-bone of my leg was broken. *c* **1250** *Gen. & Ex.* 3881 Long weiȝe and costful he ðor fond, forð bi archim ðat *meister burȝ. **1615** W. Lawson *Country Housew. Gard.* (1626) 35 Let him spread as far as he list without any *master-bough. **1642** Rogers *Naaman* To Rdr. §1 Yet they [*sc.* trees] haue some *Master and chiefe ones [*sc.* branches], into which the maine sap..is carried. **1667** Waterhouse *Fire Lond.* 131 A main Pillar and Master-branch in Englands Grandeur. **1613** Shaks. *Hen. VIII*, III. ii. 106, I would 'twer somthing y^{t} would fret the string, The *Master-cord on's heart. **1842** Tennyson *Will Waterpr.* 27 The master-chord Of all I felt and feel. **1456** Sir G. Haye *Law Arms* (S.T.S.) 47 Thair *maister citee was als mekle as Rome. **1817** Coleridge *Biog. Lit.* 120 It is connected with *master-currents below the surface. **1960** Auden *Homage to Clio* 26 Doomed to observe Beauty peck at a *master-dish. **1652** Blith *Eng. Improv. Impr.* ix. (ed. 3) 56 Thither draw a good substantial *Master-drain through all thy Lands. **1796** *Trans. Soc. Arts* XIV. 184 In carrying up the valley the master drains. **1789** T. Wright *Meth. Watering Meadows* (1790) 19 The bottom of the first work, or *master-feeder, ought to be as deep as the bottom of the river. *c* **1450** *Merlin* vii. 110 Than Bretell com to the *master forteresse where as the kynge was. **1649** Blith *Eng. Improv.* xviii. 109 A good Drayne or *Master-Furrow. **1808** J. Walker *Econ. Hist. Hebrides & Highl. Scot.* I. 168 The master-furrow at the head of the field..should be led in a very gentle slope. *c* **1450** *Merlin* xxiii. 422 He com to the *maister gate of the paleys. **1715** Leoni *Palladio's Archit.* (1742) I. 47 The chief Entry, or Master-gate. *c* **1330** *Arth. & Merl.* 5634 Her *maister gomfainoun so bar þe kinges steward, Cleodalis. **1833** Straith *Fortif.* 3 The measurements..are calculated.. from the cordon, which..is called the magistral or *master line. **1962** Y. Malkiel in Householder & Saporta *Probl. Lexicogr.* 9 Fragmentary *master-lists of the items. **1967** *N.Y. Times* (Internat. ed.) 11-12 Feb. 9/6 Master list of investment and speculative stocks—key lists for both the conservative and more speculative investor. **1671** *Phil. Trans.* VI. 2100 The ancient Tinners..affirm, that 7 Loads may lie parallel to each other in the same Hill, but yet one only *Master-Load. **1813** T. Busby tr. *Lucretius* VI. Comm. xxiii, On account of its exerting its influence upon iron (the *master-metal),..the tragedian termed it the Herculean stone. **1723** Chambers tr. *Le Clerc's Archit.* I. 75 The Corona..is the first *Master-Moulding in the Corniche. **1948** H. Hall *Home Dress-Making Simplified* xxxiii. 311 The safe plan, when remodeling, is to fit a *master pattern in muslin... This pattern is then used as a guide for fitting the section when cutting. **1960** R. Lister *Decorative Cast Ironwork* 230 *Master pattern*, a pattern from which a production work is cast. **1962** W. Nowottny *Lang. Poets Use* vi. 138 It is Eliot's peculiar insight..to have..expressed the longing for the master-pattern that will free us from the fret of a world in which there are too many equipollent patterns. *a* **1450** *Knt. de la Tour* 93 The *maister pillour of the halle, bi the whiche alle the halle was susteined. **1601** Dent *Pathw. Heaven* (1831) 29 It is a master-devil, and the *master-pock of the soul. **1654** Trapp *Comm. Job* xxxiii. 17 Which else, as a Master-pock, will break out in his forehead. **1563-87** Foxe *A. & M.* (1596) 141/2 A certeine great beame or *master post was loosed out of the place. **1677** Yarranton *Eng. Improv.* 64 The Thames and Severne are the two great *Master Rivers. **1555** Eden *Decades* 195 They sayle with two sayles as with the *master sayle and the trinkette. **1902** *Encycl. Brit.* XXXIII. 809/2 The screw is an important productive measuring instrument, whether used as a micrometer-screw of less than an inch in length, or as a *master-screw of 20 feet in length. **1712** J. James tr. *Le Blond's Gardening* 173 Bringing the two Sides as near as possible to the *Master-Shoot. *a* **1300** *Cursor M.* 527 Seuen *maister sterns er sette in heuen. **1904** W. de la Mare *Henry Brocken* vi. 62 The master-stars shone earlier here. **1601** Holland *Pliny* II. 23 If their leaves bee cropt off before the *maister stem or spire be growne big. *c* **1386** Chaucer *Knt.'s T.* 2044 The nobleste of the grekes..caryeden the beere.. Thurgh out the Citee by the *maister strete. **1713** Rowe *Jane Shore* III. i. 34 He touch'd me Ev'n on the tend'rest Point; the *Master-string That makes most Harmony or Discord to me. **1907** A. Hay *Introd. Course Continuous Current Engin.* xvi. 284 A small switch which is arranged to control simultaneously a number of larger switches is spoken of as a *master switch. **1943** *Gloss. Terms Electr. Engin.* (B.S.I.) 52 *Master switch or circuit-breaker*, a switch or circuit-breaker to which the operation or function of one or more other switches is subservient. **1975** P. Organ *House on Cheyne Walk* i. 1 The night is going. Soon someone somewhere will throw a master switch..and the lights will go out..all over London. **1954** *Master tape [see file *sb.*[2] 4 b]. **1962** *Times* 5 July 15/6 In a disc-cutting room at Decca's London studios, a master tape of a recent recording of music by Prokofiev and an ordinary commercial pressing of a disc made from it were started simultaneously. **1967** *Lebende Sprachen* XII. 137/2 *Master tape*, original recording by informant of a language laboratory drill. **1973** *Daily Tel.* (Colour Suppl.) 12 Oct. 29/2 The signals..from the master tape are then fed into the recording head that drives the cutting stylus. *c* **1385** Chaucer *L.G.W.* 1016 *Dido*, The *maystir temple of al the toun. **1896** *Allbutt's Syst. Med.* I. 161 Certain *master tissues..possess..a special function. **1601** Holland *Pliny* II. 341 The great *master teeth and grinders of a wolfe. *c* **1386** Chaucer *Sqr.'s T.* 218 (Hengwrt MS.) The Miroure, That born was vp vn to the *maister tour. **13..** *S. Erkenwolde* 26 in Horstm. *Altengl. Leg.* (1881) 266 Londone..þe metropol & þe *mayster-tone. *c* **1385** Chaucer *L.G.W.* 1591 *Hipsiph.*, Iaconitos, That was the mayster toun of al Colcos. **1733** Tull *Horse-Hoeing Husb.* x. 100 We contrive to leave the *Master-Turneps..and spare such when near one another. **1840** Marryat *Poor Jack* xlii, A *master wave, as it is termed, from being of larger dimensions than its predecessors. **1726** Leoni *Alberti's Archit.* I. 80/1 The Houses of Princes..shou'd have an entrance from the *Master Way. **1640** Bp. Reynolds *Passions* x, The *Master-wheel or first mover in all the regular motions of this passion [Love] is the Love of God. **1761** Churchill *Night* Poems 1769 I. 89 Let but the puppets move, I've my desire, Unseen the hand which guides the *Master-wire.

b. Of immaterial things, as ***master-appetite, -argument, -bias, -cause, conscience, -coup, -dream, -duty, -error, exercise, fact, -feeling, -form, -fulcrum, -genius, -idea, jest, light, -lust, -miracle, -mischief, motive, -passion, plan, -power, principle, -proof, reason, -sin, -spell, -stratagem, -tone, -vice, -virtue, -voice, -word.***

1742 Young *Nt. Th.* VII. 863 Great Nature's *Master-appetite destroy'd. **1678** Bunyan *Jerus. Sinner Saved* Wks. (1845) 73 This is Satan's *master-argument. **1807** Wordsw. *Happy Warrior* 59 A Soul whose *master-bias leans To homefelt pleasures. **1677** Horneck *Gt. Law Consid.* v. (1704) 240 The *master-cause [of misery] is the want of consideration. **1649** Milton *Eikon.* ii. 21 We may consider ..what..feeling could be in that conscience, and what fitness to be the *master conscience of three Kingdomes. **1939** R. Campbell *Flowering Rifle* vi. 148 The cynic *master-coup of propaganda. **1928** Blunden *Jap. Garland* 21 Sleep's *master-dream there stands alone: The tower of East and West! **1624** Sanderson *Serm.* I. 82 Here then the magistrate..may learn..his *master-duty. **1674** Allen *Danger Enthusiasm* 96, I deem it a Mother and a *Master-Error. **1604** Shaks. *Oth.* II. i. 268 Hard at hand comes the *Master, and maine exercise. **1831** Brewster *Newton* (1855) I. ix. 202 It is to Dr. Thomas Young..that we owe the *master fact. **1806** Surr *Winter in Lond.* II. 28 This *master feeling of his soul. **1646** Sir T. Browne *Pseud. Ep.* III. xvii. 147 Other degenerations which come up in unexpected shapes, when they want the support..of the primary and *master-formes. **1957** T. Hughes *Hawk in Rain* 11 And I.. strain towards the *master-Fulcrum of violence where the hawk hangs still. *a* **1711** Ken *Hymnotheo* Poet. Wks. 1721 III. 293 Had Athens..To our great Homer's *Master-genius bow'd..They [etc.]. **1809-10** Coleridge *Friend* (1865) 69 The three *master ideas, announced in the foregoing pages. **1678** Butler *Hud.* III. ii. 955 And who shall break the *master-jest, And what, and how, upon the rest. **1806** Wordsw. *Ode Intim. Immort.* 153 Those shadowy recollections Which..Are yet a *master light of all our seeing. **1784** Cowper *Task* v. 618 His *master-lust Falls first before his resolute rebuke. **1647** Trapp *Comm. 1 Cor.* xiii. 2 Removing of mountains is instanced, because noted by our Saviour as a *master-miracle. *a* **1709** Illidge in M. Henry *Life* (1710) 65 Atheism..is the *Master-mischief of this Age. **1860** Mill *Repr. Govt.* (1865) 51/1 The guiding and *master motives in the conduct of average human beings. **1732** Pope *Ess. Man* II. 131 One *master Passion in the breast, Like Aaron's serpent, swallows up the rest. **1935** *Master plan [see freeway]. **1939** H. M. Lewis *City Planning* xii. 128 A master plan..may be defined as a general plan for the future layout of the city. **1957** L. F. R. Williams *State of Israel* 77 The bulk of the population is being systematically spread out in accordance with a master plan drawn up by the Government. **1960** *Washington Post* 16 Nov. A. 16 The Friends, who have retained consultants to study the Zoo's problems and form a master plan, found that the institution has almost never received adequate funds. **1971** B. de Ferranti *Living with Computer* ix. 82 He therefore..gives them names so that they can be filed and described on the master plan. **1821** Hazlitt *Table-Talk* I. v. 96 His mind grappled with that which afforded the best exercise to its *master-powers. **1794** Mathias *Purs. Lit.* (1798) 118 A vindication of the great, original, *master principles on which they were founded. **1610** Bp. Hall *Apol. Brownists* v. 14, I finde these as your *Master-proofes, set as Challengers in every of your defences. **1608** Shaks. *Pericles* IV. vi. 8 Her quirks, her reasons, her *master reasons. **1607** Hieron *Wks.* I. 227 Those *master-sinnes, ignorance, contempt of the word and godlinesse. **1816** Byron *Ch. Har.* III. cvii, The lord of irony,—that *master-spell, Which stung his foes to wrath. **1647** Trapp *Comm. 2 Thess.* ii. 7 Themselves will even smile in the triumphs of their own wits..as at a *master-stratagem. **1827-35** Willis *Leper* 124 The voice was like the *master-tone Of a rich instrument. **1848** Dickens *Dombey* xlvii, Mr. Dombey's *master-vice, that ruled him so inexorably. **1833** Chalmers *Const. Man* (1835) II. x. 101 The great *master and generic virtue. **1910** W. de la Mare *Three Mulla-Mulgars* xiii. 174 Of its calm authority the *master-voice said, 'So shall it be.' **1709** Steele *Tatler* No. 17 ¶2 He is a Poet, and Merchant, which is seen in Two *Master-Words, *Credit Blossoms.*

27. Attributive, with the sense: Pertaining to, proceeding from, or characteristic of a master (in various senses), in ***master faculty, fascination,*** †***reach, throw, touch, will.*** Also ***master hand*** (see 30), masterpiece, master-stroke.

Most or all of the combinations under this head admit of being used or interpreted with the notion expressed by those under 26 b; the two meanings often blend, as both are usually applicable to the same objects.

1622 Bacon *Hen. VII* 242 Neither did hee care how Cunning they were, that hee did imploy, For hee thought himselfe to haue the Master-Reach. *a* **1674** Clarendon *Surv. Leviath.* (1676) 21 Discovers a master faculty in making easie. **1686** Ravenscroft *Titus A.* To Rdr., He only gave some Master-touches to one or two. **1710** Addison *Tatler* No. 156 ¶10, I have here only mentioned some Master-Touches of this admirable Piece. **1821** Southey in *Q. Rev.* XXV. 310 This rare dissembler..played his master-

game at once. **1825** HOGG *Q. Hynde* 324 No clamour rose, .. From such a monarch's master-throw. **1838** LYTTON *Alice* VII. vi, The master-fascination that he could command. *a***1872** J. D. AYLWARD in *Ess. Relig. & Lit.* Ser. III. (1874) III. 90 Subject themselves .. to the master-will of him whom they constitute the lord of their life. **1880** *Blackw. Mag.* Feb. 187 The master-touch interpreting all lights.

28. Objective, as ***master-killer***, ***-leaver***; instrumental, as ***master-mortified*** adj.

1606 SHAKS. *Ant. & Cl.* IV. ix. 22 But let the world ranke me in Register A Master leauer, and a fugitiue. **1608** SYLVESTER *Du Bartas* II. iv. IV. *Decay* 180 Art thou there Zimri, cursed Parricide? Fell master-killer, canst thou chuse but fear For like offence, like punishment severe? **1741** RICHARDSON *Pamela* I. xv, The poor, low, creeping, abject, self-mortified and master-mortified Mrs. Jewkes.

†**29.** In contracted forms of certain syntactical combinations used as titles of office, as **master-household** = master of the household (see 19 a); **master-voyage**, ? the commander of a fishing fleet. *Obs.*

1761 *Ann. Reg.* 188 Every boat-master, splitter, and master voyage, who are the chief people among the fisherman [French, Newfoundland] and shoremen, being the catchers and curers of fish.

30. Special comb.: **master attendant**, 'an officer in the royal dockyards appointed to assist in the fitting or dismantling, removing or securing vessels of war, &c.' (Smyth); **master-batch**, a concentrated mixture employed in the production of synthetic rubbers and plastics; hence as *v. trans.*, to mix in a master-batch; **masterbatching** *vbl. sb.*; †**master-bee**, (*a*) a queen bee (cf. KING *sb.* 8 a); (*b*) ? a worker bee; †**master-bowl** (see sense 9); **master-brain**, = MASTER-MIND *sb.* b.; **master card**, (*a*) *Bridge* (see quots.); (*b*) a record card which summarizes the information recorded on a number of other cards; **master class**, (*a*) the most powerful or influential class in society; (*b*) a class receiving instruction from a 'master' (a person of distinguished skill), esp. in *Music*; **master clock**, a clock which transmits regular pulses of electricity for controlling impulse dials or computer operations; **master-craftsman**, a craftsman thoroughly conversant with his trade; one who employs workmen; also *transf.*; hence ***master-craftsmanship***; **master fault** *Geol.*, a fault which governs the configuration of the surrounding area; †**master gunner** (see GUNNER 1 c); hence †**master gunnership**, the office of a master gunner; **master hand**, (*a*) the hand of a master, the agency of one highly skilled or one possessing commanding power; (*b*) a highly skilled worker; **master-hunt** [see HUNT *sb.*[1]], a head huntsman; **master joint** *Geol.*, a principal joint in a rock mass; **master mariner**, the commander of a ship (for mod. use see MARINER 1 b); †**master note** *Mus.*, a semibreve (see quot.); **master number** = *matrix number* (MATRIX 7); **master oscillator**, an oscillator used to produce a constant frequency, esp. the carrier frequency of a radio or television transmitter; **master race**, a race of people considered to be pre-eminent in greatness or power; *spec.* the Germans or 'Aryans' (see ARYAN *sb.* 2) regarded as a superior people (cf. HERRENVOLK) during the Nazi period; **master rod**, in a rotary or radial engine, a rod which connects one of the pistons to the crankshaft and carries the wrist pins to which the link rods are connected; **master-scene**, **shot** *Cinematography* (see quots.); †**master shipman** = *master-mariner*; **master sinew**, a main sinew; *esp.* the tendon in the hock of a quadruped, corresponding to the tendon of Achilles in man; **master-slave manipulator**, a type of manipulator (sense 2 f) which reproduces at the handling end the positions and motions of the operator's fingers; †**master water**, a liquid having powerful chemical effects; (**rattlesnake**) **master weed** *U.S.*, a plant regarded as an antidote to rattlesnake bites (cf. *rattlesnake-master*); †**master woman**, an imperious or masculine woman; **master-worker** = *master-workman*; also *spec.* in the Mint (see quot. 1670); **master workman**, a workman thoroughly conversant with his trade; one who employs workmen; also *fig.*; **master-yaw**, = *mamma-pian* (see MAMMA[1] e). See also MASTER-BUILDER, -CRAFT, -FAST, etc.

1669 PEPYS *Diary* 25 Mar., I did .. rattle the *Master-Attendants out of their wits almost. **1858** W. M. GILSON in *Merc. Marine Mag.* V. 211, I don't think there is any Master-Attendant at Trincomalee dockyard. **1937** H. BARRON *Mod. Rubber Chem.* vii. 79 Certain fundamental ingredients such as accelerators, antioxidants and sulphur are always added in small quantities. .. It is now common practice to add them as a '*masterbatch'. **1953** N. L. CATTON *Neoprenes* 32 A convenient method of making sure that mixing operations are carried out in the elastic phase is through the use of concentrated master-batches. **1959** *Times* 13 Mar. 10/2 The Cariflex range consists of hot and cold polymers, oil masterbatches, carbon black masterbatches and hot and cold latices. **1964** *Amer. Speech* XXXIX. 272 Most stocks .. in a tire are mixed in two stages. The masterbatch is the first stage, in which all the rubbers and pigments are mixed except for the curing agents. **1953** *Industr. & Engin. Chem.* May 1059/2 Copolymers of butadiene and styrene .. have been extended with various rosin-type acids in a manner similar to that employed in extending with petroleum oils (latex *masterbatching). **1971** CROWTHER & EDMONDSON in C. M. Blow *Rubber Technol. & Manuf.* viii. 269 It is generally accepted that masterbatching improves the physical properties of those compounds where a high degree of carbon black dispersion must be achieved. *Ibid.* 270 The curing ingredients themselves may be masterbatched. **1579–80** NORTH *Plutarch, Lycurgus* (1595) 61 They .. were alwaies .. together, as the bees be about their *maister bee. **1645** WALLER *Palam. to Zelinde* 8 No Honey .. But what the Master Bees have plac't In compass of their Cells. **1658** ROWLAND tr. *Moufet's Theat. Ins.* 898 Their King or Master-Bee. **1923** E. WALLACE *Missing Million* xiv. 112 The *master-brain who took his pick of the cleverest criminals at large. **1905** R. F. FOSTER *Compl. Bridge* 316 **Master card*, the best left in play of any suit which has already been led. **1937** *Times* 13 Apr. p. iv/3 A .. tabulator, which .. can collate, record and analyse 900 production facts a minute, as well as produce master cards summarizing the figures it tabulates. **1961** T. LANDAU *Encycl. Librarianship* (ed. 2) 236/2 *Master card*, a main entry in a card catalogue bearing tracings indicating all the added entries, [etc.]. **1964** COHEN & BARROW *A.B.C. of Contract Bridge* 282 *Master card*, a card that can be beaten only if it is trumped. **1970** O. DOPPING *Computers & Data Processing* iv. 72 If the machine has only one card feed, data are transferred from a master card to the following cards which are often called detail cards. **1861** MILL *Repr. Govt.* ii. 38 Slavery is .. corrupting to the *master-class when they once come under civilized influences. *c* **1926** 'MIXER' *Transport Workers' Song Bk.* 47 Note the constant drop in wages .. Endorsed by every rag-time press That the master-class command. **1930** J. DOS PASSOS *42nd Parallel* I. 104 Big Bill talked about .. sticking together in the face of the masterclass. **1963** *Ann. Reg. 1962* 446 Pablo Casals conducting a master class. **1965** *Listener* 10 June 873/2 Master-class exercises in comparative semantics and applied imagery. **1970** *Times* 26 Feb. 16/1 Old singers don't forget—they teach. And the best of them conduct master classes. **1973** *Times* 17 Apr. 32/4 Crash course on British Portraiture. .. Contact: Master Classes. **1973** *Ms.* Nov. 46/3 Ms. Rosenberger has worked out a variety of exercises like the one she suggested to the tense master-class student. **1904** *Master clock [see JOURNEYMAN 3 b]. **1922** G. L. OVERTON *Clocks & Watches* x. 108 If the master clock should have gained or lost at all, the arrangements provided for putting it right again are such that all the connected dials are at the same time automatically set to the right time. **1951** Master clock [see *impulse clock* s.v. IMPULSE *sb.* 6 b]. **1967** H. JACOBOWITZ *Electronic Computers made Simple* xiii. 261 Unless the computer is asynchronous .., all its operations are controlled by a series of equally spaced timing pulses from a master clock oscillator. **1937** G. B. BROWN *Arts in Early Eng.* VI. II. xi. 215 We are in almost complete ignorance as to the personalities of the *master craftsmen who created the schemes of enrichment. **1952** C. DAY LEWIS tr. *Virgil's Aeneid* II. 36 That master-craftsman of crime, Ulysses. *Ibid.* VIII. 177 Now there is need for Your strength, your speediest work and your master-craftsmanship. **1837** PHILLIPS *Geology* 63 The faults .. generally cross the anti-clinal axis, and terminate in a remarkable *master fault or axis of elevation. **1565** *Reg. Privy Council Scot.* I. 396 The said office of *maistir gunnarschip. **1625** in *Crt. & Times Jas. I* (1849) II. 502 Mr. Gibson .. who had in reversion the master-gunnership of England. **1709** POPE *Ess. Crit.* 145 Nameless graces .. which a *master-hand alone can reach. **1806–7** J. BERESFORD *Miseries Hum. Life* (1826) II. x, The master-hand of Tacitus. **1854** MILMAN *Lat. Chr.* IV. ii. (1883) II. 202 It might seem that, the master-hand withdrawn, all would return to the former anarchy. **1879** HOWELLS *L. Aroostook* II. xxvii, He's a master-hand to converse, any way. *c***1369** CHAUCER *Dethe Blaunche* 375 (Fairf. MS.) The *mayster hunte anoon fote hote With a grete horne blewe thre mote. **1656** EARL MONM. tr. *Boccalini's Advts. fr. Parnass.* 196 Zenofon, Apollos Master-hunt. **1839** MURCHISON *Silur. Syst.* I. xx. 244 The surprising regularity of the direction of the *master joints. **1879** *Encycl. Brit.* X. 297/2 Granite .. is traversed by two sets of chief or 'master-joints'. **13..** *Coer de L.* 1831 On the morwe he of-sent his counsellors Of the pates the *master mariners. *c* **1330** R. BRUNNE *Chron. Wace* (Rolls) 12089 Þe mayster mariner was byhynde, Þe schip to stere by þe wynde. **1838, 1886** [see MARINER 1 b]. **1662** PLAYFORD *Skill Mus.* I. vii. 23 The Semibrief .. is called the *Master Note, being of one Measure by himself; all the other Notes are reckoned by his value, by Augmentation or Diminution. **1969** *John Edwards Mem. Foundation Q.* V. IV. 146 Such documents are of great importance to the discographer who is trying to assemble the usual discographic data of *master number, recording date .. and release number. **1973** in B. Holiday *Lady sings Blues* 208 In the era of 78 rpm records most companies assigned a number to each recording they made for the sake of handy reference, called the 'master' number. **1928** STERLING & KRUSE *Radio Manual* viii. 305 The tuning of this type of circuit consists fundamentally of setting the *master oscillator at the desired wavelength and then resonating the antenna circuit for maximum antenna current. **1951** W. E. PANNETT *Radio Installations* vii. 177 The quartz crystal .. has largely superseded valve circuits as a master oscillator for controlling the frequency of a transmitter. **1971** M. G. SCROGGIE *Found. Wireless & Electronics* xv. 244 The function of what is usually called the master oscillator is to define the frequency of the station at least as accurately and constantly as the now very narrow international regulations require. **1942** J. S. HUXLEY in *South Atlantic Q.* XLI. 354 The [German] nation is formidably united behind its own ideal of an 'Aryan' *Master-Race. **1945** D. THOMSON et al. *Patterns of Peacemaking* iii. 118 Her expansionism has been due to a triple convergence of forces: the economic greed and lust for power of her ruling classes, the primitive and tribal nationalist and imperialist sentiments of her people, and hatred of the foreigner which takes the form of theories of Japanese being a 'master-race'. **1949** D. MACARDLE *Children of Europe* xiv. 212 Boys and girls who had been impregnated with the teaching of Nazi schools .. shared the overwhelming pride of the 'Master Race'. **1953** P. ABRAHAMS *Return to Goli* vi. 215 Imperceptibly, a 'master race' mentality is in the making [in Kenya]. **1974** *Times* 21 Oct. 3/4 To suggest that I [*sc.* Sir Keith Joseph] was arguing for a 'master race' .. is .. very wrong. **1922** *Encycl. Brit.* XXX. 36/2 Connecting-rods of rotary and radial engines consist usually of one *master rod, ball or roller-bearinged, with the big-end enlarged to form circular lugs to secure wrist pins carrying the plain or auxiliary type of rod of the remaining cylinders. **1928** Master rod [see *link rod* s.v. LINK *sb.*[2] 7]. **1946** J. W. VALE *Aviation Mechanic's Engine Manual* iii. 87 Constructing the crank-shaft in sections permits use of the one-piece master rod. **1960** O. SKILBECK *ABC of Film & T.V.* 83 **Master scene*, usually an establishing shot; the basic scene from which a sequence is edited by intercutting or adding closer shots. A master scene script is an optional stage in writing .. in which only the above appear. **1960** D. WILSON *Television Playwright* 16 The plays in this book are printed in 'Rehearsal Script' form, that is to say, the manuscript as the author wrote it. In the Cinema this would be called a 'Master-scene Script'. **1390** GOWER *Conf.* III. 311 The *Maister schipman cam and preide With othre suche as be therinne. *c* **1450** LOVELICH *Grail* xxxvi 499 Thanne A Maister Schipman gan forth to gon. **1953** K. REISZ *Technique Film Editing* 280 **Master shot*, single shot of an entire piece of dramatic action taken in order to facilitate the assembly of the component closer shots of details from which the sequence will finally be covered. **1959** P. BULL *I know Face* v. 94 We started .. with a 'master-shot', which means that the actors go through the entire scene from rather far off and only portions of the shot are likely to be used in the final film. **1972** R. MANVELL *Internat. Encycl. Film* 356 *Master shot*, the main shot of a complete piece of dramatic action, which facilitates the assembly of the component shots of which it will finally be composed. *a* **1300** *Cursor M.* 3941 Iacob was þan hurt wel sare, Þe *maister sinu of his the. **1607** TOPSELL *Four-f. Beasts* 402 A painefull swelling of the maister sinnew. **1952**, etc. *Master-slave manipulator [see MANIPULATOR 2 f]. **1960** *Times* 24 May 20/4 Closed-circuit stereoscopic television combined with a light-duty master-slave manipulator .. enables an operator to see the articles which he is moving in a solid radiation-proof container. **1644** NYE *Gunnery* I. (1647) 13 Take the Saltpeter out, and preserve the water that dropped, because it is *Master water. **1843** MARRYAT *M. Violet* xxiii, I beheld five or six stems of the rattlesnake *master weed. *Ibid.* xxiv, I removed .. the poultice of master weed. **1534** MORE *Comf. agst. Trib.* III. Wks. 1224/1 She is in dede a stoute *master woman. **1413** *Pilgr. Sowle* (Caxton 1483) v. xiv. 108 Yf thou wylt bylde an hows, and arte a *maister werker, couthest thou bilde withouten mater. **1622** MALYNES *Anc. Law-Merch.* 281 The Master worker .. doth put into the melting pot, two penny weight of Copper in euerie pound. **1670** PETTUS *Fodinæ Reg.* 41 The Master-worker, who receiveth the Silver from the Warden, causeth it to be melted, and delivereth it to the Moniers, and taketh it from them again when it is made. **1598** BARRET *Theor. Warres* v. iii. 134 A *maister workeman to ioyne them [boats] together. **1615** CROOKE *Body of Man* 217 The great Maister workman therefore of set purpose, made the one halfe of mankinde imperfect. **1670** EACHARD *Cont. Clergy* 118 An ordinary bricklayer, or carpenter (I mean not your great undertakers and master-workmen) .. has certainly the command of more money. **1847** EMERSON *Repr. Men, Napoleon* Wks. (Bohn) I. 368 He is .. a very consistent and wise master-workman. **1774** *Med. Ess.* V. II. 793 Sometimes after .. the Salivation is over, there remains one large Yaw, high knobbed, red and moist; this is commonly called the *Master yaw.

VI. 31. As a suffix forming compounds (mostly proprietary names) designating articles, appliances, etc., that are held to be supreme or superior in the field denoted by their first elements.

1935 *Vogue* 1 Dec. 110 Rainbow Matchmaster. **1937** *Amer. Speech* XII. 265 Then there are the *Buffet-Master*, a 'combination grill and waffle iron', *Menu-master*, *Kook-master*, and *Grill Master*, all electric grills. **1947** J. BERTRAM *Shadow of War* 334, I glanced across the lighted interior of the big Skymaster. **1955** M. MCCARTHY *Charmed Life* (1956) ii. 52 The combination waffle iron and sandwich grill, the roto-broiler, the mixmaster. **1960** *Times Lit. Suppl.* 1 July 414/2 The shops were filled with goods and buyers .. in the houses washers, dryers .. Mixmasters. **1972** M. CRICHTON *Terminal Man* I. v. 41 Robert Morris was sitting in the hospital cafeteria .. when his pagemaster went off. .. He .. went to the wall phone to answer his page.

master ('mɑːstə(r), -æ-), *sb.*[2] [f. MAST *sb.*[1] + -ER[1] 1.] A vessel having (a specified number of) masts, as in ***three-master***, ***seven-master***, etc.

1880 in WEBSTER *Suppl.* **1887** [see FIVE C. 1 c]. **1901** *Daily Chron.* 26 July 5/2 The keel of a gigantic seven-master has been laid.

master ('mɑːstə(r)), *v.* Forms: see MASTER *sb.*[1] [f. MASTER *sb.*[1] Cf. OF. *maistrier* (perh. the source in early instances), med.L. *magistrāre*, OHG. *meist(e)rôn* (G. *meistern*), Du. *meesteren*, Sw. *mestra*, Da. *mestre*.]

1. *trans.* To get the better of, in any contest or struggle; to overcome or defeat. With material or immaterial subject or object.

a **1225** *Leg. Kath.* 548 Ha wið hire anes mot meistreð us alle. *a* **1300** *Cursor M.* 25365 Quen þai faanding maister wele, Crund er þai wit mikel sele. **1303** R. BRUNNE *Handl. Synne* 7909 Y dredde hyt [synne] wlde ha maystrede me. **1375** BARBOUR *Bruce* VII. 211 The sleip masterit hym. ? *a* **1400** *Morte Arth.* 2683 He maisterede þat mane, so myghtty of strenghes. **1530** PALSGR. 633/2 Be he never so stronge I put no doutes to mayster hym. **1567** MAPLET *Gr. Forest* 83 b, [Some dogges] haue Maystred and bene good inough for the Lyon and Elephant. **1576** BAKER *Jewell of Health* 131 b, The sayd water drunck maystreth and expelleth poysons. **1591** SPENSER *Ruines of Rome* xviii, These brave Pallaces, which maystred bee Of time. *a* **1623** FLETCHER *Love's Cure* v. iii. (1647), Kings nor authority can master fate. **1647** CLARENDON *Hist. Reb.* I. §21 The King .. was very quicksighted in .. raising objections, and very slow

in mastering them. **1664** POWER *Exp. Philos.* II. 109 The smaller weight of Quicksilver is not able to master the Elastick pressure of the external Ayr. **1703** MAUNDRELL *Journ. Jerus.* (1732) 112 Here we had a very steep and rocky ascent; but however in half an hour we master'd it. **1725** DE FOE *Voy. round World* (1840) 33 The chief conspirators would be on shore..and..then I thought I could master the rest on board well enough. **1798** BERESFORD in *Ld. Auckland's Corr.* (1862) III. 414 Lord Edward was mastered, brought to the Castle, and committed to Newgate. **1838** THIRLWALL *Greece* V. xliii. 253 He resorted to new..methods of mastering his personal disadvantages. **1841** JAMES *Brigand* xx, Deep grief masters me. **1887** RIDER HAGGARD *Jess* vi, A crash that almost mastered the awful crackling of the thunder.

2. To reduce to subjection, compel to obey; to break, tame (an animal).

1423 JAS. I *Kingis Q.* clxxxi, The quhich[ë] treuly efter, day be day, That all my wittes maistrit had tofore, From hen[ne]sferth the paynis did away. **1523** LD. BERNERS *Froiss.* I. ccccxxvi. 748 The gates myght stand open..for all maner of men of warre to entre..to thentent to myster them of Parys. **1580** in *Liturg. Serv. Q. Eliz.* (1847) 573 Masters, unable to master their own affections, are become servants to other folks' servants. **1586** J. HOOKER *Hist. Irel.* in *Holinshed* II. 133/2 They..swore to be..obedient: which, so long as he maistered and kept them vnder, so long they performed it. *a* **1628** PRESTON *Breastpl. Love* (1631) 210 Doe not you reckon it a worke to breake horses, to master coltes? **1639** FULLER *Holy War* II. xxxiii. (1640) 87 Yet was he not mastered by his purse, but made it his vassal. **1725** WATTS *Logic* III. iii. §2 Every wise man masters his passions; no angry man masters his passions. **1774** GOLDSM. *Nat. Hist.* (1776) II. 393 The Zebra..could never be entirely mastered. **1844** MRS. BROWNING *Drama of Exile* Poems 1850 I. 71 This shall..master with a look Your lion at his fasting. **1876** GEO. ELIOT *Dan. Der.* IV. xxviii, He meant to be master of a woman who would have liked to master him.

3. *techn.* To temper or season; to modify. Now only in *Dyeing*, to season or age (dye stuffs), and in *Tanning*, to subject (skins) to the action of an astringent lye. (Cf. MASTERING *vbl. sb.* 2.)

1398 TREVISA *Barth. De P.R.* XIX. xxxiii. (1495) 878 And wyth Attrament ynke is tempryd and maystryd [orig. *acuitur*]. *Ibid.* 879 The colour purpura is maystred [orig. *acuitur*] and amended wyth blood that droppyth of certen shelle fysshe. *a* **1648** DIGBY *Closet Open.* (1677) 59 That the hot herbs may be mastered with the cool. **1841** in *Titles Patents* (1854) 1145 An expeditious mode of unhairing, mastering, and tanning..hides and skins. **1862** O'NEILL *Dict. Calico Print. & Dyeing* Index, Mastering or ageing of logwood.

4. To make oneself master of (an art, science, etc.); to acquire complete knowledge or understanding of (a fact, a proposition), or complete facility in using (an instrument, etc.).

1740 J. CLARKE *Educ. Youth* (ed. 3) 163 A boy has.. mastered his Syntax. **1781** COWPER *Parrot* 9 Belinda's maids are soon preferred To teach him now and then a word, As Poll can master it. *a* **1839** PRAED *Poems* (1864) II. 176 Away with ye, visions of law, Of cases I never shall master. **1865** KINGSLEY *Herew.* viii, Grammar, rhetoric, Latin prose and poetry..she mastered ere she was grown up. **1866** G. MACDONALD *Ann. Q. Neighb.* xiv. (1878) 296 When he considered that he had mastered the meaning of it. **1878** R. W. DALE *Lect. Preach.* iv. 91 The instrument you have to master stands before you—the soul of man. **1901** *Athenæum* 27 July 120/3 He has not mastered the difference between 'would' and 'should'.

†**b.** 'To execute with skill' (J.). *Obs.*

1624 BACON *Consid. War w. Spain* (1629) 3, I doe not take my selfe to bee so perfect in the customes..and priuileges of that Kingdome of Bohemia, as to be fit to handle that part; and I will not offer at that I cannot master.

5. To act the part of master towards; to rule as a master; to be the master of (a servant, scholar, house, etc.).

1611 SHAKS. *Cymb.* IV. ii. 383, I will not say Thou shalt be so well master'd. *Ibid.* 395, I good youth, And rather Father thee, than Master thee. **1711** SWIFT *Jrnl. to Stella* 2 Aug., The dog [his man Patrick] thinks he has the whip-hand of me; he begins to master me; so now I am resolved to part with him. **1715** M. DAVIES *Athen. Brit.* I. 19 He doubtless would have ordered it [St. Paul's School] to be Master'd by Learned Chaplains alone. **1790** R. TYLER *Contrast* II. ii, Father said I should come as Colonel Manly's waiter,..but no man shall master me. *a* **1845** HOOD *Lamia* i. 128, I have a house..within the walls of Corinth: Will you not master it as well as me? **1864** A. MCKAY *Hist. Kilmarnock* (1880) 366 I'm your equal: I'll be maistered nae langer. **1881** *Daily News* 14 Sept. 3/1 The estate is not well mastered. **1898** *Ibid.* 30 June 6/7 It was..a magnificent school,..magnificently mastered.

†**b.** *intr.* To act the master. Also ***to master it.***

1656 S. H. *Golden Law* 67 He..did justly master it, and rule over his masters. **1793** MME. D'ARBLAY *Diary* V. IX. 402, I have been scholaring all day, and mastering too; for our lessons are mutual.

†**6.** *trans.* To have at one's disposal; to own, possess. Also *intr.* in ***to master of.*** *Obs.*

1593 SHAKS. *Lucr.* 863 He hath it [treasure] when he cannot vse it, And leaues it to be maistred by his yong. **1596** —— *Merch. V.* v. i. 174 The wealth That the world masters. *c* **1600** —— *Sonn.* cvi, I see their antique Pen would have exprest Euen such a beautie as you master now. **1638** SIR T. HERBERT *Trav.* (ed. 2) 175 Had hee mastered any weapon, he had doubtlesse saved himselfe; but wanting it his breath failed. **1654–66** EARL ORRERY *Parthen.* (1676) 314 Bidding his Treasurer give him higher rewards, than the prisoner could Master of.

†**b.** To take possession of. *Obs.* (? *nonce-use.*)

1826 J. F. COOPER *Mohicans* xxv, The Hurons would follow up our trail, and master our scalps.

7. To address by the style of 'master'. *nonce-use.*

1583 STUBBES *Anat. Abus.* I. (1879) 122 He who hath moni enough shalbe rabbied & maistered at euery word.

masterable ('mɑːstərəb(ə)l), *a.* [f. MASTER *v.* + -ABLE.] Capable of being mastered.

1882 PROCTOR *Fam. Sci. Stud.* 1 Man might believe..that every kind of knowledge is..masterable.

'master-at-'arms. *Naut.* Formerly a warrant-officer in the navy appointed to instruct the officers and crew of a ship of war in the exercise of small arms, and to act as principal police officer on board (= MARSHAL 7 b), but now a first-class petty officer doing duty in the latter capacity only. Also *transf.*, the principal police officer on board a ship of the mercantile marine.

1748 SMOLLETT *Rod. Rand.* xxix, I was taken prisoner, and carried to the poop by the master-at-arms. **1861** THRING *Crim. Law Navy* 53 The Commander-in-Chief appoints some person (usually the master-at-arms of the flag-ship) to act as provost-marshal. **1890** W. J. GORDON *Foundry* 74, 500 cabin passengers, to look after whose comfort and conduct there are employed six dozen stewards, ..two masters-at-arms, and a surgeon. **1894** C. N. ROBINSON *Brit. Fleet* 474 A master-at-arms with a staff of ship's corporals is allowed in the larger ships.

masterate ('mɑːstərət). [f. MASTER *sb.*[1] + -ATE[1]; cf. DOCTORATE *sb.*[1]] The degree or dignity of a master (see MASTER *sb.*[1] 14).

1902 *Science* 17 Oct. 612 The masterates should, of course, be permanent, and should not involve financial relations with the Institution. **1961** *Press* (Christchurch, N.Z.) 23 Mar. 10/8 There was not enough incentive for the best students to proceed to masterate degrees. **1966** *New Statesman* 16 Sept. 411/2 (Advt.), The Department [in Massey University, New Zealand] offers courses leading to the masterate level in Arts and to the Diploma in Education. **1971** *Commonwealth Universities Yearbk.* 1408 There is no uniformity among either universities or faculties as to the stage at which honours are awarded but they are frequently deferred to the masterate.

'master-,builder. [MASTER *sb.*[1] II.]

1. One who is skilled in the art of building, an architect. Chiefly in rhetorical use or fig. context.

1557 N. T. (Genev.) *1 Cor.* iii. 10 As a skilful master builder I haue layd the foundation: and another buyldeth theron. **1594** T. B. *La Primaud. Fr. Acad.* II. 18 If we consider the ordinary generation of men, the matter is humour: naturall heate is as it were the master buylder. **1611** SPEED *Theat. Gt. Brit.* Pref., So many master-builders having in this subject gone before me. **1642** VICARS *God in Mount* (1644) 39 Our blessed Master-builders in Parliament. **1855** MISS COBBE *Intuit. Mor.* 35 The depth of the foundation shows how high the Master-builder will carry his temple. **1865** J. H. INGRAHAM *Pillar of Fire* (1872) 47 The Egyptians are not only master-builders in architecture, but [etc.].

2. One who employs workmen in building.

1714 SWIFT *Pres. St. Aff.* ¶10 When a Building is to be erected, the Model may be the contrivance only of one head; and it is sufficient that the Under-workmen be ordered to cut stones into certain shapes, [etc.]: But the several Master-builders must have some general Knowledge of the Design, without which they can give no orders at all. **1738** BIRCH *Life Milton* in *M.'s Wks.* (1738) I. 61 Anne [Milton] married a Master-Builder.

3. *Naut.* A petty officer formerly employed on the construction of ships.

1799 NELSON 11 Oct. in Nicolas *Disp.* (1845) IV. 47 My directions to the Master-builder relative to the Ships.

'mastercraft. *nonce-wd.* [f. MASTER *sb.*[1] + CRAFT.] Politic dealing characteristic of a master.

1711 HICKES *Two Treat. Christ. Priesth.* (1847) I. 140 There is no more..priestcraft in the clergy..than mastercraft in the father of a family.

masterdom ('mɑːstədəm). [f. MASTER *sb.*[1] + -DOM.]

†**1.** The office of a master or teacher; the degree of master (of divinity). *Obs. rare*$^{-1}$.

a **1050** *Liber Scintill.* xxxii. (1889) 120 *Pondus magisterii*, hefe mæʒsterdomes. *c* **1384** WYCLIF *Sel. Wks.* III. 376 What cursidenesse is þis [for a friar] to gete hym a cappe of maysterdome, by preyer of lordis, and grete giftis.

2. The position of being master; dominion, absolute control, supremacy; †victory in battle. In 1755 'Not in use' (J.).

1475 *Bk. Noblesse* (Roxb.) 7 When the duc off Burgoyn by cyvyle batayll by maisterdom expelled the duc of Orlyance partie..owt of Parys cytee. *a* **1500** *Chaucer's Dreme* 1784 And cursed the time that ever slouth Should have such masterdome of trouth. **1596** SPENSER *F.Q.* V. ii. 15 With cruell chaufe their courages they whet, The maysterdome of each by force to gaine. **1605** SHAKS. *Macb.* I. v. 71 Which shall to all our Nights, and Dayes to come, Giue solely soueraigne sway, and Masterdome. **1656** H. MORE *Enthus. Tri.* A iij, You are grown a man of strange Master-dome over your Passions. **1693** W. FREKE *Sel. Ess.* i. 4 That Body of Knowledge that has puzzl'd whole Ages of the wisest, who is so weak as to arrogate the Masterdom of it alone to himself? **1880** SWINBURNE *Stud. Shaks.* 26 The stage which he [Marlowe] was born to..re-create by the might and masterdom of his genius. **1886** BLACKIE *What does Hist. Teach?* 73 The masterdom of the Roman Pope.

†**b.** Masterful behaviour. *Obs.*

1596 SPENSER *F.Q.* IV. i. 46 For Love is free, and led with selfe delight, Ne will enforced be with maisterdome or might.

†**3.** = MASTERSHIP. *Obs.*

1588 *Marprel. Epist.* (Arb.) 3 Mine Epistle vnto your venerable masterdomes. **1589** *Pasquil's Ret.* D iv, May it please your Masterdom. **1601** CHETTLE & MUNDAY *Death Earl Huntington* D 2 b, Apolloes master doone [*read* masterdom] I inuocate.

4. ***grand masterdom***: the office of grand master.

1762 tr. *Busching's Syst. Geog.* V. 450 The administration of the grand masterdom is ever since become a mere title.

mastered ('mɑːstəd), *ppl. a.* [f. MASTER *v.* + -ED.] In senses of the vb.

1661 MORGAN *Sph. Gentry* III. ix. 112 [He] rescued the best of his former mastered french ships. **1693** DRYDEN *Juvenal* x. 151 That Monarch, whom the Master'd World obey. **1814** SCOTT *Ld. of Isles* III. xxix, The master'd felon ..gasp'd beneath a mortal wound. **1899** J. CAIRD *Univ. Addr.* 33 The mastered and established facts of knowledge.

masterer ('mɑːstərə(r)). *rare.* [f. MASTER *v.* + -ER[1].] One who masters or overcomes.

1607 HIERON *Wks.* I. 256 Who would thinke that this reiected person..should be..the conquerour of Sathan, the masterer of death. **1820** L. HUNT *Indicator* No. 23 (1822) I. 184 But oh! thou Love's and Nature's masterer.

†**'masterfast,** *a. Obs.* [f. MASTER *sb.*[1] + FAST *a.* 4.] Bound to a master.

1469 *Paston Lett.* II. 388, I wyll not make me mastyrfast with my Lord of Norff. *c* **1520** *Bk. Mayd Emlyn* 167 in Hazl. *E.P.P.* IV. 88 He that is maysterfast..dare not ronne and playe. **1526** SKELTON *Magnyf.* 2573 To day maysterfest, to morowe he hath no holde. **1542** UDALL *Erasm. Apoph.* 78 b, Whoso hath ones marryed a wife, is..in maner half maisterfast.

masterful ('mɑːstəfʊl, -æ-), *a.* [f. MASTER *sb.*[1] + -FUL.]

1. Of persons (occas. of animals) or their dispositions: Addicted to acting the part of master; accustomed to insist on having one's own way; imperious, self-willed, overbearing. Of actions: High-handed, despotic, arbitrary.

13.. *E.E. Allit. P.* A. 401 Maysterful mod & hyȝe pryde I hete þe arn heterly hated here. *c* **1374** CHAUCER *Troylus* II. 756 Elþer þey [husbands] ben ful of Ialousye, Or maisterful. **1388** WYCLIF *2 Macc.* iv. 27 Sostratus..made maisterful axing [Vulg. *exactionem*]. —— *Luke* xii. 59 To the maistirful axer [Vulg. *exactori*]. *c* **1420** *Chron. Vilod.* 2926 Þe Iaylardes ..sayden þat þey wolden þe ȝates vp barste, And other maystrefull werkus þey wold wyrche. *c* **1550** *Exam. W. Thorpe* in Foxe *A. & M.* (1583) 533 Though such tyrantes be maisterfull and cruel in boasting and manasing. **1636** SANDERSON *Serm.* (1681) II. 53 What a-do there is with him, before..his masterful spirit be soundly subdued. *a* **1639** WHATELEY *Prototypes* II. xxvi. (1640) 72 Some children are very masterfull and disobedient. **1841–4** EMERSON *Ess., Over-Soul* Wks. (Bohn 1884) I. 111 Yonder masterful cuckoo Crowds every egg out of the nest. **1860** TROLLOPE *Framley P.* (1861) III. 193 She was proud and masterful. **1899** J. HUTCHINSON in *Arch. Surg.* X. 107 This masterful disregard of logical thought.

†**b.** *Law.* (chiefly *Sc.*) Of robbers, beggars, or their actions: Using violence or threats. *Obs.*

1561 *Reg. Privy Council Scot.* I. 166 For the wranguis, violent, injust and maisterfull spolatioun. **1564** *Ibid.* 289 The maisterfull reiff and stowth fra the said Johnne, furth of his dwelling hous..of lxxx scheip. **1585** *Ibid.* III. 747 Wandering people, maisterfull beggaris, and utheris. **1747–8** *Act 21 Geo. II*, c. 34 §20 The masterful taking away or detaining the same [cattle]. **1754** ERSKINE *Princ. Sc. Law* (1809) 507 The slaughter of night-thieves, house-breakers, assistants in masterful depredations, or rebels [etc.].

†**c.** Of natural agencies: Violent, overwhelming.

1513 DOUGLAS *Æneis* v. xiii. 57 Thi self is witnes quhow, laitlie our the laif, Sa maisterfull storme amyd the Libyan see Scho raisit sone. **1641** S. MARSHALL *Peace-offering* 5 They are compared to the most masterfull and mercilesse creatures of fire and water.

†**d.** ? Strong in resistance, hard to overcome. *Obs.*

c **1470** HENRY *Wallace* IV. 159 That land is strait, and maisterfull to wyn.

2. Having the capacities of a master; qualified to command; powerful and vigorous in rule. Formerly sometimes, †having authority, in a position to rule (*obs.*).

? *a* **1400** *Morte Arth.* 3414 The ferthe was syr Judas..The maysterfulle Makabee. *c* **1470** *Rauf Coilȝear* 442, I haue na myster to matche with maisterfull men. **1608** PANKE *Fal of Babel* 116 Great Marvaile it were that Damasus should be.. growne potent, and masterfull over the bishops of the East. **1675** *Art Contentm.* III. §16 Has given us the use of reason wherewith to manage that soveraignty, without which we had only bin the more masterful sort of brutes. **1890** HOSMER *Anglo-Saxon Freedom* 165 What if the occupant of the throne had been a ruler really good and gifted.. arbitrary but masterful?

absol. **1887** G. MEREDITH *Ballads & P.* 141 Errors To be by his young masterful repaired.

b. Of language, appearances, etc.: Indicative of mastery or controlling power.

1824 MISS MITFORD *Village* Ser. I. 264 A certain triumphant masterful look in his eyes. **1862** 'SHIRLEY' (J. Skelton) *Nugæ Crit.* ix. 375 The masterful words of a great man.

3. Characterized by the skill that constitutes a master; masterly. Now only in somewhat rhetorical use, with mixture of sense 2: Characterized by commanding power.

1613 W. BROWNE *Sheph. Pipe* I. (1614) C 4 b, Not might it been hid How masterfull a leech he had him kid. **1641** MILTON *Animadv.* II. 62 Variety..erects and rouses an auditory, like the masterful running over many chords and divisions. **1733** GENT *Rippon* xi, The most masterful strokes engrav'd on Copper. **1830** *Fraser's Mag.* I. 128 The manly and masterful novels of Sir Walter Scott. **1877** MRS.

OLIPHANT *Makers Flor.* Introd., The same masterful hand which carved the lovely anguish of the Dawn. **1883** RUSKIN *Art of Eng.* ii. (1884) 65 Whether pleasing or displeasing to your taste they are entirely masterful.

masterfully ('mɑːstəfʊlɪ, -æ-), *adv.* [f. MASTERFUL *a.* + -LY[2].] In a masterful manner (see the adj.).

1388 WYCLIF *Lev.* vi. 2 A soule that synneth..ethir takith maisterfuli a thing bi violence, ether makith fals chaleng. **1457** *Act 35 Hen. VI* in Bolton *Stat. Irel.* (1621) 24 They doe ..masterfully take their goods without any pity. **1563** *Reg. Privy Council Scot.* I. 238 Violentlie, maisterfullie and unjustlie reft..and takin. *a* **1603** T. CARTWRIGHT *Confut. Rhem. N.T.* (1618) 83 Peters [heart]..was so masterfully holden by the spirit of God. *a* **1670** SPALDING *Troub. Chas. I* (1829) 24 [They] took some money frae Mr. Robert Jameson..violently and masterfully. **1695** HUMFREY *Mediocria* 39 The Masterfully Learned Bishop Forbs. **1883** A. FORBES in *19th Cent.* Oct. 723 That reproach Britain strove callously and masterfully to perpetuate. **1899** T. M. ELLIS *Three Cat's-eye Rings* 29 'I'll take it to her', shouted Polryn, laying hold of it masterfully.

masterfulness ('mɑːstəfʊlnɪs, -æ-). [f. MASTERFUL *a.* + -NESS.] The quality of being masterful.

a **1586** SIDNEY *Arcadia* III. (1590) 314 That imperious maisterfulnesse which nature giues to men aboue women. **1880** *Daily Tel.* 22 Nov., He had held..the two great law offices..with unmatched felicity of language and masterfulness in opinion. **1893** *19th Cent.* Jan. 47 Masterfulness long survives mastery.

†'**masterhead.** *Obs. rare.* [f. MASTER *sb.*[1] + -HEAD.] = MASTERHOOD.

1382 WYCLIF *Rev.* Prol., That to men not knowende desyr of seching be set, and to men sechende frut of trauaile, and to God the doctrine of maisterhed be kept.

masterhood ('mɑːstəˌhʊd). [f. MASTER *sb.*[1] + -HOOD.] The condition or quality of being a master. †*good masterhood*: patronage.

c **1454** *Paston Lett.* I. 284 Thankyng you..of your gret jentylness and good maystyrhod shewyd on to me. *a* **1586** SIDNEY *Arcadia* I. (1590) 53 Who..(like to childish maisters) thinke their masterhood nothing, without doing iniury to them, who [etc.]. **1637** EARL MONM. tr. *Malvezzi's Romulus & Tarquin* 138 A little master-hood seemes enough where there is none at all. **1864** D. W. THOMPSON *Daydreams Schoolm.* 289 My masterhood slipt off me like a loose robe. **1869** RUSKIN *Q. of Air* (1874) 200 There is entire masterhood of its business up to the required point. **1875** SCRIVENER *Lect. Text N. Test.* 18 To decipher a double palimpsest calls for the masterhood of a Tischendorf.

mastering ('mɑːstərɪŋ), *vbl. sb.* Also 6 mastringe, 8 -ing. [f. MASTER *v.* + -ING[1].]

1. The action of the verb MASTER.

1654 tr. *Martini's Conq. China* 37 Considering at how dear a rate he had bought the mastering of that City. **1740** J. CLARKE *Educ. Youth* (ed. 3) 159 As much Time..will be requisite for the mastering of them, as was..employed upon the Historians. **1874** GREEN *Short Hist.* ii. §4. 71 His life was one long mastering of difficulty after difficulty.

2. *spec.* in *Dyeing* and *Tanning* (see MASTER *v.* 3). Hence *concr.* a kind of lye made of lime or other astringent and used by tanners. Also *attrib.* as *mastering-trough*.

c **1460** *E.E. Misc.* (Warton Cl.) 89 For the masterynge, ȝe moste caste owte ȝoure olde flote of ȝoure maderynge. **1553** *Req. True-hearted Eng.* (Shaks. Soc.) 5 The best wodde that our dyars occupye is masterynge. **1586** *Will J. Palfrye, Ilminster*, My mastringe troughe, beames, working irons and all other workinge tooles belonging to my occupation of a tanner. **1797** *Encycl. Brit.* (ed. 3) XVIII. 307/1 They [skins] are put into a pit of water impregnated with pigeon dung (called a grainer or mastring) forming a strong alkaline ley. **1802** *Chron.* in *Ann. Reg.* 454 To beam or work green hides and skins out of the mastering or drench. **1825** J. NICHOLSON *Operat. Mechanic* Gloss., *Mastering*.. Preparation of lime used by tanners.

mastering ('mɑːstərɪŋ), *ppl. a.* [f. MASTER *v.* + -ING[2].] That masters, subdues, or controls. †Of an army, a garrison: Superior in force (*obs.*).

1590 SPENSER *F.Q.* III. vii. 2 Her white Palfrey, having conquered The maistring raines out of her weary wrest. **1596** —— *Hymne Heav. Beautie* 214 Ne could that Painter (had he lived yet)..Have purtrayd this, for all his maistring skill. **1599** PORTER *Angry Wom. Abingt.* (Percy Soc.) 33, I could..Carry a maistering eye vpon my maide. **1603** FLORIO *Montaigne* (1634) 462 Yet must not shee be sterne, mastring, imperious and importunate. **1633** G. HERBERT *Temple, Ch. Porch* xviii, Some great estates provide, but doe not breed A mastr'ing minde. **1694** S. JOHNSON *Notes Past. Let. Bp. Burnet* I. 58 Moses's Serpent was the Mastering Serpent and destroyed theirs. **1711** in *10th Rep. Hist. MSS. Comm.* App. v. 169 Could it be imagined that..a mastering garrison, would surrender without a blow. **1863** KINGLAKE *Crimea* II. 499 That Causeway battery which, until it was touched by the mastering key, had barred the mouth of the Pass. **1897** R. H. STORY *Apostolic Min. Scott. Ch.* viii. 291 The mastering passion.

†**b.** *mastering vein* = MASTER-VEIN. *Obs.*

1605 DRAYTON *Idea*, '*As in some countries*', First make incision on each maistring vaine.

master-key. A key that will open a number of different locks, each of which has its own key that will not open any of the rest. Also *fig.*

1576 J. DEE *Gen. & Rare Mem.* (1577) 8 This Pety Nauy Royall is thought to be the onely Maister Key wherewith to open all Locks. **1686** PLOT *Staffordsh.* 376 The Keys shall neither of them open each others lock, yet one Master-key shall open them all. **1748** HARTLEY *Observ. Man* I. iii. 352 A Master-key for unlocking the Mysteries in the Constitution of natural Bodies. **1821** SCOTT *Kenilw.* xxiii, Janet..had a master-key which opened the postern-door. **1821** HAZLITT *Table-Talk* I. xvi. 376 Affectation is the master-key to both. **1872** O. W. HOLMES *Poet Breakf.-t.* ix. (1885) 233 These same yellow disks are the master-keys that let one in. **1882** *Encycl. Brit.* XIV. 748/2 The owner..may have one master-key that will open them all. *a* **1930** D. H. LAWRENCE *Phoenix II* (1968) 101 And he, she knew to her anguish and mortification, he was still the master-key to almost all life, for her. **1934** *Planning* II. XL. 2 Self-government for industry may prove to be the master key to many of our..problems.

masterless ('mɑːstəlɪs), *a.* [f. MASTER *sb.*[1] and (sense 2) *v.* + -LESS.]

1. a. Having no master. Of animals: Deprived of a controlling hand or influence.

c **1400** *Destr. Troy* 11131 Þai mellit with the mirmydons, þat maisturles were. *c* **1420** LYDG. *Assembly of Gods* 881 Full lothe they were to be [*printed* he] mastyrles. *c* **1430** *Syr Gener.* (Roxb.) 4192 Many a feire stede went a-stray Mastirles that same day. **1590** SPENSER *F.Q.* I. vii. 19 His silver shield, now idle, maisterlesse. *a* **1600** *Flodden F.* iv. (1664) 34 And many a servant masterless. **1673** *Lady's Call.* I. ii. §12 God sets not the same value upon their [widows] being masterless, which some of them do. **1686** *Lond. Gaz.* No. 2196/1 The Grand Signior..has..turned loose his Grey-hounds to run up and down the streets Masterless. **1834** JAMES *J. Marston Hall* xiv, The Count's horse, masterless and foaming, darted into the courtyard. **1870** MORRIS *Earthly Par.* I. II. 582 Yielded towns were set aflame; For all the land was masterless. **1887** C. T. MARTIN in *Dict. Nat. Biog.* IX. 59/2 Being again left masterless, he [Carew] went over to the enemy's camp.

b. In 16–17th c. statutes, etc., used to designate one who has no reputable means of living; vagrant, vagabond. *Obs.* exc. *Hist.*

c **1471** in *Pol. Poems* (Rolls) II. 279 Like maysterles men away thay wente. **1530** PALSGR. 563/2, I loyter as an ydell or masterlesse person dothe. **1535** *Act 27 Hen. VIII*, c. 25 Such ruffelers..as..shall frequent hunt or loyter masterles and out of seruice. **1555** *Act 2 & 3 Ph. & Mary* c. 16 §1 Watermen..for the most parte been masterles men. **1626** in *10th Rep. Hist. MSS. Comm.* App. v. 474 All idle and maisterlesse personnes and such others as shall not finde maisters or men of quallitie to undertake for them. **1651** HOBBES *Leviath.* II. xviii. 94 That dissolute condition of masterlesse men. **1720** STRYPE *Stow's Surv.* (1754) II. v. xxx. 535/1 Valiant and sturdy rogues and masterless men. **1881** SHORTHOUSE *J. Inglesant* I. xvii, A number of vagrant and masterless people.

c. *transf.* Of unknown authorship or provenance.

1899 A. LANG *Homeric Hymns* 6 The conventional attribution of the Hymns to Homer..is merely the result of the tendency to set down 'masterless' compositions to a well-known name. **1903** *Library* IV. 397 It has become possible to assign to..Peter von Olpe a small group of books hitherto masterless.

†**2.** That cannot be mastered; ungovernable. *Obs.*

1619 W. SCLATER *Expos. 1 Thess.* (1630) 290 Their power masterlesse on earth, makes them forget that they also haue a Master and Iudge in heauen. **1651** N. BACON *Disc. Govt. Eng.* II. xiii. (1739) 74 The King..yielded up his Power to his Queen, (a masterless and proud woman). **1687** *Lond. Gaz.* No. 2275/2 The flame grew at last masterless. **1767** G. WHITE *Selborne, To Pennant* vii, Such vast heath-fires are lighted up, that they often get to a masterless head.

Hence '**masterlessˌness.**

1827–48 HARE *Guesses* Ser. II. (1867) 476 For Johnson to make such a parade of masterlessness as he does by prefixing these lines to the Rambler.

†'**masterlike**, *a.* and *adv. Obs.* [f. MASTER *sb.*[1] + -LIKE.] **A.** *adj.* Resembling a master, or what pertains to a master; despotic, autocratic, sovereign; authoritative, magisterial; exhibiting masterly ability or skill. **B.** *adv.* In a 'masterlike' manner.

?*a* **1500** *Chester Pl., Harrowing Hell* (Shaks. Soc.) II. 75 Who is he..That so maisterlike comes us amonge. **1580** *Ord. Prayer* in *Liturg. Serv. Q. Eliz.* (1847) 573 Servants are become master-like, and fellows with Masters. **1581** J. BELL *Haddon's Answ. Osor.* 240 Agaynst this Masterlyke sentence I will set downe the opinion of Basile. **1637** EARL MONM. tr. *Malvezzi's Romulus & Tarquin* 294 He who writ of so many things, and writ so masterlike in all. **1641** SIR F. WORTLEY *Truth Asserted* 5 Not exercising a master-like or Kingly command. **1656** EARL MONM. tr. *Boccalini's Advts. fr. Parnass.* I. xliii. (1674) 58 He would teach..how to repulse the wrestlers..; and other excellent master-like tricks. **1665–6** PEPYS *Diary* 23 Feb., I begin to doubt the picture.. is not of his making, it is so master-like.

masterliness ('mɑːstəlɪnɪs). [f. MASTERLY *a.* + -NESS.] The quality of being masterly.

1721 WODROW *Corr.* (1843) II. 590 He can lay claim to little masterliness in eloquence, who knows not how to handle his subject elegantly. **1838** J. STERLING *Ess.*, etc. (1848) I. 245 The thorough masterliness of the style. **1865** *Ch. Times* 21 Oct. 332/2 Lord Palmerston..submitted his natural good judgement to the pretended masterliness of him with the phylacteries.

masterling ('mɑːstəlɪŋ). Also *dial.* maisterlin'. [f. MASTER *sb.*[1] + -LING[1].]

†**1.** One who has the power of a master; a conqueror, a chief. *Obs.*

c **1200** *Trin. Coll. Hom.* 113 *Tollite portas, principes, uestras* ..ȝe maisterlinges of þesternesse openeð ȝiwer gaten. **13..** *K. Alis.* 400 Y have bygete on the a kyng That schal beo Phelippes maisterlyng. *a* **1400–50** *Alexander* 481 A proude feste of princes & dukis, With maisterlingis of Messadone.

2. As diminutive: A petty master.

1869 *Lonsdale Gloss.*, *Maisterlin'*, a would-be master, a petty master. **1880** L. FAGAN *Sir A. Panizzi* I. 52 Your most benign petty masterling's lawful authority.

masterly ('mɑːstəlɪ), *a.* [f. MASTER *sb.*[1] + -LY[1].]

†**1.** Belonging to, characteristic of, or resembling a master or lord; usually in bad sense, arbitrary, despotic; imperious, overbearing, domineering. *Obs.*

1531–2 LATIMER *Let.* in Foxe *A. & M.* (1583) 1750 The Galathians..were in a quiet trade vnder the dominion of maysterly Curates. **1561** T. NORTON *Calvin's Inst.* (1634) Pref., They stablished..so many canons, so many masterly [F. *magistrales*] determinations, without any word of God. *a* **1618** RALEIGH *Prerog. Parl.* (1628) 43 It was a proud and maisterly speech of the Duke. **1645** MILTON *Tetrach.* Wks. 1851 IV. 188 It gives place to maisterly power, for the Maister might take away from an Hebrew servant the wife which hee gave him. **1649** —— *Eikon.* v. ibid. III. 370 He told them with a maisterly Brow, that [etc.]. **1667** DRYDEN *Sir Martin Mar-all* IV. i, You are a saucy, masterly companion; and so I leave you. **1685** BAXTER *Paraphr. N.T.* 1 Tim. ii. 11 Let them [women]..not be over-talkative and masterly. **1766** ENTICK *London* I. 277 If he had been apprized of his masterly behaviour.

2. Of persons, their qualities, actions, etc.: Resembling or characteristic of a master or skilled workman; skilfully exercised or performed.

masterly inactivity: see INACTIVITY b.

1666 DRYDEN *Acc. Ann. Mirab.* Wks. (Globe) 40 When action or persons are to be described..how masterly are the strokes of Virgil! **1699** BENTLEY *Phal.* Introd. 2 We must expect nothing from Him, but what is masterly and great. **1713** GAY *Guardian* No. 149 ¶6 You may see the masterly hand of a painter in three or four swift strokes of his pencil. **1773** MRS. CHAPONE *Improv. Mind* (1774) II. 149, I do not wish your knowledge to be exact and masterly. **1804** *Med. Jrnl.* XII. 174 The small, but masterly work of Le Dran on Gun-shot Wounds. **1815** W. H. IRELAND *Scribbleomania* 139 *note*, She has blended truth with fiction in a masterly way. **1874** L. STEPHEN *Hours in Library* (1892) II. iii. 68 The thought is masculine and the expression masterly. **1880** McCARTHY *Own Times* IV. l. 61 The speeches themselves were masterly as mere literary productions.

3. *masterly lode* (in *Mining*): a main lode. Cf. *master lode*, MASTER *sb.*[1] 26 a.

1880 *Pioneer Mining Co., Lim., Deb. Prospectus* 1 It is traversed..by a powerful masterly lode. **1895** B. SCOTT in *Westm. Gaz.* 18 Nov. 4/1 A shaft has been sunk..on a strong masterly lode, many feet in thickness.

masterly ('mɑːstəlɪ), *adv.* [f. MASTER *sb.*[1] + -LY[2].] In a masterly manner.

c **1394** *P. Pl. Crede* 847 Y will nouȝt þis matere maistrely auouen. *a* **1400–50** *Alexander* 228 Haile, modi qwene of Messidoyne he maister-like said. *c* **1410** LYDG. *Reas. & Sens.* 2396 He kan..Maisterly revel and Daunce, Pipe and floyte lustely. **1599** NASHE *Lenten Stuffe* Wks. (Grosart) V. 233, I might enamill and hatch ouer this deuice more artificially and masterly. **1611** SHAKS. *Wint. T.* v. iii. 66 Masterly done: The very Life seemes warme vpon her Lippe. **1726** LEONI *Alberti's Archit.* II. 62 They are masterly wrought. **1887** HISSEY *Holiday on Road* 382 Its wooden gables..showed how masterly they had been carved of old.

master-man ('mɑːstəmæn). [f. MASTER *sb.*[1] + MAN *sb.*[1] Cf. MDu. *meesterman*.]

†**1.** A chief, leader (chiefly *Sc.*). *Obs.*

13.. *S. Erkenwolde* 201 in Horstm. *Altengl. Leg.* (1881) 270, I was committed & made a mayster-mone here To sytte vpone sayd causes. *c* **1375** *Sc. Leg. Saints* v. (*Johannes*) 402 He..vent þan to sterk thefis,..þare master man þai sone hym mad. **1424** *Sc. Acts Jas. I* (1814) II. 8/1 Þe quhilk sall be haldyn Dekyn or maister man oure þe layff. *c* **1470** HENRY *Wallace* IV. 87 The maistir man with sa gud will straik he [etc.]. **1616** *Orkney Witch Trial* in Dalyell *Darker Superst. Scot.* (1834) 536 Ane great number of fairie men mett her [together with] a maister man.

b. *dial.* 'The head of a household or family, a husband' (E.D.D.).

1885 HALL CAINE *Shadow Crime* I. x. 208 Towards nine the 'maister men' of Wythburn began to arrive. *Ibid.* xiii. 291 The 'maister men..made their way..to the village inn.

2. a. A person skilled in some art or craft. (Cf. MISTERMAN, with which this word was perh. sometimes confused.) *Obs.* exc. *Hist.* **b.** An employer of work-people.

c **1250** *Gen. & Ex.* 664 To maken a tur, wel heȝ & strong ..Twelwe and sexti men woren ðor-to, Meister men for to maken it so. *c* **1400** *Destr. Troy* 1599 All maister men þat on molde dwellis. **1825** BENTHAM *Offic. Apt. Maximized, Indic.* (1830) 39 Not a farthing even given to the hapless masterman. **1898** TAUNTON *Eng. Black Monks* I. 94 Among its monks were to be found master-men.

master-mason. [See MASTER *sb.*[1] 25 d.]

1. A mason who designs and carries out building in stone or who employs workmen to shape and fit stonework.

1428 in Heath *Grocers' Comp.* (1869) 6 Mason's weages with maistre mason's rewarde £5 9 2. **1560** PILKINGTON *Expos. Aggeus* (1562) 53 In buyldinges there bee maister masons and carpenters which do devise the worke. **1697** G. DALLAS *Syst. Stiles* II. 89 Gifts to be the King's Master-Printer, Master-Mason, Master-Wright, Bower, Sclater [etc.]. **1729** FENTON *Observ. Waller's Poems* 30 Stone, who was master-mason to King Charles I.

2. A fully qualified freemason, who has passed the third degree.

[*c* **1430** *Freemasonry* (Halliw.) 15 The mayster mason moste be ful securly Bothe stedefast, trusty, and trwe.] **1723** J. ANDREWS & DESAGULIERS *Constit. Free-Masons* 10 Though there were employ'd about it no less than 3,600 Princes, or Master-Masons, to conduct the Work according

to Solomon's Directions. **1737** S. PRICHARD *Masonry Dissected* (ed. 7) 25 Q. Are you a Master-Mason? A. I am; try me, prove me, disprove me if you can. **1797** *Encycl. Brit.* (ed. 3) X. 624/2 Having voted the oldest master-mason then present into the chair, constituted themselves a grand-lodge.

'master-'mind, *sb.* [MASTER *sb.*[1] 24, 26 b.] **a.** An outstanding or commanding mind or intellect; a person with such a mind. Also *transf.*

1720 POPE *Iliad* XVIII. 557 There shone the image of the master-mind. **1821** HAZLITT *Table-Talk* I. ix. 198 He shews the marks of a great moving intellect, so that we trace the master-mind, and can sympathise with the springs that urge him on. **1839** POE *William Wilson* in *Gift 1840* (Philadelphia) 235 The despotism of a master mind in boyhood over the less energetic spirits of its companions. **1841** —— *Colloquy Monos & Una* in *Graham's Mag.* Aug. 52/2 At long intervals some master-minds appeared, looking upon each advance in practical science as a retro-gradation in the true utility. **1857** DICKENS *Dorrit* II. xxiv. 529 The master-mind of the age..became mute again. **1909** WODEHOUSE *Mike* xxxii. 183 You can't expect two master-minds like us to pig it in that room downstairs. **1930** H. G. WELLS *Autocracy of Mr. Parham* III. viii. 220 This immediate personal recognition of the new régime by the master mind of Britain. **1949** E. JENKINS *Six Criminal Women* 11 Hers was one of the earliest master-minds in advertising. **1961** *Observer* 19 Feb. 5/4 An electronic master-mind called the 'Honeywell Data Centre'.

b. *spec.* Such a mind, or a person, directing a criminal enterprise.

1872 TROLLOPE *Eustace Diamonds* (1873) III. lxix. 203 The police thought that I had been the master-mind among the thieves. **1913** 'D. D. CARTER' in *Hearst's Mag.* July 137 (*title*) The master mind. **1920** 'SAPPER' *Bull-Dog Drum.* v. 121 A gang of international criminals..controlled by a master-mind. **1936** E. AMBLER *Dark Frontier* v. 80 From now on, he, Carruthers, would be the master mind. **1959** [see *crime-writing* s.v. CRIME *sb.* 4]. **1960** *Observer* 24 Jan. 5/2 These were recognised prop-men or putters up of jobs, what the mugs called master minds.

Hence **'master-,mind** *v. trans.*, to be the master-mind behind (an enterprise, a crime, etc.); to plan and direct; also occas. *intr.*; so **'master-,minding** *vbl. sb.* and *ppl. a.*

1941 *Time* 26 May 24/2 The *Telegram* hired a series of detective storytellers to mastermind the Hess case. **1941** *True Detective* June 18/3 Often suspected but never convicted of masterminding some of the plots hatched in his grog shop. **1945** *Sun* (Baltimore) 30 Nov. 8 Baseball owes him nothing much but an opportunity to retire from the strenuous side of the competition and take over the job of master-minding. **1949** R. CHANDLER *Little Sister* xxi. 151 Somebody had to master-mind this deal. **1956** W. H. WHYTE *Organization Man* (1957) vi. 75 What they mean by sales is..master-minding the work of those who do the helping. **1957** 'B. BUCKINGHAM' *Boiled Alive* xxxiii. 249 She master minded it all right, but..Pepe is not without blame. **1973** *Guardian* 29 June 15/7 A ruthless master-minding conspirator. *Ibid.* 15/8 It was possible he was..capable of master-minding a vast conspiracy. **1973** A. HUNTER *Gently French* viii. 74 Quarles has master-minded for several of the gangs. **1974** D. RAMSAY *No Cause to Kill* II. 132 Hy Goldman..was..sceptical of her master-minding potential.

†**masterous,** *a. Obs.* In 7 maistrous. [f. MASTER *sb.*[1] + -OUS.] Characteristic of a master.

1642 MILTON *Apol. Smect.* 5 Must we learne from Canons and quaint Sermonings..to wreath an Enthymema with maistrous dexterity?

masterpiece ('mɑːstəpiːs). [f. MASTER *sb.*[1] + PIECE *sb.*

Prob. after Du. *meesterstuk* or G. *meisterstück*, which occurs much earlier, and primarily denoted the piece of work by which a craftsman gained from his guild the recognized rank of 'master'. Cf. the following examples (in the former of which the Du. word appears in an adapted form):—

1579 *Aberdeen Reg.* (Spalding Cl.) II. 34 Quhill the person creven to be admittit free of his craft first compone with the said deinis of gild..the maisterstik of the person to be admittit being exhibit. **1658** A. FOX tr. *Wurtz' Surg.* I. ix. 37 Taylors..suffer none to set up his Trade, unless he have made first his Master-piece (orig. *sein Meisterstück*).]

1. a. A production of art or skill surpassing in excellence all others by the same hand; also, in wider sense, a production of masterly skill; a consummate example *of* some department of art or skill, or *of* some particular kind of excellence.

In early use, often applied to man as the 'masterpiece' of God or Nature.

1610 MARKHAM (*title*) Markhams Master-peece. Or, What doth a Horse-man lacke. **1615** CROOKE *Body of Man* 60 Beeing now to dissolue this goodly frame of Nature, and to take in pieces this Maisterpiece. **1617** *Janua Ling.* To Princc, This maisterpeece of curious schollership. **1635** QUARLES *Embl.* II. vi. (1718) 87 Man is heav'n's Master-piece. **1711** ADDISON *Spect.* No. 253 ¶5 A very fine Poem, I mean *The Art of Criticism*, which..is a Master-piece in its kind. **1749** FIELDING *Tom Jones* XVI. viii, This is indeed a master-piece of assurance. **1756–7** *Keysler's Trav.* (1760) III. 268 A crucifixion, by Guido Rheni, which is extremely admired as a real master-piece. **1790** MME. D'ARBLAY *Diary* Oct., One letter I have from him [Dr. Johnson] that is a master-piece of elegance and kindness united. **1849** MACAULAY *Hist. Eng.* i. I. 5 The master-pieces of Sophocles, of Demosthenes, and of Plato. *Ibid.* ii. 259 Speeches which ..were remembered as master-pieces of reasoning, of wit, and of eloquence. **1871** L. STEPHEN *Playgr. Eur.* ix. (1894) 203 Some masterpiece in painting. **1871** FREEMAN *Norm. Conq.* (1876) IV. xvii. 54 It was the master-piece of William's policy of outward legality. **1940** *Burlington Mag.* Sept. 93/2 Who could have ordered a cabinet made in this, apparently, needlessly expensive way? I think the only solution is that it must have been made as a 'master-piece', a test of workmanship to gain admission to a trade guild. **1951** *Oxf. Jun. Encycl.* VII. 143/2 The apprentice..was also at times required to provide a sample of his work, or 'masterpiece'. **1965** *Listener* 11 Nov. 761/1 The Mud Bath was another young man's 'masterpiece' (I am using the word 'masterpiece' in its original sense—as a test of a young painter's professional skill).

†**b.** A person's greatest achievement; an action of masterly ability. *Obs.*

1605 B. JONSON *Volpone* v. i, Here, we must rest; this is our maister-peice; We cannot thinke to goe beyond this. **1605** SHAKS. *Macb.* II. iii. 71 Confusion now has made his Master-peece. **1634** W. TIRWHYT tr. *Balzac's Lett.* 209 It is expedient to shew a Master-peece of state, to give reputation to the present current of affaires. **1702** *Eng. Theophrast.* 113 'Tis a court master-piece to draw chestnuts out of the fire with other People's fingers. *a* **1715** BURNET *Own Time* (1724) I. 254 It was certainly the master-piece of King Charles's life: And, if he had stuck to it, it would have been both the strength and the glory of his reign.

c. *colloq.* A person, thing, or action to be admired for being remarkable, singular, etc.

1906 KIPLING *Puck of Pook's Hill* 249 Ah, he was a masterpiece!..he never winked an eyelid. **1933** W. S. MAUGHAM *Sheppey* I. 20 It was a masterpiece the way I kidded him. **1963** N. MARSH *Dead Water* (1964) vii. 178 She spotted it [*sc.* sex] everywhere... She was a masterpiece. *Ibid.* viii. 223 He'm a masterpiece for holding his liquor.

†**2.** The most important feature, or the chief excellence, of a person or thing. *Obs.*

1612 DAVIES *Why Ireland*, etc. 282 This is the Maister-piece, and most excellent part, of the worke of Reformation. **1641** R. BROOKE *Eng. Episc.* 72 Wee come to Ordination;.. This is the main and Master-piece of all Episcopacy. **1644** MILTON *Educ.* Wks. 1738 I. 140 What Decorum is, which is the grand master-piece to observe. **1647** CLARENDON *Hist. Reb.* III. §81 His learning in the law being his master-piece. *Ibid.* VIII. §9 Beating up of quarters was his master-piece. **1697** G. DALLAS *Syst. Styles* III. Ep. Ded., Experience, (the great Master-peice of Humane Things).

3. The original or main piece. *rare*$^{-1}$.

1825 E. HEWLETT *Cottage Comforts* i. 4 Their clothes were so patched, that it was hard to tell which was the master-piece.

†**master-prize.** *Obs.* Also **master's prize.** = MASTERPIECE 1, 1 b.

1604 DEKKER *Honest Wh.* I. x. G 4 b, Nay, let me alone to play my maister, prize [*sic*: the speaker is an apprentice disguised as his master]. **1607** B. BARNES *Devils Charter* III. v. F 1 b, Now Frescobaldi play thy masters prize. **1615** CROOKE *Body of Man* 414 In criticall euacuations & in notable Maister-prises of Nature. **1621** QUARLES *Argalus & P.* (1678) 68 Mischief, that now was bent to play Upon the Stage her studied master-prize. **1624** MIDDLETON *Game at Chess* III. i. 213 Some notable masterprize of roguery This drum strikes up for. *a* **1635** RANDOLPH *Poems* Wks. (1875) 643 Thus have I finish'd beauty's master-prize. **1653** A. WILSON *Jas. I* 26 It behoved him to play his Master-prize in the Beginning.

†**master-root.** *Obs.*

1. The main root of a plant.

1578 LYTE *Dodoens* VI. vi. 664 Two or three foote from the principall or maister roote. **1601** HOLLAND *Pliny* I. 513 The more..safe way..was rather to cut the stocke and maister Root. **1725** BRADLEY *Fam. Dict.* s.v. *Vivacious*, They are obliged to take some [Roots] away,..to disburthen the Master-Root of them.

2. = MASTERWORT.

1599 A. M. tr. *Gabelhouer's Bk. Physicke* 221/2 In like sorte is also verye good heervnto the Masterroote.

mastership ('mɑːstəʃɪp). Forms: see MASTER *sb.*[1] and -SHIP. [Cf. G. *meisterschaft.*]

1. The condition of being a master or ruler; dominion, rule, ascendancy, control.

1387–8 T. USK *Test. Love* II. iii. (Skeat) l. 40 Whan these sely women..beleven your wordes..than graunt[en] they to you their hertes,..wherthrough their liberte in maystreship that they toforn had is thralled. *c* **1440** *Alph. Tales* 248 þer þe son hathe a reule, or a maistershupp, or a gouernans abown þe fadur. **1548** PATTEN *Exp. Scot.* Pref. b vij, Yet seke we not the mastership of you, but the felowship. **1647** N. BACON *Disc. Govt. Eng.* I. xxxviii. (1739) 58 The great men ..hereby lost..the mastership of the Life or Death of the meaner sort. **1683** KENNETT tr. *Erasm. on Folly* (1709) 44 The other..is indeed the most slavish of serving men, in being subject to the mastership of lust and sensuality. **1816** SCOTT *Old Mort.* xliii, He at once exerted that mastership over his heated..imagination [etc.]. **1894** *Daily News* 15 Nov. 5/3 That mastership..which the sea has always conferred upon its unquestioned rulers.

b. Mastery, 'upper hand'. ? *Obs.*

1573 TWYNE *Æneid* XII. N n ij, When contention falles two mightie Bulles betwixt,.. That for dominion euermore, and mastershippe do trie. **1641** BEST *Farm. Bks.* (Surtees) 123 They [swannes] beginne to strive for the mastershippe about Ladye day. **1727** *Philip Quarll* (1816) 28 An animal.. as big as himself, kept him a great while struggling for mastership. **1829** *Blackw. Mag.* XXVI. 282 Whatever were the force and power of these feelings, it was not now the time to let them get the mastership.

c. The authority of a master or teacher.

1581 MULCASTER *Positions* xxxvii. (1887) 155 So long as the child shalbe..vnder maistership in schole. *a* **1603** T. CARTWRIGHT *Confut. Rhem. N.T.* (1618) 299 They were taught of the Holy Ghost, through the immediate Mastership or Doctorship of Christ. **1865** BUSHNELL *Vicar. Sacr.* Introd. (1868) 15 The immense following that has accepted his mastership.

2. The office, function, or dignity of a 'master', or the term of office of a master, in any of the official applications of that title.

1455 *Rolls of Parlt.* V. 316/1 The Maisterships of oure Forest of Simonswode, and of oure Parkes of Croxtath. **1509** BARCLAY *Shyp of Folys* (1570) ¶¶ vj, But if that any one be in suche maner case That he will chalenge the mastership fro me [etc.]. **1591** A. NOWELL in *Lett. Lit. Men* (Camden) 87 The quietness of St. John's College duryng hys Mastershyppe there. **1609** CARLETON *Let.* 8 June in *Court & Times Jas. I*, I. 98, I hear Sir Ralph Winwood aims at a Mastership of Requests. **1626** in Rushw. *Hist. Coll.* (1659) I. 325 The chief Mastership of that Order. **1721** *Lond. Gaz.* No. 5918/1 The Pope's Bulls for the Great Mastership of St. Lazarus. **1873** *Sat. Rev.* 9 Aug. 163/1 The Mastership of the Rolls has been offered to the Attorney-General. **1882** *Society* 18 Nov. 6/2 He has accepted the Mastership of the Pau Foxhounds. **1891** *Law Times* XC. 419/2 A mastership in lunacy.

¶ *nonce-use.* The district ruled by a 'master'.

1707 (*title*) [tr. from Sp.] A Journal of the Siege of San Matheo, Capital of the Mastership of the Military Order of Montesa.

b. The position of a master in or of a school.

1806 H. K. WHITE *Let. to Sister* 25 June, The mastership of the school must be held by a clergyman. **1814** G. HARDINGE *Let.* in Nichols *Lit. Anecd. 18th C.* (1814) VIII. 544 Dr. Sumner vacated the Upper-mastership of Eton. **1881** MASSON in *Macm. Mag.* XLV. 76 The Annan mathematical mastership lasted about two years.

†**3.** With possessive pron.: The personality of a master. Often abbreviated M. (See also MASHIP.) *Obs.*

1440 in *Finchale Priory* (Surtees) 72 Whilk mater at the raverence of ȝowr maystership is fulfillid. **1526** SKELTON *Magnyf.* 1853, I pray God your maystershyp to saue. **1533** FRITH *Answ. More* D vij b, And where hys mastershyp alleageth this texte for the Sacrament that [etc.]. **1591** SHAKS. *Two Gent.* III. i. 280 How now Signior Launce? what newes with your Mastership? **1591** in *Thanes of Cawdor* (Spalding Cl.) 199 For vij quarteris of Londun claith to be your maisterchip cott and breikis. *Ibid.*, Stiffing gray to your M. doublat. *c* **1622** FORD, etc. *Witch Edmonton* I. ii, No Gentleman, I, Mr. Thorney; spare the Mastership, call me by my name, John Carter.

†**4.** ***good mastership***: patronage, protection. *Obs.*

1463 *Bury Wills* (Camden) 37, I beqwethe to William Clopton,..my best gypcer,..for a tookne he vowchesaf in tyme comyng to shewe his good maistershepe to my wil. **1465** *Paston Lett.* II. 199, I shall ly stille in pryson.. withoute your good maisterchippe shewed to me at this tyme.

5. The skill or knowledge constituting a master.

1607 SHAKS. *Cor.* IV. i. 7 Common men could beare, That when the Sea was calme, all Boats alike Shew'd Mastership in floating. **1662** GERBIER *Princ.* 42 The Grecians and Romans (who have shown their Master-ship in them [Triumphall Arches]). **1726** *Diss. Dumpling* 20 The greatest Mastership in Cookery is requir'd to make the Pudding Palatable. **1837** CARLYLE *Fr. Rev.* II. v. ii, Mastership in tongue-fence; this is the quality of qualities.

b. Mastery, thorough knowledge (*of* a subject).

a **1697** AUBREY *Lives* (1898) I. 120 He is much beholding to him for his mastership of that language. **1883** *American* VII. 184 A mastership of the technicalities of their work.

c. The status or degree of a recognized master (in a craft, a university, etc.).

1688 *True Spirit of Popery* 44 The rendred all Arts and Trades almost inaccessible to the Protestants, by the difficulties of arriving to the Mastership of them. **1831** SIR W. HAMILTON *Discuss.* (1853) 410 To commence student in Medicine, it is necessary to have obtained a Mastership in Arts. **1831** CARLYLE *Sart. Res.* III. i, An honourable Mastership in Cordwainery.

6. The existence of 'masters' or employers as the characteristic of a form of industrial organization.

1868 RUSKIN *Time & Tide* (1872) 6 The points at issue, in the comparison of this system with that of mastership, are by no means hitherto frankly stated. **1886** *Pall Mall G.* 29 Nov. 12/1 After a detailed description of the results of mastership and the effect machinery has had on the labour market..Mr. Morris spoke of the upper class.

7. *Hist.* A body of master workmen; a guild. *rare.*

1822 RANKEN *Hist. France* IX. x. i. 178 A third [decree] dissolved the corporations and masterships of towns.

master-singer ('mɑːstə,sɪŋə(r)). Now somewhat *rare*. Anglicized form of MEISTERSINGER.

1810 WEBER *Metr. Rom.* III. 335 In the time of the Mastersingers, a second German poem was written. **1871** LONGF. *Wayside Inn* II. *Cobbler of Hagenau* ii, While yet the Master-singers filled The noisy workshop..With various melodies and rhymes.

master-spring ('mɑːstəsprɪŋ). ? *Obs.* [See MASTER *sb.*[1] 26 a.] = MAINSPRING 2 (*fig.*).

a **1586** SIDNEY *Arcadia* III. (1590) 257 b, Knowing them [his men] to be the..master-spring (as it were) which makes all the rest to stir. **1682** DRYDEN & LEE *Dk. Guise* v. iii, You are the master-spring that moves our fabric. **1784** COWPER *Task* IV. 203 The slope of faces,..(As if one master-spring controll'd them all) Relax'd into a universal grin. **1816** F. H. NAYLOR *Hist. Germany* I. I. ix. 348 Religion undoubtedly formed the master-spring of all his actions. **1835** J. H. NEWMAN *Par. Serm.* (1837) I. xxii. 331 The one master spring of their whole course of life for the future.

master-stroke ('mɑːstəstrəʊk). [See MASTER *sb.*[1] 26 a. Cf. G. *meisterstreich.*]

1. A masterly line or touch (in painting, etc.); also *transf.*

1679 DRYDEN *Tr. & Cr.* Prol. 14 In this my rough-drawn play you shall behold Some Master-strokes. **1690** in E. Waller *Poems* II. Pref. sig. A5, Some Painters will hit the chief Lines, and master strokes of a Face so truly, that [etc.]. **1784** COWPER *Task* II. 398, I would trace His master-strokes, and draw from his design. **1867** EMERSON *May-Day*

108 And in their vaunted works of Art, The master-stroke is still her part.

2. A masterly exertion of skill; a surpassingly skilful act (of cunning, diplomacy, policy, etc.); one's cleverest move or device. (Cf. F. *coup de maître*.)

1711 W. KING tr. *Naude's Ref. Politics* ii. 59 In these masterstrokes of state, the thunderbolt falls before the noise of it is heard. **1712** BLACKMORE *Creat.* VI. 695 The.. stupendous Art, And Master-strokes in each Mechanick Part. **1762–71** H. WALPOLE *Vertue's Anecd. Paint.* (1786) IV. 87 The steeple.. is a master-stroke of absurdity. **1768** GOLDSM. *Good-n. Man* I. i, There's my master-stroke. I have resolved not to refuse her. **1825** COBBETT *Rur. Rides* (1885) I. 404 This was a master-stroke on the part of France. **1849** THACKERAY *Lett.* 4 Sept., A master-stroke of diplomacy.

†**master-vein.** *Obs.* [See MASTER *sb.*[1] 26 a.]

1. One of the great veins or arteries of the body; *spec.* applied to the saphena and perh. to the carotid artery or the jugular vein.

c **1400** *Laud Troy Bk.* 12604 He schet And hitte him in his gorget, That it ȝede thorow his pesayn And cut in-two his mayster-veyn. **14..** *Voc.* in Wr. Wülcker 632/8 *Sophena*, the mayster vayne. **1494** FABYAN *Chron.* VII. 300 At Yorke [Jews] to the nombre of .cccc. & mo, cutte theyr mayster veynys & bled to deth. **1683** CAVE *Ecclesiastici* Introd. 36 One of the Master-Veins breaking, all the Blood in his Body emptied it self out at his Mouth.

fig. **1647** TRAPP *Marrow Gd. Authors* in *Comm. Ep.* 732 The venome of originall lust, the master-vein wherein is Atheisme. **1677** GILPIN *Demonol.* (1867) 241 By some called the master-vein of our original corruption.

¶ *slang phrase.*

1592 GREENE *Disput. Conny-c.* C 1 b, My faire daughter was hit on the master vaine and gotten with childe.

2. A principal vein in a mine.

1670 PETTUS *Fodinæ Reg.* 42 For, say they, when we approach to the Master-vein of a Mine.. they usuallie here knocking.

master-work (ˈmɑːstəwɜːk). [See MASTER *sb.*[1] 26 a. Cf. G. *meisterwerk*.]

1. An action or procedure of chief importance.

c **1606** DANIEL *On Death of Erle of Devon.* 216 That famous seige, the Master-worke of all. **1719** YOUNG *Revenge* II, My next care is to hasten these new nuptials, And then my master-works begin to play. **1719** LONDON & WISE *Compl. Gard.* VI. 109 The Master Work of Gardening, which is Pruning.

2. A work of pre-eminent merit; a masterpiece.

1617 MORYSON *Itin.* I. 4 A.. Clocke, in the top whereof is a picture,.. which Painters esteeme a master worke. **1667** MILTON *P.L.* VII. 505 There wanted yet the Master work, the end Of all yet don. **1789** GIBBON *Autobiog.* (1854) 13 Mr. Law's master-work, the Serious Call, is still read. **1843** J. A. SMITH *Product. Farming* (ed. 2) 56 The flowers.. appear as the master-work of Nature in the vegetable kingdom. **1880** SWINBURNE *Stud. Shaks.* 74 Being thus, as he is, the English masterwork of Shakespeare's hand.

†**3.** A main channel for draining or irrigation. *Obs.*

1652 BLITH *Eng. Improv. Impr.* ix. (ed. 2) 54 Then must not of necessity all the Out-lets or Mouths of all the Master-work, and Sluces, and Water-gates be widened? **1789** T. WRIGHT *Meth. Watering Meadows* (1790) 47 The master-work which waters the highest.. part of the land.

masterwort (ˈmɑːstəwɜːt). [f. MASTER *sb.*[1] + WORT *sb.*, after G. *meisterwurz*; the same sense is expressed by the 16th c. L. name *imperātōria*, but the reason for the appellation is not clear.]

a. The umbelliferous plant *Peucedanum* (*Imperatoria*) *Ostruthium*, formerly cultivated as a pot-herb, and used in medicine. **b.** Applied to other genera, as *Astrantia* (Black Masterwort); the goutweed, *Ægopodium Podagraria* (English or Wild Masterwort); and the American plants *Angelica atropurpurea* and *Heracleum lanatum*.

1548 TURNER *Names of Herbes* (E.D.S.) 61 The seede of pilletory of Spayne called masterwurt. **1568** —— *Herbal* III. 36 It were best to call it after the Duche Maisterwort. The Physicianes of Italye call it Imperatoriam. **1578** LYTE *Dodoens* II. cix. 300 The seconde *Imperatoria*, or wylde Master-wort. **1579** LANGHAM *Gard. Health* (1633) 474 The wilde master-wort called herbe Gerard. **1597** GERARDE *Herbal* II. ccclxii. 828 *Astrantia nigra*:.. it may be called blacke Masterwoort. **1656** RIDGLEY *Pract. Physick* 141 One dram of root of Masterwort. **1715** J. PETIVER in *Phil. Trans.* XXIX. 239 Great black Masterwort. **1796** MORSE *Amer. Geog.* I. 189 Angelica, or American Masterwort (*Angelica lucida*). **1847** DARLINGTON *Amer. Weeds & Useful Pl.* (1860) 148 Woolly Heracleum.. Masterwort. **1866** *Treas. Bot.* 74/2 Masterwort, English, *Ægopodium*. **1893** McCARTHY *Red Diamonds* II. 42 Masterwort which in earlier.. days was known as 'the divine remedy'.

mastery (ˈmɑːstərɪ). Forms: 3 **meistrie, mesterie,** 3–5 **maistri, maistre,** 3–7 **maistrie,** 4 **meistri, maystri,** 4–5 **maystre, maistrye, mastrie,** 4–6 **maystery, maystry(e, masterye, mastri, mastrye,** 4–7 **mastry,** 4–7, 9 *dial.*, **maistry,** 5 **maister, mastre, maiestrie,** *Sc.* **maistir,** 5–6 **maistery,** 5–7 **masterie,** 6 **mayster, maysterie, masterc,** 6 7 **maisterie,** 5– **mastery.** [a. OF. *maistrie*, f. *maistre* MASTER *sb.*[1]: cf. Sp. *maestría*, Pg. *mestria*, It. *maestria*.

In Fr. this word was superseded by the parallel formation *maistrise* (now *maîtrise*), whence ME. MAISTRICE. From its resemblance in sound to the latter, the plural *masteries* occurs in several of the senses illustrated below.]

1. The state or condition of being master, controller or ruler; authority, sway, dominion; an instance of this.

a **1225** *Ancr. R.* 108 Muchel hofleas is þet cumen into ancre huse,.. vorte sechen eise þerinne & mesterie, & more lefdischipe þen heo muhte habben iheued, inouh reðe iðe worlde. *Ibid.* 406 Luue haueð one meistrie biuoren alle oðre þinges. *a* **1300** *Fall & Passion* 21 in *E.E.P.* (1862) 13 God ȝaf him a gret maistre of al þat was in watir an londe. *a* **1340** HAMPOLE *Psalter* ix. 20 Þe utter man haf noght maistry of þe inere. *c* **1386** CHAUCER *Doctor's T.* 58 Bacus hadde of hire mouth right no maistrie. *c* **1400** *Destr. Troy* 13662 This Merion hade maistri but a meane qwile, The lond to Laerte he leuyt as kyng. **1423** JAS. I *Kingis Q.* xxxvii, Hath he vpon oure hertis suich maistrye? *c* **1460** *Towneley Myst.* i. *Creation* 81 *Lucifer*. If that ye will behold me right, this mastre longys to me. **1535** COVERDALE *Ecclus.* xxv. 22 Yf a woman gett the maistrie, then is she contrary to hir huszbande. **1614** RALEIGH *Hist. World* III. (1634) 114 Conon the Athenian.. recovers the mastery of the Seas. **1651** HOBBES *Govt. & Soc.* xvi. §16. 285 The Priesthood was not a Maistry, but a Ministry. **1729** BUTLER *Serm.* Wks. 1874 II. 32 The appetites and passions.. often strive for mastery with judgment or reflection. **1844** H. H. WILSON *Brit. India* II. 366 They.. needed only.. guidance to dispute with the victors the mastery over Hindustan. **1874** GREEN *Short Hist.* v. §1. 221 Edward's aim.. was.. to save English commerce by securing the mastery of the Channel.

†**b.** Predominance; predominating feature; prevailing character. *Obs.*

1477 NORTON *Ord. Alch.* iv. in Ashm. *Theat. Chem. Brit.* (1652) 48 That is the Mastrie of all our intent. **1562** LEIGH *Armorie* (1597) 115 b, The mastery of colours must be tawney. *Ibid.*, The maisterie of the colour must bee Carnation. **1642** FULLER *Holy & Prof. St.* II. v. 68 A burning-fever, to which his body was naturally disposed, as appeared by the mastery of rednesse in his complexion.

2. Superiority or ascendancy in competition or strife; 'upper-hand'; victory. Now only with mixture of sense 1: Victory resulting in the subjection of the vanquished.

a **1225** *Leg. Kath.* 134 Al ha cneowen ham crauant & ouercumen, & cweðen hire þe meistrie. *c* **1290** *S. Eng. Leg.* I. 96/128 Heo ne couþen answerie hire of neuere a word and ȝeuen hire þe maistrie. **1297** R. GLOUC. (Rolls) 1147 Þoru godes grace Hii adde þe maistrie of veld. *a* **1300** *Cursor M.* 21404 Þe mastri has king constantin Thoru þe cros and cristes might. *c* **1330** R. BRUNNE *Chron.* (1810) 27 Edward had þe maistri, & þanked God. *a* **1400–50** *Alexander* 4502 Mars for his maisterris & for his many weris [etc.]. **1423** JAS. I *Kingis Q.* lix, Sum bird may cum and stryve In song with the, the maistry to purchace. *c* **1440** *Promp. Parv.* 320/2 Maystrye, or souerente, and heyare honde y(n) stryfe or werre. **1513** DOUGLAS *Æneis* v. ii. 50 First sall I ordane for my Troianis.. With all thair force to strife for the maistry. **1535** COVERDALE *2 Tim.* ii. 5 And though a man stryue for a mastrye [**1611** for masteries]. **1577** *F. de L'isle's Legendarie* G vij b, To the end in case they yet once againe got the masterie, they should not harme her. **1667** MILTON *P.L.* II. 899 Four Champions fierce Strive here for Maistrie. **1845** S. AUSTIN *Ranke's Hist. Ref.* I. 103 He.. always gained the mastery in the end.

†**b.** ***for the mastery***: as if aiming at mastery; hence, extremely, in the highest degree. Frequent in ME. poetry. (Cf. 4 b.) *Obs.*

13.. *Guy Warw.* (A.) 4961 Þe douke hadde a feir douhter for þe meistri. *c* **1400** MAUNDEV. (1839) xxvi. 268 The ȝates that Kyng Alisaundre leet make of grete Stones.. wel symented and made stronge for the maystrie. *c* **1412** HOCCLEVE *De Reg. Princ.* 1390 Whan.. pat I poore am eek for þe maystrie. *c* **1460** *Launfal* 957 Twey stones of Ynde, Gay for the maystrye.

†**3.** Superior force or power. ***to have to mastery***, to have in (one's) power. *Obs.*

1297 R. GLOUC. (Rolls) 53 Þe folc of denemarch.. þat ofte wonne englelond and helde it bi maistrie. *Ibid.* 9182 Þat he aþ inome wiþ trayson we ssolle wiþ maistrie. *c* **1340** HAMPOLE *Prose Tr.* 37, I halde it noghte spedfulle þan to a mane for to prese to mekill þare-till as if he walde gete it by maystry. *c* **1380** *Sir Ferumb.* 1904 And y wer now on þy mastrye, as þou art her in myne, Tel me.. how wostou þan do by me. **1426–7** in *Cal. Proc. in Chanc. Q. Eliz.* (1827) I. Introd. 20 Symkyn Yve.. be maistery and supportacion of lordship.. deprived and disherite John Haryngton. *c* **1483** CAXTON *Dialogues* 43/25 After that the euyll doers Haue knowlechid her euyll dedes, He hath them to mastrye. **1513** DOUGLAS *Æneis* x. i. 121 And command eyk, with gret fors and mastry The burgh of Cartage doun thring Italy. **1590** SPENSER *F.Q.* III. i. 25 Ne may love be compeld by maistery. **1818** SCOTT *Hrt. Midl.* xxxii, These wicked people.. stopped me by violence and mastery.

†**b.** *Proverb.* (Cf. OF. *la force paist le pré.*)

c **1425** WYNTOUN *Chron.* (Wemyss MS.) lxxx. 1499 It is said in commone sawis that mastry mawis þe medow doune ay.

4. The skill or knowledge which constitutes a master. *Obs.* or *arch.* exc. with mixture of sense 7. Also, in early use, †a department of skill or knowledge; an art or science (*obs.*).

13.. *K. Alis.* 3 Clerkes wel y-lerid, Faire y-dyght this myddel erde, And clepid it, in here maistrie, Europe, Affryke, and Asyghe. **1382** WYCLIF *Eccl.* I. 5 That hadde the maistrie [Vulg. *prævaluit*] to make large the cite. *c* **1386** CHAUCER *Miller's T.* 197 Somtyme, to shewe his lightnesse and maistrye He pleyeth Herodes vp on a Scaffold hye. **1460** *Lybeaus Disc.* (Kaluza) 1783 Men of maistrie, Clerkes of nigremauncie. *c* **1475** *Partenay* 188 Thys noble Erle.. Of astronemye wyse was.. So moche ther-of knew he the maistrie. **1477** NORTON *Ord. Alch.* vii. in Ashm. *Theat. Chem. Brit.* (1652) 105 Use maketh Masterie. **1597** MORLEY *Introd. Mus.* 85 This waie argueth maistrie, and.. hee who can doe it.. needeth not to stand telling his cordes. *a* **1637** B. JONSON *Underwoods, Poet to Painter*, O, had I now your manner, maistry, might,.. How I would draw. **1680** LD. ROCHESTER *Allusion to Horace* I. x. 47 With just bold Strokes he dashes here and there, Showing great Mastery with little Care. **1830** CUNNINGHAM *Brit. Paint.* II. 59 Such mastery rarely waited upon the ambition of this amiable and upright man. **1876** MORRIS *Sigurd* IV. 351 Their Gods with mastery carven. **1903** *Edin. Rev.* Apr. 464 There is a majesty and a mastery.. in the ugliness Van Eyck depicts, that redeems its homeliness.

†**b.** A rule, method, or process of an art. ***for (the) mastery***: ? as required by the rules of art. *Obs.*

c **1420** *Liber Cocorum* (1862) 44 Coloure hit with safroun for þe maystre. **1460–70** *Bk. Quintessence* 9, I wole teche ȝou þe maistrie of departynge of gold fro siluir. **1695** DRYDEN *Parallel Poetry & Painting* Ess. 1900 II. 122 Painters and sculptors.. advance their art above nature itself in her individual productions; which is the utmost mastery of human performance.

†**c.** = MAGISTERY 3. *Obs. rare*$^{-1}$.

1610 B. JONSON *Alch.* IV. i, I am the Lord of the Philosophers Stone... *Dol.* How Sir! ha' you that? *Mam.* I am the Master of the Maistry.

†**5.** An exercise or work of skill or power. ***to do, make, work,*** etc. (***a***) ***mastery*** or ***masteries***: to perform a wonderful feat or trick: to exercise one's skill or power *on* or *against* a person; to 'play the devil' (*with*). *Obs.*

a **1225** *Ancr. R.* 390 And wrouhte ueole wundres, and dude ueole meistries biuoren hire eihsihðe. *a* **1300** *Cursor M.* 12319 Iesus vp þe water heint, And bar it ham als in a ball,.. Quen maria had sene þis maistre, Sco hid it in hert priuelie. *Ibid.* 18215 Quatkin maistri mas þou on hus? **1303** R. BRUNNE *Handl. Synne* 532 Now shal y, As þou hast do, do þy maystry. **13..** *Seuyn Sag.* (W.) 2020 The king of Poile hadde gret enuie, That the Romayns made swich maistrie. *c* **1386** CHAUCER *Can. Yeom. Prol. & T.* 507 Ye shul wel seen at eye, That I wol doon a maistrie er I go. **1390** GOWER *Conf.* II. 196 The world is yit merveiled Of the maistries that he wroghte Upon the marches. *a* **1400** *Sir Perc.* 1048 Forthe rydez he thenne,.. His maystrés to make. *c* **1430** *Hymns Virg.* 20 Þe feend away from us þou dryue Whanne deeþ with us maistrie schal make. *c* **1440** *York Myst.* xxv. 64 Saie, what are ȝe þat makis here maistrie? *c* **1450** *Merlin* 78 Ther the duke a-bode, and dide many maistries in armes. *c* **1470** HENRY *Wallace* VII. 1284 Thar Cetoun met him. and mekill mastir maid. **1494** FABYAN *Chron.* VII. ccxxiv. 250 Ye Welshmen.. brake out vpon the Englysshe men in ye bordour.. and there made masteryes for a whyle. *a* **1529** SKELTON *Bowge of Courte* 329 With vs olde seruauntes suche maysters to playe. **1546** BALE *Eng. Votaries* I. (1560) 95 b, That ye maye knowe.. what masteryes they haue played. **1586** A. DAY *Eng. Secretary* II. (1625) 23 By a number of odde speeches.. you doe yet suppose to haue wrought a mastery.

†**b.** ***it is great, little, much, no mastery***: it is a great, no, (etc.) achievement, it is hard or easy (to do something). *Obs.*

1297 R. GLOUC. (Rolls) 235 Þer vore silui him let sle ac þat was lute maistrie. *a* **1300** *Fall & Passion* 50 in *E.E.P.* (1862) 14 Þat was a gret maistri þat þe doȝtir ber þe fader. **13..** *Sir Beues* (A.) 1738 'So me helpe God!' queþ Beues þo, 'Hit were no meistri, me to slo'. *c* **1412** HOCCLEVE *De Reg. Princ.* 1900 No maistri it is for þe, if þou woldist To be releeuëd. **1450–1530** *Myrr. our Ladye* 17 Yt is no more maistery to god to make of ought & to make of nought. **1456** *Paston Lett.* I. 380 It is no grete maistre to gader up that mony. **1576** FLEMING tr. *Caius' Dogs* 17 They [*sc.* duckes] go so slowely and so leasurely, that to a mans thinking it were no masteryes to take them. **1601** R. JOHNSON *Kingd. & Commw.* (1603) 157 By these helps it was no masterie to vanquish and subdue them. **1636** B. JONSON *Discov., Ingen. discrim.* i, It is a little Maistry to know them. **1652–62** HEYLIN *Cosmogr.* (1673) III. 8/2 For a man to be good in other places, is no mastery; but in Asia to lead a temperate life is indeed praiseworthy. **1667** MILTON *P.L.* IX. 29 Warrs, hitherto the onely Argument Heroic deem'd, chief maistrie to dissect With long and tedious havoc fabl'd Knights In Battels feign'd.

†**6.** A competitive or emulative feat of strength or skill; esp. in phrases ***to assay, play, prove, try masteries***, to 'try conclusions'. *Obs.*

1390 GOWER *Conf.* III. 298 Thei sholden come Unto the gamen.. To do such maistry as thei might. *c* **1450** *St. Cuthbert* (Surtees) 1028 He proued many maystryes. **1475** *Bk. Noblesse* (Roxb.) 77 King Edwarde iijde that exercised.. all his noble sonnes, in such maiestries, wherby they were more apt in haunting of armes. **1530** PALSGR. 736/1, I styckyll betwene wrastellers, or any folkes that prove mastries to se that none do other wronge. **1531** ELYOT *Gov.* I. xvii, The great game of Olympus, wherto.. came the moste actife and valiant persons to assay maistries. **1534** MORE *Comf. agst. Trib.* II. Wks. 1191/1 A iugler that would for a shew.. plai masteries at a feast. **1555** EDEN *Decades* 24 Many daunsynges.. and other tryinge of mastryes. **1594** PLAT *Jewell-ho.* I. 47 [Soil] fitter for gardens, or for the trial of maisteries, then for the enriching of arable or pasture grounds. **1606** HOLLAND *Sueton.* Annot. 30 Stage-playes, Gymnicke Exercises, and Masteries in Musicke. **1615** HEYWOOD *Foure Prentises* I. Wks. 1874 II. 237 Let vs try this maistry. **1625** BACON *Ess., Empire* (Arb.) 301 This is but to try Masteries with Fortune. **1692** R. L'ESTRANGE *Josephus, Antiq.* II. xiv. (1733) 51 He [Pharaoh] seemed to take a Vanity.. to try Masteries with God Almighty. **1697** *Phil. Trans.* XIX. 501 They were soon.. kill'd like other Venison as well for the sake of Food as Mastery and Diversion.

7. (*transf.* from 1.) Intellectual command over (a subject of study).

1668 HALE *Pref. to Rolle's Abridgm.* b j b, To get a mastery of the full knowledge of it, requires not only reason but study. *a* **1680** BUTLER *Rem.* (1759) I. 249 To commend without Desert Requires a Mastery of Art. **1828** MISS MITFORD in L'Estrange *Life* (1870) II. xi. 257 She has a mastery of the subject. **1870** DISRAELI *Lothair* lii, This consummate military leader.. was distinguished by.. a mastery of method rarely surpassed. **1880** DIXON *Windsor* III. viii. 73 His mastery of English was supreme.

b. (Influenced by MASTER *v.*) The action of 'mastering' a subject.

1797 GODWIN *Enquirer* I. vi. 48 It is essential to the just mastery of astronomy. **1823** SCOTT *Peveril* xxvi, It is matter

beyond my mastery. **1870** BALDW. BROWN *Eccl. Truth* (1871) 219 The problems of Christian ministry become more difficult of mastery year by year.

mastew, obs. Sc. form of MASTIFF.

†**'mastful**, *a. Obs. rare.* [f. MAST *sb.*² + -FUL.] Full of mast; producing mast.

1591 SYLVESTER *Du Bartas* I. iii. 560 The Mast-full Oke. **1697** DRYDEN *Virg. Georg.* II. 20 The mastful Chesnut.

masthead, *sb.* (Stress variable.) Also **mast-head.** [MAST *sb.*¹]

1. a. The head or highest part of a mast; usually, the head of the lower mast (as a place of observation or punishment), or the highest part of the whole mast as the place for the display of flags, etc.

1748 *Anson's Voy.* II. iv. 162 We had no sight of the ship from the mast-head. **1835** W. IRVING *Tour Prairies* 326 [He] took a look-out, like a mariner from the mast-head at sea. **1836** MARRYAT *Midsh. Easy* xii, Go up to the mast-head, and wait there till I call you down. **1847** TENNYSON *Princess* IV. 255 Like the mystic fire on a mast-head, Prophet of storm. *c* **1860** H. STUART *Seaman's Catech.* 74 Above the hounds is the masthead to receive the rigging. **1888** FROUDE *Eng. in W. Ind.* iii. 33 The signal to engage was flying from the masthead of..Rodney's ship.

b. *fig.* (*a*) Phr. ***to the masthead***: to the full. *Sc.* (*b*) *jocular.* (*Naut.*) A person's head.

1821 W. LIDDLE *Poems* 97 (E.D.D.) An Idiot cram'd to the mast-head Wi' that insatiate glutton weed. **1884** H. COLLINGWOOD *Under Meteor Flag* 35 Slip down to the doctor, and get him to clap a plaster over your mast-head. **1887** STEVENSON *Misadv. J. Nicholson* i, He was..enjoying to the mast-head the modest pleasures of admiration.

c. In newspapers, journals, etc., the title, colophon, motto, etc., printed in some conspicuous position, usually immediately preceding the editorial matter or at the top of the first page. orig. *U.S.*

1838 *Hennepin* (Illinois) *Jrnl.* 22 Dec. 1/1 Many of our Whig friends..were anxious that the Journal should..carry Whig colors at the mast-head. **1923** O. G. VILLARD *Some Newspapers* iii. 43 The vision of its purpose..which it now daily carries under its 'mast-head' on the editorial page. **1932** P. VAN D. STERN *Introd. Typogr.* 198 *Mast-head*, the heading on the first page of a newspaper. **1937** *Amer. Speech* XII. 13 About 35 dailies use the word *Telegram* in their masthead. **1952** S. KAUFFMANN *Philanderer* (1953) ix. 141 She was a young, bright, snub-nosed, bobbed-hair cartoon character, to appear in the masthead and all institutional advertising. **1959** *Manch. Guardian* 22 Aug. 4/1 The masthead on page one will follow the style adopted..above our principal comment of the day. **1967** *Bucks Examiner* 3 Feb. 1/7 This week the 'Bucks Examiner' has a new masthead—the name given by newspaper men to the title at the top of page one. **1973** *Guardian* 28 Feb. 13/3 Varsity, the Cambridge University newspaper..will appear next term under the mast head of its brasher rival Stop Press.

2. One who is stationed at the mast-head; a mast-head man.

In Dicts.

3. *attrib.* and *Comb.*, as ***masthead-light, man, pendant***; **masthead cutter, -sloop** (see quot. 1961); **masthead genoa**, a Genoa jib which is attached to the topmost part of the mast; **mast-head high** *adv.*, to the height of the masthead.

1949 *Yachting Monthly* LXXXVII. 235/2 Her rig is a *masthead cutter—that is to say the working jib sets to the masthead. **1961** F. H. BURGESS *Dict. Sailing* 144 *Mast-head cutter* or *sloop*, a cutter or sloop whose fore stay, on which the luff of the foresail is set, reaches up to the mast-head. **1962** J. A. S. RUSSELL in *Roving Commissions 1961* 147 Her masthead cutter rig, with the mast well inboard and a boomed staysail, is snug and versatile. **1958** *Yachting World Ann.* 115 *Springtide* has 900 sq. ft. in her working rig of main, mizzen, and boom staysail. The area may be increased by 400 sq. ft. with the *masthead genoa. **1967** J. HOWARD-WILLIAMS *Sails* vii. 102 A bending mast..will mean abandoning ideas of a masthead genoa. **1822** SCOTT *Pirate* ii, The sea-snake..with his broad glittering eyes, raised *mast-head high, looks out, as it seems..for victims. **1878** KEMP *Yacht & Boat Sailing* 358/2 **Masthead Light*, the white light which steam vessels are required to exhibit at the masthead when under way. *c* **1860** H. STUART *Seaman's Catech.* 45 The *mast head men put on a sail-tackle whip. **1867** SMYTH *Sailor's Word-bk.*, *Mast-head men*, the men stationed aloft to keep a look-out. *Ibid.*, *Mast-head pendant. **1878** KEMP *Yacht & Boat Sailing* 358/2 *Masthead Pendants*, the pendants and runners which help support the mast. **1954** D. PHILLIPS-BIRT *Rigs & Rigging of Yachts* 49 The *masthead sloop—the sloop in which a headsail may be set on a forestay from the masthead. **1958** *Yachting World Ann.* 102/2 For some reason, yachtsmen appear shy of the masthead sloop rig; yet it is difficult to see what a yacht like this would gain by the lower fore-triangle.

masthead, *v.* Also **mast-head.** [f. the sb.]

1. *trans.* To send (a sailor) to the mast-head as a punishment.

1829 MARRYAT *F. Mildmay* iv, The next morning I was..mast-headed, to do penance. *a* **1845** SYD. SMITH in Lady Holland *Mem.* (1855) I. 260 If you masthead a sailor for not doing his duty, why should you not weathercock a parishioner for refusing to pay tithes? **1884** *Century Mag.* XXIX. 172 The one-armed hero is mastheaded.

transf. and *fig.* **1861-8** LOWELL *Emerson* Pr. Wks. 1890 I. 357 The lecturer built up so lofty a pedestal under certain figures as to lift them into a prominence of obscurity, and seem to masthead them there. **1883** STEVENSON *Treas. Isl.* III. xv, They're [*sc.* the goats] all mastheaded on them mountings for the fear of Benjamin Gunn.

2. To raise (a yard, sail, etc.) to its position on the mast or at the masthead.

1840 R. H. DANA *Bef. Mast* xxv. 80 Before our yards were mast-headed, the Ayacucho had spread her wings. **1881** *Daily Tel.* 24 Feb., I waited to see the men masthead the revolving lamp. **1882** NARES *Seamanship* (ed. 6) 199 The topsails are mast-headed.

Hence **mastheaded** *ppl. a.*, **mastheading** *vbl. sb.*

1836 MARRYAT *Midsh. Easy* xii, There is not one word of mast-heading in the whole of them. **1888** STEVENSON *Black Arrow* 53 Like a mast-headed seaman. **1893** SLOANE-STANLEY *Remin. Midshipm. Life* xiii. 167 Mast-heading had been forbidden by the Admiralty.

masthede, variant of MOSTHEAD *Obs.*

†**mast-holm.** *Obs.* [f. MAST *sb.*² + HOLM².] The holm-oak, *Quercus Ilex.*

1577 B. GOOGE *Heresbach's Husb.* (1586) 101 b, The Mast-holme,..in Latine Ilex. *Ibid.*, Forrestes,..consiste of Oke, Beeche,..Mastholme. **1601** HOLLAND *Pliny* I. 458 The..mast-Holme Ilex. **1726** LEONI *Alberti's Archit.* I. 25/2 The Mast-Holm [It. *Quercia*] never consumes with Age.

masthwat, variant of MOSTWHAT *Obs.*

mastic ('mæstɪk), *sb.* Forms: 4–5 **masty(c)k, -ik,** 5 **-ykk,** 6 **mastyke, (-ike),** 6–7 **masticke,** (6 **-yc**), 6–9 **mastick, mastiche,** 7–9 **mastich** 6– **mastic.** Also in late L. form 5–8 **mastix,** (7 **-ixe**). [a. F. *mastic* masc. (from 13th c.), ad. late L. *mastichum* (also *mastix*), altered form of L. *masticha, mastichē, masticē*, a. Gr. μαστίχη. Cf. Pr. *mastic, mastec*, Pg. *mastique*, Sp. †*masticis* (also *almástiga, almástic, almáciga*, through Arab. *al-maṣṭikā, -kī*), It. *mastice, mastico*, G. *mastix*, Du. *mastik.*

The etymology of Gr. μαστίχη is somewhat obscure. As mastic is in the East commonly used as a 'chewing gum', it is not improbable that the word is (as Apollodorus suggested) from the root of μασᾶσθαι to chew; cf. μάσταξ jaw, μαστιχᾶν (once, in Hesiod) to gnash the teeth; but the formation has not been explained.]

1. A gum or resin which exudes from the bark of *Pistacia Lentiscus* and some other trees (see 2).

It is known in English commerce in the form of roundish, oblong or pear-shaped tears, transparent, and of a pale yellow or faint greenish tinge. Formerly much used in Medicine. Now used chiefly in the manufacture of varnish.

1398 TREVISA *Barth. De P.R.* XVII. xc. (1495) 657 Of the rynde [of Lentiscus] comyth Resina, that hyghte Mastyk, and this gumme mastyck hath the name of mastigando: of chewynge. *a* **1400-50** *Stockh. Med. MS.* 9 Oyle of mastyk. *c* **1450** *ME. Med. Bk.* (Heinrich) 82 Make..þy mastik..in abrasen morter. **1534** *Nottingham Rec.* III. 192 Gom Masstyc. **1579** LANGHAM *Gard. Health* (1633) 359 The Masticke is also good against spitting of bloud. **1597** GERARDE *Herbal* III. lxxviii. 1244 The Rosen is called..in Latine *Lentiscina Resina*, and likewise Mastiche: in Shops Mastix:..in English Masticke. **1602** W. VAUGHAN *Direct. Health* (1626) 169 Remember before you rest, to chew downe halfe a dozen graines of Mastike. **1712** tr. *Pomet's Hist. Drugs* I. 63 The Mastick in Tear..is a resinous Gum which drops during the great Heat. **1860** *All Year Round* No. 42. 364 Mastic resembles gum Arabic; it is crystally cracked, yellow in colour,..and has no taste at all to mention. **1883** *Encycl. Brit.* XV. 621/2 *Pistacia Khinjuk*, Stocks, and *P. cabulica*, St.,..yield a kind of mastic which..when met with in the European market is known as East Indian or Bombay mastic... Cape mastic,..not exported to England, is the produce of *Euryops multifidus*... Dammar resin is sometimes sold under the name of mastic.

fig. **1598** SYLVESTER *Du Bartas* II. i. III. *Furies* 65 And innocent Astræa did combine All with the mastick of a love divine.

2. (In full ***mastic tree.***) An evergreen shrub yielding mastic gum, *Pistachia Lentiscus* of the Levant. Applied also to other species of *Pistachia*, and to the West Indian *Bursera gummifera* and Peruvian *Schinus Molle.*

c **1420** *Pallad. on Husb.* III. 1039 And now The bones hard of mastik tre wol serue Ysowe. **1638** SIR T. HERBERT *Trav.* (ed. 2) 136 Abounding in..knotty Pines, fragrant Masticks, Kingly Oaks [etc.]. **1640** PARKINSON *Theat. Bot.* 1524 *Lentiscus Pervana.* The Indian Masticke tree. **1753** CHAMBERS *Cycl. Supp.* App. s.v., Indian Mastic, the name by which the Molle, or Peruvian Lentisk is sometimes called. **1775** R. CHANDLER *Trav. Greece* (1825) II. 181 Some boughs of green mastic served us at once for table-cloth and dish. **1864** GRISEBACH *Flora W. Ind.* 785 Mastic tree, *Bursera gummifera.* **1866** *Treas. Bot.* s.v., Barbary Mastich. *Pistacia atlantica.* **1867** LADY HERBERT *Cradle L.* ix. 233 The mastic, with its pendant white bell-shaped blossoms.

3. A valuable timber tree of the West Indies and Florida, *Sideroxylon Mastichodendron.* (Also ***mastic-tree.***)

1657 LIGON *Barbados* 73 The Mastick is a tree very tall but the body slender... The timber of this tree is rank'd amongst the fourth sort, three being better then it. **1683** J. POYNTZ *Tobago* 28 The Mastick is a Timber Tree of so fine a grain, that it plains like our English Box. **1750** G. HUGHES *Barbados* 149 The Mastich-tree; *Lat.* Calaba. **1775** ROMANS *Florida* App. 32 The peninsula affords in this place Lignum-Vitae, Mastick and Mohogany. **1830** MAYCOCK *Flora Barbad.* 111 *Sideroxylon Mastichodendron*..Mastick Tree.

†**4.** (In full **herb mastic.**) The plant *Thymus Mastichina* (see MARUM). *Obs.*

1597 GERARDE *Herbal* II. ccx. 544 Of herbe Masticke. The English and French Herbarists at this daie do call this plant Masticke or Mastiche. *Ibid.* (Table Eng. names), Bastarde Masticke, that is Goates Marierome. **1640** PARKINSON *Theat. Bot.* 12 *Marum vulgare.* Hearbe Masticke. *Ibid.* 13 *Marum Syriacum vel Creticum.* The Syrian or Candye Mastick. This Candye or Syrian Marjerome. **1741** *Compl. Fam.-Pierce* II. iii. 375 It is not yet too late to plant Slips of ..Marum, Mastick, and some other aromatick Plants. **1836** LOUDON *Encycl. Plants* 508 *Thymus Mastichina*, Mastick.

5. a. A resinous or bituminous cement. **b.** A lime cement used by builders. (Cf. *mastic cement* in 8.)

1706 LONDON & WISE *Retir'd Gard'ner* I. 85 Cover the Top of the Stem with some Mastick... This Mastick must be compounded of..Rosin,..Wax,..Pitch, and..Mutton Suet. **1713** ADDISON *Guardian* No. 156 ¶9 As for the small particles of brick or stone, the least moistness would join them together, and turn them into a kind of mastick. **1839** URE *Dict. Arts* 274 (*Cements*) Mastics of resinous or bituminous nature which must be softened or fused by heat. **1881** YOUNG *Every Man his own Mech.* 625 An asphalte composition called..Patent India Mastic. *Ibid.* 627 The..heads of the nails are afterwards to be coated with the same asphalte mastic. **1884** *Health Exhib. Catal.* 87/1 Patent Joint Mastic for making joints of all kinds.

6. A liquor, used in Turkey and Greece, made from grain-spirit or grape-juice, flavoured with gum-mastic. (Cf. *mastic-brandy* and RAKI.)

1882 E. O'DONOVAN *Merv Oasis* I. 452 In Turkey we always drank mastic on such occasions. **1887** *Pall Mall G.* 23 May 4/2 [Stamboul] Their mothers prefer mastic, the spirit that fortifies and induces the loose, indolent mood.

7. The colour of mastic; a shade of pale yellow. Also as *adj.*

1890 *Daily News* 27 Sept. 2/1 Coats and jackets in mastic, cigar-colour, and shades verging on terra-cotta. **1899** *Westm. Gaz.* 17 Aug. 3/2 A gown..of mastic cloth.

8. *attrib.* and *Comb.*, as ***mastic gum, pill, seal, timber***; ***mastic-chewing***; **mastic brandy** = sense 6 above; **mastic cement, cloth, fly** (see quots.); **mastic paint**, a kind of cement used for plastering walls; † **mastic patch**, a patch for the face (*a*) fastened on with mastic, or (*b*) composed of mastic, and worn as a remedy for the tooth ache; **mastic plant**, cat-thyme, *Teucrium Marum*; **mastic shrub** = *mastic tree*; **mastic thyme**, *Thymus Mastichina* (see 4); **mastic tree** (see 2, 3); **mastic varnish**, a fine varnish used for varnishing pictures; **mastic-wood**, the wood of the mastic tree.

1883 *Encycl. Brit.* XV. 621/2 *Mastic brandy. **1815** in *Titles Patents* (1854) 690 A *mastic cement or composition, which he denominates Dihl's mastic. **1875** *Ure's Dict. Arts* (ed. 7), *Mastic cement*, a mixture of lime, sand, litharge, and linseed-oil. **1879** GEO. ELIOT *Theo. Such* v, Preliminary media of understanding, such as pipes, chocolate, or *mastic-chewing. **1882** CAULFEILD & SAWARD *Dict. Needlework*, **Mastic Cloth*, a new variety of canvas, designed for embroidery purposes. It is woven in alternate stripes. **1700** PETIVER *Musei Petiver.* 66 *Capricornus Barbadensis major*..from..Barbadoes where they are very plentifull and call'd by them the *Mastick-fly. **1750** G. HUGHES *Barbadoes* III. 81 The Mastich-fly..derives its name from the Tree it feeds upon. **1837** *Penny Cycl.* VII. 91/1 *Mastic gum. **1884** *Health Exhib. Catal.* 87/1 Heat Resisting *Mastic Paint [cf. **1839** URE *Dict. Arts* 869 Hamelin's mastic or lithic paint to cover the façades of brick buildings, &c.]. **1597-8** BP. HALL *Sat.* VI. i. 115 Or Gellia wore a veluet *mastick-patch Upon her temples when no tooth did ach. **1639** MAYNE *City Match* III. iii, When there was not fire enough to warme a Mastick patch t' apply to his wives Temples In great extremity of toothach. **1697** GREW *Epsom Waters* 57 Take of *Mastick Pills, two Scruples. **1718** QUINCY *Compl. Disp.* 80 *Mari Syriaci*, the *Mastick Plant, as some call it. It is reckon'd a kind of Marjoram. **1837** SIR F. PALGRAVE *Merch. & Friar* i. (1844) 18 Suppose the letter completed,..and sealed with the *mastic seal. **1682** WHELER *Journ. Greece* I. 61 Lentiscus, or the *Mastick shrub. **1640** PARKINSON *Theat. Bot.* 6 *Thymum latifolium.* *Masticke Tyme. **1707** [see MARUM]. **1833** J. BENNETT *Artificer's Lex.* 228 *Mastic timber, specific gravity per foot cube, 53 lbs. **1510** in Willis & Clark *Cambridge* (1886) II. 199 *Mastyke vernysch. **1841** E. FITZGERALD *Lett.* (1889) I. 78 The picture has just been varnished with mastick varnish. **1669** H. STUBBE *Let.* in Birch *Life Boyle* (1744) 191 To let you see, what *mastick wood will do in the gout. **1699** GARTH *Dispens.* III. 90 And on the structure next he heaps a load Of ..mastic wood. **1856** MAYNE *Expos. Lex.*, *Mastich Wood*... A tincture is made from it.

†**'mastic**, *v. Obs. rare.* [f. MASTIC *sb.*] *trans.* To treat with a preparation of mastic: **a.** as a setting for a stone; **b.** as a varnish.

1688 R. HOLME *Armoury* III. 91/1 [Jewellers' terms.] Masticking, is setting a Black between the Stones to set them off. **1697** EVELYN *Numism.* vi. 217 Masticking them over very Artificially,..to elevate both the Figures and Letters with the Vernish.

masticability (ˌmæstɪkə'bɪlɪtɪ). [f. next: see -ITY.] The capability of being masticated.

1849 *Fraser's Mag.* XL. 130 The same simple expedient suffices to convert, so far as..masticability is concerned, an old fowl into a young capon. **1894** *Contemp. Rev.* LXVI. 648 You can always rely upon the masticability of the dish.

masticable ('mæstɪkəb(ə)l), *a. rare.* [f. MASTICATE *v.* + -ABLE.] That may be masticated.

1846 WORCESTER (citing *Jour. Sci.*). **1890** *Chamb. Jrnl.* 15 Mar. 162/1 Her bread is like so much masticable lead.

masticate ('mæstɪkeɪt), *v.* Also 7 **mastigate.** [f. late L. *masticāt-*, ppl. stem of *masticā-re* (4th c.) to chew, whence It. *masticare*, Sp. *mascar*, Pg. *masgar* (and the learned forms Sp. *masticar*, *mastigar*, Pg. *mastigar*), OF. *mascher* (mod.F. *mâcher*), Pr. *mastegar, maschar.*

A plausible suggestion is that late L. *masticāre* may be f. L. *mastichē* MASTIC, the assumed original sense being 'to chew

mastic', 'to treat as one treats mastic'. But it is possible that the verb may be f. Gr. μασταx-, μάσταξ jaw, or an unrecorded Latin cognate of this.]

1. *trans.* To grind (food) to a pulp with the teeth; to chew.

1649 JER. TAYLOR *Gt. Exemp.* I. Disc. iv. 128 Some chewed bitter pills and masticated gummes. **1746** R. JAMES *Moufet's Health's Improv.* Introd. 2 It is..a very great Error to swallow the Aliment before it is duly masticated. **1827** ROBERTS *Voy. Centr. Amer.* 130 Indian corn, partly boiled and masticated [in the preparation of a drink called 'mishlaw']. **1872** HUXLEY *Physiol.* vi. 139 To these ends food is taken into the mouth and masticated. **1880** GÜNTHER *Fishes* 119 Some fishes,..provided with broad molar-like teeth, masticate their food.

†**b.** *fig.* = MANDUCATE *v. Obs.*

1651 C. CARTWRIGHT *Cert. Relig.* I. 30 Except we eat the flesh of the Son of man, and drink his bloud, we have no life in us; him we must mastigate, and chew by faith.

2. To crush or knead (india-rubber or gutta-percha) to a pulp; to combine with (gutta-percha) in the process of 'mastication'.

1849 C. NICKELS in *Repert. Patent Invent.* (1850) XV. 226 The pieces of such india-rubber will admit of being kneaded or masticated. *Ibid.*, India-rubber,..manufactured by kneading or masticating therewith..flowers of sulphur.

Hence '**masticated** *ppl. a.*

1727 BAILEY vol. II, *Masticated*, chewed. **1799** *Phil. Trans.* LXXXIX. 253 This middle space..becomes filled up with the masticated food. **1849** C. NICKELS in *Repert. Patent Invent.* (1850) XV. 227 The kneaded or masticated mass [of gutta-percha]..is to be subjected to pressure.

masticating ('mæstɪkeɪtɪŋ), *vbl. sb.* [f. MASTICATE *v.* + -ING[1].] The action of the vb. MASTICATE. Also *attrib.*

1827 ROBERTS *Voy. Centr. Amer.* 129 Some few of the young men also joined in the masticating process. **1849** C. NICKELS in *Repert. Patent Invent.* (1850) XV. 224 That process of preparing and manufacturing india-rubber (caoutchouc) called grinding, masticating, or kneading. **1854** OWEN *Skel. & Teeth* in *Orr's Circ. Sci.* I. 294 A masticating apparatus, to serve the requirements of a gigantic animal..was provided by a succession of different molar teeth. **1855** BAIN *Senses & Int.* I. ii. §18 (1864) 49 The first operation upon the food in the mouth—the chewing or masticating.

masticating ('mæstɪkeɪtɪŋ), *ppl. a.* [f. MASTICATE *v.* + -ING[2].] That masticates.

1802 PLAYFAIR *Illustr. Hutton. Th.* 468 The grinder of the boar is similar to that of the elephant, in the extent of the masticating surface. **1827** HOOD *True Story* i, Some bit of masticating bone, That..only seems to gnaw itself. **1835-6** TODD *Cycl. Anat.* I. 771/1 The masticating Crustacea being the highest in point of organization.

mastication (mæstɪ'keɪʃən). Also 7 **mastucation**. [ad. late L. *masticātiōn-em*, n. of action f. *masticā-re* to MASTICATE. Cf. F. *mastication*.]

1. The action of masticating or chewing.

1565 COOPER *Thesaurus*, *Confectio escarum*..Mastication or chewing of the meate. **1615** CROOKE *Body of Man* 134 All Aliments..after mastication or chewing..are swallowed. **1658** SIR T. BROWNE *Gard. Cyrus* iii. *Hydriot.* etc. 56 After a fuller mastication, and salivous mixture. **1854** EMERSON *Lett. & Soc. Aims, Comic* Wks. (Bohn) III. 210 To put something for mastication between the upper and lower mandibles. **1880** GÜNTHER *Fishes* 329 Dentition..adapted for the prehension and mastication of crustaceous..animals.

fig. **a 1631** DONNE *Serm.* lxiii. (1640) 637 It is writ in gall and wormwood..; but if we can bring it..to that mastication, that rumination, which is [etc.].

†**b.** = MANDUCATION. *Obs.*

1601 BP. W. BARLOW *Defence* 128 They, which..haue turned..the supper into a spectacle..feeding the peoples eyes with the priestes eleuation, and sole mastucation.

2. The action or process of pulping (gutta-percha).

1881 *Times* 18 Apr. 4/6 The gutta percha is not masticated in any way, Mr. T. holding that mastication utterly destroys the material. **1885** C. G. W. LOCK *Workshop Receipts* Ser. IV. 1/2 At some works this process of 'mastication' [in waterproofing] is omitted.

masticator ('mæstɪkeɪtə(r)). [f. MASTICATE *v.* + -OR.] One who or that which masticates.

1. *pl.* The teeth or jaws. *jocular.*

1694 MOTTEUX *Rabelais* v. xxiii. (1737) 103 Her Masticators..chew'd it. **1765** STERNE *Tr. Shandy* VII. viii, Just Heaven! What masticators!—What bread! **1797** ANNA SEWARD *Lett.* (1811) IV. 311 His..preference of such impure masticator to the clean ivory supplied by the dentist. **1816** 'QUIZ' *Grand Master* III. 66 Their masticators they employ, On..beef, and goat. **1845** FORD *Handbk. Spain* I. 27 It requires powerful masticators, a vigorous appetite and digestion.

2. A person or animal that masticates or chews.

1824 W. IRVING *T. Trav.* (1850) 124 Never was there a more..thoroughly sustained attack on the trencher than by this phalanx of masticators. **1826** KIRBY & SP. *Entomol.* III. 417 Insects of late have been divided into two great tribes, *masticators* and *suckers*. **1854** BADHAM *Halieut.* 434 The Shark is not a careful masticator. **1860** TRISTRAM *Gt. Sahara* vi. 95 The dyers actually hire masticators to provide them with tannin.

3. A machine for grinding or pulping.

1858 in *Patents Specif., India Rubber* (1875) 133 The gutta percha is then..submitted to the masticator. **1875** KNIGHT *Dict. Mech.*, *Masticator*, a small machine to cut up meat for aged persons or those who have lost their teeth or the power of chewing. **1885** C. G. W. LOCK *Workshop Receipts* Ser. IV. 1/2 The rubber..is introduced into the 'masticator', which consists of a strong cylindrical box, containing a stout deeply-fluted drum, which revolves within the box.

‖**mastica'torium.** [mod.L.] = next sb.

c 1550 LLOYD *Treas. Health* F iij, Masticatorium is a confection whiche is held in the mouth & chewed to purge the head of flegme. **1592** NASHE *Summers Last Will* E i b, Physicians with their..*Masticator[i]um* and *Cataplasmata*. **1693** tr. *Blancard's Phys. Dict.* (ed. 2), *Masticatorium*, a Medicine which is to provoke spitting.

masticatory ('mæstɪkətərɪ), *a.* and *sb.* [ad. mod.L. *masticātōrius*, *-ōrium*, f. *masticāre* to MASTICATE: see -ORY [1] and [2]. Cf. F. *masticatoire* adj. and sb.] **A.** *adj.* Of, pertaining to, or concerned with mastication. ***masticatory foot*** (*Ent.*) = *foot-jaw*: see FOOT *sb.* 35.

1611 COTGR., *Masticatoire*, masticatorie, chewing, champing. **1694** MOTTEUX *Rabelais* IV. xv. (1737) 60 The molar, masticatory and canine Teeth. **1769** BANCROFT *Guiana* 262 The masticatory and digestive organs of carnivorous and granivorous animals. **1852** DANA *Crust.* II. 1035 This pair of legs is often called a pair of maxilla-feet, jaw-feet, or masticatory feet. **1862** *Jrnl. Soc. Arts* X. 324/2 The Para rubber..if not injured by masticatory processes in the manufacture,..will [etc.]. **1899** *Allbutt's Syst. Med.* VII. 680 Paralysis of the masticatory muscles.

b. Of diseases or symptoms: Affecting the organs of mastication.

1853 tr. *Romberg's Man. Nervous Dis.* (Syd. Soc.) II. 289 This serves to distinguish masticatory from histrionic paralysis. **1878** tr. *H. von Ziemssen's Cycl. Med.* XIV. 358 The so-called masticatory facial spasm.

B. *sb.* A medicinal substance to be chewed.

1611 COTGR., *Masticatoire*, a Masticatorie; a medecine for the rhewme chawed, or held betweene the teeth. **1621** BURTON *Anat. Mel.* II. iv. II. iii, Or Apophlegmatismes, masticatories to be held and chewed in the mouth. **a 1626** BACON *Med. Rem.* Wks. 1827 VII. 235 To remember masticatories for the mouth. **1733** CHEYNE *Eng. Malady* II. ix. §5 (1734) 212 Some gentle Masticatory (such as Mastick, Pellitory, Tobacco, or the like). **1880** GARROD & BAXTER *Mat. Med.* 291 It is used as a masticatory in paralysis of parts about the mouth.

mastice, mastich(e: see MASTIFF, MASTIC.

masticic (mæ'stɪsɪk), **mastichic** (mæ'stɪkɪk), *a. Chem.* [f. MASTIC *sb.* + -IC.] ***masticic acid*** (see quots.).

1845 COOLEY *Cycl. Pract. Receipts* (ed. 2) 584 Mastichic acid.. The portion of mastic soluble in alcohol. **1855** OGILVIE *Suppl.*, *Masticic acid.* **1885** T. L. BRUNTON *Pharmacol.* (1887) 897 Mastich..consists of about 90 per cent. of an acid resin (mastichic acid).

masticin ('mæstɪsɪn). *Chem.* Also **-ine**. [f. MASTIC + -IN.] The substance which remains undissolved after dissolving mastic in alcohol.

1844 in HOBLYN *Dict. Med.* **1883** *Encycl. Brit.* XV 621/2 The insoluble portion [of Mastic], Beta resin or Masticin.. is a translucent colourless tough substance.

†**masticine**, *a. Obs. rare.* [ad. late L. *masticin-us*, *mastichinus*, a. Gr μαστιχινός, f. μαστίχη MASTIC. Cf. OF. *masticin*.] Of or pertaining to mastic. In quot. *c* 1420 *absol.* = oil of mastic.

***c* 1420** *Pallad. on Husb.* IV. 144 Her seed yf me reclyne In ..Iuce of rose, other in masticyne, Or madifie hit so in oil lauryne. **1656** BLOUNT *Glossogr.*, *Masticine*, of, or pertaining to, or of the colour of mastick.

mastick(e: see MASTIC.

masticoat(e, -cot(e, -cott, -cut: see MASSICOT.

mastiff ('mɑːstɪf, -æ-), *sb.* Pl. **mastiffs**. Forms: α. 4-5, 7 **mastif**, 5-7 **mastife**, 5-6 **mastyf(e**, (5 **mestyf**, 6 **mastyve**, *Sc.* **mastew**), 6-8 **mastive**, 6-7 **masstiffe**, 7- **mastiff**; *pl.* 4-5 **masteves**, 4-6 **mastyves**, 5 **mastyfes**, **maistyves**, 6 **mastiffes**, **maistiffes**, **mastyvys**, 6-9 **mastives**, 7- **mastiffs**. β. 5-6, 9 *dial.* **mastis**, **mastice**. γ. 5-7, 9 *dial.* **masty**, 6-7, 9 *dial.* **mastie**, (6 **mastye**). [repr. OF. *mastin* (mod.F. *mâtin*) = Pr. *masti-s*, Sp. *mastin*, Pg. *mastim*, It. *mastino*:—popular L. type **mansuētinus*, f. L. *mansuētus* tame (see MANSUETE *a.*).

The form of the Eng. word is difficult to account for. Possibly the word was first known to Englishmen in the Pr. form *masti-s*; as this coincides with the form that would have been assumed in early OF. by the subject-case of a noun **mastif*, the α. forms may be due to grammatical interpretation, while the β. and γ. forms may have been taken directly from Pr. The word was more or less confused with OF. *mestif* mongrel. The form MASTIN occurs only in Caxton's translations from Fr.: cf. MÂTIN.]

A large, powerful dog with a large head, drooping ears and pendulous lips, valuable as a watch-dog. Also *mastiff dog*.

α. ***c* 1330** R. BRUNNE *Chron.* (1810) 189 On þer first eschel he smot in fulle hastif, & þorgh þam ilka del, als grehound or mastif. **1387** TREVISA *Higden* (Rolls) VIII. 187 Houndes and masteves [*MSS.* β, γ mastyves, CAXTON maistyves] beeþ i-slawe in all þe forestes of Engelond. ***c* 1400** MAUNDEV. (1839) xv. 167 There ben Rattes in that Ile, als grete as Houndes here: and men taken hem with grete Mastyfes. **1494** FABYAN *Chron.* VII. ccxxxi. 263 A mastife or great curre dogge. **1509** FISHER *Serm. Hen. VII*, Wks. (1876) 278 Euen as ye se these wood dogges these grete mastyues that be tyed in chaynes. ***a* 1529** SKELTON *Sp. Parrot* 321 Suche malyncoly mastyvys and mangye curre dogges Ar mete for a swyneherde to hunte after hogges. **1550** CROWLEY *Epigr.* 11 b, To kepe wyth daunger, a greate mastyfe dogge. **1599** SHAKS. *Hen. V*, III. vii 59 Their Mastiffes are of vnmatchable courage. **1601** HOLLAND *Pliny* I. 218 The Colophonians and Castabaleans maintained certain squadrons of mastiue dogs for their war seruice. ***a* 1652** BROME *Queenes Exch.* v. i. Wks. 1873 III. 537 There's a crust I brought To stop the open mouth of the Mastive, if he had flown at us. **1717** DE FOE *Mem. Ch. Scot.* III. 96 A Gentleman who was set upon by a Furious Mastive Dog. **1807** *Med. Jrnl.* XVII. 273 In the porch..was lying a large, savage, mastiff dog. **1809** SCOTT *Let. to Southey* 14 Jan. in *Lockhart*, We can only fight like mastiffs, boldly, blindly, and faithfully. **1812** SOUTHEY *Omniana* I. 293 Sir Thomas Roe took out some English mastives to India. **1877** *Encycl. Brit.* VII. 330/1 The Mastiff..is usually of a buff colour, with ears and muzzle darker.

β. **1483** *Cath. Angl.* 230/2 A Mastis, *liciscus*. ?***a* 1500** *Forest Laws* §12 in *Sc. Acts* (1814) I. 690/2 Ande gif ony mastice be fundyn in þe forest [etc.]. **1513** DOUGLAS *Æneis* IX. Prol. 49 The cur, or mastis, he haldis at small availl. **1869** *Lonsdale Gloss.*, *Mastice*,..corr. of mastiff. **1878** *Cumberld. Gloss.*, Mastis. **1893** *Northumbld. Gloss.*, Mastis.

γ. **1540** *St. Papers Hen. VIII*, VIII. 482 Certeyne masties ..for his hunting. **1566** DRANT *Horace Sat.* II. vi. (end), Also the vaste and ample house of mastie dogges did sounde. **1577** B. GOOGE *Heresbach's Husb.* III. (1586) 154 The mastie that keepeth the House. **1652** DOROTHY OSBORNE *Lett. to Sir W. Temple* (1888) 105 A masty is handsomer to me than the most exact little dog that ever lady played withal. **1676** WYCHERLEY *Pl. Dealer* IV. i, Surly, untractable, snarling Brute! he! a Masty-dog were as fit a thing to make a Gallant of. **1687** MIEGE *Gt. Fr. Dict.* II. s.v., A great Masty, *un gros Mâtin*. **1882** *W. Worc. Gloss.* Add., *Mastie-dog*, mastiff.

b. with an adj. prefixed, indicating a foreign variety, as ***Cuban***, ***Dutch***, ***German***, ***Tibet mastiff***.

1774 GOLDSM. *Nat. Hist.* III. 286 The Dutch mastiff. **1859** WOOD *Illustr. Nat. Hist.* I. 307 The Cuban Mastiff is supposed to be produced by a mixture of the true Mastiff with the bloodhound. **1877** *Encycl. Brit.* VII. 330/2 The Thibet Mastiff is larger than the English breed. **1883** R. GROOM *Great Dane* 4 The German Mastiff.

c. *transf.* and *fig.*

1602 *2nd Pt. Return from Parnass.* v. iv. (Arb.) 71 *Furor.* Farewell my masters, Furor's a masty dogge. **1610** B. JONSON *Alch.* I. i, May, murmuring mastiffe? I, and doe. **1781** COWPER *Table-talk* 35 To see a people scattered like a flock, Some royal mastiff panting at their heels.

d. *attrib.* and *Comb.*, as ***mastiff-bitch***, †***-cur***, ***dog*** (see 1), †***-hound***, ***mouth***, ***race***, †***strind*** (Sc.); ***mastiff-like*** adj.; **mastiff bat**, **day** *jocular* (see quots.); **mastiff-fox**, a variety of fox (see quot. 1828).

1851 GOSSE *Nat. in Jamaica* 159 The Chestnut *Mastiff-bat. **1871** *Cassell's Nat. Hist.* I. 319 The Pale Chestnut Mastiff Bat [*Nyctinomus brasiliensis*]... This species is found commonly in South America and the West Indies. *Ibid.* 320 The Smoky Mastiff Bat [*Molossus nasutus*]..is a well-known South American species. **1621** in *Naworth Househ. Bks.* (Surtees) 184 A *mastie bich. **1797** COLERIDGE *Christabel* I. 7 Sir Leoline..Hath a toothless mastiff bitch. **1522** SKELTON *Why not to Court?* 294 Our barons..Dare not loke out at dur For drede of the *mastyue cur, For drede of the bochers dogge. **1608** T. JAMES *Apol. Wyclif* 49 They did as it were so manie woolues, or mastie curs woorie them [the flock]. **1781** H. WALPOLE *Let. to H. S. Conway* 5 June, Last week we had two or three *mastiff days; for they were fiercer than our common dog-days. **1774** *Mastiff fox [see GREYHOUND 4]. **1828** J. FLEMING *Hist. Brit. Anim.* 13 Mastif-Fox.—This is of a dark brown colour, somewhat less [than the Greyhound Fox], but more strongly made. ***a* 1400-50** *Alexander* 321 A mouthe as a *mastif hunde vn-metely to shaw. **1475** *Bk. Noblesse* (Roxb.) 16 Every man kepyng the scout wache had a masty hound at a lyes. **1500-20** DUNBAR *Poems* liii. 47 Quhou *mastew-lyk [*v.r.* mastive lyk] about ȝeid he! **1851** GOSSE *Nat. in Jamaica* 293 The mastiff-like physiognomy [of the monk bat]. **1809** W. IRVING *Knickerb.* (1861) 35 He was a short, square, brawny old gentleman, with a double chin, a *mastiff mouth, and a broad copper nose. **1877** *Encycl. Brit.* VII. 330/1 The *Mastiff race of dogs..includes the Mastiff, the Bull-dog, and the Pug. **1500-20** DUNBAR *Poems* lx. 21 Mismad mandragis of *mastyf strynd [*v.r.* kynd].

†'**mastiff**, *a. Obs.* Also 5 **mestyf**. [Seems to be partly a derivative of MAST *sb.*[2], and partly a perversion of MASSIVE, in both cases due to association with MASTIFF *sb.* Cf. MASTY *a.*]

1. Of a swine: Fattened; = MASTED *a.*, MASTY *a.* 2.

***c* 1440** *Promp. Parv.* 334/2 Mestyf, hogge, or swyne, *maialis*.

2. Massive, solid, bulky.

1495 *Trevisa's Barth. De P.R.* v. lvii, Some [bones] ben.. holowy. And some mastyffe [*MS. Bodl.* massye] and sadde for the more stedfastness. **1733** CHEYNE *Eng. Malady* I. xi. §4. 101 Those [persons] of large, full, and (as they are call'd) mastiff Muscles,..are generally of a firmer State of Fibres, than those of little Muscles.

3. Burly, big-bodied; = MASTY *a.* 3.

1668 KIRKMAN *Eng. Rogue* II. xi. (1671) 96 Perceiving them to be too hard for us (for they were two stout Mastiff Queans). ***a* 1675** WHITELOCKE *Mem.* (1732) 112, I did the like to another great Mastiff Fellow, an Officer also of the King's Army, and took away his Sword from him.

†**mastigadour.** *Obs.* Also 8 **masticadour**, 9 (in Dicts.) **masticador**. [a. F. *mastigadour* (Solleysel 1682), ad. Pg. *mastigadouro* = mod.L. *masticātōrium* MASTICATORY *sb.*] (See quots.)

1720 GIBSON *Diet. Horses* vii. (1731) 103 He [Solleysell] orders the Horse to have a small Watering-bit, or Masticadour put upon him. **1727** BAILEY vol. II, *Mastigadour*, a Slabbering Bit, a Snaffle of Iron.

mastigate, rare obs. form of MASTICATE.

mastigophore ('mæstɪgəfɔə(r)). *Zool.* [ad. Gr. μαστιγοφόρος: see MASTIGOPHOROUS.]

†**1.** *Antiq.* (See quot. and next word.)

1658 PHILLIPS, *Mastigophore* (Greek), an Usher that with stripes makes way in a croud.

2. A protozoan belonging to the class *Mastigophora*, the members of which are provided with one or more flagella.

1890 in *Century Dict.*

† **mastigophorer.** *Obs.*—⁰ [formed as prec. + -ER¹.] (See quot. and prec. 1.)

1656 BLOUNT *Glossogr.*, *Mastigophorer*, a fellow worthy to be whipped; also an usher, who with whips removed the people, where there was much press.

mastigophoric (ˌmæstɪgəˈfɒrɪk), *a.* [formed as next + -IC.] = MASTIGOPHOROUS.

1816 T. L. PEACOCK *Headlong Hall* vi, He would beat his drum in Grub Street, form a mastigophoric corps of his own. **1902** WEBSTER *Suppl.*, *Mastigophoric*, .. having a lash-like cilium; flagellate;—said of the Flagellata.

mastigophorous (mæstɪˈgɒfərəs), *a.* [f. Gr. μαστῑγοφόρος scourge-bearing (f. μαστῑγ-, μάστιξ scourge + -φόρος bearing) + -OUS.]

1. That carries a scourge, scourge-bearing. Only in humorously pedantic use.

1812 PARR *Let. to C. Burney* 12 Dec., Wks. 1828 VII. 418 To meet all the mastigophorous subscribers would gladden my heart. **1826** SYD. SMITH *Wks.* (1859) II. 94/1 Not what this medium boy can do while his mastigophorous superior is frowning over him, but [etc.]. **1871** M. COLLINS *Mrq. & Merch.* II. v. 149 The sharp discipline of a mastigophorous schoolmaster.

2. *Zool.* Provided with flagella; belonging to the *Mastigophora*, a class of *Protozoa*.

1890 in *Century Dict.*, and in later Dicts.

mastigopod (ˈmæstɪgəpɒd), *sb.* and *a.* [ad. mod.L. *Mastigopoda* neut. pl. (lit. 'whip-footed' animals), f. Gr. μαστῑγ-, μάστιξ whip + ποδ-, πούς foot.] **A.** *sb.* Huxley's name for a protozoan furnished with cilia or flagella. **B.** *adj.* Furnished with cilia or flagella, or both (*Cent. Dict.* 1890).

1875 HUXLEY in *Encycl. Brit.* II. 50/1 The myxopod.. gives rise by division to bodies provided with long flagelliform cilia.. which may be termed mastigopods. **1877** —— *Anat. Inv. Anim.* ii. 76 It will be convenient to distinguish those Protozoa.. which are provided with cilia or flagella, as mastigopods. **1898** SEDGWICK *Student's Text-bk. Zool.* I. 29 Forms which pass through both the myxopod and mastigopod condition.

Hence **mastiˈgopodous** *a.* = prec. adj.

1890 in *Century Dict.*

mastigure (ˈmæstɪgjʊə(r)). [ad. mod.L. *mastigūra* (Fleming 1822), *mastigūr-us*, f. Gr. μαστῑγ-, μάστιξ whip + οὐρά tail.] 'An agamoid lizard of the genus *Uromastix*' (*Cent. Dict.* 1890).

1863 WOOD *Nat. Hist.* III. 90 The Egyptian Mastigure, or Spine-footed Stellio, is a native of Northern Africa.

mastik(e, mastilȝon, obs. ff. MASTIC, MASLIN².

mastika (mæˈstiːkə). Also **mastica, masticha.** [ad. mod.Gr. μαστίχα mastic.] = MASTIC *sb.* 6.

1926 P. M. SHAND *Bk. Wine* x. 264 Chios is also the home of the Mastic plant, whence a horrible liqueur, very popular in the Levant, called Chio-Mastica-Raki.. is made. **1930** E. WAUGH *Labels* vi. 148 He said if one ever drank *mastika* one returned to Greece. **1966** 'S. HARVESTER' *Treacherous Road* ix. 85 They were drinking mastica, the local brandy. **1967** A. LICHINE *Encycl. Wines* 346/2 *Mastika* (or *Masticha*), a favourite Greek aperitif, made on the island of Chios, from a brandy base with gum mastic added. **1968** L. DURRELL *Tunc* iii. 114 He poured me a glass of fiery mastika. **1969** *Listener* 2 Jan. 31/2 The aniseed-flavoured mastika. **1974** *Times* 21 Feb. 14 The guide maintained that, while Bulgarians were indeed virile, this was due more to drinking slivovice and mastika than to anything they ate.

†**ˈmastin.** *Obs. rare.* [a. OF. *mastin*: see MASTIFF.] = MASTIFF *sb.*

1483 CAXTON *G. de la Tour* H vij, Beholde these grete dogges that men call mastyns. **1485** —— *Chas. Gt.* 128 But rolland.. came vpon the mastyn sarasyns.

masting (ˈmɑːstɪŋ, -æ-), *vbl. sb.*¹ [f. MAST *v.*¹ + -ING¹.]

1. The action or process of fitting with masts.

1627 CAPT. SMITH *Seaman's Gram.* xi. 54 The Masting of a Ship is much to be considered, and will.. cause her to saile well or ill. **1794** *Rigging & Seamanship* I. 1 In masting.. the complete height of a mast is gained by erecting one mast on the top of another. **1870** *Daily News* 3 Oct., They considered the tripod system of masting one that answered well for the support of the masts.

b. Masts collectively.

1702 C. MATHER *Magn. Chr.* I. vi. (1852) 84 All her masting seemed blown away by the board. **1757** J. H. GROSE *Voy. E. Indies* 175 The masting generally used in the country-ship, are Pohoon-masts. **1794** *Rigging & Seamanship* II. 276 Observations on the different inclinations given to the masting of ships.

2. ? The action of felling trees for masts. *U.S.*

1792 J. BELKNAP *Hist. New Hampsh.* III. 3 Persons.. employed in surveying, masting, hunting and scouting.

3. *attrib.*, as ***masting-sheers, tree***; **masting-house** (see quot.); **masting pine,** *Pinus Strobus* of N. America.

1855 OGILVIE *Suppl.*, *Mast-house*, **Masting-house*, a place where masts, &c., are deposited. 2. A building furnished with apparatus for fixing vessels' masts. **1755** *Gentl. Mag.* XXV. 503 A white-pine or *masting-pine, .. seven feet eight inches diameter at the but end. **1760** W. DOUGLASS *Brit. N. Amer.* II. 53 The Pines may be subdivided into the masting, or white pine, the pitch pine, .. and others.. used as lumber. **1875** KNIGHT *Dict. Mech.*, **Masting-shears.* **1893** DAHLSTROM tr. *Weisbach & Herrmann's Mech. Hoisting Mach.* vi. 252 A large masting sheers designed at the machine works at Waltjen, in Bremen. **1760** W. DOUGLASS *Brit. N. Amer.* II. 53 *note*, In New Hampshire.. is much good ship timber and *masting trees.

masting (ˈmɑːstɪŋ, -æ-), *vbl. sb.*² *rare.* [MAST *sb.*²] The action of producing mast. In quot. *attrib.*

1760 W. DOUGLASS *Brit. N. Amer.* II. 375 The price of pork.. depends upon the goodness of their masting years.

mastis, mastiso, see MASTIFF, MESTIZO.

‖**mastitis** (mæˈstaɪtɪs). *Med.* [mod.L., f. Gr. μαστ-ός breast + -ITIS.] Inflammation of the female breast (in man or other mammals).

1842 in BRANDE *Dict. Sci.* etc. **1875** H. C. WOOD *Therap.* (1879) 262 In mastitis.. its local application to the breast is often very efficacious. **1899** *Allbutt's Syst. Med.* VIII. 911 Gangrenous mastitis in sheep. **1950** *N.Z. Jrnl. Agric.* Mar. 265/1 Milk from cows suffering from mastitis may be dangerous to public health. **1970** *Black's Vet. Dict.* (ed. 9) 531/2 When penicillin became available for veterinary use, it began to change the bacteriological picture of mastitis in our dairy herds.

mastive, obs. form of MASTIFF.

-mastix (ˈmæstɪks), repr. Gr. μάστιξ scourge, freq. used in the 17th c. (rarely later) in quasi-Gr. combinations formed after *Homeromastix* (Ὁμηρομάστιξ) 'scourge of Homer' (the name given to the grammarian Zoïlus on account of the severity of his censure of the Homeric poems), and designating persons violently hostile to some person or class, as ***Episcopo-mastix, Infanto-mastix, Puritano-mastix,*** etc. Also in titles of books severely attacking some person, class, institution, etc., as ***Atheomastix*** [Gr. ἄθεος atheist] (Fotherby *a* 1619), ***Histriomastix*** [L. *histrio* actor] (Prynne 1632), ***Satiromastix*** (Dekker 1602, attacking Ben Jonson).

1604 BP. W. BARLOW *Sum Conference* (1638) To Rdr., In one ranke whereof you may place our Hercules-Limbo-mastix. **1625** BP. MONTAGU *App Cæsar* 291 Incomparable Hooker, that Puritano-mastix, might well say [etc.]. **1651** H. L'ESTRANGE (*title*) Smectymnuo-mastix: or, Short Animadversions vpon Smectymnuus [etc.]. **1656** S. HOLLAND *Zara* (1719) 76 It would have puzzell'd that Female Mastix Mantuan to have limm'd this she Chymera. **1656** HEYLIN *Extraneus Vap.* 234 [St. Augustine] in condemning Infants unbaptized to the pains of Hell.. incurred the name of Infanto Mastix. **1660** GAUDEN *Serm. Funeral Brounrig* Ep. Ded., Those unreasonable Episcopomastix, whose malice is as blind, as it is bold, against all Bishops. *a* **1662** HEYLIN *Cypr. Anglicus* (1668) 50 Humphries.. got the title of a Papisto Mastyx. **1671** GLANVILL *Disc. M. Stubbe* 100 And when the Virtuoso-Mastix hath proved that these are not Complements [etc.]. **1818** F. HODGSON (title, in *Byron's Works* 1901 V. 278) Latino-Mastix **1818** —— (*Ibid.*) Sæculo-Mastix, or the Lash of the Age we live in.

†**b.** As independent sb. *Obs. rare.*

1678 CUDWORTH *Intell. Syst.* I. iv. §15. 273 Hierocles, who was the Mastix of Christianity and Champion for the gods.

mastix(e, mastizo, see MASTIC, MESTIZO.

mastless (ˈmɑːstlɪs, -æ-), *a.*¹ [f. MAST *sb.*¹ + -LESS.] Without a mast or masts.

1593 T. WATSON *Tears of Fancie* liii. Poems (Arb.) 205 Like a mastles shipe at seas I wander. **1624** HEYWOOD *Gunaik.* v. 258 [Perseus] whom Acrisius caused with his mother to be sent to sea in a mastlesse boat. **1849** ROCK *Ch. of Fathers* II. 495 The mastless vessel.. crept softly.. up the stream. **1884** *Pall Mall G.* 16 Oct. 1/2 Our mastless ironclads lie like hulks on the water, incapable of motion or direction without coal.

mastless (ˈmɑːstlɪs, -æ-), *a.*² *rare*⁻¹. [f. MAST *sb.*² + -LESS.] Without mast, without acorns.

1700 DRYDEN *Pal. & Arcite* III. 208 A crown of mastless oak adorn'd her head.

mastlin(g(e, -yn(e, -youn, obs. ff. MASLIN.

ˈmastman. *U.S.* [MAST *sb.*¹ 1.] (See quot. 1890.)

1839 C. F. BRIGGS *Adventures Harry Franco* I. xxii. 236 All hands call him dismal Jerry, except Mike, the mast man, and he calls him Sergeant Longshanks. **1890** *Cent. Dict.*, *Mastman*, a seaman stationed at a mast in a man-of-war to keep the ropes clear and in order. **1901** A. M. KNIGHT *Mod. Seamanship* 382 Caution the mastmen to keep fast the weather sheets until the yards are down.

masto- (ˈmæstəʊ), used (*Anat.* and *Path.*) **a.** to represent MASTOID *sb.*, in combinations with the general sense 'pertaining jointly to the mastoid process or bone and some other part of the skull', as ***masto-occipital, -parietal, -squamous,*** †***-tympanic*** adjs.; **b.** as combining form of Gr. μαστός breast, in names of diseases of the female breast, as ***masto-carcinoma, -chondrosis, -scirrhus*** (Mayne *Expos. Lex.* 1856); also MASTODYNIA.

1855 HOLDEN *Hum. Osteol.* (1878) 114 The mastoid part of the temporal is connected to the posterior inferior angle of the parietal bone by the *masto-parietal suture. **1858** H. GRAY *Anat.* 54 The sutures at the base of the skull are.. the petro-occipital, the *masto-occipital [etc.]. **1899** *Allbutt's Syst. Med.* VII. 599 There may be no local œdema over the mastoid, in fact no *masto-squamous abscess. **1890** *Century Dict.* (citing R. OWEN), **Masto-tympanic*, a bone of the skull of some reptiles, which should correspond to the opisthotic quadrate of modern nomenclature.

mastodon (ˈmæstədɒn). *Palæont.* [mod.L., f. Gr. μαστ-ός breast + ὀδοντ-, ὀδούς tooth.

The word was used in Fr. form (*mastodonte*) by Cuvier in 1806 in *Ann. Mus. Hist. Nat. de Paris* VIII. 270.]

A large extinct mammal resembling the elephant, characterized by having nipple-shaped tubercles in pairs on the crowns of the molar teeth.

1813 BAKEWELL *Introd. Geol.* (1815) 430 The bones of the mastodon and mammoth are found only in the upper strata. **1842** TENNYSON *Epic* 36 Nature brings not back the Mastodon. **1851** C. CIST *Sk. Cincinnati in 1851* 187 There are five other tubs, which in the aggregate, contain as much as the great mastodon just described. **1883** *Encycl. Brit.* XV. 425/2 All known Mastodons are gigantic animals. **1936** [see BLUE-PRINT, BLUEPRINT *sb.* 1 a]. **1965** *Listener* 2 Sept. 337/2 It is high time we.. began to inquire more coolly how we can expect this mastodon in our midst to behave.

fig. **1847** EMERSON *Repr. Men, Swedenborg*, One of the missouriums and mastodons of literature, he is not to be measured by whole colleges of ordinary scholars.

mastodonic (mæstəˈdɒnɪk), *a.* [f. prec. + -IC.] = MASTODONTIC *a.*

1853 KANE *Grinnell Exp.* xxxi. (1856) 269 Annette, nearly six feet high, received it with mastodonic grace.

mastodonsaurian (ˌmæstədɒnˈsɔːrɪən), *a.* [f. mod.L. *Mastodonsaur-us* (Jæger 1838, f. Gr. μαστός breast + ὀδοντ-, ὀδούς tooth + σαῦρος lizard) + -IAN.] Of or belonging to the *Mastodonsaurus*, a genus of Labyrinthodonts.

1865 LYELL *Elem. Geol.* (ed. 6) 508 Labyrinthodonts of the Mastodonsaurian type.

mastodont (ˈmæstədɒnt), *a.* and *sb.* [ad. mod.L. *mastodont-*, stem of MASTODON.] **A.** *adj.* Having teeth like a mastodon. **B.** *sb.* A mastodon.

1890 in *Century Dict.* **1897** *Nat. Science* Oct. 259 Large upper and lower tusks, as in the older Mastodonts.

mastodontic (mæstəˈdɒntɪk), *a.* [formed as prec. + -IC.] Of or belonging to a mastodon; resembling the mastodon.

1857 H. MILLER *Test. Rocks* ii. 90 The mastodontic period is removed by two great geologic eras from the present time. **1886** *Century Mag.* XXXI. 355 Some men of large size; others of mastodontic proportions. **1895** *Athenæum* 2 Mar. 285/3 The African elephant.. belongs, as regards its dentition, to an earlier and mastodontic type.

So **mastoˈdontine** *a.* = prec. (*Cent. Dict.* 1890); **mastoˈdontoid** *a.*, resembling the mastodon.

1842 OWEN in *Ann. Nat. Hist.* XI. 12 The.. collector and transmitter of the Mastodontoid fossils.

mastodonton. Incorrect var. of MASTODON.

1815 J. SCOTT *Vis. Paris* (ed. 2) App. 295 Bones of.. the American Mammoth, or Mastodonton.

‖**mastodynia** (mæstəʊˈdaɪnɪə). *Med.* Also **-dyny.** [mod.L., f. Gr. μαστ-ός breast + ὀδύνη pain.] Neuralgia of the female breast.

1802 *Med. Jrnl.* VIII. 493 Cases admitted.. Mastodynia 3. **1879** KHORY *Princ. Med.* 16 Mastodynia is often due to uterine.. irritation. **1880** WEBSTER *Suppl.*, Mastodyny.

mastoid (ˈmæstɔɪd), *a.* and *sb.* Chiefly *Anat.* [ad. mod.L. *mastoīd-ēs*, f. Gr. μαστό-ς (woman's) breast: see -OID. Cf. F. *mastoide*, 16th c. in Littré.]

A. *adj.* Shaped like a female breast.

a. *Anat.* ***mastoid process***, a nipple-shaped, conical prominence of the temporal bone. ***mastoid bone***, a bone of the skull, in fishes and reptiles, homologous with the mastoid process.

1732 MONRO *Anat. Bones* (ed. 2) 100 Into the mastoid Process the *Sterno-mastoideus* Muscle is inserted. **1841** R. E. GRANT *Compar. Anat.* 84 Anterior to the mastoid bones are the upper portions of the tympanic bones. **1878** A. HAMILTON *Nerv. Dis.* 81 Leeches being applied to both ears, and cups over the mastoid processes. **1880** GÜNTHER *Fishes* 57 The formation.. is completed by the mastoid and parietal bones.

b. *Path.* ***mastoid cancer***, a kind of firm carcinomatous growth, the section of which is thought to resemble the boiled udder of the cow.

1857 in DUNGLISON *Med. Lex.*

c. *Lichenology.* 'Teat-like'.

1873 W. A. LEIGHTON *Lichen-flora* (ed. 3).

d. *gen. rare.*

1877 CESNOLA *Cyprus* ii. 66 A mastoid or breast-shaped hill.

B. *absol.* as *sb.* = *mastoid process* or *bone*.

1842 E. WILSON *Anat. Vade M.* 24 The mastoid forms the posterior part of the bone. **1846** OWEN *Compar. Anat. Vertebr.* v. 93 The second ring of bones [of a fish's skull].. includes.. the 'parietals', and the 'mastoids'. **1899** *Allbutt's*

Syst. Med. VIII. 45 The method may be supplemented by placing a pole on each mastoid for a few minutes.

b. *attrib.* = 'of or pertaining to the mastoid process', as in ***mastoid cell, muscle.***

1800 *Phil. Trans.* XC. 9 The cavity of the tympanum, where the mastoid cells open. **1822–34** *Good's Study Med.* (ed. 4) III. 237 An excess of muscular action, particularly of the mastoid muscle. **1899** *Allbutt's Syst. Med.* VII. 276 The abscess was secondary to mastoid disease.

Hence **'mastoidal** *a.*, of or belonging to the mastoid process.

1831 R. KNOX *Cloquet's Anat.* 89 The mastoid process.. limited before by the meatus auditorius externus, and behind by the mastoidal suture. **1881** MIVART *Cat* 66 This triangular tract is the mastoidal region of the temporal bone.

mastoideal (mæ'stɔɪdɪəl), *a.* [Formed as next + -AL[1].] = next.

1848 in CRAIG; and in later Dicts.

mastoidean (mæ'stɔɪdiːən), *a.* [f. mod.L. *mastoīde-us* pertaining to the mastoid (f. *mastoīd-ēs* MASTOID) + -AN. Cf. F. *mastoïdien.*] Of or belonging to the mastoid.

1841 OWEN in *Brit. Assoc. Rep.* (1842) 75 The mastoidean angle is not uninterruptedly united with the back part of the articular process of the tympanic... The mastoidean bone has a concavity as its descending part. **1846** BRITTAN tr. *Malgaigne's Man. Oper. Surg.* 104 The second [movement] causes [the sternomastoid muscle] to project forwards.., placing its mastoidean insection on a plane anterior.

mastoidectomy (mæstɔɪ'dɛktəmɪ). *Surg.* [f. MASTOID *a.* and *sb.* + -ECTOMY.] Any operation for the relief of inflammation of or within the mastoid process (esp. within the cavities, i.e. the mastoid cells and mastoid antrum, inside this process), as by penetrating into and cleaning out these cavities; excision of the mastoid process.

1898 *Laryngoscope* IV. 365 But the now perfected mastoidectomy, even with its tympanic communication, established under the best antiseptic measures,.. left more to be desired. **1909** *Practitioner* Nov. 695, I have of late reserved the operation of mastoidectomy for cases of mastoid abscess in the acute stage with local signs. **1956** *A.M.A. Arch. Otolaryngol.* LXIII. 248/1 The surgery included both mastoidectomies (endaural and postauricular approach) and fenestrations.

‖**mastoiditis** (mæstɔɪ'daɪtɪs). *Path.* [-ITIS.] Inflammation of the mastoid process.

1890 in *Syd. Soc. Lex.* **1900** OPPENHEIM *Dis. Childh.* 618 Mastoiditis may be marked by external rupture.

mastoido- (mæ'stɔɪdəʊ), used as combining form of MASTOID, as ***mastoido-humeral*** adj., connecting the mastoid process with the humerus.

1864 *Quain's Anat.* (ed. 7) II. 193 Thus forming a mastoido-humeral muscle.

†**ma'stology.** [f. Gr. μαστός breast + -OLOGY.] A proposed substitute for MAMMALOGY.

1819 *Pantologia, Mastology*... We trust we shall not be accused of pedantry in coining this term. **1839** *Penny Cycl.* XIV. 352/2 *Mammalogy*, a hybrid word.. Accordingly M. Desmarest has proposed the term Mastology, and M. de Blainville that of Mastozoology.

Hence **masto'logical** *a.* = MAMMALOGICAL; **ma'stologist** = MAMMALOGIST.

1890 in *Century Dict.*

mastopathy (mæ'stɒpəθɪ). [f. Gr. μαστός breast + πάθος feeling, suffering: see -PATHY. Cf. F. *mastopathie.*] Disease of the female breast.

1856 MAYNE *Expos. Lex., Mastopathia*, pain in the female breast: mastopathy.

†**mastozo'ology.** *Obs.* [ad. F. *mastozoologie*, f. Gr. μαστό-ς breast + ζῷο-ν animal: see -LOGY.] = MASTOLOGY.

1839 [see MASTOLOGY].

†**mastozo'otic,** *a. Obs.* [ad. F. *mastozootique*, formed as prec. with irregular suffix.] Of a geologic formation or period: Characterized by the presence of mammalia.

1839 *Penny Cycl.* XV. 93 (art. *Mendip*) Elephants, horses, ..and other animals of the 'mastozootic' æra.

mast-quat, obs. form of MOSTWHAT.

mastras, -es(s(e, obs. forms of MISTRESS.

mastres, -ice, -is, var. ff. MAISTRICE *Obs.*

mastring, obs. f. MASTERING, kind of lye.

mastucation, rare obs. form of MASTICATION.

†**mastuprate,** *v. Obs.* Etymologizing alteration of MASTURBATE *v.* So †**mastu'pration** = MASTURBATION; **mastuprator** = MASTURBATOR.

1621 BURTON *Anat. Mel.* I. iii. II. iv. (1651) 205 Those rapes, incests, adulteries, mastuprations, [etc.]. *Ibid.* III. ii. VI. v. (1651) 581. **1623** COCKERAM, *Mastuprate.* **1647** R. STAPYLTON *Juvenal* 88 Whilst the hid knave attends, And mastuprates, mad to be so delay'd. **1855** [see MASTURBATOR].

masturbate ('mæstəːbeɪt), *v.* [f. L. *masturbāt-*, ppl. stem of *masturbārī*, of obscure origin: according to Brugmann for **mastiturbārī* f. **mazdo-* (cf. Gr. μέζεα pl.) virile member + *turba* disturbance. An old conjecture regarded the word as f. *manu-s* hand + *stuprāre* to defile; hence the etymologizing forms MANUSTUPRATION, MASTUPRATE, -ATION, used by some Eng. writers.] *intr.* To produce an orgasm by stimulation of the genitals, not by sexual intercourse; *trans.*, to cause (another person) to have an orgasm by stimulation of his or her genitals. Also *refl.* and *fig.*

1857 ACTON *Reprod. Organs* 69 *note*, He had masturbated himself. *c* **1880** H. VARLEY *Lect. Men* (1884) 30 The patients ..have at last acknowledged that they still masturbated. **1934** R. CAMPBELL *Broken Record* vi. 125 A bankclerk has to masturbate his mind all day: when he comes home he has no strength to mount the muse. **1964** H. MONTGOMERY HYDE *Hist. Pornography* i. 19 He [*sc.* Pepys] finished the book the same evening, and we now know that it excited him to masturbate. **1966** L. COHEN *Beautiful Losers* (1970) I. 36 She wanted to see me masturbate for the last time. **1968** M. COURTENAY *Sexual Discord in Marriage* vi. 61 He..had masturbated with heterosexual fantasies. **1970** B. W. ALDISS *Hand-Reared Boy* 62 During this miserable period I masturbated myself for consolation, and Ann also did it to me. **1974** *Daily Tel.* 3 Oct. 3/1 Clients at the parlour..paid £15-plus to be masturbated by young women in various stages of undress.

Hence **mastur'batic** *a.*, caused by masturbation; **'masturbator**, one who practises masturbation; **mastur'batorily** *adv.*; **'masturbatory** *a.*, pertaining to masturbation.

1855 DUNGLISON *Med. Lex.*, Masturbator, Mastuprator. **1864** tr. *Casper's Handbk. Forensic Med.* (N. Syd. Soc.) III. 334 Masturbatory pæderastia. **1868** *Index Expurgatorius of Martial* 90 Titius was a masturbator. **1874** BUCKNILL & TUKE *Psych. Med.* (ed. 3) 318 Masturbatic Insanity. **1899** *Allbutt's Syst. Med.* VII. 692 In masturbators there is more excess than in any other persons. *Ibid.* VIII. 149. **1924** J. RIVIERE et al. tr. *Freud's Coll. Papers* I. 100 The tendency to anxiety in masturbators. **1932** *Jrnl. Amer. Med. Assoc.* 24 Dec. 2201/2 Mechanical masturbators. **1948** A. C. KINSEY et al. *Sexual Behavior Human Male* II. v. 170 Many pre-adolescents take a good many years to discover masturbatory techniques. **1960** *Spectator* 3 June 809 The prose background to his [*sc.* Swinburne's] violent, cerebral, masturbatory poetry. **1963** *Listener* 24 Jan. 163/2 To be sexually attractive was one thing, but to become a sexual fetish was another. Marilyn Monroe became a pair of lips, a walk, a set of numbers, 38-24-36. The artificiality of the unresolved tension I have described finds a parallel here in this ersatz, masturbatory sex stimulus. **1967** B. BROSS *Pleasures of Love* viii. 98 These magazines are being bought by masturbators, male ones and lesbians. **1973** S. FISHER *Female Orgasm* xii. 338 If a woman wants to escape restriction and explore the new she is particularly positive toward masturbatory gratification. **1973** M. SEYMOUR-SMITH *Guide Mod. World Lit.* 225 One senses Williams hanging masturbatorily over his nasty, midcult images of evil.

masturbation (mæstəː'beɪʃən). [ad. L. *masturbātiōn-em*, n. of action f. *masturbārī* to MASTURBATE.] The action or practice of masturbating; deliberate erotic self-stimulation; **mutual masturbation**, stimulation of the genitals of one person by another in order to produce an orgasm without sexual intercourse. Also *attrib.* and *fig.*

1766 A. HUME (*title*) Onanism: or a Treatise upon the Disorders produced by Masturbation. **1851** ACTON *Urin. & Generat. Organs* (ed. 2) 232. **1897** H. ELLIS *Stud. Psychol. Sex* I. 117 The sexual relationship rarely goes beyond close physical contact, or at most mutual masturbation. **1899** *Allbutt's Syst. Med.* VIII. 382. **1924** J. RIVIERE et al. tr. *Freud's Coll. Papers* I. 90 Neurasthenics whose potency has already been seriously diminished by masturbation. **1929** D. H. LAWRENCE *Pornogr. & Obscenity* 32 The masturbation self-enclosure produces idiots. **1948** A. C. KINSEY et al. *Sexual Behavior Human Male* III. xiv. 497 As more usually employed, the word 'masturbation' refers to any self stimulation which is deliberate and designed to effect erotic arousal. *Ibid.* xxi. 616 Mutual masturbation between two males may be dismissed, even by certain clinicians, as not homosexual. **1949** M. MEAD *Male & Female* xiii. 271 The attempts of some child specialists to break down the masturbation taboo. **1951** R. CAMPBELL *Light on Dark Horse* xxiii. 346 The liberaloid mentality that they had acquired from reading the masturbations of.. Rousseau. **1954** W. FAULKNER *Fable* (1955) 59 That sort of masturbation about the human race people call hoping. **1961** R. F. C. HULL tr. *Jung's Coll. Works* IV. 212 She had induced a number of girls of her own age to perform mutual masturbation. **1967** E. LEA in R. E. L. Masters *Sexual Self-Stimulation* 325 The Dresden Criminal Museum..houses an elaborate.. masturbation machine that the user operates with a foot pedal. **1968** *Listener* 14 Mar. 350/3 It contains..many, many accounts of adventures with women, masturbation phantasies, [etc.]. **1968** M. COURTENAY *Sexual Discord in Marriage* vi. 68 He became worried about the possible harmful effects of masturbation. **1972** *Daily Tel.* 28 Nov. 17/3 Lines such as 'I like to play with my ding-a-ling' and 'Most of all with your ding-a-ling' are intended as deliberate stimulation to self and mutual masturbation. **1974** *Ibid.* 3 Oct. 3/3 For the £15 massage—with masturbation—the girls received £3 commission. *Ibid.*, He had first set up massage facilities.., but clients had wanted masturbation.

Hence **mastur'bational** *a.*, pertaining to or caused by masturbation.

1890 in *Century Dict.*

†**'masty,** *a. Obs.* [f. MAST *sb.*[2] + -Y[1].]

1. Producing mast.

1575 TURBERV. *Venerie* 217 In the vineyards in the hollow mastie woods. **1592** R. D. *Hypnerotomachia* 32 Shaddowed with greene and tender leaues of mastie Okes, Beeches [etc.]. **1611** COTGR., *Glandeux*, mastie, full of Mast. **1630** J. TAYLOR (Water P.) *Satyre* Wks. II. 259/2 The Masty Beeche.

2. Of a swine: Fattened. (Cf. MASTED *a.* and *mestif*, MASTIFF *a.* 1.)

c **1384** CHAUCER *H. Fame* III. 687 Ye masty [*Fairf. MS.* maisty] swyne, ye idyll wrechys. **1530** PALSGR. 318/1 Masty fatte as swyne be, *gras.*

3. Burly, big-bodied; = MASTIFF *a.* 3.

1665 HOOKE *Microgr.* 164 Some few of these stout and resolute soldiers with these little engines, do often put to flight a huge masty Bear. **1687** MIEGE *Gt. Fr. Dict.* II. s.v., A masty Fellow, *un gros Paisan.* **1886** *S.W. Linc. Gloss.*, *Masty*, very large and big: as 'They're a masty family'.

masty, obs. and dial. form of MASTIFF.

mastyc, -yck, -yk(e, obs. forms of MASTIC.

mastye, -yfe, -yve, obs. forms of MASTIFF.

†**masuel.** *Obs. rare.* In 14th c. texts *erron.* masnel, mansell. [a. OF. *massuelle*, f. *massue* club.] A mace used in battle.

13.. *Coer de L.* 351 Forth he toke a mansell. *Ibid.* 5660 Before his arsoun his ax off steel By that other syde hys masnel. **13..** *Sir Beues* 4503 Wiþ an vge masuel [*MS.* masnel] Beues a hite on þe helm.

masulium, masure, obs. ff. MAUSOLEUM, MAZER.

†**masures,** *sb. pl. Obs. rare.* [a. F. *masures* sb. pl.] Ruins (of buildings); squalid and tumble-down habitations.

1623 tr. *Favine's Theat. Hon.* VI. i. 103 Out of the ruines and masures [orig. *ruines et masures*] of them, foure other Moderne Citties were rebuilded. **1791** J. TOWNSEND *Journ. Spain* (1792) I. 399 We..quitted the ravin, and began crossing all the masures of the country.

masurium (mə'z(j)ʊərɪəm). *Chem.* [mod.L. (W. Noddack et al. 1925, in *Sitzungsber. d. Preuss. Akad. d. Wissenschaften* 409), f. G. *Masur-en* name of a region in NE. Poland + -IUM.] A name proposed for the element of atomic number 43 (later named TECHNETIUM), which was claimed to have been discovered spectroscopically in certain platinum ores.

1925 *Glasgow Herald* 16 June 6 These new elements have been named by their discoverers 'Masurium', after the Masurian Lake region, and 'Rhenium', after the Rhineland. **1941** *Chem. & Industry* 11 Oct. 729/2 Japanese investigators have studied the decay curves of the chemically separated masurium fraction from molybdenum after bombardment with slow neutrons and they distinguished the two masurium isotopes 99 and 101. **1947** [see ILLINIUM]. **1962** J. H. WHITE *Inorg. Chem.* xxv. 480 Technetium..has been called masurium, and it has not yet been isolated from natural minerals.

masut, var. MAZUT.

masyd, -ness, obs. forms of MAZED, -NESS.

masyl, obs. form of MEASLE.

masyn-dew(e, obs. forms of MEASONDUE.

masynry, obs. form of MASONRY.

mat (mæt), *sb.*[1] Also 1 matt (? matte), meatt, meatte, (3 *pl.* maten), 4–6 matte, 6–8 matt. [OE. (only in glossaries) *matt*, *meatt* str. (? fem.), *meatte* wk. fem., ad. late L. *matta* (4th c.), whence It. *matta*, and the Teut. forms OHG. *matta* (MHG., mod.G. *matte*, also dial. *matze*), MDu. *matte* (Du. *mat*), Sw. *matta*, Da. *matte.* A synonymous late L. *natta* (Gregory of Tours, 6th c.), whence F. *natte* (see NAT), is commonly regarded as an altered form of *matta*, with *n* for *m* as in F. *nappe* table-cloth, from L. *mappa.*]

1. a. A piece of a coarse fabric formed by plaiting rushes, sedge, straw, bast, etc., intended to lie, sit, or kneel upon, or for use as a protective covering for floors, walls, plants, etc., or in packing furniture.

c **725** *Corpus Gloss.* 487 *Spiato* [for *psiato*, ψιάθῳ], matte. *c* **1000** ÆLFRIC *Gloss.* in Wr.-Wülcker 154/2 *Storea. uel psiata*, meatta. *a* **1100** *Voc.* ibid. 328/34 *Matta*, meatte. *a* **1225** *Ancr. R.* 10 Seinte Sare, & seinte Sincletice, & monie oðre swuche weopmen & wommen mid hore greate maten & hore herde heren. *c* **1375** *S. Austin* 1490 in Horstm. *Altengl. Leg.* (1878) 87/1 In þe chirche an old monk sat, Seyinge his psauter vppon a mat. **1387** TREVISA *Higden* (Rolls) VII. 379 Þe matte [L. *matta*] þat was under hym whan he bad his bedes. **1392–3** *Earl Derby's Exp.* (Camden) 222 Item pro vj mattes ad cooperiendum le biscwhit in galeia, vj[li]. xij[s]. **1462–3** *Durham Acc. Rolls* (Surtees) 279 In duabus mattis emp. pro aula, vij. d. **1511** *Guylforde's Pilgr.* (Camden Soc.) 17 Jacobyns..brought vnto vs mattes for oure money, to lye vpon. **1553** EDEN *Treat. Newe Ind.* (Arb.) 18 Laying them on mattes or couerlettes. **1587–8** in Swayne *Sarum Churchw. Acc.* (1896) 138 A Matt for the Clarke to kneell vpon, 6d. **1626** BACON *Sylva* §696 Fleas breed Principally of Straw or Mats, where there hath beene a little Moisture. **1666** PEPYS *Diary* 15 June, A very fine African mat, to lay upon the ground under a bed of state. **1703** MAUNDRELL *Journ. Jerus.* (1721) 128 Shaded over head with Trees, and with Matts when the Boughs fail. **1716** SWIFT *Phyllis* 15 She..on the Mat devoutly kneeling, Wou'd lift her Eyes up to the Ceiling. *a* **1734** NORTH *Exam.* II. v. §118 (1740) 388 The Discovery of 80 Musquets in the Lord Grey's House, that were packed in Matts. **1766** C. BEATTY *Two Months' Tour* (1768) 44 It is covered with an handsome matt, made of

rushes. 1777 G. FORSTER *Voy. round World* I. 131 They appeared to be dressed in mats. 1830 *Encycl. Brit.* (ed. 7) II. 632/2 Mats, swung from trees serve them [S. Amer. Indians] both as seats and hammocks. 1837 J. T. SMITH tr. *Vicat's Mortars* 96 Colonel Raucourt de Charleville recommends straw-mats to be suspended in front of the walls. 1856 DELAMER *Fl. Gard.* (1861) 34 In winter, cover with mats during frosty weather.

†**b.** As the name of a material: Plaited or woven rushes, straw, etc.; matting. *Obs.* exc. *attrib.*

1523–4 *Rec. St. Mary at Hill* (E.E.T.S.) 322 Paid for ij yerdys of wykur matt for þe childrens fete, xvj d. 1555 W. WATREMAN *Fardle Facions* II. viii. 175 These are appareilled in matte, made of a certayne softe kinde of mere rushes. 1594–5 in Swayne *Sarum Churchw. Acc.* (1896) 143, 40 yeardes of matte for ye parishoners to kneele on the time of commvnion. *a*1619 FLETCHER *Bonduca* IV. ii, I defie thee, thou mock-made man of mat. 1688–9 in Willis & Clark *Cambridge* (1886) III. 348, 461 yards of Matt. 1707 MORTIMER *Husb.* (1721) II. 259 Having..ready for your Work..Woollen-Yarn, Bass-matt, or such like to bind them withal. *c*1710 CELIA FIENNES *Diary* (1888) 284 Rowles of Matt very naturall at their head and feete. 1732 POPE *Ep. Bathurst* 299 In the worst inn's worst room, with mat half-hung.

c. Applied to bast used for tying plants. Also *attrib.* in *mat-tie*. (Cf. MATTING *vbl. sb.* 3 b.)

1824 LOUDON *Encycl. Gard.* §1514 The flat-headed..nail, used either with lists, loops of cord, or mat; and the eyed.. nail, used with mat-ties. *Ibid.* 1519 When mat, bark, rush, ..or straw are used [for tying].

d. A bag made of matting, used to hold sugar, coffee, flax, etc.

1798 *Hull Advertiser* 1 Dec. 2/1, 40 mats Lexia raisins. *Ibid.* 15 Dec. 2/1, 26 matts of best Rake Liebau Flax. 1885 MRS. C. PRAED *Head Station* (new ed.) 157 Sacks of flour and mats of ration sugar.

e. *N.Z.* A type of cloak or cape worn by the Maori (cf. quot. 1777 under sense 1 a); also used allusively to refer to the Maori way of life.

1807 J. SAVAGE *Some Acct. N.Z.* viii. 50 The dress of the natives consists in a mat finely wove of the native flax. 1832 A. EARLE *Narr. Residence N.Z.* (1966) 59 They were clothed in mats, called Ka-ka-hoos. 1840 W. DEANS *Let.* 29 Mar. in J. Deans *Pioneers of Canterbury* (1937) 23 Two New Zealanders, clad in a native mat. 1849 W. T. POWER *Sketches in N.Z.* xvii. 146 New habits are rapidly modifying the old ones... In throwing off the mat and the blanket, they also dispense with shark oil and red ochre. 1874 J. C. JOHNSTONE *Maoria* i. 16 The rough *pureki*..when seen upon the men in the canoes which boarded the first vessels that visited the Island, was not inappropriately called ' a mat', and the ugly name came to be applied to any description of garment worn by the Maoris. 1905 W. B. *Where White Man Treads* 54 He is a warrior; and at any moment may cast off his mat and defend his privileges. 1947 'A. P. GASKELL' *Big Game* 92 She must have been somewhere to a Maori High School and then come back to the mat. 1970 D. M. DAVIN *Not Here, Not Now* III. vi. 197 All a man can do is go back to the mat and cry, or laugh.

f. *Bowls.* = FOOTER *sb.*[1] 4.

1892 J. BROWN *Man. Bowling* (ed. 2) 69 The mat shall be placed by the lead of the party who lost the previous head. 1910 *Encycl. Brit.* IV. 347/2 The bowler delivers his bowl with one foot on a mat or footer, made of india-rubber or cocoanut fibre, the size of which is also prescribed by rule as 24 by 16 in. 1959 *Times* 12 Aug. 4/6 Their No. 3..went to the mat. 1962 *Bowls* ('Know the Game' Series) 4 At the beginning of the first end the mat is placed lengthwise on the centre line of the rink, the back edge to be four feet from the ditch.

g. Phr. *on the mat*, orig. in army use (see quot. 1919); in trouble with some authority. Cf. *on the carpet* (s.v. CARPET *sb.* 1 b).

1898 *Pearson's Mag.* Oct. 372/2 The sergeant..shouts with military brevity: 'On to the mat, John Smith.' [*ante*, Close to the medical officer's desk is a thick padded carpet about a yard square.] 1917 A. G. EMPEY *Over Top* 302 *On the mat*, when Tommy is haled before his commanding officer to explain why he has broken one of the seven million King's regulations for the government of the Army. His 'explanation' never gets him anywhere unless it is on the wheel of a limber. 1919 *Athenæum* 1 Aug. 695/1 'He's on the mat' means the same [as 'He's for the high jump']; the pre-war orderly room was furnished with a piece of carpet, in the exact centre of which the accused stood. 1925 FRASER & GIBBONS *Soldier & Sailor Words* 154 *Mat, on the*: up for trial. In trouble. 1935 A. J. POLLOCK *Underworld Speaks* 92/2 *Put on the mat*, a thorough questioning, usually by the police. 1949 J. R. COLE *It was so Late* 62 Then I was on the mat again. Now it seems a wonder I kept out of trouble as long as I did. 1973 J. THOMSON *Death Cap* x. 136 Mrs Holbrook had been given the impression that she was on the mat in front of her husband's superior officer.

h. A piece of padded material, canvas, etc., used as a floor covering in gymnastics, wrestling, etc. Hence *fig.*, in phr. *to go to the mat*: to engage in a struggle or controversy; to argue.

1903 P. LONGHURST *Wrestling* I. 5 Ordinary gymnasium mats covered with canvas or sail-cloth form the best surface for this style of wrestling. 1924 WODEHOUSE *Leave it to Psmith* i. 28, I..heard..you and Aunt Constance going to the mat about poor old Phyllis. 1937 D. ALDIS *Time at her Heels* i. 26 She just didn't have time at the moment to call him in and go to the mat with him about it. 1950 *Oxf. Jun. Encycl.* IX. 489/1 In this type of wrestling a 'fall' is gained by bringing the opponent's two shoulders simultaneously into contact with the mat. 1967 V. L. DREHMAN *Head over Heels* i. 3 Wide mats must be used for the learner in tumbling. 1970 *New Yorker* 12 Dec. 131/1 These senators felt that the President had handed them two lemons, had gone to the mat for his choices when he didn't have to.

2. a. An article (originally such as is described in sense 1, but now more usually made of other materials) intended to be placed near a door for persons entering to wipe their shoes upon (= DOOR-MAT), or similar to those so used.

Now commonly of rectangular shape and considerable thickness; made either of some coarsely woven material (as hemp, coco-nut fibre, latterly often wire), or occasionally of perforated or corrugated indiarubber, cork, etc.

1665 HOOKE *Microgr.* 6 A very convenient substance to make Bed-matts, or Door-matts of. *a*1818 MISS ROSE in *G. Rose's Diaries* (1860) II. 75 There had been a heavy mat on the floor-cloth. 1842 BROWNING *Pied Piper* 51 Only a scraping of shoes on the mat. 1848 DICKENS *Dombey* xxiii, They found that exemplary woman beating the mats on the door-steps. 1886 FENN *Master of Ceremonies* v, He paused on the mat to draw a long, catching breath.

b. A thin flat article (originally made of plaited straw (cf. sense 1), but now of leather, oilcloth, cork, plastic, etc.) to be placed under a dish, plate, or vessel in order to protect the table from heat, moisture, etc. Also applied to various other articles of similar use, e.g. a disk or square of fancy work placed on a dressing-table to support articles of the toilet, etc., or merely for ornament.

1800 M. EDGEWORTH *Parent's Assistant* (ed. 3) V. 32 These here half dozen little mats, to put under my dishes. 1852 MRS. GASKELL *Let.* Dec. (1966) 217 The little ones had worked mats, & gathered flowers &c &c for her dressing-room. 1875 in KNIGHT *Dict. Mech.* 1904 *Pilot* 2 Apr. 307 Muslin hangings to your looking-glass, bows on your chair-rails, mats on your tables.

3. *transf.* A thick tangled mass.

1835 URE *Philos. Manuf.* 164 To break the mats of the raw wool and to render it light. 1852 MRS. STOWE *Uncle Tom's C.* ix. 77 A very heavy *mat* of sandy hair. 1872 H. C. WOOD *Fresh-w. Algæ N. Amer.* (1874) 56 A number of individuals of one or more species [of *Scytonemaceæ*] are almost always associated to form on the ground little mats. 1897 *Outing* (U.S.) XXX. 219/2 The favorite haunts of the bass are about reefs, mats of weeds [etc.] . 1898 POUND & CLEMENTS *Phytogeogr. Nebraska* iii. 53 This group is composed of acaulescent or low-stemmed plants which grow aggregated into dense cushion-like mats. 1916 B. D. JACKSON *Gloss. Bot. Terms* (ed. 3) 224/1 *Mat*, a closely intertwined vegetation, with roots and rhizomes intermixed. 1930 *Forestry* IV. 70 A 'mat' of actively growing mycelium of the parasite was present in the watering flasks of many of the cultures. 1971 *Nature* 30 Apr. 599/1 At Kariba..where the lake took 4–5 yr to fill, extensive mats of *Salvinia auriculata* and *Pistia stratiotes* accumulated over much of the lake. 1972 *Science* 27 Oct. 403/1 Microbial mats occur in Yellowstone at temperatures up to about 70°C. 1973 *Nature* 4 May 12/1 The meeting concluded with a field trip to the algal mats at the north shore of the Great Salt Lake.

4. *Naut.* A thick web of rope yarn used to protect the standing rigging from the friction of other ropes.

1497 *Naval Acc. Hen. VII* (1896) 251 Grete mattes for couerying of the seid Cordage. 1644 MANWAYRING *Sea-mans Dict.*, *Matts* are broad clowtes, weaved of synnet and thrummes, and are used in these places: To the maine and fore-yards, at the ties, (to keep the yards from galling against the mast) [etc.]. 1769 in FALCONER *Dict. Marine* (1780). 1867 SMYTH *Sailor's Word-bk.* 473 Where it is possible, rounding is now used instead of mats.

attrib. 1886 R. C. LESLIE *Sea-painter's Log* iii. 49 Were it not for the many chafing-battens, mat-service, and other gear often renewed upon them.

5. a. The coarse piece of sacking on which the feather-bed is laid (E.D.D.). **b.** A woollen bed-covering.

1702 MRS. CENTLIVRE *Beau's Duel* IV. i., I'll have no Matts, but such as lie under the Feather Beds. 1790 *Pluckley Vestry Bk.* 25 Oct. (E.D.D). Fram matt and cords. *a*1894 J. SHAW in R. Wallace *Country Schoolm.* (1899) 350 In Renfrewshire a mat meant a thick woollen covering for the bed, generally wrought into a pattern.

6. *Engineering.* A woven structure of brushwood secured by ropes and wires, used as a revetment for river banks.

1884 in KNIGHT *Dict. Mech., Suppl.*

7. *Lace-making.* (See quot.)

1882 CAULFEILD & SAWARD *Dict. Needlework*, *Mat*, a lace maker's term for the close part of a design.

8. *attrib.* and *Comb.* **a.** Simple attrib., as ***mat-awning***, ***-bag***, ***-house***, ***-hut***, ***-lodge***, ***-roof*** (hence ***mat-roofed*** adj.), ***-sail***, ***-satchel***, ***-screen***, ***-shed***, ***-skirt***, ***-work***; **b.** instrumental, as ***mat-clad***, ***-covered*** adjs.; **c.** objective, as ***mat-forming***, ***-maker***, ***-making***, ***-mender***. **d.** Special comb.: **mat-boat**, **-braid** (see quots.); **mat-canvas**, a dress material of a coarse texture; **mat-grass**, (*a*) *Nardus stricta*, (*b*) *Psamma arenaria*, the marram grass; **mat-man** *slang*, a wrestler; **mat-platting**, in *Kindergarten work*, the weaving of patterns by means of strips of coloured paper; **mat-pole** (see quot.); †**mat-reed**, the leaves of *Typha latifolia*; **mat-rush**, the bulrush, *Scirpus lacustris*; also = *matweed*; **matweed**, a name for various rush-like grasses (see quot. 1866 and cf. *mat-grass*); **mat-tree**, **-wood** [tr. F. *bois de natte*], a species of *Imbricaria* found in Mauritius; **mat-work**, (*a*) matting; anything resembling matting; (*b*) *Arch.* = NATTES (*Cent. Dict.*); (*c*) physical exercises performed on a mat.

1730 CAPT. W. WRIGLESWORTH *MS. Log-bk. of the 'Lyell'* 30 Aug., Received a New *Matt Awning and fixed it for the Main Deck. 1856 FAULKNER *Dict. Comm. Terms*, **Mat-bags*, are formed of the leaves of the date and other palm trees, and are extensively used in Bombay and many parts of India for packing goods. 1884 KNIGHT *Dict. Mech.* Suppl., **Mat boat*.., a frame of ways supported on scows, on which mat for revetment is woven. 1882 CAULFEILD & SAWARD *Dict. Needlework*, **Mat-braid*, a thick worsted Braid, woven after the manner of plaiting,..employed as a trimming. 1902 *Daily Chron.* 14 June 10/4 *Mat canvas is decidedly a fashionable fabric. 1852 G. C. MUNDY *Our Antipodes* II. xiii. 386 These are the lineal successors to the tattooed, *mat clad, cannibal old caterans. 1903 *Blackw. Mag.* Nov. 605 The cat..scrambles quickly on to the *mat-covered floor. 1951 *Dict. Gardening* (R. Hort. Soc.) IV. 1878/1 [*Saxifraga*] Section 2. Hirculus. *Mat-forming plants with undivided, deciduous, oval leaves. 1971 D. BARTRUM *Rock Gardens* vii. 162 The 'Cheddar Pink' is another very tough mat-forming plant that doesn't mind being walked upon when not in flower. 1789 J. PILKINGTON *View Derbysh.* I. 331 *Nardus stricta*, *Matgrass... This grass is stiff and hard to the touch. 1818 LATROBE *Jrnl. Vis. S. Africa* 372 [St. Helena] A peculiar kind of grass, called mat-grass, from its spreading ..over the ground in such thickness, that it forms a cover resembling thick matting. 1898 W. C. SCULLY *Between Sun & Sand* 18 (Pettman), On either side of it stood respectively, a *mat-house and a square tent. 1882 FLOYER *Unexpl. Baluchistan* 195 We found a small village of three or four families and as many *mat huts. 1807 P. GASS *Jrnl.* 203 We encamped at two *mat-lodges of the natives. 1530 PALSGR. 599/1, I knyt, as a *matte maker knytteth, *je tys*. 1881 *Instr. Census Clerks* 17 Mat maker. 1854 THOREAU *Walden* 283 Might not the basket, stable-broom, *mat-making, corn-parching, linen-spinning, and pottery business have thrived here? 1890 LD. LUGARD *Diary* 21 Feb. (1959) I. ii. 111 The Banga reed grows by the river here, but very poorly, and useless for building and mat-making. 1923 *N.Y. Times* 11 Feb. I. 11. 1/4 (*heading*) Navy *matmen on top. In a finely contested wrestling match..the Naval Academy won. 1930 *Ibid.* 16 Feb. XI. 3/5 It was..the first time in four seasons that the Midshipmen have been able to take the measure of the matmen from South Bethlehem. 1942 BERREY & VAN DEN BARK *Amer. Thes. Slang* §707/2 Matman. 1968 *Globe & Mail Mag.* (Toronto) 17 Feb. 8/3 He became one of the best known mat men in Canada. 'Wrestling always fascinated me,' he says now. 1971 *Soviet Weekly* 8 May 14 A popular group exercise among the matmen. 1880 *Plain Hints Needlework* Gloss. 76 The rudimentary teaching of this darning is taught in the Kindergarten system, under the name of '*mat platting'. 1884 KNIGHT *Dict. Mech.* Suppl., **Mat pole*.., a pole.. used in placing mats of brush for shore protection, jetties, etc. 1578 LYTE *Dodoens* IV. liii. 513 The leaues are called *Matte reede, bycause they make mattes therewith. 1897 *Daily News* 15 Jan. 5/3 The snake was sliding through the *mat roof. 1895 KIPLING *Day's Work, Maltese Cat*, Some of them were in *mat-roofed stables close to the polo-ground. 1578 LYTE *Dodoens* IV. lii. 511 The fourth is called..in English, the pole Rushe, or bull Rushe, or *Mat Rushe. 1611 COTGR., *Ionc à cabas*, the pole-rush, mat-rush, fraile-rush. 1640 [see *matweed*]. 1894 B. THOMSON *S. Sea Yarns* 80 The great *mat-sail was spread upon the sand. 1777 G. FORSTER *Voy. round World* II. 321 Most of them were married, and carried their children in a *mat-satchel on their backs. 1926 M. LEINSTER *Dew on Leaf* I. iii. 41 Warehouses, *mat-sheds, and hovels. 1939 'A. BRIDGE' *Four-Part Setting* ii. 8 To sit in a mat-shed on the sand and drink cocktails. 1908 *Daily Chron.* 15 Aug. 1/6 A Maori chief.. saying..he was to fasten the native *mat-skirt about his body. 1812 tr. *De Guigne's Observ.* in *Pinkerton's Voy.* XI. 9a Among the trees of the Isle of France must be noticed the *mat tree [orig. *bois de natte*]. 1597 GERARDE *Herbal* I. xxviii. §2. 38 Hooded *Mat weede. *Ibid.* §3. 39 English Mat weede hath a rushie roote. 1640 PARKINSON *Theatr. Bot.* XIII. xxxv. 1197 Matt weed or Mat Rushes... Our Matweed or Marram..the other of our Sea Matweedes. 1787 tr. *Linnæus' Fam. Plants* I. 41 *Lygéum*. Mat-weed. 1866 *Treas. Bot.*, Matweed, *Ammophila arenaria*, also called Sea Matweed. Hooded Matweed, *Lygeum Spartum*. Small Matweed, *Nardus stricta*. 1793 TRAPP tr. *Rochon's Voy. Madagascar* Introd. 28 [In the Isle of France are] *mat-wood, tacamacca, stinking-wood [etc.]. 1859 R. F. BURTON *Centr. Afr.* in *Jrnl. Geog. Soc.* XXIX. 290 A thick growth of aquatic vegetation, which forms a kind of *matwork. 1944 *Horizon* Jan. 48 P.T. exercises..mat work, track work.

mat (mæt), *sb.*[2] Also matt. [a. F. *mat*, subst. use of *mat*, MAT *a.*]

1. *Glass-painting.* A layer of colour 'matted' on the glass (see MAT *v.*[2] b).

1881 *Art Interchange* (N.Y.) 27 Oct. 90/3 [Painting on glass.] Laying a mat will greatly facilitate tracing... There are two kinds of mat in use, 'water mat' and 'oil mat'. 1896 H. HOLIDAY *Stained Glass* i. 23 Stipple-shading..is in common use now together with another method, consisting of a series of 'matts'.

2. a. *Gilding.* The effect of 'mat' or unburnished gold. **b.** *Metal-work.* A roughened, frosted, or figured groundwork.

1866 *Tomlinson's Cycl. Useful Arts* I. 757/2 (Gilding.) Parts of the gilding which are to be in dead gold, (called *matt*). 1887 C. L. HASLOPE *Repoussé Work* 51 These [markings] may be arranged so as to touch one another, forming a close mat, or placed a little distance apart, as an open mat, so as to form a grounding to the picture.

3. A sheet of cardboard placed on the back of a print or drawing and then covered by a mount which forms a margin round the area of the print; also used for the mount itself. Cf. MOUNT *sb.*[2] 3 a. Also *attrib.*

1845 *Pract. Hints on Daguerreotype* 37 Leather Cases, with..gilt mats and glasses complete. 1886 P. FITZGERALD in *Art Jrnl.* 327/1 It is common..to set off water-colours with a broad golden mat of pasteboard. *Ibid.*, A snow-white cardboard mat. 1890 HOWELLS *Shadow of Dream* 163 Engravings with wide mats in frigid frames of black. 1909 F. WEITENKAMPF *How to appreciate Prints* xiii. 291 Sometimes mat and mount are fastened together on all four sides, forming what is known as a 'sunk mount'. 1932 —— *Quest of Print* xii. 270 Some collectors place a sheet of celluloid, cellophane, or similar material..over the print and under

the mat. **1965** Zigrosser & Gaehde *Guide to Collecting Orig. Prints* vii. 100 Quality of Mat Board. Only 100 percent rag-fiber mat stock is to be used. **1967** *Boston Sunday Globe* 23 Apr. B. 58/7 Sometimes prints come with a mat (white space around the art), but the framed picture is much better if the mat is made from a mat board. **1973** F. Taubes *Painter's Dict. Materials & Methods* 149 Made, as a rule, from cardboards of various colours, mats serve in the framing of watercolors and all kinds of prints... The width of a mat.. should be equal on top and at the sides but somewhat greater at the bottom, or the picture will have a tendency to 'droop'. **1974** P. Highsmith *Ripley's Game* v. 50 He needed more mat paper.

4. = *matting-punch*.

1890 *Home Handicrafts* (ed. Peters) 19 (Repoussé work.) When backgrounds with patterns upon them are required, punches shaped like crescents at the point, or as circles, stars, crosses, will be required. These fancy punches.. are technically called 'mats'. **1898** T. B. Wigley *Goldsm. & Jeweller* 79 Punches of various shapes, called.. Freezer-Mat. Dead Mat. Hair Mat.

5. *attrib.*

1876 *Encycl. Brit.* V. 170/1 Matt-work is protected with one or two coats of finish-size; but burnished gold is [etc.]. **1896** H. Holiday *Stained Glass* i. 24 The painter has.. to repeat the two matt processes.

mat (mæt), *sb.*³ *Card-playing.* [Short f. MATADOR.] = MATADOR 2.

1766 [Anstey] *Bath Guide* Epil. 10 Madam Shuffledumdoo.. Has sold your poor Guide for two Fish and a Mat. **1861** *Macm. Mag.* Dec. 131 The three best trump cards.. are called Matadores.. or shortly Mats.

mat (mæt), *sb.*⁴ *dial.* [Either shortened from or cogn. with MATTOCK.] A tool for stubbing furze, ling, etc.; a mattock (E.D.D.).

mat, *sb.*⁵ Colloq. abbrev. of MATINÉE.

1914 G. Atherton *Perch of Devil* I. viii. 55 Although Mr. Compton won't take me to any balls, there are the movin' pictures and the mats—matinées. **1940** *Amer. Speech* XV. 204/2 *Mats*, matinees.

mat, *sb.*⁶ Abbrev. of MATRIX 4.

1923 M. V. Atwood *Country Newspaper* 20 Just a word should be added about matrices, or 'mats' as they are always called. **1937** E. J. Labarre *Dict. Paper* 172/1 This matrix or 'mat' is then baked and used for making a metal plate for flat or roll printing. **1942** F. Brown *Angels & Spaceships* (1955) 38 The cost of getting special Linotype mats cut would be awfully high. **1967** V. Strauss *Printing Industry* v. 225/2 Matrices, called mats by the industry, are intermediate elements in the production of stereotypes but they are also independent items of commerce. *Ibid.* 226/1 During mat-making an intaglio replica of the original relief material is produced. **1975** *Printing Historical Soc. Newslet.* No. 28. 3 A few large display matrices of the Caslon series (original founders' mats) are offered to PHS members.

mat (mæt), *v.*¹ [f. MAT *sb.*¹]

1. *trans.* To cover or furnish with mats or matting. ***to mat up***: to cover (a plant) with matting.

1549 *Privy Council Acts* (1890) II. 269 To James Rufford for matting of the chambers at Westminster. **1576–7** *Durham Acc. Rolls* (Surtees) 717 For mattinge yᵉ com'on pue, 2*s.* 8*d.* **1634** Sir T. Herbert *Trav.* 24 Temples, kept cleane and matted neatly. **1664** Evelyn *Kal. Hort.* Dec. 81 Keep the Doors and Windows of your Conservatories well matted. **1672–3** *Churchw. Acc. E. Budleigh* (1894) 13 For stopping of the presentment at the Deane Ruralls Renewing ffor nott matting the seates. **1752** Johnson *Rambler* No. 200 ¶14 He mats his stairs and covers his carpets. **1782** Miss Burney *Cecilia* I. xi, The three eldest.. were hard at work with their mother in matting chair-bottoms. **1851** *Beck's Florist* Aug. 184 It will withstand the vicissitude of our climate when planted against a wall, if matted up during severe frosty weather. **1882** Floyer *Unexpl. Baluchistan* 52 A side room.. well and neatly built of mud, and matted with pīsh matting.

2. *transf.* To cover as with a mat or matting; to cover with an entangled mass.

1577 B. Googe *Heresbach's Husb.* II. (1586) 80 The ground is matted, and as it were netted with the remaines of the olde Rootes. **1610** W. Folkingham *Art of Survey* I. vi. 13 With what Herbage the Crust or Sword is matted, mantled and swarthed. **1627** Drayton *Quest of Cynthia* 76 The Banck with Daffadillies dight, with grasse like Sleaue was matted. **1747** Franklin *Let.* Wks. 1887 II. 82 Take the whole together, it is well matted, and looks like a green corn-field. **1825** *Greenhouse Comp.* I. 167 If the ball is much matted with roots.. it is a sure indication of the vigour of the plant. **1849** Robertson *Serm.* Ser. I. xix. (1866) 243 A temple.. matted with ivy. **1901** *Scotsman* 29 Oct. 9/1 Mountain chains of Oregon and Washington, matted with the towering growth of the mighty evergreen forest.

3. To form into a mat: **a.** to entangle or entwine (*together*) in a thick mass.

1577 B. Googe *Heresbach's Husb.* II. (1586) 51 When I haue thus done, I matte it [*sc.* a plashed hedge] thicker and thicker euery yeere. **1626** Bacon *Sylva* §746 Bats haue beene found in Ouens, and other Hollow Close Places, Matted one vpon another. **1682** H. More *Contin. Remark. Stories* 35 In the night, the Daughter had.. her hair snarled and matted together in that manner, that [etc.]. **1701** Grew *Cosm. Sacr.* I. iv. §17. 19 In the Skin.. the Fibers are Matted, as Wooll is in a Hat. **1768–74** Tucker *Lt. Nat.* (1834) I. 594 To.. disentangle the boughs where they had matted themselves together. **1824** W. Irving *T. Trav.* II. 9, I sought my mother's grave: the weeds were already matted over it. **1897** *Allbutt's Syst. Med.* IV. 120 Sometimes the material which mats the intestines together can be stripped off.

b. To make by interlacing, to form into a mat.

1824 Loudon *Encycl. Gard.* §1506 Garden or bass mats are woven or matted from the bast or inner bark of.. the lime. **1865** Tylor *Early Hist. Man.* vii. 188 Weaving, which consists of matting twisted threads.

4. *intr.* To become entangled, to form tangled masses. Chiefly with *together*.

1742 *Lond. & Country Brew.* II. (ed. 2) 92 Malt.. in that Time, would grow musty, or matt together. **1763** Mills *Syst. Pract. Husb.* IV. 144 They will mat together, and rot each other. **1847** *Jrnl. R. Agric. Soc.* VIII. I 69 The [wheat] plants get too forward, and do not mat on the ground. **1851** *Ibid.* XII. I. 134 The wheat.. began then to mat and to tiller. **1879** *Cassell's Techn. Educ.* IV. 339/1 It is these proportions of the wool which interlock and mat together in the milling process. **1897** Rhoscomyl *White Rose Arno* 217 In the face of this bluff there dripped and matted a close-grown thicket of oak and ash, hazel and holly.

mat (mæt), *v.*² [a. F. *mater*, f. *mat*: see MAT, MATE *adjs.*] *trans.* To make (colours, etc.) dull; to give a 'mat' or dull appearance to (gilding, metal, etc.); to frost (glass).

1602 *Kyd's Sp. Trag.* III. xii. H 3 b, I'de haue you paint me .. In your oile colours matted. **1727–51** Chambers *Cycl.* s.v. *Gilding*, The work being thus far gilt, when dry, remains either to be burnished, or matted... To mat, is to give it a light lick in the places not burnished, with a pencil dipt in size. **1854** Reinnel *Carpenters* etc. *Comp.* 74 Those parts of your work which look dull from not being burnished, are now to be matted, that is, are to be made to look like dead gold. **1877** G. B. Gee *Pract. Gold-worker* 133 A design may be rendered more distinct after the pattern has been greatly brought out in relief by simply matting the ground. **1884** F. J. Britten *Watch & Clockm.* 173 The Swiss silver the work first and then mat it by scratch brushing. **1898** H. Maclean *Photogr. Print Process* xvi. 137 Many a time a print is distinctly improved by being on the one hand matted, or, on the other, enamelled. **1900** *Cassell's Cycl. Mech.* (1902) I. 153/2 Now pour on white acid, and let it remain until the glass is matted.

b. *Glass-painting.* 'To cover (glass) with gum or other colour, smoothed over with a badger softener' (Suffling *Glass-painting*, 1902).

1885 F. Miller *Glass-Paint.* 53 A method frequently resorted to.. to give tone and softness to white glass is to matt each square when traced, with umber or ancient brown.

mat (mæt), *v.*³ [f. MAT *sb.*⁴] *trans.* To break *up* with a mattock.

1855 *Jrnl. R. Agric. Soc.* XVI. II. 319 It is a better way to mat up the hassocks and ant-hills.

mat (mæt), *v.*⁴ [f. MAT *sb.*² 3.] *trans.* To mount a print on a cardboard backing, or to provide it with a border. So **'matted** *ppl. a.*; **'matting** *vbl. sb.*

1965 Zigrosser & Gaehde *Guide to Collecting Orig. Prints* vii. 100 The collector or owner who will have to rely on commercial framers to have his prints matted is cautioned to insist on the following points. *Ibid.* 104 If the matted print belongs to a study collection and is stored horizontally, hinging at the side is preferable because it makes for easier and safer handling. **1967** *Boston Sunday Globe* 23 Apr. B. 58/7 Oil paintings, on the other hand, do not take glass or matting. **1968** P. Nuttall *Picture Framing* ii. 24 Different papers can be used to surface the mounting (matting) boards before the window is cut.

mat: see MATE, MATT *a.*, MATTE, MAY *v.*¹, METE *v.*

mat (in Cinematography): see MATTE³.

-mat (mæt), *suffix.* [abbrev. of -MATIC *suffix.*] A terminal element in sbs. (usu. proprietary names) denoting a device that works automatically, as ROTISSOMAT, or a business that contains automatic or self-service equipment, as AUTOMAT, LAUNDROMAT. orig. *U.S.*

1935 [see -MATIC *suffix*]. **1951** *Amer. Speech* Oct. 166 Probably the 'Automat', a self-serving institution supplying food, gave special impetus to the extension of the suffix *-mat*. A 'Mail-O-Mat' is available in the Reception Section of the Pentagon building at Washington. **1971** *Amat. Photographer* 13 Jan. 78/1 (Advt.), Nikkormat FTN f2 Nikkor, £80.

Matabele (mætə'biːliː). Also 9 **Matabeli, Matabili.** [Native name.] **1.** A people of Zulu stock living in Rhodesia; also, a member of this people. Also *attrib.* or as *adj.* Cf. NDEBELE. (See also quot. 1925.)

1823 R. Moffat *Jrnl.* 27 May in I. Schapera *Apprenticeship at Kuruman* (1951) iv. 84 Several men from the Barolongs had just passed them on their way to Mahumapeloo to request their assistance.. to endeavor to make the Matabeles retreat. **1835** A. Smith *Diary* 16 June (1940) II. 75 Most of the people appeared to be the original inhabitants of the country, having a different look to the Matabeli. **1839** W. C. Harris *Wild Sports S. Afr.* iv. 22 The country of Moselekatse, king of the Abaka Zooloos, or Matabili. *Ibid.* xiv. 111 Numerous Matabili villages. **1854** R. Moffat *Matabele Jrnls.* (1945) I. 319 Scarcely a child is to be seen in a real Matabele town. **1894** *Jrnl. Anthrop. Inst.* XXIII. 83 As soon as a Matabele is dead his relations tie the corpse in a blanket. **1896** F. C. Selous *Sunshine & Storm Rhodesia* viii. 64, I should not be at all surprised to see it stated that the rebellion was caused by the inhuman behaviour of the white men in Rhodesia, who, it will be said, were in the habit of shooting down the poor, meek, inoffensive Matabele. **1919** H. H. Johnston *Compar. Study Bantu & Semi-Bantu Lang.* I. v. 798 Tebele (Sindebele). This dialect of the Matabele (Amandebele) Zulus [etc.]. **1925** A. Werner in J. A. MacCulloch *Mythol. all Races* VII. II. vii. 246 There are various tribes of ogres having only one arm and one leg, while others.. have not this peculiarity. The Basuto call the former class of beings 'Matabele'—probably from having come to look on their dreaded enemies, the Zulu tribe of that name, as something scarcely human. **1936** *Discovery* June 172/1 The Xulu-Xosa (including the so-called 'Kaffirs', and the Matabele). **1967** T. O. Ranger *Revolt in S. Rhodesia* i. 38 While the Company made use of the missionaries for its own ends, employing them to obtain a favourable press for the Matabele war, Company officials themselves shared these missionary beliefs. **1972** *Police Rev.* 24 Nov. 1521/1 Cecil John Rhodes.. began negotiating with Lobengula, king of the Matabele.

2. Matabele ant, a large, black, stinging ant, *Megaponera foetens*, found in Rhodesia.

1924 E. Step *Go to Ant* xiii. 193 One of these [stink ants] is the Stink Ant proper (*Paltothyreus tarsatus*) and the other is the Matabele Ant (*Megaponera foetens*). **1932** *Discovery* July 225/2 The big black Matabele ant, *Megaponera foetens*, often marched through our camp in military formation. **1953** S. H. Skaife *Afr. Insect Life* xxii. 361 The Matabele ant, *Megaponera foetens*, is one of the largest and best-known members of this sub-family [*sc.* the Ponerinæ].

‖**matachia.** *Obs.* [? Algonquin of Canada.] (See quot. 1613.)

1609 P. E. *Nova Francia* II. xi. 203 [The suitor] will haue a new gowne.. well garnished with Matachias. **1613** Purchas *Pilgrimage* (1614) 750 The women.. stripped themselues naked.. keeping on still their Matachia (which are Pater nosters [*marg.* Beads] and chaines, enterlaced made of the haire of the Porkespicke died of diuers colours).

matachin (mætə'ʃiːn). *Obs.* exc. *Antiq.* Forms: 6 **machachina**, 6–7 **matachine**, 7 **matachina, mattachene, -in(e, (mattasin)**, 7–8 **mattacina**, 6– **matachin.** [a. F. *matachin* (16th c.: now *matassin*), a. Sp. *matachin* (= It. *mattacino*), conjectured to be a. Arab. *mutawajjihīn*, pr. pple. plural of *tawajjaha* to assume a mask, denominative verb from *wajh* face.]

1. A kind of sword-dancer in a fantastic costume.

1582–3 *Acc. Revels Crt.* (Shaks. Soc. 1842) 177, xxjᵗⁱᵉ yards of cotten for the Matachins. **1591** Harington tr. *Ariosto* VI. lxi. 45 Monstrous of shape and of an vgly hew, Like masking Machachinas all disguised. **1622** tr. *Luna's Pursuit Lazarillo* xvi. 173 They.. looked one vpon another as if they had beene Matachines. **1807** Douce *Illustr. Shaks.* II. 435 [A dance] well known in France and Italy by the name of the dance of fools, or Matachins. **1896** *Edin. Rev.* Apr. 344.

†**2.** A dance performed by matachins. *Obs.*

App. performed by three dancers, representing a triangular duel: see quot. *a* 1586, and quot. 1624 (Smith) in 3.

a **1586** Sidney *Arcadia* I. (1590) 74 b, Who euer sawe a matachin daunce to imitate fighting, this was a fight that did imitate the matachin: for they being but three that fought, euerie one had [two] aduersaries. **1596** Harington *Anat. Metam. Ajax* L ij b, Such as I haue seene in stage-playes when they daunce Machachinas. **1606** Sylvester *Du Bartas* II. iv. II. *Magnif.* 873 Th' Antike, Morisko, and the Mattachine. **1612** Webster *White Devil* L 4 b (near end), *Lod.* We haue brought you a Maske. *Fla.* A matachine it seems, By your drawne swords. **1624** Heywood *Gunaik.* v. 215 The Matachine or sword daunce.

b. *transf.* and *fig.*

1594 Nashe *Terrors Nt.* Wks. (Grosart) III. 280 The night is for you with a blacke saunt or a matachine. **1622** Bacon *Henry VII* 36 He was taken into seruice.. to a base office in his Kitchin; so that (in a kind of Mattacina of humane fortune) Hee turned a Broach, that had worne a Crowne. *a* **1625** Fletcher *Elder Brother* v. i. But that I'me patient,.. Ide daunce a matachin with you, Should make you sweat your best blood for't. **1660** Wither *Spec. Speculat.* 26 We may thereby perchance, Ere many Springs, compelled be to dance Another Matachin. **1677** R. Cary *Chronol.* II. i. I. xiv. 129 Acting in a Matachin of Discord.

c. The music for a matachin dance.

1589 ? Lyly *Pappe w. Hatchet* Wks. 1902 III. 413, I must tune my fiddle, and fetch some more rozen, that it maie squeake out Martins Matachine.

3. *attrib.*, as ***matachin dance, suit, war.***

1584 *Acc. Revels Crt.* (Shaks. Soc. 1842) 188, xxxᵗⁱᵉ ells of sarcenet for fowre matachyne sutes. *a* **1586** Sidney *Arcadia* II. (1590) 123 One time he daunced the Matachine daunce in armour. **1624** T. Scott *Belg. Souldier* 10 They deposed one another, and as it were with a Mattachene dance of disorders many times three or foure at once followed their Competitors with whole armies of revenge. **1624** Capt. Smith *Virginia* 177 Concluding a tripartite peace of their Matachin warre.

mataco ('mætəkəʊ). Also **matacho, matico** (Dicts.). [prob. S. American.] The three-banded armadillo, *Tolypeutes tricinctus*, a small species which is able to roll itself up into a ball.

1834 *Penny Cycl.* II. 353 The Mataco.. is found in Brazil, Paraguay, and Buenos Ayres, but is nowhere very common. **1845** Darwin *Voy. Nat.* v. (1873) 96 The apar, commonly called Mataco. **1849** *Sk. Nat. Hist., Mammalia* IV. 193 The Mataco, or Bolita (little ball) as it is sometimes called.

matador ('mætədɔː(r)). Also 7–9 **matadore**, 8 **mattador(e.** [a. Sp. *matador*:—L. *mactātōr-em*, agent-n. f. *mactāre* (Sp. *matar*) to kill.]

1. a. In Spanish bull-fights, the man appointed to kill the bull.

1681 Dryden *Span. Friar* I. 10 Stranger! Cavalier.. will you not hear me? you Moore-killer, you Matador. **1797** *Encycl. Brit.* (ed. 3) III. 772 The matador at length gives the mortal blow. **1812** Byron *Ch. Har.* I. lxxiv, The light-limb'd Matadore. **1882** De Windt *Equator* 134 The bull-fighters themselves are of four grades: the espada or matador, the picadores [etc.].

b. *fig.*

1930 R. Campbell *Adamastor* 8 The matador of truth, he trails his scorn Before their lowered horns and blood-shot eyes. **1944** Auden *For Time Being* (1945) 118 George, you old matador, Welcome back to the Army.

c. Used *attrib.* to designate garments resembling those worn by a matador. Cf. TOREADOR c.

1959 M. SHADBOLT *New Zealanders* 217 She was..clad in black, in tight sweater and matador slacks. **1960** *Tamarack Rev.* XIV. 137 The girls dress mostly in matador pants and bright blouses. **1962** C. ROHAN *Delinquents* 144 She used to sit on the top of the front steps, clad in her matador pants and skin-tight sweater.

2. *Card-playing.* In some card games (as quadrille, ombre, solo), a name applied to certain principal cards.

1674 COTTON *Compl. Gamester* (1680) 70 [Ombre.] The Matadors (or killing Cards) which are the *Spadillo, Mallillio,* and *Basto* are the chief Cards. **1728** SWIFT *Jrnl. Mod. Lady* Wks. 1755 III. ii. 190 Well, if I ever touch a card! Four mattadores, and lose codill! **1778** C. JONES *Hoyle's Games Impr.* 99 Four Matadores in Hearts. **1876** CAPT. CRAWLEY *Card Players Man.* 194 [Quadrille.] There are three matadores—viz., spadille, manille, and basto.

3. *Dominoes.* (See quot.)

1865 *Compl. Domino-Player* 14 The Matadore Game. In this game, instead of fitting the same numbers together, you are only allowed to play by placing a number at one or the other end, which added to the number there, will make seven; but those dominoes which will make that number in themselves are termed matadores, and can be played at any stage of the hand,.. These are the $\frac{6}{1}$, $\frac{5}{2}$, and $\frac{4}{3}$; the double blank is also a matadore, and can be played at any time. **1897** FOSTER *Compl. Hoyle* 563.

‖**matadora** (mætə'dɔːrə). [Sp.] A woman matador.

1955 *People* (Austral.) 11 Jan. 20/2 In Mexico the girls are invading the bullrings. Pretty matadoras with flashing swords and whirling red capes are taking much of the limelight. **1956** P. MCCORMICK *Lady Bullfighter* i. 30 The words..are particularly welcome when someone substitutes the word '*matadora*' for '*señorita*'. **1968** C. CINTRON *Torera: Mem. Bullfighter* II. 70 Since they barely tolerated the idea of a gringa rejoneadora, they wouldn't even consider the possibility of an American matadora. **1974** *Publishers Weekly* 24 June 54/2 The cast includes a nervous novice matador, an ace matador,..an aspiring gypsy matadora.

mataeology (mætiː'ɒlədʒɪ). Also 7 **mateologie.** [f. Gr. μάταιος vain + -λογία discourse: see -LOGY.] Vain or unprofitable discourse.

1656 BLOUNT *Glossogr., Mateologie* (*mataeologia*) vain enquiry, or over curious search into high matters and mysteries. **1873** F. HALL *Mod. Eng.* 37 The bead-roll of mataeology embodied in the extract here following.

So †**mataeo'logian**, one who discourses vainly; †**mataeo'logical** *a.*, of or pertaining to 'mataeology', vain; †**mataeologue**, an unprofitable talker.

1653 URQUHART *Rabelais* I. xv, The doting mateologians of old time. **1716** M. DAVIES *Athen. Brit.* II. 184 The mataeological forestalling of the Apocalyptick Chronology of the end of time. *Ibid.* 168 Those Sacerdotal-Secular Mataeologues of Doway and Lisbon.

†**mataeotechny.** *Obs.* In 7 **mataeotechnia, mateotechnie, -y.** [f. Gr. μάταιο-ς vain + τέχνη art.] An unprofitable science.

1576 NEWTON *Lemnie's Complex.* To Rdr., Such a peevish practice, and unnecessary Mataeotechny. **1675** GREGORY in Rigaud *Corr. Sci. Men* (1841) II. 278, I am much mistaken if to force an equality between a negative and affirmative root be not a mere useless mataeotechnia.

matafund ('mætəfʌnd). *Antiq. rare*$^{-1}$. [ad. med.L. *matafunda* = OF. *macefonde, machefonde.*

Southey app. regarded the word as f. Sp. *matar* to kill + L. *funda* sling.]

An ancient engine of war.

[**1788** GROSE *Milit. Antiq.* II. 304 The matafunda; this was a stone-throwing machine, probably by means of a sling.] **1795** SOUTHEY *Joan of Arc* VIII. 163 That murderous sling The matafund.

matagasse, -gesse, var. ff. MATTAGESS *Obs.*

‖**matagouri** (mætə'gʊərɪ, -'gaʊrɪ). Also **matakura, matagory, -gowry.** [Corruption of Maori *tumatakuru* (Morris *Austral Engl.*).] A prickly shrub of New Zealand, *Discaria toumatou*; = IRISHMAN 2. Also *attrib.*

1859 *Otago Gaz.* 22 Sept. 280 (Morris) Much of it is encumbered with matakura scrub. **1892** W. MCHUTCHESON *Camp Life in Fiordland* 8 (Morris) Trudging moodily along in Indian file through the matagouri scrub and tussock. **1934** *Bulletin* (Sydney) 16 May 39/1 Her [*sc.* an old ewe's] long wool became entangled in the thorns of a stunted matagory bush. **1939** C. BRASCH in A. E Currie *Cent. Treas. Otago Verse* (1949) 100 Alone on the parched rise, inhuman matagowry Dry-green and fibrous. **1958** *Landfall* XII. 18 My hands were thorned with the matagauri from pulling off the finer neck wool. **1962** J. FRAME *Edge of Alphabet* xxx. 164 He remembers his last visit up Central..where the matagouri, the 'spiked plant that does not cry' grows on the hills among the snow-grass. **1963** *Times* 6 Feb. p. vii/3 What were once harsh, unlovely *matagouri* flats are now green with lucerne.

Mata Hari ('mɑːtə 'hɑːrɪ). [f. Malay *mata* eye + *hari* day.] The name taken by Margaretha Gertruida Zelle (1876–1917), used *fig.* to signify a beautiful and seductive spy; also *attrib.* and as *vb.*

1936 E. WAUGH *Waugh in Abyssinia* iii. 96 Patrick's spy.. was soon known to the European community as Mata Hari. **1947** 'N. BLAKE' *Minute for Murder* vii. 163 He's got it into his thick head that I'm a male Mata Hari. **1948** 'P. QUENTIN' *Run to Death* iii. 25 Why don't you come out from behind the Mata Hari and tell me the truth? **1962** M. CARLETON *Dread Sunset* vii. 122, I somehow can't see Miss Gantry as Jaspar's Girl Friday, let alone a Mata Hari. **1963** H. SLESAR *Bridge of Lions* (1964) i. 19 'She?' Shortlake grinned. 'Ah. Mata Hari stuff.' **1970** T. LILLEY *Projects Section* xix. 257 She was beginning to look haggard; the strain of Mata-Hari-ing was sure to tell. **1973** 'A. HALL' *Tango Briefing* xiv. 183 You wouldn't have to frisk this pint-sized Mata Hari: you could see she was armed half a mile away.

‖**matai** ('mataiː), *sb.*[1] Maori name for a New Zealand coniferous tree, *Podocarpus spicata*; the Black Pine of Otago. Also, the wood of this tree.

1835 W. YATE *Acc. N. Zealand* (ed. 2) 50 Matai (*Taxus Matai*), a plant with a small yew-tree leaf, a strong smell, and a rough bark. **1875** *Offic. Handbk. N. Zealand* 40 Valuable woods..matai (or black pine) [etc.].

‖**matai** (mataiː), *sb.*[2] [Samoan.] In a Samoan extended family, the person who is chosen to succeed to a chief's or orator's title and honoured as the head of the household.

1928 M. MEAD *Coming of Age in Samoa* (1929) iv. 40 The *matai* exercises nominal and usually real authority over every individual under his protection, even over his father and mother. **1934** F. M. KEESING *Mod. Samoa* i. 30 In general the *matais*, or titled men,..engage mostly in ceremonial activities while the work as the white man views it is done by the rest of the community. **1956** F. M. & M. M. KEESING *Elite Communication in Samoa* ii. 17 The community is made up of a series of households of 'extended family' or 'multiple family' type, each under the authority of a 'head' or '*matai*'. **1974** *Sunday Advocate-News* (Barbados) 16 Dec. 21/2 The matais usually deal out justice to law breakers in the Samoan spirit of 'forgive and forget' before the matter ever reaches the ears of the authorities. **1974** *Encycl. Brit. Macropædia* XVI. 205/2 Within the villages, close kinship ties have traditionally bound individuals into a sternly collectivist society. Elected family leaders called *matai* (titled chiefs or orators) form village or district councils to administer group affairs.

matakura, variant of MATAGOURI.

matalassé, variant of MATELASSÉ.

matalent, variant of MALTALENT *Obs.*

matalle, obs. form of METAL.

‖**matamata** (mætə'mætə). [? S. American; used as zoological Latin in 1822 by Merrem in *Isis* 690.] A South American turtle, *Chelys fimbriata.*

1840 *Cuvier's Anim. Kingd.* 272 The Matamata (*Testudo fimbria*, Gm.). **1876** *Beneden's Anim. Parasites* 58 The Matamata, a turtle living in the brackish water of Guiana.

matamoro, matamorre, var. ff. MATTAMORE.

‖**matapi** ('mætəpiː). Also **matapee.** [Arawak.] A pliable basket used in Guyana for expressing the poisonous juice from the root of the cassava or manioc.

1858 SIMMONDS *Dict. Trade.* **1899** RODWAY *Guiana Wilds* 117 The matapee for pressing out the poisonous juice.

matapo, var. MATIPO.

Matara, var. MATURA.

matata ('matata). *N.Z.* [Maori.] = *fern-bird* (FERN *sb.*[1] 2 b).

1835 W. YATE *Acct. N.Z.* (ed. 2) ii. 60 Matata—A small dusky-coloured bird, with a white and brown spotted breast. **1863** A. S. ATKINSON *Jrnl.* 29 Sept. in *Richmond-Atkinson Papers* (1960) II. 64 The korimakos in the bush and the larks and matatas in the open about us. **1882** [see *fern-bird* (FERN *sb.*[1] 2 b)]. **1966** R. A. FALLA et al. *Field Guide to Birds N.Z.* 205 Fernbird. *Bowdleria punctata.* Other names: Matata, Tataki Thrush.

Matawila, var. METAWILEH.

match (mætʃ), *sb.*[1] Forms: 1 **ȝemæcca,** (**ȝemæccea**), **ȝemecca, mæcca,** 2 **imæcca, mæcche,** 3 **meche,** 3–4 **mecche,** 3–5 **macche,** (4 **machche**), 4–5 **mach,** (5 **mehche, metche**), 5–6 **mache, matche,** 6– **match.** [OE. *ȝemæcca, ȝemecca* (for the formation see Bülbring *Ae. Elementarbuch* §177):—OTeut. type *gamakjon-, related to *gamakon-, OE. *ȝemaca,* MAKE *sb.*[1] In branch II the word inherited from OE. seems to have coalesced with a new formation from MATCH *v.*[1]]

I. One of an associated pair.

†**1.** A husband or wife, a mate, consort, a lover. Also said of animals. *Obs.*

a **831** *Charter of Oswulf* 1 in Sweet *O.E. Texts* 443 Ic osuulf aldormonn..ond beornðryð min ȝemecca sellað [etc.]. **971** *Blickl. Hom.* 23 Tweȝen turturan ȝemæccan. *c* **1000** ÆLFRIC *Saints' Lives* (1900) II. 340 His mæcca min modor. *c* **1000** *Ags. Gosp.* Matt. i. 20 Nelle þu ondrædan marian þine gemæccean to onfonne. **11..** *Voc.* in Wr.-Wülcker 537/12 Coniunx, imæcca. *c* **1160** *Hatton Gosp.* Matt. i. 24 þa aras iosepħ..& he on-feng hys mæcchen. *c* **1200** ORMIN 290 Zakariȝess macche Elysabæþ. *c* **1220** *Bestiary* 716 Vre Sowle atte kirke dure ches hire crist to meche, he is ure soule spuse. **13..** *E.E. Allit. P.* B. 695 Vch male mas his mach a man as hym-seluen. *a* **1400–50** *Alexander* 831 Philip..with a fest huge Had wed him anoþer wyfe..[Alexander says to him:] Now þou mas þe slike a mangery & macchis changis. **1558** KNOX *First Blast* (Arb.) 40 But what maketh this for Mary and her matche Phillippe? *a* **1569** KINGESMYLL *Godly Advise* (1580) 31 Suche quarrelles as the unequal matches laie one in the others dishe. **1631** WEEVER *Anc. Funeral Mon.* 853 This Heroicall Progenie of the Howards and their Matches. **1658** PHILLIPS, *Match*, A Term in Hunting, when a Wolf desires copulation, he is said to go to his match or to his mate.

†**2.** One's equal in age, rank, station, etc.; one's fellow, companion. *Obs.*

c **975** *Rushw. Gosp.* Matt. xi. 16 ȝelic is cnehtum..þæm þe clipende to heora ȝemeccum [Vulg. *coæqualibus*] cweþað [etc.]. **13..** *E.E. Allit. P.* B. 124 Vch mon with his mach made hym at ese. *c* **1440** *Promp. Parv.* 331/1 Mehche,..*par, compar.* **1533** MORE *Answ. Poysoned Bk.* Wks. 1035/1 If.. there shoulde neither felowship of their matches, nor feare of any such as are after the worldly compt accompted for theyr betters, any thing let or withstand them..to [etc.]. **1547–64** BAULDWIN *Mor. Philos.* (Palfr.) 166 Marry thy match. **1553** WILSON *Rhet.* 64 A proude disdainfull manne ..that..thinketh hymself..ouer good to haue a matche or felowe in this life. **1571** *Satir. Poems Reform.* xxvii. 66 Be thair exemple lerne experience, Ane forene mache or maister to admitt.

3. †**a.** An opponent, antagonist, rival. *Obs.*

c **1400** *Laud Troy Bk.* 9236 Eche man rides vnto his macche. *c* **1400** *Rowland & O.* 809 There es no mache un-to mee, And that me lykes ille. **1513** DOUGLAS *Æneis* V. vii. 27 Ane vthir mache to hym was socht and sperit. **1525** LD. BERNERS *Froiss.* II. xxiv. 62 Euery man with his matche. **1565** COOPER *Thesaurus, Gladiatores committere*, to sette matches of swoorde players together. *c* **1570** *Marr. Wit & Sci.* III. i, Your matche is monstrous to behoulde and full of might. **1593** SHAKS. *2 Hen. VI*, v. ii. 10 Match to match I haue encountred him.

b. A person (occasionally a number of persons, a thing) that is able to contend or compete with another as an equal. In phrases ***to find, meet one's match***; (***to be, prove oneself***) ***a match for.*** Also ***more than a match for***: able to overcome or defeat. †Rarely of two persons, ***to be matches***: to be equal in prowess.

c **1300** *Celestin* 488 in *Anglia* I. 79 Amonges vs [*sc.* the devils] shalto drecche: So longe hastou ben oure mecche, Day and ȝere. *c* **1305** *Miracle of St. James* 48 in *E.E.P.* (1862) 59þe schrewe fond his macche þo. *c* **1330** R. BRUNNE *Chron. Wace* (Rolls) 13563 þat wel couþe feighte, he fond his mecche. *a* **1450** *Le Morte Arthur* 1607 Neuyr yit er my mache I founde. **1470–85** MALORY *Arthur* X. viii. 426, I gyue you leue to goo where ye lyst. Gramercy said kyng Mark For ye & I be not matches. *a* **1568** *Knt. of Curtesy* 352 (Ritson) His mache coulde he no where finde. **1621** BURTON *Anat. Mel.* I. ii III. x. (1676) 66/1 Hannibal..met with his match, and was subdued at last. **1645** BP. HALL *Remedy Discontents* 75 Men that are not able matches to their passions. **1712** ADDISON *Spect.* No. 297 ⁋6 The Hero in the *Paradise Lost* is unsuccessful, and by no means a Match for his Enemies. **1762** GOLDSM. *Cit. W.* vii, I fancy myself at present..more than a match for all that can happen. **1833** HT. MARTINEAU *Loom & Lugger* I. iv. 58 If the rival manufactures are a match for each other, let them fight it out. **1849** MACAULAY *Hist. Eng.* v. I. 601 His followers..were no match for regular soldiers. **1871** KINGSLEY *Lett.* (1878) II. 362 The honourable man who will pay his debts is no match for the dis-honourable man who will not. **1874** GREEN *Short Hist.* vii. §1. 347 So long as Henry supported him,..he [T. Cromwell] was more than a match..for his foes.

4. A person or thing that equals another in some quality.

1470–85 MALORY *Arthur* II. v. 81 Of his strengthe and hardynesse I knowe not his matche lyuynge. **1586** A. DAY *Eng. Secretary* I. (1625) 37 The match or like of him therein, was seldome or neuer in those daies any where found. **1632** LITHGOW *Trav.* x. 499, I neuer found their matches amongst the best people of forrane Nations. **1866** MRS. GASKELL *Wives & Dau.* I. xxi. 235, I don't believe there is his match anywhere for goodness. **1888** *Daily News* 26 Sept. 6/1 Where..is there the match of this imperishable tale of the relief of Lucknow?

5. A person or thing that exactly corresponds to or resembles another, or that forms an exact pair with another.

c **1530** in Gutch *Coll. Cur.* II. 284 Oone Potte new made unto a matche. **1551** RECORDE *Pathw. Knowl.* II. iv, When two lines are drawen from the endes of anie one line, and meet in anie pointe, it is not possible to draw two other lines of like lengthe ech to his match that shal begin at the same pointes, and [etc.]. **1583** FULKE *Defence* xiv. 381 Your eies were not matches, or else they were daseled with a mist of malice, when you [etc.]. *a* **1616** BEAUM. & FL. *Wit without M.* II. ii, A maide content with one Coach and two horses, not falling out because they are not matches. **1626** BACON *Sylva* §393 Try them [Waters] in Seuerall Bottles, or Open Vessells, Matches in euery Thing else. **1674** MOXON *Tutor Astron.* II. (ed. 3) 84 You might by..looking through any Star on the Globe see its Match in Heaven. **1808** PIKE *Sources Mississ.* III. (1810) App. 22 Extraordinary matches for carriages have sold at 400 dollars per pair. **1818** J. PALMER *Jrnl. Trav.* 129 You've got two nice creatures, they are right elegant matches. **1893** STEVENSON *Catriona* 5 Ragged gillies, such as I had seen the matches of by the dozen in my Highland journey.

II. The action of matching.

†**6. a.** A matching of adversaries against each other; a contest viewed with regard to the equality or inequality of the parties. *Obs.*

?*a* **1400** *Morte Arth.* 4071 This was a mache vn-mete. *c* **1400** *Destr. Troy* 1324 Vnmete was the Macche at þe mene tyme. **1599** DRAYTON *Idea*, '*Truce, gentle Love*', Bad is the match where neither party wone. **1602** SHAKS. *Ham.* II. ii. 493 Vnequall match, Pyrrhus at Priam driues, in Rage strikes wide. **1603** DRAYTON *Bar. Wars* II. xxii. 31 Ferrer his Taberd..., well knowne in many a warlike match before. **1606** SHAKS. *Tr. & Cr.* IV. v. 46 It were no match, your naile against his horne. **1628** HOBBES *Thucyd.* (1822) 98 A profitable garland in their matches of valour.

†**b.** ***man of match***: ? a champion. *Obs.*

1640 HABINGTON *Q. Arragon* II. i. C 2 b, Seest thou that man of match Though small in stature, mighty he's in soule.

7. A contest or competitive trial of skill in some sport, exercise, or operation, e.g. in archery, cricket, football, ploughing, etc., in which two or more persons or bodies of persons are matched against each other; an engagement or arrangement for such a contest. Also applied to a contest in which animals are made to compete in a trial of speed, fighting power, or the like.

In modern sporting language a 'match' is ordinarily understood to mean a formally regulated contest between two permanent bodies (as two cricket or football clubs, two counties), or (as in billiards) between two recognized experts in a game.

1545 ASCHAM *Toxoph.* (Arb.) 91 To make matches to assemble archers togyther, to contende who shall shoote best, and winne the game, encreaseth ye vse of shotynge wonderfully amonges men. **1567** HARMAN *Caveat* (1869) 46 Where he harde..xl pence gaged vpon a matche of wrastling. **1595** SHAKS. *John* III. i. 336 Assured losse, before the match be plaid. **1611** COTGR., *Partie*,..a match, or set, at game. **1651** CLEVELAND *Poems* 44 [He] leaves it a drawn match. **1676** LADY CHAWORTH in *12th Rep. Hist. MSS. Comm.* App. v. 32 They have made four matches to be run at Newmarket. **1700** *Post Boy* 30 Mar. 2/1 A Match at Cricket, of 10 Gentlemen on each side, will Be Play'd. **1711** BUDGELL *Spect.* No. 161 ⁋3 A Foot-ball Match. **1747** *Gen. Advertiser* 4 July, Mr. Richard Newland..with two of his Brothers, and two others..having advertised that they would play a Match at Cricket..against Five of any Parish of England [etc.]. **1812** *Sporting Mag.* XXXIX. 107 [Coursing] All matches to be entered in the match book. **1847** MRS. GORE *Castles in Air* xxxiii. (1857) 326 A match was skated upon the lake. **1882** PEBODY *Eng. Journalism* xxi. 159 He speaks to his constituents..at a ploughing match.

†**8.** A suitable conjunction or pairing. Also, *above one's match*: above one's level. *Obs.*

1423 JAS. I *Kingis Q.* cix, It is no mach, of thyne vnworthynesse To hir hie birth, estate, and beautee bryght. **1542** UDALL *Erasm. Apoph.* 225 To the entente that wee may after a sorte make soome lykely matche of Roomains with the Grekes, we shall [etc.]. **1748** RICHARDSON *Clarissa* (1811) VII. 55 If I found any of them above my match.

9. *concr.* A (more or less) well-matched or accordant pair; two persons, things, or sets each the counterpart of the other.

1542 UDALL *Erasm. Apoph.* 333 Plutarchus..compareth theim twoo together as a veraye good matche and wel coupleed. **1807** PIKE *Sources Mississ.* (1810) 105 Discovered one of my sleigh dogs was missing..; this was no little mortification, as it broke the match, whose important services I had already experienced. **1838** DICKENS *Nich. Nick.* xxii, If they were a little better match—..I mean if they were a little more of a size.

10. a. A matrimonial compact or alliance; esp. one viewed as more or less advantageous with regard to wealth, rank, or social position. *to make a match*: to bring about a marriage by influence or contrivance.

1575–85 ABP. SANDYS *Serm.* xvi. 288 The common sort of men, in making their matches this way, haue chiefly two outward vntoward respects. **1599** SHAKS. *Much Ado* II. i. 315 His grace hath made the match. **1676** LADY CHAWORTH in *12th Rep. Hist. MSS. Comm.* App. v. 28 Twas a match of his friends and not his owne making. **1751** JOHNSON *Rambler* No. 182 ⁋4 Whose hope is to raise themselves by a wealthy match. **1793** MARQ. BUCKINGHAM in *14th Rep. Hist. MSS. Comm.* 390 The match which is settled between Sir W. Young and Miss Talbot. **1838** DICKENS *Nich. Nick.* xlvii, Matches are made in Heaven, they say. **1866** G. MACDONALD *Ann Q. Neighb.* v. (1878) 59 It seems to me a very good match for her. **1874** GREEN *Short Hist.* vii. §4. 378 It was by a match with Henry Stuart that Mary determined to unite the forces of Catholicism.

†**b.** A matrimonial alliance as represented heraldically. *Obs.*

1628 COKE *On Litt.* Pref., A tomb with his statue upon it together with his own match and the matches of some of his ancestors. **1640** YORKE (*title*) The Union of Honour. Containing the Armes, Matches And Issues of the Kings, Dukes, Marquesses and Earles of England. **1686** PLOT *Staffordsh.* 298 The Windows illustrated with the Armes and matches of the Chetwynds in painted glass.

†**c.** The action of marrying; relationship by marriage. *by match*: in consequence of a marriage.

1574 J. DEE in *Lett Lit. Men* (Camden) 39 In direct line, braunche, collaterall, or match. **1605** CAMDEN *Rem., Epit.* 35 Who in these 2. funerall verses, contained her princely parentage, match, and issue. *c* **1630** RISDON *Surv. Devon* §53 (1810) 58 By match, it came to Tremenet. **1655** FULLER *Ch. Hist.* III. iii. §6 He possessed fair lands in Anjou and Maine; by Match in right of Queen Elianor his Wife.

d. *concr.* A person viewed with regard to his or her eligibility (esp. on grounds of fortune or rank) as a partner in marriage.

1586 A. DAY *Eng. Secretary* I. (1625) 125 We will finde out a better match wherewith to delight thee. **1598** SHAKS. *Merry W.* III. iv. 77 She is no match for you. **1625** MASSINGER *New Way* IV. i, A maid well qualified, and the richest match Our north part can make boast of. **1688** PENTON *Guardian's Instr.* (1897) 25 When I had provided an agreeable Match, his Comrades..taught him to rail at Matrimony. **1710** SWIFT *Jrnl. to Stella* 20 Oct., Lord Ashburnham, the best match now in England. **1774** H. WALPOLE *Lett. to Mann* 28 Mar., He, the first match in England. **1809** MALKIN *Gil Blas* I. xi. ⁋1 He left me so little property, that I was a bad match. **1866** G. MACDONALD *Ann. Q. Neighb.* xxvii. (1878) 472 He's a very good match in point of property and family too. **1879** G. MEREDITH *Egoist* xxxv, He's the great match of the county.

†**11.** An agreement, an appointment; a compact, bargain. *it is a match* (or elliptically, *a match!*): said in concluding an agreement or a wager; = 'Agreed', 'Done'. *Obs.*

1569 T. PRESTON *Cambises* 250 (Manly) A match ye shall make straight with me. **1586** J. HOOKER *Hist. Irel.* in *Holinshed* II. 37/2 These things came not thus to passe, as it were by a set match, but [etc.]. **1596** SHAKS. *Tam. Shr.* V. ii. 74 A match, 'tis done. *a* **1628** PRESTON *New Covt.* (1634) 217 If a man be holy but by halves, that makes not the match, it makes not the agreement between the Lord and us. **1655** WALTON *Angler* I. iv. (1661) 74 A match, good Master, lets go to that house. **1706–7** FARQUHAR *Beaux Strat.* I. i, A Match!

III. The state of being matched.

12. *Electr.* An equality of impedance between two coupled devices (cf. MATCH *v.*[1] 5 d).

1931 *Proc. IRE* XIX. 725 By introducing capacitative elements,..a match can be obtained. **1952** D. D. KING *Measurement at Centimeter Wavelength* ii. 51 No assurance of match exists without prior knowledge of the impedance to be matched. **1962** SIMPSON & RICHARDS *Physical Princ. Junction Transistors* v. 89 The condition of conjugate match can be obtained quite readily when tuned transformer coupling is used as in many radio-frequency applications.

IV. 13. *attrib.* and *Comb.*: (sense 10) †*match-broker*, *-marring*, †*-monger*; **match ball**, a ball of the quality and dimensions specified by the laws of the game; also, in lawn tennis, a ball that may decide a match; **match-book**, (*a*) in horse racing, ? the book in which a list of the dates of matches or races is kept; (*b*) *Cricket* (see quot. 1934); **match-card** *Cricket* (see quot. 1934) (= *score-card* (a)); **match-fit** *a.*, in good physical condition for a match; also *transf.*; hence **match-fitness**; **match-game**, a game (esp. of chess) forming part of a 'match'; also *U.S.* = sense 7; †**match-horse**, a horse entered for running in a match or race; **match-play**, the play in a match (sense 7); also in *Golf*, play in which the score is reckoned by counting the holes gained on each side; so *match-player*; *match-playing* vbl. sb.; **match-point**, (*a*) the state of a game when one side or player needs only one point to win the match; also, the point itself; (*b*) in *Bridge*, a unit used in scoring in tournament play; so *match-pointed* ppl. a.; **match race**, a race run as a competition; **match-rifle**, a rifle used in firing competitions; **match-rifling** *Gun-making*, a method of rifling guns to adapt them for long-range shooting in matches; **match-winner**, one who, by his skill, makes a major contribution to the winning of a match; hence **match-winning** *ppl. a.* Also MATCH-MAKER[2], -MAKING *vbl. sb.*[2]

1849 in 'Bat' *Cricketer's Manual* (Advt.), Dark's and Duke's *Match Balls. **1895** KIPLING *Day's Work* (1898) 344 In the black jersey..of the First Fifteen, the new match-ball under his arm. **1927** *Daily Express* 5 July 2/1 They..retrieved two successive match balls in the third set. **1928** *Daily Tel.* 26 June 11/7 On the tenth game, the American had three match balls. The first time he smashed out of court. **1934** W. J. LEWIS *Lang. Cricket* 8 A match ball is one of superior quality for match-play, of the size and weight specified in the Laws. **1961** *Amer. Speech* XXXVI. 44 With a lob Fraser lifted the deciding matchball out of bounds. **1969** M. BRADY *Lawn Tennis Encycl.* 129 Match Balls. The following championships were won after the winner was match point down. **1812** *Match book [see 7]. **1845** W. DENISON *Cricketer's Compan.* p. iv, The Compiler feels it necessary to offer his thanks to the Presidents and Secretaries..for..allowing him to make extracts from their *match-books. **1900** W. A. BETTESWORTH *Walkers of Southgate* II. vii. 253 In the [Harrow] Sixth Form match-book Mr. Tremlett's score..is given as follows. **1934** W. J. LEWIS *Lang. Cricket* 161 *Match book*, a book containing the scores or tabulated records of the matches played by a club or an eleven. **1654** WHITLOCK *Zootomia* 204 What Consultations, what Embassies, and a whole Councell-Board of Banes-Wrights, or *Match-brokers, must go to the knitting of a Princes Love-Knot. **1901** H. BLEACKLEY *Tales of Stumps* iv. 96 *Match-cards with the 'order of going in' had been printed and eagerly purchased by the spectators. **1908** *Westm. Gaz.* 20 Oct. 11/2 The Jam Sahib of Nawanagar, who, however his name may be printed on the match-cards, will always be known to the cricket-loving public. **1934** W. J. LEWIS *Lang. Cricket* 162 *Match card*, a card giving the names of the players in the order of going in to bat, and a summary of the score up to the time of issue. **1960** V. JENKINS *Lions Down Under* xii. 179 Terry Davies, Tony O'Reilly and Jeff Butterfield..were still far from *match-fit. **1962** *Times* 1 Aug. 3/1 J. G. Willcox..is still not match-fit. **1967** *Listener* 24 Aug. 241/2 It took me about three months of being back in the theatre to feel match fit. **1960** V. JENKINS *Lions Down Under* xvi. 251 He..failed to reach *match-fitness in time. **1961** *Times* 1 July 3/1 It was more than the flesh and blood of a man below physical and match-fitness could stand. **1871** G. R. CUTTING *Student Life at Amherst Coll.* 113 Base ball had hardly been introduced, when certain enthusiastic students conceived the idea of a '*match game' with Williams College. **1888** *Pall Mall G.* 2 July 5/2 A champion chess player will often lose a match game to a far inferior opponent. **1607** MARKHAM *Caval.* III. (1617) 79 These Tryers..ought to ride by the *match-horses all the day long. **1890** *Athenæum* 28 June 828/2 There are four or five young people, and two old widowers do the matchmaking and the *matchmarring. **1681** RYCAUT tr. *Gracian's Critick* 250 He demanded a handsome Wife, which they sold him at the Price of an Aching-head, and the *Match-monger assured him, that [etc.]. **1886** *Pall Mall G.* 2 Aug. 3/2 There has been a revival of some of the old sporting gambits which had for long fallen into disfavour for *match play. **1893** *Baily's Mag.* Oct. 279/1 The championships are played on different principles, the amateur being by holes or 'match' play, and the open by strokes. **1920** W. T. TILDEN *Art Lawn Tennis* 67 Match play, where both men are in the same class as tennis players, resolves itself into a battle of wits and nerve. **1894** *Westm. Gaz.* 5 Apr. 2/1 Steinitz is the first *match-player living. **1909** E. H. MILES *Lessons Lawn Tennis* (ed. 3) 50 The ideal match player. *Ibid.*, Hints on *Match-playing. **1921** A. W. MYERS *20 Yrs. Lawn Tennis* 48 In the end he won the match, Dixon, after lazily reaching *match point some eight or nine times,..retiring at two sets all. **1928** *Daily Express* 22 June 1/6 The British doubles team held match point twice in the fourth set with Eames serving. **1936** E. CULBERTSON *Contract Bridge Complete* xxxiv. 371 In duplicate Contract with match-point scoring, the unit of play is not a game or a rubber, but an individual deal. **1940** *Ibid.* (ed. 2) xxxiv. 369 Top-score (7 match-points) went to the North-South pair that fulfilled a six-spade contract. **1955** *Times* 6 July 8/5 The British [bridge] team continued to disappoint..although they beat Finland to-day by 53 match points. **1965** *Listener* 30 Dec. 1091/1 Except at match-point scoring. It can be argued that at this method of scoring One No Trump is almost certain to give East-West a very good score. **1969** *New Yorker* 14 June 61/1 Pasarell can drive Graebner out of his mind, because he sometimes waits until Graebner has him at or near match point. **1973** *Country Life* 13 Dec. 2048/1 This was a good match-point result, for many pairs reached Six Diamonds. **1958** *Listener* 30 Oct. 709/2 *Match-pointed Pairs. Game All. Dealer West. **1974** *Guardian* 25 Mar. 24/7 Match-pointed pairs events require an entirely different approach from team competitions. **1804** M. CUTLER in W. P. & J. P. Cutler *Life & Corr. M. Cutler* (1888) II. 172 It was a *match race of two two-year-old colts for $1,000. **1854** W. G. SIMMS *Mellichampe* xviii. 157 If by ..a match-race on foot with an Indian runner, I could do the creature a service, I could go to work cheerfully. **1874** B. F. TAYLOR *World on Wheels* 105 The train..ran a match race with a train on the Michigan Central, and reached Chicago twenty-five minutes ahead. **1948** *Chicago Daily News* 1 Nov. 13/3 He whipped Sir Barton, a 4-year-old, in a memorable match race. **1955** *Amer. Speech* XXX. 22 The term match or match race in common acceptance encompasses any specially arranged two-horse race. R. [Rules of the N.Y. State Racing Commission] 159, however, applies the term to such a race only when the track management has added 'no money or other prize'. **1961** F. C. AVIS *Sportsman's Gloss.* 166/2 *Match Race Conditions*, those normally applied to a cycle race, and affecting the number of competitors; their positions; the start, etc. **1881** GREENER *Gun* 159 The recoil with a 10 lb. *match-rifle is inconsiderable. *Ibid.* 146 The Metford *match-rifling is very expensive to produce. **1908** *Westm. Gaz.* 21 Aug. 3/1 If you..should encounter as keen a *match-winner as yourself [at golf]. **1964** J. MERCER *Great Ones* x. 69 At Wembley nothing happened to upset matters. Reg Lewis was undoubtedly our match-winner. **1908** *Westm. Gaz.* 21 Aug. 3/1 And if you, *match-winning disciple, find yourself placed in this delicate position [etc.]. **1909** *Ibid.* 12 June 16/1 In the indefatigable Mr. Brearley they have a match-winning bowler on fast wickets. **1958** *Times* 20 Sept. 2/6 Without Wardle they have no match-winning spinner. **1960** V. JENKINS *Lions Down Under* xii. 173 The accepted New Zealand pattern for match-winning rugby. **1972** G. ROSS *Hist. Cricket* i. 16 Mynn was the greatest match-winning cricketer the game produced before W. G. Grace.

match (mætʃ), *sb.*[2] Also 4 **macche**, 4–6 **matche**, 5 **mec(c)he**, 6–7 **mache**, 7 **metch**, 6– **match**. [a. OF. *mesche*, *meiche* (mod.F. *mèche*) = Pr. *mecca*, *mecha*, Catal. *metxa*, Sp., Pg. *mecha*, It. *miccia*:—vulgar L. types **micca*, **miccia*.

The ulterior etymology is obscure. Some have attempted to connect the word with Gr. μύξα, L. *myxa* mucus of the nose, nostril, nozzle of a lamp, in med.L. lamp-wick: and with L. *muccus* mucus of the nose, whence It. *moccolo* (:—L. **mucculus*) snuff of a candle.]

†**1.** The wick of a candle or lamp. *Obs.*

1377 LANGL. *P. Pl.* B. XVII. 213 As thow seest some tyme ..a torche, The blase there-of yblowe out ȝet brenneth the weyke, With-oute leye or liȝte that the macche brenneth. **1398** TREVISA *Barth. De P.R.* XVII. clx. (1495) 708 Matches for candelles. **1422** tr. *Secreta Secret., Priv. Priv.* 237 Yf the mecche be ouer depe y-sette in the oyle, hit shall anoone be y-queynte. **1450–1530** *Myrr. our Ladye* 113 The fatnesse of oyle may not burne tyl a weyke or matche be put therto. *c* **1475** *Pict. Voc.* in Wr-Wülcker 754/20 *Hic lichinus*, meche. **1578** LYTE *Dodoens* IV. lii. 510 Pith the whiche..serueth for Matches to burne in lampes. **1601** HOLLAND *Pliny* II. 161 Of the grapes which this Palma Christi, or Ricinus doth carie, there be made excellent weiks or matches for lamps and candles. **1646** SIR T. BROWNE *Pseud. Ep.* VI. xii. 335 Nor will it [the smoke of sulphur] easily light a candle, untill.. the flame approacheth the match.

2. a. An instrument consisting of a wick, cord, or rope of hemp, tow, cotton, etc., so prepared that when lighted at the end it is not easily extinguished, and continues to burn at a uniform rate; used for firing cannon or other fire-arms, and for igniting a train of gunpowder. Also in *Mining* (see quot. 1851). †*to cock a match*: see COCK *v.*[2] 1.

The SLOW-MATCH now consists of loosely-twisted hempen cord steeped in a solution of saltpetre and lime-water, and burns at the rate of one yard in three hours. The QUICK-MATCH is a cotton wick, impregnated with saltpetre, or coated with gum and mealed gunpowder.

1549 *Privy Council Acts* (1890) II. 348 Matches, vjᶜ weight. **1573–4** in W. H. Turner *Select. Rec. Oxford* (1880) 356 Item, for a mache..jd. **1605** *His Maiesties Speach*, etc. G 4 And thereafter searching the fellow [Guido Fawkes],.. found three matches..ready vpon him. **1653** H. COGAN tr. *Pinto's Trav.* xxii. 81 Tied four and four, and five and five together with the matches of their muskets. **1657** *North's Plutarch, Add. Lives* 72 It was a Morian slave that strangled him [Atabalipa] with a match. **1797** *Encycl. Brit.* (ed. 3) VIII. 235 A musket, or musquet, is a fire-arm..formerly fired by the application of a lighted match. **1828–40** TYTLER *Hist. Scot.* (1864) III. 237 They..laid a train, which was connected with a 'lunt', or slow match. **1851** GREENWELL *Coal-trade Terms Northumb. & Durh.* 36 *Match*.—A small piece of candle end, or greased twine or tape..used to ignite the gunpowder in blasting. **1863** KINGLAKE *Crimea* (1876) I.

xiv. 240 The other was the man standing by with a lighted match and determined to touch the fuse.

fig. **1602** MARSTON *Ant. & Mel.* II. Wks. 1856 I. 19 The match of furie is lighted, fastned to the linstock or rage.

b. The material of which matches consist; cord, etc., prepared for ignition.

1572 *Nottingham Rec.* IV. 143 Gunepowder and matche that wase had at the Watch on Mydsomer Evyn. **1598** BARRET *Theor. Warres* III. i. 34 Three or foure yards of match, in seuerall peeces hanging at his girdle. **1633** T. STAFFORD *Pac. Hib.* I. vii. (1821) 97 Fiue Lasts more of powder, with Match and Lead. **1700** S. L. tr. *Fryke's Voy. E. Ind.* 47 The outward Coat of the Nutt is good to make Match. **1797** *Encycl. Brit.* (ed. 3) VIII. 195/2 When there is any apprehension of danger, his [i.e. a gunner's] field-staff is armed with match. **1866** BRANDE & COX *Dict. Sci., Lit., & Art* s.v., Before the invention of locks, small arms were fired by means of match.

3. a. An article of domestic use, consisting of a piece of cord, cloth, paper, wood, etc., dipped in melted sulphur, so as to be readily ignited by the use of a tinder-box, and serving to light a candle or lamp, or to set fire to fuel. *Obs.* exc. *Hist.*

1530 PALSGR. 243/2 Matche to lyght a candell, *alumette.* **1589** R. HARVEY *Pl. Perc.* (1590) 20 When the steele and the flint be knockde togither, a man may light his match by the sparkle. **1608** MIDDLETON *Fam. Love* v. i. 37 To light their matches at my tinder. **1695** CONGREVE *Love for L.* II. i, What a world of fire and candle, matches and tinder-boxes did you purchase! **1710** *Lond. Gaz.* No. 4677/4 There were found about them..several Fir-Matches dip'd in Brimstone. *a* **1776** R. JAMES *Diss. Fevers* (1778) 84 There are many ways of lighting a candle, by a piece of paper, by charcoal, by pit-coal or by a brimstone match. *a* **1822** SHELLEY *Hymn Merc.* xviii, Mercury first found out for human weal Tinder box, matches, fire-irons, flint and steel. **1889** J. NICHOLSON *Folk Speech E. Yorks.* 18 The present paraffin match has quite superseded the old brimstone match, made of a splinter of wood about six inches long, and dipped at both ends.

b. A similar article used for fumigation.

1703 *Art & Myst. Vintners* 23 French and Rhenish Wines are..commonly preserved by the Match. **1753** CHAMBERS *Cycl. Supp.* s.v. *Matching*, Melt brimstone.., dip into it slips of coarse linnen cloth... Take one of these matches, set one end of it on fire, and put it into the bung-hole of a cask. **1839** URE *Dict. Arts* 1303 It is useful to counteract the.. tendency to acidity, by burning a sulphur match in the casks. **1853** *Ibid.* II. 125 To make writing-paper matches, which burn with a bright flame and diffuse an agreeable odour, moisten each side of the paper with tincture of benzoin [etc.]. **1872** T. HARDY *Greenwood Tree* IV. ii, Curious objects about a foot long, in the form of Latin crosses (made of lath and brown paper dipped in brimstone —called matches by bee-fanciers).

†**c.** A small torch used for giving light. *Obs.*

c **1595** CAPT. WYATT *R. Dudley's Voy. W. Ind.* (Hakl. Soc.) 25 The which [flies] make resemblance as if they weare so manie light matches. **1615** G. SANDYS *Trav.* 118 Hanging out kindled matches to terrifie the theeues. **1638** SIR T. HERBERT *Trav.* (ed. 2) 14 Fire or a lighted matche only scaring them [*sc.* lions].

4. a. A short slender piece of wood, wax taper, or other material, tipped with some chemical composition which bursts into flame when rubbed on a rough or specially prepared surface (or, as in the earlier contrivances, when brought into contact with some chemical reagent). Now the ordinary means of producing fire. *to strike a match*: to ignite a match by friction (the verb is taken over from the earlier phrase *to strike a light*). Cf. LUCIFER 3.

paraffin match, one having the splints dipped in paraffin to facilitate ignition of the wood. *safety match*, one which can be ignited only by 'striking' on the box.

1831 T. P. JONES *New Conv. Chem.* xxiv. 245 These matches, after being covered with sulphur, are dipped into a mixture of chlorate of potassa, sugar, and sulphur, made into a paste with gum water. They are then dried, and when touched with sulphuric acid, instantaneously inflame. **1832** *Newton's Lond. Jrnl.* Conj. Ser. I. 258 [An] apparatus for producing instantaneous light, on the principle of the match and bottle has just been imported from Paris. **1845** BROWNING *Meeting at Night* 10 The quick sharp scratch And blue spurt of a lighted match. **1870** DICKENS *E. Drood* xii, [He] puts a match or two in his pocket. **1889** Paraffin match: see 3. **1903** *Longm. Mag.* July 252 He struck a match on his thole-pin.

b. Phr. (*to shatter*) *into matches*: into splinters.

1898 *Times* 10 Jan. 13/3 Captain Norie..whose left arm was shattered into matches by a bullet.

5. *attrib.* and *Comb.*, as *match-point*, *-seller*, *-selling*; **matchbook**, a 'book' containing (safety) matches; †**match-bottle**, a phial containing phosphorus, for igniting sulphur matches; **match-box**, †(*a*) *Mil.* a metal tube, pierced full of holes, for a soldier to carry his lighted match in; (*b*) a box to contain matches; (*c*) *slang* a very small house; also *attrib.*, esp. in phrases *match-box skirt* (see quot. 1968), *match-box toy*, a toy small enough to fit into a match-box; **match-box bean**, the hard seed of the Queensland Bean, *Entada scandens*, of which match-boxes are made (Morris *Austral Eng*); **match-boy**, a boy who sells matches; †**match-cock** (in a matchlock) = COCK *sb.*[1] 13 a; †**match-cord**, rope, or a piece of rope, prepared as a slow-match; **match-girl**, a girl who sells matches; **match-head**, the piece of some chemical composition with which a match (sense 4) is tipped; **match-holder**, a receptacle for a supply of matches; **match-line** = *match-cord*; **match-machine**, a machine for making matches; **match-man**, (*a*) a man who fires the match of a gun; (*b*) a man who sells matches; **match-paper**, touch-paper; **match-paste**, the paste used for making the heads of matches; **match-pipe**, a pipe used to contain a lighted match for a matchlock; **match-pot**, a small vessel for holding matches; **match-safe** *U.S.*, a box to contain matches for use (Knight *Dict. Mech.* 1875); **match-splint** = *match-stick*; **match-staff**, a staff with a slot in the upper end and a spike in the lower, used on shipboard to hold a slow-match (*Cent. Dict.*); **match-stand**, a stand for holding matches; **match-stick**, (*a*) the wood of a match (cf. *match-wood*); (*b*) *slang*, a nickname for a thin person; (*c*) *attrib.*, esp. designating simple drawings in short straight lines; **match-thread**, the thread used as match for firing guns, etc.; **match-tub**, in ships-of-war, a tub having a cover perforated with holes, in which slow-matches were hung ready for use with the lighted end downwards (Ogilvie *Suppl.* 1855); **matchwood**, †(*a*) touchwood; (*b*) wood suitable for match-sticks; (*c*) in phrase (*to break* etc.) *into matchwood*, into minute splinters.

1951 C. ARMSTRONG *Black-Eyed Stranger* (1952) iv. 31 The old *match-books in the gutter. **1966** H. WAUGH *Pure Poison* (1967) xxiii. 140 The counter..boasted a ledger..a postcard rack and a basket of matchbooks advertising the motel. **1968** MRS. L. B. JOHNSON *White House Diary* 7 Feb. (1970) 628 One table asked me for my autograph and I wrote it for them on White House matchbooks. **1839** URE *Dict. Arts* 954 Phosphoric *match-bottles. **1786** GROSE *Anc. Armour & Weapons* 65 The musqueteer should also have a little tin tube..big enough to admit a match, and pierced full of little holes, that he may not be discovered by his match..; this was the origin of the *match-boxes, till lately worn by our grenadiers. **1866** LOWELL *Wks.* (1890) II. 93 Mr. Carlyle is for calling down fire from heaven whenever he cannot readily lay his hand on the match-box. **1887** *Pall Mall G.* 9 Nov. 2/1 Twopence-halfpenny per gross is paid for matchbox-making. **1905** *Pearson's Mag.* July 103/2 Few fingers are too old and few too tiny to help the match-box maker. **1920** JOYCE *Let.* 29 Sept. (1957) I. 148 Got notice to quit this match-box and am..looking for a flat. **1946** A. J. CRUSE (*title*) Match-box labels of the world. **1962** *Harper's Bazaar* Oct. 134/2 A matchbox skirt. A flipover belt ties on the hips. **1964** *New Statesman* 10 Apr. 579/1 *Lesney Products* (matchbox toys) has reported an accelerated increase in exports, turnover and profits. **1968** J. IRONSIDE *Fashion Alphabet* 45 *Match-box*, a skirt given a squared box-like look by outside stitched seams back and front, introduced by Dior. **1969** E. H. PINTO *Treen* 211/1 A large range of German 'matchbox' wooden toys was made at that time [1930]. **1819** *Sporting Mag.* V. 122 Society of the present day, from the nobleman to the *match-boy. **1643** *Plymouth Col. Rec.* (1855) II. 65 A musket, either firelock or *matchcock. **1644** NYE *Gunnery* I. 38 The Gunner is always, when leasure will permit, to choose good *Matchcords. **1852** MME. DE CHATELAIN tr. *Andersen's Tales* 301 The Little *Match-Girl. **1898** *Westm. Gaz.* 17 Sept. 4/3 To Mr. Rosenthal belongs the credit of finding a paste for *match-heads which is not poisonous. **1884** *Harper's Mag.* Dec. 134/2 A porcelain *match holder half full of matches. **1824** MEYRICK *Anc. Armour* III. 77 The soldier is made to carry the *match-line lighted at both ends. **1875** KNIGHT *Dict. Mech.* 1410/1 Young's *match-machine cuts the splints from a block or bolt of wood [etc.]. **1815** BOWLES *Missionary* VII. 128 Last rolled the heavy guns, a sable tier, By Indians drawn, with *matchmen in the rear. **1904** T. WRIGHT in *Daily Chron.* 23 June 3/2 The match-man, with his bundles of great sulphur-tipped matches, whom 'you could smell a mile off'. **1883** *Encycl. Brit.* XV. 625/1 Instead of tinder, *match-paper or touch-paper..and amadou or German tinder..were often used. **1898** *Westm. Gaz.* 19 July 10/1 The Belgian Government has voted a sum of £2,000..to anyone who can compound a marketable *match-paste without the aid of yellow phosphorus. **1799** G. SMITH *Laboratory* I. 41 The *match pipes, the most preferable of which are either iron, lead, or wood,..should be..filled with slow charges. **1929** W. FAULKNER *Sartoris* v. 351 The thick cables along the veranda eaves would be budding into small lilac *match-points. **1856** J. C. ROBINSON *Inventory of Objects Mus. Ornamental Art* 37 Wedgwood Match-pot... Pair of *Match-pots. **1882** *Hamilton Palace Collection Catal.* No. 600 A two-handled Chinese Vase and Cover, of rock crystal, with a matchpot at the side. **1884** *Harper's Mag.* Sept. 581/2 Takes out a cigar and looks in *match-safe. **1832** MISS MITFORD *Village* Ser. V. 7 Some poor wretch, beggar or *match-seller. **1891** C. JAMES *Rom. Rigmarole* 67, I.. tried my hand at *match-selling in the East-end. **1880** M. P. BALE *Woodworking Machinery* xxviii. 252 Machines for cutting *match splints. **1873** *Young Englishwoman* July 357/2 This *match-stand is made of pasteboard, covered with velvet. **1909** *Chambers's Jrnl.* Aug. 506/1 One lot tells us of '4 silver-mounted match-stands..and a quantity of imitation jewellery'. **1791** J. LEARMONT *Poems* 24 The deil made *match-sticks o' his bains. **1901** *Wide World Mag.* VI. 449/2, I saw the vagrant telegraph-posts trailing along the horizon like a row of match-sticks. **1959** I. & P. OPIE *Lore & Lang. Schoolch.* ix. 169 Thin people inspire almost as many names and jokes as fat people..match-stick (sometimes abbreviated to 'matchy'), needles, [etc.]. **1959** HALAS & MANVELL *Technique Film Animation* 14 In France, Emile Cohl began to make his little white match-stick figures jump about against a black background as early as 1908. **1963** *Times* 22 May 3/3 One man mastered it, little Harmer, of the matchstick legs and the cool footballer's brain. **1966** *Guardian* 22 Apr. 6/5 Matchstick men—taught by adults, copied by infants—can be death to child art. **1967** J. WAINWRIGHT *Worms must Wait* i. 5 They were wasted, emaciated men... They were match-stick men... They were men who should have died, but who refused to die. **1799** G. SMITH *Laboratory* I. 40 Put in the *match-thread and stir it about, till it has drawn in all the matter. **1597** GERARDE *Herbal* Table Eng. Names, *Matchwoode, that is Touchwoode. **1838** *Civ. Engineer* I. 396/1 We wish we could see a series of experiments made upon a more enlarged scale than upon these bits of match wood. **1861** *Ann. Reg.* 21 Most of the ships that struck were broken up into match-wood. **1887** *Lady* 20 Jan. 38/3 The huts tumbled into matchwood.

match (mæʃ), *a.* [From the predicative and appositive uses of MATCH *sb.*[1]]

1. That matches; corresponding. *Obs.* exc. *techn.* in certain special collocations (usually hyphened), in most of which *match-* may be interpreted as an attrib. use of the stem of MATCH *v.*[1]: **match dissolve** [cf. DISSOLVE *v.* 7 b] *Cinemat.* (see quots. 1959, 1970); also *matched dissolve*; **match-gearing**, 'two cog-wheels of equal diameter geared together' (Knight *Dict. Mech.* 1875); **match-hook**, 'a double hook or pair of hooks in which one portion forms a *mousing* for the other' (ibid.); **match-joint**, the part by which two corresponding sections of a structure are joined; **matchmark** (see quots.); **match-plane**, either of two planes used in grooving and tonguing boards, one plane being used to form the groove, and the other to form the tongue; **match-plate** (*Founding*), 'a plate upon the opposite sides of which the halves of a pattern are placed correspondingly, to facilitate the operation of molding' (Knight 1875); †**match-term** *Math.*, one of a pair of corresponding terms in a proportion; **match-wheel**, 'a cog-wheel adapted to mesh into or work with another' (Knight 1875). Also MATCH-BOARD.

1483 CAXTON *Cato* E viij b, Thou oughtest to forbere and to favoure in tyme and place hym whyche thou knowest not matche ne lyke to the. **1551** RECORDE *Pathw. Knowl.* II. i, The whole triangles be of one greatnes, and euery angle in the one equall to his matche angle in the other. **1551** —— *Cast. Knowl.* (1556) 207 That arke of the Equinoctiall is equall with his matche arke in the Zodiacke. **1600** T. HILL *Arithm.* II. viii. 119 b, Wherefore each couple of them which so agree and match together in like sirname or quality are.. properly to be called matchtermes..; for in such cases the one couple are the antecedents and the other couple are the consequents. *Ibid.* 128 b, I see..that 2½ ells..is the third number..and that ⅓ of an ell being the matche terme thereof is the first. **1683** MOXON *Mech. Exerc., Printing* x. ¶9 Two Match half-Joynts fastned on the Frame of the Tympan. *Ibid.* xxiv. ¶7 The Frisket must be Cut: which to perform, the Press-man fits the Match-Joynts of the Frisket into the Match-Joynts of the Tympan, and pins them in with the Frisket-pins. **1833** LOUDON *Encycl. Cottage Archit.* §297 The edge of one board grooved, and the adjoining board tongued, with a pair of planes fitting into each other, called match planes. **1881** YOUNG *Every Man his own Mechanic* §395 Match planes are so called because the width of the projection left by one plane matches or tallies exactly with the width or groove cut by the other. **1918** WEBSTER Add., *Match-mark*.., a mark placed on the contiguous separable parts of any device to aid in the proper reassembling of any of those parts. **1953** K. REISZ *Technique Film Editing* II. xi. 172 When diagrams *are* used, it is most important to make exactly clear what they refer to... This is accomplished most simply by the matched dissolve. **1959** W. S. SHARPS *Dict. Cinematogr.* 110/1 *Match dissolve*, the overlapping of two *shots* so that, because of the identical positions of their subjects, only one person or object appears to be seen about the point of overlap. **1962** *Gloss. Terms Glass Industry* (*B.S.I.*) 41 *Match mark*, a line or seam on glassware formed at the join of two mould parts. **1970** W. WAGER *Sledgehammer* (1971) ix. 39 Match dissolve. That's a film term for a standard motion-picture transition, say, from the face of a clock in a police chief's office to the face of another clock in the senator's bedroom.

2. *Comb.*: **match-lined** *a.*, lined with match-board; **match-lining** = MATCH-BOARDING.

1865 *Price List of Joinery* 17 Extra for ½ in. match-lined back [of a cupboard]. *Ibid.* 19 The back lined with ⅝ match lining.

match (mætʃ), *v.*[1] Forms: 4 **mache, macche**, 6 **matche**, 6– **match**. [f. MATCH *sb.*[1]]

1. a. *trans.* To join in marriage (chiefly used with some reference to the fitness or unfitness of the conjunction); to procure a 'match' or matrimonial alliance for (e.g. a son or daughter); to connect (a family) by marriage. Also *rarely*, †to couple, mate (animals). Const. *to* (†*unto*), *with.*

1390 GOWER *Conf.* II. 308 Sche was evele macched And fer from alle loves kinde. **1513** MORE in Grafton *Chron.* (1568) II. 762 Whose bloud..was full vnmeete to be matched with hys. **1530** PALSGR. 633/2, I matche the male and the female togyther of any kynde... And you can matche this bitche you shall have pretye whelpes. **1586** J. HOOKER *Hist. Irel.* in *Holinshed* II. 137/2 They were..by waie of mariages matched and combined with honourable and great houses. **1591** SHAKS. *Two Gent.* III. i. 62, I haue sought To match my friend Sir Thurio, to my daughter. **1612** DAVIES *Why Ireland*, etc. (1747) 218 Whose sole daughter then was matcht to William de Valencia. **1667** MILTON *P.L.* XI. 681 Those ill-mated Marriages..Where good with bad were matcht. **1680** EVELYN *Diary* 6 Sept., He match'd his eldest son to Mrs. Trollop. **1703** J. TIPPER in *Lett. Lit. Men* (Camden) 305, I am heartily glad your dear Sister is so happily match'd to Mr. Stevens. **1731** FIELDING *Grub St. Op.* I. ii, Now I rely on you to match them up to one another. **1754** FOOTE *Knights* II. Wks. 1799 I. 85 Tim has fallen in love with a young woman.., and 'tis partly to

prevent bad consequences, that I am..so hasty to match him. **1842** TENNYSON *Ulysses* 3 An idle king..Match'd with an aged wife. **1849** MARRYAT *Valerie* xi. II. 140 Try if you can match her with a Duke. **1878** SIMPSON *Sch. Shaks.* I. 25 Henry II. proposed to match him with some great heiress.

†**b.** *refl. Obs.*

1362 LANGL. *P. Pl.* A. x. 193 Bote maydens and maydens maccheth ou ysamme [**1377** B. ix. 173 macche ȝow togideres]. **1581** PETTIE *Guazzo's Civ. Conv.* II. (1586) 89 Povertie bringeth.., that he is sometime driven to match himselfe in marriage with some woman of base parentage.

c. *intr.* for *refl.* To ally oneself in marriage. Const. *with.* Now *rare* exc. *dial.* † *to match into* (a family): to become connected by marriage with. †Also *rarely* of animals: To pair.

1568 GRAFTON *Chron.* II. 670 Not to be vnworthy to matche in matrimonie, with the greatest Prince of the worlde. **1586** B. YOUNG *Guazzo's Civ. Conv.* IV. 226 b, It is (saide Lord Iohn) a greate griefe of the minde, and heart breaking, to match with a foolishe Woman. **1599** SHAKS. *Much Ado* II. i. 68 Truly I hold it a sinne to match in my kinred. **1611** COTGR., *S'Apparier*, to couple, or match; as birds doe in the Spring. **1620** GATAKER *Mariage Praier* 8 They shall neuer haue my blessing..if they match without my consent. **1647** SPRIGGE *Anglia Rediv.* I. ii. 8 He matched into a most noble and martial family. **1680** DRYDEN *Span. Fryar* IV. ii. 63 Let Tygers match with Hinds, and Wolfs with Sheep. **1766** GOLDSM. *Vic. W.* iii, If he had birth and fortune to entitle him to match into such a family as ours. **1820** HAZLITT *Lect. Dram. Lit.* 348 A young woman..who would not think of matching with a fellow of low birth. **1844** MAIDMENT *Spottiswoode Misc.* I. 5 This marks rather that the Spotwoods have matched with the Gordons.

†**2. a.** *trans.* To associate, join in companionship or co-operation (persons or things); to put together so as to form a pair or set *with* (another person or thing). *Obs.* (Cf. sense 5.)

c **1470** *Gol. & Gaw.* 1159 Quhen thai war machit at mete, the mare and the myn. **1534** MORE *Comf. agst. Trib.* II. Wks. 1209/1 When god hath by suche chaunce sent hym to me, and there once matched me with him, I recken my self surely charged with him, tyl [etc.]. **1575–85** ABP. SANDYS *Serm.* iii. 47 Matching alwaies with iustice mercie. **1588** SHAKS. *L.L.L.* II. i. 49 A sharp wit match'd with too blunt a Will. **1599** —— *Much Ado* II. i. 111 God match me with a good dauncer. **1599** H. HOLLAND *Wks. R. Greenham* 1 Some busie themselues in Church-discipline, and are slender sighted in their priuie corruptions:..but it is good to match both together. **1605** BACON *Adv. Learn.* I. vii. §6 [Adrian] having his [Christ's] picture in his gallerie matched with Apollonius. **1645** USSHER *Body Div.* (1647) 68 It was matched with many infirmities and passions.

†**b.** *refl.* To make an agreement *with. Obs.*

13.. *E.E. Allit. P.* C. 99 Maches hym with þe maryneres, makes her paye, For to towe hym in-to tarce.

3. a. To encounter as an adversary. Also (now always), to encounter with equal power, prove a match for.

13.. *Gaw. & Gr. Knt.* 282 Here is no mon me to mach. *c* **1400** *Destr. Troy* 7042 Manly he macchit hom with his mayn strokes. *c* **1440** *York Myst.* xxx. 199 Oure meyne with myght At mydnyght hym mached. **1470–85** MALORY *Arthur* X. viii. 426 Ye are not able to matche a good knyght. **1587** HARRISON *England* II. iii. (1877) I. 73 The townesmen of both [Oxford and Cambridge] are glad when they may match and annoie the students. **1590** SHAKS. *Mids. N.* III. ii. 305 You perhaps may thinke, Because she is something lower then my selfe, That I can match her. **1642** ROGERS *Naaman* 39 Tell me, if God had not matched thee, who could? **1666** DRYDEN *Ann. Mirab.* 190 Sharp remembrance on the English part And shame of being matched by such a foe Rouse conscious virtue up in every heart. **1856** FROUDE *Hist. Eng.* (1858) I. ii. 173 No knight in England could match him in the tournament except the Duke of Suffolk.

†**b.** *intr.* To meet in combat, to fight (*with*). *Obs.*

a **1400–50** *Alexander* 3607 To mache with sike a multitude of men & of bestis. *c* **1400** *Destr. Troy* 9678 Thus macchit þose men till the merke night. *c* **1470** HENRY *Wallace* v. 42 Quhen xl macht [*v.r.* matchit] agayne thre hundyr men. **1559–66** *Wodrow Soc. Misc.* (1844) 69 The Congregation and the Frenchmen were often assembled, and were neare matching. **1567** MAPLET *Gr. Forest* 86 The Falcon is a bird of haughtie stomacke matching with birdes a great deale bigger and mightier then him selfe. **1595** SHAKS. *John* II. i. 330 Strength matcht with strength, and power confronted power.

4. *trans.* To array or place in opposition or conflict *with*; to 'pit' (a person or thing) *against* another. Chiefly *refl.* and *pass.* Occas. const. †*to*, †*on*.

?*a* **1400** *Morte Arth.* 1533 Þay hafe bene machede to daye with mene of þe marchez. *c* **1400** *Destr. Troy* 8288 He macchit hym to Menelay. **15..** *Scotish Fielde* 197 On who was thou mached? **1523** LD. BERNERS *Froiss.* (1812) I. cxxx. 158 He is hardely matched, wherfore he hathe nede of your ayde. **1578** *Chr. Prayers* 118 b, The sinfulnes that we haue receaued from our first Parents, hath matched the rebellious flesh against..the mind. **1667** MILTON *P.L.* VI. 631 Eternal might To match with thir inventions they presum'd So easie. **1781** COWPER *Retirement* 580 The estate his sires had owned in ancient years Was quickly distanced, matched against a peer's. **1840** DE QUINCEY *Style* I. Wks. 1862 X. 161 What if a man should match such a bauble against the Pantheon? **1855** KINGSLEY *Heroes* v. ii. (1868) 156 Let them match their song against mine. **1903** *Expositor* Aug. 113 They had to match themselves against the wily Greek or Syrian trader.

5. a. To pair or assort (persons or things) with a view to fitness or equality; to arrange in a suitable or equal pair or set; to provide with an adversary or competitor of equal power. Often in *passive* with adv., as *to be well, ill matched.*

1530 PALSGR. 633/2, I matche one with a felowe, I set one to another that be equall of power and strength. **1590** SHAKS. *Mids. N.* IV. i. 120 My hounds are bred out of the Spartan kinde,..Slow in pursuit, but match'd in mouth like bels. *a* **1645** A. STAFFORD *Fem. Glory* (1869) p. xcix, Never Prince and Church-man were better matcht then theise two. **1696** R. H. *Sch. Recreat.* 146 Match your Cock carefully. **1741** MIDDLETON *Cicero* II. x. 392 Cicero all the while, like a master of Gladiators, matching us and ordering the Combat. **1842** MISS MITFORD in L'Estrange *Life* (1870) III. ix. 142 In point of wearisome insipidity Sir Robert and Lord John are well matched one against the other. **1859** DARWIN *Orig. Spec.* i. (1873) 25 The savages in South Africa match their draught cattle by colour. **1874** SAYCE *Compar. Philol.* v. 181 Compatibility of existence on the part of two races depends upon their being more or less nearly matched in culture. **1883** FROUDE *Short Stud.* IV. I. iii. 27 The two great antagonists..were more fairly matched than Becket perhaps expected to find them.

b. To proportion, make to correspond *to* or *with.*

1680 EARL ROSCOM. *Horace's Art Poetry* 4 Let Poets match their Subject to their strength. **1708** ROWE *Roy. Convert* III. i. 29 Mine [*sc.* my hopes] have been still Match'd with my Birth. **1861** WHITTIER *Our River* 71 To match our spirits to our day And make a joy of duty. *a* **1888** M. ARNOLD *Thekla's Answ.* v, God doth match His gifts to man's believing.

c. 'To furnish with a tongue and a groove, at the edges; as to match boards' (Webster 1897).

1833 etc. [see MATCHED *ppl. a.* 2].

d. *Electr.* To equalize (two coupled impedances) so as to bring about the maximum transfer of power from one to the other; to make (a device) equal in effective impedance *to.*

1929 E. MALLETT *Telegr. & Telephony* vii. 162 Where the impedances cannot be matched transformers may be introduced to give the same effect. **1931** *Proc. IRE* XIX. 725 At high frequencies a transformer consisting of primary, secondary and mutual inductances cannot be constructed to match a generator effectively to a resistive load. **1938** Q. P. HARNWELL *Princ. Electr. & Electromagn.* iv. 114 When resistances are matched, half the power developed is delivered to the load and half is lost in the source. **1959** R. L. SHRADER *Electronic Communication* xiii. 371 The requirement is to match a 4-ohm speaker to a 4,000-ohm power tube. **1966** R. C. HANSEN *Microwave Scanning Antennas* III. ii. 186 The sinuous feed and couplers.. terminated in radiating elements which are matched to free space.

6. a. To place in competition *with*; to compare in respect of superiority. (Cf. sense 4.)

1581 MULCASTER *Positions* xxxix. (1887) 192 If in comparison ye match a toward priuate teacher with a weake publike maister. **1592** SHAKS. *Rom. & Jul.* II. Prol. 4 That faire..With tender Iuliet matcht, is now not faire. *a* **1649** DRUMM. OF HAWTH. *Conversat. betw. B. J. & W. D.* Wks. (1711) 226 The earl of Surrey, sir Thomas Wyat (whom, because of their antiquity, I will not match with our better times). **1717** POPE *Ep. to Jervas* 36 Each heav'nly piece unwearied we compare, Match Raphael's grace with thy lov'd Guido's air. **1791** COWPER *Iliad* IV. 478 Their glory then, match never more with ours. **1820** SHELLEY *Skylark* 68 Chorus Hymenæal, Or triumphal chaunt, Matched with thine would be all But an empty vaunt. **1867** HOWELLS *Ital. Journ.* iii. 29, I saw the custodian had another relic..which he was not ashamed to match with the manuscript in my interest.

†**b.** To compare in respect of similarity; to examine the likeness or difference of. *Obs. rare.*

a **1649** DRUMM. OF HAWTH. *Hist. Jas. V*, Wks (1711) 103 By matching the faces of one of those strangers with a portrait she had of King James.

†**7.** To regard, treat, or speak of as equal. *Obs.*

1580 SIDNEY *Ps.* xxvi. v, Sweete Lord, write not my soule Within the sinner's rowle: Nor my life's cause match with blood seekers case. **1595** J. KING *Queens Day Serm.* in *Jonas*, etc. (1618) 702 Whensoeuer afterwards, there was taken vppe any great lamentation, it was sampled and matched with that of Hadadrimmon, in the field of Megiddo. **1605** WILLET *Hexapla Gen.* 468 This is great presumption..to match Gods arke and Iosephs coffin together. **1606** SHAKS. *Tr. & Cr.* I. iii. 194 To match vs in comparisons with durt, To weaken and discredit our exposure.

8. a. To be equal to, to equal; to resemble sufficiently to be suitably coupled with; to correspond to, be the 'match' or counterpart of. Also *absol.* of two or more things: To be mutually equal; to be sufficiently similar to be suitably coupled together.

1592 SHAKS. *Ven. & Ad.* 1140 All loues pleasure shall not match his wo. **1603** OWEN *Pembrokeshire* iv. (1892) 40 In shorte tyme they are like to match the other inhabitaunts in nomber. **1632** LITHGOW *Trav.* III. 81 These fiue Cities are so strong, that..I neuer saw them matched. **1643** SIR T. BROWNE *Relig. Med.* I. §44 All the valiant acts of Curtius, Scevola, or Codrus, do not parallel or match that one of Job. **1663** BUTLER *Hud.* I. i. 190 For his religion, it was fit To match his learning and his wit. **1781** COWPER *Charity* 118 He..Imports what others have invented well, And stirs his own to match them or excel. **1819** SHELLEY *Cenci* III. ii. 71 Mariner's hate Matches Olimpio's. **1853** C. BRONTE *Villette* xxxvi, Life is so constructed that the event does not, cannot, will not, match the expectation. **1884** *Manch. Exam.* 17 May 4/8 There exists in no Continental country anything that can match the City and Guilds' Institute. *a* **1905** *Mod.* The colour of the carpet does not match the wallpaper. These patterns do not match.

b. *intr.* To be equal *with*; to be suitably coupled *with*; to correspond, be suitable *to.* Also (*rarely*), to fit or 'dovetail' *into.* ***to match up to***: to equal; to be comparable with.

1567 MAPLET *Gr. Forest* 32 b, But herein good heed must be taken, least we match and march with the greeke Sophister. **1577** B. GOOGE *Heresbach's Husb.* I. (1586) 39 b, It groweth..to suche a heyght, that it matcheth with indifferent Trees. **1599** SHAKS. *Hen. V*, II. iv. 130 To that end, as matching to his Youth and Vanitie, I did present him with the Paris-Balls. **1866** DK. ARGYLL *Reign Law* vii. (1871) 343 Other minds were working at the same time whose labours were to match with a curious fittingness into his. **1958** *Times* 18 Sept. 13/3 But Blanche can match up to Emily, indeed she surpasses her in the end. **1958** *Listener* 13 Nov. 800/2 This musical image..cannot match up to the breadth and immediacy of 'Mars'. **1964** M. GOWING *Britain & Atomic Energy* v. 163 Britain's manpower resources did not match up to her programmes.

c. ***to match*** (used quasi-adv. or quasi-adj. after a sb.): corresponding in number, size, style, etc. with what has been mentioned.

1838 DICKENS *O. Twist* xxxiii, A tall gentleman in..drab breeches and boots with tops to match. **1850** TENNYSON *In Mem.* i, Who shall so forecast the years And find in loss a gain to match? **1857** G. A. LAWRENCE *Guy Liv.* iii. 21 After twelve pipes over-night with gin-and-water to match. **1891** *Leeds Mercury* 27 Apr. 4/7 Theresa..was attired in wine-coloured velvet, and wore a jet bonnet, trimmed with velvet to match.

9. *trans.* To furnish with a match.

a. To find, procure, or produce an equal to.

1596 J. NORDEN *Progr. Pietie* (1847) 114 Some one of these his subtle sects in shew meeteth, and as it were matcheth every godly endeavour and sincere course that the children of God do practise. **1600** J. PORY tr. *Leo's Africa* Introd. 56 Excellent wines, and sugars which cannot be matched. **1687** A. LOVELL tr. *Thevenot's Trav.* I. 123 The body of the Pillar is of one entire piece of Garnet, so high, that the world cannot match it. **1773** JOHNSON 30 Apr. in *Boswell*, I can match his nonsense. **1842** TENNYSON *Gardener's Dau.* 31 Go and see The Gardener's daughter; trust me, after that, You scarce can fail to match his masterpiece. **1886** CONSTANCE F. WOOLSON *E. Angels* i. 15 To match it [the climate] one must seek the Madeira Islands or Algiers.

b. To fit or supply with a suitable addition or counterpart; to find, select, or obtain something sufficiently similar to or accordant with (a colour, pattern, an article of dress, etc.).

1600 SHAKS. *A.Y.L.* I. ii. 127, I could match this beginning with an old tale. **1724** SWIFT *Use of Irish Manuf.* Wks. 1755 V. II. 3 There may be room enough to employ their wit and fancy in chusing and matching patterns and colours. **1758** JOHNSON *Idler* No. 16 ¶5 Every maid.. matched her gown at Mr. Drugget's. **1770** FOOTE *Lame Lover* I. 20, [I] promised to..match a coach-horse for Brigadier Whip. **1861** WHYTE MELVILLE *Good for Nothing* I. xi. 132 Can you match me this piece of yellow silk? **1881** J. HAWTHORNE *Fort. Fool* I. xxxiv, As if it were a question of matching knitting-yarns.

c. To compare so as to select one suitable *to.*

1718 POPE *Let.* 1 Sept. in *Lady M. W. Montagu's Lett.* (1861) I. 438 John was now matching several kinds of poppies and field flowers to her complexion, to make her a present of knots for the day.

†**10.** To procure as a match. *Obs. rare*$^{-1}$.

1596 SHAKS. *Merch. V.* III. i. 81 Here comes another of the Tribe, a third cannot be matcht, vnlesse the diuell himselfe turne Iew.

match (mætʃ), *v.*² [f. MATCH *sb.*² Cf. F. *mécher.*] *trans.* To fumigate (wines or liquors, or casks) by burning sulphur matches; now chiefly in *Cider-making.* Hence '**matching** *vbl. sb.*

1703 *Art & Myst. Vintners* 28 Stum is nothing else but pure Wine kept from fretting by often racking and matching it in clean Vessels. **1753** CHAMBERS *Cycl. Supp.*, *Matching*, in the wine trade, the preparing vessels to preserve wines and other liquors, without their growing sour or vapid. **1832** *Trans Prov. Med. & Surg. Assoc.* VI. II. 200 The sweetness of the cider prepared for exportation is preserved by a process..which..is known by the term 'Matching'. **1864** *Jrnl. R. Agric. Soc.* XXV. I. 90 Most of the cider that is 'matched' in this way has a peculiar taste.

matchable ('mætʃəb(ə)l), *a.* [f. MATCH *v.*¹ + -ABLE.]

1. That can be matched, equalled, or rivalled.

a **1568** ASCHAM *Scholem.* I. (Arb.) 59 So manie notable Capitaines in warre for worthinesse, wisdome and learning, as be scarse matchable no not in the state of Rome. **1591** SPENSER *Ruins of Time* 89 To tell my forces matchable to none, Were but lost labour. **1624** HEYWOOD *Gunaik.* III. 143 A Lady scarce matchable before her time or since. **1678** *Life Black Prince* in *Harl. Misc.* (1809) III. 153 He was a prince so full of virtues as were scarce matchable by others.

†**2.** Comparable; equal; similar, analogous. Const. *to*, *with. Obs.*

1572 J. JONES *Bathes of Bath* II. 10 b, Neyther be such vapours, or dashinges, matchable to fyre in heate. *a* **1592** *Selimus* 1864 Aga, thy grief is matchable to his. **1608** DOD & CLEAVER *Expos. Prov.* xi–xii. 190 Many great pibbles are not matchable in worth with one pearle which is farre lesse then they are. **1653** GATAKER *Vind. Annot. Jer.* 149 The War.. was in divers respects not matchable onely unto, but even greater then any that had gone before it. **1695** WOODWARD *Nat. Hist. Earth* (1723) 28 [Shells] not matchable with any upon our Shores.

†**3.** Suitable, well suited, accordant. *Obs.*

1611 MARKHAM *Countr. Content.* I. xix. (1668) 81 They be ever most matchable, strong, nimble, and ready for your pleasure. **1614** D. DYKE *Myst. Selfe-Deceiuing* (1630) 297 The party affected hath pietie matchable both to person and portion. **1815** *Zeluca* III. 162 Now if you had married such a superior character as Miss Emcotts, so truly matchable with you.

Hence '**matchableness**, †'**matchably** *adv.*

1611 COTGR., *Equalite*, equalitie, euenness, matchablenesse. *Esgallement*, equally, euenly, alike, matchably. *a* **1637** B. JONSON *Eng. Gram.* Pref. 9 We shew the Copie of it, and Matchablenesse, with other tongues. **1857** C. M. YONGE *Let.* 1 Oct. in C. Coleridge *C. M. Yonge* (1903) viii. 214 A most perfect marriage..as to the matchableness of the two people.

match-board ('mætʃbɔəd), *sb. Joinery.* [f. MATCH *a.*; cf. MATCH *v.*[1]] A board which has a tongue cut along one edge and a groove in the opposite edge, so as to admit of being fitted into other similar boards to form one piece with them. Also *collect.* = *match-boarding.*

1858 SIMMONDS *Dict. Trade, Match-boards*, a kind of plank used for flooring. **1883** *Daily News* 10 Sept. 2/1 This building..is described as 'encircled by match-boards nailed to posts supporting the roof'. **18..** *Med. News* LII. 670 (Cent.) The walls..consist partly of brick piers and partly of corrugated iron lined by felt and matchboard.

Hence **'match-board** *v. trans.*, to cover or supply with match-boards; **'match-boarded** *a.*, having or composed of match-boards; **'match-boarding**, match-boards fitted together to form a material for lining walls, forming partitions or light structures such as poultry-houses, etc.

1865 *Price List of Joinery* 28 Match Boarding..forming Partitions in Bedrooms. **1882** *Garden* 18 Mar. 188/1 The house is..cased inside with match boarding. **1889** J. K. JEROME *Three Men in Boat* 81 It was expensive work. Had to match-board it all over first. **1894** *Westm. Gaz.* 16 July 8/1 What with the match-boarded character of the house and the uprush of draught by the staircase, the chances of escape would have been small indeed. **1903** *Longm. Mag.* June 126 We discovered our quarters in a bare match-boarded room with a flapping canvas ceiling.

'match-cloth. [? f. *match-* in MATCHCOAT.]

1855 OGILVIE *Suppl., Match-cloth*, a coarse woollen cloth for the Indian trade [American].

matchcoat ('mætʃkəʊt). *Obs.* exc. *Hist.* Also 7 **matchco, mach-cot,** 9 **matchicoat.** [Orig. *matchco*, prob. an American Indian word: cf. Odjibwa *matchigode* 'petticoat, woman's dress' (Baraga); afterwards corrupted by popular etymology, as if f. MATCH *sb.*[1] or *v.*[1] + COAT *sb.*]

a. A kind of mantle formerly worn by American Indians, originally made of fur skins, and afterwards of match-cloth. **b.** The material out of which matchcoats were made.

1642 in *Archives of Maryland* (1887) IV. 94, 2 rackoone matchcos and 15. armes length of ronoke. **1661** *Stat. Virginia* (1823) II. 36 He paying..for the use of those Indians thirty Matchcoats of two yards a peice. **1685** *Pennsylv. Archives* I. 94 Twenty Gunns Twenty fathom Matchcoat [etc.]. **1698** G. THOMAS *Pensilvania* 10, I..have very good Shot, with red and blue Mach-cots. **1705** BEVERLEY *Virginia* III. i. §3 (1722) 142 The proper Indian Match-coat, which is made of Skins, drest with the Fur on, sowed together... Fig. 2 wears the Duffield Match-coat, bought of the English. **1788** *New Lond. Mag.* 115 A large mantle or match-coat, thrown over all, compleats their dress. **1814** *Sporting Mag.* XLIV. 280 A matchicoat and leggins red.

matchcole, matchecold: see MACHECOLE *v.*

matched (mætʃt), *ppl. a.* [f. MATCH *v.*[1] + -ED.]

1. Having a match or equal. Chiefly in *ill-*, *well-matched*, q.v.

2. Of boards: Furnished with a tongue on one edge and a groove on the other. †*matched joint* = 'match-joint' (MATCH *a.* 1). Also *Comb.*, **matched-boarding, -lined** *a.* = *match-boarding, -lined.*

1688 R. HOLME *Armoury* III. 114/1 The several Parts of a [Printing] Press. The Matcht Joynt, is the Joynt or Hing fastned to the Timpan and hinder Raile of the Coffin. **1833** LOUDON *Encycl. Cottage Archit.* §297 Five-eighth-inch deal matched (the edge of one board grooved, and the adjoining board tongued..) and beaded boarding. **1857-9** TARBUCK *Encycl. Carpentry & Joinery* 208 In Fig. 10 the edges are shot;..in Fig. 12 matched. **1865** *Price List of Joinery* 33, 6.6¾ Matched-lined enclosure to stairs. **1873** TARN *Tredgold's Carpentry* 242 Matched-boarding.

3. ***matched orders***: the name given to systems of manipulation on the Stock Exchange, which involve artificial treatment of orders to buy and sell. Also occas. *sing.* Also called *matching orders.* orig. *U.S.*

1903 S. S. PRATT *Work of Wall St.* 146 The Syndicate may be washing sales by matched orders through curb brokers in order to market watered stock. **1908** *Westm. Gaz.* 26 Aug. 2/2 An order to buy is given to one broker and an order to sell to another, and an arrangement is made that the two brokers shall only deal with one another... The opportunity for market manipulation is obvious, and 'matched orders' have led to grave scandals. **1920** A. C. PIGOU *Econ. of Welfare* II. vi. 178 It should be observed that the device of 'matched orders' may be made difficult by a rule forbidding offers and bids for large amounts of stock on the terms 'all or none'. **1930** J. E. MEEKER *Work of Stock Exchange* (rev. ed.) xvi. 455 A..subtler evil consists of 'matching orders'... Instances where there is danger of matched orders..deserve brief explanation. **1941** DICE & EITEMAN *Stock Market* (ed. 2) 467 When a trader gives one broker orders to buy a given stock and another orders to sell a like amount of stock in a manner to either advance or depress the price artificially, such a trader is said to be giving matched orders. **1951** G. L. LEFFLER *Stock Market* xx. 327 Artificial market activity was accomplished..through matched orders and..without matched orders... Matched orders were in violation of state law and the rules of the New York Stock Exchange... The same effect as the matched order could be obtained without its actual use. **1964** P. WYCKOFF *Dict. Stock Market Terms* 163 *Matched orders.* 1. Orders to buy or sell a particular stock which are placed simultaneously with different brokers by the same person... 2. Buy and sell orders matched legitimately by the specialist in a stock in order to arrange an opening price as closely as possible to the previous close.

4. Designed to match in colour, style, etc.; matching.

1972 A. ROUDYBUSH *Sybaritic Death* (1974) vii. 70 Clare's status-conscious matched luggage. **1974** P. DE VRIES *Glory of Hummingbird* iii. 49 A matched set of luggage. **1975** P. G. WINSLOW *Death of Angel* vi. 142 He presented her with a set of matched luggage..for the weekends.

matcher ('mætʃə(r)). [f. MATCH *v.*[1] + -ER[1].]

1. One who matches, in senses of the vb.

1611 COTGR., *Marieur*, a matcher, a marier. **1628** FORD *Lovers Mel.* I. ii, A meere matcher of colours. **1682** H. MORE *Annot. Glanvill's Lux O.* 7 It would argue the wise and just God a very unequal Matcher of innocent Souls with brutish Bodies. **1896** *Daily News* 4 Jan. 5/3 An 'assortiseur', or matcher of coloured textiles.

2. 'A matching-machine' (Webster 1897). ***matcher-head***: 'the head in a planing machine which carries the cutting tool' (Knight *Dict. Mech.* Suppl. 1884).

matchet, var. form of MACHETE.

Matchevil(l)ian, obs. ff. MACHIAVELLIAN.

1632 LITHGOW *Trav.* I. 4 Simonaicall Matcheuilians.

Matchia-, Matchievillian: see MACHIA-.

matchiat, obs. form of MACHETE.

matchicoat: see MATCHCOAT.

matchination: see MACHINATION.

matching ('mætʃɪŋ), *vbl. sb.*[1] [f. MATCH *v.*[1] + -ING[1].]

1. The action of the vb. MATCH in various senses.

1562 J. HEYWOOD *Prov. & Epigr.* (1867) 180 Great patchyng, small matchyng. **1625** MANDEVILLE in *Buccleuch MSS.* (Hist. MSS. Comm.) I. 262 He propounded to me the matching with Warwick for my son. **1774** GOLDSM. *Nat. Hist.* (1776) III. 293 The greatest pains had been taken with these to enlarge the breed, both by food and matching. **1873** E. SPON *Workshop Receipts* Ser. I. 414/2 Matching is to bring different pieces of timber, in an article of furniture, to a responsive tone of colour. **1874** *Spons' Dict. Engin.* 3097 A planing machine for moulding and matching. **1889** *Athenæum* 18 May 623/2 There is like risk of bad matching when the undertaking is a poem.

2. 'A quality of wool in the best part of the fleece' (Bowman *Struct. Wool* 1885, p. 356).

1881 *Daily News* 22 Aug. 3/6 About 1,200 packs of English fleeces, matchings, skin, and other wools.

3. *attrib.*, as ***matching shop*** (nonce-wd.); **matching-machine**, a machine which tongues and grooves the respective edges of a board; **matching-plane** = *match-plane* (Knight *Dict. Mech.* 1875).

1803 tr. *P. Le Brun's Mons. Botte* I. 179 She couples ruined young men to rich widows..; and she runs away with all the business from the offices that you see at the corner of every street, called *matching shops.* **1874** *Spons' Dict. Engin.* 3097 A planing and matching machine.

matching, *vbl. sb.*[2]: see MATCH *v.*[2]

matching ('mætʃɪŋ), *ppl. a.* [f. MATCH *v.*[1] + -ING[2].] That matches; corresponding; 'to match'.

1630 *R. Johnson's Kingd. & Commw.* 97 If you will let loose the Queene of Cities, as they terme Paris, to looke bigge and angerly upon us, our London can affront her with a matching countenance. **1898** *Westm. Gaz.* 11 June 1/3 The good plain 'family' cook, with matching morals.

matchless ('mætʃlɪs), *a.* [f. MATCH *sb.*[1] + -LESS.]

1. Having no match, without an equal, peerless.

1530 PALSGR. 839/1 Matche lesse, *non pareil.* **1590** GREENE *Never too late* (1600) 68 Then should..the furrowes in my face be numberlesse, as the griefes of my hart are matchlesse. **1631** GOUGE *God's Arrows* III. §94. 360 They..plotted the matchlesse, mercilesse, devilish, and damnable gun-powder-treason. **1663** GERBIER *Counsel* a 5, The matchlesse capacity of your Highnesse. **1762-71** H. WALPOLE *Vertue's Anecd. Paint.* (1786) I. 166, I have also a matchless portrait of the king. **1871** H. AINSWORTH *Tower Hill* I. iii, There she stood before him, in all her matchless beauty. **1874** GREEN *Short Hist.* vii. §3. 374 Her matchless activity used the year to good purpose.

b. Used as *adv.*

1871 JOAQUIN MILLER *Songs Italy* (1878) 90 And men did turn and marvel so And men did say how matchless fair!

†**2.** That are not a match or pair. *Obs.*

1596 SPENSER *F.Q.* IV. i. 28 With matchlesse eares deformed and distort.

†**3.** Unmarried. (In quot. *punningly.*) *Obs.*

a **1652** BROME *Damoiselle* I. i, A matchlesse Knight Indeed, and shall be matchlesse still for me.

Hence **'matchlessly** *adv.*, in a matchless manner or degree (Bailey, fol. 1736); **'matchlessness**, the state of being matchless (Bailey vol. II. 1727).

1818 J. FERNIE *Serm.* 379 The matchlessly great and happy, holy and just God. **1884** *Cyclist's Tour. Cl. Monthly Gaz.* Mar. 78/2 A castle so matchlessly situated.

†**'matchlike,** *adv. Obs. rare*$^{-1}$. [f. MATCH *sb.*[1] + -LIKE.] In pairs.

1582 STANYHURST *Æneis* III. (Arb.) 87 Horses..Al yoked, and matchlyke teamed with common agreement.

matchlock ('mætʃlɒk). [f. MATCH *sb.*[2] + LOCK *sb.*[2]]

1. A gun lock in which slow-match is placed for igniting the powder. **b.** *attrib.*: **matchlock musket** = 2.

1698 FRYER *Acc. E. India & P.* 139 The Infantry [consists] of Gentues, with Match-Lock Muskets. **1727-52** CHAMBERS *Cycl.* s.v. *Carabine*, The carabine..was formerly made with a match-lock, but of late only with a flint-lock. **1786** GROSE *Anc. Armour & Weapons* 64 Musquets were fired with match locks. *a* **1854** H. REED *Lect. Brit. Poets* viii. (1857) 289 The clumsy matchlock musket of olden time. **1859** *All Year Round* No. 4. 87 The hand guns were used with a matchlock till the pyrites wheel lock was invented.

2. A musket having a matchlock.

1698 FRYER *Acc. E. India & P.* 99 Matchlocks, Swords, and Javelins. **1795** ANDERSON *Brit. Emb. China* 71 Others are armed with match-locks of a very rusty appearance. **1875** MAINE *Hist. Inst.* x. 290 The battle was waged out of Court with sword and matchlock.

b. *attrib.*: **matchlock-man**, a soldier armed with a matchlock.

1782 *Hist. Europe* in *Ann. Reg.* (1783) 32/1 No less than 1,800 were match-lock-men. **1893** FORBES-MITCHELL *Remin. Gt. Mutiny* 254 Some seven or eight hundred matchlock-men opened fire on them.

Hence **'matchlocked** *a.*, having matchlocks, armed with matchlocks.

1871 FORSYTH *Highl. India* 296 A whole posse of matchlocked shikáris.

'match-make, *v. rare.* [Back-formation from MATCH-MAKER[1] or -MAKING[1].] *intr.* To plot or contrive to bring about a marriage.

1865 *Cornh. Mag.* Dec. 670, I am the last person in the world to match-make. **1902** BARNES-GRUNDY *Thames Camp* 262 It..will be a lesson to me not to match-make again.

'match-maker[1]. [f. MATCH *sb.*[1] + MAKER.]

1. One who brings about or negotiates a match or marriage; usually, one who is addicted to scheming to bring about marriages.

a **1639** W. WHATELEY *Prototypes* I. xi. (1640) 102 Pray to God to give a wife or husband to your sonne and daughter, and make piety and vertue the chiefe match-makers. **1678** BUTLER *Hud.* III. i. 420 Who..would have hir'd him and his imps, To be your match-makers and pimps. **1771** SMOLLETT *Humph. Cl.* Let. i. 14 June, Perhaps the match-maker is to have a valuable consideration in the way of brokerage. **1855** MACAULAY *Hist. Eng.* xvi. III. 724 Clarendon assumed the character of a matchmaker. **1881** E. J. WORBOISE *Sissie* xi, Mrs. Williams..was frequently accused of being 'a match-maker', and bent on marrying her daughters brilliantly.

2. *Sporting.* One who enters into a match; one who arranges a match.

a **1704** T. BROWN *Table Talk* in *Collect. Poems* 123 Horse-coursers and Matchmakers make no Conscience of Cheating. **1893** *Baily's Mag.* Oct. 273/2 A match that called forth many encomiums on the match-makers.

'match-maker[2]. [f. MATCH *sb.*[2] + MAKER.]

1. One who makes match for guns.

1643 [ANGIER] *Lanc. Vall. Achor* 9 He that could finde so many Souldiers when there was none, was not to seeke for one Match-maker in time of need. **1644** PRYNNE & WALKER *Fiennes's Trial* App. 21 They had a Match-maker, a Bullet-maker in the Castle. **1723** *Lond. Gaz.* No. 6126/4 John Withers, of Black-Heath,..Matchmaker.

2. One who makes lucifer matches.

1851 *Knight's Cycl. Industry* 1182 These splints are sold by the hogshead to the lucifer match makers. **1893** *Dict. Nat. Biog.* XXXIV. 200 The match-makers of the East-end of London took fright at a suggestion which might prove fatal to their trade.

'match-making, *vbl. sb.*[1] [f. MATCH *sb.*[1]]

1. The action or practice of scheming or contriving to bring about a marriage.

1821 MISS MITFORD in L'Estrange *Life* II. vi. 125 Mrs. Dickinson has had great success in match-making lately. **1858** R. S. SURTEES *Ask Mamma* ix. 31 As well try to restrain a cat from mousing as a woman from match-making. **1887** *Poor Nellie* (1888) 82 Perfect matchmaking requires experience and practice.

attrib. **1823** 'JON BEE' *Slang* s.v., Jew-King opened a match-making office in Old Bond-street, about 1797. **1881** H. JAMES *Portr. Lady* xlix, There were people who had the matchmaking passion.

2. *Racing.* The action of arranging a match.

1812 *Sporting Mag.* XL. 282 Within fourteen days from the match-making he was backed to win.

'match-making, *vbl. sb.*[2] [f. MATCH *sb.*[2]] The process or trade of making lucifer matches.

1875 KNIGHT *Dict. Mech.* 1410/1 *Match-making Machine.* **1892** *Pall Mall G.* 16 May 7/1 Match-making has been the most successful of all the industries instituted in Japan in imitation of those existing abroad. **1898** *Cath. Bk. Notes* June 171 The recent shocking revelations with regard to the match-making and lead-glazing trades.

'match-making, *ppl. a.* [f. MATCH *sb.*[1]] Given to attempts to bring about marriages.

1700 CONGREVE *Way of World* III. xviii, Foible's a bawd, an arrant, rank, matchmaking bawd. **1886** RUSKIN *Præterita* I. v. 167 The entirely best-matched pair I have yet seen in this match-making world and dispensation.

matchy ('mætʃɪ), *a. dial.* [f. MATCH *sb.*[1] + -Y.] Suited to form a match.

1868 *Daily News* 8 Dec., Three finer, and more matchy sheep are rarely found. **1888** *Jackson's Oxford Jrnl.* 1 Sept. 3/3 They [five show ewes] were very matchy and good looking.

mate (meɪt), *sb.*[1] *Chess.* Forms: 4 **mat**, 5 **maat**, 5– **mate**. [ME. *mat*, a. OF. *mat* in *eschec mat* CHECKMATE *sb.*] The state of the king when he is in check and cannot move out of it (involving the loss of the game to the player whose king is so placed): = CHECKMATE. Also, the move by which the king is checkmated. Often in figurative contexts, with the sense of 'total defeat'. ***to give (the) mate (to)***: to checkmate. †***to take the mate***: to be checkmated.

c **1330** *Arth. & Merl.* 9346 (Kölbing) Naciens..& ek Herui .VI. heþen kinges driuen hardi..For to ȝeuen hem her mat. *c* **1407** LYDG. *Reas. & Sens.* 5903 Whan the play I-ended was..thus stood the cas Without a maat on outher syde. **1426** AUDELAY *Poems* (Percy Soc.) 23 After chec for the roke ware for the mate. *a* **1547** SURREY *To Ladie that scorned her Louer* in *Tottel's Misc.* (Arb.) 21 Although I had a check, To geue the mate is hard. **1579** LYLY *Euphues* (Arb.) 66 Sure I am at the next viewe of thy vertues, I shall take thee mate: And taking it not of a pawne but of a Prince, the losse is to be accompted the lesse. **1588** GREENE *Pandosto* (1843) 29 Fortune..began now to turne her back.. intending as she had given Fawnia a slender checke, so she would give her a harder mate. **1621** BURTON *Anat. Mel.* II. ii. IV. (1651) 275 It [chess] is a testy cholerick game, and very offensive to him that loseth the Mate. **1625** BACON *Ess., Of Boldness* (Arb.) 520 Like a Stale at Chesse, where it is no Mate, but yet the Game cannot stirre. **1626** MIDDLETON *Women Beware Women* II. ii. 310, I give you check and mate to your white king. **1647** N. BACON *Disc. Govt. Eng.* I. xvi. (1739) 32 The Church-men or Prelates checked them often, but could never give them the mate. **1735** BERTIN *Chess* 73 The knight takes that pawn, and gives a check, and mate. *Ibid.* 75 The pawn takes the white knight and gives mate.

b. with defining word.

fool's mate: a form of game in which the first player, by two unwise moves, incurs checkmate at his adversary's second move. ***scholar's mate***: a form of game in which the second player blunders so as to be mated by his adversary's fourth move. ***smothered mate*** (see quot. 1863). See also STALEMATE.

1529 MORE *Dyaloge* I. Wks. 149/1 Mary quod he, this is a blind mate indede. **1614** A. SAUL *Famous Game Chesse play* viii, The Mate at two Draughts a Fooles Mate. *Ibid.* C iij, The Mate with a Quene, a louing mate, A Mate with the Bishop, a gentle mate [etc.]. **1859** H. KINGSLEY *G. Hamlyn* vi, A simple trip, akin to scholar's mate at chess. **1863** *Handbk. Chess & Draughts* 14 Smothered Mate. This is a description of mate which can be effected only by the knight, when the adverse king is surrounded, or *smothered*, by his own forces.

mate (meɪt), *sb.*[2] Also 5–7 **mat**, 6 **maat**; *Sc.* 6 **meat**, 6–7 **mait**. [Late 14th c. *mate*, app. a. MLG. *mate* or MDu. **mate* (mod.Du. *maat*, earlier *maet*), shortened form of *gemate* (Flemish *gemaat*) = OHG. *gimazzo* (MHG. *gemazze*):—OTeut. type **gamaton-* companion, lit. 'mess-mate', f. **ga-* (see Y-) implying conjunction or participation + **mat-* (see MEAT). Cf. OE. *gemetta* (:—**gamatjon-*), ME. METTE, companion at table.]

1. a. A habitual companion, an associate, fellow, comrade; a fellow-worker or partner. Now only *colloq.* See also MESSMATE, PLAYMATE, SCHOOLMATE.

c **1380** *Sir Ferumb.* 1372 Floripe..sayde: 'Maumecet my mate y-blessed mot þou be For aled þow hast muche debate to-ward þys barnee'. *c* **1440** *Promp. Parv.* 329/2 Mate, *idem quod* Felaw. **1513** DOUGLAS *Æneis* II. xi. 83 Alkyne sterage affrayit and causit grow, Baith for my byrding and my litle mait. **1515** BARCLAY *Egloges* i. (1570) A iij, When the good is gone (my mate this is the case) Seldome the better reentreth in the place. **1521** *MS. Acc. St. John's Hosp., Canterb.*, To John Kenet & hys mate, carpenters, for ij dayes. **1568** GRAFTON *Chron.* II. 633 The Duke of Yorke and his mates were lodged within the Citie. **1583** *Leg. Bp. St. Androis* 316 He sought ane vther, Ane devill..Exceading Circes in conceattis, For chaungene of Wlisses meatis. *c* **1614** MURE *Dido & Æneas* I. 508 Parte at the ports, as sentinells abide, Vnloade their mat's and drowsie dron's do kill. **1655** FULLER *Ch. Hist.* I. i. 4 Aristobulus, though no Apostle, yet an Apostles Mate,..by Grecian Writers made Bishop of Britain. **1725** POPE *Odyss.* II. 365 Each in jovial mood his mate addrest. **1821** BYRON *Sardan.* II. i. 48 The she-king, That less than woman, is even now upon The waters with his female mates. **1845** C. GRIFFITH *Present State of Port Philip* 79 Two [bushworkers] generally travel together, who are called mates; they are partners, and divide all their earnings. **1866** MRS. GASKELL *Wives & Dau.* xxii. (1867) 223 He was inferior in education to those who should have been his mates. **1878** JEVONS *Prim. Pol. Econ.* 32 Each man usually takes one part of the work, and leaves other parts of the work to his mates. **1885** MRS. C. PRAED *Head Station* 64 I've sent my mate to prospect for a new claim. **1890** 'R. BOLDREWOOD' *Miner's Right* 136 We have been firm friends and true mates all this time. **1901** M. FRANKLIN *My Brilliant Career* i. 3 Daddy's little mate isn't going to turn Turk like that, is she? **1908** E. J. BANFIELD *Confessions of Beachcomber* I. v. 174 With a mate he had been for many months, bêche-de-mer fishing, their station..a lonely islet in Whitsunday Passage. **1911** C. E. W. BEAN *'Dreadnought' of Darling* xxxv. 311 Perhaps the strongest article in the out-back code is that of loyalty to a mate. **1942** C. BARRETT *On Wallaby* iv. 75, I told my mates some of these facts on returning. **1966** *Observer* 17 Apr. 30/1 A 17-year-old boy.. said, 'I haven't got a real mate. That's what I need.' **1968** K. WEATHERLY *Roo Shooter* 109 Old Sam, born and reared in the bush, a good mate and bushman. **1973** *Parade* (Melbourne) Sept. 34/1 An obelisk in the Jewish section of the Melbourne General Cemetery records the names of those who fought for Australia in the 1914 War. Many of them trained in the Faraday Street School cadets. They assimilated the lessons of patriotism and were great mates.

transf. and *fig.* **1669** LYBOURN (*title*) A Platform for Purchasers, a Guide for Builders, and a Mate for Measurers. **1671** MILTON *Samson* 173 Thee whose strength, while vertue was her mate Might have subdu'd the Earth.

b. Used as a form of address by sailors, labourers, etc.

c **1450** *Pilgr. Sea-Voy.* 14 in *Stac. Rome* 38 'What, howe! mate, thow stondyst to ny, Thy felow may nat hale the by;' Thus they begyn to crake. **1549** *Compl. Scot.* vi. 41 The master cryit on the rudir man, mait keip ful and by, a luf. **1582** STANYHURST *Æneis* III. (Arb.) 79 My maats skum the sea froth there in oars strong cherelye dipping. **1610** B. JONSON *Alch.* II. vi. How now! What mates? What Baiards ha'wee here? **1637** HEYWOOD *Dialogues* I. Wks. 1874 VI. 96 My Mate (It is a word That Sailors interchangeably afford To one another) speake. **1852** R. CECIL *Diary* 31 Mar. (1935) 36 When the diggers address a policeman in uniform they always call him 'Sir', but they always address a fellow in a blue shirt with a carbine as 'Mate'. 'Mate' is the ordinary popular form of allocution in these colonies. **1862** A. POLEHAMPTON *Kangaroo Land* 99 A man, who greeted me after the fashion of the Bush, with a 'Good day, mate'. **1869** *Routledge's Ev. Boy's Ann.* 554 Mates, I spoke just now. **1880** MISS BRADDON *Just as I am* i, 'Who's the magistrate hereabouts, mate?' **1974** *Sydney Morning Herald* 14 Feb. 7, I asked a station attendant (attired in a dirty open-necked shirt and trousers, recognizable only by a dirty cap) if the train was the North-West Mail. 'I wouldn't have a clue, mate,' was the reply.

†**c.** A fellow, 'chap'; often used contemptuously. *Obs.*

a **1380** *St. Bernard* in Horstm. *Altengl. Leg.* (1878) 56/2 He [*sc.* þe fend] made a mouwe, þat foule mate, And seide [etc.]. **1573** TUSSER *Husb.* (1878) 113 As for such mates, as vertue hates. **1577** G. HARVEY *Letter-bk.* (Camden) 57 Thou art a merry mate. **1584** R. SCOT *Discov. Witchcr.* VI. ii. (1886) 91 These witches are but lieng mates and couseners. **1612** T. JAMES *Jesuits' Downf.* 13 These Iesuits are cogging mates.

d. ***to go mates with***: to be an associate or partner of. Also ***to be mates with***.

1880 SUTHERLAND *Tales of Goldfields* 59 Brown lost no time in making a contract to 'go mates' with another digger. **1880** H. LAPHAM in D. M. Davin *N.Z. Short Stories* (1953) 57 At this time I was mates with a young fellow called Jim Smith, a good enough lad as a mate, and would do just as big a day's labour as any man. **1890** *Gd. Words* Mar. 211/1, I will accept his proposal to go mates with him.

e. (See quot. 1904 and cf. 4 b.)

1881 H. & C. R. SMITH *Isle of Wight Words* 21 Meyat, a mate; the carter's assistant. **1884** J. C. EGERTON *Sussex Folk & Ways* ii. 26 [A] carter-boy credited with the following.. advice to his father, whose 'mate' he was. **1904** GOODCHILD & TWENEY *Technol. & Sci. Dict.* 384 *Mate*, an assistant or subordinate who assists a more skilled workman. **1951** *Engineering* 9 Mar. 296/3 It is claimed by the strikers that a new electrician's mate..should resign. **1963** *Times* 9 Mar. 9/5 The Scottish chimney sweep..always has a mate.

2. A suitable associate (†or adversary); an equal in eminence of dignity. Now only *arch.*

1563 B. GOOGE *Eglogs*, etc. (Arb.) 126 No man so hauty lyues on earth, but ons may fynd his mate. **1577** tr. *Bullinger's Decades* (1592) 123, I am a iealous God, enuious against my riuall..nor by any meanes abyding to haue a mate. **1667** MILTON *P.L.* IV. 828 Ye knew me once no mate For you, there sitting where ye durst not soare. **1688** R. HOLME *Armoury* III. 229/2 Cardinals..now..are Mates for Kings. **1833** TENNYSON *Lady Clara Vere de Vere* 11, I know you proud to bear your name, Your pride is yet no mate for mine.

3. One of a pair. (Cf. MAKE *sb.*[1])

a. One of a wedded pair, a husband or wife. Now only, a fitting or worthy partner in marriage. †Also (*rarely*), a lover, paramour.

1549 LATIMER *1st Serm. bef. Edw. VI* (Arb.) 34 For to graunt oure kynges grace suche a mate as maye knyt hys hert and heres [etc.]. **1573** HARMAN *Caveat* (ed. 2) 41 This is their custome, that when they mete in barne at night, euery one getteth a mate [*ed.* I make] to lye wythall. **1593** SHAKS. *Lucr.* 18 What priselesse wealth the heauens had him lent, In the possession of his beauteous mate. **1615** BRATHWAIT *Strappado* 118 (A wanton Priest) there was Who made appointment with a Countrie lasse,..The place where these two louely mates should meet Was a vast forrest. **1676** TOWERSON *Decalogue* 383 Lest..men should think it enough to assume a mate..without any obligation upon themselves. **1735** SOMERVILLE *Chase* III. 174 His good old mate With choicest Viands heaps the lib'ral Board. **1786** MME. D'ARBLAY *Diary* Nov., I made a visit to Mrs. Smelt, and engaged her and her excellent mate to dinner. **1842** TENNYSON *Dora* 166 Mary took another mate; But Dora lived unmarried till her death. **1843** LYTTON *Last of Barons* II. i, Isabel of Warwick had been a mate for William the Norman. **1894** BESANT *In Deacons Orders* etc. *Peer & Heiress* 111 Happy is the man who finds his mate!

b. Of animals, esp. birds: One of a pair.

1593 *Tell-Troth's N.Y. Gift* (1876) 38 Nor fish, beast, foule, nor fruit, but takes the mate. **1611** BIBLE *Isa.* xxxiv. 15 There shall the vultures also be gathered, every one with her mate. **1667** MILTON *P.L.* VII. 403 Shoales Of Fish..part single or with mate Graze the Sea weed thir pasture. **1774** GOLDSM. *Nat. Hist.* (1776) VII. 89 Whether this proceeds from the desires of the frog, disappointed of its proper mate, or [etc.]. **1822** BYRON *Heaven & Earth* I. iii. 38 A doom which even some serpent, with his mate, Shall 'scape to save his kind to be prolong'd. **1871** R. ELLIS tr. *Catullus* lxviii. 122 Not in her own fond mate so turtle snowy delighteth.

c. Of things: The fellow of a pair; a counterpart or parallel.

1578 BANISTER *Hist. Man* v. 71 Two Nerues..beyng the mates of those Arteries. **1611** BIBLE *Isa.* xxxiv. 16 No one of these [*sc.* prophecies] shall faile, none shall want her mate. **1668** CULPEPPER & COLE *Barthol. Anat. Man.* III. i. 323 Every Nerve hath its mate or Companion. **1892** KIPLING *Barrack-r. Ballads* 81 'Ye have taken the one [a pistol] from a foe', said he; 'will ye take the mate from a friend?' *Mod. dial.* These boots are not mates.

d. *spec.* A point on tramway lines which is cast solid and pairs or 'mates' with the movable tongue or switch on the other rail; an 'open' or 'fixed' point. orig. *U.S.*

1909 in WEBSTER. **1922** *Glasgow Herald* 3 Oct. 8 The weight of the inserts varies from about 100 to 300 lb., depending on the angle of the crossing or mate.

4. Nautical uses.

a. An officer (now only on a merchant vessel) who sees to the execution of the commands of the master or commander, or of his immediate superior, and in the absence of the master takes command of the ship. In the Royal Navy the title has been changed to Sub-lieutenant; and in the merchant-sevice, mates hold functions not greatly inferior to those of lieutenants in the Royal Navy. Formerly called *master's mate* (see MASTER *sb.*[1] 2 d).

1496 etc. [see MASTER *sb.*[1] 2 d]. **1595** *Trag. Sir R. Grinuile* G ij, Th' other Maister, and the other Mat's, Disented from the honour of their minds. **1612** DRAYTON *Poly-olb.* ii. 426 The danger quite forgot wherein they were of late; Who halfe so merrie now as Maister and his Mate? **1626** CAPT. SMITH *Accid. Yng. Seamen* 2 The Maister and his Mate is to direct the course, commaund all the Saylors, for steering, trimming, and sayling the Ship. **1669** STURMY *Mariner's Mag.* II. vi. 64 Some there are that will not understand,..yet (to my knowledge) are Mates to good Ships. **1748** SMOLLETT *Rod. Rand.* xvi, The stranger..informed me that he himself had passed for third mate of a third-rate, about four months ago. **1797** *Encycl. Brit.* (ed. 3) X. 644/2 A first-rate man of war has six mates. **1835** SIR J. ROSS *Narr. 2nd Voy.* ii. 23 After some interchange of significant looks and whisperings between the mates and the men [etc.]. **1903** W. H. GRAY *Div. Shepherd* iii. 42 An old scholar, who was first mate on board a ship when a mutiny broke out.

b. An assistant to some functionary on board ship, esp. to a warrant-officer of the navy, as in *boatswain's mate*, *carpenter's mate*, *cook's mate*, *gunner's mate*, *sail-maker's mate*, etc., for which see the first words.

1610 SHAKS. *Temp.* II. ii. 49 The Gunner, and his Mate. **1702** *Royal Declar.* 1 June in *Lond. Gaz.* No. 3815/2 Carpenters Mates, Boatswains Mates, Gunners Mates,.. Quartermasters Mates. **1719** DE FOE *Crusoe* II. ii, The cook's mate of the ship. **1748** *Anson's Voy.* II. ix. 226 One of the sail-makers mates was fishing. **1753** CHAMBERS *Cycl. Supp.*, *Mates*, on board a ship, are assistants to the several officers; as *master's Mates*,..*corporal's Mates*. **1867** SMYTH *Sailor's Word-bk.*, *Mate* generally implies adjunct or assistant.

c. In the navy, an officer who assists the surgeon, usually called *surgeon's mate* (see SURGEON); in the army, an assistant who acts as dispenser and dresser. See also *hospital mate*, s.v. HOSPITAL *sb.* 6.

1612 WOODALL (*title*) The Surgeons Mate or Military & Domestique Surgery. **1758** J. S. *Le Dran's Observ. Surg.* (1771) 163 He was dressed..by the Mate of the Regiment. **1783** F. MICHAELIS in *Med. Commun.* I. 308 The medicines were..given by the mates of the hospital. **1806** *Med. Jrnl.* XV. 88 Medical Mates [in the Military Medical Department].—These are gentlemen who are supposed to be acquainted with the compounding of medicines. **1811** *Self Instructor* 577 The surgeon..is allowed a mate to assist him.

d. *U.S. Navy.* 'An officer of the navy, next below a warrant-officer, who is not in the line of promotion' (*Funk's Stand. Dict.* 1895).

1890 in *Century Dict.*

5. *attrib.* and *Comb.*, as ***mate boat***, ***fellow***, ***-hunting***; **mate fish**, a whale with calf.

1756 *Rhode Isl. Col. Rec.* (1860) V. 543 [He] represented unto this Assembly, that there is a ferry set up at the Long Wharf, in the town of Newport, which hath no *mate boat. **1887** HALL CAINE *Deemster* xxxix, If he had found me a cheerier *mate-fellow, I doubt not we should have had some cheerful hours together. **1725** DUDLEY in *Phil. Trans.* XXXIII. 261 Care is taken by those who kill these *Mate Fish..only to fasten the Calf, but not to kill her, till they have first secured the Cow. **1837** T. HOOK *Jack Brag* vi, The system of *mate-hunting through the medium of the newspapers.

‖**maté** ('mæteɪ), *sb.*[3] Also 8 **mathe**, **mathè**, 8–9 **matte**, **mati**. [Sp. *mate*, a. Quichua *mati*, explained in Gonzalez Holguin's *Vocab. de la lengua Quichua* (1608) as 'vessel or dish made of calabash'.]

1. A vessel, usually a gourd or calabash, in which the leaves of maté (see 2) are infused; also ***maté-cup***.

1717 tr. *Frezier's Voy.* 252 They put the Herb [of Paraguay] into a Cup, or Bowl, made of a Calabash, or Gourd, tipp'd with Silver, which they call *Mate*. **1826** SIR F. B. HEAD *Journ. Pampas* 87 He used to get it for me..in a little maté cup, which did not hold more than an egg-shell. **1842** *Penny Cycl.* XXIV. 135/1 It [the Maté] is drunk out of a vessel called maté. **1884** *Health Exhib. Catal.* 9/1 Specimens of Maté or Paraguay Tea, with Maté Cup.

2. a. An infusion of the leaves of the shrub *Ilex paraguayensis*; Paraguay-tea (see PARAGUAY).

1758 *Misc.* in *Ann. Reg.* 363/1 The pure leaf, the infusion of which is called mate. **1760–72** tr. *Juan & Ulloa's Voy.* (ed. 3) I. 270 Another common liquor in this country [*sc.* Quito] is the mate, which answers to tea in the East Indies. **1883** *Encycl. Brit.* XV. 627/2 Maté acts as a restorative after great

fatigue in the same manner as tea. 1901 *Brit. Med. Jrnl.* No. 2092. 301 The major part of the Estancieros (farmers) are great meat eaters and enormous consumers of maté or Paraguayan tea.

b. The shrub itself; also, its leaves prepared for infusion.

1768 J. BYRON *Narr. Patagonia* (ed. 2) 193 Matte, a herb from Paraguay. 1777 ROBERTSON *Hist. Amer.* Note ci. II. 518 From the trade of Mathè, or herb of Paraguay. 1818 T. BLAND *S. Amer.* in *Amer. St. Papers, For. Relat.* (1834) IV. 279 The young shoots and leaves of the matte, it would seem, have received the name of *yerba*, rather from [etc.]. 1859 *All Year Round* No. 32. 127 Cultivate the mati. 1866 *Treas. Bot.* 618/2 The drinking tube is then inserted, and boiling water poured on the Maté. 1879 *Cassell's Techn. Educ.* III. 186 Paraguay Tea, or Maté... A small shrub with oval, wedge-form..smooth leaves.

c. *attrib.*, as ***maté pot, wood***; **maté mangosteen**, *Garcinia purpurea* (Drury *Useful Pl. India* 1873, p. 223).

1879 J. BEERBOHM *Patagonia* iii. 30 The tobacco-pipe and the maté-pot went round the circle without any intermission. 1883 *Encycl. Brit.* XV. 627/1 A yerbal or maté wood.

†**mate**, *a. Obs.* Also 3 **matt**, 3–5 **mat**, (4 **mete**), 4–5 **maat**, 5 **maate, matte**; *Sc.* 5 **maytt**, 5–7 **mait**, 6 **mayt**. [a. OF. *mat* mated at chess, confounded, exhausted, dull (mod.F. *mat* indecl., mated, *mat*, fem. *mate*, dull, whence MAT *a.*) = med.L. *mattus* 'tristis' (*Gloss. Paris*, 10th c.), Pr. *mat*, Sp., Pg. *mate* dull, faded, It. *matto* dull, foolish. From OF. are MHG. *mat* (G. *matt*), MDu., Du. *mat*, Sw. *matt*, Da. *mat*. The Rom. word is a. Pers. *māt* at a loss, helpless (used in *shāh māt* 'the king is helpless', CHECKMATE).

Gildemeister, Dozy, and other modern scholars, dispute the customary view that the Persian word is a. Arab. *māt* 'he has died'.]

1. Mated at chess.

?1370 *Robt. Cicyle* 184 Wiþ o drauȝt he was chekmat [*H.* mate]. c1407 LYDG. *Reas. & Sens.* 10, I..Was of a Fers so Fortunat In-to a corner dryve and maat. a1500 *MS. Ashmole* 344 (Bodl.) lf. 16b, The blake kyng shalbe mate at v draughtes. *Ibid.* 18b, Then art thou mate wt hys pon. a1600 MONTGOMERIE *Misc. P.* xx. 20 That nou thair is no nek, Nor draught to mak debate, Bot let it brist or brek; For love must haif it mait.

2. Overcome, vanquished, worsted, confounded.

a1225 *Leg. Kath.* 2015 Maxence & alle hise halden ham mate. a1225 *Ancr. R.* 382 And ȝif eni mon ei swuch þing ortroweð bi him, he is more mat þen þe þeof inumen mid þeofðe. a1300 *Cursor M.* 10041 Pride..es ouercummen, and mad al matt. c1386 CHAUCER *Man of Law's T.* 837 O Golias..Hou myghte Dauid make thee so maat. c1450 *Merlin* viii. 125 And so was Claudas made pore and maat. 1513 DOUGLAS *Æneis* IV. Prol. 253 Dido..In hir faynte lust so mait, within schort quhile, That honestie [etc.].

3. Exhausted, worn out, dead tired, faint.

a1300 *Cursor M.* 15875 Mate and weri war þai þan. 13.. *Gaw. & Gr. Knt.* 1568 He was so mat, he myȝt no more renne. 1420–2 LYDG. *Thebes* II. in *Chaucer's Wks.* (1561) 366b, Tideus of bledyng was wonder feint Mate and wearie, and in greate distresse. 1490 CAXTON *Eneydos* ii. 15 Hir vysage mate by frequente sources of grete teeris. 1536 BELLENDEN *Cron. Scot.* (1821) I. 66 Mony of Gillus folkis, wery and mate.

4. Dejected, downcast, discouraged, sorrowful.

13.. *Guy Warw.* (A.) 597 He ferd as he were mat, Adoun he fel aswoune wiþ þat. c1350 *Will. Palerne* 1776 Whanne he his felawes founde of his fare þei wondred, whi he was in þat wise wexen so maat. 1375 BARBOUR *Bruce* XVII. 794 With mate cher the assalt thai left. 1390 GOWER *Conf.* III. 7 Riht so mi lust is overthrowe, And of myn oghne thoght so mat I wexe. c1460 *Towneley Myst.* xix. 245 That sorowfull sight shall make hir maytt. 1560 ROLLAND *Crt. Venus* II. 314 In all my dayis was I not half sa mayt [*rime words* dissimulat, fortunait, debait].

mate (meɪt), *v.*[1] Forms: 3 **maten**, 3–5 **mat**, 5 **maat(e, (mat(t)yn)**, 6 *Sc.* **mayt, mait**, 4– **mate**. [a. OF. *mater*, f. *mat* MATE *a.*]

1. *trans.* (*Chess.*) To checkmate. Also *absol.* Sometimes in fig. context or allusively.

c1320 *Sir Tristr.* 315 'Child, what wiltow lay?' 'Oȝain an hauke of noble air Tventi schillinges, to say Wheþer so mates oþer fair Bere hem boþe oway'. c1440 *Promp. Parv.* 329/2 Matyn at the chesse (*MS. S., P.* mattyn), *mato*. c1489 CAXTON *Sonnes of Aymon* 478 Playe well, my childe, for ye shall be mated. a1533 LD. BERNERS *Huon* xxxvi. 113 He sawe a .M. men plaing at the chesse & a nother .M. that had played & been matyd. 1563 B. GOOGE *Egloges* viii. (Arb.) 66 With costly clothes..Who then dare gyue me checke? Garments som time, so gard a knaue, that he dare mate a Knyght. 1581 PETTIE tr. *Guazzo's Civ. Conv.* I. (1586) 34b, Suffering a Gentlewoman to mate him at Chests. a1618 SYLVESTER *Mem. Mortalitie* viii. Wks. (Grosart) II. 223 The Chess-boord..Where pawns and kings have equal portion: This leaps, that limps, this checks, that necks, that mates. 1642 FULLER *Holy & Prof. St.* V. xviii. (1652) 465 Tame Traytours all! that could behold an Usurper, Mate and Check your lawfull Emperour, and neither wag hand or tongue in opposition. 1646 EARL MONM. tr. *Biondi's Civil Warres* II. 79 All the above-named were like so many paunes at Chesse, which advancing too rashly, were lost; whilst the great men..endeavouring to mate [orig. *scaccheggiando*] the King, met with the like fortune. 1864 *Field* 2 July 3/2 White to play, and mate in 3 moves. 1865 MERIVALE *Rom. Emp.* VIII. lxiii. 13 Nerva had mated his assailants; but his own game was now nearly played out. 1886 *Daily News* 19 July 3/1 Pollock was mated at the 46th move.

†**b.** *intr.* To undergo checkmate, be mated. *Obs.*

1423 JAS. I *Kingis Q.* clxviii. Help now my game, that is in poynt to mate. a1585 MONTGOMERIE *Cherrie & Slae* 216 For vnder cure I gat sik chek, Quhilk I micht nocht remuif nor nek, Bot eyther stail or mait.

†**2.** *trans.* To overcome, defeat, subdue. *Obs.*

a1225 *Ancr. R.* 98 O none wise ne muwe ȝe betere sauuen ou suluen, ant maten, & ouercumen him betere. c1320 *Cast. Love* 830 Prude..al matyd and overcome wes Thorgh bucsomnesse that sheo ches. c1450 *Mirour Saluacioun* 3281 The qwene of heven hym matid with hire sons passionne. c1500 *Melusine* 216 Your noble cheualrye & puyssaunce haue not only mated me & made lasse myn honour, but also [etc.]. c1590 MARLOWE *Faust.* Chorus 2 Not marching now in fields of Thracimene, Where Mars did mate the Carthaginians.

transf. 1625 BACON *Ess., Death* (Arb.) 385 There is no passion in the minde of man, so weake, but it Mates, and Masters, the Feare of Death.

¶**b.** App. used for: To destroy; to kill.

a1300 *Cursor M.* 21041 Þat Imperur wend him [John] to mat; In a tun was welland hat Fild of oyle he did him schott. c1400 *Destr. Troy* 9532 Fyve hundrith fully of þere fyne shippes, [hade ben] Consumet..And mony mo were þere marred, & mated with fire.

†**3.** To nonplus, baffle, render powerless (a person); to render nugatory (a design). *Obs.*

a1300 *Cursor M.* 8479 Was na clerc sa crafti kend,..þat moght þe clerc wit clerge mat þat cuth þe bokes þat he wrat. 1529 MORE *Dyaloge* I. Wks. 148/2 In what point quod he, hath that mated you? 1596 DANETT tr. *Comines* (1614) 277 They [wisdom and good government] might easily haue mated his enterprise in Italie. 1611 SPEED *Hist. Gt. Brit.* VII. xii. 262 They mated the Saxons in all their designes. 1623 FLETCHER *Rule a Wife* III. i, He stood up to me, And mated my commands! 1626 BACON *Sylva* §902 Wee see Audacitie doth almost binde and mate the Weaker Sort of Minds. 1642 CHAS. I *Mess. to Ho. Comm., & Answ.* 8 Which then would have mated and weakned the Conspirators in the beginning. 1670 COTTON *Espernon* I. II. 65 By whose assistance he thought with less difficulty to mate the ambitious Designs of the League.

†**4.** To put out of countenance; to render helpless by terror, shame, or discouragement; to daunt, abash; to stupefy. *Obs.*

c1416 HOCCLEVE *Min. Poems* xv. 23 Lat nat the strook of indigence vs mate. 1586 MARLOWE *1st Pt. Tamburl.* I. i, How now, my Lord? what, mated and amazed To heare the king thus thr[e]aten like himselfe? 1597 LYLY *Woman in Moone* IV. i. 157 O bury all thy anger in this kisse, And mate me not with vttering my offence. 1605 SHAKS. *Macb.* V. i. 86 My minde she ha's mated, and amaz'd my sight, I thinke, but dare not speake. 1632 LE GRYS tr. *Velleius Paterc.* 211 The army..being mated with his comming, his vigor and his glory rendred it selfe to him. 1636 DAVENANT *Witts* V. i, Your Wine mates them, they understand it not. 1646 EARL MONM. tr. *Biondi's Civil Warres* V. 101 This and some other losses had rather madded them then mated [orig. *sbigottiti*] the English. 1651 N. BACON *Disc. Govt. Eng.* II. xxvi. (1739) 116 The Dutchess of Burgundy..mated him with Phantoms and Apparitions of dead Bodies of the House of York. 1706 PHILLIPS (ed. Kersey), To *Mate*,..to amaze or astonish, to daunt, dash, or put out of countenance. 1827 HALLAM *Const. Hist.* x. (1854) III. 275 Twenty years of depression and continual failure mated the spirits of the cavaliers.

†**5.** To exhaust, weary; to cause to be weary or tired out; to dull or weaken (passion). *Obs.*

a1400–50 *Alexander* 1270 Mased & matid of þaire strenthes. 1489 CAXTON *Faytes of A.* I. xxiv. 77 The fyfthe that they be not mated nor traueylled nor made the more feble for honger. 1513 DOUGLAS *Æneis* IX. x. 37 Our chyldir ȝyng..Wyld deyr throu out the woddis chais and mayt [L. *Venatu invigilant pueri silvasque fatigant*]. a1693 *Urquhart's Rabelais* III. xxxi. 258 The Ardour of Lechery is very much subdued and mated by frequent Labour.

mate (meɪt), *v.*[2] [f. MATE *sb.*[2]]

1. a. *trans.* To equal, rival; to vie or cope with; to be a match for.

1509 HAWES *Past. Pleas.* xliii. (Percy Soc.) 212 Infinite I am, nothing can me mate. 1580 *Ord. of Prayer* in *Liturg. Serv. Q. Eliz.* (1847) 573 The Boy mateth the man of aged gravity. 1613 SHAKS. *Hen. VIII*, III. ii. 274 My euer Roiall Master, Dare mate a sounder man then Surrie can be. 1690 CHILD *Disc. Trade* (1698) 74 Nor ever did we greatly prosper upon it [our trade to East-India], till our interest was much abated by laws, nor ever shall mate the Dutch in it, till our interest be as low as theirs. 1697 DRYDEN *Virg. Georg.* III. 371 They [the Waves] mate the middle Region with their height. 1718 POPE *Iliad* XIII. 414 In standing fight he mates Achilles' force. 1814 SCOTT *Ld. of Isles* I. xii, In speed His galley mates the flying steed. 1874 SWINBURNE *Bothwell* I. i. 4, I might sleep well and laugh and walk at ease, With none to mate me. 1891 W. MORRIS *Poems by Way* 129 *Fig-tree.* I who am little among trees In honey-making mate the bees.

b. *intr.* To claim equality *with*. *arch.*

1692 *Vind. Carol.* iii. 40 When the safety of the Nation was at stake, [they] insolently contend, nay mate it with their Sovereign. 1702 ROWE *Tamerl.* I. ii. 678 Thou..hast dar'd To lift thy wretched self above the Stars And mate with Power Almighty. 1884 TENNYSON *Becket* I. iii, If Canterbury bring his cross to court, Let York bear his to mate with Canterbury.

2. a. *trans.* To match; to marry; to join in marriage; to take or give in marriage.

1607 SHAKS. *Timon* I. i. 140 How shall she be endowed, If she be mated with an equall Husband? 1842 TENNYSON *Locksley Hall* 47 Thou art mated with a clown. 1843 LYTTON *Last Bar.* II. iii, I fear that the king will be teased into mating my sister with the Count of Charolois. 1862 MERIVALE *Rom. Emp.* (1865) V. xl. 57 The females of ingenuous birth were not numerous enough to mate them.

refl. 1884 W. C. SMITH *Kildrostan* 55 I'd sooner mate me with A cloud,..Or wed a polar bear.

b. *intr.* for *refl.*

1589 WARNER *Alb. Eng.* VI. xxxi. (1612) 154 The gayest Females mate With Loutes as soon as Lordes. 1838 LYTTON *Leila* I. iii, Permission were easier given to thee to wed the wild tiger, than to mate with the loftiest noble of Morisca. 1862 WHITTIER *Amy Wentw.* 149 Oh, rank is good, and gold is fair, And high and low mate ill. 1895 A. C. FOX-DAVIES *Armorial Fam.* p. xx, In England men mate with whom they will.

3. a. *trans.* To pair (animals, esp. birds) for the purpose of breeding. Also with *up*.

1601 SHAKS. *All's Well* I. i. 102 The hind that would be mated by the Lion Must die for loue. 1859 DARWIN *Orig. Spec.* i. (1873) 30 Pigeons can be mated for life. 1885 *Truth* 28 May 836/1 Two of her Majesty's cows have been sent to Herefordshire to be mated with the famous bull, Lord Wilton. 1899 *Feathered World* 10 Mar. 477 The birds had been previously mated up.

transf. 1882 'OUIDA' *Maremma* I. 165 'One does not mate a trailing weed with a young oak', she said.

b. *intr.* Of animals, esp. birds: To pair.

1870, 1903 [see MATING *ppl. a.*]. 1877 BURROUGHS *Birds & Poets* (1895) 103 These birds do not mate.

4. *trans.* To join suitably *with*; to associate, couple, treat as comparable *with*. Also, †to provide with what is suitable.

1593 SHAKS. *Ven. & Ad.* 909 Her more than hast is mated with delayes. 1626 J. HAIG *Let.* in J. Russell *Haigs* (1881) 178, I pray you..write to my Colonel..desiring him..to mate me in clothes if you be not able. 1669 DRYDEN & DAVENANT *Tempest* I. i, And on a night, mated to his design, Antonio ope'd the gates of Milan. 1703 ROWE *Ulyss.* I. i. 52 'Twou'd make Comparison..monstrous seem, as if to mate A Mole-Hill with Olympus. 1891 J. WINSOR *Columbus* ii. 54 None knew this better than those, like Las Casas, who mated their faith with charity of act.

5. a. *intr.* To consort, keep company *with*.

a1832 'BARRY CORNWALL' *The Owl* 5 Not a bird of the forest e'er mates with him. 1871 B. TAYLOR *Faust* (1875) II. I. ii. 11 The judge, debarred from punishment, Mates with the felon ere he endeth. 1881 BESANT & RICE *Chapl. of Fleet* I. 160 It was a shame that a gentleman of his rank should mate with men whose proper place was among the thieves of Turnmill Street.

b. *trans.* To accompany suitably.

1870 MORRIS *Earthly Par.* I. I. 369 How sweet it would be, could I hear, Soft music mate the drowsy afternoon.

6. a. *intr.* Of an engineering part: to make a good or proper fit *with*.

1909 in WEBSTER. 1956 S. PARKER *Drawings & Dimensions* vii. 52 When considering the application of 'Go' and 'Not Go' gauges..the questions 'Will *like* mate with *like*?' and 'How much force may be used when gauging?' inevitably arise. 1959 *Motor Manual* (ed. 36) v. 132 The end of the axle hub is threaded and extends outside the wheel to take a large eared nut, which is coned internally to mate with a cone on the edge of the wheel hub. 1967 *Electronics* 6 Mar. 15/3 (Advt.), Push-pull coupling mates easily.

b. *trans.* To fit or join *with* or *to*.

1959 *Nat. Geographic* Feb. 159/1 High on skeletal service towers, we watched engineers mate, or couple, rocket stages and gingerly install the payloads containing custom-built miniaturized instruments. 1962 V. GRISSOM in *Into Orbit* 119 On 1 July the capsule was taken from the hangar..to be mated to the Redstone. 1970 N. ARMSTRONG et al. *First on Moon* iii. 55 By mid-May it was time to 'mate' the electrical systems of the rocket boosters with those of the spacecraft.

mate, obs. form of MEAT.

mate(e: see MATY.

mateco, variant of MATICO.

†'**mated**, *ppl. a.*[1] *Obs.* [f. MATE *v.*[1] + -ED[1].]

1. Confounded, amazed.

1581 T. HOWELL *Deuises* (1879) 211 The bitter smarte that straines my mated minde. 1582 STANYHURST *Æneis* II. (Arb.) 51 A feare then generals mens mated senses atached. c1586 C'TESS PEMBROKE *Ps.* XLVIII. ii, The things they see Amaze their mated mindes.

2. Checkmated.

1656 COWLEY *Pindar. Odes, Destinie* i, Here I the losing party blame For those false Moves that break the Game,.. And above all, th' ill Conduct of the mated King.

mated ('meɪtɪd), *ppl. a.*[2] [f. MATE *v.*[2] + -ED[1].]

a. Matched; married; chiefly in *ill-* or *well-mated*.

1667 [implied in *ill-mated*: see ILL- 7]. 1821 JOANNA BAILLIE *Metr. Leg., Lady G. Baillie* lii, Sweet union held of mated will. 1899 *Scribner's Mag.* XXV. 50/1 Two well-mated young lovers.

b. Fitted or fitting together.

1958 V. H. WATSON *Rover Cars* xiv. 230 Wash and examine all parts, renew as necessary, bearing in mind that the crown wheel and pinion are 'mated' parts and must be replaced as such.

matefeloun, obs. form of MATFELLON.

†**mate-griffon.** *Hist.* [repr. Pr. *matagrifun* ('Kill-Greek'), f. *matar* to kill + *Grifun* GRIFFON[1].] The name of a siege-tower used by Richard I.

c1200 RICH. DEVIZES in *Chron. Stephen, Hen. II & Rich. I* (Rolls) III. 402 Rex Angliæ..fecit castellum ligneum..juxta muros Messanæ, quod, ad opprobrium Grifonum, 'Mategrifun' nominavit. 13.. *Coer de L.* 2878 Ther leet he pyght hys pavyloun, And arerede hys Mate-gryffon. *Ibid.* 6063 The Robynet and the Mate-Griffon, Al that they hytte wente adoun. c1330 R. BRUNNE *Chron.* (1810) 157 His pele fro þat forward he [Richard I] cald it *mate Griffoun*. 1788 GROSE *Milit. Antiq.* II. 303 The robinet and mate-griffon threw both darts and stones.

matel, obs. form of METAL *sb.*

‖**matelassé** (mat(ə)lase). [Fr., f. *matelas* MATTRESS.] A French dress goods of silk, or silk

and wool, having a raised design. Also *attrib.* or *adj.* having a raised pattern like quilting.

1882 CAULFEILD & SAWARD *Dict. Needlework* s.v., Matelassé silk is employed for dresses and mantles. **1884** KNIGHT *Dict. Mech.* Suppl. 587/2 *Matelassé*, a silk-and-wool French dress goods. **1897** *Daily News* 9 Sept. 6/5 There are endless designs in matelassé cloth, a considerable mixture of silk being woven in with the wool.

matelent, variant of MALTALENT *Obs.*

mateless ('meɪtlɪs), *a.* [f. MATE *sb.*² + -LESS.]

1. Without a mate, partner, or companion.

1599 T. M[OUFET] *Silkwormes* 13 Shalt thou alone die matelesse, Thisbe mine? **1612** PEACHAM *Minerv. Brit.* II. 186 The Thrush a tenor; off a little space, Some mateless Dove doth murmur out the base. **1705** TATE *Warriour's Welc.* xliv, I'll teach you then the Charm that shall..make.. The Mateless Nightingal no more complain. **1837** *New Monthly Mag.* XLIX. 23 One mateless dove is answering. **1887** BOWEN *Virg. Æneid* IV. 553 Mateless and all unblamed, untutored in love and its pain!

†**2.** Unrivalled, matchless, unparalleled. *Obs.*

1570 B. GOOGE *Pop. Kingd.* I. (1880) 1 Good Muse declare, my force to weake can not therto attaine Ne can disclose the mysteries, of such a matelesse raigne. **1624** QUARLES *Sion's Elegies* i. 12 Say, if e're your eyes beheld.. more unparallel'd And matelesse Evills. *a* **1644** G. SANDYS *Virg. Æneis* VI. (R.), The clouds, and lightnings matelesse, To forge with brasse, and speed of horn-hooft force.

matelot ('mætləʊ). [Fr., sailor; cf. MATLO(W.]

1. A sailor. *Naut. slang.*

1911 'GUNS' & 'THEELUKER' *Middle Watch Musings* 8 You've just got two old and respected matelots well scrubbed for nuffing. **1915** *Blackw. Mag.* July 89/1 We invite the matelots to lie on their backs on the upper-deck. **1947** *Landfall* I. 283 What time we had left was spent on fruitless errands for the Pommie matelots. **1955** *Times* 10 Aug. 3/3 The Navy was there once more and so were the two matelots of Monday. **1970** [see JOCK¹ 1 b]. **1974** *Listener* 21 Nov. 672/1 Our screen matelots..should be as reticent as ..*Captain Horatio Hornblower*.

2. Applied to a shade of blue.

1927 *Daily Tel.* 26 Apr. 13/5 (Advt.), Fawn, Rose,.. Almond, Matelot. **1928** *Daily Express* 27 July 5/4 A lovely deep blue known as 'matelot'.

‖**matelote** (matlɔt), *sb.* Also 8–9 matelotte, 9 matelot. [Fr., f. *matelot* sailor.]

1. A dish of fish served in a sauce of wine, onions and other seasoning, such as mushrooms, oysters, etc.; also, a dish of other viands similarly dressed.

1730–6 BAILEY (fol.), *Matelotte* [in Cookery], victuals dressed after the seamens way. **1747** MRS. GLASSE *Cookery* 32 A Pig Matelote. **1759** W. VERRAL *Cookery* xviii. 97 This sauce may serve for several good uses; but for your matelotte prepare it with a ladle or two of your cullis, with a few nice button mushrooms. **1818** MOORE *Fudge Fam. Paris* xii. 128 The bliss Of an eel *matelote*. **1823** SCOTT *Quentin D.* Pref., The matelot of pike and eels. **1846** MRS. GORE *Eng. Char.* (1852) 47 An unctuous matelotte of eels.

2. An old sailors' dance, in duple rhythm, similar to the hornpipe. *rare*⁻⁰.

1890 in *Century Dict.*

Hence **matelote** *v. trans.*, to make into a matelote (sense 1).

1844 THACKERAY *Greenwich* Wks. 1886 XXIII. 381, I have tasted him [the eel] charmingly matelotted with mushrooms and onions.

mately ('meɪtlɪ), *a.*¹ *rare.* [f. MATE *sb.*² + -LY¹.] Friendly, sociable, intimate.

1822 T. MITCHELL *Aristoph.* II. 184 With Cleon he's friendly and mately.

mately, *a.*² *Her.* Also **mateley**. An alleged synonym for URDEE.

1688 R. HOLME *Armoury* I. 49/1 A Cross Urdee..goeth under several terms..as, a Cross Mately, a Cross Flanked [etc.]. **1889** in ELVIN *Gloss. Her.*

matens, obs. pl. form of MATIN¹.

mateo-: see MATÆO-.

‖**mater** ('meɪtə(r)). [L. = MOTHER.]

1. The thickest plate of the astrolabe. (Cf. *mother.*) *Obs.*

1594 BLUNDEVIL *Exerc.* VI. Introd. (1636) 599 The fore-part contayneth two principall parts, that is, the Mater, which is unmovable, and the Rete, which is movable. *Ibid.* 600. **1905** *Sci. Amer.* 12 Aug. 120/2 The Astrolabe of Regiomontanus... *Mater* is the name given to the large disk divided into degrees. **1974** *Ibid.* Jan. 101/1 Each plate being engraved on both sides and all being stacked in the mater, or main body, of the astrolabe.

2. *Anat.* See DURA MATER, PIA MATER.

3. Chiefly in schoolboys' slang, used familiarly for *mother*. (Cf. *pater.*)

1864 HEMYNG *Eton School Days* i. 3 'Good-bye, mater; good-bye, Letty', said Philip. 'Mind you write often', said his mother. **1888** J. PAYN *Myst. Mirbridge* xxvii, The Mater will do anything for me. **1897** *Brit. Weekly* 7 Jan. 214/3 Brydon's mater was a veritable matchmaker.

mater, obs. form of MATTER, MEHTAR.

materas, obs. form of MATTRESS.

Mater Dolorosa ('meɪtə dɒlə'rəʊsə). [med. L., lit. 'sorrowful mother'.] A title of the Virgin Mary, emphasizing her role in the Passion of Christ; a representation, in painting or sculpture, of the Virgin Mary sorrowing. Also *transf.*, a woman who has the attributes of the sorrowful mother.

The term probably originated in the medieval Latin hymn beginning 'Stabat mater dolorosa Iuxta crucem lacrimosa'.

1800 J. DALLAWAY *Anecdotes of Arts in England* 516 He has a mater dolorosa and a boy playing on a lute by Guido. *c* **1869** TAYLOR & DUBOURG in M. R. Booth *Eng. Plays of 19th Cent.* (1973) III. 308 Crosses her hands on her bosom, à la Mater Dolorosa. **1872** GEO. ELIOT *Middlem.* IV. VIII. lxxx. 283 Dorothea's face..had the pale cheeks and pink eyelids of a *mater dolorosa*. **1888** *Cycl. Painters & Paintings* III. 220/2 Mater Dolorosa.. By Murillo, Madrid Museum. .. Companion to Ecce Homo. **1892** *Servite Manual* (Servite Fathers) 200 (*heading*) Via Matris Dolorosæ or, The Stations of the Way of the Seven Dolours of Mary. **1895** *Yellow Bk.* IV. 280 A vast cape that might have enshrouded the form of a Mater Dolorosa hung by the side of a jauntily-striped Langtry-hood. **1904** G. GRONAU *Titian* vii. 147 We can follow exactly the history of this picture and of its companion, the 'Mater Dolorosa', which Titian sent off to Charles V in 1555. **1917** M. G. SEGAR *Some Minor Poems Middle Ages* xxi. 48 Old English poems on the Mater Dolorosa are always wonderfully full of feeling. **1923** M. INNES *Ten Florentine Painters* 117 This group of the 'Mater Dolorosa' and her dead Son is called a *Pietà*. **1936** R. LEHMANN *Weather in Streets* IV. ii. 398 Mrs. Cunningham stood in the double doorway..receiving with a smile of the lips, but not of the hollowed *mater dolorosa* eyes, congratulations upon Amanda. **1938** *Times Lit. Suppl.* 11 June 415/3 Patricia is the picture of the *mater dolorosa* of all time. **1942** G. D. CARLETON *Mother of Jesus* xiv. 68 The Mother of Jesus is indeed the *Mater Dolorosa*, the Sorrowful Mother. **1951** L. MACNEICE tr. *Goethe's Faust* I. 120 In a niche on the wall is an image of the Mater Dolorosa. **1955** W. SMITH tr. *Mieggé's Virgin Mary* viii. 171 All this conforms with..medieval piety..and the more recent veneration of the *Mater dolorosa*.

‖**materfamilias** (meɪtəfə'mɪlɪæs). [L., f. *māter* mother + *familiās*, old gen. of *familia* FAMILY.] The mother of a household.

1756 G. HARRIS *Justinian* 28 Denominated according to their sex, either *patres familiarum*, or *matres familiarum*. **1861** *Wheat & Tares* ii. 13 Mrs. Leslie seemed rather overpowered by her responsibilities as Materfamilias. **1891** [see PATERFAMILIAS 2].

materfil(l)on, obs. forms of MATFELLON.

†**ma'teriable**, *a.* and *sb.* *Obs. rare.* [f. L. *māteria* MATTER *sb.*¹ + -ABLE] = MATERIAL *a.* and *sb.*

1471 RIPLEY *Comp. Alch.* Ep. iii. in Ashm. (1652) 111 Reduced to theyr beginning materiable. **1652** *Zeal Examined* Add. §13. 45 Some visible and solid materiable of forcible Laws.

material (mə'tɪərɪəl), *a.* and *sb.* [ad. late L. *māteriālis*, f. *māteria* MATTER *sb.*¹: see -AL¹.

Cf. F. *matériel* adj. and sb., *matériaux* sb. pl., Sp., Pg. *material*, It. *materiale*; also the mod.Teut. forms (chiefly from Fr.), G. *materiell* adj., *material* sb., Du. *materieel* adj., *materiaal* sb.]

A. *adj.*

1. *Scholastic Philosophy* and *Theol.* (Opposed to FORMAL.) **a.** Pertaining to matter as opposed to form. ***material cause***: see CAUSE *sb.* 5. †Of number: Concrete.

c **1386**, *c* **1430** [see FORMAL A. 1]. **1447** BOKENHAM *Seyntys* (Roxb.) Introd. 1 The fyrst is clepyd cause efficyent The secunde they clepe cause materyal. **1588** KYD *Househ. Phil.* Wks. (1901) 280 Formall number may infinitly encrease, but the Materiall cannot multiply so much. **1660** JER. TAYLOR *Worthy Commun.* i. §3. 52 Not the sound, or the letters and syllables, that is, not the material part, but the formal. **1669** [see FORMAL A. 1]. **1697** tr. *Burgersdicius his Logic* I. xvi. 56 Form is..divided..into Material and Immaterial. Material Form is that which is produced out of the Power of Matter, or which dependeth upon Matter in that self same Moment and Act, by which it is made. **1713** [see FORMALLY 1]. **1827** [see FORMAL A. 1].

b. That is (so and so) merely so far as its 'matter' is concerned.

material sin: a wrong action apart from the evil intention that is necessary to constitute it a sin in the full sense of the word; so ***material heresy***, ***schism***, ***schismatic***, etc. ***material righteousness***: righteousness as definable by conduct, without regard to its motive.

1656 BRAMHALL *Replic.* ix. 341 They who separate actually without just cause, may doe it out of invincible ignorance, and consequently they are not formall but only materiall Schismaticks. **1690** NORRIS *Beatitudes* (1692) 95 The desiring material Righteousness by a direct act of the Will actually makes a man formally Righteous.

2. *Logic.* **a.** Concerned with the matter, as distinguished from the form, of reasoning. (Opposed to *formal.*)

1628 T. SPENCER *Logick* 232 A materiall Illation is when the consequent goes with the Antecedent: yet so as it followes the same, not by force thereof. **1685** tr. *Arnauld & Nicole's Logic* III. xiii. 65 The truth of a Consequence..is only propounded conditionally, and separated from the material Truth, as I may so say, of what it contains. **1697** tr. *Burgersdicius his Logic* I. xxviii. 113 The Material Modes affect the Matter of the Enunciation, viz. either Subject or Predicate. **1727–51** CHAMBERS *Cycl.* s.v. *Circle*, The material circle [in logic]..consists of two syllogisms, the former whereof proves the cause by the effect; and the latter the effect by the cause. **1727–52** *Ibid.* s.v. *Object*, Material Object..is the thing itself that is considered, or treated of.. Formal Object is the manner of considering it. **1850** WHATELY *Elem. Logic* (ed. 9) III. §3 The remaining class (*viz.* where the Conclusion does follow from the Premises) may be called the Material, or Non-logical Fallacies. **1864** BOWEN *Logic* vi. 149 The material truth of the Conclusion depends upon the material truth of the Premises. **1883** F. H. BRADLEY *Princ. Logic* 471 If 'material' is a name for what transcends mere 'concepts' and commits itself to truth, then of course all logic must be material. **1889** J. VENN *Princ. Empirical Logic* Pref., In such a province..as that of Material or Inductive Logic the case is very different. **1936** *Mind* XLV. 442 Wisdom..gives the name *Material Analysis* to the substitution, for sentences about wholes, of sentences mentioning the individual parts of the whole, where the parts are of the same order of ultimacy (as previously defined) as the whole. *E.g.*, material analysis of sentences about awe will be in terms of fear and admiration. **1937** A. SMEATON tr. *Carnap's Logical Syntax of Lang.* IV. 237 We will..assign to the material mode of speech any sentence which is to be interpreted as attributing to an object a particular property, this property being quasi-syntactical, so that the sentence can be translated into another sentence which attributes a correlated syntactical property to a designation of the object in question. **1946** *Mind* LV. 321 If we follow the material logicians in holding that universal propositions are existential as to individuals also [etc.].

b. ***material implication***: a relationship which holds between two propositions, irrespective of content, save only when the first is true and the second false.

1903 B. RUSSELL *Princ. Math.* ii. 14 How far formal implication is definable in terms of implication simply, or material implication as it may be called, is a difficult question. **1932**, etc. [see FORMAL *a.* and *sb.*¹ 1 d]. **1965** HUGHES & LONDEY *Elem. Formal Logic* iii. 17 A material implication is always true when its antecedent is false, and also when its consequent is true. That is, a false proposition materially implies any proposition; and a true proposition is materially implied by any proposition. **1974** *Encycl. Brit. Macropædia* XI. 40/2 Reading $p \supset q$ as 'If p, q'..is made convenient by the fact that 'if' is often used in English in a 'material-implication' sense (someone who asserted 'If it isn't raining, it's snowing' would usually be held to have spoken truly *unless* the antecedent were true but the consequent false; i.e., unless it was neither raining nor snowing).

3. a. Of or pertaining to matter or body; formed or consisting of matter; corporeal.

a **1340** HAMPOLE *Psalter* xlix. 4 Fire materiel or of ill consciens, sall bren. *c* **1380** WYCLIF *Eng. Wks.* (1880) 376 Whan he [Christ] was souȝte to be a kynge & to haue taake up-on hym þe materiel swerde. *c* **1386** CHAUCER *Pars. T.* ¶108 He þat is in helle hat defaut of light material. **1398** TREVISA *Barth. De P.R.* VIII. xvi. (1495) 323 Thickenes and boystousnes of materyall parties is cause and welle of heuynesse and of lyghtnesse. **1413** *Pilgr. Sowle* (Caxton) V. i. (1859) 73 Mundus is the material world, but seculum is taken for the enduryngе of the world. *c* **1440** *Gesta Rom.* xix. 66 (Harl. MS.) Þere beth two maner of medycyns, þat is to sey, material, and spirituall. *a* **1533** FRITH *Disp. Purg.* To Rdr. A vi b, I meane not his materiall crosse that he hym self dyed on, but a spretuall crosse. **1563** *Homilies* II. *Place & Time of Prayer* I. (1859) 344 God doth allow the material temple made of lime and stone..to be his house. **1655** EVELYN *Diary* (1827) II. 104 He believed the sunn to be a material fire. **1736** BUTLER *Anal.* I. iii. Wks. 1874 I. 68 The material world appears to be, in a manner, boundless and immense. *a* **1862** BUCKLE *Civiliz.* (1869) III. v. 365 While heat was supposed to be material it could not be conceived as a force.

absol. **1850** O. WINSLOW *Inner Life* i. 6 The perishing of the material is not the annihilation of the immaterial. **1874** SAYCE *Compar. Philol.* vii. 263 The analysis of the material is not the same as the analysis of the mental.

†**b.** Forming the material or substance of a thing. *Obs. rare*⁻¹.

1605 SHAKS. *Lear* IV. ii. 35 She that her selfe will sliuer and disbranch From her materiall sap.

†**c.** Applied to the terrestrial sphere. *Obs.*

1551 RECORDE (*title*) The Castle of Knowledge... Containing the explication of the sphere bothe celestiall and materiall. **1657** *North's Plutarch, Add. Lives* 6 The Mathematicians and Astrologers attribute the Invention of the Materiall Sphere to this subtill Philosopher [Archimedes].

†**d.** Of diseases: ? Organic as opposed to functional. *Obs.*

1528 PAYNEL *Salerne's Regim.* iv, If they..eyther incline to materiall sickenes or to vnmateriall. *Ibid.*, If the sickenes be materiall one maye eate the more at diner. **1541** R. COPLAND *Guydon's Quest. Chirurg.* O iv, They [cauteres] be necessary..to be gyuen in all dysposycyons of maladyes and specyall in materyal maladyes.

e. Philos. ***material object, thing***: an object considered as a physical existent independent of consciousness; hence ***material objectness***, the state of existing as a material object.

1605 BACON *Adv. Learning* I. i. §3 View and inquiry into these sensible and material things. **1649** tr. *Descartes' Discourse* 59 Imagination..is a particular manner of thinking on materiall things. **1713** BERKELEY *Three Dialogues* 61, I wou'd, therefore, fain know, what Arguments you can draw from Reason, for the Existence of what you call *real Things*, or *material Objects*. **1737** A. BAXTER *Inquiry Human Soul* (ed. 2) II. 204 He supposes that from the surfaces of all material things there are continually flying off thin membranes. **1865** MILL *Exam. Hamilton's Philos.* i. 6 We at first limit ourselves to the case of physical, or what are commonly called material objects. **1899** W. JAMES *Talks to Teachers* vii. 58 The result of all this is that intimate familiarity with the physical environment, that acquaintance with the properties of material things, which is really the foundation of human consciousness. **1912** B. RUSSELL *Probl. Philos.* iv. 58 Common sense regards tables and chairs and the sun and moon and material objects generally as something radically different from minds. **1920** A. N. WHITEHEAD *Concept of Nature* ii. 43 Thus colour is not part of the reality of the material object. **1932** H. H. PRICE *Perception* ii. 52 'Material-objectness' cannot be defined without mention of it. **1933** *Mind* XLII. 291 On the phenomenalistic view of material-objectness, there *is* evidence that material objects exist. **1940** A. J. AYER *Found. Empirical Knowl.* i. 1 It does not normally occur to us that

there is any need..to justify our belief in the existence of material things. **1941** *Mind* L. 282 The puzzle is this: if sense-data are all that we are directly aware of in perception, how have we ever acquired the concept of 'material-objectness' at all? **1959** J. L. Austin *Sense & Sensibilia* (1962) ii. 7 'Material thing' is not an expression which the ordinary man would use. *Ibid.* x. 107 The material-object language *must somehow* be 'reducible' to the sense-datum language. **1964** *Philos. Rev.* LXXIII. 324 A corpse, like a material object, is non-conscious, rather than merely unconscious.

4. a. Concerned with or involving matter or corporeal substance, its presence, use, or agency. ***material theory*** (of heat): the theory that heat is a material substance ('caloric').

1649 Jer. Taylor *Gt. Exemp.* i. v. 149 These temptations are crasse and material, and soon discernable; it will require some greater observation to arm against such as are more spiritual and immaterial. **1822** Coleridge *Table-t.* 29 Dec., Schiller has the material Sublime: to produce an effect he sets you a whole town on fire [etc.]. *a* **1824** Campbell *To Rainbow*, When Science from Creation's face Enchantment's veil withdraws, What lovely visions yield their place To cold material laws! **1863** Tyndall *Heat* ii. §17 (1870) 23 Two rival theories..which are named respectively the *material theory*, and the *dynamical*, or *mechanical, theory* of heat. **1867** H. Macmillan *Bible Teach.* Pref. (1870) 14 Agriculture, though the most material of all our pursuits, is teaching us truths beyond its own direct province. **1874** Green *Short Hist.* ix. §1. 590 The attempt to secure spiritual results by material force. **1877** Mrs. Oliphant *Makers Flor.* iv. 94 The painter's art is at once ethereal and material. **1882** T. H. Green in *Mind* No. 25. 19 The material atomism of popular science.

b. In opprobrious use, usually coupled with *gross*: Characterized by conduct, a tendency, point of view, etc. which is not elevated; unspiritual.

1588 Kyd *Househ. Phil.* Wks. (1901) 267 Not of seruile or materiall witt, but..apt to studie or contemplat. **1700** Dryden *Cymon & Iph.* 135 His gross material soul at once could find Somewhat in her excelling all her kind. **1850** Robertson *Serm.* Ser. iii. vii. (1863) 101 The Romish doctrine contains a truth which it is of importance to disengage from the gross and material form with which it has been overlaid. **1853** C. Bronte *Villette* xxxvi, What I saw struck me..as grossly material, not poetically spiritual. **1875** Manning *Mission H. Ghost* ix. 257 The gross heavy material love of the world.

c. Relating to the physical, as opposed to the intellectual or spiritual, aspect of things; concerned with physical progress, bodily comfort, or the like. ***material culture***: the physical objects (tools, articles of domestic and religious use, dwelling-places, etc.) which give evidence of the type of culture developed by a social group.

1843 Prescott *Mexico* i. iii. I. 57 *note*, The Mexican heaven may remind one of Dante's in its material enjoyments; which, in both, are made up of light, music, and motion. *Ibid.* iv. ii. II. 128 It was the material civilization, which belongs neither to the one nor the other. **1858** Mrs. Carlyle *Lett.* II. 379 Better material accommodation you could have nowhere. **1861** M. Pattison *Ess.* (1889) I. 39 The old bonds of relationship, and community of material interests. **1873–4** Dixon *Two Queens* IV. xix. iv. 25 When the fury ceased, the city was a moral and material wreck. **1879** M. Arnold *Equality* Mixed Ess. 70 France..is the country where material well-being is most widely spread. **1929** *N. & Q. Anthropol.* (ed. 5) 187 The study of the artefacts and material culture of a people should not be viewed solely from their material aspects. *Ibid.* 188 The investigator of socio-religious matters may find that he cannot get information, and he will then find that a study of material culture provides him with a convenient avenue of approach. **1931** *Encycl. Social Sci.* IV. 622/1 Material equipment of culture is not, however, a force in itself... Material culture requires a complement less simple, less easily catalogued or analyzed, consisting of the body of intellectual knowledge. **1937** R. H. Lowie *Hist. Ethnol. Theory* iii. 27 Evolution is a positive fact in material culture. **1971** *World Archaeol.* III. 119 Most items of material culture will have been removed.

d. Gram. ***material noun***, = *mass noun*.

1892 [see *class-noun* (class *sb.* 10)]. **1892** H. Sweet *New Eng. Gram.* I. 56 When a material noun is used to express an individual object of definite shape, it is no longer a material noun, but a class-noun. **1925** Grattan & Gurrey *Our Living Lang.* xviii. 110 A material-noun is a word which stands for the whole mass of matter possessing the qualities implied by the word, or for an indefinite quantity of that matter—for example, *water, iron, veal, butter*. **1969** R. Kingdon *Palmer's Gram. Spoken Eng.* (ed. 3) ii. 61 Common nouns..are subdivided into Material nouns and Class nouns. Material nouns..name substances.

5. a. Of serious or substantial import; of much consequence; important.

1529 More *Dyaloge* i. Wks. 125/1 Sith this thing is much material, as wherupon many great thynges do depende. **1605** Shaks. *Macb.* iii. i. 136 Whose absence is no lesse materiall to me, Then is his Fathers. **1625** Bacon *Ess., Cunning* (Arb.) 439 He would put that which was most Materiall in the Post-script. **1665** Glanvill *Def. Van. Dogm.* 23 'Tis a pertinent and material enquiry to ask, whence the Soul is? **1666–7** Marvell *Corr.* Wks. 1872–5 II. 209 The Poll-bill is printed, but with no materiall errors. **1709** Swift *Adv. Relig.* Wks. 1755 II. i. 117 That is no material objection against the design itself. **1719** De Foe *Crusoe* ii. xv, I have nothing material to say. **1769** *Junius Lett.* iii. 19 The last charge..is indeed the most material of all. **1769** Burke *Lett., Mrq. Rockingham* (1844) I. 211 His consequence in the India House is much more material to him than his rank in parliament. **1823** Scott *Peveril* xx, When aware of this material fact, it became Julian's business to leave Liverpool directly. **1827** Hallam *Const. Hist.* (1876) I. v. 276 In one point more material,..the commons successfully vindicated their privileges. **1847** Grote *Greece* ii. xxxv. (1862) III. 248 The Athenians had a material interest in the quarrel. **1896** *Century Mag.* Nov. 22 [He] seldom interlined a word or made a material correction.

b. Predicatively, with *inf.* or *clause* as subject.

1547 J. Harrison *Exhort. Scottes* b viij, Whether he came out of Italy or not, is not muche materiall. **1590** Spenser *F.Q.* ii. x. 74 That were too long their infinite contents Here to record, ne much materiall. **1622** Mabbe tr. *Aleman's Guzman d'Alf.* ii. 102 It is not much materiall which gate wee goe out at. **1641** Wilkins *Math. Magick* i. vii. (1648) 50 'Tis not materiall to the force of this instrument, whether the rundles of it be big or little. **1712** M. Henry *Commun. w. God* i. Wks. 1853 I. 205/2 It is essential to a letter that it be directed, and material that it be directed right. **1802** *Med. Jrnl.* VIII. 256 It is very material to distinguish them with accuracy. **1890** Ld. Halsbury in *Law Times Rep.* LXIV. 3/2 Before dealing with the particular clauses..it is material to notice the problem which the Legislature had to solve.

c. Pertinent, germane, or essential *to*.

1603 Holland *Plutarch's Mor.* 232 Those [things] that be most materiall and necessarie for mans felicitie. **1611** Shaks. *Cymb.* i. vii. 207. **1665** Manley *Grotius' Low C. Warres* 121 Nor was it a little material, to their advantage, if [etc.]. **1697** Dryden *Virg. Georg.* ii. 149, I pass the rest, whose ev'ry Race and Name, And Kinds are less material to my Theme. **1819** Scott *Ivanhoe* xxvii, Certain passages material to his understanding the rest of this important narrative. **1824** Coleridge *Table-t.* 10 June, A slight contrast of character is very material to happiness in marriage. **1876** Gladstone *Homeric Synchr.* 145 The point material to the present inquiry is that [etc.].

d. Chiefly *Law*. Applied to evidence or facts which are of such significance as to be likely to influence the determination of a cause, to alter the character of an instrument, etc. Also const. inf.: Serving materially (*to* prove).

1581 Lambard *Eiren.* ii. vii. (1588) 213 To take..the Information..(or so much thereof as shall be materiall to prooue the Felonie). **1601** R. Johnson *Kingd. & Commw.* (1603) 80 What they did one against another in the time of Charles the fift, is not much materiall to prove their courage. **1799** *Hull Advertiser* 14 Sept. 3/3 He has been twice examined, but a material witness was wanting. **1848** Arnould *Mar. Insur.* (1866) I. ii. i. 489 Facts, the statement of which may reasonably be presumed likely to have such an influence on the judgment of the underwriter are called material facts; a statement of such facts is called a material representation. **1881** Ld. Coleridge in *Times* 5 July 4/2 The alteration which vitiates a contract must be material—that is, one which alters the character of the instrument itself.

†**e.** quasi-*adv.* In an important degree. *Obs.*

1653 Holcroft *Procopius* Pref. A 2, Procopius..was a very material concerned Agent in all these Wars.

†**6.** Full of matter, sound information, or sense. *Obs.*

1600 Shaks. *A.Y.L.* iii. iii. 32 A materiall foole. **1601** B. Jonson *Poetaster* v. i, What thinks Materiall Horace of his learning? *c* **1611** Chapman *Iliad* xxiv. 566 His speech euen charm'd his eares: So orderd; so materiall. **1612** Bacon *Ess., Despatch* (Arb.) 247 Beware of being too materiall, when there is any impediment, or obstruction in mens will. **1665** J. Livingston *Mem. Charact.* in *Sel. Biog.* (1845) I. 335 Mr. James Simson, a very able and materiall preacher. **1685** Evelyn *Mem.* (1857) II. 224 Her discourse, which was always material, not trifling.

†**7.** In physical sense: Bulky, massive, solid. *Obs.*

1657 Austen *Fruit Trees* ii. 166 Wild materiall fruit-trees have no power to engraft themselves. **1715** Leoni *Palladio's Archit.* (1742) I. 11 The Tuscan is so rude and material, that it is seldom used above ground. **1735** in *Pope's Lett.* I. Suppl. 30 This was only *in ordine ad*, to another more material Volume.

B. *sb.*

†**1.** *pl.* Things that are material. *Obs.*

1587 Golding *De Mornay* xiv. 206 What doth..matter [bring forth] but matter, and materiall but materialles? **1605** Timme *Quersit.* i. iv. 14 Simples may be distinguished..into those things which are simply formals, and into those which are simply materials.

2. a. The matter from which an article, fabric, or structure is made. Chiefly *collect. pl.* or *sing.* *raw material(s*: unmanufactured material; material which is in a preparatory stage in a manufacturing process. Also *fig.*

pl. **1556** *Aberd. Reg.* (1844) I. 294 To by stanis, lyme, and all materiallis neidfull thairto. **1610** B. Jonson *Alch.* i. i, Your stills, your glasses, your materialls. **1622** Massinger *Virg. Mart.* iii. i, [He] Took from the matrons' neck the richest jewels And purest gold as the materials To finish up his work [*sc.* an image]. **1665** Boyle *Occas. Refl.* (1848) 340 This Child..despising meer Bread,..his Mother is fain to disguise the Materials of it into Cake. **1725** De Foe *Voy. round World* (1840) 329 Gunpowder..with other materials for kindling fire. **1726** Swift *Gulliver* iii. iv, A palace may be built in a week, of materials so durable as to last for ever. **1796** [see raw A. 2 e]. **1864** Burton *Scot Abroad* I. iii. 118 Adventures which would make good raw materials for several novels. **1865** Lubbock *Preh. Times* 25 Considering how perishable are the materials out of which clothes are necessarily formed. **1870** Yeats *Nat. Hist. Comm.* 2 Without a considerable knowledge of raw materials, and of their adaptations, we could not live.

sing. **1638** Junius *Paint. Ancients* 47 Art can doe nothing without the materiall; whereas the materiall without Art hath her own worthinesse. **1662** Gerbier *Princ.* (1665) 25 When Builders see their Copings [etc.]..to decay they must have patience, since there is no Meterial but is subject there unto. **1796** Hunter tr. *St.-Pierre's Stud. Nat.* (1799) III. 648 By drawing from a foreign country the raw material of their clothing. **1828** Carlyle *Misc.* (1857) I. 206 It is not the material but the workman that is wanting. **1835** Ure *Philos. Manuf.* v. 207 Flax..constitutes the material of linen cloth. **1849** Macaulay *Hist. Eng.* iii. I. 351 The ordinary material was brick. **1855** *Ibid.* III. 417 The raw material out of which a good army may be formed existed in great abundance among the Irish. **1863** P. Barry *Dockyard Econ.* 100, £1,186 12*s.* 4¾ *d.* for material, and £797 16*s.* 11*d.* for labour. **1868** [see raw A. 2 e].

b. The elements, constituent parts, or substance of something (whether physical or non-physical).

1642 Rogers *Naaman* To Rdr., As they say of the materealls of the world, they would soone dissolve if [etc.]. **1651** Baxter *Inf. Bapt.* 59 If the very materials of the Church were a Ceremony, then the Church it self should be but a Ceremony. **1662** *Bk. Com. Prayer* Pref., The Main Body and Essentials of it (as well in the chiefest materials, as in the frame and order thereof) have continued the same unto this day. **1864** Kirk *Chas. Bold* I. i. 11 The material of the character was coarser and more robust. **1878** Huxley *Physiogr.* 189 The solid materials are shot forth into the air.

c. *pl.* In Ireland: The ingredients for making whisky punch. Now 'almost always shortened to *matts*, even in a bill' (H. C. Hart).

1842 S. Lover *Handy Andy* xxxviii, She..set about getting 'the materials' for making punch. **1888** H. Smart *Master of Rakehelly* II. 53 Take my advice, leave the 'matarials' alone to-night and stick to the claret.

3. In various non-physical applications: Something which can be worked up or elaborated, or of which anything is composed; esp. documents, etc. for historical composititon; evidence from which a conclusion may be framed.

1624 Ussher in *Lett. Lit. Men* (Camden) 131 To you I must be more beholding for furnishing me with materialls. **1625** Bacon *Ess., Seditions* (Arb.) 399 Concerning the Materialls of Seditions... The surest way to prevent Seditions..is to take away the Matter of them. **1690** Locke *Hum. Und.* ii. ii. §2 The simple ideas, the materials of all our knowledge. **1713** Hearne *Rem. & Collect.* 25 June (O.H.S.) IV. 205, I have read part of the B. of St. Asaph's Life of St. Winifrid, for wch I helped him to several Materials out of Bodley. **1783** Cowper *Lett.* 7 Mar., Were my letters composed of materials worthy of your acceptance, they should be longer. **1830** D'Israeli *Chas. I*, III. Pref. 3 Research and Criticism, only furnish the materials of Meditation. **1864** Bowen *Logic* ii. 33 Perception, Memory and Imagination, through which we collect the materials for thinking. **1867** Howells *Ital. Journ.* iii. 37 Their books are material, not literature. **1877** Owen *Wellesley's Desp.* p. xlv, Wellesley..was anxious to secure fresh and malleable 'material', rather than overformed or misformed agents.

4. A stuff or fabric; in *Dressmaking*, woollen or cloth stuff as opposed to silks, etc.

1860 Dickens *Uncomm. Trav.* iv, A cool material with a light glazed surface, being the covering of the seats. **1875** *Plain Needlework* 10 The material used in the South to strain milk, called 'Cheese Cloth' in the trade.

5. Tools, implements, or apparatus for performing an action. Now only in ***writing materials***.

1731 Bailey vol. II, *Materials*, tools or stuff proper for the making or doing any thing. **1778** Pryce *Min. Cornub.* 324 *Materials*, all tools and tackle, timber and implements, that belong to a Mine; and in large Mines a person is appointed to take care of them, who is called the Material-Man. **1855** Prescott *Philip II*, ii. iii. (1857) 226 De Seso called for writing materials.

6. The *matériel* of an army. *rare*$^{-1}$.

1815 Southey in *Q. Rev.* XIII. 521 Their [*sc.* the French army's] baggage, equipage, tumbrils, artillery, the whole of what is called the *material*, were taken.

7. Preceded by a qualifying word, as ***officer material***, a person who has (or persons who have) qualities thought of as suitable for an officer; similarly ***headmaster material***, etc.; also with non-animate qualifier, as ***football material***, a person or persons potentially suitable as footballers; ***grammar-school material***, a person or persons suitable for admission to a grammar school.

1892 *College Index* (Auburn, Alabama) Nov. I. i. 23 He still kept a sharp lookout for football material. **1927** *Officers Training Corps Gaz.* Apr. 59/1 The sorely needed officer material caused by the early casualties. **1946** *Amer. Speech* XXI. 238 *Officer material*, an enlisted man short in mentality. **1951** H. Wouk *Caine Mutiny* xi. 123, I regard both those men as excellent officer material. **1964** 'E. Peters' *Flight of Witch* i. 9 Tom Kenyon, confident, clever and ambitious, was obvious headmaster material. **1968** L. Berg *Risinghill* 86 The inspector who denounced the school the first time was a man who was interested in grammar-school 'material'. **1969** M. Pugh *Last Place Left* xxvii. 194 It was difficult recruiting men... 'Some of them, well, they're not leadership material.' **1969** B. Weil *Dossier IX* ii. 4 His secretary came in. She was a tall fair girl with a tendency to stride. Wren officer material, Asher thought. **1970** 'J. Melville' *New Kind of Killer* i. 8 Her report..was, on the whole, a favourable one: 'This officer is good promotion material.' **1971** D. Eden *Afternoon Walk* viii. 109 Aren't all top executives ulcer material?

8. *attrib.*: ***materials technology***, ***material(s testing***; **material(s clerk**, a clerk who controls the supply of materials in a business house; **material(s control** (see quot. 1959); hence ***materials controller***; **material dress**, a dress made of woollen stuff; **material(s handling**, the movement and storage of materials in a factory; **material(s man**, (*a*) see quot. 1778; (*b*) one who deals in materials for building, etc.; **material(s science**, that branch of science which treats of the structure and properties of materials, esp. in so far as they are relevant to their usefulness and potential applications; so ***material(s scientist***;

material yard, a yard in which materials are stored.

1900 *Engineering Mag.* XIX. 707 It is the duty of the *material clerk to see that sufficient material is in stock, or ordered, to provide for orders in hand. **1904** *Daily Chron.* 2 June 9/3 Timekeeper and Materials Clerk required by large West-end contractors. **1918** C. E. KNOEPPEL *Organization & Administration* xv. 252 The *material control sheet takes care of pieces ordered, pieces rough, pieces in progress, and pieces finished. **1938** W. B. CORNELL *Business Organization* xvi. 318 The other important duties of the standards and methods section include..development of stores and material control and production control methods. **1959** *Gloss. Terms Work Study (B.S.I.)* 33 *Material control*, procedures and means by which the correct quantity and quality of materials and components are made available to meet production plans. **1962** A. BATTERSBY *Guide to Stock Control* 123 The Materials Control office calculated that the increase in the first-grade stock would have to be 200 items to preserve the same risk level as before. *Ibid.* x. 90 The Finance Director..will then need a subordinate who can translate his general decisions on policy into detailed instructions. The subordinate would be the *Materials Controller: this title is better than the more usual 'Stock Controller' because, as we have seen, he controls the *flow* of materials rather than the stocks themselves. **1884** *Daily News* 27 Oct. 2/1 The increasing popularity of silks as opposed to what are known as '*material' dresses. **1921** E. T. ELBOURNE *Factory Administration & Cost Accounts* (new ed.) 807 A form of production service having special reference to *material handling and custody. **1932** S. J. KOSHKIN *Mod. Materials Handling* i. 2 It is of the greatest importance that the materials-handling methods and devices should be sufficiently worked out at the time the plant is designed so as to make them an integral part of the design. **1966** A. BATTERSBY *Math. in Managem.* vii. 163 A recent paper dealing with steel fabrication showed that an extra crane costing £15,000 would not be needed in a new materials-handling system. **1778** *Material-Man [see 5]. **1819** WHEATON *Cases Supreme Court U.S.* IV. 438 Material men furnishing repairs to a domestic ship. **1832** BABBAGE *Econ. Manuf.* xx. (ed. 3) 202 A Materials-man selects, purchases, receives and delivers all articles required. **1888** BRYCE *Amer. Commw.* II. App. 679 Mechanics, material-men, artisans, and labourers..have a lien upon the property upon which they have bestowed labour or furnished material. **1961** (*title of periodical*) Progress in *materials science. **1966** P. FELTHAM *Deformation & Strength of Materials* p.v, One of the effects of the unprecedented advance in the synthesis and use of new materials in the last few decades..has been the widespread introduction of 'materials science' into curricula of university courses. **1974** *New Scientist* 9 May 349/1 (Advt.), Applicants should have a degree in physics or a material science discipline. **1974** *Nature* 16 Aug. p. vii (Advt.), A vacancy exists for a *Materials Scientist to study basic factors concerned with lubrication, wear, fatigue and corrosion of plastics and metals used in the manufacture of orthopaedic implants. **1962** *Technology* June 129/1 The course on *materials technology will draw on the methods of physics, chemistry, metallurgy and engineering. **1972** N. J. PARRATT *Fibre-Reinforced Materials Technol.* p. ix, Much of industry is concerned with making materials or with turning them into useful hardware, so that it cannot safely ignore any advances in materials technology. **1924** *Trans. Amer. Soc. Mech. Engin. Index* 124/2 (*heading*) *Materials testing. **1950** *Chem. Engin. Progress* XLVI. 110/3 Materials Testing Reactor which..will be used in studies of material to be employed in building reactors. **1969** R. F. LANG tr. *Henglein's Chem. Technol.* 315 The so-called technical laboratories..carry out the routine analyses..as well as material testing. **1901** *J. Black's Carp. & Build., Scaffolding* 89 The smaller builder, having..no *material yard, has no convenient place to store poles when not in use.

†**ma'terial**, *v.* *Obs.* [f. MATERIAL *a.* and *sb.*]

1. *trans.* To bring into material form.

1643 SIR T. BROWNE *Relig. Med.* I. §37 That the whole frame of a beast..is left in the same state after death, as before it was materialled unto life.

2. To furnish material for.

1661 GLANVILL *Van. Dogm.* 174 Comets..are materiall'd of vapours. *Ibid.* 216 Plants are partly material'd of water.

materialism (mə'tɪərɪəlɪz(ə)m). [a. mod.L. *mātēriālismus*, f. L. *mātēriāl-is* MATERIAL *a.*: see -ISM. Cf. F. *matérialisme* (1751 in Hatz.-Darm.).]

1. *Philos.* The opinion that nothing exists except matter and its movements and modifications; also, in a more limited sense, the opinion that the phenomena of consciousness and will are wholly due to the operation of material agencies. Often applied by opponents to views that are considered logically to lead to these conclusions, or to involve the attribution to material causes of effects that should be referred to spiritual causes.

1748 NEEDHAM in *Phil. Trans.* XLV. 665 Not that I imagined that..you..would think my Principles any way tending to Materialism. **1758** GRAY *Let.* 18 Aug. Wks. 1888 II. 373, I am as sorry as you seem to be, that our acquaintance harped so much on the subject of materialism. **1823** COLERIDGE *Table-t.* 3 Jan., 'And man became a living soul'. Materialism will never explain these last words. **1877** E. CAIRD *Philos. Kant* ii. 13 Sensationalism necessitates materialism, for it must explain sensations as impressions made by a material object. **1898** J. R. ILLINGWORTH *Div. Immanence* vi. 137 The mechanical automaton that materialism believes him [*viz.* man] always to be.

2. Transferred uses. **a.** Applied in reproach to theological views (e.g. on the operation of the sacraments or the nature of the future life) that are supposed to imply a defective sense of the reality of things purely spiritual.

1850 ROBERTSON *Serm.* III. vii. (1863) 103 The miserable materialism of the mass. **1898** J. R. ILLINGWORTH *Div. Immanence* vi. 143 The growth of the sacramental system was an historical necessity; which, despite of the religious materialism into which it too frequently lapsed [etc.].

b. In art, the tendency to lay stress on the material aspect of the objects represented.

1850 MRS. JAMESON *Leg. Monast. Ord.* (1863) 421, I give a sketch from a Spanish picture just to show the materialism of the conception. **1852** —— *Leg. Madonna* (1857) Introd. 33 The grand materialism of Michael Angelo is supposed to have been allied to the genius of Dante.

c. Devotion to material needs or desires, to the neglect of spiritual matters; a way of life, opinion, or tendency based entirely upon material interests.

1851 HAWTHORNE *Snow Image* (1879) 31 The stubborn materialism of her husband. **1857** TOULMIN SMITH *Parish* 505 Good old customs, which modern selfishness and cold materialism shrink from. **1899** W. R. INGE *Chr. Mysticism* viii. 317 Teutonic civilization..is prevented from sinking into moral materialism by its high standard of domestic life. **1903** A. & E. CASTLE *Star Dreamer* 24, I fear..you will never rise beyond the grossest everyday materialism.

¶**3.** *concr.* The system of material things; the material universe.

1817 CHALMERS *Astron. Disc.* vii. 231 He, who instead of seeing the traces of a manifold wisdom in its manifold varieties, sees nothing in them all but the exquisite structures and the lofty dimensions of materialism. *Ibid.* 233.

materialist (mə'tɪərɪəlɪst). [ad. mod.L. *mātēriālista*: see prec. and -IST. Cf. F. *matérialiste* (18th c.).]

I. Senses related to MATERIAL *a.*

1. An adherent of the philosophical system known as materialism.

1668 H. MORE *Div. Dial.*, The Proper Characters of the Persons in the ensuing Dialogues... Hylobares, A young, witty, and well-moralized Materialist. **1678** CUDWORTH *Intell. Syst.* I. v. 759 The Old Atheistick Materialists. **1739** HUME *Hum. Nat.* I. iv. §5 (1888) 239 The materialists, who conjoin all thought with extension. **1856** SIR B. BRODIE *Psychol. Inq.* I. ii. 38 The materialist argues that we know nothing of mind except as being dependent on material organization.

¶**b.** *fig.* with reference to disbelief in 'soul'.

1807 SOUTHEY *Spec. Later Eng. Poets* I. Pref. 31 Those who hold that poetry is an acquirable art,—the materialists of fine literature.

c. Used to render Eccl. L. *māteriārii*: see MATERIARIAN.

1702 ECHARD *Eccl. Hist.* (1710) 514 The heresiarch Hermogenes..maintained..that all evils proceeded out of matter; from whence he and his followers were called Materialists. **1730–6** in BAILEY (fol.); and in modern Dicts.

2. Applied by Berkeley to believers in the objective existence of matter.

c **1705** BERKELEY *Commpl. Bk.* Wks. 1871 IV. 472 The mind, even according to the materialists, perceiving onely the impressions made upon its brain.

3. One who takes a material view of things.

1853 LYTTON *My Novel* VII. vi, 'O materialist!' cried the boy..'you would debase the gods to a gin-palace'.

4. A believer in the materiality of heat. *rare.*

1863 TYNDALL *Heat* ii. §18 (1870) 24 The development of heat by mechanical means..was a great difficulty with the materialists.

5. *attrib.* or as *adj.* = Materialistic.

1833 LYTTON *Eng. & Engl.* (ed. 2) II. 238 He has studied Locke, and become materialist. **1869** M. PATTISON *Serm.* (1885) 172 A materialist tone is said to pervade all our reasonings about practical questions. **1876** MOZLEY *Univ. Serm.* iii. (1877) 61 This horrible materialist indifference to the extinction of our being.

II. Senses related to MATERIAL *sb.*

†**6.** A druggist; 'a merchant who sells the articles of the materia medica' (*Syd. Soc. Lex.*). [= G. *materialist*, mod.L. (Pharm.) *materialista*.] *Obs. rare*⁻⁰.

1728 BAILEY, *Materialist*, a Druggist.

7. One who mixes the 'materials' for whisky punch. ? *nonce-use.*

1843 THACKERAY *Irish Sk. Bk.* viii, There is a dirty coffee-room, with a strong smell of whisky; indeed three young 'materialists' are employed at the moment.

materialistic (məˌtɪərɪə'lɪstɪk), *a.* [f. MATERIALIST + -IC.]

1. Pertaining to, characterized by, or addicted to materialism, in any of the senses of the term.

1845 MAURICE *Mor. & Met. Philos.* in *Encycl. Metrop.* (1854) II. 45 The search for elements by the Ionic School struck Clemens as simply materialistic. **1877** DOWDEN *Shaks. Prim.* vi. 102 Sly is of the family of Sancho Panza, gross and materialistic in his tastes, and habits. **1877** E. CAIRD *Philos. Kant* ii. 13 A materialistic explanation of the universe. **1898** J. R. ILLINGWORTH *Div. Immanence* i. §3. 21 Minds of a materialistic bias.

2. Pertaining to the 'material theory' of heat. *rare.*

1860 TYNDALL *Glac.* II. xix. 331 According to the materialistic view of heat, bodies are figured as sponges, and heat a kind of fluid absorbed by them.

So **materia'listical** *a.* in the same sense (Ogilvie *Suppl.* 1855). Hence **materia'listically** *adv.*, in a materialistic manner.

1852 BUNSEN *Hippolytus* II. 60 The form of expressing the manifestation of God in the mind, as if God was Himself using human speech to man..was originally never meant to be understood materialistically. **1890** J. PULSFORD *Loyalty to Christ* I. 333 A materialistic mind will think materialistically even about the teaching of Christ. **1973** C. & R. MILNER *Black Players* v. 115 There's too much paranoia, too much greed... And suspicion, and too much materialistical fear.

materiality (mətɪərɪ'ælɪtɪ). [a. mod.L. *mātēriālitās*, f. late L. *mātēriālis* MATERIAL *a.*: see -ITY. Cf. F. *matérialité* (1690 in Hatz.-Darm.).]

1. That which constitutes the 'matter' of something: opposed to *formality*. ? *Obs.*

The first quot. is app. unmeaning, but attests the existence of the word at that date.

a **1529** SKELTON *Col. Cloute* 561 And bryng in materialites And qualyfyed qualytes Of pluralytes. **1592** G. HARVEY *Four Lett.* Wks. (Grosart) I. 229 As in other thinges, so in Artes, formality doth well; but materiality worketh the feat. **1646** H. LAWRENCE *Comm. Angells* 130 Righteousnes, which is, as I may say, the materiality of peace. **1647** TRAPP *Comm. Mark* ii. 28 The schoolmen say that God can dispense with the materiality of any precept in the decalogue, the three first excepted. **1652** L. S. *People's Liberty* xviii. 45 Whether ..God..can dispence with the Commandements of the 2d. Table, according to the materialitie of them. **1660** JER. TAYLOR *Duct. Dubit.* II. ii. Rule ii. (1676) 215 If blood be taken in its own materiality when the beast is dead.

2. The quality of being material.

1570 DEE *Math. Pref.* *j, Neither Number, nor Magnitude, haue any Materialitie. **1647** H. MORE *Poems* 108 Vitality Doth move th' inert Materiality Of great and little worlds. **1690** LOCKE *Hum. Und.* IV. iii. §6 He..will scarce find his reason able to determine him fixedly for or against the soul's materiality. **1794** G. ADAMS *Nat. & Exp. Philos.* I vii. 250 The decomposition of the rays of light proves their materiality. **1863** TYNDALL *Heat* ii. 25 The dynamical theory..of heat, discards the idea of materiality as applied to heat. **1871** TYLOR *Prim. Cult.* I. 412 Wuttke says, the ghosts of the dead have to him a misty and evanescent materiality.

b. That which is material; *pl.* things material.

1811 SHELLEY *St. Irvyne* xii, Let them suppose human nature capable of no influence from anything but materiality. **1822–34** *Good's Study Med.* (ed. 4) III. 85 To enable it to behold God in the materialities of his works. **1821** LAMB *Elia* Ser. I. *Old Benchers Inner T.*, When the grown world flounders about in the darkness of sense and materiality. **1855** *Athenæum* 3 Nov. 1267 The former believes in visions, the latter in materialities. **1880** W. WALLACE *Epicureanism* vi. 102 The soul is a subtler and more refined materiality, which is thus endowed with more ..refined perceptions than the bodily organs.

3. Material aspect or character; mere outwardness or externality.

1599 SANDYS *Europæ Spec.* (1632) 18 Their acts of Pietie, being placed more in the very massie materialitie of the outward worke, than in the puritie of the heart. **1651** JER. TAYLOR *Serm. for Year* II. ii. 15 The materiality and imperfection of the law. **1765** JOHNSON *Pref. to Shaks.* p. xxvi, It is false, that any representation is mistaken for reality; that any dramatick fable in its materiality was ever credible.

4. The quality of being material or important for the purpose contemplated. Now *legal.*

1644 VICARS *God in Mount* 96 A peece of unexpressible materiality and advantageous benefit to the whole Cause. **1780** BENTHAM *Princ. Legisl.* ix. §3 There are two points with regard to which an act may have been advised or unadvised. 1. The existence of the circumstance itself. 2. The materiality of it. **1824** H. J. STEPHEN *Pleading* 256 Rules which tend to secure the materiality of the issue. **1849** J. P. KENNEDY *W. Wirt* (1860) I. xiii. 154 The relevancy or materiality of the papers referred to was not shown. **1884** *Manch. Exam.* 29 Mar. 5/2 As he had an affidavit swearing to the materiality of the documents he asked for the order.

materialization (mətɪərɪəlaɪ'zeɪʃən). [f. next + -ATION.] The action of the verb MATERIALIZE.

1. The making a thing material (esp. as opposed to *spiritual*); the giving a material form to.

1843 *For. & Col. Q. Rev.* II. 338 Is not this symbolization or materialization necessarily connected with deism in the abstract? **1856** R. A. VAUGHAN *Mystics* (1860) II. IX. i. 125 The materialization of spiritual truth. **1899** W. R. INGE *Chr. Mysticism* VII. 263 A truer view sees in them [miracles] a materialisation of mystical symbols.

2. *Spiritualism.* The appearance of a spirit in bodily form.

1880 in WEBSTER, Suppl. **1881** *Dr. Gheist* 39 This is what Mr. Faxton calls Materialisation. **1882** *Conf. Medium* 47 We changed the form of the circle for the materialisations.

materialize (mə'tɪərɪəlaɪz), *v.* [f. MATERIAL *a.* + -IZE.]

1. *trans.* To make material or represent as material; to give or ascribe a material existence to; to invest with material attributes.

1710 ADDISON *Tatler* No. 154 ¶6 Virgil..having with wonderful Art and Beauty materializ'd (if I may so call it) a Scheme of abstracted Notions. **1713** STEELE *Guardian* No. 172 ¶4 By this means we materialize our ideas, and make them as lasting as the ink and paper. **1764** REID *Inquiry* vii. (1801) 448 These analogies will be apt to impose upon philosophers..and to lead them to materialize the mind and its faculties. **1843** HAWTHORNE *Amer. Note-Bks.* (1883) 333, I had the glimmering of an idea, and endeavoured to materialize it in words. **1848** R. I. WILBERFORCE *Doctr. Incarnation* iii. (1852) 40 Those who would materialize spirit. **1883** H. DRUMMOND *Nat. Law in Spir. W.* ii. (1884) 76 He insists on having all things materialised before his eyes in Nature.

2. *Spiritualism.* To cause (a spirit, etc.) to appear in bodily form.

1880 in WEBSTER Suppl. **1881** *Dr. Gheist* 39 Mr. Faxton firmly believed..that the spirits of the dead may become materialised. **1882** *Conf. Medium* 46 Bunches of artificial flowers were either materialised or levitated. **1885** WHITTIER

Pr. Wks. (1889) II. 314 A Newbury minister..rode..over to Hampton to lay a ghost who had materialized himself.

b. *intr.* To assume a bodily form.

1884 B. MATTHEWS in *Harper's Mag.* May 911/1 The..ghosts..gave dark séances and manifested and materialized.

c. *transf.* To come into perceptible existence; to become actual fact; to 'come off' (orig. *U.S.* in journalistic use).

1885 MISS MURFREE *Proph. Gt. Smoky Mount.* i. 18 Some fifteen or twenty hounds that suddenly materialized among the bee-hives and the althea bushes. **1887** *Boston* (Mass.) *Jrnl.* 12 Dec. 2/6 That attack upon the Interstate Commerce law, which was predicted to occur as soon as Congress met, does not materialize. **1891** *Blackw. Mag.* May 741 Year after year passed and these promises failed to materialise. **1898** *Spectator* 23 July 106 The Protestant revolters from the Unionist party failed, as the Americans say, to materialise, but instead appeared an angry crowd of Irishmen. **1900** *Ibid.* 6 Oct. 445 Out of the mist of notes and protocols..a policy seems gradually to be materialising.

3. *trans.* To make materialistic. Also *intr.* to favour materialistic views.

1820 [see MATERIALIZING]. **1836** *Fraser's Mag.* XIII. 249 The public mind is not yet so thoroughly materialised by long dealing with..exact sciences [etc.]. **1840** GLADSTONE *Ch. Princ.* 182 Those who materialise in religion. **1842** MRS. GORE *Fascin.* 144 A soul materialized by gluttony. **1866** LIDDON *Bampt. Lect.* iv. (1875) 185 There is in man unhappily a tendency to materialize spiritual truth. **1882** M. ARNOLD *Irish Ess.*, etc. 121 The system..tends to materialize our upper class, vulgarize our middle class, brutalize our lower class.

Hence **ma'terialized** *ppl. a.*, **ma'terializing** *vbl. sb.* (*attrib.*) and *ppl. a.* Also **ma'terializer**, one who materializes.

1820 RANKEN *Hist. France* VIII. iv. 370 The Epicurean or materialising tendencies of his immediate predecessor Gassendi. **1824** *New Monthly Mag.* X. 82 These materializers of the airy nothings of the mind. **1852** MRS. JAMESON *Leg. Madonna* (1857) 184 This materialised theology. **1874** GLADSTONE in *Contemp. Rev.* Oct. 677 The materializing tendencies of the age. **1882** *Conf. Medium* 44 Materialised spirits can vanish like a flash of lightning. *Ibid.* 48 This is the first materialising séance that my friend has ever attended. **1898** WATTS-DUNTON *Aylwin* II. iv, The gold which modern society finds to be more precious than..all that was held precious in less materialised times.

materially (mə'tɪərɪəlɪ), *adv.* [f. MATERIAL *a.* + -LY².]

1. Chiefly *Philos.* and *Logic.* With regard to matter as opposed to form. Also, with regard to constituent matter; in respect of material cause.

1502 *Ord. Crysten Men* (W. de W. 1506) I. iii. 22 Some thynges they make in operacyon wythout all onely, the whiche thynges are not in the soule materyally. **1646** J. WHITAKER *Uzziah* 6 Men may doe many things right materially.., and yet themselves..may not be upright. **1651** BIGGS *New Disp.* ¶250 A Catarrhe is materially from vapours out of the stomack. **1658** BAXTER *Saving Faith* iii. 18 May I not say, that materially a Ship and a Barge do differ but gradually, because *ex materia* they are not a Ship or Barge? **1675** R. BURTHOGGE *Causa Dei* 59 Though the Damned sin materially..yet 'tis a great Question whether they may be rationally affirmed formally to sin there. **1685** SOUTH *Twelve Serm.* (1692) 482 An Ill Intention is certainly sufficient to spoil..an Act in itself Materially Good. **1685, 1697** [see FORMALLY 1]. **1864** BOWEN *Logic* ii. 42 What is formally correct may be materially false. **1876** L. STEPHEN *Eng. Th. in 18th C.* II. IX. vi, The good deeds of the heathen, like the good deeds of the brutes, are materially not formally virtuous.

2. In, by, with, or in respect of matter or material substance; 'in the state of matter' (J.).

1594 BLUNDEVIL *Exerc.* III. I. (1636) 273 Superficies [are] the bounds of a body, which is that which hath imaginatively, but not materially, both length, bredth, and depth. **1646** SIR T. BROWNE *Pseud. Ep.* III. ix. 124 The generation of bodies is not effected..of soules, that is, by Irradiation,..but therein a transmission is made materially from some parts, and Ideally from every one. **1660** R. COKE *Power & Subj.* 32 All rightful Kings are so, whether they be materially anointed..or not. **1717** L. HOWEL *Desiderius* (ed. 3) 175 As he created all Men out of the same matter, they are materially equal.

†**3.** Of speaking or writing: With an appropriate or sound use of matter; soundly; to the point. *Obs.*

1605 BACON *Adv. Learn.* II. xxi. §7 There is small doubt but that men can write best and most really & materialy in their owne professions. **1607** TOPSELL *Four-f. Beasts* (1658) 266 Finding nothing of substance in him, which is not more materially, perspicuously, profitably, and familiarly..expressed by them. **1638** FEATLY *Strict. Lyndom.* I. 13 What hee materially answereth to the Knights allegations. **1646** SIR T. BROWNE *Pseud. Ep.* II. iii. 70 Bœtius de Boot,..in his Tract, *de lapidibus & gemmis*, speakes very materially hereof. **1749** CHESTERF. *Lett.* (1792) II. 282 The late Lord Townshend always spoke materially with argument and knowledge, but never pleased.

4. In a material degree; to a material or important extent; substantially, considerably.

1654 tr. *Scudery's Curia Pol.* 179 There are many Circumstances most materially considerable in them, as their age, their humour, their inclination. **1711** SHAFTESB. *Charac.* (1737) III. Misc. v. iii. 332 It is sufficient that they know that those Copys which they leave, are not materially corrupted. **1817** SHELLEY *Let. to Godwin* 7 Dec., My health has been materially worse. **1846** GROTE *Greece* I. xvii. (1862) II. 422 Tribes differing materially in habits and civilization. **1853** BRIGHT *Sp., India* 3 June (1876) 11 To comprehend how materially the great manufacturing interests are concerned. **1890** 'R. BOLDREWOOD' *Col. Reformer* (1891) 126 Short cuts, by..which the road was materially shortened.

5. In respect of material interests.

1871 MORLEY *Voltaire* (1886) 9 People with whom the world goes fairly well materially.

ma'terialness. [f. MATERIAL *a.* + -NESS.] The quality of being material.

1587 GOLDING *De Mornay* iv. 47 The imperfections which are in all things, (as chaungeablenesse, weakenesse, materialnesse, and such like). **1729** *State Trial Couns. Strange* in *Proc. agst. T. Bainbridge* (T.) This affidavit is not sufficient as to the inability or materialness of the witnesses. **1811** *Chron.* in *Ann. Reg.* 363 A sort of criterion by which to judge of the materialness of a book. **1903** A. B. DAVIDSON *Old Test. Proph.* xiii. 222 The outstanding characteristic of the Old Testament dispensation was its materialness.

‖**materia medica** (mə'tɪərɪə 'mɛdɪkə). [med.Latin, literal transl. of Gr. ὕλη ἰατρική (Galen) = medical material.]

1. The remedial substances used in the practice of medicine.

1699 M. LISTER *Journ. Paris* 244 The Arabians were wise, and knowing in the Materia Medica, to have put it in their Alkêrmes. **1752** BERKELEY *Th. on Tar-water* Wks. 1871 III. 496 Can any instance be produced in the whole materia medica..of the virtue of a medicine tried on greater numbers? **1799** *Med. Jrnl.* I. 56 The Purple Fox-glove is a medicine which, for some time, stood high in the list of the materia medica. **1817** J. BRADBURY *Trav. Amer.* 116 As I supposed this bag contained the whole *materia medica* of the nation, I examined it with some attention.

fig. **1768-74** TUCKER *Lt. Nat.* (1834) II. 97 What I may call the materia medica of morality. **1783** J. BEATTIE *Let.* 30 Mar. *Life*, etc. (1806) II. 122 It would be a valuable addition to the *materia medica* of government. **1796** BURKE *Regic. Peace* iv. Wks. IX. 124 Among other miserable remedies, that have been found in the *materia medica* of the old College, a change of Ministry will be proposed.

2. That branch of medical science which treats of these substances.

1811 A. T. THOMSON *Lond. Disp.* II. (1818) I. **1845** E. BALLARD & A. B. GARROD (*title*) Elements of Materia Medica and Therapeutics.

†**Materian.** = next *sb.*

1730-6 BAILEY (fol.), *Materians.*

‖**materia prima** (mə'tɪərɪə 'praɪmə). [L., 'first matter'; cf. Gr. ἡ πρώτη ὕλη (see HYLE).] = *first matter* (MATTER *sb.*¹ 6 c).

1551 S. GARDINER *Explication True Catholique Fayth* 137 If we agree with the Philosophers that there is (*Materia prima*)..the same (*Materia prima*) beyng as it were (substancia) that altereth not. [*a* **1586** SIDNEY *Apol. Poetrie* (1868) 55 The quiddity of..*Prima materia* will hardely agree with a Corslet.] **1603** HOLLAND tr *Plutarch's Morals* xvi. 229 The substance or matter that hath neither forme nor any colour, which they call *Materia prima*, is a subject capable of all formes. **1665** J. LOCKE *Let.* in P. King *Life of Locke* (1829) 20 Poor *materia prima* was canvassed cruelly. *Ibid.*, The young monks..dispute as eagerly for *materia prima*, as if they were to make their dinner on it. *a* **1721** PRIOR *Locke & Montaigne* in *Dialogues of Dead* (1907) 240 When he [*sc.* Descartes] gave Us his subtil matter, he only new Christened Aristotles *Materia prima*. **1905** W. JAMES in *Jrnl. Philos.* 25 May 281 'Pure experience'..was the name I gave to the *materia prima* of everything. **1961** *Times* 28 Dec. 11/4 A continuum of active or quiescent energy which..would reintroduce a *materia prima* to the satisfaction of metaphysicians.

†**Materi'arian**, *a.* and *sb. Obs.* [f. late L. *māteriāri-us* (f. *māteria* MATTER) + -AN.] Applied to ancient heretics who believed in the eternity of matter.

1678 CUDWORTH *Intell. Syst.* I. iv. §6. 197 Hermogenes and other ancient pretenders to Christianity did..assert the self-existence and improduction of the Matter, for which cause they were commonly called Materiarii, or the Materiarian Hereticks. *Ibid.*, These Materiarian Theists acknowledged God to be a Perfectly-understanding Being.

†**materiary**, *a. Obs. rare*⁻¹. [ad. L. *māteriārius*, f. *māteria*: see MATTER *sb.*¹ and -ARY.] Pertaining to matter (in quot. *ellipt.*).

1650 BULWER *Anthropomet.* 130 An excrement, not a part, and if a part, altogether an excrementitious materiarie.

†**ma'teriate**, *a.* and *sb. Obs.* [ad. L. *māteriāt-us*, f. *māteria* MATTER; see -ATE.] **A.** *adj.*

1. Produced from material; composed or consisting of matter.

1588 FRAUNCE *Lawiers Log.* I. iii. 16 b, The matter and the thing materiate. **1619** SIR A. GORGES tr. *Bacon's De Sap. Vet.* 23 They that would haue one simple beginning referre it vnto God: or if a materiate beginning, they would haue it various in power. **1686** GOAD *Celest. Bodies* III. iv. 507 The Potency..of that great Congress call'd me to look toward some materiate Cause. **1694** R. BURTHOGGE *Reason & Nat. Spirits* 157 Local Motion..is not Matter, or Materiate, but yet is in Matter, as United unto it.

b. Solid, dense.

1626 BACON *Sylva* §326 Gold (which is the most Ponderous and Materiate amongst Metalls).

2. Involved in matter: said of persons and things.

1626 BACON *Sylva* §114-5 After long Inquiry of Things, Immerse in Matter, to interpose some Subiect, which is Immateriate, or lesse Materiate. **1634** T. JOHNSON *Parey's Chirurg.* II. (1678) 46 Epicures, and other, too much natural and materiate Philosophers. **1647** J. HALL *Poems* 95 Materiate and grosse.

3. *Metaph.* 'United with matter; embodied in matter: said of an Aristotelian form' (*Cent. Dict.*).

B. *sb.* 'A material substance; a thing formed of matter' (Ogilvie 1882).

materiate (mə'tɪərɪeɪt), *v.* Now *rare* or *Obs.* [f. L. *māteriāt-*, ppl. stem of *māteriāre* (in class. Latin to construct of wood, in scholastic use as in 1 below), f. *māteria* MATTER *sb.*¹]

1. *trans.* In scholastic use. **a.** To supply or be the matter or material part of; in *passive*, to be constituted materially *by* something.

1680 BOYLE *Scept. Chem.* II. 157 When the material Parts..retain their own Nature in the things materiated, as some of the Schoolmen speak. **1691** BAXTER *Nat. Ch.* iii. 10 The Empire,..headed by one Christian Soveraign, and materiated by Christian Subjects..was all one National Church.

b. To render (a 'form') inherent in a particular 'matter'.

1653, 1654 [see MATERIATED *ppl. a.*]. **1823** DE QUINCEY *Lett. to Yng. Man* Wks. 1860 XIV. 57 *note*, The particular error by which this mere formal term of relation was *materiated* (if I may so say) in one of its accidents.

†**2.** In the class. Latin sense: To construct of wood. *Obs.* (? *nonce-use*).

a **1693** *Urquhart's Rabelais* III. lii. 429 Wooden Furniture..should be materiated of this kind of Timber.

Hence **ma'teriated** *ppl. a.*

1653 H. MORE *Antid. Ath.* II. v. §3 The effects of an inadvertent form (λόγος ἔνυλος) of materiated or incorporated art or seminal reason. **1654** WHITLOCK *Zootomia* 396 How many [elements] go to Mans Creation (or any materiated Substance)..is much debated.

†**materi'ation.** *Obs.* [ad. L. *māteriātiōn-em*, in class. Latin n. of action to *māteriārī* to procure timber, f. *māteria* timber, MATTER *sb.*¹; in scholastic Latin n. of action to *māteriāre*: see prec.]

1. (See quots.)

1623 COCKERAM, *Materiation*, the felling of timber for building. **1656** BLOUNT *Glossogr.*, *Materiation* (*materiatio*) the felling of timber for building, preparing of timber wood for service in War. Dr. Br[owne].

2. The action of MATERIATE *v.* 1.

1646 SIR T. BROWNE *Pseud. Ep.* VI. i. 274 Creation; that is,..a formation not only of matter, but of forme, and a materiation even of matter it selfe.

†**materiative**, *a. Obs.* [f. med.L. *māteriātīvus*, f. *māteriāre*: see MATERIATE *v.* and -ATIVE.] Providing the matter (of).

1652 URQUHART *Jewel* Wks. (1834) 198 An alphabet materiative of all the words the mouth of man..is able to pronounce.

materiature (mə'tɪərɪətjʊə(r)). *rare.* [f. L. *māteria* MATTER; cf. med.L. *māteriātūra* work in wood.] That which constitutes materiality.

1890 J. H. STIRLING *Philos. & Theol.* 349 As you may wash away all colour from a clot of blood, and be left at last with..a pure transparent web which held the colour, so you may discharge materiature from any particle of dust,..and be left at last with a pure diamond of fibres intellectual.

materie, obs. form of MATTER *sb.*¹

‖**matériel** (materjɛl). [Fr.: see MATERIAL *a.* and *sb.*]

1. a. The 'mechanical' or 'material' portion of an art; technique. *rare.* **b.** The 'stock-in-trade', available means or resources, for carrying on any business or undertaking.

1814 *Edin. Rev.* XXIV. 162 Mr. Hogg..is excellently well appointed as to what may be entitled the *materiel* of poetry. There is too much mere embellishment, and too little stuff or substance in his writings. **1822** DE QUINCEY *Confess.* 41 The quantity of esculent *matériel*..was little more than a roll, or a few biscuits. **1853** RUSKIN *Stones Ven.* III. vii. 212 If this be so, the question as to the materiel of education becomes singularly simplified. **1878** SIR G. G. SCOTT *Lect. Archit.* I. 156 Both [forms] should be admitted on equal terms as portions of our general *matériel*.

2. Used as a collective term for the articles, supplies, machinery, etc. used in an army, navy, or business, as distinguished from the *personnel* or body of persons employed.

1827 *Lincoln & Lincolnsh. Cabinet* 29 A more easy method of transporting the *materiel* for their army. **1856** EMERSON *Eng. Traits* xv. Wks. (Bohn) II. 117 The late Mr. Walter was printer of the 'Times', and had gradually arranged the whole *materiel* of it in perfect system. **1881** *Spectator* 15 Jan. 75 The Turkish army in Epirus is in desperate straits for matériel and money.

matering, obs. form of MATTERING.

†**ma'terious**, *a. Obs.* [ad. late L. *māteriōsus*, f. *māteria* MATTER: see -OUS.] Material.

1645 MILTON *Tetrach.* 198 This sensuous and materious cause alone can no more hinder a divorce against [etc.]. **1657** W. MORICE *Coena quasi Κοινή* x. 118 Things..having no direct concernment with faith or manners, are not so materious to be recorded.

‖**mater lectionis** ('meɪtə lɛktɪ'əʊnɪs). *Gram.* Pl. **matres lectionis.** [mod.L., lit. 'mother of reading'.] A letter which has the function of a diacritical mark; *spec.* in Hebrew writing, a sign indicating a vowel sound.

1846 B. DAVIES tr. *Gesenius's Hebrew Gram.* I. i. §8 The vowel-letters are also called by grammarians, *matres lectionis* (since they partly serve as guides in reading the unprinted

text). **1925** P. RADIN tr. *Vendryès's Lang.* v. i. 328 In the Greek alphabet the principle of the *matres lectionis* was skilfully used for the creation of a special sign for each vowel. **1962** DAVIDSON & MAUCHLINE *Introd. Hebrew Gram.* (ed. 25) 13 Thus ו would come in time to stand for long *o* and *u*, י for long *e* and *i*. ה likewise came to have a vocalic usage and the three letters are often termed vowel-letters or vocalic consonants (also *matres lectionis*).

matermone, -moyn(e, obs. ff. MATRIMONY.

matermonial, obs. form of MATRIMONIAL *a.*

†**ma'tern**, *a. Obs. rare*⁻¹. [ad. L. *mātern-us*: see next.] That is a mother, maternal.

1500–20 DUNBAR *Poems* lxxxv. 11 Ȝerne ws guberne, wirgin matern, Of reuth baith rute and ryne.

maternal (mə'tɜːnəl), *a.* (*sb.*) Also 5–7 -all, 6 -ale. [ad. F. *maternel* (Oresme, 14th c.), f. L. *mātern-us*, f. *māter* MOTHER *sb.*: see -AL¹. Cf. It. *maternale*, Sp., Pg. *maternal*.]

1. Of or pertaining to a mother or mothers; characteristic of mothers or motherhood; motherly.

1492 RYMAN *Poems* xviii. 4 in *Archiv Stud. neu. Spr.* LXXXIX. 187 This mayden..Withouten maternall doloure Oure sauyour hath borne. *Ibid.* lxxviii. 3 *ibid.* 248 The whiche thou were worthy to bere Without synne and maternall payne. **1616** BULLOKAR *Eng. Expos.*, *Maternall*, Motherly. **1654** in *Nicholas Papers* (Camden) II. 121 He told him Regall autority was above maternall and that the King was his soveraigne. **1692** DRYDEN *Eleonora* 218 At his first aptness the maternal love Those rudiments of reason did improve. **1703** MAUNDRELL *Journ. Jerus.* (1732) 64 She had her maternal fears turned into joy. **1790** COWPER *On Receipt My Mother's Pict.* 27 Ah! that maternal smile! **1858** O. W. HOLMES *Aut. Breakf.-t.* xii. 119 The great maternal instinct came crowding up in her soul just then.

b. (One's) mother's.

1605 TIMME *Quersit.* I. xi. 47 The seedes of the elements ..are coupled with the seedes of the starres, setting and putting their contayned into the maternall lappe. **1865** DICKENS *Mut. Fr.* III. iv, 'That's exactly what Ma has been doing', interposed Lavvy, over the maternal shoulder, 'ever since we got up this morning'. **1894** K. GRAHAME *Pagan P.* 106 Oblivious of..the embrace maternal, the paternal smack.

c. ***maternal language, tongue***: mother tongue, native language. Now *rare*.

The earliest recorded use both in Fr. and Eng.

1481 CAXTON *Myrr.* III. xxiv. 192, I haue presumed and emprised this forsayd translacion in to our englissh and maternal tongue. **1502** *Ord. Crysten Men* (W. de W. 1506) I. vi. 52 These crysten men ought for to knowe the Pater noster, the Aue maria, and the Credo in theyr langage maternall. **1530** PALSGR. 895 To whom the sayd tonge is maternall or naturall. **1632** LITHGOW *Trav.* x. 453 In Greeke, Latine, or their maternall tongues. **1858–9** MARSH *Eng. Lang.* i. (1860) 24 English-speaking missionaries have planted their maternal dialect at scores of important points.

¶**d.** *nonce-use.* Belonging to one's mother country.

1762–9 FALCONER *Shipwr.* (1796) I. 138 Heaven.. Restored them to maternal plains at last.

2. Of persons, animals, or personified things: **a.** That is a mother, or one's mother. Now *rare*.

1513 DOUGLAS *Æneis* VII. xiii. 137 His cheif maternall ciete full of mycht, Aricia, furth sent this worthy knycht [L. *insignem quem mater Aricia misit*]. **1659** HOWELL *Lex.*, *Brit. Prov.* To Rdr., The Cymraecan Toung, which is ranked by all Glottographers among the fourteen Maternall, and independent vernacular Languages of Europe. **1748** RICHARDSON *Clarissa* IV. 31 But paternal and maternal tyrants are the worst of all. **1873** *Sat. Rev.* 6 Sept. 309/2 The rooks bereave many a maternal pheasant that haunts the covers commanded by the rookery.

b. Having the instincts of motherhood, motherly.

1784 COWPER *Task* III. 436 As if in her [Winter] the stream of mild Maternal nature had reversed its course. **1817** SHELLEY *Rev. Islam* v. xxxiii. 7 Maternal earth, who doth her sweet smiles shed For all. **1892** GERTRUDE ATHERTON *Doomswoman* ii, She is not maternal..I never saw a baby held so awkwardly.

c. *slang.* Used *ellipt.* as *sb.* = MOTHER.

1867 *Routledge's Ev. Boy's Ann.* Dec. 728 Then is the governor driven to his wits' end..., while the maternal has to rouse herself up out of her arm-chair [etc.].

3. Inherited or derived from a mother; related through a mother or on the mother's side.

1656 BLOUNT *Glossogr.*, *Maternal*..on the mothers side. **1818** CRUISE *Digest* (ed. 2) III. 378 The same gradation takes place in the maternal line. **1828** B. B. WISNER *Mem. Susan Huntington* 1 On the maternal side Mrs. Huntington was descended from..the Rev. John Elliot. **1837** LYTTON *E. Maltrav.* I. xii, From a maternal relation, Ernest inherited an estate of about four thousand pounds a-year. **1854** THACKERAY *Newcomes* v. I. 49 When he was first brought home a sickly child, consigned to his maternal aunt. **1867** FREEMAN *Norm. Conq.* (1876) I. v. 264 Alongside of him stood his maternal uncle.

4. Of benevolent organizations: Providing for the requirements of maternity.

1856 KINGSLEY *Lect. Ladies* 57 There are clubs,—clothing-clubs, shoe-clubs, maternal-clubs. **1890** *Century Dict.* s.v., Maternal association; maternal hospital.

5. *Phys.* Of parts of the placenta: Uterine (opposed to *fœtal*).

1816 J. & C. BELL *Anat. & Physiol. Body* (ed. 4) III. 465 The maternal part of the placenta is thrown off with the other secundines. **1890** *Syd. Soc. Lex.*, *Maternal membranes*, ..the decidua vera, decidua reflexa, and decidua serotina.

6. Pertaining to the matrix of algæ.

1872 H. C. WOOD *Fresh-w. Algæ U.S.* (1874) 100 Numerous cells..are arranged on the periphery at equal distances, and are connected by the maternal jelly. **1874** *Ibid.* 16 Filaments simple..floating in a maternal jelly.

maternality (mætə'nælɪtɪ). [f. MATERNAL *a.* + -ITY.] The quality or condition of being maternal; motherhood; *pl.* (*nonce-use*) motherly remarks or discourse.

1721 BAILEY, *Maternality*, Mother-hood, &c. [*sic*]. **1865** MISS MULOCK *Chr. Mistake* iv. 90 It was worse, far worse, than poor Mrs. Ferguson's stream of foolish maternalities,—vulgar, but warm and kindly, and never ill-natured.

maternalize (mə'tɜːnəlaɪz), *v. rare.* [f. MATERNAL *a.* + -IZE.] *trans.* **a.** To make maternal. **b.** *absol.* To employ 'maternal' methods (*nonce-use*).

1877 T. SINCLAIR *Mount* (1878) 296 Comte and 'George Eliot' would methodise, paternalise, and maternalise, till there would be nothing at all wrong in their curious Eden. **1896** A. LANG in *Longm. Mag.* Jan. 315 Blanche Amory and the maternalised Laura. **1899** *Academy* 30 Sept. 331/1 The subjection of women has involved the maternalising of man. He has had to love and care for someone besides himself.

maternally (mə'tɜːnəlɪ), *adv.* [-LY².] In a maternal manner; on the maternal side; †as one's mother tongue.

1632 LITHGOW *Trav.* III. 116 They speake vulgarly and Maternally here the Hebrew tongue. **1817** G. ROSE *Diaries* (1860) I. 17, I am descended..maternally from the family of Rose of Westerclune. **1868** BROWNING *Ring & Bk.* IX. 1177 A brow maternally severe. **1902** A. LANG *Hist. Scot.* II. xiii. 355 The heir presumptive is maternally of the house of Ardkinglass.

maternalness (mə'tɜːnəlnɪs). [f. MATERNAL *a.* + -NESS.] Motherliness.

1727 BAILEY vol. II, *Maternalness*, motherliness, motherly Affection. *a* **1839** GALT *Demon of Destiny*, etc. (1840) 74 The patted cheek, the fond maternalness.

materne, obs. form of MARTEN.

†**maternine**, *a. Obs.*⁻⁰. [f. L. *mātern-us* + -INE.] Maternal.

1623 COCKERAM *Eng. Dict.* II.

maternity (mə'tɜːnɪtɪ). [ad. F. *maternité* = med.L. *māternitās*, f. L. *mātern-us*: see MATERNAL and -ITY.]

1. a. The quality or condition of being a mother; the character or relation of a mother; motherhood.

1611 COTGR., *Maternité*, maternitie. **1633** [H. HAWKINS] *Parthen. Sacra* 47 In the Violet Marie may you consider.. the golden coulour of Maternitie or Charitie in her; since her Charitie was the cause of her Maternitie. **1656** BLOUNT *Glossogr.*, *Maternity*, motherhood, the being a mother. **1847** CARDL. WISEMAN *Unreal. Anglic. Belief* Ess. (1853) 424 It is impossible to realize a belief in the maternity of the Blessed Virgin, without thus considering her. **1874** J. TAYLOR *Etrusc. Res.* 57 A state of society in which..maternity constituted the only relationship that could legally be recognised. **1879** TOURGEE *Fool's Err.* i. 9 The wife of a year, as the perils of maternity drew nigh in the absence of her husband. **1894** H. DRUMMOND *Ascent Man* 23 Even in the lowliest world of plants the labours of Maternity begin.

†**b.** As a title of the mother superior of a convent.

a **1693** *Urquhart's Rabelais* III. xxxiv. 287 The Pope did represent to their Maternities.

c. Short for *maternity hospital*. [So F. *maternité*.]

1889 *Lancet* 7 Sept. 509/2 The hospital..has also a large extern maternity attached.

2. The character or qualities properly belonging to a mother; motherliness.

1804 *Something Odd* II. 186 Mr. Macdonald was delighted at this maternity. **1823** LAMB *Elia* Ser. II. *Poor Relations*, His stars are perpetually crossed by the malignant maternity of an old woman, who persists in calling him 'her son Dick'. **1842** ORDERSON *Creol.* xv. 175 An interesting loveliness that endeared her..to the maternity of the two elderly ladies. **1883** H. DRUMMOND *Nat. Law in Spir. W.* (ed. 2) 154 The tender maternity of the bird.

3. *attrib.*: ***maternity leave***; **maternity benefit**, a welfare service payment made to women, under specified conditions, after the period of confinement; **maternity home** = *maternity hospital*; **maternity hospital**, a hospital for the reception and treatment of women during the period of confinement; so ***maternity nurse, ward***, etc; **maternity jacket** *slang* (see quot. 1925); also *ellipt.* as ***maternity***.

1911 *Q. Rev.* Oct. 561 When both husband and wife are insured, they are to be entitled, in case of the wife's confinement, to both sickness and *maternity benefit. **1911** [see BENEFIT *sb.* 3d]. **1945** *Release & Resettlement* (H.M. Govt.) xii. 40 The benefits of the National Health Insurance Scheme include..maternity benefit. **1957** BRUDNO & BOWER *Taxation in U.K.* 523/1 Maternity benefits. **1970** *National Insurance: Maternity Benefits* (Dept. Health & Social Security, NI 17A) I. i. 6 There are two maternity benefits—maternity grant and maternity allowance. Both benefits may be paid for a confinement provided the conditions are satisfied. *Ibid.* III. xxiii. 18 Any question about contributions, including whether the contribution tests for maternity benefit..are satisfied, is reserved for the Secretary of State for Social Services. **1903** *Strand Mag.* Apr. 423/1 In addition to the general wards there are..a *maternity department [etc.]. **1922** *Encycl. Brit.* XXX. 652/1 The supervision of midwifery, including the establishment of *maternity homes. **1926** *Act 16 & 17 Geo. V* c. 32 §12 The expression 'maternity home' means any premises used or intended to be used for the reception of pregnant women or of women immediately after childbirth. **1967** *Encycl. Brit.* XV. 66/1 Increasing grants have been made by some governments for the construction of free maternity homes or maternity wards in general hospitals. **1881** *Maternity hospital [see EXTERN B. 2c]. **1887** *Brit. Med. Jrnl.* 12 Mar. 591/1 Manchester has long felt the want of a maternity hospital. **1925** FRASER & GIBBONS *Soldier & Sailor Words* 154 **Maternity jacket*, the name given the double breasted tunic, worn formerly in the Royal Flying Corps. **1958** 'N. SHUTE' *Rainbow & Rose* ii. 66 A very young man in the double-breasted 'maternity' jacket of the Royal Flying Corps. *Ibid.* iii. 91 She insisted on giving me a buttonhole..but my maternity hadn't got a buttonhole to put it in. **1970** *Guardian* 21 May 13/2 At present, *maternity leave is based on the custom and practice of either individual companies or sections of industry. **1973** *Times* 17 Mar. 2/2 Mrs Christine Page..said: 'Because of the economic uncertainty of some families, we are asking for this maternity leave to be negotiated.' **1902** *Daily Chron.* 1 Mar. 4/3 Miss F., a *maternity nurse.

b. Used *attrib.* of garments spec. designed for pregnant women.

1893 *Ladies' Home Jrnl.* Apr. 28/2 Summer maternity gowns. **1907** *Dress* Jan. p. xx, My Maternity corsets are recommended by physicians everywhere. **1951** I. SHAW *Troubled Air* x. 164 She was wearing one of her shapeless tent-like maternity dresses. **1962** M. DRABBLE *Summer Bird-Cage* vi. 92 She would wear pretty maternity dresses and be an excellent mother. **1963** 'G. BAGBY' *Murder's Little Helper* (1964) ii. 14 What kind of a burglar is it that swipes maternity clothes? *Ibid.*, She hadn't splurged on maternity garments. **1964** M. DRABBLE *Garrick Year* i. 11 Three years of child-bearing and modelling maternity clothes. **1966** *Guardian* 5 Aug. 8/4 The wide coats and dresses have the ease of maternity wear. **1971** B. MALAMUD *Tenants* 211 Under a short maternity skirt her stomach is in flower. **1971** C. STORR *Thursday* vi. 63, I can just see myself in maternity smocks for the next ten years.

materteral (mə'tɜːtərəl), *a. humorously pedantic.* [f. L. *mātertera* maternal aunt.] Characteristic of an aunt. So **ma'terterine** *a.*

1823 W. TAYLOR in *Monthly Rev.* CII. 447 With maternal and materteral anxiety. **1874** M. COLLINS *Frances* II. 95 A kindly materterine message.

matery, obs. form of MATTER *sb.*¹, MATTERY.

mateship ('meɪt-ʃɪp). [f. MATE *sb.*² + -SHIP.] The condition of being a mate; companionship, fellowship; †equality.

1593 NASHE *Christ's T.* 30 Empery admitteth no mateshyppe. **1856** MRS. BROWNING *Aur. Leigh* VII. 1088, I sate among them equally, In fellowship and mateship. **1897** P. WARUNG *Tales Old Regime* 215 It was pleasant, as it was unusual, this mateship. **1905** H. LAWSON in B. Stevens *Bush Ballads* (1910) 76 The College Wreck..Tramps West in mateship with the man Who cannot write his name. **1930** W. H. HANCOCK *Australia* x. 199 Thwarted individualism found consolation in the gospel of mateship. **1960** J. FINGLETON *Four Chukkas to Austral.* xviii. 158 Benaud knew, too, that he had to cultivate mateship. **1962** *Guardian* 14 Aug. 6/5 A beery sense of 'mateship' among the men. **1968** *Courier-Mail* (Brisbane) 20 July 2/2 When I was.. Prime Minister..he gave me not only his personal co-operation, understanding and loyalty but also his mateship, often in the most difficult circumstances, even when we disagreed.

†**matesy.** *Obs.* [? var. of MATHESIS.]

c **1470** HARDING *Chron.* XCVII. xviii, Walshemen..haue suche a prophecye [*viz.* of the reconquest of England]. Thus stande they yet, in suche fonde matesye, In truste of whiche vague fantasye [etc.].

matey ('meɪtɪ), *sb.* [f. MATE *sb.*²: see -Y.] A diminutive of MATE *sb.*²; a companion, mate.

1833 MARRYAT *P. Simple* viii, I asked of a bystander who these people were, and he told me that they were dock-yard mateys. **1859** H. KINGSLEY *Recoll. G. Hamlyn* II. xiv. 277, I took him for a flash overseer, sporting his salary, and I was as thick as you like with him. And 'Matey,' says I, (you see I was familiar, he seemed such a jolly sort of bird), 'Matey, what station are you on?' **1889** P. H. EMERSON *Eng. Idyls* 56 'Good-night, matey', concluded the voice in the fast fading barge. **1909** S. WATSON *Wops the Waif* i. 2 'I say, Tickle matey, wot's all them a-readin' of on that bill over there?' interrupted Wops. **1916** 'TAFFRAIL' *Pincher Martin* ii. 16 A gray, cigar-shaped vessel lying in a dry dock, with dockyard 'maties' swarming on board her. **1931** KIPLING *Limits & Renewals* (1932) 197 Polyphemus damned back at Jemmy like a Chatham matey. **1958** E. HYAMS *Taking it Easy* I. ii. 72 The dockyard 'mateys' who had been sent us to do the work were all Bretons from the Arsenal at Brest. **1973** J. DRUMMOND *Bang! Bang! you're Dead!* xxv. 86 Right, matey, 'oo told you? **1974** 'M. HEBDEN' *Pride of Dolphins* III. iii. 232 Many of the lights in the control room were missing, probably stolen by dockyard mateys.

matey ('meɪtɪ), *a.* [f. MATE *sb.*² + -Y¹.] Like a mate or mates; friendly and familiar (*with*); sociable, companionable.

1915 [implied in MATEYNESS]. **1919** WODEHOUSE *Damsel in Distress* xv. 172 After the game he took me off to his cottage and gave me a drink... We got extremely matey. **1926** *Contemp. Rev.* June 682 The *British Worker*, an equally deplorable organ produced by *intelligentsia* trying to be 'matey'. **1929** W. DEEPING *Roper's Row* xxi. §ii, Elizabeth would..want to be matey with people. **1946** WODEHOUSE *Joy in Morning* i. 4, I..continued to tut-tut a bit at having missed the young pipsqueak, with whom my relations had always been of the matiest.

Hence **'mateyness** (also *matiness*), friendly quality or character.

1915 T. BURKE *Nights in Town* 50 You are all so—what is the word?—matey, isn't it? Yes, that's the note of the London [music] hall—mateyness. **1928** *Evening News* 28 Dec. 8/3 There is the same expansive geniality, the same

note of unassumed 'matiness'. **1950** *Landfall* IV. 345 The defensive bar-room and back-fence matiness of New Zealand life. **1958** *Times Lit. Suppl.* 20 June 347/3 When the implied mateyness is further established by such otiose asides..one stirs uncomfortably to ask why a writer who has so much that is interesting to say should waste our time with these lazy transcriptions. **1967** *Listener* 24 Aug. 244/2 Continuous pop and advertisements, presented with that bogus transatlantic mateyness which apparently 'sends' teenagers. **1974** V. GIELGUD *In Such a Night* ix. 82 She would throw a party. And in the ensuing haze of drink and mateyness grievances would..disappear.

mateyns, mateynys, obs. ff. MATINS.

matfellon ('mætfɛlən). *Obs.* exc. *dial.* Forms: 4 **matfelonn**, 5 **matefeloun**, **maidfeloun**, **matfelon(e**, **mathfelonn**, **mattefelon**, 6 **materfil(l)on**, **matfillon**, **matrefillon**, 6– **matfellon**. [a. OF. *matefelon*, app. f. *mate-r* MATE *v.* + *felon* FELON²; named from supposed curative properties.] = KNAPWEED; also ***black matfellon***.

a **1387** *Sinon. Barthol.* (Anecd. Oxon.) 24 *Jacia nigra*, matfelonn. **14..** [see KNAPWEED]. *c* **1450** *Alphita* (Anecd. Oxon.) 83/2 *Iacea nigra*, mathfelonn. **1483** *Cath. Angl.* 230/2 Mattefelon (*MS. A.* Matfelone); *iacea*, *herba est.* **1578** LYTE *Dodoens* I. lxxiii. 109 The fourth is now called on Shoppes *Iacea nigra*, and *Materfilon*: and it hath none other name knowen vnto vs. **1597** GERARDE *Herbal* II. ccxcix. 704. **1640** PARKINSON *Theat. Bot.* 469 We call it in English Bullweede, and Knapweede, as also Matfellon. **1758** MRS. DELANY in *Life & Corr.* (1861) III. 507 Matfellon and figwort flourish here remarkably. **1766** *Museum Rust.* VI. 451 Common, or Black Knapweed, Matfellon, Black Matfellon, or Bulweed. **1829** GLOVER *Hist. Derby* I. 124 *Centaurea Jacea*, common knapweed or matfellow [*sic*]. **1866** *Treas. Bot.* 724/2.

math¹ (mɑːθ, -æ-). *Obs.* exc. *dial.* (see E.D.D.). Forms: 1 **mǣþ**, 6–7 **mathe**, 6– **math**. [OE. *mǣþ* (once in Bosw.-T., gender not shown), = MHG. *mât*, *mâd-* neut. and fem. (mod.G. *mahd* fem.) f. OTeut. root *mǣ-* to MOW.

The normal mod.E. form would have been *meath* (miːθ); the existing form is due to the shortening of the vowel through loss of stress in the combinations *aftermath*, *lattermath*, *day-math*. Cf. MOWTH.]

A mowing; the amount of a crop mowed. (See AFTERMATH, DAY('S-MATH, LATTERMATH.)

963 *Lease* in Birch *Cartul. Sax.* III. 343 þæt he mid eallum cræfte twuʒa on ʒeare [? *insert* wyrce] ǣne to mæþe & oðre siðe to riþe. [**1523**, **1530**: see AFTERMATH, LATTERMATH.] **1585** HIGINS *Nomenclator* 124 *Fœnum cordum*,..late math, or lateward hay. **1601** HOLLAND *Pliny* I. 573 When this hearbe Medica or Claver grasse beginneth once to flour, cut it downe... Thus you may have sixe mathes in one yeare. **1633** BP. HALL *Hard Texts*, *Amos* vii. 557 The first mowing thereof for the King's use (which is wont to be sooner then the common mathe). *a* **1656** USSHER *Ann.* iv. (1658) 37 At the end of the spring, at the second math of grasse. **1804** COLEBROOKE *Husb. Bengal* (1806) 71 Revenue drawn from fruit-trees, pastures, and math, and rent of fisheries. **1917** MOTHER ST. JEROME *Garden of Life* 18 You feel as you lie in the math The watching unseen of his eyes. **1968** R. E. ZUPKO *Dict. Eng. Weights & Measures* 103 *Math*,..in Herefordshire equal to approximately 1 acre..or to the amount of land that a man could mow in a day.

‖**math**² (mʌth). *Indian.* Also **matha**, **muth**, **mutt**. [Hindī *maṭh*, repr. Skr. *maṭha*, hut, cottage.] A Hindu convent of celibate mendicants.

1828 H. H. WILSON in *Asiatick Researches* XVI. 103 The disciples, who are domesticated in the several *Maths*, profess also perpetual celibacy. **1834** *Baboo* II. i. 3 He was to drive to an old Muth near Garden Reach. *a* **1851** M. M. SHERWOOD *Hist. Little Henry & his Bearer* (1866) 84 This sahib..had himself built a mutt. **1862** BEVERIDGE *Hist. India* II. IV. ii. 74 They live like other mendicants collected in maths. **1877** M. WILLIAMS *Hinduism* 224 *Yatis*, monks or ascetics,..often congregate in Maṭhas or 'monasteries'. **1883** *Madras Mail* 5 Dec. 26/1 Mutts and temples are closed to him. **1885** SIR W. HUNTER *Imp. Gaz. India* XIII. 323 There are two maths or religious establishments in the village. **1913** 'A. AVALON' tr. *Tantra of Great Liberation* p. xvii, Kedarnath... A *matha* and temple dedicated to Shrī Sādāshiva. **1956** R. REDFIELD *Peasant Society & Culture* iii. 81 Some sweet-voiced, gifted expounder sitting in a temple, *mutt*, public hall or house-front.

math³ (mæθ). *U.S. colloq.* = MATHS.

Math. is used as an abbreviation in written English in the U.K. but not in speech, the normal form being *Maths.*

1890 in *Cent. Dict.* **1895** W. C. GORE in *Inlander* Nov. 64 *Math.* n. Mathematics. **1899** J. LONDON *Let.* 24 Oct. (1966) 62 She's well up in the higher math. **1916** [see *my guess is* (GUESS *sb.* 1)]. **1938** I. GOLDBERG *Wonder of Words* x. 200 He [*sc.* a student] says *math* and *ec.* **1961** C. WINSTON *Hours Together* (1962) vii. 139 There was Morton Kersh, with the math book propped against the milk bottle on the kitchen table. **1971** *Black World* June 80/2 T. J. failed Math and English. **1973** *Jrnl. Genetic Psychol.* CXXIII. 163 The follow-up results with the math-science boys. **1974** *State* (Columbia, S. Carolina) 8 Mar. 19-B/5 Parents who have children in a Title I reading, math or kindergarten program are also invited to attend.

mathe. *Obs.* (? exc. *Sc.*: see E.D.D.) Forms: 1 **maþa**, **maþu**, 2–6 **maþe**, **mathe**, 3 **meaðe**, (4 **matþe**), 5 **math**, **methe**; *Sc.* 5 **maith**, 6 **meathe**, 9 **maithe**. [OE. *maþa* wk. masc., *maþu* str. fem., cogn. w. OS. *matho* (Strasb. gl.) (MDu., MLG., mod.Du. *made*), OHG. *mado* masc. (MHG. *made* masc., mod.G. *made* fem.), Goth. *maþa*:—OTeut. **maþon-*, **maþâ*, of obscure origin: some have compared Skr. *matka* bug.] A maggot, grub, worm.

c **1000** *Voc.* in Wr.-Wülcker 205/8 *Cimex*..maþa. *c* **1000** ÆLFRIC *Gloss.* ibid. 122/3 *Cimex*, maþu. *a* **1240** *Sawles Warde* in *Cott. Hom.* 251 As meaðen iforrotet flesch. *c* **1330** *Arth. & Merl.* 484 (Kölbing) For he lete cristen wedde haþen & meynt our blod, as flesche & matþen. *a* **1380** *Minor Poems fr. Vernon MS.* 447/167 Heore bodies þat weoren so softe I-baþen..þer hit schal crepe ful of Maþen. *a* **1425** *Cursor M.* 11836 (Trin.) Maþes [*other texts* wormes] cruled in him pore. *a* **1440** *Promp. Parv.* 321/1 Make, mathe, wyrm yn þe fleshe. *c* **1460** in *Rel. Ant.* I. 302 For methys that devorith the pennys of an hawk. *c* **1470** HENRYSON *Mor. Fab.* I. (*Cock & Jasp*) xi, Riches..Quhilk maith [*v.r.* moith], nor moist, nor vther rust can screit. **1481** CAXTON *Reynard* xxviii. (Arb.) 69 Yonder lyeth a dede hare full of mathes and wormes. **1523** FITZHERB. *Husb.* §45 If a shepe haue mathes, ye shall perceyue it by her bytynge [etc.]. *a* **1585** MONTGOMERIE *Flyting w. Polwart* 319 The mair and the migrame, with the meathes in the melt.

mathe: see MATÉ, MATH¹, MAYTHE(S, MEATH.

†'**mathele**, *v. Obs.* [OE. *maðelian* (also *mæðlan*: see MELL *v.*¹), f. *mæðel* meeting, discussion = OS., OHG. *mahal* assembly, tribunal, Goth. *maþl*:—OTeut. **maþlom*.] *intr.* and *trans.* To speak; to talk, prate. Hence †**maðelung** *vbl. sb.*, †**maðelinde** *ppl. a.*; †**maðelere**, a talker; †**maðelild**, a female chatterer, gossip.

Beowulf 371 Hroðgar maþelode, helm Scyldinga: 'Ic hine cuðe cnihtwesende'. *c* **725** *Corpus Gloss.* C 854 (Hessels) *Contionatur*, maðalade *declamat.* *a* **1000** in Napier *O.E. Glosses* 38/1419 *Verbositas*, ʒewyrd, maþelung. *a* **1000** *Voc.* in Wr.-Wülcker 212/17 *Contionator*, i. *locutor*, motere, *uel* maþelere. *a* **1225** *Ancr. R.* 74 Hore muð maðeleð euer. *Ibid.* 80 Heoþ openeð hire muð mid muche maðelunge, & brekeð silence [etc.]. *Ibid.*, Ne blowe ʒe hire [hope] nout ut mid maðelinde muðe, ne mid ʒeoniinde tuteles. *Ibid.* 88 Ane maðelild [*MS. T.* maðelere] þ maðeleð hire all þe talen of þe londe.

mathematic (mæθɪ'mætɪk), *a.* and *sb.* Also 4 (*sb.* sense 1), **matematik**, 6 **methamatic**, 4–7 **mathematique**. [The adj., first recorded in the 16th c., is ad. F. *mathématique* or its source L. *mathematicus*, ad. Gr. μαθηματικός, f. μαθηματ-, μάθημα something learned, science, f. root of μανθάνειν to learn. The substantival senses B. 1 (from 14th c.) and B. 2 (from 16th c.) are, so far as Eng. is concerned, independent words, but are placed together here because they represent absol. or elliptical applications of the Gr.-Latin adj.]

A. *adj.* = MATHEMATICAL *a.*, in various senses. Now *rare.*

1549 *Compl. Scot.* vi. 62 Ptholome, auerois, aristotel, galien, ypocrites or Cicero,..var expert practicians in methamatic art. **1570** DEE *Math. Pref.* *. For the causes alleged..in respect of my Art Mathematike generall. **1593** PEELE *Hon. of Garter*, *Ad Mæcenatem Prol.* 8 That admirable Mathematique skill, Familiar with the starres and Zodiack (To whom the heauen lyes open as her booke). *a* **1609** DONNE *Lett.*, *To Sir H. Goodyere* (1651) 163 A Mathematique point, which is the most indivisible and unique thing which art can present. **1611** CORYAT *Crudities* 602 They were wise astrologers, who by the Mathematicke art (as Cyprian speaketh) knew the force and course of the planets. *a* **1619** FOTHERBY *Atheom.* II. ix. §4 (1622) 297 Like the Punctum is in Mathematicke body. **1664** H. MORE *Myst. Iniq.* 270 That the Seven-headed Beast cannot be the Turkish Empire, we may conclude with Mathematick certitude. **1670** WALLIS in Rigaud *Corr. Sci. Men* (1841) II. 519 Mathematic books..to be had very cheap. *a* **1680** BUTLER *Rem.* (1759) I. 214 The mathematic Lines, Where Nature all the Wit of Man confines. **1700** WALLIS in *Collect.* (O.H.S.) I. 320 There be mathematick lectures. **1705** *Lond. Gaz.* No. 4116/1 Isaac Newton Esq.; formerly Mathematick Professor. **1807** BYRON *Th. Coll. Exam.* i, Denouncing dire reproach to luckless fools, Unskill'd to plod in mathematic rules. **1850** LYNCH *Theo. Trin.* xii. 235 He..went to mathematic studies. **1863** LD. LYTTON *Ring Amasis* II. 266 From his earliest years, he had brought, with mathematic precision, his voice, his manners, even the lines of his face, into a harmony undisturbed by expression.

B. *sb.* **1.** [a. OF. *mathematique* (mod.F. *mathématique*) = Sp. *matemática*, Pg. *mathematica*, It. *matematica*, ad. L. *mathēmatica* (sc. *ars* or *disciplina*), Gr. μαθηματική (sc. τέχνη, θεωρία), fem. of L. *mathēmaticus*, Gr. μαθηματικός: see above. Cf. G. *mathematik*.] Mathematical science, MATHEMATICS.

The word became obs. early in the 17th c., but has been revived by some writers in the latter part of the 19th c. (? after G. *mathematik*), for use instead of *mathematics* in contexts where the unity of the science is emphasized.

c **1380** WYCLIF *Wks.* (1880) 342 þis witt þat crist spekiþ of stondeþ not in mannes lawe, ne in oþur curiouse lawes, as matematik, or lawes of kynde. **1390** GOWER *Conf.* III. 89 The thridde point of Theorique, Which cleped is Mathematique, Devided is in sondri wise... The ferste of whiche is Arsmetique, And the secounde is seid Musique, The thridde is ek Geometrie, Also the ferthe Astronomie. **1586** T. B. *La Primaud. Fr. Acad.* I. (1589) 72 Al arts and sciences handled by reason were divided into three principall kindes: into Philosophie, Rhetorike and Mathematike. **1594** R. ASHLEY tr. *Loys le Roy* 25 b, Phylosophy, Physicks and the Mathematick, were translated out of the Greeke into Arabian. **1605** BACON *Adv. Learn.* II. viii. §1 Another part of Naturall philosophie..is mathematicke. **1854** HICKOK *Mental Sci.* 125 All pure mathematic is thus a science of pure intuition. **1881** *Athenæum* 27 Aug. 269/1 Mr. Venn points out most clearly the distinction between symbolic logic and symbolic mathematic. [But Mr. Venn has 'mathematics'.]

†**2.** [ad. L. *mathēmaticus*, Gr. μαθηματικός. Cf. Sp. *matemático*, Pg. *mathematico*, It. *matematico*; also Du. *mathematicus*, G. *mathematiker*.] A mathematician. In translations from late L. often: An astrologer. *Obs.*

1547–64 BAULDWIN *Mor. Philos.* (Palfr.) 7 Archelaus..was first an hearer of Antilochus a mathematicke. **1579–80** NORTH *Plutarch*, *Solon* (1595) 87 Hippocrates the mathematike. **1587** GOLDING *De Mornay* xxvi. 403 Buteon a Mathematicke declareth expresly in a booke, what it [the Arke] contained foote by foote. **1598** SYLVESTER *Du Bartas* II. ii. III. *Colonies* 294 The Memphian Priests were deep Philosophers..and great Mathematikes. ? *c* **1600** *Distracted Emp.* I. i. in Bullen *O. Pl.* III. 169, I have seene Your conference with witches..and the damned frye Of cheating mathematicks. **1610** HEALEY *St. Aug. Citie of God* v. ix. (1620) 197 Those coniectures of the Mathmatiques he layeth flat. **1688** R. HOLME *Armoury* II. 27/2 Mathematick, one that Calculateth Nativities, an Astrologer, or a Mathematician.

†**3.** *pl.* Dice 'mathematically true'. *Obs.*

1692 *Abridgm. Specif. Patents*, *Toys*, etc. (1871) 2 A new sort of dice knowne by the name of mathematicks, cutt perfectly square by a mold. **1721** [see DOCTOR *sb.* 12].

Hence †**mathe'matic** *v. trans.*, to bring *out* with mathematical accuracy.

1627–77 FELTHAM *Resolves* II. xxix. 218 Words come not then digested and mathematic'd out, by..reason, but [etc.].

mathematical (mæθɪ'mætɪkəl), *a.* and *sb.* Also 6 **methematycall**, **mathametical**, **matematical**. [f. L. *mathēmatic-us*, see MATHEMATIC *a.* and -ICAL.]

A. *adj.*

1. a. Of, pertaining to, relating to, or of the nature of, mathematics.

1530 RASTELL *Bk. Purgat.* II. xix, The methematycall scyens. **1538** STARKEY *England* I. i. 16 The conclusyonys of artys mathematycal are euer referryd to theyr pryncypullys. **1570** BILLINGSLEY *Euclid* 357 b, The great Mechanicall vse (besides Mathematicall Considerations) which [etc.]. **1646** SIR T. BROWNE *Pseud. Ep.* II. iii. 76 A probleme Mathematicall, to finde out the difference of houres in different places. **1690** LOCKE *Hum. Und.* IV. iv. §6 (1695) 324 The Knowledge we may have of Mathematical Truths, is not only certain, but real Knowledge. **1785** REID *Intell. Powers* 607 Mathematical notions are formed in the understanding by an abstraction of another kind, out of the rude perceptions of our senses. **1843** RUSKIN *Arrows of Chace* (1880) I. 21 We will listen to no comments on Newton from people who have no mathematical knowledge.

b. Such as is recognized by mathematics; being what the name imports in mathematics. Chiefly in ***mathematical point***: see POINT *sb.*; ***mathematical model***: see MODEL *sb.* 2 e.

The scholastic term *mathematical body* was much bandied about in the transubstantiation controversies of the 16th c., and gave rise to much misunderstanding, being variously taken to mean (1) a body having spatial accidents, and (2) a body consisting of *mere* spatial accidents (without substance).

1547 HOOPER *Christ & Office* viii. H viij b, Then it is no body for a trew body phisicall and matematical: as Christes body is: cannot be except it ocopi place. **1549** BONNER in Foxe *A. & M.* (1563) 700 [Hooper] in effect denieth the verity of Christes blessed body vpon the crosse, calling it Mathematical. **1570** DEE *Math. Pref.* *j, Of Mathematicall thinges, are two principall kindes..Number, and Magnitude. **1660** JER. TAYLOR *Duct. Dubit.* II. iii. rule 11. §17 Negative precepts have no parts of duty, no degrees of obedience, but consist in a Mathematical point. **1840** LARDNER *Geom.* i. 7 If a mathematical point be conceived to move through space,..leaving..a trace..., that trace..will be a mathematical line. **1897** M. DZIEWICKI *Wyclif's De Logica* (1899) III. Introd. 26 Christ's Body..is present without either position or shape. The bread is not annihilated; what remains is a purely mathematical body, but not nothing.

c. Learned or skilled in, studying or teaching, mathematics.

1522 SKELTON *Why not to Court* 705 But let mi masters mathematical Tell you the rest. *a* **1568** ASCHAM *Scholem.* (Arb.) 34 Marke all Mathematicall heades which be only and wholy bent to those sciences. **1622** PEACHAM *Compl. Gent.* ix. (1634) 77 Mr. Doctor Hood, sometime Mathematicall Lecturer in London. **1692** LUTTRELL *Brief Rel.* (1857) II. 327 The governour of Christs hospitall waited on the king with the mathematical boys. **1713** J. WARD *Yng. Math. Guide* A 1 b, H. Ditton, Master of the New Mathematical School in Christ's Hospital. **1837** WHEWELL *Hist. Induct. Sci.* (1857) I. 253 The Science of the mathematical mechanician. **1839** *Penny Cycl.* XV. 12/1 The mathematical student. *Ibid.*, He will neither impede nor advance his mathematical career.

d. Adapted to be used in mathematical operations. ***mathematical instruments***: now usually, the instruments (such as compasses, rulers, scales, protractors) employed in drawing geometrical figures.

1625 N. CARPENTER *Geog. Del.* I. iv. (1635) 78 Philosophers haue found out by diuers Mathematicall instruments. **1663** COWLEY *College* Wks. 1721 II. 567 A Mathematical Chamber furnish'd with all Sorts of Mathematical Instruments, being an Appendix to a Library. **1678** MOXON *Mech. Dyalling* 44 Mathematical Instrument-Makers. **1696** *Lond. Gaz.* No. 3224/4 Lost.., a small Pocket-Book of Mathematical Paper. **1726** SWIFT *Gulliver* III. ii, A large table filled with globes, and spheres, and mathematical instruments. **1849** NOAD *Electricity* (ed. 3) 284 A celebrated mathematical instrument-maker.

e. ***mathematical linguistics***: a branch of linguistics concerned with the application of mathematical models and procedures to the analysis of linguistic structure; so ***mathematical linguist***; ***mathematical logic***: logic that is mathematical in its method, using symbols and following definite and explicit rules of derivation; modern logic; symbolic logic; so ***mathematical logician***; ***mathematical philosophy***: that branch of philosophy concerned with the nature of mathematics.

1951 *Language* XXVII. 221 There is a growing cleavage between the mathematical linguists, or metalinguists, and the physical linguists, whom I should call just plain linguists. **1956** J. WHATMOUGH *Lang.* xi. 220 The development of mathematical linguistics is opening a new field of inquiry, and may rightly be expected to bring greater order into a subject, which..has been and still remains chaotic. **1961** C. MOHRMANN et al. *Trends European & Amer. Ling.* 21 In his report to the 1957 Congress, Professor Joshua Whatmough mentioned the initiation of the Seminar in Mathematical Linguistics at Harvard University two years previously—the first appearance of the subject in an academic curriculum. **1964** E. BACH *Introd. Transformational Gram.* vii. 145 At several universities.. courses in 'mathematical linguistics' are offered. **1968** J. LYONS *Introd. Theoret. Ling.* ii. 71 What one might refer to loosely as 'mathematical' linguistics is now a very important part of the subject. **1972** HARTMANN & STORK *Dict. Lang. & Ling.* 137 Mathematical linguistics may be said to begin with the counting of linguistic units such as phonemes, graphemes, or vocabulary items. **1858** A. DE MORGAN *On Syllogism* (1966) 78 This *mathematical* logic..will commend itself to the educated world. **1880** J. VENN in *Princeton Rev.* 248 What with the logicians who hate mathematics, and the mathematicians who despise logic, a theory of so-called mathematical logic does not find many friends. **1908** B. RUSSELL in *Amer. Jrnl. Math.* XXX. 222 (*title*) Mathematical logic as based on the theory of types. **1940** W. V. QUINE (*title*) Mathematical logic. **1941** O. HELMER tr. *Tarski's Introd. Logic* ii. 18 Logic..has undergone a complete transformation with the effect of assuming a character similar to that of the mathematical disciplines; in this new form it is known as mathematical or deductive or symbolic logic. **1967** J. VAN HEIJENOORT *From Frege to Gödel* p. vii, Mathematical logic is what logic, through twenty-five centuries and a few transformations, has become today. **1850** A. DE MORGAN *On Syllogism* (1966) 58 There is no occasion for the mathematical logician to pay the least deference to the Christian followers of Aristotle; the master himself was a mathematician. **1883** F. H. BRADLEY *Princ. Logic* 360, I may suggest to the mathematical logician that [etc.]. **1903** B. RUSSELL *Princ. Math.* iii. 457 But now, thanks mainly to the mathematical logicians, formal logic is enriched by several forms of reasoning not reducible to the syllogism. **1879** W. JAMES *Coll. Ess. & Rev.* (1920) 141 Clifford's..chapters on the 'Philosophy of the Pure Sciences'..form as luminous an introduction to mathematical philosophy as was ever written. **1897** B. RUSSELL in *Mind* VI. 112 The problems of mathematical philosophy. **1901** *Mind* X. 30 It is..imperative, in the interests of mathematical philosophy, to supply the defect. **1919** B. RUSSELL (*title*) Introduction to mathematical philosophy.

2. *transf.* **a.** Of proofs, certitude, precision, etc.: Resembling what is found in mathematics; rigorously exact.

1662 STILLINGFL. *Orig. Sacr.* II. i. §3 To bring matters of fact into Mathematical demonstrations. **1664** H. MORE *Myst. Iniq.* iv. 10 It will follow with certitude plainly Mathematical. **1692** BENTLEY *Boyle Lect.* vii. (1693) 17, I suppose all the Particles of Matter to be..situated in an exact and mathematical evenness. **1809–10** COLERIDGE *Friend* (1865) 124 A theory conducted throughout with mathematical precision.

b. Constructed with 'mathematical' regularity.

1776 BURNEY *Hist. Mus.* I. 449 The voice varied a little up and down, and did not strictly keep to one mathematical line of tone. **1818** HAZLITT *Eng. Poets* i. (1870) 3 Plato banished the poets from his Commonwealth, lest their descriptions of the natural man should spoil his mathematical man. **1881** J. HAWTHORNE *Fort. Fool* I. xiv, Within are straight paths and mathematical grass-plots.

†**3.** Astrological. *Obs.*

1548 HOOPER *Declar. Commandm.* vi. 90 Thowghe I.. damne this damnable art Mathematicall, I do not damne souche other artes and sciences as be associatyd and annexid with this vnlawfull Astrologie. **1594** HOOKER *Eccl. Pol.* III. viii. §9 That Egyptian and Chaldæan wisedome Mathematicall, wherewith Moses and Daniell were furnished. **1674** HICKMAN *Hist. Quinquart.* (ed. 2) 90 He pretended a full perswasion of a Mathematical fate or destiny, yet..he was out of measure afraid of Thunders.

†**4.** Mechanical. *Obs.*

1565 JEWEL *Repl. Harding* 419 The Mathematical Dooue, that Architas Tarentinus made, that was hable to flie alone.

†**5.** = GEOMETRICAL. *Obs.*

1614 RALEIGH *Hist. World* II. (1634) 367 Cosmographers in their descriptions of the world..fill the same with strange Beasts, Birds, and Fishes, and with Mathematicall Lines. **1656** COWLEY *Pindar. Odes, Dr. Scarborough* vi. *note*, Archimedes..being found in his Study drawing Mathematical Lines for the making of some new Engines to preserve the Town.

B. *sb.*

1. *pl.* Mathematical objects. *rare.*

1555 EDEN *Decades* 324 Such vniforme partes as are in mathematicals. **1904** *Athenæum* 23 Apr. 521/3 Dr. Caird is ..right..in rejecting the ascription to Plato of the conception of mathematicals as an intermediate grade of being between ideas and sensibles. [Dr. Caird's own words are 'mathematical principles'.]

†**2.** *pl.* Mathematics; astrology. *Obs.*

1563 SHUTE *Archit.* A ij b, By a sertaine kinred and affinitie [it] is knit vnto all the Mathematicalles which sciences and knowledges are frendes. **1566** PAINTER *Pal. Pleas.* II. 375 b, The rare knowledge of Mathematicalls and other hydden and secrete Artes. **1594** CAREW *Huarte's Exam. Wits* (1596) 103 From a good imagination spring all the Arts and Sciences... Such are Poetrie, Eloquence, Musicke,..the Mathematicals, Astrologie [etc.]. *Ibid.* 117 They profit well in the Mathematicals, and in Astrologie, because they haue a good imagination. *a* **1619** FOTHERBY *Atheom.* II. ix. §1 (1622) 295 Mathematicals are proportioned vnto diuinitie, as the shadow to the Body.

†**3.** A mathematician or astrologer. *Obs.*

1566 PAINTER *Pal. Pleas.* II. 376 A Scholar..learneth a more cunnyng lecture of Mystresse Helena, than he didde of the subtillest Sorbone Doctor, or other Mathematicall from whence hee came. **1577** tr. *Bullinger's Decades* (1592) 116 The signes in the firmament shall be strange Gods, if wee being deceiued with the Mathematicals shall wholie hang on them. **1587** GOLDING *De Mornay* viii. 94 Protagoras was banished Athens for it, and the Mathematicals were vtterly condemned for it.

Hence †**mathematicality**, †**mathematicalness**, mathematical quality; formal accuracy.

1641 *Exam. Answ. Reas. agst. Votes Bps. Parl.* 27 If they by their Ordination bee bounded Morally, the House of Commons will never..trouble themselves about the Mathematicality of the Vow. **1698** [R. FERGUSON] *View Eccles.* 99 The Art and Mathematicalness of Thinking.

mathematically (mæθɪˈmætɪkəlɪ), *adv.* [f. MATHEMATICAL *a.* + -LY².]

1. In a mathematical manner; by mathematical methods; according to mathematical principles.

1570 DEE *Math. Pref.* a ij, A Point, by his motion, produceth, Mathematically, a line. **1579** J. JONES *Preserv. Bodie & Soule* I. xl. 90 Whether they be Mathematically measured, or Metaphisically pondered. **1668** WILKINS *Real Char.* 163 He [Joh. Buteo] proves Mathematically that there was a sufficient capacity in the Ark, for the conteining all those things it was designed for. **1730** A. GORDON *Maffei's Amphith.* 362 It being..mathematically repugnant, that part of the Arch of a Circle can be at the same time elliptical. **1847–8** H. MILLER *First Impr.* xvii. (1857) 283 If in the science of geometry, it must be settled mathematically.

2. With mathematical accuracy or exactness.

1567 MAPLET *Gr. Forest* 11 Iris is a kinde of Stone Mathematicallye wrought. **1669** STURMY *Mariner's Mag.* VII. ii. 3 Dial Planes are not Mathematically in the very Planes of Great Circles; for then they should have their Centers in the Center of the Earth. **1691** NORRIS *Pract. Disc.* 228 His Government of the World is no less Mathematically exact than his Creation of it. *a* **1715** BURNET *Own Time* (1724) I. 295 Was their opinion so mathematically certain, that they [etc.]? **1814** D. STEWART *Hum. Mind* II. ii. §3. 163 The correctness of the solution is as mathematically certain, as the truth of any property of the triangle, or of the circle.

†**3.** As regards quantity or number. *Obs.*

1607 *Schol. Disc. agst. Antichr.* I. i. 35 The chaunge..was mathematically little.

matheˈmaticaster. *rare.* [quasi-L., f. *mathēmatic-us*: see -ASTER.] A petty or inferior mathematician.

1872 DE MORGAN *Budget of Paradoxes* 483 Mr. Slum.. converted the idea into that of a hit at Mathematicasters, as easily as he turned the Warren acrostic into Jarley.

mathematician (ˌmæθɪməˈtɪʃən). Forms: 5 -icion, 6 -icien, matimatician, 6– **mathematician**. [ad. F. *mathématicien*, f. L. *mathēmaticus*, *mathēmatica* MATHEMATIC *sb.* 1 and 2: see -IAN.] One who is skilled or learned in mathematics.

1432–50 tr. *Higden* (Rolls) IV. 469 Puttenge in to exile mony mathematicions [1387 TREVISA mathematicos] and philosophres. **1570** DEE *Math. Pref.* *iij, The Rule of False positions..by two excellent Mathematiciens..enlarged. **1598** BARCKLEY *Felic. Man* (1631) 370 The Globe of the earth..is after the Mathematicians computation one and twentie thousand miles in compasse and above. **1687** LUTTRELL *Brief Rel.* (1857) I. 396 Sir Samuel Morland, the mathematician, is lately married. **1803** IMISON *Sci. & Art* I. 261 It [the pump] was first invented by Ctesibius, a mathematician of Alexandria, about 120 years B.C. **1821** J. Q. ADAMS in C. Davies *Metr. Syst.* III. (1871) 139 A committee..consisting of five of the ablest members of the academy and most eminent mathematicians of Europe.

†**b.** An astrologer. Chiefly *Hist.* as rendering of L. *mathēmaticus*. *Obs.*

1589 RIDER *Bibl. Schol.*, A Mathematician... 2. *Chaldæus*. **1591** HORSEY *Trav.* (Hakl. Soc.) 173 He..was verie inquisitive with one Elizious Bomelius..Doctor of phizicke in England, a rare matimatician 'magicion',..what years Quen Elizabeth was of. **1611** COTGR., *Mathematicien*, a Mathematician;..a caster of Natiuities. **1701** GREW *Cosm. Sacra* v. iv. 327 Mathematicians, among the Romans, were for some time, specially meant of Astrologers, or Star-Prophets. **1710** SHAFTESB. *Charac., Adv. Auth.* III. i. (1711) I. 289 Astrologers, Horoscopers, and other such are pleas'd to honour themselves with the Title of Mathematicians.

mathematicism (mæθɪˈmætɪsɪz(ə)m). *Philos.* [f. MATHEMATIC *a.* + -ISM; cf. G. *mathematizismus*.] The opinion that everything can be described ultimately in mathematical terms, or that the universe is fundamentally mathematical.

1933 *Mind* XLII. 107 Russell..is dismissed on the grounds that his subjectivism rests on a surreptitious basis of realism, that his mathematicism ignores qualities, and that his neutral monism leaves no room for mind in its indefeasible quality of awareness. **1962** L. J. COHEN *Diversity of Meaning* i. 19 Forgotten principles, like the mathematicism of Plato's *Timaeus*.

mathematicization (mæθɪˌmætɪsaɪˈzeɪʃən). [f. MATHEMATICIZ(E *v.* + -ATION.] = MATHEMATIZATION.

1952 F. X. MEEHAN in *Proc. Amer. Catholic Philos. Assoc.* XXVI. 19 Philosophy became for them a mathematicization of nature under the impetus given by Descartes and Newton. **1962** *Technology* May 12/3 The 'mathematicization' of science and technology.

mathematicize (mæθɪˈmætɪsaɪz), *v.* [f. MATHEMATIC *a.* + -IZE.] **a.** *trans.* To consider or treat in a mathematical manner. **b.** *intr.* To reason mathematically; to make mathematical calculations. Hence **matheˈmaticizing** *ppl. a.*

1849 FROUDE *Nemesis* 161 The dry mathematicizing reason. **1885** MRS. H. WARD *Amiel's Jrnl.* (13 Dec. 1859) I. 131 The mind of Naville is mathematical and his objects moral. His strength lies in mathematicising morals.

matheˈmatico-, used as combining form of L. *mathēmaticus* in hyphened compounds with the sense 'partly mathematical and partly ——'.

1830 HERSCHEL *Stud. Nat. Phil.* III. iii. 274 Their continental neighbours both in Germany and France were pushing forward in the career of mathematico-physical discovery. **1857** *Encycl. Brit.* XIII. 578/2 Now the mathematico-logical theories tend..to convert logical study into a mere cramming of the memory with formulae. **1865** MILL *Auguste Comte* 119 The sciences, all..except the mathematico-astronomical couple are still..in a very early stage. **1881** JEVONS in *Nature* XXIII. 485 Recent contributions to mathematico-logical science. **1890** W. JAMES *Princ. Psychol.* II. xxxviii. 669 Take any other mathematico-mechanical theory and it is the same. **1908** C. S. PEIRCE in *Monist* XVIII. 463 This would be very far from establishing the idea of certain mathematico-logicians that a line consists of points. **1937** [see CENTRIFUGE *sb.*]. **1940** C. L. HULL et al. (*title*) Mathematico-deductive theory of rote learning. **1965** *Math. in Biol. & Med.* (*Med. Res. Council*) IV. 135 We feel more secure when we have the guiding influence of a mathematico-physiological model in our experiments. **1973** *Nature* 6 July 60/2 Economic theorists take fairly naturally to the set-theoretic and mathematico-logical underpinning of mathematical methods.

mathematics (mæθɪˈmætɪks), *sb. pl.* [pl. of MATHEMATIC B. 1. Cf. F. *les mathématiques* (fem.).

Gr. had the neut. pl. τὰ μαθηματικά in the sense of mathematical objects, principles, facts, etc., as well as the fem. ἡ μαθηματική mathematical science, MATHEMATIC B. 1. The Fr. and Eng. use of the plural (known from the 16th c.) seems to have originated as an elliptic expression for 'mathematic sciences', and to have had at first no connexion with the Gr. use of the neuter plural. The analogy of names of sciences like *physics*, *metaphysics* (in which the pl. form is of Gr. origin) has, however, caused the sing. to be in English entirely superseded by the plural; in Fr., which has not the plural form in the other instances, the sing. *mathématique* survives in use as well as the plural.]

Originally, the collective name for geometry, arithmetic, and certain physical sciences (as astronomy and optics) involving geometrical reasoning. In modern use applied, (*a*) in a strict sense, to the abstract science which investigates deductively the conclusions implicit in the elementary conceptions of spatial and numerical relations, and which includes as its main divisions geometry, arithmetic, and algebra; and (*b*) in a wider sense, so as to include those branches of physical or other research which consist in the application of this abstract science to concrete data. When the word is used in its wider sense, the abstract science is distinguished as *pure mathematics*, and its concrete applications (e.g. in astronomy, various branches of physics, the theory of probabilities) as *applied* or *mixed mathematics*.

In early use always construed as a plural, and usually preceded by *the*. In recent use *the* is commonly omitted, and the sb. is almost always construed as a sing., exc. in (*the*) *higher mathematics*.

1581 MULCASTER *Positions* v. (1887) 35 Whose vse [*sc.* of Drawing] all modelling, all mathematikes, all manuaries do finde and confesse to be to so notorious and so needefull. **1587** HOLINSHED *Hist. Scot.* 461/1 A learned man in all philosophie, astronomie and the other mathematiks. **1596** SHAKS. *Tam. Shr.* I. i. 37 The Mathematickes, and the Metaphysickes Fall to them as you find your stomacke serues you. *Ibid.* II. i. 82 As cunning In Greeke, Latine, and other Languages, As the other in Musicke and Mathematickes. *a* **1618** RALEIGH *Mahomet* (1637) 142 He wrote divers bookes of the Mathematiques. **1641** WILKINS *Math. Magick* I. ii. (1648) 12 Mathematicks..is usually divided into pure and mixed. **1696–7** WALLIS in Hearne *R. Brunne's Langtoft* Pref. 147 Mathematicks (at that time..) were scarce looked upon as Academical studies. **1712** BENTLEY *Corr.* (1842) II. 449 Mathematicks was brought to that height, that [etc.]. **1726** SWIFT *Gulliver* I. i, Navigation, and other Parts of the Mathematics, useful to those who intend to travel. **1739** JOHNSON *Life Boerhaave* Wks. IV. 335 A very uncommon knowledge of the mathematicks. **1755** *Man* No. 35. 3 Mathematics derives its accuracy..from logic. **1838** DE MORGAN *Ess., Probab.* 68 The approximative methods of the higher mathematics. **1875** JOWETT *Plato* (ed. 2) IV. 271 By the help of mathematics, we form another idea of space.

†**mathematist.** *Obs.* [f. Gr. μαθηματ- (see MATHEMATIC) + -IST.] An astrologer.

1579 J. JONES *Preserv. Bodie & Soule* I. xliv. 115 Not regarding the words of..the Chaldean Prophetes, or rather Mathematists and Gymnosophistals.

mathematization (ˌmæθɪmətaɪˈzeɪʃən). [f. MATHEMATIZ(E *v.* + -ATION.] Mathematical treatment; the state of being mathematized.

1936 W. F. R. HARDIE *Study in Plato* v. 38 In the *Philebus* Plato refers to the discovery of the musical intervals (17[d]), and pays tribute to the inspiration derived from this example of successful mathematization. **1952** G. SARTON *Hist. Sci.* I. xvi. 416 His [*sc.* Plato's] mathematization of political thought. **1956** E. H. HUTTEN *Lang. Mod. Physics* ii. 37 There is no part of physics that can be said to be completely formalised as a system. At best, we find a 'mathematization'. **1962** L. J. COHEN *Diversity of Meaning* i. 19 He may too easily ignore what was contributed to the mathematization of science by medieval influences like Roger Bacon's stress on the need for a strictly mathematical treatment of optics. **1973** *Sci. Amer.* Dec. 101/1 In the Copernican system the planets are harmoniously ordered out from the sun so that the shorter the period, the closer the distance. It is this pattern that opened the way to the mathematization and mechanization of the universe.

mathematize (ˈmæθɪməˌtaɪz), *v.* [Formed as MATHEMATIST + -IZE.] = MATHEMATICIZE.

1719 *Freethinker* No. 117 ¶7 Persons of a Profession.. have been advised by very great Men to Mathematize a little, in order to acquire an habitual Caution in other Studies. **1833** J. H. NEWMAN *Lett.* (1891) I. 365 If, e.g., you feel disposed to mathematise. **1894** *Univ. Extension Jrnl.* 1 Oct. 11/2 The author has carefully avoided the error of needlessly mathematising what can be better described in words.

mathemeg (ˈmæθɪmɛg). [a. Cree *mathemeg*, lit. 'ugly fish', f. *mathe* ugly + *-meg*, ending of names of fishes. Watkins's Cree Dict. gives *muchemāk*, which represents a dialectal variant.] A catfish inhabiting the North American lakes.

1787 PENNANT *Arct. Zool.* Suppl. 115 Mathemeg. Inhabits the lakes of Hudson's Bay. **1836** J. RICHARDSON *Fauna Bor. Amer.* III. 135 *Silurus* (*Pimelodus*) *Borealis* (Richardson), The Mathemeg. *Ibid.*, The mathemeg or land cod of the residents of the fur countries is taken sparingly.

mathemes, obs. Sc. form of MATINS.

mathen, obs. f. MAIDEN *sb.*[1], var. MAYTHEN.

'mather(n. *dial.* Also 6, 9 **mathers**, 9 **madders, mauther(n, maythern, moithern.** [Variant or derivative of MAYTHE, MAYTHEN.] = MAYTHE.

1578 LYTE *Dodoens* II. xxx. 185 *Cotula fœtida*. Mathers or stinking Comomill. **1677** PLOT *Oxfordsh.* ix. 241 This [land] never requires a double stirring, nor must be made too fine and light, for then it runs to May-weed, or Mathern, as they call it. **1813** T. DAVIS *Agric. Wilts* 258–268 Maudlin, or Mathern, or Wild Chamomile.—These weeds usually prevail when the ground is overworked or made too light. **1842** AKERMAN *Wilts Gloss.*, *Mauthern*, the ox-eyed daisy. **1863** BARNES *Dorset Dial.*, Madders, or Mathers. The stinking chamomile (*anthemis cotula*). **1879** MISS JACKSON *Shropsh. Word-bk.*, *Maythern*... *Moithern*. **1880** JEFFERIES *Gt. Estate* 155 Last year there had been nearly as much mathern (wild camomile)..as crop.

‖**mathesis** (məˈθiːsɪs). *arch.* Also 6 **mathesi, -y.** [Gr. μάθησις action of learning, f. root of μανθάνειν to learn.]

In verse formerly often stressed 'mathesis.

Mental discipline; learning or science, esp. mathematical science. Also personified.

1426 LYDG. *De Guil. Pilgr.* 21152 Mathesis..Gaff yt [*sc.* a hand signifying chiromancy] to me. **1538** LELAND *Itin.* IV. 63 Johannes Rous..was well learned in those dayes in Mathesi. **1546** BALE *Eng. Votaries* I. (1550) 35 He sett up a great scole at Caunterbury of all maner scyences, as Rhetoryck, Logyck, Philosophy, Mathesy [etc.]. **1593** PEELE *Hon. of Garter, Ad Mæcenatem Prol.* 7 Thrice noble Earle, ..That artizans and schollers doost embrace, And clothest Mathesis in rich ornaments, That admirable Mathematique skill [etc.]. **1742** POPE *Dunc.* IV. 31 Mad *Mathesis* alone was unconfin'd, Too mad for mere material chains to bind. **1813** *Morn. Chron.* 10 Aug. in *Spirit Pub. Jrnls.* (1813) XVII. 205 As erst old Mathesis in chair of state sat. *a* **1876** M. COLLINS *Th. in Garden* (1880) II. 218 They can make immense progress in the infinite fields of mathesis.

‖**mathetic** (məˈθɛtɪk), *a.* [ad. Gr. μαθητικός pertaining to learning; cogn. with prec.] Pertaining to learning or scientific knowledge. Also (Bentham) in combining form **mathetico-**.

1816 BENTHAM *Chrestomathia* II. 1 Mathetic..exercises: exercises,..by which progress is made, proficiency obtained, or a lesson got: simply mathetic, to distinguish them from those which may be termed *mathetico-docimastic*, ..by which progress is made, and at the same time exhibited. *Ibid.* 22 During the whole of the school-time, the scholars are, all of them, employed, either in simply mathetic, in simply probative, or in organic (i.e. mathetico-probative) exercises. **1865** J. GROTE *Explor. Philos.* I. 175 Technicalism ought to stand upon a general basis of good mathetic logic.

mathfelonn, obs. form of MATFELLON.

mathiglin: see METHEGLIN.

mathingis, obs. Sc. form of MATINS.

mathook, variant of MATTOCK.

maths, colloq. abbrev. MATHEMATICS *sb. pl.*

1911 W. OWEN *Let.* 14 Sept. (1967) 81 The Answers to Maths. Ques. were given us all this morning. **1917** *Wireless World* Sept. 385 Extremely 'rusty' in 'maths'. **1931** [see DUB *sb.*[6]]. **1956** A.S.C. Ross in N. Mitford *Noblesse Oblige* 32 The U equivalent is *master, mistress* with prefixed attribute (as *maths-mistress*). **1960** M. SPARK *Bachelors* x. 155 I've got a pile of homework to do. Maths papers.

Mathurin (ˈmæθjʊrɪn). Also **Mat(h)urine.** [Said to be named from the chapel of St. *Mathurin* at Paris, near which they had a famous house.] A member of the order of regular canons (officially called Trinitarians) founded (A.D. 1198) by St. John of Matha for the redemption of Christian captives. Also *attrib.* or *adj.*

1611 COTGR., *Mathurin*,..a Mathurin Frier; (of th' Order of the Trinitie). **1693** *Emilianne's Hist. Monast. Ord.* xiv. 135 Of the Order of the Mathurines, or Trinitaries. **1727–41** CHAMBERS *Cycl.*, *Trinitarians*..vulgarly called *Mathurins*, and brothers of the *Redemption*. **1843** DYCE *Poet. Wks. Skelton* I. Introd. 37 Robert Gaguin was minister-general of the Maturines. **1900** W. WATT *Aberdeen & Banff* II. 48 King William's Maturine establishment on the bank of the Dee. **1904** WORDSWORTH & LITTLEHALES *Old Service-bks.* 289 The Trinitarian Order of St. Robert by Knaresborough (English Mathurines).

mati, obs. form of MATÉ *sb.*[3]

matias (ˈmætiæs). [Of obscure origin.] In ***matias bark*** = MALAMBO *bark.*

1844 HOBLYN *Dict. Med.*, *Malambo bark*, *Matias bark*, the bark of a tree said to be procured from Columbia, and used as a substitute for cinchona. **1890** *Syd. Soc. Lex.*

-matic (ˈmætɪk), *suffix.* [f. AUTO)MATIC *a.*] A terminal element in words (usu. proprietary names) designating devices which work automatically or mechanically, as ***Hoovermatic***, ***traffomatic***. orig. *U.S.*

1935 *Amer. Speech* Feb. 35/1 In Providence, Rhode Island *traffomatic* signals turn red lights to green as cars approach them. *Adjustomatic* and *Ceomatic* also occur, and there is a *Nickel-mat* restaurant. **1938** S. CHASE *Tyranny of Words* xiv. 173 Dial-a-matic. **1941** *Word Study* Nov. 7/1 This year bids fair to be the *-matic* year of all years. **1957** *Journal des Traducteurs* II. 50 Admen all over the continent have coined hundreds of magic brand names with this productive adaptation suffix, exploiting to the full the suggestion of 'minimum effort' it connotes..: *Accumatic* watch, *Ajustomatic* pipe, *Coffeematic* percolator. **1959** *Amer. Speech* Oct. 237 English trade names..such as *Hoovermatic* (an automatic washer and dryer) or *Sensimatic* (a Burroughs bookkeeping machine). **1966** L. COHEN *Beautiful Losers* (1970) III. 238 The Bowl-a-Matic habitually divided every strike between First and Second Player regardless of who or how many threw. **1971** *Amat. Photographer* 13 Jan. 92/2 (Advt.), Pakmatic.., Easymatic,.. Instamatic. **1972** *House & Garden* Feb. 79 'Brush-o-matic', to clean upholstery.

maticin (ˈmætɪsɪn). *Chem.* Also **-ine.** [f. MATICO + -IN.] A bitter principle obtained from the leaves of the matico plant.

1844 HODGES in *Lond.* etc. *Philos. Mag.* XXV. 206 A yellowish-brown extractive matter, maticine, remained. **1871** WATTS tr. *Gmelin's Handbk. Chem.* XVIII. 234 Maticin.

‖**matico** (maˈtiko). Also **mateco, matica.** [Sp. *yerba Matico* (*yerba* herb; *Matico* dim. of *Mateo* Matthew); alleged to be named from a Spanish soldier who discovered its styptic properties.] A Peruvian shrub, *Piper angustifolium* (*Artanthe elongata*). **b.** The leaves of this plant used as a styptic.

1838 JEFFREYS in *Lancet* 5 Jan. (1839) 567 The name of the plant from which the leaves are collected, is *Matèco*. **1842** *Provincial Med. & Surg. Jrnl.* June 209 The South American styptic 'maticó'. **1849** J. H. BALFOUR *Man. Bot.* §1034 The substance called Matico or Matica. **1880** GARROD & BAXTER *Mat. Med.* 415 Bleeding from leech-bites may be stopped..by matico.

c. *attrib.*, as ***matico leaf, oil, plant.***

1880 GARROD & BAXTER *Mat. Med.* 351 *Maticæ Folia.* *Matico Leaves. **1885** *Cassell's Encycl. Dict.*, **Matico oil.* **1871** WATTS tr. *Gmelin's Handbk. Chem.* XVIII. 234 The leaves of the *matico plant.

matico: see MATACO.

matie (ˈmeɪtɪ). Also **mattie, matje, maty.** [a. Du. *maatjes* (*haring*), earlier *maetgens-*, *maeghdekens-* (cf. MLG. *madikesherink*, mod.LG. *maidkens-hering*), f. *maagd* MAID *sb.*[1] + *-ken* -KIN. Cf. MAID *sb.*[1] 7, MAIDEN *sb.* 8; also FAIR MAID.] A herring in what is considered the best condition for food, when the roe or milt is perfectly but not largely developed.

1858 SIMMONDS *Dict. Trade*, *Maties.* **1863** *Rep. Commiss. Herring-trawling Scotl.* §51. 26 The herring is found under four different conditions: 1st, Fry or Sill; 2d, Maties or Fat Herring; 3d, Full Herring; 4th, Shotten or Spent Herring. **1864** *Macm. Mag.* Aug. 344 In the next stage [i.e. the second] of the herring, it is called a matie. **1883** S. WALPOLE *Brit. Fish Trade* (Fish. Exhib. Lit. I.) 33 'Matties', or young herrings cured. **1894** R. LEIGHTON *Wreck Golden Fleece* 38 Not many maties among 'em, eh?—Maties? No. I aren't seen a dacent-sized herrin come aboard yet.

attrib. **1883** *Fisheries Exhib. Catal.* 69, 1 Barrel Mattie Herrings. **1898** *Shetland News* 27 Aug. (E.D.D.) Excluding the Lewis and Barra matje fishings.

matier(e, obs. forms of MATTER.

‖**matière** (matjɛr). [Fr.] The quality given to his pigment by an artist. Also *fig.*

1915 W. H. WRIGHT *Mod. Painting* xiv. 320 De Vlaminck has a rich and compelling *matière* and an art sense which is almost coquettish. **1921** R. FRY *Lett.* (1972) I. 62 In the *Nature Morte*..he [*sc.* Picasso] has gained a certain plastic quality by the extraordinary contrasts of *matière*. **1936** *Burlington Mag.* July 35/1 Though the *matière* is still heavy, the paint is applied in parallel oblique strokes. **1960** *Times* 12 May 10/5 Dubuffet has experimented with the potentialities of *matière* in his paintings. **1963** *Guardian* 29 Feb. 9/2 Kossoff struggles with his grotesquely sensual matiere like a Vietnamese trooper slurping in the mud of a rice paddy. **1971** *Guardian Weekly* 7 Aug. 19 Lecture Four. The matiere of verse demonstrated further in Wallace Stevens; who isn't my poet.

Matilda (məˈtɪldə). *Austral. slang.* Also matilda. [A female Christian name.] = SWAG *sb.* 10. So ***to walk*** or ***waltz Matilda***: to carry one's swag, to travel the road (cf. WALTZ *v.*); ***Matilda-waltzer***, a tramp, traveller.

1893 *Bulletin* (Sydney) 18 Nov. 20/3 A swag is not generally referred to as a 'bluey' or 'Matilda'—it is *called* a swag. *Ibid.*, No bushman thinks of 'going on a wallaby' or 'walking Matilda'..he goes on the track. **1916** J. B. COOPER *Coo-oo-ee* i. 3 Somehow things appear different to a man on a coach to a swaggie padding the hoof along the same road with 'Matilda' slung from his shoulders. **1917** A. B. PATERSON *Waltzing Matilda* in *Saltbush Bill* (1924) 24 And he sang as he looked at his old billy boiling, 'Who'll come a-waltzing Matilda with me?' *c* **1926** 'MIXER' *Transport Workers' Song Bk.* 139 That night he packed up his 'Matilda'. **1933** *Bulletin* (Sydney) 3 May 20/2 Matilda-waltzers with one black (or brown) shoe or boot are an everyday sight. **1934** *Ibid.* 12 Dec. 25/2 He chucks Matilda into a corner and is rummaging for tucker when Old Dave comes back. **1962** MARSHALL & DRYSDALE *Journey among Men* xii. 116 It was a beautiful place for a camp. It was good to stretch out in the arms of Matilda at the end of the day, and slowly smoke a cigarette. **1965** J. S. GUNN *Terminol. Shearing Industry* II. 29 In the days of itinerant workers and wanderers the swag had many names, including 'matilda', 'bundle', [etc.].

matildite (məˈtɪldaɪt). *Min.* [a. It. *matildite* (A. D'Achiardi *I Metalli* (1883) I. 136), f. the name of the *Matilda* mine (near Morococha in the department of Junín) in central Peru: see -ITE[1].] A sulphide of silver and bismuth, $AgBiS_2$, occurring as brittle, grey to black, orthorhombic crystals that are opaque with a metallic lustre.

1892 E. S. DANA *Dana's Syst. Min.* (ed. 6) 115 Matildite. **1900** *Mineral. Mag.* XII. 313 A description is given of 128 mineral species found in Japan... The occurrence of the rare mineral matildite is recorded. **1969** *Canad. Mineralogist* IX. 655 A characteristic feature of matildite in most of its occurrences from widely separated regions of the world is its intergrowth in galena which form [*sic*] Widmanstätten-like structures.

matilent, variant of MALTALENT *Obs.*

matily (ˈmeɪtɪlɪ), *adv.* [f. MATEY *a.* + -LY[2].] In a friendly, familiar, or companionable fashion.

1973 *Daily Tel.* 10 Mar. 17/1 A squirrel chattered matily at me as I climbed the stile. **1974** *Listener* 21 Nov. 674/3 *The Hammers*..is jolly, warm-hearted,..matily naive.

matimaticion, obs. form of MATHEMATICIAN.

matin (ˈmætɪn). Pl. **matins** (ˈmætɪnz). Forms: *pl.* 3–4, 7 **matines,** 3–5 **matynes,** 4 **mateyns, matinis, matynys,** 4–5 **metenes,** 4–6 **matyns,** 5 **matens, maytenys, mayteynesse,** 6 **mattyns, mattence,** *Sc.* **matynnis, mathemes, mathingis,** 6–7 **mattens,** 4– **matins,** 6– **mattins.** *sing.* 4 **matyn,** 4–5 **matyne,** 7 **mattin, matine,** 7– **matin, mattin.** [Early ME. *matines*, a. F. *matines* fem. pl. (11th c.) = Pr. *matinas*:—Eccl. L. *mātūtīnās* (nom. *mātūtīnæ*), fem. pl. of *mātūtīnus* pertaining to the morning. The more usual forms in med.L. were the masc. sing. *mātūtīnus* (hence Sp. *maitines* masc. pl., also *matutino*) and the masc. pl. *mātūtīnī*. Cf. F. *matin*, Pr. *mati*, It. *mattino* morning:—L. *mātūtīnum* (sc. *tempus*).

With regard to the coexistence of the masc. and fem. forms in med.L., cf. the use of *vesperæ* fem. pl. and *vesperi* masc. pl., for VESPERS. Some scholars have suggested that the form *matutinæ* is ellipt. for *matutinæ vigiliæ*: cf. *vigilia matutina* 'morning watch' 1 Sam. xi. 11.]

I. In the plural form.

1. *Eccl.* **a.** One of the canonical hours of the breviary; properly a midnight office, but sometimes recited at daybreak, and followed immediately by lauds.

In modern Roman Catholic use the office as said by secular clergy is usually 'anticipated', i.e. said on the afternoon or evening before.

c **1290** *S. Eng. Leg.* I. 91/156 Ase þe Monekes weren ech-one A nyȝt at Matines. *c* **1330** *Arth. & Merl.* 6490 (Kölbing) Ich niȝt it was þe quenes maner, To chirche gon & matins here. *c* **1440** *Alphabet of Tales* 197 On a nyght as he stude at þe psalmodie at matyns. *c* **1440** *Promp. Parv.* 329/2 Mateynys, *matutine*. **1450–1530** *Myrr. our Ladye* 122 Thys versycle [*Esto nobis*] ys sayde bytwene Matyns and Lawdes. *Ibid.*, Some tyme mattyns were sayde by themselfe in the nyghte, and laudes by them selfe at morow tyde, and the same ys yet vsed of some relygyons. *c* **1483** CAXTON *Dialogues* 27/17 He ariseth alle the nyghtes For to here matynes. **1560** DAUS tr. *Sleidane's Comm.* 114 b, They came to mumble up their mattyns at mydnight, after their accustomed maner. **1601** F. GODWIN *Bps. of Eng.* 327 As he came from the morning seruice then called the Mattens which was woont to be said shortly after midnight. **1863** J. M. NEALE *Ess. Liturgiol.* 6 Matins are preceded by the Pater Noster, the Ave Maria, and the Credo. **1896** SWETE *Ch. Services* 39 The night services consisted of Nocturns, Mattins and Lauds; at daybreak came the supplementary Mattins.

†**b.** Often used as a designation for the whole of the public service preceding the first mass on Sunday. (See quot. 1904.) *Obs.*

c **1250** *Lutel Soth Serm.* 69 in *O.E. Misc.* 190 (Cott. MS.) Masses and matines ne kepeþ heo nouht. **13..** *Minor Poems fr. Vernon MS.* xxxvii. 852 ȝif þow herest matyns and masse and takest haly brede. *c* **1380** WYCLIF *Eng. Wks.* (1880) 193 ȝif prestis seyn here matynes, masse & euensong aftir salisbury vsse [etc.]. **1470–85** MALORY *Arthur* I. iii–v. 40 Whan matyns & the first masse was done. **1520** *Burgh Recs. Stirling* (1887) 5 At Mes, Mathemes and Ewinsang. *c* **1529** in Ellis *Orig. Lett.* Ser. I. I. 189 He..is alwaye present at Mattens and all Masse wᵗ evyn song. **1549** LATIMER *4th Serm. bef. Edw. VI* (Arb.) 108 Thys byshop answered hys chaplayne..as I was goynge to hys Sermon, I remembred me that I had neyther sayed masse, nor mattens. **1904** WORDSWORTH & LITTLEHALES *Old Service-bks.* 21 Then, even as now..the church was rarely used on Sundays more than three times, i.e. for Mattins at 6 or 7, for High Mass then at 9, and for Evensong at 2 p.m., 2.30 p.m., or 3 p.m. But with 'Mattins' (we conjecture) Lauds and Prime would be amalgamated.

c. The order for public morning prayer in the Church of England since the Reformation.

Structurally the service is a combination of elements of the breviary offices of matins, lauds, and prime.

1548 *Act 2 & 3 Edw. VI*, c. 1 §6 The Mattens, Evensonge, Letanye, and all other prayers. **1549** (May) *Bk. Com. Prayer* 1 An Ordre for Mattins dayly through the yere. **1559** *Act 1 Eliz.* c. 2 §2 All and singler Mynysters..shall..use the Mattens Evensong Celebracion of the Lordes Supper [etc.]. **1733** TICKELL *Her Majesty's Rebuilding* 12 To couch at Curfeu-time they thought no scorn, And froze at Matins, every winter-morn. **1863** J. M. NEALE *Ess. Liturgiol.* 7 No one, we imagine, but must have felt the lamentable want of this [Invitatory] in our own Matins. **1896** SWETE *Ch. Services* 73 Subsequent revisions of the Prayer Book have introduced into the English Mattins and Evensong elements foreign to the ancient Hours.

¶**d.** In a form of oath. (Cf. MARYMASS 2.) ? *nonce use.*

1606 *Wily Beguiled* K 1 b, Now by the Marry mattens, Peg, thou hast [etc.].

†**e.** *black matins*: at Christ Church, Oxford, the college matins (as distinguished from the cathedral matins at which surplices are worn). *Obs.*

1825 C. M. WESTMACOTT *English Spy* I. 305 If you're fond of fun, old fellow, jump up and view the Christ Church men proceeding to *black matins* this morning.

2. In various allusive and fig. uses.

a. Chiefly of birds: *to sing* (etc.) ***matins***, to sing their morning song. *poet.*

c **1530** *Crt. of Love* 1353 On May-day..To matens went the lusty nightingale... *Domine labia*, gan he crye. **1595** SPENSER *Epithal.* 80 The merry Larke hir mattins sings aloft. **1640** GLAPTHORNE *Hollander* IV. Wks. 1874 I. 133 The shrill Organd Cocke Shall cease to carroll Mattens to the morne. **1812** J. WILSON *Isle of Palms* III. 435 And kneeling there to Mercy's fane..The Maid her matins sings. **1866** NEALE *Sequences & Hymns* 81 The birds sing early Matins. **1903** *Longm. Mag.* Nov. 30 The thrushes were still at matins.

†**b.** ***Devil's matins***: a service of Satanic worship attributed to witches; *transf.* an uproar. *Obs.*

1625 MASSINGER *New Way* IV. i, Sir Giles Ouerreach Made such a plain discouerie of himselfe, And read this morning such a diuellish Matins, That [etc.]. **1634** W. WOOD *New Eng. Prosp.* II. xii, Hee [the Devil] was wont to carry away their wives and children, because hee would drive them to these Mattens. **1820** [see DEVIL *sb.* 25].

c. ***Parisian matins*** (= F. *matines de Paris*, in Cotgr. *matines parisiennes*): the massacre of St. Bartholomew (Aug. 24, 1572), which began about 2 a.m. (Cf. *Sicilian vespers.*)

1614 [see PARISIAN B]. **1683** in *Lond. Gaz.* No. 1856/5 Murders, and Massacres, not to be parallel'd by the Parisian Mattins, or Sicilian Vespers.

d. A morning duty, occupation, or performance.

1641 MILTON *Ch. Govt.* II. (1851) 142 These and such lessons as these, I know would have been my Matins duly, and my Even-song. **1814** WORDSW. *Excursion* II. 140 The music and the sprightly scene Invite us; shall we quit our road, and join These festive matins?

II. In the sing. form.

†**3.** A morning. *Obs. rare.*

In the first quot. *matine* is a trisyllable riming with *tre*, and would therefore be strictly a distinct word, ad. F. *matinée*: see MATINÉE.

[*c* **1400** *Laud Troy Bk.* 8692 The sonne schynes on euery a tre, Hit is a fair matyne.] **1602** SHAKS. *Ham.* I. v. 89 The Glow-worme showes the Matine to be neere, And gins to pale his vneffectuall Fire. **1845** DISRAELI *Sybil* (1863) 244 This morn..I learnt how your matins were now spent.

4. A morning call or song (of birds). *poet.*

1632 MILTON *L'Allegro* 114 Ere the first Cock his Mattin rings. **1742** YOUNG *Nt. Th.* I. 438 The sprightly Lark's shrill Matin wakes the Morn. **1840** J. S. POLACK *Mann. & Cust. N. Zealanders* I. 166 His shrill early matin, giving the signal to rise.

III. 5. *attrib.* and *Comb.* **a.** with *matin*: (*a*) 'pertaining to or used at the time of matins'.

c **1315** SHOREHAM *Poems* ii. 14 God and man y-take was At matyn-tyde by nyȝte. *c* **1375** *Sc. Leg. Saints* xvi. (*Magdalena*) 905 In sammyne tyme þat wont war thay In matyne offyce for to ryse. **1450–1530** *Myrr. our Ladye* 24 To saye..mattyns, at mattyn tyme, & pryme at pryme tyme. **1708** OZELL tr. *Boileau's Lutrin* 57 And call the Yawning Priests to Matin Pray'r. **1709** POPE *Jan. & May* 523 He rais'd his spouse ere Matin-bell was rung. **1796** SCOTT *Wild Huntsmen* x, To muttering monks leave matin-song. *c* **1820** S. ROGERS *Italy* (1839) 133 Those who assembled there at matin-time. **1851** LONGF. *Gold. Leg.* IV. *Refectory*, To your cells, And pray till you hear the matin-bells.

(*b*) passing into adj. in the sense 'belonging to, the early morning, morning-, matinal'.

1643 *Farington Papers* (Chetham Soc.) 99 Matin Chamber. **1667** MILTON *P.L.* v. 7 The shrill Matin Song of Birds. **1717** POPE *Eloisa* 267, I waste the Matin lamp in sighs for thee. *a* **1732** GAY *Fables* (1738) II. viii. 77 At noon (the lady's matin hour) I sip the tea's delicious flower. **1810** SCOTT *Lady of L.* II. i, All Nature's children feel the matin spring Of life reviving, with reviving day. **1863** WOOLNER *My Beautiful Lady* 45 At matin time where creepers interlace We sauntered slowly.

b. with *matins*: as ***matins book, monger, mumbling, time***; †**matins mass**, the mass before which matins is recited.

1303 R. BRUNNE *Handl. Synne* 823 þat day [Sunday] þou owyst..For to here þy seruyse al; Matyns messe here [*Dulwich MS.* matenys & messe], to rede or syngge,..Come fyrst to matyns, ȝyf þat þou may. **1395** *E.E. Wills* (1882) 5 A peyre Matyns bookis. **1484** CAXTON *Fables of Alfonce* i, The Cocke..watcheth and waketh atte matyns tyme. **1530** PALSGR. 804/2 At mattyns tyme. *Ibid.* 183 *Vnes hevres*, a primer or a mattyns boke. **1543** BALE *Yet a Course* 88 b, Mattens mongers, masse momblers, holye water swyngers. *a* **1555** G. MARSH in Foxe *A. & M.* (1583) 1565 Holy water casting, procession gadding, Mattins mumbling [etc.].

‖**mâtin** (mɑtæ̃). [Fr.: see MASTIFF.] A large French watch-dog.

1774 GOLDSM. *Nat. Hist.* (1776) III. 298 He [Buffon] bred up a young wolf..with a matin dog of the same age. **1845** YOUATT *Dog* 27 The French mâtin (*Canis laniarius*).

matinal (ˈmætɪnəl), *a.* Now *rare.* [ad. F. *matinal*, f. *matin* morning: see MATIN and -AL¹. Cf. MATUTINAL.]

1. Belonging to or taking place in the morning; early. Also, early-rising, matutinal.

1803 MARY CHARLTON *Wife & Mistress* II. i. 11 To attend the matinal *déjeuné's* of old Gruffy in town. **1819** H. BUSK *Vestriad* v. 276 The grey-ey'd Hours climb up the starry way To meet fair maidens matinal as they. **1842** MRS. F. TROLLOPE *Vis. Italy* I. xiv. 219 As if my very matinal son and myself had constituted the whole party. **1860** LD. LYTTON *Lucile* II. v. §9. 30 The matinal chirp of a bird. **1862** MRS. H. WOOD *Channings* II. 74 Believing it could be nobody less than the bishop come to alarm them with a matinal visit.

2. *Geol.* The name given by H. D. Rogers to the third of his subdivisions of the palæozoic strata in the Appalachian chain, and hence to the period at which these were formed.

1858 H. D. ROGERS *Geol. Pennsylv.* II. II. 749 These periods..are the Primal, Auroral, Matinal, Levant, Surgent [etc.]. *Ibid.* 783 Depositions and Disturbances of the Matinal Period. **1859** PAGE *Handbk. Geol. Terms.* **1863** DANA *Man. Geol.* 379 'Matinal' Limestone with blue shale.

‖**matinée** (ˈmætɪneɪ, Fr. matine). [F. *matinée* morning, what occupies a morning, f. *matin* morning.] **1.** A 'morning' (i.e. afternoon) theatrical or musical or cinema performance.

[**1848** THACKERAY *Van. Fair* lxiv, A *matinée musicale.* **1850** LONGFELLOW in *Life* (1891) II. 170 Charles Perkins gives *matinées musicales.*] **1858** *Boston Even. Gaz.* 6 Mar., A dramatic matinee is a novel idea. **1879** *Dramatic Notes* 23, I have given 379 *Matinées*, equal to one year and a quarter of night performances. **1880** *Standard* 22 Dec., The Gaiety *matinées.* **1973** P. EVANS *Bodyguard Man* i. 13 A child raised on Saturday matinée soap-operas at the local cinema.

2. A woman's lingerie jacket.

1896 *Woman's Life* 11 July 178/2 The pretty summer matinée of white cambric or lawn that accompanies this petticoat is made with full bell sleeves edged with lace. **1908** A. BENNETT *Old Wives' Tale* III. iv. 338 She sat up and managed to drag her *matinée* from a chair and put it round her shoulders. **1960** CUNNINGTON & BEARD *Dict. Eng. Costume* 134/2 *Matinee* 1851.., a hooded pardessus made of jacconet or muslin and worn outdoors over a morning dress.

3. *attrib.* and *Comb.*, as ***matinée actor, girl, public, ticket***; **matinée coat**, a baby's short outer garment; **matinée hat**, a lady's hat worn at matinées; **matinée idol**, a handsome actor of a type supposed to be especially attractive to matinée audiences.

1895 W. ARCHER in *World* 13 Feb. 25/2 He will learn next to nothing from *matinée actors and audiences. **1929** *Treasure Cot Catal.* Nov. 31 Very pretty *Matinee Coat in good quality Crepe-de-chine. **1957** W. RODWELL *Cutting & Designing Juvenile Outerwear* I. 2 Basic draft for infant's matinée coat... This draft is for the earliest type of coat worn by children. **1899** H. VAN DYKE *Fisherman's Luck* 101 The *matinée girl is not likely to have a very luminous or truthful idea of existence floating around in her pretty head. **1894** *Million* 10 Feb. 223/2 The disappearance of the **matinée* hat would be seriously felt by the writer of jokes. **1898** *St. James's Gaz.* 8 Nov. 4/1 No efforts of theatrical managers seem able to cope with the nuisance of the 'matinée hat'. **1905** G. B. SHAW *How to become Mus. Critic* (1960) 256, I once, in Drury Lane Theatre, sat behind a *matinée* hat decorated with two wings of a seagull. **1902** 'H. MCHUGH' *Back to Woods* vii. 107 Mrs. John..you should be proud of this *matinee idol husband of yours. **1909** 'O. HENRY' *Roads of Destiny* xiii. 210 Being conspirators from the cradle and matinee idols by proclamation. **1924** J. BUCHAN *Three Hostages* iv. 54 He's not in the least the ordinary matinee idol. He is..adored by women and also liked by men. **1952** GRANVILLE *Dict. Theatr. Terms* 116 A perfect example of the matinée idol was the late Owen Nares. **1973** *Times* 26 Mar. 12/5 In the heyday of the matinee idol he had commanded..a sober, serene and loyal admiration. **1919** F. HURST *Humoresque* 206 It was just their always playing in the same pictures, and that silly *matinée public..got to linking their names together. **1904** 'A. DALE' *Wanted: a Cook* 208 What do you say to mentioning *matinée tickets once a week?

ˈmatiness, var. MATEYNESS.

ˈmating, *vbl. sb.*¹ [-ING¹.] The action of MATE *v.*¹; checkmating. Also *attrib.*

c **1330** R. BRUNNE *Chron. Wace* (Rolls) 11399 At ilka mattyng [*v.r.* matyng] þei seide 'chek'. *c* **1407** LYDG. *Reas. & Sens.* 46 Ye shal fynde anoone ryght By and by in this scripture Of my matynge the Aventure. *c* **1440** *Promp. Parv.* 329/2 Matynge at the chesse, *matacio.* **1592** G. HARVEY *New Letter* Wks. (Grosart) I. 275 In a mating age, none are free from the check, but kinges. *a* **1649** DRUMM. OF HAWTH. *Fam. Epist.* Wks. (1711) 146 The mating of the king is the conclusion of the game [of chess]. **1908** *Westm. Gaz.* 12 Aug. 7/3 Mackenzie ran into a mating net with Gunsberg in a lively game. **1968** S. MORRISON *Chess* vi. 52 Black would reply 10..K–R3 and..escapes the mating net.

mating (ˈmeɪtɪŋ), *vbl. sb.*² [f. MATE *v.*² + -ING¹.]

a. The action of MATE *v.*²; matching; marrying; pairing; esp. of birds (occas. with *up*). Also *attrib.*, as ***mating-ground***.

1621 BRATHWAITE *Natures Embass. Sheph. Tales* 213 So shall we Honor'd be, In our mating, in our meeting. **1856** KANE *Arct. Expl.* I. xxi. 268 A solitary pair, who seem to have left their fellows for this far northern mating-ground. **1875** JOWETT *Plato* (ed. 2) III. 61 Do you [a breeder of birds and animals] not take the greatest care in the mating? **1888** W. DAY *Horse* xviii. 239 The management of mares at the mating season, and during the period of gestation, is a subject requiring more than mere passing notice. **1896** *Westm. Gaz.* 28 May 3/1 The mating of the blue gown with the pink or crimson hat is eminently smart. **1899** *Feathered World* 10 Mar. 474 Having described the mating-up of the breeding pens of pure brown-reds. **1905** E. WHARTON *House of Mirth* II. xiii. 500 The blind motions of her mating instinct. **1919** T. S. ELIOT *Hippopotamus* in *Poems*, At mating time the hippo's voice Betrays inflexions hoarse and odd. **1936** *Brit. Birds* XXIX. 307 The 'mating rite' is performed only on the nest. **1936** *Discovery* Oct. 307/2 During the mating season, its call is startling. **1938** *Proc. Amer. Philos. Soc.* LXXXIX. 412 As conjugation takes place usually or only between individuals of diverse types, these types will be referred to as mating types. **1953** D. A. BANNERMAN *Birds Brit. Isles* I. 78 The mating-call..can be heard all this time. **1960** G. BLANCHET *Search in North* xi. 142 The nesting season..was already ended, the mating songs were no longer heard and the young..on the wing. **1962** *Times* 30 Mar. 15/4 The mating-call or whistle of the juvenile 'wolf'. **1973** *Country Life* 29 Nov. 1848/2 The condition of the ewes by the end of mating time should be at least maintained for the first half of pregnancy.

b. *Fishing.* (See quot.)

1887 GOODE, etc. *Fisheries U.S.* Sect. v. II. 259 Sometimes two or more crews belonging to different vessels unite in the capture, and if successful an equitable division of the oil is afterward made. This is called 'mating'.

ˈmating, *ppl. a.* [f. MATE *v.*² + -ING².] That mates; pairing.

1870 F. W. H. MYERS *Poems* 100 No ringdove murmurs on the hill Nor mating cushat calls. **1903** *Westm. Gaz.* 11 Feb. 2/3 Sing more softly for his sake, you mating birds on bough. **1941** N. H. ANDERSON *Aircraft Layout* iv. 99 Dural mating parts should not be used in bearings. **1967** M. CHANDLER *Ceramics in Mod. World* iv. 129 Yet another method is to fire the rings separately, then grind the mating surfaces and join them with an epoxy resin adhesive.

†**matins**, *v. Obs.* [f. *matins*: see MATIN.] *intr.* To perform matins; also *trans.* to honour (a saint) with celebration of matins. Hence †**matinsed** *ppl. a.*, †**matinsing** *vbl. sb.* Also †**matinser** *nonce-wd.*, one who performs matins.

1543 Mattenser [see MASSER¹]. **1546** BALE *Eng. Votaries* I. (1550) 72 b, Whan theyr feastfull dayes come, they are..with no small solempnite, mattensed, massed,..sensed, smoked, perfumed and worshypped. **1547** —— *Latter Exam. A. Askew* Pref. 8 These clowted, canonysed, solempnysed, sensed, mattensed, and massed martyrs. **1553** BECON *Reliques of Rome* (1563) 141 b, Al other fashions of Mattensyng and Massyng..vtterly put away.

matipo (ˈmætɪpəʊ). *N.Z.* Also **matapo**. [Maori.] Either of two New Zealand evergreen trees, *Pittosporum tenuifolium*, of the family Pittosporaceæ, which is also called black matipo and bears clusters of purple flowers, or *Myrsine australis*, the red matipo (see MAPAU).

1866 M. A. BARKER *Let.* in *Station Life N.Z.* (1870) 94 Varieties of matapo, a beautiful shrub, each leaf a study, with its delicate tracery of black veins on a yellow-green ground. **1879** J. B. ARMSTRONG in *Trans. N.Z. Inst.* XII. 329 The tipau or matipo, Pittosporum tenuifolium..makes the best ornamental hedge I know of. **1921** H. GUTHRIE-SMITH *Tutira* vii. 51 Later, appeared slender matapo (Pittosporum tenuifolium). **1960** N. HILLIARD *Maori Girl* II. xiii. 152 Henry commented on the legs of the girls: 'Too thin! Like *matipo*.'

matir(e, obs. forms of MATTER.

matirmonye, -moyne, obs. ff. MATRIMONY.

matje, variant of MATIE.

matless (ˈmætlɪs), *a.* [f. MAT *sb.*¹ + -LESS.] Not furnished with a mat or mats.

1880 J. ROSS *Hist. Corea* x. 318 The dead body..is not, like the Chinese, put on a matless floor.

matlo(w (ˈmætləʊ). *slang.* [Phonetic ad. F. *matelot* sailor.] A sailor. Cf. MATELOT.
1903 KIPLING *Traffics & Discov.* (1904) 58 Simultaneous it hits the Pusser that 'e'd better serve out mess pork for the poor matlow. **1908** *Westm. Gaz.* 31 July 2/1 Evolutions and exercises to keep the modern 'matlow' busy and happy. **1914** 'BARTIMEUS' *Naval Occasions* xxii. 200 In less formal surroundings..he is wont to refer to himself as a 'matlow'. **1916** 'TAFFRAIL' *Pincher Martin* ii. 16 Matloes, Pincher, the same as you an' me. **1946** *News Chron.* 27 June 2 (R.N. Advt.), It's a good life and a good job, too! I'm a Matlo—Able Seaman to you. **1974** S. E. MORISON *European Discovery of America: Southern Voyages* xiii. 316 Magellan was always a sailor's sailor, and *os rudos marinheiros*, as Camoëns called the common 'matlow' of that era, always stood by him in his contests with officers.

matlockite (ˈmætləkaɪt). *Min.* [f. *Matlock*, name of a town in Derbyshire: see -ITE.] †**a.** = PHOSGENITE. *Obs.* **b.** A yellowish oxychloride of lead occurring at Cromford near Matlock.
1843 E. J. CHAPMAN *Pract. Min.* 40 Matlockite. Chloride of Lead, from Derbyshire. Kerasine, *Beud.*; Murio-Carbonate of Lead, *Phil.*; Horn-lead. **1851** R. P. GREG in *Philos. Mag.* Ser. IV. II. 120 A description of Matlockite, a new Oxychloride of Lead.

matlong, (? erron.) var. of MALTLONG *Obs.*
1614 MARKHAM *Cheap Husb.* 35 Hurts on the Cronet, as the quitterbone or Matlong. *Ibid.*, The Quitterbone is a hollow vlcer on the top of the Cronet, and so is the Matlong.

matoke (mæˈtəʊkeɪ). [Local name.] A preparation of the flesh of bananas, used as food in Uganda; also, the fruit itself. Also *attrib.*
1959 N. W. SIMMONDS *Bananas* ix. 261 In Uganda..the unripe fruit is peeled, wrapped in banana leaves and..steamed... The product is called 'matoke' and it was the basic food of the Baganda people. **1962** *Lancet* 5 May 942/1 The excretion of 5-hydroxyindolacetic acid (5-H.I.A.A.) increases after the ingestion of matoke bananas, a normal article of diet of the Baganda people of Uganda. **1966** B. KIMENYE *Kalasanda Revisited* 17 The gleaming vehicle..was only on the road when they needed fresh supplies of matoke from the market. *Ibid.* 33 Kibuka had to resort to collecting matoke peelings in an old bucket. **1969** *Reporter* (Nairobi) 16 May 39/1 For large areas of Uganda the staple food crop is bananas, or as it is known locally, matoke.

matra (ˈmɑːtrə). [Skr.] In Indian music, a beat, or a subdivision of one, within a rhythmic phrase.
1898 B. A. PINGLE *Indian Mus.* (ed. 2) v. 161 The number of Mátrás in a Tála is fixed. **1971** *Shankar's Weekly* (Delhi) 4 Apr. 24/3 The tabla player has to go through a cycle of matras, each of which is divided into a number of beats. **1972** P. HOLROYDE *Indian Mus.* v. 199 Tala (= palm of the hand) is a complex organization of rhythms or differing beats..in multiple groupings or thekas which are again subdivided by the individual components of the beat, the fractional matras. *Ibid.* 200 Matras are the smaller individual beats, each matra being determined in length by the pace of the overall rhythm.

‖**matraca** (maˈtraka). Also **mattraca.** [Sp.] In Spain: a kind of mechanical wooden rattle used instead of church bells on Good Friday.
1910 C. B. LUFFMANN *Quiet Days in Spain* i. 14 A singular contrivance in the high towers takes the place of bells on Good Friday; this is the 'mattraca'—three long boxes of heavy wood arranged round a spindle, with several roughly fashioned hammers with rings in their handles, through which a rod is run to keep them in place. At short intervals during the whole of Good Friday the mattraca is turned round, grindstone fashion, and creates a most awful din... As I can find no clue to the origin of the mattraca, I fall back on the belief that it was intended to inform the multitude of the building of, or nailing of Christ to, the cross. **1974** S. E. MORISON *European Discovery of America: Southern Voyages* v. 92 Holy Week in Seville... The supreme Passion on Good Friday when one heard the clacking of the *matraca* in place of cheerful bells.

matrace, obs. form of MATRASS, MATTRESS.

matracy, obs. form of MATRASS.

matral (ˈmætrəl, ˈmeɪtrəl), *a. rare.* [f. MATR(I- + -AL.] = MATRICENTRED *ppl. a.*
1956 [see MATRICENTRED *ppl. a.*].

‖**matranee** (məˈtrɑːniː). *Anglo-Indian.* Also **matraney.** [Corruption of Hindī *mehtarānī*, fem. of MEHTAR.] A female sweeper (of a house); a female house-servant in India whose duty it is to perform the most menial offices.
c **1804** SHERWOOD in *Life Mrs. S.* (1854) 294 A Matranee. *c* **1813** MRS. SHERWOOD *Stories Ch. Catech.* xxxvii. 376 A procession of sweeper-women, or matraneys. **1886** YULE & BURNELL *Anglo-Ind. Gloss.*, *Matranee*,..a female sweeper.

†**matrass**[1]. *Obs.* In 6 **mattresse.** [a. OF. *materas, matelas*, of obscure origin.] A quarrel or bolt for the cross-bow.
1530 PALSGR. 244/1 Mattresse for a crosbowe, *martelas.* **1867** SMYTH *Sailor's Word-bk.*

matrass[2] (ˈmætræs). Forms: 7 **matrat,** (matracy, from mod.L.), **matrace,** 7–8 **matras,** 8–9 **mattras(s,** 7– **matrass.** [a. F. *matras*, in 15–17th c. *matheras* (Hatz.-Darm.), *matraz, matrac* (Cotgr.); = Sp. *matraz*, pharmaceutical L. *matracium.*
By some considered to be a transferred use of *matras* MATRASS[1], with reference to the shape of the vessel. This view is supported by the existence of the Eng. synonym BOLT-HEAD 2, unless the latter be merely a quasi-literal translation of the Fr. word. Devic suggests adoption from the Arab. *matraʰ* leather bottle; cf. mod.L. *matracium* 'a little sack, wherein is calcinated tartar or the like, pricked here and there for the emission of liquors' (tr. *Blancard's Phys. Dict.*, ed. 2, 1693).]

1. A glass vessel with a round or oval body and a long neck, used by chemists for digesting and distilling.
1605 TIMME *Quersit.* II. v. 123 Vessels which are called matrats, like unto round globes, having straite neckes. **1657** TOMLINSON *Renou's Disp.* 592 Some include it [quicksilver] with aqua fortis in a Matracy. **1669** W. SIMPSON *Hydrol. Chym.* 166 Put a..quantity thereof in a matrass, lute it exactly [etc.]. **1681** tr. *Willis' Rem. Med. Wks.* Vocab., *Matrace*, a vessel used for chymical distillations. **1698** H. SLOANE in *Phil. Trans.* XX. 73 Put all into a Matras, and pour upon them a Quart of Brandy. **1721** W. GIBSON *Farrier's Disp.* II. i. 81 Instead of a Matrass, may be used a Florence Wine Flask. **1763** W. LEWIS *Comm. Phil. Techn.* 34 A Long necked matras or bolt head. **1811** A. T. THOMSON *Lond. Disp.* (1818) 468 Apply a moderate heat to the matrass. **1849** R. V. DIXON *Heat* I. 155 The ball of a small mattrass. **1880** GARROD & BAXTER *Mat. Med.* 48 A matrass containing twenty-two ounces of water.
attrib. **1683** PETTUS *Fleta Min.* II. 12 The word *Bell* is also applyed to a glass..which the Chimists call a matrass glass.

2. A urinal (*Syd. Soc. Lex.* 1890).
1855 DUNGLISON *Med. Lex.* (ed. 12) s.v. *Matracium.*

matrass, -at, obs. ff. MATTRESS, MATRASS.

matre, obs. variant of MEHTAR.

matrefillon, obs. form of MATFELLON.

matremoine, -mony, obs. ff. MATRIMONY.

matres, obs. form of MATTRESS.

matri- (ˈmætrɪ, ˈmeɪtrɪ), used, esp. in *Anthropol.* and *Sociol.*, as the combining form of L. *māter* (*mātr-is*) mother, in various words denoting aspects of social organization defined by relationship through women. Some examples are given below as main words. Cf. also MATRIARCH, MATRIARCHAL, etc.

matriarch (ˈmeɪtrɪɑːk). [f. L. *mātr(i)-, māter* mother: on the supposed analogy of PATRIARCH (apprehended as if f. *pater* father).] A woman having the status corresponding to that of a patriarch, in any sense of the word. In various nonce-uses, now usually jocular.
1606 BIRNIE *Kirk-Buriall* Ded., Your Spouse now the yong fruteful Matriarch of that multi-potent Marquesad. **1629** DONNE *Fifty Serm.* (1649) xliv. 417 The learnedest Nun, and the best Matriarch, and Mother of that [the Roman] Church, I think, that ever writ, Heloyssa. **1837** SOUTHEY *Doctor* cxvii. IV. 158 Dr. Southey has classed this injured Matriarch [Job's wife] in a triad with Xantippe and Mrs. Wesley. **1883** J. W. HALES in *Athenæum* 24 Feb. 248, I believe this gentleman [Father Hubbard] to be an after-thought—to be a mere weak masculine reflex of the matriarch. **1893** *Harper's Weekly* 7 Jan. 11/1 Miss Flora McFlimsey, who nowadays must be a matriarch of some thirty-five seasons' standing.
transf. **1860–1** D. COLERIDGE in *Philol. Soc. Trans.* 168 The relation which our Indian sister holds to the ancient Bactrian matriarch, nay of the great mother herself to the surrounding families.

matriarchal (meɪtrɪˈɑːkəl), *a.* [f. MATRIARCH + -AL[1], after PATRIARCHAL.] Of or pertaining to a matriarch or to maternal rule; pertaining to, of the nature of, or based on matriarchy.
1863 JOWETT in *Life & Lett.* (1897) I. xi. 363 They [Tennyson's boys] are getting too old for the matriarchal form of government. **1881** *Pall Mall G.* 12 Feb. 1/2 [In France] nothing is commoner than that two or three generations should continue to live in the same house... This little community is ordinarily rather matriarchal than patriarchal. It is the eldest of the women who usually organizes and rules it. **1884** TYLOR in *Rep. Brit. Assoc.* 905 The Indian tribes further south are largely matriarchal, reckoning descent not on the father's but the mother's side.
Hence **matri'archalism,** the condition of life under a matriarchal system. **matri'archalist,** a supporter of the theory that tribal society was primitively matriarchal.
1884 TYLOR in *Rep. Brit. Assoc.* 906 Matriarchalism has only in places yielded to the patriarchal system. **1885** —— in *Academy* 1 Aug. 67/2 The effect which the researches of the matriarchalists had on his mind.

matriarchate (meɪtrɪˈɑːkət). [f. MATRIARCH + -ATE, after G. *matriarchat.*] A matriarchal community or system. Also *attrib.*
1885 REDHOUSE in *Jrnl. Roy. Asiatic Soc. Gt. Brit.* Apr. 276 It does not even attempt to prove..that a matriarchate system was ever in existence among the Arabians. **1894** H. DRUMMOND *Ascent of Man* 401 Bachoven has familiarized us with the idea of a Matriarchate, or Maternal Family.

matriarchy (ˈmeɪtrɪɑːkɪ). [f. MATRIARCH, after PATRIARCHY.] That form of social organization in which the mother, and not the father, is the head of the family, and in which descent and relationship are reckoned through mothers and not through fathers.
1885 *Athenæum* 21 Mar. 379/3 Mr. J. W. Redhouse made a few remarks with reference to a paper he has prepared for the *Journal* of the Society..'On Matriarchy, or Mother Right'. **1892** GOMME *Ethnology in Folklore* 131 The principle of matriarchy is more primitive than that of patriarchy.

Matric (məˈtrɪk), *sb.* Also **matric.** Colloq. shortening of MATRICULATION.
1885 *Punch* 16 Mar. 233/2 Younger brother comes to-day from Harrow for Matric. **1936** AUDEN & ISHERWOOD *Ascent of F6* (1937) I. i. 18 The Crowthers' pimply son has passed Matric. **1937** A. S. NEILL *That Dreadful School* ii. 38 My staff and I have a hearty hatred of all examinations, and to us the Matric. is anathema. But we cannot refuse to teach children their Matric. subjects. **1948** [see INTER., INTER]. **1965** W. SOYINKA *Road* 83 To have served in Burma was to have passed your London Matric. **1967** D. P. CAREW *Many Years, Many Girls* vii. 135 Sixth formers took the School Leaving Certificate... Matric could be achieved on this same exam. **1971** *Sunday Express* (Johannesburg) 28 Mar. (Home Jrnl.) 14/2 My daughter is writing Matric this year. **1971** R. RUSSELL tr. *Ahmad's Shore & Wave* iv. 31 Their parents were only concerned with seeing that somehow or other they passed their matric. **1971** *Southerly* XXXI. 100 Not to mention the Matric next term. **1972** *Nature* 1 Dec. 267/2 He got a first in the London Matric, and became a 'temporary laboratory assistant' at Bradford Technical College.

matric (ˈmeɪtrɪk), *a. Math.* [f. L. *mātrīc-*, stem of *mātrix* MATRIX.] Of or pertaining to a matrix or matrices.
1921 *Proc. Nat. Acad. Sci.* VII. 84 The notion of a norm or numerical value of a complex quantity.., as it arises in algebra, has a more or less immediate generalization to more extensive matric systems. **1941** *Mind* L. 273 The total matric algebra of order sixteen over the field of complex numbers. **1952** *Electronic Engin.* XXIV. 264 The application of matric theory to networks containing thermionic valves. **1958** R. V. ANDREE *Sel. Mod. Abstr. Algebra* v. 107 The Pauli matrices form a closed set under matric multiplication. **1972** *Computer Jrnl.* XV. 228/2 Pairwise interactions..may be used to define a distance function without requiring the qualitative data themselves to constitute a matric space.

matrical (ˈmætrɪkəl, məˈtraɪkəl), *a.* [ad. late L. *mātrīcālis* (*vena matricalis*, Vegetius) f. *mātrīc-* MATRIX *sb.*: see -AL[1]. Cf. F. *matrical* (Cotgr.).]
†**1.** Pertaining to the matrix or womb. *Obs.*
1611 COTGR., *Vertiller*, to swell, or increase, as womens breasts doe when the matricall veins are stretched by the menstruall blood. **1651** *Life Father Sarpi* (1676) 34 They are presently filled with the sudden and violent motions of the matrical humours.
2. Pertaining to the matrix of algæ.
1882–4 COOKE *Freshw. Algæ* 56 Composed of very numerous cells arranged on the periphery at regular distances, connected by the matrical gelatin.

‖**matricaria** (mætrɪˈkɛərɪə). Also anglicized 6–7 **matricarye, -ie.** [med.L. *mātrīcāria* (Diefenbach), f. *mātrīc-*, MATRIX *sb.* Cf. F. *matricaire* (16th c. in Littré). (The plant was so called on account of supposed medicinal properties.)] †**a.** The plant feverfew, *Chrysanthemum Parthenium.* (*Obs.*) **b.** *Bot.* A genus (Linnæus 1735, following Tournefort) of plants, belonging to the N.O. *Compositæ*, originally including the feverfew and other species, which have since been separated and referred to other genera; a plant of this genus. (A well-known species is the wild camomile, *M. Chamomilla.*) **c.** *attrib.*, as ***matricaria-camphor.***
1599 A. M. tr. *Gabelhouer's Bk. Physicke* 220/2 Take redde Roseleaves, Camomille, & Matricarye. **1632** SHERWOOD, Matricarie. **1664** EVELYN *Kal. Hort.* Apr. (1679) 15 Transplant such Fibrous-roots..as Violets.. Hellebor, Matricaria, &c. **1706** J. GARDINER tr. *Rapin of Gardens* (1728) 49 Now on high Stems will Matricaria rear Her silver Blooms. **1767** ABERCROMBIE *Ev. Man his own Gard.* (1803) 704/1 Matricaria, or feverfew. **1885** *Cassell's Encycl. Dict.*, *Matricaria-camphor*, a camphor isomeric with laurinol, obtained from the oil of feverfew. **1890** *Syd. Soc. Lex.* s.v., *Oil of Matricaria*, a thick tenacious volatile oil obtained from the flowers of *M. chamomilla.*

matrice (ˈmeɪtrɪs, ˈmætrɪs). Also 4–5 **matris,** 5 **matryce,** 6 **mattrice.** [ad. L. *mātrīc-em* MATRIX *sb.* Cf. F. *matrice* (also in popular form OF. *marris*: see MARIS).]
†**1.** The uterus, womb (of mammals); *occas.* the ovary (of other animals); = MATRIX *sb. Obs.*
c **1400** *Lanfranc's Cirurg.* 175 þe matris of wymmen. **1471** RIPLEY *Comp. Alch.* IV. x. in Ashm. (1652) 146 That after she hath conceyved of the Man, The Matryce of her be shyt. **1561** HOLLYBUSH *Hom. Apoth.* 24 There wyth is hyr matrice or mother chafed. **1601** DOLMAN *La Primaud. Fr. Acad.* (1618) III. 821 Some are engendered..of egs, as Serpents: and also by an other manner, which is perfected in the matrice by egs, as the viper. **1661** LOVELL *Hist. Anim. & Min.* 116 It..warms the matrice, and causeth the courses. **1774** WALSH in *Phil. Trans.* LXIV. 468 In the right matrice he met with four such fetuses and nine such eggs.
†**b.** *transf.* and *fig.*
1602 FULBECKE *Pandectes* 62 Looke into the bowels & matrice of the earth, ye shall haue gold, siluer, brasse, to exceed all other mettals. **1624** FISHER in F. White *Repl. Fisher* 590 Bringing them backe againe to the Roote and Matrice of the Catholicke Church. **1669** GALE *Crt. Gentiles* I. I. xii. 76 This persuasion, of the Egyptian Tongue..being the old Matrice of the Greek, is but a dream of Kirchers. **1698** FRYER *Acc. E. India & P.* 333 For the most part this is an hospitable Soil, cherishing in its Matrice whatever is kindly sowed.

2. *Die-sinking* and *Type-founding*. = MATRIX *sb*. 4. Now *rare*; the pl. coincides graphically with that of MATRIX *sb*.

1587 in Plomer *Abstr. Wills Eng. Printers* (1903) 27 My printinge wholy furnished with presses letters caracters of cast mettell, and the mattrices. **1587-8** *Reg. Privy Council Scot.* IV. 265 James Achesoun..sinkis and makis irnes, instrumentis and matriceis, alsweill for prenting of silver as of lattoun. **1656** BLOUNT *Glossogr.* s.v., Matrices of Letters or Characters, are those moulds..in which the Letters.. which Printers use are formed. **1727-41** CHAMBERS *Cycl.* s.v., When types are to be cast, the Matrice is fastened to the end of a mould. *Ibid.*, Matrices used in coining, are pieces of steel in form of dyes. **1825** J. NICHOLSON *Operat. Mechanic* Gloss., *Matrice*, the concave form of a letter in which the types are cast. **1868** SEYD *Bullion* (1880) 278 A well made Matrice will remain in use for about 15 years.

Comb. **1683** MOXON *Mech. Exerc., Printing* xv. ¶11 Close by the..side of this Notch is a small square Wyer-staple driven, which we may call the Matrice-Check; for its Office is only to keep the Shanck of the Matrice from flying out of this Notch. **1688** R. HOLME *Armoury* III. 113/2 The Mattrice or Mould-Maker [etc.] all called Letter Founders.

†**3.** (See quots.) *Obs.*

1727-41 CHAMBERS *Cycl.*, *Matrice*, or *Matrix*, in dying, is applied to the five simple colours... These are, the black, white, blue, red, and fallow. **1731** BAILEY vol. II, *Matrice*, [with Dyers] is apply'd to the first simple colours.

4. = MATRIX *sb*. 3. *rare*.

1855 J. R. LEIFCHILD *Cornwall* 131 Man digs into darkness,..He breaks up the veins from the matrice.

matricentred (mætrɪ'sɛntəd), *ppl. a.* [f. MATRI- + CENTRED, CENTERED *ppl. a.*] Centred on the mother. Hence **matri'centric** *a.*, **matricen'tricity**.

1956 R. FIRTH *Two Stud. Kinship in London* 41 We might speak then of South Borough kinship as being *matri-centred* or *matral*. **1957** M. BANTON *W. Afr. City* xi. 205 The composition of tribal and Creole matricentric households does not differ significantly. **1957** V. W. TURNER *Schism & Continuity in Afr. Society* p. xix, Another consequence of virilocal marriage making for instability in residential structure is the measure of autonomy it confers on the matricentric family. *Ibid.* iii. 76 The transition from matricentricity to matriliny as the basis for local groupings must always be hazardous. **1963** J. J. HONIGMANN *Understanding Culture* v. 85 Matricentric households are a 'natural' solution that arises in any social system..when people occupy a very low ranking, economically hazardous position.

matrices, pl. of MATRIX *sb*.

matricidal ('meɪtrɪˌsaɪdal, 'mætrɪ-), *a.* [f. MATRICIDE[1] and [2] + -AL[1].] That kills his or her mother. Also *fig.*

1846 GROTE *Greece* I. xvi. I. 545 The remorse..of the matricidal Alcmæôn..is also mentioned by Thucydidês. **1861** HOOK *Lives Abps.* I. v. 235 A scheme most deadly, serpentine, and even matricidal. **1869** PALGRAVE *Lyr. Poems* (1871) 145 When one fair land..Saw herself rent in twain by matricidal hand.

matricide[1] ('meɪtrɪsaɪd, 'mætrɪ-). [ad. L. *mātrīcīda*, f. *mātr(i)-*, *māter* mother: see -CIDE I.] One who kills his or her mother.

1632 SHERWOOD, A Matricide (or mother-killing), *Matricide*. **1638** MAYNE *Lucian* (1664) 242 Amphilocus, the son of a wicked Matricide. **1822** T. TAYLOR *Apuleius* 232 A matricide, because he had attempted to kill his stepmother. **1879** FARRAR *St. Paul* (1883) 740 The now unchecked tyranny of the incestuous matricide.

matricide[2] ('meɪtrɪsaɪd, 'mætrɪ-). [ad. L. *mātrīcīd-ium*: see prec. and -CIDE 2. Cf. F. *matricide* (mod. rare).] The action of killing one's mother. Also *Comb.*

1594 O. B. *Quest. Profit. Concern.* 13 b, Now from viperous matricide sellers, good Lord deliuer vs. **1646** SIR T. BROWNE *Pseud. Ep.* III. xvi. 145 Nature..compensates the death of the father by the matricide or murder of the mother. **1659** T. PECKE *Parnassi Puerp.* 183 A Generation, Bald-pate Time ne're Ey'd: That durst concurre, in voting Matricide. **1846** GROTE *Greece* I. xiv. I. 381 *note*, The matricide of Orestês. **1882** FARRAR *Early Chr.* I. 64 Hers was the jealousy which had goaded Nero to matricide.

†**matricious**, *a. Obs. rare*⁻⁰. [f. L. *mātrīc-* MATRIX *sb.* + -IOUS.] = MATRICAL I.

1656 BLOUNT *Glossogr.* s.v. *Vein*, *Matricious vein* (*vena matricis*) the matrix vein, or a vein that runnes along the flank neere the Reines.

matriclan ('mætrɪklæn). [f. MATRI- + CLAN *sb.*] A matrilineal clan.

1950 D. FORDE in Radcliffe-Brown & Forde *Afr. Syst. Kinship & Marriage* 309 All members of a matriclan within a village..regard one another as kin. **1957** *Jrnl. R. Anthrop. Inst.* LXXXVII. 92 But wealth, that is money and livestock, is vested in the matriclan... The matriclan, holding only moveable property, is a non-localized descent group. **1959** G. D. MITCHELL *Sociol.* 69 Tribal offences include sexual relations between a man and a woman of the same matriclan.

‖**matricula** (mə'trɪkjʊlə). *Obs.* exc. *Hist.* Also 6 matricola. [Late L. *mātrīcula*, dim. of L. *mātrix* (see MATRIX *sb.*), which in late L. occurs in the same sense. (The development of meaning in late L. is obscure.) Cf. F. *matricule*, Sp. *matrícula*, Pg. *matricula*, It. *matricola*, G. *matrikel*.]

1. A list or register of persons belonging to an order, society, or the like. Also, a certificate of enrolment in such a register.

1555 EDEN *Decades* 348 To cause this to bee entered in the booke cauled the Matricola of owre housholde vnder the tytle of knyghtes. **1617** MORYSON *Itin.* I. 177, I shewed them my Matricula, that is, a paper, witnessing..I was a scholler of Paduoa. **1645** EVELYN *Diary* (1879) I. 254 [Padua.] I..in the afternoone (30 July) received my *matricula*, being resolved to spend some moneths here at study. **1691** WOOD *Ath. Oxon.* I. 471 His name occurs not in the Matricula, only that of John Sherley, a Sussex man. **1840** DE QUINCEY *Style* III. Wks. 1862 X. 237 It would exclude the two Plinys, the two Senecas,..and others, from the matricula of Roman eloquence. *a* **1851** *Hist. Sk. Columbia Coll.* 64 (B. H. Hall *College Words*) We find in its Matricula the names of William Watson [etc.]. **1885** *Cath. Dict.* (ed. 3) 566/2 *Matricula*, the roll containing the names of the clergy permanently attached to a cathedral, or a collegiate, or a parish church; also, the list of the names of the students regularly admitted into any university.

2. *spec.* In the Holy Roman (and later German) Empire: see quot.

1845 S. AUSTIN *Ranke's Hist. Ref.* I. 179 *note*, The Matricula..was the list of the contingents, in men and money, which the several States were bound to furnish to the empire.

matriculability (mə,trɪkjʊlə'bɪlɪtɪ). [f. MATRICUL(ATE *v.* + -AB(LE + -ILITY.] Ability or fitness to matriculate.

1927 *Camb. Univ. Reporter* 11 Oct. 142 The name of every candidate for matriculation on November 1 or 2, together with evidence of matriculability..must be sent to the Registry. **1963** *Statutes & Ordinances Univ. Cambr.* Suppl. 710 The Matriculation Registration Form when completed, together with any necessary evidence of matriculability, shall be submitted to the Registry.

matriculand (mə'trɪkjuːˌlænd). [f. MATRICUL(ATE *v.* + -AND[2].] = MATRICULANT.

1975 *Times Lit. Suppl.* 23 May 556/3 In the sixteenth century Salamanca had about 5,000–7,000 matriculands a year.

matriculant (mə'trɪkjʊlənt). [ad. med.L. *mātrīculantem*, pr. pple. of *mātrīculāre*: see MATRICULATE *v.*] One who matriculates; a candidate for matriculation.

1883 *American* V. 390 They are ready to favor the demand upon matriculants for a preliminary qualification. **1897** *Athenæum* 12 June 780 A notable increase of matriculants in the University of Wales.

matricular (mə'trɪkjʊlə(r)), *a.* and *sb.* [ad. med.L. *mātrīculāris* and *-āris*, f. *mātrīcula*: see MATRICULA and -AR. Cf. F. *matriculaire*.]

A. *adj.*

I. 1. Pertaining to, or of the nature of, a 'matricula' or official register of persons belonging to a university, an association, etc.

1575 TURLER *Traueiler* 69 Although their names be written in the Matricular bookes of students. **1611** COTGR., *Marille*, a Register, or Matricular booke. **1727** in BAILEY vol. II. **1804** in *Spirit Publ. Jrnls.* (1805) VIII. 80 Our.. Grand Officers of the Grand Legion of Honour, are ordered to insert the name of Citizen Morning Post in the Matricular Register of our said Legion.

b. With reference to Germany: Pertaining to the 'matricula' (see MATRICULA 2).

1762 tr. *Busching's Syst. Geog.* IV. 560 The Elector of Cologn has a matricular evaluation of sixty horse and two hundred and seventy-seven foot, or 1828 florins. **1894** *19th Cent.* XXXVI. 237 Prussia had to pay 211,000,000 m. of matricular contributions.

II. Used as if a derivative of MATRIX *sb.*: see -ULAR.

¶**2.** Of a language: Original; from which others are derived. *Obs.* (? *nonce-use*).

1793 HELY tr. *O'Flaherty's Ogygia* II. 89 There were seventy-two matricular Babylonian tongues. *Ibid.* 90.

3. Of or belonging to the matrix or womb.

1896 *Allbutt's Syst. Med.* I. 200 Regeneration can only occur when matricular cell elements still exist to proliferate.

†**B.** *sb.* = MATRICULA 2. *Obs.*

1603 KNOLLES *Hist. Turks* (1621) 1277 The perfecting of which Matriculer, the Emperour would haue in this assemblie to be amongst them considered of.

†**matriculary.** *Obs.* [ad. med.L. *mātrīculārius*: see prec. and -ARY.] A catalogue.

1686 GUNTON *Hist. Peterborough* 49 A publick Library.. stored with above 1700 Books, or Tractates, as by an antient Matriculary of that Library may appear.

matriculate (mə'trɪkjʊlət), *a.* and *sb.* [ad. med.L. *mātrīculāt-us*, pa. pple. of *matricul-āre*: see MATRICULATE *v.*] **A.** *adj.* = MATRICULATED.

1487 *Hen. VII* in *Epist. Acad. Oxon.* (O.H.S.) II. 514 He nethere ys contributorye unto the charge, ne yett ys matriculate. *a* **1529** SKELTON *Ph. Sparowe* 1288 Why shuld she take shame That her goodly name..Sholde be set and sorted, To be matriculate With ladyes of estate?

B. *sb.* One who has been matriculated.

1712 ARBUTHNOT *John Bull* Pref. (1755) 4 The matriculates of that famous university. **1848-9** *Cal. Univ. N. Carolina* (B. H. Hall *College Words*) The number of Matriculates has..been greater. **1887** *Pall Mall G.* 25 Aug. 9/1 [He] had been a matriculate at Trinity College, Dublin.

attrib. **1886** W. J. TUCKER *E. Europe* 376 The day following the matriculate examination.

matriculate (mə'trɪkjʊleɪt), *v.* [F. med.L. **mātrīculāt-*, ppl. stem of **mātrīculāre*, f. *mātrīcula*: see MATRICULA. Cf. Sp., Pg. *matricular*, It. *matricolare*.]

†**1.** *trans. gen.* To insert (a name) in a register or official list; usually, to admit or incorporate into a society or body of persons by insertion of the name in the register; to enrol (soldiers). *Obs.*

1577 HANMER *Anc. Eccl. Hist.* (1619) 460 For vnto that time yᵉ names of the Senators or Aldermen were matriculated. **1581** SAVILE *Tacitus Hist.* (1591) Annot. 51 Vnder the Empire..six hundreth at the least were matriculated in a Legion. **1600** HOLLAND *Livy* XXXIII. xxiv. 839 In this number [*sc.* of coloners] none of them should be matriculated, who..had beene enemies to the people of Rome. **1602** SEGAR *Hon. Mil. & Civ.* I. vii. 10 Slaues, and base people were matriculated for souldiers. **1613** R. CAWDREY *Table Alph.* (ed. 3), *Matriculate* [sic], to register or inrole. **1631** WEEVER *Anc. Funeral Mon.* 202 This murdered Bishop was..matriculated by the Pope a glorious Saint and Martyr. ?**1656** BRAMHALL *Replic.* 37 Have the English Protestants matriculated themselves into their congregational Assemblies? **1715** M. DAVIES *Athen. Brit.* I. 222 The..Church Register or Warden, who oftentimes.. would matriculate sometimes all he could hear of.

†**b.** *transf.* and *fig. Obs.*

1610 DONNE *Pseudo-martyr* 348 Wee acknowledge our selues incorporated and matriculated into that Christian warfare, wherin they entred our Names. **1638** CHILLINGW. *Relig. Prot.* I. Pref. §5 Lovers of truth (in which Company I had been long agoe matriculated). **1654** WHITLOCK *Zootomia* 188 Such as are matriculated in *Albo Sapientiæ*. ?**1656** BRAMHALL *Replic.* vi. 271 It was..their obstinacy thus to incorporate their errors into their Creeds, and matriculate their abuses among their sacred Rites. **1782** W. F. MARTYN *Geog. Mag.* I. 741 Until the boys are matriculated into the society of the men.

†**c.** In occasional uses (app. modified by quasi-etymological association with L. *māter* mother): To adopt as a child; to adopt or naturalize (an alien, a foreign custom, book, etc.); also, to consign *to* maternal care. *Obs.*

1579 J. STUBBES *Gaping Gulf* C j b, The state, which can neuer so kindly matriculate him [*sc.* an alien] as the childe which she hath born in her owne wombe. **1640** BP. HALL *Chr. Moder.* I. §5. 42 Mathew,..when he..was now to be matriculated into the family of Christ, entertained his new Master with a..banquet. **1686** F. SPENCE tr. *Varillas' Ho. Medicis* 215 Tho Luxury was sufficiently great at the Pope's court,..where they had matriculated it of late. **1704** HEARNE *Duct. Hist.* (1714) I. 136 A Work so excellent..that all Nations have chosen to Matriculate it and make it speak their own Tongue. **1768** [W. DONALDSON] *Life Sir B. Sapskull* II. xxi. 164, I was matriculated to the care of the good lady my nurse.

2. *spec.* To enter (a name) in the register of a university or college; to admit (a student) to the privileges of a university. Also *fig.*

1579 GOSSON *Sch. Abuse* (Arb.) 24, I haue bene matriculated my selfe in the schoole, where so many abuses florish. **1622** MABBE tr. *Aleman's Guzman d'Alf.* II. 286 Loue had now matriculated me in his Schoole. **1642** HOWELL *For. Trav.* (Arb.) 16, I take it for granted, hee hath been matriculated..and learn't to chop Logick. **1705** HICKERINGILL *Priest-cr.* II. v. 53 For about so long I have been matriculated in the University. **1711** HEARNE *Collect.* (O.H.S.) III. 257 Let Mr. Allen have eight Shillings to be matriculated with. **1826-7** DE QUINCEY *R. Bentley* Wks. 1857 VII. 46 Bentley was matriculated at St. John's College, Cambridge. **1904** J. T. FOWLER *Durham Univ.* 150 He entered at University College, and was matriculated in October, 1836.

b. *intr.* To be entered as a member of a university or college.

1851 DIXON *W. Penn* iii. (1872) 26 Penn the Younger went to Oxford, where he matriculated as a gentleman commoner. **1861** HUGHES *Tom Brown at Oxf.* I. Introd. 1 Tom Brown..went up to matriculate at St. Ambrose's College.

¶**c.** *trans.* To initiate as qualified. Const. *to*.

1863 GEO. ELIOT *Romola* ix, No man is matriculated to the art of life till he has been well tempted.

3. *Her.* To record (arms) in an official register.

1586 FERNE *Blaz. Gentrie* 151 It is a part of their office to register and matriculate the auntient acts of honor and the merits of gentlemen. **1809** J. HOME in *Naval Chron.* XXIV. 192 The Ensigns Armorial..are matriculated in the public registers of the Lyon Office. **1815** SCOTT *Guy M.* xlii, Mr. Cumming of the Lyon Office..being at that time engaged in discovering and matriculating the arms of two commissaries from North America [etc.].

Hence **ma'triculating** *vbl. sb.* and *ppl. a.*

a **1631** DONNE *Serm.* lxxxvii. (ed. Alford) IV. 116 A registering, a matriculating of their names in the book of the profession of the Christian religion. **1644** BULWER *Chirol.* 143 This in the sacred language of Scripture is Chirothesia ..and is a matriculating gesture.

matriculated (mə'trɪkjʊleɪtɪd), *ppl. a.* [f. MATRICULATE *v.* + -ED[1].] Admitted by enrolment, esp. as a student of a university, etc.

1642 MILTON *Apol. Smect.* Wks. 1851 III. 310 My matriculated confutant. **1771** *Act Amending Mile Ways Oxford* 65 If any matriculated Person or Persons..shall wilfully break..any of the Lamps [etc.]. **1858** (*title*) A List of the Matriculated Members of the Merchants House of Glasgow, 1768–1857. **1895** *Athenæum* 9 Nov. 647/3 It will practically have the effect of opening the College associateship to any matriculated student.

matriculation (mətrɪkjʊ'leɪʃən). [f. MATRICULATE *v.* + -ATION. Cf. It. *matricolazione*

(*matriculatione*, Florio 1611), Sp. *matriculacion*.]

1. The action of matriculating, or of registering among the members of a society, enrolling as a soldier, etc. Now chiefly in academic use, formal admission into a university or college. Sometimes used for *matriculation examination*.

1588 FRAUNCE *Lawiers Log.* Ded. ivb, Having once knowen the price of an admission, Salting, and Matriculation, with the interteyning of Freshmenne in the Rhetorike schooles, they returne whence they came. **1614** BP. HALL *Contempl. O.T.* VIII. iii, VIII. 970 Wee have no right of inheritance in..the Church of God till we have received the sacrament of our matriculation. **1633** D. ROGERS *Treat. Sacram.* I. 71 Baptisme..is called our Union with Christ,..our Matriculation, Cognizance, and Character of Christ. **1638** BRATHWAIT *Barnabees Jrnl.* II. (1818) 71 Thence to Highgate, where I viewed..th' horne of matriculation Drunk to th' freshmen of our nation. **1653** in Somers *Tracts* I. 502 No Person..shall take an Oath upon Matriculation in either of the Universities. **1711** HEARNE *Collect.* (O.H.S.) III. 257 He had 5s...to go towards his Matriculation. **1853** 'C. BEDE' *Verdant Green* I. ii, He's now quite old enough, and prepared enough for matriculation. **1881** MRS. CRAIK *Little Mother* II. (1882) 43 Papa said he must [go out to India] if he failed in his matriculation. **1900** *Oxf. Univ. Cal.* 72 These Dues are for each quarter of the first four years from Matriculation.

†**b.** A certificate of matriculation; = MATRICULA. *Obs.*

1648 J. RAYMOND *Il Mercurio Italico* 233 Our Matriculations wee had from Padua did us much service.

c. *attrib.*, in ***matriculation examination***; **matriculation book**, a book for the registration of admissions to a college or other association.

1611 SPEED *Hist. Gt. Brit.* IX. ix. §99 Those only whose names were entred into the Matriculation Booke. **1726** AYLIFFE *Parergon* 16 A Scholar, that is absent from the University for five years,..is..rased out of the Matriculation Book. *Ibid.* 384 He is presum'd to be a Merchant who is found enrolled in the Matriculation Book belonging to Merchants. **1853** *Assurance Mag.* III. 273 Institute of Actuaries..Matriculation Examination 1852.

2. *Her.* A registration of armorial bearings.

1810 *Naval Chron.* XXIV. 192 He has obtained the following copy of matriculation from the Lyon Office, Edinburgh. **1901** *Spectator* 30 Mar. 461 The doctrine..that the right to bear arms is dependent upon their matriculation in the College of Arms.

matriculator (mə'trɪkjʊleɪtə(r)). [f. MATRICULATE *v.* + -OR.] = MATRICULANT.

1869 *Globe* 13 Nov. 7 The matriculators last Michaelmas term numbered 529. **1888** *Q. Rev.* CLXVII. 209 At Oxford the matriculator subscribed the Thirty-nine Articles.

matriculatory (mə'trɪkjʊlətərɪ), *a.* [f. MATRICULATE *v.*: see -ORY.] **a.** Pertaining to the matriculation (of students, etc.). **b.** = MATRICULAR 1 b.

1884 *Athenæum* 19 July, We should like to see..the addition of a modern language to the matriculatory subjects. **1885** *Pall Mall G.* 15 Jan. 8/1 The increase in the matriculatory contributions..has to be taken into account. .. The portion of the matriculatory contributions not covered by the revenue will be met by loan.

matrifocal ('mætrɪfəʊkəl), *a. Sociol.* [f. MATRI- + FOCAL *a.*] Applied to a family in which the mother is left with the responsibility for and authority over the household; mother-centred. Hence **matrifo'cality**, the condition of a family which depends on the mother.

1952 *Internat. Afr. Inst. Memorandum* XXVI. 12 These matrifocal cells of the compound family. **1956** R. T. SMITH *Negro Family Brit. Guiana* ix. 221 We maintain that the matri-focal system of domestic relations..can be regarded as the obverse of the marginal nature of the husband–father rôle. **1969** O. LEWIS in D. P. Moynihan *On Understanding Poverty* vii. 198 For example, matrifocality, a high incidence of consensual unions, and a high percentage of households headed by women, which have been thought to be distinctive characteristics of Caribbean family organization or of Negro family life in the United States, turn out to be traits of the culture of poverty. **1969** J. & S. BARATZ in T. Kochman *Rappin' & Stylin' Out* (1972) 11 This assumption left social scientists with no other alternative than to wrongly describe..the matrifocal family unit so prevalent in lower-class black society as 'evidence of male emasculation'.

matriheritage (meɪtrɪ'hɛrɪtɪdʒ). *rare.* [f. L. *mātr(i)-*, *māter* mother + HERITAGE.] A proposed name for the system, existing in certain communities, according to which relationship through the mother, and not through the father, constitutes the title to inheritance. So **matri'herital** *a.*, pertaining to 'matriheritage'.

1886 SIR G. CAMPBELL in *Nature* 9 Sept. 455/2 The best specimen..of the matriarchal, or perhaps I should rather say matri-herital system. *Ibid.*, The result of observation of the Khassyahs has been to separate in my mind the two ideas of matri-heritage and polyandry.

matrilateral (mætrɪ'lætərəl), *a.* [f. MATRI- + LATERAL *a.*] Of or pertaining to relationship involving the mother's brother or sister, used esp. of cross-cousin marriage.

1951 *Jrnl. R. Anthrop. Inst.* LXXXI. 24/2 Matrilateral cross cousin marriage (father's sister's son—mother's brother's daughter). **1957** V. W. TURNER *Schism & Continuity in Afr. Society* viii. 254 Ndembu men appear to marry their patrilateral and matrilateral cross-cousins with equal frequency. **1963** *Brit. Jrnl. Sociol.* XIV. 23 From the point of view of this hypothetical individual, whom anthropologists for many years have called *Ego*, his non-lineage kin are *patrilateral* and *matrilateral* as the case may be. **1971** *World Archaeol.* III. 191 It is probable that this alliance..continues today due to prescribed matrilateral cross-cousin marriage.

matriline ('mætrɪlaɪn). [f. MATRI- + LINE *sb.*[2] 24.] The matrilineal line of descent.

1957 *Jrnl. R. Anthrop. Inst.* LXXXVII. 11 As Evans-Pritchard's analysis of the distribution of bride-wealth shows..there is explicit recognition of both the bride's patriline and matriline. **1963** W. J. GOODE *World Revolution & Family Patterns* v. 221 The marriage of a mother's brother's daughter to a father's sister's son repeats the relationship of deference and respect which is due from the matriline. **1965** I. M. LEWIS in M. Banton *Relevance of Models for Social Anthropol.* 109 The functional implications of descent are often much more significant than whether descent is traced in the patri- or matri-line. **1971** R. NEEDHAM *Rethinking Kinship & Marriage* i. 20 It is conceivable, and may in one alleged case be so in fact, that a terminology composed of matrilines should govern the affairs of a society that was preponderantly patrilineal. **1972** P. LASLETT *Household & Family in Past Time* 22 The daughter, not the son, brings her working class spouse into the family circle... This..occurs within a matriline, not a patriline.

matrilineage (mætrɪ'lɪnɪɪdʒ). [f. MATRI- + LINEAGE 2 c.] Matrilineal lineage.

1949 M. FORTES *Social Struct.* 60 Membership of the matrilineage is *ipso facto* membership of a widely dispersed exogamous clan. **1951** B. Z. SELIGMAN in *N. & Q. Anthropol.* (ed. 6) II. ii. 89 A matrilineage consists of all the descendants through females of a single ancestress. **1957** *Jrnl. R. Anthrop. Inst.* LXXXVII. 93 It is this group, a dispersed, basic matrilineage, which defines the extent of the lateral inheritance of wealth. **1957** V. W. TURNER *Schism & Continuity in Afr. Society* iii. 80, I regard a *minimal* matrilineage as a group consisting of the descendants through women of a common grandmother, a *minor* matrilineage as the matrilineal descendants of a common great-grandmother. **1963** W. J. GOODE *World Revolution & Family Patterns* iv. 194 The father is increasingly able to assert new rights against the traditional rights of the matrilineage.

matrilineal (mætrɪ'lɪnɪəl), *a.* [f. MATRI- + LINEAL *a.* 2.] Of, pertaining to, or based on (kinship with) the mother or the female line; recognizing kinship with and descent through females.

1904 N. W. THOMAS in *Man* LIII. 84 Mr. Hill-Tout argues that totemism originates in a patrilineal just as much as in a matrilineal state of society. **1906** —— *Kinship Organisations & Group Marriage Austral.* 30 Membership of a phratry depends on birth and is taken *directly* from the mother (matrilineal descent) or father (patrilineal descent). **1914** W. H. R. RIVERS *Kinship & Social Organisation* ii. 40 The people of Buin still practice matrilineal descent. **1921** *Edin. Rev.* July 163 His discovery of matrilineal institutions in Europe. **1946** *Nature* 28 Sept. 457/2 It is clear that the ancient Chamorro had an elaborate social organisation with matrilineal clans and village chiefs whose power was based mainly on inherited wealth and monopolies. **1951** E. E. EVANS-PRITCHARD *Social Anthrop.* ii. 29 According to Bachofen, there was first everywhere promiscuity, then a matrilineal and matriarchal social system, and only late in the history of man did this system give way to a patrilineal and patriarchal one. **1969** *Times* 22 Oct. (Ghana Suppl.) p. vii/3 The women have legal rights which would be the envy of any Englishwoman. They own property absolutely and the matrilineal system—inheritance through the women—means that the children belong to the mother's family.

Hence **matri'lineally** *adv.*

1907 *Athenæum* 20 Apr. 477/1 The method of reckoning descent matrilineally. **1937** *Nature* 20 Feb. 328/1 The husband in such a group, finding property to descend matrilineally, would try to provide for his portionless sister's family. **1964** GOULD & KOLB *Dict. Social Sci.* 367/1 In a patrilineally organized society a man must also have kinship relations through his mother, and mutatis mutandis in a matrilineally organized society.

matrilinear (mætrɪ'lɪnɪə(r)), *a.* [f. MATRI- + LINEAR *a.*] = MATRILINEAL *a.*

1910 *Manch. Guardian* 8 Aug. 5 It is said that they [*sc.* the Choctaw Indians] were governed by chiefs who succeeded by matrilinear descent. **1913** B. S. PHILLPOTTS *Kindred & Clan* 275 Kindreds organized on matrilinear or on patrilinear lines. **1926** *Contemp. Rev.* Apr. 528 That these powers are related to a previous system of matrilinear descent there can be no doubt. **1950** DARLINGTON & MATHER *Genes, Plants & People* v. 57 The historic change from matrilinear to patrilinear inheritance has also led to important conflicts.

matriliny ('mætrɪlɪnɪ). [f. MATRI- + LIN(E *sb.*[2] + -Y[3].] The observance of matrilineal descent and kinship.

1906 N. W. THOMAS *Kinship Organisations & Group Marriage Austral.* ii. 19 We may now examine the relation of matriliny to the seat of authority in the family. **1927** [see *bien entendu*]. **1937** *Nature* 20 Feb. 328/1 Though most of the tribes of Assam are now patrilineal, yet an earlier stratum of matriliny should not be overlooked. **1955** [see *father-right* (FATHER *sb.* 12)]. **1965** I. M. LEWIS in M. Banton *Relevance of Models for Social Anthropol.* 109 The lumping together of societies on the basis of patriliny or matriliny alone can only lead to confusion.

matrilocal (mætrɪ'ləʊkəl), *a.* [f. MATRI- + LOCAL *a.*] Applied to the custom in certain social groups for a married couple to settle in the wife's home or community.

1906 N. W. THOMAS *Kinship Organisations & Group Marriage Austral.* iii. 30 When the husband removes and lives in his wife's group the marriage is *matrilocal*. **1927** *Contemp. Rev.* July 84 The clan is held together by matrilocal marriage. **1933** *Times Lit. Suppl.* 8 June 390/2 Marriage is matrilocal, or, in other words, the man goes to live with his wife. **1949** M. FORTES *Social Struct.* 70 Households with female heads can be..'matrilocal', that is, made up of a woman and her dependants by marriage and motherhood. **1956** R. PIERIS *Sinhalese Social Organization* VI. i. 203 In the *binna* (matrilocal) marriage, the husband lived in his wife's parental home. **1956** J. WHATMOUGH *Lang.* 250 But the Apache 'great family', with matrilocal residence after marriage, has its special terminology. **1966** NYE & BERARDO *Emerging Conceptual Frameworks in Family Analysis* ii. 26 The extended family is a group founded on kinship and locality, and resulting from the rules of patrilocal or matrilocal marriage.

Hence **matrilo'cality**, the custom of matrilocal residence; **matri'locally** *adv.*, in a matrilocal manner.

1935 *Geogr. Jrnl.* LXXXVI. 262 The increasing amount of patrilocal marriages instead of the former pure matrilocality of the people. **1938** *Jrnl. R. Anthrop. Inst.* LXVIII. 301 The Hopi also transmit functions, such as priesthood and office, from male to male, without renouncing their matrilocality. *Ibid.*, Matrilocality here means, fundamentally, the succession of female descendants each one of whom remains her whole life in one spot. **1941** *Sudan Notes & Rec.* XXIV. 55 In a few cases the Shilluk settle matrilocally. **1963** *Economist* 13 Apr. 157/2 A mass of theorising about 'matrilocality' and the Cockney Mum.

matrimoi(g)ne, -mone, obs. ff. MATRIMONY.

matrimonial (mætrɪ'məʊnɪəl), *a.* and *sb.* [a. F. *matrimonial* (14th c. in Hatz.-Darm.) ad. late L. *mātrimōniāl-is* of or pertaining to matrimony, f. *mātrimōnium*: see MATRIMONY and -AL[1].]

A. *adj.*

1. a. Of or pertaining to matrimony.

c **1532** DU WES *Introd. Fr.* in Palsgr. 1049 The seconde love is called matrimoniall. *c* **1610** *Women Saints* 67 King Ecgfride promised him greate summes..if he could persuade the Queene to vse matrimoniall companie with him. **1675–9** MULGRAVE *Ess. Satire* 185 He lugged about the matrimonial load. **1768** BLACKSTONE *Comm.* III. 72 Matrimonial causes..are another..branch of the ecclesiastical jurisdiction. **1780** COWPER *Table-t.* 74 With close fidelity and love unfeigned, To keep the matrimonial bond unstained. **1829** LYTTON *Devereux* I. i, He had an exceeding distaste to the matrimonial state. **1884** 'RITA' *My Ld. Conceit* VII. ii, The matrimonial knot is not an easy one to slip out of.

b. *fig.*

a **1568** COVERDALE *Bk. Death* xxxix. (1579) 182 To open vnto the Lorde, to let him in, and with him to passe foorth into his royal and matrimoniall palace of the euerlastyng ioyfull kingdome. **1576** NEWTON *Lemnie's Complex.* I. ix. 75 b, To keepe..an equal poyze of matrymoniall consent and agreemente together betweene them [*sc.* mind and body].

2. Derived from marriage.

1577–87 HOLINSHED *Chron., Hist. Scot.* 365/1 The Dolphin of France..did vehementlie request that the crowne (which they terme matrimoniall) should be giuen vnto him. **1622** BACON *Hen. VII* 4 If he [Henry VII] relied vpon that Title [his marriage with Elizabeth of York], he could..but..haue rather a Matrimoniall then a Regall power.

3. a. Calculated to promote matrimony; inclining towards marriage.

1730 SWIFT *Death & Daphne*, His matrimonial spirit fled. **1749** FIELDING *Tom Jones* XI. iv, She had matrimonial charms in great abundance.

b. ***matrimonial agency, bureau*** = ***marriage bureau*** (see MARRIAGE 8); ***matrimonial agent***, one who works in a matrimonial agency.

c **1888** C. E. MORLAND *Matrimonial Agency* (1902) 3, I have always expressed myself shocked at the indelicacy of marriages arranged by Matrimonial Agencies. *Ibid.* 4 A letter of introduction from a certain matrimonial agent. **1890** W. BOOTH *In Darkest Eng.* II. vi. 233 *A matrimonial bureau*... In London at the present moment how many hundreds..of young men and young women..are practically without any opportunity of making the acquaintance of each other! **1895** [see CO-ED *a.*]. **1908** A. BENNETT *Buried Alive* ii. 51 I've been thinking for years of getting married again... And what is there except a matrimonial agency? **1917** N. DOUGLAS *South Wind* ii. 18 He..resembles a broken-down matrimonial agent. **1925** E. H. YOUNG *William* xxxvi. 308, I hope the matrimonial bureau will be a great success. **1966** K. WHITE *Lett. from Gourgounel* 40 He approaches Matrimonial Bureaux to try and find a wife. **1967** C. WATSON *Lonelyheart 4122* iii. 33 A matrimonial bureau. Well, what else could be meant by 'Handclasp House. Are you weary of the solitary path?' *Ibid.* v. 46 He has the traditional English middle-class attitude to matrimonial agencies. Terribly *infra dig.*

†**B.** *sb.* A marriage. *Obs.*

c **1475** *Partenay* 952 With great ioy made thys matrimonial.

Hence (*nonce-wds.*) **matri'monialism**, the doctrine of the excellence of matrimony. **matri'monialist**, one empowered to celebrate marriages.

1811 SHELLEY in Dowden *Life* (1887) I. 174, I will hear your arguments for matrimonialism, by which I am now almost convinced. **1834** *Fraser's Mag.* IX. 385 Some of those..gentlemen who are hoping..to exalt their sons and cousins..into a sort of official dignity, as licensed matrimonialists.

matrimonially (mætrɪˈməʊnɪəlɪ), *adv.* [f. MATRIMONIAL + -LY².]

1. According to the manner or laws of matrimony.

1606 MARSTON *Fawne* Wks. 1856 II. 75 The Romans.. thought that a woman might mixe her thigh with a stranger wantonly, and yet still love her husband matrimonially. *a* **1631** DONNE *Fifty Serm.* (1649) 16 How Matrimonially soever such persons as have maried themselves may pretend to love,..yet..all that life is but a regulated Adultery. **1726** AYLIFFE *Parergon* 123 He is so matrimonially wedded unto his Church, that he cannot quit the same. **1865** DICKENS *Mut. Fr.* I. iv, According to the principle which matrimonially unites contrasts.

2. By right of marriage.

1880 MUIRHEAD *Gaius* III. §3 The same may be said of her who is matrimonially *in manu* of a grandson.

3. As regards the state of matrimony.

1886 *Law Times* LXXX. 336/2 Both parties actually did regard themselves as matrimonially free.

†**matriˈmonious**, *a. Obs.* [f. MATRIMONY: see -OUS.] **a.** Pertaining to marriage. **b.** Conducive to matrimony.

1645 MILTON *Tetrach.* Wks. 1851 IV. 175 The miserable work that mans ignorance and pusillanimity would make in this matrimonious busines. **1837** LADY GRANVILLE *Lett.* (1894) II. 224 The green room is matrimonious.

Hence **matriˈmoniously** *adv.*, matrimonially.

1839 *Blackw. Mag.* XLVI. 28 When a man is matrimoniously inclined, let him keep his own counsel.

†**matrimonize**, *v. Obs.* [f. MATRIMONY + -IZE.] *trans.* To cause to marry.

1612 W. PARKES *Curtaine-Dr.* (1876) 12 It could not matrimonize age and youth.

matrimony (ˈmætrɪmənɪ). Forms: 4 **matirmoyne, -monye, matrimon, matermoyn(e, matremoyne, matermone, matrimoyne, -moine,** *Sc.* **matrimone,** 4–5 **matrimoigne,** 4–6 **matrymony, matrimonye,** 5 **matremony,** 6 **matrymonie,** 6–7 **matrimonie,** 4– **matrimony.** [a. OF. *matremoine, -oyne, -oigne*, a. L. *mātrimōnium* wedlock, marriage, f. *matr-em* mother: see -MONY.]

1. The rite of marriage; the action of marrying.

1303 R. BRUNNE *Handl. Synne* 11156 The syxte sacrament ys matrymony, þere hyt ys do ryȝtwusly. **1362** LANGL. *P. Pl.* A. x. 201 Seþþen lawe haþ I-loket þat vche mon haue a make In Mariage and Matrimoyne I-Medlet to-gedere. *c* **1386** CHAUCER *Knt.'s T.* 2237 Bitwixen hem was maad anon the bond, That highte matrimoigne or mariage. *c* **1440** *Gesta Rom.* xlviii. 214 (Harl. MS.) What tyme that the solempnite of the matrimonye is made, holdithe him with yow. **1508** DUNBAR *Tua mariit Wemen* 152 Sen man ferst with matrimony ȝow menkit in kirk, How haif ȝe farne be ȝour faith? **1547** *Homilies* I. *Agst. Swearing* I. (1859) 75 The sacrament of matrimony knitteth man and wife in perpetual love. **1548** CRANMER *Catech.* 70 The fayth and promise made in matrimony. **1651** HOBBES *Leviath.* IV. xlvii. 383 Teaching that Matrimony is a Sacrament, giveth to the Clergy the Judging of the lawfulnesse of Marriages. **1660** R. COKE *Power & Subj.* 78 Matrimony is the act of two free persons..mutually taking one another for husband and wife. **1765** BLACKSTONE *Comm.* I. xvi. 444 All children born before matrimony are bastards by our law. **1841** LANE *Arab. Nts.* I. 65 The tie of blood is, to him [an Arab], in every respect, stronger than that of matrimony. **1902** T. M. LINDSAY *Ch. & Ministry in Early Cent.* v. 198 In such a solemn action as matrimony the blessing of the Church should be joined to the Civil contract.

personified. **1500–20** DUNBAR *Poems* xlii. 97 Matremony, that nobill king, Was grevit.

fig. *c* **1440** *Gesta Rom.* ix. 26 (Harl. MS.), Our lord ihesu crist,..drowe matrimony with vs, þat is to say, when þat he tooke our kynde.

†**b.** A joining in wedlock; a marriage; an alliance by marriage. *Obs.*

c **1380** WYCLIF *Sel. Wks.* III. 348 Þei maken many divorsis, and many matrimonies, unleveful. *c* **1400** *Destr. Troy* 9223 A mariage & matremony hole. **1532** LATIMER *Let. to Baynton* in Foxe *A. & M.* (1583) 1751/2, I haue had more busines in my little cure since I spake with you, what with sicke folkes, and what with matrimonies, then I haue had since I came to it. **1535** CROMWELL in Merriman *Life & Lett.* (1902) I. 404 The saide Bisshop of Rome..ought to approbate and confyrme this present matrymonie. **1622** MABBE tr. *Aleman's Guzman d'Alf.* II. 253 That which they doe..is no other thing, then to dissolue a matrimonie, and to open a doore to the Devill. **1660** R. COKE *Justice Vind.* 2 If he were just, because he did adorn his Sisters with highest matrimonies [etc.]. **1737** WHISTON *Josephus, Antiq.* XX. vii. §3 He forsook at once this matrimony.

†**c.** A manner of marrying; nuptial ceremonial.

1718 LADY M. W. MONTAGU *Lett. to C'tess Bristol* (1887) I. 242 What is most extraordinary in their customs, is their matrimony.

†**d.** The marriage service. *Obs.*

1700 DRYDEN *Sigismonda* 165 The holy man..Made haste to sanctify the bliss by law; And muttered fast the matrimony o'er. **1724** MRS. M. DAVYS *Reformed Coquet* 86, I doubt not but your Chaplain has the Matrimony by heart; but, if not, pray let him con his lesson before he comes.

2. The state or condition of being husband and wife; the relation between married persons.

c **1325** *Metr. Hom.* 121 Ef Crist paied no ware Of matirmoyne [*Camb. MS.* matrimon]..he noht thar [*sc.* til Cana Galile] Cumen. *c* **1340** HAMPOLE *Prose Tr.* 11 In assys or cause of matremoyne. **1377** LANGL. *P. Pl.* B. XVI. 219 Matrimoigne with-oute moillerye is nouȝt moche to preyse. *c* **1386** CHAUCER *Pars. T.* ¶843 Matrimoyne is leefful assemblynge of man And of womman. **1422** tr. *Secreta Secret., Priv. Priv.* 192 Matremony is a dignite ordeyned of god. **1432–50** tr. *Higden* (Rolls) II. 391 Hercules gate a son ..whiche reignede after hym, not geten in trewe matrimony. **1529** MORE *Suppl. Soulys* Wks. 307/2 Then shall matrimony be much better kepte. **1643** MILTON *Divorce* I. Pref., The misinterpreting of the scripture..hath chang'd the blessing of matrimony not seldom into a familiar and co-inhabiting mischief. **1722** DE FOE *Relig. Courtsh.* I. iii. (1840) 93 The very laws of matrimony forbid it. **1829** LYTTON *Devereux* I. i, Nothing in his estimation was less becoming to a wise man than matrimony.

†**b.** Phrases. *to break matrimony*: to commit adultery. *to make matrimony*: to join in wedlock. *to make to matrimony*: to take to wife. *Obs.*

1377 LANGL. *P. Pl.* B. xv. 235 If þei lacchen syluer And matrimoigne for monye maken & vnmaken. **1432–50** tr. *Higden* (Rolls) IV. 9 Takenge the doȝhter of Darius to matrimony. **1526** TINDALE *Matt.* v. 32 Whosoever put awaye his wyfe..causeth her to breake matrimony. **1568** GRAFTON *Chron.* II. 443 Forbiddyng them aboue all thinges the brech of Matrimonie, the vse of swearyng [etc.].

†**3.** A husband or wife. *Obs.*

c **1620** FLETCHER & MASS. *Little Fr. Lawyer* IV. v, Restore my Matrimony undefil'd. **1673** DRYDEN *Marr. à la Mode* II. i, That sign of a husband there, that lazy matrimony.

†**4.** (See quot.) *Obs.*

1757 W. THOMPSON *R.N. Advoc.* 41 If these Oxen do not weigh this weight, the practice of Matrimony is then introduced... It is weighing the Fore Quarter of a heavy Ox with the Hind Quarter of a light Ox, by which conjugated State they..produce the Standard Weight.

5. A game played with a full pack of cards and resembling Pope Joan. Also, the combination of king and queen of trumps in Pope Joan, Matrimony, and other games of cards. (Cf. MARRIAGE 7.)

1801 STRUTT *Sports & Past.* IV. ii. 296 We have also the Game of Snake, and the more modern Game of Matrimony, with others of the like kind. **1830** R. HARDIE *Hoyle's Games, Pope Joan* 82 Matrimony is the king and queen, and Intrigue the knave and queen of trumps. *Ibid., Matrimony* 83 The game..consists of five chances, viz. Matrimony, which is king and queen [etc.]. **1837** DICKENS *Pickw.* vi, When the spinster aunt got 'matrimony', the young ladies laughed afresh. **1876** CAPT. CRAWLEY *Card Players' Man.* 211 Matrimony..is played with a full pack of cards. **1887** *All Year Round* 5 Feb. 66 There was Matrimony [in Pope Joan] ..the winning of which caused such delightful confusion to the ingenuous maid of the period.

6. *slang* and *dial.* A mixture of two comestibles or beverages.

1813 *Examiner* 17 May 317/1 That injudicious mixing of wines, which is called matrimony. **1882** OGILVIE, *Matrimony*..4. A name given jocularly to raisins and almonds mixed, and various other common combinations. **1892** MARIANNE NORTH *Recollect. Happy Life* I. 103 They gave us glasses of 'matrimony', a delicious compound made of star-apple sugar and the juice of Seville oranges.

7. *Comb.* in **matrimony cake** *dial.* (cf. 6), a round cake consisting of a layer of currants between two layers of pastry; **matrimony-vine**, a name for *Lycium barbarum* or *L. vulgare*.

1866 *Treas. Bot., Matrimony-vine.*

matriotism (ˈmeɪtrɪətɪz(ə)m). *nonce-wd.* [Altered from PATRIOTISM, after L. *māter* mother.] Love of one's mother country or of one's 'alma mater'.

1856 LOWELL *Lett.* (1894) I. 301, I am delighted with your *ma*triotism 'Rome, Venice, Cambridge!' **1885** H. C. BEECHING in *Academy* 14 Feb. 109/2 Though Mr. Lang's matriotism is thus divided, he has only one fatherland.

matris, obs. form of MATRICE.

†**matrisate**, *v. Obs. rare*⁻⁰. [f. ppl. stem of L. *mātrissāre*, f. *mātr-em* mother.] *intr.* To imitate a mother.

1727 in BAILEY vol. II.

matrix (ˈmeɪtrɪks), *sb. Pl.* **matrixes, matrices** (ˈmeɪtrɪsiːz). [a. L. *mātrix* (stem *mātrīc-*), in late L. womb, in older Latin pregnant animal, female animal used for breeding; app. f. *māter* mother, by change of the ending into the suffix of fem. agent-nouns. Cf. MATRICE.

The L. plural *matrices* is normally pronounced (ˈmeɪtrɪsiːz), formerly (məˈtraɪsiːz), but in the industrial sense 4 the prevailing pronunciation is (ˈmætrɪsiːz), prob. from association with the pl. of MATRICE.]

1. The uterus or womb. Also occas. used for OVARY, esp. with reference to oviparous animals.

1526 TINDALE *Luke* ii. 23 Every man chylde that fyrst openeth the matrix shalbe called holy to the lorde. **1547** BOORDE *Brev. Health* iii. 8 Abhorsion..maye come by ventositie and lubricite of humours in the matryx. **1615** CROOKE *Body of Man* 272 The partes of the Female are the wombe and the rest which by a general name are called matrices. **1655** MOUFET & BENNET *Health's Improv.* (1746) 202 The Matrix of Beasts..is but a sinewy and hard Substance. **1726–31** TINDAL *Rapin's Hist. Eng.* (1743) II. XVII. 74 *note*, The women that attended about Queen Mary alledged that her Matrix was consumed. **1765** *Treat. Dom. Pigeons* 15 The ovary, or upper matrix of the hen, or female bird. **1803** *Med. Jrnl.* IX. 57 The matrix..was uncommonly small, and the right ovarium..had attached to it small excrescences. **1816** KIRBY & SP. *Entomol.* II. 36 This part.. is now a vast matrix of eggs. **1840** *Cuvier's Anim. Kingd.* 40 The foetus, immediately after conception, descends..into the matrix.

2. a. A place or medium in which something is 'bred', produced, or developed.

1555 EDEN *Decades* 31 *margin*, Mountaynes are the matrices of golde. *Ibid.* 141 They founde certaine pearles coommynge foorthe of their matreces. **1594** PLAT *Jewell-ho.* I. 22 That which is yet chalke within the Matrix of the earth. **1641** FRENCH *Distill.* v. (1651) 161 Untill they..be received into certain matrixes in the earth which may make them put forth this potentiall saltnesse into act. **1671** J. WEBSTER *Metallogr.* iii. 46 Framed in their several seminaries, matrixes, or seed-husks. **1691** RAY *Creation* II. (1692) 82 A convenient Harbor or Matrix to cherish and hatch their Eggs. **1713** DERHAM *Phys.-Theol.* IV. xiii. 230 These Matrixes may much conduce to the Maturation and Production of the Young. **1727–52** CHAMBERS *Cycl.* s.v., The earth is the matrix wherein seeds sprout; and marcasites are by many considered as the matrixes of metals. **1853** KANE *Grinnell Exp.* xviii. (1857) 138 The question whether unmixed snow can act as a vegetative matrix. **1879** H. GEORGE *Progr. & Pov.* X. ii. (1881) 453 This is the matrix in which mind unfolds. **1880** BASTIAN *Brain* 39 This intermediate tissue is..the probable matrix wherein and from which new nerve fibres..are evolved in animals.

b. A place or point of origin and growth.

1605 CAMDEN *Rem.* (1637) 56 The old German tongue, which undoubtedly is the matrix and mother of our English. **1867** MANNING *Eng. & Christendom* 242 The root and matrix of the Catholic Church. **1896** *Peterson Mag.* VI. 263/1 The matrix of the anti-war feeling was in New England.

c. The formative part of an animal organ, e.g. the pulp and capsule of the mammalian tooth; the hair-papilla (*Syd. Soc. Lex.* 1890); the 'bed' in which the finger or toe-nails grow.

1835–6 TODD *Cycl. Anat.* I. 351/2 The matrix, or organ by which the perfect feather is produced, has the form of an elongated cylindrical cone. **1854** OWEN *Skel. & Teeth* in *Circ. Sci., Organ. Nat.* I. 280 The matrix of certain teeth does not give rise..to the germ of a second tooth. **1858** H. GRAY *Anat.* 545 The part of the cutis beneath the body and root of the nail is called the *matrix*.

d. *Bot.* The body on which a fungus or a lichen grows.

1857 BERKELEY *Cryptog. Bot.* §39. 54 The nature of the communication between the plants and matrix in the parasitic fungi. **1874** COOKE *Fungi* 25 These spores.. deposit themselves..on the surface of the *Tremella* and on its matrix.

†**e.** 'The inward, soft, pithy and spungy part of any Tree or Plant' (Phillips, ed. Kersey, 1706).

1693 tr. *Blancard's Phys. Dict.* (ed. 2), *Matrix*,..Among Vegetables it signifies the Marrow or Heart of a Plant. **1704** J. HARRIS *Lex. Techn.* I. *Matrix* of a Tree or Plant, is the same with what the Botanists call *Cor*.

3. a. An embedding or enclosing mass; esp. the rock-mass surrounding or adhering to things embedded in the earth, as metal (see GANGUE), fossils, gems and the like.

1641 FRENCH *Distill.* v. (1651) 161 Which..as yet have no saline tast, untill they meet with such principles, and be received into certain matrixes in the earth. **1756–7** tr. *Keysler's Trav.* (1760) I. 48 In the matrix of an emerald, you may see how this gem concretes. **1802** PLAYFAIR *Illustr. Hutton. Theory* 78 Some of the species of whinstone are the common matrices of agates and chalcedonies. **1871** *Trans. Amer. Inst. Mining Engin.* I. 95 Their [*sc.* ores] earthy portions we designate as their 'matrix' or 'gangue'. **1884** *Knowledge* 4 Apr. 222/2 The consolidated eruptive mud of the mines was believed by some to be the true matrix of the diamond.

b. *Biol.* The substance situated between animal or vegetable cells.

1802 *Med. Jrnl.* VIII. 300 Their vascular structure [*sc.* of bones] is enveloped in a matrix. **1875** BENNETT & DYER tr. *Sachs' Bot.* 54 The matrix which surrounds the grains of aleurone in oily seeds is..always a mixture of oily matter and albuminoids. **1881** MIVART *Cat* 17 The structureless substance and fibres form what is called the matrix of the tissue. **1890** COOKE *Introd. Fresh-w. Algæ* 156 The mucous matrix containing the families of cells seems [etc.]. **1896** *Allbutt's Syst. Med.* I. 115 The intercellular matrix undergoes modifications or degenerative changes during inflammation.

4. a. A mould in which something is cast or shaped; in *Type-founding*, a piece of metal (usually copper) on which the letter has been stamped in intaglio by means of a punch, so that it forms a mould for the face of the type; in *Coining*, the stamp and 'bed' used for striking coins; in *Stereotyping*, the paper squeeze of a form of type, serving as a mould for a type-metal cast.

1626 USSHER *Lett.* (1686) 343 His Matrices of the Oriental Tongues are bought by Elzevir the Printer. **1695** WOODWARD *Nat. Hist. Earth* (1723) 22 These Shells having served as Matrices or Moulds to them [*sc.* fossils]. **1709** TANNER 3 Oct. in *Ballard MSS.* IV. 53 They find the want of Matrices at their Press. **1832** BABBAGE *Econ. Manuf.* xi. (ed. 3) 74 Each matrix being in fact a piece of copper of the same size as the type. **1832** *Act 2 Will. IV*, c. 34 §10 Any Puncheon, Counter-puncheon, Matrix, Stamp, Die, Pattern or Mould in or upon which there shall be made or impressed..the Figure [etc.]..of any of the King's current Gold or Silver Coin. **1851** D. WILSON *Preh. Ann.* (1863) I. II. ii. 347 Moulded into form in the double matrix of stone or metal. **1859** SALA *Gas-light & D.* ii. 27 His nimble fingers are shaping out the matrix of a monstrous human face, for a pantomimic mask. **1868** *Archæol. Jrnl.* XXV. 247 Matrix of the seal of William Picard [exhibited]. **1879** J. TIMBS in *Cassell's Techn. Educ.* I. 27/2 Founding metal types in a matrix or mould. **1902** HODGKIN *Rariora* II. 52 The discovery or invention of the leaden matrix, which played.. so important a part in very early typography.

b. *Antiq.* The bed or hollowed place in a slab in which a monumental brass is fixed.

1861 HAINES *Mon. Brasses* I. cxxiii, There is the matrix of a brass at Tormarton. **1863** SIR G. G SCOTT *Glean. Westm. Abb.* (ed. 2) 150 Traces of the matrices of two brass shields. **1864** BOUTELL *Her. Hist. & Pop.* xx. 337 Deeply scored with the matrices of the lost Brasses. **1890** J. T. FOWLER in *Proc. Soc. Antiq.* Ser. II. XIII. 39 The grooves and holes for running lead to the rivets are distinctly seen in the matrices.

c. A (positive or negative) copy of an original disc recording that is used in the making of other copies; *spec.* one used as a stamper.

1904 S. R. BOTTONE *Talking Machines & Records* 86 A copper matrix is first made from it [*sc.* the original disc] by electrotyping... From the copper matrix thus produced any number of duplicates can be moulded out of ebonite by hot pressure. **1918** H. SEYMOUR *Reproduction of Sound* 175 A stamper is a working matrix for pressing records, and as such is merely a duplicate of the master matrix. *Ibid.* 310 To get an exact replica of a master matrix, an intermediate process is necessitated, in the production of a 'mother' matrix, which is a facsimile in metal of the original record.. from which the subsequent negatives can be obtained. **1922** O. MITCHELL *Talking Machine Industry* vi. 69 Several matrices are formed, which are then nickel-plated, polished and receive a strong backing of heavy steel as a support. They are then ready for the presses. **1929** *Melody Maker* Apr. 375/2 For sale. Matrices by leading U.S.A. Records Company, containing latest and biggest American successes. **1935** H. C. BRYSON *Gramophone Record* vi. 142 Negative matrices, i.e., master and stamper, may be made to reproduce by means of a special needle, the end of which is split into a tiny fork which just fits over the ridge. **1952** [see MOTHER *sb.*[1] 11]. **1964** P. J. GUY *Disc Recording & Reproduction* vi. 76 When the third shell—which is called the Matrix or Stamper—is stripped off, its ridges are nickel plated.

d. *Photogr.* A dyed print in relief used for transferring colour to a final colour print.

1947 *Van Nostrand's Sci. Encycl.* (ed. 2) 917/2 Dyed relief films or differentially hardened films are generally called matrices when used in an imbibition process. **1957** R. W. G. HUNT *Reproduction of Colour* v. 44 The matrix film is.. then washed with hot water to leave a hardened gelatin relief image. **1970** C. B. NEBLETTE *Fund. Photogr.* xxii. 312 After drying, the films, now termed matrices, are dyed in the proper colours.

5. *Dentistry.* A plate of metal or composition to serve as a temporary wall for a cavity of a tooth during filling.

1883 G. CUNNINGHAM in *Dental Record* III. 458 No matter whether one or two or even all the walls of the cavity are gone, they may be restored by a matrix. *Ibid.* 529 Ordinary tinned iron, and also dental alloy, have been used for the purpose of matrices, but have been entirely discarded by me in favour of platinum.

6. *Math.* A rectangular arrangement of quantities or symbols.

1858 CAYLEY in *Coll. Math. Papers* (1889) II. 475 The term matrix might be used in a more general sense, but in the present memoir I consider only square and rectangular matrices. **1902** *Encycl. Brit.* XXV. 277/2 A matrix has in many parts of mathematics a signification apart from its evaluation as a determinant. *Ibid.* 278/1 The matrix consists of *n* rows and *n* columns.

b. *spec.* in *Logic.* An array of symbols representing truth-values, giving the result of all possible assignments of truth-values to components of a propositional form or proposition; = *truth-table.* Also, that part of a truth-table which is an array of the total truth-possibilities (see quot. 1965). Also, a set of basic truth-tables for a particular system of logic (see quot. 1973). Also *attrib.*, as ***matrix method***, etc.

1914 C. I. LEWIS in *Jrnl. Philos., Psychol. & Sci. Methods* XI. 600 The matrix algebra for implications is useful as an instrument for investigating the interrelations of necessity, truth, possibility, falsity. **1932** —— & LANGFORD *Symbolic Logic* vii. 201 That any principle, expressible in the symbols of the system, holds or does not hold can be determined by investigating its truth-status for all combinations of the truth-values of the elements. This is the matrix method. **1955** A. N. PRIOR *Formal Logic* 243 In the other matrices, the corner values are the usual ones for the corresponding two-valued operators. **1965** HUGHES & LONDEY *Elements of Formal Logic* iii. 21 The array of possible combinations of truth-values of the variables (always set out on the left) will be called the matrix. **1973** J. J. ZEMAN *Modal Logic* v. 89 What we refer to may be called the matrix method... A truth-value system, or matrix, may be thought of as a set of tables, one for each of the primitive operators of the system, which may be used in computing a 'truth table' for any wff of the system.

c. *Logic.* An expression that would become a statement if its variables were replaced by constants, i.e. by names of individuals or classes or statements, as appropriate; = either *propositional function* or *statement-form*, depending on which type it is; *esp.*, in predicate calculus, a quantifier-free part of a formula (see quots. 1954, 1971).

1908 B. RUSSELL in *Amer. Jrnl. Math.* XXX. 238 Then p/a, which we will call a matrix, may take the place of a function. **1910** WHITEHEAD & RUSSELL *Principia Math.* I. 262 Let us give the name of matrix to any function, of however many variables, which does not involve any apparent variables. **1932** LEWIS & LANGFORD *Symbolic Logic* ix. 267 Such functions as $f(x)$ and $p \vee q$.. we may call matrices. **1954** I. M. COPI *Symbolic Logic* ix. 298 In any *wff* in prenex normal form $(Qx_1)(Qx_2)..(Qx_n)$ G the group of quantifiers $(Qx_1)(Qx_2)..(Qx_n)$ is the prefix and the quantifier-free formula G is the matrix. **1971** G. HUNTER *Metalogic* 252 A formula A is in prenex normal form iff it is of the form $Qv_1..Qv_nB$, where each Q is either $\wedge$ or $\vee$, $n \geqslant 0$, B is a wff, and no quantifiers occur in B. The B.. is called the matrix of A, and the part of A (if any) that precedes the matrix is called the prefix.

d. *Computers.* An interconnected array of diodes, cores, or other circuit elements that has a number of inputs and outputs and somewhat resembles a lattice or grid in its circuit design or physical construction.

1948 *Gloss. Computer Terms* (Mass. Inst. Technol. Servomechanisms Lab. Rep. R-138) 7 *Matrix switch*, a multi-position switch used in computers for decoding binary numbers. By mixing the output of flip-flops holding a binary number in an array of crystal rectifiers or resistors, it permits selection of one or a group of output lines. **1952** *RCA Rev.* June 185 The selected core will be magnetized in the desired direction while all other cores in the matrix will remain unaffected. The read-out is obtained by applying read-in current pulses. **1955** R. K. RICHARDS *Arithmetic Operations in Digital Computers* iii. 75 In other applications the matrix is used to 'gate' an external signal (such as a series of pulses) onto one of a multiplicity of signal lines. **1969** P. B. JORDAIN *Condensed Computer Encycl.* 315 Such a diode matrix will encode decimal into binary. **1970** O. DOPPING *Computers & Data Processing* x. 136 Cores are usually built together to form square or possibly rectangular matrices in which each matrix contains as many cores as there are words in the memory bank. Most matrices nowadays contain (64 × 64 =) 4,096 cores.

e. *Television* and *Broadcasting.* A circuit designed to accept a number of inputs and produce outputs that are linear combinations of them in different proportions. Freq. *attrib.*

1953 *Proc. IRE* XLI. 842/1 We show the pickup system giving information in the form of three channel voltages... All three of these voltages are fed to the inputs of three separate matrix or mixing units. **1954** *Ibid.* XLII. 201 (*heading*) Matrix networks for color TV. *Ibid.* 201/2 In a 3-tube video matrix with R_L and r_b equal to 5000 ohms, the gain per tube will be one third of the gain of a one-tube amplifier. **1961** CARNT & TOWNSEND *Colour Television* vii. 185 The matrix circuits, in effect, solve the three equations $R' = Y' + 0{\cdot}96\,I' + 0{\cdot}62\,Q'$, $G' = Y' - 0{\cdot}27\,I' - 0{\cdot}65\,Q'$, $B' = Y' - 1{\cdot}11\,I' + 1{\cdot}70\,Q'$, and derive their name from the matrix notation used in algebra as a form of shorthand for writing and solving such equations. **1970** *Jrnl. Audio Engin. Soc.* XVIII. 627/1 (*caption*) One form of resistive matrix employed in four-channel stereo receiver or adapter to provide electrical separation of front and rear signals in left and rear stereo channels if transmission matrix of Fig. 4 is utilized at FM broadcast transmitter. **1971** D. J. SEAL *Mazda Bk. Pal Receiver Servicing* i. 7 Two colour difference signals (R − Y and B − Y) are fed from the decoder to the matrix, where they are combined with the luminance signal (Y) to form the three primary colour signals red, green and blue. **1973** *Sat. Rev. Arts* (U.S.) 1 Apr. 49/2 *Matrix system*, the quadraphonic disc system in which four signals are fed into a circuit (matrix) that mixes (encodes) them into two signals that are inscribed on the walls of a record groove... If the disc is played on a properly equipped quad system, the signals are fed into a complementary matrix, which restores (decodes) them back to the original four, and the disc is heard quadraphonically.

7. *attrib.* and *Comb.*, as ***matrix-maker***, †***-suffocation***; ***matrix algebra***; ***matrix tin***, ***vase***; ***matrix-encircled*** adj.; **matrix mechanics** *Physics*, a form of quantum mechanics developed by W. Heisenberg in which the operators corresponding to physical co-ordinates (position, momenta, etc.) are represented by matrices with time-dependent elements; **matrix number**, a number assigned by a record company to a matrix in the manufacture of gramophone records; **matrix printer**, a printer in which each printed character is made up of dots printed by the tips of small wires selected out of a rectangular array; **matrix sentence** *Linguistics* (see quot. 1967[1]).

1930 RUARK & UREY *Atoms, Molecules & Quanta* xvii. 577 (*heading*) The laws of *matrix algebra. **1969** D. C. HAGUE *Managerial Econ.* i. 24 With complex decision problems.. calculus and matrix algebra may have to be used. **1890** 'R. BOLDREWOOD' *Miner's Right* (1899) 177/2 Many a quaint fragment, or *matrix-encircled nugget,.. was transferred.. on that auspicious day. **1656** EARL MONM. tr. *Boccalini's Advts. fr. Parnass.* 101 This Serjeant was son to a *Matrix-maker. **1926** P. A. M. DIRAC in *Proc. R. Soc.* A. CXII. 666 In Heisenberg's *matrix mechanics it is assumed that the elements of the matrices that represent the dynamical variables determine the frequencies and intensities of the components of the radiation emitted. **1966** *McGraw-Hill Encycl. Sci. & Technol.* VIII. 181/2 Matrix mechanics is disadvantageous for obtaining quantitative solutions to actual problems; because it is concisely expressed in a form independent of special coordinate systems, however, matrix mechanics is advantageous for proving general theorems. **1974** G. REECE tr. *Hund's Hist. Quantum Theory* xiii. 171 First Heisenberg showed in the language of matrix mechanics that two identical coupled systems always behaved like the two oscillators. **1965** G. MELLY *Owning-Up* xi. 129 He was a record collector who knew the *matrix number.. of every record in his immaculately filed collection. **1968** LEADBITTER & SLAVEN *Blues Records 1943–66* 7 All matrix numbers where known are given for completeness sake, even though they may only be the issue number with A or B suffixes or numbers allocated by pressing plants. **1958** GOTLIEB & HUME *High-Speed Data Processing* iii. 59 IBM has *matrix printers for use with the 702 and 705 data processors. **1964** T. W. MCRAE *Impact of Computers on Accounting* i. 17 The 'matrix' printer and the 'chain' printer can reach speeds of up to 1200 lines a minute. **1964** *Matrix sentence [see CONSTITUENT B. 5]. **1967** D. STEIBLE *Conc. Handbk. Ling.* 77 *Matrix sentence*, in transformational grammar, a basic sentence, known in traditional grammar as an independent clause, into which other structures may be embedded. **1967** *Word* XXIII. 338 The ultimate fate of an included-sentence construction, of course, is to become so thoroughly embedded in the matrix sentence as to be no longer distinguishable. **1968** *Canad. Jrnl. Ling.* XIII. 83 Infinitive phrases have a wide range of function within the matrix sentence. **1972** HARTMANN & STORK *Dict. Lang. & Ling.* 138 Matrix sentences often coincide with what is known in traditional grammar as main clauses. **1598** SYLVESTER *Du Bartas* II. i. III. *Furies* 566 Such are the fruitfull *Matrix-suffocation, The Falling-sickness, and pale Swouning-passion. **1873** C. ROBINSON *N.S. Wales* 57 Irrespective of vein or *matrix tin. **1857** BIRCH *Anc. Pottery* (1858) II. 353 This *matrix vase was made of a very fine bright red clay.

b. Applied to precious stones (see quot. 1909).

1909 *Cent. Dict.* Suppl., *Matrix-gem*, an opal, turquoise, ruby, or other gem intimately mixed with the matrix material and cut with it. **1921** *Brit. Mus. Return* 157 in *Parl. Papers* XXVII. 651 A suite of specimens of sapphire.. comprising two matrix specimens.

matrix ('meɪtrɪks), *v.* [f. prec. sb. (Orig. formed as the vbl. sb.)] *trans.* To combine (signals) in different proportions so as to obtain one or more linear combinations of them.

1969 CARNT & TOWNSEND *Colour Television* II. iii. 106 Matrixing *R–Y* and *B–Y* produces *G–Y*. **1971** D. J. SEAL *Mazda Bk. Pal Receiver Servicing* i. 7 The decoder accepts the PAL chrominance signal.., demodulates it and produces two colour difference signals to be matrixed and amplified by the colour difference amplifiers. **1972** H. F. OLSON *Mod. Sound Reproduction* ix. 188 The four inputs *LF*, *LR*, *RF*, and *RR*, representing the left front, left rear, right front, and right rear respectively, are matrixed and encoded to the left, *L*, and right, *R*, channels of the conventional two-channel stereophonic recording system. Each of the two channels *R* and *L* contains a mixture of the four channels in such a manner that the four channels can be reconstituted in reproduction by means of the decoder and matrix. **1972** *Gramophone* Jan. 1412/1 The extra channels of information intended for feeding to the back loudspeakers are simply mixed (or matrixed) with the front channel signals prior to the cutting of the disc.

So **'matrixed** *ppl. a.*, **'matrixing** *vbl. sb.*

1951 *Proc. IRE* XXXIX. 1158/2 All that is required is the addition (or subtraction..) of fractions of the camera currents to derive the currents required to control the receiver. [*Note*] This operation has been called 'matrixing' in some discussions. The analogy to the matrix operation, which is used in vector algebra to change from one system of co-ordinates to a second, is obvious. **1955** J. W. WENTWORTH *Color Television Engin.* iv. 125 Matrixing can be used to improve color fidelity only when camera signals are produced by linear devices; if the camera signals are nonlinear functions of red, green, and blue, the linear equations of the matrix process cannot be worked out properly unless the matrix circuit is preceded by linearity correctors. **1971** D. J. SEAL *Mazda Bk. Pal Receiver Servicing* v. 89 Since the luminance signal (−Y) is applied to all three cathodes, the tube performs the final matrixing, and the three gun currents are proportional to the original red, green and blue separation signals from the colour cameras. **1972** H. F. OLSON *Mod. Sound Reproduction* ix. 189 The performance, as exemplified by.. spatial effects, of a two-channel-to-four-channel coded and matrixed system is inferior to that of four discrete channels. **1972** *Observer* (Colour Suppl.) 22 Oct. 54/4 Not all the matrix systems are compatible with each other, though a machine like the Pioneer QX-8000 *is* capable of dealing with all forms of matrixed four channel.

matroclinous (mætrəʊ'klaɪnəs), *a. Biol.* [f. L. *mātr-*, *māter* mother + Gr. κλίν-ειν to lean + -OUS.] Resembling the female rather than the male parent; involving or possessing a tendency to inherit a character or characters from the female parent only. So **'matrocliny**, matroclinous inheritance.

1913 *Jrnl. Exper. Zoöl.* XV. 587 Morgan has explained the case of criss-cross inheritance on the ground that the *X*-chromosome is the carrier of all sex linked factors. The sons are matroclinous because they receive their unpaired chromosome directly from the mother, and must show all the sex linked characters which she showed. **1917** *Genetics* II. 247 But even if one hybrid should be judged to indicate patrocliny in one cross, the same hybrid appears in the reciprocal cross where it would be a case of matrocliny for the same hybrid. **1925** C. C. HURST *Exper. in Genetics* xxxviii. 535 Gametic chromosomes, male and female, are either equal with 7–14–21 or 28 each, or unequal and matroclinous with a maternal bias in the ratio of 1·5–2–3–4 or 5:1. **1939** *Nature* 14 Jan. 81/2 To account for the purely matroclinous inheritance, the following explanation is suggested. The eggs of *M. formosa* are fertilized by the other two species, but the paternal chromosomes remain inactive. **1961** A. MÜNTZING *Genetic Res.* xxvi. 257/1 F. von Wettstein.. observed that this matrocliny was clearly noticeable also in [the] F_2. **1968** R. C. KING *Dict. Genetics* 149 In *Drosophila* the daughters produced by attached-X females are matroclinous in terms of their sex-linked genes.

matron ('meɪtrən). Forms: 4–7 **matrone**, 5 **matroun**, 6– **matron**. [a. F. *matrone* (= Sp., Pg., It. *matrona*), ad. L. *mātrōna*, f. *mātr-em*, *māter* mother.]

1. a. A married woman, usually with the accessory idea of (moral or social) rank or dignity.

Roman matron: sometimes referred to as a proverbial type of feminine dignity of character or bearing. ***British matron***: in 19th-c. use, jocularly taken as the representative of certain social prejudices and rigorous notions of conventional propriety supposed to be characteristic of married women of the English upper middle-class.

c **1375** *Sc. Leg. Saints* xxxix. (*Cosme & Damyane*) 35 In þat cyte wes a matrone, þat of gret gudnes had renon. *c* **1430** LYDG. *Min. Poems* (Percy Soc.) 70 O noble matrouns, whiche have al suffisaunce Of wommanhede, yowre wittes doth up dresse. *c* **1440** *Promp. Parv.* 330/1 Matrone, eld woman, *matrona.* *a* **1548** HALL *Chron., Hen. VII* 20 b, She was layed naked in the bride bed, in the presence of diuerse noble matrones and Prynces. **1607** SHAKS. *Cor.* II. i. 279 Matrons flong Gloues, Ladies and Maids their Scarffes, and

Handkerchers, Vpon him as he pass'd. **1667** MILTON *P.L.* XI. 136 Leucothea..when Adam and first Matron Eve Had ended now their Orisons. **1695** DRYDEN *Parallel Poetry & Painting* Ess. (ed. Ker) II. 129 Neither is there any expression in that story, which a Roman matron might not read without a blush. **1766** GOLDSM. *Vic. W.* xxxii, The question was, whether my eldest daughter, as being a matron, should not sit above the two young brides. **1802** WORDSW. *Sailor's Mother*, And like a Roman matron's was her mien and gait. **1817** SHELLEY *Rev. Islam* IV. xxi. 7 Virgins bright, And matrons with their babes. **1835** THIRLWALL *Greece* I. 327 A dignity of character, which makes them worthy rivals of the Roman matrons. **1867** TROLLOPE *Chron. Barset* (1869) I. xxiv. 255 She was fat, heavy, and good-looking;..a youthful British matron every inch of her.

¶**b.** in personifications.

1581 SIDNEY *Apol. Poetrie* (Arb.) 68 So is that honny-flowing Matron Eloquence..disguised, in a Curtizan-like painted affectation. **1592** SHAKS. *Rom. & Jul.* III. ii. 11 Come ciuill night, Thou sober suted Matron all in blacke.

c. *Eccl.* As the distinctive title of a married female saint. (Cf. *virgin*.)

1519 *Aberd. Reg.* (1844) I. 96 In honor of God and the glorious matron Sanct Anne. **1862** BP. WORDSWORTH *Hymn*, '*Hark, the sound of holy voices*' ii, Saintly Maiden, godly Matron, Widows who have watch'd to prayer.

d. A female dog or horse used for breeding.

1931 A. C. SMITH *About our Dogs* vi. 67 When the matrons have been purchased..the question of finding mates for them is uppermost. **1948** C. L. B. HUBBARD *Dogs in Brit.* xxi. 365 Brood matrons were sent to Welsh Hound studs. **1966** *Telegraph* (Brisbane) 22 Jan. 5/1 King's Daughter could have been an above average stud matron. **1971** *Country Life* 11 Nov. 1267/1 The breeding of hounds ought not to be merely a question of appearance and dash... They should also be the offspring of stallions and matrons of time-honoured residence in the kennels.

2. *spec.* A married woman considered as having expert knowledge in matters of childbirth, pregnancy, etc.; now only in ***jury of matrons*** (see JURY 2 f.). †Also, applied in *plural* to married women who render assistance, or friendly offices in or after childbirth.

[So F. *matrone*; cf. also mod.L. *matrona* 'midwife' (*Syd. Soc. Lex.*).]

1491 CAXTON *Vitas Patr.* (1495) 198 The matrones or myddewyfes that were come to her for to receyve the child. **1631** MILTON *Epit. March. Winchester* 23 Once had the early Matrons run To greet her of a lovely son. **1650** WELDON *Crt. Jas. I* 79 A Jury of grave Matrons..after their inspection gave verdict, she was (*intacta virgo*).

3. A woman (not, according to present usage, necessarily a married woman) who has official charge of the domestic arrangements of a public institution such as a hospital, school, prison, etc.

1557 *Order of Hospitalls* E ij b, The Matron, in governinge the wemen and keping the provision of Bedds, Sheets, Shirts and other committed to her charge. **1706** PHILLIPS, *Matron*... Also one of the grave Women that have the Oversight of Children in an Hospital. **1780** JOHNSON *Let. to Dr. Vyse* 30 Dec., The matron of the Chartreux is about to resign her place. **1791** BENTHAM *Panopt.* I. Postscr. 43 There must be a Chaplain, a Surgeon, and a Matron. **1801** *Med. Jrnl.* V. 291 The servants of the House shall consist of a Matron, who shall superintend the domestic concerns; three ordinary nurses [etc.]. **1872** *Rep. Directors Convict Prisons* 444 Superannuated. 1 engineer, 1 matron. **1896** *Allbutt's Syst. Med.* I. 424 This power [of moving probationers] should be vested in the matron, herself a trained nurse.

4. a. *attrib.* quasi-*adj.* (pertaining to or characteristic of a matron) as ***matron air, brow, cap, cheek, face, form, grace, heart, lip, step, weed, years***; (consisting of matrons) as ***matron-train***.

1836 CAROLINE B. SOUTHEY *Poet. Wks.* (1867) 13 She, with *matron airs, Who gravely lectures her rebellious doll. **1725** POPE *Odyss.* I. 534 When the star of eve with golden light Adorn'd the *matron brow of sable night. *c* **1820** S. ROGERS *Italy* (1839) 29 Young as she was, she wore the *matron-cap. **1810** JANE PORTER *Scot. Chiefs* 338 Wallace pressed her *matron cheek to his. **1775** S. J. PRATT *Liberal Opin.* xxxviii. (1783) I. 223 The dear furrows of her *matron face. **1718** ROWE tr. *Lucan* I. 353 Her awful head Rome's rev'rend image rear'd, Trembling and sad the *Matron form appear'd. **1813** SHELLEY *Q. Mab* viii. 120 Autumn proudly bears her *matron grace. **1779** *Rocks of Meillerie* 51 Ye piteous sighs, that burst my *matron heart. **1667** MILTON *P.L.* IV. 501 He..press'd her *Matron lip With kisses pure. **1784** COWPER *Task* IV. 246 With *matron step slow moving. **1726** POPE *Odyss.* XXII. 521 The *matron-train with all the virgin band Assemble here. **1811** W. R. SPENCER *Poems* 15 To gem the *matron weeds of night. **1810** S. GREEN *Reformist* II. 7 The wanton wife, whose *matron years and situation should teach her gravity.

b. matron of honour, a chief bridesmaid who is married.

1903 *N.Y. Tribune* 20 Sept., Her only attendant, as matron of honor, wore pale blue crepe de chine. **1948** *Daily Oklahoman* (Okla. City) 9 June 13/3 The bride and I wonder whether I should be called matron of honor or maid of honor. **1961** A. BARNES *Mod. Wedding Etiquette* vii. 61 There is never more than one matron of honour and she wears, not the usual youthful style bridesmaids' dresses, but an afternoon gown with hat and gloves. Her duties are exactly the same as those of the chief bridesmaid. **1963** *Listener* 14 Mar. 473/3 The groom's brother..has to listen to the indignant and delightfully comic complaints of the matron-of-honour. **1969** EDWARDS & BEYFUS *Lady Behave* 268 If the bridesmaid is married she is known as a Matron of Honour.

matron, obs. form of MARTEN.

matronage (ˈmeɪtrənɪdʒ). [f. prec. + -AGE.]

1. A body of matrons; matrons collectively.

1771 MRS. GRIFFITH *Hist. Lady Barton* II. 56 Some sort of foundation, under the government of a respectable matronage..would certainly be an institution most devoutly to be wished for. **1796** BURKE *Regic. Peace* i. Wks. VIII. 192 His exemplary Queen, at the head of the matronage of this land. **1825** SCOTT *Betrothed* xi, The Lady of Hugh de Lacy will be one of the foremost among the matronage of England. **1860** HOOK *Lives Abps.* (1868) I. iii. 477 The matronage of England rose up in chaste indignation.

2. Guardianship by a matron.

1771 MRS. GRIFFITH *Hist. Lady Barton* II. 270, I was under the matronage of my aunt Marriot. **1774** *Westm. Mag.* II. 257 He should be able finally to place her under the safe matronage of his dear wife. **1798** CHARLOTTE SMITH *Yng. Philos.* III. 175 If you had thought proper to have transmitted your daughter to the protective matronage of your truly estimable mother. **1878** *Tinsley's Mag.* XXIII. 94 A species of..picnic, under the matronage of the volatile Rosamund. **1878** J. GRANT *Ld. Hermitage* 249 She..had only done so..under the matronage of the housekeeper.

3. The state or condition of being a matron.

1870 LOWELL *Study Wind.* (1886) 165 Underscorings in young ladies' letters [are] a wonder..to themselves under the colder north-light of matronage. **1884** MRS. F. MILLER *Ht. Martineau* 52 Matronage is a profession in itself.

matronal (ˈmeɪtrənəl), *a.* [a. F. *matronal* (Cotgr.) ad. L. *mātrōnālis*, f. *mātrōna*: see MATRON and -AL¹.]

1. Of, pertaining to, or appropriate to a matron.

1609 DOULAND *Ornith. Microl.* 36 Others do loue the decent, and as it were, matronall carriage of the eight [tone]. **1619** SIR A. GORGES tr. *Bacon's De Sap. Vet.* 19 Besydes (for her matronall chastity) shee was held venerable by Antiquity. **1622** BACON *Hen. VII* 218 He had heard of the Beautie..of the young Queene of Naples,..being then of Matronall yeares of seuen and twentie. **1777** JOHNSON *Let. to Mrs. Thrale* 19 May, When you are, with matronal authority, talking down juvenile hopes. **1822** T. TAYLOR *Apuleius* 59, I have always despised matronal embraces. **1876** BANCROFT *Hist. U.S.* V. lxvi. 285 Susanna Smith Elliott..stepped forth..in matronal beauty.

2. Having the characteristics of a matron.

1748 RICHARDSON *Clarissa* (1811) VI. 18 The dialogues between the old matronal lady and the young lady. **1847** SMEATON *Builder's Man.* 203 Draped matronal figures. **1849** CLOUGH *Amours de Voy.* I. 160 Eager for battle here Stood Vulcan, here matronal Iuno.

Hence ˈ**matronally**, *adv. rare*$^{-0}$.

1727 in BAILEY vol. II.

‖**Matronalia** (ˈmætrəˌneɪlɪə). [L. *Mātrōnālia*, neut. pl. of *mātrōnālis*: see prec.] A festival in honour of Mars celebrated by the Roman matrons.

1706 in PHILLIPS (ed. Kersey). **1869** LECKY *Europ. Mor.* (1877) I. ii. 301 The Saturnalia and Matronalia..were the most popular holidays in Rome.

matronhood (ˈmeɪtrənhʊd). [f. MATRON + -HOOD.] The state or condition of being a matron.

1836 MRS. GORE *Mrs. Armytage* I. 142 Had not matronhood and maternity chanced to recall her to the softer duties of her sex. **1868** M. COLLINS *Sweet Anne Page* III. 271 A very dainty presentment of matronhood.

matronism (ˈmeɪtrənɪz(ə)m). *rare.* [f. MATRON + -ISM.] **a.** The qualities appropriate to a matron. **b.** Guardianship by a matron.

1606 BIRNIE *Kirk-Buriall* Ded., Your Mother, the mirrour of all godly graue matronisme. **1815** *Zeluca* I. 95, I know that in this age female matronism is as serviceable as paternal vigilance can be to daughters.

matronize (ˈmeɪtrənaɪz), *v.* [f. MATRON + -IZE.]

1. *trans.* To render matronly.

1741 S. RICHARDSON *Familiar Lett.* 187 Childbed matronizes the giddiest Spirits. **1754** —— *Grandison* (1781) VII. xxxix. 190 She will be matronized now. The Mother must make her a Wife. **1797** MRS. A. M. BENNETT *Beggar Girl* (1813) II. 137 Every step taken by him, to lessen the expences of his family, and matronize his wife. **1843** CAROLINE B. SOUTHEY *Poet. Wks.* (1867) 197 Life's grave duties matronize the bride.

2. *intr.* To become or be made a matron.

1802 H. MARTIN *Helen of Glenross* I. 212, I respect matrimony, and should be sorry not to see you some day matronized. **1872** M. COLLINS *Pr. Clarice* II. xix. 216, I love Isis in its maidenhood, before it matronises into Thames.

3. a. *trans.* To act as a matron to; to chaperon.

1807–8 W. IRVING *Salmag.* (1824) 7 When young ladies used to go a sleigh-riding at night..without being matronized. **1818** MISS FERRIER *Marriage* I. 295 Lady Maclaughlan..will matronize you to the play. *Ibid.*, You are rather young to matronize yourself yet. **1881** MISS BRADDON *Asph.* II. 206, I wish we could have old Spicer in to matronise the party. **1888** *Scribner's Mag.* Oct. 455/2 Some married cousin had been found to matronize them.

b. *U.S.* To preside as a matron over, to act as hostess to (a party, etc.).

1892 *Boston* (Mass.) *Jrnl.* 17 Nov. 8/3 Members of the committee will matronize the rooms daily. **1897** HOWELLS *Landl. Lion's Head* 204 The lady who was matronizing the tea recognized him.

¶**4.** Used humorously for *patronize* when said of a feminine subject.

1830 *Blackw. Mag.* XXVIII. 893 Madam, you do not matronise—and, sir, you do not patronise—waltzing? **1833** *Ibid.* XXXIII. 146 The poetry matronized by fashion is sufficiently so-so-ish.

Hence ˈ**matronized** *ppl. a.*, ˈ**matronizing** *vbl. sb.* and *ppl. a.*

a **1825** FUSELI *Aphor.*, *Life & Writ.* (1831) III. 128 The Madonnas of Raffaelle..are uniformly transcripts..of some favourite face matronized. **1867** MRS. WHITNEY *L. Goldthwaite* iv, They were to..participate..under her matronizing, in city gayeties. **1883** *Century Mag.* XXVI. 283 The matronizing of a houseful of hungry school-boys. **1897** HOWELLS *Landl. Lion's Head* 213 They stood before the matronizing hostess.

matron-like (ˈmeɪtrənlaɪk), *a.* [f. MATRON + -LIKE.] Resembling or befitting a matron; matronly. Also *fig.*

1575–85 ABP. SANDYS *Serm.* xvi. 281 The husband shold labour to reforme his wife; to..frame her to discretion, sobrietie, al matron-like vertues, & all godlinesse. **1577** NORTHBROOKE *Dicing* (1843) 150 Their daunces were..matronelyke, mouing scarce little or nothing in their gestures at all. **1642** HOWELL *For. Trav.* (Arb.) 17 Whereas Religion should go array'd in a grave Matron like habit, they have clad her rather like a wanton Courtisane in light dresses. **1645** EVELYN *Diary* June, The heads of two matron-like servants or old women. **1710** ADDISON *Tatler* No. 120 ¶5 The Front of it was raised on Corinthian Pillars, with all the meretricious Ornaments that accompany that Order; whereas that of the other was composed of the chaste and matron-like Ionic.

matronly (ˈmeɪtrənlɪ), *a.* [f. MATRON + -LY¹.] Like a matron; characteristic of or suitable to a matron.

1656 *Artif. Handsom.* 72 Painting, polishing, and pruning (beyond a matronly comelinesse or gravity). *a* **1660** HAMMOND *Serm.* Wks. 1684 IV. 564 Noted by all the neighbourhood for an absolute Wife; a grave, solemn, matronly Christian. **1754** RICHARDSON *Grandison* (1811) II. v. 86 In every matronly lady I have met with a mother: in many young ladies,..sisters. **1824** MISS MITFORD *Village* Ser. I. 26 She was making a handsome matronly cap. **1882** MISS BRADDON *Mt. Royal* II. x. 212 The figure was a shade more matronly.

Comb. **1818** LADY MORGAN *Autobiog.* (1859) 131 *note*, This mild and matronly-looking lady.

Hence ˈ**matronliness**, matronly quality.

1852 JAMES *Pequinillo* III. 236 A certain composedness of manner and matronliness of dress. **1881** MISS G. M. CRAIK *Sydney* II. ix. 247 You have a pretty kind of matronliness about you.

matronly (ˈmeɪtrənlɪ), *adv.* [f. MATRON + -LY².] In the manner of a matron.

1590 SPENSER *F.Q.* I. x. 8 She..toward them full matronely did pace. **1824** GALT *Rothelan* I. I. xii. 109 Being ..matronly engaged..in soothing her little orphan to sleep.

matronship (ˈmeɪtrənʃɪp). [f. MATRON + -SHIP.]

1. The personality of a matron. In ***your, her matronship***, jocularly used as a title.

1591 LYLY *Endym.* II. ii, I crye your Matronship mercy. **1620** SHELTON *Quix.* III. xxxvii. 264 But for her Matronship, I like it, that ye stir not a Foot. **1718** D'URFEY *Grecian Heroine* III. ii, Is your Matronship grown mad o th' sudden. **1868** HOLME LEE *B. Godfrey* xv. 81 Which time only can answer to your judicious matronship's satisfaction.

2. = MATRONHOOD.

1831 *Fraser's Mag.* IV. 11 The above galaxy..of staid matronship, frisking maidenhood, and sweet romance.

3. The office of 'matron' in a public institution, as a hospital, workhouse, or the like.

c **1843** DICKENS *Lett.* (1880) III. 43, I can't state in figures ..the number of candidates for the Sanatorium matronship. **1888** *Scott. Leader* 5 Oct. 5 Dundee Infirmary Matronship.

matronymic (mætrəʊˈnɪmɪk). [Hybrid f. L. *mātr-*, *māter* mother, after PATRONYMIC. Cf. It. *matronimico*.] **A.** *adj.* = METRONYMIC *a.*

1874 I. TAYLOR *Etrusc. Res.* 224 The Etruscan matronymic suffix is occasionally *-nal* instead of *-al*.

B. *sb.* = METRONYMIC *sb.*

1794 MRS. PIOZZI *Synon.* II. 45 Men..were..named.. sometimes by matronymics, as Anson, Nelson, &c. **1817** COLEBROOKE *Algebra* 30 *note*, Arjuna, surnamed Párt'ha: his matronymic from Prit'há. **1888** G. DE BERNEVAL in *N. & Q.* 7 Jan. 14/1 The Spanish custom of appending the matronymic.

b. A metronymic suffix.

1874 I. TAYLOR *Etrusc. Res.* 223 *Aul*, a form which may exactly represent the sound of the Etruscan matronymic *-al*.

So †**matroˈnymical** *a.* (in quot. app. misused in the sense of 'vernacular').

c **1640** J. SMYTH *Hundred of Berkeley* (1885) 35 [There is] a little meade called Riam, whither on Sunday next after Whitsunday resorted the youthes of both sexes..a day known in all the quarters thereabouts by the matronimicall name of Riam-mead Sunday.

matross (məˈtrɒs). *Mil. Obs.* exc. *Hist.* Also 7 **matroze, montross**, 8–9 **mattross**. [a. Du. *matroos* sailor (whence G. *matrose*, Da., Sw. *matros*), app. a corruption of F. *matelot* sailor.] A soldier next in rank below the gunner in a train of artillery, who acted as a kind of assistant or mate.

In the U.S. the term was synonymous with private of artillery.

1639 in Grose *Milit. Antiq.* (1786) I. 373 Captain of the pioneers, Quarter master, Four conductors of the matrozes, Forty matrozes. **1646** in Rushw. *Hist. Coll.* IV. I. 252 To execute Martial Law..upon all Gunners Matrosses and Soldiers there in pay. **1698** FRYER *Acc. E. India & P.* 38 There being in pay..of English and Portuguez, 700. reckoning the Montrosses and Gunners. **1745** *Gentl. Mag.* 249 Artillery: Wounded—1 conductor, 2 serjeants..13

matrosses. **1787** *Kent. Trav. Companion* 24 A laboratory, where the mattrosses are employed in the composition of fireworks and cartridges. **1793** *Stat. Massachusetts* 22 June [in force until 1810], Each company of Artillery shall consist of one Captain, two Lieutenants, . . six Gunners, six Bombardiers, . . and thirty two privates or Matrosses. **1800** Dundas in Owen *Wellesley's Desp.* (1877) 564 Each company to have an additional Lieut.-Fireworker, and ten additional matrosses. **1815** *Chron. App.* in *Ann. Reg.* 212 Total of killed and wounded . . 11 mattrosses. **1876–7** J. Grant *Hist. India* I. vii. 40/1 The battery was guarded . . by only fifty sepoys and a few European matrosses.

matroun, matroze, matryce, matrys, obs. ff. MATRON, MATROSS, MATRICE, MATTRESS.

matso, var. MATZAH.

‖**matsu** (ˈmætsuː). [Japanese.] A local name for several pine trees, especially the two native to Japan, *Pinus densiflora*, the Japanese red pine, and *P. thunbergii*, the black pine, both valuable ornamental and timber trees.

1727 J. G. Scheuchzer tr. *Kæmpfer's Hist. Japan* I. I. 118 The common Fir, which they call *Matzuoki*, will come to the age of a thousand. [**1863** A. Murray *Pines & Firs Japan* 23 Pinus Massoniana. *Wo matsu.* Japon., i.e. Pinus mas, sive *Kuro matsu*, i.e. Pinus nigra.] **1884** tr. *J. J. Rein's Japan* I. vii. 151 The Aka-matsu or red pine . . and the Kuro-matsu or black pine . . are the commonest conifers in the country. **1916** E. H. Wilson *Conifers & Taxads Japan* 25 The Japanese Red Pine, or Aka-matsu, is very widely distributed in Kyushu. *Ibid.* 27 This Black Pine, or Kuro-matsu, is found in Japan. *Ibid.* 28 Another name for this pine [*sc.* Black Pine] in Japan is O-Matsu (Male Pine). **1923** Dallimore & Jackson *Handbk. Coniferæ* 466 *Pinus Thunbergii*, . . Black Pine, . . Kuro-matsu. **1938** D. T. Suzuki *Zen Buddhism & its Influence on Jap. Culture* II. iii. 247 The Japanese species of the pine known as *matsu* generally spreads its branches irregularly and the trunk is gnarled. **1965** J. Ohwi *Flora Japan* 115/2 *Pinus thunbergii*. . . Kuro-matsu, O-matsu. **1971** S. Eliovson *Gardening Jap. Way* 86 Pine (*Matsu*). This is the symbol of longevity, being hardy and evergreen during cold winters.

‖**matsuri** (mætˈsuːrɪ). [Jap.] A solemn celebration or festival held periodically at every Shintō shrine in Japan in order to deepen the consciousness of the gods in the daily lives of the worshippers.

1727 J. G. Scheuchzer tr. *Kæmpfer's Hist. Japan* I. III. 223 It is a custom which obtains in all cities and villages, to have two such Matsuri's celebrated every year with great pomp and solemnity in honour of that God, to whose more particular care and protection they have devoted themselves. **1841** *Manners & Customs of Japanese* iii. 65 Many and . . various peculiarities belong to the *Matsuri* festival. **1883** E. G. Holtham *Eight Yrs. Japan* viii. 194 The Kiyōto matsuri, specially connected with the 'Gion' quarter of the city, inhabited by singing and dancing girls and such like, . . was well worth seeing. **1928** F. A. Lombard *Outl. Hist. Jap. Drama* iii. 62 *Matsuri* . . have from ancient times in Japan been occasions of great popular rejoicing. **1964** *Asia Mag.* 20 Sept. 9 (*caption*) The winding festival or *matsuri*.

matt (mæt), *a.* Also 7, 9– matte, 9 mat. [a. F. *mat*: see MATE *a.*] Of colours, surfaces: Without lustre, dull, 'dead'.

a **1648** Digby *Closet Open.* (1677) 215 Smooth like silver between polished and matte. **1864** *Reader* 26 Nov. 675/1 The traces are made with diamond points on mat-black paper. **1876** *Encycl. Brit.* V. 170/1 Water gilding . . is finished either 'matt' or burnished. . . Matt-work is protected with one or two coats of finish-size. **1887** *Sci. Amer.* 7 May 297/2 Most kinds of varnish that will dry 'bright' under ordinary circumstances will become 'matt' if subjected to a chill. **1890** *Anthony's Photogr. Bull.* III. 14, I like a landscape photograph, if not too small, better on plain paper—as we call a mat surface print, than on a glazed surface. **1892** *Photogr. Ann.* II. 76 The metal separates in a matt grey form. **1896** *Godey's Mag.* Apr. 448/2 Others are of mat Roman gold. **1897** [see GLOSSY *a.* a]. **1909** *Chamber's Jrnl.* Oct. 684/1 Taken altogether, it cannot compare with the 'matte' appearance of the flatted enamel which is so extensively used in French decoration. **1925** *Morris Owner's Manual* 79 The operation is finished when the valve face has a clean, even, matt-surfaced ring around it. **1933** *Archit. Rev.* LXXIII. 265 To treat plastic materials without humbug so as to bring out their . . pleasant matt texture. **1944** L. MacNeice *Springboard* 32 The matt-grey iron ship, Which ought to have been the Future. **1953**, **1958** [see EGG-SHELL c]. **1967** E. Chambers *Photolitho-Offset* iii. 27 Some smooth, semi-matt prints give fair results, but, in general, sepia tone prints, matt-surface prints and hand-coloured prints should be avoided. **1969** *Sears Catal.* Spring/Summer 6 Uniquely styled in matte-finished vinyl. **1973** *Sci. Amer.* Oct. 128/1 For those who wish a definite opaque matte appearance, talc is cut to a third, and rice starch or particularly fine precipitated chalk is added to improve absorption.

matt, variant of MAT, MATE *a.*

mattachene, etc., obs. forms of MATACHIN.

mattadore, obs. form of MATADOR.

†**ˈmattagess.** *Obs.* Also 6 matagasse, 7 matagesse. [a. southern Fr. *matagasse*, a. Pr. **matagassa* lit. 'magpie-killer', f. *mata-r* to kill + *agassa* magpie (see HAGGESS).] A butcher-bird, *Lanius excubitor*.

1575 Turberv. *Faulconrie* 72 Though the Matagasse be a hawke of none accompte or price neyther with us in any use. **1678** Ray *Willughby's Ornith.* 85 The Matagesse or great Butcherbird. **1753** Chambers *Cycl. Supp.* s.v., The word *Mattagess* is borrowed from the Savoyards, and signifies the murdering pye.

‖**mattamore** (mætəˈmɔə(r)). Also 7 matamorre, 9 matamoro. [a. F. *matamore*, a. Arab. *maṭmūrah*, f. *ṭamara* to store up.] A subterranean habitation, storehouse, or granary.

1695 Motteux *St. Olon's Morocco* 73 Lodging only in Matamorres or Subterraneous places. **1849** *Southey's Comm.-pl. Bk.* Ser. II. 473 They leave stones heaped over the Mattamores as marks. **1873** Tristram *Moab* vii. 123 Several very large domed cisterns or matamoros, which have been carefully cemented.

†**matte**[1]. *Obs.* In the trivial oath *by the matte*, ? alteration of *by the mass*. (Cf. MACK *sb.*[2])

a **1553** Udall *Royster D.* IV. vii. (Arb.) 75 By the matte but I will. *Ibid.* viii. (Arb.) 77 Come away, by the matte she is mankine.

matte[2] (mæt). *Metallurgy.* [a. F. *matte*.] An impure and unfinished metallic product of the smelting of various ores, esp. those of copper.

1839 Ure *Dict. Arts* 802 *Matte* is a crude black copper reduced . . from sulphur and other heterogeneous substances. **1884** C. G. W. Lock *Workshop Receipts* Ser. III. 59/2 This matte is termed 'white metal'. **1899** *Daily News* 13 June 4/4 They ask that Canada shall not impose a duty on nickel ore or nickel matte.

attrib. **1877** Raymond *Statist. Mines & Mining* 288 The employment of the method for the purpose of matte-smelting . . is objectionable on the ground that [etc.]. *Ibid.* 391 They are melted in the matte-furnace with rich gold ores.

matte[3] (mæt). *Cinemat.* Also **mat.** [Fr.] A mask (MASK *sb.*[3] 4 e) used to obscure or shade (part of) the image shown. Also *attrib.*

1938 *Motion Pict. Sound Engin.* (*Acad. Motion Pict. Arts & Sci.*) 39 A more recent procedure is to use a W-type mat which reduces the track width from the center as well as from both . . edges. **1948** Mencken *Amer. Lang.* Suppl. II. 699 *Matte shot*, a film made with a section blocked out, to be filled later on another set. **1949** W. H. Offenhauser *16-Mm. Sound Motion Pict.* xii. 382 A traveling matte . . is merely a film interposed at the gate between the light source and the image-bearing film that alters the light intensity in the manner of a neutral density film. *Ibid.* 549/2 Matte rolls are a pair of film rolls used as light modulators. **1959** W. S. Sharps *Dict. Cinematogr.* 110/2 *Matte box*, a box fitted to the front of a camera to hold mattes. The matte box frequently combines the functions of a lens hood and filter holder as well. **1960** O. Skilbeck *ABC of Film & TV* 84 *Matte*, a specially photographed Mask which . . leaves blanks which can be correspondingly filled with something else at a second printing; e.g. adding a false Background as though seen through a window. **1972** L. D. Giannetti *Understanding Movies* 73 Mattes are used to block out certain areas of the real scene where the animated drawings will appear in the finished print.

matte, variant of MATE *a. Obs.*, obs. f. MATÉ, var. MATT *a.*

matte, var. MATT *a.*

matted (ˈmætɪd), *ppl. a.*[1] [f. MAT *v.*[2] + -ED[1].] Dulled, deprived of lustre or gloss. (See senses of the vb.)

1823 Rutter *Fonthill* 15 Lights glazed with matted glass in lozenge lattice. **1865** *Price List of Joinery* 8 Front Doors . . glazed with matted glass. **1884** F. J. Britten *Watch & Clockm.* 173 The granular surface formed on watch plates and wheels prior to gilding is spoken of indifferently as matted or frosted. **1899** *Westm. Gaz.* 27 June 1/3 A fine silver-gilt Jacobean goblet . . with foliage and cone ornament on matted ground.

matted (ˈmætɪd), *ppl. a.*[2] [f. MAT *v.*[1] + -ED[1].]

1. Laid or spread with matting or mats.

1607 Middleton *Fam. Love* IV. i. 116 Like a horsekeeper in a lady's matted chamber at midnight. **1712** Steele *Spect.* No. 429 ¶12 He has chosen an Apartment with a matted Anti-chamber. **1852** Dickens *Bleak Ho.* i, The various solicitors . . ranged in a line, in a long matted well. **1883** Stevenson *Treas. Isl.* vi, The servant led us down a matted passage.

b. Formed of mats as a covering.

1720 De Foe *Capt. Singleton* viii. (1840) 141 We pitched our matted tents. **1841** J. L. Stephens *Centr. Amer.* II. iii. 47 The little matted tents of the market-women.

c. Made of plaited rushes. Of chairs, etc.: Rush-bottomed.

1692 Dryden *Cleomenes* Prol. 6 Who . . print our matted seats with dirty feet. **1720** *Lond. Gaz.* No. 5891/4 Tho. Smith, Citizen and Turner, of that Branch called a matted Chair-maker, is in want of Journeymen . . either for Matting, Turning, Joining or Carving, in the said matted Chair business. . . Tho. Smith maketh . . all sorts of matted Work, and fine mimick Wallnut-Tree. **1745** *De Foe's Eng. Tradesman* xxvi. (1841) I. 266 The ordinary matted chairs. **1777** W. Dalrymple *Trav. Sp. & Port.* xv, We find . . matted bottom chairs, in their principal rooms. **1833** Loudon *Encycl. Cottage Archit.* §2145 A child's chair . . having . . a matted seat.

2. Of vegetable growths, also of hair or other fibre: Tangled and interlaced, or covered with tangle.

1613 Purchas *Pilgrimage* (1614) 696 The places in their Winter . . covered with water, doe grow thicke and matted with abundance of little trees, herbes and plants. **1661** K. W. *Conf. Charac., High Constable* (1860) 36 His matted noddle is so stuft with the windy conceit of his mastership, that [etc.]. **1683** Moxon *Mech. Exerc., Printing* xxiv. ¶19 [He] Teizes his Wooll, by opening all the hard and almost matted Knots he finds in it. **1697** Dryden *Virg. Past.* IV. 36 Through the Matted Grass the liquid Gold shall creep. **1745** Collins *Ode Death Col. Ross* vii, Her matted tresses madly spread. **1749** Warton *Tri. Isis* 57 Cam meandering thro' the matted reeds. **1770** Goldsm. *Des. Vill.* 349 Those matted woods, where birds forget to sing. **1832** Lytton *Eugene A.* I. vi, The grass sprung up long and matted. **1865** Dickens *Mut. Fr.* I. i, Half savage as the man showed, with no covering on his matted head. **1877** Black *Green Past.* xlii, The matted underwood and the rank green grass.

b. In names of plants, as ***matted pink, thrift.***

1625 Bacon *Ess., Gardens* (Arb.) 558 Then Pincks, specially the Matted Pinck, and Cloue Gilly-flower. **1678** Phillips, *Matted*, an Epithete given to Plants when they grow, as if they were platted together, as Matted Pink, Matweed, &c. **1706** London & Wise *Retir'd Gard'ner* I. xxi. 98 Matted Pink. **1861** Miss Pratt *Flower. Pl.* IV. 254 Matted Thrift.

c. Compressed into the semblance of a mat.

1825 *Greenhouse Comp.* I. 168 Loosen the earth and matted roots. **1831** Willis *Poem Brown University* 175 Tender moss, and matted forest leaves. **1845** *Florist's Jrnl.* 148 The roots are very apt to get matted in the pots. **1849** Murchison *Siluria* xii. 295 Such Lower Coal . . had been often transported in large matted masses from the mouths of great rivers.

d. Covered with a dense growth.

1791 E. Darwin *Bot. Gard.* I. 79 By thee the plowshare rends the matted plain. **1818** Keats *Endym.* I. 151 His eye Steadfast upon the matted turf he kept. **1877** Bryant *Song of Sower* iv, The matted sward. **1881** M. Arnold *Westm. Abbey* ii, That new Minster in the matted fen.

e. *Path.*

1897 *Allbutt's Syst. Med.* IV. 121 The ascitic fluid is sometimes loculated between the matted intestines. **1899** *Ibid.* VI. 10 The matted valves may remain rigidly fixed.

3. Enclosed or wrapped in matting. Also with *up*.

1758 Gray *Let.* 2 Dec. *Wks.* (1884) II. 388 A wainscot Chest of Drawers, matted up. *Ibid.*, If the matted things fright you on the same account [*sc.* the danger of fire], the coverings may be taken off, and laid by in some dry place. **1798** *Hull Advertiser* 15 Dec. 2/1 For Sale, . . 10 tons Riga matted flax. **1812** J. Smyth *Pract. of Customs* (1821) 86 Flax. . . In Matted Bales, with thick ropes. **1855** Mrs. Gaskell *North & S.* xxvii, The matted-up currant bushes . . at the corner of the west-wall.

Hence **ˈmattedly** *adv.*, in a matted manner.

1894 Du Maurier *Trilby* I. 87 More greasily, mattedly unkempt than even a successful pianist has any right to be.

mattefelon, obs. form of MATFELLON.

matter (ˈmætə(r)), *sb.*[1] Forms: 3–4 materie, 4 matery, 4–5 matiere, mate(e)re, matire, -yr(e, 4–6 -ir, 4–7 mater, matier, (5 mateer, mattir, 6 mattier, mattar, *Sc.* maiter), 5– matter. [ME. *materie, matere, matiere*, a. OF. *matere, matiere* (mod.F. *matière*), ad. L. *māteria* (also *māteriēs*), building material, timber, hence stuff of which a thing is made, subject of discourse or consideration, also (in philosophical use) 'matter' in contradistinction to 'mind' or to 'form'.

It has been conjectured that L. *māteria* represents a prehistoric **dmāteria*, f. **dmā-* (cf. Doric Gr. νεο-δμᾱ-τος new-built) related to the Indo-germanic root **dem-*, **dom-* (occurring, e.g. in L. *domus* house and Eng. TIMBER). The primary sense continued to be prominent in late popular Latin: cf. Sp. *madera*, Pg. *madeira* wood, and the derivative F. *merrain* timber:—late L. *māteriāmen* (Lex Salica, etc.). The sense-development of the word in Latin was influenced by that of the Gr. ὕλη, of which it was the accepted equivalent in philosophical use. In the derived senses the Latin word has been adopted in all the Rom. langs.: Sp., Pg., It. *materia*, Roumanian *materie*.]

I. In purely physical applications.

1. a. The substance, or the substances collectively, out of which a physical object is made or of which it consists; constituent material; also, a particular kind of substance serving as material. Now only with implication of sense 3 or 5.

1340 *Ayenb.* 152 Þet hi [*sc.* þe speche] by y-weȝe ase guode moneye . . þet is þet hi by of guode matire, ase of guod metal and of guode sseppe þet is of guode manere y-speke. **1390** Gower *Conf.* I. 36 If a man were Mad al togedre of o matiere Withouten interrupcioun. **1483** Caxton *Gold. Leg.* 195 b, To assemble matere wherof myght be made and edefyed a chyrche. **1540–1** Elyot *Image Gov.* 15 He vsed no golde but pure beryll and christall, and other like mattier to drinke in. **1573** G. Harvey *Common-pl. Bk.* (1884) 25 As there is matter of poison to the spider where wuld be matter of honi to the bee. **1604** E. G[rimstone] *D'Acosta's Hist. Indies* III. xxi. 187 Vpon that coast there rise no vapors, sufficient to engender raine for want of matter. **1617** Moryson *Itin.* I. 89 The glasse makers of Venice . . have a more noble matter, and thereof make much better glasse than we can. **1659** Leak *Waterwks.* 33 The matter of the Summer which ought to be of Oak. **1709** Steele *Tatler* No. 137 ¶13 In all Operas . . where it thunders and lightens . . the Matter of the said Lightning is to be of the finest Rosin. **1728** tr. *Newton's Treat. Syst. World* 1 marg., That the matter of the Heavens is fluid. **1848** Mill *Pol. Econ.* I. i. §1 (1876) 15 The matter of the globe is not an inert recipient of forms . . impressed by human hands.

†**b.** Timber, wood. *Obs. rare.* [A Latinism.]

c **1420** *Pallad. on Husb.* II. 437 Nowe matere is to falle . . For pale, or hegge, or hous, or shippe.

†**2.** A substance used or acted upon in a physical operation; *Obs.* (merged in 3).

c **1375** *Sc. Leg. Saints* xxxii. (*Justin*) 735 [He gert] . . þarein be done blak pic & . . brynstane bla, & vndir it a fyre gert ma, til þat mater wes moltyne thyne. *c* **1386** Chaucer *Can. Yeom. T.* 217 The care and wo That we hadde in our matires sublyming. *c* **1460** *Bk. Quintessence* 4 Þis is þe watri mater

fro which is drawe oure quinta essencia. **1530** PALSGR. 666/2, I make the printe of a thyng in any mater or stuffe. **1635** N. CARPENTER *Geog. Del.* I. iii. 54 Electricall bodies drawe and attract not without rubbing and stirring vp of the matter first. **1680** MOXON *Mech. Exerc.* 175 As there is different Matter or Substance to be Turned, so there is also different Ways..to be used in Turning each different Matter. **1687** A. LOVELL tr. *Thevenot's Trav.* II. 85 They beat this Stuff with one hand..stooping at every blow, and nothing but the flat side of the Club hits the matter. **1797** *Encycl. Brit.* (ed. 3) VII. 772/1 (*Glass*), He takes up a small ball of matter, which sticks to the end of the tube by constantly turning it.

3. In wider sense: Used as a vague designation for any physical substance not definitely particularized, e.g. applied in *Physiology* to the fluids of the body, excrementitious products, etc. Often with qualifying adj., as in ***colouring***, ***extractive***, ***fæcal***, etc. ***matter***.

grey matter, ***white matter*** (of the brain): see the adjs.

c **1400** *Lanfranc's Cirurg.* 93 Cankre..comeþ of a wounde yuel heelid, to whom comeþ a malancolient mater rotid. **1604** E. G[RIMSTONE] *D'Acosta's Hist. Indies* III. xxv. 196 Ther are places in th' earth, whose vertue is to draw vaporous matter, and to convert it into water. **1608** TOPSELL *Serpents* (1658) 725 There is no part of the Frog so medicinable as is the bloud, called also the matter or the juyce, and the humor of the Frog. **1664** EVELYN *Sylva* i. 16 Oaks bear also a knur, full of a Cottony matter. **1797** *Encycl. Brit.* (ed. 3) X. 684/2 The earthy and stony substances in which these metallic matters are inveloped. **1813** SIR H. DAVY *Agric. Chem.* (1814) 18 Animal matters are the soonest destroyed by the Operation of air, heat and light. Vegetable substances yield more slowly. **1825** J. NICHOLSON *Operat. Mechanic* 737 Mix these matters in a large iron or copper pan. **1851** LONGF. *Gold. Leg.* VI. *School Salerno*, To report if any confectionarius Mingles his drugs with matters various. **1891** *Law Times* XCII. 94/1 Milk which on analysis proved to be deficient in fatty matter to the extent of 33 per cent. **1897** *Allbutt's Syst. Med.* III. 794 An obstruction to the passage of matter along the intestines. **1899** *Ibid.* VIII. 730 Hyperidrosis..soaking the boots and stockings with a stinking matter.

4. *spec.* (= *corrupt matter*.) Purulent discharge, pus. [So F. *matière*.]

[*c* **1400** *Lanfranc's Cirurg.* 52 Poudre of mirtilles..castiþ to þe wounde þe corrupt mater þat is in þe place þat is brusid.] *c* **1420** *St. Etheldreda* in Horstm. *Altengl. Leg.* (1881) 293 A gret swellyng abouȝt my throte þer is,..Were hit ybroke & þe mater ouȝt y-renne,..To my body..myche eysse hit wolde do. **1486** *Bk. St. Albans* c vij, Kutt theys botches with an knyfe and let owte the mater of theym. **1523** FITZHERB. *Husb.* G 5 b, A glaunder, whan it breaketh, is lyke matter. **1641** FRENCH *Distill.* vi. (1651) 191 It..expells the matter of a carbuncle by sweat. **1722** *Lond. Gaz.* No. 6045/8 The Matter taken on a Person who has had the Small Pox by Inoculation. **1885** W. ROBERTS *Pract. Treat. Urinary Dis.* (ed. 4) III. v, She began to pass considerable quantities of what she considered 'matter' with the urine.

5. a. Physical or corporeal substance in general (of which the chemical elements and their compounds are the separate kinds), contradistinguished from immaterial or incorporeal substance (spirit, soul, mind), and from qualities, actions, or conditions.

a **1626** BACON *New Atl.* (1900) 24 Wee maintaine a Trade, not for Gold..Nor any other Commodity of Matter. **1677** GALE *Crt. Gentiles* II. IV. 307 Metaphysic mater..without the least physic extension or mater. **1690** LOCKE *Hum. Und.* IV. x. §10 Matter,..by its own strength, cannot produce in itself so much as motion. **1692** BENTLEY *Boyle Lect.* ii. 40 Matter and Motion cannot think. *a* **1721** KEILL *Maupertius' Diss.* (1734) 6 In order..for the former to be in æquilibrio with the latter, it would be necessary for it to contain a greater quantity of Matter; it ought to be longer. **1759** JOHNSON *Rasselas* xlvii, Matter is inert, senseless, and lifeless. **1802** PALEY *Nat. Theol.* xxiv. (1819) 397 The essential superiority of spirit over matter. **1846** SIR W. HAMILTON *Reid's Wks.* 935 Mind and matter exist for us only as they are known by us. **1875** JOWETT *Plato* (ed. 2) IV. 271 All our applications of mathematics are applications of our ideas of space to matter. **1885** WATSON & BURBURY *Electr. & Magn.* I. 46 Let there be at *O* a particle of matter of mass *m*.

†**b.** ***subtile matter*** [tr. *materia subtilis*]: the name given by Descartes to a fluid which he supposed to fill the whole of space. *Obs.*

1717 PRIOR *Alma* III. 55 Deny Des-cart his subtil matter, You leave him neither fire nor water.

II. *Metaph.*, *Logic*, etc.: contrasted with *form*.

6. *Philos.* **a.** In Aristotelian and scholastic use: That component of the essence of any thing or being which has bare existence, but which requires the addition of a particular 'form' (see FORM *sb.* 4 a) to constitute the thing or being as determinately existent. Also †***matter subject***: see SUBJECT *a.*

c **1374** CHAUCER *Boeth.* v. pr. iv. (Morris) 164 Þe wit comprehendiþ fro wiþ outen furþe þe figure of þe body of þe man þat is establissed in þe matere subiect [L. *in subjecta materia*]. But the ymaginacioun comprehendith only the figure with owte the matere. **138.** WYCLIF *Sel. Wks.* III. 257 Matere, and forme, and ende of her graunt. *c* **1385** CHAUCER *L.G.W.* 1582 As matier apetitith forme alwey. **1398** TREVISA *Barth. De P.R.* x. ii. (1495) 372 Matere is neuer seen wythout fourme. **1413** [see FORM *sb.* 4 a]. **1561** T. HOBY tr. *Castiglione's Courtyer* III. (1577) O iij b, It is the opinion of most wise men that man is likened to the Forme, the woman to the Mattier. **1586** T. B. *La Primaud. Fr. Acad.* I. 162 Aristotle saith, that nature in one respect is said to be the first and chiefe matter subject of every thing that hath being. **1607** WALKINGTON *Opt. Glass* 46 It is that will..that keepes a comely decorum in observing the time, the place, the matter subject, and the every singular circumstance. **1625** N. CARPENTER *Geog. Del.* I. i. (1635) 7 The principles whereof the Spheare is composed are two; viz. Matter, and Forme. **1634** CANNE *Necess. Separ.* (1849) 197 Piscator affirms 'The matter of a particular church to be a company of believers'. **1651** HOBBES (*title*) Leviathan, or the Matter, Forme, and Power of a Commonwealth. **1727–52** CHAMBERS *Cycl.* s.v., Aristotle makes three principles, matter, form, and privation. **1845** STODDART in *Encycl. Metrop.* I. 5/1 By the *form*..of language..we mean its signification; by the *matter* of language we mean the sound of words in speech [etc.].

†**b.** The result of the first creative fiat was often viewed by the scholastics as consisting in the production of matter without form. Hence Bacon speaks of 'the matter' as equivalent to 'Chaos'. *Obs.*

a **1300** *Cursor M.* 348 Þe mater first þer of he mad, þat es þe elementis to sai þat first scapless al samen lay. *a* **1340** HAMPOLE *Psalter* xxxii. 9 He sayd..& þai ere made, þat is, þai ere fourmyd of vnfourmyd matere. **1625** BACON *Ess.*, *Truth* (Arb.) 500 First he breathed Light vpon the Face of the Matter or Chaos.

c. ***first matter*** (= L. *materia prima*, Gr. ἡ πρώτη ὕλη): cf. the quots.

1619 PURCHAS *Microcosm.* lviii. 564 Vncreated Chaos, or Hyla, or first Matter. **1667** MILTON *P.L.* v. 47 One first matter all, Indu'd with various forms, various degrees Of substance. *a* **1687** H. MORE *App. to De Philos. Cabbal.* viii. (1713) 183 That Hyle or first Matter is mere Possibility of Being, according to Aristotle.

fig. **1647** N. BACON *Disc. Govt. Eng.* I. xl. (1739) 60 Though the Saxons were in name our first matter.

d. In Kantian and subsequent use, applied to that element of knowledge that is supplied by sensation, regarded apart from the 'form' which it receives from the categories of the understanding.

1838 tr. *Kant's Critick of Pure Reason* 90 Experience, which contains two very dissimilar elements, namely, a *Matter* for cognition arising out of the senses, and a certain Form to order it, arising from the internal source of pure intuition and thought.

7. *Theol.* (Sacraments are said to have matter and form: see FORM *sb.* 4 b.)

c **1315** SHOREHAM *Poems* i. 366 Ich mot of þis sacrement ȝou telle þe materie. *Ibid.* 1170 Þe matyre of þis sacrement Hys ryȝt þe oylle allone. **1548–9** (Mar.) *Bk. Com. Prayer*, With what thyng, or what matter they dyd Baptise the childe. *a* **1600** HOOKER *Eccl. Pol.* VI. iv. §3 Surely to admit the matter as a part, and not to admit the form, hath small congruity with reason. **1883** *Cath. Dict.* (1897) 812/2 The Scotists, who make absolution both the form and matter of Penance.

8. *Logic.* The particular content of a proposition or syllogism as distinguished from its form.

1697 [see MATERIAL *a.* 2]. **1827** WHATELY *Elem. Logic* II. ii. §3 (ed. 2) 81, 82 'All islands (or some islands) are surrounded by water', must be true, because the matter is necessary:..again, 'some islands are fertile', 'some are not fertile', are both true, because it is Contingent Matter. **1855** ABP. THOMSON *Laws Th.* Introd. 19 The matter of any representation is that part of it which with reference to any given law is non-formal. **1864** BOWEN *Logic* vi. 149 In respect to their Matter, both the Premises and the Conclusion may be false.

III. Material of thought, speech, or action.

9. Material for expression; something to say; fact or thought as material for a writing or speech. Also †***matter subject***: see SUBJECT *a.*

a **1300** *Cursor M.* 93 Mater fynd ȝe large and brade? Þof rimes fele of hir be made, Qua-sa will of hyr fayrnes spell, Find he sal inogh to tell. **1340** *Ayenb.* 118 Ous be-houeþ to spekene mid greate reuerence of zuo heȝe matiere ase of þe zeuen holy yefþes of þe holy gost. *c* **1450** HOLLAND *Houlate* 35, I haue mekle matir in metir to gloss Of ane nothir sentence. **1543** LELAND *N.-Y. Gift* in Strype *Eccl. Mem.* (1721) I. App. cxviii. 331, I have matter at plenty already prepared to this purpose, that is to say, to wryte an hystory. **1586** T. B. *La Primaud. Fr. Acad.* I. 28 We will intreat of the passions of the soule, as of our chiefe matter subject. **1600** SHAKS. *A.Y.L.* II. i. 68, I loue to cope him in these sullen fits, For then he's full of matter. **1605** BACON *Adv. Learn.* I. iv. §3 Here therefore, is the first distemper of learning, when men studie words and not matter. **1611** BIBLE *Job* xxxii. 18 For I am full of matter, the spirit within me constraineth me. **1634** W. TIRWHYT *Balzac's Lett.* I. 43, I will here conclude, rather out of discretion than for want of matter. **1697** DRYDEN *Virg. Georg.* III. 455 The mean Matter which my Theme affords, To embellish with Magnificence of Words. **1709** STEELE *Tatler* No. 150 ¶8 Whether they have Matter to talk of or not. **1878** HUXLEY *Physiogr.* Pref. 6 A clear line of demarcation, both as to matter and method.

†**10.** The subject of a book or discourse; a theme, topic, subject of exposition. *Obs.*

c **1330** R. BRUNNE *Chron.* (1810) 321 Turne we tille our matere, & on our gest to hie. *c* **1330** *Arth. & Merl.* 663 (Kölbing) Al hou, y no may nouȝt tellen, ywis, Mi matery wer to long. *a* **1340** HAMPOLE *Psalter* Prol. 4 The matere of this boke is crist & his spouse. *c* **1450** *Merlin* xxvii. 503 But now repeireth the tale to his mater that he hath lefte for to telle this thinge. *a* **1568** ASCHAM *Scholem.* I. (Arb.) 86 But to my matter, as I began. **1589** PUTTENHAM *Eng. Poesie* (Arb.) 161 It behooueth the maker or Poet to follow the nature of his subiect, that is if his matter be high and loftie that the stile be so to. **1590** SPENSER *F.Q.* III. iv. 3 Thee, O Queene! the matter of my song. **1625** A. GILL *Sacr. Philos.* Pref., Raimund de Sabunde though his writings be easie and quicke, yet his matiers are scattered. **1704** PRIOR *Let. Despreaux* 54 How hard is it for me To make my matter and my verse agree!

11. a. The substance of a book, speech, or the like; that which a spoken or written composition contains in respect of the facts or ideas expressed; often as opposed to the form of words ('manner') in which the subject is presented.

c **1384** CHAUCER *H. Fame* II. 353 Hard langage and hard matere Is encombrous for to here. **1592** A. DAY *Eng. Secretary* II. (1625) 62 This invective seemeth to have been over-sharpe in the matter but not in manner. **1592** SHAKS. *Rom. & Jul.* III. ii. 83 Was euer booke containing such vile matter So fairely bound? **1641** J. JACKSON *True Evang. T.* I. 5 This Text..is rich as the High Priests pectoral both for words and matter. **1695** DRYDEN *Parall. Poetry & Painting* Ess. (ed. Ker) II. 123 Though I cannot much commend the style, I must needs say, there is somewhat in the matter. **1741** WATTS *Improv. Mind* iv. Wks. (1813) 34 If the matter of a book be really valuable and deserving. **1769** BLACKSTONE *Comm.* IV. xi. 150 It is immaterial with respect to the essence of a libel, whether the matter of it be true or false. **1800** COLQUHOUN *Comm. Thames* Pref., The importance of the Work..can only be appreciated by a..Review of the various matter it contains. **1871** MORLEY *Voltaire* (1886) 9 He was always serious in meaning and laborious in matter. **1885** *Nature* 19 Mar. 453/1 When we look from the manner to the matter of his speech, we are unable to bestow such unqualified praise.

†**b.** Sense, substance (as opposed to nonsense or trifling). *Obs.*

1599 SHAKS. *Much Ado* II. i. 344, I was borne to speake all mirth, and no matter. **1605** —— *Lear* IV. vi. 178 O matter, and impertinency mixt, Reason in Madnesse.

†**c.** ***there is (a) matter in it***: some importance attaches to it. *Obs.*

1549 LATIMER *4th Serm. bef. Edw. VI* (Arb.) 110 If Salomon sayd it, there is a matter in it. **1604** SHAKS. *Oth.* III. iv. 139 There's matter in't indeed, if he be angry. **1611** —— *Wint. T.* IV. iv. 874 To him will I present them, there may be matter in it.

†**12.** That with which a science, art, law, etc. has to do; that which belongs to a subject of study; the subject-matter of a study. *Obs.*

a **1300** *Cursor M.* 28868 We find..þat almus, Es þe best biginging Of alle penances..And for þer mater es gode to knau, of almus sal i for-þer drau. **1387** TREVISA *Higden* (Rolls) IV. 403 Þis Seneca..hadde..greet knowleche of þynges, and wel nyh al matir of study [L. *omnem studiorum materiam*] of witte and of sciens. **1390** GOWER *Conf.* III. 89 Of Arsmitique the matiere Is that of which a man mai liere, What Algorisme in nombre amonteth. *c* **1391** CHAUCER *Astrol.* II. §4 Natheles, theise ben obseruauncez of iudicial matiere & rytes of payens, in which my spirit ne hath no feith. **1586** FERNE *Blaz. Gentrie* 149 The matter of all armes ..is seuered into the same three parts that the Embleme is. **1594** HOOKER *Eccl. Pol.* I. xv. §3 The subject or matter of laws in general is thus far forth constant: which matter is that for the ordering whereof laws were instituted.

13. Ground, reason, or cause for doing or being something: †**a.** Followed by an *inf.* or *clause*, or *simply*. Often qualified by an adj., as *good*, *much*, *little*. ***to seek matter***: to seek a pretext or occasion. *Obs.*

1340 *Ayenb.* 136 He [*sc.* þe milde herte] ne wille nenne zuo kuead,..þet he ne can draȝe materie god uor to herie. *c* **1375** *Cursor M.* 20080 (Fairf.) Þai me do alle þis shame, wiþ-oute mater bere I blame. **1375** BARBOUR *Bruce* III. 301 He.. fenȝeit to mak bettir cher, Then he had matir to, be fer. *c* **1400** *Destr. Troy* 2089 Thow ges matir to men mony day after, fforto speke of þi spede. *c* **1450** BURGH *Secrees* 2236 He wyl redily Seeke mateer, And soone consente to thyn destruccioun. **1532** CROMWELL in Merriman *Life & Lett.* (1902) I. 347 So his high pleasure is that ye shall do if ye see good matier to bere it. **1573** *Satir. Poems Reform.* xli. 81 Ȝit hes thow mater for to murne. **1604** E. G[RIMSTONE] *D'Acosta's Hist. Indies* II. x. 103 Having..shewed, that the burning Zone is much subiect vnto raine, it appears that there is matter in it, to temper the violence of the heat. **1607** SHAKS. *Cor.* III. iii. 58 What is the matter. That..I am so dishonour'd, that [etc.]. **1630** B. JONSON *Magn. Lady* III. iv, I have done the part of a friend..In furnishing your fear with matter first, If you have any; or, if you dare fight, To.. comfort your resolution. **1644** MILTON *Divorce* II. iii. 38 This is the matter why Interpreters..will not consent it to be a true story.

b. Const. *for*, *of*. Now only: What occasions or is fitted to occasion some specified feeling: chiefly *predicative*.

c **1420** *Ploughmans Prayer* in Foxe *A. & M.* (1583) 400/1 Here is much matter of sorow, to see [etc.]. **1509** FISHER *Wks.* (1876) 305 Yf she had contynued in this worlde, she sholde dayly haue herde & sene mater and cause of sorowe. **1625** BACON *Ess.*, *Envy* (Arb.) 512 Neither can he, that mindeth but his own Businesse, finde much matter for Enuy. **1667** MILTON *P.L.* IX. 951 Matter of scorne, not to be given the Foe. **1712** M. HENRY *Daily Comm. God* Wks. 1855 I. iii. 235 Whenever we go to bed, we shall not want matter for praise, if we did not want a heart. **1726** SHELVOCKE *Voy. World* Pref. 22 Making it a sufficient matter for his contempt of any man, that he had served in the navy. **1819** SCOTT *Ivanhoe* i, Mynheer Calf..is Saxon when he requires tendance, and takes a Norman name when he becomes matter of enjoyment. **1826** DISRAELI *Viv. Grey* v. xiii, The acquisition of which has been, to me, matter of great sorrow. **1865–6** TENNYSON '*I stood on a Tower*,' in *Gd. Words* IX. 144 Science enough and exploring..Matter enough for deploring, But aught that is worth the knowing? **1884** *Manch. Exam.* 17 June 5/2 The annual migration of the Viceroy to Simla is an old matter of complaint. **1896** A. E. HOUSMAN *Shropshire Lad* l, 'Tis sure small matter for wonder If sorrow is with one still.

c. with attributive sb. prefixed.

1676 W. ALLEN *Addr. Nonconf.* 121 They are prayer matter, and thanksgiving matter.

†**14.** Means of doing something. *Obs.*

1580 LYLY *Euphues* (Arb.) 265 They perceiued a kinde of courtly Maiestie in the minde of their host, though he wanted matter to shew it in his house. **1583** GOLDING *Calvin on Deut.* xv. 89 In all the benefites which wee haue receiued of God we must consider in what taking wee had bene if wee had gone without them: and wee shall haue

matter good store wherewith to doe that if we are not wilfully blinde.

†**15.** Material cause; element or elements of which something consists or out of which it is developed. *Obs.*

1570 BILLINGSLEY *Euclid* VII. ii. 184 Vnitie is as it were the very matter of number. **1581** J. BELL *Haddon's Answ. Osor.* 258 Voyde of all matter of probabilitie. **1607–12** BACON *Ess., Of Seditions* (Arb.) 398 Let vs..speake of the Materialls, and the causes, and the remedyes. The matter of seditions is of two kindes, Much povertye and much discontent. *a* **1619** FOTHERBY *Atheom.* II. x. §3 (1622) 304 His vncompounded simplicitie is the true matter of his Vnitie. **1751** HARRIS *Hermes* Wks. (1841) 208 To know the nature and powers of the human voice, is in fact to know the matter or common subject of language. **1825** BENTHAM *Ration. Reward* 237 There are many things which may constitute part of the matter of wealth, which, when taken separately or in small quantities, would hardly be called wealth.

16. a. In vague sense, nearly equivalent to 'things', 'something'; esp. with qualifying words (adj. or sb. prefixed, or *of* with *sb.* following), things or something of a specified kind, involving or related to a specified thing.

1449 *Rolls of Parlt.* V. 148/2 It is mater of Parlement longyng to the Kynges Highnesse. **1586** A. DAY *Eng. Secretary* II. (1625) 26 The first [Letter] whereof shall be for matter of unkindnesse. **1594** HOOKER *Eccl. Pol.* II. vii. §2 That in matter of fact there is some credite to be giuen to the testimonie of man, but not in matter of opinion and iudgement. **1599** SHAKS. *Hen. V*, v. ii. 365 The King of France hauing any occasion to write for matter of Graunt. **1601** B. JONSON *Poetaster* v. i, I haue Matter of danger, and state, to impart to Cæsar. **1605** BACON *Adv. Learn.* II. ii §11 The Chronicle..red before Ahassuerus..contained matter of affaires. **1651** G. W. tr. *Cowel's Inst.* 198 This is rather matter of fact then of Law. **1660** JER. TAYLOR *Ductor Dubit.* III. v. Rule iv *heading*, The Fathers power does not extend to matter of Religion. **1788** G. WHITE *Selborne* v, This must have been matter of mere accident. **1828** SCOTT *F.M. Perth* xiii, I have matter for thy private ear. **1873** M. ARNOLD *Lit. & Dogma* (1876) 388 Certainly in the Gospels there is plenty of matter to call out our feelings. **1884** *Manch. Exam.* 29 May 4/7 That it is eminently desirable to attain this end is not now matter of dispute.

b. *spec.* in *Law.* Something which is to be tried or proved; statements or allegations which come under the consideration of the court. ***matter in deed, matter of record, nude matter*** (see quots.).

1532 ST. GERMAN *Doctor & Stud.* II. liv. 138 It is nat alleged in the Indytement by matter in dede that he had suche weapon. **1607** COWEL *Interpr.* s.v., Mater in deede seemeth to be nothing else, but a truth to be proued, though not by any Record: and mater of Record, is that which may be proued by some Record. **1706** PHILLIPS (ed. Kersey) s.v., *Nude Matter*, is a naked Allegation of a thing done, to be prov'd only by Witnesses, and not by a Record, or other Specialty in Writing under Seal. **1727–51** CHAMBERS *Cycl.*, *Foreign Matter*, in law, is matter triable in another county; or matter done in another county. **1766** BLACKSTONE *Comm.* II. 344 Assurances by matter of record are such as do not entirely depend on the act or consent of the parties themselves. **1797** *Encycl. Brit.* (ed. 3) IX. 413/2 He may plead the general issue, and give the special matter in evidence. **1853** STOCQUELER *Milit. Encycl.*, *Matter*,..in reference to court-martials..the specific charges which are brought against a prisoner, and to which the president and members must strictly confine themselves.

†**c.** ***matter in deed***, also (? orig.) ***by matter in deed***: in point of fact, as a matter of fact; truly, really. ***matter in fact***: a matter of fact. *Obs.*

15.. *New Notbroune Mayd* 144 in Hazl. *E.P.P.* III. 7 Matter in dede, My sydes dyde blede For man. **1530** PALSGR. 833/1 By matter in dede, *par effet.* **1533** tr. *Erasmus' Expos. Comm. Crede* 78 The Iewes do graunte..that Iesus was crucified verye matter in dede. **1621** ELSING *Debates Ho. Lords* (Camden) 113 The question whether this cause had a sufficient hearinge, or noe, which is matter in facte.

17. a. Things printed or written; often with qualification, e.g. ***printed, manuscript, type-written matter.*** In *Printing* applied *techn.* to (*a*) the body of a printed work, as distinguished from the titles, headings, etc.; in newspapers, the general contents as distinguished from the advertisements; (*b*) type set up; (*c*) manuscript prepared for printing, 'copy'.

1683 MOXON *Mech. Exerc., Printing* xxii. ⁋5 He Sets the Title of the Chapter or Section in a..different Character than his Matter is Set in. *Ibid.* xxiii, The like mark he makes in Matter and Margin if two Letters are Transpos'd. *Ibid.* 386 *Open Matter.* Full of Breaks and Whites. **1824** J. JOHNSON *Typogr.* II. xviii. 588 A new mode in the arrangement of the matter. **1838** MRS. CARLYLE *Lett.* I. 106 We have printed half the matter. **1875** [see *live matter*, LIVE *a.* 9]. **1886–94** SPENCER *Autobiog.* I. xxxiii. 512 Matter which has been revised in manuscript, and again revised in proof. **1887, 1890** [see FACE *v.* 8 c].

b. (*postal*) ***matter***: whatever may be sent by post.

1891 *Century Dict.* s.v. *First-class*, First-class matter, in the postal system of the United States, matter which is in writing, or sealed against inspection. *Ibid.* s.v. *Second-class*, Second-class matter,..mail matter consisting of newspapers and other periodical publications. *Ibid.* s.v. *Third-class.* **1896** *Strand Mag.* 338/2 [Letters and other] postal matter, such as book parcels, post-cards, newspapers, circulars, telegrams, etc.

18. Idiomatic phrases. **a.** ***it makes no matter***, later ***it is*** (occas. †***skills***) ***no matter*** = it is of no consequence or importance; now often with ellipsis of the vb., ***no matter***, also ***what matter..?*** Often with dependent clause or an interrogative pronoun or adv. used *ellipt.* †(***it is***) ***no matter for***: there is no importance attaching to, (the thing in question) does not matter. Also with mixed constr. †***it is not a (one) farthing matter.***

1478 [see MAKE *v.*[1] 25]. **153.** TINDALE *Expos. Matt. v–vii.* (? 1550) 61 What mater maketh it, yf I speake wordes whych I vnderstand not? *c* **1550** BALE *K. Johan* (Camden) 14 *N.* To the church, I trust, ye wyll be obedyent. *K. J.* No mater to yow whether I be so or no. **1576** FLEMING *Panopl. Epist.* 128 My behauiour hathe not deserued, any such doggishe dealing: but makes it any great matter? **1591** SHAKS. *Two Gent.* III. i. 334 *Sp.* Item, she doth talke in her sleepe. *La.* It's no matter for that, so shee sleepe not in her talke. *Ibid.* II. vii. 66 No matter who's displeas'd, when you are gone. **1609** DEKKER *Guls Horne-bk.* vii. 33 How course soeuer the stuffe be, tis no matter so it hold fashion. **1634** SIR T. HERBERT *Trav.* 45 No great matter where. **1670** in *Cosin's Corr.* (Surtees) II. 251 It skills no matter what Neile's atturney said to you. **1678** BUNYAN *Pilgr.* I. 39 So be we get into the way, what's matter which way we get in? **1693** CONGREVE *Old Bach.* IV. xv, *Bell.* My patch, my patch. *Læt.* ..No matter for your patch. **1712–13** SWIFT *Jrnl. to Stella* 3 Mar., Tis not a farthing matter her death, I think. *a* **1774** GOLDSM. *Surv. Exp. Philos.* (1776) I. 351 But no matter for the tides in the moon; it is very well if they have satisfactorily explained the tides upon earth. **1802** MAR. EDGEWORTH *Moral T.* (1816) I. xix. 169 'He has lost the key of the trunk ..' 'No matter; we can break it open'. **1862** SPENCER *First Princ.* I. iii. §21 (1875) 66 After no matter how great a progress in the colligation of facts. **1875** JOWETT *Plato* (ed. 2) I. 18 But what matter..from whom I heard this?

b. †***to make much (no) matter of***: to make much (nothing) of (*obs.*). ***to make a matter***: to make a fuss or to-do.

a **1586** MONTGOMERIE *Misc. Poems* iii. 19 For men of merit sho [*sc.* Fortune] no mater maks. *a* **1649** WINTHROP *New Engl.* (1853) I. 175 Much matter was made of this. **1893** STEVENSON *Catriona* 82 Because you said a word too much in a friend's ear..to make such a matter!

IV. A thing, affair, concern; corresponding to L. *res*, which it is often employed to render.

19. a. An event, circumstance, fact, question, state or course of things, etc. which may be an object of consideration or practical concern; a subject, affair, business.

a **1225** *Ancr. R.* 270 Of þis ilke materie ich spec muchel þeruppe. *c* **1386** CHAUCER *Wife's Prol.* 836 Lo, goode men, a flie and eek a frere Woln falle in every dissche and matiere. **1411** *Rolls of Parlt.* III. 650/1 He knoweth wel that in the matier on hym surmetted by the sayd Bille, he ne hath noght born hym as he sholde hav doon. *c* **1450** *Merlin* vii. 114, I praye yow,..that ye will me counseile in this matere. **1560** DAUS tr. *Sleidane's Comm.* Ded. A 2, To judge by matters past, what shalbe the consequent, and end of things to come. **1611** BIBLE *Acts* xix. 39 But if yee enquire any thing concerning other matters, it shalbe determined in a lawfull assembly. **1625** BACON *Ess.*, *Truth* (Arb.) 499 One of the later Schoole of the Grecians examineth the matter, and is at a stand [etc.]. **1710** SWIFT *Jrnl. to Stella* 12 Oct., He..then falls on his sword; and, to make the matter sure, at the same time discharges a pistol through his own head. **1743** BULKELEY & CUMMINS *Voy. S. Seas* 73 Upon this we dropt the Matter, and began to discourse concerning the Provisions. **1768** STERNE *Sent. Journ.* (1778) I. 1 They order, said I, this matter better in France. **1802** MAR. EDGEWORTH *Moral T.* (1816) I. xiii. 105 The brewer cut the matter short, by saying, he had not time to argue. **1842** BORROW *Bible in Spain* xxviii, To mend the matter, the hostess was a most intolerable scold and shrew. **1856** FROUDE *Hist. Eng.* (1858) I. ii. 154 In default of help from Rome, he would lay the matter before parliament. **1883** *Manch. Exam.* 24 Oct. 4/6 One of the leading matters under consideration was the report of the Ecclesiastical Commission. **1887** E. STUART *In His Grasp* iii. 39, I tried to lead the conversation to personal matters.

b. with possessive (or equivalent): An affair or business specially belonging to some person or persons; (one's) cause, concern, or affair. ? *Obs.*

In later use app. only *collect. plural.*

c **1350** *Will. Palerne* 613, I wold meng al mi mater ȝif I miȝt for schame. *c* **1386** CHAUCER *Melib.* ⁋775. 2931 We putten..al our matere and cause al hoolly in your goode wil. *c* **1412** HOCCLEVE *De Reg. Princ.* 1794 Lordes han for to done So mych for hem-self, þat my mateere Out of hir mynde slippith away soone. *c* **1460** FORTESCUE *Abs. & Lim. Mon.* xv. (1885) 145 Thai were so occupied with thair owne maters, and with the maters off thair kynne,..þat thai entendet but litle..to þe kynges maters. **1503** HAWES *Examp. Virt.* XII. 234 By me your mater shall be well sped. **1530** PALSGR. 473/2 If thou se my lerned counsayle in Westmynster hall, call upon them to remember my mater agaynst Bulkyn [Fr. *mon proces contre Bulkyn*]. *a* **1568** ASCHAM *Scholem.* I. (Arb.) 83 Though, for their priuate matters they can follow, fawne, and flatter noble Personages. **1612** BREREWOOD *Lang. & Relig.* xv. 157 You may see them ..in Possevins book of the matters of Moscovia. **1625** BACON *Ess.*, *Envy* (Arb.) 512 To know much of other Mens Matters. *a* **1657** MURE *Psalm* xxi. 2 Lord, in thy strength the King sall joy;..To his minde Thow makst his maters goe. **1837** T. HOOK *Jack Brag* v, Take my advice, Jack,..try them both. Manage your matters well—lead them both on. **1857** BORROW *Rom. Rye* xi. 74 Let the matters of my sister and Jasper Petulengro alone, brother.

c. *pl.* (without article or qualification): Events, affairs, circumstances, etc., understood to refer to a particular occasion, but not further specified.

1570 SIR H. SIDNEY *Let.* in *Life of Sir P. Carew* (1857) 241 Thomond matters have gone verie leisurelie on. **1598** SHAKS. *Merry W.* I. i. 79 If matters grow to your likings. *a* **1649** WINTHROP *New Eng.* (1853) I. 369 At Providence matters went after the old manner. **1671** MILTON *S.A.* 1348 Matters now are strain'd Up to the highth, whether to hold or break. **1699** T. BROWN in *R. L'Estrange's Erasmus Colloq.* (1725) 390, I will take a proper occasion to discourse matters with your Husband. **1760–72** H. BROOKE *Fool of Qual.* (1809) IV. 52, I will bring you to her as a stranger, and so you may bring matters about. **1769** BLACKSTONE *Comm.* IV. 351 This seems to be carrying matters too far. **1868** *Pall Mall G.* 9 Dec. 10 Matters are very different in France. **1879** *Cassell's Techn. Educ.* IV. 235/2 A state of matters which.. was..attended with heavy loss to this country.

d. In *plural* sometimes used vaguely of concrete things. ? *Obs.*

1709 HEARNE *Collect.* (O.H.S.) II. 291 Which MS[t]. he has been pleas'd to give to the writer of these matters. **1743** BULKELEY & CUMMINS *Voy. S. Seas* 207 That we did not want great Matters, only barely enough to support Life. **1760–72** H. BROOKE *Fool of Qual.* (1809) IV. 50 After a short repast of some small matters. **1824** SCOTT *St. Ronan's* ii, She [the landlady] retired after these acts of hospitality, and left the stranger to enjoy in quiet the excellent matters which she had placed before him. **1826** DISRAELI *Viv. Grey* v. iv, Cups, balls, and rings, and other mysterious-looking matters, which generally accompany a conjuror.

20. *contextually.* A subject of contention, dispute, litigation, or the like. More explicitly ***matter in dispute, question,*** †***variance,*** †***difference.***

c **1386** CHAUCER *Melibeus* ⁋65 Thilke Iuge is wys, that sone understondeth a matere [*v.r.* matiere] and iuggeth by leyser. **1390** GOWER *Conf.* III. 181 Non withinne the cite In desorbance of unite Dorste ones moeven a matiere. **1462** *Cal. Anc. Rec. Dublin* (1889) I. 314 Hit is grawnt..that hit be lawfull to determe all maner materis and make lawes. **1470–85** MALORY *Arthur* XVIII. i. 726 And quarels and maters thow hast now a dayes for ladyes and gentilwymmen more than euer thou were wonte to haue. **1532** CROMWELL in Merriman *Life & Lett.* (1902) I. 348 Touching a certen matier in varyaunce betwixt thexecutours of Sir William Spencer disceasyd and my ladye spencer. **1535** COVERDALE *Deut.* xvii. 8 Yf a matter be to harde for the in iudgment betwixte bloude and bloude. **1597** BACON *Coulers Gd. & Evill* (Arb.) 140 If the matter should be tryed by duell betweene two Champions. **1774** [see DIFFERENCE *sb.* 3]. **1774** BURKE *Sp. Amer. Taxation* Sel. Wks. I. 147 Not being troubled with too anxious a zeal for any matter in question. **1825** [see DISPUTE *sb.* 1 b]. **1886** MRS. LYNN LINTON *Paston Carew* viii, They rarely met without crossing swords on one matter if not another.

†**b.** Phr. ***to make a matter to*** (a person), to pick a quarrel with. ***to have a matter with*** or ***against***, to have a quarrel with. *Obs.*

1530 PALSGR. 618, I make a mater to one, I pycke a quarell to him..I make no mater to hym, *je ne luy demande riens.* **1535** COVERDALE *Judg.* xii. 2, I and my people had a greate matter with y[e] children of Ammon. **1611** BIBLE *Acts* xix. 38 If Demetrius, and the craftesmen..haue a matter against any man, the law is open.

21. a. With qualification (attribute, or *of* and sb.): A thing, affair, subject, etc., of the kind denoted by or pertaining to the thing denoted by the qualification.

For the illustration of such phrases as *galley, halfpenny, hanging, laughing, massing, money matter*, see the first element. See also MATTER OF COURSE, MATTER OF FACT.

c **1425** WYNTOUN *Chron.* I. xvii. (MS. Cott.) *heading*, Þe fyrst materis of mawmentry þat clerkis callis ydolatry. **1508** DUNBAR *Tua Mariit Wemen* 122 Euer ymagynyng in mynd materis of evill. **1509** FISHER *Funeral Serm. C'tess Richmond* Wks. (1876) 292 She dyde translate dyuers maters of deuocyon out of Frensshe into Englysshe. **1549** LATIMER *5th Serm. bef. Edw. VI* (Arb.) 149 It is taken for a laughynge matter. **1590** SIR J. SMYTH *Disc. Weapons* Ded. 4 b, All their ancient orders and proceedings in matters Militarie. **1598** SHAKS. *Merry W.* I. i. 2, I will make a Star-Chamber matter of it. **1655** FULLER *Ch. Hist.* IX. 73 Matters of faith..are so plainly setled by the Scriptures, that [etc.]. **1678** WANLEY *Wond. Lit. World* v. i. §99. 468/1 Mens Consciences are not to be forced in matters of Religion. **1850** TENNYSON *In Mem.* xcvi[i]. 31 She knows but matters of the house, And he, he knows a thousand things. **1900** *Daily News* 22 Oct. 3/4 The campaign is nearly over—as a field matter it is fully at an end.

b. ***a matter of***: a circumstance which involves or brings into play..; a 'case' of.

1802–12 BENTHAM *Ration. Judic. Evid.* (1827) V. 179 When once we steer a hair's-breadth out of the sphere of every day's practice, everything is a matter of cross and pile. **1823** J. BADCOCK *Dom. Amusem.* 51 As a matter of economy, it is suggested [etc.]. **1843** GROVE *Corr. Phys. Forces* (1846) 35 This, however, must be taken merely as a matter of opinion. **1849** JAMES *Woodman* ix, This is a matter of life and death. **1868** W. K. CLIFFORD *Mental Development* Lect. & Ess. (1879) I. 104 The power of creation is not a matter of static ability;..it is a matter of habits and desires.

22. a. Used, like *thing*, as an indeterminate sb. to which to attach an epithet. Also in phrases like ***it is no such matter, another matter.***

c **1384** CHAUCER *H. Fame* III. 427 But hit a ful confuse matere Were al the gestes for to here. **14..** LYDG. *Isop.* (Zup.) 48 In matyrs þat touche poetry. **1596** SHAKS. *1 Hen. IV*, II. iv. 301 Instinct is a great matter. *c* **1600** —— *Sonn.* lxxxvii. 14 In sleepe a King, but waking no such matter. **1610** —— *Temp.* II. i. 88 What impossible matter wil he make easy next? **1611** BIBLE *Ps.* xxxv. 20 They deuise deceitfull matters against them that are quiet in the land. **1692** RAY *Disc.* (1732) Pref. 9, I had taken notice of five matters of ancient tradition. **1736** BUTLER *Anal.* II. i. Wks. 1874 I. 153 It cannot in any wise be an indifferent matter, whether we obey or disobey those commands. **1828** MISS MITFORD in L'Estrange *Life* (1870) II. 249 If actresses are bad, no manager can help it; but to take pains to turn a bad woman into an actress is another matter. **1842** BROWNING *Waring* I. iv, Truth's a weighty matter. **1847** TENNYSON *Princess* IV. 438 Who desire you more Than..dying lips, With many thousand matters left to do, The breath of life. **1876** BLACK *Madcap V.* xvii, The pronunciation of the word *allegro* is not a matter of very grave moment.

†**b.** ***all is a matter***: it is all the same. *Obs.*

1589 PUTTENHAM *Poesie* II. xii. [xiii.] (Arb.) 127 Whether we make the common readers to laugh or to lowre, all is a matter. **1682** N. O. *Boileau's Lutrin* II. 118 Let me sob, roar, or swoon, 'tis all a matter To marble-hearted John.

†**c.** (*any, some, no*) ***great matter***: (something, nothing) considerable. *Obs.*

1563–87 Foxe *A. & M.* (Cattley) (K.O.), It is no great matter. **1622** Bacon *Hen. VII* 120 It did shew manifestly vnto the World, that hee [Perkin] was some Great matter. *c* **1680** Beveridge *Serm.* (1729) II. 554 This..may seem to be no great matter at first sight. **1717** Berkeley *Jrnl. Tour Italy* Wks. 1871 IV. 528 We saw an armoury which seemed no great matter.

d. ***for that matter***: = 'for the matter of that' (see 25 e).

1673 Dryden *Marr. à-la-Mode* III. ii. 47 *Pala.* But who told you I was here?..*Rho.* O, for that matter, we had intelligence. **1693** Congreve *Old Bach.* IV. xxii, No, no, for that matter, when she and I part, she'll carry her separate maintenance about her. **1898** *Times* 10 Jan. 13/3 The.. shivering drivers..who (like every one else, for that matter) had to lie out in it [the rain] without tents.

23. a. With qualifying adj., usually *small*: A (certain) quantity or amount (*of*). ? *Obs.*

1630 *R. Johnson's Kingd. & Commw.* 265 [He] sold them their liberties for a small matter. *Ibid.* 271 It is thought that the Empire receiveth every way above seven millions, which is a great matter. **1652** Needham tr. *Selden's Mare Cl.* 472 At first an easie matter was demanded by the King of Denmark, and now more exacted than they can possibly bear. **1687** A. Lovell tr. *Thevenot's Trav.* 71 They can live upon a small matter; and provided they have Rice [etc.]. **1712** W. Rogers *Voy.* (1718) 33 It produces a small matter of Indico. **1723** *Lond. Gaz.* No. 6142/3 One sorrel Horse Colt,..with a small matter of White in his Face. **1749** Fielding *Tom Jones* IV. v, I..sent a small matter to his wife. **1760–72** H. Brooke *Fool of Qual.* (1809) III. 114 My son here has been of some little matter of use to you. *Ibid.* IV. 26 You will oblige us by.. taking some little matter of supper with us.

b. ***a small matter***, occas. ***a matter***, used advb. = Somewhat, slightly. *Obs.* or *arch.*

1690 Child *Disc. Trade* (ed. 4) 133 Very large quantities of Timber..may be had, though some small matter dearer than in Norway. **1700** Congreve *Way of World* III. xv, I have thought to tarry a small matter in town to learn somewhat of your lingo. **1703** Moxon *Mech. Exerc.* 275 Open them a small matter wider, or shut them a small matter closer. **1788** Smeaton in *Phil. Trans.* LXXIX. 4 The socket and spindle being a small matter taper. **1834** Landor *Exam. Shaks.* Wks. 1853 II. 267/1 Carnaby did quail a matter at these words.

24. ***a matter of***: used to qualify a numeral, indicating that it is not to be taken as literally exact. Also rarely ***matter of*** (? *obs.*), ***the matter of***.

c **1645** Howell *Lett.* (1655) I. 193 The French that came over with Her Majesty..are all casheer'd this week, about a matter of sixscore, wherof the Bishop of Mende was one. **1652** Gaule *Magastrom.* 360 [He] lets him have a great deal of it for a matter of a shilling. **1653** Cogan tr. *Pinto's Trav.* xi. 34 Accompanied with a matter of seven hundred men. **1771** Johnson *Let. to Mrs. Thrale* 7 July, He had had, as he phrased it, a matter of four wives. **1829** Landor *Imag. Conv.* Wks. 1853 I. 378 Hither have I been riding of matter of thirteen miles. **1843** Carlyle *Past & Pres.* II. i, Lackland.. boarded once, for the matter of a fortnight, in St. Edmundsbury Convent. **1862** Borrow *Wales* lxxxiii. (1901) 258 'Is it long since your honour was in Durham county?' 'A good long time. A matter of forty years'.

25. the matter (in various idiomatic uses).

†**a.** That which is contemplated, intended, or desired. ***to the matter***: to the point, relevant(ly); = L. *ad rem.* ***from the matter***: irrelevant(ly). ***much about the matter***: not far from the point. *Obs.*

1560 Daus tr. *Sleidane's Comm.* 30 a, Thou aunswerest Luther, more unreverently, then it becommeth thee, and not sufficientlye to the matter. **1597** Bacon *Ess., Discourse* (Arb.) 22 To vse too many circumstances ere one come to the matter is wearisome. **1611** Shaks. *Cymb.* v. v. 169. **1626** Bacon *Sylva* §326 To helpe the Matter, the Alchymists call in..many Vanities, out of Astrologie. **1658** Rowland tr. *Moufet's Theat. Ins.* 951 It shall not be from the matter to tax in brief the madnesse of the ancient Gentiles. **1669** Sturmy *Mariner's Mag.* v. xii. 55 If you take 5 parts Lead, and one part Stone, it will come very near the matter. *a* **1694** Tillotson *Serm.* (1714) I. 12 He grants it [*sc.* the deluge] to have come so near the matter, that but very few escap'd it. **1725** Bailey *Erasm. Colloq.* (1733) 483 You're much about the Matter [L. *haud multum aberras a scopo*].

b. The circumstance or state of things which actually involves or concerns some person or thing, esp. one which calls for remedy or explanation; chiefly in ***what is the matter?*** and similar expressions. Phr. (colloq.) ***what is the matter with..?*** = What ails, troubles, or is amiss with..? hence (*jocular*) What is the objection to, What is there to complain of in..?

1469 *Plumpton Corr.* (Camden) 23 Maister Rochif asked him what the matter was, if I might have any ease. **1535** Coverdale *Ecclus.* xxii. 8 Whan he hath tolde his tayle, he sayeth: what is the matter? **1560** Daus tr. *Sleidane's Comm.* 323 b, No man knew what the matter was. **1604** Shaks. *Oth.* II. iii. 163 What is the matter heere? **1605** Bacon *Adv. Learn.* I. vii. §15 Alexander happed to say: Doe you thinke these men would haue come from so farre to complaine, except they had iust cause of griefe? and Cassander answered, Yea, that was the matter, because they thought they should not be disprooued. **1682** N. O. *Boileau's Lutrin* III. 6 The Canto tells you, what's the matter. **1713** Swift *Cadenus & Vanessa*, Why she likes him, admire not at her; She loves herself, and that's the matter. **1715** De Foe *Fam. Instruct.* I. iv. (1841) I. 88, I beseech what is the matter with you. **1802** *Spirit Publ. Jrnls.* (1803) VI. 8 What's the matter with the peace? **1833** Ht. Martineau *Three Ages* ii. 75 The children..amused themselves as if nothing was the matter. **1837** [see leg *sb.* 1]. **1847–9** Helps *Friends in C.* II. (1851) 5 There was something the matter with the old man. **1885** 'F. Anstey' *Tinted Venus* 69 'What's the matter?' 'Nothing is the matter, Matilda', he said.

†**c.** ***on*** or ***upon the matter*** (also ***upon the whole m.***): taking the thing as a whole, speaking generally; for all practical purposes, practically speaking. *Obs.*

c **1560** *Misogonus* III. i. 192 (Brandl), Pounder matter, well, if she should not knowt, who showlde knowe? **1612** Bacon *Ess., Deformity* (Arb.) 254 So that vpon the whole matter [*ed.* 1625 vpon the matter], in a great wit, deformity is an aduantage to rising. **1639** Fuller *Holy War* II. xxxvii. (1640) 93 That Christians are not bound to keep faith with idolaters, the worshippers of a false god, as the Egyptian Caliph was on the matter. **1679** Moxon *Mech. Exerc.* 120 The Rules they both work by are upon the matter the same, in Sawing, Mortessing,..&c. **1689** Burnet *Tracts* I. 79 This is upon the matter a Pension paid under a more decent name to the most considerable Men of the Country. **1691** South *Serm.* (1823) II. 188 Upon the whole matter it is absurd to think that conscience can be kept in order without frequent examination. *a* **1710** Bp. Bull *Serm.* xviii. Wks. 1827 I. 439 He is upon the matter sure of a long life.

d. Phr. ***in the matter of*** (= law Latin ***in re***): in relation to, with regard to; chiefly in *Law*.

1790 Ambler *Chancery Rep.* 78 In the Matter of Annesley, a Lunatic. **1834** Adolphus & Ellis *1 K.B. Rep.* 843 In the Matter of Elmy and Sawyer. **1876** *Law Rep., Prob. Div.* I. 423 In the Matter of the Petition of Sheehy. **1881** Saintsbury *Dryden* iv, He [Dryden] had 'seen many others', as an admirable Gallicism has it, in the matter of attacks. **1882** *Times* 30 June 5 In the matter of Egypt,..the German Chancellor will leave them to act as they like. **1904** *Standard* 29 Nov. 9/7 In the Matter of an Arbitration between the Manchester Carriage and Tramways Company (Claimants) v. The Swinton and Pendlebury Urban District Council (Purchasing Authority).

e. ***for the matter of that***: as far as that goes.

1764 Foote *Mayor of G.* I. (1783) 24 For the matter of that, we can afford it well enough as it is. **1766** Goldsm. *Vic. W.* xxi, 'Consider, my dear', cries the husband, 'she is a gentlewoman'... 'As for the matter of that', returned the hostess, 'gentle or simple, out she shall pack with a sussarara'.

26. *attrib.* and *Comb.*, as ***matter-hating***, ***-moulded***, ***-woven*** adjs.; †**matter-bear** (see quot.); **matter wave** *Physics*, a de Broglie wave (see de Broglie).

1612 S. Sturtevant *Metallica* (1854) 117 The matter-beare, is a generall part of a Furnace which beereth and holdeth the substances of the Raw-matters. **1850** Tennyson *In Mem.* xc[i]v, In matter-moulded forms of speech. **1853** Kingsley *Hypatia* viii. 98 Facts, objects, are but phantoms matter-woven. **1856** R. A. Vaughan *Mystics* (1860) I. 17 The matter-hating principles of this school. **1930** Ruark & Urey *Atoms, Molecules & Quanta* xxi. 722 When electrons impinge on polycrystalline metal surfaces the fraction scattered at an angle θ with the normal to the surface does not decrease uniformly as θ increases... The results seemed likely to remain unexplained, until Einstein discussed de Broglie's matter waves, in 1924 and 1925. **1972** *Sci. Amer.* Oct. 106/3 The bombarding particles have the properties not only of particles but also of waves. Such 'matter waves' are called de Broglie waves (after Louis de Broglie, who first suggested that the wave-particle duality observed for electromagnetic radiation might also exist for matter). **1974** G. Reece tr. *Hund's Hist. Quantum Theory* xi. 141 The intuitive theory of matter waves and of fields of matter is modified to the point where there is room for the idea of particles.

†**'matter**, *sb.*[2] *Obs.* Also 7 **matteyer.** [f. mat *sb.*[1] + -er[1].] A mat-maker.

14.. *Voc.* in Wr.-Wülcker 613/38 *Storiator*, a mattere. *c* **1430** *Pilgr. Lyf Manhode* II. lxvii. (1869) 101 Whan þus hadde seid me þe mattere [F. *natier*] who he was. **1611** Cotgr., *Nattier*, a Matter; or maker of mats. **1614** *Acc. Revels at Court* (Shaks. Soc. 1842) p. xliv, To Richard Ansell Matteyer to his Ma^{ty}..for his paines and chardges in nayling downe the greene clothe in the Banquetting House ..for the Maske.

matter ('mætə(r)), *v.* Also 6 **mattre, matier.** [f. matter *sb.*[1]]

1. a. *intr.* To discharge matter or pus; to suppurate.

1530 Palsgr. 633/2 Whan thynke you that your byle wyll matter? **1544** Phaer *Bk. Childr.* (1553) S iv b, The..skin of an adder..boiled in oile..is also good for an eare that mattereth. **1658** A. Fox *Surg. Guide* III. iv. 227 Every wound mattereth, and desireth to make a separation of that which is destroyed. **1736** Ainsworth *Lat. Dict., Suppuro*, ..to matter, to suppurate. [**1875–86** Elworthy *W. Som. Gloss.*, *Mattery*, to discharge pus.]

†**b.** To exude in the form of matter or pus.

1635 Quarles *Embl.* I. xii. 49 Earth's milk's a ripen'd core That drops from her disease, that matters from her sore.

2. To be of importance; to signify: chiefly in interrogative and negative sentences. (Freq. *impersonal* with dependent clause.) Const. *to*; also (*poet. rare*) with *dative*.

1581 Savile *Tacitus, Hist.* IV. (1612) 161 Sosianus & Sagitta were men vile & of no account, neither mattered it where they liued. *a* **1617** Bayne *Lect.* (1634) 68 What those are who are not under our houshold gouernment, mattereth not to our discredit. **1633** Hall *Occas. Medit.* (1851) 18 It matters not, O God, how I am vexed here below, a while. **1711** Steele *Spect.* No. 252 ¶1 What matters it what she says to you? **1817** Southey *Wat Tyler* I. i. Poet. Wks. II. 25 What matters me who wears the crown of France? **1840** Marryat *Poor Jack* xxvi, We haven't spent any to matter. **1846** Landor *Imag. Conv.* I. 156 Nor does it matter a straw whether we use the double *e* instead of *ete* in *sweet.* **1873** Dixon *Two Queens* I. iv. i. 175 His pretext mattered little. **1878** Tennyson *The Revenge* xi, We die—does it matter when? **1884** *Law Rep. 26 Chanc. Div.* 128 It mattered nothing to them whether the other Corporators were eight or a thousand. **1885** 'F. Anstey' *Tinted Venus* 181 'It matters not', she said, calmly. **1909** H. W. C. Newte *Sparrows* xl. 505 With your appearance and talents you should be a great social success with people who matter. **1926** G. B. Shaw *Translations & Tomfooleries* II. 49 Well, what about Edith? Doesn't she matter? **1933** E. A. Robertson *Ordinary Families* x. 233 Wives still matter politically, if a man's to be offered a comfortable Conservative seat.

3. a. With a negative: To be concerned about, care for, regard, heed, mind. (Sometimes with dependent clause.) *Obs.* exc. *dial.* in the sense: To approve of, like.

1649 Blith *Eng. Improv. Impr.* (1653) 96 Let his Land be fit for one, or fit for another use, he matters it not. **1664** H. More *Myst. Iniq.* xi. 37, I matter not what careless abuses there may be put upon a word. **1720** *Humourist* Ded. 13 They matter it not of a straw. **1749** Fielding *Tom Jones* II. vi, If it had been out of doors I had not mattered it so much. **1760–72** H. Brooke *Fool of Qual.* (1809) I. 26 He did not matter cold, nor hunger, nor what he eat, nor what he drank. **1804** Eugenia de Acton *Tale without Title* I. 215 Oh! as to your fine speeches, Miss, I matter not them a straw. **1892** M. C. F. Morris *Yorksh. Folk-Talk* 89 If a workman does not take kindly to his occupation, he would say that he did not matter it much.

b. *absol.* or *intr.* To care, mind. ? *Obs.*

1677 Moxon *Mech. Exerc.* 43 Let it somewhat fall short or exceed that number they matter not. **1713** in G. Sheldon *Hist. Deerfield, Mass.* (1895) I. 350 If he would not marry them they matter'd not. **1729** Walkden *Diary* (1866) 80, I mattered not if we exchanged, so he took my box, and I his.

†**4.** To arrange the subject-matter of. *nonce-use.*

1548 Geste *Pr. Masse* Ded., Whiche I can neyther word, matier, ne reason accordynglye, and so [etc.].

†**'matterative**, *a.* *Obs.* Also 7 **mattrative.** [irreg. f. matter *sb.*[1] or *v.* + -ative, with recollection of *maturative.*] Characterized by the presence of matter or pus.

1639 T. de Gray *Compl. Horsem.* 40 The corruption which the horse venteth: if that mattrative stuffe be green [etc.]. **1727** Bradley *Fam. Dict.* s.v. *Fever*, His Eyes are so swell'd that he cannot easily open 'em for matterative Stuff. *Ibid.* s.v. *Wen*, [Wens] being as to the outward part, Flesh, but toward the Root, matterative.

†**'mattered**, *a.* *Obs. rare.* [f. matter *sb.*[1] + -ed[2], after med.L. *māteriātus.*]

1. *Metaph.* = materiated.

1620 T. Granger *Div. Logike* 57 A mattered effect, or effect of the matter, is euery thing made of some matter. **1654** Z. Coke *Logick* 159 From the common matter put or taken away,..to put or take away the mattered,..is a contingent inference: as, In Germany is much wood, therefore they have many ships.

2. Containing matter or pus.

1590 Barrough *Meth. Physick* v. vi. (1639) 278 A mattered tumour is more safely opened with a knife then with burning medicines.

matterful ('mætəfʊl), *a.* [f. matter *sb.*[1] + -ful.] Of a book, an author, or the like: Full of 'matter' or substance.

1819 Lamb *Lett.* x. *To Wordsworth* 97 From thence I turned to Vincent Bourne; what a sweet, unpretending, pretty-manner'd, matterful Creature. **1873** Miss Broughton *Nancy* I. 147 In sweet and matterful verse. **1887** *Sat. Rev.* 3 Sept. 337 The cheap little collection.. called the 'Bibliothèque utile', seldom admits numbers which are not 'matterful and factful', as some singular people say.

Hence **'matterfulness.**

1883–4 Grosart *Nashe's Wks.* I. Introd. 45 One is struck with their terseness and matterfulness.

†**'mattering**, *vbl. sb.* *Obs.* [f. matter *v.* + -ing[1].]

1. The formation of matter or pus, suppuration.

1528 Paynell *Salerne's Regim.* X iiij, Nothynge is better to heale matterynge at the eares, than the ieuse of wylowe leaues. **1631** Widdowes *Nat. Philos.* 55 Extraordinary mattering is, when..the humors or parts themselves are made full of corrupt matter. **1749** Bracken *Farriery* (ed. 6) xxx. 258 Mattering of the Yard..in Stoned Horses is often no other than a *Gonorrhœa Simplex.*

2. Caring, minding.

1693 Evelyn *De la Quint. Compl. Gard.* I. 35 The Cloth as it were, should always be laid in a fine Garden, without mattering to see what passes in the open Fields.

†**'mattering**, *ppl. a.* *Obs.* [f. matter *v.* + -ing[2].] Forming or discharging matter, purulent.

1561 Hollybush *Hom. Apoth.* 20 Scabbes,..mattering sores,..and the canker. **1589** Rider *Bibl. Schol.* s.v., A mattering, or running sore.

†**'matterish**, *a.* *Obs.* [f. matter *sb.*[1] + -ish.] Of the nature of, full of, forming, or discharging pus.

1580 Blundeville *Curing Horses Dis.* 59 A kind of Scab.. which is full of fretting matterish water. **1673** R. Head *Canting Acad.* 74 The Matterish clouts that are wrapt about [the sore]. **1725** Atkinson in *Phil. Trans.* XXXIII. 341 There had been discharg'd a small Quantity of matterish Substance.

matterless ('mætəlɪs), *a.* [f. matter *sb.*[1] + -less.]

1. Having no matter; not embodied in matter; immaterial. Now *rare.*

1548 Geste *Pr. Masse* B v, The broken bread..is material & not mattierles. **1602** J. Davies (Heref.) *Mirum in modum*

(Grosart) 20/1 Who being immateriall, cannot change, (For that's immutable thats matterlesse). *a* **1849** H. Coleridge *Ess.* (1851) I. 56 He cannot live upon matterless forms. **1890** J. H. Stirling *Gifford Lect.* xv. 304 A matterless form would vanish.

†**2.** Without materials. *Obs. rare*$^{-1}$.

14.. *Pilgr. Sowle*, No more men maye glosen withouten text than bylde materles.

†**3.** Devoid of 'matter', sense, or meaning. *Obs.*

1612 T. Taylor *Comm. Titus* To Rdr., With multiplication of matterless words. *a* **1637** B. Jonson *Hor.: Art P.* 460 All fine noise Of verse meere-matter-lesse. **1767** Mrs. S. Pennington *Lett.* III. 37 Some dissipation is necessary for you, and therefore, my matterless lines may have their use.

4. Immaterial, of no concern or importance. Chiefly *dial.*

a **1650** May *Old Couple* II. (1658) 10 'Tis matterless in goodness who excels: He that hath coyn, hath all perfections else. **1875** *Manley & Corringham Gloss.* s.v., It's matterless which waay you tak' th' watter. **1889** *Archaeol. Aeliana* (N.S.) XIII. 280 It being matterless whether a saint is incorruptible or, as in the case of Bede, corrupted.

b. Applied to persons: Of no consequence; incompetent, shiftless, helpless. *dial.*

1794 Hutchinson *Hist. Cumbld.* I. 225 *note*, Mr. Robinson..a simple matterless body. **1876** *Whitby Gloss.*

matterne, obs. form of MARTEN.

matter of course. Something which is to be expected as following the natural course or order of things.

1739 [see COURSE *sb.* 37 a]. **1809** Malkin *Gil Blas* I. xii. (1866) 27 Having as a matter of course sold my cloak-bag. **1878** S. Walpole *Hist. Engl.* II. 525 Protestants guilty of killing Roman Catholics were acquitted, as a matter of course, by Protestant juries. **1884** *Manch. Exam.* 22 May 5/2 It was a matter of course that France should retain the territory she had conquered.

b. *attrib.* or as *adj.* (written with hyphens), rarely as *predicative adj.*: Occurring or following as a matter of course; to be expected. Freq. of persons or their mode of action: Taking things as a matter of course.

1840 Dickens *Barn. Rudge* liii, The cool matter-of-course manner of this reply. **1854** Lowell *Jrnl. Italy* Pr. Wks. 1890 I. 129 A sudden change in the scenery, like those that seem so matter-of-course in dreams. **1861** Hughes *Tom Brown at Oxf.* xxx, I won't have that sort of matter-of-course acquiescence. **1865** Mozley *Mirac.* v. 100 The belief in it is so necessary and so matter-of-course an act in us, that [etc.]. **1892** W. S. Gilbert *Foggerty's Fairy* 190, I said some matter-of-course words to the effect [etc.].

Hence **matter-of-'courseness** *nonce-wd.*

1890 *Temple Bar* Sept. 78 A naturalness, a matter-of-courseness that admitted of no questioning.

matter of fact (ˌmætərəv'fækt), *sb.* and *a.* [See MATTER *sb.*^{1} 16, 21 and FACT *sb.* 6.]

A. *sb.* **a.** *Law.* That portion of a subject of judicial inquiry which is concerned with the truth or falsehood of alleged facts; a particular question or issue that is of this nature: opposed to *matter of law*. **b.** What pertains to the sphere of fact as opposed to opinion, probability, or inference; also, something which is of the nature of a fact. Phrases, ***as a matter of fact, in matter of fact***: in point of fact, really.

1581 E. Campion in *Confer.* II. (1584) M b, He speaketh of a matter of fact. **1594** Hooker *Eccl. Pol.* II. vii. §2 If it be admitted that in matter of fact there is some credite to be giuen to the testimonie of man, but not in matter of opinion and iudgement. **1605** Bacon *Adv. Learn.* I. iv. §9 It is either a beleefe of Historie (as the Lawyers speeke, matter of fact:) or else of matter of art and opinion. **1621** Elsing *Debates Ho. Lords* (Camden) 112 The House to consider of the matter of facte. **1661** Evelyn *Diary* 1 Oct., He then commanded me to draw up the matter of fact happening at the bloudy encounter. **1690** Locke *Hum. Und.* IV. xvi. (1695) 380 Some particular Existence, or, as it is usually termed, matter of fact, which falling under Observation, is capable of humane Testimony. **1709** Addison *Tatler* No. 122 ¶1 It is true in Matter of Fact, I was present at the ingenious Entertainment. **1727** A. Hamilton *New Acc. E. Ind.* II. xxxiii. 9 The Story was really true Matter of Fact. **1730** A. Gordon *Maffei's Amphith.* 289 The Matter of Fact is, that..the two Gates..will undoubtedly be found wider. **1739** Hume *Hum. Nat.* I. iii. §7 (1888) 94 All reasonings from causes or effects terminate in conclusions, concerning matter of fact; that is, concerning the existence of objects or of their qualities. **1776** —— *My own Life*, This is a matter of fact which is easily cleared and ascertained. **1793** Smeaton *Edystone L.* §119, I have strictly adhered to matter of fact. **1816-60** Whately *Comm.-pl. Bk.* (1864) 131 By a matter of fact is meant something which might conceivably be submitted to the senses, and about which it is supposed there could not be any disagreement among persons who should be present and to whose senses it should be presented. **1842** J. H. Newman *Eccl. Mirac.* (1843) 56 There exists, in matter of fact, that very connection.. between Ecclesiastical and Scripture miracles. **1849** Grote *Greece* II. lxvii. (1862) VI. 38 *note*, Great numbers of Aristophanic jests have been transcribed as serious matter-of-fact. **1888** Bryce *Amer. Commw.* II. lii. 311 They did not receive, as matter of fact, the good government which they desired. **1889** J. K. Jerome *Three Men in a Boat* 283 As a matter of fact, you are quite right. I did catch it.

B. *attrib.* passing into *adj.* (Usually written with hyphens.) Pertaining to, having regard to, or depending upon actual fact as distinguished from what is speculative or fanciful; unimaginative, prosaic.

1712 Steele *Spect.* No. 521 ¶1, I contemn the Men given to Narration under the Appellation of a Matter of Fact Man. **1787** Burns *Let.* 15 Jan., Wks. (Globe) 323 To write him a mere matter-of-fact affair, like a merchant's order. **1856** Stanley *Sinai & Pal.* i. 67 The scene is not impressive in itself,—that at Suez especially is matter-of-fact in the highest degree. **1875** Jowett *Plato* (ed. 2) II. 277 The more Callicles is irritated, the more provoking and matter of fact does Socrates become. **1887** R. N. Carey *Uncle Max* xi. (1887) 84 [She] bade her drink her tea before it got cold, in a sensible matter-of-fact way.

absol. **1870** Lowell *Among my Bks.* Ser. II. (1873) 125 Its oscillations between the ideal and the matter-of-fact.

Hence **ˌmatter-of-'factism**, the principle or practice of regarding or relying upon matter of fact only; so **ˌmatter-of-'factist**, one who regards matter of fact only; **ˌmatter-of-'factly** *adv.*, in a matter-of-fact manner; **ˌmatter-of-'factness**, matter-of-fact quality or character.

1860 Sara Hennell *Thoughts in Aid of Faith* 195 Hard *matter-of-fact-ism. *a* **1866** J. Grote *Exam. Utilit. Phil.* xviii. (1870) 283 Positivism and matter-of-factism, that is, the refusal to take account of any thing else in things except that they are. **1833** *New Monthly Mag.* XXXIX. 165 The *matter-of-factists will put down as your sober opinion.. the ἔπεα πτερόεντα inspired by the festivity of the hour. **1865** J. Grote *Explor. Philos.* I. 80 Thorough positivists..or, I may say, matter-of-factists. **1873** Miss Broughton *Nancy* I. 47 'You mean us, I suppose', I answered *matter-of-factly. **1816** J. W. Croker in *C. Papers* 28 Nov. (1884), [The] success..I attribute altogether..to the *matter-of-factness, with which it is written. **1879** W. Knight *Stud. Philos. & Lit.* 291 The infelicities..in Wordsworth's style ..its sinking from ideality into matter-of-factness.

mattery ('mætərɪ), *a.* Also 4-7 **mattry**. [f. MATTER *sb.*^{1} + -Y^{1}.]

1. Full of, forming, or discharging matter or pus; purulent.

1398 Trevisa *Barth. De P.R.* XVII. ci. (1495) 667 Oleum mirtum..clensyth mattry eerys. **1527** Andrew *Brunswyke's Distyll. Waters* I v a, Impostumes whiche roune of mattery humours and moystoures. **1666** J. H. *Treat. Gt. Antidote* 11 It brought away much mattery substance. **1871** Napheys *Prev. & Cure Dis.* III. xiii. 1070 A mattery sore. **1955** W. W. Denlinger *Compl. Boston* I. 152 Small mattery spots on the inside of the thigh..are often the first indication that a dog is suffering from distemper. **1961** S. Chaplin *Day of Sardine* i. 8 This was a sick kitten. Thin as a rake, mattery eyes, scabby eyes.

†**2.** Full of 'matter' or sense. *Obs. rare*$^{-1}$.

1601 B. Jonson *Poetaster* IV. v, Away with your Mattery Sentences..; They are to graue and wise, for this meeting.

matteyer, variant of MATTER *sb.*^{2} *Obs.*

Matthean (mæ'θiːən), *a.* Also **-æan**. [f. L. *Matthæ-us* Matthew + -AN.] Of, pertaining to, or characteristic of the evangelist St. Matthew.

1897 *Expositor* Aug. 152 The closing sentence being distinctly Matthæan. *Ibid.* Dec. 448 In two of the Matthæan logia the Lord speaks of His disciples collectively as the *ecclesia*.

Matthew Walker. *Naut.* In full ***Matthew Walker knot***, a multi-stranded rope end knot, prob. named after its originator.

[**1808** D. Lever *Young Sea Officer's Sheet Anchor* 5 Matthew Walker's knot.] **1841** R. H. Dana *Seaman's Manual* vii. 37 A Matthew Walker knot,..unlay the end of a rope [etc.]. **1856** C. Nordhoff *Man-of-War Life* xii. 212, I practised..and was soon master of long and short splices, manrope knots, turks-heads, and Matthew Walkers. **1860** *All Year Round* 28 July 382/1 'Which knot?' asked Toby... 'Matthew Walker, spritsail-sheet, stopper or shroud?' **1883** *Man. Seamanship for Boys' Training Ships R. Navy* (Admiralty) (1886) 105 A Matthew Walker knot is used for the standing part of the lanyards of lower rigging. **1953** *People* (Austral.) 26 Aug. 47/3 Mason will talk by the hour about Matthew Walker knots, bell ropes..and cross-pointing if he encounters a pair of sympathetic ears. **1961** F. H. Burgess *Dict. Sailing* 144 *Matthew Walker*, a knot, single or double, used to make a collar on a rope; the strands may be relaid when formed (a development of the wall knot). **1968** E. Franklin *Dict. Knots* 20 *Matthew Walker* and *Double Matthew Walker*, probably the best and most useful of the multistrand rope end knots. It is claimed that the unknown Matthew Walker is the only man to have a knot named after him. **1971** I. Imrie tr. *Svensson's Handbk. Seaman's Ropework* 79 The Mathew Walker knot on a three-stranded rope is the simplest of all knots with a rope's own end.

mattie, mattin: see MATIE, MATIN.

matting ('mætɪŋ), *vbl. sb.*^{1} [f. MAT *v.*^{1} and *sb.*^{1}]

1. The action of becoming or state of being matted or tangled. Also with *down, together*.

1682 H. More *Contn. Remark. Stor.* 41 This Magical matting of the Daughter's hair into a Witch-lock. **1707** Mortimer *Husb.* 570 It [*sc.* the Malt] sinks gradually, distributing its strength to your Liquor equally without matting. **1865** Gosse *Land & Sea* (1874) 19 The matting of the vegetation, impeding the flow of the water. **1884** W. S. B. McLaren *Spinning* (ed. 2) 2 The property of felting or matting, which is so characteristic of wool. **1897** *Allbutt's Syst. Med.* III. 809 Obstruction [of the bowel] by the matting together of several coils of intestine. **1899** *Ibid.* VII. 480 The..matting down of the velum interpositum.

2. a. The process of making mats or matting. **b.** The covering of a floor, etc. with matting.

a. 1720 *Lond. Gaz.* No. 5891/4 Tho. Smith..of that Branch called a matted Chair-maker, is in want of Journeymen..for Matting. **1871** Tylor *Prim. Cult.* I. 7 Among the textile arts are to be ranged matting, netting [etc.].

b. 1813 L. Hunt in *Examiner* 22 Feb. 114/1 Matting and carpeting have done much for the stone floor.

3. *concr.* A fabric composed of a coarse material, e.g., coir, bast, hemp, grass, etc., used as a covering for floors or roofs, or as material for packing, for tying plants, etc. Also *Naut.* = MAT *sb.*^{1} 4.

Different kinds of matting are known as ***Canton, Dutch, India*** (see INDIA 6), ***Russia matting***; also **coco-nut matting** (see COCO 4 e), **sword matting** (see SWORD).

1748 *Anson's Voy.* III. v. 341 The sail..is made of matting, and the mast..of bamboo. **1812** J. Smyth *Pract. of Customs* (1821) 154, 20 Rolls Dutch Matting... Matting is used by the Cabinet-makers for packing of goods. **1819** *Mem. Caled. Hort. Soc.* III. 111 Through the heads of these nails, strings or strands of matting are introduced. **1843** Mrs. Houston *Yacht Voy. Texas* (1844) I. 27 The floors..are spread with a fine matting. **1846** J. Baxter *Libr. Pract. Agric.* (ed. 4) II. 324 The scion, which you will tie to it slightly with a piece of wetted matting. **1861** Delamer *Flower Gard.* 31 The cold frame (covered with matting). **1866** Geo. Eliot *F. Holt* (1868) 10 The broad stone staircase with its matting worn into large holes. **1901** Hasluck *Bamboo Work* iii. 48 The top [of the table] is of wood covered with Japanese matting.

b. Materials for mats.

1847 in Webster; and in recent Dicts.

4. *attrib.* or as *adj.* Covered with or composed of matting.

1833 J. Bennett *Artificer's Lex.* 190 Matting hassocks,.. oval or round. **1888** *Literary World* (Boston) 4 Aug. 246/3 Matting roofs. **1895** C. Holland *Jap. Wife* 24 The matting floor. **1900** P. F. Warner *Cricket in many Climes* 219 An ideal ground as far as a matting wicket ever can be so.

5. *attrib.* and *Comb.*, as ***matting line, needle, tie*** (cf. 2 a, b); **matting-boat** = *mattress-boat*: see MATTRESS 4 (*Cent. Dict.* 1890); **matting-loom**, a loom in which matting is made; see also quot. 1875.

1862 *Catal. Internat. Exhib.* II. XIX. 10 *Matting lines, twines, coir yarn and fibre. **1853** in *Abridgm. Specif. Patents, Weaving* (1861) 423 My invention consists in making mats in a *matting loom. **1875** Knight *Dict. Mech.*, *Matting-loom* (Weaving), one in which slats are introduced into the shed to form the woof. **1688** R. Holme *Armoury* III. 273/2 Their [*sc.* Upholsterers'] Pack or *Matting Needle. **1825** *Greenhouse Comp.* I. 172 Common *matting ties.

matting ('mætɪŋ), *vbl. sb.*^{2} [f. MAT *v.*^{2} + -ING^{1}.]

1. The production of a 'mat' surface, in *Chasing, Gilding*, etc. Also, the mat surface thus produced.

1688 R. Holme *Armoury* III. 259/2 Matting or Hatching, is to make a Beast or Lion Hairy, a Bird Feathers, Fish Scales, and Flowers and Leaves, Veins and Threads. **1758** *Handmaid to Arts* 381 The deeper and obscure parts of the carving..are coloured after the gilding; which treatment is called matting. **1854** Reinnel *Carpenters' & Gilders' Comp.* 74 Matting or Dead Gold. **1885** F. Miller *Glass-Paint.* 53 If this matting [*i.e.* antiquing glass with umber or ancient brown] is done to deceive, it is certainly false. **1887** L. L. Haslope *Repoussé Work* 52 The simplest form of matting is made by dots. **1893** *Brit. Jrnl. Photogr.* XL. 800 The 'matting' of gelatine prints has become very general. **1898** T. B. Wigley *Goldsm. & Jeweller* 146 The term..'surface chasing' is generally applied to the feathering of birds,..the matting of foliage, &c.

2. The furnishing (of a picture) with a mat; *concr.* = MAT *sb.*^{2} 3.

1864 Webster, *Matting*, an ornamental border of thin rolled brass, placed between the plate and glass of a daguerreotype picture, to prevent abrasion. **1875** Knight *Dict. Mech.*, *Matting*, the passepartout over a picture. A mat. **1889** *Anthony's Photogr. Bull.* II. 141 The matting and framing of a [photographic] print.

3. *Comb.*, as ***matting-pattern, -punch, -tool***.

1877 G. B. Gee *Pract. Gold-worker* 133 An effective matting-punch was at once produced. This matting-tool appears to have been greatly used by the mediæval gold-workers. **1898** T. B. Wigley *Goldsm. & Jeweller* 120 Passing the wire through flattening rolls with matting pattern.

mattins: see MATIN.

mattock ('mætək), *sb.* Forms: 1 **mattoc, mettoc, metoc, meottuc**, 1-2 **mattuc**, 4-6 **mattok**, 4, 6 **matock**, 4-7 **matok(e**, 5 **mattoke**, 5-6 **mattokk**, 6-7 **mattocke**, (6 **mathooke**), 7-9 **mathook**, 6- **mattock**. [OE. *mattuc, meottuc* masc., of unknown origin: the Welsh *matog* and Gael. *madag* are from Eng.

The ending would appear to be the dim. suffix in OE. *bulluc* bullock. The word has not been found in continental Teut.; its relation, if any, to the synonymous Russian *motyka*, Lith. *matikkas*, is not clear.]

An agricultural tool (of which there are several varieties) used for loosening hard ground, grubbing up trees, etc. It has a socketed steel head (fixed transversely at the end of a straight handle), having on one side a blade shaped like that of an adze, and sometimes on the other side a kind of pick.

a **700** *Epinal Gloss.* 565 *Lagones*, mettocas. *a* **800** *Corpus Gloss.* (Hessels) L. 161 *Ligones*, meottucas. *c* **893** K. Ælfred *Oros.* IV. viii. §2 þonne het he hiene mid fyre onhætan, & siþþan mid mattucun heawan. *a* **1100** *Gerefa* in *Anglia* (1886) IX. 263 Mattuc, ipping-iren, scear. **1303** R. Brunne *Handl. Synne* 940 Mattok is a pykeys. **1382** Wyclif *Joel* iii. 10 Bete to gydre..ȝour pikoysis, or mattokis [**1388** mattokkis], in to speris. *c* **1420** *Pallad. on Husb.* I. 1153 Yet tolis mo, The mattok, twibil, picoys forth to go. **1494** Fabyan *Chron.* IV. lxix. 48 He..with a Pykax or Mattoke, with his owne hande, breke the grounde. *a* **1533** Ld.

BERNERS *Huon* xxx. 93 With pykes & mattokes they brake downe a corner toure. **1588** SHAKS. *Tit. A.* IV. iii. 11 'Tis you must dig with Mattocke, and with Spade. **1649** JER. TAYLOR *Gt. Exemp.* III. xiv. 13 Repentance..like a mattock and spade breaks away all the roughnesses of the passage. *a* **1734** NORTH *Exam.* III. viii. §14 (1740) 592 Spades and Mathooks. **1771** ROBERTSON *Hist. Amer.* (1778) I. IV. 335 After digging the field with wooden mattocks, they sowed or planted it. **1824** LOUDON *Encycl. Gard.* (ed. 2) §1296 The mattock..is sometimes called a crow, and also a grubbing-axe, hoe-axe, &c. **1848** *Jrnl. R. Agric. Soc.* IX. II. 537 Stony or gravelly, so as to require..to be pecked with a mathook or pick. **1851** STEPHENS *Bk. Farm* (ed. 2) II. 652/1 The common mattock which on one arm has a horizontal cutting face, and on the other a vertical one. **1874** GREEN *Short Hist.* i. §2. 13 The debtor, unable to discharge his debt..took up the labourer's mattock.

attrib. and Comb. **1855** TENNYSON *Maud* I. XVIII. iv, Born To labour and the mattock-harden'd hand. **1832** *Planting* 37 (L.U.K.) Mattock planting is confined chiefly to rocky ground. *Ibid.* 60 An active workman with a steel mattock-hoe will clean round the plants [etc.].

mattock ('mætək), *v.* [f. MATTOCK *sb.*] *trans.* To turn *up* with the mattock. Also *fig.*

1649 BLITH *Eng. Improv. Impr.* 140 Prejudice..so deeply rooted, as will aske hot water to Mattock up. **1792** A. YOUNG *Trav. France* 411, I have seen them..mattocking up every corner of a field where the plough could not come. **1840** *Cottager's Manual* 45 (L.U.K.) No plant is so much improved by deep..mattocking between the rows as the potato. **1854** *Jrnl. R. Agric. Soc.* XV. II. 274 Have all the ant-hills and hassocks mattocked up.

mattoid ('mætɔɪd), *a.* and *sb.* [ad. It. *mattoide*, f. *matto* insane: see -OID.] See quot. 1891.

1891 tr. *Lombroso's Man of Genius* iii. 209 This variety forms the link between madmen of genius, the sane, and the insane properly so called. These are what I call semi-insane persons or mattoids. *Ibid.* iii. 223 Mattoid theologians.. have unfortunately been taken so seriously as to be burned alive. **1899** *Allbutt's Syst. Med.* VIII. 196 The so-called borderland cases between sanity and insanity—for example eccentrics, cranks, mattoids.

mattraca, var. MATRACA.

mattras(s, obs. forms of MATRASS.

mattrative, variant of MATURATIVE.

mattre, obs. form of MATTER.

mattress[1] ('mætrɪs). Forms: 3–6 **materas**, 4 **matrace**, 4–5 **materace**, 6 **mattrace**, 4–6 **materes**, 5–6 **matres**, 6 **mattres**, 6–7 **mattresse**, **-iss**, **matteris**, (5 **matras(e**, **-ess**, **-ys**, **materis**, **-os**, **matteras**, 6 **mattrys**, **matrice**, 7 **matt(e)rice**), 5, 8–9 **matrass**, 9 **mattrass**, 6– **mattress**. [a. OF. *materas* (mod.F. *matelas*), ad. It. *materasso*, commonly viewed as identical (exc. for the Arab. prefixed article *al-*) with Sp. and Pg. *almadraque*, Pr. *almatrac*, ad. Arab. *al-maṭrah*, place where something is thrown, in mod. use also mat, cushion, f. root *ṭaraḥa* to throw. The MHG. *matraz* (mod.G. *matratze*) is from Fr.]

1. A contrivance used as a bed or (more commonly) as a support for a bed, consisting of a case formed by two pieces of canvas or other textile material quilted together, stuffed with hair, flocks, straw, or the like. In recent use extended to include other appliances serving the same purpose, esp. one consisting of wire cloth stretched upon a frame or containing an array of springs.

c **1290** *S. Eng. Leg.* I. 188 'Goth', he seide, 'and maketh a bed..Of quoiltene and of materasz'. **1395** *E.E. Wills* (1882) 5 My secunde best fetherbed, with caneuas materas. *c* **1425** HOCCLEVE *Minor Poems* xxiii. 779 The pilwes nesshe and esy materas. **1495** *Nottingham Rec.* III. 38 Duo matrasses, pretii vs. **1519** HORMAN *Vulg.* 24 b, The flesshe lieth bytwene the bone and the skynne lyke a mattresse of cotton. **1588** *Fitch's Voy.* in Hakl. *Voy.* (1811) II. 388 Gownes of cotton like to our mattraces and quilted caps. **1624** *Invent.* in *Archæologia* XLVIII. 136 A bedsteed, a matt, a matterice, a fetherbed. **1693** DRYDEN *Juvenal* vi. 128 She..On a hard Mattress is content to sleep. **1764** HARMER *Observ.* 82 Their beds consist of a matrass laid on a floor, and over this a sheet. **1812** *Chron.* in *Ann. Reg.* 86 He hid it between a mattrass and a bed. **1848** in *Abridgm. Specif. Patents, Furniture*, etc. (1869) 551 An elastic mattress entirely metallic. **1850** *Ibid.* 158 A very portable spring mattress. **1877** KNIGHT *Dict. Mech.* 2291 *Spring-mattress*, one having metallic springs beneath the hair or moss filling. *Ibid.* 2792 Wire-mattress... See patents:— ..79,040. June 16, 68 [etc.]. **1890** *Syd. Soc. Lex.* s.v. *Mattress, Water mattress*, a waterproof case containing water, used for the prevention of bed-sores. **1900** *Cassell's Cycl. Mech.* (1902) IV. 325 A full-size wire mattress.

†**2.** A protective covering for a floor or for plants; a MAT. *Obs.*

1644 EVELYN *Diary* 17 Oct., By their carefull covering them [*sc.* plaster floors in the palace of Negros, Genoa] with canvas and fine mattresses, where there is much passage [etc.]. **1658** —— *French Gardiner* (1675) 239 Shelter them [peas] with pannels of Reeds, or Mattrasses. **1664** —— *Kal. Hort.* Apr. 65 Covering them [delicate plants] with Mattresses supported on cradles of hoops. **1706** J. GARDINER tr. *Rapin of Gardens* (1728) 59 Your Flow'rs defend with Matresses of Straw.

3. a. *Engineering.* A strong mat consisting of brushwood bound or twisted together, used in layers in the construction of dikes, piers, etc.

1875 *Proc. Inst. Civ. Engin.* XLI. 161 In commencing the construction of the dam..the first step was to cover the entire site with a strong fascine mattrass. *Ibid.* 167 The body of the pier takes from five to six mattrasses, averaging, with the stones, about 3 feet 3 inches thick. **1886** *Encycl. Brit.* XX. 581/1 The parallel jetties [at the mouth of the Mississippi] consist of tiers of willow mattresses.

b. *U.S.* A bed of sugar-cane. Hence **mattress** *v. trans.*, to form (sugar-cane) into 'mattresses'.

1829 A. SHERWOOD *Gazetteer Georgia* (ed. 2) 255 The stacks or banks in which seed cane is preserved during winter, are called mattresses. **1833** B. SILLIMAN *Man. Sugar Cane* 12 They are cut near the ground, and carted to the vicinity of the fields where they are to be planted; being formed..into long beds about fifteen feet wide, which are called *mattresses*. **1850** *Rep. Comm. Patents: Agric. 1850* (U.S. Dept. Agric.) 423 It was..supposed that the cane was spoiled in the mattress by the continued warm weather after it was mattressed.

4. *attrib.* and *Comb.*: **a.** *attrib.* (sense 1), as ***mattress-maker***, ***-making***, ***tick***; (sense 3), as ***mattress dike***, ***sill***; **b.** special comb., as **mattress antenna**, **array** = BILL-BOARD, BILLBOARD 2, also *ellipt.*; **mattress boat**, a boat on which mattresses for dikes, etc. are made and from which they are launched; **mattress-coat**, **needle** (see quots.); **mattress-jig** *slang*, sexual intercourse; †**mattress rubber**, ? a rough mattress-cover; **mattress suture** *Surg.*, a continuous suture through both lips of a wound, in which when a stitch has been taken the thread is tied, and the needle inserted on the same side from which it emerged.

1950 *Mattress antenna [see BILL-BOARD, BILLBOARD 2]. **1947** D. G. FINK *Radar Engin.* iv. 247 The power efficiencies of properly adjusted *mattress arrays vary from 80 to 95 per cent. *Ibid.* 249 The gain of a paraboloid is generally lower than that of a mattress of the same area expressed in square wavelengths. **1961** R. L. MATTINGLY in H. Jasik *Antenna Engin. Handbk.* xxv. 26 A common transmitter-receiving antenna can be implemented with a mattress array. **1884** KNIGHT *Dict. Mech.* Suppl., *Mattress Boat. **1641** BEST *Farm. Bks.* (Surtees Soc.) 20 When woll is well risen from the skinne, the fleece is as it weare walked togeather on the toppe, and underneath it is but lightly fastened to the undergrowth; and when a fleece is thus it is called a *mattrice-coate. **1886** *Encycl. Brit.* XX. 581/1 The entrance..was contracted..by means of *mattress dykes; and mattress sills were laid right across the entrance. **1896** FARMER & HENLEY *Slang* IV. 290/2 **Mattress-jig*, copulation. **1922** JOYCE *Ulysses* 418 Smutty Moll for a mattress jig. **1381** *Rolls Parlt.* III. 112/2 Johannes Sutton, *Materas-maker. **1829** *Register of Arts* III. 51 In the manner of *mattress making. **1884** KNIGHT *Dict. Mech.* Suppl. 236/2 *Curved *Mattress Needle* (Hydraulic Engineering), a needle for sewing brush mats with No. 13 wire. *a* **1625** BEAUM. & FL. *Wit. at Sev. Weap.* II. ii. (1647) 76/1 Here's a promising palme..here's Downe compared with Flocks and quilted Straw, thy Knight's fingers Are Ieane [1679 and mod. edd. *read* lean] *mattrice rubbers to these Feathers. **1886** *Mattress sill [see *mattress dike*]. **1904** *Brit. Med. Jrnl.* 24 Dec. 1682/2 In suturing up the wound in the kidney in the ordinary way the stitches frequently, on tying them, cut through. To avoid this..I have again followed Kelly who advises the use of *mattrass sutures. **1857** *Subj.-Matter Index of Patents* 924 Weaving looms (for making..*mattress-ticks, &c.).

mattress[2], **mattriss** (mætrɪs). [Of obscure origin; cf. 18th c. Fr. *maîtresse*: see Fry loc. cit.] (See quot. 1867.)

1685 *Lond. Gaz.* No. 2500/4 Playing-Cards..the Mattriss at 10*s*. 6*d*. per Gross, Fine Mattriss at 12*s*. per Gross [etc.]. **1867** FRY *Playing-Card Terms* in *Philol. Soc. Trans.* 56 *Mattress, Mattriss*, rejected playing cards..placed at the bottom of the sorted bundle, to be..sold at a cheaper rate. .. *Fine Mattress* is..applied to cards which are less defective; *Common M.* to cards which are more defective.

mattresse: see MATRASS[1]. *Obs.*

mattrice, mattross, obs. ff. MATRICE, MATROSS.

mattry, obs. form of MATTERY.

‖**mattulla** (mæ'tʌlə). [mod.L., app. f. L. *matta* mat, after *medulla*.] (See quots.)

1849 J. H. BALFOUR *Elem. Bot.* §57 In Palms also a similar [brown chaffy] substance occurs, called *reticulum* or *mattulla* (*matta*, a mat). *Ibid.* §96 The bases of the leaves.. surrounded by the mattulla or reticulum.

matty ('mætɪ), *a. rare.* [f. MAT *sb.*[1] + -Y.] Matted. Also in Comb. ***matty-haired*** adj.

1820 CLARE *Rural Life* (ed. 3) 141 And brush the weaving branches by Of briars and thorns so matty. **1824** J. SYMMONS tr. *Æschylus' Agamemnon* 52 And, matty-hair'd, our soldiers look'd like beasts.

mattyn, obs. form of MATE *v.*[1]

matulat, variant of MALTALENT *Obs.*

Matura ('mɑːtərə). Also **Matara**. [Name of a town (now called *Matara*) in Sri Lanka.] ***Matura diamond***: a colourless variety of zircon used as a gem. Cf. JARGON *sb.*[2]

1880 *Encycl. Brit.* XIII. 532/1 The Singalese variety [of pale jargoons], found chiefly at Matura, has been termed 'Matura diamond'. **1936** L. J. SPENCER *Key to Precious Stones* xvii. 189 Much of the colourless zircon..is known as 'Matura diamond'. **1962** R. WEBSTER *Gems* I. vii. 118 The colourless stones..were..called by the misnomer 'Matara diamonds', a term which should now be forgotten.

maturable (mə'tjʊərəb(ə)l), *a.* [f. MATURE *v.* + -ABLE.] That may be matured.

1889 *Critic* in *Nation* 9 May XLVIII. p. iv, Abilities, which, if immature, are yet maturable. **1902** *Cassell's Encycl. Dict.* Suppl., *Maturable*,..specif. in Surg., used of an inflamed part that may be brought to suppuration.

†**maturant**, *a.* and *sb.* ? *Obs.* [ad. L. *mātūrant-em*, pr. pple. of *mātūrāre*: see MATURE *v.*] = MATURATIVE *a.* and *sb.*

1661 LOVELL *Hist. Anim. & Min.* 363 Inflammation..; it's cured, by..maturants, rumpents [etc.]. **1844** HOBLYN *Dict. Terms Med.* (ed. 2) s.v. *Maturation*, Applications which promote suppuration have been called *maturants*. **1856** MAYNE *Expos. Lex.*, *Maturans*..maturing: maturant.

†**maturate**, *a. Obs. rare*[−1]. [ad. L. *mātūrātus*, pa. pple. of *mātūrāre*: see MATURE *v.*] Matured.

1556 *Ann. Barber-Surg. Lond.* (1890) 312 His well defycell cures..wch can not be dooen wtout maturate judgment, and Learninge.

maturate ('mætjʊreɪt), *v.* Also 6 **maturat**. [f. L. *mātūrāt-*, ppl. stem of *mātūrāre* to ripen, f. *mātūr-us* ripe: see MATURE *a.*]

1. *trans.* (*Med.*) To cause (matter, a boil, pustule, etc.) to ripen or suppurate; to 'bring to a head'. Also *absol.*, to cause suppuration. Now *rare* or *Obs.*

1541 R. COPLAND *Guydon's Form.* R iij b, Whan they [remedies] fynde mater redy to rypenesse they do maturate and to resolue, they resolue. **1547** BOORDE *Brev. Health* cix. 41 b, Than excoriat the skyn and maturat the matter. **1665** G. HARVEY *Advice agst. Plague* 27 The said tumours being now imperfectly maturated..are to be opened. **1694** W. SALMON *Bate's Dispens.* (1713) 687/1 It is a delicate Anodyn; it lenifies or softens, and maturates. **1779** *Gentl. Mag.* XLIX. 80 [It] is frequently used to maturate boils. **1801** *Med. Jrnl.* V. 404 They [pustules] continued filling till they were completely maturated. **1890** in *Syd. Soc. Lex.*

†**2.** To mature, ripen (fruits, vegetable juices, liquors, etc.). Also *fig. Obs.*

1628 FELTHAM *Resolves* I. xix. 35 Which may strongly argue the Intentions of the Soul to be good; though unable to maturate that seed that is in it. **1655** FULLER *Ch. Hist.* I. i. 8 By powring every night warm water on the root thereof, a Tree may be maturated artificially, to bud out in the midst of Winter. **1676** WORLIDGE *Cider* ii. §3. 14 This Juice or Sap [in Fruit]..is by the continual animating heat of the Sun, maturated. **1732** BERKELEY *Minute Philos.* (1732) 36/2 Aromatic Oils maturated by great length of time turn to Salts. **1743** *Lond. & Country Brew.* III. (ed. 2) 206 It is not Boiling that maturates and preserves Malt-Liquors, but a right and due Fermentation. **1756** P. BROWNE *Jamaica* 13 Dung adds warmth to the soil, and maturates as well as it enriches the juice.

†**3.** To mature, develop, make perfect. (With object a person or personal attribute.) *Obs.*

1622 C. FITZ-GEFFRY *Elisha* 7 Yeares must maturate men to such Functions. **1662** HOPKINS *Serm.* (1685) 104 Time, to maturate these growing hopes. **1791** SMEATON *Edystone L.* Contents 8/2 Dovetailing considered... The idea of Dovetailing maturated.

†**4. a.** *Alchemy.* To purify and digest (a metal) by maturation; to exalt by purification *into*. **b.** *Metallurgy.* To bring (an ore) into the metallic state.

1641 FRENCH *Distill.* vi. (1651) 176 A perfect metall, as gold, hath [not] this impurity; I mean when it is fully maturated and melted. **1669** W. SIMPSON *Hydrol. Chym.* 58 The ripening coagulating fire of the embrionate Sulphur.. exiccates and maturates the radical Mercurial moisture, and terminates it in a Metalick species. **1686** PLOT *Staffordsh.* 160 Burning it [a stone] in a Crucible, it was quickly maturated into Iron. **1758** W. BORLASE *Nat. Hist. Cornw.* 202 The metal becomes thoroughly maturated, that is, as ductile, and free from stone [etc.]..as fire itself can make it.

†**5.** (See quot.) *Obs.*[−0]

1623 COCKERAM, *Maturate*, to hasten.

†**6.** *intr.* Of fruit: To ripen, mature. *Obs.*

1665 SIR T. HERBERT *Trav.* (1677) 388 Such [fruits] as will not maturate with us in England. **1756** P. BROWNE *Jamaica* 200 It will soften and maturate in a few days.

7. Of a pustule: To ripen, suppurate.

1746 *Brit. Mag.* 101 About 50 or 60 small Pox came out, which maturated and scabbed. **1858** J. COPLAND *Dict. Pract. Med.* III. 812/2 From the fifth to the eighth day of the eruption, the pustule maturates.

Hence '**maturated** *ppl. a.*, '**maturating** *vbl. sb.* and *ppl. a.*

1628 ALEX. LEIGHTON *Sion's Plea agst. Prelacy* (ed. 2) 26 Rather than they would suffer the plague soare of their oppressing pride to be burst by the maturating Cataplasmes of wholesom Laws. **1698** [R. FERGUSSON] *View of Ecclesiastick* 31 Maturated, Adult and Pregnant Wit. **1698** *Phil. Trans.* XX. 440, I ordered him Maturating Gargles. **1758** J. S. *Le Dran's Observ. Surg.* (1771) 96, I applied maturating Cataplasms. **1897** *Allbutt's Syst. Med.* III. 171 The addition of various..substances to the maturating medium.

maturation (mætjʊ'reɪʃən). Also 6 **maduracyon**, **maturacion**, 7 *erron.* **-ition**. [a. F. *maturation*, ad. L. *mātūrātiōn-em*, n. of action f. *mātūrāre*: see MATURATE and MATURE *vbs.*]

1. *Med.* The 'ripening' of morbific matter; the process by which matter is formed in an abscess or a vesicle becomes a pustule, suppuration; the action of causing this process.

1541 COPLAND *Guydon's Form.* S iij, The fyrste [cure] is to rype the mater. The seconde after the maduracyon to open it. **1543** TRAHERON tr. *Vigo's Chirurg.* II. i. 13 b/2 Humours ..whych nature canne not..bringe to maturation or

suppuration. **1597** A. M. tr. *Guillemeau's Fr. Chirurg.* 23/4 Perseaving it to be come to his full maturation and ripnes. **1684** tr. *Bonet's Merc. Compit.* I. 17 The parts affected may be cleared of the Thrush by maturation of it. **1791** BOSWELL *Johnson* an. 1760, Mr. Sharpe is of opinion that the tedious maturation of the cataract is a vulgar error. **1800** *Med. Jrnl.* III. 502 The progressive stages of inflammation, maturation, and scabbing. **1861** GRAHAM *Pract. Med.* 665 The period of maturation of the eruption. **1897** *Allbutt's Syst. Med.* II. 565 The maturation of the pocks.

†**2.** *Alchemy.* The operation of converting a baser metal into gold. Cf. MATURATE *v.* 4. *Obs.*

1612 WOODALL *Surg. Mate* Wks. (1639) 273 Maturation is exaltation of a substance, rude and crude to that which is mature and perfect. **1626** BACON *Sylva* §326 We conceive indeed, that a perfect good Concoction, or Digestion, or Maturation of some Metalls, will produce Gold. **1671** J. WEBSTER *Metallographia* ii. 31 Whose Art of.. Maturation of Metals he laboureth to prove to be false.

†**3.** *Physics.* The (supposed) natural ripening or development of material substances by the operation of heat and motion. *Obs.*

a **1652** J. SMITH *Sel. Disc.* IV. iii. (1821) 75 The very grass ..may..after many refinings, macerations, and maturations,..spring up into so many rational souls. **1665-6** *Phil. Trans.* I. 338 Whether..the Mine will afford Ore or Metal in tract of time,..and whether to this Maturation of the Mine, the being exposed to the free Aire be necessary. **1753** SHUCKFORD *Creation & Fall* 133 Little Particles..which have..in the Maturation of Ages, remained sandy and sabulous..or become Rocks or Minerals.

4. a. Of fruits, the juices of plants, etc.: The action or process of ripening or becoming ripe; development to ripeness; also, an instance of this.

1621 BURTON *Anat. Mel.* I. i. II. v, Maturation is especially obserued in the fruits of trees. **1770-4** A. HUNTER *Georg. Ess.* (1803) I. 49 Maturation of their seed, seems all that is required of them. **1791** HAMILTON *Berthollet's Dyeing* I. I. I. vi. 115 By maturation, the fruit from having been hard grows soft..and sweet. **1839** URE *Dict. Arts* 292 After the maturation of the fruit..they are plucked. **1882** *Garden* 7 Jan. 4/1 Perfect maturation of the foliage, which means maturation of the bulb.

b. Of liquors or other things undergoing preparation for use: The action of maturing; the process of becoming matured.

1605 TIMME *Quersitanus* II. vi. S b, So wee see, that wines in whose maturation or rypening the heate of the sunne failed are made more crude and sharpe. **1626** BACON *Sylva* §312 For the Maturation of Drinkes, it is wrought by the Congregation of the Spirits together. **1675** EVELYN *Terra* 59 If..the ground seem to require an hastier maturation, there may be a crop of Beans [etc.] sown upon it, which will mellow it exceedingly. **1707** MORTIMER *Husb.* (1721) II. 348 Ginger accelerateth the Maturation of Cyder. **1743** *Lond. & Country Brew.* III. (ed. 2) 201 The Liquor has before received due Maturation in the Copper and Mash-tun. **1778** [W. MARSHALL] *Minutes Agric.* 17 Oct. 1774 The idea of making compost useful while in a state of maturation. **1835** URE *Philos. Manuf.* 83 The downy filaments of cotton..get more or less flattened in the maturation and drying of the wool. **1902** *Daily Chron.* 7 Jan. 6/3 A lengthy process of maturation in sherry casks is required to make it [whisky] a wholesome beverage.

5. The action or process of coming to full growth or development: **a.** of man, his faculties, etc. In *Psychol.*, the physical growth which, together with learning, leads to full development. Also *transf.*

1616 J. LANE *Contn. Sqr.'s T.* v. 492 Our care to feede them [children],..our after cares, as they gaine maturation. **1660** G. FLEMING *Stemma sacrum* 6 From the first time that could begin any Maturition to his Judgement. **1693** J. TYRRELL *Law Nat.* 30 There happens to us Men.. Maturation, Decay, and Dissolution. **1820** FOSTER *Ess. Evils Pop. Ignor.* 294 The maturation of the spiritual being, to the highest attainable degree. **1834-43** SOUTHEY *Doctor* clxxxv. (1862) 483 Imputing to the decay of our nature that which results from its maturation. **1921** *Psychol. Rev.* May 196 The process runs along parallel with the process of maturation and it is not clear in any case just what is contributed by heredity and what is due to learning. **1938** R. S. WOODWORTH *Exper. Psychol.* xxix. 764 Maturation consists largely in development of the ability to learn. **1943** C. T. MORGAN *Physiol. Psychol.* vii. 124 Many experiments have been carried out on the general problem of the relative importance of maturation and learning. **1958** K. LOVELL *Educ. Psychol. & Children* vii. 103 In studying the effects of maturation on learning in children, use has been made..of identical twins. **1968** M. BUNGE in Lakatos & Musgrave *Probl. Philos. Sci.* 134 Scientific Research can pass through several phases of maturation, the degree of maturity attained depending on the depth and the logical organization of the ideas involved. **1970** D. S. WRIGHT et al. *Introducing Psychol.* iv. 70 There is still some value in contrasting maturation and learning... This is simply a convenient way of classifying different antecedent conditions of the single process of development.

b. of plants, animals, etc. *spec.* of their gametes.

1664 POWER *Exp. Philos.* I. 61 To give..vegetation and maturation to Plants. **1655-87** H. MORE *App. Antid.* xiii. (1712) 223 He found these Birds [Tree geese] in several degrees of maturation. **1755** B. MARTIN *Mag. Arts & Sci.* III. xi. 376 The Maturation, and bringing to Perfection the Chicken contained in Embryo. **1826** KIRBY & SP. *Entomol.* IV. 146 Organs..which are appropriated to the.. maturation, exclusion and deposition of their eggs. **1884** W. K. PARKER *Mammal. Descent* ii. (1885) 55 The growth and maturation of the germs. **1896** E. B. WILSON *Cell* 338 *Maturation*, the final stages in the development of the germ-cells. More specifically, the processes by which the reduction of the number of chromosomes is effected. **1904** *Brit. Med. Jrnl.* 17 Dec. 1643 The maturation and fertilization of the ovum. **1972** BALIN & GLASSER *Reproductive Biol.* v. 319 (*heading*) Maturation of epididymal spermatozoa.

c. of a disease.

1818-20 E. THOMPSON *Cullen's Nosol. Meth.* (ed. 3) 331 A vesicular disease, which..passes through a regular course of increase, maturation, and decline. **1871** DARWIN *Desc. Man* I. i. 12 That mysterious law which causes..the maturation ..of various diseases, to follow lunar periods.

d. *transf.* and *fig.* esp. the completing or perfecting (of a plan, work, etc.).

1655 *Theophania* 165 The birth, growth and maturation of our Love. **1751** JOHNSON *Rambler* No. 111 ⁋3 Time sufficient for the regular maturation of our schemes. *Ibid.* No. 156 ⁋12 A play represents some transaction, through its regular maturation to its final event. **1845** J. H. NEWMAN *Developm. Chr. Doctrine* (1878) 38 The germination and maturation of some truth. **1884** G. ALLEN *Philistia* III. xxxvii. 273 The pamphlet and the paper were in course of maturation.

†**6.** The forwarding (of a business, etc.). *Obs.*

1584 *Leycesters Commonw.* (1641) 98 It..tendeth directly to Maturation of the principall purpose. **1623** COCKERAM, *Maturation*, a hastening. **1655** FULLER *Church Hist.* IX. xvi. 173 The said Convocation met..for the maturation of business with the more expedition.

7. *attrib.*, as **maturation division** *Biol.*, either of the two divisions of meiosis.

1896 E. B. WILSON *Cell* v. 185 It is plain that the nature of the maturation-divisions can only be approached through a study of the origin of the tetrads. **1966** *Chromosoma* XIX. 99 (*heading*) The maturation divisions of the parthenogenetic stick insect *Carausius morosus* Br.

Hence **matu'rational** *a.*, of or pertaining to maturation (esp. sense 5).

1929 A. GESELL in C. Murchison *Found. Exper. Psychol.* 651 (*heading*) Maturational correspondence in identical twins. *Ibid.* 658 Maturational factors preserve his native endowment. **1953** *New Biol.* XIV. 27 Clearly this 'setting' of the perceptual and behavioural pattern in the third and fourth years must have as its base important maturational changes in the physiology and anatomy of the brain. **1961** J. BERKO in Saporta & Bastian *Psycholinguistics* VI. 372/1 Throughout childhood, girls are perhaps from a maturational point of view slightly ahead of the boys who are their chronological age mates.

maturative (mə'tjʊərətɪv), *a.* and *sb.* Also 5 **maturatif, -yf.** [a. F. *maturatif*, ad. L. *mātūrātīv-us*, f. *mātūrāre* to MATURE.]

A. *adj.*

1. *Med.* That causes maturation or the formation of pus; pertaining to or characterized by maturation. (Cf. MATTERATIVE.)

c **1400** *Lanfranc's Cirurg.* 44 He leide þerto a plastre maturatijf. **1543** TRAHERON tr. *Vigo's Chirurg.* II. i. 14/1 We haue seen that coruption of an Aposteme hath chaunced thorough defaute of appliynge conuenyent maturatyue Medicines. **1568** SKEYNE *The Pest* (1862) 42 Quhilk is maruelous maturatiue, distroyand all venome. **1620** VENNER *Via Recta* v. 88 Butter..is of a moystning, mollifying, maturatiue, and resolutiue faculty. **1725** SLOANE *Jamaica* II. 92 Birdlime is maturative. **1831** J. DAVIES *Mat. Med.* 391 Its leaves bruised and boiled are frequently used as a maturative poultice. **1858** J. COPLAND *Dict. Pract. Med.* I. 810/1 The maturative, or suppurative stage [of small-pox].

†**2.** Having the power or function of maturing or ripening (fruits, etc.); of or pertaining to maturation.

1646 SIR T. BROWNE *Pseud. Ep.* IV. xiii. 227 They..have their second Summer hotter and more maturative of fruits then the former. **1658** —— *Gard. Cyrus* iii. *Hydriot*, etc. 50 The maturative progresse of Seeds. **1685** BOYLE *Salubr. Air* 35 Some maturative power, whereby an inanimate Body may gradually admit of such a change.

B. *sb.* A maturative remedy.

1398 TREVISA *Barth. De P.R.* VII. xxi. (1495) 239 Thenne men must werke fyrste wyth colde maturatiues rypynge. *c* **1400** *Lanfranc's Cirurg.* 211 If þer haþ be leid þerto ony maturatif so þat þe mater þerof be rotid, þan opene it. **1543** TRAHERON tr. *Vigo's Chirurg.* II. i. 14/1 Auicenne.. counselleth vs, to applye colde and moyste maturatyues. **1665** G. HARVEY *Advice agst. Plague* 27 We are to give them [tumours] vent as speedily as possible, by applying.. Maturatives. **1743** tr. *Heister's Surg.* 183 These compound Maturatives. **1831** J. DAVIES *Mat. Med.* 195 It is employed as a maturative and stimulant. **1855** DUNGLISON *Med. Lex.* (ed. 12), *Maturative*, a medicine which favours the maturation of an inflammatory tumour.

mature (mə'tjʊə(r)), *a.* [ad. L. *mātūrus* ripe, timely, early. Cf. MURE.]

1. Complete in natural development or growth.

a. Of fruits, etc.: Ripe. *Obs.* in lit. use.

1599 A. M. tr. *Gabelhouer's Bk. Physicke* 58/2 When as.. the seede [of Fennell] is mature cut it there of. **1676** WORLIDGE *Cider* ii. §3. 14 Cider well made of Mature Fruits. **1791** COWPER *Yardley Oak* 33 Thou [the acorn] fell'st mature.

fig. **1850** TENNYSON *In Mem.* lxxxi, There cannot come a mellower change, For now is love mature in ear.

b. Of an embryo, fœtus, plant, etc.: Full grown.

1801 *Med. Jrnl.* V. 45 A living mature fœtus. **1845** *Florist's Jrnl.* 274 The proper season for repotting mature plants. **1882** VINES *Sachs' Bot.* 775 The green leaves do not grow after they are mature.

†**c.** 'Ripe' or ready *for*. *Obs.*

1607 SHAKS. *Cor.* IV. iii. 26 This [insurrection] lyes glowing..and is almost mature for the violent breaking out. **1667** MILTON *P.L.* XI. 537 Till like ripe Fruit thou drop.. or be..Gatherd, not harshly pluckt, for death mature.

d. Of a soil: having a fully developed profile. Of a soil profile or its parts: fully developed.

1926 C. F. MARBUT in Tansley & Chipp *Study of Vegetation* vii. 131 Mature soils..owe their essential characters to the nature of the climate in which they are developed. **1927** [see IMMATURE *a.* 2 e]. **1954** W. D. THORNBURY *Princ. Geomorphol.* iv. 76 A mature soil profile exhibits well-developed horizons. **1971** E. A. FITZPATRICK *Pedology* vii. 249/2 Marbut placed great emphasis on mature freely drained soils.

2. a. Of a person: Having the powers of body and mind fully developed. Of personal qualities, etc.: Fully developed or ripened.

1600 J. PORY tr. *Leo's Africa* Ded. A 2 M. Richard Hakluyt: who out of his mature judgement in these studies, ..was the onely man that mooved me to translate it. **1606** SHAKS. *Tr. & Cr.* IV. v. 97 The yongest Sonne of Priam;.. Not yet mature, yet matchlesse. **1667** MILTON *P.L.* x. 882 To trust thee [Eve] from my side, imagin'd wise, Constant, mature. **1697** DRYDEN *Virg. Georg.* III. 79 A Time will come, when my maturer Muse..a nobler Theme will chuse. **1718** PRIOR *Solomon* II. 164 Mature the virgin was,..Grace shap'd her limbs, and beauty deck'd her face. **1726** CAVALLIER *Mem.* IV. 310 When they came to maturer Years. **1842** COMBE *Digestion* 241 In mature and middle age..still greater caution..becomes requisite. **1870-74** J. THOMSON *City Dreadf. N.* I. ix, Mature men chiefly, few in age or youth.

b. const. *in.*

1606 SHAKS. *Ant. & Cl.* I. iv. 31 Boyes..mature in knowledge. **1682** DRYDEN *Mac Fl.* 16 Shadwell..Mature in dulness from his tender years. **1784** COWPER *Task* v. 296 When they are grown mature In wisdom. **1875** JOWETT *Plato* (ed. 2) V. 243 No animal at birth is mature or perfect in intelligence.

c. Of or pertaining to maturity or manhood. *rare.*

1611 SHAKS. *Wint. T.* I. i. 27 They were trayn'd together in their Child-hoods;..Since their more mature Dignities.. made seperation of their Societie [etc.].

d. *mature student*: an adult who undertakes a course of study at a later age than normal.

[**1924** L. G. E. JONES *Training of Teachers in Eng. & Wales* xiv. 352 The sprinkling of more mature students is a great help.] **1953** C. A. RICHARDSON et al. *Educ. of Teachers in Eng., France & U.S.A.* iii. 59 The mature student is one who..wishes to embark on a course of training as a teacher at an age considerably later than the normal age of entry to college. **1969** H. C. DENT *Educ. Syst. Eng. & Wales* (ed. 4) x. 205 From 1962–63 the Minister of Education ceased to give State scholarships (except to mature students). **1969** *Guardian* 16 Sept. 5/3 The formation of a new union for mature students has given fresh hope to people who are taking up teachers' training courses late in life. **1970** *St. Hilda's College (Oxf.) Rep. 1968–69* 21 One mature student was accepted to read for the B.A. in English. **1971** *Mod. Law Rev.* XXXIV. 652 A better solution to the problem of democratising recruitment would be to facilitate the attendance at law school of mature students.

3. (The earliest use.) Of thought or deliberation: Duly prolonged and careful. Of plans, conclusions, etc.: Formed after adequate deliberation.

1454 *Rolls of Parlt.* V. 239/2 The Justicez, after sadde communicacion and mature deliberacion hadde amonge theim, aunswered..that [etc.]. **1543** in W. H. Turner *Select. Rec. Oxf.* 170 After long and mature debating of the mattar. **1578** *Reg. Privy Council Scot.* III. 54 Eftir mature advise and deliberatioun. **1638** JUNIUS *Paint. Ancients* A 3 Things..which..in the review and more mature cogitation I wished might be altered. **1726** SWIFT *Gulliver* II. iii, Upon mature thoughts, I began to doubt whether I was injured or no. **1792** BURKE *Pres. St. Aff.* Wks. 1842 I. 585 On a full and mature view and comparison of the historical matter. **1839** JAMES *Louis XIV*, I. 389 Till his plans for revolt were mature. **1848** LYTTON *Harold* VIII. iv, The interval.. allowed no time for mature and careful reflection. **1879** FARRAR *St. Paul* xxxviii. (1883) 637 His ripest thoughts, and ..the maturest statement of the Gospel which he preached.

†**4.** That takes place early; prompt. *Obs.*

1600 FAIRFAX *Tasso* XIX. xcviii. 356 Hardly I scapt their hands by mature flight. **1672** MARVELL *Corr.* Wks. 1872–5 II. 407 Carrying things on with the maturest expedition.

†**5.** Of an event: Occurring when the fitting time has come. Of time: Due. (The opposite of 'premature'.) *Obs.*

1605 SHAKS. *Lear* IV. vi. 282 In the mature time, With this vngracious paper [Ile] strike the sight Of the death-practis'd Duke. **1667** MILTON *P.L.* v. 862 The birth mature Of this our native Heav'n.

6. *Med.* **a.** In a state of suppuration; ripe.

1828 in WEBSTER; and in later Dicts.

b. Of a progressive cataract: characterized by complete opacity.

1850 [see IMMATURE *a.* 2 d]. **1904** L. W. FOX *Dis. Eye* xii. 310 Operations should not be performed on both eyes at the same time, even though both cataracts are mature. **1970** A. H. KEENEY *Ocular Exam.* ix. 143/1 A mature cataract is one that has developed complete opacification throughout.

7. *Comm.* Of a bill, etc.: That has reached the time for payment; due.

1882 in OGILVIE.

mature (mə'tjʊə(r)), *v.* Also 6 madure. [Partly ad. obs. F. *maturer*, also *madurer*, ad. L. *mātūrāre*, f. *mātūrus* MATURE; partly f. MATURE *a.*]

1. *trans.* (*Med.*) = MATURATE *v.* I.

1541 COPLAND tr. *Guydon's Form.* S iij b, In mundyfyenge it madureth, and suffreth nat to fystule. **1599** A. M. tr. *Gabelhouer's Bk. Physic* 95/1 A potione to mature, or ripen, an Apostematione. **1898** *Allbutt's Syst. Med.* V. 39 To mature, that is to loosen the [bronchial] catarrh.

2. To bring to maturity or perfect development; to ripen (fruits, wine, etc.); to

bring (a plant or crop) to full growth. Also *pass.* = 6.

1626 BACON *Sylva* §314 Creame is Matured..by Putting in Cold Water. *Ibid.* §326 To see if the Virtuall Heat of the Wine..will not Mature it [an apple]. **1701** J. PHILIPS *Splendid Shilling* 117 Nor taste the Fruits that the Sun's genial Rays Mature. **1781** COWPER *Charity* 442 A ship, well freighted with the stores The sun matures on India's spicy shores. **1853** ROBERTSON *Serm.* Ser. III. viii. (1857) 114 Warmth..expands the leaf, matures the fruit [etc.].

fig. **1821** SHELLEY *Hellas* 575 The Greek has reaped The costly harvest his own blood matured.

absol. **1626** BACON *Sylva* §326 They are euer Temperate Heats that Digest, and Mature.

3. *transf.* To cause to develop fully (the mind, judgement, etc.); to perfect the development of (a person) mentally and physically.

1660 R. COKE *Power & Subj.* 75 Whenas judgment is matured by age. **1671** MILTON *P.R.* IV. 281 Till time mature thee to a Kingdom's waight. **1742** YOUNG *N. Th.* v. 772 Virtue, not rolling suns, the mind matures. **1766–88** GIBBON *Decl. & F.* II. xliii. 597 His prudence was matured by experience. **1842** TENNYSON '*Love thou thy land*' x, Nature ..Thro' many agents making strong, Matures the individual form. **1851** MACAULAY *Ess.*, *Fredk. Gt.* (1877) 661 Suffering had matured his understanding.

absol. *a* **1861** MRS. BROWNING *Little Mattie* ii. Poems (1862) 2 Just so young but yesternight, Now she is as old as death... An hour matures.

4. *fig.* To make ripe or ready; to perfect (a plan, work, etc.); to bring to a head.

1667 MILTON *P.L.* I. 660 But these thoughts Full Counsel must mature. **1769** ROBERTSON *Chas. V*, III. x. 222 He had leisure to mature his schemes. **1784** COWPER *Task* iii. 450 An art That toiling ages have but just matured. **1817** JAS. MILL *Brit. India* I. III. ii. 500 His vizir..matured the dissatisfaction of the Omrahs, and..dethroned..him. **1851** GALLENGA *Italy* 195 The great events that were maturing the destinies of the common country in Northern Italy. **1865** H. PHILLIPS *Amer. Paper Curr.* II. 23 The plans.. were evidently not yet matured.

b. Const. *into.*

1855 MACAULAY *Hist. Eng.* xii. III. 210 The passions.. would be at once matured into fearful vigour. **1857** BUCKLE *Civilisation* I. ix. 585 Their habits of self-reliance, enabled them to mature into a system..the right of private judgment. **1861** T. WRIGHT *Ess. Archæol.* II. xxii. 197 This taste for gallantry was matured into a system.

†**5.** To forward or hasten duly. *Obs. rare.*

1660 MARVELL *Corr.* Wks. 1872–5 II. 24 The House hath been..busied in..maturing those bills. **1661–2** *Ibid.* 77 Be maturing your own businesse hither as fast as may be.

6. *intr.* To come to maturity or perfect development; to grow ripe: **a.** of fruits, seeds, wine, etc.

1626 BACON *Sylva* §324 It is like they [*sc.* fruit] would mature more finely. **1795** NAPLETON *Adv. to Student* v. 55 It [the seed] may..grow and mature where you see it not. **1843** *Penny Cycl.* XXVII. 463/2 The wine is left in the cask..to mature. **1879** LUBBOCK *Sci. Lect.* i. 8 In some cases the stigma has matured before the anthers are ripe.

b. of animals.

1887 F. FRANCIS Jun. *Saddle & Mocassin* 163 You want the cattle that's easiest handled, and easiest sold, and that matures quickest and keeps in best condition.

c. *transf.* of persons.

1844 BROWNING *Boy & Angel* 33 The man matured and fell away Into the season of decay. **1870** DISRAELI *Lothair* xl, But what pleases me most are his manners... I never knew any one who had so matured.

d. *fig.* To 'ripen' or develop *into* or *to.*

1805 SOUTHEY *Madoc* I. xvii, Such thoughts, As might.. have matured To penitence and peace. **1875** POSTE *Gaius* I. (ed. 2) 78 Possession could not mature by usucapion into ownership.

7. *Comm.* Of a bill, sum of money, etc.: To reach the time fixed for payment; to become due.

1861 GOSCHEN *For. Exch.* 10 Those bills being all forced upon the money-market for discount at once, instead of being gradually encashed as they mature. **1892** *Daily News* 20 Feb. 2/4 In March as much as 980,000*l.* will mature. **1896** *Law Times* C. 436/2 Debentures which had matured for payment.

Hence **ma'turer** *rare*, one who matures.

1863 W. HANNA *Our Lord's Resurr.* 18 The nourisher, the maturer of that eternal life which is for our souls in him.

matured (mə'tjʊəd), *ppl. a.* [f. MATURE *v.* + -ED^1.] Ripened; fully developed or grown; perfected or completed.

1676 EVELYN *Terra* 53 On this [cast] a layer of well-matur'd Dung. **1805** A. KNOX *Rem.* (1834) I. 1 This matured state of grace. **1837** HT. MARTINEAU *Soc. Amer.* III. 75 He brought a rich and matured mind to the first employment of it. **1863** GEO. ELIOT *Romola* vi, The matured scholarship of Messere. **1882** A. W. WARD *Dickens* vi. 166 He seemed to stand erect in the strength of his matured powers. **1886** C. SCOTT *Sheep-farming* 38 Sheep prefer the fresh growth to matured blades.

maturely (mə'tjʊəlɪ), *adv.* Also 6 **maturly.** [f. MATURE *a.* + -LY^2.]

1. With full deliberation, after mature consideration.

1594 PARSONS *Conf. Next Success.* II. iv. 85 A sentence.. so maturely giuen, could not be reuoked. **1611** BIBLE *Transl. Pref.* ¶11 To haue the translations of the Bible maturely considered of. *a* **1639** SPOTTISWOOD *Hist. Ch. Scot.* II. (1677) 89 They might more maturely advise what course was fittest to be taken. **1735** BERKELEY *Free-think. in Math.* §43 Wks. 1871 III. 327, I had long and maturely considered the principles of the modern analysis. **1841** JAMES *Brigand* xxv, The rest might stand over till both you and I had thought maturely of the matter. **1865** CARLYLE *Fredk. Gt.* IX. x. III. 168 Our Crown-Prince, somewhat of a judge in after years, is maturely of opinion, That the French Lines were by no means inexpugnable.

†**2.** With due promptness: in good time; not too late; early. *Obs.*

1531 ELYOT *Gov.* I. xxii. (1546) 72 Consult before thou enterpryse any thyng, and after thou hast taken counsel, it is expedient to do it maturly. **1662** H. MORE *Antid. Atheism* III. xv. (1712) 135 They..were never able..maturely to discover the approaching dangers. **1692** BENTLEY *Boyle Lect.* iii. (1693) 17 We give him thanks for..receiving us more maturely [than the long-lived antediluvians] into those Everlasting Habitations above. **1790** COWPER *Odyss.* II. 227 But let us frame Effectual means maturely to suppress Their violent deeds.

3. With full development; ripely. Also, in a manner indicative of maturity.

1841 MYERS *Cath. Th.* III. §47. 128 The formation of a maturely Christian mind. **1886** CONST. F. WOOLSON *East Angels* ix. 176 But Garda Thorne isn't immature, she talks as maturely as I do. **1902**, **1965** [see DISSECTED *ppl. a.* 2 b]. **1965** M. SPARK *Mandelbaum Gate* iv. 108 The rest were Arabs and Jews, most of whom were maturely sixteen years of age and upward.

maturement (mə'tjʊəmənt). *rare*$^{-1}$. [f. MATURE *v.* + -MENT.] The action of maturing.

1883 D. WINGATE *Lost Laird* xviii, To do a little day by day towards the maturement of his plans.

matureness (mə'tjʊənɪs). [f. MATURE *a.* + -NESS.] The state of being mature, maturity.

1701–2 *Narr. Lower Ho. Convoc. Vind.* 51 The.. Matureness of their final Resolution. **1727** in BAILEY vol. II. **1833** G. R. PORTER *Trop. Agric.* 227 By..extracting a piece of pith, and examining its degree of matureness.

maturescence (mætjʊ'rɛsəns). [f. L. *mātūrēscentem*: see next and -ENCE.] The process of maturing.

1856 W. L. LINDSAY *Pop. Hist. Brit. Lichens* 66 The effect of maturescence of the spores.

†**matu'rescent**, *a. Obs.*$^{-0}$ [ad. L. *mātūrēscent-em*, pr. pple. of *mātūrēscĕre*, f. *mātūr-us*: see MATURE *a.* and -ESCENT.]

1727 BAILEY vol. II, *Maturescent*, waxing ripe. **1847** in WEBSTER.

†**ma'turify**, *v. Obs. rare*$^{-1}$. [ad. late L. *mātūrefacĕre* to make ripe: see -FY.] *trans.* To 'maturate' or exalt (a metal) *into* (gold).

1641 FRENCH *Distill.* v. (1651) 138 It [Oil of sand] maturifieth imperfect metals into gold.

maturing (mə'tjʊərɪŋ), *vbl. sb.* [f. MATURE *v.* + -ING^1.] The action of the verb MATURE.

1626 BACON *Sylva* §326 The Maturing of Metalls, and therby Turning some of them into Gold. **1885** *Athenæum* 25 Apr. 534/3 The gradual maturing of the young hero's mind. **1897** *Allbutt's Syst. Med.* II. 843 The maturing of wine is the process of development of these ethers.

maturing (mə'tjʊərɪŋ), *ppl. a.* [f. MATURE *v.* + -ING^2.] That matures, in the senses of the verb.

1801 SOUTHEY *Thalaba* III. xiv, His lip was darken'd by maturing life. **1820** KEATS *To Autumn* 2 Season of mists and mellow fruitfulness, Close bosom-friend of the maturing sun. **1903** *Blackw. Mag.* Jan. 44/2 A patch of maturing tobacco.

maturish (mə'tjʊərɪʃ), *a. rare*$^{-1}$. [f. MATURE *a.* + -ISH.] Somewhat mature.

1885 MEREDITH *Diana* III. xii. 244 She played..the maturish young woman smitten by an adorable youth.

maturity (mə'tjʊərɪtɪ). Also 4 **maturite**, 5 **-yte**, 6 **-itee**. [ad. F. *maturité* (15–16th c. in Hatz.-Darm.) or its source L. *mātūritās*, f. *mātūrus*: see MATURE *a.* and -ITY.]

†**1.** Deliberateness of action; mature consideration, due deliberation. *Obs.*

c **1375** BARBOUR *Bruce* XI. 583 Bot nane of thame so hardely Ruschit emang thame as did he, Bot with fer mair maturite. **1534** LD. BERNERS *Gold. Bk. M. Aurel.* (1546) B v b, A thyng that a sage personne with greatte maturitie and deliberation hath written. **1604** T. WRIGHT *Passions* II. x. 41 Yoong men and women..resolve rashly, and performe rarely, because that they concluded without maturity. **1611** BIBLE *Transl. Pref.* ¶14 Matters of such weight and consequence are to bee speeded with maturitie. **1706** tr. *Dupin's Eccl. Hist. 16th C.* II. III. xxi. 387 It shall be done, after Examination of the Case, with the utmost Maturity. **1734** tr. *Rollin's Anc. Hist.* (1827) I. Pref. 15 The study of profane history when entered upon with judgment and maturity.

†**2.** Due promptness. *Obs.*

1531 ELYOT *Gov.* I. xxii. (1546) 71 b, Yet of these two [celeritie and slownesse] springeth an excellent vertue, whervnto we lacke a name in englishe. Wherfore I am constrained to vsurpe a latine worde, callyng it Maturitie. *c* **1540** tr. *Pol. Verg. Eng. Hist.* (Camden) I. 77 Agricola.. hasted with maturitee [L. *maturat*] to resiste this eminent perrill. *Ibid.* 172 Which thing this yonge impe executed with great maturitee [L. *mature fecit*]. **1670** MARVELL *Corr.* Wks. 1872–5 II. 339 All things will be perfected doubtless with all possible maturity.

3. The state of being mature; fullness or perfection of development or growth.

a. Of a person (mentally and physically) or his attributes; also, the state of being of age.

1426 LYDG. *De Guil. Pilgr.* 23918 She was of gret sobrenesse..and of gret maturyte. **1568** GRAFTON *Chron.* II. 664 To abide and tarie the maturitie and decent full age of this noble princes. **1603** DANIEL *Panegyr. to King* lxiv, Thy full maturitie Of yeares and wisdome. **1651** G. W. tr. *Cowel's Inst.* 29 This age [one and twenty] with us is perfect and full maturity. **1796** BURKE *Regic. Peace* i. Wks. VIII. 146 When I was very young, a general fashion told me I was to admire some of the writings against that Minister: a little more maturity taught me as much to despise them. **1845** S. AUSTIN *Ranke's Hist. Ref.* I. 115 Till she reached years of maturity, she was confided to French guardianship. **1858** O. W. HOLMES *Aut. Breakf.-t.* xi. 106 Lines which embody the subdued and limited desires of my maturity. **1876** FREEMAN *Norm. Conq.* I. vi. 531 In the full maturity of life.

b. Of animals, plants, etc.: The state of being full grown.

1597 GERARDE *Herbal* clxvii. 1391 In short space after it [the barnacle-goose] commeth to full maturitie, and falleth into the sea. **1606** SHAKS. *Tr. & Cr.* I. iii. 317 The seeded Pride That hath to this maturity blowne vp In ranke Achilles, must..now be cropt. **1692** BENTLEY *Boyle Lect.* iv. 114 The inclosed Fœtus; which at the time of maturity broke through those Membranes. **1753** HOGARTH *Anal. Beauty* vi. 29 A single spreading oak, grown to maturity. **1774** GOLDSM. *Nat. Hist.* (1776) V. 328 She lays four or five eggs; of which but a part..come to maturity. **1833** G. R. PORTER *Tropical Agric.* 158 All the [tobacco] plants throughout the same field do not arrive together at their full maturity. **1879** HARLAN *Eyesight* ii. 25 Each one [eyelash] reaches maturity in about five months, and then drops out.

c. Of fruits, wine, etc.: Ripeness.

1665 BOYLE *Occas. Refl.* (1848) 68 Green Fruit..being neither sweetned nor concocted by Maturity. **1676** WORLIDGE *Cider* ii. §3. 14 The Bloud of the Grape obtains not that degree of Maturity in the Fruit, as [etc.]. **1707** MORTIMER *Husb.* (1721) II. 302 Large Shoots that impede the Fruit from its due Maturity. **1843** *Penny Cycl.* XXVII. 464/1 When wines have been kept in the wood for the period ..proper for attaining maturity.

4. Of immaterial things: The state of being complete, perfect or ready.

1625 K. LONG tr. *Barclay's Argenis* III. xi. 187 He may be sent backe..upon hope of being recalled, when things are come to better maturity. *a* **1635** NAUNTON *Fragm. Reg.* (A. b.) 36 The Secretary might have had end of discovery on a further maturity of the Treason. **1719** F. HARE *Ch. Authority Vind.* 26 Till things were come to that maturity that the dispensation of the Gospel did no longer want them. **1732** SWIFT *Repeal. Test* Wks. 1761 III. 293 They must wait maturity of time. **1785** REID *Intell. Powers* I. vi. 241 One science may be brought to a great degree of maturity. **1844** H. H. WILSON *Brit. India* III. 265 Measures which..were nearly brought to maturity. **1852** CONYBEARE & HOWSON *St. Paul* (1862) I. 54 The revolution of which Herod had sown the seeds now came to maturity.

†**b.** *pl.* Matured conditions. *Obs. rare*$^{-1}$.

1633 ADAMS *Exp. 2 Peter* i. 1 Canaan..was already furnished to their hands: Nature had enriched it with commodities, and Industry beautified it with buildings and maturities.

5. *Comm.* The state of becoming due for payment; the time at which a bill becomes due.

1815 DALLAS in Taunton *Comm. Pleas. Rep.* (1818) VI. 311 The period that intervened between the refusal to accept and the bill arriving at maturity for payment. **1860** *Commerc. Handbk.* 15 The period of the date of maturity of bills at or after sight. **1861** GOSCHEN *For. Exch.* 135 When their drafts come to maturity. **1901** *Scotsman* 30 Oct. 5/1 For six months' maturities the rate is still maintained at $3\frac{1}{2}$ to $3\frac{5}{8}$.

6. The state of an abscess in which the pus is fully formed (*Syd. Soc. Lex.* 1890).

1676 WISEMAN *Surg.* I. xvii. 79 Three or four days after they [*sc.* pustules] came to maturity, and brake.

matutinal (mætju:'taɪnəl), *a.* [ad. L. *mātūtīnālis*, f. *mātūtīnus*: see MATUTINE. Cf. F. *matutinal.*] Of or pertaining to the morning, occurring or performed in the morning, early. Also *rarely* [? after F. *matinal*], rising early.

1656 BLOUNT *Glossogr.*, *Matutinal*, belonging to the morning, or morning prayer. *a* **1800** PEGGE *Anecd.* (1814) 277 Another matutinal expression in ancient use was—'Give you (i.e. God) good Day'. **1834** JAMES *J. Marston Hall* xiv, Our household was not the most matutinal in the world. **1839** THACKERAY *Paris Sk.-bk.*, *Fr. School Paint.* (1869) 53 The matutinal dews twinkling in the grass. **1855** BRISTOWE *Th. & Pract. Med.* (ed. 2) 101 There is usually a matutinal fall, and an evening rise [of temperature]. **1869** BROWNING *Ring & Book* VI. 1443 What? Matutinal, busy with book so soon Of an April day? **1874** *Lays Mod. Oxford* 12 While undergraduates masticate The matutinal muffin. **1897** *Allbutt's Syst. Med.* IV. 192 The matutinal use of saline aperients.

Hence **matu'tinally** *adv.*, every morning.

1897 P. WARUNG *Old Regime* 107 Three workers only—and six mustered nightly—and rations for six drawn matutinally.

matutinary, *a. rare*$^{-1}$. [f. L. *mātūtīn-us* (see next) + -ARY.] Matutinal, early.

1858 HAWTHORNE *Fr. & It. Note-bks.* I. 239 We..were ready to start between five and six; being thus matutinary in order to get to Terni in time.

matutine ('mætju:taɪn), *a.* (and *sb.*) [ad. L. *mātūtīn-us*, f. *Mātūta* (occurring only as the proper name of the goddess of dawn, but prob. orig. appellative), allied to *mātūrus* early, MATURE *a.*]

1. Of or pertaining to the morning; occurring in the morning.

c **1445** LYDG. *Nightingale* 187 This ourc of morow, cleped matutyne, Falsly be-trayed. **1549** *Compl. Scot.* vi. 38 The crepusculyne lyne matutine of the norht est orizone. *a* **1602** W. PERKINS *Cases Consc.* (1619) 166 The first [canonical hour] they call the matutine, before the sunne rising. **1686** GOAD *Celest. Bodies* I. xii. 62[They] hint a Lunation following the next Feria at hor. 2 Matutine. **1848** CLOUGH *Bothie* I. 32 Hewson and Hobbes were down at the

matutine bathing. **1871** M. COLLINS *Marq. & Merch.* I. ix. 279 Covent Garden awoke to its matutine business.

b. Of a star; *spec.* in *Astron.* and *Astrol.*: That rises or is above the horizon before sunrise.

1500–20 DUNBAR *Poems* i. 4 Wp sprang the goldyn candill matutyne. **1601** HOLLAND *Pliny* I. 587 According as the said stars begin either to shine out or bee hidden in the morning before the Sun be up, or at evening after the Sunne is set, they..are named Matutine or Vespertine. **1652–62** HEYLYN *Cosmogr.* III. (1682) 109 The rising and setting of the Stars, whether..Matutine, or Vespertine, as the Artists phrase it. **1690** LEYBOURN *Curs. Math.* 449 She [Venus] is..Gibbous, ..as well when she is Vespertine as Matutine. **1819** J. WILSON *Dict. Astrol.* 286 The Moon is matutine until she has passed her first dichotome.

†**2.** *sb. pl.* Matins. *Obs.*

[Cf. *a* 1602 in sense 1.] **1655** FULLER *Ch. Hist.* VI. 287 Matutines: At the first hour, or six of the clock.

Hence ˈ**matutinely** *adv.*, in the morning.

1833 *New Monthly Mag.* XXXVIII. 442 [He] was wont to walk, matutinely, knee-deep into the sea.

mat-weed: see MAT *sb.*[1]

maty (ˈmeɪtɪ), **mate** (meɪt). *Anglo-Indian.* Also **matee.** [Of obscure origin: cf. Skr. *mētha* elephant-keeper, and Eng. MATE *sb.*[2]; see Yule.] A native servant, esp. an assistant or under-servant.

1810 T. WILLIAMSON *E. Ind. Vade M.* I. 241 In some families, *mates*, or assistants, are allowed, who do the drudgery. **1837** *Lett. fr. Madras* xii. (1843) 106 Here is our establishment:—one butler, one dress-boy, one matee, [etc.]. *Ibid.*, A cook's maty or helper. **1873** *Sat. Rev.* 6 Sept. 312/1 One of the attendants [of an elephant], who in Indian phraseology is termed 'a mate', the title of *Mahout* being reserved for the head keeper.

maty, variant of MATIE.

matyng, variant of METING *Obs.*, dream.

matzah (ˈmætsə). Also **matso** (ˈmætsəʊ), **-za, -zho, -zo, -zot, -zoth, mazzot, -oth, motso, -za, mozza.** Pl. **matzoth, -os.** [Yiddish *matse*, f. Heb. *maṣṣāh*.] (A wafer of) unleavened bread, eaten by orthodox Jews during the Passover.

1846 *Jewish Manual, or Pract. Information Jewish & Mod. Cookery* p. xiv, *Matso*, Passover cakes. **1871** E. LEVY *Jewish Cookery Bk.* 32 Soak two matzos, or crackers, in cold water. **1891** M. FRIEDLÄNDER *Jewish Relig.* II. 380 The head of the family..who reads the [Passover] Service has before him on the table..three unleavened cakes (*matsoth*). **1893** I. ZANGWILL *Childr. Ghetto* (ed. 3) xxii. 202 Now is the national salutation changed to 'How do the *Motsos* agree with you?' **1904** *Jewish Encycl.* VIII. 393/1 The eating of mazzot during the seven days of the Passover festival is intended to recall the hurried departure from Egypt. **1922** JOYCE *Ulysses* 79 Something like those mazzoth: it's that sort of bread: unleavened shew-bread. **1927** *Daily Express* 16 Apr. 9 The command concerning unleavened bread, known as 'Matzos', will be observed. **1950** G. MIKES *Milk & Honey* 152 On the feast day..matzot is eaten instead of bread. **1952** S. SPENDER *Learning Laughter* xi. 159 This night we eat *matza* and no leavened bread. **1963** *Ann. Reg. 1962* 374 In March the Soviet Government banned the making of *matzot* (unleavened bread) required for Passover observances. **1965** M. SPARK *Mandelbaum Gate* ii. 33 The unleavened bread, crisp *matzho* that made crumbs everywhere, was uncovered. **1970** L. M. FEINSILVER *Taste of Yiddish* iii. 323 Even the Air Force..has a pretty good idea of what matzo is, for a New Jersey woman reported an Unidentified Flying Object as looking like a big matzo. **1973** *Jewish Chron.* 2 Feb. 23/2 This particular hechsher only applies to matzot manufactured in Britain.

attrib.

1846 *Jewish Manual, or Pract. Information Jewish & Mod. Cookery* i. 9 *Matso soup*... Take half a pound of *matso* flour. **1906** *Mrs. Beeton's Bk. Househ. Managem.* lv. 1574 Take up a little of the motza paste..roll lightly in the motza meal. **1921** *Dict. Occup. Terms* (1927) 433 *Matzo* (or *matzoth*) *baker*..expeditiously removes circular matzo bread i.e. Jewish passover bread. **1953** W. P. MCGIVERN *Big Heat* ix. 111 He liked Jewish food..mozza ball soup. **1970** S. J. PERELMAN *Baby, it's Cold Inside* 208 The exhibit you see here..was first believed by the coroner to be a fossilized matzo ball. **1971** M. MCCARTHY *Birds of America* 36 She should be making *gefüllte* fish and matzoth balls. **1973** *Times* 3 Feb. 13/5 You can try the kneidlach soup (with matzo-meal dumplings).

mau, variant of MOWE *Obs.*, kinswoman.

maubre, obs. form of MARBLE.

mauby (ˈməʊbɪ). Also **mawby.** [See MOBBIE, MOBEE.] In Barbados, a drink made from the diluted extract of the bark of a tree or shrub of the genus *Gouania* or related plants; cf. MOBBIE, MOBEE 1.

1790 J. B. MORETON *Manners & Customs West India Islands* 105 Cool drink or mauby is a delicious nectar to them in the morning. **1954** S. M. SADEEK *Windswept & Other Stories* (1969) 25 He drank, at first sipping the tall mauby slowly. **1957** I. BAYLEY in F. A. Collymore *Notes for Gloss. Words & Phr. Barbadian Dial.* 56 Mauby is made from bark, boiled in water for about an hour, and concentrated to a basic extract. When making the drink, some of the stock is diluted with water; sugar and vanilla essence are added... The result is a bitter-sweet drink, with a frothy head, popular for quenching the thirst, and for 'cooling' the blood. **1958** J. CAREW *Black Midas* i. 17 One Friday Tanta Moore invited him in for a drink of mauby. **1962** *Listener* 16 Aug. 248/2 A man stands beside his handcart dispensing mawby or snowball, which consists of shaved ice covered with scarlet syrup. **1965** *Ibid.* 8 Apr. 523/3 Constant chatter is punctuated with the high-pitched, rather doleful cry of the 'mauby' girl: she..carries a two-gallon tank on her head, with a tap on it that she manipulates to dispense cold tea to her customers; a special kind of cold tea, brewed from the bark of the mauby plant. **1968** E. LOVELACE *Schoolmaster* i. 8 Fruit wines from cashew and guava, and sorrel and mauby. **1973** *Advocate-News* (Barbados) 15 Dec. 8/1 In short, it is like serving mauby and ginger beer in a cocktail glass. **1974** *Sunday Advocate-News* (Barbados) 10 Mar. 14/1 Formerly, mauby women walked the streets with their load on their heads, and a bench in hand. But today, some of them drive or are driven.

maucauco, obs. form of MACACO *sb.*[2]

maucherite (ˈmaʊx-, ˈmaʊk-, ˈmaʊʃəraɪt). *Min.* [ad. G. *maucherit* (F. Grünling 1913, in *Centralbl. f. Min., Geol. u. Paläont.* 225), f. the name of W. *Maucher* (1879–1930), mineral dealer of Munich; see -ITE[1].] A nickel arsenide, approximately $Ni_{11}As_8$, occurring as brittle, reddish grey tetragonal crystals that are opaque with a metallic lustre and tarnish on exposure.

1913 *Jrnl. Chem. Soc.* CIV. II. 516 Maucherite, a new nickel mineral from Thuringia... This new mineral, which was at first mistaken for rammelsbergite, occurs..in veins..in the copper-shales..at Eisleben, Thuringia. **1940** *Mineral. Mag.* XXV. 570 A physical, chemical, and preliminary structural study of maucherite..from Eisleben, Thuringia, and Sudbury, Ontario, and temiskamite..from Elk Lake, Ontario, shows that these minerals..represent a single mineral species. **1963** *Mineral. Abstr.* XVI. 263/1 Syntheses from nickel and arsenic were carried out by means of dry thermal procedures... At arsenic vapour pressure, Ni_5As_2, maucherite, niccolite, rammelsbergite or paramelsbergite [*read* pararammelsbergite], are formed depending on the temperature.

maucht, -less, etc.: see MAUGHT, -LESS, etc.

†**maud**[1]. *Obs.* [app. a use of the name *Maud* (:—*Mahald*) = Matilda.] A hag, beldam.

1532 MORE *Confut. Tindale* Wks. 685/1 So I see well Tindall meaneth for hys mother, some olde mother mawde. **1566** L. WAGER *Marie Magd.* (1904) 717 In good faith, when ye ar come to be an old maude, Then it will be best for you to play the baude.

maud[2] (mɔːd). Also 9 **mawd.** [Of obscure origin: cf. MALDY.] A grey striped plaid worn by shepherds in the South of Scotland; also a travelling rug or wrap resembling a maud.

1787 MRS. SCOTT in *Burns's Wks.* (Chamb.) 66 A' honest Scotsmen loe the maud. **1831** SCOTT *Ct. Robt.* Introd. Addr., A grey maud,..completed such an equipment as, since Juvenal's days, has been the livery of the poor scholar. **1885** *Advt.*, Rugs and Mauds of every description. **1901** *Daily Chron.* 13 July 8/3 A long 'maud', broad enough to act as a cover-all from neck to ground.

attrib. **1877** W. ROSS *Past. Work in Covenant. Times* v. 93 Shepherds with their maud plaids.

maude, obs. pa. t. of MAKE *v.*[1]

maudelard, obs. form of MALLARD.

maudle (ˈmɔːd(ə)l), *v. rare.* [Back-formation f. MAUDLIN *a.*, taken as pr. pple.] **a.** *trans.* To make maudlin. **b.** *intr.* To talk maudlinly.

1706 PHILLIPS (ed. Kersey), *To Maudle*, to besot, or put out of Order, as drinking strong Liquors does in a Morning. *Ibid.*, *Maudlin*, maudled, half drunk. **1826** *Examiner* 124/1 Leaving John Bull to suck his thumbs, and maudle about 'his good Queen Anne'.

maudlin (ˈmɔːdlɪn), *sb.* Forms: 4–5 **maudeleyne, mawd(e)leyn,** 4, 6 **maudelen,** 5 **mawdelayn, -en,** 6 **maud(e)lene, -elein, -elyn, -lein(e, mawdel(e)in, -(e)leyn,** 6–7 **maudlen, mawdlin,** 7 **maudline, mawdlen, -line.** [a. OF. *Madelaine*, semi-popular ad. L. *Magdalēna*, MAGDALEN(E.]

†**1.** As proper name: = MAGDALEN 1. *Obs.*

c **1320** R. BRUNNE *Medit.* 445 To maudelens hous Ion went. *c* **1380** WYCLIF *Serm.* Sel. Wks. I. 382 Marie Mawdeleyn. *c* **1460** *Towneley Myst.* xxviii. 67 Mawdleyn witnes beres that ihesus rose from ded. **1565** JEWEL *Repl. Harding* (1611) 257 Mary Maudlen. **1573** TUSSER *Husb.* (1878) 49 Gehezie, Lots wife,..Rough Esau, with Mawdlin.

†**b.** *transf.* A penitent resembling Mary Magdalen. (Cf. MAGDALEN 2.) *Obs.*

1602 [? BRETON] *Pass. Discont. Mind* A 3 b, To play a poore lamenting Mawdlines part, That would weepe streams of bloud to be forgiuen. **1631** BRATHWAIT *Eng. Gentlew.* (1641) 288 They fall into a poore Maudlins distemper by giving reines to passion, till it estrange them from the soveraignty of reason.

†**2.** = MAGDALEN 3. *Obs.*

1603 OWEN *Pembrokeshire* (1892) 11 Diuerse priories, ffriers, Maudlens [*printed* Mandleus], Almehouses [etc.].

3. †**a.** = COSTMARY, *Tanacetum Balsamita. Obs.* **b.** The herb *Achillea Ageratum.* (Also *sweet maudlin.*)

c **1460** J. RUSSELL *Bk. Nurture* 132 Gynger valadyne & maydelyn ar not so holsom in mete. **1548** TURNER *Names Herbes* 37 Thys is not Eupatorium Mesues, for that is called in englishe Maudlene. **1578** LYTE *Dodoens* II. lxxvi. 250 The second kinde [of Balsamynte] is called..in English Mawdelein. **1597** GERARDE *Herball* II. cxcviii. 524 Maudlein is without doubt a kinde of Costmarie. **1612** DRAYTON *Poly-olb.* xv. 197 They hot Muscado oft with milder Maudlin cast. **1640** PARKINSON *Theat. Bot.* 78 *Ageratum purpureum*, Purple sweete Maudeline. **1688** R. HOLME *Armoury* II. 98/2 Small Maudlin hath the stalk full of small slender leaves of whitish green. **1718** QUINCY *Compl. Disp.* 130 Maudlin, is a kind of Agrimony, & flowers about July. **1866** *Treas. Bot.*, Sweet maudlin, *Achillea Ageratum.*

†**4.** The name of a kind of peach (= MAGDALEN 4); also of a kind of pear (= *Magdalen pear*). *Obs.*

1664 EVELYN *Kal. Hort.* June 68 [Pears]. The Maudlin (first ripe)..&c. **1699** *Ibid.* Aug. (ed. 9) 100 Peaches and Abricots... Bourdeaux Peach,..Maudlen, Minion Peach. **1676** WORLIDGE *Cyder* 167 The Margaret, the Maudlin.. and many other early Pears are in esteem for the Table in July. **1707** MORTIMER *Husb.* (1721) II. 294 The Margaret, the Maudlin, and the Cluster Pear.

5. [From the adj.] What is maudlin; weak or mawkish sentiment.

1838 LYTTON *Alice* VI. ii, I allow that there is a strange mixture of fustian and maudlin in all these things. **1865** *Spectator* 11 Feb. 153 Let us at least have them tried like all others, with as little maudlin and romance about..withered hearts..as may be consistent with sincerity.

6. *Comb.*: †**maudlin daisy**, the ox-eye daisy, *Chrysanthemum Leucanthemum*; **Maudlin day**, = *Magdalen day*; †**maudlin pot**, ? some kind of drinking vessel; **maudlin tansy** = *sweet maudlin* (see 3 b); **maudlin tide**, the time of the feast of St. Mary Magdalen, 22 July; **maudlin-wort** (? *obs.*) = *maudlin daisy*; †also applied to the yellow ox-eye, *Chrysanthemum segetum.*

1861 MISS PRATT *Flower. Pl.* III. 312 (Great White Ox-eye)..The plant was formerly called *Maudlin Daisy. *c* **1470** HARDYNG *Chron.* clxii. (1812) 297 The kyng vpon the *Maudeleyn day, At Fowkirke fought with Scottes in great aray. **1638** *Lanc. Wills* (Chetham Soc.) III. 204 A dozen of silver spoones and a little *Maudlin pott of silver. **1856** MAYNE *Expos. Lex.*, **Maudlin Tansy.* *c* **1530** LD. BERNERS *Arth. Lyt. Bryt.* (1814) 7 Arthur..demaundyd of him yf he had receyued at yᵉ *mawdeleyn tyde yᵉ reuenewes of the forest. **1552** ELYOT *Dict.*, *Amaranthus*, an herbe, of the which be two sortes: the flower of the one is yelow,..called also..of Apothecaries *sticas citrina*, in English, *Maudelene woort or Baltasar. **1578** LYTE *Dodoens* II. xix. 169 The great wild Daysie, or Maudelynwurte..hath grene leaues. **1766** *Museum Rust.* VI. 451 Greater Daisie, Ox-eye, or Maudlin-wort. **1866** *Treas. Bot.*, Maudlinwort, *Chrysanthemum Leucanthemum.*

maudlin (ˈmɔːdlɪn), *a.* Forms: 6 **maudlayne, mawdlen,** 7 **maudline, mawd(e)lin,** 8–9 **maudling,** 7– **maudlin.** [From the attrib. use of MAUDLIN *sb.*, in allusion to the pictures in which the Magdalen was represented weeping.]

1. Weeping, tearful, lachrymose. *Obs.* or *arch.*

1607 MIDDLETON *Michaelm. Term* II. i. 137 That's a penitent maudlin dicer. *a* **1680** BUTLER *Rem.* (1759) II. 136 He laments, like Heraclitus the Maudlin Philosopher, at other Men's Mirth. **1715** ROWE *Lady J. Grey* v. i, No Maudlin Gazers, To wet their Handkerchiefs. **1847** LYTTON *Lucretia* (1853) 152 Blooming amidst those maudlin eyes.

2. Characterized by tearful sentimentality; mawkishly emotional; weakly sentimental.

a **1631** DONNE *Lett.* (1651) 145 It was matter, which I might very well have left unwritten, having too much of the Maudlin humour in it. *a* **1704** T. BROWN *Praise Poverty* Wks. 1730 I. 98 A thousand maudlin oaths of friendship. **1779** SHERIDAN *Critic* II. ii, Is this a time for maudling tenderness? **1845** DISRAELI *Sybil* (Rtldg.) 317 The mob became not only enthusiastic but maudlin. **1877** FARRAR *Days of Youth* xiii. 123 Doing right only in maudlin dreams, not in manly effort.

3. (First in *maudlin-drunk*: see 4.) Used to designate that stage of drunkenness which is characterized by the shedding of tears and effusive displays of affection. Phrase, † *to drink maudlin.*

1616 R.C. *Times' Whistle* v. 1958 The second kinde we maudline drunkards call. **1668** R. L'ESTRANGE *Vis. Quev.* (1708) 40 Am not I here, the Fifth Husband of a woman yet living in the World, that hopes to..drink Maudlin at the Fifteenth Funeral? *a* **1700** B.E. *Dict. Cant. Crew*, *Mawdlin*, weepingly Drunk, as we say the Tears of the Tankard. **1714** ADDISON *Spect.* No. 561 ⁋12 When they grow Maudlin, they are very apt to commemorate their former Partners with a Tear. **1789** E. DARWIN *Bot. Gard.* II. (1791) 110 'Drink deep, sweet youths', seductive Vitis cries, The maudlin tear-drop glittering in her eyes. **1840** DICKENS *Old C. Shop* xxiii, The maudlin state or stage of drunkenness. **1860** *All Year Round* No. 49. 533 His potations had rendered him somewhat maudlin.

4. *Comb.* (with another adj.) as ***maudlin-kind, -moral***; **maudlin-cupped**, having drunk enough to become maudlin; **maudlin-drunk**, †**drunken** [orig. a similative comb. of the sb.], in the maudlin stage of intoxication.

1627–77 FELTHAM *Resolves* II. xxix. 220 Claudius..being *Maudline cupp'd, he grew to lament the Destiny of his marriages. **1509** BARCLAY *Shyp of Folys* (1570) 33 Some *maudlayne dronke, mourning loudly and hye. **1592** NASHE *P. Penilesse* 23 b, Mawdlen drunke, when a fellow wil weepe for kindnes in the midst of his Ale and kisse you. **1709** STEELE *Tatler* No. 47 ⁋5 Such a Tragedian is only maudlin drunk. **1856** MISS MULOCK *J. Halifax* xix, Another ill-looking fellow, maudlin drunk. **1685** G. MERITON *Yorks. Ale* 8 Some *Maudlin drunken were, and wept full sore. *a* **1668** DAVENANT *Man's the Master* Wks. (1673) 367, I am *Maudlin kind, would I had one of thy Hoods to cover my face. **1842** TENNYSON *Will Waterpr.* 208 It is but yonder empty glass That makes me *maudlin-moral.

Hence ˈ**maudlinize** *v. trans.*, to make maudlin, to cause to be in a maudlin state of intoxication; ˈ**maudlinism**, the state of being maudlin-drunk.

a **1652** BROME *Covent Garden* IV. ii, I hope 'twill maudlinize him. **1837** DICKENS *Pickw.* xxxviii, Mr. Benjamin Allen had perhaps a greater predisposition to maudlinism than he had ever known before.

maudlinly (ˈmɔːdlɪnlɪ), *adv.* [f. MAUDLIN *a.* + -LY^2.] In a maudlin manner.

1854 LADY LYTTON *Behind Scenes* I. I. iv. 129 It would have been impossible to have looked more maudlingly than he did at the assembled crowd. **1882** *Fraser's Mag.* XXVI. 255 He becomes maudlinly eloquent.

maues, mauf: see MAUGH.

maufesour, variant of MALFEASOR *Obs.*

†**ˈmaufrey.** *Obs. rare*$^{-1}$. [Short for GALLIMAUFRY.] = GALLIMAUFRY 3.

1647 WARD *Simp. Cobler* 21 Such a multimonstrous maufrey of heteroclytes and quicquidlibets.

mauger, variant of MAUGRE.

†**maugh.** *Obs.* Forms: 3 **moȝ**, 4 *pl.* **maues, mohwes**; *Sc.* and *north. dial.* 4 **mawch, mach, macht**, 4, 6 **magh**, 4–6 **mawch(e**, 5 **mawich(e, maygh(e**, ? **mawth**, ? **mayth**, 6 **maich, meache, mawggh**, 7–9 **m(e)augh**, 8–9 **mauf.** [a. ON. *mág-r* son-in-law, brother-in-law, father-in-law (Sw. *måg*, Norw. *maag* son-in-law), corresp. to OE. *mǽȝ* kinsman MAY *sb.*^{1} (pl. *máȝas*, whence possibly the 14th c. form *mohwes*), OFris. *mêch*, OS. *mâg* (MDu. *maech*, mod.Du. *maag* kinsman), OHG. *mâg*, Goth. *mēg-s* son-in-law:—OTeut. **mǣgo-z*, prob. related by ablaut to **magu-z*, OE. *maȝu* boy, young man.] A near (male) connexion by marriage; a brother-in-law or a son-in-law.

The glossaries of North and Mid Yorkshire give a sense 'colleague, partner'.

c **1250** *Gen. & Ex.* 1761 [Laban calls Jacob] Min moȝ, min neue, and felaȝe. *a* **1300** *Cursor M.* 2811 (Cott.) Loth went and til his maues [*Gött.* mohwes] spak. *Ibid.* 7650 þan bade þe king.. His magh [*Trin.* sone in lawe] dauid man suld him sla. *c* **1375** *Sc. Leg. Saints* xliii. (*Cecile*) 214, I grant þis day þat þu [*sc.* her husband's brother] art my mach verray. *c* **1425** WYNTOUN *Cron.* II. xvii. 1637 (Cott.) [Turnvs] þat.. mawche [*Wemyss* mayghe] was to þis kynge Latyn And weddit his douchtyr. **1533** BELLENDEN *Livy* I. xvi. (S.T.S.) I. 89 Thare was nane fund sa wourthy to be his maich as the said Seruius, And sa þe king gaif him finalie his dochter in mariage. **1565–73** *Durham Depos.* (Surtees) 110 John Tompson, alias Percivall, is this examinate's mawggh [here = brother in law]. *c* **1600** JAS. MELVILL *Diary* (1842) 199 The Archbishopes meache and graittest associat, Mr. Alexander Home. **1674–91** RAY *N.C. Words* 55 *Meaugh*, 'my meaugh', my wives brother, or sisters husband. **1788** W. MARSHALL *Yorksh.* II. Gloss. (E.D.S.) *Mauf*, a brother-in-law. **1829** BROCKETT *N.C. Gloss.* (ed. 2) *Mauf, Maugh, Meaugh*, a brother-in-law.

maught, maucht (mɔːxt). Now only *Sc.* Forms: 3–4 **maȝt, maght**, 4 **mauȝt**, 4, 9 **macht**, 4–5 **mawcht**, 4– **maucht**, 4– **maught.** [App. a. ON. **maht-r* (Icel. *mátt-r*):—OTeut. type **mahtu-z*, a parallel formation with **mahti-z* fem.: see MIGHT *sb.*] Strength, might, power, ability.

c **1220** *Bestiary* 541 Ðis deuel is mikel wið wil and maȝt. *a* **1300** *Cursor M.* 6720 þe lord þat þat beist aght, Sal þar-for ansuer at his maght. *c* **1320** *Sir Beues* (A.) 860 A swerd of miche mauȝt. *c* **1375** *Sc. Leg. Saints* xxi. (*Clement*) 454 He.. hyre embrasit with al his macht. *c* **1425** WYNTOUN *Cron.* v. x. 3065 Wytht mekyll mawcht. **1549** *Compl. Scotl.* vi. 41 Ane lang draucht, ane lang draucht, mair maucht, mair maucht. **1768** ROSS *Helenore* (1789) 22 They had nae maughts for sick a toilsome task. *a* **1774** FERGUSSON *Poems* (1789) II. 96 Fearfu' aften o' their maught. **1825–80** JAMIESON s.v. *Maucht*, Of a person who is paralytic, or debilitated by any other malady, it is said; He has lost the machts, or his machts.

Hence **ˈmaughtless** (also **mauchless**) *a.*, powerless; **ˈmauchty** *a.*, powerful.

1768 ROSS *Helenore* (1789) 17 Jeering, they'd say, Poor Lindy's maughtless grown. *Ibid.* 22 Amo' the herds that plaid a maughty part. **1819** W. TENNANT *Papistry Storm'd* (1827) 38 Whairat the mauchty knicht took fire. **1882** J. WALKER *Jaunt to Auld Reekie*, etc. 27 Flat on the floor.. Where mauchless he in beastly stupor fell.

Maugrabee (ˈmɔːgrəbiː). Also 8 **Mogrebee.** [a. Arab. *maɣrabīy* western, f. *ɣarb* west.] An African Moor.

1704 J. PITTS *Acc. Mohammetans* vii. 101 A Turk.. ask'd me what Countryman I was; a Mogrebee (said I) *i.e.* one of the West. **1813** BYRON *Br. Abydos* I. viii, The sire.. With Maugrabee and Mamaluke, His way amid his Delis took.

Maugrabin (ˈmɔːgrəbɪn). Also **Mograbian.** [a. Arab. *maɣrabīyīn*, pl. of *maɣrabīy*: see prec.] = prec. Also *attrib.*

1823 SCOTT *Quentin D.* xvi, The men beyond our tents call me Hayraddin Maugrabin, that is Hayraddin the African Moor. **1842** BRANDE *Dict. Sci.* etc., *Mograbians*, or *men of the west*, a name formerly given to a species of Turkish infantry composed of the peasants of the Northern parts of Africa. **1889** J. PAYNE *Aladdin* 57 One day.. behold, a Maugrabin dervish came up.

maugracious, variant of MALGRACIOUS.

maugre (ˈmɔːgə(r)), *sb.* and *prep.* Forms: α. 4–5 **maugreþ, mawgrethe, malegrefe, -greue, mawgref(e**, 4–6 **maugref(e**, 5 **maugreue.** β. 4–7 **malgre**, 5–7 **malgrye**, 5–8 **maulgre.** γ. 4 **magrei, maugray, magrey**, 4–5 **maugrey, mawgr(e)y**, 4–6 **magry, maugrie, -y, magree**, 4–7 **maugree**, 4–9 **magre**, 5 **mawgre, magger**, *Sc.* **magra**, 5–8 **mauger**, 6 **mawger, mager, -ir, maugrea, mawgree, magrie**, 3– **maugre.** [a. OF. *maugré, malgré* (= Pr. *mal grat*, It. *malgrado*) f. *mal* bad, evil + *gré* (see GREE *sb.*^{2}). The mod.F. MALGRÉ has sometimes been used by Eng. writers as a foreign word; so in the 16th c. the It. MALGRADO.]

†A. *sb. Obs.*

1. Ill-will, displeasure, or spite, borne by a person towards another. Often in phr. *to can* or ***con maugre*** (see CAN *v.*^{1} 10, CON *v.*^{1} 4 b).

c **1320** *Sir Tristr.* 2017 He ne couþe him bot maugre. **13..** *E.E. Allit. P.* B. 250 þer was malys mercyles & mawgre much scheued. *c* **1422** HOCCLEVE *Learne to Die* 283 Why was y nat ferd of goddes maugree? *c* **1460** *Towneley Myst.* xxiv. 270 Take it to you with all the mawgre of myn and myght of mahowne. **1470–85** MALORY *Arthur* IX. xl. 405, I haue herd moche of your maugre ageynst me. **1485** CAXTON *Chas. Gt.* 185 Wyte it not me,.. ne conne me noo maulgre. **15..** *Curs. J. Rowlis* 161 in *Bannatyne MS.* (Hunter. Cl.) 303 Malice, rancour and invy, With magry and malancoly. **1513** DOUGLAS *Æneis* IX. Prol. 17 Wirk na malgre, thocht thou be nevir sa wyght. **1515** BARCLAY *Egloges* V. (1570) D iij b, I thought no mauger, I tolde it for a bourde. **1542** UDALL *Erasm. Apoph.* 259 Pollio.. had none other cause to surceasse his maugre.

b. Phr., ***bongre maugre*** (F. *bon gré mal gré*), whether one will or no, willy-nilly.

c **1430** *Pilgr. Lyf Manhode* III. xxxiv. (1869) 154 Thi god he shal be boongree mawgree.

2. The state of being regarded with ill-will. Chiefly in phr. ***to have, get maugre.*** Also, an instance of this.

c **1290** *St. Nicholas* 457 in *S. Eng. Leg.* I. 253 ȝif þat þou woldest þure-fore þou haue maugre. *a* **1300** *Cursor M.* 21471 Maugre [*Fairf.* maugrefe] þar-for mot þai haf. *c* **1330** R. BRUNNE *Chron. Wace* (Rolls) 12898 ȝyf hit falle wel, wel schal vs be; ȝyf hit ne do, we gete maugre. *c* **1380** WYCLIF *Wks.* (1880) 465 Heere may cristenmen soone wite which clerk or lord.. haþ wille to stonde þerfore & suffere a magrey. **1415** HOCCLEVE *Let. Cupid* 376 Wyteth the feend, and his be the maugree. *c* **1430** *How wise Man tauȝt his Son* 47 in *Babees Bk.*, And gete þee mawgre here & þeere More þan þank. **1453** in *14th Rep. Hist. MSS. Comm.* App. III. 9 Gyf ony of thaim happyns to inryn fedis or maugreis. **1470–85** MALORY *Arthur* XX. xi. 815 Here wynne ye no worshyp but maulgre and dishonoure. **1483** *Cath. Angl.* 231/1 A Mawgry, *demeritum.* **1560** ROLLAND *Crt. Venus* II. 167 ȝe haue seruit greit magrie to ȝour meid.

3. ***in (the) maugre of***: in spite of, notwithstanding; = B (below).

c **1440** *Gesta Rom.* lxiv. 277 (Harl. MS.) In malgre of þi tethe. *a* **1500** *Chevy Chase* 3 in Skeat *Spec. Eng. Lit.* III. 68 That he wold hunte In the mowntayns.. In the magger of doughtè dogles. **1535** STEWART *Cron. Scot.* II. 687 [He] wan the wod in magir of thame all. **1871** W. ALEXANDER *Johnny Gibb* vii. 50 An' we'll dee't still, i' maugre o' an Erastian Presbytery.

B. (*adv.* and) *prep.*

1. In spite of, notwithstanding; notwithstanding the power of. *arch.*

c **1264** *Song agst. King Almaigne* in *Pol. Songs* (Camden) 69 Let him habbe, ase he brew, bale to dryng, maugre Wyndesore. *c* **1350** *Will. Palerne* 3745 A kniȝt.. hade him out of þe ost mawgrey hem alle. **1377** LANGL. *P.Pl.* B. VI. 69 [To] make hem mery þere-mydde maugre who so bigruccheth it. *c* **1400** *Sowdone Bab.* 1442 Thai were agon, Magre who so wolde. **1481** CAXTON *Godfrey* xxiii. 55 Ther wente wel somtyme .X. M or more, maulgre the barons. **1581** MARBECK *Bk. of Notes* 939 He threw it into the fire, maugrie all the Cardinalls that were about him. **1596** SPENSER *F.Q.* IV. i. 48 Tell what thou saw'st, maulgre who so it heares. **1686** F. SPENCE tr. *Varillas' Ho. Medicis* 177 The quarrel, wherein they were engaged, maugre their endeavours and inclinations for peace. **1704** *Lond. Gaz.* No. 4061/3 Keeping the Mastery at Sea,.. maugre the.. Strength of the Enemy's Fleet. **1755** SMOLLETT *Quix.* (1803) IV. 202, I persevere in this career, maugre and in despite of my own understanding. **1765** *Museum Rust.* IV. xliv. 193 Maugre my most sanguine expectations, the field by no means answers. **1854** H. MILLER *Sch. & Schm.* xxii. (1857) 488, I continued my rounds, maugre the suspicion. **1892** *Nation* (N.Y.) 4 Aug. 93/3 'La Débâcle', maugre all faults, stands out as Zola's best and strongest work up to the present time.

¶ Used by Spenser for: A curse upon..!

1590 SPENSER *F.Q.* II. v. 12 [Fortune] That hath (maugre her spight) thus low me laid in dust. *Ibid.* III. iv. 39 Yett, maulgre them, farewell my sweetest sweet!

†**b.** ***maugre his, ours***, etc.: in spite of him, etc. [Cf. OF. *maugré suen, maugré vostre*, etc.] *Obs.*

a **1300** *Cursor M.* 4305 Maugre his, he dos him lute. *c* **1330** R. BRUNNE *Chron. Wace* (Rolls) 10266 Maugre oures, forsoþe hit was. **1390** GOWER *Conf.* II. 3 God wot that is malgre myn. *c* **1450** *Merlin* xiv. 214 Magre hirs thei were driven bakke. *c* **1500** *Lancelot* 115 Al magre thine a seruand schal yow bee.

†**c.** ***maugre of, to, with***: in spite of. *Obs.*

c **1470** HENRY *Wallace* VI. 393 Thow sall ws se.. Battaill to gyff, magra off all thi kyn. **1480** CAXTON *Chron. Eng.* VII. (1520) 100/2 The kynge.. gate the castell maugre of them all that were within. **1494** FABYAN *Chron.* VI. clx. 150 He than assemblyd to hym a strong hoost, and recoueryd his wyfe, malgre to all his enmyes. **1548** UDALL, etc. *Erasm. Par. Mark* iii. 30 Whose power the findes are compelled maugry of theyr headés, to geue place unto. **1646** EARL MONM. tr. *Biondi's Civil Warres* IV. 67 She was maugre with those which would have defended her, taken prisoner.

d. without regimen. (Cf. MALGRÉ, quot. 1608.)

1423 JAS. I *Kingis Q.* xxiv, So infortunate was vs that fremyt day, That maugre, playnly, quhethir we wold or no [etc.]. **1596** SPENSER *F.Q.* V. i. 29 Until that Talus had his pride represt, And forced him, maulgre, it up to reare. **1620** BP. HALL *Hon. Mar. Clergy* I. xvii. 94 He shall (maugre) be forced to confesse, that [etc.].

2. Phrases. ***maugre*** (a person's) ***teeth, head***: in spite of (his) resistance, notwithstanding all (he) can do (*arch.* and *dial.*). †Formerly also in many other forms now obs., as ***maugre (his) beard, cheeks, eyes, face, heart, mind, mouth, nose, visage, will.***

1297 R. GLOUC. (Rolls) 2090 Maximian was suþþe aslawe maugre [*MS. B* magrei] is nose. **13..** *K. Alis.* 5840 He.. maugre the teeth of hem alle, Sette his rigge to the walle. **13..** *E.E. Allit. P.* C. 44 Much maugre his mun, he mot nede suffer. *c* **1369** CHAUCER *Dethe Blaunche* 1201 Maugre myn heed, I muste haue tolde her or be deed. *c* **1380** WYCLIF *Sel. Wks.* III. 170 þe fend may not do but if þat it turne to þe worschipe of God mawgrethe hys wille. *c* **1386** CHAUCER *Wife's Prol.* 315 That oon thou shalt forgo, maugree thyne eyen. *a* **1400–50** *Alexander* 1747 Made to be meke malegreue his chekis. **1470–85** MALORY *Arthur* XX. xi. 816 Kynge Arthur shalle haue his Quene and the maulgre thy vysage. **1529** MORE *Dyaloge* IV. Wks. 274/1 So should al our dedes good or badde, ascend or descende by the violent hande of God, magre our mindes. *c* **1550** BALE *K. Johan* (Camden) 5 Quodcunque ligaveris, I trow, will playe soch a parte, That I shall abyde in Ynglond, magry your harte. **1555** [see BEARD *sb.* 1 e]. **1614** TOMKIS *Albumazar* I. iv. (1615) C, Not haue his sister? Cricca, I will haue Flavia, Maugre his head. **1860** MOTLEY *Netherl.* (1868) II. xix. 513 He may see your Highness enjoy your blessed estate, maugre the beards of all confederated leaguers. **1891** BARRIE *Little Minister* xliii, But, dominie, I couldna hae moved, magre my neck.

†**ˈmaugre,** *v. Obs.* [a. F. *maugréer*, f. *maugré* MAUGRE *sb.*] *trans.* To show ill-will to; to defy, oppose. Also with *down.*

1597 BEARD *Theatre God's Judgem.* (1612) 179 Except by horrible bannings and swearings they despight and maugre God. *c* **1609** WEBSTER *Appius & Virginia* II. iii, Whose bases are of Marble, deeply fixt To mauger all gusts and impending stormes. **1632** TATHAM *Love crowns the end* (1640) K ij, Had you smil'd as you did frowne, All his strength I'd mauger'd downe.

maukin, maukish: see MALKIN, MAWKISH.

maul, mall (mɔːl), *sb.*^{1} Forms: α. 3 **mealle**, 3, 6 **male**, 4 **mayl**, 4–7 **malle**, 5 **mal**, 5– **mall.** (See also the northern MELL *sb.*) β. 6–7 **maull, mawle, maule**, 7–8 **mawl**, 7– **maul.** [a. F. *mail* (in OF. pronounced maʎ) = Pr. *malh-s*, Sp. *mallo*, Pg. *malho*, It. *maglio*:—L. *malleum* (nom. *malleus*) hammer.]

I. 1. a. = MACE *sb.*^{1} 1. Also, a wooden club. *Obs.* exc. *arch.* and *Hist.*

a **1240** *Sawles Warde* in *Cott. Hom.* 253 Hare unirude duntes wið mealles istelet. **1297** R. GLOUC. (Rolls) 4229 Is male [*v.r.* mace] he dude ek bituene ac þat blod adoun wende. **13..** *Erasmus* in Horstm. *Altengl. Leg.* (1878) 202 These he suffred of þe turmentours.. xviii was betyng on his body withe brennyng malles. **13..** *St. Cristofer* 547 *ibid.* (1881) 461 His false goddis he smate þame alle In sondir with ane Iryne malle. *c* **1380** *Sir Ferumb.* 4653 A mayl of Ire he bar an honde. *c* **1450** *Merlin* 339 Whan Arthur saugh the Geaunte lifte vp his malle he douted the stroke. **1523** LD. BERNERS *Froiss.* I. ccccxvii. 730 They were of harnessed men.. mo than xxx. thousande, and as many with malles. **1545** ASCHAM *Toxoph.* (Arb.) 70 A leaden maule, or suche lyke weapon, to beate downe his enemyes withall. **1563–87** FOXE *A. & M.* (1596) 40/1 Felix and Philip had their braines beaten out with mawles. **1590** SPENSER *F.Q.* I. vii. 51 With mighty mall The monster mercilesse him made to fall. **1627** DRAYTON *Agincourt*, etc. 39 With Battle-axes, Halberts, Bills, and Maules. **1682** BUNYAN *Holy War* 48, I have a Maul, Fire-brands, Arrows, and Death, all good hand weapons. **1686–7** AUBREY *Rem. Gentilism & Judaism* (1881) 19 The Holy-mawle, wch (they fancy) hung behind the Church dore, wch when the father was seaventie, the sonne might fetch, to knock his father in the head, as effœte, and of no more use. **1891** *Cornh. Mag.* Oct. 444 Steel caps, mail brigandines.. completed this equipment, while in some cases the murderous maule or five-foot mallet was hung across the bow-stave.

†**b.** *pl.* A name given to the Parisian insurgents of 1 Mar. 1382, who were armed with leaden clubs.

1525 LD. BERNERS *Froiss.* II. clxxxv. [clxxxi.] 563 The sayd Constable put downe the malles of Parys, and punyshed them for their rebellyons.

2. a. In early use, a massive hammer of any kind. Now, applied to various special kinds of heavy hammers or beetles, commonly of wood, used, (e.g.) in driving piles, in shipbuilding, in mining operations, and in various operations on board ship. ***top-mall*** (*Naut.*): see TOP *sb.*

c **1400** *Lanfranc's Cirurg.* 127 þou schalt smyte wiþ a mal eiþer an hamer on þe greet eende. *c* **1420** *Chron. Vilod.* 4332 Bot his hedde was gret, leygc to a gret malle. **1432–50** tr. *Higden* (Rolls) II. 229 Tubal hauenge delectacion in the sownde of the malles [etc.]. **1460** CAPGRAVE *Chron.* (Rolls) 34 With a malle and a nayle sche smet him in the hed. ?*c* **1475** *Hunt. Hare* 91 Then euery man had a mall Syche as thei betyn clottys withall. **1485** *Naval Acc. Hen. VII* (1896) 39 Lede malles feble.. xiiij. **15..** *Smyth & Dame* 17 in Hazl. *E.P.P.* III. 202 He covde werke wyth a mall Many maner of metall. **1523** FITZHERB. *Husb.* §15 And if the barleye grounde wyll not breake with harrowes.. it wolde be beaten with malles. *Ibid.* §126 Take thy mall agayn and dryue downe the edderynges and also thy stakes. **1591** SYLVESTER *Du Bartas* I. iv. 342 Th' Iron Maule that chimes The intire Day in twice twelue equall times. **1676** WORLIDGE *Cyder* (1691) 96 Others beat them [apples] on a table with mauls. **1680** MOXON *Mech. Exerc.* 203 The Joyner's Mallet would supply the Office of this Tool; but Use has made the Mawl more handy for them. **1688** R. HOLME *Armoury* III. 312/2 The Executioner with the Violence of a Blow on the head of the Axe with his heavy Maul, forced it through the Mans

Neck. **1764** *Char.* in *Ann. Reg.* 23/1 The instruments of agriculture they use..are a spade, a mall, and a rake or harrow. **1812** *Chron.* in *Ann. Reg.* 5 The stake, with the mall, was driven through the body. **1840** R. H. DANA *Bef. Mast* ix. 20 We..stopped the mall with rope-yarns. **1874** J. H. COLLINS *Metal Mining* (1875) 61 Hammers.—The chief kinds used in metal mines are mallets or 'malls'. **1886** R. C. LESLIE *Sea-painter's Log* vii. 154 The shipwright's maul.

U.S. slang. **1872** SCHELE DE VERE *Americanisms* 616 *Maul and Wedges*..often used to denote the whole of a man's possessions, his movables.

†**b.** *trans.* and *fig.* after L. *malleus.* (Often, like *hammer*, *scourge*, applied to a person as the irresistible foe or the terrible oppressor of some person, class, or institution.) *Obs.*

c **1380** WYCLIF *Wks.* (1880) 351 þe stake is þe synne hardud in mannus hert; þe malle þat he driueþ it wiþ is newe rehersynge of synne. **1432–50** tr. *Higden* (Rolls) VI. 43 The Sawden and duke of Turkes, the grete malle of Cristen peple. **1577** VAUTROUILLIER *Luther on Ep. Gal.* 155 God must needes take this maule in hand, the lawe I meane,..to bring to nothing this beast. **1624** H. MASON *Art of Lying* iv. 59 Luther was a great mawle, that battered their Babel. **1658** ROWLAND tr. *Moufet's Theat. Ins.* 951 That flower of Knighthood, and Maul of the Spanish pride, Francis Drake. **1711** HICKES *Two Treat., Chr. Priesth.* (1847) II. 34 Optatus ..the great mall of the Donatists.

II. [From MAUL *v.*] †**3.** A heavy blow, as with a hammer. *Obs.*

1664 BUTLER *Hud.* II. i. 527 Give that Rev'rend Head a mall, Or two, or three, against a Wall.

4. *Rugby Football.* A mauling or tackling. ***maul (in goal)***: see quot. 1871.

1867 *Rugby School Football Laws* 18 Only those who are touching the ball with their hands may continue in the maul inside goal. **1871** in *Rugby U. Football Ann.* (1874–5) 6 A Maul in goal is when the holder of the ball is tackled inside goal line, or being tackled immediately outside, is carried or pushed across it, and he, or the opposite side, or both, endeavour to touch the ball down. **1874–5** *Rugby U. Football Ann.* 38 A maul occurred in the centre of the ground, from which Edinburgh emerged victorious. **1892** CAIL in *Field* 17 Sept. 458/1 This year the maul has finally been relegated to the past [by the Rugby Union]. **1960** *Times* 7 Dec. 17/1 The ability to start attacks from line-outs and loose mauls. **1973** *Times* 9 Feb. 11/2 We did not do well in the rucks and mauls against Wales.

maul (mɔːl), *sb.*[2] *dial.* Also 5 **malle**, 9 **maule**. [Variant of MALLOW.] = MALLOW.

c **1425** *Voc.* in Wr.-Wülcker 644/34 *Hec malua*, malle. **1674–91** RAY *N.C. Words* 46 *Mauls*, Mallowes. **1788** W. MARSHALL *Yorksh.* II. Gloss. (E.D.S.), *Mauls, malvæ*, mallows. **1866** *Treas. Bot.*, Maule, *Malva sylvestris.* **1876** *Mid-Yorksh. Gloss.*, *Mauls*, the herb marsh-mallows.

maul (mɔːl), *v.* Forms: *α.* 3 **meallen**, 5–6 **malle**, 4– **mall**. *β.* 6–7 **maule**, 7 **maull**, **mawle**, **mawll**, 7–9 **mawl**, 7– **maul**. [f. MAUL *sb.*[1]]

†**1.** *trans.* To beat or strike (with or as with a maul or hammer); to hammer, batter; also, to beat or knock *in*, *along*. *Obs.*

?*a* **1400** *Morte Arth.* 3038 Mynsteris and masondewes they malle to þe erthe. *c* **1420** *Pallad. on Husb.* II. 17 The cloddis malled be with mannes hond. *Ibid.* v. 516 This pece [of wood] amydde his trunke hit is to malle. **1530** PALSGR. 632/2 Nowe that he hath done with plowynge of our grounde go mall the cloddes. **1609** J. DAVIES *Holy Roode* (Grosart) 12/1 See how they mall it on, in ruthlesse rage. **1633** T. JAMES *Voy.* 51, I ordered the Cooper to..looke to all our Caske: those that were full, to mawle in the bungs of them.

fig. **1607** HIERON *Wks.* (1619–20) II. 373 A certayne hammer, which the Lord vseth in this seruice of malling and breaking the heart.

b. *U.S.* To split (rails) with a maul and wedge.

1686 in P. A. Bruce *Econ. Hist. Virginia* (1896) I. 318 *note*, Johnson..doth..impower you..to fall, mall, and set up.. 400 panels of sufficient post and rails. **1789** ANBUREY *Trav.* II. 323 Fence rails, which are made out of trees, cut or sawed into lengths of about twelve feet, that are mauld or split into rails. **1856** OLMSTED *Slave States* 207, I always have two hundred rails mauled in a day. **1896** P. A. BRUCE *Econ. Hist. Virginia* I. 317 Among the terms..in the contract..was one requiring the latter to maul six hundred fencing rails.

†**c.** *intr.* To hammer. *Obs.*

a **1375** *Joseph Arim.* 508 Miȝtful men mallen þorw scheldes. **1615** BRATHWAIT *Strappado* (1878) 113 Her hands like Fullers wheels, one vp, one downe, Which still lie malling on my costrell crowne.

†**2.** *trans.* To strike (a person or animal) with a heavy weapon; to knock *down*. *Obs.*

a **1240** *Sawles Warde* in *Cott. Hom.* 251 Deoflen þat ham meallið ant deruēð aa ant drecchēð wið alles cunnes pinen. ?*a* **1400** *Morte Arth.* 3841 And mett hyme in the myde schelde, and mallis hyme thorowe. *Ibid.* 4037, I salle evene amange his mene malle hym to dede. **1530** PALSGR. 632/1 If he mall you on the heed I wyll nat gyve a peny for your lyfe. **1537** MATTHEW *Judg.* v. 22 Then they malled the horsses legges, yͭ their myghtie coursers lefte praunsyng. **1596** SPENSER *F.Q.* v. xi. 8 The sad steele..lighting on his horses head him quite did mall. **1610** CHAPMAN *Widowes T.* v. K 3 b, *Lys.* Would not my Ghost start vp, and flie vpon thee? *Cyn.* No, I'de mall it down againe with this [*i.e.* a crowbar]. **1613** PURCHAS *Pilgrimage* VIII. xii. (1614) 805 Many Gentlewomen..while his [the king's] bodie was burning were malled with clubbes, and buried foure and foure in a graue. **1648** GAGE *West Ind.* xiii. (1655) 72 They mawled with a club those which had the Garlands.

3. To beat and bruise (a person); to maltreat; to knock about.

c **1610** MIDDLETON *Widow* v. i. 138 Your women..will so maul him With broken cruises and pitchers..He'll never die alive. **1712** SWIFT *Jrnl. to Stella* 7 Aug., My lord's business is to hasten the peace before the Dutch are too much mauled. **1748** SMOLLETT *Rod. Rand.* (1812) 314 It was proposed by Bragwell that we should..maul the watch. **1858** DORAN *Crt. Fools* 105 Thrashing the..bishop and terribly mauling his body of followers.

4. *transf.* To damage seriously; to shatter, mangle. (Said, e.g., of storms, shot, etc.; formerly of disease or the like.)

1692 SOUTH *12 Serm.* (1697) II. 41 Nor is Excess the onely thing by which Sin mauls and breaks Men in their health. **1709** STEELE *Tatler* No. 1 ¶5 This Passion has so extremely mauled him, that his Features are set and uninformed. **1758** *Ann. Reg.* 100 Her larboard side is most terribly mauled: there are seventy shot-holes on that side. **1805** in Nicolas *Disp. Nelson* (1846) VII. 190 *note*, Saw some of the Fleet at times, very much mauled and greatest part partly dismasted. **1817–18** COBBETT *Resid. U.S.* (1822) 145 America is not wholly exempt from that mortal enemy of turnips, the fly, which mawled some of mine. **1885** RUNCIMAN *Skippers & Sh.* 112 The sea was mauling her pretty badly.

5. *fig.* To subject to damaging criticism, injure by criticizing, 'cut up', 'pull to pieces'.

1593 NASHE *Four Lett. Confut.* 50 By the eternal iests he would maule thee with. **1695** CONGREVE *Prol. Hopkins' Pyrrhus* 25 Far hence they vent their Wrath, Mauling in mild Lampoon th'intriguing Bath. **1711** *Medley* No. 21. 240 The poor Whigs are every day so maul'd off by the Tories for their Fanaticism, that [etc.]. **1759** DILWORTH *Pope* 94 Finding themselves let pass free of all censure, and seeing the other sex so mauled. **1785** CRABBE *Newspaper* 412 To vex and maul a ministerial race. **1875** JOWETT *Plato* (ed. 2) I. 187 They are a class who are very likely to get mauled by Euthydemus and his friends. **1885** *Manch. Exam.* 25 Feb. 3/3 Poor Sir David Brewster, a really harmless man, is mauled in quite a wicked fashion.

6. To handle roughly or carelessly (chiefly with *about*); to damage by rough or careless handling. Also *fig.* ***to maul down*** (dial.): to lift down.

1781 COWPER *Conversat.* 290 We that make no honey, though we sting, Poets, are sometimes apt to maul the thing. **1827** CLARE *Sheph. Cal.* 156 She came smiling out, Saying she hated to be mawled about With their black faces. **1847** BUSHNELL *Chr. Nurt.* II. ii. (1861) 264 He is a man that mauls every truth of God. **1856** MRS. BROWNING *Aur. Leigh* III. 906 To see them laugh and laugh and maul their texts. **1878** T. HARDY *Ret. Native* VI. iv, Maul down the victuals from corner cupboard if canst reach, man. **1885** FORFAR *Cornish Poems* 17 You mustn't maul the fish about. **1899** *Ch. Q. Rev.* Jan. 541 We..regret..that it [the First Prayer Book of Edward VI.] was suffered to be mauled about in deference to the rather impertinent objections of foreigners.

7. *intr.* (*dial.*) To toil, work hard. [Perh. a different word: cf. MOIL *v.*]

1821 CLARE *Vill. Minstr.* I. 16 When he a ploughboy in the fields did maul. *Ibid.* 138 Huge baskets mauling on. **1871** BRIERLEY *Cotters of Mossburn* xv. 141 [She] Likes maulin' amung pigs and keaws.

8. *Football. trans.* (See quot. 1856.)

1856 *Rules Football St. Peter's Sch. York* vii, The player holding the ball may be mauled; *i.e.* he may be held and the ball if possible wrested from him. **1867** *Rugby School Football Laws* 18 When a player holding the ball is mauled by one or more of the opposite side outside goal.

9. *Comb.*, as **maul-text** *a.*, that 'mauls' his text.

1881 DU CHAILLU *Land Midnight Sun* I. 162 This maul-text preacher was reading in a loud voice verses of the Bible.

Hence **mauled** *ppl. a.*, bruised, disfigured.

a **1700** B.E. *Dict. Cant. Crew*, *Maul'd*, swingingly Drunk, or soundly Beat. **1781** MME. D'ARBLAY *Diary* June, 'Never was I so mauled in my life!' said he. **1828** CARLYLE *Misc.* (1857) II. 305 The print of six horsenails on his own mauled visage. **1854** E. FORBES *Lit. Papers* vii. (1855) 197 Though severely mauled, the huntsman was able to make his way.. to his quarters. **1904** *Daily Chron.* 2 Jan. 8/5 At this the grievously-mauled nigger began to skin him [a lion].

‖**Maulana** (maʊˈlɑːnə). Also **Maulanah**, **Mawlana**, **Mulana**. [Arab. *maulānā* our Lord: cf. MOOLVEE and MULLAH.] A title given to a learned Muslim.

1832 H. H. WILSON *Relig. Sects of Hindus* in *Asiatick Researches* XVII. 297 Maulana Rum observes—'What is the world? forgetfulness of God, not clothes, nor wealth, nor wife, nor offspring.' *a* **1846** G. OUSELEY *Biogr. Notices Persian Poets* 112 The author of this sublime poem on Divine Love and the Súfi Philosophy, was Mulána Jeláluddin. *Ibid.* 116 The Mulána was sixty-nine years of age when he closed his earthly career in Koniah. **1855** H. H. WILSON *Gloss. Judicial & Revenue Terms* 335/2 *Mauláná*,.. the title of a person of learning or respectability, teacher, doctor: in the Maratha countries, the usual designation of the Mohammadan village school-master. **1888** *Encycl. Brit.* XXIII. 656/1 Ottoman literature may be said to open with a few mystic lines, the work of Sultán Veled, son of Mauláná Jelál-ud-Dín, the author of the great Persian poem the *Mathnawí*. **1895** *Jrnl. Asiatic Soc. Bengal* LXIII. III. 54 When sixteen years of age, he studied under Mauláṇáh 'Abd-ul-'Azíz of Delhi. **1902** E. A. GAIT *Rep. Census India 1901* VI. iv. 174 Other reformers were spreading the doctrines of the Patna School, the most successful of whom was Mauláná Karámat A'li of Jaunpur. **1936** *Encycl. Islām* III. 417/2 Allāh is often called *Mawlānā* 'our Lord' in Arabic literature. *Ibid.* 418/2 Peace was negotiated..by Mawlānā Ḥamza. **1962** *Economist* 9 Mar. 889/1 The maulanas want..the kind of obscurantist stranglehold on the [Pakistani] nation..the president is determined to resist. **1975** *Bangladesh Times* 18 July 2/1 Maulana Abdur Rab.. breathed his last recently at his village home due to heart attack... The late maulana was renowned for his social services, community developments and preaching the ideals of Islam.

maular, -ard(e, obs. forms of MALLARD.

maulavi, variant of MOOLVEE.

†**maule, mawle**, *v. Obs.* [Echoic: cf. MIAUL.] *intr.* To cry like a cat; to mew.

1599 MINSHEU *Sp. Dict.*, To Maule like a cat. **1611** COTGR., *Moüaner*, to mawle, yawle, or cry like a little child.

mauler (ˈmɔːlə(r)). Also 7 **maller**. [f. MAUL *v.* + -ER[1].] **1.** One who mauls. (Sometimes used to render L. *malleus* = MAUL *sb.*[1] 2 b.)

1618 NAUNTON in *Fortesc. Papers* (Camden) 74 The maller and confounder of theyr battel. **1655** [see HAMMER *sb.* 1 b]. *a* **1661** FULLER *Worthies, Camb.* (1662) I. 178 Thomas Lord Cromwell (the Mauler of Monasteries). **1858** CARLYLE *Fredk. Gt.* III. v. (1872) I. 165 The Polish King, Casimir IV. (late mauler of the Teutsch Ritters). **1884** *Athenæum* 1 Mar. 278/2 Vice the great vampire and violence, the great mauler.

2. *slang.* A hand; a fist. Cf. MAULEY.

1820 'W. T. MONCRIEFF' *Mod. Collegians* 18 The Old Gentleman wishes to know how to put his maulers in action. **1936** 'F. GERALD' *Millionaire in Memories* vii. 193 To a young fellow who fancied himself with his 'maulers' the proposition was attractive..plenty of fighting. **1960** S. H. COURTIER *Gently dust Corpse* xii. 170 Wait till I get my maulers on Lew Boston. **1973** J. ROSSITER *Manipulators* viii. 92 You keep your big maulers off this.

mauley (ˈmɔːlɪ). *slang.* Also **maul(l)y**, **mawl(e)y**, **morley**, ? **mylier**. [? f. MAUL *v.*; but cf. Shelta (tinker's dialect) *malya*, said to be a transposition of Gaelic *lamh* hand.] A hand, a fist.

1780 G. PARKER *Life's Painter* 116, I say, how are you? Slang us your mauly. *Ibid.* 139 A Queen Elizabeth in her maully, that is, the key of the street door in her hand. **1842** DE QUINCEY *Mod. Greece* Wks. 1862 XIII. 326 Holding in his dexter 'mauley' a red herring. **1888** 'R. BOLDREWOOD' *Robbery under Arms* i, It takes a good man to..stand up to me with the gloves, or the naked mauleys. **1891** CAREW *Autob. Gypsy* xxxv. 414 Being jest a bit too 'andy with my myliers.

b. The 'hand' that one writes; handwriting.

1851 MAYHEW *Lond. Labour* I. 313 If they 'granny the mauley' (perceive the signature) of a brother officer or friend.

maulgre, variant of MAUGRE.

mauling (ˈmɔːlɪŋ), *vbl. sb.* [f. MAUL *v.* + -ING[1].] The action of MAUL *v.*[1]

c **1400** *Destr. Troy* 9520 Mallyng þurgh metall maynly with hondes. **1621** MOLLE *Camerar. Liv. Libr.* v. ii. 321 He fell a mawling of his soldiers. **1831** TRELAWNY *Adv. Younger Son* I. 129, I have never seen a fellow endure such a mauling in my life. **1864** *Field* 17 Dec. 425/3 During the whole match there was a great deal too much 'mauling'.

mauling (ˈmɔːlɪŋ), *ppl. a.* [f. MAUL *v.* + -ING[2].] That mauls.

1778 MME. D'ARBLAY *Diary* 18 June, Allowing for my mauling reading, he gave it quite as much credit as I had any reason to expect.

maulkin, maulmy: see MALKIN, MALMY.

maul oak. [? ad. Sp. *maula* imposture, sham.] An American oak, *Quercus chrysolepis*.

1884 SARGENT *Rep. Forests N. Amer.* (*10th Census* IX.) 146 *Quercus chrysolepis*... [Syn.] Live Oak. Maul Oak. Valparaiso Oak.

maulstick (ˈmɔːlstɪk). Also 7 **mol stick**, 7–8 **mostick**, 8 **mallstick**, 9 **mahlstick**. [ad. Du. *maalstok*, f. *malen* to paint + *stok* stick. Cf. G. *malerstock* (*maler* painter), *malstab* (*stab* = staff).] A light stick used by painters as a support for the right hand, and held in the left. The upper end is surmounted by a ball of cotton-wool covered with soft leather.

1658 PHILLIPS, A *Mostick* [ed. 1706 *Maul stick*], a word used in painting, being a round stick about a yard long, which the Artist doth rest upon when he paints. **1672** SALMON *Polygraphice* 165 The Stay, or Mol-stick, is a Brazil stick (or the like) of a yard long; having [etc.]. **1855** THACKERAY *Charac. Sk.* Wks. 1898 III. 537 When Titian dropped his mahlstick, the Emperor Charles V. picked it up. **1872** J. HATTON *Vall. Poppies* I. xiii. 216 In her left hand she holds a maul-stick, upon which her right arm rests. **1890** KIPLING *Light that failed* iv, I'd let you go to the deuce on your own mahl-stick.

maulvi, variant of MOOLVEE.

†**maum**, *v. vulgar. Obs.*[−1] *trans.* In phrase ***mauming and gauming***: To 'paw'.

1738 [see GAUM *v.*[1]].

maum(e, variant forms of MALM.

maum, mawm, *U.S.* varr. MA'AM or MAM[1]. Cf. MARM.

1826 A. ROYALL *Sk. Hist., Life & Manners U.S.* 121 Yes mawm, no mawm. **1835** A. B. LONGSTREET *Georgia Scenes* 110 'Aunt' and 'mauma', or 'maum', its abbreviation, are terms of respect commonly used by children, to aged negroes. **1881** *Harper's Mag.* Apr. 728/2 Maum Dulcie, is my habit ready? **1928** J. PETERKIN *Scarlet Sister Mary* ii. 14 Mary had grown up in Maum Hannah's old house in the Quarters. **1950** *Publ. Amer. Dial. Soc.* XIV. 46 Maum' Dinah.

mauma, maumer, maumie, varr. *mamma*, = MAMMY 2.

1835 W. G. SIMMS *Partisan* 141 You have told me nothing of old mauma. **1838** C. GILMAN *Recoll. Southern Matron* xv. 101 Who does not remember his youthful Christmas; the reiterated charge to his *maumer* to awaken him first? **1881** *Harper's Mag.* Apr. 737/2 Maumie, how I should like to see

a Hoodoo meeting! **1890** *Ibid.* July 232/1 Respectable colored 'maumas', ample of girth, in spotted white aprons. **1895** *Century Mag.* May 155/2 Only a few, a very few, of the faithful old 'maumers' and loyal house- and body-servants remain. **1950** *Publ. Amer. Dial. Soc.* XIV. 46 *Mauma*, . . name by which elderly Negro women were called by the children of the family with which they were connected.

Mau Mau ('maʊmaʊ). [Kikuyu.] Name of an African secret society originating among the Kikuyu, having as its aim the expulsion of European settlers and the ending of British rule in Kenya. Also *attrib.*

1950 *E. Afr. Standard* 16 June A/5 We have arrived at a state of dissatisfaction and insecurity, bitterness and delusion which has given rise to the formation of such societies as the 'Dini ya Mswambwa' and the 'Mau Mau Association'. **1952** L. S. B. LEAKEY *Mau Mau & Kikuyu* xi. 96 The Kikuyu regard the Mau Mau Association as nothing more than the old Kikuyu Central Association under another name. **1952** *N.Y. Times* 26 Oct. I. 3/2 Large groups of natives fled today to lofty mountain hideouts to escape the Government drive . . against Mau Mau terrorists, who have sworn death to the white man. **1955** *Times* 13 July 6/5 Further evidence of the infiltration of Mau Mau into tribes other than the Kikuyu, Embu, and Meru was revealed here to-day. **1960** F. D. CORFIELD *Hist. Survey Orig. & Growth Mau Mau* 78 On 21st September [1948] the Director of Intelligence and Security reported . . that a new movement, the *Mau Mau* . . had appeared in Naivasha. **1971** *Sunday Nation* (Nairobi) 11 Apr. 12/5 Events beyond human control—famine, Mau Mau, the changing environment.

Hence **'mau-mau** *v. U.S. slang*, to threaten, terrorize; so as *sb.*; **'mau-mauer**; **'mau-mauing** *vbl. sb.*

1970 T. WOLFE *Radical Chic & Mau-mauing Flak Catchers* (1971) 97 Going downtown to mau-mau the bureaucrats got to be the routine practice in San Francisco. *Ibid.* 124 In public you used the same term the whites used, namely, 'confrontation'. The term '*mau-mauing*' was a source of amusement in private. The term *mau-mauing* said, 'The white man has a voodoo fear of us, because deep down he still thinks we're savages. Right? So we're going to do that Savage number for him.' *Ibid.* 148 And it was here that Bill Jackson proved himself to be a brilliant man and a true artist, a rare artist of the mau-mau. **1971** *Harper's* June 9 His [*sc.* Norman Mailer's] demonstration of the inadequacies and distortions of Kate Millett's *Sexual Politics* is convincing and indicates that the English Department of Columbia University had been mau-maued by that termagant of Women's Lib. **1974** *Maclean's Mag.* Dec. 108/1 We've had a belly full of Indian rhetoric. After a threat is made for the fifth, twelfth or fortieth time, the excitement wears off; boredom becomes contempt when we find out that each hollow boast brings more government money tinkling into the Indian organizations' pockets. American writer Tom Wolfe calls the technique 'mau-mauing'; it's no accident that the most successful mau-mauer, Harold Cardinal, runs one of the strongest Indian organizations in Canada.

maumenye, variant of MALMENY *Obs.*

maumerye, variant of MAHOMERY *Obs.*

c **1380** *Sir Ferumb.* 2534 To þe maumerye þo sche wente.

maumet ('mɔːmɛt). *Obs.* exc. *arch.* and *dial.* Forms: α. 3 **mahimet**, (*pl.* **mawmez**, **-ex**, **maumez**), 3–4 **maumete**, 3–5 **mawmete**, 4 **-med**, **-mat**, **maunmet**, 4–5 **maummet**, **mamet**, **maumett**, 4–6 **mawmette**, 5 **mowmet(te**, **mawȝmette**, 6 **maumette**, **mawmot**, **mammot**, 6–7 **mawmett**, 9 **mom(m)et**, **mammelt**, 4– **mammet**, **mawmet**, 3– **maumet**. β. 4 **momenet(te**, **mamenet**, (*pl.* **momenes**), 4–6 **maument**, 4–6, 9 **mawment**, 5 **mamnet**, **mamente**, **mawmente**, **-mentt**, 6 **mamant**. [a. OF. *mahumet* idol; a use of *Mahumet* MAHOMET, due to the common mediæval notion that Muhammad was worshipped as a god.]

†**1. a.** A false god, or an image of one; an idol. *Obs.*

c **1205** LAY. 14585 And bilæue þe hahȝe godd, & luuie heore mahimet. *Ibid.* 29221 þer inne he hafde his maumet, þa he heold for his god. **1303** R. BRUNNE *Handl. Synne* 190, 192 She shal noght to any be sette Withoutyn leue of my maumette. The munke seyd he graunted weyl Aftyr hys maumette to do euery deyl. **1340** *Ayenb.* 6 þe ilke þet worssipeþ þe momenes. *c* **1400** MAUNDEV. (Roxb.) xix. 86 þe kirke . . es mykill and faire and full of ymagery of þaire mawmets. **14 . .** *Sir Beues* 488 Wheþure were strenger god in hevyn Or all the mawȝmettes. **1513** DOUGLAS *Æneis* x. Prol. 153 Lat Virgyll hald his mawmentis till hym self; I wirschip noder idoll, stok, nor elf. *a* **1529** SKELTON *Speke, Parrot* 395 Moloc, that mawmett, there darre no man withsay. **1529** MORE *Dialoge* I. Wks. 119/2 The ydolles and mammettes of the paganes. **1535** STEWART *Cron. Scot.* I. 99 And mamantis als he hes gart mak also, Of Phebus, Diane, and of Apollo. **1608** WILLET *Hexapla Gen.* 326 Such images and mammetts were found in Iacobs house. **1647** TRAPP *Comm. Acts* xix. 25 Wealth is the worldlings god, which he prizeth as Micah did his mawmet. [*a* **1654**: see MAUMETRY 1.]

†**b.** *transf.* A person or thing that usurps the place of God in the human affections. *Obs.*

a **1340** HAMPOLE *Psalter* xcvi. 7 Sum has syluyre his mawmet. **138.** WYCLIF *Sel. Wks.* III. 38 Lovynge moore vicis þan virtues, and so þei serven mawmetis. *c* **1386** CHAUCER *Pars. T.* 749 Euery floryn in his cofre is his Mawmet.

†**c.** Applied by Protestants to the images of Christ and the saints. *Obs.*

1581 J. BELL *Haddon's Answ. Osor.* 309 If those Mawmettes, and signes of Sainctes, be erected in their churches for none other ende, but to put the beholders in remembraunce of the Saincts themselves [etc.]. **1650** TRAPP *Comm. Deut.* vii. 5 Those mawmets and monuments of idolatry, the Rood of grace, the blood of Hales, &c.

2. a. An image, dressed-up figure; a doll, puppet; also, a person of grotesque appearance or costume, a 'guy'. Now only *dial.*

1494 FABYAN *Chron.* VII. 554 The cytie of Roan . . made them a mamet of a fatte & vnwyldely as. **1530** PALSGR. 244/1 Maument, *marmoset; poupee.* **1583** STUBBES *Anat. Abus.* (1877) 75 Mawmets of rags and cloutes compact together. **1596** SHAKS. *1 Hen. IV*, II. iii. 95 This is no world To play with Mammets. **1597–8** *Yorks. Arch. & Topogr. Jrnl.* XXXIII. 186 *note*, These havyng folowed theire vanitie al the night in sekynge there maumet, commonly called the floure of thwell, would nedes bringe the same on a barrow into ye church in prayer times. **1600** LYLY *Maydes Metam.* II. ii. 60 *Io.* What Mawmets are these? *Fris.* O they be the Fayries that haunt these woods. *a* **1608** DEE *Relat. Spir.* I. (1659) 11 There stand a great many of Mawmets, little ugly fellows at the top of the hill. **1609** *Ev. Woman in Hum.* v. i. in Bullen *O. Pl.* IV, *Julius Cæsar*, acted by the Mammets. **1642** FULLER *Answ. Ferne* 2 Hee . . sets up . . a Mawmet of his owne dressing. **1892** SARAH HEWETT *Peasant Sp. Devon* 15 It was at one time customary for village children to canvass the neighbourhood for subscriptions for materials to make a Guy Fawkes' 'momet'.

†**b.** *fig.* A person who is the 'tool' or 'puppet' of another; a 'man of straw'. *Obs.*

1460 *Paston Lett.* I. 514, I knowe wele the Juge, W. Wayte his mawment. *a* **1548** HALL *Chron., Hen. VII* (1809) 462 Wherefore she [the duchess] sent Perkyn Werbeck, her new inuented Mawmet first into Portyngall. **1593** G. HARVEY *Pierce's Super.* 141 Nash, . . Greene, . . Euphues, . . the three famous mammets of the presse.

c. A baby, child. *dial.*

1932 S. GIBBONS *Cold Comfort Farm* v. 69 Far from those that loves her and cowdled her in their bosoms when she was a mommet. **1949** *Antiquity* XXIII. 42 The poor mommet whose father was 'in trade' is discernible even on its tomb as 'a really vulgar babe'.

3. Applied to a person as a term of abuse or contempt. Now *dial.*

a **1529** SKELTON *Agst. Garnesche* 170 Thou murrionn, thow mawment, Thou fals stynkyng serpent. **1592** SHAKS. *Rom. & Jul.* III. v. 186 A wretched puling foole, A whining mammet. **1600** *Look About You* L 3 b, Downe stubborne Queene, . . Downe, Mammet. **1608** MACHIN *Dumb Knt.* III. F 4, O God that euer any man should looke Vpon this maumet and not laugh at him. **1610** B. JONSON *Alch.* v. iii, 'Slight you are a Mammet! O, I could touse you, now. **1630** MASSINGER *Picture* I. i, How the mammet twitters! **1891** HARDY *Tess* xlii, What a mommet of a maid!

†**4.** A kind of pigeon; = MAHOMET 5. *Obs.*

1678 RAY *Willughby's Ornithol.* 182 Mawmets, called (as I take it) from Mahomet. **1688** R. HOLME *Armoury* II. 244/2 Of Pigeons . . Mawmets . . exceed all others . . from their great black eyes. **1735** etc. [see MAHOMET]. **1835** P. J. SELBY *Nat. Hist. Pigeons* 164 Turkish or Mawmet Pigeon. *Columba Turcica.*

†**5.** *attrib.* and *Comb.*, as ***maumet god***, ***house***, ***place***, ***wood***, ***worshipper***.

1382 WYCLIF *2 Kings* xviii. 4 He . . hewȝ doun the mawmett wodis [Vulg. *lucos*]. **1483** *Cath. Angl.* 231/2 A Mawment place (*A.* A Mawment howse); *idolium. Ibid.* 232/1 A Mawment wyrscheper, *idolatra.* **1618** FLETCHER *Isl. Princess* IV. v, Where I meet your maumet Gods I'le swing 'em.

†**'maumeter.** *Obs.* In 5 **mawmenter**, **mawmetrer.** [f. MAUMET + -ER[1].] An idolater.

c **1440** *Promp. Parv.* 330/2 Mawmenter, or he þat dothe mawmentrye, *ydolatra.* **1496** *Dives & Paup.* (W. de W.) VI. viii. 243/1 Ne mawmetrers, ne glotons, ne wycked spekers, . . shall haue the kyngdome of heuen.

†**'maumetrous**, *a. Obs.* In 6 **mammetrouse.** [f. prec. or next + -OUS.] Idolatrous.

1546 BALE *1st Exam. Anne Askew* 21 b, Their most monstruose Masse or mammetrouse Mazon.

maumetry ('mɔːmɪtrɪ). *Obs.* exc. *arch.* Forms: see MAUMET; also 4 **mamentre**, (4–5 *pl.* **mau-**, **mawme(n)tryse**), 6 **mamoutrie**, **malmontrye**, **mammon(t)rie**, **mammitrie**, **-ye**. [f. MAUMET + -RY. Cf. MAHOMETRY.]

1. The worship of images; idolatry. Also 'false religion', heathenism.

a **1300** *Cursor M.* 6623 þai . . heild his comamentes right, ne heildid til na mametri. *c* **1330** *King of Tars* 803 Mi maumetrie ichul forsake, And Cristendom ichul take. *c* **1330** R. BRUNNE *Chron.* (1810) 320 þe Kyng said . . þe pape . . Errid mislyuyng, haunted Maumetrie. **1387** TREVISA *Higden* (Rolls) II. 279 Of þe bryngynge forþ of mawmetrie com wel nyh al þe feyninge of poetrie. *a* **1400–50** *Alexander* 4486 Maumentry, . . þat dose ȝow dompe to þe devill quen he ere dede hethen. *c* **1450** *St. Cuthbert* (Surtees) 1600 And to maumetry þai þaim graythe. ? *a* **1500** *Chester Pl., Balaam* 6, I wyll, you honour no God sauc me, ne Mawmentrye none make yee. **1530** *Compend. Treat.* (1863) 49 Kinge Antioche . . compelled yᵉ people to do maumentry. **1535** STEWART *Cron. Scot.* I. 505 All mammitrie fra he gart thame forsaik. *Ibid.* II. 180 With all thair micht . . to magnifie Mahoun thair maister with fals mamoutrie. **1552** LYNDESAY *Monarche* 235 To sic mischeand Musis nor malmontrye. **1570–6** LAMBARDE *Peramb. Kent* (1826) 268 Let the souldiours of Satan and superstitious Mawmetrie, howle, and cry out [etc.]. **1577–87** HOLINSHED *Chron.* I. 107/1 The Eastsaxons . . continued in their wicked mawmetrie. [*a* **1654** SELDEN *Table-T.* (Arb.) 88 Heretofore they call'd Images Mammets, and the Adoration of Images Mammettry: that is, Mahomet and Mahometry.]

†**b.** *pl.* Idolatrous beliefs or practices. *Obs.*

c **1340** HAMPOLE *Prose Tr.* (1866) 9 All mawmetryse, all wychecrafte and charemynge. *c* **1357** *Lay Folks Catechism* 176 (MS. T.) In this commandement is forboden us . . al mawmetries. **1550** BALE *Apol.* 142 Theyr vowes to holy churche the mother of theyr olde mammetryes. **1563–87** FOXE *A. & M.* (1596) 610/2 They falsly and cursedlie deceiue the people with their false mammetries and lawes.

†**c.** *fig.* = IDOLATRY 2. *Obs.*

a **1340** HAMPOLE *Psalter* xcvi. 7 Auerice is seruyce of mawmetry, and ilke man makis þat his mawmet þat he mast lufis. *c* **1440** *Jacob's Well* 120 þe firste fote brede of þis wose in coueytise is mawmetrye.

†**2.** Idols collectively. *Obs.*

a **1300** *Cursor M.* 11776 Hijs godds and his maumentri. *c* **1330** R. BRUNNE *Chron. Wace* (Rolls) 1337 þe folk myslyuande Worschipped . . Maumetry. *c* **1400** *Octouian* 1306 He ran with a drawe swerde To hys Mamentrye. **1526** *Pilgr. Perf.* (W. de W. 1531) 6 They be no true rychesse, but false and deceyuable mammotry of iniquite. **1567** *Gude & Godlie Ball.* 71 Stock and stane is Mammontrie.

†**b.** An idol. *Obs. rare.*

1303 R. BRUNNE *Handl. Synne* 4974 þese Phylystyens þat hadde þe maystry Beleuyd on Dagoun, a maumettry.

3. Mohammedanism; = MAHOMETRY. (In early use not distinguished from sense 1.)

c **1386** CHAUCER *Man of Law's T.* 138 In destruccioun of Maumetrye . . They ben acorded. **1600** ABBOT *Jonah* 117 Those seaven Churches . . are now the residence of the Turke, and a sincke of filthy maumetry. **1638** SIR T. HERBERT *Trav.* (ed. 2) 32 If (throwing away the raggs of Mawmetry) he roab'd his soule with true faith in Christ. **1805** SOUTHEY *Ball. & Metr. T.* Poet. Wks. VI. 239 Now shall the Crescent wane, . . Woe, woe to Mawmetry!

maumsay, obs. form of MALMSEY.

1492–3 *Med. Rec. City Ch.* (E.E.T.S.) 190.

maumy, obs. form of MALMY *a.*

maun (mɔːn), *a. Sc.* Also 8 **maan.** [? repr. attrib. use of ON. *magn* sb.: see MAIN *sb.*] Great, huge; chiefly associated with *mickle*.

17 . . *Herd's Coll.* (1776) II. 99 A meikle maan lang draket grey goose-pen. *a* **1774** FERGUSSON *Poems* (1789) II. 68 To screen their faces Wi' hats and muckle maun bongraces.

maun (mɒn, mɔːn), *v.*[1] (*pres. ind.*) *Sc.* Forms: 4– **man**, (4–6 **mane**), 9 **mann**, 6– **maun.** [a. ON. *man*, pres. t. of *munu*: see MUN *v.*] = MUST *v.*

c **1375** *Sc. Leg. Saints* iii. (*Andreas*) 1060 Sa mane we þane trew, þat [etc.]. *a* **1400–50** *Alexander* 1681 þe men of Medi man, be ȝoure leue, Lang all in oure lawe lely to-gedire. **1500–20** DUNBAR *Poems* lxxxi. 54 With sum rewaird we mane him quyt againe. **1577** in *3rd Rep. Hist. MSS. Comm.* 419/1, I man prepair me to keip the same. *c* **1620** A. HUME *Brit. Tongue* I. ii, To make a conformitie baeth in latine and English, we man begin with the latine. **1721** RAMSAY *Prospect of Plenty* 112 Maun bauld Britannia bear Batavia's yoke? **1788** BURNS *My bonie Mary*, And I maun leave my bonie Mary. **1816** SCOTT *Antiq.* xxvii, What's dune in the body maun be answered in the spirit. **1894** CROCKETT *Lilac Sunbonnet* 34 Ye maun hae been terrible bonny in thae days!

maun (mɔːn), *v.*[2] *Sc.* Also **man(n.** [a. ON. *magna*, f. *magn*: see MAIN *sb.*] To manage *to* do.

1790 A. WILSON *Poems* 202 Death's maunt at last to ding me owre. *Ibid.* (1816) 46 (Jam.) Sud ane o' thae, by lang experience, man To spin out tales. **1895** CROCKETT *Men of Moss Hags* 226 The thought of his kindness made me like him better than I had manned to do for some time.

maunance, obs. form of MENACE.

maunch, var. MANCHE[1]; obs. f. MUNCH.

†**maunche present.** *Obs.* Forms: 5 **monge presawnte**, **mawnchepresande**, 6 **maunche**, **mounch**, 7 **manch**, 7–8 (*Dicts.*) **manche-present.** [? f. *manche*, MUNCH *v.* + PRESENT *sb.*; there may have been an AF. **mange-present*, f. stem of *manger* to eat.] (See quots.)

c **1440** *Promp. Parv.* 342/2 Monge presawnte, *sichophanta.* **1480** *Cath. Angl.* 232/1 Mawnchepresande, *sicofanta.* **1530** PALSGR. 244/1 Maunche present, *briffavlt.* **1560–1** AWDELAY *Frat. Vacab.* (1869) 14 Mounch present is he that is a great gentleman, for when his Mayster sendeth him with a present, he wil take a tast thereof by the waye. **1589** RIDER *Bibl. Schol.*, A Manch-present, *Dorophagus.* **1623** COCKERAM, *Manch-presents*, notable bribe-takers.

maunchet(t, obs. forms of MANCHET.

maunciple, obs. form of MANCIPLE.

maund (mɔːnd), *sb.*[1] Forms: 1 **mond**, 1, 5–9 **mand**, 5 **mande**, **mawnde**, 5–7 **mawnd**, **maunde**, 7 **moane**, 8 **maand**, 9 *dial.* **maun**, **mawn**, **mound**, 5– **maund.** [OE. *mand*, *mǫnd* fem. = MDu., MLG. *mande* fem., masc. (Du. *mand* fem.), mod.G. dial. *mand(e.* The forms *maund(e*, *mawnd(e*, however, represent the OF. *mande* (mod.F. *manne*, dial. and techn. *mande*), adopted from Du. and LG.; it is uncertain whether the *mand* of some dialects represents the OE. word or the later adoption from OF.; as, however, the word has not been found in Eng. between the 11th and the 15th c., the latter supposition seems more plausible.]

1. A wicker or other woven basket having a handle or handles. Now only *local*, applied *spec.* in various districts to denote particular kinds of baskets (see quots. in E.D.D.).

c **725** *Corpus Gloss.* C 635 (Hessels) *Coffinus*, mand. *c* **950** *Lindisf. Gosp.* Matt. xvi. 10 Hu moniᵹ monda [L. *sportas*]. *c* **1050** *Voc.* in Wr.-Wülcker 370/19 *Coffinos*, manda. **1459** *Invent.* in *Paston Lett.* I. 481 Item, ij. maundys. ? *a* **1480** *Promp. Parv.* 330/2 (MS. S.) Mawnd, skype, *sportula.* **1489** CAXTON *Faytes of A.* II. xxxv. 152 Men may lete doune fro

the walles certayn persones in grete maundes by nyght. **1535** COVERDALE *Ecclus.* xi. 30 Like as a partrich in a maunde, so is the hert of the proude. **1546** *Kirton-in-Lindsey Ch. Acc.* in *Antiquary* Dec. (1888) 20 A mand for hully bred. **1597** SHAKS. *Lover's Compl.* 36 A thousand favours from a maund she drew Of amber, crystal, and of beaded jet. **1609** N. F. *Fruiterer's Secr.* 13 There must be prouided great baskets, or (as some call them) Maunds, of quarters or halfe quarters. **1615** SANDYS *Trav.* 260 Sweete composures Of violets haue I for thee in maunds of Osiers. **1623** R. WHITBOURNE *Newfoundland* 75 For pots and liuer Mands—*li.*000 18*s.* *od.* **1669** WORLIDGE *Syst. Agric.* (1681) 328 A *Maund*, A Basket, or rather a hand-basket with two lids to carry on ones Arm. **1678** H. MORE *Postscr.* in *Glanvill's Sadducismus* (1681) 46 Her own short Cloak, which she used with her maund under her arm to ride to Fairs or Markets in. **1721** PERRY *Daggenham Breach* 16 Great Maands, or Baskets, filled with Chalk. **1824** HITCHINS & DREW *Hist. Cornw.* II. 471 The pilchards . . are invariably carried by men . . in large maunds. **1864** BLACKMORE *Clara Vaughan* (1872) 114 After carrying into the kitchen the mighty maun. **1888** W. H. H. ROGERS *Mem. of the West* xiii. 275 A great maund of cabbages . . fills up the body of the little vehicle.

b. The contents of a 'maund'; a basketful.

1869 BLACKMORE *Lorna D.* viii, I will bring you such a maun of things. *Ibid.* lxviii, As fine a maund as need be of provisions, and money, and other comfort.

2. A measure of capacity varying with the locality and the commodity to be measured. Now *dial.*

1545 *Rates Custom-Ho.* a v, Bokes vnbounde the basket or maunde iiii*l.* *Ibid.* c viij, Trenchers the maunde or baskete xx.*s.* **1583** *Ibid.* F iv b, Glouers clippings the maund or fat. **1660** *Act 12 Chas. II*, c. 4 Sched. s.v. *Books*, Bookes unbound—the basket or maund, containing 8 bales or 2 fats. **1674** JEAKE *Arith. Surv.* (1696) 66 If the Fish be small; the Maund or Moane, holdeth about a Gallon. **1714** *Fr. Bk. Rates* 38 Coal Stone per Maund 00 04. **1727** SWITZER *Pract. Gard.* III. xxx. 154 They sell them [artichokes] from two . . to five shillings *per* maund, that does not hold above a dozen. **1833** J. BENNETT *Artificer's Lex.* 229 *Maund*, of unbound books, is 6 bales of each 1000 lbs. weight. **1884** *West. Morn. News* 4 Sept. 4/5 Thirty trawlers landed from 4 to 15 maunds of common fish per sloop.

3. *dial.* A utensil for moving grain in a barn or granary. ***hop-maund***, a vessel used in breweries.

1844 STEPHENS *Bk. Farm* II. 283 *Wechts* or *maunds* for taking up corn are made either of wood or of skin, attached to a rim of wood. **1868** *Gloss. Sussex Words* in Hurst *Horsham* (1889), Hop-mand.

4. *attrib.* and *Comb.*, as ***maund basket, form, -maker, -woman.***

c **1481** CAXTON *Dialogues* 38/19 Ghyselin the mande maker Hath sold his vannes. **1551** RECORDE *Cast. Knowl.* (1556) 147 This forme maye be called maundforme, or bellforme, bicause it is like a maunde basket, or a bell. **1678** H. MORE *Postscr.* in *Glanvill's Sadducismus* (1681) 47 A Maund-womans Cloak. **1843** *Jrnl. R. Agric. Soc.* IV. II. 581 In stacking the oats, I have a maun-basket drawn up the middle.

‖**maund** (mɔːnd), *sb.*^{2} Forms: 6 **mao, mana,** 7 **maune, mahan, mawn(d, maon, mein,** 7, 9 **man,** 8 **maun,** 7– **maund.** [English pronunciation of Hindī and Persian *man.*

According to Yule, ultimately from the Accadian *mana*, whence also the Gr. μνᾶ, the L. *mina*, and the Heb. MANEH. The early form *mao* is from a Portuguese source, the word having been, by a natural sound-substitution, adopted in Pg. as *mão* (mãu), homophonous with the Pg. word for 'hand'.]

1. A denomination of weight current in India and Western Asia, varying greatly in value according to locality. The standard maund of the Indian empire was = 100 lbs. troy, or $82\frac{2}{7}$ lbs. avoirdupois.

In India the past and present local values of the maund range from under 19 lbs. to over 163 lbs. avoirdupois. In Persia the maund of Tabriz is nearly 7 lbs., the 'royal maund' (*man shāhī*) is twice that weight.

1584 W. BARRET in Hakluyt *Voy.* (1599) II. I. 271 A Mana of Babylon is of Aleppo 1 roue 5 ounces and a halfe: and 68 manas and three seuenth parts, make a quintall of Aleppo, which is 494 *li.* 8 ounces of London. **1598** W. PHILLIP *Linschoten* I. xxxv. 69 They [of Goa] haue likewise another wayght called Mao, which is a Hand, and is twelue pounds. **1611** H. MIDDLETON in Purchas *Pilgrims* I. 270 Each maund being three and thirtie pound English weight. **1614** W. HAWKINS in Purchas *Pilgrimage* V. xvii. (ed. 2) 545 Which . . amounted to threescore maunes in gold, euery maune is fiue and fiftie pound weight. **1625** PURCHAS *Pilgrims* I. 524 The weights [of Persia] differ in diuers places: two Mahans of Tauris make one of Spahan. **1634** SIR T. HERBERT *Trav.* 65 A Mawnd is six pounds. **1665** *Phil. Trans.* I. 104 They now sell us a Maon of 6 pounds for two Rupias. **1678** J. PHILLIPS tr. *Tavernier's Trav.* II. II. 128 It [indigo] is sold by the mein which contains . . $51\frac{3}{4}$ of our pounds. **1681** FRYER *Acc. E. India & P.* IV. vii. (1698) 205 The Surat Maund . . is 40 Sear, of 20 Pice the Sear which is 37*l.* The Maund Pucka at Agra is double as much. **1687** LOVELL tr. *Thevenot's Trav.* II. 89 The Man of Ispahan is a weight of twelve pounds. **1788** *Trans. Soc. Arts* VI. 124 At the rate of twelve Rupees a Maund of nearly eighty-two pounds avoirdupois. **1863** FAWCETT *Pol. Econ.* I. v. 72 Four rupees per maund, of 83 lbs. **1909** *Chambers's Jrnl.* Oct. 665/2 The import of dyeing materials into Kashmir in one year was: Indigo, fourteen maunds, or one thousand one hundred and twenty pounds. **1955** *Times* 12 May 12/5 Throughout the Himalaya the unit of weight for barter is the load a man can carry—a maund, or 80 pounds. **1969** *Commerce* (Bombay) 26 July 188/1 Raw jute arrivals in the last week remained static at the previous level of 30,000 maunds a day. **1972** *Nat. Geographic* Oct. 532/2, I harvested about 33 maunds an acre. At a fraction more than 82 pounds to the maund that is roughly 2,700 pounds. **1975** *Bangladesh Observer* 21 July 7/3 On July 4 Bangladesh Rifles personnel chased an alleged smuggler near the border, but he fled away leaving one maund thirty seers of fertilizer.

2. As a liquid measure: see quot.

1875 BEDFORD *Sailor's Pocket Bk.* ix. (ed. 2) 323 Liquid measure. Maund = 8 Palli = 9.81 British Imperial Gallons.

†**maund,** *sb.*^{3} *Cant. Obs.* Also **mawnd.** [f. MAUND *v.*^{1}] Begging. Also, with prefixed word: A begging imposture of a specified kind.

1610 ROWLANDS *Martin Mark-all* E 3, What maund doe you beake, what kind of begging vse you? Ile myll your maund, Ile spoyle your begging. *a* **1700** B. E. *Dict. Cant. Crew, Footman's Mawnd*, an artificial Sore made with unslack'd Lime, Soap and the Rust of old Iron, on the Back of a Begger's hand, as if hurt by the bite or kick of a Horse. *Ibid., Rum-mawn'd*, one that Counterfeits himself a Fool. *Ibid., Souldiers-Mawn'd*, a Counterfeit Sore or Wound in the Left Arm. **1785** GROSE *Dict. Vulg. Tongue, Mason's mawnd*, a sham sore above the elbow, to counterfeit a broken arm, by a fall from a scaffold.

†**maund,** *v.*^{1} *Cant. Obs.* [Of obscure origin: possible sources are F. *mendier* and *quémander* to beg. Cf. also Romany *mang* in the same sense.] *trans.* and *intr.* To beg. ***to maund it***, 'to go a begging'.

1567 HARMAN *Caveat* (1869) 84 To maunde, to aske or requyre. *Ibid.* 85 Yander is the kene, dup the gygger, and maund that is bene shyp. *Ibid.* 86. **1608** DEKKER *Lanth. & Candlelight* B 2, The Ruffin cly the nab of the Harman beck, If we mawnd Pannam, lap, or Ruff-peck, Or poplars of yarum. **1610** ROWLANDS *Martin Mark-all* E 2, He maunds Abram, he begs as a madde man. **1618** B. HOLYDAY *Technogamia* II. vi, Wee had rather Mawnd then Mill to keepe vs from Trining. **1622** FLETCHER *Beggar's Bush* II. i, You must hereafter maund on your own pads, he saies. **1641** BROME *Joviall Crew* III. Wks. 1873 III. 395 Let me hear how you can Maund when you meet with Passengers. *a* **1700** B. E. *Dict. Cant. Crew, Maund-ing*, to Beg, Begging. **1720** PENNECUIK *Streams Helicon* 67 Ilk an must maund on his awn Pad. **1791–1823** [see quot. s.v. MAUNDING *vbl. sb.*].

†**maund,** *v.*^{2} *Obs. rare*$^{-1}$. [f. MAUND *sb.*^{1}] *trans.* To pack in a 'maund' or basket.

1609 N. F. *Fruiterer's Secr.* 16 How to packe or maunde apples.

maund(e, variants of MAND *v. Obs.*

1578 WHETSTONE *2nd Pt. Promos & Cass.* IV. ii, The King maunded him her strayght to marry.

maund, maunday, obs. ff. MOUND, MAUNDY.

†**'maunder,** *sb.*^{1} *Cant. Obs.* [f. MAUND *v.*^{1} + -ER^{1}.] A beggar.

1609 W. ROWLEY *Search for Money* (Percy Soc.) 40 The Divill (like a brave maunder) was rid a begging himselfe and wanted Money. **1610** ROWLANDS *Martin Mark-all* G 4 To write of his knaueries, it would aske a long time: I referre you to the old manuscript, remayning on record in maunders hall. **1641** BROME *Joviall Crew* II. Wks. 1873 III. 377 The great Commander of the Maunders, and king of Canters. **1719** D'URFEY *Pills* III. 100 A Craver my Father, a Maunder my Mother. **1829** LYTTON *Disowned* I. ii. 12 Hark ye, my maunders, if ye dare beg, borrow, or steal a single croker [etc.].

maunder ('mɔːndə(r)), *sb.*^{2} [f. MAUNDER *v.*^{2}] Idle incoherent talk or writing.

1880 *Sat. Rev.* 20 Nov. 656 *Beatrice Melton's Discipline* is not so much a story as a maunder without beginning or end. **1892** *Pall Mall G.* 22 Mar. 3/2 The discussion that followed was little better than amiable maunder.

†**'maunder,** *v.*^{1} *Cant. Obs.* [? f. MAUNDER *sb.*^{1}] *intr.* To beg.

1611 MIDDLETON & DEKKER *Roaring Girle* K 3 b, I instructed him in the rudements of roguery . . so that now he can maunder better than my selfe. *c* **1616** FLETCHER & MASS. *Thierry & Theod.* v. i, Beg, beg, and keep Constables waking, . . maunder for butter-milk.

maunder ('mɔːndə(r)), *v.*^{2} Also 7 **mander.** [Of obscure origin; perh. imitative: with senses 2 and 3 cf. *daunder*, DANDER *v.*]

†**1.** *intr.* 'To grumble, mutter or growl' (Phillips, ed. Kersey, 1706). *Obs.*

Very common in the 17th c. Quot. 1848 may belong to 3.

1621 BURTON *Anat. Mel.* III. iii. II. i, At home, abroad, he is the same, still inquiring, mandring, gazing, listening, affrighted with every small object. **1622** MABBE tr. *Aleman's Guzman d'Alf.* I. 253 When I heard them thus mutter and maunder against him, I came vnto them. *a* **1632** T. TAYLOR *God's Judgem.* iv. (1642) 55 She began to mander and murmur. *a* **1708** BEVERIDGE *Priv. Th.* I. (1816) 149 Not repining at their master's commands, not muttering and maundering against them. **1711** SWIFT *Jrnl. to Stella* 28 Apr., I hate to buy for her: I am sure she will maunder. **1740** *De Mouhy's Fort. Country-Maid* (1782) II. 286/1 The door was opened: He maunder'd; but Julia was beforehand with him. She said [etc.]. **1818** SCOTT *Hrt. Midl.* vi, What are ye maundering and greeting for? **1848** KINGSLEY *Saint's Trag.* IV. i, Let halting worldlings . . Maunder against earth's ties, yet clutch them still.

2. To move or act in a dreamy, idle, or inconsequent manner. Const. *along, away.* Cf. DANDER *v.* I.

c **1746** J. COLLIER (Tim Bobbin) *View Lanc. Dial.* Wks. (1862) 64, I maundert up on deawn hereobeawt ogen, oth' seme sleeveless arnt. **1790** MRS. WHEELER *Westmld. Dial.* (1821) 25, I lost me sel on thor plaguy Fels, an I been maunderin twoa heaal neets an twoa days. **1841** LYTTON *Nt. & Morn.* II. vi, A day-dreamer who had wasted away his life in dawdling and maundering over Simple Poetry. **1887** JESSOPP *Arcady* vii. 218 He came maundering after Miss Tasker thirty years ago. **1890** H. FREDERIC *Lawton Girl* 56 She . . maundered along wearily through such tasks of the day as forced themselves upon her.

b. quasi-*trans.* with *away*.

1867 S. WILBERFORCE *Sp. Missions* (1874) 61 To take things as they are, and not to maunder away our lives and our sympathies.

3. To talk in the dreamy and foolish manner characteristic of dotage or imbecility; to ramble or wander in one's talk. Also *trans.* to utter (something) in this manner. Cf. DANDER *v.* 2.

1831 CARLYLE *Sart. Res.* I. iv, Mumbling and maundering the merest commonplaces. **1860** W. COLLINS *Wom. White* 121 While he was maundering on in this way I was . . returning to my senses. **1860** *All Year Round* No. 74. 569 Signor Tagliafico's double maunders out good Tory port wine sentiments. **1861** HUGHES *Tom Brown at Oxf.* vi, The help . . was maundering away some . . sentimental ditty. **1865** LIVINGSTONE *Zambesi* iii. 68 We might maunder away about intellect. **1869** TROLLOPE *He Knew*, etc. lxviii, Men . . had heard the old Major maunder on for years past.

†**'maunderer**^{1}. *Cant. Obs.* [f. MAUNDER *v.*^{1} + -ER^{1}.] A professional beggar.

1611 MIDDLETON & DEKKER *Roaring Girle* K 3 b, I am . . a maunderer vpon the pad I confesse.

maunderer^{2} ('mɔːndərə(r)). [f. MAUNDER *v.*^{2}]

†**1.** 'A murmurer; a grumbler'. *Obs.*

1755 in JOHNSON.

2. One who rambles in his talk; a twaddler.

1827 *Blackw. Mag.* XXI. 783 An honorary member of the right worshipful company of Maunderers. **1864** *Morning Star* 28 May 5 The inanities of some prosy maunderer.

maundering ('mɔːndərɪŋ), *vbl. sb.* [f. MAUNDER *v.*^{2} + -ING^{1}.]

†**1.** The action of grumbling or muttering. *Obs.*

1611 MIDDLETON & DEKKER *Roaring Girle* L, *Mol.* Be sure you meete mee there. *Trap.* Without any more maundring I'le doo't. *a* **1716** SOUTH *Serm.* (1823) V. 245 The maunderings of discontent are like the voice and behaviour of a swine. **1740** tr. *De Mouhy's Fort. Country-Maid* (1741) II. 262 [She] had not digested the Blows, nor the continual Maundering she had undergone. **1816** SCOTT *Old Mort.* v, The principal object of her maundering was to display her consequence and love of power.

2. Rambling or drivelling talk; dotage.

1860 EMERSON *Cond. Life, Worship* Wks. (Bohn) II. 397 In creeds never was such levity; witness the . . maundering of Mormons. **1882** *Garden* 30 Dec. 577/3 The crazy maunderings of sentimental anti-vivisectionists. **1903** *Edin. Rev.* Oct. 282 The *non possumus* of the Vatican left an impression of senile maundering.

†**'maundering,** *ppl. a.*^{1} [f. MAUNDER *v.*^{1} + -ING^{2}.] Begging.

1630 J. TAYLOR (Water P.) *Begger* Wks. I. 100/1 Suppose a Begger to be in the shape of a maundering or wandering souldier.

maundering ('mɔːndərɪŋ), *ppl. a.*^{2} [f. MAUNDER *v.*^{2} + -ING^{2}.] † Grumbling (*obs.*); wandering aimlessly; doting, drivelling.

1848 KINGSLEY *Saint's Trag.* I. iii, Sour old maids, and maundering Magdalens. **1850** BLACKIE *Æschylus* II. 69 Lest with idiocy the thunder Harshly blast your maundering wits. **1865** TROLLOPE *Belton Est.* xvi, The squire with a maundering voice drawled out some expression of regret. **1904** *Blackw. Mag.* Feb. 191/2 Nothing is more irritating to an active long-striding sportsman . . than a sluggish maundering dog.

maunderingly ('mɔːndərɪŋlɪ), *adv.* [f. MAUNDERING *ppl. a.*^{2} + -LY^{2}.] In a maundering manner; inconsequently.

1909 I. ZANGWILL *Melting-Pot* III. 172 *David.* (. . he picks up the violin, and as his fingers draw out the broken string he murmurs) I must get a new string. (He resumes his dragging march toward the door, repeating maunderingly) I must get a new string. **1915** F. M. HUEFFER *Good Soldier* IV. vi. 282 Edward . . believed maunderingly that some essential attractiveness in himself must have made the girl continue to go on loving him. **1955** J. SLOTKIN in *Perspective* Autumn 152 He raised his head maunderingly, like a jackal from a lion's kill no longer warm.

maundful. [f. MAUND *sb.*^{1}] The amount contained in a maund.

1828 W. CARR *Dial. Craven* (ed. 2) I. 314 *Maund-ful*, a basket full. **1924** *Chambers's Jrnl.* 20 Sept. 673/2 Two maunfuls at a time, the pilchards are tipped out of the baskets.

†**'maunding,** *vbl. sb. Cant. Obs.* [f. MAUND *v.*^{1} + -ING^{1}.] The act of begging; an instance of this; an abusive demand.

1610 ROWLANDS *Martin Mark-all* G 4 b, Being borne and bred vp in the trade of maunding, nipping, and foisting. **1620** MIDDLETON & ROWLEY *World Tost at Tennis* 4 If you take me a maunding, . . let 'em show me the House of Correction. *a* **1670** HACKET *Abp. Williams* II. (1692) 116 He dealt fairly with him; not reckoning by his maundings and rough language. **1791–1823** D'ISRAELI *Cur. Lit.* (1859) II. 312 Uttering a silly maunding, or demanding of charity.

†**'maunding,** *a. Cant. Obs.* [f. MAUND *v.*^{1} + -ING^{2}.] Mendicant.

1636 W. CARTWRIGHT *Royall Slave* IV. iii, Some counterfeiting trick of such maunding people. *c* **1645** *Roxb. Ball.* (1886) VI. 321 A maunding Cove that doth it love. **1713** C'TESS WINCHELSEA *Misc. Poems* 61 My Wife, acknowledg'd such thro' maunding Tribes, As long as mutual Love . . can bind our easy Faiths.

maundrel, -il: see MANDREL.

maundy ('mɔːndɪ). Forms: 3- maunde, 4 mandee, mondee, 4-5 mande, maundee, 4-6 maundye, 5 mawnde, monde, mawndee, 5, 8 maundey, 6 mawndy(e, -daye, mawneday, 6-7 manday, maundie, 6-9 maunday, 7-8 mandy, 6- maundy. [a. OF. *mandé*, ad. L. *mandātum*, lit. 'commandment' (see MANDATE *sb.*).

The ceremony of washing the feet of poor persons on the day before Good Friday was instituted in commemoration of Christ's washing the apostles' feet at the Last Supper, and of his injunction that his disciples should in like manner wash one another's feet (John xiii. 14). The words 'A new commandment (*mandatum novum*) give I unto you, that ye love one another' (*ibid.* 34) from the discourse which followed the washing of the apostles' feet, were adopted as the first antiphon sung at the commemorative observance, which hence acquired the name of *mandatum*. (Hence OHG. *mandât*, in Otfrid's paraphrase of John xiii. 11-14.) In later use, perh. owing to the currency of *dies mandati* (lit. 'day of the commandment') as a name for the day before Good Friday, *mandatum* frequently denoted the Last Supper itself.]

1. The ceremony of washing the feet of a number of poor people, performed by royal or other eminent persons, or ecclesiastics, on the Thursday before Easter, and commonly followed by the distribution of clothing, food, or money. In England (except among Roman Catholics), the distribution of 'maundy money' (see 4) is all that remains of this ceremony. Phr. ***to make, keep, hold one's maundy.***

c **1290** *St. Brendan* 364 in *S. Eng. Leg.* 229 And sethþe he [þis procuratour] wuchs hore fet alle þe maunde for-to do huy [þe Monekes] heolden þare heore maunde. *a* **1300** *Cursor M.* 21611 A-pon þe dai o þe mande [*Gött.* mondee, *Fairf.* mandee]. **1502** *Privy Purse Exp. Eliz. York* (1830) 1 To the Quene for xxxvij^ti pore women every woman iijs. *jd.* for her maunday upon Shire Thursday. **1533** FITZWILLIAM in Ellis *Orig. Lett.* Ser. I. II. 27 That my Lady the Kings Grauntdame during her lif kept a yerely Maundy. **1577-87** HOLINSHED *Chron.* III. 914/2 Upon Maundie thursdaie he made his maundie, there hauing nine and fiftie poore men, whose feet he washed. **1667** PEPYS *Diary* 4 Apr., My wife.. had been to-day at White Hall to the Maunday,.. but the King did not wash the poor people's feet himself, but the Bishop of London did it for him. *c* **1700** in A. J. Stephens *Bk. Comm. Prayer* (1850) II. 899 *note*, The Order of the Maundy. The Sub-Dean begins the Exhortation [etc.]. **1850** A. J. STEPHENS *Bk. Comm. Prayer* II. 890 *note*, In England the rite of the Maundy continued to be performed by our sovereigns till the time of James II, who is said to have been the last sovereign who celebrated it in person. *Ibid.* 891 *note*, The 'Office for the Royal Maundy'.

b. The dole made at the ceremony.

[**1502**: see 1.] **1850** A. J. STEPHENS *Bk. Comm. Prayer* II. 893 *note*, Every recipient of the Maundy must be sixty years of age or upwards. **1865** *Pall Mall G.* 10 Apr. 7 On Thursday next Her Majesty's Royal Maundy will be given by the Lord High Almoner..to forty-six aged men and forty-six women.

†**c.** *fig.* Almsgiving, bounty, largesse. *Obs.*

1595 COPLEY *Wits, Fits & Fancies* 78 A Scriuener was writing a Marchantes last will..in which the marchant expressed many debts that were owing him... A kinsman of this Marchantes then standing by..saide vnto the Scriuener: hagh, hagh, what saith my vncle now? Doth he now make his Maundies? No (answered the Scriuener) he is yet in his demaunds. **1602** BOYS *Wks.* 396 Thy neighbour is bountiful in relieving the poor; thou seest his maundie but thou knowest not his mind. **1647** HERRICK *Noble Numbers* 43 All's gone, and Death hath taken Away from us Our Maundie; thus, Thy Widdowes stand forsaken.

†**2.** The Last Supper. *Obs.*

1377 LANGL. *P. Pl.* B. XVI. 140 The þorsday byfore þere he made his maundee, Sittyng atte sopere he seide þise wordes [etc.]. **1380** WYCLIF *Sel. Wks.* III. 415 Crist beggid a house to eete inne his maundee. **14..** *Pol. Rel. & L. Poems* 156/381 A tabull þer ys, þat men mey se That cryste made on his monde. **1533** MORE *Answ. Poysoned Bk.* Pref. *Wks.* 1038/1 The maundye of Christ with his apostles vpon sheare thursday, wherin our sauiour actually dyd institute the blessed sacrament. **1566** STAPLETON *Ret. Untruths to Jewell* i. 7 The example of the twelue at Christes maunde where that most holy mysteries were wrought. **1640** BP. HALL *Serm.* xxxi. Wks. 1837 V. 419 He should see him making his Maundy with his disciples, on the Thursday; and crucified, on Good Friday.

†**b.** The Lord's Supper or Eucharist. *Obs.*

1533 FRITH *Answ. More* H vij b, The breaking of breade at the Maundye is not the very deathe of Chrystes bodye, but onelye a Representacion of the same. *c* **1555** HARPSFIELD *Divorce Hen. VIII* (1878) 58 Nor to be secluded from the holy Maundy of the body and blood of Christ.

†**3.** A feast. ***to make one's maundy***: to feast.

[**1533** FRITH *Answ. More* M i b, Thys Lambe muste they cate hastelye and make a Merye maundye. **1545** BRINKLOW *Lament.* 102 Vnto all beleuers the ceremonye of eatinge the paschalle lambe ceassed..when Christ had chaunged it in to a maundaye of thankesgeuinge.] **1646** QUARLES *Sheph. Oracles* 66 Their flocks do fare No better than Chameleons ..Making their Maundy with an empty sent.

4. *attrib.* Applied to things distributed at a maundy, as ***maundy ale, bread, cup,*** or to people receiving them, as ***maundy man, people, woman***; also †**maundy-like** *adj.*; **maundy dish, purse**, a dish, purse used to hold the money to be distributed at a maundy (*Cent. Dict.*); **maundy money**, silver money (see quot. 1866) distributed by the royal almoner to poor people on Maundy Thursday, now usu. by the reigning monarch at Westminster Abbey; so ***maundy coin***; **maundy-supper** = sense 2; **Maundy-week**, Holy Week.

1517-18 in Swayne *Sarum Churchw. Acc.* (1896) 60 For *Mawneday ale ijs. iijd. for *Mawneday cuppys xijd. **1534-5** *Ibid.* 73 *Maundy brede, iijs. **1883** *Encycl. Brit.* XVI. 482/2 *note*, The number and weights of the fourpences, twopences, and pence, being *Maundy coins, are the same for each of the years [1871-81]:—4518 fourpences, 4752 twopences, and 7920 pence. **1534** MORE *Dial. Comfort* I. xix. (1553) E ij b, Not hys *maundy like merite, as hys passion, nor his slepe like merite, as his watche and his prayer. **1838** *Times* 16 Apr. 5/5 The Queen's Royal alms were distributed ..at the Almonry-office, to the *Maunday men and women placed on the supernumerary lists. **1856** SIMMONDS *Dict. Trade*, **Maundy money.* **1866** CRUMP *Banking* x. 231 The Maunday money consisted of 4, 3, 2, and 1 penny pieces in silver. **1887** *Roy. Procl.* in *Standard* 18 May 3/2 Pieces of Silver money called 'The Queen's Maundy Monies'. **1967** *Everyman's Encycl.* VIII. 293/1 In 1833..the dole was replaced by a money payment ('Maundy money') distributed by the sovereign in person or through a royal almoner. **1826** *Ann. Reg.* 47/2 About eleven o'clock the *Maundy people arrived. **1532** MORE *Confut. Tindale* Wks. 660/2 At the *Maundaye supper, when he [*sc.* Judas] went to betraye the headde of that churche. **1868** MORRIS *Earthly Par.* (1870) I. I. 322 As by the fire-light Peter swore of old, When in that *Maundy-week the night was cold.

Maundy Thursday. [See prec.] The Thursday next before Easter.

[**1517** TORKINGTON *Pilgr.* (1884) 66 Ther we a bode Mawdleyn thursday, Good fryday.] **1530** PALSGR. 244/1 Maundy thursday, *jevdy absolv.* **1546** LANGLEY *Pol. Verg.* 98 Washyng of feet on Maundye thursday, that the priestes vse among them selfes, and nobles to inferiour persons. **1563-83** FOXE *A. & M.* 1232/2 The Sacrament that Jesus Christ instituted at his last supper on Maundye Thursdaye. **1678** *Gunpowder-Treas.* 4 The Pope on Maunday-Thursday did censure and Condemn all Hereticks in the general. **1727-52** CHAMBERS *Cycl.*, Maundy, or Maundey Thursday, *Dies Mandati.* **1840** HOWITT *Visits Remark. Places* Ser. I. 260 On Maunday Thursday he washed and kissed the feet of fifty poor people; gave each twelve pence, three ells of good canvass, for shirts; a pair of shoes; and a cask of red herrings.

maung-: see MANG-.

maungee, obs. form of MANJEE.

1832 G. C. MUNDY *Pen & Pencil Sk. Ind.* II. 148 The Maungee gave the word of weighing.

maunkie, variant of MANCO *Sc.*

maunt-: see MANT-.

maupe. *dial.* Also 7 maulpp, malpe, 9 mwope, mawp. [Of obscure origin: cf. the synon. ALP², OLP, NOPE.] A bullfinch. Also *attrib.*

1654 *Goostrey Churchw. Acc.* in Earwaker *Sandbach* (1890) 248 For killing a dozen of maupes. **1670** *Wilmslow Churchw. Acc.* in Earwaker *E. Cheshire* (1877) I. 115 Paid for 16 maupe heads 6*d.* **1673** *Rostherne Churchw. Acc.* in *Lanc. Gloss.* (E.D.S.), Payd for maulpp taken 38 in Rostherne [etc.]..for every malpe 1*d.* **1885** SWAINSON *Prov. Names Birds* 66 *Bullfinch*..Mwope (Dorset). Mawp (Lancashire).

†**maur.** *Obs.* Forms: 5 mawr, mowr(e, mour(e, 7 maure. [a. ON. *maur-r*; for the affinities of this word see MIRE *sb.*²] An ant. Also *attrib.* in ***maur-hill, house***, an ant-hill.

c **1400** *Destr. Troy* 111 How Mawros were men made on a day At þe prayer of a prinse þat peopull hade lost. *c* **1400** MAUNDEV. (Roxb.) xxxiii. 149 When þe wedir es noȝt hate, ne mowres hydes þaim noȝt in þe erthe [etc.]. **15..** *Scott. N.T.* Matt. vi. 20 Quhar nouthir roust nor mowris destroyis. *c* **1450** *St. Cuthbert* (Surtees) 2408 For salomon biddes a slaw man ga To þe moure. **1483** *Cath. Angl.* 244 A pyss Mowre (*A.* A Mowre); *formica.* A pyss Mowre-hylle (*A.* A Mowre hylle); *formicarium.* A Mowre howse; *formicalion.* **1601** HOLLAND *Pliny* II. 379 *marg.*, Maure-hils, corruptly called Moule-hils: for Ants were in old English called Maures.

Maure, obs. form of MOOR *sb.*²

maureeyah, var. MOYA.

Mauresque, variant of MORESQUE.

Maurian, -en, var. forms of MORIAN *Obs.*

maurisk, variant of MORRIS.

Maurist ('mɔːrɪst). [f. (St.) *Maur* + -IST.] A French Benedictine monk belonging to the congregation of St. Maur, founded in 1618, famous for the learning and literary industry of its members. Also *attrib.* (quasi-*adj.*)

c **1800** C. BUTLER *Life & Writ. A. Butler* in *Lives of Saints* (1847) I. 12 Dom Ruinart, a Maurist Monk. **1893** *Dubl. Rev.* Apr. 394 The name Maurist became synonymous with a man given wholly to God and to study.

Mauritanian (mɒrɪ'teɪnɪən), *a.* and *sb.* Also **Mauretanian.** [f. *Mauretania* (see below) + -AN.] **A.** *adj.* Of or pertaining to the ancient country of Mauretania in North Africa, or the modern independent republic of Mauritania on the west coast of Africa, formerly a French colony. **B.** *sb.* A native or inhabitant of Mauritania. Also **Mauri'tanic** *a.*

1594 MARLOWE & NASHE *Dido* IV. iv. 215 And will my guard with Mauritanian darts, To waite vpon him. **1607** TOPSELL *Four-f. Beasts* 247 That same herbe (called *Doronicum*)..[is] highly esteemed among the Arabians[,] Graecians, and Mauritanians. *Ibid.* 461 These also are the Epethets of lions, wrathfull, maned..stout, great, Masilian, Mauritanian, Parthian, [etc.]. **1652** J. TAYLOR *Rule of Holy Dying* (ed. 2) iii. 95 Masinissa the Mauritanian. *a* **1680** EVELYN *Diary* an. 1645 (1955) II. 467 There were kept in it two Eagles, a Crane, a Mauritanian Sheepe, a stag, and sundry foule. **1776** [see MOOR *sb.*² 1]. **1895** [see *Afro-European* adj. and sb.]. **1911** 'I. HAY' *Safety Match* xiv. 221 Algiers—that curious combination of Mauretanian antiquity and second-rate French provincialism. **1959** *Times* 7 Jan. 11/7 The Mauritanian trader is a common sight in the markets. **1964** *Times* 29 Sept. 10/7 An attack by a gang of white youths on Mr. Youssouf Gueye, the First Secretary of the Mauritanian delegation. **1967** *Oceanogr. & Marine Biol.* V. 450 Two regions of the Atlantic Ocean, namely the Lusitanian..and the Mauritanian extending from Gibraltar to Cape Blanc, and including the Canary Islands and Madeira. **1968** *Encycl. Brit.* XIV. 1124/2 Mauretanian history really begins with the Punic Wars... Mauretanians were good military material and were used by the Romans in both Africa and other parts of the empire. **1972** *Guardian* 8 Feb. 13/1 A couple of Mauritanians selling silver spoons.

Mauritian (mɒ'rɪʃən), *sb.* and *a.* [f. MAURITIUS + -AN, -IAN.] **A.** *sb.* A native or inhabitant of the island of Mauritius in the Indian Ocean. **B.** *adj.* Of or pertaining to Mauritius.

[**1835** J. JEREMIE *Recent Events at Mauritius* i. 5 The Mauriciens are to set an example 'au monde entier'.] **1865** *Chambers's Jrnl.* Sept. 546/2 To Mauritians..this droll little Mauritian journal..may very probably appear a most influential exponent of public opinion. **1884** H. W. LITTLE *Madagascar* xiii. 280 Cheap rum..is often used..for the purchase of bullocks for the Mauritian markets. **1896** B. BURLEIGH *Two Campaigns* 60 Fiery Mauritian rum. *Ibid.* 111 The place was under a Mauritian named Hemming. **1918** L. HUXLEY *Life J. D. Hooker* II. xxviii. 12 The Mauritian Herbarium was to go back, as soon as the assistant had revised the lists. **1926** *Chambers's Jrnl.* Apr. 212/1 The Mauritian Creole is a crafty fellow. **1963** *Guardian* 26 Feb. 4/2 A young Mauritian said he would now shave off his beard. **1966** M. R. D. FOOT *SOE in France* xi. 380 The Mayer brothers,..Mauritians by origin. **1967** R. I. McDAVID in G. V. Bobrinskoy *Lang. & Areas* 86 A viable language in its own right—like..Haitian or Mauritian Creole. **1971** *Leader* (Durban) 7 May 1/2 Officials of the sports body..have already had negotiations with Mauritian football authorities. **1972** *Guardian* 8 Mar. 13/3 Ramgoolam would have to decide whether to..find a Mauritian for the top job, or (swallowing Mauritian pride..) find a suitable Englishman. **1973** *Times* 5 Mar. (Mauritius Suppl.) p. i/3 Warmed by the sun and Mauritian friendliness we relaxed. **1974** *Times* 14 Mar. 16/4 The Mauritians invited me to their binge..celebrating the sixth anniversary of their independence.

Mauritius (mɒ'rɪʃəs). [Name of an island in the Indian Ocean so called by the Dutch in 1598 after the Stadtholder Maurice.] Used *attrib.* in ***Mauritius-weed***, a lichen (*Roccella fuciformis*) from which archil is obtained.

1858 in SIMMONDS *Dict. Trade.*

Maurya ('maʊrɪə). [Skr., f. the name of Chandragupta *Maurya*, who founded the dynasty.] The name of a dynasty that ruled northern India from 321 to *c* 184 B.C.; a member of this dynasty. Also *attrib.* Hence '**Mauryan** *a.*

1870 *Jrnl. R. Asiatic Soc.* IV. 96 The celebrated Mauryan king..was not only sovereign of the valley, but of the whole of Northern India. *Ibid.* 122 (*heading*) Maurya dynasty, 130 years. **1886** *Encycl. Brit.* XXI. 272/2 The oldest hitherto known specimens of Indian writing are five rock-inscriptions, containing religious edicts in Pâli..issued by the emperor Aśoka..of the Maurya dynasty. **1910** *Ibid.* XIV. 399/1 After Asoka the Mauryas dwindled away, and the last of them..was treacherously assassinated in 184 B.C. **1935** *Times Lit. Suppl.* 4 July 434/4 The interest that the Mauryan State took in preventing famine and in relieving distress appears to have been more vigorous than in modern days. **1956** A. TOYNBEE *Historian's Approach to Relig.* vii. 90 In the age of the Maurya Emperor Açoka. **1959** *Chambers's Encycl.* VI. 553/2 About 185-175 King Demetrius conquered the Mauryan empire in north India up to Patna on the middle Ganges. **1968** I. W. MABBETT *Short Hist. India* v. 61 The Mauryan dynasty, like the rest of them, eventually became a line of kings jostling with others, a principality in the north-east. **1973** *Times* 14 Apr. (Nepal Suppl.) p. ii/2 The oldest monuments found on Nepalese soil are contemporaneous with the Mauryan empire of North India.

mauryah, var. MOYA.

Mauser ('maʊzər). [f. the name of the inventor.] (More fully ***Mauser rifle.***) A military rifle adopted by the German military experts in 1871, and perfected in 1884.

1880 *Encycl. Brit.* XI. 284/2. **1882** VOYLE & STEVENSON *Milit. Dict.* Suppl. *Mauser Rifle.* **1887** *Pall Mall G.* 25 Jan. 3/1 In the original Mauser..the soldier had to give the stock a smart stroke so as to throw out the used cartridge.

Hence **Mauser** *v.* (*nonce-wd.*) *trans.*, to shoot (a person) with a Mauser rifle.

1903 KIPLING *Five Nations* 168 When you want men to be Mausered at one and a penny a day.

†**mausole, mausolee.** *Obs.* Also 7 mausolæ, -ly. [Anglicized forms of MAUSOLEUM. (OF. had *mausole.*)] = MAUSOLEUM. Also *attrib.*

1585 JAS. I *Ess. Poesie* (Arb.) 35 The Mausole tombe the names did eternise Of Scope, Timotheus, Briace and Artemise. **1603** HEYDON *Jud. Astrol.* xiii. 325 The most sumptuous Pyramide, Mausole, Colosse, triumphant Arche, or other monument. **1605** SYLVESTER *Du Bartas* II. iii. II. *Vocation* 1424 No gorgeous Mausole, grac't with flatt'ring verse. **1614** T. WHITE *Martyrd. St. George* c 4, In which Georg had no gorgeous Mausolæ. **1618** BOLTON *Florus* (1636) 316 She betooke her selfe to the Mausoly (so call they the Sepulchers of their Kings). **1663** *Let.* in *Tavernier's Trav.* (1684) II. 94 Two wonderful Mausolees, or Tombs, that give to Agra so much advantage over Delhi.

mausoleal (mɔːsəˈliːəl), *a.* [f. MAUSOLE-UM + -AL¹.] Having the character of a mausoleum.

1883 A. J. EVANS in *Archæologia* XLIX. 53 It was in fact an example of the circular mausoleal churches.

mausolean (mɔːsəˈliːən), *a.* Also 7 **mausolæan, -lian,** 8 **-lœan.** [f. MAUSOLE-UM + -AN.]

†**1.** *Mausolean sepulchre, tomb* = MAUSOLEUM.

1607 TOPSELL *Four-f. Beasts* (1658) Pref., The Mausolean Sepulchre, the Colossus of Rhodes, or the Pyramids of Egypt might sooner be renewed. **1616** R. C. *Times' Whistle* ii. 593 The brave erect Mausolian monument. **1631** R. H. *Arraignm. Whole Creature* xii. §5. 143 The Mausolean Tombe.

transf. and *fig.* **1557** GRIMALD in *Tottel's Misc.* (Arb.) 117 No costly tomb..Nor Mausolean masse, hoong in the ayre. **1654** WHITLOCK *Zootomia* 248 Short-lived Pyramids, or Mausolæan Piles of stone. *a* **1734** NORTH *Exam.* II. v. §53 (1740) 347 He hath erected..a Mausolean Pile of Scandal.

2. Pertaining to, or resembling, mausoleums.

1785 COWPER *Task* v. 183 Some have..sought By pyramids and mausolæan pomp..to immortalize their bones. **1831** WORDSW. '*Well Sang the Bard*', That new Pile, For the departed, built with curious pains And mausolean pomp. **1871–74** J. THOMSON *City Dreadf. Nt.* x. v, These shapes lit up that mausoléan night.

mausoleum (mɔːsəʊˈliːəm). Pl. mausolea (-ˈliːə), mausoleums. Also (*erron.*) 7–8 **mausolæum,** 7 *pl.* **mausoleas.** [a. L. *mausōlēum*, ad. Gr. *μαυσωλεῖον*, f. *Μαύσωλος* Mausolus.]

1. The magnificent tomb of Mausolus, King of Caria, erected in the middle of the 4th c. B.C. at Halicarnassus by his queen Artemisia, and accounted one of the seven wonders of the world.

1546 LANGLEY *Pol. Verg.* III. vii. 71 b, Mausoleum that was the Tombe of Mausolus kynge of Caria. **1869** RAWLINSON *Anc. Hist.* 151 Artemisia II, B.C. 353, the builder of the famous 'Mausoleum'.

2. A stately edifice erected as a commemorative burial place for or by some person of distinction.

1600 HOLLAND *Livy* 1397 Augustus made a Mausoleum, to serve for a sepulchre as well to himselfe and all the Emperours, as also for his whole house and name. **1638** SIR T. HERBERT *Trav.* (ed. 2) 337 It includes many stately buildings; and Mausoleas. **1819** T. HOPE *Anast.* (1820) I. xii. 220 Aqueducts, and temples, and mausolea. **1841** ELPHINSTONE *Hist. Ind.* II. 151 Shir Sháh was buried at Sahserám, where his stately mausoleum is still to be seen.

¶ **b.** *loosely.* A stately tomb.

1688 *New Hist. China* 47 There are..six Hundred Fourscore and five Mausoleums. **1756–7** tr. *Keysler's Trav.* (1760) III. 241 Her husband Constantius, together with their son Valentinian II, in a mausoleum on the left. **1802** *Sk. Paris* II. xliv. 88 Lewis XIV never conceived the idea of erecting, in the *Hôtel des Invalides*, mausolea, with the statues of the generals who had led..the armies of the nation. **1824** in *Spirit Pub. Jrnls.* (1825) 374 His mausoleum may repose under the altar of St. Sophia.

c. *transf.* and *fig.*

1696 BROOKHOUSE *Temple Open.* 29 After some time, it comes forth of this Mausoleum a perfect New Creature of Whitish colour, with Wings and Legs. **1760–72** H. BROOKE *Fool of Qual.* (1792) IV. 175 O! London, London! thou mausoleum of dead souls! **1818** BYRON *Ch. Har.* IV. lx, The dead, Whose names are mausoleums of the Muse.

†**3.** = CATAFALQUE 1. *Obs.*

1695 *Lond. Gaz.* No. 3059/2 The Body..was deposited under a magnificent Mausoleum. **1695** LUTTRELL *Brief Rel.* (1857) III. 505 Stealing part of the fringe from the queen's mausoleum in Westminster Abbey. **1705** *Lond. Gaz.* No. 4103/1 A very magnificent Mausolæum is preparing in the ..Chapel..where the Body is to be Deposited. **1727–52** CHAMBERS *Cycl.*, s.v.

mausure, obs. form of MAZER.

mautalent, -telent, var. ff. MALTALENT *Obs.*

mauther (ˈmɔːðə(r)). *dial.* Forms: 5 **moddyr, moder,** 5–8 **modder,** 6 **moether,** 6–7 **mo(a)ther,** 7 **modher, mothther,** 9 **morther,** 8– **mawther,** 7– **mauther.** [Of obscure etymology.

Often regarded as a variant of MOTHER, on the ground that in Norwegian dialects *mor* ('mother') is often used vocatively to little girls, as *far* ('father') to boys; but this explanation is not very satisfactory. The suggestion that it may be a derivative or compound of ON. *møy-*, *mǽ-r* (see MAY *sb.*), or of some cognate of OE. *mæʒeð* (see MAIDEN) involves difficulties app. insuperable. In vocative use a shortened form *maw'r*, *mor*, is common: see E.D.D.]

A young girl.

Chiefly current in East Anglia and the adjoining counties, but instances (with the sense 'great awkward girl') are quoted in the Eng. Dial. Dict. from Gloucestershire, Herts., and Sheffield.

c **1440** *Promp. Parv.* 341/1 Moder, servaunte, or wenche (*S.* moddyr), *carisia.* **1573** TUSSER *Husb.* (1878) 37 A sling for a moether, a bowe for a boy. *Ibid.* 39 With mother or boy that Alarum can cry. **1591** FRAUNCE *Yuychurch* A iv b, Will Phillis still be a Modder, And not care to be cal'd by the deare-sweete name of a Mother? **1610** B. JONSON *Alch.* IV. vii, Away, you talke like a foolish Mauther. **1674** RAY *S. & E. C. Words* 72 *A Modher* or *Modder, Mothther*; a girle or young wench: used all over the Eastern part of England. **1787** W. MARSHALL *Norfolk* (1795) II. Gloss., *Mauther*, a little girl (in common use). **1798–1800** BLOOMFIELD *Richard & Kate* xii, When once a giggling Mawther you, And I a red-fac'd chubby Boy. **1849** DICKENS *Dav. Copp.* xxxi, 'Cheer up, my pretty mawther!' said Mr. Peggotty. **1865** W. WHITE *E. Eng.* I. 70 Throngs of noisy girls, 'factory mawthers', as they are called in Norwich. **1893** ZINCKE *Wherstead* 100 Down to thirty years ago in this neighbourhood a young woman was always spoken of as a 'mawther', or 'morther'.

mauther, mauthern: see MATHER(N.

‖**mauvais coucheur** (mɔvɛ kuʃœr). [Fr., lit. 'bad bedfellow'.] A difficult, uncooperative, or unsociable person.

1959 *Times* 19 Nov. 15/2 Brecht at best was a *mauvais coucheur*. **1960** C. P. SNOW *Affair* iv. 45 The moral roughneck, the *mauvais coucheur*, often seemed to her to have a dignity and elevation not granted to the rest of us. **1963** *Times Lit. Suppl.* 26 Apr. 297/3 Goddard was a man of talent but he was obviously a *mauvais coucheur*.

‖**mauvaise honte** (mɔvɛz ɔ̃t). [Fr., lit. = 'ill shame'.] False shame; painful diffidence.

1721 LADY M. W. MONTAGU *Lett., to C'tess Mar* (1887) I. 325 Nothing hindered me but a certain *mauvaise honte* which you are reasonable enough to forgive. **1825** BENTHAM *Ration. Rew.* 86 A kind of littleness and *mauvaise honte*, which avoids, with timid caution, everything that is bold, striking, and eccentric. **1877** L. W. M. LOCKHART *Mine is Thine* xvii, The *mauvaise honte* and artificial cynicism so constantly to be observed in the Anglo-Saxon.

‖**mauvaise langue** (mɔvɛz lɑ̃g). [Fr., lit. 'bad tongue'.] An evil or venomous tongue; a vituperative gossip; a scandal-monger.

1888 C. M. YONGE *Beechcroft at Rockstone* II. xiii. 14 The foreboding that the *mauvaises langues* would get hold of it. **1924** A. D. SEDGWICK *Little French Girl* IV. i. 304 Marigold is a wretched gossip, and worse. She's a *mauvaise langue*; I would not trust her story. **1936** 'R. WEST' *Thinking Reed* i. 18 In another moment that couple of *mauvaises langues* would have something to wag about. **1939** C. BEATON *My Royal Past* ix. 101 A lady..with a very *mauvaise langue.* **1974** *New Society* 11 Apr. 58/2 We are told that all Europe is at a standstill, until it knows who has been elected president (and those who are *mauvaise langue* will add that if it is Chaban-Delmas, there will be a further delay whilst he acquaints himself with foreign affairs).

‖**mauvais pas** (mɔvɛ pɑ). *Mountaineering.* [Fr., lit. 'bad step'.] A place that is dangerous or difficult to negotiate.

1816 SHELLEY *Let.* 25 July (1964) I. 500 The one [mule] which I rode fell, in what the guides call a *mauvais pas.* **1843** J. D. FORBES *Trav. through Alps of Savoy* iv. 67 The spot has acquired the name of the *Mauvais Pas*, which it bears more frequently than its proper one of La Roche de Moré. **1871** L. STEPHEN *Playground of Europe* v. 315 As a mere gymnast upon the mountains..in overcoming *mauvais pas* of all descriptions—the guide is incontestably superior. **1907** G. D. ABRAHAM *Compl. Mountaineer* iv. 56 The leader can retie himself on the end and scramble safely up the *mauvais pas.* **1940** F. S. CHAPMAN *Helvellyn to Himalaya* vii. 166 We decided to return once more to the couloir..thus short-circuiting the *mauvais pas* we had seen in our reconnaissance. **1971** N. TENNENT *Islands of Scotl.* i. 30 The northern section of the ridge..has some fine situations, including a tricky descent on the Iorsa side to the 'impassable' 'mauvais pas'.

‖**mauvais quart d'heure** (mɔvɛ kar dœr). [Fr., lit. 'bad quarter of an hour'.] A short period of time which is embarrassing and unnerving; a brief but unpleasant experience.

1864 M. B. CHESNUT *Diary* 8 Jan. (1949) 353 General Preston rushed in to the breach... But Mr. Willie Mountford had his *mauvais quart d'heure.* **1871** M. ARNOLD *Friendship's Garland* 95 You must needs have..a *mauvais quart d'heure.* **1883** LD. SALTOWN *Scraps* II. iii. 77 My modesty was severely tried, and I do not remember to have often spent a more *mauvais quart d'heure*, which was actually about the length of time that my martyrdom endured. **1897** J. MCCABE *Twelve Yrs. in Monastery* iv. 64 We gave him many a *mauvais quart d'heure* by running to the door when we saw his shadow near it, and chasing him through the convent. **1905** E. M. FORSTER *Where Angels fear to Tread* ii. 47 He takes it so well. But you must have had a *mauvais quart d'heure.* **1920** *Punch* 18 Feb. 138/3 Last week's programme had its *beaux moments*, but it had also at least two *mauvais quarts d'heure.* **1924** P. C. WREN *Beau Geste* I. i. 25 At the end of ten minutes, a very *mauvais quart d'heure*, I beckoned the Sergeant-Major. **1960** *Guardian* 21 Sept. 8/6 The long-term effects of a transitory *mauvais quart d'heure.* **1965** *Economist* 5 June 1125 John Kennedy had his *mauvais quart d'heure* between April and June, 1961.

‖**mauvais sujet** (mɔvɛ syʒɛ). [Fr. = 'bad subject'.] A worthless fellow, a 'bad lot'.

1793 T. FREMANTLE in *Wynne Diaries* (1952) xix. 251 Find the surgeon to be a mauvais subjet [*sic*], talk much to him. He crys, and promises to amend. **1813** A. ROMILLY *Let.* 12 Aug. in S. H. Romilly *Romilly-Edgeworth Lett.* (1936) 56 The youngest son, who was a very mauvais sujet, has just been killed in a duel. **1825** H. WILSON *Mem.* I. 179, I will lay my life, you two desperate mauvais sujets came here together! **1847** BARHAM *Ingol. Leg.* Ser. III. *Bros. Birchington*, Snob, (An obsolete term, which..We should probably render by *mauvais sujet*). **1881** FORSTER in *Standard* 25 Jan., A large proportion of them again are the *mauvais sujets* of the neighbourhood. **1897** E. A. BARTLETT *Battlefields Thessaly* viii. 171 These *mauvais sujets* had maltreated their own countrymen and women. **1945** R. HARGREAVES *Enemy at Gate* 56 Rome had failed to save one of its children, and even if that *mauvais sujet* had been guilty of recusancy, in the offspring's downfall the parent was no less undone. **1953** *Essays in Crit.* III. 217 The things in my criticism that he shakes his head over..endorsing the charges of..'bad form' and '*mauvais sujet*', *are* the effort to win that recognition. **1975** A. CHRISTIE *Curtain* v. 46 The *mauvais sujet*—always women are attracted to him.

‖**mauvais ton** (mɔvɛ tɔ̃). Now *rare.* [Fr. = 'bad taste'.] *Predicatively.* What is disapproved by good society; 'bad form'.

1784 HAN. MORE in W. Roberts *Mem.* (1834) I. 341, I know it is *mauvais ton* to have so little enthusiasm on this subject. **1814** MAR. EDGEWORTH *Patron.* xxxvi, With men of sense she found it was not *mauvais ton* to use her eyes for the purposes of instruction. **1835** *Court Mag.* VI. p. xiv/1 It would be considered *mauvais ton* to appear in any spring fashion till the season had been opened at Longchamps.

mauvaniline (məʊˈvænɪlaɪn). [f. MAUVE + ANILINE.] An aniline substance prepared by heating aniline and dry arsenic acid together, for the production of purple-red dyes.

1885 in *Cassell's Encycl. Dict.*

†**mauvasty.** *Obs.* Also 5 **mauayste.** [a. OF. *malvaistié, mauvaistié*, wickedness, f. *malveis, mauvais*, bad. Cf. MAVITE.] Wickedness, malice.

1474 CAXTON *Chesse* II. i, Thou ne say that thou shalt do it by pouerte but by euyl and mauayste. *Ibid.* II. v, A gyfte of grete felonye and of mauastrye [*sic*]. **1483** —— *G. de la Tour* xxii. L iv, In this..is not loue, but rather it is grete falshede and mauuastye.

mauve (məʊv), *sb.* and *a.* [a. F. *mauve*: see MALLOW.] **a.** *sb.* A bright but delicate purple dye obtained from coal-tar aniline; the colour of this dye. **b.** *adj.* Of the colour of 'mauve'. Also Comb. ***mauve-colour, -coloured*** adjs.; also with other colours, as ***mauve-pink, -red.***

1859 R. F. BURTON *Centr. Afr.* in *Jrnl. Geogr. Soc.* XXIX. 427 Beads..mauve-coloured round or oval. **1859** *Blackwood's Lady's Mag.* XLVI. 61 The lower part of the skirt is trimmed with ruches of mauve-colour crape. **1860** MISS YONGE *Stokesley Secret* ix. (1861) 137 Her mauve muslin..flounced up to her waist. **1861** *St. James's Mag.* I. 292 The fashionable and really beautiful *mauve* and its varieties. **1863** *Fownes's Chem.* 672 Mauve thus prepared forms a brittle substance, having a beautiful bronze-coloured surface. **1877** W. THOMSON *Voy. Challenger* I. ii. 126 Some beautiful mauve patches of almond-blossom. **1882** *Garden* 21 Oct. 353/3 A pretty variety..finely edged with pale mauve. **1899** B. W. WARHURST *Colour Dict.* 44 Lilac-rose is a dull rose..which..as a tint will appear as.. Mauve-pink. **1917** D. H. LAWRENCE *Look! We have come Through!* 57 Their mauve-red petals on the cloth. **1952** A. G. L. HELLYER *Sanders' Encycl. Gardening* (ed. 22) 92 *Catalpa Fargesii*..with its fine var. *Duclouxii* with large mauve-pink flowers.

Hence **ˈmauvish** *a.*, somewhat mauve.

1896 VIZETELLY *Zola's Rome* 187 Whose blue, mauvish eyes paling with enthusiasm he now..remarked.

mauveine (ˈməʊvɪn). *Chem.* [f. F. *mauve* mallow + -INE⁵.] The base of the purple aniline dyes.

1863 W. H. PERKIN in *Proc. Roy. Soc.* XII. 713 This substance is a base which I propose to call Mauveine. **1869** ROSCOE *Elem. Chem.* (1871) 410 It contains a base of complicated constitution, termed mauveine.

maux. *Obs.* exc. *dial.* Also **mawk(e)s, mox.** [Cf. *maukin*, MALKIN.] A low woman: **a.** a slattern (so in mod. dial.: see E.D.D.); **b.** a prostitute. Also used as *plural.*

1596 LODGE *Wits Miserie* (1879) 44 You seeme to be an honest gentleman, go prettie maid & shew him a chamber; now maux you were best be vnmanerly & not vse him well. **1677** OTWAY *Cheats of Scapin* Epil., Shall steal from th' Pit, and fly up to the Box, There hold impertinent Chat with taudry Maux. **1706** PHILLIPS (ed. Kersey), *Mawks*, as *A great Mawks*, i.e. a dirty nasty Slut. **1728** *Street Robberies Considered* 25, I had the clever'st Mauks in town. **17..** *Compl. Letter-writer* (1768) 215, I was sensible that I should appear to no Disadvantage after his former Maux. **179.** PEGGE *Derbicisms* (E.D.S.) 45 *Mox*, ..for *Maux*, by which they mean a foolish and slatternly woman.

†**mauze.** *Obs.* [Arab. *mauz.*] The plantain-tree.

1681 GREW *Musæum* II. 223 The Spike or Head of the Ægyptian Mauze. **1753** CHAMBERS *Cycl. Supp.*, *Mauz*, a name used by some authors for the *musa*, or plantain-tree.

maveis(s, obs. forms of MAVIS.

mavelard, obs. form of MALLARD.

maven (ˈmeɪvən). *U.S. colloq.* Also **mavin, mayvin.** Pl. **-im.** [ad. Heb. *mevin* understanding.] An expert or connoisseur.

1965 *Hadassah News Letter* Apr. 30 (Advt.), Get Vita at your favorite supermarket, grocery or delicatessen. Tell them the beloved *Maven* sent you. It won't save you any money: but you'll get the best herring—Vita. **1968** L. ROSTEN *Joys of Yiddish* 223 *Mavin* was recently given considerable publicity in a series of newspaper advertisements for herring tidbits. 'The Herring *Mavin* Strikes Again!' proclaimed the caption. The picture showed an empty jar. A real advertising *mavin* must have thought that up. **1969** *Time* 12 Sept. 78 Much of the credit for the Cinderella publishing story goes to Robert Gottlieb, then the editorial genie in residence at Simon & Schuster, now the mavin at Alfred Knopf. **1970** L. M. FEINSILVER *Taste of Yiddish* iii. 323 Canada Dry has been touting its product as 'Maven's Choice' in American Jewish weeklies, where Switzerland Emmentaler cheese announces itself with: 'Calling all Mayvinim!' **1972** *Publishers Weekly* 10 July 22/1 If Shawn is not exactly a boxing *maven*, he knows even less about baseball. **1973** *Milwaukee Jrnl.* 4 Mar. V. 4/1 Miss Decter (no Ms., please) is one of the culture 'mavins' of New York, to use a newly chic term borrowed from the Hebrew. **1973** *N.Y. Times* 8 July X. 31/4 Mama, who had managed

to support herself by becoming a local real estate *maven*, negotiated the purchase.

‖**maverick** ('mævərɪk), *sb.* [Samuel A. *Maverick* (1803–1870), a Texas cattle-owner who left the calves of his herd unbranded.] Also **mavorick.**

1. *U.S.* In the cattle-breeding districts, a calf or yearling found without an owner's brand.

1867 in J. G. McCoy *Hist. Sk. Cattle Trade* (1940) 83 The term maverick which was formerly applied to unbranded yearlings is now applied to every calf which can be separated from the mother cow. **1872** Schele de Vere *Americanisms* 211. **1887** F. Francis Jun. *Saddle & Moccasin* 172 Nowadays you don't dare to clap a brand on a mavorick even. **1894** Remington in *Harper's Mag.* Feb. 356 In a dell in the forest we espied some 'mavericks', or unbranded stock. **1942** S. Kennedy *Palmetto Country* 223 Most likely candidates for rustling are unbranded calves and cattle, called 'mavericks' in the West. **1974** G. Jenkins *Bridge of Magpies* xv. 229 Cowpunchers riding herd and trying to rope the most bloody-minded maverick that ever cut loose on the plains of Texas.

2. *transf.* **a.** A masterless person; one who is roving and casual; an independent person; an individualist; applied *spec.* in the U.S. to a politician who will not affiliate with a regular political party. Also *attrib.* in sense 'independent, unattached'.

1886 *Calif. Maverick* (San Francisco) 13 Feb. 4/1 People would say, 'He holds maverick views', meaning that his views were untainted by partisanship in the matter. **1892** Kipling *Life's Handicap* 195 A very muzzy Maverick smote his sergeant on the nose. **1901** *McClure's Mag.* Dec. 147 Occasionally they found a maverick legislator, or traded for one. **1903** *Critic* XLIII. 358/2, I felt as if I..for once was a happy maverick soul in the world at large. **1948** *Manch. Guardian Weekly* 8 Jan. 4/1 A few maverick liberals. **1948** *Chicago Daily News* 11 June 16/7 One Republican Senator, and not by any means a conspicuous maverick, pointed out that the Senate might have acted. **1954** *Manch. Guardian Weekly* 30 Dec. 8/3 His fellow 'maverick'..also appeared to have gone into not uncomfortable shadows. **1957** *Times Lit. Suppl.* 8 Mar. 1/3 A contrast of Maverick with Movement verse will illustrate this... To Mavericks, Movement verse expresses 'antagonism towards sensibility and sentiment'. **1957** *Oxf. Mag.* 17 Oct. 22/2 The story is not just of local boy making good, but also, and more significantly, of maverick making friends. **1963** *Listener* 17 Jan. 115/1 Neither the novelists of the central tradition of English writing, nor the great Mavericks of the nineteenth century, whose strong apprehension of evil forced them to break through the domestic web in which they wished to remain, had any clear theological pattern in which to embody their sense of evil. **1968** P. Oliver *Screening Blues* 18 Maverick lines that move from blues to blues are given new rhymes and new meanings by their juxtaposition with other ideas, while they retain the quality of surprise. **1973** *Radio Times* 4–10 Aug. 8 Ruth Inglis met the 77-year-old maverick zoologist at his Oxford base.

b. '*Western U.S.* Anything dishonestly obtained, as a saddle, mine, or piece of land' (*Cent. Dict.* 1890).

Hence **'maverick** *v.* (*a*) *trans.*, 'to seize or brand (an animal) as a maverick; hence, to take possession of without any legal claim; appropriate dishonestly or illegally' (*Cent. Dict.*). (*b*) *intr.*, to stray or wander like a maverick.

1883 in *Amer. Speech* (1958) May 141 The Indians stole them..and the Texans 'mavericked' the unbranded. **1910** W. M. Raine *Bucky O'Connor* 203 It hadn't penetrated my think-tank that this was your hacienda when I came mavericking in. **1948** J. K. Rollinson *Wyoming Cattle Trails* 139 The artful practice of burning or working over brands was resorted to, with honest mavericking as a side line.

mavis ('meɪvɪs). Now *poet.* and *dial.* Forms: 4–6 **mavys**, 5 **mawys(se, mavyce, mauvys, maviss,** 6 **mavyss,** *Sc.* **maveis, maves,** 6–7 **mavisse,** 9 *dial.* **mavish,** 6- **mavis.** *pl.* 4–6 as *sing.* (also 5 **mavies**); 7- **mavis(s)es.** [a. F. *mauvis* masc., in OF. fem. (12–13th c.), **malvis* (med.L. *malvitius*, 13th c.; Anglo-L. *maviscus*, 15th c.), = Sp. *malviz* (? from Fr.), Neapolitan *marvizzo*; the ulterior etymology is unknown.]

1. The song-thrush, *Turdus musicus*.

? *a* **1366** Chaucer *Rom. Rose* 665 Thrustles, terins, and mavys, That songen for to winne hem prys. *c* **1440** *Promp. Parv.* 330/1 Mavyce, byrde, *maviscus, merula, fallica*. *c* **1450** Holland *Howlat* 712 The Maviss and the Merle syngis. **1471** Ripley *Comp. Alch.* Ep. iii. in Ashm. (1652) 115 Crowes, Popingayes, Pyes, Pekocks, and Mavies. *a* **1529** Skelton *Ph. Sparowe* 424 The mauys with her whystell Shal rede there the pystell. **1549** *Compl. Scot.* vi. 39 The maueis maid myrtht for to mok the merle. **1595** Spenser *Epithal.* lxxxiv, So does the Cuckow, when the Mavis sings, Begin his witlesse note apace to clatter. **1604** Drayton *Owle* 113 In yonder goodly Tree, Where the sweet Merle, and warbling Mavis bee. **1626** Bacon *Sylva* §676 In Birds; Kites and Kestrels haue a Resemblance with Hawkes;..Black-birds with Thrushes, and Mauisses. **1725** Ramsay *Gentle Sheph.* II. iv, Delightfu' notes That warble through the merle or mavis' throats. **1791** Burns *Lament Mary Q. Scots* 13 The mavis mild wi' many a note, Sings drowsy day to rest. **1810** Scott *Lady of L.* IV. xii, Merry it is in the good greenwood When the mavis and merle are singing. **1830** Tennyson *Claribel*, The clear-voiced mavis dwelleth.. Where Claribel low-lieth. **1849** Dickens *Dav. Copp.* iii, 'Like two young mavishes', Mr. Peggotty said. **1876** 'Ouida' *In Winter City* viii. 237 The mavis and blackbird were singing.

transf. **1821** Scott *Kenilw.* v, I must visit this mavis [Amy Robsart], brave in apparel..and gay in temper.

2. *mavis skate*: a British species of Ray, *Raja oxyrhyncha*.

1810 Neill *Fishes* 28 (Jam.). **1828** Fleming *Hist. Brit. Anim.* 171 Sharp-nosed Ray... May Skate, Mavis Skate.

†**3.** [Perh. a different word.] Some kind of tobacco. *Obs.*

1688 R. Holme *Armoury* III. xxii. (Roxb.) 274/1 Sorts of Tobacco. Pig taile... Antago. Mavis.

†**mavite.** *Sc. Obs.* Also 4 **mawite, mawyte.** [a. OF. *mal-*, *mauvitié*, var. of *malvaistié*: see MAUVASTY.] Malice, evil intent.

1375 Barbour *Bruce* I. 126 Bot ȝe traistyt in lawte As sympile folk, but mawyte. *Ibid.* VI. 212 And he, that of thair mavite Wist na thing, his vay has tane.

‖**Mavors** ('meɪvɔːz). [L.: see Mars.] = Mars.

a **1592** Lodge & Greene *Looking-gl.* (1598) C 2, Nymphes, Knancks, sing for Mauors draweth nigh. **1602** *Narcissus* (1893) 332 The sweat hot breath of blowing Mavors. **1633** J. Fisher *Fuimus Troes* Prol., Mavors for Rome, Neptune for Albion stands. **1868** Tennyson *Lucretius* 82 Then would I cry to thee To kiss thy Mavors, roll thy tender arms Round him.

†**Ma'vortial,** *a. Obs.* [ad. L. **māvortiālis* of or belonging to Mavors, f. *Māvort-*, *Māvors*: see prec. and -IAL.] = next *adj.*

1595 *Locrine* IV. i, Once was I guarded with Mavortial bands. **1616** J. Lane *Cont. Sqr.'s T.* (Chaucer Soc.) 57 Mavortial Cambuscan. **1639** Drumm. of Hawth. *Challenge Knts. Errant* Wks. (1711) 231 Awaken your sleeping courages with mavortial greetings.

†**Ma'vortian,** *a.* and *sb. Obs.* [f. L. *Māvortius* (f. *Māvort-em* Mavors) + -AN.] **a.** *adj.* Warlike, martial. **b.** *sb.* A warrior.

1557 Grimald *Of N. Ch.* in *Tottel's Misc.* (Arb.) 115 Mauortian moods, Saturnian furies fell. **1598** Marston *Sco. Villanie* II. vii. 205 Behold yon sprightly dread Mauortian. **1600** Tourneur *Transf. Metam.* lxvi, O peerelesse worth! O worth Mavortian!

‖**mavourneen** (mə'vʊəniːn). Also 9 **mavournin.** [Irish *mo mhurnín*.] My darling.

1800 Campbell *Exile of Erin* v, Erin mavournin. **1883** H. Jay *Connaught Cousins* I. ix. 209 Hush, mavourneen, don't cry.

mavrodaphne (mævrəʊ'dæfniː). [mod.Gr., f. late Gr. μαῦρος dark (Gr. ἀμαυρός) + δάφνη laurel.] A dark-red sweet Greek wine made from the grape of the same name.

1911 in Webster. **1935** A. L. Simon *Wines & Liqueurs from A to Z* 36 *Mavrodaphne*, a sweet dessert wine from Patras (Greece). **1945** E. Waugh *Brideshead Revisited* I. ii. 52 Neither the mixture of wines, nor the Chartreuse, nor the Mavrodaphne Trifle..explains the distress of that hag-ridden night. **1958** R. Liddell *Morea* II. ii. 52 The sweet wine, *Mavrodaphne*..reminds me too often of the Looking-glass precept: 'Come fill up your glasses with treacle and ink.' **1960** M. Stewart *My Brother Michael* vi. 82, I sipped the wine. It was dark as mavrodaphne. **1972** *Times* 10 June 9/1 Mavrodaphne, the only Greek wine apart from retsina to be well-known outside its homeland, comes from the Peloponnese.

mavrone (məv'rəʊn), *int.* Anglicized form of Irish *mo bhrón* my grief (f. *brón*), used as an exclamation of sorrow.

1892 W. B. Yeats *Countess Kathleen* iii. 64 The treasure-room is broken in—mavrone, mavrone The door stands open, and the gold is gone. **1922** Joyce *Ulysses* 197 He wailed:—And we to be there, mavrone, and you to be unbeknownst. **1939** —— *Finnegans Wake* II. 232 Stop up, mavrone, and sit in my lap.

maw (mɔː), *sb.*[1] Forms: 1 **maȝa, maȝe,** 2 **mahȝe,** 3 **mahe, maugh,** 3–7 **mawe,** 4 **magh, maȝe, mau(e,** 4 **maw.** [Com. Teut.: OE. *maȝa* wk. masc. (once *maȝe* wk. fem.) = OFris. *maga*, MDu. *maghe* (mod.Du. *maag*) fem., OHG. *mago* (MHG., mod.G. *magen*) masc., ON. *mage* wk. masc. (Sw. *mage*, Da. *mave*):—OTeut. **magon-*.]

1. a. The stomach (of men and animals); the cavity of the stomach. Now only (exc. in ludicrous use) applied to the stomach of animals, esp. mammals; *spec.* the last of the four stomachs of a ruminant. † *to close the maw*, to stop looseness of the bowels. † *to chaw (one's) maw*, to fret internally.

c **725** *Corpus Gloss.* S 573 (Hessels) *Stomachum*, maȝa. *c* **1000** Ælfric *Gloss.* in Wr.-Wülcker 159/14 *Uentriculus*, maȝe. *Ibid.* 161/2 *Stomachus*, maȝa. *c* **1000** *Sax. Leechd.* II. 4 He cymð of acolodum maȝan. *a* **1225** *Ancr. R.* 370 Þe on was iwuned, uor his kolde mawe uorto nutten hote spices. *c* **1275** *XI Pains of Hell* 148 in *O.E. Misc.* 151 Gripes freteþ heore Mawen. *c* **1386** Chaucer *Man of Law's T.* 388 Who kepte Ionas in the fisshes mawe Til he was spouted vp at Nynyuee? **1393** Langl. *P. Pl.* C. XVII. 218 The man that muche hony eet his mawe hit engleymeth. *c* **1430** *Two Cookery-bks.* 39 The grete wombe of þe Schepe, þat is, þe mawe. **1513** *Bk. Keruynge* in *Babees Bk.* 266 Mylke, creme, & Iouncat, they wyll close the mawe, & so dooth a posset. **1544** Phaer *Regim. Life* (1553) E ij b, The mawe of an olde cocke dried, and made in pouder, is exceding good to drink in red wine. **1590** Spenser *F.Q.* I. iv. 30 But inwardly he chawed his owne maw At neighbours welth. **1605** Shaks. *Macb.* III. iv. 73 If Charnell houses, and our Graues must send Those that we bury, backe; our Monuments Shall be the Mawes of Kytes. **1613** Purchas *Pilgrimage* (1614) 354 Euery tenth man being by lot tithed to the shambles, and more returning in their fellowes mawes, then on their owne legges. **1706** E. Ward *Wooden World Diss.* (1708) 102 It's a plain Symptom, that his Maw's out of order. **1727–41** Chambers *Cycl.* s.v., The *Abomasus*, popularly called the *maw*, is the last of the four [*sc.* stomachs of ruminants]. **1769** Mrs. Raffald *Eng. Housekpr.* (1778) 17 Scald the maw or paunch [of the turtle]. **1819** Byron *Juan* II. xxxiv, Fright cured the qualms Of all the luckless landsmen's sea-sick maws. **1851** Mayne Reid *Scalp Hunt.* xxxviii, The night-hawk has filled his ravenous maw. **1861** J. Pycroft *Agony Point* (1862) 381 A shark with a sailor's baccy-box in his maw. **1887** W. Morris *Odyss.* IX. 296 Whenas the Cyclops had filled his mighty maw.

b. *transf.* and *fig.*: chiefly with reference to a metaphorical voracity.

(Cf. sense 3, which in figurative uses blends with this.)

c **1386** Chaucer *Shipman's Prol.* 28 Ther is but litil latyn in my mawe. **1599** Middleton *Micro-Cynicon* Wks. (Bullen) VIII. 134 The wide maws of more scopious lakes. **1607** Shaks. *Timon* III. iv. 52 Then they could smile, and fawne vpon his debts, And take downe th' Intrest into their glutt'nous Mawes. **1654** Whitlock *Zootomia* 403 Time.. whose Maw hath devoured the very Ruines of those stately Piles [etc.]. **1667** Milton *P.L.* x. 991 Death Shall..with us two Be forc'd to satisfie his Rav'nous Maw. **1742** Young *Nt. Th.* VII. 922 Pluck'd from foul Devastation's famish'd Maw. **1833** Marryat *P. Simple* xxix, Yellow Jack had filled his maw, and left the rest of us alone. **1875** Gladstone *Glean.* VI. xxxvi. 218 The devouring maw of the agents of the Popedom. **1880** 'Ouida' *Moths* III. 25 It is only the prison's maw that is never full.

†**c.** Inmost recesses. *Obs.* (? *nonce-use*.)

1630 Lord *Banians* 81 Some of the Rajahs yeelded, others flying to retyrements impregnable, lay in the Mawe of the countrey [etc.].

2. Applied to other internal parts. †**a.** The abdominal cavity as a whole; the belly. *Obs.*

1297 R. Glouc. (Rolls) 6363 Here is þat knif al blodi þat ich broȝte him wiþ of dawe & smot in þoru þe foundement & so in to þe mawe. *a* **1300** *Cursor M.* 22394 All þe filthes of his maugh sal brist vte at his hindwin. **1482** *Monk of Evesham* (Arb.) 85 The maw and inwarde bowels of him yat sate in the sadelle were sore smyt thorow.

†**b.** The womb. *Obs.*

a **1300** *E.E. Psalter* cxxxviii. 13 Fra maghe ofe mi moder me keped þou. *c* **1325** *Metr. Hom.* 124 Quen sain Thomas was in hir maw. *a* **1340** Hampole *Psalter* lvii. 3 Aliend ere synful fra maghe [*v.r.* marice].

†**c.** The liver. *Obs.*

1382 Wyclif *Exod.* xxix. 13 The calle of the mawe. **14..** *Voc.* in Wr.-Wülcker 588/36 *Jecur*, the mawe. *a* **1400–50** *Alexander* 4508 Cupido has þe custodi & cure of þe mawe. *c* **1440** *Promp. Parv.* 330/1 Maw, *jecur*. *c* **1500** *New Not-br. Mayd* 216 in Hazl. *E.P.P.* III. 10 My herte and mawe To rent and drawe..Cheseth not he?

†**d.** The honey-making apparatus of bees. *Obs.*

1577 B. Googe *Heresbach's Husb.* IV. (1586) 180 b, Beeing sucked vp from the leaues by the Bees and digested in their mawes. **1609** C. Butler *Fem. Mon.* iv. (1623) H j, You shall neuer find his [the Bee's] maw without a good drop of the purest nectar.

†**e.** The crop of a granivorous bird. *Obs.*

1658 Rowland *Moufet's Theat. Ins.* 1023 Hens feed on Earwigs:..I have found a great number of them in their Mawes. **1731** Arbuthnot *Nat. Aliments* (1735) 222 Their [*sc.* granivorous birds'] maw is the Happer which holds and softens the Grain, letting it drop by degrees into the Stomach.

f. The 'swim-bladder' or sound of a fish.

c **1430** *Two Cookery-bks.* 18 Take the Mawes of Turbut, Haddok, or Codeling. **1883** R. Haldane *Workshop Receipts* Ser. II. 355 Isinglass or fish glue, in its raw state, is the 'sound', 'maw', or swimming bladder of various kinds of fish.

3. The throat, gullet; now chiefly, the jaws or mouth (of a voracious mammal or fish). Also *fig.*

1530 Palsgr. 244/1 Mawe of a beest, *josier*. **1814** Cary *Dante, Paradise* IV. 4 A lamb between the maw Of two fierce wolves. **1818** Keats *Endymion* II. 272 Weary, he sat down before the maw Of a wide outlet. **1843** Lytton *Last Bar.* I. vii, The philosopher's hand closed on them as the fish's maw closes on the bait. **1851** H. Melville *Whale* ix. 44, I saw the opening maw of hell. **1867** F. Francis *Angling* i. (1880) 1 Within reach of its voracious maw. **1873** G. C. Davies *Mount. & Mere* ii. 9 A little black ball has gone down the hungry maw of a pike. **1931** F. Hurst *Back St.* xxxi. 277 The small vestibule where stood a row of these iron men of chance. Occasionally one of the guests, feeding coins into these metal maws, staked her. **1955** *Times* 5 Aug. 9/7 The grim realities of economics are rapidly driving the stubbornly 'independent' man into the insatiable maw of large combines.

†**4.** Used (like *stomach*) for: Appetite, inclination, liking. *Obs.*

1598 Jonson *Ev. Man in Hum.* III. iv. (1616) 38 O, I doe stomack them hugely! I haue a maw now, and't were for Sʳ Bevis his horse, against 'hem. **1602** Marston *Antonio's Rev.* IV. v, Have you no mawe to restitution? **1607** Middleton *Fam. Love* v. iii. 146 If you have any maw, feed here till you choke again. **1645** Milton *Colast.* Wks. 1851 IV. 365 Next the word Politician is not us'd to his maw, and therupon he plaies the most notorious hobbihors. **1668** R. L'Estrange *Vis. Quev.* (1708) 37, I have no great Maw to go home again. **1704** Cibber *Careless Husb.* v. (1705) 50, I have no great Maw to that Business, methinks.

5. *attrib.* and *Comb.*, as **maw-bound** *a.*, constipated (*Syd. Soc. Lex.* 1890); also †*sb.*, a constipated disease in cattle; †**maw-gut** (see quot. 1607); †**maw-mother**, a mooncalf or 'false conception' (*tumor ventris*); †**maw-skin**, the stomach of a calf which has fed on nothing but milk.

a **1722** Lisle *Husb.* (1752) 344 The distemper in cows called the *maw-bound..comes from a surfeit by being overheated by driving. **1848** *Rural Cycl.* II. 486 *Grain-sick*,

or *Maw-bound*, a great and dangerous distension of the rumen of cattle. **1607** TOPSELL *Four-f. Beasts* (1658) 153 He hath his gall in his *maw-gut. *Ibid.* 509 The maw-gut differeth from all other, for it is *Coecum*, that is, as I take it without a passage out of it into any other part then the other guts [etc.]. **1483** *Cath. Angl.* 232 *Mawmoder, *molucrum*. **1784** TWAMLEY *Dairying* 41 The *Maw-skin..is the Maw or Stomach of Calves. **1846** J. BAXTER *Libr. Pract. Agric.* (ed. 4) I. 205 The water thus impregnated with the maw-skin is passed through the sieve into the milk.

maw (mɔː), *sb.*² *Obs.* exc. *dial.* Also 5-6 **mawe**, 9 (*pl.* constr. as *sing.*) **maas, mawse, maws.** [var. of MALLOW. Cf. MAUL *sb.*] = MALLOW.

c **1425** WYNTOUN *Cron.* I. viii. 433 Froyt & gyrs thai oysyd tyll ete As kers, or mawe, or wyolete. *c* **1450** *Alphita* (Anecd. Oxon.) 23 Malva ortolana vel domestica. g. mauue, ang. mawe. **1562** TURNER *Herbal* II. 45 The vertues of mallowe or mawes. **1568** SKEYNE *The Pest* (1860) 40 Fomentit with the decoctioun of the rute of lilie, maw, althe, cammeile. **1696** in *Analecta Scot.* II. 13 Aduertes me, gif he hes the seid of al sort of mawes, purpie, and sorrelis. **1893** *Northumbld. Gloss., Maas, Mawse. Ibid., Maws,* the maws mallow or marshmallow.

maw (mɔː), *sb.*³ *Obs.* exc. *dial.* Also 6 **mau**, 7-8 **mall.** [a. ON. *má-r* (dat. *máve*, *máfe*, pl. *mávar*) = OE. *mǽw*: see MEW *sb.*¹] A gull, esp. the Common gull, *Larus canus.*

c **1450** HOLLAND *Howlat* 179 The Se Mawis war monkis, the blak and the quhyte. **1500-20** DUNBAR *Poems* xxxiii. 90 Thik was the clud of kayis and crawis, Of marleȝonis, mittanis, and of mawis. **1549** [see *gull-maw*, GULL *sb.*¹ c]. **1678** RAY *Willughby's Ornithol.* 345 The common Sea-Mall, *Larus cinereus minor.* **1698** M. MARTIN *Voy. St. Kilda* (1749) 28 The Fulmar, in Bigness equals the Malls of the second Rate. *c* **1825** *Jolly Goshawk* iii. in Child *Ballads* II. 360/1 The thing of my love's face is white It's that of dove or maw. **1852** MACGILLIVRAY *Hist. Brit. Birds* V. 593 *Gavia ridibunda*...[Syn.] Laughing Gull...Black-cap. Hooded Maw.

maw (mɔː), *sb.*⁴ *Obs.* exc. *Hist.* Also 6 **mall**, 6-7 **mawe.** [Of obscure origin.] 'An old game at cards. It was played with a piquet pack of thirty-six cards, and any number of persons from two to six formed the party' (Halliwell). ***a set at maw***: a party or game at maw. ***to set a maw***: ? to arrange a game. ***to heave at (the) maw***: a technical phrase of the game, app. designating its characteristic feature. (Cf. MAYO.)

1548 FORREST *Pleas. Poesye* xix. 58 b, At ale howse too sitt at mack or at mall. **1575** TURBERV. *Faulconrie, In Commend. Hawk.* 77 To checke at Chesse, to heaue at Maw, at Mack to passe the time. **1593** RICH in *Greene's Newes fr. Heaven & Hell* To Rdr., Although the knave of trumpes be the seconde carde at Mawe, yet the five-finger may commaunde both him and all the rest of the pack. **1594** HENSLOWE *Diary* (1845) 46 [Title of play] the mawe. *Ibid.* 47 *note*, The seat at mawe. *a* **1612** HARINGTON *Epigr.* IV. xii. (1618) K 6 b, Then thirdly follow'd heaving of the Maw, A game without Ciuility or Law. **1624** GATAKER *Wife in Deed* 62 Whom a pint of wine drunke together,..or a set at Maw maketh Friends. **1630** BRATHWAIT *Eng. Gentlem.* (1641) 126 In games at cards the Maw requires a quicke conceit or present pregnancy. **1633** FORD *Love's Sacr.* III. ii, My lord you were best to try to set a maw. **1864** *Reader* No. 105. 826/1 Primero yielded the ascendancy to Maw.

†**b.** ***a help at maw***: app. a term of this game, but occurring only *fig.* a means of evasion, a resource.

1644-7 CLEVELAND *Char. Lond. Diurn.* 7 If any thing fall out amiss, which cannot be smothered, the *Diurnall* hath a help at Maw. **1660** R. COKE *Justice Vind.* 13 But it may be our Author has a help at Mawe; for our Author Ground 8. saies It is evident [etc.]. **1678** B. R. *Let. Pop. Friends* 4 A Dispensation..is always an Infallible Help at Maw, a sure Antidote against Perjury.

†**maw**, *v. Obs. rare*⁻¹. [a. Du. *mauwen.*] *intr.* Of a cat = MEW *v.*

1481 CAXTON *Reynard* (Arb.) 22 Tybert coude not goo awaye, but he mawede and galped so lowde that [etc.].

maw: see MAUGH, MAUL, MOW.

mawa, variant of MAHWA.

1800 *Asiat. Ann. Reg., Misc. Tracts* 131/2.

mawby, var. MAUBY.

mawch(e, mawde, variant ff. MAUGH, MAUD¹.

mawdelard(e, obs. forms of MALLARD.

mawdelayn, -lein, -len, etc., obs. ff. MAUDLIN.

mawe: see MAUGH, MAUL, MOW.

mawen, 3rd pl. pres. ind. of MAY *v.*¹

mawer, obs. form of MAYOR, MOWER.

mawfesour, variant of MALFEASOR *Obs.*

mawger, -gre(e, -gref(e, etc., var. ff. MAUGRE.

mawggh, Mawhown: see MAUGH, MAHOUND.

mawich(e, obs. Sc. variant forms of MAUGH.

mawk (mɔːk). *Obs.* exc. *dial.* Also 5 **mawke**, 5, 7 **make**, 6-8 **mauk**, 7 **mauke, malke**, 8 *pl.* **mox.** [ad. ON. *maðk-r*: see MADDOCK.] = MAGGOT.

c **1425** *Voc.* in Wr.-Wülcker 643/2 *Hic cimex*, mawke. *c* **1440** *Alphabet of Tales* 332 Att þe laste mawkis bred þerin. *c* **1440** *Promp. Parv.* 321/1 Make, mathe, wyrm yn þe flesche. **1623** SANDERSON *Serm.* I. 93 He is a sorry shepherd, that is busie to kill flies and maukes in his sheep, but letteth the wolf worry at pleasure. **1641** BEST *Farm. Bks.* (Surtees) 79 In what part of the woll soever it bee, there will malkes breede immediately. **1684** G. MERITON *Praise Yorks. Ale*, etc., Clavis, Mawks are Maddocks. **1789** DAVIDSON *Seasons* 5 The cloken hen to the midden rins..To scrape for mauks. **179.** PEGGE *Derbicisms* (E.D.S.) 112 *Mox*, moths. **1894** CROCKETT *Lilac Sunbonnet* 73 A mawk on a sheep's hurdie.

mawkin, obs. form of MALKIN.

'mawkingly, *a. Obs.* exc. *dial.* [f. *mawking*, MALKIN + -LY¹.] Slovenly.

1656 *Artif. Handsom.* 87 Some silly soules are prone to place much piety in their mawkingly plainnesse, and in their censoriousnesse of others, who use more comely and costly curiosities.

mawkish ('mɔːkɪʃ), *a.* Also 7-8 **malkish, maukish.** [f. MAWK *sb.* + -ISH¹.]

†**1.** Inclined to sickness; without appetite. *Obs.*

1668 DRYDEN *Enem. Love* IV. i, I feel my Stomach a little maukish. **1706** PHILLIPS (ed. Kersey), *Mawkish*, sick at Stomack, squeamish. *a* **1745** SWIFT *Progr. Marriage* 60 The dean who us'd to dine at one, Is maukish, and his stomach gone. **1755** *Connoisseur* No. 82 (1774) III. 83 He constantly goes senseless to bed, and rises maukish in the morning. **1836** T. HOOK *G. Gurney* II. 59 The feverish, heated, mawkish, wretched state in which I was.

†**b.** Having no inclination *to. Obs.*

1679 DRYDEN *Troil. & Cress.* IV. ii, Who knows but rest may cool their brains, and make them rise mawkish to mischief upon consideration?

2. Having a nauseating taste; now, having a faint, sickly flavour with little definite taste.

a **1697** AUBREY *Nat. Hist. Surrey* (1719) I. 215 The medicated Springs here..have a maukish Taste. *a* **1700** B. E. *Dict. Cant. Crew, Wallowish*, a malkish, ill Taste. *a* **1719** ADDISON *Virg. Georg.* IV. 117 Others look loathsom and diseas'd with sloth, Like a faint traveller whose dusty mouth Grows dry with heat, and spits a maukish froth. **1728** POPE *Dunc.* III. 171 Like thine inspirer, Beer,..So sweetly mawkish, and so smoothly dull. **1786** tr. *Beckford's Vathek* (1868) 89 He regarded the ragouts of his other wives as entirely maukish. **1803** *Med. Jrnl.* IX. 492 It is without smell, has a maukish taste, and has but little consistence. **1872** *Cooper's Dict. Pract. Surg.* II. 643 Pus has a sweetish, mawkish taste.

3. *fig.* Feebly sentimental; imbued with sickly or false sentiment; lacking in robustness.

1702 *Eng. Theophrast.* 110 It is one of the most nauseous maukish mortifications under the Sun..to have to do with a punctual finical fop. **1776** FOOTE *Bankrupt* I. Wks. 1799 II. 104 His mind is so maukish, that should he be confronted with Lydia, he would betray our whole plot in an instant. **1818** KEATS *Lett.* Wks. 1889 III. 141, I hate a mawkish popularity. **1819** *Metropolis* I. 47 The mawkish tepidity of his manner. **1885** *Spectator* 8 Aug. 1048/2 The mawkish and unreal sentiment which constituted Mr. Dickens's chief fault. **1889** D. HANNAY *Capt. Marryat* viii. 125 It [*Masterman Ready*] is pathetic, and yet it is not mawkish.

†**4.** *slang.* Slatternly. *Obs. rare*⁻⁰.

1725 *New Cant. Dict., Mawkish*, Slatternly.

mawkishly ('mɔːkɪʃlɪ), *adv.* [-LY².]

1. So as to be 'mawkish' in flavour.

1758 *Monthly Rev.* 592 Swallow it neither too hot nor mawkishly cool. **1785** MARTYN *Rousseau's Bot.* xxix. (1794) 461 The berry is red, and mawkishly sweet—not poisonous.

2. In a feebly sentimental manner.

1816 J. GILCHRIST *Philos. Etym.* 230 A feeble, finical race, mawkishly puling about taste. **1853** READE *Chr. Johnstone* 279, I should have been very kind to you—mawkishly kind I fear, my sweet cousin. **1867** BUSHNELL *Mor. Uses Dark Th.* 282 Goodness is no such innocent mawkishly insipid character.

mawkishness ('mɔːkɪʃnɪs). [-NESS.]

†**1.** The condition of being sick or 'squeamish'.

1727 BAILEY vol. II, *Mawkishness*,..Sickness at the Stomach, Squeamishness.

2. Insipidity or sickliness of flavour.

1727 BAILEY vol. II, *Mawkishness*,..a nauseous Taste. **1876** BARTHOLOW *Mat. Med.* (1879) 350 Wines should have a taste free from mawkishness, and indicative of instability. **1887** BEATTY-KINGSTON *Music & Manners* II. 308 'White beer', a liquor of paramount mawkishness.

transf. **1876** MISS BRADDON *J. Haggard's Dau.* II. 70 Their music was sweet to mawkishness.

3. Sickly sentimentality.

1818 KEATS *Endymion* Pref., There is a space of life between [*sc.* boyhood and manhood] in which the soul is in a ferment,..the ambition thick-sighted; thence proceeds mawkishness. **1824** *Examiner* 595/1 The languid mawkishness of the loungers. **1833-40** J. H. NEWMAN *Hist. Sk.* (1873) II. IV. iv. 406 He is..as removed from softness and mawkishness..as any bishop among them. **1849** ROCK *Ch. of Fathers* I. 35 *note*, That mawkishness of taste..shewn by some people for what is classic.

b. Dullness of spirits, ennui. *rare.*

1861 HUGHES *Tom Brown at Oxf.* v. (1889) 44 All the companionship of boating and cricketing..won't keep him from many a long hour of mawkishness.

mawky ('mɔːkɪ), *a. dial.* [f. MAWK + -Y.]

1. a. Maggoty. **b.** Full of 'maggots' or whims; crotchety.

1790 GROSE *Prov. Gloss.* (ed. 2), *Mawky*, magotty, N. **1837** WHITTOCK, etc. *Bk. Trades* (1842) 466 We can neither understand, nor relish, this 'mauky' affectation of candour on the part of our former friend. **1855** ROBINSON *Whitby Gloss., Mawky*, maggoty, whimsical, hypochondriac.

2. = MAWKISH.

1830 'JON BEE' *Ess.* in *Foote's Wks.* I. p. xxiii, Even John Dryden penned none but mawky plays, nor did Byron succeed at all as a dramatist. **1881** *Oxfordsh. Gloss.* Suppl., *Mawky*, over-sweet.

Mawlana, var. MAULANA.

mawlard, mawl(e, obs. ff. MALLARD, MAUL.

mawley, var. MAULEY.

mawm(e, variant forms of MALM.

mawmany, -mene(e, etc.: see MALMENY.

mawment, -trie: see MAUMET, MAUMETRY.

†**'mawmer, -ar.** *Sc. Obs.* [Cf. Du. *mammiering* 'scupper-hose'.] The discharge pipe of a ship's pump. Also *attrib.* in ***mawmer-leather***.

1497 *Acc. Ld. Treas. Scotl.* (1877) I. 379 Item for ane mawmar to the pomp of Lord Kennydyis schip. **1512** *Ibid.* (1902) IV. 455 Item for mawmer ledderis for the greit schip. *Ibid.* 456 Item to the plummair for vi mawmeris to the litill bark callit the Gabriell.

mawmet: see MAUMET.

†**'mawmish**, *a. Obs.* [f. *maum* MALM *a.*: cf. MALMISH, MALMY.] Mawkish, disgusting.

1668 R. L'ESTRANGE *Vis. Quev.* (1708) 200 The Flesh was so Cursedly Mawmish and Rotten, that [etc.]. **1692** —— *Fables* cccxl. 426 One of the most Nauseous, Mawmish Mortifications under the Sun. **1866** J. SHANKS *Elgin* 43 The fear of offending mawmish delicacy.

mawnchepresande, var. MAUNCHE PRESENT.

mawnciple, -cypylle, obs. ff. MANCIPLE.

mawngery, variant of MANGERY *Obs.*

mawnge(u)r, -joure, obs. forms of MANGER.

mawp, variant of MAUPE.

†**maw-pie.** *Obs.* [The first element is of obscure origin.] The magpie, *Pica caudata.*

1615 W. LAWSON *Country Housew. Gard.* (1626) 45 Your Cheries and other Berries when they be ripe, wil draw all the Black-birds, Thrushes and Maw-pies to your Orchard.

mawseed ('mɔːsiːd). [Half-translated ad. Ger. dial. *mahsaat, mohsamen*, f. *mah, moh* (literary G. *mohn*) poppy + *saat, samen* seed.] The seed of the opium poppy, *Papaver somniferum.*

1730 SOUTHALL *Bugs* 21 The Eggs are..as small as the smallest Maw-seed. **1774** GOLDSM. *Nat. Hist.* (1776) V. 343 Feed them with..bread, maw-seed [etc.]. **1812** J. SMYTH *Pract. of Customs* (1821) 208 Maw-seed. **1866** in *Treas. Bot.*

mawth, ? obs. Sc. variant of MAUGH.

mawworm¹ ('mɔːwɜːm). ? *Obs.* [f. MAW *sb.*¹ + WORM.] A worm infesting the stomach or intestines of man and other mammals, esp. applied to species of *Ascaris* and *Oxyuris.*

1607 TOPSELL *Four-f. Beasts* (1658) 336 It will presently destroy and consume the maw or belly-worms which are within him. *a* **1619** FLETCHER *Bonduca* I. ii, Your warlike remedy against the maw-worms. **1694** SALMON *Bate's Dispens.* (1713) 672/2 If..you add Powder of Maw-Worms vj. it will be much more effectual. **1784** UNDERWOOD *Dis. Children* (1799) I. 142 The very small maw-worm, or ascarides, resembling bits of thread. **1822-34** *Good's Study Med.* (ed. 4) I. 275 The term Maw-worm, according to P. Harvey, is derived from the occasional visits which this animal makes to the maw or stomach.

fig. **1652** BENLOWES *Theoph.* III. xii, No Glutt'nies Maw-worm; nor the Itch of lust No Tympanie of Pride.

mawworm² ('mɔːwɜːm). (Properly with initial capital.) A man who resembles *Mawworm*, a character in Bickerstaffe's play *The Hypocrite*, 1769; a hypocritical pretender to sanctity.

1850 *Tait's Mag.* XVII. 547/2 Can it be that these.. wailings have in their motive something of the Maworm spirit, 'I like to be despised'. **1861** J. HOLLINGSHEAD in *Gd. Words* 441 We all know precisely what a mawworm is... He is a slimy villain. **1866** SALA *Barbary* vii. 130 There was a sanctified Mawworm expression, too, about this fellow. **1872** GEO. ELIOT *Middlem.* I. ii, He would be the very Maw-worm of bachelors who pretended [etc.]. **1891** R. BUCHANAN *Coming Terror* 353 The Scapin of Politics walks hand-in-hand with the Mawworm of Morality.

Hence **'mawwormish, mawwormy** *adjs.*, **'mawwormism** *sb.*

1850 *Tait's Mag.* XVII. 547/2 Mawormism is a thing unknown north of the Tweed. **1883** K. BLIND in *Gentl. Mag.* Nov. 488 Luther..was..no maw-wormish mar-joy. **1885** in J. R. Ware *Passing Eng.* (1909) 174/2 Without being mawwormy, I fail to see why a wreath should be presented to any man who makes a business of giving opera.

†**max.** *Obs.* [Of obscure origin.] Gin.

1811 *Lex. Balatron., Max*, gin. **1819** BYRON *Juan* II. xvi, The dying man cried, 'Hold! I've got my gruel! Oh! for a glass of max!' **1840** BARHAM *Ingol. Leg.* Ser. I. *Bagman's Dog*, Who, doffing their coronets, collars, and ermine, treat Boxers to Max, at the One Tun in Jermyn Street. **1851** MAYHEW *Lond. Labour* (1864) I. 168 The stimulant of a 'flash of lightning', a 'go of rum', or a 'glass of max',—for so a dram of neat spirit was then called.

maxhill: see MIXHILL.

maxi- ('mæksɪ), combining form of MAXIMUM 5 denoting things, esp. articles of clothing, which

are very long or large of their kind. Also as *sb.* Cf. MIDI-, MINI-.

1961 *Spectator* 30 June 965 If you get into a maxi-taxi after midnight with a companion, there is 3/3d on the clock before you start. **1966** *Times Educ. Suppl.* 24 June 2015/2 There will be Lady X in Rutland realizing with a gasp of horror that she is wearing the same maxi-skirt as Lady Y. **1966** *Daily Tel.* 24 Oct. 11/1 The maxi-bag must be the next thing. And by the natural sequence of bag fashion psychology, the manufacturers are now designing bags on briefcase lines. **1967** *Punch* 3 May 624/1 The clampdown in Greece.. may shut up those tireless critics, in our own land of the free, of mini-skirt girls and maxi-hair boys, now banned by the Greek Minister of the Interior. **1967** *Evening Standard* 7 Dec. 9/1 You're in a black crêpe maxi-skirt... If everyone is wearing maxi's, you're all right. **1968** *Daily Tel.* 18 Jan. 15/3, I doubt if we'll see the Queen in a real maxi yet awhile, but the belted emerald maxi coat sketched was certainly the Royal dressmaker's newest looking garment in the collection he showed yesterday. **1968** *Guardian* 2 May 7/4 Here are expensive clothes from 30 to 70 guineas. They are not for youngsters who wear maxis for kicks. **1970** R. LOWELL *Notebk.* 167 The girl's maxi-coat, Tsar officer's, dragged the snow. **1970** *Time* 16 Nov. 67 To relieve the sterile monotony of nurses' uniforms, Fashion Designer Pierre Cardin recently unveiled three new creations at a London showing. Two of his designs—nunlike wimples with white maxidresses—were harmless affairs that might make ward nurses look functional if not fashionable. **1971** 'V. X. SCOTT' *Surrogate Wife* 230 He was wearing a great big olive green maxicoat. **1971** *Ink* 12 June 1/2 'Have a whiff' was released by Pye on a maxi-single (two tracks on each side). **1973** S. B. JACKMAN *Guns covered with Flowers* vi. 98 Marija slipped off her tweed maxi-coat. **1975** *Daily Tel.* 4 Jan. 16 This figure is quite impressive until it is compared with the 1974–75 budget of £1,325 million, which means that it is only a 1½ per cent. mini-reduction in what promises to be a maxi-budget.

‖**maxilla** (mæk'sɪlə). Pl. maxillæ (mæk'sɪliː). [L. *maxilla* jaw.]

1. A jaw or jaw-bone, esp. the upper jaw in mammals and most vertebrate animals. ***inferior, superior maxilla***, the lower, upper jaw.

1676 WISEMAN *Surg.* I. xix. 93 The same Patient complained of a hard Tumour fixed under that Ear and *Maxilla*. **1727–41** CHAMBERS *Cycl.* s.v., The *maxillæ* are two in number, denominated from their situation, *superior*, and *inferior*. **1797** *Encycl. Brit.* (ed. 3) I. 683/1 Of these [bones] six are placed on each side of the maxilla superior. **1846** BRITTAN tr. *Malgaigne's Man. Oper. Surg.* 115 The lower border of the inferior maxilla. *Ibid.*, The inferior posterior border of the maxilla. **1888** ROLLESTON & JACKSON *Anim. Life* 92 The maxilla [*sc.* of the common perch], which is edentulous,.. lies behind and parallel to it [*sc.* the præmaxilla]. **1893** NEWTON *Dict. Birds* 539 The word Maxilla is frequently used to express the whole of the upper jaw. **1897** *Allbutt's Syst. Med.* III. 150 A simple superior maxilla is sometimes alone affected by hyperostosis.

2. One of the anterior limbs of insects and other arthropods, so modified as to serve the purpose of mastication. Also *attrib.*

1798 AFZELIUS in *Trans. Linn. Soc.* IV. 275, *c.* the tops of the maxillæ. *d.* the labium. **1826** KIRBY & SP. *Entomol.* III. 47 Both labium and maxillæ being furnished with jointed moveable organs peculiar to annulose pedate animals. **1852** DANA *Crust.* I. 20 The organ consists of two oblong flat lobes, in some Decapods, somewhat maxilla-like in form. **1896** tr. *Boas' Text Bk. Zool.* 184 The second and third [*sc.* pairs of mouth-parts in Arthropods] are known respectively as the first and second maxillæ.

†**maxillar**, *a. Obs.* [f. MAXILLA + -AR.] Of or pertaining to the jaw, esp. to the upper jaw.

1656 BLOUNT *Glossogr.*, *Maxillar*, belonging to the jaw-bone. **1682** T. GIBSON *Anat.* (1697) p. iv, The Parotides and maxillar glands convey the saliva into the mouth. **1720** HALE in *Phil. Trans.* XXXI. 5 The external Maxillar Glands in Brutes are of the Conglomerate kind.

maxillary (mæk'sɪlərɪ), *a.* and *sb.* [f. MAXILLA + -ARY. Cf. F. *maxillaire*.] **A.** *adj.*

1. Belonging to, connected with, or forming part of the jaw or jaw-bone, esp. of the upper jaw of vertebrate animals.

1626 BACON *Sylva* §747 There is the Skull of one Entire Bone; there are.. the Maxillary Bones [etc.]. **1713** DERHAM *Phys.-Theol.* IV. xi. (1714) 195 The.. Maxillary Glands. **1774** GOLDSM. *Nat. Hist.* II. 402 The horn is entirely solid, growing from the upper maxillary bone. **1804** ABERNETHY *Surg. Obs.* 36 The external maxillary artery was unavoidably divided. **1874** COUES *Birds N.W.* 135 But even the youngest specimen shows no maxillary streaks. **1883** MARTIN & MOALE *Vertebr. Dissect.* 158 The Superior Maxillary Nerve passes outward. *Ibid.*, The Inferior Maxillary Nerve.. divides into two branches. **1888** ROLLESTON & JACKSON *Anim. Life* 68 The maxillary teeth [of a snake].

2. Belonging to, connected with, or forming part of the maxillæ of arthropods. ***maxillary system***: the system of classification of insects based on the form of the maxillæ.

1826 KIRBY & SP. *Entomol.* III. 358 *Palpi Maxillares* (the Maxillary Feelers). *Ibid.* IV. 450 Which [system], from the *maxillæ* being principally employed to characterize the Classes or rather Orders, may be called the *Maxillary System*. **1878** BELL *Gegenbaur's Comp. Anat.* 246 In many Diptera the maxillary setæ are rudimentary.

B. *sb.* = *maxillary bone.*

1836–9 TODD *Cycl. Anat.* II. 211/1 The vertical plate is short to correspond with the short vertical diameter of the upper maxillary. **1854** BADHAM *Halieut.* 307 The maxillaries, prolonged into barbels, come off from the lower jaw. **1880** GÜNTHER *Fishes* 90 No part of the maxillary is situated behind the premaxillary [of fishes].

maxillated ('mæksɪleɪtɪd), *a. Zool.* [f. MAXILLA + -ATE² + -ED¹.] Furnished with maxillæ.

1852 DANA *Crust.* I. 14 The maxillated Entomostraca.

maxilliferous (mæksɪ'lɪfərəs), *a.* [f. MAXILLA + -(I)FEROUS.] Bearing maxillæ.

1826 KIRBY & SP. *Entomol.* III. xxviii. 17 Most commonly four antennæ, with a maxilliferous mouth seldom rostriform.

maxilliform (mæk'sɪlɪfɔːm), *a.* [f. MAXILLA + -(I)FORM.] Formed like a maxilla; 'having the shape or form of a cheekbone' (Cassell 1885).

1835 KIRBY *Hab. & Inst. Anim.* II. xvi. 78 The whole organ may be regarded as maxilliform. **1877** HUXLEY *Anat. Inv. Anim.* vi. 257 With Maxilliform Gnathites.

maxilliped, -pede (mæk'sɪlɪpɛd, -piːd). *Zool.* [f. MAXILLA + L. *ped-em, pēs* foot.] A 'foot-jaw' (see FOOT *sb.* 35). Cf. *jaw-foot* s.v. JAW *sb.*¹ 7.

Foot-jaw was app. the first term used, and this was rendered by *maxilliped*, which in turn was translated *jaw-foot*.

1846 DANA in *Amer. Jrnl. Sci.* Ser. II. I. 226 Order Entomostraca. Tribe Cyclopacea... Maxillipeds, one pair: sometimes simple maxillæ. **1870** NICHOLSON *Man. Zool.* 207 Two pairs of maxillipedes. **1883** PACKARD in *Ann. & Mag. Nat. Hist.* Nov. 342 They are somewhat analogous to the maxillipedes of Crustacea.

Hence **maxilli'pedary** *a.*, pertaining to maxillipedes.

1877 HUXLEY *Anat. Inv. Anim.* vi. 311 The sternal regions of the three maxillipedary somites have the same characters.

maxillo-, taken as comb. form of MAXILLA in the sense 'pertaining to the maxilla and..'; so ***maxillo-mandibular, -palatine, -pharyngeal, -premaxillary, -turbinal***, etc. (see *Syd. Soc. Lex.* 1890).

1872 MIVART *Elem. Anat.* 115 The maxillo-premaxillary suture is for a long time or permanently very evident on the face. **1875** HUXLEY & MARTIN *Elem. Biol.* (1877) 188 The nerve divides into three main branches, the orbito-nasal, the palatine and the maxillo-mandibular. **1875** C. C. BLAKE *Zool.* 46 There are no maxilloturbinals in any skulls. **1887** MARSHALL & HURST *Pract. Zool.* 371 The maxillo-palatine process. **1890** COUES *Field & Gen. Ornith.* 240 They are commonly described as if they were independent bones, under the name of the *maxillopalatines*.

maxim ('mæksɪm), *sb.*¹ Also 5–7 **maxime**, 6 *pl.* erron. **maximies**. [a. F. *maxime*, ad. L. *maxima* fem. sing. of *maximus* greatest, used *ellipt.* (see below). Cf. Sp. *máxima*, Pg. *maxima*, It. *massima*.

Boethius (6th c.) used *propositio maxima* ('greatest proposition') in the sense of 'axiom' (synonymous with *dignitas* = ἀξίωμα, but especially used with reference to rhetoric). Albertus Magnus (12th c.) used *maxima* with ellipsis of *propositio*, but applied it to a class of universal propositions not intuitively certain like the *dignitates* or axioms, but capable of being assumed as practically indisputable. Elsewhere (according to Hamilton in *Reid's Wks.* 767, where the reference is incorrect) he identifies *maxima* and *dignitas*; and Petrus Hispanus and later logicians use *maxima* in the sense of 'axiom'.]

†**1.** An axiom; a self-evident proposition assumed as a premiss in mathematical or dialectical reasoning. *Obs.*

1426 LYDG. *De Guil. Pilgr.* 5603 Thys greueth me most at al, That my maxime apryved [*sc.* that the whole is greater than its part] Ye in dede han yt reprevyd. *Ibid.* 6000. **1556** RECORDE *Castle Knowl.* 108 Then takinge that for a maxime in argumente, I annexe this minor, that [etc.]. **1690** LOCKE *Hum. Und.* IV. vii. §1. 299 There are a sort of Propositions, which under the name of Maxims and Axioms, have passed for Principles of Science. **1692** BENTLEY *Boyle Lect.* vi. 209 It is urged as an universal Maxim, That Nothing can procede from Nothing.

2. a. A proposition (esp. in aphoristic or sententious form) ostensibly expressing some general truth of science or of experience.

1594 DRAYTON *Idea* 391 In ev'ry thing I hold this Maxim still, The Circumstance doth make it good, or ill. **1605** VERSTEGAN *Dec. Intell.* iv. (1628) 98 This maxime or principle must be granted. **1606** SHAKS. *Tr. & Cr.* I. ii. 318 This maxime out of loue I teach: Atchieuement is command. **1654** WHITLOCK *Zootomia* 214 What seriously exerciseth one Mans Braine to defend as a Maxime, tickleth anothers Diaphragme no lesse than an Epigram. **1770** G. WHITE *Selborne* iii, I lay it down as a maxim in ornithology, that as long as there is any incubation going on there is music. **1827** COLERIDGE *Table-t.* 24 June, A Maxim is a conclusion upon observation of matters of fact. **1874** BLACKIE *Self-Cult.* 89 The maxim that knowledge is power is true only where knowledge is the main thing wanted.

b. *esp.* in *Law*.

1567 R. MULCASTER *Fortescue's De Laud. Leg.* (1672) 21 b, They are certaine universall propositions which they that be learned in the Laws of England, and likewise the Mathematicals, do terme Maximes. **1590** SWINBURNE *Testaments* 59 It is a maxime in the common lawes of this realme, that he that is outlawed doeth forfeite all his goods. **1628** COKE *On Litt.* 67 A maxime is a proposition, to be of all men confessed & granted. **1766** BLACKSTONE *Comm.* II. 199 It is an antient maxim of the law, that no title is completely good, unless the right of possession be joined with the right of property. **1893** *Weekly Notes* 67/2 He considered at length the meaning of the maxim, 'a man's house is his castle'.

3. A rule or principle of conduct; also, a precept of morality or prudence expressed in sententious form. *spec.* Used of precepts of morality or prudence occurring in Old English verse.

1579 G. HARVEY *Letter-bk.* (Camden) 66 Is not this the principall fundation and grande maxim of our cuntry pollicy not to be over hasty in occupying a mans talent [etc.]. **1590** SIR J. SMYTH *Disc. Weapons* Ded. 9 All great Captaines.. have holden for a Maxime, to preserue by all meanes possible the liues of their soldiers. **1640** HOWELL *Dodona's Gr.* 6 Selfe defence hath beene alwaies held the first maxime of policy. **1642** FULLER *Holy & Prof. St.* IV. v. 258 Some think it beneath a wise man to alter their opinion: A maxime both false and dangerous. **1709** STEELE *Tatler* No. 47 ¶1, I knew a Gentleman that made it a Maxim to open his Doors and ever run into the Way of Bullies. **1757** WASHINGTON *Lett.* Writ. 1889 I. 494, I have all along laid it down as a maxim, to represent facts freely and impartially. **1807** ROBINSON *Archæol. Græca* II. xvii. 173 The art of comprising moral maxims in short sentences. **1830** S. COOPER *Dict. Pract. Surg.* (ed. 6) 817 All prudent surgeons.. have laid it down as an invariable maxim, never to.. undertake lithotomy, without having first introduced a metallic instrument. **1832** HT. MARTINEAU *Hill & Valley* iii. 35 Her maxim was, that it was time enough to come when she was called. **1868** MISS YONGE *Cameos* (1877) I. xvi. 117 He wrote a book of maxims, even on etiquette. **1883** H. KENNEDY tr. *B. ten Brink's Hist. Eng. Lit.* I. 64 The poet is fond of beginning a new maxim or a chain of them with the second half of a verse. **1892** S. A. BROOKE *Hist. Early Eng. Lit.* II. 277 The *Gnomic Verses*.. consist of folk-proverbs, maxims, short descriptions of human life, [etc.]. **1896** R. G. MOULTON *Ecclesiasticus* Introd. 12 The Maxim is the prose counterpart to the Epigram. **1902** *Jrnl. Eng. & Germ. Philol.* IV. 477 The *Wife's Complaint*.. closes with a general maxim deduced from the sad experiences of the once happy couple. **1966** S. B. GREENFIELD in E. G. Stanley *Continuations & Beginnings* 143 The diction of secular gnomes or maxims.

4. *attrib.*, as ***maxim-maker, -making, -monger***.

1806 MAR. EDGEWORTH *Leonora* (1833) 47 Some maxim-maker says that past misfortunes are good for nothing but to be forgotten. **1851** HELPS *Comp. Solit.* v. (1874) 64 Cleverly put, but untrue, after the fashion of you maxim-mongers. **1895** *Daily News* 19 Apr. 5/1 Maxim-making was a favourite game in French society.

Maxim ('mæksɪm), *sb.*² [From the name of Sir Hiram S. *Maxim*, the inventor.] In full ***Maxim (machine) gun, Maxim mitrailleuse***, or ***bomb Maxim***: A single-barrelled quick-firing machine gun, the barrel of which is surrounded by an outer casing filled with water to keep the parts cool, and the mechanism so adjusted that any number of shots can be fired in a given time up to six hundred rounds a minute. Also ***Maxim-Nordenfelt gun***, a modification of the original Maxim gun.

1885 *Nature* 5 Mar. 414/2 The Maxim Gun. *Ibid.* 415 Fig. 1—Maxim Mitrailleuse. **1889** E. ROGERS *Machine Rifle-batteries* 26 The barrel of the Maxim is.. surrounded by a water jacket. **1892** GREENER *Gun* (ed. 5) 186 The Maxim machine gun. **1900** *Daily News* 19 Mar. 4/1 The Maxim-Nordenfeldt, or pom-pom, is thought very highly of. **1900** *Westm. Gaz.* 28 Aug. 2/2 Our soldiers.. had not so much as the moral support of a bomb Maxim with them.

†'**maxim**, *a.* and *sb.*³ *Obs.* [ad. L. *maximus*.]

A. *adj.* = GREATEST (in certain technical uses).

1686 GOAD *Celest. Bodies* III. iii. 442 Conjunctions maxime in the Fiery and Watry Trigons,.. are above our reach. **1694** *Phil. Trans.* XVIII. 72 He concludes this Discourse with a Table, containing all the Notes and Intervals, explaining how each of those in the Diatonick Scale are composed of those three Degrees, viz. Minor, Major, and Maxim.

B. *sb.*³ *Mus.* = LARGE *sb.* 4, MAXIMA 2.

In recent Dicts.

Maxim ('mæksɪm), *v. nonce-wd.* [f. MAXIM *sb.*²] *trans.* To kill with a Maxim gun.

1894 *Sat. Rev.* 20 Jan. 61/2, I Maxim you by three thousands, that is fair war and glorious victory. **1903** KIPLING *Five Nations* 82 Said England unto Pharaoh, 'I must make a man of you,.. That will Maxim his oppressor as a Christian ought to do'.

‖'**maxima**. *Obs.* [L., fem. sing. of *maximus* greatest, used *ellipt.* for *maxima propositio, nota*.]

1. = MAXIM *sb.*¹

1565 JEWEL *Repl. Harding* xxii. 619 This maie stande wel for a *Maxima*, as one of the greatest truethes of M. Hardinges whole booke. **1584** COGAN *Haven Health* 195 This Maxima is generally to be observed: *Sani similes* [etc.]. **1594** PARSONS *Confer. Success.* II. i. 4 The bishop alleageth many proofes that ther is no such maxima in the common lawes of England.

2. *Mus.* = LARGE C. 4, MAXIM *sb.*³

1782 BURNEY *Hist. Mus.* II. 186, 453. **1818** BUSBY *Gram. Mus.* 65 Former musicians used the *Maxima*, or *Large*.

maxima, pl. of MAXIMUM *a.* and *sb.*

maximal ('mæksɪməl), *a.* [f. MAXIMUM + -AL¹.] Consisting of, or relating to, a maximum; greatest possible; of a size or duration not to be exceeded.

1882 V. IDELSON in *Lond. Med. Rec.* No. 36. 318 The average increase is equal to 8 millimètres maximal to 17 millimètres. **1883** L. BRUNTON in *Nature* 8 Mar. 438 The maximal contraction of which the tissue is capable. **1898** *Allbutt's Syst. Med.* V. 470 It [sc. blood-pressure in the ventricle] slowly increases throughout the systole becoming maximal immediately prior to relaxation. **1955** *Bull. Atomic Sci.* Apr. 107/2 The tradition of an insistence on maximal loyalty—the tradition of hyper-patriotism—is an old one in the United States, and it becomes very demanding in

periods of crisis. **1958** E. Winter in Middleton & Tait *Tribes without Rulers* 140 What is termed the maximal lineage consists of all the descendants in the male line of a single eponymous ancestor. **1960** P. Suppes *Axiomatic Set Theory* viii. 244 A is a maximal chain in B if and only if A is a chain in B and there is no chain C in B such that $A \subset C$. **1963** W. V. Quine *Set Theory* x. 231 There are notable equivalents of the axiom of choice... One is Hausdorff's law that every partial ordering harbors a maximal ordering. **1964** E. Mendelson *Introd. Math. Logic* 10 A maximal ideal is a proper ideal which is included in no other proper ideal. **1971** D. Crystal *Ling.* 199 The investigation of grammatical models in terms of maximal units. *Ibid.* 201 The sentence is the maximal unit of grammatical analysis. **1972** *Language* XLVIII. 264 The present delayed publication is intended especially to permit me to acknowledge that before today the only adequate publication of the principle of maximal redundancy has been in the Presidential Address of December 1969.

Hence **'maximally** *adv.*, in the maximum degree.

1884 W. James in *Mind* IX. 12 Those portions of the brain that have just been maximally excited retain a kind of soreness. **1969** *Daily Tel.* 11 Jan. 5/3 The answer, as with the short-term gain.., is to tax yourself maximally. In this case you would assume that £700 would be left to you after 30 p.c. had been deducted. **1970** *Nature* 30 May 804/1 The enzyme was assayed in maximally activated conditions. **1971** *Jrnl. Gen. Psychol.* LXXXIV. 88 It has been found that the same manners of input timing that maximally increase brightness also act to affect hue and desaturation maximally. **1971** D. Crystal *Ling.* 175 Phonology deals with sounds and contrasts between sounds only within the context of some language (maximally, in any language). **1973** *Nature* 2 Mar. 68/1 Histamine is synthesized maximally in the hypothalamus.

maximalism ('mæksɪməlɪz(ə)m). [f. maximal *a.* + -ism or ad. Russ. *maksimalízm.*] The policy or theory of a 'maximum' programme of some kind. Cf. Maximalist.

1920 *Glasgow Herald* 11 May 10 Bologna is undoubtedly to-day one of the chief Italian strongholds of Maximalism. **1951** N. Gorodetzky *St. Tikhon Zadonsky* ix. 189 The tendency of many Russians to seek extremes, maximalism, paroxysms, even in spiritual matters. **1967** J. M. Cammett *Antonio Gramsci* iv. 88 Thereafter, the break between *Ordine Nuovo* and maximalism widened, eventually contributing heavily to the Socialist schism at Livorno. **1967** C. Seton-Watson *Italy from Liberalism to Fascism* xii. 524 Maximalism..provided only revolutionary talk as a substitute for revolution.

Maximalist ('mæksɪməlɪst). Also **maximalist**. [f. maximal *a.* + -ist or ad. Russ. *maksimalíst*, f. L. *maximum*, or ad. F. *maximaliste.*] A member of the more extremist 'fraction' of the Russian Socialist-Revolutionary Party which split off from the main body of the party in 1904 and which used and advocated terrorist methods. Later regarded as a translation of Russ. *bol'shevik* and used as an alternative name for a Bolshevik. Also, a member of any similar group outside Russia. Also *attrib.* or as *adj.*, of or pertaining to a policy or theory of maximum demands (of some kind specified in the context).

1907 I. Zangwill *Ghetto Comedies* 408 'Ah, you're a Maximalist,' said the beadle. 'No, I am only a Minimalist.' **1909** *Westm. Gaz.* 23 Dec. 7/4 He is said to have joined the 'Maximalists' in 1907. **1921** tr. *Trotsky's Defence of Terrorism* ix. 173 Plekhanovists, Maximalists, Anarchists... Absolutely all the 'shades of Socialism'. **1921** *Glasgow Herald* 14 Oct. 9 Forty out of 100 Deputies are Reformists ..headed by some of the best brains in the country, like Signore Turati..and Modigliani. To them are opposed an equal number of Maximalists. **1933** M. Eastman tr. *Trotsky's Hist. Russ. Revolution* II. xiii. 309 While on the right the 'democracy' was competing with the Bolsheviks, on the left too there were the anarchists, the Maximalists, the Left Social Revolutionaries, trying to crowd them out. **1933** *Mind* XLII. 181 The rule..of always acting so as to produce the greatest amount of good, which latter rule the 'Maximalists' say we ought always to follow. *Ibid.*, The 'Maximalist' Theory (this designation suggests quantity better than 'Optimific') concentrates generally upon the consideration, not of individual situations, but of what happens when a general practice, custom or institution is dropped and replaced by another. **1954** *Ann. Reg. 1953* 153 There were the 'maximalists'..who wanted a real surrender of sovereignty, and the 'minimalists'. **1955** D. W. Treadgold *Lenin & his Rivals* iv. xi. 212 They were bitterly denounced by orthodox SR's, who took fright..at 'their own reflection in the Maximalist mirror'. **1962** R. R. Abramovitch *Soviet Revolution* i. 30 This concept shocked the Russian Marxists..they considered it a betrayal of scientific Socialism, a reversion to the old, utopian, Bakuninist, maximalist-anarchist ideas. **1966** *Economist* 5 Nov. 568/1 We have moved from a position of protest to one of responsibility and have put behind us the old maximalist dreams and illusions. **1967** C. Seton-Watson *Italy from Liberalism to Fascism* xii. 511 The [Italian Socialist] party elected a 'maximalist' executive at its Rome congress in September 1918 and proclaimed the dictatorship of the proletariat to be its goal. **1969** D. M. Smith *Italy* (ed. 2) vii. xxvii. 216 The maximalists were made strong and uncompromising by the belief that history was on their side.

maximality (mæksɪ'mælɪtɪ). [f. maximal *a.* + -ity.] The property of being maximal.

1964 A. P. & W. Robertson *Topological Vector Spaces* i. 4 This would contradict the maximality of μ. **1971** D. Gorenstein in Powell & Higman *Finite Simple Groups* i. 102 But $[Q_1, Z] = Q_1$, so $Q_1 = Q$ by the maximality of Q.

maximate ('mæksɪmeɪt), *v.* [f. L. *maxim-us* greatest + -ate².] = maximize *v.*

1881 W. E. Forster *Sp. in Ho. Com.* 5 Apr., The hon. Member..said that I had in certain circumstances minimized, and in others maximated, the statements of evictions.

Hence **maxi'mation** = maximization.

1891 W. J. Greenstreet tr. *Guyau's Educ. & Heredity* 109 Herbart very clearly saw the tendency of the human mind to 'maximation'.

maximed, *a.* [f. maxim *sb.*¹] Expressed as or in a maxim.

1883 J. C. Van Dyke *Bks. & how to use Them* i. 19 There is another maximed truth in this connection..: 'Knowledge is a two-edged sword.'

ma'ximic, *a. nonce-wd.* [f. maxim *sb.*¹ + -ic.] Resembling a maxim.

1854 Lady Lytton *Behind Scenes* II. ii. viii. 33 It being a favourite 'short turn' of his to interlard his frivolities with *maximic* gems of thought.

ma'ximical, *a. nonce-wd.* [-al¹.] = prec.

1778 [W. Marshall] *Minutes Agric., Observ.* 4 Each distinct Minute, or each distinct passage of a Minute, was endeavoured to be compressed into a Maximical Sentence.

maximin ('mæksɪmɪn), *sb.* and *a.* [f. maxi(mum + min(imum *sb.* and *a.*, after *minimax.*] The largest of a set of minima; usu. *attrib.* (passing into *adj.*), *spec.* designating a strategy that maximizes the smallest gain that a participant in a game or other situation of conflict can guarantee himself. Cf. minimax *sb.* and *a.*

1954 Blackwell & Girshick *Theory of Games & Statistical Decisions* i. 27 ξ_0 is called a maximin strategy for player I. **1957** Luce & Raiffa *Games & Decisions* iv. 81 A strategy which dictates choices *c* and *g* on moves 2 and 4, respectively, cannot be maximin for this game. **1958** *Engineering* 21 Mar. 369/2 Player A will thus determine the smallest value in each row and choose the largest of these minima, the 'maximin'. **1968** G. Owen *Game Theory* vii. 140 Though it is of course impossible to determine how a person will act.., we can nevertheless set a minimum to the amount that a player will accept for himself. This is the amount that he can obtain by unilateral action, whatever the other player does. This is, of course, the maximin value of the game for that player. **1970** Beveridge & Schechter *Optimization* xii. 656 This result represents the mini-max theorem of von Neumann and Morgenstein [*sic*] (1953), which states that *A*'s expected gain is at least *P*, and *B*'s expected loss is at worst *L*, where *P* = *L*... The value of *P* (and *L*) lies between the row maxi-min and the column mini-max. **1972** J. Rawls *Theory of Justice* §26. 152 The maximin rule tells us to rank alternatives by their worst possible outcomes.

†**maximious,** *a. Obs. rare*⁻¹. [f. L. *maxim-us* greatest + -ious.] Of great power.

c **1566** *Merie Tales of Skelton* x. in *S.'s Wks.* (1843) I. p. lxiv, Coste, more pertaynyng for an emperoure or a maxymyous kynge, then for such a man as he was.

maximist ('mæksɪmɪst). [f. maxim *sb.*¹ + -ist.] One who makes maxims.

1855 in Ogilvie *Suppl.* **1889** J. M. Robertson *Ess. Crit. Method* 221 The maximist makes the subtler analyses of *amour-propre*. **1889** Earl of Desart *Little Chatelaine* II. xx. 63 When you trust one rogue you trust all roguedom, as ought to have been said by some other maximist.

maximistic (mæksɪ'mɪstɪk), *a.* [f. L. *maxim-us* greatest + -ist + -ic.] Pertaining to the school of 'maximizers'.

1888 *Dublin Rev.* July 12 *note*, Even the 'maximistic' side admitted that infallible pronouncements are 'far rarer' than other official acts of the Pope.

maximite ('mæksɪmaɪt). [f. the name of Hudson *Maxim*, the inventor + -ite.] A smokeless gunpowder composed of gun-cotton, nitro-glycerine, and castor oil.

1897 *Daily News* 9 Feb. 7/4 We call it cordite. For the purposes of the inquiry I propose to call it Maximite. **1901** *Westm. Gaz.* 5 Mar. 8/2 Mr. Hudson Maxim's new explosive, 'Maximite', is claimed to be the highest explosive yet discovered.

†**maximity.** *Obs.* [f. L. *maxim-us* greatest + -ity.] 'Exceeding greatness' (Blount *Glossogr.* 1656–61); also, maximum amount.

1651 Biggs *New Disp.* 98 The maximity or greatest quantity of it.

maximization (mæksɪmaɪ'zeɪʃən). [f. maximize *v.* + -ation.] The action of raising to the highest possible point, position or condition.

Common in Bentham.

1802 Bentham *Princ. Judic. Procedure* Wks. 1843 II. 6/1 The maximization of the happiness of the greatest number. **1854** Owen *Skel. & Teeth* in *Circ. Sci., Org. Nat.* I. 260 A particular use, dependent on the maximization of the brain. **1886** E. B. Bax *Relig. Socialism* 94 That the supreme end of life is the maximisation of labour, and the minimisation of the enjoyment of its product.

maximize ('mæksɪmaɪz), *v.* [f. L. *maxim-us* maxim *a.* + -ize.]

1. *trans.* **a.** To increase to the highest possible degree. (Common in Bentham.) Used *esp.* in *Economics.* **b.** To magnify to the utmost (in estimation or representation).

1802 Bentham *Princ. Judic. Procedure* Wks. 1843 II. 8/2 By this means, appropriate moral aptitude may be maximized. **1866** Alger *Solit. Nat. & Man* iv. 360 Instead of minimizing he maximized the distinction of himself from other men. **1899** *Allbutt's Syst. Med.* VIII. 282 The turpitude is maximised. **1902** W. James *Varieties Relig. Exp.* 130 In contrast with such healthy-minded views as these..stands a radically opposite view, a way of maximizing evil. **1943** E. R. Walker *From Econ. Theory to Policy* v. 93 He [*sc.* the businessman]..is frequently engaged in exploratory action, designed to discover methods of maximizing profit. **1968** *Listener* 28 Mar. 403/1 The evidence is not inconsistent with the hypothesis that peasants act as if they maximised profit. **1970** *Jrnl. Gen. Psychol.* LXXXII. 15 The adversarial system of justice, which demands that each litigant do whatever is necessary to maximize the probability of a favorable result. **1970** T. Lupton *Managem. & Social Sci.* (ed. 2) i. 11 So arranging spells of work and rest that output would be maximized. **1971** *Daily Tel.* 12 June 20/7, I wish to maximise my after tax income. Do you consider an investment in Guaranteed Income Bonds is a safe way of doing this? **1971** J. Z. Young *Introd. Study Man* xxv. 361 Difficulties of adjustment will be maximized by ignorance and uncertainty. **1972** *Jrnl. Social Psychol.* LXXXVI. 57 These groups were selected so as to maximize the variety of occupational areas included.

2. *intr.* To maintain the most rigorous or comprehensive interpretation possible of a doctrine or an obligation. Chiefly *Theol.*

1875 J. H. Newman *Cert. Diffic. Anglic.* (1876) 365 When I speak of minimizing, I am not turning the profession of it into a dogma; men, if they will, may maximize for me, provided they too keep from dogmatizing. **1882** W. S. Lilly in *Contemp. Rev.* Feb. 243, I am far from wishing to maximize upon this matter. **1898** Knox Little in *Our Churches*, etc. 13 The Roman Church may be said to maximise, the Anglican to minimise. The Anglican teaches just what is necessary to be believed for the salvation of souls; the Roman turns pious opinions into necessary doctrines.

3. *intr.* To attain a maximum value.

1972 *Physics Bull.* Oct. 587/3 Photons of energy $h\nu$ greater than satisfies equation (1) suffer absorption while at some energy $h\nu_{max}$ the gain maximizes. **1973** [see minimize *v.* 3]. **1974** *Globe & Mail* (Toronto) 21 Oct. 4/3 If emissions were curtailed now, the resultant ozone destruction would maximize around 1990 and would remain significant for several decades.

Hence **'maximized, 'maximizing** *ppl. adjs.*

1920 A. S. Pringle-Pattison *Idea of God* (ed. 2) 356 Eternal, not in the sense of a maximized consciousness of time, but as an apprehension different in type. **1927** N. P. Williams *Ideas of Fall & Orig. Sin* 395 The maximising and minimising versions of the Fall-Doctrine. **1949** *Mind* LVIII. 195 The concept of a maximising individual, the famous 'Economic Man', has arisen. This maximising assumption is usually held to be the fundamental assumption of Economics. **1968** *Listener* 28 Mar. 403/1 Time enough, if the peasant is already a maximising Economic Man in the Henry Ford mould.

maximizer ('mæksɪmaɪzə(r)). [f. maximize *v.* + -er¹.] One who maximizes; *spec.* one who accepts the dogma of the infallibility of the pope in its most comprehensive interpretation.

1868 E. S. Ffoulkes *Church's Creed* (ed. 2) 37, I am not aware that any demur to this conclusion..can be raised even by maximisers. **1874** *Contemp. Rev.* XXIV. 296 The Ultramontanes themselves..now are divided into Maximizers and Minimizers.

maximum ('mæksɪməm). *Pl.* **maxima**, *rarely* **-ums**. [a. L. *maximum*, neut. of *maximus*, superl. of *magnus* great. Cf. F. *maximum.*]

1. *Math.* The greatest of all the values of which a variable or a function is capable; the value of a continuously varying quantity at the point at which it ceases to increase and begins to decrease.

1743 Emerson *Fluxions* 104 In Case it..passes through one or more Maximums or Minimums; then the several Parts of the Fluent, between any given Point and each Maximum or Minimum must be separately found by distinct Operations. **1806** Hutton *Course Math.* II. 306 If we would find the quantity ax-x^2 a maximum or minimum; make its fluxion equal to nothing. **1856** Sabine in *Phil. Trans.* CXLVI. 505 The declination has two easterly and two westerly maxima in the interval between two successive passages of the moon over the astronomical meridian.

2. *gen.* The highest attainable magnitude or quantity (of something); a superior limit of magnitude or quantity.

1740 Cheyne *Regimen* 306 In the Works of the God of Nature, there is no Maximum or Minimum assignable, or conceiveable by us. **1755** Winthrop *Earthquakes* 28 Laws of this sort are sufficiently vindicated..if upon the whole they produce a maximum of good. **1806** Colquhoun *Indigence* 49 The art of conducting a nation to the maximum of happiness and the minimum of misery. **1855** Bain *Senses & Int.* ii. ii. §14 (1864) 137 The animal powers attain their maximum in cold climates. **1902** T. M. Lindsay *Ch. & Ministry in Early Cent.* vii. 279 A strange compound of minimum of fact and maximum of theory.

3. The highest amount (esp. of temperature, barometric pressure, etc.) attained or recorded within a specified period.

1850 Edmonds in *Rep. Brit. Assoc., Sections* (1851) 32 The following remarkable maxima of temperature. **1860** Maury *Phys. Geog. Sea* (Low) vii. §348 The barometer also has its maxima and minima readings for the day. **1880** *Daily News* 18 Sept. 3/7 The maxima to-day were below 60 deg. in the Shetlands and Hebrides. **1902** *Westm. Gaz.* 16 June 5/2 The years of sunspot maximum.

4. A superior limit imposed by authority; *esp.* in *French Hist.*, a limit of price for corn.

1821 Syd. Smith *Wks.* (1859) I. 352/1 The danger of insurrection is a circumstance worthy of the most serious consideration in discussing the propriety of a maximum.

1835 ALISON *Hist. Europe* (1847) IV. 164 They [the farmers, 1793] were compelled to part with their grain at the price fixed by the *maximum*, which was calculated on the scale of prices before the Revolution. **1941** R. R. PALMER *Twelve who Ruled* x. 239 The Maximum of September 29 caused trouble from the start.

5. *attrib.* **a.** quasi-*adj.* or *adj.*, with the sense: That is a maximum, or that stands at the maximum; greatest. [Cf. F. *la dépense maximum.*]

1834 MRS. SOMERVILLE *Connex. Phys. Sci.* xxvi. (1849) 297 Surround two poles of maximum cold. **1860** MAURY *Phys. Geog. Sea* (Low) ix. §430 The maximum density of average sea-water. **1861** *Times* 23 July, The maximum contract price for the conveyance of these emigrants was 25*l.* 18*s.* 4*d.* per statute adult. **1879** G. PRESCOTT *Sp. Telephone* 96 A point of maximum disturbance. **1876** GRANT *Burgh Sch. Scotl.* II. ii. 103 The heritors paying the maximum salary and the town paying £12 annually for the support of a master. **1880** C. R. MARKHAM *Peruv. Bark* 405 The latter helping to produce a maximum temperature favourable to coffee cultivation.

b. Simple attributive: Pertaining to a maximum or maxima, as ***maximum period***; **maximum thermometer**, a thermometer which records automatically the highest temperature within a given period. Also in *Comb.*, as ***maximum-security*** (used *attrib.*).

1852 *Newton's Lond. Jrnl.* Conjoined Ser. XLI. 402 An improved maximum thermometer. **1868** LOCKYER *Elem. Astron.* ii. (1879) 49 There is a minimum period, when none are seen for weeks together, and a maximum period, when more are seen than at any other time. **1966** *Punch* 28 Dec. 962/2 The family wing of every prison enjoyed maximum security arrangements. **1969** E. AMBLER *Intercom Conspiracy* (1970) ii. 27 The special maximum-security passes that would be needed to gain admittance. **1972** *Guardian* 29 Jan. 9/5 Albany, the new maximum security prison on the Isle of Wight.

maxite (ˈmæksaɪt). *Min.* [ad. G. *maxit* (Laspeyres 1872), f. name of *Max* Braun, a Belgian mining engineer: see -ITE.] = LEADHILLITE.

1885 in *Cassell's Encycl. Dict.* **1896** in A. H. CHESTER *Dict. Min.*

maxixe (maˈʃiʃə, mækˈsiːks). [Pg.] A round dance of Brazilian origin resembling the two-step.

1914 *Maclean's Mag.* Nov. 82/2 The Maxixe comes to us from Brazil. **1922** C. BELL *Since Cézanne* xx. 227 Sportsmen at the bar who like a fox-trot or a maxixe. **1925** *Chambers's Jrnl.* July 427/1 They sang..and danced the *maxixe* until cockcrow! **1954** *Ballet Ann.* VIII. 102/1 Ready to seek consolation..to the rhythm of the *maxixe*. **1969** F. RUST *Dance in Society* x. 82 In the early months of 1914, the general craze for the tango in England helped to popularize another South American dance—the Brazilian maxixe.

Maxwell[1] (ˈmækswɛl). The name of Charles *Maxwell*, 19th-century English soldier and explorer, used in the possessive to designate **Maxwell's duiker**, a small brown West African antelope, *Cephalophus maxwelli*, brought back from Sierra Leone by him.

[**1827** E. GRIFFITH et al. tr. *Cuvier's Animal Kingdom* IV. 267 Maxwell's Antelope. (*A. Maxwellii.*) A specimen somewhat inferior in size was brought home from Sierra Leone by Colonel Charles Maxwell.] **1905** SCLATER & THOMAS *Bk. Antelopes* I. 182 Maxwell's Duiker appears to extend from Senegal and Gambia all along the west coast of Africa to the mouths of the Niger. **1960** *Times* 29 Sept. (Nigeria Suppl.) p. xxi/4 The little Maxwell's duiker..is everywhere abundant.

Maxwell[2] (ˈmækswɛl). *Physics.* [The name of James Clerk *Maxwell* (1831-79), Scottish physicist.] **1.** Used in the possessive and *attrib.* to designate various concepts originated by him, as **Maxwell('s) demon**, a being imagined by Maxwell as allowing only fast-moving molecules to pass through a hole in one direction and only slow-moving ones in the other direction, so that if the hole is in a partition dividing a gas-filled vessel into two parts one side becomes warmer and the other cooler, in contradiction to the second law of thermodynamics; **Maxwell('s) distribution**, the distribution of molecular velocities predicted by Maxwell's law, the number with a velocity between v and $v+dv$ being proportional to $\exp(-\frac{1}{2}mv^2/kT)v^2dv$ (where m is the mass of a molecule, k is Boltzmann's constant, and T is the absolute temperature); **Maxwell('s) equation**, each of a set of four linear partial differential equations (first proposed by Maxwell in 1864) which summarize the classical properties of the electromagnetic field and relate space and time derivatives of the electric and magnetic field vectors, the electric displacement vector, and the magnetic induction vector, and also involve the electric current and charge densities; usu. *pl.*; **Maxwell('s) law**, a law in classical physics giving the probabilities of different velocities for the molecules of a gas in equilibrium.

1879 W. THOMSON *Pop. Lect. & Addresses* (1889) I. 137 Clerk *Maxwell's 'demon' is a creature of imagination.., invented to help us to understand the 'Dissipation of Energy' in nature. **1885** *Science* 31 July 83/1 (*heading*) Maxwell's demons. **1956** E. H. HUTTEN *Lang. Mod. Physics* iv. 152 It would require a Maxwell demon..to select the rapidly moving molecules according to their velocity and concentrate them in one corner of the vessel. **1971** *Sci. Amer.* Sept. 182/2 Maxwell's demon became an intellectual thorn in the side of thermodynamicists for almost a century. The challenge to the second law of thermodynamics was this: Is the principle of the increase of entropy in all spontaneous processes invalid where intelligence intervenes? **1899** R. E. BAYNES tr. *Meyer's Kinetic Theory of Gases* 370 If the number of particles is limited..*Maxwell's distribution cannot exist at every moment, but will occur with exactness only when the changing states which succeed each other in the course of a sufficiently long period are all taken into account together. **1955** FRIEDMAN & WEISSKOPF in W. Pauli *Niels Bohr* 138 The spectrum of neutrons and protons emitted from nuclei bombarded with neutrons of 14 Mev or with protons of similar energy fits approximately the predicted Maxwell distribution of an evaporating compound nucleus. **1907** *Sci. Abstr.* A. X. 1295 The principle of relativity in conjunction with *Maxwell's equation leads to the conclusion that the inertia of a body changes in a quite determinate manner with its energy-content. **1962** CORSON & LORRAIN *Introd. Electromagn. Fields* iii. 101 If the symmetry of the [electrostatic] field is simple and if the charge density ρ is zero, as it often is, we can usually integrate the Maxwell equation $\nabla\cdot\mathbf{D} = \rho$ to find the displacement vector **D**. **1964** E. A. POWER *Introd. Quantum Electrodynamics* i. 4 Maxwell's equations are not invariant under Galilean invariance and thus are not valid in all inertial frames. Historically this was a most important result leading to special relativity. **1899** R. E. BAYNES tr. *Meyer's Kinetic Theory of Gases* iii. 48 That this extension of *Maxwell's law to compound molecules is admissible was first recognised by Boltzmann. **1943** MARGENAU & MURPHY *Math. Physics & Chem.* xii. 432 The Maxwell law for the distribution of velocities in an ideal gas.

2. (Usu. written **maxwell.**) The unit of magnetic flux in the C.G.S. system, equal to the flux through an area of one square centimetre normal to a uniform induction of one gauss.

In the International System of Units the unit of magnetic flux is the weber (= 10^8 maxwells).

1900 *Nature* 30 Aug. 414/1 The Commission proposes to assign to the unit of magnetic flux, of which the magnitude will be subsequently defined, the name of Maxwell. **1924** A. STILL *Elem. Electr. Design* iv. 68 It is desired to estimate the total flux in maxwells carried by a closed circular iron ring. **1959** R. L. SHRADER *Electronic Communication* iii. 72 The gauss is the flux density in maxwells per square centimeter.

Maxwell-Boltzmann (ˈmækswɛlˈbɒltsmən). *Physics.* The names of J. C. *Maxwell* (see prec.) and L. *Boltzmann* (see BOLTZMANN), used (in some cases as an alternative to *Maxwell* or *Boltzmann* alone) to designate concepts arising out of their work on the kinetic theory of gases.

1901 O. LODGE in *Phil. Mag.* II. 241 Any rotational energy possessed by a dumbbell about its longitudinal axis could have no influence on smooth collisions, and accordingly could not be transferred or altered in amount; therefore such rotation ought not to be included in the partition of energy within the meaning of the Maxwell-Boltzmann law when properly stated. **1927** R. C. TOLMAN *Statistical Mech.* iv. 53 In a system containing a large number of molecules appreciable deviations from the Maxwell-Boltzmann distribution will have a very small probability of occurrence. **1951** D. BOHM *Quantum Theory* i. 16 For a perfect gas..we obtain the familiar Maxwell-Boltzmann distribution of velocities. **1968** M. S. LIVINGSTON *Particle Physics* iii. 58 In classical mechanics the distribution of thermal velocities and energies among the molecules of a gas, in thermal equilibrium due to the exchange of energy in random impacts, is described by Maxwell-Boltzmann statistics.

Maxwellian (mæksˈwɛlɪən), *a. Physics.* Also **maxwellian.** [f. MAXWELL[2] + -IAN.] Of, pertaining to, or originated by J. C. Maxwell; in accordance with Maxwell's theory.

1886 *Electrician* 26 Mar. 386/2 The Maxwellian stress. **1914** L. SILBERSTEIN *Theory of Relativity* ii. 48 In using the Maxwellian stress..in his theory, Lorentz considers it..as a system of 'merely fictitious tensions'. **1939** *Brit. Jrnl. Psychol.* XXIX. 253 The light from an electric bulb, rendered nearly parallel by a condenser, filled a large lens at whose principal focus the eye was placed. This lens appeared uniformly illuminated by the 'Maxwellian view'. **1958** H. J. GRAY *Dict. Physics* 318/1 The Maxwellian view refers to the method of making a lens apparently flooded with a uniform brightness: a real image of a source of light is formed by a lens in the pupil of the eye. An extended area of bright white light or coloured light is produced and has wide application in photometry and colorimetry. **1968** R. A. LYTTLETON *Mysteries Solar Syst.* i. 32 For a whole group of individual stars, these relative speeds are distributed rather like the maxwellian distribution of velocities for the particles of a gas.

†ˈmaxy. *dial. Obs.* [Corruption of MARCASITE.] In *Tin-Mining* = MUNDIC.

1671 *Observ. Mines Cornwal & Devon* in *Phil. Trans.* VI. 2102 And so continue sinking..till we find either the Load to grow small, or degenerate into some sort of weed, which are diverse; as Mundick or Maxy (corrupted from *Marchasite*) of 3 sorts; white, yellow, and green. **1710** J. HARRIS *Lex. Techn.* II. **1730–6** BAILEY (fol.).

may (meɪ), *sb.*[1] *poet.* (*arch.*) Forms: [? 1 **mǽȝ**], 3 **maȝȝ, mayȝ,** 3–4 **mai,** 4–6 **maye,** 5 **mey,** 4– **may.** [Perh. a. ON. *møyj-* (nom. *mǽ-r*, accus. *møy*, *mey*; Sw. *mö*, Da. *mø*) = Goth. *mawi*:—OTeut. **maujâ-*, **maᵹwjâ-*, fem. f. **magu-z* (Goth. *magu-s*) boy, son: see MAIDEN.

The OE. poet. *mǽȝ* kinswoman (cogn. with *mǽȝ* masc. MAY *sb.*[2]) often occurs with the sense 'woman', and sometimes appears to mean 'maid' or 'virgin'. This use has been commonly regarded as the source of the present word; the OE. and the ON. word may have coalesced in ME.]

A maiden, virgin.

[*a* **900** CYNEWULF *Crist* 87 (Gr.) Sio eadᵹe mæᵹ..Sancta Maria. *a* **1000** *Cædmon's Gen.* 895 (Gr.) Him þa freolecu mæᵹ [*sc.* Eve]..andswarode.] *c* **1200** ORMIN 2489 þatt clene maȝȝ þatt shollde ben Allmahhtiȝ Godess moderr. *c* **1275** LAY. 30486 þe king dude [vnwis]dom þat he þat ilke may nom [*earlier text* maide]. *c* **1290** *S. Eng. Leg.* I. 194/26 To bringue luþer þouȝt In-to þis swete ȝounge mayȝ. *a* **1300** *Cursor M.* 10267 þat man..þat has na barn, ne mai ne knaue. *c* **1330** R. BRUNNE *Chron.* (1810) 95 þe corounyng of Henry, & of Malde þat may. **1362** LANGL. *P. Pl.* A. XII. 111 Marie moder and may. *c* **1386** CHAUCER *Man of Law's T.* 753 Thow glorie of wommanhede, thow faire may. **1513** DOUGLAS *Æneis* VI. i. 22 Sibilla the may. **1579** SPENSER *Sheph. Cal.* Nov. 39 The fayrest May she was that euer went. **1590** GREENE *Mourn. Garm.* (1616) C 3 b, Nor was Phillis that fair May Halfe so gawdy or so gay. **1607** *Barley-Breake* (1877) 5 Old Elpin with his sweete and louely May Would oft prepare..To keepe their sheep. **16..** *Sir Cauline* iii. in Child *Ballads* II. 58 Deerlye [he] lovde this may. **1818** T. L. PEACOCK *Nightmare Abbey* 119 For ill beseems in a reverend friar The love of a mortal may. **1855** *Fraser's Mag.* LI. 92 The maiden is pure all mays above. **1870** MORRIS *Earthly Par.* II. III. 349 Amid these latter words of his, the may From her fair face had drawn her hands away.

†may, *sb.*[2] *Obs.* Forms: 1 **mǽȝ,** (**meeȝ, méȝ**), *pl.* **máȝas,** 2 **maiȝ,** 3 **mæi, mæȝ, mei, mey,** (**meay**), **mai, may.** [Com. Teut.: OE. *mǽȝ* = OFris. *mêch*, OS. *mâg* (MLG. *mâch*, Du. *maag*), OHG. *mâg* (MHG. *mâc*, *mâg-*), ON. *mág-r* (adopted in northern Eng. as MAUGH), Goth. *mēg-s*:—OTeut. **mǣgo-z*, prob. related by ablaut to **magu-z* son, boy (Goth. *magu-s*, ON. *mǫg-r*): see MAIDEN.] A male relative, kinsman.

Beowulf 408 Ic eom Hiᵹelaces mæᵹ and maᵹoðeᵹn. *a* **700** *Epinal Gloss.* 164 *Contribulus*, meeᵹ. *c* **1160** *Hatton Gosp.* Mark xiii. 12 þa bearn ariseð aᵹen heore maiᵹes. *a* **1200** *Moral Ode* 187 Nolde it mouwe don for mey ne suster for broþer. *c* **1205** LAY. 3838 þurh þe haueð Morgan mi mæi [*c* **1275** mey] is monschipe afallet. *a* **1300** in *E.E.P.* (1862) 17 Alle we beþ meiis and mowe.

May (meɪ), *sb.*[3] Forms: 4–5 **Maij,** 4–6 **Maii,** 5–6 **Mai,** 6 **Maie, Maye,** 3– **May.** Also in Latin form 1–4 **Maius,** (4 **Mayus**). [a. F. *mai*:—L. *Maium* (nom. *Maius*, sc. *mēnsis*). Cf. Pr. *mai*, Sp. *mayo*, Pg. *maio*, It. *maggio*; also (from Fr.) MHG. *Mei(g)e* (G. *Mai*), MDu. *mey(e*, *meide* (Du. *Mei*), Sw. *Maj*, Da. *Mai*, late Gr. *Μάϊος*.

The etymology of the Latin name is obscure; some ancient writers connected it with the name of the goddess *Maia*.]

1. a. The fifth month of the year in the Julian and Gregorian calendar.

c **1050** *Byrhtferth's Handboc* in *Anglia* (1885) VIII. 316 Nouember & december habbað fif & twentiᵹ ealdne monan ..& aprelis & maius eahta & twentiᵹ. *a* **1121** *OE. Chron.* an. 1080 (MS. E) þis dydon Norðhymbran on Maies monðe. *c* **1290** *S. Eng. Leg.* I. 26/83 (St. Austin of Canterbury) His day is toward þe ende of May. *c* **1374** CHAUCER *Troylus* II. 1098, I may not slepe neuere a Mayes morwe. *c* **1391** —— *Astrol.* I. §10 Ianuare, Februare, Marcius, Aprile, Mayus [etc.]. *a* **1400–50** *Alexander* 3699 þai made as mery melody & musik þai sanng As in þe moneths of Mai or mydsomere euyn. *c* **1430** LYDG. *Min. Poems* (Percy Soc.) 23 When the larke..Salveth the uprist of the sonne shene,..in April and in May. **1598** BARNFIELD *Ode*, As it fell vpon a Day, In the merrie Month of May. *c* **1630** MILTON *Sonn. Nightingale*, While the jolly hours lead on propitious May. **1784** COWPER *Task* VI. 62 The season smiles,..And has the warmth of May.

personified. *c* **1374** CHAUCER *Troylus* II. 50 In may þat moder is of monethes glade. **1508** DUNBAR *Gold. Targe* 82 There saw I May, of myrthfull monethis quene. **1593** SHAKS. *Rich. II*, V. i. 79 She came adorned hither like sweet May. **1630** MILTON *On May morning* 5 Hail bounteous May, that dost inspire Mirth and youth and warm desire. **1826–34** WORDSW. *To May* i, Though many suns have risen and set Since thou, blithe May, wert born.

b. In proverbial and allusive phrases.

c **1386** CHAUCER *Prol.* 92 He was as fressh as is the Monthe of May. **1508** DUNBAR *Gold. Targe* 261 Surmounting ewiry tong terrestriall, Alls fer as Mayes morow dois myd-nycht. **1588** SHAKS. *L.L.L.* IV. iii. 102. **1599** —— *Much Ado* I. i. 194 There's her cosin..exceedes her as much in beautie, as the first of Maie doth the last of December. **1600** —— *A. Y. L.* IV. i. 148. **1658** H. PLUMPTRE *Let.* in *12th Rep. Hist. MSS. Comm.* App. v. 6 Wishing that all your yeares yet to come.. may partake more of Mayes then Julyes. **1659** HOWELL *Prov.* 11/1 As welcome as Flowers in May. **1732** T. FULLER *Gnomologia* 276 Leave not off a Clout Till May be out. **1742** GRAY *Spring* 50 We frolick, while 'tis May. **1889** D. HANNAY *Capt. Marryat* 150 If he had not spent his summer while it was May—at least he had run through it far too soon.

c. *fig.* Bloom, prime, heyday. *poet.*

a **1586** SIDNEY *Astr. & Stella* xxi. (1591) B 2, If now the May of my yeeres much decline. **1599** SHAKS. *Much Ado* V. i. 76. **1602** MARSTON *Antonio's Rev.* I. i, We both were rivals in our May of blood Unto Maria. **1633** MASSINGER *Guardian* I. i, I am in the May of my abilities, And you in your December. **1847** TENNYSON *Princess* II. 439 Others lay about the lawns, Of the older sort, and murmur'd that their May Was passing. **1859** —— *Elaine* 553 A Prince, In the mid might and flourish of his May.

d. ***May and January*** or ***December***: used to describe the marriage of a young woman to an old man.

c **1386** CHAUCER *Merch. T.* 449 That she, this mayden, which þat Mayus highte..Shal wedded be vn-to this Ianuarie. *Ibid.* 642 Thilke day That Ianuarie hath wedded fresshe May. **1581** T. HOWELL *Devises* I ij, In fayth doth frozen Ianus double face, Such fauour finde, to match with pleasant Maye. **1606** DEKKER *Sev. Sins* (Arb.) 44 You doe wrong to Time, inforcing May to embrace December. **1891** R. BUCHANAN *Coming Terror* 267 When asthmatic January weds buxom May.

2. The festivities of May-day. ***Queen of the May***, † ***Queen of May***, ***Lady of the May*** (cf. MAY-LADY): a girl chosen to be 'queen' of the games on May-day, being gaily dressed and crowned with flowers. † ***King, Lord of (the) May*** = MAY-LORD.

1506 *Acc. Ld. Treas. Scot.* (1901) III. 195 Item, to ane Quene of Maij at the Abbay ȝet, be the Kingis command xiiijs. **1515** in Glasscock *Rec. St. Michael's, Bp. Stortford* (1882) 34 Item pd for brede and ale th same day that Sabysford may was whan they of Sabysford did come rydynd to the toune to sett ther may. **1568** T. HOWELL *Arbour of Amitie* 36 b, Ich beare the banner before my Lorde of May. **1577** *Gen. Assembly* in Child *Ballads* III. 45 Discharge playes of Robin Hood, King of May, and sick others, on the Sabboth day. **1611** BEAUM. & FL. *Knt. Burn. Pestle* v. iii, I..by all men chosen was Lord of the May. *a* **1634** RANDOLPH *Amyntas* Prol., How shall we talk to nymphs so trim and gay, That ne'er saw lady yet but at a May? **1673** DRYDEN *Marr. à la mode* II. 28 Then I was made the Lady of the May. **1686** *Loyal Garland* (ed. 5) B 5, Cloris Queen of all the May. **1711** STEELE *Spect.* No. 80 ¶2 The Girls preceded their parents like Queens of May, in all the gaudy Colours imaginable, on every Sunday to Church. **1802–16** MRS. SHERWOOD *Susan Gray* ix. (1869) 58 Why, Susan, you look as handsome as the queen of May in that hat. **1832** TENNYSON *May Queen* i, For I'm to be Queen o' the May, mother, I'm to be Queen o' the May.

3. Blossoms of the hawthorn (*Cratægus Oxyacantha*); hence occas., the tree itself: so called because it blooms in the month of May.

a **1548** HALL *Chron., Hen. VIII* 7 b, On May daye..hys grace..rose in the mornynge very early to fetche May or grene bows. **1592** NASHE *Summers Last Will* (1600) B 3 The Palme and May make countrey houses gay. **1604** E. G[RIMSTONE] *D'Acosta's Hist. Indies* v. xxviii. 413 In this moone and moneth, which is when they bring Maie from the fieldes into the house. **1626** JACKSON *Creed* VIII. xix. §1 By such a maner or trope of speech, as the English and French doe call the buds or flowers of haw-thorne May. **1820** SHELLEY *Question* iii, The moonlight-coloured May. **1848** J. H. NEWMAN *Loss & Gain* ii. 5 The laburnums are out, and the may. **1866** M. ARNOLD *Thyrsis* vi, With blossoms red and white of fallen May.

4. *Cambridge Univ.* **a.** (*sing.* or *pl.*) = ***May examination***; **b.** (*pl.*) = ***May races***: see 5.

1852 C. A. BRISTED 5 *Yrs. Eng. Univ.* (ed. 2) 63 The College Easter Term Examination, familiarly spoken of as 'the May'. *Ibid.* 64 The 'May' is one of the features which distinguishes Cambridge from Oxford; at the latter there are no public College examinations. **1879** 'JULIAN HOME' *Sk. Camb.* 53 And in the trials, in the Mays, From stroke to bow, ..they keep the river head. **1901** *Daily Chron.* 6 May 8/3 The annual 'Mays'—paradoxically held in June—are fixed for the 5th of the latter month and following days.

5. *attrib.* and *Comb.*, as (sense 1) ***May-born***, ***glad*** adjs., ***-hope***, ***-mess***, ***morning***, ***-night***, ***season***, ***time*** (also *attrib.*), ***-yeaned*** adj.; (also with reference to 1 c) ***May month***, ***moon***, ***morn***; (sense 2) ***May-eve***, ***feast***, ***fool***, ***-keeper***; (sense 3) ***may-bloom***, ***-blossom***, ***-blossomed*** adj., ***bough***, ***branch***, † ***busket***, ***leaf***, ***tree***; † **may ale**, ? an ale-drinking held on May-day; † **May bishop**, an opprobrious name for a titular bishop; **May-drink** [= G. *maitrank*, Du. *meidrank*], white wine medicated with woodruff, drunk in Belgium and northern Germany; **May examination**, a college examination held at the end of the Easter term at Cambridge; **May-gad** (see quot. and GAD *sb.*[1] 5); **May-Hill**, used in the phrase ***to have climbed May Hill***, to have passed through the part of the year most dangerous to health (perh. with allusion to May Hill as a local name); **May-house** (see quot.); † **May-king** = *king of the May* (see 2); **May-kitten**, ? a kitten born in May; † **May-like** *adv.*, with the freshness of May; † **May Marian** (see quot. and cf. MAID MARIAN); **May meetings**, a series of annual meetings of various religious and philanthropic societies held during the month of May in Exeter Hall, London, and other buildings; **May queen**, the Queen of the May (see 2); hence **May queenship**; **May races**, intercollegiate boat races held in the Easter term at Cambridge (now in June); † **May-roll** *v. trans.*, to roll in the grass as a May-day game; † **May-sel**, May-time; † **May skin**, ? the skin of a sheep sheared in May; **May-term**, colloq. name for the Easter term at Cambridge; **May-week**, the week of the May races at Cambridge; † **May wool**, ? wool taken from a sheep in May. Also MAY-BUTTER, -DAY, -DEW, -GAME, -LADY, -LORD, etc.

1516 in Glasscock *Rec. St. Michael's, Bp. Stortford* (1882) 35 Item resseyvyd of the *may ale above all charge ls. **1565** JEWEL *Def. Apol.* (1611) 585 Your late Chapter of Trident, with your worthie number of forty Prelates, whereof certaine were onlie *May Bishops, otherwise by you called Nullatenses. **1818** TODD, **May-bloom*, the hawthorn. **1599** B. JONSON *Cynthia's Rev.* v. ii. Wks. 1616 I. 248 *Mer.* Sweet Madames..your brests and forehead are whiter then gotes milke, or *May-blossomes. **1872** TENNYSON *Gareth & Lynette* 575 A damsel of high lineage, and a brow May-blossom, and a cheek of apple blossom. *a* **1789** MICKLE *Eskdale Braes* 29 The *May-blossom'd thorn. **1788** TURNBULL *Laura*, The sweetest *May-born flowers Paint the meadows. **1530** PALSGR. 666/1 In stede of a trapper he pricked his horse full of *maye bowes. **1560** in Sowerby *Eng. Bot.* (1864) III. 240 Those boys who choose it may rise at four oclock to gather *May branches. **1823** in Hone *Every-day Bk.* (1859) I. 565 On May morning..the girls look with some anxiety for their May-branch. **1579** SPENSER *Sheph. Cal.* May 10 To gather *may bus-kets and smelling brere. **1850** LONGF. *Gold. Leg.* I. *Court-yard of Castle*, Fill me a goblet of *May-drink, As aromatic as the May From which it steals the breath away. **16..** *Songs Lond. Prentices* (Percy Soc.) 18 Upon *May Eve As prentices on Maying went. **1825** CROKER *Fairy Leg. & Trad. S. Ireland* I. 307 May-eve is considered a time of peculiar danger. *Ibid.* 308 Another custom prevalent on May-eve is the painful and mischievous one of stinging with nettles. **1852** C. A. BRISTED 5 *Yrs. Eng. Univ.* (ed. 2) 85 After the trial heat of the first *May examination, the field of candidates for Honours begins to assume something like a calculable form. **1778** HUTCHINSON *View Northumb., Anc. Customs* 14 The syllabub, prepared for the *May feast. *a* **1591** H. SMITH *Serm.* (1594) 394 May-games, and May poales, and *May fooles, and Morris-dancers are vanitie. **1724** STUKELEY *Itin. Curios.* I. 29 Making a procession to this hill with *may gads (as they call them) in their hands, this is a white willow wand the bark peel'd off, ty'd round with cowslips. **1911** E. POUND *Canzoni* 4 No poppy in the *May-glad mead. *a* **1661** FULLER *Worthies, Derbysh.* (1662) I. 252 Whereas, in our remembrance, Ale went out when Swallows came in,..it now hopeth (having climed up *May-hill) to continue its course all the year. *a* **1889** G. M. HOPKINS *Poems* (1967) 38 *May-hope of our darkened ways! **1824** MISS MITFORD *Village* Ser. I. 89 From the trunk of the chestnut the *May-houses commence. They are covered alleys built of green boughs, decorated with garlands and great bunches of flowers..hanging down like chandeliers among the dancers. **1904** *Edin. Rev.* Jan. 55 Other *May-keepers whose symbols are now but relics. **1519** HORMAN *Vulg.* 277 b, It is the custome that euery yere we shal haue a *may kynge. **1690** DRYDEN *Amphitryon* III. 33 Blear-ey'd, like a *May-Kitten. **1844** MRS. BROWNING *Lost Bower* xxix, There fell Two white *may-leaves..From a blossom. **1592** T. L[ODGE] *Euph. Shadow* (1882) 16 When..I..*May-like young, of pleasure gan to taste. **1582** FETHERSTON *Dial. agst. Dancing* D 7, In your maygames.. you doe vse to attyre men in womans apparrell, whom you doe most commenly call *maymarrions. **1849** CLOUGH *Dipsychus* I. iv, Sweet eloquence! at next *May Meeting How it would tell in the repeating! **1877** G. M. HOPKINS *Poems* (1967) 67 Look, look: a *May-mess, like on orchard boughs! **1470–85** MALORY *Arthur* XVIII. xxv. 771 Lyke as *may moneth floreth and floryssheth in many gardens. **1600** S. NICHOLSON *Acolastus* (1876) 8 In the May moneth of my blooming yeares. **1737** FIELDING *Tumble-Down Dick* Ded., A play judiciously brought on by you in the May-month. **1576** GASCOIGNE *Steele Gl.* Ep. Ded. (Arb.) 43 In the *May-moone of my youth. **1813** MOORE *Yng. May Moon* 1 The young May moon is beaming, love. **1599** SHAKS. *Hen. V*, I. ii. 120 My thrice-puissant Liege Is in the very *May-Morne of his Youth. **1878** BROWNING *Poets Croisic* xv, On May-morns, that primeval rite Of temple-building..lingers. **1377** LANGL. *P. Pl.* B. Prol. 5 On a *May [*Text A.* Mayes] mornynge on Maluerne hulles. **1601** SHAKS. *Twel. N.* III. iv. 156 More matter for a May morning. **1859** G. MEREDITH *R. Feverel* xviii. (xv.), The hand was..white and fragrant as the frosted blossom of a *May-night. **1832** TENNYSON (*title*) The *May Queen. **1881** RUSKIN *Lett., to Faunthorpe* (1895) I. 49, I hope the *May Queenship is beginning to be thought of. **1893** in *Camb. Univ. Almanack* (1894) 209 During the Lent or *May Races. **1656** R. FLETCHER *Poems* 210 The game at best, the girls *May rould must bee. **1508** DUNBAR *Tua mariit Wemen* 24 Grein..as the gress that grew in *May sessoun. **14..** *Stockh. Med. MS.* II. 407 in *Anglia* XVIII, 3if it be gaderid in *may-sel. **1497** HALYBURTON *Ledger* (1867) 46 Item..a sek off *May skynis contenand 300. **1534–5** *Durham Acc. Rolls* (Surtees) 109 Pro xj may skynnes. **1905** *Cambr. Review* 4 May 281/1 The *May term is seldom a good time for serious concerts. *c* **1350** *Will. Palerne* (1881) 823 Alle freliche foules þat on þat friþ songe, for merþe of þat *may time þei made moche noyce. **1633** P. FLETCHER *Purple Island* XII. lxxxii. 179 More fruitfull then the May-time Geminies. **1804** WORDSW. '*She was a Phantom of delight*', But all things else about her drawn From May-time and the cheerful Dawn. **1930** T. S. ELIOT *Ash-Wednesday* 14 The broadbacked figure..Enchanted the maytime with an antique flute. **1963** A. CLARKE *Coll. Plays* 161 Who will wash them by the river's edge, Hang them unseen upon as white a hedge In Maytime? **1895** *Cassell's Fam. Mag.* June 518 So many visitors are attracted to Cambridge for the '*May week'. **1720** STRYPE *Stow's Surv.* (1754) II. v. xiv. 325/2 Fallen *May wool rotten and other ill wool. **1884** *Century Mag.* Feb. 518 In June, when the *May-yeaned lambs were skipping in the sunshine.

b. In names (chiefly *local*) of animals: **May-beetle**, the cockchafer; also, the CHOVY; **May-bird**, the whimbrel, *Numenius phæopus*; *U.S.* the bobolink (Bartlett *Dict. Amer.* 1859); **May-chafer** [cf. G. *maikäfer*] = *May-beetle* (in quot. *fig.*); † **May-chick** = *May-bird*; † **May-chit** (see CHIT *sb.*[4]); **May-curlew** = *May-bird*; **May fish**, a name for the twait shad, because of its entering rivers in May; *U.S.* a killifish, *Fundulus majalis*; **May-fowl**, **-jack** = *May-bird*; **May parr**, **peal**, local names for salmon at certain stages of growth; **May-skate**, the sharp-nosed ray, *Raia oxyrhyncha*; **May-sucker** *U.S.*, the hare-lipped sucker, *Quassilabia lacera*; † **May-worm**, an oil-beetle (genus *Meloe*). Also MAY-BUG, MAY-FLY.

1720 ALBIN *Nat. Hist. Insects* 60 In the middle of May came forth a brown Beetle called the Chafer, Oak Web, or *May Beetle. **1842** T. W. HARRIS *Insects injur. Veget.* (1862) 31 The best time..for shaking the trees on which the May-beetles are lodged, is in the morning. **1860** J. CURTIS *Farm Insects*, Index, May-bug or beetle—*Anisoplia horticola*. **1864** *E. Cornw. Words* in *Jrnl. Roy. Inst. Cornw.* Mar. 18 *May-bird, the whimbrel. **1870** H. STEVENSON *Birds Norf.* II. 199 The appearance of the main body [of whimbrels] in May..is so invariable that this species is alway spoken of as the 'May bird' by the gunners in both localities. **1827** CARLYLE *German Romance* III. 132 Your idle *May-chafers and Court-celestials. **1577** *Exp. Entert. Gorhambury* in Nichols *Progr. Eliz.* (1823) II. 57 Quails..*Maychicks.. Malards. **1885** SWAINSON *Prov. Names Birds* 200 Whimbrel. .. *May curlew..(Ireland). **1836** YARRELL *Fishes* II. 133 The Twaite Shad..in consequence of the time of its annual visit to some of the rivers of the European Continent is called the *May-fish. **1896** JORDAN & EVERMANN *Fishes N. & Mid. Amer.* I. 639 Killifish; Mayfish; Rockfish. **1852** MACGILLIVRAY *Hist. Brit. Birds* IV. 253 [Syn.] Whimbrel, Little Curlew..*Mayfowl. **1880** *Antrim & Down Gloss.*, **May jack*, the whimbrel. **1841** *Penny Cycl.* XX. 364/1 The smaller summer parrs (called, in Dumfriesshire, *May parrs). **1861** *Act 24 & 25 Vict.* c. 109 §4 All migratory fish of the genus salmon, whether known by the names..mort, peal, herring peal, *may peal, pugg peal, harvest cock,..or by any other local name. **1828** FLEMING *Hist. Brit. Anim.* 171 *Raia oxyrinchus.* Sharp-nosed Ray... White Skate, Friar Skate, *May Skate. **1884** GOODE *Nat. Hist. Usef. Aquatic Anim.* 614 The 'Rabbit-mouth', 'Hare-lip',..or '*May Sucker' is found in abundance in many rivers of Tennessee and..Ohio. **1658** ROWLAND tr. *Moufet's Theat. Ins.* 1017 They hang the *May-worm (for so he cals the Oyl-beetle) about the neck with a thred, especially in the moneth of May.

c. In names of plants and fruits: **May-bean** (see quot.); **May-blob**, the marsh marigold, *Caltha palustris*; also applied to other plants (see *Eng. Dial. Dict.*); † **May-blossom**, lily of the valley (see also 5 above); **May-cherry**, (*a*) a small early kind of cherry; (*b*) *U.S.* the fruit of *Amelanchier canadensis*, the June-berry; † **May-fern** (see quot.); **May gowan** (see GOWAN 2); † **May grapes**, *Botrychium Lunaria*; **May grass**, *Panicum latifolium* (J. T. Maycock *Flora Barbadensis* 1830, 61); **May-haw** (see HAW *sb.*[2] 3); **May lily**, lily of the valley (see LILY 2); **May-pop** *U.S.*, the fruit of the passion-flower, esp. of *Passiflora incarnata*; also, the plant itself; **May-rose**, a name for any rose flowering in May; also the guelder rose, *Viburnum Opulus*; **May-thorn**, the hawthorn; **May-wort**, *Galium cruciatum* (Treas. Bot. 1866). Also MAY-APPLE, MAY-BUSH, MAY DUKE, MAYFLOWER.

1802 *Eng. Encycl.* IV. 473/1 The *May-beans are a larger sort of ticks, and somewhat earlier ripe. **1863** *May-blob [see *granny's nightcap*]. **1881** S. EVANS *Evans's Leicestershire Words* (new ed.) 192 *May-blob*, the marsh-marigold. **1908** *Pacific Monthly* XX. 94/2 Could they or their children after them pick out a May-blob from a May-pop? **1916** D. H. LAWRENCE *Amores* 38, I can smell the gorgeous bog-end, in its breathless Dazzle of may-blobs. **1960** *Oxf. Bk. Wild Flowers* 4/2 Marsh Marigold (*Caltha palustris*)... The plant has many other names such as Kingcup and May Blobs. **1578** LYTE *Dodoens* II. xxvi. 178 Lyllie Conuall, is now called ..in English..*May blossoms. **1664** EVELYN *Kal. Hort.*, *May* (1679) 16 The *May-Cherry. **1713** ADDISON *Guardian* No. 97 ¶4 To Zelinda two sticks of May-Cherries. **1718** J. LAWRENCE *Fruit-g. Kalendar* 78 The little early May-Cherry is indeed worth nothing. **1832** L. HUNT *Sir R. Esher* (1850) 142 The finest apples and pears, strawberries, and May-cherries. **1884** SARGENT *Rep. Forests N. Amer.* (*10th Census* IX.) 84 *Amelanchier Canadensis*... May Cherry. **1658** tr. *Bergerac's Satyr. Char.* xii. 41 A girdle of *May-fearne [orig. *fougere de May*] woven in tresses. **1548** TURNER *Names of Herbes* (E.D.S.) 85 Lunaria minor, which may be called in englishe litle Lunary or *Maye Grapes, the duch cal this herbe..meydruuen. **1868** *Amer. Naturalist* II. 468 They [*sc.* deer] visit the ponds in which the *May-haw grows, the fruit of which is juicy with the flavor of the apple. **1938** M. K. RAWLINGS *Yearling* xi. 112 He concentrated on light bread and mayhaw jelly. **1851** *De Bow's Rev.* XI. 49 *May Pop, Passion Flower, is also abundant here. **1887** J. C. HARRIS *Free Joe*, etc. (1888) 200 An' I fotch you some May-pops too. **1753** CHAMBERS *Cycl. Supp.* s.v. *Rose*, The small red rose, commonly called the *May rose. **1802–16** MRS. SHERWOOD *Susan Gray* xiii. (1869) 94 In her hand she had a bunch of May-roses. **1844** MRS. BROWNING *Vis. Poets* Concl. 105, I receive The *maythorn, and its scent outgive! **1882** KEARY *Outlines Prim. Belief* 107 Even the maythorn is to be met with.

may (meɪ), *sb.*[4]: see MAY *v.*[1] 11.

may (meɪ; unstressed mɛ), *v.*[1] Forms: see below. [A Com. Teut. vb., belonging (by conjugation if not by origin) to the class of preterite-presents, in which the present tense has the inflexion of a strong preterite, while the past tense is formed from the root by means of a suffix: cf. *can*, *dare*, *dow*, *mote* (*must*), *owe*, *shall*, *wot*. The OE. *mæȝ*, *maȝon*, *meahte* (later *mihte*), correspond to OFris. *mei*, *mugun*, *machte*, OS. *mag*, *mugun*, *mahta* (Du. *mag*, *mogen*, *mocht*), OHG. *mag*, *magum* (*mugum*), *mahta* (MHG. *mag*, *magen*, *mohte*, mod.G. *mag*, *mögen*, *mochte*), ON. *má*, *megom*, *mátte* (Sw. *må*, *måtte*, Da. *maa*, *maatte*), Goth. *mag*, *magum*, *mahta*. The primary sense of the verb is to be strong or able, to have power; the root OTeut. **mag-*, OAryan **magh-*, appears in MIGHT *sb.*, OSl. *mogą* I can, Gr. *μῆχος* contrivance, *μηχανή* MACHINE, Skr. *mahan* great.

The conjugation is abnormal; according to Brugmann *Grundriss* II. §887 the verb was originally a thematic present

with weak root-vowel, and was attracted into the preterite-present class by analogy.]

A. Inflexional Forms.

†**1.** *Infinitive. Obs.* Forms: α. 1 **maȝan**, 3 **muȝen**, *Ormin* **muȝhenn**, 4 **mowen**, **mow**, 5 **mown**, 4–5 **moun**, 4–6 **mowe(n**.

c **1050** *De Consuet. Monach.* in *Anglia* XIII. 389 *Posse carere*, maȝan þolian. *c* **1200** ORMIN 3944 þatt mann-kinn shollde muȝhenn wel Upp cumenn inntill heoffne. *c* **1250** *Gen. & Ex.* 1818 Hu sal ani man ðe muȝen deren? *a* **1340** HAMPOLE *Psalter* xvii. 41 þai sall noght mow stand. *c* **1374** CHAUCER *Boeth.* IV. met. i. (1868) 110 þou..shalt mowen retourne hool & sounde. **1390** GOWER *Conf.* II. 2 Thou schalt mowe senden hire a lettre. *c* **1440** *Promp. Parv.* 346/2 Mown, or haue myȝhte.., *possum*. **1495** *Act 11 Hen. VII*, c. 5 No Ship of greate burdon shall mowe comme..in the seid Haven. **1533** MORE *Apol.* xxii. Wks. 885/1 Some waye that appered..to mow stande the realme in great stede.

β. 5–6 **may**, (5 **maye**).

1435 MISYN *Fire of Love* 15, I haue denyed hym to may be knawen. *c* **1489** CAXTON *Sonnes of Aymon* i. 26 As longe that I shalle maye bere armes. **1503** ATKYNSON tr. *De Imitatione* III. lxiv. 258 Nor stronge helpers shal nat may helpe. **1532** CRANMER *Let.* in *Misc. Writ.* (Parker Soc.) II. 233, I fear that the emperor will depart thence, before my letters shall may come unto your grace's hands. **1565** COOPER *Thesaurus*, *Possum*..To may, or can.

2. *Indicative Present.*

a. *1st and 3rd. pers. sing.* **may.** Forms: 1 **mæȝ**, **meȝ**, (**mæiȝ**, **maȝ**), 2 **mayȝ**, 2–3 **maiȝ**, **mei**, 2–4 **mai**, 2–5 **mey**, 3 **mæi**, *Ormin* **maȝȝ**, 3–6 **ma**, **maye**, 5–6 **maie**, 3– **may**.

The ONorthumbrian writers often use the subjunctive forms (*mæȝe*, *-æ*, *-o*, *-i*) instead of those of the indicative.

Beowulf 2801 (Gr.) Ne mæȝ ic her leng wesan. *c* **825** *Vesp. Psalter* lxxvii. 19 Ah meȝ god ȝearwian biod in woestenne? *a* **1100** *Gerefa* in *Anglia* IX. 261 Æfre he mæiȝ findan on ðam he mæiȝ nyt beon. *c* **1160** *Hatton Gosp.* Matt. vi. 24 Ne mayȝ nam man twam hlaferden þeowian. *c* **1175** *Lamb. Hom.* 9 Ne þe deofel mey nefre cumen inne him. *c* **1200** ORMIN 6199 þa birrþ þin macche gætenn þe All þatt ȝho maȝȝ fra sinne. *c* **1220** *Bestiary* 516 Ðe smale he wile ðus biswiken, ðe grete maiȝ he noȝt bigripen. *c* **1250** *Gen. & Ex.* 295 Ðowȝte ðis quead, 'hu ma it ben?' *c* **1275** *Passion our Lord* 68 in *O.E. Misc.* 39 As ich eu seȝȝe may. **1382** WYCLIF *Phil.* iv. 13, I may alle thingis in him that comfortith me. *c* **1430** LYDG. *Min. Poems* (Percy Soc.) 40 And my paper it conteyne ne may. **1503** in *Trans. Roy. Hist. Soc.* (1902) 152 Alex. maye I trust the? **1551** T. WILSON *Logike* (1580) 31 b, This maie bee true, and this maie bee false. **1567** *Gude & Godlie B.* (S.T.S.) 33 Bot luke on that, quhilk now ma not be sene.

b. *2nd pers. sing.* **mayest**, **mayst** (ˈmeɪɪst, meɪst). Forms: α. 1 **meaht**, *Northumb.* **mæht**, *Kent.* **meht**, 1–4 **miht**, 2–3 **myht**, 3 **maht**, (*Ormin* **mahht**), **mayhte**, **maucht**, **meiht**, **micht**, (**mith**), 4 **maiȝt**, **mait**, **mayt**, **mate**, (**mayth**), **myht**, **myȝt**, 5 **mat**, **myȝte**.

In 12th–14th c. *þ* and *s* are sometimes found for *h*, *ȝ*.

8.. *Kent. Gl.* in Wr.-Wülcker 58/11 *Si uales..*, ȝif ðu meht. *c* **950** *Lindisf. Gosp.* Luke vi. 42, & hu mæht [*c* **1000** *Ags. Gosp.* miht, *c* **1160** *Hatton* myht] ðu cuoæða broðre ðinum [etc.]. *c* **1200** ORMIN 7779 Depe sinness þatt tu mahht Wel nemmnenn dæde werrkess. *c* **1200** *Trin. Coll. Hom.* 258 Ase þu ert freo & wilt & maucht. *c* **1205** LAY. 2981 þu mith [*c* **1275** miht] me wel ileue. *a* **1225** *Ancr. R.* 276 And so þu meiht icnowen þine owune woke unstrencðe. *c* **1250** *Kent. Serm.* in *O.E. Misc.* 31 Yef þu wilt þu me micht makie hool. *c* **1275** *Luue Ron* 31 *Ibid.* 94 þus is þes world as þu mayht seo. *a* **1300** *Cursor M.* 26575 For sua þou mate noght wasch þi wite. *c* **1330** *Spec. Gy Warw.* 881 þerfore worch, while þu mait, For sodeyneliche þu might be caiht. **1362** LANGL. *P. Pl.* A. I. 146 Her thou miht [B. I. 170 myȝtow] seon ensample in hymselfe one. **1426** AUDELAY *Poems* 8 Ellys i-savyd thou mat noȝt be. *c* **1450** MYRC 15 Here thow myȝte fynde & rede.

β. 4–5 **maiste**, **mayste**, 4–7 **maist**, (5 **maxste**), 5–6 **maiest**, 4– **mayst**, 6– **mayest**, **may'st**.

[A new formation on *may*.]

c **1374** CHAUCER *Compl. Mars* 112 Wel maist thou wepe and crien. *c* **1385** —— *L.G.W.* 504 That mayst thow sen sche kytheth what sche is. **1470–85** MALORY *Arth.* IV. x. 131 Thow arte ouercome and maxste not endure. **1477** EARL RIVERS (Caxton) *Dictes* 21 b, Take not from me that that thou maiest not yeue me. **1553** EDEN *Treat. Newe Ind.* (Arb.) 7 In this Booke thou mayest reade many straunge thinges. **1640** BROME *Sparagus Garden* II. iii, Thou maist make a Country gentleman in time. **1717** POPE *Eloïsa* 325 In sacred vestments may'st thou stand. **1819** SHELLEY *Cenci* v. iv. 155 So mayest thou do as I do. **1821** —— *Hellas* 844 Thou mayst behold How cities [etc.].

γ. Chiefly *Sc.* and *north.* 4 **mai**, 4–5 **may**, 4–6 **ma**, 5 **maye**.

a **1300** *Cursor M.* 290 Behald þe sune and þou mai se. *c* **1375** *Sc. Leg. Saints* i. (*Petrus*) 380, I am Resine, as þou ma se. *a* **1400–50** *Alexander* 1090 May þou oȝt, lede, þe ȝonder lawe lyft on þi schulder? *c* **1440** HYLTON *Scala Perf.* (W. de W. 1494) I. lxxii, Thou maye [1533 mayst] not lyue wythout mete and drynke. **1500–20** DUNBAR *Poems* xc. 34 Thow ma rycht weill in thi mynde consydder That [etc.].

c. *plural.* **may.** Forms: α. 1 **maȝon**, (**un**, **-an**), **mahon**, **maȝe(n**, *Northumb.* **maȝa**, **-o**, 2–3 **maȝe(n**, 3 **mahen**, **mah**, **mawe**, 3–5 **mawen**.

c **900** tr. *Bæda's Hist.* I. i. (Schipper) 11 Oðer ealond..þæt we maȝon oft leohtum daȝum ȝeseon. *c* **950** *Lindisf. Gosp.* Matt. xx. 22 Maȝaȝe [*c* **975** *Rushw.* maȝon ȝit, *c* **1000** *Ags. Gosp.* maȝe ȝyt, *c* **1160** *Hatton* muȝen ȝyt] drinca calic ðone ic drinca willo. *a* **1122** *OE. Chron.* an. 656 (MS. E), Ealle þa þa to Rome na maȝen faren. *c* **1175** *Lamb. Hom.* 21 We ne maȝen alre coste halden crist bibode. *a* **1225** *Leg. Kath.* 361 Cleopest þeo þinges godes, þat nowðer sturien ne mahen ne steoren ham seoluen. *a* **1250** *Prov. Ælfred* 14 in *O.E. Misc.* 102 Heom he bi-gon lere so ye mawe [*other text* muȝen] i-hure. **1439** in Willis & Clark *Cambridge* (1886) I. Introd. 56 Yer is so grete scarstee of maistres of gramer, whereof as now ben almost none, nor none mawen be hade in your Universitees.

β. 1 **mæȝon**, 4 **mai**, *north.* **mais**, 4–6 **ma**, etc. as in 1st and 3rd pers. sing.

c **897** K. ÆLFRED *Gregory's Past. C.* xxiii. 176 Ða þe medomlice & wel mæȝon [*Hatton MS.* maȝon] læran. *c* **950** *Lindisf. Gosp.* John xiii. 36 Ne mæȝon [*c* **975** *Rushw.* maȝun] ȝie mec nu fylȝe. *a* **1300** *Cursor M.* 5518 We ma sua our landes tin. *c* **1375** *Sc. Leg. Saints* xxxvi. (*Baptista*) 761 Sum cristine þare wonnyne mais. **1390** GOWER *Conf.* II. 51 Men mai recovere lost of good. *c* **1400** *Cursor M.* 29132 (Cotton Galba) We mey se by saint austin lare [etc.]. *a* **1400–50** *Alexander* 684 May ȝe oȝt me in any maner to þat sterne schewe?

γ. 2–3 **muȝen**, (2 **muȝon**, **muȝe**), 3 **muhen**, **muwe(n**, **mouwen**, (*Ormin* **muȝhenn**), **muȝhe**, *Kent.* **muee**, **mohe**, **mo**, 3–4 **moȝe(n**, 3–5 **mowen**, 4 **mou**, **mu**, 4–5 **mowne**, **moun**, **mow**, 5 **mown**, **mowghe**, 6 **mowe**.

c **1160** *Hatton Gosp.* John xiv. 5 Hu muȝe we þanne wei cunnan? *a* **1175** *Cott. Hom.* 221 Ne hi muȝen ne hi nelleð nane synne ȝewercon. *Ibid.* 223 Imuȝon [= ye may] ȝecnowen eiȝðer god and euyl. *c* **1200** ORMIN 13408 We muȝhenn sen whatt itt bihallt. *a* **1225** *Ancr. R.* 44 Toward te preostes tiden herkneð se wel ȝe muwen. *c* **1230** *Hali Meid.* 43 Ne muhen ha nanes weis bedden in a breoste. *c* **1250** *Kent. Serm.* in *O.E. Misc.* 27 Ye muee wel under-stonde ..þet [etc.]. *c* **1250** *Death* 255 *Ibid.* 184 þenne mohe [*Jesus MS.* muwe] we cwemen crist at þe dom. *c* **1290** *Beket* 979 in *S. Eng. Leg.* 134 Wel ȝe mouwen i-seo þat he is prouȝt. *a* **1300** *Cursor M.* 22559 Quine mak þai, sin þai sua mu [*Gött.* mv, *Trin.* mow] Anoþer heuen and erth? **1387** TREVISA *Higden* (Rolls) I. 185 Foules mowe not lyue þere. *c* **1449** PECOCK *Repr.* II. xx. 273 Hem whiche kunnen not rede or moun not here the word of God. *c* **1475** *Partenay* 5446 And ye mow noght, Alway here byde moste ye. *c* **1485** *Digby Myst.* (1882) III. 392 In alle þe hast þat euer they mown. *a* **1553** UDALL *Royster D.* IV. iv. (Arb.) 66 Ralph Roister Doister, whome ye know well mowe [*rime* you].

3. *Subjunctive Present.* **may.** Forms: α. *sing.* 1 **mæȝe**, (**mæhȝe**, **mæȝȝe**), *Mercian* **meȝe**, *Northumb.* **mæȝæ**, **mæȝi**, *Kent.* **meiȝe**, 3 **meih**, 2– (as in Indicative). *plural.* 1 **mæȝen**, **meȝen**, *Northumb.* **mæȝi**, **maȝon**, etc.

Beowulf 680 þeah ic eal mæȝe. **8..** *Kent. Glosses* in Wr.-Wülcker 81/32 *Ne..non possis*, ðe les ðu ne meiȝe. *c* **825** *Vesp. Psalter* lxx. 8 Ðæt ic meȝe singan wuldur ðin alne deȝ. *c* **950** *Rit. Dunelm.* (Surtees) 95 Ðe mæȝi hia ædeava [*L. tibi valeant apparere*]. *c* **950** *Lindisf. Gosp.* John xxi. 25 Nidoemo ic þætti middanȝeord mæȝi bifoa ðailco ðaðe [etc.]. *c* **1205** LAY. 1206, & ȝif ich þat lond mai [*c* **1275** mawe] bi-ȝeten. *a* **1225** *Ancr. R.* 230 ȝif þu..meih. **14..** in Horstmann *Hampole's Wks.* (1895) I. 105 If þou may. *a* **1553** UDALL *Royster D.* IV. vii. (Arb.) 72 Saue thy head if thou may.

β. *sing.* 1 **maȝe**, 2–3 **maȝe**, **muȝe**, (3 *Ormin* **muȝhe**), **muhe**, **muwe**, **moȝe**, **mawe**, 3–5 **mowe**, 4 **mow**. *plural.* 1 **maȝon**, **-en**, (**mahan**), 3 *Ormin* **muȝhenn**, 4–5 **mowe(n**, etc. (as in Indicative).

c **888** K. ÆLFRED *Boeth.* vii. §3 (Sedgefield) 18 þæt him þa stormas deriȝan ne mæȝen [*v.r.* mahan]. *c* **1000** ÆLFRIC *Gen.* xv. 5 Telle þas steorran, ȝif þu maȝe. *a* **1000** *Cædmon's Gen.* 400 ȝif we hit maȝen wihte aþencan. *c* **1121** *O.E. Chron.* an. 675 (MS. E), And he ne muȝe hit forðian. *c* **1200** ORMIN 2419 Hu maȝȝ þiss forþedd wurrþenn, þatt I wiþþ childe muȝhe ben? *c* **1205** LAY. 1520 Wheðer ich maȝe [*c* **1275** mawe] þe ufere hond habben. *a* **1225** *Ancr. R.* 68 Iðen ilke huse, oðer þer he muwe [*MS. T*, muhe] iseon touward ou. *c* **1275** *Prov. Ælfred* 561 in *O.E. Misc.* 132 ȝif..þu ne moȝe mid strenghe þe selwen steren. *a* **1300** *Havelok* 675 Yif me gold and oþer fe þat y mowe riche be. **1414** *Rolls of Parlt.* IV. 59/1 That these..meschiefs..mowen ben amended. *c* **1420** *Pallad. on Husb.* I. 131 Chaunge hem yf thou mowe. *a* **1450** MYRC 95 And but scho mowe se þe hed.

4. *Indicative and Subjunctive Past.*

a. *1st and 3rd pers. sing.* **might** (maɪt). Forms: 1 **meahte**, **mehte**, *Northumb.* **mæhte**, 1–4 **mihte**, 2–3 **micte**, 2–4 **myhte**, 3 **michte**, **miitte**, **myht**, **mahte**, *Ormin* **mihhte**, 3–5 **miȝte**, **myȝte**, 3–6 **miȝt**, **myȝt**, 4–5 **mighte**, 4–6 *Sc.* **micht**, **mycht**, 4–7 **myght**, (4 **miht**, **miȝth**, *Sc.* **macht**, 4, 8–9 (chiefly *Sc.*) **mith**, 5 **meghte**, **myte**, **myth**, 6 **mythe**, 6–7 **myt**, 7 **may't**, 8–9 *Sc.* **meith**), 4– **might**.

c **975** *Rushw. Gosp.* Matt. viii. 28 Swa þætte mæniȝ mæhte faran þurh wæȝe þæm. *a* **1000** *Guthlac* 548 Hit ne meahte swa. *a* **1000** *Boeth. Metr.* xi. 102 ȝif hit meahte swa. **1154** *OE. Chron.* an. 1137 (MS. E), Ðæt he ne myhte nowiðerwardes. *c* **1205** LAY. 1205 To ane wnsume londe þer ich mihte wunien. *a* **1225** *St. Marher.* 13 Ne mahte me na mon ouercomen. **1297** R. GLOUC. (Rolls) 1483 ȝif it miȝte be ido. *a* **1300** *K. Horn* 9 Feyrore child ne myhte be born. *a* **1300–1400** *Cursor M.* 466 (Gött.) In heuen might [*Cott.* moght, *Fairf.* miȝt, *Trin.* myȝte] he no langer abide. *Ibid.* 686 Saufli mith þai samen slepe. *c* **1330** R. BRUNNE *Chron.* (1810) 3 He was of grete elde, & myght not trauaile. *c* **1375** *Sc. Leg. Saints* vi. (*Thomas*) 247 Til he thocht quhat vyse he micht torment þam. *c* **1375** *Ibid.* xiii. (*Marcus*) 180 þat stand one fut na man macht. *c* **1400** *Adam Davy's Dreams* 14 He ne miȝth þennes goo ne ride. **1415** SIR T. GREY in *43 Dep. Kpr's. Rep.* 583, I said treuly I meghte not but I wolde cum. *c* **1440** *Gesta Rom.* liii. 233 He lernid to be a phisicien, that myte be in eny place. **1470–85** MALORY *Arthur* III. xi. 111 Rydynge..as fast as she myȝt dryue. *a* **1529** SKELTON *Woffully Araid* 33 in Wks. (Dyce) I. 142 What myȝt I suffir more Than I haue don? **1536** *Anc. Cal. Rec. Dublin* (1889) I. 499 In that he mythe..obtayne the kyng hys vaverys. **1553** EDEN *Treat. Newe Ind.* (Arb.) 6 It myghte happelye haue comen to passe. **1567** *Satir. Poems Reform.* iii. 60 He mycht haue bene ane marrow to ane Quene. **1610** SHAKS. *Temp.* I. ii. 168 Would I might But euer see that man. **1819** TENNANT *Papistry Storm'd* (1827) 116 A man mith weel had heard the clutter..o'their chafts.

b. *2nd pers. sing.* **mightest** (ˈmaɪtɪst). Forms: 1 **meahtest**, (Subj. **meahte**), *Northumb.* **mæhtest**, (**mihtes**, **mæht(t)es** *ðu*), 1–3 **mihtest**, 2 **mahtest**, **myhtes**, 2–3 **myhtest**, 3 **mihtes**, *Ormin* **mihhtesst**, 4 **miȝtes**, 4–5 **miȝtest**, 5 **myȝt-**, **mightist**, **myghttyst**, 4– **mightest**.

c **888** K. ÆLFRED *Boeth.* xx. (Sedgefield) 48 Mid hu micelan feo woldest þu þa habban ȝeboht þæt ðu switole mihtest tocnawan þine frind & ðine fynd? *a* **900** CYNEWULF *Crist* 1431 þæt..þu meahte minum weorþan mæȝ-wlite ȝelic. *c* **950** *Lindisf. Gosp.* Mark xiv. 37 Ne mæhtes [*Rushw.* mæhttes, *Ags. & Hatton* mihtes] ðu an huil ȝewæccæ? **1154** *O.E. Chron.* an. 1137 (MS. E), Wel þu myhtes faren all a dæis fare sculdes thu neure finden man in tune sittende. *c* **1175** *Lamb. Hom.* 29 Hu mahtest þu gan to þine aȝene liche ȝif þin hefet were offe? *c* **1200** ORMIN 5160 ȝiff þatt tu mihhtesst lufenn Godd. *c* **1205** LAY. 28112 ȝet þu mihtest þe awreken. *c* **1275** *Passion our Lord* 168 in *O.E. Misc.* 42 Ne Myhtestu one tyde wakien myd me? *a* **1300** *Cursor M.* 13559 Art þou not he þat ȝondir day miȝtes not se? *a* **1425** *Ibid.* 9847 (Trin.) þus miȝtestou selcouþ calle If þou him say. **1509** BARCLAY *Shyp of Folys* (1570) 62 Then wouldest thou gladly (if thou might) do well. **1535** COVERDALE *Ps.* l[i]. 4 That thou mightest be iustified in thy saynges. [So **1611**.] **1567** *Satir. Poems Reform.* viii. 48 War nocht o[r] faith defendit,..Than þow myt writte in gennerall.

c. *plural* **might** (maɪt). Forms: 1 **meahton** (Subj. **-en**), **mihton**, *Northumb.* **mæhtun**, **-on**, **mæȝhton**, **mæhtes**, **mæhtæs**, (1–2 **mihte**, **myhte** *we*, etc.), 2 **mehten**, **miht(i)**, **micht(i)**, 2–4 **mihten**, (3 **mæhte**, **mahte**, **miþte**), 3–4 **myhten**, **miȝtin**, **miȝtten**, **myȝtten**, 4–5 **miȝten**, **myȝten**, **myghten**, 4– as in 1st and 3rd pers. sing.

Beowulf 314 Him þa hildedeor hof modiȝra torht ȝetæhte, þæt hie him to mihton ȝeȝnum gangan. *c* **950** *Lindisf. Gosp.* Matt. xii. 14 Huu hine mæhtes to lose ȝedoa [Vulg. *perderent*]. *Ibid.* xxvi. 40 Ne mæhto ȝie [*c* **1160** *Hatton* ne myhte ȝe] ane tid wæcca mec mið? *c* **1000** ÆLFRIC *Saints' Lives* iv. 326 And bebyriȝdon hine swa swa hie selost mihton on. **11..** *O.E. Chron.* an. 1066 (MS. C), þet hi ne micte þa brigge oferstiȝan. *c* **1175** *Lamb. Hom.* 129 And ne mehten þer naleng etstonden. *c* **1250** *Prov. Ælfred* 31 in *O.E. Misc.* 104 How ye myhte [*c* **1275** we miȝtin] worldes wrþsipes welde. **1390** GOWER *Conf.* II. 202 Wher thei the profit mihten cacche. *c* **1449** PECOCK *Repr.* III. i. 279 That in tho citees the peple of clerkis myȝten..dwelle. **1470–85** MALORY *Arthur* IV. v. 125 He was so heuy that an C men myght not lyfte hyt vp. **1508** DUNBAR *Flyting w. Kennedie* 468 Thay micht haue tane the collum at the last. **1590** SPENSER *F.Q.* I. iv. 27 Two iron Coffers..full as they might hold. **1596** DALRYMPLE tr. *Leslie's Hist. Scot.* I. 93 That.. quhen thay walde thay my[t] schote..a darte.

β. **mought** (mɔʊt). Now *dial.* and in regional English (esp. Black English) in the U.S. (This form had an extensive literary currency in the 16th and 17th c.; it is often difficult to distinguish from the archaic MOTE *v.*, which was by confusion frequently written *mought*.) Forms: 1–2 **muhte**, 4–5 **moht**, **moȝt(e**, **moghte**, **mouȝt**, **mowcht**, **muȝt**, **mught**, 4–6 **moght**, **mocht**, (4 **mouht**, **moucht(e**, **mouthe**, **mouct(h)e**, **mowcte**, 5 **mowȝt**, **mouth**, **mowth**, 6 **moughte**, 8 **mucht**, 9 **mowt**, **mout**, **mught**), 6– **mought**. Also *2nd pers. sing.* 6–7 **mought(e)st**; *pl.* 1–2 **muhton**, **-en**, 4 **moȝten**, etc.

O.E. Chron. an. 992 (MS. E), ȝif hi muhton þone here ahwær betræþþen. *Ibid.* an. 1004 He þa ȝegaderode his fyrde diȝlice swa he swyðost muhte. *Ibid.* an. 1140 þa hi ne leng ne muhten þolen þa stali hi ut & fluȝen. *a* **1300** *Cursor M.* 2085 He liued lelly quylist he moȝt. *Ibid.* 14830 And quar-for sent ye yow..Bot for to tak him if yee moght [*Trin.* mouȝt]? **13..** *Gaw. & Gr. Knt.* 1953 þay maden as mery as any men moȝten. *c* **1375** *Cursor M.* 12686 (Fairf.) His knes ware bolned squa þat he muȝt vnneþes ga. *c* **1375** *Sc. Leg. Saints* iii. (*Andreas*) 890 þat mycht na man..Sa wel do as he mowcht. *c* **1400** *Cursor M.* 23223 (Edinb.) Quil þou mouht turn þin hand about, it sud worise wit-outen dout. *c* **1450** *Ibid.* 16538 (Laud) They seid it not mowth. *c* **1475** *Rauf Coilȝear* 492, I vndertuk thay suld be brocht, This day for ocht that be mocht. **1488** *Anc. Cal. Rec. Dublin* (1889) I. 493 A yeman..keste a spere into the see..as far as he moghte. *a* **1529** SKELTON *Col. Cloute* 581 They mought be better aduysed Then to be so dysgysed. *a* **1557** MRS. M. BASSET tr. *More's Treat. Passion* M.'s Wks. 1310/1 The traytour mought haue caused hym and hys dysciples to bee taken. **1565** TURBERV. *Epit.* etc. 25 b, Thou hast fled the place.. Where thou moughtst chat with me thy fill. **1590** SPENSER *F.Q.* I. i. 42 So sound he slept, that nought mought him awake. **1605** BACON *Adv. Learn.* II. Introd. §8 Wher such as were so disposed, mought give themselves to Histories. **1638** QUARLES *Emblems*, *Hierogl.* vii. (1639) 347 There was no Cave-begotten damp that mought Abuse her beams. **1690** in Wolseley *Marlborough* II. 212 Soe that the garisons mought pay for what they take. **1718** RAMSAY *Christ's Kirk Gr.* III. xv, He..Ca'd her a jade, and said she mucht 'Gae hame'. **1810** S. GREEN *Reformist* I. 88 You mought as well, Sir, ax for one of their lives. **1849** C. BRONTË *Shirley* viii, I mught as weel tell him that at t'same time. **1872** SCHELE DE VERE *Americanisms* 508 In North Carolina '*it mout be*' is a standing phrase for perhaps. **1885** TENNYSON *Spinster's Sweet-arts* vii, Or I mowt 'a liked tha as well. **1885** MISS MURFREE *Prophet Gt. Smoky Mts.* i. 27 They mought jounce round hyar ez ef they war bereft o' reason. **1927** A. P. RANDOLPH in A. Dundes *Mother Wit* (1973) 203 You can't 'speck des 'nigger' bosses to speak up for our rights when it mought cos dey jobs. **1933** J. M. BREWER in *Ibid.* 248/2 Yuh mought as well die wid de chills. **1938** M. K. RAWLINGS *Yearling* 144 Mought be, we'll find 'em in a pen some'eres.

†**5.** *Present Participle. Obs.* Forms: 1 **maȝende**, *Kent.* **meȝende**, 4 **mowende**, 5 **mouwynge**, **mowing**, **-yng**, 6 **maeyinge**.

8.. *Kent. Glosses* in Wr.-Wülcker 61/1 *Nec ualens*, na meȝende. *c* **1000** ÆLFRIC *Gram.* (Z.) 251 *Quiens*, maȝende. **1382** WYCLIF *Prov.* vii. 11 Ne mowende in the hous abide stille with hir feet. *c* **1440** LOVE *Bonavent. Mirr.* liv. 109 Peter..noght mouwynge reste. *c* **1450** *Mirour Saluacioun* 2672 Noght mowing dye in realle clothis of his deitee. **1487** *Will Knight* (Somerset Ho.), Not mowyng for hastynesse of

deth to reforme his testament. **1556** *Aurelio & Isab.* (1608) M ix, Maeyinge suffer no more the loue & deathe of Aurelio.

†**6.** *Past Participle. Obs.* Forms: 5 **mowed, mowte, mow(e, myght,** 6 **mought.**

c **1400** MAUNDEV. (1839) xxix. 298 Wee wolde han gon toward the Trees..ȝif wee had myght. *c* **1420** LYDG. *Assembly of Gods* 1951, I wold haue be thens, yef I had mowte. **1440** in *Wars Eng. in France* (Rolls) II. 454 Whiche was not lyke mowed to be borne. **1490** CAXTON *How to Die* 7 Whan the deuyll hath not mowe ne can not induce the man to goo oute of the fayth. *c* **1500** *Melusine* 27 Thenne he had nat mow say one only word. *c* **1510** MORE *Picus* Wks. 7/2 Ye haue mought oftentimes, & yet maie desceyue me.

†**7.** *Verbal sb.* MOWING, q.v. *Obs.*

B. Signification and uses.

I. As a verb of complete predication.

†**1.** *intr.* To be strong; to have power or influence; to prevail (*over*). With adv., (*it*) ***may well with***: (it) can well support or endure. ***if I may***: if I have any power in the matter; hence, if I can avoid or prevent it. *Obs.*

In OE. *ic mæȝ wel* = I am in good health. [So MHG. *ich mag wol.*]

c **825** *Vesp. Psalter* ix. 20 Aris dryhten ne meȝ mon [Vulg. *non prævaleat homo*]. *c* **1000** *Sax. Leechd.* I. 300 Heo mæȝ wið maneȝa untrumnyssa. *c* **1000** ÆLFRIC *Gen.* xxix. 6 Þa cwæð he: Hu mæȝ he? Hiȝ cwædon þæt he wel mihte. **1154** *O.E. Chron.* an. 1137 (MS. E), Hi..ræueden munekes & clerekes & æuric man other þe ouer myhte. *c* **1200** ORMIN 8043 þatt ifell gast maȝȝ oferr þa þatt follȝhenn barrness þæwess. *c* **1375** *Cursor M.* 5869 (Fairf.) þai salle for-soþ if atte I may, wirk ij dayes werk a-pon a day. *c* **1386** CHAUCER *Frankl. T.* 690 My body at the leeste way Ther shal no wight defoulen, if I may. **1393** LANGL. *P. Pl.* C. XIII. 191 Lynne-seed and lik-seed..Aren nouht so worthy as whete, ne so wel mowen In þe feld with þe forst. **1398** TREVISA *Barth. De P. R.* XII. xxvii. (1495) 429 The kite is a byrde that maye well wyth traueylle. *Ibid.* XVIII. lxxxi. 833 Shepe that haue longe taylles may worse wyth wynter than those that haue brode taylles. *c* **1430** *Pol. Rel. & L. Poems* 197/93 For & þou ouer me myȝtist, as y ouer þee may.

†**b.** With cognate obj. (*might, power*). *Obs.*

a **1300** *Cursor M.* 7708 He him soght Wit all þe mightes [*Gött.* miht] þat he moght. *Ibid.* 18064 He þat suilkins mightes moght. *c* **1375** BARBOUR *Bruce* III. 366 God help him, that all mychtis may! *c* **1470** HENRY *Wallace* III. 396 For all the power thai mocht.

II. As an auxiliary of predication; with a following simple inf., or with ellipsis of this.

May shares with various other auxiliary vbs. (as *can, will, shall*) the characteristic that the inflected past subjunctive (though coinciding formally with the past indicative) retains its original functions. Like other past subjunctives, *might* is frequently used in a sense which differs from that of the present form not temporally but modally (partly corresponding to the 'present conditional' of Romanic grammar). The fact that *might* thus admits of three different meanings is sometimes productive of ambiguity, which has to be avoided by recourse to some different form of expression. Further, *may* agrees with certain other auxiliaries in having no pa. pple.; hence its pa. t. is used with a following perfect infinitive where logical correctness would require the plupf. tense (ind. or subj.) of the auxiliary followed by a present infinitive. Thus, in sense 3 below, *he might do* may be paraphrased either 'he was free to do' or 'he would be free to do'; and *he might have done* = either 'he had been free to do' or 'he would have been free to do'.

2. Expressing ability or power; = CAN *v.*[1] 4. *Obs.* exc. *arch.*

9.. *Durham Admon.* in *O.E. Texts* 176 ȝif men ferlice wyrde unsofte, oððe sprecan ne maeȝe. *c* **1175** *Cott. Hom.* 229 Ne michti hi alle hin acwelle. ȝef he sylf nold. *c* **1200** *Trin. Coll. Hom.* 185 Swo muchel muriðe is in þe bureh of heuene, þat eie ne maiȝ swo muchel biholden. **1297** R. GLOUC. (Rolls) 349 Corineus..so strong was of honde..him ne miȝte no man ne no geant at stonde. **1340** HAMPOLE *Pr. Consc.* 577 A best þat men Lynx calles, þat may se thurgh thik stane walles. *c* **1386** CHAUCER *Can. Yeom. Prol.* 128 We mowen nat..It ouer-take, it slit awey so faste. *c* **1440** *Gesta Rom.* xxxi. 115 (Harl. MS.) The Oynementes shal lose his tethe, In so muche that he shalle not mow fight ayenste the lenger. **1480** CAXTON *Chron. Eng.* cxxvii. 106 Charged with as moche gold and syluer as we mowe bere bitwene our handes. **1530** PALSGR. 670/1 He..shotte at me as harde as he myght drive. **1582** BENTLEY *Mon. Matrones* ii. 14 No man may separate me from thee. **1627** DRAYTON *Nymphidia* (1753) II. 460 Thy mighty strokes who may withstand? **1857** [see 9 a].

3. Expressing objective possibility, opportunity, or absence of prohibitive conditions; = CAN *v.*[1] 6. Now with mixture of sense 5.

c **888** K. ÆLFRED *Boeth.* xviii. §2 (Sedgefield) 42 Hu maȝ ðær..synderlice anes rices monnes nama cuman? *c* **975** *Rushw. Gosp.* Mark ii. 4 Hi ne mæhtun ȝebringan hine him for menȝo. *c* **1175** *Lamb. Hom.* 15 ȝe hit maȝen witen iwis þet hit is al for ure sunne. **1297** R. GLOUC. (Rolls) 9 Plente me may in engelond of alle gode ise. **1386** CHAUCER *Prol.* 301 But al þat he myghte of his freendes hente, On..lernyng he it spente. *c* **1400** MAUNDEV. (1839) ii. 10 Cedre may not, in Erthe ne in Watre, rote. *c* **1450** *Merlin* i. 22 'Alle these thynges', quod Merlyn, 'ne mowe the hynder in body, ne in sowle'. **1481** E. PASTON in *P. Lett.* III. 278 Lete me have knowlache of ȝour mynde..whan ȝe shall moun be in this cuntre. **1526** *Pilgr. Perf.* (W. de W. 1531) 5 b, For the lawe myght not delyuer them. **1623** WEBSTER *Duchess Malfi* III. i, A Count! he's a meere sticke of sugar-candy, (You may looke quite thorough him). **1678** BUNYAN *Pilgr.* I. 64 And when thou comest there, from thence,..thou maist see to the Gate of the Cœlestial City. **1781** COWPER *Hope* 209 A soldier may be anything, if brave. **1833** TENNYSON *Two Voices* 303 He knows a baseness in his blood At such strange war with something good, He may not do the thing he would. **1884** 'H. CONWAY' *Bound Together* I. 55 Different people may hold different opinions as to whether life is pleasanter in large cities or small towns. **1903** D. MCLEAN *Stud. Apostles* iv. 58 You may force fruit, but you cannot force flavour.

¶**b.** The pa. t. indicative in this sense (*he might* = 'he had opportunity to', 'it was possible for him to') is, exc. in actual or virtual obliqua oratio, now obsolete, on account of the tendency to interpret *might* as subjunctive. In poetry *might* was sometimes nearly equivalent to 'did'.

This use is strikingly characteristic of the style of Gibbon, as is also that explained under 5 c; it is often difficult to determine which of the two senses he intended.

a **1450** *Knt. de la Tour* 23 She was a ladi of Fraunce, that might spende more thanne fyue hundred pounde bi yeere. **1515** BP. WEST in Ellis *Orig. Lett.* Ser. III. I. 182 He that in a lytell tyme past myght spend a hundreth poundes by yere, may nott att thys day spend xx[ti]. **1563** B. GOOGE *Eglogs*, etc. (Arb.) 109 And there I might discerne the Byrds that songe in euery tree. **1588** SHAKS. *L.L.L.* v. ii. 92 Toward that shade I might behold addrest, The King and his companions. **1676** G. TOWERSON *Decalogue* 384 In the infancy of the world such a practice might be..necessary to the peopling of it. **1781** GIBBON *Decl. & F.* xxx. (1828) IV. 51 But the reign of Stilicho drew towards its end; and the proud minister might perceive the symptoms of his approaching disgrace.

c. Of an event or state of things.

a **1300** *Cursor M.* 18964 Hu..mai it be, þat vr langage spek þai þus? **1390** GOWER *Conf.* III. 330 Bot thei him tolde it mai noght be. **1449** *Will Dolman* (Somerset Ho.), After the discrecyon of myne Executors as þe shal mow seme most..expedient. **1590** SPENSER *F.Q.* I. vi. 39 'Ah! dearest Lord', (quoth she) 'how might that bee, And he the stoutest knight that ever wonne?' **1896** *Law Times* C. 508/2 One third, as nearly as may be, of the vestrymen first elected.

d. const. passive inf.

8.. *Kent. Glosses* in Wr.-Wülcker 56/27 *Et..non ualent comparari*, and ne maȝon bion wiðmetene. *c* **1290** *Magdalena* 102 in *S. Eng. Leg.* 465 Iudas..seide 'it mai beon i-sold ful deore to bugge with muchel mete'. **1340** HAMPOLE *Pr. Consc.* 1194 Worldes worshepe may be cald Noght elles but vanite. *c* **1386** CHAUCER *Pars. T.* ¶213 Ther is noon oother name..by which a man may be saued but oonly Ihesus. **1470–85** MALORY *Arthur* II. xv. 93 A bedde arayed with clothe of gold the rychest that myghte be thought. *c* **1560** A. SCOTT *Poems* ii. 95 Thair wes no deth mycht be devynd. **1563** *Homilies* II. *Excess of Apparel* (1859) 309 With whose traditions we may not be led, if we give ear to St. Paul. *a* **1648** LD. HERBERT *Hen. VIII* (1683) 480 We have done nothing that may not be abiden by. **1741** WATTS *Improv. Mind* ii. §1 When this observation relates to anything that immediately concerns ourselves..it may be called Experience. **1800** WORDSW. *Michael* 481 The remains Of the unfinished Sheep-fold may be seen Beside the boisterous brook of Greenhead Ghyll.

†**e.** Coupled with *can. Obs.*

1154 *O.E. Chron.* an. 1137 (MS. E), I ne can ne i ne mai tellen alle þe wunder. *c* **1380** WYCLIF *Wks.* (1880) 116 Wise clerkis..þat myȝten, couden, and wolden teche þe peple þe gospel. *c* **1386** CHAUCER *Knt.'s T.* 1454 Now helpe me, lady, sith ye may and kan. **1486** in *Four C. Eng. Lett.* (1880) 7 Or ellis resorte ageyn to seintuary, if he can or maie.

†**f.** In ME. poetry often in the formula ***as ye may hear*** (or *lere*), where *shall* would now be used.

c **1250** *Doomsday* 74 in *O.E. Misc.* 166 Wið þe sunfule also ȝe mahen ihere Goð awariede gostes feondes ifere. *c* **1330** *Assump. Virg.* 4 (B.M. MS.) ȝif ȝe wille to me here, Off owre ladi ȝe mai lere. *c* **1425** *Seven Sag.* (P.) 457 [She] went into a chambyr i-fere, And full evyly, as ȝe mowe hyre.

†**g.** occas. *might* = was 'fit' to. *Obs.*

14.. *Pol. Rel. & L. Poems* 279/138 Here tendre hert myth breste on iij Quan she sau here sone fre On rode hys lyf lete.

h. In poetry, *might* is sometimes used to express past habit = used to, 'would'.

1819 KEATS *Lamia* 18 And in those meads where sometimes she might haunt, Were strewn rich gifts.

i. *might* (subj.) is often used *colloq.* (*a*) with pres. inf. to convey a counsel or suggestion of action, or a complaint that some action is neglected; (*b*) with perf. inf. to express a complaint that some not difficult act of duty or kindness has been omitted.

1864 MEREDITH *Emilia* xxv, 'I dare say he dined early in the day', returned Emilia... 'Yes, but he might laugh, all the same.' **1894** G. M. FENN *In Alpine Valley* I. 147 'They might have offered to help us..' said Aunt Ecclesia, pettishly.

4. Expressing permission or sanction: To be allowed (to do something) by authority, law, rule, morality, reason, etc.

a **1000** *Last Judgment* 3 (Gr.) Oft mæȝ se þe wile in his sylfes sefan soð ȝeþencan. *c* **1000** *Ags. Gosp.* Luke xvi. 2 Ne miht þu lencg tun-scire bewitan. *a* **1225** *Ancr. R.* p. xxiv, Of þe þinges þe ȝe mahen underuon & hwet þinges ȝe mahen witen oðer habben. *c* **1430** LYDG. *Compl. Bl. Knt.* vi, Who-so that wolde frely mighte goon Into this park. *c* **1449** PECOCK *Repr.* I. xx. 120 Where is it in Holi Scripture groundid..that men schulden or miȝten lauȝwe? **1470–85** MALORY *Arthur* I. i. 35 And yf he wille not come at your somons thenne may ye do your best. **1550** CROWLEY *Last Trumpet* 397 Thou maist not grudge or repine Agaynst thy kynge in any wise. **1579** SPENSER *Sheph. Cal.* April 91 Pan may be proud, that euer he begot such a Bellibone. *c* **1622** FORD, etc. *Witch Edmonton* I. ii, He likes Kate well. I may tell you, I think she likes him as well. **1646** J. HALL *Horæ Vac.* 129 Illusory deceits may not bee done though to a good end. **1653** H. MORE *Conject. Cabbal.* (1662) 28 Justice did but (if I may so speak) play and sport together in the businesse. **1781** COWPER *Conversat.* 293 An argument of cogence, we may say, Why such a one should keep himself away. **1784** *Lett. Honoria & Marianne* III. 115 If one..considers the motives which influence to it, we may indeed be amazed. **1818** CRUISE *Digest* (ed. 2) III. 114 The grantor says, you may go in this particular line, but I do not give you a right to go either on the right or left. **1852** THACKERAY *Esmond* III. xiii, May we take your coach to town? I saw it in the hangar.

¶**b.** *Law.* In the interpretation of statutes, it has often been ruled that *may* is to be understood as equivalent to *shall* or *must*.

1728 SKINNER *K.B. Rep.* 370 For *may* in the Case of a publick Officer is tantamount to *shall.* **1782** ATKYNS *Chancery Rep.* III. 166 The words *shall and may* in general acts of parliament, or in private constitutions, are to be construed imperatively, they *must* remove them. **1873** BLACKBURN in *Law Rep.*, *8 Q.B.* 482 There is no doubt that 'may', in some instances, especially where the enactment relates to the exercise of judicial functions, has been construed to give a power to do the act, leaving no discretion as to the exercise of the power.

5. Expressing subjective possibility, i.e. the admissibility of a supposition.

a. (with pres. inf.) In relation to the future (*may* = 'perhaps will').

c **1205** LAY. 31098 þurh hire þu miht biwinnen lufe of hire cunnen. *a* **1300** *Cursor M.* 11963 Vr neghburs mai [*Fairf.* wil, *Trin.* wol] þam on vs wreke. *c* **1369** CHAUCER *Dethe Blaunche* 556 And telleth me of youre sorwes smerte Paravnture hit may ease youre herte. *a* **1450** *Knt. de la Tour* (1868) 88 What harmes and inconueinences mow come therof to the foule body. *a* **1533** LD. BERNERS *Huon* xci. 311 Yf ye go not to my brother for socoure ye may happe to repent it. **1592** SHAKS. *Rom. & Jul.* III. iv. 25 It may be thought we held him carelesly, Being our kinsman, if we reuell much. **1621** FLETCHER *Wild Goose Chase* IV. ii, Stick to that truth, and it may chance to save thee. **1677** FELTHAM *Resolves* I. lxxi. 109 Miseries, that but may come, they anticipate and send for. **1711** STEELE *Spect.* No. 95 ¶5 The Improvement of our Understandings may, or may not, be of Service to us, according as it is managed. **1871** MORLEY *Voltaire* (1886) 10 The violent activity of a century of great change may end in a victory.

b. (with pres. inf.) In relation to the present (*may be* or *do* = 'perhaps is' or 'does').

1390 GOWER *Conf.* I. 48 Ther is manye of yow Faitours, and so may be that thow Art riht such on. *a* **1400** *Relig. Pieces fr. Thornton MS.* 2 Perawnter þe defaute may be in thaym þat hase þaire saules for to kepe. **1707** CHAMBERLAYNE *St. Gt. Brit.* III. xi. 428 The next thing remarkable in the City of London, may be the Bridge. **1751** *Affecting Narr. Wager* 8 What I have said may seem oddly introduced here. **1855** M. ARNOLD *Summer Night* 84 A tinge, it may be, of their silent pain. **1875** JOWETT *Plato* (ed. 3) I. 463, I dare say, my friend, that you may be right.

c. In the 18th c. it was common to use *might be* or *do* in the sense of 'perhaps was' or 'did'. This is now rare.

The now current form *may have been* or *done* (5 d) is more logical, as the subjective possibility is a matter of the speaker's present.

1753 RICHARDSON *Grandison* (1811) II. xxix. 297 Your father, my dear, (but you might not know that,) could have absolved you from this promise. **1762** HURD *Lett. Chiv. & Rom.* 85 After all, these two respectable writers might not intend the mischief they were doing. *c* **1789** GIBBON *Autobiog.* (1896) 258 After the publication of my Essay, I revolved the plan of a second work; and a secret Genius might whisper in my ear that [etc.]. **1834** *Tracts for Times* No. 22. p. 3 All along the whole length of the garden (which might be perhaps nearly one hundred yards)..he had fixed ..stakes. **1862** BORROW *Wild Wales* xcv, It might be about half-past two in the afternoon when I left Lampeter.

d. (with perf. inf.) In relation to the past (***may have been*** or ***done*** = 'perhaps was' or 'did', 'perhaps has been' or 'done').

1682 PRIDEAUX *Lett.* (1875) 131 It is not Alestre, ye book-sellers son, whom you may have known. **1860** R. WILLIAMS in *Ess. & Rev.* 91 Reverence, or deference, may have prevented him from bringing his prayers into entire harmony with his criticisms. **1879** MISS BRADDON *Cloven Foot* xxxii, The husband, or lover, may have been out of the way.

6. Uses of the pa. t. subj. (in any of the senses 2–5) in the statement of a rejected hypothesis (or a future contingency deemed improbable) and its consequences.

a. in the protasis. (In poetry, sometimes with inversion: ***might I*** = ***if I might.***)

a **1175** *Cott. Hom.* 233 Mihti efre isi, Na ȝewold ham selfe to biȝeten wrldlic echte. *c* **1200** ORMIN 5160 ȝiff patt tu mihhtesst lufenn Godd Swa þatt itt wære himm cweme Wiþþutenn lufe off iwhillc mann. Þa mihhtesst tu ben borrȝhenn Wiþþutenn lufe off iwhillc mann. *a* **1300** *Cursor M.* 4123 To stint wald he, if he moght, þe foly þat his breþer thoght. **1470** *Gaw. & Gol.* 422 Gif pament or praier mught mak that purchese. **1579** SPENSER *Sheph. Cal.* March 53 Mought her necke bene joynted attones, She shoulde have neede no more spell. **1594** MARLOWE & NASH *Dido* III. iii, And mought I liue to see him sacke rich Thebes..Then would I wish me with Anchises Tombe. **1607** SHAKS. *Timon* I. ii. 90 Might we haue that happinesse..we should thinke our selues for euer perfect. **1617** HIERON *Wks.* II. 88 Dauid ..mought he haue had his choise..no doubt he would rather haue had one little drop of mercy. **1807** BYRON *Hours of Idleness*, Oh! might I kiss those eyes of fire, A million scarce would quench desire.

b. in the apodosis, *might* = would be able to, would be allowed to, would perhaps.

c **888** K. ÆLFRED *Boeth.* VII. §iii. (Sedgefield) 17 ðif þæt þine aȝne welan wæron þe þu mændest þæt þu forlure, ne meahtest þu hi na forleosan. *c* **1200** [see a]. *c* **1374** CHAUCER *Compl. Mars* 205 Yf that Ielosie hyt knewe They myghten lyghtly ley her hede to borowe. **1470–85** MALORY *Arthur* IV. xxii. 148 For and he wold haue foughte on foote he myghte haue had the better of the ten knyghtes. **1664** J. WILSON *Projectors* I, You mought have come up a pair of stairs higher if you had pleas'd. **1697** DRYDEN *Virg. Georg.* IV. 704 A Fault which easie Pardon might receive, Were Lovers Judges, or cou'd Hell forgive. **1764** FOOTE *Mayor of Garratt* I. (1783) 24 If the war had but continued awhile, I don't know what mought ha' been done. **1875** TENNYSON *Q. Mary* I. iii, So you would honour my poor house to-night, We might enliven you. **1895** R. L. DOUGLAS in *Bookman*

Oct. 23/1 Had he but shown a little more firmness and astuteness, he might have secured infinitely better terms than he did.

c. with suppressed protasis.

971 *Blickl. Hom.* 69 To hwon sceolde þeos smyrenes þus beon to lore ȝedon? eaþe heo mehte beon ȝeseald to þrim hunde peneȝa. *c* **1230** *Hali Meid.* 3 Fleschliche þohtes, þat.. maken þe to þenchen.. Hu muche god mihte of inker streon maxen. **1350** *Will. Palerne* 5354 No tong miȝt telle þe twentiþe parte Of þe mede to menstrales þat mene time was ȝeue. **1362** LANGL. *P. Pl.* A. v. 21 Of þis Matere I mihte Momele ful longe. **1477** EARL RIVERS (Caxton) *Dictes* 1 Werkes that myght be most acceptable to hym. **1576** FLEMING *Panopl. Epist.* 257, I my selfe seeme to.. consume the time, which otherwise on my booke mought be employed. **1595** SHAKS. *John* I. i. 123 Your father might haue kept This calfe.. from all the world. **1621** BP. MOUNTAGU *Diatribæ* 93 Diuers haue.. protested against the taking or holding Parsonages as Lay-fees, when they mought haue had them vpon good Purchase. **1796** HUNTER tr. *St.-Pierre's Stud. Nat.* (1799) I. 477 The same doubts might be started, respecting the nature of Water. **1809** MALKIN *Gil Blas* VI. i. ¶14 Three figures such as ours might have dumbfounded a better man. **1845** M. PATTISON *Ess.* (1889) I. 15 In the sixth century.. a conscientious bishop might be truly said to place his life in jeopardy every hour. **1860** R. WILLIAMS in *Ess. & Rev.* 92 *note*, One might ask, whether the experience of our two latest wars encourages our looking to Germany. **1891** *Speaker* 2 May 533/1 The book is very much what might have been expected from the author.

¶**d.** In the perfect tense *have* was sometimes dropped.

1440 in *Wars Eng. in France* (Rolls) II. 450 And it had ben wel gouverned, [it] might many a yeere susteyned youre werres. **1525** LD. BERNERS *Froiss.* II. 402 He might wel escaped, if he had wolde.

7. In questions, *may* with inf. is sometimes substituted for the indicative of the principal vb. to render the question less abrupt or pointed.

15.. *Kyng & Hermyt* 143 in Hazl. *E.P.P.* I. 19 The wey to the towne if I schuld wynd, How fer may it be? *a* **1721** PRIOR *Phillis's Age* 1 How old may Phillis be, you ask. **1798** WORDSW. *We are seven* 14 Sisters and brothers, little maid, How many may you be? **1886** W. J. TUCKER *E. Europe* 401 'What may you want with our schoolmaster?'

b. Similarly *might*.

1599 MASSINGER, etc. *Old Law* V. i, And which might be your faire Bride sir? **1630** DEKKER *2nd Pt. Honest Wh.* V. ii, What mought I call your name, pray?

8. As an auxiliary of the subjunctive mood.

a. Since the desire for an end involves the desire for the possibility of the end, *may* in sense 3 in combination with an inf. is used, in clauses involving the idea of purpose or contemplated result, to express virtually the same meaning as the subjunctive of the principal verb. Hence this combination has come to serve as a periphrastic subjunctive, which has in ordinary prose use superseded the simple subjunctive in final clauses.

(*a*) in final clauses introduced by *that* or *lest*; also occas. with ellipsis of *that* (e.g. after *to the end*).

c **900** tr. *Bæda's Hist.* II. i. (Schipper) 107 Onfoh þu eorþe lichaman of þinum lichaman ȝenumen, þæt þu hine eft aȝyfan mæȝe, þonne hine God liffæste. *c* **950** *Lindisf. Gosp.* Mark iii. 10 Hia raesdon on him þætte hine hie ȝehrindon *vel* hrina mæhtæs. *a* **1175** *Cott. Hom.* 229 þa wercte he fele wundra þat men mihten ȝelefen þat he was godes bearn. *c* **1275** *Sinners Beware* 30 in *O.E. Misc.* 73 Makie we us clene and skere þat we englene ivere Mawe beon. *a* **1300** *Cursor M.* 14578 þat agh þe drau þe folk emid, þat þai þe baþ mai se and here. **1422** tr. *Secreta Secret., Priv. Priv.* 205 Youre lyght so lyght afore men that thay mowen See youre goode workys. **1540–1** ELYOT *Image Gov.* 2, I wysshed that it had been published in suche a tounge, that moe men mought understande it. **1559** [see LEST 1 c]. **1652** J. WRIGHT tr. *Camus' Nat. Paradox* VIII. 176 To the end by his return thou maist give o'r complaining. **1751** JOHNSON *Rambler* No. 170 ¶7 Lest my appearance might draw too many compliments. **1807** *Med. Jrnl.* XVII. 342, I took several children to see the woman.. that they might behold the nature of the disease.

(*b*) in relative clauses with final meaning.

c **1220** *Bestiary* 627 in *O.E. Misc.* 20 For he ne hauen no lið ðat he muȝen risen wið. *c* **1250** *Gen. & Ex.* 573 Al-miȝtin god him bad it so, And mete quorbi ðei miȝten liuen. *c* **1375** *Sc. Leg. Saints* XXXV. (*Thadee*) 127 Scho.. lefit a hole quhare men mocht reke hyre mete, as þame thocht. **1638** LISLE *A.S. Monum., Lord's P.* T 3 b, Whereby they mought the better serue their God. *c* **1645** HOWELL *Lett.* (1726) 8 Then let me something bring May Handsel the new year to Charles my king. **1751** JOHNSON *Rambler* No. 170 ¶3 My mother sold some of her ornaments to dress me in such a manner as might secure me from contempt. **1849** MACAULAY *Hist. Eng.* ii. I. 201 It was not easy to devise any expedient which might avert the danger.

(*c*) in clauses depending on such vbs. as *wish, demand, desire, beseech*, and their allied sbs.

c **1000** ÆLFRIC *Hom.* (Th.) I. 152 Hwæt wylt ðu þæt ic þe do? He cwæð, Drihten, þæt ic mæȝe ȝeseon. **1390** GOWER *Conf.* I. 10 Unto the god ferst thei besoughten.. That thei mihten fle the vice Which Simon hath in his office. **1432** *Paston Lett.* I. 32 The said Erle desireth.. that he may putte hem from.. occupacion of the Kinges service. **1546** *St. Papers Hen. VIII*, XI. 162 Wischyng that, if yt shall so happen, I mought be agaynst that tyme ready armyd. **1549** *Bk. Com. Prayer, Coll. 1st Sund. after Epiph.*, Graunt that they maie both perceaue and knowe what thinges they ought to do. **1610** SHAKS. *Temp.* I. ii. 168 Would I might But euer see that man. **1670** J. SMITH *Eng. Improv. Reviv'd* 13 It is my great request to God that there might not be one Family in England want bread. **1771** [see 9 a]. **1781** COWPER *Conversat.* 124 He humbly hopes—presumes—it may be so. **1834** *Tracts for Times* No. 22. p. 11, I desired he might come to me into my Study. **1849** MACAULAY *Hist. Eng.* v. I. 572 He.. demanded that a large vessel.. might be detained.

(*d*) in clauses (introduced by *that, lest*) depending on *fear* vb. or sb., *afraid*, and the like.

1563 *Homilies* II. (1859) 375 Continually to fear, not only that we may fall as they did [etc.]. **1606** G. W[OODCOCKE] *Hist. Ivstine* III. 19 Fearing, least if the Lacedemonians shoulde be the first that violated the league, they might haue seized thereupon. **1651** C. CARTWRIGHT *Cert. Relig.* I. 67 Be not highminded, but fear.. least thou also maist be cut off. **1691** [see FEAR *v.* 4 b]. **1816** [see AFRAID 2 c].

b. In exclamatory expressions of wish, *may* with the inf. is synonymous with the simple pres. subj., which (exc. *poet.* and *rhet.*) it has superseded.

The subject normally follows *may*, but examples are found in the older lang. in which this is not so.

1586 MARLOWE *1st Pt. Tamburl.* I. i, Long liue Cosroe, mighty Emperour! *Cosr.* And Ioue may neuer let me longer liue Then I may seeke to gratifie your loue! **1593** SHAKS. *Ven. & Ad.* 505 Long may they kisse ech other for this cure! **1611** BIBLE *Transl. Pref.* ¶3 Long may he reigne. **1634** MILTON *Comus* 924 May thy brimmed waves for this Their full tribute never miss. **1647** *Fletcher's Woman's Prize* Prol., Which this may prove! **1712** TICKELL *Spect.* No. 410 ¶6 But let my Sons attend, Attend may they Whom Youthful Vigour may to Sin betray. **1717** *Entertainers* No. 2. 7 Much good may it do the Dissenters with such Champions. **1786** C. SIMEON in W. Carus *Life* (1847) 71 May this be your blessed experience and mine. **1840** DICKENS *Old C. Shop* viii, 'May the present moment', said Dick,.. 'be the worst of our lives!'

c. *might* is also used to express a wish, esp. when its realization is thought hardly possible.

This use appears to be developed from the hypothetical use (6 a).

a **1400–50** *Alexander* 1605 (Ashm.) 'Ay moȝt [*Dubl.* mott] he lefe, ay moȝt he lefe' quod ilka man twyse. **1596** SHAKS. *Merch. V.* II. ii. 98 Lord worshipt might he be, what a beard hast thou got. **1852** M. ARNOLD *To Marguerite, Cont'd* 18 Oh might our marges meet again!

d. *may* with the inf. of a vb. is used (instead of the simple indicative or subjunctive) to emphasize the uncertainty of what is referred to:

(*a*) in indirect questions depending on such verbs as *ask, think, wonder, doubt*, and their allied sbs.

a **1100** *Gerefa* in *Anglia* IX. 261 þæt he asece hu he yrde mæȝe fyrme ȝeforðian ðonne ðæs time sy. *c* **1205** LAY. 18753 þa ȝet hit weore a wene whar þu heo mihtes aȝe. *c* **1220** *Bestiary* 683 in *O.E. Misc.* 22 He.. weren in ðoȝt, wu he miȝten him helpen ovt. *a* **1250** *Owl & Night.* 1581 þat gode wif.. fondeth hu heo muhe [*Jesus MS.* mowe] Do þing þat him beo iduȝe. *c* **1386** CHAUCER *Clerk's T.* 53 Ne koude nat vs self deuysen how We myghte lyuen in moore felicitee. *c* **1530** LD. BERNERS *Arth. Lyt. Bryt.* (1814) 508 And than he demaunded of his seruauntes what it might be [Fr. orig. *que c'estoit qu'il auoit*]. **1795** COLERIDGE *Conciones* 62 On her enquiring what might be the price of the jewels, she is told, they were [etc.]. **1861** DASENT *Story Burnt Njal* II. 1 The Earl asked of what stock he might be.

(*b*) in clauses introduced by an indef. relative.

1530 PALSGR. 444/2 Be as be maye, *vaille que vaille*. **1605** SHAKS. *Macb.* I. iii. 146 Come what come may. *a* **1616** BEAUM. & FL. *Queen of Corinth* I. i, I am confirm'd Fall what may fall. **1690** [see HOWEVER 1 c]. **1711** ADDISON *Spect.* 46 ¶6 However weary I may go to Bed, the Noise in my Head will not let me sleep. **1782** COWPER *Hope* 596 He laughs, whatever weapon Truth may draw. **1861** M. PATTISON *Ess.* (1889) I. 37 The preceptor.. whatever his other qualifications may have been, had not earned his promotion by his Latin style. **1870** RUSKIN *Lect. Art* (1875) 102 Those of you who may intend passing their vacation in Switzerland. **1899** W. JAMES *Talks to Teachers* (1904) 57 A tactful teacher may get them to take pleasure.. in preserving every drawing or map which they may make.

9. With ellipsis of the infinitive.

a. In independent sentences, where the inf. is to be supplied from a prec. sentence; or (more freq.) in subord. clauses, where the inf. is to be supplied from the principal clause.

a **1000** *Guthlac* 1082 Aras ða eorla wynn heard hyȝesnottor, swa he hraþost meahte. *c* **1000** *Ags. Gosp.* Luke xvi. 26 þa ðe willað heonon to eow faran ne maȝon. *c* **1175** *Lamb. Hom.* 37 And helpen heom mid þon þe þu maȝe. *c* **1205** LAY. 3524 And help him nu for þu miht. *c* **1250** *Hymn* i. 38 in *Trin. Coll. Hom.* App., þu me sschild ȝe from þe feonde ase þu ert freo & wilt & maucht. *c* **1300** *Harrow. Hell* 141 Kepe þe ȝates whoso mai. **138.** WYCLIF *Sel. Wks.* III. 510 Oþere Crist myȝte ȝeve sich a reule.. and wolde not.. or ellis Crist wolde ordeyne sich a reule and myȝte not. *c* **1440** LOVE *Bonavent. Mirr.* xii. 29 Here frendes comforteden hem as þei myghten. **1470–85** MALORY *Arthur* X. xxxvi. 472 Kepe the as wel as euer thow mayst. **1513** DOUGLAS *Æneis* VI. v. 180 And fra his sorofull hart, as that he mocht, Sum deil expellit hes the dolorus cair. **1547** *Homilies* I. Of Charity II. (1859) 72 To all such we ought, as we may, to do good. **1599** SHAKS. *Hen. V*, II. i. 23 Things must be as they may. **1615** W. BEDWELL *Moham. Impost.* I. §29 *Ah.* I know not whether I may aske that question, or not. *Sh.* Yes, you may. **1689** A. ASHLEY in King *Life Locke* 183 So far was I from learning the discretion I mought by this that I grew worse than before. **1771** SMOLLETT *Humph. Cl.* 31 May, Perhaps I mistake his complaisance; and I wish I may, for his sake. **1796** HUNTER tr. *St.-Pierre's Stud. Nat.* (1799) III. 456 Be it as it may. **1805** SCOTT *Last Minstr.* II. xxiv, He joyed to see the cheerful light, And he said Ave Mary, as well as he might. **1851** E. FITZGERALD *Euphranor* (1904) 42 We think the world is growing wiser; it may in the end. **1857** M. ARNOLD *Rugby Chapel* 34 We.. have endured Sunshine and rain as we might. **1896** A. E. HOUSMAN *Shropshire Lad* v, 'Twill do harm to take my arm. 'You may, young man, you may'.

b. With ellipsis of a vb. of motion. Chiefly *poet.*

Beowulf 754 He on mode wearð forht on ferhðe; no þy ær fram meahte. *a* **1000** *Christ & Satan* 425 (Gr.) þæt ic up heonon mæȝe. **1154** *O.E. Chron.* an. 1131 (MS. E), þær man him held þæt he ne mihte na east na west. *c* **1330** *Arth. & Merl.* 7907 (Kölbing) For we no mow no whar oway. *c* **1386** CHAUCER *Reeve's T.* 197 For it was nyght and forther myghte they noght. **1590** SHAKS. *Mids. N.* III. ii. 433 That I may backe to Athens by day-light. **1596** —— *1 Hen. IV*, III. i. 142 The Moone shines faire, You may away by Night.

c. With ellipsis of *do* or *be*. Also in the phr. *I may not but* = 'There is nothing for me to do but. (Cf. sense 1.)

Beowulf 680 (Gr.) Ic hine sweorde swebban nelle.. þeah ic eal mæȝe. *a* **1000** *Christ & Satan* 22 (Gr.) Ðuhte him on mode, þæt hit mihte swa, þæt [etc.]. **1154** *O.E. Chron.* an. 1132 (MS. E), þa he nanmor ne mihte. *c* **1330** R. BRUNNE *Medit.* 522 þey bete hym.. Tyl þey be wery and mow no more. **1382** WYCLIF *Wisd.* xi. 24 Thou hast merci of alle, for alle thingus thou maist. **1390** GOWER *Conf.* I. 89 He was a man that mochel myhte. **1422** tr. *Secreta Secret., Priv. Priv.* 161 Who so will not whan he may, he shal not when he wille. *c* **1450** *Guy Warw.* (C.) 6947 He felle downe and myght no more. **1556** *Aurelio & Isab.* (1608) I ij, So muche mighte her malice, that not oneley she sinnede, but made hir husbande sinne. **1587** FLEMING *Contn. Holinshed* III. 1317/2 Much maie that was not yet. **1597** MORLEY *Introd. Mus.* 2 If it had beene the pleasure of him who may all things. **1604** SHAKS. *Oth.* III. i. 50 The Moore replies.. that in wholsome Wisedome He might not but refuse you. **1721** KELLY *Scot. Prov.* 169 He that may not as he will, must do as he may.

d. In † *be as be may, be that* (or *it* or *this*) *as it may, that is as may be*, and similar expressions: whether that is so or not, that may well be so: phrases used to indicate that a statement or act, etc., is perhaps true or right from one point of view but not from another, or that there are other factors to be taken into consideration.

c **1386** CHAUCER *Man of Law's Tale* (1894) 1012 Be as be may, ther was he at the leste. **1470–85** MALORY *Works* (1967) I. 73 Be as hit be may. **1530** [see MAY *v.*[1] 8 d (*b*)]. **1593** SHAKS. *3 Hen. VI* I. i. 194 But be it as it may: I here entayle The Crowne to thee. **1796** [see MAY *v.*[1] 9 a]. **1820** R. SOUTHEY *Let.* 17 Nov. in *N. & Q.* (1975) Sept. 400/1 Be that as it may, I wish you would let me know what books of mine you have not received from Longmans. **1834** M. EDGEWORTH *Tour in Connemara* (1950) i. 10 There goes a story, you know that no woman must ever appear at Ballinasloe Fair... Be this as it may, we were suffered to drive very quietly through the town. **1875** TROLLOPE *Way we live Now* I. xlix. 311 'Good news?' she asked... 'That's as may be,' he said. **1883** A. DOBSON *Old-World Idylls* 211 Rose kissed me to-day. Will she kiss me to-morrow? Let it be as it may, Rose kissed me to-day. **1910** GALSWORTHY *Motley* 168 'Yu'le tak' the ole 'arse then?' 'That's as mebbe —waal, gude naight.' **1928** F. HURST *President is Born* 14 Be that as it may, the circle of giving in Centralia was anything but a vicious one. **1935** G. HEYER *Death in Stocks* iv. 41 That's as may be, and if it's true you couldn't say but what it's a judgment. **1939** G. M. GATHORNE-HARDY *Fourteen Points & Treaty of Versailles* 14 The Fourteen Points.. has been described, by Mr. Winston Churchill, as 'certainly an accommodating document'. Be that as it may, it was presumably what the President had actually meant. **1949** F. MACLEAN *Eastern Approaches* I. viii. 133 If the authorities.. had received no instructions regarding my journey it could only be due to a most regrettable omission... To this he answered that this was as it might be; but without explicit instructions.. he could not allow me to remain on Chinese territory. **1949** H. PAKINGTON *Young W. Washbourne* vi. 51 'But if it was used as a sitting-out place it wouldn't be secluded,' said Mrs. Harbottle. 'That was as it might be,' retorted Mrs. Wilkins. **1958** *Economist* 1 Nov. 387/2 There have been reports of some exchange of views between these two formidable figures. Be that as it may, the manner in which their views have been made known shows a wide and characteristic difference. **1975** T. HEALD *Deadline* ii. 23 'I shall have to liaise with the police.' 'That's as may be,' said Lord Wharfedale.

10. For **may well, may as well**, see WELL *adv.*

11. as *sb.* An instance of what is expressed by the vb. *may*; a possibility.

1849 H. MILLER *Footpr. Creat.* 248 Even were we to permit the sceptic himself to fix the numbers representative of those several *mays* in the case. **1897** G. SAINTSBURY *Flourishing of Romance* ii. 30 These 'mays' are not evidence. **1935** G. K. ZIPF *Psycho-Biol. of Lang.* (1936) 303 From the great number of.. *mays* of today are taken those which are to belong to the matrix of *musts* of tomorrow.

†**12.** In advb. phrases of the same type as and equivalent in meaning to MAYHAP: **may chance, may-fall, may-fortune, may-tide.** *Obs.*

a **1300** *Cursor M.* 2759 If þou þar findes.. fifty or fourte o þi lele men, tuenti mai fall, or tuis fiue, ne sal þai alle haue þar-for liue? *Ibid.* 4977, etc. *c* **1375** BARBOUR *Bruce* IX. 376 Thai that war vithin, ma fall,.. slepit all. *c* **1460** *Towneley Myst.* vi. 81 May tyde he will oure giftis take. **1548** UDALL *Erasm. Par. John* 7 Mafortune as then ye tyme did not suffer so inexplycable a misterie to be put in wryting to all mens knowledge. **1556** HOBY *Castiglione's Courtier* Epist. (1561) Bj, Many yong gentlemen, which haue may chaunce an opinion that to be in me, that is not in deed. **1581** MULCASTER *Positions* xvi. (1887) 72 That [dancing] onely is reserued, which beareth oftimes blame, machance being corrupted by the kinde of musick.

may (meɪ), *v.*[2] *Obs.* exc. *arch.* in pr. pple. [f. MAY *sb.*[3]] *intr.* To take part in the festivities of May-day or in the pleasures of the month of May; to gather flowers in May. Cf. MAYING *vbl. sb.*

1470–85 MALORY *Arthur* XIX. i. 773 Soo as the quene had mayed and alle her knyghtes alle were bedasshed with herbys mosses and floures. **1508** DUNBAR *Gold. Targe* 131 Ladyes to dance full sobirly assayit, Endlang the lusty rywir

so thai mayit. **1848** KINGSLEY *Saint's Trag.* II. x. [ix.], Oh! that we two were Maying Over the fragrant leas.

†may, *v.*³ *Obs.* [Aphetic f. AMAY.] *trans.* To dismay. Also *intr.* To be dismayed.

c **1380** *Sir Ferumb.* 978 Ac wan Charlis hit wiste & seȝ for hymen hym gan to maye. *c* **1400** *Beryn* 1685 Full sore he gan to may. *a* **1400–50** *Alexander* 3010 Mayes [*Dubl. MS.* mayse] noȝt ȝour hertis. *Ibid.* 5399 Oure mode kyng was so maied myndles him semed. **1560** ROLLAND *Crt. Venus* II. 314 In all my dayis was I not half sa mayt.

may, dial. f. MAKE *v.*¹, var. MO *Obs.*, more.

may-: see MAI-.

‖maya ('mɑːjə), *sb.*¹ [Skr. *māyā.*] Illusion: a prominent term of Hindu philosophy.

1823 COLEBROOKE in *Trans. Roy. Asiatic Soc.* (1827) I. 30. **1827** *Ibid.* (1830) II. 39 The notion that the versatile world is an illusion (*máyá*). **1878–9** J. CAIRD *Philos. Relig.* (1880) 339 Religion..teaches us that only by looking on the world and the lust thereof as 'Maya', as illusion, vanity, deceptive appearance, can we get near to God.

Maya ('mɑːjə, 'maɪ(j)ə, 'meɪə), *sb.*² and *a.* Also 9 **Maye.** [Sp.] **A.** *sb.* **a.** A member of an ancient Indian people of Yucatan and Central America; these people collectively. **b.** The language of this people. **B.** *adj.* Of, pertaining to, or designating this people.

1825 J. CONDER *Mod. Traveller Mexico & Guatimala* I. 191 The number of these [Mexican] languages exceeds twenty, of which fourteen have grammars..tolerably complete; viz. the Mexican or Aztec, the Otomite,..the Maye or Yucatan. **1832** J. BELL *Syst. Geogr.* V. 584 In the space between the Rio del Norte and the American frontier, are the following tribes: 1. The *Tawakenoes*, on the *Rio Brassos*, 200 warriors, 800 souls;..5. *Mayes*, at the mouth of the Guadaloupe river, 200 warriors, 800 souls. **1845** *Trans. Amer. Ethnol. Soc.* I. 252 *K* has in the Maya a different sound from our *c* before *a, o, u.* **1875** H. H. BANCROFT *Native Races Pacific States* II. 117 This Maya culture. *Ibid.* 118 Yucatan was occupied in the sixteenth century by the Mayas proper. **1877** [see CHIBCHA]. **1914** T. A. JOYCE *Mexican Archæol.* viii. 202 Both divisions of this people originally spoke Maya. *Ibid.* 203 The Maya language as a whole exhibits certain points of similarity to that of the Mixtec and Zapotec. *Ibid.* xi. 282 Of the land system among the Maya we know very little. **1928** T. GANN *Discoveries Cent. Amer.* 89 The old man..knew no word of any language but Maya. *Ibid.* 206 In none of them [*sc.* cities] is the Maya arch found. **1959** E. TUNIS *Indians* 21/2 The Maya of Mexico were the only Indians who achieved a written language, with symbols that stood for individual words. **1974** *Nat. Geographic* Nov. 661 In Guatemala's lofty highlands..Maya Indians dwell amid the cloud-ripping hulks of dead and dormant volcanoes. *Ibid.*, Here live Maya-speaking Indians in villages that garland the lakeshore with a litany of saints' names.

Hence **'Mayan** *a.*, of, pertaining to, or designating the Mayas; *sb.*, one of the Mayan people, their language; **'Mayanist**, an expert in, or student of, Mayan culture.

1889 S. HALE *Mexico* viii. 82 The Mayan legends..tell of nothing but wars and conquests, struggles and defeats. **1911** *Encycl. Brit.* XVIII. 335/2 These Pipils..migrated into territories previously occupied by an older race of Mayan origin... The easternmost limit of prehistoric Mayan civilization, on the Pacific coast of Central America is Fonseca Bay. **1923** H. I. PRIESTLEY *Mexican Nation* ii, In the modern oil region along the Pánuco River and the coast, was a segregated group of Mayans. **1926** *Blackw. Mag.* Nov. 647/2 This man..was of pure Maya blood, and was filled..with old Mayan lore and tradition. **1933** E. PINCHON *Viva Villa!* x. 135 The craftsmanly and aristocratic Mayans and Tehuans of the south. **1950** *Caribbean Q.* II. II. 27 Later that year Dr. Linton Satterthwaite, Associate Curator of the Pennsylvania University Museum and a Mayanist of note, was put in touch with the writer. **1961** T. PROSKOURIAKOFF in L. Deuel *Conquistadors without Swords* (1967) xxvii. 384 We Mayanists spend an inordinate amount of time deciphering half obliterated hieroglyphic texts. **1962** L. KEMP tr. *Leon-Portilla's Broken Spears* iii. 31 By the time Cortes ransomed him from the natives eight years later he spoke Mayan fluently. **1965** B. ROSS *Mexico* i. 21 They asked him where he had obtained the cloth and the pottery? The Mayan said that it came from a land not very far away. **1968** *Listener* 11 July 53/3 They describe the attempts of Olson, newly arrived in Yucatan, to come to terms with Mayan culture. *Ibid.* 54/1 He takes off for Yucatan unprepared for his task, learning Mayan as he goes, and from inadequate books. **1973** *New Yorker* 24 Mar. 116/2 He got the word in Mayan for 'road' or 'journey'. *Ibid.* 116/3 One can thus understand the interest among Mayanists when..it was announced that a wholly unknown fourth codex had come to light. **1973** *Listener* 7 June 746/1 The Mayans..invented essentially the same way of writing large numbers as a sequence of digits that we use.

May-apple. *U.S.* [MAY *sb.*³]

1. An American herbaceous plant, *Podophyllum peltatum*, bearing a yellowish, egg-shaped fruit, which appears in May.

Called also *duck's foot, hog apple, wild lemon, mandrake.*

1733 MILLER *Gard. Dict.* (ed. 2), *Anapodophyllon*, Duck's foot, or *Pomum Maiale*, i.e. May-apple... This Plant was brought from America. **1788** J. MAY *Jrnl. & Lett.* (1873) 97, I ate frequently of the May-apple, which is of a very agreeable flavor, and resembling pine-apple. **1876** HARLEY *Mat. Med.* (ed. 6) 777 The May Apple is common..along the eastern side of North America.

2. = *honeysuckle-apple*: see HONEYSUCKLE 8.

1872 SCHELE DE VERE *Americanisms* 400 The same term of *May-Apple* is not unfrequently applied to a large, globular excrescence produced by the sting of a wasp on the miniature flowers of the Swamp Honeysuckle, and..occasionally to the shrub itself.

may-be, maybe ('meɪbiː), *adv.*, *sb.*, and *a.* Also *dial.* **mebbe, mebbies**, etc. (see E.D.D.). [Shortened from *it may be*: cf. MAY-FALL, MAYHAP, and F. *peut-être.*]

A. *adv.* Possibly, perhaps. Sometimes used like a conj. with a dependent *that* (cf. F. *peut-être que*). Also phr. ***and I don't mean maybe***: I am positive (*colloq.*).

a **1425** *Cursor M.* 17553 (Trin.) May be [*Cott.* mai fall] sum goost awey him ledde. **1599** MASSINGER, etc. *Old Law* III. ii, May-be, some fairy's child..Has pissed upon that side. **1661** GLANVILL *Van. Dogm.* 175 This, may be, was the reason some imagin'd Hell there. **1733** SWIFT *Apol.* Wks. 1755 IV. I. 209 Impossible! it can't be me. Or may be I mistook the word. **1848** THACKERAY *Lett.* 28 July, Our Lord speaking quite simply to simple Syrian people, a child or two maybe at his knees. **1866** DASENT *Gisli* 22 Maybe that others than Arnor utter this. **1871** R. ELLIS tr. *Catullus* lxii. 46 Maybe for all they chide, their hearts do inly desire thee. **1897** KIPLING *Capt. Cour.* vii. 147 Don't want nothin', 'less, mebbe, an anchor that'll hold. **1926** MAINES & GRANT *Wise-Crack Dict.* 5/1 And I don't mean maybe, jazz form of putting one's self on oath. **1930** JOYCE *Anna Livia Plurabelle* 23 I'll make it worth your while. And I don't mean maybe. **1931** E. LINKLATER *Juan in Amer.* v. v. 401 When a guy..tries to get fresh..a girl's justified in giving him the razz—and I don't mean maybe! **1933** E. CALDWELL *God's Little Acre* viii. 110 We've sunk a hole twenty feet since this morning, and I don't mean maybe, either. **1953** *Manch. Guardian Weekly* 20 Aug. 7 Except maybe a guy had been there two years. **1968** B. FOSTER *Changing Eng. Lang.* i. 30 Some years ago a song popular in this country bore the title 'Maybe', and on consulting the *O.E.D.* one finds this word described as archaic and dialectal! Yet by now it is in everyday use in Britain. **1968** *New Society* 29 Aug. 305/1 The *Oxford English Dictionary* describes 'maybe' as archaic and dialectal. But within the last generation it has been re-instated in England, obviously as a result of its popularity in the American vocabulary, where 'perhaps' is a very rare bird. Yet all this time 'maybe' (or 'mebbe') has been thriving in northern England, Scotland and Ireland. **1975** *New Yorker* 13 Jan. 36/1, I wanted to think maybe she was different now.

B. *sb.* What may be; a possibility, possible contingency.

a **1586** SIDNEY *Sonn.* in *Arcadia* etc. (1629) 525 And thus might I for feare of may be, leaue The sweet pursuit of my desired prey. **1603** N. BRETON *Post with a Mad Packet* I. xlii, May be is a doubt, but what is must be regarded. **1615** DAY *Festivals* xii. 335 Without all Maybees, the Lord is never more gracious to his Servants. **1756** *Monitor* No. 9. II. 9, I will not..be scared out of my senses by improbabilities and maybe's. **1892** A. BIRRELL *Res Judic.* vi. 168 [He] objected to our carrying on a flirtation with mystic maybe's and calling it Religion.

Proverbs (*punningly*). **1721** KELLY *Scot. Prov.*, Maybes are no aye honey-bees. **1738** SWIFT *Pol. Conversat.* i. 19 May-bees don't fly now, Miss.

C. *adj.* Which are possibly to come.

1687 DRYDEN *Hind & P.* III. 294 Those may-be years thou hast to live.

'May-bug. [MAY *sb.*³] The cockchafer; also the CHOVY.

1698 FROGER *Voy.* 48 The Colibrie is a small bird, no bigger than a May-bugg. **1712** [see COCKCHAFER]. **1774** GOLDSM. *Nat. Hist.* (1862) II. IV. vi. 542 The May-bug, or dorr-beetle. **1884** *Christian World* 18 Sept. 697/2 The sparrow..eats 'chovies', or May bugs.

May-bush. [MAY *sb.*³] **a.** A branch of hawthorn. **b.** The hawthorn or may-tree.

1579 SPENSER *Sheph. Cal.* May 34 O that I were there, To helpen the Ladyes their Maybush beare. **1597** GERARDE *Herbal* III. xxii. 1146 Many do call the tree it selfe the May bush, as a chiefe token of the comming in of May. **1598** FLORIO, *Bagaia*, the white-thorne, hawthorne tree, or landouers maie bush. **1727** W. MATHER *Yng. Man's Comp.* 126 Scandalous Sports and Pastimes, such as May-Bushes, Morris-Dancing. **1781** C. JOHNSTON *Hist. J. Juniper* II. 136 His tawney face looked just like that of a chimney-sweeper's boy peeping through his may-bush. **1861** NEALE *Notes Eccl. & Pict. Dalmatia*, etc. 164 Red May-bushes sending out their fragrance.

May-butter. [MAY *sb.*³: cf. F. *beurre de mai.*] **a.** Unsalted butter preserved in the month of May for medicinal use (see quot. 1615).

1584 COGAN *Haven Health* cxcvi. (1612) 157 Yet would I wish that such as haue children to bring vp, would not be without May butter in their houses. **1614** MARKHAM *Cheap Husb.* I. lx. 37 Take the leaues of wilde Nepe..and beating them in a mortar with May-Butter, apply it. **1615** —— *Eng. Housew.* II. iv. 113 If during the month of May before you salt your butter you saue a lumpe thereof and put it into a vessell, and so set it into the sunne the space of that moneth, you shall finde it exceeding..medicinable for wounds. **1660** M. R. *Exact Acc. Receipts* 10 A pound of May-butter. **1812** J. J. HENRY *Accurate Acct. Heroes Campaign against Quebec* 23 We gave salted pork, and they returned two fresh beaver tails, which when boiled, renewed ideas, imbibed with the May-butter of our own country.

b. In fig. and proverbial use.

1601 DEACON & WALKER *Answ. Darel* 224 Not any other but May-butter it selfe could possiblie melt in their mouthes. *a* **1625** FLETCHER *Noble Gent.* I. i, Mad as May-butter. **1653** WALTON *Angler* iv. 115 You see it rains May-butter.

maychance: see MAY *v.*¹

maycock ('meɪkɒk). *U.S.* Forms: 6 **macocqwer**, 7 **macokos, macocquer,** 8 **macoquer,** 7– **macock,** 8–9 **maycock.** [Algonquin (Powhatan dialect) *mahcawq* (vocabulary in Strachey *Virginia* 1612).] A kind of melon.

1588 T. HARIOT *Virginia* II. C 2 b, They set..Beanes and Peaze..among the seedes of Macócqwer Melden, and Planta solis. **1612** CAPT. SMITH *Map Virginia* 17 A fruit like vnto a muske millen,..which they call Macocks. **1612** STRACHEY *Virginia* (Hakl. Soc.) 119 The macokos is of the forme of our pumpeons. **1633–6** *Gerarde's Herbal* II. cccxlv. 919 Macocks Virginiani, sive Pepo Virginianus, The Virginian Macocke, or Pompion. **1681** GREW *Catal. Rarities* II. 195 The Macocquer. A Virginian Fruit. **1705** BEVERLY *Virginia* 27 Their macocks are a sort of melo-pepones, or lesser sort of pompion. **1872** SCHELE DE VERE *Americanisms* 60 The..name survives in its Anglicized form of Maycock. **1896** P. A. BRUCE *Econ. Hist. Virginia* I. 98 There were muskmelons,..macocks or squashes, gourds,..beans and pumpkins.

maycock, variant of MEACOCK.

'May-day¹. [MAY *sb.*³] **a.** The first day of May.

Ill (or *Evil*) *May-day*: 'the 1st of May, 1517, when the apprentices of London rose against the privileged foreigners, whose advantages in trade had occasioned great jealousy' (Nares).

1438 in Gross *Gild Merch.* (1890) II. 65 On Mayday the yerre of our lorde Kyng Henry þe Seixt xvi., anno Dom. 1438. **1541** *Nottingham Rec.* III. 382 Peyd for wyne on May Dey when we rode Mey. **1609** B. JONSON *Sil. Wom.* IV. ii, Out of my doors, you sons of noise and tumult, begot on an ill May-day. **1645** EVELYN *Diary* 1 May, On May-day the greate procession of the Universitie and the Mulatiers at St. Antonie's. **16..** *Songs Lond. Prentices* (Percy Soc.) 17 How Ill May-day first got the name. **1863** *Chambers's Bk. Days* I. 571/1 The observances of May Day.

b. *attrib.*, as ***May-day games, garland, morning***; **May-day sweep**, a chimney-sweeper decorated with ribbons and flowers at the London sweeps' May-day festival.

1613 SHAKS. *Hen. VIII*, v. iv. 15 'Tis as much impossible..To scatter 'em, as 'tis to make 'em sleepe On May-day Morning. **1615** HEYWOOD *Four Prentices* I. B 2 b, Hee will not let mee see a mustering, Nor in a May-day morning fetch in May. **1832** MARRYAT *N. Forster* xl, The frolic gambols of the may-day sweep. **1843** JAMES *Forest Days* iv, The May-day games of old England. **1850** GOSSE *Rivers Bible* (1878) 160 *note*, As sometimes two hoops are fastened, to carry May-day garlands.

c. *attrib.*, *spec.* of political processions, celebrations, etc., on the first day of May.

1906 [see COMMUNISM 1 b]. **1930** I. LOW *His Master's Voice* x. 120 Scaffolding began to appear in the Red Square for May Day celebrations. **1939** [see *hunger-march*]. **1973** *Listener* 9 Aug. 184 In 1890, during the first of the big May Day demonstrations, we read of trade-union branches assembling from every quarter of London.

May-day². Also **Mayday, mayday.** [Phonetic repr. of F. *m'aider* imper. inf. 'help me!', or shortening of *venez m'aider.*] An international radio-telephone signal of distress. Also *transf.* and *attrib.*

1927 *Internat. Radio Telegraph Convention* 51 Rules apply to the radio telephone distress call which consists of the spoken expression MAYDAY, (corresponding to the French pronunciation of the expression 'm'aider'..). **1929** *Times* 18 June 16/1 The pilot, after wirelessing the S.O.S. of the Air Service 'May Day'..endeavoured to return to Lympne aerodrome with the power still at his disposal. **1930** *B.B.C. Year-Bk.* 399 *Aircraft and Wireless...* In case of distress, due to engine failure over the sea, the word 'Mayday'—equivalent to the S.O.S. used by ships—transmitted through the microphone, will summon immediately all possible help. **1951** O. BERTHOUD tr. *Clostermann's Big Show* I. 30 If you can't get back to the coast, bale out after calling 'May Day' on frequency D. **1962** *Listener* 1 Mar. 370/2 With the onset of lambing time the farmers' 'Mayday' signal begins to hum along the network of telephone wires. **1962** *Sunday Express* 5 Aug. 1/2 Her first 'Mayday' distress message came soon after midday. **1971** *Islander* (Victoria, B.C.) 16 May 13/1 When her topmast chains snapped, she radioed a mayday signal. **1971** *Daily Tel.* 23 Aug. 1/5 The radio operator sent a Mayday distress call before the sea rushed into the cabin.

maydese, variant of MAIDEUX *Obs.*

'May-dew. [MAY *sb.*³] Dew gathered in the month of May, supposed to have medicinal and cosmetic properties.

c **1430** LYDG. *Min. Poems* (Percy Soc.) 217 Whan buddys first appeere, And the May-dewhe round lik perlys fyne. **1602** PLAT *Delights for Ladies* (1611) H 8 b, Some commend May-dew gathered from Fennell and Celandine, to be most excellent for sore eyes. **1626** BACON *Sylva* §781, I suppose, that he that would gather the best May-Deaw, for Medicine, should gather it from the Hills. **1667** PEPYS *Diary* 28 May, To Woolwich, to lie there tonight, and so to gather May-dew tomorrow morning. **1751** JOHNSON *Rambler* No. 130 ⁋5 A regular lustration performed with bean-flower water and May-dews. **1849** JAMES *Woodman* xviii, I have ordered my knave to bring you a furred dressing gown and a bottle of essence of maydew.

may duke, mayduke ('meɪdjuːk). [Cf. *May-cherry* (MAY *sb.*³ 5 c) and *Duke cherry* (DUKE *sb.* 6), both in Evelyn 1664.

The statement that this cherry was introduced from *Médoc* in France, and thence named, seems to be unfounded.]

A variety of sour cherry.

1718 BRADLEY *Improv. Plant. & Gard.* III. 43 All sorts of Cherries, excepting the small May, and the May-Duke-Cherries, prosper best when they have Liberty. **1820** H. MATTHEWS *Diary* (ed. 2) 465 *Medoc*—whence by the way comes our cherry whose name we have corrupted into May Duke. **1828** MISS MITFORD *Village* Ser. III. 28 He would persuade you that brill was turbot, and that black cherries

were Maydukes. **1841** *Knickerbocker* XVII. 154 The air is impregnated with the fragrances..of the blossoming may-dukes. **1874** *Rep. Vermont Board Agric.* II. 359 This variety, and the..May Duke, Late Duke, and other Dukes,..are hardly less hardy than plums.

mayed, obs. form of MAID *sb.*[1]

mayer (ˈmeɪə(r)). [f. MAY *v.*[2] + -ER[1].] One who 'goes a-maying'.
1756 TOLDERVY *Hist. 2 Orphans* II. 152 They set out on foot to join the merry mayers. **1825** HONE *Every-day Bk.* I. 566 Parties of these Mayers are seen dancing. **1893** 'Q.' *Delect. Duchy* 23 All but a few of the mayers had risen from the table.

mayer, -ery: see MAYOR, MAYORY.

†**ˈMayey**, *a. Obs. rare.* Also -ie. [f. MAY *sb.*[3] + -ey, -Y.] Flowering in the month of May.
1604 T. WRIGHT *Passions* I. iii. 14 To..enioy the roses till they flourish, not to let wither the Mayie flowres of their flesh. *a* **1618** SYLVESTER *Maiden's Blush* 470 And up hee comes as fresh as Mayey-Rose.

Mayfair (ˈmeɪfɛə(r)). [MAY *sb.*[3] + FAIR *sb.*[1]] **a.** A fair held in May, esp. that held annually from the 17th century until the end of the 18th century in Brook fields near Hyde Park Corner. **b.** The district of London, very fashionable since the 19th century, between Oxford Street and Piccadilly, occupying the site of the old fairground. Also as quasi-*adj.*
1701 B. FAIRFAX in *Tatler* (1786) I. Notes 418, I wish you had been at May-fair, where the rope-dancing would have recompensed your labour. **1709** *Tatler* 24–26 May, The Crowd of the Audience are fitter for Representations at May-fair, than a Theatre-Royal. **1748** H. WALPOLE *Let.* 3 Sept. (1903) II. 336 A chosen committee waited on the faithful pair to the minister of May-fair. **1754** *Connoisseur* 17 Oct. 227 Catalogue of Males and Females to be disposed of in Marriage to the Best Bidder, at Mr. Keith's Repository in May Fair. **1848** THACKERAY *Van. Fair* li. 453 Yesterday, Colonel and Mrs. Crawley entertained a select party at dinner at their house in May Fair. **1874** H. C. PENNELL (*title*) The Muses of Mayfair: selections from *vers de société* of the nineteenth century. **1933** J. BUCHAN *Prince of Captivity* II. i. 146 Clothes slightly astray from the conventions of Mayfair. **1953** A. CHRISTIE *Pocket Full of Rye* i. 8 Miss Grosvenor..wailed in a voice whose accent was noticeably less Mayfair than usual.
c. *attrib.* and *Comb.*
1752 H. WALPOLE *Let.* 27 Feb. (1903) III. 85 They were married with a ring of the bed-curtain..at Mayfair chapel. **1843** CARLYLE *Past & Present* III. ix. 252 Patent-Digester, Spinning-Mule, Mayfair Clothes-Horse. **1866** M. MACKINTOSH *Stage Reminisc.* vi. 74 So elegant and comfortable that even luxurious west-enders might have fancied themselves at home in their own May-Fair drawing-rooms. **1940** N. MARSH *Surfeit of Lampreys* (1941) ii. 31 The twins were saying..that..the only thing..was for them to turn crooks and be another lot of Mayfair boys. **1943** I. BROWN *Just Another Word* 24 'She got terribly akimbo'..a species of Mayfair slang for what was earlier called 'high horse'. **1957** R. W. ZANDVOORT *Handbk. Eng. Gram.* v. ii. 225 It's such a bore, don't you know. In the..example (which really represents 'Mayfair' English) the tag practically ceases to be a question. **1962** J. D. SALINGER *Franny & Zooey* 155 He was still for a moment. Then, in an almost unintelligibly thick Mayfair accent: 'I'd rather like a word with you, Miss Glass.' **1967** K. GILES *Death in Diamonds* i. 21 He's insolent, smooth and tough, very hip in his talk. Like the Mayfair boys in the thirties. **1970** C. DRUMMOND *Stab in Back* iv. 88 They 'ad a saying when we were young about 'Mayfair Boys', meaning gentlemen crooks.
Hence **ˈMayfairish** *a.*, of the nature or character of Mayfair.
1938 G. ALLIGHAN *Sir John Reith* iv. 235 The B.B.C. organisation..is too isolated from the common people. There is a West End outlook, a Mayfairish idea of the elite, an everlasting implication of superiority. **1967** [see *ideal home*].

mayflower (ˈmeɪflaʊə(r)). [f. MAY *sb.*[3] + FLOWER *sb.* Cf. G. *maiblume*, Du. *meibloem* lily of the valley; so *may-blossom* (MAY *sb.*[3] 5 c).]
1. A flower that blooms in May: used locally as a specific name for various plants, as the Cowslip (*Primula veris*), the Lady's Smock (*Cardamine pratensis*); see Britten & Holland *Plant-n.*
1626 BACON *Sylva* §507 They are commonly of rancke and fulsome Smell; As May-Flowers, and White Lillies. [**1659** HOWELL *Prov.* 12/1 April showers bring forth May flowers.] **1688** R. HOLME *Armoury* II. 70 The Cowslip..we call it a May-flower. **1776** MICKLE tr. *Camoens' Lusiad* I. 24 May-flowers crouding o'er the daisy-lawn. **1817** KEATS '*I stood tiptoe*' 29 A bush of May-flowers with the bees about them. **1853** G. JOHNSTON *Bot. E. Bord.* 33 *Cardamine pratensis*... In Roxburghshire..it is called the May-flower.
fig. **1576** GASCOIGNE *Steele Glass* (Arb.) 119, I hope very shortly to see the May flowers of your fauour.
2. A variety of apple.
1664 EVELYN *Kal. Hort.* Aug. 72 Apples... Cushion Apple, Spicing, May-flower.
3. *N. America.* **a.** *Azalea nudiflora.* **b.** The trailing arbutus, *Epigæa repens.*
1838 LOUDON *Arboretum* II. 1140 *Rhododendron nudiflorum* Torr. (*Azalea nudiflora* L.)..the American Honeysuckle; May Flowers. **1853** W. H. BARTLETT *Pilgr. Fathers* iii. 182 The beautiful May-flower—with its delicate roseate blossom and delicious scent. **1882** *Garden* 13 May 323/1 The May-flower..is the emblem of Nova Scotia, with the motto, 'We bloom amid the snow'.
4. The West Indian *Dalbergia Brownei* and *Ecastaphyllum Brownei.*
1864 GRISEBACH *Flora W. Ind.* 785.
5. The South American *Lælia majalis.*
1894 WRIGHT & DEWAR *Johnson's Gard. Dict.*

ˈmay-fly. [f. MAY *sb.*[3] + FLY *sb.*]
1. An insect of the family *Ephemeridæ*; esp. as an angler's name for *Ephemera vulgata* and *E. dania* or an artificial fly made in imitation of either of these.
1651–3 T. BARKER *Art of Angling* 6 As for the May-Flie you shall have them alwayes playing at the River side. **1653** WALTON *Angler* iv. 115 First for a May-flie, you may make his body with greenish coloured crewel. **1769** G. WHITE *Selborne* (1789) 68 What time the may-fly haunts the pool or stream. **1856** 'STONEHENGE' *Brit. Rural Sports* §650 Caddies are the larvæ of the ephemera, or May-fly, as well as the stone-fly and the caddis-fly. **1867** F. FRANCIS *Angling* vi. (1880) 223 The May Fly or Green Drake, called in Wales the Cadow.
2. An insect of the family *Phryganeidæ* or *Sianidæ* (e.g. *Sialis lutaria*); the caddis-fly.
1816 KIRBY & SP. *Entomol.* ix. (1818) I. 282 *Phryganeæ* [in their imago state are called] may-flies (though this last denomination properly belongs only to the *Sialis lutaria*.. and *Ephemeræ*. *Ibid.* II. 295 [The larvæ] of the true may-fly (*Semblis lutaria*, F.)..use their legs in swimming.
†**3.** A dragon-fly. *Obs.*
1744 COLLINSON in *Phil. Trans.* XLIV. 329 The May Flies, a Species of Libella. **1750** *Ibid.* XLVI. 400 A further Account of the Libellæ or May-flies, from Mr. John Bartram of Pensylvania.
4. *attrib.*, as ***may-fly season, tribe.***
1816 KIRBY & SP. *Entomol.* xxi. (1818) II. 240 The May-fly tribe (*Phryganea*, L., *Trichoptera*, K.). **1857** HUGHES *Tom Brown* I. ix, But now came on the may-fly season.

ˈMay-game. [MAY *sb.*[3]]
1. a. *pl.* The merrymaking and sports associated with the first of May. **b.** *sing.* A set performance or entertainment in the May-day festivities.
1549 COVERDALE, etc. *Erasm. Par. 1 Tim.* 8 In such maner of apparaill, as the commen sorte of vnfaithfull women are wonte to goe forth vnto weddynges and maygames. **1583** R. ROBINSON *Anc. Order Pr. Arthur* L 4 b, A May game was of Robyn-hood, and of his traine that time. **1589** GREENE *Menaphon* (Arb.) 56 He was chosen Lord of the May game, king of their sports, and ringleader of their reuils. **1641** HINDE *J. Bruen* iii. 12 The holy Sabbaths of the Lord were ..spent..in May-poles and May-games. **1888** CHILD *Eng. & Sc. Ball.* III. 46 Maid Marian is a personage in the May-game and morris.
2. *transf.* and *gen.* Merrymaking, sport, frolic, entertainment; foolish or extravagant action or performance, foolery.
1571 GOLDING *Calvin on Ps.* lxxiii. 1 He cryed out..that the endever of living well was but a Maygame. **1660** R. COKE *Power & Subj.* 50 It were a fine may-game to be a King, if Kings might make their Will the rule of their actions. **1768–74** TUCKER *Lt. Nat.* (1834) I. 357 The vulgar [have] their..coarse jokes, and may-games. **1843** CARLYLE *Past & Pr.* III. xiii, Life was never a May-game for men.
3. An object of sport, jest, or ridicule; a laughing-stock. Also in phr. ***to make a May-game of.***
1569 J. SANFORD tr. *Agrippa's Van. Artes* 158 A manifest foolishnes, and a maie game to the multitude. **1583** FULKE *Defence* iv. 137 Whereas in one translation we vse the worde Generall for Catholike, you make a greate maygame of it. **1644** QUARLES *Barnabas & B.* 253 What is man but..the spoil of time, the may-game of fortune? *a* **1739** JARVIS *Quix.* I. III. xxv. (1885) 146 She..makes a jest and a may-game of everybody.
4. *attrib.*, as ***May-game king, lord, morris, pastime***; also as adj. with the sense 'trivial'.
1586 J. HOOKER *Hist. Irel.* in *Holinshed* II. 79/2 This maigame lord, named indeed Peter (in scorne Perkin) Warbecke. **1602** I. R[HODES] *Answ. Rom. Rime* C 3, Your May-game pastimes. **1614** RALEIGH *Hist. World* IV. ii. §4. 148 In this sort came the Maygame-King into the field, incumbred with a most vnnecessary traine of Strumpets. **1653** DELL *Tryal Spirits* 86 School Doctors, that is, Trifling or May-game Doctors. **1888** CHILD *Eng. & Sc. Ball.* III. 45 The relation of Robin Hood, John, and the Friar to the May-game morris is obscure.
Hence †**Maygamester**, one who takes part in May-games.
c **1585** R. BROWNE *Answ. Cartwright* 37 Drunkardes, Maygamesters, blasphemers.

maygh(e, variant forms of MAUGH.

maygne, -gnelle, obs. ff. MEINIE, MANGONEL.

mayhap (meɪˈhæp, ˈmeɪhæp), *adv.* Now *arch.*, *rhetorical* and *dial.* Also 8 **mehap**, 8–9 **mayhaps**. [The phrase (*it*) *may hap* (see HAP *v.*), taken as one word.] Perhaps, perchance.
a **1536** *Interl. Beauty & Gd. Prop. Women* A v, May hap ye stomble Quod he on the trewth, as many one doth. **1575** *Gamm. Gurton* v. ii. (Manly), There is a thing you know not on, may hap. **1706** MRS. CENTLIVRE *Basset-Table* IV, Sir Richard, mehap a woman may not like me. **1718** MOTTEUX *Quix.* (1733) III. 67 I'll trust no longer to Rewards, that mayhaps may come late, and mayhaps not at all. **1840** DICKENS *Barn. Rudge* lxxii, Mayhap she's hungry. **1870** MORRIS *Earthly Par.* II. III. 37 Or hast thou mayhap wandered wide? **1900** HOPE in *Yorks. Arch. Jrnl.* XV. 300 Pins or hooks, mayhap for hanging curtains from.

mayhappen, *adv.* Now *arch.* and *dial.* Also **mappen**, etc. (see E.D.D.). [The phrase (*it*) *may happen* (see HAPPEN *v.*), taken as one word.] = prec.
c **1530** H. RHODES *Bk. Nurture* 747 in *Babees Bk.* 102 Another tyme were he may happen he may doe as much for thee. *a* **1843** SOUTHEY *Doctor* Interch. xxiv. (1847) VII. 83 Mappen they'll sarra us. **1887** W. MORRIS *Odyss.* x. 269 Let us..flee; if yet mayhappen we may 'scape our evil day.

mayhem (ˈmeɪhɛm), *sb. Old Law.* Forms: 5 **mahyme**, 5–7 **mayme**, 6 **mayom**, **maiheme**, **mayheme**, **mahym**, 6–7 **maime**, 6–8 **mayhim**, 7 **mahin**, 7–8 **maim**, 7–9 **maihem**, **mahim**, 7– **mayhem**. [a. AF. *mahem*, *mahaym*, *maiheme*, *maheyng*, etc.: see MAIM *sb.*] The crime of violently inflicting a bodily injury upon a person so as to make him less able to defend himself or annoy his adversary.
1472–3 *Rolls of Parlt.* VI. 54/2 For the punycion of the said murdre and maymes. **1503** *Ibid.* 550/1 The same Sir William, suyde Appele of Mayme ayenst the said Sir Edward. **1523** in W. H. Turner *Select. Rec. Oxford* (1880) 33 Morders, fellonyes, mayoms. **1529** S. FISH *Supplic. Beggers* (1871) 8 Robbery, trespas, maiheme, dette or eny other offence. **1620** J. WILKINSON *Coroners & Sherifes* 22 Mayhem is properly said where any member of a man is taken away. **1641** *Termes de la Ley* 198 The cutting off of an eare or nose, or breaking of the hinder teeth, or such like, is no Maihem. **1765** BLACKSTONE *Comm.* I. 130 Those members which may be useful to him in fight, and the loss of which only amounts to mayhem by the common law. **1802–12** BENTHAM *Ration. Judic. Evid.* (1827) V. 139 All imaginable crimes,—rape, robbery, burglary, mayhem, incendiarism. **1853** T. WHARTON *Digest Cases Pennsylv.* (ed. 6) 486 An indictment for maihem which does not contain the words 'lying in wait' is bad.
fig. **1868** LANIER *Jacquerie* II. 44 Thou felon, War, I do arraign thee now Of mayhem of the four main limbs of France. **1894** *Critic* (U.S.) 30 June 444/1 The literary mayhem becomes as inexplicable as it is unpardonable.
Hence **mayhem** *v. trans.*, to inflict mayhem on.
1534 *Act 26 Hen. VIII*, c. 11 Diuers..haue beaten, mayhimed..and somtimes murdered diuerse of the same pursuers. **1743** *Conn. Col. Rec.* (1874) VIII. 579 For that he ..did feloniously mayhem the body of one Thomas Allyn. **1879** TOURGEE *Fool's Err.* xxxix. (1883) 251 To buy, to sell, to task, to whip, to mayhem this race at will.

mayhime, mayhme, obs. forms of MAIM *v.*

mayht, obs. form of MIGHT *sb.*

Mayie, variant of MAYEY *a.*, *Obs.*

maying (ˈmeɪɪŋ), *vbl. sb.* [f. MAY *v.*[2]] The celebration of or participation in the festivities of May-day or the month of May. Chiefly in phr. ***to go a maying***, † ***to ride on maying.***
1470–85 MALORY *Arthur* XIX. i. 772 That erly vpon the morowe she wold ryde on mayeng in to woodes. **1598** STOW *Surv.* 74 These great Mayinges and Maygames were made by the gouernors..of the Citie. **1632** MILTON *L'Allegro* 20 Zephir with Aurora playing, As he met her once a Maying. **1674** PLAYFORD *Skill Mus.* I. 64 Now is the Month of Maying. **1712** BUDGELL *Spect.* No. 365 ¶ 10 Proserpine was out a Maying, when she met with that fatal Adventure. **1824** MISS MITFORD *Village* Ser. I. 81 A country Maying is a meeting of the lads and lasses of two or three parishes, who assemble in certain erections of green boughs called May-houses, to dance. **1899** 'Q.' *Ship of Stars* x. 79 It had been a grand Maying.
b. *attrib.* in **maying-party** *U.S.*, a party making an excursion for gathering flowers.
1853 W. H. BARTLETT *Pilgrim Fathers* iii. 182 It is a favourite pastime to make Maying parties in the woods.

mayl, obs. f. MAUL *sb.*[1]

mayl-: see MAIL-.

ˈMay-lady. *Obs.* exc. *Hist.* [MAY *sb.*[3]] A Queen of the May. Also, a puppet in a May-day game (see quot. 1802).
1560 BECON *Catech.* VI. Wks. 1564 I. 516 b, To be decked and trimmed like a Marelady [*sic: ? misprint for* Maie-], or the Quene of a game. *Ibid.* 533 As though they were mareladies [*sic*] or Popets in a game. **1619** FLETCHER *M. Thomas* II. ii, Or you must marry Malkyn the May Lady. **1621** BURTON *Anat. Mel.* III. ii. II. iii. 573 Some light huswife belike, that was dressed like a may lady, and as most of our gentlewomen are. **1802** AUDLEY *Comp. to Almanack* 21 The custom..of children having a figure dressed in a grotesque manner, called a May-lady; before which they set a table, having on it wine, &c. They also beg money of passengers,..their plea to obtain it is, 'Pray remember the poor May-lady'.

mayll easse, variant of MALEASE.

mayllet, obs. form of MALLET *sb.*[1]

ˈMay-lord. [See MAY *sb.*[3] and LORD *sb.* 14 a.] A young man chosen to preside over the festivities of May-day; *transf.* one whose authority is a matter of derision.
1599 NASHE *Lenten Stuffe* 9 Cerdicus..was the first may-lord, or captaine of the morris daunce that [etc.]. **1622** WITHER *Mistr. Philar.* in *Juvenilia* (1633) 741 Wealth and Titles would hereafter Subjects be for scorn or laughter, All that Courtly stiles affected Should a May-Lords honour have. **1633** P. FLETCHER *Purple Isl.* I. ii, The Shepherd-boys who with the Muses dwell Met in the plain their May-lords new to choose,..to order well Their rural sports. **1639** SHIRLEY & CHAPMAN *Ball* III. iii, [I] blush within to think How much we are deceived; I may be even With this May-

lord. *a*1670 HACKET *Abp. Williams* I. (1692) 40 [They] will prove to be May-lords in Fortune's interlude.

maymot, obs. form of MAIMED *ppl. a.*

mayn: see MAIM, MAIN, MOAN.

maynat, obs. form of MINA[2].

† **mayne**, *v. Obs.* Also 5 mene, 6 mayn, meyne, meane. [a. OF. *meine-*, str. stem of *mener* to lead. Cf. DEMEAN *v.*[1]]

1. *trans.* To lead (a horse).

*a*1400 *Sir Perc.* 711 The childe gone his mere mayne After the stede. *Ibid.* 1402.

2. *to mayne evil* [= F. *malmener*]: to maltreat.

1481 CAXTON *Godfrey* cxxxix. 208 The Archiers.. that so fledde were so euyl mened that they were but a fewe whan they retorned in to thoost.

3. To conduct, direct, manage (an affair).

1520 in *Edinb. Burgh Rec.* (1869) I. 200 And gif ony truble or debait happinis amangis ony of the saidis craftis, thai till meyne the samyn amangis tham self in cheritable maner. 1537 CROMWELL in Merriman *Life & Lett.* (1902) II. 92 It is Bruted that there shuld be a communication of a peax to be mayned by others. 1541 HEN. VIII in *St. Papers* III. 332 Howe We thinke you maye best mayn thinges there to our purpose. 1546 *Ibid.* XI. 225, I will do what I can to meane the thing: if there be no remedye, then must Godd worcke. 1549 in Strype *Eccl. Mem.* II. App. 117 Beseching God to give you the grace to mayne and conduct them, as I do wish.

4. *refl.* To conduct or demean oneself (in a particular way).

1352 MINOT *Poems* i. 29 Of Scotland had þai neuer sight Ay whils þai war of wordes stout. þai wald haue mend þam at þaire might And besy war þai þareobout. *c*1400 *Destr. Troy* 11313 How may ye þus meane you with malis, for shame!

Hence † '**mayning** *vbl. sb.*

1527 WOLSEY in *St. Papers Hen. VIII*, I. 200 The universal peace, which is now in mayning and treating. 1550 in Strype *Eccl. Mem.* (1822) II. App. PP. 139 The mayning and directing of our affairs.

mayne, mayneal, obs. ff. MEINIE, MENIAL.

maynerey, variant of MANGERY *Obs.*

mayngate, maynhe, obs. ff. MANCHET, MAIM *v.*

maynor, -oure, -oyre, etc., obs. ff. MANURE.

mayntelle, mayny, obs. ff. MANTEL, MEINIE.

maynyseynge, obs. form of MENACING.

† **Mayo**[1]. *Obs. rare*$^{-1}$. Some game.

Possibly = MAW *sb.*[4] which is often mentioned in connexion with 'Primero'.

?*c*1650 SIR G. RADCLIFFE in *Strafforde's Lett. & Disp.* (1739) II. 433 He [Strafford] played excellently well at Primero and Mayo.

mayo[2] ('meɪəʊ), colloq. abbrev. of MAYONNAISE.

1960 WENTWORTH & FLEXNER *Dict. Amer. Slang* 335/1 *Mayo*, mayonnaise. Common lunch-counter use since *c*1930. 1969 L. HELLMAN in *Atlantic* Apr. 118 Run down to the corner and get me a ham and cheese on rye and tell them to hold the mayo. 1971 *New Yorker* 10 July 20 We were sitting at a luncheonette counter the other day, just about to bite into a b.l.t. down, with mayo, when a familiar voice addressed us from an adjacent stool.

† **mayo(c)k**. *Sc. Obs.* ? Arbitrary alteration of MAKE *sb.*[1]

*c*1600 MONTGOMERIE *Cherrie & Slae* (2nd version) ii, The painted pawn with Argos eyis Can on his mayock call. 1638 H. ADAMSON *Muse's Thren.* (1774) 160 Balthyock, Where many peacock cals upon his mayok.

Mayologist (mɑːˈjɒlədʒɪst). [f. MAYA *sb.*[2] + -OLOGIST (see -OLOGY).] A student of Maya antiquities.

1926 *Glasgow Herald* 18 May 9 Mr. Joyce, perhaps the ablest of living Mayologists, has been sent.. on a mission of inspection.

‖ **mayonnaise** (meɪəˈneɪz, Fr. majɔnɛz). [F. *mayonnaise*, also *magnonaise*, *mahonnaise*, the latter being prob. fem. of *mahonnais* of Port *Mahon*, capital of Minorca, taken by the duc de Richelieu in 1756.] **1.** A thick sauce consisting of yolk of egg beaten up with oil and vinegar, and seasoned with salt, etc., used as a dressing for salad, cold meat, or fish; also, a dish (of meat, etc.) having this sauce as a dressing. Also with defining word, as ***egg***, ***fish***, ***lobster***, ***salmon mayonnaise***.

See quots. s.v. LOBSTER[1] 5.

1841 THACKERAY *Mem. Gormand.* Misc. Ess. (1885) 396 A mayonnaise of crayfish. 1861 MRS. BEETON *Bk. Househ. Managem.* 225 For a fish Mayonnaise, this sauce may be coloured with lobster-spawn, pounded. 1883 *Chamb. Jrnl.* 316 The dressing, or mayonnaise, of the salad is then commenced. 1910 *Encycl. Brit.* VII. 74/2 The mayonnaise (originally *mahonnaise*) is ascribed to the duc de Richelieu. 1975 D. BLOODWORTH *Clients of Omega* xvi. 153 The partners.. began to eat salmon mayonnaise off the altar.

2. *Contract Bridge* = GOULASH 2.

1927 M. WORK *Contract Bridge* 138 *Mayonnaise*, old name of Goulash.

Hence **mayo'nnaised** *a.*

1968 C. DRUMMOND *Death & Leaping Ladies* i. 7 A hearty trencherman himself, a victor over many a mayonnaised lobster. 1972 P. A. WHITNEY *Listen for Whisperer* vii. 130 An array of tiny mayonnaised shrimps.

mayor (mɛə(r), mɛə(r)). Forms: 3 mer, 3–7 (latterly *Sc.*) mair, 4 meire, 4–5 meir, meyr, 4–6 mayr, meyre, 4–7 maire, mayre, 5 maieur, mere, majer, maiere, meer, mar, mawer, 5–6 mayer, maier, meyer, 5–7 mare, 6–7 maio(u)r, 6–8 major, 6– mayor. [Early ME. *mair*, *mer*, a. F. *maire* (from 13th c.):—L. *mājor* nom., properly adj., greater (see MAJOR). OF. had also a form *maor*, *meor*:—L. *mājōrem* acc., which may be represented in some of the ME. forms. The spelling *maio(u)r*, common in the 16th c., seems to be intended to represent the L. *major*, but as the *i* could be read as a vowel, this form became phonetically nearly coincident with those adopted from Fr. The substitution of *y* for *i* was in accordance with the orthographical habits of the 16–17th c., and need not be ascribed to imitation of the Sp. form *mayor*.

The med. L. *mājor* as a title was adopted as OHG. *meiur*, whence MHG. *meier*, *meiger*, mod.G. *meier* farm bailiff, farmer. Du. *meier* has both senses, 'mayor' and 'farmer'.]

1. The head or chief officer of the municipal corporation of a city or borough.

The title is used in England and Ireland (see also LORD MAYOR), in the British Commonwealth, and in the U.S. It was formerly borne by the heads of certain royal burghs in Scotland, but has there been long superseded by *provost*. It occasionally renders its etymological equivalent (F. *maire*) as the title of a similar municipal officer in French towns, though the Fr. word is now more commonly used; similarly, *mayor* was formerly used occas. to designate certain administrative officers in Holland and Switzerland (cf. MAYORALTY 3, MAYORY).

The continued practice of electing mayors in some decayed boroughs (e.g. Queenborough in Sheppey) which had become mere villages or hamlets is a common matter of jesting allusion in the literature of the 17th c. There are also in various parts of the country instances in which a so-called 'mayor' is or was elected periodically with burlesque ceremonies; of these mock-dignitaries the 'Mayor of Garratt', near Wandsworth, is the best-known example.

1297 R. GLOUC. (Rolls) 11226 þe mer [of Oxford] was viniter. *c*1330 R. BRUNNE *Chron. Wace* (Rolls) 8031 þe Meyre of Kermerdyn. 1386 *Rolls of Parlt.* III. 225/1 When free men of the Citee [*sc.* London] come to chese her Maire. 1415 *Procl.* in *York Myst.* Introd. 34 Ye Mair and ye Shirefs of yis Citee. *c*1450 *Lay Folks Mass Bk.* 69 We sall pray especially for þe meer. *c*1460 J. RUSSELL *Bk. Nurture* 1137 in *Babees Bk.*, þe meyre of london, notable of dignyte, and of queneborow þe meire, no þynge like in degre. *c*1488 *Plumpton Corr.* (Camden) 87 To the behaufe of the mawer of the Cyte of Yorke & his bredren. 1537 WRIOTHESLEY *Chron.* (Camden) I. 31 Sir John Allen, maiour, being also one of the Kinge's Counsell. 1555 *Inv. Ch. Goods* (Surtees Soc., No. 97) 157 One of the attorneys within the mayeres courte. 1599 *Broughton's Let.* ii. 9 As the runn-away apprentice thought, the bels recalling him, told him he should be Maior of London. *a*1627 MIDDLETON (*title*) The Mayor of Quinborough. 1654 WHITLOCK *Zootomia* 311 Hee were an arrant Mayor of Quinborrow, that should send to the Indies for Kentish Oysters. 1764 FOOTE (*title*) The Mayor of Garratt. 1765 T. HUTCHINSON *Hist. Mass.* I. 176 A corporation, consisting of a mayor, eight aldermen and a recorder. 1818 CRUISE *Digest* (ed. 2) V. 115 The mayor of the said city shall have full power.. to receive and record all and every such fine and fines. 1902 *Westm. Gaz.* 22 May 2/3 A boatman on the Bolton and Bury Canal has been selected as 'Lord Mayor of the village of Ringley'. *Ibid.*, In some parts the burlesque civic official was designated 'Mayor of the Pig Market', and in Dublin 'Mayor of the Bull Ring'.

† **b.** *mayor's peer*: app. a person eligible for the office of mayor. *Obs.*

1560 in Picton *L'pool Munic. Rec.* (1883) I. 33 Every Mayor and Mayors peer.

† **c.** In Ireland, app. applied to several members (? chief or capital burgesses) of the municipal body of which the mayor properly so called was the head.

1557 in *10th Rep. Hist. MSS. Comm.* App. v. 416 That ther be no more but twelve Mayors and the Mayor for the tyme beinge.

d. ***Mayor of the Staple***: see STAPLE.

† **2.** Used *gen.* for one in high judicial office. *Obs.*

*a*1300 *Cursor M.* 7036 þair leder and þair maister mair. 1362 LANGL. *P.Pl.* A. VIII. 171 ȝe meires and ȝe maister iuges. *c*1440 CAPGRAVE *Life St. Kath.* v. 1241 There was a man in Alisaundre.. Meyer and leedere of alle the puple there.

† **3.** In Scotland (ordinarily spelt **mair**), formerly the title of various officers differing widely in rank, having delegated jurisdiction or executive functions, either under the sovereign or under some judicial authority. ***mair of fee***: a 'king's mair' holding his office as a heritable possession. *Obs.*

Hence Gaelic *maor*, steward, policeman.

1429 *Sc. Acts Jas. I* (1814) II. 17/2 A mayr of fee quheþer he be mayr of þe hail schirefdome or of part sal haf powere [etc.]. *c*1470 HENRY *Wallace* IV. 359 The mar kepyt the port of that willage, Wallace knew weill. 1522–3 *Ld. Treas. Acc. Scot.* V. 209 Deliverit to the lord Zesteris heid mare our soverane lordis lettrez. 1544 in E. D. Dunbar *Docum. Moray* (1895) 67 Principal Mair off the lands after specefied, viz. the Thayndaine [etc.]. 1609 SKENE *Reg. Maj., Stat. Alex. II* 17 b, He [the Earle of Fife] may not enter as Earle; bot as Mair to the king of the Earledom of Fife. 1703 FOUNTAINHALL in M. P. Brown *Suppl. Decis.* (1826) IV. 564 The malversations of their mairs or messengers.

† **b.** ***mayorsfeud***: the fee of a 'mair'. *Obs.*

1608 in E. D. Dunbar *Docum. Moray* (1895) 69 The said office of Mairsfeod of the forsaid earldom of Murray is held in chief of James Earl of Murray.

4. ***Mayor of the Palace*** (Hist.): = F. *maire du palais*, a mod. translation of med.L. *major domus* (occas. *m. palatii*), the title borne by the prime ministers (under the later Merovingians the virtual sovereigns) of the Frankish kingdoms. Also ***Mayor of Austrasia***, ***of Neustria***.

1529 RASTELL *Pastyme* (1811) 77 Cloyter son of Clouis.. ordeynyd mayrs of yᵉ palys. 1711 W. KING tr. *Naude's Ref. Politics* v. 171 The Majors of the palace.. in France.. embroiled the kingdom to make themselves necessary. 1818 HALLAM *Mid. Ages* (1841) I. i. 5 Ebroin and Grimoald mayors of Neustria and Austrasia. 1875 MAINE *Hist. Inst.* v. 139 The Mayor of the Frankish Palace became King of the Franks.

5. *attrib.* and *Comb.*, as ***mayor-choosing***; † **mayor-corn**, an ancient Scottish tax of corn given to the 'mair'; † **mayor-town**, a town ruled by a mayor, a municipal town; also *Sc.* a farm or piece of land held by a 'mair' in right of his office.

1823 T. BOND *E. & W. Looe* 277 *Mayor-choosing Days. The following Table.. shews the Days of the Mayor-choosing at East Looe. 1606 in E. D. Dunbar *Docum. Moray* 68 The haill *Mair cornes, reik hens, and uther casualities and feis quatsumevir of the tounis and lands of Tarress [etc.]. 1623 J. TAYLOR (Water-P.) *Discov. Lond. Salisb.* A4 Then downe to Erith, 'gainst the tyde we went, Next London, greatest *Mayor [1630 Maior] towne in Kent. *c*1710 CELIA FIENNES *Diary* (1888) 4 Yᵉ Assizes is allwayes kept at Salsebury and is a Major town though Wilton about 2 mile off is yᵉ County town. 1778 *Eng. Gazetteer* (ed. 2) s.v. *Sittingborn*, In the reign of Elizabeth this was made a mayor-town. 1798 W. ROBERTSON *Index Charters* 120 Carta to William Herowart, of the office of Mairship of the east quarter of Fife, with the land called the Mairtoun, whilk William Mair resigned.

‖ **mayoral** (majoˈral), *sb.* Forms: 6 mayorall, 7 maioral, 9– mayoral. [Sp., f. *mayor* greater (see MAJOR *a.* and *sb.*, MAYOR).] A conductor in charge of a train of beasts of burden; also, a head shepherd; *occas.* the conductor of a diligence.

1598 BARRET *Theor. Warres* v. iv. 136 A Harbenger, and a Mayorall, which goeth with euery thousand beasts. 1622 F. MARKHAM *Bk. War* III. ii. 85 The Master Gunner.. is.. to command all the inferior Gunners, Clerkes, Harbengers, Maiorals, Gill-Masters and other depending vpon the Ordnance. 1833 LONGF. *Outre Mer* Prose Wks. 1886 I. 138 Here our conversation was cut short by the Mayoral of the diligence. 1845 FORD *Handbk. Spain* I. 18 The 'Mayoral' or 'conductor'.. is responsible for the whole conduct of the journey. 1879 *Cassell's Techn. Educ.* I. 149 A mayoral or chief shepherd at their head.

mayoral (ˈmeɪərəl, ˈmɛərəl), *a.* [f. MAYOR + -AL[1].] Pertaining to a mayor or mayoralty.

1698 SWIFT *Let. to Winder* 13 Jan., Wks. 1841 II. 436, I was at his mayoral feast. 1703 W. PENN in *Pa. Hist. Soc. Mem.* IX. 181, I hope Randall carries a hat for Edward Shippen of a mayoral size. 1869 *Daily News* 30 Mar., The Mayoral order was that certain leading thoroughfares were to be closed. 1885 *Standard* 14 Apr. 5/2 Mr. Alderman Fowler, M.P., has consented to serve for the remainder of the Mayoral year.

mayoralty (ˈmɛərəltɪ). Forms: 4 mairaltee, 5 mayraltye, 5–6 mairalte, mayraltie, 5–7 mairaltie, 6 merialtie, meralty, mayralte, mayreraltie, 6–7 maioraltie, 7 majorality, mairoltie, myraltie, maioralty, mearaltie, 8 may'ralty, mayorality, majoralty, 7– mayoralty. [ad. OF. *mairalté*, f. *maire* MAYOR, after *principalté*, mod. *principauté*.]

1. The office of a mayor.

1386 *Rolls of Parlt.* III. 225/1 The eleccion of Mairaltee is to be to the Fre men of the Citee. 1438 in *10th Rep. Hist. MSS. Comm.* App. v. 330 Ony citsaine bering office of Mairaltie or of balifs. 1534 WHITINTON *Tullyes Offices* I. (1540) 65 Pericles sayd well whan he had a felowe in offyce in his mayraltie [orig. in *prætura*] called Sophocles poete. 1571 CAMPION *Hist. Irel.* II. vii. (1633) 96 This Majorality both for state and charge of that office.. exceedeth any Citty in England, except London. 1702 *Toleration* 17 The May'ralty and other Offices are confin'd to their City Councils. 1851 D. G. MITCHELL *Fresh Gleanings* 75 The office of Mayoralty in the.. American cities. 1890 GROSS *Gild Merch.* I. 97 The mayoralty, which gave them a chief officer of their own election.

2. The period during which a mayor holds office.

1494 FABYAN *Chron.* VII. (1533) II. 30/2 The mayraltie of John Tolesham. 1540 in W. H. Turner *Select. Rec. Oxford* (1880) 159 Hys ij yeres mayreraltie. 1632 in *10th Rep. Hist. MSS. Comm.* App. v. 480 The yeare of the myraltie of Sir Vallentin Blake. 1727 W. MATHER *Yng. Man's Comp.* 105 Nor has the Lord Mayor of London, during his Mayorality, a less Title than Right Honourable. 1870 LOWELL *Study Wind.* 108 Of his mayoralty we have another anecdote.

† **3.** The district over which a 'mayor' has jurisdiction. *Obs. rare*$^{-1}$.

1705 *Lond. Gaz.* No. 4113/3 The Mayoralty of Boisleduc.. and the Country beyond the Maese, are directed to have in a readiness 1700 Wagons.

4. *attrib.*

1573 in *10th Rep. Hist. MSS. Comm.* App. v. 423 Mr. Andrew Brown.. beinge then in his Meralty office. 1647 *Ibid.* 496 Wee.. thought fitt to record the same in the Mearaltie booke of this Corporation. 1822 C'TESS BLESSINGTON *Magic Lantern* 22 The Lord Mayor's coach, with all the paraphernalia of mayoralty finery. 1887 *Dict.*

Nat. Biog. XI. 102/2 The mayoralty pageant provided [1635] by the Ironmongers' Company for Clitherow.

Hence † **mayoraltyship**, the office of a mayor.

1582 in *10th Rep. Hist. MSS. Comm.* App. v. 432 The office of Meraltyship. **1600** *Ibid.* 459 The office of Maioraltishipp or Baillifshipp.

mayordom ('mɛədəm). *Obs.* exc. *Hist.* See quot. 1611; also *Sc.* the office of a 'mair of fee'.

1611 COTGR., *Mairerie*, a Maiordome; the office, or place of a Mayor; also, his iurisdiction, or the precincts thereof. **1872** COSMO INNES *Lect. Scot. Legal Antiq.* ii. 78 We had numerous mairdoms or subdivisions of sheriffdoms, and several mairs of fee, that is, hereditary mairs.

mayordom(e, -domo, obs. ff. MAJOR-DOMO.

mayoress ('mɛərɪs). Forms: 5 **meyresse**, 5, 7 **mayresse**, 6 **mayras, majoris, maiores**, 7 **mai-, majoresse**, 8–9 **may'ress**, 7– **mayoress**. [f. MAYOR + -ESS. Cf. F. *mairesse* (now only jocular).]

1. The wife of a mayor.

Also sometimes applied, when a mayor is unmarried or a widower, to a lady of his family who fulfils the ceremonial duties normally belonging to the mayor's wife.

The wife of a LORD MAYOR is called *Lady Mayoress*.

c **1430** *Pilgr. Lyf Manhode* II. viii. (1869) 78 What is this? Art thou meyresse? **1494** FABYAN *Chron.* VII. (1533) II. 223 b/2 The kynge..sent vnto the mayresse and her systers, aldermennes wyfes two hartes and .vi. buckes, wyth a tonne of wyne. **1541** *Cal. Anc. Rec. Dublin* (1889) I. 410 Such obprobrious words..spokyn by Maisteras Mayras. **1558** *Reg. St. George's, Canterb.*, M'res Agnes May, Majoris, buried in the Church. **1587** in Picton *L'pool Munic. Rec.* (1883) I. 105 She whose husband..hath been Mayor of this said town..shall take her place..nearest to M^{ris} Maiores for the time being. **1619** MIDDLETON *Tri. Love & Antiq.* C 3 This king..sent to the Lady Maioresse..2 Harts [etc.]. *a* **1637** B. JONSON *Underwoods* lx. *Elegy*, The Lady Mayresse. **1702** *Lond. Gaz.* No. 3842/2 She was pleased to admit Mrs. Mayoress..to the Honour of kissing Her Majesty's Hand. **1778** *Eng. Gazetteer* (ed. 2) s.v. *Westbury on Trin*, William Cannings..built an alms-house here, allowing the mayor of Bristol to put in one of the men, and Mrs. mayoress one of the women. **1824** BYRON *Juan* XVI. xlv. *note*, The mayoress of a provincial town.

2. A woman holding the office of mayor. *U.S.*

1884 *Chicago Tribune* 5 May 4/3 She cannot under the laws monopolize the holding of nice special offices like Mayoress. **1895** *N. Amer. Rev.* Sept. 267 When women shall have become..mayoresses and alderwomen. **1947** *Chicago Sun* 4 Nov. 16/5 The dish..will be delivered..by Mrs. Margaret Craig, mayoress of Twickenham.

3. A person appointed to assist a female mayor.

1932 *Times* 10 Nov. 8/6 Mrs. Emily F. George, the Labour Mayor of Bermondsey, has appointed her daughter ..to be Mayoress.

† **'mayorhood.** *Obs.* In 6 **mayrehod**. [f. MAYOR + -HOOD.] The office of a mayor.

1586 *Chron. Gr. Friars* (Camden) 5 This year [40 Edw. III] in Januarij Adam Bury was dyschargyd of hys mayrehod.

mayorlet ('mɛəlɪt). *rare*$^{-1}$. [f. MAYOR + -LET.] A petty mayor.

1837 CARLYLE *Fr. Rev.* II. III. iv, The Patriotic Mayor or Mayorlet of the Village of Moret tried to detain them.

mayorship ('mɛəʃɪp). [f. MAYOR + -SHIP.]

1. The office, position, or dignity of a mayor.

1485 *Rolls of Parlt.* VI. 357/1 The Offices of Maireshipp of Glawdstre in Radmoresland. **1544** in E. D. Dunbar *Docum. Moray* (1895) 67 The service of the foresaid office of Mairship vseit and wont to Marie Queen of Scotts. **1578** in W. H. Turner *Select. Rec. Oxford* (1880) 395 Suche parsons as have borne thoffice of Mayorshippe. **1611** COTGR., *Mairie*, a Maiordome, or Maiorship; the office, or place of a Maior, or of a village-Maior. **1801** RANKEN *Hist. France* I. 259 Clotaire consented to confirm him for life in his mayorship.

2. *nonce-use.* As a mock title: ***Your Mayorship***.

1822 SCOTT *Pirate* xxxiv, If it please your noble Mayorship's honour and glory.

‖ **mayory.** *Obs.* Also 7 **-ery**. [f. MAYOR + -Y, after F. *mairie*, Du. *meierij*.] The district over which a mayor (Dutch or Swiss) has jurisdiction.

1679 *Lond. Gaz.* No. 1393/3 The French..are resolved to exact the Contributions they demand from the Mayery of Bolduc. **1705** *Ibid.* No. 4146/3 The Enemy's Parties..infest the Mayory of Boisleduc. **1796** MORSE *Amer. Geog.* II. 322 This republic [Neuchâtel] is divided into four chatellanies, and 15 mayories.

mayple, obs. form of MAPLE.

maypole ('meɪpəʊl). [f. MAY *sb.*^{3} + POLE *sb.*]

1. A high pole, painted with spiral stripes of different colours and decked with flowers, set up on a green or other open space, for the merrymakers to dance round on May-day.

In quot. 1597 applied for the nonce to a barber's pole.

1554 in *Vicary's Anat.* (1888) App. iii. 176 That no..persones..cause to be..sett vpp eny maner of maye pole.. in any opyn streat. **1597** G. HARVEY *Trimming T. Nashe* Wks. (Grosart) III. 25 My shoppe in the towne, the teeth that hange out of my Windowe, my painted may-poole. **1642** MILTON *Apol. Smect.* Wks. 1851 III. 306 He had the whole bevie at command whether in morrice or at May pole. **1702** *Lond. Gaz.* No. 3783/4 The Wine-Cellar under the Flower-de-Luce against the May Pole in the Strand. **1863** *Chambers' Bk. Days* I. 572/2 The May Queen..was placed in a sort of bower or arbour near the maypole, there to sit in pretty state.

b. *transf.* Applied jocularly to a tall object, esp. a tall slender man or woman.

1590 SHAKS. *Mids. N.* III. ii. 296 How low am I, thou painted May-pole? **1611** RICH *Honest. Age* (Percy Soc.) 37 Such monstrous May-powles of hayre. **1648** J. RAYMOND *Il Merc. Ital.* 201 This Place is much frequented by the Venetian walking May Poles, I meane the women. **1765** E. THOMPSON *Meretriciad* (ed. 6) 33 Maypoles love you because you're wonderous small. **1773** GOLDSM. *She stoops to Conq.* I. ii, The daughter, a tall, trapesing, trolloping, talkative maypole. **1871** MRS. H. WOOD *Dene Hollow* i, He was turned sixty, a lean maypole of a man.

2. a. The American Aloe, *Agave americana*. **b.** The tree *Spathelia simplex* of Jamaica (*Treas. Bot.* 1866).

1750 G. HUGHES *Barbados* 223 The May-Pole; *Lat.* Aloe Americana muricata. **1769** E. BANCROFT *Nat. Hist. Guiana* 46. **1848** SCHOMBURGK *Hist. Barbados* 588.

3. *attrib.*, as ***maypole dancer, green***; ***maypole-like*** adj.; also quasi-adj. = (1) very tall, as ***maypole figure, freshman***; (2) such as are associated with maypole festivities, as ***maypole face, virtue***.

1610 in *3rd Rep. Hist. MSS. Comm.* 57/2 Acting a stage play..upon a Maypole green. **1632** LITHGOW *Trav.* IX. 406 What a May pole Dauncer, was Iohn 12...who made the Lateran..a playne Stewes or Brothel house. *a* **1634** RANDOLPH *Muses' Looking-glass* v. i, Will virtues dance? O vile, absurd, maypole, maid-marian virtue! **1647–8** WOOD *Life* (O.H.S.) I. 140, I am none of those May-pole freshmen, that are tall cedars before they come to be planted in the academian garden. **1670** J. SMITH *Eng. Improv. Reviv'd* 74 So many May-pole-like-Trees. **1789** CHARLOTTE SMITH *Ethelinde* (1814) II. 222 That maypole-like figure. **1902** LOWNDES *Camping Sk.* 85 We soon descried his maypole figure on the opposite side against the sky.

mayr(e, obs. ff. MAYOR, MERE *sb.*^{1}; Sc. ff. MORE.

mays: see MAKE *v.*^{1}, MAIZE.

mayse: see MAZE, MEASE.

maysilles, obs. pl. form of MEASLE.

mayson-dew(e, etc., obs. forms of MEASONDUE.

mayss, mayst: see MAKE *v.*^{1}, MAY *v.*^{1}, MOST.

mayster, -ir, -ry, etc.: see MASTER, etc.

† **'maystrial**, *a.* *Obs.* *rare*$^{-1}$. = MAGISTRAL.

1576 BAKER *Jewell of Health* 126 b, A maystrial baulme of unknowne Aucthour.

maystries, etc., **mayt, mayth**: see MAISTRICE, MATE, MAUGH.

† **mayth.** *Obs.* In 1 **mǽgð**, 3 *Ormin* **maȝȝþ**. [OE. *mǽgð* str. fem.] A family, race, tribe.

c **1000** ÆLFRIC *Num.* i. 4 þæra mægða ealdras [Vulg. *principes tribuum*]. *c* **1200** ORMIN 7678 Hire faderr Fanuæl Wass off Assæress maȝȝþe.

† **maythe(s.** *Obs.* Forms: α. 1 **maȝoþe, -eþe, -aþe, maȝþa**, 5 **mawth**. β. 1 **mæȝeþe, mæȝþa**, 4, 6 **mathe**, 4, 8 **maithe**, 4–7 **maythe**, 5 **mathge** (?), 6–7 **mayth**. [OE. *maȝoþe* wk. fem., *mæȝþa* wk. masc., of obscure origin; some have suggested connexion with OE. *mæȝeð* maiden.]

1. Stinking Camomile, *Anthemis Cotula*. Applied also to various other composite plants resembling this, as *Anthemis nobilis, Matricaria Chamomilla, M. inodora, Chrysanthemum Leucanthemum, Pyrethrum Parthenium*.

c **1000** *Sax. Leechd.* I. 120 Ðas wyrte þe man camemelon & oðrum naman maȝeþe nemneð. *Ibid.* II. 140 þa readan maȝoþan. *Ibid.* 206 Wermod & wildre maȝþan wyrttruman. *c* **1050** *Voc.* in Wr.-Wülcker 296/29 *Beneolentem*, maȝaðe, *uel camemelon*. *Ibid.* 297/3 *Bucstalmum* [read *Buoftalmum*], hwit mæȝeðe. *Ibid.*, *Obtalmon*, maȝeðe. *a* **1387** *Sinon. Barthol.* (Anecd. Oxon.) 10/2 *Amarusca*, maythe. *Ibid.* 16/2 *Cocula fetida*, maythes. **14..** *Sloane MS.* 5 in *Promp. Parv.* 321 *note*, *Amarusca calida, Gall. ameroche, Ang.* maithe. **14..** *Voc.* in Wr.-Wülcker 563/23 *Amarusa*, a mathge. *c* **1450** *Alphita* (Anecd. Oxon.) 45/2 *Consolida media*,..whit-bothel uel seynt Mary maythe. **14..** in *Archæologia* XXX. 410 Mawth. **1523** FITZHERB. *Husb.* §20 Doggefenell and mathes is bothe one. **1578** LYTE *Dodoens* II. xxx. 186, I haue Englished it Unsauerie Camomill, foolish Mathes, and white Cotula without sauour. **1597** GERARDE *Herbal* Table Eng. Names, Stinking Mayth, that is Maie weed. **1614** MARKHAM *Cheap Husb.* I. Table of Hard Words, *Maythe*, is a weede that growes amongst corne, and is called of some Hogs-Fennell.

2. ***red maythe(s***: Red or Purple Camomile, *Adonis autumnalis*.

1548, **1551** [see MAIDWEED]. **1597** GERARDE *Herbal* II. lxxiv. 310 Adonis flower is called in Latine *Flos Adonis*..in English we may call it red Maythes. **1713** PETIVER *Catal. Ray's Eng. Herbal* §v. Pl. xxxix. 8 Red Maithes.

maythen ('meɪð(ə)n). *Obs.* exc. *dial.* Forms: 4 **maþen**, 6 **maythen, mawthen**, 8 **maithen**, 9 **mathen, -an**. [Repr. OE. *mæȝ(e)þan, maȝoþan*, oblique case and pl. of *mæȝeþa, maȝoþe*: see prec. Cf. MATHER(N.) = prec.

c **1325** *Gloss. W. de Bibbesw.* in Wright *Voc.* 162 Ameroke e gletoner [*glossed* mathen (maythe) and cloten]. **1524** *Grete Herball* cxxxvii, *Consolida media*. Maythen. **1597** GERARDE *Herbal* App., Mawthen is *Cotula fœtida*. **1845** *Jrnl. R. Agric. Soc.* V. II. 431 The mathen and crow-needles grow more thickly. **1883** *Hampsh. Gloss.*, Mathan, *Anthemis Cotula*.

maythern, variant form of MATHERN.

may-tide: see MAY *v.*^{1} 12.

mayweed ('meɪwiːd). [For ****maythe-weed***: see MAYTHE and cf. MAIDWEED.] = MAYTHE 1.

1551 in Strype *Eccl. Mem.* II. App. A. 145 That ground, which..was most to be nobly adorned with corn,..now.. replenished with mayweed, thistles, docks. **1573** TUSSER *Husb.* (1878) 112 The May weed doth burn and the thistle doth freat. **1597** GERARDE *Herbal* II. ccxlix. 617, 1 *Cotula fœtida*. Maie weede. 2 *Cotula lutea*. Yellow Maie weede. **1657** C. BECK *Univ. Charac.* I iv b, Oxe-eye, vid. may weed. **1672** JOSSELYN *New-Eng. Rarities* 86 May-weed, excellent for the Mother; some of our English Housewives call it Iron Wort. **1758** R. BROWN *Compl. Farmer* (1759) 94 Rub the place with wormwood, nettles, may-weed. **1892** JEFFERIES *Toilers of Field* 310 The mayweed fringes the arable fields with its white rays and yellow centre.

mazagan ('mæzəgæn). [Said to be named from *Mazagan* in Morocco, where it grows wild.] In full ***mazagan bean***: a small early variety of the broad bean, *Faba vulgaris*.

1754 JUSTICE *Scots Gardiners Director* 190 The Mazagan and the early Lisbon are the earliest kinds; but I prefer the Mazagan Bean. **1759** MILLER *Gard. Dict.* (ed. 7) s.v. *Faba*, The Mazagan Bean is the first and best Sort of early Beans at present known; these are brought from a Settlement of the Portuguese on the Coast of Africa, just without the Streights of Gibraltar. **1846** J. BAXTER *Libr. Pract. Agric.* (ed. 4) II. 425 Sow.—Melons, cucumbers, peas, beans, the broad sorts, or the mazagans, if wanted early.

Mazahbi, var. MAZHABI.

mazal tov, var. MAZEL TOV.

mazame (mə'zeɪm). Also **mazama**. [a. F. *mazame* (Buffon), a. Mexican *maçame* (cited in the Sp. transl. of Hernandez, 1615), pl. of *maçatl* deer, mistaken for a sing.

The U.S. Dicts. give the above pronunciation; the original word is (ma'same).]

1. Used as a name for various American species of deer; also applied to the Pronghorn.

By some recent zoologists the mod.L. *mazama* is used as the name of a genus including all the American Cervidæ.

1791 SMELLIE tr. *Buffon* (ed. 3) VII. 31 These roebucks, or mazames and temamaçames of Mexico. **1890** *Century Dict.*, *Mazame*. 1. The North American pronghorn. 2. The pampas-deer of South America.

2. The antilopine Rocky Mountain goat, *Oreamnus* or *Haplocerus montanus*.

Hence the name of 'The Mazamas', given to a society of mountain-climbers organized on the summit of Mount Hood 19 July 1894 (*Gd. Words* Feb. 1901, p. 101).

1852 J. E. GRAY *Catal. Specim. Mammalia Brit. Mus.* III. 114 *Mazama Americana*, The Mazame or Spring-buck. **1871–82** *Cassell's Nat. Hist.* III. 27 The Mazama or Mountain Goat of California and the Rocky Mountains.

mazapane, obs. form of MARZIPAN.

mazar, obs. form of MAZARD *sb.*^{2}, MAZER.

mazard ('mæzəd), *sb.*^{1} Also 7 **mazerd**, 7–9 **mazzard**. [app. an alteration of MAZER, by association of the ending with the suffix -ARD.]

† **1.** A mazer; a cup, bowl, drinking vessel. Also *attrib.* *Obs.*

1601 FULBECKE *1st Pt. Parall.* 86 The Bæotians did giue.. Bacchus his mazard with a cluster of grapes. **1632** *Proc. Star Chamb.* (Camden) 303 In Salisbury they have digged up an old Bishop out of his grave and have made a mazzard of his scull. **1696** AUBREY *Misc.* (1857) 213 They..drank good ale in a brown mazard.

2. *jocular. arch.* **a.** The head.

1602 SHAKS. *Ham.* v. i. 97 Knockt about the Mazard with a Sextons Spade. **1621** MOLLE *Camerar. Liv. Libr.* v. xiv. 376 Certaine young men, hauing their mazerds well heated with drinking. **1624** MIDDLETON *Game at Chess* III. i. 306 The red hat, fit for the guilty mazzard. **1709** *Brit. Apollo* II. No. 39. 3/1 A..Fellow..takes me o'er the Mazard. **1876** BROWNING *Pacchiarotto* iv, With fancy he ran no hazard: Fact might knock him o'er the mazard.

b. The face, countenance, 'phiz'.

1762–71 H. WALPOLE *Vertue's Anecd. Paint.* (1786) IV. 103 His countenance harmonized with his humour, and Christian's mazard was a constant joke. **1820** MOORE *Fables* ii. 82 In vain the Court, aware of errors In all the old established mazards, Prohibited the use of mirrors, And tried to break them at all hazards.

3. *slang.* (*Anglo-Irish.*) The 'head' of a coin.

1802 MAR. EDGEWORTH *Irish Bulls* 129 'Music!' says he —'Skull!' says I—and down they come three brown mazzards.

Hence † **mazard** *v. trans.*, to knock on the head.

a **1616** B. JONSON *Love Restored*, The rogues let a huge trap-dore fall o' my head. If I had not been a spirit, I had been mazarded.

mazard ('mæzəd), *sb.*^{2} *dial.* Forms: 6–7 **mazar, mazer**, 7 **massard**, 7– **maz(z)ard**. [Of obscure origin: possibly a use of prec.] In the s.w. counties, a kind of small black cherry; in some other localities applied to the wild cherry; also *attrib.* as ***mazard cherry***.

1578 LYTE *Dodoens* VI. I. 723 The common small Cherries, or Mazars. **1579** LANGHAM *Gard. Health* (1633) 136 The gumme of the mazer or wilde Cherytree. *c* **1630** RISDON *Surv. Devon* §322 (1810) 332 A fruit, called mazards here, elsewhere black cherries. **1676** LADY FANSHAWE *Mem.* (1830) 70 They have, near this town [Barnstaple], a fruit

called a massard, like a cherry, but different in taste. **1782** M. CUTLER in *Life*, etc. (1888) I. 90 Set out some mazzard cherries I brought from Mr. Balch's, at Newbury. **1790** GROSE *Prov. Gloss.* (ed. 2), *Mazards*, black cherries. Glouc. **1855** KINGSLEY *Westw. Ho!* i, 'Red quarrenders' and mazard cherries.

mazare, obs. form of MAZER.

†**mazarine**, *sb.*[1] *Obs.* Also 7 **mazerine**, 8 **massereen, mazareen.** [Of obscure history.

Phillips 1706 mentions a phrase *à la mazarine* (not given by Fr. lexicographers), used to designate a particular mode of dressing fowls, and possibly f. the name of Cardinal Mazarin (*died* 1662) prime minister of France, or of the Duchesse de Mazarin, who died at Chelsea in 1699. *Mazarine dish, plate*, may perh. be attributive uses of this word.]

a. In early use also ***mazarine dish, plate***: A deep plate, usually of metal. **b.** (See quot. 1706.)

1673 MARVELL *Reh. Transp.* II. Wks. (Grosart) III. 451 What ragousts had here been for you to have furnish'd the Mazarines on your table! **1674** *Lond. Gaz.* No. 863/4 Stoln ..Seven Mazarine Plates, One Mazarine Plate of a smaller size, Ten Pottage Plates [etc.]. **1687** *Ibid.* No. 2237/4 Stolen .. 18 Plates, 4 deep ones or Mazarines. **1688** *Ibid.* No. 2315/8 There has been lately stolen out of Her Majesty's Kitchen, a Silver Mazarine Dish. **1706** PHILLIPS (ed. Kersey), *Mazarines*, a kind of little Dishes to be set in the middle of a large Dish for the setting out of Ragoos, or Fricassies; also a sort of small Tarts fill'd with Sweet-meats. **1736** BAILEY *Housh. Dict.* 234 Put them on a mazarine and bake them. **1747** MRS. GLASSE *Cookery* xiv. (1796) 224 When that is done, set it into a massereen, throw sugar all over, and garnish with orange. **1773** *Lond. Chron.* 7 Sept. 248/3 Mazareens.

mazarine (mæzə'ri:n), *sb.*[2] and *a.* Also 7 **mazarien,** 8 **mazerene, mazarene,** 7–9 **mazarin.** [Perh. from the name either of Cardinal Mazarin or of the Duchesse de Mazarin (see prec.); but evidence is wanting. (Not in Fr. Dicts.)]

1. In full ***mazarine blue***: A deep rich blue.

1686 *Lond. Gaz.* No. 2150/4 The other [saddle] with Gold, Silver, and Silk, of several Colours, upon Mazarine Blue Velvet. **1753** *Discov. J. Poulter* (ed. 2) 16 We sold .. the Mazerene blue Coat for one Pound. **1819** SAMOUELLE *Entomol. Compend.* 381 Mazarine blue moth (*Lycæna Cymon*). **1879** J. J. YOUNG *Ceram. Art* 132 The mazarine blue is similarly treated.

2. A stuff or a garment of a mazarine blue colour.

1694 *Lond. Gaz.* No. 3003/4 The Coach was lined with blue Shag or Mazarien. **1766** [ANSTEY] *Bath Guide* ix. 92 Bring my silver'd mazarine, Sweetest gown that e'er was seen.

b. A London common-councilman; so called from his mazarine blue gown.

1761 *Ann. Reg.* 238 Mr. ——, who was .. a *mazarine*... It is a sort of nick-name given to the common-councilmen on account of their wearing mazarine blue silk gowns upon this occasion [Lord Mayor's day].

3. as *adj.* Of a mazarine blue colour.

1684 *Lond. Gaz.* No. 1959/4 He hath on a Nutmeg colored Coat, faced with Mazarine Shag at the hands. **1688** *Ibid.* No. 2405/4 A bay Nag .. with a Mazarene Saddle. **1866** GEO. ELIOT *F. Holt* xxxi, Some with the orange-coloured ribbons and streamers of the true Tory candidate, some with the mazarine of the Whig.

†**mazarine**, *v. Obs.* In 7 **mazzarine.** [Prob. from the name of the Duchesse de Mazarin: see MAZARINE *sb.*[1]] *trans.* To decorate with lace in some particular manner.

1694 *Acct. for lace supplied to Q. Mary* in *Mrs. Palliser's Hist. Lace* (1902) 343 Three yards of lace to mazzarine ye pinners at 25 shillings.

†**mazarine hood.** *Obs.* (See quot. 1708.)

1689 SHADWELL *Bury Fair* II. i., *Millener*. What d'ye lack, Ladies? fine Mazarine Hoods, Fontanges, Girdles [etc.]. **1708** KERSEY, *Mazarine-hood*, a hood made after a particular fashion, such as was us'd by the Duchess of Mazarine.

Mazaroth, obs. form of MASORITE.

Mazatec ('mæzətɛk), *sb.* and *a.* **a.** (A member of) an Indian people inhabiting northern Oaxaca in southern Mexico. **b.** The language of this people. Also *attrib.* or as *adj.* Hence **Maza'tecan** *a.*

1909 WEBSTER, *Mazatec*, one of a tribe of Zapotecan Indians of northeastern Oaxaca, Mexico. They raise silk and are noted for gorgeous silken fabrics. **1949** E. A. NIDA *Morphol.* (ed. 2) II. 24 Mazatec, a language of Mexico. **1957** *Encycl. Brit.* V. 138/2 *Mazatec* (Guerrero, Puebla, Oaxaca; includes *Trique* and *Chocho*). **1958** J. BERRY in J. A. Fishman *Readings Sociol. of Lang.* (1968) 751 One of the Mazatec dialects. **1962** D. H. HYMES in *Ibid* 111 The Mazatecs of Mexico. *Ibid.* 129 Neighboring dialects may differ, as when one group of Mazatec abstract the tones of their language for a whistled code, while the Soyaltepec Mazatec do not. **1963** *Times* 27 April 9/7 Land where heron live at peace with primitive Mazatecan Indians. **1967** S. C. GUDSCHINSKY *How to learn Unwritten Lang.* ii. 19 Transitive relationship is expressed in Mazatec by a transitive verb followed by a noun object and a noun subject. *Ibid.* 22 Mazatec possessive phrases are quite different from English. **1974** *Encycl. Brit. Micropædia* VI. 728/1 The Mazatec language is most closely related to Chocho, Ixcatec, and Popoloca. *Ibid.*, The Mazatec are Roman Catholic with syncretistic elements.

Mazbi, var. MAZHABI.

Mazdaism ('mæzdəɪz(ə)m). Also **Mazdeism.** [f. Avestic *mazda*, the name of the good principle (Ahura-mazda, Ormuzd) of ancient Persian theology.] The ancient Persian religion as taught in the Avesta; Zoroastrianism.

1871 P. SMITH *Anc. Hist. East* III. xviii. 384 The Zendavesta claims to be the revelation of *Mazdeism*. **1886** *Encycl. Brit.* XX. 360 Zarathustric religion (Mazdaism).

So **Maz'dean, -'dæan** *a.*, pertaining to the religion of the Avesta; *sb.* an adherent of this religion.

1880 DARMESTETER tr. *Zend-Avesta* I. Introd. 42 There was a Mazdean literature in existence in those times. **18..** J. MILNE *Relig. Persia* in *Cycl. Sci.* I. 601 The Mazdean's idea of the resurrection glorified man's body as his eternal companion.

Mazdaist ('mæzdəɪst). [f. as MAZDAISM + -IST.] An adherent of Mazdaism.

1920 in WEBSTER. **1932** *Antiquity* VI. 277 Where Mazdaists and Christians were found together, there must certainly have been adherents of the Manichæan creed. **1941** *Burlington Mag.* Aug. 59/1 Mohammedans .. Mazdaists .. Christians, Buddhists and perhaps Jews as well had their own temples.

maze (meɪz), *sb.* Forms: 3–8 **mase,** 4 **masse,** 4– **maze.** [See MAZE *v.*]

†**1.** ***the maze.*** (The use of the article is somewhat difficult to account for, but cf. the similar use with names of diseases.) *Obs.*

a. Delirium, delusion; disappointment.

1297 R. GLOUC. (Rolls) 6585 Wite he sede alle men þat an erþe wonieþ her þat it nis bote þe pure mase [*B.* masse] eni kinges poer. *c* **1305** *Judas Iscariot* 14 in *E.E.P.* (1862) 107 þis wyf was wel sore adrad: to hire louerd heo tolde [her dream] anon ȝe, he seide, hit is þe mase. **1362** LANGL. *P. Pl.* A. III. 155 Heo ledeþ þe lawe as hire luste and loue-dayes makeþ, þe Mase for a Mene mon þauȝ he mote euere. **1377** *Ibid.* B. Prol. 196 Better is a litel losse þan a longe sorwe þe mase amonge vs alle þouȝ we mysse a schrewe.

b. Vanity, vain amusement, dissipation.

1362 LANGL. *P. Pl.* A. I. 6 Sixt þou þis peple Al hou bisy þei ben aboute þe mase? **14..** *How Goode wyfe* 62 in *Q. Eliz. Acad.* 46 Go not as it wer A gase Fro house to house, to seke þe mase.

†**2. a.** A delusive fancy. **b.** A trick, deception.

c **1374** CHAUCER *Troylus* v. 468 Al this nas but a mase [*v.r.* maze]. *c* **1386** —— *Nun's Pr. T.* 273 Men dreme al day of Owles or of Apes, And of many a maze ther-with-al. **1412–20** LYDG. *Chron. Troy* v. xxxvii. (1555), All was done for an ydell mase. **14..** *Kyng & Hermit* 417 in Hazl. *E.P.P.* I. 29 Hopys thou, I wold for a mase Stond in the myre there?

3. a. A state of bewilderment. *Obs.* exc. *dial.*

In early examples it is uncertain whether *a maze* or AMAZE *sb.* is intended.

1430 [see AMAZE *sb.* 1]. *c* **1489** CAXTON *Blanchardyn* liv. 221 The faire Beatrix .. stood in a maze. **1535** JOYE *Apol. Tindale* (Arb.) 48 Orels leue the reder as yt were in hys Maze. **1577–87** HOLINSHED *Chron.* III. 1139/2 The maze was such, that besides his sonne maister Arthur Greie.. not a man else did follow him. **1631** HEYWOOD *2nd Pt. Faire Maid of West* III. Wks. 1874 II. 374 Six, to the maze Of all the rest, were slain. **1653** *Cloria & Narcissus* 274 Admiration stands at a maze. **1666** BUNYAN *Grace Ab.* §20 (1900) 302 At this I was put to an exceeding Maze. **1722** SEWEL *Hist. Quakers* (1795) I. IV. 271 That he came to a perfect recovery from his having been in a maze seems to appear plainly. **1819** W. TENNANT *Papistry Storm'd* (1827) 136 [He] up the street Rade on—in mickle maze I ween, For fient ae face was to be seen.

¶**b.** Used by Scott for: Confusing haze.

1813 SCOTT *Trierm.* Concl. i, When a pilgrim strays, In morning mist or evening maze, Along the mountain lone.

4. a. A structure consisting of a network of winding and intercommunicating paths and passages arranged in bewildering complexity, so that without guidance it is difficult to find one's way in it; a labyrinth; *occas.* in *plural*, the windings of a labyrinth. Also in *fig.* context. *spec.* in *Psychol.*, a device, consisting of a correct path concealed by blind alleys, used to study human and animal intelligence and learning. Also *attrib.* and *Comb.*

Sometimes loosely applied to a structure in which there is a single path winding in such a manner that the distance from the entrance to the end is enormously greater than it would be in a direct line. (So in quot. 1903.)

c **1385** CHAUCER *L.G.W.* 2010 *Ariadne*, The hous is krynkeled two & fro, And hath so queynte weyis for to go For it is shapyn as the mase is wrought. **1432–50** tr. *Higden* (Rolls) I. 311 In that yle is also oon of the iiij. mases [L. *de quatuor labyrinthis*]. **1534** MORE *Comf. agst. Trib.* II. Wks. 1202/2 They walke round about as it were in a round mase. **1577** B. GOOGE *Heresbach's Husb.* II. (1586) 66 Roses growing in Borders, and made in a maze. **1590** SHAKS. *Mids. N.* II. i. 99. **1615** BRATHWAIT *Strappado* (1878) 104 There doth grow, A groue of fatall Elmes, wherein a maze, Or labyrinth is fram'd. **1762** FALCONER *Shipwr.* II. 207 Such arduous toil sage Daedalus endur'd, In mazes self-invented long immur'd. **1835** THIRLWALL *Greece* V. I. 133 He vanquished the monster of the labyrinth, and retraced its mazes. **1836–9** DICKENS *Sk. Boz, Seven Dials*, The gordian knot was all very well in its way: so was the maze of Hampton Court: so is the maze at the Beulah Spa. **1901** W. S. SMALL in *Amer. Jrnl. Psychol.* XII. 228 The process of learning the way through this maze is adequately described as a gradual establishment of direct associations by profiting by chance experience. **1903** G. E. JEANS *Handbk. Linc.* 222 A maze, called *Julian's Bower*, is cut in the grassy brow of the cliff. **1914** F. A. C. PERRIN (*title*) An experimental and introspective study of the human learning process in the maze. **1921** *Lancet* 19 March 597/2 The .. Porteous maze tests which, testing as they do the foresight, the capacity to plan, the practical judgment and concentration of the child, supply a marked lack of the Binet scale. **1940** *Brit. Jrnl. Psychol.* Jan. 191 Many maze workers have noted the fact of variability in performance from day to day. **1951** G. HUMPHREY *Thinking* viii. 257 Verbal instruction improves the score in stylus-maze running. **1958** *Spectator* 8 Aug. 201/1 The obsessional maze-running experiments of the American rat-psychologists. **1964** M. ARGYLE *Psychol. & Social Probl.* v. 67 [Areas in which delinquents differ from non-delinquents] Impulsiveness, weakness of 'ego-control', tendency to cut corners in maze tests.

b. *transf.* and *fig.*

In 16–17th c. often in phr. ***to tread a maze***, perhaps with allusion to 4 c.

1542–5 BRINKLOW *Lament.* (1874) 106 Leadynge them in an endlesse mase of dyrtye tradicyons and folyshe ceremonyes. **1578** *Chr. Prayers* 17 To the intent we should not wander any longer vp and down in the mazes of this world. **1596** KEYMIS *2nd Voy. Guiana* G 4 In the discouerie of Guiana, you may read both of Oreliano .. and of Berreo, with others that haue trode this maze, and lost them selues in seeking to find this countrie. **1605** BACON *Adv. Learn.* II. xi. §1 The trauaile therein taken seemeth to haue ben rather in a Maze, then in a way. **1615** CROOKE *Body of Man* 15 The Labyrinthæan Mazes and web of the small arteries. **1646** SIR. T. BROWNE *Pseud. Ep.* I. x. 42 To lose us in this maze of error. **1781** CRABBE *Library* 121 Whether 'tis yours to lead the willing mind Through History's mazes, and the turnings find. **1837** DISRAELI *Venetia* IV. ii, They were lost in a delicious maze of metaphor and music. **1849** MACAULAY *Hist. Eng.* iii. I. 347 Bath was .. a maze of only four or five hundred houses. **1872** BLACK *Adv. Phaeton* vi. 74 A tangled maze of bracken and briar.

c. A winding movement, esp. in a dance.

1610 *Histrio-m.* III. 232 The world doth turn a maze in giddy round. **1617** B. JONSON *Vision of Delight* (near end), In curious knots and mazes so The Spring at first was taught to go. **1704** POPE *Windsor For.* 122 To plains with well-breath'd beagles we repair, And trace the mazes of the circling hare. **1742** YOUNG *Nt. Th.* IX. 9 Dancing, with the rest, the giddy Maze, Where Disappointment smiles at Hope's Career.

†**d.** ? A mode of plaiting the hair. *Obs.*

1657 R. LIGON *Barbadoes* 16 Their haire not shorne .. close to their heads; nor in quarters, and mases.

5. *attrib.*, as ***maze-like*** adj. and adv.; **Maze-Monday** *dial.* (Cornw.), the Monday after pay-day at a mine (cf. *Mazed Monday*, MAZED *ppl. a.*) (E.D.D.); †**Maze-Sunday** *dial.* (Devon), some particular Sunday set apart for feasting.

1598 SYLVESTER *Du Bartas* II. ii. IV. *Columnes* 749 The Maze-like Mean that turns and wends so fair. **1700** T. BROWN *Acc. Journ. Exon* Wks. 1709 III. 103. I arrived at Exon... The next Day being Sunday, call'd by the Natives of this Country Maze-Sunday, (and indeed not without some Reason, for the People look'd as if they were Gallied) I was waked by [etc.]. **1889** PATER *G. de Latour* (1896) 35 Its maze-like crypt, centering in the shrine of the sibylline Notre-Dame. **1904** *Westm. Gaz.* 15 Mar. 1/3, I looked down on to rows of clipped, regular, hornbeam hedges, with grass paths between them, maze-like.

maze (meɪz), *v.* Forms: 3–6 **mase,** 5 **mayze,** 6 **mayse,** 4– **maze.** [The vb. and the related MAZE *sb.* appear before 1300; OE. may have had **masian* vb. or **mæs, *mase* sb.; a compound *ámasod* (= AMAZED) occurs once in the alliterative phrase 'ámasod and ámarod' (*Be Domes Dæge* 125, whence quoted by Wulfstan *Hom.* 137).

Possible cognates are Norw. dial. *mas* exhausting labour, annoying pertinacity, whim, fancy, idle chatter; *masa* to be busy, toil, to pester, worry, to chatter, *passive* to fall into a doze; Sw. *mas* sluggard, *masa* to crawl, walk lazily, *refl.* to bask, sun oneself.]

1. *trans.* To stupefy, daze; to put out of one's wits; †to craze, infatuate. Chiefly in *passive*. Now *arch.* and *dial.*

a **1300** *E.E. Psalter* lxxvii[i]. 71 [65] And wakened es lauerd als slepand, Als mased [Vulg. *crapulatus*] of wine mightand. *c* **1374** CHAUCER *Anel. & Arc.* 322, I am so mased þat I deye, Arcyte hathe borne aweye þe keye Of all my worlde, and my goode Aventure! *c* **1386** —— *Man of Law's T.* 428 She seyde, she was so mazed in the see That she forgat hir mynde, by hir trouthe. *a* **1400** *Cursor M.* 27891 (Cott. Galba) Dronkinhede .. mase a man .. bod for to speke and do foly; .. so es his minde mased and mad. *c* **1400** *Destr. Troy* 13280 Folis .. þat heron the melody [of the Sirens], so mekill are masit in hert, Lettyn sailis doun slyde, & in slym fallyn. *c* **1425** [see MAP *v.*[2]]. **1530** PALSGR. 633/2 You mased the boye so sore with beatyng that he coulde nat speake a worde. **1563** B. GOOGE *Sonn.* (Arb.) 88 Gorgon .. Who with her Beautie mazed men, and nowe doth raygne in Hell. **1591** *Troub. Raigne K. John* II. (1611) 79, I am mad indeed, My heart is maz'd, my sences all foredone. **1610** B. JONSON *Alch.* v. v, Finding This tumult 'bout my dore (to tell you true) It somewhat maz'd me. **1658** MANTON *Exp. Jude* 16 Wks. 1871 V. 318 This is the devil's device, first to maze people, as birds are with a light and a bell in the night, and then to drive them into the net. **1716** B. CHURCH *Hist. Philip's War* (1865) I. 21 The Pilot yet sat his Horse, tho' so maz'd with the Shot, as not to have sense to guide him. **1725** BRADLEY *Fam. Dict.* s.v. *Milk*, Neither should the Milk-maid .. affright the Cow or maze her. **1820** SCOTT *Abbot* xix, 'The lad is mazed!' said the falconer to himself. **1855** A. MANNING *O. Chelsea Bun-house* xiv. 232 My head was mazed with my journey. **1863** MRS. GASKELL *Sylvia's L.* III. 100, If I could but think; but it's my head as is aching so; doctor, I wish yo'd go, for I need being alone, I'm so mazed. **1870** MORRIS *Earthly Par.* III. IV. 295 Then said the King, 'The man is mazed with fear'.

†**2.** *intr.* To be stupefied or delirious; to wander in mind. *Obs.*

c **1350** *Will. Palerne* 438 A fers feintise folwes me oft, .. þat i mase al marred for mournyng neiȝh hondes. *c* **1386** CHAUCER *Merch. T.* 1143 'Ye maze, maze, goode sire', quod

she. *a* **1568** ASCHAM *Scholem.* II. (Arb.) 159 All men may stand still to mase and muse vpon it.

3. *trans.* To bewilder, perplex, confuse. Often with some notion of a figurative maze or labyrinth.

1482 CAXTON *Trevisa's Higden* I. xxx. 40 b, Who that gooth in to that hows [a labyrinth] & wolde come out agayn . . shal be so mased that out can he not goo. *a* **1500** *Assemb. Ladies* 38 Other ther were, so mased in her mind, Al wayes [of a maze] were good for hem, bothe eest and west. **1768** JOHNSON *Pref. Shaks.* Wks. IX. 245 He who has mazed his imagination in following the phantoms which other writers raise up before him, may here be cured of his delirious ecstacies. **1868** ROGERS *Pol. Econ.* Pref., The historian who is ignorant of the interpretations of political economy is constantly mazed in a medley of unconnected and unintelligible facts.

refl. **1627** W. SCLATER *Exp. 2 Thess.* (1629) 73 Wee maze our selues sometimes in following Schoolemen.

4. *intr.* To move in a mazy track. †Also *to maze it.*

1591 SYLVESTER *Du Bartas* I. iii. 86 Like as moulten Lead being poured forth Upon a levell plat of sand or earth, In many fashions mazeth to and fro. **1756** LANGHORNE *Poems* (1760) 44 Thus silver Wharf . . Still, melancholy-mazing, seems to mourn. **1767** H. BROOKE *Fool of Qual.* (ed. 2) II. xi. 179 Walter led his . . patron through this field and that field; . . till, having mazed it and circled it for . . three hours, he finally conducted the serjeant to the very gate at which he had first entered. **1865** CARLYLE *Fredk. Gt.* XIX. i. (1872) VIII. 108 They struck their tents everywhere, . . and only went mazing hither and thither.

†**b.** *trans.* To involve in a maze or in intricate windings; to form mazes upon. *Obs.*

1606 SYLVESTER *Du Bartas* II. iv. I. *Tropheis* 1003 Meander-like . . Thou run'st to meet thy self's pure streams behind thee Mazing the Meads wher thou dost turn & wind thee. **1654** WHITLOCK *Zootomia* To Author A iv, Some maze their Thoughts in Labyrinths, and thus Invoke no Reader, but an Oedipus.

maze, obs. form of MAIZE; var. MEASE.

mazed (meɪzd), *ppl. a.* [f. MAZE *v.* + -ED[1].] In senses of the verb: Stupefied, dazed, crazed; bewildered, confused; †terrified.

Mazed Monday (dial. Cornw.): (*a*) = *Maze-Monday* (MAZE *sb.* 5); (*b*) the Monday before Christmas (E.D.D.).

c **1350** *Will. Palerne* 884 So witerly was þat word wounde to hert, þat he ferd as a mased man an marred neiȝ honde. **1493** *Festivall* (W. de W. 1515) 71 b, They . . walked up & downe in yᵉ countre lyke mased beestes. **1596** SPENSER *F.Q.* V. viii. 38 Like mazed deare . . they flew. **1613** SHAKS. *Hen. VIII*, II. iv. 185 Many maz'd considerings, did throng And prest in with this Caucion. **1755** WESLEY *Wks.* (1872) II. 342, I said 'To be sure it is some mazed man'. **1830** MRS. BRAY *Fitz of F.* iii. (1884) 28 He had very much the appearance of what the country people here call a mazed man. **1836** KEBLE in *Lyra Apost.* (1849) 222 The voice ineffable Wakening your mazed thoughts with an Almighty spell.

Hence †**'mazedly** *adv.*, †**'mazedness.**

c **1386** CHAUCER *Clerk's T.* 1005 She ferde as she had stert out of a sleepe, Til she out of hire mazednesse abreyde. **14** . . HOCCLEVE *Min. Poems* (1892) 44 Syn my spirit nat dar putte vp his bille, . . But in his mazidnesse abydith stille. **1530** PALSGR. 243/2 Masydnesse, *musardie, desuere, effroy.*

mazeful ('meɪzfʊl), *a. Obs.* exc. *arch.* [f. MAZE *sb.* + -FUL.] Bewildering, confounding.

1595 SPENSER *Epithal.* 190 And stand astonisht lyke to those which red Medusaes mazeful hed. **1897** F. THOMPSON *New Poems* 3 It was a mazeful wonder.

mazels, obs. pl. of MEASLE *sb.*

‖**mazel tov** ('mazəl toːv, tɒf). Also **mazal tov, mazel tov**, etc. [ad. mod.Heb. *mazzāl ṭōḇ* good luck, f. Heb. *mazzālōth* pl., constellations.] As a salutation: good luck, congratulations.

1862 *Once a Week* VII. 192/2 Whereupon all present wish him *mazal tov* (good speed), and the ceremony is at an end. **1892** I. ZANGWILL *Childr. Ghetto* I. 37 There was a hubbub of congratulation ('*Mazzoltov, Mazzoltov*', 'Good Luck'). **1932** L. GOLDING *Magnolia St.* III. iv. 520 The air pattered like hail with their good luck wishes . . *Mazel tov, mazel tov!* **1957** L. STERN *Midas Touch* III. xx. 149 '*Mazeltof*, father,' he said. **1959** B. KOPS *Hamlet of Stepney Green* II. ii, Going to have another one? . . Mazeltoff, darling. **1970** *New Yorker* 19 Sept. 32/1 'Uri is going to be a father.' Yigael . . said, 'He told me. *Mazel tov.*' **1972** 'H. HOWARD' *Nice Day for Funeral* x. 138, I said, 'Mazeltov. I hope you're both very happy.' **1973** *Jewish Chron.* 2 Feb. 19/3 Mother and baby . . are . . doing well. A hearty mazzeltov to them!

mazelyn, variant of MASELIN *Obs.*, a mazer.

mazement ('meɪzmənt). Also 6 **masement.** [f. MAZE *v.* + -MENT.] Stupor; a state of stupor or trance. Also = AMAZEMENT.

c **1580** MUNDAY *View Sundry Examples* (Shaks. Soc. 1851) 97 Call to mind the greevous and suddain Earthquake . . which caused such a mazement through the whole Citie. **1598** TOFTE *Alba* (1880) 72 Though that it be such As euery eye with masement it doth fill. **1727** BAILEY vol. II, *Mazement*, amazement. **1890** W. A. WALLACE *Only a Sister* 167 Just wait till I get near you, and we'll see if I can't find another mazement for you. **1901** KIPLING *Kim* xi. 264 A very few white people, but many Asiatics, can throw themselves into a mazement as it were by repeating their own names over and over again to themselves.

mazer ('meɪzə(r)), *sb. Obs.* exc. *Hist.* Forms: 3– **mazer**, 4–9 **maser.** Also 2–3 **mazere**, 4 **mazre**, 4–5 **maseer(e**, 5 **mausure, masour, masowyr**, 5–6 **masar, masere**, 6 **meyser, mas(s)or, masser, masure, mazur, mazare**, 6–7 **mazor, mazar.** [a. OF. *masere, masre* (*masdre, madre*, whence F. *madré* veined, variegated) used in senses 1 and 2; of Teut. origin: cf. OHG. *masar* excrescence on a tree (glossing L. *tuber, nodus*), MHG. *maser* excrescence on a tree, maple, drinking cup, mod.G. *maser* markings in wood; MDu. *maeser* maple; ON. *mǫsur-r* maple (:—**masur-oz*).

The Teut. root **mas-*, **mǣs-*, expressing the notion of 'spot' or 'excrescence', is found also in OHG. *mâsa* (MHG. *mâse*) cicatrix, spot on the body, early mod.Du. *mase, maese* spot, mesh (Du. *maas* mesh, *maashout* maplewood); Norw. dial. *masa* to grain, paint in imitation of the grain of wood; and the words cited s.v. MEASLE.

The Welsh *masarn* maple, sycamore, is certainly from English, though the evidence of the use of *mazer* in this sense in Eng. is somewhat scanty.]

1. A hard wood (? properly maple; but cf. quot. *c* 1500 in b) used as a material for drinking cups.

c **1200** *Trin. Coll. Hom.* 163 Ðe caliz [is] of tin; and hire [the priest's concubine's] nap of mazere. **1419** *Will of Mounford* (Somerset Ho.), Ciphum de mazer legatum cum argento. **1593–1656** *Rites & Mon. Ch. Durh.* (Surtees 1903) 80 The goodly Cup called Sᵗ Beedes Bowl, the outside whereof was of black Mazer.

†**b.** The tree yielding this wood. *Obs. rare.*

14 . . *Metr. Voc.* in Wr.-Wülcker 629 [In list of trees] *Iuniparus, labruscaque, mirra*, jenupyrtre wyld vyne masere. **1483** *Cath. Angl.* 229/2 A Maser, *cantarus, murra*; *murreus*; *murpis* (A. *murrus*) *Arbor est.* *c* **1500** in Turner *Dom. Archit.* I. 144 *note*, Take many rype walenottes and water hem a while, and put hem in a moiste pytt, and hile hem, and ther shalbe grawe therof a grett stoke that we calle masere. **1547** SALESBURY *Welsh Dict.*, *Masarn*, Masar.

2. A bowl, drinking-cup, or goblet without a foot, originally made of 'mazer' wood, often richly carved or ornamented and mounted with silver and gold or other metal. Often applied to bowls entirely of metal or other material.

1311 in *Archæol.* (1887) L. I. 176, j mazer cum pede argenteo. *c* **1330** R. BRUNNE *Chron. Wace* (Rolls) 11418 He gaf . . Somme masers of riche pris. **1420** *E.E. Wills* (1882) 46 Also .i. bord mausure with a bond of seluer. **1424** *Ibid.* 56, I wull he haue my maser of a vine rote. **1530** *Burgh Rec. Edinb.* (1871) II. 39 A masser of siluer ourgilt. **1555** W. WATREMAN *Fardle Facions* II. ix. 193 Of the Skulles of the heades thus slaine, thei [Scithians] make masures to drincke in. **1579** SPENSER *Sheph. Cal.* Aug. 26 A mazer ywrought of the Maple warre. **1645** EVELYN *Diary* 25 Jan., They shew'd us . . mazers of beaten and solid gold set with diamonds, rubies, and emeralds. **1697** DRYDEN *Virgil* (1721) I. Ded. 13 One of his Shepherds describes a Bowl, or Mazer, curiously carved. **1814** SCOTT *Ld. of Isles* V. xxxiv, 'Bring here', he said, 'the mazers four'. **1851** D. WILSON *Preh. Ann.* (1863) II. IV. ix. 488 The royal Mazer, or convivial bowl.

fig. **1629** Z. BOYD *Last Battell* 1123 Take now the Cuppe of Saluation, the great Mazer of his mercie.

†**3.** The head; = MAZARD *sb.*[1] 2. *Obs.*

1581 J. BELL *Haddon's Answ. Osor.* 77 b, Being imagined in your own braynsicke mazer. *a* **1652** BROME *Love-sick Court* IV. iii, So wilt thou whilst thou canst lift thy bottle To that old Mazer.

b. *transf.* A helmet.

1591 SYLVESTER *Du Bartas* I. iv. 614 Hardy Lælius . . All in gilt armour, on his glistring Mazor A stately plume, of Orange mixt with Azur.

4. *attrib.* and *Comb.*: †**mazer-band**, the silver binding of a mazer; **mazer bowl, cup, -dish** = 2; †**mazer tree** = 1 b; **mazer wood**, = sense 1.

1441 in *Archæol.* (1887) L. I. 187 Unum *maserband. **1562–3** *Ibid.* 193 A *masar bole wᵗʰ a border of sylver and gilt abowt ytt. **1590** SPENSER *F.Q.* II. xii. 49. **1686–7** AUBREY *Rem. Gentilism & Judaism* (1881) 35 A Mazar-bowle of maple (Gossips bowle) full of beer. **1434** *E.E. Wills* (1882) 101 A litil *maser coppe. **1656** TRADESCANT *Mus. Tradesc.* 52 *Mazer dishes. ? *c* **1475** *Sqr. Lowe Degre* 689 She . . closed hym in a *maser-tre. **1595** DUNCAN *App. Etymol.* (E.D.S.) 66 *Acer*, the maser tree. **1656** TRADESCANT *Mus. Tradesc.* 44 The plyable *Mazer wood, being warmed in water will work to any form.

Hence †**mazer** *v. trans.*, = MAZARD *v.*

1596 NASHE *Saffron-Walden* V 4 He terrefies mee with insulting 'hee was Tom Burwels the Fencers Scholler, and that he will squeaze and mazer me whensoeuer he met me'.

mazer, mazerd, obs. ff. MAZARD *sb.*[2] and *sb.*[1]

mazerine, obs. form of MAZARINE *sb.*[2]

mazey, mazi, variants of MAZY *a.* and *sb.*

Mazhabi ('mʌzhɑːbiː). *India.* Also **Maz(ah)bi, Muzbi, Muz(hu)bee.** [Hindi, f. Arab. *mazhab* religion.] A convert to the Sikh religion from Islam, *spec.* in the Punjab; a converted Chuhra or member of the sweeper caste.

1849 J. D. CUNNINGHAM *Hist. Sikhs* 379 *Muzhŭbee*, converts from Mahometanism are so called. **1858** R. TEMPLE *Let.* 25 May in Yule & Burnell *Hobson-Jobson* (1886) 464/1 To the same destination (Delhi) was sent a strong corps of Muzhubee (low-caste) Sikhs, numbering 1200 men, to serve as pioneers. **1908** KIPLING *Lett. of Travel* (1920) 162 A fair sprinkling of Punjabis—ex-soldiers, Sikhs, Muzbis, and Jats—are coming in on the boats. **1917** *Encycl. Relig. & Ethics* IX. 608/2 Such converts may form new castes, like the Mazbi or Mazhabi Sikhs, who were by origin Chūhrās, or scavengers, outside the Hindu pale. **1923** *Chambers's Jrnl.* 20 Jan. 113/1 He was not going to give his daughter in marriage to a *Muzbee.* **1965** SHER SINGH *Sansis of Punjab* ix. 188 If a Sansi takes food from a Choohra, Mazahbi, Chamar or other lower castes, he is outcast and fined.

mazil, obs. form of MEASLE.

mazily ('meɪzɪlɪ), *adv.* [f. MAZY *a.* + -LY[2].] In a mazy manner.

a **1225** *Ancr. R.* 272 Þe bimasede Isboset, lo! hwu he dude maseliche [*MS. T.* masedliche]. **1839** BAILEY *Festus* xviii. (1852) 226 While six sister goddesses mazily tread The bright fields of air. **1855** S. BROOKS *Aspen Crt.* I. x. 144 Those mazily cut Valentines one sees in windows. **1864** TENNYSON *Milton*, The brooks of Eden mazily murmuring.

maziness ('meɪzɪnɪs). [f. MAZY *a.* + -NESS.] The state or condition of being mazy.

1847 in WEBSTER. **1857** R. H. PATTERSON *Ess. Hist. & Art* (1862) 435 This peculiar feature . . gives to Indian mythology a haziness and maziness which set arrangement and strict definition at defiance.

'mazing, *vbl. sb.* [f. MAZE *v.* + -ING[1].] The action of causing amazement, astonishment.

1600 S. NICHOLSON *Acolastus* (1876) 39 Sweeping they came, and seemd to brush the ground, Their tipto-tripping pace bred double mazing, Their ratling silkes my sences did confound.

mazing ('meɪzɪŋ), *ppl. a.* [f. as prec. + -ING[2].] Causing confusion, bewilderment, or perplexity.

c **1449** PECOCK *Repr.* II. xiv. 230 He schal ful ofte bi masing studie be ful idil, whanne he myȝte be weel and fruytfulli occupied. **1556** J. HEYWOOD *Spider & F.* lviii. 30 This ant . . Hath cast manie masing mists before your iyse. **1623** tr. *Favine's Theat. Hon.* VI. v. 132 Clewes, to guide us out of these mazing Labyrinths. **1833** *Philol. Museum* II. 442 The mazing and dazzling power of a rich system of harmonies.

mazo- ('meɪzəʊ), used as comb. form of mod.L. *māza* placenta, a. Gr. μᾶζα cake.

‖**mazocacothesis** (ˌmeɪzəkæ'kɒθɪsɪs) [Gr. κακός bad + θέσις a placing], malposition of the placenta; hence ˌ**mazocaco'thetic** *a.* ‖**mazolysis** (meɪ'zɒlɪsɪs) [Gr. λύσις a loosing], the separation or detachment of the placenta; hence **mazo'lytic** *a.* ‖**mazopathia** (meɪzə'pæθɪə) [Gr. πάθος suffering, feeling: see -PATHY], a disease of, or originating from, the placenta; hence **mazo'pathic** *a.*

1856 in MAYNE *Expos. Lex.*

‖**mazodynia** (meɪzə'daɪnɪə). *Med.* [mod.L., f. Gr. μαζ-ός breast + ὀδύνη pain.] = MASTODYNIA.

1850 BIRKETT *Dis. Breast* 18 The severe neuralgic affection comprehended under the term mazodynia.

†**ma'zology.** [f. Gr. μαζό-ς breast + -LOGY. Cf. MASTOLOGY.] Brewster's substitute for MAMMALOGY.

1807–29 *Edinb. Encycl.* XIII. 393/1 *Mazology* . . is that branch of zoology which treats of the class of mammiferous animals. **1828–32** WEBSTER, *Mazology*, . . the doctrine or history of mammiferous animals.

Hence **mazo'logical** *a.* = MAMMALOGICAL; **ma'zologist** = MAMMALOGIST.

1807–29 *Edinb. Encycl.* XIII. 393/2 The two most eminent mazologists of antiquity are Aristotle and Pliny. **1828–32** WEBSTER, *Mazological*, . . *Mazologist.*

mazor, obs. form of MAZER.

Mazorete, -etical, obs. ff. MASORETE, -ETICAL.

mazouelle. *Antiq.* = MASUEL.

1857 *Archæol. Jrnl.* XIV. 281 A German mazouelle of steel.

mazoun, obs. form of MASON *sb.*[1]

mazourca, -ka, obs. forms of MAZURKA.

mazout, var. MAZUT.

Mazuca, mazur: see MASOOKA, MAZER.

mazuma (mə'zuːmə). *U.S. slang.* Also **mazume.** [Yiddish.] Money, cash.

1904 G. V. HOBART *Jim Hickey* i. 15 We're a sad bunch . . when we haven't a little mazume in the vest pocket. **1906** 'O. HENRY' *Four Million* (1916) 131 Burn a few punk sticks in the joss house to the great god Mazuma. **1907** C. E. MULFORD *Bar-20* viii. 90 When th' mazuma is divided up it won't buy a meal. **1913** —— *Coming of Cassidy* xii. 191 'What's this?' he demanded. . . 'Money,' replied Hopalong. 'It's that shiny stuff you buy things with. Spondulix, cash, mazuma.' **1926** *Amer. Speech* May 456/1 How many of those using the word *mazuma* know its meaning? As originally used by the Jewish people it is '*m'zumon*' and is a Chaldean word meaning in literal translation the 'ready necessary'. It is employed in the Talmud which is written in Chaldean and not Hebrew. **1941** *Amer. Mercury* May 615/1 When you die, you have to leave your mazuma behind. **1943** W. H. CHASE *Sourdough Pot* xvi. 97 A sign tacked on a tent pole, informed the public, that 'No Credit—You must product the mazuma. We are not in business for our health.' **1972** *Times Lit. Suppl.* 29 Sept. 1154/3 Likewise piling up its mazuma by legerdemain.

mazurka (mə'zɜːkə, mə'zʊəkə). Also 9 **mizurko, mazourca, mazourka.** [a. Polish *mazurka* woman of the Polish province Mazovia. In Fr. *masurka, mazurka, -ourka, -urke*, Ger. *masurka.*]

1. A lively Polish dance resembling the polka; the music is in triple time.

1818 T. CREEVEY in Sir H. Maxwell *Papers* etc. (1904) I. 283 My delight was to see the Mizurko danced by Madame Suwarrow and her brother the Prince Nariskin. **1831**

Society I. 306 A large party had assembled there..to practice the Mazourca. **1842** MOTLEY *Corr.* (1889) I. iv. 116 He is at all the parties perpetually, and perpetually dancing the mazurka. **1885** MABEL COLLINS *Prettiest Woman* x, The after-supper-dance is called the White-Mazurka, because it is kept up till the daylight is broad and clear.

2. A piece of music intended to accompany this dance, or composed in its rhythm.

1854 THACKERAY *Newcomes* xxviii, The Austrian brass band..plays the most delightful mazurkas and waltzes.

mazut (mə'zuːt). Also **masut, mazout.** [Russ. *mazút*, ad. Arab. *makhzulat* refuse, waste.] The viscous liquid left as residue after the distillation of Russian petroleum, used as fuel oil and a coarse lubricant.

1897 *Chambers's Jrnl.* 19 June 393 Masut, the new substitute for coal. **1907** *Times Engin. Suppl.* 16 Oct. 4/2 Among liquid fuels which may be employed that known as 'masut' will help to supply the increasing demand. **1924** J. A. HAMMERTON *Countries of World* II. 1277/1 'Crude oil'..is refined into benzine, petrol and kerosene, the refuse or 'mazout' being consumed for common fuel and furnaces. **1924** *Blackw. Mag.* Feb. 152/1 They caught the sickly sweet smell of half-burnt 'Mazut' fuel. **1951** R. CAMPBELL *Light on Dark Horse* xx. 288 The oil, or mazout, has also spoilt the quality of the red-mullet. **1974** P. HIGHSMITH *Ripley's Game* v. 47 He tackled with broom and dustpan the exterior of the pipes and the floor around their *mazout* furnace.

mazy ('meɪzɪ), *a.* Forms: 6 **macy,** 6–7 **mazie,** 7 **mazi,** 7, 9 **mazey,** 7– **mazy.** [f. MAZE *sb.* + -Y^1.]

1. Resembling or of the nature of a maze; full of windings and turnings.

1579 SPENSER *Sheph. Cal.* Dec. 25, I wont to raunge amydde the mazie thickette. **1598** SYLVESTER *Du Bartas* II. i. I. *Eden* 510 Not treading Sin's false mazy measures. **1615** CROOKE *Body of Man* 465 A mazey laberynth of small veines and arteries. **1667** MILTON *P.L.* IX. 161, I..prie In every Bush and Brake, where hap may finde The serpent sleeping, in whose mazie foulds To hide me. **1714** POPE *Rape of Lock* II. 139 Some thrid the mazy ringlets of her hair. **1728** —— *Dunc.* I. 68 Pleas'd with the madness of the mazy dance. **1797** COLERIDGE *Kubla Khan* 25 Five miles meandering with a mazy motion..the sacred river ran. **1844** HOOD *Haunted Ho.* xxxiii, The cobweb hung across in mazy tangle. **1888** BRYCE *Amer. Commw.* (1890) II. lxi. 434 It is hard to keep one's head through this mazy whirl of offices, elections [etc.].

b. Moving in a maze-like course.

1725 POPE *Odyss.* XVII. 355 With him the youth pursu'd the goat or fawn, Or trac'd the mazy leveret o'er the lawn.

c. as *sb. jocular.* Short for 'the mazy dance'.

1840 DICKENS *Old C. Shop* lvi, In remembrance of her with whom I shall never again thread the windings of the mazy.

2. *spec.* in *Min.* Having convoluted markings.

1811 PINKERTON *Petral.* I. 465 Mazy alabastrite, of a deep brown, with lighter veins.

3. Giddy, dizzy, confused in the head. *dial.*

c **1510** *Songs* (MS. Royal, App. 58) in *Anglia* XII. 268 My hed is all macy and meruelowsly dothe werke. *c* **1746** COLLIER (Tim Bobbin) *View Lanc. Dial.* Wks. (1862) 45 Sumheaw it made meh meazy. **1896** *Daily News* 5 Sept. 2/4 Deceased seemed to have accidentally fallen in [the water], probably during a 'mazy bout', she being subject to severe headaches.

4. *Comb.*

1728–46 THOMSON *Spring* 576 Oh pour The mazy-running soul of melody Into my varied verse.

mazzard, mazzarine: see MAZARD, MAZARINE *v.*

mazzel tov, var. MAZEL TOV.

Mazzinian (mæt'siːnɪən), *sb.* and *a.* [f. the name of Giuseppe *Mazzini* (1805–72), Italian patriot and revolutionary + -AN.] **A.** *sb.* An adherent of Mazzini. **B.** *adj.* Of, pertaining to, supporting, or resembling Mazzini or his policy. So **Maz'zinianism, Maz'zinism,** the principles or methods of Mazzinians; **Maz'zinist** = MAZZINIAN A.

1850 J. MILEY *Hist. Papal States* III. VIII. iv. 644 They..have loaded the memory of Gregory XVI., just as much as the Mazzinians, with every species of libellous invective. **1860** *Illustr. London News* 7 Jan. 18/3 Even the Mazzinists claim him at times as their own. **1861** tr. *A. Bresciani's Jew of Verona* p. iv, Misrepresentation which had been so assiduously thrown around the recent events by the Mazzinian press. **1862** *Dublin Rev.* Feb. 203 The universal dread which Mazzinism inspired. **1866** H. E. MANNING in S. Leslie *Life H. E. Manning* (1921) xiii. 195 Mazzinianism and Fenianism are one in principle. **1875** P. K. O'CLERY *Hist. Italian Revolution* v. 165 The Mazzinian programme was the establishment of a single republic... The literary propaganda of Mazzinianism. *Ibid.* 187 They were no less revolutionists than the Mazzinians. **1932** G. F.-H. BERKELEY *Italy in Making* I. xiv. 209 Aurelio Saffi, the well-known Mazzinian, who lived in Forlì. **1937** *Times Lit. Suppl.* 1 May 322/4 Meredith's attack..was a satire of social extravagances tinged with Mazzinian idealism. **1965** C. HIBBERT *Garibaldi & his Enemies* I. x. 140 Louis Napoleon could not free himself so easily..from the indiscretions of the Mazzinians. *Ibid.*, The Mazzinian *L'Italia e Popolo* of Genoa. **1967** C. SETON-WATSON *Italy from Liberalism to Fascism* xi. 422 The militant irredentists from Istria and Dalmatia..cared nothing for the Mazzinian dream of Italo-Slav friendship.

mazzot, mazzoth, varr. MATZAH.

M.B. (ɛm biː). [Abbreviation of 'Mark of the Beast' (see MARK *sb.*^{1} 11 c, BEAST *sb.* 7), used with jocular allusion to the popular view that this garment was a badge of 'Popery'.] ***M.B. waistcoat***: a kind of waistcoat with no opening in front, worn by Anglican clergymen (originally, *c* 1840, only by adherents of the Tractarian party, but afterwards by many belonging to other schools).

1853 CONYBEARE in *Edinb. Rev.* Oct. 315 Who does not recognise..the stiff and tie-less neckcloth, the M.B. coat and cassock waistcoat [etc.]. **1874** [see MARK *sb.*^{1} 11 c]. **1876** MRS. OLIPHANT *Phœbe Jun.* xvi. (1877) 114 He smiled superior at the folly which stigmatised an M.B. waistcoat.

M.B., abbreviation of L. *Medicinæ Baccalaureus* bachelor of medicine: see B (the letter) III. 1.

‖**mbongo** (m'bɒŋgəʊ). *S. Afr.* Also **imbonga, imbongo, mbonga, mbongi.** [Zulu.] An official who sings the praises of the (Zulu) king; hence applied to any flatterer of a high personage or institution.

1839 W. C. HARRIS *Wild Sports S. Afr.* xiv. 116 We..were accordingly preparing to start when a herald, called, in the Matabili language, *Imbongo*, a proclaimer of the king's titles, suddenly made his appearance outside the kraal. **1871** in T. Baines *Northern Goldfields Diaries* (1946) III. 687 His *Imbonga*, or court flatterer..recounted the battles of the Matabele. **1945** *Cape Times* 29 May, Municipal mbongo... The Mayor made quite a good case for the appointment of an official who would be a sort of professional praiser. **1948** *Cape Argus* 16 Sept. 7 Government supporters have danced around their Ministers like dutiful, adoring and disciplined mbongos. **1957** *Ibid.* 15 June 1/7 They were..a lot of mbongas to hymn the praises of the incompetent Nationalist hierarchy. **1973** *Drum* 8 Mar. 53 The mbongis..climb up his ancestral tree singing the praise poems of Vorster's illustrious forebears.

Mbret, var. MPRET.

Mc. All words of Scottish or Irish origin beginning with *Mc* (e.g. MCCARTHYISM, MCCOY) are placed alphabetically as if spelt *Mac-*.

M.D. Abbreviation of Latin *Medicinæ Doctor* doctor of medicine: see D (the letter) III. 3. Often used *colloq.* (pronounced (ɛm diː)) for: One holding the degree of M.D., a physician.

1755 in JOHNSON. **1766** REID *Let.* Wks. I. 47/1, I think our surgeons eclipse our M.D.'s. **1883** MAPLESON *Mem.* (ed. 2) I. 209 She gave bonds for her appearance when called upon, in order to save her trunks from seizure, which the M.D. had threatened.

Mdlle: see MADEMOISELLE 1.

Mdme: see MADAME 1.

me (miː, mɪ), *pers. pron.*, 1st *pers. sing.*, *acc.* and *dat.* Forms: 1– **me**; also 1 (acc.) **mec**, *Northumb.* **mech, meh,** 3–4 **mi,** 4–7 **mee,** 8–9 *dial.* (unstressed) **ma.** [The OE. *mē̆* accus. represents, like OFris. *mi*, OS. *mī*, *mē* (Du. *mij*), L. *mē*, Gr. ἐμέ, με, OIrish *mē* (mod.Irish *mi*), Welsh *mi*, the bare stem, OAryan *eme-, *me-, from which in all the Indogermanic langs. the oblique cases of the pronoun of the 1st pers. sing. are formed. OE. had also a form *mec* (which did not survive into ME.), corresp. to OFris. *mich*, OS. *mik* (MDu. *mik*), OHG. *mih* (MHG., mod.G. *mich*), ON. *mik* (Sw., Da. *mig*), Goth. *mik*:—Pre-Teut. **mege* (= Gr. ἐμέγε), in which a limiting particle **ge* (= Gr. γε, 'at least') is added to the simple accus. The OE. *mē̆* dative corresponds to OFris. *mi, mir*, OS. *mī* (MDu. *mî*, mod.Du. *mij*), OHG., mod.G. *mir*, ON. *mér*, Goth. *miz*:—Pre-Teut. **mes*; the final *s*, which is the sign of the dative also in the Teut. pronouns of the 2nd pers. sing., has not been explained with certainty, but Brugmann has suggested that it may have arisen from the analogy of the Pre-Teut. **nes* (Skr. *nas*), the stem of the 1st pers. plural, which was used uninflected as a dative, and of which Teut. **uns* (Eng. US) is an ablaut-variant.]

I. The accusative and dative form of the pronoun of the first person *I*.

1. *Accusative*, as direct object.

Beowulf 447 ʒif mec deað nimeð. *c* **950** *Lindisf. Gosp.* Matt. x. 32 Eghuelc..seðe ʒe-ondetas meh [*c* **975** *Rushw.* mec, *c* **1000** *Ags. Gosp.* me] before monnum. *a* **1250** *Owl & Night.* 160 Ich wiste wel þat þou me misraddest. **1362** LANGL. *P. Pl.* A. VII. 88 He is holden, Ich hope to haue me in Muynde. **1470–85** MALORY *Arthur* VII. xxxii. 264 Spare me not to morne when I haue restyd me. **1535** FISHER *Wks.* (E.E.T.S.) I. 382 He wil not forsake me nor suffer mee to perish. **1611** BIBLE *Ruth* i. 20 Call me not Naomi, call mee Marah. **1762** BICKERSTAFF *Love in Village* I. x. (1765) 20 Well, my lad, are you willing to serve the king? *Countryman.* Why, can you list ma? **1832** TENNYSON *Œnone* 38 Hear me, for I will speak.

2. *Dative.* **a.** As indirect obj.; also (now *rare* exc. *arch.*) in dependence on certain impers. vbs. (cf. MESEEMS, METHINKS, LIST *v.*^{1}), adjs., and advs.

Beowulf 2155 Me ðis hildesceorp Hroðgar sealde. *c* **1175** *Lamb. Hom.* 113 Her is min child þe me is swiðe leof. *a* **1300** *Cursor M.* 3611 þar-efter now mi langes sare. **1390** GOWER *Conf.* I. 45 So hard me was that ilke throwe That [etc]. *c* **1440** *York Myst.* viii. 15 Me repentys and rewys for-þi. **1533** MORE *Debell. Salem* Wks. 1024/1 Me nedeth neuer to loke more for that matter. **1654–66** EARL ORRERY *Parthen.* (1676) 343 Those strange Accidents which had arrived me. **1666** BOYLE *Orig. Formes & Qual.* 395 The quantity presented me was less inconsiderable. **1898** RIDER HAGGARD *Dr. Therne* 21 Will you lend it me?

b. As dat. of interest (= *for me*), chiefly in commands. *arch.*

c **950** *Lindisf. Gosp.* John xiii. 8 Ne ðuoas ðu me [Vulg. *mihi*] foet. *c* **1385** CHAUCER *L.G.W.* 46 In myn bed there dawith me no day That I ne am vp. **14..** *Tundale's Vis.* 87 Loke me my sparthe, where ever it stonde. **1603** SHAKS. *Meas. for M.* II. i. 121 Come me to what was done to her. **1712** ADDISON *Spect.* No. 488 ⁋2 A large Family of Daughters have drawn me up a very handsome Remonstrance. **1765** STERNE *Tr. Shandy* VII. xliii, Tie me up this tress instantly. **1849** M. ARNOLD *Sick King in Bokhara* 45 Prick me the fellow from the path!

c. Used expletively in passages of a narrative character. (The so-called ethical dative.) *arch.*

Formerly often in vulgar or colloq. phrases (now obs.) such as 'then says me I', 'what did me I but', etc.

13.. *Gaw. & Gr. Knt.* 1905 þay fel on hym alle, & woried me þis wyly wyth a wroth noyse. **1535** *Goodly Primer, Passion* IV, But Peter..cometh me back again unto the fire. *c* **1500** *Robyn Hode* II. st. 100 (Child) Here be the best coresed hors That euer yet sawe I me. **1596** SHAKS. *Merch. V.* I. iii. 85 The skilfull shepheard pil'd me certaine wands. **1697** VANBRUGH *Æsop* I. II. 1 I'se get our wife Joan to be the queen's chambermaid; and then—crack says me I! and forget all my acquaintance. **1724** SWIFT *Prometh.* Wks. 1755 III. II. 151 Prometheus once this chain [of gold] purloin'd, Then whips me on a chain of brass. **1820** LAMB *Elia* Ser. I. *Oxf. in Vac.*, With great exactitude of purpose he enters me his name in the book.

3. Governed by a *preposition*.

c **950** *Lindisf. Gosp.* John vi. 35 Seðe ʒelefes on mech [*Rushw.* mec]. *c* **1200** ORMIN 237 þuss hafeþþ Drihhtin don wiþþ me. *a* **1250** *Owl & Night.* 367 þu liest on me hit is isene. *c* **1375** *Canticum de Creatione* 11 in Horstm. *Altengl. Leg.* (1878) 124/1 þe rode treo þat god on deyde for ȝow & meo. **1470–85** MALORY *Arthur* VIII. xxiii. 307, I pray to god that he neuer be..shamed for me. **1616** B. JONSON *Forest* ix, Drink to me, onely, with thine eyes. **1642** CHAS. I *Sp.* Wks. 1662 I. 401 You see that My Magazine is going to be taken from Me. **1711** STEELE *Spect.* No. 79 ⁋2 The Writer will do what she pleases for all me. **1816** J. WILSON *City of Plague* I. i. 101 A voice comes to me from its silent towers.

4. Qualified by an adj.

a **1586** SIDNEY *Arcadia* II. (1590) 179 b, Vntil you came, after so many victories to make a conquest of poore me. **1608** SHAKS. *Per.* I. iv. 69 To..make a conquest of vnhappie mee. **1646** CRASHAW *Poems* 149 And full of nothing else but empty me. **1809** MALKIN *Gil Blas* x. x, As for poor little me,..I was sent to the foundling hospital. **1814** JANE AUSTEN *Let.* 2 Mar. (1932) II. 92, I am to call upon Miss Spencer: Funny me! **1895**, etc. [see *little me* s.v. LITTLE *a.* 13]. **1961** 'P. DENNIS' (*title*) Little me: the intimate memoirs of that great star..Belle Poitrine. **1973** 'D. HALLIDAY' *Dolly & Starry Bird* viii. 111 'As Timothy would say, silly me,' Johnson said in a voice as hard as his bifocals.

5. *Reflexive* (= myself, to or for myself) *arch.* and *poet.* exc. in U.S. colloq. usage.

a **1000** *Juliana* 452 (Gr.) þær ic swiþe me þyslicre ær þraʒe ne ʒewende. *a* **1200** *Moral Ode* 6 þenne ich me bi-þenche wel sare ich me adrede. *a* **1225** *Leg. Kath.* 480 Ich..toc me him to lauerd. *c* **1386** CHAUCER *Pars. T.* ⁋235, I purposed fermely to shryue me. *c* **1570** *Pride & Lowl.* (1841) 61 Thinking to me they meant to gone us by. **1665** HOOKE *Microgr.* Pref. f, I provided me a Tube of Brass. **1703** ROWE *Ulyss.* II. i, Methought I found me by a murm'ring Brook. **1819** KEATS *La Belle Dame* 44 And I awoke, and found me here. **1821** W. SEWALL *Diary* (1930) 75 Purchased me some linens. **1859** TENNYSON *Marr. Geraint* 281 Where can I get me harbourage for the night? **1867** MACFARREN *Harmony* vi. (1876) 209, I must content me with the bare statement. **1874** *Rep. Vermont Board Agric.* II. 512 In 1861 I built me a horse barn, twenty-eight by forty. **1916** 'B. M. BOWER' *Phantom Herd* iii. 42 I'm going to make me one. **1972** *'Gramophone' Pop. Record Catal.* Dec. 129/2 (*song-title*) I'm gonna get me a gun. **1974** M. HASTINGS *Dragon Island* xv. 129 I'll grab me the first-aid box and..see how my patients are doing.

6. For the *nominative*. **a.** Chiefly predicative; as subject now only *dial.* and *vulgar*.

In uneducated speech commonly used where the pron. forms with another pron. or a sb. the subject of a plural verb.

a **1500** in Arnolde *Chron.* (1811) 108 Be it knowen to al men by theis presentis me, T. H. of Oxenford glouar, ordeyne [etc.]. **1519** in *Charters*, etc. *Peebles* (1872) 49 Be it kennit tyll all men be thir present letteres, me James Baroune..grantis me to haif rasawit [etc.]. **1591** SHAKS. *Two Gent.* II. iii. 25 Oh, the dogge is me, and I am my selfe. **1733** SWIFT *Apol.* Wks. 1755 IV. I. 209 To dine with her! and come at three! Impossible! it can't be me. **1758** GOLDSM. *Mem. Prot.* (1895) I. 201 There was left surviving only me. **1865** DICKENS *Mut. Fr.* I. viii, Me and Mrs. Boffin stood the poor girl's friend. **1886** BESANT *Childr. Gibeon* II. xxvii, We're an easy-going lot, me and my friends. **1893** [see HIM 3]. **1903** *Dialect Notes* II. 320 *Me and you*,..almost universal for 'you and I'. **1905** *Westm. Gaz.* 11 Nov. 3/1, I can foresee..that unless me and Ellen advise you, you'll become simply——. **1936** MENCKEN *Amer. Lang.* (ed. 4) ix. 457 Him and me are friends. **1966** 'J. HACKSTON' *Father clears Out* 50 Me an' me mate's eyes was dancin' out of our 'eads.

b. After *as, than.*

1606 SHAKS. *Ant. & Cl.* III. iii. 14 Is she as tall as me? **1748** RICHARDSON *Clarissa* I. x. 58, I am fitter for this world than you, you for the next than me. **1804** BYRON *Let.* 2 Nov., Lord Delawarr is considerably younger than me.

†**c.** In the absolute participial construction. *Obs.*

c **1450** tr. *De Imitatione* III. v. 69 These folke, me beyng displesed [L. *me eis adversante*], ofte tymes fallen into gret temptacions. **1671** MILTON *Samson* 463 Dagon hath presum'd, Me overthrown, to enter lists with God.

7. In various exclamatory uses, without definite syntactical relation to the context.

a. In interjectional phrases, as ***ah me! ay me! o me! dear me! †fore me! †God's me!*** etc.

See also BODY *sb.* 4, GOD *sb.* 8 b.

1589 GREENE *Menaphon* (Arb.) 66 Ay me vnhappie. **1591–1860** [see AY 2]. **1601** B. JONSON *Poetaster* I. i, Gods a' me! **1607** SHAKS. *Cor.* I. i. 124 What then? Fore me, this Fellow speakes. **1610** [see O 2]. **1632** ROWLEY *Wom. never vext* IV. 59 *Rob.* O me my shame! I know that voyce full well. *Ibid.* 60 O me, mine Vncle sees me! **1798** in *Spirit Pub. Jrnls.* (1799) II. 216 Dear me! O la! Good me! **1819** KEATS *St. Agnes* xii, Alas me! flit! Flit like a ghost away.

b. In imitation of Latin uses (e.g. *me miserum!*).

1667 MILTON *P.L.* II. 73 Me miserable! which way shall I flie Infinite wrauth, and infinite despaire? **1889** BROWNING *Pope & Net* iii, 'Unworthy me!' he sighs: 'From fisher's drudge to Church's prince—it is indeed a rise'.

c. In surprised interrogation = 'Do you mean me?'

1600 SHAKS. *A.Y.L.* I. iii. 44 And get you from our Court. *Ros.* Me Vncle. *Duk.* You Cosen. **1760** FOOTE *Minor* III. (1767) 72 What says your father! *Sir Will.* Me! Oh, I'll shew you in an instant. **1782** MISS BURNEY *Cecilia* IV. vii, Then, turning to Miss Larolles, 'Don't you dance?' he said. 'Me?' cried she, embarrassed, 'yes, I believe so.'

d. Vulgarly, ***and me***... = 'especially considering that I am...'.

Cf. the similar use of *I*, as in Burns *Banks o' Doon*, And I sae weary, fu' o' care.

1812 MAR. EDGEWORTH *Absentee* xi, Which would be hard on us and me a widow. **1864** G. MEREDITH *Emilia* xv, And twenty shindies per dime we've been havin', and me such a placable body, if ye'll onnly let m' explode.

e. Followed by an inf. in exclamations of surprise or indignation at some proposal or statement. Also used intensively like French *moi*.

The nom. *I* is considered more grammatical.

1885 J. K. JEROME *On the Stage* 16 'Me! me pay!' I exclaimed, rendered ungrammatical by surprise. 'What for?' **1923** *Dialect Notes* V. 244, I am not going to-day, *me.* **1963** *Listener* 20 June 1041/3 Me, I like fighting, too.

8. quasi-*sb.* Personality, individuality; EGO.

1828 CARLYLE *Misc.* (1857) I. 86 Haunted and blinded by some shadow of his own little Me. **1855** BAIN *Senses & Int.* II. i. §12 A *not me* as opposed to the *me* of passive sensibility and thought.

9. With the verb *to be*: suited to or representative of my tastes, ability, personality, etc.; appropriate for me; my real self.

1899 J. LONDON *Let.* 29 July (1966) 47 This is me all the time and all over. **1905** A. BENNETT *Sacred & Profane Love* I. v. 83 But that poor little book isn't *me*... I shall never write another like it. **1925** R. HALL *Saturday Life* vii. 79 Nothings, just nothings, they didn't count; this is the thing that's *me.* **1938** J. CARY *Castle Corner* 557 The house has got to be contemporary, it's got to be art..and it's got to be me. **1949** R. CHANDLER *Little Sister* xxviii. 209, I don't like the script... It just isn't me, if you know what I mean. **1957** P. WILDEBLOOD *Main Chance* 56 Cardigans are not.. particularly *me.* **1963** F. T. VISSER *Hist. Syntax Eng. Lang.* I. iii. 240, I like this dress, it's me!

II. 10. Used *colloq.* and *dial.* (also *Austral.* and *N.Z.*) as a poss. adj.

The origin of this use is probably the unstressed form of the possessive adj. (see MY *poss. adj.* 1β), but it is now apprehended as a levelling of functions under a single inflexional form.

1862 G. MEREDITH *Let.* 23 June (1970) I. 152 B. Wyse came the other day..and hoped for forgive *miss*: 'Me deer Mardith', etc.! **1901** M. FRANKLIN *My Brilliant Career* x. 84 Now it's your turn, me fine lady. *Ibid.* xxvi. 220 A couple of letters..stuffed in me pocket. **1911** W. OWEN *Let.* 20 Sept. (1967) 83 Love to Mary and me brethren twain. **1946** K. TENNANT *Lost Haven* (1968) i. 20 Me own mother sent me word he wants to see me! *Ibid.* ii. 39 Me granddaughter's coming to stay with me. **1960** G. SLATTER *Gun in my Hand* ii. 21 An' it ran like a hairy goat an' I did me chips. **1966** F. SHAW et al. *Lern Yerself Scouse* 20 *Me dollypegs*, my legs... *Me webs*, my feet. **1968** K. WEATHERLY *Roo Shooter* 21 'Cost you a night's shooting, me backside,' roared the driver. **1972** *Southerly* XXXII. 6 Me motorbike's out at the station. **1973** *Sunday Express* (Trinidad & Tobago) 1 Apr. (Suppl.) 13/1 Ah on de road, Putting out me hand Like a mas in a band.

†me, *indef. pron. Obs.* Also 4 **ma.** [A further reduced form of MEN *pron.*, weakened from MAN *pron.*] = ONE 21.

c **1175** *Lamb. Hom.* 17 Hit is riht þet me hem spille. *a* **1225** *Ancr. R.* 54 Þus, ofte, ase me seið, of lutel wacseð muchel. *c* **1380** *Sir Ferumb.* 2828 Ma calþ me Gyoun of Borgoygne. **1426** AUDELAY *Poems* 9 To do as thou woldest me dud by the. *c* **1483** CAXTON *Dialogues* 6/20 Thinges That ben vsed after the hous, Of whiche me may not be withoute.

†me, ? *int.* or *conj. Obs.* [Of obscure origin: some have compared the MDu., MLG. *men*, 'but' (whence Da. *men*, Sw. *män* in the same sense), but it is doubtful whether this is connected.] A particle (exclamatory or adversative) employed (mainly in texts of the 'Katherine group') to introduce a question, or (less commonly) a statement: = 'lo', 'now', 'why'.

a **1225** *Leg. Kath.* 327 Me hwat is mare madschipe þen for to leuen on him. *a* **1240** *Ureisun* in *Cott. Hom.* 185 Me nis he fol chapmon þe buþ deore a wac þing [etc.].

mea, Sc. variant of MO (= more) *Obs.*

meace, meach, obs. ff. MESS *sb.*, MITCH.

meach, var. MEECH *v.*

meachin(g), varr. MEECHING *ppl. a.*

†'meacock. *Obs.* Forms: 6 **maycocke, meycocke, mecock(e, meicocke, 6–7 meacock(e.** [Of obscure origin: perh. orig. a name of some bird (cf. quot. 1575). (The suggestion that it is f. MEEK *a.* is untenable.)]

1. An effeminate person; a coward, weakling.

1526 *Pilgr. Perf.* (W. de W. 1531) 69 b, He sholde be no cowarde, no maycocke, no fearfull persone that dare nothynge enterpryse. **1563–87** FOXE *A. & M.* (1596) 394/2 [The bishop] rebuked the maior and his brethren for mecocks and dastards. **1575** R. B. *Appius & Virginia* B, As stout as a Stockefish, as meeke as a mecocke. **1590** *Tarlton's News Purgat.* 39 Shee found fault with him, because he was a meacocke and a milkesoppe. **1640** GLAPTHORNE *Hollander* II. Wks. 1874 I. 98 They are like my husband, meere meacocks verily. **1719** D'URFEY *Pills* (1872) IV. 14 For my part I will no more be such a Meacock To deal with the plumes of a Hyde-Park Peacock. **1834** SIR H. TAYLOR *Artevelde* III. ii, A bookish nursling of the monks—a meacock!

2. *attrib.* passing into *adj.* Effeminate; cowardly.

1587 CHURCHYARD *Worth. Wales* (1876) 41 Yonder effeminate and meycocke people. **1601** CHESTER *Love's Mart.* (N. Shaks. Soc.) 59 Let vs giue onset on that meacocke Nation. **1639** G. DANIEL *Vervic.* 176 Shall.. Warwicke keepe The strength of Callice? meacocke King, you sleepe.

‖mea culpa ('meɪɑ 'kʊlpɑ, 'miːə 'kʌlpə). [L., lit. 'through my own fault'.] A phrase from the prayer of confession in the Latin liturgy of the Church; used *lit.* and *transf.* as an exclamation of repentance, and as the name of such an exclamation; also ***mea maxima culpa.*** See CONFITEOR.

c **1374** CHAUCER *Tr. & Cr.* (1894) II. 525 Now, *mea culpa*, lord! I me repente. **1602** W. WATSON *Decacordon* 40 Shall lay their hands a little heavier on their hearts with *Mea maxima culpa.* **1818** LADY MORGAN *Florence Macarthy* IV. v. 208 Mingled a broken *ave-maria* and *mea-culpa*, in utter consternation and superstitious fear. **1891** E. DOWSON *Let.* 7 Feb. (1967) 184 Today, mea culpa, mea maxima culpa, I have done nothing. **1922** JOYCE *Ulysses* 279 He beat his hand upon his breast, confessing: *mea culpa.* **1948** R. BUTLER *Words of Mass* I. 10 The striking of the breast at the *mea culpa* is an emphatic recognition of guilt and expression of sorrow. **1958** *Times* 17 Oct. 17/1 Eisenstein made a public *mea culpa* at the time in the form of an open letter to the Committee. **1960** [see *guilt-complex*]. **1974** 'D. SHANNON' *Crime File* (1975) v. 79 *Mea culpa*... We all do stupid things sometimes.

mead[1] (miːd). Forms: α. 1 **medo, meodu, 3–7 mede, 4 meed, meode, 5 med, meyde, 6 meade, 6–7** *Sc.* **meid, 6– mead.** β. **3–4 meth, 4–5 meeth, 4–6 methe, 6 meedth, 6–7 meathe, 6–8 meath.** [Com. Teut. and Aryan: OE. *meodu* str. masc. = OFris., MLG., MDu. *mede* (Du. *mede, mee*), OHG. *metu, mitu* (MHG. *mete, met*, mod.G. *met*), ON. *mjǫð-r* (Da. *miød*, Sw. *mjöd*), Gothic **midu-s* (not recorded exc. in Gr. transcription as μέδος, given by Priscus as the name at the Hunnish court A.D. 448 for the drink which there took the place of wine):—OTeut. **medu-z*:—OAryan **medhu-s*; cf. Skr. *mádhu* neut., honey, sweet drink, OSl. *medŭ* honey, wine, Lith. *midù-s* mead, *medùs* honey, Gr. μέθυ wine, OIrish *mid*, genit. *meda*, Welsh *medd*. The word may have been orig. an elliptical use of an adj. meaning 'sweet' (= Skr. *mádhu* adj.).

The β forms may be partly from ON. and partly from Welsh; with regard to the latter cf. the adoption from Welsh of the synonymous (but unrelated) METHEGLIN.]

a. An alcoholic liquor made by fermenting a mixture of honey and water: also called *metheglin*.

The distinction alleged in quot. 1609 (under β) was prob. merely a figment of the writer's own.

α. *Beowulf* 604 (Gr.) Gæþ eft, se þe mot, to medo modig. *a* **1000** *Riddles* xxi. 12 (Gr.) Þær hy meodu drincað. *c* **1205** LAY. 6928 Ah longe leouede here Cherin, muchel he dronk mede [*c* **1275** meþ] and win. **1390** *Earl Derby's Exped.* (Camden) 43, xxiiij barellis de meed. *c* **1460** *Towneley Myst.* xxviii. 111 It is swetter then med. **1483** *Cath. Angl.* 232/2 *Meyde* (*A.* Methe), *idromellum, medus, medo.* **1625** K. LONG tr. *Barclay's Argenis* I. xviii. 49 By occasion of their Mead, they fell into talke of Bees. **1712** ADDISON *Spect.* No. 383 ¶6 A Masque..asked him if he would drink a Bottle of Mead with her? **1767** MRS. GLASSE *Cookery* App. 353 How to make mead. *Ibid.* 374 To make white mead. **1891** T. HARDY *Tess* II. 62, I found the mead..extremely alcoholic.

β. *c* **1275** [see α]. *c* **1386** CHAUCER *Miller's T.* 194 He sente hire pyment Meeth and spyced Ale. *c* **1449** PECOCK *Repr.* I. xx. 121 Without sidir and wijn and meeth, men and wommen my3te lyue ful long. **1577** B. GOOGE *Heresbach's Husb.* II. (1586) 58 b, They say they will be verie pleasant, if the seede be steeped in meedth. **1609** C. BUTLER *Fem. Mon.* (1634) 162 Meth or Hydromel is of two sorts, the weaker and the stronger (Mede and Methæglen). *a* **1674** MILTON *Hist. Mosc.* i. Wks. 1851 VIII. 480 Thir Drink is better, being sundry sorts of Meath. **1747** MRS. DELANY *Life & Corr.* (1861) II. 463 He begs a thousand acknowledgements to you for all favours, particularly the meath.

b. *transf.* (*a*) *poet. nonce-use* (see quot.). (*b*) Now applied to several made beverages, esp. *U.S.* 'a sweet drink charged with carbonic gas, and flavored with some syrup, as sarsaparilla' (*Cent. Dict.* 1890).

1667 MILTON *P.L.* V. 345 For drink the Grape She crushes, inoffensive moust, and meathes From many a berrie.

c. *attrib.* and *Comb.*, chiefly *arch.* or *Hist.* in terms relating to Teutonic antiquities, as ***mead-horn***; **mead-bench** (OE. *medubenc*), a seat at a feast when mead was drunk; **mead-hall** (OE. *meduheall*), a banqueting hall. Also **† mead-inn,** an inn where mead is the beverage sold; **mead-wine,** a home-made 'wine' prepared from mead.

1860 HOOK *Lives Abps.* I. v. 181 Nobles left their halls and the *mead-bench. **1959** A. G. BRODEUR *Art of Beowulf* 16 A mead-bench is a seat in a royal hall, where the dispensing of good drink symbolizes the warm relationship between lord and retainer. **1881** GREEN *Making of Eng.* 173 The leader.. gave them..a seat in his *mead hall. **1903** L. F. ANDERSON *Anglo-Saxon Scop* 36 Personal valour and prowess on the field of battle, courage.., hardihood.., these were the all-absorbing topics of conversation in the mead-hall. **1968** E. B. IRVING *Reading of Beowulf* v. 242 The clustering of the clan family in the lighted mead-hall. **1870** MORRIS *Earthly Par.* II. III. 391 Shun the *mead-horn. **1621** BURTON *Anat. Mel.* I. ii. II. ii. (1651) 74 Be merry together..as our modern Muscovites do in their *Mede-Inns. **1804–6** SYD. SMITH *Mor. Philos.* (1850) 248 Every clergyman's wife makes *mead-wine of the honey.

mead[2] (miːd). Now *poet.* and *dial.* Forms: 1 **mǽd,** *Anglian* **méd,** 3 **med,** 3–6 **mede,** 4 **maied,** 4, 6 **meed(e,** 5 *Sc.* **meide,** 5–6 *Sc.* **meid,** 6 **mydde,** 6–7 **meade,** 6– **mead.** [OE. *mǽd* str. fem.:—OTeut. type **mǣdwâ*: see MEADOW.

By phonetic law the *w* was dropped in the nom. sing. in OE., and retained in the other forms. Although the regular inflexion is the more common, the oblique cases and pl. are sometimes found assimilated to the nom. sing., as gen. and dat. *mǽde* (dat. also *méda* as from a *u*-stem), pl. *mǽda.*]

= MEADOW 1.

c **1000** in Napier *O.E. Glosses* 5/138 *Prata, i. uiriditates,* mæda. *a* **1250** *Owl & Night.* 438 Þe blostme ginneþ springe and sprede Beoþe ine treo and ek on mede. *c* **1290** *Becket* 1722 in *S. Eng. Leg.* I. 156 In ane Mede þat men cleopiez 3uyte 'þe traitores mede'. **1297** R. GLOUC. (Rolls) 11255 Sir Ion giffard fram brumesfeld þuder sone com To þe castle med wiþoute toun. *c* **1386** CHAUCER *Prol.* 89 Embrouded was he, as it were a mede Al ful of fresshe floures, whyte and rede. **1508** DUNBAR *Tua mariit Wemen* 514 And all remuffit the myst, and the meid smellit. **1551** TURNER *Herbal* I. B v, The second [kind of garlick] groweth in myddes and feldes in euery cuntre. **1573** TUSSER *Husb.* (1878) 195 Riuers sweete along the meedes. **1605** SHAKS. *Lear* I. i. 66 Of all these bounds..With plenteous Riuers, and wide-skirted Meades We make thee Lady. **1612** DRAYTON *Poly-olb.* xii. 160 A goodly mead, which men there call the Hide. **1713** C'TESS WINCHILSEA *Misc. Poems* 292 The loos'd Horse.. Comes slowly grazing thro' th' adjoining Meads. **1799** W. TOOKE *View Russian Emp.* I. 73 Artificial meads, as not deemed necessary, are unusual. **1812** BRACKENRIDGE *Views Louisiana* (1814) 105 These natural meads. **1896** A. E. HOUSMAN *Shropshire Lad* v, Oh may I squire you round the meads And pick you posies gay?

†b. Meadow-land; = MEADOW 1 b. *Obs.*

1297 R. GLOUC. (Rolls) 3887 In þe oþer half beþ grete wodes lese & mede al so. **1455** *Rolls of Parlt.* V. 313/1, vii acres of Mede, liggyng in the Mede beside the Brigge. **1670** *Conn. Col. Rec.* (1852) II. 133 This Court grants Mr. Benjamin Fenn, two hundred and fifty acres of land, whereof there may be thirty of mead.

c. *attrib.* and *Comb.*, as **† mead-gavel,** a rent for meadow land; **mead grass,** meadow grass, esp. *Poa pratensis*; **mead ground,** meadow land; **mead-month,** quasi-*arch.*, an alleged OE. name for July; **†mead-rattle,** app. ground ivy or speedwell; **† mead silver** (see quot.).

1235–53 *Rentalia Glaston.* (Somerset Rec. Soc.) 54 Hii qui solvunt *Medgavel. **1778** [W. MARSHALL] *Minutes Agric., Digest* 66 Cut Clover early,—*Meadgrass late. **1453** in *Trevelyan Papers* (Camden) 22 With viij acr. of *meade grounde. **1571** in W. H. Turner *Select. Rec. Oxford* (1880) 336 Fyve acres of meade ground lying in Botley meade. **1681** W. ROBERTSON *Phraseol. Gen.* (1693) 584 In *mede month; Hay time. **1714** FORTESCUE-ALAND *Fortescue's Abs. & Lim. Mon.* Notes 116 July was called Mæde-monað, *Mead-Month.* **1849** LYTTON *K. Arthur* VIII. xiv, Roved the same pastures when the Mead-month smil'd. *c* **1450** *Alphita* (Anecd. Oxon.) 28/1 *Camepiteos..uel germandria maior..angl.* *mederatele. **1778** *Eng. Gazetteer* (ed. 2) s.v. *Cobham*, The parishioners pay no tithe-hay, but a composition..of 1*d.* an acre, which is called *Mead Silver.

mead, obs. form of MEED *sb.*

meaddowe, obs. form of MEADOW.

meader ('miːdə(r)). *dial.* [repr. OE. *mǽðere* = MDu., MLG. *mader, meder*, OHG. *mâdari* (MHG. *mâdære*, mod.G. *mahder, mähder*):—OTeut. type **mǣþarjo-z*, f. the sb. represented in OE. *mǽð* MATH *sb.*[1]] A mower.

a **1000** *Gloss.* in Wr.-Wülcker 235/3 *Falcarius, i. falciferens, uel falcifera,* siþberend, *uel* mæpre. *Ibid.* 237/35 *Fenisece,* mæperas. ? **18..** *Old Song* in *N. & Q.* 1st Ser. (1854) X. 480 The meader walks forth with his scythe on his shoulder. **1864** *E. Cornw. Words* in *Jrnl. Roy. Inst. Cornw.* Mar. 18, *Meader*, a mower.

meader, obs. form of MADDER *sb.*[2]

meadow ('mɛdəʊ), *sb.* Forms: 1 *sing.* (oblique cases) **mǽdwe, médwa,** *pl.* **mǽdwa,** 3 **meduwe, 3–4 midu, 3–5 medwe, 3–6 medewe, 4–5 medou, medoe, medew, 4–6 medo, 4–7 medow(e, 5 medue,**

meedewe, mydew(e, 5–6 middow, 6 medoy, me(a)ddowe, myddoe, 6–7 middow, meadowe, 7 *Sc.* **meadou, 6– meadow.** [repr. OE. *mǽdwe* oblique case of *mǽd* str. fem. (see MEAD²):—OTeut. type **mǣdwâ*:—pre-Teut. **mētwā́*, f. root **mē-* (whence MOW *v.*).

The precise formal equivalent does not occur in any other Teut. lang., but cognate words of similar meaning are OFris. *mêde*, ODu. *mada* (Franck), MDu., MLG. *made*, early mod.Du. *matte* (now *mat*), MHG. *mate, matte* (mod.G. *matte*). See also MATH *sb.*¹]

1. a. Originally a piece of land permanently covered with grass which is mown for use as hay. In later use often extended to include any piece of grass land, whether used for cropping or pasture; and in some districts applied esp. to a tract of low well-watered ground, usually near a river.

969 *Lease* in Birch *Cartul. Sax.* III. 532 An medwa beneoðan þæm hliþe. *c* **1205** LAY. 1942 Cornes heo seowen medewen heo meowen. *Ibid.* 4817 Meduwen and mores & þa hæ ȝe muntes. *c* **1290** *S. Eng. Leg.* I. 214/491 A fair Medwe he saiȝ with swete floures. *a* **1300** *Cursor M.* 4573 In þat medu sa lang þai war þat etten þai had it erthe bare. **13..** *E.E. Allit. P.* B. 1761 Þe myst dryues þorȝ þe lyst of þe lyfte, bi þe loȝ medoes. **1390** GOWER *Conf.* II. 327 Nature..Wole..With herbes and with floures bothe The feldes and the medwes clothe. *c* **1400** *Song Roland* 306 Amonge medos, and moris, & evyll bankis. *c* **1400** MAUNDEV. (Roxb.) xxxiii. 148 All þe tymes of þe ȝere er..þaire mydews grene. *c* **1430** *Syr Gener.* (Roxb.) 5653 Comen was the king of kinges And armed in the middow rode. **1463** *Bury Wills* (Camden) 34 The medwe at Babwelle. **1488** *Act 4 Hen. VII*, c. 15 §2 Divers pastures and medues. **1526** *Pilgr. Perf.* (W. de W. 1531) 74 The dayes of this worlde be but transitory, as the floure of yᵉ medowe. **1551** TURNER *Herbal* I. B viij, Althea.. groweth naturally in watery & marrish myddoes. **1560** DAUS tr. *Sleidane's Comm.* 220 Beyng brought foorthe into a meddowe and stripped naked, they were slayne eche one. **1588** SHAKS. *L.L.L.* v. ii. 907 Ladie-smockes all siluer white, Do paint the Meadowes with delight. **1589** in *Exch. Rolls Scotl.* XXII. 26 The landis of the Kingis medo besyde Edinburgh. **1611** MURE *Misc. Poems* i. 53 A blooming meadou. **1634** W. TIRWHYT tr. *Balzac's Lett.* (vol. I.) 77, I march into a Meddow. **1717** LADY M. W. MONTAGU *Let. to Abbé Conti* 29 May, The rest of our journey was through fine painted meadows. **1846** J. BAXTER *Libr. Pract. Agric.* (ed. 4) I. 370 The proper grasses which constitute the produce of the richest permanent pastures and meadows.

transf. and *fig.* **1588** SHAKS. *Tit. A.* III. i. 125 Looking all downewards to behold our cheekes How they are stain'd in meadowes, yet not dry With miery slime left on them by a flood. **1777** [see MEANDER *v.* 1 b].

b. Land used for meadows; 'meadow land'.

c **1122** *O.E. Chron.* an. 777 (MS. E), Mid læswe & mid mædwe. *c* **1330** R. BRUNNE *Chron.* (1810) 75 Alle mad he wasteyn, pastur, medow, & korn. **1532** *Test. Ebor.* (Surtees) VI. 31, 16 acres of meadow in Kellome. **1636** *Rec. Dedham, Mass.* (1892) III. 21 He shall haue for a Fearme..soe much medowe & vpland as shalbe sufficient. **1799** J. ROBERTSON *Agric. Perth* 204 It is perhaps more proper to name all land, from which hay is taken, meadow. **1846** MCCULLOCH *Acc. Brit. Empire* (1854) I. 181 Above 500,000 [*sc.* acres] are arable, meadow, and pasture.

2. *N. America.* **a.** A low level tract of uncultivated grass land, esp. along a river or in marshy regions near the sea.

1670 D. DENTON *Descr. New York* (1845) 14 After-skull River puts into the main Land on the West-side,..There is very great Marshes or Medows on both sides of it, excellent good land. **1778** T. HUTCHINS *Descr. Virginia*, etc. 14 On the North-west and South-east sides of the Ohio..are extensive natural meadows, or Savannahs. **1779** D. LIVERMORE *Jrnl.* in *Coll. N. Hampshire Hist. Soc.* (1850) VI. 316 The intervale or meadow extends four miles from the banks of the river. **1881** E. H. ELWELL in *Coll. Maine Hist. Soc.* (1887) IX. 214 It was the fertility of these meadows which attracted the adventurers of a century ago.

b. *beaver meadow*: the rich, fertile tract of land left dry above a demolished beaver dam.

1784 M. CUTLER in *Life*, etc. (1888) I. 100 A swamp, or beaver meadow, in which Ellis river takes its rise. **1836** *Backwoods of Canada* 144 All these are found on the plains and beaver-meadows. *Ibid.* 239. **1863** MISS E. H. WALSHE *Cedar Creek* xii. 92 Why is that green flat called a beaver meadow?..Well, they say that long ago beavers dammed up the current in such places as this [etc.].

3. a. 'An ice-field or floe on which seals herd'. **b.** 'A feeding ground of fish' (*Cent. Dict.* 1890).

1877 *Rep. U.S. Fish. Commiss.* (1879) 541 The 'fishing grounds', 'cod-meadows', have an extent of about 200 geographical miles in length, and 67 miles in breadth.

4. *attrib.* and *Comb.*

a. Obvious combinations, as ***meadow-base, -croft, -down, -farmer, -field, -flower, -gale, -hay, -leet, -lot, -man, -road, -side, -swell, -verse, -watering.***

1832 TENNYSON *Pal. of Art* ii, A huge crag-platform,.. whose rangèd ramparts bright From great broad *meadow-bases of deep grass Suddenly scaled the light. **1812** W. TENNANT *Anster F.* II. lxvii, Anon uprises..On the green loan and *meadow-crofts around, A town of tents. **1877** G. M. HOPKINS *Poems* (1967) 71 *Meadow-down is not distressed For a rainbow footing it. **1742** W. ELLIS *Mod. Husbandman* II. III. 109 There are two Sorts of Farmers, who carry on this Business..*viz.* the Grass, or *Meadow-farmer, and the Plough-farmer. **1884** R. JEFFERIES *Life of Fields* 139 The meadow-farmers, dairymen, have not grubbed many hedges. **1822** J. WILSON *Lights & Shad. Scot. Life* 37 Dancing all day like a butterfly in a *meadow-field. **1492** RYMAN *Poems* lxxxiv. 2 in *Archiv Stud. neu. Spr.* LXXXIX. 253 As *medowe floures of swete odoures. **1798** COLERIDGE *Anc. Mar.* VI. xii, It fann'd my cheek, Like a *meadow-gale of spring. **1733** TULL *Horse-Hoeing Husb.* xiv. 180 If *Meadow-Hay cannot have good Weather to be cut [etc.]. **1856** *Farmer's Mag.* Jan. 36 As much phosphate of lime..as though he consumed meadow-hay. **1877** BLACKMORE *Erema* II. xl. 288 The *meadow-leet..was dry as usual. **1637** *Boston Rec.* (1877) II. 21 It is agreed that Mr. Atherton Haulgh shall have..the rest of Bretheren's *meadow Lotte there. **1880** *World* 29 Sept. 15 The farmers and *meadow-men seem to entertain no objection to people wandering..amongst the mowing-grass. **1879** GEO. ELIOT *Coll. Breakf. P.* 825 Watched with half closed eyes The *meadow-road. **1523** LD. BERNERS *Froiss.* I. xcviii. 119 They lay alonge by a fayre *medowe syde, and made a great dyke about their host. **1835** BROWNING *Paracelsus* v. 137 The gulf rolls like a *meadow-swell, o'erstrewn With ravaged boughs. **1648** HERRICK *Hesper.*, *Parting Verse* Poems (1869) 149 Herrick shall make the *meddow-verse for you. **1813** SIR H. DAVY *Agric. Chem.* i. (1814) 24 *Meadow-watering..acts not only by supplying useful moisture to the grass, but [etc.].

b. Prefixed to the names of animals regarded as denizens of meadow land; as **meadow ant**, the small British ant, *Lasius flavus*; **meadow bird** = BOBOLINK (Bartlett *Dict. Amer.* 1859); **meadow brown (butterfly)**, a common British butterfly, *Maniola jurtina*; **meadow chicken** (see quot.); **meadow clapper**, the salt-water marsh-hen (*Cent. Dict.* 1890); **meadow crake, drake** = CORN-CRAKE; **meadow crane-fly** = DADDY-LONG-LEGS; **meadow fly**, an American fire-fly; **meadow gallinule** = CORN-CRAKE; **meadow-hen** (see quot. for *meadow-chicken*); **meadow-lark**, (*a*) = TITLARK; (*b*) *U.S.* the grackle, *Sturnella magna* or *ludoviciana*; **meadow mouse**, any field vole (*Arvicola*); **meadow mussel**, a mussel found in American salt meadows, *Modiola plicatula* (Cent. Dict.); **meadow pipit** = TITLARK; †**meadow rat**, the field vole, *Arvicola agrestis*; **meadow snipe**, (*a*) = *grass bird* (see GRASS 13); (*b*) *U.S.* the common American snipe, *Gallinago Wilsoni*; **meadow titling** = TITLARK; **meadow vole** = *meadow mouse*; **meadow worm**, the common earthworm, *Lumbricus terrestris* or *Agricola*.

1879 LUBBOCK *Sci. Lect.* iv. 136 The yellow *meadow-ant keeps the underground kinds [of Aphides]. **1720** ALBIN *Nat. Hist. Insects* 53 On the 11th of June came the *Meadow Brown Butterfly. **1819** SAMOUELLE *Entomol. Compend.* 396 Meadow brown butterfly, *Hipparchia Janira.* **1930** *Times Educ. Suppl.* 4 Oct. p. iv/4 The meadow-brown's heavy, indolent flight. **1974** *Lady* 1 Aug. 169/1 Butterflies abound ..from the innumerable brown ringlets, 'gate-keepers', speckled woods and meadow browns, to various beauties like the common blues. **1893** NEWTON *Dict. Birds* 539 **Meadow-chicken* and *Meadow-hen*, names given in North America to more than one species of Rail or Coot. **1833** SELBY *Illustr. Brit. Ornith.* II. 177 The *Meadow Crake.. affecting rich meadows [etc.]. **1847** TENNYSON *Princess* IV. 105 Marsh-divers, rather, maid, Shall croak thee sister, or the meadow-crake Grate her harsh kindred in the grass. **1802** BINGLEY *Anim. Biog.* (1813) III. 310 The *Meadow Crane-fly, or Long-legs. **1867** EMERSON *Lett. & Soc. Aims* vii. (1875) 180 Fresh and delicate as the bonfires of the *meadow-flies. **1843** YARRELL *Brit. Birds* I. p. xxiii, *Meadow Gallinule. *a* **1841** W. P. HAWES *Sporting Scenes* (1842) I. 18 The principal inhabitants are gulls, and *meadow-hens. **1863** 'G. HAMILTON' *Gala-Days* 97 You know you didn't scare a little meadow-hen. **1611** COTGR., *Alouette de pré*, the chit, or small *meadow-larke. **1775** B. ROMANS *Conc. Nat. Hist. E. & W. Florida* 114 Meadow larks, fieldfares, rice birds, &c. are very frequently had. **1863** LONGF. *Wayside Inn* I. *Birds Killingw.* 142 Is this more pleasant to you than the whirr Of meadow-lark and her sweet roundelay? **1893** NEWTON *Dict. Birds* 512 The Meadow-Lark of America..is an Icterus. **1948** H. JACOBS *We chose Country* 161 Birds were everywhere, first killdeers, making a din in the fields at dusk, then meadowlarks, caroling in the morning sun. **1963** G. H. THOMSON *Crocus Country* xx. 131 The bird we loved most..was the meadow lark. **1969** N. W. PARSONS *Upon Sagebrush Harp* viii. 42 There were many birds, but the meadowlark moved me most. **1801** SHAW *Zool.* II. I. 81 *Meadow Mouse. **187.** *Cassell's Nat. Hist.* III. 117 The most abundant North American species is the Meadow-mouse (*Arvicola riparius*). **1893** *Leaflets Board of Agric.* (1894) 35 *Arvicola agrestis.* Locally known as..Meadow Mouse. **1825** SELBY *Illustr. Brit. Ornith.* I. 216 *Meadow Pipit or Tit. **1781** PENNANT *Hist. Quadrup.* II. 460 *Meadow [Rat]. *Mus agrestis.* **1828** FLEMING *Hist. Brit. Anim.* 75 *A*[*nthus*] *pratensis.* *Meadow Titling. **1863** C. ST. JOHN *Nat. Hist. Moray* Index, *Arvicola riparia.* *Meadow vole. **1787** BEST *Angling* (ed. 2) 16 Marsh, or *Meadow-worm.

c. Prefixed to names of plants, to denote varieties or species growing in meadows: often in book-names as a rendering of the Latin specific name *pratensis*, *-ense*, as in ***meadow barley, clover, crane's bill, dock, pea, sage, trefoil, vetchling***; also in **meadow beauty** (see quot.); **meadow-bell**, the harebell; **meadow campion**, the Ragged Robin, *Lychnis Flos-cuculi* (Britten & Holland 1886); **meadow cress** (see CRESS 1 b); **meadow crocus** = *meadow saffron* (Britten & Holland); **meadow fern**, a North American shrub, *Myrica Comptonia* (Cent. Dict. 1890); **meadow fescue** (see FESCUE 4); **meadow gowan** = MARSH MALLOW (Britten & Holland); **meadow grass**, any one of the grasses of the genus *Poa*, esp. *P. pratensis*; **meadow lily**, a common lily of the eastern U.S., *Lilium canadense*; also, formerly used for lily-of-the-valley, *Convallaria majalis*; **meadow mushroom**, *Agaricus campestris*; **meadow orchis**, *Orchis Morio*; **meadow parsnip** (see PARSNIP 2); **meadow pine**, *Pinus cubensis* (of the southern U.S.); **meadow pink**, (*a*) = RAGGED ROBIN; (*b*) = *maiden pink* (see MAIDEN 10 b); **meadow('s) queen** = MEADOW-SWEET (cf. *queen of the meadow(s*, QUEEN *sb.* 6 b); **meadow rhubarb, rue**, *Thalictrum flavum* (Britten & Holland); also **alpine meadow rue** = *feathered columbine* (see COLUMBINE *sb.*² 3); **meadow saffron**, *Colchicum autumnale*; **meadow (pepper) saxifrage** (see SAXIFRAGE).

1866 *Treas. Bot.* 727/1 **Meadow Beauty*, an American name for *Rhexia*. *Ibid.* 972/2 Commonly called Deer-grass, or Meadow-beauty. **1827** G. DARLEY *Sylvia* 136 Like soft winds jangling *meadow-bells. *c* **1275** *Luue Ron* 16 in *O.E. Misc.* 93 Vnder molde hi liggeþ colde and faleweþ so doþ *medewe gres. **13..** *Minor Poems fr. Vernon MS.* xxxvii. 537 Þe eorþe ȝeldeþ not fruit as hit wont was, Of corn of þe feld ne of þe medewe-gras. **1597** GERARDE *Herbal* I. i. 1 Common Medow grasse hath very small tufts of rootes. **1840** J. BUEL *Farmer's Comp.* 232 The red meadow-grass (*Poa aquatica*). **1832** W. D. WILLIAMSON *Hist. State Maine* I. 125 [We have] two varieties of *meadow-lilies,..May-lily, or 'lily of the valley'; and nodding-lily. **1894** *Jrnl. Amer. Folk-Lore* VII. 102 *Lilium Canadense*,..meadow lily, nodding lily. **1946** E. HODGINS *Mr. Blandings builds his Dream House* (1947) viii. 104 When the bluebells and the columbine faded, the meadow lilies and the wild geranium took up the torch... August was well along. **1884** *Leisure Hour* Nov. 703/2 The popular name of the common edible agaric is everywhere 'the *meadow mushroom'. **1866** *Treas. Bot.*, *Meadow-orchis. **1882** *Garden* 4 Feb. 81/1 The common Meadow Orchis..is not to be found wild everywhere. **1896** G. HENSLOW *How to Study Wild Flowers* 98 *Lathyrus pratensis*, *Meadow Pea. This genus resembles vetches, but has fewer leaflets. **1960** *Oxf. Bk. Wild Flowers* 22/2 Meadow Vetchling or Meadow Pea (*Lathyrus pratensis*). Although this Pea has thin, rather weak stems, it may reach up to 3 feet in height by scrambling over other plants. **1884** SARGENT *Rep. Forests N. Amer.* (*10th Census* IX.) 202 *Pinus Cubensis*..Slash Pine... *Meadow Pine. **1785** MARTYN *Rousseau's Bot.* xix. (1794) 276 *Meadow Pink. *Lychnis flos cuculi.* **1625** B. JONSON *Pan's Annivers.*, Star'd with yellow-golds, and *Meadowes Queene. **1668** WILKINS *Real Char.* II. iv. §4. 83 *Meadow Rue. **1863** BARING-GOULD *Iceland* 190 The tremulous dancing flowers of the Alpine meadow rue. **1884** *Gardening Illustr.* 8 Nov. 425/2 Allied to Columbines are the Meadow Rues. **1578** LYTE *Dodoens* III. xxxv. 367 *Medowe Saffron..is found.. about Bath in Englande. **1878** tr. *H. von Ziemssen's Cycl. Med.* XVII. 734 Some seed-capsules of the meadow-saffron. **1629** J. PARKINSON *Parad.* I. lxxix. 341 The Medica's are generally thought to feede cattell fat much more then the *Medow Trefoile, or Clauer grasse. **1686** PLOT *Staffordsh.* 356 Produces the Meddow-trefoile.

d. Special Comb.: **meadow green** (see quot.); **meadow ground**, (*a*) ground laid down in meadow; (*b*) prairie land; **meadow land** = *meadow ground*; **meadow-ore**, bog iron ore (cf. LIMONITE); **meadow thatch**, coarse grass or rush used for thatching.

1794 KIRWAN *Elem. Min.* (ed. 2) I. 28 *Meadow green —lively green, in which however the yellow predominates. **1523** FITZHERB. *Surv.* 2 b, Lowe groundes *medowe groundes and marsshe groundes for hey. **1667** MILTON *P.L.* XI. 644 A Band..drives A herd of Beeves..From a fat Meddow ground. **1802** WORDSW. *Sonn.* '*Here, on our native soil*', Those boys who in yon meadow-ground In white-sleeved shirts are playing. **1653** *Early Rec. Lancaster, Mass.* (1884) 29 Wee Covenant to lay out *Meddow Lands. **1844** DISRAELI *Coningsby* IV. iii, A broad meadow land. **1817** THOMSON *Syst. Chem.* (ed. 5) III. 478 *Meadow Ore. **1430–31** *Durham Acc. Rolls* (Surtees) 231 Empcio tignorum, straminis, et *Medewthak.

meadow ('mɛdəʊ), *v.* [f. prec.] *trans.* To devote (land) to the production of grass.

1768 [W. DONALDSON] *Life Sir B. Sapskull* II. xxiv. 191 By meadowing a great deal, and feeding a little, they impoverish the land. **1865** TROLLOPE *Belton Est.* iii, I didn't know you ever meadowed the park. **1885** *Law Times* 28 Mar. 384/2 During this period they [grass lands] were neither meadowed, grazed, nor cropped.

†**'meadowage.** *Obs.* [f. MEADOW *sb.* + -AGE.] (See quot.)

1611 COTGR., *Preage*, Medowage; or, a freedome to put cattell into other mens medowes.

meadowed, *ppl. a.* [f. MEADOW *sb.* or *v.* + -ED.] Having, or cultivated as, meadow land.

Tennyson (*Morte d'Arthur* 262) has *deep-meadow'd*, parasynthetically f. MEADOW *sb.*, in imitation of Gr. *βαθυλείμων*.

1670 *Mass. Col. Rec.* IV. II. 461 Plantation..exceeding well meadowed. **1831** J. WILSON *Unimore* ii. 177 That meadow'd plain as green as emerald. **1888** *Harper's Mag.* Apr. 735 The Gulf has eaten three miles into her meadowed land.

meadower ('mɛdəʊə(r)). [f. MEADOW *sb.* or *v.* + -ER¹.] 'One who waters meadow-lands to increase or preserve their verdure' (Ogilvie *Suppl.* 1855).

meadowing ('mɛdəʊɪŋ), *vbl. sb.* [f. MEADOW.]

1. Land used or suitable for the growth of a crop of grass. Also *attrib.*

c **1598** in Harwood *Lichfield* (1806) 385, ij closes and j piece of meadowing. **1611** COTGR., *Preir*, to make Medowing of; to turne into Medow. **1639** *Plymouth Col. Rec.* (1855) I. 110 Prouided he be allowed meddowing elswhere in lieu thereof. **1732** *Pennsylv. Gaz.* 31 July–7 Aug. 4/1 A very good Plantation..with plentiful Meadowing fit

for the Scythe. **1844** *Jrnl. R. Agric. Soc.* V. I. 108 On leaving Dunham I observed some good meadowing.

attrib. **1611** SPEED *Theat. Gt. Brit.* xix. (1614) 37/1 Meadowing-pastures upon both sides of the river Came. **1675** *Providence (R.I.) Rec.* (1893) IV. 39 Ye two shares of ye meaddoing ground.

2. The action of cultivating meadow land.

1735 *Pennsylv. Gaz.* 15–22 Mar. 2/2 Several Tracts of good Land..good Part of it fit for Meadowing. **1894** *Morning Post* 3 Feb. 2/1 Less valuable land, worthless for the purpose of meadowing, would be left.

attrib. **1796** WASHINGTON *Let.* Writ. 1892 XIII. 259, I am altogether in the farming and meadowing line

†'meadowish, *a. Obs.* [f. MEADOW *sb.* + -ISH.] Resembling meadow.

1668 *1st Cent. Hist. Springfield, Mass.* (1899) II. 98 The Town granted unto Abell Wright..ffourteen acres of Meddowish Land up the Little River. **1681** *Plymouth Col. Rec.* (1857) VII. 238 Which fence stood on the said Woodworth swampy, meddowish land.

meadowless ('mɛdəʊlɪs), *a.* [f. MEADOW *sb.* + -LESS.] Lacking meadows.

1887 *Century Mag.* Dec. 171 The bare rocks, meadowless inclines, and treeless shores of Galilee.

meadow-sweet ('mɛdəʊswiːt). [f. MEADOW *sb.* + SWEET *a.* (The earlier form was MEADSWEET.)] The rosaceous plant *Spiræa Ulmaria*, common in moist meadows and along the banks of streams, growing on erect, rigid stems to a height of about two feet, with dense heads of creamy white and highly fragrant flowers. In the U.S. applied to another species, *S. salicifolia*.

1530 PALSGR. 244/1 Medowe swete herbe. **1597** [see MEADSWEET]. **1688** R. HOLME *Armoury* II. 97/1 Queen of the Meadows, or Meadow sweet, or Mead sweet. **1856** LEVER *Martins of Cro' M.* 306 The odour of the white thorn and the meadow-sweet.

attrib. **1840** HOOD *Kilmansegg, Honeymoon* xxi, O blessed nature..Who does not sigh for its meadow-sweet breath?

meadow-wink ('mɛdəʊwɪŋk). *U.S. local.* [f. MEADOW *sb.* + *wink* (? echoic).] = BOBOLINK.

1884 COUES *Key N. Amer. Birds* (ed. 2) 400 *Dolichonyx oryzivorus*..Bobolink. Meadow-wink. Skunk Blackbird.

meadowy ('mɛdəʊɪ), *a.* [f. MEADOW *sb.* + -Y[1].] Resembling a meadow.

1598 FLORIO, *Piaggioso*, medowie, large, bleach, fieldie. **1612** DRAYTON *Poly-olb.* x. 94 Thy full and youthfull breasts, which in their meadowy pride, Are brancht with riuery veines, Meander-like that glide. **1774** PENNANT *Tour Scotl. in 1772*, 328 This terminates in a meadowy plain. **1805** WORDSW. *Waggoner* IV. 40 Yon meadowy bottom. **1871** PALGRAVE *Lyr. Poems* 80 Miles of meadowy splendour.

meadsman ('miːdzmən). *dial.* [f. *mead's*, genitive of MEAD *sb.*[2] + MAN.] = HAYWARD.

1893 MRS. STAPLETON *Three Oxfordsh. Parishes* 311 Boats using this towing-path pay toll to the meadsman.

meadstead: see MERESTEAD.

†'meadsweet. *Obs.* Forms: 5 **medeswote, -swete**, 6 **-swete, -sweete**, 8 **meadsweet**, 6–8 *corruptly* **maidsweet**. [app. f. MEAD[2] + SWEET *a.*; but it is possible that, as in MEADWORT, the first element may originally have been MEAD[1].

The MDu. *medesoete* has the appearance of being etymologically equivalent (*mede* occurs both for MEAD[1] honeydrink and for MEAD[2] meadow), but it meant 'marigold', an application difficult to reconcile with either of these etymologies. Zedler *Universal-lex.* 1733, s.v. *Barba-Capræ*, gives *Medesüss* and *Medkraut* as Ger. names for meadow-sweet, and also cites a latinized form *medesusium* from Cordus (16th c.).]

= MEADOW-SWEET.

14.. *Voc.* in Wr.-Wülcker 595/29 *Melessa*, medeswote. *Ibid.* 607/20 *Regina prati*, medesewte. *c* **1450** *Alphita* (Anecd. Oxon.) 40/2 *Citria, mellissa idem. anglice* medswete *uel* bonrefair. **1578** LYTE *Dodoens* I. xxix. 41 Medesweete or Medewurte..hath great, long brode leaues like Egrimonie. **1597** GERARDE *Herbal* II. ccccii. 886 Of Medesweete, or Queene of the medowes... It is called..in English Maidesweete [(1636) 1043 Meades-sweet], Medowsweete, and Queene of the medowes. **1736** AINSWORTH *Lat. Dict.*, *Ulmaria*..Meadsweet, or medewort [ed. 1783 meadwort] goat's beard. **1750** W. ELLIS *Country Housew.* 252 Maidsweet that grows like a Kecks in wet Meadows.

†'meadwort. *Obs.* Forms: 1 **medo-, medewyrt**, 3 **medwurt**, 4, 8 **medewort**, 5 **-wourth**, 6 **-wurt**, 5 **medwor, -wert**, 6 *Sc.* **meduart, -wart**, 6 **medæwart, medow wurt**, 7 **medowort**, 8 **meadwort**. [OE. *medowyrt*, f. *medo* MEAD[1] + *wyrt* WORT, plant; corresponding to Sw. dial. *mjödört* (and equivalents in Norw., Da., mod.Icel.); possibly the flowers may have been used for flavouring mead. The first element was, however, early associated with MEAD[2] (= MEADOW), the confusion being helped by the circumstance that another name for the plant was 'queen of the meadow' (L. *regina prati*, F. *reine des prés*, G. *wiesenkönigin*, Da. *engdronning*).

With regard to the possible use of meadow-sweet for flavouring mead, cf. the statement in Zedler *Universal-lex.* (1733) s.v. *Barba-capræ*, that the flowers were used to give to wine a flavour like that of malmsey.]

1. = MEADOW-SWEET.

c **1000** *Sax. Leechd.* II. 70 ȝenime neoþowearde medowyrt, & lustmocan. *c* **1265** *Voc. Plants* in Wr.-Wülcker 555/8 *Regina*, reine, medwurt. *a* **1387** *Sinon. Barthol.* (Anecd. Oxon.) 29/2 *Melissa*,..medewort. *c* **1450** *Alphita* (ibid.) 115/1 *Mellissa*,..medwor. *Ibid.* 156/2 *Reginela*, ..mede-wort. *Ibid.* 177/2 *Scrophularia*,..medwert. **1549** *Compl. Scot.* vi. 42 Than the scheiphyrdis vyuis..gadrit mony fragrant grene meduart. **1568** TURNER *Herbal* III. 8 Of Mede-wurt, or Medow wurt, or Medeswete... It groweth about watersydes. *a* **1578** LINDESAY (Pitscottie) *Chron. Scot.* (S.T.S.) I. 336 The fluir laid witht greine cherittis witht sprattis med-wartis and flouris. **1579** LANGHAM *Gard. Health* (1633) 388 Medowort: Drinke the decoction or powder of it to stop the laske. **1590** SPENSER *F.Q.* II. viii. 20 The metall first he mixt with Medæwart, That no enchauntment from his dint might save. **1736–83** [see MEADSWEET].

†2. ? Watercress. Also ***women's meadwort***. *Obs.*

a **1400–50** *Stockholm Med. MS.* fol. 209 Freynch cresse or wymmannys medewourth: *nascorium gallicanum.* ? **14..** *MS. Harl.* 3388 in *Sax. Leechd.* II. 399 *Nasturtium ortolan[um]*, medwort.

meady ('miːdɪ), *a. rare.* [f. MEAD[1] + -Y[1].] Resembling or suggestive of mead.

1887 G. MEREDITH *Ballads & Poems Tragic Life* 102 Yellow flamed the meady sunset. **1900** *Sydney Mail* 31 Mar. 777 If you simply let it stand it will usually work up into the meady beverage.

meag, obs. form of MEAK *dial.*

meagre ('miːgə(r)), *a.* (*sb.*) Forms: 4–7 **megre**, 5 **megire, meger(e**, 6 **meiger**, *Sc.* **megir**, 6–7 **maigre, megar**, 6–9 **meager**, 7 **meaguer**, 6– **meagre**. [ME. *megre*, a. OF. *megre*, *maigre* (mod.F. *maigre*) = Pr. *magre*, *maigre*, Sp., Pg., It. *magro*, Roumanian *macru*:—L. *macrum* (*macer*), cogn. with Gr. μακρός long, μακεδνός tall, slender, μῆκος length. The synon. Teut. **magro-* (OE. *mæȝer*, MLG., Du. *mager*, OHG. *magar*, mod.G. *mager*, ON. *magr*, Sw., Da. *mager*; wanting in Goth.) may represent a pre-Teut. **makró-* = L. *macro-*, Gr. μακρό-; the nature of the sense renders this more likely than the alternative supposition that the Teut. word was adopted from Latin.]

1. Of persons and animals, their limbs, etc.: Having little flesh; lean, thin, emaciated.

13.. *Coer de L.* 1079 The lyoun was hungry and megre. **13..** *E.E. Allit. P.* B. 1198 Fro þat mete was myst, megre þay wexen. **1470–85** MALORY *Arthur* X. lxxxvii. 568, I am megre and haue ben longe seke for the loue of la Beale Isoud. **1591** SPENSER *M. Hubberd* 599 Thou art so leane and meagre waxen late. **1596** —— *F.Q.* IV. viii. 12 With heary glib deform'd, and meiger face. **1603** DEKKER *Wonderful Year* B j b, She..was deliuered of a pale, meagre, weake childe. **1634** W. TIRWHYT tr. *Balzac's Lett.* (vol. I.) 151 There are others..who make use of all the secrets in Physicke to have a megar aspect. **1673** O. WALKER *Educ.* I. ix. 95 [They] are alwaies lean, maigre and consumptive. **1748** *Anson's Voy.* II. xiii. 275 The wan and meager countenances of the crew. **1820** SCOTT *Monast.* ix, The meagre condition of his horse. **1822** W. IRVING *Braceb. Hall* ii. 13 A meagre wiry old fellow. **1872** BLACKIE *Lays Highl.* Introd. 55 As for us, meagre mountaineers, we shall continue..to make the best of our granite rocks. **1883** F. M. WALLEM *Fish-Supply Norway* 29 (Fish. Exhib. Publ.) The Italians prefer meagre fish to plump.

b. with personifications, esp. Famine, Envy.

1594 KYD *Cornelia* I. i. 176 Maigre famin, which the weake foretell. *a* **1625** FLETCHER *Cust. Country* V. i, Maugre [*? read* maigre] palenesse Like winter nips the roses and the lilies. **1784** COWPER *Task* II. 185 He calls for Famine, and the meagre fiend Blows mildew from between his shrivelled lips. **1809** HEBER *Palestine* 13 Lawless force, and meagre want are there.

¶c. Applied to what produces emaciation.

1612 DEKKER *If it be not good* Wks. 1873 III. 282 Your order..Tyed to religious fasts, spends the sad day Wholy in meager contemplation.

†d. *absol.* as *sb.* Leanness, emaciation.

a **1400–50** *Alexander* 1164 Slik mischife in þe mene quile emang his men fallis For megire [*Dubl. MS.* meger] & for meteles ware mervaile to here. **1530** PALSGR. 244/1 Megre a sicknesse, *maigre*.

2. Deficient or mean in quantity, size or quality; wanting in fullness or richness; poor, scanty.

a. of material things; esp. of soil, vegetation.

†In the first quot. without disparaging implication: ? small in size; ? delicate in sound.

1501 DOUGLAS *Pal. Hon.* I. xxxv, Quhairfra dependant hang thir megir bellis. **1595** SHAKS. *John* III. i. 80 The glorious sunne..playes the Alchymist, Turning..The meager cloddy earth to glittering gold. **1596** —— *Merch. V.* III. ii. 104 But thou, thou meager lead..Thy palenesse moues me more then eloquence. **1681** CHETHAM *Angler's Vade-m.* xxxix. 286 Cankered, and very Maigre, Hungry Soil. **1806** *Gazetteer Scot.* (ed. 2) 136 A sandy plain.. covered with a meagre, green, benty pasture. **1848** DICKENS *Dombey* xxxiv, An old woman..sat..crouching over a meagre fire. **1856** STANLEY *Sinai & Pal.* xiv. (1858) 465 On its shabby roof a meagre cupola. **1871** BLACKIE *Four Phases* i. 41 A meagre plant growing up in a bad climate. **1872** JENKINSON *Guide Eng. Lakes* (1879) 71 Little Langdale Tarn lies close below..looking very meagre.

b. Of food, fare, diet: Scanty; deficient in quantity or goodness.

1663 COWLEY *Verses & Ess.* (1669) 123 We must excuse her for this meager entertainment. **1831** LAMB *Elia* Ser. II. *Ellistoniana*, The meagre banquet. **1856** KANE *Arct. Expl.* I. vi. 56 The meagre allowance of two pounds of raw flesh every other day. **1898–9** J. A. WYLIE *Hist. Protestant.* 237 The meagre meals he allowed himself.

c. Of literary composition or material, information, subject-matter, artistic treatment, or the like: Wanting in fullness or elaboration; jejune.

1539 CROMWELL in Merriman *Life & Lett.* (1902) II. 193, I haue caused them [*sc.* letters] to be writen in suche a maigre sorte as I thought the case required. **1582** STANYHURST *Æneis* Ep. Ded. (Arb.) 4 Oure Virgil not content wyth such meigre stuffe. **1696** PHILLIPS s.v., Figuratively we say a Meager Stile, a Meager Subject. **1794** SULLIVAN *View Nat.* IV. 353 All we have is a meagre fragment, a traditionary tale. **1841** D'ISRAELI *Amen. Lit.* (1867) 112 The continuation of a meagre chronicle. **1898** J. MURRAY in *Westm. Gaz.* 14 June 8/2 Collecting the best stories and stringing them together with the very meagrest amount of comment.

d. Of pleasures, intellect, ideas; also of resources, possessions.

1638 BAKER tr. *Balzac's Lett.* (vol. II.) 53 The pleasures of the Country are too gross and meager for a taste that is used to more delicate and solid pleasures. **1755** YOUNG *Centaur* iii. Wks. 1757 IV. 169 It is one of their minute, and meagre pleasures. **1862** J. MARTINEAU *Ess.* (1866) I. 199 It is but a meagre and imperfect form of faith. **1871** R. ELLIS tr. *Catullus* lxviii. 33 Books—if they're but scanty, a store full meagre, around me. **1875** JOWETT *Plato* (ed. 2) IV. 397 Their meagre minds refuse to attribute anything to anything. **1893** SALTUS *Madam Sapphira* 19 There was the house, the meager income and his professional hopes.

e. *Min.* Harsh, dry. ? *Obs.*

1794 KIRWAN *Elem. Min.* (ed. 2) I. 12 Calcareous earths feel dry, meagre, and harsh. *Ibid.* 116 Meagre lime takes up less sand. **1844** E. J. CHAPMAN *Char. Minerals* 53 This sensation [touch] may be either *very greasy*, ex. talc; *greasy*, ex. steatite; *rather greasy*, ex. asbestus; or *meagre*, ex. chalk.

3. = MAIGRE. ***soup meagre*** tr. F. *soupe maigre*.

1705 ADDISON *Italy* 474 (*Switzerland*) The best meagre Food in the World. **1756–7** tr. *Keysler's Trav.* (1760) I. 331 On meagre days the Roman-catholics here fare very badly. **1796** SOUTHEY *Lett. fr. Spain* (1799) 352 After doing penance for forty days on fish and soup meagre, they [etc.]. **1832** *Veg. Subst. Food* 222 The church enjoins a number of meagre days. **1855** DELAMER *Kitch. Gard.* (1861) 55 The Red cabbage..is generally eaten..during Lent, when it forms an excellent meagre dish.

b. *absol.* as *sb.* 'Maigre' diet. Phrases, ***to eat, make meagre***. (Cf. MAIGRE *a.* 3.)

1770 BARETTI *Journ. Lond. Genoa* III. lxv. 220 The Spaniards do not eat meagre on Saturdays. **1834** BECKFORD *Italy* I. 335 Every thing..which..the rules of meagre could allow. **1851** J. H. NEWMAN *Cath. in Eng.* 326 Prejudice.. which would..call it Popish persecution, to be kept on meagre for a Lent. **1852** THACKERAY *Esmond* II. iii, We make meagre on Fridays always.

4. *Comb.*, as ***meagre-hued, faced, minded***, etc. adjs.

1596 R. L[INCHE] *Diella* (1877) 58 That pale leane-fac'd meager-hewed enuie. **1644** HOWELL *Eng. Teares* Ded., Methinks I spie meagre-fac'd Famine making towards thee. **1865** TROLLOPE *Belton Est.* xx. 230 Cold-hearted, thankless, meagre-minded creature as I know he is.

†meagre ('miːgə(r)), *v. Obs.* [f. MEAGRE *a.* Cf. F. *maigrir*.] *trans.* To make meagre or lean.

1563–87 FOXE *A. & M.* (1596) 1696/2 So weried and megered for want of sustenance, that [etc.]. **1700** DRYDEN *Æsacus Transf.* 54 His ceaseless sorrow for the unhappy maid Meagred his look, and on his spirits preyed. **1807** SIR R. WILSON *Jrnl.* 16 June, I am meagred to a skeleton.

meagre, variant of MAIGRE *sb.*

meagrely ('miːgəlɪ), *adv.* [f. MEAGRE *a.* + -LY[2].] In a meagre manner.

a **1586** SIDNEY *Arcadia* IV. (1598) 430 Alas thou helpest meagerly, When once one is for Atropos distrained. **1616** J. LANE *Cont. Sqr.'s T.* XI. 334 Next came a knight..vppon a pale horse, meagerlie bestridd in armor, plumes, caparisone all pale. **1833** HT. MARTINEAU *Three Ages* ii. 71 An hospital, meagrely supplied with the comforts. **1878** F. HARRISON in *Fortn. Rev.* Nov. 689 Austin has treated these questions somewhat meagrely. **1886** W. J. TUCKER *E. Europe* 179 A meagrely furnished room.

meagreness ('miːgənɪs). [+ -NESS.]

1. Leanness, emaciation.

1599 T. M[OUFET] *Silkwormes* 55 Lest belly break, or meagernesse ensewe, By giuing more or lesse then was their due. *a* **1656** HALES *Gold. Rem.* (1688) 58 His ill Colour and Meagerness. **1756** W. DODD *Fasting* (ed. 2) 9 This paleness and meagerness of visage. **1830** D'ISRAELI *Chas. I*, III. vi. 112 The reason which induces me to consider this portrait as an original, is the meagreness of the countenance.

transf. **1875** MASKELL *Ivories* 44 The figures in Byzantine work..begin to be characterised by sharpness and meagreness of form, and lengthiness of proportion.

2. Scantiness, lack of fullness; poorness of quality.

1622 BACON *Hen. VII* 138 The Meagernesse of his Seruice in the Warres. **1798** FERRIAR *Illustr. Sterne, Eng. Hist.* 230 The most striking defect..is not meagreness, but inflation. **1831** J. JEBB in C. Forster *Life* (1834) II. 593 An ante-script, which will indemnify you for the meagreness of this [letter]. **1876** SMILES *Sc. Natur.* xiv. (ed. 4) 279 The meagreness of the list of Crustacea and Testacea. **1884** CHURCH *Bacon* ix. 215 [The Essays] are austere even to meagreness.

†b. Littleness (of heart). *Obs.*

1501 DOUGLAS *Pal. Hon.* I. xxi, Had not bene that, certes my hart had brokin For megirnes and pusillamitie.

meagrim, variant of MEGRIM.

|ˈmeagry, *a. Obs. rare.* [f. MEAGRE *a.* + -Y.] Having a meagre appearance.
1603 DEKKER *Wonderf. Yeare* B b, She was deliuered of a pale, meagry, weake child, named Sicknesse.

meaguer, obs. form of MEAGRE *a.*

meak (miːk). *dial.* Also 5 meeke, meyke, 6 meake, 7, 9 meag, 8–9 make. An implement with a long handle and crooked iron or blade used to pull up or cut down peas, bracken, reeds, etc. Also *pea-meak* (see PEA[1] 7), *pease-meak* (see PEASE *sb.* 5).
1478 *Maldon* (Essex) *Court Rolls* Bundle 50 No. 10[v], Holwell come out with a wepen called a meyke. 1481–90 *Howard Househ. Bks.* (Roxb.) 113, I paid Gravely for vj. meekes. 1573 TUSSER *Husb.* (1878) 37 A meake for the pease, and to swinge vp the brake. 1674 RAY *Collect. Words* 71 A *Meag* or *Meak*, a Pease-hook. 1865 W. WHITE *Eastern Eng.* I. vii. 100 We..cuts the reeds down as deep as we can with a make, a kind o' short-bladed, long-handled scythe. 1895 P. H. EMERSON *Birds*, etc. *Norf. Broadland* 74 Disturbed by meak or crome that drags forth the lamb's-tail.
Hence **meak** *v.*, *trans.* to cut with a meak. *dial.* *absol.* 1892 P. H. EMERSON *Son of Fens* xiii. 99 Which are you going to do—meag or mow? Well, we'd better meag, now the water is up.

meaken, obs. form of MEEKEN.

meakenes, obs. form of MEEKNESS.

meaking (ˈmiːkɪŋ), *vbl. sb. Naut.* Also 9 meeking. [? f. MEAK + -ING[1].] Only in *meaking iron*: 'The tool used by caulkers to run old oakum out of the seams before inserting new' (Smyth 1867).
According to information supplied by Mr. G. Crocker, of H. M. Dockyard, Devonport, the term is now often misapplied to the *making-iron* (MAKING *vbl sb.* 10); the first quot. is an example of the erroneous use.
[1852–4 *Cycl. Usef. Arts* (ed. Tomlinson 1866) II. 511/1 Two men, one of whom holds..the meeking or making iron to the caulked seam, while the other man drives it in with the beetle.] 1878 D. KEMP *Yacht & Boat Sailing* 358 *Meaking iron*, an instrument used to extract old caulking from seams.

meakle, obs. dial. form of MICKLE, *Sc.*

meal (miːl), *sb.*[1] Forms: 1 melu, -o, -a, meolo, meala (*inflected* melw-, melew-, -ow-, -uw-, meolw-, mealew-); 3–4 mel, 3–6 mele, 4 meel, melow(e, 4, 6 meill, melle, 4–6 meele, 5 meyle, 6 meell, *Sc.* maill, meil, 6–7 meale, 7– meal. [Com. Teut.: OE. *melo, melw-* str. neut. = OFris. *mel*, OS. *melo* (MDu. *mele*, Du. *meel*), OHG. *melo, melaw-* (MHG. *mel, melw-*, mod.G. *mehl*), ON. *mjǫl, mjǫlv-* (Sw. *mjol*, Da. *meel*, now *mel*):—OTeut. *melwo[m]*, f. root *mel-, mal-, mul-* (pre-Teut. *mel-, mol-, ml̥-*), whence Com. Teut. *malan* to grind (found in all Teut. langs. exc. Eng.), cogn. w. L. *molĕre*, OSl. *mlěti*, Lith. *málti*, OIrish *melim*; further cognates are L. *mola, molīna* (see MILL *sb.*), Gr. *μύλη, μύλος* mill, millstone.]

1. a. The edible part of any grain or pulse ground to a powder. Now commonly understood to exclude the product of wheat (this being called FLOUR). Also *spec.* in Scotland and Ireland = OATMEAL; in the U.S. the meal of Indian corn (= *Indian meal*: see INDIAN *a.* 3). *whole meal*: see WHOLE.
c888 K. ÆLFRED *Boeth.* xxxiv. §11 Swa swa mon meolo syft. c1000 *Sax. Leechd.* II. 134 ȝenim merce nioþoweardne & huniȝ & hwætenes meluwes smedman. c1200 ORMIN 1552 þu sammnesst all þin mele inn an & cnedest itt togeddre. c1300 *Havelok* 780 Hise pokes fulle of mele an korn. 1382 WYCLIF *Num.* v. 15 The tenthe part of a busshel of barly melowe [1388 barli meele]. 1398 TREVISA *Barth. De P.R.* IV. iv. (1495) 84 Branne of whete or of rye,..and also sope and meele of beenes wasshe awaye the fylthe of the face and of all the body. c1440 *Promp. Parv.* 331/2 Meele of corne growndyn, *farina*. 1508 DUNBAR *Flyting w. Kennedie* 147 As gredy gleddis, ȝe gang With polkis to mylne, and beggis baith meill and schilling. 1546 in W. H. Turner *Select. Rec. Oxford* (1880) 179 The untrue and excessyve tollinge of certayne quarters of wheate meale. 1556 *Chron. Gr. Friars* (Camden) 57 The howse for the markyt folke in Newgate market for to waye melle in. 1611 BIBLE *2 Kings* iv. 41 He said, Then bring meale. 1707 MORTIMER *Husb.* (1721) I. 257 Some..feed them with Curds, Barley-meal, Bran, &c. 1775 JOHNSON *Journ. W. Isles* 68 Her two next sons were gone to Inverness to buy meal, by which oatmeal is always meant. 1832 TENNYSON *Miller's Dau.* 104 The very air about the door Made misty with the floating meal. 1844 H. STEPHENS *Bk. Farm* I. 137 A third lot was fed on..turnips and bean-meal. 1884 *Health Exhib. Catal.* 159/1 Chick Pea Meal, Mais Cariaro Meal.

b. Applied to the finer part of the ground grain, in contrast with *bran*. Often *fig.* ? *Obs.*
1579 LYLY *Euphues* (Arb.) 123, I haue thorowly sifted the disposition of youth, wherein I haue founde more branne then meale, more dowe then leauen. 1607 SHAKS. *Cor.* III. i. 322 He..is ill-school'd In boulted Language: Meale and Bran together He throwes without distinction. 1611 —— *Cymb.* IV. ii. 27 Nature hath Meale, and Bran; Contempt, and Grace.

†**c.** Phr. *of the same meal*: of the same kind or quality; = L. *ejusdem farinæ*. *Obs.*
1611 B. JONSON *Catiline* IV. ii, Except he were of the same Meal and Batch. 1677 GALE *Crt. Gentiles* III. 155 Thomas Aquinas, Bonaventura, and others of the same meal did many and wonderful things at Paris.

2. *transf.* A powder produced by grinding (e.g. in *linseed meal*); a powdery substance resembling flour. In *Bot.* applied to the powder covering the surface of the leaves, petals, etc., of certain plants.
1549 *Privy Council Acts* (1890) II. 348 Brymston in meale, ij barrelles. 1561 HOLLYBUSH *Hom. Apoth.* 14 Take fyne mustard sede mele. 1627 CAPT. SMITH *Seaman's Gram.* xiv. 71 Serpentine powder in old time was in meale, but now corned. 1728–46 THOMSON *Spring* 536 Auriculas, enrich'd With shining meal o'er all their velvet leaves. 1784 COWPER *Task* III. 538 The bee transports the fertilizing meal From flow'r to flow'r. 1796 KIRWAN *Elem. Min.* (ed. 2) II. 436 The arsenic rises in the form of a white meal. 1870 HOOKER *Stud. Flora* 300 [*Primula farinosa*] Glabrous above, meal below white or sulphur-coloured.

3. *attrib.* and *Comb.* **a.** Obvious combinations, simple attrib., as *meal-ark* dial., *-bag, -barrel, -chest, -drift, -dust, -girnal* Sc., *-husk, -kist* Sc., *-market, -mill* Sc., *-pap, -poke, -sack, -sieve, -trough*; *meal-dusty, -white* adjs.; objective, as *meal-†maker, -miller* Sc., *-monger* Sc., *-seller, -sifter, -weigher*.
1594 *Knaresb. Wills* (Surtees) I. 199 One *meale arke. 1814 SCOTT *Wav.* x, When a Whiggish mob destroyed his meeting-house,..intromitting also with his mart and his meal-ark. 1644 *Essex County, Mass. Probate Rec.* (1916) I. 46 Too *meal baggs. 1738 *New Hampsh. Probate Rec.* (1914) II. 622 He knows of no meal Bag that his son had but what he borrowed of him. 1876 *Wide Awake* 72/1 She was bundled up so you would hardly have known her from one of the meal-bags. 1968 E. R. BUCKLER *Ox Bells & Fireflies* ii. 34 Father puts three basketsful [of potatoes] into each meal bag. 1840 J. BUEL *Farmer's Comp.* 65 The *meal-chest must be occasionally replenished. 1877 G. M. HOPKINS *Poems* (1967) 70 What lovely behaviour Of silk-sack clouds! has wilder, wilful-wavier *Meal-drift moulded ever and melted across skies? 1535 COVERDALE *Isa.* xxix. 5 For the multitude of thine enemies shalbe like *meal-dust. 1902 CORNISH *Naturalist Thames* 101 Meal-dust hung from every nail, peg, and rope-end on the walls. 1951 W. DE LA MARE *Winged Chariot* 40 *Meal-dusty polls, glossed plumage. 1548 *Aberd. Reg.* (1844) I. 259 Thre *meill girnalis, out of my loft, xxx s. 1839 CARLYLE *Chartism* v. (1840) 45 Peasants living on *meal-husks and boiled grass. 1856 J. AITON *Clerical Econ.* v. (ed. 2) 304 Muck is the mother of the *meal-kist. a1400 in *York Myst.* Introd. 40 *Mele-makers. 1721 WODROW *Ch. Hist.* I. 288 John Bryce, Mealmaker, in Cambusnethan parish. 1555–6 in *Edinb. Burgh Rec.* (1871) II. 366 For the irnis at the kirk dur, *meill merkat, flesche merkat. 1705 *Lond. Gaz.* No. 4169/3 They intend to Let to Farm the Tolls..of the Meal-Market at Fleet-Chanel. 1793 *State, Leslie of Powis* etc. 67 (Jam.) A small island lying between the *meal-mill race, and the north grain of the river. 1892 R. LOVETT *J Gilmour of Mongolia* i. 18 Our maternal grandfather..was a farmer and *meal-miller on the estate of Cathkin. 1766 NICOL *Poems* 165 Just like a covetous *meal-monger. 1818 SCOTT *Br. Lamm.* xxix, The match between the laird of Kittlegirth's black mare and Johnston the meal-monger's four-year-old colt. 1799 *Underwood's Syst. Med.* (ed. 4) I. 154 Violent convulsions, which disappeared entirely, upon the prohibition of *meal-pap. 17.. *Robin Hood & Beggar* v. in Child *Ballads* III. 160 His *meal-pock hang about his neck, Into a leathern fang. 1818 SCOTT *Br. Lamm.* v, Shame be in my meal-poke, then. c1400 *Ywaine & Gaw.* 2032 That da he kest than in his sek, Als it was a *mele-sek. 1820 SCOTT *Monast.* xxxvii, It is always best to be sure, as I say when I chance to take multure twice from the same meal-sack. 1552 HULOET, Mealeman or *meale-seller, *suffarraneus*. 1565 COOPER *Thesaurus*, *Farinarium cribrum*, a *meale sieue. 1624 in *Archæologia* XLVIII. 148 A meale sive. 1552 HULOET, *Mealesifter, *pollintor*. 1623 MINSHEU, A *Meale trough, *harinal*. 1825 J. NICHOLSON *Operat. Mechanic* 100 The buckets, dipping into the meal-trough, convey the flour to the upper story. 1671 F. PHILLIPS *Reg. Necess* 363 Three *Meal-Weighers. 1812 *Examiner* 19 Oct. 662/2 The Lord Mayor, after inspecting the Meal Weighers Return,..ordered the price of Bread to fall 3*d.* in the peck-loaf. 1938 W. DE LA MARE *Memory* 95 This *meal-white snow.

b. Special Comb.: **meal-bark**, a name for certain species of *Cycas*, so called on account of the starchy matter in the trunk; **meal-beetle**, a coleopterous insect (*Tenebrio molitor*), which infests granaries, etc., and is injurious to flour; **meal-berry**, the Red Bearberry, *Arctostaphylos uva ursi* (Treas. Bot. 1866); †**meal-house**, a place where meal is stored; †**meal-malt**, malt ground to a powder (as for use in distilling); **meal-mite**, the *Acarus farinæ* (Syd. Soc Lex. 1890); **meal-Monday**, a Monday given as a holiday in Scottish universities, formerly for the purpose of allowing the students to go home to fetch enough meal to last till the end of the session; **meal-moth**, a book-name for two species of moth, *Asopia farinalis* and *Pyralis farinalis*, the larvæ of which feed on meal or flour; **meal-powder**, finely ground gunpowder; **meal-tree**, the wayfaring-tree, *Viburnum Lantana* (called also *mealy tree*); **meal-tub**, a tub for containing meal; also *attrib.* in *Meal-tub Plot*, the pretended conspiracy of the Duke of Monmouth in 1679, the evidence for which consisted of papers found in a meal-tub; **meal-worm**, the larva of the meal-beetle; **meal-worm beetle** = *meal-beetle*.
1822 GOOD *Study Med.* I. 4 The..*meal-bark (*cycas circinalis*). 1836–9 TODD *Cycl. Anat.* II. 863/2 The *meal-beetles, *Tenebrionidæ*. c1050 *Suppl. Ælfric's Gloss.* in Wr.-Wülcker 185/27 *Farinale*, *mealehus. c1330 *Durham Acc. Rolls* (Surtees) 518 In j sera emp. pro le Melhous iij*d.* 1582 BRETON *Fl. Fansie* (Grosart) 16/1 The Pastrie, Mealehouse, and the roome wheras the Coales do ly. 1702 O. HEYWOOD *Diaries*, etc. (1885) IV. 293 Mr. Oats man with *meal-malt. 1842 T. W. HARRIS *Insects injur. Veget.* (1862) 475 The *meal-moth (*Pyralis farinalis*). 1781 THOMPSON in *Phil. Trans.* LXXI. 260 *Meal-powder is more inflammable than that which is grained. 1796 CUTLER in Morse *Amer. Geog.* I. 338 *Mealtree (*Viburnum Lantana*). 1614 RALEIGH *Hist. World* III. viii. §11. 104 A lewd fellow was brought forth, who said, That he himselfe escaping in a *mealetubbe, had beene [etc.]. 1681 BAXTER *Answ. Dodwell* iv. 53 If this *Hypothesis*..come out of the Meal-Tub, or forge of Inventers, what shall such men be called? a1715 BURNET *Own Time* III. (1724) I. 476 They found a paper that contained the scheme of this whole fiction, which because it was found in a Meal tub came to be called the Meal-tub plot. 1658 SIR T. BROWNE *Pseud. Ep.* III. xxi. (ed. 4) 193 That Cameleon had been observed to drink water, and delight to feed on *Meal-worms. 1774 GOLDSM. *Nat. Hist.* V. 265 But meal-worm insects they..swallowed..most greedily. 1863 WOOD *Nat. Hist.* III. 474 The Meal-worm..is the larva of a beetle named *Tenebrio molitor*. 1860 J. CURTIS *Farm Insects* 334 The *Meal-worm Beetle.

meal (miːl), *sb.*[2] Forms: 1 mǽl, mél, 2–3 mel, 3 mæl, 3–6 mele, 4 male, 4–6 meel(e, 5 maile, *Sc.* maill, mell, 6–9 meale, 7 meall, 3– meal. [Com. Teut.: OE. *mǽl* neut., mark, sign, measure, fixed time, occasion, meal = OFris. *mêl, mâl* (in phr. *al to mâl* always, *etmâl* space of 12 or 24 hours), OS. *-mâl* sign, measure (MDu. *mael* masc., fem., neut., mark, sign, landmark, fixed time, meal-time, Du. *maal* neut., meal, masc., time), OHG. *mâl* neut., time (MHG. *mâl* neut., spot, point of time, meal, mod.G. *mal* time, *mahl* meal), ON. *mál* neut., mark, measure, point or portion of time, meal-time (Sw. *mål* mark, measure, meal, Da. *maal* mark, measure), Goth. *mēl* time (pl. *mēla* marks, writing):—OTeut. *mǣlo[m]*, f. Indogermanic root *mē-* (Skr. *mā-*) to measure.]

†**1.** A measure. *Obs.*
c1000 *Sax. Leechd.* II. 184 Diles þreo cucler mæl. c1382 WYCLIF *Ex.* xxv. 2 [A] coroun with foure fingur mele heiȝt [Vulg. *altam quatuor digitis*]. c1400 *Lanfranc's Cirurg.* 154 Al maner wounde þat is madd in þe extremitees of þe lacertis as .iij. fyngir mele brede vndir þe schuldris.

2. a. Any of the occasions of taking food which occur by custom or habit at more or less fixed times of the day, as a breakfast, dinner, supper, etc.
c897 K. ÆLFRED *Gregory's Past. C.* xliii. 316 þe ðæt nyle ðearfum sellan ðæt he ðonne on mæle læfð. c1175 *Lamb. Hom.* 31 He wule festen and eaten ȝif he mei et ane mele swa muchel swa et twam. c1205 LAY. 19690 Ælche dæie on a mæl ure mete truked. a1225 *Ancr. R.* 428 Bitweonen mele ne gruselie ȝe nouðer frut, ne oðerhwat. c1290 *S. Eng. Leg.* I. 469/232 þo it was time of mele huy wenden to heore mete. 1390 GOWER *Conf.* III. 25, I have at every meel Of plente more than ynowh. 14.. *Dietary* 67 in *Barbour's Bruce* (S.T.S.). Betuix malys drink nocht for na plesand delit. 1463 *Bury Wills* (Camden) 21 He to prey for my soule at euery meel, mete or sopeer. 1540–1 ELYOT *Image Gov.* 45 b, There shuld be at the leaste .vi. houres betwene euery meale. 1617 MORYSON *Itin.* I. 61 They give good fare for foure grosh a meale. 1778 MISS BURNEY *Evelina* xviii, Our breakfast was the most agreeable meal..that we have had since we came to town. 1842 A. COMBE *Physiol. Digestion* (ed. 4) 193 Meals, then, ought to be early or late in proportion to the habits of the individual. 1860 TYNDALL *Glac.* I. xi. 72 We set about preparing our evening meal. 1897 W. RYE *Norfolk Songs* 25 'He don't like working between meals' is a succinct description of a lazy man.

b. Without reference to time: An occasion of taking food, a repast. Also, the material of a repast; the food eaten at or provided for a repast. *meals-on-wheels*: a service, usually provided by a women's voluntary organization, whereby meals are taken by car to old people, invalids, etc. Also *attrib.*
c1200 ORMIN 4959 ȝiff itt iss in þin herrte, To shunenn.. derewurrþe mæless. c1250 *Gen. & Ex.* 1484 Ðe fader luuede esau wel, for firme birðe & swete mel. 1297 R. GLOUC. (Rolls) 4204 He wole þe limemele To drawe & uorsuolwe þar auenture at one mele. 1398 TREVISA *Barth. De P.R.* VI. xx. (1495) 207 Meete shall be lyke and of one manere whyche that men ete atte one meele. c1400 *Gamelyn* 636 He was sore alonged after a good meel. 1481 CAXTON *Reynard* (Arb.) 13, I shal do late you haue so moche that ten of yow shold not ete it at one mele. 1590 SHAKS. *Com. Err.* V. i. 74 Vnquiet meales make ill digestions. 1727–46 THOMSON *Summer* 1025 Their mangled limbs Crashing at once, he dyes the purple seas With gore, and riots in the vengeful meal. 1767 JAGO *Edge Hill* IV. 77 The lusty Steers ..leisurely concoct their grassy Meal. 1853 M. ARNOLD *Scholar-Gipsy* xii, The blackbird, picking food, Sees thee, nor stops his meal. 1857 *G. Bird's Urin. Deposits* (ed. 5) 274 The earthy phosphates are always abundant after a meal. 1902 T. M. LINDSAY *Ch. & Ministry in Early Cent.* ii. 51 They ate together a meal which they themselves provided. 1961 *Times* 17 Jan. 7/1 Of those who get meals-on-wheels, less than 10 per cent have adequate meals on week days when there is no delivery. 1961 *Guardian* 19 Apr. 2/5 The need for an extension of the meals-on-wheels schemes as a contribution to the care of the home-bound. 1966 'O. MILLS' *Enemies of Bride* xii. 106 Having just completed a tour with a Meals-on-Wheels van to less fortunate old ladies, she was dressed in a green, shirt-waister dress of the Women's Voluntary Services. 1966 'K. A. SADDLER' *Gilt Edge* i. 22 I'm on National Assistance. I get Meals-on-Wheels twice a week. 1970 J. FLEMING *Young Man, I think*

you're Dying ii. 25 On weekday mornings the meals-on-wheels service would bring hot food for the invalid.

transf. **1772** C. JENNER *Town Eclogues* ii. 8 When..cits take in their weekly meal of air.

c. † ***at meal*** (*obs.*), ***at meals***: at table; at dinner, breakfast, supper, etc. Similarly †(*to go*) ***to meal.***

1362 LANGL. *P. Pl.* A. I. 24 That on clothing is from chele ow to saue: And that othur mete at meel for meseise of thiseluen. **1533** ELYOT *Cast. Helthe* 42 b, For moche abundance of drinke at meale, drowneth the meate eaten. **1565** COOPER *Thesaurus, Accubare apud aliquem*, to be at the table in a mans house: to sitte at meale with him. **1620** VENNER *Via Recta* viii. 185 The wholesomnesse of wine.. moderately taken at meale..is..well knowne. **1635** PAGITT *Christianogr.* I. iii. (1636) 205 They which fast may goe to meale at ten, eleven, or twelve of the clocke. **1710** STEELE *Tatler* No. 235 ¶3 It was an unspeakable Pleasure to visit or sit at Meal in that Family. **1818** KEATS *Isabella* i, They could not sit at meals but feel how well It soothed each to be the other by.

d. ***to make a meal of***, † ***to make one's meal on***: to devour; also, to treat in an over-fussy or laborious manner.

1610 SHAKS. *Temp.* II. i. 113 O thou mine heire..what strange fish Hath made his meale on thee? **1827** POLLOK *Course T.* VIII, Slander early rose, And made most hellish meals of good men's names. *a* **1832** 'BARRY CORNWALL' *Eng. Songs* 143 Have I..Preyed on my brother's blood, and made His flesh my meal to-day? **1961** C. WILLOCK *Death in Covert* iv. 93 Dyson..was making a meal of everthing. He had carefully paced the distance... He had stuck sticks in the ground. **1968** *Guardian* 22 Aug. 7/2 When university people get on to fashion they make a meal of it. **1970** *Ibid.* 5 Dec. 8/5 He had as one of his guests Inia Te Wiata, whose name has been pretty familiar to radio listeners for some years now but Mr Murray still made a meal, if not a light snack, of promoting it. **1970** *N. Z. News* 21 Jan. 16/4 New Zealand scored 325 for six wickets declared—everyone except M. G. Burgess and G. E. Vivian making a meal of University bowlers. **1971** M. POLLAND *Package to Spain* vii. 95 His small sharp face was full of righteous outrage... Henry was making a meal of it. **1972** J. EASTWOOD *Henry in Silver Frame* xxiii. 191, I wouldn't want the gutter-press to make a meal of me.

e. meal's meat, later **meal of meat**: = sense 2 b. Now *dial.* (see E.D.D.).

13.. *Guy Warw.* (A.) 6845 A meles mete ȝif thou me. **1393** LANGL. *P. Pl.* C. XVI. 36 Crauede..A meles mete for a poure man. *c* **1410** *Sir Cleges* 347 For my labor schall I nott get But yt be a melys mete. *c* **1440** *Promp. Parv.* 321/2 Meel of mete.., *commestio.* **1511** *Plumpton Corr.* (Camden) p. cxviii, Sir Robert Plomton..paid for every maile of meate..iiij^d for himselfe, & ii^d for his servant. **1530** PALSGR. 454/2 In this sence I fynde also *je inuite* but properly to a meales meate, or to eate. **1613** FLETCHER, etc. *Honest Man's Fort.* II. iii, You never yet had a meales meat from my Table. **1693** J. DRYDEN in *Dryden's Juvenal* xiv. Notes (1697) 366 King Saturn..gave this Example by making a Meals-meat of his own Children. **1717** *Entertainer* No. 6. 36 The Parasite may smell a Feast at C—t, and go flatter Some-body there for a Meals-meat.

†**f.** The phrases ***a merry meal, a sorry meal***, were in ME. sometimes used *fig.* for: Something joyful or the contrary. *Obs.*

13.. *E.E. Allit. P.* A. 23 O moul þou marrez a myry mele. **14..** *King & Hermit* 425, I..haue hade many merry mele. *c* **1440** LOVELICH *Merlin* 2754 Also sone as the dragouns togyderes fele, be-twixen hem schal be-gynnen a sory mele.

3. a. The quantity of milk given by a cow at one milking; also, the time of milking.

1613 W. BROWNE *Brit. Past.* I. iv, Each shepheard's daughter with her cleanly peale Was come afield to milke the morning's meale. **1670** CAPT. J. SMITH *Eng. Improv. Reviv'd* 176 Northern Milch Cows, one of the least of which shall give 2 Gallons of Milk at one Meal. **1727** BRADLEY *Fam. Dict.* s.v. *Cheese*, To make a Cheese of two Meals, as of the Morning's new Milk, and the Evening's Cream-milk, you must do also the same. **1775** JOHNSON *Journ. Hebrides* 187 A single meal of a goat is a quart. **1805** R. W. DICKSON *Pract. Agric.* I. 58 It may be fitted up with such..coolers as are sufficient to contain a meal's milk. **1844** H. STEPHENS *Bk. Farm* II. 459 The milk drawn from the udder at one milking, or *meal*, as it is termed.

b. *dial.* (See quot.)

c **1830** *Glouc. Farm Rep.* 33 in *Libr. Usef. Knowl., Husb.* III, The cheeses pass through the three presses in this order, advancing a step in their progress at each 'meal' or making.

4. *attrib.* and *Comb.*: **meal-break**; **meal-going**, used *attrib.* (after *church-going*); **meal-hour, -tray**; **meal-pendant, -pennant**, *U.S. Navy*, a red pennant displayed during meal-times (*Cent. Dict.* 1890); **meal-settle**, a seat at meals (? *Obs.*); **meal ticket** *orig. U.S.*, (*a*) a ticket entitling a person to a meal; (*b*) *fig. slang*, a source of income or livelihood (esp. a husband or wife regarded as such).

1958 *Guardian* 20 Aug. 1/1 The central committee's advice to busmen..was to insist on full *meal breaks. **1971** 'H. CALVIN' *Poison Chasers* ix. 112 Ronnie Samson had to stop me to let the boys off for a meal break. **1858** HOGG *Life Shelley* II. 295 Startled at his books by the sound of the *meal-going bell. **1802** MRS. E. PARSONS *Myst. Visit.* IV. 92 He seldom saw her but at *meal hours. **1899** *Scribner's Mag.* XXV. 89/2 The quartermaster..hauled down the *meal pennant. *a* **1225** *St. Marher.* 11 *Mel seotel softest ant guldene ȝerde alre gold smeatest. **1870** O. LOGAN *Before Footlights* 248 The rather scrubby party who occasionally purchases..a '*Meal Ticket', and thus gets entrance to the festive dining hall. **1899** 'J. FLYNT' *Tramping with Tramps* 395 *Meal-ticket*, a person 'good' for a meal. **1912** *Collier's* 23 Nov. 38/2 I've been doin' a lot for her—a regular meal ticket an' ticket agency for her. **1926** [see GOOD A. *adj.* I f.]. **1929** T. WOLFE *Look Homeward, Angel* (1930) xxvii. 377 She can't bear to give him up... He's her meal-ticket. **1939** ADE *Let.* 7 July (1973) 214 The play remained at the Garden until the following summer and next year it was being played by three companies. It turned out to be my meal ticket. **1972** 'H. HOWARD' *Nice Day for Funeral* iii. 40 He was her meal-ticket. Why should she want him sent to the pen? **1972** *Lebende Sprachen* XVII. 34/1 US meal ticket—BE [*sc.* British English] luncheon voucher. **1973** *Jewish Chron.* 2 Feb. 23/5 Our young women do not look for 'meal-ticket' marriages. **1905** *19th Cent.* Jan. 92 She gets ready the patients' *meal-trays in a tasteful manner.

†**meal**, *sb.*^{3} *Obs.* Forms: 1 méli, meeli, méle, -mæle, 3–6 mele, 4 miele, 4–5 meel, 5–6 meyle, 6 meale, meele. [OE. *méle*, (*wæter*)-*mæle* str. masc., prob. repr. OTeut. type **mêljo-z*, and so corresponding to ON. *mæli-r* measure; see MEAL *sb.*^{4}] A tub, bucket. Also used as a measure.

In OE. sometimes used to gloss L. *patera, carchesium, cyathus*, which mean bowl, dish, or cup.

a **700** *Epinal Gloss.* 56 *Alvium*, meeli. *c* **1000** *Sax. Leechd.* II. 86 Do þonne mele fulne buteran on. *c* **1290** *S. Eng. Leg.* I. 240/6 þat child..Ase it was in ane mele i-baþed al one upriȝt it stod. *a* **1300** *Cursor M.* 3306 Wantes ves here na uessell, ne mele, ne bucket, ne funell. **1357–8** *Durham Acc. Rolls* (Surtees) 124 In j Mele empt. pro carbonibus portandis. **1370–71** *Ibid.* 263 In una mele lingnea pro pedibus lavandis. **1390** GOWER *Conf.* III. 21 Thei in hope to assuage The peine of deth..Of wyn let fille full a Miele, And dronken til [etc.]. **1408** tr. *Vegetius* (MS. Douce 291, lf. 47 b), Bokettis, meles, and payles. **1440** *Durham Acc. Rolls* (Surtees) 410, viij meel calcis extinctæ empt...ad xijd. **1459–60** *Ibid.* 89, j kyrn, j meyle, ij Chesfattez. **1565** COOPER *Thesaurus, Alueus*..a meele or vessell to washe in. **1567** *Wills & Inv. N.C.* (Surtees) I. 278, iij milk meales.

meal (miːl), *sb.*^{4} *Sc.* Forms: 5, 8 meel, 6 meale, 7 maile, meill, mell, 8 mail, miel, 9 meil. [a. ON. *mæli-r* measure (Norw. *mæle* a measure of capacity varying in different localities):—OTeut. type **mæljo-z*, f. **mælo*^{m} measure: see MEAL *sb.*^{1}] 'A relative weight used in Orkney' (Jam.).

1597 SKENE *De Verb. Sign.* s.v. *Serplaith*, Item [in Orknay], 6 settings maks ane mail. Item 24 meales makis ane Last. **1624** *Witch Trial* in *Abbotsford Club Misc.* I. 148–9 His brother haid twa mells [of corn]. **1629** *Witch Trial* in *County Folklore* (1903) III. 78 She wantit the proffeitt of ane meill of malt that she was brewing. **1698** M. MARTIN *Voy. St. Kilda* (1749) 48 Ancient Measures, as the Maile..: this Maile contains ten Pecks. **1793** *Statist. Acc. Scotl.* V. 412 The stipend consists of 86 mails malt (each mail weighing about 12 stones Amsterdam weight). *Ibid.* VII. 477, 6 settings make 1 meel. *Ibid.* 563 On the first is weighed settings and miels. **1805** FORSYTH *Beauties Scotl.* V. 52 Six setteens or lispunds make a meil.

meal (miːl), *sb.*^{5} *dial.* Also 8 male, 8–9 meale, 9 miol, miel. [a. ON. *mel-r* sandbank, also bentgrass (the latter is prob. the original sense; for the development cf. MARRAM).] A sand-dune.

1706 PHILLIPS, *Meals* or *Males*, the Shelves or Banks of Sand on the Sea-coasts of Norfolk: Whence *Ingom-meals*, the Name of a Sandy Shore in Lincoln-shire. **1778** *Eng. Gazetteer* (ed. 2) s.v. *Edmond's-Chapel*, The coast here is secured against the incursions of the sea, by sand heaps, commonly called Meales. **1839** *Penny Cycl.* XVI. 258 Sand-hills..locally termed 'meals', or 'marum hills'. **1867** SMYTH *Sailor's Word-bk.*, *Meales*, or *Miols*, immense sandbanks thrown up by the sea on the coasts of Norfolk, Lancashire, etc. **1897** *Spectator* 209 At present only the highest tides ever cover the surface of the 'meals'.

Comb. a **1893** in Cozens-Hardy *Broad Norf.* 77 Mielbanks, banks of sand blown up by the wind and consolidated by the marum grass—also called 'meal-banks'. **1899** CORNISH in *Cornhill Mag.* Mar. 313 The fascinating but little known region of the 'meal marshes' which fringe the North Norfolk coast.

meal (miːl), *v.*^{1} Somewhat *rare.* [f. MEAL *sb.*^{1}]

1. *trans.* To cover with meal; to powder with meal.

1611 BEAUM. & FL. *Knt. Burning Pest.* v. i, Enter Jasper with his Face mealed. **1882** *Garden* 21 Jan. 33/3 All their flowers will be more or less mealed on the surface.

b. *fig.* ***to meal one's mouth***: to become 'mealy-mouthed'; to speak in gentle terms. ? *nonce-use.*

1826 SOUTHEY in *Corr. w. C. Bowles* (1881) 96 Though there is as much civility as can be desired..yet I have neither mealed my mouth nor minced my words.

2. a. *trans.* To grind into meal; to reduce to a fine powder. **b.** *intr.* To become reduced to meal or powder.

1669 STURMY *Mariner's Mag.* v. xiii. 89 Meal all these very fine, and mix them together. *Ibid.*, It will Meal presently.

3. *intr.* To yield or be plentiful in meal.

1799 J. ROBERTSON *Agric. Perth* 155 It is a little earlier than the old Polish oat, and meals equally well.

meal (miːl), *v.*^{2} [f. MEAL *sb.*^{2}]

1. *intr.* To make a meal; to eat meals; to feed.

1628 O. FELLTHAM *Resolves* (ed. 3) lxxvi. 236 With Earthen Plate, *Agathocles* (they say) Did vse to meale. **1827** HONE *Every-day Bk.* II. 218 There were..worms there.., which would have mealed handsomely upon him. **1840** R. H. DANA *Bef. Mast* xxx. 109 *Mess*, any number of men who meal together. **1886** M. K. MACMILLAN *Dagonet the Jester* 5, I will not meal with a churl, nor moil with a churl. **1891** H. C. BUNNER *Zadoc Pine* 201 A lodging-house for those who 'mealed' at the hotel. **1918** *Jrnl. Friends' Hist. Soc.* 7 John Lecky..generally arranged to meal at Friends' houses. **1960** A. POWELL *Casanova's Chinese Restaurant* 113 'Doesn't Carolo ever eat himself?'..'He often meals with us as a matter of fact.'

2. *trans.* To feed, give fodder to (cattle). ? *Obs.*

1630 WINTHROP *Let.* in *New Eng.* (1825) I. 378 Some more cows would be brought, especially two new milch, which must be well mealed and milked by the way.

†**meal**, *v.*^{3} *Obs. rare*$^{-1}$. [Identical with OE. *mǽlan*, f. *mál* spot, stain, MOLE *sb.*^{1}

(Northern dialects have *mail* vb., to spot, stain, f. *mail*, northern form of *mole*: see E.D.D.)]

trans. To spot, stain; by Shaks. used *fig.*

1603 SHAKS. *Meas. for M.* IV. ii. 86 Were he meal'd with that Which he corrects, then were he tirrannous.

meal, obs. form of MAIL *sb.*^{2}

-meal, *suffix*, forming advs. (all obs. exc. *piecemeal*), repr. ME. *-mele* (down to the 14th c. sometimes *-melum*), OE. *-mǽlum*. The OE. advs. in *-mǽlum* are in form the instrumental case plural of compounds of *mǽl* MEAL *sb.*^{2}, in the sense of 'measure', 'quantity taken at one time', as in *cuclérmǽl* spoonful (as a measure), the instr. pl. of which would be **cuclérmǽlum* by spoonfuls. The particular compounds of this formation actually recorded in the instr. pl., however, do not occur in the other cases, and already in OE. *-mǽlum* had come to be a mere suffix with the sense expressed in Latin by *-ātim, -tim*, and in mod.Eng. by the repetition of the sb. preceded by *by*. Examples which existed in OE. are *dropmǽlum* DROPMEAL, *floccmǽlum* FLOCKMEAL, *fótmǽlum* FOOTMEAL, *héapmǽlum* HEAPMEAL, *limmǽlum* LIMBMEAL, *scéafmǽlum* sheaf by sheaf, *stemmǽlum* turn by turn, alternately, *stundmǽlum* STOUNDMEAL, *styccemǽlum* bit by bit, *ȝéarmǽlum* year by year. The suffix continued to be productive in ME., among the formations dating from that period being *cantlemeal, cupmeal, gobbetmeal, littlemeal, parcelmeal, pennymeal, piecemeal, poundmeal*, and the Latinisms *ravishmeal* (Wyclif) 'raptim', *table-meal* 'tabulatim'. A remarkable survival of the OE. inflexion appears in Wyclif's *hipyllmelum* (see HIPPLE). To the 16th c. belong *fitmeal, inchmeal, jointmeal, lumpmeal*; in later Eng. the suffix has not been productive, though nonce-words such as *pagemeal* have occasionally been formed, more or less playfully. A trace of the originally substantival character of the suffix remains in the use of *by piecemeal* as a synonym of the simple adv. (cf. the obs. *by flockmeal, by pennymeal*, etc.).

1493 *Festivall* (W. de W. 1515) 8 b, Hymselfe with his owone handes kest away the fleshe lompe mele. **1827** *Blackw. Mag.* XXI. 884 How pleasant it would be to tear it pagemeal, and fling it in the author's face.

mealable ('miːləb(ə)l), *a.* [f. MEAL *v.*^{1} + -ABLE.] Capable of being mealed.

1823 *Mech. Mag.* No. 9. 138 Satisfied with having their corn reduced to a mealable form. **1885** A. STEWART *'Twixt Ben Nevis & Glencoe* xxv. 181 So much mealable grist.

meale, variant of MELE *v. Obs.*, to speak.

mealed (miːld), *ppl. a.* [f. MEAL *v.*^{1} + -ED^1.] Finely pulverized; *spec.* of gunpowder.

1692 *Capt. Smith's Seaman's Gram.* II. xxxi. 150 Fine Mealed Powder. **1859** F. A. GRIFFITHS *Artil. Man.* (1862) 89 A hole is bored through the mealed powder at the top.

mealer^1 ('miːlə(r)). [f. MEAL *sb.*^{2} and *v.*^{2} + -ER^1.]

1. In parasynthetic derivatives (*nonce-wds.*): One who eats (one, half a) meal in the day.

1849 D. J. BROWNE *Amer. Poultry Yd.* (1855) 48 Certain hens..are called Monositæ (that is, one-mealers, or such as eat only once a day). **1899** R. WHITEING *5 John St.* 111 The half-mealers, who always leave off with a hungry belly.

2. *U.S. colloq.* One who takes his meals at one place and lodges at another; a 'table-boarder'.

1883 M. F. SWEETSER *Summer Days* 126 That class of the community known as 'hauled mealers'. **1887** A. A. HAYES *Jesuit's Ring* 52 You are a 'mealer' here.

3. *slang.* One pledged to take alcoholic drink only at meals.

1890 in BARRÈRE & LELAND *Dict. Slang.*

mealer^2 ('miːlə(r)). [f. MEAL *v.*^{1} + -ER^1.] A wooden rubber for mealing powder.

1875 in KNIGHT *Dict. Mech.*

mealer, variant of MAILER^1.

mealie ('miːlɪ). Also 9 (from *pl.*) milice. [a. Cape Du. *milje* (pronounced 'mili), a. Pg. *milho* MILLET^1, used also (with defining words *milho grande, m. da India*) for maize.] **1.** A South African name for maize; chiefly used in the *pl.* Freq. *attrib.* Cf. MIELIE.

1853 GALTON *Tropical S. Afr.* vi. 182 The Ovampo had little pipkins to cook in, and eat corn (milice) steeped in hot water. **1855** J. W. COLENSO *Ten Weeks in Natal, Hist. Sk.* p. vi, The second range of land..furnishing abundant crops of hay, oats, mealies, or Indian corn, and barley. **1855** W. C. HOLDEN *Hist. Natal* x. 282 The consumption of mealie (maize) meal in D'Urban has increased. **1879** *Cape Argus* 5 June (Cent.), A bivouac was made near a deserted kraal, there being..a mealie-field hard by... A volley was fired

from the adjacent mealie-garden. **1884** E. P. MATHERS *Glimpse of Gold Fields* 29 At one of our camps I tried to get some mealie porridge made. **1893** *Westm. Gaz.* 10 Oct. 2/1 Their staple diet then being 'mealie' meal porridge made with water. **1901** *Scotsman* 11 Mar 8/1 For eight days they had to live on half a pound of mealie a day, with very little meat. **1925** P. SMITH *Little Karoo* 18 Just outside the door was the worn mealie-stamper, cut out of a tree-trunk and shaped like an hour-glass, in which the mealies were pounded into meal. **1928** R. CAMPBELL *Wayzgoose* i. 27 Your notice boards like mealie-stems are stripped. **1929** D. REITZ *Commando* xiv. 129 Rations were chiefly game and mealie-meal. **1944** M. DE B. NESBITT *Road to Avalon* (1949) xiv. 113, I sit on the mealie planter, control the levers and see that the hoppers are well filled as they drop mealies in the furrows. **1956** N. GORDIMER *Six Feet of Country* 9 The girl catching her stockings on the mealie-stooks. **1962** *Cape Times* 13 June 1/4 A Harvard aircraft.. crashed in a mealie land near Dunnottar. **1971** *Sunday Times* (Johannesburg) 28 Mar. 12/5, I made all sorts of things like mealie bread to make a bit of money for my poor old husband to buy a piece of industrial ground. **1973** *Times* 28 Nov. 8/7 Mealie-meal, the staple food, was.. in short supply. **1974** G. JENKINS *Bridge of Magpies* iii. 51 A slovenly breakfast of half-burnt mealie-meal porridge and boiled penguin eggs.

2. mealie-cob, a corn cob; **mealie-cob worm**, the caterpillar of *Heliothis armigera*, a noctuid moth; **mealie-pap** = *mieliepap* (MIELIE).

1859 R. J. MANN *Natal* 137 (Pettman), The young *mealy-cob is generally preferred to bread. **1932** S. ZUCKERMAN *Social Life Monkeys* xii. 195 The meally cobs and fruit it [*sc.* chacma] plunders from cultivated lands. **1911** J. D. F. GILCHRIST *S. Afr. Zool.* 150 (Pettman), The *Mealie-cob worm.. does extensive damage to mealies, peas, tomatoes, and lucerne. **1880** E. F. SANDEMAN *Eight Months in Ox Waggon* xxvii. 273 Guinea fowls.. form a very relishing change from the never-varying *menu* of bôk or *mealie pap. **1902** J. H. M. ABBOTT *Tommy Cornstalk* 28 A few Kaffir transport drivers.. are boiling their 'mealie-pap' in three-legged pots. **1903** J. Y. F. BLAKE *West Pointer with Boers* iii. 49 We had to come down to straight mealie pap (corn meal mush), and fresh beef. **1922** J. BUCHAN *Bk. Escapes* vi. 120 For food he had to trust to mealie-pap at Kafir kraals. **1966** D. VARADAY *Gara-Yaka's Domain* xii. 135 Mealie-pap—maize-porridge—the bush substitute for bread was cooking.

mealiness (ˈmiːlɪnɪs). [f. MEALY *a.* + -NESS.] The quality or condition of being mealy.

1609 C. BUTLER *Fem. Mon.* (1634) 127 They [teredines] offend the Bees also with their mealiness, as the Snails do with their sliminess. **1776** WITHERING *Brit. Plants* (1796) IV. 69 Leaves covered with a kind of ash-coloured mealiness. **1820** L. HUNT *Indicator* No. 37 (1822) I. 294 There was a sort of exquisite silver clearness and soft mealiness in her utterance of these verses. **1844** STEPHENS *Bk. Farm* II. 666 The mealiness consists of a layer of mucilage immediately under the skin, covering the starch or farina. **1876** ABNEY *Instr. Photogr.* (ed. 3) 125 The cause of mealiness or 'measles' in the print. **1886** BESANT *Childr. Gibeon* II. ii, To bring out the full mealiness of a potatoe.

mealing (ˈmiːlɪŋ), *vbl. sb.*¹ Also 5 **melwynge**. [f. MEAL *v.*¹ + -ING¹.]

1. The action of grinding meal; also, the action of finely pulverizing gunpowder. Chiefly *attrib.*, as in ***mealing trade***; **mealing stone**, a stone used for grinding meal; **mealing table**, a slab for mealing gunpowder upon.

14.. *Voc.* in Wr.-Wülcker 582/19 *Farracio*, Melwynge. **1805** A. EDLIN (*title*) On the Art of Bread-making, wherein the Mealing Trade.. is Examined. **1828** J. M. SPEARMAN *Brit. Gunner* (ed. 2) 78 Mealing Tables. **1866** *Reader* 22 Sept. 307 A mealing stone with a hollow in which the corn was bruised. **1880** DAWKINS *Early Man* 268 Two concave stone grain-rubbers or 'mealing-stones'.

2. The action of covering with meal.

a **1810** *Robin Hood & Beggar* lxxix. in Child *Ballads* (1888) III. 163/2 He thought, if he had done them wrong In mealing of their cloaths [etc.].

mealing (ˈmiːlɪŋ), *vbl. sb.*² [f. MEAL *v.*² + -ING¹.] The action of taking meals; *U.S.* the action of taking meals at a boarding-house.

1659 H. L'ESTRANGE *Alliance Div. Off.* 188 The junketings, comessations, and mealing together were soon laid aside. **1887** A. A. HAYES *Jesuit's Ring* 55 She must draw the line.. when the hauling cost more than the mealing.

mealing, obs. form of MAILING.

meall(e, obs. ff. MAUL *sb.*¹, MEAL *sb.*²

mealless (ˈmiːllɪs), *a.* [f. MEAL *sb.*² + -LESS.] Without a meal.

1894 *Season* X. 57/2 Many men unnecessarily exhaust themselves by going a whole day mealless.

meally, obs. form of MEALY.

mealman (ˈmiːlmən). [f. MEAL *sb.*¹ + MAN.] One who deals in meal.

1552 HULOET, Mealeman or meale seller, *suffarraneus*. **1556** *Chron. Gr. Friars* (Camden) 77 Alle save only the melemen. **1679** *Lond. Gaz.* No. 1407/4 Mr. Acres Meal-man. **1778** *Eng. Gazetteer* (ed. 2) s.v. *Henley*, The inhabitants are generally maltsters, mealmen and bargemen. **1802** in *Spirit Publ. Jrnls.* (1803) VI. 89 All our meal-men and millers are Esquires.

†**ˈmealmouth**, *sb.* and *a.* *Obs.* [f. MEAL *sb.*¹ + MOUTH.] **a.** *sb.* A mealy-mouthed person. **b.** *adj.* Mealy-mouthed.

1546 J. HEYWOOD *Prov.* (1867) 19 When the meale mouth hath woon the bottome Of your stomake, than will the pickthanke it tell. **1575** G. HARVEY *Letter-bk.* (Camden) 92 [Written to a miller] Those same fine.. milltermes wherewith your mealemowthe the letter and whitebred sonett ar.. illuminate. *a* **1700** B. E. *Dict. Cant. Crew*, *Meal-mouth*, a sly, sleepish Dun, or Sollicitor for Money.

†**ˈmeal-mouthed**, *ppl. a.* *Obs.* [Formed as prec. + -ED².] = MEALY-MOUTHED.

1576 FLEMING *Panopl. Epist.* 155 Saying, that you had flatterers & meal-mouthed merchants in high estimation. **1686** WOOD *Life* 5 Nov. (O.H.S.) III. 199 Dr. Reynell.. in his sermon was meale-mouthed and timorous.

mealt(e, obs. forms of MELT *v.*

†**ˈmealtide.** *Obs.* exc. *Sc.* *Sc.* meltith (ˈmɛltɪθ). Forms: α. 3 **mel tid**, 4 **meel-tyd**, 5 **melltyde**, 6 **meale tyde**, **meltyd**, 7 **mealtide**. β. 6 **mailteth**, **melteithe**, 6–9 **melteth**, 7 **mealtite**, 8 **mealtith**, **meltet**, 8–9 **meltit**, **meltith**, 9 **mealtaith**. [f. MEAL *sb.*² + TIDE *sb.*: cf. G. *mahlzeit*, Du. *maaltijd*, late ON. *máltíð* (Da. *maaltid*).]

1. = MEAL-TIME. Also, a meal, food.

c **1200** *Trin. Coll. Hom.* 13 þe man þe suneð aleð gestninge .. and haueð riht mel tid and nutteð timeliche metes. *c* **1374** CHAUCER *Troylus* II. 1556 The morwen com and neyhen gan þe tyme Of meltid. **1485** *Cely Papers* (Camden) 177 Item I pᵈ to my noste Gyllam de la Towr for howr melltydes from Sonday tyll Fryday viˢ viiiᵈ. **1534** MORE *Comf. agst. Trib.* II. Wks. 1185/1 He wold not for breaking of his penance, take anye praye for hys meale tyde, that shuld passe the prise of syxe pence. **1563–7** BUCHANAN *Reform. St. Andros* Wks. (1892) 7 Every man ane eg at the mailteth. **1588** A. KING tr. *Canisius' Catech.* 162 b, We.. ar content onelie with ane melltyd on the day. **1614** B. JONSON *Barth. Fair* I. ii, A Suitor that puts in here at Meal-tide. **1655** CULPEPPER, etc. *Riverius* XV. v. 419 A Bath, into which Blood-warm let the Patient enter.. far from meal-tide. **1728** RAMSAY *Daft Bargain* 12 [He] seem'd right yap His mealtith quickly up to gawp. *c* **1826** HOGG in J. Wilson *Noct. Ambr.* Wks. 1855 I. 212 Tam lo'ed his meltith and his clink.

2. The quantity of milk given by a cow at one milking. = MEAL *sb.*²

1633 *Orkney Witch Trial* in *Abbotsford Club Misc.* 153 Alse mony mealtitis off milk. **1839** J. M. WILSON *Tales Borders* V. 96/1 She, accordingly brought her evening's meltith, and skimmed it into his dish.

ˈmeal-time. [f. MEAL *sb.*² + TIME.] The usual time for eating a meal.

c **1175** *Lamb. Hom.* 115 He scal hine ibidan on a-sette tidan and her meltiman metes ne arinan. **13..** *Minor Poems fr. Vernon MS.* xxxvii. 937 Whon mon haþ at meeltyme such as he wile, Tak þat he haþ neode of. **1377** LANGL. *P. Pl.* B. v. 500 Aboute mydday whan most liȝte is and mele tyme of seintes. **1611** BIBLE *Ruth* ii. 14 And Boaz sayde vnto her, At meale time come thou hither. **1704** M. HENRY *Commun. Comp.* iii. Wks. 1853 I. 306/1 The great Master of the family would have none of his children missing at meal-time. **1860** S. WILBERFORCE *Addr. Ordination* 134 We must not break in on the meal-time of the poor.

mealy (ˈmiːlɪ), *a.* Also 6–7 **mealie**, 7–9 **meally**. [f. MEAL *sb.*¹ + -Y.]

1. Resembling meal, having the qualities of meal, powdery. Of fruits: (see quot. 1725). Of potatoes when boiled: Forming a somewhat dry and powdery mass, resembling flour (considered to be a good quality: opposed to *waxy*).

1533 ELYOT *Cast. Helthe* (1541) 88 b, Some groundes or residence [in urine] is like to meale, wheate, or barley, and may be named mealy residence. **1658** SIR T. BROWNE *Gard. Cyrus* iii. *Hydriot.* etc. 58 Though the regular spots in their [*sc.* butterflies] wings seem but a mealie adhesion.. yet [etc.]. **1672–3** GREW *Anat. Roots* II. §30 Many Apples, after Frosts, eat mealy. **1725** BRADLEY *Fam. Dict.*, *Mealy*; a Term used concerning certain Pears, which having generally surpassed their Ripeness, or growing in an ill Soil, have not that Quantity of Juice and fine Pulp, which they should have: Thus they say of the Lansac, Dean, &c. this Pear is mealy, this Pear has a mealy Taste. **1758** REID tr. *Macquer's Chem.* I. 35 By which means its crystals lose their transparency, become, as it were, mealy, and fall into a fine flour. **1795** *Hull Advertiser* 5 Dec. 4/3 Mealy potatoe. **1818–20** E. THOMPSON tr. *Cullen's Nosol. Method.* (ed. 3) 203 Small clustering pimples.. after three days go away in a small mealy desquamation. **1840** PEREIRA *Elem. Mat. Med.* II. 661 Many druggists prefer mealy sarsaparilla, that is, sarsaparilla whose cortex is brittle and powdery, and which, on being fractured transversely, throws out a white dust.

2. Containing meal or farina; farinaceous. ***mealy pudding*** = ***white pudding*** (WHITE *a.* 11 e).

1591 SYLVESTER *Du Bartas* I. iii. 832 Our mealy grain Our skillfull Seedman scatters not in vain. **1667** *Phil. Trans.* II. 485 A Farinaceous or Mealy Tree, serving to make bread of it. **1694** SALMON *Bate's Dispens.* (1713) 591/1 The meally Julep. **1732** ARBUTHNOT *Rules of Diet* 267 Decoctions of mealy Vegetables lubricate the Intestines. **1890** *Syd. Soc. Lex.*, *Mealy albumen*, the albumen of seeds which contains many starch granules, as in wheat. **1914** F. B. JACK *Cookery for every Household* 517/1 *Mealy Puddings.* 1 lb. oatmeal. ½ lb beef suet... When the puddings are required, toast them a few minutes in front of the fire. **1946** F. M. MCNEILL *Recipes from Scotland* 65 *White or Mealie Puddings*... The puddings will keep for months if hung up. **1951** *Good Housek. Home Encycl.* 550/1 *Mealy Pudding*, an oatmeal pudding which is served with grilled sausages, bacon, herrings, etc.

3. Covered with flour.

1704 N. N. tr. *Boccalini's Advts. fr. Parnass.* I. 233 That some sort of People should be so foolish, to expect to come, as meally out of the Mill, when they had staid there but a quarter of an Hour, as the Miller himself. **1773** FERGUSSON *Poems* (1789) II. 68 Mealy bakers, Hair-kaimers [etc.]. **1832** TENNYSON *Miller's Dau.* i, The wealthy miller's mealy face. **1883** H. W. V. STUART *Egypt* 113 He emerged from the mills as white as the clown in a pantomime, nor were we less mealy.

transf. **1591** SYLVESTER *Du Bartas* I. iv. 672 The mealie Mountains (late unseen) Change their white garments into lustly green. **1839** LONGF. *Hyperion* I. vi, Winter.. will come down at last in his old-fashioned mealy coat.

4. **a.** Covered with or as if with a fine dust or powder. Chiefly in *Bot.* and *Ent.*

1567 MAPLET *Gr. Forest* 34 b, Britannick or English Herb, hath the very looke of the greatest Sorrell, but in Colour a little more black, somewhat Mossie or Mealie. **1606** SHAKS. *Tr. & Cr.* III. iii. 79 Men like butter-flies, Shew not their mealie wings, but to the Summer. **1870** HOOKER *Stud. Flora* 316 Chenopodium album.. more or less mealy. **1890** *Syd. Soc. Lex.*, *Mealy hairs*, term applied by De Bary to the capitate hairs, presenting a powdery aspect, found on the under surface of various ferns belonging to the species *Gymnogramma Pteris* and *Nothochlæna* [etc.].

Comb. **1646** SIR T. BROWNE *Pseud. Ep.* III. xv. 141 Some flye with two wings,.. some with foure, as all farinaceous or mealy winged animals, as Butter-flies and Moths.

b. In various specific designations of animals, plants, and minerals: **mealy-bug**, a scale insect of the family Pseudococcidæ, esp. one of the genus *Pseudococcus*; **mealy centaury**, *Centaurea dealbata* (Sanders *Encycl. Gard.*, ed. 2, 1896); **mealy duck** (see quot.); **mealy insect** = *mealy bug*; **mealy parasol**, an esculent fungus, *Agaricus granulosus*; **mealy redpoll, -pole**, see REDPOLL¹; **mealy starwort**, *Aletris farinosa* (*Syd. Soc. Lex.* 1890); **mealy tree**, the wayfaring tree, *Viburnum Lantana*; **mealy zeolite**, an obs. synonym of both natrolite and mesolite (A. H. Chester).

1824 LOUDON *Encycl. Gard.* §3059 M'Phail [*c.* 1800] observes, that the red spider, the *mealy white bug, and the brown turtle insect are the most injurious to the vine. **1840** *Cuvier's Anim. Kingd.* 573 The Mealy-bug, *C. adonidum*, is somewhat of a rosy hue, with the body covered with a white mealy powder. **1927** *Chambers's Jrnl.* Aug. 502/1 The mealybug, so called from its white waxy or mealy coating, belongs to the big family of scale insects known as the Coccidae. **1953** S. H. SKAIFE *Afr. Insect Life* xi. 122 Mealy bugs are small insects, the largest being only about one-eighth of an inch long, pink or purplish in colour but appearing to be white because their bodies are covered with a waxy powder. **1971** *Daily Colonist* (Victoria, B.C.) 5 May 27/5 The Comstock Mealybug, also known as the Pseudococcus Comstocki, is a serious threat to citrus, sugar beets, grapes, apples and other crops. **1885** SWAINSON *Prov. Names Birds* Index, *Mealy bird or -duck. **1890** *H. Stevenson's Birds Norfolk* III. 219 The immature long-tailed duck is known to the Blakeney gunners as the 'little mealy duck'. **1815** *Trans. Horticult. Soc.* I. 297 *Coccus Adonidum*, the *Mealy Insect. **1887** HAY *Brit. Fungi* 73 *Agaricus granulosus*... The *Mealy Parasol. **1706** PHILLIPS (ed. Kersey), *Mealy Tree or Wild Vine. **1760** J. LEE *Introd. Bot.* App. 319 Mealy-tree, Pliant, *Viburnum*.

5. **a.** Of colour: Spotty, uneven. In *Photography* = MEASLY *a.* 3.

1784 J. BARRY in *Lect. Paint.* vi. (1848) 216 To give a richness and depth to the dark colours, by preventing that mealy appearance which results from the light resting and glittering on their surfaces. **1804** TINGRY *Varnsher's Guide* (1816) 3 The use of camphor for varnish is limited; too great a quantity would render it mealy. **1876** [see MEASLY *a.* 3]. **1890** *Anthony's Photogr. Bull.* III. 86 My greatest trouble has been mealy prints.

b. Of colours of horses: Spotty, interspersed with whitish specks. Also *Comb.*, as ***mealy-buttocked***, ***-flanked***, ***-mouthed***, ***-nosed*** adjs. (Cf. MAILY *a.*)

1675 *Lond. Gaz.* No. 980/4 Stolen.., a black brown Nag, .. with a star in the Forehead, a light brown mealy mouth. **1677** *Ibid.* No. 1198/4 A brown bay Gelding, with a shorn Mane, mealy mouth'd,.. 'twixt 14 and 15 hands. **1691** *Ibid.* No. 2692/4 Stolen.., a black brown Nag,.. mealy Buttock'd, and mealy Nosed with a Star on his Snip. **1703** *Ibid.* No. 3978/4 A brown Nag.. mealy Flank't. **1708** *Ibid.* No. 4438/4 A Black Mare of about five years old,.. a small meally Slip under her Right Nostril. **1861** WHYTE MELVILLE *Mkt. Harb.* 19 A mealy bay cob.

6. Of complexion: Floury, pale. Also *Comb.*, as ***mealy-complexioned***, ***-faced*** adjs.

1838 DICKENS *O. Twist* xiv, I only know two sorts of boys. Mealy boys, and beef-faced boys. **1840** BARHAM *Ingol. Leg.* Ser. I. *Hamilton Tighe*, They bring her a little, pale, mealy-faced boy. **1860** *All Year Round* No. 66. 367 The boys of these London schools are thin and long: white, mealy, and flaccid. **1876** GEO. ELIOT *Dan. Der.* xxxvi, A mealy-complexioned male. **1883** F. M. CRAWFORD *Dr. Claudius* viii, A mealy-faced, over-cerebrated people are springing up.

7. Of the flavour of tea: Soft, not harsh.

1892 WALSH *Tea* (Philad.) 98 Clear and bright in liquor, and mellow or 'mealy' in flavor.

8. Soft-spoken, given to mince matters; mealy-mouthed.

1600 [see MEALY-MOUTH]. **1697** C. LESLIE *Snake in Grass* (ed. 2) 173 Therefore, George, notwithstanding all thy meally modesty, it is [etc.]. **1720** AMHERST *Ep. Sir J. Blount* 12 If you don't straitway find out what The meally Rascals would be at. **1824** MISS FERRIER *Inherit.* xxvii. (1882) I. 241 A little squeaking mealy voice. **1854** DICKENS *Hard T.* II. viii, I didn't mince the matter with him. I am never mealy with 'em.

mealy (ˈmiːlɪ), *v.* *Bleaching.* [f. MEALY *a.*] *trans.* = BRAN *v.*; to 'clear' maddered goods by boiling in bran-water.

1811 *Self Instructor* 537 Bran liquors are used to meally dying-stuffs.

mealy-dew, obs. form of MILDEW.

mealy-mouth ('mi:lɪ'maʊθ). [MEALY *a.* 8; cf. MEALY-MOUTHED *a.*] **1.** A mouth which never utters plain terms; a soft, indirect, or reticent manner of speaking; hence a mealy-mouthed person. Also ironically: see quot. 1941. *slang.*

1600 DEKKER *Gentle Craft* i. (1862) 9 This wench with the mealy mouth, is my wife I can tell you. **1828** CARLYLE *Misc.* (1857) IV. 140 Bless its mealy mouth! **1862** J. C. JEAFFRESON *Bk. abt. Doctors* xiii. (1862) 156 Well-fed Vicars of Bray.. with mealy mouths and elastic consciences. **1808** B. KIRKBY *Lakeland Words* 100 *Mealy-Mooth*,.. eny body 'at's mealy-moothed's o' that sooart. **1919** J. C. SNAITH *Love Lane* xlvii. 254 It was no use having a divided mind, it was no use having a mealy-mouth. **1941** J. SMILEY *Hash House Lingo* 37 *Mealy mouth*, fault finding customer. **1942** *Scrutiny* X. 400 Iudushka, the chief character, is the apotheosis of the mealy-mouth.

2. *dial.* Applied to various birds, as the willow warbler, *Phylloscopus trochilus*, or the whitethroat, *Sylvia communis*.

1885 C. SWAINSON *Provincial Names & Folklore Brit. Birds* 26 Willow Warbler.. Mealy mouth (Craven). **1961** *Countryman* LVIII. 468 A missel thrush is a 'greybird'.. the whitethroat a 'mealymouth' [in S. Pembrokeshire].

mealy-mouthed ('mi:lɪ'maʊðd), *a.* [Cf. MEALY *a.* 8.] Soft-spoken; not outspoken; afraid to speak one's mind or to use plain terms.

c **1572** GASCOIGNE *Fruites Warre* lxxxvi, So were more meete for mealy mouthed men. **1606** DAY *Ile of Guls* IV. iv, And ile not be mealely mouthed, I warrant em. **1679** 'T. TICKLEFOOT' *Trial Wakeman* 7 He was not mealy mouth'd, but would.. have talked his mind to Knights, or any Body. **1788** WESLEY *Wks.* (1872) VII. 106 Carry your point, whatever it costs. Be not mealy-mouthed. **1855** TENNYSON *Brook* 94 Mealy-mouth'd philanthropies. **1887** BESANT *The World went* xvi. 138 None of your mincing, mealy-mouthed, fine ladies.

¶ Used for: Over scrupulous.

1809 MALKIN *Gil Blas* XII. xiv, You are not mealy-mouthed about receiving a commoner into your pedigree.

Hence **mealy-mouthedly** *adv.*, **mealy-mouthedness**.

1727 BAILEY vol. II, *Mealy-mouthedness.* **1838** SOUTHEY *Doctor* (1848) 382 He is not given to speak, as his friends the Portuguese say, enfarinhadamente—which is, being interpreted, mealy-mouthedly. **1894** *Sat. Rev.* 24 Mar. 304 School Boards and other engines of mealy-mouthedness have laid a ban upon some of our old plant names.

† **mean,** *sb.*[1] *Obs.* Forms: 3-5 **mene**, 6, 9 **meane**, 9 **meen.** [f. MEAN *v.*[2]] A lament, complaint.

12.. *Prayer to Virg.* 34 in *O.E. Misc.* 196 To þe ne dar i clepien noht to hire ich make min mene. **1300-1400** *Cursor M.* (Gött.) 19758 Widuten ani mene or sare. *c* **1470** HENRY *Wallace* IV. 153 Thar petuous mene as than couth nocht be bett. *a* **1578** LINDESAY (Pitscottie) *Chron. Scot.* (S.T.S.) I. 286 This bischope.. maid his meane and complent to the lord Home. **18..** in *Kinloch's Sc. Ballads* (1827) 131 She heard a puir prisoner making his meane. **18..** *Mary Hamilton* xiii. in Child *Ballads* III. 389 'Make never meen for me', she says.

mean (mi:n), *sb.*[2] Forms: 4-6 **mene**, 4-7 **meane**, 5-6 **meyne**, 5 **meene**, 6- **mean**. [Partly the absolute use of MEAN *a.*[2], and partly adopted from the similar substantival use in OF.]

I. That which is in the middle.

1. a. That which is intermediate; a condition, quality, disposition, or course of action, that is equally removed from two opposite (usually, blamable) extremes; a medium. Often with laudatory adj., as GOLDEN, *happy*, †*merry mean*.

c **1374** CHAUCER *Boeth.* IV. Pr. vii. 146 Occupy þe mene by stedfast strengþes [L. *firmis medium viribus occupate*]. **1399** [see MERRY *a.*]. *c* **1400** *Rom. Rose* 6527 Richesse and mendicitees Ben cleped two extremitees; The mene is cleped suffisaunce. *c* **1420** *Pallad. on Husb.* II. 27 Demene hit in the mene of moyst and drie. *Ibid.* 127 The mene is best thyn ayer to qualifie. **1529** *Supplic. to King* (1871) 45 Betwene these extreame contraries there is no meane. **1580** LYLY *Euphues* (Arb.) 337, I haue hard that extremities are to be vsed, where the meane will not serue. **1587**, etc. [see GOLDEN *a.* 5c]. **1596** SPENSER *Hymn Hon. Love* 87 Tempering goodly well Their contrary dislikes with loved meanes. **1654-66** EARL ORRERY *Parthen.* (1676) 5 There was no mean between my misery and her favour. **1690** W. WALKER *Idiomat. Anglo-Lat.* 297 In apparel the mean is the best. **1727** SWIFT *Poisoning E. Curll* Wks. 1755 III. I. 152 There is a mean in all things. **1732** BERKELEY *Alciphr.* v. §6 Religion is the virtuous mean between incredulity and superstition. **1849** MACAULAY *Hist. Eng.* vii. (ed. 5) II. 234 It is not easy.. to preserve with steadiness the happy mean between these two extremes. **1879** *Cassell's Techn. Educ.* IV. 24/2 A mean between the darkest and lightest tint used.

†**b.** Absence of extremes; moderation, measure. *in a mean*: with moderation. *to use a mean*: to exercise moderation. *Obs.*

1545 ASCHAM *Toxoph.* (Arb.) 17, I woulde desire all.. to vse this pastime in suche a mean that the outragiousnes of great gamyng, should not hurte the honestie of shotyng. **1556** *Aurelio & Isab.* (1608) Diij, The Kinge.. axede them what meane one oughte to keape in suche a case. **1579** GOSSON *Sch. Abuse* (Arb.) 23 So they [versifying, dancing and singing] bee vsed with meane, and exercised in due tyme. **1607** NORDEN *Surv. Dial.* II. 103, I wish, that Lords and their ministers would vse a meane in exacting. **1621** FLETCHER *Wild Goose Chase* II. ii, I will be what I please, Sir, So I exceed not Mean. **1625** BACON *Ess., Adversity* (Arb.) 504 But to speake in a Meane. **1655** CULPEPPER, etc. *Riverius* I. i. 4 Use a mean in sleep and waking. **1718** POPE *Iliad* XVII. 573 When he seeks the prize War knows no mean.

2. *Mus.* †**a.** A middle or intermediate part in any harmonized composition or performance, esp. the tenor and alto. Also, a person performing that part or the instrument on which it is played.

The use app. survived in dialects until recently: see E.D.D.

c **1330** R. BRUNNE *Chron. Wace* (Rolls) 11263 Þo clerkes þat best couþe synge, Wyþ treble, mene, & burdoun. *c* **1400** *Laud Troy Bk.* 6599, I schal the teche bothe burdoun and mene. *c* **1500** in Burney *Hist. Mus.* (1782) II. 435 There are 3 degrees of Discant, that is to say Mene, Treble, and Quadrible. The Mene beginneth in the 5, abowvyn the Playn Songe in voys [etc.]. *Ibid.* And so the Discant of the Mene Salbegynne hys Discant about the Playne Songe in Syght. **1526** SKELTON *Magnyf.* 138 All trebyllys and tenours be rulyd by a meyne. **1611** TOURNEUR *Ath. Trag.* III. iii, Trebles and bases make poore musick without meanes. **1698** WALLIS in *Phil. Trans.* XX. 302 Several Parts or Voices (as Bass, Treble, Mean, &c. sung in Consort).

fig. *c* **1430** LYDG. *Min. Poems* (Percy Soc.) 54 The [nasal] organys.. begynne to syng ther messe, With treble meene and tenor discordyng. **1590** SPENSER *F.Q.* II. xii. 33 On the rocke the waves breaking aloft A solemne Meane unto them measured. **1616** GOODMAN *Fall of Man* 78 The little chirping birds.. they sing a mean.

†**b.** A name for the second and the third string of a viol or lute. *Obs.*

1879 CHAPPELL *Pop. Mus.* I. 317 *note*, If there were two means, as in the lute, the lower was called the greater; the upper, the lesser mean. **1880** GROVE *Dict. Mus.* II. 242/2.

†**c.** ? = NATURAL *sb. Obs.*

1675 COCKER *Morals* 20 Grace.. tunes Natures Harp, And makes that Note a Mean, which was a Sharp.

†**3.** The middle (of anything). *Obs.*

c **1420** *Pallad. on Husb.* III. 398 He seyd ereithe[r] sappe wol condescende Vnto that mene, & glew hem self in fere. *c* **1440** *Promp. Parv.* 332/1 Meene, myddys (*H.P.* medyl), *medium.* **1688** R. HOLME *Armoury* II. 79/1 This leaf is.. heart-like in the mean, or part next the stalk.

†**4.** *Logic.* The middle term of a syllogism. *Obs.*

1605 BACON *Adv. Learn.* II. xiv. §1 It is in proofe by Syllogisme; for the proofe being not immediate but by Meane: the Inuention of the Meane is one thinge [etc.].

†**5.** *Gram.* A 'mean' or 'middle' verb (see MEAN *a.*[2] 8): = REFLEXIVE *sb.* B. 2. *Obs.*

1530 PALSGR. Introd. 35 All whiche differences of conjugation betwene the actyve verbes and theyr meanes I declare at length in my seconde boke.

†**6.** Something interposed or intervening. ***by means***: through intermediate links (of descent). ***without any mean*** (= F. *sans moyen*): directly, immediately, unconditionally. *Obs.*

c **1340** HAMPOLE *Prose Tr.* 16 All menes lettande be-twyx þe saule and þe clennes of angells es brokene and put awaye fra it. **1425** *Rolls of Parlt.* IV. 270/2 Of whiche Doughter by menes is comen ye Erle. **1523** LD. BERNERS *Froiss.* I. lxiii. 85 It was determyned, that bothe parties.. shulde sende foure or fyue personages, as their embassodours, and to mete at Arras; and the pope in likwyse to sende thyder foure, and ther to make a full confirmacyon without any meane. *Ibid.* cccli. 564 All the gentylmen of Flaunders sware to hym to be good and true.. without any meane, wherfore therle was greatly reioysed. **1548-77** VICARY *Anat.* ii. (1888) 18 That the grystle should be a meane betweene the Lygament and him [*sc.* the bone]. **1593** SHAKS. *3 Hen. VI*, III, ii. 141 So doe I wish the Crowne, being so farre off, And so I chide the meanes that keepes me from it.

†**7.** ***in the mean***: in the meantime. *Obs.*

1565 STAPLETON tr. *Bede's Hist. Ch. Eng.* 27 In the meane suffering no remedies to be applied vnto his owne infirmities. **1590** SPENSER *F.Q.* II. i. 58 In the meane, vouchsafe her honorable toombe. *a* **1657** R. LOVEDAY *Lett.* (1663) 193* In the mean, I shall.. read over your Translation with the Originall. **1793** JEFFERSON *Writ.* (1859) IV. 59 Time in the mean will be lost.

8. a. *Math.* [= F. *moyenne*, ellipt. for *quantité moyenne*.] The term (or, in plural, the terms) intermediate between the first and last terms (called the extremes) of a progression of any kind (distinctively, ***arithmetic(al***, ***geometric(al***, ***harmonic(al mean***). Also, in a wider sense, a quantity so related to a set of n quantities that the result of operating with it in a certain manner n times is the same as that of operating similarly with each of the set. In this sense the *arithmetic(al mean* (commonly called simply the *mean*) of a set of n quantities is the quotient of their sum divided by n; the *geometric(al* mean is the nth root of their product.

1571 DIGGES *Pantom., Math. Treat.* def. iv. Tjb, When foure magnitudes are.. in continual proportion, the first and the fourth are the extremes, and the second and thirde the meanes. **1660** R. COKE *Justice Vind.* 23 Nor [in harmonical proportion] do the extremes added or multiplied produce the like number with the mean. **1674** JEAKE *Arith.* (1696) 570 If between 2 and 54 two proportional Means be sought, the Lesser will be 6 and the Greater 18. **1709** J. WARD *Yng. Math. Guide* I. vi. (1734) 73 If any Four Numbers are in Arithmetical Progression, the Sum of the Two Extreams will be Equal to the Sum of the Two Means. **1881** J. CASEY *Sequel Euclid* 88 The Arithmetic mean is to the Geometric mean as the Geometric mean is to the Harmonic mean.

b. An average amount or value; used for ***mean pressure, temperature***, etc.

1803 SYD. SMITH *Catteau's États Danois* Wks. (1850) 51 Upon a mean of twenty-six years, it has rained for a hundred and thirty days every year. **1855** J. R. LEIFCHILD *Cornwall* 182 The temperature of the adit.. is on an average more than 12° above the mean of the climate. **1893** W. L. DALLAS in *Indian Meteorol. Mem.* IV. 516 The means of pressure have been obtained [etc.].

II. An intermediary agent or instrument.

†**9. a.** One who acts as mediator, 'go-between', or ambassador between others; one who intercedes for a person or uses influence on behalf of an object. ***to be good mean***, to act as intercessor. *Obs.*

c **1374** CHAUCER *Troylus* III. 205 (254) For þe am I becomen.. swych a mene As maken wommen vn-to men to comen. **1377** LANGL. *P. Pl.* B. I. 158 A mene, as þe Maire is bitwene þe kyng and þe comune. *c* **1386** CHAUCER *Miller's T.* 189 He woweth hire by meenes and brocage. *c* **1440** *Promp. Parv.* 332/2 Meene, massyngere,.. *internuncius. Ibid.*, Meene, or medyatowre,.. *mediator.* **1455** *Rolls of Parlt.* V. 285/1 It myght lyke the said Lieutenaunte and all the Lordes, to be goode meanes unto the Kynges Highnesse, that suche a persone myght be purveide fore. **1538** in Ellis *Orig. Lett.* Ser. I. II. 90 That it might please your Lordship to be a meane for us to our Soveraign Lorde the Kynge is Highenes. **1562** *Child-Marriages* 71 This deponent was desired of both parties, to be a meane that they might marie before the day appointed. **1606** J. CARPENTER *Solomon's Solace* xii. 47 She would be a meane for him to the king. **1612** BACON *Ess., Suitors* (Arb.) 47/1 Let a man, in the choise of his meane, rather chuse the fittest meane then the greatest meane.

†**b.** in pl. form, with sing. sense and const.

1554 CRANMER *Misc. Writ.* (Parker Soc.) II. 445 In most humble wise Sueth unto your right honourable lordships, Thomas Cranmer, late Archbishop of Canterbury; beseeching the Same to be a means for me unto the queen's highness. **1559-66** in *Wodrow Soc. Misc.* (1844) 74 The Marques of D'Albuef, the subtill meanes of the Duke of Guise. **1585** T. WASHINGTON tr. *Nicholay's Voy.* I. xx. 25 He being by them praied to be a meanes towards the Bascha. **1611** COTGR., *Moyenneur*, a means, mediator.

†**c.** *spec.* A mediator between God (or Christ) and man. *Obs.*

1362 LANGL. *P. Pl.* A. VIII. 183, I counseile alle cristene to crie crist merci, And Marie his Moder to beo mene bitwene. **1377** *Ibid.* B. xv. 535 þus in a faith lyueth þat folke and in a false mene [i.e. Mohammed]. *c* **1380** WYCLIF *Wks.* (1880) 409 A prest shulde be a mene bitwixe god & þe puple. **1508** FISHER *Penit. Ps.* xxxviii. Wks. (1876) 54 O blyssed lady be thou meane & mediatrice between thy son and wretched synners. **1570** T. NORTON tr. *Nowel's Catech.* (1853) 186 We need not then, for access to God, some man to be our mean. **1597** HOOKER *Eccl. Pol.* v. l. §3 There is no union of God with man without that mean between both which is both.

10. An instrument, agency, method, or course of action, by the employment of which some object is or may be attained, or which is concerned in bringing about some result. Often contrasted with *end*. Often predicatively (of persons as well as things), ***to be the means*** (or †***the mean***) ***of***.

a. in sing. form. Now only *arch.*

c **1374** CHAUCER *Troylus* v. 1551 The fate wold his soule sholde vnbodye, And shapen hadde a mene it out to dryue. **1444** *Rolls of Parlt.* V. 104/2 Be which subtile meene ye lose gret part of your custumes. **1539** CROMWELL in Merriman *Life & Lett.* (1902) II. 226 This.. sheweth a meane howe.. you may make them yet better. **1611** SHAKS. *Wint. T.* IV. iv. 90 Yet Nature is made better by no meane, But Nature makes the Meane. **1611** W. SCLATER *Key* (1629) 243 Vncharitable is that sentence of Papists; that Baptisme is necessarie as a meane to saluation. **1635** J. HAYWARD tr. *Biondi's Banish'd Virg.* 114 Dariacan himselfe had beene the instrumentall meane of my flight. **1785** T. BALGUY *Disc.* 31 Let us consider it as a mean, not as an end. **1814** W. BROWN *Propag. Chr. among Heathen* II. 402 The Mission to the South Sea Islands.. has.. been a powerful mean of promoting the interests of Christianity. **1881** SWINBURNE *Mary Stuart* II. i, God.. procure Some mean whereby mine enemies craft and his May take no feet but theirs in their own toils.

b. in plural form and plural or doubtful sense. ***by fair means***: see FAIR *a.* 15. ***ways and means***: see WAY *sb.*

c **1380** WYCLIF *Wks.* (1880) 121 þei comen bi false menys as ypocrisie & lesyngis to þes grete lordischipes. *c* **1386** CHAUCER *Friar's T.* 186 We been goddes Instrumentz, And meenes to doon hise comandementz. **1420** in Ellis *Orig. Lett.* Ser. I. I. 6 Lettres.. chargyng me to assaye by all the menesse that I kan to exyte and stirre sych as bene able gentilmen. **1549** COVERDALE, etc. *Erasm. Par. Rom.* 28 The eares, throughe whom as meanes the gospell of Christ is powred into the obedient soule. **1600** J. PORY tr. *Leo's Africa* III. 180 [He] left no meanes unattempted for the recouerie of this citie. *a* **1625** FLETCHER *Cust. Country* v. iv. Wonders are ceas'd Sir, we must work by meanes. **1733** POPE *Ess. Man* III. 82 And find the means proportioned to their end. **1888** BRYCE *Amer. Commw.* III. xcvi. 341 Vehement declaimers hounded on Congress to take arbitrary means for the suppression of the practice.

c. in pl. form, with sing. sense and const.

1512 in Ellis *Orig. Lett.* Ser. II. I. 192 A good meanys to know the trowthe.. were to gyve in commandement to John Style secretli to write the trowthe. **1606** G. W[OODCOCKE] *Hist. Ivstine* XXXVIII. 120 Being.. a means to train them vp in a secure experience to make themselues waye. **1652** H. L'ESTRANGE *Amer. no Jewes* 6 To be dashed and defeated by so weak a seeming means. **1750** BEAWES *Lex Mercat.* (1752) 2 Commerce.. is now become an universal means.. for the improvement of.. fortune. **1843** BETHUNE *Sc. Fireside Stor.* 28 You were indirectly the means of getting me introduced. **1843** MILL *Logic* Introd. §1 Writers have availed themselves of the same language as a means of delivering different ideas. **1863** C. REDDING *Yesterday & To-day* III. 142 *note*, I was the means of this being done.

d. Phrases. †***to make mean(s***: to take steps, use efforts (*obs.*). ***to find (the) means*** (or †***mean***): to find out a way, contrive, manage (now only const. *inf.*).

c **1386** CHAUCER *Frankl. T.* 155 How thanne may it bee That ye swiche meenes make it to destroyen, Whiche meenes do no good, but euere anoyen? **1461** *Paston Lett.* II.

35 That Richard Calle fynde the meane that a distresse may be taken of such bestes as occupie the ground at Stratton. c1462 *Ibid.* 107 Or hise wryting cam, Wydwell fond the meanys..that we had a discharge for hym out of the Chauncery. 1551 ROBINSON tr. *More's Utop.* II. (1895) 257 They make all the meanes and shyftes that maye be, to kepe themselfes from the necessitye of fyghtynge. 1568 GRAFTON *Chron.* II. 45 Then meanes was made vpon either side for the deliuery and exchaunge of prisoners. 1585 T. WASHINGTON tr. *Nicholay's Voy.* I. viii. 8b, I founde the meanes for moneye and white fayre woordes to hyre a.. Spaniarde. 1617 MORYSON *Itin.* I. 259 We..found meanes to pierce the vessell, and get good Wine to our ill fare. 1631 WEEVER *Anc. Funeral Mon.* 562 A man much renowned for ..the charges he was at, and the meanes he made, to adorne ..his Church.

e. ***means of grace*** (*Theol.*): the sacraments and other religious agencies viewed as the means by which divine grace is imparted to the soul, or by which growth in grace is promoted: in 'Evangelical' use often employed as a synonym for public worship. Also occas. with sing. sense, an agency conducive to spiritual improvement. ***under the means of grace*** (formerly often †*under means*): subject to the operation of the means of grace.

1642 ROGERS *Naaman* 5 Shall rise up and convince all beleevers, I meane such as live under meanes in that day. 1650 BAXTER *Saint's R.* IV. (1651) 8 Do we not miss Ministry and Means more passionately, then we miss our God? *Ibid.* 20, I know the means of grace must be loved and valued, and the usual enjoyment of God is in the use of them. 1662 *Bk. Com. Prayer, Thanksgiving*, For the means of grace, and for the hope of glory. 1771 WESLEY *Wks.* (1872) V. 187 By 'means of grace' I understand outward signs, words, or actions, ordained of God,..to be the ordinary channels whereby he might convey to men, preventing, justifying, or sanctifying grace. 1833 *Tracts for Times* No. 11. 2 The same company that are under the means of grace here. *Ibid.* 6 The Sacraments, which are the ordinary means of grace, are clearly in possession of the Church. 1841 A. R. C. DALLAS *Past. Superintend.* 185 The number of persons above the age of education, who ought to attend the means of grace. 1891 BESANT *St. Katherine's* x, The discourse of the preacher was on the fearful condition of those who disobey the discipline of the Church and refuse the means of Grace.

†**f.** *pl.* and *collect. sing.* Stratagem, trickery. *Obs.*

c1460 *Towneley Myst.* xxiv. 386 By hir meanes she makys dysers to sell. c1470 HENRY *Wallace* VII. 1116 Bot he be meyne gat his castell agayne. 1537 *St. Papers Hen. VIII*, I. 548 Ne any brogges or meanes, that any of those borderers or any other, canne make. 1602 WARNER *Alb. Eng.* IX. liii. (1612) 237 Nor is through Meed, or Means, the weak betraied to the strong.

g. ***means-end(s)*** (used *attrib.*): of or pertaining to the ways of achieving a result considered together with the result.

1933 *Psychol. Rev.* XL. 60 The 'means-end-readiness' Tolman defined as a certain selectivity as regards stimuli, and as regards the responses..to such stimuli. 1951 R. FIRTH *Elem. Social Organiz.* iii. 85 Structural change implies that there was some imperfection in the previous means-ends schedule of a substantial number of members of the society. 1958 *Listener* 5 June 931/2 We must look at the contexts where the means-end model *is* appropriate... The second means-end context is that of making or producing things. We mix the flour in order to make a cake. 1963 A. KAPLAN in P. A. Schilpp *Philos. R. Carnap* 840 If there were a final end it could not have the derived cognitive meaning of a means-end implication. 1965 H. I. ANSOFF *Corporate Strategy* ii. 24 The two sets of rules have a means-ends relationship; objectives set the goals, and strategy sets the path to the goals. 1965 *Language* XLI. 80 Aiming towards a means-ends model of language.

†**11.** A condition that permits or conduces to something; an opportunity; in early use *pl.* conditions, offered terms (of peace). Also in phrase ***in means, in a mean***: 'in a fair way' *to do* something. *Obs.*

1430-1 *Rolls of Parlt.* IV. 371/2 To refuse Pees offred with menes resonable. *Ibid.*, Yf yeim thynke ye menys of Pees offred. *Ibid.*, To offre for ye Kyngges partie menis yat shal be thought. a1552 LELAND *Itin.* VI. 2 Asscheforde Churche was in a meane to be collegiatyd by the Reqwest of one Fogge. 1590 SHAKS. *Com. Err.* I. ii. 18 Many a man would take you at your word, And goe indeede, hauing so good a meane. 1592 tr. *Junius on Rev.* xii. 2 She seemed near unto death, and in meanes ready to give up the Ghost. 1592 R. D. *Hypnerotomachia* 81b, My secret thoughts consented therunto, consygning a free meane and large entrance for the discovery of my desire. a1613 OVERBURY *Charact.*, *Worthy Commander* Wks. (1856) 07 He understands in warre, there is no meane to erre twice.

12. a. *pl.* [= F. *moyens.*] The resources at (one's) disposal for effecting some object; chiefly, (a person's) pecuniary resources viewed with regard to their degree of adequacy to (his) requirements or habits of expenditure: sometimes more explicitly ***means of living, of subsistence***. In early use sometimes more widely: = 'money', 'wealth'. ***man of means***: one possessing a competency.

1603 SHAKS. *Meas. for M.* II. ii. 24 Let her haue needfull, but not lauish meanes. 1605 BACON *Adv. Learn.* I. iii. §2 Iudging that meanes were to be spent vpon learning, and not learning to be applyed to meanes. 1606 G. W[ODCOCKE] *Hist. Ivstine* XVI. 66 Having meanes to corrupt tharmy of Demetrius with great rewardes. 1609 SIR E. HOBY *Let. to T. H[iggons]* 66, I know no man so respectlesse of himselfe, but would willinglie part with one moytie of his meanes, for his future reliefe. a1625 FLETCHER *Cust. Country* V. v, And when thou went'st, to Imp thy miserie, Did I not give thee meanes? 1630 *R. Johnson's Kingd. & Commw.* 50 If hee be a man of meanes, and likely hereafter to beare charge in his Countrey..I wishe him to Historie. 1660 F. BROOKE tr. *Le Blanc's Trav.* 284 Two children, who lived there upon their mothers means. 1775 SHERIDAN *Duenna* II. iii, He has never sullied his honour, which, with his title, has outlived his means. 1823 SCOTT *Peveril* ii, We are great enough for our means, and have means sufficient for contentment. 1859 TENNYSON *Enid* 455 My means were somewhat broken into. 1894 WILKINS & VIVIAN *Green Bay Tree* I. 11 It was very wrong for a man to live beyond his means.

†**b.** Formerly sometimes construed as sing.; rarely in particularized use, a livelihood. *Obs.*

1615 WITHER *Sheph. Hunt.* v. in *Juvenilia* (1633) 439, I waste my Meanes which of itself is slender. 1615 BRATHWAIT *Strappado* (1878) 52 They're..men that get A slauish meanes out of a seruile wit. c1642 R. HARRIS *Hezekiah's Recovery* 27 All that meanes..is little enough to buy a constant Preacher bookes and physicke.

13. Intermediary agency or condition.

†**a.** (Cf. sense 9.) Mediation, intercession; exercise of influence to bring about something, instigation. ***to make mean(s***: to intercede, make interest; to negotiate *with*; to make overtures *to*. *Obs.*

sing. 1432-50 tr. *Higden* (Rolls) IV. 239 He was sente ageyne the kynge of Araby thro meane of Cleopatra [L. *ad petitionem Cleopatræ*]. 1477 EARL RIVERS (Caxton) *Dictes* 1 Thurgh the meane of the Mediatrice of Mercy. 1510 *Hours Bl. Virgin* 91 Give us the life that ever doth excell, Through thy prayer & speciall meane. 1535 *Goodly Prymer* L iij, They must nedes fyrst make meane vnto hym [a temporal prince] by some man that is in his fauour. 1565 *Satir. Poems Reform.* i. 567 The mr Maxwell..to reconcile my meane, on his knees entreated me to hear [etc.]

pl. c1400 *Three Kings Cologne* 131 Sche made grete menes to þe chefe lordys of þis yle. 1526 *Pilgr. Perf.* (W. de W. 1531) 164b, By whose suffrage, intercession & meanes we be holpen in this lyfe. 1536 *Cal. Anc. Rec. Dublin* (1889) I. 498 Youre grase hys good mens. 1591 UNTON *Corr.* (Roxb.) 237 Great meanes have been made for him. 1594 SHAKS. *Rich. III*, I. iii. 78 Our Brother is imprison'd by your meanes. 1656 FINETT *For. Ambass.* 191 Sir Henry Mildmay had made his meanes to the Duke of Buckingham..for carriage ..of the Present designed to the Ambassador.

b. (Cf. sense 10.) Instrumentality, operation as an instrument, method, or proximate cause. Only in certain phrases: see 14.

14. Adverbial, prepositional, and conjunctional phrases.

a. ***by all (manner of) means***: (*a*) in every possible way; (*b*) at any cost, without fail; (*c*) used to emphasize a permission, request, or injunction, = 'certainly'.

(*a*) 1491 *Act. 7 Hen. VII*, c. 11 §1 Ye verily intendyng.. to aredie yourself by all meanes to you possible..to invade upon your and our auncien ennemyes. c1520 BARCLAY *Jugurth* (1557) 70b, He..by all maner meanes made prouysion for hym selfe. 1596 DALRYMPLE tr. *Leslie's Hist. Scotl.* I. 129 To this end they labouret be al meines possible.

(*b*) 1611 BIBLE *Acts* xviii. 21, I must by all meanes keepe this feast. 1754 CHATHAM *Lett. Nephew* 35 The trick of laughing frivolously is by all means to be avoided.

(*c*) 1693 *Humours Town* 31 By all means, Sir, Object and Return, as often as you please. 1774 FOOTE *Cozeners* II. Wks. 1799 II. 168 *Flaw.* I'll run before, and prepare Mrs. Fleece'em. *Mrs. Air.* By all manner of means. 1844 DISRAELI *Coningsby* III. iii, Tell it us by all means. 1874 RUSKIN *Fors Clav.* xlii. 125 Yes, in God's name, and by all manner of means. 1895 *Law Times* C. 101/2 By all means let the [County] Council drift rudderless.

b. ***by any (manner of) means*** (or †*mean*): (*a*) in any way, anyhow, at all; †(*b*) by all means.

(*a*) c1470 HENRY *Wallace* XI. 207 A band thai maid..to wyrk his confusioun, Be ony meyn. 1474 *Rolls of Parlt.* VI. 117/2 Undelyvered by any meane unto you. c1520 BARCLAY *Jugurth* (1557) 57b, He lost more people by this way than by any other meane before. 1537 in *Lett. Suppress. Monast.* (Camden) 153 In as large and ample maner and forme as ever I had or aught to have of and in the same or any part or parcell therof by ony maner of meanes. 1567 J. SANFORD *Epictetus* 24 Occasion cannot be giuen by any maner of meanes, nor any arte. 1611 BIBLE *Ps.* xlix. 7 None of them can by any meanes redeeme his brother. 1809 W. IRVING *Knickerb.* v. iv. (1849) 278, I do not by any means pretend to claim the merit. 1873 RUSKIN *Fors Clav.* xlv. 193 Not by any manner of means. 1893 R. WILLIAMS in H. D. Traill *Soc. Eng.* i. 32 She was not, however, by any means the only female deity.

(*b*) 1610 B. JONSON *Alch.* v. ii, Yes, tell her, She must by any meanes addresse some present To th' cunning man. 1616 —— *Devil an Ass* v. v, *Mer.* Yes, Sir, and send for his wife. *Eve.* And the two Sorcerers, By any meanes!

c. ***by no means*** (or †*mean*), ***by no manner of means*** (or †*mean*), † ***by no manner mean***: (*a*) in no way, not at all; (*b*) on no account.

(*a*) 1442 T. BECKINGTON *Corr.* (Rolls) II. 214 Your said adversary by no manner of meen may be induced to graunte us his lettres of saufcondeuct. 1472 J. PASTON in *P. Lett.* III. 35, I can not yet make my pesse wyth my Lord of Norffolk ..by no meane. c1520 BARCLAY *Jugurth* (1557) 40 This town could by no meanes be well besyged nor taken. 1564 *Brief Exam.* ****ij, They are not to be reiected, as yf they were by no maner of meanes in the worde of God. 1782 MISS BURNEY *Cecilia* IX. i, I am by no means an approver of that mode of proceeding. 1893 GUNTER *Miss Dividends* 102 The young men are looking at each other with by no means kindly eyes. 1893 SWINBURNE *Stud. Prose & Poetry* (1894) 111 *Basil* is by no manner of means an impeccable work of imperishable art.

(*b*) 1509 BARCLAY *Shyp of Folys* (1570) 123 And if hir husbande to any thinge agree By no maner meane will she therto encline. 1600 J. PORY tr. *Leo's Africa* III. 161 They will by no meanes vouchsafe to marie their daughters vnto them. 1625 BACON *Ess., Gard.* (Arb.) 563 But these to be, by no Meanes, set too thicke. 1711 STEELE *Spect.* No. 51 ¶1 Such an Image as this ought, by no means, to be presented to a Chaste and Regular Audience. 1864 J. H. NEWMAN *Apol.* 35 What word should I have used twenty years ago instead of 'Protestant?' 'Roman' or 'Romish?' by no manner of means. 1879 M. ARNOLD *Mixed Ess.*, *Falkland* 232 Shall we blame him for his lucidity of mind, and largeness of temper? By no means.

d. ***by this*** or ***that means*** (or †*mean*): (*a*) by means of this or that; in this or that way; thus.

c1520 BARCLAY *Jugurth* (1557) 117 By this meanes shal they be muche beholden to you. 1568 GRAFTON *Chron.* II. 11 That he might preferre Normans to the rule of the Church..and by that meane stand in the more suretie of his estate. 1629 MAXWELL tr. *Herodian* (1635) 372 By that meanes you shall take away that most odious and hideous tyrant Maximine. 1667 SPRAT *Hist. R. Soc.* 100 By this means, they will accomplish their main Design. 1750 BEAWES *Lex. Mercat.* (1752) 1 When by this means an aggregated number swelled to too great a magnitude..they were compelled to seek for remoter helps by commerce. 1825 COLERIDGE *Aids Refl.* (1848) I. 31 By this mean, and scarcely without it, you will at length acquire a facility in detecting the *quid pro quo*.

†(*b*) In consequence, consequently.

c1520 BARCLAY *Jugurth* (1557) 52 Because Iugurth was on the small hyll before hym, and by that meane on the hyer ground.

†**e.** ***by some manner of means***: 'by hook or by crook'. *Obs.*

1573 TUSSER *Husb.* (1878) 88 Friend, harrow in time, by some maner of meanes, not onely thy peason, but also thy beanes.

f. ***by*** or ***through*** (†***the***) ***means*** (or †*mean*) ***of***: (*a*) by the instrumentality of (a person or thing).

1427 *Rolls of Parlt.* IV. 326/2 Hit belanged unto you of rygȝt, as wel be ye mene of your birth. c1450 *Merlin* 20 Thow purchacest a-corde be-twene the and thi husbonde, by mene of the person hym-self, for to hyde yowre counseill. 1530 PALSGR. 611/2 Se how moche this chambre is lyghtenned by meane of one torche. 1560 A. L. tr. *Calvin's Foure Serm. Songe Ezech.* Epist., By meane of whose aide.. he findeth himselfe holpen. 1611 BIBLE *Heb.* ix. 15 By meanes of death..they which are called, might receiue the promise of eternall inheritance. 1653 LD. VAUX tr. *Godeau's St. Paul* A ij, Having obtained by meanes of your most noble Lady, a view of this choise piece [etc.]. 1736 BUTLER *Anal.* I. ii. Wks. 1874 I. 35, I know not, that we have any one kind ..of enjoyment, but by the means of our own actions. 1749 FIELDING *Tom Jones* VIII. xiii, He had succeeded so far as to find me out by means of an accident. 1807 MISS MITFORD in L'Estrange *Life* (1870) I. 67, I hoped that through his means you would get acquainted with Walter Scott.

†(*b*) In consequence of, by reason of, owing to.

1439 *Rolls of Parlt.* V. 32/2 Hynderyng and clamour of the said diverse of your communes, be mene of the said purvyance. 1526 SKELTON *Magnyf.* 1441 That was by the menys of to moche lyberte. 1568 GRAFTON *Chron.* I. 151 He also amended many things..that had beene long time out of frame, by meane of the Danes. a1626 BACON *New Atl.* (1900) 11 By meanes of our solitary Situation..we know well most part of the Habitable World, and are our selues vnknowne. 1688 R. HOLME *Armoury* III. 320/2 By means of this cover he is very rarely wet on his Body. 1726 G. ROBERTS *Four Years' Voy.* 13 He could not yet hold a Pen in his Hand by means of his late Sickness.

†**g.** ***by (the) means (that)***: for the reason that, because, since. *Obs.*

1550 CROWLEY *Last Trumpet* 1083 White meate beareth a greate pryce Which some men thinke is by the meane That fermes be found such marchaundise. 1565 SPARKE in *Hawkins' Voy.* (1878) 24 But sure we were that the armie was come downe, by means that in the euening we sawe such a monstrous fire. 1596 HARINGTON *Apology* (1814) 36, I guessed at his meaning by means I had once some smattering of the Latin tongue. 1599 —— *Nugæ Ant.* (1804) I. 257 By means the weather falls out so monstrous wet as the like hath not been seen.

15. *attrib.* and *Comb.* as (in sense 10c) ***means-maker, -using***; †**mean-keeper** (cf. sense 1b), one who observes moderation; †**mean-keeping**, moderation; †**means-making** (cf. sense 13b), intercession, use of interest or influence on a person's behalf; **means test**, an official inquiry into an applicant's private resources, determining or limiting a grant or allowance from public funds; also (with hyphen) as *vb.*; hence **means-testable** *a.*; **means-tested** *ppl. a.*; **means testing** *vbl. sb.*

1553 GRIMALDE *Cicero's Offices* I. (1558) 62 In which thynges ther must doutlesse be used a measure that to a meankepyng [L. *ad mediocritatem*] muste be reduced. *Ibid.* II. 98 Soon after Lucius Crassus with Quinctus Mutius, the greatest meanekeeper [L. *moderatissimo*] of all men, kept the time of their Edile office most royally. 1617 BACON *Sp. on taking his place in Chancery* in *Resuscit.* 84 It will also avoid all Means-making, or Labouring; For there ought to be no Labouring in Causes but the Labouring of the Counsell at the Barr. 1625 —— *Apoph.* §8 Wks. 1825 I. 351 His wife, by her suit and means making, made his peace. 1640 FULLER *Joseph's Coat*, etc. 172 Looke not..on the meanes but on the Meanes-maker. 1642 ROGERS *Naaman* 146 What, but our ascribing to ourselves in our means-using, makes them so unfruitful? 1930 *Economist* 7 June 1263/2 We should not cavil greatly at the principle of granting, on the basis of a means test, maintenance allowances for children compelled to attend school. 1935 *Planning* II. 11 A system of Transitional Payments was introduced..subject, however, to a household 'Means Test' administered by the local Public Assistance Committees. 1940 *Manch. Guardian Weekly* 23 Feb. 153/3 Non-contributory pensions, to which alone the household means test was to apply, had been conditioned by the applicant's means ever since 1908. 1957 *Times* 31 Dec. 11/5 Provision should be made in the new scholarship scheme for giving adequate assistance to students who would be debarred under 'means tests' from accepting scholarships offered by the State and other

sources. **1963** *Economist* 1 June 882/2 All university awards are means-tested now. **1966** *Ibid.* 29 Jan. 388/1 The genuinely poor long-term sick should be generously treated, preferably through generous means-tested national assistance. **1970** *Guardian* 29 Oct. 13, 1971 is going to be a record year for means-testing... Millions of new means-test forms will have to be designed... More people.. will.. make the sudden move from means-tested exemption from Health Service charges to paying the full rate. **1970** *Daily Tel.* 12 Dec. 2/6 Many of them are now living on fixed private incomes or with the aid of supplementary benefits which are means-tested. **1972** *Times* 30 Sept. 15/4 The poorest being supported by means testable benefits. **1973** *Times* 13 Feb. 16/7 Means-testing over a wide range of social benefits has been introduced on a scale unprecedented since the war.

mean (miːn), *sb.*^{3} *colloq. rare.* [*sb.* use of MEAN *a.*^{1} 5.] A mean person; = MEANY.

1938 E. BOWEN *Death of Heart* II. iv. 241 You *are* a mean, Dickie!

mean (miːn), *a.*^{1} and *adv.*^{1} Forms: 3 **meane**, 3–4 **mene**, 4–5 **meen**, 5 **mean**. [App. repr. (with normal loss of prefix) the earlier I-MENE, OE. *ȝemǽne* = OFris. *gemêne*, OS. *gimêni* (MLG. *gemeine*, MDu. *gemêne*, Du. *gemeen*), OHG. *gimeini* (MHG. *gemeine*, mod.G. *gemein*; Sw., Da *gemen* from Ger.), Goth. *gamains*:—OTeut. **ga-maini-*, f. *ga-* copulative prefix (synonymous with L. *com-*) + **maini-*:—pre-Teut. **moini-* in L. *commūnis* (:—**com-moini-s*) COMMON *a.*

The pre-Teut. **moini-* is believed to be a ppl. derivative of the root **mei-, moi-* (as in L. *mūtāre*:—**moitāre*) to change, whence L. *mūnus* (:—**moinos-*) reward, gift, and perh. (with the notion of change for the worse) OTeut. **maino-* wicked, MAN *a.*

The primary sense of Teut. **gamaini-*, as of L. *commūnis*, is 'possessed jointly', 'belonging equally to a number of persons'. In OE., and in the early stages of the other Teut. languages, this was substantially the only sense; but in ME., as in Du. and Ger., it underwent a development corresponding to that of COMMON *a.*, so that it acquired the senses of 'ordinary', 'not exceptionally good', 'inferior'. In English this development was furthered by the fact that the native word coincided in form with the word adopted from OF. *meien, meen* (see MEAN *a.*^{2}) middle, 'middling', which was often used in a disparaging or reproachful sense. The uses in branch II below might be referred almost equally well to the native and to the foreign adj.; the truth is prob. that they are of mixed ancestry.

It is often supposed that the sense-development of the word has been influenced by OE. *mǽne* false, wicked (cogn. w. *mân* MAN *sb.*^{2} and *a.*); but this does not seem possible, as this adj. did not survive into ME., while the moral senses of *mean* do not appear before the mod.Eng. period.]

A. *adj.* **I. 1.** Common to two or more persons or things; possessed jointly. ***in mean***: in common. ***to go mean***: to act as partners, to share. *Obs.* exc. *dial.* (see E.D.D.).

c **1200** *Trin. Coll. Hom.* 179 Al þat hie bi ben, hie hauen of here [*sc.* underlinges] mene swinche. *a* **1240** *Sawles Warde* in *Cott. Hom.* 261 Sei us nu hwuch blisse is to alle iliche meane. *c* **1400** MAUNDEV. (Roxb.) xiii. 59 þai hald a lawe in meen betwene vs and þe Grekez. *a* **1598** D. FERGUSON *Prov.* (1785) 6 A mein pot plaid never even. **1730** WALKDEN *Diary* (1866) 94 That we would go mean at ploughing. *Ibid.* 116 We concluded to get John Dickenson to measure our ground we had plowed mean.

II. Inferior in rank or quality.

†**2. a.** Of persons, their rank or station: Undistinguished in position; of low degree; often opposed to *noble* or *gentle*. (Cf. COMMON *a.* 12.) *Obs.*

a **1300** *Cursor M.* 13272 Nu ches felaus wil he bigin, Bot noght o riche kinges kin,.. Bot mene men o pour lijf. *c* **1330** R. BRUNNE *Chron.* (1810) 168 þe mene folk (comonly fulle gode men & wise) Com to his mercy. —— *Chron. Wace* (Rolls) 11202 þe legat; and oþer bischopes of mener stat. *c* **1420** *Liber Cocorum* (1862) 7 Take black sugur for mener menne. **1483** CAXTON *G. de la Tour* A viij b, Therfor my fayre daughters shewe your curtosye unto the mene and smal peple. **1568** GRAFTON *Chron.* II. 154 The Commons (specially such as were of the meaner sort) cryed vpon Thomas fitz Thomas. **1586** J. HOOKER *Hist. Irel.* in *Holinshed* II. 128/1 The opinion.. and judgement of a meane burgesse, is of as great availe as is the best lords. **1600** DEKKER *Gentle Craft* Wks. 1873 I. 19 O love, how powerfull art thou, that canst change.. a noble mind To the meane semblance of a shoomaker. **1606** SHAKS. *Ant. & Cl.* II. v. 82 These hands do lacke Nobility, that they strike A meaner then my selfe. *a* **1626** BACON *Chr. Paradoxes* Wks. 1879 I. 341 He bears a lofty spirit in a mean condition. **1675** EVELYN *Diary* 22 Mar., Sir William [Petty] was the sonn of a meane man some where in Sussex. **1701** DE FOE *True-born Eng.* 35 The meanest English Plowman studies Law. **1774** *Chesterfield's Lett.* (1792) I. xliv. 141 A mean fellow.. is ashamed when he comes into good company. **1827** ROBERTS *Voy. Centr. Amer.* 225 The meanest persons smoke tobacco.

transf. **1752** HUME *Ess. & Treat.* (1777) I. 198 Where women.. are bought and sold, like the meanest animal. **1774** GOLDSM. *Nat. Hist.* (1776) II. 9 As to animals of a meaner rank.. they very soon alter their natures with the nature of their nourishment.

†**b.** Poor, badly off. *Obs.*

1362 LANGL. *P. Pl.* A. Prol. 18 Alle maner of men the mene and the riche. **1558** in Strype *Ann. Ref.* (1709) I. App. iv. 5 Of.. Men meaner in substance. **1685** BUNYAN *Bk. Boys & Girls* (repr.) 1 Thou shalt not steal, though thou be very mean. *a* **1707** BP. PATRICK *Autobiog.* (1839) 11 My father was so mean then, he could not otherwise maintain me. **1776** ADAM SMITH *W.N.* I. xi. (1869) I. 162 The circumstances of gardeners, generally mean, and always moderate.

c. Inferior, 'poor', in ability, learning, etc. *Obs.* exc. in phr. (*to*) ***the meanest understanding*** (***capacity***, etc.) and as in 4.

1387 TREVISA *Higden* (Rolls) III. 93 þe comyn lettre of Mathew is ful skars for mene men myȝte vnderstonde. **1590** STOCKWELL *Rules Construct.* A iv, Most cleare and easie for the capacitie of the verie meanest. **1621** BRATHWAIT *Nat. Embassie* Ded., The meanest Menalchas that is able to play upon an oaten pipe. **1678** (*title*) Cockers Arithmetick, being a plain and familiar Method suitable to the meanest capacity. **1711** HEARNE *Collect.* (O.H.S.) III. 133 A mean man, and.. altogether unqualify'd for a Critick. **1719** F. HAER *Ch. Authority Vind.* 39 Many [parts of Scripture] are plain and easy to the meanest understanding. **1738** NEAL *Hist. Purit.* IV. 347 Most of them were very mean Divines.

†**d.** Of conditions: Abject, debased. *Obs.*

c **1680** BEVERIDGE *Serm.* (1729) II. 547 Our frail and mean condition.. requires us to pray always.

e. ***mean white***: a term of contempt applied to the poor and landless white men in the Southern United States, who in the days of slavery were regarded by the negroes as inferior to themselves.

1837 HT. MARTINEAU *Soc. Amer.* II. 311 There are a few, called by the slaves 'mean whites', signifying whites who work with the hands.

transf. **1887** RIDER HAGGARD *Jess* iv, You must have a gentleman. Your mean white will never get anything out of a Kafir.

f. *U.S. colloq.* In low spirits or poor state of health; poorly, not quite well.

1857 'DOW, JR.' *Dow's Patent Sermons* 1st Ser. 7 As mean.. as a rooster in a thundershower. **1911** H. S. HARRISON *Queed* vii. 90 Mebbe you could do better writing and harder writing if only you didn't feel so mean. **1911** J. F. WILSON *Land Claimers* i. 21 'Feel pretty mean,' the packer asked him kindly.

3. Of things: **a.** Poor in quality; of little value; inferior. Now chiefly *N. Amer.* (*colloq.*), of domestic animals or things in general: poor in quality or condition; comparatively worthless; unpleasant, disagreeable.

1377 LANGL. *P. Pl.* B. VI. 185 Lete hem ete with hogges, .. Or elles melke and mene ale. **1647** CLARENDON *Hist. Reb.* VII. §24 The Fortifications were very mean to endure a form'd siege. **1669** WORLIDGE *Syst. Agric.* (1681) 260 Although the Bream be esteem'd as a mean Fish. **1766** *Compl. Farmer* s.v. *Vinegar*, The cyder (the meanest of which will serve the purpose) is first to be drawn off fine. **1770** LANGHORNE *Plutarch's Lives* (1879) II. 1059/1 Those poor Caunians had about two quarts of bad water in a mean bottle. **1817** in *Trans. Illinois State Hist. Soc. 1910* 148 Hogs in this Country are the meanest that I have ever seen... I do not believe you ever see half so mean hogs as we have here. **1823** W. FAUX *Memorable Days Amer.* 219 The horses here are nearly all mean,.. dwarfish things. **1842** C. M. KIRKLAND *Forest Life* I. 140 You've had a pretty mean time, I reckon. *a* **1890** in Barrère & Leland *Dict. Slang* (1890) II. 49/1 The night was dark and stormy, about as mean a night as was ever experienced in Washington. **1936** ADE *Let.* 29 Apr. (1973) 192 We arrived home on the 17th without mishap and almost immediately ran into mean weather including one snow fall which completely covered the ground. **1948** 'N. SHUTE' *No Highway* ix. 245 Eight handles it [*sc.* a coffin] had, for carrying, but gee, that was a mean load. **1973** *Kingston* (Ontario) *Whig-Standard* 11 Aug. 7/5 That was just about the meanest electric storm I ever sat through.

b. Petty, unimportant; inconsiderable. ? *Obs.*

1585 T. WASHINGTON tr. *Nicholay's Voy.* II. viii. 41 Foure other officers.. to looke vnto the old and new buildings, and other meane & pollitike affayres [Fr. *et autres menuz affaires politiques*]. **1599** *Warn. Faire Wom.* II. 1510 For such a fault too meane a recompence. **1726** LEONI *Alberti's Archit.*, *Life* 2 He cou'd discourse.. of common and mean things with.. pleasantness. **1745** *De Foe's Eng. Tradesman* II. xlix. 220 The cider trade may perhaps be thought a trifle too mean to be mentioned here. **1754** GRAY *Pleasure* 49 The meanest flowret of the vale. [**1807** WORDSW. *Ode Intim. Immort.*, The meanest flower that blows.]

c. Undignified, low. Of literary style, etc.: Wanting in elevation; formerly sometimes without reproachful sense, †unambitious, unadorned.

a **1400–50** *Alexander* 3464 Al be þe metire bot mene þus mekill haue I ioyned. *a* **1568** ASCHAM *Scholem.* II. (Arb.) 144 The meter and verse of Plautus and Terence be verie meane. **1586** A. DAY *Eng. Secretary* I. (1625) 8 An Epistle.. should .. be simple, plaine, and of the lowest & meanest stile. **1610** SHAKS. *Temp.* III. i. 4. **1650** MARVELL *Horatian Ode* 57 He nothing common did or mean, Upon that memorable scene. **1659** HAMMOND *On Ps.* lx. 6 The wash-pot, we know, is a mean part of household-stuffe. **1676** EVELYN *Diary* 19 July, Sir William Sanderson.. author of two large but meane histories of King Iames and King Charles the First. **1751** JOHNSON *Rambler* No. 168 ¶3 A mean term never fails to displease him to whom it appears mean. **1789** BURNEY *Hist. Mus.* III. i, In these Lamentations.. the poetry is too mean and gloomy for any but modern saints or methodists. **1823** LAMB *Elia* Ser. II. *Poor Relations*, He will thrust in some mean and unimportant anecdote of the family.

d. Of buildings, attire, ornament, personal appearance, etc.: The reverse of imposing, shabby.

1600 J. PORY tr. *Leo's Africa* III. 156 A suburbe.. the houses whereof are but meane, and the inhabitants base. **1769** *De Foe's Tour Gt. Brit.* (ed. 7) II. 4 Camelford is a mean but ancient Borough-town. **1855** S. BROOKS *Aspen Crt.* I. x. 142 Around which the meaner houses and shops of the present day clustered. **1871** FREEMAN *Norm. Conq.* (1876) IV. xvii. 92 The robes of state.. made all that France .. had beheld of the same kind seem mean by comparison. **1874** MICKLETHWAITE *Mod. Par. Churches* 245 Let not your altar be mean and your stove conspicuous.

¶**4.** ***no mean*** ——: often = 'no contemptible', applied eulogistically to a person or thing.

1596 SHAKS. *Merch. V.* I. ii. 7 (1st Qo 1600) It is no meane [1623 smal] happinesse therefore to be seated in the meane. **1611** BIBLE *Acts* xxi. 39 A citizen of no meane citie. **1678** BUTLER *Hud.* III. iii. 245 Hence timely Running's no mean part Of Conduct, in the Martial Art. **1708** J. PHILIPS *Cyder* I. 589 The Roman Legions and great Cæsar found Our Fathers no mean Foes. **1791** BOSWELL *Johnson* (1831) I. 136 His correspondence with him, during many years, proves that he had no mean opinion of him. **1875** E. WHITE *Life in Christ* II. xvii. (1878) 224 *note*, Mr. Cox, himself no mean Rabbinical scholar, adds [etc.].

5. a. Of persons, their characters and actions: Destitute of moral dignity or elevation; ignoble, small-minded.

1665 BOYLE *Occas. Refl.* IV. xii. (1848) 243 The Sublimity of such a Condition would make any Soul, that is not very mean, despise many mean things. **1724** RAMSAY *Vision* xi, He.. did me rebuke, For being of sprite sae mein. **1734** POPE *Ess. Man* IV. 282 Think how Bacon shin'd, The wisest, brightest, meanest of mankind. **1741** MIDDLETON *Cicero* I. vi. 449 A mean submission to illegal power. **1768** STERNE *Sent. Journ.* (1778) II. 39 (*Address*), How many mean plans .. did my servile heart form! **1771** *Junius Lett.* xlix, The meanest and the basest fellow in the kingdom. **1815** W. H. IRELAND *Scribleomania* 25 Rhymsters who.. meanest actions eulogize. **1830** D'ISRAELI *Chas. I*, III. viii. 187 Charles the Second.. was mean enough to suspend her pension. **1874** GREEN *Short Hist.* viii. §2. 469 James had meaner motives for his policy of peace than a hatred of bloodshedding. **1888** BRYCE *Amer. Commw.* III. xcv. 336 Good citizens who were occupied in.. more engrossing ways, allowed politics to fall into the hands of mean men.

b. orig. *U.S. colloq.* In trivial applications: 'Disobliging, pettily offensive or unaccommodating' (*Cent. Dict.*). Also, ***to feel mean***: to feel ashamed of one's conduct, to feel guilty of unfairness or unkindness.

(*a*) **1839** MARRYAT *Diary Amer.* Ser. I. II. 224 Mean is occasionally used for ashamed. 'I never felt so mean in all my life'. **1841** 'DOW, JR.' *Short Patent Sermons* 78 [One girl] thought me real mean for uttering such super-diabolical sentiments. **1891** R. T. COOKE *Huckleberries* 14 It would be awful mean of me to leave you here alone.

(*b*) **1862** R. H. NEWELL *Orpheus C. Kerr Papers* 1st Ser. ii. 21 I see he felt powerful mean, so I walked up to him. **1884** 'MARK TWAIN' *Huck. Finn* xli. 421 [She] tucked me in, and mothered me so good I felt mean.

c. *U.S. slang.* Of a horse, etc.: Vicious.

1848 *Georgia Scenes* 27 He'll cut the same capers there as here. He's a monstrous mean horse. **1887** F. FRANCIS Jun. *Saddle & Mocassin* 146 He [a cowboy] gets all-fired mean sometimes when he's full. **1888** ROOSEVELT in *Century Mag.* Oct. 836/1 There can be no greater provocation than is given by a 'mean' horse or a refractory steer.

d. *colloq.* (orig. *U.S.*). Remarkably clever, adroit, etc.; excellent; formidable.

1920 H. C. WITWER in *Collier's* 15 May 6/3 Everything was jake until K. O. Krouse shook a mean dice and win $28 from Battlin' Lewis on the way to Toledo. *Ibid.* 57/2 You never heard tell of Kane Halliday?.. The big.. football star, the weights thrower.. what they call a round-about athalete? *You* know, one of them bimbos which flings a wicked spear and hurls a mean hammer and that there stuff, get me? *Ibid.* 62/2 Your wonder child may pack a mean wallop. **1924** *Ladies' Home Jrnl.* Feb. 21/1 'That Lucy Layman sure does shake a mean foot,' began Edmond airily. **1931** D. RUNYON *Guys & Dolls* (1932) iii. 64 She swings a very mean skillet, and gets me up some very tasty fodder. **1963** *Economist* 23 Nov. 775/2 Mr. Ronnie Scott.. plays a mean saxophone. **1968** *Globe & Mail* (Toronto) 13 Jan. 34/7 He blows a mean trumpet and sings well, too. **1973** *Observer* 9 Sept. 30/3 Does a mean goulash, taught him by his grandmother and perfected in Hungary. **1973** *Listener* 25 Oct. 578/2 Jack Palance smokes a mean cigar in *Oklahoma Crude.*

6. Penurious, wanting in liberality, 'stingy'.

1755–1822 [implied in MEANNESS^1 5]. **1860** in WORCESTER. **1872** T. L. CUYLER *Heart-Culture* 96 The meanest of misers is he who hoards a truth. **1876** GEO. ELIOT *Dan. Der.* xxxv, At least he is not mean about money.

7. a. *Comb.*: parasynthetic, as ***mean-apparelled***, ***-conditioned***, ***-faced***, ***-gifted***, ***-souled***, ***-spirited***, ***-witted*** adjs.; whence ***mean-spiritedness***, etc.; predicative, as ***mean-born***, ***-looking*** adjs; adverbial, as †***mean-dressed*** adj.

1534 MORE *Comf. agst. Trib.* I. xii. (1847) 40 Mean-witted men. **1593** SHAKS. *2 Hen. VI*, III. i. 335 Let pale-fac't feare keepe with the meane-borne man. **1596** —— *Tam. Shr.* III. ii. 75 Oftentimes he goes but meane-apparel'd. *a* **1620** J. DYKE *Worthy Commun.* (1640) 81 Shall a poore, mean conditioned woman refuse the offer of a Rich husband. *a* **1683** OLDHAM *Poet. Wks.* (1686) 103 Mean-soul'd offenders now no honours gain. **1694** F. BRAGGE *Disc. Parables* viii. 293 Away with that mean-spirited religion. **1699** M. HENRY *Meekness of Spirit* (1822) 63 Meekness is commonly despised as a piece of cowardice and mean-spiritedness. **1740–87** *Lett. Miss Talbot* etc. (1808) 19 A mean dressed man got into a tree, and from thence harangued them. **1782** MISS BURNEY *Cecilia* v. vi., Here a mean-looking man.. came up to Mr. Hobson. **1824** T. FENBY *Refl.* iii, Fortune's meaner-gifted, homely maids. **1918** MRS. BELLOC LOWNDES *Out of the War?* 211 Thin, mean-faced, yet sharply intelligent-looking man. **1953** E. S. GRENFELL in C. K. Stead *N.Z. Short Stories* (1966) 69 A shiftless, mean-faced fellow.

†**B.** *adv.*^{1} = MEANLY. *Obs.*

a **1626** BACON *Chr. Paradoxes* Wks. 1879 I. 341 When he is ablest, he thinks meanest of himself. **1719** DE FOE *Crusoe* II. (Globe) 553 If he fed them meaner than he was fed himself.. they must fare very coarsely indeed. **1861** O. W. NORTON *Army Lett.* (1903) 26 Virginia has acted meaner than South Carolina.

mean (miːn), *a.*² and *adv.*² Forms: 4–6 **men**, 4–5 **meene**, 4–6 **mene**, 4–7 **meane**, 5 **meen**, **meyn**, 5–6 **meyne**, **mæne**, **meaine**, *Sc.* **meine**, 6–7 *Sc.* **mein**, 5– **mean**. See also MESNE, MOYEN. [a. OF. *men*, *meen*, *meien*, *moien* (mod.F. *moyen*) = Pr. *meian*, Sp., Pg. *mediano*, It. *mezzano*:—late L. *mediānus* that is in the middle, f. *medius* middle: see MID *a.*]

A. *adj.*

†**1. a.** Occupying a middle or an intermediate place in order of enumeration or in spatial position. ***mean term*** (Logic) = 'middle term'. *Obs.*

1340 *Ayenb.* 122 And al alsuo ase ine heuene heþ þri stages of uolke..huer-of þe on is heȝere þe oþer men þe þridde loȝest. *c* **1380** WYCLIF *Wks.* (1880) 270 Crist, mene persone in trinyte. **1435** *Rolls of Parlt.* IV. 493/1 To repaire unto Pruce, and to the Townes of the mene Hans. **1541** R. COPLAND *Guydon's Quest. Chirurg.* E ij, The places called lacune..be in the meane ventrycle. **1541** *Act 33 Hen. VIII*, c. 15 Al places meane betwene Manchester and Westchester. **1727–52** CHAMBERS *Cycl.*, *Medium*, in logic, or medium of a syllogism, called also the *mean*, or *middle term*. **1822** G. ROLANDO *Fencing* (ed. Forsyth) 100 The Counter of Carte parade..parries, the wrist in the mean position inclined outside the arm, the following thrusts.

†**b.** *Mus.* Applied to the tenor and alto parts and the tenor clef, as intermediate between the bass and treble. *Obs.*

1597 MORLEY *Introd. Mus.* 17 An example of augmentation..in the Treble and Meane parts. **1674** PLAYFORD *Skill Mus.* I. i. 2 Three several Parts of Musick, into which the Scale is divided, first the Bass,..secondly, the Mean, or middle part, and thirdly the Treble. **1721** A. MALCOLM *Treat. Mus.* xi. 333 The Treble or *g* Clef is ordinarily set on the 2*d* Line..and the mean or *c* Clef on the 3*d* Line... The mean Clef which most frequently changes Place.

†**c.** ***in the mean way***: on the way, in the course of one's journey. *Obs.*

1568 GRAFTON *Chron.* II. 559 The Erle of Arundell.. departed to Mauns, and in the meane way, tooke the Castels of Mellay and saint Laurence. *Ibid.* 563 In the meane way they encountered with syr Thomas Kiriell [etc.]. **1613** PURCHAS *Pilgrimage* (1614) 837 In the meane way they passed by the Tapemiry Paraibæ [etc.].

2. Intermediate in time; coming between two points of time or two events; intervening. Now only in phrases ***in the mean time***, ***while*** (see MEANTIME, MEANWHILE); formerly, in the same sense, †***in the mean season***, ***space***, ***way***. Also with omission of prep., †***the mean season***, †***mean space***; and MEANTIME, MEANWHILE *advs.*

1464 *Rolls of Parlt.* V. 569/2 Aswell for the sustentation of youre people of the seid Townes, as of all youre people of youre Shires in the mean waye. *c* **1500** *Melusine* 347 And þat meane sayson came two knightes to Lucembourgh. **1519** *Interl. Four Elem.* (Percy Soc.) 50 And for lacke of mynstrelles, the mean season, Now wyll we begyn to syng. **1532** MORE *Conf. Tindale* Wks. 460/1 In the meane waye marke me this. **1539** CROMWELL in Merriman *Life & Lett.* (1902) II. 216, I have in this meane space devised a fourme of Instructions for Mr. Sadleyer. **1600** *Maydes Metam.* v. in Bond *Lyly's Wks.* (1902) III. 386 Meane space, vpon his Harpe will Phœbus play. **1606** G. W[OODCOCKE] *Hist. Ivstine* VI. 32 Meane space word was brought that Agesilaus was very neere at hand. **1627** J. CARTER *Plain Expos.* 112 When the performance of Gods promise is long delayed, and nothing almost appeareth in the meane season,..then [etc.]. *a* **1677** HALE *Prim. Orig. Man.* 305 There was no mean portion of Time between their Formation and Animation,.. they were living Beings..as soon as they were formed. **1760–72** H. BROOKE *Fool of Qual.* (1809) III. 83 In the mean space..Jenkins had his right leg..carried off by a cannon shot.

3. *Law.* Intermediate, either in time or status. Usually spelt MESNE.

1439 *Rolls of Parlt.* V. 15/2 To be holden mene betwene ye date of ye seide Writ, and ye day of ye returne yerof. **1509–10** *Act 1 Hen. VIII*, c. 12 §2 They..shall nott be restored to any meane issues or Profyttes of Landes. **1535** *Act 27 Hen. VIII*, c. 22 The lordes immediat & thother meane lords haue not put the..acte in dewe and plaine execucion. **1548** STAUNFORD *King's Prerog.* (1567) 84 b, The king shal haue the meane issues. **1670** PETTUS *Fodinæ Reg.* 20 It is good for Princes, and even for mean Lords, to keep a Claim to their Prerogatives and Customes. **1700** *Col. Rec. Pennsylv.* II. 9 Griffith Jones, first purchaser and Henry Elfrith mean purchaser under him complain. **1707** E. CHAMBERLAYNE *Pres. St. Eng.* II. ii. 78 If the mean Patron present not in due Time.., the Right of Presentation comes to the King.

†**4.** Intermediary; employed as an agent or 'go-between'; serving as a means or instrument; done for an ulterior end; intervening as part of a process. Also ***mean way***: the course adopted to achieve an end. *Obs.*

1377 LANGL. *P. Pl.* B. IX. 112 Þe wyf was made þe weye for to help worche, And þus was wedloke ywrouȝt with a mene persone. *c* **1380** WYCLIF *Wks.* (1880) 278 Þat þe sotil amortasynge of seculer lordischipis þat is don bi menene [? *read* mene] hondis in fraude of þe statute be visely enquyred. **1382** —— *Gen.* xlii. 23 Bi a mene persone vndoynge both the langagis [L. *per interpretem*]. *c* **1440** *Jacob's Well* 205 Bothe þe theef & þe rauenere owyn to aske forȝifnesse slely be hem-self, or be an-oþer meen persone. *c* **1449** PECOCK *Repr.* III. ix. 332 Crist ȝaf mediatli, (that is to seie, bi meene ȝiftis to his clergie,) the endewing of immouable godis. **1451** *Paston Lett.* I. 215, I proferid hym..ye wold..leve a summe if he wold a named it in a mene mannys hand, and seche as he hath trust to. **1509** FISHER *Funeral Serm. C'tess Richmond* Wks. (1876) 296 Oftentymes by herself she wolde..courage euery of them to doo well. And somtyme by other meane persones. **1549** RIDLEY *Let. to Somerset* in R. Potts *Liber Cantabr.* (1855) I. 245–6 No faut can be found ether in hir entent or in the mean ways whearby she wrought to accomplishe the same. **1563** *Homilies* II. *Peril of Idolatry* III. (1859) 228 To be mean intercessors and helpers to God. **1615** CROOKE *Body of Man* 55 The mutation or change of bloud into a bone, cannot be accomplished but by long interpolation and many meane alterations.

5. a. Intermediate in kind, quality, or degree. Now *rare.*

1340 HAMPOLE *Pr. Consc.* 3187 Þa er veniel synnes þat may falle, Bathe grete and smale, and men with-alle. **1375** BARBOUR *Bruce* VI. 347 For-thi has vorschip sic renoune That it is mene [*ed. Hart* mid] betuix thai tua [*sc.* 'fule-hardyment' and 'cowardiss']. **1398** TREVISA *Barth. De P.R.* XIX. vii. (1495) 865 Aristotle rehercith thise fyue meane coloures by name: and callith the fyrste yelowe and the seconde cytryne and the thyrde red the fourth purpure and the fyfthe grene. **1551** TURNER *Herbal.* I. (1568) 12 Venus heyre is in mean tempre betwene hote and colde. **1587** HARRISON *Eng.* I. vi. 14/1 in *Holinshed*, Ours is a meane language, and neither too rough nor too smooth in vtterance. **1601** HOLLAND *Pliny* II. 328 Of this Sinopis..there be three kindes, the deepe red, the pale or weake red, and the meane between both. **1610** WILLET *Hexapla Dan.* 297 The meane opinion betweene these is the best. **1656** STANLEY *Hist. Philos.* IV. (1701) 134/2 Of affections, some are pleasant, some harsh and troublesome, some mean:..the mean are neither good nor ill. **1703** T. N. *City & C. Purchaser* 131 Sculpture..wherein the Figure sticks out from the Plain whereon it is Engraven,..according as it is more or less protuberant, is call'd..Bas-relief, Mean-relief, or High-relief. **1871** MORLEY *Crit. Misc.* Ser. I. *Vauvenargues* (1878) 20 We must take them in pairs to find out the mean truth. **1888** BRYCE *Amer. Commw.* III. c. 414 Many experiments may be needed before the true mean course between these extremes is discovered.

†**b.** ***mean way*** [= L. *via media*]: a middle course (as an escape from a proposed alternative).

c **1374** CHAUCER *Anel. & Arc.* 286 Ther ben non other mene weyes newe. *c* **1400** *Rom. Rose* 4844 Men this thenken ..That lasse harm is..Disceyve them, than disceyved be.. wher they ne may Finde non other mene wey. *c* **1407** LYDG. *Reas. & Sens.* 4667 Ther was non other mene weye. **1706** Z. CRADOCK *Serm. Charity* (1740) 17 All the mean way partakes more or less..of both the opposite extreams.

†**c.** *spec.* (*a*) said of the middle condition between extremes of fortune; (*b*) said of the married state as contrasted with continence on the one hand and unchastity on the other. *Obs.*

c **1540** R. MORICE in *Lett. Lit. Men* (Camden) 24 If he coulde not lyve chast..he shoulde tak a wif and lyve a meane lyf. *a* **1541** WYATT in *Tottel's Misc.* (Arb.) 83 (*title*) Of the meane and sure estate.

6. Not far above or below the average; moderate, mediocre, middling.

†**a.** Of or with reference to size, stature, or age.

c **1374** CHAUCER *Troylus* V. 806 Criseyde mene was of here stature. **1398** TREVISA *Barth. De P.R.* V. xxv. (1495) 134 In foure foted beestes wyth thycke bodyes and meane thyes, the necke is shorte grete and moche strengthe of suche bestes is in the necke. **1484** CAXTON *Fables of Æsop* VI. xvi, A man of a meane age whiche tooke two wyues. **1490** —— *Eneydos* xxix. 112 A meane noose, not to grete nor to lytell, wythout ouer grete openynge. **1544** PHAER *Regim. Lyfe* (1553) H viij, Geue..at euery time the quantity of a meane chesnutte. *a* **1548** HALL *Chron. Hen. IV* 32 b, This kyng was of a mean stature wel proporcioned and formally compact. **1575–6** in Nichols *Progr. Eliz.* (1823) II. 2, Two mene perles pendaunte. **1579–80** *Ibid.* 290 A snake with a meane white saphire on the hedd. **1577** B. GOOGE *Heresbach's Husb.* I. (1586) 13 b, Of a meane age, that he be not vnwylling to woorke for youth, nor vnable to trauayle for age. **1657** W. COLES *Adam in Eden* liii, It is of the height and bignesse of a mean tree. **1697** DAMPIER *Voy.* (1729) I. 395 Their Noses of a mean bigness.

†**b.** Having some quality in moderate degree. Of wines: ? Moderate in alcoholic strength. Of the voice: Moderately loud. Of soil: Moderately fertile. *Obs.*

c **1420** *Pallad. on Husb.* I. 79 Yf hit [mould] be lene, hit gooth in al and more; Yf hit be mene [L. *mediocris*], hit wol be with the brinke. *c* **1450** LYDG. & BURGH *Secrees* 2647 Meene in voys neythir to grete nor smalle, Signe is of trewthe and rightwysnesse. **1542** BOORDE *Dyetary* x. (1870) 255 Meane wynes, as wynes of Gascony, Frenche wynes, & specyally Raynysshe wyne that is fyned, is good with meate. **1577** B. GOOGE *Heresbach's Husb.* I. (1586) 25 After a croppe of Rye in meane ground, you shall haue the same yeere great Rapes. **1607** NORDEN *Surv. Dial.* v. 233, I have seene thistles in meane ground. **1679** PULLER *Moder. Ch. Eng.* (1843) 115 A voice mean and grave, fit to excite devotion

†**c.** Moderate in amount, or in degree of excellence; tolerable, mediocre. (In later use only with disparaging implication, and so coincident with MEAN *a.*¹) *Obs.*

c **1460** *Towneley Myst.* ii. 111 My wynnyngis ar bot meyn, No wonder if that I be leyn. **1494** FABYAN *Chron.* VI. cxciv. 197 She was..but of meane fayrenesse as other women were. **1546** *Yorks. Chantry Surv.* (Surtees) II. 213 Of honest qualities and condicions, and meane lerenyng. **1551** ROBINSON tr. *More's Utop.* II. (1895) 171 The resydewe they sell at reasonable and meane price. **1580** LYLY *Euphues* (Arb.) 308 Let thy apparell be but meane, neyther too braue ..nor too base. **1600** HOLLAND *Livy* XLII. lxvi. 1155 The Consull contenting himselfe with a meane good hand.. retired with his forces into the campe. **1604** E. G[RIMSTONE] *D'Acosta's Hist. Indies* IV. xxxiii. 299 In that countrie it is but a meane wealth. *a* **1628** PRESTON *New Covt.* (1634) 24 It is better for thee..to have meane gifts, than to have high gifts. **1719** DE FOE *Crusoe* II. ii, My own house..where I should see there had been but mean improvements.

†**d.** Using moderation; temperate. *Obs.*

c **1425** *Eng. Conq. Irel.* 88 He was..[of] mete, & of drynke ful meen & for-berynge.

7. *Math.* **a.** Of an amount or value: Having such a relation to the amounts or values occurring in a given set of instances that the algebraical sum of their differences from it is zero; that is an arithmetical mean. Hence used (as in ***mean motion***, ***diameter***, ***distance***, ***temperature***, etc.) in concord with a designation of variable concrete quantity, to express the mean value of this. ***mean sun***: a fictitious sun, supposed for purposes of calculation to move in the celestial equator at the mean rate of the real sun. ***mean*** (***solar***) ***time***: the time of day as it would be shown by the 'mean sun' (the time shown by an ordinary correctly regulated clock); so ***mean noon***, etc. ***mean square***: the (arithmetical) mean of the squares of a set of numbers; ***mean-square deviation*** (***mean-square error***, †***error of mean square***): the mean of the squares of the differences between a set of numbers and some fixed number; usu. identical with the variance; formerly, †the square root of this (usu. identical with the standard deviation). Cf. MEAN TONE (*Mus.*).

c **1391** CHAUCER *Astrol.* II. §44 The residue is the mene mote for the same day and the same houre. **1694** HOLDER *Disc. Time* 20 According to the Mean Motion of the Sun. **1704** J. HARRIS *Lex. Techn.* I, *Mean Motion* or *Mean Longitude of the Sun*, in the Ptolomaick Hypothesis, is an Ark of the Ecliptick, reckoned from the Beginning of Aries to the Line of the Sun's Mean Motion. **1709** J. WARD *Yng. Math. Guide* (1734) 455 By the Bung and Head Diameters, find such a mean Diameter as you judge will Reduce the propos'd Cask to a Cylinder. **1742–3** LD. HERVEY in *Johnson's Debates* (1787) II. 309 The produce of the customs was the last year less by half a million than the mean revenue. **1743** EMERSON *Fluxions* 299 If the mean Radius of the Earth be 21000000, then [etc.]. **1798** MALTHUS *Popul.* (1817) I. 470 In the Pays de Vaud the lowest mean life..is 29½ years. **1845** *Encycl. Metrop.* II. 460, *k'* and *k''* are approximately found by taking the actual mean, and the actual mean square, of a large number of observed durations. Again, the mean risk of error in estimating a single duration is $\cdot 39894\sqrt{[(k'' - k'^2) \div s]}$. **1860** MAURY *Phys. Geog. Sea* (Low) v. §282 Rain-gauges will give us the mean annual rain-fall. **1878** HUXLEY *Physiogr.* 200 The constant temperature being nearly the mean temperature of the surface. **1878** PETRIE in *Jrnl. Anthrop. Inst.* (1879) VIII. 113 The circle divided into equal squares is apparently not so accurate, the mean error being 7 inches on 130 feet. **1894** Error of mean square [see DEVIATION 2 d]. **1956** A. A. TOWNSEND *Struct. Turbulent Shear Flow* iii. 44 The contributions to the mean-square rate of strain of the eddies larger than $1/k$ come mostly from values of $E(k')$ for k' near k. **1968** R. A. LYTTLETON *Mysteries Solar Syst.* vii. 245 This regrouping of the equations of condition..results in a further reduction of the number of unknowns at the price.. of increasing the mean-square error associated with each equation. **1970** S. BRANDT *Statistical & Computational Methods* vi. 83 A sum of squares..divided by the number of degrees of freedom is called the mean square or more explicitly the mean-square deviation... Its square root (which has the dimension of the measured quantity, i.e. the mean) has the lengthy name root-mean-square deviation.

b. ***mean proportional***: the middle one of three quantities, of which the first has the same ratio to the second as the second has to the third. ***extreme and mean ratio*** (or †***proportion***): see EXTREME *a.* 1 b.

Originally *mean* was the sb. and *proportional* the adj. (cf. F. *moyenne proportionnelle*); but as the expression is now apprehended the functions of the words are reversed.

1571 DIGGES *Pantom.*, *Math. Treat.* viii. X iij b, The Ooctaedrons side is meane proportionall betweene the diameter and semidiameter of the circumscribing sphere. **1608** R. NORTON tr. *Stevin's Disme* D iij b, Seeke the meane proportionall betweene BM and his 10 part BR.

†**8.** *Gram.* Of a verb: In the middle voice, reflexive. *Obs.*

1530 PALSGR. Introd. 33 The mean verbes have also thre dyvers sortes of conjugations. *Ibid.* 632/2. **1583** FULKE *Defence* v. 151 Πληροῦμαι..is often taken passiuely: But seeing it is also found to be a verbe meane, who neede to be afraide to vse it actiuely?

B. *adv.*

†**1.** Moderately; also, comparatively less. *Obs.*

1398 TREVISA *Barth. De P.R.* XVII. ii. (1495) 595 By crafte of tyllynge..pome garnade is made meane soure. **1535** JOYE *Apol. Tindale* (Arb.) 20 Printed the new testament in a mean great volume. **1565** JEWEL *Def. Apol.* (1611) 101 A mean learned man may vnderstand it wel enough. **1576** BAKER *Jewell of Health* 231 b, When out of this you shall have drawne a cuppe meane full,..distyll it againe in Balneo Mariæ. **1612** W. SCLATER *Minister's Portion* 42 The meane wealthy amongst their people.

2. Intermediately (in time or character).

1548 STAUNFORD *King's Prerog.* (1567) 47 For that that hee that is outlawed was emprisoned meane betweene the awardynge of the exigent and the outlawrie pronounced. **1561** T. NORTON *Calvin's Inst.* I. 54 They in going meane betwene the Philosophers opinions and the heauenly doctrine are plainly deceiued. **1577–87** HOLINSHED *Chron.* III. 1243/1 Which office it seemeth that he had, meane betweene the twelfe and the foureteenth yeare of the said king. *a* **1625** SIR H. FINCH *Law* (1636) 46 Any such thing done meane betwixt the verdict and the iudgement. **1642** tr. *Perkins' Prof. Bk.* xi. §837. 38 If meane, after the first demand and before the latter end of the moneth the lessor doe happen to come.

mean (miːn), *v.*¹ Pa. t. and pa. pple. **meant** (mɛnt). Forms: 1 **mǽnan**, 3 **mæinen**, 3–7 **mene**, **meane**, 4 **men**, **meen**, 4–5 **meene**, 4–6 **meine**, *Sc.*

meyn(e, 5 menne, 6–7 mein, 6– mean. *Pa. t.* α. 1 **mǣnde,** 3 **mende,** 4 **meenede, mennede,** 4–5 **mened,** 4–6 *Sc.* **menit, -yt,** 5 **menyd,** 6 *Sc.* **meynd, meind, me(i)nit,** 6–9 **meaned,** (6 *Sc.* **-it**); β. 4–5 **mente,** 4–7 **ment,** 6– **meant.** *Pa. pple.* α. 1 **(ȝe)mǣned,** 5 **meened,** 6–9 **meaned;** β. 4–5 **yment,** 5 **imente, imeynt;** 4–5 **mente,** 4–7 **ment,** 6– **meant.** [Com. WGer.: OE. *mǣnan* = OFris. *mêna* to signify, OS. *mênian* to intend, signify, make known (MLG., MDu. *mênen*, mod.Du. *meenen*), OHG. *meinen* to have in mind (hence also, to love), to intend, signify, make known, mention (MHG. and mod.G. *meinen*, now chiefly, to have in one's mind, to hold or express an opinion); cf. the compounds, OS. *gimênian* to make known, OHG. *gemeinen* to proclaim, show forth, *bimeinen* to decree, destine, dedicate (whence *bimeinida* testament). The Scandinavian forms, Icel. *meina*, Sw. *mena*, Da. *mene*, are from Low German.

The W.Ger. **mainjan* is cogn. w. OFris. *mêne* opinion, OHG. *meina* fem., ? opinion (found only in Otfrid in certain phrases, *thia meina, bî thia meina*, etc., meaning 'verily', 'forsooth'). Outside Teut., the OSl. formal equivalent, *měniti*, exhibits an extraordinarily close parallelism of meaning, having all the varied senses of the OE. and OS. verb. The ultimate etymology and the order of sense-development are doubtful; the prevailing view that the root is **men-* to think (see MIND *sb.*) would account plausibly for all the recorded senses, but involves phonological difficulties that have not been satisfactorily disposed of.]

1. a. *trans.* To have in mind as a purpose or intention; to purpose, design. Chiefly with *inf.* as obj., less frequently with *clause* or *sb.*

In modern colloquial use sometimes: To intend with determined purpose.

For *to mean business, mischief*, see the sbs.

c **888** K. ÆLFRED *Boeth.* xxxix. §5 Þa ongan he sprecan swiðe fiorran ymbutan, swilce he na þa spræce ne mænde, & tiohhode hit ðeah þiderweardes. *c* **1300** *Leg. St. Gregory* 742 Þan alon sche left þer inne, Non wist what sche ment. **13..** *K. Alis.* 5942 Thoo had kynge Alisaunder y-ment.. The cee haue y-passed ayein. *c* **1374** CHAUCER *Troylus* II. 532 (581) And syn ye woot þat myn entent is clene, Tak hede þer-of, for I noon yuel mene. *c* **1440** *York Myst.* xxx. 494 A! mercy, lorde, mekely, no malice we mente. **1560** DAUS tr. *Sleidane's Comm.* 70 b, The Duke of Saxon, and the Lantgrave,.. ment to go home. **1567** *Reg. Privy Council Scot.* I. 515 Hir Majestie menit to subvert the lawis. **1612** BACON *Ess., Wisd. for Man's Self* (Arb.) 184 Except they meane their seruice should bee made but the accessary. **1617** MORYSON *Itin.* I. 40 These cut-throates.. meant presently to returne. **1692** DRYDEN *Cleomenes* II. i. 11 Thou art only Misplanted in a base degenerate Soil; But Nature when she made thee, meant a Spartan. **1773** GOLDSM. *Stoops to Conq.* IV, You only mean to banter me. **1845** SIR C. J. NAPIER *Conq. Scinde* II. viii. 455 The Beloochs certainly meaned to break out with a counter attack. **1895** KEKEWICH in *Law Times Rep.* LXXIII. 663/2 We must not jump to the conclusion that the Legislature meant to interfere with contracts. **1904** MAJ. A. GRIFFITHS *Fifty Yrs. Publ. Service* ii. 22 Even to my young and inexperienced eyes it seemed that the attack [on the Redan] was never 'meant'.

†**b.** with ellipsis of vb. of motion. *Obs.*

c **1470** HARDING *Chron.* IX. i, With shyppes .xii. to Italy had they mente.

†**c.** To aim at, direct one's way to. *Obs. rare.*

c **1400** *Laud Troy Bk.* 4172 Gret schame it is.. That we durst neuere Troye mene. **1633** G. HERBERT *Temple, Ch. Porch* lvi, Who aimeth at the sky Shoots higher much than he that means a tree. **1706** WATTS *Horæ Lyr.* I. 100 The muse ascends her heavenly car, And climbs the steepy path and means the throne divine.

d. To design (a thing) for a definite purpose; to intend or destine (a person or thing) to a fate or use. Const. *against, for,* †*to*; rarely *dative.* †Also with complement, to destine to be (*obs.*).

a **1400** *Octouian* 1953 The old emperesse.. hadde the same jugement That sche to Florance hadde y-ment. **1560** DAUS tr. *Sleidane's Comm.* 242 b, This warre is not ment nor prepared against the Cyties. **1580** SIDNEY *Ps.* XXVII. v, When greate griefes to me be ment, In tabernacle his, he will Hide me. **1611** BIBLE *Gen.* l. 20 God meant it vnto good. **1634** MILTON *Comus* 765 She [*sc.* Nature] good cateress Means her provision onely to the good That live according to her sober laws. **1639** SHIRLEY *Gent. Ven.* v. ii, Providence.. made me worth a strangers piety, Whom your cho[i]ce meant the ruine of my honor. **1643** DENHAM *Cooper's Hill* 325 Fair Liberty pursu'd, and meant a Prey To lawless power, here turn'd. **1792** J. BARLOW *Conspir. Kings* 83 Why to small realms for ever rest confin'd Our great affections, meant for all mankind? **1842** BROWNING *Through the Metidja* v, Ere I pried, she [Fate] should hide.. All that's meant me. **1884** W. C. SMITH *Kildrostan* 57, I think Fate meant us for each other. **1896** A. E. HOUSMAN *Shropshire Lad* lxii, Say, for what were hop-yards meant, Or why was Burton built on Trent?

e. To intend (a remark, allusion, etc.) to have a particular reference. Const. †*at,* †*by, of,* †*to.* Also †absol. ***to mean by*** = to intend to refer to.

In the 16th c. *to mean* (a remark or a designation) *by* (a person) was the usual expression where we now say 'to mean (such or such a person) by (a remark, etc.)', the vb. being then in sense 2.

1513 MORE *Edw. V*, Wks. 55/2 That ment he by the lordes of the quenes kindred that were taken before. **1542** UDALL *Erasm. Apoph.* 230 b, He saied that he would leaue.. suche a successour... Menyng by Tiberius. **1570** *Satir. Poems Reform.* xix. 8 Gone is the Joy and gyde of this Natioun; I mene be James, Regent of Scotland. **1596** SPENSER *State Irel.* Wks. (Globe) 621, I do not meane this by the Princes wardes. **1641** SANDERSON *Serm.* (1681) II. 184 A flaunting hyperbole, far beyond the merit of the Party he meant it to. **1749** CHESTERF. *Lett.* (1792) II. 230 He.. thinks every thing that is said meant at him. **1753** *Ibid.* IV. 13 They are convinced that it was meant at them. *a* **1906** *Mod.* I wonder whether he meant it of any one in particular.

f. *intr.* To be (*well, ill,* etc.) intentioned or disposed. Const. *to, by,* or *dative.* ***to mean well*** (used ironically).

c **1374** CHAUCER *Troylus* III. 115 (164) By-sechyng hym.. þat he wolde.. eke mene wel to me. *c* **1412** HOCCLEVE *De Reg. Princ.* 1986 But how I speke, algate I mene weel. *c* **1440** *Promp. Parv.* 332/2 Menyn yn herte, wel or evyl, *intendo.* *c* **1450** tr. *De Imitatione* I. xii. 13 Þouȝ we do wel & mene wel. *c* **1590** GREENE *Fr. Bacon* vi. 9 Now shall Edward trie How Lacy meaneth to his Soueraigne Lord. **1601** SHAKS. *Twel. N.* IV. iii. 22 If you meane well Now go with me. **1628** EARLE *Microcosm., Reseru'd Man*, He.. puts himselfe to a great deale of affliction to hinder their plots, and designes where they meane freely. *a* **1680** BUTLER *Rem.* (1759) I. 58 The purest Business of our Zeal Is but to err, by meaning well. **1719** DE FOE *Crusoe* II. xi, You seem to mean honestly. **1771** *Junius Lett.* xlv. (1820) 243 They who object to [his] last letter, either do not mean him fairly, or [etc.]. **1802** BEDDOES *Hygëia* II. 34 The projector of a new domestic medicine, meaning well by himself and the public. **1813** JANE AUSTEN *Pride & Prej.* III. v. 108 Perhaps she *meant* well, but, under such a misfortune as this, one cannot see too little of one's neighbours. **1884** RIDER HAGGARD *Dawn* ii, I do not think that your cousin means kindly by you. **1889** F. ANSTEY in *Granta* 17 May 9/2 Still, with all their presumption, they meant well, poor fellows! **1910** R. BROOKE *Let.* 9 Jan. (1968) 206 He *is* a silly man... Yet he means well. **1961** G. SMITH *Business of Loving* ix. 206 Felix obviously meant well. **1973** S. B. JACKMAN *Guns covered with Flowers* x. 159 He smiled apologetically, 'He means well'. Stevens grinned. 'And you can't say worse than that about anyone.'

2. a. *trans.* To intend to indicate (a certain object), or to convey (a certain sense) when using some word, sentence, significant action, etc. Sometimes with *clause* as obj. In mod. use often const. *by.*

c **888** K. ÆLFRED *Boeth.* xxxviii. §2 ȝif he þara nan nyte, þonne nat he hwæt he mænð. *c* **1000** ÆLFRIC *Gen.* xviii. 20 God þa ȝeopenude Abrahame, hwæt he mid þære spræce mænde. *c* **1200** *Trin. Coll. Hom.* 11 Wat þe holie apostle meneð þo he nemnede niht and niehtes dede. *c* **1275** *Wom. Samaria* 27 in *O.E. Misc.* 85 Heo nuste hwat heo mende heo wes of wytte poure. *a* **1300** *Cursor M.* 12631 Quat he wit þis wordes ment, Graithli wist þai noght þe entent. *c* **1375** *Sc. Leg. Saints* xv. (*Barnabas*) 89 Gyf ȝe will wit quhat ve meyne. *c* **1380** WYCLIF *Sel. Wks.* II. 6 And sum men seien þat Crist meenide þat he himsilf.. is more þan Joon Baptist. **1415** HOCCLEVE *To Sir J. Oldcastle* 1 The laddre of heuene, I meene charitee. **1513** DOUGLAS *Æneis* I. Prol. 387 Tuichand our tongis penurite, I mene onto compair of fair Latyne [etc.]. **1530** PALSGR. 444/2 He becked at me, but I wyste nat what he ment. **1617** MORYSON *Itin.* I. 68 The twelfth day.. wee rode foure miles (meaning Dutch miles). **1644** DIGBY *Nat. Bodies* xviii. §2. 158 When we have examined this, we shall vnderstand in what sense it is meaned that Nature abhorreth from Vacuity. **1671** MILTON *P.R.* II. 6, I mean Andrew and Simon. **1711** STEELE *Spect.* No. 136 ⁋4, I mean by this Town the Cities of London and Westminster. **1782** MISS BURNEY *Cecilia* IV. x, In both which [*sc.* reproof and compliment] more seemed meant than met the ear. **1825** COBBETT *Rur. Rides* 442 And what is meaned by 'The fear of the Lord'? **1895** KEKEWICH in *Law Times Rep.* LXXIII. 663/1 The Act does not mean literally what it says.

b. *transf.* in questions of the form ***what does*** (a person) ***mean*** (***by*** certain conduct)? i.e. 'what motive or justification has he for it?'

1854 THACKERAY *Newcomes* I xxix. 287 What the devil do you mean about your Chimène and your Rodrigue? **1892** MRS. H. WARD *D. Grieve* II. iii, What, no top-coat in such weather! What do you mean by that, sir? You're wet through. **1930** G. B. SHAW *Apple Cart* I. 16 What do you mean? Isn't it what I have always said?

c. (***if***) ***you know, see, understand, what I mean,*** i.e. 'have I made it clear?'

1846 G. E. JEWSBURY *Sel. Lett. to Mrs. Carlyle* (1892) 203 There would be a want of reverence in it, if you understand what I mean. **1968** *Guardian* 24 Apr. 9/8 If I thought.. he was going to back-chat me like he does now.. I'd half-kill him now, you know what I mean? **1968** *Listener* 30 May 711/3 A braying Brooklyn accent studded with 'You know what I means'. **1974** *Sunday Times* 20 Jan. 12/4 [He'll] be only too keen to get back to his boat, if you see what I mean.

3. a. Of things, words, statements: To have a certain signification; to signify or import; to portend.

a **1000** *Sal. & Sat.* (Kemble) 472 Saȝa hwæt ic mæne. *c* **1200** ORMIN 5502 Swa þatt teȝȝ muȝhenn shæwenn ȝuw All whatt itt seȝȝþ & meneþþ. *c* **1330** R. BRUNNE *Chron.* (1810) 8 Þei wist what it ment. *a* **1400** *Cursor M.* 25395 (Cott. Galba) 'Amen', þat menes, 'so mot it be'. **1475** MARG. PASTON in *P. Lett.* III. 135 Some of them.. wote full lytyll what yt meneth to be as a sauger. **1557** NORTH *Gueuara's Diall Pr.* 345 From the time I knew what meaned to governe a common weale, I have alwayes [etc.]. *a* **1584** MONTGOMERIE *Cherrie & Slae* 605 Experience came in, and speirit Quhat all the matter meind. **1611** BIBLE *Gen.* xxi. 29 What meane these seuen ewe lambes, which thou hast set by themselues? **1622** BACON *Hen. VII* 234 His Armes were neuer Infortunate; neither did hee know what a Disaster meant. **1648** GAGE *West Ind.* x. (1655) 35 They knew not what money meaned. **1667** MILTON *P.L.* III. 275 Admiration seis'd All Heav'n, what this might mean. *Ibid.* XI. 875 But say, what mean those colourd streaks in Heavn. **1828** SCOTT *F.M. Perth* xxxvi, Eachin MacIan—what means all this?

b. Of a person or thing: to be of some account or importance, to 'matter' *to* (someone); to be a source of benefit, or an object of regard, affection, or love *to* (someone).

1888 MRS. H. WARD *R. Elsmere* II. III. xxvi. 279 It was only by a great effort that he could turn his thoughts from the Squire, and all that the squire had meant to him during the past year. **1912** *Red Mag.* 1 Mar. 515/1 It came over me how much she meant to me and how hard a wrench it was going to be to live along without her. **1914** *Times Lit. Suppl.* 8 Jan. 12/1 Comprehension of what Lady Gregory has meant to him and to others who worked with her. **1922** JOYCE *Ulysses* 356 He would never understand what he had meant to her.

c. *pass.* To be destined (by providence); to have special significance.

1897 KIPLING *Captains Courageous* viii. 169 It couldn't have been *meant*. It was only the tide. **1956** M. STEWART *Wildfire at Midnight* i. 16 So *handy* having that address. It's as if it were *meant*. **1962** M. ALLINGHAM *China Governess* (1963) xii. 151 That's miraculous! That's what people mean when they say a thing is 'meant'. **1974** I. MURDOCH *Sacred & Profane Love Machine* 239 When I need you, you are here. You must see how *meant* it all is.

†**4. a.** *trans.* To have in mind, to remember. *Obs.*

1303 R. BRUNNE *Handl. Synne* 6674 Sone! menest þou nat what y er seyde? *c* **1420** *Anturs of Arth.* 229 Gyffe me grace for to.. mene [*Douce MS.* mynge] the with messes and matynnes one morne. *c* **1440** *York Myst.* xii. 1 Grete meruell is to mene Howe man was made.

†**b.** *refl.* and *intr.* Const. *of, on, upon.* *Obs.*

a **1300–1400** *Cursor M.* 5274 (Gött.) Ne menis ȝou noght, nou mani a day, Of a drem ful lang siþen gan? *c* **1330** R. BRUNNE *Chron. Wace* (Rolls) 1838 He recouered his strengþe for tene, Of skaþe wold he hym no more mene. **1375** BARBOUR *Bruce* XII. 269 Menys on ȝour gret manheid. *c* **1425** *Thomas of Erceld.* 30 The Mawys menyde hir of hir songe. **1438** *Bk. Alexander Gt.* (Bann. Cl.) 67 Mene vpon ȝour hecht. **1442** *Aberdeen Reg.* (1844) I. 397 It is to mene apon that.. Robert Masoun, and Gilbert Masoun, oblist them.. til a honourable knight. **1513** DOUGLAS *Æneis* XI. Prol. 172 Allthocht his lord wald meyne On his ald seruis.

†**c.** impers. ***me meaneth*** = I remember. Const. *of, on.* *Obs.*

a **1300** *Cursor M.* 16889 Vs meins quils he was in lijf þat we herd him sai þat [etc.]. *c* **1375** *Sc. Leg. Saints* xvi. (*Magdalena*) 881 Menis þe nocht of þe ewangel, þat in þe kirk is red vmquhile of mary. *c* **1425** *St. Elizabeth of Spalbeck* in *Anglia* VIII. 118/7 Atte a dewe oure, and, as me meniþ, bytwix sexte and noon.

†**5.** *intr.* To hold or entertain an opinion; to think, imagine. *Obs.*

a **1300** *Cursor M.* 14686 'Þou mas þe godd, and þou art man'. 'Soth it es', coth iesus þan, 'Bath i am, qua right wil men'. *c* **1330** R. BRUNNE *Chron. Wace* (Rolls) 6888 'Lord', he seyde, 'ȝow þar nought wene, Why y am comen ȝe may wel mene'. *c* **1449** PECOCK *Repr.* III. xvii. 391 Ellis Crist in the alleggid xe. chapiter of Luk schulde haue meened aȝens him silf in the other now alleggid placis. **1533** GAU *Richt Vay* (1888) 51 Ciprianus menit that ye quyk suld be the saulis. *a* **1578** LINDESAY (Pitscottie) *Chron. Scot.* (S.T.S.) I. 31 Evirie man menit that it sould redound to his gret hurt. **1637** RUTHERFORD *Lett.* (1862) I. 221 Knots of straw and things (as they mean) off the way to heaven.

†**6. a.** *trans.* To say, tell, mention. *Obs.*

Beowulf 857 Ðær wæs Beowulfes mærðo mæned. *c* **1205** LAY. 16333 Wel ȝe hit maȝen imunen þat ich wulle mæinen. *a* **1225** *Ancr. R.* 316 Inouh hit is to siggen so þet þe schrift feder witterliche understonde hwat tu wulle menen. *a* **1300** *Cursor M.* 12498 (Cott.) He had þar-for wel gret pite, And þus to ioseph it mened he. **1387** TREVISA *Higden* (Rolls) II. 345 Þey poetes mene þat Iupiter gildede Saturnus. *c* **1450** HOLLAND *Howlat* 756 Menstralis and musicianis, mo than I mene may. *c* **1460** *Towneley Myst.* xiv 37 The myght of me may no man mene. **1494** FABYAN *Chron.* II. xxxiv. 26 Gaufride meneth yt this Sicillius was but .vii. yeres of age when his Fader dyed.

†**b.** *intr.* (rarely *refl.*) To speak, tell. Chiefly const. *of, on,* Sc. and north. *by.* Cf. 1 e *absol.* *Obs.*

a **1300** *Cursor M.* 24878 Hir succur son to ham sco sent, Þat in sli murning on hir ment. *c* **1350** *Will. Palerne* 1925, I wol minge of a mater i mennede of bi-fore. *a* **1400–50** *Alexander* 1615 (Dubl. MS.) Þai amervale þaime mekyll as menys me þe writtes [*Ashm. MS.* As þe buke tellis]. *c* **1470** HARDING *Chron.* LXXXVII. vii, All these were called Westsex, as Bede ment. ? *a* **1500** *Chester Pl., Purif.* 217 Mary, of mirth we may us meane. **1500–20** DUNBAR *Poems* lxiv. 12, I dout that Merche, with his cauld blastis keyne, Hes slane this gentill herbe, that I of mene. **1535** STEWART *Cron. Scot.* II. 219 Richt so did he, as my author did meyne. **1562** WINȜET *Cert. Tract.* i. Wks. 1888 I. 3 We mein of the pastores of the Kirk. **1625** BP. MOUNTAGU *App. Cæsar* 196 S. Paul speaketh of Iustification in the attayning it... But S. Iames meaneth of Iustification had and obtained.

7. *Comb.*: †**mean-nothing,** a meaningless, insincere phrase.

1654 WHITLOCK *Zootomia* 387, I tell you for your good, and, what is it to me?.. with many such non-significants, or mean-nothings.

†**mean,** *v.*[2] *Obs.* (After 15th c. only *Sc.* and *north. dial.*) Forms: 1 **mǣnan,** 2–7 **mene,** 3 **mæne, maine, meane,** 5 **meene,** 5–6 *Sc.* **meyn(e,** 6–7 *Sc.* **meine,** 6– **mean.** [OE. *mǣnan*: see MOAN *sb.*]

1. *trans.* To complain of, lament (something); to lament for (a dead person).

c **888** K. ÆLFRED *Boeth.* iv. (*heading*), Hu Boetius hine singende ȝebæd, & his earfoðu to Gode mænde. *c* **1175** *Lamb. Hom.* 33 Gif þu me dest woh.. ic hit mene to mine lauerde. *c* **1205** LAY. 2438, & swiðe heo hit mænde to alle monnen. *a* **1225** *Ancr. R.* 224 Ȝif heo edmodliche mened hire neode. **1375** BARBOUR *Bruce* IX. 300 Eftir that, neir fifty ȝheir, Men menyt the heirschip of Bouchane. *c* **1375** *Sc. Leg. Saints* xii. (*Mathias*) 203 Scho menyt ofte rycht sare hyr a sowne. *c* **1400** *Rom. Rose* 2596 My greet unese ful ofte I mene. **1513** DOUGLAS *Æneis* IX. v. 157 The Troianis.. With tender hartis menand Ewrialus. **1536** BELLENDEN *Cron. Scot.* (1821) II. 289 Becaus this Duncane wes ane tyrane.. few menit his slauchter. **1599** JAS. I *Βασιλ. Δωρον* (1682) 20 His fall is but little meaned by the rest of his subjects.

b. With cognate obj.: *to mean* (one's) *moan*, (one's) *complaint*.

a **1300** *Cursor M.* 4277 (Cott.) Oft sco meind til him hir mane. *a* **1300–1400** *Ibid.* 8159 (Gött.) Unese had he menid his mode, þat a lem fra þe wandes stode. *c* **1330** R. BRUNNE *Chron. Wace* (Rolls) 2440 [Lear] ment his mone euen & morwe. **14..** HARDING *Chron.* Pref. (1812) 5 To none other my complaynte can I mene.

c. To pity.

c **1440** *Pol. Rel. & L. Poems* (1903) 186 If þou be sijk, y schal þee hele; If þou moorne ouȝt, y schal þee meene. **1508** DUNBAR *Tua mariit Wemen* 501, I am so mercifull in mynd, et menys all wichtis. **1535** STEWART *Cron. Scot.* II. 541 The husband men full lytill now ar ment, Quhome be we ar vphaldin and sustent. *c* **1560** A. SCOTT *Poems* (S.T.S.) xxvi. 32 Thay wald be menit, and no man menis. **1603** *Philotus* clxv, I grant indeid thair will na man me meine, For I my self am authour of my greif.

d. in predicative phrase, *to mean*: to be deplored or pitied.

c **1330** R. BRUNNE *Chron.* (1810) 335 Allas! it was to mene, his vertuz & his pruesse So fele in him were sene, þat perist for falsnesse. **1535** STEWART *Cron. Scot.* (1858) I. 16 Quhairfoir thair mister wes the moir to mene. **1719** RAMSAY *3rd Answ. Hamilton* x, An fowk can get A doll of rost beef.. And be na sick.. They're no to mean. **1788** R. GALLOWAY *Poems* 132 Yes, said the king, we're no to mean, We live baith warm, and snug, and bien.

2. *intr.* To lament, mourn; to complain.

c **888** K. ÆLFRED *Boeth.* xi. § 1 þu simle mid wope & mid unrotnesse mænst ȝif þe ænies willan wana bið. *c* **1205** LAY. 29613 þa wolde he þer after sone wenden to Rome and menen to Gregorie. *a* **1225** *Ancr. R.* 274 So þet heo mei weopen & menen ase sori mon, mide þe salmwuruhte. *a* **1300–1400** *Cursor M.* 3059 (Gött.) Quilys scho menyd in hir mode, Confort com hir sone ful gode. *c* **1375** *Sc. Leg. Saints* vi. (*Thomas*) 513 Carisius.. for his vif gretly can men. *c* **1420** *Anturs of Arth.* (MS. I) 110 Hyt menet, hit musut, hyt marret. *c* **1430** *Syr Tryam.* 28 Ofte tyme togedur can they meene, For no chylde come them betwene. *c* **1560** A. SCOTT *Poems* (S.T.S.) xx. 22 Off all thy wo and cair It mends the no^t to mene. *a* **1800** *Proud Lady Marg.* v. in Scott *Minstr. Scott. Bord.* (1803) III. 276 If you should die for me, sir knight, There's few for you will meane.

b. To complain *of* (an offender).

a **1225** *Ancr. R.* 362 Uor þe ueond is affuruht and offered of swuche and forði þet Job was swuch he mende of him. *a* **1250** *Owl & Night.* 1257 Hwi wulleþ men of me mene.. þah ic hi warny al þat yer.

c. impers. ***me meaneth*** = I mourn.

13.. *Guy Warw.* (A.) 433 Sore me meneþ, for me smert, Miche care is in mine hert.

d. *refl.* in the same sense.

c **1175** *Lamb. Hom.* 17 Men þe to halie chirche, þet is to þan preoste and to þan folke. *c* **1205** LAY. 31504 And heo gunnen wenden to þan Kinge Pendan and menden heom to Pendan. *a* **1225** *Ancr. R.* 98 Meneð ou to his earen. *c* **1320** *Sir Tristr.* 1135 Til mark he gan him mene. **1362** LANGL. *P. Pl.* A. III. 163 Thenne mornede Meede and menede hire to the kyng. *c* **1400** *Destr. Troy* 7612 The grekes for þe greuaunce.. Made myche murmur & menit hom sore. *c* **1450** *St. Cuthbert* (Surtees) 4174 Gretely he him mened. **1790** MRS. WHEELER *Westmld. Dial.* (1821) 62 Awr lass hed been ath shop, for a quartern ea hops, en hard him mean hissel.

3. *trans.* To state as a grievance; to represent by way of formal complaint or petition. *Sc.*

1475 *Aberdeen Reg.* (1844) I. 33 Fersamekil as it is lammentabilly menit till ws be our louit Johne of Spens, litster,.. that [etc.]. **1525** *Ibid.* I. 110 Forsamekill as it is humelie meynit and schewin to ws be ane reverend fader in God [etc.]. **1560** in Spottiswood *Hist. Ch. Scot.* III. (1677) 144 They were forced to mean our estate to the Queen of England. **1569** *Reg. Privy Council Scot.* II. 61 Ordaining baith the parties,.. to meyne the mater to the said Generall Assembly. **1752** LOUTHIAN *Form of Process* (ed. 2) 25 It is humbly meaned and shown to Us, by Our Lovit, C.D. That [etc.].

b. *refl.* To present a complaint.

1551 *Reg. Privy Council Scot.* I. 114 Thai menit thame diverse tymes to the Lordis of Sessioun. *a* **1670** SPALDING *Troub. Chas. I* (Spalding Cl.) II. 72 To stramp it out he meinis him self to the Parliament.

mean, *v.*³ Also 5 **meen**, 5–6 **mene**, 6 *Sc.* **meyne**. [a. OF. *meenner*, *moiener*, f. *meien* (see MEAN *a.*). Cf. MEAN *sb.*² 9.]

† **1.** *trans.* To mediate. *Obs. rare.*

c **1440** *Promp. Parv.* 332/2 Menyn, or goon be-twene ij. partyes for a-corde.. *medio.* *c* **1449** PECOCK *Repr.* II. xix. 263 If Iohun be a prouoking meene that the King ȝeue to me xx^li. pound of ȝeerli fee,.. it mai be seid.. that Iohun dooth and ȝeueth to me thilk fee,.. in this vndirstonding, that Iohun meneth or helpith, and fortherith in meenyng that the ȝeuyng be doon. *c* **1522** DOUGLAS in *Wks.* (1874) I. p. cx, Causing thame mene and procure so that the remayning with hir husband was not payit of her dower. **1654** H. L'ESTRANGE *Chas. I* (1655) 138 Nor was any assistance more like to mean and procure his Restauration then theirs.

† **2.** To moderate (by intervention). *Obs. rare.*

1500–20 DUNBAR *Poems* lxxxv. 47 Our teyne to meyne, and ga betweyne, Ane hevinle oratrice.

3. *trans.* [f. MEAN *a.*² 7 or *sb.*² 8.] To calculate the arithmetical mean of. Also with *up*.

1882 W. J. L. WHARTON *Hydrogr. Surveying* 210 We need not mean up each column of times. *Ibid.* 213 When working several sets, calculate them simultaneously as far as this, and mean the results. *a* **1888** P. F. SHORTLAND *Naut. Surveying* (1890) 64 The permanent errors will destroy each other in the results of all.. observations so meaned.

† **'meanably**, *adv. Obs. rare*⁻¹. [f. MEAN *a.*² + -ABLY.] In a mean or medium degree.

1577 FRAMPTON *Joyfull Newes* II. 48 b, Giuying to the Cholerike lesse seethyng,.. and to the Flegmaticke more seethyng,.. and to the Sanguine meanablie [Sp. orig. *medianamente*].

meanashing, obs. form of MENACING.

meander (mɪ'ændə(r)), *sb.* Also (6 **meandor**), 6–9 **mæander**. [a. L. *mæander*, Gr. μαίανδρος, appellative use of the name of a river in Phrygia noted for its winding course. Cf. F. *méandre* (1582 in Hatz.-Darm.), Sp., Pg., It. *meandro*.]

1. *pl.* Sinuous windings (of a river); turnings to and fro (in its course); flexuosities. Rarely in *sing.*, the action of winding; one of such windings.

1599 NASHE *Lenten Stuffe* 14 In all which foords or Meandors.. if any drowne themselues in them, their Crowners sit vpon them. **1646** SIR T. BROWNE *Pseud. Ep.* VI. viii, The River Niger.. deflecting after Westward, without meanders, continueth a strait course about 40 degrees. **1796** W. COOMBE *Boydell's Thames* II. 67 The stream loses itself in a distant meander. **1825** WATERTON *Wand. S. Amer.* I. i. 118 Probably.. these apparently four creeks are only the meanders of one. **1834** BECKFORD *Italy* I. 166 Springs whose frequent meanders gave to the whole prospect the appearance of a vast green carpet shot with silver. **1876** BANCROFT *Hist. U.S.* III. xv. 235 The river now flowed in gentle meanders.

transf. and *fig.* **1638** BRATHWAIT *Barnabees Jrnl.* II. G iij, When my head feels his [*sc.* Ale's] Mæander, I am stronger than Lysander. **1784** COWPER *Task* IV. 65 Here rills of oily eloquence in soft Mæanders lubricate the course they take. **1820** SCOTT *Abbot* i, The boy.. lay.. half drowned in the meanders of the fluctuating delirium.

2. *pl.* Crooked or winding paths (of a maze); labyrinthine passages; windings or convolutions (of a vein, fissure, line, etc.).

1598 SYLVESTER *Du Bartas* II. i. I. *Eden* 561 Round-winding rings, and intricate Meanders.. of an end-less Maze. **1603** J. SAVILE *K. Jas. Entertainm. Theobalds* B b, Hee went into the Laberinth-like garden to walke, where hee recreated himselfe in the Meanders compact of Bayes, Rosemarie, and the like. **1610** SHAKS. *Temp.* III. iii. 3. **1615** CROOKE *Body of Man* 94 Intercepted and deteined within those Meanders [*sc.* the guts]. **1666** G. HARVEY *Morb. Angl.* iv. 34 The effuges, or mæanders of the central.. parts of the brain. **1699** GARTH *Dispens.* I. 25 Now she [Nature] unfolds.. How ductile Matter new Meanders takes. **1750** JOHNSON *Rambler* No. 65 ¶ 2 The new path, which he supposed only to make a few meanders. **1799** KIRWAN *Geol. Ess.* iv. 141 The fibres of the rind.. and the meanders of the fibrillae being equally discernible. **1801** J. JONES tr. *Bÿgge's Trav. Fr. Rep.* xii. 238 The inextricable windings and meanders of those caves.

† **b.** *fig.* Confusing and bewildering ways; intricacies (of affairs, the law, a subject, etc.). *Obs.*

1576 FLEMING *Panopl. Epist.* 285 They being ouerwhelmed in Mæanders of mischiefes. **1631** R. H. *Arraignm. Whole Creature* i. 5 He was in such Meanders of miserie and labyrinths of troubles. **1652** H. L'ESTRANGE *Amer. no Jewes* 71 There are many Meanders and windings in this question of Plantation. **1712** ARBUTHNOT *John Bull* I. vi, Ten long years did Hocus steer his Cause through all the meanders of the Law. **1759** FRANKLIN *Ess.* Wks. 1840 III. 132 In this purpose I am ready.. until by better information out of England, we shall be led out of these state meanders.

† **c.** *sing.* A winding or labyrinthine course or plan; a labyrinth, maze. *lit.* and *fig. Obs.*

c **1586** C'TESS PEMBROKE *Ps.* CXLIII. v, Lest awry I wander In walking this meander. **1610** HEYWOOD *Lanc. Witches* IV. Wks. 1874 IV. 226 The more I strive to unwinde My selfe from this Meander, I the more Therein am intricated. **1645** EVELYN *Diary* Apr. (1879) I. 211 After wandering two or three miles in this subterranean meander [the catacombs]. **1651** BIGGS *New Disp.* 46 [They] have made of Physick a Meander,.. and wild labirynth of incertainty. **1796** W. COOMBE *Boydell's Thames* II. 3 The garden.. retains its early form, and the lesser walks preserve their original meander.

3. A circuitous journey or movement; a deviation; a winding course (as in the dance); chiefly *pl.*

1631 WEEVER *Anc. Funeral Mon.* 241 For building Churches sure he goes to Christ without Meander. **1634** SIR T. HERBERT *Trav.* 20 Dancing many times, a great multitude passe together, and in mæanders turne and winde themselves. **1713** YOUNG *Last Day* II. 50 So swarming bees, that.. In airy rings, and wild meanders play. **1719** DE FOE *Crusoe* I. xix, He made so many Tours, such Meanders, and led us by such winding ways. **1891** T. HARDY *Tess* xliv, Her journey back was rather a meander than a march.

4. *Art.* An ornamental pattern composed chiefly of lines winding in and out with rectangular turnings or crossing one another at right angles.

It is used chiefly as a border ornament on walls, pottery, etc.

1706 PHILLIPS (ed. Kersey), *Mæander*,.. a Fret-work in arched Roofs. **1737** WHISTON *Josephus, Antiq.* XII. ii. § 8 On the table itself they engraved a meander. **1851** C. NEWTON in Ruskin *Stones Ven.* I. App. 401 Two conventional imitations [of water], the wave moulding and the Mæander, are well known. **1857** BIRCH *Anc. Pottery* (1858) II. 196 The exterior has been ornamented with a mæander, in white paint.

5. *attrib.* and *Comb.*, as ***meander pattern***, ***walk***; ***meander-like*** adv.

[**1598** SYLVESTER *Du Bartas* II. iv. I. *Tropheis* 1000 Now, like thy Jordan, (or *Meander-like) Round-winding nimbly with a many-Creek.] **1612** DRAYTON *Poly-olb.* x. 94 Riuery veines, Meander-like that glide. **1851** C. NEWTON in Ruskin *Stones Ven.* App. 401 In the *Mæander pattern [of water] the graceful curves of nature are represented by angles. **1766** *Museum Rust.* VI. 80 Lay out the ground in some gentle *meander-walks.

meander (mɪ'ændə(r)), *v.* [f. MEANDER *sb.*]

1. a. *intr.* Of a river, stream, etc.: To flow in meanders; to wind about in its course.

c **1612** DRUMM. OF HAWTH. *Tears Death Mœliades* (1614) A 3, Forth where thou first didst passe Thy tender Dayes,.. Meandring with her Streames. **1738** GLOVER *Leonidas* VIII. 149 Soft streams mæander'd. **1894** RIDER HAGGARD *People of Mist* xxxvi, Rivers that.. meandered across the vast plains.

indirect passive. **1731** POPE *Ep. Burlington* 85 Beds.. With silver-quivering rills mæander'd o'er.

b. *transf.* and *fig.*

1777 SHERIDAN *Sch. Scand.* II. i. (ed. Rae 1902), When you shall see in a beautiful Quarto Page, how a neat rivulet of Text shall meander thro' a meadow of margin. **1784** COWPER *Task* III. 202 Pierce my vein, Take of the crimson stream meandering there. **1835–6** TODD *Cycl. Anat.* I. 462/2 Blue veins are seen meandering on its [the skin's] surface. **1853** FELTON *Fam. Lett.* xxix. (1865) 257 The smoke.. meandered in graceful curls among the timbers.

2. Of a person: To wander deviously or aimlessly. (? Partly suggested by MAUNDER *v.*² 2.) Also *fig.*

1831 S. LOVER *Leg. & Stories Irel.* 151 He wint meandherin' along through the fields. **1872** CALVERLEY *Fly Leaves* (1903) 101, I meandered Through some chapters of Vanity Fair. **1875** HELPS *Soc. Press.* v. 71 They will have.. meandered about the flower-garden in a listless way.

† **3.** *trans.* To entangle as in a labyrinth. *Obs.*

1652 URQUHART *Jewel* 95 [They devised questions, arguments, etc.] thereby to puzzle him in the resolving of them, Meander him in his answers.. and drive him to a non-plus.

4. *U.S.* To pass or travel deviously along or through (a river, etc.).

1821 in *Missouri Hist. Soc. Coll.* (1906) II. 61 We still continued meandering the Arkansas. **1831** J. O. PATTIE *Personal Narr.* 13 We crossed the Missouri.. and meandered the river as far as Pilcher's fort. **1839** Z. LEONARD *Adventures* (1904) 69 We separated, each party to meander the rivers that had been respectively allotted to them. **1839** in *Trans. Mich. Agric. Soc.* (1856) VII. 360 Branches of Swan creek meander this track in such manner as to facilitate drainage.

Hence **'meandered** *ppl. a.*, winding, labyrinthine. Also **'meanderer**, one who meanders.

1612 DRAYTON *Poly-olb.* I. 158 Those armes of Sea,.. By their Meandred creeks indenting of that Land. **1622** *Ibid.* XXII. 19 Ouze.. in Meandred Gyres doth whirle herselfe about. **1708** *Brit. Apollo* No. 43. 3/1 Love's meander'd Paths. **1887** T. N. PAGE *Ole Virginia* (1889) 188 The meanderer was Drinkwater Torm.

meandering (mɪ'ændərɪŋ), *vbl. sb.* [f. MEANDER *v.* + -ING¹.] The action of the vb. MEANDER; an instance of this.

1652 A. WILSON in Benlowes *Theoph.* To Author, Or can the crawling Worm.. With its Meandrings finde the center out? **1807–8** W. IRVING *Salmag.* (1824) 382 The grove must be a paradise that is refreshed by thy meanderings! **1865** GROTE *Plato* III. 45, I here repeat the precise state of the question, which is very apt to be lost amidst the mæanderings of a Platonic dialogue.

'meandering, *ppl. a.* [f. MEANDER *v.* + -ING².] That meanders; flexuous, winding.

1680 MORDEN *Geog. Rect.* Introd. (1685) 6 Winding Bays, Creeks and meandring Inlets. **1748** RICHARDSON *Clarissa* (1811) III. iii. 29 Flesh.. so clear that every meandring vein is to be seen. **1846** DANA *Zooph.* (1848) 174 The tentacles.. margin the meandering cell. **1878** HUXLEY *Physiogr.* 142 The river flows in a meandering course.

Hence **'meanderingly** *adv.*

1887 STOCKTON in *Century Mag.* Mar. 886 Through which a narrow path meanderingly ran.

† **meandrated**, *ppl. a. Obs.*⁻⁰ In 8 **mæandrated**. [f. L. *mæandrāt-us* full of curves like the Mæander + -ED¹.] (See quot.)

1727 BAILEY vol. II, *Mæandrated*, turned, intricately wrought.

† **meandrian**, *a. Obs. rare.* [f. L. *mæandri-us* (f. *mæander*: see MEANDER *sb.*) + -AN.] Like the meanders of a river; flexuous, winding.

1608 J. KING *Serm.* 5 Nov. 27 This serpent surrepent generation, with their Mæandrian turnings & windings. **1656** S. H. *Golden Law* 81 Religion's rigidness and Meandrian intricacies are too hard for most of them.

meandrically (mɪ'ændrɪkəlɪ), *adv.* [f. L. *mæandric-us* (F. *méandrique*), f. *mæander* + -AL¹ + -LY².] In a meandrous manner.

1886 R. VON LENDENFELD in *Proc. Zool. Soc.* 21 Dec. 590 Meandrically winding tubes.. *Meandrospongidæ*.

meandriform (mɪ'ændrɪfɔːm), *a.* [f. L. *mæandri-* MEANDER *sb.* + -FORM.] Having a winding form, labyrinthine.

1898 *Nat. Sci.* Sept. 227 This is covered above and below by a layer of vermiform and meandriform chambers.

‖ **Meandrina** (miːæn'draɪnə). [mod.L. *Mæandrīna*, fem. of *mæandrīnus adj.: see next. Cf. F. *méandrine*.] A genus of corals the surface of which somewhat resembles the convolutions of the human brain; also, a polype of this genus.

1838 BAKEWELL *Introd. Geol.* (ed. 5) 638 Where the laminæ take a serpentine direction, they are called Meandrina, or brain stone. **1860** MAURY *Phys. Geog. Sea* (Low) xiii. § 560 Dense masses of Meandrinas and Astraeas.

meandrine (miːˈændrɪn), *a.* Also **mæandrine.** [ad. mod.L. **mæandrinus*, f. L. *mæandr-* MEANDER *sb.*] Characterized by windings; said esp. of corals belonging to the genus MEANDRINA.

1846 DANA *Zooph.* (1848) 155 There are thus the simple and meandrine forms of the calicularly branched species. **1884** J. COLBORNE *Hicks Pasha* 13 Rounded masses of meandrine coral with its brain-like convolutions.

† **meandrite** (miːˈændraɪt). *Obs.* Also **mäandrite.** [f. L. *mæandr-* MEANDER *sb.* + -ITE. Cf. G. *mäandrit*, F. *méandrite* (Humboldt).] A coral belonging to the genus MEANDRINA.

1802-3 tr. *Pallas's Trav.* (1812) I. 147 Its cells and tubes extend, as is the case with *mäandrites* or *madreporites*, in a parallel line from the surface. **1819** HELEN M. WILLIAMS tr. *Humboldt's Trav.* xvi. IV. 200 Small rocks of meandrites, madreporites, and other corals.

meandrous (miːˈændrəs), *a.* Also 7 **mæandrous.** [f. MEANDER + -OUS.] Full of or characterized by windings and turnings; *esp.* of a river.

1656 BLOUNT *Glossogr.* s.v. *Meander*, ..Meandrous is used for crooked, or full of turnings. *a* **1657** R. LOVEDAY *Lett.* (1663) 268 With whose vertuous rectitude Meandrous falshood is inconsistent. *a* **1661** FULLER *Worthies, Bedfordsh.* I. (1662) 114 Ouse..in this Shire, more Mæandrous then Mæander. *a* **1734** NORTH *Exam.* II. iv. §86 (1740) 274 That, in the Prosecution of this meandrous Labyrinth,..I may not ..be thought tedious. **1836** *Tait's Mag.* III. 561 A river, flowing in a meandrous course. **1892** LD. LYTTON *Marah* 118 Desire's meandrous labyrinths among.

† ˈ**meandry**, *a. Obs. rare*$^{-1}$. [f. MEANDER + -Y.] = prec.

1614 SIR A. GORGES tr. *Lucan* I. 14 The Trumpets (with their dreadfull notes Drawn through their hoarse Meandry throats..). **1619** —— tr. *Bacon's Wisdom Anc.* v. 15.

me-and-you. *slang.* [Jocular adaptation of colloq. pronunc. (ˈmiːnjuː) of MENU.] = MENU 2.

1932 P. P. *Rhyming Slang* 23 Me and you..Menu. **1943** N. MARSH *Colour Scheme* iv. 68 Come on, Beautiful. Let's have a slant at the me-and-you.

meane, obs. f. MAIN *sb.*^{4}, MEAN, MESNE, MIEN.

† **meaned**, *a. Obs. rare*$^{-1}$. [f. MEAN *sb.* + -ED^{2}.] Furnished with or having means. Only with qualifying word, as ***better meaned.***

1605 CHAPMAN, etc. *Eastw. Hoe* I. i, There's thy fellowe-Prentise, as good a Gentleman borne as thou art: nay, and better mean'd.

† **meanel.** *Obs.* See quot. (and cf. MENALD *a.*).

?*a* **1685** T. MORE in *Ray's Collect.* (E.D.S.) 55 *Meanels*, spots called flea-bits in white-coloured horses.

† **meaner**^{1}. *Obs.* In 4 **mener**, 5 **menowre, menar.** [a. OF. *meneur, moieneor, moyenneur.*] A mediator; an interpreter.

1387 TREVISA *Higden* (Rolls) IV. 409 Mark þe gospellour, Paule his disciple and his mener [L. *interpres Petri*]. *Ibid.* V. 397 Austyn..com alonde wiþ fourty felawes and som meners [*interpretibus*]. *c* **1440** *Promp. Parv.* 333/1 Menowre, or medyatowre. *c* **1450** HOLLAND *Howlat* 747 Thow moder of all mercy, and the menar.

meaner^{2} (ˈmiːnə(r)). ? *Obs.* [f. MEAN *v.*^{1} + -ER^{1}.] One who means, intends, or purposes. Chiefly with qualifying adj. prefixed.

1580 LUPTON *Sivqila* 138 We haue the faithfullest meaners, and truest dealers, that are in all the world. **1590** SPENSER *F.Q.* III. v. 25 So mischief fel upon the meaners crowne. **1604** HIERON *Wks.* I. 490 If the meaner be not assured of the goodnesse of it..his meaning is naught. *a* **1616** BEAUM. & FL. *Scornf. Lady* I. i, A *Simile* seruant? This roome was built for honest meaners, that deliuer themselues hastily and plainely, and are gone. **1634** A. WARWICK *Spare Min.* (1637) 18 The good meaner hath two tongues. **1712** STEELE *Spect.* No. 504 ¶2 Your double Meaners are dispersed up and down thro' all Parts of Town or City where [etc.].

† ˈ**meaner**^{3}. *Obs. rare.* [? Subst. use of comparative of MEAN *a.*^{1}; or perh. f. MEAN *a.*^{1} + -ER: cf. *commoner*.] One of the humbler class.

1602 WARNER *Alb. Eng.* XII. lxx. (1612) 293 But of some meaners, that their liues haue ventured no lesse, Perform'd as much [etc.]. **1642** ROGERS *Naaman* 383 Lawyer, Justice, Gentleman or meaner do within the compasse of their places [etc.].

meaneschot, obs. Sc. form of MANCHET.

† **meaness.** *Obs. rare*$^{-1}$. In 6 **menesse.** [f. MEAN *sb.*^{2} (9) or MEANER^{1}: see -ESS. Cf. OF. *moieneresse.*] A mediatress.

1450-1530 *Myrr. our Ladye* 306 *Mediatrix*, Menesse of men, and wassher of synnes, heyle kyngly virgyn.

meanesse, obs. form of MEANNESS.

meanie, obs. f. MANY; var. MEINIE *Obs.*

meanie, var. MEANY.

meaning (ˈmiːnɪŋ), *vbl. sb.*^{1} Forms: 3-6 **mening(e**, 4-6 **menyng(e, meanyng(e**, (4 **mennyng, meneyng**, 5 **menying, meenyng**, 7 **meaninge**), 6- **meaning.** [f. MEAN *v.*^{1} + -ING^{1}: cf. OHG. *meinunga* (mod.G. *meinung*), MDu. *meninge* (mod.Du. *meening*).]

1. Intention, purpose. *arch.* † ***upon a meaning***: with the intention. † ***a good meaning***: (*a*) a good intention, friendly disposition; (*b*) a 'good mind', a strong inclination (to do something).

c **1385** CHAUCER *L.G.W.* Prol. 474 It was myn entente To forthere trouthe..And to be war from falsenesse..this was myn menynge. **1390** GOWER *Conf.* III. 254 Whan Collatin hath herd hire telle The menynge of hire trewe herte. *c* **1412** HOCCLEVE *De Reg. Princ.* 2315 þe kyng..knewe him and his menynge. **1526** TINDALE *1 Cor.* i. 10 Be ye perfecte in one mynde, and one meanynge. **1585** SIR A. POULET *Let. to Walsingham* 27 Apr. in *Letter-Bks.* (1874) 11 This cloth of Estate was set up at the first coming hither of this Queen, upon a meaning that she should dine and sup ordinarily in that chamber. *c* **1592** MARLOWE *Jew of Malta* IV. ii, Yet, if he knew our meanings, could he scape? **1592** GREENE *Groat's W. Wit* (1617) 13 Lucanio..had a good meaning to vtter his mind. **1605** SHAKS. *Lear* I. ii. 190, I am no honest man, if ther be any good meaning toward you. **1633** FORD *Broken H.* IV. i, A man of single meaning. **1781** COWPER *Ep. Lady Austen* 98 A..visit..made almost without a meaning, Produced a friendship. **1814** WORDSW. *Excursion* IV. 1150 You..Adore, and worship, when you know it not; Pious beyond the intention of your thought; Devout above the meaning of your will. **1847** TENNYSON *Princess* III. 206 Since we learnt our meaning here, To lift the woman's fall'n divinity. **1896** A. E. HOUSMAN *Shropshire Lad* xxxiii, Sure, sure, if stedfast meaning, If single thought could save, The world might end to-morrow, You should not see the grave.

2. That which is intended to be or actually is expressed or indicated. (See also DOUBLE MEANING.)

a. Of language, a sentence, word, etc.: The signification, sense, import; a sense, interpretation. Also, the intent, spirit as apart from the 'letter' (of a statement, law, etc.). † ***(that) is to meaning***: (that) means.

1303 R. BRUNNE *Handl. Synne* 611 þe menyng ys,..ȝyf þou sweryst fals [etc.]. **1398** TREVISA *Barth. De P.R.* II. xvii. (1495) 41 Raphael is to meanynge the medycine of god. **1401** *Pol. Poems* (Rolls) II. 85 If we taken the gospel aftir the menynge. *a* **1450** *Knt. de la Tour* xxxiv. 48 'Doughter, loue and worship youre husbonde..'; that is to menying that ye shulde loue and doute youre husbonde. *c* **1491** *Chast. Goddes Chyld.* 21 The fyrst feuer is callid a cotydian in whiche is properly in ghostly menyng a varyaunce of the herte. **1560** DAUS tr. *Sleidane's Comm.* 12 b, If this be the meaning of the lawe, then can no more the Spaniarde be chosen, then the Frencheman. **1625** BACON *Ess., Unity in Relig.* (Arb.) 429 Termes, so fixed, as whereas the Meaning ought to gouerne the Terme, the Terme in effect gouerneth the Meaning. **1671** MILTON *P.R.* IV. 516 That I [Satan] might learn In what degree or meaning thou art call'd The Son of God, which bears no single sence. **1736** BUTLER *Anal.* I. iii. Wks. 1874 I. 63 Difficulties may be raised about the meaning, as well as the truth, of the assertion. **1843** MILL *Logic* (1865) II. 233 It may be good to alter the meaning of a word, but it is bad to let any part of the meaning drop. **1876** JEVONS *Logic Prim.* 23 The confusion which arises between the different meanings of the same word.

b. That which a speaker or writer intends to express; the intended sense of (a person's) words.

c **1330** R. BRUNNE *Chron. Wace* (Rolls) 16709 After hym in Englische y hit brought; Of his meninge y wot þe weye, But his fair speche can y nought seye. *a* **1533** FRITH *Disput. Purgat.* (1829) 101, I will briefly declare the meaning of the Apostle. **1621** T. WILLIAMSON tr. *Goulart's Wise Vieillard* A iv b, I hope I haue hit of his meaning, though I vary from his wordes. **1841** J. H. NEWMAN *Lett.* (1891) II. 336 The Articles are to be interpreted, not according to the meaning of the writers, but..according to the sense of the Catholic Church. **1878** R. W. DALE *Lect. Preach.* vi. 161 You will be good enough not to misunderstand my meaning.

c. Of a dream, symbol, phenomenon, etc. † ***in meaning that***: as a sign or token that. *Obs.*

1377 LANGL. *P. Pl.* B. xv. 301 Ac god sent hem fode bi foules and by no fierse bestes, In menynge [cf. 1393 C. XVIII. 33 In tokenynge] þat meke þinge mylde þinge shulde fede. **1382** WYCLIF *Dan.* ii. 5 No bot ȝe shuln shewe to me the sweuen, and the coniecturyng, or menyng, therof. **1597** HOOKER *Eccl. Pol.* v. lxvii. §11 If he haue no such Being, neither can the Sacrament haue any such meaning as wee all confesse it hath. **1611** BIBLE *Dan.* viii. 15 When I..had seene the vision, and sought for the meaning. **1702** ADDISON *Dial. Medals* ii. Wks. 1721 I. 457 What is the meaning that this transparent Lady [*sc.* Hope] holds up her train in her left hand? for I find your women on Medals do nothing without a meaning. **1885** CLODD *Myths & Dr.* I. iv. 66 The Greeks had sought out the meaning of their myths.

d. Of an action, a state of things, etc.

1828-32 WEBSTER s.v., What is the meaning of all this parade? **1877** FROUDE *Short Stud.* (1883) IV. I. iii. 29 What could be the meaning of so sudden and so startling a transformation? **1878** T. HARDY *Ret. Native* I. iv, What's the meaning of this disgraceful performance?

e. In generalized use: Significance. ***no-meaning***: nonsense.

1690 LOCKE *Hum. Und.* III. xi. (1695) 288 He that hath Names without Ideas, wants Meaning in his Words. **1735** POPE *Ep. Lady* 114 True No-meaning puzzles more than Wit. *a* **1800** COWPER *Ode to Apollo* i, Those luckless brains That..Indite much metre with much pains, And little or no meaning. **1865** KINGSLEY *Herew.* i, As he passed the young lord he cast on him a look so full of meaning, that [etc.].

† **3.** Remembrance; only in phr. ***to have, make meaning.*** Also, a commemoration, memorial. *Obs.*

Cf. MINNING, often occurring in ME. as a variant reading for this word.

a **1300** *Cursor M.* 24748 Quen i ma mening o þat mild, Quat blis sco bred again vr bale. **1303** R. BRUNNE *Handl. Synne* 5208 Lorde, have on me menyng. **1340** HAMPOLE *Pr. Consc.* 8320 When þou has of þi syns meneyng. **1503** *Aberdeen Reg.* (1844) I. 72 Atour he sal nocht ring Laurence at the saule messe nor menyngis, bot for the nobill and honorabill personis of the town.

† **4.** Mention. Only in phr. ***to make meaning.***

a **1300-1400** *Cursor M.* 8518 (Gött.) Childer..Of þe quilk i make na mening here. *c* **1330** R. BRUNNE *Chron.* (1810) 26 þei mak no menyng whan, no in what date. *c* **1375** *Sc. Leg. Saints* xiii. (*Marcus*) 14 Vthire twa, of quhame I wel here menyng ma.

† **5.** Knowledge, understanding. *Obs. rare*$^{-1}$.

1393 LANGL. *P. Pl.* C. II. 138 'Ich haue no kynde knowyng', quaþ ich, 'ȝe mote kenne me bettere, By what wey hit wexith, and (wheder) out of my menyng'.

6. *attrib.* and *Comb.*, *as* ***meaning-analysis, -area, -change, -content, -relation, -relationship, -unit; meaning-bearing, -carrying*** adjs.

1936 WIRTH & SHILS tr. *Mannheim's Ideology & Utopia* i. 46 There are..vast possibilities of precision in the combination of *meaning-analysis and sociological situational diagnosis. **1966** C. G. HEMPEL *Philos. of Nat. Sci.* viii. 103 The characterization of these substances by their molecular structure is arrived at, not by meaning analysis, but by chemical analysis. **1958** C. RABIN in *Aspects of Translation* vii. 124 The object in question has to be assigned either to the *meaning-area of *watch* or to that of *clock*. **1957** N. CHOMSKY in Saporta & Bastian *Psycholinguistics* (1961) 266/2 We have counter examples to the suggestion..that morphemes be defined as minimal *meaning-bearing elements. **1972** *Archivum Linguisticum* III. 83 Generativists have attempted to remove all meaning-bearing elements from transformations into the deep structure. **1965** H. A. GLEASON *Ling. & Eng. Gram.* 192 We might have had the *meaning-carrying verb *washed*. **1954** F. G. CASSIDY *Robertson's Devel. Mod. Eng.* (ed. 2) ix. 232 The various types of *meaning-change. **1968** M. BLACK *Labyrinth of Lang.* vii. 163 A reasonably adequate account of the nature of such meaning-changes..is bound to be very complicated. **1949** PRIEBSCH & COLLINSON *German Lang.* (ed. 2) II. iii. 234 In several Indo-European languages are types of compounds in which the *meaning-content or 'determination' is left unexpressed. **1948** *Mind* LVII. 80 Each separately is intelligible by itself and has its own meaning-content independently of the other. **1934** PRIEBSCH & COLLINSON *German Lang.* II. iii. 208 From the point of view of the *meaning-relation of their component words compounds fall into several well-marked classes. **1963** J. LYONS *Structural Semantics* ii. 28 The only meaning-relation that is relevant in the case of phonemes is sameness and difference of meaning. **1961** R. B. LONG *Sentence & its Parts* i. 11 *Meaning relationships are obviously varied. **1966** *English Studies* XLVII. 256 We find the same meaning-relationship between the adjunct clause and its verb. **1938** I. GOLDBERG *Wonder of Words* xvi. 323 The smallest *meaning-unit of a word is called a semanteme. **1962** W. NOWOTTNY *Lang. Poets Use* vii. 162 What we call the 'same word' is not a single meaning-unit.

† ˈ**meaning**, *vbl. sb.*^{2} *Obs.* [f. MEAN *v.*^{2} + -ING^{1}.] The action of the vb. MEAN; moaning, lamentation.

c **1200** *Trin. Coll. Hom.* 63 On fuwuer wise us bihoueð turnen to him; on heorte, on festene, on wope, on meninge. **13..** *Guy Warw.* (A.) 4803 Biside him he herd a mening, Also it were a woman schricheing. *c* **1470** HENRY *Wallace* VIII. 734 Madennys murnyt with gret menyng amang. **1572** *Satir. Poems Reform.* xxx. 27 Dowglas..& gude Westiraw.. with lytill meaning, fra the men be past.

meaning (ˈmiːnɪŋ), *sb.*^{3} *Astr.* [f. MEAN *a.*^{2} + -ING^{1}.] The motion of the sun in mean longitude.

1884 E. J. STONE in *Observatory* 1 Jan. 3 And as we make no distinction in our theories between the real motion of the sun in longitude and that of the mean sun, the meaning of the real sun is fixed when [etc.].

meaning (ˈmiːnɪŋ), *ppl. a.* [f. MEAN *v.*^{1} + -ING^{2}.]

1. Having intention or purpose. Usually with qualifying word, as ***better, well meaning***, etc.

1581 MULCASTER *Positions* iii. (1887) 8 Some well meaning man. **1633**, **1681** Ill-meaning [see ILL- B]. **1748** RICHARDSON *Clarissa* (1768) IV. 343 At first..(and till I observed her meaning air, and heard her speak) I supposed that she had no very uncommon Judgment. **1760-72** H. BROOKE *Fool of Qual.* (1809) I. 134 One of them..is..as little meaning of harm to any one as his mother.

2. That conveys or expresses meaning or thought; expressive, significant.

1728 YOUNG *Love of Fame* v. (ed. 2) 110 The motion of her lips, and meaning eye Pierce out the Idea her faint words deny. **1838** DICKENS *Nich. Nick.* ii, 'Had done business with him', said Mr. Bonney with a meaning look. **1865** W. G. PALGRAVE *Arabia* I. 115 The thoughtful expression of his large forehead and meaning eye. **1885** *Manch. Exam.* 10 July 5/5 At this frank confession a meaning smile passed between Mr. Gladstone and Mr. Childers.

meaningful (ˈmiːnɪŋfʊl), *a.* [f. MEANING *vbl. sb.*^{1} + -FUL.] **a.** Full of meaning or expression; significant. **b.** Amenable to interpretation; having a recognizable purpose or function; *spec.* in *Logic*, resulting from the application of the rules of a language or sign system; able to function as a term in such a system.

1852 *Tait's Mag.* XIX. 552 All the little meaningful gifts. **1879** G. MACDONALD *Sir Gibbie* xiii, It was a..meaningful smile. **1922** *Times Educ. Suppl.* 29 Apr. 200/2 The pupils see at once that their studies are meaningful. **1934** COHEN & NAGEL *Introd. Logic* ix. 185 It has been said that to the two alternatives *true* and *false*, there is a third, the *meaningless*... The question of what constitutes a meaningful expression is a large one. **1940** W. V. QUINE *Math. Logic* iv. 164 Under Russell's scheme an abstraction prefix..can be applied outright to any meaningful formula. **1942** T. C. POLLOCK *Nature of Lit.* ix. 192 If the charge is made that a particular

work..is..'meaningless'..a good critic may be able to discriminate privately..that it is..highly meaningful. **1952** C. P. BLACKER *Eugenics* ix. 203 It is a different matter to test the tests and to prove them to be meaningful and workable. **1953** *Mind* LXII. 8 We often ask what a word means, but we do not ordinarily ask whether a word is meaningful or not. If it were not meaningful we would not call it a word. **1954** *Essays in Crit.* IV. 349 Tragedy affirms a cosmos of which man is a meaningful part. **1959** B. WOOTTON *Social Sci. & Social Path.* iii. 92 Meaningful conclusions are, moreover, inhibited by the inadequacy of the available evidence. **1970** O. DOPPING *Computers & Data Processing* i. 18 We can add the information contents from different parts of the message and obtain a meaningful result from the addition. **1971** *Sat. Rev.* (U.S.) 18 Dec. 59/1 All of us..see a need to be related in a meaningful way to the black experience. In our case, this means teaching black people. **1973** *Times* 9 Feb. 24/4 Federation met again last month to try to get meaningful talks going again on a new disputes machinery. **1973** *Physics Bull.* May 281/3 The phoneme is the smallest meaningful unit of sound a listener can perceive.

Hence **ˈmeaningfully** *adv.*

1890 SARAH J. DUNCAN *Soc. Departure* 262 Orthodocia glanced at me..meaningfully. **1937** *Mind* XLVI. 385 The finitist must hold..that of 'the sequence of time intervals' also, it cannot meaningfully be supposed that it denotes an infinite extension. **1955** *Sci. Amer.* Aug. 84/2 We cannot meaningfully look for any further sense of 'rational'. **1961** J. McCABE *Mr. Laurel & Mr. Hardy* (1962) vi. 122 He must arrange the sequence of action clearly, meaningfully, dramatically.

meaningfulness (ˈmiːnɪŋfʊlnɪs). [f. MEANINGFUL *a.* + -NESS.] The fact or quality of being meaningful.

1919 R. H. FISHER *Outside of Inside* 105 In mystical trance he discerned the meaningfulness of the third heaven **1922** J. Y. SIMPSON *Man & Attainment of Immortality* xiv. 320 The exquisite sensitivity of their minds to the meaningfulness of his language. **1935** *Mind* XLIV. 426 'Redness' is a concept which has application in experience, and this is all that is required for meaningfulness. **1940** W. V. QUINE *Math. Logic* iii. 147 The meaningfulness of an expression—the eligibility of an expression to occur in statements at all, true or false—is a matter over which we can profitably maintain control. **1941** A. D. WOOZLEY in T. Reid *Ess.* p. xxix, He is far more interested in..universals as related to words—*i.e.* in the meaningfulness of language. **1951** *Trans. Philol. Soc.* 43 Here also the fundamental argument is meaningfulness. **1953** *Essays in Crit.* III. 107 Verification of meaningfulness in literature must lie, in the last analysis, outside literature. **1959** *Cambr. Rev.* 30 May 567/2 Whether or not the verifiability criterion is a criterion of the meaningfulness of a statement or of the scientific character of a statement, the defects which it has in either case can be reproduced *quid pro quo* for the falsifiability criterion. **1959** H. GARDNER *Business of Crit.* II. iii. 131 Our first step towards making it [*sc.* a play or poem] meaningful to us is to be aware of the meaningfulness of the images to men of its own day. **1971** *Human World* Nov. 40 The question of the meaningfulness of religious utterances.

meaningless (ˈmiːnɪŋlɪs), *a.* [f. MEANING *vbl. sb.*[1] + -LESS.] Without meaning or signification; devoid of expression; without purpose. Also, not 'meaningful' (cf. MEANINGFUL *a.* b).

1797 LAMB *Let. to Coleridge*, Ill-digested, meaningless remarks. **1810** SOUTHEY *Kehama* XVI. xi, Rayless eyes.. Glazed, fix'd, and meaningless. **1876** FOX BOURNE *Locke* II. x. 138 Locke had a healthy contempt for the meaningless definitions..of the scholastic writers. **1890** W. JAMES *Princ. Psychol.* I. xvi. 676 He learned lists of meaningless syllables by heart. **1934, 1942** [see MEANINGFUL *a.*].

Hence **ˈmeaninglessly** *adv.*; **ˈmeaninglessness**.

1849 RUSKIN *Sev. Lamps* i. §7. 16 The expense which is sacrificed in domestic vanities, if not absolutely and meaninglessly lost..would [etc.]. **1853** —— *Stones Ven.* III. i. §39. 26 The modern decorative system..united the meaninglessness of the veined marble with the evanescence of the fresco. **1894** H. DRUMMOND *Ascent Man* 436 It is not the monotony of life which destroys men, but its pointlessness..its meaninglessness crushes them.

meaningly (ˈmiːnɪŋlɪ), *adv.* [f. MEANING *ppl. a.* + -LY[2].] In a meaning manner; †in one's purpose or intention (*obs.*); intentionally, purposely; in mod. use chiefly, with significance of look, tone, gesture, etc.

c **1449** PECOCK *Repr.* IV. iv. 444 Who euer biddith openli ouȝwhere eny thing to be doon for a cause..wole priueli and menyngli in the same bidding lijk thing be doon in othere placis..where is the same cause. **1862** MRS. H. WOOD *Channings* i, He spoke meaningly, as if preparing them for a surprise. **1866** G. MEREDITH *Vittoria* xxxv, I do not believe that he..ever had the intention to betray us, or has done so in reality, that is, meaningly, of his own will. **1894** H. NISBET *Bush Girl's Rom.* 56 Fixing his eyes meaningly upon her.

meaningness (ˈmiːnɪŋnɪs). [Formed as prec. + -NESS.] The attribute of having a meaning or intention; significance, expressiveness.

1754 RICHARDSON *Grandison* (1781) VI. li. 313 She.. looked..so silly! and so full of unmeaning meaningness. **1816** J. SCOTT *Vis. Paris* (ed. 5) 108 Their [French ladies'] beauty..consists rather in expression than in feature; but what with meaningness of look [etc.]. **1901** *Blackw. Mag.* Nov. 678/2, I was more than usually sensitive to the meaningness of their words.

meanish (ˈmiːnɪʃ), *a.* [f. MEAN *a.* + -ISH.] Somewhat mean.

1831 DE QUINCEY *Whiggism* Wks. 1857 VI. 42 Dr. Parr.. lost nothing in our esteem by shewing a meanish exterior.

†**ˈmeanless**, *a.*[1] *Obs. rare.* [f. MEAN *sb.*[2] + -LESS.] Having no mean: **a.** Immoderate, extreme. **b.** Performed without the aid of means or instrumentality.

1587 T. HUGHES *Misf. of Arthur* I. ii, Loe, here the loue that stirres this meanelesse hate. **1593** NASHE *Christ's T.* (1613) 130 Since his [Christ's] ascention into heauen, meanlesse miracles are ceased.

meanless (ˈmiːnlɪs), *a.*[2] ? *Obs.* [f. MEAN *v.*[1] + -LESS.] Meaningless.

1739 G. OGLE *Gualtherus & Griselda* 69 With sundry meanless Items, quaint and old. **1832** J. M. REYNOLDS *Miserrimus* (1833) 29 The most meanless phrases of formal intercourse.

†**ˈmeanly**, *a.*[1] *Obs.* In 2 mænelik, 3–4 menelich. [aphetic f. OE. *ȝemǽnelic*, f. *ȝemǽne* (see I-MENE) + *-lic* -LY[1].] Common, general.

c **1200** ORMIN 2503 All wass mænelike þing Whatt littless se þeȝȝ haffdenn. *a* **1300** in *Rel. Ant.* I. 282 Ich i-leve..in Ihesu Crist oure meneliche loverd.

†**meanly**, *a.*[2] *Obs. rare*[−1]. [f. MEAN *a.*[2] + -LY[1].] Moderate.

c **1374** CHAUCER *Boeth.* I. pr. vi. 19 (Camb. MS.) By lyghte and Meenelyche remedyes [L. *mediocribus fomentis*].

meanly (ˈmiːnlɪ), *a.*[3] *rare*[−1]. [f. MEAN *a.*[1] + -LY[1].] = MEAN *a.*[1]

1827 CAPT. HARDMAN *Waterloo* 2 Away I ran into his meanly old hoard.

meanly (ˈmiːnlɪ), *adv.*[1] [f. MEAN *a.*[1] + -LY[2].]

1. Indifferently, ill, poorly, badly; with mean attire or equipment.

1587 FLEMING *Contn. Holinshed* III. 1959/2 Sir William Hamilton, and James Leirmonth..whose message was so meanlie liked, that they were faine to send an herald into Scotland for other ambassadors. **1600** J. PORY tr. *Leo's Africa* III. 170 They are passing rich, yet go they very meanly attired. **1670** DRYDEN *2nd Pt. Conq. Granada* (1672) 163 [Many of Shakspere's plays] were..so meanly written, that the Comedy neither caus'd your mirth, nor the serious part your concernment. **1748** RICHARDSON *Clarissa* IV. 55, I think, my dear, I am not meanly off. **1757** BURKE *Abridgm. Eng. Hist.* II. vi, Their towns were meanly built and more meanly fortified. **1783** —— *Sp. Fox's E. India Bill* Wks. 1842 I. 300 Ministers..caused persons meanly qualified to be chosen directors. **1851** BORROW *Lavengro* lxviii, A rather pretty-looking woman, but..meanly dressed.

2. With reference to rank, state in life, etc.: Basely, lowlily.

1594 SHAKS. *Rich. III*, IV. iii. 37 His daughter meanly haue I matcht in marriage. **1674** EVELYN *Diary* 22 July, She was much censur'd for marrying so meanly, being herselfe allied to the Royal family. **1765** BICKERSTAFF *Maid of Mill* I. v. 10 To what purpose could a man of his distinction cast his eyes on a girl, poor, meanly born? **1869** BROWNING *Ring & Bk.* IX. 1135 I' the very breast of Jove, no meanlier throned!

3. In a way that shows a mean or base disposition, or a small mind; shabbily; sordidly, niggardly, stingily, illiberally.

1602 MARSTON *Antonio's Rev.* IV. ii, He that's a vilaine, or but meanely sowl'd. **1687** DRYDEN *Hind & P.* I. 436 Nor will I meanly tax her constancy. **1784** MANN in *Lett. Lit. Men* (Camden) 428 That M. Lavoisier..should meanly appropriate to himself Mr. Cavendish's excellent discovery. **1876** GEO. ELIOT *Dan. Der.* iv, We cannot speak a loyal word and be meanly silent..in the same moment.

4. *to think meanly of*: to have a mean estimate of; to characterize in one's thought as of little worth.

1642 ROGERS *Naaman* 387 Thinke the meanlier of us when we thinke the highliest of ourselves. **1768** GOLDSM. *Good-n. Man* I. i, Can Olivia think so meanly of my honour?

†**meanly**, *adv.*[2] *Obs.* Forms: see MEAN *a.*[2] Also 4 **menly**, 6 **mennly**. [f. MEAN *a.*[2] + -LY[2].]

1. In the mean or middling degree or manner; half way between two extremes; moderately, tolerably; fairly, moderately well.

c **1380** WYCLIF *Wks.* (1880) 31 He..synneþ not menely but greuously. *c* **1450** LYDG. & BURGH *Secrees* 2694 Fleshe soffte of disposicioun, Or meenely sharp and of mene stature. **1533** MORE *Confut.* Wks. 808/2 A church of folke, not menely good, but of folk so good, so pure, & so cleane, that [etc.]. **1548–77** VICARY *Anat.* ii. (1888) 20 Strong, and tough, meanly betweene hardenes and softnes. **1599** PORTER *Angry Wom. Abingt.* (1841) 42 Canst thou read? *Nich.* Forsooth, though none of the best, yet meanly. **1641** MILTON *Reform.* II. Wks. 1851 III. 41 He that is but meanly read in our Chronicles, needs not to be instructed. **1763** MURDOCH in *Phil. Trans.* LIII. 182 When a meanly-refrangible ray passes from water into air.

b. At a moderate speed, neither fast nor slow.

1625 PURCHAS *Pilgrims* II. 1141, I asked them how many leagues from Toro to Cairo,—they told me 7 days journey going meanly.

2. With express or implied limitation: Only moderately; not above the average; hence (coalescing with MEANLY *adv.*[1] 1), slightly, indifferently, poorly.

1600 SURFLET *Country Farm* I. xv. 101 They are set on a row..in an ouen verie meanly warme. **1695** DRYDEN tr. *Du Fresnoy's Art Paint.* Pref. 30 In the Reign of Domitian,.. Poetry was but meanly cultivated, but Painting eminently flourish'd. **1707** HEARNE *Collect.* (O.H.S.) I. 327 He shews himself..to be very meanly skill'd in the Fathers.

b. *not meanly*: in no slight degree. So also *more than meanly*.

1590 SHAKS. *Com. Err.* I. i. 59 My wife, not meanely prowd of two such boyes. **1656** EARL MONM. tr. *Boccalini's Advts. fr. Parnass.* II. xiv. (1674) 159 It would have been more than meanly pleasing to the Literati. *a* **1662** HEYLIN *Laud* II. (1671) 242 Laud..was not meanly offended, as he had good reason to be.

meanness[1] (ˈmiːnnɪs). [f. MEAN *a.*[1] + -NESS.]

1. The condition of being mean; lowness or humbleness of rank, birth, etc.; lowliness; insignificance.

1583 GOLDING *Calvin on Deut.* cxcvii. 1226 Let vs learne to acknowledge our meanesse with all humilitie. **1653** MILTON *Hirelings* (1659) 97 Without soaring above the meannes wherein they were born. **1776** GIBBON *Decl. & F* xiii. I. 358 The rusticity of his appearance and manners still betrayed in the most elevated fortune the meanness of his extraction. **1886** SPURGEON *Treas. Dav.* Ps. cxxxvi. 170 Reaching downward even to beasts and reptiles, it is, indeed, a boundless mercy, which knows no limit because of the meanness of its object. **1900** H. W. C. DAVIS in *Eng. Hist. Rev.* July 561 The meanness of his birth.

2. Weakness, deficiency, inferiority; slightness, scantness. Of physical things: Littleness, smallness. Also *pl.*

1556 ROBINSON tr. *More's Utop.* (Arb.) 19 To the meanesse of whose learning I thoughte it my part to submit my stile. **1597** HOOKER *Eccl. Pol.* v. xxxi. §3 The Ministers greatnes or meanesse of knowledge to do other things. **1682** NORRIS *Hierocles* 28 Nor to scoff at the meanness of his understanding. *a* **1716** SOUTH *Serm.* (1744) II. 82 The great purpose that brought Christ out of his Father's bosom, and clothed him with the infirmities and meannesses of our nature. **1774** GOLDSM. *Nat. Hist.* (1776) IV. 64 We suffer greater injuries from the contemptible meanness of the one [the mouse], than the formidable invasions of the other [the elephant]. **1833** LAMB *Elia* Ser. II. *Product. Mod. Art*, The large eye of genius saw in the meanness of present objects their capabilities of treatment. **1858** HAWTHORNE *Fr. & It. Note-Bks.* I. 84 The associations of moral sublimity and beauty seem to throw a veil over the physical meannesses.

3. Want of mental or moral elevation or dignity; littleness of character or mind; baseness.

1660 R. COKE *Power & Subj.* 263 This doth not proceed from any abject baseness or meanness of spirit. **1718** POPE *Iliad* XIV. 103 Lives there a Man so dead to Fame, who dares To think such Meanness? **1878** M. C. JACKSON *Chaperon's Cares* II. viii. 91 His dastardly soul would stoop to the lowest depths of meanness.

b. In *pl.* Instances of this; mean acts.

1726 DE FOE *Hist. Devil* I. iv, To descend to the meannesses of frightening children and old women. **1879** E. GARRETT *House by Works* I. 23 The little one never told him about sharp words and petty meannesses.

4. Poorness of appearance or equipment. Of literary or artistic production: Poverty of style, execution, or design; want of grandeur, nobility, etc.

a **1656** BP. HALL *Anthem Christmas Day* Rem. Wks. (1660) 436 The King of Gods in meanness drest. **1672** DRYDEN *Def. Epil.* Ess. (ed. Ker) I. 173 [Jonson] when he trusted himself alone, often fell into meanness of expression. **1705** ADDISON *Italy* 419 (Florence), I doubt however whether this Figure be not of a later Date..by the Meanness of the Workmanship. **1816** J. SCOTT *Vis. Paris* (ed. 5) 104, I found their students..assiduously copying the hard atrocities and cold meannesses of their own David. **1832** G. DOWNES *Lett. Cont. Countries* I. 155 Richtenschwyl and its precincts are very pretty, notwithstanding the meanness of most of the houses. **1852** DICKENS *Lett.* (1880) I. 285 Its intrinsic meanness as a composition.

5. Sordid illiberality; niggardliness, stinginess.

1755 in JOHNSON. **1821** LAMB *Elia* Ser. I. *Old & New Schoolm.*, All this [is] performed with a careful economy, that never descends to meanness. **1822** J. MACDONALD *Mem. J. Benson* 520 He carefully shunned both meanness and imprudent expenditure.

†**ˈmeanness**[2]. *Obs.* [f. MEAN *a.*[2] + -NESS.] The condition of being between two extremes; moderateness in size or other qualities.

1398 TREVISA *Barth. De P.R.* XIX. ii. (1495) 861 Yf the matere of clerenesse is meane it chaungeth somtyme to thyknesse and drynesse of erthe: soo that it passe not and gooth not beyonde meanesse of erthe. *c* **1450** LYDG. & BURGH *Secrees* 2555 Visage rounde boody hool and right, With meenesse of the heed is good in ech wyght. **1598** FLORIO, *Tepidezza*, luke warmth,..meannes, between hot and cold.

†**meanor.** *Obs. rare*[−1]. Aphetic f. DEMEANOUR.

a **1670** HACKET *Abp. Williams* I. (1693) 108 If the Testimony of that Lady be true..I do not shuffle it over as if his Meanor to the Lord Marquess were not a little culpable.

meano(u)r, obs. forms of MANURE *sb.*

†**means**, *sb. Obs. rare*[−1]. [f. MEAN *v.*[1]; the form perh. represents the 3rd pers. sing.] Meaning.

1656 EARL MONM. tr. *Boccalini, Pol. Touchstone* 404 The means of this was soon understood by the French, English and Italians.

means: see MEAN *sb.*[2]

meant (mɛnt), *ppl. a.* [pa. pple. of MEAN *v.*[1]] In senses of the vb. (q.v. for the predicative uses); *rarely* attributive, exc. with prefixed adv. (usually hyphened) as in *well-*, *ill-*, *kindly-meant.*

1729 SAVAGE *Wanderer* II. 284 Wrath yet remains, tho' strength his fabric leaves, And the meant hiss, the gasping mouth deceives.

†**b.** (Well) intentioned. *Obs. rare.*

c **1470** HENRY *Wallace* XI. 1041, I haiff spokyn with lord Clyffurd that knycht, Wyth thair chyftanys weill menyt for your lyff.

mean time, ˈmeantime, *sb.* and *adv.* [Properly two words (see MEAN *a.*[2] and TIME *sb.*), and still often so written in the phrases, less frequently when used alone as an adv.]

A. as *sb.*, chiefly in various adverbial phrases.

1. ***in the mean time.*** **a.** During or within the time which intervenes between one specified period or event and another; while something is going on, 'at the same time', 'all the while'. †Also, in the same sense, ***in mean time, in that*** (*this, which,* etc.) ***mean time.*** †***in the mean time of***: during.

1340 *Ayenb.* 36 Hi [*sc.* hire bestes] sterueþ ine mene-time: do oþre ine hare stede ase moche worþ. **1382** WYCLIF *1 Macc.* ix. 1 In the mene tyme [Vulg. *interea*]. *c* **1420** LYDG. *Assembly of Gods* 946 In thys mene tyme whyle [etc.]. **1447** BOKENHAM *Seyntys* (Roxb.) 20 In the mene tyme of hyr preyer They rent hyr flesh on every syde. **1502** in *Lett. Rich. III & Hen. VII* (Rolls) II. 108 In the moyne time he wold commune with the lord Nasso. *c* **1520** BARCLAY *Jugurth* (1557) 42 Wherfore (in meane tyme while they were counselling) he [etc.]. **1526** *Pilgr. Perf.* (W. de W. 1531) 12 b, In the whiche meane tyme not one of them all miscaryed. **1575–6** *Reg. Privy Council Scot.* II. 479 Eftir the committing of the foirsaidis oppressionis in the menetyme of his being at the said Lord Regent complening thairupoun. **1638** H. SPELMAN in *Lett. Lit. Men* (Camden) 155 In the mean tyme you would applie your self to the antientest Authors. **1740** tr. *De Mouhy's Fort. Country-Maid* (1741) I. 112 In mean time the People, surpris'd at what had happened, crowded to the Altar. **1818** CRUISE *Digest* (ed. 2) IV. 264 The uses..which only take place in the meantime, and until the appointment is made. **1849** MACAULAY *Hist. Eng.* iv. I. 467 In the meantime the king would be an object of aversion and suspicion to his people.

b. Used (like ***at the same time,*** etc.) in adversative or concessive sense: While this is true; still, nevertheless. ? *Obs.*

1633 BP. HALL *Occas. Medit.* (1851) 141 If ought hurt us, the fault is ours; in mistaking the evil for good: in the mean time, we owe praise to the Maker. **1638** JUNIUS *Paint. Ancients* 82 Some who making a shew of..pastimes, doe in the meane time under that pretence entertaine..most dangerous plottes. **1809** SYD. SMITH *Serm.* II. 113 In the mean time, there are many habits of thought [etc.]. **1843** BETHUNE *Sc. Fireside Stor.* 49 In the meantime, you know that my father [etc.].

†**2.** Without prep. ***the mean time, this mean time***: = 'in the mean time', 1 a. *Obs.*

c **1375** *Sc. Leg. Saints* xvi. (*Magdalena*) 986 þe mentyme þe magdelaine criste in his luf sa cane inflame, þat [etc.]. *c* **1450** *Life St. Cuthbert* (Surtees) 1745 Bot all þis meen tyme, nyghtes and dayes, Cuthbert for þair heele prayes. **1597** J. KING *On Jonas* (1618) 533 To be iustified the meane-time, or hereafter to bee glorified and liue by them. **1606** SHAKS. *Ant. & Cl.* III. iv. 25. **1700** BLACKMORE *Job* 91 While the mean time the just and godlike kind From heav'n and earth alike hard measure find.

3. ***for the mean time***: so long as the interval lasts. Also predicatively: Intended to serve for the interim.

1480 CAXTON *Chron. Eng.* ccxxxviii. 263 Whan he was yeue to ony occupacion he left al other thyng for the mene tyme and tendid therto. **1509** FISHER *Funeral Serm. C'tess Richmond* Wks. (1876) 305 Tho the rysynge of the body be delayed for a season, the soule neuertheles shall for the meane tyme haue a pleasaunt & a swete lyfe. **1897** *Daily News* 17 Feb. 3/2 This order was for the meantime.

4. *attrib.* Provisional, temporary. *rare.*

1840 BROWNING *Sordello* II. 755 Praise and blame Of what he said grew pretty nigh the same—Meantime awards to meantime acts. **1873** —— *Red Cott. Nt.-cap* 1322 The lost sheep's meantime amusements.

B. *adv.*

1. = ***in the mean time,*** A. 1 a.

1588 SHAKS. *L.L.L.* II. i. 169 Meane time, receiue such welcome at my hand, As Honour..may Make tender of, to thy true worthinesse. **1597** J. KING *On Jonas* (1618) 501 What auaileth it to abstaine from eating and drinking, if meane time we eate and deuour vp our brethren? **1632** HOLLAND *Cyrupædia* 144 Meane time whiles they came togither, those foreriders who had skowred the plaines, brought with them certaine men. **1782** MISS BURNEY *Cecilia* VI. vii, Mean-time, evidently offended..[he] conversed only with the gentlemen. **1824** SOUTHEY *Ess.* (1832) II. 201, I..trusted that, meantime, a kind and generous heart would resist the effect of fatal opinions. **1842** ORDERSON *Creol.* viii. 76 The ladies, meantime, were on the *qui vive.* **1879** MCCARTHY *Own Times* II. 259 Meantime where was Lord Palmerston?

†**2.** = ***in the mean time,*** A. 1 b. *Obs.*

1593 SHAKS. *Lucr.* Ded. 5 Were my worth greater, my duety would shew greater, meane time, as it is, it is bound to your Lordship. **1681** tr. *Belon's Myst. Physick* 64 Mean time, it may be said in general, that part of those Rules [etc.].

mean tone, ˈmeantone. *Music.* [MEAN *a.*[2]]

a. (As two words.) The averaged or standard interval (half-way between a greater and less major second) which is the basis of the system of tuning in vogue before the introduction of 'equal temperament'. **b.** *attrib.* or *adj.* (= MESOTONIC), as in ***meantone interval, system, temperament.***

1799 YOUNG in *Phil. Trans.* XC. 150 The system of mean tones, the *sistema participato* of the old Italian writers, still frequently used in tuning organs. **1884** J. LECKY in Grove *Dict. Mus.* IV. 72 It will be convenient to take equal temperament as the standard of comparison, and to measure the meantone intervals by the number of equal Semitones they contain. *Ibid.*, In the meantone system the interval G♯—E♭ is sharper than the perfect Fifth by nearly one-third of a Semitone.

meanus, obs. form of MENACE *sb.*

mean while, ˈmeanwhile, *sb.* and *adv.* [Properly two words (see MEAN *a.*[2] and WHILE *sb.*), and still often so written (cf. MEAN TIME).]

A. *sb.*, chiefly in advb. phrases.

1. ***in the mean while.*** **a.** = 'in the mean time' as in MEAN TIME A. 1 a. Also †***in*** (*that, this, which,* etc.) ***mean while,*** †***in mean while,*** †***in the mean(s whiles.***

c **1350** *Will. Palerne* 1148 þan boþe partiȝes..made hem alle merie in þe mene while. *c* **1386** CHAUCER *Man of Law's T.* 570 On this book he swoor anoon She gilty was, and in the meene whiles An hand hym smoot vpon the nekke boon. —— *Friar's T.* 147 In this meene while, This yeman gan a litel for to smyle. *c* **1400** *Destr. Troy* 3102 Ho..staryt O þat stoute with hire stepe Ene, There most was hir mynd in þat mene qwhile. *c* **1540** tr. *Pol. Verg. Eng. Hist.* (Camden) I. 286 In the mean whiles it fortuned that [etc.]. **1570–6** LAMBARDE *Peramb. Kent* (1826) 285 Archbishop Baldwin went into the Holy Lande and died without returne in which meane while the Chapele of Hakington..was..demolished. **1581** J. BELL *Haddon's Answ. Osor.* 147 b, And where in the meanes whiles lurketh then the law that is written within, in the hartes of the faythfull? **1590** MARLOWE *Edw. II,* IV. v, We in meanwhile, madam, must take advice How [etc.]. **1595** DANIEL *Civ. Wars* IV. xxxiv, Yet now in this so happie a meane while. **1606** HOLLAND *Sueton.* 11 And in this meane while,..when the Senate thought good there should be but one Consul created, namely Cn. Pompeivs. **1628** E. BLOUNT in Earle *Microcosm.* To Rdr. (Arb.) 18 In the meanwhile, I remaine Thine. Ed. Blovnt. **1707** FREIND *Peterborow's Cond. Sp.* 235 In the mean while, my Lord pursu'd the Enemies Army. **1818** COBBETT *Pol. Reg.* XXXIII. 101 Upon this subject I will in my next Number make an appeal. .. In the meanwhile let me pride myself a little on the circumstance [etc.]. **1908** H. G. WELLS *First & Last Things* III. viii. 123 The organized state..has not arrived..and in the meanwhile they must act like its anticipatory agents. **1960** G. SANDERS *Mem. Professional Cad* II. viii. 170 In the meanwhile the boat..evidently decided to end it all. **1972** *Listener* 1 June 705/2 In the meanwhile sanctions would be continued.

†**b.** ***in the mean while that***: during the time that. *Obs.*

1480 CAXTON *Chron. Eng.* cxxxix. 118 The emperesse in the mene whyle that the batayll dured escaped fro thens and went vnto oxenford.

c. In adversative or concessive use; cf. MEANTIME 1 b.

1597 HOOKER *Eccl. Pol.* v. xlviii. §13 We pray..that God would turne them away from vs, owing in the meane while this deuotion to the Lord our God, that [etc.]. **1879** MCCARTHY *Own Times* II. xxix. 368 In the meanwhile we may regard him simply as a great author.

†**2.** ***the mean while*** = 'in the mean while', A. 1 a. Also ***this, that mean while(s, all this mean while, all that mean while during.*** *Obs.* exc. *arch.*

c **1374** CHAUCER *Troylus* III. 50 Lay al þis mene while Troylus, Recordynge his lesson in þis manere. **14..** *Voc.* in Wr.-Wülcker 590/14 *Interea,* the mene whyle. **1470–85** MALORY *Arthur* II. iii. 79 The meane whyle that this knyght was makyng hym redy to departe [etc.]. **1548** UDALL *Erasm. Par. Luke* 20 b, Al that meane while duryng, [they] had a priest that could not speake. **1654** EARL MONM. tr. *Bentivoglio's Warrs Flanders* 363 But the United Provinces lost not the opportunity this mean whiles which offered it self so favourably to them. **1658** —— tr. *Paruta's Wars Cyprus* 40 Generall Zaune, was this mean while gone from Corfu. **1922** JOYCE *Ulysses* 381 This meanwhile this good sister stood by the door.

3. ***for the mean while*** = 'for the mean time': see MEAN TIME A. 3.

c **1386** CHAUCER *Man of Law's T.* 448 Ther was hir refut for the meene while.

4. Subst. use of the adv. (see B. 1). *rare*$^{-1}$.

1872 W. R. GREG *Enigmas Life* 191 The long ages of the Meanwhile.

B. *adv.* (Cf. MEAN TIME.)

1. = ***in the mean while,*** A. 1 a.

c **1440** *Promp. Parv.* 332/2 Mene whyle, *interim.* *c* **1586** C'TESS PEMBROKE *Ps.* LXVIII. i, The just meane while shall in Jehovah's presence Play, sing, and daunce. **1588** SHAKS. *Tit. A.* I. i. 408 Let the lawes of Rome determine all, Meane while I am possest of that is mine. **1678** BUTLER *Hud.* III. i. 99 Meanwhile the Squire was on his way, The Knight's late Orders to obey. **1713** ADDISON *Cato* II. vi, Mean while I'll draw up my Numidian Troops, And, as I see Occasion, favour thee. **1877** FROUDE *Short Stud.* (1883) IV. I. x. 113 The archbishop meanwhile had returned from his adventurous expedition.

2. = ***in the mean while,*** A. 1 c.

1597 J. KING *On Jonas* (1618) 539 Meane-while, the time, and cause, and measure of this anger in Ionas, I thinke, are worthie to be blamed. **1837** G. S. FABER *Prim. Doctr. Justif.* 277 Meanwhile, the really primitive and apostolic and catholic doctrine was that of the Reformers. **1876** L. STEPHEN *Eng. Th. 18th C.* II. 443 Meanwhile, however, one characteristic of the English sentimentalists must be noticed.

meany (ˈmiːnɪ). *colloq.* Also **meanie.** [f. MEAN *a.*[1] + -Y[6], -IE.] A mean-minded or stingy person.

1927 H. C. BROWN *In Golden Nineties* iii. 107 It was whispered by some old meanies that many of the five-foot floral offerings were purchased by the actors themselves and sent to the theatre with fictitious names attached. **1928** J. P. MCEVOY *Showgirl* xiii. 212/1 This old meany..last night..found himself, much to his aged surprise, in the Klaw Theatre. **1936** L. C. DOUGLAS *White Banners* xiv. 315 Colonel Livingstone was an old meanie. **1951** J. B. PRIESTLEY *Festival at Farbridge* II. i. 34 He was at heart, she felt, a cunning old meanie. **1974** *Times* 15 Feb. 4/4 A bunch of local 'baddies' reinforced by 'meanies'.

meany(e, obs. ff. MANY; var. ff. MEINIE.

†**meapte.** *Obs.* [? A blundered adaptation of L. *meātus* or F. *méat.*] = MEATUS.

1572 J. JONES *Bathes Buckstone* 11 Of the more vehement force, of the breath, followeth necessarily, all the meaptes to be clenzed. *Ibid.* 13 b, Keepe your bedde for two or three houres after, lest the small meaptes being opened, a soddaine alteracion may happen.

mear(e: see MARE *sb.*, MERE *sb.*, *a.*, and *v.*

mearaltie, obs. form of MAYORALTY.

mearch, obs. form of MARCH *sb.*[1] and *v.*[1]

meari, obs. form of MARROW.

mearing: see MERING *vbl. sb.*

mearl(e, variants of MERLE *sb.*

mearlew muse, variant of MURLIMEWS *Obs.*

mearmayde, obs. form of MERMAID.

meary, obs. form of MERRY *a.*

mease (miːz). Forms: 5–6 **mayse,** 5, 6, 9 **meise,** 6–8 **mese,** 6, 9 **maise,** 6–9 **meaze,** 7 **maze, mes,** 7–9 **mesh, maze,** 9 **mais, maize, mase, meas, meash,** 7– **mease.** [a. OF. *meise, maise* barrel (or some other receptacle) for herrings (in 14th c. latinized *meisa*); of Teut. origin: cf. OHG. *meisa* bundle, box (MHG. *meise* barrel for herrings, mod.G. dial. *meise* basket), MLG., MDu. *mêse* barrel for herrings, ON. *meiss* box, basket (MSw. *mes, mese,* Sw. dial. *mes, meis,* MDa. *mees*), ? cogn. w. Lith. *máisza-s* bag.] A measure for herrings, equal to five 'hundreds' (usually 'long hundreds' varying in different localities: see quots.).

In N. Devon the number is 612, i.e. four times 153, app. suggested by John xxi. 11 (see E.D.D.).

1469 in *10th Rep. Hist. MSS. Comm.* App. v. 306 He shal pay for every meise so solde xii.*d.* **1535** in *Mem. Fountains Abb.* (Surtees) 259, x mayses allic. rub. distribut' dictis pauperibus. **1597** SKENE *De Verb. Sign.*, *Mese,* of herring, conteinis fiue hundreth. **1603** OWEN *Pembrokeshire* (1892) 122 Such store of fishe as pleaseth god to send, sometimes x meises, sometimes xij. xvj. or xx meises. **1613** in *Lex Scripta of Isle of Man* (1819) 100 An anncyent Statute in this Isle for paying of Custom Heyrings (called Castle Mazes). *c* **1682** J. COLLINS *Salt & Fishery* 107 [They] take sometimes 60 Mesh at a Tide, which are three Lasts of Herrings. **1780** A. YOUNG *Tour Irel.* I. 190 A boat will catch 6 maze of herrings in a night, each 500. **1883** S. WALPOLE *Brit. Fish Trade* (Fish. Exhib. Lit. I.) 37 In Ireland and the Isle of Man herrings are measured by the mease, which contains 525 fish. **1887** HALL CAINE *Deemster* xxxviii, I took more fish by many meshes than I could ever consume. **1894** —— *Manxman* 226 Ten maise of this sort for the last lot. **1905** *Whitaker's Alm., Weights & M.*, Herrings are sold..on the ..Isle of Man, and in Ireland, by the Maze, which contains 5 long hundreds of 123 each.

mease, var. MESE *Obs.*, MESS *sb.* and *v.*

measelen, -line, obs. forms of MASLIN[1] and [2].

measb, obs. form of MASH, MEASE, MESH.

meashie, obs. form of MESHY.

measle (ˈmiːz(ə)l), *sb.* Forms: 5 **masyl, mazil, meselle, -ylle,** 6 **measel, meazell,** 7 **meazil, -le,** 9 **measle.** *Pl.* 4 **maseles,** 4–6 **mesels,** 5 **meazeles, meseles,** 6 **maisils, massels, maysilles, meselles,** 6–7 **masels, measel(l)s,** 7 **maisels, mazels, measil(l)s,** 7–8 **meazels, -les,** 7– **measles.** [ME. *maseles* pl., cogn. w. OHG. (? and OS.) *masala,* occurring as gloss to L. *flemen,* i.e. *phlegmon* blood-blister (MHG. *masel(e,* MLG. *masele, massele,* MDu. *masel* fem., blood-blister, pustule, spot on the skin; also in pl. measles; mod.Du. *mazelen* measles); a related form occurs in MDu. and mod.G. *masern* pl., measles; for the Scandinavian forms see MEASLINGS. For other derivatives of the Teut. root **mas-*, **mǣs-*, expressing the notion of 'spot' or 'excrescence', see MAZER.

It is possible that the word may have come into Eng. from continental LG. For its existence in OE. there is no other evidence than the occurrence, in a 12th c. MS., of *mæslesceafe* as a spelling of *mælsceafa* MALSHAVE. The phonetic development is irregular: normally the modern form should be **mazel* (cf. HAZEL[1], for which spellings like *hesel, heasle* occur in the 15–16th c.). That the dialectal form *measle* appears in literary English may be due to a mistaken association of this word with MESEL leper; a similar confusion occurred in MHG., where *maselsucht* (etymologically 'measles') was often used for *miselsucht* leprosy.]

1. a. *pl.* (rarely *sing.*). A specific infectious disease of man (in medical Latin called *Rubeola* and *Morbilli*), characterized by an eruption of rose-coloured papulæ arranged in irregular circles and crescents, preceded and accompanied by catarrhal and febrile symptoms; it rarely attacks the same person twice. (Often referred to as one of the diseases

incident to childhood, although it frequently attacks adults.) The plural form is now usually construed as a *sing*.

German (formerly also ***false, French, hybrid***) ***measles***: a contagious disease (*Roseola epidemica* or *Rubella*) distinct from measles, but resembling it in some of its symptoms.

c **1325** *Gloss W. de Bibbesw.* (MS. Arundel 220) in Wright *Voc.* 161 *Rugeroles*, maseles [*c* 1300 *MS. Camb.* maselinges]. **14..** *Nom.* in Wr.-Wülcker 707/25 *Hec serpedo*, a mesylle. *c* **1440** *Promp. Parv.* 328/2 *Masyl*, or *mazil*, sekenesse. **1483** *Cath. Angl.* 237/1 A Meselle; *serpedo.* **1489** *Plumpton Corr.* (Camden) p. cxiv, At that season ther wer the Meazelles soo strong, & in especiall amongis Ladies & Gentilwemen, that sum died of that sikeness. **1533** Elyot *Cast. Helthe* (? 1541) 80 b, Purpilles, measels, and small pockes. *c* **1560** *Misogonus* III. iii. 49 (Brandl), I can cure the Agwe, the Massels and the french pocke. **1578** Lyte *Dodoens* I. xvii. 27 It is good.. against.. the small Pockes and Meselles. **1601** Dolman *La Primaud. Fr. Acad.* (1618) III. 813 Fumitory.. is good against the mezels. **1663** Butler *Hud.* I. iii. 1248 From whence they start up chosen vessels, Made by contact, as men get measles. **1696** *Lond. Gaz.* No. 3224/3 The Princess of Piedmont is fallen ill of the Meazles. **1732** Arbuthnot *Rules of Diet* in *Aliments*, etc. I. 250 The Small Pox, Meazles, and pestilential Fevers. **1802** *Med. Jrnl.* VIII. 28 The Measles usually makes its appearance at the commencement of the year. **1877** Roberts *Handbk. Med.* (ed. 3) I. 143 Measles is decidedly infectious. **1924** Galsworthy *White Monkey* I. iii. 21 Fleur knew how catching the word was; it would run like a measle round the ring. **1948** Mencken *Amer. Lang.* Suppl. II. 383 False singulars, made by back formation, are numerous, *e.g.*,.. *measle*, nor are they confined to the untutored.

attrib. **1843** R. J. Graves *Syst. Clin. Med.* xiv, The measles like eruption [of typhus fever] appeared about the fifth day. **1897** *Allbutt's Syst. Med.* II. 148 The rash for a time may be suggestive of Scarlet Fever, but sooner or later it usually conforms more to the measles type.

b. *pl.* The pustules characteristic of this disease; †formerly sometimes applied to the pustules of eruptive diseases generally.

1398 Trevisa *Barth. De P.R.* XIX. ix. (1495) 870 Colour of skynne chaungyth for streyte contynuaunce of the skynne: as it fareth ofte in Mesels: Pockes: woundes: botches and brennynge. **1599** A. M. tr. *Gabelhouer's Bk. Physicke* 277/2 Others take a fether, and dippe it in the saide water, and therwith they annoynte all the Measells of the Face when they are come forth. **1685** *Cooke's Mellif. Chirurg.* VI. II. ix. (ed. 4) 214 Those little Pustles in the skin, with a deep redness.. are called Measles. **1789** W. Buchan *Dom. Med.* (1790) 241 About the sixth or seventh day from the time of sickening, the measles begin to turn pale on the face.

¶**c.** In exclamatory phrase. ? *nonce-use.*

1614 B. Jonson *Barth. Fair* III. iv, Why the measills, should you stand heere, with your traine [etc.].

2. a. *pl.* (†formerly also *sing.*) A disease in swine, produced by the scolex of the tapeworm; in later use, a similar disease in other animals.

[This application of the word arose from a misinterpretation of the adj. *mesel* 'leprous' (see measle *a.*) as used to designate swine suffering from this disease.]

1587 Mascall *Govt. Cattle, Hogges* (1627) 273 Poultry dung, which also is ill for hogs, and will increase a measel among them. **1615** Latham *Falconry* (1633) 107 Such setled curnels like vnto the mazels of a swine. **1636** B. Jonson *Discov.* Wks. (1640) 93 The Swyne dyed of the Measils. **1793** A. Young *Ann. Agric.* XIX. 299 Is the small pox known among sheep? It is a little known, but not at all common.—Called the measles. **1844** Stephens *Bk. of Farm* II. 245 Pigs are subject to a cutaneous disease called measles, which is supposed to render the flesh unwholesome.

b. The scolex or cysticercus which produces this disease. Also *attrib.* in ***measle-disease.***

1863 Aitken *Sci. & Pract. Med.* (ed. 2) II. 94, 95 The first animal he experimented on died from a violent attack of the measle disease; and on dissection the muscles were found filled with measles, or imperfectly developed *scolices.* **1901** Osler *Princ. & Pract. Med.* (ed. 4) 367 The measles are more readily overlooked in beef than in pork, as they do not present such an opaque white colour.

3. *pl.* 'A disease of trees which causes the bark to become rough and irregular, and the branch finally to die' (*Syd. Soc. Lex.*). Also *sing.* a blister or excrescence on a tree. ? *Obs.*

1601 Holland *Pliny* I. 539 Oliue.. hath another greefe and sorance called in Latin Clavus, Fungus or Patella (*i.* a Knur, Puffe, Meazil or Blister). **1611** Florio, *Chiauo*, a meazell or blister growing on trees. **1674** Josselyn *Voy. New Eng.* 190 Their fruit-trees are subject to two diseases, the Meazels,.. and lowsiness. **1679** Evelyn *Sylva* xxvii. (ed. 3) 141 Trees (especially Fruit-bearers) are infested with the Measels. **1707** Mortimer *Husb.* 392.

4. *pl.* In *Photography.* Cf. measly *a.* 3.

1876 [see mealiness].

†'measle, *a. Obs.* Forms: 5-6 **mesel,** 6 **masyl, meazel, messell(e, mesyl, mys(s)ell,** 7 **meazell, measle.** [A particular application of mesel *a.*, leprous; the later spelling proceeds from association with measle *sb.*] Of swine, their flesh: Affected with 'measles', measly.

[**1398**: see measled *a.*] *c* **1460** *Towneley Myst.* ii. 264 Yit teynd thou not thi mesel swyne? **1519** in *Surtees Misc.* (1888) 33 For sellyng messell pork xxd. **1547** Boorde *Introd. Knowl.* xxviii. (1870) 195 Masyl baken, and sardyns, I do eate and sel. **1598** Kitchin *Courts Leet*, etc. (1675) 347 Where Meazel Porks are sold at Rumford. *a* **1652** Brome *City Wit* v. Wks. 1873 I. 363 The kell of a meazell hog.

measle ('mi:z(ə)l), *v.* Also 7 **meazel, meazle, mezle.** [f. measle *sb.*]

1. *trans.* To infect with measles.

1611 Cotgr. s.v. *Pied d'oison*, Goose-foot, wild Orache; called also Swinesbane, because it kills, or measels, the Swine which eat of it. *a* **1845** Hood *Tale of Trumpet* lv, Though the wishes that Witches utter Can.. Send styes in the eye—and measle the pigs. **1890** *Syd. Soc. Lex.*, *Measle*, to infect with measles.

2. *transf.* To cover as with 'measles' or spots.

In quot. 1678 there is a reference to mesel *sb.*, leper.

1638 Wentworth 23 May in *Strafforde Lett.* (1739) II. 173, I was so damnably bitten with Midges, as my Face is all mezled over ever since. **1885** D. Ker in *Libr. Mag.* (U.S.) Sept. 219 A tall, sallow fellow, measled all over with brass buttons.

absol. **1678** Butler *Hud.* III. i. 319 With Cow-itch meazle like a Leper.

3. *intr.* To develop the eruption of measles. *colloq.*

a **1906** *Mod.* 'The child is measling nicely'. 'The baby measled at the same time' (Dr. W. Sykes).

4. *fig.* To be full of or teem *with* (objectionable things). *rare.*

1856 C. Reade *Never too Late* II. xxv. 245 All this.. in thieves' cant, with an oath or a nasty expression at every third word. The sentences measled with them.

measled ('mi:z(ə)ld), *ppl. a.* Forms: 4 **meselyd,** 5 **maselyd, meselled,** 6 **meseld, -led, mezeled,** 6-7 **measeled,** 6-8 **meazeled,** 7 **messeled, miselled,** 7-8 **meazled,** 6- **measled.** [f. measle *sb.*, *a.*, and *v.* + -ed.]

1. Infected with measles.

1398 Trevisa *Barth. De P.R.* VII. lxiv. (1495) 281 Meete that is soone corrupte as of meselyd hogges. *c* **1440** *Promp. Parv.* 329/1 Maselyd, *serpiginosus.* **1499** *Maldon, Essex, Court Rolls* (Bundle 58, no. 1ᵛ), Meselled hog. **1573** Tusser *Husb.* (1878) 52 Thy measeled bacon. **1647** *New Haven Col. Rec.* (1857) I. 342 [He] obiected against on of the hoggs wᶜʰ was misellled. **1713** C'tess Winchelsea *Misc. Poems* 214 A Pestilential Sow, a meazeled Pork, On the foundation has been long at work. **1820** J. Jekyll *Corr.* (1894) 144 We dined at A. Ellis's last week with the Poodle who has buried his measled Majesties. **1876** tr. *Wagner's Gen. Pathol.* (ed. 6) 114 By the use of measled meat.

2. Spotted.

1634 Sir T. Herbert *Trav.* 213 One speckled fish.. is called the poyson fish, tis shaped like a Tench, but meazled. **1706** Phillips, *Meazled*, full of Meazles, Spots, or Blotches.

†**3.** *fig.* Poor, 'scurvy'. (Cf. measly 4.)

1596 Nashe *Saffron-Walden* Wks. (Grosart) III. 191 That meazild inuention of the Goodwife my mothers finding her daughter in the ouen, where [etc.].

Hence †**'measledness,** measled condition.

1611 Cotgr., *Sursemure*, the measeldnesse of Hogs.

†**'measling,** *vbl. sb.* [f. measle *v.* + -ing¹.] Infection with measles.

1573 Tusser *Husb.* (1878) 41 And diligent Cislye, my dayrie good wench, make cleanly his cabben, for measling and stench.

measlings ('mi:zlɪŋz), *sb. pl. Obs.* exc. *dial.* Also 4 **maselinges,** 7 **meslings,** 9 **mezlings, mizzlings.** (See E.D.D.) [Early ME. *maselinges*, f. (? Eng. or LG.) *masel* measle *sb.* + -ing¹. Cf. Da. *mæslinger* pl. (recorded from the 16th c.), Sw. *messling, mässling*, mod.Icel. *mislingar* pl., measles.

The formation has not been found exc. in Eng. and in Scandinavian; it is unlikely to have arisen independently in those two branches of Teut.; it may have belonged to early MLG., and thence have passed into Eng. and Da.]

The measles.

c **1300** *Gloss W. de Bibbesw.* (MS. Camb.) in Wright *Voc.* 161 *Rugeroles* [glossed] maselinges [*c* 1325 *MS. Arundel* 220 maseles]. **1671** Skinner *Etymol. Ling. Angl.* I. ii, *Meslings*, vox agro Linc. usitatissima.. vide *Measels.* **1890** *Syd. Soc. Lex.*, *Measlings*, measles.

measly ('mi:zlɪ), *a.* Also 8 **meazly,** 8-9 **measley.** [f. measle *sb.* + -y.]

1. Of or pertaining to measles; resembling measles.

1782 W. Heberden *Comm.* vii. (1806) 20 Distinguished from the measley efflorescence. **1822-34** *Good's Study Med.* (ed. 4) I. 356 The measley tubercles which form the second [kind of hydatids, in swine]. **1897** *Allbutt's Syst. Med.* III. 576 A dark measly rash.

2. Of swine, their flesh: Affected with measles. (Cf. measle *a.*, measled *ppl. a.*)

1687 A. Lovell tr. *Thevenot's Trav.* I. 89 She saw a Measly Hog come and Wash in the Water. **1747** Mrs. Glasse *Cookery* xxi. 161 If you find little Kernels in the Fat of the Pork, like Hail-shot.. 'tis measly, and dangerous to be eaten. **1885** Runciman *Skippers & Sh.* 5 What's the grub to-morrow? Measly pork again.

3. Spotty. In *Photography.* (See quot. 1876.)

1876 Abney *Instr. Photogr.* (ed. 3) 110 The result would be 'measly' or mealy prints—i.e. prints in which minute red spots alternate with darker ones in the shadows after fixing. **1891** *Anthony's Photogr. Bull.* IV. 254 The remainder, after even an hour's soaking were only a very measley brown. **1898** Talmage in *Chr. Herald* (N.Y.) 5 Jan. 4/4 The slushy custards; the jaundiced or measly biscuits.

4. *slang.* Poor, contemptible, of little value.

1864 M. E. Braddon *Henry Dunbar* II. xi. 212 The audacity to offer a measly hundred pounds or so for the discovery of a great crime! **1872** *Punch* 27 July 39/2 That was a fine old hen.. but.. the others were a measly lot. **1892** Zangwill *Childr. Ghetto* I. 302 Greenwich, where they take you girls for a measly day's holiday once a year. **1905** *Dialect Notes* III. 14 *Measly*,.. poor. 'I don't want that *measly* stuff.' **1919** E. O'Neill *Ile* in *Moon of Caribbees* (1923) 13 Did you ever hear o' me pointin' s'uth for home with only a measly four hundred barrel of ile in the hold? **1973** J. Porter *It's Murder with Dover* vi. 55 Ten measly years in the nick doesn't worry anybody. **1974** *Sunday Tel.* 9 June 34/4 A spineless exhibition by the early Yorkshire batting—they have mastered only a measly five batting points all season—put them on the rack yet again.

Comb. **1869** Aldrich *Story of Bad Boy* 29 A measly-looking little boy with no shoes.

measne, obs. form of mesne.

meason, ? variant of maison *Obs.*, house.

a **1550** *Image Ipocr.* in *Skelton's Wks.* (1843) II. 423/1 [A bishop ought] To spende in tyme and season, And so to kepe his meason.

meason, obs. Sc. form of mason *sb.*

'measondue. *Obs.* exc. *Hist.* Forms: 4 **masondewe,** 4-5 **mesondieu,** (*pl.* **-deux, -dieux**), 5 **mayson-, mesondewe,** 5-6 **masendewe, maysyndew,** 6 **masone dew, massindewe, meason de dieu, masoun de Dieu,** 6-8 **measondue,** 7-9 **maisondieu,** 8 **massondew, measondieu.** [a. OF. *meson-dieu, maison-Dieu*, lit. house of God. Cf. F. *hôtel-Dieu* (hotel 1 c.).] A hospital or poorhouse.

1354-5 *Durham Acc. Rolls* (Surtees) 555 Rogero de Esshe cooperienti super le Mesondieu. **1362** Langl. *P. Pl.* A. VIII. 28 Treuþe.. Bad hem.. make Meson deu [**1377** B. VII. 26 mesondieux] þer-with Meseyse to helpe. ? *a* **1400** *Morte Arth.* 3038 Mynsteris and masondewes they malle to the erthe. **1429-30** *Wills & Inv. N.C.* (Surtees) I. 78 To ye mesondieu of sint kateryne.. for yair enoʳments xxl. **1455** *Rolls of Parlt.* V. 315/2 A meson Dewe founded by him by oure licence, in the seid Toune of Bockyng. **1470** *Will* in *Ripon Ch. Acts* (Surtees) 144 Pauperibus manentibus in Masyndew. **1546** *Yorks. Chantry Surv.* (Surtees) 468 There is a Bedehouse or Massindewe of poure folkes. **1558** *Act 1 Eliz.* c. 21 §34 Any Hospitall, Measondue, or Spittel House. **1597-8** *Act 39 Eliz.* c. 5 To erecte, founde, and establysh one or more Hospitalls, Measons de Dieu. **1630** *Acts of Sederunt* (1790) 43 Aganis unlawfull dispositiouns of whatsomevir landes, teinds, or rentes, dottit to hospitallis or massondewis. **1631** T. Powell *Tom All Trades* (1876) 170, I find not any *Meson de dieu* for relieving of mayned Marriners. **1641** *Termes de la Ley*, Measondue is an appellation of divers Hospitalls in this Kingdome. **1842** Barham *Ingol. Leg.* Ser. II. *Old Woman in Grey*, Where can I find out the old *Maison Dieu*?

measque, rare obs. form of mask *sb.*²

measse, obs. form of mess.

meastling, obs. form of maslin¹.

measura'bility. [f. next + -ity.] Capability of being measured.

1697 J. Sergeant *Solid Philos.* 105 Many other.. Attributes, are given to Quantity; such as are Divisibility, Impenetrability, Space, and Measurability. **1955** W. Pauli *Niels Bohr* 71 Measurability of electro-magnetic fields. **1957** *Times Lit. Suppl.* 18 Oct. 620/2 A chapter on 'Illusionism and Perspective' deals with.. measurability in quattrocentro compositions. **1969** *Nature* 14 June 1033/1 Though a physical quantity is considered primarily an attribute of the object under investigation, the need for measurability implies that the characteristic features of the relevant instruments of observation are an integral part of the quantity. **1975** *Times* 26 May 6/2 The main cause of this domination is measurability. Money provides an incontrovertible unit of measurement.

measurable ('mɛʒ(j)ʊərəb(ə)l), *a.* Also 4-6 **mes-.** [a. F. *mesurable*:—late L. *mensūrābilis*, f. *mensūrāre* to measure. In sense 3 directly f. the Eng. vb.]

†**1.** Of persons, their actions, etc.: Characterized by moderation; moderate, temperate; *occas.* modest.

13.. *K. Alis.* 7050 They beon treowe, and stedefast, Mesureabele, bonére, and chest. *c* **1386** Chaucer *Prol.* 435 Of his diete mesurable was he. —— *Parson's T.* ¶862 A wyf sholde eek be mesurable in lokinge and in beringe and in laughinge. *c* **1430** Lydg. *Min. Poems* (Percy Soc.) 67 Curteys of language, in spendyng mesurable. **1540** Hyrde tr. *Vives' Instr. Chr. Wom.* (1592) F vj, Follow his [Christ's] sober & measurable mother. **1595** Southwell *Tri. Death* (1596) 6 Of feeding shee was very measurable, rather too sparing, than too liberall a diet. **1608** T. James *Apol. Wyclif* 35 Abstinence with prudence was needeful, that is.. measureable fasting, both of bodie and soule.

2. Of moderate size, dimensions, quantity, duration, or speed. *Obs.* exc. as implied in 3.

a **1340** Hampole *Psalter* xxxviii. 7 Lo mesurabils þou sett my dayes. **1362** Langl. *P. Pl.* A. III. 241 þat laborers and louh folk taken of heore Maystres, Nis no Maner Meede bote Mesurable huyre. **1426** Lydg. *De Guil. Pilgr.* 22613, I sawgh oon.. Goon a mesurable paas. **1494** Fabyan *Chron.* VII. 413 The Kynge.. assembled a mesurable hoost of people. *a* **1548** Hall *Chron.*, *Hen. VII*, 3 b, Luke warme drynke, temperate heate, and measurable clothes. **1594** Carew *Huarte's Exam. Wits* iii. (1596) 28 The braine should be tempered with measurable heat.

3. That can be measured; susceptible of measurement or computation; of such dimensions as to admit of being measured; *spec.* (of rainfall) not less than $\frac{1}{100}$ inch.

1599 Hakluyt *Voy.* II. I. 273 Any measurable wares. **1690** Locke *Hum. Und.* II. xvi. §8 Number.. is that which the Mind makes use of, in measuring all things that by us are measurable. **1780** Marsham in *Phil. Trans.* LXXI. 451 The annual increase of very old trees is hardly measurable with a string. **1837** Carlyle *Fr. Rev.* I. VII. x, The fire of Insurrection gets damped.. into measurable, manageable heat. **1876** Bristowe *Theory & Pract. Med.* (1878) 480 The descent of the diaphragm.. causes measurable enlargement of the upper region of the abdomen. **1893** *Times* 4 May 10/4

A measurable quantity of rain fell over the western parts of England.

b. Phrase, ***to come within a measurable distance of*** (some undesirable condition or event).

1890 *Guardian* 19 Nov. 1825/1 Reckless dealing in South American securities brought them..within measurable distance of bankruptcy.

c. *Math.* (See MEASURE *v.* 7 b.)

1667 *Phil. Trans.* II. 572 A Multiplex of the Product or least Dividend measurable by those Divisors.

†**4.** Characterized by due measure or proportion.

1563 *Homilies* II. *Coming down of Holy Ghost* I. (1859) 458 All which gifts..are..given to man according to the measurable distribution of the Holy Ghost.

†**b.** Proportionate *to*. *Obs. rare*—[1].

1533 ELYOT *Cast. Helthe* (1541) 40 b, The dyner moderate, and the drynke therunto mesurable, according to the drynesse or moystnesse of the meate.

†**5.** Measured, uniform in movement; metrical, rhythmical. *Obs.*

1569 J. SANFORD tr. *Agrippa's Van. Artes* 30 b, To daunce with framed gestures, and with measurable pases. **1586** W. WEBBE *Eng. Poetrie* (Arb.) 22 The force of this measurable or tunable speaking. **1597** BEARD *Theatre God's Judgem.* (1612) 435 The graue behauior, the measurable march, the pompe and ostentation of women dancers.

b. *Mus.* = MENSURABLE.

1614 RAVENSCROFT *Brief Discourse* I The Definitions and Diuisions of Moode, Time, and Prolation in Measurable Musick. [**1879** HELMORE *Plain-Song* 11 Portions of Plain-Song often fall into strictly measurable forms.]

†**6.** as *adv.* Moderately. *Obs.*

1542 in Hodgson *Hist. Northumbld.* (1828) III. II. 214 *note*, A lytle town in measurable good reparacions. **1551** TURNER *Herbal* I. K v, The leues are..mesurable roughe.

ˈmeasurableness. [f. prec. + -NESS.]

†**a.** Moderation (*obs.*). **b.** Capability of being measured.

c **1511** COLET in Lupton *Life* (1887) 301 The lawes that commaunde sobernes, and a measurablenes in aparayle. **1563** *Homilies* II. *Of Matrimony* (1859) 303 If he [*sc.* the husband] will use measurableness and not tyranny, and if he yield some things to the woman. **1697** J. SERGEANT *Solid Philos.* 182 The same way gives us the plain Notion of Immensity, by joining a Negation to Measurableness. **1727** BAILEY vol. II, *Measurableness*, capableness of being measured.

measurably (ˈmɛʒ(j)ʊərəblɪ), *adv.* [f. MEASURABLE + -LY[2].]

†**1.** Moderately, in moderation. *Obs.*

c **1380** WYCLIF *Wks.* (1880) 433 Hou þey & herne shulen first take mesurably of þes godis. *c* **1386** CHAUCER *Melib.* ¶639 Vse hem by mesure, that is to seyn, spende hem mesurably. *c* **1491** *Chast. Goddes Chyld.* xxv. 72 Mete whan it is mesurably taken and well defyed: it maketh a man hole in body. **1535** COVERDALE *Ecclus.* xxxi. 28 Wyne measurably dronken [*similarly* **1611**] is a reioysinge of the soule. **1579** LANGHAM *Gard. Health* (1633) 254 An ounce of the iuice of the root [etc.] purgeth the body measurably.

2. In due measure or proportion; proportionably.

c **1400** *Destr. Troy* 3985 Ho was mesurably made. *c* **1449** PECOCK *Repr.* III. xiii. 358 Constantyn endewid not..eny chirche in Rome with eny greet habundaunt immouable possessiouns, but oonli with possessiouns competentli and mesurabily. **1572** J. JONES *Bathes Buckstone* 4 Measurably qualifyinge the ouerheated members, and drying such as bee ouer moyste. **1607** J. CARPENTER *Plaine Mans Plough* 176 He may be able to draw forth of his full vessel measurably unto his flocke. **1701** WHITEHEAD *Truth Prevalent* 20 If a thirsty Man comes to Drink at a Well..he drinks measurably as much as he needs.

3. In some measure, to some extent; 'in a measure'. *U.S.*

1756 J. WOOLMAN *Jrnl.* (1840) 30 The public meetings were large and measurably favoured with divine goodness. **1848** LOWELL *Biglow P.* Ser. I. *Introd.* Poet. Wks. (1879) 174 If I know myself, I am measurably free from the itch of vanity. **1875** WHITNEY *Life Lang.* xii. 254 Until the anomalies of Semitic language are at least measurably explained.

4. To an extent which admits of being measured.

1866 RUSKIN *Eth. Dust* 127 Other such phenomena, quite measurably traceable within the limits even of short life. **1897** *Allbutt's Syst. Med.* IV. 374 The primary renal arteries are measurably thickened in both their coats.

†**measurage.** *Obs.* [a. F. *mesurage* (13th c.), f. *mesurer* to MEASURE: see -AGE.] A duty payable on the cargo of a ship.

Cf. *Droict de mesurage* in Cotgr.

1460 *Maldon, Essex, Liber B.* lf. 6 b, Mesurage and other dewtees. *a* **1676** HALE *Narr. Customes* iv. in S. A. Moore *Foreshore* (1888) 356 Busselage, measurage, prises, and tolls of various sorts. **1744** *Admiralty Minute* 29 Dec. (MS., P.R.O.), For demanding the duty and measurage of all foreign ships.

measure (ˈmɛʒ(j)ʊə(r)), *sb.* Forms: 3–6 mesur(e, 4–6 mesour(e, -ore, (5 meser, *Sc.* 6 myssour, myssuyr, 7 meassour, missour), 6– measure. [a. F. *mesure*:—L. *mēnsūra*, n. of action f. *mēns-*, ppl. stem of *mētīrī* to measure. Cf. Pr. *me(n)sura*, Sp., Pg. *mesura*, It. *misura*. Many of the senses below were developed in Fr., and adopted.]

I. Action, result, or means of measuring.

1. a. The action or process of measuring, measurement. Now *rare*.

c **1400** *Rom. Rose* 5026 So litel whyle it doth endure That ther nis compte ne mesure. **1530** PALSGR. 442/1, I awme, I gesse by juste measure to hytte or touche a thyng. **1557** RECORDE *Whetstone* Pref. b ij b, Measure is but the nombryng of the partes of lengthe, bredthe, or depthe. **1607** J. NORDEN *Surv. Dial.* III. 150 Doe you imagine that the truest measure is by triangles? **1650** J. WYBARD *Tactometria* 3 Every continuall or continued Quantity falling under Measure (in practicall Geometry) is referred..to the discrete. **1774** MASKELYNE in *Phil. Trans.* LXIV. 167 The formula, for the measure of heights, may also be changed. **1875** *Encycl. Brit.* II. 380/2 [Archimedes] The Measure of the Circle (*κύκλου μέτρησις*).

b. ***by measure***: as determined by measuring (in contradistinction to weighing or counting).

1553 EDEN *Treat. Newe Ind.* (Arb.) 22 It is solde there by measure, as wheat is with vs, and not by weight. **1715** *Lond. Gaz.* No. 5309/4 The Page Galley,..burthen about 301 Tons by Measure. **1844** STEPHENS *Bk. Farm* II. 394 In Scotland, grain used to be sold by measure alone. **1863** *Fownes's Chem.* (ed. 9) 144 Composition of the Atmosphere. Nitrogen. By weight 77 parts. By measure 79·19.

2. a. Size or quantity as ascertained or ascertainable by measuring. Now chiefly in phrase (***made***) ***to measure***, i.e. (made) in accordance with measurements taken (said of garments, etc., in contradistinction to 'ready-made'). Also *transf.* and *fig.*: fashioned to fulfil specified requirements; appropriate for a particular purpose; chiefly *attrib.*

to know the measure of (a person's) ***foot***: see FOOT *sb.* 26 c.

a **1300** *Cursor M.* 1668, I sal þe tell hou lang, hou brade, O quat mesur it sal be made. **1382** WYCLIF *Ex.* xxvi. 2 Of o mesure shal be made alle the tentis. *c* **1440** *Alphabet of Tales* 32 A stake of þe same mesur & lenthe. **1576** FLEMING *Panopl. Epist.* 58 Hee suffered not..the fourme and measure of his members to be made in metall. **1668** WILKINS *Real Char.* 163 Therefore the measure of the cubit must be larger. **1703** MOXON *Mech. Exerc.* 126 Their measure they note down upon a piece of paper. **1851** MAYHEW *Lond. Lab.* I. 476/2 The suit is more likely to be bought ready-made than 'made to measure'. **1857** *G. Bird's Urin. Deposits* (ed. 5) 61 It is much easier to obtain the measure than the weight of urine passed in a given time. **1928** *Punch* 11 July p. xix/1 (Advt.), It is to give all the benefits of made-to-measure shoes..that these Lotus Bespoke Models have been created. **1937** *Evening News* 5 Feb. 8/2 We shall have made-to-measure houses..with provision for adding rooms as families grow. **1958** *Listener* 9 Oct. 563/2 The new knowledge..may ultimately enable us to produce made-to-measure mutant viruses. **1959** *Ibid.* 2 Apr. 608/1 The Boat Race..made to measure for television.

b. ***full, good, short*** etc. ***measure*** (see the adjs.): ample or deficient quantity in what is sold or given by measure. Also *fig.*

Full, good measure are also appended to designations of measured quantity, to indicate something in excess of the stated amount.

1382 [see GOOD *a.* 19]. **1581**, etc. [see OVER-MEASURE *sb.*]. **1706** E. WARD *Wooden World Diss.* (1708) 68 What's wanting in his Guns is made up in his Cups, which are sure to have full measure. **1887** LOWELL *Democracy*, etc. 6 His audience would feel defrauded of their honest measure.

c. ***to take measures*** (†***measure***): to ascertain the different dimensions of a body. So, ***to take the measure of*** a person for clothes, etc.

c **1430** LYDG. *Min. Poems* (Percy Soc.) 11 Euclyde toke mesures, be craft of Gemytré. **15..** *Adam Bel* 283 in Hazl. *E.P.P.* II. 150 To take the mesure of that yeman, And therafter to make hys graue. **1520** GRESHAM in Ellis *Orig. Lett.* Ser. III. I. 234, I have takyn the measures of xviij. Chambres at Hamton Cortte and have made a Boke of them. **1580** LYLY *Euphues* (Arb.) 290 Like the Taylours boys, who thinketh to take measure before he can handle the sheeres. **1590** SHAKS. *Com. Err.* IV. iii. 9. **1647** WARD *Simp. Cobler* 28 He that makes Coates for the Moone, had need take measure every noone. **1793** SMEATON *Edystone L.* §97 The difficulty I had to get the proper measures taken. **1834** MARRYAT *P. Simple* ii, The man..took my measure, and departed.

d. *techn.* The width of a printed page; the width of an organ pipe.

1683 MOXON *Mech. Exerc., Printing* xxii. ¶4 So many Words as will fill up the Measure pretty stiff, viz. Justifie the Line. *Ibid.* xxiv. ¶7 A second Form of the same Volumne, Measure and Whites. **1824** JOHNSON *Typogr.* II. 93 After having made the measure for the work, we set a line of the letter that is designed for it. **1852** SEIDEL *Organ* 76 The width of a pipe is called its measure.

e. *Fencing.* The distance of one fencer from another as determined by the length of his reach when lunging or thrusting. (In first quot. *fig.*) Also, in military drill.

1591 SHAKS. *Two Gent.* V. iv. 127 Come not within the measure of my wrath. **1692** SIR W. HOPE *Fencing-Master* 95 Break his measure, or make his thrust short of you. **1696** R. H. *Sch. Recreat.* 67 Measure. This is only a distance between you and your Adversary, which must be cautiously and exactly observed when he is Thrusting at you; so that you may be without his measure or reach. **1833** *Reg. Instr. Cavalry* I. 144 As soon as the Attacking File has passed on, and is out of measure, both Files will 'Slope Swords'. *Ibid.* 146 The opposing Files should..circle 'Right' within measure. **1868** T. GRIFFITHS *Mod. Fencer* 69 The Measure ..must be determined by the length of the foil and the height of your opponent.

†**f.** Duration (of time, of a musical note). *Obs.*

1662 PLAYFORD *Skill Mus.* I. viii. 26 Pauses or Rests are silent Characters, or an Artificial omission of the Voyce or Sound, proportioned to a Certain Measure of Time. *Ibid.* xi. 36 Hold..is placed over the Note which the Author intends should be held to a longer Measure then the Note contains. **1696** PHILLIPS, *Measure of time*, is much to be regarded in handling Nativities, that when you have a Direction, you may know how long it will be before it operates. **1706** [see *measure-note* in 23].

3. *fig.* **a.** In the phrases under 2 c. †***to take measure(s***: to form an opinion or opinions; also, †***to take a fair, wrong*** (etc.) ***m. of***. ***to take the measure of***, formerly ***to take m. of***: to form an estimate of; now *esp.* to weigh or gauge the abilities or character of (a person), with a view to what one is to expect from him.

1650 JER. TAYLOR *Holy Living* ii. §7 (1686) 118 He onely lived according to Nature, the other by pride and ill customs, and measures taken by other mens eyes and tongues. **1659** *Burton's Diary* (1828) IV. 458, I know nothing of it, and therefore must take measure by what is before me. **1677** HALE *Prim. Orig. Man.* 245 They thought it more sutable to take their Measures, and make their Conclusions consonant to the course of Nature. **1790** BURKE *Fr. Rev.* Wks. V. 58 If we take the measure of our rights by our exercise of them at the revolution. **1795** —— *Th. Scarcity* Wks. 1842 II. 253 We cannot assure ourselves, if we take a wrong measure, from the temporary necessities of one season. **1875** JOWETT *Plato* (ed. 2) I. 84, I have encountered a good many of these gentlemen in actual service, and have taken their measure. **1889** DOYLE *Micah Clarke* 113 Our hostess..bustled off..to take the measure of the new-comer. **1893** *Nation* 5 Jan. LVI. 4/1 The people have taken the measure of this whole labor movement.

†**b.** Hence, An estimate, opinion, or notion. *Obs.*

1665 GLANVILL *Scepsis Sci.*, *Addr. Roy. Soc.* A 3 b, I can expect no other from those, that judge by first sights and rash measures, then to be thought fond or insolent. **1670** in *Buccleuch MSS.* (Hist. MSS. Comm.) I. 487 He has given the King of France the character of all our Court..as he himself thinks of them; so that he has..given us wrong measures here as he has given you. *a* **1678** H. SCOUGAL *Life of God*, etc. (1735) 79 All who are enemies to holiness have taken up false measures and disadvantageous notions of it. **1691** T. H[ALE] *Acc. New Invent.* 20 Be pleased to receive the Measures of this Companies judging therein.

4. An instrument for measuring.

a. A vessel of standard capacity used for separating and dealing out fixed quantities of various substances (as grain, liquids, some vegetables, coal).

1297 R. GLOUC. (Rolls) 8834 False elnen & mesures he broȝte al clene adoun. **1398** TREVISA *Barth. De P.R.* XIX. cxxviii. (1495) 932 That is properly callyd mesure by whom fruyte and corne and lycour and other thynges moyste and drye ben mette. *c* **1440** *Alphabet of Tales* 330 If I hafe right-wuslie..mesurd with thies mesurs to þaim at I selde ale to. **1508** *Acc. Ld. Treas. Scot.* (1902) IV. 137 For ane mesure to the Kingis gun of silvir. **1694** HOLDER *Disc. Time* 3 A Concave Measure, of known and denominated Capacity, serves to measure the Capaciousness of any other Vessel. **1865** DICKENS *Mut. Fr.* I. v, A little wooden measure which had no discernible inside.

b. A graduated rod, line, tape, etc., used by builders, tailors, etc. for taking measurements; †also (see quot. 1688). See also TAPE-*measure*, YARD-*measure*.

1555 EDEN *Decades* (Arb.) 240 The streates were also directed with corde, compase and measure. **1595** SHAKS. *John* IV. ii. 196 [A tailor] with his Sheeres, and Measure in his hand. **1688** R. HOLME *Armoury* II. 464/1 Instruments used by Perawick Makers... Measures, are lengths of Paper or Parchment, with Figures on, by which the Hair is Woven in the rounds, according as it is to fall in the Wig, whether long or short. **169.** *Ad Populum Phaleræ* i. 24 Our ancient Rolls, grown useless to preserve Our Rights, may then for Taylors Measures serve.

5. a. A unit or denomination of measurement.

1535 COVERDALE *1 Chron.* xxiii[i.] 29 For all maner of weight and measure [**1611** measures and size]. **1555** EDEN *Decades* (Arb.) 257 They vse waightes and measures. **1559** W. CUNNINGHAM *Cosmogr. Glasse* 56 A Barly corne (being the least measure). **1650** J. WYBARD *Tactometria* To Rdr., The Standard-measures for Wine and Ale or Beer. **1688** [see DRY *a.* 10]. *a* **1696**, **1848** [see LINEAL 1 b]. **1710** J. HARRIS *Lex. Techn.* II, *Measures of Capacity*. **1765** BLACKSTONE *Comm.* I. I. vii. 305 Superficial measures are derived by squaring those of length. **1842–59** GWILT *Archit.* §2316 The common measure for tiling is a square of 10 feet. **1843** *Penny Cycl.* XXVII. 196/2 The measures of time..are the only usual ones in which a natural standard exists. *Ibid.* 203/1 All the multiples and subdivisions of every measure [in the metrical system] are decimal.

b. Used for some specific unit of capacity (formerly also of length) understood from context or usage; in England often applied to the bushel. Also, such a quantity of anything as is indicated by this unit. In translations from foreign langs. sometimes used to render the name of some definite unit: e.g. in the Bible of 1611 as translation of SEAH, COR, and BATH.

1382 WYCLIF *Luke* xvi. 7 An hundrid mesuris [1388 coris] of whete. **1494** *Will Joan Wynne* in *Somerset Med. Wills* (1901) 322, ij mesers of Ode [? = woad]. **1535** COVERDALE *1 Sam.* xxv. 18 Fyue measures of firmentye. **1604** SHAKS. *Oth.* IV. ii. 73, I would not doe such a thing for a ioynt Ring, nor for measures of Lawne, nor for Gownes. **1605** —— *Macb.* III. iv. 11 Anon wee'l drinke a Measure The Table round. **1606** —— *Ant. & Cl.* II. vi. 37 To send Measures of Wheate to Rome. **1688** R. HOLME *Armoury* III. 337/2 A Measure, an Hoop, or a Strick, is 4 Pecks, or 9 Gallons. Yet some reckon but 8 gallons to the Measure, which in some places is also called a Bushel. **1787** WINTER *Syst. Husb.* 194 This field used commonly to be sowed with twenty measures of wheat, each measure containing one hundred and six pounds of eighteen ounces. **1805** FORSYTH *Beauties Scotl.* II. 253 Between 20,000 and 30,000 measures in shells..the measure containing two Winchester bushels. **1870** BRYANT *Homer* I. VII. 234 These Brought wine, a thousand measures.

c. *Chem.* A unit of volume used in ascertaining the quantity of a gas or liquid, usually indicated by graduations on a tube (as an alkalimeter or

eudiometer) or other vessel. Also, the quantity measured by such a unit.

1807 T. THOMSON *Chem.* (ed. 3) II. 149 The gas amounted to 16 very small measures. **1845** PARNELL *Chem. Anal.* 416 Each measure of the alkalimeter represents half a grain of chloride of lime.

d. In descriptions of mixture or composition: One of a number of equal volumes indeterminate in quantity; a 'part' as estimated by measurement.

1837 *Civil Eng. & Arch. Jrnl.* I. 33/2 The concrete..is to consist of six measures of gravel and sand to one of ground lime. **1863** *Fownes's Chem.* (ed. 9) 144 Carbonic acid, from 3·7 measures to 6·2 measures, in 10,000 measures of air.

6. A method of measuring; *esp.* a system of standard denominations or units of length, surface, or volume.

Chiefly with qualifying word denoting the class or kind of system, the substances to which it is applied, or the locality in which it is used or originated; e.g. ***linear, long, square, cubic measure; liquid, dry, ale, corn measure; Irish, London measure.***

1439 *Rolls of Parlt.* V. 30/2 There as any Merchaunt.. excepte at London, will make a Clothe in measuring XXIIII yerdes, they woll make therof XXII or lasse, seyinge that it is the mesure of London. **1455** *Cal. Anc. Rec. Dublin* (1889) I. 288 Al maner of women that syllyn ale..syll aftyr the Kyng's ale mesure. **1670** CAPT. J. SMITH *Eng. Improv. Reviv'd* 25 The content of the whole fence by the said Wood measure is 1466 Perch 12 foot. **1672** PETTY *Polit. Anat. Irel.* in *Tracts* (1769) 299 A perch or pole Irish measure, is 21 foot. **1709** J. WARD *Yng. Math. Guide* I. iii. (1734) 34 That there should be but one Measure for Wine, Ale and Corn, throughout this Realm. *Ibid.* 36 Dry Measure is different both from Wine and Ale Measure. **1842–59** GWILT *Archit.* §2303 In lime measure, what is called a hundred is 100 pecks, or 25 striked bushels (old measure). **1843** *Penny Cycl.* XXVII. 200/2 Apothecaries' fluid measure. **1898** *Engineering Mag.* XVI. 95 The completed raft contains 450,000 lineal feet of timber, or in the neighborhood of 3,000,000 feet, board-measure.

7. a. That by which anything is computed or estimated, or with which it is compared in respect of quantity. Chiefly in phr. ***to be the measure of.*** [Cf. Gr. use of μέτρον.]

c **1580** SIDNEY *Ps.* VI. i, Lord,..let [not] thy rage of my due punishment Become the measure. **1612** BACON *Ess., Of Despatch* (Arb.) 244 Time is the measure of businesse, as money is of wares. **1635** WELLS *Sciographia* 113 The tangent of SG [the subtending arc] the measure of the angle Z. **1706** PHILLIPS (ed. Kersey) s.v., In Philosophy, Time is the Measure of Motion; but in Mechanicks, Motion is the Measure of Time. **1852** C. W. H[OSKYNS] *Talpa* 19 The weakest link of a chain is the measure of its strength. **1865** BRANDE *Dict. Sci.*, etc. III. 606/1 The reciprocal of the radius of a circle is a measure of its curvature. **1892** KIPLING *Barrack-r. Ball.* 65 And the measure of our torment is the measure of our youth.

b. A standard or rule of judgement; a criterion, test; also, a standard by which something is determined or regulated. Now *rare*.

1641 in *Rushworth's Hist. Coll.* (1692) III. I. 555 Having.. no measure of happiness or misfortune in this world, but what I derive from your Majesties value of my affection and fidelity. **1660** STANLEY *Hist. Philos.* XI. *Protagoras* ii. (1687) 768 He began one of his Books thus: Man is..the measure of all things. **1690** LOCKE *Hum. Und.* III. vi. §22 Our abstract ideas are to us the measures of species. **1785** PALEY *Mor. Philos.* II. ix, The will of God is the measure of right and wrong. **1830** TENNYSON *Poems* 153 Man is the measure of all truth Unto himself.

c. In collocation with RULE *sb.* (q.v.).

8. *Math.* A quantity which divides or is contained in another quantity some number of times without remainder; a submultiple. Thus, 2, 3, 4, and 6 are all *measures* of 12. [After Gr. μέτρον.]

common measure = common divisor (see DIVISOR 1 b). Also *fig.* or allusively. ***greatest common measure*** (abbreviated G.C.M.): the greatest quantity that divides each of a number of given quantities exactly.

1570 DEE *Math. Pref.* 5 In pure Arithmetike, an Vnit, is the common Measure of all Numbers. **1570** BILLINGSLEY *Elem. Geom.* 234 b, It is required of these three magnitudes to finde out the greatest common measure. **1656** HOBBES *Six Less.* Wks. 1845 VII. 196 One quantity is the measure of another quantity, when it, or the multiple of it, is coincident in all points with the other quantity. **1727–52** CHAMBERS *Cycl.* s.v., 9 is a measure of 27. **1870** J. H. NEWMAN *Gramm. Assent* I. iv. 80 The establishment of a common measure between mind and mind. **1875** COLENSO *Elem. Alg.* v. 48 We may sometimes find by inspection the G.C.M. of two quantities.

9. [? *concr.* of sense 2.] A stratum or bed of mineral; now only *pl.* (*Geol.*) in ***coal-measures, culm measures*** (see CULM[1] 3).

1665 [see COAL-MEASURE]. **1686** PLOT *Staffordsh.* 158 The other Iron Ores..which lye in some places but thin, others thicker, and as the coal is, divided into measures of different denominations. **1795** AIKIN *Manchester* 523 The measures or strata, by which the beds of coal are divided. **1837** [see CULM[1] 3]. **1865** LYELL *Elem. Geol.* 532 The Devonian group ..its relations to the overlying Carboniferous rocks or 'Culm Measures'. **1881** RAYMOND *Mining Gloss., Measures*, strata of coal, or the formation containing coal beds.

II. Prescribed or limited extent or quantity.

†**10.** What is commensurate or adequate; satisfaction (of appetite, desire, need). *Obs.*

c **1200** *Trin. Coll. Hom.* 55 And he sette muðes mesure on his ferde þat he gaderede [L. *et fecit gulam militiæ suæ principem*]. **13..** *E.E. Allit. P.* A. 224 A mannez dom moȝt dryȝly demme, Er mynde moȝt malte in hit mesure. **1593** SHAKS. *3 Hen. VI*, II. iii. 32 Till either death hath clos'd these eyes of mine, Or Fortune giuen me measure of Reuenge. **1607** —— *Cor.* II. ii. 127 He cannot but with measure fit the Honors which we deuise him.

11. †**a.** Proportion; due proportion, symmetry.

c **1400** *Destr. Troy* 806 Sho gafe hym a glasse with a good lycour, And bade..To werke it in mesure. *Ibid.* 1648 The windowes, worthely wroght in a mesure. *c* **1407** LYDG. *Reas. & Sens.* 58 Wyth the which she dooth gouerne Euery maner creature, With-oute[n] ordre or mesure. **1597** HOOKER *Eccl. Pol.* v. lv. §2 Measure is that which perfecteth all things. **1600** E. BLOUNT tr. *Conestaggio* 25 For being an exercise that requireth order and measure, all things were there disordered and confused. **1662** EVELYN *Chalcogr.* Table, Measure and proportion have Influence on all our Actions.

b. ***in measure as***: in proportion as. [A Gallicism: cf. F. *á mesure que.*]

1789 COWPER *Let. to Newton* 16 Aug. *Wks.* (1836) VI. 256 [Fame] is a commodity that daily sinks in value, in measure as the consummation of all things approaches. **1894** G. MOORE *Esther Waters* 332 His irritability increased in measure as he perceived the medicine was doing him no good.

†**c.** ***to hold measure with***: to be proportionate to or commensurate with. *Obs.*

1611 TOURNEUR *Ath. Tragedie* I. i, Now let thy trust.. Hold measure with thy amplitude of wit.

12. a. An extent not to be exceeded; a limit. Now only in certain phrases, as ***to set measures to, to know no measure*** (see also b and c).

1390 GOWER *Conf.* III. 234 That he schal mesure His bodi, so that no mesure Of fleisshly lust he scholde excede. **1514** BARCLAY *Cyt. & Uplondyshm.* (Percy Soc.) 30 Thou pasest mesure, Faustus. **1530** PALSGR. 572/1 This mater gothe out of mesure, *ceste matiere se desmesure*. **1604** E. G[RIMSTONE] tr. *Acosta's Hist. Indies* I. vi. 19 Although the great Ocean stretcheth farre, yet doth it never passe this measure. **1633** G. HERBERT *Temple, Ch. Porch* xix, If thy sonne can make ten pound his measure. **1659** PEARSON *Creed* (1839) 272 What bounds can we set unto that grief, what measures to that anguish? **1667** MILTON *P.L.* v. 517 Full to the utmost measure of what bliss Human desires can seek or apprehend. **1710** PHILIPS *Pastorals* i. 14 Fond Love no Cure will have..nor any Measure knows. *a* **1716** SOUTH *Twelve Serm.* (1744) XI. 162 To determine and give measures to the divine bounty and wisdom, to tell it what it ought to do.

b. In advb. phr. ***beyond (above,*** †***without,*** †***over) measure***, also † ***out of measure, out of all measure*** (arch.): beyond all bounds, excessively. †Formerly (esp. Sc.) used also predicatively = boundless, unlimited, excessive.

c **1375** BARBOUR *Bruce* I. 570 He wes angry out of mesur. *Ibid.* XVII. 810 The laiff our mesur war wery. *c* **1400** MAUNDEV. (Roxb.) xxx. 137 On lenth it es withouten mesure. **1470–85** MALORY *Arthur* II. i. 77 The damoysel made grete sorow out of measure. **1513** DOUGLAS *Æneis* VII. vi. 59 Abufe myssuyr forsuth thai chaistyit war. **1530** PALSGR. 418/2 This adversite hath anguissed me beyonde measure. **1565** *Reg. Privy Council Scot.* I. 370 A thing sa far beyond all measour that [etc.]. **1642** ROGERS *Naaman* To Rdr. §2 So Selfe encountered with a Law, proves out of measure sinfull. **1665** SIR T. HERBERT *Trav.* (1677) 356 The air is usually warm, and at some time above measure. **1706** E. WARD *Wooden World Diss.* (1708) 73 He's so often out of Measure in his Drinking. **1856** R. A. VAUGHAN *Mystics* (1860) I. VI. iii. 166 He was full of Eckart's doctrine, out of all measure admiring the wonderful man. **1872** BLACK *Adv. Phaeton* xxxi 414 My Lady was once vexed beyond measure.

c. ***to keep*** or ***observe measure(s***: to be moderate or restrained in action. †***to keep measures with***: to use consideration towards (a person).

1551 R. ROBINSON tr. *More's Utopia* II. (Arb.) 135 In rewardes they kepe no measure. **1710** SHAFTESB. *Charac.* (1737) II. 266 Our Author..endeavours to shew Civility and Favour, by keeping the fairest Measures he possibly can with Men of this sort. **1734** tr. *Rollin's Rom Hist.* (1827) III. 69 He thought fit to observe measures with him in the beginning, hoping, perhaps, by gentle methods to bring him back to his duty. *Ibid.* 74 He no longer observed any measures and reigned like a true tyrant. **1792** W. ROBERTS *Looker-On* No. 7 (1794) I. 93 If his taylor continue to disappoint him, I promise to keep no measures with the delinquent. *a* **1832** MACINTOSH *Life More* Wks. 1846 I. 493 More, having no longer any measures to keep, openly declared, that [etc.]. **1852** M. ARNOLD *Second Best* i. 2 Quiet living, strict-kept measure. **1863** COWDEN CLARKE *Shakesp. Char.* viii. 198 He keeps no measure in his contempt for him.

d. In Biblical phrases. ***by measure, in measure***: to a limited extent, in part. ***to fill up the measure of***: to complete the sum of (one's iniquities), to add what is wanting to the completeness of (a person's misfortunes). [A blending of Matt. xxiii. 32 with Gen. xv. 16; cf. F. *combler la mesure.*]

1382 WYCLIF *Ezek.* iv. 11 And thou shalt drynke water in mesure [Vulg. *in mensura*] the sixt part of hyn. [**1382** —— *Matt.* xxiii. 32 Ȝe fulfillen the mesure of ȝoure fadris.] **1535** COVERDALE *John* iii. 34 God geueth not the sprete (vnto him) by measure. **1581** N. BURNE *Disputation* 143 The mesour of impietie begun be him is nocht zit fullie accomplished. **1611** BIBLE *Jer.* xxx. 11, I will correct thee in measure, and will not leaue thee altogether vnpunished. *a* **1716** BLACKALL *Wks.* I. 66 To obtain that Righteousness which they desire, (here in good measure, and hereafter to the full). **1820** W. IRVING *Sk. Book* II. 267 To fill up the measure of his misfortunes. **1846** TRENCH *Mirac.* xvi. (1862) 276 The prophets having grace only in measure, so in measure they wrought their miracles. **1856** FROUDE *Hist. Eng.* (1858) I. ii. 91 The church was allowed a hundred and fifty more years, to fill full the measure of her offences.

†**13. a.** Moderation, temperance. ***of measure***: moderate, temperate. ***by measure, in measure***: in moderation. *Obs.*

a **1225** *Ancr. R.* 74 Vt of god into vuel, & from mesure into unimete. **13..** *E.E. Allit. P.* B. 247 Al in mesure & meþe was made þe vengaunce. **1390** GOWER *Conf.* II. 112 Slep.. helpeth kinde..Whan it is take be mesure. *a* **1400** *Sir Perc.* 397 Luke thou be of mesure Bothe in haulle and in boure. *c* **1430** LYDG. *Min. Poems* (Percy Soc.) 81 Iche thynge is praysed if it in mesure be. **1548** CRANMER *Catech.* 182 Yf we wyll be contente with a meane dyet, and kepe a measure in our apparell. **1583** BABINGTON *Commandm.* 194 It hath euer been helde, that blushing in measure, modestie, and silence haue been commendable tokens in yong yeeres. **1593** SHAKS. *Rich. II*, III. iv. 7 My Legges can keepe no measure in Delight, When my poore Heart no measure keepes in Griefe. **1667** MILTON *P.L.* VII. 128 Knowledge..needs.. Her Temperance over Appetite, to know In measure what the mind may well contain.

personified. **1377** LANGL. *P. Pl.* B. XIV. 70 If men lyued as mesure wolde. *c* **1412** HOCCLEVE *De Reg. Princ.* 502 Mesure is out of londe on pylgrymage. *a* **1510** DOUGLAS *K. Hart* ii. 511 That fayr sweit thing [Chastity]..That..euirmore is mareit with mesour.

b. Proverbs.

1362 LANGL. *P. Pl.* A. I. 33 Mesure is Medicine þauh þou muche ȝeor[n]e. **1399** —— *Rich. Redeles* II. 139 Mesure is a meri mene. *c* **1430** LYDG. *Min. Poems* (Percy Soc.) 208 Men wryte of oold how mesour is tresour. *a* **1529** SKELTON *Sp. Parrot* 64 In mesure is tresure. ? **1570** *Satir. Poems Reform.* xvii. 44 Thinkand alwayis that mesure was ane feist. *a* **1598** FERGUSSON *Prov.* (1785) 13 He that forsakes missour, missour forsakes him.

†**c.** ? A compromise. *Obs.*

1425 *Paston Lett.* I. 21 If this mesure be accepted.

14. a. A quantity, degree, or proportion (of something), esp. as granted to or bestowed upon a person.

1610 GUILLIM *Heraldry* III. xiv. (1660) 171 The Buck.. hath a degree and measure of all the properties of the Stag. **1671** MILTON *Samson* 1439 For never was from Heaven imparted Measure of strength so great to mortal seed. **1674** W. ALLEN *Danger Enthus.* 105 Mens differences about these points proceed..from their different measures of Light and understanding. **1784** COWPER *Task* v. 309 In whom lust And folly in as ample measure meet As in the bosoms of the slaves he rules. **1850** SCORESBY *Cheever's Whalem. Adv.* xiii. (1859) 181 We had a good measure of these contingents of successful enterprise. **1875** JOWETT *Plato* (ed. 2) III. 680 Critias..begs that a larger measure of indulgence may be conceded to him. **1877** 'H. A. PAGE' *De Quincey* I. x. 200 To do some measure of steady work.

b. In advb. phr. formed with preps. ***in a great*** or ***large measure*** (†***in good m.***, †***after some large m.***): to a considerable extent or degree, largely. ***in some*** or ***a measure***: to a certain extent, in some degree, somewhat. ***in*** (†***upon***) ***the same measure***: to the same extent.

138. WYCLIF *Sel. Wks.* III. 360 þei [*sc.* curatis] shulden lyve on þe puple in good mesure as Poul biddiþ. **1590** SHAKS. *Mids. N.* I. ii. 30, I will condole in some measure. **1611** BIBLE *Ps.* lxxx. 5 Thou..giuest them teares to drinke in great measure. **1632** LITHGOW *Trav.* x. 493 The recouery (after some large measure) of my health. **1662** STILLINGFL. *Orig. Sacr.* I. I. §20 Which difference of writing is in a great measure the cause of the different dialect between the Athenians and Ionians. **1664** EVELYN *Pomona* Gen. Advt. (1729) 91 Cider cannot be unwholesome upon the same Measure that stummed wine is so. **1736** BUTLER *Anal.* II. iii. Wks. 1874 I. 180 Objections against Christianity itself are, in a great measure, frivolous. **1871** SMILES *Charac.* I. (1876) 8 Goodness in a measure implies wisdom. **1895** R. L. DOUGLAS in *Bookman* Oct. 22/2 Louis [XIV] was in a large measure responsible for the horrors of the Revolution.

15. Treatment (of a certain kind) 'meted out' to a person, esp. by way of punishment or retribution. *Obs.* or *arch.* exc. in ***hard measure***.

1593 SHAKS. *3 Hen. VI*, II. vi. 55 In stead whereof, let this supply the roome, Measure for measure, must be answered. **1601** —— *All's Well* II. iii. 273 This is hard and vndeserued measure. **1603** —— *Meas. for M.* III. ii. 257 He professes to haue receiued no sinister measure from his Iudge. **1611** BIBLE *Transl. Pref.* ¶3 This is the measure that hath been rendred to excellent Princes in former times, euen..For their good deedes to be euill spoken of. **1667** MILTON *P.L.* I. 513 He from mightier Jove..like measure found. *a* **1715** BURNET *Own Time* (1724) I. 558 He thought he had met with hard measure. **1784** COWPER *Ep. Jos. Hill* 55 O happy Britain! we have not to fear Such hard and arbitrary measure here. **1887** A. BIRRELL *Obiter Dicta* Ser. II. 67 It is certainly hard measure on the poor fellow.

III. 'Measured' sound or movement.

16. Poetical rhythm, as 'measured' by quantity or accent; a kind of poetical rhythm; a metrical group or period; = METRE. *spec.* applied to Old English verse.

long measure (in hymns): see LONG *a.*[1] A. 18.

c **1450** LYDG. & BURGH *Secrees* 1530 Or of metrys the feet to make equal, be tyme and proporcion kepying my mesurys. **1589** PUTTENHAM *Eng. Poesie* II. iii. (Arb.) 81 Meeter and measure is all one, for what the Greekes called μετρον, the Latines call *Mensura*, and is but the quantitie of a verse, either long or short. **1599** SHAKS. *Hen. V*, v. ii. 139. **1699** BENTLEY *Phal.* 198 It is an Iambic Verse; and it was a good while after the invention of Comedy and Tragedy, before that Measure was used in them. **1706** A. BEDFORD *Temple Mus.* vi. 115 The..Verse consisted of Two Measures, and each of them of Ten Syllables. **1774** R. HENRY *Hist. Gt. Brit.* II. 432 The kinds and measures of their [*sc.* Saxon and Danish poets'] verses. **1778** JOHNSON *L.P., Cowley* (1868) 23 To the disproportion and incongruity of Cowley's sentiments must be added the uncertainty and looseness of his measures. **1802** J. SIBBALD *Chron. Scottish Poetry* IV. p. lviii, In the same kind of measure [as the Fragment of the genuine Cædmon] are almost all the popular rhymes which still continue to be repeated by children in their ring-dances. **1820** HAZLITT *Lect. Dram. Lit.* 73 It is beautiful prose put into heroic measure. **1869** A. J. ELLIS *E.E. Pronunc.* iv. §4. 333 Chaucer's verse seems to consist generally of five measures.

1873 H. MORLEY *First Sk. Eng. Lit.* 20 There is one measure for Beowulf, Cædmon's Paraphrase, and all subsequent First English poems. **1877** H. REHRMANN *Ess. Anglo-Saxon Poetry* 10 A foot or measure is made up..of one accented syllable and its connected unaccented syllable, or syllables. **1942** J. C. POPE *Rhythm of Beowulf* 44 According to Heusler, alliteration must introduce the first measure in the second half-line.

17. An air, tune, melody. Now *poet.*

1390 GOWER *Conf.* III. 301 Bot if ye the mesure pleide, Which, if you list, I schal you liere. *c* **1461** *E.E. Misc.* (Warton Club) 50 A pype, boy, thou schalt have also, True of measure schall it go. **1595** SHAKS. *John* III. i. 304 Shall braying trumpets, and loud churlish drums..be measures to our pomp. **1774** BRYANT *Mythol.* I. 445 A great musician, and particularly expert in all pastoral measure. **1842** LYTTON *Zanoni* 22 He would pour forth..strange wild measures, on his violin. **186.** BRYANT *Sella* 361 They called for quaint old measures.

18. *Mus.* **a.** The relation between the time-values of a note of one denomination and a note of the next, determining the kind of rhythm (duple, triple, etc.); hence, the time of a piece of music. (Also called MODE.)

1597 MORLEY *Introd. Mus.* Annot. *4 This [triple time] is the common hackney horse of all the Composers, which is of so manie kindes as there be maners of pricking,..and yet all one measure. **1601** SHAKS. *Twel. N.* v. i. 41 The triplex, sir, is a good tripping measure. **1662** PLAYFORD *Skill Mus.* I. vii. 23 Measure..is a Quantity of the length and shortness of Time, either by Natural Sounds pronounced by the Voyce, or by Artificial upon Instruments; which Measure is by a certain Motion of the Hand expressed in a varietie of Notes. **1727–52** CHAMBERS *Cycl.* s.v. *Time*, The mode or measure of two times, or the dupla measure. **1797** *Encycl. Brit.* (ed. 3) XII. 533/1 There are properly two kinds of measures or modes of time: the measure of two times, or of common time ..and the measure of three times, or of triple time. **1840** *Penny Cycl.* XVIII. 207/1 It admits but one measure, the duple. **1901** H. E. WOOLDRIDGE *Oxf. Hist. Mus.* I. 102 A special name, *Cantus mensurabilis*, was indeed often adopted by many authors, to describe the music in which measure was present throughout.

b. Each portion of a musical composition comprising a group of notes beginning with a main accent, and commonly included between two vertical lines or bars; a 'bar' (see BAR *sb.*[1] 16).

1667 C. SIMPSON *Pract. Mus.* I. §10. 30 The Mood.. called Perfect of the Less, in which three Semibreves went to a Measure. **1878** F. TAYLOR in Grove *Dict. Music* I. 136 The word bar is also commonly, though incorrectly, applied to the portion contained between any two such vertical lines [bars], such portion being termed a 'measure'.

¶ **c.** Inaccurately used for L. *modus* as transl. of Gr. τρόπος, ἁρμονία: see MODE.

1635 CARPENTER *Geog. Del.* II. xiv. 247 The Northerne mans humour consortes best with the Phrygian measure, a loud and stirring harmony. **1776** BURNEY *Hist. Mus.* I. iii. 60 The Lydian measure was appropriated to..songs of sorrow.

19. Rhythmical motion, esp. as regulated by music; the rhythm of a movement. ***to keep measure***: to observe strict time.

1576 FLEMING tr. *Caius' Dogs* 35 Dogges..which are taught..to daunce in measure at the musicall sounde of an instrument. **1623** BINGHAM *Xenophon* 104 All this is performed in measure to the Flute. **1655** STANLEY *Hist. Philos.* I. vii. (1687) 25/1 He first taught Soldiers to march by the sound of Fifes and Harps, observing a kind of measure in their pace. **1694** ADDISON *St. Cecilia's Day* Wks. 1726 I. 33 The Bears in aukward measures leap. *a* **1704** T. BROWN *On Beauties* Wks. 1730 I. 44 May she in measure like Clarinda move. **1704** PRIOR *To Mrs. Singer* 14 If Amaryllis breathes thy secret pains, And thy fond heart beats measure to thy strains. **1800–24** CAMPBELL *Pilgrim of Glencoe* 8 Whose crews..Keep measure with their oars. **1864** D. G. MITCHELL *Sev. Stor.* 253 He would beat the measure of a light polka on his pallet.

20. a. A dance, *esp.* a grave or stately dance; often in phr. ***tread a measure***. Now *arch.*

1509 [see DANCE *v.* 4]. **1584** LYLY *Campaspe* IV. iii, To tread the measurs in a daunce. **1590** MARLOWE *2nd Pt. Tamburl.*, v. i, Where fair Semiramis..Hath trod the measures. **1671** MILTON *P.L.* I. 170 All Heaven..in Celestial measures mov'd Circling the Throne and Singing. **1808** SCOTT *Marmion* v. xii, Now tread we a measure! said young Lochinvar. *a* **1839** PRAED *Poems* (1864) II. 44 And dancers leave the cheerful measure To seek the Lady's missing treasure. **1888** W. E. HENLEY *Bk. Verses* 28 Kate the scrubber..treads a measure.

†**b.** ***to lead*** (a person) ***the measures***: to 'lead him a dance'. *Obs.*

1594 NASHE *Unfort. Trav.* K4b, Hee stript her, and scourged her from top to toe tantara. Day by day he disgested his meate with leading her the measures.

IV. 21. A plan or course of action intended to attain some object. **a.** *pl.* esp. in phrases ***to take, adopt, †follow, pursue*** (certain) ***measures***. † ***to break*** (a person's) ***measures*** [= F. *rompre* (*ses*) *mesures*]: to frustrate his plans. † ***in the measures of***: privy to the plans of.

This sense of 'to take measures' (*prendre des mesures*) is adopted from Fr.; Littré regards it as developed from the sense 'to form an estimate of a situation', in which the phrase also occurs. Cf. 3 above.

1698 FRYER *Acc. E. India & P.* 51 By the Measures they follow, this also in time must fall into their hands. **1700** S. L. tr. *Fryke's Voy. E. Ind.* 185 We agreed there in an instant to take our measures about it. **1704** TRAPP *Abra-Mulé* I. i. 323 On purpose to defeat My close Contrivances, and break my Measures. **1708** PARTRIDGE *Bickerstaff detected* in *Swift's Wks.* (1755) II. I. 168 [He] has paid his visits to St. Germains, and is now in the measures of Lewis XIV. *a* **1715** BURNET *Own Time* (1724) II. 360 He pursued the Measures, which he had begun to take, of raising new Divisions in that Kingdom. **1719** DE FOE *Crusoe* II. (Globe) 594 My Measures being fix'd..for Arch-Angel, and not to Muscovy. **1767** T. HUTCHINSON *Hist. Prov. Mass. Bay* iii. 297 This rupture with the Indians broke his measures. **1817** JAS. MILL *Brit. India* II. v. v. 476 Pondicherry was the object of importance; and it was resolved to lose no time in taking measures for its reduction. **1874** J. R. GREEN *Short Hist.* viii. §4 (1882) 494 The measures of Laud soon revived the panic of the Puritans. **1899** *Allbutt's Syst. Med.* VIII. 604 To assist the external measures by internal medication.

b. *sing.*

1767 A. YOUNG *Farmer's Lett. to People* 36 Every just argument that can be urged for or against any measure. **1833** HT. MARTINEAU *Charmed Sea* i. 7 Before..any measure of prevention..could be taken. **1841** BREWSTER *Mart. Sci.* II. iii. 170 His first plan was to remove every thing from Huen, as a measure of security. **1842** BORROW *Bible in Spain* xxxviii, This measure by no means took me by surprise.

22. a. *spec.* A legislative enactment proposed or adopted.

1759 ROBERTSON *Hist. Scot.* I. Wks. 1851 I. 64 In none of our historians do we find an instance of any opposition formed against the court in parliament, or mention of any difficulty in carrying through the measures which were agreeable to the king. **1839** KEIGHTLEY *Hist. Eng.* II. 57 The great measure of this parliament was that respecting religious doctrines. **1879** MCCARTHY *Own Times* II. xviii. 27 This measure was passed rapidly through all its stages.

b. Phrase, ***measures, not men***.

1742 LD. CHESTERFIELD 6 Mar. *Lett.* (1845) III. 138, I have opposed measures, not men. **1769** *Junius Lett.* xxvi. note (1788) 141 Measures, and not men, is the common cant of affected moderation. **1792** *Anecd. W. Pitt.* (1797) I. x. 224 Some disliked the measures, others disliked the men. **1839** BAILEY *Festus* (1852) 113, I care for measures more than men.

V. 23. *attrib.* and *Comb.*: **measure-filling** *a.*, filling up the measure (of iniquity); **measure-full**, as much as will fill a measure; **measure-glass**, a graduated glass for measuring drugs, medicine, etc.; †**measure-keeping**, moderation; †**measure line**, a measuring line; **measure-moth**, a geometer moth (*Cent. Dict.*); †**measure-note**, a semi-breve; also, the length of note indicated by the lower figure in the rhythmical signature of a piece; †**measure pot**, a pot used for measuring out liquids; **measure-strip**, a strip of paper used by tailors in taking measures; †**measure time**, the slow time of the dances called 'measures'; **measure-work**, piece work (cf. *measured work*).

1713 M. HENRY *Ordin. Serm.* Wks. 1857 II. 510/2 Jerusalem's *measure-filling sin. **1851** BORROW *Lavengro* lxviii, 'The largest *measure-full in your house', said I. ..'This is not the season for half-pint mugs'. **1899** tr. *R. von Jaksch's Clinical Diagnosis* (ed. 4) vii. 36 Ten or twenty cc. ..each of solutions j and ij are mixed together in a *measure-glass. **1553** GRIMALDE *Cicero's Offices* III. (1558) 165b, Semelinesse, *measurekeping [L. *moderatio*], sobermode, stayednesse. **1535** COVERDALE *Zech.* II. 1 A man with a *measure lyne in his honde. **1706** PHILLIPS (ed. Kersey), **Measure-Note*..the Semibreve..so call'd because it is of a certain determinate Measure, or Length of Time by itself. **1809** CALLCOTT *Mus. Gram.* (ed. 2) 36 Compound Triple Time is formed by dividing the Measures of simple Triple into nine parts, and by dotting the Measure Note of the original Time. **1562** R. WEST in *Hist. Comp. Pewterers* (1903) I A ffalse maker of *measure pottes. **1887** HALLIWELL *Life Shaks.* II. 382 Some deeds had been given to a tailor for conversion into *measure-strips. **1626** BACON *Sylva* §113 As when Galliard Time, and *Measure Time, are in the Medley of one Dance. **1852** C. W. H[OSKYNS] *Talpa* 25 Furrows are avoided as a nuisance and a loss, except as a mark for *measure-work.

measure (ˈmɛʒ(j)ʊə(r)), *v.* Forms: see prec. sb. [a. F. *mesure-r*, f. *mesure* MEASURE *sb.* Cf. L. *mēnsūrāre*.]

†**1. a.** *trans.* To regulate, moderate, restrain. *Obs.*

a **1300** *Cursor M.* 28918 þat þou can mesure þe quen þat þou giues þi charite. *c* **1375** *Sc. Leg. Saints* ii. (*Paulus*) 166 Nero, mesure þi gret foly. *c* **1400** *Destr. Troy* 3928 Troilus ..mesuret his maners, þof he þe myrth vsid. *c* **1485** *Digby Myst.* (1882) IV. 264 Gud Mawdleyn, mesure youre distillinge teres! *a* **1500** *Mankind* 227 (Brandl) Mesure yowur sylf: euer be ware of excesse! **1574** tr. *Marlorat's Apocalips* 40 Too measure our sorow, so as wee giue not our selues ouer too it.

†**b.** To limit or restrict (a person). *Obs. rare*⁻¹.

1560 DAUS tr. *Sleidane's Comm.* 149b, It was lawful neither for him nor no man els to prescribe or measure them in this behalf.

2. a. To ascertain or determine the spatial magnitude or quantity of (something); *properly*, by the application of some object of known size or capacity. Also, in extended sense, to ascertain the quantity of (e.g. force, heat, time) by comparison with some fixed unit.

a **1340** HAMPOLE *Psalter* lix. 6 The dale of tabernacles I sal mesour [L. *metibor*]. *c* **1375** *Sc. Leg. Saints* xxii. (*Laurentius*) 552 He gert mesoure þe tre sone, & fand It mare be quantyte þane to þe wark nedit be. **1481** CAXTON *Myrr.* I. xi. 37 Thus is by geometrye mesured alle thingis. **1530** PALSGR. 634/1, I mesure clothe with a yerde. **1535** COVERDALE *Ezek.* xlii. 15 When he had measured all the ynnermer house. **1688** R. HOLME *Armoury* III. 260/2 Some measure..Salmons and Eels by Ale Measure. **1732** POPE *Ess. Man* II. 20 Go, measure earth, weigh air, and state the tides. **1774** GOLDSM. *Nat. Hist.* (1862) I. xx. 124 Those Instruments called anemometers, which are made to measure the velocity of the wind. **1816** PLAYFAIR *Nat. Phil.* II. 41 The angles of these triangles are to be measured. **1844** STEPHENS *Bk. Farm* II. 276 Corn is measured up direct from the fanners in this way. **1860** TYNDALL *Glac.* I. xxi. 149, I..endeavoured to measure some of the undulations.

b. With clause as obj.

1611 SHAKS. *Cymb.* I. ii. 25 Till you had measur'd how long a Foole you were vpon the ground.

c. To take (a person's) measure *for* clothes, etc. Also *transf.* and *fig.*

1824 R. HUMPHREYS *Mem. J. Decastro* 156 Mr. Cross.. when he wrote a character for a person, measured the extent of his genius the same as a tailor does the body for a garment, and was generally very successful in making a *good* fit. **1836** MARRYAT *Japhet* xvi, I ordered a suit of the most fashionable clothes,..being very minute in my directions to the foreman, who measured me. **1848** DICKENS *Dombey* ii, You have been already measured for your mourning, haven't you? **1859** B. JERROLD *Life D. Jerrold* vi. 94 The pig was to be measured for his part. **1880** 'OUIDA' *Moths* I. 57 Measure me for my clothes. *a* **1890** in Barrère & Leland *Dict. Slang* (1890) II. 49/1 He had been measured for a funeral sermon three times, he said, and had never used either one of them. **1896** FARMER & HENLEY *Slang* IV. 296 *To have been measured for a new umbrella*..(American), -(1) To appear in new but ill-fitting clothes; whence (2) to pursue a policy of doubtful wisdom. **1942** BERREY & VAN DEN BARK *Amer. Thes. Slang* §117/16 Be buried,..be measured for a new overcoat.

d. *fig.* To take the measure of (a person); to look (a person) up and down. (Cf. F. *mesurer*.)

1747 RICHARDSON *Clarissa* (1768) I. viii. 48 My Brother.. having measured me, as I may say, with his eyes..from head to foot. **1896** A. E. HOUSMAN *Shropshire Lad* xli, In many an eye that measures me.

e. With dimensions or amounts as obj. Also, to mark or lay off (a line of definite length) in a certain direction.

1382 WYCLIF *Ezek.* xlviii. 30 Fro the north coost thou shalt mesure fyue hundrid and foure thousandis. **1535** COVERDALE *Num.* xxxv. 5 Ye shal measure without the cite on yᵉ East syde, two thousand cubites. **1611** BIBLE *Ruth* iii. 15 He measured sixe measures of barley, and laide it on her. **1844** MRS. BROWNING *Drama Exile* 10 Whence to mark despair, And measure out the distances from good! **1853** SIR H. DOUGLAS *Milit. Bridges* (ed. 3) 61 Having measured a line, as A E,..in any convenient direction. **1882** MINCHIN *Unipl. Kinemat.* 210 By measuring from P along the lines PA_1, PA_2, PA_3,..lengths, Pa_1, Pa_2, Pa_3.

f. ***to measure*** (†***out***) ***one's length***: to fall prostrate.

Cf. **1611** BIBLE *1 Kings* xvii. 21 He stretched [*margin* Hebr. measured] himselfe vpon the childe. [The Vulgate has *mensus est*, whence Wyclif *mesurede*.]

1590 SHAKS. *Mids. N.* III. ii. 429 Faintnesse constraineth me, To measure out my length on this cold bed. **1605** —— *Lear* I. iv. 100 If you will measure your lubbers length againe, tarry. **1838** DICKENS *Nich. Nick.* xix, He lost his balance, and measured his length upon the ground. **1853** W. STIRLING *Cloister Life Chas. V* 163 Many of his cedars.. measured their length upon the discomfited parterres.

†**g.** To form of, raise or reduce to, certain dimensions or proportions. *Obs.*

a **1300** *Cursor M.* 22952 [God] mai..Mak a wel fairer licam, And if þar-of was mar or less, To mesure [*a* **1425** *Trin.* To mesure hit] als his will es. *c* **1400** *Destr. Troy* 3033 With browes full brent..Full metly made & mesured betwene. **1513** DOUGLAS *Æneis* XII. iv. 35 The forrettis of thir beistis toppis baith They clip and missour, as tho was the gys.

h. *absol.* or *intr.* To take measurements; to use a measuring instrument.

1611 BIBLE *Deut.* xxi. 2 They shall measure vnto the cities which are round about him that is slaine. **1875** JOWETT *Plato* (ed. 2) V. 36 The young carpenter should be taught to measure and use the rule.

i. *intr.* (in *pass.* sense). To admit of measurement.

1765 *Museum Rust.* III. 222 My malt..does not shrink so much when it comes to be laid on the kiln; of course it measures to more advantage.

j. ***to measure swords***: *lit.* of adversaries in a duel, to ascertain that their swords are of equal length. Hence, to contend in battle, try one's strength *with* (cf. sense 10).

Cf. F. *mesurer les épées, mesurer son épée avec.*

1600 SHAKS. *A.Y.L.* v. iv. 91 And so wee measur'd swords, and parted. **1852** THACKERAY *Esmond* II. ii, You.. wanted to measure swords with Mohun, did you? **1878** BOSW. SMITH *Carthage* 267 Four times over he had now measured his sword with the future conquerors of the world.

3. *trans.* Chiefly with *out*: To mark the boundary or course of; to delimit. *poet.*

1513 BRADSHAW *St. Werburge* I. 200 The..ryuer and water of Mersee..Mesurynge and metynge the bondes.. Bitwene chesshyr & lancashyr. **1600** SHAKS. *A.Y.L.* II. vi. 2 Heere lie I downe, And measure out my graue. **1781** COWPER *Expost.* 177 A cloud to measure out their march by day.

4. a. To have a measurement of (so much).

1671 MILTON *P.R.* I. 210 E're yet my age Had measur'd twice six years. **1823** H. J. BROOKE *Introd. Crystallogr.* 198 The planes M on M′, measure 120°. **1833** LOUDON *Encycl. Cottage Archit.* §297 Each shutter measuring four feet six inches superficial. **1899** *Allbutt's Syst. Med.* VII. 540 The circumference of his head measures 22 inches.

b. *intr.* To vie in measurement *with*. Also, to be comparable *with*.

1712 ARBUTHNOT *John Bull* I. xi, The prodigious dimensions of them. In short, they would have measured with the best bale of cloth in John's shop. **1904** G. PARKER *Ladder of Swords* vi. 61 Her words for the great cause had measured well with her deeds. **1907** *Smart Set* Mar. 126/2 The dog moved a cat-like step forward, making up the interval, and the man made a mental note that its single stride measured with his.

c. fig. ***to measure up to***: to be equal (in ability, etc.) to; to match (cf. *match up to* s.v. MATCH *v.*[1]

8 b); to have the necessary qualifications for. orig. *U.S.*

1910 *N.Y. Even. Post* 16 Dec. 8 A man should be found for Senator who in ability and character will measure up to the just demands of such a situation. **1930** J. W. JOHNSON *Black Manhattan* xiv. 177 These plays..made a high demand on the versatility of the company... The demand was fully measured up to. **1931** G. T. CLARK *Leland Stanford* xii. 405 Stanford..had in mind the problem of selecting some one who measured up to his ideal. **1958** *Spectator* 7 Feb. 181/2 The later period, however, does not measure up to the earlier in the originality or interest of its political literature.

5. *trans.* To estimate the amount, duration, value, etc. of (an immaterial thing) by comparison with some standard.

1667 MILTON *P.L.* XII. 554 How soon hath thy prediction, Seer blest, Measur'd this transient World, the Race of time, Till time stand fixt. **1695** LOCKE *Further Consid. Value Money* 5 'Tis by the quantity of Silver he gets for it in Exchange..that he measures the value of the Commodity he sells. **1790** COWPER *Catharina* 48 And by Philomel's annual note To measure the life that she leads. **1837** LYTTON *E. Maltrav.* (1851) 40 We may measure our road to wisdom by the sorrows we have undergone.

6. To judge or estimate the greatness or value of (a person, a quality, etc.) by a certain standard or rule; to appraise by comparison with something else.

c **1374** CHAUCER *Boeth.* III. pr. ii. 51 (Camb. MS.), Many folk mesuren and gessen þat souereyn good by Ioye and gladnesse [L. *Plurimi vero boni fructum gaudio lætitiaque metiuntur*]. **1509** HAWES *Past. Pleas.* XXI. (1555) 100 Who of this science dooth know the certaynte All maysteries might measure perfytely. **1586** B. YOUNG *Guazzo's Civ. Conv.* IV. 195 b, We ought perfectlie to..understand the sentences of our auncestors, and measure them with their customes. **1597** SHAKS. *2 Hen. IV*, v. ii. 65. **1605** —— *Macb.* v. viii. 45. **1617** MORYSON *Itin.* I. 199 It is great injustice, that our actions should be measured by opinion, and not by reason. **1622** BACON *Hen. VII* 45 In all which the King measured and valued things amisse. **1651** HOBBES *Leviath.* I. ii. 4 Men measure, not onely other men, but all other things, by themselves. *c* **1655** MILTON *Sonn., to C. Skinner*, To measure life, learn thou betimes. **1784** COWPER *Task* I. 396 Measure life By its true worth, the comfort it affords. **1879** FROUDE *Cæsar* viii. 71 Sylla had measured the difficulty of the task which lay before him. **1884** GILMOUR *Mongols* 78 Measuring me by himself he supposed that I was merely telling a lie.

7. a. To be the measure of, or a means of measuring.

1590 SHAKS. *Com. Err.* III. ii. 113 An Ell and three quarters, will not measure her from hip to hip. **1667** MILTON *P.L.* v. 581 Time..measures all things durable By present, past, and future. **1775** HARRIS *Philos. Arrangem.* (1841) 338 *note*, The measurer and the thing measured should reciprocate; so that while the gallon measures the wine, the wine should measure the gallon. **1821** LAMB *Elia* Ser. I. *Old Benchers I.T.*, The..sun-dials..seeming coevals with that Time which they measured. **1842–59** GWILT *Archit.* §917 The angle formed by a tangent and chord is measured by half the arc of that chord. **1868** LOCKYER *Elem. Astron.* v. (1879) 190 For common purposes, time is measured by the Sun.

absol. **1614** RAVENSCROFT *Brief Discourse* 3 The Minime is the first Note that Measureth (being in it selfe indiuisible) and the Semibreue the first note Measured.

b. *Math.* Of a quantity: To be a measure or submultiple of (another quantity); †*refl.* to be exactly divisible *by*. †Also *absol.*

1570 BILLINGSLEY *Euclid* 126 The other kinde of a part, is any lesse quantitie in comparison of a greater, whether it be in number or magnitude, and whether it measure or no. *Ibid.* 234 If a magnitude measure two magnitudes, it shall also measure their greatest common measure. **1709–29** V. MANDEY *Syst. Math., Arith.* 6 Every number measures it self by unity; so 7 measures it self by 1.

8. a. To apportion by measure; to mete or deal *out*. (Also *absol.* or *intr.*, and in indirect pass.) *arch.*

a **1300** *Cursor M.* 27159 Preist..þat mesurs oft-sithes vr penances. **1452** in Gross *Gild Merch.* (1890) II. 67 The sayde..wardens shall mesure & devyde trulye to ewry of theme after harr degree. **1530** PALSGR. 635/1 By the same mesure that you mesure to other men wyll men mesure by to you. **1579** LYLY *Euphues* (Arb.) 92 That thou maist be mesured vnto, with the lyke measure that thou hast meaten vnto others. **1674** BREVINT *Saul at Endor* 241 If you be not pleased with this Mesuring Indulgences. **1790** GOUV. MORRIS in Sparks *Life & Writ.* (1832) II. 117 Each district measures out its obedience by its wishes. **1818** CRUISE *Digest* (ed. 2) VI. 165 To measure out the quantity of estate that the devisee was to take. **1876** L. STEPHEN *Eng. Th. in 18th C.* II. XII. vi. 429 Sermons were measured out with no grudging hand.

†**b.** To deal blows upon, to strike. (Cf. F. *mesurer un coup*.)

1652 J. WRIGHT tr. *Camus' Nat. Paradox* VI. 132 Hee had his Arm already up to measure Pisides o're the Shoulders.

9. a. To proportion, adjust (something) *to* an object, or by a standard.

1590 SPENSER *F.Q.* II. xii. 33 On the rocke the waves breaking aloft A solemne Meane unto them measured. **1642** FULLER *Holy & Prof. St.* III. i. 153 Measure not thy entertainment of a guest by his estate, but thine own. **1650** JER. TAYLOR *Holy Living* ii. §7 (1686) 117 If you will secure a contented spirit, you must measure your desires by your fortune,..not your fortunes by your desires. **1732** POPE *Ess. Man* I. 71 His knowledge measur'd to his state and place.

†**b.** To be commensurate with. *Obs.*

1576 FLEMING *Panopl. Epist.* 43 Your promise was, that your dealing shoulde measure their deseruing. **1633** G. HERBERT *Temple, 23rd Psalm*, Thy sweet and wondrous love Shall measure all my days.

10. To bring into competition, opposition, or comparison *with*. Also *refl.* to try one's strength *against*.

1715–20 POPE *Iliad* XXIII. 888 All start at once; Oïleus led the race; The next Ulysses, measuring pace with pace. **1784** COWPER *Task* IV. 337 To measure lots With less distinguish'd than ourselves. **1817** JAS. MILL *Brit. India* II. IV. v. 187 He was pleased to measure dignities with his king. **1838** PRESCOTT *Ferd. & Is.* II. xiv. III. 181 He was compelled to measure his genius with that of the greatest captain of the age. **1869** FREEMAN *Norm. Conq.* (1875) III. xii. 192 Herbert was not afraid to measure himself against a much more dangerous enemy.

11. a. To travel over, traverse (a certain distance, a tract of country); also, †to peruse or read through. Chiefly *poet.*

After uses of L. *metiri, emetiri*.

c **1374** CHAUCER *Boeth.* v. pr. i. 116 (Camb. MS.), So þat þou ne mayst nat suffice to mesuren the ryht wey [L. *ad emetiendum rectum iter*]. **1579** SPENSER *Sheph. Cal.* Sept. 21 Since when thou hast measured much ground. **1590** —— *F.Q.* I. i. 32 The Sunne, that measures heaven all day long. *Ibid.* III. xii. 36 Full dreadfull thinges out of that balefull booke He red, and measur'd many a sad verse. **1596** SHAKS. *Merch. V.* III. iv. 84 For we must measure twentie miles to day. **1682** N. O. *Boileau's Lutrin* III. 25 With equal pace the Temples Nave they measure! **1725** POPE *Odyss.* I. 339 He..measur'd a length of seas, a toilsome length, in vain. **1835** WORDSW. *Extemp. Eff. Death J. Hogg* 13 Nor has the rolling year twice measured, From sign to sign, its steadfast course, Since [etc.].

b. *to measure back*: to retrace (one's steps, the road). ? *Obs.*

1595 SHAKS. *John* v. v. 3 When English measure backward their owne ground In faint Retire. **1610** —— *Temp.* II. i. 259 A space, whose eu'ry cubit Seemes to cry out, how shall that Claribell Measure vs backe to Naples? **1697** DRYDEN *Æneid* x. 932 The Vessel..measures back with speed her former Way. **1758** SMOLLETT *Hist. Eng.* III. 150 They measured back their ground with some disorder. **1797** BURKE *Regic. Peace* III. (1st par.), With a sort of plodding perseverance, we resolve to measure back again the very same joyless, hopeless,..track. **1809** MALKIN *Gil Blas* x. ix. (Rtldg.) 360 Measure back your steps..to Lirias, and stay quietly there.

†**12.** To turn into metre. *Obs.*

c **1586** C'TESS PEMBROKE *Ps.* XLIX. i, Wordes shall from my mouth proceed, Which I will measure by melodious eare. *a* **1774** GOLDSM. tr. *Scarron's Com. Romance* (1775) I. 278 All nature lay hushed in sleep..except some poets, who had cramp verses to measure [F. *des vers difficiles à tourner*].

†**13.** To encircle, encompass. *Obs.*

c **1425** *Found. St. Bartholomew's* (E.E.T.S.) 63 She beganne..with a long threid to compasse the howse... And ..the howse that was mesurid with the threid, hit [the fire] myght nat hurte. **1680** MOXON *Mech. Exerc.* 210 The String that comes down every Tread, measures a small Circumference oftner than it does a greater Circumference.

measured ('mɛʒ(j)ʊəd), *ppl. a.* [f. MEASURE *sb.* and *v.* + -ED.]

†**1.** Moderate, temperate. (Also *well measured*.)

c **1400** *Rule St. Benet* 2328 A Priores..Aw to be mesured euermair To bind non als bot þai may bere. **1456** SIR G. HAYE *Law Arms* (S.T.S.) 300 To be wele mesurit in..eting and drinking. **1483** CAXTON *Cato* F vij b, To be temperate and mesured in alle thynges.

2. a. Determined, apportioned, or dealt out by measure. *measured mile*: a distance of one mile carefully measured, esp. such a distance used for determining the speed of a ship; also *attrib.* *measured work*, piece-work.

c **1440** *Promp. Parv.* 335/1 Mesuryd wythe mesure, *mensuratus*. **1608** J. CHAMBERLAIN *Let.* 15 July (1939) I. 262 A gentleman wan a great wager for riding five measured miles..twenty times over in lesse than five howres. **1614** RAVENSCROFT *Brief Discourse* 11 The breaking of the Measur'd Notes. **1666** P. HENRY in M. Henry *Life* M. H's Wks. 1853 II. 666/2 The scripture speaks of measured miles in a law-case, Deuteronomy xxi. 2. *a* **1700** DRYDEN *Cymon & Iph.* Fables 553 Scarce the third Glass of measur'd Hours was run. **1720** *Britannia Depicta, or Ogilby Improved* (title-page), Wherein are..Engraven, All yᵉ Cities..scituate on or near the Roads, with their respective Distances in Measured and Computed Miles. **1784** COWPER *Task* III. 424 The rest ..he disposes neat At measured distances. **1822** GALT *Provost* xxxviii. (1868) 110 Two measured glasses of whisky in an old doctor's bottle. **1834–47** J. S. MACAULAY *Field Fortif.* (1851) 57 It is..cheaper to pay a high price for measured work, than to employ them by the day. **1843** *Pract. Mechanic* June 358/2 The *Mermaid* then..performed the measured mile at the rate..of above thirteen miles through the water per hour. **1901** *Trans. Inst. Naval Archit.* XLIII. 23 The whole idea of the design has been, not so much to procure a very high measured-mile speed for a few hours, as to assure a good, continuous ocean speed. **1950** *Engineering* 10 Feb. 147/1 Measured-mile posts were in existence at Hartley..prior to 1884.

b. Accurately regulated or proportioned.

1605 BACON *Adv. Learn.* I. To the King §2 This which I shall say is no amplification at all, but a positiue and measured truth. **1748** GRAY *Alliance Educ. & Govt.* 40 Here measured Laws and philosophic Ease Fix and improve the polish'd Arts of Peace. **1901** J. WATSON *Life of the Master* xxi. 198 For their toil and work they will receive a measured wage.

†**c.** Limited, finite. *Obs. rare*⁻¹.

1653 ROUSE *Myst. Marr.* 328 As much as a poor measured creature may resemble that which is unmeasurable.

3. a. Consisting of 'measures' or metrical groups; written in metre; metrical. (Cf. F. *mesuré*.)

1581 SIDNEY *Apol. Poetrie* (Arb.) 50 In ryme or measured verse. **1682** SOAMES & DRYDEN tr. *Boileau's Art Poetry* II. 21 Closing the Sence within the measur'd time, 'Tis hard to fit the Reason to the Rhyme. **1704** PRIOR *Let. Boileau* 50 That we poetic folks, who must restrain Our measur'd sayings in an equal chain. **1850** TENNYSON *In Mem.* v, For the unquiet heart and brain, A use in measur'd language lies. **1871** PALGRAVE *Lyr. Poems* Ded., The sweet propriety of measured phrase.

b. *gen.* Of motion, sound, flow of language, etc.: Having a marked rhythm; rhythmical; regular in movement.

1633 MILTON *Arcades* 71 And the low world in measur'd motion draw After the heavenly tune. **1725** POPE *Odyss.* I. 196 They all advance And form to measur'd airs the mazy dance. **1812** BYRON *Ch. Har.* II. lxxx, Music..timely echo'd back the measured oar. **1837–9** HALLAM *Hist. Lit.* II. II. vii. §34. 310 It is in many parts very well written, in a measured prose. **1855** MRS. CARLYLE *Lett.* II. 253, I heard a measured tread; and then..advanced on me eight soldiers. **1891** T. HARDY *Tess* xliii, It [winter] came on in stealthy and measured glides, like the moves of a chess-player.

c. *Mus.* = MENSURABLE.

1782 BURNEY *Hist. Mus.* II. 180 Franco [in his *Ars Cantus Mensurabilis*] only intends to treat of Measured Music, of which, he piously observes, plain-chant has the precedence. **1880** ROCKSTRO in Grove *Dict. Mus.* II. 415 *Musica Mensurata* or *Cantus Mensurabilis.* (Measured Music). **1901** H. E. WOOLDRIDGE *Oxf. Hist. Mus.* I. vi. (*heading*) Discant or Measured Music. The Measured Notation and its Relation to Fixed Rhythms.

4. Chiefly with reference to language: Carefully weighed or calculated; deliberate and restrained. (Cf. sense 1.)

1802 WORDSW. *Resol. & Independ.* xiv, Choice word and measured phrase. **1847–54** WEBSTER s.v., In no measured terms. **1898** BODLEY *France* II. III. iii. 140 Men..tell the same story in more measured language. **1903** MORLEY *Gladstone* III. VIII. x. 176 In the debate, said Mr. Gladstone, Lord Hartington restated with measured force the position of the government.

Hence '**measuredness**.

1854 FABER *Growth in Holiness* xiv. (1872) 201 How the world admires..measuredness of words!

measuredly ('mɛʒ(j)ʊədlɪ), *adv.* [f. MEASURED *ppl. a.* + -LY².]

1. With measured movement or pace.

1826 J. BANIM *Tales O'Hara F.* Ser. II. II. 263 He..gave, slowly and measuredly, his 'Sarvent, Miss'. **1865** CARLYLE *Fredk. Gt.* XVIII. ix. (1872) VII. 263 That..advances with its eyes open, measuredly, counting its steps. **1872** LEVER *Ld. Kilgobbin* liv, His heart could beat more measuredly.

2. In some measure. *rare.*

1860 RUSKIN *Mod. Paint.* V. IX. viii. §1. 281, I can enter measuredly into the feelings of Correggio.

measureless ('mɛʒ(j)ʊəlɪs), *a.* [f. MEASURE *sb.* + -LESS.] Having no bounds or limits; unlimited, immeasurable, infinite.

1362 LANGL. *P. Pl.* A. III. 231 Þer is a Meede Mesureles þat Maystrie desyret. *a* **1541** WYATT *Ps.* cii. Prol. 18 Here hath he comfort when he doth measure Measureless mercye to measureless faulte. **1591** SPENSER *Tears of Muses* 516 To see thee, and thy mercie measurelesse. **1607** SHAKS. *Cor.* v. vi. 103 Measurelesse Lyar. **1797** COLERIDGE *Kubla Khan* 29 The caverns measureless to man. **1866** LIDDON *Bampt. Lect.* vi. (1875) 307 God is parted from the highest forms of created life by a measureless interval. **1887** MORRIS *Odyss.* IX. 537 He..put forth his measureless might.

Hence '**measurelessly** *adv.*, immeasurably, infinitely; '**measurelessness**, immeasurableness.

1839 BAILEY *Festus* vi. (1852) 77 Joy even in thine anguish; —such was His, But measurelessly more. **1854** J. S. C. ABBOTT *Napoleon* (1855) II. xiii. 235 The measurelessness of the calamity. **1863** GEO. ELIOT *Romola* I. xix, Feigned and preposterous admiration varied by a corresponding measurelessness in vituperation. **1887** DOWDEN *Shelley* I. ix. 435 The man whose life—measurelessly dear to her—seemed to be placed in her hands.

†'**measurely**, *a. Obs. rare.* [f. MEASURE *sb.* + -LY¹.] **a.** Moderate. **b.** ? Symmetrical.

1573 TUSSER *Husb.* (1878) 21 Yet measurely feasting with neighbors among, shal make thee beloued. **1829** LANDOR *Imag. Conv., Steele & Addison* Wks. 1853 II. 152/2 His wig even and composed as his temper, with measurely curls and antithetical top-knots.

'**measurely**, *adv.* Orig. *U.S.* (long *rare*). In 5 mesur(e)ly, -li, -le, -like. [Formed as prec. + -LY².] Moderately.

c **1400** *Cato's Morals* 85 in *Cursor M.* p. 1670 Loke þou spende mesureli þe gode þat þou liuis bi. *c* **1400** *Rule St. Benet* 8 Ye ne sal noht be prude in herte; Ne ete ourmikil;.. Mesurlike slepe. *a* **1460** *How Good Wif thaught hir Doughter* 53 in Hazl. *E.P.P.* I. 183 Mesurely take ther offe, that the falle no blame. **1878** J. H. BEADLE *Western Wilds* xiv. 222 It is measurely free from winter storms.

measurement ('mɛʒ(j)ʊəmənt). [f. MEASURE *v.* + -MENT. Cf. OF. *mesurement*.]

1. The action or an act of measuring; mensuration.

1751 LABELYE *Westm. Br.* 88, I was exempted..from having any Concern with Measurements. **1776** GIBBON *Decl. & F.* xi. I. 304 The extent of the new walls..is reduced by accurate measurement to about twenty-one miles. **1843** *Penny Cycl.* XXVII. 196/2 A greater uniformity has prevailed in the measurement of angular magnitude than of any other whatsoever. **1866** CRUMP *Banking* viii. 160 A commodity employed for the measurement of the value in exchange of all other articles.

2. A dimension ascertained by measuring; size or extent measured by a standard.

1756 BURKE *Subl. & B.* III. iv, It seems amazing to me, that artists..have not by them at all times accurate measurements of all sorts of beautiful animals to help them to proper proportions. **1823** J. BADCOCK *Dom. Amusem.* 21

Iron vessels, within the measurement allowed by law. **1880** HAUGHTON *Phys. Geog.* ii. 30 This measurement is very important, as shewing the deep soundings which occur close to the western coasts of both Americas.

3. A system of measuring or of measures.

1867 BRANDE & COX *Dict. Sci.* etc. III. 808/1 The new measurement is universally adopted for vessels registered under the Board of Trade; .. but pleasure yachts still .. cling to the O.M. or old measurement. **1872** [see LINEAL *a.* 1 b].

4. *attrib.*: **measurement goods**, goods upon which the freight is charged by measurement instead of by weight; so ***measurement cargo***.

1858 SIMMONDS *Dict. Trade.* **1896** *Daily News* 9 Nov. 7/6 The measurement cargo which the vessel will carry is 18,000 tons, while her dead-weight cargo is down at 11,500 tons.

measurer (ˈmɛʒ(j)ʊərə(r)). [f. MEASURE *v.* + -ER[1].]

1. a. One who measures or takes measurements; *esp.* one whose duty or office it is to see that goods or commodities are of the proper measure.

1552 HULOET, Measurer, *dimensor.* **1570** DEE *Math. Pref.* a iij b, To vnderstand .. how Farre, a thing seene .. is from the measurer. **1616** SURFL. & MARKH. *Country Farm* 519 The second instrument verie necessarily required for the Measurer to measure assuredly withall .. is the Richards chayne. **1636** *Early Rec. Dedham, Mass.* (1892) III. 36 We doe order yt all high wayes .. he orderly set out by our Measurer. **1641** *Rec. Colony & Plantation New Haven* (1857) I. 51 Bro: Pecke chosen measurer for the towne to fill and strike all the corne. **1706** PHILLIPS (ed. Kersey) s.v. *Alnager*, There are three distinct Officers, known by the Names of Searcher, Measurer and Alnager. **1706** *Rec. Early Hist. Boston* (1882) VIII. 37 Allexander Seers, Samuell Bridge, .. to serve as Measurers of board, Timber, and Plank. **1827** DRAKE & MANSFIELD *Cincinnati in 1826* vi. 51 The council have power to appoint .. Measurers of wood and coal. **1841** in C. Cist *Cincinnati in 1841* (Advt.), George Warren, Measurer of Stone-work, Birch-work, and Plastering. **1875** PROCTOR *Expanse Heav.* 241 The measurer of the moon's distance. **1916** BLUNDEN *Harbingers* 24 The binman found the measurer pleased, For hops were clean and work was through. **1972** *Classification of Occupations* (Dept. of Employment) III. 408/2 Workers in this group weigh and otherwise measure materials, goods and products, .. for example: .. Measurers.

b. *fig.* (Said esp. of the sun, as measuring time.)

1556 J. HEYWOOD *Spider & F.* xcii. 76 This mayde right mesurer to me is, As I to other haue mesurde wrong. **1576** FLEMING *Panopl. Epist.* 352 The foure quarters [of the year] .. whiche we knowe to be the measurer and meater of our life. **1641** HOWELL *Vote, Poem to Chas. I* 1 The world's bright Ey, Time's measurer. **1874** SAYCE *Compar. Philol.* viii. 333 When we call the moon 'the measurer' we at once personify it.

c. That which is the measure of (something).

1775 [see MEASURE *v.* 7].

2. An instrument used for measuring, as a rain-gauge, an hour-glass.

1764 HARMER *Observ.* i. 2 The flat-roof of any building that hath but one spout for carrying off the water, might be a measurer of the different quantities of the fallen rain. **1771** BARKER in *Phil. Trans.* LXI. 227 The height my rain measurer stands above the ground. **1821** CLARE *Vill. Minstr.* II. 162 [An hour-glass] Old-fashioned uncouth measurer of the day. **1877** Heat-Measurer [see HEAT *sb.* 14 b].

3. A measuring-worm; = GEOMETER 4.

(Cf. LAND-MEASURER 2.)

measuring (ˈmɛʒ(j)ʊərɪŋ), *vbl. sb.* [f. MEASURE *v.* + -ING[1].]

1. The action of the vb. MEASURE; the process of taking measurements; measurement, mensuration.

1340 HAMPOLE *Pr. Consc.* 7692 Bot swa sutelle and wise may na man be, þat þat mesuryng knawes swa wele als he. **1461** in *10th Rep. Hist. MSS. Comm.* App. v. 301 The wakman of the saide citie .. shall have the mesuring of salte and corne. **1598** SHAKS. *Merry W.* II. i. 215. **1656** H. PHILLIPS *Purch. Patt.* (1676) B viij, This measuring by the Pole .. is very inconvenient. **1709** J. WARD *Introd. Math.* I. ii. (1734) 21 Division is by Euclid fitly termed the measuring of one Number by another. **1844** STEPHENS *Bk. Farm* II. 275 The measuring up of grain. **1893** *Athenæum* 23 Sept. 423/3 The yearly measurings and observations.

†**2.** Dimension. *Obs.*

1529 MORE *Dyaloge* II. Wks. 188/1 Thei be not cyrcumscribed in place, for lack of bodily dymencion and measuring. **1597** A. M. tr. *Guillemeau's Fr. Chirurg.* 2/1 Shee hath a threefoulde measuringe, in length, bredthe, and debthe.

†**3.** Dancing of 'measures'. *Obs.*

1599 MARSTON *Sco. Villanie* I. i, Hath been at feasts, and led the measuring At Court.

4. *attrib.* esp. in the names of various instruments and vessels graduated for purposes of measurement, as ***measuring-chain***, ***-foot***, ***-glass***, ***-line***, ***-pole***, ***-reed***, ***-rod*** (also fig.), ***-rule***, ***-staff***, ***-tape***, †***-yard***; †**measuring-money** (see quot.); **measuring-wheel**, (*a*) = ODOMETER; (*b*) = CIRCUMFERENTOR 2 (Knight *Dict. Mech.* 1875).

1875 KNIGHT *Dict. Mech.* 1413/2 **Measuring-chain*, the Surveyor's chain. **1665** J. WEBB *Stone-Heng* (1725) 24 The Difference between our measuring Foot, and the Vicentine. **1842** FRANCIS *Dict. Arts*, **Measuring Glass.* **1870** DICKENS *E. Drood* xiii, The small squat measuring glass in which little Rickitts took her steel drops daily. **1611** BIBLE *Zech.* ii. 1 A man with a *measuring line in his hand. **1706** PHILLIPS (ed. Kersey), **Measuring-Money*, a certain Duty formerly laid upon Cloth besides Alnage. **1774** M. MACKENZIE *Maritime Surv.* 104 At the End of each Chain, or *Measuring-pole. **1611** BIBLE *Ezek.* xlii. 17 Hee measured the North side fiue hundreth reedes, with a *measuring reed round about. **1656** H. PHILLIPS *Purch. Patt.* (1676) 197 Your *measuring Rod. **1870** J. H. NEWMAN *Gram. Assent* II. 476 Does Gibbon think to sound the depths of the eternal ocean with the tape and measuring-rod of his merely literary philosophy? **1842–59** GWILT *Archit.* §2212 The plumber's *measuring rule is 2 feet long. **1884** *Athenæum* 8 Nov. 586/3 The theodolites, *measuring-staves, and plane-tables. **1823** P. NICHOLSON *Pract. Build.* 386 The *Measuring-tape is a kind of strong tape, graduated, marked, and coiled up by a little winch into a cylindrical box. **1728** R. MORRIS *Ess. Anc. Archit.* Advt., Plane-Tables, Water-Levels, *Measuring-Wheels. **1842** FRANCIS *Dict. Arts*, *Perambulator*, or *Measuring Wheel*, an instrument which being run along a road or other level surface indicates and registers the exact distance it passes over. **1760–72** H. BROOKE *Fool of Qual.* (1809) III. 19 She whipt up the *measuring yard, and .. flew to the door.

b. measuring cast: (*a*) *lit.* in the sport of throwing the bar, a throw so nearly equal to another that measurement is required to decide the superiority (? *obs.*); (*b*) *fig.* a nice question, a ticklish point; a 'toss-up' (*arch.*).

1632 STRAFFORD in Browning *Life* (1892) 301 As if it weare a measuring cast, betwixt them, whoe weare like to proue the greater loosers vpon the parting. **1645** WALLER *On Fletcher's Plays* Poems 179 When lusty shepheards throwe The barre by turnes, and none the rest out goe So farre but that the best are measuring casts. *a* **1661** FULLER *Worthies* (1840) III. 161 It is a measuring cast, whether this proverb pertaineth to Essex or this county. **1712** ADDISON *Spect.* No. 538 ¶5 Yet I thought some in the Company had been endeavouring who should pitch the Bar farthest; that it had for some time been a measuring Cast, and at last my Friend .. had thrown beyond them all. **1898** SIR W. HARCOURT in *Times* 18 Jan. 10/3 That majority you have succeeded in reducing to a measuring cast.

ˈ**measuring**, *ppl. a.* [-ING[2].] **a.** That measures.

1570 BILLINGSLEY *Euclid* 126 The number 5. is a part of the number 15. .. And this kynde of part is called commonly *pars metiens* or *mensurans*, that is, a measuryng part.

b. measuring-worm: the larva of a geometrid moth; a geometer or looper.

1843 J. E. DEKAY *Zool. N.Y.* VI. 41 It walks after the manner of some caterpillars called Measuring worms. **1859** CLEMENS in *Ann. Rep. Smithson. Inst.* 186 The geometers, properly so called, or measuring worms. **1884** *Riverside Nat. Hist.* (1888) II. 445. **1903** W. J. HOLLAND *Moth Bk.* 323 The larvæ, which are commonly known as 'measuring-worms', 'span-worms', or 'loopers', have the power in many cases of attaching themselves by the posterior claspers to the stems and branches of plants, and extending the remainder of the body outwardly at an angle. **1939** DUNCAN & PICKWELL *World of Insects* x. 172 Certain large measuring-worms, of the family Geometridae, have the ability, when danger threatens, to stiffen themselves out at angles to the stem on which they have been feeding or crawling, and thereafter for several minutes or hours to resemble perfectly bare and lifeless twigs. **1956** W. R. BIRD *Off-Trail in Nova Scotia* viii. 215, I saw some of those long 'loopers' or 'measuring worms' that I hadn't seen since a boy.

Hence ˈ**measuringly** *adv.*, as if taking a person's 'measure'.

1879 MISS BIRD *Rocky Mountains* 44 A hard, sad-looking woman looked at me measuringly.

meat (miːt), *sb.* Forms: 1 **mete, mæt(e, mett,** 2–8 **mete,** 3 **mæte,** 4–5 **meite, mett, meyte,** 4–6 **meet(e, met(te,** 4–7 **meyt,** 5 **maite, mate, meett,** (*pl.* **meyttes, -is**), 5–7 **meate, meit,** 6 *Sc.* **meitt,** 5– **meat.** [OE. *mẹte* str. masc. = OFris. *met(e, meit*, OS. *meti* masc., *mat* neut., OHG. *maz* neut., ON. *mat-r* masc. (Sw. *mat*, Da. *mad*), Goth. *mat-s*:—OTeut. types **mati-z*, **mato-*, prob. repr. an original neuter **matoz-*, *-iz-*:—pre-Teut. **mados-*, *-es-*, perh. f. root **mĕd-* to be fat: see MAST *sb.*[2]

The LG. and Du. *met* minced meat (whence Du. *metworst*, G. *mettwurst* sausage) is prob. unconnected; cf. med.L. *matia* pl., tripe.]

1. a. Food in general; anything used as nourishment for men or animals; usually, solid food, in contradistinction to *drink*. Now *arch.* and *dial.*

green meat: grass or green vegetables used for food or fodder (see GREEN *a.* 4). See also HARD MEAT, HORSEMEAT, WHITEMEAT. ***meal of meat***, ***meal's meat***: see MEAL *sb.*[2] 1 e.

a **900** tr. *Bæda's Hist.* v. iv. (Schipper) 568 He eode on his hus & þær mete [*v.r.* mæte] þyȝede. *c* **975** *Rushw. Gosp.* Luke xii. 23 Sawel mara is ðonne mett. *a* **1050** *Liber Scintill.* xlvii. (1889) 153 Nys rice godes meta & drinc. *c* **1175** *Lamb. Hom.* 135 Ne sculen ȝe nawiht ȝimstones leggen Swinen to mete. *c* **1200** ORMIN 3213 Hiss drinnch wass waterr aȝȝ occ aȝȝ, Hiss mete wilde rotess. *a* **1240** *Lofsong* in *Cott. Hom.* 205 Ich habbe i-suneged ine mete and ine drunche. *a* **1300** *Cursor M.* 898 Mold sal be þi mete for nede. *c* **1380** WYCLIF *Wks.* (1880) 206 Alas, þat so gret cost & bisynesse is sette abouten þe roten body, þat is wormes mete. *c* **1440** *Pol. Rel. & L. Poems* (1903) 185 Thy mete shall be mylk, honye, & wyne. **1477** NORTON *Ord. Alch.* v. in Ashm. (1652) 76 Without Liquor no Meate is good. **1578** LYTE *Dodoens* II. xlvi. 205 These kindes of lillies are neither used in meate nor medicine. **1623** COCKERAM II, *Meate of the Gods*, Ambrosia, Manna. **1693** TATE in *Dryden's Juvenal* xv. (1697) 378 Who Flesh of Animals refus'd to eat, Nor held all sorts of Pulse for lawful Meat. **1775** JOHNSON *Journ. W. Isl.* 86 Our guides told us, that the horses could not travel all day without rest or meat. **1794** C. SMITH *Wanderings of Warwick* 66 Sending out women and children, after a hard day's work, to collect meat for the cattle. **1819** SHELLEY *P. Bell* VII. v. 4 He had .. meat and drink enough. **1844** STEPHENS *Bk. Farm* II. 709 Meat is then set down to them on a flat plate, consisting of crumbled bread and oatmeal. **1893** STEVENSON *Catriona* xxi. 253 When .. my father and my uncles lay in the hill, and I was to be carrying them their meat. **1902** *Daily Chron.* 12 Dec. 5/6 Imports of fruit and other choice green-meat.

b. *fig.* in various applications. (Also in many passages of the Bible, e.g. John iv. 32, 34, 1 Cor. iii. 2, Heb. v. 12, and in allusions to these.) ***to be meat and drink to*** (a person): to be a source of intense enjoyment to.

c **1200** *Trin. Coll. Hom.* 27 Þe þridde is for mete þat ilch man agh mid him to leden þan he sal of þesse liue faren, þat is cristes holie licame. *a* **1340** HAMPOLE *Psalter* vii. 5 Synful mannys lif is the deuels mete. **1497** BP. ALCOCK *Mons Perfect.* C j b/2 Obedyence is .. the meete and comforte of all sayntes. **1533** FRITH *Answ. More* E j, It ys meate and drinke to this childe to plaie. **1600** SHAKS. *A.Y.L.* v. i. 11 It is meat and drinke to me to see a Clowne. **1620** T. GRANGER *Div. Logike* 20 Idlenes is the meate of lust. **1693** *Humours Town* 5 Petty-foggers, and their Meat and Drink, the Litigious. **1837** CARLYLE *Misc.*, *Mirabeau* (1840) V. 139 But then his style! .. Strong meat, too tough for babes. **1855** BROWNING *Fra Lippo* 315 To find its meaning is my meat and drink.

c. Proverbs and phrases.

a **1529** SKELTON *Col. Cloute* 450 Swete meate hath soure sauce. **1546** J. HEYWOOD *Prov.* (1867) 8 God neuer sendth mouth, but he sendeth meat. **1597** SHAKS. *2 Hen. IV*, II. iv. 135, I am meat for your Master. **1616** T. DRAXE *Bibl. Scholast.* 127 One mans meate is another mans poyson. *a* **1623** FLETCHER *Love's Cure* III. ii, What's one mans poyson, Signior, Is anothers meat or drinke. **1749** FIELDING *Tom Jones* XI. viii, My lady is meat for no pretenders. **1809** MALKIN *Gil Blas* X. ix, Why must one man's meat be another man's poison? **1853** MRS. GASKELL *Cranford* xv. 296. After that she acknowledged that 'one man's meat might be another man's poison'. **1902** J. CONRAD *End of Tether* xiv, in *Youth* 370 One man's poison, another man's meat. **1905** A. BURVENICH *Eng. Idioms* 240 It is nuts to him; meat and drink to him, viz. the very sort of thing he likes. **1914** G. B. SHAW *Misalliance* 17 Whats one woman's meat is another woman's poison. **1929** J. B. PRIESTLEY *Good Companions* I. iii. 82 She had a trick of repeating phrases, raising her voice the second time, that had been meat and drink to mimics at Washbury for years. *a* **1930** D. H. LAWRENCE *Phoenix* (1936) 701 In the free, spontaneous self, one man's meat is truly another man's poison. And therefore you *can't* draw any average .. unless you are going to poison everybody. **1937** PARTRIDGE *Dict. Slang* 515 *Meat, the nearer the bone the sweeter the*, a .. low catch-phrase applied by men to a thin woman. **1939** F. THOMPSON *Lark Rise* i. 20 In spite of their poverty and the worry and anxiety attending it, they were not unhappy, and, though poor, there was nothing sordid about their lives. 'The nearer the bone the sweeter the meat', they used to say. **1939** N. MARSH *Overture to Death* xxii. 254 I'm no psycho-analyst, but I imagine she'd be meat and drink to any one who was.

†**d.** Phr. ***to carry meat in one's*** (or ***the***) ***mouth***, to bring in money, be a source of profit; *occas.* to afford entertainment or instruction. *Obs.*

Perh. originally said of a hawk.

1580 G. HARVEY *Three Lett.* Wks. (Grosart) I. 92 Those studies and practizes, that carrie, as they saye, meate in their mouth, hauing euermore their eye vppon the Title *De pane lucrando*, and their hand vpon their halfpenny. **1582** STANYHURST *Æneis* Ded. (Arb.) 7, I neauer .. omitted yt [*sc.* Virgil's epithet *Saturnia* applied to Juno], as in deede a terme that carieth meate in his mouth. **1592** GREENE *Disput. Conny-catchers* Wks. (Grosart) X. 269 The oldest lecher was as welcom as the youngest louer, so he broght meate in his mouth. **1599** B. JONSON *Cynthia's Rev.* v. ii, A gentleman of so pleasing and ridiculous a carriage, as, euen standing, carries meat in the mouth, you see. **1668** KIRKMAN *Eng. Rogue* II. xxxvii. (1671) 356 He bringing meat in his mouth, good store of Gold in his pocket, which he willingly and freely gave me.

e. The edible part of fruits, nuts, eggs, etc.: the pulp, kernel, yolk and white, etc. in contradistinction to the rind, peel, or shell. ? Now only *U.S.* exc. in proverbial phrase (see quot. 1592). Also, the animal substance of a shell-fish.

c **1420** *Pallad. on Husb.* III. 708 A stanry pere is seyd to chaunge his mete In esy lond ygraffed yf he be. **1530** PALSGR. 245/1 Meate of any frute, *le bon.* *a* **1562** G. CAVENDISH *Wolsey* (1893) 30 A very fayer orrynge wherof the mete or substaunce within was taken owt. **1592** SHAKS. *Rom. & Jul.* III. i. 25 Thy head is as full of quarrels, as an egge is full of meat. **1613** PURCHAS *Pilgrimage* (1614) 506 Of the meat of the Nut dried, they make oyle. **1679** J. SKEAT *Art Cookery* 30 First take all the meat out of the lobster. **1766** *Museum Rust.* I. lxxxiii. 370 Low or swampy grounds don't answer well for potatoes, .. the meat being generally scabby, close, wet and heavy. **1802** PALEY *Nat. Theol.* xx. (1819) 313 *note*, The meat of a plum. **1900** *Boston Even. Transcr.* 29 Mar. 7/3 Force through a meat chopper with one-half pound nut-meats, using English walnut meats, pecan-nut meats. **1902** *Fortn. Rev.* June 1012 A bit of crab-meat.

†**2.** A kind of food, an article of food, a 'dish'. ***white meat***, an article of food made with milk. *Obs.* (Cf. BAKE-MEAT, MILK-MEAT, SWEET-MEAT.)

c **897** K. ÆLFRED *Gregory's Past. C.* xliii. 318 Ða mettas þe God self ȝesceop to etonne ȝeleaffullum monnum. *c* **1200** ORMIN 11540 Þatt time þatt himm ȝet wass ned To metess & to drinnchess. **1340** *Ayenb.* 51 A god huet we hedde guod wyn yesteneuen and guode metes. *c* **1374** CHAUCER *Boeth.* II. met. v. 35 (Camb. MS.), They heldyn hem apayed with the metes þat the trewe feeldes browten forth. *c* **1470** HENRY *Wallace* III. 315 He .. Maide him gud cheyr of meyttis fresche and fyne. **1519** *Interl. Four Elem.* (Percy Soc.) 34 Of all metes in the worlde that be By this lyght, I love best drynke. **1565** COOPER *Thesaurus*, *Coccetum*, a meate made of honie and popie seede. **1598** FLORIO, *Geladia*, .. the meate we call gellie. **1613** PURCHAS *Pilgrimage* (1614) 200 They must not vse the same knife to meats made of milk, which they vsed in eating flesh. **1667** PEPYS *Diary* 2 Sept., In discourse at dinner concerning the change of men's humours and fashions touching meats. **1726** SWIFT *Gulliver* IV. vi, He desired I would let him know, what these costly meats were.

fig. **1601** B. Jonson *Poetaster* v. i, Shun Plavtus and old Ennivs; they are meates Too harsh for a weake stomacke.

3. a. The flesh of animals used for food; now chiefly in narrower sense = butcher's meat, flesh *sb.* 4, in contradistinction to fish and poultry. Also, *local U.S.*, confined to certain types of meat, usu. pork.

dark meat (U.S.): 'all the meat of chickens and turkeys, except the breast and wings, these being called light meat' (Webster *Suppl.* 1880).

13.. *E.E. Allit. P.* B. 637 Þe burne..by þe bred settez Mete. *c* **1460** Fortescue *Abs. & Lim. Mon.* x. (1885) 132 In Fraunce the peple salten but lytill mete, except thair bacon. **1590** Shaks. *Com. Err.* II. ii. 57 *S. Dro.* I thinke the meat wants that I haue. *Ant.*..What's that? *S. Dro.* Basting. **1656** Stanley *Hist. Philos.* VIII. (1701) 298/1 He Water drinks, then Broth and Herbs doth eat, To Live, his Scholars teaching, without Meat. **1727** Arbuthnot *Tables Anc. Coins*, etc. xviii. 190 The *Vectigal Macelli*, a tax upon Meat. **1793** Beddoes *Sea Scurvy* 59 Considering fresh meat, or the muscular part of animals, chemically, I [etc.]. **1828** Lytton *Disowned* Introd. 8 And, harkye, Bedos..if you eat a grain of *meat* I discharge you. A valet, Sir, is an ethereal being, and is only to be nourished upon chicken! **1832** J. K. Paulding *Westward Ho!* I. 124 Nothing is called meat in these parts but salt pork and beef. **1845** C. M. Kirkland *Western Clearings* 93 Venison is not 'meat' to be sure, in our parlance; for we reserve that term for pork, *par excellence*. **1856** 'Stonehenge' *Brit. Sports* 182 Thickened milk and broth, the latter with the meat of the sheep's head broken up in it. **1881** *Daily News* 16 Sept. 5/4 Wild ass and antelope meat are also brought in for sale. **1883** Moloney *Fisheries W. Afr.* 56 The cleaning, pickling, and drying process only requires ten days, when the fish, sometimes two or three inches thick in the meat, is ready for export. **1891** *Fur, Fin & Feather* 182 A bearskin is worth $5 to him..besides, he likes the flesh if meat (i.e. pork) is 'skeerse'. **1902** *Dialect Notes* II. 239 *Meat*, bacon always understood. **1903** *Ibid.* 320 *Meat*,..pork. Not often applied to beef, mutton, etc. **1927** *Ibid.* V. 469 *Meat*,..ham; —used only of the hog.

b. *pl.* Different kinds of meat.

1693 Congreve in *Dryden's Juvenal* xi. 22 In Shambles; where with borrow'd Coin They buy choice Meats, and in cheap plenty dine. **1841** Lane *Arab. Nts.* I. 110 And took to him wine to drink, and boiled meats. **1902** *Westm. Gaz.* 4 June 7/3 Within a fortnight the price of meats all over the country will be reduced.

c. *colloq.* or *slang.* (*a*) ***to make meat of***: to kill. (*b*) Something enjoyable or advantageous. Also, matter of importance or substance; the gist or main part (of a story, situation, etc.). Cf. meaty *a.* 1 b.

a **1848** Ruxton *Life in Far West* (1849) 4 Poor Bill Bent! them Spaniards made meat of him. **1886** *Century Mag.* XXXII. 701/1 There was meat in the idea, and the professor chewed it. **1897** *Westm. Gaz.* 28 Dec. 7/1 There is a good deal of meat for the actors. **1901** Kipling *Kim* xv. 390 At evening time..she won to the meat of the matter, explained low-voicedly by the lama. **1937** *Jrnl. R. Aeronaut. Soc.* XLI. 1025 There was so much real meat in this paper that it was impossible to enter into any long discussion about it. **1942** *Tee Emm* (Air Ministry) II. 129 Delving into detail, digging out the meat, and giving your advice. **1951** in M. McLuhan *Mech. Bride* (1967) 36/4 It is not only full of meat, but so interestingly written that I am going to loan it around the store. **1955** *Bull. Atomic Sci.* June 226/3 But the real meat of the book is in the depiction of the moral conflicts keenly felt by these men. **1960** *Times* 23 June 3/4 This makes the meat of Wimbledon. **1970** *Nature* 12 Sept. 1092/2 Shift registers..perform the meat of a computer calculation.

d. Applied proleptically to living animals such as are killed for food; in early use chiefly in † ***wild meat*** = 'game'. In modern hunting use (*U.S.*) one's quarry or prey.

1529 *Edinb. Burgh Rec.* (1871) II. 9 Nochtwithstanding William Cawder has..coft certane pluveris and vther wild meit incontrare the said statutis. **1550** *Reg. Privy Council Scot.* I. 95 The gret and exhorbitant derth of the wyld mete of this realme. **1624** *Aberdeen Reg.* (1848) II. 390 Great superfluitie of vennisone and wyld meat of all sortis. **1851** Mayne Reid *Scalp Hunt.* iv. 26 Others, old hunters, had the 'meat' in their eye. **1884** *Century Mag.* Dec. 198/2 The ram was my meat.

transf. **1872** 'Mark Twain' *Roughing It* l. 357 Come along—you're my meat *now*, my lad. **1907** S. E. White *Arizona Nights* I. vii. 136 'Whew!' I whistles, 'That's a large order—But I'm your meat.' **1917** A. G. Empey *From Fire Step* xvi. 103, I gleefully fell in with the scheme, and told Cassell I was his meat. **1922** A. Bennett *Let.* 14 Nov. (1966) I. 319 It was not everybody's meat, but it was in my opinion somebody's meat. **1922** E. O'Neill *Hairy Ape* (1923) iii. 29 Say, dis is a cinch! Dis was made for me! It's my meat, get me! **1942** W. E. Johns *Biggles sweeps Desert* v. 66 The way you snaffled my Hun! I call that a bit thick... He was my meat, absolutely, yes by Jingo. *Ibid.* 67 'You were jolly nearly his meat,' Biggles pointed out, coldly. **1956** B. Holiday *Lady sings Blues* (1973) iv. 46 'I Cried' was my damn meat, just like 'Rhythm' was Lester's. **1972** *Dict. Contemp. & Colloq. Usage* (Eng.-Lang. Inst. Amer.) 19 *Meat*,..one's field of interest;..as: Math, that's my *meat*.

e. *coarse slang.* The penis; the female genital organs; the human body regarded as an instrument of sexual pleasure; a prostitute.

1595 Gosson *Pleasant Quippes* sig. B2 That you should coutch your meat in dish, And others feele, it is no fish. **1597** Shakes. *Henry IV: Part Two* (1623) II. iv. 83/1 Away you mouldie Rogue, away; I am meat for your Master. **1611** L. Barry *Ram-Alley* v. sig. H4ᵛ Faith take a maide, and leaue the widow, Maister. Of all meates I loue not a gaping oyster. **1664** T. Killigrew *Parson's Wedding* v. ii, in *Comedies & Tragedies* 142 Your bed is big enough for two, and my meat will not cost you much. **1860-1** W. Whitman *Leaves of Grass* (ed. 3) 301 Feeling with the hand the naked meat of his own body. **1923** J. Manchon *Le Slang* 192 *A bit of meat*, une putain. **1967** G. Davis in W. King *Black Short Story Anthol.* (1972) 341 Maxine's mother was never home on Saturday mornings, so I kept Maxine's three younger brothers outside while Teddy slipped the meat to her in the bedroom. **1970** G. Greer *Female Eunuch* 265 It would be unbearable, but less so, if it were only the vagina that was belittled by terms like *meat*. **1971** B. Malamud *Tenants* 31 I'm not saying I don't appreciate her company, especially when my meat's frying, but not when I have something I got to write. *Ibid.* 136 Sam wanted the brothers to beat up on you and crack your nuts for putting the meat to his bitch. *Ibid.* 143 I got you in bed with nothin on you You gonna eat my meat. **1971** *Black Scholar* Sept. 36/1 She was in his arms ..and gabbing his erect meat. **1973** D. Barnes *See Woman* (1974) 94 I've tried the white meat..so I can understand why you might be wondering if the dark meat isn't better.

f. The centre (of a cricket bat, of the head of a golf club, etc.), esp. in phr. ***to hit*** (a ball) ***on*** or ***with the meat.*** *slang.*

1909 *Westm. Gaz.* 15 Jan. 4/2 If you did not take the gutta-percha ball right in the middle of the club (right 'on the meat', according to the modern abominable phrase) it declined to go at all. **1922** Wodehouse *Clicking of Cuthbert* ix. 203 You think..that lovely woman loses in queenly dignity when she fails to slam the ball squarely on the meat? **1925** *Country Life* 11 July 48/2 It is easy to drive a lob bowler ..on the 'meat' or drive of the bat. **1959** R. Fuller *Ruined Boys* II. ix. 143 Wilkes hit the second ball of the over with the meat of the bat. **1963** *Times* 28 Jan. 4/3 It was apparent that here was the severest and purest hitter in the game at the pinnacle of his form, tuning up as though the ball were tied to the meat of his racket by a string of elastic. **1974** *Guardian* 6 Aug. 23/2 Kitchen was well held, full off the meat, by Younis at forward short leg in Arnold's first over.

†4. a. A meal, repast, feast. Sometimes used for the principal meal, dinner. *Obs.* exc. as in b.

a **1175** *Cott. Hom.* 237 Ȝief he frend were me sceolde ȝief him his morȝe mete þat he þe bet mihte abide þane more mete. **1303** R. Brunne *Handl. Synne* 6632 Þou shuldest nat forgete þe pore man at þy mete. **1382** Wyclif *Luke* xiv. 12 Whanne thou makist a mete ether souper, nyle thou clepe thi frendis [etc.]. *c* **1386** Chaucer *Prol.* 348 After the sondry sesons of the yeer, So chaunged he his mete and his soper. **1432-50** tr. *Higden* (Rolls) II. 167 Whiche vse mony diversities of meites at a meite. *a* **1483** *Liber Niger* in *Househ. Ord.* (1790) 32 At the furst or latter mete. **1868** Morris *Earthly Par.*, *Man born to be king* Argt. 50 And presently, the meat being done, He bade them bring him to his throne.

b. In various prepositional phrases (now somewhat *arch.*): ***at meat*** (ME. *at þe, at te mete*), † ***at meat and meal***: at table, at one's meals. Similarly, ***after meat, before meat***, † ***to go to meat***, etc.

a **1175** *Cott. Hom.* 231 Ǣer þanne we mid ure frienden to ðe mete go. *c* **1200** *Trin. Coll. Hom.* 67 Drinke o tiȝe atte mete and noht þer after. **1297** R. Glouc. (Rolls) 1217 After mete as riȝt was þe menestraus eode aboute. *c* **1386** Chaucer *Sqr.'s T.* 165 This knyght..is vnarmed and vnto mete yset. **1390** Gower *Conf.* I. 205 He sente Unto the Senatour to come..and..sitte with him at the mete. **1425** in Entick *London* (1766) IV. 354 Every day, both at meet and soupier, they eat..within the said almes-house. **1470-85** Malory *Arthur* x. lxxviii. 551 Whyle we ar at oure mete. **1596** Bp. W. Barlow *Three Serm.* iii. 117 At sitting downe and rising from meat, they give him thankes. **1599** Nashe *Lent. Stuffe* 47 And then they might be at meate and meale for seuen weekes togither. **1607** Shaks. *Cor.* IV. vii. 3 Your Soldiers vse him as the Grace 'fore meate, Their talke at Table, and their Thankes at end. **1611** Bible *Luke* xxii. 27 For whether is greater, hee that sitteth at meat, or hee that serueth? **1621** Fletcher *Pilgrim* II. ii, He's within at meat, sir; The knave is hungry. **1853-8** Hawthorne *Eng. Note-bks.* II. 135 Those who sit at meat. **1880** Howells *Undisc. Country* ii. 44 She sat long at meat, morning, noon, and night.

5. *attrib.* and *Comb.*: **a.** simple attrib. as ***meat-axe, -broth, can, -cupboard, -diet, -dish, -extract, -hook, -inspection, -jack*** (= Jack *sb.*[1] 7), ***-juice, -pie, -platter, -pudding, -salesman, -saw, -solution, -stock,*** † ***-stomach, -supper, -tin, -trade, -trough, -tub, vat, -vessel.*** **b.** objective, as ***meat-chopper, -eater, -eating*** *sb.* and *adj.*, ***meat-freezer, -freezing, -hungry*** adj., † ***keeping, -packer, -packing, -producer, -producing*** adj., ***meat rationing,*** † ***-reiver, -tenderizer.*** **c.** instrumental, as ***meat-fed*** adj. **d.** similative, as ***meat-faced, -pink*** adjs.

1835 Haliburton *Clockm.* Ser. I. (1862) 237 She was..as wicked as a *meat-axe. **1890** *Syd. Soc. Lex.*, **Meat broth*,.. the fluid obtained by boiling meat for many hours in water. **1897** *Outing* XXX. 284/1 For active service..the two regiments would need to be supplied with..*meat cans. **1868** *Mich. Agric. Rep.* VII. 348, 1 lightning *meat chopper. **1922** Joyce *Ulysses* 302 In the course of the argument.. meatchoppers..were resorted to. **1956** *Amer. Speech* XXXI. 87 Back-formations from nouns in *-er* indicating agents, such as..*meat chopper.* **1610-11** in *Anc. Invent.* (Halliw. 1854) 75 The *meat cubberd, with plate. **1564** P. Moore *Hope Health* I. ii. 3 A *mete diet may sone bee serched out. **1879** *St. George's Hosp. Rep.* IX. 601 The patient..was ordered meat-diet. **14..** *Nom.* in Wr.-Wülcker 729/8 *Hic escarinus*, a *metdysch. **1899** *Allbutt's Syst. Med.* VIII. 557 The worst instances are found..in large *meat-eaters and topers. **1853** *Trans. Mich. Agric. Soc.* IV. 154 The Americans are notoriously a *meat eating people. **1905** *Vegetarian Messenger* Jan. 14 Vegetarianism *v.* meat-eating. **1921** G. B. Shaw *Back to Methuselah* II. 77 One of his sons invented meat-eating. **1939** Dylan Thomas *Map of Love* 24 Sewing a shroud for a journey By the light of the meat-eating sun. **1958** A. R. Radcliffe-Brown *Method in Social Anthropol.* I. v. 115 The two chief meat-eating birds. **1899** *Allbutt's Syst. Med.* VI. 342 Beef-tea, *meat extracts and essences..should be sparely used. **1922** Joyce *Ulysses* 33 The *meatfaced woman, a butcher's dame. **1896** Kipling *Seven Seas* 51 To our five-meal, *meat-fed men. **1909** *Daily Chron.* 2 Nov. 5/4 Australian globe-trotters, *meat-freezers, financiers. **1908** *Westm. Gaz.* 14 Dec. 2/1 The *meat-freezing works employ over 3,000 men. **1909** *Chambers's Jrnl.* Jan. 23/1 Argentina..had in 1884 the first meat-freezing works established. **1842** Emerson *Lect. Transcend.* Wks. (Bohn) II. 289 The martyrs were sawn asunder, or hung alive on *meat-hooks. **1873** E. W. Tarn *Tredgold's Carpentry* 286 Meat-hooks are large wrought-iron hooks, generally tinned over, having a screw on one end, which is driven into a beam in the ceiling of a larder. **1893** Selous *Trav. S.E. Africa* 73 Crowds of *meat-hungry Mashunas. **1843** Carlyle *Past & Pr.* III. iv, An unfortunate rusty *Meat-jack, gnarring and creaking with rust and work. **1890** *Syd. Soc. Lex.*, **Meat juice*, the red fluid obtained by squeezing raw flesh; used as a nutrient. *c* **1440** *Promp. Parv.* 10/1 Almery of *mete kepynge, or a saue for mete, *cibutum.* **1903** E. Johnson *Amer. Railway Transportation* 131 The large *meat-packers..own their own cars. **1921** *Daily Colonist* (Victoria, B.C.) 7 Apr. 8/1 The strike situation between the meat packers and their employees remained unchanged this morning. **1973** *Guardian* 23 Feb. 18/1, I finally got a job as a meat packer on £18 a week. **1873** *Rep. Iowa Agric. Soc. 1872* 175 The panacea for all these ills is to be found in tanneries..*meat packing and curing houses, [etc.]. **1891** J. J. Flinn *Chicago* 330 Meat packing is the oldest of Chicago's industries. **1907** G. B. Shaw *Major Barbara* Pref. 179 Who chips a corner of the veneering from the huge meat packing industries of Chicago. **1974** *Daily Colonist* (Victoria, B.C.) 28 July 16/8 Meatpacking companies have reaped most of the benefits of the present subsidy while producers received very little. **1773** Johnson in *Boswell* 9 Apr., I generally have a *meat pye on Sunday. **1852** Dickens *Bleak Ho.* xl, He retires to the servants' hall to regale on cold meat-pie and ale. **1860** O. W. Holmes *Elsie V.* vii. (1891) 97 A mince pie,—or meat-pie, as it is more forcibly called in the..villages. **1939** Auden & Isherwood *Journey to War* i. 31 Hairy, *meat-pink men. **1863** 'G. Hamilton' *Gala-Days* 75, I decided upon a *meat-platter. **1916** *Daily Colonist* (Victoria, B.C.) 2 July 7/1 (Advt.), Large Meat Platters, regular value 60 c. July Clearance each 35 c. **1909** *Westm. Gaz.* 14 Dec. 2/1 The consumer is called upon to pay £5,600,000, in order that..the Colonial *meat-producer may receive the negligible gift of £350,000. **1932** J. S. Huxley *Probl. Relative Growth* vi. 202 Animals cannot show their full potentialities as meat-producers if kept in unfavourable nutritive conditions. *Ibid.* iii. 90 Meat-producing animals. **1858** Simmonds *Dict. Trade*, *Meat-pie*, **Meat-pudding*, meat covered or encased with dough. **1918** *Times* 7 Feb. 3/1 Should the currency coupon become the basis of *meat rationing, it is probable that [etc.]. **1500-20** Dunbar *Poems* lxiii. 44 Innoportoun askaris of Yrland kynd; And *meit revaris. **1851** in *Illustr. Lond. News* 5 Aug. (1854) 119/2 *Meat-salesman. **1875** Knight *Dict. Mech.*, **Meat-saw*, a saw with a thin blade strained in an iron frame, used by butchers. **1877** tr. *von Ziemssen's Cycl. Med.* VII. 458 Only the most easily digestible diet, such as milk, *meat-solution, &c. should be allowed. **1883** 'Annie Thomas' *Mod. Housewife* 53 Half-a-pint of any kind of *meat-stock. **1592** Nashe *P. Penilesse* (Shaks. Soc.) 48 There being one joynt of flesh on the table for such as had *meate stomackes. **1577** tr. *Bullinger's Decades* v. 1064 It [the Lord's Supper] differeth from our ordinarie *meate suppers..for yᵗ it is specially instituted by the sonne of God. **1969** *New Yorker* 27 Sept. 122/2 Unite, slaves of the steam kettle and the shakers of *meat tenderizer and MSG. **1970** M. Slater *Caribbean Cooking* 12 The pulp [of pawpaw] contains pepsin and the skin and seeds are useful as meat tenderisers. **1889** *Century Mag.* Apr. 909/2 They say that he sometimes fills an old *meat-tin with water in anticipation of a long march. **1902** E. Banks *Autobiogr. Newspaper Girl* 64, I would have been capable of going into the street and knocking down any little butcher's boy who refused peaceably to deliver up to me the contents of his wooden *meat-trough. **1779** E. Parkman *Diary* (1899) 171 We are unhappily low in ye *Meat Tub. **1875** Knight *Dict. Mech.*, *Meat-tub*, a tub for holding pickled meat. **1847** *Rep. Comm. Patents 1846* (U.S.) 310 The mode by which I obtain a vacuum in *meat vat A. for curing meat. **1483** *Cath. Angl.* 238/2 A *Mete wesselle, *escale.*

6. Special comb.: † **meat-ambry**, a cupboard for keeping food; a meat safe; **meat-ant**, a name used in Australia for an ant of the genus *Iridomyrmex*, esp. *I. detectus*, a large copper-coloured ant; **meat ball** (see quot. 1970); also *fig.*; also used *attrib.* to designate a type of landing system for aircraft (*U.S. slang*); **meat-biscuit**, a biscuit made with concentrated meat; **meat-block**, a block of wood on which meat is cut up; **meat-breakfast**, a breakfast that includes a meat dish; **meat card**, a card entitling the holder to a ration of meat; **meat-chamber**, a refrigerating chamber in ocean steamships for the purpose of transporting fresh meat to Europe (*Cassell's Encycl. Dict.*, 1885); † **meat-cloth**, ? a table-cloth; **meat coupon**, one of the coupons of which a meat card is made up; **meat-crusher**, 'a pair of rollers for tendering steak' (Knight *Dict. Mech.* 1875); **meat cube**, a small cube of concentrated meat extract; **meat-earth** *dial.*, good and fertile soil; † **meat-failer** [cf. quots. under fail *v.* 7], one who lacks meat, a starveling; † **meat-fellow**, † **-fere**, a companion at meat, a guest; **meat-flour**, beef dried at a low temperature and ground into a fine powder (*Syd. Soc. Lex.* 1890); **meat-fly**, a blue-bottle fly; † **meat-form**, a form on which to sit at one's meals; **meat-fruit**, the fruit of *Artocarpus incisa* (*Syd. Soc. Lex.*); † **meat-giving**, the providing of meals; † **meat-grace**, a grace used before or after meat; **meat-grinder**, a mincing machine; also *fig.*; **meat-hale** *Sc.* and *north. dial.* = *meat-whole* (see E.D.D.); † **meat-hanger**, ? a hanging shelf for a larder; **meat-head** *slang* (chiefly *U.S.*), a stupid person; so **meat-headed** *a.*, stupid; † **meat-herring** ? = matie; **meat hog**, a hog intended for food (*U.S.*, *rare*); **meat-hook**,

(*a*) see sense 5 a; (*b*) an arm or hand *slang*; **meat-house**, (*a*) a house in which meat is hung; (*b*) *dial.*, 'a larder; *fig.* a house where a liberal allowance of good food is given' (E.D.D., *q.v.*); (*c*) *slang*, a brothel; **meat-hunter** *U.S.*, one who hunts game for profit; **meat jelly**, a jelly prepared from meat; †**meat-like** *a. Sc.*, having the appearance of being well-fed; **meat loaf** = LOAF *sb.*[1] 2 e; **meat lozenge**, a lozenge made with concentrated meat; †**meat lust** (*-list*), appetite for food; **meat maggot**, the larva of the meat-fly; **meat man, meatsman**, †(*a*) one who provides food, a caterer; †(*b*) one who eats meat; (*c*) one who sells meat; (*d*) a man responsible for supplying meat to a camp; **meat-market**, †(*a*) a market where food of any kind is sold; (*b*) a market for butcher's meat; (*c*) *slang*, a rendezvous for prostitutes, homosexuals, etc.; **meat meal**[1], a meal of which meat forms the chief part; **meat-meal**[2], meat dried and ground into powder for cattle; **meat-offering**, a sacrifice consisting of food; in versions of the Bible from the 16th c. used to render Heb. *minḥāh*, which meant an offering consisting of fine flour or parched corn and oil (R.V. 'meal-offering'); †**meat pipe**, the œsophagus; †**meat-place**, a place for eating, a refectory; **meat-poisoning**, poisoning by eating decomposed meat; **meat rack** = *meat-market* (*c*); **meat-rail**, a wooden rail for supporting meat in a larder; **meat rocker**, a mincing knife having a handle at each end, and worked by a rocking motion (Knight *Dict. Mech. Suppl.* 1884); **meat safe**, (*a*) a cupboard for storing meat, usually made of wire gauze or perforated zinc; also sometimes applied to a wire gauze cover for meat; (*b*) *transf.* a name given to a kind of hat; **meat screen**, a metal screen placed behind roasting meat to reflect back the heat of the fire; †**meat table**, (*a*) a dining-table; (*b*) a table on which meat is cut up in preparation for cooking; †**meat-taking**, the taking of food, eating; **meat tea**, a tea at which meat is served, a high tea; **meat ticket**, (*a*) *Mil. slang*, an identity disc; (*b*) = *meal ticket* (*b*); †**meat time** = MEALTIME; **meat tool** *coarse slang*, the penis; **meat train**, the men, horses, etc., conveying meat to a party; **meat-wagon** *slang* (chiefly *U.S.*), (*a*) an ambulance; (*b*) a police van, 'black Maria'; (*c*) a hearse; **meat-washing** *attrib.* or *adj.* (*Path.*), applied to the appearance of the stools in the second stage of dysentery, when they assume the character of a reddish fluid containing small flesh-like lumps; †**meat-while**, the time of taking food; meal time; †**meat whitch**, a chest or box for keeping meat; **meat-whole**, *dial.* having a good appetite for food; †**meat-will**, a craving for food; **meat-works** chiefly *Austral.* and *N.Z.*, an establishment where meat is processed and packed; also, a slaughterhouse; †**meat-worth** *a. Sc.* = *meat-like*. Also MEAT-BOARD.

1457 *Peebles Charters*, etc. (1872) 119 Alssua a *met amri and wessal ammari. **1548** *Burgh Rec. Edinb.* (1871) II. 136 Ane meit almarye to xiiiis. **1907** W. W. FROGGATT *Austral. Insects* 95 Most of them [*sc.* ants of the genus *Iridomyrmex*] are small, except our 'Mound Ant', sometimes known as the '*Meat Ant', *Iridomyrmex detectus*, which is the commonest and most widely distributed ant in Australia. **1952** *Coast to Coast* 101 The ant-lion had seized the meat-ant by one leg. **1970** BROWN & TAYLOR in *Insects of Australia* (Commonwealth Sci. & Industr. Res. Organization) xxxvii. 958/1 The meat ants (*Iridomyrmex* spp.) can be a serious pest around homes and food-processing plants. *c* **1838** C. MATHEWS in M. R. Booth *Eng. Plays of 19th Cent.* (1973) IV. 138 You must be content with pâté or forced *meat ball. **1877** *Cassell's Dict. Cookery* 413/1 *Meat Balls, Minced, Fried.*—Take some roast mutton, some chestnuts, and neck of veal boiled in water with salt and vinegar. **1941** P. GALLICO in *Sat. Even. Post* 14 June 110/2 As for that revolting meat-ball, I never wish to see him again. **1957** *Economist* 31 Aug. 688/2 The mirror reflects a bright light astern and upward into a beam which the pilot follows straight to a landing by keeping the 'meatball' light precisely centred in the mirror. **1957** *New Yorker* 5 Oct. 82/3 I'll polish off a meatball sandwich. **1960** *Aeroplane* XCIX. 65/1 The equipment evaluated by the F.A.A. included the U.S.A.F. 'Meat Ball' system, the U.S. Navy mirror system. *Ibid.* 401/1 The pilot aligns the 'meatball', or blob of reflected light, in the centre of the deck-landing mirror. **1962** *Flight Internat.* LXXXII. 100/1 A steady descent at 250kt to 1,000 ft..would be followed by a further descent to 600 ft, with the talkdown continuing until the pilot picked up the 'meatball' light of the mirror sight. **1969** R. AIRTH *Snatch!* iv. 36 He looked a very tough meatball. **1970** SIMON & HOWE *Dict. Gastron.* 262/2 *Meat balls*, any combination of meat, raw or cooked, shaped into balls. **1852** J. BELL in *Lect. Gt. Exhib.* 141 Mr. Borden's *meat-biscuit—a convenient form of animal food in a concentrated and portable state. **1838** E. FLAGG *Far West* II. 59 Mr. W...was on the stump, in shape of a huge *meat-block at one corner of the market-house. **1857** GEO. ELIOT *Scenes Clerical Life* (1858) I. 105 The unpleasant circumstances..together with heavy *meat breakfasts, may..have contributed to his desponding views. **1910** *Bradshaw's Railway Guide* Apr. 1149 *Hotel Bedford —Paris*... Room, meat breakfast, electric light.., from 6s. **1870** *Food Jrnl.* 1 Dec. 622 The restaurateurs are compelled to ask for their customers' '*meat card'. **1918** *Times* 6 Feb 8/2 (*heading*), The London meat card. *Ibid.* 25 Feb. 9/5 Only three coupons each week of a meat card can be used for butcher's meat. **1499** *Yatton Churchw. Acc.* (Som. Rec. Soc.) 122 A *mete clothe and a ryng. **1494** in *Somerset Med. Wills* (1901) 323 A Mete cloth and iij tuels. **1918** *Times* 25 Feb. 9/5 You must not tear off *meat coupons yourself. This duty rests with the retailer. **1919** 'I. HAY' *Last Million* 97 'Got my meat coupons?' They shook their heads... 'Better have bacon and eggs,' announced Hebe. 'They're not rationed.' **1951** *Good Housek. Home Encycl.* 392/2, 1 *meat cube, or 1 tsp. meat extract. **1971** *Guardian* 19 May 8/2 Make stock with a meat cube, sieve in left-over vegetables and you have an economical soup. **1778** PRYCE *Min. Cornub.* 324 **Meat-Earth*, soil; the superficial earth, fit for agriculture. **1860** *Eng. & For. Min. Gloss.* (Cornw. Terms), *Meat earth*, the vegetable mould. **1599** PORTER *Angry Wom. Abingt.* (Percy Soc.) 21 Oh, this *meate failer Dicke! **1382** WYCLIF *2 Sam.* xix. 28 Forsothe thou puttist me thi seruaunt among thi *meetfelawis [1388 gestis] of thi bord. —— *Dan.* xiv. 1 Danyel was *meete feere of the kyng. **1840** *Cuvier's Anim. Kingd.* 633 *Musca vomitoria*, Linn., the Common *Meat Fly. **1861** HULME tr. *Moquin-Tandon* II. IV. i. 237 The Blue or Meat Fly (Calliphora Vomitoria) is one of the largest species found in France. *a* **1400** *Octavian* 1245 Whene his swerde brokene was, A *meteforme he gatt par cas. **1382** WYCLIF *Ecclus.* xxxvii. 32 Wile thou not ben gredy in alle plenteuous *mete ȝyuyng [Vulg. *in omni epulatione*]. *a* **1225** *Ancr. R.* 426 Ȝif heo ne kunnen nout þe *mete graces, siggen in hore stude Pater noster & Aue Maria biuoren mete. **1951** M. MCLUHAN *Mech. Bride* (1967) 128/1 That man.. whose school training wins him the privilege of getting at once into the technological *meat grinder. **1969** R. & D. DE SOLA *Dict. Cooking* 150/1 *Meat grinder*, utensil or attachment for grinding meat, usually provided with a variety of cutting blades for different grinds. **1970** W. BURROUGHS JR. *Speed* vii. 145 I'd be sucked right into the actual meatgrinder of another reel. **1972** *Listener* 17 Aug. 199/1 The North Vietnamese..managed to tie down South Vietnam's strategic reserve..in a gruesome 'meat-grinder'. **1626** in *Anc. Invent.* (Halliw. 1854) 99 Item, a square *meate hanger. **1945** H. I. PHILLIPS *Private Purkey's Private Peace* i. 8 'Harriet!' mocked a battered buddy. 'Honey bunch! Lissen to the *meathead.' **1967** *Boston Globe* 18 May 27/3 It seems to this meat-head that the building of a branch of the state university..gives all of us a great chance to upgrade some area which needs a little up-grading. **1971** *Newsweek* 29 Nov. 52/1 Archie Bunker, the middle American hero of 'All in the Family'..sees himself menaced by a rising tide of spades,..meat-heads,..fags and four-eyes. **1949** W. R. BURNETT *Asphalt Jungle* (1950) vi. 72 Some *meat-headed tart. **1758** *Descr. Thames* 227 The *Meat Herring, which is likewise large, but not so thick nor so fat as the former [Fat Herring]. **1856** G. N. JONES *Florida Plantation Rec.* (1927) 169, I doe not see but verry few of the shoats that I turned out for *meat hogs this year. **1919** W. H. DOWNING *Digger Dial.* 33 **Meat-hook*, arm. **1932** *Amer. Speech* VII. 334 *Meat hooks*, hands. **1945** L. SHELLY *Jive Talk Dict.* 29 *Meat hooks*, the hands. **1805** W. CLARK in Lewis & Clark *Orig. Jrnls. Lewis & Clark Expedition* (1905) III. 284 Had the *Meet house covered and the Meat all hung up. **1831** J. M. PECK *Guide for Emigrants* II. 126 Around it [*sc.* the cabin] are put a meat or smoke house [etc.]. **1862** R. HENNING *Let.* 28 Aug. (1966) 95 The woolshed, meathouse..and dwelling-house are so very well put up. **1896** FARMER & HENLEY *Slang* IV. 296/2 *Meat-house*, a brothel. **1906** *Dialect Notes* III. 146 *Meat-house*,..smoke-house; a wooden shed in which smoked and preserved meats are kept. **1923** J. MANCHON *Le Slang* 192 *Meat-house*,..maison publique. **1937** PARTRIDGE *Dict. Slang* 515/1 *Meat-house*, a brothel. **1889** *Harper's Mag.* May 878/1 The *meat-hunters are still devoting their attention to the killing of larger game. **1381** *Forme of Cury* (1780) xxxvi. 103 For to make *mete Gelee that it be wel chariaunt. **1865** MRS. STOWE *House & Home Papers* 248 Those fine, clear meat-jellies which form a garnish.. palatable to the taste. **1965** V. HOLLAND tr. *A. Escoffier's Ma Cuisine* 67 Beef tea and meat jelly for invalids. **1762** BP. FORBES *Jrnl.* (1886) 216 You see I am *meat-like and cloath-like, as we say in Scotland. **1932** E. CRAIG *Cooking with E. Craig* 58 (*heading*) Banana and *meat loaf. **1939**, etc. Meat loaf [see LOAF *sb.*[1] 2 e]. **1903** *Longm. Mag.* July 129, I took only some tins of Brand's essence of beef, chocolate, *meat-lozenges [etc.]. **1578** LYTE *Dodoens* v. xxxv. 597 The Rampion eaten with vinegar and salt stirreth up appetite or *meate-lust. **1746** *Exmoor Courtship* 560 (E.D.S.) And cham come to my Meat list agen. **1567** MAPLET *Gr. Forest* 89 He is as good a *meates man and Catour for him selfe, as any thing liuing is. **1606** HOLLAND *Sueton.* 220 A great feeder and meate-man by report he was. **1831** R. COX *Adventures Columbia River* II. x. 222 The meat-men did not return until nine this morning..but at eleven the hunter's signal drew us to the shore, and the meat-men were despatched. **1910** *Dialect Notes* III. 445 *Meat-man*,..butcher, or driver of a butcher's wagon. **1920** *Ibid.* V. 83 *Meat man*, for butcher. **1551** ROBINSON tr. *More's Utop.* II. (1895) 157 *Meate markettes, whether be brought not onlye all sortes of herbes, and the fruites of trees with breade, but also fishe. **1856** *Farmer's Mag.* Jan. 9 The Christmas meat-markets. **1896** FARMER & HENLEY *Slang* IV. 296/2 *Meat-market*,..any *rendezvous* of public women. **1937** PARTRIDGE *Dict. Slang* 515/1 *Meat-market*, a rendezvous of harlots. **1957** J. OSBORNE *Entertainer* i. 18 Every tart and pansy boy in the district are in that place... It's just a meat-market. **1973** *Amer. Speech* 1970 XLV. 58 *Meat market* n., street on which homosexuals gather, cruise, and pick up tricks. **1896** *Allbutt's Syst. Med.* I. 465 A substantial *meat meal should be provided for breakfast and dinner. **1898** *Westm. Gaz.* 8 Oct. 4/2 The residue is dried and ground into *meat meal for cattle feeding. **1535** COVERDALE *Num.* vii. 13 Full of fyne floure myngled with oile for a *meatofferinge. **1611** BIBLE *Lev.* ii. 14. **1633** P. FLETCHER *Purple Isl.* II. xxxi. *marg.*, The Oesophagus or *meat-pipe. **1755** JOHNSON, *Gullet*..the meat-pipe. **1483** *Cath. Angl.* 238/1 A *Mete place, *esculentum*. **1875** tr. *von Ziemssen's Cycl. Med.* I. 50 There is a particular disease produced by *meat-poisoning. **1972** B. RODGERS *Queens' Vernacular* 132 **Meat rack*, outdoor setting..where homosexuals gather to parade their wares. **1842** GWILT *Archit.* §2285. 614 Fittings for larder, Two *meat rails, 6 feet long, of wrought fir...suspended from wrought iron stirrups. **1836–9** DICKENS *Sk. Boz, Boarding-ho.* i, There were *meat-safe-looking blinds in the parlour windows. **1840** —— *Old C. Shop* xxxvi, The candle-box, the salt-box, the meat-safe, were all padlocked. **1860** *Heads & Hats* 23 Various strong-minded heads have presented to our startled and derisive gaze, sundry 'tiles', 'wide-awakes', 'meat-safes', and a variety of things by courtesy called 'hats'. **1830** MARRYAT *King's Own* xli, Knife-tray, *meat-screen. **14..** *Nom.* in Wr.-Wülcker 729/7 *Hec escaria*, a *mettabylle. **1485** *Naval Acc. Hen. VII* (1896) 51 Moldyng trowghes..j, lanteres..x, Mete tables..iij. **1435** MISYN *Fire of Love* II. x, God we awe to loyf, And in tyme of our *meet takynge & space be-twix morsels to ȝeild him loueyngis with honily swetnes. **1860** SALA *Baddington Peerage* I. xi. 193 A good, hearty *meat tea. **1885** BLACK *White Heather* xxv, This high occasion was to be celebrated by a 'meat-tea'. **1919** W. H. DOWNING *Digger Dial.* 33 **Meat Ticket*, (or Dead Meat Ticket)—an identification disc. **1925** FRASER & GIBBONS *Soldier & Sailor Words* 154 *Meat ticket*, the identity disc. **1929** *Papers Mich. Acad. Sci., Arts & Lett.* X. 307 *Meat-ticket*, wrist-tag for purposes of identification; 'dog-tag'. **1936** P. BOTTOME *Level Crossing* xvi. 192 He'd better not try to settle too much on my meat ticket! **1948** PARTRIDGE *Dict. Forces' Slang* 117 *Meat ticket*, identity disc. *c* **1400** *Rule St. Benet* 150 Þair sal scho sit in hir prayers vnto þe *mete-tym. **1971** B. MALAMUD *Tenants* 88 What do you do..with your *meat tool? You got no girl, who do you fuck other than your hand? **1845** J. C. FRÉMONT *Rep. Exploring Expedition* 234 The *meat train did not arrive this evening, and I gave Godey leave to kill our little dog. **1925** J. H. TABER *Story of 168th Infantry* I. xvi. 189 By this time all of the old members of the regiment..cheerfully referred to the ambulance as the '*meat wagon'. **1939** *Forum* (N.Y.) July 42/1 He must have pulled his rip cord because he woke up in the meatwagon. **1942** BERREY & VAN DEN BARK *Amer. Thes. Slang* §81/13 *Hearse*, meat cart, -crate, or wagon. **1943** R. CHANDLER *Lady in Lake* (1944) xvi. 95 Murder-a-day Marlowe, they call him. They have the meat wagon following him around to follow up on the business he finds. **1954** *Britannica Bk. of Year* 637/1 The meat-wagon was the police-van in which the criminal rode to captivity. **1956** S. LONGSTREET *Real Jazz* 7 The band would march out behind the meat-wagon, black plumes on the hearse horses. **1964** *Listener* 31 Dec. 1055/2 The bogeys..bundle us into the back of a meat-wagon. **1971** 'E. MCBAIN' *Hail, Hail, Gang's all Here* i. 15 We'll need a couple of meat wagons. The minister and two other people were killed, and..there're a lot of injured. **1973** 'H. HOWARD' *Highway to Murder* xiii. 153 She hadn't deserved to become a parcel of broken flesh and bone in the meat wagon. **1897** *Allbutt's Syst. Med.* III. 940 In any case the '*meat-washing' character of the stools ..should prevent a mistake. **1435** MISYN *Fire of Love* II. x, With desire in *meet qwhiel to ȝerne. *c* **1460** *Emare* 229 When the mete-whyle was doun, Into hys chambur he wente soun. **1468** *Medulla* in *Promp. Parv.* 335 *note*, *Cibutum*, a *mete whycche. **1599** *True Report* etc. in *Hakluyt's Voy.* (1812) V. 36 In all but seven men aboord the shippe that were *meat-whole. **1643** in Dalyell *Darker Superst. Scotl.* (1834) 492–3 Ye sall have such ane *meit-will and sall have nothing to eat. [**1895** T. A. COGHLAN *Wealth & Progress New South Wales* I. 367 All the cattle killed, except 27,891 treated in the meat-preserving works, were required for local consumption.] **1934** WEBSTER, **Meat works*. **1948** V. PALMER *Golconda* ii. 9 Driving them across country to the meatworks at Wyndham. **1960** B. CRUMP *Good Keen Man* 46 The hut stank like a meat works. **1968** *Times* 23 Jan. (Austral. Suppl.) p. xiv/3 In one year before the meatworks opened a large property shot 10,000 scrub bulls (not branded or castrated). **1576** in Pitcairn *Crim. Trials* (Bann. Cl.) I. 53 Seis thow nocht me, baith *meit-worth, claith-worth, and gude aneuch lyke in persoun?

meat (miːt), *v.* Now *dial.* [f. prec. sb. Cf. late OE. *mętian* to supply with food.]

1. *trans.* To feed, supply with food or provender.

1568 *Jacob & Esau* II. iii. C iv, Well ywisse Esau, ye did knowe well ynouw That I had as muche nede to be meated as you. **1573** TUSSER *Husb.* (1878) 139 Good husbandrie meateth his friend and the poore. *c* **1611** CHAPMAN *Iliad* XIX. 196 Haste then, and meate your men. **1641** BEST *Farm. Bks.* (Surtees) 55 Those that trail the sweathrake have usually 6*d.* a day, if they meate themselfes. **1686** tr. *Chardin's Trav. Persia* 385 They meat their Horses with Barley. **1776** C. KEITH *Farmer's Ha'* lix, But gae awa' e'now (quo' he) And meat the horse. **1866** *Rachel's Secret* I. 105 Besides their own family, there were the five men whom they had to 'meat'. **1895** 'Q' *Wandering Heath* 26 My father..went out to meat the pig.

2. *intr.* To feed, partake of food.

c **1410** *Master of Game* (MS. Digby 182) xxv, And euere, as he stereth and passeth forth metynge, þei do drawe hem nere hym [etc.]. **1889** *Jokes* Ser. I. 11 (E.D.D.) In Aberdeenshire where farm-servants 'meat' in the house.

meat, obs. Sc. form of MATE *sb.*[2]

meat(e, obs. forms of MEET *a.*

†'**meatable**, *a. Obs.* [f. MEAT *sb.* + -ABLE.] That can be used for food, edible.

1610 W. FOLKINGHAM *Art of Survey* I. ii. 36 These Meateable Rootes, Parsnep, Carrot, Skirrot, Radish.

meatal (miːˈeɪtəl), *a.* [f. MEAT-US + -AL[1].] Of or pertaining to a meatus.

1868 OWEN *Anat. Vertebr.* III. 230 In the Hare the meatal part of the tympanic is long. *Ibid.* 244 The meatal cartilage. **1899** *Allbutt's Syst. Med.* VIII. 108 We should expect..that the perosseous hearing should be affected step by step with the meatal.

†**meat-board.** *Obs.* [f. MEAT *sb.* + BOARD *sb.*] A table for food, a dining-table.

c **1205** LAY. 3638 Alle þai mete-burdes [*c* **1275** mete-bordes] ibrustled mid golde. **1382** WYCLIF *Exod.* xxv. 23 Thow shalt make a meet bord [Vulg. *mensam*] of the trees of Sichym. **1387** TREVISA *Higden* (Rolls) III. 475 Þe wode is my mete borde [L. *silvam pro mensa*]. **1488** *Durham Acc. Rolls* (Surtees) 99, j mete-bord. **1572** *Rec. Elgin* (New Spald. Cl. 1903) I. 135 Ane metbuird with the treslis and furmis thairof.

meate, obs. form of METE *sb.* and *v.*

meated ('miːtɪd), *a.* [f. MEAT *sb.* + -ED².] In Comb. **well-meated**, (*a*) of animals, having plenty of flesh; (*b*) of cheese, rich in nutriment; **open-meated**, of cheese, juicy.

1573 TUSSER *Husb.* (1878) 37 Strong oxen and horses, wel shod and wel clad, wel meated and vsed. **1600** SURFLET *Countrie Farme* I. xiii. 87 A good bull for breed must be fat, well set togither, and well meated. **1896** *Daily News* 26 Dec. 2/6 Canadian [cheese] as a rule, is wholesome, well-meated, and fat. *Ibid.*, The early ripened, open-meated Cheshire cheese.

'meater. [f. MEAT *v.* + -ER¹.]

†**1.** One who provides or gives meat or food. *Obs. rare.*

1649 R. HODGES *Plain. Direct.* 13 [Homonyms.] A meater that giveth meat to the cattel. A corn-meter.

2. *rare.* One who eats (butcher's) meat; a meat-eater.

1920 *Contemp. Rev.* Dec. 819 The 'meater' lives at higher pressure and exhausts his energy quicker than the non-meat-eater.

meater, obs. form of METER.

†**'meat-giver.** *Obs.* [f. MEAT *sb.* + GIVER *sb.*] A giver of food, a hospitable person.

1377 LANGL. *P. Pl.* B. xv. 143 Men..bymeneth good mete-ȝyueres and in mynde haueth, In prayers [etc.]. *a* **1483** *Liber Niger* in *Househ. Ord.* (1790) 18 The fame of an excellent mete giver. [**14..** *Nom.* in Wr.-Wülcker 688/37 *Hic dapifer*, mettes gyffer.] **1567** *Sc. Acts Jas. VI* (1814) III. 31/2 The ressettar,..meit geuar, & intercommonar with sic personis, salbe [etc.].

meath(e, obs. forms of MEAD *sb.*¹

meathe, obs. variant of MATHE.

†**'meatified**, *ppl. a. nonce-wd.* [f. MEAT *sb.* + -(I)FY + -ED¹.] ? Corpulent.

1607 DEKKER & WILKINS *Jests* Wks. (Grosart) II. 356 So that to a man that is meatefyed in flesh, and whose state (in this world) is desperate, a Sergiant may serue instead of a Deathshead, to put him in minde of his last day.

†**'meating**, *vbl. sb. Obs.* [f. MEAT *v.* + -ING¹.] The action of the vb. MEAT; feeding. Of animals, pasturing. Also *concr.*

c **1410** *Master of Game* (MS. Digby 182) ii, After þei secheth good cuntre of metyng of corne, of appulles, of vynes. *Ibid.* xxv, Neuerthelesse it were good redinesse to loke if þei myght se ony deere at is metynge. **1561** HOLLYBUSH *Hom. Apoth.* 10 Beware..of thynges that cause euell humores and of inordinate meatinge or drinkinge.

meating, obs. form of MEETING.

meatless ('miːtlɪs), *a.* [f. MEAT *sb.* + -LESS.]

1. Having no food.

a **900** CYNEWULF *Elene* 612 þæm..þe on westenne meðe & meteleas morland trydeð. **1297** R. GLOUC. (Rolls) 5036 Þei folc was meteles. **1362** LANGL. *P. Pl.* A. VIII. 130 Meteles and Moneyeles on Maluerne hulles. *a* **1440** *Sir Eglam.* 887 Sche was meteles vj. dayes. **1529** MORE *Suppl. Soulys* Wks. 302/1 Is not thys a royall feast to leue these beggers meateles, & then send mo to dynner to theim. **1607** TOPSELL *Four-f. Beasts* (1658) 271 Let him be..suffered to stand on the bit meatlesse two or three hours after. **1646**, **1860** [see DRINKLESS].

2. Without meat. *spec.* Of foods specially prepared or supplied for vegetarians: containing no butcher's meat.

1845 LEWES *Hist. Philos.* II. 24 Growling over his unenvied virtue as a cur growls over his meatless bone. **1909** C. H. SENN (*title*) Meatless fare and lenten cookery. **1909** *Daily Chron.* 2 Nov. 7/3 Even that anomaly—to most people—'the meatless meal' is included. **1969** *Daily Tel.* 9 Oct. 16/4 The era of meatless meat, chickenless chicken and cheeseless cheese is already dawning in America. **1972** *Guardian* 8 June 7/5 Some of them [*sc.* countries] had their meatless days. *Ibid.* 31 July 2/4 The city's three big department stores..decreed meatless menus.

Hence **'meatlessness.**

1918 *Punch* 27 Mar. 206/2 If he [*sc.* our butcher] were removed we should be plunged into absolute meatlessness.

meato-, used as combining form of MEATUS, in some names of surgical instruments, etc. **meatometer** (miːə'tɒmɪtə(r)), an instrument for measuring the meatus urinarius (*Cent. Dict.*). **meatoscope** (miː'eɪtəskəʊp) [see -SCOPE], a speculum for examining the urethra near the meatus (*Syd. Soc. Lex.* 1890). **meatotome** (miː'eɪtətəʊm) [Gr. -τόμος that cuts], a spring knife for the cutting of a contracted meatus urinarius (*Ibid.*). **meatotomy** (miːə'tɒtəmɪ) [Gr. -τομία cutting], section of the meatus urinarius to make a larger opening (*Ibid.*).

1895 ERICHSEN *Surg.* (ed. 10) II. 1160 Meatotomy being, ..performed to allow its [*sc.* a bougie's] introduction. **1895** *Arnold & Son's Catal. Surg. Instr.* 573 Meatoscope.

meatu(a)re, obs. forms of METEOR.

‖**meatus** (miː'eɪtəs). Pl. **meatus** (miː'eɪtjuːs), **meatuses.** [L. *meātus* (*u*-stem), f. *meāre* to flow, run.]

†**1.** A natural channel or tubular passage. *Obs.*

1665 SIR T. HERBERT *Trav.* (1677) 187 This Caspian hath some secret meatus or intercourse with some Sea. **1675** EVELYN *Terra* (1776) 34 Clay is of all others a curst Stepdame to almost all vegetation as having few or no Meatus's for the percolation of the alimental showers or expansion of the roots. **1698** E. LHUYD in *Ray's Disc.* (1713) 190 The Chinks and other Meatus's of the Earth.

2. *spec.* in *Anat.* †**a.** = PORE (*obs.*). **b.** With qualifying word expressed or understood, applied to certain passages in the body.

auditory meatus (L. *m. auditorius*): the channel of the ear. ***nasal*** or ***olfactory meatus***: the passage of the nose. ***urinary meatus***: the external orifice of the urethra.

1665 GLANVILL *Scepsis Sci.* iv. §3. 18 The *meatus*, or passages, through which those subtill emissaries are conveyed to the respective members. **1708** KERSEY, *Meatus*, a Movement, or Course, a Passage, or Way; also the Pores of the Body. **1800** SIR A. COOPER in *Phil. Trans.* XC. 152 A membrane which has been generally considered, from its situation in the meatus..as essentially necessary to the sense of hearing. **1878** HOLDEN *Hum. Osteol.* 132 The three 'meatus' or passages of the nose. **1899** *Allbutt's Syst. Med.* VII. 540 Over the vertex [of the head] from meatus to meatus measures 15⅝ in.

meatwand, obs. form of METEWAND.

meaty ('miːtɪ), *a.* [f. MEAT *sb.* + -Y¹.]

1. Full of meat; fleshy.

1787 W. MARSHALL *Norfolk* (1795) II. Gloss., *Meaty, adj.* fleshy, but not 'right fat'. **1865** *Reader* No. 144. 363/2 A very meaty egg. **1883** G. ALLEN in *Knowledge* 20 July 34/1 In a crab..the meatiest part..consists of [etc.]. **1900** *Andover Advertiser* 19 Oct., Meaty steers.

b. *fig.* (chiefly *U.S.*) Full of substance.

1881 G. S. HALL *German Culture* 105, I think any discussion of it would be likely to be rather more meaty than ..inane speculations about the nature of the Beautiful and Sublime. **1896** *Advt. of Preacher's Compl. Homilet. Comm.* (N.Y.), The Index suggests thousands of meaty themes for sermons. **1902** *Academy* 13 Dec. 655/2 The sentences are really too 'meaty'.

2. Of or pertaining to meat; having the flavour of meat.

1864 SALA in *Daily Tel.* 27 Sept., Inhaling the glorious aroma of the meaty Eden. **1865** DICKENS *Mut. Fr.* I. v, Meaty jelly.

Hence **'meatiness.**

1873 TROLLOPE *Australia* I. 57, I felt as though I were pervaded by meatiness for many hours.

meaugh: see MAUGH.

meaul, meawl(e: see MIAUL.

meaw(e: see MIAOW.

†**meaze.** *Obs. rare*⁻¹. App. a variant of or mistake for MEUSE, misused for: The 'form' of a hare.

1602 *2nd Pt. Return fr. Parnass.* II. v. 791 A hare that wee found this morning musing on her meaze.

meaze, var. MEASE (measure of herrings)

meazel, var. MEASLE *a. Obs.* and MEASLE *v.*

meazle, variant of MESEL (leper).

meazling, obs. form of MIZZLING.

'mebbe, 'mebby, *colloq.* and *dial.* variants of MAY-BE, MAYBE (*see E.D.D.*).

1844 'J. SLICK' *High Life N.Y.* I. vi. 65 Mebby I'll mention where I got them. **1886** H. BAUMANN *Londinismen* 106/2 Mebbe. **1906** W. CHURCHILL *Coniston* I. x. 119 Mebbe I be, and mebbe I hain't. **1910** R. BROOKE *Let.* 8 June (1968) 240 Jacques'll be here about then, mebbe. **1948** E. POUND *Pisan Cantos* (1949) lxxxi. 110 A vacant lot where you'd occasionally see a wild rabbit Or mebbe only a loose one. **1961** S. CHAPLIN *Day of Sardine* vii. 148 'We're goin' to the pictures and mebbe afterwards we'll fill up with some fish and chips. **1972** *Last Whole Earth Catalog* (Portola Inst.) 152/1 I read in *Newsweek* or somewhere that this is the New Renaissance—Mebbe so.

mebile, meble, variants of MOBLE *Obs.*

mebos ('miːbɒs, *Afrikaans* 'meːbɔs). *S. Afr.* Also **meebos.** [Afrikaans, prob. ad. Jap. *umeboshi*, a dried, preserved plum.] A confection made from apricots dried, flattened or pulped, and preserved in salt and sugar.

1793 tr. *C. P. Thunberg's Trav. Europe, Afr. & Asia* III. 120, I saw several kinds of fruit, the produce of this country [*sc.* Japan], either dried or preserved in yeast, in a mode which is, I fancy, only practised at Japan or China. The fruit that was only dried, such as plumbs and the like, was called *Mebos*. **1899** *Answers* 18 Nov. 7/2 The best sort of preserve is called *mebos*, and is made of stoned and sun-dried apricots, flattened out, and pickled with salt and sugar. **1912** *Northern Post* 27 Sept. (Pettman), I have now come to the conclusion that our old navigators became acquainted with this delicacy in Japan, learned to like it, and afterwards at the Cape attempted to imitate it, but used the fruit of apricot trees.., and that the word *Meibos* or *Meebosje* had its origin in [Jap.] *Umeboshi*. **1939** S. CLOETE *Watch for Dawn* iii. 39 He had mebos and raisins and sun-dried peaches. **1954** M. KUTTEL *Quadrilles & Konfyt* i. 9 Have a jar of mebos handy on board..in case of sea-sickness. **1959** J. COLLIER *Stellenbosch Revisited* ii. 45 A delicacy called 'mebos' which consisted of apricots dried, flattened and treated with salt and sugar. **1974** *Eastern Province Herald* 27 Nov. 37 Mevrou Van Niekerk..fed them on mebos and honey cakes in her big farm kitchen.

Mebyon Kernow ('mɛbjɒn 'kɜːnəʊ). [Cornish.] 'Sons of Cornwall', the name of a Cornish party of independence.

1962 *Rep. Comm. Broadcasting 1960* 224 in *Parl. Papers 1961–2* (Cmnd. 1753) IX. 259 We note..a submission entered by Mebyon Kernow (Sons of Cornwall) advocating a service of broadcasting for Cornwall. **1963** *Guardian* 8 Apr. 3/6 Mebyon Kernow, the Cornish home rule movement. **1967** *Ibid.* 5 Dec. 3/2 Mebyon Kernow (Sons of Cornwall) are to put forward candidates in the next general election. **1975** *Isis* 17 Oct. 9/3 Mebyon Kernow (The Sons of Cornwall), the nationalist organisation, has never demanded autonomy but the more reasonable 'self-government in domestic affairs' within the United Kingdom.

Mecænas, bad form of MÆCENAS.

mecamylamine (ˌmɛkə'maɪləmiːn). *Pharm.* [f. ME(THYL + **cam*(*phane* + -YL + AMINE.] A potent ganglion-blocking drug, 3-methyl-aminoisocamphane, $C_{11}H_{21}N$, which is used in treating hypertension.

1955 *Sci. News Let.* 29 Oct. 281/1 A nerve-blocking drug called mecamylamine. **1956** *Arch. Internal Med.* XCVII. 561/1 Such side effects as constipation were just as prominent with the small completely absorbed doses of mecamylamine as with the relatively large poorly absorbed doses of other ganglion-blocking agents. **1968** L. GYERMEK in A. Burger *Drugs Affecting Cent. Nervous Syst.* I. iv. 290 Mecamylamine depresses the vasomotor center independently of its ganglionic blocking action. **1971** *Nature* 17 Sept. 207/1 Previous work in this laboratory with monkeys trained to puff cigarette smoke showed that mecamylamine, a nicotinic-blocking agent, reduced their smoking. **1974** M. C. GERALD *Pharmacol.* viii. 159 Ganglionic blocking agents such as mecamylamine (Inversine)..prevent cholinergic transmission at the autonomic ganglia.

mecanyc, -yke, -ycall: see MECHANIC, -ICAL.

‖**mecate** (meɪ'kɑːteɪ). [Aztec *mecatl* 'corde, fouet, discipline' (Siméon *Dict. Nahuatl*).]

1. A rope made of the fibre or hair of the maguey.

1877 in BARTLETT *Dict. Amer.* **1880** in WEBSTER *Suppl.*; and in recent Dicts.

2. 'A Mexican square measure, equal to about one-tenth of an acre' (*Cent. Dict.* 1890).

Mecca ('mɛkə). [The name (repr. Arab. *Makkah*) of the birthplace of Mohammed, the great place of pilgrimage of the Mohammedans.]

1. *transf.* and *fig.* Applied to a place which one regards as supremely sacred, or which it is the aspiration of one's life to be able to visit.

1850 BOKER *Anne Boleyn* I. iii, Make to the Mecca of our hopes, the king, A solemn pilgrimage. **1887** *Times* (weekly ed.) 21 Oct. 9/1 Stratford..is the Mecca of American pilgrims. **1890** 'R. BOLDREWOOD' *Col. Reformer* (1891) 379 He..was..free once more to turn his brow erect and undaunted towards the Mecca of his dreams.

2. *attrib.* in ***Mecca balm, balsam*** = BALM, BALSAM of Mecca.

1823 in CRABB *Technol. Dict.*; and in recent Dicts.

Meccan ('mɛkən), *a.* and *sb.* [f. MECCA + -AN.]

A. *adj.* Of or pertaining to Mecca.

1687 DRYDEN *Hind & P.* III. 1098 Such as the Meccan Prophet us'd of yore. **1898** *Eng. Illustr. Mag.* Feb. 511 A crowd of Meccan pilgrims.

B. *sb.* An inhabitant or native of Mecca.

1855 BURTON *El-Medinah & Meccah* II. 280 The Meccans, a dark people, say of the Madani that their hearts are black and their skins are white. **1902** A. B. DAVIDSON *Biblical & Lit. Ess.* 224 This appellation being derived from an attack made on the Meccans that year.

Meccano (mɪ'kɑːnəʊ). Also **meccano.** The proprietary name of a set of metal pieces, nuts, bolts, etc., and tools, specially designed for constructing small models of buildings, machines, or other engineering apparatus; any portion of such a set. Also *attrib.* and *fig.*

1907 *Trade Marks Jrnl.* 23 Oct. 1893 Meccano... Constructional toys. Frank Hornby,..Liverpool; manufacturer of constructional models. **1908** (*title*) Meccano (mechanics made easy): manual of instructions for the whole series of models. **1924** H. DE SÉLINCOURT *Cricket Match* iii. 56, I shall make a prison cell of meccano, and pretend you're locked..inside. **1927** *Sunday at Home* Aug. 675/1 There was meccano in the goldfish bowl. **1928** *Television* May 20/1 String, cardboard, and pieces of rough wood with Meccano parts;..all combined to make the television machine. **1928** 'R. WEST' *Strange Necessity* ii. 199 The complete meccano set for the mind that is in The First Men in the Moon. **1930** J. B. PRIESTLEY *Angel Pavement* vi. 307 It seemed only yesterday when he was..putting the Meccano set by the boy's bedside. **1934** *Amer. Speech* IX. 167/1 An economy may be made for the foreigner by presenting to him the elementary words only, thereby substituting a linguistic Meccano for the expense of ready-made models. **1945** J. BETJEMAN *New Bats in Old Belfries* 45 Pressed 'neath the box of his Meccano set. **1957** *New Scientist* 25 Apr. 9/2 The vocabulary is largely a 'Meccano' vocabulary; it is built up from bits and pieces which can be stuck together in twos, threes and fours. **1960** S. R. RANGANATHAN *Colon Classification* (ed. 6) 13 The Meccano feature makes it necessary to give, in addition to the unit-schedules, a set of Rules for constructing Class Numbers with the aid of the unit-schedules. **1965** *Listener* 23 Sept. 464/3 In crisp Technicolor images and prose painstakingly constructed on a Meccano-like principle. **1970** J. A.

HOWARD *Aerial Photo-Ecol.* xi. 122 The mechanical or spider templates are provided by 'meccano' type strips. **1972** R. PERRY *Fall Guy* iii. 48 The suspension bridge was still standing, its graceful lines making Sydney harbour bridge look like a clumsy piece of Meccano. **1972** *Guardian* 14 Oct. 3/2 The Eiffel Tower..is quite a piece of Meccano: there are more than 18,000 structural components in the 985 ft high tower. **1973** *Ibid.* 10 Feb. 10/2 He's the sort of uncle who'd give you a Meccano set for Christmas and then stay all afternoon and tinker with it. **1974** *Trade Marks Jrnl.* 30 May 939/2 Meccano Multikit... Toys and playthings, all sold in kit form. Meccano Limited,..Liverpool,..manufacturers and merchants.

mecche, obs. form of MATCH *sb.*[1]

Mecenas, bad form of MÆCENAS.

mech (mɛk), colloq. abbrev. of MECHANIC *sb.* 3.
1951 PARTRIDGE *Dict. Slang* (ed. 4) 1107/2 *Mech*, mechanic; esp. in the old *air mech* of the R.F.C. and the current *flight mech* of the Air Force: coll.: since ca. 1912. **1968** J. SANGSTER *Touchfeather* xvi. 191 Bud carries a heater, the mechs don't. **1973** A. HUNTER *Gently French* iii. 23 Hanson called over a mech. The mech started it for us and drove it out.

mech, mechacan, obs. ff. MUCH, MECHOACAN.

†**'mechal**, *a. Obs.* In 7 mechall, michall. [f. L. *mœch-us* (a. Gr. μοιχός) adulterer + -AL[1].] Adulterous. (Only in Heywood.)
1606 HEYWOOD *Challenge for Beauty* v. i, Her owne tongue Hath publish'd her a mechall prostitute. **1624** —— *Gunaik.* IV. 195. **1633** —— *Eng. Trav.* Fj, Pollute the Nuptiall bed with Michall sinne.

‖**mechameck** ('mɛtʃəmɛk). [? American Indian.] The wild potato-vine; = MECHOACAN.
1828 RAFINESQUE *Medical Flora* I. 123 (heading) Convolvulus Panduratus, English name, Mechameck bindweed... The native name of mechameck ought to be given to it as a distinctive appellation. **1890** in *Syd. Soc. Lex.*

mechanic (mɪ'kænɪk), *a.* and *sb.* [ad. L. *mēchanic-us*, a. Gr. μηχανικός (adj. and sb.), f. μηχανή MACHINE. Cf. F. *mécanique* (from 14th c.: perh. the source in early instances), Pr. *mechanic*, Sp. *mecánico*, Pg. *mechanico*; also OE. *mechanisc*, Ger., Du. *mechanisch*, Sw., Da. *mekanisk*.
The adj. was introduced much later than MECHANICAL, which in early uses is somewhat closer to the sense of the Latin word.]

A. *adj.*

1. a. Pertaining to or involving manual labour or skill. Now *rare*: cf. MECHANICAL 1 b.
1549 *Compl. Scotl.* Prol. 8 To leyrne sciens, craftis, ande mecanyke occupations. **1622** PEACHAM *Compl. Gent.* xiii. (1634) 129 Painting in Oyle..is..of more esteeme then working in water colours; but then it is more mechanique, and will robbe you of over much time from your more excellent studies. *a* **1631** DONNE *80 Serm.* (1640) xxxvii. 364 When we see any man doe any work well, that belongs to the hand, to write, to carve, to play, to doe any mechanique office well. **1677** YARRANTON *Eng. Improv.* 187 The persons working in the Mechanick-Arts. **1770** LANGHORNE *Plutarch* (1879) I. 175/2 If a man applies himself to servile or mechanic employments. **1838** PRESCOTT *Ferd. & Is.* (1846) I. ii. 132 He was a considerable proficient in music, painting, and several mechanic arts.

†**b.** Pertaining to mechanical arts; industrial.
1721 BRADLEY *Philos. Acc. Wks. Nat.* 7 It is a hard Coal for Mechanick Uses.

2. Of persons: Having a manual occupation; working at a trade. Now blended with the attributive use of the sb.
1549 *Compl. Scot.* ii. 25 Ande mecanyc lauberaris sal reproche gentil men. **1655** STANLEY *Hist. Philos.* IV. *Menedemus* i, Though noble by descent, Mechanick by profession and indigent. **1678** R. BARCLAY *Apol. Quakers* x. xxiii. 316 Most..are Labouring and Mechanick men. **1719** DE FOE *Crusoe* I. i, The Labour and Sufferings of the mechanic Part of Mankind. **1837** HT. MARTINEAU *Soc. Amer.* III. 48 Are the mechanic and farming classes satisfied? **1845** R. W. HAMILTON *Pop. Educ.* iii. (ed. 2) 56 If mechanic life be miserable, if the crowded population which it collects is degraded.

†**3.** Belonging to or characteristic of the 'lower orders'; vulgar, low, base. *Obs.*
1599 MARSTON *Sco. Villanie, In Lect. prorsus indignos*, Each mechanick slaue, Each dunghill pesant. **1606** SHAKS. *Ant. & Cl.* IV. iv. 32 To stand On more Mechanicke Compliment. **1642** CHAS. I *Declar.* Wks. 1662 II. 170 Suffering Mechanick, Ignorant fellows to preach and expound the Scripture. **1676** ETHEREDGE *Man of Mode* IV. i, Writing, Madam's a Mechanick part of Witt! A Gentleman should never go beyond a Song or a Billét. **1705** VANBRUGH *Confed.* I. iii, A woman must indeed be of a mechanic mould, who is either troubled or pleased with anything her husband can do for her. **1762** LLOYD *Actor* 40 The Play'r's profession (though I hate the phrase, 'Tis so mechanic in these modern days).

4. a. Of the nature of, or pertaining to, a machine or machines; also, worked by machinery. Now *poet.* or *rhetorical*: cf. MECHANICAL *a.* 3.
1625 N. CARPENTER *Geog. Del.* I. iv. (1635) 74 A Ballance, and other such mechanicke instruments. **1696** MANDEY & MOXON (*title*) Mechanick-powers: or, the Mistery of Nature and Art unvail'd, shewing what great things may be performed by Mechanick Engines, etc. **1788** *Gentl. Mag.* LVIII. I. 77/1 A man of war hove 3 inches by mechanic force. **1876** GEO. ELIOT *Dan. Der.* III. xxxvii. *heading*, Fine mechanic wings that would not fly.

b. *mechanic powers* or †*faculties*: = *mechanical powers* (see MECHANICAL *a.* 3 c). ? *Obs.*
1648 BP. WILKINS *Math. Magick* I. xii, Concerning the force of the Mechanick faculties, particularly the Ballance and Leaver. **1701** MOXON *Math. Dict.*, *Mechanick Powers*, or Mechanick Faculties are Six. **1825** J. NICHOLSON *Operat. Mechanic* 11 The pulley is the third mechanic power. **1856** EMERSON *Eng. Traits, Literature* Wks. (Bohn) II. 112 They [*sc.* Englishmen] are incapable of an inutility, and respect the five mechanic powers even in their song.

5. a. Worked or working like a machine; having a machine-like action or motion; acting mechanically. Somewhat *arch.*; cf. MECHANICAL *a.* 4.
1697 CONGREVE *Mourning Bride* II. viii, O impotence of sight! mechanic sense,..Not seeing of election but necessity. **1762** LLOYD *Actor* 2 Acting,..its perfection draws From no observance of mechanic laws. **1850** TENNYSON *In Mem.* v, The sad mechanic exercise, Like dull narcotics, numbing pain. **1863** KINGLAKE *Crimea* (1876) I. iv. 68 That branch of industry which seeks to give uniformity and mechanic action to bodies of men.

†**b.** Involuntary, automatic. *Obs.*
1723 LD. BOLINGBROKE in *Pope's Pr. Wks.* (1741) II. 26 Good digestions, serene weather, and some other mechanic springs. **1741** BETTERTON *Eng. Stage* vi. 102 Nature by a sort of mechanic Motion throws the Hands out as Guards to the Eyes on such an Occasion.

6. Of agencies, forces, principles: Such as belong to the subject-matter of mechanics; = MECHANICAL *a.* 5. Now *rare* or *Obs.*
1664 POWER *Exp. Philos.* I. 3 So great is the mechanick power which Providence has immur'd within these living walls of Jet [*viz.* a flea]. **1683** T. HOY *Agathocles* 18 The Mechanique Power, by which they move, It self is guided by some Hand above. **1712** *H. More's Antid. Ath.* II. i. *Schol.* 153, I..perceiv'd the motion of the World to be no ways mechanick. **1844** DISRAELI *Coningsby* II. i, The supreme control obtained by man over mechanic power.

†**7.** Of theories and their advocates; = MECHANICAL *a.* 6. *Obs.*
1691 RAY *Creation* I. (1692) 28 These mechanick Theists have here quite outstripped and outdone the Atomick Atheists. **1790** BURKE *Fr. Rev.* Wks. V. 152 On the principles of this mechanick philosophy, our institutions can never be embodied, if I may use the expression, in persons.

†**8.** Of persons and their aptitudes: Skilled in mechanical contrivance. *Obs.*
1713 STEELE *Guardian* No. 1 ¶3, I am..convinced of the importance of mechanick heads. **1714** GAY *Trivia* I. 272 A new Machine Mechanick Fancy wrought. **1748** *Anson's Voy.* III. x. 411 The mechanic dexterity of the Europeans.

B. *sb.* (See also MECHANICS.)

†**1. a.** Manual labour or operation. *Obs.*
1390 GOWER *Conf.* III. 142 Of hem that ben Artificier, Whiche usen craftes and mestiers, Whos Art is cleped Mechanique. **1605** BACON *Adv. Learn.* II. viii. §3 He..may superinduce upon some metall the Nature and forme of Gold by such Mechanique as longeth to the production of the Natures afore rehearsed.

†**b.** A mechanical art. *Obs.*
1604 R. CAWDREY *Table Alph.*, *Mechanick*, handycraft. **1655** in Hartlib *Ref. Commw. Bees* 33 There is not any one Mechanick, which hath its Basis on Phylosophy, in which there are not many errors, into which an Artist, that hath been long versed in the Practique, may hap to fall. **1656** [? J. SERGEANT] tr. *T. White's Peripat. Inst.* 387 Consider the honour of..the Mechanicks, 't is the work that's most proper to mankind. **1691** RAY *Creation* II. (1704) 245 Besides the known uses [of plants]..in Building, in Dying, in all Mechanicks, there may be as many more not yet discover'd.

†**c.** Mechanism, mechanical structure. *Obs.*
1605 BACON *Adv. Learn.* x. §5 The fault being in the very frame and Mechanicke of the parts.

2. a. One who is employed in a manual occupation; a handicraftsman.
mechanics' institute or *institution*: the designation adopted by a class of societies, established (in 1823 and subsequently) in London and most other towns of England to afford their members facilities for self-education by classes and lectures. In many of these institutions, only a small proportion of the members belonged to the 'mechanic' or artisan class. See also INSTITUTE *sb.*[1] 4.
1562 A. SCOTT *Poems* (S.T.S.) i. 174 Merchandis to trafique and travell to and fro, Mechanikis wirk. **1607** TOPSELL *Four-f. Beasts* (1658) 341 Houses or yards, where Carpenters or such Mechanicks work. **1638** SIR T. HERBERT *Trav.* (ed. 2) 163 These people are most of them mechanicks and husbandmen. **1713** SWIFT, etc. *Frenzy of J. Dennis* Wks. 1755 III. I. 142 My friend an apothecary! a base mechanic! **1777** FLETCHER *Bible Calvinism* Wks. 1795 IV. 244 An industrious sober mechanic can hardly pay for a mean lodging in a garret. **1825** HONE *Every-day Bk.* I. 1549 On the 2d of December, 1823, the London Mechanics' Institution was formed. **1849** MACAULAY *Hist. Eng.* iii. I. 418 An English mechanic,..instead of slaving like a native of Bengal for a piece of copper, exacted a shilling a day. **1891** LECKIE *Life & Relig.* 71 He [St. Paul] was an itinerant mechanic.

b. Used *contemptuously*. Now *rare*.
1607 SHAKS. *Cor.* v. iii. 83 Do not bid me..capitulate Againe, with Romes Mechanickes. **1768** HORNE *Disc.* ix. Wks. 1818 II. 171 The meanest mechanic takes place of the nobles and kings of the earth, if he were a better Christian than they were. **1828** SCOTT *F.M. Perth* xxiii, This fellow is a wretched mechanic. **1842** TENNYSON *Walking to Mail* 67 Lest..his nice eyes Should see the raw mechanic's bloody thumbs Sweat on his blazon'd chairs.

†**c.** A low or vulgar fellow. *Obs.*
a **1700** B. E. *Dict. Cant. Crew*, *Mechanic*,..a mean,..contemptible Fellow. **1733** FIELDING *Intrig. Chambermaid* II. ix, I am glad you have taught me at what distance to keep such mechanics for the future.

d. One who cheats at gambling games, *spec.* cards; a card-sharp. *U.S.* and *Austral. slang*.
1909 in *Cent. Dict.* Suppl. **1944** D. RUNYON in *Collier's* 12 Feb. 12/4 What I must know is are you a mechanic at gin? **1949** J. SCARNE *On Cards* i. 1 To the average card player the man who makes his living by cheating at cards is a sharper, sharp or shark, but to card hustlers and house men he is known as a *mechanic*. *Ibid.* ii. 10 Some mechanics keep two fingers curled around the long edge of the deck and two around the short upper edge. **1953** BAKER *Australia Speaks* v. 121 *Mechanic*, a person who cheats at cards, especially a professional card sharp (Americans use *mechanic* for a dishonest player at faro). **1966** K. GILES *Provenance of Death* v. 146 The games were straightish, no real mallarky, though Jack himself was a 'mechanic' with the cards if necessary. **1966** *Daily Tel.* (Colour Suppl.) 30 Sept. 27/2 As croupier..always on guard for the sharps—the mechanics. **1970** R. & J. PATERSON *Cranberry Portage* vii. 40 He was what other gamblers called a 'mechanic', an expert manipulator of playing-cards.

3. In restricted sense: A skilled workman, esp. one who is concerned with the making or use of machinery.
In some English manufacturing districts the term denotes a man who has the management and repairing of the machinery in a factory.
1662 HOBBES *Consid.* (1680) 53 What is here said of Chymists is applicable to all other Mechaniques. **1681** *Lond. Gaz.* No. 1643/4 His Majesty having sent for Sir Samuel Morland..was Graciously pleased to Declare, that he was highly satisfied with all the late Experiments and extraordinary Effects of Sir Samuels new Water-Engine... After which, the Lord Chamberlain..caused him to be Sworn Master of the Mechanicks. **1719** DE FOE *Crusoe* II. i, A very handy ingenious Fellow, who was a Cooper by Trade, but was also a general Mechanick; for he was dexterous at making Wheels [etc.]. **1835** MISS MITFORD in L'Estrange *Life* (1870) III. iv. 31 Captain Gore is, amongst his other excellences, a great mechanic, and a capital working carpenter. **1870** EMERSON *Soc. & Solit.*, *Work & Days* Wks. (Bohn) III. 64 The apprentice clings to his foot-rule, a practised mechanic will measure by his thumb.

4. One who holds mechanical theories; a mechanical physiologist. *rare.* (Cf. MECHANIST 3.)
a **1776** R. JAMES *Diss. Fevers* (1778) 86, I might produce the causes of fevers according to the various principles of the Galenists, the Chymists, the Mechanics.

mechanical (mɪ'kænɪkəl), *a.* and *sb.* [f. late L. *mēchanic-us*: see prec. and -ICAL.] A. *adj.*

1. Of arts, trades, occupations: Concerned with machines or tools. Hence,

a. Concerned with the contrivance and construction of machines or mechanism.
1432-50 tr. *Higden* (Rolls) VII. 73 Certeyne instrumentes of his makynge made by arte mechanicalle, and specially organes. **1626** BACON *New Atl.* 38 Wee haue also diuerse Mechanicall Arts, which you haue not; and Stuffes made by them; as Papers, Linnen [etc.]. **1756-7** tr. *Keysler's Trav.* (1760) IV. 395 Those who are fond of mechanical arts, manufactures, &c. **1815** J. SMITH *Panorama Sci. & Art* I. 124 To make any useful proficiency in mechanical pursuits. **1872** YEATS *Techn. Hist. Comm.* 367 Machine-making..belongs to a high order of mechanical art.

b. Concerned with manual operations; of the nature of handicraft.
c **1450** LYDG. & BURGH *Secrees* 2097 Whoom his ffadir..Boonde and dysposyd to crafft mechanycalle. **1477** NORTON *Ord. Alch.* iv. in Ashm. *Theat. Chem. Brit.* (1652) 49 Handie-crafte called Arte Mechanicall. **1586** A. DAY *Eng. Secretary* II. (1625) 106 A seruant, meanly trained in some Mechanicall Science. **1605** BACON *Adv. Learn.* II. To King §13 Arts Mechanicall contract Brotherhoods in communalties. **1706** PHILLIPS (ed. Kersey) *title-p.*, The Arts and Sciences, either Liberal or Mechanical. **1753** HOGARTH *Anal. Beauty* 4 Many other little circumstances belonging to the mechanical part of the art. **1834** MACAULAY *Ess., Pitt.* (1899) 288 Almost every mechanical employment ..has a tendency to injure some one or other of the bodily organs of the artisan. **1837-9** [see ILLIBERAL *a.* 1]. **1841** EMERSON *Method Nat.* Wks. (Bohn) II. 220, I look on trade and every mechanical craft as education also.

†**c.** *transf.* Pertaining to the mere technicalities of a profession or art. *Obs.*
a **1648** LD. HERBERT *Hen. VIII* (1683) 325 Other Laws also were enacted, which for being meerly legal, and there fore relative chiefly to the Masters of the Law, or otherwise Mechanical, or at least so particular that they belong, not properly to History. **1681** NEVILE *Plato Rediv.* 103 The Mechanical part of their Callings (which is to assist Clients with Counsel, and to plead their Causes). *a* **1763** SHENSTONE *Ess.* (1765) 5 The vulgar may not indeed be capable of giving the reasons why a composition pleases them. That mechanical distinction they leave to the connoisseur.

2. a. Of persons: Engaged in manual labour; belonging to the artisan class. Now *rare*. †Hence, characteristic of this class, mean, vulgar (*obs.*).
1589 *Late Voy. Sp. & Port.* (1881) 102 Wherein mechanicall and men of base condition doo dare to censure the dooings of them, of whose acts they be not worthie to talke. **1591** HORSEY *Trav.* (Hakl. Soc.) App. 302 Thearby [*sc.* by commerce] your marchantes growe riche, your mecanycall peoples sette a worke. **1597** SHAKS. *2 Hen. IV*, v. v. 38 Hall'd thither by most Mechanicall and durty hand. **1646** EARL MONM. tr. *Biondi's Civil Warres* IX. 182 Born at Corneto a poor village in Toscany, of mean mechanical parentage. **1695** CIBBER *Love's Last Shift* III, 'Tis mechanical to marry the Woman you love; Men of Quality should always marry those they never saw. **1730** FIELDING *Author's Farce* I. v, These are represented as mean and mechanical, and the others as honourable and glorious. **1830** GALT *Lawrie T.* v. ii, Settlers of the mechanical orders. **1880** E. WHITE *Cert. Relig.* 31 Among the peasantry and mechanical orders.

†**b.** Occupied with or skilled in the practical application of an art or science; practical as opposed to speculative. *Obs.*

1570 DEE *Math. Pref.* a iij b, A speculative Mechanicien.. differreth nothyng from a Mechanicall Mathematicien. **1633** T. STAFFORD *Pac. Hib.* III. viii. (1810) 567 If they had been as good Mechanicall Cannoniers, as they were Commaunders.

3. †**a.** Of the nature of a machine or machines (*obs.*). **b.** In modern use: Acting, worked, or produced by a machine or mechanism: often in contrast to what is produced by hand-labour.

1567 MAPLET *Gr. Forest* 2 Albeston is a stone of Archadie ..whereof in olde time was built that kind of worke Mechanicall. **1579–80** NORTH *Plutarch, Marcellus* (1595) 335 Instruments and engines (which are called mechanicall, or organicall). **1648** BP. WILKINS *Math. Magick* II. vi. 191 The *volant* or flying *Automata* are such Mechanicall contrivances, as have a self-motion [etc.]. **1839** *Penny Cycl.* XV. 49/1 The centre of gravity might by mechanical means be made to rise continually higher. **1860** FARADAY *Lect. Forces Matter* 170 An instrument wrought only by mechanical motion. **1875** WHYTE MELVILLE *Riding Recoll.* vi. (1879) 98 The mechanical horse exhibited in Piccadilly some ten or twelve years ago. **1902** *Daily Chron.* 7 Apr. 3/2 The invention and practical perfectioning of the mechanical pianoforte player.

c. ***mechanical powers*** or †***faculties***: the six 'simple machines'. (Cf. MECHANIC *a.* 4 b.)

1648 BP. WILKINS *Math. Magick* I. iii, Of the first Mechanical faculty, the Ballance. **1727–41** CHAMBERS *Cycl.* s.v., The mechanical powers, are the balance, lever, wheel, pully, wedge, and screw.

d. ***mechanical drawing***: drawing performed with the help of instruments, as compasses, rulers, etc. ***mechanical construction*** (of curves): construction by the use of some apparatus, as distinguished from 'tracing' by calculation of successive points.

1842–59 GWILT *Archit.* §995 Practical Geometry..has been defined as the art which directs the mechanical processes for finding the position of points, lines, surfaces [etc.].

e. ***mechanical (wood) pulp*** (see quot. 1926).

1888 CROSS & BEVAN *Text-bk. Paper-Making* vi. 105 Mechanical Wood Pulp.—A very large quantity of pulp is used in the commoner kinds of paper, such as cheap news, etc., which is obtained by disintegrating wood by mechanical means alone. **1890** A. WATT *Art of Paper-Making* x. 113 Mechanical wood pulp is also used in a moderate degree. **1926** *Paper Terminol.* (Spalding & Hodge) ii. 17 *Mechanical wood*, the lowest grade of wood pulp prepared by the purely mechanical process of grinding. **1936** *Economist* 8 Feb. 304/1 Of sulphate as well as of mechanical pulp, both annual production and stocks have been sold out. **1937** [see GROUND *ppl. a.* 4]. **1953** *Economist* 26 Sept. 883/1 Mechanical pulp, from which newsprint is made, is about 10s. a dry ton higher [than chemical pulp]. **1963** R. R. A. HIGHAM *Handbk. Paper-Making* v. 129 Mechanical pulp is an important cheap grade used in the manufacture of papers such as newsprint, wallpaper, [etc.].

f. ***mechanical twin*** (Metallurgy): a twinned crystal produced by mechanical deformation; so ***mechanical twinning***.

1913 *Engineering* 10 Oct. 510/3 There is now good reason to doubt that mechanical twinning ever occurs in metals. **1923** GLAZEBROOK *Dict. Appl. Physics* V. 344/1 These internal stresses cause internal straining of the metal, which in turn causes the formation of numerous mechanical twins. **1935** G. E. DOAN *Princ. Physical Metall.* iii. 77 In mechanical twinning, each atom moves a certain distance relative to the neighboring plane. **1966** *McGraw-Hill Encycl. Sci. & Technol.* VIII. 293/1 Typical phenomena observable are...effects of deformation—strain markings, ..mechanical twins, and microcracks. **1966** W. J. McG. TEGART *Elem. Mech. Metall.* v. 121 Another important mode of deformation is that of mechanical twinning.

4. Of persons, their actions, etc.: Resembling (inanimate) machines or their operations; acting or performed without the exercise of thought or volition; lacking spontaneity or originality; machine-like; automatic.

1607 TOPSELL *Four-f. Beasts* (1658) 271 Our Mechanical Horse Farriars, who cure many times what they know not, and kill where they might cure, knew they the cause. **1663** BP. PATRICK *Parab. Pilgr.* xxi. (1668) 210 The Mechanical Christian will here find himself to be dead and void of Christ. **1711** STEELE *Spect.* No. 152 ¶2 None of these Men of Mechanical Courage have ever made any great Figure in the Profession of Arms. **1766** GOLDSM. *Vic. W.* iv, I always thought fit to keep up some mechanical forms of good breeding. **1788** REID *Active Powers* III. v. 613 The one we may for distinctions sake, call mechanical government, the other moral. **1818** HAZLITT *Eng. Poets* ii. 64 Versification is a thing in a great degree mechanical. **1841** MYERS *Cath. Th.* III. §36. 131 Is not the notion of a mechanical rule—a rule ever ready and ever applicable—in spiritual things, altogether out of place? **1871** MORLEY *Condorcet* in *Crit. Misc.* Ser. I. (1878) 66 The official religion of the century was lifeless and mechanical.

5. a. Of agencies, operations, and principles: Such as belong to the subject-matter of mechanics; in modern use often opposed to *chemical*. ***mechanical equivalent of heat***: see EQUIVALENT *sb.* 2 c.

1626 BACON *Sylva* §98 The Cause of all Flight of Bodies thorow the Aire, and of other Mechanicall Motions. **1662** STILLINGFL. *Orig. Sacr.* III. ii. §1 To explain the Origine of the Universe..meerly by the Mechanical Laws of the motion of matter. **1698** KEILL *Exam. Th. Earth* Introd. (1734) 17 The World..did exist from all eternity, without any change, or alteration, but such as happened from pure Mechanical principles, and causes. **1805–17** R. JAMESON *Char. Min.* (ed. 3) 151 If we have recourse to mechanical division, in order to obtain the cubic nucleus from this kind of octahedron. **1839** *Penny Cycl.* XV. 291/1 Liquid medicines consisting of several ingredients..in a state of mechanical suspension in some viscid medium. **1842–59** GWILT *Archit.* Gloss., *Mechanical Carpentry*. That branch of carpentry which relates to the disposition of the timbers of a building in respect of their relative strength and the strains to which they are subjected. **1863** TYNDALL *Heat* i. §9 (1870) 8 The sea is rendered warmer by a storm, the mechanical dash of its billows being..converted into heat. *Mod.* Common air is a mechanical mixture, not a chemical compound.

fig. **1875** JOWETT *Plato* (ed. 2) II. 201 The distinction between the mere mechanical cohesion of sounds or words and the chemical combination of them into a new word.

b. *Geol.* Applied to formations in which the ingredients have undergone no alteration in their chemical constitution or molecular structure.

1833 LYELL *Princ. Geol.* III. Gloss. 73 *Mechanical Origin*, Rocks of. When rocks are composed of sand, pebbles, or fragments, to distinguish them from those of an uniform crystalline texture, which are of chemical origin. **1878** HUXLEY *Physiogr.* xvii. 293 The mere mechanical detritus of siliceous rocks.

6. Of theories and their advocates: Explaining phenomena by the assumption of mechanical action.

1692 BENTLEY *Boyle Lect.* v. 145 The Mechanical Atheist. **1704** J. HARRIS *Lex. Techn.* I, *Mechanical Philosophy*, is the same with the Corpuscular, which endeavours to explicate the Phænomena of Nature from Mechanical Principles. **1707** FLOYER *Pulse Watch* I. II. ii. 205 Which Method of Physic is both Mechanical and Philosophical. **1771** T. PERCIVAL *Ess.* (1777) I. 21 The mechanical hypothesis concerning the operation of medicines, which is supposed to depend upon the size, figure, and gravity of their constituent particles. **1860** TYNDALL *Glac.* I. i. 5 The mechanical theory of slaty cleavage. **1880** HUXLEY in *Nature* No. 615. 345 The mechanical physiologists, who regarded these operations as the result of the mechanical properties of the small vessels, such as the size, form, and disposition of their canals and apertures.

7. Concerned with or involving material objects or physical conditions.

1664 POWER *Exp. Philos.* 104, I have an Experiment in Banco which will give some Mechanical Evidence of this great Mystery. **1665** GLANVILL *Def. Vanity Dogm.* 28 There are Mechanical difficulties in the way of his Solutions. **1675** TRAHERNE *Chr. Ethics* 148 In physical goodness there is a mechanical fitness, and dead convenience. **1860** MILL *Repr. Govt.* (1865) 4/1 Besides these moral hindrances, mechanical difficulties are often an insuperable impediment to forms of government.

8. a. Pertaining to mechanics as a science.

1648 BP. WILKINS *Math. Magick* I. i. 3 Art may be said.. to overcome, and advance nature, as in these Mechanicall disciplines. **1827** JAMIESON (*title*) A Dictionary of Mechanical Science. **1861** W. FAIRBAIRN *Pres. Addr. to Brit. Assoc.* p. lviii, The mechanical sciences..may be divided into Theoretical Mechanics and Dynamics..and Applied Mechanics.

b. Having to do with machinery.

1793 SMEATON *Edystone L.* §122 Subjects of mechanical invention and investigation. **1863** FAWCETT *Pol. Econ.* I. iv. (1876) 33 The foremost mechanical genius of this mechanical age is devoted to the production of weapons of death. **1881** *Instr. Census Clerks* (1885) 42 Mechanical Engineer, Inventor, Draughtsman, Student. **1897** MARY KINGSLEY *W. Africa* 669 The great inferiority of the African to the European lies in the matter of mechanical idea.

c. ***mechanical advantage*** (of a machine): the ratio of the load to the force applied to the machine; ***mechanical zero*** (see quot. 1971²).

1894 W. J. LINEHAM *Textbk. Mech. Engin.* ix. 481 The first is the principle of virtual velocities, and the second mechanical advantage. **1962** A. NISBETT *Technique Sound Studio* v. 94 A reversed-reading instrument is used: it has its mechanical zero at the right-hand end of the scale and is deflected back to the scale zero (its 'electrical zero') by a steady current. **1971** B. SCHARF *Engin. & Its Lang.* ix. 68 To calculate the efficiency of a machine we divide the real mechanical advantage by the ideal mechanical advantage and multiply the result by 100%. **1971** *Gloss. Electrotechnical, Power, Terms (B.S.I.)* I. iv. 9 *Mechanical zero*, equilibrium position which the index will approach when the measuring element..is de-energized.

9. *Math.* **a.** Applied to curves not expressible by equations of finite and rational algebraical form; = TRANSCENDENTAL.

So called as admitting of production only by 'mechanical construction': see 3 d.

1727–41 CHAMBERS *Cycl.* s.v. *Curve*, These [*sc.* transcendental] curves, Des Cartes, &c. call mechanical ones. **1743** EMERSON *Fluxions* ii. 139 Mechanical or transcendent curves. **1847** J. DWYER *Princ. & Pract. Hydraulic Eng.* 75 A cycloid..is a mechanical curve of.. curious properties.

b. ***mechanical solution*** (of a problem): see quot.

1704 J. HARRIS *Lex. Techn.* I, *Mechanical Solution* of a Problem in Mathematicks, is either when the Thing is done by repeated Tryals, or when the Lines made use of to solve it are not truly Geometrical.

10. *Comb.*, as ***mechanical-minded*** adj.

1947 J. STEINBECK *Wayward Bus* xvii. 223, I suppose people really think they are mechanical-minded.

B. *sb.*

1. = MECHANIC B. 2. *arch.* (as echo of Shaks.).

1590 SHAKS. *Mids. N.* III. ii. 9 A crew of patches, rude Mechanicals, That worke for bread vpon Athenian stals. **1603** HOLLAND *Plutarch's Mor.* 211 These covetous misers gather wealth together like mightie magnificoes, but they spend like beggerly mechanicals. **1647** LILLY *Chr. Astrol.* clx. 676 It..expresseth in Mechanicalls, great Custome and Trade; in men otherwise qualified, Preferment, Office. **1830** *Westm. Rev.* XIII. 211 Socrates! we hear all the vulgar mechanicals exclaim,..a poor, mean, pitiful, pennyless fellow! **1963** *Times* 20 Apr. 4/1 The play scene is omitted and the rest of the mechanicals, a couple of fellows boldly designated on the programme as 'Bottom's Friends', are left deliberately vague. **1968** *Listener* 1 Feb. 148 Frivolity seems to me the only, precarious excuse for this novel—a let-out, for instance, for treating the income-earning group as characters and the rest as 'mechanicals'.

2. *pl.* †**a.** The science which relates to the construction of machines. *Obs.*

1605 BACON *Adv. Learn.* II. xxi. §6 In mechanicalls, the direction how to frame an Instrument or Engyne, is not the same with the manner of setting it on woorke.

b. Details of mechanical construction. *rare.*

1821 T. G. WAINEWRIGHT *Ess. & Crit.* (1880) 146 This class of subjects demands the greatest attention to mechanicals. **1843** LYTTON *Last Bar.* I. ix, 'They were indifferently well wrought, specially a chevesail, of which the'—'Spare me the fashion of thy mechanicals, and come to the point', interrupted Marmaduke.

3. *Printing.* The artwork and 'copy' as finally assembled. Also *transf.*

1967 V. STRAUSS *Printing Industry* xi. 744/2 At its simplest, the mechanical is a piece of artists' illustration board, somewhat larger than the final size of the printed piece. To this board are attached, by cementing or pasting .., a number of line images, all in the same focus and, of course, of inspected quality. This board bears, furthermore, all notations that will enable it to serve as the blueprint of the job. **1967** KARCH & BUBER *Offset Processes* iii. 47 This final assembly of reading matter and artwork for the printer is called a *mechanical*. **1967** *Britannica Bk. of Year* (U.S.) 66 Many regulations, particularly in relation to TV, prevented advertisers from using international campaigns if the basic mechanicals—artwork, films, and so on—were not produced in Italy by Italians. **1973** *Publishers Weekly* 12 Mar. 38 The layout [of an advertisement] was changed at the last minute, and the mechanical bearing [the publisher] Quadrangle's name either was not replaced, or it fell off.

mechanicalism (mɪˈkænɪkəlɪz(ə)m). [f. MECHANICAL + -ISM.] **a.** The philosophic doctrine that all the phenomena of the universe, or some particular class of phenomena indicated by the context, are mechanically caused. **b.** 'Mechanical' or routine procedure.

So **meˈchanicalist**, one who favours mechanicalism.

1877 T. SINCLAIR *Mount* (1878) 71 A mechanicalist would put one's thoughts very quickly into his shape, no doubt. **1893** *Nation* (N.Y.) 3 Aug. 88/2 These two things, mechanicalism and infallibilism, are the great obstacles to any common understanding between religious thinking and scientific thinking. **1903** *Speaker* 30 May 201/2 Others.. have lost all touch with human nature, the slaves of an academic mechanicalism.

mechanicality (mɪˌkænɪˈkælɪtɪ). [f. MECHANICAL *a.* + -ITY.] The quality of being mechanical, or like a machine; chiefly *fig.*

1778 [W. MARSHALL] *Minutes Agric., Observ.* 117 This construction was adopted on account of its Simplicity, and, at the same time, its Mechanicality. **1871** *Contemp. Rev.* XIX. 86 Sermons..exhibit a sameness and mechanicality. **1890** ABP. BENSON in *Life* II. 307 By much conversation I do believe I have prevailed on Wyon to depart much from mechanicality of touch.

mechanicalization (mɪˌkænɪkəlaɪˈzeɪʃən). [f. MECHANICALIZE *v.* + -ATION.] The being or becoming mechanical in character or in means of operation; *esp.* in military terminology.

1922 *Glasgow Herald* 5 Jan. 4 A record of experimental progress towards mechanicalisation of wireless telegraphy in as simple and portable a form as possible. **1924** *Westm. Gaz.* 26 Mar., Colonel Rudkin..proved himself an expert on mechanicalisation—the new word to indicate army tendencies. **1924** *Times Lit. Suppl.* 16 Oct. 654/4 The mechanicalization of the army. **1926** *Glasgow Herald* 27 Aug. 11 Military minds turn to 'mechanicalisation', an ugly word but an indication of the abolition of what Tommy Atkins terms 'foot-slogging'. **1927** *Sunday Times* 6 Mar. 20/3 The real benefits that result from a mechanicalisation of industry.

mechanicalize (mɪˈkænɪkəˌlaɪz), *v.* [f. MECHANICAL *a.* + -IZE.] *trans.* To render mechanical (in any sense of the adj.); formerly, †to degrade to the rank or character of a mechanic; 'to render mean or low' (Todd 1818). Also **meˈchanicalized** *ppl. a.*, **meˈchanicalizing** *vbl. sb.*

1611 COTGR., *Mechanizé*, Mechanicalized; made, or growne base, vile, ordinarie, meane. **1892** *Cosmopolitan* XIII. 155/2 Even utilitarianism and the mechanicalizing of labor have failed entirely to take away its significance. **1903** *Daily News* 4 Mar. 3/1 The tendency of modern industry to 'mechanicalise men.' **1924** *Army Q.* Oct. 39 The first step suggested is that the divisional transport should be mechanicalized. **1926** *Glasgow Herald* 9 Sept. 9 One of the problems studied..was the landing of a mechanicalised force on an open beach in the face of opposition.

mechanically (mɪˈkænɪkəlɪ), *adv.* [f. MECHANICAL *a.* + -LY².]

1. By mechanical art, contrivance, or methods; by the use of machinery or instruments.

1570 DEE *Math. Pref.* c ij b, Thus, may you Double your Cube Mechanically. *Ibid.* c iij, Though it be Naturally done and Mechanically: yet hath it a good Demonstration Mathematicall. **1656** tr. *Hobbes' Elem. Philos.* (1839) 315 The ancients pronounced it impossible to exhibit in a plane the division of angles,..otherwise than mechanically. **1737** BRACKEN *Farriery Impr.* (1749) I. 329 A silly Man carrying

two Buckets of Water upon his Shoulders with a round Pole, instead of a flattish one hollowed and mechanically fitted to receive his Shoulders. **1856** KANE *Arct. Expl.* I. xxix. 401 To lift her mechanically above her line of flotation. **1893** *Atlantic Monthly* Feb. 192/2 Large crowds gathered in the mechanically flooded fields.

2. By mechanical (as opposed to chemical, vital, etc.) agencies or processes; as a mechanical agent; in respect of mechanical properties.

1684–5 BOYLE *Min. Waters* 23 Whether any thing..can be ..discover'd..by Chymically and Mechanically examining the Mineral Earths [etc.]. **1691** RAY *Creation* II. (1704) 415 They suppose even the perfect Animals..to have been formed Mechanically among the rest. **1794** KIRWAN *Elem. Min.* (ed. 2) I. 186 The calx and magnesia may be chemically combined with the argill, and not merely mechanically mixed as in marls. **1823** J. BADCOCK *Dom. Amusem.* 25 Being itself insolvable in any known menstruum, and acting mechanically only, it neither destroys nor is destructible. **1860** TYNDALL *Glac.* I. xxv. 177 The dust and thin smoke mechanically suspended in a London atmosphere.

3. As by machinery or mechanical action; without spontaneous or conscious exercise of will or thought; automatically.

1692 BENTLEY *Boyle Lect.* 202 If atoms formed the world according to the essential properties of bulk, figure, and motion, they formed it mechanically; and if they formed it mechanically without perception and design, they formed it casually. **1741** tr. *D'Argens' Chinese Lett.* xiii. 85 With Men who act in a Manner mechanically, who behave so and so to Day only because they did so yesterday, there is [etc.]. **1800** MRS. HERVEY *Mourtray Fam.* II. 91 Emma, almost indifferent to every thing, followed her mechanically. **1853** C. BRONTE *Villette* xxxviii, The place could not be entered. Could it not? a point worth considering; and while revolving it, I mechanically dressed. **1865** DICKENS *Mut. Fr.* II. i, He could do mental arithmetic mechanically.

4. By reference to mechanical causes or principles.

1737 BRACKEN *Farriery Impr.* (1757) II. 88 We ought to explain the Thing mechanically. **1861** H. SPENCER *Educ.* (1888) 18 The mechanically-justified wave-line principle.

5. With mechanical tastes or aptitudes.

1726 SWIFT *Gulliver* I. vi, Having a head mechanically turned,.. I had made for myself a table and chair. **1890** *Anthony's Photogr. Bull.* III. 201 Any mechanically inclined man can make one in a day.

†**6.** In a 'mechanical' or ungentlemanly manner; meanly. (Cf. MECHANICAL *a.* 2, MECHANIC *a.* 3.) *Obs.*

1613 CHAMBERLAIN *Let.* in *Crt. & Times Jas. I* (1848) I. 224 But his [Sir T. Bodley's] servants grumble and murmur very much, with whom he hath dealt very mechanically, some of them having served him..above two and twenty years.

7. *Comb.*, as ***mechanically-minded*** adj.

1922 *Guardian* 19 May, Any mechanically-minded person can make a simple receiving set for a pound or two. **1937** B. H. L. HART *Europe in Arms* xvii. 231 Some doubt must remain..as to the ability of horse-minded soldiers to become mechanically minded. **1972** G. DURRELL *Catch me a Colobus* ii. 45 Oscar the orang-utan,..the most mechanically-minded of all the apes.

mechanicalness (mɪˈkænɪkəlnɪs). [-NESS.] The quality of being mechanical.

1611 COTGR., *Mecaniquerie*, Mechanicallnesse; basenesse of humor. **1691–8** NORRIS *Pract. Disc.* (1711) III. 18 Men not perceiving the Mechanicalness of its operation, are apt to have recourse to some inherent Quality. **1874** *Contemp. Rev.* XXV. 95 Science does not affirm..mechanicalness in Nature. **1900** *Conferences on Books & Men* xiii. 229 The very mechanicalness of the routine seems to have soothed and numbed Cowper's too irritable sensibilities.

mechanician (mɛkəˈnɪʃən). Also 6–7 -icien, 7 -itian. [f. MECHANIC + -IAN. Cf. F. *mécanicien.*]

a. One who practises or is skilled in a mechanical art; a mechanic, artisan. Now *rare*. **b.** One who is skilled in the construction of machinery.

1570 J. DEE *Math. Pref.* aiij b, A Mechanicien, or a Mechanicall workman is he, whose skill is, without knowledge of Mathematicall demonstration, perfectly to worke and finishe any sensible worke, by the Mathematicien principall or deriuative, demonstrated or demonstrable. **1621** BURTON *Anat. Mel.* I. ii. III. ii. (1651) 94, I appeal to Painters, Mechanicians, Mathematicians. **1671** BOYLE *Usef. Exp. Nat. Philos.* II. III. 11 By frequenting the Shops and Work-houses of Mechanitians. **1759** DA COSTA in *Phil. Trans.* LI. 187 There are even mechanicians in that kingdom [France], who seriously doubt, whether the fire engine is anywise useful. **1819** *P.O. Lond. Direct.* 144 Wm. Hawks, Mechanician and Optician to their Majesties. **1863** FAWCETT *Pol. Econ.* I. v. (1876) 58 The mechanician upon whose skill the accuracy of a chronometer depends.

meˈchanicism. [f. MECHANIC + -ISM.] = MECHANISM 2.

1710 DE FOE in *Review* No. 119. VI. 474 They would denude us of the beautiful Garment of Liberty, and prostitute the Honour of the Nation to the Mechanicism of Slavery! **1962** W. STARK *Fund. Forms of Social Thought* II. xii. 176 A fresh high-water mark of mechanicism was reached in the eighth decade of the nineteenth century. **1971** *Archivum Linguisticum* II. 115 But if to avoid the limitations of Kurylowicz's method, we have to admit that a form passes arbitrarily from one function to another, not taking into account the facts of polarization, attraction, etc., then we fall into mechanicism.

mechanicist (mɪˈkænɪsɪst). [f. MECHANIC *a.* and *sb.* + -IST.] = MECHANICALIST.

1934 *Mind* XLIII. 248 'Mechanical' is a highly ambiguous term, and many who call themselves mechanicists would not deem it inconsistent with their principles to recognise in the molecule a different unit from the atom, with different properties. **1936** *Nature* 4 Apr. 559/2 Haldane asserts that the real universe is a universe of personality and the manifestation of God... No doubt materialists and mechanicists would take exception to some of the arguments. **1939** *Ibid.* 8 July 52/2 Controversies about the philosophy of animate Nature..keep alive the old feud between vitalists and mechanicists. The latter favour the view that life is a by-product of blind processes of dead matter.

mechanicize (mɪˈkænɪsaɪz), *v.* [f. MECHANIC + -IZE.] *trans.* To render mechanical.

18.. *American* X. 39 (Cent.) No branch of the race was more mechanicized by Lockianism than the American.

meˈchanico-, used as comb. form of L. *mēchanicus* (see MECHANIC), in hyphened combinations with the sense 'partly mechanical and partly something else', as ***mechanico-acoustic***, ***-intellectual***, ***-material***, ***-merciful*** adjs.; **mechanico-chemical** *a.*, comprising mechanics and chemistry; (of phenomena) pertaining partly to mechanics and partly to chemistry; **mechanico-corpuscular** *a.*, an epithet applied to the philosophy which views all phenomena, material and spiritual, as explicable by the movement of atoms according to mechanical laws; **mechanico-morphic** *a.* = MECHANOMORPHIC *a.*; **mechanico-morphism** = *mechanomorphism*; **mechanico-physical** *a.*, of or pertaining to the philosophy which explains all phenomena as the outcome of the physical laws of the motions and interactions of matter.

1964 Y. R. CHAO in D. Abercrombie et al. *Daniel Jones* 39 The *mechanico-acoustic set-up for recording speech on wax masters. **1840** SMART s.v. *Mechanic*, The **Mechanico-chemical* sciences are magnetism, electricity, galvanism, &c. **1825** COLERIDGE *Aids Refl.* (1848) I. 327 The utter emptiness..of the vaunted *Mechanico-corpuscular philosophy. **1870** EMERSON *Soc. & Solit.* vii. 131 [Steam] is yet coming to render many higher services of a *mechanico-intellectual kind. **1920** D. H. LAWRENCE *Touch & Go* 9 The strike situation..is a *mechanico-material struggle, two mechanical forces pulling asunder from the central object, the bone. **1866** G. MACDONALD *Ann. Q. Neighb.* vi. (1878) 70 Stepping over many single leaves in a *mechanico-merciful way. **1937** *Mind* XLVI. 176 We wish to stress here what we conceive to be the inadequacy of all '*mechanico-morphic' representations of concrete becoming in nature. **1935** J. MURPHY tr. *Schrödinger's Sci. & Human Temperament* Introd. 19 We must..abandon the mechanical structure. We must turn to the statistical concept... In other words, Schrödinger pleads for the abandonment of what may be called *mechanico-morphism in the pursuit of natural science,..the casting aside of all models and the wholesale employment of mathematical formulas in their stead. **1890** W. JAMES *Princ. Psychol.* II. xxviii. 666 The modern *mechanico-physical philosophy..which.. includes the nebular cosmogony, the conservation of energy, the kinetic theory of heat and gases, etc.,..begins by saying that..the only laws [are] the changes of motion which changes in collocation bring.

mechanics (mɪˈkænɪks). [In form a pl. of MECHANIC: see -IC 2.

Gr. had both ἡ μηχανική and τὰ μηχανικά; hence in late L. *mēchanica* fem. sing., mechanical science, *mēchanica* neut. pl., works of mechanical art. The Rom. langs. use the fem. sing.: Fr. *mécanique* (in 18th c. also *les mécaniques* fem.), Sp. *mecánica*, Pg. *mechanica*, It. *meccanica*; cf. G. *mechanik*, Du. *mechanica*, Da., Sw. *mekanik*.]

1. a. Originally (and still in popular use): That body of theoretical and practical knowledge which is concerned with the invention and construction of machines, the explanation of their operation, the calculation of their efficiency. **b.** That department of applied mathematics which treats of motion and tendencies to motion: comprising (according to the division now generally received) *kinematics*, the science of abstract motion, and *dynamics* (including *statics* and *kinetics*), the science of the action of forces in producing motion or equilibrium in bodies.

analytical mechanics: mechanics treated by the differential and integral calculus. ***animal mechanics***: mechanics as applied to the study of the movements of animals.

1648 BP. WILKINS *Math. Magick* I. ii. 12 Astronomy handles the quantity of heavenly motions, Musick of sounds, and Mechanicks of weights and powers. **1671** BOYLE *Usef. Mech. Discipl. Nat. Philos.* 1, I do not here take the Term, *Mechanicks*, in that stricter and more proper sense, wherein it is wont to be taken, when tis us'd onely to signifie the Doctrine about the Moving Powers, (as the Beam, the Leaver, the Screws, and the Wedg) and of framing Engines to multiply Force; but I here understand the word *Mechanicks* in a larger sense, for those Disciplines that consist of the Applications of pure Mathematicks to produce or modifie Motion in inferior Bodies. **1770** LANGHORNE *Plutarch* (1879) I. 342/1 The first that turned their thoughts to mechanics..were Eudoxus and Archytas. **1828** HUTTON *Course Math.* II. 139 Mechanics is the science of equilibrium and of motion. **1841** W. SPALDING *Italy & It. Isl.* I. 118 Archimedes..devoted the best efforts of his skill in mechanics to the defence of his native town.

†**2.** *pl.* Manual operations. *Obs. rare*⁻¹.

1726 SWIFT *Gulliver* IV. x, I shall not trouble the Reader with a particular Description of my own Mechanics; let it suffice to say, that in six Weeks Time..I finished a Sort of Indian Canoo.

3. *transf.* The procedural or operational details (*of* something).

1925 E. B. WILSON *Cell* (ed. 3) ii. 172 This fact is fundamentally important for the mechanics of mitosis. **1930** *Writer* Sept. 265/2 Is the playwright perpetually making references in his dialogue to the mechanics of his craft? **1932** *Punch* 13 Jan. 55/1 Miss E. B. C. Jones is well up in the mechanics of psycho-analysis. **1940** *Punch* 10 Apr. 407/3 It is a pity the mechanics of the story take up so much of the time. **1960** L. PICKEN *Organization of Cells* viii. 373 (*heading*) The mechanics and energetics of changes in cell shape. **1974** *Nature* 22 Mar. 280/3 Speakers at current meetings in the field generally give little information on how their results are actually obtained, that is, the pure mechanics of the business.

mechanism (ˈmɛkənɪz(ə)m). [ad. mod.L. *mēchanismus*, f. Gr. μηχανή MACHINE: see -ISM. Cf. F. *mécanisme*, Sp. *mecanismo*, Pg. *mechanismo*, It. *meccanismo*; also G. *mechanismus* (pl. *mechanismen*). Late Latin had *mēchanisma* contrivance.

The mod. L. word was chiefly used to denote the mechanical structure and action of nature according to the Cartesian philosophy.]

1. a. The structure, or mutual adaptation of parts, in a machine or anything comparable to a machine, whether material or immaterial. (In early use chiefly with reference to natural objects.)

1662 STILLINGFL. *Orig. Sacr.* III. §15. 401 To impute that rare *mechanism* of the works of nature to the blind and fortuitous motion of some particles of matter? **1685** BOYLE *Enq. Notion Nat.* 73, I shall express, what I call'd General Nature, by Cosmical Mechanism, that is, a Comprisal of all the Mechanical Affections (Figure, Size, Motion, &c.) that belong to the matter of the great System of the Universe. **1722** WOLLASTON *Relig. Nat.* v. 100 He..knows the make of their bodies, and all the mechanism and propensions of them. **1776** G. CAMPBELL *Philos. Rhet.* (1801) I. 241 The wonderful mechanism of our mental frame. **1833** HT. MARTINEAU *Briery Creek* iv. 85 The mechanism of society thus resembles the mechanism of man's art. **1854** BREWSTER *More Worlds* xvii. 256 The wonderful mechanisms of animal and vegetable life. **1855** BAIN *Senses & Int.* II. i. §1 The mechanism or anatomy of movement in the animal frame. **1862** DARWIN *Fertil. Orchids* iii. 100 The mechanism of the flower. **1867** LADY HERBERT *Cradle L.* iii. 96 The door was a marvel of mechanism.

†**b.** In somewhat wider sense (see quot. 1755).

1712 *Spectator* No. 518 ¶8 The Contour of his Person, the Mechanism of his Dress, [etc.]. **1715** DESAGULIERS *Fires Impr.* 154 The whole Mechanism of it [viz. a chimney] will be easily understood by a sight of the Figures. **1755** JOHNSON, *Mechanism*,..2. Construction of parts depending on each other in any complicated fabrick.

2. *concr.* **a.** A system of mutually adapted parts working together mechanically or in a manner analogous to mechanical action; a piece of machinery; the machinery (*lit.* or *fig.*) by means of which some particular effect is produced. Also, machinery or mechanical appliances in general. Also used, esp. *Psychol.*, of the means or agency by which mental processes and bodily actions are caused to take place (cf. quot. 1885).

a **1677** HALE *Prim. Orig. Man.* I. ii. 48 That Opinion that depresseth the natures of sensible Creatures below their just value..rendring them no more but barely Mechanisms or Artificial Engins. **1758** REID tr. *Macquer's Chym.* I. 129 This is brought about by a mechanism to which we are strangers. **1802** PALEY *Nat. Theol.* xxiii. (ed. 2) 447 Mechanism is not itself power. Mechanism, without power, can do nothing. **1814** D. STEWART *Hum. Mind* II. ii. §2. 143 The wonderful mechanism of speech. **1822** IMISON *Sci. & Art* I. 94 The part of the mechanism of a watch which shows the hour of the day. **1876** A. B. KENNEDY *Reuleaux' Kinem. Machinery* 47 A closed kinematic chain, of which one link is thus made stationary, is called a mechanism. **1879** *St. George's Hosp. Rep.* IX. 809 The vascular dilatation must be considered as the result of the morbid condition of the mechanism of the circulation. **1885** tr. *Lotze's Micro-cosmos* I. II. iv. 232 The mind is not content to have connections of ideas imposed on it by the mechanism of perception and memory. **1903** HEYWOOD *Music in Churches* 7 Average choir boys cannot recite on a low note without being liable to use the..chest voice..and the use of their lower mechanism is usually accompanied with flatness. **1910** G. N. CALKINS *Protozool.* i. 29 Bodies closely associated with the mechanism of nuclear division and of locomotion. **1913** J. S. HALDANE *Mechanism, Life & Personality* I. 9 Descartes, in his writings about the nervous system,..suggested nervous mechanisms. *Ibid.* II. 58 The real difficulty for the mechanistic theory is that we are forced..to postulate that the germ-plasm is a mechanism of enormous complexity and definiteness, and..that this mechanism..can divide and combine with other similar mechanisms. **1921** H. C. MILLER *New Psychol. & Teacher* 161 This mental mechanism [*sc.* the complex] lies at the root of all bias, all injustice, and all inability to think clearly. **1924** *Brit. Weekly* 28 Aug. 471/3 He will see strange recesses in human personality and unsuspected mechanisms fashioning religious beliefs. **1929** K. S. LASHLEY (*title*) Brain mechanisms and intelligence. **1941** *Psychosomatic Med.* July 227/1 The adaptive mechanisms by means of which the organism strives to achieve this goal. *Ibid.* 233/1 By 'cognitive field' or 'practical insight' we mean a mechanism capable of registering and integrating stimuli. **1958** *Amer. Jrnl. Psychiatry* Sept. 204/2 The brain, unlike a machine into which any mechanism can be set, appears to have mechanisms of its own. **1964** COFER & APPLEY *Motivation* xi. 573 Conceptions of learned drive basically assert that responses which produce strong stimuli are the mechanisms of such drives. **1968** M. BUNGE in Lakatos & Musgrave *Probl. Philos. Sci.* 128 Something mediating between inputs and outputs, i.e. a mechanism triggered by the inputs and which has the required outputs. **1972** *Physics Bull.* Mar.

141/1 Furthermore some mechanism must be found for judging the quality of the work done by the chief scientist and the controller.

b. *spec.* in musical instruments.

1825 CROSSE *York Festival* 154 The admirable mechanism by which it [*sc.* an organ] was made available on this occasion. 1871 *Abridgm. Specif. Patents, Music* 163 The invention consists in so arranging the mechanism of a flute that the closing of the C sharp and the B natural holes may be simultaneous by the action of the second finger. 1876 STAINER & BARRETT *Dict. Mus. Terms, Mechanism,* that part of an instrument which forms the connection between the player and the sound-producing portion.

c. *Kinematics.* 'An ideal machine, a combination of movable bodies constituting a machine, but considered only with regard to relative movements' (Webster 1897).

†**3.** Mechanical action; 'action according to mechanick laws' (J.). *Obs.*

1671 S. PARKER *Def. Eccl. Pol.* 342 The Philosophy of a Phanatick being as intelligible by the Laws of Mechanism, as the Motion of the Heart, and Circulation of the Bloud. 1692 BENTLEY *Boyle Lect.* iii. 32 He acknowledges nothing besides Matter and Motion; so that all that he can conceive to be transmitted hither from the Stars, must needs be perform'd either by Mechanism or Accident. 1704 NORRIS *Ideal World* II. ii. 90 The most that use them [movements] are utterly ignorant of the laws of mechanism and yet order their footing as artificially as the most skilful. 1731 ARBUTHNOT *Aliments* (1735) 34 After the Chyle has pass'd through the Lungs, Nature continues her usual Mechanism, to convert it into Animal Substances. 1748 HARTLEY *Observ. Man* I. iv. 500 The Mechanism or Necessity of human Actions, in Opposition to what is generally termed Free-will. 1794 SULLIVAN *View Nat.* IV. 5 Mechanism has become a learned word. But, does it mean any more than that one particle of matter is impelled by another,.. and that still by another, until we come to the particle first moved?

†**4.** A contrivance, artifice. *Obs. rare.*

1670 W. CLARKE *Nat. Hist. Nitre* 92 It is also a pretty Mechanism in Cookery.. which is this, Nitre giveth a Red Colour to Neats-Tongues, [etc.] 1688 EVELYN in Gutch *Coll. Cur.* I. 414 All their [the Jesuits'] other mechanismes and arts having fail'd them.

†**5.** Mechanical operations; mechanical art. *Obs.*

1710 STEELE *Tatler* No. 209 ¶2 Painting is Eloquence and Poetry in Mechanism. 1736 AINSWORTH *Lat. Dict.*, Talus.. who first invented the saw.. grew such an artist, that Dædalus fearing to be outdone in mechanism put him to death.

6. The opinion that everything in the universe is produced by mechanical forces.

1690 LOCKE *Hum. Und.* I. iii. 22 Thereby making Men no other than bare Machins... And upon that ground they must necessarily reject all Principle of Vertue, who cannot put Morality and Mechanism together. 1777 PRIESTLEY *Matt. & Spir.* (1782) I. Introd. 5 Mechanism is the undoubted consequence of materialism. 1902 BALDWIN *Dict. Philos. & Psychol.* II. 59/1 In biology: mechanism is opposed to vitalism, and in more recent controversy to neo-vitalism. 1909, 1917 [see FINALISM 2]. 1956 O. L. ZANGWILL in A. Pryce-Jones *New Outl. Mod. Knowl.* 170 *Mechanism* has sought to account for all behaviour in terms of the quasi-automatic activities of the central nervous system.

7. *Art.* **a.** The mechanical execution of a painting, sculpture, piece of music, etc.; technique. (Opposed to *style* or *expression*.)

1843 RUSKIN *Mod. Paint.* II. §1. vii. 94 *note*, Canaletti's mechanism is wonderful. Prout's the rudest possible; but there is not a grain of feeling in the one, and there is much in the other. 1860 *Ibid.* V. IX. viii. §1. 281 [Teniers and Wouvermans] seem never to have painted indolently, but gave the purchaser his thorough money's worth of mechanism. 1876 STAINER & BARRETT *Dict. Mus. Terms, Mechanism*, the physical power of performance, as distinguished from the intellect or taste which directs it.

b. 'Mechanical' quality (of literature); the following of set methods for producing effect.

1903 LD. ROSEBERY in *Daily News* 27 Nov. 5/5 Lord Macaulay's works.. are charged now with a certain amount of mannerism and a certain amount of mechanism.

mechanist ('mɛkənɪst). [f. MECHAN-IC + -IST.]

1. †**a.** A mechanic, handicraftsman (*obs.*). **b.** One who constructs machinery; a machinist.

1606 J. KING *Serm.* Sept. 32 They will turn.. Princes into mechanistes and artificers. 1718 J. CHAMBERLAYNE *Relig. Philos.* (1730) I. x. §17. 92 Adapted by Mechanists to other sort of uses. 1759 JOHNSON *Rasselas* vi, Having seen what the mechanist had already performed. *a*1761 CAWTHORN *Poems* (1771) 200 Observing this unlucky railer Was neither mechanist, nor taylor. 1806 *Edin. Rev.* IX. 210 The mechanist could have very little to do with the success of the play. 1852 GROTE *Greece* II. lxxxii. X. 664 He collected.. all the best engineers, mechanists, armourers, artisans, etc., whom Sicily or Italy could furnish.

2. One versed in mechanics; a mechanician.

1704 NORRIS *Ideal World* II. ii. 90 Placing their bodies in the aptest postures for their preservation, such as the wisest mechanist cannot correct. 1751 JOHNSON *Rambler* No. 117 ¶1 The Mechanist will be afraid to assert.. the Possibility of tearing down Bulwarks with a Silkworm's thread. *a*1774 GOLDSM. *Surv. Exp. Philos.* (1776) I. 212 It is called by mechanists the center of gravity. 1809–10 COLERIDGE *Friend* (1865) 160 One state possesses chemists, mechanists, mechanics of all kinds, men of science. *a*1822 SHELLEY *Def. Poetry* Pr. Wks. 1888 II. 28 Poets have been challenged to resign the civic crown to reasoners and mechanists.

3. One who holds a mechanical theory of the universe. (Cf. MECHANIC B. 4.) Also as *adj.*

1668 H. MORE *Div. Dial.* Characters, Cuphophron, A zealous.. Platonist and Cartesian, or Mechanist. 1913 J. S. HALDANE *Mechanism, Life & Personality* I. 6 The constant controversies.. between mechanists and non-mechanists. 1919 G. B. SHAW *Heartbreak House* p. xv, Their mechanist theory taught them that medicine was the business of the chemist's laboratory, and surgery of the carpenter's shop. 1925 C. D. BROAD *Mind & its Place* 43 One feels that the disputes between Mechanists and Vitalists are unsatisfactory. 1931 *Brit. Jrnl. Psychol.* Oct. 137 Those whom their opponents call 'vitalists' can see in the relationship an attribute of something living. Those whom their opponents dub 'mechanists' can see in the relationship [between association processes and neuronic excitation] a property they attribute to mechanism. 1965 *Listener* 19 Aug. 286/2 Pain due to emotional disturbance.. arises in the mind (or in the brain if you tend to be a mechanist).

mechanistic (mɛkə'nɪstɪk), *a.* [f. prec. + -IC.] Of, pertaining to, or connected with mechanics or mechanism. Also, pertaining to or holding mechanical theories in biology, philosophy, psychology, or linguistics.

1884 *Nature* 21 Aug. 383/1 The series of curves of velocity given for different mechanistic combinations. 1893 BURDON-SANDERSON in *Athenæum* 16 Sept. 375/2 The mechanistic view of the phenomena of life. 1904 *Westm. Gaz.* 3 Dec. 16/3 The mechanistic school. 1915 B. HOLMES in *Chicago Med. Recorder* Mar. 2 (*heading*) The Mechanistic view of Dementia Precox. 1923 W. MCDOUGALL *Outl. Psychol.* i. 30 All the varieties of psychology which propose .. to replace the hypothesis of a mind, a soul, a self, [etc.].., by that of a brain or a bodily organism working on strictly mechanical or physical principles.. may be conveniently classed together as mechanistic psychologies. 1924 W. B. SELBIE *Psychol. Relig.* 278 On the negative side they have adduced evidence of a kind which makes a merely mechanistic explanation of the universe impossible. 1933 L. BLOOMFIELD *Lang.* 33 The *materialistic* (or, better, *mechanistic*) theory supposes that the variability of human conduct, including speech, is due only to the fact that the human body is a very complex system. 1939 *Ann. Reg. 1938* 301 The Government's revenue would be so great that extinction of the debt would be automatic. This 'mechanistic' theory was severely ridiculed. 1952 J. DREVER *Dict. Psychol.* 163 *Mechanistic theory*,.. the interpretation of psychological processes on a mechanical basis, and denial of the reality or efficacy of ends and purposes. 1963 MARX & HILLIX *Syst. & Theories Psychol.* II. ix. 203 One man, Gustav Fechner, seems to have shared the mechanistic-romantic conflict with Freud. 1966 M. PEI *Gloss. Ling. Terminol.* Mechanistic theory,.. an approach to language and linguistics based on objective methodology in recording and classifying language phenomena. 1967 R. A. WALDRON *Sense & Sense Devel.* ix. 201 The rather more austere and mechanistic tendency of twentieth-century linguistics has given such phraseology a quaint, old-fashioned air. 1968 M. BUNGE in Lakatos & Musgrave *Probl. Philos. Sci.* 128 The first approach can be called phenomenological or global, the second mechanistic or atomistic.

mecha'nistically, *adv.* [f. MECHANISTIC *a.*] In a mechanistic manner; on mechanistic principles.

1923 W. MCDOUGALL *Outl. Psychol.* vi. 189 One attempt to explain mechanistically this fundamental type of profiting by experience has been widely accepted. 1925 C. D. BROAD *Mind & its Place* ii. 77 The attempts which have been made .. to treat mental phenomena mechanistically. 1935 *Mind* XLIV. 88 If you show that mental activity has independent causal powers, and that it works purposively and not mechanistically, surely [etc.]. 1947 J. C. RICH *Materials & Methods of Sculpture* xi. 350 Metal negative molds.. are used commercially for mechanistically manufacturing papier mâché reproductions in large quantities. 1961 *N. & Q.* June 237/2 Mr. White's method is usually to utter a few simple principles about the art of fiction.. and then test them rather mechanistically against his author's four novels. 1971 *Nature* 25 June 495/2 This situation looks unlikely to change, unless there is more collaboration in the design of mechanistically meaningful experiments. 1974 FRITH & MCLAUCHLAN in R. K. Harris *Nucl. Magn. Resonance* III. xii. 393 CIDNP is normally most useful mechanistically when performed in the high field of a normal spectrometer.

mechanize ('mɛkənaɪz), *v.* [f. MECHAN-IC + -IZE; cf. obs. F. *méchaniser*.]

1. *trans.* To make or render mechanical; to import or attribute a mechanical character to; to bring into a mechanical state or condition; to work out the mechanical details of (a design, idea, etc.). Also, to change (an industry, etc.) to a mechanical form of working; to provide with machines; spec. *Mil.*, to equip with mechanical weapons and vehicles, as tanks, armoured cars, etc.

1678 [implied in MECHANIZING *vbl. sb.*]. 1704 NORRIS *Ideal World* II. ii. 99 God can so mechanize matter, as to make it capable of doing some things that [etc.]. 1795 COLERIDGE *Conciones* 32 A system of fundamental Reform will scarcely be effected by massacres mechanized into Revolution. 1831 CARLYLE *Sart. Res.* III. iii, Cannot he.. mechanise them [*sc.* motives] to grind the other way? 1843 J. MARTINEAU *Chr. Life* (1867) 201 You cannot mechanize benevolence. 1870 EMERSON *Soc. & Solit., Art.* Wks. (Bohn) III. 21 Raphael paints wisdom: Handel sings it,.. Shakspeare writes it,.. Watt mechanizes it. 1879 BARING-GOULD *Germany* I. 127 He [the artisan] is mechanised. 1942 E. WAUGH *Put out More Flags* i. 21 The yeomanry.. had recently been mechanized, in the sense that they had had their horses removed; few of them had ever seen a tank. 1952 *Oxf. Jun. Encycl.* VI. 286/2 The spreading of farmyard manure and other winter jobs have been mechanized. 1957 *Encycl. Brit.* II. 412/2 The Germans had broken abruptly with the past by mechanizing their artillery.

2. *intr.* (*nonce-uses.*) To work as a mechanic; to move mechanically.

1886 T. HARDY *Mayor Casterbr.* xxxvi, Rural mechanics too idle to mechanise, rural servants too rebellious to serve. 1902 —— *Mother Mourns* Poems 71 Why loosened I olden control here To mechanize skywards.

Hence '**mechanized** *ppl. a.*, spec. *Mil.*, of, pertaining to, equipped with, or using mechanical vehicles and weapons; '**mechanizing** *vbl. sb.* (in quot. used *attrib.*). Also ˌ**mechani'zation**, the action of the verb MECHANIZE; '**mechanizer**, one who mechanizes, a believer in mechanical order or system = MECHANIST 3.

1678 CUDWORTH *Intell. Syst.* I. iii. §38. 175 Some of the ancient religious atomists were also too much infected with this mechanizing humour. 1813 SHELLEY *Q. Mab.* III. 180 A mechanized automaton. 1831 CARLYLE *Sart. Res.* III. v, Our European Mechanisers are a sect of boundless diffusion, activity, and co-operative spirit. 1839 J. STERLING *Ess.*, etc. (1848) I. 297 The mechanization of the mind. 1842 *Ibid.* 393 Genius.. cannot be prevented by the happiest mechanization of man. 1891 *Longm. Mag.* Aug. 431 By force of conscious and unconscious repetition of the phrase, it became mechanised. 1915 A. W. GOUGH *God's Strong People* 32 A tyranny built.. on a degradation and mechanization of the personal power. 1928 *Daily Mail* 7 Feb. 7/5 The 'mechanisation' of the army. 1928 *Daily Mail* 8 Feb. 7/5 The fast two-seater tanks of the mechanised army. 1937 *Daily Express* 11 Jan. 10/2 Mechanisation has come to the farmer. 1939 *Punch* 8 Nov. 504/1 Their plan.. was to attack.. the Maginot line.. along the whole extent from North to South, at the same time executing a turning mechanized movement through.. Switzerland. 1941 *Picture Post* 3 May 19/1 Mechanised warfare and careful preparation have again defeated flesh and blood. 1941 *Punch* 16 July 59/2 Enemy mechanized units penetrated our defences. 1942 *Times* (Weekly ed.) 7 Jan. 4 The conscience of humanity is still a factor of which even the lords of mechanized war may have to take account. 1942 *R.A.F. Jrnl.* 16 May 9 A vital means of countering the German Panzer and mechanised troops. 1954 [see AUTOMATION]. 1960 *Post Office Electr. Engineers' Jrnl.* LIII. II. 75/2 The mechanization of the trunk service, involving the installation of automatic trunk exchanges.. is now well advanced. 1968 R. M. OGORKIEWICZ *Design & Devel. Fighting Vehicles* i. 30 Some of the new ideas were explored in a series of experiments which began with the Experimental Mechanised Force assembled in 1927 on Salisbury Plain. 1970 MACKSEY & BATCHELOR *Tank* 33/1 It is one of the paradoxes of early mechanised warfare that the technologists not only produced the machines but also foresaw their tactical possibilities ahead of the soldiers.

mechano- ('mɛkənəʊ), repr. Gr. μηχανο-, comb. form of μηχανή MACHINE *sb.*, and used in the senses (*a*) 'machine(s)', as in MECHANOLOGY, (*b*) 'mechanical (and)', as in MECHANOTHERAPY, MECHANOCHEMICAL *a.* Also ˌ**mechano'caloric** *a.* *Physics* [CALORIC *a.*], applied to the phenomenon by which a flow of the superfluid form of liquid helium (helium II) generates a difference in temperature between the sending and receiving ends; ˌ**mechano-e'lectric**, **-e'lectrical** *adjs.*, pertaining to or producing a conversion of mechanical movements into corresponding electrical effects; also ˌ**mechano-elec'tronic** *a.* (*rare*).

1939 MENDELSSOHN & DAUNT in *Nature* 29 Apr. 720/1 The mechano-caloric effect is evidently the reverse of the 'fountain phenomenon', for whereas the latter means that the setting up of a temperature difference results in a flow of liquid helium II, the mechano-caloric effect shows that a flow of liquid helium II is accompanied by a development of heat (or cold). 1964 *New Scientist* 24 Sept. 773/1 Shortly after the discovery of this 'thermo-mechanical' effect the complementary 'mechano-caloric' phenomenon was observed. 1958 *Jrnl. Gen. Physiol.* XLI. 1245 (*heading*) The sites for mechano-electric conversion in a pacinian corpuscle. *Ibid.* 1263 The simplest interpretation of our results would seem to be that the entire mechano-electric transducer lies in the membrane of the non-myelinated ending. 1974 *Nature* 1 Mar. 69/2 Isometric tension was measured with two RCA 5734 mechano-electric transducers. 1961 M. L. GAYFORD *Acoustical Techniques & Transducers* VI. 279 Trying to obtain a perfect electrical copy of the groove excursion by the mechano-electrical groove-following means provided by a gramophone pick-up. 1974 *Nature* 20–27 Dec. 728/1 The muscle fibre was.. mounted horizontally with one of its tendons hooked to the anode of a RCA 5734 mechano-electrical transducer tube. 1950 *18th Internat. Physiol. Congr. Copenhagen* 171 The movements of the membrane.. are communicated to the plate of a mechano-electronic transducer (R.C.A. 5734), a triode which by means of a pivoted anode translates mechanical movements into electric current variations.

mechanochemistry (ˌmɛkənəʊ'kɛmɪstrɪ). [f. prec. + CHEMISTRY.] The study or phenomenon of mechanochemical processes.

1928 P. M. TRAVIS *Mechanochemistry* 3 This new science of mechanical dispersion, involving the principles of physical chemistry, I am calling 'Mechanochemistry', because it involves dispersion or deflocculation by mechanical means rather than by chemical. 1951 *Jrnl. Polymer Sci.* VII. 407 A simplified model which discloses the principles of the mechanochemistry of polyelectrolytes will be shown here. 1961 *New Scientist* 2 Mar. 548/3 In the USSR.. the field of investigation has been aptly named 'mechanochemistry', in line with 'electrochemistry' and 'photochemistry'. 1972 *Science* 3 Nov. 460/2 A complete understanding of the sliding filament model for generating flagellar bending waves must include an understanding of the mechanochemistry of the active sites at the molecular level.

Hence ˌ**mechano'chemical** *a.*, pertaining to both mechanics and chemistry; *spec.* able to convert chemical energy directly into mechanical energy; ˌ**mechano'chemically** *adv.*

1949 W. GARNER *Textile Laboratory Manual* i. 14 (*heading*) Mechano-chemical methods for single fibres. 1949

A. KATCHALSKY in *Experientia* V. 320/1 In the phenomena discussed here the chemical ionization energy is transformed directly into mechanical energy. We may therefore regard them as the first synthetic examples of mechanochemical systems. **1961** *New Scientist* 2 Mar. 549/2 The action of an internal combustion engine causes substantial changes in lubricating oil viscosity due to mechanochemical breakdown of the polymer being sheared between the narrow clearances. *Ibid.* 550/3 Mechanochemically initiated polymerization has been found to occur with a large variety of polymerizable substances using substrates other than rubber. **1964** *Oceanogr. & Marine Biol.* II. 198 Takata suggested that in *Acetabularia* there may be an ATP sensitive protein that forms a mechanochemical system controlling protoplasmic streaming. **1972** *Science* 3 Nov. 460/2 The basic mechanochemical process by which energy from ATP dephosphorylation is used to produce mechanochemical work may be very similar to the active sliding process. **1974** *Nature* 31 May 475/2 Exergonic band cleavage would therefore occur in the mechanochemically coupled step.

mechanograph (mɪˈkænəgrɑːf, -æ-). *rare*⁻⁰. [f. Gr. μηχανο-, μηχανή machine + -GRAPH.] One of a set of copies of a work of art, writing, etc. multiplied by mechanical means.

1885 in *Cassell's Encycl. Dict.*; and in recent Dicts.

mechanographic (ˌmɛkənəʊˈgræfɪk), *a. rare.* [f. Gr. μηχανο-, μηχανή machine + -GRAPHIC.]

1. Treating of mechanics.

1830 MAUNDER *Treas. Knowl.* I.

2. Pertaining to mechanography (Ogilvie *Suppl.* 1855).

mechanography (mɛkəˈnɒgrəfɪ). *rare*⁻⁰. [ad. mod.L. *mēchanographia*, f. Gr. μηχανο-, μηχανή machine: see -GRAPHY.] The art of copying or reproducing a work of art or writing by mechanical means. Hence **mechaˈnographist**, one who practises this art.

[**1826** ELMES *Dict. Fine Arts, Mechanographia.*] **1840** SMART, s.v. *Mechanic, Mechanography*, is the art of imitating paintings by mechanical means. **1847** WEBSTER, *Mechanographist.*

mechanology (mɛkəˈnɒlədʒɪ). *rare.* [f. Gr. μηχανο-, μηχανή machine + -LOGY.] The science of, or a treatise on, machines or mechanism.

1840 DE QUINCEY *Style* Wks. 1859 XI. 194 The science of style, considered as a machine,..might be called the mechanology of style. **1876** DUNGLISON *Med. Lex.*, *Mechanology*, a description of, or treatise on machines, or apparatus used in medicine or surgery.

mechanomorphic (ˌmɛkənəʊˈmɔːfɪk), *a.* [f. MECHANO- + Gr. μορφή form + -IC.] Having the form or qualities of a machine or mechanism; of or pertaining to the Deity regarded as a mechanical force. Hence **ˌmechanoˈmorphism**, the concept of something (esp. the Deity) as mechanomorphic.

a **1885** D. D. WHEDON *Ess., Rev. & Discourses* (1887) 265 A still more curious notion of dignity..rejects the *anthropomorphic* and substitutes therefor a *mechanomorphic* theory. **1926** B. H. STREETER *Reality* i. 2 Materialism pictures the Universe as an Infinite Machine; this by analogy may be called mechanomorphism. *Ibid.* 22 Mechanomorphic materialism. **1937** A. HUXLEY *Ends & Means* ix. 124 They have felt the effects of mechanomorphism. **1950** —— *Themes & Variations* 197 Cubists, who liked to paint machines or to represent human figures as though they were parts of machines..representation of human beings in a mechanomorphic guise.

mechanoreceptor (ˌmɛkənəʊrɪˈsɛptə(r)). *Physiol.* Also **mechano-receptor.** [f. MECHANO- + RECEPTOR.] A sensory receptor which responds to mechanical stimuli, such as pressure changes resulting from touch or sound.

1927 J. H. PARSONS *Introd. Theory Perception* i. 7 Receptors which are found in animals may be classified into three groups..chemo-receptors, mechano-receptors, and radio-receptors. *Ibid.* 9 Mechano-receptors can be divided into two classes, contact and distance receptors. **1951** *Sci. Amer.* Jan. 17/2 Among these mechano-receptors are the receptor organs for rotatory and translatory motion in the inner ear, the receptors responsible for the pressure sense of the skin, the muscle spindles imbedded in all muscles that fix and move bodily masses, and the so-called Pacinian or Vater's corpuscles found throughout the connective tissues. **1970** *Nature* 28 Mar. 1263/2 These passive movements are perceived by mechanoreceptors of the pedicel.

Hence **ˌmechanoreˈception**, the process by which a mechanical stimulus is converted by a mechanoreceptor into a nervous impulse; **ˌmechanoreˈceptive** *a.*, capable of performing mechanoreception.

1951 *Jrnl. Physiol.* CXV. 16 The mechanoreceptive area was localized by touching the tongue with a thin wire while listening to the pressure impulses in the loudspeaker. **1958** *Jrnl. Gen. Physiol.* XLI. 1249 (*heading*) Mechano-reception after excision of capsular structure. **1968** R. T. VERRILLO in D. R. Kenshalo *Skin Senses* vii. 139 (*heading*) A duplex mechanism of mechanoreception. **1974** *Nature* 26 Apr. 740/2 Neuromas in man must..contain mechano-receptive endings since they are always tender when gently palpated.

mechanotherapy (ˌmɛkənəʊˈθɛrəpɪ). Also in Lat. form **-therapia.** [ad. mod.L. type **mēchanotherapia*, f. Gr. μηχανο-, μηχανή machine + θεραπεία healing.] Cure by mechanical means.

1890 in *Syd. Soc. Lex.* **1896** *Allbutt's Syst. Med.* I. 373 The practice of 'mechano-therapy' by manipulators usually quite ignorant of medicine. **1901** *Westm. Gaz.* 16 May 2/1 The Zander Institute at Paris is the home of mechanotherapia, or cure by mechanical means.

‖**méchant** (meʃɑ̃), *a.* Also fem. **méchante** (meʃɑ̃t). [Fr. See also MESCHANT.] Malicious, spiteful, wayward, worthless, wicked.

1813 BYRON 26 Nov. in Moore *Lett. & Jrnls.* (1830) I. 453 She has much beauty,—just enough,—but is, I think, *méchante*. **1849** THACKERAY *Pendennis* xlvi, Mr. Pendennis was wicked, *méchant*, perfectly abominable. **1865** 'OUIDA' *Strathmore* I. ix. 145 That light, *méchante* voice that had mocked him from the mask.

mechant, variant of MESCHANT *Obs.*

mechanurgy (ˈmɛkənɜːdʒɪ). [As if ad. Gr. *μηχανουργία, f. μηχανο-, μηχανή machine + ἔργ-ον work.] That branch of mechanics which treats of moving machines.

1864 in WEBSTER; and in recent Dicts.

†**meˈchation.** *Obs. rare*⁻⁰. [ad. L. *mœchātiōn-em*, f. *mœchārī* to commit adultery, f. *mœchus*, a. Gr. μοιχός adulterer.] Adultery.

1656 BLOUNT *Glossogr.*, *Mechation*, fornication, Whoredom, strumpeting.

meche, obs. form of MATCH *sb.*¹, MUCH.

mechef, obs. form of MISCHIEF *sb.*

mechel, mecher, etc.: see MICKLE, MICHER.

mechient, variant of MESCHANT *Obs.*

mechil(l, obs. forms of MICKLE.

Mechitarist: see MEKHITARIST.

Mechlin (ˈmɛklɪn), *a.* and *sb.* Forms: 5 **meighlyn,** 7 **mecklen,** 8 **mechlen, mecklin, mechline, macklin,** 8– **mechlin.** [The name of a town in Belgium, used *attrib.* and *ellipt.*]

†1. ***Mechlin black***: a black cloth made at Mechlin.

1483 *Wardr. Acc.* in Grose *Antiq. Rep.* (1807) I. 61 ij pair of hosen made of..broode meighlyn blac.

2. In full ***Mechlin lace***: lace produced at Mechlin. †***Mechlin cravat***: a neckerchief made of Mechlin lace. ***Mechlin embroidery*** (see quot. 1882).

1699 *Lond. Gaz.* No. 3525/4 A Wastcoat and Holland Shift, both laced with Mecklen Lace. **1706** FARQUHAR *Recruiting Officer* III. i, Right Mechlin, by this light! Where did you get this Lace? **1714** GAY *Araminta*, The Silver Knot o'erlooks the Mechlen Lace. **1716** POPE *Basset-t.* 91 With eager beats his Mechlin Cravat moves. **1728** YOUNG *Love of Fame* v. (ed. 2) 105 Mecklin the queen of lace. **1728** SWIFT *Jrnl. Mod. Lady* Wks. 1751 VII. 192 Fresh Matter for a World of Chat, Right Indian this, right Macklin that. **1748** SMOLLETT *Rod. Rand.* xxxiv. (1760) I. 265 His shirt which was of the finest cambric, edged with right Mechline. **1865** MRS. PALLISER *Lace* 31 All the laces of Flanders, with the exception of those of Brussels and the point double, were known at this period [1665] under the general name of Mechlin. **1882** CAULFEILD & SAWARD *Dict. Needlework*, *Mechlin Embroidery*, a term applied to Mechlin Lace, as the thread that was inserted round the outlines of that lace gave it somewhat the look of Embroidery. *Ibid.*, *Mechlin Lace Wheel*,..formed with a number of Bars crossing each other, with a circle or wheel ornamented with Picots in the centre of the space. **1888** MISS BRADDON *Fatal Three* I. i, The flowing garment..was to be changed presently for white satin and old Mechlin lace.

†**mechloic** (miːˈkləʊɪk), *a. Chem. Obs.* [f. ME(CONIN) + CHLO(RINE) + -IC.] ***mechloic acid***: a crystallized acid produced by the action of chlorine gas on fused meconin.

1836 J. M. GULLY *Magendie's Formul.* (ed. 2) 35 Chlorine at the fusing point of meconine..transforms it into an acid, to which the name of mechloic has been given. **1838** T. THOMSON *Chem. Org. Bodies* 103 Mechloic Acid was discovered by M. Couerbe. **1839** *Penny Cycl.* XV. 50/2.

mechloˈrinic, *a.* = prec.

1890 [see MECONIN.]

mechoacan (mɛˈtʃəʊəkən). Also 6 **mechoicana,** 7 **mechoacham, mechacan, mechocan, mechoacauna,** (**mecoacan**), 7–9 **mechoachan.** [Called from the Mexican province *Mechoacan.* (Hence often written with capital M.)]

1. The root of a Mexican species of bindweed, *Ipomæa* (*Batatas*) *Jalapa*, formerly used in medicine as a purgative; also, the plant itself. Also called ***white mechoacan.***

1577 FRAMPTON *Joyfull Newes* 23 b, The *Mechoacan* is a Roote..brought from a countrie..called Mechoacan. **1594** BLUNDEVIL *Exerc.* v. xi. (1636) 555 The chiefe Merchandizes that come from Mexicana..are these, Gold, Silver,..the root Mechoicana. **1597** GERARDE *Herbal* II. cccviii. 723 That plant..called Mechoacan, or Bryonie of Mexico. *Ibid.*, The Bryonie, or Mechoacan of Peru groweth vp [etc.]. **1672** JOSSELYN *New-Eng. Rarities* 58 Briony of Peru..; some take it for Mechoacan. **1676** T. GLOVER in *Phil. Trans.* XI. 630 Here [Virginia] grow two Roots, which some Physicians judg, the one to be Turbith, the other Mechoacan. **1688** R. HOLME *Armoury* II. 95/2 Mechacan of Peru..groweth up like hops, by help of a pole. **1703** DAMPIER *Voy.* (1729) III. 453 Mechoacan. A Sort of blush-coloured Bindweed. **1741** *Compl. Fam.-Piece* I. i. 34 The Root of Mechoacan. **1768** W. LEWIS *Mat. Med.* (ed. 2) 375 Mechoacan scarcely yields one sixth part so much [resin] as jalap does. **1840** PEREIRA *Elem. Mat. Med.* II. 893 The roots of several others have been employed in medicine on account of their purgative properties; as the root called Mechoacan... Their use is now obsolete. **1856** MAYNE *Expos. Lex.*, *Mechoacanna*,..the plant mechoacan. **1872** SCHELE DE VERE *Americanisms* 410 Wild Potato Vine (*Convolvulus panduratus*), also known by its Indian name of Mechoachan, which grows in sandy soil all over the United States. **1890** *Syd. Soc. Lex.*, *Mechoacan, white*, same as *Mechoacan.*

2. With qualifying words, applied to various other plants of similar properties.

1890 *Syd. Soc. Lex.* s.v., *Black Mechoacan*, a synonym of Jalap. *Grey Mechoacan*, the root of *Myrabilis* [sic] *longiflora. Mechoacan of Canada*, the root of *Phytolacca decandra.*

†3. A purgative drug obtained from the roots of *Ipomæa* (*Batatas*) *Jalapa* and other plants. *Obs.*

1610 [see KERMES 1]. **1626** BACON *Sylva* §36 The Qualitie of the Medicine..is..of secret Malignity, and disagreement towards Mans Bodie..; As in Scammony, Mechoacham, Antimony, &c. **1681** tr. *Willis' Rem. Med. Wks.* Vocab., *Mechoacan*, a purging drug brought from the Indies. **1768** W. LEWIS *Mat. Med.* (ed. 2) 375 The dose of the mechoacan in substance is from one dram to two or more.

4. *attrib.*, as ***mechoacan root***; †**mechoacan-ale,** a drink medicated with mechoacan; **mechoacan jalap** (see JALAP 2).

1696 SALMON *Fam.-Dict.* 203 Spring and Fall purge with *Mecoacan-Ale. **1632** SHERWOOD *s.v.*, The (Indian) *Mechoacan root, *Rhamindique.* **1866** TREAS. BOT. 727/1 Mechoacan root. *Batatas Jalapa.*

mecistocephalic (mɪˌkɪstəʊsɪˈfælɪk), *a.* [f. Gr. μήκιστος longest + κεφαλή head.] Longest-headed: applied by Huxley to skulls with the highest cephalic index (69 and under).

1866 HUXLEY *Preh. Rem. Caithn.* 115 The large increase in the percentage of meco- and mecistocephalic skulls.

So ‖**mecistoˈcephali** (-aɪ), *sb. pl.* [mod. Latin], men with mecistocephalic skulls. **mecistoˈcephalous** *a.* = MECISTOCEPHALIC. **mecistoˈcephaly,** the condition or quality of being mecistocephalic.

1866 HUXLEY *Preh. Rem. Caithn.* 112 There is every stage from brachistocephaly to mecistocephaly to be met with between Switzerland and Scandinavia. **1878** BARTLEY tr. *Topinard's Anthrop.* II. ii. 238 In Mr. Huxley's system the terms themselves are altered. His mecistocephali are 69 and under. **1890** *Syd. Soc. Lex.*, *Mecistocephalous.*

meck (mɛk). [a. Du. *mik* forked stick.]

1867 SMYTH *Sailor's Word-bk.*, *Meck*, a notched staff in a whale-boat on which the harpoon rests.

Meckelian (meˈkiːlɪən), *a. Anat.* [f. *Meckel* + -IAN.] The designation of certain structures discovered by J. F. Meckel (1714–74), or his grandson J. F. Meckel (1781–1833). ***Meckelian arch, bar, cartilage, rod***: the cartilaginous rod or bar which is temporarily developed in the mandibular arch of the fœtus. ***Meckelian ganglion***, the spheno-palatine ganglion.

More commonly these structures are known as *Meckel's arch, cartilage, ganglion*, etc.

[**1836–9** *Todd's Cycl. Anat.* II. 285/1 The ganglion..has also received the title of *Meckel's ganglion.*] **1858** HUXLEY in *Proc. Roy. Soc.* IX. 397 The Meckelian cartilage. [**1864** *Quain's Anat.* (ed. 7) I. 66 The remaining part..is named Meckel's cartilage after its first describer.] **1890** *Syd. Soc. Lex.*, *Meckelian bar.* **1890** *Century Dict.*, *Meckelian ganglion, rod*, etc.

meckenynge, obs. form of MEEKENING.

Mecklin, obs. form of MECHLIN.

meclozine (ˈmɛkləzɪn, -iːn). *Pharm.* Also **meclizine.** [f. ME(THYL + C(H)LO(RINE *sb.* + PIPERA)ZINE.] A piperazine derivative, $C_{25}H_{27}N_2Cl$, which is an antihistamine drug used mainly as an anti-emetic, esp. in preventing motion-sickness, and is usu. given as the dihydrochloride, a white crystalline compound.

Meclozine is the name in the *British Pharmocopœia*, *meclizine* that in the *Pharmacopeia of the U.S.A.*

1955 *Jrnl. Pharmacol. & Exper. Therap.* CXV. 483 From a perceptual-motor viewpoint there would seem to be no valid reason why operating personnel could not take advantage of the beneficial effects which cyclizine, meclizine and promethazine have upon motion sickness. **1957** *Brit. Pharmaceut. Codex 1954* Suppl. 39 Meclozine hydrochloride has the properties of the anti-histamine drugs. **1959** *Which?* July 69/1 The 1 mg. of hyoscine protected over 80 per cent of the subjects from sea-sickness, and..this dose, for one hour, was significantly more effective than the cyclizine and meclozine. **1963** *Times* 27 May 18/4 (Advt.), The thalidomide tragedy did not directly affect your Company, but one of our most widely prescribed products, which contains meclozine, is for use in pregnancy sickness... Near the end of the year meclozine itself came under criticism. **1965** *New Scientist* 4 Nov. 328/2 Anti-histamines, containing meclizine, cyclizine and chlorcyclizine must now carry a strong warning label. **1971** J. J. BURNS in B. N. La Du et al. *Fund. Drug Metabolism & Drug Disposition* xvii. 361 Although large doses of chlorcyclizine and meclizine can induce malformations in

laboratory animals, no evidence of harm to the human fetus has been reported.

mecnesse, obs. form of MEEKNESS.

mecocephalic (ˌmiːkəʊsɪˈfælɪk), *a.* [f. Gr. μῆκος length + κεφαλή head.] = DOLICHOCEPHALIC.
1866 [see MECISTOCEPHALIC].

mecock(e, variant forms of MEACOCK *Obs.*

mecodont (ˈmiːkəʊdɒnt), *a.* [f. Gr. μῆκο-ς length + ὀδοντ-, ὀδούς tooth.] Having long teeth.
1875 HUXLEY in *Encycl. Brit.* I. 760/2 This 'mecodont' arrangement is strikingly exemplified by Salamandra maculosa.

mecography (miːˈkɒgrəfɪ). *rare.* [f. Gr. μῆκο-ς length + -GRAPHY.] †**a.** (See quot. 1603.) *Obs.* **b.** (See quot. 1890.)
1603 (*title*) *The Mecographie of ye Loadstone* [tr. Nautonnier *Mecographie de l'Eymant*], tat is to say ane Description of the lenthes or longitudes, quhikis ar fon be ye observations of ye loadstone. **1890** *Syd. Soc. Lex.*, *Mecography*, the graphic investigation of the dimensions and weight of the body.

mecometer (miːˈkɒmɪtə(r)). [f. Gr. μῆκο-ς length + -METER, after F. *mécomètre*.] An instrument for measuring length; *spec.* a graduated instrument for measuring the length of new-born infants, used at the Hospice de la Maternité, Paris.
1855 DUNGLISON *Med. Lex.* (ed. 12) *Mecometer.* **1867** DE MORGAN in *Athenæum* 19 Jan. 89 In fact, he did his very best to get larger 'mercy'. And he shall have it; and at a length which will content him, unless his mecometer be an insatiable apparatus.

†**meˈcometry.** *Obs. rare.* [f. Gr. μῆκος length + -METRY.] Measurement of length.
1570 DEE *Math. Pref.* a iij b, To be certified, either of the length, perimetry, or distance lineall: . . is called Mecometrie. **1618** M. BARET *Hippon.* xxxviii. 117 How can a man . . learne the knowledge of Mechometry, whereby lengths and distances are measured, if not [etc.].

meconate (ˈmiːkənət). *Chem.* Earlier meconiate. [f. MECON-IC + -ATE.] A salt of meconic acid.
1833 *Lond. & Edinb. Philos. Mag.* II. 156 These crystals are brownish, and consist of meconine, meconiates, and other substances. **1836** J. M. GULLY *Magendie's Formul.* (ed. 2) 38 To separate the meconate of lime. **1874** GARROD & BAXTER *Mat. Med.* (1880) 192 The meconate and lactate of morphia and codeia.

†**meˈconia.** *Chem. Obs.* [f. Gr. μήκων poppy + -IA.] = MECONIN.
1836 BRANDE *Chem.* (ed. 4) 1019 Meconia. This substance was discovered by Dublanc and Couerbe. *Ibid.* The quantity of meconia in opium is so small, that [etc.].

meconial (miːˈkəʊnɪəl), *a. Med.* [f. MECONIUM + -AL¹.] 'Pertaining to, or due to, meconium; as, meconial colic' (Webster *Suppl.* 1902).

meconiasin: see MECONISIN.

meconic (miːˈkɒnɪk), *a. Chem.* [f. Gr. μήκων poppy + -IC.] ***meconic acid***: a white crystalline acid obtained from opium. So ***meconic ether***.
1819 J. G. CHILDREN *Chem. Anal.* 277 Meconic acid is obtained from opium. **1865** WATTS *Dict. Chem.* III. 861 Meconic Ethers. **1884** BOWER & SCOTT *De Bary's Phaner.* 184 Morphin combined with meconic acid in opium.

meconidine (miːˈkɒnɪdɪn). *Chem.* Also -in. [f. Gr. μήκων poppy + -ID- + -INE⁵: cf. *quinidine.*] An amorphous alkaloid found in opium; discovered by Hesse in 1870.
1871 WATTS tr. *Gmelin's Handbk. Chem.* XVIII. 199 Meconidine . . . Contained in the aqueous extract of opium.

‖**meconidium** (miːkəʊˈnɪdɪəm). *pl.* -ia. [mod.L., as if ad. Gr. *μηκωνίδιον, dim. of μήκων poppy.
For the reason for the name see quot. 1871; the dim. termination was suggested by *gonidium, biastidium,* etc.]
One of the fixed medusoid buds produced by certain Hydroids, which contain the reproductive elements; a gonophore.
1849 ALLMAN in *Ann. Nat. Hist.* Ser. III. IV. 137 The extra-capsular medusiform sporosacs ('meconidia') of Laomedea. **1871** —— *Gymnobl. Hydroids* Introd. 16 Meconidium, peculiar sporosacs, somewhat resembling a poppy capsule in form. **1884** *Riverside Nat. Hist.* (1888) I. 85 The cavity of the blastostyle is directly continuous with a central cavity in this meconidium.

meconin (ˈmiːkənɪn). *Chem.* Also -ine. [ad. F. *méconine*, f. Gr. μήκων poppy: see -IN¹.] A white, crystalline, neutral compound existing in opium, regarded as an anhydride of meconic acid. Cf. MECONIA.
1833 *Lond. & Edin. Philos. Mag.* II. 156 Meconine was discovered in opium, by M. Couerbe in 1830. **1874** GARROD & BAXTER *Mat. Med.* 202 Meconine or Opianyl acts on man as a mild hypnotic. **1890** *Syd. Soc. Lex.*, *Meconin resin*, a resin which falls on the addition of water to the chlorine-holding fluid from which mechlorinic acid has been obtained.

meconioid (miːˈkəʊnɪɔɪd), *a. Med.* [f. MECONIUM + -OID.] Resembling, of the nature of, pertaining to, or obtained from meconium.
1856 in MAYNE *Expos. Lex.* s.v. *Meconioides.*

meconisin (miːˈkɒnɪsɪn). *Chem.* Also -iasin. [Arbitrarily varied from MECONIN.] (See quots.)
1887 BRUNTON *Pharmacol.* (ed. 3) §5. xxxi. 846 The neutral substances [in opium] are meconin and meconiasin. **1890** BILLINGS *Nat. Med. Dict.* II. 122 Meconisin $C_8H_{10}O_2$. A crystallizable neutral principle discovered in opium by T. and H. Smith (1878).

‖**meconium** (miːˈkəʊnɪəm). [L. *mēcōnium* (Pliny), a. Gr. μηκώνιον (in senses 1 and 2 below), f. μήκων poppy.]
†**1.** The inspissated juice of the poppy; opium.
1601 HOLLAND *Pliny* II. 68. **1681** tr. *Willis' Rem. Med. Wks.* Vocab., *Meconium*, the juice of the leaves and heads of poppy. **1783** JUSTAMOND tr. *Raynal's Hist. Indies* II. 147 The meconium, or common opium is prepared by pressing the poppy heads that have been already cut. **1804** *Med. Jrnl.* XII. 470 Meconium or poppies.—For excessive fluxes, and pains in the uterus.
2. The dark excrementitious substance in the large intestines of the fœtus; hence, the first fæces of a new-born infant.
1706 in PHILLIPS (ed. Kersey). **1732** ARBUTHNOT *Rules of Diet* in *Aliments*, etc. 404 All of them [*sc.* new-born Infants] have a Meconium, or sort of dark colour'd Excrement in the Bowels. **1899** CAGNEY tr. *Jaksch's Clin. Diagn.* (ed. 4) 244 The term 'meconium' is applied to the substance discharged from the rectum of the child immediately after birth.
3. *Ent.* The fæces of an insect just transformed from the pupa.
1789 *Trans. Soc. Arts* VII. 131 The elasticity of the silk, as the moths creep through, has the effect of pressing out a kind of red meconium. **1890** in *Century Dict.*
4. 'Applied to the black pigment of the choroid' (*Syd. Soc. Lex.* 1890).

meconology (miːkəˈnɒlədʒɪ). *rare*—⁰. [ad. mod.L. *meconologia*, f. Gr. μήκων poppy + -OLOGY.] A treatise on the poppy or opium.
[**1693** tr. *Blancard's Phys. Dict.* (ed. 2), *Meconologia*, a Description of Opium.] **1721** BAILEY, *Meconologia*, a Description or Treatise of Opium. **1856** MAYNE *Expos. Lex.*, *Meconologia*, . . meconology. [In recent Dicts.]

meconophagism (miːkəˈnɒfədʒɪz(ə)m). *Med.* [f. Gr. μηκων(ο)-, μήκων poppy + -φάγος that eats + -ISM.] Opium-eating. So **mecoˈnophagist**, an opium-eater.
1886 *Alien. & Neurol.* VII. 463 The death of the patient being attributed to causes which are supposed to be disconnected from the meconophagism. *Ibid.* 471 If they happen to find solace in opium readily, they become meconophagists. **1893** DUNGLISON *Med. Dict.* (ed. 21) *Meconophagism*, opium-eating.

‖**meconopsis** (miːkəˈnɒpsɪs). *Bot.* [mod.L., f. Gr. μήκων poppy + ὄψις appearance.] A genus of plants of the N.O. *Papaveraceæ*; also, a plant of this genus.
1836 LOUDON *Encycl. Plants* 462 Welsh Meconopsis. **1905** *Westm. Gaz.* 3 Jan. 9/1 The remarkable meconopsis recently sent from the Thibetan highlands.

†**mecop.** *Obs.* [a. Flem. *mekop*, f. **mēn* = MDu. *maan*, G. *mohn* poppy + *kop* head.] The poppy.
c **1481** CAXTON *Dialogues* 20/11 Oyle of mecop.

†**mecubalist.** *Obs.* [f. late Heb. *mequbbāl* what is received, pa. pple. of *qibbēl* to receive (whence CABBALA) + -IST.] ? One versed in Jewish traditions.
1653 R. SANDERS *Physiogn.* 202 By searching into the ancient Cabalists, Mecubalists, and Massorets, I find [etc.].

mecul(le, obs. forms of MICKLE.

Mec Vannin (mɛk ˈvænɪn). [Manx, lit. 'sons of (the Isle of) Man'.] Name of a Manx nationalist party.
1966 *Isle of Man Weekly Times* 7 Jan. 8/2 (*heading*) Mec Vannin. . . Manx Nationalists could not be fully convinced by the argument that . . the banks and the houses . . are still Manx . . even though their ownership and administration is increasingly passing out of native hands. *Ibid.* 8/3 The man who comes to open a shop, or a boarding-house or a factory, which will be run by himself in the Island, is a candidate for Mec Vannin. **1974** *Times* 8 Apr. 4/6 Mec Vannin . . intends to field candidates for all the Tynwald seats at the next general election.

med.¹, med (mɛd). (*a*) Abbrev. of MEDIC *sb.* or MEDICAL *sb.* 1; (*b*) abbrev. of MEDICAL *a.*; (*c*) abbrev. of MEDICINE *sb.*¹
(*a*) **1851** [see MEDIC *sb.*]. **1853** in Farmer & Henley *Slang* (1896) IV. 298/1 Take . . Sixteen interesting meds, With dirty hands and towzeled heads. **1899** A. H. QUINN *Pennsylvania Stories* 19 The Meds waited till the visitors were opposite them. **1942** [see (*b*) below].
(*b*) **1933** PARTRIDGE *Slang To-day & Yesterday* III. iii. 190 Of the 'plural' variety [of abbreviation] is *med. lab.*, medical laboratory. **1942** BERREY & VAN DEN BARK *Amer. Thes. Slang* §529/2 Doctor; physician, . . *med*, . . *med man*. *Ibid.* §529/5 Medical student, . . *med*. *Ibid.* §530/9 Medical college, . . *med college* or *school*. *Ibid.* §534/1 *Med business*, the medical profession. **1955** in *Amer. Speech* (1956) XXXI. 233 The law students began the boress by storming the Medical Building singing about the evils of the med students. **1974** *Spartanburg* (S. Carolina) *Herald* 18 Apr. A3/2 The lawmakers from Charleston County, site of the existing med school, are opposed to the move.
(*c*) **1942** BERREY & VAN DEN BARK *Amer. Thes. Slang* §531/8 Medicine; drugs, *dope*, *med*. *Ibid.* §831/22 *Courses of study*. . . Medicine, *med*. **1962** 'E. MCBAIN' *Like Love* (1964) xi. 158 A page out of a textbook, elementary stuff, we had this in first-year med. **1973** H. MCCLOY *Change of Heart* vii. 71, I want to study psychiatry when I get through med.

Med² (mɛd). Abbrev. of MEDITERRANEAN *sb.* 1. Also *attrib.*
1948 in PARTRIDGE *Dict. Forces' Slang*. **1955** G. FREEMAN *Liberty Man* I. i. 14 We went all round the Med., Istanbul, Capri, Gib. **1960** 'S. HARVESTER' *Chinese Hammer* ii. 26 He is off-course over the Med heading for Turkey. **1962** *Punch* 3 Oct. 486/1 Hoardings are turning Med-blue. **1971** *Guardian* 6 July 11/5 The summer cruise of the Med Fleet was a grand affair.

med, obs. form of MEAD, MEED.

medæwart, variant of MEADWORT.

medagle, medaglion, medaillon, obs. ff. MEDAL *sb.*, MEDALLION *sb.*

‖**médaillon** (medajɔ̃). [Fr., lit. = medallion.] A small, flat, round or oval-shaped cut of meat or fish.
1900 [see ESCALOPE]. **1921** W. J. LOCKE *Mountebank* xvi. 207 A *médaillon de veau périgourdine*, a superimposition of toast, *foie gras*, veal and truffles. **1964** L. JOYCE-COWEN *Million Menus* 90 a Lobster médaillons with Gruyère cheese soufflé topping. **1971** *Guardian* 4 June 11/4 Medaillons of Pork Tenderloin.

medal (ˈmɛdəl), *sb.* Forms: 6–7 **medaill(e, 7 medall, -ull, meddal(l, medaile, -el, 7– medal.** Also 7 **medagle,** *pl.* **-glies.** [a. F. *médaille* (15th c. in Hatz.-Darm.), ad. It. *medaglia* = OF. *meaille*, *maille* (see MAIL *sb.*⁴), Sp. *medalla*, Pg. *medalha*:—Com. Rom. **medallia*:—popular L. type **metallea*, f. *metallum* METAL *sb.* In early Rom. use the word meant a coin of minute value; cf. MAIL *sb.*⁴
The Rom. word passed into OHG. as *medilla*, rendering the Latin *as*; in MHG. *medile*, *medele* occurs for (the widow's) mite. Mod.G. has adopted the Fr. word as *medaille*; so also Du., Da. *medaille*, Sw. *medalj*.]
1. A metal disk bearing a figure or an inscription used as a charm or trinket.
a **1586** SIDNEY *Arcadia* III. (1598) 342 He gaue Dametas certaine Medailles of gold hee had long kept about him. **1611** SHAKS. *Wint. T.* I. ii. 307 He that weares her like her Medull, hanging About his neck. **1642** HOWELL *For. Trav.* (Arb.) 36 Lewis . . had . . an humour of his own, to weare in his hat a Medaille of Lead. **1674** BREVINT *Saul at Endor* 250 Any Meddal when rightly consecrated can do as much. **1922** JOYCE *Ulysses* 622 A pious medal he had that saved him. **1972** *Sci. Amer.* Feb. 57/2 (Advt.), Medals are recognized as a beautiful medium for artistic expression, as will be exemplified in this fine art series.
2. a. A piece of metal, usually in the form of a coin, struck or cast with an inscription, a head or effigy of a person, or other device or figure to commemorate a person, action, or event; also as a distinction awarded to a soldier, etc. for a heroic deed or other service rendered to a country, etc. In collectors' use, extended to include coins possessing artistic or historical interest.
1611 COTGR., *Manieur de sable*, a Moulder, or caster of Medalls, or prizes in sand. **1647** CLARENDON *Hist. Reb.* I. §119 He . . had a rare Collection of the most curious Medals. **1658** W. BURTON *Itin. Anton.* 142 The Coyns and medaglies of all the Emperours. **1709** STEELE *Tatler* No. 65 ¶2 Medals had been struck for our General's Behaviour. **1712** SWIFT *Let. Eng. Tongue* Wks. 1751 IV. 256 If any such persons were above Money, . . a Medal, or some mark of distinction, would do full as well. **1756–7** tr. *Keysler's Trav.* (1760) I. 285 The king had formerly a very valuable collection of medals. **1813** *Gen. Order* 7 Oct. in *Lond. Gaz.* 9 Oct., One Medal only shall be borne by each Officer. **1839** ALISON *Hist. Europe* (1849–50) VIII. liii. §50. 447 Two medals were unanimously voted to record the memorable acts of Bayonne. **1899** *Westm. Gaz.* 1 June 7/1 The members of the Mission will be decorated with commemoration medals.
b. As a reward for merit, or for proficiency, skill, or excellence in any art or subject. Freq. with a defining word indicating the degree of excellence attained, as in ***gold medal*** (see GOLD¹ 8 d), ***silver medal*** (see SILVER *sb.* and *a.* IV. 21), ***bronze medal***.
1751 BERKELEY *Let. to Archdall* 22 Nov., Wks. 1871 IV. 329 Gold medals for encouraging the study of Greek. **1839** *Jrnl. Geog. Soc.* IX. p. ix, The gold medals, awarded respectively to Dr Rüppell . . and Mr. Thomas Simpson. **1852** C. FOX *Let.* 29 Sept. in *Jrnls.* (1972) 207 They have not hesitated to give Anna Maria two bronze medals. **1892** *Field* 16 Apr. 573/2 After the match the Mayor . . presented the cup and medals to the winning team. **1904** *Athenæum* 24 Dec. 880/3 An engraved silver medal awarded by the Plymouth Independent Rangers . . for 'skill at arms'. **1908** T. A. COOK *Olympic Games* i. 16 For all these gold, silver, and bronze prize medals have been allotted. **1973** P. O'DONNELL *Silver Mistress* vii. 133 That may not be a hundred percent right, but do I get a bronze medal for trying?
†**3.** *fig.* **a.** in various uses: An image, representation (cf. MODEL *sb.*); something beyond the common run (as a medal compared with current coin). ***medals of creation***: a

rhetorical term applied to fossils, as commemorating events in the history of the globe (cf. quot. 1768 s.v. MEDALLIC).

a **1613** OVERBURY *Characters, Prison* Wks. (1856) 155 It [a prison] comes to be a perfect medall of the iron age, sithence nothing but gingling of keyes, rattling of shackles,..are here to be heard. **1653** H. MORE *Antid. Ath.* I. xi. (1712) 36 This little Meddal of God, the Soul of Man. **1656** *Artif. Handsom.* 129 Neither the wit nor tongue..can be a mint capable to coyne the least farthing sin, much less so large a piece and medaile as this man pretends to make of any helping our complexion. **1751** EARL ORRERY *Remarks Swift* (1752) 165 As their letters were not intended for the public, perhaps I was unreasonable in looking for medals, and not being contented with the common current species. **1804** PARKINSON *Org. Rem.* I. 7 The illustrious Bergmann elegantly describes fossils as the medals of creation. **1844** MANTELL (*title*) Medals of Creation.

b. Phrases. † ***the medal is reversing*** [cf. Fr. *la médaille est renversée*]: things or events are changing for the worse. ***the reverse of the medal***: the other side of the question.

1641 EVELYN *Diary* 28 June, The medaill was reversing, and our calamities were but yet in their infancy. **1690** *Dialogue betw. Francesco* &c., *Harl. Misc.* (Park) IX. 455 To show you the reverse of the medal. Is it not a pity that [etc.]. **1868** GRANT DUFF *Pol. Surv.* 195 Then for the reverse of the medal, you have Mr. Christie's *Notes on Brazilian Questions*.

4. *attrib.* and *Comb.*, as ***medal-casting, -hunter, -hunting, -inscription, -monger, -striker, -tract***; **medal chief** *U.S.*, an Indian chief who received a medal from the Colonial or U.S. authorities; **medal-cup**, 'a drinking vessel of metal, usually of silver, in which coins or medallions are incrusted and form a part of the decoration' (*Cent. Dict.* 1890); **medal-machine** (see quot.); **medal-play** *Golf*, play in which the score is reckoned by counting the number of strokes taken to complete a round by each side (*Cent. Dict.* 1890); **medal ribbon**, a ribbon of specific colours and design for attaching a particular medal or for wearing without a medal; **medal round** *Golf*, a round of medal-play; **medal-tankard** = *medal-cup* (*Cent. Dict.* 1890).

1847 LD. LINDSAY *Chr. Art* I. p. ccix, A complete classification should include artists..in *medal-casting, gem and seal-cutting [etc.]. **1772** D. TAITT *Let.* in N. D. Mereness *Trav. Amer. Colonies* (1916) 518 [Letter] To the Great and Small *medal chiefs. **1813** *Niles' Reg.* V. 270/2 At this moment a medal chief of the Choctaw nation is soliciting to be employed. *a* **1816** B. HAWKINS *Sk. Creek Country* (1848) 27 He is one of the great medal chiefs. **1893** *Brit. Jrnl. Photog.* XL. 795 The army of exhibition and *medal-hunters. **1902** L. S. AMERY etc. '*Times*' Hist. War II. 26 It [*sc.* fighting against inferior foes] conduces to ..*medal-hunting. **1658** SIR T. BROWNE *Hydriot.* i. (1736) 12 As testified by History and *Medal-Inscription yet extant. **1875** KNIGHT *Dict. Mech.* 1418/1 **Medal-machine*, a machine for making copies of medals and raised or sunk works on a scale larger or smaller than the original. **1764** FOOTE *Patron* I. (1781) 10 What, old Martin, the *medal-monger?.. Martin! why he likes no heads but upon coins. **1899** *Westm. Gaz.* 27 Sept. 4/3 In *medal play a player who drives from outside the teeing-ground is to be disqualified. **1909** *Westm. Gaz.* 4 Oct. 1/3 The *medal-ribbon which a soldier tore off his tunic. **1944** *R.A.F. Jrnl.* Aug. 286, I did not recognize his medal-ribbon, so asked what it was. **1971** *Daily Tel.* (Colour Suppl.) 16 July 5/3 The steward...looked too distinguished with his medal ribbons to be tipped. **1898** W. A. MORGAN '*House*' *on Sport* I. 180 It does not at all follow that the man who can play a match can also play a *medal round. **1909** *Westm. Gaz.* 27 Aug. 12/3 It was arranged to play a medal round in the forenoon. **1872** SYMONDS *Introd. Study Dante* 185 No *medal-striker ever made his outlines sharper or his shadows deeper. **1716** M. DAVIES *Athen. Brit.* III. 73 Great Brittain has produc'd the fewest of *Medal-Tracts and Numismatical Collectors.

medal ('mɛdəl), *v.* [f. MEDAL *sb.*] *trans.* To decorate or honour with a medal; to confer a medal upon as a mark of distinction.

1822 BYRON *Let. to Scott* 4 May, He was medalled. **1860** THACKERAY *Round. Papers, Nil nisi Bonum* (1899) 174 Irving went home medalled by the King. **1900** *Nation* (N.Y.) 4 Oct. 269/2 It would have been much more to the point, anyway, had he [Herr Menzel] exhibited and been medalled [at the Paris Exhibition] as illustrator.

medalet ('mɛdəlɪt). Also **medallet**. [f. MEDAL *sb.* + -ET[1].] A small or diminutive medal; also applied to small medals bearing the figures of saints, worn by Roman Catholics.

1789 PINKERTON *Ess. Medals* I. xiii. 227, I shall beg leave to give this class the appellation of medalets. **1799** J. CONDER (*title*), An Arrangement of Provincial Coins, Tokens, and Medalets. **1897** W. C. HAZLITT *Four Generations* II. 227 A medalet with the three sisters of Napoleon as the Three Graces.

medallary ('mɛdələrɪ). *rare*[−1]. [f. MEDAL *sb.* + -ARY[1].] A collection or set of medals.

1882 R. F. BURTON in *Athenæum* 28 Jan. 125/2 The medallary struck for the ter-centenary festival.

medalled ('mɛdəld), *ppl. a.* [f. MEDAL *v.* + -ED[1].] Adorned, furnished, or decorated with a medal. Of a picture, etc.: For which a medal has been awarded.

1857 EMERSON *May-day* (1867) 25 The high-school and medalled boy. **1889** *Pall Mall G.* 23 Oct. 1/3 There has been a good deal of ill-feeling..in regard to affixing to 'medalled' pictures the labels explanatory of the nature of the award. **1900** *Ch. Times* 2 Feb. 136/4, I communicated over seventy around a tent..this morning, from medalled general to private Atkins.

medallic (mɛ'dælɪk), *a.* [f. MEDAL *sb.* + -IC.]

1. Pertaining or relating to, characteristic of, or of the nature of a medal; represented on a medal.

1702 ADDISON *Dial. Medals* I. (1766) 13, I am afraid you will never be able, with all your Medallic eloquence, to [etc.]. **1768** A. CATCOTT *Treat. Deluge* 407 Neither do the fossil reliquiæ of plants and animals..yield in elegancy and exactness to medalic insignatures. **1778** PENNANT *Tour Wales* (1883) I. 17 In the library is a..numerous collection of books..which comprehend the medallic history. **1876** HUMPHREYS *Coin-coll. Man.* xxvi. 396 We have modern examples of medallic caricatures. **1885** *Athenæum* 1 Aug. 149/3 Recent productions of medallic art.

2. Resembling a medal.

1806 HARWOOD *Lichfield* 367 Small medallic tokens.. have been stamped. **1875** JEVONS *Money* vii. 63 Such medallic coins would become the most durable memorials.

medallically (mɛ'dælɪkəlɪ), *adv.* [f. MEDALLIC + -AL[1] + -LY[2].] By the evidence of medals.

1842 DE QUINCEY *Pagan Oracles* Wks. 1858 VIII. 180 Which..historically and medallically can be demonstrated to have availed [etc.].

medallion (mɪ'dæljən), *sb.* Also 7–8 meda(g)lion, 8 medaillon. [a. F. *médaillon*, ad. It. *medaglione*, augmentative of *medaglia* MEDAL *sb.*]

1. A large medal.

Erroneously explained in Blount *Glossogr.* 1661 as 'a little medal', after Cotgrave's erroneous rendering of *médaillon*.

1658 SIR T. BROWNE *Gard. Cyrus* ii. *Hydriot.* etc. 41 In this figure the sitting gods and goddesses are drawn in medalls and medallions. **1701** W. WOTTON *Hist. Rome* 253 Morellius produces a beautiful Medaglion of Commodus. **1799** G. SMITH *Laboratory* II. 13 The large sort, which are called medallions, are but seldom struck, except intended for particular presents. **1876** HUMPHREYS *Coin-coll. Man.* vi. 57 Of the finest epoch (of Syracusan coins) the celebrated and highly prized medallions, bearing the head of Ceres or Proserpine are the most remarkable.

2. Anything resembling this; applied to various objects resembling a large medal, in decorative work, as a tablet or panel usually of an oval or circular shape, bearing objects or figures in relief; a portrait; also a decorative design resembling a panel or tablet, as in a carpet, a window, or title-page of a book, etc.

1762–71 H. WALPOLE *Vertue's Anecd. Paint.* (1786) I. 277 A medallion of him in marble. **1768** BOSWELL *Corsica* (ed. 2) 373 Le Brun..has given this story as a medaillon on one of the compartments of the great gallery at Versailles. **1849** *Guardian* 7 Nov. 733/2 The tympanum..is filled with a.. window, and internally with two medallions. **1862** *Catal. Internat. Exhib.* II. xxx. 9 Circular incised group, on stone —a replica of one of the medallions for the pavement of Lichfield Cathedral.

3. *attrib*, and *Comb.*, as ***medallion figure, machine, portrait, size***; **medallion carpet**, a carpet containing a large prominent central design or figure (*Cent. Dict.* 1890); **medallion pattern**, 'a design for the ornamentation of a surface of which a medallion or medallions form an important part' (*Ibid.*); **medallion window** (see quot.).

1875 W. McILWRAITH *Guide Wigtownshire* 56 A circular *medallion figure. **1859** *Handbk. Turning* p. xxiii, The *medallion machine requires much labour and very expensive apparatus. **1902** ELIZ. L. BANKS *Newspaper Girl* 292 He gave me a *medallion portrait of himself. **1774** J. BRYANT *Mythol.* II. 231 [These coins] were of brass, and of the *medaglion size. **1847** C. WINSTON *Inq. Anc. Glass Paint.* I. 32 *Medallion windows..are principally filled with medallions, or panels, containing coloured pictures.

medallion (mɪ'dæljən), *v.* [f. MEDALLION *sb.*] *trans.* To ornament with medallions, or to make to resemble a medallion.

1861 NEALE *Notes Dalmatia* etc. 81 On the vertex of the arch is our Lord's monogram, also medallioned and surrounded by acanthus leaves. **1893** *Daily News* 7 Apr. 5/3 The invitation and the portraits [of an invitation card] are medallioned upon a coloured ground.

Hence **me'dallioned** *ppl. a.*

1888 *Athenæum* 21 Apr. 503/1 An elaborate medallioned title-page of birds, by Mr. J. G. Millais.

medallionist (mɪ'dæljənɪst). [f. MEDALLION *sb.* + -IST.] A worker of medallions.

1892 *Sat. Rev.* 15 Oct. 435/2 Mr. Woolner, R.A., a sculptor, especially a medallionist. **1894** J. M. GRAY *J. & W. Tassie* 60 *note*, James Tassie, the Glasgow Medallionist.

medallist ('mɛdəlɪst). Also **medalist**. [f. MEDAL *sb.* + -IST.]

1. One who is skilled or interested in medals.

1682 WHELER *Journ. Greece* III. 281 This is a Medal hath been valued much by the Medalists beyond the Seas. **1828** SCOTT *Jrnl.* (1890) II. 135 The General is a medallist, and entertains an opinion that the bonnet-piece of James V. is the work of some Scottish artist who died young.

2. An engraver, designer, or maker of medals.

1756–7 tr. *Keysler's Trav.* (1760) II. 149 The Pretender had a medal struck on this occasion, by Hamerani, the pope's medalist. **1849** MACAULAY *Hist. Eng.* vii. (ed. 5) II. 160 Sculptors, painters, and medallists exerted their utmost skill in the work of transmitting his features to posterity. **1851** in *Illustr. Lond. News* 5 Aug. (1854) 119/2 Medallist and medal-maker. **1885** *Athenæum* 14 Feb. 220 The medalists of the Renaissance.

3. A recipient of a medal awarded for merit. Also in parasynthetic derivatives as ***gold medallist***.

1797 *Cambr. Univ. Calendar* 214 List of Medallists from their first Institution to the present Time. **1864** *Q. Jrnl. Sci.* I. 211 The Gold Medallists of the Science and Art Department. **1898** RIDER HAGGARD *Dr. Therne* 9, I was gold medallist of my year. **1968** *Times* 18 Oct. 12/1 Tommie Smith, together with the bronze medallist, John Carlos, has made sporting history. **1973** M. MACKINTOSH *King & Two Queens* xvi. 220 Don't be a heroine. I didn't choose an Olympic gold medallist.

medallize ('mɛdəlaɪz), *v. rare.* [f. MEDAL *sb.* + -IZE.] *trans.* †**a.** To illustrate by reference to medals (*obs.*). **b.** To represent on a medal.

1716 M. DAVIES *Athen. Brit.* III. 75 The History of Julius Cæsar has been also Medaliz'd by Mr. l'Abbé de Camps. **1882** *Mag. Art* 221 Mr. Legros has also medallised Mr. Constantine Ionides, and medals of John Mill, Carlyle, and Robert Browning, are expected from him very shortly.

medallurgy ('mɛdəlɜːdʒɪ). Also **medalurgy**. [f. MEDAL *sb.* + *-urgy*, after METALLURGY.] The art of designing and striking or engraving medals.

1842 BRANDE *Dict. Sci.* etc., *Medallurgy*.., the art of making and striking medals and coins. [In recent Dicts.]

‖**medano** ('medano). [Sp. *médano*.] 'A hill of pure sand; a dune' (*Webster's Suppl.* 1902).

1851 BOLLAERT in *Jrnl. Geog. Soc.* XXI. 101 In these desert plains [of Peru] may be seen the 'Medanos', or moving semicircular sand-hills. **1897** *Geogr. Jrnl.* IX. 307 The barchanes, or, as we call them, medanos.

medarsa, var. MADRASAH.

medcin, -cyn(e, etc., obs. ff. MEDICINE, etc.

meddar, obs. form of MADDER *sb.*[2]

1689 FAREWELL *Irish Hudibras* 79 A Meddar..Which tho 'twas reckon'd but a small one, Contain'd Three halfs of a whole Gallon. *Ibid.* 82.

meddel(l, -er, obs. ff. MEDDLE, MEDLAR.

meddernex: see MEDRINACKS.

meddes, meddick, obs. ff. MIDST, MEDICK.

†'**meddle**, *sb. Obs. rare.* [f. MEDDLE *v.*] The action, or an act, of meddling or interfering.

1600 W. WATSON *Decacordon* (1602) 338 The priests found more fauour at the ciuill magistrates hands, than they [the Jesuits] could find, bicause they had cleered themselues of all state meddles. [**1864** EARL DERBY in Hansard *Parl. Deb.* Ser. III. CLXXIII. 28 The foreign policy of the noble Earl,..may be summed up in two short homely but expressive words—'meddle and muddle'.]

meddle ('mɛd(ə)l), *v.* Forms: 4–7 **medle**, 4–5 **medele**, 4–6 **medel**, 5–6 **medell**, **meddel**, **medyll(e**, **medul(l**, 5 **medill**, **medyl**, 6 **meddell**, **meddyl(l**, **middle**, *Sc.* **mydle**, 8 *Sc.* **midle**, 4– **meddle**. [a. OF. *medler*, *mesdler*, a variant (with euphonic insertion of *d* between *s* and a liquid: see the parallel instances cited under ISLE) of OF. *mesler* = Pr. *mesclar*, Sp. *mezclar*, It. *mescolare*, *meschiare*, *mischiare*:—popular L. **misculāre*, f. L. *miscēre* to mix. Cf. MELL *v.*]

†**1.** *trans.* To mix, mingle; to combine, blend, intersperse; *esp.* to mix (one thing) *with* (another), or (two or more things) *together*. Also const. *among*, *in*, *to*. *Obs.*

a **1325** *Prose Psalter* lxxiv. (lxxv.) 7 Grace ys in þe honde of our Lord ful of sharpenes medeled wyþ lyþenes. **1362** LANGL. *P. Pl.* A. x. 3 Of Erþe and Eir hit is mad I-medelet to-gedere. *c* **1375** ? HYLTON *Mixed Life* (MS. Vernon) in *Hampole's Wks.* (ed. Horstm.) I. 267 Thow schalt medle þe werkes of actif lyf wiþ gostly werkes of contemplatyf lyf, and þen dost þou wel. *c* **1385** CHAUCER *L.G.W.* 874 *Thisbe* (Fairf. MS.), And how she wepe of teres ful his wounde, How medeleth she his blood with her compleynte. *c* **1400** MAUNDEV. (1839) vii. 76 It is a Roche of white Colour, and a lytille medled with red. **1450–1530** *Myrr. our Ladye* 22 They are also blamefull that..medel other prayers, or other besynes with these holy houres. **1486** *Bk. St. Albans* B vj b, Medill the blode of the pecoke among the poudre. **1563** T. GALE *Antidot.* II. 86 He shall in his daylye drynke meddle three or foure droppes of the same. **1572** MASCALL *Plant. & Graff.* vii. 45 If ye do then meddle about eache tree of good fat earth or dung,..it shall be good. **1601** HOLLAND *Pliny* II. 438 Take the ashes of 3 frogs..meddle them with hony. **1627** BP. HALL *Heav. upon Earth* xi, Thy prosperity is idle and ill spent if it be not medled with such fore-casting.. thoughts. **1658** tr. *Porta's Nat. Magic* I. iii. 4 The Elements ..are all changed, every one of them being more or less medled with one another.

†**b.** To mix (wares) fraudulently. *Obs.*

1393 LANGL. *P. Pl.* C. VII. 260 Ich haue.. Meddled my marchaundise, and mad a good moustre; The werst lay with-ynne. **1463–4** *Rolls of Parlt.* V. 501/2 That noo persone ..medell, or put in or uppon the same Cloth,..eny Lambes wolle. *a* **1500** in Arnolde *Chron.* F iij b/1 Where as marchauntis haue vsed moche false pakyng of ther wood medlyng y[e] better w[t] y[e] worse. **1622** BP. ANDREWES *Serm.* (1629) 231 Thus doth he medle his chaffe; mold in his soure levin into Christ's *nova conspersio*.

†**c.** To prepare by mixing. *Obs.*

c **1374** CHAUCER *Boeth.* iv. pr. iv. 95 (Camb. MS.) Certes.. medleth to hire newe gestes drynkes..maked with enchauntmentz. **1382** WYCLIF *Rev.* xviii. 6 In the drinke that she medlide [Vulg. *miscuit*] to ȝou, menge ȝe double to hir.

†**2.** *intr.* for *refl.* Of things: To mingle, combine. Also *refl. Obs.*

c **1315** SHOREHAM *Poems* i. 760 [Þat sacrement] ne defiþ nauȝt, ase þy mete Wyþ þyne flesch medlyþ. *c* **1384** CHAUCER *H. Fame* III. 1012 We [*sc.* a lesing and a soth-sawe] wil medle us eche with other, That no man.. Shal han on (of) two, but bothe At ones. **1390** GOWER *Conf.* III. 138 Whan wordes medlen with the song, It doth plesance wel the more. **1610** SHAKS. *Temp.* I. ii. 22 More to know Did neuer medle with my thoughts.

†**3.** *trans.* To mix or mingle (persons) *with*, *among* (others) or *together*. Chiefly *pass.* Also *refl.* to mix oneself *in*, *among*. *Obs.*

c **1290** *St. Brandan* 281 in *S. Eng. Leg.* I. 227 In-to þe freytore he ladde heom þo: and sette heom wel heiȝe, I-medlede with heore owene couent. *c* **1330** R. BRUNNE *Chron. Wace* (Rolls) 13524 Kynge & prynces of Payen Were medled among Cristen. **1387** TREVISA *Higden* (Rolls) II. 149 Þere þey wonede long tyme afterwarde i-medled wiþ Britouns. *c* **1489** CAXTON *Sonnes of Aymon* i. 43 So medled theymself the one partye among the other. **1513** DOUGLAS *Æneis* I. vii. 127 Himself alsua, mydlit, persavit he, Amang princis of Grece. **1598** GRENEWEY *Tacitus Ann.* II. xviii. (1622) 59 By sorting and medling together the runnagates, the new and raw souldier lately taken [etc.]..he marshalled them in forme of a legion. **1600** HOLLAND *Livy* XXXVII. xxxix. 967 Thus you see all the forces that the Romanes had besides two thousand Thracians and Macedonians medled and blended together.

†**4.** *intr.* for *refl.* To mix or join in company; to mingle, associate *with*. *Obs.*

c **1375** ? HYLTON *Mixed Life* (MS. Vernon) in *Hampole's Wks.* (ed. Horstm.) I. 269 O tyme he [our Lorde] comuned & medled wiþ men. *a* **1425** *Cursor M.* 5690 (Trin.) Soone he meleded [*Cott* menged] hem amonge. **1463** *Bury Wills* (Camden) 38 Alle the persony s, man, woman, or chyld generally that ever I medlyd with. **1513** DOUGLAS *Æneis* IV. iii. 43, I affeir me les the fatis onstable..consent nocht, ne aggre, That [etc.] Or list appreif thai peplis all and summyng Togiddir middle, or jone in lige or band.

†**5.** To have sexual intercourse (*with*). Also *refl.*

1340–70 *Alisaunder* 964 Dame,.. Þou haste medled amis, methynk, by thy chere. **1377** LANGL. *P. Pl.* B. XI. 335 Bothe horse and houndes..Medled nouȝte wyth here makes þat with fole were. *c* **1400** *Destr. Troy* 10811 Wemen allone, Withouten mon, owther make, to medill hom with. **1573** L. LLOYD *Pilgr. Princes* 75 b, Their women [are] commen for all men at al tymes to medle [**1583** medle with]. **1655** FULLER *Ch. Hist.* VI. 315 Making her believe that..as ofte as they shold medle together, if she were..confessed by him,..she shold be cleere forgiven of God.

†**6.** To mingle in fight; to engage in conflict, to contend. *Obs.*

1340–70 *Alisaunder* 93 That hee ne myght with þo menne medle no while. **1377** LANGL. *P. Pl.* B. XII. 178 'Now I see', seyde lyf, 'þat surgerye ne Fisyke May nouȝte a myte auaille to medle aȝein elde'. **1470–85** MALORY *Arthur* IX. xxxv. 395 For and I had sene his black sheld I wold not haue medled with hym. *c* **1489** CAXTON *Sonnes of Aymon* iii. 100 Whan Alarde and Guycharde..saw that they myght not passe but that they muste medle they spored theyr horses. *a* **1533** LD. BERNERS *Gold. Bk. M. Aurel.* (1546) R v b, They medled so one with an other..that there was slaine .v. capitaynes. **1568** GRAFTON *Chron.* II. 242 But when the Normans sawe them recule back..some sayde they are afrayde to medle wyth vs. **1601** SHAKS. *Twel. N.* III. iv. 275 Therefore on, or strippe your sword starke naked: for meddle you must that's certain.

†**7.** *refl.* To concern or busy oneself. Const. *with*, *of*, *after*. *Obs.*

c **1350** *Will. Palerne* 2492 Many man by his miȝt medled him þer-after. **1377** LANGL. *P. Pl.* B. XII. 16 And þow medlest þe with makynges. **1426** LYDG. *De Guil. Pilgr.* 10845 Medle the ryht nouht Tarest pylgrymes by vyolence. **1442** *Rolls of Parlt.* V. 54/2 Some haven Shippes of here owne, and some medle hem of freight of Shippes. **1470–85** MALORY *Arthur* XX. viii. 809, I wyl not medle me therof. **1530** PALSGR. 634/1 You medyll you with maters that you have naught to do with. *a* **1553** UDALL *Royster D.* I. iii. (Arb.) 20 Nourse medle you with your spyndle. **1562** WINȜET *Wks.* (1888) I. 50, I wes almaist astoneist..that sa obscuir men durst presume to medle thame aganis all auctoritie.

8. *intr.* To concern or busy oneself, to deal *with*, †*of*; to interpose, take part *in*. Now always expressive of disapprobation, to concern oneself or take part interferingly.

1415 HOCCLEVE *To Sir J. Oldcastle* 137 Lete holy chirche medle of the doctryne Of Crystes lawes. *c* **1430** *Freemasonry* 220 Yn suche a case but hyt do falle, Ther schal no mason medul withalle. *c* **1483** CAXTON *Dialogues* 18/6 Ony ware Of whiche I medle with, Or that I haue under hande. **1526** TINDALE *1 Thess* iv. 11 We beseche you..that ye studdy to be quyet and to medle with your owne busynes. **1528** GARDINER in Pocock *Rec. Ref.* I. 123 It should be well done your grace meddled not as judge in the matter. **1545** in *Vicary's Anat.* (1888) App. xv. 288 The Bochers..haue..inhaunsed the prices of all kyndes of vytales that they medle withall & putt to sale. **1574** tr. *Littleton's Tenures* 107 A perpetual chauntry wherof the ordinary hathe nothinge to medle nor to do. **1622** R. HARRIS *Serm.* 8 Happie that State wherein the Cobler meddles with his last, the Tradesman with his shop. **1638** BAKER tr. *Balzac's Lett.* (vol. II) 154 He meddles in an infinite number of things with equal capacitie. **1694** RAY in *Lett. Lit. Men* (Camden) 200 The slender-bill'd [birds]..seldome meddle with dry seeds unlesse driven by hunger. **1774** FRANKLIN *Ess.* Wks. 1840 II. 401 It would be better if government meddled no farther with trade than to protect it. **1790** BURKE *Fr. Rev.* Sel. Wks. II. 13 Wholly unacquainted with the world in which they are so fond of meddling. **1818** CRUISE *Digest* (ed. 2) II. 462 It [the statute] does not meddle with wills. **1852** MRS. STOWE *Uncle Tom's C.* xvii. 161 Some evil persons..might be disposed to meddle with us if they saw our wagon. **1853** J. H. NEWMAN *Hist. Sk.* (1876) II. III. v. 328 His enemies accused him..of ..meddling in matters which did not belong to him. **1865** GROTE *Plato* I. ii. 95 Philosophers who meddled less with debate and more with facts.

b. without const.

1555 EDEN *Decades* 9 They shuld meddle no further than their commission. **1686** F. SPENCE tr. *Varillas' Ho. Medicis* 22 There are Connexions..in point of Traffick, which are only well known by those that meddle that way. **1711** SWIFT *Jrnl. to Stella* 28 Aug., I was advising him to use his interest to prevent any misunderstanding between our ministers; but he is too wise to meddle. **1859** MISS CARY *Country Life* (1876) 303 She had better attend her own affairs, and I will tell her so if she comes here meddling. **1860** EMERSON *Cond. Life* iii. (1861) 65 Do not legislate. Meddle, and you snap the sinews with your sumptuary laws.

c. Phrases and proverbial sayings. ***neither make nor meddle***, etc.: see MAKE *v.* 71.

1562 HEYWOOD *Prov.* II. iii. G, Who medleth in all thyng, maie shooe the goslyng. **1598** B. JONSON *Ev. Man in Hum.* III. ii, Nay, he will not meddle with his match, I warrant you. **1721** KELLY *Sc. Prov.* 200 It is ill medling between the Bark and the Rind. *Ibid.* 246 Meddle with your Match... You dare not meddle with your Match.

†**d.** *trans.* (with omission of preposition). To deal with; interfere with. *Obs. rare.*

1461 *Paston Lett.* II. 51, I der say I should have had as speciall and as gode a maister of you, as any pour man..yf ye had never medulled the godes of my maister F. **1523** in *10th Rep. Hist. MSS. Comm.* App. v. 400 No town dweller shall meddell nor interrupte nor occupie no mans occupacion or sience..but only his own sienc. **1573** [see 5].

Hence †**'meddled** *ppl. a.*, mixed.

c **1375** ? HYLTON *Mixed Life* (MS. Vernon) in *Hampole's Wks.* (ed. Horstm.) I. 268 To þise also longeþ þis medled lyf, þat is boþe actyf & contemplatyf. **14..** *Voc.* in Wr.-Wülcker 625/14 *Mixtilioque*, medylde corne. **1573** T. CARTWRIGHT *Repl. Answ. Whitgift* I. 131 A medled & mingled estate of the order of the gospell & the ceremonies of popery. *a* **1641** BP. MOUNTAGU *Acts & Mon.* (1642) 88 A medled company of all the Tribes of Israel. **1736** W. THOMPSON *Epithalamium* [An imitation of Spenser] xv. 1 And lo! what medled passions in him move.

meddle, obs. form of MEDLEY.

meddle-come. *dial.* One who comes meddling or interfering; a meddler.

1857 KINGSLEY *Two Y. Ago* xv, We'm old-fashioned folks here..and don't like no new-fangled meddlecomes.

meddlement ('mɛd(ə)lmənt). *nonce-wd.* [f. MEDDLE *v.* + -MENT.] Meddling, interference.

1842–3 THACKERAY *Fitzboodle's Prof* Misc. Wks. IV. 10 For once my sister in law was on my side, not liking the meddlement of the elder lady.

†**meddleous**, *a. Obs. rare.* In 5 medel(o)us. [f. MEDDLE *v.* + -OUS.] Meddlesome.

c **1430** *A.B.C. of Aristotle* in *Babees Bk.* 12 [Be not] To medelus, ne to myrie, but as mesure wole it meeue. *a* **1470** TIPTOFT *Tulle on Friendsh.* (Caxton 1481) B v b, And [it is] to peyneful to be medelous in other mennes maters [orig. *alienis nimis implicari*].

meddler ('mɛdlə(r)). [f. MEDDLE *v.* + -ER[1].] One who meddles, in the senses of the verb.

1388 WYCLIF *Bible, Pref. Ep.* vi, I holde my pees of gramariens, and of medelerïs of retorik. **1522** CLERK in Ellis *Orig. Lett.* Ser. III. I. 314 John Matheo, secretary vnto the said Cardinall, and chief medillar in all affaires her' aboute the Pope. **1571** GOLDING *Calvin on Ps.* iv. 5 They which erst were medlers with euerything, lerne to bee sober & quiet. **1612** T. TAYLOR *Comm. Titus* i. 6 (1619) 108 What if he will not speak the truth, because he will not be a meddler? **1730** SWIFT in *Portland Papers* VI. (Hist. MSS. Comm.) 28 He is distinguished as an unfortunate meddler in poetry. **1852** THACKERAY *Esmond* I. xiii, And this is the good meddlers get of interfering. **1895** C. R. B. BARRETT *Surrey* iv. 111 The unfortunate clerical meddler in politics.

meddler, obs. form of MEDLAR.

meddlesome ('mɛd(ə)lsəm), *a.* [f. MEDDLE *v.* + -SOME.] Given to meddling or interfering. ***Meddlesome Matty*** (or ***Mattie***): a nickname for a meddlesome person (allusively, from quot. 1814).

1615 G. SANDYS *Trav.* 238 A people..talkative, meddlesome, dissentious. **1743** BLAIR *Grave* I. 179 Honour! that meddlesome officious Ill, Pursues thee ev'n to Death. **1814** A. & J. TAYLOR *Orig. Poems* (ed. 11) II. 3 (*title*) Meddlesome Matty. [Not in 1805 ed.] **1861** PEARSON *Early & Mid. Ages Eng.* 141 The story is a fair instance of the meddlesome legislation of those times. **1874** GREEN *Short Hist.* viii. §5. 505 The Queen, frivolous and meddlesome as she was, detested him [Strafford]. **1889** W. S. PLAYFAIR *Midwifery* (ed. 7) II. III. ix. 4 The time-honoured maxim that 'meddlesome midwifery is bad'. [**1923** D. H. LAWRENCE *Kangaroo* xi. 230 Jaz is a meddlesome-Patty.] **1927** *Times* 17 Aug. 11/5 My warning was addressed to those who would make of the League 'a kind of international Meddlesome Matty'. **1938** A. G. MACDONELL *Autobiogr. of Cad* xxi. 259 Every reformer finds his obstructionists... In both cases Meddlesome Matties were to blame. **1960** D. HOLMAN-HUNT *My Grandmothers & I* iv. 92 Good gracious, child, what a meddlesome matty you are.

Hence **'meddlesomely** *adv.*, **'meddlesomeness**.

a **1677** BARROW *Serm.* Wks. 1716 I. 209 Meddlesomeness is commonly blameable. **1858** CARLYLE *Fredk. Gt.* x. iv. (1872) III. 246 A Hofkriegsrath..poking too meddlesomely into his affairs. **1875** JOWETT *Plato* (ed. 2) III. 325 A meddlesomeness, and interference, and rising up of a part against the whole of the soul.

meddling ('mɛdlɪŋ), *vbl. sb.* [f. MEDDLE *v.* + -ING[1]]

†**1.** The action or process of mixing, blending or combining, admixture; the state of being mixed or combined. *Obs.*

? *a* **1366** CHAUCER *Rom. Rose* 896 His garnement was..y-wrought with floures, By dyvers medling of coloures. *a* **1400** HYLTON *Scala Perf.* (W. de W. 1494) II. iv, For thenne shall the soule receyue..the full felynge of god in all myghtes of it, wythoute medelynge of ony other affeccyon. **1548–77** VICARY *Anat.* v. (1888) 50 The senewes..with the Lygamentes..in their medling together..are made a Corde or a Tendon.

†**b.** *quasi-concr.* The result of the action; a joining, combination, mixture. *Obs.*

1382 WYCLIF *Matt.* ix. 16 Sothely no man sendith ynne a medlynge of rudee, or newe, clothe in to an olde clothe. **14..** *Voc.* in Wr.-Wülcker 605/45 *Pula*, medlyng of water and wyne. **1482** *Monk of Evesham* (Arb.) 110 Trewly yn thys pele and rynging..a variant medelyng of melody sownyd wyth alle.

†**c.** Fraudulent mixing (of goods). *Obs.*

1495 *Act 11 Hen. VII*, c. 23 §1 It shuld be well and truly packed, that is to sey, the greate Salmon by it self without medeling of any Grilles..with the same.

†**2.** Of persons: The action of mingling together in a fight or brawl; also, an instance of this. *Obs.*

c **1450** *Merlin* xiii. 199 And than be-gan the meddelynge amonge hem full crewell and fell. **1481** CAXTON *Godeffroy* xix. 49 Yf they wold goo in peas without medlynges and oultrages. *a* **1533** LD. BERNERS *Gold. Bk. M. Aurel.* (1546) R v b, There was medlyng on bothe parties, the one to bear awaie, and the other to defend. **1616** T. DRAXE *Bibl. Scholast.* 128 It is no medling with short daggers.

†**3.** Sexual intercourse. *Obs.*

1388 WYCLIF *Gen.* xxx. 42 Whanne the late medlyng [1382 comyng togidere] and the laste conseyuyng weren. **14..** LYDG. *Life Our Lady* xx. v. (MS. Rawl. poet. 140, fol. 31), Eke serteyn briddes called vultures Wiþ oute medelinge [MS. Ashmol. 39 fol. 32 mellyng] conseyue by nature. **1450–1530** *Myrr our Ladye* 326 *Que sine*, whiche hathe begotte wythoute medlynge of man.

4. The action of taking part; dealing; management. Now only in bad sense: The action of taking part officiously in the affairs of others; interference. Const. *with*. Also, an instance of this.

c **1374** CHAUCER *Troylus* IV. 167 And seyn þat þorugh þi medlyng is y-blowe Yowre bothere loue, þere it was erst vnknowe. **1426** LYDG. *De Guil. Pilgr.* 3229 He ys nat wys, That in medlyng ys mor large Than the boundys of hys charge. **1536** *Act 28 Hen. VIII* in Bolton *Stat. Irel.* (1621) 179 Every such person and persons before any actual or reall possession or medling with the profites,..shall [etc.] *a* **1548** HALL *Chron., Hen. VIII* 150 He [the French king] thought ..yet again once to haue a medelyng in Italy. **1676** WISEMAN *Surg.* IV. iv. 286 But I, being at that time much indisposed in my health, declined the meddling with it [a Tumour] **1795** BURKE *Th. Scarcity* Wks. 1842 II. 257 This most momentous of all meddling on the part of authority; the meddling with the subsistence of the people. **1877** FROUDE *Short Stud.* (1883) IV. I. x. 112 [He] had been moved to volunteer..by another instance of Becket's dangerous meddling. **1884** *Athenæum* 29 Mar. 400/2 The limits of needless meddling with the text of Sophocles seemed to have been reached.

Proverb. **1539** TAVERNER *Erasm. Prov.* (1545) 57 In litle medlinge lyeth greate ease. **1546** J. HEYWOOD *Prov.* (1867) 47 For of little medlyng cometh great reste.

meddling ('mɛdlɪŋ), *ppl. a.* [f. MEDDLE *v.* + -ING[2].] That meddles, in the senses of the verb.

a **1529** SKELTON *Sp. Parrot* 63 To wyse is no vertue, to medlyng, to restless. **1530** PALSGR. 318/1 Medlynge, *entremetteux*. *c* **1586** C'TESS PEMBROKE *Ps.* CXXXI. i, Never.. have I borne in things to hygh A medling mind. **1629** EARLE *Microcosm.* (Arb.) 88 A medling man Is one that has nothing to do with his businesse, and yet no man busier then hee. **1634** MILTON *Comus* 846 And ill luck signes That the shrewd medling Elfe delights to make. **1798** WORDSW. *Tables Turned* 26 Our meddling intellect Misshapes the beauteous forms of things. **1830** MACAULAY *Ess., Southey* (1850) 112 A meddling government, a government which tells them what to read, and say, and eat, and drink, and wear. **1859** JEPHSON *Brittany* v. 57 That meddling personage Mrs. Grundy.

Hence **'meddlingly** *adv.*

1755 JOHNSON, *Pragmatically*, meddlingly; impertinently.

meddly, obs. form of MEDLEY.

meddowe, obs. form of MEADOW.

meddyl(l, obs. forms of MEDDLE.

Mede (miːd), *sb.* [ad. L. *Mēdus*, a. Gr. Μῆδος.]

1. A native or inhabitant of Media; = MEDIAN[2] B.

1382, etc. [see LAW *sb.*[1] 1 c]. *c* **1384**, [see ELAMITE *sb.* and *a.*]. **1568**, etc. [see PERSIAN *sb.*[1]]. **1632** LE GRYS tr. *Velleius Paterc.* 15 Pharnaces the Mede. **1930** J. D. DUFF tr. *Rostovtzeff's Hist. Anc. World* (ed. 2) viii. 123 The Iranian tribes of Medes and Mannai..grew stronger by degrees, and their pressure upon Assyria steadily increased. **1969** J. CONWAY tr. *Bengtson's Greeks & Persians* i. 5 Cyaxares the Mede seized the last, ephemeral Assyrian kingdom. *Ibid.*, Greek tradition mentions the Medes and the Assyrians in one breath.

†**2.** A precious stone described by ancient writers, said to be found in Media. *Obs.*

The description in the quot. is taken from Bartholom. Angl. *De Proprietatibus Rerum* XVI. lxvii.

1601 CHESTER *Love's Martyr* (1878), P, The Meade stone coloured like the grassie greene, Much gentle ease vnto the Goute hath donne, And helpeth those being troubled with the Spleene, Mingled with Womans milke bearing a Sonne.

†**mede**, *a. Obs. rare.* [ad. L. *medius*: see MEDIUM.] Middle, mean.

1706 A. BEDFORD *Temple Mus.* vi. 111 The Mede Voice is ..a great advantage to the Greeks. 1709 *Brit. Apollo* II. No. 68. 1/2 It's Mede Length contains..2280 Miles.

mede, obs. form of MAID, MEAD, MEED.

medeen, variant of MEDINE.

medel, obs. form of MEDDLE, MIDDLE.

medele, var. MELL *v. Obs.*; obs. f. MEDLEY.

medeler, obs. form of MEDLAR.

medell, obs. f. MEDAL, MEDDLE, MIDDLE.

medel(o)us, variant forms of MEDDLEOUS.

medely, obs. form of MEDLEY.

mederatele, variant of *meadrattle*, MEAD² c.

mederinax, medernex: see MEDRINACKS.

medersa, var. MADRASAH.

medevac (ˈmɛdɪvæk). *U.S.* Also **medivac.** [f. MED(ICAL *a.* + EVAC(UATION.] A military helicopter for transporting wounded soldiers to hospital. Hence **Medevac, Med-Evac** *v. trans.*, to transport by medevac.

1966 [see HELI-]. 1967 *Harper's Mag.* Jan. 77 The two wounded Aid Men continued to crawl about and administer care. There would be no medevac; there was no landing zone for it. 1969 *Time* 28 Nov. 23 At My Lai, Ridenhour reported, one soldier shot himself in the foot so that he would be Medevacked out of the area. 1973 *Washington Post* 13 Jan. A. 3/3 You look at an NLF (National Liberation Front) soldier who can't get Med-Evac'ed in 20 minutes. 1973 *Maclean's Mag.* July 17/3 While McCoy attended his patients, and the nurses and Thomas stood by, Logozar and Hartwell debated who would fly the medivac.

medew, obs. form of MEADOW.

†**medewax, medwex.** *Obs.* [f. *med.* (? = MEAD¹ or ²) + WAX *sb.*] Some kind of wax.

*c*1450 *ME. Med. Bk.* (Heinrich) 172 *note*, For to make a gomed cloth Tak half a quartron of mede wax, half a quarteron of terpentyn [etc.]. *Ibid.* 174 Entret pur bocches, biles..& huiusmodi. Tak of medwex I lī, of barowes grece ..as muche [etc.].

medewife, obs. form of MIDWIFE.

medewort, -wurt, -wyrt, var. ff. MEADWORT.

medful(l, medi, obs. ff. MEEDFUL, MEED *v.*

medi- (ˈmiːdɪ). *Zool.* = MEDIO-.

1903 *Amer. Anthropologist* V. 627 The meditemporal [fissure] consists of a segment in the cephalic region of the lobe, 6 cm. in length. *Ibid.* 631 The medifrontal [fissure] springs from the orbitofrontal.

‖**media¹** (ˈmiːdɪə). Pl. (in sense 1) **mediæ** (ˈmiːdiiː). [L., fem. of *medius* middle, used elliptically.]

1. *Phonetics.* [Applied by Priscian I. xxvi. (with ellipsis of *littera*) to *b, g, d* as intermediate in sound between the tenues (*leves*) and the aspirates.] A voiced or 'soft' mute; = MEDIAL *sb.* 2.

1841 LATHAM *Eng. Lang.* 103 The *Tenues* of the Classics ..are sharp, the *Mediæ* flat. 1848 E. GUEST in *Trans. Philol. Soc.* III. 176, 1st, the mediæ *b, g, d*,; 2ndly, the tenues *p, k, t*; and 3rdly, the aspirates. 1890 CONWAY in *Amer. Jrnl. Philol.* XI. 304 The invention of G to denote the voiced media as distinguished from C.

2. *Biol.* [Short for L. *tunica* or *membrana media.*] The middle tunic or membrane of an artery or vessel.

1876 tr. *H. von Ziemssen's Cycl. Med.* VI. 411 In many cases aneurism seems to be produced by a primary disease of the media. 1889 LEIDY *Anat.* (ed. 2) 580 The media is composed of transverse muscle-fibres with some elastic fibres.

media² (ˈmiːdɪə), *sb. pl.* [Pl. of MEDIUM *sb.*⁵, prob. after *mass media.*] Newspapers, radio, television, etc., collectively, as vehicles of mass communication. Freq. *attrib.* or as *adj.*

Also erron. as sing. in same sense.

1923 [see MASS MEDIUM]. 1927 *Amer. Speech* III. 26 It was finally decided to allot a definite media to each member. *Ibid.*, One of the best advertising medias in the middle west. 1929 E. O. HUGHES *Outl. Advertising* v. 82 The advertising *media* to which reference will be made..are newspapers, journals, magazines and such-like printed publications. 1958 *Times Lit. Suppl.* 5 Dec. 698/5 The media which appeal to our visually conscious age call for organizing ability as well as individual talent. 1962 M. MCLUHAN *Gutenberg Galaxy* 246 Is not the essence of education civil defence against media fall-out? 1966 K. AMIS in *New Statesman* 14 Jan. 51/3 The treatment of *media* as a singular noun..is spreading into the upper cultural strata. 1966 *Economist* 10 Dec. 1166/1 In any recession, media buyers, never a very adventurous lot, stay with the safest bets in any advertising medium. 1968 *Sun* (Baltimore) 4 July A16/3 Then there is 'media coordinator', that is, a tape recorder operator. 1969 T. PARSONS *Politics & Social Struct.* III. x. 250 Different media (or often the same media) carry qualitatively different content. 1971 *Daily Tel.* 4 Nov. 17/4 Decrees laid down in 1965 formally forbid direct contact between the [Dutch] Royal House and the publicity media. 1971 *Radio Times* 18 Nov. 82 The media have an ambiguous relationship with the radical left. 1972 *Guardian* 16 May 16/6 McGovern..occasionally stages a 'media event' which uses the unwitting people as props for TV news footage. 1972 *Times* 19 July 13/6 Miss Allen seems to be under the impression that the media is confined to newspapers. 1973 *Black World* Mar. 80 The theme of the poem deals with the white backlash, a media term describing the hostile reactions of white folks to civil-rights activities. 1973 'R. MACDONALD' *Sleeping Beauty* i. 9 'You from a media?' 'No, I'm just a citizen.' 1974 *Listener* 28 Feb. 260/1 The impartial experts and media-men. 1975 *Atlantic Monthly* Jan. 29/2 'Media' is itself a code name for a stereotype. *Ibid.*, Enemies of journalism..refer to the profession as the 'media' in disdain.

mediacy (ˈmiːdɪəsɪ). [In sense 1 prob. ad. L. *mediātio* MEDIATION, on the analogy of sbs. in -ACY (cf. OF. *mediatie*); in sense 2 f. MEDIATE *a.*: see -ACY.]

†**1.** The function of a mediator; mediation. *Obs.*

1400 *Prymer* in Maskell *Mon. Rit.* II. 34 Graunte us..that thurȝ hir deseruyngis and hir mediacie we be worthi to come to the hil that is crist.

2. *Logic* and *Philos.* Mediateness.

1853 SIR W. HAMILTON *Discuss.* (ed. 2) 663 Were there in these syllogisms no occult conversion of an undeclared consequent, no mediacy from the antecedent, they could not [etc.]. 1864 BOWEN *Logic* viii. 250 The mediacy being concealed by the concealment of the mental inference which really precedes. 1865 J. GROTE *Explor. Philos.* I. 119 How do presentation and representation thus viewed, stand related to the notions of mediacy and immediacy of knowledge?

mediad (ˈmiːdɪæd), *adv.* [f. MEDI-AL + *-ad* (see DEXTRAD).] Towards the middle line or plane (of a body); mesiad.

1878 BELL tr. *Gegenbaur's Comp. Anat.* §260 Two pairs of ..gills..an inner pair, which are placed mediad [etc.].

mediæval, medieval (mɛdɪˈiːvəl, miːdɪˈiːvəl), *a.* and *sb.* [f. L. *medius* middle + *ævum* age + -AL¹.]

A. *adj.* Of, pertaining to or characteristic of the Middle Ages. Of Art, Religion, etc.: Resembling or imitative of that of the Middle Ages.

1827 *Gentl. Mag.* XCVII. II. 490 The sculptured representations of the latter part of the mediæval æra. 1876 STUBBS *Early Plantag.* 6 Weapons drawn from the storehouse of medieval English history. 1879 SIR. G. G. SCOTT *Lect. Archit.* I. i. 7 Mediæval architecture..being the last link of the mighty chain which had stretched unbroken through nearly 4000 years.

b. ***mediæval embroidery***: a name given to a particular style of modern embroidery, worked with floss and purse silks and gold thread. ***mediæval guipure***: an earlier name for MACRAMÉ.

1882 in CAULFEILD & SAWARD *Dict. Needlework.*

B. *sb.* One who lived in the Middle Ages.

1856 RUSKIN *Mod. Painters* IV. xiii. §27 III. 193 The elements of their minds by which..they are connected with the mediævals and moderns. 1894 PARRY *Stud. Gt. Composers, Palestrina* 3 Though their music was so limited the mediævals contrived to make some fine effects with it.

mediævalism, medievalism (mɛdɪ-, miːdɪˈiːvəlɪz(ə)m). [f. prec. + -ISM.] The system of belief and practice characteristic of the Middle Ages; mediæval thought, religion, art, etc.; the adoption of or devotion to mediæval ideals or usages; *occas.* an instance of this.

1853 RUSKIN *Lect. Archit.* iv. (1854) 194 You have, then, the three periods: Classicalism, extending to the fall of the Roman empire; Mediævalism, extending from that fall to the close of the 15th century; and Modernism. 1873 SYMONDS *Grk. Poets* ix. 301 Renan regards the 'sentiment of the infinite' as the chief legacy of mediaevalism to modern civilization. 1886 *19th Cent.* May 665 It is a pity to have our language interlarded with Orientalisms and Mediævalisms. 1890 STUBBS *Primary Charge, Oxford* 55, I am sick of hearing about sacerdotalism and mediævalism from men who scarcely know how to spell the words.

mediævalist, medievalist (mɛdɪ-, miːdɪˈiːvəlɪst). [f. MEDIÆVAL + -IST. Cf. F. *médiéviste.*]

1. One who studies or is skilled in mediæval history or affairs; one who practises mediævalism in art, religion, etc.

1874 RUSKIN *Val D'Arno* (1886) App. 137 These outlines will..show my pupils what is the real virtue of mediæval work:—the power which we mediævalists rejoice in it for. 1874 L. STEPHEN *Hours in Library* (1892) I. vi. 232 He heartily despises the modern mediævalists.

¶**2.** One who lived in the Middle Ages.

1855 M. BRIDGES *Pop. Mod. Hist.* 445 Such observations ..would probably be made by any intelligent mediævalist, could he return to these sublunary scenes.

mediævalize, medievalize (mɛdɪ-, miːdɪˈiːvəlaɪz), *v.* [f. MEDIÆVAL + -IZE.] **a.** *trans.* To make mediæval in character. **b.** *intr.* To favour mediæval ideas or usages.

1854 J. L. PETIT *Archit. Stud. France* 173 He tries to mediævalize himself and his ideas. 1859 KINGSLEY *Let.* 23 Jan. in *Life* (1877) II. 77 Some illustrators..have tried to medievalize them [Bunyan's characters]. 1874 J. FERGUSSON in *Contemp. Rev.* Oct. 765 Views opposed to the Paganism of St. Paul's or to the attempt to mediævalize it.

Hence **mediˈævalized** *ppl. a.*; **mediˈævalizing** *vbl. sb.* and *ppl. a.*

1881 SYMONDS *Renaiss. Italy* IV. iv. 247 The 'Mort d'Arthur'..has become the plaything of medievalising folk in modern England. 1897 *Edin. Rev.* Jan. 76 The poet's [*sc.* Wm. Morris] mediævalised mind and turn of thought..are more in accordance with the mediæval character of the subject. 1900 J. L. DAVIES in W. E. Bowen *Crisis Eng. Ch.* Introd. 7 The mediævalising movement in the Church of England. *Ibid.* 12 If his whole soul is in the mediævalising of the Church of England.

mediævally, medievally (mɛdɪ-, miːdɪˈiːvəlɪ), *adv.* [f. MEDIÆVAL + -LY².] In a mediæval manner; in mediæval times; in accordance with mediævalism.

1882 *Century Mag.* XXIII. 654, I did not feel mediaevally inclined that night. 1883 SALA in *Illustr. Lond. News* 11 Aug. 131/1 The..Miracle Plays for which Coventry was medievally so renowned.

medial (ˈmiːdɪəl), *a.* and *sb.* [ad. late L. *mediālis*, f. *medius* middle: see MEDIUM. Cf. F. *médial.*]

A. *adj.*

1. a. Occupying a middle or intermediate position; middle; (of a letter, etc.) occurring in the middle of a word. ***medial to***: situated in the middle of; intermediate between.

1721 BAILEY, *Medial*, belonging to the middle. 1741 BOYSE *Patience* 235 Beneath the scorching of the medial line [i.e. the equator]. 1807 F. WRANGHAM *Serm. Transl. Script.* 14 This province may be regarded as medial to Persia, Tartary, Tibet. 1824 J. JOHNSON *Typogr.* II. xii. 309 The characters assume a different shape according to their situation, whether initial, medial, final, or single. 1829 COLERIDGE in *Lit. Rem.* (1839) IV. 28 The understanding is in all respects a medial and mediate faculty, and has therefore two extremities or poles, the sensual..and the intellectual. 1881 TYNDALL *Floating Matters Air* 228 In regard to the supply of oxygen, there is a medial zone favourable to the play of vitality, beyond which, on both sides, life cannot exist. 1902 *Encycl. Brit.* XXV. 360/2 A great extension of Medial plains, stretching in moderate altitude from the Arctic Ocean to the Gulf of Mexico.

b. *spec.* in *Anat., Zool.*, etc. (Cf. MEDIAN *a.*¹)

1803 BARCLAY *New Anat. Nomencl.* 7 What I should call the proximal, medial, and distal phalanges. 1846 DANA *Zooph.* (1848) 284 A continuous medial line of large polyps, with others smaller, scattered on each side. 1880 GÜNTHER *Fishes* 313 Medial and paired fins. 1899 *Allbutt's Syst. Med.* VII. 390 One set of these vessels, the medial, enters the medulla in the middle line.

2. Pertaining to a mathematical mean or average. ***medial line***: a line which is a mean proportional between two other lines; also ***medial area*** (see quot.).

1570 BILLINGSLEY *Euclid* X. xxiii, A right line commensurable to a mediall line, is also a mediall line. 1704 J. HARRIS *Lex. Techn.* I, *Alligation Medial*, teaches how to find a Mean in the Price, Quantity, or Quality between the Extreams. 1811 PINKERTON *Petral.* I. 345 According to a medial sum of many analyses. 1908 T. L. HEATH tr. *Euclid's Elements* III. x. 50 A medial straight line..is so called because it is a mean proportional between two rational straight lines commensurable in square only. *Ibid.* 55 It is in the Porism that we have the first mention of a medial area. It is the area which is equal to the square on a medial straight line.

3. Of average or ordinary dimensions; *occas.* of ordinary attainments.

1778 [W. MARSHALL] *Minutes Agric.* 18 Aug. an. 1775, The distance was medial—not half a mile. 1804 C. B. BROWN tr. *Volney's View Soil U.S.* 113 The general or medial temperature of a country. 1830 LYELL *Princ. Geol.* I. 185 The united waters have only..a medial width of about three quarters of a mile. 1894 *Harper's Mag.* Jan. 273/2 Exceptional qualifications..are lacking to the medial man.

4. *Mus.* **medial accent** (see quot. 1879). **medial cadence**, in the ecclesiastical modes, a cadence closing with the mediant of a mode (Grove *Dict. Mus.* 1880); in modern music, a cadence in which the leading chord is inverted. **medial consonances** (see quot. 1885).

1809 CALLCOTT *Mus. Gram.* (ed. 2) 221 When the leading Harmony of any Cadence is not radical, but inverted, the Cadence is, in this Work, termed Medial, and is used to express an incomplete Close. 1879 HELMORE *Plain Song* 105 The Medial Accent is the fall of a minor third from the dominant or reciting note. 1885 A. J. ELLIS tr. *Helmholtz' Sensations of Tone* 194 The major Sixth and the major Third, which may be called medial consonances.

†**5.** *Phonetics.* (See B. 2.) *Obs.*

1833 *Penny Cycl.* I. 379/2 The middle (or medial) letters, *g, d, b.*

B. *sb.*

1. A medial letter; a form of a letter used in the middle of a word.

1776 J. RICHARDSON *Arab. Gram.* 17 The initial of the first, a medial of the second, and the final of the third [letter] are generally taken. 1817 COLEBROOKE *Algebra*, etc. Dissert. p. xii, Diophantus employs the inverted medial of ἔλλειψις, defect or want..to indicate a negative quantity. He prefixes that mark *ψ* to the quantity in question.

†**2.** *Phonetics.* A voiced mute; = MEDIA 1. *Obs.*

1833 *Penny Cycl.* I. 380/2 The three medials, *β, γ, δ.* 1848 E. GUEST in *Trans. Philol. Soc.* III. 174 Three medials, as they are called *b, g, d.* 1880 EARLE *Philol. Eng. Tongue* (ed. 3) 5 If the Classical word begins with an aspirate, the English word begins with a medial.

medially ('miːdɪəlɪ), *adv.* [f. MEDIAL *a.* + -LY^2.] In a medial or central position.

1861 *Macm. Mag.* IV. 472/2 A tract..lying medially between the Atlantic and the Mississippi. **1883** *Athenæum* 29 Dec. 870/2 The peculiarity being the manner in which the solid part of the web was medially swung.

‖**mediamne.** *Obs. rare.* [ad. late L. *mediamna*, f. *medius* middle + *amnis* river.] An island in the middle of a river.

a **1552** LELAND *Itin.* II. 31 Diverse Armelettes breaking out of the 2 streames and making Mediamnes. *Ibid.* 41.

median ('miːdɪən), *a.*^{1} and *sb.*^{1} Also 6 **-ane.** [ad. L. *mediān-us* (cf. MEAN *a.*^{2}), f. *medius* middle: see -AN. Cf. F. *médian*, Sp., Pg., It. *mediano.*]

A. *adj.*

1. a. Occupying a middle or intermediate position; middle; †neutral.

1645 *Sacred Decretal* 11 Not knowing which way the Dice would fall, we kept ourselves in a direct Median Posture, that wee might be sure notwitstanding, which way soever it went. **1656** BLOUNT *Glossogr.*, *Median*, the middle, half, mean; not deserving praise or dispraise. **1771** *Antiq. Sarisb.* 13 The Gates and the median rampart. **1877** J. SULLY *Pessimism* 244 In the lower and median latitudes of our emotional life.

b. ***median strip***, a strip of ground, paved or landscaped, dividing a street or highway. *N. Amer.*

1954 J. C. INGRAHAM *Mod. Traffic Control* ii. 31 Choice of the type of median strip—solid concrete, grass and curbing or grass alone. **1967** *Boston Sunday Herald* 7 May 1/1 A fence erected on the median strip to discourage the road-crossings. *Ibid.*, The need for the closing of dangerous, life-taking crossovers in the median strip. **1968** *Globe & Mail* (Toronto) 3 Feb. 31/4 A street of exceptionally broad sidewalks and a median strip for trams. **1971** *Fremdsprachen* XV. 67/1 The city of Lawndale, Calif., recently installed nearly two miles of man-made turf on its traffic median strips.

2. Special scientific uses.

a. *Anat.*, as ***median artery, nerve, vein,*** now chiefly applied to certain structures in the arm; formerly in various other applications.

median line: any line in the median plane. **median plane**: the plane which divides any body into two equal and symmetrical parts; the mesial plane or meson.

1592 NASHE *Strange News* K 2 b, This I will proudly boast ..that the vaine which I haue (be it a median vaine, or a madde man) is of my owne begetting. **1597** A. M. tr. *Guillemeau's Fr. Chirurg.* 30 The fourth is the mediane, or kidneyevayne, situated belowe the foote. **1629** BP. HALL *Serm. to Lds. of Parlt.* 18 Feb., God and his divine phisician doe still let bloud in the median vein of the heart. **1831** R. KNOX *Cloquet's Anat.* 85 The last-mentioned suture, designated by the name of the Median or Frontal,..is generally indistinct. **1835–6** *Todd's Cycl. Anat.* I. 217/2 The median nerve. **1840** G. V. ELLIS *Anat.* 25 The anterior median fissure of the medulla spinalis.

b. *Zool.*, as ***median crest, fin, line*** (see a), etc.

1835–6 *Todd's Cycl. Anat.* I. 706/1 The median parts of the lobes of the mantle [in *Conchifera*] are extremely thin. **1840** *Cuvier's Anim. Kingd.* 197 The Great Tit..with a black median list down the belly. **1861** HULME tr. *Moquin-Tandon* II. III. ii. 112 The median line of the abdomen. **1894** R. B. SHARPE *Handbk. Birds Gt. Brit.* I. 35 The lesser and median wing-coverts white.

c. *Bot.*

[**1852** HENSLOW *Dict. Bot. Terms* 105 *Medianus*, when some part originates or is connected with the middle of some other.] **1884** BOWER & SCOTT *De Bary's Phaner.* 160 The median plane of the lens-shaped double cavity. **1900** JACKSON *Gloss. Bot. Terms*, *Median Line*, the central line of a bilateral organ, as the midrib of a symmetric leaf. *Ibid.*, *Median Wall*, in Archegoniates, the wall in a plane at right angles to the basal wall dividing the proëmbryo into lateral halves.

d. *Surg.* Of an incision: Made through the middle of a tumour. ***median lithotomy***: that method in which the incision is made through the median line of the perinæum (opposed to *lateral*).

1854 ALLARTON *Lithotomy Simplif.* 42 The spot selected for the incision in the median operation. **1863** —— *(title)* A Treatise on Modern Median Lithotomy. **1891** *Lancet* 18 Apr. 907/1 He makes a median incision over the tumour.

e. *Geography*, etc.

median line, the line along the middle of the calm belt between the north and south trade winds. ***median zone***, a zone along the sea-bottom between 50 and 100 fathoms in depth.

a **1854** E. FORBES *Nat. Hist. Europ. Seas* (1859) 100 The inhabitants of the median or coralline zone around the British shores. **1875** CROLL *Climate & Time* xiv. 229 During a glacial period in the northern hemisphere the median line between the trades would be shifted..south of the equator.

3. *Statistics.* **a.** Used to designate that quantity which is so related to the quantities occurring in a given set of instances that exactly as many of them exceed it as fall short of it. ***median dose***, a dose which is effective in half of those receiving it.

Thus, 6 is the median number of the set 1, 1, 2, 6, 20, 20, 27.

1882 F. GALTON in *Rep. Brit. Assoc. Adv. Sci. 1881* 245 The Median, in height, weight, or any other attribute, is the value which is exceeded by one-half of an infinitely large group, and which the other half falls short of. **1894** *Times* 19 Dec. 12/2 If graphically arranged, they would present a 'curve of error', the 'median ordinate' of which (to use a phrase familiar to the new school of statisticians) would yield a sentence far more satisfactory and just than many that are every week awarded. **1900** *Boston* (Mass.) *Transcript* Mar., The average age of the population of the United States..is twenty-five years; the median age is twenty-one years. The latter means the point at which there are as many people above as below. **1929** KELLEY & SHEN in C. Murchison *Found. Exper. Psychol.* 838 Some investigators have often preferred the median to the mean as a measure of central tendency. **1947** *Radiology* XLIX. 302/2 Most of the following data were obtained after median lethal and lower doses of radiation. **1973** *Daily Tel.* 30 Jan. 7/1 The Statistical Office report shows the median wage for Northamptonshire as £1,260.

b. (See quot.)

1901 *U.S. 12th Census Rep.* I. p. xxxvi, The median point is the point of intersection of the line dividing the population equally north and south with the line dividing it equally east and west.

B. *sb.*

1. *Anat.* The median vein, nerve, etc.

1541 R. COPLAND *Guydon's Quest. Chirurg.* M iij, Howe many and what veynes are to be let blode in the body?.. there be .xij amyd the armes that is to wyte two medyans, two cephalykes [etc.]. **1564–78** BULLEYN *Dial. agst. Pest.* (1888) 41 Fower vnces [of blood must be letten]..sometyme in the Median, sometyme in the Basilica. **1660** CULPEPPER *Two Treat.* (1672) 10 In Summer open still the Liver-vein, In Spring that of the Heart called Median. **1899** *Allbutt's Syst. Med.* VIII. 9 The simultaneous examination of the medians can only be made by crossing the hands.

†**2.** Something which is in an intermediate condition. *Obs.*

1635 PERSON *Varieties* I. v. 16 Fumes are medians betwixt fire and earth, in respect that they are easily transmuted or changed in the one or the other.

3. *Math.* A line drawn from a vertex of a triangle to the midpoint of the opposite side.

1883 *Encycl. Brit.* XVI. 15/1 If *a*, *b*, *c* be the three sides of a triangle, and α, β, γ the three medians, i.e., the lines drawn from the angles to the middle points of the opposite sides. **1888** [see COSYMMEDIAN]. **1888** HALL & STEVENS *Text-bk. Euclid* (1894) 105 The medians of a triangle are concurrent.

4. *Statistics.* A median quantity (see A. 3).

1902 F. Y. EDGEWORTH in *Encycl. Brit.* XXVIII. 287/1 The median (that point which has as many of the given observations above as below it).

Median ('miːdɪən), *a.*^{2} and *sb.*^{2} [f. *Media* + -AN, or MEDE *sb.* + -IAN.] **A.** *adj.* **a.** Of or belonging to the ancient kingdom of Media, or the Medes.

1601 HOLLAND *Pliny* XII. iii. 359 The Citron tree, called.. by some, the Median Apple-tree. **1685** BP. KEN in W. Hawkins *Life*, etc. (1713) 88 Either the Babylonian, or the Median, or the Persian Idolatries. **1839** *Penny Cycl.* XV. 54/2 Pharaortes..greatly extended the Median empire.

b. *allusively.* Unchanging. (Cf. *Dan.* vi. 8.)

1882 H. S. HOLLAND *Life & Logic* (1885) 2 A Median kingdom..whose laws..never know..change.

B. *sb.* **1.** An inhabitant of Media; a Mede.

1601 HOLLAND *Pliny* VI. xv. 122 Two cittles of the Parthians, built sometimes as forts opposite against the Medians. **1901** *Expositor* Nov. 344 Gobryas, the general of Cyrus, a Median, appeared before Sippara.

2. The language of ancient Media, a dialect related to Old Persian; = MEDIC *sb.*^{2}

1813 [see KURD]. **1841** R. G. LATHAM *Eng. Lang.* I. i. 3 The Ossetic, a language spoken by an insulated tribe of Mount Caucasus, and a supposed remnant of the Ancient Median, is Indo-European. **1848** *Trans. R. Irish Acad.* XXI. II. 241 In Median..sounds were sometimes confounded. *Ibid.* 244, I..observed some Median words transcribed in one of the inscriptions, and a few other words that, though altered, appeared to be of Persian or Median origin. **1908** T. G. TUCKER *Introd. Nat. Hist. Lang.* 189 It has, however, been argued strongly that the Avestic language is in reality Old Median. **1939** L. H. GRAY *Foundations of Lang.* 32 From the New Testament..we know that in the first century A.D. Parthian, Median, Elamite, Cappadocian, Pontic, Phrygian, Pamphylian, Cretic.., and Arabic were spoken. **1950** R. H. KENT *Old Persian* I. i. 6/2 Among the less known Old Iranian languages the most important was Median.

ˌmediaˈnimic, *a.* *Spiritualism.* [f. MEDI-UM + L. *anima* soul + -IC.] Pertaining to mediumship. So **ˌmediaˈnimity**, mediumship.

1876 ANNA BLACKWELL *Kardec's Medium's Bk.* 388–9.

medianly ('miːdɪənlɪ), *adv.* [f. MEDIAN *a.*^{1} + -LY^2] In a median direction or position.

1872 MIVART *Elem. Anat.* iii. (1873) 76 A large aperture medianly divided by a vertical partition. **1875** —— in *Encycl. Brit.* II. 151/1 The laryngeal sac [of the *Semnopithecinæ*] opens medianly into the front of the larynx.

mediant ('miːdɪənt), *sb.* *Mus.* [ad. It. *mediante*, repr. late L. *mediantem*, pr. pple. of *mediāre* to be in the middle, f. *medi-us* middle: see MEDIUM. Cf. F. *médiant.*] **a.** In ecclesiastical music: One of the 'regular modulations' of a mode; in the authentic modes, it lies about midway between the final and the dominant; in the plagal modes, it varies in position. **b.** In modern music, the third of any scale, lying midway between the tonic and the dominant.

[**1727–41** CHAMBERS *Cycl.* s.v. *Mode*, The fundamental [note] is also called the *final*; the fifth the *dominante*; and the third, as being between the other two, the *mediante*.] **1753** —— *Cycl. Supp.* s.v. *Mediante*, The Mediant of a mode is that note which is a third higher than the final; or that which divides the fifth of every authentic mode into two thirds. **1818** BUSBY *Gram. Mus.* 314 The Triad may have its mediant either two whole tones, or a tone and a semi-tone, above its Root.

attrib. **1880** STAINER *Composition* § 18 The seventh degree of the scale can be part either of the dominant or mediant chords. **1885** A. J. ELLIS tr. *Helmholtz' Sensations of Tone* 462 Modulation into the Mediant Duodene.

'mediant, *a.* *rare*$^{-1}$. [ad. late L. *mediant-em*, pr. pple. of *mediāre*: see prec.] Intervening.

1853 MISS SHEPPARD *Ch. Auchester* III. 150, I..set off on foot along the sun-glittering road..till through the mediant chaos of brick-fields..I entered the dense halo surrounding London.

mediastinal (miːdɪəˈstaɪnəl), *a.* *Anat.* [f. MEDIASTIN-UM + -AL^1.] Of or pertaining to a mediastinum, or partition, *esp.* that of the thorax.

1826 KIRBY & SP. *Entomol.* III. 376 *Neura Mediastina* (Mediastinal Nervure). **1831** R. KNOX *Cloquet's Anat.* 189 The mediastinal surface of the sternum. **1835–6** *Todd's Cycl. Anat.* I. 193/2 The posterior mediastinal arteries are numerous and small. **1899** *Allbutt's Syst. Med.* VI. 64 Mediastinal diseases.

†**mediastine**^{1}. *Obs.* Also 7 -in. [Anglicized form of MEDIASTINUM. Cf. F. *médiastin.*] = MEDIASTINUM.

1631 WIDDOWES *Nat. Philos.* 60 The lesse principall parts of breathing, are the midriffe, and the mediastin. **1653** URQUHART *Rabelais* I. xxvii, He did transpierce him, by running him in at the breast, through the mediastine and the heart. **1732** ARBUTHNOT *Rules of Diet* in *Aliments*, etc. 339 There is none of the Membranes..but may be the Seat of this Disease, the Mediastine as well as the Pleura.

†**mediastine**^{2}. *Obs.* *rare*$^{-1}$. Also -in. [ad. L. *mediastīn-us*.] 'A drudge, or kitchin slave' (Phillips 1658); also quasi-*adj.*

1716 M. DAVIES *Athen. Brit.* II. 139 A certain mediastin Genius, porcupin'd all over with all the three.

‖**mediastinitis** (miːdɪæstɪˈnaɪtɪs). *Path.* [mod.L., f. MEDIASTIN-UM + -ITIS.] Inflammation of the areolar tissue around the organs of the mediastinum.

1858 COPLAND *Dict. Pract. Med.* II. 825 The Causes of mediastinitis are chiefly external injuries. **1898** *Allbutt's Syst. Med.* V. 783 These exo-pericardial adhesions..may possibly result from a mediastinitis.

‖**mediastino-** (miːdɪəˈstaɪnəʊ). Used as the combining form of MEDIASTINUM. **mediastino-callous** *a.*, descriptive epithet of 'the form in which the pericardium becomes thickened' (*Syd. Soc. Lex.* 1890). **mediastino-pericardial** *a.*, pertaining to the mediastinum and the pericardium. **mediastino-pericarditis**, inflammation affecting both these structures.

1876 tr. *H. von Ziemssen's Cycl. Med.* VI. 649 Indurated mediastino-pericarditis. **1897** *Allbutt's Syst. Med.* III. 45 Cases of mediastino-pericardial fibrosis.

‖**mediastinum** (ˌmiːdɪəˈstaɪnəm). *Anat.* Pl. **-a.** [mod.L., neut. of med.L. *mediastinus*, medial, intermediate, f. *medius* middle, after the classical L. *mediastīnus* (also *mediastrīnus*) sb., inferior servant, drudge.] A membranous middle septum or partition between two cavities of the body; *esp.* that formed by the two inner walls of the pleura, separating the right and left lungs.

anterior mediastinum: the part of the mediastinum extending from the pericardium to the sternum. ***middle m.***: 'the enlarged central portion of the whole space between the pleuræ' (Syd. Soc. Lex.). ***posterior m.***: the portion of the mediastinum between the pericardium and the lower dorsal vertebræ. ***superior m.***: the space between the manubrium of the sternum and the upper dorsal vertebræ.

In medical Latin the name is used, with qualifications, to denote certain other structures to which its etymological meaning is appropriate; as ***mediastinum auris***, the membrane of the drum of the ear; ***m. cerebri***, ***m. cerebelli***, synonyms of *falx cerebri* and *cerebelli* (see FALX); ***m. testis***, Sir Astley Cooper's name for the septum of the testicle (*Corpus Highmori*).

1541 R. COPLAND *Guydon's Quest. Chirurg.* H j, With the mediastinum wherwith it [the hert] is steyed and strengthed. **1615** CROOKE *Body of Man* 360 The Pericardium toucheth not the Lunges but by the interposition of the Mediastinum. **1797** M. BAILLIE *Morb. Anat.* (1807) p. xxv, The Posterior Mediastinum. **1878** T. BRYANT *Pract. Surg.* I. 49 Pericarditis or suppurative inflammation of the mediastinum.

mediate ('miːdɪət), *a.* Also 6 *Sc.* **mediat.** [ad. late L. *mediāt-us*, pa. pple. of *mediāre*: see MEDIATE *v.* Cf. F. *médiat.*]

1. a. Intermediate; intervening or interposed in position, rank, quality, time, or order of succession. Now *rare*.

1432–50 tr. *Higden* (Rolls) II. 179 The membres inferialle supporte and do seruyce, the meane other membres mediate [of the body], receyve, and refunde. **1547** *Reg. Privy Council Scot.* I. 78 The mediat air that is to succeid to the persoun that happynnis to deceis. **1655** FULLER *Ch. Hist.* VIII. iii. Ded., I may wish you and yours less mediate trouble then he had in the course of his Life. *a* **1661** —— *Worthies, Suffolk* (1662) II. 59 After many mediate preferments..at last he became Arch-bishop of Canterbury. **1707** PRIOR *Charity* 49 But soon the mediate clouds shall be dispell'd. **1829** [see MEDIAL *a.* 1]. **1840** *Cuvier's Anim. Kingd.* 169 The Marsh-eagles hold a sort of mediate station between the Ernes, the Ospreys, and the Buzzards. **1857–8** SEARS *Athan.* III. ii. 262 There are three conditions after death, heaven and hell, and a state mediate between them.

†**b.** Of a person: Intermediary. *Obs.*

1571–2 *Reg. Privy Council Scot.* II. 121 Na maner of persoun..sall pay or procure to be payit of thair awin substance or be mediat personis. **1582–8** *Hist. James VI* (1804) 290 Quhen he sawe sick apparand disgrace, he trauellit be some mediat persouns to mak satisfactioun. **1604** EDMONDS *Observ. Cæsar's Comm.* 63 These [the Tribunes and Centurions] were mediate officers between the Generall and them [the soldiers]. **1655** in *Proc. Soc. Antiq. Scot.* XXX. (1896) 18 The saids goods ar to be put in a mediate man's hands, who sall be answerable for them. **1660** R. COKE *Power & Subj.* 193 It will not follow that the Bishop is the Kings mediate officer in all things and cases which relate to his Episcopal function and jurisdiction.

c. Serving as a means to an end. †Also, conducive, serviceable. *Obs.*

1502 ATKYNSON tr. *De Imitatione* II. xii. 195 He exorted his disciples..to take the crosse as the moost medyate meane to folowe hym. **1741** WARBURTON *Div. Legat.* II. 634 The..supposition of a mediate and an ultimate religion. **1845** THORPE *Lappenberg's Hist. Eng.* Introd. 53 A temple of Diana was mediate to the faith of so many people.

d. *nonce-use.* That is in the middle of his course. In quot. *absol.*

1839 BAILEY *Festus* xxviii. (1852) 474 Death divine alone can perfect both, The mediate and initiate.

2. Acting or related through an intermediate person or thing; opposed to *immediate*.

a. *Feudal Law.* Said of a superior and of a tenant or vassal, when the latter holds of the former not directly but through a mesne lord. Also applied to the relation between the two parties, as in ***mediate holding***, ***sovereignty***, ***tenure***.

1454 *Rolls of Parlt.* V. 272/2 To paye..their rentes and dewtees to their Lordis mediates and immediates. **1529** MORE *Suppl. Soulys* Wks. 333/2 Yᵉ king or any other Lorde mediate or immediate, that [etc.]. **1601** R. JOHNSON *Kingd. & Commw.* 84 As touching his mediat soueraigntie. **1614** SELDEN *Titles Hon.* 229 To be free from either a mediat, or immediat Tenure of him. **1818** HALLAM *Mid. Ages* (1841) I. v. 452 Those which had depended upon mediate lords became immediately connected with the empire. **1845** STEPHEN *Comm. Laws Eng.* (1874) I. 186 The holding might also be mediate, that is, in the way of subinfeudation.

fig. **1839** POE *Island of Fay* Wks. 1864 I. 361 [A planet] whose mediate sovereign is the sun.

b. *gen.* Of a person or thing in relation to another: Connected with the correlate not directly but through some other person or thing.

Now *rare*; many expressions formerly common (e.g. *mediate cause*) are now avoided as ambiguous, the adj. being liable to be taken in the directly opposite sense 1.

1626 BACON *Sylva* §400 The Immediate Cause of Death, is the Resolution or Extinguishment of the Spirits; And..the Destruction or Corruption of the Organs is but the Mediate Cause. **1655** FULLER *Ch. Hist.* III. ii. §69 Stephen Langton, his [*sc.* Becket's] mediate successor, removed his body [etc.]. **1718** *Wodrow Corr.* (1843) II. 370 Our sponsors are what I cannot away with, when parents, mediate or immediate, can be had. **1752** HUME *Ess. & Treat.* (1777) II. 109 Nor is it possible to explain distinctly how the Deity can be the mediate cause of all the actions of men.

c. Of an action, relation, or effect: Involving or dependent on some intermediate agency or action. Also *Psychol.* (See quot. 1897.)

mediate inference (Logic): an inference arrived at through a middle term. ***mediate knowledge*** (Philos.): knowledge which is not the direct result of intuition, but is obtained by means of inference or testimony.

1588 J. HARVEY *Disc. Probl.* 36 Either by Mediate apparance, and reuelation of some vision; or by Imediate..illumination from God. **1641** H. AINSWORTH *Orth. Found. Relig.* 18 Mediate creation is the making of things of some former matter. **1642** WOTTON *Life & D. Buckingham* 13 The most..pressing care of a new and Vigorous King was his marriage, for mediate establishment of the Royall lyne. **1646** P. BULKELEY *Gospel Covt.* III. 231 This mediate witnesse of the spirit..is not to be harkened unto, untill the immediate witnesse hath spoken. **1704** NORRIS *Ideal World* II. iii. 145 Perception is either immediate or mediate... Mediate, as when we perceive how they [Ideas] are related to each by comparing them both to a third. **1790** PALEY *Horæ Paul.* i. 3 Although..the agreement in these writings be mediate and secondary. **1817** COLERIDGE *Biog. Lit.* xii. I. 264 All truth is either mediate,..derived from some other truth..or immediate and original. **1836–7** SIR W. HAMILTON *Metaph.* (1859) I. 218 What is called mediate knowledge. **1842** ABP. THOMSON *Laws Th.* §83 (1860) 146 This is mediate inference. **1868** M. PATTISON *Academ. Org.* v. 224 The principle of mediate election is not commonly practised in this country. **1888** BRYCE *Amer. Commw.* II. xl. 83 They are all copies, some immediate, some mediate, of ancient English institutions. **1897** C. H. JUDD tr. *Wundt's Outl. Psychol.* iii. 239 'Mediate recognition'..consists in the recognition of an object, not through its own attributes, but through some accompanying mark or other. **1912** *Amer. Jrnl. Psychol.* Jan. 106 The cases of true mediate association found in these experiments.

d. *Law.* Of evidence: Directed to the establishment of some intermediate fact which is to serve as a ground of argument for the fact to be proved.

1848 WHARTON *Law Lex.*, *Mediate testimony*, secondary evidence.

e. Med. ***mediate auscultation***: auscultation performed with the interposition of some object (as a stethoscope) between the body and the ear. ***mediate percussion*** (see quot. 1843).

R. T. H. Laennec's *De l'Auscultation Médiate* appeared in 1819, and P. A. Piorry's *De la Percussion Médiate* in 1828.

1821 J. FORBES tr. *Laennec's Dis. Chest*, etc. (1834) 27 The signs afforded by mediate auscultation in the diseases of the lungs. **1843** SIR T. WATSON *Princ. & Pract. Physic* xlvii. II. 10 More recently mediate percussion has been introduced..by M. Piorry. In mediate percussion, some solid substance is placed upon the spot, the resonance of which is about to be explored, and the blow is made upon that substance, which is called a pleximeter. **1870** S. GEE *Auscult. & Percuss.* I. iv. 62 Auenbrugger's glove was obviously an approach to that mediate percussion which was first systematically practised by Piorry.

†**3.** ? Conciliated, propitious. *Obs. rare*⁻¹.

14.. *Why I can't be a Nun* 98 in *E.E.P.* (1862) 140 Lord to my mornyng be mediate.

mediate ('mi:dɪeɪt), *v.* [f. late L. *mediāt-*, ppl. stem of *mediāre* (used in various senses derived independently from the etymology: to divide in the middle, halve; to transact as an intermediary; to occupy a middle position; etc.), f. *medi-us* middle: see MEDIUM. Cf. obs. F. *médier*.

In English the verb is of late emergence, and may have originated by back-formation from *mediation* and *mediator*.]

†**1.** *trans.* To divide into two equal parts. *Obs.*

1542 RECORDE *Gr. Artes* H vj b, If you wold mediat or diuid into 2, this sum. **1610** W. FOLKINGHAM *Art of Survey* II. vi. 57 The Diameter that mediates the Arch of each Sector is the Meridian.

2. a. *intr.* To occupy an intermediate or middle place or position; to be between; usually, to form a connecting link or a transitional stage between one thing and another.

1642 R. CARPENTER *Experience* v. xix. 322 There mediates no reall tie betwixt you and me, but the worne and old tie of old Acquaintance. **1644** DIGBY *Nat. Bodies* iii. §7. 21 By theire being crowded together, they exclude all other bodies that before did mediate betweene the litle parts of theire maine body. **1646** H. LAWRENCE *Comm. Angells* 72 Betweene the temptation of the Divell and sin there ever mediates, or goes betweene, cogitation, or thought, in which the temptation properly and formally lyes. **1850** MRS. BROWNING *Poems* II. 388 No twilight in the gateway To mediate 'twixt the two. **1862** STANLEY *Jew. Ch.* (1877) I. xviii. 343 To mediate between the old and the new..is the mission of institutions like ours. **1872** E. TUCKERMAN *Gen. Lichenum* 11 Evernia vulpina must be admitted to mediate, ..in an important detail of thalline structure, between the other northern species and *Usnea*.

†**b.** To take a moderate position; to avoid extremes. *Obs. rare.*

1612 WEBSTER *White Devil* I. i, The law doth somtimes mediate, thinkes it good Not euer to steepe violent sinnes in blood.

3. To act as a mediator or intermediary; to intercede, or intervene for the purpose of reconciling.

1616 BULLOKAR *Eng. Expos.*, *Mediate*, to deale betweene two, to make meanes of agreement, as an indifferent party to both. **1618** EARL OF SUFFOLK in *Fortescue Papers* (Camden) 75, I must fly to you as to my pryncipall advocate to medyate to his Majestie for my coming to hys presence. *c* **1620** CAMDEN in *Lett. Lit. Men* (Camden) 124 Yff you will mediate with my L. Burghley for the Loane of Chrisostomes Greeke Copie. **1635** PAGITT *Christianogr.* I. ii. (1636) 58 Interpreters to mediate between the people and the Governour. **1712** SWIFT *Jrnl. to Stella* 24 Dec., I have been ..mediating between the Hamilton family and Lord Abercorn, to have them compound with him. **1837** MACAULAY *Ess.*, *Bacon* (1899) 363 Bacon attempted to mediate between his friend [the Earl of Essex] and the Queen. **1861** M. PATTISON *Ess.* (1889) I. 43 In vain Cabinets endeavoured to mediate. **1892** M. DODS *Gosp. John* II. xiv. 209 He [the Holy Spirit] was to mediate and maintain communication between the absent Lord and themselves.

4. a. *trans.* 'To effect by mediation' (J.); to bring about (a peace, treaty, etc.) by acting as mediator; to procure by intercession.

c **1592** MARLOWE *Jew of Malta* v. iv, Let me go to Turkey, In person there to mediate your peace. **1600** E. BLOUNT tr. *Conestaggio* 139 To mediate with the King a suspension of armes. **1617** MORYSON *Itin.* II. 79 Beseeching him to use his power, in mediating licence unto him, that he might come over for a short time to kisse the Queenes hand. **1718** *Freethinker* No. 15 The Friends, on both sides, thought, they might mediate a Peace with as much Ease as a Truce. **1754** HUME *Hist. Eng.* I. vi. 142 Anselm..mediated an accommodation between them. **1838** PRESCOTT *Ferd. & Is.* II. xiii, It is singular that the last act of his political life should have been to mediate a peace between the dominions of two monarchs who had united to strip him of his own.

†**b.** To intercede on behalf of. *Obs.*

1621 FLETCHER *Pilgrim* I. ii, In your prayers..mediate my poor fortunes.

c. To settle (a dispute) by mediation. †Also, ? to mitigate (an evil) by mediation. *Obs.*

1568 T. NORTH tr. *Gueuara's Diall Pr.* IV. 99 The miseries wee suffer..haue for the most part proceeded from our parents, and afterwards by our frends haue been mediated and redressed. **1623–4** MIDDLETON & ROWLEY *Sp. Gipsy* II. ii, No friends Could mediate their discords. **1856** KANE *Arct. Expl.* II. xxii. 222 His companions indulged in a family conflict..which was only mediated, after much effort.

5. To be the intermediary or medium concerned in bringing about (a result) or conveying (a gift, etc.); *passive*, to be communicated or imparted mediately. Spec. in *Psychol.*, to bring about (a result) by acting as a mediating agency between an idea, intention, etc., and its realization; to act as such a mediator.

1630 LORD *Banians* Introd., Who, to give this undertaking [the book] the better promotion, interested himselfe in the worke, by mediating my acquaintance with the Bramanes. **1644** DIGBY *Nat. Bodies* xxv. §1. 227 An immediate working of God..without conuenient and ordinary instruments to mediate and effect this configuration. **1846** G. S. FABER *Lett. Tractar. Secess.* 224 Moses..mediated an inferior covenant between God and the Israelites. **1856** R. A. VAUGHAN *Mystics* (1860) II. VIII. vi. 67 Ten years after the first manifestation he believed himself the recipient of a second, not, like the former, mediated by anything external. **1861** GOSCHEN *For. Exch.* 18 A country which, like England, mediates the transactions of many others. **1903** J. CONN *Fulness of Time*, etc. vi. 77 Everything we know of Him who is the Light of the World has been mediated to us through men. **1931** G. STERN *Meaning & Change of Meaning* xiv. 388 The comprehension of *Buchmacher* was mediated by the English word. **1942** COFER & FOLEY in *Psychol. Rev.* XLIX. 522 Behavioral generalization in children was found to be mediated by verbal responses. **1957** B. F. SKINNER in Saporta & Bastian *Psycholinguistics* (1961) 67/2 Instead of going to a drinking fountain, a thirsty man may simply 'ask for a glass of water'... The consequences of such behavior are mediated by a train of events no less physical or inevitable than direct mechanical action. **1958** B. BERNSTEIN in J. A. Fishman *Readings Sociol. of Lang.* (1968) 227 The working-class child has to translate and thus *mediate* middle-class language structure through the logically simpler language structure of his own class to make it personally meaningful. **1968** M. BUNGE in Lakatos & Musgrave *Probl. Philos. Sci.* 128 [A] theory that takes the risk of hypothesizing something mediating between inputs and outputs. **1971** SUTHERLAND & MACKINTOSH *Mechanisms Animal Discrimination Learning* I. ii. 5 The behaviorists in general have denied the existence of the process of selective attention in animals except where the process could be mediated by overt orientation responses. **1972** *Jrnl. Social Psychol.* LXXXVII. 129 Of particular interest to the present investigators was the extraction of the dimensions actually used by individuals in mediating similarity. **1974** *Nature* 1 Mar. 73/1 Cholera enterotoxin mediates specific biochemical events in both intestinal and non-intestinal tissues by stimulating adenyl cyclase and cyclic AMP. **1974** *Author* Summer 89/2 People wanted direct, authentic communication that had not been mediated by sub-editors or script writers. The tape recorder made this new authenticity possible.

mediated ('mi:dɪeɪtɪd), *ppl. a.* [f. prec. + -ED¹.] Interposed, intervening. Also *Psychol.*, arrived at by mediation; involving mediation (MEDIATION 3 b).

1832 AUSTIN *Jurispr.* (1879) II. 926 The right or duty is not created or divested by a law without the intervention of a fact distinct from the law itself but is really created or divested by a law through a mediated or intervening fact. **1942** COFER & FOLEY in *Psychol. Rev.* XLIX. 514 A theoretical analysis of mediated generalization as a specific conditioned response phenomenon. **1950** KELLER & SCHOENFELD *Princ. Psychol.* v. 161 (*caption*) Mediated generalization in the conditioning of the galvanic skin response to verbal stimuli. **1971** A. PAIVIO *Imagery & Verbal Processes* ix. 319 Mediated transfer studies generally involve the learning of two or more lists.

mediately ('mi:dɪətlɪ), *adv.* [f. MEDIATE *a.* + -LY².] In a mediate way: opposed to *immediately*.

1. By the intervention of an intermediary or medium; (in feudal law) through a mesne lord; through a medium or mediator, or by a means; by indirect agency, or by mediation, in indirect connexion; indirectly.

1526 *Pilgr. Perf.* (W. de W. 1531) 125 Whether it be immediatly of yᵉ holy goost, or els mediatly, as by yᵉ mynistracyon of some good aungell. **1550** LATIMER *Last Serm. bef. Edw. VI* (1584) 107 She [*sc.* the woman] is not immediately under God, but mediately. **1596** BACON *Max. & Use Com. Law* II. (1635) 30 All lands are holden of the crowne either mediately or immediately. **1604** E. G[RIMSTONE] *D'Acosta's Hist. Indies* VI. iv. 439 For if they signifie things mediately they are no more letters nor writings, but ciphers and pictures. *a* **1661** FULLER *Worthies, Worc.* (1662) II. 174, I confess he might be mediatly of Welch extraction, but born in this County. *a* **1703** BURKITT *On N.T.* Matt. v. 8 They shall see him spiritually and mediately in this life: gloriously and immediately in the life to come. **1823** J. MARSHALL *Const. Opin.* (1839) 276 Persons who claimed immediately from the crown, or mediately, through its grantees or deputies. **1855** SIR W. HAMILTON *Metaph.* App. (1859) II. 520 Something different from the realities externally existing, through which, however, they are mediately represented. **1874** SULLY *Sensation & Intuition* 45 We compare the sensations mediately, by means of the average strength of either class. **1889** PATER *G. de Latour* (1896) 50 He derived his impressions of things not directly from them, but mediately from other people's impressions about them.

2. With a person or thing intervening in time, space, order, or succession.

1620 T. GRANGER *Div. Logike* 223* Here the particle (not) is mediately prefixed before (perisheth). **1794** MORSE *Amer. Geog.* 139 Running waters, when turbid, will deposit, first, the coarsest and heaviest particles, mediately, those of the several intermediate degrees of fineness, and ultimately.. the most light. **1818** CRUISE *Digest* (ed. 2) IV. 370 An estate is limited, either mediately or immediately, to his heirs in fee, or in tail. **1890** *Sat. Rev.* 13 Sept. 326/2 A day spent.. mediately in pursuit of sport, it may be immediately in mountain-climbing.

mediateness ('mi:dɪətnɪs). [f. MEDIATE *a.* + -NESS.] The quality of being mediate.

1704 NORRIS *Ideal World* II. iii. 146 The..mediateness of our conception. **1860** WORCESTER (cites *Bannister*).

‖**mediateur.** ? *Obs.* [F. *médiateur* 'sorte de jeu de quadrille' (Littré): etymologically = MEDIATOR. Cf. Sp. *mediator*, according to the *Dicc. de la Academia* a name for ombre.] A term in a variety of the game of quadrille: see quot. 1830.

1797 *Encycl. Brit.* (ed. 3) XV. 732/2 A king is the mediateur, which is demanded of the others by one of the

players, who has a hand he expects to make five tricks of; and through the assistance of this king he can play alone and make six tricks. *Ibid.* 733/1 A fish extraordinary is given to him who plays the mediateur, and to him who plays sans prendre. **1830** 'EIDRAH TREBOR' *Hoyle made Familiar* 38 (*Quadrille*) In order to vary this game, some introduce the *Mediateur* or *Roy Rendu*, which is a king demanded of the others by one of the players, who having a hand by which he expects to make five tricks, can, with the assistance of this king, get six, and so plays alone, or sans appeller.

mediating ('mi:dɪeɪtɪŋ), *ppl. a.* [f. MEDIATE *v.* + -ING².] That mediates.

1. Of opinions and their advocates: Tending to mediate between extremes.

a **1729** J. ROGERS 19 *Serm.* (1735) 309 That Corruption of Manners we lament in the World, we shall find..owing to some mediating Schemes, that offer to comprehend the different Interests of Sin and Religion. **1885** *Athenæum* 4 July 10/3 Dr. Salmon, being no mediating scholar, accepts the last twelve verses of St. Mark's Gospel.

2. a. Acting as a mediator.

1749 FIELDING *Tom Jones* VII. iii, Regard to my family hath made me take upon myself to be the mediating power. **1817** *Parl. Deb.* 1351 A mediating party between the zealous friends of the practice and the public. **1866** LIDDON *Bampt. Lect.* vi. (1875) 306 St. Paul dwells often and earnestly upon our Lord's mediating Humanity.

b. *Psychol.* Interposing between an idea, intention, etc., and its result; acting as a mediator (sense 6).

1953 C. E. OSGOOD *Method & Theory Exper. Psychol.* III. ix. 401 Certain stimulus patterns..are variably associated with systems of mediating reactions. **1963** W. W. GRINGS in M. H. Marx *Theories Contemp. Psychol.* xxxi. 517 The lack of a clear-cut basis for deducing the nature of the mediating response. **1966** W. N. RUNQUIST in J. B. Sidowski *Exper. Methods Psychol.* 503/2 A common mediating association ('army-ocean', mediated by 'navy'). **1968** K. DUNCKER in Wason & Johnson-Laird *Thinking & Reasoning* ii. 34 The final form of a solution is typically attained by way of mediating phases of the process. **1971** SUTHERLAND & MACKINTOSH *Mechanisms of Animal Discrimination Learning* IX. ii. 309 The nature of the 'mediating processes' possibly available to children but not to animals.

Hence '**mediatingly** *adv.*

1841 *Blackw. Mag.* XLIX. 466 To go mediatingly.. between others.

mediation (mi:dɪ'eɪʃən). Forms: 4–5 **mediacioun**, 4–6 **-cion**, 5 **medyacyoun**, 5–6 **-cion**, 6 **medea-**, **mediacyon**, **mediatioun**, 5– **mediation**. [a. OF. *mediacion* (mod.F. *médiation*), ad. late L. *mediātiōn-em* (*c* 500 in Quicherat), n. of action f. *mediāre*: see MEDIATE *v.* Cf. Sp. *mediacion*, Pg. *mediação*, It. *mediazione*]

†**1. a.** Division by two; division into two equal parts; halving, bisection. *Obs.*

c **1425** *Craft Nombrynge* (E.E.T.S.) 14 Mediacion is a takyng out of halfe a nombre out of a holle nombre. **1542** RECORDE *Gr. Artes* H vj, Mediation..is nothyng els but deuidyng by 2. **1674** JEAKE *Arith.* (1696) 33 To take the half of any Number called Mediation, Bipartition, or Division by 2. **1727** BAILEY vol. II, *Mediation* (in *Geom.*) with respect to lines, is called bissection or bipartition.

†**b.** *Mus.* [= med.L. *mediatio octavæ.*] The division of the octave at the arithmetical or harmonic mean. *Obs.*

1597 MORLEY *Introd. Mus.* Annot., The fourth may be set in the eight, either aboue the fift, which is the harmonicall diuision or mediation (as they tearme it) of the eight, or vnder the fift, which is the Arithmeticall mediation.

†**c.** Astron. ***mediation of heaven*** [med.L. *mediatio cæli*]: the southing of a heavenly body.

1426 LYDG. *De Guil. Pilgr.* 16668 The loode sterre, which off his nature abydeth ffyx in hys spere, and neuere draweth ffor to declyn by medyacion. **1633** H. GELLIBRAND in *T. James' Voy.* R iij, At the instant of the Moones Culmination or Mediation of Heauen.

2. Agency or action as a mediator; the action of mediating between parties at variance; intercession on behalf of another.

c **1386** CHAUCER *Man of Law's T.* 136 By the popes mediacion..They been acorded. **1431** in *Eng. Gilds* (1870) 280 If these men so chosen, with good mediacion of the alderman, mowe not brynge hem to acorde. **1447** BOKENHAM *Seyntys* (Roxb.) Introd., Be the blyssyd medyacyoun Of this virgyne. **1572** *Reg. Privy Council Scot.* II. 134 Be freindlie mediatioun and laubouris. **1662** *Bk. Com. Prayer* Prayer High Crt. Parl., These and all other necessaries..we humbly beg in the Name and mediation of Jesus Christ. **1667** MILTON *P.L.* III. 226 All mankind Must have bin lost,..had not the Son of God,..His dearest mediation thus renewd. **1788** GIBBON *Decl. & F.* xlv. IV. 462 As a Christian bishop, he [Gregory] preferred the salutary offices of peace; his mediation appeased the tumult of arms. **1844** THIRLWALL *Greece* lxiii. VIII. 243 Envoys.. had been sent to offer their mediation for the purpose of terminating the war.

attrib. **1857** M. PATTISON *Ess.* (1889) II. 241 The Mediation-Theology itself does not shrink from engaging the Christological problem.

3. a. Agency as an intermediary; the state or fact of serving as an intermediate agent, a means of action, or a medium of transmission; instrumentality.

c **1391** CHAUCER *Astrol.* Prol. 1 By mediacion of this litel tretis, I purpose to teche thee a certein nombre of conclusiouns apertening to the same instrument. **1560** DAUS tr. *Sleidane's Comm.* 21 His fellowes at home..wrot to Lewis the Frenche kinge, by the mediation of Erarde Marchiane Byshoppe of Liege. **1615** G. SANDYS *Trav.* 168 Not to be touched but by the mediation of a sticke prepared for the purpose. **1646** H. LAWRENCE *Comm. Angells* 38 The understanding receives things by the mediation, first of the externall sences, then of the fancy. **1648** *Hamilton Papers* (Camden) 205, I intend to corresponde with you by her mediation. **1796** BURKE *Regic. Peace* i. Wks. VIII. 156 To seek for peace..through the mediation of a vigorous war. **1796** KIRWAN *Elem. Min.* (ed. 2) II. 269 By the mediation of nickel it will unite to Bismuth. **1860** TYNDALL *Glac.* I. iii. 23 Through his mediation I secured a chamois-hunter.

b. *Psychol.* (See quot. 1934.) Also *attrib.*

1912 *Amer. Jrnl. Psychol.* Jan. 102 The occurrence of associations whose mediation does not come into consciousness in any recognizable manner is certainly an interesting and well-attested phenomenon. **1934** H. C. WARREN *Dict. Psychol.* 162/1 *Mediation*, the interposition of one or more ideas or acts between an initial stimulus or idea and a given end result whose genesis is under investigation. **1953** C. E. OSGOOD *Method & Theory Exper. Psychol.* III. ix. 395 Short circuiting enters into all behavior, and its most important role lies in formation of those representational mediation processes. **1963** ERVIN & MILLER in J. A. Fishman *Readings Sociol. of Lang.* (1968) 91 While there is overlap..with American studies in verbal mediation, the experimental questions have been quite different. **1970** *Jrnl. Gen. Psychol.* LXXXIII. 53 Osgood..developed it [*sc.* the Semantic Differential] and rationalized it in terms of mediation theory. **1971** A. PAIVIO *Imagery & Verbal Processes* ix. 320 The experimental and language-habit approach to the investigation of mediation paradigms.

4. *Mus.* That part of a plain-song or an Anglican chant which lies between the two reciting-notes.

The mediation of a plain-song chant is regarded by some as including the reciting-note, and is then taken to be all that part of the first half of the chant following the 'intonation'.

1845 J. JONES *Man. Instr. Plain-Chant* 10 When, at the mediation of the 1st, 3d, 6th, and 7th tones, the last word is a monosyllable, it is joined to the preceding syllable. **1879** HELMORE in Grove *Dict. Mus.* I. 337/2 In the modern Anglican chants the Intonation has been discarded, and the chant consists of the Mediation and Termination only. **1893** J. HEYWOOD *Art of Chanting* viii. 21 Most of the early Anglican chants seem to require two accents in their mediation.

mediational (mi:dɪ'eɪʃənəl), *a.* [f. MEDIATION + -AL.] Of or pertaining to mediation; mediating.

1951 PARSONS & SHILS *Toward Gen. Theory Action* III. i. 280 One can assume, within reasonable limits (without, that is, detailed psychophysiological, 'mediational' investigation), what potential 'perceptions' are possible. **1953** C. E. OSGOOD *Method & Theory Exper. Psychol.* III. ix. 404 Mediational modification is indicated..by a single asterisk. **1956** *Scottish Jrnl. Theol.* IX. 228 The leading mediational theologian [*sc.* J. Baillie] of our time. *Ibid.* 234 That supreme sensitivity and mediational quality which have always marked his thought and outlook. **1964** *Language* XL. 211 'Operant' is one of those psychological terms (together with 'latency' and 'mediational') which recur frequently in psycholinguistics. **1968** M. BLACK *Labyrinth of Lang.* vii. 158 Causal theories..insist upon the importance of the 'mediational process' induced by perceiving the sign. **1971** *Jrnl. Gen. Psychol.* LXXXV. 125 A mediational process involving colour cues.

mediative ('mi:dɪətɪv), *a. rare.* [f. MEDIATE *v.* + -IVE.] That has the quality of mediating; pertaining to mediation or a mediator.

1813 SHELLEY *Q. Mab* v. 232 This commerce of sincerest virtue needs No mediative signs of selfishness. **1860** WESTCOTT *Introd. Study Gosp.* v. (ed. 5) 303 In the Synoptists faith is the mediative energy in material deliverances as the types of higher deliverance. **1890** FAIRBAIRN *Catholicism* (1899) 299 All means were inadequate, and so divisive; as mediative they held the spirit out of the immediate Presence.

mediatization (ˌmi:dɪətaɪ'zeɪʃən). [f. next + -ATION.] The action of the verb MEDIATIZE; the state of being mediatized.

1818 *Edin. Rev.* XXIX. 349 Mediatisation and confederacy are courtly and diplomatic terms. **1844** DISRAELI *Coningsby* II. i, The mediatization of the petty German princes. **1887** *Cornh. Mag.* Aug. 202 Mediatisation means retention of princely title, and surrender of princely independence and sovereignty.

mediatize ('mi:dɪətaɪz), *v.* [ad. F. *médiatiser*, f. *médiat*: see MEDIATE *a.* and -IZE. Cf. G. *mediatisiren.*]

1. *trans. Hist.* In Germany under the Holy Roman Empire: To reduce (a prince or state) from the position of an immediate vassal of the Empire to that of a mediate vassal. Hence, in later times: To annex (a principality) to another state, leaving to its former sovereign his titular dignity, and (usually) more or less of his rights of government. Also *transf.* and *fig.*

1830 *Fraser's Mag.* I. 158 If Prince Paul..did such a thing, he would be mediatised in his princedom of fashion. **1843** THACKERAY *Irish Sk. Bk.* ix, Let us trust that the Prince..was at least restored to his family and decently mediatised. **1849** J. M. KEMBLE *Saxons in Eng.* II. iv. 149 The ducal families were in direct descent from the old regal families, which became mediatized, to use a modern term. **1876** J. MARTINEAU *Ess.*, etc. (1891) IV. 257 It [intellectual purpose] is liable to be deposed and 'mediatized' by advancing knowledge.

2. *intr.* To mediate, take up a mediating position.

1885 *Unitarian Rev.* Aug. XXIV. 114 A creed of reconciliation which attempts to mediatize between two opposite parties can never hope for success, if [etc.].

Hence '**mediatized** *ppl. a.*

1826 DISRAELI *Viv. Grey* VI. iv, His Highness has the misfortune of being a mediatised prince. **1841** W. SPALDING *Italy & It. Isl.* III. 102 The mediatized principalities in Germany. **1887** *Westm. Rev.* June 334 The mediatized Bey.

mediator ('mi:dɪeɪtə(r)). Also 4–6 **medyat-**; 4–5 **-ure**, 4–6 **-oure**, 4–7 **-our**, 5 **-owr(e**, **-er**, (6 **medeator**). [a. F. *médiateur*, ad. late L. *mediātōr-em*, f. *mediāre* to MEDIATE. Cf. Sp. *mediador*, Pg. *mediador*, *mediator*, It. *mediatore*.

The Lat. word, though formally implying the vb., was perh. formed directly on *medius* middle, in imitation of Gr. μεσίτης (f. μέσος middle). The early examples, exc. one in Appuleius (2nd c.), are all Christian and theological, representing μεσίτης as used in the N.T.]

1. One who intervenes between two parties, esp. for the purpose of effecting reconciliation; one who brings about (a peace, a treaty) or settles (a dispute) by mediation.

1387 TREVISA *Higden* (Rolls) VII. 125 Mediatours goynge bytwixe, pees was made. **1413** *Pilgr. Sowle* (Caxton 1483) IV. xxxi. 80 These Royal lordes ben menes and medyatours bytwene the kyng and his peple in euery nede that may befalle. **1554** *Act 1 & 2 Phil. & Mary*, c. 8 §9 It maie please yoʳ Majesties to be Intercessours and Mediatours to.. Cardinall Poole. **1606** PULTON *Kalender of Stat.* 18 b (27 *Edw. III*, c. 24), And two English men, two of Lombardie, and two of Almaigne shall chosen to be Mediators of questions between sellers and buiers. *c* **1615** BACON *Adv. Sir G. Villiers* Wks. 1879 I. 509/1 The trouble of all men's confluence..to yourself, as a mediator between them and their sovereign. **1769** ROBERTSON *Chas. V.* x. III. 251 The Princes who were present..acted as intercessors or mediators between them. **1853** J. H. NEWMAN *Hist. Sk.* (1873) II. II. iv. 258 He claimed for himself especially the part of mediator between political rivals. **1855** MILMAN *Lat. Chr.* x. iv. (1864) VI. 172 The lofty station of the mediator of such peace became his sacred function.

fig. **1609** DANIEL *Civ. Wars* VIII. liii, And in deliv'ring it, lifts vp her eyes, (The mouingst Mediatours shee could bring).

2. *Theol.* One who mediates between God and man; applied esp. to Jesus Christ (cf. 1 Tim. ii. 5).

a **1300** *Cursor M.* 27503 Þou has me [the confessor] made als mediator, Als medioter and messager, Tuix þe and þam þair errand bere. *c* **1375** *Sc. Leg. Saints* xxxvi. (*Baptista*) 629 Medyature als wes he betwene ws & þe trinite. **1382** WYCLIF *1 Tim.* ii. 5 O God and mediatour of God and men. **1526** *Pilgr. Perf.* (W. de W. 1531) 190 b, Sauyour & mediatour of mankynde. **1649** BP. REYNOLDS *Hosea* i. 41 The Prophet here secretly leadeth us to Christ the Mediatour. **1667** MILTON *P.L.* XII. 240 Instructed that to God is no access Without Mediator. **1736** BUTLER *Anal.* II. v. (Bohn) 240 There is then no sort of objection, from the light of nature, against the general notion of a mediator between God and man. **1902** A. B. DAVIDSON *Biblical & Lit. Ess.* 247 These saints as intercessors and mediators bridge over the chasm that separates God from man.

†**3.** A go-between; a messenger or agent. *Obs.*

c **1375** *Sc. Leg. Saints* iii. (*Andreas*) 1063 Þane he þat mediatoure had bene, and hard þis answere all bedene, recordyt it to þe bischope. *c* **1386** CHAUCER *Pars. T.* ¶893 The fourthe circumstance is, by whiche mediatours or by whiche messagers, as for enticement, or for consentement to bere campainye with felaweshipe. *c* **1470** *Gol. & Gaw.* 400 Our souerane Arthour..Has maid ws thre as mediatour, His message to schaw. **1576** FLEMING *Panopl. Epist.* 331 Your highnesse, whom it hath pleased..voluntarily (without the helpe of any mediatour) to graunt mee free..accesse to your friendshippe. **1622** MALYNES *Anc. Law-Merch.* 98 A Merchant, hauing many of these Billes..will resort vnto.. another Merchant, commonly accompanied with a Mediator or Broker. **1697** in *Syllabus Rymer's Fœd.* (1869) Pref. 112 The French had received our ratification under the signett, and putt it collationed into the mediatours hands.

4. *Path.* Applied to those constituents of a serum which actively produce hæmolysis.

1903 A. S. GRÜNBAUM in *Brit. Med. Jrnl.* 21 Mar. 654 Ehrlich..recognized..that Bordet was right in assuming the existence of two bodies for the production of this phenomenon [*sc.* hæmolysis], and that one body (mediator, amboceptor) was present in quantity in the serum of immunized animals only, while the other (the complement) occurred in the serum of normal untreated animals. *Ibid.* 4 Apr. 784 The immune serum merely contains an excess of normal mediators and not new ones.

5. A variation in the games of ombre and quadrille. [= Sp. *mediator.* Cf. MEDIATEUR.]

1902 LD. ALDENHAM *Ombre* 6 Quadrille, Quintille, Piquemedrille, Tredrille, Sextille, and Mediator, which are all variations of the Game of Ombre.

6. That which effects a transition between one stage and another; *spec.* in *Psychol.*, that which acts as an agent in mediation (sense 3 b). Also *attrib.*

1953 C. E. OSGOOD *Method & Theory Exper. Psychol.* III. ix. 402 The self-stimulation produced by mediators. *Ibid.* 404 (*caption*) A change in the instrumental sequence elicited by a mediator. **1965** *Language* XLI. 139 Such words as *istorik, istorija*.., which appear already in Old Russian literature, are justly regarded by her as direct borrowings from Greek or Latin, and not as mediated by other languages... On the other hand, the more detailed data obtained on foreign words have enabled Mrs. Worth to correct and to define more precisely the role of the mediator languages, especially that of Polish. **1967** *Word* XXIII. 14 Among the numerous 'mediator' languages suggested so far those based on the symbols of mathematical logic are of especial interest to modern interlinguistics. **1969** [see *E.S.T.* (*E. III)]. **1970** N. E. SPEAR in M. R. D'Amato *Exper. Psychol.* xii. 604 S's consequential use of potential mediators for learning. **1970** *Jrnl. Gen. Psychol.* LXXXIII. 5 Rhine also furthers his analysis to the affect-arousal components that certain verbal mediators may eventually elicit. **1971** A. PAIVIO *Imagery & Verbal Processes* ix. 319 Potential mediators are either inferred from association norms or are 'built in' experimentally.

mediatorial (ˌmiːdɪəˈtɔːrɪəl), *a.* [f. L. type **mediātōri-us* (see MEDIATORY) + -AL¹.] Of, pertaining to, resembling, or characteristic of a mediator or mediation.

1650 W. PYNCHON in *First Cent. Hist. Springfield, Mass.* (1898) I. 81 There is no need that our blessed Mediator should pay both the price of his Mediatorial obedience, and also [etc.]. **1708** *Brit. Apollo* No. 91. 1/2, I have not yet Discharg'd my Mediatorial Office. **1742** YOUNG *Nt. Th.* IX. 272 No Patron! Intercessor none! Now past The sweet, the clement, Mediatorial Hour! **1876** MOZLEY *Univ. Serm.* v. 106 A mediatorial function..pervades the whole dispensation of God's natural providence, by which men have to suffer for each other.

Hence **media'torially** *adv.*, as a mediator; **media'torialism**, mediatorial attitude or position.

1774 A. M. TOPLADY *Gd. News fr. Heaven* Wks. 1794 III. 208 Christ shall reign..mediatorially. **1827** CH. WORDSWORTH *Chas. I* (1828) 151 And, because, at the same time they [two Presbyterians] were 'moderate and mediatorial', [they may] have stuck one Episcopalian between them, as a voucher of their moderation and mediatorialism.

† **media'torian**, *a. Obs. rare.* [Formed as prec. + -AN.] = MEDIATORIAL. So **media'torious** *a.*

a **1659** BP. BROWNRIG *Serm.* (1674) II. xv. 187 The Arrians blaspheme of his Deity, 'tis as false also of his Mediatorious Efficacy. **1676** CUDWORTH *Serm. on 1 Cor.* xv. 57 (ed. 3) 72 Christ after His Resurrection..having a mediatorious Kingdom bestowed upon Him. **1692** BEVERLEY *Disc. Dr. Crisp* 18 There is a Mediatorian Law and Covenant in the Hand of the Mediator.

'mediatorship. [See -SHIP.] The office of a mediator.

a **1600** HOOKER *Eccl. Pol.* VIII. iv. §6 Government doth belong to his kingly office, mediatorship, to his priestly. **1693** LUTTRELL *Brief Rel.* (1857) III. 242 Their masters had undertaken the mediatorship of a general peace. **1876** MOZLEY *Univ. Serm.* viii. (1877) 181 The mediatorship of Christ.

mediatory (ˈmiːdɪətərɪ), *a.* [ad. L. type **mediātōri-us*, f. *mediātor* MEDIATOR: see -ORY.] Having the function of mediating; pertaining to, or of the nature of, mediation.

1619 W. SCLATER *Exp. 1 Thess.* (1630) 51 Christ's actions ..were..some Mediatory. **1665** J. SPENCER *Vulg. Proph.* 120 The solemn Inauguration of our Saviour to his Mediatory Kingdom. **1677** GALE *Crt. Gentiles* III. 182 The Philosophers' Demons or Mediatorie Lords, which were the original Exemplars of Antichrist's Mediatorie Saints. *a* **1711** KEN *Christophil* Poet. Wks. 1721 I. 447 Our humble King began to rear His Mediatory Realm. **1765** BLACKSTONE *Comm.* I. 51 If the supreme power were lodged..in the king and commons, we should want that circumspection and mediatory caution, which the wisdom of the peers is to afford. **1806** G. S. FABER *Diss. Prophecies* (1814) I. 280 The excessive veneration of supposed mediatory saints and angels. **1836–7** SIR W. HAMILTON *Metaph.* xxxii. (1859) II. 245 The mediatory agency of latent thoughts in the process of suggestion. **1885** *L'pool Daily Post* 25 Apr. 4/9 Austria and Germany are evincing an increased disposition to dictate terms, but rather of a selfish than a mediatory nature.

¶ Used = MEDIATE *a.* 1.

1651 BIGGS *New Disp.* 169 To avell the pleura or lining of the Thorax from the ribs, which is firmely annexed and immediately adheres unto them, by the mediatory ligation of numerous solid fibres.

mediatress (ˈmiːdɪeɪtrɪs). Now *rare.* [f. MEDIATOR + -ESS.] = MEDIATRIX.

1616 R. SHELDON *Surv. Miracles Ch. Rome* 125 Neither dare wee associate her as a secondarie Mediatrisse with her sonne. **1748** RICHARDSON *Clarissa* xlii. (1811) III. 249 How shall two such come together—no kind mediatress in the way? **1867** *Contemp. Rev.* V. 57 He does not hesitate to employ her as mediatress.

mediatrice (ˈmiːdɪeɪtrɪs). Now *rare* (or only as Fr.). [a. F. *médiatrice*, ad. L. *mediātrix* (see next).] = MEDIATRIX.

The pl. form *mediatrices* is, so far as spelling is concerned, common to this word and the next: the example placed here may belong to MEDIATRIX.

c **1375** *Sc. Leg. Saints* xxxiv. (*Pelagia*) 361 As medyatrice hyr wil I sende to god. **1447** BOKENHAM *Seyntys* (Roxb.) 270 Thorgh goddys grace ordeynyd to be A medyatryce for this cyte. **1500–20** DUNBAR *Poems* lxxxv. 67 Oratrice, mediatrice, salvatrice, To God gret suffragane! **1540** HYRDE tr. *Vives' Instr. Chr. Wom.* (1592) N vij, God is the overseer, the church is the mediatrice in mariage. **1686** *Speculum Beatæ Virginis* 17 They desire her to interceed with God for them, which also makes her a joynt Mediatrice with Christ. **1842** AGNES STRICKLAND *Queens Eng.* II. 291 The French monarch..proposed to make the queen-dowager of France and Isabella the mediatrices of a peace. **1891** *Cath. News* 24 Jan. 6/6 Our advocate, our mediatrice with Him.

mediatrix (miːdɪˈeɪtrɪks). Pl. **mediatrices** (miːdɪəˈtraɪsiːz): see prec. [a. L. *mediātrix*, fem. of *mediātor*, MEDIATOR.] A female mediator. (Often applied to the Virgin Mary.)

1462–3 *Pol. Poems* (Rolls) II. 270 Pray the vierge immaculat To be good mediatrix. **1577–87** HOLINSHED *Chron.* III. 1183/2 As a meane or mediatrix betweene the parties, there was Christierna dutchesse of Loraine. **1651** tr. *De-las-Coveras' Don Fenise* 39 She having confessed herselfe the mediatrix of their loves. **1738** OZELL *Cervantes* 9 Certain..Knights..invoking them [their Ladies]..as so many Advocates and Mediatrixes in their Conflicts and Encounters. **1753** RICHARDSON *Grandison* IV. iv. 21 War seems to be declared: And will you not turn mediatrix? *Ibid.* IV. xxviii. 175 Mediators and mediatrices. **1781** WARTON *Hist. Eng. Poetry* III. 493 The mediatrix of the factions of France. **1846** PUSEY *Let.* in Liddon, etc. *Life* II. 505 The [Roman] system as to the Blessed Virgin as the Mediatrix and Dispenser of all present blessings to mankind. **1848** THACKERAY *Van. Fair* xi, The friendship..lasted as long as the jovial old mediatrix was there to keep the peace. **1880** MEREDITH *Tragic Com.* xi (end), Here was the mediatrix—the veritable goddess with the sword to cut the knot!

‖ **media vuelta** (ˈmedia ˈvwelta). Also **media-vuelte.** [Sp., lit. 'half turn'.] In bullfighting, a method of killing the bull by approaching from behind (see quot. 1962).

1932 [see BANDERILLA *v.*]. **1934** R. CAMPBELL *Broken Record* viii. 183 Don Simao uses a *media-vuelte* in sticking in his banderillas from horseback; that is, he takes the bull while it is turning, citing it from behind. **1962** B. CONRAD *Encycl. Bullfighting* 163/1 *Media vuelta*... A way of placing *banderillas* in which the *torero* comes at the bull from behind, forcing the animal into a *media vuelta* as the man approaches. **1967** MCCORMICK & MASCAREÑAS *Compl. Aficionado* iv. 121 Once in a great while..you will see an aging matador, green with fear, killing *a la media vuelta.*

medic (ˈmɛdɪk), *a.*¹ and *sb.*¹ (See also MEDICS.) [ad. L. *medic-us* adj. and sb., f. root of *medērī* to heal. Cf. OF. *medique* sb., physician, Sp. *médico*, Pg., It. *medico* adj. and sb.]

A. *adj.* = MEDICAL. Only *poet.*

1700 POMFRET *Reason* 84 Should untun'd Nature crave the Medic Art, What Health can that contentious Tribe impart? **1769** *Poetry* in *Ann. Reg.* 242 Order Drops, ye Medic Dunces, Order Scruples, Drams, and Ounces. **1873** W. S. MAYO *Never Again* xxxii. 417 Thy medic touch becalms my throbbing brow.

B. *sb.* A physician, 'medical man'; a medical student.

1659 T. PECKE *Parnassi Puerp.* 16 The Medic heals the Body. **1661** BLOUNT *Glossogr.* (ed. 2), *Medick*, a Physitian. **1694** MOTTEUX *Rabelais* v. (1737) 232 Your Medic's Friend. **1696** J. EDWARDS *Exist. & Provid. God* II. 136 This author ..was most bitter..not only against physicians, but all medicks. **1823** *The Crayon* (Yale Coll.) 23 (Farmer) Who sent The medic to our aid! **1851** B. H. HALL *College Words* 198 *Med, Medic*, a name sometimes given to a student in medicine. **1885** B. G. WILDER in *Jrnl. Nervous Dis.* XII. 281 Medic is the legitimate paronym of *medicus*, but is commonly regarded as slang. **1895** W. C. GORE in *Inlander* Nov. 64 *Medic*, a student in the medical department. **1902** W. W. HALL *Appl. Relig.* I. 22 For ages medics have been laying down rules for the regimen of diseased people. **1925** FRASER & GIBBONS *Soldier & Sailor Words* 154 *The Medics*, R.A.M.C. [Royal Army Medical Corps]. **1945** *Finito! Po Valley Campaign* 61 (*caption*) Our medics treat German wounded. **1968** MRS. L. B. JOHNSON *White House Diary* 17 Jan. (1970) 618 He was a Medic and, although twice wounded, he had gone on..to save life after life, crawling across the battlefield. **1970** *Oxford Mail* 21 Feb. 12/3 (*heading*) The 'medics' are fast movers. **1973** *Black Panther* 3 Mar. 6/2, I was a member of the U.S. Army from 1967 to 1970. During the Tet offensive of 1968, I served as a combat medic with the 101 ABN. Div. at Hue, South Vietnam. **1974** *Evening Standard* 1 Mar. 48/3 Dr Brian Warren, Mr Heath's personal physician, called to see him at Downing Street—but as a friend, not as a medic.

Medic (ˈmiːdɪk), *a.*² and *sb.*² [ad. L. *Mēdic-us*, Gr. Μηδικός Median.] **A.** *adj.* = MEDIAN *a.*²

1888 G. BERTIN *Abridged Gram. Lang. Cuneiform Inscriptions* 81 Medic Grammar. **1889** *Jrnl. Anthrop. Inst.* Aug. 31 The Medic language is not the same as the Akkadian, though in syntax and in vocabulary it presents a very marked connection. **1912** H. G. RAWLINSON *Bactria* ii. 25 A treaty was made between the rival nations, and ratified by a marriage between the Medic king and a Lydian princess. **1933** C. DAWSON *Enquiries Relig. & Culture* ii. 80 Assyria was at the height of her power..but her pitiless militarism was gradually ruining..Asia and prepared the way for a new series of barbarian invasions—Cimmerian, Scythian and Medic.

B. *sb.* = MEDIAN *sb.*² 2.

1894 A. H. SAYCE *Primer of Assyriology* ii. 20 The script and language of Elam—sometimes, but incorrectly, called Scythian, Medic, or Protomedic.

medic, var. form of MEDICK.

† **'medica.** *Obs.* [a. L. *mēdica*: see MEDICK.] = MEDICK.

1577 B. GOOGE *Heresbach's Husb.* I. (1586) 37 Amongst all sortes of fodder, that is counted for the cheefe..which..the Italians at this day call *Medica.* **1651** R. CHILD in *Hartlib's Legacy* (1655) 71 The plants which are usually called Medicaes with us, are annual plants. **1664** EVELYN *Kal. Hort.*, Apr. (1679) 15 Sow..Medica, Holy-hocks, Columbines [etc.]. **1712** tr. *Pomet's Hist. Drugs* I. 12 A species of Trefoil,..to which some have given the Name of Medica, or Median Hay. **1753** CHAMBERS *Cycl. Supp.* s.v., The sea Medica... The great prickly sea Medica.

medicable (ˈmɛdɪkəb(ə)l), *a.* [ad. L. *medicābilis*, f. *medicāre, medicārī*: see MEDICATE *v.* and -ABLE. Cf. OF. *medecable, medicable* (in sense 2), Sp., Pg. *medicable*, It. *medicabile.*]

1. Admitting of cure or remedial treatment.

1616 BULLOKAR *Eng. Expos.*, *Medicable*, which may be healed. **1744** ARMSTRONG *Preserv. Health* III. 516 For want of timely care Millions have died of medicable wounds. **1816** WORDSW. *Ode*, 1815, 81 For them who bravely stood unhurt, or bled With medicable wounds. **1834** *Tait's Mag.* I. 15/2 Of the more enduring and less medicable ailments of his patient, the surgeon knew..nothing. **1871** NAPHEYS *Prev. & Cure Dis.* I. i. 43 Medicable wounds.

† **2.** Possessing medicinal properties. *Obs.*

1658 PHILLIPS, *Medicable*, able to heal. **1666** BOYLE *Orig. Formes & Qual.* (1667) 293 Wine obtains divers medicable Vertues (as that of cooling, dissolving Coral, Pearle, &c.).

Medicaid (ˈmɛdɪkeɪd). Also **medicaid.** [f. MEDIC(AL *a.* + AID *sb.*] Name given in the United States to a scheme making available state and federal funds for the use of persons judged to require assistance with medical expenses, and provided for under Title XIX of the Social Security Act, 1965. Also *attrib.*

1966 *Life* 29 July 4/1 The word we are going to be hearing a lot more is something called 'Medicaid'—also known as Title 19. **1967** *Economist* 2 Dec. 960/2 The states have until 1970 to set up their Medicaid schemes, but 33 have already done so, attracted by the generous federal contribution. **1972** *Daily Colonist* (Victoria, B.C.) 6 Jan. 1/7 Nearly $1 billion in medicaid payments 'went down the drain' in New York City through medical malpractice. **1973** *Interfaces* May 44 The launching of the Medicare and Medicaid programs..created a need for new technical words. **1974** *Spartanburg* (S. Carolina) *Herald* 22 Apr. B4/6 If you can be paid you will also be eligible for Medicaid provided through the South Carolina Department of Social Services.

medical (ˈmɛdɪkəl), *a.* and *sb.* [a. F. *médical*, = Sp., Pg. *medical*, It. *medicale*, ad. late L. *medicālis*, f. *medic-us* physician: see MEDIC.]

A. *adj.*

1. a. Pertaining or related to the healing art or its professors. Also, in a narrower sense, Pertaining or related to 'medicine' as distinguished from surgery, obstetrics, etc.

medical man: used as a general term including 'physician', 'surgeon', 'accoucheur', etc.

1646 SIR T. BROWNE *Pseud. Ep.* To Rdr. a 4, In this work attempts will exceed performances: it being composed by snatches of time, as medicall vacations,..would permit us. *a* **1682** —— *Tracts* 22 Not onely in medical but dietetical use and practice. **1753** *Phil. Trans. R. Soc.* XLVII. 399 Every body has consider'd what the Italians printed..upon the subject of medical electricity, as too hasty a publication. **1760–72** H. BROOKE *Fool of Qual.* (1809) II. 99, I summoned the chief medical artists, and got the precious remains.. embalmed. **1776** T. PENNANT *Tour in Scotl. & Voy. Hebrides 1772* II. 247 The number of medical students are now annually reckoned at about 300. **1777** T. CAVALLO *Compl. Treat. Electr.* x. 287 *Medical Electricity*, a practical method of applying Electricity to the human body, when affected with different distempers. **1778** T. A. MANN in *Lett. Lit. Men* (Camden) 416 We are here occupied and divided upon Medical Electricity. **1799** *Med. Jrnl.* I. 364 Such an excess of acid is therefore useless, especially in medical practice. *Ibid.*, The Medical Society also desired the Citizens Bouillon-La Grange, and Chaussier, to examine [etc]. **1814** G. J. SINGER *Elem. Electr.* III. iv. 286 Mr. Partington, whose experience as a medical electrician is considerable. **1835** F. D. MAURICE *Let.* 6 Oct. in J. F. Maurice *Life F. D. Maurice* (1884) I. xiii. 186 If I could get any influence over the medical students, I should indeed think myself honoured. **1849** MACAULAY *Hist. Eng.* iv. I. 432 All the medical men of note in London were summoned. **1864** MRS. GASKELL *Wives & Daughters* (1866) I. iii. 26 He went very steadily to work..advertising in medical journals, reading testimonials, sifting character and qualifications. **1878** W. JAMES in R. B. Perry *Tht. & Char. W. James* (1935) II. IV. liii. 29 The degrading sophistries of medical materialists. **1885** *Househ. Words* 20 June 155 (Farmer), Medical students have liberally assisted in the formation of slang, their special department thereof being known as medical Greek. **1895** *Arnold & Sons' Catal. Surg. Instruments* 19 Field Medical Paniers, fitted complete with instruments..etc. **1899** *Allbutt's Syst. Med.* VIII. 778 Neither the patient nor the medical attendant. **1902** W. JAMES *Varieties Relig. Experience* i. 13 Medical materialism finishes up Saint Paul by calling his vision on the road to Damascus a discharging lesion of the occipital cortex, he being an epileptic. **1935** *Economist* 7 Sept. 456/2 The [National Health Insurance] scheme provided for the payment of cash benefit in time of sickness, for medical benefit..and sanatorium benefit. **1945** *Release & Resettlement* (H.M. Govt.) xii. 40 The benefits of the National Health Insurance Scheme include medical benefit (i.e. free treatment by an insurance doctor and medicine). **1966** I. JEFFERIES *House-Surgeon* ii. 20 'I know you've *graduated*,' she interposed, 'but at heart you're still a medical student.' **1975** M. DUKE *Death of Holy Murderer* i. 15, I put aside the medical journal I'd been trying to read.

b. Proper or appropriate to a medical practitioner.

1809 MALKIN *Gil Blas* II. iii. ¶2 He had got into reputation with the public by a certain professional slang, humoured by a medical face.

c. Of diseases: Requiring medical as distinguished from surgical treatment or diagnosis.

1885–8 FAGGE & PYE-SMITH *Princ. Med.* (ed. 2) I. 74 Internal, or as it may be styled 'medical' pyæmia. **1899** *Allbutt's Syst. Med.* VI. 174 The preceding remarks..relate only to the medical thromboses, and not to the septic and suppurative thrombo-phlebitides of the surgeon. **1904** *Hospital* 11 June, Suppl. 14 By medical diseases is meant those diseases which are situated either as to their source or their origin in one or other of the three great cavities of the body.

d. Special collocations: **medical board** [BOARD *sb.* 8 b], a body of medical men responsible for the medical examination of soldiers, the maintenance of public health, etc.; hence ***medical-board*** vb. trans., to refer for consideration by a medical board (*rare*); **medical certificate**, a certificate from a doctor, attesting the state of a person's health, etc.; **medical examiner**, (*a*) a doctor who carries out an examination for physical fitness; (*b*) *U.S.*, a medically qualified public officer whose duty is to investigate deaths that occur under unusual

or suspicious circumstances, to perform post-mortems, and sometimes to initiate inquests; hence **medical examination**, an examination to establish the degree of a person's physical fitness, etc.; †**medical finger** = LEECH-FINGER; **medical garden**, a garden appropriated to the cultivation of medicinal plants; a 'physic-garden'; **medical hall** *Ireland*, a pharmacy, a chemist's shop; **medical jurisprudence**, the law as it relates to the practice of medicine; also = *forensic medicine*; †**medical month** (see quot.); **medical officer**, a doctor appointed by a public authority or company to attend to matters relating to health (in Gt. Britain in the public sphere the post of 'medical officer of health' was abolished on 1 Apr. 1974); **medical register**, a register, in Britain kept by the General Medical Council, of all doctors legally in practice; so ***medical registration***; also *attrib.*; **medical school**, (a school or faculty of) a college or university in which medicine is studied.

1814 *Niles' Reg.* VI. 36/2 A *Medical Board is now sitting at the city of Washington, by order of the secretary of war. **1843** *Times* 29 Nov. 4/3 Two distinct medical boards have declared themselves satisfied as to his sound state of health. **1922** *Encycl. Brit.* XXXI. 898/2 Every medical board paper was a kind of forecast. **1947** L. HASTINGS *Dragons are Extra* iii. 63 He was then medical-boarded and sent to the nursing-home in England. **1973** 'R. MACLEOD' *Burial in Portugal* i. 18 The last medical board had cut his army pension, reckoning his back was improving. **1838** DICKENS *Nickleby* (1839) xv. 131 A very little more and it [*sc.* a back comb] must have entered her skull. We have a *medical certifiket that if it had, the tortershell would have affected the brain. **1853** C. SCHREIBER *Jrnl.* (1952) 12 The medical certificate would be quite sufficient, and..without his appearing the fellowship was safe. **1914** KIPLING *Lett. of Travel* (1920) 210 One could eat..in one's cabin without a medical certificate from the doctor. **1971** J. CLEGG *Dict. Social Services* 96 A medical certificate (on the official form) must be sent to the local social security office. **1973** E. MCGIRR *Bardel's Murder* ii. 35 'Did you get a medical certificate?' 'That and pain killers.' **1974** *Times* 23 Sept. 2/3 She had attempted suicide five years ago..but she had medical certificates that said she was now all right. **1898** F. DE H. HALL (*title*) *Medical examination for life assurance. **1916** *Brit. Med. Jrnl.* 26 Aug. 300/2 (*heading*) Medical examination of recruits. **1935** S. G. LEIGH *Guide to Life Assurance* (ed. 4) viii. 92 Many people have an aversion from the medical examination. **1848** *Risks of Life Assurance* 5 Dr. Ingleby..then the *medical examiner for the Norwich Office. **1877** *Acts & Resolves Gen. Court of Massachusetts 1877* 580 The governor shall nominate..able and discreet men, learned in the science of medicine, to be medical examiners. **1889** POLLOCK & CHISHOLM *Med. Handbk. Life Assurance* p. viii, Plain instructions for the guidance of the medical examiner, to afford him a ready handbook of reference on insurance rules. **1928** *Bull. Nat. Research Council* LXVI. 13 Only in New York City and Boston, where the medical examiner's system prevails, is the bulk of the work done in the properly equipped morgues. **1937** T. A. GONZALES et al. *Legal Med. & Toxicol.* ii. 9 The coroner has investigative and judicial powers; the medical examiner can conduct only an investigation. **1973** *Times* 5 June 6/4 No official ruling on the cause of death has yet been given by the medical examiner, the equivalent of the coroner. **1653** URQUHART *Rabelais* I. viii, On the *medical finger of his right hand he had a Ring made Spire wayes. *a* **1706** J. EVELYN *Diary* an. 1658 (1955) III. 217, I went to see the *Medical Garden, at Westminster, well stored with plants, under Morgan, a very Skillful Botanist. **1838** *Civil Engineer* I. 362/2 Four acres are devoted to a medical garden. **1922** JOYCE *Ulysses* 669 Purchased by him at 10.20 a.m. on the morning of 27 June 1886 at the *medical hall of Francis Dennehy. **1938** J. CARY *Castle Corner* 279 Ah, ye dirty devil, and what sort of a drip are ye to be dropped in a medical hall. **1788** S. FARR (*title*) Elements of *medical jurisprudence. **1845** [see FORENSIC *a.*]. **1937** T. A. GONZALES et al. *Legal Med. & Toxicol.* p. vii, The section on legal medicine is concerned with the principal pathologic conditions encountered in cases of forensic importance,..and medical jurisprudence or that part of the law which deals with the practice of the physician. *Ibid.*, The subjects which are considered a part of medical jurisprudence, such as the corpus delicti,.. malpractice, insanity, and insurance. **1646** SIR T. BROWNE *Pseud. Ep.* IV. xii. 213 Which..makes 26. dayes and 22. howres, called by Physitians the *medicall month; introduced by Galen..for the better compute of Decretory or Criticall dayes. **1835** *Times* 2 Nov. 7/1, I have only heard of two unions, in which the number of *medical officers is equal to the number employed before the formation of these unions. **1841** DICKENS *Let.* 29 Oct. (1969) II. 414 With regard to the Medical officers it will be best to say that I am going out of town. **1860** F. NIGHTINGALE *Notes on Nursing* i. 10, I have known a medical officer keep his ward windows hermetically closed. **1916** W. OWEN *Let.* 10 Feb. (1967) 379 The Medical Officer says I should get them removed. **1964** *Times* 22 Feb. 6/2 Medical officers of health should be more closely concerned with the functions of their local authority that had a bearing on health in any way. **1974** *Daily Tel.* 1 Apr. 6/6 Regional hospital boards, executive health councils and local authority departments with health responsibilities will disappear. So too will medical officers of health, some of whom will now become 'community physicians'. **1886** *Act 49 & 50 Vict.* c. 48 §14 The *medical register shall contain a separate list of the names and addresses of the colonial practitioners. **1926** *Brit. Med. Jrnl.* II. 430/1 A few years ago the Government of the Irish Free State announced that it had decided to establish a separate Medical Register. **1973** *Times* 26 July 2/4 Dr —— was suspended from the medical register yesterday for professional misconduct in prescribing drugs for other than bona-fide treatment. **1886** *Lancet* 10 July 85/2 The great importance of due *medical registration. **1926** *Brit. Med. Jrnl.* II. 322/2 A decision on the medical registration question has not yet been reached. **1765** in J. Carson *Hist. Med. Dept. Univ. of Pennsylvania* (1869) 55 The institution of *Medical Schools in this country has been a favorite object of my attention. **1841** *Southern Lit. Messenger* VII. 550/2 We had lighted upon the University, in the act of organizing an extensive Medical School. **1909** J. S. FLETCHER in H. Greene *Crooked Counties* (1973) 228 He was anxious to see one or two experiments.. being carried on in some of the medical schools. **1973** *Guardian* 25 Jan. 15/6 The shortage of doctors in some regions is directly related to the absence of a regional medical school.

2. Curative; medicinal. *rare.*

1646 SIR T. BROWNE *Pseud. Ep.* V. xxi. 269 The membranous covering, commonly called the silly how..is.. preserved with great care, not onely as medicall in diseases, but [etc.]. **1811** A. T. THOMSON *Lond. Disp.* (1818) 462 Medical properties and uses. **1830** HERSCHEL *Stud. Nat. Phil.* III. iv. 303 The essential medical principles in vegetables.

B. *sb.*

1. A student or practitioner of medicine. *colloq.*

1823 HAWTHORNE in *H. & Wife* (1885) I. 111 He is the best scholar among the medicals. **1834** J. HALLEY in *Life* (1842) 15 He determined..as he said 'to beat the medicals'. **1903** *Midland Inst. Mag.* Feb. 113 The..only medical elected to a University headship since William Harvey was warden of Merton in 1644.

2. ? *U.S.* 'A small bottle or vial made of glass tubing' (*Cent. Dict.* 1890).

3. A medical examination for fitness.

1917 'TAFFRAIL' *Sub* i. 27 It was neither the *x* and *y* part of the business nor the 'medical' which caused me qualms. It was the dreaded interview. **1938** N. MARSH *Death in White Tie* x. 103 He wanted me to go to Edinburgh to take my medical... I wanted to go to Thomas's. **1946** H. WAYNE *Two Odd Soldiers* i. 7 The Recruiting Officer welcomed and encouraged us..and told us to present ourselves on the following Tuesday for our 'medical'. **1968** *Listener* 8 Feb. 187/3 Mr Scannell's adolescence appeared to be no more remarkable than a hundred others. He coughed at his RAF medical; he spouted Yeats to a literal-minded girl. **1973** *Times* 1 June 5/6 (*heading*) Medicals for drivers urged.

medical, obs. var. MISKAL, an Oriental weight.

medically ('mɛdɪkəlɪ), *adv.* [f. MEDICAL + -LY².] In a medical manner; with respect to medical science or practice, or the medical profession.

1646 SIR T. BROWNE *Pseud. Ep.* IV. xiii. 227 That which chiefly promoted the consideration of these dayes, and medically advanced the same, was the doctrine of Hippocrates. **1805** *Med. Jrnl.* XIV. 393, I was willing to hope that the case, not viewed medically, might be rendered more formidable than it really was. **1887** *Homeop. World* 1 Nov. 523 These clubs are medically officered by an allopathic practitioner. **1902** *Daily Chron.* 8 May 6/2 Educated and medically-trained women as workhouse inspectors.

medicament (mɪ'dɪkəmənt, 'mɛdɪkəmənt), *sb.* [a. F. *médicament*, ad. L. *medicāmentum*, f. *medicārī*: see MEDICATE *v.* and -MENT. Cf. Sp., Pg., It. *medicamento*.] A substance used in curative treatment.

1541 R. COPLAND *Galyen's Terap.* 2 C iv, It semeth that he had neuer experyence..of any medicamentes, whiche is a manyfest thynge of the boke that he hath made of medycamentes. **1597** A. M. tr. *Guillemeau's Fr. Chirurg.* 16/2 Some resolvinge and strengtheninge medicamentes. **1650** BULWER *Anthropomet.* 160 He speaks of Cosmetique medicaments, or the Art of Decoration. **1750** tr. *Leonardus' Mirr. Stones* 96 In these they strew soporiferous medicaments. **1831** J. DAVIES *Manual Mat. Med.* 61 Some medicaments which are commonly used as astringents. **1899** *Allbutt's Syst. Med.* VIII. 922 Certain drug eruptions ..have their greatest intensity round the part to which the medicament is applied.

b. *transf.* and *fig.*

1614 W. BARCLAY *Nepenthes* A 4, [Tobacco] is the only medicament in the world ordained by nature to entertaine good companie. **1654** HAMMOND *Fundamentals* xix. §32. 235 First, the admonitions..of his fellow Christians, then more publike reprehensions..and upon the unsuccessfulness of all these milder medicaments, the use of that stronger Physick, the Censures of the Church. **1824** A. HENDERSON *Wines* 45 It was only for the inferior wines, however, that such medicaments were used. **1872** M. COLLINS *Two Plunges for Pearl* III. viii. 183 There are few medicaments equal to walking at your fastest pace.

me'dicament, *v.* [f. the sb. Cf. F. *médicamenter.*] *trans.* To administer medicaments to. Hence **me'dicamenting** *vbl. sb.*

1823 GALT *R. Gilhaize* xxxvii, But for many a day all the skill and medicamenting of Doctor Callender did him little good. **1849** THACKERAY *Pendennis* liii, He..had been treated and medicamented as the doctor ordained.

medicamental (,mɛdɪkə'mɛntəl), *a.* Now *rare.* [f. MEDICAMENT *sb.* + -AL¹.] Having the nature of a medicament; medicinal.

1657 TOMLINSON *Renou's Disp.* 26 Aconitus..and many others are both medicamental and poysonous. **1670** MAYNWARING *Vita Sana* xiii. 119 Sallads of Lettuce..are medicamental aliment. **1755** in JOHNSON; in mod. Dicts.

medicamentally (,mɛdɪkə'mɛntəlɪ), *adv.* [f. prec. + -LY².] After the manner of medicaments.

1646 SIR T. BROWNE *Pseud. Ep.* II. v. 85 The substance of gold is indeed invincible by the powerfullest action of naturall heat,..not only alimentally..but also medicamentally. **1884** *N. & Q.* 15 Mar. 210 The fish is.. more wholesome medicamentally, but not so toothsome.

medicamentary (,mɛdɪkə'mɛntərɪ), *a.* [f. MEDICAMENT *sb.* + -ARY.] Having the nature of a medicament; curative. Also, of a book, treating of medicaments.

1590 BARROUGH *Meth. Phisick* VIII. (1596) 484 Neither was it necessarie to stuffe this Medicamentarie booke with vnusuall..compositions. **1656** RIDGLEY *Pract. Physick* 286 We..must rather fight with medicamentary aliments, then with Medicaments. **1881** *Nature* 15 Sept. 480/2 Certain toxical or medicamentary substances..are not absorbed.

medicamentation (,mɛdɪkəmɛn'teɪʃən). [f. MEDICAMENT *sb.* + -ATION.] The action of 'medicamenting'; remedial treatment.

1885 *Public Opin.* 9 Jan. 30/1 The crisis of our interests has passed far beyond the medicamentation of mere talk.

medicamentous (,mɛdɪkə'mɛntəs), *a.* [f. MEDICAMENT *sb.* + -OUS.] = MEDICAMENTAL.

1684 tr. *Bonet's Merc. Compit.* xv. 524 The new-born Infant..requires a Medicamentous Milk. **1861** *Technologist* II. 30 It reaches the druggist, who has to prepare from it his medicamentous extract.

Medicare ('mɛdɪkɛə(r)). Also **medicare**. [f. MEDI(CAL *a.* + CARE *sb.*¹ 4.] **a.** Name given in the United States to a scheme of health insurance for the elderly, provided for under Title XVIII of the Social Security Act, 1965; cf. MEDICAID. **b.** Name of a similar scheme in Canada. Also *attrib.*

1962 *Economist* 16 June 1099 Ailing Medicare. **1963** *Times* 25 Feb. (Canada Suppl.) p. vi/6 The Canadian medicare problem must be seen against Canada's geographical, economic and political background. **1963** *Punch* 16 Oct. 577/3 The cost of providing Medicare..would be less than the annual cost of burying them. **1965** *New Statesman* 6 Aug. 177/1 Last week he [*sc.* President Johnson] signed the medicare bill. **1968** *Globe & Mail* (Toronto) 13 Feb. 1/7 Under the federal medicare legislation starting July 1, Ottawa will pick up half the average per capita cost. **1970** *Ibid.* 28 Sept. 17/1 A meeting of the Quebec Cabinet in Montreal tonight to discuss the possibility of passing emergency legislation to implement medicare. **1971** *Maclean's Mag.* Oct. 65/3 However he discharges his other campaign promises from abolishing deterrent fees for users of Medicare to renegotiating the pulp-mill deal, [etc.]. **1971** *Optometry Today* (Amer. Optometric Assoc.) 22 At present, optometrists..cannot provide optometric services to American senior citizens under the Medicare program. **1973** [see MEDICAID]. **1974** *Globe & Mail* (Toronto) 2 Mar. 8/3 Saskatchewan, which introduced medicare amid stormy and turbulent summer days in 1961, is embarking on a denticare programme.

medicaster ('mɛdɪkæstə(r)). Also 8 **medicastor**. [a. assumed L. **medicaster* (whence also It. *medicastro*, F. *médicastre*), f. *medicus* physician: see MEDIC and -ASTER.] A pretender to medical skill; a quack, charlatan. So †**medi'castra**, a female 'medicaster'.

1602 F. HERING *Anat.* 28 An other Medicastra, a ratling Gossip..commended a Drench. **1612** WOODALL *Surg. Mate* Wks. (1653) 244 Andreas Libavius, doth report of a certain Medicaster of his time [etc.]. **1706** BAYNARD in Sir J. Floyer *Hot & Cold Bath.* II. 393, I could say much more..to the Shame..of this sorry Medicaster. **1835** J. M. WILSON *Tales of Borders* (1857) I. 59 Doctors are quacks and medicasters to us. **1881** DUFFIELD *Don Quixote* I. 337 A queen may be leman to a medicaster.

†**'medicate**, *a.* *Obs.* [ad. L. *medicāt-us*, pa. pple. of *medicāre* (see next).] = MEDICATED.

1638 T. WHITAKER *Blood of Grape* 41 Not but that I take notice of medicate Wines, and their excellencies.

medicate ('mɛdɪkeɪt), *v.* [f. L. *medicāt-*, ppl. stem of *medicāre*, *-ārī*, f. *medicus*: see MEDIC.]

1. *trans.* To treat medically; to administer remedies to; to heal, cure.

1623 COCKERAM, *Medicate*, to heale or cure. **1691** BAXTER *Nat. Ch.* x. 48 All the Physicions Medicate all England. **1757** DYER *Fleece* I. 374 To soil Thy grateful fields, to medicate thy sheep,..Thy vacant hours require. **18..** SHELLEY *Ess. & Lett.* (1852) I. 256 He postponed all other purposes to the care of medicating himself. **1833** CHALMERS *Const. Man* (1835) I. 237 Which mars instead of medicates. **1880** BARWELL *Aneurism* 94 To feed, and if desirable also to medicate, the patient in such manner that [etc.].

fig. **1807** tr. *Three Germans* I. 68 What can medicate the wounds of the mind? **1860** EMERSON *Cond. Life* iv. (1861) 83 What we call our root-and-branch reforms of slavery, war [etc.] is only medicating the symptoms.

†**b.** To treat (a thing) with drugs or other substances for any purpose. *Obs.*

1644 EVELYN *Diary* Apr., His collection of all sorts of insects..is most curious; these he spreads and so medicates that no corruption invading them, he keepes them in drawers. **1775** G. WHITE *Selborne* 1 Nov. (1789) 198 A pound of rushes, medicated [*i.e.* steeped in tallow] and ready for use, will cost three shillings.

fig. **1839** DE QUINCEY *Philos. Rom. Hist.* Wks. 1890 VI. 431 Did ever Siren warble so dulcet a song to ears already prepossessed and medicated with spells of Circean effeminacy?

2. To impregnate with a medicinal substance.

1707 [see MEDICATING *vbl. sb.*]. **1753** *Scots Mag.* XV. 40/2 When a course of milk is ordered..may it not be thus *medicated* much to the advantage of the patient? **1898** *Allbutt's Syst. Med.* V. 37 The inhalation of steam medicated with terebene.

fig. **1751** JOHNSON *Rambler* No. 150 ¶3 The antidotes with which philosophy has medicated the cup of life. **1809** SYD. SMITH *Wks.* (1859) I. 185/2 You are multiplying..the chances of human improvement, by preparing and

medicating those early impressions, which always come from the mother.

†**b.** In wider sense [after L. *medicāre*]: To impregnate or mix with drugs or deleterious substances; to 'doctor' (liquors, etc.). *Obs.*

1662 GRAUNT *Bills Mortality* 68 The Fumes, Steams, and Stenches of London, do so medicate and impregnate the Air about it, that [etc.]. **1684** BAXTER *Twelve Argts.* Pref. F j b, They medicate their Wines with Arsenick and Mercury. **1744** BERKELEY *Siris* §11 Wines in the time of the old Romans were medicated with pitch and resin. **1791** COWPER *Odyss.* x. 291 She..medicated with her pois'nous drugs Their food.

3. *intr.* To practise the art of healing. *rare.*

1835 *Tait's Mag.* II. 17 Skilled in herbs too, he medicates successfully for man and beast.

medicated ('mɛdɪkeɪtɪd), *ppl. a.* [f. MEDICATE *v.* + -ED.[1]] Charged or impregnated with medicinal substances, drugs, or the like. Also *fig.*

1625 BP. HALL *Serm. Thanksgiving* (1626) 52 If some infrequent passenger crossed our streets, it was not without his medicated Posie at his nose. **1676** WISEMAN *Surg.* IV. v. 316, I..prescribed her a medicated Ale..for her constant Drink. **1781** GIBBON *Decl. & F.* xxxi. III. 206 *note*, The beautiful faces of the young slaves were covered with a medicated crust..which secured them against the effects of the sun. **184.** MRS. BROWNING *Sonn. fr. Portuguese* xvii, Antidotes Of medicated music. **1899** *Allbutt's Syst. Med.* VIII. 525 Medicated soaps.

medicating ('mɛdɪkeɪtɪŋ), *vbl. sb.* [f. MEDICATE *v.* + -ING[1].] = MEDICATION 1 b.

1707 MORTIMER *Husb.* (1721) II. 6 The medicating or steeping of Seeds.

'medicating, *ppl. a.* [-ING[2].] Healing.

1831 CARLYLE *Sart. Res.* III. iii, Leave him to Time, and the medicating virtue of Nature. **1879** STEVENSON *Trav. Cevennes, Florac*, The race of man..has medicating virtues of its own.

medication (mɛdɪ'keɪʃən). [ad. L. *medicātion-em*, n. of action f. *medicāre, medicārī*: see MEDICATE *v.* Cf. F. *médication.*]

1. The action of treating medically or subjecting to the action of medicaments.

1603 SIR C. HEYDON *Jud. Astrol.* ii. 99 So doth Galen attribute much to Homericall medication. **1646** SIR T. BROWNE *Pseud. Ep.* IV. xiii. 222 During those dayes, all medication or use of Physick is to be declined. **1831** J. DAVIES *Manual Mat. Med.* 225 Hemorrhage, agitation, fever, &c. &c. often attend this medication. **1848** THACKERAY *Van. Fair* xli, She hoped that her body might escape medication. **1899** *Allbutt's Syst. Med.* VIII. 604 It is better to assist the external measures by internal medication. *fig.* **1804** MITFORD *Inquiry* 158 Rarely indeed more than three lines together, even of Chaucer's, are found wholly unwanting medication.

b. Applied to treatment of plants. Also *concr.*, something used for 'medication'. ? *Obs.*

1626 BACON *Sylva* §500 The Watering of the Plant oft, with an Infusion of the Medecine. This..may have more force than the rest; Because the Medication is oft renewed. **1796** *New Ann. Reg.* 137 The cure [for animalcules]..is rubbing off with the lard medication. *Ibid.*, I have formerly quite removed the canker from some nonpareils, which, after three years medication, threw out shoots a yard long.

2. 'The act of tincturing or impregnating with medicinal ingredients' (J.); the infusion of medicinal substances.

1755 in JOHNSON. **1898** *Allbutt's Syst. Med.* V. 37 Meanwhile arrangements are to be made for..the occasional supply of steam and for its medication with eucalyptus.

medicative ('mɛdɪkətɪv), *a.* [f. MEDICATE *v.* + -IVE. Cf. med.L. *medicātīvus.*] Having the function or power of curing; curative.

1644 DIGBY *Nat. Bodies* xviii. §9. 165 If those vapors be ioyned with any medicatiue quality or body. **1814** D. STEWART *Hum. Mind* II. iv. §6. 471 Those physicians who profess to follow Nature..by watching and aiding her medicative powers. **1866** R. CHAMBERS *Ess.* Ser. II. 111 Oh, Nature,..Thy breath, thy voice, thy placid face, how truly medicative they are.

'medicator. *rare.* [f. MEDICATE *v.* + -OR. Cf. late L. *medicātor*, medical practitioner.] One who prepares potions.

1830 SCOTT *Demonol.* I. 67 The art of a medicator of poisons.

medicatory ('mɛdɪkeɪtərɪ), *a.* *rare*$^{-1}$. [f. L. *medicāt-*, ppl. stem of *medicāre*: see MEDICATE *v.* and -ORY.] Medicinal, healing.

1864 MRS. H. WOOD *Trev. Hold* III. ix. 123 Not all the medicatory drugs..can prevent the diseased vagaries of the imagination.

Medicean (mɛdɪ'siːən), *a.* [f. mod. L. *Medice-us* (f. It. *Medici*, surname) + -AN. Cf. F. *médicéen.*] Pertaining to the family of the Medici, who ruled Florence during the 15th c., and to whom belonged Popes Leo X (1513–21) and Clement VII (1523–34). Used as the designation of the library at Florence (otherwise called Laurentian) founded by Lorenzo de' Medici, and of MSS. there preserved; also, of various works of ancient art contained in the Florentine collections founded by the Medici.

1741 J. MARTYN *Virg. Georg.* IV. 262 *note*, Pierius found *aut* in the Medicean manuscript. **1835** *Penny Cycl.* IV. 5/2 The celebrated Medicean and Borghesan vases. **1893** GOW *Comp. Sch. Classics* vi. (ed. 3) 45 The sole authority for the letters *ad Familiares* is in the Medicean library. **1904** *Pilot* 9 Apr. 338/1 A description of Medicean Rome.

medicerebellar (miːdɪsɛrɪ'bɛlə(r)), *a.* *Anat.* [f. L. *medi-us* middle + CEREBELLAR.] Situated in the middle of the cerebellum.

1890 J. S. BILLINGS *Nat. Med. Dict.* II. 124 Medicerebellar Artery. Cerebellar Artery, anterior inferior.

medicerebral (miːdɪ'sɛrɪbrəl), *a.* *Anat.* [irreg. f. L. *medi-us* middle + CEREBRAL.] Lying about the middle of each cerebral hemisphere. Also *absol.* the medicerebral artery.

1889 *Buck's Handbk. Med. Sci.* VIII. 234 The Medicerebral [artery]. The vessel represents the most direct continuation of the cerebral carotid. *Ibid.*, The medicerebral in its further course yields two classes of branches.

Medici ('mɛdɪtʃɪ), *a.* [It. surname: cf. MEDICEAN *a.*] = MEDICEAN *a.*, esp. ***Medici collar*** (see quot. 1968); ***Medici lace*** (see quot. 1969), ***Medici porcelain*** (or ***china***), a type of porcelain produced under the patronage of Francesco de' Medici; ***Medici print, reproduction***, etc., one produced by the Medici Society, Ltd., London. Also *ellipt.*

1799 N. W. WRAXALL *Mem. Courts* II. xxi. 114 A broad Medicis of Dresden lace surrounded her bosom and shoulders. **1868** J. MARRYAT *Hist. Pott. & Porc.* (ed. 3) xiv. 456 (*caption*) Brocca of Medici Porcelain, 15 inches high. **1873** *Young Englishwoman* May 234/1 The Medici's collarette..is..becoming only to those ladies who have a slender swan-like neck. **1890** *Amer. Mail Order Fashions* (1961) 13 [Drawers] Cambric, ruffle of Medici lace, 75 c. **1900** F. LITCHFIELD *Pott. & Porc.* ii. 18 It was of soft paste, is extremely rare, and is known as 'Medici china'. **1902** JOURDAIN & DRYDEN *Palliser's Hist. Lace* (rev. ed.) iv. 56 The Medici collars were supported by fine metal bars called 'verghetti'. **1906** *Burlington Mag.* Oct. 47/1 If their quality can be maintained the *Medici* prints now being issued by Messrs. Chatto and Windus, of which the first three plates now lie before us, will undoubtedly represent a great advance upon anything which has yet been done in colour reproduction. **1908** BEERBOHM in *Around Theatres* (1924) II. 405 Nor was I embarrassed by the hoop and Medici collar that Dalila wore. **1936** *Catal. Medici Prints* 3 This Series has now attained a world-wide reputation under the title of 'Medici Prints'. **1940** *Burlington Mag.* May p. x/2, Medici porcelain. *Ibid.*, A 'Medici' plate, marked with the letter F and the dome of the Cathedral of Florence. **1949** F. TOWERS *Tea with Mr. Rochester* 24 The study with its Axminster carpet and Medici prints and rows of encyclopædias. **1957** J. BRAINE *Room at Top* vi. 60, I was..looking at the Medici reproduction of Olympe. **1960** R. G. HAGGAR *Conc. Encycl. Cont. Pott. & Porc.* 306/1 With one exception, all the known pieces of Medici porcelain are painted in blue, or blue and manganese purple. **1963** A. GERNSHEIM *Fashion & Reality* II. 79 Many capes had a small Medici collar. Such upstanding collars were worn on evening dresses, 1888–92 ..and fur Medici collars on coats and jackets during the winter of 1889–90. **1964** M. CLIVE *Day of Reckoning* iv. 42 There was a gap between those large, pale, repellant Victorian Arundel prints and the neat Medici reproductions which took their place. **1968** J. IRONSIDE *Fashion Alphabet* 51 *Medici collar*, a stiffened collar usually of lace, fan-shaped; high at the back of the neck and tapering away at the sides. **1969** R. T. WILCOX *Dict. Costume* (1970) 206/1 *Medici lace*, French bobbin-lace similar to Cluny lace, but of finer thread. Woven closely and open in intricate pattern with one edge scalloped.

†**medician.** *Obs.* [f. L. *medicus* (see MEDIC) + -IAN. Cf. *physician.*] A physician.

1597 in *Spalding Club Misc.* I. 133 Scho is altogiddir conswmit away; and na mediciane nor phisitian that will tak on hand to cure.

†**me'dicianer.** *Obs.* In 6 **medicianar**, 7 **medicioner.** Cf. MEDICINER. [f. MEDICIAN + -ER[1].] A physician.

a **1578** LINDESAY (Pitscottie) *Chron. Scot.* (S.T.S.) I. 362 They war certiffieit be the doctouris medicianaris that no successioun wald come of hir body. **1634** Medicioner [see MEDICINE *sb.*[2], quot. 1545].

medicinable ('mɛdsɪnəb(ə)l), *a.* and *sb.* Forms: 4–7 **medycinable**, 4–6 **medicynable**, 5 **medecynnabil**, **medycynable**, 6 **medcynable**, **medsonable**, **mediscenable**, 7 **medicineable**, 6–9 **med'cinable**, 4– **medicinable.** [a. OF. *medecinable*, f. *medeciner*: see MEDICINE *v.* and -ABLE.]

A. *adj.*

1. Having healing or curative properties; = MEDICINAL. *Obs.* exc. *poet.* or *arch.*

1398 TREVISA *Barth. De P.R.* XIV. xxi. (Tollem. MS.), Olyues and medicynable herbes and swete spices. *c* **1407** LYDG. *Reason & Sens.* 5630, I saugh the..herbes ful medycynable. *c* **1425** *St. Christina* xi. in *Anglia* VIII. 124/1 Hee bonde vppe hir legge wiþ medecynnabil cloþes. **1547** BOORDE *Introd. Knowl.* xxii. (1870) 177 Welles of water the whych..be mediscenable for sycke people. **1577** B. GOOGE *Heresbach's Husb.* III. (1586) 146 Cowe milk is most medicinable. **1604** SHAKS. *Oth.* V. ii. 351 Drop teares as fast as the Arabian Trees Their Medicinable gumme. **1634** W. WOOD *New Eng. Prosp.* (1865) 10 Many..haue beene restored by that medicineable Climate to their former..health. **1796** COLERIDGE *To J. Cottle*, Herbs of medicinable powers. **1842** SIR A. DE VERE *Song of Faith* 72 Paradise Of priceless and most medicinable fruits. **1885** PATER *Marius* II. 218 Soothing fingers had applied to his hands and feet..a medicinable oil.

b. *fig.* and in figurative context.

c **1400** *Apol. Loll.* 21 Medicinable comyning wiþ þe kirk or sacraments of it. *c* **1440** *Alphabet of Tales* 422 Be þi medycynable tong I trow at God shall delyver me from my moste errour. **1556** J. HEYWOOD *Spider & F.* ii. 150 Pacience the medsonable meane, To take all fautles falles, reioisinglie. **1611** SHAKS. *Cymb.* III. ii. 33 Some griefes are medcinable, that is one of them, For it doth physicke Loue. **1798** J. HUCKS *Poems* 146 In memory's stores, I seek the med'cinable balm.

†**2.** Of or belonging to medicine. *Obs.*

1530 PALSGR. 318/1 Medcynable belongyng to physicke. **1586** BRIGHT *Melanch.* xl. 268 It yeeldeth no medicinable tast to the mouth. **1607** MARKHAM *Caval.* I. (1617) 57 Then you shall seek by medicinable means to recouer them.

†**3.** ***medicinable finger*** = LEECH-FINGER; ***medicinable ring***, app. a blessed ring supposed to cure diseases. *Obs.*

1432–50 tr. *Higden* (Rolls) II. 313 The iiij[the] fynger, which is callede the fynger medicinable. *a* **1483** *Liber Niger* in *Househ. Ord.* (1790) 23 Item, to the king's offerings to the crosse on Good Friday, out from the Countyng-house, for medycinable rings of gold & sylver.

†**B.** *sb.* A medicinal substance. *Obs.*

1683 TRYON *Way to Health* 560 A great number of Medicinables..of our own growth, proper for the Cure of those Diseases that are generated in our Elevation.

Hence †**medicinableness.**

1660 INGELO *Bentiv. & Ur.* I. (1682) 167 The medicinableness of every one [of these fruits] is so affix'd to its own Branch that it is not communicated to another.

medicinal (mɪ'dɪsɪnəl), *a.* and *sb.* [a. L. *medicīnāl-is* of or pertaining to medicine: see MEDICINE and -AL[1]. Cf. F. *médicinal.*]

A. *adj.* **1.** Having healing or curative properties or attributes; adapted to medical uses. Const. *against, for.*

a **1340** HAMPOLE *Psalter* l. 8 Ysope is a medicynall erbe. **1422** tr. *Secreta Secret., Priv. Priv.* 245 Medycinal Purgacions sholde bene y-makyd in this tyme. **1525** in *Vicary's Anat.* (1888) App. VIII. 214 It may be by the College considered whether the bill were medecynall, or hurtfull, to the siknes. *c* **1540** tr. *Pol. Verg. Eng. Hist.* (Camden) I. 295 His..ringe was..medicinalle againste..the fallinge sickenes. **1617** MORYSON *Itin.* I. 116 Most of the waters are medicinall. **1671** MILTON *Samson* 627 Dire inflammation which no cooling herb Or medcinal liquor can asswage. **1717** LADY M. W. MONTAGU *Let. to P'cess of Wales* 1 Apr., Here are hot baths, very famous for their medicinal virtues. **1899** *Allbutt's Syst. Med.* VI. 429 The medical and medicinal treatment of aortic aneurysm.

b. *fig.*

c **1400** *Wyclif's Bible* Tit. ii. 8 (MS. *M*) Word medicynal [1382 an hool word, 1388 an hoolsum word, Vulg. *sanum*]. **1502** ARNOLDE *Chron.* 174 As in the councel of Oxenford it is..decreed that the sentence of excommunication whiche is sayd medecinall iiij tymes in the yere to be pronounced. **1561** T. NORTON *Calvin's Inst.* III. 213 All this misery of mankinde..is a medicinal sorrow, and not a penall sentence. **1672** CAVE *Prim. Chr.* III. v. (1673) 374 The medicinal vertue of Repentance, lying not in the duration, but the manner of it. **1794** COLERIDGE *To a Friend* 11 Soothing each pang with fond solicitude, And tenderest tones medicinal of love. **1870** EMERSON *Soc. & Solit., Bks.* Wks. (Bohn) III. 81 Plutarch cannot be spared from the smallest library..because he is so..medicinal and invigorating. **1903** *Hibbert Jrnl.* Mar. 583 The preaching of Christianity as medicinal for soul and body brought success.

†**2.** Of or relating to the science or the practice of medicine. *Obs.*

1387 TREVISA *Higden* (Rolls) III. 363 He made problems medicinal of phisik. *c* **1400** *Lanfranc's Cirurg.* 7 (Add. MS.) Surgerie..is a medycineal sciense. *c* **1400** tr. *Secreta Secret., Gov. Lordsh.* 66 Y wyl delyure to þe techinge Medicynal. **1563** T. GALE *Antidot.* Pref. 1 Suche medicinall instruments, as..are mentioned in the same bookes. *a* **1641** BP. MOUNTAGU *Acts & Mon.* (1642) 171 Certain medicinall books and writings of Trismegistus. **1685** DRYDEN *Thren. August.* v. 170 They min'd it near, they batter'd from afar With all the Cannon of the Med'cinal War. **1755** J. SHEBBEARE *Lydia* (1769) I. 178 As nonsense and medicinal knowledge are equally intelligible to most people [etc.]. **1804** *Miniature* No. 20 (1806) I. 267 The medicinal art.

b. Resembling medicine.

1824 A. HENDERSON *Wines* 344 [It] is apt to infect the liquor with a medicinal taste.

†**3.** ***medicinal-finger*** = LEECH-FINGER. ***medicinal day, hour, month***, times when the administration of medicine was deemed proper. *Obs.*

1597 A. M. tr. *Guillemeau's Fr. Chirurg.* 12 b/1 The Medicinalle finger, or Ringe finger, betweene the little finger and the middle finger. **1623** tr. *Favine's Theat. Hon.* I. v. 48 The medicinall finger of the left hand. **1674** JEAKE *Arith.* (1696) 229 The time when most proper to administer Physick, called the Medicinal Moneth. **1722** QUINCY *Lex. Phys.-Med.* (ed. 2) s.v. *Medicine*, Medicinal Days, such are so called by some Writers, wherein no Crisis or Change is expected, so as to forbid the use of Medicines..: but it is most properly used for those Days, wherein Purging or any other Evacuation is most conveniently comply'd with. *Ibid.*, Medicinal Hours are commonly reckoned in the Morning fasting, about an Hour before Dinner [etc.]. **1747** tr. *Astruc's Fevers* 120 The antients divided the days of an acute fever into critical, indicatory, intercalary, and medicinal.

B. *sb.* **a.** A medicinal substance. †**b.** *pl.* Matters pertaining to medical science (*obs.*).

1382 WYCLIF *Rev.* iii. 18 Anoynte thin iȝen with colirie, [*gloss*] that is, medicynal for yȝen, maad of diuerse erbis. *a* **1657** R. LOVEDAY *Lett.* (1663) 191 'Tis possible Mr. R's directions, as one well skill'd in such medicinals, may prove

available. **1667** H. Oldenburg in *Phil. Trans.* II. 410 In Medicinals we have now and then..inquired after some rarities. **1716** M. Davies *Athen. Brit.* III. *Diss. Physick* 12 The knowledge of all the Medicinals, that they could come any way to be acquainted with. *Ibid.* 36 Searching into the Oriental..Medicinals. **1813** *Examiner* 15 Feb. 99/2 Brandy, medicinals, &c. **1862** Lytton *Str. Story* II. 5 The remarkable cures he had effected by the medicinals stored in the stolen casket.

medicinally (mɪˈdɪsɪnəlɪ), *adv.* [f. prec. + -ly².]

1. With the purpose or effect of a medicine.

1607 Topsell *Four-f. Beasts* (1658) 65 They gave it medicinally to them which were sick of the Ptisick. **1682** Dryden *Medal* 150 The Witnesses, that, Leech-like, liv'd on bloud, Sucking for them were med'cinally good. **1725** Bradley *Fam. Dict.* s.v. *Wormwood*, That which is commonly made Use of Medicinally. **1836** J. M. Gully *Magendie's Formul.* (ed. 2) 23 It is now..fifteen years since I first used..the muriate of morphia medicinally. **1899** *Allbutt's Syst. Med.* VI. 795 The internal administration of specific remedies..is all that can be done medicinally.

fig. *a* **1711** Ken *Anodynes* Poet. Wks. 1721 III. 452 Thy Love, Lord, I in Pains perceiv'd, And sing thy Love when med'cinally griev'd.

2. †**a.** From the point of view of the science of medicine (*obs.*). **b.** *nonce-use.* In the practice of medicine.

1621 Burton *Anat. Mel.* Democr. to Rdr. 69 My purpose ..is..to Anatomise this humour of Melancholy..and that philosophically, medicinally, to shew the causes..and seuerall cures of it. **1846** Poe *J. W. Francis* Wks. 1864 III. 38 Connected in some manner with everything that has been well said or done medicinally in America.

meˈdicinalness. *rare*⁻⁰. [-ness.] Medicinal quality.

1727 Bailey vol. II, *Physicalness*, Naturalness, also Medicinalness.

†**meˈdicinary**, *a.* *Obs.* [f. medicine *sb.* + -ary.] Possessing healing properties.

1607 Walkington *Opt. Glass* 3 The wise Physitians medicinary prescript. **1638** *Anat. Woman's tongue* in *Harl. Misc.* (1809) II. 187 Among these weeds, to supply men's wants, There grew some medicinary plants. **1657** Tomlinson *Renou's Disp.* 664 Medicinary Oyls are neither all, nor alwayes elicited out of Plants.

medicine (ˈmɛds(ə)n, ˈmɛdɪsɪn, -s(ə)n), *sb.*¹ Forms: 3 medicin, 4 medisine, 4–5 medcyne, 4–6 medycine, 4–6 medycyne, medicyne, 5 medcyn, -ycyn, -esyn, metycyne, mettecyn, medcoyne, 5–6 medecyn(e, medicyn, 6 medecin, -yson, -ysyne, medsin, -syn, meddicine, metson, 6–9 medecine, medecen, 7 medcin, 3– medicine. [a. OF. *medecine*, *medicine* (mod.F. *médecine*), ad. L. *medicīna* (1) the art of the physician, (2) a physician's laboratory, (3) a medicament, remedy, f. *medic-us* physician: see medic. Cf. Pr. *medecina*, *medicina*, *metzina*, Sp., Pg., It. *medicina*, G. *medizin*, Du. *medicijn*, Da., Sw. *medicin*.

For the formation of the L. word cf. *officīna* (for **opificina*), *ruina*, *rapīna*. There seems to be no sufficient ground for the common view that *medicīna* is the fem. of an adj. *medicīnus* used with ellipsis (in the three senses respectively) of *ars* art, *officina* workshop, *rēs* thing. The adj. occurs in late L., but otherwise only in one passage of Varro (in the phrase *ars medicina*), and its formation may have been suggested by the existence of the sb.

The disyllabic pronunciation (recognized by Johnson 1755) has existed at least from the 14th c., as occasional spellings indicate. The trisyllabic pronunciation is less common in England, and is by many objected to as either pedantic or vulgar; in Scotland and in the U.S. it is app. the prevailing usage; examples of it occur in verse of all periods, from the 14th c. onwards.]

1. That department of knowledge and practice which is concerned with the cure, alleviation, and prevention of disease in human beings, and with the restoration and preservation of health. Also, in a more restricted sense, applied to that branch of this department which is the province of the physician, in the modern application of the term; the art of restoring and preserving the health of human beings by the administration of remedial substances and the regulation of diet, habits, and conditions of life; distinguished from Surgery and Obstetrics.

c **1320** *Sir Tristr.* 1204 Þe fair leuedi, þe quene, Louesom vnder line And sleiȝest had y bene, And mest couþe of medici[n]e. *c* **1374** Chaucer *Troylus* i. 659 Phebus þat first fond art of medecyne. **1484** Caxton *Fables of Auian* v, I am a maystresse in medecyne, and canne gyue remedy to al manere of sekenes by myn arte. **1500–20** Dunbar *Poems* xxxiii. 30 He murdreist mony in medecyne. **1550** Lyndesay *Sqr. Meldrum* 1446 And, als, be his naturall ingyne, He lernit the Art of Medicyne. **1641** Wilkins *Math. Magick* i. i. (1648) 3 Art may be said, either to imitate nature, as in limming and pictures, or to help nature, as in medicine. **1725** Watts *Logic* i. vi. §10 Medicine is justly distributed into Prophylactick..and Therapeutick. **1828** Scott *F.M. Perth* vii, The peaceful man of medicine. **1866** A. Flint *Princ. Med.* (1880) 17 Medicine, in the largest sense of the term, comprehends everything pertaining to the knowledge and cure of disease. In a more restricted sense, the term is used in contradistinction to Surgery and Obstetrics. **1891** C. James *Rom. Rigmarole* 93, I took up medicine again in England.

2. a. Any substance or preparation used in the treatment of disease; a medicament; also, medicaments generally, 'physic'. Now commonly restricted to medicaments taken internally.

a **1225** *Ancr. R.* 178 Þu seist þet te nis no neod medicine. **1297** R. Glouc. (Rolls) 3073 Vor in þe verroste stede of affric geans wule vette þulke stones vor medicine..Vor hii wolde þe stones wasse & þer inne baþie. *a* **1300** *Cursor M.* 1378 Cedre,ciprese, and pine, O þam sal man haue medicen. **1398** Trevisa *Barth. De P.R.* vii. lxix. (1495) 288 Medycyne maye neuer be sykerly take, yf the cause of the euyll is vnknowe. *c* **1440** *Alphabet of Tales* 93 He had burnyd his hand ill, & his brethir come & made a medcyn & layd þervnto. **1464** M. Paston in *P. Lett.* II. 160 For Goddys sake be war what medesyns ye take of any fysissyans of London. **1513** Bradshaw *St. Werburge* ii. 853 All phisike and medicyns were founde to her in vayne. **1565** T. Stapleton *Fortr. Faith* 110 b, The more he fancieth his metson, the better it shall proue with him. **1612** Woodall *Surg. Mate* Wks. (1653) 3 Have ready your medicines to bind up the wound again. **1657** Trapp *Comm. Job.* xvi. 3 If the eye be inflamed, the mildest Medicine troubleth it. **1697** Dryden *Virg. Georg.* iii. 685 From the Founts where living Sulphurs boil, They mix a Med'cine to foment their Limbs. **1741–3** Wesley *Extract of Jrnl.* (1749) 15 One of the mistresses lay ..near death, having found no help from all the medicines she had taken. **1842** A. Combe *Physiol. Digestion* (ed. 4) 369 The action of the bowels may be restored with little or no aid from medicine. **1850** Tennyson in H. Tennyson *Mem.* (1897) I. 334 Having heard that Henry Taylor was ill, Carlyle rushed off from London to Sheen with a bottle of medicine.

transf. **1613** Purchas *Pilgrimage* (1614) 600 Their old men ..they strangle with an Oxe-taile, which medicine they minister likewise to those that have grieuous diseases.

b. Colloquially used *spec.* for: 'A purging potion' (Dunglison *Med. Lex.*, 1857). Chiefly in ***to take*** (†***a***) ***medicine***. Cf. F. *prendre* (*une*) *médecine*.

1830 Southey in *For. Rev. & Cont. Misc.* V. 290 On the day when signal was made for sailing, he had taken a medicine, which was in those times considered a more serious affair than it is now.

†**c.** A method or process of curative treatment.

1390 Gower *Conf.* I. 267 So longe thei togedre dele, That thei upon this medicine Apointen hem..That..Thei wolde him bathe in childes blod. **1575** Laneham *Let.* (1871) 35 Kings & Queenz of this Realm, withoout oother medsin (saue only by handling & prayerz), only doo cure it [the king's evil].

†**d.** An effectual remedy, cure. *Obs.*

1390 Gower *Conf.* I. 47 Ne hyd it noght, for if thou feignest, I can do the no medicine. *c* **1450** *St. Cuthbert* (Surtees) 6140 Scho gat sone medecyne Of þe sekenes þat had hir pynde. **1529** Rastell *Pastyme* (1811) 32 Arnold.. was etyn with lyse, and coud have no medecin, and dyed.

e. *fig.* In 14–15th c. often applied to Christ or the Virgin Mary.

a **1225** *Ancr. R.* 164 Þuruh medicine of schrifte, & þuruh bireousunge. *c* **1315** Shoreham ii. 136 Suche a deaþ a [*sc.* he, Christ] vnder-ȝede, Of lyf þe medicine. **1362** Langl. *P. Pl.* A. i. 33 Mesure is Medicine þauh þou muche ȝeorne. *c* **1380** Wyclif *Serm.* Sel. Wks. II. 224 Medicyne for alle siche synne is, to be clopid in Jesus Crist. *c* **1440** *Jacob's Well* 157 Medycyne here-of is, ferst to caste out þe wose of glotonye. *c* **1450** Holland *Howlat* 719 Haile moder of our maker, and medicyn of myss! **1522** More *De quat. Noviss.* Wks. 93/1 To putte in proofe..thoperacion..of this medicine, the remembraunce of these foure last thinges. **1603** Shaks. *Meas. for M.* iii. i. 2 The miserable haue no other medicine But onely hope. **1638** *Penit. Conf.* vii. (1657) 161 If any of their sins were deemed fit by the Confessor to come abroad in publick, they were admitted to that publick Medicine. **1787** Jefferson *Writ.* (1859) II. 194 It is, indeed, a strong medicine for sensible minds, but it is a medicine. **1842** Miss Mitford in L'Estrange *Life* (1870) III. ix. 157 He finds in constant employment a medicine for great grief.

f. ***to take one's medicine***, to submit to or endure something disagreeable; to learn a lesson; ***a dose, taste***, etc., ***of one's own*** (***kind of***) ***medicine***, repayment or retaliation in kind; 'tit for tat'.

1865 A. D. Richardson *Secret Service* v. 75 The leaders refused to take their own medicine. **1894** P. L. Ford *Hon. Peter Stirling* xxvii. 150 'He snubbed me..,' explained Miss De Voe, smiling slightly at the thought of treating Peter with a dose of his own medicine. **1903** *N.Y. Times* 21 Sept., Canada can do nothing—she must take her medicine and make the best of it. **1904** 'O. Henry' *Cabbages & Kings* xvii. 299 You go back and take your medicine like a man. **1939** T. S. Eliot *Family Reunion* i. i. 18 Make him feel that what has happened doesn't matter. He's taken his medicine, I've no doubt. **1941** V. Perdue *Singing Clock* (1945) viii. 52 It was only fair for them to get a taste of their own medicine. **1961** L. van der Post *Heart of Hunter* i. vii. 111 Giving him some of his own medicine, I said: 'How very charming of you!' **1961** C. Willock *Death in Covert* xii. 217, I set the spring-guns, sir... I'm willing to take my medicine for that... If it's found out..it'll make the other things look black for me. And them I did not do. **1968** E. Gaines in A. Chapman *New Black Voices* (1972) 102 He ain't the first one they ever beat and he won't be the last one, and getting in it will just bring you a dose of the same medicine.

†**3.** Applied to drugs used for other than remedial purposes: e.g. to the philosopher's stone or elixir, to cosmetics, poisons, philtres, etc. *Obs.*

c **1400** Maundev. (Roxb.) vii. 24 If þaim think þam noȝt blak ynough when þai er borne, þai vse certayne medecynes for to make þam black withall. **1477** Norton *Ord. Alch.* i. in Ashm. (1652) 20 But to make trew Silver or Gold is noe ingin, Except only the Philosophers medicine. **1555** W. Watreman *Fardle Facions* ii. ix. N ij, Then enoint thei both that [*sc.* the body] and their face with certaine medicines.. whereby thei become..slicke and smothe. *Ibid.* App. X viij b, No Israelite shall haue any medecine of death, ne otherwise made to do anye maner of hurte. **1580** Lyly *Euphues* (Arb.) 337 Knowest thou not, that Fish caught with medicines, and women gotten with witchcraft are neuer wholesom? **1596** Shaks. *1 Hen. IV*, ii. ii. 19 If the Rascall haue not giuen me medicines to make me loue him, Ile be hang'd. **1601** —— *All's Well* v. iii. 102. **1604** —— *Oth.* i. iii. 61. **1615** Chapman *Odyss.* xii. 368 And as an Angler medcine for surprise Of little fish, sits powring from the rocks.

fig. *c* **1380** Wyclif *Wks.* (1880) 463 God haþ ordeyned medicyn to knowe falsed of anticrist.

4. a. Used to represent the terms applied in their native languages by North American Indians to denote any object or ceremony supposed by them to possess a magical influence; a spell, charm, fetish; sometimes = Manitou. Hence used, by later writers, to express the same or similar meanings as current among other primitive peoples. Also *colloq.* in phr. ***bad medicine***, something or someone sinister or ill-fated.

As primitive peoples usually regard the operation of medicines as due to what we should call magic, it is probable that their words for magical agencies would often be first heard by outsiders as applied to medicine, and hence it would be natural that 'medicine' should be regarded as their primary sense.

1805 Pike *Sources Mississ.* (1810) 17 This they called their great medicine; or as I understood the word, dance of religion. **1807** P. Gass *Jrnl.* 44 He told them..he had more medecine..than would kill twenty such nations in one day. **1825** G. Simpson *Jrnl.* in *Fur Trade* (1931) 136 Some of them have it that I am one of the 'Master of Life's Sons' sent to see 'if their hearts were good' and others that I am his 'War Chief' with bad medicine if their hearts were bad. **1841** Catlin *N. Amer. Ind.* (1844) I. vi. 35 The word medicine.. means mystery, and nothing else. **1850** R. G. Cumming *Hunter's Life S. Afr.* (ed. 2) I. 274 They [the Bechuana tribes] also believe that for every transaction there is a medicine which will enable the possessor to succeed in his object. **1851** Mayne Reid *Scalp Hunt.* xxvi, All these are their 'coats' of arms, symbolical of the 'medicine' of the wearer. **1869** *Harper's Mag.* Jan. 151/2 Will Comstock was sure that it was bad 'medicine' (luck) to camp on the Stinking Water. **1870** Lubbock *Orig. Civiliz.* vii. (1875) 323 When he sleeps the first animal of which he dreams becomes his 'medicine'. **1877** Dodge *Hunting Grounds Gt. West* 399 It [a 'scalp'] had been carefully cured, and peculiar value was set upon it as 'big medicine'. **1945** P. Cheyney *I'll say she Does!* ii. 38 I'd like to talk to him. He's bad medicine. **1964** 'E. Peters' *Flight of Witch* i. 25 'Did you know that outcrop of rock is known locally as the Altar?'..'So that's it,' he said. 'Just bad medicine.' **1969** 'J. Morris' *Fever Grass* xxiii. 214 When people like me..get together we can be bad medicine fer anybody from outside. **1973** P. O'Donnell *Silver Mistress* xiii. 216 Momma's gotta go redundant. She's a great kid..but she's gonna be bad medicine on the run.

b. = *medicine-man*.

1817 J. Bradbury *Trav. Amer.* 70 Eleven Sioux Indians, who had given or devoted their clothes to the medicine, ran into the camp. **1827** J. F. Cooper *Prairie* II. xii. 199 The incantations of the medecine.

5. *slang.* Intoxicating drink. (Cf. *lotion*, *poison*.)

1851 Mayhew *Lond. Labour* (1864) II. 24/1 As long as you can find young men that's conceited about their musical talents, fond of taking their medicine (drinking). **1891** Farmer *Slang* s.v. *Drinks*, What's your medicine?

6. *attrib.* and *Comb.*

a. In sense 2: ***medicine bottle, cabinet, chest, cupboard, -dropper, -mixer, -monger, -taker; medicine-like*** adj.; **medicine ball**, a stuffed leather ball which is thrown and caught to provide exercise; **medicine glass**, a small drinking-glass graduated for use in measuring medicines; **medicine seal, stamp**, a name for small cubical or oblong stones with inscriptions in intaglio, found among Roman remains, which seem to have been used by physicians for marking their drugs (also called *oculist-stamp*, *oculist's stamp*); **medicine show** *N. Amer.*, a travelling show, in which entertainers attract customers to whom medicine can be sold; **medicine tree**, the horse-radish tree (see horse-radish 3).

1895 *Crescent* (Brooklyn, N.Y.) 1 Nov. 14/1 While Charlie Notman opines that the 'gym' needs more *medicine ball, the few inoffensive ones now on hand are kicking for more 'gym'. **1903** W. L. Savage in *Athletics & Outdoor Sports for Women* 49 The illustrations below show two of the methods for passing medicine balls. **1930** *Bulletin* 13 Feb. 8/2 The Prince of Wales..instead of indulging in..tennis and quoits, preferred to devote the time after tea to throwing the medicine ball. **1965** G. McInnes *Road to Gundagai* x. 156 Down the middle of the hall three teams were competing at medicine ball. **1974** J. Heller *Something Happened* 314 It was a relay race, and he was ten yards ahead,..carrying a heavy medicine ball. **1852** Dickens *Bleak Ho.* (1853) v. 35 Quantities of dirty bottles: blacking bottles, *medicine bottles, [etc.]. **1862** *Chambers's Encycl.* IV. 777/1 Medicine bottles. **1899** *Montgomery Ward Catal.* 576/2 *Medicine cabinet, made of oak. **1922** S. Lewis *Babbitt* i. 14 Above the set bowl was a..medicine cabinet. **1955** W. Gaddis *Recognitions* ii. vii. 572 Esther set off with her to the bathroom, where they interrupted someone who was looking through the medicine cabinet. **1974** M. Babson *Stalking Lamb* xiv. 93 The sleeping tablets..in the bathroom medicine cabinet. **1731** in E. Singleton *Social N.Y. under Georges* (1902) 85 A very fine *Medicine Chest with great variety of valuable Medicines. **1828** Rymer (*title*) A Treatise on Diet and Regimen..To which are added a Posological Table, or medicine chest directory [etc.]. **1841** Marryat *Masterman Ready* xiii, The grindstone and Mrs. Seagrave's medicine chest were then landed. **1957** P. Kemp *Mine were of Trouble* i. 6, I remember a bulky 'medicine chest' which seemed to contain chiefly iodine, quinine and

cascara. **1907** *Yesterday's Shopping* (1969) 131/3 Fumed oak *Medicine Cupboard..4/7. **1966** A. E. Lindop *I start Counting* xiii. 151, I fled to the bathroom. I yanked open the medicine cupboard so hard that the mirror came off its hinges. **1898** *Allbutt's Syst. Med.* V. 565 At short intervals by a spoon or *medicine-dropper, [he] should have small quantities of his mother's milk. **1853** *Medicine glass [see *bed table* s.v. BED *sb.* 19]. *c* **1555** Lady Vane *Let.* in Foxe *A. & M.* (1583) 1829 His sweetenesse..maketh al these poticary druggs of yͤ world, euen *medicinelike in my mouth. **1860** J. C. Jeaffreson *Bk. about Doctors* I. 79 The mean *medicine-mixers..dashing by in their carriages. **1651** Wittie tr. *Primrose's Pop. Err.* I. iv. 13, I see no reason ..that some divines may not be more learned than some *Medicine-mongers. **1795** *Fortnight's Ramble* 33 Uncounted are the candidates for fame, who humbly crouched to this mock medicine-monger. **1851** Simpson in *Monthly Jrnl. Med. Sci.* XII. 238 Roman *medicine-seals. **1938** H. Asbury *Sucker's Progress* 355 Minnie and Colorado Charley then organized a *medicine show with which they traveled through Mexico and Central America. **1958** P. Gammond *Decca Bk. Jazz* ix. 117 Thelonious Monk, passing through with a travelling medicine show, was once heard as an uncomplicated swing stylist there. **1962** E. Lucia *Klondike Kate* 7 They travelled with medicine shows, carnivals, [etc.]. **1970** P. Oliver *Savannah Syncopators* 96 With the demise of the work song, the blues became the song vehicle to accompany labour and, in earlier years, for the medicine show or the barber shop. **1849** C. Roach Smith in *Jrnl. Brit. Archæol. Assoc.* IV. 280 On a Roman *medicine stamp..found at Kenchester. **1851** Simpson in *Monthly Jrnl. Med. Sci.* XII. 39 Notices of ancient Roman Medicine-stamps..found in Great Britain. **1422** tr. *Secreta Secret., Priv. Priv.* 87 Yf þe sonne and þe mone bothe be yn tokenynge fleumatyk, lightly þe *medicyn takere shal forth lede. **1902** Webster *Suppl.*, **Medicine tree*, the horse-radish tree.

b. In sense 4: ***medicine animal, arrow, bag, bundle, chief, dance, fast, hunt, lodge, pipe, pouch, sack, song, stone***; **medicine line**, a name given by American Indians to the border between Canada and the United States; **medicine man**, a magician or shaman among American Indians and other peoples; hence *colloq.*, a doctor (cf. sense 2 a above); also *transf.* and *fig.*; **medicine murder**, murder committed to obtain parts of the body for 'medicine'; ritual murder; **medicine wolf** *U.S.* = COYOTE; **medicine woman**, an Indian woman dealing in magic.

1871 Tylor *Prim. Cult.* xv. II. 211 The worship paid by the North American Indian to his *medicine animal [etc.]. **1877** W. Matthews *Ethnogr. Hidatsa* 69 They stuck their *medicine-arrows in the ground. **1797** C. Chaboillez *Jrnl.* in B. C. Payette *Northwest* (1964) [I] made him consent to go for his *Medicine Bag. **1801** A. Henry *Jrnl.* in E. Coues *New Light Hist. Greater Northwest* (1897) I. 162 The fellow came accordingly with his drum and medicine bag. **1809** A. Henry *Trav.* 122 One, who was a physician, immediately withdrew, in order to fetch his *penegusan*, or medicine-bag. **1865** Milton & Cheadle *N.W. Passage by Land* iv. 66 The chief..dressed in a spangled shirt, a cap covered with many-coloured ribbons, and an elaborately-worked medicine-bag, rose and made an oration. **1971** J. McDougall *Parsons on Plains* xix. 180 With their medicine-bags in hand they stood like statues. **1936** *Canad. Geogr. Jrnl.* XII. 98/2 Wherever they went they carried with them a *medicine pipe and bundle upon the back of a milk-white steed. **1952** *Beaver* Sept. 27 Medicine bundles, both personal and tribal, were of great importance. **1969** *Ibid.* Summer 49/1 Each member had his own medicine bundle containing various items. **1851** Mayne Reid *Scalp Hunt.* xl. 312 One was the *medicine chief as I could tell by the flowing white hair. **1808** Pike *Sources Mississ.* (1810) 132 Dr. Robinson and myself went to the Grand Village, at which we saw the great *medecine dance. **1855** Longf. *Hiaw.* xv. 145 Then they.. Danced their medicine-dance around him. **1898** A. Lang *Making Relig.* iii. 61 The *medicine-fast, at the age of puberty. **1887** —— *Myth, Ritual, & Relig.* II. 74 The ritual ..is a mere *medicine-hunt. **1910** A. L. Haydon *Riders of Plains* 95 The Indians..called the International Boundary the '*Medicine Line', assuming that in the absence of any agreement between the two Governments relative to this crime, they were perfectly safe on one side of the line with regard to what had been done on the other. **1913** L. V. Kelly *Range Men* 143 In their own tongue they [*sc.* Indians] called it the 'medicine line', and were very well pleased with the condition of affairs. *Ibid.* 162 The Canadian Indians were not entirely disappointed at the results of their own forays south of the 'medicine line'. **1962** W. Stegner *Wolf Willow* II. vii. 96 By that time Crow and Gros Ventre and Sioux and Blackfoot and Assiniboin would already know that the 'Medicine Line', as they called it, was something potent in their lives. **1970** *Beaver* Winter 28/1 In 1801 he was..just across the North Dakota medicine line, the magical boundary between Canada and the States. **1973** R. D. Symons *Where Wagon Led* I. vii. 110 The various ranch outfits would make up big trail herds and move them across the Medicine Line. **1808** C. Mackenzie in L. R. Masson *Les Bourgeois* (1889) I. 354 The women were directed to go into the woods for branches to cover the *Medecine lodge. **1814** Brackenridge *Jrnl.* in *Views Louisiana* 258 A great number of girls were collected before the medecine lodge or temple. **1901** F. H. Giddings *Inductive Sociol.* 207 Religious Societies—..In North American Indian tribes, they are known as Medicine Lodges. **1944** *Beaver* June 35 At the end of the medicine lodge inside, Moanday erects two poles, a cross-bar between. At the foot of each pole he lays the body of a dog he has killed. **1801** A. Henry *Jrnl.* in E. Coues *New Light Hist. Greater Northwest* (1897) I. 162 An Indian who pretended to be a *medicine man was employed by Maymiutch to cure his sick brother. **1817** J. Bradbury *Trav. Amer.* 116, I was accosted by the Medicine Man, or doctor. **1855** Longf. *Hiaw.* xv. 87 The medicine-men, the Medas. **1890** E. Dowson *Let.* 10 Oct. (1967) 170 In spite of my rooted aversion to the genre I shall have to call in a medicine-man. **1898** G. B. Shaw *Doctors' Delusions* (1932) 107 Out of sheer credulity as to the infallibility of the medicine man, we are drifting into a legal procedure which relieves them from all necessity to gain our confidence by the good they do us. **1922** Joyce *Ulysses* 16 She bows her old head to a voice that speaks to her loudly, her bonesetter, her medicine-man. **1939** J. Dillard in A. Dundes *Mother Wit* (1973) 278/2 Medicine men..falsify their experience..in order to qualify for their craft. **1947** Auden *Age of Anxiety* (1948) iii. 72 The medicine men who keep this body Politic free from fevers, Cancer and constipation. **1961** *Listener* 20 Apr. 683/2 He [*sc.* a foreign correspondent] has, like a medium or a circus medicine man, simply to go into a trance to pronounce what '*the*' American people feel about it all. **1965** R. & D. Morris *Men & Snakes* ii. 46 A double-sexed two-headed snake named Sachan..was the typical emblem of the Near Eastern and Mediterranean medicine man. **1966** B. Kimenye *Kalasanda Revisited* 92 The medicine man at Nakivubo bus park had a fresh supply of snuff. **1974** Wodehouse *Aunts aren't Gentlemen* iii. 17, I was a bit early for my appointment, and was informed on arrival that the medicine man was tied up for the moment with another gentleman. [**1947** *Times* 25 Oct. 3/5 Seventeen Africans were sentenced to death in two cases..here today for committing murder for 'medicine'.] **1952** *Basutoland 1951* (H.M.S.O.) ix. 57 During 1951 fourteen trial cases..were heard by the High Court. Two of these cases dealt with the crime known as *Medicine Murder. **1966** *New Statesman* 25 Feb. 265/1 A chapter..on the abominations of 'medicine murder'. **1833** G. Catlin *N. Amer. Indians* (1841) I. 111 At that hour.., with *medicine-pipes in his hands and foxes tails attached to his heels, entered Mah-to-he-hah (the old bear). **1971** J. McDougall *Parsons on Plains* xii. 110 First, The oldest conjuror took the big medicine pipe with the long stem. **1855** Longf. *Hiaw.* xv. 143 Then they shook their *medicine-pouches O'er the head of Hiawatha. *a* **1831** J. Smith *Jrnl.* in M. S. Sullivan *Trav. J. Smith* (1934) 5 You observe at the door [of the Indian Lodge] three straight and handsome poles set up in a triangular form and joined together at the top, on which is suspended the *medicine sack of the owner, consisting of such things as he fancies to possess a certain undefined charm. **1883** 'Mark Twain' *Life on Mississippi* 613 See my medicine-sack and my war club tied to it. **1809** A. Henry *Trav.* 119 In his hand, he had his *shishiquoi*, or rattle, with which he beat time to his *medicine-song. **1885** Henshaw in *Amer. Jrnl. Archæol.* I. 110 The use of the *medicine-stones among the San Buenaventura Indians. **1837** W. Irving *Capt. Bonneville* II. xv. 147 This little, whining, feast-smelling animal, is.. called among Indians the '*medicine wolf'. **1846** [see COYOTE]. **1860** E. J. Lewis in *Colorado Mag.* (1938) XV. 30 Went up town and saw a young grizzly bear, a young swift or medicine wolf much resembling a fox. **1834** *Knickerbocker* IV. 372 The mother evinced her sagacity, as a diviner or *medicine woman. **1836** *Ibid.* VIII. 152 It was at the wigwam of an old Indian 'medicine-woman' that I stopped.

†'**medicine**, *sb.*² *Obs.* [a. F. *médecin*, ad. late L. *medicinus* adj. (see prec.) used *absol.* as *sb.*] A medical practitioner. Also *fig.*

a **1450** *Knt. de la Tour* 137 She hadde her medicines and surgens forto hele and medicine alle such as were needfulle. **1484** Caxton *Fables of Æsop* (1889) 66, I dyssymyled and fayned my self to be a medycyn. **1545** Raynold *Byrth Mankynde* 92 Aske, and vse the aduyse of some wel learned medicine [*ed.* 1634 II. vii. 139 medicioner]. **1601** Shaks. *All's Well* II. i. 75, I haue seen a medicine That's able to breath life into a stone. **1632** Lithgow *Trav.* VIII. 370 [There] flourished the most famous medicines, and Philosophers.

medicine ('mɛds(ə)n, 'mɛdısın, -s(ə)n), *v.* Forms: see MEDICINE *sb.*¹ [a. OF. *medeciner* (mod.F. *médeciner*), f. *medecine* MEDICINE *sb.*¹]

1. *trans.* To heal or cure by medicinal means; to administer medicine to.

a **1450** [see MEDICINE *sb.*²]. **1484** Caxton *Fables of Æsop* (1889) 62 He desyred to be medycyned and made hole of his foote. **1577** B. Googe *Heresbach's Husb.* (1586) 149 Afore they go to pasture, they [pigs] must be medecined. **1595** Spenser *Col. Clout* 877 Being hurt, seeke to be medicynd Of her that first did stir that mortall stownd. **1605** Bacon *Adv. Learn.* II. xxii. §6 As in medicining of the body, it is in order first to know the divers complexions and constitutions..; so in medicining of the mind [etc.]. **1877** Ruskin *Fors Clav.* lxxv. VII. 75 It [a dog] was warmed and medicined as best might be. **1889** J. Masterman *Scotts of Bestminster* III. xiv. 29 She could medicine the sick.

b. *nonce-use.* To bring by medicinal virtue *to.*

1604 Shaks. *Oth.* III. iii. 332 Not Poppy, nor Mandragora ..Shall euer medicine thee to that sweete sleepe Which thou owd'st yesterday. **1820** Shelley *Witch Atl.* xvii.

2. *transf.* and *fig.*

1593 Abp. Bancroft *Daung. Posit.* III. xv. 127 To medicine these mischiefes. **1601** Holland *Pliny* I. 544 All remedies to others are mischiefs to it [the cypress tree], and in one word, go about to medicine it you kil it. **1611** Shaks. *Cymb.* IV. ii. 243 Great greefes I see med'cine the lesse. **1645** Milton *Tetrach.* Wks. 1851 IV. 201 Thus med'cining our eyes we need not doubt to see more into the meaning of these our Saviours words. *c* **1750** Shenstone *Elegies* xx. 68 Where ev'ry breeze shall med'cine ev'ry wound. **1868** E. Edwards *Ralegh* I. xxii. 504 Cares, as usual with Ralegh, were medicined by strenuous and varied labour.

3. *nonce-use.* To employ as medicine.

1654 Gayton *Pleas. Notes* III. iii. 78 Get me these ingredients..Such as the bearded sonne of the smooth-chinn'd Father Apollo us'd and medicin'd.

Hence †**medicined** *ppl. a.*, medicated, drugged.

1558 Phaer *Æneid.* VI. Argt., Æneas..casting Cerberus in a sleape with a medcined soppe. *a* **1637** B. Jonson *Underwoods* lviii, As men drinke up In hast the bottome of a med'cin'd Cup, And take some sirrup after.

mediciner (mı'dısınə(r), 'mɛdsınər). *arch.* (in early use chiefly *Sc.*) Also 6 **medycyner**, 4 **medycinar**, 4–7 **medicinar**, 5 **medicinare**, 6 **medcinar**, **metsouner**. Cf. MEDICIANER. [f. MEDICINE *sb.*¹ or *v.* + -ER¹: cf. OF. *medecineur.*]

1. A physician, 'medical man', 'leech'.

c **1375** *Sc. Leg. Saints* xxxvi. (*Baptista*) 1071 þan come diuerse medicinaris nere, for wynninge of his stat to spere. **1456** Sir G. Haye *Law Arms* (S.T.S.) 138 A medicinare may geve hele till a man that askis it nocht. **1533** (*title*) Pronostycacyon of Mayster John Thybault, medycyner and astronomer of the Emperyall maiestie. *a* **1578** Lindesay (Pitscottie) *Chron. Scot.* (S.T.S.) II. 127 Lord James..quha was hangit be the heillis be the metsouneris to caus the poysone to drop out. *a* **1670** Spalding *Troub. Chas. I* (1829) 87 Dr. Gordon, medicinar in Old Aberdeen. **1828** Scott *F.M. Perth* xv, 'He who lacks strength', said the wily mediciner, 'must attain his purpose by skill'. **1873** Ruskin *Fors Clav.* xxxi. 20 How many second-rate mediciners have lived on..prescriptions of bread pills.

2. *nonce-uses.* **a.** Used to translate Gr. φαρμακεύς, poisoner, sorcerer. **b.** Used for *medicine man.*

1845 J. H. Newman *Ess. Development* iv. §1. 224 'Wizard, mediciner, cheat, rogue, conjurer', were the epithets applied to him by the opponents of Eusebius. *Ibid.* 225 St. Anastasia was thrown into prison as a mediciner. **1859** R. F. Burton *Centr. Afr.* in *Jrnl. Geog. Soc.* XXIX. 271 His forehead is adorned with the two little antelope-horns worn by sultans and mediciners.

medicining ('mɛds(ə)nıŋ), *vbl. sb.* [f. MEDICINE *v.* + -ING¹.] The action of the vb. MEDICINE.

1577 B. Googe *Heresbach's Husb.* III. (1586) 139 It behoooueth the shepeheарde to be skilfull in medcening of his cattell. **1601** Holland *Pliny* II. 167 If they [*sc.* figs] be brought unto their maturitie by medicining, that is to say, by caprification, then they are never good. **1611** Cotgr., *Pharmacie*: a curing, or medecining with drugs. **1633** T. Adams *Exp. 2 Peter* ii. 22. 1089 The medicining of the one, and cleansing of the other, did not take away their nature; still the one remained a Dogge, the other a Hogge. **1867** Carlyle *Remin.* II. 135 She..having..a turn herself for medicining. **1876** Ruskin *Fors Clav.* lxvii. 204 They.. propose to themselves the general medicining..of the population.

medicioner, variant of MEDICIANER *Obs.*

medick ('miːdık). Also 5 **medike**, 6–7 **medicke**, 6–9 **medic**, 8 **meddick**. [ad. L. *mēdica*, ad. Gr. Μηδική (πόα), lit. 'Median grass'.] Any plant of the genus *Medicago*, esp. *M. sativa*, Purple medick or LUCERNE. (Also ***medick fodder, trefoil.***) ***black*** or ***hop medick*** = NONESUCH.

c **1420** *Pallad. on Husb.* v. 1 At Auerel medike is forto sowe. **1562** Turner *Herbal* II. 52, I haue found no name as yet in England for it [*Medica*]: but it may be called horned clauer or medic fother. **1616** Surfl. & Markh. *Country Farme* 147 The flowers of Medicke fodder. **1733** Miller *Gard. Dict.* (ed. 2), *Medica marina*..Sea Medick or Snail-Trefoil. **1764** *Museum Rust.* II. xlvii. 139 The new lucern is a kind of medick trefoil. **1816–20** T. Green *Univ. Herbal* II. 102 *Medicago Falcata*, Yellow Medick. *Ibid.*, *Medicago Lupulina*, Hop or Black Medick. **1839** *Penny Cycl.* XV. 58/2 Purple medick. **1912** W. Somerville *Agric.* iii. 69 Species standing wide apart, like beans and medick, have no mutual interest in any particular organism. **1960** *Oxf. Bk. Wild Flowers* 20/2 Spotted Medick or Calvary Clover... The leaflets are much bigger than those of other Medicks.

medico ('mɛdıkəʊ). Pl. **medicoes**, **medicos**. [a. It. *medico* or Sp. *médico*: see MEDIC.]

1. A medical practitioner; also, a medical student. Now *slang* or *jocular.*

1689 G. Harvey *Curing Dis. by Expect.* xv. 115 It is in the power of the Medico, to oblige the Husband. **1844** Kinglake *Eothen* xviii. 308 The Medico held my chin in the usual way, and examined my throat. **1896** *Field* 1 Feb. 173/2 Again did the Medicos force the ball down. **1915** A. Conan Doyle *Valley of Fear* I. iv. 53 The medicos will have a word to say before we finish. **1923** A. Bennett *Riceyman Steps* I. x. 46 Dr. Raste would sometimes say with a dry, brief laugh, 'we medicoes'. **1943** A. Huxley *Let.* 7 May (1969) 489 One can only..pray that the army doctors aren't merely pumping him full of toxic sulfanilamide..which is what so many medicos do. **1951** E. Paul *Springtime in Paris* xv. 284 Leaving Hortense to the medicos, young and old, I went with Busse to the Gare de Lyon. **1971** *Lancet* 23 Oct. 919/1 We really need a new word for doctor. Perhaps the Common Market will insist on a common term—medico perhaps? **1973** *Nature* 6 Apr. 377/2 The twenty thousand or so scientists, engineers, medicos and so on on the staff of British universities.

‖**2.** *Sp. Amer.* The surgeon fish.

1902 in Webster *Suppl.*

medico- ('mɛdıkəʊ), used as combining form of L. *medicus* to form combinations denoting the application of medical science to various subjects of research, as ***medico-botanic(al, -chirurgical, -culinary, -electric, -galvanic, -judicial, -legal*** (hence ***-legally*** adv.), ***medico-moral, -pedagogic, -philosophical, -physical, -psychological, -social, -statistical, -zoological*** adjs.; or (rarely) describing a person who regards a subject from a medical standpoint, as in †***medico-theologue***; also **medico-mania**, 'a mania for the science of medicine without the necessary study' (Dunglison 1876).

1838 *Prospectus Gardens Roy. Bot. Soc.* in *Civil Engineer* I, *Medico-Botanic Garden. **1838** *Civil Engineer* I. 361/2 Having passed under the promenade, we reach the *medico-botanical garden. **1809** (*title*) *Medico-chirurgical Transactions, published by the Medical and Chirurgical Society of London. Volume the First. **1858** Gen. P. Thompson *Audi Alt.* II. lxxviii. 32 *Medico-culinary

philosophers of great mark. **1875** T. P. SALT (*title*) *Medico-Electric Apparatus and How to Use it. **1862** *Catal. Internat. Exhib.* II. xvii. 129/1 Galvano-Piline for *medico-galvanic purposes. **1835** I. TAYLOR *Spir. Despot.* III. 97 The delicate offices entrusted to them [*sc.* professors of medicine] in several *medico-judicial instances. **1835** *Cycl. Pract. Med.* IV. 558/1 Circumstances affecting the *medico-legal character of wounds. **1870** M. GONZALEZ ECHEVERRIA (*title*, New York), The trial of 'John Reynolds' *medico-legally considered. **1866** READE *G. Gaunt* (ed. 2) II. 265 A sort of *medico-moral diary. **1904** *Brit. Med. Jrnl.* 17 Sept. 679 Many of the children had much improved under the *medico-pedagogic treatment to which they had been subjected. **1698** TYSON in *Phil. Trans.* XX. 132 Two *Medico-Philosophical Dissertations about these Tophi. **1720** QUINCY (*title*) Medicina Statica,..to which is added ..*Medico-Physical Essays on Agues [etc.]. **1890** *Syd. Soc. Lex.*, **Medico-psychological*, relating to the department of medicine which treats of mental disorders. **1961** *Lancet* 29 July 259/1 (*heading*) *Medicosocial aspects. **1967** *Times* 20 Feb. 13/4 Everything is to be gained by the widest publicity being given to these serious medico-social problems affecting all sections of the community. **1896** *Allbutt's Syst. Med.* I. 30 The *medico-statistical point of view. **1712** *H. More's Antid. Ath.* III. xi. *Scholia* 174 He professes himself a *Medico-Theologue. **1861** HULME tr. *Moquin-Tandon* Pref. 6 An arrangement founded upon the characters of the animal, or its *medico-zoological relations.

medicommissure (miːdɪˈkɒmɪsjʊə(r)). *Anat.* Also **medio-**. [f. L. *medi-us* middle + COMMISSURE.] The middle commissure of the brain.

1882 WILDER & GAGE *Anat. Techn.* 446 The mediocommissure. **1885** B. G. WILDER in *Jrnl. Nerv. Dis.* XII. 287. **1890** in *Syd. Soc. Lex.*

†ˈ**medics**, *sb. pl. Obs.* [pl. of MEDIC: see -IC 2.] The science of medicine.

1663 J. SPENCER *Prodigies* (1665) 402 In Medicks, we have some confident Undertakers to rescue the Science from all its reproaches and dishonors. **1695** J. EDWARDS *Perfect. Script.* 180 Apollo was..made by the antient sages the God of medicks as well as musick. **1737** STACKHOUSE *Hist. Bible* (1752) II. VII. i. 1018/2 The Masters of the Medicks who have treated of this Kind of Madness [etc.].

†**medie**, *v. Obs. rare.* [ad. late L. *mediāre*: see MEDIATE *v.*] *trans.* To divide into two equal parts; to halve.

c **1425** *Craft Nombrynge* (E.E.T.S.) 15 þen medye 4 & þen leues 2. *Ibid.* 16 þou schalt..do away þat figure þat is medied, & sette in his styde halfe of þat nombre.

mediety (mɪˈdaɪɪtɪ). [ad. L. *medietās* (whence OF. *moietié* MOIETY; OF. had also the learned form *medieté*), f. *medius* middle: see -TY.]

1. †**a.** *gen.* A half. *Obs.*

c **1420** *Pallad. on Husb.* XI. 288 The muste, decoct to his mediete Or thridde part, they casteth to their wyne. **1571** DIGGES *Pantom.* II. iv. M ij b, 140 whose medietie being 70, diuided by 14, yeldeth 5. **1590** BARROUGH *Meth. Physick* V. xxiv. (1596) 343 The common measure or quantity therof [*sc.* of the dose of arsenic], is the mediety of one graine of wheate. **1603** SIR C. HEYDON *Jud. Astrol.* xxi. 449 The medietie of the Moones globe was allwaies illustrated which is towardes the sunne. **1686** GOAD *Celest. Bodies* I. xvi. 106 Let us consider the Occidental Mediety of Heaven.

b. *spec.* in *Law.* = MOIETY. Chiefly with reference to ecclesiastical benefices.

a **1661** FULLER *Worthies, Warw.* (1662) II. 126 That good Mannour (with the alternate gift of the Mediety of the rich Parsonage therein). **1834** SOUTHEY *Doctor* xlii. (1862) 100 A rectory of two medieties, served by two resident rectors. **1877** J. C. COX *Ch. Derbysh.* III. 212 Sir Henry Chandos succeeded to the mediety of the Mugginton manor. **1894** A. JESSOPP *Random Roaming*, etc. 186 This benefice consists of two medieties.

†**2.** Middle or intermediate state, position, or quality. *Obs.*

1573 G. HARVEY *Letter-bk.* (Camden) 135 A very compounde of contrarietyes In thinges indifferent and medietyes. **1610** HEALEY *St. Aug. Citie of God* IX. xiii. (1620) 333 In seeking a mediety betweene immortality blessed and mortality wretched. *a* **1639** WOTTON in *Reliq.* (1685) 661 The Pope means..to carry himself as it were in a Mediety between the King of Spain, and the great Duke. *c* **1645** HOWELL *Lett.* (1655) I. VI. xiv. 258 This Cabal..was reveal'd..to Solomon in a dream, wherby he came to know the beginning, mediety, and consummation of times. **1651** BIGGS *New Disp.* §183 It ought to consist in a mediety, betwixt corrupt and very sound bloud.

†**3.** Moderation. (Cf. MEAN *sb.*[2]) *Obs.*

1583 STUBBES *Anat. Abus.* I. sig. I *marg.*, Medietie to be obserued in meats.

†**4.** *Math.* The quality of being a mean between two quantities; hence = MEAN *sb.*[2] 8. *Obs.*

1598 J. D. tr. *L. Le Roy's Aristotle's Polit.* V. 250 Similitude or likenesse of proportions, and equality, and mediety. **1603** HOLLAND *Plutarch's Mor.* 1255 Three sorts of primitive Medieties there be,..to wit, Arithmeticall, Geometricall, and Harmonicall. **1678** CUDWORTH *Intell. Syst.* I. iv. §20. 376 The Tetrad is an arithmetical mediety betwixt the Monad and the Hebdomad. **1694** HOLDER *Harmony* iv. 47 Now in 4 to 2 the Mediety is 3. *Ibid.* vii. 168 These two divide Diapason, 64 to 32, by the Mediety of 45; And they divide it so near to Equality, that in Practice they are hardly to be distinguished.

medifixed (ˈmiːdɪfɪkst), *a. Bot.* [f. L. *medi-us* middle + FIXED; after mod.L. *medifixus*, F. *médifixe*.] Fixed by the middle; said of anthers.

1880 A. GRAY *Struct. Bot.* 253 Adnate anthers are perhaps as frequently extrorse as introrse. Others, whether basifixed or medifixed, are more commonly introrse.

‖**medifurca** (miːdɪˈfɜːkə). *Ent.* [mod.L., f. L. *medi-us* middle + *furca* fork.] The middle forked apodeme which serves for the attachment of the muscles by which the midlegs of insects are moved. Hence **mediˈfurcal** *a.* (*Cent. Dict.*).

1826 KIRBY & SP. *Entomol.* III. 379 *Medifurca* (the Medifurca). A branching vertical process of the endosternum.

†**medify**, *v. Obs. rare.* [Badly f. L. *medicus* physician + -FY.] *trans.* To heal, cure.

c **1470** HARDING *Chron.* LXXII. xiii, All his sores to be medifyed. *Ibid.* LXXXIV. ii, But this Mordred gaue Arthure deaths wond, For which he gode his woundes to medifie.

mediglacial (miːdɪˈgleɪʃəl), *a. rare*$^{-1}$. [f. L. *medi-us* middle + GLACIAL *a.*] Mid-glacial; in the midst of glaciers.

1823 SCORESBY *North. Whale Fishery* 50 During the next day we traced the limits of our mediglacial sea.

medil(l, obs. forms of MEDDLE, MIDDLE.

medimn (mɪˈdɪm). *Antiq. rare.* Also 7 **medimne**. [ad. L. *medimnus*, a. Gr. μέδιμνος. Cf. F. *médimne*. English writers usually employ the Latin form; pl. *medimnī*.] An ancient Greek measure of capacity, equal to about 12 gallons.

1600 HOLLAND *Livy* XXXVIII. xiii. 990 The Consull imposed upon them a paiment of..10000 medimnes of wheat. **1658** PHILLIPS, *Medimne*, a certain measure, containing six bushels. **1807** ROBINSON *Archæol. Græca* I. ii. 23 Those who were worth five-hundred medimns of commodities were placed in the first class. [**1847** GROTE *Greece* II. xi. III. 155 Those whose annual income was equal to 500 medimni of corn..and upwards, one medimnus being considered equivalent to one drachma in money.]

medina (mɪˈdiːnə). Also **Medina**. [Arab., 'town'.] The non-European section of a North African town.

1906 D. SLADEN *Carthage & Tunis* II. i. 330 Inside, these great houses of the Medina are just as stately. **1935** G. GORER *Africa Dances* I. vii. 76 The dispossessed negroes went to live in the Medina, a geometrical ghetto of one-room stone huts. **1950** R. LANDAU *Invitation to Morocco* iii. 28 Leaving the native *medina* surrounded by its ancient walls untouched, he erected outside it an entirely new town. **1961** J. ANTHONY *About Tunisia* i. 28 My favourite walks were in the residential quarters high in the Medina. **1972** *Country Life* 13 Jan. 86/2 The crowded Medinas of Islamic cities. **1972** W. MCGIVERN *Caprifoil* (1973) x. 174 He never made the mistake of pretending he understood Arabs. He had grown up with them..listened in the *medinas* to the rise and fall of the wise men's prayers.

Medinal (ˈmɛdɪnəl). *Pharm.* Also **medinal**. A proprietary name for the sodium salt, $C_8H_{11}N_2O_3Na$, of barbitone; it is a hypnotic of similar action to barbitone.

1908 *Trade Marks Jrnl.* 12 Aug. 1319 Medinal... Medicines for human use. Chemische Fabrik auf Actien (Vorm. E. Schering),..Berlin, Germany, manufacturers. **1922** *Daily Mail* 16 Dec. 7 The verdict was Death from an Overdose of Medinal taken by Misadventure. **1946** J. B. PRIESTLEY *Bright Day* vii. 217 As I undressed I chewed two tablets of medinal... I knew that medinal acts slowly with me, but it was all I had there. **1965** J. POLLITT *Depression & its Treatment* v. 66 As these patients are already retarded it is rarely necessary to give tranquillisers or sedatives during the day, but barbitone sodium (Medinal) at night is often most effective in preventing early waking.

‖**medine** (mɛˈdiːn). Also 6, 9 **medin**, 6 **madyne, madayne, madien**, 7 **madin, madein, meydine, meidin**, 8 **medina**, 9 **medeen, medino**. [a. F. *medin* (Cotgr.), a. vulgar Arab. *mayyidī*, corrupt form of *mu'ayyidīy*, from the name *Mu'ayyad*: see below.] Originally, a silver half-dirhem first issued by the Sultan al-Mu'ayyad (15th c.); latterly, a copper coin current in Egypt, Syria, etc., valued at $\frac{1}{40}$ of a piastre, or $\frac{1}{20}$ of a penny. (The Turkish name is PARA; in Egyptian Arabic it was commonly called *faḍḍa*^{h}, i.e. 'silver'.)

1583 J. NEWBERY in *Hakluyt's Voy.* (1599) II. I. 247, 40 medins maketh a duckat. —— *Let.* in Purchas *Pilgrims* (1625) II. IX. 1643 Nutmegs fortie fiue Madynes, Ginger the Batman, one ducket Pepper seuentie fiue Madaynes. **1584** W. BARRET in *Hakluyt's Voy.* (1599) II. I. 271, 47 medines passe in value as the duckat of gold of Venice. **1615** G. SANDYS *Trav.* (1621) 153 Paying by the way two Medines a head. **1753** BP. CLAYTON *Jrnl. fr. Cairo to Sinai* 5 Sept. 1722 *note*, A medina is 1d$\frac{1}{5}$ English money. **1819** T. HOPE *Anastasius* (1820) II. ii. 38 My Coobtic writer, who, with a salary of six medeens a day,..had become..as rich as a Sultan's seraf. **1833** J. BENNETT *Artificer's Compl. Lex.*, *Medin*, in Egypt 3 aspers; at Aleppo is [etc.].

‖**medio** (ˈmedio). Also **medio real**. [Sp. *medio* half.] An obsolete Mexican coin, also used in Cuba, worth half a *real fuerte* or $6\frac{1}{4}$ *centavos*.

1824 J. R. POINSETT *Notes on Mexico* 141 A *medio*, the sixteenth of a dollar. **1844** G. W. KENDALL *Santa Fé Expedition* II. xii. 239 One of the lads [handed] each of the unfortunate prisoners a medio. **1845** T. J. GREEN *Jrnl. Texian Expedition* 246 One medio would buy a leaden rivet. **1859** R. H. DANA *To Cuba* 47 As there is no coin in Cuba less than the medio, $6\frac{1}{4}$ cents, the musicians get a good deal or nothing. **1897** T. A. JANVIER *Mexican Guide* vii. 81 Medio real = $6\frac{1}{4}$ centavos. **1909** 'O. HENRY' *Roads of Destiny* xxi. 358 I've got one Chili Dollar, two *real* pieces, and a *medio*.

medio- (ˈmiːdɪəʊ), used as combining form of L. *medius* middle: **1.** In *Zool.* and *Bot.* in various adjs. descriptive of parts and organs of animals and plants, with the sense either 'relating to the middle of' (an organ or part), as in ***medio-carpal, -colic, -digital, -dorsal*** (hence ***medio-dorsally*** adv.), ***-frontal*** (also *absol.* = 'medio-frontal suture'), ***-lateral*** (hence ***medio-laterally*** adv.), ***-occipital, -palatine*** (also *absol.* = 'medio-palatine bone'), ***-pontine, -stapedial*** (*absol.* in quots.), ***-tarsal, -ventral***; or 'in the middle', as in ***medio-depressed, -perforate***; also in **medio-inferior, -posterior** = 'lower middle', 'posterior-middle' (margin).

1890 *Syd. Soc. Lex.*, **Medio-carpal*, relating to the middle of the carpus. **1871** W. A. LEIGHTON *Lichen-Flora* 78 Subpeltate, *medio-depressed, margin white crenulate [etc.]. **1852** DANA *Crust.* I. 625 Species with a *medio-dorsal spine. **1882** VINES *Sachs' Bot.* 449 The first leaf is the scutiform leaf..which is placed *medio-dorsally. **1865** THURNAM in *Nat. Hist. Rev.* Apr. 246 The almost infallible closure of the *medio-frontal. **1849** DANA *Geol.* App. I. (1850) 698 [The] straight *medio-inferior margin, parallel with the dorsal. **1854** OWEN *Skel. & Teeth* in *Circ. Sci., Org. Nat.* I. 214 The *medio-lateral pieces as..developments of the ribs. **1971** *Nature* 20 Aug. 542/2 The nucleus is crescent shaped in cross section and extends 1·4 mm rostrocaudally and *mediolaterally. **1890** *Syd. Soc. Lex.*, **Medio-occipital*, relating to the middle of the occipital region. **1884** COUES *Key N. Amer. Birds* (ed. 2) 173 The most marked *medio-palatine ossification... Such are..formations which, like the medio-palatine, serve to bind the palate halves together. **1879** W. A. LEIGHTON *Lichen-Flora* (ed. 3) 516 **Medio-perforate*, perforated in the centre. **1890** *Syd. Soc. Lex.*, **Medio-pontine*, relating to the middle of the pons varolii. **1852** DANA *Crust.* I. 625 *Medio-posterior spine small, very remote from posterior margin. **1875** W. K. PARKER in *Encycl. Brit.* III. 702/2 The bar itself is the '*medio-stapedial'..; it will soon segment itself off from the ear-capsule. **1890** *Syd. Soc. Lex.*, *Medio-stapedial*, the middle third of the columella of the ear in the frog. **1884** COUES *Key N. Amer. Birds* (ed. 2) 121 *note*, A bird's ankle-joint is.. between proximal and distal series of tarsal bones, and therefore **medio*-tarsal as in reptiles. **1870** ROLLESTON *Anim. Life* Introd. 40 Reflected upwards from the *medio-ventral line.

2. In *Philol.*, as **medio-palatal** *a.*, articulated with the tongue against the middle part of the hard palate; **medio-passive** *a.*, of the voice of a verb, intermediate between active and passive (cf. MIDDLE *a.* 4a); also as *sb.*; hence ***medio-passivization***.

1902 E. W. SCRIPTURE *Elem. Exper. Phonetics* xvii. 297 Roof articulations are indicated by the names..pre-, medio-, postpalatal. **1942** BLOCH & TRAGER *Outl. Ling. Analysis* 15 Different points of articulation are designated by the terms prepalatal, mediopalatal, and postpalatal, indicating that the front [of the tongue] touches or approaches respectively the anterior, the middle, or the posterior part of the hard palate. **1949** R.-M. S. HEFFNER *Gen. Phonetics* vi. 148 In Midwest American pronunciations of English there is an open *r* sound, which is formed by raising the middle region of the dorsum of the tongue towards the mediopalatal junction between the hard palate and velum. **1962** CHAVARRIA-AGUILA & PENZL in Householder & Saporta *Probl. Lexicogr.* IV. 241 A contrasting pair of voiced and voiceless medio-palatal fricatives occur. **1921** E. SAPIR *Lang.* iv. 74 Of the seven suffixes..*-o(ht)* -indicates activity done for the subject (the so-called 'middle' or 'medio-passive' voice of Greek). **1933** E. H. STURTEVANT *Compar. Gram. Hittite Lang.* vi. 250 Hittite has a medio-passive, which has the same uses as the Gk. middle voice. It most frequently represents the subject as acting upon or in respect of himself. **1934** PRIEBSCH & COLLINSON *German Lang.* II. vi. 296 Germanic retained in Gothic an inflected medio-passive present from Indo-European. **1952** O. R. GURNEY *Hittites* vi. 118 The verb has two voices—active and medio-passive. **1968** *Encycl. Brit.* XI. 558/1 Besides the active there survives a medio-passive voice [in Hittite] characterized in the present by a somewhat loose *-r(i)* attached to the old middle endings. **1972** *Language* XLVIII. 393 A reflexive—hence, by ergative criteria, mediopassive—form of the verb. *Ibid.* 395 In keeping with the ergative focus, the object (non-ergator) is retained formally in an intransitive, mediopassive form, there being no external agent of the action described. **1973** A. H. SOMMERSTEIN *Sound Pattern Anc. Greek* ii. 13 The infinitive ending in all medio-passive senses is /-sthay/. **1975** *Language* LI. 97 Ambiguity between reflexive and medio-passive constructions is possible (e.g. 'I got out' vs. 'I cut myself'); but in practice this is not much of a problem, since many verbs do not undergo medio-passivization.

†**mediˈocral**, *a. Obs.* [f. MEDIOCRE + -AL[1].]

1. 'Being of a middle quality; indifferent; ordinary; as *mediocral* intellect' (Webster 1828–32 citing Addison).

2. *Ent.* Of middle size; *spec.* (see quot.).

1826 KIRBY & SP. *Entomol.* IV. 317 *Mediocral*, when [the antennæ are] of the length of the body.

mediocre (ˌmiːdɪˈəʊkə(r)), *a.* and *sb.* [a. F. *médiocre*, ad. L. *mediocris* of middle degree, quality, or rank, f. *medi-us* middle.

Formerly often printed in italics and with accent as Fr.]

A. *adj.* Of middling quality; neither bad nor good; indifferent. Said chiefly of literary or artistic works, ability, or knowledge, and hence of persons considered with reference to their mental power or skill.

1586 A. DAY *Eng. Secretary* I. (1625) 10 Mediocre [*sc.* style] a meane betwixt high and low, vehement and slender. **1659** MACALLO *Can. Physick* 97 A larger diet must be

granted to children then to old folks, and a mediocre to those of a middle age. 1742 POPE *Let. to Warburton* 27 Nov., A very mediocre poet, one Drayton, is yet taken some notice of, because Selden writ a few notes on one of his poems. 1797 *Monthly Mag.* III. 29 There are four silver clasps..the style of the engraving of which is but *médiocre*. 1815 JANE AUSTEN *Emma* II. xiv, My performance is *médiocre* to the last degree. 1829 LYTTON *Devereux* I. iii, His talent was of that mechanical, yet quick nature, which makes wonderful boys, but *médiocre* men. 1847–8 H. MILLER *First Impr.* iii. (1857) 34 We enter the suburbs, and pass through mediocre streets of brick. 1865 CARLYLE *Fredk. Gt.* XXI. iv. (1872) X. 17 It is thus that mediocre people seek to lower great men. 1880 VERN. LEE *Stud. Italy* III. ii. 104 He held up to contempt all that was mediocre in his art. 1884 *Graphic* 18 Oct. 410/3 Captain Ross's Welsh cow gave 46 lb. of mediocre milk. *absol.* 1884 SIR R. HARRINGTON in *Law Times* LXXVII. 393/2 The mediocre..always form numerically the largest portion of every profession. 1903 *Speaker* 17 Oct. 61/1 The result would be a kind of nightmare of the mediocre, a universal Brixton.

B. *sb.* Only *pl.* Mediocre persons. *rare.*

1834–43 SOUTHEY *Doctor* (ed. 2) I. 187 The mediocres in every grade aim at pleasing the public. 1893 D. PRYDE *Pleas. Mem.* ix. 131 You must bring forward the whole rank and file—duxes, mediocres, dullards, and dunces.

'mediocrist. Now *rare.* [f. MEDIOCRE + -IST.] A person of middling talents or ability.

1787 HAWKINS *Johnson* 271 If he be but a mediocrist, he is surely not a subject of imitation; it being a rule, that of examples the best are always to be selected. 1797 MRS. A. M. BENNETT *Beggar Girl* (1813) I. 211 They danced well, sung a little..and were indeed mediocrists in all female accomplishments. 1818 TODD [quotes Swift *Let. Pope* 3 Sep. 1735; but the early edd. have 'among the *mediocribus*']. 1823 in *Spirit Pub. Jrnls.* 170 Warburton draws a very just distinction between a man of true greatness and a mediocrist. 1903 *Sat. Rev.* 12 Dec. 722 Mr. —, the cultured mediocrist, so rarely relaxes the firm hold he has on commonplace,..that [etc.].

mediocritization (mi:dɪˌɒkrɪtaɪ'zeɪʃən). orig. *U.S.* [f. MEDIOCRIT(Y: see -IZE.] The action or process of rendering mediocre; reduction to a common level of mediocrity.

1970 *Esquire* Aug. 124/4, I subscribe more to my own theory of our general mediocritization (or would if the word itself were less unwieldy). 1985 *N.Y. Times* 15 Sept. I. 58/1 It had..led to what he called the 'academic consumptive disease called mediocritization'. 1986 *Christian Science Monitor* 17 Apr. 29/3 It leads to mediocritization and trivialization of theater.

Hence [as back-formation] **medi'ocritize** *v. trans.*, to render mediocre.

1972 *N.Y. Times Mag.* 10 Sept. 50/2 The banal patter on the show is appalling... Everything is mediocritized.

†mediocriture. *Obs.* [irreg. f. L. *mediocris* MEDIOCRE + -TURE.] Moderation.

1574 NEWTON *Health Magist.* 77 An expedient Mediocriture of seasonable exercise.

mediocrity (mi:dɪ'ɒkrɪtɪ). Also 5–6 -crite, 6 -critye, 6–7 -critie. [a. F. *médiocrité*, ad. L. *mediocritās*, f. *mediocris*: see MEDIOCRE and -ITY.]

1. The quality or condition of being intermediate between two extremes; mean state or condition, mediety. Also, something (a quality, position, etc.) equally removed from two opposite extremes; a mean. (Chiefly as a quasi-technical term, with reference to the Aristotelian theory of 'the mean'. Now *rare.*)

1531 ELYOT *Gov.* III. viii, Fortitude..is a Mediocritie or meane betwene two extremities. 1532 SIR B. TUKE in Thynne *Chaucer's Wks.* A ij, Such sensyble and open style, lackyng neither maieste ne mediocrite couenable in disposycion. 1579 E. K. in *Spenser's Sheph. Cal.* July *Embl.*, Albeit all bountye dwelleth in mediocritie, yet perfect felicitye dwelleth in supremacie. 1609 OVERBURY *Observ.* Wks. (ed. Rimbault) 251 At fifteene they quit bookes, and begin to live in the world, when indeed a mediocritie betwixt their forme of education and ours would doe better then either. 1645 MILTON *Tetrach.* Wks. 1851 IV. 233 As the offence was in one extreme, so the rebuke, to bring more efficaciously to a rectitude and mediocrity, stands not in the middle way of duty, but in the other extreme. 1650 HOBBES *De Corp. Pol.* 41 The common Opinion, that Virtue consisteth in Mediocrity and Vice in Extreams. 1759 ADAM SMITH *Mor. Sent.* I. iii. 49 The propriety of every passion excited by objects peculiarly related to ourselves,..must lye, it is evident, in a certain mediocrity. 1768 [W. DONALDSON] *Life Sir B. Sapskull* II. xxii. 168 His temper was a mediocrity of chearfulness and solemnity. *a* 1871 GROTE *Eth. Fragm.* v. 163 When he places virtue in a certain mediocrity between excess and defect [etc.].

†b. *golden mediocrity* = *golden mean* (see GOLDEN 5 c). *Obs.*

c 1510 MORE *Picus* Wks. 15/1 The golden mediocrite, the meane estate is to be desired. 1605 BACON *Adv. Learn.* II. xxv. §4. 1661 COWLEY *Cromwell* Wks. (1688) 76 Was ever Riches gotten by your Golden Mediocrities?

†c. *Geom.* = MEAN. *Obs.*

1726 LEONI *Alberti's Archit.* II. 89/2 These the Philosophers call Mediocrities or Means,..of all which the purpose is, that the two extreams being given, the middle mean or number may correspond with them in a certain determined manner.

†2. A middle course in action; measured conduct or behaviour; moderation, temperance. Phr. *to keep* or *observe a mediocrity*. *Obs.*

1531 ELYOT *Gov.* I. xxvii, Some men wolde saye, that in mediocritie, whiche I haue so moche praised in shootynge, why shulde nat boulynge, claisshe, pynnes, and koytyng be as moche commended? 1564 ABP. PARKER *Corr.* (Parker Soc.) 215 He noted much and delighted in our mediocrity, charging the Genevians and the Scottish of going too far in extremities. 1565 COOPER *Thesaurus* s.v. *Modus*, *Statuere modum inimicitiarum*, to kepe a mediocritie or measure in hatinge. 1594 HOOKER *Eccl. Pol.* I. xvi. §7 That law of reason, which teacheth mediocritie in meates and drinkes. 1597 A. M. tr. *Guillemeau's Fr. Chirurg.* 14/1 The Chirurgiane must, in sowinge, vse mediocritye, and not take to great a qvantitye of the fleshe. 1621 BURTON *Anat. Mel.* II. ii. IV. (1651) 286 Body and mind must be exercised, not one, but both, and that in a mediocrity. 1637 R. HUMPHREY tr. *St. Ambrose* II. 41 A mediocrity is to be kept in liberality. 1670 G. H. *Hist. Cardinals* I. I. 30 If the Popes had been contented to carry themselves with mediocrity, they had never run that hazard of losing all. 1774 PENNANT *Tour Scotl. in 1772*, 135 Reformation in matters of religion, seldom observes mediocrity.

†3. The condition of possessing attributes in a medium or moderate degree; moderate degree or rate, average quality or amount; tempered condition. *Obs.*

1598 BARCKLEY *Felic. Man* (1631) 505 The temperate zone where..men..live in a pleasant mediocritie, voide of both extremities. 1612 BACON *Ess.*, *Youth & Age* (Arb.) 260 Men of age..seldome driue businesse home to the full period; but content themselues with a mediocrity of successe. 1659 MACALLO *Can. Physick* 56 Sleep likewise surpassing the bounds of mediocrity, is in like manner evil. 1665 NEEDHAM *Med. Medicinæ* 265 There are in the Bloud, much Water and Spirit, a Mediocrity of Salt and Sulphur, and some little of Earth. 1683 TRYON *Way to Health* 292 Let them beware of strong Drinks, because they heat the blood & body beyond Mediocrity. 1733 CHEYNE *Eng. Malady* II. v. §11 (1734) 170 To ascertain the Mediocrity of such a Diet as neither makes the Salts and Oils too many [etc.]. 1744 BERKELEY *Siris* §89 We enjoy a great mediocrity of climate. 1753 HANWAY *Trav.* (1762) II. II. i. 65 Whether we..enjoy a profusion, or mediocrity of the gifts of providence.

b. Medium size. *rare.*

1653 R. SANDERS *Physiogn.* a iij, To the predicament of Quantity, appertain magnitude, parvity, and mediocrity of parts. 1841 CATLIN *N. Amer. Ind.* (1844) II. lvii. 220 In stature he is about at mediocrity.

†4. Moderate fortune or condition in life. *Obs.*

c 1450 tr. *De Imitatione* I. xxii. 28 It is [not] mannys felicite to haue temporall godes in abundaunce, but mediocrite sufficiþ him. *a* 1591 R. GREENHAM *Wks.* (1599) 50 Which thing ought to humble vs in the desire of outward things, and to make vs thankfull for a mediocritie. 1681 FLAVEL *Meth. Grace* xxviii. 478 A mediocrity is the Christian's best external security. 1784 COWPER *Task* I. 50 These for the rich; the rest, whom fate had placed In modest mediocrity, ..sat on well-tanned hides. 1816 SINGER *Hist. Cards* 125 John Gænsfleisch..was constrained by the mediocrity of his means to quit his native city of Mentz.

5. The quality or condition of being mediocre; *spec.* a moderate or average degree of mental ability, talents, skill, or the like; middling capacity, endowment, or accomplishment. Now chiefly with disparaging implication, in contrast with excellence or superiority.

1588 *Marprel. Epist.* (Arb.) 11 Secondly, you haue to your mediocritie written against the Papists. 1589 NASHE *Pref. Greene's Menaphon* (Arb.) 14 Which makes me thinke that either the louers of mediocritie are verie many, or that the number of good Poets, are very small. 1605 BACON *Adv. Learn.* II. ii. §8 For Moderne Histories..there are some fewe verie worthy, but the greater part beneath Mediocritie. 1624 FISHER in F. White *Repl. F.* 300, I am persuaded no vnlearned man that hath in him any sparke of humilitie, or any mediocritie of Iudgement, will vndertake it. 1656 SANDERSON *Serm.* (1689) 440 If a man have once attained to a good mediocrity in this Art. 1709 LADY M. W. MONTAGU *Let. to Miss A. Wortley* 21 Aug., Leave me my own mediocrity of agreeableness and genius. 1776 ADAM SMITH *W.N.* I. x. (1869) I. 111 To excel in any profession, in which but few arrive at mediocrity, is the most decisive mark of what is called genius. 1822 IMISON *Sci. & Art* II. 391 The way to avoid mediocrity, is by the study..of beautiful productions. *a* 1859 MACAULAY *Biog.* (1867) 212 The most important offices in the state were bestowed on decorous and laborious mediocrity. 1878 BOSW. SMITH *Carthage* 141 He who would attempt it must be either a fool or a military genius... A respectable mediocrity has hitherto been the order of the day.

6. *concr.* A person of mediocre talents or ability.

1694 CONGREVE *Double Dealer* II. i, Methinks he wants a manner,..some distinguishing quality..; he is too much a mediocrity, in my mind. 1840 MILL *Diss. & Disc.* (1859) II. 408 He [the American President] is now always either an unknown mediocrity, or a man whose reputation has been acquired in some other field than that of politics. 1874 GREEN *Short Hist.* x. §4. 801 Spencer Perceval, an industrious mediocrity of the narrowest type.

†'medious, *a. Obs. rare.* [f. L. *medi-us* middle + -OUS.] Intermediate in degree.

1657 W. MORICE *Coena quasi Κοινή* Pref. 20 Some..out of a medious complyance, hoping by going on part of the way to draw them another. *Ibid.* xv. 233 They impetrate medious, though not the highest mercie.

†medioxumate, *a. Obs. rare*[−1]. [f. L. *medioxum-us* of middle rank or position, applied to gods ranking between those of heaven and those of hell, or according to others to demi-gods.] Only in *medioxumate gods* (misused by Rowlands: see quot.).

1723 H. ROWLANDS *Mona Antiq. Rest.* 63 The Stream of Idolatry..deflected them [the Druids] from their profess'd Monotheism, to give Divine Worship to Medioxumate Gods; such as Taranis, or Jupiter; Hesus, or Mars [etc.].

†medioxumous, *a. Obs. rare*[−1]. [Formed as prec. + -OUS.] = prec.

1664 H. MORE *Myst. Iniq.* 40 Mercury and the whole order of the medioxumous or internuntial deities or dæmons.

‖medipectus (mi:dɪ'pɛktəs). *Ent.* [mod.L., f. L. *medi-us* + *pectus* breast. Cf. F. *médipoitrine*.] The underside of the mesothorax. Hence **medi'pectoral** *a.*, of or pertaining to the medipectus.

1826 KIRBY & SP. *Entomol.* III. 378 *Medipectus* (the *Mid-breast*). The underside of the first segment of the alitrunk. *Ibid.* IV. 344 *Medipectoral*. The mid-legs, affixed to the *Medipectus*. 1848 MAUNDER *Treas. Nat. Hist.* 794 *Medipectoral*.

†medisance. *Obs.* [a. F. *médisance*, f. *médis-*, *médire* to speak evil.] Evil speaking, detraction.

1656 BLOUNT *Glossogr.*, *Medisance*, reproach, obloquy, detraction. 1664 BULTEEL *Birinthea* 49 Medisance and slander. [1812 *Edin. Rev.* XX. 103 That gift of sportive but cutting *medisance*.]

medisect (mi:dɪ'sɛkt), *v. rare.* [f. L. *medi-us* middle + *sect-*, ppl. stem of *secāre* to cut.] *trans.* To divide (a body) along the median line; to cut into equal right and left halves. Hence **medi'section**, the action of 'medisecting'.

a 1890 B. G. WILDER (Cent. Dict.).

Medism ('mi:dɪz(ə)m). [ad. L. *mēdismus*, Gr. μηδισμός, f. μηδίζειν to MEDIZE.] *Gr. Hist.* **a.** Sympathy with the 'Medes': used to describe the attitude of those Greeks in the 6th and 5th c. B.C. who were said to favour unpatriotically the interests of the Persians. **b.** A word or idiom belonging to the language of the Medes.

1849 GROTE *Greece* II. xliv. V. 359 Medism (or treacherous correspondence with the Persians). 1864 PUSEY *Lect. Daniel* i. 34 Chaldaisms, Medisms, Persisms could, accordingly, be nothing strange in the Hebrew portion of his book.

†meditabund, *a. Obs. rare*[−1]. (*humorously pedantic.*) In 7 **-abound**. [ad. L. *meditābund-us*, f. *meditārī* to MEDITATE.] Absorbed in meditation.

1681 COLVIL *Whigs Supplic.* (1751) 120 On the ground He groveling lies meditabound. 1727 BAILEY vol. II, *Meditabund*.., pondering,..musing, in a brown Study.

†meditance. *Obs. rare*[−1]. [f. next: see -ANCE.] Meditation.

1612 *Two Noble K.* I. i, Your first thought is more Then others laboured meditance.

meditant ('mɛdɪtənt), *a.* and *sb. rare.* [ad. L. *meditant-em*, pr. pple. of *meditārī* to MEDITATE.]

a. *adj.* Meditating. In quot. 1614 *jocular* (quasi- *Her.*). **b.** *sb.* One who meditates.

1614 B. JONSON *Barth. Fair* Induct., A wise Iustice of Peace meditant. 1748 in *Hervey's Medit.* To Auth. (ed. 4) I. p. xii, Celestial Meditant! whose Ardours rise Deep from the Tombs, and kindle to the Skies. 1898 *Dublin Rev.* July 177 Untrained meditants outside conventual life.

†'meditate, *a. Obs.* [ad. L. *meditātus*, pa. pple. of *meditārī*: see next.] = MEDITATED.

1581 LAMBARDE *Eiren.* II. vii. (1588) 250 The law deemeth that he doeth it..with a meditate hatred. 1854 S. DOBELL *Balder* iii. 18 My early planned, Long meditate..epic!

meditate ('mɛdɪteɪt), *v.* [f. L. *meditāt-*, ppl. stem of *meditārī*, a frequentative f. the root *mĕd-*, whence many words expressing the notion of thought or care, as Gr. μέδεσθαι to think about, care for, μήδεσθαι to care for, L. *medērī* to cure.

The Latin uses (which are reproduced approximately in Eng.) seem partly due to association with Gr. μελετᾶν (f. μελέτη care, study, exercise), from which the word was anciently believed to be derived.]

1. *trans.* To muse over or reflect upon; to consider, study, ponder. Now *rare.*

c 1580 SIDNEY *Ps.* v. i, O Lord,.. Consider what I meditate in me. 1695 ADDISON *King* Misc. Wks. 1726 I. 9 Our British Youth..Had long forgot to Meditate the Foe. 1791 BURKE *Let. Memb. Nat. Assembly* 31 Him [Rousseau] they study; him they meditate. 1837–9 HALLAM *Hist. Lit.* I. I. iii. §111. 222 Alberti had deeply meditated the remains of Roman antiquity. *a* 1871 GROTE *Eth. Fragm.* ii. (1876) 40 If they thoroughly meditated the circumstances of the case.

b. To fix one's attention upon; to observe with interest or intentness. Now *rare.*

1700 DRYDEN *Sigism. & Guisc.* 244 Like a lion..With inward rage he meditates his prey. 1754 RICHARDSON *Grandison* IV. xvii. 108 He bowed his head upon his pillow, and meditated me. *Ibid.* (ed. 2) VI. xlv. 230 She seeing.. that I meditated the seal with impatience, begged me to read it then. 1851 G. W. CURTIS *Nile Notes* xlv. 219 At the doors of their cliff-retreats, sit sagely the cormorants, and meditate the passing Howadji.

¶c. *to meditate the Muse* (nonce-use, after L. *Musam meditari*, Virg. *Ecl.* i. 2): to occupy oneself in song or poetry.

1637 MILTON *Lycidas* 66 What boots it..To tend the homely slighted Shepherds trade, And strictly meditate the thankles Muse?

2. To plan by revolving in the mind; to conceive, plan or design mentally.

1591 SHAKS. *1 Hen. VI*, II. iv. 60 *Yorke.* Now Somerset, where is your argument? *Som.* Here in my scabbard, meditating, that Shall dye your white Rose in a bloody red. **1651** HOBBES *Leviath.* I. xv, It is also a law of nature, that all men that meditate peace, be allowed safe conduct. **1715** ROWE *Lady J. Grey* I. i. 11 Ev'n now she seems to meditate her flight. **1774** GOLDSM. *Nat. Hist.* (1776) VII. 167 A creature meditating mischief. **1820** L. HUNT *Indicator* No. 54 (1822) II. 15 Kubla Khan, which was meditated under the effects of opium. **1879** FROUDE *Cæsar* xi. 135 Catiline was meditating a revolution. **1885** *Manch. Exam.* 6 Nov. 5/2 They are meditating a reimposition of the tax on corn.

†**b.** with *inf.* as obj.

1794 GODWIN *Cal. Williams* 283, I meditated to do you good. **1834** A. F. TYTLER *Univ. Hist.* (1850) I. III. vii. 352 The Latins..meditated to shake off the Roman yoke.

†**3.** To entertain as an opinion, think. *Obs.*

1585 T. WASHINGTON tr. *Nicholay's Voy.* Ep. Ded., What is..more vnbeseeming..than alwaies to abide at home..and not to meditate and thinke that at one time or other it is meete..to flie abroade. **1609** BIBLE (Douay) Pref., What shal we therefore meditate of the especial prerogative of English Catholiques at this time?

4. *intr.* To exercise the mental faculties in thought or contemplation; *spec.* in religious use (see MEDITATION 2).

1594 SHAKS. *Rich. III*, III. vii. 75 He is..meditating with two deepe Diuines. **1611** BIBLE *Gen.* xxiv. 63 And Isaac went out, to meditate in the field, at the euentide. **1644** MILTON *Areop.* (Arb.) 56 When a man writes to the world, ..he searches, meditats, is industrious. **1847** TENNYSON *Princess* I. 95 While I meditated A wind arose. **1897** *Cath. Dict.* (ed. 5) 618/1 The understanding considering this truth in its application to the individual who meditates.

b. const. *on, upon, over,* †*of;* (Hebraism) †*in.*

1560 BIBLE (Geneva) *Ps.* i. 2 In his Law doeth he meditate day and night. **1594** T. B. *La Primaud. Fr. Acad.* II. 163 The better to haue them in memorie, it often thinketh and meditateth of those things. **1601** SHAKS. *Twel. N.* III. iv. 219, I wil meditate the while vpon some horrid message for a Challenge. *a* **1618** W. BRADSHAW *Medit. Man's Mortal.* (1621) 30 When God in any judgement..shewes his wrath, wee should thinke and meditate of this. **1630** PRYNNE *Anti-Armin.* 195 He then that shall vnfainedly meditate on all these Texts. *a* **1716** SOUTH *Serm.* (1744) X. i. 19 He that accustoms himself to meditate upon the greatness of God, finds [etc.]. **1834** JAMES *J. Marston Hall* ix, Leaving me to meditate over the future. **1877** MONIER WILLIAMS *Hinduism* vi. 76 A Buddhist..only meditates on the perfections of the Buddha.

Hence '**meditating** *vbl. sb.* and *ppl. a.* Also '**meditatingly** *adv.*, meditatively.

1643 MILTON *Divorce* x. Wks. 1851 IV. 49 Those divine meditating words. **1645** —— *Tetrach.* Introd., Some of our severe Gnostics, whose little reading, and lesse meditating holds ever..that which it took up. **1753** RICHARDSON *Grandison* III. i. 2 He enquired..Why she looked so meditatingly? *a* **1873** LYTTON *Ken. Chillingly* v. vii, Meditatingly propped on his elbow.

meditated ('mɛdɪteɪtɪd), *ppl. a.* [f. MEDITATE *v.* + -ED[1].] Contemplated, intended; also, thought out, produced or prepared by meditation.

1736 GRAY *Statius* II. 22 'Twas there he aim'd the meditated harm. **1760** C. JOHNSTON *Chrysal* (1822) II. 120 Walking a meditated turn or two across the tent. **1814** WORDSW. *Excurs.* IX. 21 The food of hope Is meditated action. **1841** MACAULAY *Ess., Leigh Hunt* (ed. Montague) III. 43 The Way of the World, the most deeply meditated and the most brilliantly written of all his works. **1855** MILMAN *Lat. Chr.* IX. ii. IV. 49 Already there were dark rumours of his treachery and meditated revolt.

meditater, variant of MEDITATOR.

meditation (mɛdɪ'teɪʃən). [a. F. *méditation* or ad. L. *meditātiōn-em*, n. of action f. *meditārī* to MEDITATE.]

1. The action, or an act, of meditating; continuous thought or musing upon one subject or series of subjects; serious and sustained reflection or mental contemplation.

1390 GOWER *Conf.* I. 256 Fro hevene as thogh a vois it were, To soune of such prolacioun That he his meditacioun Therof mai take. *a* **1460** *Pol. Poems* (Rolls) II. 242 That the heyere herd with good medytacioun May the pore peple swych wyse avaunce [etc.]. **1526** *Pilgr. Perf.* (W. de W. 1531) 233 Meditacyon is a profounde or studyous cogitacyon about ony certeyn thynge. **1588** FRAUNCE *Lawiers Log.* I. i. 1 Reasoning may be..in solitary meditations and deliberations with a mans selfe. **1590** SHAKS. *Mids. N.* II. i. 164 The imperiall Votresse passed on, In maiden meditation, fancy free. **1633** EARL MANCH. *Al Mondo* (1636) 5 Meditation, I saw, was but a reiterated thought, proper to production of good or evill. **1712** LADY M. W. MONTAGU *Let. to Mr. W. Montagu* 9-11 Dec., The terrace is..consecrated to meditation..gay or grave. **1820** BYRON *Mar. Fal.* II. i, My lord, pray pardon me For breaking in upon your meditation. **1831** LYTTON *Godolphin* vi, After a fortnight's delay and meditation, he wrote. **1848** DICKENS *Dombey* i, His meditations on the subject were soon interrupted, by the rustling of garments on the staircase.

†**b.** Thought or mental contemplation *of* something. *Obs.*

1534 MORE *Comf. agst. Trib.* III. Wks. 1235/1 The fleshe shrinckynge at the meditacion of payne and deathe. **1672** MARVELL *Reh. Transp.* I. 81 It is the wisdome of Cats to whet their Claws..in meditation of the next Rat they are to encounter.

2. *spec.* in religious use: That kind of private devotional exercise which consists in the continuous application of the mind to the contemplation of some religious truth, mystery, or object of reverence, in order that the soul may increase in love of God and holiness of life.

a **1340** HAMPOLE *Psalter* Prol., þare in is discryued..þe meditacioun of contemplatifs. *c* **1491** *Chast. Goddes Chyld.* 7 Thenne cometh so mery meditacyons wyth plente of teres of compascyon. **1590** SPENSER *F.Q.* I. x. 46 Of God and goodnes was his meditation. **1641** HINDE *J. Bruen* xlv. 145 His first dayly duty, namely his holy and religious Meditation. **1704** M. HENRY *Commun. Comp.* vi. Wks. 1853 I. 330/1 In meditation we converse with ourselves; in prayer we converse with God. **1893** PATMORE *Relig. Poetæ* 34 The hour or half-hour of daily 'meditation'..is now unheard of. **1897** *Cath. Dict.* (ed. 5) 618/1 It was St. Ignatius of Loyola who reduced the rules of meditation to a system.

b. Used for: The theme of one's meditation.

1560 BIBLE (Geneva) *Ps.* cxix. 97 Oh how loue I thy Law! it is my meditacion continually. *Ibid.* 99, I haue had more vnderstanding then all my teachers: for thy testimonies are my meditacion.

3. A discourse, written or spoken, in which a subject (usually religious) is treated in a meditative manner, or which is designed to guide the reader or hearer in meditation.

a **1225** *Ancr. R.* 44 Redinge of Englichs, oðer of Freinchs, holi meditaciuns. *c* **1320** R. BRUNNE (*title*) Here bygynneþ meditacyuns of the soper of oure lorde Ihesu. *c* **1386** CHAUCER *Pars. Prol.* 55 But nathelees, this meditacion I putte it ay vnder correccion Of clerkes. **1612** A. STAFFORD (*title*) Meditations and Revolutions, moral, divine, politicall. **1710** SWIFT (*title*) A meditation upon a broom-stick. **1746** HERVEY (*title*) Meditations among the Tombs.

attrib. **1711** SHAFTESB. *Charac.* (1737) III. 95 The essay-writers,..reflection-coiners. meditation-founders, and others of the irregular kind of writers.

medi'tationist. *nonce-wd.* [f. prec. + -IST.] One who writes meditations.

1834-43 SOUTHEY *Doctor* Interch. xxii. (1847) VI. 380 Jeremy Taylor's is both a flowery and a fruitful stile: Hervey the Meditationist's a weedy one.

meditatist ('mɛdɪteɪtɪst). *rare.* [f. MEDITATE + -IST.] One who makes a business of meditating.

1860 in WORCESTER (citing *Ec. Rev.*). **1873** H. W. BEECHER in *Chr. World Pulpit* IV. 388/3 Thirdly, there are the meditatists..thousands meditate when they have nothing to meditate on.

meditative ('mɛdɪtətɪv, 'mɛdɪteɪtɪv), *a.* and *sb.* [ad. late L. *meditātīv-us*, f. ppl. stem of *meditārī* to MEDITATE: see -IVE. Cf. F. *méditatif.*]

A. *adj.*

1. Of persons, their dispositions or state of mind: Inclined or accustomed to meditation.

1656 BLOUNT *Glossogr.*, *Meditative*, apt to meditate, or cast in the mind. **1683** HOWE *Union Among Prot.* Wks. (1846) 108 His musing meditative mind. **1784** BERINGTON *Hist. Abeillard* IV. 198 Abeillard..was pious, reserved, meditative. **1798** COLERIDGE *Fears in Solitude* 23 And he, with many feelings,..Made up a meditative joy. **1874** GREEN *Short Hist.* vii §7. 426 The melancholy and meditative Jaques. **1885** J. MARTINEAU *Types Eth. Th.* I. I. ii. §8. 194 The highest calls of meditative piety.

b. Inclined to meditate or engaged in meditating (something specified). Const. *of.*

1876 M. COLLINS *Fr. Midnight to Midn.* II. ii. 223 There ..is our ontologic poet, meditative of incisive analytic unscannable blank verse.

2. Of actions, manner, appearance, etc.: Accompanied by meditation; indicative of meditation.

1756-7 tr. *Keysler's Trav.* (1760) II. 43 He used to take his meditative walks. **1903** *T. P.'s Weekly* 6 Nov. 724/2 After a dozen meditative pulls of his pipe, Harry proceeded.

3. Conducive to meditation.

1868 HAWTHORNE *Amer. Note-Bks.* II. 64 A stone wall, when shrubbery has grown around it,..becomes a very pleasant and meditative object.

†**4.** *Gram.* = DESIDERATIVE. *Obs.*

1755 JOHNSON, *Meditative*, expressing intention or design.

†**B.** *sb.* A desiderative word. *Obs.*

1612 BRINSLEY *Pos. Parts* (1669) 127 What Verbs do you call Meditatives? **1635** *Grammar Warre* B viij, Other Adverbs: as Meditatives, Deminutives, and Denominatives. **1726** S. LOWE *Lat. Gram.* 12 Meditatives in *-urio.* **1845** STODDART *Gram.* in *Encycl. Metrop.* (1847) I. 50/1 Most of the verbs in *rio* are meditatives.

meditatively ('mɛdɪtətɪvlɪ), *adv.* [f. prec. + -LY[2].] In a meditative manner.

1825 COLERIDGE *Aids Refl.* (1848) I. 305 Then.. meditatively contemplate..the beautiful effects of this ordinance. **1893** SALTUS *Madam Sapphira* 41 Mrs. Nevius ..for a while puffed meditatively.

meditativeness ('mɛdɪtətɪvnɪs). [f. MEDITATIVE + -NESS.] The condition of being meditative.

1860 in WORCESTER (citing COLERIDGE). **1877** 'H. A. PAGE' *De Quincey* II. xix. 221 Dreamy meditativeness.

meditator ('mɛdɪteɪtə(r)). Also 9 -er. [f. MEDITATE *v.* + -OR.] One who meditates.

1665 BOYLE *Occas. Refl.* IV. i. (1848) 46 It is wont to suggest variety of Notions to the Meditator. **1712** LADY M. W. MONTAGU *Let. to Mr. W. Montagu* 9-11 Dec., I would publish a daily paper called the *Meditator.* **1822** COLERIDGE *Table-t.* 29 Dec. (1835) I. 3 Lear is the most tremendous effort of Shakespeare as a poet; Hamlet as a philosopher or meditater. *a* **1859** DE QUINCEY *Conversation* Wks. 1860 XIV. 153 The mere meditators..may finally ripen into close observers. **1894** T. WATTS in *Athenæum* 20 Oct. 530/1 He had the mind..of the meditater upon nature.

†**medite**, *v. Obs.* [ad. F. *méditer* or L. *meditārī.*] *trans.* and *intr.* = MEDITATE *v.*

1483 CAXTON *Gold. Leg.* 442/1 The preest medytyng and thynkyng on the passyon of our lord..sayth [etc.]. **1606** SYLVESTER *Du Bartas* II. iv. II. *Magnif.* 770 Who, mediting the sacred Templ's plot, By th' other twin..is shot.

†**Mediterrane**, *a.* and *sb. Obs.* Also -an, -ayne, -en, -ean. [ad. L. *mediterrān-eus*: see MEDITERRANEAN.] **A.** *adj.*

1. = MEDITERRANEAN A. 2.

c **1425** WYNTOUN *Cron.* I. xiii. 1249 Fra þe Mer Mediterrayne Lyis souythe on to þe Occiane. **1598** HAKLUYT *Voy.* I. 588 He that neuer saw the sea will not be persuaded that there is a mediterrane sea. **1621** AINSWORTH *Annot. Pentat.*, *Numb.* xxxiv. 6 This great sea is commonly called the Mediterrane Sea. **1632** LITHGOW *Trav.* I. 25 The Riuiera of Genoa, along the Mediterrean sea. *Ibid.* III. 77 Now Creta comes, the Mediterren Queene.

2. Inland, interior; = MEDITERRANEAN A. 1.

1598 in *Hakluyt's Voy.* (1904) VI. 357 They that have seene the mediterran or inner parts of the kingdom of China, do report [etc.]. **1608** BACON *Sp. Gen. Natural.* Wks. 1826 V. 54 It is the mediterrane countries, and not the maritime, which need to fear surcharge of people. **1660** R. COKE *Power & Subj.* 262 It were a most unreasonable thing that the same Lawes should be imposed upon Mediterrane places, where are observed in Maritime.

B. *sb.* **a.** An enclosed piece of water. **b.** The Mediterranean Sea.

1658 R. FRANCK *North. Mem.* (1821) 197 By what means then was she moved into this small Mediterrane? **1662** OGILBY *King's Coronation* 18 We'll whip him like a Gig About the Mediterrane.

†**Medite'rraneal**, *a. Obs.* Also 7 -nell. [f. L. *mediterrāne-us* (see next) + -AL[1].] **a.** Inland, interior. **b.** *spec.* Mediterranean (sea).

1598 BARRET *Theor. Warres* Gloss. 251 *Mediterraneall*, is Inland countrie, or countries distant from the sea. **1609** BIBLE (Douay) *Num.* xxxiv. Comm., Mediterraneal sea, called great in respect of the lakes in the holie Land. **1622** F. MARKHAM *Bk. War* v. vii. §3. 186 All places whatsoeuer, whether Mediterranell or Maritime.

Mediterranean (mɛdɪtə'reɪnɪən), *a.* and *sb.* [f. L. *mediterrāne-us* (f. *medi-us* middle + *terra* land, earth) + -AN.] **A.** *adj.*

1. Of land: Midland, inland, remote from the coast; opposed to *maritime.* Also, intermediate (between two areas). †Applied also to the inhabitants of a region so situated.

1601 HOLLAND *Pliny* I. 501 The Mediterranean or midland parts of any country are..preferred before the maritime or sea-coasts. *a* **1691** BOYLE *Hist. Air* (1692) 197 The more mediterranean parts of Russia. **1756** C. LUCAS *Ess. Waters* II. 54 Sea water differs..not essentially, from the waters of our mediterranean salt springs. **1773** JOHNSON *Let. to Mrs. Thrale* 28 Aug., Craggy rocks, of height not stupendous, but to a Mediterranean visitor uncommon. **1869** RAWLINSON *Anc. Hist.* 12 The rivers of the central tract are continental or mediterranean; i.e. they begin and end without reaching the sea. **1875** J. H. BENNET *Winter Medit.* II. xi. 340 There is a highland country, an elevated mediterranean area of mountains and valleys.

transf. **1603** DEKKER *Wonderf. Yr.* D 4 How nimble is Sicknes,..The greatest cutter that takes vp the Mediterranean Ile in Powles for his Gallery to walke in, cannot ward off his blowes.

2. a. Of water surfaces: Nearly or entirely surrounded or enclosed by dry land; land-locked. ***Mediterranean Sea***, the proper name of the sea which separates Europe from Africa.

The notion expressed by the proper name (late L. *mare Mediterrāneum*, 7th c.; F. *Mer Méditerranée*; Sp. *Mar Mediterráneo*; It. *Mare Mediterraneo*) may originally have been 'the sea in the middle of the earth' rather than 'the sea enclosed by land'.

1594 R. ASHLEY tr. *Loys le Roy* 75 b, All those which are within the mediterranean sea. **1615** G. SANDYS *Trav.* 51 The Pirats..doe rob on the Ægean and Mediterranean seas. **1813** BAKEWELL *Introd. Geol.* 182 The boundary of a mediterranean sea or lake of fresh water. **1846** DARWIN *Geol. Observ. S. Amer.* 235 *note*, The theory that rock-salt is due to the sinking of water, charged with salt, in mediterranean spaces of the ocean. **1862** DANA *Man. Geol.* III. 301 The great mediterranean sea of the Silurian age.

b. Pertaining to 'mediterranean' waters. (See also B. 1 b.)

1830 LYELL *Princ. Geol.* I. 245 The delta of the Mississippi has somewhat of an intermediate character between an oceanic and mediterranean delta.

B. *sb.*

1. a. An inland sea or lake; a water area nearly or entirely surrounded by dry land; *spec.* the Mediterranean Sea.

1652-62 HEYLIN *Cosmogr.* III. 9 A man of perspicuous eyes may discern the Euxine on the one hand, and the Mediterranean on the other. **1661** LOVELL *Hist. Anim. & Min.* Introd., Some [fishes] are better in the ocean than in the mediterranean, and the contrary. **1704** ADDISON *Italy* (1705) 4 There is nothing more undetermined among the Learned than the Voyage of Ulysses; some confining it to the Mediterranean; others [etc.]. **1853** KANE *Grinnell Exp.* (1856) 544 The North Polar Ocean is a great mediterranean. **1875** S. COX in *Expositor* 251 The blue waters of the Mediterranean.

b. *attrib.*, passing into *adj.* (Cf. A. 2 b.) Pertaining to the Mediterranean Sea. Also, pertaining to the lands or countries in or around the Mediterranean Sea; spec. ***Mediterranean anæmia*** or ***disease***, thalassæmia, esp. thalassæmia major; ***Mediterranean climate***, the climate of lands around the Mediterranean Sea, characterized by hot, dry summers and mild, wet winters; also applied to any similar climate in other regions, as parts of California, Chile,

South Africa, and southern Australia; ***Mediterranean fever*** = *Malta fever* (see MALTA); ***Mediterranean pine*** = *maritime pine* (MARITIME *a.* 6), or STONE-PINE.

1599 NASHE *Lenten Stuffe* Wks. (Grosart) V. 229 In M. Hackluits English discoueries I haue not come in ken of one mizzen mast of a.. mediteranean sternebearer sente from her [Yarmouth's] Zenith or Meridian. **1678** YOUNG *Serm. at Whitehall* 29 Dec. 27 One of the Mediterranean Pirates. **1760** G. WASHINGTON *Diaries* (1925) I. 145 Planted 4 nuts of the Mediterranean Pine in the Pen. **1816** SIR. W. BURNETT (*title*) A Practical Account of the Mediterranean Fever [etc.]. **1896** *Jrnl. R. Microsc. Soc.* 324 (*heading*) Influence of the Mediterranean climate on plants. **1897** M. L. HUGHES (*title*) Mediterranean, Malta or Undulant Fever. **1899** *Daily News* 14 Jan. 6/4 The whole costume is in Mediterranean blue cloth. **1908** R. DE C. WARD *Climate* v. 124 The sub-tropical belt is exceptionally wide... The fact that the Mediterranean countries are so generally included in this belt has led to the use of the name 'Mediterranean climates'. **1924** *Scottish Geogr. Mag.* XL. 150 (*heading*) The Mediterranean climates of Eurasia and the Americas. **1933** Mediterranean pine [see CORONILLA]. **1936** WHIPPLE & BRADFORD in *Jrnl. Pediatrics* IX. 279 (*heading*) Mediterranean disease—thalassemia (erythroblastic anemia of Cooley). *Ibid.*, This interesting disease presents three important abnormalities together characterizing a syndrome which may be designated 'Mediterranean disease'. *Ibid.* 292 The clinical diagnosis was Mediterranean anemia, pericardial effusion, bronchopneumonia terminal. **1953** A. SMITH *Blind White Fish in Persia* iii. 51 Truly the Elburz mountains divide the arid heat of Tehran from the Mediterranean climate of the Caspian. **1954** *Blood* IX. 648 The term Mediterranean anemia is used in this paper to encompass the entire group of diseases characterized by microcytosis, hypochromia, ovalocytosis, anisocytosis and poikilocytosis, and, most prominently, targeting, together with certain familial hereditary patterns and clinical features. It is recognized that this group covers the spectrum from the most benign to the most severe forms clinically, and the range from hypochromic polycythemia to the severe Cooley's anemia hematologically. **1961** R. D. BAKER *Essent. Path.* xviii. 494 In thalassemia (Cooley's or Mediterranean anemia) there is an inherited anomaly of the red blood corpuscles consisting of flat 'target' cells. **1969** NEUBERGER & CAHIR *Princ. Climatol.* vi. 81 Climates having dry summers and wet winters as a result of the shifts of the subsidence belts are said to be 'Mediterranean' or 'California' climates. **1971** F. A. WARD *Primer of Haematol.* vi. 54 If,.. in Mediterranean anaemia, it can be shown that excessive destruction of red cells is taking place almost exclusively in the spleen, then splenectomy will relieve but, of course, not cure the condition.

†**2.** An inhabitant of an inland region. *Obs.*

1654 H. L'ESTRANGE *Chas I.* (1655) 131 Again the Mediterraneans the Highlanders muttered at the Imposition.

3. A racial type found especially in countries bordering on the Mediterranean sea; a person of this racial type. Also *attrib.* passing into *adj.* (Cf. EURAFRICAN *a.* and *sb.*)

1888 C. MORRIS *Aryan Race* i. 13 The hair of the Mediterraneans is not so long or so cylindrical in section as in the Mongolians. **1899**, **1910** [see EURAFRICAN *a.* and *sb.* 1]. **1921** *19th Cent.* May 896 It would be difficult to deny that the latinised 'Mediterraneans' are the most finely tempered peoples of Europe. **1921** *Man* CVII. 180 The brown dolichocephals called Mediterraneans. **1928** [see EURAFRICAN *a.* and *sb.* 1]. **1935** HUXLEY & HADDON *We Europeans* iv. 137 The Nordic, Eurasiatic, and Mediterranean types which are now scattered through the European population. *Ibid.* vi. 172 The Mediterranean type is much more widely distributed than the Mediterranean area. **1939** C. S. COON *Races of Europe* iv. 83 Some Mediterraneans were probably white skinned, and others brown. *Ibid.*, The Mediterranean group seems to be of purely *sapiens* ancestry, without Neanderthaloid or other mixture. **1959** *Chambers's Encycl.* XI. 433/1 Caspians.. are taller and less glabrous than the European Mediterraneans. **1960** J. COMAS *Man. Physical Anthropol.* ix. 602 This is the Dinaric race, which seems to be a Mediterranean type brachycephalized by some non-Mediterranean agency. **1962** C. S. COON *Orig. Races* (1963) i. 19 Races like the.. Mediterranean, East Baltic, and Dinaric, which loom large in the Europe-centred literature of anthropology, are neither subspecies nor, in a strict sense, local races. **1971** J. C. KING *Biol. of Race* vi. 114 For the European populations one began to hear of Nordic, Alpine, Mediterranean.. and God alone knows how many other races and subraces. **1974** N. FREELING *Dressing of Diamond* 11 He didn't look the part... A round Mediterranean head, and coarse black hair... A slightly Slav face. **1974** I. MURDOCH *Sacred & Profane Love Machine* 288 He.. looked into the big dark eyes.. Mediterranean eyes, African eyes.

Medite'rraneanize, *v.* [f. MEDITERRANEAN *a.* + -IZE.] *trans.* To make Mediterranean in character or attributes.

So **Mediter,raneani'zation**.

[**1896** T. COMMON tr. *Nietzsche's Case of Wagner* iii. 9 *Il faut méditerraniser la musique*: I have reasons for using this formula. The return to nature, to health, to gaiety, to youth, and to *virtue*!] **1915** *Nation* (N.Y.) 6 May 485/3 The Greeks are Mediterraneanized Slavs whose only heritage is a language which Demosthenes could neither have pronounced nor understood. **1921** *19th Cent.* May 894 The ancient Alpine race has been mediterraneanised, latinised, slavonised, and teutonised in Europe, and the Teuton in his turn has undergone mediterraneanisation, latinisation and slavonisation. **1947** N. CARDUS *Autobiogr.* III. 244 He mediterraneanises Wagner, to use Nietzsche's term.

mediterranell, obs. variant of MEDITERRANEAL.

†**mediterraneous**, *a. Obs.* [f. L. *mediterrāne-us* (see MEDITERRANEAN) + -OUS.]

1. Inland, remote from the coast.

1646 SIR T. BROWNE *Pseud. Ep.* II. iv. 82 It is found in mountaines and mediterraneous parts. **1692** RAY *Disc.* iii. (1732) 31 The mediterraneous Places above the Shores.

2. In the middle of the earth; subterranean.

1668 *Palp. Evid. Witchcr.* 102 The bituminous matter brought from the mediterraneous Vaults.

†**Mediterrany**, *a.* and *sb. Obs.* [ad. F. *méditerrané* or L. *mediterrāne-um*.] = MEDITERRANEAN.

c **1400** MAUNDEV. (Roxb.) xxxiii. 150 It rynnez in to þe see Mediterrany. **1432-50** tr. *Higden* (Rolls) I. 53 Of the grete see or Mediterranye.

meditrunk ('miːdɪtrʌŋk). *Ent.* [ad. mod.L. *meditruncus*, f. L. *medi-us* middle + *truncus* TRUNK.] (See quot.)

1826 KIRBY & SP. *Entomol.* III. xxxv. 532 If terms be thought necessary to designate the two intire segments into which the alitrunk is resolvable, the first may be the meditrunk (*meditruncus*), and the other the potrunk (*potruncus*).

‖**meditullium** (medɪ'tʌlɪəm). [L., f. *medi-us* middle; the second element is prob. cogn. w. *tellus* earth.]

†**1.** The middle (of anything). *Obs.*

1611 CORYAT *Crudities* 396 Baden.. lyeth in the very meditullium of Heluetia. **1638** SIR T. HERBERT *Trav.* (1677) 48 That Meditullium of the earth [India].

2. *spec.* The cellular or reticulated bony substance between the inner and outer laminæ of the cranium; = DIPLOE 1. ? *Obs.*

1693 tr. *Blancard's Phys. Dict.* (ed. 2), *Meditullium*, that Spungy Substance betwixt the Two *Lamina* [sic] of the Scull.

3. *Bot.* The interior parenchyma of the leaves and other parts of plants; = DIPLOE 2.

1840 PEREIRA *Elem. Mat. Med.* II. 661 The meditullium has frequently a reddish tint. **1880** GARROD & BAXTER *Mat. Med.* 374 The roots are seen to consist of a cortex or rind, and a ligneous cord or meditullium inclosing the pith.

Hence †**medi'tullian** *a. Obs.*, pertaining to the middle (of the earth).

1670 PETTUS *Fodinæ Reg.* Introd., As if they were but the soft Products of those Meditullian Petrefactions.

medium ('miːdɪəm), *sb.* and *a.* Pl. **media**, **-iums**. [a. L. *medium*, neuter of *medius* middle, cogn. with MID *a.*] **A.** *sb.*

1. a. A middle quality, degree, or condition. Formerly also, †something intermediate in nature or degree. †*in a medium*, intermediate (*between*).

1593 *Tell-Troth's N.Y. Gift* (1876) 29 There is no concorde betweene water and fire, nor any medium betweene loue and hatred. **1618** E. ELTON *Exp. Rom. vii.* (1622) 362 There is no medium: no middle nor indifferent state and condition betweene these two. **1626** BACON *Sylva* §293 This Appetite is in a Medium between the other two. **1649** BLITH *Eng. Improv. Impr.* (1653) To Husb., There is a Medium in all things. **1651** FRENCH *Distill.* v. 111 A saltish slime, and in tast.. a Medium betwixt salt, and Nitre. **1663** *Flagellum, or O. Cromwell* (ed. 2) Pref., I place and reckon this Cromwell as a Medium or Mean, betwixt.. Wallenstein .. and Thomas Anello. **1752** J. GILL *Trinity* vi. 116 Between God and a creature there is no medium. *a* **1770** JORTIN *Serm.* (1771) VII. vi. 108 There is a medium between frantic zeal and sinful compliance. **1811** BUSBY *Dict. Mus.* (ed. 3), *Recitative*, a species of musical recitation forming the medium between air and rhetorical declamation. **1811** BYRON *Hints fr. Hor.* lvii, Poesy between the best and worst No medium knows. *a* **1820** I. MILNER in Mary Milner *Life* (1842) 510 Is there no medium between going to Court, and going a hunting? **1869** SPURGEON *J. Ploughm. Talk* 28 There is a medium in all things, only blockheads go to extremes.

†**b.** Moderation. *Obs.*

1693 *Humours Town* 88 They are generally Men of no Medium, but continually in Extreams. **1748** SMOLLETT *Rod. Rand.* (1812) I. 4 He determined.. to observe no medium but.. sent her a peremptory order. **1780** W. PITT in Ld. Stanhope *Life* I. 35 The use of the horse I assure you I do not neglect, in the properest medium.

†**c.** A middle course, compromise. *Obs.*

1719 DE FOE *Crusoe* I. (Globe) 33 When I let him know my Reason, he own'd it to be just, and offer'd me this Medium, that he [etc.].

†**d.** Something intermediate in position. *Obs.*

1726 LEONI *Alberti's Archit.* I. 12/1 That the Inhabitants may not be obliged to pass out of a cold Place into a hot one, without a Medium of temperate Air.

†**2.** *Logic.* The middle term of a syllogism; hence, a ground of proof or inference. *Obs.*

1584 FENNER *Def. Ministers* (1587) 62 Let him.. conclude the Apostles question, with his medium, argument, and reason. **1630** RANDOLPH *Aristippus* Wks. (1875) 19 Your drinking is syllogism, where a pottle is the *major terminus*, and a pint the *minor*, a quart the *medium*. **1641** *Vind. Smectymnuus* v. 61 This we evinced by foure mediums out of Scripture. **1751** WESLEY *Wks.* (1872) XIV. 168 An equivocal medium proves nothing. **1757** SIR J. DALRYMPLE *Hist. Feudal Property* (1758) 147 They had refused to subject estates tail to forfeiture, and on this medium, that who cannot alienate cannot forfeit. **1817** JAS. MILL *Brit. India* III. i. 33 To trace the media of proof from one link to another.. is not, say the lawyers, the way to justice.

†**3.** A (geometrical or arithmetical) mean; an average. *Obs.*

1612 DAVIES *Why Ireland*, etc. 39 The reuenew.. did not rise vnto 10000. li. per annum, though the Medium be taken of the best seauen years. **1638** WILKINS *New World* III. (1707) 30 Betwixt two Extreams there can be but one Medium. *a* **1687** PETTY *Pol. Arith.* (1690) 55 At a medium I reckon that the whole Fleet must be Men of three or four years growth. **1727** SWIFT *Mod. Proposal* Wks. 1755 II. II. 62, I have reckoned upon a medium, that a child just born will weigh 12 pounds. **1731** BAILEY vol. II. s.v., Arithmetical Medium, is that which is equally distant from each extreme. *Ibid.*, Geometrical Medium, is [etc.]. **1788** LD. AUCKLAND *Corr.* (1861) II. 84 The medium of the thermometer continues here at about 70°. **1793** SMEATON *Edystone L.* §113 The medium of half an inch on a side. **1817** JAS. MILL *Brit. India* I. II. i. 94 Only thirty-three years, as a medium, are assigned to a reign.

4. a. Any intervening substance through which a force acts on objects at a distance or through which impressions are conveyed to the senses: applied, e.g., to the air, the ether, or any substance considered with regard to its properties as a vehicle of light or sound. Often *fig.*

1595 CHAPMAN *Ovids Banq. Sence* D 2 *margin*, Sight is one of the three sences that hath his medium extrinsecally. **1621** BURTON *Anat. Mel.* I. i. II. vi. 33 To the Sight three things are required, the Obiect, the Organ, and the Medium. **1643** A. ROSS *Mel Heliconium* 27 The air, which is the medium of musick and of all sounds. *a* **1652** J. SMITH *Sel. Disc.* i. 25 They shall no more behold the Divinity through the dark mediums that eclipse the blessed sight of it. **1709** *Phil. Trans.* XXVI. 368 Air is the only Medium for the Propagation of Sound. **1711** ADDISON *Spect.* No. 257 ¶8 He therefore who looks upon the Soul through its outward Actions, often sees it through a deceitful Medium. **1742** YOUNG *Nt. Th.* VIII. 243 The Truth, thro' such a Medium seen, may make Impression deep. **1768-74** TUCKER *Lt. Nat.* (1834) II. 443 Both visible and sonorous bodies act equally by mediums, one of light and the other of air, vibrating upon our organs. **1794** G. ADAMS *Nat. & Exp. Philos.* II. xv. 136 By a medium.. is meant any pellucid or transparent body, which suffers light to pass through it. **1815** J. SMITH *Panorama Sci. & Art* I. 422 In passing into a denser medium, light is refracted towards the perpendicular. **1851** SIR F. PALGRAVE *Norm. & Eng.* I. 189 The liability incurred by the nation is refracted through so many media. **1875** *Encycl. Brit.* I. 100/1 The air around us forms the most important medium of sound to our organs of hearing. **1880** BASTIAN *Brain* iii. 60 To rudimentary aggregations of pigment, in some animals transparent media are added, serving to condense the light thereon.

b. The application of the word in sense 4 to the air, ether, etc. has given rise to the new sense: Pervading or enveloping substance; the substance or 'element' in which an organism lives; hence *fig.* one's environment, conditions of life.

[**1664** POWER *Exp. Philos.* Pref. 11 The aetherial Medium (wherein all the Stars and Planets do swim).] **1865** GROTE *Plato* I. v. 201 You cannot thus abstract any man from the social medium by which he is surrounded. **1873** HAMERTON *Intell. Life* IX. v. (1875) 320 The general talk, which is nothing but a neutral medium in which intelligences float. **1876** L. STEPHEN *Eng. Th. 18th C.* I. i. 6 The gradual adaptation of the race to its medium. **1878** *Encycl. Brit.* VIII. 36/2 When the insulating medium, or, as it is called, the 'dielectric', is shellac. **1880** M. ARNOLD *Lett.* (1895) II. 184-5 The medium in which he [Burns] lived, Scotch peasants, Scotch Presbyterianism, and Scotch drink, is repulsive. Chaucer.. pleases me more and more, and his medium is infinitely superior. **1886** *Encycl. Brit.* XXI. 406/1 Thoroughly conducted cultivations should decide in what medium the Schizomycete flourishes best.

5. a. An intermediate agency, means, instrument or channel. Also, intermediation, instrumentality: in phrase ***by*** or ***through the medium of***. *spec.* of newspapers, radio, television, etc., as vehicles of mass communication. Also *attrib.* and in *pl.* (see MEDIA[2]).

1605 BACON *Adv. Learn.* II. xvi. §2 But yet is not of necessitie that Cogitations bee expressed by the Medium of Wordes. **1614** RALEIGH *Hist. World* II. v. §10. 309 Moses.. wrought.. by the medium of mens affections. **1659** T. PECKE *Parnassi Puerp.* 179, I know the Medium to let you see A wonder. **1726** DE FOE *Hist. Devil* II. vi. (1840) 249 The devil has managed several secret operations by the medium or instrumentality of the cloven foot. **1775** BURKE *Sp. Conc. Amer.* Wks. III. 31 The proposition is peace. Not peace through the medium of war. **1795** *Gentl. Mag.* 544/1 Some useful information.. may.. be hoped for through the medium of your curious Publication. *c* **1811** FUSELI in *Lect. Paint.* iv. (1848) 438 They are the end, this the medium. **1856** SIR B. BRODIE *Psychol. Inq.* I. v. 186 The seal.. except through the medium of his whiskers,.. may be said.. [to have] no sense of touch at all. **1866** FELTON *Anc. & Mod. Gr.* I. I. 16 They [Latin and Greek] were the media of the scholarship, the science, the theology of the Middle Age. **1880** *Coach Builders' Art Jrnl.* I. 63 Considering your Journal one of the best possible mediums for such a scheme. **1883** S. R. GARDINER *Hist. Eng.* II. xvi. 184 *note*, It seems.. more probable that the tarts went backwards and forwards as media of a correspondence. **1898** ILLINGWORTH *Div. Immanence* vi. 136 He [Christ] ordained sacraments; selecting, as their media, the two.. most universal religious rites. *a* **1906** *Mod.* The ——shire *Gazette* is the best advertising medium in the country. **1967** M. MCLUHAN (*title*) The medium is the massage. **1968** *Listener* 28 Mar. 394/3 My recent visits to the theatre, together with my colour television set, have convinced me that McLuhan has it wrong. The medium *impedes* the message.

b. ***medium of circulation*** or ***exchange***, ***circulating medium***: something which serves as the ordinary representative of exchangeable value, and as the instrument of commercial transactions; in civilized countries usually coin or written promises or orders for the delivery of coin. †In the American colonies often simply

medium, chiefly used in speaking of the local paper currency.

1740 *Conn. Col. Rec.* (1874) VIII. 318 The expences of this government are likely to be very heavy..by reason..of a great scarcity of a medium of exchange. **1740** W. DOUGLASS *Disc. Curr. Brit. Plant. Amer.* 6 Upon cancelling this Paper Medium all those Inconveniences did vanish. **1758** in B. P. Smith *Hist. Dartmouth Coll.* (1878) 16 The discredit of our medium. **1828** P. CUNNINGHAM *N.S. Wales* (ed. 3) II. 101 Bullion and paper, as mediums of circulation. **1833** HT. MARTINEAU *Charmed Sea* Summary 135 The adoption of a medium of exchange. **1838** PRESCOTT *Ferd. & Is.* (1846) II. xvii. 128 The only medium for representing their property was bills of exchange. **1884** *Rep. Brit. Assoc.* 837 Media of Exchange: some Notes on the Precious Metals and their Equivalents.

6. a. *Painting.* Any liquid 'vehicle' (as oil, water, albumen, etc.) with which pigments are mixed to render them capable of being used in painting. Also, any of the varieties of painting as determined by the nature of the vehicle employed, as oil-painting, water-colour, tempera, fresco, etc.

1854 FAIRHOLT *Dict. Art*, *Medium*, the menstruum, or liquid vehicle, with which the dry pigments are ground and made ready for the artist's use. **1892** *Nation* (N.Y.) 15 Dec. 477/2 There is no man to-day who understands his medium [viz. water-colour] more perfectly. **1903** *Edin. Rev.* Apr. 454 If his colours, his gilding, his mediums were of inferior quality, they were confiscated.

b. *Photogr.* A varnish used as a vehicle in 'retouching' (see quots.).

1890 J. HUBERT *Retouching* (1903) 23 If your medium will not take the blacklead readily, the former may be thickened. **1892** *Phot. Ann.* II. 201 The simplest medium to render the surface of the negative suitable for marking upon is made by dissolving white powdered resin in turpentine... The negative to be retouched is prepared by rubbing upon it..a drop of the medium.

7. *Theatr.* A screen fixed in front of a source of light in order to throw a coloured light upon the stage.

1859 G. A. SALA *Gas-light & D.*, *Getting up Pantomime*, Gas pipes with coloured screens called 'mediums'. **1873** *Routledge's Yng. Gentl. Mag.* 282/1 Fish-tail burners, guarded by curved metal reflecting hoods on the back and by wire work on the front side..so as to allow of red or green tammy mediums being dropped over each row. **1933** P. GODFREY *Back-Stage* vii. 90 'Two more floods up-stage, Bill,' says the stage-manager. 'What mediums, sir—amber or pink?'

8. Applied to a person. **a.** *gen.* An intermediary agent, mediator.

1817 BOWDICH, etc. *Mission to Ashantee* i. iii. (1819) 63 This man..is our only safe medium, and interprets to the King anxiously and impressively.

b. *Spiritualism*, etc. A person who is supposed to be the organ of communications from departed spirits. Hence also applied to a clairvoyant or a person under hypnotic control.

1853 H. SPICER *Sights & Sounds* 88 This lady was a medium, and as the subject of 'spirit rappings' was already [etc.]. **1854** MISS MITFORD in L'Estrange *Life* (1870) III. xiv. 303 Bulwer is in the hands of a set of mediums, and passes his time in conversation with his dead daughter. **1888** BRYCE *Amer. Commonw.* III. 639 Attempts to pry by the help of 'mediums' into the book of Fate.

9. Senses derived from the adj. **a.** *nonce-use.* A person of the middle class.

1837 T. HOOK *Jack Brag* ii, The tip-toppers are livelier than the mediums.

b. A soldier of 'medium' equipment, between 'light' and 'heavy'. (Cf. quot. 1876 in B. 1.)

1889 *N. & Q.* 7th Ser. VIII. 111/1 The 4th Dragoon Guards are no longer 'Heavies', but 'Mediums'. *Ibid.*, Thirteen regiments of 'Mediums', comprising the seven regiments of Dragoon Guards, numbered 1 to 7 [etc.].

c. A kind of cotton goods.

1777 in *Essex Inst. Hist. Coll.* (1906) XLII. 319 There cargo is Salt..37 bales, cases, hhds of mediums [etc.]. **1862** *Catal. Internat. Exhib.* II. XVIII. 4 India twills, silicias, casbans, and mediums.

10. A medium-dated security.

1968 [see *medium-dated* adj., sense B. 3 below]. **1974** *Daily Tel.* 25 May 20/6 The popularity among high tax-payers of low coupon mediums such as Treasury 3 p.c. 1979 is not all that difficult to comprehend. **1975** *Times* 25 Apr. 24/7 'Shorts', after being $\frac{1}{2}$ point higher at one stage, ended mixed... 'Longs' and 'mediums' were up to $\frac{3}{4}$ point up.

B. *attrib.* and *adj.*

1. a. Intermediate between two degrees, amounts, qualities, or classes.

1796 C. MARSHALL *Garden.* ix. (1813) 114 A good medium way is to plant the deciduous sorts [of trees] the beginning of March. **1859** DARWIN *Orig. Spec.* iv. (1873) 92 A medium form may often long endure. **1876** VOYLE & STEVENSON *Milit. Dict.* s.v. *Cavalry*, In the British army cavalry is classed as heavy, medium, and light cavalry. **1884** *Bath Herald* 27 Dec. 6/5 The offal..is separated into broad bran, medium bran, and sharps. **1903** *Edin. Rev.* Apr. 493 There is a tendency for land to get into the hands of medium and large proprietors. **1905** J. HEYWOOD *Mus. Churches* 17 Average choir boys cannot recite on a low note without being liable to use the thick register or chest voice instead of the medium register.

b. *Fencing.* **medium guard**: see quot. 1767.

1747 J. GODFREY *Sci. Defence* 21 Here are four Guards, viz. Inside, Outside, Medium, and Hanging. *Ibid.* 22 The Medium is the Small-Sword Posture, and that alone may properly be called a guard. **1767** FERGUSSON *Dict. Terms Small Sword* 13 *Medium Guard*, the arm, wrist, and sword in this guard ought to be kept in the same height as the Quarte, and the edge of the sword perpendicular to the ground.

c. The designation of a size of paper between royal and demy.

The sheet of medium writing and drawing paper usually measures 22 × $17\frac{1}{2}$ inches; in U.S., 23 × 18. The sheet of medium printing paper is usually 24 × 19.

1711 *Act 10 Anne* c. 18 §37 For..all Paper..called..Medium Fine..the Summe of Six Shillings for every Reame... Genoa Medium..Two Shillings and Six Pence for every Reame. **1774** M. MACKENZIE *Maritime Surv.* 105 A Folio Observation book of 4 Quires medium Paper. **1859** *Stationer's Handbk.* 20, 73.

d. Of sherry, wine, etc., having a flavour intermediate between dry and sweet. So ***medium dry***, ***medium sweet*** adj. phrs.

1906 *Hatch, Mansfield Price List* 11 *First Quality*, Extra or Medium Dry. *Ibid.* 20 *Light*, Medium Sweet. **1933** H. W. ALLEN *Sherry* iii. 46 This medium wine is likely to find its way into a blend of Amoroso. **1951** R. POSTGATE *Plain Man's Guide to Wine* iii. 57 Their labels contain nothing more informative than 'Best South African Sherry: Medium Dry', or some such phrases. **1960** I. JEFFERIES *Dignity & Purity* i. 18, I expect you'd like sherry, wouldn't you? Medium? **1961** *Twining Bros. Wine List* 2 Amontillado Rico (Medium Dry)... Ancient Browne Rednutt (Medium Sweet). **1969** *Guardian* 13 Feb. 9/1 The medium dry white wine. **1972** A. HUNTER *Vivienne* viii. 101 The waiter..remembered the Major's buying Mrs. Selly a drink, a medium sherry. **1972** *Country Life* 23 Mar. 673/3 One can make it [*sc.* mead] very dry or quite sweet... I intended to make mine medium sweet. **1973** J. PORTER *It's Murder with Dover* v. 45 He sipped his medium sweet cider. **1974** 'A. GILBERT' *Nice Little Killing* iv. 61 Maybe a Dubonnet or a medium sherry—spirits never.

e. The designation of meat cooked between 'well done' and 'rare'. So ***medium done***, ***medium rare*** adj. phrs. (cf. RARE *a.*[2] b).

1939 P. K. NEWILL *Good Food* iv. 72 Beef..medium..22–25 [minutes per pound]. **1953** J. & M. ROBERSON *Meat Cookbk.* ii. 47 Beefsteaks...medium 1 in. 7 min. on each side. **1968** L. O'DONNELL *Face of Crime* (1969) vii. 104 His own steak was just as ordered: medium rare and delicious. **1972** 'E. MCBAIN' *Sadie when she Died* iv. 45 Carella ordered prime ribs, medium rare. **1972** *House & Garden* Feb. 111/1 Steak au poivre was ordered *bleu*..but arrived medium done. **1975** M. KENYON *Mr Big* xix. 176, I never saw myself ..tellin' Jeeves to do the steak medium.

†**2.** Average, mean. *Obs.*

1670 PETTUS *Fodinæ Reg.* 9 Two Tun and a quarter of Oar make a Tun of Metal at a medium rate 3*l.* 10*s.* **1748** *Anson's Voy.* II. v. 182 The medium heat all the year round will be 66°. **1799** *Hull Advert.* 14 Sept. 3/2 Both of which may be accounted medium years. **1800** *Misc. Tracts in Asiat. Ann. Reg.* 72/2 The medium height of a Fahrenheit's thermometer was between 80° and 82°.

3. *Comb.* **a.** With sbs. used *attrib.*, forming adjs., as ***medium-grade***, ***-haul***, ***-heel***, ***-pace***, ***-range***, ***-rise***, ***-term***, ***-weight*** adjs.; **b.** parasynthetic, as ***medium-coloured***, ***-paced***, ***-powered***, ***-priced***, ***-sized***, adjs.; **medium-dated** *a.* (see quots. 1958 and 1968).

1891 C. JAMES *Rom. Rigmarole* 75 *Medium-coloured hair. **1948** *Financial Times* 5 May 1/6 Among *medium-dated stocks War Loan $3\frac{1}{2}$ per cent was a good spot. **1953** *Economist* 25 July 287/3 In the gilt-edged market interest at first was concentrated upon the 'shorts' and the medium dated issues. **1958** 'NEDLAW' *Your Guide to Stocks & Shares* III. 78 *Medium dated*, a gilt-edged security having more than five years but less than ten years to run to its final maturity or redemption date. **1968** P. A. S. TAYLOR *Dict. Econ. Terms* 70 *Medium-dated, 'mediums'.* Securities with a life of between five and fifteen years. **1877** RAYMOND *Statist. Mines & Mining* 174 A stratum of *medium-grade ore. **1963** *Punch* 4 Sept. 352/3 The new *medium-haul Trident. **1965** 'W. HAGGARD' *Hard Sell* iii. 31 SAGA was building a medium-haul aircraft. **1974** *Times* 14 Mar. 5/4 The new dishes now being served on all medium-haul flights. **1973** A. ROY *Sable Night* iii. 24 Dark red suède *medium-heel shoes. **1898** *Westm. Gaz.* 16 May 4/2 Slow and *medium-pace bowlers. **1884** *Lillywhite's Cricket Ann.* 103 A straight *medium-paced bowler. **1963** BIRD & HUTTON-STOTT *Veteran Motor Car* 41 Georges Richard himself was more interested in the *medium-powered, medium-priced car. **1895** *Montgomery Ward Catal.* 15/3 The most satisfactory *medium-priced cottons on the market. **1972** E. HARGREAVES *Fair Green Weed* v. 67 They were booked in at a medium-priced hotel. **1943** *Sun* (Baltimore) 24 Aug. 2/6 But it could be of real value to *medium and short-range planes. **1974** 'F. CLIFFORD' *Grosvenor Square Goodbye* II. 166 The provision of a medium-range aircraft at Heathrow. **1968** *Guardian* 19 June 3/3 '*Medium-rise' housing—flats going up to only four or five stories. **1972** *Times* 17 June 8/8 Aaron Wallis lived in Battersea, in a medium-rise block of no great character. **1882** J. HAWTHORNE *Fort. Fool* I. xiv, He was a *medium-sized, full-bodied man. **1958** *Spectator* 15 Aug. 216/3 A high credit rating for *medium-term loans. **1965** *McGraw-Hill Dict. Mod. Econ.* 321 A medium-term forecast made in July, 1963, could cover the period from January, 1965, through 1967. **1969** *Times* 5 May 22/2 The Midland Bank Finance Corporation..specialises in medium-term credit. **1971** *Jrnl. Gen Psychol.* LXXXIV. 243 Span memory is distinct from medium-term memory in the case of semantic material. **1895** *Montgomery Ward Catal.* 282/3 Men's *medium weight, natural wool color undershirts. **1964** *McCall's Sewing* i. 11/1 Select medium-weight fabrics which drape nicely and add roundness. **1968** M. S. LIVINGSTON *Particle Physics* i. 5 Medium-weight nuclei are the most tightly bound and the most stable.

c. *attrib.* and *Comb.* in sense 8 b.

1872 SCHELE DE VERE *Americanisms* 245 A Circle is held for Medium Developments and Spiritual Manifestations at Bloomfield-street every Sunday. **1886** W. JAMES in *Proc. Amer. Soc. Psychical Res.* 105 Her pupils contract in the medium-trance. **1919** J. M. KEYNES *Econ. Consequences Peace* iii. 37 Mr. Lloyd George's unerring, almost medium-like, sensibility to every one immediately round him. **1972** A. FORD *Life beyond Death* i. 49 'I'm willing to go along with this stuff,' a medium baiter said one time, 'if you'll positively guarantee to bring me Socrates.'

d. Special collocations: **medium bomber**, a bomber intermediate between the heavy and the light; **medium close-up** *Cinematogr.*, a cinematographic or television shot intermediate between a medium shot (see below) and a close-up; also called ***medium-close shot***; **medium frequency**, an intermediate frequency (of oscillation); *spec.* in *Broadcasting*, a frequency of a medium wave, viz. one between 300 kilohertz and three megahertz; **medium shot** *Cinematogr.*, a cinematographic or television shot intermediate between a close-up and a long shot; **medium wave** *Broadcasting*, a radio wave with wavelength between a hundred metres and a kilometre (see quot. 1929 for former limits); freq. *attrib.* (usu. hyphenated).

1935 *Flight* 22 Aug. 204a/2 The specialized light bomber ..may..be supplanted eventually by the very fast *medium bomber. **1938** *Encycl. Brit. Bk. of Year* 161/1 A medium bomber can carry enough incendiary bombs to start 150 separate simultaneous fires. **1956** *U.S. Air Force Dict.* 321/2 *Medium bomber*,..currently (1956), a bomber having a gross weight, including bomb load, of between 100,000 and 250,000 pounds..; a medium bomber is thought of as having medium range, and as being best used at medium altitudes, as well as having a medium gross weight. **1971** E. LUTTWAK *Dict. Mod. War* 45/2 'Medium' bombers and 'light' bombers retain a residual role in 'tactical' situations. **1957** MANVELL & HUNTLEY *Technique Film Music* ii. 34 Long track, mostly in medium or *medium-close shot, with one large pull-back during the market-place scene. **1933** A. BRUNEL *Filmcraft* 147 Scene 168. *Medium close up. The slave-driver father looks desperately round again. **1948** E. LINDGREN *Art of Film* v. 82 A medium close-up of his body on which shadows of the prison bars form a pattern. **1950** E. E. BRODBECK *Handbk. Basic Motion-Pict. Techniques* 103 *Medium close up*... Such a scene shows the most vital part of the subject plus some of that part's surrounding area. **1969** W. RUTHERFORD *Gallows Set* vi. 77 David in medium close up came on the monitor screens. **1920** *Whittaker's Electr. Engineer's Pocket-Bk.* (ed. 4) 348 The result..has been the adoption of two frequencies, a *medium frequency for general power and lighting, and a low frequency for systems supplying rotary converters. **1946** *Happy Landings* (Air Ministry) July 9/1 The radio compass, when tuned to any medium frequency, was seriously affected by thunderstorms... The compass pointer did not point towards the M/F station selected. **1966** *McGraw-Hill Encycl. Sci. & Technol.* I. 363/2 European medium-frequency (mf) broadcasting channels are assigned at 9-kc intervals rather than the 10-kc intervals used in the Western hemisphere. **1933** A. BRUNEL *Filmcraft* 150 Scene 488. *Medium shot. The waiter pouring out champagne into the glasses on Pauline's table. **1937** *Discovery* Nov. 330/2 The [television] cameras are also fitted with lenses of suitable focal length for getting long-shots, medium-shots and close-ups as desired. **1953** K. REISZ *Technique Film Editing* ii. 81 In a long-lasting shot (33) Bill slows down as he approaches the camera and finally comes to rest in medium shot. **1966** H. P. MANOOGIAN *Film-Maker's Art* vi. 219 In traditional editing the scene is established, usually in a long shot, and as the action within the scene proceeds a number of medium shots and close-ups are taken to relate that action. **1975** *New Yorker* 26 May 32/3, I think we can get around the full lotus by having a stunt man do it, and using medium and long shots in a half-lit room. **1928** *Wireless World* 7 Nov. 626/2 It will..be best to concentrate on maximum efficiency in *medium-wave transformers. **1929** *Jrnl. Inst. Electr. Engin.* LXVIII. 22/2 The definitions were fixed as follows [by the International Radio Technical Committee]... Medium waves: kilocycles/sec 1500 to 100; m 200 to 3000. **1938** D. H. SURGEONER *Aircraft Radio* iii. 23 Medium waves are.. suitable for both communications and direction-finding and these can be transmitted over reasonable distances. **1961** *Radio Times* 6 Apr. 9/1 The Network Three transmitters, both medium-wave and VHF, will be used for one channel ..and the BBC's television sound transmitters for the other. **1974** Medium wave [see *long wave* s.v. LONG *a.*[1] 18].

mediumism (ˈmiːdɪəmɪz(ə)m). [f. prec. + -ISM.] The practices of spiritualistic 'mediums'.

1864 A. LEIGHTON *Myst. Leg. Edin.* (1886) 121 The spirit-rapping miracles of mediumism. **1880** HOWELLS *Undisc. Country* xii. 181 A mercenary professional mediumism.

mediumistic (ˌmiːdɪəˈmɪstɪk), *a.* [f. MEDIUM + -ISTIC.] Relating to 'mediumism'; having the characteristics of a 'medium'.

1868 *Harper's Mag.* July 193/2, I should think they were both highly mediumistic. **1869** GREGORY in *Eng. Mech.* 3 Dec. 281/1 Many persons do not possess the necessary mediumistic qualification. **1876** SAINTSBURY in *Academy* 16 Dec. 582 Maud is a pretty girl, of supposed 'mediumistic' powers. **1896** H. R. HAWEIS *Dead Pulpit* vi. 117 He is for the time, in fact, highly sensitized and mediumistic. **1920** D. H. LAWRENCE *Lost Girl* xv. 344 The terror, the agony, the nostalgia of the heathen past was a constant torture to her mediumistic soul. **1941** L. A. G. STRONG *John McCormack* xiv. 217 That almost mediumistic quality which enabled the singer to surrender to the song and yet keep his own individuality. **1954** A. HUXLEY *Let.* 5 Dec. (1969) 717 Huene's reactions were wholly aesthetic; Gerald's mainly verbal and mediumistic—with other personalities talking through him from a variety of mental levels. **1974** *Times Lit. Suppl.* 27 Sept. 1046/3 What relation do they bear to mediumistic trances?

mediumize (ˈmiːdɪəmaɪz), *v.* [f. MEDIUM + -IZE.] *trans.* To convert into a (spiritualistic) 'medium'. Hence ˌ**mediumiˈzation**.

1880 *Argosy* XXIX. 460 He need have laid no command on the Captain, for the poor man was planted there: chloroformed, mesmerised, mediumised. **1880** HOWELLS *Undisc. Country* ii. (1881) 29 The crude and unsettled spiritual existence reached by our present system of mediumisation.

mediumly (ˈmiːdɪəmlɪ), *adv.* [f. MEDIUM *a.* + -LY².] Moderately; to a medium or average extent.

1909 *Nation* (N.Y.) 16 Dec. 598 An excellent anthology, for old as well as for the 'mediumly' young. **1958** *Times Lit. Suppl.* 30 May 301/4 Well-known names and personalities even to the mediumly informed. **1961** A. WILSON *Old Men at Zoo* iv. 213 I'm wedged as hell and mediumly happy there.

mediumship (ˈmiːdɪəmʃɪp). [f. MEDIUM + -SHIP.]

1. Intervening agency, instrumentality.

1882 L. WINGFIELD *Gehenna* II. ix. 274 Subterranean convulsions, through whose mediumship volcanic flames.. would purify the heavens. **1882** RIDER HAGGARD *Cetywayo* 198 The government announced through the mediumship of the Queen's Speech that [etc.]. **1890** 'ANNIE THOMAS' *On Children* I. vii. 131 He had been made known to them through the mediumship of an Aldermanic friend.

2. *Spiritualism.* The attribute of being a 'medium'; action as a 'medium'.

1868 *Law Rep., Equity Cases* VI. 663 The wonderful things done by the spirits through the Defendant's mediumship. **1875** *Q. Jrnl. Sci.* XII. 48 As an instance of hereditary mediumship, 'the same man had four daughters, virgins, which did prophesy'. **1881** PEMBER *Earth's Earliest Ages* (1893) 329 A séance held through the mediumship of Mr. Bastian. **1898** A. LANG *Making Relig.* viii. 169, I cannot feel.. as if the case of physical mediumship itself, as a freak of nature, were definitely closed.

medius (ˈmiːdɪəs). *Mus.* [a. L. *medius* middle.]

†**1.** An alto or tenor voice or part: = MEAN *sb.*² 2.

1565 (*title*) Mornyng and Euenyng prayer and Communion, set forthe in foure partes, to be song in churches. [title of Part] Medius. **1609** RAVENSCROFT *Deuteromelia* 17 Freemens Songs of 4. Voices. Treble.. Medivs.. Tenor.. Bassvs. **1758** (*title*) Divine Melody in twenty-four choice Hymns; the first fifteen were set to Music, in two Parts, by Mr. Prelleur, the rest chiefly by Mr. Moze, who hath also composed a Medius to every Hymn.

2. In ecclesiastical music = MEDIANT.

1782 BURNEY *Hist. Mus.* II. 583 The Mode, the Dominant, and Medius, are all the same [in the three chants].

medivac, var. MEDEVAC.

Medize (ˈmiːdaɪz), *v.* [mod. ad. Gr. Μηδίζ-ειν, f. Μῆδοι the Medes: see -IZE.] *intr.* To be a Mede in manners, language and dress; to side with the Medes. Of a Greek of the 6th and 5th c. B.C.: To favour the interests of the 'Median' or Persian enemies of his country. Also *trans.* To make like a Mede. Hence **ˈMedizing** *vbl. sb.* and *ppl. a.*

1849 GROTE *Greece* II. xl. V. 101 The leading men of Thebes.. decidedly *medised*, or espoused the Persian interest. *a* **1873** LYTTON *Pausanias* III. iii. (1876) 248 They would rather all Hellas were Medised than Pausanias the Heracleid. *Ibid.* iv. 265 The Medising traitor is here. *Ibid.* IV. iv. 341 They accuse him of medising. **1901** *Contemp. Rev.* Feb. 176 The Greek thought of 'Medizing' as the sum of all possible offences.

medjelis, medjliss, varr. MAJLIS.

‖**medjidie** (mɛˈdʒiːdɪeɪ). Also **Medjidy, -deh.** [Turkish (Arabic) *mejīdie*, f. the name *Abdu'l Majīd*.]

1. A Turkish silver coin first minted by the Sultan Abdul-Medjid in 1844, equal to 20 piastres (about 3*s.* 8*d.*).

1882 *Macm. Mag.* XLVII. 191 He kindly offered these eggs at a medjidy apiece. **1902** *19th Cent.* Aug. 233 There are as yet no taxes but a poll tax of a medjideh.

2. *the Medjidie*: a Turkish order or decoration instituted in 1851 by the Sultan Abdul-Medjid.

1856 *Ann. Reg., Chron.* (1857) 291 The Imperial Order of the Medjidie of the First Class. **1888** *Hazell's Ann. Cycl.* 36/1 He [Sir Samuel Baker] has received the Order of the Grand Cordon of the Medjidie.

medjidite (ˈmɛdʒɪdaɪt). *Min.* [f. name of the Sultan Abdul-*Medjid*: see -ITE.] A hydrous sulphate of uranium and calcium, first found near Adrianople.

1848 J. L. SMITH in *Amer. Jrnl. Sci.* Ser. II. V. 336.

†**medkniche.** *local. Obs. rare*⁻¹. [f. *med* (? MEED *sb.*, or MEAD²) + KNITCH.] (Explained in the context as the quantity of hay to be given in reward to the hayward, being as much as he could lift with his middle finger as high as his knee.)

1235–52 *Rentalia Glaston.* (Somerset Rec. Soc.) 85 Et die quando levat Langhemede, debet habere medkniche.

medlar (ˈmɛdlə(r)). Forms: 4–7, 9 **medler**, 5 **meddeller, medeler**, 5 **medlier**, 5–6 **meddeler**, 6 **medlor**, 5– **medlar**. [a. OF. *medler* (Godefr. *Compl.* s.v. *Nesplier*), f. **medle* (var. of *mesle*) medlar (fruit): see MEDLE.

Although the word primarily denoted the tree, it is in our earliest quot. already applied to the fruit. In present use sense 2 is the more common, the tree being usually called 'medlar-tree'; but Johnson 1755 (who was prob. not influenced by etymological considerations), and later lexicographers give sense 1 the first place.]

1. The fruit-tree *Mespilus germanica.*

The chief varieties in cultivation are the *Dutch*, *Nottingham*, and *stoneless medlar*.

c **1420** *Pallad. on Husb.* III. 1041 The meddeler to graffe ek tol[d] is how. *Ibid.* IV. 493 Now meddellers in hoot lond gladdest be, So hit be moyst. *a* **1450** *Fishing with Angle* (1883) 8 Take a feyr schoyt of blake thorne crabtre medeler or geneper. *a* **1500** in *Arnolde's Chron.* 63/2 The medlar wyl bere welle yf he bee plantyd. **1578** LYTE *Dodoens* VI. xliii. 713 Our common Medlers doo flower in Aprill and May. **1664** EVELYN *Kal. Hort.* Nov. (1729) 222 Graff the Medler on the White-Thorn. **1741** *Compl. Fam.-Piece* II. iii. (ed. 3) 374 There are several other Trees and Shrubs which are now in Flower, as.. dwarf Medlar. **1796** C. MARSHALL *Garden.* xvii. (1813) 283 The sorts are, the German, the Italian, and the English or Nottingham Medler. **1881** *Encycl. Brit.* XII. 271/2 The Medlar, *Mespilus germanica*, is a deciduous tree, native of the middle and south of Europe, and found in hedges and woods in England.

b. Applied to other trees, as ***Neapolitan*** or ***Oriental medlar***, the AZAROLE, *Cratægus Azarolus*. ***Japan medlar***, the LOQUAT.

1718 R. BRADLEY *New Improv. Plant. & Gard.* III. 18 The L'Azzarole or Neapolitan Medlar is a kind of Service... Of late Years it has been brought into England [from Italy]. **1753** CHAMBERS *Cycl. Supp.* s.v. *Cratægus*, 4. The jagged-leav'd cratægus, called parsley-leav'd medlar. **1797** *Encycl. Brit.* (ed. 3) V. 513/2 [*Cratægus Azarolus*, variety] the oriental medlar. **1866** *Treas. Bot.* 727/2 Japan Medlar, *Eriobotyra japonica.*

2. The fruit of the medlar tree, resembling a small brown-skinned apple, with a large cup-shaped 'eye' between the persistent calyx-lobes. It is eaten when decayed to a soft pulpy state.

? *a* **1366** CHAUCER *Rom. Rose* 1375 And many hoomly trees.. That.. bere, Medlers, ploumes, peres, chesteynes. *c* **1483** CAXTON *Dialogues* 13/7 Of fruit.. Pesshes, medliers [F. *nesples*]. **1533** ELYOT *Cast. Helthe* (1539) 21 Medlars ar cold and dry, and constrictife. **1600** SHAKS. *A.Y.L.* III. ii. 125 You'l be rotten ere you bee halfe ripe, and that's the right vertue of the Medler. **1755** GRAY *Let.* in *Poems* (1775) 232 If there were nothing but medlars and black-berries in the world, I could be very well content to go without any at all. **1858** GLENNY *Gard. Every-day Bk.* 248/2 Medlars should be gathered, and laid by to rot.

fig. **1791** WOLCOT (P. Pindar) *Rights of Kings* xix, The heart should be a medlar, not a crab.

3. *attrib.* and *Comb.*, as ***medlar-jelly***; ***medlar-like*** adj.: **medlar tree** = 1.

1881 BLACKMORE *Christowell* xxxvi, We will take her some *medlar jelly. **1567** MAPLET *Gr. Forest* 42 The Fig tree is of no high growth.. his flower *Medlerlike. **1548** TURNER *Names of Herbes* (E.D.S.) 53 Mespilus.. is called in englishe a *medler tree. **1592** SHAKS. *Rom. & Jul.* II. i. 34 Now will he sit vnder a Medler tree. **1873** MISS THACKERAY *Wks.* (1891) I. 70 A medlar-tree.

medlay, obs. form of MEDLEY.

†**medle.** *Obs.* Forms: 4–5 **medle, meyle**, 5 **mele, mel, merle**, 6 **marle**. [ME. *medle, mele, merle*, a. OF. **medle, meele, merle, mesle* (Godefr. *Compl.* s.v. *Nesple*):—L. *mespila, -us, -um*, a. Gr. μεσπίλη, μέσπιλον.

A late L. altered form **nespila* is represented by OF. *nesple* (mod.F. *nèfle*), Sp. *néspera*, Pg. *nespera*, It. *nespola* (cf. also Sp. *níspero*, It. *nespolo* medlar-tree). The L. word passed into Teut. as OHG. *mespila, nespila* (MHG. *mespel, mispel, nespel*, mod.G. *mispel*), MDu. *mispele* (mod.Du. *mispel*), Sw., Da. *mispel*; the Slavonic and other eastern European langs. have forms chiefly adopted from Ger.]

The fruit of the medlar-tree, a medlar. Also *attrib.* in ***medle-tree.***

13.. *Sir Beues* (A.) 1287 A sat and dinede in a wede Vnder a faire medle tre. *a* **1387** *Sinon. Barthol.* (Anecd. Oxon.) 29/2 *Mespyla sunt fructus*, meyles. *c* **1425** *Voc.* in Wr.-Wülcker 646/28 *Hec mesculus*, meletre. **14..** *Nom.* ibid. 716/37 *Hec mespulus*, a meltre. *a* **1500** *Flower & Leaf* 86, I was ware of the fairest medle-tree That ever yet in al my lyf I sy. *a* **1500** in *Arnolde's Chron.* 64 b/2 Chese a graf of a good merle tree. **1573** TUSSER *Husb.* (1878) 76 Medlars or marles.

medle, obs. form of MEDDLE; var. MELL *v.*¹

medle(e, medler, obs. ff. MEDLEY, MEDLAR.

medlert, variant of MIDDLE-EARTH.

medles, variant of MEEDLESS *a. Obs.*, MILDS.

medley (ˈmɛdlɪ), *sb.* and *a.* Forms: 4 **medlay**, 4–5 **medlee**, 4–5, 7 **medle**, 5 **medele**, 5–8 **medly**, (5 **medely**, 6 **medleye**), 6–7 **medlie**, 7–8 **meddly**, 5– **medley**. [a. OF. *medlee*, var. of *meslee* (mod.F. *mêlée*: see MÊLÉE):—vulgar L. type **misculāta*, f. **misculāre* to mix: see MEDDLE *v.* Cf. Sp. *mezclada*, It. *mescolata*. The primary sense is thus 'mixture', but in Eng. the word occurs first in the sense of mingling in combat.]

A. *sb.*

1. Combat, conflict; fighting, esp. hand-to-hand fighting between two parties of combatants. Now only *arch.* Cf. MELLAY, MÊLÉE.

13.. *K. Alis.* 4612 His folk weore sone, in that medláy, Parforce y-dryven al away. *Ibid.* 6532 The olifans, in medlé, And theo lyouns he [the rinocertis] wol sle. **1340** *Ayenb.* 41 Huanne me makeþ medles ine cherche zuo þet þer ys blod yssed. **1470–85** MALORY *Arth.* I. xv. 56 Lucas and Gwynas & bryaunte & Bellyas of Flaundrys helde strong medle ayenst vj kynges. **1490** CAXTON *Eneydos* xi. 41 Ne seche nothyng but thyssue for to flee, yf there were ony medlee. **1586** WARNER *Alb. Eng.* I. vi. 21 The medly ended, Hercules did bring the Centaure bound To Prison. **1601** R. JOHNSON *Kingd. & Commw.* (1603) 197 When the warre was made in these poppulous countries.. every man made one in the medle. **1653** H. COGAN tr. *Pinto's Trav.* vii. (1663) 19 Stepping before him with 2000 men, he cut off his way.. in so much that the medly grew to be the same as it was before, and the fight was renewed. **1839** THIRLWALL *Greece* III. 301 Cleon.. sent all the men who survived the first medley.. prisoners to Athens. **1862** MERIVALE *Rom. Emp.* (1865) V. xlii. 168 Broken by repeated defeats,.. he was.. less conspicuous in the medley.

fig. **1791** BURKE *App. Whigs* Wks. 1808 VI. 26 In the press and medley of such extremities.

2. A combination, mixture.

†**a.** without disparaging sense. *Obs.*

c **1440** *Promp. Parv.* 331/1 Medle, or mengynge to-gedur of dyuerse thyngys, *mixtura*. *a* **1529** SKELTON *Agst. Scottes* 87 A medley to make of myrth with sadnes. **1577** B. GOOGE *Heresbach's Husb.* I. (1586) 9 b, This kinde of building hath an equall medlie of the winter windes and sommer windes. *Ibid.* 32 b, A medley of sundry sortes of seedes. **1601** HOLLAND *Pliny* I. 501 He that shall set vines there.. shall make an excellent medley between the temperature of that aire and the nature of soile together. **1626** BACON *Sylva* §528 The Making of some Medley or Mixture of Earth, with some other Plants Bruised or Shauen. **1650** FULLER *Pisgah* III. xii. 346 Graves and green herbs make a good medly seeing all flesh is grass. **1712** tr. *Pomet's Hist. Drugs* I. 8 The Perfumers keep it.. to mix among a variety of other Aromaticks, which is what we properly call a Medley.

b. in disparaging sense: A heterogeneous combination or mixture (of things); a mixed company (of persons differing in rank, occupation, etc.).

1652–62 HEYLIN *Cosmogr.* IV. (1682) 5 An hochpot or medly of many nations. **1668–9** PEPYS *Diary* 18 Jan., To the Duke of York's playhouse and there saw 'The Witts', a medley of things. **1683** T. HOY *Agathocles* 5 A wretched Medley betwixt Priest and Layman. **1755** SMOLLETT *Quix.* (1803) IV. 190 Leaving Don John and his companion astonished at the medley of sense and madness they had observed in his discourse. **1859** REEVE *Brittany* 236 A medley of shining brass pans, bellows, and tubs, are exposed for sale. **1865** GROTE *Plato* II. xxiv. 256 Principles which are a medley between philosophy and rhetoric. **1879** CHURCH *Spenser* 38 The Shepherd's Calendar,.. an early medley of astrology and homely receipts.

3. A cloth woven with wools of different colours or shades; = *medley-cloth* (see B. 4).

1438 *E.E. Wills* (1882) 111, 1 gowne of Russet medley. **1502** *Privy Purse Exp. Eliz. of York* (1830) 70 Item for making of a gowne of tawny medley. **1609** *Stat. Laws Isle of Man* (1821) 79 Every Woolen Weaver shall have.. for every Yard of Medlie 1*d.* Qs. *a* **1661** FULLER *Worthies, Wilts.* III. (1662) 143, I am informed that as Medleys are most made in other Shires, as good Whites as any are woven in this County. **1778** *Eng. Gazetteer* (ed. 2) s.v. *Frome-Selwood*, The cloths made here for the most part, are medleys of 7 or 8*s.* a yard. **1851** *Illustr. Catal. Exhib.* I. 98/1, XII. Woollen and Worsted. A. Broad Cloths. 1... Medleys... N.B. The term 'Medleys' includes all Wool-dyed Colours, excepting Blue and Black.

†**4.** A 'mixed' colour. *Obs. rare*⁻⁰.

1499 *Promp. Parv.* 331/1 (Pynson), Medle[,] coloure, *mixtura*. **1530** PALSGR. 244/1 Medley[,] colour, *mellé*. **1556** WITHALS *Dict.* (1568) 34 b/2 Medley, *color mixtus*.

†**5.** = MASLIN¹ 1. *Obs. rare.* (Cf. B. 2.)

1601 HOLLAND *Pliny* II. 487 The Corinthian medley.

6. A musical composition consisting of parts or subjects of a diversified or incongruous character.

1626 BACON *Sylva* §113 As when Galliard Time, and Measure Time, are in the Medley of one Dance. **1811** BUSBY *Dict. Mus.* (ed. 3), *Medley*... With the moderns, a medley is a humorous hotch-potch assemblage of the detached parts or passages of different well-known songs, so arranged that [etc.]. **1864** in WEBSTER; and in later Dicts.

7. As the title of a literary miscellany.

? **1630** M. P. (black-letter sheet), An excellent new Medley. ? **1640** —— A new Medley, or Messe of All-together. **1710** (*title*) The Medley. No. 1. Oct. 5. **1728–42** POPE *Dunc.* I. 42 Hence Journals, Medleys, Merc'ries, Magazines. **1826** (*title*) The Entertaining Medley; being a collection of true histories and anecdotes.

B. *adj.*

†**1.** Of a mixed colour; variegated, motley. *Obs.*

c **1386** CHAUCER *Prol.* 328 (Ellesm.) He rood but hoomly in a medlee cote. **14..** *Voc.* in Wr.-Wülcker 597/7 *Multicolor*, Medle. *c* **1515** *Cocke Lorell's B.* 8 A ryche pal.. Made of an old payre of blewe medly popley hosone. **1595** in *Hist. MSS. Comm.* (1894) XLVIII. 309 A tall man.. wearing a medly russet mandilliane of red and blue, with.. a pair of medley russet venetians. **1622** HAKEWILL *David's Vow* vii. 252 Hee would not haue his family like a motley cloth, or a meddly colour. **1681** W. ROBERTSON *Phraseol. Gen.* (1693) 876 A medley colour; *color mixtus*.

b. *medley cloth*: see quot. 1837.

a **1661** FULLER *Worthies, Wilts.* III. (1662) 158 And such a *Medly*-Cloth, is the Tale-story of this Clothier. **1712** *Lond. Gaz.* No. 5008/2 The Woollen Manufacture of Mixt or Medley Broad Cloath. **1769** *De Foe's Tour Gt. Brit.* II. 25 These fine Spanish Medley Cloths are the mix'd coloured Cloths, which all the Persons of Fashion in England wear. **1837** YOUATT *Sheep* vi. 222 What are now called medley-cloths, different coloured wools being mixed together in the thread... These.. were first made in Gloucestershire.

†**2.** ***medley brass*** = MASLIN¹. *Obs.* (Cf. A. 5.)

1600 *Acc. Bk. W. Wray* in *Antiquary* XXXII. 279 One medle brasse potte.

3. Composed of diverse or incongruous parts or elements; mixed, motley.

1594 NASHE *Terrors Night* Wks. (Grosart) III. 229 A Medley kinde of licor called beere. **1597** J. KING *On Jonas* (1599) 99 A garment of divers stuffes as of linnen and wollen, shall not come vpon thee... [May] such medly garments sit vpon the backes of our enemies. **1624** WOTTON *Archit.* in *Reliq.* (1672) 58, I could wish such medly and motly Designs

confined only to the Ornament of Freezes. **1642** Fuller *Holy & Prof. St.* iii. vii. 167 A medly view (such as of water and land at Greenwich) best entertains the eyes. **1708** J. Philips *Cyder* ii. 55 This the Peasants blithe Will quaff, and whistle,.. Pleas'd with the medly Draught. **1745** Eliza Heywood *Female Spect.* (1748) II. 288 That strange, squeaking, meddly thing of the doubtful gender, Mr. Mollman. **1798** Wordsw. *Peter Bell* i. xxiii, Of courage you saw little there, But, in its stead, a medley air Of cunning and of impudence. **1838** Dickens *Nich. Nick.* xxiii, Who could do anything, from a medley dance to Lady Macbeth. **1878** Stubbs *Const. Hist.* III. xxi. 557 The medley multitude that held up their hands for or against the nominees of the hustings.

b. in chance-medley, q.v.

4. *Comb.*, as ***medley-coloured*** adj.

1611 Speed *Hist. Gt. Brit.* v. ii. §7. 8 As the Latine Poets describe them [the Britaines] hauing their backes pide or medlycoloured. **1701** *Lond. Gaz.* No. 3758/8 A brownish medly coloured streight Coat.

medley (ˈmɛdlɪ), *v.* [f. medley *sb.*] *trans.* To make a medley or mixture of; to intermix. Chiefly in **ˈmedleyed, ˈmedlied** *pa. pple.* and *ppl. a.*

c **1483** Caxton *Dialogues* 14/34 Clothes medleyed [F. *draps mesles*], Red cloth or grene [etc.]. **1657** W. Morice *Coena quasi Κοινή* iii. 43 The common fate of men that compound and medly themselves to comply with several Interests. **1679** L. Addison *Mahumedism* xvi. 83 The things taught by Mahumed are so mixt and confused... And yet they are not more medly'd in themselves, than disadvantageously represented by Writers. **1710** Philips *Pastorals* iv. 8 Lo! here the King-Cup of a Golden Hue, Medley'd with Daisies white, and Endive blue. **1746** W. Horsley *Fool* (1748) II. 78 This Dish.. was so odly medly'd, with Dutch, French, and Jacobite Materials, as to give universal Distaste. **1855** Singleton *Virgil* I. 297 And stones from stones asunder wrenched, and smoke Billowing with medlied dust. **1904** *Blackw. Mag.* July 87/1 Till we came to the medlied establishments of the native chiefs.

medlie, obs. form of medley.

medlier, medlor, obs. forms of medlar.

†**medlure.** *Obs. rare*$^{-1}$. [ad. OF. **medlure*, var. of *meslure*, f. *medler*, *mesler* to mix: see meddle *v.*] Mixing, mixture.

1413 *Pilgr. Sowle* (Caxton 1483) iv. xxxiii. 82 This syluer must ben withouten medlure of ony corrupte metal.

medly, medo, obs. forms of medley, meadow.

Medo- (ˈmiːdəʊ), combining form of Mede *sb.* (L. *Mēdus*, Gr. Μῆδος), used parasynthetically with terms denoting other peoples or countries, esp. ***Medo-Persian*** adj.

1769 J. Brown *Dict. Bible* II. 381/2 The three kingdoms .. conquered by Cyrus and his Medo-Persian troops. **1835** J. B. Robertson tr. *Schlegel's Philos. of Hist.* I. vii. 272 The Assyro-Babylonian empire which preceded the Medo-Persian. **1869** G. Rawlinson *Man. Anc. Hist.* ii. 9 A revolution in the Medo-Persian capital. **1875** *Encycl. Brit.* I. 604/2 The name for God in Medo-Scythic is *Annap*. **1899** *Captain* Apr. 96/2 There are certain Medo-Persian laws pertaining to a successful stamp collection. **1938** *Times Lit. Suppl.* 1 Jan. 14/2 For a long period the technique of American journalism has been almost Medo-Persian in its rigidity.

Médoc, Medoc (meɪˈdɒk, Fr. medɔk). [a. F. *médoc* from *Médoc* a district in S.W. France.] A general name for the red wines produced in Médoc, comprising all the best growths of 'claret'.

[**1824** A. Henderson *Wines* 180 The fine perfume by which the Medoc wines are distinguished.] **1833** C. Redding *Mod. Wines* 52 The wines thus embodied are excellent Medoc. **1842** Thackeray *Miss Löwe* Misc. Ess. (1885) 313 He would send some excellent Médoc at a moderate price. *a* **1849** Poe *Cask of Amontillado* Wks. 1865 I. 348 A draught of this Medoc will defend us from the damps.

medoe, medon, obs. ff. meadow, maidan.

medou, medow(e, obs. ff. meadow.

medowort, medow wurt: see meadwort.

medoy, obs. form of meadow.

†**medreie.** *Sc. Obs. rare*$^{-1}$. [App. an OF. semi-popular ad. L. *metrēta*, a certain denomination both of liquid and dry measure.] A certain measure used for corn.

c **1375** *Sc. Leg. Saints* xxvi. (*Nycholas*) 219 þane askit he þame to sel vitale, a hundre medreiis [orig. Latin *modiis*] at þe lest of ilke schipe at his request.

medres(s)e(h), -ressa, obs. ff. madrasah.

medrick (ˈmɛdrɪk). *U.S.* Also **madrick**. A tern or sea-swallow (according to U.S. Dicts.).

1869 Lowell *Pict. fr. Appledore* 65 The medrick that makes you look overhead With short, sharp scream, as he sights his prey.

†**medrinacks.** *Obs.* Forms: 6 **methernix, meddernix, me(d)dernex, mederinax,** 7 **mildernix, medrinack(e)s, medrianack(e)s, midri(a)nack(e)s, medrinacles.** [Of obscure origin; presumed to be ultimately indentical with next.

There is nothing to show whether the Eng. word was adopted from Sp. or the Sp. word from Eng., or whether both come from a common source. The 16th c. forms bear some resemblance to the place-names *Metternich* (Westphalia), and *Medernach* (Luxemburg), but no evidence of connexion with those places has been found.]

A kind of canvas (see quots.).

1588 in *St. Papers* Dom. CCXV. 75 Imprimis, for 6. methernixes for the Roebuck £7 4*s.* 0*d.* **1588** *Ibid.* CCXVIII. 24 Here is.. not a cable, nether ropes.. Speks, naills, but vij bolts meddernexes. **1603–4** *Act 1 Jas. I*, c. 24 Preamble, The Clothes called Mildernix and Powle Davies, where of Saile Clothes.. ar made, were heretofore altogether brought out of Fraunce and other partes beyond the Seas. **1611** Cotgr., *Aulonnes*, Ouldernes, Medrinacks, Poule-dauies, the canuas whereof sayles for ships are made. **1617** Minsheu *Ductor*, *Medrinacles*, a course canuas that Tailors stiffen doublets, and collers withall. *Ibid.*, *Poule-dauies*, Ouldernes, Medrinackes, the course canvas which taylors stiffen doublets with, or whereof sayles of ships are made. **1632** Sherwood, Medrianackes... Midrinackes... Ouldernesse (or Midrianacks). **1658–1706** Phillips, *Medrinacles*.

‖**medrinaque.** ? *Obs.* Also 8 **madrenaque.** [Sp. *medriñaque*, 'Philippine stuff for stiffening women's skirts; short skirt' (Cuyás *Appleton's Sp.-Eng. Dict.*, N.Y., 1903); of obscure origin.

The Sp. word occurs in A. de Morga *Sucesos de las Islas Filipinas* (1609) in the forms *medrinaque* (p. 136) and *mendriñaque* (p. 138). It appears not to be, as might be supposed, a Tagal word, for in Santos' *Vocab. Tagalo* 1794 it is given as Spanish with various Tagal renderings. (Cf. medrinacks.)]

(See quots.).

1704 tr. *Gemelli-Carperi's Voy.* v. in *Churchill's Voy.* IV. 442 [The Philippine islanders make] of the Thread of the Coco-Tree, a sort of Cloth they call *Madrenaque*, with the warp of Cotton. **1851** MacMicking *Recoll. Manilla* 217 In Luzon.. the natives make a species of cloth from the plantain-tree, known by the names of *Medrinaque* and *Guiara* cloths. *Ibid.*, The bulk of all the Medrinaque exported goes to the United States. **1866** *Treas. Bot.* 728 *Medrinaque*, a coarse fibre from the Philippines, obtained from the Sago palm, and used chiefly for stiffening dress linings, &c. [In later Dicts.]

medsin, obs. form of medicine *sb.*

medsonable, obs. form of medicinable.

meduart, variant of meadwort *Obs.*

medue, obs. form of meadow.

medul(l, obs. forms of meddle, middle.

‖**medulla** (mɪˈdʌlə). *Biol.* [L. *medulla* pith, marrow, prob. cogn. w. *medius* middle.]

1. *Anat.* The marrow of bones; also, the spinal marrow. Also, †the substance of the brain.

1651 *Raleigh's Ghost* 87 The inward medulla or marrow of the brain. **1668** *Phil. Trans.* III. 889 He affirms, that the whole Substance called the Medulla of the Brain and the After-brain is a Heap of Fibres or Vessels. **1813** J. Thomson *Lect. Inflam.* 393 The inner surface of the new bone.. is lined with a membrane containing medulla. **1845** Todd & Bowman *Phys. Anat.* I. 103 The cancelli are filled with fat, or medulla, the marrow of bone. **1854** Jones & Siev. *Pathol. Anat.* (1875) 147 These tumours always arise either from the inner layer of the periosteum or from the medulla of bone. **1873–5** Nicholson *Zool.* Glossary, *Medulla*. Applied to the marrow of bones; or to the spinal cord, with or without the adjective '*spinalis*'.

attrib. **1904** *Brit. Med. Jrnl.* 17 Sept. 649, I put her on red medulla tabloids.

b. (More fully ***medulla oblongata***: lit. 'prolonged marrow'.) The hindmost segment of the brain, or continuation of the spinal cord within the cranium.

1676 Glanvill *Ess.* iii. 5 Those Nerves, which.. are found by late Anatomists to proceed from the Medulla Oblongata. **1722** Quincy *Lex. Physico-Med.* (ed. 2) 51 The third [process] goes backwards on the upper side of the *Medulla*. **1878** Bartley tr. *Topinard's Anthrop.* 103 Section of the spinal cord where it joins the medulla oblongata. **1899** *Allbutt's Syst. Med.* VII. 222 A softening patch on the left side of the medulla.

c. The central parts of certain organs (*esp.* the kidney) as distinguished from the cortex.

1878 Bristowe *Theory & Pract. Med.* 841 The vessels —and more especially those of the medulla, the Malpigian tufts, and the stellate veins on the surface [of the kidney] —become more or less deeply congested.

d. The soft fatty substance (the 'white substance' of Schwann) which forms the sheath of a nerve.

1839–47 Todd *Cycl. Anat.* III. 592/2 The real structure of the primitive nerve fibre appears to be a tube composed of homogeneous membrane, containing a delicate, soft, pulpy, semi-fluid, and transparent medulla. **1873** A. Flint *Physiol. Man, Nerv. Syst.* i. 19 These [nerve] fibres.. contain, enclosed in a tubular sheath, a soft substance called the medulla.

e. The nerve cord in certain worms.

1878 Bell tr. *Gegenbaur's Comp. Anat.* 167 A median one [sinus].. embraces in Clepsine and Piscicola, the alimentary canal and the ventral medulla.

f. The 'pith' of mammalian hair. Also, the soft fibrous substance which occupies the axis of the capsule of a growing feather.

1826 Prichard *Researches Phys. Hist. Man.* (ed. 2) I. 136 The pith or medulla [of hair] appears to be endowed with a species of vitality. **1835–6** Owen in *Todd's Cycl. Anat.* I. 353/1 When the quill of the feather has acquired due consistence, the internal medulla becomes dried up. **1842** Prichard *Nat. Hist. Man.* (ed. 2) 95 Weber declares the human hair to consist of a homogeneous substance, in which no distinction of cortex and medulla can be perceived.

g. The endosarc of protozoa.

1888 Rolleston & Jackson *Anim. Life* 833 The protoplasm is either similar throughout, or it is divisible into an exoplasm (cortex) and endoplasm (medulla).

2. *Bot.* The pith or soft internal tissue of plants.

1651 *Raleigh's Ghost* 96 In the Medulla or marrow of the Plant there is a genital power or vertue. **1760–72** tr. *Juan & Ulloa's Voy.* (ed. 3) I. 286 The pod [of the guava], opened longitudinally, is found divided into several cells, each containing a certain spungy medulla. **1880** Gray *Struct. Bot.* iii. §3. 75 The Pith or Medulla, consisting entirely of soft.. thin-walled cells.

b. = medullin.

1819 J. G. Children *Chem. Anal.* 298 Medulla was obtained by Dr. John, from the pith of the sunflower.

†**3.** *fig.* The 'pith' or 'marrow' of a subject. Often in mod.L. titles of books (cf. marrow *sb.*[1] 1 d); hence used for: A compendium, abridgement, summary. *Obs.*

1643 Milton *Divorce* Introd., Wks. 1851 IV. 12 Their youth run ahead into the easy creek of a System or a *Medulla*, sails there at will. **1660** South *36 Serm.* (1720) II. 17 Their preaching Tools, their Medulla's Notebooks, their Mellificiums, Concordances, and all. **1704** Swift *T. Tub* v. Wks. 1755 I. 97 An infinite Number of Abstracts, Summaries, Compendiums,.. Medullas.. and the like. **1769** Bush *Hibernia Cur.* To Rdr. 12 The abridgers, who.. engage to furnish you, at a very easy expence, with the *medullam* of your civil history.

medullar (mɪˈdʌlə(r)), *a.* ? *Obs.* [ad. late L. *medullār-is*, f. *medulla*: see medulla and -ar.] = medullary.

1541 R. Copland *Guydon's Quest. Chirurg.* E ij b, Woundes of the scalpe.. be moste peryllous... y[t] toucheth the substaunce medulare. **1670** *Phil. Trans.* V. 2062 The Medullar Mass of the Brain. **1715** Cheyne *Philos. Princ. Relig.* i. vi. 340 Nerves in the Medullar Part.

medullary (mɪˈdʌlərɪ, ˈmɛdələrɪ), *a.* [ad. late L. *medullāris*: see prec. and -ary[2].]

1. *Anat.* Of, pertaining to, of the nature of, or resembling marrow. Also, pertaining to the medulla or central portion (of an organ or structure); occasionally, pertaining to the *medulla oblongata*.

1677 Plot *Oxfordsh.* 302 His assigning.. the Medullary [*sc.* part of the brain], or *Corpus callosum*, for the operations of the Phantasie. **1704** J. Harris *Lex. Techn.* I, *Medullary Oil*, is the finer and more subtile part of the Marrow of the Bones. **1715** Cheyne *Philos. Princ. Relig.* i. vi. §43 That Medullary Substance, that runs down its Cavity. **1748** Hartley *Observ. Man* i. i. 7 The Nerves arise from the medullary, not the cortical Part, every-where, and are themselves of a white Medullary Substance. **1828** Fleming *Hist. Brit. Anim.* 553 The whole colour [of a mollusc] is pink, with a dark medullary band. **1847–9** *Todd's Cycl. Anat.* IV. i. 233/1 The kidneys of reptiles.. have no distinction of cortical and medullary substance. **1871** Tyndall *Fragm. Sci.* (1879) II. xiv. 352 The human organism is provided with long whitish filaments of medullary matter. **1878** Bell tr. *Gegenbaur's Comp. Anat.* 42 The medullary tube or spinal cord [in *Vermes*]. *Ibid.* 512 The primitive medullary cavity.. remains open in the lumbar swelling of Birds. **1878** tr. *H. von Ziemssen's Cycl. Med.* XIII. 863 Diseases which are proper to each occur in the medulla [oblongata]. This gives the medullary pathology a very varied character. **1886** *Buck's Handbk. Med. Sci.* III. 174/1 As the medullary groove deepens, its edges become more sharply defined.

b. Pertaining to the medulla of hair.

1844 Carpenter *Hum. Phys.* (ed. 2) 550 Most Human hairs consist of two distinct substances; an external, cortical, hard, and fibrous part; and an internal, medullary, granular portion. **1862** H. Macmillan in *Macm. Mag.* Oct. 462 The medullary portion, or pith of the hair.

c. *Path.* An alternative epithet for encephaloid or soft cancer or sarcoma.

1804 Abernethy *Surg. Observ. Tumours* (1816) 57 The disease is usually of a pulpy consistence; and I have, therefore, been induced to distinguish it by the name of medullary sarcoma. **1852** Jas. Miller *Pract. Surg.* (ed. 2) vi. 139 The medullary and malignant nasal polypi may be regarded as incurable. **1870** T. Holmes *Syst. Surg.* (ed. 2) I. 564 Medullary cancer at first spreads chiefly through the loose cellular tissue.

2. †**a.** Pertaining to the soft internal substance or pulp (of plants). *Obs.* **b.** *Bot.* Of, relating to, or connected with the pith of plants. ***medullary ray***: one of the wedge-shaped cellular processes which divide the vascular bundles and connect the pith with the bark in exogens. ***medullary sheath***: see quot. 1849.

1620 Venner *Via Recta* (1650) 133 The pulp or medullary substance of the Orange is not good to be eaten. **1812** J. Smyth *Pract. of Customs* (1821) 69 Colocynth, is the dried medullary part of a.. Gourd. **1830** Lindley *Nat. Syst. Bot.* Introd. 19 Plates of cellular tissue.. called medullary rays. **1849** Balfour *Man. Bot.* §76 The Medullary-Sheath, is the fibro-vascular layer immediately surrounding the pith. **1882** *Encycl. Brit.* XIV. 553/2 The rest of the thallus consists of the medullary system.

†**3.** *transf.* Pertaining to the inner part of a mineral formation. *Obs.*

1778 Pryce *Min. Cornub.* 79 Thus, the medullary or inner part of a Fissure, in which the Ore lies, is all the way environed and bounded by two walls or coats of Stone.

†**4.** *fig.* Pertaining to the 'marrow' or inmost nature of something. *Obs.*

1651 Biggs *New Disp.* ⁋198 This indication is peculiar, naturall, medullary, and intirely proper to it.

†**medullate**, *v. Obs.*—⁰ [f. MEDULL-A + -ATE³. (Late L. had *medullāre* to fill with marrow.)] 'To take out the marrow' (Bailey vol. II, 1727).

medullated (mɪˈdʌleɪtɪd), *ppl. a.* [f. late L. *medullāt-us* having a marrow (f. *medulla*: see -ATE²) + -ED¹.] Having a medulla.
1867 J. MARSHALL *Outl. Physiol.* I. 55 These medullated tubular nerve-fibres compose the white part of the brain and spinal cord. **1899** *Allbutt's Syst. Med.* VI. 499 The medullated tracts of the cord.

medulle, obs. form of MIDDLE.

medullin (mɪˈdʌlɪn). *Chem.* [Used in German by John (1814); f. L. *medulla*: see MEDULLA and -IN.] A form of lignin derived from the pith of certain plants, esp. the sunflower.
1817 T. THOMSON *Chem.* (ed. 5) IV. 182 Of Medullin. This is the name given by Dr. John to the pith of the sunflower, &c. **1830** LINDLEY *Nat. Syst. Bot.* 200.

†**medulline**, *a. Obs.* [f. MEDULL-A + -INE.] = MEDULLARY.
1620 VENNER *Via Recta* vii. 120 The medulline part of the Grape. **1727** BAILEY vol. II, *Medulline*, of or belonging to marrow.

meˌdulliˈspinal, *a. Anat.* [f. MEDULLA + SPINAL.] Pertaining to the spinal cord.
1858 H. GRAY *Anat.* 416 The Veins of the Spinal Cord (medulli spinal). **1884** *Holden's Man. Dissect.* (ed. 5) 782 The medulli-spinal or proper veins of the spinal cord lie within the dura mater.

medullitis (mɛdəˈlaɪtɪs). *Path.* [f. MEDULL-A + -ITIS.] **a.** Inflammation of the spinal cord; myelitis. (Mayne *Expos. Lex.* 1856.) **b.** Inflammation of the marrow of bone; osteomyelitis. (Treves *Man. Surg.* 1889 II. 114.)

medulloblastoma (mɪˌdʌləʊblæˈstəʊmə). *Path.* Pl. **-blastomas, -blastomata.** [f. MEDULL(A + -O + BLAST(O- + -OMA.] A malignant tumour of the central nervous system that usually occurs in the cerebellum of children.
1925 BAILEY & CUSHING in *Arch. Neurol. & Psychiatry* (Chicago) XIV. 193 We shall adopt for our cases the term *Medulloblastoma* as appropriate to the particular tumors to which we independently wish to call attention. **1926** —— *Classification Tumors of Glioma Group* 118 Medulloblastomas..are rapidly growing, soft, malignant tumors which not infrequently, when they reach the leptomeninges, disseminate themselves through the subarachnoid spaces. **1974** PASSMORE & ROBSON *Compan. Med. Stud.* III. xxxiv. 75/1 Medulloblastomata usually arise from the inferior vermis and involve the flocculus and nodule. Hence the presentation is often difficulty in walking, truncal ataxia and a tendency to sudden falls.

medullose, *a. rare*—⁰. [f. MEDULL-A + -OSE.] Having the texture of pith.
1866 in *Treas. Bot.*; and in mod. Dicts.

†**medullous**, *a. Obs.* [f. MEDULL-A + -OUS.] Marrowy; pithy; medullary.
1578 BANISTER *Hist. Man* I. 2 The Vertebres, and other small bones,..not beyng much medullous. **1615** CROOKE *Body of Man* 947 Platerus saith it containeth a medullous substance. **1684** tr. *Bonet's Merc. Compit.* I. 18 The medullous substance of the Cerebrum and Cerebellum.

Medusa (mɪˈdjuːsə). Also 4 **Meduse.** [a. L. *Medūsa*, a. Gr. *Μέδουσα*.]
1. *Gr. Myth.* One of the three Gorgons whose head, with snakes for hair, turned him who looked upon it into stone; she was slain by Perseus, and her head fixed on the ægis or shield of Athene. Hence used *allusively*.
1390 GOWER *Conf.* I. 56 Cast noght thin yhe upon Meduse, That thou be torned into Ston. **1594** GREENE & LODGE *Looking Glasse* (1598) G 1, She is faire Lucina to your King, But fierce Medusa to your baser eye. **1598** HAKLUYT *Voy.* I. 222 Being as it were astonished with the snaky visage of Medusa. **1667** MILTON *P.L.* II. 611 Medusa with Gorgonian terror guards The Ford. **1753** RICHARDSON *Grandison* (1811) IV. xxvi. 207 But, after what Emily told me, she appears to me as a Medusa. **1882** M. ARNOLD *Irish Ess.* 179 And the true and simple reason against inequality they avert their eyes from, as if it were a Medusa.
attrib. **1876** GEO. ELIOT *Dan. Der.* VI. xlviii, The Medusa-apparition was made effective beyond Lydia's conception by the shock it gave Gwendolen. **1901** *Harper's Mag.* Apr. 684/1 Medusa-like locks fell in wild profusion over his bare shoulders. **1903** *Edin. Rev.* Apr. 407 The tragic beauty of a Medusa head.
2. *Zool.* (Pl. *medusæ*, *-as.*) **a.** A jelly-fish or sea-nettle; any one of the soft gelatinous discophorous hydrozoans. **b.** One of the two types of reproductive zooids in hydrozoans: opposed to *hydroid*.
Applied by Linnæus as the L. name of a genus (from the resemblance of certain species to a head with snaky curls). Now disused as a term of classification, but still employed descriptively, esp. as denoting one of the types recurring in the alternation of generations of certain hydrozoa.
1758 BORLASE *Nat. Hist. Cornw.* 256 The *Urtica marina*.. is called *Medusa*. *Ibid.* 257 Another variety of the medusa's. **1832** MACGILLIVRAY tr. *Humboldt's Trav.* i. 28 The whole sea was covered with a prodigious quantity of medusæ. **1835** KIRBY *Hab. & Inst. Anim.* I. vii. 222 They [*sc.* Salpes] are gelatinous like the medusas and beroes. **1848** E. FORBES (*title*) A monograph of the British naked-eyed Medusæ. **1888** ROLLESTON & JACKSON *Anim. Life* 752 The ovum is marked, as it always is in Craspedote Medusae. *Ibid.* 753 In C[*unina*] *proboscidea* the young sexually mature Medusa differs entirely from its parent.
c. *attrib.*, as ***medusa-bud, -budding, form, generation, -larva, -type***; ***medusa-like, -shaped***, adjs.
1851 *Edinb. New Philos. Jrnl.* L. 268 The *Medusa-bud falls off before its full development. **1871** ALLMAN *Gymnobl. Hydroids* 82 The phenomenon of *medusa-budding does not necessarily find its extreme term in the formation of the medusa itself. **1878** BELL tr. *Gegenbaur's Comp. Anat.* 95 Swimming Hydroid colonies, all the persons of which have passed into the *Medusa form. **1855** W. S. DALLAS in *Syst. Nat. Hist.* I. 254 A *Medusa generation may go on producing Medusa generations. **1888** BROOKS in *Stud. Biol. Labor. Johns Hopkins Univ.* IV. 148 The hydranth is essentially a *medusa-larva. **1848** E. FORBES *Naked-eyed Medusæ* 81 Mr. Lister..describes and figures *Medusa-like animals in course of production from *Campanulariæ*. **1846** DANA *Zooph.* iii. (1848) 23 The *medusa-shaped young. **1871** ALLMAN *Gymnobl. Hydroids* 84 A very different *medusa-type.

†**Medusæan**, *a. Obs.* [f. L. *Medūsæus* MEDUSA + -AN.] Of, pertaining to, or resembling Medusa.
1608 TOPSELL *Serpents* (1658) 628 The Adder..hath many epithets; as..hurtful, Medusæan, Cyniphian. **1656** BLOUNT *Glossogr.*, *Meducean* [sic].

medusal (mɪˈdjuːsəl), *a. Zool.* [f. MEDUSA + -AL¹.] Pertaining to, or of the nature of, a medusa.
1847 TULK tr. *Oken's Physiophilos.* 591 Fam. 9. Medusal Worms, *Asteriadæ*. **1859** ALLMAN in *Ann. Nat. Hist.* Ser. III. IV. 144 The polypal and the medusal terms of this series. **1888** *Nature* 9 Aug. 356/2 Its endoderm has no direct communication with the medusal endoderm.

medusan (mɪˈdjuːsən), *a.* and *sb. Zool.* [f. MEDUS-A + -AN.] **a.** *adj.* Of or pertaining to the medusæ, or to medusoid animals. **b.** *sb.* A medusan animal. (In recent Dicts.)
1847 DALYELL *Rare & Remark. Anim. Scot.* I. 123 The expanding Medusan lobes. *Ibid.*, Thus the Medusan circle is of larger diameter than the tentacular circle. **1888** ROLLESTON & JACKSON *Anim. Life* 761 The Medusan eye consists of sense-cells with pigmented..supporting cells.

†**meduˈsarian**, *a.* and *sb. Zool. Obs.* [f. mod.L. *Medūsāria* neut. pl. (f. MEDUSA) + -AN.]
a. *adj.* Of or belonging to the (now disused) family *Medusaria*, consisting of the medusæ or jelly-fishes. **b.** *sb.* An animal of this family.
1841 *Penny Cycl.* XIX. 119/2 The *Pulmograda*, or *Medusarians*. **1847** DALYELL *Rare & Remark. Anim. Scot.* I. 68 The Medusarian race. *Ibid.* 70 The legions of the Medusarian family.

Medusa's head. Also, when used attrib., **Medusa head.**
1. *Astr.* A cluster of stars including the bright star Algol, in the constellation Perseus.
1706 PHILLIPS (ed. Kersey), *Algol*, or *Medusa's Head*. **1819** J. WILSON *Dict. Astrol.*
2. a. An ophiuran echinoderm of either of the genera *Astrophyton* and *Euryale*; a basket-fish or sea-basket. **b.** An extant crinoid, *Pentacrinus caput-medusæ*.
1784 *Cook's Voy.* (1790) IV. 1292 Upon the beach were found many pretty Medusa's-heads. **1848** MAUNDER *Treas. Nat. Hist.* 414 *Medusa's Head*, a name sometimes applied to those species of Star-fishes which have the rays very much branched. *Ibid.* 225 [*Euryale*] sometimes known by the name of Medusa's heads. **1863** WOOD *Nat. Hist.* III. 738 Medusa's Head—*Pentacrinus Caput Medusæ*.
3. a. A kind of spurge, *Euphorbia Caput-Medusæ*. **b.** A species of orchid, *Cirrhopetalum Medusæ*. **c.** A species of agaric, *Hydnum Caput-Medusæ*.
1760 J. LEE *Introd. Bot.* App. 319 Medusa's Head, *Euphorbia*. **1822–34** *Good's Study Med.* (ed. 4) I. 181 The bulbous agaric, the Medusa's head [etc.]. **1866** *Treas. Bot.* 728/1 Medusa's Head. *Euphorbia Caput Medusæ*; also *Cirrhopetalum Medusæ*. **1871** COOKE *Handbk. Fungi* 297 *Hydnum caput-medusæ* Bull. Medusa-head Hydnum.

medusian (mɪˈdjuːsɪən), *a.* and *sb. Zool.* [f. MEDUS-A + -IAN.] = MEDUSAN.
In mod. Dicts.

medusid (mɪˈdjuːsɪd), *sb.* and *a. Zool.* [ad. mod.L. *Medūsidæ* pl., f. MEDUSA: see -ID.]
a. *sb.* A jelly-fish of the family *Medusidæ*. **b.** *adj.* Belonging to the *Medusidæ*.
1861 J. R. GREENE *Man. Anim. Kingd., Cœlent.* 61 The adult Medusid. *Ibid.* 63 Some true Medusids. *Ibid.* 118 A group of Medusid forms.

medusidan (mɪˈdjuːsɪdən), *a.* and *sb. Zool.* [f. *Medūsid-æ* (see prec.) + -AN.] **a.** *adj.* Of or belonging to the *Medusidæ* or jelly-fishes (*Cassell's Encycl. Dict.* 1885). **b.** *sb.* One of the *Medusidæ* (Webster, 1847–54).

meduˈsiferous, *a. Zool.* [f. MEDUS-A + -(I)FEROUS.] Bearing or producing a medusa.
1859 ALLMAN in *Ann. Nat. Hist.* Ser. III. IV. 50 A verticil of medusiferous gonophores.

medusiform (mɪˈdjuːsɪfɔːm), *a. Zool.* [f. MEDUS-A + -(I)FORM.] Resembling a medusa; medusoid.
1848 E. FORBES *Naked-eyed Medusæ* 80 An account of the production of medusiform bodies in a Zoophyte of the Adriatic. **1881** *Encycl. Brit.* XII. 554/1 The medusiform persons being early produced did not separate themselves from the colony.

medusite (mɪˈdjuːsaɪt). [ad. mod.L. *Medūsītēs*: see MEDUSA and -ITE.] A fossil medusa.
In recent Dicts.

medusoid (mɪˈdjuːsɔɪd), *a.* and *sb. Zool.* [f. MEDUS-A + -OID.]
A. *adj.* Resembling a medusa; medusa-like.
1848 E. FORBES *Naked-eyed Medusæ* 83 Zoophytic and Medusoid forms would have regularly alternated. **1870** ROLLESTON *Anim. Life* 162 The 'medusoid-bud' presented to us in the 'gonophore' of the Sea-Fir.
B. *sb.* **1.** The medusa-like generative bud of a fixed hydrozoan.
1848 E. FORBES *Naked-eyed Medusæ* 72 The full-grown medusoid of the *Corymorpha*. **1870** NICHOLSON *Man. Zool.* I. 87 These being developed into the sexless *Hydrozoön* by which the medusoid was produced.
2. A medusa or medusa-like animal.
1882 *Cassell's Nat. Hist.* VI. 282 One of the prettiest free-swimming Medusoids is more or less bell-shaped. **1890** FOTHERGILL *Zool. Types & Classif.* 12 Free swimming 'Medusoids' or Craspedota with velum.

medusome (mɪˈdjuːsəʊm). *Zool.* [f. MEDUSA (? + Gr. σῶμα body).] A modified medusoid.
1892 J. A. THOMSON *Outl. Zool.* 143 Free-swimming colonies of modified medusoid persons (medusomes).

meduwe, medwe, obs. forms of MEADOW.

medwart, -wert, etc.: see MEADWORT.

medwif, -wyfe, obs. forms of MIDWIFE.

medyl(l(e, obs. forms of MEDDLE, MIDDLE.

medyng(e, obs. ff. MEEDING *ppl. a.*, MIDDEN.

medys, variant of MIDS.

mee (miː). [ad. Chinese *mien* flour, noodles, dough, prob. via the Hokkien pronunc. (min).] A Chinese dish popular in Malaysia, consisting basically of noodles, with a variety of other ingredients.
1935 A. DIXON *Singapore Patrol* xiii. 107 We were confronted by a large dish piled with a startling mixture of spaghetti, bamboo shoots, sliced prawns, and tiny cubes of pork. The concoction was well seasoned with garlic, chillies, and soya-bean sauce. Its name..was *mee*. *Mee* is a favourite dish of the Chinese, and is on sale at all hours of the day and night. **1955** P. ANDERSON *Snake Wine* II. vi. 163 A Chinese cook tosses a handful of bean-sprouts, a bundle of pale yellow *mee*. **1963** J. KIRKUP *Tropic Temper* viii. 82, I had some nice fried mee at a Chinese stall. **1965** C. SHUTTLEWORTH *Malayan Safari* v. 72 They sit..wrestling manfully with knives and forks over English lamb chops, with their stomachs clamouring for Chinese *mee* or *kuay teow*. **1966** D. FORBES *Heart of Malaya* ii. 31 One could get a plate..of the noodles called *mee*, for a few cents.

meeble, variant of MOBLE *sb. Obs.*

meece, obs. plural of MOUSE.

meech, *v.* Chiefly *U.S.* Also **meach.** [Dial. var. of MITCH *v.*] *intr.* To retire from view; to slink *off*; to skulk *around*.
1833 S. SMITH *Life & Writings J. Downing* 176 The old man hauled in his horns and meeched off looking shamed enough. **1857** 'DOW, JR.' *Dow's Patent Sermons* 1st Ser. 203 When you fall short of the object for which you jump, you go meechin off, like a cat that has missed her mouse. **1902** H. L. WILSON *Spenders* xxxi. 366 I'd hate to have you come meachin' around after that stock has kited.

meech, -er, etc., var. ff. MITCH, MICHER, etc.

meeching, *ppl. a.* Also **meaching, meachin, me(e)chin.** [var. of MITCHING *ppl. a.*; now dial. and the preferred spelling in the U.S.] Skulking, furtive; mean.
1610 BEAUMONT & FLETCHER *Scornf. Lady* (1616) v. i. 9 Sure shee has some Meeching raskall in her house. **1792** *Mass. Spy* 22 Mar. 1/1 There is a kind of meaching souls in the world. *a* **1800** *Spirit of Farmer's Museum* (1801) 287 We observed, however, that he had lantern jaws and a meaching look. **1836** T. C. HALIBURTON *Clockmaker* 1st Ser. (1837) xv. 140 Father goes up to him, lookin as soft as dough, and as meechin as you please. **1844** 'J. SLICK' *High Life N.Y.* II. 219, I gin her hand a leetle mechin shake. **1869** *Harper's Mag.* 193/2 Of old the contrast between the Southerner's proud self-assertion and the Northerner's meeching humility was inexpressibly mortifying to every thoughtful inhabitant of the free States. **1884** W. D. HOWELLS *Rise S. Lapham* (1885) ix. 153 I'm not going to have you do anything that will make you feel meeching afterward. **1944** H. WENTWORTH *Amer. Dial. Dict.* 383/1 *Meech*,..1926, Maine, 'He was so meechin' that butter wouldn't melt in his mouth.' Common.

meed (miːd), *sb.* Forms: 1 **méd**, 2–7 (9 *arch.*) **mede**, 3 (? *pl.*) **meda**, 4 **meode**, 4–5 **med**, 4–7 **meede**, 4–8 *Sc.* **meid**, 7 **meade**, 5– **meed.** [OE. *méd* fem. = OFris. *mêde*, *mîde*, *meide*, OS. *mêda*, *mieda*, *meoda* (MLG. *mêde*, *meide*, MDu. *miede*),

OHG. *mêta, miata, mieta* (MHG., mod.G. *miete*):—WGer. *mêda* str. fem., cogn. w. OE. *meord* fem., reward, pay, Goth. *mizdô* wk. fem., reward (:—OTeut. **mizdâ, -ôn-*), Gr. μισθός, OSl. *mĭzda*, Zend *mīzda* reward, Skr. *mīḍhá* prize, contest:—Indo-germanic type **mizdho-, -dha-*.

The exact nature of the relation between the WGer. **mêda* and the OTeut. **mizdâ* is disputed. According to some scholars the former represents a Pre-Teut. type **mēizdhā* (ablaut-var. of **mizdhā*), the disappearance of the *z* being due to the long diphthong.]

1. In early use: That which is bestowed in requital of labour or service, or in consideration of (good or ill) desert; wages, hire; recompense, reward. Now only *poet.* or *rhetorical*, in narrower sense: A reward, guerdon, or prize awarded for excellence or achievement; one's merited portion *of* (praise, honour, etc.).

Beowulf 2134 He me meda ȝehet. **971** *Blickl. Hom.* 45 Þonne onfoh hi from Gode maran mede. *c* **1200** ORMIN 4381 Siþþenn shall þe Laferrd Crist Uss ȝifenn ure mede. *c* **1205** LAY. 17646 What scal beon mi mede ȝif ic þider ride? *c* **1275** *Passion our Lord* 61 in *O.E. Misc.* 39 Vor alle þe gode þat he heom dude hi yolde him luþre mede. *a* **1330** *Otuel* 858 Such cas may fallen in sum neede, He mai quiten vs oure mede. *c* **1350** *Will. Palerne* 5355 No tong miȝt telle þe twentiþe parte Of þe mede to menstrales þat mene time was ȝeue. *c* **1374** CHAUCER *Anel. & Arc.* 305 A scorne shall be my mede. *c* **1380** *Sir Ferumb.* 2392 Þov schalt haue an hundred pound of golde for þy mede. *c* **1449** PECOCK *Repr.* I. xv. 83 Forto serue God and deserue meede in hevene. **1509** BARCLAY *Shyp of Folys* (1570) 49 He that lendeth to haue rewarde or mede..may of hell payne haue dread. **1563** BECON *Wks.* III. Pref. AAAA iij, In the kepyng of them there is great mede. **1570** *Satir. Poems Reform.* xx. 105 That man in deid is worth sum meid, His fault that dois confes. **1590** SPENSER *F.Q.* I. ii. 37 A Rosy girlond was the victors meede. **1613** HEYWOOD *Silver Age* I. i. Wks. 1874 III. 90 As thy guilt's meede, by that monster die. **1637** MILTON *Lycidas* 14 He must not flote upon his watry bear..Without the meed of som melodious tear. **1658** PHILLIPS, *Meed*, (old word) merit, or reward. *a* **1677** BARROW *Serm.* Wks. 1716 II. 158 A long and prosperous enjoyment of the Land of Canaan was the meed set before them. **1725** POPE *Odyss.* XIV. 177 If so, a cloak and vesture be my meed; Till his return, no title shall I plead. **1769** SIR W. JONES *Palace Fortune* Poems (1777) 19 Let falling kings beneath my javelin bleed, And bind my temples with a victor's meed. **1814** SCOTT *Ld. of Isles* III. iv, A lordly meed To him that will avenge the deed! **1830** D'ISRAELI *Chas. I*, III. v. 66 The office of Lord High Treasurer, to which..the nobility looked as their meed of honour and power. **1854** S. DOBELL *Balder* xxiii. 125 Rich loves that, as they list, Exchange and take and give Unmeted mede and debts for ever due. **1877** SPARROW *Serm.* xix. 251 The exacting of God's meed of praise is only postponed for a little while. **1885–94** R. BRIDGES *Eros & Psyche* Apr. viii, To be praised for beauty and denied The meed of beauty.

†**b.** in *collective plural*. *Obs.*

a **900** tr. *Bæda's Hist.* IV. iii. (Schipper) 358 Þa me to þam heofonlican medum cyȝdon & laþedon. *c* **1205** LAY. 2987 God scal beon þi meda for þira gretinge. *a* **1225** *Leg. Kath.* 38 Summe þurh muchele ȝeouen & misliche meden. *a* **1300** *Cursor M.* 2353 Lang he led him with delay To mare þe medes of his fai. **1382** WYCLIF *Gen.* xxxi. 8 The dyuers colourid shulen be thi medis. *a* **1400–50** *Alexander* 2428 Ȝit rad for all þaire rebelte resayued þai þaire medis. **1500–20** DUNBAR *Poems* xvi. 2 Sum gevis for mereit and for meidis. **1590** SPENSER *F.Q.* II. ii. 31 She..winnes an Olive girlond for her meeds. **1592** CONSTABLE *Sonn.* xiii, If Love be ledd by hope of future meedes. [**1613** HEYWOOD *Silver Age* III. i. Wks. 1874 III. 127 Theseus, Perithous, Philoctetes, take Your valours meeds. *a* **1616** B. JONSON *Poetaster, Dial. Hor. & Trebatius*, Then dare to sing vnconquer'd Caesars deeds; Who cheeres such actions, with aboundant meeds.]

c. *to meed* (in ME also *to medes* OE. *tó médes*): as a reward. *Obs.* exc. *arch.* Also †*to* (*one's*) *meed*.

In the OE. form *médes* is an irregular genitive sing., owing its inflexion to the analogy of neuter nouns used in similar advb. phrases; in ME. it was doubtless taken as a plural.

c **1000** ÆLFRIC *Saints' Lives* (Skeat) I. 270 God him sylð to medes þæt ece lif. *c* **1175** *Lamb. Hom.* 155 Þet we moten.. habbe to mede endelese blisse. *c* **1200** *Trin. Coll. Hom.* 67 Ure louerd ihesu crist..giueð hem to medes eche lif and blisse. **1297** R. GLOUC. (Rolls) 3150 Wat woste..pulke mon to is mede ȝiue uawe, þat þe king aurely broȝte sone of lifdawe? *c* **1374** CHAUCER *Troylus* II. 1152 (1201) My-self to medes wole þe lettre sowe. *a* **1400** *Celestin* 75 in *Anglia* I. 69 To meodes I wile bicom þi man at þi somoun. *Ibid.* 611 *ibid.* 82 Wratthe and enuie, haue þis to meode. *c* **1440** *Cast. Persev.* 603 To medys þou ȝeue me howse and londe. **1870** MORRIS *Earthly Par.* III. IV. 186 Those who pleasure had to meed Upon a day when all were glad.

†**d.** *for any meed*: from any motive. *for no* (*kin*) *meed*: on no account, not at all. *Obs.*

13.. *Coer de L.* 5404 Off Kyng Richard myght they nought spede, To take trewes for no mede. *a* **1330** *Syr Degarre* 614 Lo, what chaunse and wonder strong, Bitideth mani a man with wrong; That..spouseth wif for ani mede. *a* **1400–50** *Alexander* 3120 Me wondirs, I-wisse if he it wete wald, For any mede a-pon mold his meneyhe to lyuire. *c* **1407** LYDG. *Reson & Sens.* 6248 For age taryeth for no mede. *c* **1450** *Bk. Curtasye* 135 in *Babees Bk.*, Ne spit not lorely, for no kyn mede, Before no mon of god for drede. *c* **1460** *Launfal* 363, I warne the, That thou make no bost of me, For no kennes mede.

†**e.** A gift. *Obs. rare.*

1607 SHAKS. *Timon* I. i. 288 No meede but he repayes Seuen-fold aboue it selfe.

¶**f.** Adjudged character or title. *rare.*

1833 TENNYSON *Œnone* 85 Pallas and Aphrodite, claiming each This meed of fairest. **1868** MISS YONGE *Cameos* (1877) I. xxxiv. 291 Even the world itself could hardly award the meed of unprofitable to the studies of Roger Bacon.

†**2.** Reward dishonestly offered or accepted; corrupt gain; bribery. *Obs.*

1362 LANGL. *P. Pl.* A. III. 241 Þat laborers and louh folk taken of heore Maystres, Nis no Maner Meede bote Mesurable huyre. *c* **1380** WYCLIF *Wks.* (1880) 247 False curatis þat ȝeuen mede or hire to comen in-to siche worldly offices. *c* **1386** CHAUCER *Pars. T.* ¶ 521 Thow shalt nat swere for enuye, ne for fauour ne for meede. ? **1423** *Rolls of Parlt.* V. 407/1 For affection, love, mede, doubte or drede. **1436** *Libel Eng. Policy* in *Pol. Poems* (Rolls) II. 184 That they take mede wythe pryvé violence, Carpettis, and thynges of price and pleysaunce. **1523** LD. BERNERS *Froiss.* I. xviii. 25 He toke mede and money of the Scottis. **1549** COVERDALE, etc. *Erasm. Par. Gal.* 20 He that for corrupte teachyng the gospel receiueth mede of him, whom he so teacheth [etc.]. **1550** CROWLEY *Epigr.* 196 It is a packe of people that seke after meede. **1591** FLORIO *2nd Fruites* 93 Golden meedes doo reach al heights. **1633** T. STAFFORD *Pac. Hib.* I. i. (1821) 33 For any respect of Favour, Meade, Dreade, Displeasure, or Corruption. **1765** BLACKSTONE *Comm* I. 230 Without partiality through affection, love, meed, doubt, or dread. **1808** SCOTT *Marm.* II. xxii, Her comrade was a sordid soul, Such as does murder for a meed.

personified. **1362** LANGL. *P. Pl.* A. II. 16 'Þat is Meede þe mayden', quod heo, 'þat hath me marred ofte'. *c* **1381** CHAUCER *Parl. Foules* 228 Fool hardynesse & flaterye & desyr, Messagerye, & meede & oþer thre.

†**3.** Merit, excellence, worth. *Obs.*

a **1375** *Lay Folks Mass Bk.* App. iv. 20 Þat is the Meedes of þe Masse. *c* **1380** WYCLIF *Wks.* (1880) 476 And siþ it is greet meede to do almes for a tyme, it were myche more meede to contynue perpetual almes. **1387** TREVISA *Higden* (Rolls) V. 149 A man of grete meryt and mede. **1493** *Festivall* (W. de W. 1515) 47b, Fayth hath no mede ne meryte Where mannes wytte gyueth experyence. **1509** BARCLAY *Shyp of Folys* (1570) 42 It is mede, To geue it to such as haue necessitie. **1565** JEWEL *Repl. Harding* 375 They say, It is a mater of special meede: and hable to Confounde Heresies. **1593** SHAKS. *3 Hen. VI*, IV. viii. 38 My meed hath got me fame. *a* **1600** *Floddan F.* i. (1664) 2 Thou imp of Mars thy worthy meeds, Who can discourse with due honour. **1623** COCKERAM, *Meed*, desert. **1714** GAY *Sheph. Week* Wed. 17 Thou bard of wond'rous meed. (*Note*, Meed, an old word for Fame or Renown.)

†**b.** *to do meed*: ? to do one's duty. *Obs.*

c **1400** *Melayne* 1017 Sen ilke a man feghtis for his saule I sall for myn do mede.

4. *Comb.* †**medȝeorn** *a.* [see YERN *a.*; cf. MHG. *metegern*], desirous of bribes.

a **1200** *Moral Ode* 256 Medȝeorne [*v.rr.* -ierne, -ȝierne, -yorne] domes men.

† **meed**, *v. Obs.* Forms: 2 meaden, 3–6 mede, 3 medin, 4 med, myde, medi, 4–7 meed(e. [f. MEED *sb.* Cf. OS. *mêdan* (MLG., MDu. *mieden*), OHG. *miaten* (MHG., mod.G. *mieten*).]

1. *trans.* To reward, recompense. In bad sense, to bribe.

a **1175** *Cott. Hom.* 243 We scule bien imersed alle [*read* alse] gode cempen and imeaded mid heahere mede. *a* **1225** *Leg. Kath.* 415 He bihet to medin ham mid swiðe heh mede. **1340** *Ayenb.* 146 He [God]..alle ssel deme communliche and alle medi largeliche þo þet habbeþ y-hyealde his hestes. *c* **1350** *Will. Palerne* 4646 He..meded hem so moche wiþ alle maner þinges,..So þat þei him bi-hiȝt bi a schort terme, Þat þei prïueli wold enpoyson þe king & his sone. **1387** TREVISA *Higden* (Rolls) III. 421 Þanne Alisaundre mededε [L. *subornabat*] þe bisshoppes, and warned hem what answere he wolde have. *c* **1400** tr. *Secreta Secret., Gov. Lordsh.* 107 It fallys þat þou mede his werkys, aftyr his seruyce þat he doos to þe. **1496** *Dives & Paup.* (W. de W.) IX. xiv. 367/2 They shal be thanked & be meded therfore as I sayd fyrste. *a* **1542** WYATT in *Tottel's Misc.* (Arb.) 223 Mine Anna..My loue that medeth with disdaine.

2. To deserve, merit. *nonce-use.*

1613 HEYWOOD *Silver Age* I. Wks. 1874 III. 89 Thy body meedes a better graue.

meed(e, obs. forms of MEAD.

†'**meeder.** *Obs.* [f. MEED *v.* + -ER[1].] One who gives bribes.

1556 J. HEYWOOD *Spider & F.* vii. 19 Meede, Judgth the meeder, more, then Justice conteinse.

meedewe, obs. form of MEADOW.

†'**meedful**, *a. Obs.* Also 4–5 med-, 4–6 mede-, meede-. [f. MEED *sb.* + -FUL.] Deserving of reward, meritorious.

a **1340** HAMPOLE *Psalter*, etc. 499 Þe froyte of goed werke & of medful meditacioun. **1465** *Paston Lett.* II. 224 It is merytory, nedefull and medefull to bere witnesse of trought. **1530** PALSGR. 318/1 Medefull, *meritable*. **1573** TUSSER *Husb.* (1878) 177 True pittie is meedeful.

Hence †**meedfully** *adv.*, †**meedfulness**.

c **1340** HAMPOLE *Prose Tr.* 23 So shalt þou goo from the oone to the othir medefully, and fulfille hem both. *c* **1440** *Jacob's Well* 276 It techyth how..þou schalt medefully mynystryn..þi temperall godys. **1530** PALSGR. 244/1 Medefulnesse, *merite*.

†'**meeding**, *vbl. sb. Obs.* [f. MEED *v.* + -ING[1].]

1. The action of the vb. MEED; rewarding.

c **1380** WYCLIF *Sel. Wks.* III. 7 For he [*sc.* Christ] failiþ no tyme, here in helpinge, ne in hevene of meedynge.

2. In phr. *to meeding*: as a reward.

a **1300** *Siriz* 271 Have her twenti shiling, This ich ȝeve the to meding, To buggen the sep and swin. **13..** *K. Alis.* 5533 The lettre was onon y-write. Kyng Alisaunder it underfynge, And golde and silver to medyng.

†'**meeding**, *ppl. a. Obs.* [? f. **meede* v., ad. L. *medērī* to heal + -ING[2].] ? Healing.

1599 T. M[OUFET] *Silkwormes* 31 With their friendly hands and meeding art To hasten that which ready was to part.

meedles, obs. form of MILDS.

†'**meedless**, *a. Obs. rare.* [f. MEED *sb.* + -LESS.] Having no meed; undeserving; unrewarded.

1435 MISYN *Fire of Love* 67 In kyngis seruis or grete lordis grete gyftis meydles þa haue resauyd. **1783** J. YOUNG *Crit. Gray's Elegy* 70 Yet glows not, meedless quite, the warm desire.

meedth, meef(e, obs. ff. MEAD *sb.*[1], MOVE *v.*

meek (miːk), *a.* Forms: 3 meoc, muk, 3–4 mec, 3–5 mek, meok(e, muke, 3–6 meke, 4–5 mieke, meyk, myke, (*superl.* mekerst(e), 4–7 meeke, (6 myck), 5–7 *Sc.* meik(e, 4– meek. [Early ME. *meoc*, a. ON. *miúk-r* soft, pliant, gentle (Sw. *mjuk*, Da. *myg*); related by ablaut to Goth. **mūk-s* in *mūka-mōdei* meekness (Gr. πραότης); also to early mod.Du. *muik* soft (:—**mūko-*).

According to some scholars the same root is found in ON. *myki* (see MUCK) and, outside Teut., in OIrish *mocht* (:—**mukto-*) soft, Welsh *mwytho* to soften.]

1. †**a.** Gentle, courteous, kind. Of a superior: Merciful, compassionate, indulgent. *Obs.*

c **1200** ORMIN 2501 Eȝȝþerr [*sc.* Mary and Joseph] wass wiþþ oþerr mec. **1303** R. BRUNNE *Handl. Synne* 12254 Newe þy shryfte euer ylyke, hyt makeþ Iesu cryst to þe meke [*v.r.* myke]. *c* **1350** *Will. Palerne* 412 Haue here þis bold barn & be til him meke. **1362** LANGL. *P. Pl.* A. I. 150 Þeiȝ ȝe ben miȝty to mote beþ meke of ȝour werkis. **1375** BARBOUR *Bruce* I. 390 Quhen he wes blyth, he wes lufly, And meyk and sweyt in cumpany. *c* **1400** *Destr. Troy* 215 It Ioyes me, Iason, of þi just werkes, þat so mighty & meke & manly art holdyn. *c* **1450** *Cov. Myst.* (Shaks. Soc.) 201 Every man..Be meke and lowe the pore man to. **1530** PALSGR. 318/2 Meke pityfull, *clement*. **1557** GRIMALD in *Tottel's Misc.* (Arb.) 97 Then, for our loue, good hope were not to seek: I mought say with myself, she will be meek. **1567** *Gude & Godlie B.* (S.T.S.) 115 The Lord is meik, and mercyfull is he. **1601** SHAKS. *Jul. C.* III. i. 255, I am meeke and gentle with these Butchers. **1609** BIBLE (Douay) *Ps.* lxxxv. Comm., He is meeke to remitte offences.

b. As connoting a Christian virtue (= Vulgate *mansuetus*, Biblical Gr. πρᾶος): Free from haughtiness and self-will; piously humble and submissive; patient and unresentful under injury and reproach.

c **1200** ORMIN 667 Godess enngell iss full meoc, & milde, & soffte, & bliþe. *a* **1225** *Leg. Kath.* 103 Ðeos milde meke meiden. *c* **1290** *S. Eng. Leg.* I. 47/14 He [Edward the Martyr] was meoke and milde inouȝ. *c* **1380** WYCLIF *Wks.* (1880) 460 Crist..was porerste man of lif & mekerste & moost vertuous. **1382** —— *Matt.* xxi. 5 Lo! thi kyng cometh to thee, homly [*gloss*] or meke, sittynge on an asse. *a* **1400** *Transl. N.T.* (Selwyn MS.) *2 Tim.* iii. 4 (Paues 119) Incontynent, noȝ[t] muke, with-outen benygnyte. *c* **1491** *Chast. Goddes Chyld.* xxi. 60 He that is not meke is proude. **1526** *Pilgr. Perf.* (W. de W. 1531) 10b, With a clene herte & meke spiryte. **1535** COVERDALE *1 Pet.* iii. 4 A meke & a quyete sprete. **1590** SHAKS. *Com. Err.* II. i. 33 Patience vnmou'd, no maruel though she pause, They can be meeke, that haue no other cause. **1637** MILTON *Lycidas* 177 In the blest Kingdoms meek of joy and love. **1667** —— *P.L.* III. 266 His words here ended, but his meek aspect Silent yet spake. **1766** FORDYCE *Serm. Yng. Wom.* (1767) II. xiii. 227 A proud Character was never a meek one. **1838** LYTTON *Alice* 31 'God is good to me', said the lady, raising her meek eyes. **1860** WARTER *Sea-board* II. 158 Bold bad men far outnumber the meek ones of the earth.

absol. *c* **1200** ORMIN 9613 Drihhtin hateþþ modiȝ mann, & lufeþþ alle meoke. **1382** WYCLIF *Luke* i. 52 He puttide doun myȝty men fro seete, and enhaunside meke. **1535** COVERDALE *Matt.* v. 5 Blessed are the meke: for they shall inheret the erth. **1567** *Gude & Godlie B.* (S.T.S.) 96 Till slay the meik and Innocent. *c* **1580** SIDNEY *Ps.* XXV. vi, The meeke he doth in judgment leade. **1798** PORTEUS *Lect. Matt.* vi. (1802) 139 These [blessings], I apprehend, are the peculiar portion and recompence of the meek.

c. Submissive, humble (occas. †const. *to*). In unfavourable sense: Inclined to submit tamely to oppression or injury, easily 'put upon'; now often in a tone of ironical commendation, with allusion to 1 b.

1340–70 *Alisaunder* 953 Hee..made all þe menne meeke too his wyll. **1362** LANGL. *P. Pl.* A. x. 83 Drede is such a Mayster þat he makeþ Men Meoke and Mylde of heore speche. *c* **1386** CHAUCER *Clerk's T.* 85 Hir meeke preyere and hir pitous cheere. *a* **1400–50** *Alexander* 1747 Made to be meke malegreue his chekis. *c* **1450** *Bk. Curtasye* 179 in *Babees Bk.*, Be not to meke, but in mene þe holde, For ellis a fole þou wylle be tolde. **1536** R. BEERLEY in *Four C. Eng. Lett.* (1880) 34 My lowly and myck scrybulling. *c* **1560** A. SCOTT *Poems* (S.T.S.) ii. 142 Than every man gaif Will a mok, And said he wes our meik. **1590** SPENSER *F.Q.* I. x. 44 He humbly louted in meeke lowlinesse. **1741** RICHARDSON *Pamela* (1824) I. 180 When I have asked thee, meek-one, half a dozen questions together, I suppose thou wilt answer them all at once! **1835** LYTTON *Rienzi* I. i, The boy was of a meek and yielding temper. **1868** BROWNING *Ring & Bk.* I. 976 He feels he has a fist, then folds his arms Crosswise and makes his mind up to be meek. **1884** W. C. SMITH *Kildrostan* 92, I hate Your meek and milky girls that dare not kiss A burning passion, clinging to your lips. **1891** *Spectator* 4 July, [They] put up with angry opposition in a way which, if English statesmen did it, would be denounced as 'meek'.

d. Proverbial phr. (in the various senses above) *as meek as a lamb, a maid*, etc., *as Moses*.

c **1330** *Spec. Gy de Warewyke* 260 He þat was woned to be Meke as a lomb, ful of pite. *c* **1386** CHAUCER *Miller's T.* 16 He was..lyk a mayden meke for to see. *c* **1470** HENRY *Wallace* IX. 1937 In tym off pes, mek as a maid was he. **1860** GEO. ELIOT *Mill on Fl.* I. xii, Mr. Glegg,..though a kind man..was not as meek as Moses.

†**e.** Used as *adv.* = MEEKLY.

c **1330** R. BRUNNE *Chron.* (1810) 167 Ageyn R. he ferd, to fote he felle fulle meke. a **1425** *Cursor M.* 18982 (Trin.) Boþe on mon & wommon eke Of prophecie shul þei speke meke. **1605** SHAKS. *Macb.* I. vii. 17 Besides, this Duncane Hath borne his Faculties so meeke.

2. Of animals: Tame, gentle, not fierce.

c **1200** ORMIN 1312 Forr lamb is soffte & stille deor, & meoc, & milde, & liþe. c **1325** *Metr. Hom.* 158 Douf a ful mec fuel is. c **1375** *Sc. Leg. Saints* xxxiii. (*George*) 278 He folouyt hyre as it had bene þe mekeste quhelpe wes euir sene. c **1450** HOLLAND *Howlat* 240 Thir ar na fowlis of reif,..Bot mansweit,..manerit and meike. **1500–20** DUNBAR *Poems* xlviii. 111 The meik pluch ox. **1530** PALSGR. 318/2 Meke nat wylde, *doulx*.

†**3. a.** In physical applications: Not violent or strong; mild, gentle. *Obs.* or *arch.*

c **1420** *Pallad. on Husb.* XII. 192 His translacion The pynys fruyt [wol] esy make and meke [L. *fructum pineum translatione mitescere*]. **1525** LD. BERNERS *Froiss.* II. ii. 6 It was in the monethe of Maye, whan the waters be peaseable and meke. **1564** P. MOORE *Hope Health* II. xii. 49 Then must that superfluous humour be pourged out..with a meke medicine. **1781** COWPER *Conversat.* 268 Venus..with a quiet, which no fumes disturb, Sips meek infusions of a milder herb. **1824** MISS FERRIER *Inher.* xlv, A meek, gray, autumnal day.

†**b.** ***meek mother*** (tr. PIA MATER): see MOTHER.

4. *Comb.* chiefly parasynthetic adjs., as ***meek-browed, -eyed, -faced, -hearted*** (hence ***meek-heartedness***), ***-mild, -spirited, -swarded***; also adverbial, as ***meek-dropt*** adj.

1863 I. WILLIAMS *Baptistery* I. ii. (1874) 22 The *meek-brow'd child of truth, Humility. c **1829** MRS. HEMANS *Child's Last Sleep* 14 Love..hath press'd Thy *meek-dropt eyelids and quiet breast. **1629** MILTON *Hymn Nativity* iii, But he her fears to cease, Sent down the *meek-eyd Peace. **1818** BYRON *Ch. Har.* IV. cxvi, The meek-eyed genius of the place. **1871** J. G. WHITTIER *Miriam* 29 That lean, fierce priest..*Meek-faced, barefooted. **1933** W. DE LA MARE *Fleeting* 92 Meek-faced, they snuff the air. **1535** COVERDALE *Ps.* cxlix. 4 The Lorde..helpeth the *meke-harted. **1849** ROCK *Ch. of Fathers* II. 309 In her *meek-heartedness, the royal Ædilthryda desired, and was buried in a wooden coffin. **1951** W. DE LA MARE *Winged Chariot* 23 *Meek-mild as chickweed. **1535** COVERDALE *Ps.* xxxvi. 11 The *meke spreted shal possesse the earth. **1759** STERNE *Tr. Shandy* I. x. (1760) 40 A meek-spirited jade of a broken-winded horse. **1953** C. DAY LEWIS *Italian Visit* I. 24 Immortal landscape of a day..*Meek-swarded, comely pastoral.

Hence †**'mekelac** (*meocleȝȝc, meokelec*) [see -LAIK], meekness, gentleness, lowliness.

c **1200** ORMIN 2535 Annd soþ meocleȝȝc wass opennliȝ Inn hire anndswere shæwedd. a **1225** *Leg. Kath.* 1240 þæt he þæt ouercom mon, were akast þurh mon, wið meokelec & liste, nawt wið luðer strencðe. c **1230** *Hali Meid.* 676 (Titus MS.) For mi lauerd biseh his þufftenes mekelac.

†**meek,** *v. Obs.* Forms: 3–4 meoke(n, 3–6 **meke,** 4–6 **meeke,** (4 **mike, myke,** 5 **mekyn,** 6 *Sc.* **meik**), 6–7 **meek.** [f. MEEK *a.*]

1. *trans.* To make meek in spirit, to humble; *occas.* to appease, mollify.

c **1200** ORMIN 9385 Forr swa to meokenn þeȝȝre lund & teȝȝre modess wille. a **1300** *Cursor M.* 4299 Strenger þen euer sampson was, þat luue ne mai him mike wit might. ?**1370** *Robt. Cicyle* 62 He ete and laye with howndys eke, Thogh he were prowde, hyt wolde hym meke. **1387** TREVISA *Higden* (Rolls) VII. 27 By þat word he meked [*MS. γ* mykede] so þe kynges herte, þat was to swolle for wrethe, þat [etc.]. c **1400** *Rom. Rose* 3394 To preve if I might meke him so. c **1450** tr. *De Imitatione* I. xiii. 14 Temptacions are ofte tymes riȝt profitable to man,..for in hem a man is mekid, purged & sharply tauȝt. **1528** TINDALE *Obed. Chr. Man* Pref. 5 b, To humble, to meke and to teach him Gods wayes. **1680** MRS. ELIZ. NIMMO *Diary* in W. G. Scott-Moncrieff *Narr. J. Nimmo* (1889) Introd. 16 There was much of the Lord's goodness to be seen in supporting her, and in meeking her spirit.

b. To 'bring low', abase, humiliate.

a **1340** HAMPOLE *Psalter* xvii. 30 All that dyes in thaire pride he [god] mekis thaim in til the lawe pitt of hell. **1483** CAXTON *Gold. Leg.* 38/1 By cause she synned in pryde he meked her seyeng Thou shalt be under the power of man. **1554–9** in *Songs & Ball.* (1860) 12 Withe miche soar hongger our bodis that he meikys.

c. *refl.* (also ***to meek one's heart, soul, mind,*** etc.): To humble or abase oneself.

c **1200** ORMIN 13950 All forr nohht uss haffde Crist Utlesedd fra þe defell, ȝiff þatt we nolldenn mekenn uss To follȝhenn Cristess lare. a **1225** *Ancr. R.* 278 O þisse wise makieð edmod & meokeð our heorte. a **1300** *Cursor M.* 17578 For him to find qua will him seke, þair mode til him þai most meke. **1362** LANGL. *P. Pl.* A. IV. 81 þenne Meede Meokede hire And Merci bi-souhte. **1387** TREVISA *Higden* (Rolls) V. 423 þe kyng meked hym and ȝeede barfoot. c **1400** *Rom. Rose* 2244 He that pryde hath, him withinne, Ne may his herte, in no wyse, Meken ne souplen to servyse. c **1450** tr. *De Imitatione* III. lii. 124 þou woldist meke þiself unto þe erþe. **1508** FISHER *7 Penit. Ps.* vi. Wks. (1876) 19 The lyon ..wyll not hurte the beest that falleth downe and meketh hymselfe vnto hym. **1509** BARCLAY *Shyp of Folys* (1570) 186 O men meke your mindes. **1533** MORE *Apol.* xiii. Wks. 873/1, I wisse tyll you meeke your selfe and amende [your conditions], thys anger of your husband will neuer be well appeased. **1563–83** FOXE *A. & M.* 148/1 But the sayde Constantine meeked himselfe so lowly to the King, that [etc.].

2. *trans.* To tame (an animal).

c **1450** *Mirour Saluacioun* 5067 Thow meked the felle pantere. **1526** TINDALE *Jas.* iii. 7 All the natures off beastes and off byrdes and off serpentes and thynges of the see ar meked and tamed off the nature off man. **1653** H. WHISTLER *Upshot Inf. Baptisme* 50 The generation of Vipers and other sort of cruel beasts, meeked with Infants at the Ensign of Christ's Kingdom.

3. *intr.* To become meek, to be meek.

a **1300** *E.E. Psalter* xxxiv. 14 Als wepand, and als dreri, Swa meked I witterli. a **1300** *Cursor M.* 12373 þe bestes mekand knaus me. **1377** LANGL. *P. Pl.* B. xx. 35 Ac nede is next hym for anon he meketh, And as low as a lombe for lakkyng of þat hym nedeth. c **1400** *Rom. Rose* 3541 His herte is hard, that wole not meke, Whan men of mekenesse him biseke. c **1400** *Destr. Troy* 1952 He mekyt to þat mighty, and with mowthe said His charge full choisly, chefe how he might.

Hence †**'meeked** *ppl. a.*, †**'meeking** *vbl. sb.*

a **1340** HAMPOLE *Psalter* liv. 21 Noght anly that i pray for my heghynge bot alswa that i pray for mekynge of thaim. c **1400** *Prymer* in Maskell *Mon. Rit.* II. 147 Meekid boonys [L. *ossa humiliata*] shulen ioie to the lord. c **1450** tr. *De Imitatione* II. ii. 42 To þe meke man he grauntiþ gret grace, and after his meking liftiþ him in glory. *Ibid.* III. lvii. 135 þou hast neuere despised þe contrite & þe meked [L. *humiliatum*] herte.

meeken ('miːk(ə)n), *v.* Now *rare.* Also 4–6 **meken,** 6 **mekyn, meaken.** [f. MEEK *a.* + -EN⁵. Cf. Norw., Sw. *mjukna.*]

1. *trans.* To make meek; to humble, soften, tame; †to mitigate, assuage; to lessen the violence of (a fire); to 'bring low', abase.

13.. *E. E. Allit. P.* B. 1328 Ofte hit mekned his mynde, his maysterful werkkes. **1502** ATKYNSON tr. *De Imitatione* I. xiii. 161 Therby man is mekende, pourged, & infourmed by experyence. **1547–64** BAULDWIN *Mor. Philos.* (Palfr.) 11 He meekneth the mighty, & exalteth the lowly. **1587** GOLDING *De Mornay* xii. (1617) 176 Basenesse to humble them, sicknes to meeken them. **1591** R. TURNBULL *Exp. St. James* 160 b, Snakes haue beene so meekened, as that men haue carried them without danger in their bosomes. **1647** TRAPP *Comm. Matt.* v. 46 Thou shalt melt these hardest metals.. thou shalt meeken their rancour. **1662** J. SPARROW tr. *Behme's Rem. Wks., 1st Apol. B. Tylcken* 33 Its Fire became allayed or Meekened. **1728–46** THOMSON *Spring* 265 This when..The glaring lion saw, his horrid heart Was meekened. a **1788** WESLEY '*Saviour, on me the want bestow*' ii, Meeken my soul, thou heavenly Lamb, That I in the new earth may claim My hundred-fold reward. **1856** MRS. BROWNING *Aur. Leigh* II. 564, I was quelled before her, Meekened to the child she knew.

†**b.** *refl. Obs.*

c **1440** *Alphabet of Tales* 284, I mekend me befor þe bedels & þe messangiers of allmighti God. **1537** MATTHEW *2 Chron.* xxxiii. 23 Amon..mekened not him selfe before the Lord as Manasseh his father had mekened himselfe.

2. *intr.* To become meek or submissive; to submit meekly (*to* something).

1844 MRS. BROWNING *Brown Rosary* II, And she so mild? ..As spirits, when They meeken, not to God but men. **18..** —— *Wisdom Unapplied* viii, If I were thou, O gallant steed, ..I would not meeken to the rein, As thou.

Hence **'meekened** *ppl. a.*; **'meekening** *vbl. sb.* and *ppl. a.*

1537 MATTHEW *Ps.* li. 19 *marg.*, The mortifynge of the fleasshe and meakenynge of the hert. **1539** TONSTALL *Serm. Palm Sund.* (1823) 93 Thou God wylte not despyse a harte contryte and mekened. **1597** J. PAYNE *Royal Exch.* 46 No less rightlie illumininge, then as trulie..humblinge and mekeninge. **1616** W. BROWNE *Brit. Past.* II. i. 22, I.. climb'd Mountaines..Then with soft steps enseal'd the meekned Vallyes In quest of memory. **1698** M. HENRY *Meekness & Quietn. Spirit* (1822) 166 Repentance..is very meekening. **1728–46** THOMSON *Spring* 944 Her eyes, Where meekened sense and amiable grace And lively sweetness dwell. **18..** MRS. BROWNING *Isobel's Child* xxxv, I changed the cruel prayer I made, And bowed my meekened face, and prayed That God would do His will. **1859–60** J. HAMILTON *Moses* v. (1870) 86 The meekening process in the mind of God's destined agent.

†**'meekhead.** *Obs.* Also 3 **mek-, meok-, mukhede.** [f. MEEK *a.* + -HEAD.] = MEEKNESS.

1297 R. GLOUC. (Rolls) 8004 Milce nas þer mid him non ne no Manere Mekhede [*v.rr.* meok hede, mukhede]. a **1350** *Birth Jesu* 391 (Egerton MS.) Vor he [God] haþ þe mek hede biholden of his hine. **1672** CRESSY in Stillingfl. *Idol. Ch. Rome* (ed. 2) 224 Our being beclosed in..his [God's] meek-head.

meekle, obs. form of MICKLE.

†**'meekless,** *a. Obs.* [f. MEEK *v.* + -LESS.] That cannot be appeased or rendered meek.

1587 *Mirr. Mag., Madan* iv, No counsayle could my meekelesse minde asswage.

†**'meekly,** *a. Obs.* In 4 **mekliche.** [f. MEEK *a.* + -LY¹.] = MEEK *a.*

a **1350** *Birth Jesu* 400 (Egerton MS.) Mekliche men iheiȝed he haþ also.

meekly ('miːklɪ), *adv.* Forms: see MEEK *a.*; also 4 **mekkeli, mikelik, muekliche, mukly.** [f. MEEK *a.* + -LY².] In a meek or humble manner.

c **1200** ORMIN 11392 þe birrþ biforr þin Laferrd Godd Cneolenn meoclike & lutenn. a **1225** *St. Marher.* 14 þis beoð þe wepnen..eoten meokeliche and druncken meokeluker. a **1300** *Cursor M.* 1304 Quen cherubin þis errand herd Mikelik he him answard. c **1380** *Sir Ferumb.* 1945 Loke þat þou þan mukly speke & to hym mercy crye. c **1450** *Mirour Saluacioun* 4511 Iesu of thi seruants wesshe thowe the fete mekely. **1547–8** *Order Commun.* 12 Mekely knelyng vpon your knees. **1641** J. JACKSON *True Evang. T.* II. 131 He.. answered meekely as a Lamb. **1745** W. ROBERTSON in *Transl. & Paraphr. Scot. Ch.* (1786) xxv. ix, Wrong'd and oppress'd how meekly he in patient silence stood. **1849** MACAULAY *Hist. Eng.* iv. I. 503 They had..submitted themselves meekly to the royal authority.

meekness ('miːknɪs). Forms: see MEEK *a.*; also 4 **mikeness, mueknesse,** 6 **meacknesse, meakenes, mykenes.** [f. MEEK *a.* + -NESS.] The quality of being meek; gentleness of spirit; humility.

c **1200** ORMIN 3612 þatt dide he forr to shæwenn swa Unnseȝȝendliȝ meocnesse. a **1240** *Wohunge* in *Cott. Hom.* 273 Meknesse and mildschipe makes mon eihwer lued. a **1300** *Cursor M.* 9996 Sco serued in vr lauerd dright, In mikenes suet, bath dai and night. **1340** *Ayenb.* 65 God þet loueþ Mueknesse and zoþnesse. c **1400** *Destr. Troy* 3941 Eneas was..A man full of mekenes & mery of his chere. c **1440** *Promp. Parv.* 331/2 Mekenesse, and softenesse, *mansuetudo, clemencia.* **1542–5** BRINKLOW *Lament.* (1874) 108 Yet for all their outwarde meakenes and holynes, they be within rauenynge wolues. **1556** *Aurelio & Isab.* (1608) N vij, You shall use towardes me suche meacknesse, lyke as God usethe unto all sinnars. **1613** SHAKS. *Hen. VIII*, v. iii. 62 Loue and meekenesse, Lord, Become a Churchman, better then Ambition. **1741** RICHARDSON *Pamela* II. 310 It must be owing to my Meekness, more than his Complaisance. **1860** WARTER *Sea-board* II. 161 Gentle natures in which grace has kindled meekness.

†**'meekship.** *Obs.* [+ -SHIP.] Meekness.

c **1230** *Hali Meid.* 659 (Bodley MS.) Miltschipe & meokeschipe of heorte.

meel(e, meell, obs. forms of MEAL.

meeling, obs. variant of MAILING, a farm.

1595 DUNCAN *App. Etymol.* (E.D.S.) 69 *Fundus*, a meeling.

meelte, meen(e, obs. ff. MELT *v.*, MEAN, MIEN.

meemies ('miːmɪz), *sb. pl. slang.* [Origin obscure.] In full, ***screaming meemies.***

1. Hysterics; a hysterical person. (See also quot. 1927.)

1927 *New Republic* 9 Mar. 72 The following is a partial list of words denoting drunkenness now in common use in the United States... To have the screaming meemies [etc.]. **1942** *Ibid.* 19 Jan. 78 If the mother gets the screaming meemies every time the siren growls, this deep and damaging fear is reflected and associated with all sirens, and all talk of bombs. **1946** MEZZROW & WOLFE *Really Blues* (1957) xvii. 323 The jangled nerves, the reefer flights, the underworld meemies. **1970** *N.Z. Listener* 12 Oct. 13/3 Thunderclap. Gets the screaming meemies. I couldn't help hearing her shouting, in the next room. **1973** GAGNON & SIMON *Sexual Conduct* (1974) v. 151 We've got a nice circle of friends that aren't a bunch of screaming meemies.

2. Also *sing.* **meemie, mimi.** (See quots.)

1944 *Infantry Jrnl.* Sept. 23 In Sicily it was the Nebel-werfer mortar, nicknamed the 'woof-woof' or 'screaming mimi'. **1945** *N.Y. Herald Tribune* 4 Feb. 3 The nebel-werfer is a six-barreled projector firing six-inch rockets... The rockets, not very accurate, are variously called 'screaming meemies' and 'moaning Minnies', but, like most Army slang terms, these names are also applied to other enemy explosives. **1945** *Sat. Rev. Lit.* 3 Nov. 7 The Screaming Meemie is a German multi-barreled rocket-mortar (so named for the sound it makes going off).

meende, meeng(e: see MIND, MENG.

meer, var. MIR *sb.*¹

meer(e: see MARE¹, MAYOR, MERE, MORE.

meercere, -cery, obs. ff. MERCER, MERCERY.

meerkat ('mɪəkæt). Also 5 **mercatte,** 9 **meercat,** 20 **mierkat.** [a. Du. *meerkat* monkey (= G. *meerkatze*), app. f. *meer* sea + *kat* cat.

Cf., however, Hindī *markaṭ*, Skr. *markaṭa* ape. Can the European word (already found in OHG. as *mericazza*) be an etymologizing perversion of an Oriental name?]

†**1.** A monkey. *Obs.*

1481 CAXTON *Reynard* (Arb.) 98, I wende hit had be a mermoyse a baubyn or a mercatte for I sawe neuer fowler beest. **1559** W. CUNNINGHAM *Cosmogr. Glasse* 191 There are diuerse straunge beastes bred in Assia,..Mercattes.

2. A name given in S. Africa to two small mammals: **a.** *Cynictis penicillata*, allied to the ichneumon. **b.** The suricate, *Suricata tetradactyla*, which is tamed as a pet.

1801 J. BARROW *Trav. S. Africa* I. 231 Upon those parched plains are also found a great variety of small quadrupeds that burrow in the ground, and which are known to the colonists under the general name of *meer-cats*. **1826** A. SMITH *Catal. S. Afr. Mus.* 32 Meer Kat of the Dutch. Ryzæna Surikatta of the Naturalists. **1833** OGILBY in *Trans. Zool. Soc.* (1835) I. 34 The name *Meer-kat*..is of very general acceptation in South Africa, being applied indifferently to the present species [*Cynictis*], the Cape Herpestes, Ground Squirrels, and various other burrowing animals. **1890** MRS. A. MARTIN *Home Life Ostrich Farm* 158 There are two kinds of meerkats; one red, with a bushy tail like that of a squirrel, the other grey, with a pointed tail, and it is this latter kind which makes so charming a pet. **1901** O. SCHREINER *Thoughts on S. Afr.* (1923) 19 There was a possibility that the red African mier-kat might ultimately creep back into its hole in the red African earth. **1949** *Cape Argus Mag.* 3 Sept. 1/9 To most people it is just a 'mierkat', but in reality it is a rodent, a squirrel, and quite different from the insect-eating, slender-tailed mierkat that is to be found in the same vicinity.

attrib. **1897** ANNE PAGE *Afternoon Ride* 62 Meerkat skins sewn together, as pouches for tobacco.

meerschaum ('mɪəʃɔːm, -ʃəm). Forms: 8 ?**myrsen,** 8–9 **meershaum,** 9 **meerchum, mereschaum, merschaum,** 8– **meerschaum.** [a. G. *meerschaum*, lit. 'sea-foam', f. *meer* sea + *schaum*

foam (a literal transl. of the Persian name *kef-i-daryā*), alluding to its frothy appearance.]

1. A popular synonym of sepiolite, a hydrous silicate of magnesium occurring in soft white clay-like masses.

1784 [see KEFFEKILL]. **1794** KIRWAN *Elem. Min.* (ed. 2) I. 145 Keffekill or myrsen, which the Germans corruptly call Meerschaum, is said to be when recently dug of a yellow colour. **1812** J. NOTT *Dekker's Gull's Horn-bk.* 176 *note*, Those tobacco-pipes which they manufacture of a species of earth, of the magnesious genus combined with silex, denominated meerschaum. **1891** *Daily News* 26 Oct. 5/6 He bought wholesale little blocks of flawed meerschaum, polished them, and made them up into pipes.

attrib. **1823** DE QUINCEY *Mr. Schnackenberger* vi, The great meerschaum head of his pipe.

2. (In full ***meerschaum pipe.***) A tobacco-pipe, the bowl of which is made of meerschaum.

1799 COLERIDGE *Let.* 14 Jan., A pipe of a particular kind, that has been smoked for a year or so, will sell here [at Ratzeburg] for twenty guineas... They are called Meerschaum. **1812** J. NOTT *Dekker's Gull's Horn-bk.* 176 *note*, A meerschaum pipe nearly black with smoking is considered a treasure. **1818** *Blackw. Mag.* III. 404 Bobwigs and meerschaums, petticoats and sabres. **1858** O. W. HOLMES *Aut. Breakf.-t.* xi, One Stradivarius, I confess, Two Meerschaums, I would fain possess. **1884** *Graphic* Christmas No. 5/3 He produced an enormous meerschaum. **1887** G. R. SIMS *Mary Jane's Mem.* 145 He sent me back the meerschaum-pipe.

mees(e: see MESE, MESS.

†**meese.** *Obs.* [a. Du. *mees* = ME. MOSE, whence corruptly *-mouse* in TITMOUSE.] A tom-tit.

c **1481** CAXTON *Dialogues* 10/35 Wodecoks, nyghtyngalis, Sparowes, meesen, Ghees [etc.].

meest, obs. f. MOST.

meet (miːt), *sb.* [f. MEET *v.*] **1. a.** The meeting of hounds and men in preparation for a hunt. Also, by extension, applied to other kinds of sporting meetings (e.g. of coaches, cyclists).

1831-4 R. S. SURTEES *Jorrock's Jaunts* (1838) 39 They overtook a gentleman perusing a long bill of the meets for the next week, of at least half a dozen packs. **1854** WARTER *Last of Old Squires* vi. 58 If it so happened that the fox-hounds did not make their usual meets in the neighbourhood. **1893** *Times* 4 May 12/1 The interesting meet of the stage-coaches to be held to-day. **1897** *Outing* (U.S.) XXX. 493/2 For 16 years the club's meet has been one of the most popular cycling events.

b. *slang.* A meeting; an assignation or appointment, esp. a meeting with a supplier of drugs; a meeting-place, esp. one used by thieves.

1879 *Macm. Mag.* Oct. 503/1 At six I was at the meet (trysting-place). **1889** 'MARK TWAIN' *Lett.* (1917) II. 512 We'll manage a meet yet. **1893** L. W. MOORE *His Own Story* xxxvii. 460 Where he could see the 'meet'. *Ibid.* 461 He made a 'meet' for the following day. **1916** C. J. DENNIS *Songs Sentimental Bloke* 23, I dunno 'ow I 'ad the nerve ter speak, An' make that meet wiv 'er fer Sundee week! **1929** *Chicago Tribune* 11 Oct. 14/3 The [drug-] peddler takes his stock to a point on the street or possibly a pool hall. The place where he meets his customer is called a 'meet' or a 'stand'. **1930** *Amer. Speech* VI. 118 Coast dental meet set for July 8–12. **1938** D. RUNYON *Take it Easy* xv. 291 He finally arranges a personal meet with the Judy. **1944** [see GROUSE *a.*]. **1955** W. GADDIS *Recognitions* II. v. 490 I'm going to make a meet, he answered..—I'm going out to meet a passer, to hand this stuff over to him. **1962** K. ORVIS *Damned & Destroyed* xxv. 183 Your man made a meet... No drugs changed hands. **1967** J. MORGAN *Involved* 26 I've made the meet with Alfie Stride for twelve-thirty. **1970** G. F. NEWMAN *Sir, You Bastard* vi. 180 Manso was considering trying to make a meet with you.

2. a. *Geom.* A point, line, or surface of intersection.

1893 J. W. RUSSELL *Pure Geom.* 156 The meets of opposite sides of a hexagon..inscribed in a conic are collinear. *Ibid.* 236 Given five points on each of two conics, to construct the conic which passes through the four meets of these conics and also touches a given line. **1958** A. BARTON *Introd. Coordinate Geom.* viii. 147 (*heading*) Meet of two tangents. *Ibid.* x. 213 Find the equation of the lines joining O to the meets of $4x - 3y = 10$ and $x^2 + y^2 + 3x - 6y - 20 = 0$.

b. *Algebra.* The intersection of two or more sets; also, the infimum of two or more elements of a lattice.

1933 G. BIRKHOFF in *Proc. Cambr. Philos. Soc.* XXIX. 441 Let Π be any collection of subalgebras S_k... By the meet $\Delta\{\Pi\}$ of Π we mean the set of elements in every S_k of Π. **1933** H. F. BAKER *Princ. Geom.* VI. ii. 70, [*h*] and [*k*] have a common space [*m*], which we may call their meet. **1938** T. G. ROOM *Geom. of Determinantal Loci* i. 6 The join of two spaces is defined as the space of least dimension which contains all the points of each of them, and the meet (or intersection) of the two spaces as the space of least dimension containing all points common to both of them. **1965** D. E. RUTHERFORD *Introd. Lattice Theory* i. 3 We frequently call the l.u.b. of a subset the union of the elements which compose the subset, and correspondingly we call the g.l.b. of the subset the intersection or meet of its elements. **1972** A. G. HOWSON *Handbk. Terms Algebra & Analysis* xv. 76 Every two elements of *P* have a meet and a join, e.g. $12 \wedge 30 = 6$, $3 \vee 5 = 15$, and so *P* is a lattice.

meet (miːt), *a.* and *adv.* Now *arch.* Forms: 1 (**ʒe**)**mǽte, méte,** 4 **met,** 4–6 **mete,** 5–7 **meete,** (6 **mytt, meat(e,** *Sc.* **meit, meyit**), 6– **meet.** Also 2–3 I-METE. [ME. *mēte* (with close *ē*, riming with *swēte*, etc.); prob. repr. OE. (Anglian) **ʒeméte*, WS. *ʒemǽte* (early southern ME. I-METE) with normal loss of the prefix. The OE. *ʒemǽte*:—OTeut. **gamǽtjo-* (OHG. *gamâzi* equal, MHG. *gemæze*, mod.G. *gemäsz*), f. **ga-* (Y-) prefix synonymous with L. *com-* + **mǽtā* measure, f. **mǽt-*, ablaut-var. of **met-* (see METE *v.*¹). The etymological sense is thus 'commensurate'.

OE. had *mǽte* adj. of similar formation without the prefix, but it occurs only in the senses 'small, inferior'. The formally equivalent ON. *mǽt-r*, 'valuable, excellent, lawful', may possibly be the source of some of the Eng. senses. The alleged OE. *ʒemet* adj., sometimes assigned as the etymon, appears to be merely a predicative use of *ʒemet* sb., measure, what is fitting; and if the adj. existed its ME. form would not have had close *ē*.]

A. *adj.*

†**1.** Having the proper dimensions; made to fit. In later use: Close-fitting, barely large enough. Also Comb. ***meet-bodied.*** *Obs.*

[*c* **961** ÆTHELWOLD *Rule St. Benet* lv. (Schröer 1885) 89 Besceawiʒe se abbod and hate besidian þæra reafa ʒemet, þæt hy ne synd to scorte, ac ʒemæte þam, þe hyra notiað. *a* **1300** in *Leg. Holy Rood* (1871) 30 Þo was it bi a fot to schort ..hi ne miȝte it make Imete.] *a* **1300** *Cursor M.* 8809 Son þe tre was heun dun, And squir on-laid and scantlian, þe tre was als mete and quem, Als animan þar-to cuth deme. *c* **1375** *Sc. Leg. Saints* xii. (*Mathias*) 50 Þar-for of spechis a cowyne þa mad til hyme met. **1500–20** DUNBAR *Poems* xxviii. 13 Sowtaris, with schone weill maid and meit, ȝe mend the faltis of ill maid feit. **1513** DOUGLAS *Æneis* VIII. viii. 10 Apon his feyt his meyit schois hoit War buklit. **16..** *Will Stewart & John* lxi. in Child *Ballads* II. 436 Iohn he gott on a clouted cloake, Soe meete and low then by his knee. **1727** *Burgh Rec. Stirling* (1889) 200 They will allow him [the towns pyper] a meet bodied coat with the towns livery thereon. *a* **1763** *Sweet William's Ghost* xiii. in Child *Ballads* II. 229 There's no room at my side..My coffin's made so meet. **1825–80** JAMIESON, *Meet-coat*, a term used by old people for a coat that is exactly meet for the size of the body, as distinguished from a long coat.

†**2.** Equal, on the same level. Const. *to.* Also *absol.* as *sb.*, an equal. *Obs.*

c **1369** CHAUCER *Dethe Blaunche* 484 Of al goodenesse she had none mete. *c* **1400** *Ywaine & Gaw.* 2114 Thar es na sorow mete to myne. *c* **1440** *York Myst.* xvii. 281 Hayll! man þat is made to þin men meete [*MS.* mette, *rime* feete].

†**b.** *to be meet with*: to be even or quits with; to be revenged upon. *Obs.*

1599 SHAKS. *Much Ado* I. i. 47 You taxe Signior Benedicke too much, but hee'l be meet with you. **1603** HOLLAND *Plutarch's Mor.* 187 The foule ill take me if I be not revenged and meet with thee. **1687** *Death's Vis.* Pref. (1713) 12 An Unjust, Terrible Devil..that..will be severely meet with them for all the..Scorn they have cast even on his Being and Power.

3. Suitable, fit, proper (for some purpose or occasion, expressed or implied). Const. *for, to*; also *to* with *inf.*

13.. *Gaw. & Gr. Knt.* 71 Alle þis mirþe þay maden to þe mete tyme. *c* **1385** CHAUCER *L.G.W.* 1043 (*Dido*) There nis no womman to him half so mete. *c* **1386** —— *Knt.'s T.* 773 Two harneys..Bothe suffisaunt and mete to darreyne The bataille. *c* **1460** J. RUSSELL *Bk. Nurture* 832 Mustard is metest with alle maner salt herynge. **1481** CAXTON *Reynard* xv. (Arb.) 32 Hadde we an halter which were mete for his necke and strong ynough. **1530** PALSGR. 574/1 Of all monethes Marche is the metest to set yonge plantes and to graffe in. **1547–8** *Order of Communion* 10 So shall ye bee mete partakers of these holy misteries. **1552** in *Vicary's Anat.* (1888) App. iii. 151 A gate or dore..for the Apte, commodyous, and meate passage of the gouernours. **1557** *Tottel's Misc.* (Arb.) 245 For to deceiue they be most mete That best can play hypocrisy. **1563** SHUTE *Archit.* B ij, Whose names also I thought not altogyther the metest to be omitted. **1616** BOYLE in *Lismore Papers* (1886) I. 129, I am to pass back a lease of 40 yeares to Capⁿ Tynt at a meet Rent. *a* **1661** FULLER *Worthies* (1840) II. 448 He was happy in a meet yoke-fellow. **1692** BENTLEY *Boyle Lect.* iii. 8 The Eye is very proper and meet for seeing. **1820** SCOTT *Monast.* xviii, To transmew myself into some civil form meeter for this worshipful company. **1852** M. ARNOLD *Empedocles* 68 Not here, O Apollo! Are haunts meet for thee. **1898** *Allbutt's Syst. Med.* V. 372 Thrombosis meet to explain the death is not always found.

b. Predicatively of an action: Fitting, becoming, proper. Chiefly in ***it is meet that..., as*** (or ***than***) ***is meet.***

a **1300** *Cursor M.* 3675 Sco..cled him, sum it was mete, Wit his broþer robe þat smelled suete. *c* **1485** *Digby Myst.* (1882) IV. 686 O swete child! it was nothinge mete..To let Iudas kisse thes lippes so swete. **1548–9** (Mar.) *Bk. Com. Prayer, Communion*, It is mete and right so to do. **1611** BIBLE *Jer.* xxvi. 14 Doe with mee as seemeth good and meet vnto you. **1652** NEEDHAM tr. *Selden's Mare Cl.* 56 Using far less diligence here than was meet. **1752** YOUNG *Brothers* I. i, My cities, which deserted in my wars, I thought it meet to punish. **1833** TENNYSON *Poems* 116 This is lovelier and sweeter, Men of Ithaca, this is meeter, In the hollow rosy vale to tarry. **1846** TRENCH *Mirac.* Introd. (1862) 38 It was only meet that this Son should be clothed with mightier powers than theirs.

†**4.** Mild, gentle. *Obs.*

1433 LYDG. *S. Edmund* 1007 in Horstm. *Altengl. Leg.* (1881) 394 Most temperat he was of his dieete,..To foryefnesse most mansuet and meete. **1535** STEWART *Cron. Scot.* (Rolls) I. 320 Mansweit and meit, and full of gentres. **1598** GRENEWEY *Tacitus Ann.* III. vii. 73 The Senators.. thought Lepidus rather meete [L. *mitem*] then a coward.

†**B.** *adv.* In a meet, fit, or proper manner; meetly, fitly; sufficiently. Also, exactly (in a certain position). ***meet to***: in close contact with.

1390 GOWER *Conf.* III. 183 His skyn was schape al meete, And nayled on the same seete. *c* **1470** HENRY *Wallace* x. 149 That taill full meit thow has tauld be thi sell. **1542** RECORDE *Gr. Artes* G vij b, In them the two fyrste fygures wer set euer mete one vnder the other. **1589** R. ROBINSON *Gold. Mirr.* (1851) 1 Gasing in the cloudes, these countreys for to vew, Meete underneath, the mountaine where I was. *a* **1600** MONTGOMERIE *Misc. Poems* xxxv. 68 Diana keeps this Margarit, Bot Hymen heghts to match hir meit. **1601** SHAKS. *All's Well* v. iii. 333 All yet seemes well, and if it end so meete, The bitter past, more welcome is the sweet. **1632** LITHGOW *Trav.* x. 465 The cords being first laid meet to my skin. **1688** SHADWELL *Sqr. Alsatia* III. i, You have given me so many bumpers I am Meet drunk already.

meet (miːt), *v.* Inflected **met.** Forms: 1 **métan,** *Northumb.* **moeta,** 3 **meten,** 3–4 **miete(n,** 3–6 **mete,** 4–7 *Sc.* **meit(e,** 5–7 **meete,** (4 **meyt, met,** 5 **mett,** 6 **might,** 7 **meat**), 4– **meet.** *Pa. t.* 1 **métte,** 3–6 **mette,** 4 **meyt,** 4–7 **mett,** 5 *Sc.* **meit,** 4– **met.** *Pa. pple.* 4 **mett, mete,** 4–6 **mette,** 5 **meyt,** 4– **met;** 4–5 **ymette,** 4–7 **ymet,** 5 **imett(e.** [OE. *métan* (Northumb. *mœ́ta*), also with prefix *ʒemétan*, wk. vb., corresponds to OFris. *mêta*, OS. *môtian* (MLG. *môten*, *gemôten*, Du. *moeten*, ON. *mœ́ta* (Sw. *möta*, Da. *möde*), Goth. *gamōtjan*:—OTeut. *(*ga*)*mōtjan*, f. **mōtoᵐ* coming together, encounter, meeting. See MOOT *sb.*]

I. Transitive senses.

1. To come or light upon, come across, fall in with, find. Now only *dial.* exc. with person as obj., in which use it is merged in 4; otherwise superseded by *meet with.*

c **888** K. ÆLFRED *Boeth.* xxx. §2 Hwi ofermodiʒe ʒe þon ofer oðre men for eowrum ʒebyrdum buton anweorce, nu ʒe nanne ne maʒon metan unæþelne? **971** *Blickl. Hom.* 217 Ða he eft ham com, þa mette he ðane man forðferedne. ? *a* **1400** *Arthur* 343 Þe ferst lond þat he gan Meete, Forsoþe hyt was Bareflete. *c* **1400** MAUNDEV. (1839) xv. 164 Summe of hem worschipe the Sonne,..summe Serpentes, or the first thing that thei meeten at morwen. **1590** SHAKS. *Com. Err.* III. ii. 188, I see a man heere needs not liue by shifts, When in the streets he meetes such golden gifts. **1676** WISEMAN *Surg.* II. iii. 174 Of this Intemperies you will find an Observation in Herpes... And whereever you meet it, you shall find difficulty. **1760–72** H. BROOKE *Fool of Qual.* (1809) III. 61, I had not gone..a mile, when, meeting a dirty road, I turned over a stile. *Mod. Pembrokeshire* (E.D.D.), I met this glove on the road.

2. a. To come face to face with, or into the company of (a person who is arriving at the same point from the opposite or a different direction).

c **1205** LAY. 18127 In are brade strete he igon mete þreo cnihtes & heore sweines. *c* **1290** *S. Eng. Leg.* I. 54/7 Ase he cam a day bi þe wei he gan mieten bi cas Ane kniȝt. **1362** LANGL. *P. Pl.* A. v. 82 Whon I mette him in þe Market þat I most hate, Ich heilede him as hendely as I his frend weore. *c* **1475** *Rauf Coilȝear* 606 He met ane Porter swayne Cummand raith him agayne. **1530** PALSGR. 635/1, I mette hym a myle beyonde the towne. **1693** CONGREVE *Old Bach.* IV. v, I would have overtaken, not have met my Game. **1824** HOGG *Conf. Sinner* 130 They perceived the two youths coming, as to meet them, on the same path.

b. To arrive in the presence of (a person, etc., approaching) as the intended result of going in the opposite direction: often in phrases ***to come, go, run,*** etc. ***to meet.*** Hence, to go to a place at which (a person) arrives, in order e.g. to welcome, communicate with, accompany, or convey (him). Similarly, ***to meet a coach, a train***, etc.

a **1300** *Cursor M.* 10555 Þi lauerd es comand als suith, Ga to mete him. *c* **1470** HENRY *Wallace* I. 62 Till Noram kirk he come with outyn mar, The consell than of Scotland meit hym thar. **15..** *Sir A. Barton* in *Surtees Misc.* (1888) 74 To might my Lord came the kinge and quen. **1598** SHAKS. *Merry W.* IV. ii. 96 Ile appoint my men to carry the basket againe, to meete him at the doore with it. **1599** —— *Much Ado* I. i. 97 Good Signior Leonato, you are come to meet your trouble: the fashion of the world is to auoid cost, and you encounter it. **1666** DRYDEN *Ann. Mirab.* cx, As in a drought the thirsty creatures cry And gape upon the gathered clouds for rain, And first the martlet meets it in the sky. **1667** MILTON *P. L.* x. 103 Where art thou Adam, wont with joy to meet My coming seen far off? **1710** BERKELEY *Princ. Hum. Knowl.* §97 Bid your servant meet you at such a time. **1808** SCOTT *Marm.* I. xiii, Then stepp'd to meet that noble Lord, Sir Hugh the Heron bold. **1894** DOYLE *S. Holmes* 49 I'll meet the seven o'clock train and take no steps till you arrive. *Mod.* An omnibus from the hotel meets all trains. I was met at the station by my host with a carriage.

c. Phr. ***to meet half-way***: chiefly in figurative uses, †to forestall, anticipate (*obs.*); to respond to the friendly advances of; to make concessions to (a person) in response to or in expectation of equal concessions on his part; to come to a compromise with. ***to meet trouble half-way***: to distress oneself needlessly with anticipations of what may happen.

1594 NASHE *Unfort. Trav.* B, Presently he remembred himselfe, and had like to fall into his memento againe, but that I met him halfe waies, and askt his Lordship [etc.]. **1625** BACON *Ess., Judicature* ¶3 Let not the Iudge meet the Cause halfe Way; Nor giue Occasion to the Partie to say; His Counsell or Proofes were not heard. **1638** BAKER tr. *Balzac's Lett.* (vol. III) 112, I like this popular Divinitie, which meets us halfe way, and stoops a little, that we may not strayne our selves too much. **1706** FARQUHAR *Recruit. Officer* III. i, We lov'd two Ladies, they met us half way, and [etc.]. **1799** NELSON in Nicolas *Disp.* (1845) IV. 66 There is not a thing that the Admiral could propose that I would not meet him half-way. **1821** LAMB *Elia* Ser. I. *Valentine's day*, The world meets nobody half-way. **1884** *Times* (weekly ed.) 5 Sept. 12/2 The Polish peasantry..will meet the Czar halfway in whatever he does for their good.

d. *transf.* with inanimate things as subj. or obj.: To come into contact, association, or junction with (something or some one moving in a different course). Also, of things that have attributed motion, as a line, road, etc.: To arrive at a point of contact or intersection with (another line, etc.).

a **1300** *Cursor M.* 23161 Oft i was wit malisce mette. **1590** SPENSER *F.Q.* III. iii. 21 Let no whit thee dismay The hard beginne that meetes thee in the dore. **1602** *2nd Pt. Return fr. Parnass.* II. i. (Arb.) 22 Where so ere we run there meetes vs griefe. **1833** TENNYSON *Lady of Shalott* i. 3 Long fields of barley and of rye, That clothe the wold and meet the sky. **1842** —— *Sir Galahad* vi, I yearn to breathe the airs of heaven That often meet me here. **1849** MACAULAY *Hist. Eng.* v. I. 663 The gibbet was set up where King Street meets Cheapside. **1898** *Encycl. Sport* II. 297 (*Rowing*) *Meeting the oar*, bringing the body up to the oar at the close of the stroke in place of bringing the hands strongly up into the chest.

e. Of an object of attention: To present itself before, to come under the observation of. ***to meet the eye*** (***sight, view***), ***the ear***: to be visible, audible. ***to meet the eye of***: to happen to be seen by. ***more than meets the eye***: greater significance than is at first apparent.

1632 MILTON *Penseroso* 120 Of Forests, and inchantments drear, Where more is meant then meets the ear. **1667** —— *P.L.* VI. 18 Chariots and flaming Armes, and fierie Steeds Reflecting blaze on blaze, first met his view. **1781** COWPER *Progr. Err.* 48 Where'er he turns, enjoyment and delight.. meet his sight. **1853** 'P. PAXTON' *Stray Yankee in Texas* 308 There might be more in it than at first met the eye. **1876** TREVELYAN *Macaulay* I. 363 All that met his ear or eye. **1883** GILMOUR *Mongols* xviii. 211 Striking pious attitudes at every object of reverence that meets his eye. *a* **1906** *Mod. Advt.* If this should meet the eye of A. B., he is requested [etc.]. **1906** GALSWORTHY *Man of Property* III. viii. 368 There's more here, sir, however, .. than meets the eye. I don't believe in suicide, nor in pure accident, myself. **1911** BEERBOHM *Zuleika D.* xvi. 247 Quick in more than meets the eye, John. Spiritually quick. You saw me putting on my hat; you did not see love taking on the crown of pity. **1923** WODEHOUSE *Inimitable Jeeves* ii. 21 'There is more in this than meets the eye,' I said. 'Why should your uncle ask a fellow to lunch whom he's never seen?' **1943** F. W. CROFTS *Affair at Little Wokeham* ii. 21 There's more in most things than meets the eye.

f. ***to meet*** a person's ***eye, gaze***, etc.: to perceive that he is looking at one; also, to submit oneself to his look without turning away.

1670 DRYDEN *Tyr. Love* v. i. 48 So much of guilt in my refusal lyes, That Debtor-like, I dare not meet your eyes. **1847** TENNYSON *Princess* IV. 177, I.. Not yet endured to meet her opening eyes. **1883** FRANCES M. PEARD *Contrad.* xxxii, As she turned her head.. she met his eyes.

g. Naut. ***to meet*** (***her, the ship***): see quots. 1776 and 1948.

1776 W. FALCONER *Universal Dict. Marine* (Phr. French Marine), s.v. *Rencontre*! The order to the helmsman, to meet the ship, right the helm, or put it towards the opposite side, in order to check the ship's sheer. **1841** R. H. DANA *Seaman's Manual* 183 If the order is.. 'Ease her!' 'Meet her!' or the like, the man should answer by repeating.. the order. **1856** C. NORDHOFF *Merchant Vessel* 233 The obstinate craft takes a mighty, almost resistless sweep to the other side, and 'meet her', is the cry, while poor Jack tugs desperately at the heavy-moving wheel. **1902** B. LUBBOCK *Round the Horn* 187 Occasionally he says sharply, 'Meet her! Meet her!' and sometimes he jumps to the wheel and gives us his powerful aid in grinding it up and down. **1948** R. DE KERCHOVE *Internat. Maritime Dict.* 461/1 *Meet her*, an order given to the helmsman to shift the rudder so as to check the swing of the vessel's head in a turn. **1968** H. F. CHASE *Boatswain's Manual* (ed. 3) xi. 255 If given too much wheel, .. her head may start to fall off to port. When this is about to happen the helmsman will 'meet her' by putting the wheel to starboard for a few moments.

3. a. To encounter or oppose in battle. Also (after F. *rencontrer*), to fight a duel with.

c **1275** LAY. 16366 Ten þusend Scottes he sende bi-halues þe heaþene to mete [*c* 1205 to imete]. *c* **1330** *Amis & Amil.* 1114 Yif Y may mete him aright, With mi brond that is so bright. **1375** BARBOUR *Bruce* XII. 226 Meit thame with speris hardely. *c* **1400** *Destr. Troy* 6527 All þat met hym with malis .. Auther dyet of his dynttes, or were ded wondit. **1596** DALRYMPLE tr. *Leslie's Hist. Scot.* II. 159 At thair cuming baldlie and wᵗ scharpe weiris thay meit thame. **1671** MILTON *Samson* 1123, I only with an Oaken staff will meet thee. **1771** *Junius Lett.* lxiii. (1820) 323 His opponents.. never meet him fairly upon his own ground. **1847** TENNYSON *Princess* IV. *song*, Like fire he meets the foe. **1855** SMEDLEY *H. Coverdale* lii, I suppose I should be forced to meet him.. if he were to challenge me.

†**b.** To be 'meet' or even with; = 11 i. *Obs.*

1613 FLETCHER, etc. *Hon. Man's Fort.* III. iii, I have heard of your tricks, .. well I may live To meet thee. **1623** FLETCHER *Rule a Wife* v. iii, Some trick upon my credit, I shall meet it.

c. To encounter or face the attacks of (something impersonal); to oppose, cope or grapple with (an objection, difficulty, evil). (Cf. 11 h.)

1745 *De Foe's Eng. Tradesman* (1841) I. vii. 53 Not be afraid of meeting the mischief which he sees follow too fast for him to escape. **1837** J. H. NEWMAN *Par. Serm.* (ed. 2) III. xi. 166 Who does not see, that to bear pain well, is to meet it courageously? **1854** BREWSTER *More Worlds* xv. 221 It is vain to argue against assertions like these which can only be met by an equally positive denial of them. **1855** BAIN *Senses & Int.* II. ii. §11 The impetus of a push or a squeeze received on the hand is measured by the muscular exertion induced to meet it. **1874** GREEN *Short Hist.* i. §4. 40 The threats of Charles were met by Offa with defiance. **1884** *Punch* 22 Nov. 252/1 Seen my last pamphlet, 'How to Meet the Microbe'?

†**d.** With simple *refl. pron.* in reciprocal sense: To encounter each other; = sense 9. *Obs.*

1297 R. GLOUC. (Rolls) 1950 Bi side winchestre in a feld to gadere hii hom mette. *c* **1320** *Sir Tristr.* 3325 Þai metten hem in asty Bi o forestes side.

4. a. To come (whether by accident or design) into the company of, or into personal intercourse with; to 'come across' (a person) in the intercourse of society or business. Freq. used in the imperative as part of a formula of introduction.

c **1374** CHAUCER *Compl. Mars* 138 Alas when shal I mete yow, herte dere? **1607** SHAKS. *Cor.* II. iii. 149 Remaines, that, in th' Officiall Markes inuested, You anon doe meet the Senate. **1676** WISEMAN *Surg.* I. xxi. 114 The next day in the afternoon the two Physicians and some of the Chirurgeons met me at the Patient's Chamber. **1676** DRYDEN *State Innoc.* v. i, And not look back to see, When what we love we ne'er must meet again. **1767** *Woman of Fashion* I. 127, I was.. struck with the Person, but much more with the good Sense, of the young Creature I accidently met. **1849** MACAULAY *Hist. Eng.* vi. II. 81 It was not strange that the king did not then wish to meet them. **1855** TENNYSON *Maud* II. IV. xiii, I loathe the squares and streets, And the faces that one meets. **1887** BEATTY-KINGSTON (*title*) Monarchs I have met. *a* **1906** *Mod.* His medical colleagues refuse to meet him in consultation. **1920** C. E. MULFORD *Johnny Nelson* vi. 37 'Meet th' Doc, Nelson,' said Dave. Johnny turned. 'Glad to meet you, Doctor.' **1926** A. A. THOMSON (*title*) Meet Mr. Huckabee. **1933** 'HAY' & 'ARMSTRONG' *Orders are Orders* II. 46 Waggermeyer (*breezy as ever*) Good morning, boys! Meet Miss Marigold, my secretary and continuity girl. **1961** T. HUGHES (*title*) Meet my folks!

b. Phrase, ***to be well, happily***, etc., ***met***. Also *ellipt.*, ***well met!*** (as an expression of welcome).

c **1460** *Play Sacram.* 237 A petre powle good daye & wele imett. **1470–85** MALORY *Arthur* II. vii. 83 Now go we hens said balyn & wel be we met. **1526** SKELTON *Magnyf.* 461 What, wanton, wanton, nowe well ymet! **1590** SHAKS. *Com. Err.* IV. iii. 45 Well met, well met, Master Antipholus. *a* **1592** GREENE *James IV*, IV. ii, Widow Countess, well y-met. **1596** SHAKS. *Tam. Shr.* IV. iv. 19 You are happilie met. **1834** LYTTON *Pompeii* I. i, Ho, Diomed, well met.

†**c.** With simple *refl. pron.* (cf. 3 d): To encounter each other; = sense 8. *Obs.*

c **1290** *S. Eng. Leg.* I. 354/302 Bi þe watere of pireford þis two schirene hem mette, And conteckeden for þis holie bodie. *a* **1300** *Cursor M.* 10563 Quen þis seli mett þam same, Þai grett þam-self wit gastli game.

5. To encounter, experience (a certain fortune or destiny); to receive (reward, punishment, or treatment of a certain kind). Now *rare* or *poet.*, superseded by ***meet with*** (11 g).

c **1440** *York Myst.* xi. 288 Mo mervaylles mon he mett. **1591** SHAKS. *Two Gent.* I. i. 15 Wish me partaker in thy happinesse, When thou do'st meet good hap. *a* **1631** DONNE *Lett., To Sir T. Lucy* (1651) 11, I have a little satisfaction in seeing a letter written to you upon my table, though I meet no opportunity of sending it. **1661** BOYLE *Style of Script.* (1675) 243 Those.. met a destiny not ill resembling that of Zacheus. **1667** MILTON *P.L.* IX. 271 As one who loves, and some unkindness meets. *a* **1677** BARROW *Serm.* xvii. Wks. 1687 I. 243 Whoever hath in him any love of truth.. shall hardly be able to satisfie himself in the conversations he meeteth; but [etc.]. **1697** DRYDEN *Virg. Georg.* IV. 655 Thy great Misdeeds have met a due Reward. **1726** SWIFT *Gulliver* II. v, In this Exercise I once met an Accident. **1808** MACKINTOSH *Let.* 28 Sept. in *Life* (1836) I. 437 'Meet your approbation' is a slang phrase, not fit for public despatches or letters. **1833** HT. MARTINEAU *Fr. Wines & Pol.* iv. 61 He met only threats and laughter. **1845** M. PATTISON *Ess.* (1889) I. 19 This generous appeal met no response. **1847** TENNYSON *Princess* IV. 309, I fear'd To meet a cold 'We thank you'. **1855** M. ARNOLD *Balder Dead* 24 He has met that doom which long ago The Nornies.. spun.

6. To come into conformity with (a person's wishes or opinions).

1694 CONGREVE *Double Dealer* v. xiii, By Heav'n he meets my wishes! **1784** COWPER *Task* III. 788 He.. leaves the accomplished plan Just when it.. meets his hopes. **1842** BISCHOFF *Woollen Manuf.* II. 69 Such duties on the importation of foreign woollen manufactures as would meet their views. **1849** MACAULAY *Hist. Eng.* vi. II. 120 The Estates.. would go as far as their consciences would allow to meet His Majesty's wishes. **1864** HAWTHORNE *S. Felton* (1883) 273 If her thoughts.. had settled on that.. wholesome young man, instead of on himself, who met her on so few points. *Mod.* (*Comm.*) I will do my best to meet you in the matter.

7. To satisfy (a demand or need); to satisfy the requirements of (a particular case); to be able or sufficient to discharge (a pecuniary obligation). ***to meet a bill*** (Comm.): to pay it at maturity.

1833 MARRYAT *P. Simple* xi, The money.. was.. not more than sufficient to meet one of the demands. **1837** SIR F. PALGRAVE *Merch. & Friar* (1844) 187 No body is ever unable to pay his debts; he is only unable to meet his engagements. **1847** MARRYAT *Childr. N. Forest* iv, His widow sold the gun to meet her wants. **1876** MACLEOD *Elem. Banking* 167 Even under the best circumstances, an acceptor may fail to meet his bill. **1884** SIR E. E. KAY in *Law Times Rep.* 10 May 322/2 A remedy which exactly meets the necessities of the case. **1884** *Manch. Exam.* 16 May 5/1 This view of the question gets rid of.. all mere wrangling, while no other adequately meets the case. **1891** *Law Rep.* Weekly Notes 78/1 The course suggested on the part of the Comptroller was necessary to meet the justice of the case. **1894** BARING-GOULD *Kitty Alone* II. 84 Five hundred pounds will not suffice to meet all claims.

II. Intransitive senses.

8. a. [From the earlier reciprocal use: see 4 c.] Of two or more persons: To come from opposite or different directions into the same place or so as to be in each other's presence or company, whether by accident or by design; to come face to face. Often with *together*. Sometimes conjugated with *be*.

a **1300** *Cursor M.* 22963 Þe stede o dome quar all sal mete. *c* **1374** CHAUCER *Compl. Mars* 72 The grete Ioye that was betwix hem two Whan they be met. *c* **1450** *St. Cuthbert* (Surtees) 889 Þai met neuer eftir whils þai leued. *c* **1475** *Rauf Coilȝear* 250 Baith the King and the Quene meitis in Paris, For to hald thair ȝule togidder. **1538** STARKEY *England* I. ii. 27 Seying that we be now here mete.. accordyng to our promys. **1605** SHAKS. *Macb.* I. i. 1 When shall we three meet againe? In Thunder, Lightning, or in Raine? **1628** J. MEAD in *Crt. & Times Chas. I* (1848) I. 314 One bade him come to the lord mayor; he answered, my lord mayor might come to him: but in fine they agreed to meet half way. **1720** GAY *Sweet Wiliam's Farew.* iv, We only part to meet again. **1781** J. LOGAN in *Sc. Paraphr.* LIII. viii, Where death-divided friends at last shall meet, to part no more. *c* **1830** T. H. BAYLY *Song*, We met—'twas in a crowd—and I thought he would shun me. **1859** THACKERAY *Virgin.* II. xix. 158 The two gentlemen, with a few more friends, were met round General Lambert's supper-table. **1870** E. PEACOCK *Ralf Skirl.* II. 259 They had not met for years.

b. Of the members of a more or less organized body, a society, or regular assembly: To assemble for purposes of conference, business, worship, or the like. Often with collect. noun as subj.

1530 PALSGR. 635/2 Whan they mete to gyther I wyll put them in mynde of your mater. **1560** DAUS tr. *Sleidane's Comm.* 10b, These beynge called to an assemblie.. mette at Franckefourt. **1607** SHAKS. *Cor.* II. iii. 152 The People.. are summon'd To meet anon, vpon your approbation. **1611** BIBLE *2 Macc.* xiv. 21 And [they] appointed a day to meet in together by themselues. **1711** STEELE *Spect.* No. 49 ¶4 When this Assembly of Men meet together. **1711** SWIFT *Jrnl. to Stella* 1 Dec., The Parliament will certainly meet on Friday next. **1791** HAMPSON *Mem. J. Wesley* III. 82 Many of these [classes] are subdivided into smaller companies called bands, which also meet once a week. **1845** M. PATTISON *Ess.* (1889) I. 17 The bishops.. were summoned to meet in synod, at Paris. **1874** GREEN *Short Hist.* viii. §2. 469 The Parliament.. met in another mood from that of any Parliament which had met for a hundred years.

†**c.** To come to or be present at a meeting; to keep an appointment. *Obs.*

c **1300** *Rom. Rose* 4571 Expectant ay tille I may mete, To geten mercy of that swete. *a* **1400–50** *Alexander* 770 Aithire with a firs flote in þe flide metis. **1470–85** MALORY *Arthur* IV. xxvi. 156 Soo he departed to mete at his day afore sette. **1598** SHAKS. *Merry W.* III. iii. 5 'Tis past the howre (Sir) that Sir Hugh promis'd to meet. **1603** —— *Meas. for M.* IV. i. 18. **1717** ADDISON tr. *Ovid's Met.* IV. *Salmacis* 43 She fain wou'd meet him, but refus'd to meet Before her looks were set with nicest care.

d. To arrive at mutual agreement.

1851 PUSEY *Let. Bp. London* (ed. 3) 127/1 Devout minds, of every school, who meditate on the Passion, meet at least in this.

†**9.** To come together in the shock of battle. ***to meet on***: to come into conflict with. *Obs.*

c **1400** *Destr. Troy* 7815 Bothe þe grekis on þe grene, & þe grym troiens, Mettyn with mayne þaire myghtis to kythe. *Ibid.* 8288 He macchit hym to Menelay, & met on þe kyng. **1460** *Lybeaus Disc.* 1638 The styward.. Fell of hys stede bakward, So harde they two metten. *Ibid.* 2012 As þey togeder sette, Har boþe swerdes mette. [**1782** COWPER *Friendship* 137 How fiercely will they meet and charge! No combatants are stiffer.]

10. a. Of inanimate objects: To come into contact; to come together so as to occupy the same place, or follow the same line or course.

to make both ends meet: see END *sb.* 24.

a **1300** *Siriz* 358 Loke hou hire heien greten, On hire cheken the teres meten. *c* **1400** MAUNDEV. (1839) xvii. 185 Alle the Lynes meeten at the Centre. **1530** PALSGR. 635/1 Hylles do never mete, but acquayntaunce dothe often. **1560** DAUS tr. *Sleidane's Comm.* 412 Where the Rhine and Moselle mete. **1666** PEPYS *Diary* 4 Nov., My vest being new and thin, and the coat cut not to meet before upon my breast. **1667** MILTON *P.L.* IV. 784 Our circuit meets full West. **1719** DE FOE *Crusoe* (1840) II. xiv. 286 It was very hard to see where the tiles met. **1771** SMOLLETT *Humph. Cl.* 3 Oct., He .. discovered that his waistcoat would not meet upon his belly by five good inches at least. **1774** PORTEUS *Serm.* v. (1797) I. 116 How two mathematical lines, indefinitely produced, can be for ever approaching each other, and yet never meet. **1781** COWPER *Hope* 49 The blue rim, where skies and mountains meet. —— *Expost.* 22 Her vaults below, where every vintage meets. **1810** SCOTT *Lady of L.* I. xii, Where seemed the cliffs to meet on high. **1833** TENNYSON *May Queen* Concl. 22 There came a sweeter token when the night and morning meet. **1871** R. ELLIS tr. *Catullus* lxii. 52 Look as a lone lorn vine.. Bows, till topmost spray and roots meet feebly together. **1892** KIPLING *Barrack-r. Ball.*, etc. 75 Oh, East is East, and West is West, and never the twain shall meet.

b. Of eyes, glances, etc. (cf. 2 f).

1859 TENNYSON *Elaine* 1303 He raised his head, their eyes met and hers fell.

c. Said of qualities, etc., uniting in the same person, etc.

1581 PETTIE tr. *Guazzo's Civ. Conv.* II. (1586) 114 Al the three beauties meet together.. in young men. **1662** STILLINGFL. *Orig. Sacr.* II. vi. §9 The uniformity and perfect harmony of all these several Prophecies.. all giving light to each other, and exactly meeting at last in the accomplishment. **1697** CHETWOOD *Dryden's Virgil* Life ** 3 It being rarely found that a very fluent Elocution, and depth of judgment meet in the same Person. **1781** COWPER *Charity* 37 In baser souls unnumbered evils meet. **1842** TENNYSON *Morte d'Arthur* 125 Thou, the latest-left of all my knights, In whom should meet the offices of all. **1894** J. T. FOWLER *Adamnan* Introd. 57 The nobility of two races met in the child.

†**d.** To lie or fit close *to*. (Cf. MEET *a.*) *Obs.*
1568 *Satir. Poems Reform.* xlviii. 30 It meites lyk stemmyne to 3or theis.

†**e.** To agree or tally. *Obs. rare.*
1579 GOSSON *Sch. Abuse* (Arb.) 27 He that compareth our instruments, with those that were vsed in ancient times, shall see them agree like Dogges and Cattes, and meete as iump as German lippes. **1662** STILLINGFL. *Orig. Sacr.* I. vi. §1 It was yet greater difficulty to regulate it by the course of the Sun, and to make the accounts of the Sun and Moon meet. **1823** LAMB *Elia.* Ser. II. *Old China*, It is mighty pleasant at the end of the year to make all meet—and much ado we used to have every Thirty-first Night of December to account for our exceedings.

11. meet with.

a. To come across, light upon; = sense 1, which it has superseded in common use.
c **1275** LAY. 1426 Hii mette wid [*earlier text* Imetten heo faren] Numbert þeos kinges sonde of þan erþ. *a* **1300** *Cursor M.* 19604 Saulus soght aiquar and thrett All þe cristen he wit mett. *c* **1450** *St. Cuthbert* (Surtees) 4327 Þai spared nouthir kynn na kyth, Man na woman þat þai mett with. **1596** SPENSER *State Irel.* Wks. (Globe) 640/2 When he cometh to experience of service abroade..he maketh as woorthy a souldiour as any nation he meeteth with. *a* **1626** BACON *New Atl.* 21 And continually we mett with many things, worthy of Observation, and Relation. **1638** JUNIUS *Paint. Ancients* 14 Others..wander up and downe to meet somewhere with a refreshing shade. **1662** J. DAVIES tr. *Olearius' Voy. Ambass.* 158 They make a shift to live upon any thing they can meet withall. **1761** HUME *Hist. Eng.* III. lxi. 318 This was the first public opportunity he had met with. **1782** JOHNSON *Lett. to Mrs. Thrale* 13 June, In the penury of fuel ..I have yet met with none so frugal as to sit without fire. **1830** D'ISRAELI *Chas. I*, III. vi. 94 We cannot read a history of foreign art without meeting with the name of Charles. **1875** DAWSON *Dawn of Life* iv. 84, I have occasionally met with instances. **1899** *Allbutt's Syst. Med.* VII. 592 Though abscess beneath the tentorium usually occurs in the substance of the hemisphere it may be met with in other situations.

†**b.** To come into the presence of; = sense 2. *Obs.*
a **1300** *Cursor M.* 20145 In þe temple wit her he met, Anurd hir and tar hir grette. *c* **1380** *Sir Ferumb.* 3778, & euene to þe pauyllouns þay gunne go, & meteþ with þe Amyrel. *c* **1477** CAXTON *Jason* 89 Whan Jason was come to this temple medea cam and mette with him. **1526** *Pilgr. Perf.* (W. de W. 1531) 21 b, His grace preuenteth vs, before we mete with it. **1542** UDALL *Erasm. Apoph.* 27 Socrates mette full butte with Xenophon, in a narrowe backe lane, where he could not stert from hym. **1686** tr. *Agiatis or Civ. Wars Lacedemonians* 59 As he returned, he was met with by an Achaian. **1816** CHALMERS in *Life* (1850) II. 78 We fell in with Mr. Cook, who came out to meet with me.

†**c.** To encounter (an enemy); = sense 3. *Obs.*
1297 R. GLOUC. (Rolls) 3205 Vter..wende toward seint dauid to mete wiþ is fon. *c* **1386** CHAUCER *Pard. T.* 365 Is it swich peril with him for to meete? I shal hym seke by wey and eek by strete. *c* **1470** HENRY *Wallace* IV. 250 Thus Wallace sone can with the capteyn meite. **1596** SHAKS. *1 Hen. IV*, IV. iv. 13 At Shrewsbury..The King, with mightie and quick-raysed Power, Meetes with Lord Harry. **1664** BUTLER *Hud.* II. iii. 993 How in fight you met, At Kingston, with a May-pole idol.

†**d.** To come into or be in physical contact with. Of a garment: To reach exactly to (a certain point).
a **1300** *Cursor M.* 9915 O thre colurs..þe grund neist þar es ful tru, Metand wit þat rochen stan. **13..** *E. E. Allit. P.* B. 371 When þe water of þe welkyn with þe worlde mette. *c* **1430** *Syr Gener.* (Roxb.) 4460 Ful litle wanted the soket That with the throte it had y-met. **1480** *Robt. Devyll* 328 in Hazl. *E.P.P.* I. 232 With hys shyelde Robert mette playne. **1574** tr. *Marlorat's Apocalips* 22 A long garment..[which] meteth iust with the feete. **1604** R. CAWDREY *Table Alph.* (1613) A iv, One lands end meets with another. **1745** P. THOMAS *Jrnl. Anson's Voy.* 145 In its Fall, meeting with the Fore-yard broke it in the Slings.

†**e.** To have carnal knowledge of. *Obs.*
a **1300** *Cursor M.* 1197 Adam..suld wit his wijf yete mete For ur lord had aghteld yete A child to rais of his oxspring.

†**f.** To agree or accord with. *Obs.*
a **1586** SIDNEY *Apol. Poetrie* (Arb.) 24 Wherein I know not, whether by lucke or wisedome, wee Englishmen haue mette with the Greekes, in calling him a maker. **1655** FULLER *Ch. Hist.* IX. ii. §15 Lords of right noble extraction ..(whose titles met with their estates in the Northern Parts).

g. To experience, undergo (a particular kind of fortune or treatment); = sense 5.
c **1435** *Torr. Portugal* 2109 God that died vppon the Rode, Yff grace that she mete with good! **1593** SHAKS. *Rich. II*, III. iv. 49 He that hath suffer'd this disorder'd Spring, Hath now himselfe met with the Fall of Leafe. **1596** —— *Tam. Shr.* IV. iii. 6 Elsewhere they meet with charitie. **1660** BLOUNT *Boscobel* 3 At Warrington Bridge [he] met with the first opposition made by the Rebels. *a* **1692** POLLEXFEN *Disc. Trade* (1697) 100 These Manufactured Goods from India, met with such a kind reception, that [etc.]. **1693** CREECH *Dryden's Juvenal* xiii. (1697) 326 A little Sum you Mourn, while Most have met With twice the Loss, and by as Vile a Cheat. **1711** ADDISON *Spect.* No. 122 ¶9 In our Return home we met with a very odd Accident. **1718** *Freethinker* No. 75. 137 It has always met with the Approbation of the Wisest Men. **1771** GOLDSM. *Hist. Eng.* II. 176 Sir William Gascoigne..met with praises instead of reproaches. **1843** BORROW *Bible in Spain* xxvi, I have..never met with ill-usage, except once..amongst the Papists. **1873** BLACK *Pr. Thule* xix, Mariners..who had met with their death on this rocky coast. **1893** EARL DUNMORE *Pamirs* II. 311 This system of semi-official marauding met with the approval of the Czar.

†**h.** To oppose, grapple with (an error, objection, malpractice), take precautions against (a danger); to provide for (an emergency). Also, to cope with (a person). *Obs.*
1529 MORE *Dyalogue* IV. Wks. 285/1 And all this good fruite woulde a fewe mischieuous persons..vndoutedlye bring into thys realme, if the prince and prelates..did not in the beginnyng mete with their malice. **1575–85** ABP. SANDYS *Serm.* xi. 172 Paul, in this treatie of a magistrate, meeteth with both these errors. **1600** in *Liturg. Serv. Q. Eliz.* (Parker Soc.) 694 Meet with the purposes and practices of all ambitious Absalons. **1603** H. CROSSE *Vertues Commw.* (1878) 8 A prudent man..meeteth with euerie mischiefe, and is not ouertaken, with *non putaui*, had I wist. **1668** *Rolle's Abridgment* Publ. Pref., The body of Laws..consists of infinite particulars, and must meet with various Emergencies. **1692** SOUTH *12 Serm.* (1698) III. 524 To meet with their doubts, and to answer their Objections. **1712** ARBUTHNOT *John Bull* IV. iv, Let it suffice, at present, that you have been met with.

†**i.** To be even with; to requite or 'pay out'.
c **1590** MARLOWE *Faust.* x, I'll meet with you anon for interrupting me so. **1601** DENT *Pathw. Heaven* 307 God.. though he meet with some in this life, yet he lets thousands escape. **1667** WATERHOUSE *Fire Lond.* 129 For which sins God may meet with you also.

j. *Sc.* To pay (a creditor).
1854 H. MILLER *Sch. & Schm.* (1858) 288 They had been unable, term after term, to meet with the laird, and were now three years in arrears.

12. Sc. ***to meet in with***, to encounter (a person); = sense 4.
1825 JAMIESON Suppl., *To meet in wi'*, to meet with. S.B. **1828** D. M. MOIR *Mansie Wauch* xi. 96, I..advised him to take a step in at his leisure to St. Mary's Wynd, where he would meet in with some merchants in scores. **1878** R. CUDDIE *Corstorphine Lyrics* 18, I met my auld frien' Tam. Wha had met in wi' some guid chiel' and tasted half a dram. **1889** R. L. STEVENSON *Master of Ballantrae* ix. 247, I was not always as I am today; nor (had I met in with a friend of your description) should I have ever been so.

13. ***to meet up with***: to overtake or fall in with; to meet, encounter; to become acquainted with. *colloq.* (orig. *U.S.*). Also *absol.*, ***to meet up***.
1837 A. SHERWOOD *Gazetteer Georgia* (ed. 3) (Provincialisms), *Met up with*, for overtook. **1889** K. MUNROE *Golden Days* ix. 96 They'd meet up with you somewheres along Coloma way. **1905** *Dialect Notes* III. 87 He started before I did, but I met up with him before we got to town. **1919** F. HURST *Humoresque* 297 Tell him his little Sid is here with thirty minutes before she meets up with the show on the ten-forty. **1935** [see GET *v.* 74c]. **1949** G. DAVENPORT *Family Fortunes* I. i. 10 It was better than staying at home and they would probably meet up with friends. **1955** E. HILLARY *High Adventure* vi. 104 We.. there met up with Evans and his two Sherpas. **1959** *N.Z. Listener* 12 June 5/4 It was there that I met up with Lowry again. **1972** D. HASTON *In High Places* xi. 116 Everyone met up on Pokhara airstrip. **1972** *Daily Tel.* 13 May 20/8 The Sun Life is a very competitive office and would seem to meet up with your requirements. **1973** C. BONINGTON *Next Horizon* v. 92, I met up with Mick Burke in the camp site.

14. Comb. ***meet-the-people***: phr. used *attrib.* to describe a tour, etc., made by an eminent person to meet members of the general public (in quot. 1943 of a hamburger with 'popular' appeal). orig. *U.S.*
1943 *Amer. Speech* XVIII. 148 *Meet-the-People burger* (musical comedy 'Meet the People' Los Angeles 1940). **1959** *Economist* 30 May 820/2 Their 'meet-the-people' tours of factories and shipyards. **1959** *Punch* 16 Sept. 160/2 His colleagues mysteriously disappeared during a 'meet the people' tour of the Isle of Wight. **1975** *Times* 2 July 6/2 The Belgian Prime Minister..continued his meet-the-people tour in Edinburgh yesterday.

meet(e, obs. forms of MET, METE.

meetel(e)s, var. forms of METELS *Obs.*, dream.

meeten ('miːt(ə)n), *v.* [f. MEET *a.* + -EN[5].] *trans.* To make meet or fit (*for*).
1807 C. WINTER in W. Jay *Life* (1843) 173 That you..may be richly accommodated with grace till you are meetened for glory. **1879** A. REED *Alice Bridge* 272 These trials will meeten us for whatever the future unfolds.

meeter ('miːtə(r)). [f. MEET *v.* + -ER[1].] One who attends or takes part in a meeting; †*spec.* in Quaker phraseology, a member of a particular 'meeting' or congregation.
1646 *Mass. Col. Rec.* (1853) II. 185 Ye maior pt of those first meeters. **1682** W. ROGERS *7th Pt. Chr., Quaker* 82 G. W. a Member of the Second-days Meeting..smooth'd up the Barbadoes Meeters with this Expression. *a* **1713** ELLWOOD *Autobiog.* (1765) 251 The whole Fines of such and so many of the Meeters as they should account poor. **1887** E. F. BYRRNE *Heir without Heritage* II. xi. 219 These early torchlight-meeters.

meeter, obs. form of METER, METRE.

'**meeterly**, *a.* and *adv. north. dial.* Also [? 4–5 materly], 9 **meterly**. [app. related to MEET *a.*, but the formation is obscure: possibly influenced by *witterly* or some similar word. The *materly* of the first quotation is difficult to connect with the other forms: cf. ON. *mátalega*, *mátulega*, f. *máte* measure, moderation.
A synon. *meetherly*, *meederly*, *meeverly* occurs in dialects (see E.D.D.), and may possibly be referable to METHE *sb.*]

a. *adj.* Moderate, middling, fairly good. **b.** *adv.* 'Tolerably, moderately, fairly; handsomely, modestly, agreeably' (E.D.D.).
[*c* **1400** *Rule St. Benet* 2306 Þus bi ensaumpil sal scho take Materly al thinges to make (= L. *sic omnia temperet*, etc.).] **1674** RAY *N. C. Words*, *Meeterly*, *Meetherly*, *Meederly*: handsomely, modestly; As bow meeterly, from meet, fit. *c* **1746** COLLIER (Tim Bobbin) *View Lanc. Dial.* Wks. (1862) 54 *M*... Is Seroh o Rutchots so honsome? *T.* Eigh, hoos meeterly. **1847** E. BRONTË *Wuthering Heights* I. xiii. 321 They's a pack uh corn i' t' corner, thear, meeterly clane. **1865** B. BRIERLEY *Irkdale* II. 99 I'm metterly..for an 'owd body.

meeth: see MEAD[1] (the drink), METHE (measure).

†**meet-help.** *Obs.* [orig. two words like *help meet* in Gen. ii. 18, 20: subseq. combined as in *sweet heart*, *good wife*, etc.] A fitting helper; = HELPMEET.
[**1641** J. SHUTE *Sarah & Hagar* (1649) 18 The end of her Creation; which was, to be a meet help for him. *a* **1656** BP. HALL *Rem. Wks.* (1660) *Life* 15 Enjoying the comfortable Society of that meet Help for the space of fourty nine years.] **1696** WHISTON *Th. Earth* II. (1722) 96 Among all these Creatures there was not a Meet-help, or suitable Companion for him.

So **meet-helper**; also **meet-helping**, the condition of being a helpmeet.
1636 W. STRODE *Floating Isl.* IV. iii, Recreation much consisteth in The yoak of a meet helper. **1869** BUSHNELL *Wom. Suffrage* iv. 74 Woman is created to be the meet-helper of man. *Ibid.* i. 18 The husbanding and meet-helping of the marriage bond itself.

meeting ('miːtɪŋ), *vbl. sb.* [f. MEET *v.* + -ING[1]. OE. had *ȝeméting*, glossing L. *conventio*, *conventus*, *concilium*, *synagoga*.]

1. a. The action of coming together from opposite or different directions into one place or into the presence of each other, of assembling for the transaction of business, etc. Now somewhat *rare* exc. in gerundial use; formerly in phr. ***in meeting***, ***at*** (***next***, etc.) ***meeting***, ***till meeting***.
a **1300** *Cursor M.* 5846 His broþer aaron he mett, þat drihtin self has meting set. *c* **1320** *Sir Tristr.* 181 Swiche meting nas neuer made Wiþ sorwe on ich aside. *c* **1400** MAUNDEV. (1839) xv. 166 There ben also sum Cristene men, that seyn, that summe Bestes han gode meetynge, that is to seye, for to meete with hem first at morwe. *c* **1440** LOVELICH *Merlin* 4580 The kyng, that aȝens Merlyne went in metyng. **1485** in Jupp *Acc. Carpenters' Comp.* (1887) 35 Reseyvyd in the Barge at the metyng of the Kyng on the Water vij[s] vij[d]. **1559** BP. SCOT in Strype *Ann. Ref.* (1709) I. App. vii. 14 At Peter's first metinge with our Savyour Christe. **1639** *Hamilton Papers* (Camden) 95 Muche more of this kynd that past betwixt one of ther number and me this day..at meating. **1771** SMOLLETT *Humph. Cl.* 2 Apr., I desire you will lock up all my drawers, and keep the keys till meeting. **1844** LD. BROUGHAM *Brit. Const.* ix. (1862) 119 The people's right of Meeting in large bodies. **1903** *Edin. Rev.* Apr. 314 These old makers..do not dwell on meetings in heaven.

b. ***to give*** (a person) (***the*** or ***a***) ***meeting*** [after F. *donner rendez-vous*]: to appoint a time and place for meeting with him. ? *Obs.*
1632 J. HAYWARD tr. *Biondi's Eromena* 25 A friend.. whom they were to procure to come disguised, and give them the meeting. **1638** MAYNE *Lucian* (1664) 161 At length, with much intreaty, he gave her a meeting. *a* **1648** LD. HERBERT *Hen. VIII* (1683) 35 Promising that he would not only give him meeting, but take pay under him. **1771** SMOLLETT *Humph. Cl.* 30 Sept., That..he would come to Bath in the winter, where I promised to give him the meeting. **1833** MACAULAY *Ess.*, *War Succession* (ed. Montague) I. 509 The King resolved to give her the meeting in Catalonia. **1840** DICKENS *Barn. Rudge* xii, You ask me to give you a meeting.

†**2. a.** An encounter in arms; a fight, battle. *Obs.*
13.. *K. Alis.* 2696 Com, and geve us on justyng, And thow schalt have hard metyng. *c* **1330** R. BRUNNE *Chron. Wace* (Rolls) 1011 At þat metyng..Taken was sire Antygoun. **1596** DALRYMPLE tr. *Leslie's Hist. Scot.* II. 148 Vncertane victorie at bathe the meitings.

b. Used euphemistically for: A duel. (After F. *rencontre*: cf. RENCOUNTER *sb.* 1 b.)
1812 *Chron.* in *Ann. Reg.* 31 A meeting took place.. between Mr. O. Joynt and Mr. P. McKim..when, on the first fire, the latter was struck in the forehead. **1838** MACAULAY in Trevelyan *Life* II. 6, I had..no notion that a meeting could be avoided.

3. a. A gathering or assembly of a number of people for purposes of intercourse, entertainment, discussion, legislation, and the like. Now chiefly restricted to gatherings of a public character, and assemblies of some organized society; formerly used to include private gatherings or parties, as in *card-meeting*.
1513 MORE in Grafton *Chron.* (1568) II. 766 They assembled by and by together, to common of thys matter at London: At which meeting, the Archebishop of Yorke.. secretly sent for the great Seale agayne. **1611** BIBLE *Isa.* i. 13 The calling of assemblies I cannot away with; it is iniquitie, euen the solemne meeting. **1693** *Humours Town* 59 To Ogle the Nymphs in the Boxes or Musick-Meetings. **1712** SWIFT *Prop. Correct. Eng. Tongue* 29 Since they [*sc.* ladies] have been left out of all Meetings, except Parties at Play. **1849** MACAULAY *Hist. Eng.* vi. II. 95 He was no longer summoned to any meeting of the board. **1886** STEVENSON *Dr. Jekyll* 1 At friendly meetings, and when the wine was to his taste.

b. An assembly of people for purposes of worship: in England from the 17th c. applied almost exclusively to gatherings of nonconformists, and now *rare* exc. with reference to Quakers. (Sometimes used, after prep., without article, esp. in ***to go to meeting***.) Hence, a nonconformist congregation; also, †a nonconformist place of worship, a dissenting chapel or meeting-house (*obs.*).

1593 [see CONVENTICLE 4 b]. **1677** W. HUBBARD *Narrative* II. 51 September the twenty fourth, being Lords day, as he was going home from the Meeting. **1679** *Establ. Test* 23 A.. Jesuit takes a Lodging at a Quakers,..goes to the Silent meeting with his Landlord. **1688** PENTON *Guard. Instruct.* (1897) 33, I went to a notorious Meeting, upon the fame of an extraordinary gifted Preacher. **1710** PALMER *Proverbs* 375 The pharisees cry was, The temple! the temple! and the modern hypocrites is, The church! and The meeting! **1750** *Nova Scotia Archives* (1869) 618 A Meeting for Dissenters, a Court House and Prison. **1774** J. ADAMS in *Fam. Lett.* (1876) 10 We went to meeting at Wells. **1781** HUTTON *Hist. B'ham.* 117 Another was erected in the reign of King William, now denominated The Old Meeting. **1815** W. F[IELD] *Warw. & Leamington* 140 Wesleian Methodist Meeting. This is situated in Gerard Lane, small in extent, and humble in appearance. **1834** *Tracts for Times* No. 29. 3 There is something so fine in the prayers without book, as they are offered at meeting. *Ibid.* 5 [The Church] had been in the country many, many years, whereas all the meetings about are (so to say) of yesterday. **1855** OGILVIE, Suppl., *Meeting*. In England, a conventicle; an assembly of Dissenters.—In the United States, an assembly for public worship generally. **1889** MARY HOWITT *Autobiog.* I. 4, I use here the phraseology of Friends, 'meeting' in this sense being equivalent to church or religious body.

c. = *race-meeting* (RACE *sb.*^{1} 11).

1764 *App. to Chron.* in *Ann. Reg.* 128/1 Westminster Races...Spring Meeting. **1859** *Ann. Reg.* 73 Magnificent weather and excellent sport made the great people's meeting [the Derby] pass off with great *éclat*.

4. a. Of inanimate objects: Joining, junction; confluence (of rivers).

1530 PALSGR. 527/1, I drawe nere, as a shyppe dothe lande, or any other thynges whan they come to the metyng. **1606** G. W[OODCOCKE] *Hist. Ivstine* IV. 21 The meetings of the waters. *c* **1639** SUCKLING *Brennoralt* III. (1648) 32 Her face is like the milky way i' th' sky, A meeting of gentle lights without name. **1807** MOORE *Irish Melodies*, (*title*) The Meeting of the Waters.

b. A joint in carpentry or masonry.

1656 H. PHILLIPS *Purch. Patt.* (1676) B viij b, In the square meeting of the Table. **1663** GERBIER *Counsel* 7 Which will hinder the Rain..to peirce..through the meeting of the Brickwork and Stone. *c* **1860** H. STUART *Seaman's Catech.* 70 What are the 'end boards'? They are boards which cover and form the ends of the meetings.

c. *Mining*. The passing of ascending and descending cars; hence, the place at which they pass.

1830 T. WILSON *Pitman's Pay* (1843) 26 We'd pass'd the meetin's aw've ne doubt. **1860** *Eng. & For. Min. Gloss., Newc. Terms, Meetings*, the middle of a pit or inclined plane. **1875** R. F. MARTIN tr. *Havrez' Winding Mach.* 36 If these moments be equal at meetings and at the landing of the cage.

†**5.** ? An average value. *Obs.*

1711 W. SUTHERLAND *Shipbuild. Assist.* 14 The Method of buying a quantity of Timber is to add the Contents together of the several Pieces; the Quotient thereof is call'd the Meeting of that Timber, and accordingly thereto the Value of the whole Quantity is sold.

6. = MEETING-PLACE. *poet.*

1596 SHAKS. *1 Hen. IV*, III. ii. 174 On Thursday, wee our selues will march. Our meeting is Bridgenorth. **1801** SOUTHEY *Thalaba* III. i, The Domdaniel caverns,..Their impious meeting.

7. *attrib.*, as ***meeting acquaintance, bonnet, clothes, coat, -day, gown, hat, -point, -room, -stead*** (arch.), ***-time***; **meeting-folks**, dissenters; **meeting seed** (see quot. 1851). Also MEETING-HOUSE, -PLACE.

1792 MME. D'ARBLAY *Diary* V. VII. 299 Mrs. Kennedy.. with whom I renewed a *meeting acquaintance, but evaded a visiting one. **1867** J. R. LOWELL *Biglow Papers* 2nd Ser. p. lxxix, Her new *meetin'-bunnet Felt somehow thru' its crown a pair O' blue eyes sot upon it. **1775** in O. E. Winslow *Amer. Broadside Verse* (1930) 141/2 He got him on his *meeting clothes. **1867** 'T. LACKLAND' *Homespun* I. 63 The 'meetin clothes' of the children are laid away for another week, and the old ones got out again. **1887** M. E. WILKINS *Humble Romance* 139 An thar was Israel in his *meetin coat, an' me in my best gown. **1644** *Early Rec. Portsmouth, Rhode Island* (1901) 32 It is..ordered that the businesse of such *metinge dayes shal be specified. **1686** S. SEWALL *Diary* (1878) I. 146 Mr. Moodey exercises at our House being our meeting-day. **1776** T. PENNANT *Tour in Scotl. & Voy. Hebrides 1772* II. 364 After three market-days or meeting-days within the town of Halifax. **1835** *Gentl. Mag.* Nov. 491 My father drank to Church and King, And the *Meeting-folks love no such thing. **1856** M. J. HOLMES *'Lena Rivers* 30 Nobody'd think any better of them for being rigged out in their very best *meetin' gowns. **1887** M. E. WILKINS *Humble Romance* 300 Hatty in her meeting-gown of light-brown delaine, and her white *meeting-hat..was not pretty. **1818** BUSBY *Gram. Mus.* 152 Those notes of the passage immediately under the *meeting points of the sign [for diminuendo-crescendo]. **1872** LIDDON *Elem. Relig.* ii. 75 Miracle is the meeting-point between intellect and the moral sense. **1761** FITZGERALD in *Phil. Trans.* LII. 154, I.. have placed the instruments for the inspection of the gentlemen of the Royal Society, in their *meeting-room. **1851** *Knickerbocker* XXXVIII. 372 (Th.), Some people call it 'caraway' and 'aniseseed', but we call it '*meetin'-seed', 'cause we cal'late it keeps us awake in meetin'. **1889** R. T. COOKE *Steadfast* xxxix. 414 Mothers of young families distributed fragrant bunches of dried 'meetin' seed' among their flocks. **1905** E. U. VALENTINE *Hecla Sandwith* 25 [He] sat contentedly munching 'meeting seed' which Molly Tucker..had given him. **1940** E. EARLY *New England Sampler* 319 In old New England gardens there grew three plants called *Meetin' Seed*—Fennel, Dill, and Caraway. **1887** W. MORRIS *Odyss.* II. 147 Zeus..sent him two ernes to fly Adown..that *Meeting-stead to find. **1639** *Rec. Colony & Plantation New Haven* (1857) I. 26 On the Lords Day in the *meeting time. **1881** MRS. STOWE *Sam Lawson's Oldtime Fireside Stories* 200 We were in disgrace, we boys; and the reason of it was this: we had laughed out in meeting-time!

'meeting, *ppl. a.* [f. MEET *v.* + -ING^2.]

1. That meets.

1592 SHAKS. *Ven. & Ad.* 820 The wilde waues..Whose ridges with the meeting cloudes contend. **1606** —— *Tr. & Cr.* I. iii. 7 As knots by the conflux of meeting sap, Infect the sound Pine. **1720** GAY *Fan* II. 156 Where meeting beeches weave a grateful shade. *a* **1881** ROSSETTI *House of Life* xii, Still glades; and meeting faces scarcely fann'd.

b. In *Joinery*. Often hyphened with the sb.

1825 J. NICHOLSON *Operat. Mechanic* 590 The staff stile, which imitates the meeting-stiles. *Ibid.* 625 The common rafters..must be so arranged that a rafter shall lie under every one of the meeting-joints. **1844** STEPHENS *Bk. Farm* II. 538 The three equal wheels..are set in the sheers—the first of the three being upon the carriage-axle, which is in halves as before, and the meeting-ends supported on the sheers. **1875** KNIGHT *Dict. Mech.*, *Meeting-post*..that stile of a canal-lock gate which meets the corresponding stile of the other gate at the mid-width of the bay.

†**2.** Coming forward in response or welcome; responsive. *Obs.*

1548 UDALL, etc. *Erasm. Par. 1 Tim.* i. 15 The thing that they renounce, is withal studious endeuoure to be embraced (as they saye) with meting armes [L. *obuiis, ut aiunt, ulnis amplectendum*]. **1632** MILTON *L'Allegro* 138 Married to immortal verse Such as the meeting soul may pierce. **1639** SALTMARSHE *Pract. Policy* 122 Bee not too meeting, and seeme not too hasty in accepting graces and favours. **1664** SOUTH *Serm.* (1823) I. xiv. 385 He..offers himself to the visits of a friend with facility, and all the meeting readiness of appetite and desire.

meetinger ('mi:tɪŋə(r)). [f. MEETING *vbl. sb.* + -ER^1.] One who 'goes to meeting'; a dissenter.

1810 S. GREEN *Reformist* I. 185, I plainly see, Sir, you are a methodist, or a meetinger, I believe you call it. **1890** JESSOPP *Trials Country Parson* 68 The Meetinger keeps himself posted up with the last clerical escapade.

'meeting-house.

†**1.** A (private) house used for a meeting. *Obs.*

1658 WOOD *Life* 14 July (O.H.S.) I. 256 They had entertain'd him with most excellent musick at the meeting house of William Ellis.

2. a. A place of worship: in the general sense, now only *U.S.* In England from the 17th c. always a nonconformist or dissenting place of worship, a conventicle: now only (exc. with reference to the Quakers) in jocular or disparaging use.

1632 *Rec. Cambridge, Mass.* (1901) 4 Every person..shall [be]..within [the] meeting-house in the Afternoone. **1634** *Rec. Watertown, Mass.* (1894) I. 1 The charge of the Meeting House shal be gathered by a Rate justly levied. **1636** *Plymouth Col. Rec.* (1855) I. 41 There to build a meeting howse and towne. **1687** EVELYN *Diary* 10 Apr., There was a wonderful concourse of people at the Dissenters' Meeting-house in this parish. **1766** WESLEY *Jrnl.* 10 Apr., It [a deed] everywhere calls the house a Meeting-House, a name which I particularly object to. **1809** KENDALL *Trav.* I. xii. 132 Two meeting-houses, one belonging to quakers, and the other to baptists. **1847** W. E. FORSTER in Reid *Life* (1888) I. vii. 207 Last evening I deluded them into a Methody meeting-house. **1896** MRS. H. WARD *Sir G. Tressady* 140 The brick meeting-houses in which they [the villages] abounded. **1910** *Dialect Notes* III. 445 *Meeting house*,..church. Older generation. **1959** *Amer. Speech* XXXIV. 9 Around the turn of the nineteenth century, Baptists,..and others began dropping the term *meetinghouse* and replacing it with *church*.

b. *Polynesia*. A tribal hall (see quot. 1949).

1865 L. ANDREWS *Dict. Hawaiian Lang.* 144/1 *Ha-le-ha-la-wai, s. Hale* and *halawai*, to meet; assemble. A meeting house; a synagogue; a place of meeting. **1897** A. HAMILTON *Maori Art* (1901) II. 112 *Whare-matoro*, a large meeting house. **1944** D. STEWART in D. M. Davin *N.Z. Short Stories* (1953) 267 The young Maori..led me over to the meeting-house, a long, low, gusty barn of a building. **1949** P. BUCK *Coming of Maori* (1950) III. iv. 374 The meeting houses formed the social focus of the tribe, hence they were generally named after tribal ancestors. When the people assembled within its walls for tribal discussions, the orators were justified when they said, 'We have gathered together within the bosom of our ancestor.' The carved meeting houses were a source of pride to the people and they gave an atmosphere to the village that nothing else could equal. **1960** N. HILLIARD in C. K. Stead *N.Z. Short Stories* (1966) 239 There I go walking into the meeting-house with my shoes on. **1974** *N.Z. Listener* 20 July 10/4 They are clustered, the kuia, around the tent in which the body lies alongside the meetinghouse.

3. *attrib.*, as ***meeting-house chamber, ground, land, lot, post, rate, yard***; †**meeting-house man**, a nonconformist or dissenter.

1651 *Official Rec. Springfield, Mass.* (1898–9) I. 200 The above mentioned bargain about the *meeting house chamber. **1689** S. SEWALL *Diary* (1878) I. 286 Paid 40 £.. for the Releases of *Meetinghouse Ground. **1690** *Ibid.* 334 Mrs. Judith Winthrop's Deed of the *Meeting-house Land in Boston. **1735** *New Hampsh. Probate Rec.* (1914) II. 523, I give to my son..a lot of land lying in the *Meeting house lot. **1711** *Countrey-Man's Let. to Curat* 22 These were not *Meeting-House-Men in whose Favours the Councel thus Wrote,..but some of 'em Parsons, some Vicars, some Curats, &c. **1647** *Rec. Watertown, Mass.* (1894) I. 11 A wrighting shall be sett upon the *meting-house-post, to give Warning [etc.]. **1656** *Ibid.* 48, 2ly [that] ye give acompt of the *meeting howse rate. **1712** *New Hampsh. Probate Rec.* (1907) I. 687 Northerly on the fence by the *metinge house yard. **1808** *Beverley Lighting Act* 27 Any meeting-house, chapel, church yard, and meetinghouse yard.

'meeting-place.

A place in which a meeting occurs or is held; †a meeting-house.

1553 *Reg. Privy Council Scot.* I. 149 Nocht half ane Scottis myle fra the said metynge place. **1589** NASHE *Anat. Absurd.* (1590) B iij b, They will include it [the name of the Church] onely in their couenticles, and bounde it euen in Barnes, which many times they make their meeting place. **1659–60** PEPYS *Diary* 7 Feb., I saw Monk's soldiers abuse Billing and all the Quakers that were at a meeting-place there. *c* **1710** CELIA FIENNES *Diary* (1888) 58 The Church is neate and pretty..here is also a good large Meeteing place. **1897** *Allbutt's Syst. Med.* IV. 338 The organ thus lies at the meeting-place of the hypochondriac, right lumbar, and epigastric regions.

†**'meetly**, *a. Obs.* Forms: 4 **metli**, 4–6 **meteli**, 4–7 **metely**, 6 **metly**, **meetelie**, **-ly**, 6–7 **meetly**. [f. MEET *a.* + -LY^1. (But the early form *metli* may represent OE. *ȝemetlic*, f. *ȝemet* measure, moderation.)]

1. Moderate; of moderate size or quantity.

a **1300** *Cursor M.* 18847 Metli har was on his chin. ? *a* **1366** CHAUCER *Rom. Rose* 822 With metely mouth and yen greye. *c* **1500** MEDWALL *Nature* (Brandl) I. 317 Leue thyn hawt conceytys and take a metely way. **1505** in *Mem. Hen. VII* (Rolls) 232 The fingers of the said queen be right fair and small, and of a meetly length and breadth before, according unto her personage very fair handed. **1523** LD. BERNERS *Froiss.* I. xvi. 18 Wherof they were well served for their horses, and at a metly price. **1600** HOLLAND *Livy* x. xii. 359 After he had left at Falerii all his bag and baggage with a meetly garrison [L. *cum modico præsidio*]. **1620** VENNER *Via Recta* iv. 73 Mullet..is of pleasant taste, and of meetly nourishment.

2. Fitting, proper, suitable, meet.

1426 AUDELAY *Poems* 4 Fore love together thus cum thai schal be, Fore this makus metely maryage. **1492** *Rolls of Parlt.* VI. 455/1 Here is the place most metely for you, and where ye shall lak nothing. **1579–80** NORTH *Plutarch, Lysander* (1595) 492 It was better, and meetelier for the Spartans that they should choose them for their kinges, whom they found the meetest men of all their magistrates. **1633** GERARD *Part. Descr. Somerset* (1900) 182 The most refined and meetly English now spoken.

meetly ('mi:tlɪ), *adv.* Forms: 5 **metly**, 5–6 **mete-**, 6 **meate-**, **meete-**, 6– **meetly**. [f. MEET *a.* + -LY^2. (But perh. partly repr. OE. *ȝemetlíce*, f. *ȝemet*: see prec.)]

1. Moderately, fairly, tolerably. (Common in the 16th c.)

c **1400** *Destr. Troy* 3069 Full metely made of a meane lenght. **1476** *Paston Lett.* III. 157 He is well spokyn in Inglyshe, metly well in Frenshe, and verry perfite in Flemyshe. **1551** RECORDE *Pathw. Knowl.* I. Defin., Nowe haue you heard as touchyng circles meetely sufficient instruction. **1609** HOLLAND *Amm. Marcell.* 402 Tall of stature, and faire of complexion, their haire meetly yellow. **1657** HOWELL *Londinop.* 339 A fine and meetly large Church.

2. Fitly, suitably; as is meet.

1502 HEN. VII in Ellis *Orig. Lett.* Ser. I. I. 55 The King both with men and money metely and conveniently..wol yeve assistence. **1656** SANDERSON *Serm.* (1689) 323 Then are we meetly prepared for his service. **1813** SCOTT *Trierm.* I. xx, The monarch meetly thanks express'd. **1857** H. MILLER *Test. Rocks* iii. 138 And with this ancient elephant there were meetly associated in Britain..many other mammals of corresponding magnitude. **1878** BROWNING *La Saisiaz* 72 How I may..fix where change should meetly fall.

meetness ('mi:tnɪs). [f. MEET *a.* + -NESS.] The condition of being meet; fitness, suitableness.

c **1449** PECOCK *Repr.* III. xi. 347 Certis this fadir were not to be blamed, if he wolde ordeyne that these schoon be notabli widdir than the meetenes of hem wolde aske, as for the firste dai in which thei schulden be worne. **1586** W. WEBBE *Eng. Poetrie* (Arb.) 46 Ye meetnesse of our speeche to receiue the best forme of Poetry. *c* **1600** SHAKS. *Sonn.* cxviii, And, sicke of wel-fare found a kind of meetnesse To be diseas'd ere that there was true needing. **1758** S. HAYWARD *Serm.* xiv. 409 Holiness is a meetness for heaven. **1867** H. MACMILLAN *Bible Teach.* x. (1870) 202 They have no title to heaven and no meetness for it.

meetre, obs. form of METRE.

meeve, mefe, meffynge: see MOVE, MOVING.

mefeesh, var. MAFEESH *a.* and *int.*

‖**méfiance** (mefjɑ̃s). [Fr.] Mistrust.

1876 H. JAMES *Let.* 8 Feb. in R. B. Perry *Tht. & Char. W. James* (1935) I. 366 Touches that are too raffiné, words and phrases that are too striking, or too complete, inspire him with an instinctive *méfiance*. **1921** D. H. LAWRENCE *Sea & Sardinia* vii. 285 Partly it is barbaric *méfiance*. **1938** E. BOWEN *Death of Heart* II. vi. 280 'Oh, did you,' said Dickie, with a certain *méfiance*.

Meg^1 (mɛg). [var. of MAG *sb.*^{2}] A pet form of the female name *Margaret*, used *dial.* to indicate a hoyden, coarse woman, etc.; also in the proverbial phrases ***Meg's delight*** or ***diversions***, 'the deuce and all', 'the very mischief' (see E.D.D. and cf. MAG *sb.*^{2} 1). ***Long Meg, Meg of Westminster***, the appellation of a virago whose exploits were famous in the 16th c.; hence proverbially in allusive uses.

c **1538** LYNDESAY *Supplic. Syde Taillis* 67 Ane mureland Meg, that mylkis the ȝowis. **1572** *Satir. Poems Reform.* xxxii. 37 And we, agane, wald by ane Fraer of Fegges,..and sell to landwart Megges. **1582** (*title*) The life and pranks of Long Meg of Westminster. **1593** NASHE *Strange News* Wks. (Grosart) II. 223 Thou art a puissant Epitapher. Yea? thy Muses foot of the twelues; old long Meg of Westminster? Then, I trowe thou wilt stride ouer Greenes graue and not stumble. **1602** DEKKER *Satiro-mastix* F ij b, Tis thou makst me so, my Long Meg a Westminster, thou breedst a scab, thou ——. **1611** MIDDLETON & DEKKER *Roaring Girl* K j b,

Was it your Megge of Westminsters courage that rescued mee? *a* **1700** B. E. *Dict. Cant. Crew, Long-meg*, a very tall Woman. **1725** RAMSAY *Gentle Sheph.* I. i, Then fare ye weel Meg-Dorts. **1813** W. BEATTIE *Yule Feast* (1871) 11 Twa bunching megs. **1834, 1849** [see MAG *sb.*² 1]. **1874** S. BEAUCHAMP *Grantley Grange* I. 202 Well, it were Meg's delight, sir; and in the middle on it all..he roars out [etc.].

b. The great 15th c. gun in Edinburgh Castle was called ***Mons Meg*** (? from having been cast at Mons in Flanders), ***Muckle, Great Meg***. Also ROARING MEG.

1650 in Scott *Prov. Antiq. Scot.* (1826) p. xxi *note*, The great iron murderer called Muckle Megg. **1650** *Art. Rendition Edinb. Castle* 4 Three Iron Guns, besides the Great Mag. **1753** MAITLAND *Hist. Edinb.* 164 A huge Piece of Ordnance, resembling an old-fashioned Mortar.. denominated Mounts-Megg.

meg² (mɛg). *slang* and *dial.* [Of obscure origin. Cf. MAG *sb.*³ and MAKE *sb.*³]

† **1.** A guinea. *Obs.*

1688 SHADWELL *Sqr. Alsatia* I. i, *Sham.* No, no; Meggs are Guineas, Smelts are half-guineas. **1691** *Islington Wells* 12 To see a Town not far from Dover, Butter'd with Megs and Smelts all over. *c* **1742** in Hone *Every-day Bk.* II. 527 Tickets to be had, for three Megs a Carcass.

2. A half-penny: = MAG *sb.*³, MAKE *sb.*³

1781 [see MAG *sb.*³]. **1872** in Hartley *Yorks. Ditties* (ed. 2) 90 He wodn't pay a meg.

Meg³: see MEGGER.

mega- (ˈmɛgə), before a vowel **meg-**, repr. Gr. μεγα-, comb. form of μέγας great, used esp. in many scientific terms (often having correlatives f. MICRO-, and sometimes also synonyms f. MACRO-), as **megabacteria** *pl.* [BACTERIUM]; **ˈmega-city**, a very large city; **megaˈcocci** *pl.* [Gr. κόκκος a berry], names of two stages in the development of Billroth's *Coccobacteria septica*; **megaˈcolon** *Path.* [COLON¹], gross dilatation and hypertrophy of the colon; a colon in this condition; **megaˈfrustule** [FRUSTULE] *Biol.*, a frustule of comparatively large size; **megaˈgamete** [GAMETE], one of the larger motile sexual (female) cells of algæ; **megaˈkaryocyte** (also **-caryo-**) *Biol.* [KARYO- + -CYTE], any of the giant cells with large multilobar nuclei which are found in small numbers in normal blood marrow and which are believed to give rise to blood platelets by their fragmentation; so **ˌmegakaryoˈcytic** *a.*; **megallantoid** *a.* [ALLANTOID], having a large allantois; *sb.*, an animal so characterized; **ˈmega-machine**, a social system dominated by technology and functioning without regard for specifically human needs; **mega-millionaire**, a multi-millionaire; **megaˈnucleus** [NUCLEUS], the nucleus proper as distinguished from the micronucleus or paranucleus; **meˈgaphyllous** *a. Bot.* [Gr. φύλλον leaf], having large leaves; **ˈmegaripple** *Geol.*, an extensive undulation of the surface of a sandy beach or sea bed that is typically tens of metres from crest to crest and tens of centimetres in height, but may be much larger; **ˈmegashear** *Geol.* [SHEAR *sb.*²], a transcurrent fault in which the displacement is very large (of the order of a hundred kilometres); **ˈmegasporange, -spoˈrangium** (pl. -ia) *Bot.* [SPORANGIUM], a sporangium containing megaspores; **ˈmegaspore** *Bot.* [SPORE], the larger of the two kinds of spores in heterosporous cryptogams; later, extended to the homologous structure in seed plants (i.e. the immature embryo sac); **megaˈsporophyll** *Bot.* [SPOROPHYLL], any leaf or modified leaf which bears megasporangia; **megaˈtechnics**, the extensive mechanization of a society with a highly developed technology; **megaˈvitamin** *attrib.*, based upon the administration of large doses of vitamins; **megaˈzoosporange** *Bot.* [ZOOSPORANGIUM], the special sporangium in *Hydrodictyon* which contains a swarm of megazoospores; **megaˈzoospore** *Bot.* [ZOOSPORE], a zoospore of relatively large size. Also MEGABASITE, MEGACEPHALIC, etc. Cf. MEGALO-.

1883 MACALISTER tr. *Ziegler's Path. Anat.* I. §185. 265 According to size we may distinguish them as micrococci, mesococci, and *megacocci, and microbacteria, mesobacteria, and *megabacteria. **1968** *Harper's Mag.* Feb. 61 The noisy, ugly, chaotic, increasingly dangerous and ever-spreading *mega-cities. **1975** *N.Y. Times* 20 Aug. 37/2 Or, as the Mailer-Breslin platform said, 'New York will become the first insane asylum of the megacity.' **1906** DORLAND *Med. Dict.* (ed. 4) 419/2 *Megacolon. **1908** *Practitioner* Sept. 459 True congenital idiopathic megacolon, or Hirschsprung's disease. **1949**, etc. Megacolon [see HIRSCHSPRUNG]. **1895** *Naturalist* 260 Drawings made with the camera lucida..of the conjugating process showing the *megafrustules. **1891** HARTOG in *Nature* 17 Sept. 484 The smaller (micro-)gamete is male, the larger *(mega-)gamete, female. **1897** PARKER & HASWELL *Text-bk. Zool.* I. 71 Union always taking place between a large cell or megagamete and a small cell or microgamete. **1890** W. H. HOWELL in *Jrnl. Morphol.* IV. 118, I shall speak of them hereafter as *megakaryocytes, or large nucleated giant cells. **1938** H. DOWNEY *Handbk. Hematol.* I. vii. 449 (*heading*) Blood platelets and megacaryocytes. **1966** *Lancet* 24 Dec. 1416/1 There was virtual absence of erythroid precursors in the bone-marrow, with normal myeloid series and megakaryocytes. **1938** H. DOWNEY *Handbk. Hematol.* I. vii. 482 Many of the blood platelets of the peripheral blood were rather large *megacaryocytic fragments. *Ibid.*, Wuyts produced a marked megacaryocytic reaction in rabbits. **1972** *Nature* 7 Apr. 293/3 Erythroid, granulocytic or megakaryocytic cells. **1877** W. TURNER *Hum. Anat.* II. 869 So large and persistent is the sac of the allantois in the ordinary Ruminantia [etc.], that M. H. Milne-Edwards has grouped them together as *Megallantoids. **1967** L. MUMFORD *Myth of Machine* i. 12 Cosmic order was the basis of this new human order. The exactitude in measurement, the abstract mechanical system, the compulsive regularity of this '*megamachine', as I shall call it, sprang directly from astronomical observations and scientific calculations. **1967** *Harper's Mag.* Oct. 110 The mega-machine was 'invisible' because its tens of thousands of interacting parts were human. **1970** L. MUMFORD in *New Yorker* 31 Oct. 85 What is needed to save mankind from the megamachine—or whatever controls the megamachine—is to displace the mechanical world picture with an organic world picture, in the center of which stands man himself. **1973** *Physics Bull.* Jan. 5/2 The sophisticated industrial megamachines of the present century are also based on system centred technology, and the troubles they have led us into are only too clear. **1968** *Time* 8 Mar. 21 Nelson Aldrich Rockefeller, 59, a *megamillionaire via the Rockefellers, a political patrician through the Aldriches. **1973** *Observer* 12 Aug. 11/1 He has managed to reach the near top of the mega-millionaire league table. **1897** PARKER & HASWELL *Text-bk. Zool.* I. 84 The *meganucleus in *Paramœcium* is ovoid. **1903** S. J. HICKSON in E. R. Lankester *Zool.* I. *Protozoa* 372 The Meganucleus (= Macronucleus). **1904** *Science* 21 Oct. 529/1 The pteridophytes..may be disposed according to the prevalent size of their leaves in a series, leading from microphyllous to *megaphyllous types. **1909** D. H. SCOTT in A. C. Seward *Darwin & Mod. Sci.* 203 A large proportion of the higher plants are microphyllous in comparison with the highly megaphyllous fern-like forms from which they appear to have been derived. **1953** L. M. J. U. VAN STRAATEN in *Geol. en Mijnbouw* XV. 3/1 Initial stages of transverse *megaripples covered with the common small scale current ripples are frequently seen on the large, sandy tidal flats. **1968** *New Scientist* 18 Apr. 113/1 The strange features that have come to be known as megaripples—regularly formed giant undulations, measured by echo sounders, that straddle the ocean floor with distances of three to four miles between crest and crest. **1954** S. W. CAREY in *News Bull. Geol. Soc. Austral.* July 1 The known *megashears, where orogens are displaced hundreds of km., were next examined. **1971** *Nature* 2 July 23/1 We regard these two [American] plates as distinct entities separated mainly by the Cayman-Puerto Rico megashear. **1889** BENNETT & MURRAY *Cryptog. Bot.* 11 It [*i.e.* a spore-case] is a *megasporange or a microsporange, according as it contains megaspores or microspores. **1886** *Athenæum* 10 Apr. 491/2 Mr. Bennett has made use of the term *Megasporangia in describing the heterosporous vascular cryptogams. **1858** CARPENTER *Veg. Phys.* §734 Three or four roundish fleshy bodies (*megaspores). **1889** BENNETT & MURRAY *Cryptog. Bot.* 11 Two different kinds of spore,.. megaspores and..microspores. **1900** *Jrnl. R. Microsc. Soc.* 605 The division of the megaspore of *Erythronium* is.. essentially the same as in *Lilium philadelphicum*. **1965** K. ESAU *Plant Anat.* (ed. 2) xviii. 563 The ovule developing from the placenta of the ovary is the seat of formation of the megaspores (or macrospores). **1902** *Encycl. Brit.* XXV. 432/2 The microsporophylls (stamens) and the *megasporophylls (carpels). **1967** L. MUMFORD *Myth of Machine* ix. 189 When all the components, political and economic, military, bureaucratic and royal, must be included, I shall usually refer to the 'megamachine': in plain words, the Big Machine. And the technical equipment derived from such a megamachine thence becomes '*mega-technics'... At its inception no inferior chief could organize the megamachine and set it in motion. **1967** *Harper's Mag.* Oct. 108 Under the impulsion of unprecedented 'mega-technics'—'nuclear energy, supersonic transportation, cybernetic intelligence, and instantaneous distant communication'—the far-flung settlement patterns of Megalopolis are resistlessly expanding in many parts of the world, transforming man and the earth. **1970** *New Yorker* 10 Oct. 76/2 The idea of universal mechanization (mega-technics) was established in the megamachine of Egypt. **1970** L. PAULING *Vitamin C & Common Cold* 70 The use of very large amounts of vitamins in the control of disease has been called *megavitamin therapy. Megavitamin therapy is one aspect of orthomolecular medicine. It is my opinion that in the course of time it will be found possible to control hundreds of diseases by megavitamin therapy. **1972** *Daily Colonist* (Victoria, B.C.) 20 Feb. 19/2 Dr. Abram Hoffer, a Saskatchewan psychiatrist who pioneered megavitamin therapy for schizophrenia. **1975** *Nature* 14 Aug. 529/3 Efforts of the FDA to regulate megavitamin promotion, however, were set back by a court decision and by the passage last year of a bill in the US Senate that specifically prevents the FDA from classifying high-potency vitamin preparations as drugs. **1889** BENNETT & MURRAY *Cryptog. Bot.* 297 Fig. 260..C. *megazoosporange..D. *megazoospores.

b. Prefixed to names of units of measurement, force, resistance, etc., *meg(a-* is used to denote 'a million times'; e.g. ***megabar*** [BAR *sb.*⁶ 1, 2], ***megabit*** [BIT *sb.*⁴], ***megabyte, megacurie, megadalton*** [DALTON²], ***megadyne, meg(a)erg*** (cf. *megalerg* s.v. MEGALO-), ***megafarad, megahertz, meg(a)joule, megametre, meganewton, megaparsec, megapone, megarad, megavolt*** (hence ***megavoltage***), ***megawatt, megaweber, megohm***; also **ˈmegabuck** *colloq.* [BUCK *sb.*⁸], a million dollars; **ˈmegacorpse**, a million dead bodies, a term used in estimating the possible effects of nuclear warfare; **ˈmegadeath**, the death of a million persons, as a unit in estimating the possible effects of nuclear warfare; **megaunit** (ˈmɛgəjuːnɪt) *Biol.* and *Med.*, a million international units.

1903 RICHARDS & STULL *New Method determining Compressibility* 43 The pressure of a megadyne per square centimeter would be called a *megabar. **1925** J. JOLY *Surface-Hist. Earth* iii. 55 The megabar is one million dynes per sq. cm. It is nearly one atmosphere. **1969** *New Scientist* 9 Jan. 81/3 The pressure needed to produce metallic hydrogen may well be less than a megabar. **1957** *Electronics* 1 Oct. 163 (*heading*) High-speed computer stores 2·5 *megabits. **1972** *Sci. Amer.* Sept. 139/2 A broadcast-quality color-television signal in digital code calls for 90 megabits per second. **1946** *Picture Post* 7 Dec. 10/1 Atomic research is so expensive that American scientists have ceased to use the dollar as their unit. They have laughingly coined the term '*megabuck'—one megabuck equals a million dollars. **1952** *Galaxy* June 16/2, I had already pencilled in a tentative campaign in the budget well under a megabuck. **1968** *Amer. Anthropologist* LXX. 608/2 He certainly had no megabuck research grant. **1973** *Nature* 12 Jan. 86/1 The diamond project was not cheap (I think I first heard the word 'megabuck' in connexion with diamond synthesis). **1973** *Megabyte [see *kilobyte* s.v. KILO- b]. **1958** *Tuscaloosa* (Alabama) *News* 4 Sept. 4/5 The eeriest new word coined in the space age is '*Mega-corpse'. **1968** *Economist* 13 Apr. 29/2 Dr. Kahn, a controversial figure best known for his calculations on thermo-nuclear war and his invention of the term 'megacorpse', has begun to broaden the institute's scope. **1947** *Radiology* XLIX. 326/1 The amount of radioactivity from these fission products with moderately long half-lives was in the range of hundreds of *megacuries. **1957** *New Scientist* 10 Oct. 28/3 Large amounts of radioactivity can be measured in megacuries: one megacurie is the equivalent of one [metric] ton of radium. **1960** *New Biol.* XXXI. 121 The weight of 1 per cent of the particle [*sc.* T2 phage] is 1·2 Md. [*Note*] Md = *megadaltons or 1,000,000 molecular weight units. **1973** *Sci. Amer.* Apr. 22/2 The molecular weight of the *E. coli* chromosome is 2,500 megadaltons. **1953** *Birmingham* (Alabama) *News* 21 June E3/1 He does not deal in numbers of atomic bombs or precise methods of delivery, in kilotons or *megadeaths. **1959** *New Statesman* 21 Nov. 693/3 Mr Krushchev's announcement that a single Soviet factory is producing 250 megadeath weapons a year is a timely reminder of the risks of delay. **1962** R. E. LAPP *Kill & Overkill* viii. 100 '55 megadeaths' does not sound as bad as 55 million Americans dead. **1971** *Islander* (Victoria, B.C.) 5 Dec. 15/4 The brain that was good enough to produce the skilled hunter was also good enough to produce huge empires, noble causes to die for, vast armies, and megadeath. **1871** *Brit. Assoc. Rep.* II. 29 The author [Everett] proposed..that the names *kilodyne*, *megadyne, *kilopone*, *megapone be employed to denote a thousand and a million dynes and pones. **1891** L. CLARK *Dict. Metric. Meas.*, *Meg-erg, or *Megalerg* = one million ergs... *Meg-joule* = one million joules. **1868** L. CLARK *Electr. Meas.* 44 *Megafarad. **1941** *Chem. Abstr.* XXXV. 2159 (*heading*) Molecular changes following irradiation with hertzian waves of a frequency of 1875 *megahertz. **1966** *Electronics* 3 Oct. 171 Transatlantic airliners will communicate with the satellite on the 118 to 136 Megahertz band. **1971** D. W. SCIAMA *Mod. Cosmol.* iv. 52 The revised 3C catalogue gives a virtually complete list of the [radio] sources between declinations −5° and +90° that are brighter than 9 flux units at 178 megahertz. **1892** B. SMITH & HUDSON *Arith.* 147 A million joules make a *megajoule. **1902** *Encycl. Brit.* XXXIII. 812/1 *Megametre (astronomy) ..1,000,000 metres. **1970** *Sci. Jrnl.* June 16/1 It is possible to transform maraging steels with a high content of embrittling components..into fine wire having a tensile strength of about 5200 *meganewtons per square metre. **1975** *Physics Bull.* Apr. 165/1 Traditionally, standard forces up to meganewtons are produced on deadweight machines. **1933** *Proc. Nat. Acad. Sci.* XIX. 1001 At the distance of three *megaparsecs, the largest galaxies in the Virgo group have linear diameters of approximately six kiloparsecs. **1938**, etc. Megaparsec [see HUBBLE]. **1973** *Physics Bull.* Nov. 674/1 There is evidence for an intergalactic [magnetic] field of order 10^{-13} T which seems to be uniform over scales of several thousand megaparsecs. **1958** *Times Rev. Industry* July 25/3 For many applications the *megarad (one million rads) is more suitable. **1960** A. CHARLESBY *Atomic Radiation & Polymers* iv. 65 A reactor running at 100 megawatts power output could provide 30 megarads to 1 ton of material. **1953** *Economist* 31 Jan. 307/2 During last summer, British production [of penicillin] fell below the 1951 weekly average of 1,216,000 *mega units. **1970** *New Scientist* 19 Mar. 543/1, 2.4 megaunits of long acting benzathine penicillin can maintain a treponemicidal blood and tissue level for three weeks or more. **1868** L. CLARK *Electr. Meas.* 43 *Megavolt. **1924** C. R. UNDERHILL *Magnets* i. 11 The volt per microcoulomb or the megavolt per coulomb. **1957** *Technology* July 181/1 A research physicist at work on the 450 megavolt synchro-cyclotron. **1961** *Lancet* 16 Sept. 616/2, 3 patients with a recurrent infiltrating neoplasm after *megavoltage therapy were included. **1961** D. W. SMITHERS in Tanner & Smithers *Tumours Oesophagus* xxi. 265 The next step forward came with the introduction of megavoltage [X-ray] apparatus. **1900** WEBSTER, *Megawatt. **1955** *Times* 16 July 6/4 The first atomic stations of the Central Electricity Authority will have two nuclear reactors each, together providing a net output of electricity of 100 to 200 megawatts. **1969** P. W. MCDANIEL in D. Z. Robinson et al. *Nucl. Energy Today & Tomorrow* (1971) II. iv. 210 In 1962 the largest U.S. power reactor was 180 megawatts. **1868** L. CLARK *Electr. Meas.* 43 One million ohms = 1 *megohm. **1902** *Encycl. Brit.* XXVIII. 4/2 Convenient multiples and subdivisions of the ohm are the microhm and the megohm.

megabasite (mɛgəˈbeɪsaɪt). *Min.* [a. G. *megabasit* (Breithaupt 1852), f. Gr. μέγα-ς great + βάσι-ς base: see -ITE.] A synonym of HÜBNERITE.

The name is meant to express the fact that the mineral contains more basic matter than wolframite.

1868 DANA *Syst. Min.* (ed. 5) 604.

megacephalic (mɛgəsɪˈfælɪk), *a. Anat.* [f. Gr. μέγα-ς great + κεφαλή head: cf CEPHALIC.] Large-headed; *spec.* (see quot. 1882).

1879 FLOWER *Catal. Mus. Coll. Surg.* I. 10 Crania of unusually large size (Megacephalic). **1882** *Quain's Anat.* (ed. 9) I. 80 Those [skulls] exceeding 1450 cubic centimeters in capacity are megacephalic.

So **megaˈcephalous** *a.*, large-headed.

1856 in MAYNE *Expos. Lex.* **1890** in *Syd. Soc. Lex.*

‖**megaceros** (mɛˈgæsərɒs). *Palæont.* [mod.L., f. Gr. μέγα-ς great + κέρας horn, after ῥινόκερως RHINOCEROS.] The extinct Irish elk.

1865 PHILLIPS *Addr. Brit. Assoc.* 32 Can our domestic cattle..be traced back to..contemporaries of the urus, megaceros, and hyæna?

megacerotine (mɛgəˈsɛrəʊtaɪn), *a. Zool.* [f. mod.L. *megacerōt-*, MEGACEROS + -INE.] Of or pertaining to the megaceros.

1884 FLOWER *Catal. Mus. Coll. Surg.* II. 307 Megacerotine Group.

megacerous (mɛˈgæsərəs), *a.* [Formed as MEGACEROS + -OUS.] 'Having very large horns, as the extinct Irish elk' (*Cent. Dict.*).

1856 MAYNE *Expos. Lex.*, *Megacerus*..megacerous.

megacheilous (mɛgəˈkaɪləs), *a. Ent.* [f. Gr. μέγα-ς great + χεῖλ-ος lip + -OUS.] Having a large labrum.

1890 *Syd. Soc. Lex.*

megacheiropteran (mɛgəkaɪˈrɒptərən), *a.* and *sb. Zool.* [f. mod.L. *Megacheiroptera* (see MEGA- and CHEIROPTERA) + -AN.] **a.** *adj.* Pertaining to the group *Megacheiroptera* or fruit-eating bats. So **megacheiˈropterous** *a.* with the same sense. **b.** *sb.* A bat of this group.

1890 in *Century Dict.*

megacosm (ˈmɛgəkɒz(ə)m). [f. Gr. μέγα-ς great + κόσμος world, COSMOS.] = MACROCOSM.

1617 MIDDLETON & ROWLEY *Fair Quarrel* Ded., If..this Megacosme, this great world, is no more then a Stage. **1624** [T. SCOTT] *Vox Dei* 48 As thus it is, in the microcosme of priuate estates, so it is, in the megacosme of publique wealths also. **1711** *Brit. Apollo* No. 137. 2/1 Supposing the Microcosm to be as well the Subject of your Contemplations as the Megacosm. **1851** G. S. FABER *Many Mansions* 157 As Light was let in upon the darkened Megacosm: so [etc.].

megacycle (ˈmɛgəsaɪk(ə)l). [f. MEGA- b + CYCLE *sb.*] **a.** One million cycles (of an oscillation or other periodic phenomenon). **b.** *ellipt.* One million cycles per second; = *megahertz* (MEGA- b).

1928 STERLING & KRUSE *Radio Manual* 45 The frequency of 1,000,000 cycles can then be expressed as 1,000 kilocycles or 1 megacycle. **1936** A. HUND *Phenomena High-Frequency Syst.* ii. 56 It may be assumed from the theory of the ionized layer that for waves below 10 m in length (above 30 megacycles/sec) the sky wave passing toward this layer will never be returned. **1955** *Radio Times* 22 Apr. 3/1 The BBC decided..to build..short-range V.H.F. stations operating on frequencies around 90 megacycles per second. **1959** [see KILOCYCLE]. **1971** C. BONINGTON *Annapurna South Face* iii. 38 Kelvin plunges into details of frequencies, megacycles and all the other gibberish of technical experts.

megaderm (ˈmɛgədɜːm). *Zool.* [ad. mod.L. *Megaderma*, f. Gr. μέγα-ς great + δέρμ-α skin.] A horse-shoe bat of the genus *Megaderma*.

1840 *Cuvier's Anim. Kingd.* 72 The Megaderms.

megadont (ˈmɛgədɒnt). *Ethnology.* [Badly f. Gr. μέγα-ς great + ὀδοντ-, ὀδούς tooth.] Having teeth of large size, esp. as measured by a recognized dental index. (Cf. MACRODONT.)

1884 FLOWER in *Jrnl. Anthrop. Inst.* XIV. 185 The first three species are therefore strongly megadont. *Ibid.*, The Megadont section, being composed exclusively of the black races. *Ibid.* 186 Megadont Races. Melanesians [etc.].

megagametophyte (mɛgəgæˈmiːtəʊfaɪt). *Bot.* [f. MEGA- + *gametophyte* (s.v. GAMETE).] A gametophyte that develops from a megaspore; a female gametophyte.

1933 *Amer. Jrnl. Bot.* XX. 217 (*heading*) Morphology of the megagametophyte and the embryo sporophyte of *Isoetes lithophila*. **1964** H. J. DITTMER *Phylogeny & Form Plant Kingdom* xxi. 487 A single megagametophyte may contain several archegonia with ripe eggs.

megagnathous (mɛˈgægnəθəs), *a. Anat.* [f. Gr. μέγα-ς great + γνάθ-ος jaw + -OUS.] Having a large jaw (*Syd. Soc. Lex.* 1890); = MACROGNATHOUS.

‖**megalacria** (mɛgəˈlækrɪə). *Path.* [mod.L., f. Gr. μεγαλο- great + ἄκρα, ἄκρον extremity: see -IA.] A morbid condition in which the hands and feet and the face, esp. the bones of the face, are abnormally enlarged.

1891 CUNNINGHAM in *Trans. R. Irish Acad.* XXIX. 611 Dr. Haughton and Dr. Ingram have furnished me with the much more correct term of 'megalacria'.

megalæsthete (mɛgəˈliːsθiːt). *Biol.* [f. Gr. μεγαλο- great + αἰσθητής 'one who perceives' (here used for 'organ of sense').] A supposed tactile organ occupying the megalopore of chitons.

1884 MOSELEY in *Rep. Brit. Assoc.* (1885) 781 A series of elongate cylindrical organs of touch ('megalæsthetes'). **1885** —— in *Q. Jrnl. Micr. Sci.* XXV. 43 To which I shall apply the name megalæsthetes, believing that they are peculiar organs of touch and are at all events peculiar to Chitonidæ.

megaleme (ˈmɛgəliːm). *Ornith.* [ad. mod.L. *Megalæma* (G. R. Gray 1842 *Megalaima*), f. Gr. μέγα-ς great + λαιμός throat.] A bird of the genus *Megalæma* of scansorial barbets.

1890 in *Century Dict.*

megalith (ˈmɛgəlɪθ). *Antiq.* [Back-formation from MEGALITHIC.] A stone of great size used in construction, or for the purpose of a monument.

1853 LUKIS in *Archæologia* XXXV. 233 Celtic Megaliths. **1872** J. FERGUSSON *Rude Stone Monum.* 181 *note*, Hundreds of our countrymen rush annually to the French megaliths. **1894** *Chamb. Jrnl.* 555 A circle comprising..thirty freestone megaliths.

megalithic (mɛgəˈlɪθɪk), *a. Antiq.* [f. Gr. μέγα-ς great + λίθος stone + -IC.] **1.** Consisting or constructed of great stones. Hence, of a period, a people, etc.: Characterized by the erection of megalithic monuments.

1839 A. HERBERT (*title*) Cyclops Christianus, or an Argument to disprove the supposed Antiquity of Stonehenge and other Megalithic Erections. **1865** LUBBOCK *Preh. Times* 53 This appears to have been the finest megalithic ruin in Europe. **1867** SIR J. Y. SIMPSON *Archaic Sculpt.* 144 A race of Megalithic Builders—if we may so call them. **1875** D. WILSON in *Encycl. Brit.* II. 338/1 The rudiments of architectural skill pertaining to the Megalithic Age.

2. Special collocations, as **megalithic fathom**, a name given to a measure of length equal to 5·44 ft., used in the construction of certain British megalithic monuments; **megalithic yard**, half a megalithic fathom (2·72 ft.).

1961 A. THOM in *Math. Gazette* XLV. 83 The unit of length used was the same from Land's End to John o' Groats... This unit was 5·44 ft... Half of this, 2·72 ft., might be called the Megalithic Yard, but whether this or the Megalithic Fathom (5·44 ft.) was the length of the standard rod carried about the country it is not possible to say. **1962** —— in *Jrnl. R. Statistical Soc.* A. CXXV. 243 In an earlier paper (Thom, 1955) it was shown that in a statistically significant number of cases the diameters of stone circles were multiples of 5·44 ft. This might be called the megalithic fathom. *Ibid.* 246 About 55 per cent. of all circles have the diameter an even number of fathoms. In setting out a circle it is the radius rather than the diameter which has to be measured out on the ground, so that where the diameter is an odd number of fathoms, that is, in about 45 per cent. of all circles, the constructors used a half fathom. Thus for our present purpose it seems better to take as the unit a length of half a fathom (2·72 ft) and for convenience call it the megalithic yard. **1967** —— *Megalithic Sites in Britain* v. 36 We first demonstrate that there is a presumption amounting to a certainty that a definite unit was used in setting out these rings. It is proposed to call this the Megalithic yard (MY). Two of these might be called the Megalithic fathom... It will appear that the Megalithic yard is 2·72 ft and so the Megalithic fathom is 5·44 ft. **1975** *Country Life* 16 Jan. 134/2 The megalithic yard of 2·72 ft that Professor Thom has recently so convincingly shown to have been used by the builders of Stonehenge, Avebury, Carnac.

megalo- (ˈmɛgələʊ), before a vowel **megal-**, a. Gr. μεγαλο-, combining form of μέγας great (cf. the equivalent MEGA-), used in many scientific terms; **megalenceˈphalic** *a.* [ENCEPHALIC], pertaining to or affected with hypertrophy of the encephalon or cerebrum; **ˈmegalerg** *Physics* = *megerg* [see MEGA- b]; **ˈmegaloblast** *Path.* [-BLAST], one of the nucleated red blood-disks found in the blood of anæmic persons (*Syd. Soc. Lex.*); hence **megaloˈblastic** *a.*, containing megaloblasts; ‖**megaloˈcardia** *Path.* [Gr. καρδία heart], the condition of having an abnormally large heart (Dunglison *Med. Lex.* 1855); **megaloˈcarpous** *a. Bot.* [Gr. καρπός fruit], having large fruit (Mayne); **megaloceˈphalic** *a.* = MEGACEPHALIC; so **megaloˈcephalous** *a.* (*Cent. Dict.* 1890); **megaloˈcephaly**, the condition of being megacephalic; also *Path.*, an enlargement of the head occurring in *Leontiasis ossea* (Osler *Princ. & Pract. Med.*, ed. 4, 1901, p. 1145); **megaloˈchirous** *a.* [Gr. χείρ hand], having large hands or large tentacles (Mayne); **ˈmegalocyte** *Path.* [Gr. κύτος a hollow], one of the large red blood-corpuscles seen in anæmia (*Syd. Soc. Lex.*); **megaloˈdontous** *a. Anat.* [Gr. ὀδούς tooth], large-toothed (*ibid.*); ‖**megaloˈgastria** *Path.* [Gr. γαστ(ε)ρ-, γαστήρ stomach + -IA], the condition of possessing great stomach capacity; **megalogoˈnidium** *Bot.*, a gonidium larger than others produced by the same species (*Cent. Dict.*); = *macrogonidium*; **ˈmegalopod** *a.* and *sb.* [Gr. πούς foot], (*a*) *adj.* having large feet, megalopodous; (*b*) *sb.* a person with large feet; **megaˈlopodous** *a.* [Gr. πούς foot], having a long foot (*Syd. Soc. Lex.*); **ˈmegalopore**, one of the larger pores in the dorsal shell of certain chitons; **ˈmegalosphere** [SPHERE], the initial chamber of a megalospheric foraminifer; hence **megaloˈspheric** *a.*, applied to certain foraminifera having a large initial chamber and a single large nucleus.

1856 MAYNE *Expos. Lex.*, *Megalanthus*..*megalanthous. **1900** FLETCHER in *Lancet* 2 June 1589/1 *Megalencephalic would be a more suitable name [*sc.* for cerebral hypertrophy]. **1873** *Brit. Assoc. Rep.* 225 The mechanical equivalent of one gramme-degree (Centigrade) of heat is 41.6 *megalergs, or 41,600,000 ergs. **1899** CAGNEY tr. *Jaksch's Clin. Diagn.* i. (ed. 4) 43 Microcytes, *megaloblasts and nucleated red corpuscles are also not of rare occurrence. **1900** ELDER in *Lancet* 28 Apr. 1199/2 The majority of the cells being of the *megaloblastic type. **1904** *Brit. Med. Jrnl.* 10 Sept. 584 A stage when almost all the red cells are nucleated, and most of them megaloblastic. **1876** DUNGLISON *Med. Lex.*, **Megalocephalic*, having an unusually large head. **1878** BARTLEY tr. *Topinard's Anthropol.* I. v. 176 Megalocephalic, skull of very large capacity. *Ibid.* 543 *Index*, *Megalocephaly. **1889** D. J. HAMILTON *Text-bk. Pathol.* I. 462 Giant blood corpuscles or *megalocytes running up to 14 μ in diameter. **1897** *Allbutt's Syst. Med.* III. 485 A stomach otherwise normal, may yet be of extraordinary capacity—a condition which has received such names as megastria and *megalogastria. **1909** *Cent. Dict.* Suppl., *Megalopod, *a.* and *n.* **1951** AUDEN *Nones* (1952) 40 The basalt Tombs of the sorcerers shatter And their guardian megalopods Come after you pitter-patter. **1884** MOSELEY in *Rep. Brit. Assoc.* (1885) 781 A series of pores ('*megalopores') by which this surface is covered. **1894** LISTER in *Phil Trans.* CLXXXVI. 406 The parent shell is *megalospheric, the *megalosphere being pear-shaped.

megalograph (ˈmɛgələʊgrɑːf, -æ-). [f. MEGALO- + -GRAPH. In Fr. *mégalographe*.] (See quot. 1876.)

[**1876** *Sci. Amer.* XXXV. 345/2 In this exhibit is an admirably designed camera lucida, or, as it is here called, *megalographe*... It differs from the ordinary camera lucida, inasmuch as it admits of drawing directly from the objects under the microscope. **1884** KNIGHT *Dict. Mech.* Suppl., *Megalographe*.] **1890** *Century Dict.*, *Megalograph*.

†**megaˈlography.** *Obs.* [f. MEGALO- + -GRAPHY.] 'A drawing of pictures at large' (Bailey 1731).

megalomania (mɛgələʊˈmeɪnɪə). *Nosology.* [f. MEGALO- + MANIA.] The insanity of self-exaltation; the passion for 'big things'. Often *transf.*

1890 in *Syd. Soc. Lex.* **1892** *Contemp. Rev.* Feb. 166 Here again megalomania—the desire to 'do the great'—had the upper hand. **1895** *Spectator* 2 Mar. 291 The patient exhibits erotomania or megalomania, or a maudlin..liability to emotion. **1897** MARQ. SALISBURY in *Daily Chron.* 17 Nov. 8/2 A common intellectual complaint..which I may name (as I see Mr. Gladstone has consecrated the word) megalomania—the passion for big things simply because they are big. **1904** A. GRIFFITHS *Fifty Years Public Service* xiv. 222 Megalomania was strangely prevalent among these criminal lunatics.

Hence **megaloˈmaniac** *a.* and *sb.*; **megalomaˈniacal** *a.*

1890 *Syd. Soc. Lex.* s.v. *Megalomania*, Many megalomaniacs are illegitimate children. **1892** *Contemp. Rev.* Feb. 167 A sort of megalomaniacal aberration. **1899** *Pall Mall Gaz.* 14 Feb. 2/3 A megalomaniac world is always apt to regard a waistcoat-pocket community as a joke. **1899** *Speaker* 29 July 105/1 He [Signor Crispi] was neither himself a megalomaniac nor the framer of the Triple Alliance. **1929** W. J. LOCKE *Ancestor Jorico* 29 They had to attribute the great fortune to the megalomaniac dreams of a dying man. **1974** J. POPE HENNESSY *R. L. Stevenson* xii. 226 A project emanating from Fanny's now megalomaniac brain.

megalomartyr (mɛgələʊˈmɑːtə(r)). *Eccl. Hist.* [a. late Gr. μεγαλόμαρτυρ: cf. MEGALO- and MARTYR.] (See quot. 1756.)

1756 A. BUTLER *Lives Saints* 7 Feb. (1821) II. 90 Among those holy martyrs whom the Greeks honour with the title of Megalomartyrs (*i.e.* great martyrs) as St. George, St. Pantaleon, &c. **1840** I. TAYLOR *Anc. Chr.* (1842) II. 186 The 'Megalomartyrs' or Dii Selecti.

megalonyx (mɛgəˈlɒnɪks). *Palæont.* [mod.L., f. Gr. μεγαλο- great (see MEGALO-) + ὄνυξ claw.] A large fossil sloth-like edentate from the post-pliocene strata of North America.

1797 JEFFERSON *Writ.* (1859) IV. 195 The Megalonyx, as we [? *sc.* the American Philosophical Society] have named him. **1813** BYRON in Moore *Lett. & Jrnls.* (1830) I. 461 The Mammoth and Megalonyx. **1839** *Penny Cycl.* XV. 73/1 The Megalonyxes were provided with a tail.

attrib. **1887** *Amer. Naturalist* XXI. 459 The Megalonyx Beds.

megalopa (mɛgəˈləʊpə). *Zool.* [mod.L., fem. of **megalōpus*, a. Gr. μεγαλωπός large-eyed, f. μεγαλο- MEGALO- + ὠπ-, ὤψ eye.] = MEGALOPS 1.

1815 W. E. LEACH *Malacostraca Podophth. Brit.* Plate xvi, Megalopa *Leach*. **1862** W. B. CARPENTER *Microsc.* §408 (ed. 3) 659 In which stage the [crab-] larva is remarkable for the large size of its eyes, and hence received the name of *Megalopa* when it was supposed to be a distinct type. **1880** HUXLEY *Crayfish* 284 The Megalopa stage of the crab.

megalophonic (mɛgələˈfɒnɪk), *a.* [f. Gr. μεγαλόφων-ος, f. μεγαλο- great + φωνή voice, sound: see -IC.] Having a loud strong voice.

1856 MAYNE *Expos. Lex.* **1890** *Syd. Soc. Lex.*

megalophonous (mɛgəˈlɒfənəs), *a.* [Formed as prec. + -OUS.] **a.** Of imposing sound. (*Burlesque nonce-wd.*)
1819 SHELLEY *Peter Bell* Prol. 36 *note*, The oldest scholiasts read 'A dodecagamic potter': this is at once more descriptive and more megalophonous.
b. Having a great voice (Crabb 1823).

megalopic (mɛgəˈlɒpɪk), *a.* *Zool.* [f. Gr. μεγαλωπ-ός or mod.L. *megalōp-*: see MEGALOPS.] Resembling a megalops.
In mod. Dicts.

megalopine (ˈmɛgələʊpaɪn), *a.* (and *sb.*) [ad. mod.L. *megalōpin-us*, f. *megalōp-*, MEGALOPS.]
1. Of or pertaining to the megalops stage of decapod crustaceans (Webster *Suppl.* 1902).
2. Pertaining to, or connected with, the sub-family *Megalopinæ* of fishes. As *sb.*, a fish of this sub-family. (*Cent. Dict.* 1890.)

megalopolis (mɛgəˈlɒpəlɪs). [f. Gr. μεγαλο- great + πόλις city; see MEGALO-, -POLIS.] Used (freq. with capital initial) as a designation of a very large city or its way of life; also, the practice of building large cities. Also *attrib.* Cf. †MEGAPOLIS.
The normal Eng. pl. (after METROPOLIS) would be *megalopolises*, but the irregular formation *megalopoli* occurs occasionally.
1832 WEBSTER, Megalopolis. **1869** M. COLLINS *Ivory Gate* II. 211 Paul and his wife are back in the precincts of Megalopolis. **1945** *Archit. Rev.* XCVII. 5/1 Normal impulses, suppressed and frustrated in Megalopolis, return in the form of collective aggressions. **1951** M. MCLUHAN *Mech. Bride* (1967) 38/2 Megalopolis is both humanly and economically wasteful. **1959** *Economist* 25 Apr. 330/1 The dream of a massive shift of the American economy to the Great Lakes, and the growth of a vast new megalopolis along their shores. **1964** *Economist* 12 Sept. 1010/2 'Megalopolis'—or excessive urbanisation resulting from modern technology. **1968** C. A. DOXIADIS *Between Dystopia & Utopia* 4 The city turned into a metropolis, which has now grown into a megalopolis. **1969** *Daily Tel.* 29 May 16/3 Los Angeles..is a vast megalopolis of over 10 million, not so much a city as an endless sprawling suburb without a centre ..and criss-crossed with multi-lane freeways. **1970** *New Scientist* 5 Feb. 259/1 From the mud hut level of Indian villages and towns to the concrete towered megalopoli of Europe and North America. **1972** *Listener* 9 Mar. 293 Big money is unlikely to be made except perhaps in a very few megalopolis centres.

So **megaloˈpolitan** *sb.* and *a.*, (*a*) *sb.* an inhabitant of a megalopolis; (*b*) *adj.* of or pertaining to a megalopolis or the way of life characteristic of large cities.
[**1633** E. GRIMSTONE tr. (*title*) The History of Polybius the Megalopolitan.] **1926** *Brit. Weekly* 29 July 355/3 Follows the winter season, with its dawning of 'megalopolitan civilization', its extinction of spiritual creative force. **1930** E. WAUGH *Labels* I. 15 After the exaggerated cleanliness and sparkle of the preceding country, this exaggerated sombreness and squalor, called up..all the hatred and weariness which the modern megalopolitan sometimes feels towards his own civilization. **1946** *Theology* XLIX. 94 The report deplores the sprawl of houses but not that of megalopolitan culture. **1957** R. HOGGART *W. H. Auden* 15 Auden's interest is in men in urban societies, in men now living through their perennial moral and metaphysical problems in megalopolitan settings. **1971** *Daily Tel.* 30 Nov. 10/4 The same international, megalopolitan forces, rolling over everything in their path, threaten Welsh and English alike. **1974** *Listener* 10 Jan. 53/2 Megalopolitan life brings with it anonymity and bewilderment.

‖**megalops** (ˈmɛgəlɒps). *Zool.* [mod.L. *megalōps*, altered form of MEGALOPA; cf. L. *Cyclōps*, Gr. Κύκλωψ.]
1. Originally, the name of a supposed genus of crustaceans (characterized by eyes of enormous size), now known to represent merely a particular stage in the development of crabs. Now retained as a descriptive term for a crab in this 'large-eyed' stage of development.
1855 W. S. DALLAS in *Syst. Nat. Hist.* I. 312 In this form the young animals have received the name of *Megalops*. **1896** KIRKALDY & POLLARD tr. *Boas' Text Bk. Zool.* 226 There is no mysis-stage, but the young one passes through a prawn-stage (the so-called megalops).
2. The typical genus of the sub-family *Megalopinæ* of the family Elopidæ of clupeoid fishes.
1840 *Cuvier's Anim. Kingd.* 321. **1880** GÜNTHER *Fishes* 661.

‖**megalopsia** (mɛgəˈlɒpsɪə). *Path.* [mod.L., f. Gr. μεγαλο- great (see MEGALO-) + -οψία, in nouns of agency f. combs. of ὀπ- to see: cf. AUTOPSY *sb.*] A pathological condition of the eyes in which objects appear enlarged.
1890 *Syd. Soc. Lex.*

megalopsychic, *a.* *nonce-wd.* [f. Gr. μεγαλό-ψυχ-ος 'great-souled' (f. μεγαλο- great + ψυχ-ή soul) + -IC.] Magnanimous.
1896 *Spectator* 7 Mar. 337/1 The megalopsychic monster whose immaculateness is so uninteresting that [etc.].

†**megalopsychy**. *Obs.* *rare*⁻⁰. [ad. Gr. μεγαλοψυχία, noun of quality f. μεγαλόψυχος: see prec.] 'Magnanimity' (Blount *Glossogr.* 1656).

‖**megalosaurus** (ˌmɛgələʊˈsɔːrəs). *Palæont.* Pl. -i. [mod.L., f. Gr. μεγαλο- great (see MEGALO-) + σαῦρος lizard.] An extinct genus of gigantic terrestrial carnivorous lizards, the remains of which have been found in the Oolite; an animal of this genus. Also anglicized **ˈmegalosaur**.
1824 BUCKLAND in *Trans. Geol. Soc.* Ser. II. I. 391, I have ventured, in concurrence with my friend and fellow-labourer, the Rev. W. Conybeare, to assign to it the name of Megalosaurus. *Ibid.* 392 The megalosaurus itself was probably an amphibious animal. **1841** OWEN in *Brit. Assoc. Rep.* (1842) 104 The carnivorous Megalosaur. **1844** ANSTED *Geol., Introd.* etc. I. 409 The Megalosaurus was a carnivorous reptile, closely allied to some existing lizards. **1864** MISS YONGE *Trial* I. 87 He is physically as strong as a young megalosaur.

Hence **megaloˈsaurian** (*a*) *adj.*, having the character of a megalosaurus; (*b*) *sb.*, a megalosaurus or similar animal. Similarly **megaloˈsauroid** *a.* and *sb.*
1841 OWEN in *Rep. Brit. Assoc.* (1842) 109 Their Megalosaurian character. **1844** ANSTED *Geol., Introd.* etc. I. 410 When first the Megalosaurian remains were described by Dr. Buckland. **1890** *Century Dict.*, Megalosauroid *a.* and *n.*

†**megaloscope**. *Obs.* Also *erron.* 8 **megalascope**, 9 **megalscope**. [f. MEGALO- + -SCOPE.]
1. A hand lens for examining small but not microscopic objects.
c **1790** IMISON *Sch. Art* I. 227 This is an optical instrument that may be properly called a megalascope for the hand; because it is adapted for viewing all the larger sort of small objects. **1815** J. SMITH *Panorama Sci. & Art* I. 476 The Hand Megalscope.
2. An endoscope with a magnifying apparatus.
1902 in WEBSTER Suppl.

megameter (mɛˈgæmɪtə(r)). [a. F. *mégamètre*: see MEGA- and -METER.] **a.** An instrument for measuring large objects. **b.** An instrument for taking astronomical measurements.
1767 *Ann. Reg.* (1772) 96 To make trial of some instruments designed to facilitate the determination of the longitude by sea, and particularly..the megametre or grand measurer of the Sieur de Charnieres. **1777** *Phil. Trans.* LXVII. 789 An Account of a new Micrometer and Megameter [was] read June 19. **1875** KNIGHT *Dict. Mech.* 1419/1 *Megameter*, an instrument for determining the longitude by observation of the stars.

†**meganology**. *Obs.* *rare*⁻⁰. [Badly f. μέγα-ς great + -OLOGY.] (See quot.)
1656 BLOUNT *Glossogr.*, *Meganologie*, a speaking or discourse of magnitude or greatness.

Meganthropus (mɛˈgænθrəʊpəs). [mod.L. (G. von Koenigswald, 1942), f. Gr. μεγα- great + ἄνθρωπος man.] A large fossil hominid of the genus so called, esp. *Meganthropus palæojavanicus*, fragments of whose remains were first discovered by G. von Koenigswald in Java in 1941. Also *attrib.*
1942 G. VON KOENIGSWALD *Let.* 15 Jan. in *Anthropol. Papers Amer. Mus. Nat. Hist.* (1945) XL. 16/1 *Meganthropus* is a newly discovered fossil hominid perhaps related to *Australopithecus*. **1944** *Science* 16 June 480/2 The *Meganthropus* jaw is much too large and massive. **1959** J. D. CLARK *Prehist. S. Afr.* iii. 73 It has been suggested that the *Meganthropus* form living in Java at this time is another early hominid of the Australopithecine group. **1967** M. H. DAY *Guide to Fossil Man* (ed. 2) 238 (*caption*) The Meganthropus II mandibular fragment.

megaphone (ˈmɛgəfəʊn), *sb.* [f. Gr. μέγα-ς great + φωνή voice, sound.]
1. An instrument for carrying sound a long distance, invented by T. A. Edison.
1878 *Sci. Amer.* XXXIX. 111/3 Now, at last, we have a megaphone, which is to the ear almost what the telescope is to the eye. **1879** PRESCOTT *Sp. Telephone* 561 One of the most interesting experiments made by Mr. Edison..is that of conversing through a distance of one and a half to two miles, with..a few paper funnels. These funnels constitute the megaphone.
2. A large speaking trumpet. Also *attrib.* and *fig.*
1896 *Boston* (Mass.) *Jrnl.* 5 Nov. 6/4 The Society for the Suppression of Needless Noise should regulate the use of the megaphone. **1898** *Westm. Gaz.* 25 Apr. 7/2 Captain Bob Evans..shouted through the megaphone. **1905** 'O. HENRY' *Trimmed Lamp* (1907) 180 The megaphone man roars out at you to observe the house of his uncle. **1909** *Daily Chron.* 7 June 5/1 They felt sure that the British Press were not the paid megaphones of financial buccaneers. **1951** M. MCLUHAN *Mech. Bride* (1967) 138/1 Is there any role left for the individual in a world of collective megaphone personalities? **1960** V. NABOKOV *Invitation to Beheading* xvi. 162 The director..examined a piece of paper, and in a megaphone voice addressed Cincinnatus. **1968** *Listener* 20 June 803/1 Tell Joanna she must stop being a megaphone for a negative tendency in a parent-child participating democracy.
Hence **megaˈphonic** *a.*
1881 MRS. LYNN LINTON *My Love* I. xvi. 290 She had escaped even the microscopic research and the megaphonic talk of a small country place like Highwood.

megaphone (ˈmɛgəfəʊn), *v.* [f. the sb.] *intr.* and *trans.* To speak or utter (as) through a megaphone. Hence **ˈmegaphoned**, **ˈmegaphoning** *ppl. adjs.*
1901 *Daily Colonist* (Victoria, B.C.) 30 Oct. 1/7 The Cufic ..megaphoned the lightship asking to be reported. **1901** R. C. LEHMANN *Anni Fugaces* 70 The air grows blue with loud reproaches Hurled at the crews by megaphoning coaches. **1912** J. H. MOORE *Ethics & Educ.* 97 Long ago she [*sc.* a dog] and her associates were accustomed to megaphone to each other in this way. **1920** *Glasgow Herald* 21 Apr. 8 The captain megaphoned an invitation to come on to the flag deck. **1927** H. G. WELLS in *Sunday Express* 2 Oct. 12/7 The impressive gatherings.., the megaphoned and broadcast speeches. **1963** A. SMITH *Throw out Two Hands* iv. 46 Aldermanic individuals had to be given captive ascents on a long rope while they megaphoned their impressions to the gaping faces down below. **1967** *Punch* 26 July 121/2 The compere's megaphoned voice could be heard from the concert hall.

ˈmegaphonist. [f. MEGAPHONE 2.] One who speaks through a megaphone.
1906 'O. HENRY' *Four Million* 203 'What's eatin you?' demanded the megaphonist. **1949** *Box Office* 5 Nov. 20 Elliot Nugent is the megaphonist and William H. Wright the producer. *Ibid.* 21 As the month began, no megaphonist had been set for 'Jet Pilot'.

megapode (ˈmɛgapəʊd), **megapod** (-pɒd). *Ornith.* [ad. mod.L. *Megapodius*, f. Gr. μέγα-ς great + ποδ-, πούς foot.] Any bird of the genus *Megapodius* or of the family *Megapodiidæ*, a mound-bird or mound-builder, native of Australia and the Malay Archipelago. Also *attrib.*
1857 *Carpenter's Zool.* I. 484 The family of Megapodidæ, or Megapodes, is peculiar to Australia and the adjacent islands. **1880** A. R. WALLACE *Isl. Life* i. 4 The strange mound-building megapodes. **1900** *Edin. Rev.* Apr. 500 The remarkable Megapode birds.
Hence **meˈgapodan**, (*a*) *adj.* of or belonging to the megapodes; (*b*) *sb.* a megapode (*Cent. Dict.* 1890).

†**meˈgapolis**. *Obs.* [f. Gr. μέγα-ς + πόλις city.] A chief city.
1638 SIR T. HERBERT *Trav.* (ed. 2) 61 [Amadavad is] at this present the Megapolis of Cambaya. **1855** I. C. PRAY *Mem. J. G. Bennet* 450 Capital alone is wanting to make this city in point of influence..the megapolis of the world.

megar, obs. form of MEAGRE *a.*

Megarian (mɛˈgɛərɪən), *a.* and *sb.* Also **Megarean**. [f. L. *Megara*, Gr. Μέγαρα (neut. pl.), a city in Greece + -IAN; also f. L. *Megarē-us* + -AN.]
A. *adj.* **a.** Pertaining to the school of philosophy founded c. 400 B.C. by Euclides of Megara.
1878 *Encycl. Brit.* VIII. 578/1 Four distinct philosophical schools trace their immediate origin to the circle that gathered round Socrates—the Megarian, the Platonic, the Cynic, and the Cyrenaic.
b. Applied to a type of bowl of the Hellenistic period, usu. hemispherical and with relief ornament.
[**1874** A. DUMONT *Peintures Céramiques* vi. 50 On leur a donné en Grèce le nom de Mégare, parce qu'elles se rencontrent..sur le territoire de cette ville.] **1905** H. B. WALTERS *Hist. Anc. Pott.* I. xi. 499 A series of vases known as Megarian or Homeric bowls, of hemispherical form, without handles. **1960** R. M. COOK *Greek Painted Pott.* vii. 215 The so-called 'Megarian' bowls, commercially the most successful relief ware of the Greeks, extend through most of the Hellenistic world and age. The shape is roughly hemispherical with or without a low ring foot. **1961** *Oxf. Univ. Gaz.* 10 Mar. 832/2 A 'Megarian' bowl with figures of Pan and (?) Heracles and Auge.
B. *sb.* A member or adherent of the Megarian school.
1603 HOLLAND *Plutarch* Explan. Words, *Megarian questions*, that is to say, such as were propounded and debated among the Philosophers Megarenses. **1656** STANLEY *Hist. Philos.* IV. *Euclid* ii. 28 Litigious Euclid.. Who the Megareans mad contention taught. **1838** MORRISON tr. *Ritter's Anc. Philos.* II. 131 This doctrine had been previously attributed to the Megarians by Aristotle. **1848** *Schools Anc. Philos.* 110 The Megareans.

Megaric (mɛˈgærɪk), *a.* and *sb.* [ad. Gr. Μεγαρικ-ός belonging to Megara.] = prec.
1656 STANLEY *Hist. Philos.* IV. *Euclid* i. 27 Euclid (instituter of the Megarick Sect). **1744** BERKELEY *Siris* §312 In consequence of that Megaric doctrine, we can have no sense but while we actually exert it. **1845** LEWES *Hist. Philos., Anc.* II. 7 The Megaric doctrine is therefore the Eleatic doctrine, with an Ethical tendency borrowed from Socrates. **1867** —— *Ibid.* (ed. 3) I. 175 The Megarics.

‖**megaron** (ˈmɛgərən). [Gr. μέγαρον hall.] The great central hall of a type of house characteristic esp. of the Mycenæan period. Also *attrib.*
1877 *Architect* 4 Aug. 54/2 Palace of Ulysses at Ithaca... Within was another portico and a stately doorway, admitting to the *megaron*; this was a large apartment, unfloored, but lofty, roofed, and used as a dining hall by the men. **1906** *Ann. Brit. Sch. Athens* XII. 253 A fixed central hearth was introduced into the megaron to suit the needs of a more rigid climate than the original Africo-Aegean one. **1907** T. D. SEYMOUR *Life Homeric Age* vi. 188 The great hall or *megaron* is the centre of the life of the household—not unlike the baronial halls of the old English castles. **1928** C. DAWSON *Age of Gods* iii. 58 They brought with them a new

type of house, with a pillared porch opening into a single large room or hall. This is the so-called Megaron hall, which was characteristic of the early Greeks. **1950** H. L. LORIMER *Homer & Monuments* i. 6 A form of the megaron house, rectangular, with a single entrance to the main room and a more or less central hearth standing clear of the walls. **1963** *New Scientist* 9 May 301 Evidence which strongly suggests that the 'megaron' was an Anatolian rather than a Greek invention.

megarrhine (ˈmɛgəraɪn), *a.* *Zool.* Also **megarhine**. [ad. mod.L. *megarrhinus*, f. Gr. μέγα-ς great + ῥῑν-, ῥίν, ῥίς nose.] 'Great-nosed'; the distinctive epithet of an extinct species of rhinoceros.

1865 DAWKINS in *Nat. Hist. Rev.* July 403 All the three species [of Rhinoceros]—the megarhine, leptorhine, and tichorhine, are found together at Crayford and Ilford. **1895** LYDEKKER *Brit. Mammalia* 304 Both the Leptorhine (*R. leptorhinus*) and Megarhine (*R. megarhinus*) Rhinoceroses.. differ essentially from the woolly kind.

megascope (ˈmɛgəskəʊp). [f. MEGA- + -SCOPE.] **1.** A modification of the camera obscura or magic lantern for throwing a reflected magnified image of an object upon a screen.

1831 BREWSTER *Optics* xl. §192 A modification of the camera obscura called the megascope is intended for taking magnified drawings of small objects placed near the lens. **1879** *Sci. Amer.* XLI. 63 An improved megascope,..in which the object to be viewed is firmly fixed upon a sliding screen [etc.]. **1893** *Brit. Jrnl. Photogr.* XL. 798 Pictures projected upon the screen by means of the megascope or aphengescope lantern.

2. (See quot.)

1875 KNIGHT *Dict. Mech.* 1419/1 *Megascope.* 1. A solar microscope in which the objects are opaque and illuminated in front by reflecting mirrors.

megascopic (mɛgəˈskɒpɪk), *a.* [Formed as prec. + -IC.]

1. Visible to the naked eye without the aid of a microscope; = MACROSCOPIC.

1879 RUTLEY *Study Rocks* xi. 194 Crystals, both megascopic and microscopic, occur..in some perlites. **1890** BILLINGS *Nat. Med. Dict.*, *Megascopic*, macroscopic.

2. a. Of or pertaining to the megascope or to the projection of images of opaque objects upon a screen. **b.** Enlarged or magnified, *spec.* of photographic pictures, images, etc. (Webster 1902).

Also **mega'scopical** *a.*; **mega'scopically** *adv.*

1890 in *Century Dict.* **1894** H. S. WASHINGTON *Volcanoes Kula Basin* 21 Megascopically it is much more frequent and prominent than either the augite or the olivine. **1909** J. P. IDDINGS *Igneous Rocks* I. II. iii. 445 Coarse-grained rocks.. must be measured megascopically on the surface of proper-sized specimens. **1938** A. JOHANNSEN *Descr. Petrogr. Igneous Rocks* IV. 377 Megascopically, laths of black pyroxene up to 2 cm. in length are seen. **1943** *Amer. Mineralogist* XXVIII. 499 The material under the botryoidal surface is also megascopically crystalline. **1970** K. C. JACKSON *Textbk. Lithology* iv. 214 Epidote..is difficult to recognize megascopically because of small grain size and masking by associated micaceous minerals.

megasea (mɛˈgæsɪə). [mod.L. (A. H. Haworth *Saxifragëarum Enumeratio* (1821) 6), f. Gr. μέγας large, in reference to the large leaves of the plants.] A perennial herb of the genus formerly so called; = BERGENIA.

1886 [see BERGENIA]. **1914** G. JEKYLL *Colour Schemes for Flower Garden* (ed. 3) 96 The Megaseas persist the whole year round. **1962** R. PAGE *Educ. Gardener* I. iv. 135 The bergenias which we used to call saxifrage or megasea are handsome through the twelve months of the year with their bold leathery leaves.

megaseme (ˈmɛgəsiːm), *a.* and *sb.* *Anat.* [a. F. *mégasème* (Broca), f. Gr. μέγα-ς great + σῆμα sign.] **a.** *adj.* Having a large orbital index; *spec.* having an orbital index over ·89. **b.** *sb.* A skull having a large orbital index.

[**1878** BARTLEY tr. *Topinard's Anthrop.* II. ii. 258 M. Broca has created three general terms..bearing reference to this [orbital] index,..namely, mégasème when the index is large [etc.].] **1879** FLOWER *Catal. Mus. Coll. Surg.* I. 256 The females are all megaseme. **1882** *Quain's Anat.* (ed. 9) I. 83 If above 89, it [the orbital index] is megaseme.

megasine, obs. form of MAGAZINE.

1616 BULLOKAR *Eng. Expos.*, *Megasine*, a storehouse for warre.

‖**megass** (mɛˈgæs). Also **megasse**. [Of unknown origin: cf. BAGASSE.] The fibrous residue after the expression of sugar from the cane. Also *attrib.*

1847 *Simmonds's Colonial Mag.* June 187 The megass is carried to the megass-house, and from there to the fire-place, all by manual labour. **1887** *Encycl. Brit.* XXII. 625/2 In a three-roller [sugar-] mill they consist of a cane, top, and megass roller respectively. **1887** MOLONEY *Forestry W. Afr.* 453 Megasse or Bagasse, the refuse cane after the juice has been extracted.

megasthene (ˈmɛgəsθiːn). [ad. mod.L. *megasthena* neut. pl. (see definition), f. Gr. μέγα-ς great + σθέν-ος strength.] A member of the *Megasthena* or second order of Mammalia in Dana's classification, comprising the largest and most powerful mammals. Hence **megasthenic** *a.*, of or pertaining to this order; also used by Dana in etymological sense, 'having great strength'.

1863 DANA in *Amer. Jrnl. Sci.* Ser. II. XXXV. 71 There is a close parallelism with the Mutilates, the lowest of the Megasthenes. *Ibid.* XXXVI. 8 Among Crustaceans, the megasthenic and microsthenic divisions of which..stand widely apart. *Ibid.* 327 The Megasthenic-type.

megastructure (ˈmɛgəˌstrʌktjʊə(r)), *sb.* [f. MEGA- + STRUCTURE *sb.* 5.] A massively large construction or complex, esp. one consisting of many buildings. Hence ˌ**mega'structural** *a.*

1965 *Life* 24 Dec. 146 Other planners foresee skeletal Megastructures of enormous, light-weight 'space frames'—grid-works towering high in the air. **1967** *Listener* 6 July 12/2 Those temporary heavens of exhibition and transport—the Victorian megastructures—..have acquired a permanence in people's minds out of all proportion to the functions they originally housed. *Ibid.* 20 July 73/3 The megastructural schemes by Corbusier's followers in Japan. **1968** *Daily Tel.* (Colour Suppl.) 13 Dec. 30/1 Rudolph's design..truly qualifies as a 'megastructure', a city-within-a-city. **1973** *Observer* (Colour Suppl.) 2 Dec. 33/3 An early attempt to blend housing, commerce and townscape in one huge building—the lumpish description, 'urban megastructure', has been much used.

megathere (ˈmɛgəθɪə(r)). *Palæont.* Anglicized form of MEGATHERIUM.

1839 OWEN in *Trans. Geol. Soc.* (1842) VI. 93 The external cuneiform bone of the Megathere differs [etc.]. **1887** SIR H. H. HOWORTH *Mammoth & Flood* 346 Great mylodons and thickly-hided megatheres.

megatherial (mɛgəˈθɪərɪəl), *a.* [f. MEGATHERIUM + -AL[1].] Resembling the megatherium; in quots. *fig.*, ponderous, unwieldy.

1894 *Nature* 26 July 301 The disorderly offspring of a quite megatherial wit. **1898** H. G. WELLS *Cert. Personal Matters* 82 A vast edifice..with which a Megatherial key was identified.

mega'therian, *a.* and *sb.* [f. MEGATHERIUM + -AN.] **a.** *adj.* Pertaining to the megatherium. **b.** *sb.* A megatherium or kindred animal.

1842 OWEN *Descr. Skel. Mylodon* 161 The extinct race of Megatherians. *Ibid.*, Generations of the Megatherian race.

megatherioid (mɛgəˈθɪərɪɔɪd), *a.* and *sb.* Also **-roid**. [f. next + -OID.] **a.** *adj.* Resembling the megatherium. **b.** *sb.* A megatherium or any similar edentate animal.

1839 OWEN in *Trans. Geol. Soc.* (1842) VI. 98 The Megatherioid families of Edentata. **1839** *Penny Cycl.* XV. 65/2 *Megatheriidæ*, Megatheroids of Owen. *Ibid.* 70/1 *Mylodon.* A genus of Edentate Megatherioids. **1872** NICHOLSON *Palæont.* 416 The gigantic Megatheroids.

megatherium (mɛgəˈθɪərɪəm). *Palæont.* Pl. **-ia**. [mod.L. (Cuvier), as if Gr. μέγα θηρίον 'great beast': see MEGA-.] An extinct genus of huge herbivorous edentates resembling the sloths, the fossil remains of which are found in the upper tertiary deposits of South America; an animal of this genus.

1826 PRICHARD *Res. Phys. Hist. Man.* (ed. 2) I. 64 They have been termed megalonyx and megatherium. **1832** CLIFT in *Trans. Geol. Soc.* (1835) III. 437 The Remains of the Megatherium described in this paper. **1856** EMERSON *Eng. Traits, Stonehenge* Wks. (Bohn) II. 124 Professor Sedgwick's Cambridge Museum of megatheria and mastodons.

b. *transf.* Something of huge or ungainly proportions.

1850 H. ROGERS *Ess.* (1874) II. iv. 190 Those huge megatheria among particles, 'peradventure', 'notwithstanding', and 'nevertheless'. **1870** DISRAELI *Lothair* xxvi, The wild panting of the loosened megatheria [locomotives] who drag us.

megatherm (ˈmɛgəθɜːm). *Bot.* [f. Gr. μέγα-ς great + θέρμη heat, θερμός hot.] A plant requiring great heat. Cf. MEGISTOTHERM, MEIOTHERM.

1879 STORMONTH *Man. Sci. Terms*, *Megatherms*, plants requiring a high temperature; also called 'macrotherms'.

megathermic (mɛgəˈθɜːmɪk), *a.* [f. MEGATHERM + -IC.] Pertaining to, connected with, or consisting of megatherms.

1903 W. R. FISHER tr. *Schimper's Plant Geogr.* 226 The megathermic flora is already perceptibly impoverished.

megaton (ˈmɛgətʌn). [f. MEGA- b + TON[1].]

a. A unit of explosive power, equal to that of one million tons of T.N.T. Freq. *attrib.*

1952 *N.Y. Herald-Tribune* 18 June 23/7 The first true super-bomb to be detonated is expected to have a power of two megatons. **1955** *Times* 30 May 7/7 The Pacific tests in 1952 and 1954 showed that a hydrogen bomb equivalent to 10 to 15 million tons of T.N.T. (commonly called 10–15 megatons) dropped on the centre of an ordinary city would cause total destruction within a circle of four to five miles. **1957** *Oxford Mail* 20 Aug. 1/5 Britain, he said, was concentrating on ballistic missiles because aircraft were unable to have 100 per cent success against an enemy equipped with megaton bombs. **1959** *Listener* 2 Apr. 613/3 The force of each detonation is believed to have been in the kiloton rather than the megaton range. **1962** *Newnes Conc. Encycl. Nucl. Energy* 48/1 A Bikini-type megaton bomb would destroy completely most ordinary buildings in an area of 84 square miles. **1965** *New Statesman* 21 May 810/2 Six megatons were used in the whole of the Second World War. **1972** [see MAGNITUDE 2 c].

b. *fig.*

1957 M. SHULMAN *Rally round Flag, Boys!* (1958) vi. 74 A broth of a woman..filled with energy in the megaton range. **1963** *Daily Tel.* 9 July 1 Another British spy scandal of 'megaton proportions' was forecast yesterday. **1969** N. COHN *AWopBopaLooBop* (1970) ix. 86 Music splintering and feet shuffling, butts twitching by the megaton.

Hence **'megatonnage**, explosive power of nuclear weapons, as expressed in megatons.

1963 *Economist* 23 Nov. 746/2 Nato is probably much closer to equality with the Warsaw alliance, in numbers of footsloggers as well as in nuclear megatonnage, than used to be thought. **1967** *Listener* 9 Feb. 186/2 The Russians have not been very explicit..about doubling the megatonnage of their warheads. **1971** *Guardian* 3 Aug. 11/5 The deliverable megatonnage of nuclear weapons. **1971** *Nature* 24 Dec. 493/2 The Soviet Union has already substantially overtaken the United States in numbers of ICBMs, in megatonnages, and in underground tests of large nuclear devices.

megatype (ˈmɛgətaɪp). [f. MEGA- + -TYPE.] An enlarged copy of a picture or negative produced by photography (*Cent. Dict.* 1890).

Hence **'megatypy**, the process of photographic enlargement of pictures or negatives (Webster 1902).

megazin(e, obs. forms of MAGAZINE.

meger(e, obs. forms of MEAGRE *a.*

†**megetho'logical**, *a.* *Obs.* [f. Gr. μέγεθος magnitude: see -LOGICAL.] Pertaining to the calculation of magnitudes.

1570 DEE *Math. Pref.* a iij, The helpe of Megethologicall Contemplations.

meggatapye: see MAGGOT[2].

Megger (ˈmɛgə(r)). The proprietary name of apparatus designed esp. for measuring electrical insulation resistance. Also **megger**. Also **Meg**[3], a type of Megger.

1903 *Trade Marks Jrnl.* 2 Sept. 962 Megger... Electric testing apparatus..and scientific instruments..Evershed and Vignoles, Limited,..London,..manufacturers. **1920** *Whittaker's Electr. Engineer's Pocket-Bk.* (ed. 4) 282 *Evershed's Megger.* The Megger insulation testing set contains in one case a hand-driven magneto generator and a direct reading moving coil ohmmeter. **1923** *Nature* 13 Jan. 63/2 The 'Meg' insulation tester.., a remarkably light and cheap megger running to 10,000 mgo. which should prove a boon to linemen. **1923** [see *insulation tester*]. **1924** *Trade Marks Jrnl.* 28 May 1189 Megger... All goods included in class 6 [Machinery of all kinds, and parts of machinery, except agricultural and horticultural machines]. Evershed & Vignoles, Limited,..London,..electrical engineers. **1928** *Naval Electr. Manual* (Admiralty) I. ix. 204 The 'Megger' is a direct-reading ohmmeter for the measurement of high resistances, such as the insulation resistance wiring, etc. **1930** *Engineering* 31 Jan. 129/3 A demonstration model of their megger earth tester. **1936** *Discovery* July 220/2 This instrument [*sc.* the Timber Humidity Meter]..has the appearance of a Megger. **1942** *Trade Marks Jrnl.* 11 Nov. 468/1 Meg... Electrical apparatus for testing insulation resistance and electrical apparatus for testing earth resistance, each comprising an electric generator and an electric measuring instrument. Evershed & Vignoles Limited,..London,..electrical and mechanical engineers. **1942** *Tee Emm* (Air Ministry) II. 84 Always remember the importance of megger-testing the insulation. **1950** *Engineering* 14 Apr. 404/1 The same firm were showing a new pattern of Megger insulation tester. **1957** G. CLARK *Archæol. & Society* (ed. 3) ii. 63 By using a 'Megger' Earth Tester, and measuring resistivity at intervals, it is possible to contour degrees of resistivity and so to detect areas of ancient disturbance, in the form of ditches.

Meghelmes, obs. form of MICHAELMAS.

Megillah (məˈgɪlə). Also †**meghillah**, **megilla(h)**, **megille**. Pl. **megil(l)oth**, **megil(l)a(h)s**. [Heb. *megillah* roll, scroll.] **a.** Each of five books of the Old Testament, namely S. of S., Ruth, Lam., Eccles., and Esther, appointed to be read by adherents of the Jewish faith on certain feast days; freq. with particular reference to the book of Esther, read at the feast of Purim. Also, a copy of any one, or all, of these books.

1650 E. CHILMEAD tr. *Leon Modena's Hist. Rites of Jews* III. x. 165 They read..the whole book of Esther; which they have..in a long Roll:..and this they call..*Meghillah*, that is to say, *Volumen*, a Volume, or Roll. **1652** E. BARGISHAI *Brief Compendium Vain Hopes of Jews Messias* 17 In the same *Talmuth* and book *Megilla*..saith *Chennina*, when the *Messias* shall appear, then shall God..shew great honours to the Jews. **1818** *Jewish Preceptress* 85 After the usual service, the Megilla, or book of Esther, is read. **1836** *Nethiboth Olam* (*Old Path*) 26 Feb. 27/1 We request the attention of our readers to the reason given why the reading of the Megillah is more important than any of the commandments. **1857** C. D. GINSBURG *Song of Songs* p. vii, The following is an exposition of the first of the five books called Megilloth. *Ibid.* 2 This Song is the first of the..five Megiloth, or books which are annually read in the Synagogues. **1926** 'R. LEARSI' tr. *Ash's Kiddush Ha-Shem* 89 Young men drew artistic designs in colors for..*Megillahs.* **1932** A. Z. IDELSOHN *Jewish Liturgy* 391 Mĕgilla chanting. **1957** *Oxf. Dict. Chr. Ch.* 882/1 *Megilloth* (Heb..., 'rolls'), the name given to five Books in the OT, all of them in the third and latest section of the OT canon known as the 'Hagiographa', which were read by the Jews on certain feast days. **1968** L. ROSTEN *Joys of Yiddish* 230 *Megillah*... Hebrew: 'scroll'. 1. *Megillah* usually describes the Book of Esther..; also the Book of Ruth. (There are five *megillahs* in all.) **1973** *Synagogue Light* Sept. 12/2 We read in Megilas Ruth [etc.].

1974 *Jewish Chron.* 13 Sept. 17/1 A megilla in an engraved casket.. was presented to the Brighton and Hove Hebrew Congregation.

b. *slang.* With allusion to the length of the Megillah: a long, tedious, or complicated story; freq. in phr. ***a whole Megillah*** (Yiddish *a gantse Megillah*).

1957 L. M. FEINSILVER in *Chicago Jewish Forum* Summer 228/1 *A gantse Megillah* or 'a whole *Megillah*' has been thrown around by a number of TV personalities.. presumably with little idea of the origin of the phrase. **1968** L. ROSTEN *Joys of Yiddish* 230 *Megillah*... 2. Anything very long, prolix; a rigmarole... 3. In popular parlance: Anything complicated, boring, overly extended, fouled up. **1968** *Punch* 1 May 626/1 Feeding all the *megillah* to the papers about his family of Irish Polacks who came over with the Pilgrim Fathers. **1970** L. M. FEINSILVER *Taste of Yiddish* i. 28 The *Megille*, or scroll, of Esther which is read aloud on Purim, and which takes some time to read, gave rise to the humorous description of a long story as *a gantse megille* (a whole *megille*). **1970** S. SHELDON *Naked Face* (1971) x. 110 'Do you know the most peculiar thing about this whole megillah?' queried Moody thoughtfully.

megilp (mɪˈgɪlp), *sb.* Forms: see quot. 1854; also **majellup, macgellup, meggellup, McGilp, megilph, meguilp.** [Of obscure origin: the suggestion that it is from a surname is improbable.]

1. A preparation (consisting usually of a mixture of linseed oil with turpentine or mastic varnish) employed as a vehicle for oil colours.

1768 [W. DONALDSON] *Life Sir B. Sapskull* I. x. 116 The magilp was a nostrum known only to the ancients; but our modern artists.. have labour'd.. to find out this valuable mystery, and as they say with some degree of success... The magilp produces that warmth and serenity which characterizes the peculiar merit of Claude Lorraine. **1803** *Edin. Rev.* II. 458 By the pulp, he meant to express some of the drying oils, or perhaps macgellup. *a* **1821** FARINGTON in Wright *Life R. Wilson* (1824) 20 A magylph or majellup of linseed-oil and mastic varnish.. was his [Richard Wilson's] usual vehicle. **1854** FAIRHOLT *Dict. Art* s.v. *Gumption*, note, In the different treatises on painting and in the colourmen's catalogues we find it thus variously named... Magelp, magelph, magilp, magylp, magylph, megilp, megelp, megylp, megylph, macgelp, macgelph, macgilp, macgilph, macgylph, macgulp, magulp, megulph, mygelp, mygelph, mygilp, mygilph, mygulp, mygulph.

2. A composition used by grainers (see quot.).

1827 WHITTOCK *Painters' & Glaz. Guide* I. ii. 21 The graining colour.. is.. a compound of various ingredients, mixed together to the consistence of thick treacle: this is called megilp.

megilp (mɪˈgɪlp), *v.* [f. prec.] *trans.* To varnish with megilp; to give to (oil colours) the quality which megilp is used to impart.

1873 E. SPON *Workshop Receipts* Ser I. 420/1 If it [water] is well mixed with the oil colour, it megilps it sufficiently to hold the combing. **1875** E. A. DAVIDSON *House-paint.*, etc. 110 The work.. must be varnished or 'megilped'.

megir(e, obs. forms of MEAGRE *a.*

megistotherm (mɪˈgɪstəʊθɜːm). *Bot.* [f. Gr. μέγιστο-ς, superl. of μέγας great + θέρμη heat.] A plant requiring a very high temperature for growth. Cf. MEGATHERM, MEIOTHERM.

1879 STORMONTH *Man. Sci. Terms, Megistotherms*, plants requiring extreme or a very high degree of heat.

megne, obs. variant of MEINIE.

megohm: see MEGA- b.

megre, obs. form of MEAGRE *a.*

megrim[1] (ˈmiːgrɪm). Forms: α. 5 mygrane, -ene, -eyn, 6 -ayne, megryne, 7 migrane. β. 4 mygrame, 5 -greyme, migrym, my(e)grym, midgrame, -grym, 6 migramme, -grym(me, mygrim, magryme, maigram, meigryme, megrym(e, 6–7 megrime, migram, meigrim, megrum, 7 megro(o)me, -greme, -grimme, mygram, migrim, migrame, migraim, meigram, 7–9 meagrim, 6– megrim. [a. F. *migraine* (13th c.), semi-popular ad. late L. *hēmicrānia*: see HEMICRANE. Cf. Sp. *migraña*, It. *magrana*. The Fr. MIGRAINE is now the most ususal synonym of HEMICRANIA; mod.G. has *migräne*, Sw. *migrän*.]

1. Hemicrania; a form of severe headache usually confined to one side of the head; nervous or sick headache; an attack of this ailment.

α. *c* **1420** *Chron. Vilod.* 4584 A feruent mygreyn was in þe ry3t syde of hurre hedde. *c* **1440** *Promp. Parv.* 337/1 Mygreyme, sekenesse (*S.* mygrene), *emigranea.* **1483** *Cath. Angl.* 239/1 þe Mygrane; vbi emigrane. *c* **1530** *Hickscorner* (Manly) 292, I sayd, that in my heed I had the megryne. **1541** R. COPLAND *Guydon's Form.* Xj, The seconde fourme is of mygrayne. **1603** FLORIO *Montaigne* III. xiii. (1632) 617 The mind is.. confounded by a migrane.

β. **1398** TREVISA *Barth. De P.R.* IV. v. (1495) 87 The mygrame and other euyll passyons of the heed. *c* **1460** *Play Sacram.* 613 For.. alle maner red eyne bleryd eyn & þe myegrym also [etc.]. *c* **1566** *Merie Tales of Skelton* in *Skelton's Wks.* (1893) I. p. lx, Other whyle he woulde saye hee had the megrym in hys head. **1579** GOSSON *Sch. Abuse* (Arb.) 58 It is not a softe shooe that healeth the Gowte.. nor a crown of Pearle that cureth the Meigrim. **1634** T. JOHNSON *Parey's Chirurg.* XVII. iv. (1678) 376 The Megrim is properly a disease affecting the one side of the head, right or left. **1668** R. L'ESTRANGE *Vis. Quev.* (1708) 268 By how much it is more Honourable to Dye upon a Swords-point.. than for a Man to snivel and sneeze himself into another World; or to go away in a Meagrim. **1713** *Phil. Trans.* XXVIII. 229 For the Megrim, they smoak.. the dried Bark of a Pomegranate Tree. **1871** NAPHEYS *Prev. & Cure Dis.* III. x. 1005 Brow-ague, or megrims, as it is sometimes called. **1899** *Allbutt's Syst. Med.* VI. 543 Attacks of megrim are often accompanied by.. contraction of the temporal artery.

b. = VERTIGO.

1595 DUNCAN *App. Etymol.* (E.D.S.) 75 *Vertigo*, dizzinesse, the migramme. **1626** BACON *Sylva* §725 In every Megrim, or Vertigo, there is an Obtenebration joyned with a Semblance of Turning Round. **1679** 'EPHELIA' *Female Poems* 7 A giddy Megrim wheel'd about my head. **1804** *Med. Jrnl.* XII. 109 A gentleman.. was suddenly attacked with a severe pain in his forehead, accompanied with so much megrim and stomach sickness, as would have caused him to fall, had he not received support.

c. *fig.*

a **1536** TINDALE *Exp. Matt. v-vii.* (?1550) 50 The weake and feble eyes of the world deseased with the mygrym and accustomed to darcknesse. **1634** W. TIRWHYT tr. *Balzac's Lett.* (Vol. I.) 228 Send me something to rid me of the Megreme I have taken in reading the sotteries of these times. ?*c* **1660** R. WILD *Poems* (1670) 27 The meagrim of opinions, new or old, The colic in the conscience, he could cure. **1685** SIR G. MACKENZIE *Relig. Stoic* 42 Finding that Fortunes megrim could not be cured.

2. A whim, fancy, fad.

1593 R. HARVEY *Philad.* 23 Iago.. died of a frensie, as he liued with a megrim. **1631** BRATHWAIT *Whimzies, Traveller* 91 Hee is troubled with a perpetuall migrim; at sea hee wisheth to bee on land, and on land at sea. **1711** E. WARD *Quix.* I. 235 With Fifty Meagrims in his Head. **1716** ADDISON *Drummer* I. i, Whims! freaks! megrims! indeed Mrs. Abigal. **1866** GEO. ELIOT *F. Holt* xi, Can't one work for sober truth as hard as for megrims? **1884** *Harper's Mag.* Aug. 466/2 What confounded megrim has seized you?

3. *pl.* 'Vapours'; 'blue devils'; low spirits.

1633 FORD *Broken H.* III. ii, These are his megrims, firks, and melancholies. **1754** RICHARDSON *Grandison* (1781) VI. xlv. 286 If these megrims are the effect of Love, thank Heaven, I never knew what it was. **1823** in *Spirit Pub. Jrnls.* 451 A very fine lady, and subject to the meagrims. **1887** G. R. SIMS *Mary Jane's Mem.* 214 Nurses.. having as many dislikes as a fashionable lady with the megrims.

4. *pl.* The staggers or vertigo (in animals).

1639 T. DE GRAY *Compl. Horsem.* 69 These paines in the head.. breed megrims. **1765** *Treat. Dom. Pigeons* 39 The next.. distemper incident to this kind of birds is the vertigo, or (as generally styled by the fancy) the megrims. **1849** D. J. BROWNE *Amer. Poultry Yd.* (1855) 261 This is evidently the same disorder which Dr. Bechstein terms *epilepsy*, and Mr. Clater, the *megrims* or *giddiness*. **1850** COL. HAWKER *Diary* (1893) II. 321 The poor mare was suddenly seized with megrims, or mad staggers.

Hence †**meˈgrimical** *a.*, of or belonging to megrim; **ˈmegrimish** *a.*, inclined to megrim.

1661 K. W. *Conf. Charac., Detracting Empirick* (1860) 65 This quackroyall is never.. so happy as when he's.. telling them [his patients].. how many megrimicall and hypocondriacal humors he hath dissipated. **1855** R. REDGRAVE in *Memoir* vi. (1891) 160 The maid was summoned to dress her mistress. She found her languid and megrimish.

megrim[2] (ˈmiːgrɪm). *dial.* Also **megrin.** The scald-fish, *Arnoglossus laterna.*

1836 YARRELL *Brit. Fishes* II. 254 The Scaldfish, or Megrim, as it is called in Cornwall. **1881** *Cassell's Nat. Hist.* V. 69 The Scald-fish, or Megrim, or Smooth Sole (*Arnoglossus laterna*). **1900** *Dundee Advert.* 5 Jan. 2 When whitches and megrins have arrived in any great quantity, values have speedily dropped. **1901** *Scotsman* 14 Mar. 4/4 Aberdeen.. prices,.. megrims., 20s. to 22s. per box.

megrin, obs. form of MEGRIM[2].

meguilp, megylp(h, variant forms of MEGILP.

mehap, obs. f. MAYHAP.

mehari (məˈhɑːrɪ). Also **maharee, mahari, maherry, mehara, meheri,** etc. [F. *méhari*, f. Algerian Arab. *mehrī*, Class. Arab. *mahrī*, of Mahra, a province in South Arabia.] An Arabian, single-humped camel, used for riding.

1738 T. SHAW *Travels or Observations relating to Barbary & Levant* 240 That species of the Camel-kind, which is known to us by the name of the *Dromas* or Dromedary, is here called *Maihāry*; though it is much rarer in Barbary than in the Levant. **1821** G. F. LYON *Narr. Trav. N. Afr.* i. 23 A small Kafflé passed us, consisting of ten or twelve camels, and amongst them one or two Maherries. **1826** DENHAM & CLAPPERTON *Narr. Trav. & Discoveries in N. & Cent. Afr.* i. 22 A marauding party was sent out to plunder some maherhies. *Ibid.*, Nine camels of the maherhy species were brought in. **1848** J. RICHARDSON *Travels in Great Desert of Sahara* I. iii. 87 The two races, the coast-camel, and the Maharee or desert-camel... The most fierce and dominant was the Maharee. **1854** J. R. MORELL *Algeria* 480 The mahari supports fatigue better than the camel, and never betrays an ambuscade. **1857** H. BARTH *Trav. N. & Cent. Afr.* I. viii. 178 Riding my own méheri, I was quite at liberty to go before or fall behind. **1863** J. HUTTON tr. *Daumas's Horses of Sahara* II. 342 Fetoum remounted her *mahari* and gave the signal for retreat. **1904** R. HICHENS *Garden of Allah* II. viii. 113 'He who smokes the keef is like a Mehari with a swollen tongue,' he rejoined. **1921** M. W. HILTON-SIMPSON *Among Hill-Folk Algeria* 120 In the great desert he rides the 'mehari', or trotting camel. **1923** G. CASSERLY *Algeria To-Day* 235 A Targui's *mehara* (riding camel) is usually white, is speedy and full of endurance. **1926** *Contemp. Rev.* Oct. 425 Captain Domèvre of the Spahis.. after being severely wounded in action with his *méhari*, is transferred to the military intelligence section at Beyrout.

mehche, obs. f. MATCH *sb.*[1]

†**mehe, me3he.** *Obs.* [OE. *mǽge* wk. fem.: related to MAY *sb.*[2]] A kinswoman.

c **1000** *Ags. Gosp.* Luke i. 36 Nu elizabeth þin mæge sunu on hyre ylde ʒe-eacnode. *c* **1200** ORMIN 3178 Hire me3he Elysabæþ Wass gladd inoh & bliþe Off hire dere child Johan. *a* **1225** *St. Marher.* 16 Meies ba ant mehen. *a* **1225** *Ancr. R.* 76 Hire oðre wordes weren þoa heo com & grette Elizabeð hire mowe [*MS. T.* mehe, *MS. C.* meðʒe].

‖**mehmandar** (ˈmeɪmændɑː(r)). Forms: 7 **mehmander, mehemandar, -er, mammandore, -dar, ma(h)mendar,** 9 **mehmandar, -daur.** [Pers. *mihmāndār*, f. *mihmān* stranger, guest.] In Persia and India, an official appointed to act as courier to a traveller of distinction.

1623 *St. Pap. Col., E. Indies* 1622–4 (1878) 161 Our mehmander or presenter. **1634** SIR T. HERBERT *Trav.* 51 Our Mammandore or Harbinger, prouiding for vs. **1638** *Ibid.* 132 Our Ambassadour.. sent his Mammandar to the Governour.. to demand fresh horses. **1662** J. DAVIES tr. *Olearius' Voy. Ambass.* 369 The Mehemandar, who conducts Ambassadors from one Province to another till they come to Court. **1687** A. LOVELL tr. *Thevenot's Trav.* II. 103 The Mahmendar Bassa, Master of the Ceremonies. **1840** J. B. FRASER *Koordistan* I. vi. 172 A dispute between our mehmandar and the villagers regarding a supply of corn for our horses. **1842** ELPHINSTONE *Caubul* I. 29 The necessity.. of waiting for a Mehmandaur from his Majesty, to accompany the mission.

‖**mehtar** (ˈmeɪtə(r)). Also 7 **meheter, mehater,** 9 **mater, matre, mehter.** [a. Urdū *mehtar*, a. Pers. *mihtar* head man, prince, occurring in many titles like *mihtar-i-asp*, master of the horse, *m.-i-raχt*, master of the household; comparative of *mih* great.]

1. a. In Persia: Originally, the title of certain great officers of the royal household. Now, a groom, a stable-boy.

1662 J. DAVIES tr. *Olearius' Voy. Ambass.* 272 Near the Pages stood the Meheter, or Groom of the Chamber, who hath the ouer-sight of them. *Ibid.* 286 The King.. would have kill'd him, if a Mehater, or Gentleman belonging to his Chamber had not prevented him. **1828** MORIER *Hajji Baba in Eng.* I. 60 Besides many mehters or stable-boys.

b. In Bengal: A house sweeper and scavenger; the lowest of the menial house-servants.

1810 WILLIAMSON *E. India Vade M.* I. 276 The *Mater*, or sweeper, is considered the lowest menial in every family. **1811** MRS. SHERWOOD *Henry & Bearer* 26, I gave all my last sweetmeats to the matre's boy. **1886** YULE & BURNELL *Anglo-Ind. Gloss.* s.v. *Bungy*, In the Bengal Pry. he is generally called mehtar.

2. A title borne by the ruler of Chitral. Hence **ˈmehtarship,** the office of mehtar.

1892 *Pall Mall G.* 21 Dec. 4/3 Nizam-ul-Mulk, the new Mehtar of Chitral. **1895** *Westm. Gaz.* 22 Mar. 7/1 The Amir ul Mulk,.. who recently usurped the Mehtarship by killing his brother.

mehte, obs. f. MIGHT sb. and *might* pa. t. of MAY *v.*[1]

Mehumitanisme, obs. form of MAHOMETANISM.

meibomian (maɪˈbəʊmɪən), *a.* *Anat.* [f. *Meibomius* (see below) + -AN.] The distinguishing epithet of certain sebaceous glands in the human eyelid, discovered by H. Meibom (Meibomius) of Helmstadt (died 1700).

1813 J. THOMSON *Lect. Inflam.* 161 When scrophula attacks the eye-lids, it has usually its seat in the Meibomian glands. **1858** H. GRAY *Anat.* 565 The Meibomian glands are situated upon the inner surface of the eyelids.

meiching, variant of MITCHING.

meicock, variant of MEACOCK *Obs.*

meid(e, obs. forms of MEAD *sb.*[1], *sb.*[2], MEED *sb.*

meidan, variant of MAIDAN *Indian.*

meiden, obs. form of MAIDEN.

meidin, variant of MEDINE.

meidle, meiger, obs. ff. MIDDLE *a.*, MEAGRE *a.*

meighlyn, obs. form of MECHLIN.

meigne(e, meigniall, obs. ff. MEINIE, MENIAL.

meigrim, -ym, obs. forms of MEGRIM.

Meiji (ˈmeɪdʒɪ). [Jap., 'enlightened government'.] The name given to the period of the rule of the Japanese emperor Mutsuhito (1868–1912), which was marked by the modernization and westernization of Japan. Freq. *attrib.*

1873 E. M. SATOW tr. *Kinsé Shiriaku: Hist. Japan* 125 The chronological period was also changed to Meiji (Enlightened Government), and an imperial proclamation was published making it a rule for all time that there should be only one chronological period for each reign. **1894** D. MURRAY *Japan* xv. 378 The year-period, which from January 1865, had borne the name of Keiō, had been changed to *Meiji* (Enlightened Peace), and was fixed to begin from January, 1868. **1901** C. LOWE tr. *A. von Siebold's Japan's Accession to Comity of Nations* p. vi, The writer..

felt particularly called upon to contribute to an appreciation of the magnificent achievements of the statesmen and diplomatists of the *Meiji* Era. **1931** I. Nitobé *Japan* iv. 225 The two great reforms of Japanese history—those of the Taika and Meiji eras. **1936** J. A. B. Scherer *Three Meiji Leaders* i. 1 Hirobumi Ito..became Japan's first Premier under the new Meiji government. *Ibid.* xiv. 133 The three Meiji leaders differed widely from one another, but each was of a classic grandeur. **1957** *Encycl. Brit.* XII. 967/1 During the first years of the Meiji period, when western ideas were being adopted in the newly re-opened Japan, the European style of painting was more cultivated than any other. **1961** A. M. Craig *Chōshū in Meiji Restoration* i. 6 Chōshū and Satsuma, han whose samurai were subsequently to carry out, as the dominant center of the new Meiji government, the revolution of the early Meiji period. **1972** M. Kochan tr. *P. Akamatsu's Meiji 1868* ii. ii. 258 As far as government accounts in the early years of Meiji can be known, nine and a half million *yen* are said to have been devoted to military expenditure in the period between November 13, 1871, and December 31, 1872. **1974** G. Jenkins *Bridge of Magpies* xiii. 206 My grandfather..lived at the time of the Meiji Revolution which made Japan into a modern state.

meik(e, obs. Sc. forms of MEEK *a.* and *v.*

meikill, meikle, obs. forms of MICKLE.

meil, obs. form of MEAL *sb.*¹ and *sb.*⁴

meild, meile, var. ff. MELD, MELE, *vbs. Obs.*

‖**meiler** (ˈmaɪlə(r)). [Ger.; orig. a pile of wood for making charcoal.] A charcoal-kiln.

1839 Ure *Dict. Arts* 996 Fig. 873. represents a simple coking *meiler* or *mound*. **1854** Ronalds & Richardson *Chem. Technol.* (ed. 2) I. 65 (*heading*) Preparation of Charcoal in Meiler.

meill, obs. f. MEAL *sb.*¹ and *sb.*⁴; var. MELE *v.*

mein, obs. f. MAIN, MIEN, MINE *pron.*, MING *v.*

†**meindre**, *a. Obs. rare*⁻¹. [a. AF. *meindre* (= mod.F. *moindre*):—L. *minor* MINOR *a.*] In phr. *meindre age*, minority.

a **1461** *Rolls of Parlt.* V. 394/1 By reason of the meyndre age of his seid Heire.

[**meine**, *v.*, a spurious verb inferred from *meind*, pa. t. of MENG *v.*

1736 in Ainsworth *Eng.-Lat. Dict.* Hence **1755** in Johnson; and in later Dicts.]

meine, obs. form of MEAN.

‖**mein Gott** (maɪn gɔt), *int.* [G., = my God.] Used as a typically German exclamation corresponding to *My God* (GOD 7).

c **1838** C. J. Mathews in M. R. Booth *Eng. Plays of 19th Cent.* (1973) IV. 130 Oh mine Got, mine Got, when I tink of zat bewitching Miss Parker! **1867** Trollope *Claverings* I. xix. 239 'Yes, yes;—mein Gott, yes,' said Schmoff. **1891** Kipling *Life's Handicap* 261 Mein Gott! I would sooner collect life red devils than liddle monkeys. **1924** 'Sapper' *Third Round* vi. 142 And think—five, ten minutes more and I also to pieces would have been blown. *Mein Gott!* it makes me sweat. **1968** R. Sawkins *Snow along Border* iv. 33 Oh, mein Gott, I've just remembered something odd.

‖**mein Herr** (maɪn hɛr). [G., = my lord.] Used in a jocular or ironic tone in addressing a German man; so as *sb.*, a male German.

1922 Joyce *Ulysses* 202 The gross virgin who inspired *The Merry Wives of Windsor* let some meinherr from Almany grope his life long for deephid meanings in the depth of the buckbasket. **1967** [see Herr]. **1975** J. Blackburn *Mister Brown's Bodies* xxii. 185 Very clever, *mein Herr*, though the real prize will excape you.

meinie (ˈmeɪnɪ). *Obs.* exc. *arch.* Forms: 3 **maynee, meingne, menyeie,** 3–4 **meigne,** 3–5 **maine, mayne, meine, meynee,** 3–6 **menye, meyne, menȝe,** 3, 5, 7, 9 **menie,** 4 **meygne, megne, mengȝe, mengne, meynne, meyneȝ, meyney, meinee,** 4–5 **meignee, meynye, mene, meneyhe, meynȝe, menȝey, menȝhe, meneȝe,** 4–6 **mayny,** 4–7 **meny,** 4–9 **meyny,** 5 **meneȝee, menne, maygne, menyhe, meneya, meneyay, meyni,** 5–6 **maynye,** 5–9 **meynie,** *Sc.* **menȝie,** 6 **mainy, meany(e, meini, meniey, meignye, menyei,** 6–7 **meiney,** 6–8 **meiny,** 7 **meney, meanie,** *Sc.* **meinzie,** 9 **meisny,** *Sc.* **mengyie, manzy,** 6– **meinie.** [a. OF. *meyné, mesnie*, earlier *mesnede* = Pr. *mesnada, maisnada, mainada* (whence Sp. *mesnada, manada*, It. *masnada*):—popular Latin type **mansiōnāta*, f. L. *mansiōn-em* (see MANSION), whence F. *maison* house.

In English the word was in some of its applications confused with MANY *sb.*]

1. A family, household.

c **1290** *S. Eng. Leg.* I. 480/3 Seint ypolyt þe Martyr..þat wuste seint laurence in prisone..And þoruȝh him turnde to cristindom and his maine al-so. *a* **1300** *Cursor M.* 12271 Þan went ioseph and mari bun Wit iesu til a-noiþer tun, Þat meingne was sa mild and meth. **13..** *E. E. Allit. P.* B. 331 Þis meyny of aȝte I schal saue of monnez saulez. *c* **1380** Wyclif *Wks.* (1880) 32 No weddid man owiþ to leue his wife & children & meyne vngouerned. **1481** Caxton *Reynard* (Arb.) 98, I sawe neuer a fowler meyne, they [the ape and its young] laye on fowle heye whiche was al be pyssed. **1532** Hervet *Xenophon's Househ.* (1768) 78 For a man that is at great costes..in his house, and can not gette as moche..as wyll fynde hym and his meyny. **1587** *Durham Depos.* (Surtees) 327, I will command my menyei (which, as this examinate thinketh, he ment his wife and children) that they will be good to the. **1667** Cotton *Scarron.* iv. 105 A Farm lies ready cut and dry'd, Will hold both me, and all my meany.

2. a. A body of retainers, attendants, dependents, or followers; a retinue, suite, train.

1297 R. Glouc. (Rolls) 3484 Þat so moche folc to him com of kniȝtes ȝonge & olde Þat he nadde noȝt wel war wiþ such menie up to holde. *a* **1300** *Cursor M.* 20579 Þan com ihesus wit his meigne. *c* **1330** R. Brunne *Chron. Wace* (Rolls) 2388 Þey sette hym honurable to be, Wiþ fourty knyghtes of meygne. *c* **1400** Maundev. (Roxb.) xxx. 135 When he rydes in tyme of peesse with his priuee menȝee. *c* **1400** *Rom. Rose* 7156 Thus Antecrist abyden we, For we ben alle of his meynee. *c* **1415** *Pol. Poems* (Rolls) II. 124 Ther all the ryall powere of Frensshemen come aȝenst owre kynge and his litill meyné. **1423** *Rolls of Parlt.* IV. 248/2 For the expens resounable of hir, and of a certein meyne that shuld abide aboute hir. *c* **1460** *Godstow Reg.* (E.E.T.S.) 182 Hys meyny of woluerton sholde haue fre & full power to lede her bestys to the welle. **1470–85** Malory *Arthur* x. xi. 430 Kynge marke rode froward them with alle his mayneal meyny. *c* **1500** *Gest Robyn Hode* 335 in Child *Ballads* III. 72 Fonde she there Robyn Hode, And al his fayre mene. **15..** *Chevy Chase* 6 Then yᵉ perse owt off banborowe cam, wᵗ him A myghtee meany. **1513** Douglas *Æneis* iii. i. 25 Furth sail I, ..With my ȝoung son Ascanius and our menȝe. **1605** Shaks. *Lear* ii. iv. 35 They summon'd vp their meiney, straight tooke Horse, Commanded me to follow. *c* **1640** J. Smyth *Lives Berkeleys* (1883) I. 214 Wherto eleven knights were wittnesses, then of his meiny or houshold seruants. **1728** Ramsay *To D. Forbes* vii, What gars thee look sae big and bluff? Is't an attending menzie? **1904** Saintsbury *Hist. Crit.* III. 426 Titania and her meyny.

†**b.** Used as a *plural*: Servants. *Obs.*

c **1450** *Bk. Curtasye* 604 in *Babees Bk.*, Now let we þes officers be, And telle we wylle of smaller mené. *c* **1450** *St. Cuthbert* (Surtees) 252 Þe lady, þe menȝe, grete and small.

†**c.** *God's meinie*: applied (*a*) to the angels; (*b*) to the poor, as objects of his special care. *Obs.*

a **1300** *Assump. Virg.* (Camb. MS.) 110 He wile senden after þe, Fram heuene adun of his meigne. **1496** *Dives & Paup.* (W. de W.) ix. xiv. 367/1 For why wycked doers & synful poore men ben called the leste of goddes menye.

†**3.** A company of persons employed together or having a common object of association; an army, ship's crew, congregation, assembly, or the like. *Obs.*

a **1300** *Cursor M.* 17288 + 440 Ȝit apon þe same day he schewd to þis menȝe. *c* **1330** R. Brunne *Chron.* (1810) 97 He gadred grete mayne of alle þat he mot hent. **1375** Barbour *Bruce* xvi. 375 Of archeris a gret menȝhe Assemblit. *c* **1400** *Destr. Troy* 5243 Mony fallyn were fey of þe fell grekes, But mo of the meny, þat mellit hom with. *c* **1400** *Beryn* 1581 For there nas Shippis meyne for auȝt that they could hale That myȝte abuten of the Shipp the thiknes of a skale. **1598** *Nottingham Rec.* IV. 247 To requyre the Burgesses in his Ward to mete a meny of honest Burgesses.

†**4.** The collection of pieces or 'men' used in the game of chess. *Obs.*

[**1322** in *Rolls Parlt.* III. 363 Escheqirs..ove tres peirs meines de cristall, et tables de ivoir, ove la meine d'ivoire et d'eban.] **13..** *Guy Warw.* (A.) 3195 Þe cheker þai oxy & þe meyne. *c* **1330** R. Brunne *Chron. Wace* (Rolls) 11396 Meyne for þe cheker Wyþ draughtes queinte of knight & rok. *c* **1400** *Beryn* 1733 The ches was al of yvery, the meyne fressh and newe. **14..** *Voc.* in Wr.-Wülcker 609/41 *Scaccus*, the meny of the cheker. *c* **1450** *Merlin* xxi. 362 The pownes, and all the other meyne were golde and yvory freshly entailled.

5. a. A multitude of persons; chiefly in disparaging use, a 'crew', 'set'. Also, the common herd, the masses.

13.. *E.E. Allit. P.* B. 454 He..wysed þeroute A message fro þat meyny hem moldez to seche. *c* **1440** *Alphabet of Tales* 121 A grete meneyay of pylgrams. *c* **1440** *York Myst.* xi. 277 Lord, whills we with þis menyhe meve, Mon never myrthe be vs emange. **1529** Rastell *Pastyme* (1811) 268 A meanye of rascall and euyll disposed people. **1529** Skelton *Dethe Erle Northumb.* 46 A mayny of rude villayns made hym for to blede. **1533** More *Answ. Poysoned Bk.* Wks. 1119/2 Mayster Walker and al the meany of them. **1609** Day *Festivals* (1615) Ep. Ded., If we account them not more Religious, then the Meyny, or Multitude, are. **1640** Brathwait *Two Lanc. Lovers* 99 One, whom the rest of that miserable meniey..called Spurcina. *a* **1670** Spalding *Troub. Chas. I* (1829) 41 A menzie of miscontented puritans. **1788** Shirrefs *Poems* (1790) 346 What gart you pit them [critics] in my head? That menzie, Sir, are a' my dread. **1819** W. Tennant *Papistry Storm'd* (1827) 140 The meikle menzie on ilk side Did break in twa. **1970** J. Wain *Winter in Hills* iv. 361 A speech was now made by McAlister, the Scotch poet in whose ostensible support this meinie was assembled.

†**b.** (Common) people. *Obs.*

1387–8 T. Usk *Test Love* i. vi. (Skeat) l. 145 Notwithstandinge that in the contrary helden moche comune meyny.

†**6.** Of animals: A herd, drove, flock, etc.; a number, multitude. *Obs.*

1484 Caxton *Fables of Æsop* vi. ix. (1889) 204 Ones amonge a grete meyny of ghees and cranes [a labourer] took a pyelarge. **1522** Skelton *Why not to Court?* 241 A mayny of marefoles. *Ibid.* 292 They wolde Rynne away and crepe, Lyke a mayny of shepe. **1530** Palsgr. 475/1 They can no more skyll of it than a meany of oxen. **1556** Olde *Anti-christ* 12 b, You are muche more worthe than a great meignye of sparrowes.

7. Of things: A number, a numerous collection or aggregation. *Obs.* exc. *Sc.*

c **1440** *Alphabet of Tales* 294 A grete meneya of palmelevis. **1530** Palsgr. 244/2 Meny of plantes, *plantaige*. *Ibid.* 721/1 As thoughe there were a menye of brokes [F. *vng tas de ruisseaux*] had their springes there. **1896** Barrie *Marg. Ogilvy* iv. 76 You get no common beef at clubs; there is a manzy of different things all sauced up to be unlike themsels.

meinie, obs. form of MANY.

meiobenthos (ˌmaɪəʊˈbɛnθɒs). [f. Gr. μείων smaller + BENTHOS.] The section of the benthos that includes animals neither small enough to be grouped with the microfauna nor large enough to be grouped with the macrofauna. So **ˌmeioˈbenthic**.

1942 M. F. Mare in *Jrnl. Marine Biol. Assoc.* XXV. 519 A new terminology is needed, and these groups are here designated the macrobenthos, meiobenthos, and microbenthos. The macrobenthos is equivalent to the macrofauna of the bottom... The meiobenthos here comprises the fauna of intermediate size, such as small crustacea (copepods, cumaceans, etc.) small polychaetes and lamellibranchs, nematodes and foraminifera. The microbenthos comprises all the small organisms. **1967** *Oceanogr. & Marine Biol.* V. 522 The number of individuals given by Kiseleva has the great merit of taking into account the meiobenthos. **1969** *Nature* 15 Nov. 720/2 Nematodes are among the commonest meiobenthic animals. **1971** *Ibid.* 28 May 260/1 (*heading*) Deficiency of gravity corers for sampling meiobenthos and sediments. **1973** *Ibid.* 30 Mar. 324/1 Where hydrodynamic conditions and bottom configuration are so subdued that meiobenthic bioturbation becomes a locally prominent sedimentological process.

meiocene: see MIOCENE.

meiofauna (ˈmaɪəʊfɔːnə). [f. Gr. μείων smaller + FAUNA.] = MEIOBENTHOS. So **ˌmeioˈfaunal** *a.*

1967 M. L. Wass in Olson & Burgess *Pollution & Marine Ecol.* vi. 272 Benthic animals under stress may be meiofaunal in size. *Ibid.*, An extensive study has been done ..on a group of protozoan meiofauna. **1973** *Nature* 30 Mar. 323/2 Ostracods and nematodes were the most widely distributed and active members of the meiofaunas. *Ibid.* 324/1 Data confirming..the complete disappearance of some meiofaunal groups, in sediments of the deeper seafloor.

meiogyrous (maɪəˈdʒaɪrəs), *a. Bot.* [irreg. f. Gr. μείων smaller, less + γῦρος (see GYRE) + -OUS.] 'Rolled inwards a little' (Jackson *Gloss. Bot. Terms.* 1900).

meiolithic: see MIOLITHIC.

meionite (ˈmaɪənaɪt). *Min.* Also **mionite**. [a. F. *meionite* (Haüy), f. Gr. μείων smaller: see -ITE. Meant to indicate that the crystals are smaller than those of vesuvianite.]

A white or colourless silicate of aluminum and calcium found in lava.

1808 *Nicholson's Jrnl.* XXI. 191 Does the mineral mentioned by the name of meïonite in the *Tableau méthodique* of Mr. Haüy constitute a distinct species? *Ibid.* 199, I have yet compared the meïonite with the feldspar only in respect to form. **1879** Rutley *Stud. Rocks* x. 112 The species meionite and marialite are closely related to scapolite.

meiophylly (ˈmaɪəfɪlɪ). *Bot.* Also **mio-**. [irreg. f. Gr. μείων less + φύλλον leaf + -Y. Cf. MEIOSTEMONOUS.] The suppression of one or more leaves in a whorl.

1869 Masters *Veget. Terat.* 396 Meiophylly. A diminished number of leaves in a whorl, occasionally takes place. **1879** in Stormonth *Man. Sci. Terms.*

‖**meiosis** (maɪˈəʊsɪs). Also 7 **miosis**. Pl. **meioses**. [Gr. μείωσις lessening, f. μειοῦν, to lessen, f. μείων less.]

1. *Rhet.* †**a.** A figure of speech by which the impression is intentionally conveyed that a thing is less in size, importance, etc., than it really is.

1586 A. Day *Eng. Secretary* ii. (1625) 84 *Meiosis*, a manner of disabling, as when we say, Alas Sir, it is not in my power to doe it. **1589** Puttenham *Eng. Poesie* III. xvi[i]. (Arb.) 195 If you diminish and abbase a thing by way of spight.., such speach is by the figure *Meiosis* or the disabler spoken of hereafter. *a* **1716** South *Serm.* (1717) IV. 32 Their whole Discourse being one continued *Meiosis* to diminish, lessen, and debase the great Things of the Gospel.

b. = LITOTES.

1642 Fuller *Holy & Prof. St.* ii. vii. 73 Some condemne Rhetorick as the mother of lies, speaking more then the truth in Hyperboles, lesse in her Miosis. **1655** —— *Ch. Hist.* viii. iii. §32 The foresaid Author..termeth Him..Pedantick enough, that is too much, to such as understand his Miosis. *a* **1716** South *Serm.* (1727) IV. x. 434 The Words are a *Meiosis*, and import much more than they express. **1903** *Speaker* 16 May 159/1 Self-assertiveness, Mr. Sheppard observes with a pleasing meiosis, is not required.

2. *Path.* The stage of a disease in which the symptoms begin to abate.

1857 Dunglison *Med. Lex.* 577. **1890** in *Syd. Soc. Lex.*

3. *Biol.* (Formerly also **maiosis**.) The division of a diploid cell nucleus into four haploid nuclei, which offsets a doubling of chromosome numbers at a subsequent fertilization and normally comprises a reduction division (meiosis I) followed by an equational division (meiosis II); commonly used to include also the accompanying division of the cytoplasm.

1905 Farmer & Moore in *Q. Jrnl. Microsc. Sci.* XLVIII. 489 We propose to apply the terms Maiosis or Maiotic phase to cover the whole series of nuclear changes included in the two divisions that were designated as Heterotype and Homotype by Flemming. **1907** *Rep. Brit. Assoc. Adv. Sci.* 689 There is reason to believe that a sorting of the chromosomes, analogous to that seen in meiosis, takes place

in the third division of the ascus. **1925** E. B. WILSON *Cell* (ed. 3) vi. 576 Meiosis brings about two additional results... One is to establish new haploid combinations of the original maternal and paternal chromosomes in the germ-cells... Not less important is the reorganization of the chromosomes, individually considered, that takes place during meiosis, by means of 'crossing-over'. **1934** L. W. SHARP *Introd. Cytol.* (ed. 3) xvi. 254 Meiosis involves two nuclear divisions but only one chromosomal division. **1949** DARLINGTON & MATHER *Elem. Genetics* i. 34 Since crossing-over can probably take place between any two chromomeres, it will be rare indeed for two identical haploid nuclei to be produced from different meioses. **1971** *Sci. Amer.* Aug. 56/3 Without mitosis there could be no meiosis, the type of cell division that gives rise to eggs and sperm.

meiostemonous (maɪəʊ'stiːmənəs), *a. Bot.* Also mio-. [irreg. f. Gr. μείων less + στημον-, στήμων stamen + -OUS.] Having fewer stamens than petals.

1832 LINDLEY *Introd. Bot.* 400 Meiostemonous would be said of a plant the stamens of which are fewer in number than the petals. **1849** BALFOUR *Man. Bot.* §392 Miostemonous.

meiotaxy ('maɪətæksɪ). *Bot.* Also **mio-**. [irreg. f. Gr. μείων less + τάξις arrangement. Cf. prec. and MEIOPHYLLY.] The suppression of an entire whorl of floral organs.

1869 MASTERS *Veget. Terat.* 403 Meiotaxy of the calyx... This term is here employed to denote those illustrations in which entire whorls are suppressed. **1879** in STORMONTH *Man. Sci. Terms.*

meiotherm ('maɪəʊθɜːm). *Bot.* [irreg. f. Gr. μείων less + θέρμη heat, θερμός hot.] A plant of a temperate habitat. (Cf. MEGATHERM, MEGISTOTHERM.) Also *attrib.*

1875 J. G. BAKER *Bot. Geog.* 48 Meiotherm, characteristic of the cool-temperate zone, and therefore quite hardy in the open air in England. *Ibid.* 95 Meiotherm types. **1884** *Trans. Victoria Inst.* 38 Meiotherms—plants inhabiting cool temperate zones.

meiotic (maɪ'ɒtɪk), *a.* [f. Gr. μειωτικ-ός diminishing (see MEIOSIS).] **1.** *Rhet.* That represents things as less than they really are; characterized by meiosis or litotes.

1907 *Westm. Gaz.* 17 June 2/2 Is there not..a good deal to be said for the meiotic method [of portraying the Caesars] preferred by Sir Lawrence Tadema? **1915** *Oxf. Mag.* 18 June 38/2 We have occasionally mentioned in mild meiotic terms that the Oxford roads do not wholly satisfy our ideal of perfection.

2. *Biol.* (Formerly also **maiotic.**) That is characterized by meiosis (sense 3); of, pertaining to, or occurring at meiosis.

1905 [see MEIOSIS 3]. **1913** W. BATESON *Mendel's Princ. Heredity* (rev. ed.) 270 This differentiation will come about at this reduction, or meiotic division, as it is called. **1952** SRB & OWEN *Gen. Genetics* vii. 119 The period between the two meiotic divisions is designated by the special term interkinesis. It may be rather long, but typically it is very short. **1962** *Lancet* 15 Dec. 1270/1 Three types of meiotic non-disjunction have been recognised. **1973** *Nature* 5 Oct. 261/2 For spermatozoa and meiotic preparations, ripening testes were removed.

Hence **mei'otically** *adv.*

1676 R. MEGGOTT *Sermon preached on St. Paul's Day* 6 This is that which according to the Hebrew way of speaking is here meiotically expressed by *It is not good.* **1959** *Times* 7 Oct. 4/1 To put it meiotically, the match was rather one-sided. **1966** *Times* 28 Mar. (Austral. Suppl.) p. xiv/5 A *y* chromosome might..be attached to another meiotically driven chromosome. **1968** R. RIEGER *Gloss. Genetics & Cytogenetics* 274 Thus, the zygotic (diploid) chromosome number is meiotically reduced to the gametic (haploid) number. **1973** *Nature* 5 Oct. 259/1 When the brandspore germinates its nucleus divides meiotically to re-establish the haploid sporidial phase.

‖**mei p'ing** (meɪ pɪŋ). Also **mei ping** and with capital initials. [Chin., lit. = prunus vase.] A Chinese porcelain vase with a narrow neck designed to hold a single spray of flowers.

1915 R. L. HOBSON *Chinese Pott. & Porc.* v. 79 A vase of the form known as *mei p'ing* with green Imperial dragons in a yellow ground and the Wan Li mark. **1953** S. JENYNS *Ming Pott. & Porc.* iv. 39 Other blue and white pieces..are the *mei ping* vases decorated with sages. **1968** J. UPDIKE *Couples* ii. 152 An empty but perfect blue vase of *mei ping* form. **1972** *Country Life* 21 Dec. 1715/3 The Mei Ping (a vase designed with an aperture to hold a single flower). **1973** *Ibid.* 2 Aug. 290/1 A Mei-P'ing, literally 'plum blossom vase', a shape which first appeared in the 10th century..small mouth, wide shoulders and tapering body. **1974** *Times* 3 Apr. 1/5 She paid £160,000 for an early Ming blue-and-white *mei p'ing* and cover.

meir, meir(e, obs. ff. MERE, MAYOR.

meir-maid, -swyne, ob. ff. MERMAID, -SWINE.

†**meirre, meire,** *a. Her. Obs.* [Of obscure origin: cf. F. *moire, moiré* watered silk, also OF. *meire* 'sorte de vêtement' (Godefr.).] (See quot.; Leigh's figure identifies it with COUNTER-POTENT.)

1562 LEIGH *Armory* 191 He beareth Meirre Argent, and Azure. Some olde Hereaughtes haue taken this for a dublinge, and yet they wolde call it varry cuppe, & varrey tassa, which is asmuche to saye, as furre of Cuppes, or of goblettes... Well let that blazonne goo, and vse this worde Meire, for so is it well blazed, and very auncient and is a Spanishe Cote moste commonly.

meis(e, variant forms of MEASE.

meish(e, obs. forms of MESH.

meisie, meisje ('meɪsɪ). *S. Afr.* [Afrikaans *meisie*, f. Du. *meisje*, cogn. w. Eng. MAIDEN *sb.*] Girl; young lady or woman.

1890 *Digger's Doggerel* 27 Romeo Troilus Giddy McSmack Has been granted, secure from all legal attack, The sole right to practise and use osculation On the 'meisjes' and 'vrauws' of the Transvaalsche Nation. **1895** H. A. BRYDEN in *Blackw. Mag.* July 131/1 A little wizened Hottentot has been..making coffee for the *baas* and *meisje*. **1910** *Cape Times* 7 Oct. 10 There is enough to be done before nightfall for an idle meisje to bestir herself without waiting to be called. **1927** W. PLOMER *I speak of Afr.* 47 He was stared at, especially by fat meisjes here and there, flappers with matronly figures. **1934** 'N. GILES' *Ridge of White Waters* II. ii. 207 That child of Isaak Prinsloo's grows into a pretty meisje. **1953** J. COLLIN-SMITH *Locusts & Wild Honey* II. iv. 146 The lass loves you; which is more than can be said for me of that wilful 'meisjie' your sister. **1965** *Economist* 17 Apr. 339 Milling about in front as well as behind the open counters are the attractive *meisies*, known as hostesses.

meiss, obs. form of MEASE *v.*, MESS *sb.*

Meissen ('maɪsən). The name of a town near Dresden used *attrib.* or *absol.* to designate a hard-paste porcelain made there since 1710; Dresden porcelain (DRESDEN). Also *fig.*

1863 W. CHAFFERS *Marks Pott. & Porc.* 176 *Dresden.* Meissen. The two swords crossed..; used about 1730. **1882** 'OUIDA' *Bimbi* 50 A lovely little lady..made of the very finest and fairest Meissen china. **1938** *Burlington Mag.* Dec. p. xvii/2 Pieces of Meissen and other porcelains. **1951** 'J. TEY' *Daughter of Time* i. 11 People wouldn't send you a lot of fool nonsense when you were flat on your back, and bossy bits of Meissen wouldn't expect you to read them. **1951** [see CHANTILLY 1]. **1961** J. WADE *Back to Life* xiv. 195 Her face ..had the smooth, pleased prettiness of Meissen. **1964** MRS. L. B. JOHNSON *White House Diary* 5 June (1970) 156, I recognize it as Meissen from Germany. **1968** *Michelin Guide N.Y. City* 52 German stoneware, faience and porcelain (Meissen, Nymphenburg and Hochst). **1970** *Canad. Antiques Collector* May 29/1 Meissen was the first true porcelain made in Europe. It was produced in a factory at Meissen, about 10 miles from Dresden, from about 1710 onwards.

Meissner effect ('maɪsnə(r)). *Physics.* [named after Fritz Walther *Meissner* (1882–1974), German physicist, who with R. Ochsenfeld published an account of the phenomenon in *Naturwissenschaften* (1933) XXI. 787.] The existence of zero, or very low, magnetic induction in a superconducting material even in the presence of a magnetic field; esp. the (partial or complete) expulsion of magnetic flux when the material becomes superconducting in a magnetic field.

[**1935** *Proc. R. Soc.* A. CXLIX. 73 Equation (6) says more than (2), so far as it includes Meissner's effect.] **1935** *Ibid.* CLII. 10 The magnetization curve for decreasing fields is in striking contradiction to the classical electro-magnetic description of a Supraconductor, and provides an independent confirmation that B = 0 is characteristic of the ideal supraconducting state (Meissner effect). **1953** C. F. SQUIRE *Low Temperature Physics* vii. 116 The complete Meissner effect (B = 0) is difficult to obtain experimentally. *Ibid.* 117 (*heading*) A permanent magnet floats above the superconducting tin dish because of the Meissner effect. **1968** C. G. KUPER *Introd. Theory Superconductivity* iii. 44 It is rather unusual in physics for purely topological properties of a body to be important, but superconductivity provides an example. In a multiply-connected superconducting body, although the Meissner effect ensures that the magnetic flux will be expelled from the material of the body, flux may be trapped in the holes.

meist ('miːɪst). *nonce-wd.* [f. ME *pron.*: see -IST.] An egoist.

1737 *Common Sense* I. 311 His Works hereafter will be more favourably receiv'd..by the Meists and Selfists.

meister, var. MASTER, MISTER *sb.*[1], trade.

Meistersinger ('maɪstəˌzɪŋə(r), -sɪŋ-), *sb. pl.* and *sing.* [G.: cf. MASTER-SINGER.] German lyric poets and musicians in the 14th to 16th centuries organized in guilds and having an elaborate technique; (*sing.*) a member of such a guild.

1845 LONGFELLOW *Poets & Poetry of Europe* (1847) 373/2 These Chambers [of Rhetoric] were to Holland, in the fifteenth century, what the Guilds of the Meistersingers were to Germany. [**1854** A. G. HENDERSON tr. *Cousin's Philos. of Kant* i. 5 The poetry of this period is to be found in the songs of the *Minnesängers* and the *Meistersängers*.] **1954** *Grove's Dict. Mus.* (ed. 5) VII. 912/2 The Meistersinger were either preoccupied with the observance of rules or were rarely visited with inspiration. **1968** *Encycl. Brit.* XV. 118/2 The *Meistersinger* were not popular figures, as Wagner's opera *Die Meistersinger* suggests; they were largely ignored by professional men.

fig. **1924** R. CAMPBELL *Flaming Terrapin* iv. 56 Across the night with dismal hum The hurricanes, your meistersingers, come.

meit(e, obs. forms of MEAT, MEET, METE.

meith (miːθ), *sb. Sc.* Forms: 6 **meithe**, 6–7 **meth**, 8 **myth, meeth**, 9 **meethe, meath**, 6– **meith**. [app. a. ON. *mið* a mark, a fishing-bank 'indicated by prominences or landmarks on shore' (Vigf.); but associated with L. *mēta* boundary, goal, METE *sb.* The OE. *mǣþ*, ME. METHE, due measure, moderation, seems to be unconnected.]

1. A landmark or sea-mark; a boundary, goal.

1513 DOUGLAS *Æneis* v. iv. 1 With this thai gan towart the meithe approche. *Ibid.* xiv. 16 The donk nycht had rone almaist evin Hir myd cours or methis in the hevin. **1579** *Burgh Rec. Edin.* (1882) IV. 124 To vesy thair meithis and boundis. *a* **1680** DALLAS *Stiles* (1697) 710 The old Bounds, Marches and Meiths of the same [Lands]. **1701** BRAND *Descr. Orkney*, etc. (1703) 145 The House of Mey formerly mentioned is a Myth, Sign or Mark, much observed by Saillers. **1813** BEATTIE *Poems* (1871) 35 Mark nor meith ye wadna ken. **1824** SCOTT *St. Ronan's* iii, They had been ower the neighbour's ground they had leave on up to the march, and they werena just to ken meiths when the moor-fowl got up. **1899** J. SPENCE *Shetl. Folk-lore* 130 A given straight course, indicated by meiths or marks on the land.

2. A measurement.

1726 *Burgh Rec. Stirling* (1889) 189 There shall be two foot more deepness..after meiths taken at the beg stone. **1819** W. TENNANT *Papistry Storm'd* (1827) 189 As they look't up ilk lofty wa', Takin' their meiths for its downfa', That they may strike and stroy.

meith (miːθ), *v. Sc.* Also 6 **meth**, 7 **meath**, 9 **mith.** [f. prec. Cf. ON. *miða* to mark the position of something.] *trans.* To bound or mark out.

c **1575** *Balfour's Practicks* (1754) 438 Landis..merchit and meithit be trew and leill men of the countrey. **1679** in Cramond *Ann. Banff* (1891) I. 158 That the said common way be meithed and merched on the south syde of the Colle-hill. **1899** J. SPENCE *Shetl. Folk-lore* 47 A landmark at sea for *meithing* (marking) the Burgascurs.

meizin, obs. form of MUEZZIN.

meizoseismal (maɪzəʊ'saɪsməl), *a.* and *sb.* [irreg. f. Gr. μείζων greater + σεισμός earthquake: see -AL[1] and SEISMIC.]

a. *adj.* Pertaining to the points of maximum disturbance in an earthquake. **b.** *sb.* A curve traced through these points.

1859 MALLET in *Admiralty Man. Sci. Enq.* (ed. 3) 351 This may be called the Meizoseismal Circle or Zone.

meizoseismic (maɪzəʊ'saɪsmɪk), *a.* [f. as prec.: see -IC.] = prec. adj.

1877 RUDLER in *Encycl. Brit.* VII. 610 The line indicating this maximum is termed the *meizoseismic curve.*

mejliss, var. MAJLIS.

mek(e, meken, etc., obs. ff. MEEK, MEEKEN, etc.

mekel(l, obs. forms of MICKLE *adv.*

Mekhitarist ('mɛkɪtɑːrɪst), *sb.* and *a.* Also **mechitarist.** [f. *Mekhitar* (see below) + -IST.]

A. *sb.* One of a congregation of Armenian monks of the Roman Catholic church originally founded at Constantinople in 1701 by Mekhitar, an Armenian, and by him in 1717 finally established in the island of San Lazzaro, south of Venice.

1834 *Penny Cycl.* II. 364/1 They..call themselves Mekhitaristes. **1882–3** SCHAFF *Encycl. Relig. Knowl.* II. 1457 The Mekhitarists form one of the noblest congregations of the Roman Catholic Church.

B. *adj.* Of or belonging to the Mekhitarists.

1874 *Supernat. Relig.* II. II. ix. 184 In the Mechitarist library at Venice. **1884** *Catholic Dict.* (1897) 617/1 The books..which are printed in the Mechitarist presses of Vienna and Venice are carried far beyond Persia.

Hence **Mechita'ristican** *a.* = prec.

1825 A. GOODE (*title*) A brief Account of the Mechitaristican Society.

mekil(e, mekill(e, obs. forms of MICKLE.

†**mekilwort.** *Sc. Obs.* [app. f. *mekil* MICKLE *a.* + WORT.] The deadly nightshade.

1536 BELLENDEN *Cron. Scot.* (1821) II. 257 The Scottis tuk the jus of mekilwort berries, and mengit it in thair wine [etc.]. **1633** *Orkney Witch Trial* in Dalyell *Darker Superstit. Scot.* (1834) 153 Ane litle pig of oyle, maid of mekillwort.

†**mekin.** *Obs.* A herb used for salad.

1706 LONDON & WISE *Retir'd Gard.* I. 95 *Sallad Seeds...* Mekin.

mekle, obs. form of MICKLE.

mekometer (miː'kɒmɪtə(r)). *Mil.* [f. Gr. μῆκος length + -METER. Cf. MECOMETER.] **a.** An instrument for finding the range for infantry fire.

1894 *Times* 1 Mar. 6/5 The mekometer, the new English infantry range-finder. **1900** *Daily News* 12 Sept. 6/3 The Watkin mekometer.

b. Also **Mekometer.** A device for the accurate measurement of distances in which light elliptically polarized at a microwave frequency is beamed at a reflector at the distance to be measured and the polarization of the reflected light analysed to find the amount by which the distance of the reflector exceeds a whole number of modulation half-wavelengths.

1961 FROOME & BRADSELL in *Jrnl. Sci. Instruments* XXXVIII. 458/1 The paper describes an experimental equipment (known as the 'N.P.L. Microwave Mekometer') using elliptical polarization modulation of a light beam at 9·4

Gc/s (9400 Mc/s) and intended for the accurate measurement of distances of the order of 50 m. **1962** *New Scientist* 26 July 207/2 At the NPL the Mekometer is to be used for the verification of surveyors' precision tapes. **1964** *Trans. Soc. Instrument Technol.* XVI. 31 By September 1960 patents had been filed and in early 1961 the mekometer had become a reality using the Pockels effect at 9·375 Gc/s in a device for the accurate measurement of distance. **1970** *Physics Bull.* Aug. 349/2 Prof R G Mason and his collaborators at Imperial College used a new electromagnetic distance measuring instrument, the mekometer, developed by Dr K D Froome..and in the course of nearly two years detected movements of a few centimetres.

mekul(l, mekyl(l, obs. forms of MICKLE.

mekyn, obs. form of MEEKEN.

mel (mɛl). *Acoustics.* [f. MEL(ODY *sb.*] A unit of subjective pitch, defined so that the number of mels is proportional to the pitch of a sound, and the pitch of a 1000-hertz note (often, one forty decibels above the listener's threshold of hearing) is 1000 mels.

1937 S. S. STEVENS et al. in *Jrnl. Acoustical Soc. Amer.* VIII. 188/1 The numbers on the pitch scale are related to each other as the subjective magnitudes of the pitches. A pitch of 1000 units (mels) is subjectively twice as high as a pitch of 500 units... The name *mel* was chosen as a name for the subjective pitch unit. **1957** J. L. HUNTER *Acoustics* viii. 249 A tone having an apparent pitch twice as high has a pitch of 2,000 mels..regardless of its frequency. **1962** P. LADEFOGED *Elem. Acoustic Phonetics* vi. 79 Frequency data about speech sounds are often converted into mel units before being presented graphically. **1966** R. L. SURI *Acoustics* I. ii. 21 The unit of pitch has been given the name 'mel' such that the pitch at 1000 cycles is 1000 mels.

mel, obs. f. MEAL; variant of MEDLE, MELL.

‖**mela** ('meːlə). [Hindī *mela*:—Skr. *mēlā* assembly, f. root *mil* to meet.] A religious fair and festival amongst the Hindus.

1800 *Misc. Tracts* in *Asiat. Ann. Reg.* 245/2 This Mela, or fair, is an annual assemblage of Hindus. **1894** *19th Cent.* XXXVI. 284 The great annual meeting, or mela, at the shrine of Janakpur. **1896** N. DAVIS *Three Men & a God* 157 Poor wretches who at the Mela time stand in the court-yard and have the sacred water poured over them.

†**melaconise.** *Min. Obs.* [a. mod.F. *mélaconise*, f. Gr. μέλα-ς black + κόνις dust.] = next.

1839 URE *Dict. Arts* 336 Oxide of Copper..Black, or Melaconise; a black earthy looking substance found at Chessy and other places.

melaconite (mɪ'lækənaɪt). *Min.* [Altered from prec.: see -ITE.] An earthy black oxide of copper, found also in crystals. See TENORITE.

1850 DANA *Syst. Min.* (1854) II. 518. **1865** *Rep. Brit. Assoc., Sections* 33 Crystals of oxide of copper (melaconite).

melacotone, obs. form of MELOCOTON.

melada (mɛ'leɪdə). [a. Sp. *melada*, f. *melar* to boil sugar a second time, f. *miel* honey. Cf. Sp. *melaza* MOLASSES.] (See quot.)

1875 *U.S. Statutes* XVIII. III. 340 Melada shall be.. defined as an article made in the process of sugar-making, being the cane-juice boiled down to the sugar point and containing all the sugar and molasses resulting from the boiling process and without any process of purging or clarification.

melæna (mɪ'liːnə). *Path.* [a. mod.L. *melæna*, a. Gr. μέλαινα, fem. of μέλας black.] In early use, the name of a disease (now no longer recognized), characterized by the evacuation from the bowels and vomiting from the stomach of dark bloody matter. Now used to designate these symptoms occurring in any disease.

1800 *Cullen's Nosol.* 226 Melæna. **1827** ABERNETHY *Surg. Wks.* I. 34 There is great reason for ascribing the discharges in the diseases called melæna to a vitiated secretion from the surface of the alimentary canal. **1834** *Good's Study Med.* (ed. 4) I. 339 *note*, We mean therefore by melæna, the occurrence, as a symptom, in any disease, of very dark-coloured, grumous, pitchy, often highly fetid evacuation by stool..or we use the word as the name of a disease, in which such evacuations..constitute the characteristic symptom. **1905** H. D. ROLLESTON *Dis. Liver* 272 Melæna in cirrhosis may depend on hæmorrhages from the mucosa of the intestines.

b. *concr.* (See quot. 1858.)

1858 COPLAND *Dict. Pract. Med.* II. 827 *Melæna*.., discharges from the bowels, or from the stomach, or both by stool and by the mouth, of a black, or nearly black matter, consequent upon visceral or constitutional disease. **1897** *Allbutt's Syst. Med.* III. 530 In other cases the blood..is passed out per rectum as melæna.

melainotype, erron. form of MELANOTYPE.

‖**melaleuca** (mɛlə'l(j)uːkə). *Bot.* [mod.L. (Linnæus), f. Gr. μέλας black + λευκός white.] A genus of plants; a plant of this genus.

1822 *Med. Botany* II. 129 Cajeput Tree, or Aromatic Melaleuca. **1825** *Greenhouse Comp.* I. 131 Proteas, acacias, melaleucas, and a few other Cape and Botany Bay plants.

‖**melalgia** (mɛ'lældʒɪə). *Path.* [mod.L., f. Gr. μέλος limb + ἄλγος pain.] Pain in the limbs.

1890 in *Syd. Soc. Lex.* **1898** *Allbutt's Syst. Med.* V. 222 Beau grouped these [cases] together under the name 'melalgia'.

melam ('mɛlæm). *Chem.* [Named in 1834 by Liebig (*Ann. d. Pharmacie* X. 12); he declines to give an etymology, preferring that the word should be regarded as an arbitrary coinage; for the ending *-am* cf. MELAMINE.] A buff-coloured, insoluble amorphous substance obtained by the distillation of sulphocyanide of ammonium.

1835 *Rec. Gen. Sci.* I. 185. **1838** T. THOMSON *Chem. Org. Bodies* 772. **1889** MUIR & MORLEY *Watts' Dict. Chem.* II. 323 Melam, $C_6H_9N_{11}$.—Crude melam is obtained by the action of heat on ammonium thiocyanide.

melamed (mɪ'lɑːmɪd). Also **melammed**. Pl. **melamdim**. [Heb.] A teacher of elementary Hebrew.

1892 I. ZANGWILL *Childr. Ghetto* II. 16 A *Melammed*, or Hebrew teacher. **1902** H. HAPGOOD *Spirit of Ghetto* i. 19 He is carried by his father to the school and received there by the 'melamed', or teacher. **1968** L. ROSTEN *Joys of Yiddish* 232 Pitying, even derogatory, tales about *melamdim* abound among Jews. In all of them, the *melamed* is not the hero but the goat—hapless, unlucky, unresourceful. **1970** L. M. FEINSILVER *Taste of Yiddish* ii. 233 Where the melamed used the ruler and threatened with his strap, the modern Hebrew teacher takes all he can and then sends the kid to the office. **1972** F. B. MAYNARD *Raisins & Almonds* 163 A world peopled by rabbis, starving *melameds* (teachers), matchmakers, [etc.].

melamine ('mɛləmiːn, -aɪn). *Chem.* Also **-in**. [Named by Liebig in 1834; f. MEL(AM) + AMINE.] **1.** A crystalline substance obtained by boiling melam with potassic hydrate, or by heating cyanamide to 302°; called also *cyanuramide*.

1835 *Rec. Gen. Sci.* I. 185 Melamine. **1836–41** BRANDE *Chem.* (ed. 5) 577 Melamin. **1844** FOWNES *Chem.* 468 Melamine.

2. Also **Melamine**. Melamine resin, or a plastic derived from it.

1940 *Plastics* IV. 162/3 The Westinghouse panels for refrigerators making use of the new plastic were made, initially at least, with a white 'Melamine' coating over phenolic laminated sheet. **1943** *Jrnl. Oil & Colour Chem. Assoc.* XXVI. 187 There has been some tendency to regard melamine and melamine resin as meaning the same thing. **1958** *Spectator* 26 Sept. 406/3 Much of the tough new plastic tableware is made of melamine. **1972** *Daily Tel.* 6 June 13/4 Young couples usually eat in the kitchen, and kitchen/dining tables with white melamine tops are attractive. **1973** 'D. HALLIDAY' *Dolly & Starry Bird* ii. 20 Charles.. poured him a noggin..into a yellow Melamine cup.

3. *attrib.* and *Comb.*: ***melamine-formaldehyde, -surfaced*** adjs.; **melamine resin**, any of the synthetic resins made by the condensation of melamine with an aldehyde, used in making tableware, as coatings for working surfaces, in adhesives, and for treating cloth and paper.

1941 *Industr. & Engin. Chem.* June 771/2 In order that melamine-formaldehyde resins are to be of use to the paint and varnish industry. **1962** J. T. MARSH *Self-Smoothing Fabrics* vi. 81 Melamine-formaldehyde finishes suffer little loss in strength on chlorination but the fabric becomes yellow. **1967** *Times Rev. Industry* June 74/3 No kitchen interior is acceptable to-day without its melamine-formaldehyde laminated surfaces. **1939** *Brit. Plastics* June 28/2 (*heading*) Creaseless fabrics containing melamine resin. **1943** *Jrnl. Oil & Colour Chem. Assoc.* XXVI. 192 The American paint industry is showing a great interest in melamine resins. **1966** *McGraw-Hill Encycl. Sci. & Technol.* XIV. 216/2 Melamine resins are especially valuable as adhesives for laminates of paper or fabrics. **1960** *Times* 16 Mar. (Canberra Suppl.) p. viii/5 Bulkheads and deckheads ..will be covered in either melamine-surfaced laminated plastic, or the softer material commonly known as P.V.C. **1971** *Woman's Own* 27 Mar. 53/3 Elegant shelves can be made from white melamine-surfaced Contiplas.

†**melampod.** *Obs.* Also 6 **melampode, -podi**, 9 in Latin form **melampodium**. [ad. L. *melampodium, -ion*, a. Gr. μελαμπόδιον black hellebore, f. μελαν-, μέλας black + ποδ-, πούς foot.] Black Hellebore, *Helleborus officinalis*.

1579 SPENSER *Sheph. Cal.* July 85 Here grows Melampode every where. **1592** R. D. *Hypnerotomachia* 32 Heleborous [*sic*] Niger or Melampodi. **1643** *Parables reflecting on Times* 12 Briony, Wormwood, Wolfebane, Rue, and Melampod (the emblems of Sedition, Malice, Feare, Ambition and Iealousie). **1656** BLOUNT *Glossogr.*, Melampod (*melampodium*), the hearb called *Hellebore*. **1822–34** *Good's Study Med.* (ed. 4) IV. 284 The melampodium or black hellebore was at one time a favourite cathartic in dropsies.

melampyre ('mɛlæmpaɪə(r)). [f. mod.L. *Melampyrum*, the generic name of cow-wheat: see MELAMPYRIN.] = COW-WHEAT.

1905 E. PHILLPOTTS *Secret Woman* III. v. 244 The melampyre's lemon blossoms and the orange stars of the woody loosestrife mingled close at hand.

melampyrin (mɛlæm'paɪərɪn). *Chem.* [f. mod.L. *Melampȳrum* (a. Gr. μελάμπυρον 'cow-wheat', f. μελαν- black + πυρός wheat), the name of a genus of plants in which the substance is found.] = DULCITE. Also **Melam'pyrite**.

1844 HOBLYN *Dict. Med.*, *Melampyrin*, a substance obtained from the *Melampyrum nemorosum*. **1865** WATTS tr. *Gmelin's Handbk. Chem.* XV. 389 Melampyrin. *Ibid.*, Melampyrite.

†**mela'næma.** *Path. Obs.* [mod.L., a. Gr. μέλαν αἷμα black blood: see next.] A condition of suffocation in which the blood throughout the body assumes a dark or black colour.

1788 GOODWYN *Connex. Life with Respiration* 95 This disease..might with more propriety be named Melanæma. **1822** GOOD *Study Med.* III. 551. **1890** in *Syd. Soc. Lex.*

melanæmia (mɛlə'niːmɪə). *Path.* [mod.L., f. Gr. μελαν-, μέλας black + αἷμα blood. Cf. G. *melanàmie* (Frerichs in *Günsb. Ztschr.* 1855).] A morbid condition, associated with severe forms of malarial fever, in which the blood contains granules and flakes of black or brown pigment.

1860 *N. Syd. Soc. Year Bk. Med.* 254 Cases of Morbus Addisonii, Melanæmia [etc.]. **1898** P. MANSON *Trop. Dis.* i. 2 Those absolutely characteristic features of malarial disease —melanæmia and malarial pigmentation of viscera.

melanæmic (mɛlə'niːmɪk), *a. Path.* [f. prec. + -IC.] Relating to or affected with melanæmia.

1878 tr. *H. von Ziemssen's Cycl. Med.* VIII. 558 At the next febrile attack..the patient becomes again.. melanæmic. **1899** CAGNEY tr. *Jaksch's Clin. Diagn.* i. (ed. 4) 40 Melanæmic Blood..from a Case of Malarial Cachexia.

†**melanagogue.** *Med. Obs.* Also erron. 8 **melano-**. [a. F. *mélanagogue*, f. Gr. μελαν-, μέλας black + ἀγωγός leading, drawing.] A medicine supposed to expel 'black bile'. Hence †**melana'gogal** *a.*, having the property of expelling 'black bile'.

[**1657** *Phys. Dict.*, *Melanogogon*, purgers of melancholy.] **1657** TOMLINSON *Renou's Disp.* 115 Other [pills are called] Melanagogall which purge and move Melancholicall succe. **1683** SALMON *Doron Med.* I. iii. 34 Sena..is one of the best Melanagogues in Nature. **1737** BRACKEN *Farriery Impr.* (1757) II. 250 Melanagogues, which are supposed to draw or carry off the black Matter.

melanasphalt (mɛlə'næsfælt). *Min.* [f. Gr. μελαν-, μέλας black + ἄσφαλτ-ος: see ASPHALT.] = ALBERTITE.

1852 WETHERILL in *Trans. Amer. Philos. Soc.* (1853) X. 353 On a New Variety of Asphalt: (Melan-asphalt).

melanate ('mɛlənət). *Chem.* [f. MELAN-IC + -ATE.] A salt of melanic acid (*Cassell's Encycl. Dict.* 1885).

melanchlor(e ('mɛlənklɔər). *Min.* [Named 1839 by Fuchs (*Melanchlor*), f. Gr. μελαν-, μέλας black + χλωρός green.] A blackish-green hydrous phosphate of iron.

1854 DANA *Syst. Min.* (ed. 4) II. 428 Melanchlor. **1865** WATTS *Dict. Chem.* III. 866 Melanchlor.

†**melancholeric**, *a. Obs. rare*—[1]. [f. Gr. μελαν-, μέλας black + χολέρα CHOLER + -IC.] = MELANCHOLIC *a.*

1650 VENNER *Tobacco* in *Bathes of Bathe* 415 Tobacco any way, or any time used, is most pernicious unto dry melancholerick bodies.

‖**melancholia** (mɛlən'kəʊlɪə). *Nosology.* Pl. **-iæ**. [late Latin: see MELANCHOLY.] 'A functional mental disease, characterised by gloomy thoughtfulness, ill-grounded fears, and general depression of mind' (*Syd. Soc. Lex.* 1890); a species or a case of this disease.

1693 tr. *Blancard's Phys. Dict.* (ed. 2). **1814** SYD. SMITH *Wks.* (1859) I. 232/2 The number of recoveries, in cases of *melancholia*, has been very unusual. **1886** HALL & JASTROW in *Mind* Jan. 60 In certain melancholiæ and other mental disorders. **1899** *Allbutt's Syst. Med.* VIII. 373 Grayness [of the hair] often increases rapidly in melancholia.

melancholiac (mɛlən'kəʊlɪæk), *a.* and *sb.* [f. MELANCHOLIA + -AC, after *maniac*.]

a. *adj.* Affected with melancholia. **b.** *sb.* One suffering from melancholia.

1863 READE *Hard Cash* III. 100 In short, she gave them the impression that Alfred was a moping melancholiac. *Ibid.* 123 A lunatic of the unhappiest class, the melancholiac. **1897** A. R. URQUHART in *Dict. Nat. Biog.* LII. 320/2 Separating the insane into groups of maniacs, melancholiacs, and so on.

†**melan'cholian**, *a.* and *sb. Obs.* Also 4 **malen-, malancolien, melanconien.** [f. MELANCHOLY + -AN.] **a.** *adj.* Having the atrabilious temperament; also, addicted to 'melancholy' or causeless anger. **b.** *sb.* One suffering from melancholia. Also, one of an atrabilious temperament.

1340 *Ayenb.* 157 Þe dyeuel..asayleþ..þane sanguinien mid ioliuete and mid luxurie..þane melanconien mid enuie and mid zorȝe. **1390** GOWER *Conf.* I. 287 He which Malencolien Of pacience hath no lien, Wherof his wrathe the he mai restreigne. **1632** tr. *Bruel's Praxis Med.* 102 Melancholians feare much and are sad. **1681** COLVIL *Whigs Supplic.* (1751) 119 Sanguinians did only laff, Cholerick Melancholians chaff. *a* **1695** J. SCOTT *Wks.* (1718) II. 125 You may observe, in the Modern Stories of our Religious Melancholians, that they commonly pass out of one Passion into another.

†**melan'choliant**, *a. Obs.* In 4 **malancolient, -lyent.** [a. OF. *melancoliant*, pr. pple. of *melancolier* to affect with or suffer from

melancholy, f. *melancolie* sb.] Of blood: Affected with 'melancholy'; atrabilious.

c **1400** *Lanfranc's Cirurg.* 84 Or ellis þe splene is to feble to purge þe malancolient [*Add. MS.* malancolyent] blood.

melancholic (mɛlən'kɒlɪk), *a.* and *sb.* Forms: 4–5 **malencolik, -colyk, malancolike, melancolyk, -colik,** 6 **-ic, -yk(e, -cholyke, -chollike,** 6–7 **-cholik(e, -icke, -ique,** 7 **-chollique,** 7– **melancholic.** [ad. late L. *melancholicus*, a. Gr. μελαγχολικός, f. μελαν- black + χολή bile: see MELANCHOLY and -IC. Cf. F. *mélancolique* (from 14th c.), Pr. *melancolic*, Sp. *melancólico*, Pg. *melancolico*, It. *melancolico*, *malinconico*; also G. *melancholisch*.]

A. *adj.*

†**1.** Pertaining to or containing 'melancholy' or 'black bile'; atrabilious. Of food, atmospheric or planetary influences, etc.: Tending to produce 'melancholy' or atrabilious disorder. *Obs.*

c **1386** CHAUCER *Knt.'s T.* 517 Manye Engendred of humour malencolik. **1398** TREVISA *Barth. De P.R.* VII. lxiv. (1495) 281 Somtyme lepra comyth of euyll dyete as Melancolyk meete to colde and drye. *c* **1532** DU WES *Introd. Fr.* in *Palsgr.* 1071 All suche byrdes ben of nature melancolyke. **1549** *Compl. Scot.* vi. 61 The..northin vynd ..is cald and dry, of ane melancolic natur. *c* **1550** LLOYD *Treas. Health* L viij, Much melancholyke bloud conteynyd in the lyuer. **1578** LYTE *Dodoens* 377 All diseases springing of melancholique, adust, and salt humours. **1631** WIDDOWES *Nat. Philos.* 10 Hee is a Planet masculine, of cold and dry nature, therefore melancholicke.

2. Of persons, their attributes, actions, etc.

†**a.** Having the atrabiliar temperament or constitution (*obs.*). **b.** Constitutionally liable to (formerly also, †affected with) melancholy or depression of spirits; gloomy, depressed, melancholy.

†*melancholic gentleman*: see MELANCHOLY *a.* 6 (quot. 1629).

?*a* **1400** LYDG. *Isopus* 61 (Zupitza) By whyche he [the cock] haþe.. corage and hardynes, And of hys berde melancolyk felnes. *c* **1430** —— *Min. Poems* (Percy Soc.) 197 Malencolik of his complexioun. **1471** CAXTON *Recuyell* (ed. Sommer) 105 He..becam all melancolik with out takyng Ioye ne plaisir in ony thyng that he sawe. **1570–6** LAMBARDE *Peramb. Kent* (1826) 125 King Canutus..departed all wroth and melancholike into Denmark. **1647** CLARENDON *Hist. Reb.* VI. §386 No man had more melancholic apprehensions of the issue of the war. **1693** CONGREVE *Old Bach.* III. x, I am melancholic when thou art absent. **1708** GAY *Wine* 60 In melancholic mood Joyless he wastes in sighs the lazy hours. **1717** PRIOR *Alma* I. 210 Just as the melancholic eye Sees fleets and armies in the sky. **1876** BANCROFT *Hist. U.S.* I. x. 362 'Religion', said the melancholic Norton, 'admits of no eccentric motions'. **1900** MORLEY *Cromwell* i. 15 Oliver was of the melancholic temperament.

transf. **1612** WEBSTER *White Devil* F 4, And like your melancholike hare Feed after midnight.

absol. **1594** CAREW *Huarte's Exam. Wits* (1616) 148 He.. was not verie prompt of speech, which Aristotle affirmeth to be a propertie of the melancholicke by adustation.

†**3.** Resulting from, or of the nature of, 'melancholy' or atrabilious disorder. *Obs.*

1652–62 HEYLIN *Cosmogr.* III. (1682) 188 He contracted some melancholick distempers. **1683** SALMON *Doron Med.* I. ix. 61 In melancholick Tumors.

†**4.** Causing melancholy or depression of spirits; saddening. *Obs.*

1612 WEBSTER *White Devil* H 4, The blacke, and melancholicke Eugh-tree. **1615** G. SANDYS *Trav.* 83 Keeping time with the melancholicke musicke. **1693** DRYDEN *Let.* 30 Aug., Pr. Wks. 1800 I. II. 28, I was tempted to it, by the melancholique prospect I had of it. **1723** MATHER *Vind. Bible* 360 No public sorrow should be expressed on so melancholick an occasion. **1812** G. CHALMERS *Dom. Econ. Gt. Brit.* 139 Such is the melancholic picture.

†**5.** Expressive of melancholy or sadness. *Obs.*

1671 MILTON *Samson* Introd., In Physic, things of melancholic hue and quality are us'd against melancholy. **1757** MRS. GRIFFITH *Lett. Henry & Frances* (1767) II. 295, I wrote a long, and of course, a melancholic letter to you.

6. In mod. use: Pertaining to, or affected with, melancholia.

1866 W. H. O. SANKEY *Lect. Mental Dis.* iii. 74 The case, commencing by a melancholic stage,..the melancholic and maniacal symptoms blend in different cases.

B. *sb.*

1. †**a.** One who is affected with mental depression or sadness (*obs.*). **b.** One suffering from melancholia; = MELANCHOLIAC *sb.*

1586 BRIGHT *Melancholy* xxxix. 256 With such like ornament of iewell as agreeth with the habilitie and calling of the melancholicke. **1645** RUTHERFORD *Tryal & Tri. Faith* (1845) 394 The Soul..is put to silence before God, and sitteth alone, as melancholics do. **1681** GLANVILL *Sadducismus* (1682) Ded., The discontented Paradox of a melancholick, vext, and of mean condition. **1755** *Man* No. 29. 3 Two famous sects of philosophers, which..still continue to divide the world into melancholics, and men of pleasure. **1870** MAUDSLEY *Body & Mind* 95 Should he do injury to himself or others, as hypochondriacal melancholics sometimes do. **1899** *Allbutt's Syst. Med.* VIII. 371 One melancholic swam across a canal to throw himself under a train.

†**2.** Used by Clarendon for: Depression of spirits, melancholy. *Obs.*

1647 CLARENDON *Hist. Reb.* I. §62 He continued in this melancholic and discomposure of mind many days. *a* **1674** —— *Life* II. (1759) 69 My Condition..will very well justify the Melancholick that, I confess to you, possesses me.

Hence †**melan'cholical** *a.*, melancholy; **melan'cholically** *adv.*, in a melancholy manner.

1657 TOMLINSON *Renou's Disp.* 115 Which purge and move melancholicall succe. **1882** B. NICHOLSON in *N. Shaks. Soc. Trans.* 349 He..became melancholicaly mad immediately on the shock of these revelations. **1889** *Harper's Mag.* Apr. 767/2 Its walls of rammed clay frittering away melancholically in the sun.

†**melan'cholicly**, *adv. Obs.* [f. MELANCHOLIC *a.* + -LY².] In a melancholy manner.

1607 WALKINGTON *Opt. Glasse* xii. 130 An aliment vnto the parts which are melancholikly qualified, as the bones, grisles, sinewes, &c. **1631** R. BOLTON *Comf. Affl. Consc.* (1640) 202 Men are melancholikely grieved.

‖**melan'cholico.** *Obs.* [It. *melancolico*: see MELANCHOLIC.] A hypochondriac.

1676 *Doctrine of Devils* 156 Or of the Monstrous Credulity, some besotted Melancholicoes may be inveigled into.

melancholily ('mɛlənkɒlɪlɪ), *adv.* [f. MELANCHOLY *a.* + -LY².] In a melancholy manner.

1536 CROMWELL in Merriman *Life & Lett.* (1902) II. 23 Applieng the same if not colerikly I must nedes thinke melancoulily, to your purpose. **1647** COWLEY *Mistress, Maidenhead*, No wonder 'tis..thou shouldst be Such tedious..Company, Who liv'st so Melancholily. **1846** THACKERAY *Laman Blanchard* Wks. 1900 XIII. 470 Laman Blanchard, who passed away so melancholily last year. **1891** *Harper's Mag.* Aug. 434/1 Others big and wavering float melancholily.

†'**melancholiness.** *Obs.* [f. MELANCHOLY *a.* + -NESS.] The condition of being melancholy.

1528 PAYNEL *Salerne's Regim.* B, In this doctrine be comprehended melancolynes and heuines. *a* **1697** AUBREY *Lives, Hobbes* (1898) I. 329 When he was a boy he was playsome enough, but withall he had even then a contemplative melancholinesse. **1715** M. DAVIES *Athen. Brit.* I. Pref. 4 A Vent to Melancholiness.

melancholious (mɛlən'kəʊlɪəs), *a.* Now *rare.* Forms: 4–5 **malan-, malencolious, -ius, malen-, melancolyous(e, (5 malencolyows, malecoliowus),** 5–6 **malincolyous,** 6 **malacolious, melancolyouse, -colius, melencolous,** 7 *Sc.* **melancholiows,** 4–7 **melancolious,** 6– **melancholious.** [a. OF. *melancolieus*, f. *melancolie* MELANCHOLY: see -OUS.]

1. Constitutionally inclined to melancholy; †atrabilious in constitution (*obs.*); affected with melancholy, gloomy. Also, of sounds, etc.: Expressive or suggestive of melancholy.

c **1380** WYCLIF *Wks.* (1880) 215 Whanne þei ben out of reson as wroþ & malencolious. *c* **1384** CHAUCER *H. Fame* I. 30 Somme man is to curiouse In studye, or melancolyouse. **1433** LYDG. *St. Edmund* 465 in Horstm. *Altengl. Leg. N.F.* (1884) 405 Malencolius of face, look and cheer. **1471** CAXTON *Recuyell* (ed. Sommer) 24 Sorowfull syghes and melancolyous fantasies. **1523** LD. BERNERS *Froiss.* I. cccxlvi. 547 This pope..was a fumisshe man and malincolyous. **1568** GRAFTON *Chron.* II. 816 Whether it were by the inspiracion of the holy ghost, or by Melencolous disposition, I had diuers and sundrie imaginations howe [etc.]. **1610** BARROUGH *Meth. Physick* I. xxviii. (1639) 45 They that be melancholious have strange imaginations. **1637–50** Row *Hist. Kirk* (Wodrow Soc.) 368 The King was sad and melancolious. **1783** BURNS *Poor Mailie's Elegy* 8 Come, join the melancholious croon O' Robin's reed! **1848** THACKERAY *Van. Fair* xi, The Rector..added, in a melancholious tone [etc.]. **1897** CROCKETT *Lads' Love* iii. 31 The sufferer..from whom .. most melancholious sounds .. continually proceeded.

†**2.** Tending to cause, or of the nature of, 'melancholy' or atrabilious disorder. *Obs.*

c **1400** *Lanfranc's Cirurg.* 171 þoruȝ þat oon pore he drawiþ malancolious blood of þe lyuere. *Ibid.* 273 Varicosa schal be curid..wiþ purgaciouns of malancholious blood. **1456** SIR G. HAYE *Law Arms* (S.T.S.) 76 The tane [star or planet] is sangwyne, the tothir is malancolius. **1562** BULLEYN *Bulwark, Bk. Simples* 78 b, It bredeth choler adust, and melancholious diseases.

Hence **melan'choliousness.**

1610 BARROUGH *Meth. Physick* I. xxviii. (1639) 45 There be three diversities of melancholiousnes, according to the three kinds of causes.

†**melancholish**, *a. Obs.* [f. MELANCHOLY + -ISH.] **a.** = MELANCHOLIC *a.* 1. **b.** Inclined to be melancholy or depressed.

1562 TURNER *Herbal* II. 54 b, Mynt..leueth still it that is grosse and melancholishe. **1775** S. J. PRATT *Liberal Opin.* xcv. (1783) III. 198 Miss is a little melancholish.

melancholist ('mɛlənkəlɪst). Now *rare* or *Obs.* [f. MELANCHOLY + -IST.] †One of a 'melancholic' constitution (*obs.*); one affected with melancholia; in the 17th c. often applied contemptuously to religious enthusiasts.

1599 H. BUTTES *Dyets drie Dinner* L iv b, Doth helpe melanchollists onely, by moistning their dry constitution. **1676** GLANVILL *Ess.* VI. 29 The proud and fantastick Pretences of many of the conceited Melancholists in this Age. **1749** LAVINGTON *Enthus. Meth. & Papists* I. (1754) 2 Montanus..drew after him several religious Melancholists. **1806** *Med. Jrnl.* XV. 212 Dr. G...visited the male ideots and melancholists. **1858** BURTON in *Blackw. Mag.* LXXXIII. 276 Our gallant captain, a notable melancholist, sat up till dawn.

melancholize ('mɛlənkəˌlaɪz), *v.* Now *rare* or *Obs.* [f. MELANCHOLY + -IZE.]

1. *intr.* and *refl.* To be or become melancholy.

1597 A. M. tr. *Guillemeau's Fr. Chirurg.* 52/2 They doe so melancholize themselves therin, that they doe wholy neglect themselves. **1621** BURTON *Anat. Mel.* I. ii. III. vi. 134 They dare not come abroad all their liues after, but melancholize in corners. **1794** COLERIDGE *Let.* 22 July in *Biog. Lit.* (1847) II. 339 From Oxford..have I journeyed, now philosophizing with hacks, now melancholizing by myself. **1801** LAMB *Ess., Cur. Fragm.* [imitating Burton] ii. in *John Woodvil*, etc. (1802) 119 Melancholising in woods where waters are. **1863** K. H. DIGBY *Chapel St. John* (ed. 2) 395 Others were melancholizing in woods, and sighing in gardens.

2. *trans.* To make melancholy.

1642 H. MORE *Song of Soul* I. III. xl, Like faithlesse wife that..Doth inly deep the spright melancholize Of her aggrieved husband. **1668** —— *Div. Dial.* II. xiv. (1713) 129 There's nothing does more contristate and melancholize my Spirit than any reflexions upon such Objects.

Hence **'melanchoˌlized** *ppl. a.*, rendered melancholy; **'melanchoˌlizing** *vbl. sb.*

1621 BURTON *Anat. Mel.* Democr. to Rdr. 7 They get their knowledge by bookes, I mine by melancholising. **1642** H. MORE *Song of Soul* Ded., Nor can ever that thick cloud ..of melancholized old age..dark the remembrance of your pristine Lustre. **1678** CUDWORTH *Intell. Syst.* Contents I. v, Our own Imaginations [are] taken for sensations and realities in sleep, and by melancholized persons when awake.

melancholy ('mɛlənkəlɪ), *sb.* Forms: 4 **malyncoly,** 4–5 **malycoly, malencoli(e, -colye, malicoli,** 4–6 **malancoly, -encoly, melancoly(e, -lie,** 5 **mali(n)coly, -yncolie, malencholye, malancoli(e, -lye, melancholye,** 5–6 **mallancoly,** 5–7 **melancholie,** 6 **melacholy, melancholi,** *Sc.* **-kolie,** 6–7 **melancholly, -olye,** 6– **melancholy.** [a. OF. *melancolie*, *melencolie*, *malencollie*, etc. (mod. F. *mélancolie*), ad. L. *melancholia*, a. Gr. μελαγχολία lit. 'condition of having black bile', f. μελαν-, μέλας black + χολή bile. Cf. Pr. *melancolia*, Sp. *melancolía*, It. *melancolia*, *malinconia*; also G. *melancholie*, Du. *melankolie*, Da., Sw. *melankoli*.]

Down to the 17th c. the poetical examples commonly indicate stress on the second or fourth syllable.

†**1.** The condition of having too much 'black bile' (see b); the disease supposed to result from this condition; in early references its prominent symptoms are sullenness and propensity to causeless and violent anger, and in later references mental gloom and sadness. From the 17th c. onwards the word was used without its ætiological implication as the name of the mental disease now called in technical language MELANCHOLIA. *Obs.*

Quot. 1866 is an exceptionally late instance of the sense: cf. quot. 1859 in 3.

1303 R. BRUNNE *Handl. Synne* 3710 þe man wraþþyþ hym lyghtly, For lytyl as yn malyncoly, þat synne ne ys ryght gref þat sone ys wroþe, and lyghtly lef. *c* **1374** CHAUCER *Troylus* v. 360 Thy sweuenes ek and [al] swich fantasye Dryf out, and lat hem faren to myschaunce; For þey proceden of þi malencolye. **1471** CAXTON *Recuyell* (ed. Sommer) 21 After many right sorowful syghes engendrid in þe roote of malencolie. **1578** LYTE *Dodoens* I. lvii. 84 The dissease called choler or melancholy. **1615** G. SANDYS *Trav.* 99 That windy malancholy arising from the shorter ribs, which so saddeth the mind of the diseased. **1677** J. WEBSTER (*title*) The Displaying of supposed Witchcraft, wherein is affirmed that there are many sorts of Deceivers and Impostors, and Divers persons under a passive Delusion of Melancholy and Fancy. But that [etc.]. **1722** QUINCY *Lex. Phys.-Med.*, Melancholy [is] supposed to proceed from a Redundance of black Bile; but it is better known to arise from too heavy and too viscid a Blood. **1866** W. H. O. SANKEY *Lect. Ment. Dis.* ii. 33 There are cases of melancholy which are accompanied by great restlessness.

†**b.** *concr.* The 'black bile' itself: one of the four chief fluids or 'cardinal humours' of the ancient and mediæval physiologists. *Obs.*

1398 TREVISA *Barth. De P.R.* IV. xi. (1495) 95 Malencoly is bred of trowbled drast of blode and hath his name of melon that is blak and calor that is humour, so is sayd as it were a blak humour, for the colour therof lynyth toward blackenes. *c* **1400** *Lanfranc's Cirurg.* 202 þer is engendrid anoþer substaunce þat is sumwhat stynkyng & is clepid malancoli. **1533** ELYOT *Cast. Helth* (1541) 8 In the body of Man be foure principall humours: Bloudde: Fleume: Choler: Melancoly. **1578** BANISTER *Hist. Man* v. 70 A short vessel, whereby the splene belcheth vp melancolye into the ventricle. **1610** BARROUGH *Meth. Physick* III. xxx. (1639) 149 The Iaundeis is nothing else but a shedding either of yellow choler, or of melancholy all over the body. **1653** H. MORE *Antid. Ath.* II. vi. (1712) 56 There are receptacles in the Body of Man and Emunctories to drain them of superfluous Choler, Melancholy, and the like.

†**2.** Irascibility, ill-temper, anger, sullenness.

c **1350** *Will. Palerne* 4362 Meke þe of þi malencoli for marring of þi-selue. **1375** BARBOUR *Bruce* XVI. 128 Vith that the king come hastely, And in his gret malancoly,..To schir Colyne sic dusche he gave. *c* **1386** CHAUCER *Wife's Prol.* 252 And if she be riche, of heigh parage, Thanne seistow it is a tormentrie To soffren hire pride and hire malencolie. *a* **1400–50** *Alexander* 1981 þat I mete þe in my malicoly my meth be to littill. **14..** *Tundale's Vis.* 76 (Wagner) Tundale gruched and wex wrothe..þe man speke to hym curtesly And brought hym out of his malycoly. **1525** LD. BERNERS *Froiss.* II. xv. 29 The kynge beyng in his malencoly, assone as he sawe hym he sayd in great yre, certesse vncle of Lancastre, ye shall nat attayne as yet to your entent. **1530**

PALSGR. 244/1 Melancoly testysnesse, *melencolie*. **1567** in *Satir. Poems Reform.* vii. 191 For wickit lyfe imprisont was Ferquhaird, Quha slew him self of proude melancolie.

personified. **1390** GOWER *Conf.* I. 280 Malencolie..which in compaignie An hundred times in an houre Wol as an angri beste loure. *c* **1400** *Rom. Rose* 4998 Malencoly, that angry sire. **1595** SHAKS. *John* III. iii. 42 If that surly spirit melancholy, Had bak'd thy blood, and made it heauy, thicke.

3. Sadness and depression of spirits; a condition of gloom or dejection, especially when habitual or constitutional.

In the early quots. with mixture of sense 2. In the Elizabethan period and subsequently, the affectation of 'melancholy' was a favourite pose among those who made claim to superior refinement; see, e.g. Jonson *Every Man in his Humour* (passim), and quots. under MELANCHOLY *a.* 3; cf. also 3 d below.

c **1374** CHAUCER *Troylus* v. 1216 Bycause he wolde soone dye, He ne eet ne dronk, for his malencolye. **14..** *Sir Beues* 582 (MS. M) Iosyan..Toke hym vp and kyssud hym swete, His malincoly there to abate. **1485** CAXTON *Chas. Gt.* 168 Whyche also slewe my cosyn the kyng Claryon, for whome I am in grete melancolye. *a* **1586** SIDNEY *Arcadia* III. (1598) 386 The Hare [gave] her sleights; the Cat, his melancholy. **1590** SPENSER *F.Q.* I. xii. 38 Musicke did apply Her curious skill the warbling notes to play, To drive away the dull Melancholy. **1593** SHAKS. *2 Hen. VI*, v. i. 34 My minde was troubled with deepe Melancholly. **1593** DRAYTON *Sheph. Garland* (Roxb. Club) 68 And, being rouzde out of melancholly, Flye, whirle-winde thoughts, vnto the heavens, quoth he. **1692** DRYDEN *Cleomenes* I. i. 2 This Melancholly Flatters, but Un-mans you. What is it else, but Penury of Soul; A Lazie Frost, a numness of the Mind? **1716** LADY M. W. MONTAGU *Let. to Lady X—* 1 Oct., It gives me too much melancholy to see so agreeable a young creature buried alive. **1842** BORROW *Bible in Spain* xxxiv, A morbid melancholy seized upon the Irishman. **1859** BUCKNILL *Psychol. Shaks.* 240 Care should be taken..to distinguish between melancholy and melancholia. **1899** *Allbutt's Syst. Med.* VIII. 372 The melancholy associated with general paralysis is commonly marked by great exaggeration.

personified. **1601** SHAKS. *Jul. C.* v. iii. 67 O hatefull Error Melancholies Childe. **1632** MILTON *L'Allegro* 1 Hence loathed Melancholy, Of Cerberus and blackest midnight born. **1750** GRAY *Elegy* Epit., And Melancholy mark'd him for her own. **1819** KEATS *Melancholy* iii, In the very temple of Delight Veiled Melancholy has her sovran shrine.

†**b.** A cause of sadness, an annoyance or vexation. Chiefly in *plural*. *Obs.*

1477 EARL RIVERS (Caxton) *Dictes* (*c* 1490) F vj, The maistre of a grete house hath many melancolyes. **1644** MILTON *Areop.* (Arb.) 57 Which to a diligent writer is the greatest melancholy and vexation that can befall.

c. A state of melancholy. †Also, a melancholy fit or mood (often in *plural*). *Obs.*

a **1586** SIDNEY *Arcadia* I. (1590) 17 b, Two or three straungers, whom inwarde melancholies hauing made weery of the worldes eyes, haue come to spende their liues among the countrie people. **1587** FLEMING *Contn. Holinshed* III. 1319/2 Entring by litle and litle out of his present melancholies into his former misfortunes. **1650** JER. TAYLOR *Holy Living* ii. § 5 (1727) 107 If we murmur here, we may at the next melancholy be troubled that God did not make us to be Angels or Stars. **1774** BURKE *Corr.* (1844) I. 480 In spite of all my efforts, I fall into a melancholy which is inexpressible. **1798** CHARLOTTE SMITH *Yng. Philos.* I. 64 A deep yet soft melancholy succeeded.

d. In a lighter sense: A tender or pensive sadness.

1614 DRUMM. OF HAWTH. *Madrigal*, '*When as she smiles*', A sweet melancholie my sences keepes. **1632** MILTON *Penseroso* 12 But hail thou Goddes, sage and holy, Hail divinest Melancholy. **1634** —— *Comus* 546, I..began Wrapt in a pleasing fit of melancholy To meditate my rural minstrelsie. **1796** COLERIDGE *Sonn. to Bowles* [2nd vers.] 8 Their mild and manliest melancholy lent A mingled charm, which oft the pang consigned To slumber. **1844** A. B. WELBY *Poems, Melancholy* 117 Love's delicious melancholy.

†**e.** A short literary composition (usually poetical) of a sad or mournful character. *Obs.*

1596 LODGE *Marg. Amer.* L i b, Another melancholy of his, for the strangenesse thereof, deserueth to be registred. *Ibid.*, Another [*sc.* poem]..hauing the right nature of an Italian melancholie, I haue set down in this place.

4. Comb., as ***melancholy-purger***; ***melancholy-mad***, ***-sick*** adjs.; †**melancholy water**, a decoction recommended as 'good for women if they are faint'.

1660 *Trial Regic.* 171 He was melancholly sick. **1676** J. COOKE *Marrow Chirurg.* 812 Of Melancholy Purgers, Simple and Compound. **1684** HAN. WOOLLEY *Queen-like Closet* (ed. 5) 15 The Melancholly Water. Take of [etc.]. **1853** HICKIE tr. *Aristophanes* (1872) II. 683 He has sent away my master melancholy-mad.

melancholy (ˈmɛlənkəlɪ), *a.* Forms: 6 **malancoly, malincolye, melancholie,** 6–7 **malancholy, melencholly,** 7 **melancholly,** 6– **melancholy.** [From the attrib. use of the sb.]

†**1.** Affected with or constitutionally liable to the disease of melancholy. Also *absol. Obs.*

1526 *Pilgr. Perf.* (W. de W. 1531) 233 b, The contemplacyon of suche turneth eyther to supersticyousnes..or to a melancoly folysshnes. **1542** BOORDE *Dyetary* viii. (1870) 245 Melancoly men may take theyr pleasure. **1612** WOODALL *Surg. Mate* Wks. (1653) 190 It is also effectual to be given to melancholy people, which are void of reason. **1698** M. HENRY *Meekness & Quietn. Spirit* (1822) 80 The quietness of spirit will help..to suppress melancholy vapours. **1732** ARBUTHNOT *Rules of Diet* in *Aliments*, etc. 260 All Spices are bad for melancholy people.

†**b.** Of or affected by the melancholy 'humour'.

1604 T. WRIGHT *Passions* I. ix. 35 A little melancholly blood may quickly change the temperature, and render it [the hearte] more apt for a melancholly Passion. **1610** MARKHAM *Masterp.* II. cxii. 404 It proceedeth from melancholy and filthy bloud. **1655** STANLEY *Hist. Philos.* III. *Socrates* xiv. (init.), As to his person, he was very unhandsome, of a melancholy complexion. **1656** RIDGLEY *Pract. Physick* 306 A crooked melancholy vein under the Tongue. **1667** *Phil. Trans.* II. 493 'Tis vulgarly said that this black part of the bloud is Melancholy bloud.

†**c.** Producing the disease of melancholy. *Obs.*

1650 BAXTER *Saints' R.* II. vii. § 3 Sauls Melancholy Devil would be gone, when David played on the Harp.

†**2.** Irascible, angry; sullen. *Obs.*

1575–6 *Durham Depos.* (Surtees) 290 Sir Richerd is a very earnest malincolye man, and some tyme gyven to be angrye. **1579** TOMSON *Calvin's Serm. Tim.* 191/1 When wee come to make our prayers to God, wee must not bring thither with vs, our melancholy passions and fretting and fuming. **1604** CHAPMAN *Byron's Conspir.* II. i. (1608) D 2 b, Duke Byron Flowes with adust and melancholy choller.

3. Of persons, their actions, attributes, feelings, state, etc.: Depressed in spirits; sad, gloomy, dejected, mournful; *esp.* of a constitutionally gloomy temperament.

1588 SHAKS. *L.L.L.* I. ii. 2 Boy, What signe is it when a man of great spirit growes melancholy? **1592** LYLY *Midas* v. ii. 104 (Bond), Melancholy is the creast of Courtiers armes, and now euerie base companion, beeing in his muble fubles, sayes he is melancholy. **1598** B. JONSON *Ev. Man in Hum.* I. iv, I will be more proud and melancholie, and gentleman-like then I haue beene, I doe ensure you. *c* **1598** SIR J. DAVIES *Epigr.* No. 47 See yonder melancholy Gentleman, Which hood-wink'd with his hat, alone doth sit. **1744** HARRIS *Three Treat.* Wks. (1841) 40 A funeral will much more affect the same man if he see it when melancholy, than if he see it when cheerful. **1753** CHAMBERS *Cycl. Supp.* s.v. *Mania*, Some are dull and stupid, others very sorrowful and melancholy. **1774** BURKE *Sp. Amer. Tax.* Sel. Wks. I. 136, I remember, Sir, with a melancholy pleasure, the situation [etc.]. **1824** W. IRVING *T. Trav.* I. 293 There is no more melancholy creature in existence than a mountebank off duty. **1884** F. M. CRAWFORD *Rom. Singer* I. i. 17 If I am sad and inclined to melancholy humours.

absol. **1759** JOHNSON *Rasselas* xlvi, For this reason the superstitious are often melancholy, and the melancholy almost always superstitious.

transf. (of animals). **1593** NASHE *Christ's T.* 25 b, The mellancholy Owle, (Deaths ordinary messenger). **1612** DRAYTON *Poly-olb.* ii. 204 The melancholie Hare. **1787** BEST *Angling* (ed. 2) 42 He is a solitary, melancholy, and bold fish, always being by himself.

b. Pensive, thoughtful; sadly meditative.

1632 MILTON *Penseroso* 62 Sweet Bird that shunn'st the noise of folly, Most musicall, most melancholy! **1659** WOOD *Life* Feb. (O.H.S.) I. 270 To refresh his mind with a melancholy walke. **1748** THOMSON *Cast. Indol.* I. xl, A certain music, never known before, Here soothed the pensive, melancholy mind. **1792** S. ROGERS *Pleas. Mem.* II. 190 The tender images we love to trace Steal from each year a melancholy grace. **1821** LAMB *Elia* Ser. I. *All Fools' Day*, We will drink no wise, melancholy, politic port on this day.

†**c.** in proverbial and other similes. *Obs.*

1592 LYLY *Midas* v. ii. 100 (Bond), I am as melancholy as a cat. **1596** SHAKS. *1 Hen. IV*, I. ii. 83–8. **1599** —— *Much Ado* II. i. 221, I found him heere as melancholy as a Lodge in a Warren. **1606** *Wily Beguiled* Prol. A 2 b, Why, how now, humorous George? What, as melancholy as a mantle tree? **1607** DEKKER *Northw. Hoe* I. Wks. 1873 III. 11 I'me as melancholy now as Fleet-streete in a long vacation. *a* **1732** GAY *New Song of New Similies*, I, melancholy as a cat Am kept awake to weep.

4. Of visible objects, sounds, places, etc.: Suggestive of sadness, depressing, dismal. Also, of sounds, words, looks, etc.: Expressive of sadness.

†*melancholy hat* (? jocular nonce-use, or slang), app. applied to a mourning hat (but cf. quot. *c* 1598 in sense 3).

1592 SHAKS. *Rom. & Jul.* IV. v. 86 Melancholy Bells. **1600** —— *A. Y. L.* II. vii. 111 Vnder the shade of melancholly boughes. **1614** J. COOKE *Greene's Tu Quoque* B 1 b, Go to the next Haberdashers & bid him send me a new melancholy hat. **1632** LITHGOW *Trav.* I. 43 Padua is the most melancholy City of Europe. **1697** DRYDEN *Virg. Georg.* IV. 747 Melancholy Musick fills the Plains. **1718** LADY M. W. MONTAGU *Let. to C'tess Bristol* 10 Apr., Eight or ten of them make a melancholy concert with their pipes. **1725** SLOANE *Jamaica* II. 307 It loves low melancholly places. **1728–46** THOMSON *Spring* 612 The stock-dove breathes A melancholy murmur thro' the whole. **1833** L. RITCHIE *Wand. by Loire* 197 You glide in a canoe-like boat..shut in by melancholy banks. **1835** LYTTON *Rienzi* I. i, The thick and melancholy foliage. **1843** BORROW *Bible in Spain* x, With here and there a melancholy village. **1860** TYNDALL *Glac.* I. xxvii. 198 The fountain made a melancholy gurgle. **1897** MARY KINGSLEY *W. Africa* 475 Negro children..with ..immense melancholy deer-like eyes.

Comb. **1877** BLACK *Green Past.* v, He was a melancholy-faced man.

†**b.** In the 17th c.: Favourable to the pensive mood. (Cf. 3 b.) *Obs.*

1641 EVELYN *Diary* 8 Oct., So naturally is it [the Parke] furnish'd with whatever may render it agreeable, melancholy and country-like. **1644** *Ibid.* 30 Sept., The house is moderne, and seemes to be the seate of some gentleman, being in a very pleasant though melancholy place.

5. Of a fact, event, state of things: Saddening, lamentable, deplorable.

1710 WODROW *Analecta* (1842) I. 308 It was one of the melancholyest sights to any that have any sense of our antient Nobility, to see them going throu for votes, and making partys. **1763** C. JOHNSTON *Reverie* II. 44 You are affected with this melancholy detail. **1768** STERNE *Sent. Journ., Remise Door*, Melancholy! to see such sprightliness the prey of sorrow. **1807** *Med. Jrnl.* XVII. 247 The most serious and melancholy effect ensued. **1886** *Q. Jrnl. Microsc. Sci.* XXVIII. 291 A melancholy instance of the extent to which Dr. P. acts upon the principle of bending facts to theory.

6. In certain book-names of plants, as **melancholy gentleman**, a kind of rocket, *Hesperis tristis*; **melancholy (plume) thistle**, *Carduus heterophyllus*; **melancholy tree**, the Night Jasmine, *Nyctanthes Arbor-tristis*.

1629 PARKINSON *Parad.* Table, The Melancholy [*text* p. 260 Melancholick] Gentleman. **1690** RAY *Syn. Stirp. Brit.* 52 The great English soft or gentle Thistle or Melancholy Thistle. **1760** J. LEE *Introd. Bot.* App. 319 Melancholy Thistle, *Carduus*. Melancholy-tree, *Nyctanthes*. **1861** MISS PRATT *Flower. Pl.* III. 237 *Cnicus heterophyllus* (Melancholy Plume Thistle).

Hence **ˈmelancholyish** *a. nonce-wd.*

1837 LYTTON in *Fonblanque's Life & Lab.* (1874) 53, I had a melancholyish letter from Lady Blessington.

†**ˈmelancholy,** *v. Obs.* [ad. OF. *melancolier*, f. *melancolie* MELANCHOLY *sb.*] *trans.* To make melancholy.

1491 CAXTON *Vitas Patr.* (W. de W. 1495) II. 290 b/2 The pleasure of god is that; of whiche thou melancolyest thy selfe to be soo doon. **1541** R. COPLAND *Guydon's Quest. Chirurg.* Q iij b, It brenneth the blode & melancolyeth it. **1567** PAYNEL tr. *Herberay's Treas. Amadis of Gaule* 78 Ye melancholy your selfe..for the mariage that I have found out for you. *a* **1657** R. LOVEDAY *Lett.* (1663) 165, I am extremely melancholy'd at your dilated resolutions of seeing London.

Melanchthonian (mɛləŋkˈθəʊnɪən), *a.* and *sb.* [f. name of Philipp *Melanchthon* (Gr. transl. of Schwarzerd 'black earth'), a German reformer (1497–1560) + -IAN.] **a.** *adj.* Of or pertaining to Melanchthon or his opinions. **b.** *sb.* A follower of Melanchthon.

1755 CARTE *Hist. Eng.* IV. 137 The Melanctonian doctrine of predestination. **1765** MACLAINE tr. *Mosheim's Eccl. Hist.* II. i. § 11 (1833) 480/1 There arose..three philosophical sects, the Melanchthonian, the Aristotelian, and the Scholastic. **1863** W. C. DOWDING *Life & Corr. Calixtus* iii. 20 We have described him as a Melanchthonian both in taste and principle. **1882–3** SCHAFF *Encycl. Relig. Knowl.* I. 474 It [the Anglican Church] is yet Melancthonian in its assertion of the visibility of the Church.

melanchyme (ˈmɛlənkaɪm). *Min.* [G. *melanchym* (Haidinger 1851), f. Gr. μελαν-, μέλας black + χυμός juice (see CHYME).] = ROCHLEDERITE.

1868 DANA *Syst. Min.* (ed. 5) II. 744.

melancoli(e, -ien, -(i)ous, obs. forms of MELANCHOLY, etc.

†**melancounterous,** *a. Obs.* [For ***malencounterous**, ad. F. *malencontreux*, f. *mal* ill + *encontrer* to ENCOUNTER: see -OUS.] Ill-timed.

a **1610** SIR J. SEMPLE in *Sempill Ballatis* (1872) 244 The never ceasing feide of melancounterous faites Ouer haistnit this abortiue birth of Importune regrates.

melander, obs. form of MALANDER, MALLENDER.

melanellite (mɛləˈnɛlaɪt). *Min.* [Obscurely f. Gr. μελαν-, μέλας black: see -ITE.] A black hydrocarbon forming part of rochlederite.

1868 DANA *Syst. Min.* (ed. 5) II. 750 Melanellite... Black and gelatinous.

Melanesian (mɛləˈniːʃ(ɪ)ən, -ˈniːʒ(ɪ)ən), *a.* and *sb.* [f. *Melanesia* (see below: f. Gr. μέλα-ς black + νῆσος island) + -AN.

The name, modelled after *Polynesia*, was intended to mean 'the regions of islands inhabited by blacks'.]

A. *adj.* Of or pertaining to Melanesia (a group of islands in the western Pacific, including Fiji, New Caledonia, etc.), its inhabitants, language, etc. **B.** *sb.* **a.** A native of Melanesia. **b.** The language of the Melanesians.

1849 SELWYN in Tucker *Mem.* (1879) I. 302 The Melanesian (Anaijom) *aijeama*, we, but not you. *Ibid.*, The Melanesian dialects. **1898** A. LANG *Making Relig.* viii. 167 Cases in which the rod acts like those of the Melanesians, Africans, and other savages. **1904** *Athenæum* 9 Apr. 460/3 Words in this Melanesian language which have cognates in Malay and Malagasy.

Melanesoid (mɛləˈniːzɔɪd), *a.* [f. *Melanes(ia* (see MELANESIAN *a.* and *sb.*) + -OID.] Similar in racial type to the Melanesian; resembling a Melanesian.

1932 *Man* Dec. 283 The term Melanesoid was used to indicate the offspring of tribes from Southern China (Yunnan) and Northern Indo-China (Tonkin). **1939** F. WEIDENREICH in *Peking Nat. Hist. Bull.* XIII. 170 The morphological analysis of the three skulls..led to the result that they typify three different racial elements, best to be classified as primitive Mongoloid, Melanesoid and Eskimoid types. **1943** —— *Skull of Sinanthropus Pekinensis* 251 Skull of a female... The female, B, shows the greatest similarity to the Melanesians of today. For this reason I have designated the type as 'Melanesoid'. **1946** [see ESKIMOID *a.*].

‖**mélange** (melɑ̃ʒ) *sb.* Also 7 **meslange,** 7–9 **melange.** [F. *mélange* mixture, f. *mêler* to mix: see MEDDLE *v.*

Often written without accent, but (at least in sense 1) perh. always regarded as a foreign word.]

1. A mixture; usually, a congeries of heterogeneous elements or constituents, a medley.

1653 J. HALL *Paradoxes* 112 The sweetnesses and killing languors of their eyes, the meslange and harmony of their colours. **1697** EVELYN *Numism.* vi. 213 Many exquisitely wrought Vessels..of that precious Melange. **1711** LADY M. W. MONTAGU *Let. to Mrs. Hewet*, A bad peace, people I love in disgrace [etc.]..I believe nobody ever had such a *mélange* before. **1729** SWIFT *Let. to Bolingbroke* 21 Mar. in *Pope's Wks.* (1741) II. 85, I come from looking over the Melange above-written, and declare it to be a true copy of my present disposition. **1811** SHELLEY *Let.* in Hogg *Life* I. 397 A strange melange of maddened stuff, which I wrote by the midnight moon last night. **1840** B. E. HILL *Pinch—of Snuff* 33 The pleasant melange sold but a few years since as 'The Speaker's', is very different from 'Lord Canterbury's Mixture'. **1859** *Gentl. Mag.* June 606 He professes that the present Part is 'taken from Usher, Ware [etc.]', and a very curious *melange* he has made of it. **1887** A. M. BROWN *Anim. Alkal.* 36 The melange of ferricyanide and ferrochloride gives feebly the bluish tint.

2. a. A dress fabric of cotton chain and woollen weft (Knight *Dict. Mech.* Suppl. 1884). **b.** A kind of woollen yarn of mingled colours. Also *attrib.* and *Comb.*

1881 *Instr. Census Clerks* (1885) 144/2 Mèlange Weaver—Woollen Cloth Manuf. **1886** *Daily News* 20 Sept. 2/4 An active demand continues in twofold yarns, in mottles, and melanges. **1897** *Allbutt's Syst. Med.* II. 551 If bales of dry wools and hairs were placed in steamers—as is done in the melange printing process—and submitted [etc.].

3. (See quot. 1935.)

1922 JOYCE *Ulysses* 245 I'll take a *mélange*, Haines said to the waitress... He sank two lumps of sugar deftly long-wise through the whipped cream. **1935** H. SIMPSON *Cold Table* 264 Café Mélange. Ingredients: Coffee, milk; water; whipped cream; castor sugar. **1971** *Guardian* 27 Feb. 7/4 The famous Viennese coffee houses where you can sip your *melange* (or a dozen other varieties of coffee).

melange (melɑ̃ʒ), *v.* [a. F. *mélanger*, f. *mélange*: see prec.] *trans.* To mix (wool of different colours). Hence **me'langer**.

1880 *Times* 28 Dec. 8 A dyer or melanger sued to recover £85 for melanging wool. **1881** *Instr. Census Clerks* (1885) 144/2 Mèlanger—Woollen Cloth Manuf.

Melanian (mɪˈleɪnɪən), *a.*[1] and *sb.*[1] *Anthropology.* [ad. F. *mélanien* (Bory de Saint-Vincent). f. Gr. μελαν-, μέλας black: see -IAN.] Originally = NEGRITO *a.* and *sb.*; later, used as = NEGROID.

1861 HULME tr. *Moquin-Tandon* I. vi. 36. **1868** OWEN *Anat. Vert.* III. 145 We know not the size of brain in the Melanian inventor of the 'throwing-stick'. **1885** W. H. FLOWER in *Jrnl. Anthrop. Inst.* XIV. 381 To begin with the Ethiopian, Negroid or Melanian, or 'black' type.

melanian (mɪˈleɪnɪən), *a.*[2] and *sb.*[2] *Zool.* [f. mod.L. *Melania*, the typical genus of the *Melaniidæ* (f. Gr. μελαν-, μέλας black) + -AN.]

a. *adj.* Of or belonging to the *Melaniidæ*, a family of fresh-water snails. **b.** *sb.* A member of this family.

1839 *Penny Cycl.* XV. 76 *Melanians*, Lamarck's name for a family of fluviatile, testaceous, operculated Mollusks.

melanic (mɪˈlænɪk), *a.* (*sb.*) [f. Gr. μελαν-, μέλας black + -IC.]

1. *Ethnology.* Having black hair and a black or dark complexion. Cf. MELANOCOMOUS, MELANOUS.

1826 PRICHARD *Res. Phys. Hist. Man.* (ed. 2) I. 139 These three varieties are the melanic, including all individuals or races who have black hair; the xanthous..; and the albino. **1829** T. PRICE *Physiogn. & Physiol. Inhabit. Brit.* 109 Whether I should attribute the few melanic countenances, I noticed in the South of Ireland, to a Spanish origin.

2. a. Of animals: Affected by melanosis. Esp. in reference to the darker varieties of moths and other animals that have developed in certain industrial areas. Also as *sb.*, an animal characterized by melanism.

1882-4 *Yarrell's Brit. Birds* (ed. 4) III. 665 The melanic varieties occasionally found in our northern Skua. **1894** *Naturalist* 333 A melanic form of the Pipistrelle. **1903** *Daily Chron.* 30 Dec. 3/3 The melanic variety of the common leopard. **1915** R. C. PUNNETT *Mimicry in Butterflies* viii. 101 In some parts of England the common peppered moth, *Amphidasys betularia*, has been almost entirely supplanted by the darker melanic form *doubledayaria*. **1940** H. B. COTT *Adaptive Coloration in Animals* I. i. 17 The distribution of such melanic varieties, coinciding as it often does with industrialism, is very significant. So is the fact that the melanic forms have not..become established, even though they are present, in rural districts. **1958** H. B. D. KETTLEWELL in *New Scientist* 3 July 298/2 New theories were evoked to account for the rapid spread of species [of moths] changing from light coloration to black—the 'industrial melanics'. **1970** *Nature* 12 Sept. 1155/1 The murk of nineteenth century Manchester fostered the melanic form *carbonaria* of the peppered moth, *Biston betularia* (L.). **1971** *Ibid.* 29 Oct. 586/3 The value of smoke abatement is demonstrated by the almost immediate decline in the frequency of the melanics where smoke control zones are introduced. **1973** *Ibid.* 21/28 Dec. 535/1 Intensive selective predation by birds on moths, which largely accounts for the presence of melanics in both industrial and some non-polluted rural areas. **1975** *Sci. Amer.* Jan. 90/2 The first [problem] is the question of why there is a difference in the proportion of melanics found among populations of various moth species that share the same environment. *Ibid.* 95 (*caption*) Frequency of melanic form is different in various species.

b. Used as the distinctive epithet of the black pigment occurring in melanosis, and of the cells containing it.

1847-9 *Todd's Cycl. Anat.* IV. 116/1 Melanic pigment is essentially composed of extremely minute granules. *Ibid.* 116/2 Melanic cells never exhibit any tendency even to cohere—much less to form the basis of a stroma. **1855** DUNGLISON *Med. Lex.* (ed. 12), *Melanic*, of or belonging to Melanosis; as *Melanic deposit*, a black colouring matter deposited from the blood under special circumstances.

3. ***melanic acid.*** †**a.** Prout's name for indican of urine (see INDICAN b). *Obs.*

1822 *Medico-Chirurg. Trans.* XII. I. 45 *note*, Dr. Prout would propose to distinguish this new substance, on account of its black colour, by the name of Melanic acid.

b. (See quot.)

1844 FOWNES *Chem.* 434 In a humid state they [*sc.* crystals of salicylite of potassium]..eventually change to a black, soot-like substance..called *melanic acid.*

melaniline (mɛˈlænɪlaɪn). *Chem.* [f. Gr. μελαν-, μέλας black + ANILINE.] A basic substance obtained from chloride of cyanogen and aniline.

1852 *Fownes' Chem.* (ed. 4) 557 The above salt furnishes melaniline in the form of an oil.

melanin (ˈmɛlənɪn). *Chem.* and *Phys.* [f. Gr. μελαν-, μέλας black + -IN[1].] The black pigment in the retina, choroid, hair, epidermis, etc. of coloured races of man or melanic varieties of animals. Also, the black pigment developed in certain diseases. Also *attrib.* and *Comb.*

1843 OWEN *Lect. Invertebr. Anim.* 355 It [the secretion in the ink-bag of a cephalopod] is affirmed by some chemists to contain a peculiar animal principle, which Vizio has termed 'melanine'. **1855** tr. *C. Wedl's Pathol. Histol.* (Syd. Soc.) II. i. 118 Black pigment (melanin) appears in the form of reddish brown molecules. **1871** WATTS tr. *Gmelin's Handbk. Chem.* XVIII. 417 Melanin. L. Gmelin's Black Pigment of the Eye. **1874** BARKER tr. *Frey's Histol. & Histochem.* 53 We must be on our guard, however, not to confound the ordinary black pigment found in the human lungs with melanin. **1898** P. MANSON *Trop. Dis.* i. 2 Melanæmia and malarial pigmentation are fully accounted for by the melanin-forming property of the plasmodium. *Ibid.* 6 The melanin particles, so characteristic of the malaria germ.

melanism (ˈmɛlənɪz(ə)m). [f. Gr. μελαν-, μέλας black + -ISM.]

1. Darkness of colour resulting from an abnormal (but not morbid) development of black pigment in the epidermis or other external appendages (hair, feathers, etc.) of animals; opposed to *albinism.*

1843 PRICHARD *Nat. Hist. Man* (1845) 39 Throughout intertropical America, both melanism and albinism, as he [M. Roulin] terms the black and white varieties, make their appearance very frequently in warm-blooded animals. **1882** TIEMANN in *Field Naturalist* July 32 Melanism occurs in various species of animals, but is far rarer than albinism.

b. A melanic variety (of some recognized species).

1863 J. R. WISE *New Forest* 309 Mr. Rake informs me that a Sabine's snipe..which is now generally regarded as only a melanism of this species was shot at Picket Post, Jan., 1859. **1889** H. SAUNDERS *Man. Brit. Birds* 12 An example of the Siberian Thrush..originally supposed to be a melanism of the Redwing.

2. *Bot.* 'A disease producing blackness in plants' (*Cassell's Encycl. Dict.* 1885).

melanistic (mɛləˈnɪstɪk), *a.* [f. Gr. μελαν-, μέλας black + -ISTIC.] Characterized by melanism.

1874 COUES *Birds N.W.* 357, I took no specimens in the melanistic state of plumage. **1888** O. THOMAS *Catal. Marsupialia Brit. Mus.* 266 In the black melanistic variety every part of the body is deep black.

†**melanite**[1]. *Obs.* [Perh. some error: cf. med. L. *melonītēs* corrupt form of *malochītes* malachite (Schade, *Altd. Wb.* Suppl. s.v. *Melochites*): the description in Maplet is prob. evolved from a pseudo-derivation from L. *mel* honey.] (See quot.)

1567 MAPLET *Gr. Forest* 15 The Melanite is a Stone, which distilleth & droppeth that iuice which is verie sweete and honie like; wherfore it may well be called Melanite as you would say Honistone,..on the one side it is greene, on the other side yellow.

melanite[2] (ˈmɛlənaɪt). *Min.* [ad. G. *melanit* (Werner 1799), f. Gr. μελαν-, μέλας black: see -ITE[1].] A velvet-black variety of andradite.

1807 AIKIN *Dict. Chem. & Min.* II. 68 Melanite...Black garnet. **1854** DANA *Syst. Min.* (ed. 4) II. 192.

melanite[3] (ˈmɛlənaɪt). *Conch.* [f. mod.L. *Melania* (see MELANIAN) + -ITE[1].] A fossil melanian (*Cent. Dict.*).

melanitic (mɛləˈnɪtɪk), *a.* [f. MELANITE[2] + -IC.] Pertaining to, resembling, or containing melanite.

In recent Dicts.

melanization (mɛlənaɪˈzeɪʃən). [f. MELANIZ(E *v.* + -ATION.] The process or result of becoming melanized.

1945 W. M. KROGMAN in R. Linton *Sci. Man in World Crisis* 47 A possible exception may be found in the 'protective' melanization or skin coloring of tropic-dwelling peoples. **1954** *Sci. News* XXXIV. 94 The pink and brown colour of insectorubin is completely obscured by the melanization of the outer cuticle. **1974** *Nature* 10 May 187/1 The epidermal cells..showed progressive granulation and melanisation.

melanize (ˈmɛlənaɪz), *v.* [f. Gr. μελαν-, μέλας + -IZE.] *trans.* To produce melanism in.

1885 *Standard* 7 Aug. 5/1 The black Jews in Cochin.. were native converts, not Hebrews who had become melanised under the Indian sun.

melano (mɪˈlɑːnəʊ). [f. Gr. μελαν-, μέλας black: after ALBINO.] An animal distinguished by an abnormal development of black pigment in the epidermis, hair, feathers, etc.; opposed to ALBINO.

1902 *Ann. & Mag. Nat. Hist.* IX. 59 Spotted tiger-cats of the *F. Macrura* group. The small specimen is a melano, but shows indications of the normal spotted condition.

melano- (ˈmɛlənəʊ), a. Gr. μελανο-, combining form of μέλας black, as in **melanoblast** (ˈmɛlənə-, mɪˈlænəblɑːst) *Zool.* [a. G. *melanoblast* (S. Ehrmann *Das melanotische Pigment* (1896) viii. 20): see -BLAST], a cell that produces melanin; also, a precursor of a melanin-forming cell. **melanocarciˈnoma** *Path.* = MELANOMA (Mayne *Expos. Lex.* 1856). **melanoˈcratic** *a. Petrol.* [ad. G. *melanokrat* (W. C. Brögger *Eruptivgesteine des Kristianiagebietes* (1898) III. 263), f. Gr. κρατ-εῖν to rule, prevail)], (of a rock) dark-coloured; rich in dark-coloured minerals. **ˈmelanoderm** (also **Melano-**) *sb.* and *a.* [Gr. δέρμ-α skin], (of, pertaining to, or being) a person of a dark-skinned (negroid) race; ‖**melanoˈderma, -ˈdermia** *Path.* [Gr. δέρμα skin: see -IA] = MELASMA; hence **melanodermic** *a.*, (*a*) relating to melanodermia; (*b*) (naturally) dark-skinned, negroid. **melanoˈgallic** *a. Chem.* [GALLIC] = METAGALLIC. **melanoˈgenesis** *Physiol.* [-GENESIS], the formation of melanin. **melanoˈglossia** [Gr. γλῶσσα tongue + -IA], the condition of having a black tongue. ‖**melanoˈpathia** *Path.* [see -PATHY] = MELASMA; also anglicized **melaˈnopathy.** **melanophore** (ˈmɛlənə-, mɪˈlænəfɔːə(r)) *Zool.* [ad. G. *melanophor* (R. Keller 1895, in *Arch. f. Physiol.* LXI. 141): see -PHORE], a cell containing melanin; esp. such a cell in the lower vertebrates which is contractile and confers the ability to change the depth of colour (see quot. 1953). **melanosarˈcoma** *Path.*, sarcoma characterized by the presence of black pigment cells. **ˈmelanosome** *Physiol.* [-SOME[4]], a particle in the cytoplasm of melanocytes in which melanin is thought to be formed from tyrosine (see quot. 1961). **melanoˈtannic** *a. Chem.* (see quot. 1866).

1902 *Encycl. Medica* XI. 182 Ehrmann.., from his investigations of amphibians and reptiles, concludes that the epithelial colouring matter is elaborated in special connective tissue corpuscles (chromatoblasts or *melanoblasts), from material derived from the red blood corpuscles. **1942** G. H. BOURNE *Cytol. & Cell Physiol.* viii. 329 A spread of melanin formation from the melanoblasts to similar but non-pigmented dendritic cells of the white area of the skin. **1953** *Science* 5 June 640/1 The term melanoblast is used by medical investigators for the mature cell elaborating melanin, whereas in biology the term melanoblast refers to an immature pigment cell during its migration from the neural crest. *Ibid.* 640/2 The term melanoblast for the mature pigment-forming cell as originally suggested by Bloch is objectionable. *Ibid.* (*table*) Recommended terminology of pigment cells. Immature melanin-forming cell: Melanoblast. **1968** H. HARRIS *Nucleus & Cytoplasm* i. 11 Enucleate fragments of prospective pigment cells (melanoblasts) from the developing neural crest of urodele embryos also survive for long periods *in vitro.* **1909, 1954** *Melanocratic [see *leucocratic* adj. s.v. LEUCO-]. **1963** D. W. & E. E. HUMPHRIES tr. *Termier's Erosion & Sedimentation* 411 *Peridotite*, an ultrabasic (melanocratic) crystalline rock. **1924** A. C. HADDON *Races of Man* (ed. 2) 13 Among the xanthoderms and *melanoderms the irides are almost uniformly dark brown in colour. **1927** H. H. WILDER *Pedigree of Human Race* vi. 345 The Melanoderm Race has developed several moderately high civilizations, especially on the west of the Sahara. **1935** *Jrnl. R. Anthrop. Inst.* LXV. 123 The three main divisions of mankind Leukoderms (Caucasians), Xanthoderms (Mongolians) and Melanoderms (Western and Eastern Negroes)—did not prove to have a blood-group factor of their own. **1901** OSLER *Princ. & Pract. Med.* (ed. 4) viii. 831 Lastly, with arterio-sclerosis and chronic heart-disease there may be marked *melanoderma. **1886** FAGGE *Princ. & Pract. Med.* II. 755 *note*, A remarkable case of perfectly symmetrical leuco- and *melano-dermia. **1899** *Allbutt's Syst. Med.* VIII. 707 So-called syphilitic 'leucoderma' is usually a melano-dermia. **1890** *Syd. Soc. Lex.*, *Melanodermic. **1924** A. C. HADDON *Races of Man* (ed. 2) 144 A tropical jungle may have been a refuge for an indigenous melanodermic folk from fairer intruders into the country. **1852** MORFIT *Tanning & Currying* (1853) 63 *Melanogallic acid. **1928** *Funk's Stand. Dict.*, *Melanogenesis. **1964** *Oceanogr. & Marine Biol.* II. 409 An interesting feature of melanogenesis in the ophiuroids is that in light-coloured individuals which are regenerating arm-tips the regenerate is dark, suggesting that under conditions of wound-healing and repair the normal inhibitor of melanogenesis..is overcome or absent. **1898** P. MANSON *Trop. Diseases* iv. 88 *note*, This condition, *melanoglossia, is

racial and not pathological. **1847** E. WILSON *Dis. Skin* (ed. 2) 328 Cases illustrative of *Melanopathia. **1876** DUNGLISON *Med. Lex.*, *Melanopathia*, *Melanopathy, Nigritism... A disease of the skin, which consists in augmentation of black pigment; generally in patches. **1903** *Proc. Amer. Acad. Arts & Sci.* XXXIX. 261 The conspicuous black bodies of Anolis.. well buried in the derma and sending branching processes outward toward the epidermis, correspond to the *melanophores described by Keller. **1946** *Nature* 7 Sept. 344/1 The pigmentary hormone of *Dixippus*, the regulator of colour change in this animal, activates the melanophores of frogs.. by causing expansion of them. **1953** *Science* 5 June 640/1 Investigators in biology and medicine at the present time are using different terms for the same cell. For example, the term melanophore which has long been used by biologists refers to certain dendritic-shaped cells in the skin of fish, amphibians and reptiles which have 'contractile' properties. The melanin contained in the melanophores may, in response to certain stimuli, disperse into the dendrites or concentrate in the perikaryon, thus accounting for the color change. In human cytology and pathology the term melanophore is a macrophage. *Ibid.* 640/2 (*table*) Recommended terminology of pigment cells. 'Contractile' cell: Melanophore. **1965** LEE & KNOWLES *Animal Hormones* x. 128 A characteristic feature of hormonally controlled melanophores is that colour change takes hours to occur, whereas this is achieved in minutes if there is nervous control. **1875** H. WALTON *Dis. Eye* (ed. 3) 988 The sarcoma is usually of the pigmented form, *melano-sarcoma. **1900** *Brit. Med. Jrnl., Epit. Curr. Med. Lit.* 42 The case was one of melanosarcoma of wide distribution. **1961** M. SEIJI et al. in *Jrnl. Investigative Dermatol.* XXXVI. 251/2 Because the melanin granule has been shown by electronmicroscopy to be structurally distinct from mitochondria, to be unique in its localization within the cytoplasm of mammalian melanocytes, and to contain a specialized metabolic pathway that converts tyrosine to melanin, we would like to suggest that during its enzymically active stages it be called a *melanosome... The term 'melanin granule' could be reserved for the mature, fully melanized particle which has lost its tyrosinase activity and is no longer confined to the cytoplasm of the melanocyte. **1973** *Nature* 26 Oct. 436/3 The melanocyte's contribution [to pigmentation] begins with the synthesis of melanosomes, and the oxidation of tyrosine to melanin. **1852** MORFIT *Tanning & Currying* (1853) 63 *Melanotannic acid. **1866** BRANDE & COX *Dict. Sci.*, etc. II. 489/2 *Melanotannic Acid*, the black substance formed by the action of excess of potassa upon tannic or gallic acid.

melanocerite (mɛlənəʊ'sɪəraɪt). *Min.* [First in G. *melanocerit* (W. C. Brögger 1887), f. MELANO- + CERITE.] A fluo-silicate of cerium and yttrium found in black tabular crystals (Chester *Dict. Min.* 1896).

† **melanochal'cographer.** *Obs.* [f. MELANO- + CHALCOGRAPHER.] An engraver of copper plates for printing.

1697 EVELYN *Numism.* viii. 283 The late Melanochalcographer, N. de Seigen, who first produced the Mezzo-Tinto Graving.

melanochin (mɪ'lænəʊtʃɪn). *Chem.* [f. MELANO- + mod.L. CHIN-A quinine.] A product of the action of ammonia and chlorine on quinine.

1865 WATTS *Dict. Chem.* III. 867.

melanochlorous (mɛlənəʊ'klɔərəs), *a.* [f. Gr. μελανο-, μέλας black + χλωρός yellow: see -OUS.] Having the body variegated with black and yellow (Mayne *Expos. Lex.* 1856).

‖ **melanochroi** (mɛlə'nɒkrəʊaɪ), *sb. pl.* *Anthropology.* [mod.L.; formed by Huxley, who seems to have meant it as a transliteration of an assumed Gr. μελάνωχροι, f. μελαν-, μέλας black + ὠχρός pale. (On this view the correct mod.L. form would have been *melanōchri*; the irregularity occurs also in the other terms of Huxley's classification, *Xantho-melanoi* and *Melanoi*.) By subsequent writers, and in Dicts., the word has been taken as mod.L. *melanŏchroī* (sing. *-ous*), ad. Gr. μελανόχροος (= μελάγχροος), f. μελανο- (= μελαν-, μέλας) + χρόα skin.] In Huxley's classification of the varieties of mankind: A subdivision of the *Leiotrichi* or smooth-haired class, having dark hair and pale complexion.

1866 HUXLEY *Preh. Rem. Caithn.* 132 The Leiotrichi may be best subdivided, according to their complexion, into Xanthochroi, Melanochroi, Xanthomelanoi, and Melanoi. **1875** TYLOR in *Encycl. Brit.* II. 113/2 The Melanochroi or dark whites. **1878** RAMSAY *Phys. Geog.* xxxiv. 580 Dark-complexioned, black-haired and black-eyed Melanochroi.

Hence **melano'chroic**, **melanochroid**, **melanochrous** *adjs.*, pertaining to or resembling the *Melanochroi*.

1865 HUXLEY *Crit. & Addr.* vii. (1873) 157 Among Europeans, the melanochrous people are less obnoxious to its [yellow fever's] ravages than the xanthochrous. **1871** *Ibid.* viii. 180 The melanochroic or dark stock of Europe. **1878** BARTLEY tr. *Topinard's Anthrop.* II. i. 202 The melanochroid group: pale-complexioned, dark eyes, hair long and black. Example: Iberians [etc.]. **1899** W. CROOKE in *Jrnl. Anthropol. Inst.* XXVIII. 228 A fusion of Melanochroid Caucasic and Austral-negro blood.

melanochroite (mɛlənəʊ'krəʊaɪt). *Min.* [First in G. *melanochroit*, f. Gr. μελανόχροος black-coloured + -ITE.] = PHŒNICOCHROITE.

1835 *R. D. Thomson's Rec. Gen. Sci.* I. 273. **1836** T. THOMSON *Min., Geol.*, etc. I. 561. **1837** DANA *Syst. Min.* 234.

melanocomous (mɛlə'nɒkəməs), *a.* [f. Gr. μελανοκόμ-ης (f. μελανο-, μέλας black + κόμη hair) + -OUS.] Black-haired.

1836 PRICHARD *Res. Phys. Hist. Man* (ed. 3) I. 220 The black-haired or melanocomous or melanous variety [of complexion], characterised by black or very dark hair. **1849–52** TODD *Cycl. Anat.* IV. 936/2 The melano-comous or dark races.. are mostly of the melancholic temperament. **1851** H. W. TORRENS in *Jrnl. Asiat. Soc. Bengal* 38 The melano-comous character of complexion.

melanocyte ('mɛlənəʊ-, mɪ'lænəʊsaɪt). *Zool.* [f. MELANO- + -CYTE.] A mature melanin-forming cell; also, a melanophore.

1890 in BILLINGS *Med. Dict.* II. 128/1. **1935** *Chem. Abstr.* XXIX. 8125 Melanocyte reaction of the preparations of pituitary body and the urine of cancer patient. **1953** *Science* 5 June 640/2 (*table*) Recommended terminology of pigment cells. Mature melanin-forming cell: Melanocyte. **1957** *Times* 4 Oct. 5 There are 500 to 2,000 melanocytes per square millimetre of skin surface, except on the face, forehead and behind the ears, where there are 1,500 to 4,000 per square millimetre. **1971** *New Scientist* 12 Aug. 366/1 It is difficult to understand why MSH is still secreted by the pituitary gland of birds and mammals, when these animals have lost the capacity for varying the colour of their body through the movements of pigment granules in melanocytes.

Hence **melanocyte-stimulating hormone**, a hormone that stimulates melanocytes or melanophores and causes darkening of the skin; abbrev. *MSH*.

1953 LERNER & FITZPATRICK in M. Gordon *Pigment Cell Growth* 329 There are many indications that the pituitary gland produces a melanocyte-stimulating hormone (MSH) Rattner *et al.*). **1954** A. B. LERNER et al. in *Jrnl. Clin. Endocrinol. & Metabolism* XIV. 1465 We have called the pituitary factor which darkens skin the melanocyte-stimulating hormone or MSH, a term first suggested by W. H. Rattner. Names used previously include melanophore hormone, melanophore-dilating principle, intermedin, and others. **1956** *Jrnl. Biol. Chem.* CCXXI. 958 Two distinct melanocyte-stimulating hormones (α- and β-MSH) are present in hog pituitary gland. **1964** [see INTERMEDIN]. **1971** *New Scientist* 12 Aug. 365/2 Melanocyte-stimulating hormone and corticotrophin.. are two of the many polypeptide hormones secreted by the pituitary gland.

melanogen (mɪ'lænədʒɛn). *Phys.* [f. Gr. μελανο-, μέλας black: see -GEN 1.] A substance capable of yielding melanin.

1899 CAGNEY tr. *Jaksch's Clin. Diagn.* vii. (ed. 4) 321 The reaction occurs in presence of melanin or melanogen.

melanogogue, erron. form of MELANAGOGUE.

‖ **melanoi**, *sb. pl.* *Anthropology.* [Intended as mod.L.; formed irregularly by transliteration of Gr. μελανοί, pl. of μελανός, var. of μέλας black.] Huxley's name for the black-haired and dark-complexioned division of his class *Leiotrichi* or smooth-haired peoples.

1866 [see MELANOCHROI].

melanoid ('mɛlənɔɪd), *a.* *Path.* [f. Gr. μελανοειδ-ής, 'black-looking' (L. & Sc.), f. μελανο-, μέλας black + εἶδος form.] Of morbid growths: Characterized by the presence of black pigment.

1854 JONES & SIEV. *Pathol. Anat.* 183 Melanoid cancer is ..encephaloid structure, with the addition of black pigment. **1898** P. MANSON *Trop. Diseases* xxxvii. 572 We have the white, or ochroid, the black, or melanoid, and the red forms of mycetoma.

‖ **melanoma** (mɛlə'nəʊmə). *Path.* Pl. **melanomata** (mɛlə'nəʊmətə). [mod.L., a. Gr. type μελάνωμα (occurring in late Gr. with the sense 'blackness'), f. μελανοῦσθαι: see MELANOSIS, and cf. *carcinoma* and other names for kinds of cancerous or morbid growths.] A melanotic growth; *esp.* a tumour consisting largely of black pigment.

183. CARSWELL *Path. Anat.*, *Melanoma* 1, I include under the title of Melanoma all melanotic formations, black discolourations or products, described by Laennec and other authors. **1847–9** *Todd's Cycl. Anat.* IV. 128/2 Growths, more or less deeply tinged by [melanic cell-pigment], have been distinguished.. under the title of Melanotic Tumours or Melanomata. **1875** H. WALTON *Dis. Eye* (ed. 3) 1006 Simple benign pigmented tumour of the iris, melanoma. **1876** tr. *Wagner's Gen. Path.* (ed. 6) 316 Pure pigment tumors or melanomata. **1877** tr. *H. von Ziemssen's Cycl. Med.* XII. 235 Melanoma is a very rare pigmented tumour.

melanophlogite (mɛlə'nɒflədʒaɪt). *Min.* [a. G. *melanophlogit* (Lasaulx 1876), f. Gr. μελανο-, μέλας black + φλογ-, φλόξ flame; indicating that the mineral turns black when heated.] An impure form of silica found in minute cubes on sulphur.

1879 DANA *Man. Min. & Lithol.* (ed. 3) 241.

melanoscope ('mɛlənəʊskəʊp). [ad. G. *melanoskop*: see MELANO- and -SCOPE.] A combination of coloured glasses, devised by Lommel in 1871 (*Pogg. Ann.* CXLIII. 489) for exhibiting certain optical properties of chlorophyll; by intercepting nearly all except the middle red rays of the spectrum, it causes green plants seen through it to appear almost black.

1876 *Catal. Spec. Collect. Sci. Appar. S. Kens. Mus.* (ed. 3, 1877) 247 Melanoscope. Prof. Dr. Lommel, Erlangen. **1884** in KNIGHT *Dict. Mech.* Suppl. (with incorrect explanation, followed in later Dicts.).

melanose ('mɛlənəʊs), *sb.* [ad. F. *mélanose*, the Fr. form of MELANOSIS.] A fungoid growth on grape-vines produced by *Septoria ampelina*.

1890 in *Century Dict.*

melanose ('mɛlənəʊs), *a.* *Path.* [f. Gr. μελαν-, μέλας black + -OSE; but app. suggested by MELANOSIS.] Containing, or of the nature of, the black pigment occurring in melanosis.

1823 CULLEN & CARSWELL in *Trans. Edin. Med.-Chir. Soc.* (1824) 265 The peritonæum had melanose matter lying upon it in streaks. **1829** *Good's Study Med.* (ed. 3) III. 339 The pleura was studded with melanose tubercles. **1834** J. FORBES *Laennec's Dis. Chest* (ed. 4) 361 The melanose affection.. tends to produce cachexy and anasarca. **1835–6** *Todd's Cycl. Anat.* I. 64/1 Cases in which the osseous system appears to be stained with the melanose deposit. **1890** in *Syd. Soc. Lex.*

melanosed (mɛlə'nəʊst), *ppl. a.* *rare*$^{-1}$. [f. *melanose* vb. (f. MELANOS-IS) + -ED[1].] Permeated with melanotic matter.

1829 *Good's Study Med.* (ed. 3) III. 340 The substance of both mammæ and of both ovaries were completely melanosed.

ˌ**melano'siderite.** *Min.* [f. MELANO- + SIDERITE.] An iron hydrate containing silica.

1875 J. P. COOKE in *Proc. Amer. Acad.* X. 451 Melanosiderite, a new mineral species from Mineral Hill, Delaware County, Pennsylvania.

‖ **melanosis** (mɛlə'nəʊsɪs). *Path.* Pl. **-oses** (-'əʊsiːz). [mod.L., a. late Gr. μελάνωσις blackening, f. μελανοῦσθαι to become black, f. μελαν-, μέλας black.]

1. Morbid deposit or abnormal development of a black pigment in some tissue; occas. *concr.* a discoloration due to this.

1823 CULLEN & CARSWELL in *Trans. Edin. Med.-Chir. Soc.* (1824) 264 We observed in a horse the disease termed Melanosis, developed to a remarkable degree. **1829** *Good's Study Med.* (ed. 3) III. 341 In the cutaneous texture, says Brescher, melanoses are common. **1843** GRAVES *Lect. Clin. Med.* xxx. 382 In some whites this tendency to secrete black matter becomes excessive and gives rise to certain forms of melanosis. **1871** SIR T. WATSON *Lect. Princ. & Pract. Physic* (ed. 5) lii. 251 It [a certain morbid state] has been sometimes called spurious melanosis, sometimes colliers' phthisis. **1899** *Allbutt's Syst. Med.* VIII. 700 Freckles may be considered as actinic melanoses. *Ibid.* 844 Chronic melanosis of the skin is a malady to which hitherto little attention has been drawn.

2. Black cancer.

1834 J. FORBES *Laennec's Dis. Chest* (ed. 4) 355 Melanosis is one of the rarest species of cancer. **1877** ROBERTS *Handbk. Med.* (ed. 3) I. 277 Melanosis and colloid are generally regarded as forms of cancer which [etc.].

melanosity (mɛlə'nɒsɪtɪ). [f. MELANOUS *a.*: see -OSITY.] Melanous character.

1885 BEDDOE *Races Brit.* 5, I double the black, in order to give its proper value to the greater tendency to melanosity shown thereby.

melanosperm ('mɛlənəʊspɜːm). *Bot.* [f. mod.L. *Melanosperm-eæ*, f. Gr. μελανο-, μέλας black + σπέρμα seed.] An alga belonging to the *Melanospermeæ*, a division or sub-order characterized by dark olivaceous spores. Hence **melano'spermous** *a.*

1856 CARPENTER *Microsc.* §205. 367 The group of Melanospermous or olive-green Sea-weeds. **1884** *Public Opinion* 3 Oct. 426/1 The melanosperms.. are found chiefly within high- and low-water mark.

melanotekite (ˌmɛlənəʊ'tiːkaɪt). *Min.* [ad. Sw. *melanotekit* (G. Lindström 1880, in *Öfversigt af K. Vetenskaps-Akad. Förhandl.* XXXVII. vi. 56), f. Gr. μελανο- MELANO- + τήκ-ειν to melt, dissolve: see -ITE[1].] A black to dark grey silicate of lead and iron (see quot. 1962).

1882 *Jrnl. Chem. Soc.* XLII. 291 Melanotekite, so called from its behaviour before the blowpipe (fusion to a black bead),.. is a black to blackish-grey mineral, often with a bluish tinge. **1962** *Arkiv för Mineral. och Geol.* III. 143 Kentrolite and melanotekite are isostructural. They form a series with the end-members $Pb_2Mn_2Si_2O_9$ and $Pb_2Fe_2Si_2O_9$... Kentrolite can be defined as those members of this series which contain more than 50 mol per cent $Pb_2Mn_2Si_2O_9$, and the others are called melanotekite. **1968** *Amer. Mineralogist* LIII. 1278 The synthesis of melanotekite ($Pb_2Fe_2Si_2O_9$), kentrolite ($Pb_2Mn_2Si_2O_9$) and of intermediate members of this complete solid solution series has been reported elsewhere (Ito and Frondel, 1967). Using similar procedures, we have synthesized the Sc, Ga and Cr analogues of these compounds.

melanotic (mɛlə'nɒtɪk), *a.* [Formed after MELANOSIS: see -OTIC.]
1. *Path.* Characterized by melanosis; of the nature of melanosis.
1829 *Good's Study Med.* (ed. 3) III. 331 The melanotic deposit takes place in three distinct forms. **1843** GRAVES *Lect. Clin. Med.* xxx. 382 The melanotic patches are, no doubt, often of a different shade. **1873** T. H. GREEN *Introd. Pathol.* (ed. 2) 116 Osteoid-sarcoma, melanotic-sarcoma, and cystic-sarcoma, have been described as distinct varieties. **1875** H. WALTON *Dis. Eye* (ed. 3) 981 All melanotic growths are sarcomatous.
2. *Zool.* = MELANISTIC.
1874 COUES *Birds N.W.* 304 The same rufescent phase.. is apparently analogous to the melanotic condition of many Hawks.

melanotype (mɪ'lænətaɪp). Also incorrectly **me'lainotype.** [f. MELANO- + -TYPE.] A kind of ferrotype: see FERROTYPE 2.
1864 WEBSTER, *Melanotype.* **1867** SUTTON & DAWSON *Dict. Photogr., Melainotype.* This positive process is of American origin. **1890** *Anthony's Photogr. Bull.* III. 302 These tin or melainotypes were taken everywhere. **1892** WOODBURY *Encycl. Photogr., Melainotype,* or *Melanotype.*

melanous ('mɛlənəs), *a. Anthropology.* [f. Gr. μελαν-, μέλας black + -OUS.] With reference to hair and complexion: Blackish, dark; *spec.* in Huxley's use, belonging to the variety of mankind called by him MELANOI.
1836 PRICHARD *Res. Phys. Hist. Man* (ed. 3) I. 227 The Greeks were probably, in Homer's time as now, in general of a melanous variety. **1843** —— *Nat. Hist. Man* (1845) 78 As we know of no expressions in English precisely correspondent with these names, blonde and brunette, I have adopted those of xanthous and melanous as distinguishing terms. **1859** R. F. BURTON *Centr. Afr.* in *Jrnl. Geog. Soc.* XXIX. 315 The skin, like the hair, is of the melanous order. **1865** HUXLEY *Crit. & Addr.* vii. (1873) 153 The 'melanous', with black hair and dark-brown or blackish skins.

melanovanadite (ˌmɛlənəʊ'vænədaɪt). *Min.* [f. MELANO- + VANAD(IUM + -ITE[1].] A black opaque oxide of calcium and vanadium that occurs as bunches of acicular monoclinic crystals.
1921 W. LINDGREN in *Proc. Nat. Acad. Sci.* VII. 249 In 1920 Mr. W. Spencer Hutchinson, Consulting Engineer for the Vanadium Company of America, brought to my attention three specimens of a mineral collected by him at Mina Ragra, Peru. He suspected that it was a new mineral, and this opinion was proved correct by chemical and optical examination. The formula is $2CaO.3V_2O_5.2V_2O_4$ and I wish to propose for it the name of melano-vanadite, in allusion to it being practically the only vanadium mineral of a deep black color. **1956** *Science* 1 June 990/3 Along fractures in the ore-bearing sandstone there is commonly a thin massive coating of an undescribed vanadium oxide. On this coating duttonite occurs as crusts and coatings... Associated minerals are melano-vanadite and abundant crystals of hexagonal native selenium. **1968** I. KOSTOV *Mineral.* II. 470 Simplotite and melanovanadite have perfect {010} cleavage.

melanterite (mɪ'læntəraɪt). *Min.* Also **-therite.** [ad. F. *mélanthérite* (in Littré), f. Gr. μελαντηρία black metallic dye or ink: see -ITE.] Native copperas.
1839 *Penny Cycl.* XV. 78/2 *Melanterite.* **1843** E. J. CHAPMAN *Pract. Min.* 14 Melantherite.

melanth ('mɛlænθ). [Shortened from the mod.Latin name.] Lindley's name for a plant of the N.O. *Melanthaceæ.*
1845 LINDLEY *Sch. Bot.* 138 *Melanthaceæ.*—Melanths.

melanthaceous (mɛlæn'θeɪʃəs), *a. Bot.* [f. mod.L. *Melanthace-æ* + -OUS.] Of or belonging to the N.O. *Melanthaceæ,* which is now included in the N.O. *Liliaceæ,* and contained the meadow saffron or colchicum, white hellebore, etc.

†**melanthy.** *Obs.* [ad. Gr. μελάνθιον.] = GITH.
1595 CHAPMAN *Ovid's Banq. Sence* B2 Where grew Melanthy, great in Bees account.

melanure ('mɛlənjʊə(r)). *Zool.* [ad. mod.L. *melanūrus,* a. Gr. μελάνουρος, f. μελαν-, μέλας black + οὐρά tail.] A small fish of the genus *Sparus,* native of the Mediterranean (Webster 1828–32 citing *Dict. Nat. Hist.*).

‖**melanuria** (mɛlə'njʊərɪə). *Path.* [mod.L., f. Gr. μελαν-, μέλας black + οὖρον urine: see -IA.] A pathological condition in which the urine assumes a black or dark blue colour.
1890 CAGNEY tr. *Jaksch's Clin. Diagn.* vii. 249 A test for melanuria. **1905** H. D. ROLLESTON *Dis. Liver* 511 Melanuria very seldom or never occurs without secondary growths being found in the liver.

melanuric (mɛlə'njʊərɪk), *a.*[1] *Chem.* [Based on G. *melanurensäure,* Liebig's alteration of Henneberg's term (1850) *mellanurensäure,* f. *mellan* mellone + *uren* a supposed base of urea + *säure* acid.] ***melanuric acid,*** a white chalky powder, obtained by heating urea.
1852 W. GREGORY *Handbk. Org. Chem.* 96 This product .. is intermediate between ammelide and cyanuric acid. It is now called mellanuric [*ed.* **1856** melanuric] acid. **1877** ROSCOE & SCHORLEMMER *Chem.* I. 677 Melanuric Acid .. is produced, together with cyanuric acid, when urea is heated.

melanuric (mɛlə'njʊərɪk), *a.*[2] *Path.* [f. MELANURIA + -IC.] Pertaining to or characterized by melanuria. ***melanuric fever,*** malarial fever with melanuria, black-water fever.
1881 PEABODY *Suppl. H. von Ziemssen's Cycl. Med.* 132 The melanuric or hæmaturic form of the fever produced by the malarial agent. *Ibid.* 137 Malarial hæmaturia, or melanuric fever.

melanurin (mɛlə'njʊərɪn). *Chem.* Also **-ourine.** [f. Gr. μελαν-, μέλας black + οὖρον urine: see -IN.] Braconnot's term for indican of urine.
1844 G. BIRD *Urin. Deposits* 219 Melanourine and melanic acid. **1845** tr. *Simon's Anim. Chem.* (Syd. Soc.) I. 45 The blue and black pigments that.. have received the names of cyanurin and melanurin. **1880** tr. *H. von Ziemssen's Cycl. Med.* IX. 387 A pigment which becomes black by oxidation on exposure of the urine to the air, and on addition of nitric acid (melanin, melanurin).

melaphyre ('mɛləfaɪə(r)). *Petrology.* [a. F. *mélaphyre* (Brongniart), f. Gr. μέλα-ς black + (*por*)-*phyre* PORPHYRY.] A species of black or dark-coloured porphyry.
1841 *Penny Cycl.* XX. 56/2 Melaphyre (Trap porphyry). Black petrosilicious hornblende, with crystals of felspar. **1867** *Murchison's Siluria* xiii. 332 Chocolate-coloured.. melaphyres. **1879** RUTLEY *Study Rocks* xiii. 260 Melaphyres possess a vitreous, or a devitrified magma which allies them more to basalt than to diabase.

mela-rosa, mella-rosa (mɛlə'rəʊzə). [It. *melarosa,* f. *mela* apple + *rosa* rose.] A variety of *Citrus Bergamia* or *C. Limetta.*
1837 *Penny Cycl.* VII. 215/2 The Mellarosa of the Italians is a variety [of *Citrus Bergamia*] with ribbed fruit. **1866** *Treas. Bot.* 730, 733 *Mela-rosa, Mella-rosa.*

melasma (mɪ'læzmə). *Path.* [mod.L., a. Gr. μέλασμα black spot, black dye, related to μελαίνειν to blacken, f. μελαν-, μέλας black.] A morbid condition in which there is an excess of the black pigment in the human skin; *spec.* a skin disease differing from CHLOASMA in the dark colour of the pigment. Also applied to a dark livid spot which occurs on the tibia of old persons.
1817 GOOD *Syst. Nosol.* 489 Ecthyma... Melasma, Plenck, Linn. Vog. **1854** JONES & SIEV. *Pathol. Anat.* 164 The local discolorations, termed 'melasma'. **1899** *Allbutt's Syst. Med.* VIII. 701 Diffuse forms of pigmentation.. which are sometimes described under the name of Melasma.
Hence **me'lasmic** *a.,* affected by, of the nature of, melasma.
1865 WILSON *Cutan. Med.* 401 A peculiar discoloration of the eyeball, which we termed melanæmic or melasmic eye.

melasses, obs. form of MOLASSES.

melassic (mɪ'læsɪk), *a. Chem.* [ad. F. *mélassique.*] ***melassic acid,*** an acid produced by heating glucose with caustic alkalis.
1839 *Hooper's Med. Dict.* (ed. 7). **1865** WATTS *Dict. Chem.* III. 868.

‖**melastoma** (mɪ'læstəmə). *Bot.* Pl. **-æ, -as.** [mod.L., f. Gr. μέλα-ς black + στόμα mouth: in allusion to the fact that the fruit of some species blackens the mouth when eaten.] A tropical genus of shrubs, the type of the N.O. *Melastomaceæ* and sub-order *Melastomeæ;* a plant of this genus.
1753 CHAMBERS *Cycl. Supp.* **1832** MACGILLIVRAY tr. *Humboldt's Trav.* xxiii. 324 Forests of oaks, melastomæ and cinchonæ. **1871** KINGSLEY *At Last* xi, Nowhere did I see the Melastomas more luxuriant.
So **melasto'maceous** *a.,* belonging to the N.O. *Melastomaceæ.* **me'lastomad,** Lindley's name for any plant of this order.
1836 LOUDON *Encycl. Plants* 300 Melastomaceous plants. **1846** LINDLEY *Veg. Kingd.* 731 Melastomaceæ—Melastomads. **1880** C. R. MARKHAM *Peruv. Bark* 384 A melastomaceous tree, with beautiful purple flowers. **1882** *Garden* 1 Apr. 214/1 Most of the cultivated Melastomads are handsome flowers.

melasus, obs. form of MOLASSES.

melatonin (mɛlə'təʊnɪn). *Biochem.* [f. Gr. μέλα-ς black + SERO)TONIN.] An indole derivative, $CH_3O{\cdot}C_8H_5N{\cdot}CH_2{\cdot}CH_2{\cdot}NH{\cdot}CO{\cdot}CH_3$, which is formed in the pineal gland in various mammals (principally from serotonin) and may be concerned with the regulation of certain physiological activities, esp. the reproductive cycle.
1958 A. B. LERNER et al. in *Jrnl. Amer. Chem. Soc.* LXXX. 2587/1 We wish to report isolation from beef pineal glands of the active factor that can lighten skin color and inhibit MSH. It is suggested that this substance be called melatonin. *Ibid.* 2587/2 In preventing darkening of frog skin by MSH, melatonin.. was at least.. 5,000 times as active as serotonin. **1965** *Sci. Amer.* July 60/3 The ability of melatonin to modify gonadal function suggests, but does not prove, that its secretion may have something to do with the timing of the estrus and menstrual cycles. **1968** PASSMORE & ROBSON *Compan. Med. Stud.* I. xxiv. 36/1 Evidence from experiments in rats has led to the discovery that the pineal produces a hormone named melatonin, capable of antagonizing the effects of gonadotrophic hormones, slowing the oestrous cycle and reducing the weight of the ovaries. Production of melatonin falls when a rat is in a constantly lit environment... How far these findings relate to man is uncertain; but secreting tumours of the pineal in children lead to delayed sexual development, as if too much melatonin were being released. **1970** *Nature* 30 May 804/1 Melatonin controls diurnal and seasonal adjustments of activity in many species. **1974** *Sci. Amer.* June 62/3 The pineal.. makes a hormone called melatonin that inhibits the activity of sex glands.

melatto, obs. form of MULATTO.

Melba ('mɛlbə). The stage name Nellie *Melba* (adopted from *Melbourne,* Australia, by Helen Mitchell (1861–1931), an Australian operatic soprano): used to designate certain foods, etc., named in her honour, as **peach Melba** (also **melba, pêche à la Melba, pêche Melba** (pɛʃ 'mɛlbə)), a confection of ice-cream and peaches flavoured with raspberry sauce, etc.; **Melba sauce** (see quot. 1951); **Melba toast** (or **toast Melba**), thinly-sliced bread toasted to crispness.
1905 [see COUPE[1]]. **1907** G. A. ESCOFFIER *Guide Mod. Cookery* xx. 778 *Pêches Melba.* Poach the peaches in vanilla-flavoured syrup. Dish them in a timbale upon a layer of vanilla ice-cream, and coat them with a raspberry purée. **1907** *Yesterday's Shopping* (1969) 33/2 *Sauces*..Melba (Escoffier's)—1/6. [**1909** A. G. MURPHY *Melba* xxiii. 141 Melba's.. tour for 1898–99. By this time innumerable soaps and sauces, ribbons and ruffles, had been named after her.] **1909** W. J. LOCKE *Septimus* iii. 40 The spoonful of peach Melba which she was going to put in her mouth. **1923** *Mrs. Beeton's All about Cookery* 418/1 Peach Melba... Halve and peel the peaches. ..serve them piled around a mould of vanilla ice cream... pour over a rich raspberry syrup. **1925** I. C. B. ALLEN *Mrs. Allen on Cooking* xii. 222 Patti Bread or Melba Toast. **1926** KIPLING *Debits & Credits* 28 Filet béarnaise, Woodcock and Richebourg '74, Pêches Melba, Croûtes Baron. **1928** D. L. SAYERS *Unpleasantness at Bellona Club* xviii. 214 You're as cold as a *pêche Melba.* **1938** *Times* 19 Aug. 7/3 Future generations may want more chickens and more peach melbas and less bread and cheese. **1938** M. L. RITZ *César Ritz* xiv. 204 Toast thin slices of bread once, then cut it through again, and again toast it... The result was Escoffier's justly famous *toast Melba*... During that year [*sc.* 1897] Melba had returned from America very ill... I had heard Escoffier discuss her *régime.* Dry toast figured on it... 'Call it *toast Melba,*' I said. **1951** *Good Housek. Home Encycl.* 552/1 *Melba Sauce,* a bright-red sweet sauce made from fresh raspberries and served with fruit sundaes, peach melba and similar desserts. **1953** E. TAYLOR *Sleeping Beauty* ix. 161 Sundaes, shakes, parfaits, whips, melbas. **1964** A. LAUNAY *Caviare & After* 137 *Melba,* large or small cuts of meat garnished with truffles, mushrooms, [etc.].. and served with a Port-flavoured sauce. *Also* fruit served with vanilla ice-cream and thick raspberry syrup. **1970** SIMON & HOWE *Dict. Gastron.* 292/2 The peach is historically associated with ice-cream because when Dame Nellie Melba, the great Australian singer, gave a party at the Savoy Hotel in London in 1892, Escoffier, who was then the chef at the Savoy, created the famous *Pêche Melba* in her honour. **1972** S. ATTERBURY *Waste Not—Want Not* 142 The Slow Cooking Method is ideal for Melba toast. **1972** *Vogue* June Special 128/3 *Melba sauce.* Blend 8 oz. fresh raspberries and pass through a sieve. Mix in 4 tablespooons icing sugar and add Kirsch to taste.

melch: see MELSH *a. dial.*

melch(e, obs. forms of MILCH *a.*

Melchite ('mɛlkaɪt). *Eccl.* Also **Malkite, Melkite.** [ad. L. *Melchīta,* repr. Syr. *mal'kåyē* pl., 'royalists' (i.e. adherents of the party of the Roman emperor), f. *malkå* king; the Arabic form is *malakīy.*] Originally, the designation applied by the Syrian Monophysites and Nestorians, and after their example by the Mohammedans, to those Eastern Christians who adhered to the orthodox faith as defined by the councils of Ephesus (A.D. 431) and Chalcedon (A.D. 451). In later use, applied to those orthodox Eastern Christians who use an Arabic version of the Greek ritual, and esp. to those of them who have been united to the communion of the Roman church, while retaining their separate organization.
1619 PURCHAS *Microcosmus* lxviii. 686 These Surians, or Melchites. **1635** PAGITT *Christianogr.* I. ii. (1636) 53 The Christians under the Patriarch of Antioch are called Syrians ..; And Melchites of the Syrian word מלכא which signifieth a King. **1788** GIBBON *Decl. & F.* xlvii. (1828) VI. 62 Their numbers.. bestowed an imperfect claim to the appellation of Catholics: but in the East, they were marked with the less honourable name of Melchites, or Royalists. **1883** I. TAYLOR *Alphabet* I. 294 The alphabet used by the Melchites of Palestine. **1885** *Catholic Dict.* (1897) 619/1 In fact, both from a dogmatic and liturgical point of view, the Melchites are simply Greeks living in Egypt and Syria. **1902** *Encycl. Brit.* XXVII. 237/2 The emperor appointed a new bishop of Alexandria, whose adherents the Copts styled Melkites or Imperialists. **1927** B. J. KIDD *Churches Eastern Christendom* xviii. 460 Originally a 'Melkite' meant a Christian who accepted the Emperor's religion. **1933** *Times Lit. Suppl.* 14 Dec. 890/2 They [*sc.* Christians] actually tended to welcome the Moslem conquest as releasing them from the persecution of the Melkite Church. **1947** G. EVERY *Byzantine Patriarchate* xii. 158 In Palestine.. most Syrian Christians were Melkites. **1961** N. ZERNOV *Eastern Christendom* ii. 68 The official hierarchy.. was nicknamed *Melkites* (King's men).
b. *attrib.* (quasi-*adj.*) and *ellipt.*

1883 I. Taylor *Alphabet* I. 295 The uncial Melchite [alphabet] goes generally by the name of Syro-Palestinian. *Ibid.*, The later cursive Melchite is wholly unlike the Syro-Palestinian. **1901** Hunter-Blair in *Daily Chron.* 12 Nov. 5/7 The Patriarch of the..influential Melchite Church. **1909** A. S. Lewis *Codex Climaci Rescriptus* p. xiii, As this version was adopted by the Malkite Church, it cannot be older than the Council of Chalcedon (A.D. 451).

melchoir, = MAILLECHORT.
1892 *Pall Mall G.* 3 Dec. 7/2.

†**meld**, *v.*[1] *Obs.* Also 4 meild. [OE. *meldian*, *meldan* = OS. *meldon* (Du. *melden*), OHG. *meldôn*, *meldên* (MHG., mod.G. *melden*) :—WGer. **melþōjan*, *-ējan*, f. **melþā* sb. fem. (OHG. *melda*, OE. *meld*), information, announcement. Cf. OE. *melda* informer, betrayer.] *trans.* To speak of, show forth, make known. Also, to inform (a person) *of*.
a **1000** *Riddles* xxix. 12 (Gr.) þonne æfter deaþe deman onginneð, meldan mislice. *c* **1000** *Ags. Ps.* (Th.) cxxxiv. 16 þa muð habbeð, and ne meldiað wiht. *a* **1300** *Cursor M.* 27830 O couaitise..cums..strenth, þat lauerding agh to meild, þat o þair men tas wrangwis yeild. *c* **1325** *Old Age* 3 in *E.E.P.* (1862) 148 Eld nul meld no murþes of mai. *c* **1325** *Metr. Hom.* 42 My consciens gan me meld. *Ibid.* 166 Dede war me leuer to be, Than thou of my dede melded me.

meld (mɛld), *v.*[2] and *sb.* *Cards.* [app. ad. G. *melden*: see prec.] *trans.* In the game of pinocle and other card games, esp. canasta and rummy: Equivalent to DECLARE *v.* in bezique. Also as *v. intr.* Hence **meld** *sb.*, a group of cards to be melded; ˈ**melding** *vbl. sb.*
1897 *Foster's Compl. Hoyle* 361 The various combinations which are declared during the play of the hand are called melds. *Ibid.* 363 A player has melded and scored four kings, and on winning another trick he melds binocle. **1952** *Times Rev. Year* 1 Jan. p. v/2 Canasta has begun to influence the language, if slightly. It has spread the use of natural..as a noun, and figurative jobs have been found for meld, a combination of three or more cards of the same rank. **1958** 'J. Welcome' *Run for Cover* iv. 83 He melded several more times—small melds which did not look dangerous from a canasta point of view. **1964** A. Wykes *Gambling* vii. 163 In most card games, players aim either to make specific card combinations (or 'melds') as in rummy, or to take tricks, as in whist. *Ibid.* 164 Games in which 'melding' (making specific combinations of cards) is a basic principle. These are the *rummy* games, which include all forms of *poker*.

meld (mɛld), *v.*[3] orig. and chiefly *U.S.* [perh. a blend of MELT *v.*[1] and WELD *v.*; but cf. E.D.D. *melder* entanglement, mental confusion; *meldered*, mixed, entangled.] *trans.* and *intr.* To merge, blend; to combine, incorporate. Hence as *sb.* and ˈ**melding** *vbl. sb.*
1939 *New Yorker* 23 Sept. 31 (Advt.), Schenley's exclusive process—melding—which 'marries' the whiskey blend so perfectly that it retains its rich flavor. **1952** *N.Y. Times* 18 Jan. 4/6 (*citing W. S. Churchill's Address to U.S. Congress*) What matters most is not the form of fusion, or melding—a word I learned over here. **1952** *Time* 29 Dec. 37/1 Taylor hopes to remodel the entire museum... He has plans to meld his eleven departments into five. **1959** M. Steen *Tower* I. iii. 50 Our small..existence couldn't meld with his design for living. **1960** S. Plath *Colossus* (1967) 14 Then I was seeing A melding of shapes in a hot rain. **1971** *Nat. Geographic* Oct. 560/2 Then clouds and gray sea melded and a steady rain slanted across the dry sides of the island. **1973** *Times Lit. Suppl.* 3 Aug. 911/5 The craft..of melding brisk jollity with real death. **1974** *Spartanburg* (S. Carolina) *Herald* 21 Apr. A6 (Advt.), A lovely cushioned group that offers a compatible meld of Ivy Leaves and light scrollwork. **1975** *New Yorker* 19 May 12/3 Jones' meld of traditional techniques with radical conceptions is in itself a radical conception, and gives the photographs their special, quiet interestingness.

melded (ˈmɛldɪd), *ppl. a.* [Blend of MELT *v.*[1] and WELDED *ppl. a.*: cf. prec.] Formed from or using man-made fibres that have an outer sheath which has been melted to bind the fibres together into a fabric.
1969 *Sci. Jrnl.* July 77 (*caption*) New possibilities have now been opened up by side by side or core/sheath bi-component fibres which, when heated enough to melt one component, result in 'melded' (melt welded) fabric. **1970** *Cabinet Maker & Retail Furnisher* 23 Oct. 174/1 The most recent development of durable non-woven fabrics for upholstery is the production of melded fabrics. **1972** *Guardian* 5 Apr. 9 Melded fabrics have arrived from ICI Fibre.

melder (ˈmɛldə(r)). *Sc.* Also 5 meltyre, 6 meldir, 8 meldar. [a. ON. *meldr*:—prehistoric **malidro-z*, f. root of *mala* to grind.] A quantity of meal ground at one time.
By Douglas used to render L. *mola* (*salsa*), the mixture of meal and salt with which Roman sacrifices were sprinkled.
14.. *Nom.* in Wr.-Wülcker 725/9 *Hoc emolimentum*, a meltyre. **1513** Douglas *Æneis* II. ii. 138 Quhen that of me suld be maid sacrifice, With salt meldir. **1715** Pennecuik *Descr. Tweeddale* Wks. (1815) 87 The seeds, from the different makings of meal (melders) through winter, are preserved. **1790** Morison *Poems* 110 Our simmer meldar niest was mil'd. **1820** Scott *Monast.* viii, I have often thought the miller's folk at the Monastery-mill were far over careless in sifting our melder. **1882** J. Walker *Jaunt to Auld Reekie*, etc. 23 Yestreen he cam doon wi' a melder to brie.
b. An occasion of taking corn to be ground.
1790 Burns *Tam O' Shanter* 23 That ilka melder, wi' the miller, Thou sat as lang as thou had siller.

meldew, obs. form of MILDEW *sb.*

meldometer (mɛlˈdɒmɪtə(r)). [irreg. f. Gr. *μέλδ-ειν* to melt + -METER.] (See quot.)
1885 Joly in *Nature* 5 Nov. 15/2 The Meldometer. The apparatus which I propose to call by the above name (*μέλδω*, to melt) consists of an adjunct to the mineralogical microscope, whereby the melting points of minerals may be compared or approximately determined.

ˈ**meldrop.** *Sc.* and *north. dial.* Also 5 myl-, 9 mildrop. [a. ON. *mél-dropi* drop or foam from a horse's mouth.]
1. A drop of mucus at the nose; also, the foam which falls from a horse's mouth (see Jamieson).
c **1480** Henryson *Test. Cres.* 158 Out of his nois the meldrop [*v.r.* myldrop] fast can rin. **1829** Brockett *N.C. Wds.*, *Mell-drop*, the least offensive species of mucus from the nose.
2. A dew drop.
1802 T. Paine *Writ.* (Conway) III. 390 Birthday addresses..should not creep along like mildrops down a cabbage leaf, but roll in a torrent of poetical metaphor.

†**mele**, *sb. Obs.* [var. of MALE *sb.*[1]; but the origin of the form is obscure: cf. It. *melo*, Gr. *μῆλον*.] An apple; an apple-tree.
c **1420** *Pallad. on Husb.* III. 891 The meles round, ycald orbiculer [L. *mala rotunda*], Withowton care a yer may keped be. *Ibid.* IV. 517 In hymsylf graffe hym in ffeueryere, In mele also; ek graffe hym in the pere [L. *inseritur..in se et in pyro et in malo*].

†**mele**, *v. Obs.* Forms: 1 mǽlan, 3 *Ormin* mælenn, 3–4 meile, (4 meille, 5 meill), 3–5 mele, (3 meale). [OE. *mǽlan* = ON. *mǽla* (Da. *mæle*):—**mǣljan*, f. OE. *mǽl*, ON. *mál* speech: see MAIL *sb.*[2]] *intr.* and *trans.* To speak, tell.
c **1000** *Ags. Ps.* (Th.) lxxxiv. 7 Hwæt me haliȝ God, on minum mod-sefan, mælan wille. *c* **1200** Ormin 2919 Off all þatt tatt he wile don & tatt he wile mælenn. *a* **1225** *Leg. Kath.* 1245 Hwil þis eadi meiden motede & mealde þis & muchele mare. *a* **1300** *Cursor M.* 27214 And þar him-self wit word he meild bath of his youthed and his eild. *c* **1350** *Will. Palerne* 621 What man so ich mete wiþ or mele wiþ speche. *c* **1470** Henry *Wallace* x. 1063 Off king Eduuard ȝeit mar furth will I meill.
Hence †**meling** *vbl. sb.*, talking, conversation.
c **1350** *Will. Palerne* 760 ȝif meliors wiþ hire maydenes in meling þere sete.

mele: see MEAL, MEDLE, MELL.

Melean, var. MELIAN *sb.* and *a.*

‖**mêlée** (ˈmɛleɪ, ˈmeɪ-). Also **melée, melee.** [Fr.: see MEDLEY, MELLAY.] **1.** A mixed or irregular fight between two parties of combatants, a skirmish. Also *transf.*, a lively contention or debate.
a **1648** Ld. Herbert *Autobiog.* in *Life* (1886) 74, I cannot deny but a demivolte with courbettes, so that they be not too high, may be useful in a fight or *mêlée*. **1765** H. Walpole *Lett.* (1857) IV. 346, I almost wish for anything that may put an end to my being concerned in the *mêlée*. **1837** W. Irving *Capt. Bonneville* II. 100 In this mêlée, one white man was wounded. **1871** J. Leighton *Paris under Commune* lxviii. 243 Already, yesterday the mêlée of a battle could be distinguished from the fort of Vauves.
2. [perh. a different word.] Small diamonds less than about a carat in weight.
1911 L. Cohen *Reminisc. Kimberley* 267 (Pettman), On a certain day I had entrusted him with two or three hundred carats of melée—small stones—to sell. **1920** *Daily Tel.* 22 June 1/2 Stones of various weights from 1⅛ carats downwards, and a quantity of melee. **1962** R. Webster *Gems* I. ii. 39 Farther down the scale are mêlée which are crystals less than 1 carat in weight. **1972** *Daily Tel.* (Colour Suppl.) 30 June 10/2 Stones under one carat, known as Melée, are divided into fewer categories, but with subdivisions of these main ones according to colour, quality .., and of course size, there are well over 2,000 kinds.

meleguet(t)a, variant forms of MALAGUETTA.

melene (ˈmɛliːn). *Chem.* [f. MEL(ISSYL) + -ENE.] An olefine obtained by the distillation of bees-wax. Called also **melissylene.**
1848 Brodie in *Phil. Trans.* CXXXIX. 101 The hydro-carbon of the wax-alcohol.., to which may be given the name of melen. **1884** Roscoe & Schorlemmer *Chem.* III. II. 286 Melissylene or Melene, $C_{30}H_{60}$.

†**melet**, Some kind of fish.
c **1475** *Pict. Voc.* in Wr.-Wülcker 765/9 *Nomina piscium marinorum*, *Hic molanus*, a melet. *a* **1672** Willughby *Hist. Pisc.* (1686) 210 In litore nostro raro capitur, dicitur que Melet.

†**meleˈtetics**, *sb. pl. Obs. rare.* [ad. Gr. *μελετητικά*, neut. pl. of *μελετητικός* pertaining to meditation, f. *μελετᾶν* to meditate.] Rules or methods of meditation.
1665 Boyle *Occas. Refl.* I. iii. 8 Nor will the Meleteticks (or way, and kind of Meditation) I would perswade, keep Men alone from [etc.]. *Ibid.* III. v. 46 The usefulness of our Meleteticks towards the improvement of Men's parts.

meletre: see MEDLE(*-tree*).

meleward, var. MILLWARD.

melewell, obs. f. MULVEL.

meleyn, obs. form of MILAN[1].

melezitose (mɪˈlɛzɪtəʊs). *Chem.* [f. F. *mélèze* larch, after MELITOSE.] A sugar, isomeric with cane-sugar, discovered by Bonastre in larch-manna.
1862 Miller *Elem. Chem.* (ed.2) III. 96. **1876** tr. *Schutzenberger's Ferment.* 33 Melezitose, melitose, and lactine.

melfoil, obs. form of MILFOIL.

‖**melia** (ˈmiːlɪə). *Bot.* [mod.L. (*Linnæus*), a. Gr. *μελία* ash-tree; the leaves of the azedarac resemble those of the ash.] A genus of trees (typical of the N.O. *Meliaceæ*), of which the best known species is the AZEDARAC; ; a tree of this genus.
1753 Chambers *Cycl. Supp.*, *Melia*, in botany, the name by which Linnæus calls the *azedarach*. **1838** *Penny Cycl.* XI. 73/1 Magnolias, melias, robinias.
Hence **meliˈaceous** *a.*, pertaining to the *Meliaceæ*; ˈ**meliad**, a plant of this order (*Syd. Soc. Lex.*); ˈ**melial** *a.*, in *melial alliance*, Lindley's name for an alliance embracing this and some other orders.
1836 Lindley *Nat. Syst. Bot.* (ed. 2) 92 The highest alliances in regard to structure are the Malval and Melial. **1846** —— *Veg. Kingd.* 463 Meliaceæ—Meliads.

Melian (ˈmiːlɪən), *sb.* and *a.* Also **Melean.** [f. *Melos* (Gr. *Μῆλος*), the name of an island in the Ægean Sea + -IAN.] **a.** *sb.* An inhabitant of Melos. **b.** *adj.* Of or pertaining to the island of Melos.
1550 T. Nicolls tr. *Thucydides' Hystory* [*Peloponnesian War*] v. xi. sig. Bb3ᵛ The Meliens..refused to be under the obeissaunce of the Athenyans. **1629** T. Hobbes tr. *Thucydides' Peloponnesian Warre* v. 341 Dialogue betweene the Athenians and Melians. **1709** I. Littlebury tr. *Herodotus' Hist.* II. VIII. 300 The Hermionians..were ejected by Hercules and the Melians out of that Country which is now call'd Doris. *Ibid.* 302 The Melians..arriv'd in Gallies of fifty Oars. **1832** J. Bell *Syst. Geogr.* II. 513 Marbles of many varieties are abundant in Greece... Another variety was..the Melian. **1887** L. E. Upcott *Introd. Greek Sculpture* viii. 110 The statue of Aphrodite in the Louvre, called the 'Melian Venus' (Venus de Milo), found in 1820 in the island of Melos. **1910** W. James *Mem. & Stud.* (1911) 270 The Meleans say that sooner than be slaves they will appeal to the gods. **1936** *Discovery* Oct. 325/1 One of the finest Egyptian masterpieces in the world, a royal portrait, was actually executed in Melian obsidian. **1946** G. Murray *Euripides & his Age* v. 128 The Melians.. answer as best they can. **1968** *Encycl. Brit.* XV. 132/1 The Melian earth was employed as a pigment by ancient artists. *Ibid.* 132/2 In 416 B.C. the Athenians attacked the island and compelled the Melians to surrender.

‖**melianthus** (mɛlɪˈænθəs). *Bot.* [mod.L. (Tournefort 1700), f. Gr. *μέλι* honey + *ἄνθος* flower.] A genus of flowering plants, the type of the N.O. *Melianthaceæ*; now including only the five South African species known as HONEYFLOWER; formerly much more extensive.
1733 Miller *Gard. Dict.* (ed. 2), *Melianthus*,..Honey-Flower. **1741** *Compl. Fam.-Piece* II. iii. 401 Myrtles,.. Meleanthus,..and such tender Greens as remain yet abroad. **1751** J. Hill *Gen. Nat. Hist.* II. *Hist. Plants* 517 The pinnated-leaved Melianthus with serrated pinnulæ... It is a native of Virginia. *a* **1876** M. Collins *Th. in Garden* (1880) II. vi. 225 How would it be for fruit-growers to plant thyme,.., melianthus, and mignonette near their southern walls?

melibiose (mɛlɪˈbaɪəʊz, -s). *Chem.* [a. G. *melibiose* (Scheibler & Mittelmeier 1889, in *Ber. d. Deut. Chem. Ges.* XXII. 1684), f. G. *meli-tose* MELITOSE: see BI-[2] and -OSE[2].] Glucose-6-α-galactoside, $C_{12}H_{22}O_{11}$, a crystalline sugar obtained from raffinose.
1889 *Jrnl. Chem. Soc.* LVI. 953 This disaccharide is, therefore, not lactobiose (lactose), which it closely resembles, but a new carbohydrate, for which the author proposes the name *melibiose*. **1948** [see DIOSE]. **1970** G. C. Whiting in A. C. Hulme *Biochem. Fruits* I. i. 8 Kliewer.. detected trace amounts of maltose and melibiose in the grape. **1975** *Sci. Amer.* Jan. 82/3 The molecule bears a close resemblance to two common plant galactosides: melibiose, a disaccharide (two-sugar compound), and raffinose, a trisaccharide.
Hence **meliˈbiase** [a. G. *melibiase* (A. Bau 1895, in *Chemiker-Zeitung* 16 Oct. 1874/1): see -ASE], an enzyme which brings about the hydrolysis of melibiose.
1899 J. R. Green *Soluble Ferments* ix. 136 Barr [*sic*] has extracted the enzyme from low fermentation Froberg yeast but he attributes it only to the final stage in the hydrolysis, the conversion of melibiose into glucose and galactose, and he has named it melibiase in consequence. **1943** H. Tauber *Enzyme Technol.* i. 28 Ale yeast does not contain melibiase, whereas lager yeast does. **1956** *Nature* 25 Feb. 383/1 (*heading*) Complementary action of melibiase and galactozymase on raffinose fermentation.

melibœan (mɛlɪˈbiːən), *a.*[1] [f. L. *Melibœ-us* the epithet of a purple dye) + -AN.] Pertaining to Melibœa, a Syrian island (colonized from Thessaly), famous for its purple dye.
1667 Milton *P.L.* XI. 242 Over his lucid Armes A Militarie Vest of purple flowd, Livelier then Melibœan.

meli'bœan, *a.*[2] [f. *Melibœus*, the name of one of the two interlocutors in the first eclogue of Virgil + -AN.] Used by Carlyle for: AMŒBÆAN.

1837 CARLYLE *Misc.* (1872) V. 224 In vain preached this apostle and that other simultaneously or in Melibœan sequence. —— *Fr. Rev.* III. I. viii, In rapid Melibœan stanzas, only a few lines each, they propose motions not a few.

melic ('mɛlɪk), *sb.* Also **melick.** [ad. mod.L. *melica*, of obscure origin.] A genus (*Melica* Linn.) of grasses of the tribe *Festuceæ*; a grass of this genus. Also ***melic-grass.***

1787 tr. *Linnæus' Fam. Plants* I. 46 *Melica.* Melic-grass. **1804** CHARLOTTE SMITH *Conversations*, etc. II. 108 In a few short months.. Would velvet moss and purple melic rise. **1854** S. THOMSON *Wild Fl.* III. (ed. 4) 193 The mountain or wood melic-grass (*Melica nutans*). *a* **1863** JEAN INGELOW *High Tide on Linc. Coast*, From the meads where melick groweth.

melic ('mɛlɪk), *a.* [ad. Gr. μελικός, f. μέλος song.] Of poetry: Intended to be sung; applied *spec.* to the strophic species of Greek lyric verse. Hence applied to poets who compose such verse. Also *absol.* = melic poetry.

1699 BENTLEY *Phal.* xv. 484 Stesichorus a Melic or Lyric Poet. **1850** MURE *Lit. Greece* III. 28 The more delicate varieties of melic rhythm. *Ibid.* 56 Strophic odes.. may be classed under two heads, Melic and Choric. **1886** F. B. JEVONS *Greek Lit.* 123 The history of melic begins for us with Terpander. *Ibid.* 160 Theognis was an elegiac and not a melic poet.

melicaris, obs. form of MELICERIS.

meliceratous, *a.* *Obs.* [Badly f. MELICERIS.] = MELICERIC.

1755 GUY in *Phil. Trans.* XLIX. 35 A meliceratous fluid.

meliceric (mɛlɪ'sɪərɪk), *a.* [f. MELICER-IS + -IC.] Pertaining to meliceris.

1835-6 *Todd's Cycl. Anat.* I. 788/2 Those subcutaneous tumours.. which contain meliceric.. matter. **1847-9** *Ibid.* IV. 97/2 The most common seats of atheromatous and meliceric cysts are the scalp and eyelids.

‖**meliceris** (mɛlɪ'sɪərɪs). *Path.* Pl. **melicerides** (mɛlɪ'sɛrɪdiːz). Also 6 **meliciris, meliceres,** 8–9 **mellіceris.** [mod.L., a. Gr. μελικηρίς some eruptive disease, f. μελίκηρον honeycomb, f. μέλι honey + κηρός wax.]

1. An encysted tumour containing matter which resembles honey.

1562 TURNER *Herbal* II. 121 b, Melicirides which are apostemes.. haue an oylish thyng within them lyke vnto honye. **1597** A.M. tr. *Guillemeau's Fr. Chirurg.* 18 The vlceration Meliceres differeth from the Ateroma. **1762** R. GUY *Pract. Obs. Cancers* 31 Melliceris. **1847-9** *Todd's Cycl. Anat.* IV. 97/2 The chief varieties of these [cysts] are *atheroma*,.. *meliceris*,.. and *steatoma*.

attrib. **1739** SHARP *Operat. Surg.* 128 The Ganglion of the Tendon is an Encysted Tumour of the Meliceris kind.

2. 'The fluid contents of a distended joint when yellow and honey-like' (*Syd. Soc. Lex.* 1890).

1870 PAGET *Lect. Surg. Pathol.* xxi. (ed. 3) 672 [Synovial cysts.] Their contents possess a gelatinous or even a honey-like consistency which constitutes a form of Meliceris.

†**meliceritous**, *a.* *Obs.* [Badly f. MELICERIS.] = MELICERIC.

1804 ABERNETHY *Surg. Obs.* 88 The contents [of a wen] were of the consistence which is termed meliceritous.

melicerous (mɛlɪ'sɪərəs), *a.* [f. MELICER-IS + -OUS.] = MELICERIC.

1828-32 in WEBSTER (who names *Hosack*). **1846** in *Todd's Cycl. Anat.* IV. 1114/2 Melicerous degeneration of the thyroid. **1890** *Syd. Soc. Lex.*, *Melicerous cyst.*

melicertan (mɛlɪ'sɜːtən). *Zool.* Also **-ian.** [f. *Melicerta* (from L. *Melicerta*, Gr. Μελικέρτης, name of a sea-god) + -AN.] A rotifer of the genus *Melicerta* of family *Melicertidæ*.

1856 CARPENTER *Microsc.* §281. 498 The first group.. includes two families, the Floscularians and the Melicertians. **1884** C. T. HUDSON in *Q. Jrnl. Microscop. Sci.* XXIV. 343 In all other Melicertans the row of smaller cilia encloses the row of larger ones.

meliciris, obs. form of MELICERIS.

melicoton(ie, -y, var. ff. MELOCOTON *Obs.*

†'**melicrate.** *Obs.* Also 6 **melicrat, mellicrate.** [ad. late L. *melicrātum*, ad. Gr. μελίκρατον (-κρητον), f. μέλι honey + κρᾶ-, κεραννύναι to mix.] A drink made with honey and water.

1563 HYLL *Art Garden.* (1593) 80 A spoonfull of mellicrate. **1578** LYTE *Dodoens* I. xviii. 28 The leaues.. dronken with Meade or Melicrat.. it healeth the Sciatica. **1584** COGAN *Haven Health* (1636) 198 Eat nothing at all, or else, but a little melicrate. **1775** SIR E. BARRY *Obs. Wines* 389 Its comparative strength with that of melicrate, or water and honey.

Hence †**melicrated** *a.*, made by mixing water and honey.

1657 TOMLINSON *Renou's Disp.* 100 The rule of confecting Melicrated mulsa.

melik, var. MALIK.

melilite ('mɛlɪlaɪt). *Min.* Also **mellilite.** [a. F. *mélilite* (Delamétherie 1795), mod.L. *melilithus*, f. Gr. μέλι honey + λίθος stone: see -LITE.]

1. A silicate of calcium, aluminium and other bases, found in honey-yellow crystals.

1821 JAMESON *Man. Min.* 325 Mellilite... Strikes fire with steel. **1823** W. PHILLIPS *Introd. Min.* (ed. 3) 208 Melilite.. has only been found at Capo di Bove near Rome, in the fissures of a compact black lava. **1836** T. THOMSON *Min., Geol.*, etc. I. 207 Mellilite. **1879** RUTLEY *Stud. Rocks* xiii. 255 Apatite,.. melilite and garnet are among the more common accessory minerals [in nepheline basalt].

2. = MELLITE (after Kirwan).

1796 KIRWAN *Elem. Min.* II. 68 Mellilite, Honigstein, of Werner. **1821** JAMESON *Man. Min.* 296 Pyramidal Mellilite, or Honeystone. **1837** DANA *Syst. Min.* 438 Mellite.. Mellilite. Honey Stone.

†**melilithic**, *a.* *Chem.* *Obs.* [f. MELILITH-US + -IC.] ***melilithic acid***, an acid found in mellite.

1803 *Med. Jrnl.* IX. 474 Chemical Analysis of the Honey-stone... 106 parts of it contain 46 melilithic acid.

‖**melilithus.** *Min.* *Obs.* [mod.L.: see MELILITE.] = MELILITE 2, MELLITE.

1800 *Med. Jrnl.* III. 583 Mr. Klaproth, of Berlin, has enriched chemistry with the discovery of a new acid, which he obtained by the analysis of the honey stone, or melilithus.

melilot ('mɛlɪlɒt). Forms: 5–8 **mellilot,** 6 **mellylot(e, melli-, millelote,** 6–9 **melilote,** 6– **melilot.** [a. OF. *melilot* (mod.F. *mélilot*), ad. late L. *melilōtos*, a. Gr. μελίλωτος, -ον, a sweet kind of clover, f. μέλι honey + λωτός: see LOTUS. Cf. Sp., Pg. *meliloto*, It. *mel(l)iloto*.] A plant of the leguminous genus *Melilotus*, esp. *M. officinalis* or Yellow Melilot, the dried flowers of which were formerly much used in making plasters, poultices, etc.

c **1410** *Master of Game* (MS. Digby 182) xii, Oyle of camamylle and of mellilot. **1533** ELYOT *Cast. Helthe* (1541) 11 Meates inflatynge or wyndye: Beanes: Lupines:.. Mellylote. **1541** R. COPLAND tr. *Guydon's Quest. Chirurg.* Y iv b, Yᵉ decoction of moleyn, camomille, millelote. **1548** TURNER *Names Herbes* (E.D.S.) 52 *Melfrugum*... It may be called in englishe whyte melilote. **1587** MASCALL *Govt. Cattle, Horses* (1596) 154 One ounce of the powder of mellilot. **1728** J. GARDINER tr. *Rapin's Of Gardens* 18 Sweet-scented Mellilot. **1778** *Eng. Gazetteer* (ed. 2) s.v. *Horsheath*, This part of the county abounds with melilot, whose seeds mix so much with the corn.. that it gives a taste to their bread, which is very disagreeable to strangers. **1864** SWINBURNE *Atalanta* 1354 Every holier herb, Narcissus, and the low-lying melilote. **1883** *Encycl. Amer.* I. 480/1 Such plants as white or alsike clover, or melilot, catnip.. etc.

fig. **1748** RICHARDSON *Clarissa* VII. 330 Will not some serious thoughts mingle with thy melilot, and tear off the callus of thy mind?

b. *attrib.*, as †***melilot-emplaster, -flower, -plaster***; **melilot trefoil,** *Medicago lupulina.*

1676 WISEMAN *Surg.* v. i. 351 To which purpose Sponges were prest out of *Melilot Emplaster, and the Wound fill'd with them. **1694** SALMON *Bate's Dispens.* (1713) 205/1 A Melilot Emplaster or Colewort-leaf may be applied. *c* **1540** in *Vicary's Anat.* (1888) App. ix. 226 The pouldre of *mellilote flowres. **1826** *Sporting Mag.* XIX. 27 Water distilled from the melilot flowers has been held to improve the flavour of other substances. **1712** SWIFT *Jrnl. to Stella* 24 Apr., At last I advised the doctor to use it like a blister, so I did with *melilot plasters, which still run. **1795** BURKE *Corr.* (1844) IV. 276, I would not put my melilot plaister on the back of the hangman. **1760** J. LEE *Introd. Bot.* App. 319 *Melilot Trefoil, *Trifolium.*

†**meline**, *a.*[1] *Obs.* *rare*$^{-1}$. [ad. L. *mēlinus*, a. Gr. μήλινος, f. μῆλον apple, quince.] Quince-yellow.

1398 TREVISA *Barth. De P.R.* XVII. cxci. (1495) 730 Of vyolets is thre manere of kynde. purpure whyte and melyne, that is a manere whyte colour that comyth out of the ylonde Melos.

meline ('miːlaɪn), *a.*[2] [ad. L. *mēlīnus*, f. *mēlēs* 'marten or badger' (L. & Sh.), in mod. zoological Latin the generic name of the badger: see -INE.] Of or pertaining to the genus *Meles*; badger-like.

1891 FLOWER & LYDEKKER *Mammals* 567 Divided.. into the Otter-like (Lutrine), Badger-like (Meline), and Weasel-like (Musteline) forms.

meling, var. MELLING; and see under MELE *v.*

melinite[1] ('mɛlɪnaɪt). [Named by E. F. Glocker in 1847, f. Gr. μήλιν-ος (see MELINE *a.*[1]) + -ITE.] A clay resembling yellow ochre. Also '**melinine.**

1868 DANA *Syst. Min.* (ed. 5) II. 477 Melinite. **1896** CHESTER *Dict. Min.*

melinite[2] ('mɛlɪnaɪt). [a. F. *mélinite*, f. Gr. μήλινος: see prec.] A French explosive, said to be composed of picric acid, guncotton, and gum arabic.

1886 *Daily News* 2 Dec. 5/2 France and Germany are lavishing money upon repeating rifles, melanite [*sic*] shells, and iron-plated forts. **1887** *Chicago Advance* 3 Feb. 78/4 The new French explosive, melenite,.. resembles yellow clay. **1887** *Nature* 17 Mar. 472/2 The new gunpowder melinite has already begun its work of destruction.

melinophane, earlier name of MELIPHANITE.

melioidosis (ˌmɛlɪɔɪ'dəʊsɪs). *Path.* [mod.L., f. Gr. μηλί-ς a distemper of asses, prob. glanders + -OID + -OSIS.] An infectious disease similar to glanders which is caused by the bacterium *Pseudomonas pseudomallei*, is endemic in rodents in certain (chiefly tropical) regions, and is occas. transmitted to man (in whom it is usu. fatal) and to other animals.

1921 STANTON & FLETCHER in *Trans. 4th Congr. Far Eastern Assoc. Trop. Med.* 197 The Greek physicians described under the name 'Melis' a variety of conditions resembling glanders. We propose for this disease of such varied form the name 'Melioidosis'. **1925** —— in *Lancet* 3 Jan. 10/2 Melioidosis.. apart from one case in Singapore, has been recognised nowhere except in the towns of Rangoon and Kuala Lumpur. **1939** *Nature* 11 Nov. 801/1 The great plague of Athens in 430 B.C. may, Scott believes, have been melioidosis. **1952** M. E. FLOREY *Clin. Applic. Antibiotics* I. viii. 237 Five West African soldiers employed in Burma were found to be suffering from melioidosis. **1970** JUBB & KENNEDY *Path. Domestic Animals* (ed. 2) I. iii. 162/2 Outbreaks of melioidosis, as well as isolated cases, occur in sheep, goats, and pigs.

†'**melion.** *Obs.* *rare*$^{-1}$. = MELILOT.

c **1420** *Pallad. on Husb.* XI. 358 An vnce of melion [L. *meliloti*].

melior, obs. variant of MULIER.

meliorability. *rare.* [f. *meliorable adj., f. late L. *meliōrāre*: see MELIORATE *v.* and -ABLE] Capacity of being improved. (Only in Bentham.)

1811-31 BENTHAM *Language* Wks. 1843 VIII. 297/2 Meliorability.

meliorant ('miːlɪərənt). [ad. late L. *meliōrantem* pr. pple. of *meliōrāre*: see MELIORATE *v.*] Something that makes better; an improver.

1920 G. SAINTSBURY *Notes on Cellar-Bk.* 102, I am afraid that the 'whets' of our ancestors were rather stimulants to drinking.. than meliorants of appreciation.

meliorate ('miːlɪəreɪt), *v.* [f. late L. *meliōrāt-*, ppl. stem of *meliōrāre*, f. L. *meliōr-*, *melior* better.]

1. *trans.* To make better, to improve; = AMELIORATE *v.* Also, †to mitigate (suffering, ill-feeling).

a **1552** LELAND *Itin.* (1768) III. 65 This Joannes Grandisonus chaungid an hold Fundation of an Hospital of S. John's in Excester and melioratid it. **1598** in Row *Hist. Kirk* (Wodrow Soc.) 190 If he hes meliorat or deteriorat his benefice any way to the prejudice of his successor. **1620** VENNER *Via Recta* ii. 41 They are meliorated, by putting to them sugar, nutmeg, and.. ginger. **1647** JER. TAYLOR *Lib. Proph.* xix. 248 Religion is to meliorate the condition of a people. **1702** W. J. *Bruyn's Voy. Levant* xli. 166 A Fatness which so far Meliorates the Lean and Sandy Soil of this Country. **1782** MISS BURNEY *Cecilia* I. vii, She pleased herself with the intention of meliorating her plan in the meantime. **1796** MRS. HOWELL *Anzoletta Z.* I. 125 These sentiments her brother.. had meliorated, by proposing that a ball should be given [etc.]. **1802** *Noble Wanderers* II. 6 It would have meliorated his sufferings. **1854** H. MILLER *Sch. & Schm.* i. (1857) 6 The mutiny at the Nore had not yet meliorated the service to the common sailor. **1894** W. J. DAWSON *Making of Manhood* 29 Every movement which seeks to meliorate the common lot.

b. *absol.*; *spec.* in Scots law, to effect 'meliorations' (see MELIORATION 2 b).

a **1701** SEDLEY *Grumbler* I. i, Nothing is more dangerous than chastisement *sine causa*; instead of meliorating, it pejorates. **1769** ROBERTSON *Chas. V*, III. (1796) I. 121 To squeeze and to amass, rather than to meliorate, was their object. **1838** W. BELL *Dict. Law Scot.* 641 An obligation on the tenant to meliorate or repair, if not implemented by himself, falls upon his representatives. **1845** R. HUNTER *Landlord & Tenant* (ed. 2) II. 220 By the contract, stipulations to meliorate and preserve may bind either the lessor or lessee, or both.

2. *intr.* To grow better. = AMELIORATE *v.* 2.

1654 H. L'ESTRANGE *Chas. I.* (1655) 166 The Scot'sh Revolters in the state I left them, were not like to meliorate nor to goe lesse in animosity. **1681** NEVILE *Plato Rediv.* 269 That we can never Meliorate, but by some such Principles, as we have been here all this while discoursing of. **1764** GOLDSM. *Hist. Eng. in Lett.* (1772) II. 76 British ferocity [began] to meliorate into social politeness. **1793** J. TURNBULL in Sparks *Corr. Amer. Rev.* (1853) IV. 443, I hope.. that circumstances in that distressed city may continue to meliorate. **1849** H. MILLER *Footpr. Creat.* xii. (1874) 219 When the climate had greatly meliorated. **1860** EMERSON *Cond. Life* i. (1861) 13 The face of the planet cools and dries, the races meliorate, and man is born.

Hence '**meliorated** *ppl. a.*; '**meliorating** *vbl. sb.* and *ppl. a.*

1649 BLITH *Eng. Improv. Impr.* xx. (1652) 132 All which as to all sorts of Land, they are of an exceeding Meliorating nature. **1665** HOOKE *Microgr.* 246 Promoted by the meliorating of Glasses. **1692** R. L'ESTRANGE *Josephus, Wars of Jews* III. ii. (1733) 663 Great Plenty of Fruits, both wild, and meliorated or domestick. **1766** *Complete Farmer* s.v. *Husbandry*, To return the meliorated earth to the corn. **1783** WASHINGTON *Circular* 18 June, The free culivation of letters, the unbounded extension of commerce,.. have had a meliorating influence on mankind. **1789** BURNEY *Hist. Mus.* IV. 350 The first movement in the overture is grave and grand, in Lulli's meliorated style, by Handel.

melioration (miːlɪə'reɪʃən). [n. of action f. late L. *meliōrāre* to MELIORATE.]

1. The action of making better, or the condition of being made better; amelioration, improvement.

1626 BACON *Sylva* §855 You must ever resort to the beginning of things for Melioration. *a* **1682** SIR T. BROWNE *Tracts* (1684) 47 A notable way for melioration of the Plant. **1772** PRIESTLEY in *Phil. Trans.* LXII. 184, I could not .. effect any melioration of the noxious quality of this kind of air. **1796** BURNEY *Mem. Metastasio* II. 280 Persevere in your melioration, till you are perfectly cured. **1827** STEUART *Planter's G.* (1828) 205 All soils are susceptible of melioration. **1876** BANCROFT *Hist. U.S.* III. i. 7 The generations of men are not like the leaves on the trees, which fall and renew themselves without melioration or change.

2. An instance of meliorating; a change for the better; a thing or an action by which something is made better; an improvement.

1647 LILLY *Chr. Astrol.* xxviii. 183, I concluded, that about two yeers after .. he should sensibly perceive a melioration in Estate by meanes of a Wife. **1661** BOYLE *Cert. Phys. Ess.* (1669) 120 By an Insight into Chymistry one may be enabl'd to make some Meliorations (I speak not of Transmutations) of Mineral and Metalline Bodies. **1796** MORSE *Amer. Geog.* II. 568 Transplanting, engrafting, and other meliorations [in horticulture]. **1878** EMERSON *Sovereignty of Ethics* in *North Amer. Rev.* CXXVI. 406 The civil history of man might be traced by the successive meliorations as marked in higher moral generalizations.

b. *Scots Law.* In *plural*, applied *spec.* to improvements effected by a tenant upon the land rented by him.

1838 W. BELL *Dict. Law Scot.* 644 A clause binding the landlord to make the necessary meliorations. **1845** R. HUNTER *Landlord & Tenant* (ed. 2) II. 232 A proprietor stipulated in the lease to make certain meliorations, and to pay to the lessee the expense of meliorations made by him.

'meliorative, *a.* (*sb.*) [f. late L. *meliōrāre* to MELIORATE: see -ATIVE.] **a.** That meliorates; improving. *spec.* in *Linguistics*, giving or acquiring a more favourable meaning or connotation (opp. *pejorative*).

1808 G. EDWARDS *Pract. Plan* iii. 30 We .. become savage in our hatred to the various meliorative processes. **1841** R. OASTLER *Fleet Papers* I. xl. 314 Peel has no meliorative and restorative principle to propose. **1902** *Encycl. Brit.* XXXI. 678/1 The so-called meliorative and pejorative developments in word-meaning. **1916** F. SWINNERTON *Chaste Wife* xvii. §2. 254 Its note had been meliorative rather than optimistic. **1933** G. A. VAN DONGEN *Amelioratives in Eng.* I. 146 A meliorative sense-development can be shown to have taken place in a far greater number of words than is generally supposed. **1954** PEI & GAYNOR *Dict. Ling.* 134 *Meliorative suffix*, a suffix which gives a word a more favorable or flattering connotation. **1967** R. A. WALDRON *Sense & Sense Devel.* vii. 159 *Shrewd* is certainly most often a term of praise nowadays, though it comes from ME *shrewede* 'wicked, vicious' .. and passes through the 'cunning, crafty' stage before reaching its present mainly meliorative sense. **1971** *Archivum Linguisticum* II. 36 Not only is *silly old* —— recognizably an example of a 'meliorative-pejorative' adjectival compound in English but, more generally, the example has .. been shown to be ambiguous. **1973** *Times Lit. Suppl.* 8 June 647/3 His qualities were British, in the meliorative sense.

b. As *sb.* A word which has had a meliorative sense-development.

1933 G. A. VAN DONGEN *Amelioratives in Eng.* I. 115 The delimitation of the scope of content displayed by those words .. may result in the word becoming a meliorative or a pejorative.

meliorator, meliorater ('miːlɪəreɪtə(r)). *rare.* [agent-n. f. MELIORATE *v.*: see -OR, -ER[1].] One who or something which meliorates.

1855 in OGILVIE *Suppl.* **1870** EMERSON *Soc. & Solit., Work & Days* Wks. (Bohn) III. 68 The greatest meliorator of the world is selfish, huckstering Trade.

meliorism ('miːlɪərɪz(ə)m). [f. L. *melior* better + -ISM.]

1. The doctrine, intermediate between optimism and pessimism, which affirms that the world may be made better by rightly-directed human effort.

As used by some writers, the term implies further the belief that society has on the whole a prevailing tendency towards improvement.

[**1858**: cf. MELIORIST.] **1877** GEO. ELIOT *Let. J. Sully* 1 Jan. in Cross *Life* (1885) III. 301 The doctrine of meliorism. **1877** J. SULLY *Pessimism* 399 Our line of reasoning provides us .. with a practical conception .. which, to use a term for which I am indebted to .. George Eliot, may be appropriately styled Meliorism. By this I would understand the faith which affirms not merely our power of lessening evil—this nobody questions—but also our ability to increase the amount of positive good. **1885** J. H. CLAPPERTON (*title*) Scientific Meliorism and the Evolution of Happiness.

2. Used as the designation of a principle of action in dealing with the evils of society (see quot.).

1883 L. F. WARD *Dynam. Sociol.* II. 468 Meliorism .. may be defined as humanitarianism *minus* all sentiment... It implies the improvement of the social condition through cold calculation, through the adoption of indirect means. It is not content merely to alleviate present suffering, it aims to create conditions under which no suffering can exist.

meliorist ('miːlɪərɪst). [f. L. *melior* better + -IST.] One who believes in meliorism.

1858 J. BROWN *Horæ Subsec., Locke & Sydenham* Pref. 19, I am not however a pessimist, I am, I trust, a rational optimist, or at least a meliorist. **1877** GEO. ELIOT in Cross *Life* (1885) III. 301, I don't know that I ever heard anybody use the word 'meliorist' except myself. **1890** G. B. SHAW in *Fab. Ess. Socialism* 28 The Socialist came forward as a meliorist on these lines.

attrib. **1884** H. SPENCER in *Contemp. Rev.* July 39 The meliorist view— .. that life .. is on the way to become such that it will yield more pleasure than pain.

melioristic (miːlɪə'rɪstɪk), *a.* [f. MELIORIST + -IC.] Of or pertaining to meliorism.

1888 *Academy* 3 Mar. 148/1 Perhaps too scientifically melioristic for the common herd.

meliority (miːlɪ'ɒrɪtɪ). [ad. med.L. *meliōritās*, f. L. *meliōr-*, *melior* better: see -ITY.] The quality or condition of being better; superiority.

1578 SIDNEY *Wanstead Play* in *Arcadia*, etc. (1605) 574 [Pedant *loq.*] Either according to the penetrancie of their singing, or the melioritie of their functions, or lastly the superancy of their merits. **1597** BACON *Coulers Good & Evill* No. 1 So that this couler of melioritie and preheminence is oft a signe of eneruation and weakenesse. **1640** BP. HALL *Episc.* II. xi. 154 This meliority therefore, or betternesse above the Priests and Deacons, is ascribed to the Bishop. **1715** CHEYNE *Philos. Princ. Relig.* Contents *5 Some more particular Reflections, upon the Meliority of the Frame and Constitution of the Celestial Bodies. **1845** A. DUNCAN *Disc.* 139 They may point out such a meliority of disposal, figure and size, as ever converts its essential properties to the most useful purposes.

†**meliori'zation.** *Obs.* [f. MELIORIZE *v.* + -ATION.] Melioration; improvement.

1599 A. M. tr. *Gabelhouer's Bk. Physicke* 38/1 Till such time as we perceaue some meliorization, or amendment.

†**'meliorize,** *v. Obs.* [f. L. *melior* better + -IZE.] **a.** *trans.* To make better; to improve. **b.** *intr.* To grow better.

1597 A. M. tr. *Guillemeau's Fr. Chirurg.* *v, I desire that they woulde vouchsafe to meliorize the same. **1599** —— tr. *Gabelhouer's Bk. Physicke* 115/1 Till shee beginne to meliorise, and waxe lesse.

meliphagan (mɛ'lɪfəgən). *Ornith.* Also *erron.* melli-. [f. mod.L. *Meliphaga* (f. Gr. μέλι honey + -φάγ-ος that eats) + -AN.] A bird belonging to the Australian genus *Meliphaga* or family *Meliphagidæ* (see next).

1842 BRANDE *Dict. Sci.* etc., *Melliphagans*, a family of Tenuirosters, comprising the birds which feed on the nectar of flowers. In mod. Dicts.

meliphagidan (mɛlɪ'fædʒɪdən), *a.* and *sb.* [f. mod.L. *Meliphagid-æ* (f. *Meliphaga*: see prec. and -ID) + -AN.] **a.** *adj.* Belonging to the *Meliphagidæ*, a family of Australian birds which extract honey from plants. **b.** *sb.* A bird of this family.

In recent Dicts.

meliphagine (mɛ'lɪfədʒɪn), *a.* and *sb. Ornith.* [ad. mod.L. *Meliphagin-us*, f. *Meliphaga*: see MELIPHAGAN and -INE.] **a.** *adj.* Of or pertaining to the *Meliphaginæ*, a sub-family of the *Meliphagidæ* (see prec.). Also used for MELIPHAGIDAN. **b.** *sb.* A bird of this sub-family.

1884 *Ibis* July 340 The two genera *Melithreptus* and *Plectorynchus* are obviously Meliphagine. **1890–99** S. B. WILSON & A. H. EVANS *Birds Sandwich Isl.* Introd. 21 It is a very old supposition that some of the Finch-like forms were Meliphagine.

meliphagous (mɛ'lɪfəgəs), *a. Ornith.* Also *erron.* melli-. [f. mod.L. *Meliphaga* (see MELIPHAGAN) + -OUS.] Belonging to the *Meliphagidæ* or honey-eating birds.

1826 VIGORS & HORSFIELD in *Trans. Linnean Soc.* XV. 311 There are many species .. which have been ranked as *Meliphagous* in consequence of the alleged filamentous conformation of their tongue. **1837** SWAINSON *Nat. Hist. Birds* II. 146 The plumage of the meliphagous birds of New Holland is almost universally dull.

meliphanite (mɛ'lɪfənaɪt). *Min.* Also **'meliphane.** [f. Gr. μέλι 'honey' + φαν-, φαίνεσθαι to appear + -ITE.

Named by Dana, in allusion to its colour, after LEUCOPHANE, -PHANITE; the earlier name (Scheerer 1852) was *melinophan*, prob. f. μήλινος MELINE *a.*[1]]

Fluo-silicate of glucinum, calcium and sodium.

1867 DANA in *Amer. Jrnl. Sci.* Ser. II. XLIV. 405 *note*, Meliphane (melinophane) appears to bear the same relation in form and constitution to phenacite, as Leucophane to Chrysolite. **1868** —— *Syst. Min.* (ed. 5) II. 263 Meliphanite.

‖**melisma** (mɪ'lɪzmə). *Mus.* Pl. **melismata, melismas.** [Gr. μέλισμα song, air, melody.] (See quot. 1880.) Also, in singing, the prolongation of one syllable over a number of notes.

[**1611** T. RAVENSCROFT (*title*) Melismata; Musical Phansies fitting the Court, Citie, and Countrey Humours.] **1880** W. S. ROCKSTRO in Grove *Dict. Mus.* II. 248/2 *Melisma.* Any kind of Air, or Melody, as opposed to Recitative, or other music of a purely declamatory character. Thus, Mendelssohn employs the term in order to distinguish the Mediation and Ending of a Gregorian Tone from the Dominant, or Reciting Note. Other writers sometimes use it (less correctly) in the sense of *Fioritura*, or even *Cadenza.* **1881** MRS. WODEHOUSE *ibid.* III. 618/2 These melodic melismas also allow the voice great scope in the so-called 'kehrreim' or refrain. **1938** *Oxf. Compan. Mus.* 557/1 The melisma is a feature of eighteenth-century vocal music, often used merely for display purposes but also descriptively and for emotional expression (Handel, 'Rejoice greatly' and 'Thou shalt break them' in *Messiah*; Bach in such words as 'wept' and 'scourged' in his Passions). **1957** *Times* 22 Oct. 3/1 Some of the tunes were of considerable interest, varying from oriental melismata to a modal melody like an English folksong. **1959** *Listener* 8 Jan. 80/2 The opening cantabile theme .. continuously flows into more ornate melismata. *Ibid.* 15 Jan. 145/2 Little arabesques and melismas. **1962** A. HUXLEY *Island* xiv. 242 Long-drawn, almost bird-like melismata on a single vowel sound. **1963** *Times* 27 Dec. 4/7 The melismas with altered vowels ('I saw her yesterday-ee-ay') which have not quite become mannered. **1965** *Observer* 5 Sept. 24/8, I enjoy the graceful vocal melisma of the improvisations. **1971** *Daily Tel.* 25 June 10/4 The melismata of Boulez' 'Pli selon Pli' are wearing well. **1972** E. T. SITHOLE in T. Kochman *Rappin' & Stylin' Out* 70 The black man .. appreciates the rhythm of his speech and retains it in his songs by avoiding the melisma (many notes to one syllable of a word), as most of the Negro spirituals illustrate.

Hence **me,lis'matic** *a.*, ornate or florid in melody; also **melis'matics** *sb. pl.*, the art of florid or ornate vocalization. (*Cent. Dict.*).

1909 C. H. H. PARRY *J. S. Bach* 99 A recitative for soprano with a beautiful melismatic close. **1936** *Jrnl. Theol. Stud.* XXXVII. 165 Does that mean that these sequences were originally intended to be sung as they stand, and that afterwards the melismatic form was combined with the syllabic? **1971** *Daily Tel.* 6 May 14/6 The English performances .. entirely lacked the minute melismatic ornaments .. that gave the Greek singers' performances their idiomatic character. **1972** *Times* 29 May 5/4 The sopranos, soaring effortlessly through melismatic phrases like 'music', 'praise' and 'rejoice'.

melissa (mɪ'lɪsə). *Med.* [mod.L. generic name (Tournefort), a. Gr. μέλισσα bee.] The herb balm (*Melissa officinalis*). ***melissa oil***, a volatile oil obtained from this plant. ***melissa water***, a distillation in water of the leaves of the plant, balm-water.

a **1593** J. HESTER 114 *Exper. Paracelsus* (1596) 4 A girle .. whom I cured with the Oyle of Camomell, in the water of Melissa and Valerian. **1881** tr. *Trousseau & Pidoux' Treat. Therap.* III. 198 Melissa is proclaimed as one of the best exhilarants. **1887** *Brunton's Text-bk. Pharmacol.* etc. (ed. 3) 1007 U.S.P. Melissa .. Balm—The leaves and tops of *Melissa officinalis* .. used in the form of warm infusion or tea as a diaphoretic in slight febrile conditions.

†**melissæan,** *a. Obs.* [f. Gr. μελισσαî-ος (f. μέλισσα bee) + -AN.] Pertaining to bees.

1609 C. BUTLER *Fem. Mon.* (1634) 44 The Melissæan year is most fitly measured by the Astronomicall months.

melissic (mɪ'lɪsɪk). *a. Chem.* [formed as next + -IC.] ***melissic acid***: an acid obtained from melissin. ***melissic alcohol***: = MELISSIN.

1848 BRODIE in *Phil. Trans.* CXXXIX. 95 This acid I call Melissic Acid. **1852** *Fownes' Chem.* (ed. 4) 471 Mr. Brodie has prepared two alcohols, cerotylic and melissic, from bees' wax.

melissin (mɪ'lɪsɪn). *Chem.* Also **melissine.** [f. Gr. μέλισσα bee + -IN.] A substance obtained by boiling a mixture of myricin (myricyl palmitate) and potash; called also *melissic*, *melissyl*, *myricic* or *myricyl alcohol.*

1848 BRODIE in *Phil. Trans.* CXXXIX. 93 This substance I propose to call Melissin. **1880** GARROD & BAXTER *Mat. Med.* 410 An acid, the melissic, which bears the same relation to melissine that acetic acid does to alcohol.

melissyl (mɪ'lɪsɪl). *Chem.* [formed as prec. + -YL.] The hypothetical radical ($C_{30}H_{60}$) of certain compounds derived from wax; called also *myricyl.* ***melissyl alcohol***: = MELISSIN.

1852 *Fownes' Chem.* (ed. 4) 592 Hence myricin is likewise a compound ether, namely palmitate of oxide of melissyl. **1869** ROSCOE *Elem. Chem.* (1871) 325 Melisyl [*sic*] Alcohol, a solid white substance contained in beeswax.

melissylene: see MELENE.

melissylic (mɛlɪ'sɪlɪk), *a. Chem.* [f. prec. + -IC.] ***melissylic alcohol***: = MELISSIN.

1862 MILLER *Elem. Chem.* (ed. 2) III. 264 Another wax alcohol, melissylic alcohol, or melissin, is liberated.

melitagrous (mɛlɪ'teɪgrəs), *a.* [f. mod.L. *melitagra* a synonym of IMPETIGO (f. Gr. μελιτ- honey + -αγρα after ποδάγρα gout) + -OUS.] A term applied to the honey-like secretion from the skin which occurs in such diseases as favus and is produced by some irritating ointments. (*Syd. Soc. Lex.* 1890.)

†**Melitane,** *a. Obs.* [as if ad.L. **Melitānus*, f. *Melita* Malta.] = MALTESE.

1600 THYNNE *Emblems* xxv. 1 The melitane dogge, bredd onlie for delight, whose force is smale, though voice be lowde and shrill.

†**'melitism.** *Obs.* [app. ad. Gr. μελιτισμός, f. μελιτ- honey; but the Gr. word is known only in the sense 'use of honey in plasters'.] (See quot.)

1656 BLOUNT *Glossogr.*, Melitism (*melitismus*), a drink made of honey and wine.

melitose ('mɛlɪtəʊs). *Chem.* [f. Gr. μελιτ-, μέλι honey + -OSE.] A kind of sugar obtained from the manna of Eucalyptus.

1861 *Fownes' Chem.* (ed. 8) 410 The Australian manna, which is the produce of *Eucalyptus mannifera*, according to

recent researches of Berthelot, contains two different isomeric sugars, called melitose and eucalyne.

†**meliturgy.** *Obs. rare.* In 7 melliturgie. [a. F. *melliturgie* (Cotgr.), ad. Gr. μελιτουργία honey-making (but the true reading is perh. μελιττουργία bee-keeping).] (See quot. 1656.)

1620 T. GRANGER *Div. Logike* 180 [Subjects of Virgil's Georgics] Georgie, dendrographie, Ktenotrophie, melliturgie. **1656** BLOUNT *Glossogr.*, *Melliturgie* (Fr.), the making of honey, Bees-work.

‖**melituria** (mɛlɪˈtjʊərɪə). *Path.* Also mell-. [mod.L., f. Gr. μελιτ-, μέλι honey + οὖρ-ον urine + L. suffix *-ia*.] The presence of sugar in the urine; = *diabetes mellitus* (but see quot. 1877).

1856 in MAYNE *Expos. Lex.* [as L.]. **1863** AITKEN *Sci. & Pract. Med.* (ed. 2) II. 335 Any agents or conditions which cause a suspension of the functions of animal life, while the purely nutritive or organic functions remain intact, may bring about *melituria*. **1877** tr. *H. von Ziemssen's Cycl. Med.* XVI. 858 By the constant excretion of sugar, diabetes mellitus is distinguished from those..conditions in which appreciable quantities of sugar appear in the urine *at times*—conditions which have..been specially designated as *melituria* or *glycosuria*.

melk, obs. form of MILK *sb.* and *v.*

melkbos (ˈmɛlkbɔs). *S. Afr.* Also **melkbosch**. [Afrikaans, f. *melk* milk + *bos* bush.] A deciduous shrub or small tree, *Diplorhynchus condylocarpon*, of the family Apocynaceæ, which has a milky latex; also = *milk-bush* (*d*) s.v. MILK *sb.* 10 b. Also *attrib.*

1862 'A LADY' *Let.* 23 Apr. in L. G. Ross *Life at Cape* (1963) ix. 100 Here also you find tufts of reed called the 'melkbosch', which are full of a milky fluid, only grateful to goats, for sheep will not touch it. **1898** in T. R. Sim *Forests & Forest Flora Cape Good Hope* (1907) 316 The local name of the plant [*sc. Euphorbia cervicornis*] is Olifant Melkbosch. **1939** 'D. RAME' *Wine of Good Hope* I. vii. 92 They camped below melk-bosch trees. **1951** L. G. GREEN *Grow Lovely* xxiv. 199 An even more historic landmark..is the gnarled melkbos tree known as 'the old slave tree'. **1957** *Cape Times* 18 Feb. 2/3 Seedlings from the old Melkbos tree at Mossel Bay should be cultivated. *Ibid.* 12 Sept. 2/4 The Board decided to give a melkbosch tree for an afforestation scheme. **1973** PALMER & PITMAN *Trees S. Afr.* III. 1911 One of the features of the tree [sc. *Diplorhynchus condylocarpon*] is its milky latex which when 'dry' is soft, sticky and rubber-like and which gives it the common names of 'rubber tree' or 'melkbos'.

Melkite (ˈmɛlkaɪt), var. MELCHITE.

melktert (ˈmɛlktɛərt). *S. Afr.* [Afrikaans, f. *melk* milk + *tert* tart, pie.] A kind of pie with a cinnamon-flavoured custard filling.

1944 I. D. DU PLESSIS *Cape Malays* 42 Many old Cape dishes such as *melktert*..are still to be found in the Malay home. **1947** *Cape Argus* 22 Feb. 2 Melktert, which the Queen enjoyed at Paarl this week, is one of those old Cape afternoon tea dishes which are as popular to-day as they were two centuries ago. **1949** L. G. GREEN *In Land of Afternoon* iv. 61 She was able to bake a cake and prepare *melktert* and *poffertjies* for Queen Mary. **1958** *Cape Argus* 1/2 Dr. and Mrs. Verwoerd gave them tea, melktert and sandwiches. **1972** *Good Housek. World Cookery* 406/2 (*heading*) Melktert (Dutch Milk Tart).

mell (mɛl), *sb.*[1] Now only *Sc.* and *dial.* [Northern var. of *mall*, MAUL *sb.*[1]]

1. A heavy hammer or beetle of metal or wood (= MAUL *sb.*[1] 2); †a mace or club (*obs.*); also, a chairman's hammer.

a **1300** *Cursor M.* 23240 Þaa dintes ar ful fers and fell, Herder þan es here irinn mell. **1340** HAMPOLE *Pr. Consc.* 7048 Þarfor þe devels salle stryk þam þare, With hevy melles ay. *c* **1440** *Alphabet of Tales* 353 Swilk a sownd like as þe bed had bene dongen on with mellis. **1563** WINȜET *Vincent. Lirin.* Ded., Euery kind of necessar waippin and werklume ..as habirione, scheild, suord, bow, speir, spade, mattok, and mell, &c. **1641** BEST *Farm. Bks.* (Surtees) 107 Theire manner is for one to stande with a mell and breake the clottes small [etc.]. **1768** ROSS *Helenore* III. 109, I hae..A..quoy.. She's get the mell an' that sall be right now, As well's a quoy altho she were a cow. **1864** A. MCKAY *Hist. Kilmarnock* (1880) 326 The mell used on the occasion was one that had been handled by Burns. **1897** CROCKETT *Lad's Love* v, A mason had gaun hame wi' his square and mell ower his shooder.

b. Phrases. ***as dead as a mell***, quite dead. ***mell and wedge*** (***work***): used by miners for work done with those tools as opposed to 'blasting'. ***to keep mell in shaft*** (Sc.): to 'keep things going'; to be able to maintain oneself; also allusively.

1798 D. CRAWFORD *Poems* 54 They'll think you're as dead as a mell, Or my ern-tangs. **1811** PINKERTON *Petral* I. 271 The clay-bed..varies from the softness of tough clay, to the hardness of striking fire with steel; in the language of miners, from mell and wedge to blasting. **1824** MACTAGGART *Gallovid. Encycl.* (1876) 339 When a person's worldly affairs get disordered, it is said the mell cannot be keeped in the shaft. **1830** T. WILSON *Pitman's Pay* (1843) 33 A' bein' mell-and-wedge wark then. **1831** MRS. CARLYLE *Let.* 6 Oct. in *New Lett. & Rem.* (1903) I. 38 Carlyle is reading to-day with a view to writing an Article—to keep mall in shaft. **1850** J. STRUTHERS *Life* vii. p. cviii. in *Poet. Wks.*, He had gained something in the way of experience, and had been able still to keep the shaft in the mell.

2. *Sc.* and *north. dial.* (See quots. and E.D.D.)

a **1743** J. RELPH *Misc. Poems* (1747) 5 And still still dog'd wi' the damn'd neame o'mell? *Gloss.*, A *mell*, a beetle, signifies here the hindmost, from a custom at Horse-races of giving a mell or beetle to the hindmost. Hence they call the hindmost the *Mell*. **1837** HOGG *Sheph. Wedd.* Tales II. 161 Now for the mell! now for the mell! Deil tak the hindmost now! *Ibid.*, He..thus escaped the disgrace of winning the mell. **1869** *Lonsdale Gloss.* s.v. *Mell*, To get the mell is to obtain a mallet in prize ploughing, as a prize for the worst ploughing.

3. *Comb.*: **mell-headed** *a. Sc.* and *north. dial.*, having a head like a mell, *i.e.* large, thick, etc.

1500–20 DUNBAR *Poems* lx. 60 Mell-heidit lyk ane mortar-stane. **1878–99** DICKINSON *Cumberld. Gloss.*, *Mell-heedit*.

†**mell** (mɛl), *sb.*[2] *Obs.* Forms: 6, 9 **mel**, 6–7 **mell**. [a. L. *mell-*, *mel*, = Gr. μελιτ-, μέλι, Goth. *miliþ*, O. Irish *mil*.] Honey.

a **1575** GASCOIGNE *Dan Bartholomew* Posies *Flowers* 98 That bitter gall was mell to him in tast. **1584** LODGE *Truth's Compl.* (Shaks. Soc. 1853) 119 The drones from busie bee no mel could drawe. **1586** WARNER *Alb. Eng.* IV. xx. 86 Her.. lookes were..such as neither wanton seeme, nor waiward, mell, nor gall. **1648** HERRICK *Hesper.*, *Pray & prosper*, The spangling Dew dreg'd o're the grasse shall be Turn'd all to Mell, and Manna. **1864** BAMFORD *Rhymes* 181 Adieu to the ..lip that is sweet as the mel of the bee.

b. *attrib.* (***mel-dew*** = honey-dew.)

1606 SYLVESTER *Du Bartas* II. iv. I. *Tropheis* 1053 Th' Heav'n..Pours-forth a Torrent of mel-Melodies [Fr. *vn roux torrent de miel*], In David's praise. *a* **1643** BROWNE *Brit. Past.* III. (Percy Soc.) 27 Some choicer ones, as for the king most meet, Held mel-dewe and the hony-suckles sweet.

†**mell**, *sb.*[3] *Obs. rare*[−1].

1726 *Dict. Rust.* (ed. 3) s.v. *Colick*, Tying down his [the horse's] Mell or Tail close between his Legs.

mell (mɛl), *sb.*[4] *Sc.* and *north. dial.* The last sheaf of corn cut by the harvesters. Also *attrib.*, as **mell-day**, **-doll**, **-sheaf**, **-supper**, (see quots).

1777 BRAND *Pop. Antiq.* xxxi. 303 A plentiful Supper for the Harvest-men..; which is called a Harvest-Supper, and in some places a Mell-Supper. **1832** J. HODGSON *Northumbld.* II. II. 2 *note*, The mell-doll or corn-baby is an image dressed like a female child, and carried by a woman on a pole, in the midst of a group of reapers. **1846–59** *Denham Tracts* (1895) II. 2 The last day of reaping..is known throughout the north by the appellation of 'Mell Day'. **1878** *Cumberld. Gloss.*, *Mell*, the last cut of corn in the harvest field... [It] is commonly platted, enclosing a large apple. **1892** M. C. F. MORRIS *Yorksh. Folk-Talk* 212 The last sheaf gathered in is, in the North and East Ridings, called the 'mell sheaf'.

†**mell**, *v.*[1] *Obs.* Forms: 1 **meðlan**, **mæðlan**, 3–6 **mell**, 4–5 **melle**, 4 **medle**, **medele**. [OE. *meðlan*, f. *mæðel* discourse; a parallel formation with *mæðelian* MATHELE *v.* Cf. MELE *v.*] *intr.* and *trans.* To speak, tell, say.

a **900** CYNEWULF *Crist* 1338 (Gr.) Þær he [Christ]..to þam eadȝestum ærest mæðleð. *a* **1000** *Andreas* 1440 (Gr.) Ær awæȝed sie worda æniȝ, þe ic þurh minne muð meðlan onȝinne. *a* **1300** *Cursor M.* 26657 Dute o brath on hell, þat reues man þe tung to mell. **13..** *E.E. Allit. P.* A. 797 Þe profete ysaye of hym con melle. **1377** LANGL. *P. Pl.* B. III. 36 Þanne come þere a confessoure..To Mede þe mayde he mellud [*MS. O* medelede] þis wordes. *c* **1387** *Ibid.* A. xI. 93 (Vernon MS.) He bi-com so confoundet he couþe not medle [*other MSS.* mele]. *c* **1400** *Destr. Troy* 109 More of thies Mirmydons mell I not now. *c* **1460** *Towneley Myst.* xvi. 195, I haue maters to mell with my preuey counsell.

mell (mɛl) *v.*[2] Now chiefly *arch.* and *dial.* Also 4–6 **mel**. [a. OF. *meller*, var. of *mesler*: see MEDDLE *v.*]

1. *trans.* To mix, mingle, combine, blend. Also with *together*, *up*.

a **1340** HAMPOLE *Psalter* ix. 9 When god melles sorow anguys & trauaile till his flescly lykynge. **1375** BARBOUR *Bruce* XVI. 65 Quhen byrdis syngis on the spray, Melland thair notys with syndry sowne. *c* **1400** MAUNDEV. (Roxb.) x. 38 Þat es whyt of colour and a lytill reed melled þerwith. *a* **1500** *Ratis Raving* 675 A man..suld..mell Justice and mercy to gider in Jugment. **1605** SYLVESTER *Du Bartas* II. iii. I. *Vocation* 918 [He] That with his Prowesse Policy can mell. **1633** T. ADAMS *Exp. 2 Peter* i. 5 Both these knowledges must be so melled together, that they be not severed. **1748** THOMSON *Cast. Indol.* I. xliii, And oft' began..wintry storms to swell, As heaven and earth they would together mell. **1888** *Reports Provinc.* (E.D.D.), Us mell up one bushel o'lime to two o'sand. *a* **1889** G. M. HOPKINS *Poems* (1967) 185 May Mells blue and snowwhite through them, a fringe and fray Of greenery. **1959** *Encounter* Aug. 60/2, I published an excerpt from *Road* (melling it with parts of *Visions of Neal*).

†**2.** *intr.* for *refl.* To mingle, combine, blend.

a **1300** *Cursor M.* 22641 Þan sal þe rainbou descend,..Wit þe wind þan sal it mell, And driue þam [þe deuels] dun all vntil hell. **1390** GOWER *Conf.* II. 222 Whan venym melleth with the Sucre.

3. *trans.* To mix or mingle (persons). Const. *with*, *together*. Also *pass.*

c **1300** *St. Brandan* 276 And sette hem ther wel heȝe I-melled with his owe covent. **1387** TREVISA *Higden* (Rolls) II. 155 Normans and Englischemen [ben] i-medled [*MS. a* i-melled] in alle þe ilond. *c* **1400** *Song Roland* 647 Let us now our men melle to-gedur. **1570** BUCHANAN *Admonitioun* Wks. (1892) 24 How yai ar mellit wt godles papistes. **1895** CROCKETT *Men of Moss-Hags* vii, I wonder..if it would be possible to transplant you Gordons... Here ten score King's men melled and married would settle the land.

4. *intr.* for *refl.* To mix, associate, have intercourse *with*, to associate.

c **1350** *Ipomadon* 1663 (Kölbing) Thy brother schall the know there by, Yf ever god wolle, þat ye melle. *c* **1515** A. WILLIAMSON *Let.* in Douglas *Wks.* (1874) I. Introd. 24 She may cowrs the tyme that euer she mellyt with your blood. *c* **1557** ABP. PARKER *Ps.* lix. 2 From workers bad O saue my lyfe, wyth them no tyme to mell. *a* **1600** MONTGOMERIE *Sonn.* lxvii. 13 Mell not with vs, vhose heads weirs l[aurel]. **1785** *Poems Buchan Dial.* 24 But Diomede mells ay wi' me, An' tells me a' his mind. **1880** WEBB *Goethe's Faust* Prol. in Heaven 23 With the dead in churchyard hidden I never care to mell or mingle. **1896** CROCKETT *Grey Man* vi. 39 None of us..desired to mix or to mell with loose company.

†**5.** *intr.* To copulate. *Obs.*

c **1375** *Sc. Leg. Saints* xxi. (*Clement*) 406 Of my wyf þis case þane fel, þat cane hyre with hyre serwandis mel. *c* **1450** *Cov. Myst.* 215 A talle man with her dothe melle. **1508** DUNBAR *Tua Mariit Wemen* 56 God gif matrimony were made to mell for ane ȝeir! *a* **1555** RIDLEY in Coverd. *Lett. Martyrs* (1564) 100 And with thys whore doth spiritually mell..all those Kinges and Princes. **1594** WILLOBIE *Avisa* lviii. (1605) 49 b, Their feet to death, their steps to hell Do swiftly slide that thus do mell. **1641** BROME *Joviall Crew* II. (1652) G, If you are..Dospos'd to Doxie, or a Dell, That never yet with man did Mell.

6. To mingle in combat.

c **1320** *Sir Tristr.* 3270 Þe cuntre wiþ hem meld. *c* **1350** *Will. Palerne* 3325 Þei..hadden gret ioye, þa so manli a man wold mele in here side. *c* **1400** *Beryn* 2648 Who makith a fray, or stryvith auȝt, or mel to much, or praunce. *c* **1470** *Gol. & Gaw.* 543 Forthi makis furth ane man,..That for the maistry dar mell With schaft and with scheild. **1513** DOUGLAS *Æneis* X. xiv. 116 To mell with me, and to meyt hand for hand. **1594** *Battell of Balrinness* in *Scot. Poems 16th C.* (1801) II. 353 Lat sie how we can mell wt them Into thair disaray. **1823** SCOTT *Quentin D.* xxxvii, Draw in within the court-yard—they are too many to mell with in the open field. **1838** *Blackw. Mag.* XLIII. 205 Beware..how ye mell among these hosts—their darts are sharp.

7. *refl.* To concern or busy oneself. *Obs.* exc. *arch.*

c **1350** *Will. Palerne* 1709 And manly sche melled hire þo men forto help. *c* **1386** CHAUCER *Melib.* ¶ 575 (Harl. MS.) He is coupable þat entremettith him or mellith him with such þing as aperteyneþ not vnto him. *c* **1400** *Destr. Troy* 3783 Telamon..mellit hym with musike & myrthes also. **1456** SIR G. HAYE *Law Arms* S.T.S. 161 Thai mell thame nocht tharewith. **1540** JAS. V in *St. Papers Hen. VIII*, V. 173 And quhat falt ony freir..committis..supponand it concerne Our self, We mel Ws nocht. **1600** HAMILTON *Facile Traictise* in *Cath. Tract.* (S.T.S.) 226 Thair first mother Eua, for melling hir self with maters of religion,.. procurit..a curs of God to hir and al woman kynd. **1941** E. R. EDDISON *Fish Dinner* (1968) vii. 92, I find close harbours of discontentment:..foolish and furious designs. Go, I'll mell me with no flirtations but them as end in bed.

8. a. *intr.* To busy, concern, or occupy oneself; to deal, treat; to interfere, meddle. Const. *in*, †*of*, *with*.

c **1400** *Destr. Troy* 9577 As þe maner is of men, þat mellyn with loue. **1465** *Paston Lett.* II. 202, I canne not have no knowlych that Haydon mellyth in the mater of Drayton. **1516** *Will of Rich. Peke of Wakefield* 4 June, And no ferder to mell nor hurtt hir. **1550** CROWLEY *Epigr.* 496 When none but pore Colyars dyd with coles mell. **1557** *Tottel's Misc.* (Arb.) 105 And, after, in that countrey lyue,..Where hoonger, thirst, and sory age, and sicknesse may not mell. **1590** SPENSER *F.Q.* I. i. 30 With holy father sits not with such thinges to mell. **1605** SYLVESTER *Quadrains* lxviii, To some one Art apply thy whole affection; And in the Craft of others seldome mell. **1786** BURNS *Scotch Drink* xvi, It sets you ill, Wi' bitter, dearthfu' wines to mell. **1819** SCOTT *Ivanhoe* xxxii, I will teach thee..to mell with thine own matters. **1851** C. L. SMITH tr. *Tasso* IX. lix, Go; tell them, thou, no more henceforth to mell With war, which warriors only should sustain. **1893** SNOWDEN *Tales Yorksh. Wolds* 122 They tucked them [the bed clothes] well in, so that they would be sure to 'feel her if shoo melled agean'.

b. Phrase. ***to mell or make*** (with), ***to make or mell*** (with). *dial.* Cf. MEDDLE *v.* 8 c.

1825 J. JENNINGS *Obs. Dial. w. Eng.* 139 Ther war naw need To mell or make wi' thic awld Creed. **1871** W. ALEXANDER *Johnny Gibb* xix. 144 There's some fowk wud never mak' nor mell wi' naething less nor gentry.

mell (mɛl), *v.*[3] Now only *dial.* [f. MELL *sb.*[1]] *trans.* To beat with a mell; hence, to beat severely.

? *a* **1400** *Morte Arth.* 2950 Thane sir Gawayne..Metes þe maches of Mees and melles hym thorowe. *c* **1400** *Destr. Troy* 10994 Pirrus þis prowes pertly beheld, How his Mirmydons with might were mellit to ground. **1824** HOGG *Conf. Sinner* 332 To entertain a stranger, an' then bind him in a web wi' his head down, an' mell him to death!

mell, obs. form of MEAL *sb.*[2] and *sb.*[4]

mellacatton, variant of MELOCOTON.

mellaginous (mɛˈlædʒɪnəs), *a.* [f. mod.L. *mellāgin-*, *mellāgo* a preparation resembling honey (f. *mell-*, *mel* honey) + -OUS.] Pertaining to or of the nature of honey.

1681 GREW *Musæum* II. 208 The Oil or Mellaginous Succus betwixt the Rind and the Kernel is that which is called *Mel Anacardinum*. **1833** F. v. MUELLER in *Chemist & Druggist* (Melbourne), The mellaginous exudations of the trusses of flowers attract..a number of honey-sucking birds.

mellah (ˈmɛlə). [Etym. unknown.] The Jewish quarter in a Moroccan or Turkish city; cf. GHETTO.

1874 tr. *G. Rohlfs's Adventures Morocco* vi. 105 There is a Jew's quarter (Mälha) or Ghetto, for there is no town in Morocco, and scarcely an oasis in the desert where Jews are not to be found. **1893** S. BONSAL *Morocco* xvii. 315 In the large towns the Jews are obliged to reside in a separate quarter called the Mellah, the gates of which are closed and placed under guard at night. **1925** P. GUEDALLA *Napoleon & Palestine* v. 41 Old men in Turkish *mellahs* muttered the undying *Esperança de Israel*. **1963** *Guardian* 17 July 8/6 The mellahs, as the ghettoes of Morocco are called. **1972** *Country Life* 17 Feb. 414/3 The different quarters of the town: the kasba or quarter of government officials and

Europeans; the Medina or Moorish quarter and the Mellah or Jewish town.

mella-rosa: see MELA-ROSA.

mellate (ˈmɛleɪt). *Chem.* Earlier **-at.** [a. F. *mellat* (Klaproth), f. *mell(itique)*: see MELLITIC and -ATE.] A salt of mellic or mellitic acid; = MELLITATE.

1794 G. ADAMS *Nat & Exp. Philos.* I. App. 547 Mellats—neutralized by potass, crystallize in long prisms. **1802** T. THOMSON *Chem.* III. 527 *Aluminous salts*..Mellite—Honeystone—Mellate of Alumina.

†**meˈllation.** *Obs. rare*$^{-0}$. [ad. L. *mellātiōn-em*, n. of action f. *mellāre* to make or collect honey.] (See quots.)

1623 COCKERAM, *Mellation*, the driuing of Bees to get out the Honie. **1656** BLOUNT *Glossogr.*, *Mellation*, the time of taking honey out of the Hives.

mellay (ˈmɛleɪ), *sb.* and *a.* Forms: 4–6 **melle**, 5–6 **mely**, 5–6, (9) **melly**, (6 **mellie**, **-ye**, 9 **-ey**), 6, 9 **mellay**. [a. OF. *mellée*, *meslée*: see MÊLÉE.]

A. *sb.*

†**1.** Mixture. *Obs. rare*$^{-1}$.

1375 BARBOUR *Bruce* V. 404 Syne of the tunnys the hedis out-strak, A foull melle thair can he mak.

2. †Contention, fight, quarrel (*obs.*); *spec.*, an engagement in which the two parties or combatants are mixed together in a close hand to hand fight. Cf. MÊLÉE. *arch.*

13.. *Gaw. & Gr. Knt.* 342, I be-seche now with saȝez sene, þis melly mot be myne. **1375** BARBOUR *Bruce* XVII. 120 Thar wes gret melleis twa or thre. *c* **1400** *Ywaine & Gaw.* 504 Woso flites, or turnes ogayne, He bygins al the mellè. **1508** DUNBAR *Lament Makaris* 23 Wictour he is at all melle. **1513** DOUGLAS *Æneis* VII. x. 5 Als sone as this gret melly begunne, The erd littit wyth blude. **1819** SCOTT *Ivanhoe* xxix, The love of battle is the food upon which we live—the dust of the mellay is the breath of our nostrils! **1847** TENNYSON *Princess* v. 491 As here and everywhere He rode the mellay, lord of the ringing lists. **1875** KINGLAKE *Crimea* (1877) V. i. 152 So that Russians..and men of the Scots Greys and men of the 5th Dragoon Guards, were here forced and crowded together in one indiscriminate melley. **1881** GREEN *Hist. Eng.* I. IV. ii. 419 The Welshmen stabbed the French horses in the melly.

†**3.** A cloth of a mixture of colours or shades of colour; also a 'mixed' colour. (Cf. MEDLEY.)

1381–4 *Durham Acc. Rolls* (Surtees) 592 In di. panno de Melle. **1420** *Will* in *Trevelyan Papers* (Camden) 18 Item lego Matild'..unam togam de violet, aliam de melly... Item lego Johanne.. unam togam russetam & aliam togam de mely. **1587** *Acc. Bk. W. Wray* in *Antiquary* XXXII. 118, iij yeardes white mella', xijs. **1593** *Ibid.*, iij yeardes & a q'ter fyne mella', xiiis.

†**4.** ? A kind of brass. In quot. *attrib.* (Cf. MASLIN^{1}.) *Obs.*

1545 *Richmond Wills* (Surtees) 56 A mellay pot with a kylp, a chaffer, a brewyng leyyd [etc.].

†**B.** *adj.* Of a mixed or variegated colour. *Obs.*

1515 *Will of R. West* (Somerset Ho.), My melly tawny gowne. **1551** *Aberdeen Reg.* XXI. (Jam.) The price litting of the stane of mellay hew xxxii sh. *Ibid.* XXIV. (Jam.) Ane mella kirtill. **1558** *Wills & Inv. N. C.* (Surtees) I. 173 It'm I giue to my curate..my mellye gowne.

b. *Comb.*: †**melly parted** *a.*, parti-coloured.

1418 *E.E. Wills* (1882) 37 A furre of beuer and oter medled; also a Hewk of grene and other melly parted.

Hence †**mellay** *v. intr.*, to contend.

c **1425** WYNTOUN *Cron.* VIII. xv. 19 Ðare Willame Walays tuk on hand, Wyth mony gret Lordys of Scotland, To mellay wyth þat Kyng in fycht.

melle, obs. form of MEAL *sb.*^{1}, MELLAY, MILL.

Melle, Melli, varr. MALI *a.* and *sb.*^{2}

†**mellean**, *a. Obs. rare*$^{-0}$. [f. L. *melle-us* (f. *mel*: see MELL *sb.*^{2}) + -AN.] 'Of or like honey, sweet, yellow' (Blount *Glossogr.* 1656).

†**melled**, *ppl. a.*^{1} *Obs.* Also 5 **-yde**, **-ide**, 6 **-yd.** [f. MELL *v.*^{1} + -ED^{1}.] Mixed.

1390 GOWER *Conf.* III. 256 He, which hath his lust assised With melled love and tirannie. **1393** *Will of Organ or Atte Stone* (Somerset Ho.), Gonnam de viridi mellet. *c* **1400** *Rowland & O.* 1254 A nobill suerde the burde not wolde, Now for thi Mellyde hare. **1449–50** *Durham Acc. Rolls* (Surtees) 632 In iij pannis integris blodei mellide. **1562** *Richmond Wills* (Surtees) 152 Inprimis, iij mellyd russetts xlij^{s}.

†**ˈmelled**, *ppl. a.*^{2} *Obs. rare*$^{-1}$. [f. MELL *sb.*^{2} + -ED^{2}.] Sweet as honey; honeyed.

1605 SYLVESTER *Du Bartas* II. iii. III. *Law* 841 Thou.. That has the Ayre for farm, and Heav'n for field (Which, sugred Mel, or melled sugar yeeld).

mellefoly, obs. form of MILFOIL.

mellegette, -ghete, obs. ff. MALAGUETTA.

melleous (ˈmɛlɪəs), *a.* [f. L. *melle-us* (see MELLEAN) + -OUS.] Of the nature of or resembling honey; containing honey.

1656 BLOUNT *Glossogr.*, *Melleous*, of or like honey, sweet, yellow. **1657** TOMLINSON *Renou's Disp.* I. iv. xxxix. 317 Apiastrum or Melissophyllon, which is a melleous leaf. **1664** BOYLE *Exp. Colours* II. vii. 145, I shall not Examine which of the Slow wayes may be best Employ'd, to free Wax from the Yellow Melleous parts. **1760** J. LEE *Introd. Bot.* II. xx. (1765) 116 A melleous Liquor.

mellet, melley, var. ff. MELLIT, MELLAY.

†**mellfluvious**, *a.*, blundered f. MELLIFLUOUS.

1600 ROWLANDS *Lett. Humours Blood* iv. D8 Mellfluuious, sweete Rose watred elloquence.

mellic (ˈmɛlɪk), *a.*^{1} *rare*$^{-0}$. [f. L. *mell-*, *mel* honey + -IC.] Of or pertaining to honey.

In some recent Dicts.

mellic (ˈmɛlɪk), *a.*^{2} *Chem.* [Shortened from MELLITIC, on the analogy of MELLATE.] *mellic acid*: = MELLITIC *acid.*

1837 DANA *Min.* 438 Mellite... According to Klaproth.. and Wohler, it contains..Mellic Acid.

melliceris, variant of MELICERIS.

mellicoton, variant of MELOCOTON.

mellicrate, obs. variant of MELICRATE.

†**ˈmellie, melly.** *Obs. rare*$^{-1}$. = MELL *sb.*^{2}

1614 J. DAVIES *Eclog.* 19 in W. Browne *Sheph. Pipe* G 3 b, For, fro thy Makings milke and mellie [*ed.* 1620 melly] flowes To feed the Songster-swaines with Arts soot-meats.

mellie, obs. form of MELLAY.

melliferous (mɛˈlɪfərəs), *a.* [f. L. *mellifer* (f. *mell(i)-*, *mel* honey + *-fer* bearing) + -OUS. Cf. F. *mellifère.*] Yielding or producing honey.

1656 BLOUNT *Glossogr.*, *Melliferous*, that bringeth or beareth honey. **1701** GREW *Cosm. Sacra* IV. ii. §22. 149 Judæa..could not but abound with Melliferous Plants of the best kind. **1816** KIRBY & SP. *Entomol.* (1818) I. 296 Insects attracted by the melliferous glands of the flower. **1861** HULME tr. *Moquin-Tandon* II. iii. 196 The most perfect melliferous animals are the Bees. **1895** KERNER & OLIVER *Nat. Hist. Plants* II. 128 [These] in the case of melliferous flowers preserve..the honey from being spoilt by the wet.

fig. **1772** *Birmingham Counterfeit* I. vi. 97 The stings of Cupid's melliferous darts.

†**mellific**, *a. Obs. rare*$^{-0}$. [ad. L. *mellific-us* f. *mell(i)-*, *mel* honey + *-ficus*: see -FIC. Cf. F. *mellifique.*] 'That makes honey'.

1706 in PHILLIPS (ed. Kersey). **1856** in MAYNE *Expos. Lex.*

†**mellificate**, *v. Obs. rare*$^{-0}$. [f. L. *mellificāt-* ppl. stem of *mellificāre*, f. *mellificus*: see prec.] *intr.* To make honey.

1623 in COCKERAM. **1656** in BLOUNT *Glossogr.*

†**mellifiˈcation.** *Obs.* [ad. L. *mellificātiōn-em*, n. of action f. *mellific-āre*: see MELLIFICATE *v.* and -ATION. Cf. F. *mellification.*] The action or process of making honey. (Said of bees.)

1655 G. S. in Hartlib *Ref. Commw. Bees* 31 Mellification, respects the work and labour of this Insect, not its Physical virtues. **1733** ARBUTHNOT *Ess. Effects Air* ix. 223 In judging of the Constitution of the Air, many things besides the Weather ought to be observ'd:..the Silence of Grashoppers; Want of Mellification in Bees [etc.].

†**ˈmellified**, *ppl. a. rare*$^{-1}$. [f. MELLIFY + -ED^{1}.] Sweetened with honey.

1597 A. M. tr. *Guillemeau's Fr. Chirurg.* 49/2 We may vse mellifyed or Honyed-water.

†**mellifluat(e**, *a. Sc. Obs.* Also 6 **melle-**. [f. L. *melliflu-us* (f. *mell-*, *mel* honey + *fluĕre* to flow) + -ATE.] Mellifluous.

1508 DUNBAR *Gold. Targe* 265 Your angel mouthis most mellifluate Our rude langage has clere illumynate. **1560** ROLLAND *Crt. Venus* I. 147 He bair ane plesant flour..: With Cinamone mixt, and mellifluat.

†**mellifluе**, *a. Obs. rare.* Also **-flwe.** [a. OF. *melliflue*, ad. L. *mellifluus.*] Mellifluous.

c **1450** *Mirour Saluacioun* 3690 Hire dere son melliflwe presence. **1456** in *Coventry Corpus Chr. Plays* (E.E.T.S.) 110 The mellyflue mekenes of your person shall put all wo away.

mellifluence (mɛˈlɪfluːəns). [f. next: see -ENCE.] The state or quality of being mellifluent.

a **1631** DONNE *Serm.* (1640) 806 In which, (as S. Bernard also expresses it, in his mellifluence) *Mutua* [etc.]. **1779–81** JOHNSON *L. P.*, *Dryden* Wks. II. 418 The English ear has been accustomed to the mellifluence of Pope's numbers. **1841** D'ISRAELI *Amen. Lit.* (1867) 304 The mellifluence and flexibility of the vowelly language were favourable to unrhymed verse.

mellifluent (mɛˈlɪfl(j)uːənt), *a.* [ad. late L. *mellīfluent-em* adj., f. L. *mell(i)-*, *mel* honey + *fluent-em* pr. pple. of *fluĕre* to flow. Cf. F. *mellifluant* (Godef.).] = MELLIFLUOUS.

1601 WEEVER *Mirr. Mart.* Bj, Descending..Like the mellifluent brooke of Castilie. **1622** AILESBURY *Serm.* (1623) 16 It was *Opus sine exemplo*.., saies mellifluent Bernard. **1634** SIR T. HERBERT *Trav.* 14 The ground by Floraes mellifluent vertue, was ore-spread with Flowres. **1764** J. G. COOPER *Ep. Friends in Town* iii. *Apol. Aristippus* 175 Gresset's clear pipe..Symphoniously combines in one Each former bard's mellifluent tone. **1888** *Harper's Mag.* Apr. 763 A profound, mellifluent, booming horn-tone.

mellifluous (mɛˈlɪfluːəs), *a.* [f. L. *melliflu-us* (f. *mell-*, *mel* honey + *flu-ĕre* to flow) + -OUS.]

1. Flowing with honey, honey-dropping; sweetened with or as with honey. Now *rare.*

1485 CAXTON *Chas. Gt.* 36 By the sauour of tho mellyfluous flowres alle the cytee was puryfyed. **1536** *Primer Hen. VIII* 146 In the mouth honie so mellifluous. **1658** ROWLAND *Moufet's Theat. Ins.* 919 The increase of Bees is more in regard of..the plenty of mellifluous dews. **1667** MILTON *P.L.* v. 429. **1725** POPE *Odyss.* IX. 239 Twelve large vessels of unmingled wine, Mellifluous. **1849** THACKERAY *Dr. Birch* 41 And no one lacked, neither of raspberry open-tarts, nor of mellifluous bull's-eyes.

2. *fig.* Sweetly flowing, sweet as honey. Chiefly of eloquence, the voice, etc.

1432–50 tr. *Higden* (Rolls) I. 3 Thei [the nowble wryters of artes] ar to be enhauncede and exaltede..as makenge a commixtion of a thynge profitable with a swetenesse mellifluous. *c* **1485** *Digby Myst.* (1882) III. 1446 O Iesu! þi mellyfluos name Mott be worcheppyd with reverens! **1573** L. LLOYD *Marrow of Hist.* (1653) 59 Such mellifluous words and sugred sentences proceeded out of his mouth that they were amazed. **1601** SHAKS. *Twel. N.* II. iii. 54 A mellifluous voyce, as I am true knight. **1671** MILTON *P.R.* IV. 277 Wisest of men; from whose mouth issu'd forth Mellifluous streams. **1791** BOSWELL *Johnson* 20 Mar. an. 1776, A work..written in a very mellifluous style. **1834** R. MUDIE *Brit. Birds* (1841) I. 243 Its note is not so mellifluous and varied as that of the song thrush. **1838–9** HALLAM *Hist. Lit.* IV. vi. §42 A smoothness of cadence, which though exquisitely mellifluous, is perhaps too uniform. **1874** MOTLEY *Barneveld* I. iv. 167 The not very mellifluous title of Craimgepolder.

b. of a speaker, writer or singer.

1483 CAXTON *Gold. Leg.* 264b/1 Saynt Bernard the mellifluous doctor. **1598** F. MERES *Pallad. Tamia* II. 281 b, Mellifluous and hony-tongued Shakespeare. *c* **1709–10** HENLEY in *Swift's Lett.* (1767) I. 17 As that mellifluous ornament of Italy, Franciscus Petrarcha, sweetly has it. **1837** CARLYLE *Fr. Rev.* II v. ii. 283 Most mellifluous yet most impetuous of public speakers. **1873** SYMONDS *Grk. Poets* xi. 373 The most mellifluous of all erotic songsters.

Hence **meˈllifluously** *adv.*, **meˈllifluousness.**

1812 R. H. in *Examiner* 30 Nov. 763/2 The versification of Pope is mellifluously flowing. **1820** BYRON *Juan* v. i, In liquid lines mellifluously bland. **1821** *New Monthly Mag.* III. 445/1 A head by Corregio..abounding in that feminine loveliness and blending mellifluousness of colour and *chiaro oscuro*, which [etc.]. **1886** RUSKIN *Præterita* I. iv. 136 The little Elise, then just nine, set herself deliberately to chatter to me mellifluously for an hour and a half.

melliform (ˈmɛlɪfɔːm), *a.* [as if ad. mod.L. *melliformis*, f. *mell(i)-*, *mel* honey: see -FORM] Resembling honey.

1890 in *Syd. Soc. Lex.*

†**mellify**, *v. Obs. rare.* [ad. L. *mellificāre* to make honey: see -FY.] **a.** *intr.* To make honey. **b.** *trans.* To sweeten with honey.

c **1420** *Pallad. on Husb.* v. 151 Place apte is ther swete herbes multiplie And bees the welles haunte, & water cleche; Utilite is there to mellifie. **1597** [see MELLIFIED.]

melligenous (mɛˈlɪdʒɪnəs), *a. Obs. rare*$^{-0}$. [Two formations: (1) f. pseudo-L. *melligin-us* (a false reading in Pliny) + OUS; (2) L. *mell(i)-*, *mel* honey + -GEN- + -OUS.] **a.** 'Of the same kind with honey' (Bailey 1721). **b.** 'Producing honey' (*Syd. Soc. Lex.* 1890).

†**melligineous**, *a. Obs. rare*$^{-1}$. [f. mod.L. *melligine-us* (f. L. *mellīgin-*, *mellīgo* honey-like juice, f. *mell-*, *mel* honey) + -OUS.] Resembling honey.

1684 tr. *Bonet's Merc. Compit.* XVII. 591 Sometimes a Melligineous matter..is contained within the Bladder.

mellilet, obs. form of MELILOT.

mellilite, less correct form of MELILITE.

†**melliloquent**, *a. Obs. rare*$^{-0}$. [f. L. *mell(i)-*, *mel* honey + *loquent-em*, pr. pple. of *loquī* to speak.] 'That speaketh sweetly'.

1656 in BLOUNT *Glossogr.* **1658** in PHILLIPS.

†**mellinder.** *Obs.* [a. Sp. *melindre.*] A kind of pastry.

1604 E. G[RIMSTONE] *D'Acosta's Hist. Indies* IV. xvi. 255 A certaine kinde of paste, they doe make of this flower mixt with sugar, which they call biscuits and mellinders.

†**melling** (ˈmɛlɪŋ), *vbl. sb. Obs.* Also 4 **meling.** [f. MELL *v.*^{2} + -ING^{1}.] The action of the vb. MELL.

1. Blending, combining; mixture.

c **1350** *Will. Palerne* 5257, & to meliors his quene bi messageres nobul, as to here lege lord lelli bi riȝt, þurth meling of þe mariage of meliors þe schene. *c* **1375** *Sc. Leg. Saints* xxi. (*Clement*) 399, & of þe planetis sic mellynge In þe tyme of engendryng gerris weman do adultery. **1375** BARBOUR *Bruce* v. 406 Mcill, malt, blude, and vyne Ran all to-gidder in a mellyne.

2. Copulation.

c **1375** *Sc. Leg. Saints* xxxii. (*Justin*) 339 For gyf sic mellyng suld nocht be..al kynd of man..suld falȝe. **14..** LYDG. *Life Our Lady* xx. vi. (MS. Ashm. 39. lf. 32), Eke certeyn birdes called vultures W^{t} outten mellyng [*v.r.* medelinge] conceyven by nature.

3. The action of mixing in fight or joining in combat. *melling while*, time of combat.

c **1350** *Will. Palerne* 3858 Meliadus in þat meling while a sturne strok set William on his stelen helm. **1375** BARBOUR *Bruce* VII. 481 It is hard till vndirtak Sic mellyng vith ȝow for to mak. *c* **1475** *Partenay* 1326 Ther full gret affray was at ther mellyng.

4. Dealing; intercourse; meddling.

c **1440** *W. Hylton's Mixed Life* (MS. Thornton) in *Hampole* (ed. Horstman) I. 276 By-cause of mellynge [*c* **1375** *MS. Vern*, medlyng] with swilke besynes. **1564** *Reg. Privy*

Council Scot. I. 279 Nane of oure Soverane Ladiis liegis have traffique, cumpany, or melling with thame. **1579** *Sc. Acts Jas. VI* (1814) III. 182/1 Inhibiting the personis now displacet of all further melling and intromissioun with the saidis rentis. **1596** SPENSER *F.Q.* v. xii. 35 That euery matter worse was for her melling. **1603** *Philotus* (1835) cxlv. Than how could wee twa disagree, That neuer had na melling.

melliot, obs. form of MELILOT.

†**melliphill.** *Obs. rare*$^{-1}$. [app. ad. Gr. μελίφυλλον, name of a plant, ? balm; lit. 'honey-leaf', f. μέλι honey + φύλλον leaf: cf. *melisphylla* (pl.) Virg. *Georg.* IV. 63.]

1595 CHAPMAN *Ovid's Banq. Sence* B 2 b, White and red Iessamines, Merry, Melliphill: Fayre Crown-imperiall, Emperor of Flowers [etc.].

mellisonant (mɛˈlɪsənənt), *a. arch.* [f. L. *mell(i)-*, *mel* honey + *sonant-em*, pres. pple. of *sonāre* to sound.] Sweet-sounding.

a **1634** RANDOLPH *Amyntas* v. iv, I'le have't no more a sheep-bell; I am Knight Of the Mellisonant Tingletangle. **1893** SWINBURNE *Stud. Prose & Poetry* (1894) 46 It was doubtless in order to relieve this saccharine and 'mellisonant' monotony that [etc.].

†**mellit.** *Obs.* Also 7 **mellet**. A disease incident to horses (see quots.).

1610 MARKHAM *Masterp.* II. lxix. 333 A Mellet is a dry scabbe that groweth vpon the heele [of a horse]. **1704** *Dict. Rust. et Urban.*, *Mellet* [ed. 1726 *Mellit*], a dry Scab that grows upon the Heel of a Horse's Fore-feet.

mellitate (ˈmɛlɪteɪt). *Chem.* [f. MELLIT(IC) + -ATE[1].] A salt of mellitic acid; = MELLATE.

1828 *Philos. Mag.* IV. 229 The mellite (mellitate of alumina). **1894** *Athenæum* 25 Aug. 260/2 Mellite, or honey-stone, which is aluminium mellitate.

mellite (ˈmɛlaɪt), *sb. Min.* [First in mod.L. *mellītēs* (Gmelin 1793), f. L. *mell-*, *mel* honey: see -ITE.] Native mellitate of aluminium, occurring in honey-yellow octahedral crystals. See also MELILITE 2, HONEY-STONE 2.

First found in brown-coal seams in Thuringia.

1801 *Nicholson's Jrnl.* IV. 516 Honigstein..has a light yellow colour, which has caused it to obtain the name of mellite, or honey stone. **1823** W. PHILLIPS *Introd. Min.* (ed. 3) 374. **1878** LAWRENCE tr. *Cotta's Rocks Class.* 66 Mellite occurs as an accessory ingredient in Brown Coal.

†**mellite**, *a. Obs. rare*$^{-1}$. [ad. L. *mellīt-us*, f. *mell-*, *mel* honey.] Honeyed, sweet.

c **1420** *Pallad. on Husb.* II. 262 Summe..honge hem [services] vp in place opake and drie; And wyn mellite [L. *sapa*], as seid is, saue hem shall.

mellitic (mɛˈlɪtɪk), *a. Chem.* [f. MELLITE *sb.* + -IC, after F. *mellitique* (Klaproth).] *mellitic acid* ($C_{12}H_6O_{12}$), the peculiar acid of mellite. (Also called MELLIC.)

1794 G. ADAMS *Nat. & Exp. Philos.* I. App. 542. **1802** T. THOMSON *Chem.* III. 527 Klaproth found the mellite composed of alumina and a peculiar acid to which he gave the name of *mellitic* acid. **1844** FOWNES *Chem.* 373 Mellitic acid..is soluble in water and alcohol.

mellitimide (mɛˈlɪtɪmaɪd). *Chem.* [f. MELLIT(IC) + IMIDE.] A compound obtained from mellitate of ammonium.

1865 WATTS *Dict. Chem.* III. 873 Paramide or Mellitimide.

melliturgie: see MELITURGY.

mellituria, less correct form of MELITURIA.

mellivorous (mɛˈlɪvərəs), *a.* [f. mod.L. *mellivor-us* (f. L. *mell-*, *mel* honey + *vor-āre* to devour) + -OUS. Cf. F. *mellivore*.] Feeding on honey.

1801 LATHAM *Gen. Syn. Birds* Suppl. II. 166 *marg.*, Mellivorous Creeper. **1822** —— *Gen. Hist. Birds* IV. 161 Mellivorous Honey-eater. **1878** RILEY in *Amer. Naturalist* XII. 215 A..partly carnivorous, partly mellivorous diet.

mellodion: see MELODEON.

mellon, obs. form of MELON[1].

mellone (ˈmɛləʊn). *Chem.* Also **mel(l)on**. [Named by Liebig in 1834; f. *mel-* (as in MELAM) + -ONE.] A compound of carbon and nitrogen obtained as a yellow powder by the action of heat on certain cyanogen-compounds.

1835 *R. D. Thomson's Rec. Gen. Sci.* I. 185 Liebig terms this citron-coloured powder *mellon*. **1838** T. THOMSON *Chem. Org. Bodies* 2 The richest body in azote known is melon, which is composed of C^6 Az^4. *Ibid.* 768 Mellon.

mellonide (ˈmɛlənaɪd). *Chem.* [f. MELLONE + -IDE.] A compound of mellone with a metal.

1845 W. GREGORY *Outl. Chem.* II. 311 Mellonide of potassium. **1862** MILLER *Elem. Chem.* (ed. 2) III. 697.

mellonuret (mɛˈlɒnjʊərɛt). *Chem.* [f. MELLONE + -URET.] = MELLONIDE.

1841 BRANDE *Chem.* (ed. 5) 575 Mellon..combines directly with potassium;..a mellonuret of potassium [is] formed.

mellophone (ˈmɛləʊfəʊn). Chiefly *U.S.* [f. MELLO(W *a.* + -PHONE.] A type of brass instrument similar to the orchestral horn; an alto or tenor horn.

1927 *Melody Maker* May 491/1 The Mellophone has a distinct tone of its own; mellow, as its name implies. In colour I can only liken it to a cross between the tone of the French horn and trombone. In looks the instrument..closely resembles a French horn. **1929** *Ibid.* Apr. 369/3 A mellophone is used and scored for..as part of the brass section. **1946** R. BLESH *Shining Trumpets* (1949) vii. 166 The brass section was rounded out by Isidore Barbarin on mellophone (alto horn). **1958** P. GAMMOND *Decca Bk. Jazz* xix. 229 He was mainly featured on an E-flat tenor horn, which produced a mellophone-like sound. **1966** *Crescendo* Sept. 35/2 Roy Fox's *Whispering* (with Nat himself soloing on mellophone).

Hence **meˈllophonist**, one who plays a mellophone; **melloˈphonium**, a mellophone.

1962 *Melody Maker* 7 July 9 The Stan Kenton-Tex Ritter Capitol album soon to be released, has mellophoniums, trombones, and rhythm only, plus the hawaiian guitar. *Ibid.* 21 July 5 Two odd instruments currently in London. Above,..the skoonum... Below, Jimmy Deuchar with his new mellophonium. **1975** *New Yorker* 5 May 7/1 (Advt.), Mellophonist Don Elliot's quartet is on hand Wednesday and Thursday.

Mellotron (ˈmɛlətrɒn). *Mus.* [f. *mellow* + *electronic*.] (See quots.)

1969 *Britannica Bk. of Year* (U.S.) 800/2 *Mellotron*, an electronic musical instrument programmed to imitate the sounds of orchestral instruments. **1970** *Times* 22 Dec. 11 The cold, windswept string tone of the Mellotron, a keyboard instrument which simulates—but not quite—the sound of an orchestra. **1974** *Melody Maker* 20 Apr. 46 The Mellotron, which was first introduced in 1963, cannot be slotted into any known category, but is best described as a series of controlled tape machines manipulated by a single keyboard. Each key relates to a tape on which has been pre-recorded a single note of an orchestral instrument. When the key is depressed the tape is played.

mellow (ˈmɛləʊ), *a.* Forms: 5 **melwe**, 5–6 **melowe**, 6 **mellowe**, 6– **mellow**. [First appears in the 15th c.; perh. developed from some unrecorded attributive use of OE. *melo* (stem *melw-*), ME. *melowe*, MEAL *sb.*[1] Cf. mod. Flemish *meluw* soft, mellow (Franck s.v. *Mollig*).

In sense the adj. corresponds strikingly with early ME. MEROW, OE. *mearu* (a Com. Teut. word), which may possibly have influenced its development.]

1. a. Of fruit: Soft, sweet, and juicy with ripeness. Also *fig.*

c **1440** *Promp. Parv.* 332/1 Melwe, or rype (*P.* melowe), *maturus*. **1526** *Pilgr. Perf.* (W. de W. 1531) 106 b, Thynke how god may make of that grene apple a swete fruyte full melowe. **1530** PALSGR. 318/2 Melowe as fruyte is, *meur*. **1589** NASHE *Anat. Absurd.* 32 This greene fruite, beeing gathered before it be ripe, is rotten before it be mellow. **1607** SHAKS. *Cor.* IV. vi. 100 As Hercules did shake downe Mellow Fruite. **1611** COTGR. s.v. *Paré, Pomme parée*, ripened in straw, &c.; made mellow by art. **1623** COCKERAM, *Mellow*, ripe. **1681** DRYDEN *Span. Friar* III. iii. 42 Nature drops him down, without your Sin, Like mellow Fruit, without a Winter Storm. **1719** D'URFEY *Pills* (1872) I. 266 Women, like some other Fruit, Lose their relish when too mellow. **1756** LADY M. W. MONTAGU '*Good madam*', But the fruit that can fall without shaking Indeed is too mellow for me. **1806–7** J. BERESFORD *Miseries Hum. Life* (1826) VI. xxxiv, One dish of mellow apples. **1814** SCOTT *Ld. of Isles* III. xxi, Mellow nuts have hardest rind.

b. Of colour, odour, taste: Indicative of ripeness.

1563 *Homilies* II. *Alms-deeds* II. 174 b, So doth the crabbe and choke pere, seeme outwardlye to haue sometyme as fayre a redde, and as melowe a colour, as the fruite which is good in deede. **1644** DIGBY *Nat. Bodies* i. (1645) 3 My eye telleth me it [an apple] is green or red; my nose that it hath a mellow sent.

c. Of landscape, seasons, etc.: Characterized by ripeness.

1819 KEATS *To Autumn* 1 Season of mists and mellow fruitfulness. *a* **1845** HOOD *Poems* (1846) II. 49, Twas in that mellow season of the year When the hot Sun singes the yellow leaves Till they be gold. **1862** B. TAYLOR *Poets Jrnl.* i, A moment she the mellow landscape scanned.

d. Of wines or their flavour: Well-matured; free from acidity or harshness. Also *fig.*

a **1700** B. E. *Dict. Cant. Crew*, *Mellow*,..smooth, soft Drink. **1787** J. CROFT *Treat. Wines Portugal* 7 The Port Wines..being less racey and mellow than the Alicants from Spain. **1853** C. BRONTË *Villette* xix, His spirit was of vintage too mellow and generous to sour.

2. *transf.* **a.** Of earth: Soft, rich, loamy.

1531 ELYOT *Gov.* I. iv, The most melowe and fertile erth. **1577** B. GOOGE *Heresbach's Husb.* I. (1586) 25 If the ground be mellowe, after Barley in some places they sowe Millet. **1664** EVELYN *Kal. Hort.*, *Mar.* (1729) 195 Sow Skirrets in rich, mellow, fresh Earth. **1697** DRYDEN *Virg. Georg.* II. 356 Hoary Frosts..will rot the Mellow Soil. **1777** A. HUNTER *Georg. Ess.* 168 *note*, In the North of England, when the earth turns up with a mellow and crumbly appearance, and smoaks, the farmers say the earth is *brimming*. **1815** J. SMITH *Panorama Sci. & Art* II. 632 It delights most in a stiff, mellow, well pulverized soil. **1879** JOAQUIN MILLER *Nicaragua* in *Poems of Places, Brit. Amer. etc.* 175 My father old He turns alone the mellow sod.

b. In various applications: Soft; soft and smooth to the touch.

1797 *Encycl. Brit.* (ed. 3) III. 544/2 This frequent turning it over, cools, dries, and deadens the grain; whereby it becomes mellow. **1844** STEPHENS *Bk. Farm* III. 836 [Young cattle.] To be a good thriver..the hair should feel mossy, and the touch of the skin mellow. **1875** *Encycl. Brit.* I. 390/2 Young cattle..are at 18 months old already of great size, with open horns, mellow hide [etc.].

3. *fig.* (from sense 1). Mature, ripe in age. Now chiefly, softened or sweetened by age or experience; having the gentleness or dignity resulting from maturity.

1592 KYD *Sp. Trag.* I. iii. 41 My yeeres were mellow, his but young and greene. **1611** MIDDLETON & DEKKER *Roaring Girle* I. D.'s Wks. 1873 III. 145 Maister Greene-wit is not yet So mellow in yeares as he. **1749** SMOLLETT *Regicide* v. iv, In florid youth, or mellow age, scarce fleets One hour without its care! **1855** M. ARNOLD *Sonn. to Friend* 13 The mellow glory of the Attic stage. **1893** GOLDW. SMITH *United States* 63 He [Benjamin Franklin] was an offspring of New England Puritanism grown mellow.

4. Of sound, colour, light, etc.: Rich and soft; full and pure without harshness.

a. of sound, musical instruments, singers.

1668 H. MORE *Div. Dial.* III. xxxvi. (1713) 284 How sweet and mellow, and yet how Majestick, is the Sound of it! **1700** DRYDEN *Ovid's Met.* XII. 218 The mellow harp did not their ears employ. **1722** SNAPE in *Swift's Lett.* (1766) II. 27 His voice, since its breaking, is somewhat harsh, but I believe will grow mellower. **1728–46** THOMSON *Spring* 604 The mellow bullfinch answers from the grove. **1742** BERKELEY *Let. to Gervais* 2 Feb., Wks. 1871 IV. 284 A six-stringed bass viol of an old make and mellow tone. **1746** COLLINS *Ode Passions* 61 Pale Melancholy..Pour'd thro' the mellow Horn her pensive soul. **1821** BYRON *Juan* IV. lxxxvii, Who swore his voice was very rich and mellow. *a* **1849** POE *The Bells*, Hear the mellow wedding bells, Golden bells. **1863** LEVER *Barrington* xviii, The hardy old squire, whose mellow cheer was known at the fox-cover. **1863** GEO. ELIOT *Romola* lxi, There was silence when he began to speak in his clear mellow voice.

b. of colour, light, drawing, etc., or coloured objects. Sometimes with additional notion: Softened in colour by age.

1706 *Art of Painting* (1744) 342 His pencil was light and mellow. **1766** GOLDSM. *Vic. W.* xx, The colouring of a picture was not mellow enough. **1784** COWPER *Task* IV. 314 The golden harvest, of a mellow brown. **1815** WORDSW. *Excursion* I. 958 The sun declining shot A slant and mellow radiance. **1842** TENNYSON *Locksley Hall* 9 Many a night I saw the Pleiads, rising through the mellow shade. **1859** GEO. ELIOT *A. Bede* vi, Pleasant jets of light were thrown on mellow oak and bright brass. **1880** MISS BRADDON *Just as I am* ii, Time had toned down every colour inside and outside the good old house to mellowest half tints.

5. a. Good-humoured, genial, jovial.

1711 ADDISON *Spect.* No. 68 ¶3 In all thy Humours, whether grave or mellow. **1824** W. IRVING *T. Trav.* I. 7 The Baronet was..as merry and mellow an old bachelor as ever followed a hound. **1871** M. COLLINS *Mrq. & Merch.* II. viii. 234 When..their glasses were filled with..port, Mowbray grew a trifle mellower in mood.

b. *U.S. slang.* Satisfying, attractive, skilful, pleasant.

1942 Z. N. HURSTON in A. Dundes *Mother Wit* (1973) 224/2 If they's white, they's right! If they's yellow, they's mellow! If they's brown, they can stick around. **1944** D. BURLEY in *Ibid.* 207/1 The whole town's copping the mellow jive. **1945** L. SHELLY *Jive Talk Dict.* 15/1 *Mellow* (adj.) superlative. *Ibid.* 29/1 *Mellow fellow*, a satisfactory person. *Mellow mouse*, attractive female. **1960** WENTWORTH & FLEXNER *Dict. Amer. Slang* 336 *Mellow*,..skillful; sincere, heart-felt; said of a jazz performance. **1970** C. MAJOR *Dict. Afro-Amer. Slang* 81 *Mellow*, gentle, sincere, satisfying; cool. **1973** *To our Returned Prisoners of War* (Office of U.S. Secretary of Defense) 7 *Mellow*, pleasant or satisfied. Just good.

6. a. Affected with liquor, partly intoxicated.

1611 COTGR. s.v. *Enyvrer*, *S'enyvrer*, to be drunke, or in drinke; to be mellow, tipled, flusht, ouerseene. **1638** BRATHWAIT *Barnabees Jrnl.* III. (1818) 85 For the world, I would not prize her,..Had she in her no good fellow That would drinke till he grew mellow. **1775** SHERIDAN *Duenna* II. iii, The hateful fellow That's crabbed when he's mellow. **1895** SCULLY *Kafir Stories* 193 The beer was not in sufficient quantities to cause intoxication, but nevertheless all were somewhat mellow when the sun went down.

b. *U.S. slang.* (See quot.)

1946 MEZZROW & WOLFE *Really Blues* (1957) 376 *Mellow*: feeling good, especially after smoking marihuana.

7. a. *Comb.*, chiefly parasynthetic and advb., as ***mellow-breathing***, ***-coloured***, ***-deep***, ***-eyed***, ***-lighted***, ***-mouthed***, ***-ripe***, ***-tasted***, ***-tempered***, ***-toned*** adjs.

a **1777** FAWKES *Epithalamic Ode* 19 The merry pipe, the *mellow-breathing flute. **1895** CLIVE HOLLAND *Jap. Wife* 70 Countless numbers of paper lanterns, which throw a *mellow-coloured radiance on the faces of the passers-by. **1832** TENNYSON *Eleänore* 67 A sweep Of richest pauses, evermore Drawn from each other *mellow-deep. **1866** HOWELLS *Venet. Life* x. 139 *Mellow-eyed dun oxen. **1892** PATER *Wks.* (1901) VIII. 209 The melodious, *mellow-lighted space. **1604** T. WRIGHT *Passions* v. §3. 182 A preacher,..knowing his auditours wallowed in sinne, ought not with..*mellow-mouthed words tickle their eares. **1579** SPENSER *Sheph. Cal.* Dec. 107 Ere they were halfe *mellow ripe. **1730–46** THOMSON *Autumn* 705 The *mellow-tasted burgundy. **1873** E. BRENNAN *Witch of Nemi*, etc. 85 *Mellow-toned laughter.

b. ***mellow yellow*** (*U.S. slang*), banana peel used as an intoxicant; also as *adj.*

1967 *Boston Sunday Herald Mag.* 30 Apr. 28/3 So I offered him—grass, acid, speed, magic—mushrooms, DMT, hash, and mellow yellow. **1968–70** *Current Slang* (Univ. S. Dakota) III–IV. 82 *Mellow yellow*, intoxicated from smoking a banana peel.

mellow (ˈmɛləʊ), *v.* [f. MELLOW *a.*]

1. *trans.* To render mellow; to ripen and render soft and juicy (fruits); to mature (wines or liquors), to free from harshness or acidity. Also *fig.*

1572 GASCOIGNE *Counc. Withipoll* Posies (1575) Hearbes 155 Those sunnes do mellowe men so fast, As most that trauayle come home very ripe. **1590** GREENE *Orl. Fur.* (1599) 47 Me thinks I feele how Cynthya.. meloweth those desires Which phrensies scares had ripened in my head. **1594** SHAKS. *Rich. III* III. vii. 168 The Royall Tree hath left vs Royall Fruit, Which mellow'd by the stealing howres of time, Will well become the Seat of Maiestie. **1630** DONNE *Lett.* (1651) 317 All this mellows me for heaven. **1697** DRYDEN *Virg. Georg.* II. 758 Winter Fruits are mellow'd by the Frost. **1701** ADDISON *Let. to Halifax* 132 On foreign mountains may the Sun refine The Grape's soft juice, and mellow it to wine. **1754** RICHARDSON *Grandison* IV. xxxii. 203 Yours is Love mellowed into Friendship. **1781** COWPER *Conversation* 644 Age,.. As time improves the grape's authentic juice, Mellows and makes the speech more fit for use. **1818** SOUTHEY *Lett., to H. H. Southey* II. 115 Generous minds and tempers.. are mellowed, like wine, as they grow older. **1848** LYTTON *Harold* III. v, The year.. had mellowed the fruits of the earth.

b. *intr.* Of fruit, wines, etc.: To become mellow; to ripen, mature. Also *fig.*

1594 SHAKS. *Rich. III* IV. iv. 1 So now prosperity begins to mellow, And drop into the rotten mouth of death. *a* **1631** DONNE *On Himself* 6 Till death us lay To ripe and mellow here we are stuborne Clay. **1638** SIR T. HERBERT *Trav.* (ed. 2) 297 From a dark-greene, [they] mellow into a flaming yellow. **1693** EVELYN *De La Quint. Compl. Gard.* Pref., Exactly when to gather both those which ripen on the Tree, and those which attain not their full ripeness there, but must be laid up to mellow in the House. **1768–74** TUCKER *Lt. Nat.* (1834) II. 343 Their juices will mellow by mingling together. **1830** M. DONOVAN *Dom. Econ.* I. 21 These were often hung in the smoke of a chimney, at some distance above the fire, in order to mellow. **1884** W. C. SMITH *Kildrostan* 74 Unripe fruit is bitter oft i' the mouth, Yet mellows with the months.

2. *trans.* To make (soil) soft and loamy.

1577 B. GOOGE *Heresbach's Husb.* I. (1586) 23 b, The land it selfe is also called grosse and rawe, that is not well mellowed. **1634** SIR T. HERBERT *Trav.* 115 A small streame, which.. meloes most of the Gardens and Groues. **1707** MORTIMER *Husb.* (1721) I. 52 Wind, Sun and Dews, all which sweeten and mellow the Land very much. **1846** J. BAXTER *Libr. Pract. Agric.* (ed. 4) II. 288 Their surfaces soon become mellowed by the action of the air.

b. *intr.* Of soil: To become soft and loamy.

1815 J. SMITH *Panorama Sci. & Art* I. 184 The earth.. should have sufficient time to mellow and ferment. **1895** *Tablet* 9 Nov. 739 Then the soil will have mellowed sufficiently to bear wheat and potatoes.

3. *trans.* To impart softness and richness (of flavour, colour, tone, etc.) to; to soften, sweeten, free from harshness or crudity. Also (*nonce-use*), to drive (something) *out of* (a person) by a process of mellowing.

1593 NASHE *Christ's T.* 16 b, As Archesilaus ouer-melodied, and too-much melowed and sugred with sweet tunes,.. caused his eares to be new relished with harsh sower and vnsauory sounds. **1596** —— *Saffron Walden* 113 The Page was easily mellowd with his attractiue eloquence. **1693** DRYDEN *To Sir G. Kneller* 178 Time shall.. Mellow your colours. **1742** BLAIR *Grave* 102 The sooty blackbird Mellow'd his pipe, and soften'd every note. **1761** HUME *Hist. Eng.* III. xlvii. 36 In order to mellow these humours. **1786** S. ROGERS *Sailor* 8 Its colours mellow'd, not impair'd, by time. **1810** SCOTT *Lady of L.* II. xvii, At first the sounds, by distance tame, Mellowed along the waters came. **1871** L. STEPHEN *Playgr. Eur.* ii. (1894) 49 Lichens mellow the scarred masses of fallen rock. **1887** SAINTSBURY *Ess. Eng. Lit., Jeffrey* (1891) 102 The priggishness which he showed early, and never entirely lost, till fame, prosperity, and the approach of old age mellowed it out of him. **1902** A. THOMSON *Lauder & Lauderdale* x. 102 The King.. visited him.. to endeavour by personal interview to mellow his manners.

b. *intr.* To soften, become toned down or subdued; to become free from harshness.

1737 M. GREEN *Spleen* 711 Unhurt by sickness' blasting rage And slowly mellowing in age. **1777** ROBERTSON *Hist. Amer.* (1778) II. v. 4 The impetuosity of his temper, when he came to act with his equals, insensibly abated.. and mellowed into a cordial soldierly frankness. **1823** BYRON *Island* II. xv, The broad sun set, but not with lingering sweep, As in the north he mellows o'er the deep. **1840** DICKENS *Barn. Rudge* xi, The very furniture of the room seemed to mellow.. in its tone. **1861** J. BROWN *Horæ Subs.* (1863) 64 His character mellowed and toned down in his later years. **1902** A. E. W. MASON *Four Feathers* xvii. 165 The sunlight mellowed and reddened.

4. *trans.* To bring under the influence of liquor.

a **1761** CAWTHORN *Poems* (1771) 189 Gods.. will, like mortals, swear and hector, When mellow'd with a cup of nectar. **1836** W. IRVING *Astoria* II. 13 When he thought him sufficiently mellowed, he proposed to him to quit the service of his new employers. **1855** TENNYSON *Brook* 155 There he mellow'd all his heart with ale.

mellow ('mɛləʊ), *sb. U.S. slang.* [perh. *catachr.* f. MELODY *sb.*] (See quots.)

1942 BERREY & VAN DEN BARK *Amer. Thes. Slang* §568 *Mellows*, spirituals or religious songs. **1958** P. GAMMOND *Decca Bk. Jazz* i. 21 There were sustained 'mellows'—hollers in which a single idea or phrase might be repeated with numerous variations until the singer tired of it or thought of another.

mellowed ('mɛləʊd), *ppl. a.* [f. MELLOW *v.* + -ED[1].] In senses of the vb.: Rendered mellow.

1575 GASCOIGNE *Gloze Text 2* Posies Hearbes 145 My riper mellowed yeares beginne to follow on as fast. **1593** SHAKS. *3 Hen. VI*, III. iii. 104 Call him my King, by whose iniurious doome My elder Brother.. Was done to death?.. Euen in the downe-fall of his mellow'd yeeres. **1798** BLOOMFIELD *Farmer's Boy, Spring* 63 Wide o'er the fields, in rising moisture strong, Shoots up the simple flower, or creeps along The mellow'd soil. **1830** M. DONOVAN *Dom. Econ.* I. 155 This water, present in exposed or mellowed malt, tends to lower the resulting temperature. *a* **1853** ROBERTSON *Lect.* (1858) 247 Ripened with the mellowed strength of manly life. **1889** *County* vi. in *Cornh. Mag.* Feb., The fine old room with its mellowed walls and priceless brocades.

mellowing ('mɛləʊɪŋ), *vbl. sb.* [f. MELLOW *v.* + -ING[1].] The action of the vb. MELLOW.

1528 PAYNEL *Salerne's Regim.* Hij, The operations of dulce wynes are digestion, mellowyng, and encressynge of nourishement. **1621** FLETCHER *Pilgrim* II. i, Fling him i' th' hay-mow, let him lie a-mellowing. **1675** GREW *Tastes Plants* iv. §11 Sower apples, by mellowing, and harsh pears, by baking, become sweet. **1845** *Encycl. Metrop.* XXV. 1286/2 The mellowing of wine by time is a process which has baffled hitherto all scientific inquiry. **1897** *Allbutt's Syst. Med.* II. 845 Some amylic alcohol, which tends, however, to disappear in the process of mellowing.

attrib. **1871** GLADSTONE in Morley *Life* (1903) II. VI. viii. 382 In his character the mellowing process has continued to advance.

mellowing ('mɛləʊɪŋ), *ppl. a.* [f. MELLOW *v.* + -ING[2].] That mellows (in senses of the vb.).

1637 MILTON *Lycidas* 5, I com to.. Shatter your leaves before the mellowing year. **1725** POPE *Odyss.* III. 504 Late from the mellowing cask restor'd to light. **1807** CRABBE *Par. Reg.* II. 454 And their full autumn felt the mellowing frost. **1894** *Athenæum* 2 June 702/3 [It] became afterwards poetized by the mellowing sun of his genius.

mellowly ('mɛləʊlɪ), *adv.* [f. MELLOW *a.* + -LY[2].] In a mellow manner.

1806 J. GRAHAME *Birds of Scot.* 90 Mildly the sun, upon the loftiest trees, Shed mellowly a sloping beam. **1833** TENNYSON *Poems* 106 The luscious fruitage clustereth mellowly.

mellowness ('mɛləʊnɪs). [f. MELLOW *a.* + -NESS.] The quality or state of being mellow, in various senses of the adj.

1530 PALSGR. 244/2 Melownesse, *mevreté.* **1647** TRAPP *Comm. 2 Pet.* iii. 18 Grow.. as an apple doth in mellownesse. **1707** MORTIMER *Husb.* (1721) I. 350 This perfects the Sweetness and Mellowness of the Malt. **1742** ABP. HORT *Instr. Clergy of Tuam* 9 *Suaviloquentia*, that mellowness and sweetness of speaking so much praised in some of the Roman orators, in opposition to the rusticity of noisy declaimers. **1777** SHERIDAN *Sch. Scand.* I. i. (ed. Rae) 148 She wants that delicacy of Tint—and mellowness of sneer—which distinguish your Ladyship's Scandal. **1787** J. CROFT *Treat. Wines Portugal* 5 Red Wines of a superior mellowness or body. **1805** W. IRVING in *Life & Lett.* (1864) I. 157 In the tender scenes he [Kemble] wanted mellowness. **1882** TRAILL in Morley *Gladstone* (1904) III. VIII. vi. 91 The tang of the wood brings out the mellowness of a rare old wine. **1884** *Harper's Mag.* Feb. 349/1 A mellowness of light and shade unattainable in marble.

mellowy ('mɛləʊɪ), *a.* [f. MELLOW *a.* + -Y.] = MELLOW *a.*, in various senses.

c **1420** *Pallad. on Husb.* IV. 523 Ypuld not melowy but grene. **1612** DRAYTON *Poly-olb.* x. 97 Whose mellowy gleabe doth beare The yellow ripened sheafe that bendeth with the eare. **1816** L. HUNT *Rimini* III. 428 A pavilion,.. Small, marble, well-proportioned, mellowy white.

melltyde, variant of MEALTIDE *Obs.*

mellwell, obs. form of MULVEL.

melly, obs. f. MELLAY; var. MELLIE *Obs.*

mellylot(e, obs. forms of MELILOT.

melner, obs. form of MILLER[1].

melo ('mɛləʊ), colloq. abbrev. of MELODRAMA.

1889 E. DOWSON *Let.* 24 Mar. (1967) 54, I could no more go *twice* than I could to an Adelphi *melo. Ibid.* 24 Dec. 121 Even bad melo doesn't cause me to vomit as it did of old. **1920** A. HUXLEY *Let.* 23 Apr. (1969) 183 What one wd call a West End melodrama as opposed to a Lyceum melo. **1971** *Radio Times* 26 Aug., True life was *melo* about the first woman to win the George Cross. (As a stump word, '*melo*' is short for '*melodrama*'.) **1973** *Ibid.* 20 Dec. 18/4 *The Roots of Heaven*.. John Huston's melo about elephant conservation.

‖**melocactus** (mɛləʊ'kæktəs). *Bot.* [mod.L. (Tournefort 1700) f. late L. *mēlo* MELON + CACTUS.] A genus of cactaceous plants, natives of Central and South America (popularly called *melon-thistle*); a plant of this genus.

1733 MILLER *Gard. Dict.* (ed. 2), *Melocactus*.. Melon-Thistle. **1853** TH. ROSS tr. *Humboldt's Trav.* III. xxvi. 114 The agaves and melocactuses half-buried in the sand. **1871** KINGSLEY *At Last* i, We saw our first Melocactus, and our first night-blowing Cereus creeping over the rocks.

melochite, obs. form of MALACHITE.

†**melocoton.** *Obs.* Forms: 7 malacaton, -catoon, -katoone, -cotoon, -malecotone, mali-, mallagatoon, melacatoon, -cotone, melicot(t)on, melicotonie, mellacat(t)on, mellicoton, melocotone, -cotune, 7–8 malacoton, malecotoon, melicotoon(e, 8 malacotoune, malocotoon, melacotoon, melicotony, melococoon, -coton, -cotony, -cotoon. [a. Sp. *melocoton*, ad. It. *melocotogno*, ad. med.L. *mēlum cotōneum* (= late L. *mālum cotōneum*), ad. Gr. μῆλον κυδώνιον 'Cydonian apple': see COYN, QUINCE. Cf. F. *mirecoton, mirelicoton* (Cotgr.).] A peach grafted on a quince. Also *melocoton peach.*

The more original sense of 'quince', which occurs in Sp. and It., does not seem to have existed in Eng.

1611 COTGR., *Mirecoton*, the delicate yellow Peach, called a Melicotonie. **1614** B. JONSON *Barth. Fair* I. ii, A wife heere with a Strawbery-breath, Chery-lips,.. and a soft veluet head, like a Melicotton. **1661** RABISHA *Cookery Dissected* 8 To pickle Mallagatoons. **1688** R. HOLME *Armoury* III. 80/2 Sweetnings, as.. Oranges and Lemmons and them candied, Mellacattons. **1704** *Collect. Voy.* (Churchill) III. 46/1 Melicotoons, Peaches, Auberges. **1719** LONDON & WISE *Compl. Gard.* p. iii, The Malecotoon Peach, which is not worth any ones planting. **1744** A. DOBBS *Countries Adjacent to Hudson's Bay* 144 A Fruit they called Obi, like to Melacotoons. **1745** P. THOMAS *Jrnl. Anson's Voy.* 95 Peaches, Nectarines, Melococoons, Apricots.. grow plentifully.

melodeon, melodion (mɪ'ləʊdɪən). [In sense 1, an altered form of MELODIUM, with a quasi-Gr. ending; in sense 2 perh. f. MELODY in imitation of ACCORDION.]

1. A wind instrument, furnished with a keyboard, the bellows being moved by means of pedals worked by the feet of the performer; an earlier form of the 'American organ'.

1847 W. G. HAMMOND *Jrnl.* 30 Sept. in G. F. Whicher *Remembrance Amherst* (1946) 183 Under the lead of Goodale with his melodeon [they] sing 'Sparkling and Bright'. **1850** *Rep. Comm. Patents 1849* (U.S.) 278 Improvement in Melodeons. **1858** SIMMONDS *Dict. Trade, Melodeon.* **1872** 'MARK TWAIN' *Innoc. Abr.* ii. 17 Our parlour organ and our melodeon were to be the best instruments of the kind. **1891** *Scribner's Mag.* Sept. 356/2 A.. broken-down melodeon. **1964** *Amer. Folk Music Occasional* I. 39 As a youngster he heard his father's fiddle and listened to his mother's singing of the old songs to the strain of a wheezy melodeon.

2. A kind of accordion.

1880 (*title*) The Art of playing the Melodion, or German accordion, without a Master. **1886** *Pop. Self-Instructor for the Melodeon* 4 The Melodeon, or improved German Accordion.

3. A music-hall. *U.S.*

1840 *Boston Transcript* 1 Jan. 3/1 A grand vocal and instrumental concert will be given by Mr. John Bartlett, at the Melodeon, Washington street, on Saturday evening. **1861** E. COWELL *Diary* (1934) 283 Hattie James.. was burned to death, lately at the Gayities or Melodeon. **1864** in WEBSTER. **1948–9** *Northwest Ohio Q.* Winter 19 Parker occupied Cleveland's Melodeon again on June 12, 1854, when he delivered 'The Progress of Mankind' to a 'crowded house'.

melodial (mɪ'ləʊdɪəl), *a.* [f. L. *melōdia* MELODY + -AL[1].] Of or relating to melody.

1818 BUSBY *Gram. Mus.* 111 *note*, So rare.. is the command of melodial modulation, that the greatest masters cannot always exhibit felicitous examples of its excellence. **1902** *Durham Exam. Papers* 174 (*For the degree of D.Mus.*) Make your work interesting in a melodial sense.

Hence **me'lodially** *adv.*

1818 BUSBY *Gram. Music* 365 Modulation.. Harmonically and melodially exhibited.

melodic (mɪ'lɒdɪk), *a.* [ad. F. *mélodique* = Sp. *melódico*, It. *melodico*, ad. late L. *melōdicus* (Cassiodorus), a. Gr. μελῳδικός, f. μελῳδία: see MELODY and -IC.] Of or pertaining to melody.

melodic minor scale: see MINOR *a.*

1823 *New Monthly Mag.* VIII. 132 We should not.. hesitate to risk a comparison between the best Greek melodic concert, and the melharmonic strains and combinations of a modern performance. **1864** in WEBSTER. **1868** H. SPENCER *Princ. Psychol.* (1872) II. 641 The melodic element in music. **1893** *Athenæum* 23 Dec. 890/2 Scale is the accepted foundation of all music, melodic or harmonic.

†**me'lodical**, *a. Obs.* [f. late L. *melōdic-us* MELODIC + -AL[1].] Melodious.

1596 FITZ-GEFFRAY *Sir. F. Drake* (1881) 24 Fetch Orpheus harpe with strings harmonicall; And musicke from the Spheares melodicall. **1601** WEEVER *Mirr. Mart., Sir. J. Oldcastle* B viij, Strayned ditties most melodicall.

melodically (mɪ'lɒdɪkəlɪ), *adv.* [Formed as prec. + -LY[2].] In a melodic manner; with regard to melody.

1876 STAINER & BARRETT *Dict. Mus. Terms* (1898) 394 Form of minor mode sometimes used melodically. **1887** E. GURNEY *Tertium Quid* II. 18 The form may be far from melodically inventive.

melodicon (mɪ'lɒdɪkən). [ad. Gr. μελῳδικόν neut. of μελῳδικός pertaining to melody, f. μελῳδία: see MELODY *sb.*] (See quot.) ***psalm melodicon***: see PSALM *sb.* 3.

1876 STAINER & BARRETT *Dict. Mus. Terms* 285/2 *Melodicon*, an instrument made of steel bars in different lengths tuned to the diatonic scale, struck with hammers held in the hand. **1938** *Oxf. Compan. Mus.* 789/1 Grenié's invention, the *Orgue Expressif*, became the parent of a progeny including the.. Melodicon.

melodics (mɪ'lɒdɪks). [See MELODIC *a.* and -IC[2].] The branch of musical science that is concerned with melody.

1864 in WEBSTER; and in later Dicts.

melodiograph (mɪ'ləʊdɪəgrɑːf, -æ-). [f. MELODY + -GRAPH.] A contrivance to record the notes of tunes played upon an instrument. Cf. MELOGRAPH.

1884 KNIGHT *Dict. Mech.* Suppl. 592/2 In the melodiograph of Zigliani, a double flat spring placed under

each key is connected with a battery and with a recording apparatus.

† **me'lodion**[1]. *Obs.* [A pseudo-Gr. formation on MELODY.] (See quot.) A musical instrument consisting of a series of metal rods, actuated by being pressed against a rotating cylinder.

1830 *Edinb. Encycl.* XVII. 563 This musical instrument was invented..by M. Dietz, a German, and he has given it the name of melodion from the sweetness and harmony by which it is characterized.

melodion[2]: see MELODEON.

melodious (mɪ'ləʊdɪəs), *a.* Forms: 4–6 **melodyous(e, 5 melodiose, -dyows, 6 mellodi(o)us, -dyous, melodyus.** [ad. OF. *melodieus* (mod.F. *mélodieux*), = Sp., Pg., It. *melodioso*, med.L. *melōdiōsus*, f. L. *melōdia*: see MELODY and -OUS.]

1. Characterized by melody or pleasing succession of sounds; sweet-sounding, tuneful.

c **1374** CHAUCER *Troylus* v. 577 Herde I myn alderleuest lady dere, So wommanly wiþ voys melodious, Syngen so wel. *c* **1430** LYDG. *Min. Poems* (Percy Soc.) 80 Thus thay songe..This melodious ympne. *a* **1533** LD. BERNERS *Huon* xxii. 66 He..blewe so melodyous a blast. **1629** MILTON *Hymn Nativ.* xiii, Ring out ye Crystall sphears,..And let your silver chime Move in melodious time. *c* **1700** DRYDEN *Charac. Gd. Parson* 22 A music more melodious than the spheres. **1713** BERKELEY *Guardian* No. 27 ⁋7 A melodious consort of vocal and instrumental music. **1797** *Encycl. Brit.* (ed. 3) XI. 375/2 That an air which was never set or intended for words, however melodious, cannot be imitative. **1836** EMERSON *Nature, Discipline* Wks. (Bohn) II. 156 Man..forges the subtile..air into wise and melodious words. **1865** DICKENS *Mut. Fr.* I. iv, Melodious sounds were not long in rising from the frying-pan on the fire.

2. Producing melody; singing sweetly.

1588 SHAKS. *Tit. A.* III. i. 85 Where like a sweet mellodius bird it sung. **1589** PUTTENHAM *Eng. Poesie* I. iii. (Arb.) 22 By his discreete and wholesome lessons vttered in harmonie and with melodious instruments. **1697** DRYDEN *Virg. Georg.* IV. 697 The lovely Bride In safety goes, with her Melodious Guide [Orpheus]. **1784** COWPER *Task* IV. 574 The walk..unconscious once Of other tenants than melodious birds. **1847** EMERSON *Repr. Men, Swedenborg* Wks. (Bohn) I. 333 Melodious poets shall be hoarse as street ballads, when [etc.].

3. *nonce-use.* Susceptible to melody.

c **1586** C'TESS PEMBROKE *Ps.* XLIX. i, Wordes shall from my mouth proceed, Which I will measure by melodious eare.

4. Having a melody; pertaining to or of the nature of melody.

1727–52 CHAMBERS *Cycl.* s.v. *Melody*, Yet so far as the bass may be made airy, and to sing well, it may be also properly said to be melodious. **1818** BUSBY *Gram. Mus.* 59 The first rudiments of the simplest province of musical composition, and musical performance,—melodious succession.

melodiously (mɪ'ləʊdɪəslɪ), *adv.* [-LY[2].] In a melodious manner.

c **1430** LYDG. *Min. Poems* (Percy Soc.) 157 The yelwe swan famous and aggreable, Ageyn his dethe melodyously syngyng. **1597** HOOKER *Eccl. Pol.* v. lxvii. §12 Their discourses are heauenly,..their tongues melodiously tuned instruments. **1616** SURFL. & MARKH. *Country Farm* 715 Birds which sing melodiously with sweet and pleasant songs. *a* **1711** KEN *Hymnotheo* Poet. Wks. 1721 I. 253 Ferventio's Song..Instructive, and melodiously grave. **1810** SOUTHEY *Kehama* x. vii, Ganges..rippled round melodiously. **1903** *Blackw. Mag.* June 743/1 His melodiously delivered sermons..were distinctly popular.

melodiousness (mɪ'ləʊdɪəsnɪs). [-NESS.] The quality of being melodious.

1530 PALSGR. 244/1 Melodyousnesse, *melodie.* **1727** in BAILEY vol. II. **1904** *Edin Rev.* Jan. 116 Herrick owed most to his beloved 'Ben', whose full melodiousness emboldened his follower to rise above conceits.

melodist ('mɛləʊdɪst). [f. MELODY + -IST.]

1. A singer.

In the first half of the 19th c. somewhat frequently used in the titles of collections of songs with music.

1789 *Trifler* No. 33. 419 Often I am constrained to listen to the broken notes of ignorant, but presumptuous melodists. **1817** (*title*) The Melodist..an excellent collection of..songs. Selected and compiled by R. L. I. **1819** KEATS *Ode Grecian Urn* iii, Happy melodist, unwearied, For ever piping songs for ever new. **1840** SIR H. BISHOP in Grove *Dict. Mus.* III. 249, I hail the establishment of the Melodists' Club..as essentially calculated to aid the cause of the musical art in this country. **1852** HAWTHORNE *Blithedale Rom.* xxiii. (1885) 226 The choir of Ethiopian melodists. **1892** W. H. HUDSON *Natur. La Plata* 28 The rufous tinamou—sweet and mournful melodist of the eventide.

2. A composer of melodies; one skilled in melody.

1826 M. KELLY *Remin.* I. 225, I compare a good melodist to a fine racer, and counterpointists to hack post horses. **1872** LOWELL *Milton* Prose Wks. 1890 IV. 96 Milton was a harmonist rather than a melodist. **1893** W. GRAHAM in *19th Cent.* Nov. 765 As an absolute melodist—I mean a master of word-music as distinct from other qualities—I consider Swinburne unequalled.

melodium (mɪ'ləʊdɪəm). [A quasi-L. formation on MELODY.] = MELODEON I.

1847 *Illustr. Lond. News* 7 Aug. 95/2 Pianos, melodiums, harmoniums, eolinas, &c., too dear at any price. **1878** GROVE *Dict. Mus.* I. 61 The instruments first made in America were known as 'Melodeons', or 'Melodiums'.

melodize ('mɛləʊdaɪz), *v.* [f. MELODY + -IZE.]

1. *intr.* To make melody; *occas.* somewhat jocularly, to play (*on* an instrument). Also *poet.* to blend melodiously *with.*

1662 J. SPARROW tr. *Behme's Rem. Wks., Apol. conc. Perfect.* 42 A Harmony of God, upon which the Spirit of God would melodise. **1794** SOUTHEY *Let. to H. Bedford* 24 Jan. in *Life* (1849) I. 203 Lightfoot still melodises on the flute. **1811** SCOTT *Roderick* Introd. ii, Yes! such a strain with all o'er-pouring measure, Might melodize with each tumultuous sound. **1813** SHELLEY *Q. Mab* VIII. 69 To murmur through the heaven-breathing groves And melodize with man's blest nature there. **1886** T. HARDY *Mayor Casterbr.* viii, As the Scotchman again melodised with a dying fall.

2. *trans.* To make melodious.

1759 J. LANGHORNE *Ode to River Eden* 44 Whose murmurs melodize my Song. **1766** H. WALPOLE *Let. to Lady Hervey* 11 Jan., Thy enchanting look Can melodize each note in Nature's book. **1841** D'ISRAELI *Amen. Lit.* II 253 These repeated attempts of the learned English..to melodise our orthoepy. **1869** RUSKIN *Q. of Air* (1874) 60 Music in which the words and thought lead, and the lyre measures or melodizes them.

3. To compose a melody for (a song).

1881 DORAN *Drury Lane* II. 191 He penned and melodised hundreds of popular songs.

Hence **'melodized** *ppl. a.*, made melodious; **'melodizing** *vbl. sb.* and *ppl. a.* Also **'melodizer**, one who melodizes.

1811 BUSBY *Dict. Mus.* Introd. 14 This art of *melodizing*, if I may so call it, seems in the present age to have reached its acmé. *a* **1821** KEATS *Sonn. on reading K. Lear* 3 O golden tongued Romance, with serene lute!..Leave melodizing on this wintry day. **1841** HOR. SMITH *Moneyed Man* III. ix. 240 Her bird-like singing is the melodised cheerfulness of her heart. **1890** *Temple Bar* Dec. 588 Romance!..O golden melodizer of sweet dreams!

melodram: see MELODRAME.

melodrama ('mɛləʊdrɑːmə, mɛləʊ'drɑːmə). [Alteration of MELODRAME, after DRAMA.]

1. In early 19th c. use, a stage-play (usually romantic and sensational in plot and incident) in which songs were interspersed, and in which the action was accompanied by orchestral music appropriate to the situations. In later use the musical element gradually ceased to be an essential feature of the 'melodrama', and the name now denotes a dramatic piece characterized by sensational incident and violent appeals to the emotions, but with a happy ending.

1809 SOUTHEY *Lett.* (1856) II. 181 They have made a melo-drama of 'Mary the Maid of the Inn'. **1818** C. E. WALKER *Sigesmar the Switzer* Pref., The following trifle was written two years back, during the rage for Melo-dramas. **1836** *Gentl. Mag.* Apr. 423 It [a 'comœdietta'] is one of those tissues of domestic calamities..which..were a few years since denominated melodramas. **1883** D. COOK *Nts. Play* II. 333 Mr. Sims's 'Lights o' London', is a five-act melodrama of the good old Adelphi pattern.

attrib. **1879** STEVENSON *Trav. Cevennes, Cheylard & Luc*, The kitchen..was the very model of what a kitchen ought to be; a melodrama kitchen, suitable for bandits or noblemen in disguise.

b. The species of dramatic composition or representation constituted by melodramas; the mode of dramatic treatment characteristic of a melodrama.

1814 *New Brit. Theatre* I. 216 In tragedy and comedy the final event is the effect of the moral operations of the different characters, but in the melo-drama the catastrophe is the physical result of mechanical stratagem. **1838** DICKENS *Nich. Nick.* xxx, This Mr. Crummles did in the highest style of melo-drama. **1889** D. HANNAY *Capt. Marryat* viii. 122 Amine [in *The Phantom Ship*] is a very acceptable heroine of melodrama. **1902** *Daily Chron.* 22 Aug. 8/7 Melodrama thrives solely upon exaggeration.

2. *transf.* A series of incidents, or a story true or fictitious, resembling what is represented in a melodrama; also, in generalized sense, melodramatic behaviour, occurrences, etc.

1814 SIR R. WILSON *Priv. Diary* (1861) II. 306 The world will approve the catastrophe of the melodrama which metes out signal punishment to Joachim the first in the last act of his life. **1816** SCOTT *Antiq.* xii, She beheld..the old beggar who had made such a capital figure in the melo-drama of the preceding evening. **1854** EMERSON *Lett. & Soc. Aims, Immort.* Wks. (Bohn) III. 285 My idea of heaven is that there is no melodrama in it at all. **1891** J. LECKIE *Life & Relig.* 117 Open your eyes and look round you on the strange melodrama of life.

melodramatic (mɛləʊdrə'mætɪk), *a.* [f. MELODRAMA, after DRAMATIC.] Of or pertaining to melodrama; having the characteristics of melodrama. Often in depreciative sense: Characterized by sensationalism and spurious pathos.

1816 *Edin. Rev.* XXVII. 79 This siege abounded in melodramatic situations. **1831** TRELAWNY *Adv. Younger Son* III. 218 Her melo-dramatic fury augmented to such a pitch..that [etc.]. **1873** J. HANNAY in *Cornh. Mag.* Feb. 189 Sometimes his tragedy degenerates into the melodramatic. **1897** MARY KINGSLEY *W. Africa* 13 Whenever and however it may be seen, soft and dream-like in the sunshine, or melodramatic and bizarre in the moonlight, it is one of the most beautiful things the eye of man may see.

melodramatical (mɛləʊdrə'mætɪkəl), *a. rare.* [f. MELODRAMATIC *a.* + -AL[1].] = MELODRAMATIC.

1890 in *Century Dict.*

melodra'matically, *adv.* [Formed as prec. + -LY[2].] In a melodramatic manner.

1837 DICKENS *Pickw.* xiii, The Honourable Samuel Slumkey..melodramatically testified by gestures to the crowd, his ineffaceable obligations to the *Eatanswill Gazette.* **1873** 'ANNIE THOMAS' *Two Widows* I vii. 145 Whose manner had struck Gilbert as..melodramatically pretentious.

melodramaticism (mɛləʊdrə'mætɪsɪz(ə)m). [f. MELODRAMATIC *a.* + -ISM.] Preference for what is melodramatic.

1878 T. SINCLAIR *Mount* 152 Their high art is nerve stretching, a kind of spiritual melodramaticism.

melodramatics (mɛləʊdrə'mætɪks), *sb. pl.* [f. MELODRAMATIC *a.*] Melodramatic behaviour, action, or writing.

1915 *Nation* (N.Y.) 11 Feb. 161/2 We do not know when we have witnessed so disgusting a misuse of Federal authority, heightened as it was by the melodramatics with which Dr. Allen took the stand on his own behalf. **1929** J. C. POWYS *Meaning of Culture* 374 No tricky affectations or morbid self-consciousnesses, no melodramatics with regard to art or with regard to one's own originality. **1959** *Economist* 7 Feb. 493/1 The melodramatics of 'massive resistance'. **1959** *Times* 19 Oct. 6/7 Then it [*sc.* a film] falls back defeated, although the melodramatics are exciting enough. **1963** *Guardian* 18 Sept. 20/4 No melodramatics had followed Mr. Macmillan's receipt of the Denning report.

melodramatist (mɛləʊ'dræmətɪst). [f. MELODRAMA, after DRAMATIST.] A writer of melodramas.

1873 W. MATHEWS *Getting on in World* 27 Perils greater than any which the most daring romance writer or melodramatist ever imagined for his hero. **1883** *Contemp. Rev.* June 892 Shakespeare is..almost the first, and quite the greatest of English melodramatists.

melodramatize (mɛləʊ'dræmətaɪz), *v.* [f. MELODRAMA, after DRAMATIZE. Cf. F. *mélodramatiser* (Daudet 1876).] *trans.* To make melodramatic; also, to convert the story of (a novel) into a melodrama. Hence **melo'dramatized** *ppl. a.*

1820 *Examiner* No. 613. 25/2 Booth's appearance in a melo-dramatised *Richard the Third. Ibid.*, Elliston..melodramatised both *Richard the Third* and *Macbeth.* **1892** *Sat. Rev.* 29 Oct. 507/1 Webster melodramatizes and almost burlesques his theme by the introduction of physical terrors. **1900** *Academy* 21 July 54/1 His book was melo-dramatised very successfully for Mr. Benson.

melodrame ('mɛləʊdræm), *sb.* Now *rare* or *Obs.* Also **melodram.** [a. F. *mélodrame* (1781 in Hatz.-Darm.), f. Gr. *μέλο-ς* song, music + F. *drame* DRAMA. Cf. Sp. *melodrama*, It. *melodramma*, G. *melodram* (from Fr.).]

1. = MELODRAMA 1, 1 b.

1802 *Sk. Paris* II. lxx. 390 Melo drames and pieces connected with pantomime. **1803** in *Spirit Pub. Jrnls.* (1804) VII. 68 The Melo-drame, which was performed..upon the re-opening of this [the National] Theatre. **1814** *New Brit. Theat.* III. 255 (*Remarks on 'The Spaniards; an Heroic Drama'*) Had it [this piece] been condensed into three acts, and called a melo-dram, it might have, even in the opinion of the managers, served the interests of their concern [etc.]. **1815** HELEN M. WILLIAMS *Narr. Events France* xii. 254 Strangers seem to arrive in France, as they would go to a melo-drame, prepared for extraordinary events. **1818** LADY MORGAN *Autobiog.* (1859) 212 Shakspeare is supreme in melodrame, and he is its founder; and the melo-drame of Macbeth is finer than any modern exhibition which has followed it. **1825** *Gentl. Mag.* XCV. I. 362 The scenery, as usual in melo-drames, was very beautiful. **1835** J. P. KENNEDY *Horse Shoe R.* xxxiii. (1860) 372 It [the bugle] was displayed as ostentatiously as if worn by the hero of a melodrame. **1841** GEN. P. THOMPSON *Exerc.* (1842) VI. 186 Might not there be hope for the ministry, if it were to..send its adherents to make progresses by threes and fours throughout the country, to 'solemn music' as the melodrames have it.

2. *transf.* = MELODRAMA 2.

1817 LADY MORGAN *France* (1818) II. 346 To perform a subordinate part in this splendid melo-drame of the elements. **1822** BYRON *Vis. Judgem.* x, The torches, cloaks, and banners..Form'd a sepulchral melodrame. **1842** J. STERLING *Ess.*, etc. (1848) I. 430 The ostentatious emptiness of the charitable melodrame. **1845** *Q. Rev.* LXXV. 234 All this melodram of Mullaghmast was but a prelude to a design of unmixed gravity.

† **'melodrame**, *v. Obs. rare*[−1]. [f. the sb.] = MELODRAMATIZE *v.*

1836 *New Monthly Mag.* XLVII. 235 We have seldom read a novel more suited to be melodramed.

† **melodramic**, *a. Obs. rare.* [f. MELODRAME + -IC.] = MELODRAMATIC *a.*

1852 *Blackw. Mag.* LXXI. 374 The public appetite is not to be sated..with mere melodramic romance.

melody ('mɛlədɪ), *sb.* Also 4 **melodi, meloudie,** 4–6 **melodye,** 4–8 **melodie,** 6 **mellodie.** [a. OF. *melodie* (mod.F. *mélodie*), ad. late L. *melōdia*, a. Gr. *μελῳδία* singing, chanting, also 'a choral song, both words and air' (L. & Sc.), f. *μελῳδός* singing songs, musical, also as sb., lyric poet, f.

μέλ-ος song + *ᾠδ-* contracted form of *ἀοιδ-*, ablaut- var. of *ἀείδ-ειν* to sing (cf. *ἀοιδός* singer, *ἀοιδή*, *ᾠδή* song, ODE).

In Eccl. Latin *melodia* was applied to the singing of the sequences, 'proses', or rhythmical hymns, and was also used as a general term for a Gregorian 'mode'. The word also occurs frequently in med.L. with the sense 'sweet sound', 'music' (cf. the frequent glosses, *dulcis cantus*, OHG. *suozsanc*, etc.); it was prob. influenced in meaning by etymologizing associations with *mel*, honey. It is now used in all the Rom. and Teut. langs.: cf. Sp. *melodia*, Pg., It. *melodia*, G. *melodie* (poet. *melodei*), Du. *melodie, melodij*, Da., Sw. *melodi*.]

1. a. Sweet music, whether vocal or instrumental; beautiful arrangement of musical sounds; beauty of musical sounds, tunefulness.

c **1290** *St. Christopher* 18 in *S. Eng. Leg.* I. 271 Þe kyng louede muche Melodie of fieþle and of songue. *a* **1300** *Leg. Rood* (1871) 28 Wiþ gret melodie of is harpe. *a* **1300** *Cursor M.* 7431 Gleuand he sang be-for þe king, And gert him wit his melodi Fal on-slepe. *c* **1386** CHAUCER *Knt.'s T.* 2239 Thus with alle blisse and melodye Hath Palamon ywedded Emelye. *c* **1430** *Life St. Kath.* (1884) 17 She herde a merueylous melodye of swetnes which passed alle hertes to descriue. **1526** *Pilgr. Perf.* (W. de W. 1531) 7 b, They shall ..se dayly theyr holy & blessed conuersacyon, & here theyr songe & melody. *a* **1533** LD. BERNERS *Huon* lii. 175 It was grete melody to here it. **1588** SHAKS. *Tit. A.* II. iii. 12 The Birds chaunt melody on euery bush. **1590** —— *Mids. N.* II. ii. 13 Philomele with melodie, Sing in your sweet Lullaby. **1597** HOOKER *Eccl. Pol.* v. xxxviii. §2 Dauid..was..the author of adding vnto poetrie melodie in publique prayer, melodie both vocall and instrumentall for the raysing vp of mens harts. **1604** R. CAWDREY *Table Alph., Melody*, sweete sounding, or sweete musick. **1667** MILTON *P.L.* VIII. 528 The melodie of Birds. **1728-46** THOMSON *Spring* 576 Lend me your song, ye nightingales; oh pour The mazy-running soul of melody Into my varied verse. **1819** SHELLEY *Prometh. Unb.* II. v. 77 Whilst all the winds with melody are ringing. **1870** EMERSON *Soc. & Solit, Art* Wks. (Bohn) III. 19 We are like the musician on the lake, whose melody is sweeter than he knows.

b. Phrase. *to make melody*. Now *arch.*

a **1330** *Otuel* 631 Þe king took otuwel a non, & to his paleis made him gon, & makeden murthe & meloudie. *c* **1388** CHAUCER *Prol.* 9 Smale foweles maken melodye. *c* **1440** *York Myst.* xv. 83 Make myrthe and melody. **1525** LD. BERNERS *Froiss.* II. lxxxix. [lxxxv.] 264 They were ryght ioyous..and made grete chere and melody. **1535** COVERDALE *Eph.* v. 19 Synginge and makynge melody vnto the Lorde in youre hertes. *a* **1548** HALL *Chron., Hen. VI* 108 To tel you..what melody was made in Tavernes..it were a long woorke. **1778** FLETCHER *Lett.* Wks. 1795 VII 222 Attempting to make such melody as you know is commonly made in these parts.

c. *transf.* 'Musical' quality, beauty of sound in the arrangement of words, *esp.* in poetical composition.

1789 BELSHAM *Ess.* I. xii. 224 [The] exquisite beauties of which blank verse is susceptible..are majesty, melody, and variety. **1871** SWINBURNE *Ess. & Stud.* (1875) 304 In the verse of neither is there that instant and sensible melody which comes only of a secret and sovereign harmony of the whole nature.

†**2.** A song or other musical performance. *Obs.*

c **1290** *S. Eng. Leg.* I. 16/510 Al folk onourede al-so þe croiz..With offringues and with song and with opur melodies al-so. *c* **1400** MAUNDEV. (Roxb.) xxv. 116 Þe mynstrallez begynnez to do þaire melodys agayn. **1413** *Pilgr. Sowle* (Caxton) II. xlvi. (1859) 52 Yellyng with a carful melodye. **1530** PALSGR. 244/1 Melody played in a mornynge, *reueil*.

3. a. A series of single notes arranged in musically expressive succession; a tune: = AIR *sb.* 19.

1609 DOULAND *Ornithop. Microl.* 31 The Melodie of the Verses in the answeres off the first Tone. **1752** AVISON *Mus. Express.* 67 By a Diversity of Harmonies, the Chain and Progression of Melodies is also finely supported. **1792** THOMSON *Let. to Burns* Sept., I have..employed many leisure hours in selecting and collating the most favourite of our national melodies for publication. **1806** CALLCOTT *Mus. Gram.* II. i. 85 A particular succession of single sounds forms a melody or Tune. **1819** KEATS *Grecian Urn* ii, Heard melodies are sweet, but those unheard Are sweeter. **1860** TYNDALL *Glac.* I. iii. 24 My guide kept in advance of me singing a Tyrolese melody.

b. The principal part in a harmonized piece of music; = AIR *sb.* 20.

1880 W. S. ROCKSTRO in Grove *Dict. Mus.* I. 761/2 Arrangements [of metrical psalms] with the melody, as usual, in the Tenor..published at Leyden in 1633.

c. *transf.* Applied to poems written to be sung to particular melodies. Also (*nonce-use*), a melodious poem or passage, an instance of verbal melody.

1807 MOORE (*title*) Irish Melodies. **1814** BYRON (*title*) Hebrew Melodies. **1842** W. CARLETON *Irish Peasantry* (1843) I. Introd. 4 The touching and inimitable Melodies of my countryman Thomas Moore. **1872** LOWELL *Milton* Writ. 1890 IV. 96 There are..some exquisite melodies (like the 'Sabrina Fair') among his earlier poems.

d. Applied to pictorial combinations of colour thought to be analogous in mental effect to melodies.

1830 GALT *Lawrie T.* III. v. (1849) 100 The rising sun was beginning to silver the leaves,..a visible melody,..like the song of early birds. **1843** RUSKIN *Arrows of Chace* (1880) I. 23 [Turner's pictures] are studied melodies of exquisite colour. **1856** MCCOSH & DICKIE *Typical Forms* II. iii. 155 Colours are said to be in Melody when two contiguous tints ..run insensibly into each other.

4. That element of musical form which consists in the arrangement of single notes in expressive succession; contradistinguished from *harmony*.

1727-41 CHAMBERS *Cycl.*, Melody is the effect only of one single part, voice, or instrument. **1752** AVISON *Mus. Express.* Advt., Melody may be defined the Means or Method of ranging single musical Sounds in a regular Progression, either ascending or descending, according to the established Principles. **1782** BURNEY *Hist. Mus.* II. 155 Thus far Melody and Harmony..had been cultivated for the use of the church. **1880** C. H. H. PARRY in Grove *Dict. Mus.* II. 250 Melody is the general term which is vaguely used to denote successions of single notes which are musically effective.

†**5.** A pretended name for a company of harpers.

1486 *Bk. St. Albans* F vj b, A melody of Harpers.

6. *Comb.*

1876 STAINER & BARRETT *Dict. Mus. Terms, Melody Organ* or *Harmonium*, a harmonium so constructed that the upper note of the chords played is louder than the rest of the sounds. **1879** A. J. HIPKINS in Grove *Dict. Mus.* I. 667 The melody-attachment..has the effect of making the melody-note, or air, when in the highest part, predominate. **1934** S. R. NELSON *All about Jazz* i. 27 In his melody section, Whiteman had a complement of violins, 'cellos, saxophones, trumpets and trombones. *Ibid.* ii. 56 The more attractive section in the orchestra, in which we have the melody instruments. **1955** L. FEATHER *Encycl. Jazz* (1956) 64 The slide trombone was at first considered no less a rhythm than a melody instrument in jazz.

Hence **'melodyless** *a.*, without melody.

1832 *Examiner* 213/2 Music..passionless, melodyless, unrememberable.

melody ('mɛlədɪ), *v. rare.* [f. the sb. Cf. med.L. *melōdiāre*, OF. *melodier*.] *intr.* To make melody; to sing. Hence **'melodying** *vbl. sb.*

1596 FITZ-GEFFRAY *Sir F. Drake* (1881) 24 While with teares you sit melodying, Shee shall weepe with you, though she cannot sing. **1895** *Chamb. Jrnl.* XII. 748/2 He could hear something athwart the melodying which made him put his pipe away.

‖**meloe** ('mɛləʊiː). *Ent.* [mod.L. *Meloē* (see quot. 1650), of unknown origin; applied by Linnæus as a generic name.

Paracelsus *Op.* (1603) III. 220 has (in a prescription) a genitive *melloes*, which Mouffet interprets as identical with this word. Cf. MELOLONTHA.]

The typical genus of the family *Meloïdæ*; an insect of this genus, an oil-beetle.

[**1650** J. F. *Chym. Dict., Melaones* or *Meloes* are Beetles that fly, and are of a golden colour, and being rubbed make a sweet smell; they are commonly found in Meadows in the moneth of May.] **1658** ROWLAND tr. *Moufet's Theat. Ins.* II. xvii. 1080 Of the Gloworm, and the female Melo [orig. (1634) *De Cicindela, & Meloe Femina*]. *Ibid.*, The oyl Beetle or Meloe [orig. (1634) *Proscarabeum, sive Meloen*]. **1797** *Encycl. Brit.* (ed. 3) XI. 376 Larvæ, which pass through the state of chrysalids in order to attain to that of meloes. **1826** KIRBY & SP. *Entomol.* IV. 226 Acrid plants, which the *Meloe* likewise feeds upon.

melograph ('mɛləʊgrɑːf, -æ-). [mod. f. Gr. *μέλο-ς* song + -GRAPH.] An apparatus for automatically recording music played on the organ or pianoforte.

The name was first given to an invention of Euler in the 18th c. (see Grove *Dict. Mus.* I. 499); subsequently to an electrical contrivance invented by J. Carpentier in 1887.

1888 *Sci. Amer.* 15 Dec. 376/3.

melographic (mɛləʊ'græfɪk), *a.* [f. Gr. *μέλο-ς* song + -GRAPHIC.] (See quot.)

1863 *Jrnl. Soc. Arts* 16 Oct. 747/1 Electro-magnetic phonograph. This machine is capable of being attached to.. keyed musical instruments, by means of which they are rendered melographic, that is, capable of writing down any music that is played upon them.

meloid ('mɛlɔɪd), *sb.* and *a.* [ad. mod.L. *Meloïdæ*, f. *Meloē*: see MELOE.] **a.** *sb.* Any member of the family *Meloidæ* of parasitic insects. **b.** *adj.* Pertaining to the *Meloidæ*.

1878 RILEY in *Amer. Naturalist* XII. 218 A very interesting and anomalous Meloid (*Hornia minutipennis* Riley). *Ibid.* 290 What is known of the Larval Habits of other Meloid genera. **1881** *Cassell's Nat. Hist.* V. 339 Another parasitic Meloïd..infesting the cells of Mason Bees.

melologue ('mɛləʊlɒg). [f. Gr. *μέλο-ς* song + *λόγος* speech (see -LOGUE). Cf. F. *mélologue* (Berlioz 1832).] A musical composition, in which some of the verses are sung and others recited.

18.. MOORE *A Melologue upon National Music* Advt., It may not be superfluous to say, that by 'Melologue' I mean that mixture of recitation and music, which is frequently adopted in the performance of Collins's Ode on the Passions. **1881** SHEDLOCK in *Academy* 5 Nov. 354/2 Mr. Manns was..fully justified in giving the work at a concert as a 'melologue', for in this he only followed the example of Berlioz himself.

‖**melolontha** (mɛləʊ'lɒnθə). *Ent.* [mod.L. *mēlolontha*, ad. Gr. *μηλολόνθη* cockchafer.] A genus of lamellicorn beetles, typical of the family (or sub-family) *Melolonthidæ*, and including the common cockchafer, *M. vulgaris*. Hence **melo'lonthian** [+ -IAN], **melo'lonthidan** [+ -ID + -AN], **melolonthidian** [+ -ID + -IAN] *adjs.*, belonging to the (sub) family *Melolonthidæ*; also *sbs.*, a beetle of this (sub) family; **melolonthid** *a.*, pertaining to the *Melolonthidæ*; **melo'lonthine** *a.*, pertaining to the genus Melolontha. (In recent Dicts.)

1706 PHILLIPS, *Melolontha*, the Beetle or May-bug; an Insect. **1842** T. W. HARRIS *Insects injur. Veget.* (1862) 30 We have several Melolonthians whose injuries in the perfect and grub state approach to those of the European cock-chafer. **1900** *Ibis* Apr. 240 A single melolonthid beetle.

melomane ('mɛləʊmeɪn). [a. F. *mélomane*, f. Gr. *μέλος* song + *-μανής* mad: see -MANE.] = MELOMANIAC.

1890 in *Century Dict.*

melomania (mɛləʊ'meɪnɪə). [ad. F. *mélomanie*, f. Gr. *μέλο-ς* song, music + *μανία* madness: see -MANIA.] A mania for music. Hence **melo'maniac**, one who has a craze for music.

1880 VERN. LEE *Stud. Italy* III. ii. 115 The Florentine aristocracy had the fashionable melomania to almost as great an extent as the Milanese. **1880** *Pall Mall Budget* 3 Dec. 10/2 M. Grévy is a melomaniac. **1921** W. J. TURNER *Mus. & Life* 18 It seems characteristic of that bogus science rampant among us to call persons fond of music 'melomaniacs'. **1926** C. GRAY in Gray & Heseltine *Carlo Gesualdo* I. 46 This musical education and culture was by no means confined to the male sex... Lucrezia d'Este, afterwards Duchess of Urbino, was a veritable melomaniac. **1973** *Times Lit. Suppl.* 17 Aug. 955/5 A silent musical feast, this one, but a must for all connoisseurs and melomaniacs.

melomanic (mɛləʊ'mænɪk), *a. rare.* [Formed as MELOMANIA + -IC.] Characterized by melomania.

1822 *New Monthly Mag.* VI. 391 Volunteers of promising ability might, in the present melomanic times, be abundantly procured.

melomany. *rare*$^{-0}$. = MELOMANIA.

1890 in *Century Dict.*

melon[1] ('mɛlən). Forms: 4-6 **melone, -oun**, 6 **millian, milon, myl(l)on, milion, mylyon**, 6-7 **mellon, millon**, 7 **millen**, 6-8, 9 *dial.* **million**, 7 **mealon, meloune, milleon**, 5- **melon**. [a. F. *melon* = Sp. *melon*, Pg. *melão*, It. *melone*, ad. late L. *mēlōn-em, mēlo*, prob. a colloquial formation on the first element of L. *mēlopepo*: see MELOPEPON.]

1. a. A name common to several kinds of gourds, esp. the MUSK MELON, *Cucumis Melo*, and the WATER MELON, *Citrullus vulgaris*. (Applied both to the fruit and to the plant producing it.)

a **1387** *Sinon. Barthol.* (Anecd. Oxon.) 33/2 *Pepones*, melones. **1388** WYCLIF *Num.* xi. 5 Gourdis, and melouns [Vulg. *pepones*], and lekis,..comen in to mynde to vs. *c* **1400** *Lanfranc's Cirurg.* 190 Do þerto seed of melonis maad clene. *c* **1420** *Pallad. on Husb.* v. 94 Cucumber now is sowe; Melones, peletur, cappare, and leek. **1530** PALSGR. 245/1 Myllon a frute, *melon*. **1542** BOORDE *Dyetary* xxi. (1870) 285 Mylons doth ingender euyl humoures. **1563** HYLL *Art Garden.* (1593) 147 Melons, and all kindes of the Pompions, desire..the same earth and aire which the Citrones and Cucumbers doe. **1657** W. COLES *Adam in Eden* xcix, Citruls or Turkey Millions are of the same temperature as the Gourd. **1691** *Lond. Gaz.* No. 2724/2 A piece of pure Gold in form of a Mellon. **1748** CHESTERF. *Let.* 13 Dec. Misc. Wks. 1777 II. 347 Could you send me..some seed of the right canteloupe melons? **1824** LOUDON *Encycl. Gard.* III. I. (ed. 2) 4208 *The pumpkin, pumpion*, or more correctly, *pompion*... This is the melon or millon of our early horticulturists, the true melon being formerly distinguished by the name of musk-melon. **1847** TENNYSON *Princess* Conclus. 87 A raiser of huge melons and of pine. **1855** DELAMER *Kitch. Gard.* (1861) 118 A pretty little old-fashioned variety,—Queen Anne's Pocket Melon.. produces green-fleshed well-flavoured fruit, the size of a large orange.

b. *prickly melon*: the DURIAN.

1640 PARKINSON *Theat. Bot.* 1640 *Duriones*, the prickly fruitfull Melon. **1688** R. HOLME *Armoury* II. 83/1 The prickly Melon.

c. *to cut the melon*, to decide a question.

1911 H. QUICK *Yellowstone Nights* xii. 308 The O.M. as usual cuts the melon with a word.

d. Abundant profits to be shared among a number of people. Esp. in phr. *to cut the melon*. Hence **melon-cutting** *vbl. sb.*, in Stock Exchange and Betting slang, the dividing up or sharing of profits.

1908 *Daily Report* 24 Aug. 2/4 The theory that any prospective melon-cutting will be postponed until next year. **1909** *N.Y. Even. Post* (Semi-Weekly ed.) 7 Oct. 2 A purse of $25,000 will be distributed among employees. About 8,000 men will participate in the cutting of the melon. **1911** *Daily Colonist* (Victoria, B.C.) 11 Apr. 14/2 The Suez Canal..has been earning a gross revenue of upward of $20,000,000 a year, forming one of the juiciest melons every year anywhere in the world. **1927** C. A. & M. R. BEARD *Rise Amer. Civilization* II. xx. 203 All went well until The Credit Mobilier in 1868 'cut a melon' in the form of dividends composed of the stocks and bonds of the Union Pacific. **1927** *Sunday Express* 24 July 6/4 As the company distributed some Preference shares only a short while ago we should think it unlikely there will be any further melon-cutting yet. **1928** *Weekly Dispatch* 24 June 6/4 The Union Pacific's portfolio [of outside investments] is one of the biggest potential 'melons' on the American horizon. **1939** *New Statesman* 7 Jan. 7/1 The enemy could practically destroy our commerce and industry... Every nation of the world would have an incentive to have a free cut at the melon. **1941** DICE & EITEMAN *Stock Market* (ed. 2) 462 *Cutting a melon*,

the declaration of a large extra dividend. **1942** BERREY & VAN DEN BARK *Amer. Thes. Slang* §734/6 *Melon cutting*, the division of heavy winnings by a group of bettors. *Ibid.* §745/7 *Melon cutting*, the division of heavy winnings by a group of gamblers. **1948** *Aurora* (Illinois) *Beacon News* 7 Nov. (Suppl.) 39/2 This year, a record number of your friends and neighbors will split a record 'melon' in our 1948 savings clubs. **1964** P. WYCKOFF *Dict. Stock Market Terms* 163 *Melon*, slang expression referring to the sum total of extraordinary profits waiting to be divided.

e. = *melon pink* below.

1930 MAERZ & PAUL *Dict. Color* 199/1 Melon... *Melon Yellow.* **1975** *Harper's & Queen* June 172/3 Striped swimsuit... Cassis, citron, melon,.. chocolate.

2. *Conch.* The shell of a mollusc of the genus *Melo*. Also ***melon-shell, -volute*** (see 4 d).

1840 SWAINSON *Malacology* 67.

3. A hemispherical mass of blubber taken from the top of the head of certain cetaceans.

1887 G. B. GOODE, etc. *Fisheries U.S.* Sect. v. II. 299 About 30 gallons of oil.. being obtained from each fish, besides about 6 quarts of extra oil from the melon. The melons are taken from the top of the head [etc.].

4. *attrib.* and *Comb.* **a.** simple attributive, as ***melon-bank, -bed, -flower, -frame, -garden, -ground, -harvest, -infusion, -leaf, -merchant, -monger, -patch, -pit, -plant, -plot, -seed, -vine.*** **b.** parasynthetic, as ***melon-formed, -shaped*** adjs. **c.** similative, as ***melon-yellow*** adj. **d.** Special Comb.: **melon-beetle**, a beetle of the genus *Diabrotica*, esp. *D. vittata* and *D. duodecimpunctata*, injurious to melons (Webster 1897 and *Suppl.* 1902); **melon-blubber** = MELON[1] 3 (*Cent. Dict.*); **melon-cactus** = MELOCACTUS; **melon-caterpillar**, the larva of an American moth, *Phacellura* (*Eudioptis*) *hyalinata*, destructive to melons; † **melon-feast**, a rustic gathering at which prizes were offered for the finest melons; **melon-fruit**, the papaw, *Carica Papaya*, called also Tree-Melon (Bartlett *Dict. Amer.* 1859); **melon-hood**, a kind of fungus, *Hygrophorus pratensis*; **melon-oil**, the oil of the melon of a cetacean; **melon pink**, a yellowish-pink colour; † **melon-pompion** (*obs.*), **melon-pumpkin**, *Cucurbita maxima* or *C. Melopepo*; **melon-seed bodies** *Path.* (see quot. 1890); **melon-shell** = sense 2; **melon-thick** (*W. Indian*), **melon-thistle** = MELOCACTUS; **melon-tree**, the papaw (*Cassell's Encycl. Dict.* 1885); **melon-volute**, a melon-shell; **melon-ware** (see quot.); **melon-wood**, a yellow Mexican wood, which resembles sanders-wood, used for furniture (*Treas. Bot.* 1866); **melon-worm** = *melon-caterpillar* (*Cent. Dict.* 1890).

1707 MORTIMER *Husb.* (1721) II. 174 They thrive best.. in such places as they have not grown in before, especially on the sides of *Melon Banks. **1622** MABBE tr. *Aleman's Guzman d'Alf.* I. (1630) 25, I call my selfe his sonne,.. since that from that *Mellon-bed I was made legitimate by the holy right of Matrimony. **1794** MCPHAIL *Cult. Cucumber* 83 The seeds are sown some time about the middle of April in a cucumber or melon bed. **1857** A. GRAY *First Less. Bot.* (1866) 47 In *Melon-Cactuses.. with their globular or bulb-like shapes. **1885** *Riverside Nat. Hist.* (1888) II. 444 The *melon-caterpillar, *Eudioptis hyalinata*, which occurs throughout the greater portions of North America and South America. **1826** MISS MITFORD *Village* Ser. II. 4 Lending his willing aid in waiting and entertaining.. at pink-feasts and *melon-feasts. **1845** BROWNING *Home Thoughts*, The buttercups, the little children's dower—Far brighter than this gaudy *melon-flower! **1819** *Hermit in London* III. 170 Her *melon-formed head and double chin. **1793** *Trans. Soc. Arts* XI. 120 Over the whole, [I] placed a large *melon-frame. ? *a* **1642** KILLIGREW *Parson's Wedd.* v. i. (1663) 138 One of the Watermen is gone to the *Mellon Garden. **1733** MILLER *Gard. Dict.* (ed. 2), Melonry or *Melon-ground. **1774** *Heroic Epist. to Sir W. Chambers* (ed. 13) 9 From his melon-ground the peasant slave Has rudely rush'd. **1849** M. ARNOLD *Strayed Reveller* 24 Worms I' the unkind spring have gnaw'd Their *melon-harvest to the heart. **1887** HAY *Brit. Fungi* 99 *Hygrophorus pratensis*, the *Melon-hood. **1881** TYNDALL *Ess. Floating Matter Air* 173 The tubes in one of the chambers containing *melon-infusion had become rapidly turbid. **1868** BROWNING *Ring & Bk.* I. 98 A broad *melon-leaf. **1727** S. SWITZER *Pract. Gard.* II. vii. 55 Good glasses, without which the *melon-merchant can't effect his purpose. **1622** MABBE tr. *Aleman's Guzman d'Alf* II. 59, I am like a *Melon-mongers Knife cutting here a slice and there a slice. **1887** G. B. GOODE, etc. *Fisheries U.S.* Sect. v. II. 309 The *melon oil of the black-fish. **1838** GOSSE in E. Gosse *Life* (1890) 136 At length we reached the *melon-patch. **1949** *Dict. Colours for Interior Decoration* (Brit. Colour Council) III. 17/2 **Melon pink*,.. a descriptive colour name, from the fruit, used in the textile trade. **1975** *Country Life* 6 Mar. 561/2 Daylilies.. provide a show of yellows, melon pinks and apricots. **1824** LOUDON *Encycl. Gard.* III. I. (ed. 2) §2684 Knight's *melon-pit,.. which may also be applied to the culture of cucumbers. **1739** MILLER *Gard. Dict.* II. s.v. *Melo*, The Papers.. may be used for covering your *Melon-plants. **1577** B. GOOGE *Heresbach's Husb.* (1586) 63 When they grow rounde, they are *Melon-pompeons. **1840** PAXTON *Bot. Dict.*, **Melon-pumpkin* see *Cucurbita Melopepo*. *c* **1420** *Pallad. on Husb.* IV. 176 Now *melon seed too foote atwene is sette. **1879** *St. George's Hosp. Rep.* IX. 261 An incision was made into the ..tumour,.. and a quantity of clear fluid containing numbers of 'melon-seed' bodies pressed out. **1890** *Syd. Soc. Lex.*, *Melon seed bodies*, small, white, or brownish-looking bodies resembling melon seeds in shape. They are found in the sheaths of tendons which have been inflamed and in adventitious.. bursæ. **1832** LINDLEY *Introd. Bot.* 374 *Melon-shaped, irregularly spherical, with projecting ribs; as the stem of Cactus melocactus: a bad term. **1840** SWAINSON *Malacology* 100 The pre-eminently typical volutes, or *melon-shells. **1864** GRISEBACH *Flora W. Ind.* 785 *Melon-thick, *Melocactus communis*. **1731-3** MILLER *Gard. Dict.* (ed. 2), *Melocactus*.. *Melon-Thistle. The whole Plant hath a singular Appearance. **1763** MILLS *Syst. Pract. Husb.* IV. 182 The *melon vines will waste themselves by running out in length. **1840** SWAINSON *Malacology* 99 The truncated and wide-mouthed helmet-shells, among the *Muricidæ*, find their prototypes in the *melon volutes. **1883** SOLON *Art O. Eng. Potter* 101 The pieces upon which this fruit was introduced all went by the name of *melon-ware, and so were styled also the generality of pieces mottled green and yellow. **1773** *Phil. Trans.* LXIII. 391 An Anemone, whose limbs are of the *melon-yellow colour.

‖ **melon**[2] ('miːlɒn). *Path.* [= F. *melon*, a. Gr. μῆλον apple, protuberance of the eye (Paulus Ægineta).] A kind of exophthalmus or staphyloma.

1676 J. COOKE *Marrow Chirurg.* 713 If the protuberance be.. great, 'tis called *Staphyloma*... If it thrust out more, that it over-reaches the Eye-lid, 'tis called *Melon*, like an Apple hanging by the Stalk. **1802** TURTON *Med. Gloss.*, *Melon*.. a protuberance of the ball of the eye from its socket. **1890** in *Syd. Soc. Lex.*

melon[3] ('mɛlən). *Australian.* Short for PADDYMELON. Also *attrib.*, in ***melon-hole***.

1847 LEICHHARDT *Jrnl.* iii. 77 The shallow depressions of the surface of the ground, which are significantly termed by the squatters 'melon-holes'. **1898** MORRIS *Austral Eng.*, *Melon*. Besides its botanical use, the word is applied in Australia to a small kangaroo, the *Paddy-melon*. *Melon-hole*, a kind of honey-combing of the surface in the interior plains, dangerous to horsemen, ascribed to the work of the Paddy-melon... The name is often given to any similar series of holes, such as are sometimes produced by the growing of certain plants.

melon, variant of MELLONE *Chem.*

melongena (mɛlən'dʒiːnə). Also 8 **melinzane**, 9 **melangeno**. [a. mod.L. *melongēna*, It. *melanzana*: for the history of the word see BRINJAL.] The mad-apple or egg-plant, *Solanum Melongena*.

1775 R. CHANDLER *Trav. Asia M.* (1825) I. 341 The garden furnished.. a species of fruit called melinzane. **1785** MARTYN *Rousseau's Bot.* xvi. (1794) 202 Melongena or Mad-Apple, is also of this genus. **1819** *Banquet* 91 From Iceland lichens, and St. Kitt's tomato; From Cuba melangeno and potato.

melongene ('mɛləndʒiːn). [ad. F. *mélongène* aubergine.] A West Indian name for the aubergine, *Solanum melongena*, or its fruit; = MELONGENA.

1939 *Nature* 29 July 178/1 The very general use to which the [Trinidad Low Temperature Research] Station could be put was recognized.. and.. work was.. extended to tomatoes, limes,.. melongenes, cucurbits of various kinds, and to the assortment of vegetables that can be grown in the tropics. **1952** S. SELVON *Brighter Sun* ii. 37 Lettuce taking good... But ochro and melongene would take good. **1969** G. SIMS *Sand Dollar* iv. 50 We might.. fry some jacks and melongene, that's a kind of egg-plant. **1973** *Express* Trinidad & Tobago) 26 June 3/6 Outside of the same building melongene is offered at 20 cents a pound.

melon-hole: see MELON[3].

‖ **meloniere**. *Obs.* [F. *melonnière*, f. *melon* MELON[1].] A melonry.

1658 EVELYN *Fr. Gard.* (1675) 138 Heaped up together in some place near your meloniere. **1718** J. LAWRENCE *Fruit-g. Kalendar* 60 To see what his Servants have been doing in other Parts of the Kitchen-Garden, Meloniere, &c.

meloniform (mɪ'lɒnɪfɔːm), *a. Bot.* [ad. mod.L. type **mēlōniform-is*, f. *mēlōn-*, *mēlo*, MELON[1] + *form-a*: see -FORM.] Melon-shaped.

1866 *Treas. Bot.*, *Melon-shaped*, *Meloniform*, irregularly spherical, with projecting ribs.

melonist ('mɛlənɪst). [f. MELON[1] + -IST.] One who cultivates melons.

1669 *Phil. Trans.* IV. 901 Concerning his way of ordering Melons; now communicated in English for the satisfaction of several curious Melonists in England. **1727** S. SWITZER *Pract. Gard.* II. vi. 49 At their first coming into England, there were but two kinds that our melonists.. took notice of.

melonite ('mɛlənaɪt). *Min.* [Named by F. A. Genth in 1868 after the Melonese mine, Calaveras Co., Cal., its locality.] Nickel telluride, of a reddish-white colour.

1868 GENTH in *Amer. Jrnl. Sci.* Ser. II. XLV. 313 Melonite, a new mineral, $Ni_2 Te_3$?, hexagonal.

melonry ('mɛlənrɪ). [f. MELON[1] + -RY.] A place for the cultivation of melons.

1727 S. SWITZER (*title*) Practical Kitchen Gardiner, or System for Employment in the Melonry, Kitchen Garden, and Potagery. **1824** LOUDON *Encycl. Gard.* (ed. 2) §2479 The situation of the melonry is generally in the slip.

† **me'lopepon**. *Obs.* [ad. L. *mēlopepon-em*, *-pepo*, a. Gr. μηλοπέπων, f. μῆλο-ν apple + πέπων a kind of gourd (orig. an ellipt. use of πέπων ripe).

In the quots. *melopepones* may be the Latin plural.]

A kind of melon.

1555 EDEN *Decades* 81 An other frute.. in tendernes equal to melopepones. **1705** BEVERLEY *Hist. Virginia* iv. (1722) 124 Their Macocks are a sort of Melopepones, or lesser sort of Pompion. **1727** BAILEY vol. II, Melopepon.

melophone ('mɛləʊfəʊn). [f. Gr. μέλο-ς song, music + φωνή sound.] **a.** = *melophonic guitar*. **b.** A kind of accordion.

1859 WRAXALL tr. *R. Houdin* xii. 169 The melophone, a species of accordion recently invented. **1879** A. J. HIPKINS in Grove *Dict. Mus.* I. 667 The only maker of melophones in 1855. **1883** *Ibid.* III 97 Regondi.. on the former of these tours [in 1841].. played both the guitar and the melophone (whatever that may have been).

melophonic (mɛləʊ'fɒnɪk), *a.* [Formed as prec. + -IC.] **a.** In ***melophonic guitar*** (see quot. 1842). **b.** Used, app. with the sense 'musical', in the title of a society founded in 1837 (see quot. 1880).

1842 *Mech. Mag.* XXXVII. 160 The Melophonic Guitar, is the very appropriate name of a new instrument which was introduced to the musical public, a few days ago, by the inventor, M. Barelli. **1880** MACKESON in Grove *Dict. Mus.* II. 252 The Melophonic Society, established 1837, 'for the practice of the most classical specimens of choral and other music,' by band and choir.

melophonist ('mɛləʊfəʊnɪst). *rare*[−1]. [Formed as prec. + -IST.] A melodist.

1847 THACKERAY *Dinner in the City* iii. Wks. 1898 VI. 560 Here, as in the case of the Hebrew melophonists, I would insinuate no wrong thought.

melopiano (mɛləʊpɪ'ænəʊ). [f. Gr. μέλο-ς song, melody + PIANO.] (See quots.)

1876 STAINER & BARRETT *Dict. Mus. Terms*, *Melopiano*, an invention by which sustained sounds can be produced on a pianoforte. **1880** A. J. HIPKINS in Grove *Dict. Mus.* II. 252 *Melopiano*, a grand piano with a *sostinente* attachment, the invention of Signor Caldera.

meloplast ('mɛləʊplæst). [a. F. *méloplaste*, f. Gr. μέλο-ς song, music + πλαστής moulder, f. πλάσσειν to mould.] (See quot.)

1820 *Ann. Reg.* II. 1365 M. Galin.. has lately introduced a new instrument for teaching music, called the *meloplast*. M. Galin's ingenious method consists in making his pupils sing from a stave, without either clefs or notes, according to the movements of a portable rod.

meloplasty ('mɛləʊplæstɪ). *Surg.* [f. Gr. μῆλο-ν apple, in late Gr. used poet. for 'cheek' (perh. through influence of the L. *māla*) + -πλαστος moulded + -Y.] The operation of restoring a cheek which has been injured or destroyed by grafting new tissue. Hence **melo'plastic**, of or pertaining to meloplasty (Dunglison *Med. Lex.* 1857).

1883 HOLMES & HULKE *Syst. Surg.* (ed. 3) III. 681 Plastic Operations on the Cheek (Meloplasty).

‖ **melopœïa** (mɛləʊ'piːɪə). *Antiq.* [a. Gr. μελοποιία, f. μελοποιός maker of songs, f. μέλο-ς song + ποι-, ποιεῖν to make.] The art of composing melodies; the part of dramatic art concerned with music.

1759 SIR F. H. E. STILES in *Phil. Trans.* LI. 698 By this school harmonic was divided into these seven parts; 1. of sounds.. 7. of melopœïa. **1776** BURNEY *Hist. Mus.* I. v. 65 Of Melopœia. **1878** *N. Amer. Rev.* CXXVI. 51 This part of a drama, called the *melopœia*, is ranged by Aristotle on a level with the diction.

melopœic (mɛləʊ'piːɪk), *a.* [f. MELOPŒ(IA + -IC.] Of, pertaining to, or characterized by melopœia.

1927 *Contemp. Rev.* July 73 Wagner.. turned to the melopœic chant, dramatised but not lyricised, for the expression of the words. **1940** *Burlington Mag.* Oct. 109/2 This melopoeic pattern is the chief beauty of Augustan verse.

melos ('mɛlɒs, 'miːlɒs). *Mus.* [a. Gr. μέλος song, tune.] Song, melody; *spec.* the succession of tones considered apart from rhythm; an uninterrupted flow of melody.

1740 J. GRASSINEAU *Mus. Dict.* 129 *Melos*, is no more than a song or piece of melody. **1811** BUSBY *Dict. Mus.* (ed. 3), *Melos*, a term applied by the ancients to the sweetness of any melody; or to that quality or character by which a melody was rendered agreeable. **1876** STAINER & BARRETT *Dict. Mus. Terms* 286/2 Melos... A succession of musical sounds as opposed to *noises*. A tune. A song. **1887** E. DANNREUTHER tr. *Wagner's On Conducting* 18 He [*sc.* a conductor] found the right tempo whilst persistently fixing the attention of his orchestra upon the *melos* of the symphony. The right comprehension of the *melos* is the sole guide to the right tempo. **1903** A. W. PATTERSON *Schumann* 205 The tasteful *melos* or *arioso* which, throughout, takes the place of recitative. **1947** *Penguin Music Mag.* II. 13 The 'melos' by which he [*sc.* Wagner] means the unifying thread of line that gives a work its form and shape. **1963** *Times* 5 June 15/4 Size and melos and purposeful rhythm are the chief characteristics of Professor Josef Krips's Beethoven readings. **1964** C. HOWELL tr. *Gélineau's Voices & Instruments Christian Worship* i. 20 By means of melos he lets the words take on the colors of the prism of sentiments which illuminates them.

† **melote**. *Obs.* Also 6 **melotte**. [ad. L. *mēlōta*, *mēlōtē*, a. Gr. μηλωτή sheepskin.] A garment made of skins, worn by monks.

1491 CAXTON *Vitas Patr.* (W. de W. 1495) I. xxxvi. 37 b/2 Nexte his flesshe he ware the hayre; and ther upon a vestement of hayre namyd Melote. *Ibid.* II. 196 b/2 He asked

of them where theyr melotes were; that is to saye theyr habytes made of skynnes that they were wont to be clothed withall. *a* **1529** SKELTON *Col. Cloute* 866 Some walke aboute in melottes [cf. Vulg. Hebr. xi. 37 *circuierunt in melotis*], In gray russet and heery cotes.

melo-'tragedy. *rare.* [f. Gr. μέλο-ς song + TRAGEDY.] A tragedy in which songs occur; an operatic tragedy.

Alfieri called his play of *Abel* a 'tramelogedia', inserting *melo-* in the middle of *tragedia*, to express the intimate mixture of the lyric and dramatic element in the piece.

1818 HOBHOUSE *Hist. Illustr. Ch. Har.* etc. (ed. 2) 402 He [Alfieri] composed a sort of drama, altogether new, which he called a melo-tragedy. **1905** *Westm. Gaz.* 7 Mar. 2/3 Michael Faraday, according to tradition, would leave his investigations at the sound of the pan-pipes and see the melo-tragedy [Punch and Judy] once more.

Hence **melo'tragic** *a.*

1872 C. KING *Mountain. Sierra Nev.* ix. 193 Nothing more effectually banishes a melotragic state of mind, than the obtrusive ugliness.. of this plant.

melotrope ('mɛləʊtrəʊp). [f. Gr. μέλο-ς song, melody + τροπή turning.] A piano fitted with a mechanical device for automatically reproducing a piece of music by means of a melograph stencil.

1888 *Sci. American* 15 Dec. 376/3 The melotrope is merely mechanical in its operation, and is intended, as far as possible, to imitate the motion of the fingers in playing upon the keys of the instrument.

melotto, meloun(e, obs. ff. MULATTO, MELON.

melow(e, melowe, obs. ff. MEAL *sb.*[1], MELLOW *a.*

†**mel-pell,** *adv. Obs.* [a. OF. *melle pelle*, inversion of *pelle-melle*] = PELL-MELL.

a **1600** HOOKER *Eccl. Pol.* VIII. ix. §5 Theodosius.. slew mel-pell both guilty and innocent, to the number of 7000.

†**mel'pomenish,** *a. Obs.* [f. *Melpomenē*, the Muse who presided over tragedy + -ISH.] Tragic.

1801 SURR *Splendid Misery* II. 170 Why so melpomonish, Julia?

†**melrose.** *Obs.* [ad. pharmaceut. L. *mel rosæ* honey of the rose.] A preparation composed of powdered rose-leaves with honey and alcohol.

1790 FORDYCE *On Muriatic Acid* 8 What I used was a mixture of mel-rose with sixteen drops of the muriatic acid.

melsh, melch (mɛlʃ), *a.* Now *dial.* Also 4 **melsch,** 5 **melissche.** [Perh. repr. OE. *męlsc*, *mylsc*, **mielisc* mellow (in *melsc æppla*, mellow apples), ?cogn. w. Goth. *(ga)malwjan* to crush. The OE. word seems to have been confused with *milisc* honeyed, cogn. w. Goth. *miliþ* honey. Cf. MULSH.] Mellow, soft, tender. Of weather: Mild and 'soft'.

1398 TREVISA *Barth. De P.R.* XVII. cxvi. (1495) 679 In grounde that is melch and sondy [*MS. Bodl. E. Mus.* melissche, L. *in terra leni sabulosa*]. **1737** J. BROADHEAD in *N. & Q.* 8th Ser. (1895) VII. 405/1 Very fine melch weather. **1874** E. WAUGH *Chimney Corner* (1879) 113 Nice melch mak o' a mornin'.

Comb. **1647** TRAPP *Comm. Tit.* i. 13 A metaphor from Chyrurgeons, who must not be melch-hearted, saith Celsus, but pare away the dead flesh. **1782** ELIZ. BLOWER *Geo. Bateman* II. 111 'Dad', (said the glassman.. pulling out his pocket-handkerchief) 'I didn't used to be so melch-hearted.'

Hence †**melshhead, -hood,** ripeness.

a **1325** *Prose Psalter* cxviii. [cxix.] 147 Ich com forþe in melshede [*v.r.* melschhode, Vulg. *præveni in maturitate*].

†**melt,** *sb.*[1] *Obs.* [Fr., a. Mexican *metl.*] = MAGUEY.

1598 SYLVESTER *Du Bartas* II. i. I. *Eden* 606 There mounts the Melt [Fr. *Là se pousse le Melt*] which serves in Mexico For weapon, wood, needle, and thread (to sowe).

†**melt,** *sb.*[2] *Obs.* (See quot.)

1688 R. HOLME *Armoury* II. 177/1 Melt of Sheep, an abundance of Blood which must be taken from them.

melt (mɛlt), *sb.*[3] [f. MELT *v.*[1]]

1. Phr. *on the melt*: in the process of melting.

1897 BLACKMORE in *Blackw. Mag.* Sept. 362 The rush of two streams into one another, both being buxom with snow on the melt.

2. Metal or other substance in a melted condition. Also *fig.*

1854 *Pharmac. Jrnl.* XIII. 432 The 'melt' obtained in the manufacture of Ferrocyanide of Potassium. **1868** WHITMAN *To Working Men* 6 Iron works.. men around feeling the melt with huge crowbars. **1886** E. KNECHT tr. *Benedikt's Coal-tar Colours* 216 Melting with caustic acid... The melt is then allowed to cool. **1962** SIMPSON & RICHARDS *Physical Princ. Junction Transistors* iii. 39 A small single crystal, known as the seed crystal, is inserted in the melt and withdrawn slowly in the vertical direction... A large single crystal having the same orientation as the seed is thus formed. **1966** *New Statesman* 22 Apr. 591/2 Pan American has now chucked a large, expected crystal into the melt by ordering 25 jumbo-jets from Boeing. **1971** *Nature* 8 Jan. 80/3 In the Vale of York, the most densely populated area liable to flooding discussed in the report, the chief culprits are snow melt.. and violent thunderstorms. **1971** I. G. GASS et al. *Understanding Earth* i. 17/1 The composition of the olivine formed by crystallization from a silicate melt is of course a function of the availability of the two elements.

3. A quantity of metal melted at one operation.

1886 *Rep. Sec. of Treasury* 175 (Cent.) 12,867 melts of ingots were made for coinage during the year. **1890** HIORNS *Mixed Metals* 309 The 75,000 ounces of gold were divided into 14 'melts' of 5,400 ounces each, and each melt separately toughened. **1904** *Internat. Libr. Technol., Specif.* 61 *Melt*, a charge of metal placed in a cupola or pot for melting. The product of such a charge is also called a melt.

4. The quantity melted within a certain period.

1903 *Daily Rec. & Mail* 28 Dec. 2/3 The melt of this class of iron, especially in Scotland, has been exceptionally heavy.

5. Special Comb.: **melt spinning,** the process of extruding a substance (esp. a polymer) which has been softened by heat through a spinneret so as to form a fibre; hence (as back-formations) **melt-spin** *v. trans.*, **melt-spun** *ppl. a.*; **melt-water** *Geol.*, water resulting from the melting of ice or snow, esp. that of a glacier.

1950 R. W. MONCRIEFF *Artificial Fibres* xvii. 197 Nylon is *melt spun. **1973** *Materials & Technol.* VI. iv. 325 The molten polymer produced is melt-spun directly. **1939** W. W. TRIGGS *Brit. Pat. 528,455* 27 Apr., In *melt spinning, the spinneret is generally placed so that the filaments fall vertically from the spinneret. **1963** A. J. HALL *Textile Sci.* ii. 75 With the introduction of nylon an entirely new method of fibre-spinning was established—so-called melt-spinning in which the polymer.. is melted in a novel device above the spinneret so that it can by means of a pump be extruded through the multi-holed spinneret into cold air to ensure the immediate solidification of the issuing fluid streams into filaments. **1973** *Materials & Technol.* VI. iv. 297 Melt spinning is used for the majority of thermoplastic man-made fibre-forming materials. **1948** SCHMIDT & MARLIES *Princ. High-Polymer Theory & Pract.* viii. 340 Nylon, polyvinylidene-vinyl chloride (e.g. saran), and Fiberglas are commercially important examples of *melt-spun fibers. **1962** *Economist* 20 Jan. 241/1 Part of the industry where there was overlapping of effort, namely the melt-spun fibre field. **1934** *Geogr. Jrnl.* LXXXIII. 79 The amount of *melt-water is so great that temporary rivers and lakes form. **1970** *Nature* 24 Oct. 352/1 Because most of the volcano is covered by glaciers, a great deal of melt-water has caused floods. **1973** C. BONINGTON *Next Horizon* x. 144 The face of the Pillar was sheer, clean and dry, but the slabby flanks were dotted with snow patches and running with melt water.

melt (mɛlt), *v.*[1] *Pa. t.* **melted.** *Pa. pple.* **melted, molten.** Forms: 1 **melt-, mielt-, milt-, myltan,** 2–3 **mealten, melten,** 3 **i-multen,** *Orm.* **melltenn,** 3–6 **melte,** 4 **meelte,** 4–5 **malt(e,** 4–6 **mylt(e,** (5 **molte, multe,** 6 **mealt, moult),** 4– **melt.** *Pa. t.* 1 **mealt** (*pl.* **multon**), **(ȝe)melte,** 3–5 **malt(e,** 4 **meltit, moltid,** 5 **meltid,** 5–6 **molte,** 6 **moulte, molted,** 6– **melted.** *Pa. pple.* 1 **ȝemolten, ȝemylted,** 3 **imealt, imelte, imolte,** 4 **meltid(e, meltyn, moltid, multen, mylt,** 4–5 **moltyn(e,** 4–6 **molte,** 5 **molton, moltynnyd, multyn,** 5–7 **melt,** 6 **melten, molted,** *arch.* **ymolt,** 5–7 **molt, moult,** 7 **moulten,** 8 *arch.* **ymolten,** 4– **molten,** 6– **melted.** [Originally two distinct vbs.: (1) the intransitive strong vb. OE. *meltan* (pa. t. *mealt*, pl. *multon*, pa. ppl. *ȝemolten*); (2) the weak vb. (causative of the former) OE. *mieltan*, *myltan* (:—prehistoric **mealtjan*, **maltjan*) corresponding to ON. *melta* to digest, to malt (grain), Goth. **maltjan* to dissolve, whence *gamalteins* vbl. sb., dissolution (transl. of ἀνάλυσις 2 Tim. iv. 6). In OE. the strong vb. was always intransitive; the weak vb. was normally transitive, but sometimes intransitive. In ME. the strong and weak inflexions were used indiscriminately, the former becoming gradually less frequent. In the 16th c. the strong pa. t. (in the form *molte*, from the analogy of the pa. pple.) was used *poet.* by a few writers, but was not generally current. The strong pa. pple. is now only poet. and rhetorical exc. as adj. (see MOLTEN *ppl. a.*), and even in that use is merely literary.

The root OTeut. **melt-* (: *malt-*: *mult-*), whence also MALT *sb.*[1], represents an Indogerm. **meld-* (: *mold-*: *mld-*), whence Gr. μέλδειν to melt, Skr. *mṛdu* soft, L. *mollis.* It is prob. a variant of OTeut. *smelt-* (: Indogerm. **smeld-*): see SMELT *v.*]

I. Intransitive senses.

1. a. To become liquefied by heat. *to melt away*: be destroyed or wasted by being melted.

Beowulf 3011 Ne scel anes hwæt meltan mid þam modiȝan. *a* **900** *O.E. Martyrol.* 9 Mar. 38 Þa on niht com leoht of heofonum swa hat swa sunne bið on sumera, ond þæt is ȝemelte, ond þæt wæter wearð wearm. *c* **1000** *Ags. Ps.* (Th.) lvii. 7 Swa weax melteð. *a* **1225** *Juliana* 20 His mod feng to heaten ant his meari to melten [*Bodl. MS.* mealten]. *c* **1290** *St. Christopher* 200 in *S. Eng. Leg.* I. 277 Þo he was i-leid þar-on, As wex þat gredile malt awei. **1382** WYCLIF *Exod.* xvi. 21 Whanne the sunne bigan to heet, it moltid [**1530** TINDALE, it moulte]. **1387** TREVISA *Higden* (Rolls) VII. 355 Whanne þat frost gan to þawe and to melte [*v.rr.* multe, molte, mylte]. *c* **1450** *Two Cookery-bks.* 86 Take faire grece.. and sette ouer þe fyre til hit mylte. *c* **1460** *Launfal* 740 Hyt malt as snow ayens the sunne. **1575** GASCOIGNE *Fruits of Warre*, xlviii, *Flowers* 123 Whose greace hath molt all caffed as it was. **1617** MORYSON *Itin.* I. 206 When the snow melts from the Mountaines. **1753** CHAMBERS *Cycl. Supp.* s.v. *Metals*, When the copper and arsenic are mixed, the tin is to be put in; this soon melts. **1860** TYNDALL *Glac.* II. iii. 241 Ice before it melts attains a temperature of 30° Fahr.

b. In jocular hyperbole: To perspire excessively, to suffer extreme heat.

1787 COLMAN *Inkle & Yarico* III. i, A.. black boar.. came down the hill in a jog trot! My master melted as fast as a pot of pomatum. **1820** KEATS *Lett., to Miss F. Brawne* Mar. (1895) 476, I have no need of an enchanted wax figure to duplicate me, for I am melting in my proper person before the fire.

2. a. To become disintegrated, liquefied, or softened, e.g. by the agency of moisture; to be dissolved. *to melt in the mouth*: said of articles of food that are extremely tender. †In OE. of food: To be digested.

a **1000** *Voc.* in Wr.-Wülcker 235/33 *Fatiscit,.. dissoluitur,* ..mylt. *c* **1000** *Sax. Leechd.* II. 196 Late mylt hryþeres flæsc. **1523** FITZHERB. *Husb.* §16 The clottes kepe the wheate warme all wynter, and at Marche they wyll melte and breake, and fal in manye small peces. **1693** EVELYN *De La Quint. Compl. Gard., Melons* I [Melons] which be.. dry, yet melting in the Mouth. **1852** MRS. STOWE *Uncle Tom's C.* iv. 19 Can she make your real flecky paste, as melts in your mouth and lies all up like a puff?

†**b.** Of the body: To undergo corruption, to waste *away. Obs.*

c **1290** *S. Eng. Leg.* I. 76/198 A slouȝ feuere.. made is bodi to melte a-wei. **1398** TREVISA *Barth. De P.R.* VII. lxvi. (1495) 283 He that is bytten of a Cokatryce meltyth and swellyth and castyth venym and deyeth sodaynly.

c. Of clouds, vapour: To dissolve, be evaporated or dispersed; to break or dissolve *into* rain.

13.. *Gaw. & Gr. Knt.* 2080 Mist muged on þe mor, malt on þe mountez. **1604** E. G[RIMSTONE] *D'Acosta's Hist. Indies* II. vii. 98 A great aboundance of vapours from the Earth and Ocean.. melt into water. **1814** BYRON *Lara* II. i, The vapours round the mountains curl'd Melt into morn, and Light awakes the world. **1860** TYNDALL *Glac.* I. xiv. 96 The dense clouds which had crammed the gorge.. melted away. **1873** BLACK *Pr. Thule* xxiv, The clouds had melted into a small and chilling rain.

d. To vanish, disappear. Also const. *away.*

1611 SHAKS. *Wint. T.* III. iii. 37 With shriekes She melted into Ayre. **1611** —— *Cymb.* I. iii. 20, I would haue.. followed him, till he had melted from The smalnesse of a Gnat, to ayre. **1852** MRS. STOWE *Uncle Tom's C.* xiv. 123 When caught, she melted from them again like a summer cloud. **1934** A. THIRKELL *Wild Strawberries* vi. 118 David.. melted from the room. **1957** C. MACINNES *City of Spades* I. viii. 58, I could see no sign of Hamilton, and hoped he'd melted. **1959** M. DOLINSKY *There is no Silence* iv. 61 What friends?.. They melted with the first headline. **1970** 'D. HALLIDAY' *Dolly & Cookie Bird* vii. 72 People had started to melt, walking fast round the side of the house. **1975** P. SOMERVILLE-LARGE *Couch of Earth* iii. 48 Otway came bursting out... The girl melted away immediately.

3. Of a person, his 'soul' or 'heart', feelings, etc.

†**a.** To be overwhelmed with dismay or grief.

The idiom is app. native, though the examples in the versions of the Bible are literal translations from the Hebrew.

c **1000** *Ags. Ps.* (Th.) lxx. 8 Þonne me mæȝen and mod mylte on hreðre, ne forlæt þu me, lifiende God. *c* **1350** *Will. Palerne* 434, & seþþe sike i & sing samen to-gedere, & melt neiȝh for mournying & moche ioie make. ? *a* **1366** CHAUCER *Rom. Rose* 276 She is in so greet turment.. whan folk doth good, That nigh she melteth for pure wood. *c* **1375** *Sc. Leg. Saints* xxxviii. (*Adrian*) 470 þat his hart for dred suld melt. **1546** J. HEYWOOD *Prov.* (1867) 75 My herte for wo molte. **1560** BIBLE (Genev.) *Ps.* cxix. 28 My soule melteth [1535 COVERDALE, melteth away] for heauines. **1611** BIBLE *Josh.* ii. 11 Our hearts did melt.

b. To become softened by compassion, or love; to yield to entreaty; to 'dissolve' *in* or *into* tears.

c **1200** *Vices & Virtues* 145 Þat hie mihte nexxin and mealten and ut-sanden sume tear. *a* **1225** *Ancr. R.* 110 Þet on was his moderes wop, & þe oðres Maries, þæt fleoweden & melten al of teares. **13..** *Cristene-mon & Jew* 97 (Vern. MS.) Þe cristen mon mildely gon malt. *c* **1374** CHAUCER *Troylus* IV. 339 (367) Troylus, þat felte His frend Pandare y-comen hym to se Gan as þe snow a-yen þe sonne melte. **1509** HAWES *Past. Pleas.* xvi. (Percy Soc.) 71 Harde is the heart that no love hath felt Nor for to love wyl than encline and melt. **1563** SACKVILLE *Induct.* lxxviii. in *Mirr. Mag.* R iv b, My hart so molte to see his griefe so great. **1590** SPENSER *F.Q.* I. ii. 22 Melting in teares, then gan shee thus lament. **1595** SHAKS. *John* V. ii. 47 My heart hath melted at a Ladies teares. **1637** MILTON *Lycidas* 163 Look homeward Angel now, and melt with ruth. **1647** SPRIGGE *Anglia Rediv.* II. ii. (1854) 80 And the governor so far melted as to send forth Tom Elliot in haste. **1709** STEELE *Tatler* No. 104 ¶7 She melted into a Flood of Tears. **1857** READE *Course True Love* 178 His resolve melted at this. **1862** CARLYLE *Fredk. Gt.* XIV. viii. (1872) V. 249 Each had his own causes of regret, and each melted into tears. **1888** BURGON *Lives 12 Gd. Men* I. III. 341 At sight of the dusty.. urchins, his heart evidently melted.

c. *to melt away*: To be 'dissolved' in ecstasy.

1711 ADDISON *Spect.* No. 159 ¶2 (*Vis. Mirza*), My Heart melted away in secret Raptures. **1746** COLLINS *Ode to Pity* vii, There let me oft, retir'd by day In dreams of passion melt away. *a* **1761** CAWTHORN *Poems* (1771) 58 How weak fair faith and virtue prove When Eloisa melts away in love!

4. a. To waste away, become gradually smaller; to dwindle. Now chiefly with *away.* †Occas. of a swelling, *to melt down.*

a **1225** *Ancr. R.* 268 Herdeliche ileueð þet al þe deofles strencðe melteð þuruh þe grace of þe holi sacrament. *a* **1225** *St. Marher.* 6 Þi mihte schal unmuchelin ant melten to riht noht. *a* **1250** *Prov. Ælfred* 385 in *O.E. Misc.* 126 And vyches cunnes madmes to mixe schulen i-Multen. *a* **1400** *St. Erkenwolde* 158 in Horstm. *Altengl. Leg.* (1881) 269 He has not layne here so longe, to loke hit by kynde, To malte so out of memorie. *c* **1586** C'TESS PEMBROKE *Ps.* CVII. ix, Their might doth melt, their courage dies. **1606** SHAKS. *Ant. & Cl.* III. xiii. 90 Authority melts from me of late. **1629** MILTON *Hymn Nativ.* 138 Leprous sin will melt from earthly mould, And Hell it self will pass away. **1665** SIR T. HERBERT *Trav.* (1677) 166 His huge Army melted away, and quickly became

less numerous. **1762** R. GUY *Pract. Obs. Cancers* 156 By Degrees the hard Tumour entirely melted down. **1794** BURKE *Corr.* (1844) IV. 213 The body of his party is melting away very fast. **1818** BYRON *Ch. Har.* IV. xii, Nations melt From power's high pinnacle, when they have felt The sunshine for a while. **1855** MACAULAY *Hist. Eng.* xiii. III. 377 The host which had been the terror of Scotland melted fast away. **1860** READE *Cloister & H.* lxxviii. (1896) 223 While her heart was troubled, her money was melting. **1891** *Leeds Mercury* 27 Apr. 5/2 There was a surplus of fifty-seven million dollars when President Harrison took office, and it has all melted away. **1897** *Allbutt's Syst. Med.* II. 279 Tumours in muscle, which will wholly melt away under the influence of iodide of potassium, are sometimes [etc.].

b. *slang.* Of money: To be spent on drink. (Cf. 13.)

1765 FOOTE *Commissary* I. i, Give him the sixpence; there, there, lay it out as you will. *Coachm.* It will be to your health, mistress; it shall melt at the Meuse, before I go home.

5. To filter in, become absorbed *into*. Also *fig.*

13.. *E.E. Allit. P.* B. 1566, & make þe mater to malt my mynde wyth-inne. **1590** SPENSER *F.Q.* I. ix. 31 His subtile tong like dropping honny mealt'h Into the heart, and searcheth every vaine. **1776** GIBBON *Decl. & F.* ii. I. 40 It was by such institutions that the nations of the empire insensibly melted away into the Roman name and people. **1821** SHELLEY *Epipsych.* 110 Like fiery dews that melt Into the bosom of a frozen bud.

6. Of sound: To be soft and liquid.

1626, etc. [see MELTING *ppl. a.* 1 c]. **1713** YOUNG *Force Relig.* I, She clasps her lord, brave, beautiful, and young, While tender accents melt upon her tongue. **1792** S. ROGERS *Pleas. Mem.* II. 38 With rapt ear drink the enchanting serenade, And as it melts along the moonlight-glade [etc.].

7. To pass by imperceptible degrees *into* something else.

1781 COWPER *Retirement* 424 Downs..That melt and fade into the distant sky. **1820** W. IRVING *Sketch Bk., Rip Van Winkle* ¶ 2 Where the blue tints of the upland melt away into the fresh green of the nearer landscape. **1865** J. THOMSON *Sunday up River* III. ii, The vague vast grey Melts into azure dim on high.

II. Transitive senses.

8. a. To reduce to a liquid condition by heat.

a **1000** *Elene* 1311 (Gr.) Gold..þurh ofnes fyr eall ȝeclænsod amered & ȝemylted. *c* **1000** *Sax. Leechd.* I. 366 Nim leon ȝelynde & heortes mearȝ mylt & ȝemeng tosomne. *c* **1200** ORMIN 17415, & badd he shollde melltenn brass & geten himm a neddre. *a* **1225** *Ancr. R.* 284 þe caliz was imelt iðe fure & stroncliche iwelled. *c* **1374** CHAUCER *Troylus* v. 10 The goldtressed Phebus heighe on lofte Thries hadde al with his bemes clere The snowes molte. *c* **1375** *Sc. Leg. Saints* xx. (*Blasius*) 237 þe presydent with fellone will gert melt leyd in fusione. *c* **1384** CHAUCER *H. Fame* II. 414 Nyse ykarus, That fleegh so high that the hete Hys wynges malte. *c* **1425** WYNTOUN *Cron.* IV. xxi. 1895 All the metall moltynnyd than In tyll a qwerne togydder ran. **1444** *Rolls of Parlt.* V. 109/1 That no white money..be broke nor molte for the cause above said. **1474** CAXTON *Recuyell* (ed. Sommer) 18 Saturne..malte and fyned gold and metalles. *a* **1562** G. CAVENDISH *Wolsey* (1893) 267 Rather than I wold ..embesell or deceyve hyme of a myght, I wold it ware molt and put in my mouthe. **1565** COOPER *Thesaurus, Aurum.. fusile*, that may be molted. **1590** SPENCER *F.Q.* III. xi. 25 As a thonder-bolt..doth displace The soring clouds into sad showres ymolt. **1593** B. BARNES *Parthenophil* (Arb.) Sonn. xliv, Whose might all metals' mass asunder moults! **1614** *Sco. Venus* (1876) 35 Or had the bed bene burnt with wilde fire all, And thereby moult the heauens golden frame. **1647** H. MORE *Poems* Notes 362 *note*, Ice..once melt by the warmth of the Sunne it becomes one with the rest of the Sea. **1667** MILTON *P.L.* XI. 562 One who..two massie clods of Iron and Brass Had melted. **1681** HICKERINGILL *Black Non-Conf.* Postscr., Wks. 1716 II. 171 Go, then, you subtile Persecutors! fret, and be molt in your own fat. *a* **1756** MRS. HAYWOOD *New Present* (1771) 43 Till the butter is all melted. **1871** TYNDALL *Fragm. Sci.* (1879) I. i. 5 A sun or planet once molten, would continue for ever molten. **1874** TAIT *Rec. Adv. Phys. Sci.* (1876) 45 Davy showed..that the mere rubbing together by proper mechanical force of two pieces of ice was sufficient to melt the surface of each.

absol. **1535** COVERDALE *Jer.* vi. 29 The melter [1611 founder] melteth in vayne. **1683** PETTUS *Fleta Min.* IV. ix. 304, I conclude it better to melt with Coals, than with Moll.

†**b.** To melt and refashion *into*; also, to form (an image, etc.) out of molten material. *Obs.*

c **1440** *Alphabet of Tales* 273 He prayed þat all his tresurs, þat war of grete valow, mott be molten in-to a grete mace. **1560** BIBLE (Genev.) *Isa.* xl. 19 The workeman melteth an image. **1573** CARTWRIGHT *Reply to Whitgift* 28 The Jewes when they molted a golden calfe..did neuer thinke that to be God. **1577–87** HOLINSHED *Chron.* I. 113/1 A brasen image by maruelous art melted and cast. **1582** G. MARTIN *Manif. Corrupt. Script.* iii. 56 Behold Eunomius, how he molted and cast a false image, and bowed down to that which he had molten. **1611** BIBLE *Isa.* xl. 19.

c. With advs. *to melt away*: to remove, destroy, or waste by melting. *to melt down*: to melt (coin, plate, or other manufactured articles) in order that the metal may be used as raw material. Hence (*jocularly*), to convert (property) into cash. Also, less frequently, *to melt up*. *to melt in*: to melt (a substance) so that it becomes an ingredient of a mixture.

c **1375** *Sc. Leg. Saints* xxxii. (*Justin*) 394 He sonnere but delay meltit þane wax in fyre away. *c* **1384** CHAUCER *H. Fame* III. 59 Thoo gan I in myn herte cast, That they were molte awey with hete, And not awey with stormes bete. **1633** T. STAFFORD *Pac. Hib.* II. iv. (1821) 267 Meet to be moulten downe and brought into her majesties mint. *a* **1704** T. BROWN *Sat. Fr. King* Wks. 1730 I. 60 Old Ierom's volumes next I made a rape on, And melted down that father for a capon. **1721** BERKELEY *Prev. Ruin Gt. Brit.* Wks. 1871 III. 202 A private family in difficult circumstances,..ought to melt down their plate. **1868** JOYNSON *Metals* 115 The solder is then..melted in, either with a blow-pipe or by being placed in a charcoal fire. **1874** MICKLETHWAITE *Mod. Par. Churches* 226 How many bronzes have been melted down to make guns. **1888** J. A. SPARVEL-BAYLY in *Antiquary* Dec. 238 Church bells shared the general fate of other church-furniture, and hundreds were sold and melted up.

d. in jocular hyperbole.

1677 W. HUBBARD *Narrative* 40 While Capt. Mosely took a little breath, who was almost melted with labouring, commanding, and leading his men.

9. a. To dissolve, make a solution of. †Also, in OE., to digest.

c **897** K. ÆLFRED *Gregory's Past. C.* xxxvi. 259 Sua sua sio wamb ȝemielt ðone mete. *c* **1420** *Liber Cocorum* (1862) 6 Malt hit [*sc.* salt] in bryne. **1610** BARROUGH *Meth. Physick* VII. v. (1639) 388 A Syrupe is of medicines a juyce with Sugar or Hony molten therin. **1707** *Curios in Husb. & Gard.* 136 Nitre melted in Water..mixes itself with the Water. **1805** R. W. DICKSON *Pract. Agric.* II. 1012 This re-union, or in the dairy phrase, melting the cream, is probably the best method practised.

†**b.** To disintegrate, loosen (soil). *Obs.*

1615 W. LAWSON *Country Housew. Gard.* (1626) 3 The soile is made better by deluing, and other meanes, being well melted. **1708** J. C. *Compl. Collier* (1845) 21 If the Feeders be of any considerable Quantity, it will melt, or dissolve the Earth.

10. To disperse, cause to disappear. Also with *away*.

a **1300** *Cursor M.* 24470 þi saul es molten [*Gött.* multen] al to ded. **1602** MARSTON *Antonio's Rev.* I. v, Comfort's a parasite, a flattering Jack: And melts resolv'd despaire. **1820** SHELLEY *Sensitive Plant* III. 73 [77] At night they [the vapours] were darkness no star could melt. **1865** PARKMAN *Huguenots* i. (1875) 8 Cold, disease, famine, thirst, and the fury of the waves, melted them away.

11. a. To soften or make tender; to 'touch' the feelings of (a person). † *to melt down*: to subdue by softening.

1377 LANGL. *P. Pl.* B. XVII. 226 þanne flaumbeth he as fyre on fader & on filius, And melteth her myȝte in-to mercy. *a* **1400** *Octouian* 249 With that anoon hys herte was mylt. **1434** MISYN *Mending Life* xii. 129 Many truly ar multyn in teris & aftirwarde has turnyd to yll. **1608** SHAKS. *Per.* IV. i. 7 Nor let pittie..melt thee, but be a souldier to thy purpose. **1668** R. STEELE *Husbandman's Calling* x. (1672) 251 You would be melted into submission, not forced: do you the like to them, melt them rather than force them. *a* **1716** SOUTH *Serm.* (1744) VII. vii. 153 Nothing could have been spoke more gently, and yet more forcibly, to melt him down into a penitential sorrow for, and an abhorrence of those two foul deviations from the law of God. **1738** WESLEY *Hymns, Infinite Power, Eternal Lord* vii, Melt down my Will, and let it flow, And take the Mould divine. **1748** THOMSON *Cast. Indol.* I. viii, Till clustering round th' enchanter false they hung, Ymolten with his syren melody. **1847** TENNYSON *Princess* VI. 103 Her noble heart was molten in her breast. **1849** MACAULAY *Hist. Eng.* iv. I. 434 His solemn and pathetic exhortation awed and melted the bystanders to such a degree that [etc.]. **1891** HAN. LYNCH *G. Meredith* 88 Rhoda, melted to him, calls her sister down to happiness.

absol. **1818** BUSBY *Gram. Mus.* 483 A manly, yet tender quality of tone,..which melts and cheers at the same moment.

b. *to melt away*: to 'dissolve into ecstasies'.

c **1320** R. BRUNNE *Medit.* 1001 Now certes my soule ys melted awey. **1713** ADDISON *Cato* I. iv. 11 Alas, thy Story melts away my Soul.

†**12.** To weaken, enervate. Also, *to melt down*.

1599 SHAKS. *Much Ado* IV. i. 321 Manhood is melted into cursies, valour into complement. **1607** —— *Timon* IV. iii. 256 Thou would'st haue..melted downe thy youth In different beds of Lust. **1632** LE GRYS tr. *Velleius Paterc.* 15 Pharnaces the Mede, deprived Sardanapalus, melted with easefull delicacies [L. *mollitiis fluentem*],..both of his Empire and life. *a* **1704** T. BROWN *Persius' Sat.* i. Prol., Nor Virgils great majestick lines Melted into enervate Rhimes.

13. a. To spend, squander (money). Chiefly *slang* (*spec.*, with notion of sense 9, to spend on drink); also † *to melt away*. **b.** *slang.* To cash (a cheque or bank-note).

a **1700** B.E. *Dict. Cant. Crew* s.v., *Will you Melt a Bord?* Will you spend your Shilling? **1705** PENN in *Pa. Hist. Soc. Mem.* X. 71 The vast sum of money I have melted away here in London to hinder much mischief against us. **1756** TOLDERVY *Hist. 2 Orphans* IV. 45 They had the ambition.. to melt it [a crown] at Ashley's punch-house upon Ludgate-Hill. **1807** E. S. BARRETT *Rising Sun* I. 134 If Moses [money-lender] does not come soon, all the money will be melted before he brings it. **1868** READE & BOUCICAULT *Foul Play* lii, I had him arrested before he had time to melt the notes. **1897** *Daily News* 5 Oct. 3/5 Another of the 100*l.* notes was, according to the prisoner's expression, 'melted' (i.e. cashed).

14. To blend *into* one mass of colour, etc.

1778 SIR J. REYNOLDS *Disc.* viii. (1876) 456 This effect is produced by melting and losing the shadows in a ground still darker. **1823** F. CLISSOLD *Ascent Mt. Blanc* 23 The glassy pinnacles of the..Alps,..melting their outlines in the softer tints of evening. **1860** HAWTHORNE *Marb. Faun* (1879) II. iv. 49 The words..being softened and molten..into the.. richness of the voice that sung them. **1872** BLACK *Adv. Phaeton* xvii, A grey mist..melted whole mountains into a soft dull grey. **1900** JULIA WEDGWOOD in *Contemp. Rev.* Mar. 336 In him there was a strong revolutionary element, and it is difficult in looking back not to melt it in with the other revolutionary manifestations of the time.

15. [= ON. *melta.*] To make (malt); to prepare (barley) for fermentation. *Obs.* exc. *dial.* (Yorks.): see E.D.D.

1615 MARKHAM *Eng. Housew.* II. vii. (1668) 169 The Art of making, or (as some term it) melting of Malt.

melt, *v.*[2] *Sc.* ? *Obs. trans.* 'To knock down; properly by a stroke in the side, where the *melt* or spleen lies' (Jam.).

a **1585** POLWART *Flyting w. Montgomerie* 762 Skade scald, ouerbald! soone fald, or I melt thee. **1785** FORBES *Ulysses' Answ.* in *Poems Buchan Dial.* 36 But I can..melt them ere they wit; An' syne fan they're dung out o' breath They hae na maughts to hit.

melt, obs. and dial. variant of MILT *sb.*

meltable ('mɛltəb(ə)l), *a.* [f. MELT *v.*[1] + -ABLE.] Capable of being melted, in senses of the vb.

1610 W. FOLKINGHAM *Art of Survey* I. ii. 3 These are either Liquable or Not-Meltable. *a* **1661** FULLER *Worthies* (1840) III. 52 It is the most impure of metals, hardly meltable. **1852** R. S. SURTEES *Sponge's Sp. Tour* xxix. 176 Money's like snow,..a very meltable article.

Hence **melta'bility** *rare*, capacity of being melted.

1865 DICKENS *Mut. Fr.* IV. vii, The brittleness and meltability of wax.

meltaith, Sc. variant of MEALTIDE.

meltdown ('mɛltdaʊn). [f. vbl. phr. *to melt down* (MELT *v.*[1] 8 c).] **a.** The process of melting.

1937 *Ice Cream Trade Jrnl.* Mar. 36/1 The Sod. Alg. ice cream melts down cleanly in the mouth... Due to the clean melt-down..a cooler sensation results in the mouth than with gelatin ice cream. **1965** *New Scientist* 15 Apr. 161/3 Overheated fuel may result in 'meltdown' and general contamination of the reactor system. **1975** *New Yorker* 12 May 98/2 He was worried about loss-of-coolant accidents, core meltdowns, and breaches of containment walls.

b. A melted mass.

1973 *Sci. Amer.* Aug. 114/2 They recycle..bottles into gemlike necklaces, the meltdown fanned by the bowl bellows of ancient Egypt.

melte, obs. form of MILT *sb.*

melted ('mɛltɪd), *ppl. a.* [f. MELT *v.*[1] + -ED[1].] In senses of the verb.

1. That has been liquefied by heat. (Cf. MOLTEN.) ***melted butter***: see BUTTER I. 1 d.

1599 SHAKS. *Hen. V*, III. v. 50 Rush on his Hoast, as doth the melted Snow Vpon the Valleyes. **1660** F. BROOKE tr. *Le Blanc's Trav.* 366 The chaldron full of rich melted mettle. **1683** TRYON *Way to Health* 302 All kind of melted Butter and fryed Foods..are hurtful to the Health of all People. **1797** tr. *C. De Massoul's Treat. Art Paint.* 44 This melted glass in Enamel, produces the same effect, that oils, gums or glues produce in the other processes of Painting. **1815** J. SMITH *Panorama Sci. & Art* I. 5 Upon the surface of melted lead. **1861** FAIRBAIRN *Iron* 159 The silicium thus formed alloying the steel, gives that quietness and freedom from boiling known in the trade as 'dead melted'. **1870** J. H. FRISWELL *Mod. Men of Lett.* iii. 65 A spectacle to gods and men in these melted-butter days.

†**2.** Of corn: That has sprouted in harvesting.

1799 *Hull Advertiser* 26 Oct. 3/2 Every bushel of melted wheat.

†**3.** 'Dissolved' in emotion. *Obs.*

1628 *Brittain's Ida* vi. 9 Bathing in liquid ioyes his melted sprite.

Hence '**meltedness.** *rare.*

1852 J. D. MACLAREN in *Mem.* (1861) 78 There would be only more meltedness of heart.

melteithe, variant of MEALTIDE.

meltemi (mɛl'tɛmɪ). Also **meltem.** [a. mod. Gr. μελτέμι, Turk. *meltem.*] A wind experienced in the north-eastern Mediterranean; etesian wind.

1921 *Handbk. Macedonia* (Admiralty, Naval Intelligence Div.) ii. 50 At the coast of the Aegean Sea, and at Constantinople, the northerly and north-easterly winds (the 'Etesian' winds of the Greeks and the 'Meltemi' of the Turks) become more definitely the prevailing wind. **1942** *Turkey* (Admiralty, Naval Intelligence Div.) I. v. 196 The west coast also has north-west (*etesiae* or *meltemi*) winds in summer. **1957** L. DURRELL *Bitter Lemons* 73, I will take you to a special place of mine to taste the *meltemi* wind. **1958** *Times* 20 Sept. 9/6 In Aegina the *meltemi* will be blowing, a fresh salty breeze which tempers the noonday heat. **1959** *Chambers's Encycl.* VII. 775/2 The prevailing wind [in Istanbul]..in summer..is the *meltem*, a refreshing breeze. **1967** J. RATHBONE *Diamonds Bid* xx. 171 The gusty dry wind, which the Turks call 'meltemi', sending clouds of dust down the boulevards.

melter ('mɛltə(r)). [f. MELT *v.*[1] + -ER[1].]

1. One who or that which melts, in various senses of the vb.

1581 *Act 23 Eliz.* c. 8 §1 The said Melter, Myngler or Corrupter,..shall forfeyte [etc.]. *c* **1586** C'TESS PEMBROKE *Ps.* CXLVII. vi, Abroad the southern wind, his melter goes. *c* **1620** FLETCHER & MASS. *False One* II. iii, Thou melter of strong mindes, dar'st thou presume To smother all his triumphes with thy vanityes? **1695** LOCKE *Short Observ. Pr. Paper* 19 The melter of our mill'd money. *a* **1764** LLOYD *On Rhyme* Poet. Wks. 1774 II. 123 The..charming melter of his purse. **1824–9** LANDOR *Imag. Conv.* Wks. 1846 I. 204, I keep both out of the crucible and out of the *aqua regia*, another great melter and transmuter. **1856** KANE *Arct. Expl.* I. xvii. 201 One of our deck-watch, who had been cutting ice for the melter.

2. *spec.* One whose trade or office it is to melt metals or other substances; esp. a workman so employed in a factory or in the Mint; also, formerly, †the designation of an officer of the Exchequer.

1535 COVERDALE *Jer.* vi. 29 The lead is consumed, the melter melteth in vayne. **1567** *Reg. Privy Council Scot.* I. 556 All Meltaris, Forgearis, and Prentaris within the said

cunyehous. **1670** PETTUS *Fodinæ Reg.* 41 Then the Melters, that melt the Bullion before it come to the Coining. **1697** LUTTRELL *Brief Rel.* (1857) IV. 191 Then they heard the accusation against major Barton, the chief melter of York mint. **1708** MADOX tr. *Dial. de Scacc.* I. iii. 4 b, The under exchequer..has..two officers,..one who presides over the examinations, and the melter... The melter also examines the silver. **1883** P. L. SIMMONDS *Usef. Anim., Melter*, a tallow chandler. **1884** C. G. W. LOCK *Workshop Rec.* Ser. III. 254/1 The foreman may have various reasons for wanting his melter to make all these changes.

3. A small furnace or melting-pot.

1883 HALDANE *Workshop Rec.* Ser. II. 103 An improved form of melter..consists of a small furnace [etc.].

4. A variety of the peach in which the flesh parts freely from the stone when ripe; = FREE-STONE^{2}.

1766 *Complete Farmer* s.v. *Peach-tree*, The nivette; this is a melter, and ripens in September. **1840** *Penny Cycl.* XVII. 347. **1866** [see CLINGSTONE].

melter, obs. form of MILTER.

meltet(h, meltid, Sc. variants of MEALTIDE.

melting (ˈmɛltɪŋ), *vbl. sb.* [f. MELT *v.*^{1} + -ING^{1}.]

1. The action of the vb. MELT; an instance of this.

1390–1 *Earl Derby's Exp.* (Camden) 86 Et pro meltyng de sepo et iiij lb. pinguedinum, vj s. pr. **1444** *Rolls of Parlt.* V. 109/1 The maistr' of his mynt..to have and take for his labour of double meltyng, blaunchyng, wast and other costs VII d in nombre. **1483** *Cath. Angl.* 234/1 A Meltynge, *deliquium, liquamen, liquefaccio.* **1526** *Pilgr. Perf.* (W. de W. 1531) 150 There foloweth the moost blessed effecte, that is a liquefaction or a meltynge of the soule. **1722** BP. E. GIBSON tr. *Camden's Brit.* (ed. 2) I. p. clxxiii, *Ley, lee, lay*, are all from the Saxon Leaȝ, a field or pasture; by the usual melting of the letter ȝ. **1740** W. SEWARD *Jrnl.* 13 There was much melting under both Sermons. **1775** S. J. PRATT *Liberal Opin.* lxxx. (1783) III. 94, I shall be with you and your good man again, in the melting of a lump of sugar. **1797** tr. *C. De Massoul's Treat. Art Paint.* 57 If, after every melting, you perceive that any air-bubbles have arisen, or [etc.]. **1822–34** *Good's Study Med.* (ed. 4) II. 20 Even in abscesses, where there is a loss of substance, it is not the melting down of the solids that gives rise to the pus. **1868** JOYNSON *Metals* 68 The strength is increased up to a certain number of meltings. **1897** *Allbutt's Syst. Med.* IV. 477 The injections [of thyroid gland extract]..were found to bring about a rapid melting away of the swelling.

†**b.** ***Surveyor of the Meltings***: the former designation of a certain officer of the mint. Hence ***the Meltings***: the office of the Surveyor of the Meltings.

1684 E. CHAMBERLAYNE *Pres. St. Eng.* II. 224 The Surveyor of the Melting. **1766** ENTICK *London* IV. 341 Surveyor of the meltings, clerk of the irons. **1807–8** SYD. SMITH *Plymley's Lett.* iii. Wks. (1850) 497 Suppose the person to whom he [*sc.* the Chancellor of the Exchequer] applied for the Meltings had withstood every plea of wife and fourteen children, no business, and good character, and refused him this paltry little office [etc.]. *Ibid.*, But do not refuse me the Irons and the Meltings now.

2. *concr. pl.* That which has been melted; a substance produced by melting. ? *Obs.*

1558 WARDE (*title*) The Secretes of the reverende Maister Alexis of Piemovnt. Containyng excellente remedies against diuers diseases,..with the manner to make distillations,.. fusions and meltynges. **1712** J. JAMES tr. *Le Blond's Gardening* 188 Such Waters..are no more than a Collection of Rain-Water, and the Meltings of Snow.

3. *attrib.* and *Comb.* **a.** Simple attributive, as ***melting chamber, -furnace, -oven, -pan, -place, -shop***. **b.** Special comb.: **melting-book**, an account-book kept to record quantities of metal melted; **melting-cone** (see quot.); **melting-heat**, the degree of heat which is necessary to melt a given substance; **melting-house**, a building in which the process of melting is carried on, *esp.* at the Mint; **melting-point** (see quot. 1842); **melting-pot**, a vessel in which metals or other substances are melted (phrases, ***to put*** or ***cast into*** the ***melting pot***; often *fig.* with reference to thorough remodelling of institutions, etc.).

1622 MALYNES *Anc. Law-Merch.* 283 As for your *Melting booke where the allay is entred, if you will charge the Mint-master thereby, let it be done distinctly for siluer, and copper, or [etc.]. **1890** W. J. GORDON *Foundry* 14 Into these red-hot chambers the fresh gas and air are turned and heated before they enter the *melting-chamber. **1753** CHAMBERS *Cycl. Supp.*, **Melting Cone*, in assaying, is a small vessel made of copper or brass, of a conic figure, and of a nicely polished surface within. **1758** REID tr. *Macquer's Chym.* I. 187 The *melting furnace is designed for applying the greatest force of heat to the most fixed bodies, such as metals and earths. **1868** JOYNSON *Metals* 102 The *melting heat is 442° Fahr. **1431** *Test. Ebor.* (Surtees) II. 16 Lego.. Johanni Beverlay omnia instrumenta et necessaria shopæ meæ ad le *meltynghouse. **1647** HAWARD *Crown Rev.* 23 Surveyor of the melting-house. **1778** J. MILLER in Grose *Antiq. Repert.* (1807) I. 241, I should refer the three Roman numerals as a melting-house mark..to the number of Pigs melted. **1854** *Hull Improv. Act* 33 Any candle-house, melting-house, melting-place or soap-house. **1683** PETTUS *Fleta Min.* III. x. 247 The *melting Oven to try the Copper Oars from the copper-stone. **1884** *Imp. & Mach. Rev.* 1 Dec. 6711/1 The sugar..passes..into the 'blow-ups' or *melting pans. **1483** *Cath. Angl.* 234/1 A *Meltynge place, *conflatorium*. **1842** FRANCIS *Dict. Arts* etc., s.v., That point of the thermometer which indicates the heat at which any particular solid becomes fluid, is termed the *melting point of that solid. **1898** *Rev. Brit. Pharm.* 51 Solubilities and melting-points are given in much fuller detail than in the last edition. **1545** *Rates Custom-ho.* b viij, *Meltynge pottes for goldsmethes. **1679** DRYDEN *Pref. to Tr. & Cr.* Ess. (ed. Ker) I. 227 If his embroideries were burnt down, there would still be silver at the bottom of the melting-pot. **1855** MILMAN *Lat. Chr.* XIV. ix. IX. 311 The avarice which cast all these wonderful statues into the melting pot to turn them into money. **1861** FAIRBAIRN *Iron* 181 These are melted in steel melting-pots. **1887** J. MORLEY in *Pall Mall G.* 10 Feb. 11/2, I think it will be best for the Constitution of this country not to send it to the melting-pot. **1555** EDEN *Decades* Pref. (Arb.) 54 In the two *meltynge shoppes of the gold mines of the Ilande of Hispaniola is molten yearely three hundreth thousande pounde weyght. **1892** *Labour Commission* Gloss., *Melting Shop and Plant*, the furnaces used in the melting and converting of iron into steel and the producers for the making of gas for such furnaces.

melting (ˈmɛltɪŋ), *ppl. a.* [f. MELT *v.*^{1} + -ING^{2}.] That melts, in senses of the vb.

1. In intransitive senses: **a.** That is in process of liquefaction; †capable of liquefaction, fusible (*obs.*). Also, †decaying.

1398 TREVISA *Barth. De P.R.* XVI. vii. (1495) 556 The element and mater of whiche all meltyng metall is made [L. *omnium liquidabilium metallorum*]. **1577** HANMER *Anc. Eccl. Hist.* (1650) 161 His whole body larded and distilled much like unto..melting wax. **1605** *1st Pt. Ieronimo* III. ii. 163 Honord Funerall for thy melting corse. **1799** G. SMITH *Laboratory* I. 76 The whole is to be kept in a melting state for some minutes.

b. Yielding to tender emotion; feeling or expressing tenderness or pity; tearful. Often in phr. ***the melting mood***, after Shaks.

1593 SHAKS. *Lucr.* 1227 Each flowre moistned like a melting eye. **1597** —— *2 Hen. IV*, IV. iv. 32 A Hand Open (as Day) for melting Charitie. **1601** —— *Jul. C.* II. i. 122 To steele with valour The melting spirits of women. **1604** —— *Oth.* V. ii. 349 Albeit vn-vsed to the melting moode. **1658** *Whole Duty Man* XV. §3 Our compassions are to be most melting towards them of all others. **1712–14** POPE *Rape Lock* I. 71 What guards the purity of Melting maids In courtly balls, and midnight masquerades? **1879** FROUDE *Cæsar* viii. 72 He was a high-spirited ornamental youth, with soft melting eyes.

c. Of sound: Liquid and soft, delicately modulated. Also of form, colour, etc.

1626 BACON *Sylva* §223 No Instrument hath the Sound so Melting and prolonged as the Irish Harp. **1632** MILTON *L'Allegro* 142 The melting voice through mazes running. **1713** GAY *Fan* II. 14 And thus in melting sounds her speech began. *a* **1761** CAWTHORN *Poems* (1771) 37 That step, whose motion seems to swim, That melting harmony of limb. **1849** RUSKIN *Sev. Lamps* iv. §39. 129 The most exquisite harmonies..soft and full, of flushed and melting spaces of colour. **1885** G. ALLEN *Babylon* v, Her pretty, melting native dialect.

d. That 'melts in the mouth', tender. Said esp. of varieties of pear; also of those varieties of peach that part easily from the stone: cf. MELTER.

1605 B. JONSON *Volpone* I. i. (1607) B b, You shall ha' some will swallow A melting heire, as glibly, as your Dutch Will pills of butter. **1753** CHAMBERS *Cycl. Supp.* s.v. *Nectarine*, This is a very well flavoured nectarine, of a soft, melting juice, and parts from the stone. **1766** *Complete Farmer* s.v. *Stock*, Summer peaches (commonly distinguished by the appellation of melting peaches). **1859** DARWIN *Orig. Spec.* i. (1872) 27 No one would expect to raise a first-rate melting pear from the seed of the wild pear.

2. In transitive senses: **a.** That liquifies or dissolves (*rare*). **b.** That softens the heart; deeply touching or affecting.

1611 BIBLE *Isa.* lxiv. 2 As when the melting fire burneth, the fire causeth the waters to boyle. **1656** J. OWEN *Mortif Sin* Wks. 1851 VI. 77 God's peace is humbling, melting peace. **1695** J. EDWARDS *Perfect. Script.* 439 The charms of a most melting and affectionate rhetorick. **1715–20** POPE *Iliad.* XXI. 83 While thus these melting words attempt his heart. **1739** *Joe Miller's Jests* No. 118 A melting Sermon being preach'd in a Country Church. **1826** E. IRVING *Babylon* II. 409 When Jeremy the prophet poured over them his melting lamentations in vain.

3. Comb.: ***melting-hearted*** adj., ***-heartedness***.

1593 NASHE *Christ's T.* 31 Exclayming, for some melting-harted man, to come and rydde them out of theyr lingring-lyuing death. **1647** TRAPP *Comm. 1 Cor.* xi. 11 There must be all mutuall respects and melting-heartednesse betwixt married couples.

meltingly (ˈmɛltɪŋlɪ), *adv.* [f. MELTING *ppl. a.* + -LY^{2}.] In a melting manner.

a **1586** SIDNEY *Arcadia* II. (1590) 176 Lying..with her face so bent ouer Ladon, that (her teares falling into the water) one might haue thought, that she began meltingly to be metamorphosed to the vnder-running riuer. **1680** *Revenge* I. i. 7 Kiss him as you do me, as soft and meltingly. **1827** SCOTT *Jrnl.* 30 July, Ballantyne marched on too, somewhat meltingly, but without complaint. **1888** R. DOWLING *Miracle Gold* II. xix. 107 That wonderful, irresistible, meltingly affectionate voice.

meltingness (ˈmɛltɪŋnɪs). [f. MELTING *ppl. a.* + -NESS.] The quality or state of being melting.

1622 MABBE tr. *Aleman's Guzman d'Alf.* II. 38 With the.. meltingnesse of their language, they moue many to pity. **1879** G. MEREDITH *Egoist* III. x. 204 She ran through her brain for a suggestion to win a sign of meltingness if not esteem from her father.

meltit(h, Sc. variants of MEALTIDE.

Melton (ˈmɛltən). The name of a town in Leicestershire (more fully Melton Mowbray), a famous hunting centre. Used *attrib.* in ***Melton jacket***, a kind of jacket formerly worn by hunters; ***Melton pad***, a hernia truss specially suited to be worn on horseback. Also in ***Melton cloth*** (see quot. 1882) and ***ellipt.*** as *sb.*

1823 BYRON *Juan* XIII. lxxviii, Even Nimrod's self might leave the plains of Dura, And wear the Melton jacket for a space. **1858** SIMMONDS *Dict. Trade, Melton*, a kind of broadcloth. **1882** CAULFEILD & SAWARD *Dict. Needlework, Melton cloth*, a stout make of cloth suitable for men's wear, which is 'pared', but neither pressed nor 'finished'. **1891** *Times* 7 Oct. 4/4 The output of printed meltons at present is a good deal above the average of a year ago.

Meltonian (mɛlˈtəʊnɪən), *a.* and *sb.* [f. *Melton* (see prec.) + -IAN.] **a.** *adj.* Pertaining to Melton Mowbray. ***Meltonian cream***, the name of a polish for boot-tops. **b.** *sb.* One who hunts at Melton Mowbray, an adept at hunting.

1825 H. ALKEN (*title*) A Few Ideas, being Hints to all Would-be Meltonians. All is not gold that glitters; Neither does Keeping Horses at Melton, and mounting the scarlet, Make The Real Meltonian. **1840** BLAINE *Encycl. Rural Sports* §1637 All riders are not Meltonians. **1901** *Edin. Rev.* Jan. 100 The red evening coat in which fox-hunters dine may be traced to the Meltonian dandies.

meltre: see MEDLE-*tree*.

meltyd, meltyre, var. ff. MEALTIDE, MELDER.

melub, variant of MAHALEB.

melusine (mɛl(j)uːˈsiːn). Also **Melusine**. [a. Fr. *mélusine*, a kind of felt. Connection w. *Mélusine*, the name of a fairy in French folk-lore, is likely.] A silky, long-haired felt, used for making hats. Also *attrib.*

1908 *Westm. Gaz.* 24 Oct. 19/2 The Parisienne's latest love in millinery is the hat of silky beaver felt that she calls melusine. **1952** C. W. CUNNINGTON *Eng. Women's Clothing* ii. 62 Toques in Melusine beaver. **1959** *Housewife* June 98 My white melusine hat is now a little soiled. **1962** A. SOUTHERN *Millinery* ii. 29 Melusine is a high-grade fur felt which is made in a range of beautiful colours.

†**ˈmelvie**, *v. Sc. Obs.* [f. Sc. *melvie* adj. mealy (Jam.), for **melwie*, f. *melw-*, OE. and ME. stem of MEAL *sb.*] *trans.* To cover with meal.

1785 BURNS *Holy Fair* xxv, Sma' need has he to say a grace, Or melvie his braw claithing!

melwe, melwell, obs. ff. MELLOW *a.*, MULVEL.

melwynge, obs. form of MEALING *vbl. sb.*^{1}

mely, melyone, obs. ff. MELLAY, MILLION.

melzie, melȝie, obs. Sc. form of MAIL *sb.*^{4}

1535 STEWART *Cron. Scot.* (1858) I. 68 [*rime* assailzie]. **1568** in *Satir. Poems Reform.* xlviii. 83 [*rime* felȝie = *failȝie*, FAIL *v.*].

mem., *sb.* Abbreviation of MEMORANDUM, placed in front of a note of something to be remembered.

Colloq. and in humorous verse often treated as a word, pronounced (mɛm). Cf. MEMO.

1818 MOORE *Fudge Fam. Paris* ix. 234 Mem. too—when Sid. an army raises, It must not be 'incog.' likes Bayes's. **1827** WADD (*title*) Mems. Maxims, and Memoirs. **1861** CALVERLEY *Dover to Munich* 19 Tickets to Königswinter (mem. The seats objectionably dirty). **1892** J. PAYN *Mod. Whittington* II. 63 Mr. Robert made a mem. in his mind that an ample provision should now be made.

mem, *v.* [f. the sb.] *trans.* To note or write down as a memorandum.

1915 W. J. LOCKE *Jaffery* v. 61 Once having 'mem-ed' an unpleasant thing in my diary, the matter is over.

mem, vulgar variant of MA'AM.

mem: see MEM-SAHIB.

member (ˈmɛmbə(r)), *sb.* [ME. *membre*, a. F. *membre* (11th c. in Littré) (= Sp. *miembro*, Pg., It. *membro*):—L. *membrum* limb, part of the body, constituent part of anything.

By many philologists considered to represent a prehistoric **mems-ro-*, cogn. with Goth. *mimz* flesh.]

1. a. A part or organ of the body; chiefly, a limb or other separable portion (as opposed to the trunk). *arch.*

privy member or ***members***, †***carnal member***: the secret part or parts. ***the unruly member*** (after James iii. 5–8): the tongue. ***virile member***: see VIRILE *a.* and *sb.* 3.

1297 R. GLOUC. (Rolls) 11731 Þat is priue membres hii ne corue of iwis. *c* **1325** *Song of Merci* 152 in *E.E.P.* (1862) 123 His hert al-so And alle þe Membres þat we con mynge. **1382** WYCLIF *Jas.* iii. 5 The tunge sotheli is a litel membre. **1393** LANGL. *P. Pl.* C. XI. 156 Man is hym most lyk of membres and of face. *c* **1430** *Life St. Kath.* (1884) 55 Þat..she scholde by meuyng of þe wheles be rent membre from membre. *c* **1430** LYDG. *Min. Poems* (Percy Soc.) 44 If ye mowe chastise your carnal membre. **1495** *Act. 11 Hen. VII*, c. 3 §3 Any other offence wherfor any persone shall lose life or member. **1548–9** (Mar.) *Bk. Com. Prayer, Collect Circumcision*, That our hertes, and al our membres..may.. obey thy blessed wil. **1585** T. WASHINGTON tr. *Nicholay's Voy.* IV. xxv. 145 Exceeding all others in bignesse of body and force of members. **1611** BIBLE *Deut.* xxiii. 1 Hee that.. hath his priuie member cut off. **1660** F. BROOKE tr. *Le Blanc's Trav.* 61 They tye a cloth only to hide their privie members. **1697** DRYDEN *Virg. Georg.* III. 424 Their Masters mangl'd Members they devour. **1715–20** POPE *Iliad* XXII. 575 All her members shake with sudden fear. **1756** NUGENT *Gr. Tour, Italy* III. 316 Artificial noses, lips, ears, and other members. **1823** J. F. COOPER *Pioneers* v. (1869) 24/2 There was something noble in the rounded outlines of his head and brow. The very air and manner with which the member haughtily maintained itself [etc.].

b. *spec.* (after L.): = 'privy member'.

c **1290** *S. Eng. Leg.* I. 306/249 Heore membres to-swellez sone. **1297** R. GLOUC. (Rolls) 10524 Ȝe þat vil it is to telle, some hii lete honge Bi hor membres an hey. *c* **1330** *Arth. & Merl.* 3472 (Kölbing) Vlfin him ȝaue a dint of wo þurch out þe membre & sadel also. *c* **1386** CHAUCER *Pars. T.* ⁋256 They sowed of fige leues a maner of breches to hiden hire membres. **1582** N. LICHEFIELD tr. *Castanheda's Conq. E. Ind.* I. ii. 6 They trusse up and hide theyr members in certeine Cases made of woode. **1966** L. COHEN *Beautiful Losers* (1970) I. 24 This member of mine rigid as a goal post.

c. *Biol.* In extended use: Any part of a plant or animal viewed with regard to its form and position.

1875 BENNETT & DYER tr. *Sach's Bot.* 130 It is obviously best to speak in this sense not of Organs, but of Members. The term Member is used when we speak of a part of a whole in reference to its form or position and not to any special purpose it may serve. In the same manner, from a morphological point of view, stems, leaves, hairs, roots, thallus-branches, are simply members of the plant-form. **1890** *Syd. Soc. Lex., Member*... A part of a plant or animal, such as a root, stem, leaf, or hair in a plant, or an arm or leg in an animal; a segment which can be studied in a purely morphological point of view, apart from its physiological function.

2. *fig.* with reference to a metaphorical 'body'; chiefly in ***member of Christ, of Satan.*** (Cf. LIMB *sb.*[1] 3 a, b.)

13.. *E.E. Allit. P.* A. 458 Al arn we membrez of Ihesu kryst. *c* **1375** *Sc. Leg. Saints* xvi. (*Magdalena*) 301 þe membyre of sathane. **1382** WYCLIF *Eph.* v. 30 We ben membris of his body, of his fleisch and of his boones. **1483** CAXTON *Cato* G iij b, To do therwith almesses to the poure members of Yhesu cryst. **1548-9** (Mar.) *Bk. Com. Prayer, Catechism*, Wherein I was made a member of Christe. **1582** *Reg. Privy Council Scot.* III. 493 Enemie to Chryst and to all his faithful members. **1711** ADDISON *Spect.* No. 21 ⁋3 The Body of the Law is no less encumbered with superfluous Members.

3. *transf.* **a.** Each of the constituent portions of a complex structure.

c **1391** CHAUCER *Astrol.* Prol. 3 The figures & the membres of thin Astrolabie. **1669** STURMY *Mariner's Mag.* v. xii. 48 *plate*, Yᵉ names of yᵉ members of a pece of Ordnance. **1688** R. HOLME *Armoury* III. 321/2 In it [the Vice] there are several parts and Members. **1855** BAIN *Senses & Int.* I. ii. §11 Each couple [of nerves] contains a right and a left member. **1890** W. J. GORDON *Foundry* 45 There is not a perpendicular line in any of the cantilevers... The rising members, the members that withstand the compressing, are ..all tubes. **1901** *Black's Illustr. Carp. Man., Scaffolding* 64 The horizontal members of the brackets extend out 5ft. at right angles to the uprights.

b. *Arch.* 'Any part of an edifice, or any moulding in a collection of mouldings, as those in a cornice, capital, base, &c.' (Gwilt).

1679 MOXON *Mech. Exerc.* ix. 154 Architecture considers the best forming of all Members in a Building. **1849** RUSKIN *Sev. Lamps* ii. §8. 35 In later Gothic the pinnacle became gradually a decorative member. **1862** MERIVALE *Rom. Emp.* (1865) V. xli. 72 The whole space was..decorated with all the forms and members of Roman architecture.

†**c.** Of a range of mountains, buildings, etc.: An outlying portion. *Obs.*

1601 HOLLAND *Pliny* I. 125 As for the hils Imaus, Emodisus, Paropamisus, as parts all and members of Caucasus. **1628** VENNER *Baths of Bathe* (1650) 347 The Queens Bath is a member of the Kings Bath.

4. a. Each of the individuals belonging to or forming a society or assembly. Also formerly, †an inhabitant or native (of a country or city).

c **1330** R. BRUNNE *Chron.* (1810) 130, I þe forbede to chalenge any clerke In lay courte.. Bot tille þat courte com to, of whilk he is membre calde. **1521** WARHAM in Ellis *Orig. Lett.* Ser. III. I. 240 Seyng your Grace is the moost honorable membyr that ever was of that Universitie. **1560** DAUS tr. *Sleidane's Comm.* 314 b, And with his protection to defend the members of the church. **1588** SHAKS. *L.L.L.* IV. i. 41 Here comes a member of the common-wealth. **1697** DRYDEN *Virg. Past.* IX. 44 Yet have the Muses made Me free, a Member of the tuneful trade. **1711** ADDISON *Spect.* No. 34 ⁋1 The Club of which I am a Member. **1802** M. EDGEWORTH *Moral T., Forester* viii. (1806) I. 63, I should be happy, if I were a useful member of society. **1842** ALISON *Hist. Europe* lxxviii. X. 983 The state becomes poor, and its members rich. **1891** *Law Times* XCII. 123/2 The Lord Chancellor need not be a member of the House of Lords of which he is the Speaker.

b. Used *absol.* for: A 'member of the community', a person. Now *slang* and *dial.*

1525 LD. BERNERS *Froiss.* II. ccxxxv. [ccxxxi.] 729 Where as therle and his chyldren shulde be great membres in Englande. **1603** SHAKS. *Meas. for M.* v. i. 237 These poore informall women, are no more But instruments of some more mightier member That sets them on. *c* **1613** BEAUM. & FL. *Coxcomb* I. v, You'll keep no whores, rogue, no good members. **1888** J. RUNCIMAN *Chequers* 187 You're a red-hot member! **1891** *Sporting Life* 28 Mar. 3/5 But, warm a member as our hero was, standing in front of a blazing furnace for hours..was too hot even for Jem's *sanguinary* temperament. **1922** JOYCE *Ulysses* 298 Gob, he's a prudent member and no mistake. *Ibid.* 228 Hot members they were all of them, the Geraldines.

†**c.** One who takes part in an action, participates in a benefit, etc. *Obs.*

1554-9 in *Songs & Ball. Philip & Mary* (1860) 3 To be members of mersye he hathe us up lyfft. **1569** *Reg. Privy Council Scot.* II. 66 The authoris and members of the said commotioun. **1597** SHAKS. *2 Hen. IV*, IV. i. 171 All members of our Cause, both here, and hence. **1604** —— *Oth.* III. iv. 112 That.. I may againe Exist, and be a member of his loue.

d. Usu. *attrib.*, applied to a country, nation, state, etc., belonging to an international organization.

1931 *Times Lit. Suppl.* 28 May 429/4 Common action by a society of States against a member-State. **1959** *Ibid.* 13 Feb. 79/2 The member-nations' extra-European commitments. **1959** A. H. ROBERTSON *European Institutions* iv. 93 The Member States would consult together. **1962** *B.S.I. News* June 11/2 Copies of the national standards.. would go to each member-country. **1971** W. LAQUEUR *Dict. Politics* 361 Departmental ministers of member countries. *Ibid.* 362 Representatives of the member states' Chiefs of Staff. *Ibid.* 525 All member nations have one voice and one vote.

e. *U.S. slang.* A Negro.

1964 L. HAIRSTON in J. H. Clarke *Harlem* 290 Three more, one of 'em a member,..sailed over. **1970** H. E. ROBERTS *Third Ear* 10/1 Member, a fellow black person.

5. One who has been formally elected to take part in the proceedings of a parliament: in full ***Member of Parliament*** (abbreviated M.P.), in U.S. ***Member of Congress*** (M.C.).

1454 *Rolls of Parlt.* V. 240/1 Any persone that is a membre of this high Court of Parlement. **1477** *Ibid.* VI. 191/2 All the membres usually called to the forseid Parlementes. **1603** *Jrnls. Ho. Comm.* I. 141/1 The Intrusion of sundry Gentlemen, his Majesty's Servants, and others (no Members of Parliament) into the Higher House. **1648** *Eikon Bas.* iii. 12 My going to the Hous of Commons to demand Justice upon the five Members, was an act, which My enemies loaded with all the obloquies and exasperations they could. **1711** SWIFT *Jrnl. to Stella* 8 Dec., I dined with Dr. Cockburn, and after, a Scotch member came in, and told us that the clause was carried against the Court in the house of lords. **1774** WASHINGTON *Writ.* (1889) II. 438 Dined at the State House, at an entertainment given by the city [of Philadelphia] to the members of the Congress. **1822** LD. J. RUSSELL in *Select. Sp. & Desp.* (1870) I. 205 My hon. Friend the member for Winchelsea. **1849** MACAULAY *Hist. Eng.* ii. I. 175 The Commons began by resolving that every member should [etc.].

6. A component part, branch, of a political body.

1386 *Rolls of Parlt.* III. 225/1 The folk of the Mercerye of London, as a member of the same Citee. **1414** *Ibid.* IV. 22/2 The comune of youre lond, the whiche that is, and ever hath be, a membre of youre parlement. **1673** RAY *Journ. Low C., Venice* 192 The Council of Ten, though it be a member of great importance, yet is it rather accessary..than principal. **1818** HALLAM *Mid. Ages* (1878) III. 106/1 *note*, By estates of the realm they meant members, or necessary parts, of the parliament. **1871** FREEMAN *Norm. Conq.* (1876) IV. xviii. 208 A member, doubtless the foremost member of the Danish Civic Confederation, it still kept a Danish patriciate of twelve hereditary Lawmen.

†**7.** A branch, department (of a trade, art, profession); a branch, species, subdivision of a class.

1463-4 *Rolls of Parlt.* V. 502/2 That..it may please unto your seid Highnes, to ordeyn..that every..Clothmaker.. pay to the Carders, Spynners, and all other the Laborers of eny membr' therof, lawfull money for all their lefull wages ..uppon peyne of forfeiture to the same Laborer, of the treble of his seid wages..as ofte as the seid Clothmaker refuseth to pay..to eny such Laborer by hym put to occupacion in eny of the seid membres of makyng of Cloth. **1540** *Act 32 Hen. VIII*, c. 40 §3 The science of phisike doth ..include..the knowledge of surgery as a speciall membre and parte of the same. *a* **1614** DONNE *Βιαθανατος* (1644) 132 The next Member and species of Homicide, which is, Assistance.

8. a. A section or district, esp. an outlying part, of an estate, manor, parish, or the like.

1450 *Rolls of Parlt.* V. 187/2 Havyng estate in the seid Castell, Lordship, Maner, and Membres. **1485** *Ibid.* VI. 357/2 Oure Honour of Walingford, with the members, in the Countie of Berks. *a* **1645** HABINGTON *Surv. Worcs.* in *Worcs. Hist. Soc. Proc.* III. 405 Werneleg a member of Owld Swinford. **1730** *Magna Brit.* I. 755/2 Crimscote... Peter de Montfort held it with Whitchurch, of which it was originally a Member. **1778** *Eng. Gazetteer* (ed. 2) s.v. *Halton*, Halton, or Haulton..is a member of the duchy of Lancaster. **1891** E. PEACOCK *N. Brendon* I. 339 Thurlford was a small hamlet, a member of a very large parish.

b. of a port.

1485 *Rolls of Parlt.* VI. 341/1 Men of the v Portes, or of any their members. **1676** *Lond. Gaz.* No. 1084/1 If any of the said Ships shall be in any Port of this Kingdom, or in any Member or Creek thereof. **1769** *De Foe's Tour Gt. Brit.* (ed. 7) II. 364 Swanzy..is a Member of the Port of Caerdiff. **1789** *Public Papers* in *Ann. Reg.* 132 The member is distinguished by a subordination to, and dependence upon the head-port. **1813** *Beawes's Lex. Mercat.* (ed. 6) I. 246 (Wharton) *Members*, places where anciently a custom house was kept, with officers or deputies in attendance. They were lawful places of exportation or importation.

9. *Math.* **a.** A group of figures or symbols forming part of a numerical expression or formula.

1608 R. NORTON *Stevin's Disme* A iij, Every three Characters of a Number is called a Member..as in the number 357,876,297, the 297 is called the first Member. **1685** WALLIS *Algebra* xxiii. 102 And here for every Figure or Member of the Root, we are to seek not only the several Members of the Cube, but of the Square also. **1875** *Chem. News* 9 Apr. 154 Its symbol will be {h k l, e f g}, where the second member of the symbol represents the poles equidistant with the poles {h k l} [etc.].

b. *Algebra.* Either of the sides of an equation.

1702 J. RALPHSON *Math. Dict., Equation*, (in Algebra) is a Comparison between two Quantities (or Members of the Equation,) to make them equal. **1903** WALKER *Introd. Physical Chem.* (ed. 3) xxvi. 307 Eliminating what is common to both members of the equation.

10. a. A division or clause of a sentence; a 'head' of a discourse; a branch of a disjunctive proposition.

1534 MORE *Comf. agst. Trib.* I. Wks. 1148/1 We shall therefore to gyue it lyght wythal touch euery member somewhat more at large. **1641** J. JACKSON *True Evang. T.* I. 8, I have..cast the Text according to the number of the verses, into three plain and conspicuous members. **1654** Z. COKE *Logick* 215 Under-titles also of Controversies must be disposed according the members of the Probleme to be handled. **1659** PEARSON *Creed* (1839) 7 As, for the other member of the division, we may now plainly perceive that it is thus to be defined. **1741** WATTS *Improv. Mind.* I. xiii. §12 The opponent must directly prove his own proposition in that sense, and according to that member of the distinction in which the respondent denied it. **1762** LOWTH *Eng. Gram.* (1763) 170 The Colon, or Member, is a chief constructive part, or greater division, of a Sentence. **1824** L. MURRAY *Eng. Gram.* (ed. 5) I. 270 The simple members of compound sentences. **1891** DRIVER *Introd. Lit. O.T.* (1892) 429 The verse itself may consist of one or more members; but each member..is divided by a *cæsura* into two unequal parts.

†**b.** in *Music.*

1782 BURNEY *Hist. Mus.* II. 171 Music..is now become a rich, expressive, and picturesque language in itself; having its forms, proportions, contrasts, punctuations, members, phrases, and periods. **1811** BUSBY *Dict. Mus.* (ed. 3) s.v. *Passage*, Every member of a strain or movement is a passage.

11. a. Each of the items forming a series.

1851 LYELL *Elem. Geol.* (ed. 3) 354 The *Orthoceras Ludense*..is peculiar to this member of the series. **1873** RALFE *Phys. Chem.* Introd. 17 Series of this kind are termed homologous series, and the members are said to be homologues of one another. **1884** BOWER & SCOTT *De Bary's Phaner.* 165 The division walls between the members of the series.

†**b.** ***member by member***: seriatim. (The first quot. prob. belongs to sense 1.)

[**1483** *Cath. Angl.* 234 Membyr be membyr, *membratim*.] **1726** LEONI *Alberti's Archit.* I. 43 We shall treat..of all Public Works Member by Member.

12. *Comb.*: **member bank** *U.S.*, a bank which holds shares in, and has representation on the board of directors of, a Federal Reserve Bank (see also quot. 1930); †**member-like** *a.*, befitting a member; **member-mug** *slang* and *dial.* (see *E.D.D.*) [f. sense 1 b + MUG *sb.*[1]], a chamber-pot; †**member-port** = 8 b.

1914 *Federal Reserve Act* §1 The term '*member bank' shall be held to mean any national bank, state bank, or bank or trust company which has become a member of one of the reserve banks created by this Act. **1923** E. A. SALIERS *Accountants' Handbk.* 865 Member banks may rediscount short-time commercial notes with federal reserve banks. **1930** J. M. KEYNES *Treat. Money* I. 9 The typical modern Banking System consists of a Sun, namely the Central Bank, and Planets, which, following American usage, it is convenient to call the Member Banks. **1948** G. CROWTHER *Outl. Money* (ed. 2) ii. 43 The banks other than the Central Bank are usually called 'joint-stock banks' in Great Britain and 'member banks' in the United States (i.e. members of the Federal Reserve System). **1649** *N. Eng. Hist. & Gen. Reg.* (1869) XXIII. 167 The Ch[urch]..ordered, that he be cast out of the body, till..he be brought into a more *member-like frame. **1649** J. ELLISTONE tr. *Behmen's Epist.* I. 1 From a member-like obligation (as one branch on the Tree is bound to doe to the other)..I wish unto you [etc.]. **1699** B. E. *New Dict. Canting Crew*, **Member-mug*, a Chamber-pot. **1785** GROSE *Dict. Vulgar T.*, *Member Mug*, a chamber pot. **1932** AUDEN *Orators* III. 104 The war-memorials decorate with member-mugs. *a* **1623** CAMDEN in Hearne *Collect.* (O.H.S.) II. 279 Sandwich & the *Member-Portes in Kent. **1656** TUCKER *Rep.* in *Misc. Sc. Burgh Rec. Soc.* 24 A checque, and three wayters, some of which are still sent into the member ports.

†**'member**, *v. Obs.* [a. OF. *membrer*:—L. *memorāre*: see MEMORATE.] **1.** *trans.* To mention; to remember. Hence **membered** *ppl. a.*

1382 WYCLIF *Tobit* iv. 22 The above membrid [Vulg. *ante memoratum*] weiȝte of siluer. —— *Wisd.* xi. 14 Thei membreden the Lord. **1589** WARNER *Alb. Eng.* v. xxiv. 108 They Carles garre syke a dinne, That more we member of their iapes [ed. 1602 they member vs of iapes] than mende vs of our sinne. *Ibid.* VI. xxx. 131, I member scarce thy arging.

2. Aphetic form of REMEMBER *v.* Freq. written as **'member**.

1899 KIPLING *Stalky & Co.* 254 'Member the snow all white on his eyebrows, Tertius? **1936** M. MITCHELL *Gone with Wind* lxi. 1009, I gave him to you, once before—'member?—before he was born. **1945** 'O. MALET' *My Bird Sings* II. x. 167 '*I* remember Papa!' shouted out Amaryllis.. 'So do I 'member Papa!' said Acanthus. **1971** *Black World* June 72/2 You member the day I left, Carrie Jean? **1973** *Amer. Speech 1970* XLV. 76 'Member the day I saw you on Broad Street?

memberal, obs. form of MEMBRAL.

membered ('mɛmbəd), *a.* [f. MEMBER *sb.* + -ED[1].] Having members (chiefly in parasynthetic combinations, = having members of a specified kind or number); divided into members; †consisting of links or segments.

a **1225** *Ancr. R.* 420 Ring, ne broche nabbe ȝe ne gurdel i-membred [*MSS. T., C.* i-membret], ne glouen. **1398** TREVISA *Barth. De P.R.* v. v. (Tollem. MS.), To þe ye so desposid and perfitly membrid [L. *perfecte organizatum*]. *c* **1477** CAXTON *Jason* 21, I am not grete ne membred as a geant. **1589** PUTTENHAM *Eng. Poesie* III. xxiii. (Arb.) 268 If ..the shape of a membred body [be] without his due measures and simmetry. **1630** *R. Johnson's Kingd. & Commw.* 58 Strong-membred, and blacke haired. **1832** *Fraser's Mag.* VI. 335 It is only assumed that a quantity may be divided into members *ad infinitum*—it does not follow that it is really membered to infinity. **1854** *Pereira's Pol. Light* 195 The four-membered or two- and one-axed.. system. **1878-9** J. CAIRD *Philos. Relig.* (1880) 108 Instead of

the parts being used up for the production of the end, we have a membered totality in the production and maintenance of which the parts have their own natural fulfilment or realisation.

b. *spec.* in *Her.* Said of a bird, when the legs are of a different tincture from the body. †Also (see quot. 1610).

1572 BOSSEWELL *Armorie* II. 114b, He beareth Argent, a fesse Gules, betwene three Eaglettes Sable, membred and beaked of the second. **1610** GUILLIM *Heraldry* III. xvii. (1611) 155 All those that either are whole-footed or haue their feet diuided and yet haue no Talants should be termed membred. **1718** NISBET *Ess. Armories, Terms Her., Membred*, is said of the Legs of Birds, when they are of a different Tincture from the Body. **1763** *Brit. Mag.* IV. 238 An eagle with two heads displayed, sable, armed and membered, or. **1864** BOUTELL *Her. Hist. & Pop.* xvii. (ed. 3) 280 Two storks arg., beaked and membered gu.

memberess (ˈmɛmbərɪs). Also **membress.** [f. MEMBER *sb.* + -ESS[1].] A female member; *spec.* a female member of Parliament. (Not in freq. use.)

1867 J. MACGREGOR *Rob Roy on Baltic* x. 126 It would.. be worth while being an M.P... to see the Chancellor of the Exchequer badgered.. by Dr. Emma Blew, Memberess for Honiton. **1876** C. M. YONGE *Three Brides* I. xix. 338 You proved yourself the fittest memberess for the future parliament. **1933** H. BELLOC in *G. K.'s Weekly* 7 Dec. 212/1 Your member, or membress, of Parliament is all for what he or she will call temperance.

†**ˈmembering.** *Her. Obs.* [f. MEMBER *sb.* + -ING[1]: cf. MEMBERED *a.*] The manner in which a heraldic bird is 'membered'; the tincture of the legs.

1610 GUILLIM *Heraldry* III. xx. (1611) 156 You shall not need to mention either the metall of these necks being argent or yet their membring, being gules, because they bee both naturall to the Swanne.

memberless (ˈmɛmbəlɪs), *a.* [-LESS.] Having no member or members.

1611 COTGR., *Tronçonner*.. to make headlesse, branchlesse, memberlesse. **1638** SIR T. HERBERT *Trav.* (ed. 2) 158 A troop of leane fac't, beardlesse, memberlesse Eunuchs. **1863** DANA in *Amer. Jrnl. Sci.* Ser. II. XXXVI. 337 Thus the Crab has a very small memberless abdomen. **1866** *Sat. Rev.* 28 Apr. 494/2 Three months of a new session are not yet over; yet already not a few boroughs have been pronounced memberless.

membership (ˈmɛmbəʃɪp). [f. MEMBER *sb.* + -SHIP.]

1. The condition or status of a member of a society or (organized) body. (Cf. CHURCH-MEMBERSHIP.)

1647 WARD *Simp. Cobler* (1843) 43, I should wish him a Membership in a strict Reformed Church. **1648** J. BEAUMONT *Psyche* x. cclxxviii. (1702) 155 Men, whose mystick obligation Of mutual Membership doth them invite To careful tenderness, and free compassion. **1861** E. GARBETT *Boyle Lect.* 16 The creeds did not add anything to Scripture that was not in it before, but were tests of membership. **1903** *Edin. Rev.* Apr. 454 The oath of membership required fidelity.. to the Church as well as the State.

2. The number of members in a particular body.

1850 'BAT' *Crick. Man.* 87 The.. club.. compris[es] in its membership several promising young players. **1884** *Harper's Mag.* June 148/1 A large membership is necessary. **1884** *Manch. Exam.* 4 Dec. 5/4 The necessity of adding to the membership of the House.

‖**membra disiecta, disjecta,** varr. DISJECTA MEMBRA *Lat. phr.*

1957 N. R. KER *Catal. Manuscripts containing Anglo-Saxon* p. liv, One volume of **29** belonged to Cotton, as well as *membra disiecta* of **22, 83** [etc.]. *Ibid.* p. lxii, The *membra disiecta* have come into existence for various reasons and especially because one part of a manuscript seemed more important than another part or had a different sort of interest. **1963** A. E. ELSEN *Rodin* 175 Vitrines filled with the sculptor's arsenal of membra disjecta. **1970** *Times Lit. Suppl.* 23 July 787/1 As they fed wanly on their ration of membra disjecta, they had scant hope of introduction to the more invigorating study of the specifically human phenomenon of language as a whole.

membral (ˈmɛmbrəl), *a.* Also 7 **memberal.** [f. L. *membr-um* MEMBER + -AL[1].] Pertaining to or characteristic of a member or members (in various senses). Now *rare* exc. *Anat.* and *Zool.* = appendicular.

1603 FLORIO *Montaigne* III. xii. (1632) 596 An unnaturall ill-favourdnesse, and membrall deformity. **1650** HUBBERT *Pill Formality* 63 [Judas] was a member of the Church, and not cast out, and so had a memberal right unto it. **1804** LARWOOD *No Gun Boats* 27 The limb, though amputated, has its membral portion of parental blood still flowing through its arteries. **1827** G. S. FABER *Sacr. Cal. Prophecy* (1844) II. 25 He seems.. to have enjoyed full membral liberty, not being subjected to any other confinement than that of an inclosed park. **1882** WILDER & GAGE *Anat. Techn.* 87 A membral ('appendicular') portion, including the bones of the arms and legs.

Hence †**ˈmembrally** *adv.*, in respect of a member.

1643 R. O. *Man's Mort.* iii. 14 If Nature be deprived more or lesse in her worke of conception of her due,.. her Effect is accordingly: If membrally impedited, a membrall impediment. *Ibid.* 16.

membranaceo- (ˌmɛmbrəˈneɪʃɪəʊ), taken as combining form of MEMBRANACEOUS.

1854 BUSK *Catal. Mar. Polyzoa Brit. Mus.* II. 55 Polyzoary membranaceo-calcareous or calcareous. **1871** W. A. LEIGHTON *Lichen-flora* 3 Thallus membranaceo-lobate.

membranaceous (mɛmbrəˈneɪʃəs), *a.* [f. late L. *membrānāceus*, f. *membrāna* MEMBRANE: see -ACEOUS.]

1. *Nat. Hist.* Resembling or of the nature of a membrane; membranous. In *Bot.* (see quot. 1832).

1684 tr. *Bonet's Merc. Compit.* VII. 253 Men observe the membranaceous Stalk.. where the Ganglium rises. **1713** DERHAM *Phys.-Theol.* IV. xi. 199 Where teeth are wanting.. the Defect is abundantly supplied by one thin membranaceous Ventricle. **1753** CHAMBERS *Cycl. Supp.* s.v. *Leaf*, Membranaceous Leaf, one merely composed of membranes with no pulp between. **1832** LINDLEY *Introd. Bot.* 397 Membranaceous..; thin and semitransparent, like a fine membrane; as the leaves of Mosses. **1871** HARTWIG *Subterr. W.* ii. 11 The soft membranaceous swimming feet. **1874** H. C. WOOD *Fresh-w. Algæ N. Amer.* 14 Thallus membranaceous.

2. Printed on vellum. *nonce-use.*

1824 DIBDIN *Libr. Comp.* 621 *note*, The unique copy.. on vellum, in the matchless membranaceous Alduses of Spencer House.

membraˈnaceously, *adv.* [f. MEMBRANACEOUS *a.*] With membranaceous material.

1821 W. P. C. BARTON *Flora N. Amer.* I. 14 Stem erect,.. four-sided, membranaceously winged on the angles, smooth, nearly naked.

membranate (ˈmɛmbrənət), *a. rare.* [ad. mod.L. *membrānātus*, f. *membrāna* MEMBRANE.] (See quots.)

1777 ROBSON *Brit. Flora* iii. 7 Of stems... Surface... *Membranate*, covered with thin membranes. **1895** *Funk's Stand. Dict., Meˑmbranate*, having the characters of a membrane.

membranated, *a.* [f. mod.L. *membrānāt-us* (f. *membrāna* MEMBRANE) + -ED.] (See quot.)

1776 J. LEE *Introd. Bot.* Explan. Terms 380 *Membranatus*, membranated, flat like a thin pellucid Leaf.

†**membranatic,** *a. Obs.*$^{-0}$ [ad. mod.L. *membrānātic-us*, f. *membrāna*.] (See quot.)

1656 BLOUNT *Glossogr., Membranatick* (*membranaticus*), of or pertaining to a membrane.

†**ˈmembrance.** *Obs.* [a. OF. *membrance*, f. *membr-er* MEMBER *v.*] = REMEMBRANCE.

14.. *Customs of Malton* in *Surtees Misc.* (1890) 63 The qwyche tyme is w[t] owtyn man's membraunce or mynde. **1650** GENTILIS *Considerations* 6 The renoune which remained of Alcibiades, the membrance of his Country, Parents, Nurse and Tutors.

membrane (ˈmɛmbreɪn). Also 6 **-aan,** 7 **-an.** [ad. L. *membrāna* membrane, parchment (whence late Gr. μεμβρᾶνα, μέμβρᾶνον, F. *membrane*, Sp., Pg., It. *membrana*), f. *membrum* MEMBER *sb.*

The etymological sense appears to be 'that which covers the members of the body'.]

1. A thin pliable sheet-like tissue (usually fibrous), serving to connect other structures or to line a part or organ. Also *collect. sing.* = membranous structure.

a. in an animal body.

1615 CROOKE *Body of Man* 77 A Membrane ingirting the whole cauity of the lower belly. **1679** M. RUSDEN *Further Discov. Bees* 5 A Horny membrane or tunicle. **1788** J. C. SMYTH in *Med. Commun.* II. 210 The membrane of the nose, commonly known by the name of Schneiders membrane. **1831** BREWSTER *Nat. Magic* ii. (1833) 10 Behind the vitreous humour, there is spread out on the inside of the eye-ball a fine delicate membrane, called the retina. **1859** J. R. GREENE *Protozoa* 34 The 'dermal membrane' of the Sponge. **1896** KIRKALDY & POLLARD tr. *Boas' Text-bk. Zool.* 336 Just below the portion of skin covered by the eyelids there is usually a thin and soft membrane, which is termed the *conjunctiva bulbi*.

fig. **1626** B. JONSON *Staple of News* III. ii, Vertue and honesty; hang 'hem; poore thinne membranes Of honour; who respects them?

b. in a vegetable body.

1656 BLOUNT *Glossogr., Membrane*,.. the pill or pilling between the bark and the tree. **1681** GREW *Musæum* II. 213 A short Fibrous Lobe... Lined within with a most smooth and thin Membrane. **1835** LINDLEY *Introd. Bot.* (1848) I. 9 Membrane, as true cellulose, may be regarded as being in the beginning, a gelatinous precipitate from the organic mucus of vegetation. **1846-50** A. WOOD *Class-bk. Bot.* 21 The organic basis [of vegetable tissues] is simple membrane and fibre. **1852** HENSLOW *Dict. Bot. Terms, Membrane*... A delicate pellicle of homogeneous tissue. Also a very thin layer composed of cellular tissue. **1890** *Syd. Soc. Lex., Membrane*,.. the thin testa of a seed.

c. *Ent.* The terminal part of a hemielytrum.

1826 KIRBY & SP. *Entomol.* III. 618 The Apical Area is usually most distinguished by nervures..; the object of this is doubtless to strengthen the membrane.

d. *Path.* A morbid formation in certain diseases.

Also *false membrane, pseudo-membrane*, etc.

1765 F. HOME *Croup* 16 The.. surface of the *Trachea* was covered with a white soft thick preternatural coat or membrane. **1797** UNDERWOOD *Disorders of Childh.* I. 346 That tough membrane found in those who have died of the inflammatory croup. **1834** *Cycl. Pract. Med.* III. 488/2 Membranes expelled in dysmenorrhœa. **1835** *Ibid.* IV. 176/1 A more severe form of pharyngeal inflammation is that which is accompanied by the formation of a false membrane. **1905** H. D. ROLLESTON *Dis. Liver* 603 Cases of gall-stone colic accompanied by membranes in the stools.

2. †Parchment (*obs.*); in modern palæography, a 'skin' of parchment forming part of a roll.

1519 HORMAN *Vulg.* 80b, That stouffe that we wrytte vpon: and is made of beestis skynnes: is somtyme called parchement, somtyme velem, somtyme abortyue, somtyme membraan. **1601** in Nichols *Progr. Q. Eliz.* (1823) III. 552 Her rolls, bundells, membranes, and parcells that be reposed in her Majestie's Tower at London. **1651** BOATE in *Ussher's Lett.* (1686) 564 The bare transcription of the Obelisks and Asterisks out of the Membranes. **1656** BLOUNT *Glossogr., Membrane*,.. a skin of parchment. **1870** MISS TOULMIN SMITH in *Eng. Gilds* Introd. 44 'Miscellaneous Rolls, Tower Records'; they consist of three bundles, containing in all 549 skins or membranes. **1890** GROSS *Gild Merch.* II. 137 The third membrane of this Roll.

3. *attrib.* and *Comb.*, as ***membrane-like*** adj., ***membrane plaster***; **membrane-bone** *Ichthyol.*, a bone originating in membranous tissue; **membrane filter**, any of various filters made of cellulosic material and capable of retaining objects as small as bacteria; so ***membrane filtration***.

1880 GUNTHER *Fishes* 91 The principal *membrane-bone of the mandible is the dentary. **1951** *Jrnl. Amer. Water Works Assoc.* XLIII. 975/1 It appears reasonably certain that *membrane filters have approached a degree of refinement that suggests their extended application. **1969** *Methods in Microbiol.* I. vii. 207 Membrane filters, as manufactured by the Millipore Corporation. **1951** *Jrnl. Amer. Water Works Assoc.* XLIII. 945/2 Recent German development in the field of *membrane filtration. **1957** G. E. HUTCHINSON *Treat. Limnol.* I. ix. 646 The probability.. that seston collected by membrane filtration or centrifugation is very largely detritus. **1765** F. HOME *Croup* 54 After a severe fit of coughing a *membrane-like substance.. had been thrown out. **1822-34** *Good's Study Med.* (ed. 4) I. 460 In the disease before us we have neither inflammation nor membrane-like secretion. **1862** *Catal. Exhib.* II. XVII. 128 Liston's *membrane plaster.

Hence **ˈmembraned** *a.*, having or consisting of a membrane; **ˈmembraneless** *a.*, devoid of a membrane.

1872 BROWNING *Fifine* Prol. iv, The membraned wings So wonderful, so wide. **1876** tr. *Wagner's Gen. Pathol.* (ed. 6) 295 Membraneless, nuclear heaps of fine fat-globules.

‖**membranella** (mɛmbrəˈnɛlə). *Zool.* [mod. L., dim. of *membrāna* MEMBRANE.] The long flattened modification of cilia in some infusorians.

1880 SAVILLE-KENT *Infusoria* I. 65 These modified cilia are much flattened or compressed, and appropriately receive from him [Sterki] the distinctive title of 'membranellæ'. **1896** KIRKALDY & POLLARD tr. *Boas' Text-bk. Zool.* 92 *note*, In some Infusoria there are the so-called membranellæ, vibrating, laminating structures, each of which is regarded as a short row of fused cilia.

membraneous (mɛmˈbreɪnɪəs), *a.* [f. late L. *membrāneus*, f. *membrāna* MEMBRANE: see -EOUS.] = MEMBRANOUS.

1633 P. FLETCHER *Purple Isl.* iii. Notes, Choledochus, or the gall, is of a membraneous substance. **1688** BOYLE *Final Causes Nat. Things* iv. 195 The want of feathers in the wings is supplyed by a broad membraneous expansion. **1763** EHRET in *Phil. Trans.* LIII. 130 Leaves, having membraneous ciliated footstalks. **1836-9** *Todd's Cycl. Anat.* II. 536/2 The membraneous labyrinth (*labyrinthus membranaceus*). *Ibid.* 537/1 The membraneous ampullæ.

membraniferous (mɛmbrəˈnɪfərəs), *a. rare*$^{-0}$. [f. MEMBRANE + -(I)FEROUS.] 'Having or producing membranes' (Ogilvie *Suppl.* 1855).

membraniform (mɛmˈbreɪnɪfɔːm), *a.* [f. MEMBRANE + -(I)FORM. Cf. F. *membraniforme*.] Having the character or structure of a membrane.

1828-32 WEBSTER, *Membraniform*, having the form of a membrane or of parchment. **1830** R. KNOX *Béclard's Anat.* 249 The Membraniform Cartilages. **1859** SEMPLE *Diphtheria* 37 Other membraniform fragments.. are also expectorated.

memˈbrano-, taken as combining form of MEMBRANE, with the sense 'consisting of membrane and' (something else denoted by the adj. with which it is joined), as ***membrano-calcareous***, ***-cartilaginous***, ***-coriaceous***, ***-corneous***, ***-nervous***. Also **membranoˈgenic** *a.*, producing membrane.

1835-6 *Todd's Cycl. Anat.* I. 744/2 A membrano-cartilaginous lamina. **1836-9** *Ibid.* II. 537/1 An extremely delicate.. membrano-nervous apparatus. **1838** G. JOHNSTON *Brit. Zooph.* 289 *Flustra tuberculata*, membrano-calcareous. **1850** ALLMAN in *Brit. Assoc. Rep.* (1851) 328 Cœnœcium composed of membrano-corneous branched tubes. **1885** GOODALE *Physiol. Bot.* (1892) 227 *note*, Substances which by their mutual contact give rise to such precipitation-membranes are termed membranogenic. **1890** *Century Dict., Membrano-coriaceous*, of a thick, tough, membraneous texture or consistency, as a polyzoan.

membranoid (ˈmɛmbrənɔɪd), *a.* [f. MEMBRANE + -OID.] Resembling membrane.

1856 MAYNE *Expos. Lex.* **1897** *Allbutt's Syst. Med.* III. 482 The behaviour of the bowels is often irregular..; membranoid shreds, if present, must not be overlooked.

membranology (mɛmbrəˈnɒlədʒɪ). *rare*$^{-0}$. [See -OLOGY.] The science of the membranes.
1775 MOTHERBY *New Med. Dict.*, *Membranologia*, membranology. It treats of the common integuments, and of particular membranes.

membranophone (mɛmˈbreɪnəfəʊn). [f. MEMBRANO- + -PHONE.] A musical instrument which employs a stretched membrane to produce the sound.
1937 *Times Lit. Suppl.* 17 Apr. 288/2 Those [instruments] which employ a stretched membrane (membranophones), such as drums. **1958** *Oxf. Univ. Gaz.* 10 Mar. 772/1 Membranophones, instruments with taut membranes made to vibrate by percussion, friction, or sympathetically. **1960** *Times* 18 Mar. 4/6 But aerophones, idiophones, membranophones..are universal and they are the concern of organology. **1971** *Sci. Amer.* Dec. 90/3 A drum is a membranophone.

membranous (ˈmɛmbrənəs), *a.* [ad. F. *membraneux* (16th c.), f. *membrane* MEMBRANE.] Consisting of, resembling, or of the nature of membrane; membranaceous. In *Bot.*, thin and more or less translucent.
1597 A. M. tr. *Guillemeau's Fr. Chirurg.* 48/1 Certayne membranouse pellicles intermixed with the excrementes. **1646** SIR T. BROWNE *Pseud. Ep.* III. xx. 155 Two black filaments or membranous strings which extend into the long and shorter cornicle upon protrusion. **1756** BURKE *Subl. & B.* IV. xi, The ear drum and the other membranous parts. **1765** F. HOME *Croup* 28 The *mucus*..was formed into a membranous crust. **1811** LETTSOM in Pettigrew *Mem. Life & Writ.* (1817) III. 5 This [croupy] exudation consists of a membranous substance. **1832** LINDLEY *Introd. Bot.* 86 These [modifications] arise either from the addition of parenchyma, when leaves become *succulent*, or from the non-development of it, when they become *membranous*. **1867** J. MARSHALL *Outl. Physiol.* I. 505 The essential parts of the organ of hearing, viz., the membranous labyrinth and the cochlea. **1875** BUCKLAND *Log-bk.* 149 The stomach of the bittern is a membranous bag.

b. Of diseases: Pertaining to or involving the formation of a membrane (see MEMBRANE 1 d).
1875 tr. *von Ziemssen's Cycl. Med.* X. 334 Membranous dysmenorrhœa. **1876** BRISTOWE *Theory & Pract. Med.* (1878) 209 Although membranous croup occurs in adults, it is mainly children who suffer. **1897** *Allbutt's Syst. Med.* III. 943 Dyspeptic membranous colitis.

Hence ˈ**membranously** *adv.*, like membranes.
1750 G. HUGHES *Barbadoes* 293 The leaves..somewhat resemble those of a small curled lettuce, but are far more membranously thin.

‖**membranula** (mɛmˈbreɪnjʊlə). Also anglicized **membranule**. [L. *membrānula*, dim. of *membrāna* MEMBRANE.] A little membrane. **a.** *Anat.* In the eye (see quot. 1840). **b.** *Bot.* In ferns and mosses (see quot. 1821). **c.** *Ent.* 'A small triangular flap or incurved portion on the posterior part of the base of the wings, seen in certain dragon-flies' (*Cent. Dict.*).
1821 S. F. GRAY *Nat. Arr. Brit. Pl.* I. 221 Involucrum, Indusium, Membranula, Glandulæ squamosæ [in ferns]. A membrane that covers the sori, when young. *Ibid.* 222 Membranula [in mosses]. The fine membrane that supports the teeth of the peristome. **1840** G. V. ELLIS *Anat.* 112 The folds and striæ of pigment that compose the corona ciliaris being part of a distinct structure,—the 'membranula', applied on the hyaloid membrane. **1856** MAYNE *Expos. Lex.*, *Membranula*, *Membranulum*,..a little membrane,..a membranule. **1861** HAGEN *Syn. Neuropt. N. Amer.* 133 *Macromia taeniolata*..membranule cinereous.

Hence **memˈbranulet**, in the same sense (*Syd. Soc. Lex.* 1890); **memˈbranulous** *a.*, membranous.
1704 TYSON in *Phil. Trans.* XXV. 1752 The one having Membranulous Scales, the other Bony.

†**membratly**, *adv.* [? Modelled on L. *membrātim*.] Limb from limb.
c **1450** *Mirour Saluacioun* 4362 Some with sawes did he kitte, some with knyves membratly.

†**membrature**. *Obs.*$^{-0}$ [ad. late L. *membrātūra*, f. *membrāre* to furnish with limbs, f. L. *membrum* MEMBER *sb.*] 'A setting or ordering of members or parts' (Blount *Glossogr.* 1656).

†**membrifiˈcation**. *Obs. rare*$^{-1}$. [as if ad. L. **membrificātiōn-em*, f. *membrum*: see MEMBER *sb.* and -FICATION.] Formation of members.
1670 MAYNWARING *Vita Sana* xv. (ed. 2) 136 Membrification or Assimilation is now changed for a Cachectick..habit. **1731** BAILEY vol. II, *Membrification*, a making or producing members or limbs.

‖**membrillo** (memˈbriʎo). [Sp. *membrillo* quince.] A preserve of quinces.
1920 A. E. W. MASON *Summons* viii. 75, I..made money ..by selling dulces and membrilla and almond rock. **1935** M. HUXLEY *Let.* 4 May in A. Huxley *Lett.* (1969) 393 Cherries..have been preserved in all ways possible. Bottled, made into jams, made into queso, like membrillo, under alcohol. **1947** M. LOWRY *Under Volcano* vii. 239 There were big green barrels of jerez, habanero, catalán, parras, zarzamora, malaga, durazno, membrillo, raw alcohol at a peso a litre. **1966** P. V. PRICE *France: Food & Wine Guide* 263 A thick quince jelly, like the Spanish *membrillo*. **1970** *Guardian* 20 Nov. 11/1 *Membrillo*..is the famous Spanish quince cheese.

†**membrose**, *a. Obs.*$^{-0}$ [ad. late L. *membrōsus*, f. *membrum*: see MEMBER *sb.* and -OSE.] Having large members (Bailey vol. II, 1727). Also †**membrosity** [ad. med.L. *membrōsitas*], 'the largeness or hugeness of members' (Bailey 1721).

†**membrous**, *a. Obs.* [ad. late L. *membrōsus*: see prec. and -OUS.] Having a large 'member.'
1613 PURCHAS *Pilgrimage* (1614) 570 Their membrous monster Priapus.

memento (mɪˈmɛntəʊ). Pl. **mementoes**, **mementos** (7-8 **memento's**). [Imperative of *meminisse* to remember, a reduplicated formation on the root **men-*: see MIND *sb.*]

1. *Eccl.* Either of the two prayers (beginning with *Memento*) in the Canon of the Mass, in which the living and the departed are respectively commemorated.
1401 *Pol. Poems* (Rolls) II. 103 Thanne was the memento put fally in the masse. **1433** LYDG. *St. Giles* 227 in Horstm. *Alteng. Leg.* (1881) 374 Beyng at thy masse,..[thou] praidest for the kyng In thy Memento. **1549** LATIMER *3rd Serm. bef. Edw. VI* (Arb.) 86 When I shuld saye masse, I haue put in water twyse or thryse for faylynge, in so muche when I haue bene at my Memento, I haue had a grudge in my conscyence, fearynge that I hadde not putte in Watter ynoughe. **1593** *Rites & Mon. Ch. Durh.* (Surtees) 82 He that sunge masse hadde alwaies in his Memento all those that had geven any thinge to that Church. **1883** *Cath. Dict.* (1897) 287 After the consecration, in the fifth prayer of the Canon, the priest makes a memento of the dead. Both mementos in some MS. Missals retain the title 'oratio super' or 'supra diptycha'.

2. a. A reminder, warning, or hint as to conduct or with regard to future events. ? *Obs.*
1582 STANYHURST *Æneis* I. (Arb.) 22 Bee sure, this practise wil I nick in a freendlye memento. **1603** SIR C. HEYDON *Jud. Astrol.* xx. 412, I must needes giue him another memento and tell him, that he [etc.]. **1658** SIR T. BROWNE *Hydriot.* 45 Since the brother of death daily haunts us with dying mementos. *a* **1711** KEN *Lett.* Wks. (1838) 82 God..enable us to improve all the mementoes he is pleased to give us of eternity. **1769** BLACKSTONE *Comm.* IV. 85 This is a great security to the public,..and leaves a weighty *memento* to judges to be careful. **1791** BOSWELL *Johnson* an. 1779 (end), That this *memento*..must be in every letter that I should write to him, till I had obtained my object. **1814** *Edin. Rev.* XXIV. 243 That what we have to say may..be recorded..as a *memento* against future errors.

b. *concr.* An object serving to remind or warn in this way.
1580 G. HARVEY *Three Proper Lett.* 34 Maruell not, what I meane to send these Verses at Euensong: On Neweyeeres Euen, and Oldyeeres End, as a Memento. *a* **1623** FLETCHER *Wife for Month* I. ii. Rings, deaths heads, and such mementoes. **1658** SIR T. BROWNE *Hydriot.* Ep. Ded., Artificial Mementos, or Coffins by our Bed-side, to mind us of our Graves. **1719** DE FOE *Crusoe* I. 229, I have been, in all my Circumstances, a Memento to those who are touch'd with the general Plague of Mankind. **1839** MURCHISON *Silur. Syst.* I. v. 73 Our only present memento of the existence of volcanic action beneath us, consisting in very slight shocks of earthquake. **1885** RIDER HAGGARD *K. Solomon's Mines* (1889) 100 There he sat, a sad memento of the fate that so often overtakes those who would penetrate into the unknown.

3. a. Something to remind one of a past event or condition, of an absent person, of something that once existed; now chiefly, an object kept as a memorial of some person or event.
1768 C. SHAW *Monody* viii. 76 Where'er I turn my eyes, Some sad memento of my loss appears. **1791** COWPER *Lett.* Wks. 1837 XV. 226, I cannot even see Olney spire,..and still less the vicarage, without experiencing the force of those mementos, and recollecting a multitude of passages, to which you and yours were parties. **1826** KIRBY & SP. *Entomol.* III. xxx. 211 It will not suffer this memento of its former state [a cast-off skin] to remain near it. **1862** SALA *Seven Sons* II. x. 263 She came upon some boyish memento of him who was gone.

†**b.** A memory or remembrance. *Obs. rare*$^{-1}$.
1796 BURNEY *Mem. Metastasio* I. 179 It has awakened in my mind a croud of delightful mementos of laughable adventures.

¶**4.** Humorously misused for: **a.** A reverie, 'brown study'; hence, a doze; **b.** (One's) memory.
1587 GREENE *Tritam.* II. H3, Panthia..seeing that Aretino his choller was not yet digested, willing with some discourse to bring him out of his memento,..saide [etc.]. **1593** NASHE *Christ's T.* (1613) 164 Dormatiue potions..that when [she] lies by him,..she may steale from him, whiles he is in his deepe memento. **1594** —— *Unfort. Trav.* 7 Presently he remembred himselfe, and had like to haue fallen into his memento againe. **1619** CHAPMAN *Two Wise Men* IV. i. 43, I heare it well Sir, and haue lock'd it vp safely in my memento.

‖**5. memento mori** (ˈməʊraɪ, ˈmɔːrɪ). [L. = 'remember that you have to die'.] **a.** A warning of death. **b.** *concr.* A reminder of death, such as a skull or other symbolical object.
[**1592** NASHE *Summers Last Will* Wks. VIII. 48 Whateuer you do, memento mori, remember to rise early in the morning.] **1596** SHAKS. *1 Hen. IV*, III. iii. 34, I make as good vse of it, as many a man doth of a Deaths-Head, or a *Memento Mori*. **1597** *Pilgr. Parnass.* II. 214 (Macray), If I doe not..Ile give my heade to anie good felowe to make a *memento mori* of! **1641** in W. W. Wilkins *Pol. Ballads* (1860) I. 3 Memento Mori, I'll tell you a strange story. *a* **1680** ROCHESTER *Let. fr. Artemiza in Town*, Now scorn'd by all, forsaken, and opprest, She's a *Memento mori* to the rest. **1738** G. LILLO *Marina* I. ii, Thy face is a *memento mori* for thy own sex. **1850** THACKERAY *Pendennis* II. xxiii. 229 A great man must keep his heir at his feast like a living *memento mori*.
attrib. **1877** W. JONES *Finger-ring* 372 In the same collection is a 'memento mori' ring, of bronze.

6. ‖**memento vivere** [L. = 'remember (that you have) to live' (used in conscious opposition to *memento mori*)]: a reminder of life; a reminder of the pleasure of living.
1928 BLUNDEN *Undertones of War* ii. 17 Sitting in the headquarters dugout with 'La Vie Parisienne' as a *memento vivere*. **1931** A. HUXLEY *Cicadas* 8 Rosy among the funeral black (*Memento Vivere*) a naked girl. **1966** *Punch* 19 Oct. 603/2 A *memento vivere* from an asylum sought, found, but ultimately rejected.

memer(e, variants of MAMMER *Obs.*, to stammer.

†**memerill**. *Obs. rare*$^{-1}$. Also **meimerill**, **memerel**. [represents *memerylo* in the Italian original.] An arbutus.
1592 R. D. *Hypnerotomachia* 34 b, The leaffy Memerill or Arbut. *Ibid.*, Betwixt the comare Meimerill or Arbut, and the Satire, were two little Satires. *Ibid.* 93 Fruitefull memerels.

meminiscent, *a.* Blunder (after L. *meminisse*: see MEMENTO) for REMINISCENT.
1812 L. HUNT in *Examiner* 7 Dec. 770/1 A voice meminiscent of mouthful and burly with luxury. **1847** —— *Jar Honey* i. (1848) 2 The word 'Sicilian'—a very musical and meminiscent word.

Memlo(o)k, obs. forms of MAMELUKE.

Memnonian (mɛmˈnəʊnɪən), *a.* [f. L. *Memnoni-us* (a. Gr. *Μεμνόνειος*, f. *Μεμνον-*, *Μέμνων* Memnon) + -AN.] **a.** Pertaining to the demigod Memnon, traditionally said to have erected the citadel or palace at Susa; hence used as an epithet of Susa or Persia generally. **b.** Having the property of the statue at Thebes in Egypt, believed by the Greeks to represent Memnon, and said to give forth a musical sound when touched by the dawn.
1614 SIR A. GORGES tr. *Lucan* III. 96 So huge a masse of Martiall bands Came not from the Memnonian lands, When Cyrus [etc.]. **1667** MILTON *P.L.* x. 308 Xerxes,..From Susa his Memnonian Palace..Came to the Sea. **1843** LD. HOUGHTON *Poems Many Years* (1844) 251 When my Memnonian lyre Welcomed every rising sun.

Memnonist, -ite: see MENNONIST, -ITE.

memo (ˈmɛməʊ). Abbreviation of MEMORANDUM; *colloq.* treated as a word. Cf. MEM.
1889 SIR P. WALLIS in Brighton *Life* (1892) 217 You have not received a memo. card which I posted you last week. **1903** *Blackw. Mag.* Feb. 162/2 This person annotates reports, writes memos.

memoir (ˈmɛmwɑː(r), -wɔː(r), ˈmɛmɔɪə(r)). Also 6 **memoyr**, **memor**, 7-9 **memoire**, (7 **memoyre**, **mesmoire**). [a. F. *mémoire* masc., a specialized use, with alteration of gender, of *mémoire* fem., MEMORY. The change of gender is commonly accounted for by the supposition that the word in this use is elliptical for *écrit pour mémoire*; Sp., Pg., and It. have *memoria* fem. in all senses.
The quasi-Fr. pronunciation, which is still most frequently heard, is somewhat anomalous, as the word is fully naturalized in use, and has been anglicized in spelling; its continued currency is prob. due to the fact that *-oir* is unfamiliar as an ending of English words.]

†**1.** A note, memorandum; record; *pl.* records, documents. *Obs.*
1567 in *6th Rep. Hist. MSS. Comm.* 643/2 Memoyr off the silwer veschell delyverit be me to the lard of Drumblanryk. **1580** *Reg. Privy Council Scot.* III. 335 Quhairof ordanis the said maser to deliver the said Johnne sum memor in write, quhilk gif he find different from his awin speking that then he pen and put in write the same his speking. **1659** WOOD *Life* 16 Sept. (O.H.S.) I. 283 Georg Wharton..did take notice of this matter in his almanack anno 1661,..but puts the memoire under the XI of Sept. which is false. **1727** ARBUTHNOT *Tables Anc. Coins*, etc. 188 There is not in any Author a Computation of the Revenues of the Roman Empire, and hardly any Memoirs from whence it might be collected. **1755** MAGENS *Insurances* II. 261 That the Master be provided with a Memoir of Signals from the Commander of the Convoy.

2. In diplomatic and official use: = MEMORANDUM. *rare.* †Also in *pl.* official reports of business done.
1696 PHILLIPS, *Memoirs*..are papers deliver'd by Embassadore to the Princes or States to whom they are sent, upon occasions of Business. **1700** ASTRY tr. *Saavedra-Faxardo* I. 222 Examine diligently all the Qualities of your Subjects, and after having given them any Place, look now and then into their Actions, and not be presently taken with, and deluded by the Draught of their Memoirs. **1829** B'NESS BUNSEN in Hare *Life* (1879) I. ix. 323 Charles, at his request, wrote a memoir on the subject of the negociations of Protestant Powers with the Court of Rome.

3. *collect. pl.* **a.** A record of events, not purporting to be a complete history, but treating of such matters as come within the personal knowledge of the writer, or are obtained from certain particular sources of information.

1659 Pearson *Creed* (1839) 282 *note*, Pontius Pilate kept the memoirs of the Jewish affairs, which were therefore called *Acta Pilati*. *a* **1661** Fuller *Worthies, Devon.* I. (1662) 260 But abler Pens, will improve these Short Memoires into a large History. **1746** A. Collins (*title*) Letters and Memorials of State... Also Memoirs of the Lives and Actions of the Sydneys. **1762** Sterne *Tr. Shandy* VI. xxxvi, The following memoirs of my Uncle Toby's courtship. **1769** N. Nicholls in *Gray's Corr.* (1843) 97 Why then a writer of memoirs is a better thing than an historian. **1790** Paley *Horæ Paul.* i. 1 To deliver the history, or rather memoirs of the history, of this same person. **1860** Westcott *Introd. Study Gosp.* vii. (ed. 5) 347 Their whole structure.. serves to prove that they [the Synoptic Gospels] are memoirs and not histories.

b. A person's written account of incidents in his own life, of the persons whom he has known, and the transactions or movements in which he has been concerned; an autobiographical record.

1673 Evelyn *Diary* 18 Aug., Nor could I forbeare to note this extraordinary passage in these memoires. **1676** Wycherley *Pl. Dealer* Ded., Your virtues deserve.. a volume entire to give the world your memoirs, or life at large. **1700** Prior *Carmen Seculare* 426 To write his own memoirs, and leave his heirs High schemes of government, and plans of wars. **1710** (*title*) Memoirs of an Unfortunate Young Lady. **1818** Syd. Smith *Wks.* (1867) I. 237 Any one who provides good dinners for clever people, and remembers what they say, cannot fail to write entertaining memoirs. **1841** Elphinstone *Hist. Ind.* II. 117 His Memoirs are almost singular in their own nature.

4. A biography, or biographical notice.

1826 *Life Dr. Franklin* i. 6 (Stanf.) The subject of our memoir was born at Boston in New England. **1839** G. Taylor (*title*) Memoir of Robert Surtees Esq. **1866** Cates *Maunder's Biog. Treas.* Pref., The space thus gained is more usefully occupied, partly by re-written and fuller notices of names more generally interesting, and partly by entirely new memoirs.

5. An essay or dissertation on a learned subject on which the writer has made particular observations. Hence *pl.* the record of the proceedings or transactions of a learned society.

a **1680** Butler *Rem.* (1759) I. 14 Whilst the chiefs were drawing up This strange Memoir o' th' Telescope. **1687** A. Lovell tr. *Thevenot's Trav.* I. 103, I shall here.. relate what I have learned of some Islles of the Archipelago, where I have not been, as well by what has been told me, as by a memoire that hath come to my hands. **1731** Bailey vol. II, *Memoi'rs*,.. a journal of the acts and proceedings of a society, as those of the royal society, &c. **1787** Jefferson *Writ.* (1859) II. 247 A memoire on a petrifaction mixed with shells. **1845** G. Busk *Steenstrup's Altern. Gener.* 102 Miescher's interesting memoir on the forms which the genus *Tetrarhynchus* passes through. **1865** (*title*) Memoirs read before the Anthropological Society of London. 1863-4.

†**6.** A memento, memorial. *Obs. rare*⁻¹.

a **1711** Ken *Christophil* Poet. Wks. 1721 I. 518 Of Friends whom Death lays fast asleep, They Memoirs keep.

7. *Comb.*, as ***memoir-writer***, ***-writing***.

1711 Shaftesb. *Charac.* (1737) I. 224 The raw memoir-writings and unform'd pieces of modern statesmen, full of their interested and private views. **1762** *Ann. Reg.* II. 32 Count Zinzendorf is celebrated for his profound ministerial abilities by all the memoir writers of the present age. **1860** W. G. Clark *Vac. Tour* 44 When two memoir-writers had told the same tale, they [Suetonius and Tacitus] accept it and endorse it, without a suspicion that both may be lying.

memoir(e, obs. forms of memory.

memoirist (ˈmɛmwɑːrɪst, -wɔːr-). [f. memoir + -ist.] A writer of memoirs, or of a memoir.

1769 R. Griffith *Gordian Knot* I. 154 (F. H.). **1839** Taylor *Mem. Surtees* in *Surtees' Durham* 95 *note*, Memoranda.. which the Memoirist was allowed to read. **1889** G. W. Cable *Strange True Stories Louisiana* ii. 48 Carlo was beginning to swear 'fit to raise the dead', writes the memoirist, at the tardiness of the Norman pair. **1907** *Daily Chron.* 11 Jan. 3/2 In almost every section of the volume he advances, as a memoirist, a moralist,.. or a translator.., someone whose name deserves to be rewritten over a faded tomb. **1914** *N.Y. Times* 31 May, These memoirists are as frankly revealing as any that described the daily life of the Grand Monarch's Court. **1970** *Daily Tel.* (Colour Suppl.) 13 Nov. 54/4 Hack memoirists often describe [Greta] Garbo as 'lonely' or 'loveless'.

So ˈ**memoirism**, the practice of writing memoirs.

1833 Carlyle *Misc. Ess., Diderot* (1872) V. 63 Towards reducing that same Memoirism of the Eighteenth Century into History.

memomotion (ˈmɛməʊməʊʃən). [f. memo (?repr. L. *memor* mindful, and derived words) after micromotion.] A term used (usu. *attrib.*) in place of micromotion when time-lapse photography is used in place of ordinary cinematography.

1950 M. E. Mundel *Motion & Time Study* xiii. 253 Memomotion study is the name given to the special form of micromotion study in which the pictures are taken at unusually slow speeds, one frame per second being the most common. **1961** *Engineering* 6 Oct. 449 Both memo-motion and micromotion filming have developed into very useful study aids. **1967** G. Wills in Wills & Yearsley *Handbk. Managem. Technol.* x. 183 With techniques from work study using memo-motion cameras and a variety of other photographic techniques, an accurate picture of behaviour can be deduced. **1970** R. Hammell in D. Baker et al. *Physical Design Electronic Syst.* I. xi. 507 A highly precise form of activity sampling, called memomotion study, employs a motion picture camera.

memor, obs. form of memory.

‖**memorabilia** (ˌmɛmərəˈbɪlɪə). [neut. pl. of L. *memorābilis* memorable.] Memorable or noteworthy things. Also (rare) *sing.* ‖**memorabile** (mɛməˈreɪbɪliː), something memorable.

The currency of the word in Eng. may be due to its use as the Latin title of Xenophon's 'Recollections' ('Ἀπομνημονεύματα') of Socrates.

1806-7 J. Beresford *Miseries Hum. Life* (1826) ii. Introd., Let us at once produce our memorabilia and proceed to exchange their contents. **1826** Scott *Diary* 14 Sept. in *Lockhart*, I should not have forgotten, among the *memorabilia* of yesterday, that two young Frenchmen made their way to our sublime presence. **1830-2** Memorabile [see memorable B. quot. 1823]. **1878** Spurgeon *Treas. Dav.* Ps. cxi. 4 The coming out of Egypt, the sojourn in the wilderness, and other memorabilia of Israel's history.

memorability (ˌmɛmərəˈbɪlɪtɪ). [f. next: see -ity.] The quality of being memorable. Also, a person or thing worth remembering.

a **1661** Fuller *Worthies, Kent* II. (1662) 85 And how abundantly intituled [she was] to Memorability, the ensuing Epitaph.. will sufficiently discover. **1834** Southey *Doctor* xlvii. (1848) 111 The first years of Daniel's abode in Doncaster were distinguished by many events of local memorability. **1855** Carlyle *Prinzenraub* Misc. 1857 IV. 351 There is one memorability of his last sad moments. **1866** —— *E. Irving* 145 Frank was a notable kind of man, and one of the memorabilities, to Irving as well as me. **1903** Myers *Hum. Personality* I. 36 The memorability of an act is, in fact, a better proof of consciousness than its complexity.

memorable (ˈmɛmərəb(ə)l), *a.* and *sb.* [ad. L. *memorābilis*, f. *memorāre*: see memorate *v.* and -able. Cf. F. *mémorable*, Sp. *memorable*, Pg. *memoravel*, It. *memorabile*.] **A.** *adj.*

1. Worthy of remembrance or note; worth remembering; not to be forgotten.

1483 *Rolls of Parlt.* VI. 241/1 The memorable and laudable Acts in diverse Batalls. **1585** T. Washington tr. *Nicholay's Voy.* I. xv. 16 b, A succinct description of the yland, and memorable things thereof. **1650** Marvell *Horatian Ode* 58 He nothing common did or mean, Upon that memorable scene. **1709** Steele *Tatler* No. 86 ⁋3 It is memorable of the mighty Caesar, that when he was murdered in the Capitol.. he gathered his Robe about him, that he might fall in a decent Posture. **1820** Hazlitt *Lect. Dram. Lit.* 40 It hardly contains a memorable line or passage. **1858** Carlyle *Fredk. Gt.* III. v. (1872) I. 163 That is his one feat memorable to me at present. **1895** *Law Times* C. 3/1 An interesting record of a most memorable and successful innovation in our legal system.

2. Easy to be remembered. *rare.*

1599 Shaks. *Hen. V*, II. iv. 53 Witnesse our too much memorable shame. **1658** Phillips, *Memorable*, easie to be remembred. **1881** Ruskin *Love's Meinie* I. iii. 99 The easily memorable root 'dab', short for dabble. **1882** S. Cox *Miracles* (1884) 14 Hence it [the Mosaic account of the Creation] must of necessity be concise, simple, memorable.

3. Awakening memories *of*. *rare.*

1872 Howells *Wedd. Journ.* 248 The marshy meadows beyond, memorable of Recollets and Jesuits.

B. *sb. pl.* = memorabilia. Also (rare) *sing.*

1611 Coryat *Crudities* 470 These memorables of Germany. **1613** Jackson *Creed* I. xxviii. §1 Recorded.. as one of the chiefe memorables in his raigne. **1702** C. Mather *Magn. Chr.* III. I. (1852) 251 If no speedy care be taken to preserve the memorables of our first settlement. **1813** Scott *Fam. Lett.* 13 July, I spent part of Sunday in showing them the Abbey and other memorables. **1823** —— *St. Ronan's Well* xxvi. (near end), The other memorable [1830-2 memorabile] is of a more delicate nature, respecting the conduct of a certain fair lady. **1856** Hawthorne *Eng. Note-Bks.* (1879) II. 237 These were all the memorables of our visit.

Hence ˈ**memorableness**, memorability; ˈ**memorably** *adv.*, in a memorable manner; so as to be remembered.

1727 Bailey vol. II, *Memorableness.* **1755** Johnson, *Memorably*, in a manner worthy of memory. **1832** Carlyle in *Fraser's Mag.* V. 259 It is well worth the Artist's while to examine for himself what it is that gives such pitiful incidents their memorableness. **1832** —— *J. Carlyle* 34, I never saw him but once, and then rather memorably. **1885** *Manch. Exam.* 12 Aug. 3/1 The power of so conceiving characters as to impress us strongly and memorably with their varied individualities.

†ˈ**memoral**, *a. Obs.* [ad. med.L. *memorālis* (OF. *memoral*), f. L. *memor* mindful: see -al¹.] ? Remembering, monumental. Hence ˈ**memorally** *adv.*, by way of reminder.

1513 Bradshaw *St. Werburge* I. 207 As Chester, Stafford, Lytchefelde, Couentre memorall [*rime* withall]. *c* **1530** *Pol. Rel. & L. Poems* (1903) 72/23 Bothe Ioye and sorowe in woo memorall [*rime* fantasticall]. *a* **1645** Habington *Surv. Worc.* III. 550 On the south side of the Chancell are these memorally of our mortality. *O esca vermium* [etc.].

†**memorance.** *Obs.* [as if ad. L. type **memorantia*, f. *memorāre*: see memorate *v.* and -ance.] Memory.

c **1320** [see next B. 1]. **1480** *Charters* etc. *Peebles* (1872) 187 The quhylkis sall reman in memorans of the samyn. **1662** Forbes *Aberdeen Cantus* in *Herd's Songs* (1904) 95 So that your soverance.. Mark in your memorance, mercie and ruth.

†**memorand**, *a.* and *sb. Obs.* [ad. L. *memorandus*, *-um*: see memorandum.]

A. *adj.* Serving as a memorial.

c **1320** R. Brunne *Medit.* 32 A soper he made to his deciples.. A memorand þyng to haue yn mynde.

B. *sb.*

1. A memorial.

c **1320** R. Brunne *Medit.* 195 Yn a memorand [*v.r.* In memoraunce] of hym with outyn ende.

2. = memorandum.

1686 Goad *Celest. Bodies* I. xv. 99 God hath imprinted on the Universe.. some Memorands or Signatures of his Creation. *Ibid.* III. ii. 406 Though I was no Eye-Witness of these Hail-Storms so many years ago, yet I am sure their Memorand is True. **1711** Madox *Hist. Exchequer* xxii. 619 The Records or Bundles made up by the two Remembrancers of the Exchequer have been usually called Memoranda, the Memorands or Remembrances.

memoˈrandist. *rare*⁻¹. [f. memorand-um + -ist.] One who writes memoranda.

1866 R. Chambers *Ess.* Ser. I. 210 Johnson was also a great memorandist.

memorandize (mɛməˈrændaɪz), *v.* [f. memorand(um *sb.* + -ize.] *trans.* and *intr.* To make memoranda (of).

1881 W. Whitman *Specimen Days* (1882-3) 178 Now he is sitting on the limb of an old tree.. —seems to be looking at me while I memorandize. **1912** G. Mallory *Boswell* ix. 246 Miss Burney has left us an admirable account of Boswell's deportment when in the act of 'memorandising' Dr. Johnson's conversation.

memorandum (mɛməˈrændəm), *sb.* (Also 7 -dome.) Pl. **memoranda** (-ˈændə), **memorandums** (-ˈændəmz). [L., neut. sing. of *memorandus*, gerundive of *memorāre* (see memorate *v.*).]

1. '(It is) to be remembered': placed (like 'Nota bene') at the head of a note of something that is to be remembered or a record (for future reference) of something that has been done. Now only *legal.*

1433 *Rolls of Parlt.* V. 423/1 Memorand', yat ye xxiiii day of Novembr', ye Communys [etc.]. **1465** *Paston Lett.* II. 175 Memorandum to Thomas More that because ye myzt foryete myne erand to Maister Bernay, I pray you rede hym my bille. **1506** *Guylforde's Pilgr.* (Camden) 15 Memorandum, that vpon Tewysday.. we come to Jaffe. **1567** in *6th Rep. Hist. MSS. Comm.* 643/2 Memorandum deliuerit to the lard of Drumlenrik thir pieces off siluer work efter following. **1655** in *Z. Boyd's Zion's Flowers* (1855) App. 29/2 *Memorandum*, that the whol is to repay to the Colledge, the half of the above mentioned 66 lib. 03 sh. 4d. **1763** Sterne *Let.* 12 June, Memorandum! I am not to forget how honest a man I have for a banker at Paris. **1820** Gifford *Compl. Eng. Lawyer* (ed. 5) 664 An Agreement for letting a First and Second Floor, Garret, and Kitchen, unfurnished. Memorandum, That it is hereby declared and agreed by and between [etc.].

2. a. 'A note to help the memory' (J.); by extension, a record of events, or of observations made on a particular subject, esp. when intended for the writer's future consideration or use.

1542-3 *Act 34 & 35 Hen. VIII*, c. 16 §1 Diuers summes.. as in the rolles, & Memorandum of the.. Escheker more plainly it may appere. **1596** Shaks. *1 Hen. IV*, III. iii. 179 If there were any thing in thy Pocket but Tauerne Recknings, Memorandums of Bawdie-houses. **1622** Bacon *Hen. VII* 212 And ouer against this Memorandum (of the Kings owne hand) *Otherwise satisfied.* **1726** Swift *Gulliver* II. vi, Taking Notes of what I spoke, and Memorandums of what Questions he intended to ask me. **1813** *Aubrey's Lett.* I. Advt., The Lives.. were originally designed as memoranda for the use of Anthony a Wood, when composing his Athenæ Oxonienses. **1854** J. Martineau *Ess.* (1869) II. 307 The few lines and points that are jotted down may serve, perhaps, as indicative memoranda to those who know the ground. **1903** *19th Cent.* June 961 He awoke and made a memorandum of the day and the hour and the smell.

b. *spec.* A record of a pecuniary transaction.

[**1607** *Lingua* III. i, *Memorandum* that I owe; that he owes.] **1607** Middleton *Michaelm. Term* v. i, Ile heartilye set my hand to a Memorandum. **1664** Pepys *Diary* 30 Sept., I had not fulfilled all my memorandums and paid all my petty debts. **1711** M. Henry *Forgiveness of Sin* Wks. 1853 II. 326/1 The memorandum of a debt is blotted out when it is paid. **1865** Dickens *Mut. Fr.* I. iv, I suppose a memorandum between us of two or three lines, and a payment down, will bind the bargain.

c. *Law.* The writing or document in which the terms of a transaction or contract are embodied. In *Marine Insurance*, a clause in a policy enumerating the articles in respect of which underwriters have no liability.

memorandum of agreement, the heading of certain forms of agreement. ***memorandum of association***, a document required, under the Companies Acts, for the registration of a joint stock company, containing the name of the company, its object, capital, etc. ***memorandum in error***, 'a document alleging error in fact, accompanied by an affidavit of such matter of fact' (Wharton); abolished 1875.

1591 Greene *Art Conny Catch.* II. (1592) 23 A Memorandum drawn in some legall forme. **1677** *Act 29 Chas. II* c. 3 §4 Unlesse the Agreement.. or some Memorandum or Note thereof shall be in Writeing. **1771** Burrow *K. B. Rep.* III. 1551 This Clause, or Memorandum was introduced, He said, to deliver the Insurers from small Averages. **1802** S. Marshall *Insur.* I. 139 In the common policies, used in London by private underwriters, the memorandum runs thus: N B. Corn, fish, salt, fruit, flour and seed, are warranted free from average, unless general, or the ship be stranded [etc.]. **1820** Gifford *Compl. Eng. Lawyer* (ed. 5) 661 Agreement to grant a Lease of a House. Memorandum made this day of 1819, between A.B. of of the one part, and C.D. of of the other part, as follows. **1836** R. Thomson *Bills of Exch.* etc. (ed. 2) 12 Conditions of payment.. contained in a separate memorandum on the bill or note. **1852** *Act 15 & 16 Vict.* c. 76 §158 Either Party alleging Error in Fact may deliver to One of the Masters of the Court a Memorandum in Writing,

in the Form [etc.]. **1862** *Act 25 & 26 Vict.* c. 89 §6 Subscribing their Names to a Memorandum of Association.

d. 'In diplomacy, a summary of the state of a question, or a justification of a decision adopted' (Ogilvie 1882).

1658 *Mercurius Polit.* 7–14 Oct. 908 To whom cause and Reason was shewed about the non-satisfactory proffer made lately by the Portugal Ambassador, who intends to put in another Memorandum. **1853** Malmesbury *Mem. Ex-Minister* (1884) I. 402 Sir Robert Peel.., the Duke of Wellington, and Lord Aberdeen..drew up and signed a memorandum, the spirit and scope of which was to support Russia in her legitimate protectorship of the Greek religion and the Holy Shrines. **1885** Lowe *Bismarck* II. 77 Their deliberations..resulted in the preparation of the so-called Berlin Memorandum.

†**3.** An injunction to remember something. *Obs.*

1586 B. Young *Guazzo's Civ. Conv.* IV. 191 A certaine memorandum, that he gaue mee, which was, That..I should haue an especiall care, not to incurre at anie time the daunger of water. **1610** Day *Festivals* iii. (1615) 70 Remember saith the Apostle St. Paul among his many Memorandums unto Timothy [etc.]. **1643** Sir T. Browne *Relig. Med.* §45, I have therefore enlarged that common *Memento mori*, into a more Christian memorandum, *Memento quatuor Novissima.*

†**4. a.** A reminder; also, a memento, souvenir. *Obs.*

a **1591** H. Smith *Serm.* (1624) 18 Some sentence which you haue heard, shall gnaw you at the heart with a memorandum of hell. *a* **1618** W. Bradshaw *Medit. Mans Mort.* (1621) 34[Every day] bringing with it some judgement and Memorandum or other of Gods anger for sin. **1659** Stokes *Explic. Min. Proph.* 577 They shall walk about like living carcases, ugly, noisome spectacles of misery, and memorandums of divine vengeance. **1679** *Exec. Bury* 4 He was found Guilty of Manslaughter, and carries a Memorandum in his Hand, to make him and others more wary for the future. **1760–72** H. Brooke *Fool of Qual.* (1809) IV. 91 Ye precious relics, ye delicious memorandums. **1808** Pike *Sources Mississ.* I. App. 3 Some other trifling things, as a memorandum of my good will. **1847** De Quincey *Sp. Mil. Nun* §8 That pocket-handkerchief which he had left at St. Sebastian's fifteen years ago,..and which..was the one sole memorandum of papa ever heard of at St. Sebastian's.

†**b.** A mark or sign serving to identify. *Obs.*

1760–72 H. Brooke *Fool of Qual.* (1792) II. 129 Had you any particular memorandum or mark whereby you would know him to be your child?

5. *Comm.* An informal epistolary communication, without signature or formulæ of address or subscription, usually written on paper with a printed heading bearing the word 'Memorandum' and the name and address of the sender.

6. *attrib.*, as ***memorandum book, paper,*** †***ring, tablet***; also ***memoranda rolls***; **memorandum articles**, the articles enumerated in a marine insurance memorandum (*Cent. Dict.*); **memorandum check**, 'a brief informal note of a debt of the nature of a due bill' (Ogilvie 1882); **memorandum head**, † (*a*) a head clever at making mental memoranda (? *nonce-use*); (*b*) *Comm.* the printed heading of a 'memorandum' (see 5).

1748 S. Richardson *Clarissa* V. xlii. 301 On which she observes in her *memorandum-book as follows. **1753** *Scots Mag.* XV. 36/2 She was..entering some particulars in her memorandum-book. **1843** Mrs. Carlyle *Lett.* I. 223 Having bethought me of a pretty memorandum-book in my reticule. **1830–57** Paige *Rep.* II. 612 (Bartlett) *Memorandum check. **1732** Lady B. Germain *Let.* 23 Feb. *Swift's Wks.* (1841) II. 667, I wish I had my dame Wadgar's, or Mr. Ferris's *memorandum head, that I might know whether it was 'at the time of gooseberries'. **1710** Swift *Jrnl. to Stella* 3 Nov., I have put MD's commissions in a *memorandum paper. **1794–6** E. Darwin *Zoon.* (1801) I. 179 As we talk of *memorandum-rings, and tie a knot on our handkerchiefs to bring something into our minds. **1886** *Encycl. Brit.* XX. 312/2 [An] important class of documents belonging to the Court of Exchequer..is the *memorandum rolls. *Ibid.*, The 'brevia regia' endorsed on the memoranda rolls. **1774** *Westm. Mag.* II. 560, I dropt my ivory *Memorandum-tablet in the Bedford Coffee-house.

Hence **memo'randum** *v. trans.*, to make a memorandum of; **memo'randumer** *nonce-wd.*, one who makes memoranda.

1787 Mme. D'Arblay *Diary* 26 Feb., I feel sorry to be named..by that biographical, anecdotical memorandummer [Mr. Boswell]. **1805** T. Holcroft *Bryan Perdue* III. 94 The moneybills..were addressed to me, that I might memorandum their amount. **1816** Scott *Antiq.* xli, Which business will in future be carried on under the firm of Greenhorn and Grinderson, (which I memorandum for the sake of accuracy in addressing your future letters). **1817** Fosbrooke *Brit. Monarchism* 348 The Scribes also memorandumed their interlineations.

†**'memorate**, *v. Obs.* [f. L. *memorāt-*, ppl. stem of *memorāre*, f. *memor* mindful: see memory.] *trans.* To bring to mind; to mention, recount, relate. Hence **'memorated** *ppl. a.*

1623 Cockeram, *Memorate*, to make mention of a thing. **1631** Heylin *St. George* 17 In his so memorated Storie of St. George and of the Dragon. **1647** Trapp *Marrow Gd. Authors* in *Comm. Ep.* 649 That so memorated jest of Tully. **1686** Goad *Celest. Bodies* II. ii. 176 An. 1501, where the Ebb overflow'd, memorated by Lye.

†**memo'ration**. *Obs.* [ad. late L. *memorātiōn-em*, n. of action f. *memorāre* (see prec.).]

1. Mention; commemoration.

1553 Becon *Reliques of Rome* (1563) 132 This constitution concerning yͤ memoration and prayer for yͤ dead. **1627** Speed *England* xxxviii. §9, I will forbeare to be prolixe..in the particular memoration of places in a Prouince so spatious.

2. The process of remembering.

1573 W. Fulwod tr. *Gratarolus' Castel of Memorie* vi. E vj b, Aristotle thought good, to assigne two actes of Memoration: to wit, Memorye and Remembraunce.

memorative ('mɛmərətɪv), *a.* and *sb.* ? *Obs.* [ad. med.L. **memorātīvus* (perh. through F. *mémoratif*, 13–14th c.), f. *memorāre*: see memorate *v.* and -ative.] **A.** *adj.*

1. Reminding one of something; preserving or reviving the memory of some person or thing; commemorative.

1448–9 J. Metham *Amoryus & Cleopes* D iv b (MS.), Yͤ memoratyf dart had wounded hym so sore Off Cleopes bryght chere. *c* **1557** Abp. Parker *Ps.* lxix. 191 No where in booke memorative wyth just men have they place. *a* **1603** T. Cartwright *Confut. Rhem. N.T.* (1618) 402 Melchisedec, which figured out this memoratiue sacrifice, brought forth bread and wine. **1777** Nicolson & Burn *Westm. & Cumb.* II. 193 A memorative epitaph for the worthy and loving Colonel Thomas Barwise. **1835** Carlyle in Froude *Life in Lond.* (1884) I. i. 20 Vernal weather of all kinds,..to me most *memorative.*

2. Of or pertaining to the memory, esp. in ***memorative faculty, power, virtue.***

1481 Botoner *Tulle on Old Age* (Caxton) C 4, The vertue memoratyf callyd remembraunce. *a* **1586** Sidney *Arcadia* v. (1598) 445 Voide of sensible memory, or memoratiue passion. *a* **1677** Hale *Prim. Orig. Man.* 8 How the Species, Order, and Circumstances of things are preserved in the Memorative Faculty or Organ. **1706** Phillips, *Memorative*, belonging to the Memory; as *The memorative Power.*

b. In ***art memorative*** (= med.L. **ars memorativa*, Gr. τέχνημα μνημονικόν).

1576 Fleming *Panopl. Epist.* 303 *margin*, This Simonides was the first inuenter of the Art memoratiue. **1597** J. King *On Jonas* (1618) 383 Many haue..made a memoratiue art, appointing places and their furniture, for the helpe of such as are vnexperienced. *a* **1628** Sir J. Doderidge *Eng. Lawyer* (1631) 23 The precepts of Art Memorative.

3. Having a good memory; retentive.

1481 Caxton *Myrr.* III. xxiii. 186 Thaugh he had..a thousand hertes within his body the most subtyle and the most memoratyf that myght be taken. **1610** Healey *St. Aug. Citie of God* VII. vii. (1620) 252 A respectiue memory and a memoratiue prouidence must of force goe together. **1695** tr. *Martial* I. xxvii. 38 A memorative drunkard all men hate [orig. Μισῶ μνάμονα συμπόταν].

B. *sb.* Something to put one in mind of a thing; a memorial.

1597 J. King *On Jonas* (1618) 396 Short sentences and memoratiues, as *Know thy selfe, Vse moderation, Beware of suretishippe*, and the like. **1631** J. Burges *Answ. Rejoined* 137 As Rites, as helpes, as memoratiues of such duties. **1690** E. Gee *Jesuit's Mem.* Pref. 1 The Notes and Observations of this Memorative following were gathered and laid together in time of Persecution.

†**memore**, *a. Obs. rare*⁻¹. [a. L. *memor* mindful.] Mindful *of.*

1500–20 Dunbar *Poems* lxxxv. 53 Memore of sore, stern in Aurore, Lovit with angellis stevyne.

memore, obs. form of memory.

†**memoriable**, *a. Obs. rare*⁻¹. [a. OF. *memoriable*, f. *memorie* memory: see -able.] = memorable.

1436 *Libel Eng. Policy* in *Pol. Poems* (Rolls) II. 194 [King Edgar was not] lasse memoriable Than Cirus was to Perse by puissaunce.

memorial (mɪ'mɔərɪəl), *a.* and *sb.* [a. OF. *memorial* (mod.F. *mémorial*) = Sp., Pg. *memorial*, It. *memoriale*, ad. L. *memoriālis* adj. (neut. *memoriāle*, used in late Latin as sb.), f. *memoria* memory.] **A.** *adj.*

1. Preserving the memory of a person or thing; often applied to an object set up, a festival (or the like) instituted, to commemorate an event or a person.

c **1374** Chaucer *Anel. & Arc.* 18 Thow Polymea..that.. Syngest with vois memorial in þe shade. **1426** Lydg. *De Guil. Pilgr.* 16923 Thylke Memoryal wrytyng off thy Secretys, which thyn owne Secretarye, Seynt Bernard, wroot. **1535** Coverdale *Mal.* iii. 16 It is before him a memoriall boke written for such as feare the Lorde. **1606** Shaks. *Tr. & Cr.* v. ii. 80 Thy Maister..takes my Gloue, And giues memoriall daintie kisses to it. **1725** Pope *Odyss.* XIII. 180 A memorial stone. **1866** Rogers *Agric. & Prices* I. xix. 476 The memorial windows set up to some of Edward the Third's children and relations. **1877** W. Jones *Finger-ring* 375 A..memorial ring in connection with the death of Nelson. **1885** *Times* 29 July 10/3 A memorial service for General Grant will be held in Westminster Abbey.. simultaneously with the funeral service at Mount Macgregor in America.

†const. *of.* **1725** Pope *Odyss.* I. 412 Gifts, memorial of our friendship. **1726** Broome *Pope's Odyss.* XXIV. Notes V. 286 May I..at the conclusion of a work, which is a kind of monument of his partiality to me,..place the following lines, as an Inscription memorial of it?

†**2.** Of which the memory is preserved; remembered; also, worthy to be remembered, memorable.

1390 Gower *Conf.* III. 383 Wherof his name schal be blessid, For evere and be memorial. **1503** Hawes *Examp. Virt.* VII. xlvi, They made theyr dedes to be memoryall. *c* **1566** J. Alday tr. *Boaystuau's Theat. World* L viij, In the knowledge of Histories or memoriall things done in our time. **1631** Fosbroke *Solomons Charitie* (1633) 1 The memoriall and infallible necessity of death.

3. a. Of or pertaining to memory. †**b.** Intended to assist the memory, mnemonic. †**c.** Done from memory.

c **1400** *Lanfranc's Cirurg.* 120 Not oonly animal vertues.. ben I-chaungid, also naturel vertues..also memorial. *a* **1734** North *Exam.* Pref. (1740) 1 To apply his rational as well as memorial Faculties in Opposition to those false and unjust Reflections upon the aforesaid Reign. **1735** B. Martin (*title*) The Young Student's Memorial Book or Patent Library. **1745** J. Mason *Self-Knowl.* I. xv. (1853) 117 Your Minutes or memorial Aids. **1774** M. Mackenzie *Maritime Surv.* p. xiv, A Memorial Sketch is, a Delineation of a Harbour, or any Part of a Coast, from the Memory only. **1821** R. Turner *Arts & Sci.* (ed. 18) 299 The Memorial lines stand thus. **1830** H. N. Coleridge *Grk. Poets* (1834) 43 One of the best instances of the memorial power in composition that I have found. **1847** Grote *Greece* II. xxxvii. (1862) III. 339 We hear of his memorial discipline. **1891** S. W. Mitchell in *Century Mag.* Dec. 287/2 The man thus imprisoned within himself recovers by effort a vast amount of memorial property presumed to have been lost. **1920** *Times Lit. Suppl.* 20 May 320/2 A link of material transmission..which..puts the theory of simple memorial piracy definitely out of court. **1959** F. Bowers *Textual & Lit. Crit.* iii. 71 A memorial lapse, but not a misreading, must be posited. **1963** *Medium Ævum* XXXII. 23 It is often impossible to be sure whether scribal or memorial transmission has produced a given cluster of variants.

†**4.** Mindful. Const. inf. *rare*⁻¹.

1494 Fabyan *Chron.* VII. 590 His soule to endowe, he was memoryall.

B. *sb.*

†**1.** = memory. **a.** The bearing of something in mind; remembrance, recollection. Phr. ***in (the) memorial of***: in memory or remembrance of.

1382 Wyclif *Ps.* ci. 13 Lord, in to withoute ende abidist stille; and thi memorial [Vulg. *memoriale*] in to ieneracioun and in to ieneracioun. **1390** Gower *Conf.* II. 70 An old Cronique..The which into memorial Is write. *c* **1480** Henryson *Test. Cress.* 519 For knichtly pity and memoriall Of fair Cresseid, ane girdill can he tak. **1532** More *Confut. Tindale* Wks. 471/2 A bare simple signe, and sette but onely to signify the memoriall of Christes passion. **1605** *Play Stucley* in Simpson *Sch. Shaks.* (1878) I. 265 In memorial of this victory. **1696** Tate & Brady *Ps.* cxii. 6 The sweet Memorial of the Just Shall flourish when he sleeps in dust. **1701** *Lond. Gaz.* No. 3770/2 Thy Memorial will be renowned to Posterity. *a* **1716** South *Serm.* (1744) IX. i. 19 That man who has tears to spend at the memorial of a lost friend, but none to shed at the thoughts of a lost innocence, ..has but too much cause to suspect the truth of his sorrow. **1774** J. Bryant *Mythol.* II. 277 The term..was a proper name bestowed in memorial of a person.

†**b.** The faculty of remembering; (a person's) memory or power of recollection. *Obs.*

1390 Gower *Conf.* II. 19 On..Which lost hath his memorial, So that he can no wit withholde. **1412–20** Lydg. *Chron. Troy* I. i. (1555), Bothe minde and memoriall Fordulled wer. **1538** Bale *God's Promises* in Dodsley *O.P.* (1780) I. 39 The matters are such as..ought not to slyde from your memoryall. **1567** *Gude & Godlie Ball.* 32 Quhair na myndis memoriall Can think, nor tung can tell the tryne.

2. A memorial act; an act of commemoration; *spec. Eccl.* = commemoration 2 b.

1468 *Paston Lett.* II. 312 Wyth moch lesse cost he myght make som othyr memorialle also yn Cambrygge. **1492** *Rolls of Parlt.* VI. 444/2 Dedes of Charite and memorialls to be doon for him. **1548–9** (Mar.) *Bk. Com. Prayer, Communion*, We..make here before thy diuine Maiestie, with these thy holy giftes, the memoryall whyche thy sonne hath wylled us to make. **1560** Daus tr. *Sleidane's Comm.* 313 b, The memorial, invocation and intercession of saintes. **1613** Purchas *Pilgrimage* (1614) 623 To meete, and make memoriall of their deceased friends with remembrance of their vertues. **1866** *Direct. Angl.* (ed. 3) 355 When two holidays fall together, the service of the superior one is used, and the collect of the inferior day is said after that of the Office of the Feast as its memorial.

3. Something by which the memory of a person, thing, or event is preserved, as a monumental erection, a custom or an observance. Phr. ***for a memorial*** (cf. 1 a).

1382 Wyclif *Exod.* iii. 15 This is name to me withouten ende, and this my memoriale in generacioun and into generacioun. *c* **1430** Lydg. *Min. Poems* (Percy Soc.) 61 These iiij. figures, combyned into one, Sette on thy mynde for a memorial. *c* **1440** *Promp. Parv.* 332/1 Memoryal on a grawe..in remembrawnce of a dede body. *c* **1449** Pecock *Repr.* Prol. 4 The memorialis or the mynde placis of Seints. **1530** Tindale *Prol. Lev.* Wks. (1573) 14/1 Baptisme is our common badge, and sure earnest, and perpetual memoriall that we pertaine vnto Christ. **1611** Bible *Mark* xiv. 9 This also that she hath done, shall be spoken of for a memoriall of her. **1648** *Bury Wills* (Camden) 202 To buy him a ring for a memoriall of me. **1726** Swift *Gulliver* IV. xii, They set up a rotten Plank or a Stone for a Memorial. **1849** Macaulay *Hist. Eng.* v. I. 613 The plough and the spade have not seldom turned up ghastly memorials of the slaughter. **1853** J. H. Newman *Hist. Sk.* (1873) II. 168 The memorials of the rule of the Pharaohs are still engraved on the rocks of Libya. **1857** Ruskin *Arrows of Chace* (1880) I. 44 Every day renders the destruction of historical memorials more complete in Europe.

†**4. a.** A note or memorandum. *Obs.*

1577 [Dee] (*title*) General and Rare Memorials pertayning to the Perfect Arte of Navigation. **1622** Bacon *Hen. VII* 243 Full of Notes and Memorialls of his owne Hand, especially touching Persons. **1726** Swift *Gulliver* III. x, These Struldbrugs and I would mutually communicate our Observations, and Memorials through the Course of Time. **1732** —— *Beasts' Confess.* Wks. 1755 IV. I. 271 His promises he ne'er forgot, But took memorials on the spot. **1817** *Parl.*

Deb. 1879 That Mr. Harmer drew his petitions from memorials by T.E.

†**b.** A book of memoranda; a day book. *Obs.*

1588 J. Mellis *Briefe Instr.* Bivb, The Memorial is a booke where-in a marchaunt discrieueth and writeth all his daily businesse.

c. *Law.* An abstract of the particulars of a deed, etc., serving for registration.

1813 *Act 53 Geo. III*, c. 141 §2 A Memorial of the Date of every such Deed..shall be enrolled in the High Court of Chancery. **1818** Cruise *Digest* (ed. 2) II. 61 Before the registering of the memorial of the deed.

d. *Scots Law.* A statement of facts drawn up to be submitted for counsel's opinion. Also, an advocate's brief.

1752 *Acts of Sederunt* (1760) 462 The Lords, having taken into consideration the bad practice of giving in long memorials before advising prepared states, They from this day forward discharge the giving in any such memorials, and that short cases..be made by each party, and put into the Lords boxes. **1815** Scott *Guy. M.* xxxvi, 'Give me the memorial, and come to me on Monday at ten', replied the learned counsel. *a* **1822** in *Kay's Portraits* (1838) II. 278 It's no in your memorial (brief).

5. A record, chronicle, or memoir; now chiefly *pl.*, a record, often containing personal reminiscences, of the history of a person, place, or event.

1513 Bradshaw *St. Werburge 200 An other Balade* 1 O frutefull histore o digne memoriall. *c* **1515** (*title*) The Auchinleck Chronicle: ane Schort Memoriale of the Scottis Corniklis for Addicioun [1436–1461], printed from the Asloan MS. **1667** Milton *P.L.* I. 362 Though of their Names in heav'nly Records now Be no memorial. *a* **1671** Ld. Fairfax *Mem.* (1699) 1 A short Memorial of the northern actions in which I was engaged. **1748** H. Walpole *Lett.* (1846) II. 228, I am a little pleased to have finished a slight memorial of it [*sc.* Houghton]. **1843** Sir T. D. Lauder (*title*) Memorial of the Royal Progress in Scotland in 1842. **1872** Hare (*title*) Memorials of a Quiet Life.

6. In diplomatic use: A general designation for various classes of informal state papers, either presented by an ambassador to the representative of the Power to which he is accredited, and embodying statements of facts, claims, or propositions made on behalf of his government, or sent by the ministry of foreign affairs to one of its own agents abroad, containing instructions relative to some matter of negotiation.

1536 in Strype *Eccl. Mem.* I. App. lxxvi. 182 *heading*, A memorial of such articles as were..treated of between the kings highnes counsailers &..the French ambassadors. **1561** *Reg. Privy Council Scot.* I. 194 To gif in befoir the Quenis Grace..ane formal and sufficient roll and memorial. **1680** (*title*) The two memorials delivered by Mr. Sidney his majesty of Great Britains Envoy extraordinary to induce the States-general not to enter into a league defensive with the French king. **1696** Phillips, *Memorial*,..a Writing delivered in by a Publick Minister about some part of his Negotiation. **1758** *Ann. Reg.* 187 A memorial presented..to the dyet of the empire, by Baron Gimmengen, electoral minister of Brunswick Lunenbourg. **1833** Alison *Hist. Europe* (1848) I. iii. §19. 230 The king,..unable to make up his mind on the subject, had it repeatedly debated, both orally in the council, and in written memorials of no common ability.

7. A statement of facts forming the basis of or expressed in the form of a petition or remonstrance to a person in authority, a government, etc.

1713 Steele *Guardian* No. 128 ¶2 A most humble address, or memorial, presented to her majesty. **1769** Robertson *Chas. V*, iv. Wks. 1813 V. 393 They drew up and published a memorial, containing all their demands. **1832** Ht. Martineau *Demerara* ii. 15 They met from time to time to..draw up memorials to Government.

8. *attrib.*: **memorial day**, a day on which a memorial is made; *U.S.* (with initial capitals) the day (in the Northern States 30 May; in the Southern States at various dates) set apart for honouring the memory of those who fell in the civil war of 1861–65.

1836 Keble *Serm.* xi. (1848) 276 There seems a propriety in reading on his memorial-day in particular the account of their common calling and adherence to Christ. **1897** Kipling *Captains Courageous* 245 And Monday's Memorial Day.

memorial (mɪˈmɔərɪəl), *v.* [f. memorial *sb.*]

1. *trans.* **a.** To address a memorial to (a person); to memorialize.

1768 Sir W. Johnson in F. Chase *Hist. Dartmouth Coll.* (1891) I. 80 They had even the face..to memorial me, praying that the Indians might not be allowed to give up far to the north or west. **1778** *Phil. Surv. S. Irel.* 352 Birmingham, Sheffield and other inland towns memorial government not to execute a scheme so big with ruin. **1831** Doyle in W. J. Fitz-Patrick *Life* (1880) II. 440 Would not the proper mode of proceeding, in the case of the soldier, be to memorial the commander-in-chief? **1894** W. O'Brien in *Daily News* 25 Dec. 6/5 The tenants..meekly memorial his lordship for some consideration.

b. To denounce in a memorial.

1731 *N. Hampshire Prov. Papers* (1870) IV. 614 In order to memorial the Governour to the Right Honourable the Lords of Trade & Plantations, as a Person not a friend to the Province.

2. *intr.* To draw up a memorial; to petition *for*.

1764 P. Skene in *N. York Col. Doc.* (1856) VII. 615 The Hon[ble] Board of Trade directed that the above lands memorialed for, should not be granted. **1821** Col. Hawker *Diary* (1893) I. 242 My brother officers..expressed a wish (and even wanted to memorial) for my promotion.

3. *Law.* To enter in a memorandum.

1824 *Ann. Reg.* 64 All transfers should be null and void until so memorialled and enrolled.

memorialist (mɪˈmɔərɪəlɪst). [f. memorial *sb.* + -ist.]

1. One who addresses or presents a memorial.

1713 Steele *Guardian* No. 128 ¶2 The nauseous memorialist, with the most fulsom flattery tells the queen of her thunder. **1741** in G. Sheldon *Hist. Deerfield, Mass.* (1895) I. 491 Your Memorialist Humbly prays that a consideration of the sd affair may be had. **1858** Greener *Gunnery* 345 And memorialist, as in duty bound, will ever pray.

2. A writer of biographical or historical memorials.

1766 *Ann. Reg.* ii. 29 The pains..the celebrated memorialist takes to gloss over her actions. **1832** *Blackw. Mag.* XXXII. 559 We purpose to collect from these obscure, but most interesting memorialists, a few sketches and biographical portraits of these great princes. **1903** Morley *Gladstone* I. i. 1 In one sense a statesman's contemporaries..must be the best if not the only true memorialists and recorders.

†**3.** One who has a good memory. *Obs.*

1719 *Freethinker* III. 40 Others..look on a mere Memorialist as an ill-digested Commonplace Book.

memorialize (mɪˈmɔərɪəlaɪz), *v.* [f. memorial *v.* + -ize.]

1. *trans.* To preserve the memory of; to be or supply a memorial of: to commemorate.

1798 T. Green *Diary Lover of Lit.* (1810) 82 A stone, memorialising the spot of a 'barbarous murder'. **1822–56** De Quincey *Confess.* Wks. 1890 III. 255 Those '*grammatici*' whom he [Suetonius] memorialises as an order of men flocking to Rome in the days of the Flavian family. **1892** *Blackw. Mag.* CLI. 58/1 Five arches, probably meant to memorialise the five arches of the Pool of Bethesda.

2. To address a memorial to. Also *absol.*

1798 *Hull Advertiser* 14 Apr. 2/4 The Deputies..continue to memorialize the French Plenipotentiaries. **1855** Mrs. Gore *Mammon* II. 154 Last year, I memorialised the bishop. **1880** Disraeli *Endym.* III. xxxi. 310 The counties met, the municipalities memorialised.

Hence **meˈmorialized**, **meˈmorializing** *ppl. adjs.*; **memorialiˈzation**, the action of memorialize *v.*; **meˈmorializer**, one who memorializes.

1803 *Man in Moon* (1804) 113 Memorialized. **1807** Bentham *Mem. & Corr.* Wks. 1843 X. 424 An arrangement which..J. B. has the satisfaction of seeing proposed by the memorializing Judges. **1837** T. Hook *Jack Brag* (L.), The memorializers had taken the precaution to put their memorial in the form of a round-robin. **1874** Piazzi Smyth *Our Inheritance* ii. x. 193 Those..Egyptians..delighted in ..architectural memorialization of bulls and goats and.. every bestial thing.

memorially (mɪˈmɔərɪəlɪ), *adv. rare.* [f. memorial *a.* + -ly[2].]

1. By heart; = memoriter.

1660 J. Lloyd *Prim. Episc.* 33 A premeditated and memorially delivered prayer. **1866** *Public School Latin Primer* Pref., A concise manual of facts and codes of rules in Latin, to be memorially learnt.

2. As a memorial; so as to preserve a memory.

1876 Lowell *Among my Bks.* Ser. ii. 314 Not so much living in his poems as memorially recording his life in them.

‖**memoria technica** (mɪˈmɔərɪə ˈtɛknɪkə). [L. = 'technical memory'.] A method by which the memory is assisted by artificial contrivances; a system of mnemonics; a mnemonic contrivance.

1730 [R. Grey] (*title*) Memoria Technica; or, a new method of Artificial Memory. **1843** R. J. Graves *Syst. Clin. Med.* Introd. Lect. 32 Must an artificial method of forgetting become even more necessary than a memoria technica? **1864** Pusey *Lect. Daniel* vi. 295 Such were the 22 Books intended by Josephus, so numbered by a sort of memoria technica, in conformity to the 22 Hebrew letters.

memoried (ˈmɛmərɪd), *a.* [f. memory + -ed[2].]

1. Having a memory (of a specified kind), as ***long-***, ***short-memoried***.

1573 L. Lloyd *Pilgr. Princes* 138b, The well memoried man. **1610** Healey *St. Aug. Citie of God* (1620) 249 Plato in his Theætetus saith that the cholericke person is the best memoried. **1877** Long-memoried [see long *a.*[1] 16].

2. Full of or fraught with memories. *rare.*

1851 C. T. d'Eyncourt *Eustace* (ed. 2) 18 It is such house-hold scenes as these which form The memoried World of Youth. **1898** W. K. Johnson *Terra Tenebr.* 141 And be the memoried tomb with rose-leaves spread. **1951** N. M. Gunn *Well at World's End* i. 9 She had a rosy wrinkled face like some memoried moony fruit.

memorious, *a. Obs.* or *arch. rare.* [ad. med.L. *memoriōsus* (OF. *memorieux*), f. *memoria* memory: see -ous.]

1. Having a good memory; mindful *of*.

1599 R. Linche *Fount. Anc. Fict.* Liijb, If by the Tyrannie of fore-passed times, the memorious notes of such industrious fathers were not blotted out. *c* **1600** *Timon* ii. i. (Shaks. Soc.) 26 *Pseud.* Dos't thou remember? *Gelas.* I am memorious. **1603** Florio *Montaigne* iii. viii. 563 Learned, wise and memorious [orig. *memorieux*]. **1621** G. Sandys *Ovid's Met.* xiv. (1626) 296 Memorious [orig. *memores*] of the Trojan woes. **1656** Blount *Glossogr.*, *Memorious*, that hath a good memory.

2. Memorable.

1883 Burton & Cameron *Gold Coast* I. 19 Shaggy Cintra ..with its memorious convent and its Moorish castle.

memorist (ˈmɛmərɪst). *rare.* [f. memory or memorize *v.*: see -ist.]

†**1.** One who prompts the memory. *Obs.*

1682 Sir T. Browne *Chr. Mor.* i. §21 Conscience the punctual Memorist within us.

2. One who memorizes or commits to memory; one who has a retentive memory. Orig. *U.S.*

1872 *New Cycl. Illustr. Anecd.* 9/2 Fame has given me the report of being a memorist. **1920** H. G. Wells *Outl. Hist* 115/2 Here we have..the medicine-man, the shrine-keeper, and the memorist, developed, with the development of the community.

‖**memoriter** (mɪˈmɒrɪtə(r)), *adv.* [L., f. *memor* mindful, remembering.] From memory, by heart.

1612 Brinsley *Lud. Lit.* xiii. (1627) 178 All the Theames of this Author being then written of and pronounced by them memoriter. **1766** T. Clap *Hist. Yale Coll.* 82 Twice a Week five or six deliver a Declamation memoriter from the oratorical Rostrum. **1890** J. Pulsford *Loyalty to Christ* I. 330 Any man of the world with ordinary intelligence might learn it, and express it memoriter.

b. as *adj.* Spoken or speaking 'memoriter'.

1802–12 Bentham *Ration. Judic. Evid.* (1827) III. 461 In the case of memoriter evidence of this description. **1896** *Daily News* 11 Jan. 6/4 The mere memoriter preacher.

memorize (ˈmɛməraɪz), *v.* [f. memory + -ize.]

1. *trans.* To keep alive the memory or recollection of; to cause to be remembered, make memorable. Now *rare* or *Obs.*

1594 J. Dickenson *Arisbas* (1878) 58 His fortune or rather misfortune..is memorized by vs in a prouerbial byword. **1605** Shaks. *Macb.* i. ii. 40 Except they meane to.. memorize another Golgotha. *a* **1639** Spottiswood *Hist. Ch. Scot.* ii. (1677) 28 To memorize this victory, the King did found an Episcopal See. **1657** R. Vines *Lord's Supper* (1677) 162 Memorizing him in a piece of bread and cup of wine. **1846** Landor *Hellenics* Wks. II. 484 Muses..Who from your sacred mountain..hear and memorise The crimes of men and counsels of the Gods.

b. Said of impersonal subjects. Also *intr.* To be a memorial or memento.

1593 Nashe *Christ's T.* 36 Eate of my sonne one morsel yet, that it may memorize against you, ye are accessary to his dismembering. **1622** Drayton *Poly-olb.* xxi. 160 Nothing.. Except poore widdowes cries to memorize your theft. **1654–66** Earl Orrery *Parthen.* (1676) 621 The Hellespont, memorized by the famous death of Hero and Leander. **1822** *Blackw. Mag.* XII. 412 A Cenotaph to memorise our grave.

2. To perpetuate the memory of in writing; to put on record; to relate, record, mention. Now *rare*.

1591 Spenser *Ruines of Time* 364 Because they living cared not to cherishe No gentle wits..Which might their names for ever memorize. **1632** Lithgow *Trav.* i. 11, I arriued at Rome, of the which I will memorize, some rarest things. **1652–62** Heylin *Cosmogr.* i. (1682) 88 Here flourished the exact Martial discipline, so memorized by ancient Historiographers. **1701** J. Prince (*title*) Danmonii Orientales Illustres...A Work wherein the Lives and Fortunes of the Most famous Divines,..Natives of that most noble Province..are memoriz'd. **1831** Lamb *Let. to Moxon* in *Final Mem.* viii, The R.A. here memorised, was George Daw. **1869** Browning *Ring & Bk.* ix. 1345 Like the strange favour, Maro memorized As granted Aristæus. *with clause.* **1619** Wither *Vox Pacif.* ii. 45 You have not memorized..How God..against your Enemies hath fought.

3. To commit to memory. Chiefly *U.S.*

1856 Olmsted *Slave States* 552 His power of memorizing and improvising music. **1878** W. H. Daniels *That Boy* ix. 140 He had even taken the pains to memorize a number of hymns and sonnets. **1894** Maskelyne *Sharps & Flats* vi. 150 The sharp..should be able to memorise instantly as many cards as possible.

Hence **ˈmemorized** *ppl. a.*, **ˈmemorizing** *vbl. sb.* and *ppl. a.*; **ˈmemorizable** *a.*, that may be memorized or committed to memory; **memoriˈzation**, the action of the verb memorize; **ˈmemorizer**, one who memorizes.

1600 Tourneur *Transf. Metam.* Wks. 1878 II. 211 Who vow'd his name should be æternized..In memorizing lines. **1634** Sir T. Herbert *Trav.* 135 A place scarce worth the memorizing. **1839** J. Rogers *Antipopopr.* iii. §2. 145 Jerome had more learning, Augustine had more logic; the former being the greater memorizer. **1884** *American* VIII. 396 Any good memorizable series. **1886–7** T. Grady *Proc. Amer. Instruct. Deaf* 261 A vast process of memorization. **1889** *Anthony's Photogr. Bull.* II. 297 An easily memorized series of shop sizes. **1890** J. G. Fitch *Notes Amer. Schools & Training Coll.* 50 What is oddly called 'memorizing'..is often confined to the reproduction of scraps of information or short passages from text-books.

†**ˈmemorous**, *a. Obs.* [ad. med.L. *memorōsus* (OF. *memoreux*), f. L. *memor* mindful: see -ous.] Memorable.

1513 Bradshaw *St. Werburge* i. 159 Whiche realme by processe and power vyctoryous Subdued all other to hym, full memorous. *Ibid.* 283 Whiche ladyes were buryed full memorous At Peturborowe abbay.

memory (ˈmɛmərɪ), *sb.* Forms: α. (chiefly *Sc.* and *north.*) 4–6 **memoire, memore, memour,** 5–6 **-oyre,** 6 **memor, memoir.** β. 4–6 **memorye,** 4–7 **memorie,** (6 **memoree, -i**), 4– **memory.** [a. OF. *memorie, memoire, memore* (mod.F. *mémoire*) = Sp., Pg., It. *memoria*, ad. L. *memoria*, noun of quality or condition f. *memor* mindful, remembering, a reduplicated formation on the

root **mer-*, Indogermanic **smer-* (Skr. *smar-*) to remember.

There is no etymological connexion between L. *memor* and the vb. *meminī* I remember.]

1. a. The faculty by which things are remembered; the capacity for retaining, perpetuating, or reviving the thought of things past. ***to commit*** or **†*commend to memory***: see the vbs. In *Psychol.* freq. sub-categorized according to its manifestation or the bodily process with which it is believed to be connected.

1340 *Ayenb.* 107 Ac y-yeue is þe herte parfitliche and yconfermed, uor þe memorie is zuo cleuiynde ine him þet ne of no þing þenche bote ine him. *c* **1375** *Sc. Leg. Saints* vi. (*Thomas*) 395 For in til a man visdome Is, & of þat ane þare procedis vndirstandynge, memore, & wite. **1413** *Pilgr. Sowle* (Caxton 1483) IV. xxv. 71 God made man ryght as a Trynyte, he yaf him memory, vnderstandyng and wylle. **1513** DOUGLAS *Æneis* x. Prol. 70 Rayson decernis, memor kepis the consait. **1530** PALSGR. 666/2, I commende it to memorie. *c* **1540** BOORDE *The boke for to Lerne* C iij b, It doth acuat, quycken, and refreshe, the memorye. **1690** LOCKE *Hum. Und.* I. iv. (1695) 35 By the memory it [an idea] can be made an actual perception again. **1718** LADY M. W. MONTAGU *Let. to Lady Rich* 16 Mar., The memory can retain but a certain number of images. **1828** SCOTT *F.M. Perth* xxiv, Our memory is, of all our powers of mind, that which is peculiarly liable to be suspended. **1855** H. SPENCER *Princ. Psychol.* (1872) I. IV. viii. 483 The subject-matter of Memory is retrospective. **1883** F. GALTON *Inquiries into Human Faculty* 106 One favourite expedient was to associate the sight memory with the muscular memory. **1897** tr. *T. Ribot's Psychol. of Emotions* 153 Others..recall the circumstances *plus* the revived condition of feeling. It is these who have the true 'affective memory'. **1899** *Amer. Jrnl. Psychol.* XI. 7 He found that recollection could be mediated..(1) through visual images, (*a*) successive in time or space, or (*b*) grouped..*plus* motor memory. **1906** C. S. SHERRINGTON *Integrative Action Nervous Syst.* ix. 330 The relative haste with which an animal when hungry approaches food..suggests that conation attaches to the visual reaction by association through memory with affective tone. **1921** B. RUSSELL *Analysis of Mind* ix. 157, I shall attempt the analysis of memory-knowledge..because memory, in some form, is presupposed in almost all other knowledge. **1955** H. E. GARRETT *Gen. Psychol.* x. 381 The phenomena of memory may be classified under the four headings *fixation* or acquisition, *retention, recall,* and *recognition*... Each of these four processes is a necessary part of memory. **1961** F. H. GEORGE *Brain as Computer* viii. 280 The hippocampus and hippocampal gyrus are therefore important features in recent memory. **1967** M. B. ARNOLD in Appley & Trumbull *Psychological Stress* 139 How intensely we experience stress may depend on the strength of this affective memory. **1969** T. FREEMAN *Psychopathol. of Psychoses* viii. 134 Sometimes the patient appears to have no capacity for short-term recall and yet at other times this function is quite intact. Similar inconsistencies of performance affect long-term and immediate memory.

personified. **1618** BP. HALL *Righteous Mammon* 95 Memory, the Great keeper or Master of the rolles of the soule. **1831** WORDSW. *Bothwell Castle*, Memory, like sleep, hath powers which dreams obey..; How little that she cherishes is lost!

b. ***art of memory, artificial memory***: mnemonics; a system of mnemonic devices.

[**1491** PETRUS RAVENNAS (*title*) Foenix; seu artificiosa memoria.] **154.** R. COPLAND (*title*) The Art of Memory, that otherwyse is called the Phenix. **1573** W. FULWOD tr. *Gratarolus' Castel of Memorie* vii. F v b, Artificiall Memorie is a disposyng or placing of sensible thinges in the mynde by imagination, whereunto the naturall Memorie hauing respect, is by them admonished. **1594** NASHE *Unfort. Trav.* 70 It is not possible for anie man to learne the Art of Memorie,..except he haue a naturall memorie before. **1647** COWLEY *Mistress, Soul* iii, So that thy Parts become to me A kind of Art of Memory. **1653** R. SANDERS (*title*) Physiognomie..Whereunto is added the Art of Memorie. **1747** HOYLE (*title*) A Short Treatise On the Game of Whist ..To which is added, An Artificial Memory: Or, An easy Method of assisting the Memory of those that play at the Game.

c. The capacity of a body or substance for manifesting effects of its previous state, behaviour, or treatment; the effects themselves.

1887, etc. [see *magnetic memory* (MAGNETIC *a.* and *sb.* A. 5)]. **1935** *Proc. R. Soc.* A. CXLIX. 72 The [magnetic] field ..is to be regarded as 'frozen in' and represents a permanent memory of the field which existed when the metal was last cooled below the transition temperature. **1949** *Proc. Internat. Congr. Rheology 1948* i. 5 In the usual form of the theory of viscosity it is assumed that the rate of deformation is so slow compared with the relaxation process, that only slight deviations from the equilibrium state will be found... When the relaxation-time is large and the rate of deformation high..the deviation from the equilibrium state will then show traces of a more distant past. Here we see manifested a kind of 'memory' on the part of the flowing medium. **1950** *Physical Rev.* LXXVIII. 341/2 (*heading*) Memory in simple ferromagnetic domain crystal. **1964** J. M. BLATT *Theory Superconductivity* ix. 332 Since the supercurrent acts in such a direction as to make the total flux approach more closely to an integral number of flux quanta, this initial value of m_0 remains unchanged..and preserves a 'memory' for the initial, external flux. **1971** *Nature* 5 Mar. 28/1 The palaeomagnetic memory of most igneous rocks resides in grains of magnetite and titanomagnetite which are chemically unstable. *Ibid.* 30/2 Titomagnetite retains a memory of its original magnetization after oxidation.

d. The capacity of a body or substance for returning to a previous state when the cause of the transition from that state is removed.

1956 *Chem. Abstr.* L. 4577 The conversion of a naturally occurring twinned quartz crystal to single crystals by torsion often results in the formation of an unstable state, and the crystal reverts to its original twinned state. Natural crystals exhibiting 'memory' usually contain large amounts of impurities. **1961** *Chem. & Industry* 12 Aug. 1261/2 [This] could have accounted for that part of the diameter increases observed when the polymer solution flowed out of a capillary, which could not be attributed to memory of the convergent flow at the entrance to the capillary. (This memory could not account for all the diameter increase because as the length of the capillary was increased, the diameter increase decreased, but did not tend to zero.) **1964** A. S. LODGE *Elastic Liquids* x. 236 'Bouncing putty'..may be said to have a 'memory' of a few seconds in the sense that if a sample is first rapidly elongated and then held at constant length for a few seconds, no recovery occurs on release; whereas, on immediate release following the initial elongation, appreciable recovery (i.e. decrease in length..) occurs.

2. a. This faculty considered as residing in a particular individual; often with epithet denoting the extent to which the faculty is developed or the department in which it is most active.

c **1374** CHAUCER *Anel. & Arc.* 14 This old story..That eeld, which þat all can frete and bite,..hath negh devoured oute of my memory. **1484** CAXTON *Fables of Æsop* II. ix, Good children ought..to..put in theyr hert & memory the doctryne..of theyr parentes. **1597** MORLEY *Introd. Mus.* 5, I should haue a verie good wit, for I haue but a bad memorie. **1624** HEYWOOD *Gunaik.* III. 125 For this appear'd the blazing Star Yet fresh in our memory. **1692** R. L'ESTRANGE *Fables* ccclііі. 323 Wherefore Parasites and Lyers had need of Good Memories. **1705** ADDISON *Italy* Pref., I took care to refresh my Memory among the Classic Authors. **1826** DISRAELI *Viv. Grey* VI. iii, A good memory is often as ready a friend as a sharp wit. **1852** MRS. STOWE *Uncle Tom's C.* xx. 213 Topsy had an uncommon verbal memory.

b. In the language of wills, etc., ***of †good, sane, †safe, sound, †whole memory***.

1402 *E.E. Wills* (1882) 10, I, Iohn Girdeler of Harfeld, in god mynde and saf memorye, make my testement. **1483** *Act 1 Rich. III*, c. 7 §3 Persons..within Age..or not of whole Memory at the Time of such Fine levied. **1642** tr. *Perkins' Prof. Bk.* i. §22. 10 If a man being of good memorie make a Charter of Feofment. **1820** GIFFORD *Compl. Eng. Lawyer* (ed. 5) 672, I, John Mills,..linen-draper, being of sound and disposing mind, memory, and understanding. **1826** W. ROBERTS *Wills & Codicils* (ed. 3) I. 32 No person who is not of a reasonable mind and sane memory can make any disposition by will.

†c. ***to come to one's memory***: to recover from unconsciousness. [Cf. OF. *revenir en sa mémoire*.]

1754 RICHARDSON *Grandison* V. xxviii. 174, I have endeavoured to account for the noble behaviour of your sister; and am the less surprised at it, now she is come to her memory.

d. A device (usu. part of a computer) in which data or program instructions may be stored and from which they may be retrieved when required. Freq. *attrib.* (see 12).

1946 *N.Y. Times* 15 Feb. 16/4 Numerical values covering a wide range of scientific 'constants' are interjected as and when they are needed. There are four kinds of 'memory' in the Eniac to accomplish this. **1946** *Nature* 20 Apr. 527/2 The units in which addition is carried out provide a 'memory' with a capacity of about twenty numbers. **1948** *Math. Tables & Other Aids to Computation* III. 123 The instructions governing the routine operations that the machine is to perform can be stored in the memory in exactly the same manner in which the numbers on which the machine is to operate are stored. **1959** *Listener* 25 June 1109/1 In a typical ferrite-core memory several thousand tiny ferrite rings..are threaded on to thin copper wires. **1959** *Times* 13 Oct. 11/7 Data are stored in an electronic 'memory' or 'information bank', using digital techniques. **1962** F. I. ORDWAY et al. *Basic Astronautics* iv. 137 When a particle traverses the two scintillators..the pulse height from one of the counters is processed by a channel analyzer. Data are accumulated in the analyzer's magnetic core memory and then read out serially. **1970** O. DOPPING *Computers & Data Processing* x. 134 A secondary memory.. cannot exchange data directly with any unit other than primary memory... In an external memory..the information contents can be changed not only by programmed operations, but also by manual operations... However, many people use the word external memory for what has been called secondary memory in this book.

3. a. Recollection, remembrance. Chiefly in phrases, as ***from memory; to come to*** (a person's) ***memory; to bear, have, keep in memory. †to draw*** or ***take into*** or ***to memory***: to recollect, remember. **†*to have memory*** (***of***): to recollect (trans. and intr.). **†*out of memory***: forgotten.

c **1369** CHAUCER *Bk. Duchesse* 945 Hir throte, as I haue now memoyre, Semed a round tour of yvoyre. *c* **1386** —— *Miller's Prol.* 4 It was a noble storie And worthy for to drawen to memorie. **1390** GOWER *Conf.* I. 37 Who so drawth into memoire What hath befalle of old and newe. *Ibid.* II. 22 Bot al was clene out of memoire. *Ibid.* III. 166 Tak into memoire, For al this pompe and al this pride Let no justice gon aside. *c* **1400** *Rom. Rose* 5752 Sich as..toward god have no memorie. **1500–20** DUNBAR *Poems* lxxii. 5 Having his passioun in memorye. **1550** CROWLEY *Last Trumpet* 1021 Se thou cal to memori The ende wherfore al men are made. **1553** EDEN *Treat. Newe Ind.* (Arb.) 15 This beaste..doth wonderfulli beare in memorie benefytes shewed vnto him. **1570–6** LAMBARDE *Peramb. Kent* (1826) 156 Whilest each man was guiltie of the fault, and had fresh memorie thereof. **1590** SIR J. SMYTH *Disc. Weapons* 2 The most of the which that shall fall into my memorie. **1606** SHAKS. *Ant. & Cl.* IV. ix. 7 When men reuolted shall vpon Record Beare hatefull memory. **1611** BIBLE *1 Cor.* xv. 2 If yee keepe in memorie what I preached vnto you. *a* **1626** BACON *New Atl.* (1900) 21 Wee haue memory not of one Shipp that euer returned. **1638** SIR T. HERBERT *Trav.* (ed. 2) 25 Suffer me (whiles in memory) to tell you of a fish or 2 which in these seas were obvious. **1802** WORDSW. *Sonn.*, When I have borne in memory what has tamed Great Nations. **1856** GROTE *Greece* II. xcviii. XII. 647 A considerable portion of the Greeks of Olbia could repeat the Iliad from memory. *Mod.* The portrait was painted from memory.

b. An act or instance of remembrance; a representation in the memory, a recollection.

1817 SHELLEY *Rev. Islam* VII. iii, She told me a strange tale .., Like broken memories of many a heart Woven into one. **1833** TENNYSON *Lady Clara* iv, You put strange memories in my head. **1854** MRS. STOWE (*title*) Sunny Memories of Foreign Lands.

c. A person or thing held in remembrance.

1842 TENNYSON *Gardener's Daughter* (end), The darling of my manhood, and, alas! Now the most blessed memory of my age. **1886** A. BIRRELL in *Contemp. Rev.* L. 28 The first great fact to remember is, that the Edmund Burke we are all agreed in regarding as one of the proudest memories of the House of Commons was an Irishman.

4. a. The fact or condition of being remembered; 'exemption from oblivion' (J.). ? *Obs.* exc. as in b.

c **1375** *Sc. Leg. Saints* xl. (*Ninian*) 1086 Þis sa schort tyme gane ves þat ȝet it is in memor fresch. **1375** BARBOUR *Bruce* I. 14 To put in wryt a suthfast story, That it lest ay furth in memory. **1523** LD. BERNERS *Froiss.* I. i. 1 To thentent that the..featis of armes..shulde..be..put in perpetuall memory. **1579–80** NORTH *Plutarch, Theseus* (1595) 15 And this is that which is worthy memorie..touching the wars of these Amazones. **1591** SHAKS. *1 Hen. VI*, IV. iii. 51 That euer-liuing man of Memorie, Henrie the fift. **1644** MILTON *Educ.* Wks. (1847) 98/1 To say or do aught worthy memory. **1656** STANLEY *Hist. Philos.* VI. (1701) 243/2 Mortal Nature ..obtaineth Eternal Memory by the greatness of such works.

b. ***in memory of, †to the memory of***: so as to keep alive the remembrance of; as a record of. Also **†*in memory***, for a memorial.

a **1340** HAMPOLE *Psalter* xxvi. 9 In memore of his passion. ? **1370** *Robt. Cicyle* 63 Thys storye ys, withowten lye, At Rome wretyn in memorye. *c* **1375** *Sc. Leg. Saints* xiv. (*Lucas*) 31 In lofe & in memore of þare name. *a* **1400–50** *Alexander* 1118 In mynde & in memory of him to make a cite. **1509** HAWES *Past. Pleas.* xlv. (Percy Soc.) 220 Makyng great bokes to be in memory. **1640** BP. HALL *Chr. Moder.* I. xii. 127 A yearely fast called Arzibur, in the sad memory of the dog of Sergius. **1653** *Nissena* 154 A Livery which they wore to the memory of the deceased King. **1769** GOLDSM. *Hist. Rome* II. 490 He removed, for change of air, to Helenopolis, a city which he had built to the memory of his mother. **1781** J. MORISON in *Sc. Paraphrases* xxxv. vi, Through latest ages let it pour In mem'ry of my dying hour.

5. a. The recollection (*of* something) perpetuated amongst men; what is remembered *of* a person, object, or event; (good or bad) posthumous repute.

c **1450** *St. Cuthbert* (Surtees) 495 Þe whilk place, for þe childes memour, Es halden ȝit in grete honour. **1490** CAXTON *Eneydos* xxvii. 102 Memore shalbe therof as longe as heuyn & erthe shall last. **1597** SHAKS. *2 Hen. IV*, IV. iv. 75 Their memorie Shall as a Patterne, or a Measure, liue. **1611** BIBLE *Prov.* x. 7 The memorie of the iust is blessed. **1625** BACON *Ess., Great Place* (Arb.) 293 Vse the Memory of thy Predecessor fairly, and tenderly. **1662** J. DAVIES tr. *Olearius' Voy. Ambass.* 125 Cyril of Alexandria, whose memory the Greeks celebrate on the 9. of June. **1711** SWIFT *Jrnl. to Stella* 28 May, I..promised to do what I could to help him to a service, which I did for Harry Tenison's memory. **1781** GIBBON *Decl. & F.* xvii. II. 44 The memory of Constantine has been deservedly censured for another innovation which corrupted military discipline. **1838** ARNOLD *Hist. Rome* (1846) I. vi. 213 His father's memory.. was regarded with respect and affection. **1868** FREEMAN *Norm. Conq.* (1877) II. vii. 45 He has left a dark and sad memory behind.

b. ***of blessed, happy, famous*** (etc.) ***memory***: a formula used after the names of sovereigns, princes, or other notable persons who have been distinguished for their actions or virtues.

[**1432–50** tr. *Higden* (Rolls) V. 149 Seynte Gregory.. callethe Constantyne a man of goode memory.] **1485** *Rolls of Parlt.* VI. 288/2 The most famous Prince of blessed memorie King Herrie the VIth. **1509** FISHER *Funeral Serm. C'tess Richmond* Wks. (1876) 289 A comynycacyon betwyxt the woman of blessed memory called Martha and our sauyour Ihesu. **1605** CAMDEN *Rem.* 3 Our late Soveraigne, of most deare sacred and ever-glorious memorie Queene Elizabeth. **1660** LD. BRUDNELL in *Buccleuch MSS.* (Hist. MS. Comm.) I. 313 When his late Majesty of glorious memory was intended to go against the Scots. **1738** SWIFT *Pol. Conversat.* Introd. 4 His late Majesty King William the Third, of ever glorious and immortal Memory. **1762** BP. FORBES *Jrnl.* (1886) 176 The widow of Sutherland of Bogsie, of facetious memory.

6. a. The length of time over which the recollection of a person or a number of persons extends; chiefly in phr. ***beyond, †past, †out of, within the memory*** (***of man***). **†*through all memory***: for all time.

1530 TINDALE *Pract. Prelates* D vij, And in his lawe he [the pope] thrust in fayned gyftes of old emperours that were out of memorye, sayenge that [etc.]. **1542** *Aberdeen Reg.* (1844) I. 439 Vsit and perseruit all tymes bigane, past memor of man. **1555** EDEN *Decades* I. IV. 21 b, The same yeare, the sea..rose higher than euer it dyd before by the memory of man [orig. *more maiorum*]. **1570–6** LAMBARDE *Peramb. Kent* (1576) 9 Within memorie almost the one halfe of the first sorte be disparked. **1643** MILTON *Divorce* II. xi, Why then is Pilat branded through all memory? **1667** —— *P.L.* VII. 637 How first this World and face of things began, And what before thy memorie was don From the beginning. *a* **1676** HALE *De Jure Maris* I. vi. in *Hargrave's Law Tracts* (1787) I. 35 That the river of the Severn *usque filum aquæ* was time out of memory parcell of that manor. **1711** ADDISON *Spect.* No. 13 ¶4 He..has drawn together greater Audiences than have been known in the Memory of Man. **1849** MACAULAY *Hist. Eng.* i. init., I purpose to write the history of England from the accession of king James the

Second down to a time which is within the memory of men still living. **1870** TOULMIN SMITH *Eng. Gilds* 213 *margin*, The gild was begun at a time beyond the memory of man.

b. *Law. time of* (*legal*) *memory*: see quots.

Cf. the corresponding phrase 'Time Immemorial, or Time whereof the Memory of Man runneth not to the contrary', *Act 2 & 3 Will. IV*, c. 71 §1.

1642 tr. *Perkins Prof. Bk.* ii. §120. 54 If a Deed bear date before time of memory it is not pleadable. **1766** BLACKSTONE *Comm.* I. 31 Time of memory hath been long ago ascertained by the law to commence from the reign of Richard the first.

7. *Eccl.* A commemoration, esp. of the departed. *Obs.* exc. *Hist.*

1303 R. BRUNNE *Handl. Synne* 7957 þe þryde [part of the Host] he offreþ to haue memory For soules þat are yn purgatory. **1362** LANGL. *P. Pl.* A. vii. 88 He is holden.. to.. munge me in his memorie Among alle cristene. **1463** *Bury Wills* (Camden) 18 And after the seid messe to sey a memorie of requiem for vs. **1558** in Strype *Ann. Ref.* I. App. iv. 6 If there be some other devout sort of prayers or memory said. **1591** SPENSER *M. Hubberd* 454 Their memories, their singings, and their gifts. **1853** ROCK *Ch. of Fathers* IV. xii. 125 After the collect for the day.. came the 'memories', or, as we now call them, 'commemorations'. **1885** R. W. DIXON *Hist. Ch. Eng.* xviii. III. 283 (tr. *Bucer*), And I am told that there are women of title who boldly demand memories to be celebrated when there are no communicants.

†**8.** *to make memory of*: to preserve a record or memorial of; to record, mention. *Obs.*

c **1375** *Sc. Leg. Saints* xxv. (*Julian*) 31 Of wthyre Iulyanis sere mencione I sal mak ȝou here, & als sume memor sal I ma of Iulyane apostata. *c* **1420** LYDG. *Assembly of Gods* 1515 For on the walles was made memory Singlerly of euery creature That there had byn. **1590** SPENSER *F.Q.* III. ii. 1 To whom no share in armes and chevalree They doe impart, ne maken memoree Of their brave gestes. *a* **1643** LD. FALKLAND, etc. *Infallibility* (1646) 85 There is no memory made how the sentence was received.

†**9.** A memorial writing; a historical account; a record of a person or an event; a history. *Obs.*

1432–50 tr. *Higden* (Rolls) II. 269 Cambises,.. vnder whom the memory [L. *historia*] of that woman Iudith happede. *c* **1470** HARDING *Chron.* CV. iii, The kyng came home with honour and victorye, As Flores saieth right in his memorye. *a* **1540** BARNES *Wks.* (1573) 183 Wee doe not read in any memoryes, that our fathers haue left vs, that [etc.]. **1572** R. H. tr. *Lauaterus' Ghostes* (1596) 69 Immediately after this Historie, he putteth na other more worthie memorie than the foremost. **1604** E. G[RIMSTONE] *D'Acosta's Hist. Indies* v. xii. 359 There are certaine memories and discourses which say, that in this Temple the Divell did speake visibly. **1673** RAY *Journ. Low C.* 6 There is no memory that these places were part of the Continent. **1730** A. GORDON *Maffei's Amphith.* 57 There is no Memory of any other [Amphitheatre] to be found on Medals.

†**10.** An object or act serving as a memorial; a memento. *Obs.*

c **1470** HARDING *Chron.* CXXI. iii, The Abbay of Batayle.. He called it so then for a memorye Of his batayle. **1483** CAXTON *Gold. Leg.* 231/1 They fond hys rynge and one gloue whiche they brought agayn and that other the Sextayn reteyned for a wytnes and memorie. **1547** *Injunc. Edw. VI*, xxviii. cij b, That they shall take awaie.. all shrines [etc.],.. so that there remain no memory of the same, in walles, glasses, windowes, or els where. **1548–9** (Mar.) *Bk. Com. Prayer, Communion*, And did institute, and in his holy Gospell commaund us, to celebrate a perpetuall memory of that his precious death. **1575** in W. H. Turner *Select. Rec. Oxford* (1880) 367 To remaine as a perpetuall memory and record of such orders. **1605** SHAKS. *Lear* IV. vii. 7 These weedes are memories of those worser houres. **1624** BEDELL *Lett.* xi. 150 It is a memorie and representation of the true Sacrifice.. made on the Altar of the Crosse.

†**11.** A memorial tomb, shrine, chapel, or the like; a monument. *Obs.*

c **1400** *Apol. Loll.* 49 Men bigging þe memoryes of martres. **1579** FULKE *Refut. Rastel* 797 Miracles worked at their chappelles or memorie. **1641** MEDE *Apost. Latter T.* 120 Those who approached the shrines of Martyrs, and prayed at their memories, and sepulchers. **1656** EVELYN *Diary* 8 July, King Coilus.. of whom I find no memory save at the pinnacle of one of their wool-staple houses, where is a statue. **1691** WOOD *Ath. Oxon.* I. 541 Jackson.. was buried in the Inner Chappel.. but hath no memory at all over his grave.

12. *attrib.* and *Comb.*, as (sense 1) ***memory-bowed, -haunted, -haunting, -lit, -masking, -moving, -sweet*** adjs.; ***memory-cell, hole, -idea, -image, -judgement, -knowledge, lane, -mirror, -picture, -process, sketch, -stone, -trace, work***; (sense 2 d) ***memory device, disc, element, store, unit***; **memory bank**, the memory device of a computer; also *fig.* of the human memory; **memory-belief**, the faith, probably unverifiable, that a person has in the truth of his memories; **memory book** *U.S.*, a blank book in which cuttings from newspapers and the like are pasted for preservation; a scrap-book; **memory cycle** *Computers*, (the time taken by) the process of replacing one unit of data in a memory by another; **memory drug**, a drug supposed to improve the memory; **memory drum**, (*a*) *Psychol.*, a revolving device on which material to be learnt appears; also *transf.*; (*b*) a drum-shaped memory device in a computer; **memory effect**, an effect arising from 'memory' (senses 1 c, d); **memory-man**, a professor of mnemonics; †**memory-mountebank**, a quack exponent of mnemonics; **memory span** *Psychol.*, the amount of material learnt under controlled conditions which is capable of being recalled; so ***memory-span test***; **memory trace** *Psychol.*, a trace hypothetically left in the nervous system by the act of memorizing.

1955 *Astounding Sci. Fiction* Jan. 56 The *memory banks of the computers would still contain all data pertaining to the course set for the EDS. **1970** E. TIDYMAN *Shaft* (1971) i. 16 Every face that passed him on the street became a deposit of his memory bank. **1971** J. H. SMITH *Digital Logic* vi. 119 A shift register is a memory bank in which the numbers may be moved. **1972** J. D. BUCHANAN *Professional* v. 63 He ran the last two or three assignments through his memory bank to see whether or not they bore a residual potential for violence. **1921** B. RUSSELL *Analysis of Mind* ix. 159 Everything constituting a *memory-belief is happening *now*. *Ibid.*, It is not logically necessary to the existence of a memory-belief that the event remembered should have occurred. **1925** C. D. BROAD *Mind & its Place* v. 233 Memory-beliefs.. are not reached by inference. **1948** *Mind* LVII. 17 According to this theory a memory-belief has an 'intrinsic' probability; it carries its evidence, as it were, on its face. **1931** *Publishers' Weekly* 14 Feb. 843/1 Another demand.. is that for inexpensive *memory books used by grammar school children. **1925** BLUNDEN *Eng. Poems* 28 And to my spirit *memory-bowed The world with all its wars and wails Seems turning slow. **1892** VAN LIEW & BEYER tr. *Ziehen's Introd. Physiol. Psychol.* 156 These numerous sensory cells transmit their excitation further to one other ganglion-cell, a *memory-cell. **1964** *Ann. N.Y. Acad. Sci.* CXV. 655 Most of the LINC's instructions require from one to four *memory-cycle times of eight microseconds each for execution. **1970** O. DOPPING *Computers & Data Processing* x. 136 In a memory cycle, the computer can either erase the contents of a cell and write new information into it, or read the content of a cell and re-write it. **1959** *Times* 9 Oct. 7/4 On a *memory device within the machine are stored details of the votes going to each candidate in each constituency in 1955. **1969** J. J. SPARKES *Transistor Switching* v. 118 The commonest memory device nowadays is the ferrite magnetic core. **1961** *Flight* LXXIX. 464/1 The equipment contains 10,000 diodes, 1,500 transistors, 3,500 resistors, 670 capacitors and a *memory disc. **1965** M. SPARK *Mandelbaum Gate* v. 129 Are these the *memory drugs? **1966** *New Scientist* 4 Aug. 249/3 The new memory drug.. is said to increase brain RNA production by 30 to 40 per cent. **1951** E. R. HILGARD in S. S. Stevens *Handbk. Exper. Psychol.* 547 (*caption*) *Memory drum... The material to be memorized appears in the small aperture as the drum revolves. **1953** C. E. OSGOOD *Method & Theory Exper. Psychol.* III. xii. 502 Lists of 12 nonsense syllables.. are learned in constant order on a memory drum. **1962** [see *fish-finder* (FISH *sb.*[1] 7)]. **1964** C. DENT *Quantity Surveying by Computer* iii. 22 The memory drum of a Pegasus computer. **1971** *Jrnl. Gen. Psychol.* LXXXV. 137 Whether the results would be similar to those found with the use of the more.. traditional memory drum. **1957** *Jrnl. Chem. Physics* XXVII. 93/2 '*Memory' effects.. can occur particularly in nucleation processes involving condensed phases. **1971** *Physica* LXII. 393 (*heading*) Memory effects and dynamical correlations in liquid argon and sodium. **1972** *Sci. Amer.* Nov. 40/2 Hysteresis arises because of memory effects in the magnetic materials surrounding the coil. **1958** *Electronic Engin.* XXX. 1/1 Although considerable research on switching and *memory elements is still proceeding the basic design of the digital and analogue computer is fairly well established. **1848** DICKENS *Dombey* lix, *Memory-haunted twilight. **1882** 'OUIDA' *Maremma* I. 151 The wondrous, mysterious, memory-haunted land. **1899** E. J. CHAPMAN *Drama Two Lives* 14 Many a *memory-haunting face. **1949** 'G. ORWELL' *Nineteen Eighty-Four* I. 40 When one knew that any document was due for destruction, or even when one saw a scrap of waste paper lying about, it was an automatic action to lift the flap of the nearest *memory hole and drop it in, whereupon it would be whirled away on a current of warm air to the enormous furnaces which were hidden somewhere in the recesses of the building. **1894** CREIGHTON & TITCHENER tr. *Wundt's Lect. Human & Animal Psychol.* xix. 282 *Memory-ideas are aroused by sense-perceptions, and again interrupted by new impressions. **1890** W. JAMES *Princ. Psychol.* I. xv. 620 He thinks it is almost entirely the amount to which the *memory-image of the first impression has faded when the second one overtakes it, which makes us feel how wide they are apart. **1895** R. P. HALLECK *Psychol. & Psychic Culture* 106 Memory images are those which most nearly represent existing things. **1904** G. S. FULLERTON *Syst. Metaphysics* iii. 37 He may easily introduce into the memory-image elements.. not present.. in the original. **1921** B. RUSSELL *Analysis of Mind* 207 A memory-image of a particular occurrence. **1964** M. CRITCHLEY *Developmental Dyslexia* viii. 52 Orton believed that during the normal processes of early visual education, storage of memory-images of letters and words takes place in both hemispheres. **1896** L. T. HOBHOUSE *Theory of Knowl.* I. i. 35, I substitute for the *memory-judgment proper.. the apprehension of the content of the memory judgment as an idea. **1937** *Mind* XLVI. 211 The only natural interpretation is to take it as questioning not the accuracy of memory-judgments but the worth of clear and distinct perception itself. **1931** *N. & Q.* 5 Sept. 180/1 The position is illustrated and supported by comparison of our knowledge of the physical world with our *memory-knowledge. **1943** *Mind* LII. 192 We do possess both knowledge of the past generally and memory knowledge in particular, even though we may be mistaken in particular cases. **1954** DANNETT & RACHEL (*title*) *Down memory lane. **1958** *Times* 5 June 16/6 *Liberty Hall*, an unhappily managed trip down memory lane. **1967** A. WILSON *No Laughing Matter* IV. 422 You were all down Memory Lane, no doubt, judging by the laughter. **1970** R. HILL *Clubbable Woman* vii. 203, I don't live down memory lane. What this photograph says to me is not that happiness is gone for ever, but that it's repeatable. **1973** *Ottawa Jrnl.* 5 Feb. 11/3 It was a journey down memory lane, full of anecdotes of the good old days. **1933** W. DE LA MARE *Fleeting* 72 Those eyes that, *memory-lit, Now ponder on my own. **1815** MOORE *Epil. to 'Ina'* 35 Nothing can surpass the plan Of that Professor—(*trying to recollect*) psha!—that *Memory-man. **1923** BLUNDEN *To Nature* 37 I'm not rejected then, my mind's delight Was not a play of *memory-masking fancy. **1938** R. GRAVES *Coll. Poems* 163 Where port in Limerick glasses Glows twice as red reflected In the *memory-mirror of the waxed table. **1642** FULLER *Holy & Prof. St.* III. x. 174 The artificiall rules which.. are delivered by *Memory-mountebanks. **1908** HARDY *Dynasts* III. v. v. 212 Amid no *memory-moving urgencies. **1887** F. FRANCIS *Saddle & Mocassin* 267 One of those *memory pictures that form the pleasantest relics of travel. **1897** C. H. JUDD tr. *Wundt's Outl. Psychol.* 241 The process that arises under such circumstances is a *memory-process. **1906** *Daily Chron.* 16 Apr. 3/5 Some clever memory sketches of the Franco-British Exhibition. **1925** R. FRY *Let.* 7 Sept. (1972) II. 581, I managed to do one picture... This is a memory sketch of the composition. **1917** H. J. HUMPSTONE (*title*) Some aspects of the *memory span test. **1930** R. S. WOODWORTH *Psychol.* (ed. 8) iii. 76 If the list of numbers to be memorized exceeds the memory span, several readings are necessary before it can be recited. **1951** E. R. HILGARD in S. S. Stevens *Handbk. Exper. Psychol.* 547/2 Related to what has sometimes been called the span of attention or the span of apprehension is the immediate memory span—the number of items that can be learned in one trial when they are presented serially at a controlled rate. **1955** H. E. GARRETT *Gen. Psychol.* x. 386 One of the simplest ways of determining the efficiency of immediate memory (fixation) is to test the memory span. **1969** C. N. COFFER in Talland & Waugh *Path. of Memory* 219, I would anticipate that the first locus of pathology would lie in the memory span, that is, the size of the core of actually retained list members. *a* **1847** ELIZA COOK *To Mem. Burns* ii, None that deck thy *memory-stone. **1964** C. DENT *Quantity Surveying by Computer* iii. 19 For the computer's main *memory store, magnetic core storage is now frequently used. **1938** W. DE LA MARE *Memory* 3 Still *memory-sweet its old decoy. **1924** J. RIVIÈRE et al. tr. *Freud's Coll. Papers* I. 63 Both the *memory-trace and the affect attached to the idea are there once and for all. **1951** C. T. MORGAN in S. S. Stevens *Handbk. Exper. Psychol.* 781/1 Learning problems in which memory traces had to last some time in order for the animal to make the correct choice. **1953** C. E. OSGOOD *Method & Theory Exper. Psychol.* III. xiii. 588 The gestalt theory.. must make two predictions: (1) The modifications within the memory trace for visual forms must be in the direction of reducing the stresses present in the original perception. **1967** HILGARD & ATKINSON *Introd. Psychol.* (ed. 4) xii. 321/2 This particular hypothetical construct means that the memory trace does exist and that we may some day discover its nature... Hydén has proposed the theory that ribonucleic acid (RNA) might well be the complex molecule that serves as a chemical mediator for memory. **1959** *Science* 16 Oct. 957/1 Although tables of probabilities.. containing over 300 items were used in the present study, they did not exhaust the capacity of the computer's *memory unit. **1966** C. R. TOTTLE *Sci. Engin. Materials* vi. 141 Application of ferroelectrics includes memory units in computers and in capacitors. **1939** F. J. BROWN *Sociol. Childhood* 456 It has.. encouraged or even compelled him to do '*memory work'.

'memoryless, *a.* [-LESS.] Having no memory.

1857 LOWELL in *Atlantic Monthly* Dec. (1892) 755/1, I am glad you do not forget me, though I seem so memoryless and ungrateful.

memour, -oyre, obs. forms of MEMORY.

Memphian ('mɛmfɪən), *a.* and *sb.* [f. *Memphi-s* + -AN.] **a.** *adj.* Pertaining to Memphis, a city of ancient Egypt; often used vaguely for 'Egyptian'. ***Memphian stone***: Pliny's *lapis Memphites* (cf. MEPHIS). **b.** *sb.* An inhabitant or native of Memphis; an Egyptian.

1591 SYLVESTER *Du Bartas* I. i. 783 One,.. a fearfull slaughter made Of all the First-born that the Memphians had. **1605** *Ibid.* II. iii. III. *Law* 895 They long For Memphian hotch-potch, Leeks, and Garlick strong. **1635** RUTTER *Shepheards Holy day* v. ii. F 5 b, A Memphian stone, that has the power To bring a deadly sleepe on all the senses. **1667** MILTON *P.L.* I. 307 Busiris and his Memphian Chivalrie. **1752** FOOTE *Taste* II. Wks. 1799 I. 19 Indisputable antiques, and of the Memphian marble. **1821** BYRON *Juan* III. lxv, Like skulls at Memphian banquets **1827** POLLOK *Course T.* VII, The Memphian mummy now shook off its rags.

Memphitic (mɛm'fɪtɪk), *a.* [ad. Gr. Μεμφιτικός, f. Μεμφίτης inhabitant of Memphis: see -ITE and -IC.] Pertaining to Memphis, or to the dialect of Coptic spoken there. Also † **Mem'phitical** *a.*

1581 J. BELL *Haddon's Answ. Osor.* 492 b, You builde not the consciences of men, but highe steepe Memphyticall Steeples (as I may tearme them).. of lofty speeches. **1861** *Chamber's Encycl.* II. 78/1 The duplex Egyptian [version].. the one being in the language of Lower Egypt, and termed the Coptic or Memphitic [etc.]. **1875** LIGHTFOOT *Comm. Col.* (ed. 2) 312 *note*, The readings of the Memphitic Version.

mempris, -yse, obs. forms of MAINPRIZE.

Mem-sahib ('mɛmsɑːɪb). *Anglo-Indian.* Also **memsahib** and abbrev. **mem.** [See quot. 1886 and SAHIB.] A European married lady; also, one who behaves like a European woman.

1857 *Househ. Words* 19 Dec. 16/1 An Affghan.. inquired if the Sahib or Mem-sahib was in want of any of these commodities. **1886** YULE & BURNELL *Hobson-Jobson*, *Mem-Sahib.* This singular example of a hybrid term is the usual respectful designation of a European married lady in the Bengal Presidency; the first portion representing *ma'am*. *Madam Sahib* is used at Bombay. **1873** C. M. YONGE *Pillars of House* III. xxxii. 205 She.. heard that 'it was but a few steps, and the Mem Sahib was waiting'. **1884** KIPLING *Plain Tales from Hills* (1888) 236 The half-caste woman that we call the *Mem Sahib*... The *Mem Sahib* looks very old now. **1939** 'N. BLAKE' *Smiler with Knife* i. 19 Snug little billet, this. How does the Mem like country life? **1971** N. BARBER *War of Running Dogs* xi. 124 The mems met at tea-parties to roll bandages. **1971** R. DENTRY *Encounter at Kharmel* iii. 45 'Memsahib!' he exclaimed incredulously. 'Correct,' said Pepper. 'One memsahib, two memsahibs.' She held up two fingers. *Ibid.* 47 Respectfully, mem, you are tired. You come to the rest-house. **1971** R. RUSSELL tr. *Ahmad's Shore & Wave* ii. 23 These nawabs are turning their daughters into

mem-sahibs. 1971 *Femina* (Bombay) 30 Apr. 23/1 The shopkeeper is all smiles at having produced something exactly that the *mem-sahib* wanted. 1972 A. Christie *Elephants can Remember* x. 151 You are speaking of what you might call the memsahib days..when there were Service communities in Malaya. 1972 'J. Ross' *Here lies Nancy Frail* ix. 114 The room was a monument to a long-dead British Raj.. She had the demeanour of a mem sahib in the making.

†**men**, *indef. pron. Obs.* See also ME *indef. pron.* [Weakened form of MAN *indef. pron.*; cf. Du. *men.*] = ONE 21.

c1175 *Lamb. Hom.* 33 þis beot þa twa sunne þe men fulieð alra swiðest. a1225 *Leg. Kath.* (Abbotsf.) 1372 As men [*v.r.* me] droh ham to hare deað. c1250 *Gen. & Ex.* 1293 And morie, men seið, was ðat hil. c1385 Chaucer *L.G.W.* Prol. 205, I bad men sholde me my covche make. 1398 Trevisa *Barth. De P.R.* ii. vii. (1495) 33 Of the other two Ierarchyes men shall speke innermore in theyr owne place. 1483 Caxton *G. de la Tour* f v b, Men ought not to susteyne his lord in his wrathe and yre. 1484 —— *Fables of Æsop* v. vii, Men muste putte hym self at the vpper syde of hym.

men, plural of MAN *sb.*

men, obs. f. MEAN.

†**menable**, *a. Obs.* [a. OF. *menable*, f. *mener* to lead: see -ABLE.] **a.** Having the quality of leading; fit to lead or guide. **b.** Capable of being, or liable to be, led; amenable.

1390 Gower *Conf.* I. 197 And tho began to blowe A wynd menable fro the lond. *Ibid.* 292 Thogh a man be resonable, Yit after kinde he is menable To love.

†**menacane**. *Min. Obs.* [a. G. *menacan* (Werner), f. the place-name *Menachan.*] = MENACHANITE. Hence (by back-formation) †**menac**, as a name for a genus including 'menacane'.

1803 G. Mitchel in *Trans. R. Irish Acad.* X. 11 Of the genus Menac we are already acquainted with five species or ores. *Ibid.* 23 Menacane.

menaccanite: see MENACHANITE.

menace ('mɛnəs), *sb.* Now *literary*. Forms: α. 4 **manasce, -aase**, 4–5 **manas(se**, 4–6 **manace**, 5 **menys**, 5, 7 **manesse**, 6 **mannace, -asshe, meanus, menasse, manasshe**, 5– **menace**. β. *north.* and *Sc.* 4 **manaunce, -anss**, 4–5 **man(n)ance**, 5 **manans**. [a. OF. *manace*, *menace* (mod. F. *menace*), a Com. Rom. word, = Pr. *menassa*, Sp. *(a)menaza*, Pg. *(a)meaça*, It. *minaccia*:—L. *minācia*, f. *mināc-*, *minax* adj. threatening, f. *minārī* to threaten.

The β forms prob. arose from association with words in *-ance*. Editors have commonly printed *manauce*, etc., but the *-ance* is in several instances authenticated by rimes.]

a. A declaration or indication of hostile intention, or of a probable evil or catastrophe; a threat.

a1300 *Cursor M.* 1834 For quils þat godd þam raght his grace, Littel roght þam of his manance [*other MSS.* manace]. 1390 Gower *Conf.* I. 340 He bad hem trete, And stinte of the manaces grete. c1450 *St. Cuthbert* (Surtees) 5032 He had mare drede of his trespas þan of þe Erlis manas. 1484 Caxton *Fables of Æsop* ii. xvi. (1889) 54 Somme maken grete menaces whiche haue no myghte. 1523 Ld. Berners *Froiss.* I. cccxxvii. 207 b, Suche wordes and manasshes abasshed greatly yᵉ cardynals. 1584 R. Scot *Discov. Witchcr.* ix. vii. (1886) 142 They stand in more awe of the manacies of a witch than of all the threatnings.. pronounced by God. 1664 H. More *Myst. of Iniq.* 281 Those powerful and affrightful words of Excommunication, that Menace of committing men to Hell-fire. 1682 N. O. *Boileau's Lutrin* iii. 134 And scorn their proudest braves, their stern Menaces! [*rime* faces]. 1768 Blackstone *Comm.* III. 120 A menace alone, without a consequent inconvenience, makes not the injury. 1820 Byron *Mar. Fal.* iv. i, What means this menace? 1867 Froude *Short Stud.* (1883) IV. i. ix. 106 The fierce menace was delivered amidst frowning groups of..nobles.

b. In generalized use: The action of threatening.

a1300 *Cursor M.* 27439 He dredis manas or tresum. c1380 Wyclif *Wks.* (1880) 63 A pore man þei constreynen to synne bi manas. c1430 Lydg. *Min. Poems* (Percy Soc.) 5 A sturdy champion..His swerd upreryd, proudly gave manace. c1447 in *Jarrow & Wearmouth* (Surtees) 243 Wᵗ mony other wirdis of menys. 1470 *Gaw. & Gol.* 446 Withoutin menance [*rimes* legiance, plesance]. 1508 Dunbar *Flyting w. Kennedie* 4 Had thay maid of mannace ony mynting. 1781 Gibbon *Decl. & F.* xli. (1869) II. 511 The voice of menace and complaint was silent. 1797 Mrs. Radcliffe *Italian* iii, The Marchese persisted in accusation and menace. 1874 Green *Short Hist.* viii. §2. 477 The English fleet..was cruising by way of menace off the Spanish coast.

†**c.** Phr. ***to make (much, great, no) menace***.

a1300 *Cursor M.* 28517 In gang, in chere, in contenance, þat i to men ha mad manace. 1375 Barbour *Bruce* xvii. 664 Thai..gret mananss till him mais. ?a1400 *Morte Arth.* 3383 All hir mode chaungede, And mad myche manace with mervayllous wordez. c1470 *Gol. & Gaw.* 355 And mak him na manance, bot al mesoure. 1634 Milton *Comus* 654 Though he and his curst crew Feirce signe of battail make, and menace high.

d. Attributed to impersonal agents.

c1374 Chaucer *Boeth.* i. met. iv. 7 (Camb. MS.) The Rage ne the manesses of þe see commoeuynge or chasinge vpward heete. 1697 Dryden *Æneid* ix. 38 The dark Menace of the distant War. 1824 Byron *Def. Transf.* i. ii. 195 Wilt thou Turn back from shadowy menaces of shadows? 1841 James *Brigand* i, If yonder frowning cloud fulfil one half its menaces. 1871 Palgrave *Lyr. Poems* 19 The sudden war and menace of the skies.

e. Said of a state of things, etc., which threatens danger or catastrophe.

1857 Gallenga *Italy* 373 It was an insult to the republicans,..it was a menace to the aristocracy of Turin. 1874 Green *Short Hist.* vii. §3. 362 The old social discontent ..remained a perpetual menace to public order.

f. *colloq.* Applied to a person.

1936 D. Carnegie *How to win Friends and influence People* 63 A few doors down the street lived a 'menace', as they say out in Hollywood—a bigger boy who would pull the little boy off his tricycle and ride it himself. 1942 Berrey & Van den Bark *Amer. Thes. Slang* §583/16 *Villain*..menace. *Ibid.* §636/23 *Formidable opponent*..menace. 1944 J. H. Fullarton *Troop Target* iii. xiii. 95 That B.S.M.'s a bloody menace.

menace ('mɛnəs), *v.* Forms: α. 4 **manysche**, *Sc.* **maynysse**, 4–5 **manaas(s)e, manesse**, 4–6 **manas(s)e, mannasse**, 4–7 **manace**, 4–5 **manasce, -ashe, meanashe**, 5 **manece**, 5–6 **manasshe, -ysshe**, 6 *Sc.* **manes(s)e, -is(s)e, -ische, -yse, -yssyche, mannese, -esche, minisse, mynace**, 6–7 chiefly *Sc.* **menasse, minace, -ase, myn-, minasse**, 5– **menace**. β. *north.* and *Sc.* 4 **man(n)ance, mananse, -aunce, -aunse, -aunze**. [a. F. *menacer* (11th c.), also *manecier*, *-echier*, AF. *manasser* (Wadington) = Pr. *menassar*, Sp. *(a)menazar*, Pg. *(a)meaçar*, It. *minacciare*:—popular L. **mināciāre*, f. *minācia* MENACE *sb.*]

1. *trans.* To utter or hold out menaces against; to threaten.

1303 R. Brunne *Handl. Synne* 3681 Ȝyf þou any man manasse þurgh force or power þat þou hasse. a1340 Hampole *Psalter* xxvii. 10 God manaunsid þaim with hell. 1375 Barbour *Bruce* xi. 150 Thai..Mannausit [*read* Mannansit] the Scottis men halely With gret vordis. 1472–3 *Rolls of Parlt.* VI. 54/1 The said Thomas Trethenry and Elizabeth his wyfe,..have thretted and manassed the Tenauntes. 1523 Ld. Berners *Froiss.* I. xxvii. 40 These infidels sore dyd manysshe Christendome. 1545 *Burgh Rec. Stirling* (1887) 41 Contrair the will of the wache, manisand and boistand thaim. 1632 Heywood *1st Pt. Iron Age* iii. i. Wks. 1874 III. 304 The boldest Greeke That euer manac'd Troy. 1739 Cibber *Apol.* (1756) I. 262 When he is compell'd or menac'd into any opinion that he does not readily conceive. 1828 Macaulay *Ess., Hallam* (1851) I. 54 Her subjects were incited to rebellion; her life was menaced. 1840 Dickens *Barn. Rudge* xvii, 'Hear me', he replied, menacing her with his hand.

b. Said of impersonal agents.

1377 Langl. *P. Pl.* B. xiii. 6 How þat elde manaced me. 1483 Caxton *Cato* 4 How the foure elementes menace alle men that [etc.]. 1594 Shaks. *Rich. III*, i. iv. 175 Your eyes do menace me: why looke you pale? a1649 Drumm. of Hawth. *Poems* Wks. (1711) 4 High woods, whose mounting tops menace the spheres. 1790 Burke *Fr. Rev.* 306 These evils are great... Sooner or later they may menace the nation itself. 1840 Macaulay *Ess., Clive* (1851) II. 523 A new and formidable danger menaced the western frontier.

†**c.** Const. inf. *Obs.*

c1325 *Song of Yesterday* 158 in *E.E.P.* (1862) 137 Wel þou wost..þat deþ haþ manast þe to die. 1429 *Rolls of Parlt.* IV. 345/2 [They] hem maneshud to bee dede if they made any resistence. a1450 *Knt. de la Tour* (1868) 118 Thei toke hym and menaced hym to stone hym vnto dethe.

2. *intr.* To utter menaces; to be threatening.

c1330 R. Brunne *Chron. Wace* (Rolls) 8853 So longe he manased & þret, Atte laste to-gydere þey met. c1430 Lydg. *Min. Poems* (Percy Soc.) 159 O man is meeke, anothir doth manace. 1513 Douglas *Æneis* ii. iv. 74 Furtht drawin haldis this subtell hors of tree, And manysand strydis throw the myd cietie. 1601 Shaks. *Jul. C.* i. iii. 44 Who euer knew the Heauens menace so? a1700 Dryden *Fables, Pythag. Philos.* 36 'Twas Death to go away, And the God menac'd if he dar'd to stay. 1774 Burke *Sp. Amer. Tax.* Sel. Wks. I. 135 Earth below shook; heaven above menaced. 1858 Froude *Hist. Eng.* III. xii. 1 It was idle to menace while he was unable to strike.

3. *trans.* To hold out as a punishment, penalty, or danger; to threaten to inflict.

a1340 Hampole *Psalter* Prol. 3 Now manassand hell til wyckyd. c1375 *Sc. Leg. Saints* xxiii. (*VII Sleperis*) 51 þame manesand ded in þat place. 1529 More *Dyaloge* iv. Wks. 265/2 God, yᵗ manasseth vnto them y paines of hel. 1621 G. Sandys *Ovid's Met.* v. (1626) 89 Such as menace warre. 1796 Morse *Amer. Geog.* I. 219 Their eyes..and their brandishing forked tongues,..menaces [*sic*] a horrid death. 1822–34 *Good's Study Med.* (ed. 4) IV. 134 The chief symptoms, menacing abortion, are transitory pains in the back..or [etc.]. 1854 Milman *Lat. Chr.* vii. iii. (1864) IV. 137 No threatened excommunication is now menaced.

b. with *inf.* or *clause* as object.

c1375 *Sc. Leg. Saints* xli. (*Agnes*) 123 He..manesit hire to bet & bynd. c1412 Hoccleve *Reg. Princes* 5292 Thi self manaseth þi self for to dye. 1565 Cooper *Thesaurus* s.v. *Denuntio*, To manase that he will bryng him before a iudge. 1620 Quarles *Jonah* C 1 b, Great Ashur minaces with whip in hand, To entertaine thee (welcome) to his land. 1632 Lithgow *Trav.* i. 12 The Riuer Tyber..often Manasseth to drowne the whole Mansions. 1883 J. Martine *Reminisc. Old Haddington* 73 The solitary dissentient was menacing to leave the meeting-house.

†**4.** To use threateningly. *Obs. rare*$^{-1}$.

1649 Milton *Eikon.* 23 Swords and Pistols cockt and menac'd in the hands of about three hundred..Ruffians.

Hence '**menaceable** *a.*, capable of being put down by threats; '**menaceful** *a.*, threatening; '**menacement**, menacing, threatening; '**menacer**, one who menaces or threatens.

1613 Wotton in *Reliq.* (1672) 416 Which feminine menacement did no doubt incite him to do it. 1642 W. Bird *Mag. Hon.* 46 The Menacer..standeth in the face of his enemy. 1746 Turnbull *Justin* xxviii. iii. 222 Antigonus.. being besieged in his palace by a menaceful mob of the Macedonians. 1802–12 Bentham *Ration. Judic. Evid.* (1827) III. 70 A threat, an act of menacement. 1864 Carlyle *Fredk. Gt.* xvii. vii. (1872) VI. 203 The malpractice seems to have proved menaceable in that manner. 1891 *Gd. Words* Aug. 556/1 Did it acquire its menaceful character because it had been placed on the head of Medusa?

menaced ('mɛnəst), *ppl. a.* [f. MENACE *v.* + -ED^1.] **a.** Assailed by menaces or threats. **b.** Held out or indicated as an intended or probable evil or catastrophe.

c1440 *Promp. Parv.* 324/1 Manassyd, or thret, *minatus*. 1567 Golding *Ovid's Met.* viii. (1593) 205 The manast oke did quake and sigh. 1644 Vicars *God in Mount* 204 Our menaced Arke was borne up above the..waves. 1738 Glover *Leonidas* i. 10 How best their menac'd liberties to guard. 1803 *Times* 3 Oct., The accounts from France relative to the menaced invasion. 1860 Mill *Repr. Govt.* (1865) 60/2 Injured or menaced interests.

menachanite (mə'nækənaɪt). *Min.* Also 8 **menack-, man-**, 8–9 **menaccanite**. [f. *Menachan*, in Cornwall + -ITE.] A variety of ILMENITE. Hence **menacha'nitic** *a.*, containing menachanite.

1795 E.S. *Let.* in Polwhele *Trad. & Recoll.* (1826) II. 427 The Manaccanite, a mineral or semi-metal resembling gunpowder. 1796 Kirwan *Elem. Min.* (ed. 2) II. 326 Menachanite. *Ibid.* 327 The Menachanitic Calx. 1845 Newbold in *Jrnl. Asiat. Soc. Bengal* XIV. 291 Gold-dust is found associated with..menaccanite.

menacing ('mɛnəsɪŋ), *vbl. sb.* Now *rare*. [f. MENACE *v.* + -ING^1.] The action of the verb MENACE; threatening; menace.

1352 Minot *Poems* i. 49 Ma manasinges ȝit haue thai maked. 1451 in *10th Rep. Hist. MSS. Comm.* App. v. 330 For the meanashing done in the Maire [h]is presennce, that he wolde kyll and take certain men. 1533 Bellenden *Livy* ii. xvii. (S.T.S.) I. 197 Howbeit þow was full of mynassing [*v.r.* minissing]. 1549 *Compl. Scot.* xi. 24 The thretnyng ande menassing of Gode contrar obstinat, vicius pepil. 1656 *Artif. Handsom.* 66 These..fall to cavillings and menacings. 1866 Carlyle *Inaug. Addr.* 199 Tell them..to disregard.. the temporary noises, menacings, and deliriums.

menacing ('mɛnəsɪŋ), *ppl. a.* [-ING^2.] That menaces or threatens; threatening.

1549 Coverdale, etc. *Erasm. Par. Heb.* 19 To heare these manassyng wordes of the prophecie. 1570–6 Lambarde *Peramb. Kent* (1826) 149 He mooveth the King by minacing letters to admit Stephan. 1774 Burke *Sp. Amer. Tax.* Sel. Wks. I. 134 There were in both Houses new and menacing appearances. 1867 Lady Herbert *Cradle L.* viii. 212 The population..gathered in menacing attitude.

menacingly ('mɛnəsɪŋlɪ), *adv.* [f. prec. + -LY^2.] In a menacing manner; threateningly.

1581 Savile *Tacitus' Hist.* (1612) 78 Setting vpon Verginius menacingly they besought him [etc.]. 1738 H. Brooke *Tasso* ii. 45 With awful Grace superior Godfrey smiled, And thus rejoin'd more menacingly mild. 1874 Green *Short Hist.* iv. §3. 179 The English fortress of Edinburgh looked menacingly across the Forth.

menaciously, -acy: see MINACIOUSLY, MINACY.

menad, menadic, var. MÆNAD, MÆNADIC.

1831 Carlyle *Sart. Res.* iii. x, The rites..supposed to be of the Menadic sort. 1863 Geo. Eliot *Romola* i. xviii. I. 309 Dances of satyrs and menads.

menadione (mɛnə'daɪəʊn). *Pharm.* orig. *U.S.* [f. ME(THYL + NA(PHTHALENE + -DIONE.] 2-Methyl-1, 4-naphthoquinone, $C_{11}H_8O_2$, a yellow crystalline powder which is a synthetic analogue of vitamin K and is used, often in the form of its sodium bisulphite compound, in treating hæmorrhage due to hypoprothrombinæmia. In the *British Pharmacopœia* called MENAPHTHONE.

1941 *Jrnl. Amer. Med. Assoc.* 15 Mar. 1054/1 The Council has adopted the term 'menadione'..and has authorized its use as a nonproprietary name to describe the substance 2-methyl-1, 4-naphthoquinone. 1942 T. Sollmann *Man. Pharmacol.* (ed. 6) 496 Various other naphthoquinone derivatives have the same action, for instance ..'menadione', N.N.R. (menaquinone),..which is three or four times more potent than the K vitamin. 1955 J. G. Davis *Dict. Dairying* (ed. 2) 566 It has been claimed that feeding menadione..to lactating cows will increase the keeping quality of the milk. 1968 J. H. Burn *Lect. Notes Pharmacol.* (ed. 9) 83 Menaphthone (menadione or methylnaphthoquinone) is a substance which..increases the production of prothrombin in those deficient. It is commonly given to mothers a day or two before the baby is born.

†**menadry**. *Obs.* (See quots.)

1570 Dee *Math. Pref.* Dj, Menadrie, is an Arte Mathematicall, which demonstrateth, how, aboue Natures vertue and power simple: Vertue and force may be multiplied: and so, to direct, to lift, to pull to, and to put or cast fro, any multiplied or simple, determined Vertue, Waight or Force: naturally not so directible or mouable. 1620–55 I. Jones *Stone-Heng* (1725) 23 Menadry, or Art of ordering Engines for raising Weights. 1665 J. Webb *Stone-Heng* (1725) 218 It is a Maxim as well in Menadry as War, ..a true and equal Draught..raiseth up mightly Weights.

ménage, menage (meɪ'nɑːʒ). Now only as Fr. Also 4 **mayngnage, manage**, 5 **maynage,**

manyage, meynage, menaige. [a. OF. *manaige*, *menaige* (mod.F. *ménage*):—popular L. **mansiōnāticum*, f. L. *mansiōn-em* dwelling (see MANSION), whence F. *maison* house. Cf. MESNAGE.]

†**1.** The members of a household; a man's household or 'meinie'. *Obs.*

1297 R. GLOUC. (Rolls) 3799 Al þe bachelerie þat aȝt was in þe lond he nom in is compaynie & of is mayngnage [*v. rr.* maynage, manyage]. **13..** *K. Alis.* 2087 Darye.. With his children, and with his wyve, And with his suster, and his menage. **1490** CAXTON *Eneydos* vi. 29 Jubyter.. wyth his wyf and meynage, wente anone wyth theym.

2. a. The management of a household, housekeeping; hence, a domestic establishment (often *concr.* or semi-*concr.*).

1698 W. KING tr. *Sorbière's Journ. Lond.* 3 In Paris, there are from Four to Five, and to Ten menages or distinct Families in many Houses. **1790** SIR S. ROMILLY in *Life* (1842) I. 297, I long to.. see you in your *ménage*, which I cannot express in English, because we have no word for it. **1808** HAN. MORE *Cœlebs* (1809) I. iii. 32 Nothing tended to make ladies so.. inefficient in the menage as the study of the dead languages. **1842** DE QUINCEY *Mod. Greece* Wks. 1863 XIII. 460 No single Greek nuisance can be placed on the same scale with the dogs attached to every *menage*, whether household or pastoral. **1848** THACKERAY *Van. Fair* lxiv, She tried keeping house with a female friend; then the double *ménage* began to quarrel and get into debt. **1887** DOWDEN *Shelley* II. iv. 115 An annual sufficiency to support a little ménage would be desirable.

¶**b.** *transf.* Applied to the staff or company of a theatre. ? *nonce-use.*

1746 H. WALPOLE *Lett. to Mann* 12 Aug., Lord Middlesex took the opportunity of a rivalship between his own mistress, the Nardi, and the Violette,.. to involve the whole ménage of the Opera in the quarrel, and has paid nobody.

3. *Sc.* and *northern.* **a.** 'A friendly society, of which every member pays in a fixed sum weekly, to be continued for a given term' (Jamieson 1825). **b.** (See quot. 1829.) Hence *Comb.* **menage-man**, an itinerant vendor of goods which are to be paid for by instalments. (See also *Eng. Dial. Dict.*)

1829 BROCKETT *Gloss. N.C. Words* (ed. 2), *Manadge*, a box or club instituted by inferior shop-keepers—generally linen-drapers—for supplying goods to poor or improvident people, who agree to pay for them by instalments. **1866** MITCHELL *Hist. Montrose* ix. 85 They would have got their clothing by joining a menage to which they paid 1/- in the week. **1893** *Newcastle Even. Chron.* 11 Dec. 2/4 He gave his wife to understand that she had to contract no debts with the menage-man. **1904** A. GRIFFITHS *50 Years Public Service* xix. 283 *note*, The number of debtors was always large at York on account of the widespread practices of the 'menage men' as they were called.

4. ‖**ménage à trois** [Fr., lit. 'household of three'], an arrangement or relationship in which three people live together, usually consisting of a husband, his wife, and the lover of one of these. Also *transf.* and *fig.* Cf. À TROIS. Hence ‖**ménage à deux**, an arrangement of two people living together.

1891 G. B. SHAW *Quintessence of Ibsenism* 116 An elderly gallant who quite understands how little she cares for her husband, and proposes a *ménage à trois* to her. **1911** — *Getting Married* 114 Nelson.. formed a *menage à trois* with Sir William and Lady Hamilton. **1929** D. H. LAWRENCE *Lovely Lady* (1932) 106 The scheme of a *ménage à deux* with her mother had not succeeded. **1933** *Times Lit. Suppl.* 19 Oct. 713/3 He meets, and marries.. a highly sexed waitress, who inevitably tires of.. the mother's dominance of the *ménage à trois*. **1944** H. G. WELLS *'42 to '44* 102 They [*sc.* a Roman Catholic husband and wife].. submit to a domestic *ménage à trois*, with the priest as controlling intervener. **1958** P. KEMP *No Colours or Crest* xii. 249 That curious *ménage à trois*, the Anglo-American honeymoon with Russia. **1959** N. MAILER *Advts. for Myself* (1961) 285 A *ménage-à-trois* was completed—the bohemian and the juvenile delinquent came face-to-face with the Negro, and the hipster was a fact in American life. **1959** *Times* 28 Dec. 3/6 This happy *ménage-à-trois*—the errant wife, the lover and the unsuspecting husband. **1960** *Times* 30 Apr. 9/2 Primarily it [*sc.* a song] is a marriage of voice and verse, but since an instrument is soon added it turns the relationship into a *ménage à trois*. **1973** *Country Life* 14 June 1768/3 Pauline Viardot.. the opera singer who with her husband and Turgenev formed a *ménage à trois*.

menage, etc.: see MANAGE, etc.

menagerie (məˈnædʒərı). Also 8–9 **-ery**, (8 **managerie**, **menegerie**). [a. F. *ménagerie* domestic administration, management of cattle, building of a cattle-farm, now chiefly in sense 1 below; f. *ménage*: see MÉNAGE and -ERY. Cf. MANAGERY.]

1. A collection of wild animals in cages or enclosures, esp. one kept for exhibition, as in zoological gardens or a travelling show. Also, the place or building in which they are kept.

1712 J. JAMES tr. *Le Blond's Gardening* 23 Menagery is a Place where they keep Animals of several Kinds for Curiosity. **1762–71** H. WALPOLE *Vertue's Anecd. Paint.* (1786) IV. 8 Laguerre's father.. became master of the menagerie at Versailles. **1829** LANDOR *Imag. Conv., Albani & Pict.-Dealers* Wks. 1853 II. 12/2 As to the lion, he has been in the menagery from his birth. **1886** J. G. WOOD in *Leis. Hour* 445 From early childhood I have been in the habit of frequenting menageries.

b. *transf.* and *allusively.*

1784 COWPER *Tiroc.* 293 What causes move us, knowing as we must That these *Menageries* all fail their trust, To send our sons to scout and scamper there? **1850** CARLYLE *Latter-d. Pamph.* vii. (1872) 241 Our menagerie of live Peers in Parliament. **1854** MACAULAY *Biog., Johnson* (1860) 121 An old quack doctor named Levett.. completed this strange menagerie.

†**2.** An aviary. *Obs.*

1749 LADY LUXBOROUGH *Lett. to Shenstone* 29 Aug., I have reared but one single Guinea-chick this year.—If I had such a command of corn and of water as you have, I should be apt to fall into the expense of a *Ménagerie*. **1757** MRS. DELANY in *Life & Corr.* 461 The menagerie is not stored with great variety, but great quantities of Indian pheasants. **1830** 'B. MOUBRAY' *Dom. Poultry* (ed. 6) 129 The Noblemen and Gentlemen who have private menageries for pheasants.

Hence **meˈnagerist**, a keeper of a menagerie.

1850 in Cansick *Epitaphs Middlesex* (1872) II. 130 To the Memory of George Wombwell (Menagerist),.. died.. 1850.

menagerie, -ery, variant forms of MANAGERY.

ˈ**menagogue.** *rare*⁻⁰. [= F. *ménagogue* (Littré), f. Gr. μήν month + ἀγωγός leading, bringing in.] = EMMENAGOGUE.

1755 in JOHNSON; and in mod. Dicts.

menagry, menal: see MENAGERIE, MENIAL.

menald (ˈmɛnəld), *a.* Forms: 7 **menel(e)d, menelled, menild,** 9 **mennal, menald.** [? f. MEANEL + -ED².] Of animals: Spotted, speckled. Of a deer: Of a dappled chestnut colour. Also as *sb.*, a deer of that colour.

1611 COTGR., *Grivelé*, peckled, speckled; meneld, mayled, (blacke, and white). *Ibid.*, *Perdrix maillée*, a Menild, or spotted Partridge. **1693** RAY *Syn. Quadrup.* 86 Sunt.. albis maculis pariter variegatæ,.. ut à D. Robinson habeo, *Menal'd Deer* vocant. **1902** *Field* Aug. 285/3 In 1863 the following colours and shades were to be seen in Garendon Park,.. viz:—.. black, fallow, dappled fallow,.. mennal (Col. B.'s dappled chestnut), strawberry mennal (dappled roan) [etc.]. *Ibid.*, All the light colours.. were not so hardy as the blacks, dark duns, fallows and mennals.

†**menalty.** *Obs. rare*⁻¹. [f. *mene*, MEAN *a.*² + -AL¹ + -TY. Cf. MESNALTY.] The middle class.

a **1548** HALL *Chron. Hen. IV* 10 b, The euill parliament for the nobilitee, the worse for the menaltie, but worste of all for the commonaltee.

menalty: see MENIALTY, MESNALTY.

Menangkabau, var. MINANGKABAU *a.* and *sb.*

menaphthone (məˈnæfθəʊn). *Pharm.* [f. ME(THYL + NAPHTH(ALENE + -DI)ONE.] The name of MENADIONE in the *British Pharmacopœia*.

1943 *Brit. Pharmacopœia 1932* Add. VI. 19 Menaphthone should be kept in a well-closed container, protected from light. **1954** *Thorpe's Dict. Appl. Chem.* (ed. 4) XI. 369 Menaphthone, B.P.,.. has outstanding activity, being several times as active as the natural vitamin-K. **1962** J. H. BURN *Drugs, Med. & Man* v. 60 It is fortunately possible to restore the prothrombin in the blood by giving vitamin K, or, as an alternative, a synthetic substance menaphthone, which is allied to vitamin K in composition. **1968** [see MENADIONE].

menar, menaret, menas(s, menatair, menavelings, menawe: see MANURE, MINARET, MENACE, MINOTAUR, MANAVILINS, MINNOW.

menarche (məˈnɑːkiː). [a. G. *menarche* (E. H. Kisch 1895, in *Berl. klin. Wochenschr.* 30 Sept. 848/1), f. Gr. μήν month + ἀρχή beginning.] The first appearance of menstruation.

1900 in DORLAND *Med. Dict.* **1905** *Index-Catal. Library Surg.-General's Office* X. 670/1 (*heading*) Menarche. *See* Menstruation (Commencement of). **1910** M. E. PAUL tr. *Kisch's Sexual Life of Woman* i. 83 The diseases of the female genital organs at the time of the menarche are very various. **1949** E. B. HURLOCK *Adolescent Development* ii. 41 It may be only a few days or it may be nearly a year after the menarche before the pubescent girl menstruates again. **1949** M. MEAD *Male & Female* III. viii. 178 In Samoa, there is no social stress on menarche. **1966** *Lancet* 31 Dec. 1453/2 No significant association was found between cervical cancer and abstinence from intercourse during or shortly after the menses; median age at menarche; regularity of the menstrual cycle, [etc.].

menazon (ˈmɛnəzən). [f. ME(THYL + *n* (in AMINO-) + AZ(O- + *thi*)*on*(*ate* (s.v. THIO-1).] An organophosphorus compound, $(CH_3O)_2PS{\cdot}S{\cdot}CH_2{\cdot}C_3N_3(NH_2)_2$, which is used as an insecticide for aphides (see quot. 1961).

1961 A. CALDERBANK et al. in *Chem. & Industry* 13 May 630/1 A new class of heterocyclic thiophosphate ester has been prepared which combines outstanding aphicidal properties with low toxicity to other insect species and to mammals... One of the most active members is *S*-(4, 6-diamino-1, 3, 5-triazin-2-ylmethyl)*O*, *O*-dimethyl phosphorothiolothionate.., which has been given the common name 'menazon'. **1964** *Which?* Apr. 114/1 The organophosphorus compounds, such as dimethoate, malathion, menazon, are mainly poisonous to sucking insects, such as greenfly. **1972** *Bull. Entomol. Res.* LXII. 177 In order to ensure protection from secondary spread of rosette virus on the sprayed plots, menazon was applied five times at weekly intervals.

mence, menchen, -on (etc.), **mencion, -ioun** (etc.): see MENSE, MINCE, MINCHEN, MANSION, MENTION.

mench: see MENSH.

mend (mɛnd), *sb.* Also 4–6 **mende**; 6–9 *Sc. pl. as sing.* **mense**, (6 **mens**). [Partly aphetic for *amend* (see AMENDS); partly f. MEND *v.*]

†**1.** Recompense, reparation; also, something given as compensation. *Obs.*

a. *pl.* in form; usually construed as *sing.*

a **1300** *Cursor M.* 23152 Vnnethes sal man find an in lede þat wel will scriue þam o þis sake, ne for na consail mendes mak. **1399** LANGL. *Rich. Redeles* 292 Men myȝtten as welle have huntyd an hare with a tabre, as aske ony mendis ffor that thei mysdede. *c* **1450** HOLLAND *Howlat* 72 Bot quha sall mak me ane mendis of hir worth a myte? *a* **1578** LINDESAY (Pitscottie) *Chron. Scot.* (S.T.S.) II. 19 He.. promissit that he suld haue ane suffiecent mense of the quene. *Ibid.* 147. **1590** SPENSER *F.Q.* II. i. 20 All wrongs haue mendes. **1592** KYD *Sol. & Pers.* II. i. 46 Why then the mends is made, and we still friends. **1670** LASSELS *Voy. Italy* II. 268 This country made us a full mends for all the ill way we had had before. *a* **1733** *Shetland Acts* in *Proc. Soc. Ant. Scot.* (1892) XXVI. 200 That no mends be made for corn eaten within cornyards. **1779** D. GRAHAM *Writ.* (1883) II. 21 That's better mense for a fault, than a' your mortifying o' your members. **1816** SCOTT *Bl. Dwarf* x, Westburnflat hasna the means.. to make up our loss; there's nae mends to be got out o' him, but what ye take out o' his banes.

b. *sing. for, to* (a person's) *mend*: for his reparation or restoration (from sin). ***to mend***: as a recompense.

a **1300** *Cursor M.* 6723 (Cott.) If he sla animans thain, Thritti schiling o siluer again Sal man giue þe lord to mend [*a* 1300–1400 *Gött.* to mendes]. *c* **1315** SHOREHAM *Poems* ii. 128 And ase he þoled þane deþ, Leuedy, for oure mende. *Ibid.* vii. 831 To mannes mende. *c* **1330** R. BRUNNE *Chron.* (1810) 302 To mak mende & mak alle stable. **1646** *Deposit. York Castle* (Surtees) 9 *note*, And pray to God for mend.

†**2.** *pl.* Means of obtaining restoration or reparation; remedy. *Obs.*

c **1450** HOLLAND *Howlat* 29 Mendis and medicyne for mennis all neidis. **1530** PALSGR. 666/1 If I pricke you with my daggar you have your mendes in your hande. **1606** SHAKS. *Tr. & Cr.* I. i. 68. **1655** GURNALL *Chr. in Arm.* I. 53 If any mischief befalls him, the mends is in his own hands.

†**3.** *pl.* Improvement in health. *Obs.*

1624 *Witch Trial* in *Abbotsford Club Misc.* I. 137 The said Margaret Corstoun haueing contractit seiknes, dwyned be the space of foure monethis, and could get no mendis.

†**4.** ***to the mends***: 'to boot'. *Sc. Obs.*

1636 RUTHERFORD *Lett.* (1862) I. lxxi. 185, I will verily give my Lord Jesus a free discharge of all that I.. laid to His charge, and beg Him pardon, to the mends.

5. Phr. ***on the mend***: (of a person, his health, etc.) recovering from sickness; (of affairs, trade, etc.), improving in condition.

1802 COLERIDGE in Mrs. Sandford *T. Poole & Friends* (1802) II. 77 [My] health has been on the mend ever since Poole left town. **1897** *Daily News* 27 July 11/4 Home trade in finished linens is perhaps on the mend.

6. An act of mending, a repair; a repaired hole, etc., in a fabric.

1888 *Housewife* III. 436/1 If the mend is dampened and pressed with a hot iron it is almost unnoticeable. **1900** *Daily News* 28 Nov. 10/2 Mrs. A. is reluctant to let her clothes be seen by Mrs. B., for fear that lady should notice the rents and mends. **1903** *Blackw. Mag.* Dec. 803/2 A mend in the sole [of a stocking].

†**7.** *Comb.*: **mends-making**, reparation, atonement. *Obs.*

c **1400** *Cursor M.* 28617 (Cott. Galba) Schrift aw to be thrinfalde, with rewth in hert, and schewing to preste, and mendes making. **1530** TINDALE *Answ. More* IV. ii. Wks. (1573) 320/1 And as for mendes making with worldly things, that do to thy brother whom thou hast offended.

mend (mɛnd), *v.* [aphetic f. AMEND *v.*

The aphetic form, however, occurs in our quots. earlier than the original form. Cf. AF. *mender* in one MS. (St. John's, Camb.) of Wadington's *Manuel des Pechiez* l. 10.]

I. To remove or atone for defects.

1. a. *trans.* To free (a person, his character or habits) from sin or fault; to improve morally; to reform; *occas.* to cure *of* (a fault). Now *arch.* or *dial.* exc. in phr. ***to mend one's manners, ways.***

c **1200** *Trin. Coll. Hom.* 217 On þe helde laȝe het ure drihten þat me ne sholde none man bitechen, bute he were teid to menden chirche. *a* **1300** *Cursor M.* 22436 þar es nam[an].. þat he ne his liif agh to mend. *Ibid.* 26507 Quen þou art mendid o þi sin. *c* **1430** *ABC of Aristotle* in *Babees Bk.*, It schal neuere greue a good man þouȝ þe gilti be meendid. **1562** J. HEYWOOD *Epigr.* i. R, If euery man mende one, all shall be mended. **1679** PENN *Addr. Prot.* I. ix. Wks. 1825 III. 39 A descreet and cool hand may direct the blow right.. when men of fury rather ease their passion, than mend their youth. **1711** ADDISON *Spect.* No. 112 ¶7 If he does not mend his Manners. **1766** GOLDSM. *Vic. W.* xxvii, Though the instruction I communicate may not mend them [prisoners], yet it will assuredly mend myself. **1868** FREEMAN *Norm. Conq.* (1877) II. viii. 211 That turbulent prelate had mended his ways. **1891** BARING-GOULD *Urith* xxxix, Have you seen how a little dog is mended of lamb worrying?

†**b.** *refl.* To reform oneself. *Obs.*

a **1300** *Cursor M.* 25548 Þou send vs, lauerd! wijt and will to mend us of vr dedis ill. **14..** *Tundale's Vis.* 2326 (Wagner) He warned alle.. To mende hem here, before her dede. **1596** HARINGTON *Metam. Ajax* (1814) 134 Let both the writer and the readers endeavour to mend ourselves. **1601** SHAKS. *Twel. N.* I. v. 50 Bid the dishonest man mend himself.

c. *intr.* for *refl.* Now *rare* exc. in the proverb ***it is never too late to mend.***

a **1300** *Cursor M.* 23264 For þai mai haf na might to mend. ? **1404–8** *26 Pol. Poems* v. 22 [He] þat nyl not mende, but ay

don ylle. **1550** Crowley *Last Trump.* 1436 Their conscience ..saieth thei were Told of their fault, & woulde not mende. **1605** Shaks. *Lear* II. iv. 232 Let shame come when it will, I do not call it... Mend when thou can'st, be better at thy leisure. *c* **1645** Howell *Lett.* (1655) IV. xxxviii. 92 It is never over-late to mend. **1785–6** Burns *Addr. to Deil* xxi, O wad ye tak a thought an' men'! **1842** S. Lover *Handy Andy* xxi, 'She's very young, Sir'. 'She'll mend of that, ma'am. We were young once ourselves'. **1873** Black *Pr. Thule* ix, I am afraid that you are a very foolish boy..but I hope to see you mend when you marry.

2. a. To remove the defects of (a thing); to correct (what is faulty); to improve by correction or alteration. Now only *occas.* as a transf. use of sense 5.

† *to mend* (*one's*) *mood*: to become more cheerful.

a **1300** *Cursor M.* 10434 Leuedi, sco said, for drightin dere, þou mend þi mode and turn þi chere. *c* **1330** R. Brunne *Chron.* (1810) 69, I salle þe make..my chefe Justise, þe lawes to mend & right. *c* **1420** *Pallad. on Husb.* XII. 530 For brousty oil, whit wex is to resolue In fynest oil [etc.]. So wol hit mende odour and taast also. **1461** *Cal. Anc. Rec. Dublin* (1889) I. 309 The sayd lawe was mendyt by autorite of a semble. **1577** B. Googe *Heresbach's Husb.* I. (1586) 19 Heathy, Brushy, & Grauelly ground: may these be made fruitefull, and mended [L. *corrigi & fœcundari*] by arte. **1631–2** *High Commission Cases* (Camden) 237, I wish that you..that are soe ready to fynd faultes were sett to mend the booke of common prayer. **1697** Dryden *Virg. Georg.* II. 324 Salt Earth and bitter are not fit to sow, Nor will be tam'd and mended by the Plough. **1707** Mortimer *Husb.* 74 So where Marle is not laid too thick..it will often mend Clays. **1724** A. Collins *Gr. Chr. Relig.* 20 Divines; who seem to pay little deference to the Books of the New Testament, whose text they are perpetually mending in their sermons, commentaries, and writings, to serve purposes. **1820** Cobbett *Gram. Eng. Lang.* xiv. (1847) 89 Never think of mending what you write. Let it go. No patching; no after pointing. **1872** Skeat *Chaucer's Astrolabe* (E.E.T.S.) 87, I have mended the text as well as I could by words, &c., inserted between square brackets. **1901** T. R. Glover *Life & Lett. 4th C.* 90 The last three books [of Q. Smyrnaeus].. are beyond revision. To be mended they must be re-written.

b. *intr.* To become less faulty. Of conditions: To become less unfavourable, improve.

a **1300–1400** *Cursor M.* 24490 (Gött.) All mi licam bigan to light, And mi mode to mend. **1546** J. Heywood *Prov.* (1867) 75 As sowre ale mendth in summer. *c* **1645** Howell *Lett.* (1655) II. xlix. 58, I hope the times will mend. **1708** Prior *Turtle & Sparrow* 416 Matters at worst are sure to mend. **1736** Berkeley *Querist* II. §5 Wks. 1871 III. 519 Whether..our State will mend, so long as property is insecure among us? **1826** Penn in *Pa. Hist. Soc. Mem.* I. 418 Our condition here..mends upon us. **1876** Trevelyan *Life & Lett. Macaulay* II. 2 Things did not mend as time went on.

3. a. *trans.* To rectify, remedy, remove (an evil); to correct, put right (a fault, anything amiss).

a **1300** *Cursor M.* 644 Here [*sc.* the garden of Eden] lastes lijf wit-oten end, Her es nathing for to mend. *Ibid.* 5417 Bath he [Ioseph] did his lauerd byyate, And mended nede in þair state. *c* **1374** Chaucer *Troylus* v. 1425 She wolde come, and mende al that was mis. *c* **1400** *26 Pol. Poems* iv. 137 Thouȝ holy chirche shulde fawtes mend, Summe put hem of for mede. **1500–20** Dunbar *Poems* xxviii. 14 Sowtaris, with schone weill maid and meit, Ȝe mend the faltis of ill maid feit. **1590** Shaks. *Com. Err.* III. ii. 107 She sweats... That's a fault that water will mend. **1677** Moxon *Mech. Exerc.* 20 You must examine where the fault is, and taking the Pin out, mend the fault in the Joynt. **1710** Steele *Tatler* No. 168 ¶4 There is no Way of mending such false Modesty. **1816** Scott *Bl. Dwarf* x, But how ye are to put yoursells up, I canna see! And what's waur, I canna mend it. **1819** Shelley *Cenci* III. i. 302 Poverty, the which I sought to mend By holding a poor office in the state.

†**b.** To correct (a mistake, something erroneous). *Obs.*

1563–7 Buchanan *Reform. St. Andros* Wks. (1892) 9 Na man sal mend otheris faltis [*sc.* mistakes in a lesson] vntil they cum to the regent. **1711** Swift *Jrnl. to Stella* 17 Dec., I have mistaken the day of the month, and been forced to mend it thrice.

c. *intr.* Of a fault: To undergo rectification.

1712 Pope *Spect.* No. 408 ¶7 The Fire of Youth will of course abate, and is a Fault,..that mends every Day.

4. *trans.* To make amends or reparation for, atone for (a misdeed, an injury); also *absol.* to make reparation. Occas. const. *dat.* of person. *Obs.* exc. in the proverb, ***least said soonest mended***.

a **1300** *Cursor M.* 20251 If I haf anithing mis-wroght,..I wil it mend. *Ibid.* 26223 And he þat bath [church & man] þair bleith has blend, A-gains bath be-hous him mend. *c* **1330** R. Brunne *Chron.* (1810) 303 To while pape Boniface duellid opon þis, To gyue dome þorgh grace, to mende boþe þer mys. **1426** Audelay *Poems* 12 Ȝif thai wyl mend that thai do mys, to have remyssyon. **1546** J. Heywood *Prov.* (1867) 29 Ye maie syr (quoth he) mend three naies with one yée. **1607** Shaks. *Cor.* III. ii. 26 Come, come, you haue bin too rough,..you must returne, and mend it. **1670** Ray *Prov.* 285 Little said, soon mendit. [Cf. **1659** Howell *Prov.* 9/1 Little said soon amended.] **1733** in *Swift's Lett.* (1766) II. 185 One soon learns to stop when it is wished, or to mend what is said amiss. **1841** Lytton *Nt. & Morn.* IV. viii, At present, 'least said soonest mended'.

5. a. To restore to a complete or sound condition (something broken, decayed, worn, etc.); to repair or make good (the defective part). Also ***to mend up***. Phr. ***to mend one's fences***: see fence *sb.* 5 c.

Now the prevailing sense: the others, so far as they survive, being more or less coloured by this. The vb. is now ordinarily used only with such objects as are commonly said to be 'worn', 'broken', or 'torn' (e.g. articles of clothing or furniture, tools, fences); e.g. we do not speak of 'mending' a house. *To mend a road*, however, is still current.

1362 Langl. *P. Pl.* A. III. 53 þer nis nouþur Wyndou ne Auter, þat I ne schulde maken oþur mende. *c* **1375** *Sc. Leg. Saints* xiii. (*Marcus*) 81 þe bochoure wes mendand þe scho. **1487** in T. Gardner *Hist. Dunwich* (1754) 153 Payd the Glas-wryȝte for mendyng Seynt Krysteferys Wyndown. **1535** Coverdale *Mark* i. 19 As they were in the shyppe mendynge their nettes. **1617** Moryson *Itin.* I. 186 As if I had been so good a husband, as to mend my own clothes. **1639** in *Coll. Conn. Hist. Soc.* (1897) VI. 5 All the fences.. shall be mended vp. **1747** in *Amer. Speech* (1940) XV. 228/2, I went to mamacock & Crossman Lot & mended up fence. **1756–7** tr. *Keysler's Trav.* (1760) I. 229 The rough and stony roads have been mended. **1833** S. Smith *Life & Writings J. Downing* lvi. 192 They've got their clothes pretty much mended up, and they look quite tidy. **1854** M. L. Charlesworth *Ministering Children* ii. 19 Mamma is going to give me all Edward's old warm stockings, if I mend them up quite neat! **1878** Jevons *Prim. Pol. Econ.* 29 Hedges and ditches are mended when there is nothing else to do. **1888** *Housewife* III. 436/2 After mending the holes, the thin places..should be run thickly backwards and forwards.

transf. and *fig.* (cf. 2). **1500–20** Dunbar *Poems* xxviii. 22 And ȝe tailȝouris, with wellmaid clais Can mend the werst maid man that gais. **1597** Shaks. *2 Hen. IV*, III. ii. 176.

b. To repair the garments of (a person). *colloq.*

1876 W. S. Gilbert *Sorcerer* II. (1886) 24 She will tend him, nurse him, mend him, Air his linen [etc.]. **1881** *Gd. Words* 844/2 She 'washed and mended' him to the envy of the neighbours.

c. To adjust, set right. *Obs.* exc. *Naut.*

c **1515** *Cocke Lorell's B.* 12 Some yᵉ longe bote dyde launce, some mende yᵉ corse. **1601** Shaks. *All's Well* III. ii. 7 Why he will looke vppon his boote, and sing: mend the Ruffe and sing. **1606** —— *Ant. & Cl.* v. ii. 322. **1682** Dryden & Lee *Duke of Guise* II. ii. (1683) 16 Yes, I wou'd make every Glance a Murder. Mend me this Curle. **1832** Marryat *N. Forster* xxvi, He therefore turned the hands up, 'mend sails', and took his station amidship on the booms, to see that this the most delinquent sail, was properly furled. **1867** Smyth *Sailor's Word-bk.*, *To mend sails*, to loose and skin them afresh on the yards.

d. † ***to mend the lights***: to trim the lamps, or snuff the candles (*obs.*). ***to mend a fire***: to add fuel to it (cf. the earlier beet *v.*). ***to mend a pen***: to cut a worn quill pen so as to make it fit for its purpose.

c **1480** Henryson *Test. Cress.* 36, I mend the fyre and beikit me about. **1625** B. Jonson *Staple of News* Induct., *Book-holder.* Mend your lights, Gentlemen, Master Prologue, beginne. *marg.*, The Tiremen enter to mend the lights. **1720** Petrie *Rules Deportm.* iii. Wks. (1877) 21 Do not spit in the Fire, nor offer to mend it. **1820** Keats *Lett.* (1958) II. 262, I have been writing with a vile old pen the whole week... The fault is in the Quill: I have mended it. **1834** Ht. Martineau *Farrers* i. 15 Jane shook her head as she carefully mended the fire. **1863** A. Blomfield *Mem. Bp. Blomfield* I. viii. 223 We all sit and mend our pens and talk about the weather.

6. a. *trans.* To restore to health, cure, heal. *arch.*

13.. *St. Nicholas* 349 in Horstm. *Altengl. Leg.* (1881) 15 þai praid all to saint Nicholas þat [dede] man þore forto rays & mend. **13..** *St. Lucy* 8 ibid. 17 Scho..fand no medcyn hir might mend. **1523** Fitzherb. *Husb.* §46 There be dyuers waters, & other medicyns, that wolde mende hym. **1697** Dryden *Virg. Georg.* III. 113 Yearly thy Herds in Vigour will impair, Recruit and mend 'em with thy Yearly Care. **1736** in *Swift's Lett.* (1766) II. 235, I daily see such numbers of people mended by them [these waters], that [etc.]. **1883** R. W. Dixon *Mano* I. v. 14 And slowly some we mended of their ill, And pitied all.

transf. and *fig.* **1831** Lamb *Elia* Ser. II. *Ellistoniana*, Sir A—— C——..who mends a lame narrative almost as well as he sets a fracture. **1870** Morris *Earthly Par.*, *Son of Croesus* (1903) 153/2 And August came the fainting year to mend With fruit and grain.

b. *intr.* To regain health; to recover from sickness. †Const. *of*. Also ***to mend up***.

1500–20 Dunbar *Poems* xxii. 59 May nane remeid my melady Sa weill as ȝe..And gif I mend nocht hestely. **1523** Fitzherb. *Husb.* §46 There be some shepe that wyll be blynd a season, and yet mende agayn. **1663** Chas. II in Julia Cartwright *Henrietta of Orleans* (1894) 149 She mends very slowly. **1712–13** Swift *Jrnl. to Stella* 22 Feb., The Queen is slowly mending of her gout. **1810** Shelley *Zastrozzi* xi, The health of Verezzi, meanwhile, slowly mended. **1840** Dickens *Barn. Rudge* v, The fever has left him, and the doctor says he will soon mend. **1877** A. Sewell *Black Beauty* (*c* 1878, ed. 5) xlv. 217 The farrier said he [*sc.* a horse] might mend up enough to sell for a few pounds. **1897** Hughes *Medit. Fever* v. 194 One day of injudicious dietary ..in a case that is mending, may cause a serious relapse.

c. Of a wound, etc.: To heal. Of a malady: To abate. Now *dial.*

1607 Shaks. *Timon* v. i. 190 My long sicknesse Of Health, and Liuing, now begins to mend. **1804** Abernethy *Surg. Obs.* 140 An ulcer mends in one part though it may spread in another. **1869** A. C. Gibson *Folk-Sp. Cumbld.* 163 His hand mendit weel—(He hed gud healin flesh,..hed Joe).

II. Without distinct reference to defect: To make better, ameliorate, improve.

7. a. *trans.* To improve the condition or fortune of. Now *rare* or *Obs.* exc. *refl.*, to better oneself, make an advantageous change in one's condition.

c **1330** R. Brunne *Chron.* (1810) 244 Wardeyns gode he sette, to stabille þe lond & mende [orig. *Establye ses lays, fet l'estat melliour*]. *c* **1330** —— *Chron. Wace* (Rolls) 6552 Wiþ waryson he schold þem [marriageable maidens] mende. **1558** *Richmond Wills* (Surtees) 122, I wyll yᵗ the pore folkes of the church rawe be mended with bygge. **1625** Bacon *Ess., Innov.* (Arb.) 527 Whatsoeuer is New is vnlooked for; And euer it mends Some, and paires Other. **1632** Lithgow *Trav.* III. 84 He could not mend himselfe, in regard of my shelter. **1678** Bunyan *Pilgr.* I. (1862) 58 Your service was hard.. therefore..I did as other considerate persons do, look out, if perhaps I might mend myself. **1719** De Foe *Crusoe* (Globe) 390 Whether it was by Negligence in guarding them, or that they thought the Fellows could not mend themselves, I know not, but one of them run away. **1790** Burke *Fr. Rev.* (ed. 2) 40 How either he or we should be much mended by it, I cannot imagine. **1876** J. Richardson *Cummerl. Talk* Ser. II. 183 If..he duddent know what way to gang to mend his-sel, he hed to grub away fra leet to dark for a canny laal.

†**b.** *Sc.* To profit, advantage (a person); *absol.* to avail. (In negative and interrogative contexts.)

c **1470** *Gol. & Gaw.* 1069 It may nocht mend the ane myte to mak it so teugh. *c* **1475** *Rauf Coilȝear* 653 He saw thair was na meiknes nor mesure micht mend. *c* **1560** A. Scott *Poems* (S.T.S.) xx. 22 Off all thy wo and cair It mends the noᵗ to mene. **1572** *Satir. Poems Reform.* xxx. 126 Quhat will it mend to murne thy senses out?

†**8.** To improve (a person) physically. Also *intr.* (of a child) to thrive (cf. 10 b). *Obs.*

a **1400–50** *Alexander* 464 Outhire mete has mendid þe full mekill..Or ane has stollen in my stede. *c* **1500** *Melusine* 103 Melusyne..had so grete care for her children that they mended & grewe so wel that euery one that saw them meruaylled. **1810** Hogg *Birniebouzle* 8 I'll hunt the otter an' the brock,..An' pu' the limpet aff the rock, To batten an' to mend ye.

†**9. a.** To improve by additions (*e.g.* wages, prices).

c **1440** *Pol. Rel. & L. Poems* 272 Fals iudas, to mendyn hys purs, To ded hath hym sold. *c* **1470** Harding *Chron.* (1812) 366 The market he so mended manyfolde. **1510** *Extracts Aberd. Reg.* (1844) I. 81 Thai sall caus him be pait yerlie of tene pundis..quhill thai be of puyschance to mend him his fee. **1583** Stubbes *Anat. Abus.* II. (1882) 88 If his liuing be too little, then ought the church to mend it. **1600** Shaks. *A.Y.L.* II. iv. 94 And we will mend thy wages. **1697** Dryden *Virg. Georg.* IV. 196 Sometimes white Lillies did their Leaves afford, With wholsom Poppy-flow'rs to mend his homely Board.

b. *intr.* To improve in amount or price.

1602 *2nd Pt. Return fr. Parnass.* H 2, Then let vs leaue this baser fidling trade, For though our purse should mend, our credit fades. **1812** *Examiner* 7 Sept. 563/2 Wool mending in price.

†**c.** *trans.* To supplement, make up the deficiency of. (See also 12 a.) *Obs.*

1590 Shaks. *Com. Err.* IV. iii. 60 Wee'll mend our dinner here. **1638** in Birch *Life Milton* M.'s Wks. 1738 I. 16, I would have been bold, in our vulgar phrase, to mend my draught, for you left me with an extreme Thirst. **1711** Swift *Jrnl. to Stella* 9 Oct., I was forced to lie down at twelve to-day, and mend my night's sleep.

10. a. To improve in quality; to render more excellent; to ameliorate (conditions, etc.). Now *rare*.

1603 Florio *Montaigne* II. Epist., So neyther is one vertue fit for all, nor all fit for one vertue: nor is that one so excellent, but by more it might be mended. **1605** Bacon *Adv. Learn.* II. xxii. §5 Tacitus observeth how rarely raising of the fortune mendeth the disposition. **1615** W. Lawson *Country Housew. Gard.* (1626) 19 Trees..as they grow in yeeres, bignesse, and strength; so they mend their fruit. **1672** Grew *Anat. Plants* §43 Some Vegetables lose their Smell,..others, keep it,..others, mend it. **1700** Dryden *Fables* Pref. *D, Chaucer..has mended the Stories which he has borrow'd, in his way of telling. **1712** Addison *Spect.* No. 383 ¶4 The fifty new Churches will very much mend the Prospect. **1781** W. Blane *Ess. Hunting* (1788) 21 Directions for mending and improving the Breed [of dogs]. **1781** Cowper *Hope* 451 The Sacred Book..speaks, with plainness art could never mend. **1796** Morse *Amer. Geog.* II. 47 Cattle are small... And they would be more so, were not the breed mended by a mixture with those of other countries. **1847** L. Hunt *Men, Women, & B.* II. x. 208 The Fieldings, till Henry came up to mend the reputation, were not thought very clever. **1854** Tennyson *To F. D. Maurice* x, How best to help the slender store, How mend the dwellings, of the poor.

†**b.** *intr.* To grow better in quality, improve. *Obs.*

1546 J. Heywood *Prov.* (1867) 75 Than wolde ye mend.. as sowre ale mendth in summer. **1601** Shaks. *Twel. N.* I. v. 80 What thinke you of this foole Maluolio, doth he not mend? **1705** Addison *Italy* (*Rome to Naples*) 174 St. Peters seldom answers Expectation at first entering it, but..mends upon the Eye every Moment. **1712** —— *Spect.* No. 543 ¶1 Though it [the human body] appears formed with the nicest Wisdom, upon the most superficial Survey of it, it still mends upon the Search.

c. To recover from, get better *of*, grow out *of*.

1881 J. Fothergill *Kith & Kin* III. ii. 43 He had always trusted that the boy would mend of such outlandish indifference.

11. *trans.* To improve upon, surpass, better. In early use with personal obj. Now only *colloq.* to produce something better than.

c **1320** *Sir Tristr.* 555 Bot y þe mendi may, Wrong þan wite y þe. **1588** Shaks. *L.L.L.* v. ii. 329 In Vshering Mend him who can. *Mod.* A very good story: I don't think I can mend it.

III. Phrases and Combinations.

12. Phrases. **a.** ***to mend*** (a person's) ***cheer***: †(*a*) to cheer, comfort (cf. cheer *sb.*[1] 3); (*b*) to improve the fare of (cf. cheer *sb.*[1] 6).

a **1300** *Cursor M.* 4232 His oþer suns com ilkan sere For to mend þair fader chere. *c* **1350** *Will. Palerne* 647 þanne þis maiden melior gan menden here chere. **1727** Boyer *Dict. Royal* s.v. *Mend*, I'll try if I can mend your Chear, *J'essayerai..de vous mieux regaler.* **1814** Scott *Ld. of Isles* III. xii, A bow full deftly can he bend, And if we meet a herd, may send A shaft shall mend our cheer.

†**b.** In asseverative phrases, esp. ***so God mend me***. Also in pious wishes, as ***God mend all***. *Obs.*

c **1400** *Laud Troy Bk.* 433 Lordynges, so god me mende, Lamedon me to ȝow sende. **1568** *Jacob & Esau* I. iii. B j b, The most gentle yong man aliue, as God me mende. **1592** SHAKS. *Rom. & Jul.* I. v. 81 Youle not endure him, God shall mend my soule. **1600** —— *A.Y.L.* IV. i. 193. **1611** —— *Cymb.* V. v. 68 Heauen mend all. **1789** WOLCOT (P. Pindar) *Subj. for Painters* Wks. 1812 II. 136 Where'er they go, poor imps God mend 'em!

c. ***to mend or end***: either to improve or (if that be impossible) to put an end to; in early use chiefly = 'to kill or cure'; also, †to correct or finish (a work). †Formerly also *intr.*, either to die or recover.

1578 T. WILCOCKS *Serm. Pawles* 74 Plague: what hathe it done? it hathe mended as manye as it hathe ended. **1603** FLORIO *Montaigne* II Epist., That perfect-vnperfect Arcadia, which..your all praise-exceeding father..lived not to mend or end-it. **1613** PURCHAS *Pilgrimage* 805 When the King of Mexico sickened, they vsed to put a Visor on the face..of some..Idol, which was not taken away till he mended or ended. **1648** *Eikon Bas.* xv. 123, I had the Charitie to interpret, that most part of My Subjects fought against My supposed Errors, not My Person; and intended to mend Mee, not to end Mee. *c* **1680** HICKERINGILL *Hist. Whiggism* Wks. 1716 I. I. 21, I had rather we should mend than end. **1884** J. MORLEY in *Times* 31 July 11/4 The..question of mending or ending the House of Lords.

d. ***to mend the matter, to mend matters***: to improve the state of affairs concerning a person or thing. Often used *ironically*.

1690 LOCKE *Hum. Und.* II. xvii. §16, I suppose they will thereby very little mend the matter, or help us to a more clear and positive idea. **1719** DE FOE *Crusoe* (Globe) 295 To mend the Matter,..it continued snowing. **1869** FREEMAN *Norm. Conq.* (1875) III. xii. 253 No one will argue that he would have mended matters had he fulfilled his promise.

e. ***to mend (one's) pace***: to travel faster.

1602 SHAKS. *Ham.* V. i. 64 Your dull Asse will not mend his pace with beating. **1667** MILTON *P.L.* x. 859 Justice Divine Mends not her slowest pace for prayers or cries. **1781** COWPER *Expost.* 151 Judgment, however tardy, mends her pace When Obstinacy once has conquered Grace. **1851** D. JERROLD *St. Giles* vii. 66 He mended his pace, and..jerked the pony into a trot.

†**f.** ***to mend one's hand***: to improve one's work or conduct. *Obs.*

1685 DRYDEN *Alb. & Alban.* Pref., Ess. (ed. Ker) I. 280 If it finds encouragement, I dare promise myself to mend my hand, by making a more pleasing fable. **1781** C. JOHNSTON *Hist. J. Juniper* I. 65 His nurse..being threatened to be turned off, if she did not mend her hand.

g. ***to make or mend*** (*absol.*): see MAKE *v.*[1] 1 c.

†**13.** *Comb.* with sbs. (often as quasi-proper names) with the sense 'one who mends...', as ***mend-all, mendbreech, mend-fault, mend-market***.

c **1470** HARDING *Chron.* CCVIII. Argt. (1812) 366 Howe syr Robert Vmgreuile brent Pebles on there market daye..and after the Scottes called hym Robyne Mendmarket. **1573** TUSSER *Husb.* (1878) 179 Feare flea smocke and mendbreech, for burning their bed. **1643** BAKER *Chron.* (1674) 190 Jack Cade..styling himself Captain Mend-all, marched..to Blackheath. **1654** WHITLOCK *Zootomia* 174 The Commonwealth might better spare many famous for feats of Armes, than these Learned Mend-faults (in men, or States).

mend, obs. form of MIND.

mendable (ˈmɛndəb(ə)l), *a.* [f. MEND *v.* + -ABLE.] That can be mended; capable of improvement.

1533 MORE *Apol.* xlviii. Wks. 925/2 And those extreme vices..diligently refourme & amende in such as are mendable. **1638** in *Buccleuch MSS.* (Hist. MSS. Comm.) I. 282 The locks..are not mendable when out of tune. **1890** *Graphic* 11 Oct. 405/3 If I thought there was aught mendable in thee that could be shaped by the hands of a good wife.

†**mendaciloquent**, *a. Obs. rare*⁻⁰. [f. L. *mendāciloqu-us* (f. *mendāci-*, *-mendax* mendacious + *loqu-i* to speak) + -ENT: cf. *grandiloquent*.] Speaking lies. So †**menda'ciloquence**, lying.

1656 BLOUNT *Glossogr.*, *Mendaciloquent*, that tels lies.. false speaking. *c* **1710** *Hist. London Clubs* I. 2 A witty and famous Gentleman in the Art of Mendatiloquence [*sic*].

mendacious (mɛnˈdeɪʃəs), *a.* [f. L. *mendāc-em*, *mendax* (:—**mentnax*, f. root of *mentīrī* to lie) + -IOUS.] Lying; untruthful; false.

1616 R. SHELDON *Miracles Antichr.* 63 A mendacious Legend of Ignatius his miracles. **1654** COKAINE *Dianea* IV. 266 Fame, that mixing Truth with Falsehood, renders the one and the other equally mendacious. **1840** CARLYLE *Heroes* (1858) 189 [The Pagan ages] were not mendacious and distracted, but in their own poor way true and sane! **1885** *Truth* 28 May 838/1 The..mendacious garbage that is being published in the *Nouvelle Revue*.

Hence **men'daciously** *adv.*, in a mendacious or lying manner; **men'daciousness**, mendacity.

1802–12 BENTHAM *Ration. Judic. Evid.* (1827) I. 544 The supposed mendaciously-disposed witness. **1873** *Brit. Q. Rev.* LVII. 222 Throughout it is one long record of ambitious rapacity, mendaciousness, and crime.

mendacity (mɛnˈdæsɪtɪ). [ad. late L. *mendācitās*, f. *mendāc-em*: see MENDACIOUS *a.* and -ITY.] The quality of being mendacious; the tendency or disposition to lie or deceive; habitual lying or deceiving.

1646 SIR T. BROWNE *Pseud. Ep.* I. vi. 22 If wee call to minde the mendacity of Greece. **1660** *State Trials, John Cook* (1730) II. 344/2 In that Sense it must have the Operation of Mendacity;..there must be a Lie told in it. **1877** A. B. EDWARDS *Up Nile* ix. 245 Notwithstanding his mendacity—(and it must be owned that he is the most brilliant liar under heaven). **1895** *Bookman* Oct. 26/2 The fathers, whose rhetorical exaggeration amounts to innocent mendacity.

b. An instance of this; a lie or falsehood.

1646 SIR T. BROWNE *Pseud. Ep.* I. i. 2 There were no lesse then two mistakes, or rather additionall mendacites [*sic*]. **1868** FARRAR *Seekers* III. i. (1875) 270 The age of spiritual impotencies and mendacities.

c. *attrib.* and *Comb.*

1802–12 BENTHAM *Ration. Judic. Evid.* (1827) I. 191 A motive..may be termed a mendacity-prompting..motive. *a* **1845** SYD. SMITH *Ballot* Wks. 1859 II. 316/2 The period for lying arrives, and the mendacity machine is exhibited to the view of the Wigginses.

Mendæan, -aite: see MANDÆAN, MANDAITE.

mendang (mɛnˈdæŋ). Also **mendong, mendung**. [Tibetan.] A sacred wall composed of flat stones carved with Buddhas or religious texts. Also *attrib.*

1925 J. A. HAMMERTON *Countries of World* VI. 3946/2 The mendangs—long walls in the middle of the road composed for the most part of inscribed stones. **1939** M. PALLIS *Peaks & Lamas* vi. 65 Each entrance to a village is marked by a *mendong* or *Mani* wall, a low cemented breast-work upon which innumerable flat stones carved with sacred texts in low relief have been laid, the accumulated offerings of local piety. **1952** H. W. TILMAN *Nepal Himalaya* I. iv. 39 These walls or 'mendongs', which are seven or eight feet high, must be passed on the left. **1960** 'S. HARVESTER' *Chinese Hammer* x. 94 A *mendang* wall in the town, the sacred wall. **1972** J. & R. GODDEN *Shiva's Pigeons* II. 88 Mendungs—low stone walls—carved..are built beside mountain tracks and along the trade routes of the north-eastern passes. *Ibid.*, It is reverent to pass a mendung on the right-hand side.

†**men'dation**. *Obs. rare*⁻¹. [app. for MANDATION (not found in this sense, but cf. MANDATARY, MANDATE 2 b).] The granting of papal mandates.

1561 *Godly Q. Hester* (1873) 24 And what by mendation, and dyspensation, they gat the nomynation, of euery good benefyce.

Mende (ˈmɛndiː), *sb.* and *a.* Also **Mendi**.

A. *sb.* **a.** A group of Negro peoples inhabiting Sierra Leone and Liberia; a member of this group. **b.** The language of the Mende. **B.** *adj.* Of or pertaining to the Mende or their language.

1887 *Encycl. Brit.* XXII. 44/2 The following are the more important races [of Sierra Leone] that can be distinctly classified..Mendis, 3088. **1908** T. G. TUCKER *Introd. Nat. Hist. Lang.* 147 *Mende*, of Upper Guinea, including dialects of Mandingo, Bambara, etc. **1911** *Encycl. Brit.* XVI. 542/1 Some of the Krumen are coarse and ugly, and this is the case with the Mende people. **1936** G. GREENE *Journey without Maps* I. iii. 62 He could speak Mende; he was picking up Buzie. **1948** —— *Heart of Matter* I. i. 7 His Mende sergeant clicked his heels. **1957** C. MACINNES *City of Spades* 216 Mr. Karl Marx Bo..planned to send..a tendentious report on the trial to the Mendi newspaper of which he was part-time correspondent. **1970** P. OLIVER *Savannah Syncopators* 112 *Mende*, Sierra Leone tribe situated near the coast. **1971** E. JONES in J. Spencer *Eng. Lang. W. Afr.* 68 The official news bulletin put out daily over the Sierra Leone Broadcasting Service by the Ministry of Information, as well as other important government statements, are broadcast in Krio as well as English, Mende and Temne. **1972** J. L. DILLARD *Black English* iii. 130 There will probably never be any reliable evidence as to whether the slaves themselves differentiated between the Vai-Hausa forms and the Mende form in pronunciation. **1974** *Times* 4 May (Suppl.) p. i/6 Typically a [Sierra Leonean] minister will be a Mende or a Temne with a Creole permanent-secretary.

mende, obs. form of MIND.

mended (ˈmɛndɪd), *ppl. a.* [f. MEND *v.* + -ED[1].] Repaired, improved.

1595 SHAKS. *John* V. vii. 75 Shew now your mended faiths. **1859** TENNYSON *Enid* 718 So clothe yourself in this, that better fits Our mended fortunes and a Prince's bride. **1861** THACKERAY *Four Georges* i. 67 Mended morals and mended manners. **1895** *Daily News* 17 Dec. 6/4 Whether the voice of a mended bell is ever equal to that of one unmended.

‖**mendee** (ˈmɛndiː). Also **mindy, mhendee, mendi, -y.** [Hindī *mendhī*.] An Indian name for a variety of henna, *Lawsonia alba*. Also *attrib.* as ***mendee-hedge***.

c **1813** MRS. SHERWOOD *Ayah & Lady* x. 63 She..caused her to stain the palms of her hands and feet with the juice of mindy. —— *Stories Ch. Catech.* x. 71 His garden..was well fenced round with a ditch and mindy hedge. **1839** *Penny Cycl.* XIII. 367/2 The natives of North India distinguished the unarmed species by the name *phoolke*, or flowering *mhendee*... The thorny species is called *mhendee*. **1866** *Treas. Bot.* 734/2 *Mendee*. **1886** YULE & BURNELL *Hobson-Jobson, Mendy*.

mendelevium (mɛndəˈliːvɪəm, -ˈeɪvɪəm). *Chem.* [f. the name of Dmitri Ivanovich *Mendeleev* (1834–1907), Russian chemist + -IUM.] An artificially produced transuranic element, the longest-lived isotope of which has a half-life of two months. Atomic number 101; symbol Md (formerly Mv).

1955 A. GHIORSO et al. in *Physical Rev.* XCVIII. 1519/2 We would like to suggest the name mendelevium, symbol Mv, for the new element in recognition of the pioneering role of the great Russian chemist, Dmitri Mendeleev. **1967** *New Scientist* 21 Sept. 598/2 The new mendelevium isotope, with 101 protons and 157 neutrons, falls into the odd-odd class... The long half-life will enable quite large quantities of mendelevium to be made. **1971** C. KELLER *Chem. Transuranium Elements* II. ix. 596 Six isotopes of mendelevium are known with mass numbers 252 and 254–258... They can be produced by the bombardment either of uranium or plutonium with heavy ions, or of einsteinium with α particles. *Ibid.* 597 Since ^{258}Md can only be obtained by nuclear reactions with accelerated ions, it is impossible to produce weighable quantities. Consequently, the chemical investigation of mendelevium is restricted to tracer work.

Mendelian (mɛnˈdiːlɪən), *a.* and *sb. Biol.* [f. the name of Gregor Johann *Mendel* (1822–84) + -IAN.] **A.** *adj.* Of or pertaining to Mendel, or following his law or theory of heredity.

1901 BATESON, etc. *Rep. to Evol. Comm. Roy. Soc.* (1902) 15 Cases which follow Mendelian principles. **1902** BATESON *Mendel's Princ. Heredity* 114 The Mendelian principle of heredity asserts a proposition at variance with all the laws of ancestral heredity, however formulated. **1902** *Nature* 9 Oct. 573/1 The Mendelian theory.

B. *sb.* One who adheres to or supports Mendel's principles of heredity.

1903 K. PEARSON in *Phil. Trans. R. Soc.* A. CCIII. 57 If we were 'pure Mendelians' we should for the purpose of character classification make $v = w$. **1907** *Nature* 23 May 73/1 It would be regarded as a demonstration of the falsity of the doctrine of gametic purity by everyone who was not a Mendelian. **1925** A. HUXLEY *Let.* 25 Feb. (1969) 242 You Mendelians have made all that..philosophy look..dubious. **1941** J. S. HUXLEY *Uniqueness of Man* ii. 82 Twenty-five years ago..the field of heredity was still a battle-field. The Mendelians and the Biometricians were disputing for its possession. **1972** *Science* 12 May 623/3 The Mendelians, with their insistence upon large mutations as the agent of evolutionary change, undercut the Darwinian assumption of insensibly graded variation.

Mendelianism (mɛnˈdiːlɪənɪz(ə)m). *Biol.* [f. MENDELIAN *a.* + -ISM.] = MENDELISM.

1903 K. PEARSON in *Biometrika* II. 251 Mendelianism fails also for skin-colour in crosses between the black and white races of man. **1906** *Mem. & Proc. Manch. Lit. & Philos. Soc.* L. XI. 11 What is the essential feature of that which is called Mendelism by those who believe in it, and Mendelianism by those who do not? **1947** JACOBS & STERN *Outl. Anthropol.* 309 *Mendelianism*, the theory regarding the process of inheritance of characters, first published by Gregor Mendel in the 1860's and rediscovered about 1900. **1965** J. D. WATSON *Molecular Biol. of Gene* i. 27 All four wrote major works, each showing..how Mendelianism and Darwinism were indeed compatible.

Mendelism (ˈmɛndəlɪz(ə)m). *Biol.* (now chiefly hist.). [f. the name *Mendel* (see MENDELIAN *a.*) + -ISM.] The theory that discrete bodies (now called genes) control the inheritance of any particular character and that these are inherited in accordance with certain simple laws first propounded by Mendel; the body of knowledge (forming the basis of the modern science of genetics) founded on the experiments performed and laws propounded by Mendel.

1903 *Science* 20 Mar. 451/2 The breeder wants to preserve the desirable characters or traits and eliminate the undesirable ones, but under the strict interpretation of Mendelism this is difficult. **1905** R. C. PUNNETT (*title*) Mendelism. **1906** L. H. BAILEY *Plant Breeding* (ed. 4) 168 Already so many adjustments have been made of the Mendelian principles that it is becoming difficult to determine what Mendelism is. **1920** *Edin. Rev.* July 135 Mendelism promises to furnish the stock-breeder with better and more certain means of increasing the economic value of his stock. **1927** HALDANE & HUXLEY *Animal Biol.* ii. 62 The comparatively new science called Mendelism. **1942** [see BIOMETRY 2]. **1966** E. A. CARLSON *Gene* ii. 11 If Weldon had stopped here he might have won the battle and delayed the inevitable victory of Mendelism for more years than it took.

Mendelist (ˈmɛndəlɪst). *rare.* [f. as prec. + -IST.] = MENDELIAN *sb.*

1910 H. WALKER *Lit. Victorian Era* I. iii. 230 There are Mendelists and Mutationists as well as Darwinians. **1951** *Biol. Abstr.* XXV. 657/1 The author opposes what he describes as the 'theories of the Mendelists and the Morganists' that the origin of life on earth is an extraordinarily rare occurrence.

Mendelize (ˈmɛndəlaɪz), *v.* Also **mendelize.** [f. as prec.: see -IZE.] *intr.* To behave or be transmitted in accordance with Mendel's laws of inheritance.

1906 L. H. BAILEY *Plant Breeding* (ed. 4) 171 We do not know what plants will Mendelize until we try. **1913** M. HARTOG *Probl. Life & Reproduction* vii. 190 He found the characters thus acquired behaved as unit ('allelomorph') hereditary characters to the normal ones, and Mendelised just as do the unit characters which have arisen spontaneously, or have been transmitted for generations. **1924** E. W. MACBRIDE *Introd. Study Heredity* viii. 212 'Sports'..which breed true when crossed with their like, but which 'mendelize' when crossed with the type. **1973** *Sci. Amer.* Apr. 8/2 Mendel repeated Nägeli's work with seeds supplied by him and to his disappointment found that they did not Mendelize.

Hence '**Mendelizing** *ppl. a.*

1918 BABCOCK & CLAUSEN *Genetics Rel. Agric.* 286 Those changes in specific factors which result in the appearance of new Mendelizing characters. **1952** *Amer. Scientist* XL. 89 The differences between subspecies are hereditary and they are based upon mendelizing differences. **1969** *Nature* 14

June 1101/2 Their results..constitute the first thorough genetic analysis of a maternally determined Mendelizing character.

Mendelssohnian (mɛndəl'səʊnɪən), *a.* [f. the name of the German composer Felix *Mendelssohn*-Bartholdy (1809–47) + -IAN.] Of, pertaining to, or characteristic of Mendelssohn, or his musical productions.

1887 G. B. SHAW *How to become Mus. Critic* (1960) 132 The modern Mendelssohnian 'culture', with all its refinement, its elegance, its reticence, and its 'chastity'. **1900** *Musical Standard* LIX. 283/1 The second movement was rendered with a Mendelssohnian elegance. **1909** H. G. WELLS *Ann Veronica* iii. 60 The organ..was, in its Mendelssohnian way, as glad as ever it could be. **1928** *Observer* 29 Jan. 14/4 A clearly conceived and agreeable piece of music with Mendelssohnian orchestration. **1974** *Daily Tel.* 28 Oct. 11/1 Helen Donath's singing of the consolatory, very Mendelssohnian soprano solo gained in security after a nervous opening.

Also **Mendel'ssohnic** *a.*

1889 G. B. SHAW *London Music 1888–89* (1937) 164 Her Mendelssohnic sense of form in composition. **1890** *Ibid.* 300 This Mendelssohnic curse of speed for speed's sake. **1928** *Observer* 4 Mar. 14/5 Ask yourself what are the real Beethoven touches in the Mendelssohnic finale.

mender ('mɛndə(r)). [f. MEND *v.* + -ER¹.] One who mends; a repairer or improver.

a **1380** *Minor Poems fr. Vernon MS.* xxviii. 52 Heil mender of euen monnes mynde. **1552** [see PATCHER]. **1601** SHAKS. *Jul. C.* I. i. 15. **1774** GOLDSM. *Retaliation* 62 The Terence of England, the mender of hearts. **1836** E. HOWARD *R. Reefer* xxvi, The mender of pens groaned. **1875** JOWETT *Plato* (ed. 2) I. 295 A mender of old shoes, or a patcher up of clothes. **1894** ROSEBERY in *Times* 25 May 8/3, I have always been rather a mender than an ender.

† **mendiant**, *sb.* and *a.* *Obs. rare.* In 5 **mendiaunte**, 6 **-yante**. [a. F. *mendiant*, pr. pple. of *mendier* to beg (:—L. *mendīcāre*: see MENDICANT).] = MENDICANT.

1483 CAXTON *Gold. Leg.* 124b/1 They ben they that ye calle poure & mendiauntes. **1535** *Act 27 Hen. VIII*, c. 25 Fryers mendyantes, haue littell or nothinge to liue vpon.

'mendicable, *a.* *rare*⁻⁰. [ad. L. type **mendīcābilis*, f. *mendīcāre*: see MENDICANT and -ABLE.] 'That may be begged' (Bailey vol. II, 1727).

mendicancy ('mɛndɪkənsɪ). [f. next: see -ANCY.] The state or condition of being a mendicant or beggar; the habit or practice of begging.

1790 BURKE *Fr. Rev.* 197 Nothing..can exceed the shocking and disgusting spectacle of mendicancy displayed in that capital. **1893** STEVENSON *Catriona* xxv, I began to pull on my hose, recalling the man's impudent mendicancy at Prestongrange's.

mendicant ('mɛndɪkənt), *a.* and *sb.* [ad. L. *mendīcant-em*, f. *mendīcare* to beg, f. *mendīcus* beggar. Cf. MENDIANT, MENDINANT.]

A. *adj.* Begging; given to or characterized by begging. Also, characteristic of a beggar.

1613 R. CAWDREY *Table Alph.*, *Mendicant*, begging. **1631** B. JONSON *Underw.* lxxxix. (*heading*), To the Right Honourable, the Lord high Treasurer of England. An Epistle Mendicant. **1655** FULLER *Hist. Cambr.* (1840) 81 Begging Scholars..must be vicious, or else cannot be necessitous to a mendicant condition. **1753** RICHARDSON *Grandison* IV. viii. 71 And with that dejected air and mendicant voice. **1862** *Guardian* 1 Jan. 20/3 Keziah Kadge, the lady who..intended to follow the mendicant profession till she could secure an annuity of £50 a year. **1875** JOWETT *Plato* (ed. 2) III. 234 Mendicant prophets go to rich men's doors.

b. *spec.* Applied to those religious orders which lived entirely on alms.

The members of these orders were known as *Friars*. The most important (often referred to as the 'Four Orders') were the Franciscans, Dominicans, Carmelites, and Augustinian Hermits.

1547 BOORDE *Brev. Health* 4 They dyd I go amonges the fryers mendicantes. **1626** L. OWEN *Spec. Jesuit.* (1629) 27 This proud vpstart society was declared by Pope Pius Quintus to bee of the number of the Mendicant or Begging Friers. **1868** J. H. BLUNT *Ref. Ch. Eng.* I. 395 A mendicant friar of St. Mary Spital.

B. *sb.* A beggar; one who lives by begging.

1474 CAXTON *Chesse* III. vii. 124 Haue no despyte vnto the poure mendycants. **1597–8** BP. HALL *Sat.* v. i, And but for that, whatever he may vaunt, Who now's a monk, had been a mendicant. **1643** SIR T. BROWNE *Relig. Med.* II. §2 There is surely a Physiognomy, which those..Master Mendicants observe, whereby they instantly discover a merciful aspect. **1791** COWPER *Odyss.* XVII. 264 This morsel hunting mendicant. **1863** GEO. ELIOT *Romola* xxii, They..looked like vulgar, sturdy mendicants.

fig. **1742** YOUNG *Nt. Th.* VI. 288 What is Station high? 'Tis a proud Mendicant; it boasts, and begs.

b. A begging friar.

1530 PALSGR. 244/2 Mendycant an order of freres, *mendicant*. **1561** T. NORTON *Calvin's Inst.* IV. v. (1634) 535 Of the Mendicants some doe preach, all the other Monkes either sing or mumble up Masses in their dennes. **1606** WARNER *Alb. Eng.* XIV. lxxxix. 361 A youthfull Gentleman, enamoured on her [*sc.* a nun]..thus did his Sute preferre Faining himselfe a Mendicant (Nunnes might with Friers conferre). **1846** HOOK *Ch. Dict.* (ed. 5) 611 Mendicants or Begging Friars.

c. Applied to Brahmin, Buddhist, etc. priests who beg for food.

1613 PURCHAS *Pilgrimage* (1614) 454 Next..are certaine Mendicants, which liue of Rice and Barley, which any man at the first asking giueth them. **1841** ELPHINSTONE *Hist. Ind.* II. XI. ii. 479 He..put on the dress of a Hindú religious mendicant. **1848** H. H. WILSON *Brit. India* III. III. viii. 447 A sect of religious mendicants or Jogis.

mendicanting, *a.* [f. prec. + -ING².] Begging.

1630 J. TAYLOR (Water P.) *World runs on Wheeles* Wks. II. 239/1 The foolish women..gaue all their mony to the mendicanting Canters.

mendicate ('mɛndɪkeɪt), *v.* *rare.* [f. L. *mendīcāt-*, ppl. stem of *mendīcāre*: see MENDICANT.]

1. *trans.* To beg for, ask for like a beggar.

1618 *Barnevelt's Apol.* Dj, I..maruaile, why you should so carefully search, and as it were mendicate these things. **1826** SCOTT *Jrnl.* I. 288, I have seen..papers distributed in the boxes to mendicate a round of applause. **1865** *Pall Mall G.* 23 Sept. 1/1 A loan must be had on any terms, and is now being almost *mendicated*.

2. *intr.* To beg. *rare*⁻⁰.

1623 COCKERAM, *Mendicate*, to beg. **1721**, etc. in BAILEY. **1755** in JOHNSON. Hence in mod. Dicts.

b. quasi-*trans.* with *out of*.

1768 W. LIVINGSTON *Let. Bp. Llandaff* 19 People..may be mendicated or sermonized out of their money.

Hence **'mendicated** *ppl. a.*

1641 J. SHUTE *Sarah & Hagar* (1649) 142 To be beholden to this borrowed, yea mendicated and begged dignity. **1819** *Blackw. Mag.* V. 571 The..squalid establishments for mendicated instruction had become loathsome in his eyes.

mendication (mɛndɪ'keɪʃən). [ad. late L. *mendīcātiōn-em*, f. *mendīcāre* to beg.] Begging.

1646 SIR T. BROWNE *Pseud. Ep.* VII. xvii. 375 Cedrenus and Zonaras..omit the history of his [*sc.* Belisarius'] mendication. **1849** I. TAYLOR *Loyola & Jes.* 69 The perpetual labour of providing, by mendication, not merely for his own wants, but for those of his companions.

† **mendicatory**, *a.* *Obs. rare*⁻¹. [f. L. *mendīcāt-* (see MENDICATE) + -ORY.] Begging.

1627–77 FELTHAM *Resolves* II. liv. 271 Mendicatory or fishing Gifts..the generous have ever disdained.

† **mendiciary**, *a.* *Obs. rare*⁻¹. [f. L. *mendīcus* begging + -(I)ARY.] Appropriate to beggars.

1652 URQUHART *Jewel* Wks. (1834) 279 Like so many varlets, in mendiciary and gausapinal garments.

mendicity (mɛn'dɪsɪtɪ). [a. F. *mendicité* (from 13th c.), ad. L. *mendīcitās*, f. *mendīcus*: see MENDICANT and -ITY. Cf. Sp. *mendicidad*, Pg. *mendicidade*, It. *mendicità*.]

1. The state or condition of a mendicant or beggar, beggary. Also, now usually, the existence or numbers of the mendicant class.

c **1400** *Rom. Rose* 6525 For richesse and mendicitees Ben clepid, II. extremytees. *Ibid.* 6534 God thou me kepe for thi pouste Fro Richesse and mendicite. **1490** CAXTON *Eneydos* xviii. 68 Pigmalion, my cruelle brother,..shalle comme take my cyte, and put alle to destructyon, and brynge me to mendycyte. **1611** COTGR., *Mendicité*, mendicitie, beggarie, beggarlinesse. **1812** G. CHALMERS *Dom. Econ. Gt. Brit.* 401 He [Arthur Dobbs] complained, that there were 34,425 strolling beggars, in that kingdom. He explained this striking instance of mendicity [etc.]. **1815** (*title*) Report from Committee on the State of Mendicity in the Metropolis. [Parl. Paper.] **1864** H. AINSWORTH *John Law* VI. i. (1881) 293 During the reign of Louis XIV, mendicity had existed to a frightful extent.

2. The practice or habit of begging.

1801 *13th Rep. Soc. for Poor* 22 *note*, Some workhouses are rather seminaries of mendicity, than preservatives against it. **1884** *American* VIII. 105 With a view to the regular exercise of mendicity, pillage and murder.

3. *attrib.*

1819 *1st Rep. Soc. Suppress. Mendicity* 27 The Mendicity Societies at Bath, Edinburgh, Oxford, and Dublin. **1824** T. HOOK *Say. & Do.* Ser. I. III. 329 Mr. Harding was a subscriber to the Mendicity Society, an institution which proposes to check beggary by the novel method of giving nothing to the poor. **1884** *Century Mag.* XXIX. 163 To set up a library, a 'mendicity institution', or a bank.

† **mendience**. *Obs. rare.* [a. OF. *mendience*, *-ance*, f. *mendiant*: see MENDIANT and -ANCE.] Mendicity.

c **1400** *Rom. Rose* 6657 (*Glasgow MS.*) He wolde not therfore that he lyue To seruen hym in mendience. *Ibid.* 6707 And for ther hath ben gret discorde..Vpon the estate of mendiciens [*sic*; Thynne 1532 mendicience].

mendifaunte, variant of MENDIVAUNT *Obs.*

mendil, obs. form of MANDIL.

† **'mendinant**, *sb.* and *a.* *Obs.* Also **mendyna(u)nt**, **-ynante**, **-enaunt**, **-inaunt**, **meyndenaunt**. [a. OF. *mendinant*, pr. pple. of *mendiner*, *mendienner* to beg, f. *mendien* (fem. *-enne*), an altered form, due to confusion of suffix, of *mendiant* (see MENDIANT). Cf. MENDIVAUNT: in 14th c. texts the two words cannot with certainty be distinguished.] = MENDICANT.

1362 LANGL. *P. Pl.* A. XI. 198 For mendynauntz at mischief þe men were dewid. *c* **1386** CHAUCER *Sompn. T.* 198 We mendynantz, we sely freres, Been wedded to pouerte and continence. *c* **1400** MAUNDEV. (1839) xv. 167 There ben manye religious men, and namely of Mendynantes.

'mending, *vbl. sb.* [f. MEND *v.* + -ING¹.]

1. The action of the vb. MEND in various senses. **a.** Amendment, correction, improvement.

a **1300** *Cursor M.* 26867 [þou agh to] here his scrift and giue him rede þat to sum mendyng him mai lede. **13..** *E.E. Allit. P.* A. 452 Bot vchon..wolde her coroun ez wern worþe þe fyue, If possyble wer her mendyng. **1599** SHAKS. *Much Ado* II. iii. 239 Happy are they that heare their detractions, and can put them to mending. **1631** *Star Chamb. Cases* (Camden) 55 If a man soe enter his children's names into the Church booke it is noe offence, and it is not like the mending of a sealed Indenture or a Record. **1896** A. E. HOUSMAN *Shropshire Lad* xliv, Yours was not an ill for mending, 'Twas best to take it to the grave.

b. †The action of healing (*obs.*); the action or process of advancing towards recovery. Also *attrib.*, esp. in phrase † ***on*** (***upon, in, of***) ***the mending hand*** (see HAND *sb.* 4 b). So also † ***at a mending hand*** (obs.), ***in a mending way***.

c **1375** *Sc. Leg. Saints* xli. (*Agnes*) 10 Al sekmen of his tweching of verray heile gettis mending. **1534** MORE *Comf. agst. Trib.* II. ii. (1847) 90, I look every day to depart, my mending days coming very seld. **1658** A. FOX tr. *Wurtz' Surg.* III. xxiii. 291 Go on..till you see and perceave that the member is at a mending hand. **1710–11** SWIFT *Jrnl. to Stella* 10 Mar., He has no fever, and the hopes of his mending increase. **1753** N. TORRIANO *Gangr. Sore Throat* 23 She was repurged with Success, whence they judged her in a mending Way.

c. The action or process of repairing (something decayed, worn, etc.); an instance of this. Also *techn.* (see quot. 1891) and *attrib.*

1395 *E.E. Wills* (1882) 11 Y bequeth to þe Mendyng of þe heye way..xl.s. **1429–30** *Rec. St. Mary at Hill* (1904) 72 Also for mendynge of þe sepulcre xvj d. **1596** SHAKS. *Merch. V.* v. i. 263 Why this is like the mending of high waies In Sommer. **1869** PHILLIPS *Vesuv.* ii. 33 The pavement except by occasional mendings may be readily believed to have been laid by Pelasgian hands. **1891** *Labour Commission* Gloss., *Mending*, replacing (in woven worsted-coating pieces) threads of warp or of weft dropped by the weaver. *attrib.* **1856** C. M. YONGE *Daisy Chain* I. vii. 63 Ethel had to fetch her mending-basket. **1863** 'G. HAMILTON' *Gala-Days* 41, I find myself in a mending-basket. **1867** A. D. WHITNEY *Summer in L. Goldthwaite's Life* viii. 165 What should we do without our mending-day? **1882** CAULFEILD & SAWARD *Dict. Needlework* s.v., Mending Cottons..may be had both white and unbleached. **1885** *Army & Navy Co-op. Soc.* Price List 1385 Silks... Spun Mending, Black and Colours. **1899** A. NICHOLAS *Idyl of Wabash* 18 Taking his hose from the mending basket and darning them. **1966** *Olney Amsden & Sons Ltd. Price List* 28 Mending cotton, white only. **1974** J. STUBBS *Painted Face* vii. 107 Bessie..opened her mending basket.

2. *concr.* **a.** *pl.* Articles to be repaired. *rare.* (Also in *sing.*)

1863 W. B. JERROLD *Signals Distress* 98 Workmen were busy over 'boys'' strong boots and mendings. **1891** *Harper's Mag.* Sept. 579/1 Mrs. Dorset was on the bench in the porch, the basket of mending by her.

b. *pl.* Short for *mending yarns*.

1882 CAULFEILD & SAWARD *Dict. Needlework*, *Mendings*, these yarns are composed of a mixture of cotton and wool, and designed for the darning of Merino stockings.

c. A repaired place; a 'mend'. *rare.*

1886 *Housewife* I. 109/2 [Darning.] Grafting can only be done when the new piece matches the old..and the mending is to be of large size.

† **3.** = MENDMENT 2. *dial.*

1707 MORTIMER *Husb.* 13 Which [*sc.* overflowing of rivers] brings the Soil of the Up-lands upon them, so that they need no other mending. **1855** MORTON *Cycl. Agric.* II. 724 *Mending*, (Lanc.), manuring.

4. ***mending up***: see quot. 1892. Also *attrib.*

1885 [HORNER] *Pattern Making* 225 Mending up with sweeps becomes necessary... We then have an unbroken lower edge by which to guide the mending up sweep. **1892** — *Princ. Pattern Making* 156 *Mending up*, the necessary repairs done to a mould after it has become damaged by the rapping and the withdrawal of the pattern. *Mending up piece*, any strip, sweep, or block, which is used as a guide to obtain or to restore the damaged contour of a section of a sand mould.

mendipite ('mɛndɪpaɪt). *Min.* [ad. G. *mendipit* (Glocker, 1839), f. the name of the *Mendip* Hills (Somerset) where it was found: see -ITE.] Oxychloride of lead, found in white masses.

1851 WATTS tr. *Gmelin's Handbk. Chem.* V. 147 Mendip Lead-ore or Mendipite... This mineral is likewise found, and in a state of greater purity, at Brilow near Stadtbergen.

† **mendivaunt**. *Obs.* Also **mendyfaunte**, **-vaunt**. [f. OF. (chiefly AF.) *mendif*, altered form of *mendi*:—L. *mendīcus* (see MENDICANT).

As *mendyuaunt* and *mendynaunt* would usually be indistinguishable in the MSS., it is possible that some or all of the examples under MENDINANT may belong to this word. In those given below the MSS. have *f* or *v*, not *u*.]

= MENDICANT *sb.*

c **1400** MAUNDEV. (1839) xix. 210 There duellen many religious men, as it were of the ordre of Freres: for thei ben Mendyfauntes. **1426** LYDG. *De Guil. Pilgr.* 541 Other ordrys vertuous. Mendyvauntys ful nedy. *c* **1430** *Pilgr. Lyf Manhode* I. lix. (1869) 35, j make him yiue and departe that he hath to the needy and to mendivauns.

mendment ('mɛndmənt). [Aphetic f. AMENDMENT. Cf. OF. *mendement* (once in Godef., written *mandement*).]

1. = AMENDMENT; improvement, reparation, correction, reformation.

a **1300** *Cursor M.* 23744 Þis lijf he [crist] has vs lent.. To hald ai wel his comament, If we do mis, do mendement. ? *a* **1400** *Morte Arth.* 989, I am comyne fra the conquerour.. for mendemente of the pople. **1559** *Mirr. Mag., Edw. Dk. Somerset* xxv. (1563) 167 He.. would have all thing mended, But by that mendment nothyng els he ment, But to be kyng. **1612** DEKKER *If it be not good* Wks. 1873 III. 298 *Bar.* Well, well, the world will mend. *Bra.* The pox of mendment I see.

2. Improvement of the soil; *concr.* manure; = AMENDMENT 6. Now *dial.*

1644 G. PLATTES in *Hartlib's Legacy* (1655) 289 If the mendment of their own lands were the cheapest purchase to the owner [etc.]. **1798** J. MIDDLETON *View Agric. Mdlsx.* 305 Manure is undoubtedly the great cause of fertility. (The Middlesex farmer says 'there is nothing to be done without "mendment"'.) ?**1842** LANCE *Cottage Farmer* 13 Potash and saltpetre would invigorate corn crops more than any other artificial mendment. **1883** *Hampshire Gloss.*

†**'mendnis.** *Obs.* [f. MEND *v.* + *-nis*, -NESS.] Amendment.

c **1400** *Rule St. Benet* 4 A stresce will I make in mendnis of ȝoure sinne.

mendole ('mɛndəʊl). [a. It. (Venetian) *mendole.* Cf. F. *mendol(e.*] = CACKEREL I.

1854 BADHAM *Halieut.* 276 The bream is as worthless a fish as the mendole. **1862** COUCH *Brit. Fishes* I. 206 In its native waters the Mendole is an exceedingly prolific fish.

mendong, var. MENDANG.

mendopo, var. PENDOPO.

†**mendose,** *a. Anat. Obs. rare*⁻¹. [ad. L. *mendōsus* faulty (f. *mendum* fault), in med.L. anatomy used to render Gr. νόθος spurious, as applied to the 'false' ribs, 'false' sutures, etc.]

c **1400** *Lanfranc's Cirurg.* 110 [Þo boonys Þat vndir setten ben clepid ossa mendosa]. *Ibid.*, ij. boonys Þat ben clepid mendose. *Ibid.* 111 WiÞ .ij. semes mendose. [**1855** OGILVIE *Suppl., Mendose*, false, spurious.]

†**men'doza.** *Obs.* [? The (Spanish) surname of the inventor.] In full ***mendoza wheel***, one of the wheels of a spinning-mule.

1803 *Specif. Wood's Patent* No. 2711. 2 The wheel G acts in the mendoza, called the drawing-out wheel. **1818** *Specif. of Eaton's Patent* No. 4272. 4 When the carriage [of the spinning mule] is quite out the mendoza wheel O is disengaged from the pinion. **1836** URE *Cotton Manuf.* II. 158 The large horizontal bevel-wheel 12, called the mendoza.

mendozite (mɛn'dəʊzaɪt). *Min.* [Named by Dana from *Mendoza*, Argentine Republic, where it is found: see -ITE².] A hydrous sulphate of alumina, occurring in white fibrous masses; = ALUNOGEN.

1868 DANA *Syst. Min.* (ed. 5) II. 653.

mendung, var. MENDANG.

mendy, variant of MENDEE.

†**mene.** *Obs.* [repr. OE. *ȝemǽne*, subst. use of *ȝemǽne* adj.: see I-MENE *a.*] Intercourse, fellowship.

c **1200** ORMIN 1948 Þatt nan ne shollde filedd ben Þurrh hæÞenn macchess mæne. *c* **1250** *Gen. & Ex.* 501 For alied god self him toch fro mannes mene in to ðat stede ðat adam forles for iuel dede.

mene: see MAN, MEAN, MEINIE.

menealtie, obs. form of MESNALTY.

meneer, var. MYNHEER.

meneghinite (mɛnɪ'gi:naɪt). *Min.* [f. name of Prof. J. *Meneghini*, of Pisa + -ITE.] A sulph-antimonide of lead, occurring in prismatic crystals and in fibrous masses.

1852 *Amer. Jrnl. Sci.* Ser. II. XIV. 60 The Meneghinite is a new species, established by M. Bechi. It occurs in compact fibrous forms, very lustrous [etc.].

meneisoun, menekin, menel(e)d, meneliche: see MENISON, MINIKIN, MENALD, MEANLY.

meneress, menese, menesinge, meneson, menester, menestral, meneuer: see MINORESS, MENISE, MINISHING, MENISON, MINISTER, MINSTREL, MINIVER.

meneuerance, obs. form of MANURANCE.

1473-5 in *Cal. Proc. Chanc. Q. Eliz.* II. (1830) Pref. 57 To have the meneuerance and occupacion.. of the said mese lond mede and wode.

Menevian (mə'ni:vɪən), *a.* and *sb. Geol.* Also **Min-, Mæn-.** [f. *Menevia*, med.L. name of St. David's + -AN.] **a.** *adj.* Of or pertaining to a very ancient group of rocks found near St. David's in South Wales, and also near Dolgelly and Maentwrog in North Wales, containing a large number of different species of fossils. **b.** *sb.* The Menevian formation.

1865 SALTER & HICKS in *Rep. Brit. Assoc.* (Hardwicke) 147 The authors propose the term 'Minevian' for the lowest division of the 'Lingula flag'. **1865** HICKS in *Q. Jrnl. Geol. Soc.* XXI. 477 *note*, The new term 'Mænevian Group'. **1867** SALTER & HICKS *Ibid.* XXIII. 339 The Menevian group. **1882** A. GEIKIE *Text-bk. Geol.* 654 The Menevian beds. **1894** *Geol. Mag.* Oct. 442 At this time the upper portion only of the Menevian (then called Lower Lingula Flags) had yielded any fossils.

menew, menew(e)s: see MINNOW, MENISE.

'men-folk(s. [See MAN *sb.*¹]

1. The male sex; also *dial.* (see quot. 1886).

1802 R. ANDERSON *Cumbld. Ball.* 38 I've wonder'd sin I kent mysel, What keeps the men-fwok aw frae me. **1824** SCOTT. *St. Ronan's* xxxviii, 'Mr. Tyrrel', she said, 'this is nae sight for men folk—ye maun rise and gang to another room'. **1886** ELWORTHY *W. Somerset Word-bk., Men folks*, usually the male labourers on a farm. Males in general, as distinct from 'women folks'. **1896** BLACK *Briseis* xx, Some of us Gordons about Dee-side—I mean the men-folk of us—are said to be rather quick in the temper.

2. Human beings. *rare.*

1870 MORRIS *Earthly Par., Golden Apples* (1890) 328/2 Slipping through the seas Ye never think, ye men-folk, how ye seem From down below through the green waters' gleam.

meng, *v. Obs.* exc. *dial.* Forms: *Inf.* 1 men(c)gan, mængan, 3 mengen, mengge, (*3rd pres. sing.* meinÞ), 3-7, 9 menge, 5 (mengyn), meenge, meynge, 3- meng; 3-5 myng, 3- ming, (5 mynge, 6, 9 minge). *Pa. t. Ind.* α. 1-4 mengde, 3 mengte, meng(u)d, 3-5 menged, 4 menhed, mengede, *Sc.* mengȝeit, 4-5 mengid, -it, 5 mengyd, 6 menkit; 4 mynged(e, -ide, 5 mynget, -it. β. 4 meynt, 6 ment. *Pa. pple.* α. 2-5 imengd, 3 imænged, imenget, imeingt, mengt, 3-8 menged, 4 ymengd, imengde, mengyt, -ede, 4-5 ymenged, mengid, meyng(i)d, 4-6 mengyd, 5 ymengyd, -id, mengit, menkyd, 6 menket, menkte; 5 mynged, -et, -it, -yd, mingit, 6 minged, mingde. β. 2-4 meind, 3 imeind(e, meynde, ime(y)nd, 3-4 ymeynd, 3-5 meynd, 4 mynd, yment, 4-5 ymeynt, 5-6 meynt, 6-7 ment, meint, 7 ymeint, imeint. γ. 3 imeng(e, ymeng. [OE. *męngan* = OFris. *mengia*, *menzia*, OS. *mengian* (Du. *mengen*), OHG. (MHG., mod.G.) *mengen*, ON. *menga* (Sw. *mänga*, Da. *mænge*):—OTeut. **mangjan*, f. the root of OE. *ȝe-mang*: see AMONG.

The normal form in mod. standard English would be *minge* (mɪndʒ): cf. *singe*. Forms with *i* occur both in literature (down to the 17th c.) and in mod. dialects: but the form *meng* has been adopted here as that occurring in the best-known instances.]

1. *trans.* To mix, mingle, blend: **a.** one thing *with* (†Sc. *into*) another.

c **725** *Voc.* in Wr.-Wülcker 15/15 *Confundit*, menget. *c* **1000** *Ags. Gosp.* Luke xiii. 1 Þare blod pilatus mengde [*Lindisf.* ȝemengde] mid hyra offrungum. *a* **1200** *Moral Ode* 142 in *Cott. Hom.* 169 Betere is wori water drunch Þen atter meind [*later versions* meynd, imengd, imenge] mid wine. *c* **1375** *Sc. Leg. Saints* xxvii. (*Machor*) 584 Poysone.. myngyt into drink. *Ibid.* xxxiii. (*George*) 505 Þane with wyne mengȝeit he poyson. **1390** GOWER *Conf.* II. 262 Warm melk sche putte also therto With hony meynd. *c* **1460** *Towneley Myst.* xxvi. 270 In stede of drynk thay gaf me gall, Asell thay menged it withall. **1562** TURNER *Baths* 1, I founde.. marquesites and stones menged with copper. **1579** SPENSER *Sheph. Cal.* July 84 Till with his elder brother Themis His brackish waves be meynt. **1633** P. FLETCHER *Purple Isl.* III. xx, The third bad water.. with good liquors ment. **1677** NICOLSON *Cumb. & Westm. Gloss.* in *Trans. R. Soc. Lit.* (1870) IX. 315 *Meng*, to mix.

b. two or more things (*together*).

a **1225** *Leg. Kath.* 1674 Deorewurðe stanes, of misliche heowes, imenget togederes. *c* **1410** *Master of Game* (MS. Digby 182) xii, And put alle Þise Þinges togidres and menge hem vpoun Þe fyre and stere hem wele. **1567** TURBERV. *Ovid's Epist.* L iij b, Incense I yeeld with intermedled teares, Which mingde doe surge as wine ycast in flame. **1596** SPENSER *F.Q.* V. v. 12 Bath'd in bloud and sweat together ment. **1622** DRAYTON *Poly-olb.* xxvi. 35 Till both within one bank, they on my North are meint.

c. With immaterial objects and *fig.*

a **1225** *Ancr. R.* 332 Auh hope & dred schulen euer beon imeind togederes. *a* **1250** *Owl & Night.* 870 Al my song is of longinge And ymeynd [*MS. Cott.* imend] sumdel myd woninge. **1375** BARBOUR *Bruce* VI. 360 This nobill kyng.. Mengit all tyme vith vit manheid. **1426** LYDG. *De Guil. Pilgr.* 19596 The pley ther-off ys meynt with wo. **1555** W. WATREMAN *Fardle Facions* I. ii. 30 Heate meint with moisture is apt to engendre. **1589** WARNER *Alb. Eng.* V. xxv. 111 Then taking Scottish othes, which they did breake, and he [Edw. I] reuenge, With those Exploytes he French attempts as gloriously did menge. **1608** SYLVESTER *Du Bartas* II. iv. IV. *Decay* 253 Their Country-gods with the true God they ming. **1642** H. MORE *Song of Soul* II. ii. I. viii, When that those rayes.. be closely meint With other beams of plain diversity.

2. To make a mixture of; to produce by mixing.

1375 *Sc. Leg. Saints* ii. (*Paulus*) 700 A fellone poyssone, myngit and mad be tresone. *a* **1547** SURREY *Descr. Spring* 11 in *Tottel's Misc.* (Arb.) 4 The busy bee her honye now she minges. *c* **1570** *Pride & Lowl.* (1841) 59 Their good drinke as I sayd is ming and blenne. **1730** (Som.) *Churchw. Acc.* (E.D.D.), To minging lime, and to tile pins. **1807** STAGG *Poems* 140 An' meng us up thar glasses. **1825** JAMIESON s.v., 'To meng tar', to mix it up into a proper state for smearing sheep, greasing carts, &c.

3. To stir up; after OE. only in fig. applications: To disturb, trouble, confound. Also *intr.* for *pass.*

Beowulf **1449** Se Þe meregrundas mengan scolde. *a* **1225** *Leg. Kath.* 606 Nes Þis meiden nawiht herfore imenget in hire mod inwið. *a* **1250** *Owl & Night.* 945 (MS. Cott.) For wraÞÞe meinÞ [*MS. Jesus* meynÞ] Þe horte blod. *a* **1300** *Cursor M.* 27770 And sua he mengges him wit ire, Þat brennes mans mede als fire. *c* **1460** *Towneley Myst.* xxiii. 437 Now thay meng my moode ffor grace thou can me hete. **1560** ROLLAND *Crt. Venus* iv. 370 Allace, now mingis my mane and mude.

b. *to meng with mirths*: to cheer.

a **1400** *Sir Perc.* 1327 The maydene mengede his mode With myrthes at the mete. *c* **1460** *Towneley Myst.* xvi. 1 Moste myghty mahowne meng you with myrth!

4. a. *trans.* To bring (living creatures) together; to join (the male *with* the female).

13.. *E.E. Allit. P.* B. 337, & ay Þou meng with Þe malez Þe mete ho-bestez. *c* **1400** *Destr. Troy* 6546 There mynget Þai Þere men, machit hom to-gedur; Mony dedly dint delt hom amonge!

b. *refl., pass.*, and *intr.* Of persons: To be mingled *together* in intercourse, or *with*, *among* others; to be joined in battle; to have sexual intercourse; to be united by marriage.

refl. *a* **900** tr. *Bæda's Hist.* I. xxvii. §11 Swelce is eac bewered Þæt mon hine menge wið his brodorwiife. *c* **1000** *Ags. Ps.* (Th.) cv. 26 Hi.. hi wið manfullum megndan [*sic*] Þeode. *a* **1300** *Cursor M.* 26253 O man Þat menges him wit best For his flexs lust to ful-fill.

pass. *c* **1205** LAY. 15249 Þa weoren Bruttes imænged wið Þan Saxes. **1382** WYCLIF *1 Cor.* v. 9 That ȝe be not meynd [*v.r.* meyngd], or comunen not, with lecchours. *c* **1400** *Apol. Loll.* 109 Lok Þat ȝe be not menkyd wiÞ him. *c* **1420** LYDG. *Assembly of Gods* 361 And ones in the moneth with Phebus was she meynt. **1590** SPENSER *F.Q.* III. xi. 36 When she with Mars was meynt in joyfulnesse.

intr. *c* **1250** *Gen. & Ex.* 544 He chosen hem wiwes of caym, And mengten wið waried kin. *a* **1300** *Cursor M.* 19271 Fra Þan durst na man wit Þam meng. *c* **1330** R. BRUNNE *Chron.* (1810) 298 With Þe Scottis gan he menge, and stifly stode in stoure. **1435** MISYN *Fire of Love* II. iii. 73, I lufyd not with Þame to menge.

5. *intr.* Of things: To be or become mixed.

a **1000** *Cædmon's Satan* 132 Hwæt her hat and ceald hwilum mencgaÞ. *a* **1300** *Cursor M.* 9952 Þe leme o light .. Þat menges with Þaa colurs hew. *c* **1400** *Destr. Troy* 12495 Sodonly the softe winde vnsoberly blew; A myste & a merkenes myngit to-gedur. **1614** SIR A. GORGES tr. *Lucan* VI. 233 And from his springs A vertue takes, which neuer mings With other streame. **1825** JAMIESON, *To meng*, to become mixed. 'The corn's beginnin to meng', the standing corn begins to.. assume a yellow tinge; Berwicks.

meng(e, variants of MING *v. Obs.*, to remember.

†**menged,** *ppl. a. Obs.* Forms: see MENG *v.* [f. MENG *v.* + -ED¹.] Mixed; disturbed, confused.

a **1250** *Owl & Night.* 823 Þenne is Þes hundes smel fordo: He not Þurh Þe meynde smak HweÞer he schal vorÞ Þe abak. *a* **1300** *Cursor M.* 7420 He es ai vte o wite als wode, Hu sal we meke his menged mode? **1428** in *Surtees Misc.* (1888) 1, xxxiij gyrdels of menged metaill. **1494** FABYAN *Chron.* VII. 665 A woman.. was.. punysshed for sellyng of false myngyd butter.

mengel, -ill, obs. forms of MINGLE *v.*

†**menging,** *vbl. sb. Obs.* [OE. *męnging*, f. *męngan*: see MENG *v.* and -ING¹.] Mingling, mixture; confusion or disturbance (of mind).

a **1000** *Aldhelm Glosses* in *Zeitschr. f. deutsches Alterthum* IX. 450 *Confectio*,.. mencingc. **1297** R. GLOUC. (Rolls) 2098 Conan.. Among hom nolde of Þulke lond abbe non menging. *a* **1300** *Cursor M.* 27739 Menging o mode Þat coms o gall. *c* **1380** WYCLIF *Wks.* (1880) 475 Þe myngING of Þes Þingis is unholsom to man to take. *a* **1485** *Promp. Parv.* 332/2 (MS. S.) Mengynge, *mixtura*, *commixtio*. **1562** TURNER *Baths* 9 With some menginge with mixture of brimstone. **1818** HOGG *Brownie of Bodsbeck* I. 288 The meinging of repentance.

‖**mengkuang** (mɛŋ'kwæŋ). [Malay.] A tree belonging to one of the larger species of *Pandanus*, providing leaves that can be woven into matting, etc. Also *attrib.*

1900 H. N. RIDLEY in *Jrnl. Straits Branch Roy. Asiatic Soc.* XXXIII. 170 *Pandanus atrocarpus* Griff. 'Meng-kuang'. The biggest species here, often 40 feet high with very long leaves. **1908** L. WRAY in A. Wright *20th Cent. Impressions Brit. Malaya* 235/3 Of late years a fairly large industry has sprung up in Negri Sambilan in the manufacture of mat hats... The finer are of *Pandan* leaves, and the coarser of *Mengkuang* leaves. **1935** I. H. BURKILL *Dict. Econ. Products Malay Peninsula* II. 1644 Such species [of *Pandanus*] as are used for matting are called by the Malays 'mĕngkuang'. **1947** R. O. WINSTEDT *Malays* 175 Dish covers are sometimes made of this mad plait, or they are made of strips of the white inner sheath of bamboo.. stuck over a conical *meng-kuang* lining shaped like Chinese hats. **1954** R. E. HOLTTUM *Plant Life Malaya* ii. 23 The big swamp Pandan called Mengkuang, with trunks sixty feet or more high and leaves twenty feet long, rivals most palms in bulk. **1965** C. SHUTTLEWORTH *Malayan Safari* ii. 29 A patch of earth near the cooking fires was swept clean and laid with broad *mengkuang* leaves. **1972** M. SHEPPARD *Taman Indera* 158 Coarser matting for everyday household use and sacking are made of *mengkuang*. Pandan is frequently dyed and woven into elaborate patterns. *Mengkuang* is more often used in its natural form.

mengkulang ('mɛŋku:laŋ). [Malay.] A timber tree belonging to the Malaysian genus *Tarrietia*, esp. *T. simplicifolia*, or its wood.

1940 E. J. H. CORNER *Wayside Trees Malaya* I. 622 The species of Tarrietia are mostly timber-trees known to Malays as Mengkulang. **1956** *Handbk. Hardwoods* (Forest Prod. Res. Lab.) 150 Locally, mengkulang is used for interior construction, flooring and furniture. **1972** *Timber Trades Jrnl.* 13 May 39/2 Mengkulang is not easy [to obtain], presumably because of the competition from the plywood mills.

mengle, obs. form of MINGLE *sb.* and *v.*

mengue, mengyd, obs. ff. MANGO, MANCHET.

menhaden (mɛnˈheɪdən). Also **manhad(d)en**. [Corrupted or cognate form of Narragansett Indian *munnawhatteaûg*, 'a fish somewhat like a herring' (R. Williams *Key Lang. America*, 1643).

The fish was used by the Indians for manure, and the name seems to be connected with the vb. *munnohquohteau*, (Eliot's Indian Bible) 'he enriches the land, fertilizes'.]

A fish of the herring family, *Brevoortia tyrannus*, common on the east coasts of the United States; it is much used for manure and produces a valuable oil.

1792 *Descr. Kentucky* 42 In 1787 were exported Barrels of manhadden 236. **1792** HOMMEDIEU in *Proc. Amer. Assoc.* (1880) XXVIII. 436 *note*, The fish called menhaden or mosbankers. **1880** GOODE (*title*) in *Rep. 28th Meeting Amer. Assoc. Adv. Sci.* 425 A Short Biography of the Menhaden.

b. *attrib.* as ***menhaden fishery***, ***oil***.

1883 C. A. MOLONEY *W. Afr. Fisheries* 64 (Fish. Exhib. Publ.) The American menhaden fisheries. **1883** *Fisheries Exhib. Catal.* 202 Menhaden oil, used in currying leather.

Hence **men'hadener**, a steamer engaged in fishing for menhaden.

1905 E. MARSHALL *Middle Wall* 447.

menheir, obs. variant of MYNHEER.

menhir (ˈmɛnhɪə(r)). *Archæol.* Also *erron.* **menzhir**. [a. Breton *men hir* 'long stone' (*men*, *mean* stone, *hir* long: = Welsh *maen hir*, Cornish *medn hir*).] A tall upright monumental stone, of varying antiquity, found in various parts of Europe, and also in Africa and Asia.

1840 T. A. TROLLOPE *Summer in Brittany* II. 300 The menhir of Plouarzel. **1851** [see PEULVAN]. **1870** LUBBOCK *Orig. Civiliz.* vi. (1875) 302 Circular marks closely resembling those on some of our European menhirs. **1904** WINDLE *Rem. Preh. Age* viii. 192 The Dartmoor row begins with a circle and ends with a menhir.

meni, obs. form of MANY.

menial (ˈmiːnɪəl), *a.* and *sb.* Forms: α. 4 **meynal(l, -el, 5 meygnall, menal(l.** β. 4–5 **meyneal, meynyal, 5 menyal, mayneal, meyneyall, 6 maneall, meneal, meigniall, 7 mæniall, meniall, 7– menial.** [a. AF. *meignal*, *menial*, f. *meiniee* MEINIE.] **A.** *adj.*

†**1.** Pertaining to the household, domestic. Also *transf. Obs.*

1387 TREVISA *Higden* (Rolls) II. 215 A mannes owne meynal wittes [L. *domestici sensus ejus*] beeþ his owne enemyes. **1388** WYCLIF *Rom.* xvi. 5 Grete ȝe wel her meyneal [*v.r.* meynyal, Vulg. *domesticam*] chirche. *c* **1400** *Plowman's T.* 322 The tything of *Turpe lucrum* With these maisters is meynall. **1709** MRS. MANLEY *Secret Mem.* (1720) III. 17 He had exchang'd his own Property, his very menial Necessaries for Bread to support them.

2. Of a servant: Forming one of the household; domestic. Now only in contemptuous use: see B.

1427 *Will of Sir E. Braybroke* in *Bedford. N. & Q.* (1889) II. 224, I wol that after my deces my meyne meygnall be kepte to-geder in houshold. **1444** *Close Roll, 23 Hen. VI*, The said Geffrey was a menall man of the worshipful household of our Sovereign Lord the King. **1450** *Rolls of Parlt.* V. 179/2 The wages and fees of youre menyall servauntez. *c* **1475** *Partenay* 900 To gret and smal menal persones. **1516** *Will R. Peke of Wakefield* 4 June, Every one of my maneall servantes. **1642** CHAS. I in Clarendon *Hist. Reb.* v. §396 And all this, whilst his Majesty had no other attendance than his own Menial Servants. **1675** *Essex Papers* (Camden) I. 294 That none shall heare Masse either at the Queen's or any Ambass^rs Chappell but their owne meniall Servants. **1765** BLACKSTONE *Comm.* I. xiv. 413 The first sort of servants therefore, acknowledged by the laws of England, are menial servants; so called from being *intra moenia*, or domestics. **1776** ADAM SMITH *W.N.* II. iii. (1869) I. 332 The labour of a menial servant..adds to the value of nothing. **1791** MRS. INCHBALD *Simple Story* I. iv. 32 She felt herself but as a menial servant.

3. Of service or employment: Proper to or performed by a menial or domestic servant. Now only with disparaging implication: Of the nature of drudgery; servile, degrading.

1673 TEMPLE *United Prov.* ii. 113 His [De Wit's] Train.. was only one man, who performed all the Menial service of his House at home. **1726** SWIFT *Gulliver* II. iii, A maid to dress her and two other servants for menial offices. *c* **1829** VISCT. PALMERSTON in Lytton *Life* (1870) I. vi. 317 *note*, The wives are forced to wash and perform all menial offices. **1836** W. IRVING *Astoria* II. 39 As to the Indian, he is a game animal, not to be degraded by useful or menial toil. **1840** DICKENS *Barn. Rudge* xxiv, The menial offices..the numerous degrading duties..that I've had to do for him. **1899** T. NICOL *Recent Archaeol. & Bible* iv. 153 The menial character of the labour [*sc.* brickmaking].

4. Of temper, spirit, occupations: Servile, sordid.

1837 [see MENIALISM]. **1839** BAILEY *Festus* xiii. (1852) 151 Nor cold insurgent heart, nor menial mind Can compass this. **1875** JOWETT *Plato, Gorgias* (ed. 2) II. 399 All other arts which have to do with the body are servile and menial and illiberal. **1891** *Edin. Rev.* CLXXIII. 400 Devoted only to the menial care of building a fortune.

B. *sb.* A 'menial' servant (see A. 2). Now only *contemptuous*, applied chiefly to liveried menservants kept for ostentation rather than use; often suggesting an imputation of pomposity or arrogance.

1388 WYCLIF *2 Sam.* xvi. 2 The assis ben to the meyneals of the kyng [Vulg. *domesticis regis*]. **1650** BP. HALL *Balm Gilead* xii. §4 Surely the great Housekeeper of the World.. will never leave any of his menials without the bread of sufficiency. **1755** JOHNSON, *Menial*, one of the train of servants. **1768** T. MOSS *The Beggar* 15 A pamper'd menial forc'd me from the door, To seek a shelter in an humbler shed. **1805** SCOTT *Last Minstr.* Introd. 39 The Duchess.. bade her page the menials tell That they should tend the old man well. **1820** BYRON *Mar. Fal.* IV. i, Dismiss This menial hence; I would be private with you. **1850** PRESCOTT *Peru* II. 76 The most common soldier was attended by a retinue of menials that would have better suited the establishment of a noble. **1854** THACKERAY *Newcomes* I. vii. 68 A hot menial in a red waistcoat came and opened the door. **1901** J. WATSON *Life Master* xviii. 170 The servants..allowed Him to pass with a menial's disdain for the poor.

Hence **'menialism**, the condition of a menial; a menial act; **meni'ality**, menial character; *pl.* menial conditions; **'menially** *adv.*, like a menial.

1837 *New Monthly Mag.* L. 132 Menial in soul, he may as well have the hire of menialism. **1846** MRS. GORE *Eng. Char.* (1852) 105 And is such a man to be abased to the menialities of the servants' hall? **1848** *Blackw. Mag.* LXIV. 344 Lady Suffolk..had been bedchamber woman, and of course had performed this menialism! **1882** STEVENSON *New Arab. Nts.* (1884) 169 The Prince..handed his hat to Mr. V., his cane to Mr. R., and, leaving them..thus menially employed upon his service, spoke.

†**'menialty**. *Obs.* Also 6 **menaltie**. [f. MENIAL + -TY.] The condition of being a menial. Also, *collect.* persons of menial rank.

1581 MULCASTER *Positions* xxxviii. (1887) 176 From the lowest in menaltie, to the highest in mistriship. **1593** NASHE *Christ's T.* 91 The vulgar menialty conclude, therefore it [*sc.* the Plague] is like to encrease.

menie, obs. form of MANY, MEINIE.

Ménière (‖menjɛːr). *Path.* The name of Prosper *Ménière* (1799–1862), French physician, used in the possessive to designate a disease of the membranous labyrinth of the ear associated with dizziness, tinnitus, etc., and causing progressive deafness in the ear affected (described by Ménière in 1861).

Accentuation of the name varies. The forms *Menière*, used by the physician himself, and *Ménière*, used by many writers about him and by his descendants, are both common. The unaccented form *Meniere* is used in some modern English works.

1876 *Edin. Med. Jrnl.* XXI. 716 (*heading*) Case of Menière's disease. **1885** *Encycl. Brit.* XIX. 39/1 A diminution of the power of co-ordinated action, as in Menière's disease. **1907** *Brit. Med. Jrnl.* 11 May 1107/2 Ménière's disease..is a rare disease, while cases exhibiting Ménière's symptoms are not by any means uncommon. **1938** *Proc. R. Soc. Med.* XXXI. 1317 (*heading*) Observations on the pathology of Ménière's syndrome. **1955** W. GADDIS *Recognitions* III. i. 732 If it is Ménière's syndrome, we'll have you up staggering around in no time. **1968** HARRISON & NAFTALIN (*title*) Menière's disease. **1968** J. L. PULEC (*title*) Meniere's disease. **1971** *Daily Tel.* 30 Jan. 3/2 Grounded by Ménière's syndrome, a malady of the inner ear which was causing increasing deafness, he secretly went into hospital.

menild, variant of MENALD.

menilite (ˈmɛnɪlaɪt). *Min.* [a. F. *ménilite* (H. B. de Saussure, 1795), from *Ménil(montant)*, a quarter of Paris where it is found: see -ITE.] A variety of opal of a dull greyish or brownish colour, occurring in kidney-shaped masses.

[**1801** *Encycl. Brit.* Suppl. II. 205/2 *Pitchstone. Menelites.* .. A specimen of Pitchstone from Mesnil-montant near Paris..261 (Index to Mineralogy) Menalites.] **1811** PINKERTON *Petral.* I. 550 As common flint becomes menilite, from the unctuous and magnesian marl in which it is deposited.

attrib. **1829** URE *Geol.* 324 The menilite silex.

menilla, menille, obs. ff. MANILLA[1], MANILLE.

1781 *Gentl. Mag.* LI. 616 *Menille* seems to be a corruption of the Spanish *malilla*, a wicked woman capable of any kind of mischief.

menin, variant of MENNOM *dial.*, minnow.

meningeal (mɪˈnɪndʒɪəl), *a. Anat.* and *Path.* [f. mod.L. *mēninge-us* (f. *mēning-*, MENINX: cf. F. *méningé*, It. *meningeo*) + -AL[1].] Of or pertaining to the meninges. ***meningeal artery***: one of the arteries supplying the dura mater of the brain.

1829 C. BELL *Anat. & Phys.* (ed. 7) I. 119 Groove of the meningeal artery. **1877** tr. *von Ziemssen's Cycl. Med.* XII. 171 Meningeal hæmorrhages.

meninges, pl. of MENINX.

meningic (mɪˈnɪndʒɪk), *a. rare. Path.* [f. mod.L. *mēning-* MENINX + -IC.] = MENINGEAL *a.*

1822 GOOD *Study Med.* III. 599 He [M. Serres] proposes to call the first *meningic* and the second *cerebral* apoplexy. *Ibid.* 600 Meningic or brain fever.

meningioma (mɛnɪndʒɪˈəʊmə). *Path.* Pl. **-omas, -omata**. [mod.L., f. by shortening *mening(othel)ioma*, f. MENINGO- + ENDO)THELIOMA.] A tumour, usu. benign, arising from the meninges (esp. those of the brain).

1922 H. CUSHING in *Brain* XLV. 282 (*heading*) The meningiomas (dual endotheliomas): their source, and favoured seats of origin. *Ibid.* 285 The term *meningothelioma* was first proposed, but it has, on further consideration, been shortened to *meningioma*. This word, consequently, will be used to indicate the entire group of tumours which appear to arise from the pachymeninx. **1961** *Lancet* 16 Sept. 656/2 Of particular interest was the activity of the cells comprising the whorls of a meningioma. **1974** PASSMORE & ROBSON *Compan. Med. Stud.* III. xxxiv. 110/2 About 18 per cent of intracranial tumours are meningiomata.

meningism (mɪˈnɪndʒɪz(ə)m). *Path.* [Formed as MENINGIC *a.* + -ISM.] Tendency to meningitis.

1901 *Brit. Med. Jrnl.* 5 Jan. *Epit. Curr. Med. Lit.* 1 Galli has collected observations of a number of cases of meningitis and meningism.

meningitic (mɛnɪnˈdʒɪtɪk), *a. Path.* [f. MENINGIT-IS + -IC.] Pertaining to meningitis.

1890 in *Syd. Soc. Lex.* **1899** *Allbutt's Syst. Med.* VII. 546 The meningitic exudation.

‖**meningitis** (mɛnɪnˈdʒaɪtɪs). *Path.* [mod. L., f. *mēning-* MENINX + -ITIS.] Inflammation of the membranes of the brain or spinal cord.

1828 ABERCROMBIE *Dis. Brain* 51 To prevent circumlocution, I shall employ the term *Meningitis* to express the disease, meaning thereby the inflammation of the arachnoid, or pia mater, or both, as distinct from inflammation of the dura mater. **1899** *Allbutt's Syst. Med.* VII. 546 In most cases not due to injury meningitis..is caused by an invasion of micro-organisms.

Hence **menin'gitiform** *a.* [-FORM], **menin'gitophobia** [-PHOBIA], see quots.

1890 BILLINGS *Nat. Med. Dict.* II. 133 *Meningitophobia*, ..symptoms of cerebro-spinal meningitis produced from fear of the disease. *c* **1893** F. P. FOSTER *Illustr. Med. Dict.* III. 2276 *Meningitiform*,..resembling meningitis.

meningo- (mɪˈnɪŋgəʊ), combining form of Gr. μῆνιγξ MENINX in a number of pathological and other terms, of which the following are the most important: **me'ningocele** (-siːl) [cf. CELE *sb.*], hernia of the meninges of the brain or spinal cord; **me,ningo-cere'britis** = *meningo-encephalitis*; **me,ningo'coccal, -'coccic** *adjs.*, of, pertaining to, involving, or caused by a meningococcus; **meningo-coccus**, a coccus supposed to be the cause of cerebro-spinal fever; **me,ningo-encepha'litis**, inflammation of the membranes of the brain and the adjoining cerebral tissue; **me,ningo-en'cephalocele** [ENCEPHALOCELE], the protrusion of brain substance and meninges through a hole in the skull; the mass so protruded; **me,ningo-en,cephalomye'litis** [*encephalomyelitis* s.v. ENCEPHALO-], inflammation of the meninges, brain, and spinal cord; †**meningo-'gastric fever** *Obs.* = *gastric fever*; **me,ningo-ma'lacia**, 'softening of the membranes of the brain' (Mayne *Expos. Lex.* 1856); **me,ningo-mye'litis**, inflammation of the spinal cord and its membranes; hence **me,ningo-mye'litic** *a.*; **me,ningo-'myelocele**, a hernial tumour of the spinal cord (*Syd. Soc. Lex.* 1890); = MYELOMENINGOCELE; **me,ningo-ra'chidian** *a.* [RACHIS], pertaining to the meninges and the spine; **meningo'rrhagia**, hæmorrhage of the meninges of the brain. (*Syd. Soc. Lex.*).

1867 *Bienn. Retrosp. Med.*, etc. (Syd. Soc.) 423 A case of *meningocele in the occipital region. **1899** *Allbutt's Syst. Med.* VI. 499 The chronic *meningo-cerebritis of general paralysis. **1907** *Edin. Med. Jrnl.* LXIV. 227 One case.. associated with tubercular meningitis..clearly falls..into line with *meningococcal arthritis. **1949** H. W. FLOREY in H. W. Florey et al. *Antibiotics* I. i. 23 Meningococcal carriers were successfully cleared of micro-organisms. **1966** *Jrnl. Amer. Med. Assoc.* 2 May 391 (*heading*) Meningococcal disease, 1965. **1907** *Jrnl. Med. Res.* XVII. 229 Seven different antigonococcic serums and a *meningococcic serum. **1950** *Amer. Jrnl. Med.* VIII. 468 (*heading*) Cause of death in meningococcic infection. **1893** DUNGLISON *Med. Dict.* (ed. 21), **Meningo-coccus*. **1897** *Trans. Amer. Pediatric Soc.* IX. 189 An organism resembling the meningococcus was found. **1872** COHEN *Dis. Throat* 206 Consecutive *meningo-encephalitis. **1891** F. P. FOSTER *Med. Dict.* III. 2277/1 **Meningo-encephalocele*, a tumour of the head analogous to hydro-myelocele. **1901** *Brit. Med. Jrnl.* 22 June 1542/1 (*heading*) Case of meningo-encephalocele treated by excision of the mass. **1964** S. DUKE-ELDER *Parson's Dis. Eye* (ed. 14) xxxiii. 529 Clinically they [*sc.* dermoid cysts of the orbit] may be mistaken for meningo-encephaloceles, protrusions of the cerebral contents, which usually occur at the upper and inner angle where there are most sutures between bones. **1900** DORLAND *Med. Dict.* 381/1 *Meningo-encephalomyelitis. **1966** WRIGHT & SYMMERS *Systemic Path.* II. xxxiv. 1199 Myalgic Meningoencephalomyelitis. An extensive epidemic of a benign myalgic encephalomyelitis occurred among the staff of the Royal Free Hospital in London, in 1955. **1899** *Allbutt's Syst. Med.* VI. 887 Any chronic *meningo-myelitic process. **1897** *Ibid.* III. 68 A case in which *meningo-myelitis was found at the autopsy. **1885** *Trans. Clin. Soc.* XVIII. 340 Protrusion of the membranes together with the spinal cord and its appertaining nerves, *meningo-myelocele. **1966** WRIGHT & SYMMERS *Systemic Path.* II. viii. 1234/2 In its least serious form, spina bifida occulta, there is

incomplete closure of one or more of the vertebral arches... In a more serious and commoner variety, meningomyelocele, the spinal cord is involved, and portions of its posterior columns may be stretched out in the wall of the subcutaneous cystic swelling. **1842** E. WILSON *Anat. Vade M.* (ed. 2) 351 The *Meningo-rachidian veins are situated between the theca vertebralis and the vertebræ.

‖**meninguria**, (mɛnɪŋˈgjʊərɪə). *Path.* [mod.L., f. Gr. μηνιγγ- MENINX + οὖρον urine: see -IA.] The passing of urine containing membranous shreds. Hence **meninˈguric** *a.*

1856 MAYNE *Expos. Lex.*

‖**meninx** (ˈmiːnɪŋks). Chiefly pl. **meninges** (mɪˈnɪndʒiːz); also 7 **menings.** [mod.L., a. Gr. μῆνιγξ membrane, esp. of the brain. (Late L. had *mēninga*; cf. F. *méninge*.)] Any of the three membranes enveloping the brain and spinal cord (*viz.* the dura mater, arachnoid, and pia mater).

1616 BULLOKAR *Eng. Expos.*, *Meninges*, thinne skins in which the braine is contained. **1638** A. READ *Chirurg.* xvii. 124 In the suture there is a ligament, by which the menings are tyed to the pericranium. **1666** *Phil. Trans.* I. 397 He.. inquires, whether the Nerve proceed from the Medulla itself, or its Meninx. **1747** tr. *Astruc's Fevers* 202 As to the phrenzy, it is an inflammation of the meninges, or dura and pia mater. **1839–47** *Todd's Cycl. Anat.* III. 627/2 The cerebral and spinal meninges. **1884** M. MACKENZIE *Dis. Throat & Nose* II. 370 Congestion of the meninges was found at the base of the brain.

¶**b.** The drum of the ear. [So in Gr.] *nonce-use.*

1630 RANDOLPH *Aristippus* 28 The Meninx of his eare is like a cut Drum, and the hammers lost.

menis, obs. gen. pl. MAN; obs. f. MINISH *v.*

meniscal (mɪˈnɪskəl), *a. rare*⁻⁰. [f. MENISCUS + -AL[1].] Of the form of a meniscus.

1860 WORCESTER (cites *Enfield*).

meniscate (mɪˈnɪskət), *a. Bot.* [f. MENISCUS + -ATE[2].] Resembling a meniscus in form.

1866 *Treas. Bot.* 735/1 *Meniscate*, a cylinder bent into half a circle.

menisch(e, obs. forms of MINISH *v.*

meniscoid (mɪˈnɪskɔɪd), *a. Bot.* [f. MENISC-US + -OID.] Resembling a meniscus in form; of the form of a watch-glass.

1821 tr. *Decandolle & Sprengel's Philos. Plants* 28 The higher degree of the shield-shaped passes into the meniscoid (*meniscoideus*). **1832** LINDLEY *Introd. Bot.* 380 *Meniscoid*;.. resembling a watch-glass. **1863** BERKELEY *Brit. Mosses* iii. 22 In *Sphagnum* the spore-sac.. consists of.. a meniscoid cyst at the top.

So **meniˈscoidal** *a.* = MENISCOID.

1881–2 SAVILLE-KENT *Infusoria* II. 870.

‖**meniscus** (mɪˈnɪskəs). Pl. menisci (mɪˈnɪsaɪ); also 8 **meniscusses.** [mod.L., a Gr. μηνίσκος crescent, dim. of μήνη moon.] A crescent-shaped body.

1. A crescent moon. *rare.*

1706 PHILLIPS (ed. Kersey), *Meniscus*, a little Moon. **1881** MISS A. D. KINGSTON tr. *J. Verne's Tigers & Traitors* v. 89 Thus the meniscus.. shed a few faint beams after midnight.

2. A lens convex on one side and concave on the other; *properly*, the convexo-concave form (i.e. the one which is thickest in the middle, and thus has a crescent-shaped section), but often applied also to the concavo-convex, the two being sometimes distinguished as *converging* and *diverging meniscus* respectively.

1693 E. HALLEY in *Phil. Trans.* XVII. 969 In a Meniscus the Concave side towards the Object encreases the focal length, but the Convex towards the Object diminishes it. **1794** G. ADAMS *Nat. & Exp. Philos.* II. xiv. 85 Infinitely thin meniscusses do not sensibly change the course of the rays of light. **1879** HARLAN *Eyesight* vii. 99 The periscopic glass is what opticians call a meniscus. One surface is convex and the other concave, according as one or the other of these surfaces has the sharper curvature.

3. The convex or concave upper surface of a liquid column, caused by capillarity.

1812–16 PLAYFAIR *Nat. Phil.* (1819) I. 189 The little meniscus of water.. which terminates the column. **1883** W. H. RICHARDS *Text Bk. Milit. Topogr.* 218 The 'meniscus' should be decidedly rounded; if it appears flat the barometer should be tapped [etc.].

4. *Math.* A figure of the form of a crescent.

1885 WATSON & BURBURY *Math. Theory Electr. & Magn.* I. 117 Instead of the figure formed by the two external segments, we may take.. the meniscus formed by one internal and one external segment.

5. *Anat.* A disk-like interarticular fibrocartilage situated in the interior of some joints to adapt the articular surfaces to each other, as in the wrist- and knee-joints.

1830 R. KNOX *Béclard's Anat.* 239 The menisci, or interarticular ligaments. **1877** BURNETT *Ear* 74 The articulation between the malleus and incus is a true joint, in which is found a meniscus.

6. An organ of doubtful function in *Echinorhyncus*, a genus of acanthocephalous entozoa.

1877 HUXLEY *Anat. Invert. Anim.* 647.

7. *attrib.* and *Comb.*, as ***meniscus form, glass, lens; meniscus-shaped*** adj.

1787 tr. *Linnæus' Fam. Plants* I. 70 Seeds.. *meniscus-form. **1878** ABNEY *Photogr.* (1881) 203 All single lenses.. have the meniscus form given to them. **1704** J. HARRIS *Lex. Techn.* I, **Meniscus Glasses* are those which are Convex on one side, and Concave on the other. **1833** N. ARNOTT *Physics* (ed. 5) II. 203 A lens may be convex on one side and concave on the other,.. called a *meniscus lens. **1851–6** WOODWARD *Mollusca* 74 Specimens frequently occur in the lias, with the *meniscus-shaped casts of the air-chambers loose, like a pile of watch-glasses.

†**menise.** *Obs.* Forms: 5 **menuse, -ce, menese, menys(e**, 6 **menew(e)s, menues**, 7 **men(u)ise.** [a. OF. *menuise, menuse* (mod.F. *menuise*):—L. *minūtia*: see MINUTIA.] Small fry.

*c***1430** *Two Cookery-bks.* 104 Menese or loche boiled. Take Menyse or loche, and pike hem faire. *c***1460** J. RUSSELL *Bk. Nurture* 819 Flowndurs, gogeons, muskels, menuce in sewe. **1508–13** *Bk. Keruynge* in *Babees Bk.* (1867) 280 Menewes in sewe of porpasor of samon. **1585** HIGINS *Junius' Nomencl.* 62 *Pisciculi minuti.. Poissons menus, menuise.* Small fishes called menues. **1613** J. D[ENNYS] *Secr. Angling* II. xi. C 4 b, The little Roach, the Menise biting fast. **1616** SURFL. & MARKH. *Country Farm* 507 The small fish, which is called white, are the.. Loach, Menuise, and the Trout.

†ˈ**menison.** *Obs.* Forms: 3 **menison(e**, 3–4 **meneisoun**, 4–5 **menysoun**, 5 **menyson, -isoun, -eson, mensone, mensoun**, 6 **mensyn, menson.** [a. OF. *menison, meneison, menoison*:—late L. *mānātiōnem* flowing, n. of action f. *mānāre* to flow.] Dysentery.

*c***1290** *Beket* 2367 in *S. Eng. Leg.* I. 174 Toward þe deþe he drouȝ And fur-pinede in þe menisone þat is lif him þouȝte long. *c***1305** *St. Lucy* 6 in *E.E.P.* (1862) 101 For four ȝer heo hadde.. þe meneisoun stronge. **1377** LANGL. *P. Pl.* B. XVI. 110 Bothe meseles and mute and in þe menysoun blody, Ofte he heled suche. *c***1465** *Eng. Chron.* (Camden) 35 Meny men deide on the blody mensoun. **1556** WITHALS *Dict.* (1562) 76 The bloudy menson, *discenteria.*

menisperm (ˈmɛnɪspɜːm). *Bot.* [ad. mod.L. *Mēnispermum* (Tournefort), f. Gr. μήνη moon + σπέρμα seed: cf. the Eng. name *moonseed*, referring to the crescent-shaped seeds.] A plant of the N.O. *Menispermaceæ*, of which *Menispermum* is the typical genus; the most widely known species are the Cocculus indicus, *Anamirta* (formerly *Menispermum*) *Cocculus*, and the Calumba. Also **menisperˈmaceous** *a.*, belonging to the N.O. *Menispermaceæ*; **meniˈspermad**, Lindley's term for a plant of this order; **meniˈspermal** *a.*, in ***menispermal alliance***, Lindley's term for an 'alliance' or group of orders including the *Menispermaceæ.*

1837 *Penny Cycl.* VII. 305/2 *Cocculus*, a genus of Menispermaceous plants. **1846** LINDLEY *Veg. Kingd.* 297 Menispermales—The Menispermal Alliance. *Ibid.*, The Order of Menispermads. **1880** GARROD & BAXTER *Mat. Med.* 187 The root of the Frasera Walteri, and of a Menisperm from Ceylon, have been substituted for true calumba.

menispermine (mɛnɪˈspɜːmɪn). *Chem.* Also **-ina, -in.** [f. mod.L. *Mēnisperm-um* (see MENISPERM + -INE[5].] An alkaloid obtained from the shells of the fruit of the Cocculus indicus, *Anamirta* (formerly *Menispermum*) *Cocculus.* Also †**meniˈspermia.**

1837 *Penny Cycl.* VII. 306/2 The kernel [of the fruit of *Cocculus indicus*] contains about one part in the hundred of picrotoxia, or menispermia, as some term it. **1838** T. THOMSON *Chem. Org. Bodies* 224 Menispermina.. is white and opaque, and has very much the external appearance of cyanodide of mercury. **1852** J. BELL in *Lect. Gt. Exhib.* 141 Menispermin. **1880** GARROD & BAXTER *Mat. Med.* 188 An alkaloid, Menispermine.

Menitto, meniver(e, meniye: see MANITOU, MINIVER, MANYIE.

menked, -et: see MENG *v.*

men-kind. Now *rare.* Also 5 **men kyn.** [See MAN *sb.*[1] 22.] The male sex; men-folk.

1387 TREVISA *Higden* (Rolls) II. 145 He schulde raþer chese hem a kyng.. of þe wommen kyn raþer þan of þe men kyn. **1559** in Neal *Hist. Purit.* (1732) I. 153 When the name of Jesus shall.. be pronounced in the church, due reverence shall be made.. with.. uncovering the heads of the Menkind. **1674** GOOKIN in *Coll. Mass. Hist. Soc.* (1806) I. 183 The menkind sitting by themselves and the womenkind by themselves. **1697** in C. Mather *Magn. Chr.* VI. 12, I had breakfasted with the Family, and the Men-kind were gone abroad. **1898** *Month* June 637 Where the family meals take place, and where the Basque menkind are served first.

menkit, menkte, menkyd: see MENG *v.*

menly, mennage, mennal, mennam: see MEANLY *adv.*[1], MANAGE, MENALD, MENNOM.

mennard (ˈmɛnəd). *dial.* Also 8 **mennot**, 9 **menner, mennad, menot.** [Formation obscure: perh. connected with MINNOW.] = MINNOW.

1796 MARSHALL *Rur. Econ. Yorks.* II. 333 *Mennot*,.. the minnow. **1869** *Lonsdale Gloss.*, *Menner, Mennard*, a minnow. **1904** menot [see MENNOM].

menne, obs. pl. of MAN; obs. form of MEINIE.

Mennecy (ˈmɛnəsɪ), *a.* Also **Menecy.** [Name of a town in France, near Paris.] The designation of a soft-paste porcelain made at Mennecy. Also *absol.*

1863 W. CHAFFERS *Marks Pott. & Porc.* 203 Menecy, marked in blue on a soft paste egg cup, of very early manufacture. **1869** C. SCHREIBER *Jrnl.* Aug. (1911) I. 32 Mennecy china box. **1870** *Ibid.* 71 We found a.. Mennecy basket and cover with coloured flowers in relief. **1874** *Ibid.* 255 A small piece of Mennecy at Van Houtum's. **1957** *Encycl. Brit.* XVIII. 351/2 At its best, Mennecy porcelain is of unsurpassed quality, mellow in tone and texture and of a warm white colour. **1960** R. G. HAGGAR *Conc. Encycl. Cont. Pott. & Porc.* 314/1 The Mennecy porcelain manufacture originated in the rue de Charonne, Paris.. in 1734. **1960** H. HAYWARD *Antique Coll.* 181/2 Mennecy porcelain, soft-paste porcelain.. made at Mennecy, Ile-de-France, between 1735 and 1785. **1972** *Country Life* 8 June (Suppl.) 58/1 An ormolu birdcage with Mennecy flowers.

mennelled, mennesc: see MENALD, MANNISH.

†ˈ**mennesse.** *Obs. rare.* [Aphetic for I-MENENESSE: cf. MEAN *a.*[1] I.] Communion, fellowship.

1340 *Ayenb.* 14 Ich y-leue holy cherch generalliche and þe mennesse of halȝen. *Ibid.* 268.

mennesse, variant of MANNESS *Obs.*

mennisc, mennly: see MANNISH, MEANLY.

Mennist (ˈmɛnɪst). *U.S.* [irreg. f. *Menno* (see MENNONITE) + -IST.] = MENNONIST, MENNONITE. Also *attrib.*

1771 G. TAYLOR *Voy. N. Amer.* 170 In the City of Philadelphia you see Churchmen, Quakers, Lutherans, Calvinists, Moravians, Catholics, Menists, [etc.]. **1869** *Atlantic Monthly* Oct. 474/1 The Mennists in many outward circumstances very much resemble the Society of Friends. *Ibid.*, In the interior of the Mennist meeting, a Quaker-like plainness prevails.

mennom (ˈmɛnəm). *dial.* Forms: 7–8 **minum**, 7–9 **minim**, 8 **menin**, 8–9 **mennin**, 9 **mennom, -on, -im, -um, -am**, etc. (see E.D.D.) [? A corruption of MINNOW, due to association with MINIM.] = MINNOW.

1654 FULLER *Ephemeris* Pref. 7 Minums will get through the holes thereof [*sc.* a drag-net]. **1674** RAY *Collect. Words, Fresh-water Fish* 111 The Minow, Minim or Pink. **1794–6** E. DARWIN *Zoon.* (1801) I. 251 A great number of little fish called minums or pinks. **1806** in *Archæologia* XV. 352 *note*, The minnow still called.. 'mennom' in the north of England. *a***1810** TANNAHILL *Poems* (1846) 76 Up frae the mennon to the whale. **1838** HALIBURTON *Clockm.* Ser. II. xix. 294 Little ponds never hold big fish; there is nothing but pollywogs, tadpoles, and minims in them. **1893** *Northumbld. Gloss.*, *Mennim, Mennam, Menowm, Mennem.* **1904** *Spectator* 28 May 847/2 Minnow, pink,.. meaker, menot, minim, peer,.. and minnin are all synonymous.

attrib. **1725** RAMSAY *Gentle Sheph.* III. iii, The saughtree shades the menin pool.

Mennonist (ˈmɛnənɪst). Also 7–9 **Menonist.** [Formed as MENNONITE + -IST.] = MENNONITE

1645 PAGITT *Heresiogr.* (1646) 30 Menonists, so called of Menon, a Frisian, by whose name the Anabaptists were generally called. **1776** J. ADAMS *Wks.* (1854) IX. 403 At present some colonies have.. bodies of Quakers, and Mennonists, and Moravians, who are principled against war. **1866** H. PHILLIPS *Amer. Paper Curr.* II. 72 The Menonists refuse to sell their produce unless for hard cash.

So ˈ**Mennonism**, the doctrines of the Mennonites.

1684 *Answ. Remarks More's Expos.* Pref. a 4 b, All which is done in favour of his beloved Mennonism, that Christ may not be held to begin his reign where there is any visible Monarch or Civil Magistrate that rules.

Mennonite (ˈmɛnənaɪt). *Eccl.* Also 6 *erron.* **Memnonite**, 8 **Menonite.** [f. *Menno* + -ITE.] A member of a sect of Christians which was founded in Friesland by Menno Simons (1492–1559). They are opposed to infant baptism, the taking of oaths, military service, and the holding of civic offices.

1565 T. STAPLETON *Fortr. Faith* 9 b, Memnonites and Zuenckfeldians haue ben stirring. **1684** *Answ. Remarks More's Expos.* Pref. a 2 b, Which is the opinion of Daniel Brenius a Mennonite. **1876** BARCLAY *Inner Life Relig. Soc. Commw.* 73 The doctrines.. of the Mennonites.

attrib. **1727–41** CHAMBERS *Cycl.* s.v., M. Herman Schin, a Mennonite minister. **1864** EVANS *E. Eng. Baptists* 21 The Mennonite Church in Holland. **1876** BARCLAY *Inner Life Relig. Soc. Commw.* 77 Many of them.. held to the Mennonite faith and practice.

mennot, mennow, mennum, menny: see MENNARD, MINNOW, MENNOM, MANY.

mennys, obs. gen. pl. of MAN.

meno (ˈmeɪnəʊ), *adv. Mus.* [It.] Less; used in musical directions, as ***meno mosso***, rather slower, less animated (lit. 'less moved').

1876 STAINER & BARRETT *Dict. Mus. Terms* 286/2 *Men, meno...* Less; as *meno forte*, not so loud. **1880** GROVE *Dict. Mus.* II. 311/2 *Meno mosso*, a direction, which, like Più lento, generally occurs in the middle of a movement. *Ibid.* 312/1 Beethoven uses 'Meno mosso e moderato' in the Fugue for strings in B♭, op. 133, and 'Assai meno presto' —'very much less quick'—in the Trio of Symphony No. 7.

‖**menobranchus** (mɛnəʊ'bræŋkəs). [mod.L.; irregularly f. Gr. μέν-ειν to remain + βράγχος gills.] **a.** A genus of tailed amphibians (also called *Necturus*), having permanent external gills. **b.** An animal of this genus; in this sense also in anglicized form **menobranch** ('mɛnəʊbræŋk).

1845 J. F. SOUTH *Zool.* in *Encycl. Metrop.* VII. 305/1 The Menobranch, Axolotl and Menopome. **1854** OWEN *Skel. & Teeth* in *Orr's Circ. Sci.* I. *Org. Nat.* 188 The menobranchus has four fingers and four toes. **1878** BELL tr. *Gegenbaur's Comp. Anat.* 432 The notochord..is alternately constricted and widened out in Menobranchus, Siredon, and Menopoma.

‖**menolipsis** (mɛnəʊ'lɪpsɪs). *Path.* [mod.L., f. Gr. μηνο-, μήν month + λεῖψις failure, omission, f. λείπειν to leave, fail.] The failure, retention, or cessation of the menses.

1856 in MAYNE *Expos. Lex.*, and in recent Dicts.

†**menologe.** *Obs.* Also **menologue.** [ad. Eccl. L. *mēnologium*: see MENOLOGY.] = MENOLOGY.

1626 T. H[AWKINS] tr. *Caussin's Holy Crt.* 538 In the Menologe of the Grecians, and the Roman Martyrologe. **1653** LD. VAUX tr. *Godeau's St. Paul* 316 The Greek Menologue saies, he was Bishop of Golophones. **1661** BLOUNT *Glossogr.* (ed. 2) s.v., The Greek Menologe (a book so called) is their Martyrologe, or a Collection of the Saints days of every moneth in their Church.

menologist (mɪ'nɒlədʒɪst). [f. MENOLOGY: see -IST.] A compiler of a menologium.

1895 F. TUPPER in *PMLA* X. 224 The Menologist (*Cælendcwide*, 56) ushers in Easter thus: 'Aprelis monað on þam oftust cymð [etc.]'. **1948** K. MALONE *Middle Ages* I. 35 For sources the menologist presumably used church calendars and the like... In any case the menologist was no mere clerk, learned in Church Latin only. He was steeped in classical Old English poetry, as his style and choice of words reveal.

menology (mi:'nɒlədʒɪ). Also in Gr. and Lat. forms **menologion, menologium.** [ad. mod.L. *mēnologium*, ad. late Gr. μηνλόγιον, f. μηνο-, μήν month + λόγος account: see LOGOS. Cf. *martyrology*.] A calendar of the months.

1. *spec.* **a.** The distinctive title of the calendar of the Greek church, containing biographies of the saints in the order of the dates on which they are commemorated.

1610 HOLLAND *Camden's Brit.* I. 68 They report..upon the authority..of the Greeks Menology, that St. Peter came hither. **1740** A. CLARKE *Hist. Bible* II. 321 The Greek Menologies intimate that he was shot. **1881** WESTCOTT & HORT *Grk. N. T.* App. 84 The Menologium or system of saints' days.

b. *transf.*; applied esp. to the OE. metrical church calendar first printed by Hickes in 1705. Now usu. in form *menologium*.

1709 E. ELSTOB tr. *Ælfric's Homily on St. Gregory* App. 26 The Original MS. of the Menologium is in the Cottonian Library. **1735** M. SHELTON tr. *Wotton's Short View G. Hickes's Anc. Northern-Lang.* 20 The first of these is a Poetical Calendar, translated into Latin, wherein it is observable, that this Menology, wrote at the Command of some Anglo-Saxon Bishop, or King, who reigned after the Dissolution of the Heptarchy, makes mention of no Saints except Pope Gregory, and Austin the Monk. **1807** S. TURNER *Hist. Anglo-Saxons* (ed. 2) II. 280 The elegant Menology in the Cotton Library. **1830** B. THORPE tr. *Rask's Gram. Anglo-Saxon Tongue* 138 Another remarkable instance of this [lack of strophic or stanzaic divisions] is the conclusion of the *Menologium Saxonicum*. **1844** LINGARD *Anglo-Sax. Ch.* (1858) II. x. 83 To search in the Anglo-Saxon menology for the most distinguished patrons of the monastic profession. **1887** STANTON (*title*) A menology of England and Wales, or, brief memorials of the ancient British and English saints, arranged according to the calendar. **1888** (*title*) A menology or record of departed friends [compiled by M. E. Barrow]. **1892** C. PLUMMER *Sax. Chron.* Expl. Gloss. 297 The Menologium or Metrical Calendar contained in Appendix A. **1905** E. D. HANSCOM in *Jrnl. Eng. & Germ. Philol.* V. 441 The *Menologium* preserves the popular names of October and November, *Winterfylleð* (184) and *Blotmonað* (195). **1932** CHADWICK & KERSHAW *Growth of Lit.* I. 380 The *Menologium* or metrical calendar at the beginning of MS. C of the *Saxon Chronicle*.

2. *gen.* An almanac. ? *Obs. rare*$^{-0}$.

1727 BAILEY vol. II, *Menologion*, an Account of the Course of the moon, an Almanack.

¶**3.** The department of knowledge that relates to the months.

[Properly another word, repr. an assumed Gr. type in -λογία: see -LOGY.]

1807 S. TURNER *Anglo-Sax.* VII. iv. (ed. 2) II. 24 On the Menology and Literature of the Pagan Saxons.

Menominee (mɪ'nɒmɪni:). *U.S.* Also **Menomini, -onee.** [ad. Ojibwa *manōmini*, lit. 'wild-rice people'.] **1.** The name of a tribe of Algonquian Indians first discovered near the mouth of the Menominee River in Michigan and Wisconsin; also *attrib.*; also applied to the language spoken by this people.

1762 T. HUTCHINS *Jrnl.* 26 June in *Mich. Hist. Mag.* (1926) X. 369, I delivered the same Message to the Meynomeneys that I had done to the Sax and Reynard Nations. **1830** [see HALF-BLOOD 4]. **1835** C. F. HOFFMAN *Winter in West* II. 3 The Mè-no-mé-né, or wild-rice-eaters, is a broken band that served with effect against the Sauks and Foxes in the Indian difficulties of 1832. **1920** L. BLOOMFIELD in C. F. Hockett *Leonard Bloomfield Anthol.* (1970) 90 Have been writing down Menominee words and stories. They are a delightful people, of good culture: it must have been an elaborate and beautiful culture 200 years ago. **1922** —— in *Ibid.* 99 These stems are a living (freely formed) derivation in Menomini. **1953** A. HUXLEY *Let.* 17 Aug. (1969) 683 The Menomini are Indians in a reservation in Wisconsin. **1964** E. BACH *Introd. Transformational Gram.* i. 2 To learn Greek or Menomini..it is not enough to read through a compact presentation of paradigms or rules. **1975** *Times* 8 Jan. 6 Troops of the Wisconsin National Guard were called out today to deal with a group of Menominee Indians occupying a large estate... The Menominees have a reservation near by.

2. In full, ***Menominee whitefish.*** The round whitefish, *Prosopium cylindraceum*, found in lakes of northern North America.

1884 G. B. GOODE *Fisheries U.S.: Nat. Hist. Aquatic Animals* 541 *Coregonus quadrilateralis*. The only name which I have heard applied to this fish is that of 'Menomonee White-fish'. **1902** *Rep. U.S. Comm. Fisheries 1901* 653 Table showing, by States, the products of the fisheries of the Great Lakes in 1899..White-fish (Menominee) fresh ..White-fish (Menominee) salted. **1944** G. L. NUTE *Lake Superior* 186 Menominees, a kind of whitefish, are listed at 14,940 pounds, all caught in American waters.

Menonist, -ite, obs. forms of MENNONIST, -ITE.

menopausal (mɛnə'pɔ:zəl), *a.* [f. MENOPAUSE + -AL.] Of, pertaining to, or connected with the menopause. Also *fig.*

1910 *Practitioner* June 787 Permanent cessation of the menses, so long as the ovaries have been conserved, is not associated with so-called 'menopausal' symptoms. **1964** L. MARTIN *Clin. Endocrinol.* (ed. 4) vii. 233 If human menopausal gonadotrophin units (HMG) are used, the average normal result is 30 units and values above this may be found in cases of malignant testicular tumours. **1969** D. WIDGERY in Cockburn & Blackburn *Student Power* 126 It was inevitable that students would eventually come to revolt against the menopausal leadership of NUS and its flaccid policies. **1974** M. SPARK *Abbess of Crewe* iii. 83 She is behaving in a most menopausal way, and she claims there is a plot against her to prevent her being elected Abbess.

menopause ('mɛnəpɔ:z). *Phys.* [ad. mod.L. *mēnopausis*, f. Gr. μηνο-, μήν month + παῦσις cessation, PAUSE. Cf. F. *ménopause*.] The final cessation of the menses. Also *fig.*

1872 PEASLEE *Ovar. Tumors* 2 The 30 or 35 years of menstrual life, i.e. from puberty to the menopause. **1899** *Allbutt's Syst. Med.* VIII. 302. **1954** W. FAULKNER *Fable* 69 It was winter again now, the long unbroken line from Alps to sea lying almost quiescent in mud's foul menopause. **1962** J. H. BURN *Drugs, Med. & Man* xv. 152 Stilboestrol is also used at the menopause when menstruation ends. **1970** JENNER & SEGAL *Men & Marriage* 144 In the nineteen-fifties a spate of 'popular medicine' articles flooded the press bearing the news that men, too, suffered from the Change of Life and middle-aged men found themselves swamped with sympathy over their newly recognised menopause. **1972** F. WARNER *Lying Figures* III. 19 Having your mental menopause?

Hence **meno'pausic** *a.*, having symptoms of the menopause.

1889 H. CAMPBELL *Causation Disease* viii. 55 Those menopausic patients who seek medical relief.

‖**menophania** (mɛnəʊ'feɪnɪə). *Phys.* [med.L., f. Gr. μηνο-, μήν month + -φανία appearance, φαίνειν to appear.] The first appearance of the menses.

1857 DUNGLISON *Med. Lex.* 583.

‖**menoplania** (mɛnəʊ'pleɪnɪə). *Path.* [mod.L., from Gr. μηνο-, μήν month + -πλανία, πλάνη wandering.] A discharge of blood, at the catamenial period, from some other part of the body than the uterus.

1845 S. PALMER *Pentaglot Dict.* In some recent Dicts.

‖**menopoma** (mɛnəʊ'pəʊmə). Also anglicized **menopome** ('mɛnəpəʊm). [mod.L., irreg. f. Gr. μένειν to remain + πῶμα lid.] A genus of amphibians characterized by the persistence of the branchial apertures; an amphibian of this genus, a hellbender.

1835–6 *Todd's Cycl. Anat.* I. 91/1 The *amphiuma* and *menopoma* have not as yet been observed to possess branchiæ. **1842** *Penny Cycl.* XX. 342/1 *Salamandrops*, Wagler's name for the Menopome. **1863** WOOD *Nat. Hist.* III. 185 The Menopome inhabits the Ohio and Alleghany rivers.

menor, obs. form of MINOR.

menorah (mə'nəʊrə, -'ɔərə). [Heb. *mĕnōrāh* sabbath or festival candelabrum.] A holy candelabrum having seven branches used in the ancient temple in Jerusalem; also a candelabrum having any number of branches used in modern synagogues.

1888 (*title*) Menorah monthly. **1936** *Jews in Palestine Campaign* (Menorah Club) 41 A Club under the name of Menorah (seven branched candlestick)..was established. **1958** B. MALAMUD *Magic Barrel* (1960) 128 Don't those peaks..look like a Menorah?.. Like a seven-branched candalabrum..? **1966** L. DAVIDSON *Long Way to Shiloh* ii. 31 The great seven-branched lamp, the Menorah, has been the symbol of Judaism for some thousands of years; of.. Israel, for the past fifteen or so... Titus took the lamp when he destroyed the Temple in August of 70. **1970** L. M. FEINSILVER *Taste of Yiddish* 247 The Sabbath menorah has seven holders, to accommodate a candle for each day of the week. The Chanuka menorah has nine holders. **1973** *Jewish Chron.* 2 Feb. 16/5 The Mayor of Hackney..was presented with an Israeli-made menorah. **1973** *Country Life* 20 Sept. 784/2 The symbol of the Menorah, the seven-branched candelabrum, was originally placed in the tabernacle in the Sinai Desert and in the First Temple in Jerusalem, and was carried away by Titus. Today the Menorah, framed by two olive branches, is the emblem of the modern state of Israel.

menorhynchous (mɛnɒ'rɪŋkəs), *a. Ent.* [f. mod.L. *Menorhyncha* (irreg. f. Gr. μένειν to remain + ῥύγχος snout, proboscis) + -OUS.] Belonging to or having the character of the *Menorhyncha* (in Brauer's classification of insects, those taking food by suction in the larval and imaginal state).

1899 D. SHARP *Insects* II. (Camb. Nat. Hist.) 542 According to Brauer's generalisations they [Hemiptera] are Menorhynchous, Oligonephrous Pterygogenea.

‖**menorrhagia** (mɛnɒ'reɪdʒɪə). *Path.* Also anglicized **menorrhagy** ('mɛnəreɪdʒɪ). [mod.L., f. Gr. μηνο-, μήν month + -ραγία, f. ῥαγ-, ῥηγνύναι to break, burst forth.] Excessive or long-continued menstruation.

1776–84 CULLEN *First Lines Pract. Physic* (1808) II. 4, I treat of menorrhagia here as an active hæmorrhagy, because I consider menstruation, in its natural state, to be always of that kind. **1856** MAYNE *Expos. Lex.*, *Menorrhagia Abortus*, term for menorrhagy attendant on abortion. **1872** T. G. THOMAS *Dis. Women* (ed. 3) 261 Menorrhagia may occur without pain.

Hence **menorrhagic** (mɛnɒ'rædʒɪk) *a.*, pertaining to or suffering from menorrhagia.

1844 ASHWELL *Dis. Women* 147 She has been menorrhagic for several years. **1873** E. H. CLARKE *Sex in Educ.* 62 Menorrhagic, dysmenorrhoeic girls and women. *c* **1893** F. P. FOSTER *Med. Dict.* III. 1576 Menorrhagic fever.

‖**menorrhœa** (mɛnɒ'ri:ə). *Path.* [mod.L., f. Gr. μηνο-, μήν month + ῥοία flow, flux] **a.** The ordinary flow of the menses. **b.** Long-continued, though moderate, flow of the menses. **c.** A too frequent return of the menses. (*Syd. Soc. Lex.*)

1856 MAYNE *Expos. Lex.* **1889** J. M. DUNCAN *Lect. Dis. Women* xv. (ed. 4) 107 There is not amenorrhœa, but menorrhœa into the passages, not farther.

Hence **meno'rrhœic** *a.*, pertaining to or characterized by menorrhœa.

1856 in MAYNE *Expos. Lex.*

‖**menostasis** (mɪ'nɒstəsɪs). *Path.* [mod.L., f. Gr. μηνο-, μήν month + στάσις standing.] **a.** The suppression or retention of the menses. **b.** The acute pain preceding the menses in some women (Dunglison 1855). Hence **meno'static** *a.*, pertaining to menostasis.

1839 *Hooper's Med. Dict.* (ed. 7). **1856** in MAYNE *Expos. Lex.*; and in mod. Dicts.

menostation (mɛnə'steɪʃən). *Path.* [ad. mod.L. *mēnostatiōn-em*, f. Gr. μηνο-, μήν month + L. *statiōn-em* a standing.] = MENOSTASIS.

1822 GOOD *Study Med.* IV. 46 Yet menostation may take place from a suppression of the menses after they have become habitual. **1844** HOBLYN *Dict. Med.*, *Menostation*, a suppression or retention of the catamenial discharge.

menot: see MENNARD *dial.*, a minnow.

menour, -ess, obs. forms of MINOR, -ESS.

menow(e, obs. forms of MINNOW.

†**menow weed.** *West Indian. Obs.* [Cf. *many-root* (MANY 6c), applied to the same plant; Browne's *menow weed* may be a mistake for this, or possibly both names may be distortions of some foreign word.] The plant *Ruellia tuberosa*.

1756 P. BROWNE *Jamaica* 268 Menow weed..is very common in most parts of Jamaica.

menprise, variant of MAINPRIZE *v. Obs.*

men's: see MAN *sb.*[1] 23.

‖**mensa** ('mɛnsə). [L. *mensa* table.]

1. *Eccl.* The upper surface, esp. the top slab, of an altar: an altar-table.

1848 B. WEBB *Continental Ecclesiol.* 45 An original altar of solid masonry with moulded mensa and plinth. **1904** *Athenæum* 20 Aug. 250/1 In the chancel of Car-Colston.. rests the uprooted headstone of Dr. Thoroton,..it was originally the mensa of the high altar.

2. The grinding surface of a molar tooth.

1693 tr. *Blancard's Phys. Dict.* (ed. 2), *Mensa*, the broader part of the Teeth called Grinders, which Chaws and Minces the Meat. **1856** MAYNE *Expos. Lex.*

3. (With capital initial.) Adopted as the name of an organization of people with above-average intelligence quotients. Also *attrib.*

Members qualify by passing a test equivalent to an I.Q. of 148 or more on the Cattell scale.

1962 *Mensa Register* p. ii, The Mensa Register is published to satisfy members' curiosity as to who the other members are, and to allow such individual contact to be made as is desired. **1968** *Brit. Mensa* Dec. 6/2 Mensa is essentially a social organisation, designed to bring mutually congenial people together. *Ibid.*, Examination of the Bulletin will show thriving Mensa groups in every geographic region. **1971** *Sear* (Manch. Branch Brit. Mensa) Nov., Mensa is a social club with the entry requirement that

members have an IQ higher than 98% of the general population. **1972** *Times* 2 Nov. 9/4 All participants have mensa minds that have read Wittgenstein. **1972** W. Garner *Ditto, Brother Rat!* vi. 46 Mensa is a sort of high IQ élite. Anyone can try their tests. Very few pass.

mensal ('mɛnsəl), *a.*[1] and *sb.*[1] Also 8 **mensale**. [ad. late L. *mensālis*, f. *mensa* table: see -AL[1].]

A. *adj.*

1. Pertaining to or used at the table; table-.

c **1440** *Promp. Parv.* 333/1 Mensal knyfe, or borde knyfe. **1656** Blount *Glossogr.* **1748** Richardson *Clarissa* (J.), Conversation either mental or mensal. **1778** Dr. Warner *Let.* in Jesse *Selwyn's Corr.* (1844) III. 335 The common things, mental or mensal, which I grubbed on with contentedly.

b. *mensal bed*: a couch used (as by the ancient Romans) for reclining at meals.

1675 Brooks *Gold. Key* Wks. 1867 V. 543 It is an allusion to their conjugal and mensal beds, on which the guests are so bestowed, that the first laid his left hand under the head of him that was next.

2. a. In Irish (and early Scottish) history, *mensal land*: land set apart for the supply of food for the table of the king or prince.

1607 Davies *1st Let. to Earl Salisbury* Hist. Tracts (1787) 245 The Mensall land of M'Guire. **1689** R. Cox *Hist. Irel.* I. Expl. Index, *Logh tee*, Demeasn or Mensal Lands, for House-keeping. **1880** W. F. Skene *Celtic Scot.* III. 148 The office or mensal land set apart for the maintenance of the Ri or Toisech.

b. In Scotland and Ireland before the Reformation, applied to a church, benefice, etc., appropriated to the service of the bishop for the maintenance of his table. Also similarly used in the modern Roman Catholic church in Ireland.

1605 T. Ryves *Vicar's Plea* (1620) 114 All manner of Benefices as well mensall as other. **1663** *Jrnls. Irish Ho. Lords* (1779) I. 375 That Bishops that are well settled do build a Mensal-House. **1775** L. Shaw *Moray* (1827) 360 The churches of St. Andrews, Ugston, and Laggan were Mensal. **1813** Carlisle *Topog. Dict. Scot.* II, *Hoddom*, in the Shire of Dumfries: formerly a Mensal Church to the See of Glasgow. **1861** Fitzpatrick *Dr. Doyle* (1880) I. 379 As this was a mensal parish, Dr. Doyle often visited it officially.

3. *Palmistry. mensal line*, the 'line of fortune', the table-line. [Cf. OF. *mensale* sb.]

1602 *Narcissus* (1893) 230 Thy mensall line is too direct and cragged. **1675** Salmon *Polygraph.* v. xxxix. 489.

B. *sb.*

1. *Hist.* A mensal church or benefice.

1710 J. Harris *Lex. Techn.* II, *Mensalia, Mensals*, were such Personages or Livings as were united formerly to the Tables of Religious Houses. **1847** W. Reeves *Eccles. Antiq. Down & Connor* (1867) 115 *note*, This parish was, of old, a mensal of the Bishop of Dromore.

†2. *Irish Antiq.* The provision of the royal table (see A. 2 a). *Obs.*

1782 *Vallancey's Collect. De Rebus Hibern.* III. x. 94 Lands assigned for the mensal of the chief.

mensal ('mɛnsəl), *a.*[2] and *sb.*[2] [f. L. *mēns-is* month + -AL[1]. Cf. *mensual.*] A. *adj.* Monthly.

1860 Worcester (citing *Month. Rev.*). **1888** J. Nelson in *Amer. Jrnl. Psychol.* I. 390 In the male as in the female, the maturation of the reproductive elements is a continuous process, though we may hardly say that it is not influenced by the mensal periodicity.

†B. *sb.* A monthly account. *Obs.*

a **1483** *Liber Niger* in *Househ. Ord.* (1790) 60 The cofferer hathe..one under clerke..to make the mensall and many othyr wrytings for the Thesaurere his accompt. **1526** *Ibid.* 220 Within three dayes of the expirement of every moneth to bring in his mensall.

mensalize ('mɛnsəlaɪz), *v.* [f. MENSAL[1] + -IZE.] *trans.* To convert into a 'mensal' parish, etc.

1893 Fahey *Hist. Diocese Kilmacduagh* 406 The parish was mensalised on the appointment of Dr. Archdeacon.

mensanger, obs. form of MESSENGER.

‖**mensch** (mɛnʃ). Also **mensh**. [Yiddish, a. G. *mensch* person.] A person of integrity or rectitude; one who is morally just, honest, or honourable.

1953 S. Bellow *Adventures A. March* 43, I want you to be a *mensch*. **1959** H. Pinter *Birthday Party* III. 55 You'll be a mensch... You'll be a success. **1968** L. Rosten *Joys of Yiddish* 234 The key to being 'a real *mensh*' is nothing less than—character: rectitude, dignity, a sense of what is right, responsible, decorous. Many a poor man, many an ignorant man, is a *mensh*. **1970** *New Statesman* 30 Oct. 556/1 Mr Nixon is seen as an essentially decent man,..but not as a *mensch* on the scale of Roosevelt, Eisenhower, Kennedy. **1972** *New Yorker* 24 June 26 What is a *mensch*?.. It means you're a substantial human being.

mense (mɛns), *sb. Obs.* exc. *Sc.* and *north. dial.* [Sc. pronunciation of MENSK: cf. *buss* = *busk* bush, *ass* = *ask* ashes, etc.] Propriety, decorum; neatness, tidiness.

c **1500** *Priests of Peblis* (Laing) 313 Thair manheid, and thair mense, this gait they murde; For mariage thus unyte of ane churle. **1567** *Satir. Poems Reform.* viii. 10 War ȝour richt reknit to þe croun It mycht be laid with litill menss. **1737** Ramsay *Scot. Prov.* (1797) 46, I ha'e baith my meat and my mense. [Used by one who has given an invitation that has not been accepted.] **1783** Burns *Poor Mailie's Elegy* iv, I wat she was a sheep o' sense, An' could behave hersel wi' mense. **1788** W. Marshall *Yorks.* II. 342 *Mense*, manners, creditableness. **1818** Scott *Rob Roy* vi, But we hae mense and discretion, and are moderate of our mouths.

mense (mɛns), *v. Obs.* exc. *dial.* Also **mence**. [Sc. var. of MENSK *v.*] *trans.* To grace; to adorn or decorate; to be a credit or to do honour to.

1535 Lyndesay *Satyre* 4088 Cum heir, Falset, & mense the gallows. **1606** Birnie *Kirk-Buriall* (1833) 35 Lyke Hophnees with elcrookes to minche and not Samueles to mense the offerings of God. **1780** J. Mayne *Siller Gun* III, Convener Tamson mensed the board, Where sat ilk deacon like a lord. **1818** Hogg *Brownie of Bodsbeck*, etc. II. 164 They'll..leave the good..ait-meal bannocks to..be pouched by them that draff an' bran wad better hae mensed! **1863** in Robson *Bards Tyne* 135 O bonny church! ye've studden lang, To mence our canny toon.

mense, obs. Sc. form of *mends*: see MEND *sb.*

menseful ('mɛnsfʊl), *a. Sc.* and *north. dial.* [f. MENSE *sb.* + -FUL.] Proper, decorous; neat, tidy; discreet.

1674 Ray *N.C. Words* 32 *Menseful*: comely, graceful, crediting a man, *York-sh.* **1720** Ramsay *Wealth* 119 Thus with attentive look mensfou they sit. **1816** Scott *Old Mort.* vi, Put on your Raploch grey; it's a mair mensfu' and thrifty dress. **1822** —— *Pirate* xxiii, Menseful maiden ne'er should rise, Till the first beam tinge the skies. **1891** A. J. Munby *Vulgar Verses* 191 'Bud, Gaffer', said the menseful maid—.

menseless ('mɛnslɪs), *a. Obs.* exc. *Sc.* [f. MENSE *sb.* + -LESS.] Destitute of propriety, decorum or seemliness.

15.. *Colkelbie Sow* in *Bannatyne MS.* (Hunter. Club) 1026 This cursit company And mensles mangery. **1593** B. Barnes *Parthenophil* Sonn. xv, O, but I fear mine hopes be void, or menceless! **1787** Burns *Death Poor Mailie* 50 An warn him..no to rin an' wear his cloots Like ither menseless, graceless, brutes. **1858** M. Porteous *Souter Johnny* 32 The menseless fry Gie out its for your fame they pry, To mak it strunt, an' sten' mair high.

‖**menses** ('mɛnsiːz), *sb. pl. Path.* [L. *mēnsēs*, pl. of *mēnsis* month.] = CATAMENIA.

1597 Gerarde *Herbal* I. li. 72 The seede of Darnell.. prouoketh the flowers or menses. **1607** Topsell *Four-f. Beasts* (1658) 431 A Musk-cat..is very profitable..for the bringing forth of those Womens menses or fluxes which are stopped. **1718** Quincy *Compl. Disp.* 92 Myrrh provokes the Menses, and forwards Delivery. **1896** Allbutt & Playfair *Syst. Gynæcology* 345 The suppression of the menses that occurs in young obese women is to be accounted for in the same way.

mensh (mɛnʃ). Also **mench**. Colloq. abbrev. of MENTION *sb.* and *v.*; freq. in phr. *don't mensh*, = *don't mention it* (see MENTION *v.* 1 c).

1937 in Partridge *Dict. Slang* 517/1. **1955** 'G. Carr' *Corpse at Camp Two* iii. 40 'Pray forgive my tactlessness.'.. 'Don't mench, sir.' **1961** J. Dawson *Ha-Ha* ii. 31 'I'm sorry to hear it.' 'Thank you, not at all, don't mensh.' **1968** C. Watson *Flaxborough Crab* iii. 35 'Thank you very much.' 'Don't mensh.' **1973** *Times* 27 Apr. 4/3 One little boy asked if we could 'have a mensh [mention] for Aunty Dora who fell down the stairs and broke her leg'. **1974** F. Nolan *Oshawa Project* iii. 24 'Thanks, Lucky.' 'Don't mensh, don't mensh,' Luciano said.

Menshevik ('mɛnʃɪvɪk), *a.* and *sb.* [a. Russ. *men'shevík*, f. *mén'she*, compar. of *málÿĭ* little. The Russ. pl. *men'sheviki* has been used by some English writers.] A. *adj.* Of, pertaining to, or characteristic of, the Mensheviks or Menshevism.

1907 [see Bolshevik B. *adj.*]. **1919** J. Reed *Ten Days that shook World* iii. 47 Said the Menshevik *Dien*, 'The Government ought to defend itself and defend us.' *Ibid.* iv. 91 Raising his voice to a shout he [*sc.* Khintchuk] read the Menshevik declaration. *Ibid.* viii. 204 The familiar faces of the Menshevik and Socialist Revolutionary intellectuals. **1920** *Glasgow Herald* 14 Oct. 9 Martov (Zedarbaum), who headed the Menshevik opposition when Lenin broke up the Russian Social Democratic Party in 1903. **1923** E. A. Ross *Russ. Soviet Republic* 323 The imprisonment of the Menshevik members of the Moscow printers' union. **1971** D. Smith *Russia of Tsars* viii. 128 The Petrograd Soviet was equally hesitant... Alexander Kerensky, its Menshevik vice-president,..used his influence. **1975** *Times Lit. Suppl.* 4 July 740/5 When accused..of holding menshevik positions, he replies..that revolutionary virginity is not worth preserving at the price of inaction.

B. *sb.* A member of the political group or party forming the smaller part of the Russian Social-Democratic Party after the split with the Bolsheviks in 1903 and denounced as counter-revolutionaries after the 'October' Revolution of 1917. Cf. BOLSHEVIK *sb.* Also *transf.* and *fig.*

1917 [see Bolshevik *sb.*]. [**1919** J. Reed *Ten Days that shook World* p. xiv, *Russian Social Democratic Labour Party*. Originally Marxian Socialists. At a party congress held in 1903, the party split, on the question of tactics, into two factions—the Majority (Bolshinstvo) and the Minority (Menshinstvo). From this sprang the names 'Bolsheviki' and 'Mensheviki'—'members of the majority' and 'members of the minority'.] **1923** E. A. Ross *Russ. Soviet Republic* 322 The Mensheviks can get no paper, which is a government monopoly, for pamphlets or leaflets at election time. **1926** *Contemp. Rev.* Sept. 274 He was an outsider—a 'menshevik' (the 'minority' man). **1935** N. Mitchison *We have been Warned* I. 67 Idlers, parasites, mensheviks, defeatists. **1973** *Listener* 1 Feb. 135/3 The Provisionals..by playing the Bolsheviks to the Officials' Mensheviks—though not in ideology of course—have indeed become the party of the majority.

Menshevism ('mɛnʃɪvɪz(ə)m). [a. Russ. *men'shevizm*: see MENSHEVIK *a.* and *sb.*] The doctrines and practices of the Mensheviks.

1920 *Glasgow Herald* 14 May 9 Communism as it is offered to Trans-Caucasia has assumed the form of Menshevism. **1926** *Contemp. Rev.* Sept. 275 Marx would prove it: but that would be 'Menshevism'. **1928** *Observer* 1 July 9/2 Comrade Trotsky's theory of permanent revolution is a variety of Menshevism.

Menshevist ('mɛnʃɪvɪst). [a. Russ. *men'shevíst* (now disused) MENSHEVIK *a.* and *sb.*] A Menshevik; a supporter of Menshevism. Also *attrib.* or as *adj.*

1919 *Times Lit. Suppl.* 14 Aug. 432/3 A pleasing description of the Menshevists. **1926** *Contemp. Rev.* Sept. 274 He was known to return in all intricate cases to his menshevist fallacies. **1931** *Times* 7 Mar. 12/2 The Menshevists had always been opposed to the violent overthrow of the Bolshevists. *Ibid.*, Documentary evidence of the alleged Menshevist propaganda all, strangely enough, got destroyed.

†'**mension.** *Obs.*—0 [ad. L. *mēnsiōn-em*, n. of action to *mētīri* (ppl. stem *mēns-*) to measure.] The action of measuring.

1623 Cockeram, *Mension*, a measuring. **1658** Phillips, *Mensuration*, the same as *Mension*, or measuring.

mension, obs. form of MENTION.

†**mensk**, *sb. Obs.* Forms: 3 **mensca**, **mensce**, **menke**, 3–6 **mensk**, **menske**, 5 **menseke**. (See also MENSE *sb.*) [a. ON. *mennska* humanity (Sw. *menniska*, Da. *menneske*), corresponding (exc. for declension) to OE. *menniscu* = OS., OHG. *mennisk*î:—OTeut. type **manniskîn-* wk. fem., f. **mannisko-*: see MANNISH *a.*]

1. Humanity, kindness; graciousness, courtesy.

a **1240** *Wohunge* in *Cott. Hom.* 269 Menske and mildeschipe and debonairte of herte and dede. *c* **1350** *Will. Palerne* 313 Moch is þi mercy & þi miȝt, þi menske, & þi grace! **13..** *E.E. Allit. P.* A. 163 A mayden of menske, ful debonere. *a* **1440** *Sir Degrev.* 83 He lovede welle almosdede, Powr men to cloth and ffede, Wyth menske and manhede.

2. Honour, dignity, reverence; *pl.* honours, dignities.

c **1205** Lay. 2535 Ah fourti wintre heore fader mid mensca heold his riche. *Ibid.* 2681. *a* **1225** *Ancr. R.* 192 Mid more menke, not ich non ancre þet habbe al þet hire neod is þene ȝe þreo habbeð. *a* **1300** *Cursor M.* 4245 Putifer..held ioseph in mensk and are. *c* **1320** *Sir Tristr.* 2118 More menske were it to þe Better for to do. **13..** *Gaw. & Gr. Knt.* 2410 Sele you bytyde, & he ȝelde hit yow ȝare, þat ȝarkkez al menskes! **1375** Barbour *Bruce* XVI. 621 Men sall se Quha lufis the kyngis mensk to-day! *a* **1400** *Sir Perc.* 1423 If..we foure kempys agayne one knyght, Littille menske wold to us lighte, If he were sone slayne. *c* **1460** *Towneley Myst.* xx. 175 Mensk be to this meneye! **1508** Dunbar *Tua Mariit Wemen* 352, I maid that wif carll to werk all womenis werkis, And laid all manly materis and mensk in this eird. **1509** *Test. Ebor.* (Surtees) V. 3 Ȝe shall have moch menske thereof.

b. An honour, credit, ornament.

a **1225** *Ancr. R.* 276 Þe meste menkes [*C.* menske] of þine nebbe, þet is, þet feirest del bitweonen smech muðes & neoses smel. *a* **1240** *Wohunge* in *Cott. Hom.* 281 Þu þat menske art of al mon kin, of alle bales bote, mon for to menske swuch schome þoledes.

†**mensk**, *a. Obs.* [a. ON. *mennisk-r* = OE. *męnnisc*: see MANNISH *a.*] Worshipful, honourable.

13.. *Gaw. & Gr. Knt.* 964 A mensk lady on molde.

†**mensk**, *v. Obs.* [f. MENSK *sb.*]

1. *trans.* To reverence or honour; to dignify, grace, favour.

a **1225** *Juliana* 7 He hire walde menskin wið al þat he mahte. *a* **1300** *Cursor M.* 2432 Þe king..commaunded thoru-out al his land Men suld him mensk and hald in hand. **1362** Langl. *P. Pl.* A. III. 177 For ȝit I may as I mihte menske þe wiþ ȝiftes And Meyntene þi Monhede more þen þou knowest. *c* **1400** *Destr. Troy* 1855 Send hom þat semly þat I sew fore, That he may menske hur with mariage. *c* **1460** *Towneley Myst.* ix. 140 Mahowne the menske, my lord kyng. *c* **1470** *Gol. & Gaw.* 446 Hym to mensk on mold withoutin manance.

2. To adorn; to render graceful.

13.. *E.E. Allit. P.* B. 141 Þe abyt þat þou has vpon, no halyday hit menskez. **13..** *Gaw. & Gr. Knt.* 153 A mere mantile abof, mensked with-inne, With pelure pured apert þe pane ful clene. *c* **1330** R. Brunne *Chron. Wace* (Rolls) 12460 To menske hit [a cloak] þer hit was wane. *c* **1375** *Sc. Leg. Saints* xxviii. (*Margaret*) 525 One þe morne, quhen sown was brycht, þat menskis al þe warld of lycht [etc.].

†'**menskful**, *a. Obs.* [f. MENSK *sb.* + -FUL. Cf. MENSEFUL.] Worshipful, honourable; gracious. Of a building: Stately.

a **1225** *Ancr. R.* 358 Iðe menske of þe dome þet heo schulen demen is heihschipe menskeful ouer al understonden, aȝean scheome. *a* **1300** *Cursor M.* 9878 A castel,..a worthy sted menskful to hald. *a* **1310** in Wright *Lyric P.* 51 Menskful maiden of myht. *c* **1350** *Will. Palerne* 508 His maners were so menskful a-mende hem miȝt none. *c* **1460** *Towneley Myst.* xxix. 389 Was neuer madyn so menskfull here apon molde As thou art. *c* **1470** *Gol. & Gaw.* 408 Maneris full menskfull, with mony deip dike.

absol. **13..** *Gaw. & Gr. Knt.* 555 Syr Boos, & sir Byduer, big men boþe, & mony oþer menskful.

b. Used as *adv.* = MENSKFULLY.

a **1310** in Wright *Lyric P.* 52 Middel heo hath menskful smal; Hire loveliche chere as cristal.

† **'menskfully**, *adv.* *Obs.* [f. prec. + -LY[2].] Honourably; manfully; with grace or propriety.

c **1350** *Will. Palerne* 1143 Ful menskfully to þe messangeres þemperour þan seide, he wold be boun bleþeli þe bold batayle to hold. **13..** *S. Erkenwolde* 50 in Horstm. *Altengl. Leg.* (1881) 267 Metely made of þe marbre & menskefully planede. ? a **1400** *Morte Arth.* 4076 Sir Ewayne, and sir Errake,..Demenys the medilwarde menskefully thare-aftyre. **1483** *Cath. Angl.* 234/2 Menskfully, *honeste*.

† **mens-kind, -kins**: see MAN *sb.*[1] 23.

† **'mensking**, *vbl. sb.* *Obs.* [f. MENSK *v.* + -ING[1].] Honour, worship; courtesy.

a **1300** *Cursor M.* 5304 Knele i sal be for þe king, And thank him of his grett mensking. *Ibid.* 15048 Þou tak to thanc þat we þe mak Sli mensking als we mai.

† **'menskless**, *a.* *Obs. rare.* In 6 -les. [f. MENSK *sb.* + -LESS. Cf. MENSELESS.] Ungracious.

1513 DOUGLAS *Æneis* IV. v. 41 This menskles goddes in euery mannis mouth Skalis thir newis est, west, north, and south.

† **'menskly**, *adv.* *Obs.* [f. MENSK *sb.* + -LY[2].] Courteously; reverently; honourably, with dignity.

a **1225** *Ancr. R.* 316 ȝif þu hatest þine sunne, hwui spekes tu menskeliche bi hire? a **1240** *Wohunge* in *Cott. Hom.* 269 Þat leuer is menskli to ȝiuen þen cwedli to wiðhalde. **13..** *Gaw. & Gr. Knt.* 1312 Þenne he meued to his mete, þat menskly hym keped. **1340–70** *Alisaunder* 173 The Marques of Molosor menskliche hee aught. **1375** BARBOUR *Bruce* XIX. 86 He broucht him menskly till erding. c **1450** *Bk. Curtasye* 291 in *Babees Bk.*, Drynk menskely and gyf agayne.

menslauȝt, variant of MANSLAUGHT *Obs.*

1387 TREVISA *Higden* (Rolls) V. 309 In þat stryf were meny menslauȝtes in þe citee.

mensless, variant of MENSELESS.

Men's Lib.: see MAN *sb.*[1] 23.

† **mensoigne, mensonge.** *Obs. rare*$^{-1}$. [a. OF. *mençoigne, mensonge*:—popular L. **mentitiōnica*, f. *mentīrī* to lie.] Falsehood.

c **1430** *Pilgr. Lyf Manhode* III. xxix. (1869) 151 My tunge, whiche is mesel, is cleped periurement, and my mouht j clepe mensoige [*Sic: corrected in the MS. from* mensonge].

menson(e, -soun, variants of MENISON *Obs.*

‖ **mens rea** (mɛnz 'riːə). *Law.* [mod.L., lit. 'guilty mind'.] The criminal state of mind accompanying an act which condemns the perpetrator of the act to criminal punishment; criminal intent.

1861 LEIGH & CAVE *Crown Cases Reserved* (1866) 53 The *mens rea* is an essential ingredient in every offence. **1914** D. A. STROUD *Mens Rea* i. 14 There is no real contradiction in describing a mere absence of mind as a *mens rea* or guilty mind. **1955** *Times* 15 July 11/6 If the customer used it to apply to some other dress she would be guilty of fraud. One is not anxious to multiply criminal offences in which there is no *mens rea*. **1959** *Chambers's Encycl.* IV. 241/1 Drunkenness may render the accused incapable of forming the specific intent necessary to commit the crime—when *mens rea* will not be present and the accused must be acquitted. **1965** *Listener* 16 Dec. 1006/2 The compulsory death penalty for murder, which led to a special interpretation of *mens rea*, has been abolished. **1972** *Police Rev.* 10 Nov. 1446/3 The prosecution has failed to adduce sufficient evidence of the presence of *mens rea* (or guilty knowledge).

men's room: see MAN *sb.*[1] 23.

‖ **mens sana in corpore sano.** Lat. phr. (occurring in Juvenal *Satires* x. 356): a sound mind in a sound body, esp. regarded as the ideal of education. Also *ellipt.*, as ***mens sana***.

c **1605** J. HARINGTON or S. DANIEL *Prayse of Private Life* in J. Harington *Lett. & Epigrams* (1930) iii. 329 Desyrynge of God noe more than the Satericke Poet wished, *Mens Sana, in Corpore Sano*. **1629** in *Camden Misc.* (1854) III. 10 To beare *mens sana in corpore sano*, a valient heart in such a body..wch hath never bene debilitated. **1749** CHESTERFIELD *Let.* 2 Oct. (1932) IV. 1415 *Mens sana in corpore sano*, is the first and greatest blessing. **1824** J. WIGHT *Mornings at Bow Street* 55 The General angrily declared he was altogether *mens sana in corpore sano*. **1851** GEO. ELIOT *Let.* 11 Sept. (1954) I. 359, I am really strong and healthy and hope to bring a mens sana in corpore sano to London. **1966** 'K. NICHOLSON' *Hook, Line & Sinker* xiii. 159 Cold bath first thing: *mens sana*, and all that. **1967** S. JOHNSON *Gold Drain* ii. 22 [They] accused him of suffering from the effects of a public-school education, from the *mens sana* approach. **1973** *Listener* 23 Aug. 260/1 One lady, supporting *mens sana in corpore sano* against Jo Grimond, wrote that Christ must have kept himself fit.

menstracie, -asy, etc., obs. ff. MINSTRELSY.

menstraill, -al(e, -alle, obs. ff. MINSTREL.

menstre, -strell, obs. ff. MINSTER, MINSTREL.

menstrew, variant of MENSTRUE *Obs.*

menstrua, pl. of MENSTRUUM.

menstrual ('mɛnstrʊəl), *a.* and *sb.* [a. F. *menstruel*, ad. L. *mēnstruāl-is*, f. *mēnstru-us*, *mēnstru-um*: see MENSTRUUM and -AL[1].] **A.** *adj.*

1. Monthly; happening once in a month, varying in monthly periods. Now only *Astr.*, esp. in ***menstrual parallax***, the difference produced by the moon in the apparent position of the sun and the primary planets.

1594 R. ASHLEY tr. *Loys le Roy* 2 The causes both of these cotidian, menstruall, annuall, and other the rarest mutations.., are attributed to the celestiall motions. **1664** EVELYN *Kal. Hort.* (1729) 187 Any Thing we have here alledg'd concerning these Menstrual Periods. **1665** WALLIS in *Phil. Trans.* I. 286 There is no other connexion between the Moon's motion and the Tydes Menstrual period, than a casual Synchronism. **1768** SMEATON *Ibid.* LVIII. 157 The difference thus produced in the apparent place of the Sun.. may..be..called the menstrual parallax. **1780** HERSCHEL *Ibid.* LXXI. 116 We have..no cause to suspect any very material periodical irregularity, either diurnal, menstrual, or annual. **1823** J. MITCHELL *Dict. Math. & Phys. Sci.* 343 Menstrual Parallax of the Sun is [etc.]. **1833** HERSCHEL *Treat. Astron.* §451 (1839) 289 An apparent monthly displacement of the sun..which is called the menstrual equation. **1872** O. SHIPLEY *Gloss. Eccl. Terms* s.v. Epact, It [an Epact] is therefore both annual and menstrual.

b. Lasting or extending over a month; esp. *Bot.* of a plant, remaining in bloom or foliage for a month (*Treas. Bot.* 1866).

2. Of or pertaining to the catamenia.

1398 TREVISA *Barth. De P. R.* VI. vii. (1495) 194 The moders wombe is fedde wyth blode menstruall. **1561** T. NORTON *Calvin's Inst.* II. 152 Some..do to lewdly ask, whether we will say that Christ was engendred of the menstruall sede of the Virgin. **1607** TOPSELL *Hist. Four-f. Beasts* (1658) 308 Aristotle and others do not let to write, that menstrual bloud doth naturally void from the Mare. **1718** QUINCY *Compl. Disp.* 92 A Provoker of the menstrual Discharges. **1876** BRISTOWE *Theory & Pract. Med.* (1878) 885 Inflammation..is most apt to occur during the menstrual period. **1896** ALLBUTT & PLAYFAIR *Gynæcology* 367 It may continue during the menstrual life of the patient.

† **b.** Suffering from ailments connected with menstruation. *Obs.*

1669 W. SIMPSON *Hydrol. Chym.* 73 An hysterical (or I rather think menstrual) woman.

† **3.** Of parts of the body: Produced from the menstrual blood of the mother; opposed to *spermatical*. *Obs.*

1626 BACON *Sylva* §58 Some Entrails..are hard to repaire: though that Diuision of Spermaticall, and Menstruall Parts, be but a Conceit.

† **4.** Pertaining to, or of the nature of, a menstruum. *Obs.*

1471 RIPLEY *Comp. Alch.* Pref., in Ashm. (1652) 126 Understond thy Water menstruall.

B. *sb.*

† **1.** *pl.* = CATAMENIA. *Obs.*

1597 A. M. tr. *Guillemeau's Fr. Chirurg.* 12 b/1 We apply the boxes to suscitate the menstrualles of women. **1599** —— tr. *Gabelhouer's Bk. Physicke* 135/1 It helpeth woemen when their menstrualles flowe to superfluouslye.

† **2.** *Alch.* The 'menstrual' element (see A. 4, and cf. A. 3, and note s.v. MENSTRUUM) supposed to be added to metal in the process of its conversion into gold. *Obs.*

1471 RIPLEY *Comp. Alch.* Pref., in Ashm. (1652) 125 For invysible ys truly thys Menstruall. **1477** NORTON *Ordin. Alch.* v. Ibid. 90 The seminall seed Masculine, Hath wrought and won the Victory, Upon the menstrualls worthily.

† **menstruant**, *a.* *Obs. rare*$^{-1}$. [ad. L. *mēnstruant-em*, pr. pple. of *mēnstruāre* to menstruate.] Subject to the catamenia.

1646 SIR T. BROWNE *Pseud. Ep.* IV. xii. 210 Women are menstruant and men pubescent at the year of twice seven. **1656** in BLOUNT *Glossogr.*

† **menstruate**, *a.* *Obs.* [ad. late L. (Vulg.) *mēnstruātus*, f. *mēnstru-um*: see MENSTRUUM.] Menstruous.

1382 WYCLIF *Ezek.* xxii. 10 Thei meekeden in thee the vnclennes of the menstruate womman. c **1425** *Found. St. Barthol.* 18 That welle of pyte, that was and is opyne to the menstruat womane and synful man.

menstruate ('mɛnstruːeɪt), *v.* [f. L. *mēnstruāt-*, ppl. stem of *mēnstruāre*, f. *mēnstrua* monthly courses: see MENSTRUUM and -ATE[3].]

1. *intr.* To discharge the catamenia.

1800 *Med. Jrnl.* IV. 529 Has never menstruated. **1866** TANNER *Pregnancy* i. 8 Some few girls, however, menstruate as early as the 11th, 12th, or 13th year.

2. *trans.* To pollute as with menstrual blood.

16.. CLEVELAND *On O.P. sick* 8 Wks. (1687), The reeking Steam of thy fresh Villanies Would spot the Stars, and menstruate the Skies.

Hence **'menstruating** *ppl. a.*

1872 F. G. THOMAS *Dis. Women* (ed. 3) 60 Evil often results to a menstruating woman thus constantly exposed. **1901** *Brit. Med. Jrnl.* No. 2097. 593 The changes in the menstruating uterus.

menstruated ('mɛnstruːeɪtɪd), *ppl. a.* [f. MENSTRUATE *a.* + -ED[1].] Applied to women in whom the menstrual flow is established (*Syd. Soc. Lex.* 1890).

menstruation (ˌmɛnstruː'eɪʃən). [ad. L. type **mēnstruātiōnem*, f. *mēnstruāre*: see MENSTRUATE *v.* and -ATION. Cf. F. *menstruation*, Sp. *menstruacion*, It. *menstruazione*.] The act or process of discharging the catamenia.

1776–84 [see MENORRHAGIA]. **1799** *Med. Jrnl.* I. 294 Women during menstruation, were [etc.]. **1896** ALLBUTT & PLAYFAIR *Gynæcology* 339 Menstruation usually begins in the fifteenth year.

† **menstrue.** *Obs.* Also 5 menstrewe, 6 menstrew. [a. F. *menstrue*, ad. L. *mēnstruum*: see MENSTRUUM.]

1. The catamenia; = MENSTRUUM 1.

c **1400** *Lanfranc's Cirurg.* 55 A womman in tyme of menstrue [*v.r.* menstrewe]. c **1440** *Wyclif's Isa.* lxiv. 6 Menstrue, or unclene blood. **1550** BALE *Apol.* 57 b, Our vniuersall ryghteousnesses are afore God as clothes stayned with menstrue. **1674–7** MOLINS *Anat. Obs.* (1896) 11 A Servant Maid with a suppression of the Menstrue.

attrib. c **1400** *Lanfranc's Cirurg.* 21 Þe fleisch & þe fatnes is mad of menstrue blood.

b. *pl.* In the same sense.

1579 LANGHAM *Gard. Health* (1633) 22 Anoint the breast to purge vpward, and the nauill to purge downward, and three fingers lower to prouoke menstrews. **1590** P. BARROUGH *Meth. Phisick* liii. 185 Of stopping of menstruis. **1684** tr. *Bonet's Merc. Compit.* I. 2 These symptoms had happened..at the time when she us'd to have her Menstrues.

2. = MENSTRUUM 2.

1471 RIPLEY *Comp. Alch.* Pref., in Ashm. (1652) 124 Raymond his Menstrues doth them call. **1605** TIMME *Quersit.* I. xiii. 61 The heauenly menstrueese to dispoyle metals of their colours and sulphures naturall is this [etc.]. **1610** B. JONSON *Alch.* II. iii, Are you sure, you loos'd 'hem I' their owne menstrue? **1664** EVELYN *Sylva* (1679) 6 They flatter their hopes..with fructifying liquors, Chymical Menstrues and such vast conceptions.

† **menstru'osity.** *Obs.* [ad. L. type **mēnstruōsitās*, f. **mēnstruōsus*: see MENSTRUOUS.] The condition of being menstruous; *concr.* the menstrual discharge. ***white menstruosity***, leucorrhœa.

1597 A. M. tr. *Guillemeau's Fr. Chirurg.* 32 b/2 When as there [women's] menstruositye too superfluouslye floweth from them. **1599** —— tr. *Gabelhouer's Bk. Physicke* 220/1 For the whyte menstruosytyes of a Woman. Take whyte horehownde [etc.]. **1634** H. R. *Salernes Regim.* 195 When the menstruosity keepeth due course..letting of bloud should not be done. **1653** SCLATER *Funeral Serm.* 25 Sept. (1654) 16 It is but as a defiled, nasty, and polluted menstruosity.

menstruous, *a.* [ad. OF. *menstrueus*, ad. L. type **mēnstruōsus*, f. *mēnstruum*: see MENSTRUUM and -OUS.]

1. Of a female: Having the catamenia.

1535 COVERDALE *2 Esdras* v. 8 Menstruous wemen shal beare monsters. **1615** CROOKE *Body of Man* 667 A menstruous woman doth infect a looking glasse as it were with some materiall corruption. **1638** G. SANDYS *Par. Lam.* i. 70 Jerusalem, O thou of late belov'd, Now like a Menstruous Woman art remov'd. **1752** T. DALE tr. *Freind's Emmenol.* viii. (ed. 2) 55 The same is also testified by Anatomists who have dissected menstruous Women.

2. Pertaining to the catamenia.

1599 T. M[OUFET] *Silkwormes* 67 From menstruous blasts and breathing keep them freed. **1613** PURCHAS *Pilgrimage* (1614) 599 Their troublesome menstruous purgation. **1646** SIR T. BROWNE *Pseud. Ep.* III. xvii. 147 At the first point of their menstruous eruptions. **1752** T. DALE tr. *Freind's Emmenol.* i. (ed. 2) 1 The menstruous Purgation. **1834** *Good's Study Med.* (ed. 4) IV. 35 *note*, This blood has been taken for the menstruous fluid.

† **b.** Produced from menstrual blood. (Cf. MENSTRUAL *a.* 2 c.) Also, secreting menstrual blood. *Obs.*

1626 BACON *Sylva* §900 Therefore all Sperme, all Menstruous Substance, [etc.] haue euermore a Closenesse, Lentour, and Sequacity. **1782** A. MONRO *Compar. Anat.* (ed. 3) 60 The only organs of generation..are two menstruous bags.

† **3.** Defiled with, or as with, menstrual blood (in the Old Testament referred to as the type of horrible pollution). Hence, in the 17th c. often: Horribly filthy or polluted. *Obs.*

1560 BIBLE (Genev.) *Isa.* xxx. 22 Ye shal..cast them away as a menstruous cloth. *Ibid.*, *Isa.* lxiv. 6 *marg.*, Our righteousnes and best vertues are before thee as vile cloutes, or, (as some read) like the menstruous clothes of a woman. a **1626** SCLATER *Serm. Exper.* (1638) 103 Shall man compared with God be righteous? Mans righteousnesse is more then menstruous in that comparison. a **1631** DONNE *Serm.* lxxvi. 768, I must carry into his presence a menstruous conscience and an ugly face. **1685** BUNYAN *Pharisee & Publ.* 53 All our Righteousnesses are as menstruous Rags.

† **4.** Lasting for a month; = MENSTRUAL *a.* 1 b. *Obs. rare.*

1657 W. BLOIS *Mod. Policies* (ed. 7) E 8, Conscience, which the Politician hath so much abused by an inveterate neglect, that it is become Menstruous, Ephemeral. **1866** in *Treas. Bot.*

Hence † **'menstruousness**, menstruous condition.

1597 A. M. tr. *Guillemeau's Fr. Chirurg.* 30/1 Ther monthlye sicknes, or menstruousnes. **1642** J. EATON *Honey-c. Free Justif.* 374 The filthy menstruousnesse of our sanctification. **1682** tr. *Erastus' Treat. Excomm.* 10 Women in their menstruousness, or men having a Gonorrhea. **1727** in BAILEY vol. II.

‖ **menstruum** ('mɛnstruːəm). *Pl.* menstrua ('mɛnstruːə). Also 7 *erron.* menstrum. [L., neut.

of *mēnstruus* adj., monthly, f. *mēns-*, *mēnsis* month. Cf. F. *menstrue* sing., menstruum, solvent, *menstrues* pl., monthly courses (also OF. *menstre*), Pr. *mestruas* pl., Sp., It. *menstruo*.
In classical Latin the sb. occurs only in the pl. *menstrua* (= sense 1). The development (in med. Latin) of sense 2 is to be explained by the fact that in alchemy the base metal undergoing transmutation into gold was compared to the seed within the womb, undergoing development by the agency of the menstrual blood. The medical writers spoke of the human fœtus as consisting of a 'spermatic' and a 'menstrual' part, derived from the two parents respectively; the alchemists employed this language in a transferred sense, the 'menstruum' with them being the solvent liquid. Cf. quot. 1477 s.v. MENSTRUAL B. 2, and the 14th c. quot. given by Littré under *Menstrue*.]

†**1.** The secretion produced in the womb and discharged at the monthly periods. Also *pl.* menses, catamenia. *Obs.*
1398 TREVISA *Barth. De P.R.* v. xlix. (1495) 166 That superfluyte hythe menstruum for it flowyth in the cours in the mone lyght. **1527** ANDREW *Brunswyke's Distyll. Waters* A iii, An ounce therof dronke at nyght causeth women to have her flowres named menstruum. **1650** BULWER *Anthropomet.* 222 The Maids are not to be married, till their Menstrua or natural purgation testifie their abilitie for Conception. **1726** LEONI *Alberti's Archit.* II. 127 A Tree touched with the Menstrua will lose its leaves.

†**b.** Menstrual blood as the nourishment of the fœtus; also *transf. Obs.*
1669 WORLIDGE *Syst. Agric.* (1681) 586 The Discovery and Application of what may be this proper Menstruum wherein each Seed most rejoyceth in. *a* **1677** HALE *Prim. Orig. Man.* III. iii. 264 The Semina..of the greater Animals required a..more effectual preparation of the Matter, or a Menstruum for their production out of those Semina.

2. A solvent; any liquid agent by which a solid substance may be dissolved.
[**1610** B. JONSON *Alch.* II. iii, Take your *lutum sapientis*, Your *menstruum simplex*.] **1612** WOODALL *Surg. Mate* Wks. (1639) 183 If the vehicle or menstrum you give it [medicine] in be also good. *a* **1626** BACON *Art. Enq. Metals* in *Sylva* (1661) 226 We are to enquire what is the proper Menstruum to dissolve any Metall,..and what severall Menstrua will dissolve any Metall. **1646** SIR T. BROWNE *Pseud. Ep.* II. i. 53 Powerfull menstruums are made for its emolition [*sc.* of crystal]. **1713** CHESELDEN *Anat.* III. iv. (1726) 165 Our digestion is performed by a Menstruum which is chiefly saliva. **1763** W. LEWIS *Commerc. Phil.-Techn.* 95 The most effectual menstruum of gold is a mixture..called *aqua regia*. **1800** VINCE *Hydrost.* v. (1806) 52 Solids are supposed to be dissolved in menstruums. **1881** B. W. RICHARDSON in *Med. Temp. Jrnl.* 72, I have given up the employment of alcohol as a menstruum for amyl nitrite in angina. **1898** *Rev. Brit. Pharm.* 33 Moisten the drug with the prescribed quantity of the menstruum.

b. *fig.*
1654 WHITLOCK *Zootomia* 406 Death is a preparing Deliquium, or melting us down into a Menstruum, fit for the Chymistry of the Resurrection to work on. **1691–8** NORRIS *Pract. Disc.* (1711) III. 138 This Union will not last always, Death, that Universal Menstruum, will dissolve it. **1863** HOLLAND *Lett. to Joneses* xxi. 304 In overflowing animal spirits is to be found..the menstruum of all social materials. **1890** *Illustr. Lond. News* 26 Apr. 535/3 Paradoxes ..are menstruums of friendship, they disintegrate regard.

mensual ('mɛnsju:əl, 'mɛnʃ(j)u:əl), *a.* [a. F. *mensuel*, a. late L. *mēnsuāl-is*, irreg. f. *mēns-is* month, on the analogy of *annuālis* annual.] Of or relating to a month; occurring or recurring monthly; monthly.
1794 DK. PORTLAND in *Earl Malmesbury's Diaries & Corr.* III. 124 Most averse..from withholding the mensual payments. **1893** F. ADAMS *New Egypt* 86 These seasons must..have dominated the life of this people, and prescribed its mensual, annual, and almost diurnal process.

mensuer, -ir, obs. forms of MANSWEAR *v.*

‖**mensur** ('mɛnsu:r). [G.] In Germany, a fencing duel between students fought with partially blunted weapons.
1911 L. KNOWLES *Day with Korps-Students in Germany* (ed. 2) 6 My visit was not to admire Heidelberg, but to see my *Korps*-student friends,..for on the morrow there was to be a *Mensur*, or fighting-bout. *Ibid.* 4 Even to Germans, these *Mensuren*, or lighter student-duels,..have their humorous side. **1960** *Times* 17 Sept. 9/7 The *Mensur* or duel ..is, however, frowned upon by officialdom. **1967** A. ARENT *Gravedigger's Funeral* xiii. 221 That final accolade of Teutonic narcissism, the face scars or *Mensur* marks of the military caste. **1970** 'M. HEBDEN' *Mask of Violence* (1971) xxv. 219 Anarchical young men of..the older universities, with the *Schmisse*—the duelling scars—on their cheeks, were already shouting the old *Mensur* wish before the commencement of a fight: '*Waffenschein!*' **1972** *House & Garden* May 142/4 Over the river, Hirchgasse where the 'mensor' [*sic*] duel is still fought.

mensurability (mɛnsjʊərə'bɪlɪtɪ, mɛnʃ(j)ʊər-). *rare.* [f. MENSURABLE + -ITY.] The state or quality of being mensurable.
1678 CUDWORTH *Intell. Syst.* 66 Whatsoever is, is Extended or hath Geometrical Quantity and Mensurability in it. **1814** D. STEWART *Philos. Hum. Mind* Note (G) II. 511 The common quality which characterizes all of them is their mensurability.

mensurable ('mɛnsjʊərəb(ə)l, mɛnʃ(j)ʊər-), *a.* [a. F. *mensurable*, ad. late L. *mēnsūrābil-is*, f. *mēnsūrāre* to measure, f. *mēnsūra* MEASURE *sb.*: see -ABLE.]

1. Capable of being measured; hence, having assigned limits.
1604 T. WRIGHT *Clymact. Years* 5 Loe thou hast put my dayes mensurable. **1694** HOLDER *Disc. Time* 19 The Solar Month..[is] not easily Mensurable. **1794** G. ADAMS *Nat. & Exper. Philos.* III. xxiv. 20 Every atom..has extension, which we may suppose to have mensurable proportions. **1829** SOUTHEY *Sir T. More* II. 32 It is only our mortal duration that we measure by visible and mensurable objects. **1881** FAIRBAIRN *Stud. Life Christ* 146 It was altogether a most manifest and mensurable thing.

†**2.** Just, fair: cf. MEASURABLE *a.* 1. *Obs.*
1633 J. DONE *Hist. Septuagint* 150 It [hospitality] is to shewe ones selfe not to be ingratfull but mensurable and equitable to all the world.

3. *Mus.* Having 'measure' and fixed rhythm, with notes and rests indicating a definite duration: used to denote the style (*cantus* or *musica mensurabilis*, 'descant') which succeeded the period of simple plain-song, and in which a combination of independent voice-parts was first employed.
Cf. MEASURED 3 c, MEASURABLE 5 b, MENSURAL 2.
1782 BURNEY *Hist. Mus.* II. 179 Ravenscroft..tells us boldly that he [*sc.* Franco] was the inventor of the four first simple notes of Mensurable Music. **1893** SHEDLOCK tr. *Riemann's Dict. Mus.*, *Mensurable Music*. **1901** WOOLDRIDGE *Oxf. Hist. Mus.* I. 169 Mensurable melody.

Hence **'mensurableness**, mensurable quality.
1727 in BAILEY vol. II.

†**'mensurage.** *Obs.* [f. L. *mēnsūra* measure + -AGE.] = MEASURAGE.
a **1676** HALE *Narr. Customes* vi. in S. A. Moore *Foreshore* (1888) 357 Other dutyes paid there, vizt. chalkinge, mensurage, wharfage, 1[d] a diem.

mensural ('mɛnsjʊərəl, 'mɛnʃ(j)ʊərəl), *a.* [a. med.L. *mensūrāl-is*, f. L. *mēnsūra* MEASURE *sb.*: see -AL[1].]

1. Pertaining to measure.
1651 WITTIE tr. *Primrose's Pop. Err.* IV. xxv. 301 There were among the Ancients as well pounds in measure, as in weight, for their vessels were drawn about with lines..and whatsoever they measured after this manner, they called Mensurall: As for example, a mensurall pound of oyle or wine. **1861** L. L. NOBLE *Icebergs* 245 Do not these fifty bergs ..speak more a living language to the creative, than to the mensural faculty?

2. *Mus.* = MENSURABLE 2.
1609 DOULAND *Ornith. Microl.* 39 Mensurall Musicke is a knowledge of making Songs by figures. **1893** SHEDLOCK tr. *Riemann's Dict. Mus.*, *Mensural Note*, the note of definite duration..invented about the commencement of the 12th century. **1901** WOOLDRIDGE *Oxf. Hist. Mus.* I. 114 The mensural system. *Ibid.* 174 The kind of part-writing which is characteristic of the early mensural period.

mensuralist ('mɛnsjʊərəlɪst, 'mɛnʃ(j)ʊər-). [a. F. *mensuraliste*: cf. MENSURAL *a.* 2 and -IST.]

1. A composer of measurable music.
1901 WOOLDRIDGE *Oxf. Hist. Mus.* I. 132 The figures adopted by the earlier mensuralists.

2. An advocate of a style of plainsong in which the rhythm depends on using notes of fixed length. Also *attrib.*
1905 *Grammar of Plainsong* I. i. 3 The 14th century brought a further falling off in the chant. At that time..the harmonists and mensuralists were making their mark even on the Church's song, and destroying its rhythm. **1911** *Catholic Encycl.* XII. 147/1 The mensuralists.., with Decheurens as their principal representative, hold that the notes of plain chant are subject to strict measurement. **1929** *Music Q.* XV. 18 Even the mensuralist..expressed the opinion that the Gregorian composers probably were not clearly conscious of writing metric arrangements. **1954** *Grove's Dict. Mus.* (ed. 5) VI. 820/1 The Mensuralists, in so far as they agree among themselves, hold that the notes in early medieval manuscripts are not..of approximately equal duration, but that they represent longs and shorts, the longs always being twice the duration of the shorts. **1959** *Times Lit. Suppl.* 13 Feb. 83/4 For more than fifty years many books and articles have been published expounding the 'mensuralist' view with great ingenuity. **1964** E. CARDINE *Is Gregorian Chant Measured Mus.?* 10 The *a priori* mensuralist appears perfectly clearly from the Introduction [of Vollaerts' book] onwards.

mensurate ('mɛnsjʊəreɪt, 'mɛnʃ(j)ʊəreɪt), *v. rare.* [ad. L. *mēnsūrāt-us*, pa. pple. of *mēnsūrāre* to measure, f. *mēnsūra* MEASURE *sb.*: see -ATE[3].] *trans.* To measure; to ascertain the size, extent or quantity of.
1653 R. SANDERS *Physiogn.* 274 Those 9 dimensions by which the longitude of the whole body is mensurated. **1829** LANDOR *Imag. Conv.*, *Epicur.*, *Leont. & Tern.* V. 223 We.. mensurate the fitness and adaptation of one part to another. **1897** *Daily News* 28 Jan. 7/2 Dr. Bertillon, the discoverer of the system of mensurating criminals.

mensuration (mɛnsjʊə'reɪʃən, mɛnʃ(j)ʊə'reɪʃən). [a. late L. *mēnsūrātiōn-em*, f. L. *mēnsūrāre*: see MENSURATE *v.* Cf. F. *mensuration*, Pr. *mensuratio*, Sp. *mensuracion*.]

1. The action, or an act, of measuring (anything).
1571 DIGGES *Pantom.* I. xxi. F iv b, If there happen any error in the situation thereof, great inconuenience maye followe in your mensurations. **1635** SWAN *Spec. M.* (1670) 174 In these mensurations we must not think to come so near the truth as in those things which are subject to sense. **1704** HEARNE *Duct. Hist.* (1714) I. 400 The Waters.. destroying all their Land Marks, new Mensurations were necessary every recess of the River. **1751** JOHNSON *Rambler* No. 103 ¶5. 204 Who can believe that they who first watched the course of the stars, foresaw the use of their discoveries to the facilitation of commerce, or the mensuration of time? **1777** M. CUTLER in *Life*, etc. (1888) I. 64 A map the Doctor had procured from actual mensuration.

b. *Med.* A system of comparative measurement of each side of the chest by which the thoracic cavities of the body may be explored.
1821–34 FORBES *Laennec's Dis. Chest* 409 The..signs afforded by ægophony, percussion, and mensuration. **1877** ROBERTS *Handbk. Med.* (ed. 3) II. 7 Mensuration merely gives more accurate information with regard to form and size.

†**c.** The result of measurement; size as measured. *Obs.*
1675 COCKER *Morals* 50 Then take thy Shadows length; see how much more Its Mensuration exceeds that before.

2. *Math.* That branch of mathematics which gives the rules for ascertaining the lengths of lines, the areas of surfaces, and the volumes of solids.
1704 J. HARRIS *Lex. Techn.* I, *Mensuration*, or Measuring, is to find the Superficial Area, or Solid Content, of all Surfaces and Bodies. **1855** BREWSTER *Life Newton* II. xiv. 5 He studied the mensuration of round solids.
attrib. **1859** GEO. ELIOT *A. Bede* iv, With a little blue bundle over his shoulder, and his 'mensuration book' in his pocket.

Hence **mensu'rational** *a.*, concerned with measuring.
1880 PIAZZI SMYTH in *Nature* 1 July 193/2 Three years' experimenting in mensurational spectroscopy.

mensurative ('mɛnsjʊərətɪv, 'mɛnʃ(j)ʊər-), *a.* [f. MENSURATE *v.* + -IVE.] Capable of measuring; adapted for taking measurements.
1831 CARLYLE *Sart. Res.* III. iii, Our Logical, Mensurative faculty. **1860** J. MARTINEAU *Ess.* (1891) III. 151 Let the mensurative and deductive calculus work out its results.

mensurator ('mɛnsjʊəreɪtər, 'mɛnʃ(j)ʊər-). *rare.* [a. L. *mēnsūrātor*, agent-n. f. *mēnsūrāre*: see MENSURATE *v.*] An apparatus for measuring (*Syd. Soc. Lex.* 1890).
1711 E. WARD *Vulgus Brit.* v. 61 So in they heav'd Time's Mensurator Who never mov'd one Moment a'ter.

†**men'surnal**, *a. Obs.* [irreg. f. L. *mēnsis* month, on the analogy of *diurnal*.] Monthly; from month to month.
1603 SIR C. HEYDON *Jud. Astrol.* xx. 417 We find the effects to answer, annuall, mensurnall, diurnall, and horarie profections. **1659** H. L'ESTRANGE *Alliance Div. Off.* 316 Our Church commands no such mensurnal forbearance.

men's wear, menswear: see MAN *sb.*[1] 23.

mensweare, -eir, obs. forms of MANSWEAR *v.*

mensyn, variant of MENISON *Obs.*

mensyngere, obs. form of MESSENGER.

ment: see MEAN *v.*[1], MENG *v.*, and MINT.

-ment (mənt), *suffix*, forming sbs. Originally occurring in adopted Fr. words in *-ment*, either representing Latin sbs. in *-mentum*, or formed in Fr. on the analogy of these by the addition of the suffix to verb-stems. The Latin *-mentum* was added to verb-stems, and the resulting sbs. sometimes expressed the result or product of the action of the verb, as in *fragmentum* fragment, and sometimes the means or instrument of the action, as in *alimentum* aliment, *ornāmentum* ornament. In late popular Latin, and hence in French, the suffix, while retaining its original functions, came (through sense-development in some of the older words) to be also a formative of nouns of action. In AF. the suffix was still more frequently employed than in continental OF. Of the many words in *-ment* adopted into English from French, some have concrete senses, as *garment*, *habiliment*; the majority are nouns of action, as *abridgement*, *accomplishment*, *commencement*. In most of the instances the Fr. verb has been adopted into English as well as the sb. derived from it. Hence the suffix came to be treated as an English formative. Early examples of its use as appended to native English verb-stems are *onement* (Wyclif's rendering of L. *unio*), and *hangment* (in the Promptorium *c* 1440 given as the equivalent of L. *suspendium*, *suspencio*). In the 16th c. the suffix was very freely added to English verb-stems, not only to those of Romanic etymology (as in *banishment*, *enhancement*, *excitement*), but also to those of native origin; examples of the hybrid formations of this period still surviving in use are *acknowledgement*, *amazement*, *atonement*, *betterment*, *merriment*, *wonderment*. Since the 16th c. many new derivatives in *-ment* have been formed from verbs of obvious French origin. Among verbs of native English etymology, those with the Romanic prefix *en-* (*em-*), and

those with the native prefix *be-*, seem to have given rise to derivatives of this form with especial frequency: examples are *embankment*, *embodiment*, *enlightenment*, *entanglement*; *bedazzlement*, *bedevilment*, *bedragglement*, *bereavement*, *beseechment*, *besetment*, *bewilderment*. Of formations in *-ment* from other native verbs there are few instances since Shakspere's time. It is rarely that the suffix has been appended to any other part of speech than a verb, as in *dreariment*, *funniment*, *oddment*.

The letter *y* (after a consonant) ending a verb is changed into *i* when the suffix is appended, as in *accompaniment*.

‖**mentagra** (mɛn'tægrə). *Path.* [L. (Pliny) *mentagra*, f. *ment-um* chin, after *podagra* gout.] An eruption about the chin, caused by inflammation of the hair follicles of the beard; sycosis.

1802 TURTON *Med. Gloss.*, *Mentagra*, the tetter or ringworm under the chin. **1829** T. BATEMAN *Pract. Synops. Cutan. Dis.* (ed. 7) 404 Sycosis menti .. Mentagra (Plenck). **1842** BURGESS *Man. Dis. Skin* 160 Mentagra is an essentially pustular affection.

mental ('mɛntəl), *a.*¹ and *sb.* [a. F. *mental*, ad. late L. *mentālis*, f. *ment-*, *mens* mind: see -AL¹. Cf. Sp., Pg. *mental*, It. *mentale*.] **A.** *adj.*

1. a. Of or pertaining to the mind.

mental aberration, alienation: see the sbs.

c **1425** HOCCLEVE *Min. Poems* i. 203 But now y see with myn yen mental Thestat of al an-othir world than this. **1606** SHAKS. *Tr. & Cr.* II. iii. 184 'Twixt his mental and his active parts Kingdom'd Achilles in commotion rages. **1667** MILTON *P.L.* XI. 418 The inmost seat of mental sight. **1782** V. KNOX *Ess.* xv. (1819) I. 87 Mental food is also found .. to .. delight the longest, when it is not lusciously sweet. **1802** *Med. Jrnl.* VIII. 356 Avoid excess in eating, drinking, and in mental exertion. *a* **1820** T. BROWN *Lect. Philos. Human Mind* I. 240 We shall now proceed to observe .. the mental phenomena. **1843** MILL *Logic* II. VI. iv. 506 These differences of mental susceptibility .. may be consequences of the previous mental history of those individuals. **1874** J. SULLY *Sensation & Intuition* i. 7 To understand fully all the facts of a single mental history. **1879** LINDSAY *Mind Lower Anim.* I. 56 The intelligence, .. cunning, and other mental qualities of spiders are well known. **1879** W. JAMES *Coll. Ess. & Rev.* (1920) 139 Ever some vital factor of our mental life will rebel and refuse to be dragged the same way with the rest. **1883** F. H. BRADLEY *Princ. Logic* 182 If we say, 'I wish S-P were a fact', .. the judgment .. is concerned with nothing but my mental attitude. **1890** W. JAMES *Princ. Psychol.* I. ii. 48 A most interesting effect of cortical disorder is *mental blindness*. This consists not so much in insensibility to optical impressions, as in *inability to understand them*. *Ibid.* II. xx. 205 Sounds certainly play a far more prominent part in the mental life of the blind than in our own. **1892** ANSTEY *Voces Populi* Ser. II. 98 Too severe a mental strain to be frequently cultivated. **1897** C. H. JUDD tr. *Wundt's Outl. Psychol.* 326 The law of mental growth is as little applicable to all contents of psychical experience as any other psychological law of development. **1900** *Daily News* 1 Aug. 5/7 His mental state was inherited from long-past generations. **1919** L. M. TERMAN *Measurement of Intelligence* i. 6 The large majority of these belong to the moron grade; that is, their mental development will stop somewhere .. between 9 and 12. **1921** B. RUSSELL *Analysis of Mind* i. 25, I should say that images belong only to the mental world. *Ibid.* iii. 68 Since Kant it has been customary to recognize three great divisions of mental phenomena, which are typified by knowledge, desire and feeling. *Ibid.* vi. 109 When you realize that you are glad to meet him, you acquire knowledge of a mental fact. *Ibid.* viii. 141 The sensation, as a mental event, will consist of awareness of the colour. **1932** *Mind* XLI. 137 A man whose whole life had been devoted to thought, and whose intense mental energy came out all the more clearly as his bodily powers declined. **1936** *Discovery* Jan. 22/2 Only in this way is it possible to render intelligible the mental attitude of the Chinese to other peoples. **1949** G. RYLE *Concept of Mind* i. 16, I shall probably be taken to be denying well-known facts about the mental life of human beings. *Ibid.* vi. 163 The argument, then, that mental events are authentic .. must be rejected. **1949** R. G. SIMPSON *Fund. Educ. Psychol.* ii. 22 Growth of mental functions is not as easily traced as that of physical abilities, primarily because mental growth is composed of many characteristics. **1958** K. LOVELL *Educ. Psychol. & Children* x. 127 The effects of training would be transferred from one mental function to another of the same type. **1966** *Guardian* 16 May 3/7 The students at Lancaster confess to a mental block about using nuclear weapons in any circumstances. **1968** J. A. SHAFFER *Philos. of Mind* i. 5 The only evidence we have for the existence of these faculties is the existence of the very mental phenomena they were intended to explain. **1969** C. HODDER-WILLIAMS *98·4* iv. 41 Having a mental block about one's past is all right... Security work makes a virtue out of forgetting things. **1970** K. CAMPBELL *Body & Mind* vi. 113 The new view allows, indeed requires, that mental states be causes. *Ibid.* 125 Mental objects such as images and dreams .. resist being brought within the fold of Materialism. **1973** A. KENNY *Wittgenstein* viii. 142 When we hear a sentence in a language we know, there are mental events—feelings, images, etc.

b. (*a*) ***mental breakdown, deficiency, derangement, disease, disorder, handicap, illness, incapacity, retardation, subnormality***, etc.: general terms indicating temporary or permanent impairments of the mind, due to heredity, birth injury, environment, or accident, which usually need special care; ***mental health***, health of mind as distinct from physical health; ***mental hygiene***, mental health; measures directed towards the preservation or improvement of mental health;

(*b*) ***mental case, defective, incapable, patient***, etc.: persons suffering from some kind of mental impairment; persons under medical care for mental illness;

(*c*) ***mental home, hospital, institution, ward***, etc.: places where those with mental disorders are confined or treated;

(*d*) ***mental nurse, specialist***, etc.: persons specializing in the treatment or care of those with mental disorders.

(*a*) **1794** H. L. PIOZZI *Brit. Synonymy* II. 6 Phrenzy, madness and distraction are the poetical expressions of what we call mental derangement, or disordered spirits, in elegant conversation. **1833** MILL *Lett.* (1910) I. 38, I .. am so far from being in better mental health than yourself, that I need sympathy quite as much. **1839** POE *Fall House of Usher* in *Burton's Gentleman's Mag.* Sept. 150 And now, some days of bitter grief having elapsed, an observable change came over the features of the mental disorder of my friend. **1848** GEO. ELIOT *Let.* *c* 14 May (1954) I. 261 Study *mental hygiene*—take long doses of 'dolce far niente'. **1856** *Educ. of Imbecile* (Home for Invalid & Imbecile Children, Edinburgh) 11 His appearance and bearing gave evidence of great mental deficiency. **1869** GEO. ELIOT *Let.* 21 Sept. (1956) V. 56, I have such a horror of a mental breakdown. **1902** B. RUSSELL *Let.* in A. Wood *B. Russell* (1957) viii. 79 Since I finished my book, I have devoted myself to what you [*sc.* Beatrice Webb] would call mental hygiene, with good results so far. Beyond reading a mathematical MS. of Whitehead's, I have done no work for the last fortnight, but have spent my whole days out of doors basking in the return of summer. **1904** *Lancet* 27 Aug. 598/2 Scientific views regarding mental disease have .. been undergoing great changes. *Ibid.* 17 Sept. 838/1 Those cases of mental incapacity arising from incipient or oncoming insanity. **1907** [see BREAK-DOWN 1 c]. **1908** *Lancet* 12 Sept. 812/2 It was difficult .. to secure effective treatment for early undeveloped cases of mental disorder. **1913** *Act 3 & 4 Geo. V* c. 28 (*title*) Mental Deficiency Act. **1914** W. B. DRUMMOND tr. *Binet & Simon's Mentally Defective Children* ii. 16 Some heads of schools .. have fixed to almost a year the mental retardation of the child as compared with normal children of the same age. **1921** C. BURT *Mental & Scholastic Tests* ii. 163 The central problem of this memorandum—the line of demarcation for mental deficiency. **1946** C. P. BLACKER (*title*) Neurosis and the mental health services. **1946** *Amer. Jrnl. Psychiatry* CIII. 323/1 At the present time it cannot be said that we *cure* any of the more important and more fixed mental diseases. **1957** S. H. KRAINES *Mental Depressions* xv. 422 The goal of such mental hygiene is to remove and correct those unhealthy attitudes which add to the physically based tension. **1960** *Guardian* 16 Mar. 4/6 The most important change in terminology made by the new Act [*sc.* Mental Health Act, 1959] is that the expressions 'mental deficiency' and 'mental defectives' should be abolished... 'Mental disorder' is introduced as a new term covering all forms of mental ill health. **1962** E. CLEAVER in A. Dundes *Mother Wit* (1973) 10/2 The continued application of these judgments is the cause of an untold amount of mental illness and frustration. **1964** J. TIZARD *Community Services for Mentally Handicapped* I. ii. 18 There is a statutory obligation placed upon the local authorities in Britain to ascertain cases of mental subnormality .. and to make provision for them. **1970** 'T. COE' *Wax Apple* (1973) vi. 50, I automatically *had* felt superior. After all, I'd never had a mental breakdown. **1970** L. J. KARMEL *Measurement & Evaluation in School* III. vii. 182 Some states will use 75 or even 80 as the cut-off point for mental retardation. **1971** *Rand Daily Mail* 4 Sept. 2/1 Nothing he had heard in court suggested that Muller has ever had a mental disorder. **1971** *Guardian* 18 Oct. 10/3 Mental illness is an *illness* needing therapeutic treatment... Mental handicap .. is an innate condition for which there is no cure. **1972** R. QUILTY *Tenth Session* 58 A lifetime in mental-health nursing. **1973** *Black World* May 7/1 A crucial matter here is the role The Black Church can play in our mental hygiene and group advancement. **1974** *Guardian* 28 Jan. 6/7 The patient is no longer suffering from mental illness and .. [should] be discharged.

(*b*) **1899** *Pop. Sci. Monthly* Apr. 747 (*title*) Mental defectives and social welfare. **1904** *Lancet* 17 Sept. 838/1 The Home Secretary .. has at last been impressed with the total inadequacy of the provision made for .. mental incapables. **1908** *Ibid.* 12 Sept. 813/2 Dr. W. C. S. Clapham .. had many suspected mental cases sent to his out-patient department. **1913** E. MEYNELL *Life F. Thompson* 279 Many a time I've asked him to have his bit of lunch with me and the other 'mental'—O yes, she's a mental case, as I may have told you. **1922** W. R. INGE in *Edin. Rev.* July 34 The Eugenics Education Society .. actively supported the Act for the compulsory segregation of mental defectives. **1938** *Brit. Jrnl. Psychol.* July 37 The implications of Wiersma's results obtained from mental patients have therefore been shown to hold for normal subjects. **1944** H. G. WELLS *'42 to '44* 182 The highly bred dogs are mostly physical and mental defectives. **1970** 'T. COE' *Wax Apple* (1973) iv. 33 The majority of mental patients who have been hospitalized once will be hospitalized several times more. **1973** 'D. SHANNON' *No Holiday for Crime* (1974) iv. 61 If you're going to say a mental patient, I don't think it was that kind of hospital.

(*c*) **1898** H. MORTEN *Compl. Syst. Nursing* 249 A year's training in a general hospital, and two years' training in a mental hospital, would be the proper scheme to turn out the best mental nurse. **1908** *Lancet* 26 Dec. 1943/1 (*heading*) Mental observation wards in Glasgow Parish Hospital. **1928** *Daily Mail* 25 July 8/3 One in ten of the people who reach the age of 40 in the State of New York will already have passed some time in a mental home or institution. **1932** KIPLING *Limits & Renewals* 151 They pushed him into a Mental Home, And that is like the grave. **1958** 'N. SHUTE' *Rainbow & Rose* v. 182 He had three young children and disliked the thought of bringing them up in the surroundings of a mental home. **1964** *Penguin Bk. Austral. Ballads* 18 The discharged mental-hospital patient .. with a certificate to *prove* that he was sane. **1970** 'T. COE' *Wax Apple* (1973) ii. 17 The Midway was a haven for people recently out of mental institutions. **1972** R. BLOCH *Night-World* (1974) viii. 49 The mental wards were like a prison, only worse. **1974** N. FREELING *Dressing of Diamond* 74 We're looking at every affair .. linked to mental homes, prison releases .. psychopathic anything. **1974** *Guardian* 24 Jan. 15/8 The 'oriental girl' .. had been led down from her ledge and taken off to mental hospital.

(*d*) **1898** [see sense 1 b (*c*) above]. **1922** *Lancet* 5 Aug. 290/1 The two duties of mental nurses. **1932** *Daily Tel.* 25 Apr. 9/3 Dr. Caton, the eminent mental specialist, .. has completed his findings of the state of Lt. Massie's mind at the time.

c. *colloq.* Mentally disordered or defective. Also in phr. ***to go mental***, to become mentally disordered.

1927 D. L. SAYERS *Unnatural Death* iv. 41, I gather she was a little queer towards the end—a bit mental, I think you people [*sc.* nurses] call it? **1930** J. B. PRIESTLEY *Angel Pavement* ii. 68, I don't care if Mr. Dersingham goes mental, we're going to be lucky. **1958** 'N. SHUTE' *Rainbow & Rose* iv. 151 Everybody goes a bit mental in a war. **1959** S. GIBBONS *Pink Front Door* iv. 48 They had the same round eyes, only his hadn't got that almost mental look. **1973** 'J. PATRICK' *Glasgow Gang Observed* iii. 34 They must be mental... Shit-bags the lot o' them. **1974** N. FREELING *Dressing of Diamond* 65 There's somebody mental floating about.

2. Carried on or performed by the mind; taking place in the mind. ***mental arithmetic***: the art of performing arithmetical operations within the mind, without the use of written figures or other visible symbols. ***mental reservation***: see RESERVATION.

1526 *Pilgr. Perf.* (W. de W. 1531) 159 b, To .. use yᵉ maner of prayer, whether it be mentall or vocall in yᵉ whiche he fyndeth moost swetnes. **1651** HOBBES *Leviath.* I. iii. 8 By Consequence, .. I understand that succession of one Thought to another, which is called Mentall Discourse. **1676** LOCKE *Jrnl.* 26 Aug. in *Ess. Law Nature* (1954) 278 The thing to be believed was a proper object of faith and not of sense, a mental proposition, viz. that the God of the three children was the true God. **1809–10** COLERIDGE *Friend* (1865) 12 A lazy half-attention amounts to a mental yawn. **1839** J. P. FROST (*title*) A course of mental arithmetic, in three parts. **1843** MILL *Logic* I. I. iii. 66 His mental image .. of the sun, and his idea of God, are thoughts. **1850** McCOSH *Div. Gov.* III. i. (1874) 287 The mental process .. by which the distinction between vice and virtue is observed. **1854** DICKENS *Hard T.* I. ix, She would burst into tears on being required (by the mental process) immediately to name the cost of two hundred and forty-seven muslin caps at fourteenpence halfpenny. **1865** —— *Exam. Hamilton's Philos.* vi. 72 The belief is without understanding, for we form no mental picture of what we believe. *c* **1873** W. JAMES in R. B. Perry *Tht. & Char. W. James* (1935) I. 499 Under each and all of these formulations lurks the same mental act, that of insisting that things do not exist, so to speak, only once, but are in a manner duplicated. **1880** —— *Coll. Ess. & Rev.* (1920) 161 This complex aggregate of afferent feelings .. renders absolutely precise and distinctive our mental image of the exact strength of movement to be made. **1882** L. STEPHEN *Sci. of Ethics* vi. 231 And thus the same words may call up the mental images which would be generated in the most and in the least sympathetic witness. **1889** Mental arithmetic [see GUESSING *vbl. sb.*]. **1921** B. RUSSELL *Analysis of Mind* i. 19 The whole question of the relation of mental occurrences to objects grows very complicated. *Ibid.* vi. 109 'Introspection' is supposed to furnish data for knowledge of our mental processes. **1925** J. RIVIERE et al. tr. *Freud's Coll. Papers* IV. 14 In the psychology which is founded on psycho-analysis we have accustomed ourselves to take as our starting-point the unconscious mental processes. **1932** *Mind* XLI. 37 There are four corresponding 'mental experiences' (παθήματα ἐν τῇ ψυχῇ, 511 D). **1935** C. BURT *Subnormal Mind* i. 41 The reading test and the mental arithmetic test .. will yield a fair estimate of the child's educational level. **1944** J. S. HUXLEY *On Living in Revolution* iv. 56 The deliberate 'mental operation' of psycho-analysis or other form of psychotherapy. **1949** G. RYLE *Concept of Mind* 8 The logical categories in terms of which the concepts of mental .. operations have been co-ordinated have been wrongly selected. *Ibid.* vii. 200 Stomach-aches .. have physiological attachments which threaten to sully the purity of the brook of mental experiences. *Ibid.* viii. 254 In short, there are no such objects as mental pictures. **1963** R. CARNAP in P. A. Schilpp *Philos. R. Carnap* 8 All mental processes are intimately connected with the brain. **1971** P. A. CHILTON tr. *Piaget & Inhelder's Mental Imagery in Child* p. xiii, Having attempted to analyse some of the characteristics of perceptual development, it was necessary to go on to tackle the question of the evolution of mental images. **1972** W. C. COE *Challenges Personal Adjustment* iv. 76 Mental telepathy is the transfer of thought from one person to another without overt communication.

3. Relating to the mind as an object of study; concerned with the phenomena of mind.

a **1820** T. BROWN *Lect. Philos. Human Mind* I. 8 There is, in short, a science that may be termed *mental physiology*. **1828** G. PAYNE (*title*) Elements of Mental and Moral Science. **1831** T. C. UPHAM (*title*) Elements of Mental Philosophy. **1860** J. MARTINEAU *Ess.* (1866) I. 248 Mental Science is Self-knowledge.

¶**4.** Characterized by the possession of mind, intellectual. *rare.*

1840 B. E. HILL *Pinch—of Snuff* 96 Platonically enamoured of the beauteous, mental, and excellent wife to a very jealous moralist.

5. Special collocations: **mental age**, the degree of mental development of a person, expressed as the age at which a similar level is attained by an average person; **mental chemistry** *Psychol.*, J. S. Mill's term for the psychological processes by which complex ideas, sensations, etc., are formed from an aggregate of simple ones; **mental cruelty**, conduct which inflicts suffering on the mind of another person, esp. *U.S.* as constituting grounds for legal separation or divorce; **mental healing**, healing effected solely

by the mind of the healer; so ***mental healer***; **mental ratio** = *intelligence quotient* (s.v. INTELLIGENCE *sb.* 8); **mental set**, the set (SET *sb.*^{1} 12) or predisposition of the mind which governs reactions to stimuli; **mental test** = *intelligence test*; so ***mental tester***, ***testing***; **mental year**, the average mental attainment of each year of growth, used as a unit of measurement of mental development.

1912 *Pedagogical Seminary* XIX. 189 Table I. *Mental Ages..showing the chronological and mental age distribution of the two thousand public school children graded by the Binet tests. **1919** L. M. TERMAN *Measurement of Intelligence* iii. 40 A mentally defective child of 9 years may have a 'mental age' of only 4 years, or a young genius of 9 years may have a mental age of 12 or 13 years. **1937** 'M. INNES' *Hamlet, Revenge!* III. iii. 259 His mental age's about eight. **1972** J. AIKEN *Died on Rainy Sunday* 88 Really Ellie *is* a child, she thought; in some ways her mental age can't be more than twelve or thirteen. **1843** MILL *Logic* II. VI. iv. 503 These therefore are cases of *mental chemistry: in which it is proper to say that the simple ideas generate, rather than that they compose, the complex ones. **1890** W. JAMES *Princ. Psychol.* II. xx. 202 Discrimination, association, [etc.]..are quite capable of giving us all the space-perceptions we have so far studied, without the aid of any mysterious 'mental chemistry'. **1929** W. McDOUGALL *Mod. Materialism* v. 119 J. S. Mill's use of the expression 'mental chemistry' had suggested some analogy between such mental and such physical syntheses. **1948** R. S. WOODWORTH *Contemp. Schools Psychol.* (ed. 2) iii. 44 This idea of a 'mental chemistry' reappeared from time to time in later psychological theories. **1928** *Harper's Mag.* July 159/1 The Nevada laws..necessitate a minimum of fraud... The judges demand very slight evidence to prove *mental cruelty. A woman may obtain her freedom on the ground that her husband has..told her to go to hell once too often. **1936** M. ALLINGHAM *Flowers for Judge* vii. 125 Not a care in the world except Mr. Brande's neglect and mental cruelty to her. **1967** R. S. MASTER *Elem. Psychiatry* xx. 398 The petitioner has to prove..that the spouse can differentiate between right and wrong and understand the nature of the mental cruelty. **1968** *Globe & Mail* (Toronto) 17 Feb. 29/1 The third wife of wealthy playboy John Jacob Astor III was granted a divorce yesterday on grounds of mental cruelty. **1920** in WEBSTER, *Mental healer. **1957** O. NASH *You can't get there from Here* 67 The characters in many of our popular songs are fair game for the nearest mental healer. **1970** T. S. SZASZ *Ideology & Insanity* (1973) xiii. 240 The precise activities of the various 'mental healers' are rarely defined by their practitioners. **1888** L. E. WHIPPLE (*title*) *Mental healing. **1902** W. JAMES *Varieties Relig. Experience* iv. 121 Their savage and primitive philosophy of mental healing. **1924** GALSWORTHY *White Monkey* I. xii. 100 No need of any of these vitamins, false teeth, mental healing. **1921** C. BURT *Mental & Scholastic Tests* ii. 151 If a child's mental age be divided by his chronological age, the quotient will state what fraction of ability the child actually possesses... This fraction may be termed..the child's 'intelligence quotient' or, more euphoniously.., his '*mental ratio'. **1927** A. HUXLEY *Proper Stud.* 67 A mental ratio is obtained by dividing the child's mental by his chronological age. **1934** *Brit. Jrnl. Psychol.* Jan. 312 Not all candidates with high mental ratios succeed. **1913** E. L. THORNDIKE *Educ. Psychol.* II. xii. 356 In the case of alternative systems of bonds there is then often an inhibition for a time, reducing to zero as the two systems of bonds get organized in connection with two systems of *mental sets. **1922** R. S. WOODWORTH *Psychol.* iv. 72 Much used also are 'adjustment' and 'mental set', the idea here being to liken the individual to an adjustable machine which can be set for one or another set of work. **1934** H. C. WARREN *Dict. Psychol.* 164/2 *Mental set*,..the attitude or determination of an individual before receiving an expected stimulus or with reference to a problem or general situation. **1953** *Jrnl. Exper. Psychol.* XLVI. 50 The aspect of directed thinking commonly called 'mental set'. **1963** J. LYONS *Structural Semantics* ii. 35 He [*sc.* the hearer] must be thought of as being in a certain state of 'expectancy' (or 'mental set'), in which he is disposed to hear certain units rather than others. **1890** J. M. CATTELL in *Mind* XV. 373 Psychology cannot attain the certainty and exactness of the physical sciences, unless it rests on a foundation of experiment and measurement. A step in this direction could be made by applying a series of *mental tests and measurements to a large number of individuals. **1934** H. C. WARREN *Dict. Psychol.* 165/1 Mental test. **1958** M. ARGYLE *Relig. Behaviour* vi. 58 A child's mental age is the average chronological age of children showing the same degree of intelligence, as measured by mental tests. **1972** L. S. HEARNSHAW in Cox & Dyson *20th-Cent. Mind* I. vii. 234 Francis Galton..attempted..to devise techniques for measuring intelligence. These techniques were christened 'mental tests' by the American psychologist, J. M. Cattell, in 1890. **1952** *Brit. Jrnl. Psychol.* Feb. 23 When the subjects are in full sympathy..but the *mental tester rarely has such a favourable situation. **1959** *Chambers's Encycl.* XII. 655/1 *Mental testing began with the testing of intelligence (i.e. of general intellectual capacity). **1921** C. BURT *Mental & Scholastic Tests* ii. 147 The estimate for the intelligence of every child has been converted into terms of *mental years. **1942** F. J. SCHONELL *Backwardness in Basic Subjects* iv. 74 Rene C. was, in arithmetic, almost two mental years ahead of her achievements in reading.

B. *sb.* †**a.** *pl. nonce-use.* Intellectual faculties. *Obs.* †**b.** *pl. nonce-use.* Mental reservations. *Obs.*

1676 *Phil. Trans.* XI. 554 The intrinsick mentals or intellectuals of Mankind. **1712** ARBUTHNOT *John Bull* IV. iv, Hast thou laid aside all thy equivocals and mentals in this case?

c. *colloq.* A mentally-deranged person; a mental patient.

1913 [see 1 b (*b*) above]. **1937** PARTRIDGE *Dict. Slang* 517/1 *Mental*, a person mentally deranged, mad. **1942** BERREY & VAN DEN BARK *Amer. Thes. Slang* §529/16 Mental, nut, psycho, psychot, *a psychopathic case.* **1973** F. DE FELITTA *Oktoberfest* (1974) xiv. 162 'What's to prevent him from going?' 'He is a mental.'

mental ('mɛntəl), *a.*^{2} [a. F. *mental*, f. L. *mentum* chin: see -AL^1.] Pertaining to the chin.

1727 BAILEY vol. II, *Mental*, belonging to the Chin. **1829** BELL *Anat. & Physiol.* I. 159 The second hole in the lower jaw..is named the mental hole. **1836–9** *Todd's Cycl. Anat.* II. 213/2 This line terminates below in a triangular eminence (the mental process). **1866** HUXLEY in *Preh. Rem. Caithn.* 91 The lower jaw has a well developed mental prominence.

b. *Zool.* Pertaining to or situated on the mentum.

1853 BAIRD & GIRARD *Catal. N. Amer. Reptiles* Introd. 7 The inframaxillary or mental scutellæ or shields. **1855** GOSSE in *Phil. Trans.* CXLVI. 424, I shall call..the anterior termination of the venter, the mental edge. **1890** COUES *Field & Gen. Ornithol.* II. 144 Mental or gular lines.

mentalism ('mɛntəlɪz(ə)m). *rare.* [f. MENTAL *a.*^{1} + -ISM.]

1. A process of the nature of mental action.

1874 MAUDSLEY *Mental Dis.* vii. 243 Deranged nervous function—a deranged mentalism, if I may be permitted to coin such a word—of an epileptic or allied nature. **1885** McCOOK *Tenants of an Old Farm* 134 An order of mentalism which seems to differ from human thinking more in degree than in kind.

2. (See quot. *a* 1900.) Esp. the theory that physical and physiological phenomena are ultimately only explicable in terms of a creative and interpretative mind.

a **1900** SIDGWICK in *Mind* (1901) Jan. 20 It may be held broadly that 'matter in ultimate analysis is a mode of mind or consciousness', without raising the question of a conscious self or subject... Such view I think is often called Idealism. I propose to label it 'Mentalism' in broad antithesis to 'Materialism'. If, again, the 'Mentalist's' ontology expressly excludes the notion of self or subject.. then perhaps we may designate him as an atomistic Mentalist. **1917** A. S. PRINGLE-PATTISON *Idea of God* xx. 392 The position is open..to the general objections which have been brought against Monadism and Mentalism. **1932** *Times Lit. Suppl.* 28 Apr. 314/4 Scientists who repudiate mechanism only to involve themselves in thoroughpaced mentalism. **1954** *Essays in Crit.* IV. 235 But MacNeice has tried mentalism and so raged against it..that he nearly knocked his brains out with rhyme. Therefore we must settle for monadism. **1964** *Language* XL. 124 Linguists who conceive of their science as a discipline..often pride themselves on their freedom from mentalism. But freedom from mentalism is an inherent feature of the taxonomic conception of linguistics. **1972** *Ibid.* XLVIII. 418 Writing grammars..was motivated for Boas by a theoretical concern, a 'mentalism' derived partly from the German tradition of Herder, Humboldt, [etc.]. **1973** *Word 1970* XXVI. 93 We can arrive at a knowledge of the *signifié* independently of the particular *signifiant* under study, yet still avoid mentalism.

mentalist ('mɛntəlɪst). [f. MENTAL *a.*^{1} + -IST.]

1. *rare.* In nonce-uses: **a.** One whose tastes are for mental rather than for material pleasures. **b.** One whose artistic aim is the expression of thought.

1790 CATH. GRAHAM *Lett. Educ.* 75 The mentalist, whose enjoyments depend more on those delights, which are adapted to soothe his imagination,..will find [etc.]. **1840** *Blackw. Mag.* XLVIII. 278 A purpose which is distinct both from that of the mentalists and the materialists of the [*sc.* painting] art.

2. One who maintains the doctrine of 'mentalism'. Also *attrib.* or as *adj.*

a **1900** [see MENTALISM 2]. **1927** B. RUSSELL *Outl. Philos.* xxvii. 303 Idealists in the technical sense, or mentalists, as Dr. Broad more appropriately calls them. **1933** L. BLOOMFIELD *Lang.* ix. 142 For the mentalist, language is the expression of ideas, feelings, or volition. **1966** *Philos.* XLI. 141 We must give a sense to this mentalist and substance vocabulary. **1972** *Language* XLVIII. 418 A mentalist tradition more recent than the 'Cartesian'.

mentalistic (mɛntəˈlɪstɪk), *a.* [f. MENTALIST + -IC.] **1.** Of or pertaining to the processes of the mind or to processes of a similar nature. *rare.*

1962 *Listener* 29 Mar. 568/3 Other practitioners may turn it [*sc.* treatment of insanity] into a purely mentalistic and verbal technique, letting slip all the gains which psychoanalysis has achieved by its attention to physical processes.

2. Of or pertaining to mentalism (sense 2). Hence **mentaˈlistically** *adv.*

1917 A. S. PRINGLE-PATTISON *Idea of God* x. 191, I feel it to be important..to free the position I am defending from any supposed dependence on the Mentalistic doctrines which have often been used to support it. **1925** C. D. BROAD *Mind & its Place* xiv. 611, I class these two alternatives together under the name of 'Mentalistic Neutralism'. **1927** *Mod. Philology* Nov. 225 This theory..makes the hitherto otiose mentalistic factors play an actual part in linguistic change. **1950** D. JONES *Phoneme* vii. 23 This is evidence in favour of a mentalistic view of the phoneme. **1965** N. CHOMSKY *Aspects of Theory of Syntax* i. 4 Hence, in the technical sense, linguistic theory is mentalistic, since it is concerned with discovering a mental reality underlying actual behavior. **1967** [see *identity theorist* (IDENTITY 10 b)]. **1971** D. CRYSTAL *Ling.* 95 Very little of language..can be tested in the same way as material objects.., as mentalistically-inclined linguists have been quick to point out. **1973** *Word 1970* XXVI. 150 The chapter on Syntax gives a traditional mentalistic statement of the function of the cases and moods.

mentality (mɛnˈtælɪtɪ). [f. MENTAL *a.*^{1} + -ITY.]

1. That which is of the nature of mind or of mental action.

1691 BAXTER *Rep. Beverley* 15 But tell us whether it be only a Spiritual Mentality, superangelical, or the Soul and Body of a Man at his Incarnation. **1890** A. R. WALLACE in *Nature* 24 July 291 An insect's very limited mentality. **1899** GRIFFITH-JONES *Ascent thro. Christ* III. iii. 385 There is a vast store of mentality even in the higher animals which has not yet been brought to perfection.

2. Intellectual quality, intellectuality.

1856 EMERSON *Eng. Traits* xiv. *Lit.* Wks. (Bohn) II. 104 Hudibras has the same hard mentality. **1900** G. SANTAYANA *Poetry & Relig.* 258 Pope..is too intellectual and has an excess of mentality.

3. Mental character or disposition; outlook; kind or degree of intelligence.

1895 *Funk's Stand. Dict.*, *Mentality*..cast or habit of mind. **1911** BEERBOHM *Zuleika D.* viii. 132 Your words show up your good heart... Your mentality, too, is bully, as we all predicate. **1922** JOYCE *Ulysses* 132, I speak the tongue of a race the acme of whose mentality is the maxim: time is money. **1926** FOWLER *Mod. Eng. Usage* 348/1 'The mentality of the politician is a constant source of amazement to the engineer.' Twenty years ago, no-one would have written that. **1931** L. WATT *Future of Capitalism* ii. 23 It is useless to pretend that there will be anything but hostility between the partners in industry so long as this mentality persists. **1958** R. F. C. HULL tr. *Jung's Coll. Works* XI. vii. 480 Something of the kind happens as soon as we are confronted with the Eastern mentality.

mentalization (ˌmɛntəlaɪˈzeɪʃən). [Formed as next + -ATION.] Mental action or process.

1883 E. C. MANN *Psychol. Med.* 101 (Cent.) Previous to the establishment of complete delirium or delusions there may be traced deviations from healthy mentalization.

mentalize ('mɛntəlaɪz), *v.* [f. MENTAL *a.*^{1} + -IZE.] **a.** *trans.* To develop or cultivate mentally. **b.** To stimulate the mind. *nonce-use.* **c.** To realize mentally or invest with mental qualities. *nonce-use.* So **'mentalized** *ppl. a.*, **'mentalizing** *vbl. sb.*

1807 T. CAMPBELL *Let.* 6 July in W. Beattie *Life & Lett. T. Campbell* (1849) II. iv. 110, I sometimes call on the satirical Gifford..who *mentalises* me for a few moments, but the impression lasts too short. **1837** H. SMITH *Let.* 2 Oct. in A. Mathews *Mem. Charles Mathews* (1839) IV. xviii. 447 While others satisfied themselves with endeavouring to *embody* their originals, he made it his study to *mentalize* them. I am obliged to coin a word, but my meaning is, that while he surpassed all competitors in the mere mimicry of externals, he was *unique* in the subtlety, acuteness, and truth with which he could copy the *mind* of his prototype. **1885** G. S. HALL in *N. Amer. Rev.* Feb. 145 The only thing that can ever undermine our school system in popular support is a suspicion that it does not moralize as well as mentalize children. **1927** D. H. LAWRENCE *Let.* 28 May (1962) II. 981 One emerges with a body all right—but a different one, perhaps, not so mentalised. **1935** W. DE LA MARE *Early One Morning* II. 404 Seeming stupidity may be due to a highly individualised way of mentalizing things. **1936** *Downside Rev.* LIV. 551 The body continues to produce its own characteristic actions, but along with these it produces a new action—thought. Body becomes mind, or rather mentalised. **1936** J. R. KANTOR *Objective Psychol. Gram.* v. 66 We react to printed words..as though they were words heard in conversation... It is precisely the mentalizing procedure that produces the confusion of responses to language activity. **1973** D. RAMSAY *Deadly Discretion* 76 Want to try mentalizing?.. First empty your mind... Then wait for me to send you the message.

mentally ('mɛntəlɪ), *adv.* [f. MENTAL *a.*^{1} + -LY^2.] **a.** In the mind, by a mental operation; often with reference to unuttered thoughts, resolves, judgements, etc. **b.** As regards the mind.

1661 BOYLE *Physiol. Ess.* (1679) 208 There is no assignable portion of matter so minute that it may not at least, Mentally, (to borrow a School term) be further divided. **1688** —— *Final Causes Nat. Things* iv. 129 If they be so [*i.e.* useful to us] in any Measure (as for example Mentally) they are So, for what we know, as much as He design'd they should be. **1838** LYTTON *Alice* II. ii, Such, mentally, morally, and physically, was the Reverend Charles Merton. **1848** RIMBAULT *Pianoforte* 31 When a passage is acquired.. it should then be counted mentally, that is, silently. **1879** LINDSAY *Mind Lower Anim.* I. 40 Such animals must be considered mentally and morally the superiors of the human infant and child. **1885** *Law Times* LXXVIII. 296/1 He is not mentally competent to form and express a wish for an inquiry before a jury. **1892** ANSTEY *Voces Populi* Ser. II. 7 John..wonders mentally if he can get away in time. **1894** *Psychol. Rev.* I. 425 It is..the mission of the mentally defective to give us..object lessons in psychology. **1934** H. S. SULLIVAN in H. S. Perry *Fusion of Psychiatry & Social Sci.* (1964) 9 Disorder of the emotional life of the mentally deranged is too striking to be ignored. **1964** J. TIZARD (*title*) Community services for the mentally handicapped. **1970** L. J. KARMEL *Measurement & Evaluation in School* III. vii. 182 The lowest 2 per cent of the population..could be justifiably described as mentally defective.

mentation (mɛnˈteɪʃən). [f. L. *ment-*, *mens* mind + -ATION.] Mental action, esp. as attributed to the agency of the brain or other nervous organ; also, a product of 'mentation', a state of mind.

1850 KINGSLEY *Alton Locke* iv, The cerebration of each in the prophetic sacrament of the yet undeveloped possibilities of his mentation. **1876** MAUDSLEY *Physiol. of Mind* ii. 133 That substratum of mentality, which is beneath mentation, or conscious mental function. **1900** *Contemp. Rev.* Oct. 537 Successive mental images, successive 'mentations' if I may be allowed to introduce a most useful word, made in America. **1903** *Dublin Rev.* Oct. 269 *note*, Subliminal mentation is oftenest exhibited in literary composition.

mente: see MEAN *v.*^{1} (pa. t. and pple.) and MINT.

mentel, obs. form of MANTLE.

†**'mentery.** *Obs.* Also 5 -erye, -irye. [a. F. *menterie*, f. OF. *mentere*, *menteur* liar, f. *mentir*:—L. *mentīri* to lie: see -ERY.] Lying.

c **1430** *Pilgr. Lyf Manhode* III. xxix. (1869) 151 Bi menterye [Fr. orig. *menterie*] is also periurement born and engendred. *Ibid.* xxx. 152 Mentirye. **1592** G. HARVEY *Four Lett.* Sonn. xix, Lowd Mentery small confutation needes.

‖**mentha** ('mɛnθə). *Bot.* [L., ad. Gr. μίνθη: see MINT *sb.*] A genus of fragrant herbaceous plants of the family *Labiatæ*; a plant of this genus. (The popular name of the genus is MINT.)

1846 *Penny Cycl.* Suppl. II. 272/1 The odour of the leaves, somewhat resembling a mentha.

b. ***mentha camphor*** = MENTHOL (Webster 1902).

menthene ('mɛnθiːn). *Chem.* [a. G. *menthen*, F. *menthène*, f. L. *mentha* mint: see -ENE.] A liquid hydro-carbon obtained from peppermint oil.

1838 *Brit. Ann.* (ed. R. D. Thomson) 359 Menthene.—Walter obtained this substance by distilling crystals of essence of mint over chloride of calcium. **1849** KANE *Elem. Chem.* (ed. 2) 866 Menthen.

menthol ('mɛnθɒl). *Chem.* [a. G. *menthol* (Oppenheim 1861, in *Ann. der Chem. u. Pharm.* CXX. 352), f. L. *mentha* mint: see -OL.] A crystalline camphor-like substance obtained by cooling various mint-oils, esp. oil of peppermint. ***menthol cigarette***: a cigarette flavoured with menthol. ***menthol cone*** or ***pencil***: an appliance for the relief of facial neuralgia, consisting of a conical piece of mixed menthol and spermaceti, which is rubbed on the part affected.

1876 HARLEY *Mat. Med.* 473 Oil of Peppermint deposits hexagonal crystals of menthol or peppermint camphor. **1888** *Pall Mall G.* 30 June 5/1 Menthol cones. **1889** *Ibid.* 5 July 2/1 Menthol and pyrine are sometimes useful for headaches. **1891** F. P. FOSTER *Med. Dict.* III. 2281 Menthol Pencil. **1897** *Allbutt's Syst. Med.* IV. 860 Locally a menthol spray may be used. **1952** M. TRIPP *Faith is Windsock* i. 10 He threw a packet of American menthol cigarettes across the hut. **1962** L. DEIGHTON *Ipcress File* xx. 131 She offered me one of those menthol cigarettes that taste like paint remover. **1969** O. HESKY *Sequin Syndicate* xi. 114 She..might have been an advertisement for some brand of menthol cigarette.

mentholated ('mɛnθəleɪtɪd), *ppl. a.* [f. MENTHOL + -ATE³ + -ED¹.] Treated or impregnated with menthol; containing menthol.

1933 *Tobacco World* 1 May 13 (Advt.), And now say 'hello' to KOOL, B & W's mild mentholated new cigarette. **1962** P. MOYES *Death on Agenda* ix. 149 He was lighting up yet another mentholated cigarette. **1970** G. GREER *Female Eunuch* 259 One vaginal deodorant is..flavoured with peppermint... Others are mentholated.

menthone ('mɛnθəʊn). *Chem.* [f. L. *menth-a* mint + -ONE.]

3-Methyl-6-isopropylcyclohexanone, $C_{10}H_{18}O$, an optically active cyclic ketone whose lævorotatory form is a liquid with an odour of peppermint and occurs in American peppermint, geranium, and other oils.

1889 ROSCOE & SCHORLEMMER *Treat. Chem.* III. v. 470 Menthone, $C_{10}H_{18}O$, is formed by heating menthol with sulphuric acid and potassium bichromate. **1929** *Org. Syntheses* IX. 53, *l*-Menthone can be prepared by the oxidation of rhodinol with a chromic-sulphuric acid mixture. **1969** W. TEMPLETON *Introd. Chem. Terpenoids & Steroids* iii. 53 Menthone..is found in oils of peppermint, geranium and pennyroyal, mainly in its (–)-form. **1970** [see *isovaleraldehyde* (ISO- b)].

menticide ('mɛntɪsaɪd). [f. L. *menti-*, *mens* mind + -CIDE 2.] A word coined by J. A. M. Meerloo to designate the undermining or destruction of a person's mind or will by 'psychological intervention and judicial perversion'; also in extended use. Cf. BRAINWASHING.

1951 J. A. M. MEERLOO in *Amer. Jrnl. Psychiatry* Feb. 595/1 Such an organized system of psychological intervention and judicial perversion, in which a powerful tyrant synthetically injects his own thoughts and words into the minds and mouths of the victims he plans to destroy by mock trial, may well be called menticide. **1957** —— *Mental Seduction & Menticide* Pref., The modern words 'brainwashing', 'thought-control', and 'menticide' serve to provide some indication of the..methods by which man's integrity can be violated. **1973** *Black Panther* 20 Oct. 17/1 No treatise on prisons in 1973 can possibly be complete and up-to-date without dealing with the scientifically modernized versions of these conditions and practices as they are manifested in the forms of menticide and genocide.

menticultural (ˌmɛntɪ'kʌltjʊərəl), *a. rare.* [f. next + -AL¹.] Relating to the cultivation of the mind.

1830 MAUNDER *Treas. Knowl.* I, *Menticultural*, cultivating the mind. **1842** PUNSHON in *Life* (1887) 34, I have..established a Menticultural Society in Sunderland. **1893** G. HUNTINGTON in *Advance* (Chicago) 19 Oct., A sort of menticultural prize-animal.

menticulture ('mɛntɪkʌltjʊə(r)). [f. L. *menti-*, *mens* mind + *cultūra* CULTURE, after *agriculture*.] The cultivation of the mind.

1830 MAUNDER *Treas. Knowl.* I, *Menticulture*, improvement of the mind. **1895** HOR. FLETCHER (*title*) Menticulture or the A-B-C of true living.

men'tiferous, *a.* [Formed as prec. + -FEROUS.] Proposed as the epithet of an imagined 'ether' in which 'thought-waves' are propagated.

1884 GURNEY & MYERS in *Proc. Soc. Psych. Research* I. VI. 135 The transformation [by Dr. Maudsley] of 'brain-wave' into the more ambitious 'mentiferous ether'.

†**'mentiform**, *a. Obs.* [f. L. *menti-*, *mens* mind + -FORM.] Resembling the mind.

1721 BELLAMY *Th. Trinity* 31 The Spirit is mentiform, or like the Son i.e. the Understanding from which he proceeded.

mentigerous (mɛn'tɪdʒərəs), *a. Ent.* [f. L. *ment-um* (see MENTUM) + -GEROUS.] Bearing the mentum. (*Cent. Dict.* 1890.)

‖**mentigo.** *Path. Obs.* [L. *mentīgo* (Columella), f. *ment-um* chin.] **a.** A pustular eruption on the mouth and lips of sheep. **b.** = MENTAGRA (*Syd. Soc. Lex.* 1890).

1706 PHILLIPS (ed. Kersey), *Mentigo*, a Scab among Sheep, about their Mouths and Lips, call'd *The Pocks*. **1890** in *Syd. Soc. Lex.*

mentil(e, obs. forms of MANTLE.

†**mentimu'tation.** *Obs. rare*⁻¹. [f. L. *menti-*, *mens* mind + MUTATION.] A change of mind.

1650 B. *Discolliminium* 45, I..shall be allowed the full benefit of all the..illaqueations, extrications,.. mentimutations, rementimutations,..that I..can devise.

mention ('mɛnʃən), *sb.* Forms: 4 mencyun, 4–5 -cioun(e, 4–6 -cione, -sion(e, 4–7 -cion, 5 -syon, -sioun, -cyoun(e, 5–6 -cyon, 6 -tyon, -tioun, -tione, 6– mention. [a. F. *mention* (= Sp. *mencion*, Pg. *menção*, It. *menzione*), ad. L. *mentiōn-em*, *mentio*, f. the root *men-* of *menti-*, *mens* mind, *meminisse* to remember.]

†**1.** Bearing in mind, consideration. *Obs.*

c **1300** *Gregorleg.* (Vernon MS.) 749 in *Archiv Stud. neu. Spr.* LV. 438 Alle þat herden þis storie rede wiþ herte and deuocioun, And in herte taken heede wiþ good Mencioun, þe pope haþ granted hem to mede and [*v.rr.* ane, an] hundred dawes to pardoun.

2. a. In early use, the action of commemorating or calling to mind by speech or writing. Now in more restricted sense, the action, or an act, of incidentally referring to, remarking upon, or introducing the name of (a person or thing) in spoken or written discourse. Orig. in phrase ***to make mention of*** (= Fr. *faire mention de*), which is now slightly *arch.* or *literary*, exc. in negative contexts.

1303 R. BRUNNE *Handl. Synne* 10496 Yn þat messe, þey hem affye,..For hyt makeþ mencyun of þe passyun As Iesu cryst to deþ was doun. **1377** LANGL. *P. Pl.* B. x. 448 Dauyd maketh mencioun he spake amonges kynges. *c* **1420** LYDG. *Assembly of Gods* 2054 Wherfore I toke pen and ynke And paper to make therof mencion In wrytyng. **1459** SIR JOHN FASTOLF *Will* in *Paston Lett.* I. 454 With a scripture aboute the stoon makynge mencion the day and yeer of hise obite. *c* **1470** HENRY *Wallace* VII. 757 Mencione off Bruce is oft in Wallace buk. **1542** UDALL *Erasm. Apoph.* 76 He..maketh mencion and rehersall of diuerse the wandreynges of Ulysses. **1559** BP. SCOT in Strype *Ann. Ref.* I. App. vii. 15 Without any mencyon of their conversation and livinge. **1603** OWEN *Pembrokeshire* (1892) 7 Doctor Powell..maketh mencion of an Ancient Author. *c* **1665** MRS. HUTCHINSON *Mem. Col. Hutchinson* 9, I have heard very honourable mention of him. *a* **1716** SOUTH *Serm.* (1727) V. i. 22 So that their Blood may rise, and their Heart may swell at the very mention of it. **1738** SWIFT *Pol. Conversat.* Introd. 8, I shall make honourable Mention of their Names in a short Preface. **1758** JOHNSON *Idler* No. 47 ¶11 He grows peevish at any mention of business. **1849** MACAULAY *Hist. Eng.* iv. I. 482 The mention of their names excites the disgust and horror of all sects and parties. **1868** MISS YONGE *Cameos* I. 268 He never heard from him one careless mention of the name of God. **1875** JOWETT *Plato* (ed. 2) I. 338 These two passages are the only ones in which Plato makes mention of himself. **1877** MAJOR *Disc. Prince Henry* xii. 190 The Camaldolese geographer makes no mention of the sources from which he derived his information. **1891** LOUNSBURY *Stud. Chaucer* II. v. 236 It will explain the two mentions of Lollius in 'Troilus and Cressida'.

b. *Comb.* in †***mention making***, mentioning.

1534 MORE *Treat. Passion* Wks. 1292/1 These wordes.. be the wordes of..three of the .iiii. euangelistes, which by the mencion makynge of the Pascha..geue vs here.. occasyon to speake of the poynte whiche I before towched. **1583** STOCKER *Civ. Warres Lowe C.* I. 21 Without anye mention making of our mutual assurance. **1679** KID in Hickes *Spir. Popery* (1680) 5, I bless him,..that ever such a poor and obscure person as I am, should be thus priviledged by him for mentionmaking of his grace.

†**c.** ***in the mention of***: 'apropos of'. *Obs.*

1638 JUNIUS *Paint. Ancients* 149 There is in the mention of Picture a pretie tale divulged of Lepidus, who [etc.].

†**d.** ***of no mention***: not worthy of mention, undistinguished.

1622 FLETCHER & MASSINGER *Prophetess* v. iii, 'Tis true, I have been a Rascall, as you are, a fellow of no mention, nor no mark.

e. ***honourable mention*** (rarely, after Fr. use, simply *mention*): a distinction accorded to exhibited works of art, etc., or to candidates at an examination that are considered to possess exceptional merit, but are not entitled to a prize.

1892 MRS. H. WARD *David Grieve* II. 248 'If I don't get my "mention"', she would say passionately, 'I tell you again it will be intrigue'.

f. *Mil.* A commendatory reference made to a person in an official military dispatch (abbrev. of *mention in dispatches*).

1915 A. N. LYONS *Kitchener Chaps* 81 No, sir, there's no particular cop about these 'mentions'; only something for your pals to read. **1921** S. C. JOHNSON *Medal Collector* viii. 180 No more than one leaf, however, may be fixed to the ribbon even though the wearer may have been the subject of several mentions. **1958** M. DICKENS *Man Overboard* iii. 35 Other people came out of the war with Mentions and worthwhile gongs. **1964** T. WHITE tr. *Leulliette's St. Michael* 221 I've got the Médaille Militaire, the Croix de Guerre and seven mentions.

†**3.** In occasional uses: A statement, narrative; a record, memorial; a memorial inscription. *Obs.*

c **1470** HARDING *Chron.* XCVII. iii, Of whiche came then.. batayles greate and fell discencions, As Bede wryteth amonge his mencyons. **1470–85** MALORY *Arthur* II. xii. 90 Kyng Arthur lete berye thys knyght rychely and made a mensyon on his tombe. *Ibid.* XI. i. 571 Whan this hermyte had made this mensyon he departed from the courte of kynge Arthur.

†**4.** Indication, evidence; a vestige, trace, remnant. *Obs.*

1567 in Bateson's *Hist. Northumbld.* (1893) I. 352 Westwarde by an old mencon of a dyke. *Ibid.*, Ye mencyon of an olde dike. ? *a* **1600** *Hodgson MS.* in *Northumbld. Gloss.* 475 The march..between England and Scotland..goeth by an old mension of a dycke called the Marche dyke. **1600** J. PORY tr. *Leo's Africa* I. 31 The verie trees are so drowned and ouerwhelmed therein [in snow], that it is not possible to finde any mention of them. **1601** HOLLAND *Pliny* I. 110 The rest that Homer so much speaks of..there is no mention or token remaining of them. **1601** YARINGTON *Two Lament. Trag.* E 2 b, Harke Rachel: I will..fling this middle mention of a man, Into some ditch... *Rach.* Where haue you laide the legs and battered head? **1613** PURCHAS *Pilgrimage* (1614) 532 It [the earthquake] brought vp the Sea a great way vpon the maine Land, which is carried backe with it into the Sea, not leauing mention that there had beene Land. *Ibid.* 814 Scarce any mention of the houses remained. **1633** BP. HALL *Hard Texts O.T.* 161 Where he moves in the sea he causeth a mention of his way in the waters.

mention ('mɛnʃən), *v.* Also 6 mencyon, -cion, -sion, -sin. [a. F. *mentionner* (= Sp. *mencionar*, It. *menzionare*, med.L. *mentiōnāre*), f. *mention*: see prec. *sb.*]

1. a. *trans.* To make mention of; to refer to or remark upon incidentally; to specify by name or otherwise.

The parenthetical infinitive phrase ***not to mention*** (*so-and-so*) is used as a rhetorical suggestion that the speaker is refraining from presenting the full strength of his case; †***not to mention it***: used parenthetically for 'not in any degree worth mention'; ***to be mentioned in dispatches***: to receive a 'mention' (see MENTION *sb.* 2 f); also *transf.*

1530 PALSGR. 634/2, I mencyon, I make rehersall or remembraunce of a thyng paste or a person absent, *je mencionne*. **1535** JOYE *Apol. Tindale* (Arb.) 32 Wherof Frith wrote thys warnyng to Tin[dale] whyche he here mencyoneth. **1552–3** *Inv. Ch. Goods, Staffs.* in *Ann. Lichfield* IV. 55 Md. that ij ameses mensioned in the old inventorey be stolne. *Ibid.* 67 Md. that parcells followynge ar mensined in the olde inventore. **1611** BIBLE *1 Chron.* iv. 38 These mentioned by their names were Princes in their families. **1692** WOOD *Life* (O.H.S.) III. 405 It rain'd and drisled most of the morning, having not rain'd, not to mention it, for a month. **1702** ADDISON *Dial. Medals* Misc. Wks. 1736 III. 15 Not to mention several others, Carracio is said to have assisted Aretine. **1705** —— *Italy* Pref., I think I have mention'd but few Things..that are not set in a new Light. **1729** BUTLER *Serm.* Wks. 1850 II. Pref. 5 Not to mention the multitudes who read merely for the sake of talking [etc.]. **1751** LABELYE *Westm. Br.* 25 By Means too well known to require my mentioning them. **1839** BLACKIE in *For. Q. Rev.* XXIII. 279 How the finest lines in Milton (not to mention Southey, Wordsworth, and Coleridge) have been smothered and mangled by this curious race of syllable counters, no student of English poetry requires to be told. **1849** JAMES *Woodman* v, Let us mention no names. **1858** CONINGTON *Pope* Misc. Writ. I. 18 It would be a great mistake to suppose that Pope's 'Pastorals' are worthy of being mentioned in the same day with any genuine work of Virgil's. **1875** JOWETT *Plato* (ed. 2) V. 130 The science of dialectic is nowhere mentioned by name in the Laws. **1915** A. HUXLEY *Let.* June (1969) 73 Poor Bob Gibson is killed. He was as good a soldier as he was a don. He was mentioned in dispatches. **1922** JOYCE *Ulysses* 449, I fought with the colours..and was disabled at Spion Kop and Bloemfontein, was mentioned in dispatches. **1961** PARTRIDGE *Dict. Slang* Suppl. 1182/2 *Mentioned in despatches.* To have one's name appear in a newspaper, a parish magazine, or even on a notice board: jocular. **1975** *Times* 27 Aug. 20/3 In proud and loving memory of Captain Jocelyn Fulke Dalrymple Radice, The Queen's Bays, mentioned in British and French Army dispatches,..who died of wounds on August 27, 1944.

b. With clause as obj.: To state incidentally.

1617 MORYSON *Itin.* I. 60 Give me leave to mention that there lies a City not farre distant. **1714** LADY M. W. MONTAGU *Lett.* II. lxxxviii. 143, I am surprised you do not mention where you mean to stand. **1818** CRUISE *Digest* (ed. 2) V. 594 This case is also reported by Style, who mentions that Lord Ch. J. Roll said [etc.]. **1863** G. MACDONALD *D. Elginbrod* III. III. ix. 158 He mentioned to Miss Talbot that he had been his guest that night. *a* **1906** *Mod.* It ought here to be mentioned that I had never met the man before. **1929** C. K. S. MONCRIEFF tr. *Proust's Cities of Plain* I. II. ii. 268,

I mentioned to him that I had thought I heard him come upstairs.

c. ***don't mention it***: a colloquial phrase used in deprecating offered thanks or apology.

1841 LYTTON *Night & Morning* I. II. ii. 264 'I am going to leave your house, ma'am; and I wish to settle any little arrears of rent, &c.' 'Oh! sir! don't mention it,' said the landlady. **1854** W. COLLINS *Hide & Seek* III. iv. 84 'I was just going to swab up that part of the carpet when you came in', said Zack, apologetically... 'Oh don't mention it', answered Valentine, laughing. 'It was all my awkwardness'. **1873** HOWELLS *Chance Acquaintance* iv, Oh, don't mention that! I was the only one to blame.

†**2.** *intr.* To speak or make mention *of*. Also in *indirect passive*. *Obs.*

1560 DAUS tr. *Sleidane's Comm.* 102 In their letters they mentioned of the obedience unto Magistrates. *Ibid.* 176 b, In the last boke before this, I mentioned of this duke's invectives against the Duke of Saxon. **1599** HAKLUYT *Voy.* II. I. 199 A Pyramide mentioned of in Histories. **1609** B. JONSON *Masque of Queens* B 4 b, Their little Masters or Martinets, of whom I haue mention'd before. **1667** MILTON *P.L.* x. 1041 No more be mention'd then of violence Against our selves. **1792** *Elvina* I. 32, I mentioned in my last of the kind attention that Mr. Falkland had shewn.

mentionable ('mɛnʃənəb(ə)l), *a.* [f. MENTION *v.* + -ABLE.] That can or may be mentioned; worthy of mention.

1833 *Fraser's Mag.* VII. 116 All sorts of accidents, mentionable and unmentionable. **1858** CARLYLE *Fredk. Gt.* IX. ix. (1872) III. 148 In Germany the mentionable events are still fewer. **1871** L. STEPHEN *Playgr. Eur.* viii. (1894) 178 Our only mentionable adventure was the inevitable quarrel with the porter.

†'**mentionate**, *pa. pple.* *Obs.* [ad. med.L. *mentiōnātus*, pa. pple. of *mentiōnāre*: see MENTION *v.*] Mentioned, recorded.

c **1525** WARHAM in Ellis *Orig. Lett.* Ser. III. II. 11, I thanke your Grace for your singular goodenes afor mentionate. **1561** *Reg. Privy Council Scot.* I. 189 For reformyng of the irrelevance of the summondis mentionat in the secund exceptioun. **1678** *Contract* in *Proc. Soc. Ant. Scot.* (1896) XXX. 20 During the tyme above mentionat.

†'**mentionate**, *v.* *Obs.* [f. prec.: see -ATE[3].] *trans.* To mention, speak of. Also *intr.* (const. *of*).

1550 HOOPER *Jonas* vi. 152 It is not wythoute a synguler councell of the holye goste that thys kynge is mencionated of so copiously. *c* **1600** *Short Cath. Confess.* in *Cath. Tractates* (S.T.S.) 256/9 The fruites..of thir tokens aboue mentionated.

mentioned ('mɛnʃənd), *ppl. a.* [f. MENTION *v.* + -ED[1].] Of which mention has been made. Now *rare* exc. in Combs. ***before-mentioned***, ***under-mentioned***, etc.

1592 CHETTLE *Kind-harts Dr.* C 4 Mopo and his mentioned companions. **1611** COTGR., *Mentionné*, mentionned; nominated, named. **1667** DUCHESS NEWCASTLE *Life of Duke* I. (1886) 53 The mentioned town of Gainsborough. **1706** S. SEWALL *Diary* 24 Dec. (1879) II. 175 He is to send me 15 Fountains, which are paid for in the mention'd Sum. **1733** TULL *Horse-Hoeing Husb.* xxi. 306 Which makes the mention'd Angle more acute. **1865** J. H. STIRLING *Sir W. Hamilton* 73 In reference to the mentioned doctrines of Kant.

mentioner ('mɛnʃənə(r)). [f. MENTION *v.* + -ER[1].] One who mentions.

1607 *Scholast. Disc. agst. Antichrist* I. ii. 111 The highest mentioner of it is Vincentius. **1611** SPEED *Hist. Gt. Brit.* VI. xix. 104 We will adde somewhat to wash off those false aspersions, both from the Record and from the mentioners thereof. **1660** HEXHAM, *Een melder*, a Mentioner, a Rehearser, a Recounter, or a Teller.

mentioning ('mɛnʃənɪŋ), *vbl. sb.* [f. MENTION *v.* + -ING[1].] The action of the verb MENTION.

1603 KNOLLES *Hist. Turkes* (1638) 48 The men..both dismaid at the very mentioning of the matter,..said [etc.]. **1654** tr. *Scudery's Curia Pol.* 104 The very mentioning and remembrance thereof, may amaze with horrour. **1749** FIELDING *Tom Jones* VIII. x, You have made my blood run cold with the very mentioning the top of that mountain. **1817** BYRON *Beppo* lxxxvi, Nauseous words past mentioning or bearing. **1868** G. STEPHENS *Runic Mon.* I. p. viii, Many such mentionings occur in Anglo-Scandic skinbooks. **1901** *N. & Q.* 9th Ser. VII. 470/1, I find many mentionings of Haydons in the parish registers of Hinton Blewitt.

mentionless ('mɛnʃənlɪs), *a.* *rare*[−1]. [f. MENTION *sb.* + -LESS.] Not calling for mention.

1611 SPEED *Hist. Gt. Brit.* VII. vii. (1623) 225 Famous in his issue, though mentionlesse for action in himselfe.

mentism ('mɛntɪz(ə)m). *Path.* [a. F. *mentisme*, f. L. *ment-em*, *mens* mind: see -ISM.] Disturbance of mental action produced by passion or an excited imagination (*Syd. Soc. Lex.* 1890).

†**mentition.** *Obs.* *rare*[−0]. [ad. L. *mentītiōn-em*, f. *mentīrī* to lie.] The action of lying.

1656 BLOUNT *Glossogr.*, *Mentition*, a lying, forging or telling untruths.

mento- ('mɛntəʊ), used as combining form of L. *mentum* chin, in anatomical terms, as ***mento-bregmatic***, ***-condylial***, ***-gonial***, ***-labial***, etc. (see *Syd. Soc. Lex.* 1890); ˌ**mento-'hyoid**, (*a*) *adj.* pertaining to the chin and the hyoid bone; (*b*) *sb.* an occasional muscle in man passing from the body of the hyoid bone to the chin; so ˌ**mento-hy'oidean** *a.*; ˌ**mento-Me'ckelian** *a.*, in ***mento-Meckelian bone*** or ***element***, a small bone formed by the ossification of portions of Meckel's cartilage and the lower labial cartilage; also as *sb.*, a small bone formed by the ossified end of Meckel's cartilage.

1856 MAYNE *Expos. Lex.*, *Mentolabialis*..mentolabial. **1857** DUNGLISON *Med. Lex.* 585 Mento-Labial Furrow. **1866** MACALISTER in *Proc. R. Irish Acad.* IX. 451 A small muscular mento-hyoidean band..existed single in one subject. *Ibid.* 468 Mento-hyoid muscle. **1867** —— *Ibid.* X. 163 The platysma myoides, the mento-hyoid, Lucas' fibres in the axilla [etc.]. **1877** HUXLEY & MARTIN *Elem. Biol.* 172 The mento-Meckelian element of the mandible. **1883** HUXLEY *Pract. Biol.* 220 At the..symphysial end it [Meckel's cartilage] is ossified to form the mento-Meckelian bone. **1892** J. A. THOMSON *Outl. Zool.* 449 The mento-meckelians seem to arise from two lower labial cartilages. **1925** J. S. KINGSLEY *Vertebr. Skeleton* 71 The other cartilage bone is a mentomeckelian, best known in Anura, at the symphysis of the lower jaw.

menton ('mɛntən). *Anat.* [a. F. *menton* chin:—L. ***mentum***.] = GNATHION.

1937 *Amer. Jrnl. Physical Anthrop.* XXII. 483 Menton... By all authors, this is designated as the lowest point on the lower border of the mandible in the median plane. **1954** T. C. WHITE et al. *Orthodontics* ix. 165 The Mandibular Plane passes from the menton (lowest point on the cross-section of the mandibular symphysis)..to the lowest point on the angle of the mandible. **1968** [see GNATHION]. **1974** *Nature* 8 Mar. 165/1 Six bilateral and four single roentgenographic landmarks were delineated. The single landmarks were: sella; anterior nasal spine; incisal point; menton.

mentonniere (mɛn'tɒnɪɛə(r)). *Antiq.* [a. F. *mentonnière* (16th c. *mentoniere*), f. *menton* chin.] A piece of armour covering the chin or lower part of the face and neck, attached either to the helmet or to the upper part of the body-armour.

1824 MEYRICK *Anc. Arm.* II. 247 On this is a protuberance and two rings to hold a shield, made also with a mentoniere. *Ibid.*, They have grand guards with mentonieres and coursing-hats. **1884** *St. James's Gaz.* 20 June 11/2 A Mentonnière, engraved with the royal arms of Spain.

mentor ('mɛntɔː(r)). [a. F. *mentor*, appellative use of the proper name *Mentor*, Gr. *Μέντωρ*. The name admits of the etymological rendering 'adviser', having the form of an agent-n. from the root **men-* (: *mon-*) to remember, think, counsel, etc. (cf. L. *monitor*); possibly it may have been invented or chosen by the poet as appropriately significant.]

1. a. With initial capital: The name of the Ithacan noble whose disguise the goddess Athene assumed in order to act as the guide and adviser of the young Telemachus; *allusively*, one who fulfils the office which the supposed Mentor fulfilled towards Telemachus. **b.** Hence, as common noun: An experienced and trusted counsellor.

The currency of the word in Fr. and Eng. is derived less from the Odyssey than from Fénelon's romance of *Télémaque*, in which the part played by Mentor as a counsellor is made more prominent.

1750 LD. CHESTERF. *Lett. to Son* 8 Mar., The friendly care and assistance of your Mentor. **1784** COWPER *Task* II. 595 The friend Sticks close, a Mentor worthy of his charge. **1814** SIR R. WILSON *Priv. Diary* II. 329 The same Mentor, who really is a most sincere friend, begged me to [etc.]. **1873** DIXON *Two Queens* III. XIII. vi. 36 'Too much learning is not needed in a prince', replied his mentor. **1890** GUNTER *Miss Nobody* ii. (1891) 28 Phil..is helped in the selection by the experience of his mentor.

¶**c.** Applied to a thing (more or less personified).

Littré quotes from Rousseau an example of the similar use of F. *mentor* applied to a book.

1823 BYRON *Island* II. viii, The deep..The only Mentor of his youth. **1869** SPURGEON *Treas. David* (Ps. xix. 11) I. 309 The Bible should be our Mentor. **1879** *Expositor* IX. 462 The *δαίμων* which Socrates spoke of as his mentor.

2. *attrib.* and *Comb.*

1778 ABIGAIL ADAMS in *Fam. Lett.* (1876) 338 Your venerable colleague, whose Mentor-like appearance, age [etc.]. **1811** W. SPENCER *Poems* 214 To smooth Reflection's mentor-frown. **1837** MISS SEDGWICK *Live & let Live* 76 This made it easy for her to adopt the Mentor style.

Hence **men'torial** *a.*, 'containing advice' (Smart *Dict.* 1836); '**mentorism**, guidance by a mentor; '**mentorship**, the office or function of a mentor.

1882 SIR W. HARCOURT in *Daily News* 23 Jan. 2/5, I wholly reject the mentorship of the noble lord. **1889** *Jrnl. Educ.* 1 Dec. 620/2 What a tragedy of mentorism is that of 'Robert Elsmere'! **1905** *Blackw. Mag.* Jan. 71/2 His occasional boredom and irrepressibly assertive mentorship.

‖**mentri** ('mɛntrɪ). Also 9– **mantri**. [Mal. *mentri*, ad. Skr. *mantri* MANTRI.] A title used in the Malay states for a minister. Also **mentri besar**, a title for the chief minister of a Malay state.

Mentri was used *spec.* of a Perak territorial chief in the 19th century.

1839 T. J. NEWBOLD *Pol. & Statistical Acct. Straits of Malacca* I. v. 239 The Mantris were the privy councillors to the Panghúlus, two in number. **1880** F. A. SWETTENHAM *Some Acct. Independent Native States Malay Peninsula* i. 7 He had..got the Mĕntri to assist him in farming the revenues of Krîan, a Province claimed by the Mĕntri. **1900** W. E. MAXWELL in W. W. Skeat *Malay Magic* iii. 65 The grave was discovered..by workmen employed by the Mĕntri of Perak. **1907** F. A. SWETTENHAM *Brit. Malaya* vi. 118 The Malay chief of the Lârut district was styled the Mantri, and he was one of the four high officers of state. **1955** *Times* 1 Aug. 6/6 They would be the symbol of loyalty of all classes and of all races loyal to Malaya. 'I only hope that in a short time their highnesses will see fit to appoint as their mentris besar (chief ministers) elected members of state councils.' **1958** J. SLIMMING *Temiar Jungle* ii. 27 *Mentri* is a Malay title superimposed on the Temiar system of leadership. **1972** *Straits Times* (Malaysian ed.) 4 May 6/4 Malaysia and Indonesia will be closer, and grow better in education when a common spelling system is used by both governments, Mentri Besar Inche Ja'afar bin Hassan said yesterday.

mentulate ('mɛntjʊleɪt), *a.* [ad. L. *mentulāt-us*, f. *mentula* penis: see -ATE.] Having a very large penis (*Syd. Soc. Lex.* 1890). Also '**mentulated** *a.* in the same sense (Bailey vol. II, 1727).

‖**mentum** ('mɛntəm). [L. *mentum* chin.]

1. *Anat.* The anterior and inferior margins of the mandible or lower jaw; the chin.

[**1693** tr. *Blancard's Phys. Dict.* (ed. 2), *Mentum*, the Chinn.] **1855** DUNGLISON *Med. Lex.* **1866** in BRANDE & COX *Dict. Sci.*, etc. In mod. Dicts.

2. *Ent.* A term variously applied to different parts of the labium; by recent entomologists commonly used for the median portion. Also *attrib.*

1826 KIRBY & SP. *Entomol.* III. 355 *Mentum*, the lower part of the *labium*, where it is jointed; in other cases its base. *Ibid.* 356 *note*, Our [i.e. the authors'] Mentum may generally be known by its situation between the hinges and base of the *Maxillæ*. **1828** STARK *Elem. Nat. Hist.* II. 281 Mentum large; maxillary palpi long. **1839** WESTWOOD *Classif. Insects* I. 1 Mentum-tooth triangular. *Ibid.* 4 Mentum-lobe entire. **1888** ROLLESTON & JACKSON *Anim. Life* 141 A palpiger borne on the external angle of the mentum.

3. *Bot.* 'A projection in front of the flowers of some orchids, caused by the extension of the foot of the column' (*Treas. Bot.* 1866).

menu ('mɛnjuː, ‖məny). [F. *menu* adj., small (:—L. *minūtus* MINUTE *a.*), used as sb. with the sense of detail, details collectively, detailed list.]

†**1.** Short for F. *menu peuple*: the common people. *Obs. rare*[−1].

1658 OSBORN *Adv. Son* (1673) 2 The Sons of the Menu lying so long under this lazie course. *Ibid.* 190 Which..may better become the Gentry, than the Sons of the Menu.

2. A detailed list of the dishes to be served at a banquet or meal; a bill of fare. Also, the viands so served. ***menu card***, the card upon which a menu is written.

1837 C'TESS BLESSINGTON in *Heath's Bk. Beauty* 198 Did you not examine the *menu*? **1849** THACKERAY *Pendennis* xxii, It was a grand sight to behold him in his dressing-gown composing a *menu*. **1881** C. C. HARRISON *Woman's Handiwork* II. 124 A menu card, with gilded edge and lettering. **1883** F. M. CRAWFORD *Dr. Claudius* (1892) 38 He was thinking out a *menu* for dinner. **1896** W. BLACK in *Harper's Mag.* Apr. 746/2 The long tables..with..their glossy menu-cards, and their floral decorations.

transf. **1889** *Pall Mall G.* 4 Nov. 3/1 To gain this they must qualify in Latin, Greek, Mathematics, Natural Philosophy, Logic,..[etc.]—a pretty good menu. **1922** JOYCE *Ulysses* 161 Maul her a bit. Then the next thing on the menu. **1940** H. G. WELLS *Babes in Darkling Wood* II. iii. 206 All the intelligent ones feel baffled at the menu of these degree courses. **1974** *Some Technical Terms & Slang* (Granada Television), *Menu*, a list of items read out at the start of a magazine programme.

3. *Computing.* A computer-generated list of options, usu. displayed on a screen, any of which can be conveniently selected and entered into the computer; *spec.* such a list of available commands or facilities.

1967 *Proc. IEEE* LV. 1551/2 Software function buttons, displayed on the CRT as a 'menu' of commands available to the user. **1971** *Computers & Humanities* VI. 104 The musical symbols at the top of the workscope are the 'menu'. **1977** *Sci. Amer.* Aug. 50/1 A simple menu helps you enter your data parameters on the keyboard, after which a single keystroke plots the data instantly. **1982** *Which Computer?* June 48/1 The operator can re-configure the operating parameters. This is done by a yes/no key located on the enclosure and a menu printed out on paper. **1984** J. HILTON *Choosing & using your Home Computer* 125/2 The button is pressed once to select an 'icon' (or symbol) from a screen menu, and twice to open out that particular application. **1986** *Keyboard Player* Apr. 3/3 The sophisticated edit facilities allow complicated musical forms to be created.. with the aid of on-screen menus.

4. Special Comb.: **menu-driven** *a.*, (of a program or computer) used by making selections from menus.

1979 *Proc. 12th Hawaii Internat. Conf. System Sciences* I. 158 A particular menu driven user interface is presented as an example of a successful interface. **1984** *Austral. Micro Computerworld* Feb. 13/2 The PCjr is menu-driven, using icons to identify the programs available.

menuce, variant of MENISE *Obs.*

†**menudes.** *Obs.* [app. ad. Sp. *menudos*, pl. of *menudo*, absol. use of *menudo* small (:—L. *minūtus* MINUTE *a.*).] ? Mincemeat.
1585 T. WASHINGTON tr. *Nicholay's Voy.* I. xi. 13 b, Meat dressed according to their fashion, which was a kinde of Menudes made in paste with onions.

menues, menuise, var. ff. MENISE *Obs.*

menuet: see MINUET *sb.*

‖**menura** (mɪ'n(j)ʊərə). *Ornith.* [mod.L. (Davies 1800, in *Trans. Linn. Soc.* VI), f. Gr. μήνη crescent moon + οὐρά tail, so called from the 'crescent-shaped spots' (*loc. cit.*) on the tail.] An Australian genus of birds, popularly called Lyre-birds; any bird of this genus, esp. *Menura superba*.
1839 *Penny Cycl.* XIV. 274/2 (tr. *Lesson*), The Mænura [*sic*] has then been arranged sometimes among the gallinaceous birds under the name of Lyre-Pheasant or Pheasant of the Woods. **1874** WOOD *Nat. Hist.* (1885) 337 The Menura seldom, if ever, attempts to escape by flight. **1884** WHYMPER in *Girl's Own Paper* 28 June 614/2 The superb menura, or lyre-bird.

menurance, obs. form of MANURANCE.

menure, obs. form of MAINOUR.
a **1436** *Domesday Ipswich* in *Blk. Bk. Admir.* (Rolls) II. 21 Theves taken with litell menure or with gret menure.

menure, obs. form of MANURE *v.*

menuse, variant of MENISE *Obs.*, MINISH.

‖**menus plaisirs** (məny plɛzir), *sb. pl.* [Fr., lit. 'small pleasures'; pocket-money.] Simple pleasures; small personal expenses or gratifications; fanciful or trifling objects bought with one's pocket-money. Also *attrib.*
1697 VANBRUGH *Relapse* I. ii. 8, I shall see you stand in damnable need of some Auxiliary Guineas, for you[r] *Menu Plaisirs*. **1779** H. WALPOLE *Let.* 14 Jan. (1904) X. 363 My *menus plaisirs*, a few sprinkled visits of charity from a few friends that remained in town. **1814** JANE AUSTEN *Mansf. Park* II. v. 114 He will have a very pretty income..and as..he will still live at home, it will be all for his *menus plaisirs*. **1883** M. E. BRADDON *Golden Calf* II. xi. 293 Whatever honorarium he received for his work was expended upon his *menus plaisirs*. **1915** F. M. HUEFFER *Good Soldier* III. v. 193 He may have had five hundred pounds a year English, for his menus plaisirs. **1966** 'M. INNES' *Change of Heir* v. 40 'It's in her letter. The bit about..*menus frais*.' 'What's that?' 'The same as *menus plaisirs*. Pocket-money on the scale appropriate to an English gentleman.'

menuver, obs. form of MINIVER.

menuze, menwu, obs. ff. MINISH, MINNOW.

meny, menyal(l, obs. ff. MANY, MENIAL *a.*

meny(e, obs. forms of MEINIE.

menyanthin (mɛnɪ'ænθɪn). *Chem.* Also -ine. [f. mod.L. *Menyanthēs* (Tournefort 1700), the name of a genus of plants + -IN.
The etymology of the mod.L. generic name is obscure: it has been variously conjectured to be a mistake for **Minyanthēs* (a. Gr. μινυανθής adj., blooming a short time), and to be an irregular formation on Gr. μήν month + ἄνθος flower.]
A bitter principle contained in the buckbean, *Menyanthes trifoliata*.
1842 FRANCIS *Dict. Arts*, *Menyanthin*, the peculiar principle of *menyanthes trifoliata*, or bog bean. **1850** OGILVIE s.v. *Menyanthes*, It contains an extractive called menyanthine. **1897** *Naturalist* 45 The most palpable ingredient of the plant is a bitter principle menyanthin.

menyie, variant of MANYIE *sb. Sc. Obs.*

menykinge, obs. form of MINIKIN.

menyng(e, obs. ff. MEANING, MINNING.

menys, obs. gen. pl. of MAN, obs. f. MENACE.

menyso(u)n, variants of MENISON *Obs.*

menyuer, -yver(e, obs. forms of MINIVER.

menzie, variant of MANYIE *v.*

menzil, variant of MANZIL.
1687 A. LOVELL tr. *Thevenot's Trav.* II. 148 Commonly they make it a Menzil or days Journey from Chadgegih to Destberm. **1869** TOZER *Highl. Turkey* I. 195 We were now travelling by the Menzil or Turkish post... The charge for menzil horses is three piastres and a half..an hour. **1888** DOUGHTY *Trav. Arabia Deserta* II. 179 The drone of mill-stones may be heard before the daylight in the nomad menzils.

Meo ('mi:əʊ). Also 9 **Mewoh.** [Native name.] An Indian people of Rajasthan and the Punjab, whose religion is a blend of Hinduism and Islam; a member of this people. Also as *adj.* Cf. MEWATI *sb.* and *a.*
1832 J. TOD *Ann. Rajast'han* II. 393 At this period..the mountainous region, called Méwat, was inhabited by a daring and ferocious banditti, called Mewohs, who pillaged in gangs. **1855** H. H. WILSON *Gloss. Judicial & Revenue Terms* 339/2 *Meo*, (?) H. A class of cultivators in the province of Dehli. **1873** E. BALFOUR *Cycl. India* (ed. 2) III. s.v., Meo, cultivators in the Delhi province, are a tribe of people inhabiting the low hills about Gurgaon. **1880** P. W. POWLETT in *Rajputana Gazetteer* III. 201 Meos do not marry into their own pál, or clan, but are lax about forming connections with women of other castes, whose children they receive into the Meo community. **1885** G. C. WHITWORTH *Anglo-Indian Dict.* 204/2 *Mewáti*, the name of a branch of the Jádon Rájputs;..they rule in Alwar, and are connected with the Meo tribe of the same country. **1896** W. CROOKE *Tribes & Castes N.-W. Provinces & Oudh* III. 487 Whatever their connection with the Mînas may be, the Meos themselves pretend to be of Râjput descent. **1916** R. V. RUSSELL *Tribes & Castes Cent. Provinces India* IV. 235 Abu Fazl writes that the Meos were in his time famous runners, and one thousand of them were employed by Akbar as carriers of post. **1970** D. G. MANDELBAUM *Society in India* II. xxix. 558 This intensified Islamization is shown by the Meos, the dominant jati in some two thousand villages on the borderlands of Rajasthan and Punjab. *Ibid.* 559 The Meos have adopted more of Muslim practices in the last 17 years than they had in the previous 450 years.

Meo, var. MIAO *sb.* and *a.*

meoble, variant of MOBLE *sb. Obs.*

meoc, obs. form of MEEK *a.*

meode, obs. form of MEAD *sb.*[1], MEED *sb.*

meok(e, obs. forms of MEEK *a.* and *v.*

†**meon.** *Obs.* See also MEUM. [a. late Gr. μῆον.] The herb Spignel, *Meum athamanticum*.
1562 TURNER *Herb.* II. 56 Meon or Mew..is lyke vnto dill in yᵉ stalk and lefe. **1617** MINSHEU *Ductor*, *Mewe* or meon.

meorknesse, obs. form of MURKNESS.

meovable, -ve, obs. forms of MOVABLE, MOVE.

meow, var. MIAOW *int.* and *sb.*

mepacrine ('mɛpəkrɪn, -i:n). *Pharm.* [perh. f. ME(THYL + PA(LUDISM + A)CR(ID)INE.] A tricyclic base, $C_{23}H_{30}N_3OCl$, derived from acridine and usually administered in the form of its dihydrochloride dihydrate salt, which is a yellow crystalline compound formerly widely used in the treatment of malaria and now used mainly as an anthelmintic. Cf. ATEBRIN, QUINACRINE.
1943 *Lancet* 29 May 699/1 The only synthetic anti-malarial compound of any real value so far in general use is mepacrine. **1956** W. SLIM *Defeat into Victory* xvi. 352 The jaundice yellow of all our complexions as a result of the daily dose of mepacrine. **1962** *Lancet* 29 Dec. 1387/2 A related drug, chloroquine, has proved superior to mepacrine in the suppressive treatment of malaria, rheumatoid arthritis, lupus erythematosus, and light eruptions. **1971** B. W. ALDISS *Soldier Erect* 74 The site where hundreds of BORs had pretended to swallow the morning mepacrine tablet and instead had ground it underfoot, happily risking malaria in the exercise of their own free will.

meperidine (mə'pɛrɪdi:n). *Pharm.* Chiefly *U.S.* [f. ME(THYL + PI)PERIDINE.] = PETHIDINE.
1947 *Jrnl. Amer. Med. Assoc.* 25 Jan. 243/2 In this country only 1 case of spontaneous addiction to meperidine hydrochloride is reported. **1962** J. H. BURN *Drugs, Med. & Man* x. 104 The disadvantage can however be countered by choosing one of the substitutes for morphine which have been made in the laboratory in the last twenty years. The first of these was meperidine (in Britain called pethidine). **1971** J. J. BURNS in B. N. La Du et al. *Fund. Drug Metabolism* xvii. 343 The rhesus monkey and the dog metabolize..meperidine and antipyrine much more rapidly than does man.

mephenesin (mə'fɛnəsɪn). *Pharm.* [f. ME(THYL + PHEN(YL + CR)ES(OL + -IN[1].] A colourless crystalline compound, $CH_3{\cdot}C_6H_4O{\cdot}CH_2CH(OH)CH_2OH$, which is used as a muscle-relaxant in the treatment of spastic, hypertonic, and hyperkinetic conditions, and as a tranquillizer.
1952 *Brit. Pharmaceut. Codex 1949 Suppl.* 40 Mephenesin consists of 3-(2-methylphenoxy)propane-1:2-diol. **1955** *Sci. News Let.* 16 July 40/3 In the great majority of 109 cases [of cerebral palsy] treated before dental surgery with mephenesin,..the drug produced feelings of well-being and relaxation, and nervousness diminished or disappeared. **1962** J. H. BURN *Drugs, Med. & Man* xii. 127 Another study was made by other workers to test the claim that the drug mephenesin exerts a specific effect on subjective anxiety and feeling of tension, and also on objective manifestations of this state. **1972** *Neuro-pharmacology* XI. 733 Amino-oxyacetic acid did not protect rats against the audiogenic seizures that constitute the barbiturate abstinence syndrome whereas mephenesin..did provide protection.

†**mephis.** *Obs.* [Blundered form of L. *memphītēs* (Pliny), Gr. μεμφίτης (Dioscorides).] A stone said to have anæsthetic properties. Cf. MEMPHIAN.
1584 R. SCOT *Discov. Witchcr.* XIII. vi. (1886) 240 Mephis, being broken into powder, and droonke with water, maketh insensibilitie of torture.

Mephistopheles (mɛfɪ'stɒfɪli:z). Also 6–7 **Mephas-, Mephis-, Mephostophilis, Mephas-, Mephes-, Mephostophilus,** 7 **Mephistophilus, Mephostophiles;** 9 in shortened form **Mephisto.** [Appears first in the Ger. *Faustbuch* 1587 as *Mephostophiles*; of unknown origin. The now current form *Mephistopheles*, and the abbreviation *Mephisto*, come from Goethe's *Faust*.] The name of the evil spirit to whom Faust (in the German legend) was represented to have sold his soul. Hence applied allusively to persons (in the 17th c. with reference to the character presented in Marlowe's *Doctor Faustus*, in recent use to that presented by Goethe).
[*c* **1590** MARLOWE *Faustus* (1604) B 1 b, How pliant is this Mephastophilis? *Ibid.*, Enter Mephostophilis. *Ibid.* B 4 Mephastophilus.] **1598** SHAKS. *Merry W.* I. i. 132 *Pist.* How now, Mephostophilus. **1598–9** B. JONSON *Case is Alter'd* II. iv, Thou art not lunatike, art thou? and thou bee'st auoide Mephostophiles. **1620** MELTON *Astrol.* 8 There came running down the stayres..(the little Mephistophiles) his Boy demanding with whom I would speake. **1624** FLETCHER *Wife for a Month* v. ii, A Mephestophilus, such as thou art. **1629** MASSINGER *Picture* v. iii, You know How to resolue your selfe what my intents are, By the help of Mephostophiles [*i.e.* Baptista]. **1818** LADY MORGAN *Autobiog.* (1859) 201 That Mephistopheles of diplomacy, Talleyrand. **1903** *Westm. Gaz.* 22 Aug. 2/1 It changes them mostly into Machiavels and Mephistopheleses.
Hence **Mephistophe'lean, Mephisto'phelian, Mephisto'phelic, Mephistophe'listic** (*rare*), *adjs.*, pertaining to or resembling Mephistopheles or his actions.
1837 *Fraser's Mag.* XVI. 92 We have heard some ascribe a Mephistophelistic spirit to Mr. Carlyle. **1851** H. MELVILLE *Whale* xxxi. 154 He carries an everlasting Mephistophelean grin on his face. **1853** GEO. ELIOT in Cross *Life* (1885) I. 307, I am very hard and Mephistophelian just now. **1873** LELAND *Egypt. Sketch-bk.* 102 The Mephistophelic who quiz all that they cannot compass. **1887** F. FRANCIS Jun. *Saddle & Mocassin* 209 These Apaches..were handsome, too, in a Mephistophelean style. **1888** J. MARTINEAU *Study Relig.* I. I. iv. 135 The very same Mephistophilean [*sic*] agility.

mephites, erron. form of MEPHITIS.

mephitic (mɪ'fɪtɪk), *a.* [ad. late L. *mephīticus* (whence F. *méphitique*, Sp. *mefítico*, Pg. *mephitico*, It. *mefitico*), f. L. *mephītis*: see MEPHITIS and -IC.] Pertaining to mephitis; offensive to the smell; (of a vapour or exhalation) pestilential, noxious, poisonous. †***mephitic air, acid, gas***: carbonic acid.
1623 COCKERAM, *Mephiticke*, stinking. **1656** in BLOUNT *Glossogr.* **1773** T. PERCIVAL *Ess.* II. 57 This celebrated spring abounds with a mineral spirit, or mephitic air, in which its stimulus, and indeed its efficacy resides. **1773** BRYDONE *Sicily* ii. (1809) 125 So mephitic a vapour that birds were suffocated in flying over it. **1775** BEWLY in Priestley *Exper. and Observ. Air* II. 339 The Mephitic Acid, as I shall already venture to call it. **1793** BEDDOES *Calculus* 250 The affinity which this mephitic gaz has for oxygene. **1832** *Veg. Subst. Food of Man* 212 This mephitic gas. **1899** *Allbutt's Syst. Med.* VIII. 393 Hallucinations of smell are also offensive. Patients complain of mephitic fumes,..chloroform and other volatile poisons.
absol. **1818** II. BEST *Italy* 399 Other spiracles of mephitic might probably be found here.
fig. **1887** HUXLEY in *19th Cent.* Feb. 195 The schools kept the thinking faculty alive and active, when..the mephitic atmosphere engendered by the dominant ecclesiasticism..might well have stifled it.
b. ***mephitic weasel***: the skunk, *Mephitis mephitica*.
1837 DONOVAN *Dom. Econ.* II. 85 The Skunk, or mephitic weasel of North America.
Hence **me'phitical** *a.* in the same sense.
1704 J. HARRIS *Lex. Techn.* I, *Mephitical Exhalations* are poisonous or noxious ones, issuing out of the Earth. **1741** BROWNRIGG in *Phil. Trans.* LV. 238 The mephitical air of oak, which extinguishes flame. **1842** SIR A. DE VERE *Song of Faith* 206 Our very chambers clogged with steams mephitical. **1930** D. L. SAYERS *Strong Poison* viii. 95 In one corner an anthracite stove, glowing red and mephitical, vied with a roaring gas-oven in another corner. **1933** *Punch* 6 Dec. 641/3 In the sphere of things political An atmosphere malign, mephitical, Infects the universe.

‖**mephitis** (mɪ'faɪtɪs). [L. *mephītis* noxious vapour; also personified, as the name of a goddess who averts pestilential exhalations.]
1. A noxious or pestilential emanation, esp. from the earth; a noisome, or poisonous stench.
1706 PHILLIPS (ed. Kersey), *Mephitis*, a Damp, or strong Sulphureous Smell,..a Stench, Stink, or ill Savour. **1750** *Phil. Trans.* XLVII. 53 *note*, Mephitis, a deadly or very dangerous exhalation. **1781** PENNANT *Tour Wales* II. 190 A mephites [*sic*], or pestilential vapour. **1793** BEDDOES *Calculus* 250 The mephitis, which exhales from putrefied animal substances. **1817** COLERIDGE *Satyr. Lett.* i. in *Biog. Lit.* II. 197 My nostrils, the most placable of all the senses, reconciled to or indeed insensible of the mephitis. **1856** EMERSON *Eng. Traits, Voy. to Eng.* Wks. (Bohn) II. 12 Nobody likes to be..suffocated with bilge, mephitis, and stewing oil.
2. *Zool.* A genus of skunks, typical of the family *Mephitinæ*.
1848 in CRAIG. In mod. Dicts.
Hence '**mephitism** *sb.*, mephitic poisoning of the air; †'**mephitized** *ppl. a.*, charged with mephitis; ***mephitized nitrous acid*** = next.
1794 G. ADAMS *Nat. & Exp. Philos.* I. xii. 497 Mephitized inflammable gas. **1796** KIRWAN *Elem. Min.* (ed. 2) II. 521 Mephitized Nitrous Acid. **1801** *Repert. Arts & Manuf.* XV. 425 To destroy the mephitism of the walls in the asylums of industry, indigence, and misfortune. **1813** FORSYTH *Excurs.*

Italy 269 *note*, The *campus martius* is sheltered..from the winds which bring mephitism. **1890** *Syd. Soc. Lex.*, *Mephitism.*

† **mephito-nitrous**, *a. Chem. Obs. rare*$^{-1}$. In ***mephito-nitrous acid***, ? = NITROGEN.

1796 KIRWAN *Elem. Min.* (ed. 2) II. 211 Neither the pure nor Mephito-Nitrous Acid, hot or cold, has any action on it.

† **meprize**, *v. Obs. rare*$^{-1}$. [? ad. F. *mépriser*: see MISPRIZE *v.*] *trans.* ? To despise.

1633 J. DONE *Hist. Septuagint* 133 What is that he ought to doe to meprize his Enemies? [= Gr. πῶς ἂν καταφρονοιη τῶν ἐχθρῶν;]

meprobamate (mɛˈprəʊbəmeɪt). *Pharm.* [f. ME(THYL + PRO(PYL + *car*)*bamate* (s.v. CARBAMIDE).] A colourless crystalline compound, $CH_3CH_2CH_2C(CH_2O{\cdot}CO{\cdot}NH_2)_2CH_3$, which is a mild tranquillizer used in the treatment of motion sickness, neuroses, and insomnia.

1955 *Dispensatory U.S.A.* (ed. 25) 1861/1 Meprobamate. Equanil (Wyeth). Miltown (Wallace).—This is 2-methyl-2-*n*-propyl-1,3-propanediol dicarbamate. **1962** A. HUXLEY *Island* xiii. 201 Mass opiates in the form of television, meprobamate, positive thinking and cigarettes. **1965** J. POLLITT *Depression & its Treatment* iv. 48 When tension is more prominent than depression, chlordiazepoxide, meprobamate or even amylobarbitone in average doses will help tide the patient over difficult phases. **1965** *Evening Standard* 13 Sept. 10/3 He had an envelope full of pep pills—amphetamine—in his left coat pocket and an envelope full of Equanils—meprobamate—in his right pocket. **1967** *Martindale's Extra Pharmacopoeia* (ed. 25) 391/2 Suicide attempts with meprobamate are not infrequent... There is a serious addiction risk. **1969** *Punch* 5 Mar. 340/3 The classic example was the test of the tranquilliser meprobamate, sold here under the brand names Miltown and Equanil. It had been one of the most profitable drugs ever marketed—but in the trials, the placebo proved just as effective.

mepyramine (mɛˈpɪrəmiːn). *Pharm.* [f. ME(THYL + PYR(IDINE + AMINE.] A crystalline substituted amine, $C_{17}H_{23}N_3O$, or its maleate, which is an antihistamine drug used in treating allergic conditions.

1949 *Lancet* 9 July 47/2 The histamine antagonist, N(2-dimethylaminoethyl)N(*p*-methoxybenzyl)2-aminopyridine maleate..later known on the continent as 'Neoantergan' and in this country as 'Anthisan' or mepyramine maleate..was soon recognised as the most powerful and specific of the histamine antagonists. **1964** W. G. SMITH *Allergy & Tissue Metabolism* v. 61 One of these was histamine whose actions could be blocked by mepyramine. **1972** *Nature* 21 Apr. 369/1 Certain responses ..are not antagonized by the classical antihistaminic drugs, such as mepyramine.

mer (mɜː(r)). *Chem.* [f. POLY)MER.] The repeating unit of a polymeric molecule.

1936 W. O. CAROTHERS in *Trans. Faraday Soc.* XXXII. 49 Assume that the weight of the mer or unit is 100. **1947** R. L. WAKEMAN *Chem. Commercial Plastics* xx. 554 The word 'mer'..has..been used by Carothers to designate the individual unit of repetition in both addition and condensation polymers (as distinguished from the monomeric substances themselves from which the polymer is produced). **1952** *Jrnl. Polymer Sci.* VIII. 258 The slight variability in composition and chemical structure permitted ..for high polymers results from the presence of end groups, occasional branches, variation in orientation of the mers (monomeric units), irregularity in the sequence of different types of mers (in copolymers), and sometimes other irregularities. **1967** MARGERISON & EAST *Introd. Polymer Chem.* i. 3 As soon as more than one mer is involved, a wide diversity of polymer structure and type becomes possible.

mer, obs. form of MAR, MARE, MAYOR, MERE.

mer-, used in various combinations (chiefly nonce-wds.) formed after MERMAID, denoting imaginary beings of the mermaid kind, as ***mer-baby***, ***-child***, ***-dog***, ***-folk***, ***-lady***, ***-monster***, ***-people***, ***-wife***. Cf. MERMAN, MERWOMAN.

1894 J. GEDDIE *Fringes of Fife* 150 The radiant young rogue,..fearless as a *Mer-Baby, grins at us..from his rocking craft. **1881** *Proc. Soc. Antiquaries* 19 May, Seal... Subject, a mermaid holding her *merchild to her breast. **1895** 'Q.' *Wandering Heath* 97 Change, O change him [*sc.* a drowned dog] to a *mer-dog! **1863** BARING-GOULD *Iceland* xx. 349 With regard to the appearance of the *merfolk in other countries, I may state [etc.]. **1822** HIBBERT *Descr. Shetl. Isl.* 570 The *merlady, perceiving that she must become an inhabitant of the earth, found [etc.]. **1620** *Hic Mulier* A4b, These Meare-maids or rather *Meare-Monsters. **1882** *Spectator* 16 Dec. 1618 The idea of the 'child of earth..' carried away to consort with *Mer-people is as old as Hylas. **1822** HIBBERT *Descr. Shetl. Isl.* 570 The Shetlander's love for his *merwife was unbounded.

-mer (mə(r)), terminal element repr. Gr. μέρος part, occurring in various chemical terms: orig. in *polymer* and *isomer*, and usu. in words denoting particular kinds of polymer (as *dimer*, *elastomer*) or isomer (as *epimer*).

merabolan, obs. form of MYROBALAN.

† **meˈracious**, *a. Obs. rare*$^{-1}$. Also (in Dicts.) -aceous. [f. L. *merāc-us* (f. *merus*: see MERE *a.*) + -IOUS.] Pure, unmixed. So † **meˈracity**, purity, unmixed condition (*Obs.*$^{-0}$).

1657 REEVE *God's Plea* 130 We must drink of the sweet, and it is well, if any thing be dulcy, and meracious enough for us. **1656** BLOUNT *Glossogr.*, *Meracity*, clearness, or pureness, without mixture. **1727** BAILEY vol. II, *Meraceous*, *Meracity*.

meracle, merakil(l, obs. forms of MIRACLE.

meraltie, -alty, obs. forms of MAYORALTY.

meranti (məˈræntɪ). [Malay.] A hardwood timber produced by trees of the genus *Shorea*, belonging to the family Dipterocarpaceæ, and native to Malaya, Sarawak, and Indonesia; also, a tree yielding this wood.

1783 W. MARSDEN *Hist. Sumatra* 130 *Maranti maracooly* and *murbow*, are in much estimation for building. **1839** T. J. NEWBOLD *Pol. & Statistical Acct. Straits of Malacca* I. vii. 442 The trees chiefly in use for purposes of house and ship are the Chingei,..the red and white Meranti for planks, etc. **1900** W. W. SKEAT *Malay Magic* 109 The *mĕranti* is a fine hard-wood forest tree. **1935** I. H. BURKILL *Dict. Econ. Products Malay Peninsula* II. 2002 Red Mĕranti is the commonest Malayan timber. **1955** *Nomencl. Commercial Timbers (B.S.I.)* 74 For the light to medium-weight timbers it should be noted that *meranti* is the group name for species of *Shorea* in Malaya, Sarawak, Brunei and Indonesia. **1956** *Archit. Rev.* CXX. 117 All windows and doors are framed in red meranti hardwood. **1956** *Handbk. Hardwoods* (Forest Prod. Res. Lab.) 150 In Malaya this timber is commonly classified for export mainly on the basis of colour and weight as light red meranti (the most important), dark red meranti, yellow meranti and white meranti. **1966** D. FORBES *Heart of Malaya* x. 113 Their box-like wooden houses..are dull and plain in contrast with the charming thatched cottages of red meranti wood, in which the Malays live. **1971** *Timber Trades Jrnl.* 14 Aug. 42/2 Malaysian and Singapore plywoods, of which meranti and mengkulang are the most important, accounted for 11·9% of deliveries of 102 500m^3.

merbau (ˈmɜːbəʊ). Also **marbow, merabau, murbow**. [Malay.] A hardwood timber obtained from *Intsia bijuga* or *I. palembanica*, of the family Leguminosæ, trees native to Malaysia and Indonesia; also, the tree itself.

1783 [see MERANTI]. **1836** J. LOW *Diss. Soil & Agric. Penang* v. 202 *Marbow*— this is a high tree, affording large planks. **1911** *Encycl. Brit.* XVII. 472/2 Good hard-wood timber is found in plenty, the best being the *merabau*, *penak*, *rasok* and *chengal*. **1935** I. H. BURKILL *Dict. Econ. Products Malay Peninsula* II. 1243 Mĕrbau is used for all kinds of high-grade construction on land, for furniture, and for sleepers. **1940** E. J. H. CORNER *Wayside Trees Malaya* I. 396 This small genus [sc. *Intsia*] includes the well-known timber-tree *Merbau*. **1958** J. SLIMMING *Temiar Jungle* iv. 60 The children play with spinning tops, made of *Merbau* wood. **1965** C. SHUTTLEWORTH *Malayan Safari* i. 16 There are heavy hardwoods such as merbau, balau and chengal. **1972** *Timber Trades Jrnl.* 13 May 39/2 Of the lesser species merbau and kapur are readily available.

merbel, -ul, -yl, obs. forms of MARBLE.

† **ˈmercable**, *a. Obs.*$^{-0}$ [ad. L. *mercābil-is*, f. *mercārī* to buy: see MERCHANT.] That may be bought.

1656 in BLOUNT *Glossogr.*

‖ **mercadore.** *rare*$^{-1}$. [Sp. *mercader*.] A merchant, tradesman.

1595 *Maroccus Ext.* (Percy Soc.) 9 A mercadore,..that for one or two tearmes arraie, a shall for his lives tearme.. become beggeries bondmen and usuries vassall.

‖ **mercal**[1] (ˈmɜːkəl). *Indian.* Also **mercall, marcal.** [Eng. pronunciation of Tamil *marakkāl*.] A measure for grain used in Madras.

1776 T. BROOKS *Coins E. Indies*, etc. 7, 8 Measures are equal to 1 Mercal, 400 Marcals..1 Garse. **1803** WELLINGTON in Gurw. *Desp.* (1837) II. 85 The small bags.. filled up each to the full amount of three Mercalls or seventy two pounds. **1864** W. A. BROWNE *Money, Weights & Meas.* 51, 8 Puddies = 1 Marcal, 5 Marcals = 1 Parah.

mercal[2] (ˈmɜːkəl). *Sc.* Also 9 **markal**. In Orkney and Shetland: The piece of timber carrying the plough-share, which was fastened into the lower end of the beam of a wooden plough.

1793 *Statist. Acc. Scot.* VII. 585 A square hole is cut through the lower end of the beam, and the mercal, a piece of oak about 22 inches long, introduced. **1822** SCOTT *Pirate* xviii, What manners are to be expected in a country where folk call a pleugh-sock a markal?

Mercalli (mɜːˈkælɪ). *Seismology.* The name of Giuseppe *Mercalli* (1850–1914), Italian geologist, used *attrib.* to designate an arbitrary 12-point scale he devised (in 1897) to express the intensity of an earthquake at any place.

1921 C. DAVISON *Man. Seismol.* iii. 45 The Mercalli scale ..is suitable for strong earthquakes and is adopted in Italy. **1927** —— *Founders Seismol.* vi. 106 Mercalli found that the higher degrees of the Rossi-Forel scale were insufficient... His modification of that scale contains the germs of the Mercalli scale now so widely used. **1972** *Times* 28 Nov. 5/2 The tremor (eight on the 12-point Mercalli scale) damaged many buildings in the old part of the city. **1973** *Daily Colonist* (Victoria, B.C.) 8 Apr. 10/5 An earthquake can have only one magnitude but it can have several intensities and these are registered on what is known as the modified Mercalli intensity scale.

mercantant: see MARCANTANT *Obs.*

mercantile (ˈmɜːkəntaɪl, -tɪl), *a.* (and *sb.*) Also 7 **merchantile, mercantil,** 8 **-iel.** [a. F. *mercantile*, ad. It. *mercantil*, f. *mercante*: see MERCHANT. Cf. Sp. and Pg. *mercantil*.]

1. Of or belonging to merchants or their trade; concerned with the exchange of merchandise; of or pertaining to trade or commerce; commercial.

1642 HOWELL *Instr. For. Trav.* (Arb.) 61 Navigation and Mercantile Negotiation, are the two Poles whereon that State [*sc.* Holland] doth move. *c* **1645** —— *Lett.* I. xxix. (1655) I. 43 The only procede (that I may use the mercantil term) you can expect, is thanks. **1727** ARBUTHNOT *Coins* 224 The Expedition of the Argonauts..was partly mercantile, partly military. **1759** *Book of Fairs* 54 Black cattle, sheep, horses, and mercantile goods. **1849** MACAULAY *Hist. Eng.* vi. II. 51 Bonrepaux..was esteemed an adept in the mystery of mercantile politics. **1856** E. A. BOND *Russia* (Hakl. Soc.) Introd. 130 By joining in his mercantile ventures in Russia. **1897** WEBSTER (*citing* McElrath), *Mercantile paper*, the notes or acceptances given by merchants for goods bought, or received on consignment; drafts on merchants for goods sold or consigned.

b. ***mercantile system*** (also ***m. doctrine, theory***): a term used by Adam Smith and later Political Economists for the system of economic doctrine and legislative policy based on the principle that money alone constituted wealth. Hence ***mercantile school***: those who upheld this system.

1776 ADAM SMITH *W.N.* IV. i. (*heading*) Of the Principle of the commercial, or mercantile System. **1848** MILL *Pol. Econ.* I. 2 The set of doctrines designated, since the time of Adam Smith, by the appellation of the Mercantile System. *Ibid.* 7 The Mercantile Theory could not fail to be seen in its true character. **1881** *Contemp. Rev.* Nov. XL. 806 The 'mercantile' school was right in maintaining that an influx of precious metal stimulates commerce and industry. **1885** J. K. INGRAM in *Encycl. Brit.* XIX. 354/2 The mercantile doctrine, stated in its most extreme form, makes wealth and money identical.

c. That deals with, investigates or controls commercial affairs.

1841 W. SPALDING *Italy & It. Isl.* III. 332 There are three courts,..a civil, a criminal, and a mercantile. **1848** MILL *Pol. Econ.* III. xvii. §4 Leaders of opinion on mercantile questions. **1858** HOMANS *Cycl. Comm.* s.v., The Mercantile Agency is a name applied to various houses in the leading cities of the United States, and in Montreal and London. The principal object of the Agency is to supply, to annual subscribers, information respecting the character, capacity and pecuniary condition of persons asking credit... The Agency was first established in 1841 in the city of New York. **1861** GOSCHEN *For. Exch.* 113 Putting aside..the..subject of the currency altogether, and confining ourselves to the more mercantile part of the question.

2. Engaged in trade or commerce. ***mercantile marine***, the shipping collectively employed in commerce (see MARINE *sb.* 2).

c **1645** HOWELL *Lett.* II. xv. (1655) I. 94 Amsterdam..is one of the greatest mercantil Towns in Europ. **1662** J. DAVIES tr. *Mandelslo's Trav.* II. 140 The scituation of this town is upon a fair River, with a good harbour that renders it very Merchantile. *a* **1734** NORTH *Exam.* III. viii. §29 (1740) 604 His [Fairclough's] son was then mercantiel servant to Mr. North. **1838** DICKENS *Nich. Nick.* i, Ralph Nickleby.. had been some time placed in a mercantile house in London. **1841** ELPHINSTONE *Hist. India* I. 213 The Jáins..are generally an opulent and mercantile class. **1889** *Act 52 & 53 Vict.* c. 45 §1 The expression 'mercantile agent' shall mean a mercantile agent having..authority either to sell goods, or [etc.].

3. Having payment or gain as the motive; mercenary; also, simply, disposed for bargaining.

1756 WARTON *Ess. Pope* I. 260 The mercantile bard [Dryden]. **1856** EMERSON *Eng. Traits, Lit.* Wks. (Bohn) II. 103 He [the Englishman] loves the axe, the spade, the oar, the gun, the steampipe... He is materialist, economical, mercantile. **1860** RUSKIN *Unto this Last* ii. (1862) 41 The two economies, to which the terms 'Political' and 'Mercantile' might not unadvisedly be attached... Mercantile economy, the economy of 'merces' or of 'pay', signifies the accumulation, in the hands of individuals, of legal or moral claim upon, or power over, the labour of others.

4. Of or proper to a merchant.

1819 CRABBE *T. of Hall* VII, A bill That was not drawn with true mercantile skill. **1839** ALISON *Hist. Europe* xlix. §9 (1849–50) VIII. 9 A nation in which the chivalrous and mercantile qualities are strangely blended.

† **5.** quasi-*sb.* A merchant. *Obs. rare*$^{-1}$.

1813 JANE AUSTEN *Lett.* (1884) II. 178 A great rich mercantile, Sir Robert Wigram.

Hence **ˈmercantilely** *adv.*, from a mercantile point of view; with regard to business transactions.

1827 *Examiner* 433/1 It is, mercantilely speaking, not obvious how a present expense can be met by merely possible funds. **1838** *Fraser's Mag.* XVII. 185 Before the arrest he might have been deemed mercantilely solvent.

mercantilism (ˈmɜːkəntaɪlɪz(ə)m). [f. MERCANTILE + -ISM. Cf. F. *mercantilisme*.]

1. The mercantile spirit; devotion to trade or commerce; the principles or practice characteristic of merchants; commercialism.

1873 P. FITZGERALD *Dumas* II. 105 *note*, The picture of 'literary mercantilism', described by this great writer [Balzac], shows that Dumas had only borrowed his system from journalism and social life. **1885** *Century Mag.* XXXI. 311/1 Mercantilism is drawing into its vortex the intellectual strength of the nation. The energies of its most promising

young men are enlisted in the pursuit of wealth. **1888** *Harper's Mag.* Jan. 272 The mercantilism which succeeded ..feudalism.

2. *Pol. Econ.* The principles of the 'mercantile system'.

1881 *Contemp. Rev.* Nov. XL. 792 Is it possible that merchants, bankers, [etc.]..should all be led astray by the sophism of 'mercantilism'? **1885** *Encycl. Brit.* XIX. 364/2 It has been justly observed that there are in him [Hume] several traces of a refined mercantilism.

mercantilist (ˈmɜːkəntaɪlɪst), *sb.* and *a.* [Formed as prec. + -IST.]

A. *sb.* An advocate of the 'mercantile system'.

1854 MICHELSEN *England* 253 The physiocrats occupy a far superior position to the mercantilists. **1891** CUNNINGHAM in *Economic Rev.* 16 The mercantilists held that the direction in which capital was used should be controlled so that the power of the state might be maintained.

B. *adj.* Of or pertaining to mercantilism or the 'mercantile system'.

1881 *Contemp. Rev.* Nov. XL. 806 But from these true observations..the 'mercantilist' reasoners have deduced erroneous conclusions. **1896** CUNNINGHAM *Growth Eng. Indust.* 562 The Doctor takes the mercantilist position as distinguished from the bullionist.

Hence ˌ**mercantiˈlistic** *a.* = prec. adj.

1881-4 *Lalor's Cycl. Pol. Sci.* II. 197 (Cent.) From the seventeenth century mercantilistic views began to exercise a more and more marked influence upon financial literature.

mercantility (mɜːkənˈtɪlɪtɪ). [Formed as prec. + -ITY.] The quality of being mercantile; devotion to mercantile pursuits.

1860 READE *Cloister & H.* (1861) IV. 76 'Let us make a bargain;..what say you to that?' And his eyes sparkled, and he was all on fire with mercantility.

mercaptal (mɜːˈkæptəl). *Chem.* [f. MERCAPT-AN + AL-DEHYDE.] A compound of a mercaptan with an aldehyde.

1892 MORLEY & MUIR *Watt's Dict. Chem., Mercaptals*... They may be viewed as thio-acetals or as the sulphur-compounds corresponding to the alkyl derivatives of ortho-aldehydes.

mercaptan (mɜːˈkæptən). *Chem.* [f. L. *mercurium captans* 'catching mercury' (see quot. 1834).] A sulphur alcohol; any one of a series of compounds resembling the alcohols, but containing sulphur in place of oxygen.

[**1834** ZEISE in *Ann. Phys. & Chem.* XXXI. 378 Nenne ich den vom Quecksilber aufgenommenen Stoff Mercaptum (von: Corpus mercurio aptum) und den andern Hydro-Mercaptum, oder besser..Mercaptan (d.h. Corpus mercurium captans).] **1835** *R. D. Thomson's Rec. Gen. Sci.* I. 110 Mercaptan when obtained pure from the mercaptide of mercury, is colourless, with a smell of assafœtida. **1865** WATTS *Dict. Chem., Mercaptans*, sulphydrates of the alcohol-radicles.

mercaptide (mɜːˈkæptaɪd). *Chem.* [f. prec. + -IDE.] A compound formed by the substitution of a metal for hydrogen in a mercaptan.

1835 [see prec.]. **1836** BRANDE *Chem.* 1109 When mercaptan is acted on by potassium, hydrogen is evolved, and a mercapturet or mercaptide of potassium is formed.

mercapto(-) (mɜːˈkæptəʊ). *Chem.* [f. MERCAPT(AN + -O.] **a.** As an inseparable formative element in chem. names indicating the presence of the radical –SH, as ***mercapto-acetic*** adj., ***mercaptoethanol***; **mercaptoˈpurine** *Pharm.*, any of the monomercapto derivatives of purine, *spec.* 6-mercaptopurine, $C_5H_4N_4S$, which is a yellow crystalline powder and is a cytotoxic agent used chiefly in treating leukæmia in children.

1971 *Nomencl. Org. Chem.* (I.U.P.A.C.) (ed. 2) C. 211 When –SH is not the principal group, the prefix 'mercapto-' is placed before the name of the parent compound to denote an unsubstituted –SH group. **1884** ROSCOE & SCHORLEMMER *Treat. Chem.* III. II. 88 Thioglycollic acid, or mercapto-acetic acid, $CH_2(SH)CO_2H$, is obtained by the addition of chloracetic acid to an aqueous solution of potassium hydrosulphide. **1947** *Biochem. Jrnl.* XLI. 49/2 BAL is also effective in detoxicating this arsenical, whereas a concentration of 2-mercaptoethanol equivalent to twice that of BAL is almost completely inactive. **1965** PEACOCKE & DRYSDALE *Molecular Basis Heredity* vii. 73 By inhibiting nuclear division in sea urchin eggs with mercaptoethanol, Mazia provided evidence that the prophase chromosome contains at least four strands. **1954** *Amer. Jrnl. Med. Sci.* CCXXVIII. 376/2 We have in mercaptopurine a new type of agent which has demonstrated activity against experimental tumors and leukemias in the mouse and against leukemia in man. **1961** *Lancet* 7 Oct. 821/1 Methotrexate..and mercaptopurine.. are folic-acid antagonists, which..interfere with nucleic-acid synthesis by inhibiting folic-acid reductase. **1965** Mercaptopurine [see *immunosuppressant* s.v. IMMUNO-]. **1973** *Arthritis & Rheumatism* XVI. 139 Thirteen patients with psoriasis and arthritis were treated with 6-mercaptopurine in dosages ranging from 20 to 150 mg/day.

b. As an independent word, usu. *attrib.* and sometimes joined by a hyphen to the second element: the radical –SH, present in mercaptans; sulphydryl.

1896 *Jrnl. Chem. Soc.* LXX. I. 412 Unsymmetrical homologues of thiodiglycollic acid..are prepared by the interaction of the neutral sodium salts of mercapto-acids and those of haloid fatty acids. **1930** *Chem. Rev.* VII. 511 Mercapto acids may be made in the same way as hydroxy acids. **1957** R. H. BARRY in E. Sagarin *Cosmetics* xx. 468 These inventors obtained coverage also in Great Britain for other organic mercapto compounds which function in alkaline-reacting media as depilatories.

mercapturic (mɜːkæpˈtjʊərɪk), *a.* *Chem.* [ad. G. *bromphenyl)mercaptur(säure* bromophenyl-mercapturic acid (Baumann & Preusse 1879, in *Ber. d. Deut. Chem. Ges.* XII. 807), f. *mercapt(an* MERCAPTAN + *ur(in* URINE *sb.*[1]: see -IC.] ***mercapturic acid***: any of the acids of the formula $RSCH_2CH(NH{\cdot}CO{\cdot}CH_3)COOH$ (where R is an aryl radical), some of which are excreted in the urine, probably as detoxication products of aromatic compounds.

1879 *Jrnl. Chem. Soc.* XXXVI. 803 An examination of the urine of a dog, to which 3 to 4 grams of bromobenzene had been daily administered for six months, showed... The urine contains bromophenyl-mercapturic acid. **1884** *Ibid.* XLVI. 1395 A body strongly lævorotatory, which on treatment with acids yields mercapturic acid. **1934** *Times Lit. Suppl.* 9 Aug. 555/2 Naphthalene is detoxicated in the rabbit partly by conjugation with cysteine and subsequent excretion as the mercapturic acid. **1971** H. G. MANDEL in B. N. La Du et al. *Fund. Drug Metabolism* x. 168 Acetylation takes place in the liver..and the resulting mercapturic acid is then excreted in the urine.

mercat(e, obs. forms of MARKET.

mercatante: see MARCANTANT *Obs.*

†**merˈcation.** *Obs.*$^{-0}$ [a. L. *mercātiōn-em*, n. of action f. *mercārī* to trade.] (See quot.)

1623 COCKERAM, *Mercation*, a buying.

†**mercative**, *a.* *Obs.*$^{-0}$ [As if ad. L. **mercātīv-us*, f. *mercārī* to trade: see -ATIVE.]

1656 BLOUNT *Glossogr., Mercative*, belonging to Chapmanry.

Mercator (mɜːˈkeɪtə(r)). Also **mercator**. [L., = 'merchant'.] **a.** The name of Gerhardus *Mercator* (= L. equivalent of Gerhard Kremer) (1512–94), Flemish cartographer, used *attrib.* and in the possessive with reference to the orthomorphic cylindrical map projection first used by him in 1568, in which meridians are represented by equidistant straight lines at right angles to the equator and any course that follows a constant compass bearing is represented by a straight line.

1669 Mercator's projection [see PROJECTION *sb.* 7b]. *a* **1877** KNIGHT *Dict. Mech.* II. 1419/2 *Mercator-chart*, a mode of projection invented by Gerald Mercator, in which the meridians and parallels are straight and parallel lines. **1883** *Encycl. Brit.* XV. 520/2 By 1601 Mercator's projection was in use for all sea charts. **1908** G. R. PUTNAM *Naut. Charts* 9 The Arcano del Mare, 1646, was the first marine atlas in which all the maps were drawn on the mercator projection. **1912** A. R. HINKS *Map Projections* iii. 29 The great distortion in the north and south makes Mercator's projection altogether unsuitable for a land map. **1938** L. M. MILNE-THOMSON *Theoret. Hydrodynamics* v. 138 An illustration of conformal mapping is afforded by an ordinary map on Mercator's projection. **1960** C. ECKART *Hydrodynamics of Oceans & Atmospheres* 280 The vertical co-ordinate, μ, on a Mercator chart of the Sphere is defined by $d\phi = \cos\phi d\mu$.

b. *absol.* (A map drawn on) Mercator's projection.

1879 *Encycl. Brit.* X. 208/2 The meridian Mercator drawn as described in the last paragraph..may be made to serve the important purpose of enabling one to trace on the ordinary Mercator's chart the track of a great circle joining any two places. **1953** A. H. ROBINSON *Elem. Cartogr.* iii. 43/1 The poles cannot be represented for they are 'at' infinity on the conventional Mercator.

mercatorial (mɜːkəˈtɔərɪəl), *a.*[1] Now *rare.* [f. L. *mercātōri-us* (f. *mercātor* merchant, agent-n. f. *mercārī*: see MERCHANT) + -AL[1].] Of or pertaining to merchants or merchandise; mercantile.

mercatorial guild (Antiq.): transl. of med.L. *gilda mercatoria*, more commonly rendered 'guild merchant'.

? *c* **1700** J. BENNET (*title*) The National Merchant,..being an Essay for Regulating and Improving the Trade and Plantations of Great Britain, by Uniting the National and Mercatorial Interests. **1796** BAGE *Hermsprong* lii. 231 Whose father..had sent this son upon a mercatorial tour to Europe. **1817–23** J. H. HANSHALL *Hist. Co. Chester* 490-1 in Gross *Gild Merch.* (1890) II. 174 There was established here [*sc.* Nantwich] soon after the Conquest a Mercatorial Guild. **1823** *Blackw. Mag.* XIV. 541 A country whose mercatorial advantages he so highly extols.

Mercatorial (mɜːkəˈtɔərɪəl), *a.*[2] Also **mercatorial**. [f. prec. + -IAL.] Of, pertaining to, or derived from Mercator or Mercator's projection or chart.

a **1888** P. F. SHORTLAND *Naut. Surveying* (1890) 144 Their Mercatorial meridians will be inclined to each of them respectively about 1'·2. *Ibid.* 346 To reduce a plane sheet to a Mercatorial projection proceed as follows. **1942** *Jrnl. R. Aeronaut. Soc.* XLVI. 21 It is..possible to include these scales in certain navigational devices, so that rhumb lines and mercatorial bearings may be projected if required without the aid of an actual graticule.

†**mercatory**, *a.* *Obs. rare*$^{-1}$. [ad. L. *mercātōri-us*: see -ORY.] = prec.

1654 FULLER *Two Serm.* 49 Mercatorie transactions betwixt Buyer and Seller. **1656**, **1862** [see GUILD 4].

†**mercatour.** *Sc.* *Obs.* [a. L. *mercātor*: see MERCATORIAL. Cf. OF. *mercatour.*] A merchant, shopkeeper.

1508 *Extracts Aberd. Reg.* (1844) I. 79 Andro Gordoun, mercatour.

mercatte, obs. form of MEERKAT.

†**mercature.** *Obs.* [ad. L. *mercātūra*, f. *mercārī* to trade.] Trading, commerce.

a **1620** J. DYKE *Purch. & Poss. Truth* Serm. (1640) 367 That's commendable in wordly mercature: To be sure so men deale here. **1639** HEYWOOD *London's Peaceable Est.* Wks. 1874 V. 357. **1647** LILLY *Chr. Astrol.* clxxxv. 803 Our Native may expect good encrease..in that way of Mercature or course of life he shall then lead. **1755** JOHNSON, *Mercature*, the practice of buying and selling.

†**merce**, *v.* *Obs.* Also 6 **merse**. Aphetic form of AMERCE.

1483 *Plumpton Corr.* (Camden) 43 Ye clame suyt, service & feute, of ther maner of Colthorpe, & for the same merce him in your court at Plompton. **1530** TINDALE *Exod.* xxi. 22 Then shall he be mersed, accordynge as the womans husbonde will laye to his charge. **1563-87** FOXE *A. & M.* (1596) 253/2 Walter treasurer of the kings house, was.. merced at an hundred pounds. **1607** G. WILKINS *Miseries of Inforst Marr.* B4, Then hath he power To Merce your purse. *a* **1661** FULLER *Worthies, Norfolk* II. (1662) 249 Ralph was merced in seven thousand marks, for bribery.

merce, obs. form of MERCY.

merceament, variant of MERCIAMENT.

‖**merced** (mɛrˈθeð). Also 7 **mercede**. [Sp. *merced* honour, honorarium:—L. *mercēd-em* reward: see MERCY.] A gift.

[**1589** PUTTENHAM *Eng. Poesie* (Arb.) 302 In Spaine it is thought very vndecent for a Courtier to craue..: therefore the king of ordinarie calleth euery second, third or fourth yere for his Checker roll, and bestoweth his *mercedes* of his owne meere motion, and by discretion.] **1622** MABBE tr. *Aleman's Guzman d'Alf.* I. I. 99 Daraxa..did sollicit the life of her espoused husband, begging it by the way of merced and grace. *Ibid.* I. II. 356 That I might procure some mercede or favour from him. **1855** MOTLEY *Dutch Rep.* VI. i. III. 393 On promise..of a 'merced' large enough to satisfy his most avaricious dreams. **1881** RAYMOND *Mining Gloss.*, *Merced*,..a gift. This term is applied to a grant which is made without any valuable consideration.

†**mercedary**, *a.* *Obs.*$^{-0}$ [ad. L. *mercēdāri-us*, f. *mercēd-*, *mercēs* hire, pay: see -ARY.] (See quot.)

1656 BLOUNT *Glossogr., Mercedary* is used both of him that gives wages for labor, or for him that receives it.

†**mercede.** *Obs. rare*$^{-1}$. [ad. L. *mercēd-em* (nom. *mercēs*) wages.] Pay, reward, wage.

1393 LANGL. *P. Pl.* C. IV. 292 Ac þer ys mede [and] mercede and boþe men demen A desert for som doynge derne oþer elles. *Ibid.* 306 And þat ys no mede bote a mercede, A maner dewe dette for þe doynge.

†ˈ**mercement.** *Obs.* Also 4 **mersy-**, 4–5 **merci-**, **merse-**, 4–6 **mercy-**, 6 **marsement**. [Aphetic f. AMERCEMENT. Cf. MERCIAMENT.]

1. = AMERCEMENT. Also, in wider sense, doom, adjudged punishment.

1303 R. BRUNNE *Handl. Synne* 5496 Þy mercyment shal be þe pyne of helle. **1387** TREVISA *Higden* (Rolls) I. 95 Blodwyte, mersement for schedynge of blood. *c* **1449** PECOCK *Repr.* III. xiv. 367 Forfetis, eschetis, and mercimentis, and fynys. *c* **1557** ABP. PARKER *Ps.* cxxx. 383 Because with God is ruefulnes, He oft redeemth his mercyment. *a* **1572** KNOX *Hist. Ref.* Wks. (1846) I. 361 Thay..committed the hole to the merciment of fyre. **1598** GRENEWEY *Tacitus, Ann.* XIII. vi. (1622) 187 That the Quæstors of the treasurie should not enter into record before foure months were past, the mercements adiudged by them.

2. *Sc.* ***to stand to the merciment of***: to abide the judgement of.

1560 ROLLAND *Crt. Venus* Prol. 316, I may weill thole,.. That this small Wark stand to the mercyment Of Gentilmen, and byde at thair subiectioun.

mercenarian (mɜːsɪˈnɛərɪən), *a.*[1] and *sb.*[1] *rare.* [f. L. *mercēnāri-us* (see MERCENARY) + -AN.]

†**a.** *sb.* A mercenary, hired soldier (*obs.*). **b.** *adj.* Of or belonging to mercenary soldiers.

1598 MARSTON *Pygmal.*, *In prayse of prec. Poem*, And then ensues my stanzaes, like odd bands Of voluntaries, and mercenarians. **1886** SHELDON tr. *Flaubert's Salammbo* iv. 72 A mercenarian camp.

mercenarian (mɜːsɪˈnɛərɪən), *a.*[2] and *sb.*[2] [f. med.L. *Mercēnārius* + -AN.] **a.** *adj.* Pertaining to the Spanish religious order called in Sp. *la Orden de la Merced*. **b.** *sb.* A friar of this order.

1648 GAGE *West Ind.* 10 There are Dominicans, Franciscans,..Mercenarians [etc.]. *Ibid.* 15 Mercenarian Fryers. **1740** PINEDA *Span. Dict.*, *Mercèd*, the religious Order of the Mercenarians first instituted in Aragon by King Jayme for Redemption of Captives.

mercenarily (ˈmɜːsɪnərɪlɪ), *adv.* [f. MERCENARY + -LY[2].] In a mercenary manner.

1612 T. TAYLOR *Comm. Titus* ii. 13 But doe the godly worke mercenarily? **1711** STEELE *Spect.* No. 145 ¶6 We are ..obliged by the mercenary Humour of the Men to be as Mercenarily inclined as they are.

mercenariness ('mɜːsɪnərɪnɪs). [f. MERCENARY + -NESS.] The quality of being mercenary.

a **1624** BP. M. SMYTH *Serm.* (1632) 94 Who can impeach or blemish Gods bounty and liberality, with the least note of mercinarinesse. **1752** H. WALPOLE *Lett. H. Mann* (1834) III. ccxxxix. 14 To have one's favourite author convicted of mere mortal mercenariness. **1808** LAMB *Lett.* (1888) I. 243 Mary is very thankful..; and with the less suspicion of mercenariness, as the silk..has not yet appeared. **1883** STEPNIAK in *Contemp. Rev.* Sept. 323 The mercenariness of the officials is the only guarantee against oppression.

†**mercenariously**, *adv. Obs. rare*⁻¹. [f. L. *mercēnāri-us* (see next) + -OUS + -LY².] Mercenarily.

1659 *Invisible John made Visible* 1 The old Roman Law.. was not more mercenariously devoted to serve the will and lust of Cæsar.

mercenary ('mɜːsɪnərɪ), *a.* and *sb.* Also 4-7 **mercenarie**, (5 **-ye**), 6 **mercennary**, **mercionary**, 6-7 **mercinary**, (7 **-ie**). [ad. L. *mercēnārius*, earlier *mercennārius*, f. *mercēd-*, *mercēs* reward, wages: see MERCY. Cf. F. *mercenaire* (OF. also *mercenier*), Sp., Pg., It. *mercenario*.

The sb. occurs in Eng. earlier than the adj.: the oldest uses refer to the 'hireling' (Vulg. *mercenarius*) of John x. 12.]

A. *adj.*

1. Of persons: Working merely for the sake of monetary or other reward; actuated by considerations of self-interest. Hence of motives, dispositions, etc.

1532 MORE *Confut. Tindale* Wks. 507/2 A mercennary preacher and an hired, which seketh his own temporal aduauntage & commoditie. **1596** SHAKS. *Merch. V.* IV. i. 418 And I deliuering you, am satisfied, And therein doe account my self well paid, My mind was neuer yet more mercinarie. **1616** SIR R. DUDLEY in *Fortesc. Papers* (Camden) 17 And that, whether you move this suite or noe, for I am not mercenarie. **1662** STILLINGFL. *Orig. Sacr.* III. iii. §1 Without any such mercenary eye (as those who serve God for their own ends). **1762** GOLDSM. *Cit. W.* xiii, Such wretches are kept in pay by some mercenary bookseller. **1865** DICKENS *Mut. Fr.* III. iv, Haven't I told you what a mercenary little wretch I am?

b. Of conduct, a course of action, etc.: That has the love of lucre for its motive.

1532 MORE *Confut. Tindale* Wks. 362/2 They holde that it is not lawfull to loue..God..for obteining of reward, calling this maner of loue..seruile bonde and mercennary. **1680-90** TEMPLE *Ess. Learning* i. Wks. 1731 I. 168 Learning has been so little advanced since it grew to be mercenary. **1711** SHAFTESBURY *Charac.* II. iii. (1737) I. 97 They have made Virtue so mercenary a thing, and have talk'd so much of its Rewards. **1837** HT. MARTINEAU *Soc. Amer.* III. 128 The disgusting spectacle of mercenary marriages. **1861** DICKENS *Lett.* 6 Nov., They are all old servants,..and..are under the strongest injunction to avoid any approach to mercenary dealing.

2. Hired; serving for wages or hire. Now only of soldiers. (Cf. B. 2.)

1589 GREENE *Tullies Love* (1616) G 4, A simple shepheard, who was a mercenary man. **1590** SIR J. SMYTH *Disc. Weap.* 49 b, They..began..to go ouer to serue as mercenarie soldiers in the Low Countries. **1599** SHAKS. *Hen. V*, IV. vii. 79 Many of our Princes..Lye drown'd and soak'd in mercenary blood. **1611** CORYAT *Crudities* (1776) I. 214 Of these Gondolas..sixe thousand are priuate..and foure thousand for mercenary men, which get their liuing by the trade of rowing. **1640** WALTON *Life Donne, 80 Serm.* A 6 He continued that employment.., being daily usefull (and not mercenary) to his friends. **1871** FREEMAN *Norm. Conq.* (1876) IV. xviii. 232 William at this time dismissed the mercenary part of his army.

†**b.** Of services, an office, etc.: Salaried, stipendiary. Of a profession, etc.: Carried on for the sake of gain. *Obs.*

1656 STANLEY *Hist. Philos.* VI. *Aristotle* xv. 27 He shut up his poor shop, and gave over his mercenary profession. **1664** EVELYN *Diary* 5 Feb., I saw 'The Indian Queene' acted, a tragedie..so beautified with rich scenes as the like had never ben seene..on a mercenary theater. **1726** AYLIFFE *Parergon* 319 Such Things..the Judge may despatch by his mercenary Office. **1782** PENNANT *Journey* 96 These livings at that time were good rectories; now poor vicarages, or mercenary curacies, annexed to the bishoprick.

B. *sb.*

1. One who labours merely for hire; a hireling, a mercenary person. ? *Obs.*

c **1386** CHAUCER *Prol.* 514 He [the parson] was a shepherde and noght a Mercenarie [cf. *John* x. 12]. ?*c* **1430** LYDG. *St. Giles* 183 in Horstm. *Altengl. Leg.* (1881) 373 Pastor callid, nat a mercenarye. **1643** SIR T. BROWNE *Relig. Med.* I. §52 Mercenaries that crouch unto him in feare of Hell..are indeed but slaves of the Almighty. **1805** TOOKE *Purley* II. 3 Punish the wickedness of those mercenaries who utter such atrocities. **1844** LINGARD *Anglo-Sax. Ch.* (1858) II. xii. 238 The monastic institute was looked upon with scorn, as calculated only for mercenaries and slaves.

2. One who receives payment for his services; chiefly, and now exclusively, a professional soldier serving a foreign power.

1523 LD. BERNERS *Froiss.* I. ccv. 242 The Almaygnes, and mercenaryes of strange countreis. **1583** STUBBES *Anat. Abus.* II. (1882) 74 The reading ministers, after they be hired of the parishes (for they are mercenaries). **1638** G. SANDYS *Paraphr., Job* vii. 10 He a poore mercenary serves for bread. **1687** DRYDEN *Hind & P.* II. 290 Like mercenaries, hired for home defence, They will not fight against their native prince. **1776** JEFFERSON *Wks.* (1859) I. 23 He is at this time transporting large armies of foreign mercenaries. **1840** BROWNING *Sordello* IV. 51 Lean silent gangs of mercenaries ceased Working to watch the strangers. **1849** GROTE *Greece* II. lx. (1862) 279 Greeks continental and insular.. volunteers and mercenaries..were all here to be found.

fig. **1861** J. PYCROFT *Ways & Words* 285 Literary mercenaries, ready to serve under friend or foe.

mercer ('mɜːsə(r)). Also 4 **mercere**, 5 **meercere**, 5-6 **merser**, 6 **marsar**. [a. F. *mercier* (from 13th c.) = Pr. *mercier*, *mercer*, Sp. *mercero*, Pg. *merceiro*, It. *merciajo*:—popular L. **merciārius*, f. L. *merci-*, *merx* merchandise.] One who deals in textile fabrics, *esp.* a dealer in silks, velvets, and other costly materials (in full *silk-mercer*). Also, *occas.* (as in Fr.) a small-ware dealer. (For an obsolete use, see quot. 1696.)

[*c* **1123** in *Eng. Hist. Rev.* (1899) July 429 Stephanus mercer.] *a* **1225** *Ancr. R.* 66 Þe wreche peoddare more noise he makeð to ȝeien his sope, þen a riche mercer al his deorewurðe ware. **1377** LANGL. *P. Pl.* B. VII. 255, I haue.. ymade many a knyȝte bothe mercere and drapere. **1464** *Mann. & Househ. Exp.* (Roxb. Cl.) 248 Payd ffor x. ȝerdys sarsynet to Thomas Rowson merser in Chepesyde, xx. s. **1526** *Pilgr. Perf.* (W. de W. 1531) 152 Neyther marchaunt ne mercer, groser, draper, ne yet ony other crafte. **1554** MACHYN *Diary* (Camden) 71 The compene of the Clarkes, and of the Marsars. **1603** SHAKS. *Meas. for M.* IV. iii. 11 Then is there heere one Mʳ Caper, at the suite of Master Three-Pile the Mercer, for some foure suites of Peach-colour'd Satten. **1696** PHILLIPS (ed. 5), *Mercer*, in the City one that deals only in Silks and Stuffs; In Country Towns, one that Trades in all sorts of Linen, Woollen, Silk, and Grocery Wares. **1778** MISS BURNEY *Evelina* x. (1791) 20 The shops are really very entertaining, especially the mercers. **1851** MAYHEW *Lond. Labour* (1864) II. 539 A row of pins, arranged as neatly as in the papers sold at the mercers'. **1872** GEO. ELIOT *Middlem.* II. IV. 196 This second cousin was a Middlemarch mercer.

†**b.** *the mercer's book*: proverbial in the Elizabethan period with reference to the debts of a gallant.

1591 NASHE *Prognost.* D 1 b, Diuers young Gentlemen shall creepe further into the Mercers Booke in a Moneth, then they can get out in a yere. **1591** GREENE *Farew. Follie* To Gent. Stud. (1617), Such Wagges as..haue marched in the Mercers booke to please their Mistris eye with their brauery. **1592** —— *Quip Upst. Courtier* D, A clownes sonne must be clapt in a veluet pantophle, and a veluet breech, though the presumptuous asse be drownd in the Mercers booke. **1601** B. JONSON *Poetaster* III. i, How many yards of veluet dost thou thinke they containe? *Hora*... Faith, sir, your mercers booke Will tell you with more patience, then I can.

merceress ('mɜːsərɪs). *rare.* [f. MERCER + -ESS.] A female mercer.

1840 *Tait's Mag.* VII. 264 Madame Ramsden, milliner and merceress. **1872** CUTTS *Scenes Middle Ages* 509 This is a mercer's and the merceress describes her wares.

mercerize ('mɜːsəraɪz), *v.* [f. the proper name *Mercer* (see below) + -IZE.] *trans.* To prepare (cotton goods) for dyeing by treating with a solution of caustic potash or soda, or certain other chemicals. Hence '**mercerized** *ppl. a.*, '**mercerizing** *vbl. sb.* (also *attrib.*). Also '**mercerization**, the process of mercerizing.

John Mercer, an Accrington dyer, is said to have discovered the process in 1844. He patented it in 1850, but the process was not made use of in the trade until *c* 1895.

1859 *Abridg. Specif. Patents, Bleaching* etc. Index 748 Mercerising: Various modes of. **1862** O'NEILL *Dict. Calico Print.* etc., *Mercerised cloth.*—The process called mercerising. **1886** E. A. PARNELL *Life J. Mercer* Contents 11 Chapter x... Process of mercerising with soda—Increased strength of mercerised cloth—..Mercerising by sulphuric acid, and by chloride of zinc. *Ibid.* 317 The mercerising process. **1899** *Warehouseman & Draper* 3 June 789 Mercerised yarn. **1902** *Westm. Gaz.* 6 Jan. 2/1 Cellulose treated with cold concentrated soda lye, or mercerisation, as the process is called.

†'**mercership.** *Obs. rare*⁻¹. [f. MERCER + -SHIP.] The trade of a mercer.

c **1645** HOWELL *Lett.* (1650) II. lxiv. 101 He confesseth himself to be an egregious fool to leave his Mercership, and go to be a Musqueteer.

mercery ('mɜːsərɪ). Forms: 3-6 **mercerie**, 4-5 **merceryе**, (4 **marcerye**, 5 **merceyre**, **meercery**, 5-6 **mers(s)ery**), 5- **mercery**. [a. F. *mercerie* (from 13th c.), f. *mercier* MERCER. Cf. Sp. *merceria*, Pg., It. *merceria*.]

1. *collect. sing.* (rarely *pl.*) The wares sold by a mercer.

c **1290** *S. Eng. Leg.* I. 356/20 He founde Marchauns at rome with Mercerie wel hiende. **13..** *Metr. Hom.* (Vernon MS.) in *Archiv Stud. neu. Spr.* LVII. 313 He..bad him take ten pound and buye Marchaundise and Merceryе. **1382** *Pol. Poems* (Rolls) I. 264 Thai..dele with dyvers marcerye, right as thai pedlers were. **1436** *Libel Eng. Policy* in *Pol. Poems* (Rolls) II. 179 Wee bene ageyne charged wyth mercerye, Haburdasshere ware, and wyth grocerye. **1468** *Burgh Recs. Edinb.* (1869) I. 23 Item of all mersery or merchandice..to costome it be the crowne [ij d.]. **1542** *Galway Arch.* in *10th Rep. Hist. MSS. Comm.* App. v. 410 The said merchantes.. ys bounde to bringe the same merssery and packes to the costome housse. **1594** BLUNDEVIL *Exerc.* v. ii. (1597) 256 b, Bombazine, Fustian, Suile, Armour, all sorts of workes made of Iron, or brasse, and other merceries. **1766** ENTICK *London* IV. 309 Tradesmen..in cloth, mercery, and linnen. **1839-41** S. WARREN *Ten Thous. a Year* viii. I. 242 She had once accompanied her sister-in-law..to purchase some small matter of mercery.

†**2.** *the Mercery*: the Mercers' Company. Also, the trade in mercery-ware; the part of a city where this is carried on. *Obs.*

1386 *Rolls of Parlt.* III. 225/1 The folk of the Mercerye of London. **1425** in Entick *London* (1766) IV. 354 Maisters.. of the Mercery. *c* **1440** *Promp. Parv.* 333/1 Meercery, place or strete where mercerys syllen here ware. **1494** FABYAN *Chron.* VII. 630 This was done by thassent of the masters and housholders of the mercerye. **1518** COLET in Lupton *Life Colet* (1887) 281 A Cofer of Iren gevyn of me to the mercery standing in theyr hall. **1651** *Life Father Sarpi* (1676) 34 At the Sign of the Cock, in the Mercery. **1662** J. GRAUNT *Observ. Bills of Mortality* ix. §12. 56 Canning-street, and Watlin-street have lost their Trade of Woollen-Drapery to Paul's Church-Yard..; the Mercery is gone from out of Lombard-street..into Pater-Noster-Row.

3. A mercer's shop.

1879 SALA in *Daily Tel.* 21 July, I stand before the mighty mercery of Shoolbred.

4. *attrib.*, as *mercery-ware*.

1429 *Rolls of Parlt.* IV. 352/1 Mercery ware. **1542** *Galway Arch.* in *10th Rep. Hist. MSS. Comm.* App. v. 410 If any.. merchantes bringith with them merssery warres and packes. **1671** CHARENTE *Let. Customs* 43 Merchants trade thither.. with..Mercery-ware. **1712** ARBUTHNOT *John Bull* I. ii, Next day he would be dealing in mercery-ware.

merch, obs. form of MARCH, MARROW *sb.*¹

merchall, obs. form of MARSHAL.

merchand, obs. form of MERCHANT.

merchandable, -dice, -die, -dies, obs. ff. MERCHANTABLE, MERCHANDY, -DISE.

†**merchandisable**, *a. Obs. rare.* [f. MERCHANDISE *v.* + -ABLE.] Of a saleable quality or condition; merchantable.

1482 *Rolls of Parlt.* VI. 221/2 Broken belyed Samon, which is not merchaundizable. *Ibid.*, Good and merchaundizable Heryng. **1499** in G. Schanz *Engl. Handelspolitik* (1881) II. 425 The saide cloathes were.. neyther their merchandize nor merchandizable till suche time as they were shorne.

merchandise ('mɜːrtʃəndaɪz), *sb.* Forms: α. 3-7 **marchandise**, 3-6 **-dis**, **marchaundise**, 4 **marchauntyse**, *Sc.* **-andiss**, 4-6 **-aundyse**, 4- 7 **-andize**, 5 **-tyse**, **-endise**, **-anddysse**, 5-6 **-andyse**, **-aundys**, 5-7 **-andies**, 6 **-aundies**, **-dize**, **-auntdyse**, 6-7 **-andice**, **-ize**. β. 3 **mercandise**, 5 **merchauntyse**, **-antdyse**, **-andyse**, **-aundys**, 5-6 **-dyse**, 6 **merchandice**, **-dys**, 6- **merchandize**, 3- **merchandise**. [a. F. *marchandise* (from 12th c.), f. *marchand* MERCHANT.]

†**1.** The action or business of buying and selling goods or commodities for profit; the exchange of commodities for other commodities or for money. *to be of good merchandise*, to be easily marketable. *to go a merchandise*, to go trading. *Obs.* exc. *arch.*

1297 R. GLOUC. (Rolls) 2199 Ȝe beþ men bet iteiȝt to.. hamer & to nelde & to mercandise al so þan wiþ suerd oþer hauberc eny bataile to do. *c* **1320** *Sir Tristrem* 1383 A schip ..Wiþ alle þing..þat pende to marchandis. **1382** WYCLIF *John* ii. 16 Nyle ȝe make the hous of my fadir an hous of marchaundise [L. *negotiationis*]. **1393** LANGL. *P. Pl.* C. IV. 110 What manere mester oþer merchaundise he vsede. **1428** in *Surtees Misc.* (1888) 10 To..by and sell after treu cource of merchantdyse. **1452** in Gross *Gild Merch.* II. 67 He that hawe bene aprentyse with a marchaunte at marchanddyssis. **1523** LD. BERNERS *Froiss.* I. ccccviii. 710 Ther was made a commandement yᵗ non shuld go a marchandise into Flaunders. **1534** in W. H. Turner *Select. Rec. Oxford* 121 No person..shall use eny maner of marchauntdyse or marchauntdysyng. **1553** EDEN *Treat. New Ind.* (Arb.) 21 There is little trafficque or marchaundise in this region. **1585** T. WASHINGTON tr. *Nicholay's Voy.* II. xiii. 49 To exercise..their handicrafts and merchandises. **1652-62** HEYLIN *Cosmogr.* I. (1682) 100 He fell from Merchandize, which was his first Profession, unto the study of Religion. **1685** BAXTER *Paraphr. N.T., Mark* ii. 17 These use Merchandize here. **1725** DE FOE *Voy. round World* (1840) 85, I produced three bales of English cloth, and said they would be of good merchandise at Gombaroon. **1731** (*title*) An Essay on the Merchandise of Slaves and Souls of Men. **1817** JAS. MILL *Brit. India* I. II. ii. 116 Their duties are to tend cattle, to carry on merchandize, and to cultivate the ground.

†**b.** *transf.* and *fig.*

a **1300** *Cursor M.* 16471 Quen þat he sagh his maister sua be-casten al to care..þan him reud his marchandis. *c* **1380** WYCLIF *Wks.* (1880) 63 Þes synnes of robberie & sathanas marchaundise. *c* **1400** *Apol. Loll.* 10 O maruelous marchaundies! Þe Maker of man kynd takyng a soulid body of þe virgyn. **1523** LD. BERNERS *Froiss.* I. cclxxxviii. 431 Or we make yᵗ marchandyse, we shall sell ourselfe so derely that it shall be spoken of a hundred yeres after our dethes. **1560** DAUS tr. *Sleidane's Comm.* 56 b, They establishe the marchandise of massing, and other abhominations. **1577** NORTHBROOKE *Dicing* (1843) 119 These are the fruits, and reuenues, of that wicked merchandice of dice playing. **1656** EARL MONM. tr. *Boccalini's Advts. fr. Parnass.* II. xiv. (1674) 156 [They] have turned the administration of sacred Justice into an execrable Merchandize. **1822** LAMB *Elia* Ser. I. *Distant Corresp.*, This sort of merchandise [*sc.* puns] above all requires a quick return.

c. Phr. *to make* (*a* or *one's*) *merchandise*, †to carry on or conclude a bargain (*obs.*); also (*arch.*) const. *of* = to traffic in (usually in bad sense).

c **1290** *S. Eng. Leg.* I. 53/3 His Marchaundise he maude a-day in þe cite of Asise. *a* **1300** *Cursor M.* 16490 'All for noght', coth þai, 'iudas þi marchandis es made'. *c* **1300** *Harrowing of Hell* 98 Hou mihtest þou on ani wise Of oþer

mannes þing make marchandise? *c* **1400** *Laud Troy Bk.* 9673 Thei made a schrewed marchaundise: Eche slo other. *c* **1440** *York Myst.* XXVI. 215 But I wolde make a marchaundyse. **1483** *Cath. Angl.* 235/1 To make Merchandyse, *mercari, mercandizari, & cetera.* **1531** TINDALE *Expos. 1 John* 28 They made marchaundise of open penaunce. **1565** *Reg. Privy Council Scot.* I. 332 Nane of thame sall brek bouk, nor mak marchandice quhill the tyme that thair gudis be housit. **1611** BIBLE *Deut.* xxi. 14 Thou shalt not make merchandize of her. **1642** FULLER *Holy & Prof. State* v. xiv. 413 [They] will rather suffer their daughter to make merchandise of her chastity, than marry the richest merchant. **1774** FRANKLIN *Ess.* Wks. 1840 II. 394 Coin may be liable, in the fluctuation of trade, to be made a merchandise of. **1814** CARY *Dante, Par.* XVII. 50 There [at Rome] Where gainful merchandize is made of Christ. **1863** FROUDE *Hist. Eng.* VIII. 182 She said she would make no merchandise of her conscience.

2. The commodities of commerce; movables which are or may be bought and sold.

petty merchandise (16th c. *pitimarchandis*): small wares. *c* **1290** *S. Eng. Leg.* I. 53/3 In almesdede he spendede an on pouere Men muchedel is Marchaundise. *a* **1300** *Cursor M.* 14723 He mani chapmen fand Serekin marchandis chepand. *c* **1380** *Sir Ferumb.* 4348 Þe somers schulleþ byforn ous gon, Wyþ grete pakkes euerechon, As it were marchaundyse. **1432–50** tr. *Higden* (Rolls) I. 145 Gothia is a region of Scythia..copious of alle kyndes of marchandise. **1522** in *10th Rep. Hist. MSS. Comm.* App. v. 327 Other habordasher [? = haberdash ware] and pitimarchandis broght by marchant estrangers commyng to this citie. **1523** *Act 14 & 15 Hen. VIII*, c. 1 Any vitail, or other marchaundise. **1624** CAPT. SMITH *Virginia* II. 29 Ships of warre or marchandize. **1635** R. N. *Camden's Hist. Eliz.* I. 57 Wooll and other English Marchandies. **1651** HOBBES *Leviath.* II. xxii. 119 Where but one selleth, the Merchandise is the dearer. **1734** SALE *Koran* Prelim. Disc. §1. 4 A great fair or mart for all kinds of merchandize. **1825** BENTHAM *Ration. Reward* 238 When an article of the produce of land or labour..is offered in exchange, it then becomes an article of commerce: it is merchandise. **1852** MRS. STOWE *Uncle Tom's C.* xii, A black woman..threw her arms round that unfortunate piece of merchandise before enumerated, 'John, aged thirty'. **1903** *Edin. Rev.* Apr. 490 Small quantities of merchandise.

†b. With plural construction. *Obs.*

1588 KYD *Househ. Philos.* Wks. (1901) 276 Heereof speaketh Tully,..that Merchandize, if they were small, were base and but of vile account; if great, not much to be dislyked. **1606** SHAKS. *Ant. & Cl.* II. v. 104 The Marchandize which thou hast brought from Rome Are all too deere for me. *c* **1610** BACON *Impos. Merchandises* Wks. 1778 II. 223 You shall find, a few merchandise only excepted, the poundage equal upon alien and subject. **1633** MASSINGER *Guardian* Epil., I am left to enquire..at what rate His marchandise are valued.

†c. A kind of merchandise; a saleable commodity, an article of commerce. *Obs.*

c **1400** MAUNDEV. (1839) xxvii. 270 The Marchauntes come not thidre so comounly, for to bye Marchandises. **1439** *Rolls of Parlt.* V. 24/1 Chese and Buttur is a Merchaundise that may not wele be kept. **1577** B. GOOGE *Heresbach's Husb.* I. (1586) 20 b, Marle..whiche caried vppon the sea in vessels is sold as a great marchandize. **1643** EVELYN *Diary* 14 Nov., They brought us choice of guns and pistolls,..being here a merchandise of greate account. **1704** ADDISON *Italy* (1733) 58 The Duties are great that are laid on Merchandises. **1758** *Descr. Thames* 211 Cavear or Kavia is a considerable Merchandize among the Turks. **1853** WHEWELL tr. *Grotius* III. 372 Nor ought there to be urged ..the cases of merchandises which..are carried past the place where dues are to be paid.

d. *attrib.* in ***merchandise exports, imports, mark, traffic.***

1887 *Act 50 & 51 Vict.* c. 28 §1 This Act may be cited as the Merchandise Marks Act, 1887. **1892** *Daily News* 22 July 2/4 Till 1st January, 1893, on which date the new classification of merchandise traffic..will come into force on all the railways. **1898** *Ibid.* 1 Feb. 5/2 The figures show an increase of 14,700,000*l*...in merchandise imports and an increase of 17,700,000*l*...in merchandise exports.

merchandise ('mɜːtʃəndaɪz), *v.* [f. prec.]

1. *intr.* To trade, traffic; †also, to make merchandise *of*. *arch.*

1382 WYCLIF *Luke* xix. 13 And he seide to hem, Marchaundise ȝe [Vulg. *negotiamini*] til I come. *Ibid. 2 Pet.* ii. 3 Thei shulen marchaundise of ȝou [Vulg. *de vobis negotiabuntur*]. **1433** *Rolls of Parlt.* IV. 475/1 He sende..his Servant, Factour and Attournay, to marchandise ther with Wollen Cloth. **1523** LD. BERNERS *Froiss.* I. ccccviii. 711 They of Tourney durst nat marchaundyse with them of Flaunders. **1633** T. STAFFORD *Pac. Hib.* I. xii. 77 Such further mischiefes, as might arise by his Subjects merchandizing with the Rebels. **1673** *Ess. to Revive Educ. Gentlew.* 35 She could not Merchandize, without knowledge in Arithmetick. **1679** PENN *Addr. Prot.* II. (1692) 179 Who hath merchandized in Souls of Men. **1706** VANBRUGH *Mistake* II. 283 He that merchandises thus must be undone at last. **1737** [S. BERINGTON] *G. di Lucca's Mem.* 215 This they are doing perpetually..rather visiting than merchandizing. **1862** SALA *Ship Chandler* iv. 65 For how many years had they not merchandised together? **1890** GROSS *Gild Merch.* I. 37 Anyone who is not of that Gild may not merchandise with them.

2. *trans.* To buy and sell; to barter; to traffic in. *arch.*

1538 ELYOT *Dict.*, Add., *Aginor*, to marchandyse vyle thinges, or of small value. **1592** *Conspir. Pretended Reform.* 21 Thus..they merchandized the hasard of their friends life. *c* **1600** SHAKS. *Sonn.* cii, That loue is marchandiz'd, whose ritch esteeming, The owners tongue doth publish euery where. **1629** MAXWELL *Herodian* (1635) 115 The Romans call upon me..not [to] permit so..glorious an Empire to bee basely merchandized. **1631** MASSINGER *Emperor East* III. ii, Must I..like A prostituted creature, merchandize Our mutuall delight for hire? **1684** W. PENN in *Academy* 11 Jan. (1896) 36/1 If it be below great men to be kind for recompence, and marchandize their Powr, it is [etc.]. **1715** ROWE *Lady J. Grey* v. ii, Think'st thou that princes merchandize their grace, As Roman priests their pardons?

3. a. To put on the market; to promote the sale of (goods, etc.).

1926 *Publishers' Weekly* 22 May 1687/2 When an author suddenly springs into prominence with a best seller..I would make that best seller work retroactively and I would merchandise all of his preceding books. **1959** I. ROSS *Image Merchants* (1960) xv. 270 A new breakfast food or a new form of aspirin can easily be merchandised. **1970** R. LOWELL *Notebk.* 43 This typing paper..only merchandised in Maine. **1971** *Daily Tel.* 9 June 5/3 Books can be merchandised like other products.

b. *transf.* To advertise (an idea or person); to publicize; to 'put over'.

1973 J. RYDER *Trevayne* (1974) xxxix. 309 Andrew Trevayne could be merchandised with extraordinary effect. He has all the qualifications. **1974** *Radio Times* 20 Jan. 9/3, I was never merchandised in my career as any kind of symbol. **1974** *Saturday* (Charleston, S. Carolina) 20 Apr. 1-A/3 Paul said the effect of trouble will depend on how the 'unfortunate situation' is merchandised.

†'merchandised, *a. Obs.* [f. MERCHANDISE *sb.* + -ED².] Abounding in commercial activity.

1619 MILLES tr. *Mexia's* etc. *Treas. Anc. & Mod. T.* II. 364/2 A goodly..country..greatly merchandized, in regard of the sea.

merchandiser ('mɜːtʃəndaɪzə(r)). [f. MERCHANDISE *v.* + -ER¹.] A dealer in commodities; one who traffics. Also *fig.*

1597 J. KING *Jonas* (1618) 6 The commission..is most requisite to be weighed, that we may discerne the..faithfull dispensers from marchandisers of the word of God. **1616** R. CARPENTER *Past. Charge* 36 Christian loue..whippeth anger ..out of the heart, as Christ did the prophane Marchandizers out of the Temple. **1678** BUNYAN *Pilgr.* I. (1900) 84 That which did not a little amuse the Merchandizers, was, that these Pilgrims set very light by all their Wares. **1887** N. D. DAVIS *Cavaliers & Roundheads* 59 A luckless merchandizer who had sold goods for cotton. **1965** F. SARGESON *Mem. Peon* iv. 68 A merchandiser of building material. **1971** *Daily Tel.* 10 June 25 (Advt.), We are seeking to appoint Merchandisers who will be responsible within a Sales Team for maximising the Company's sales in cash and carries and supermarkets. **1973** *Ibid.* 3 Jan. 19 (Advt.), A vacancy exists for a Merchandiser to develop fashion ranges of men's shirts.

merchandising ('mɜːtʃəndaɪzɪŋ), *vbl. sb.* [f. MERCHANDISE *v.* + -ING¹.] The transaction of mercantile business; trafficking. Also, the promotion of sales (of goods, etc.) by advertising and publicity; the process of selling goods (see MERCHANDISE *v.* 3).

1382 WYCLIF *Ezek.* xxvii. 15 Manye ilis [weren] the marchaundisynge of thin hoond. *c* **1449** PECOCK *Repr.* II. iv. 158 The vsing of profitable craftis and marchaundising. **1561** T. NORTON *Calvin's Inst.* IV. 88 [They] with carying about the reliques of martyrs dyd vse filthy merchandisynges. **1625** BACON *Ess., Usury* (Arb.) 546 Certaine Principall Cities and Townes of Merchandizing. **1656** SIR E. NICHOLAS in *N. Papers* (Camden) III. 265 The recompense will be deservedly the more advantageous to him if it shall be effected without any merchandising. **1769** BLACKSTONE *Comm.* IV. 63 The laws of king Athelstan forbad all merchandizing on the lord's day. **1840** CARLYLE *Heroes* (1858) 221 There were yearly fairs, and there, when the merchandising was done, Poets sang for prizes. **1904** *Athenæum* 18 June 788 Commerce comprises goods, transportation, exchange or merchandizing, money, and advertising. **1922** S. LEWIS *Babbitt* iv. 39, I guess that'll show Chan Mott..something about modern merchandizing! **1940** *Economist* 11 May 860/1 The distinctive feature of the chain stores' success is the wedding of efficient merchandising with the control of production from the retail end. **1958** *Ibid.* 18 Oct. 200 (Advt.), Merchandising..means following up your advertising. It means getting retailers on your side, and giving them all they need to help you sell. **1968** *Globe & Mail* (Toronto) 17 Feb. B 6 (Advt.), Must be experienced in all areas of supermarket operations and merchandising. **1971** *Daily Tel.* 10 June 25 (Advt.), Candidates should be in their twenties with good education and preferably have experience in selling or merchandising in the Grocery field. **1973** *Times* 10 Mar. 14/6 In the past two decades the merchandizing of Disney's cartoon creations in a plethora of T-shirts, key-rings and assorted trivia may have obscured their creator's rightful claim to be regarded as one of the most original film producers in cinema history.

attrib. **1665** E. TERRY *Voy. E. India* 368 But further, for the merchandizing Commodities the Mogul's Provinces afford, there is Musk..to be had in good quantity. **1759** *Book of Fairs* 44 Messingham, Lincolnshire, Trinity Mond. for merchandizing goods. **1926** *Publishers' Weekly* 16 Jan. 171/1 His frank criticism of 'price-cutting for bait' indicates that he has found other merchandising practices of more value in business building. **1930** *Daily Express* 9 Sept. 2/6 A wide assortment of issues rose from 1 to 3 points, with utilities, merchandising stocks, coppers, and specialities prominent.

merchandising ('mɜːtʃəndaɪzɪŋ), *ppl. a.* [f. MERCHANDISE *v.* + -ING².] Engaged in trade.

1624 CAPT. SMITH *Virginia* VI. 218 Citizens (whose merchandizing thoughts were onely to get wealth). **1757** DYER *Fleece* (1807) 110 Thro' Tyne, and Tees..and merchandizing Hull. **1868** BROWNING *Ring & Bk.* I. 903 The motley merchandizing multitude.

†merchandrise. *Sc. Obs.* Also 6 **marchantdreis, marchandreise, merschandrise, merchandrice, -ryce.** [app. from the pl. of *marchandrie* MERCHANDRY, the ending *-ies* having been associated with the suffix -ISE 2.] Trade; merchandise, goods.

c **1375** *Sc. Leg. Saints* xliv. (*Lucy*) 98 Lucy in merchandrise had fundine a thing for to by. ? **1495** *Ld. Treas. Acc. Scotl.* (1877) I. 219 The Charge of it that was tane fra Jhonne Williamsoune, at the Kingis command, in woll and merchandreis. **1535** STEWART *Cron. Scot.* II. 491 Rycht mony Dene that in the toun wes than In merschandrice, tha slew thame euerie man. **1549** *Compl. Scot.* vii. 69, I beheld..al sortis of cornis,..grene treis, schips, marchantdreis [etc.]. **1561** *Aberdeen Reg.* (1844) I. 330 The wairis and merchandrices of quhatsumeuer schip. *Ibid.* 334 The wairis and merchandrises thairof. **1562** WINȜET *Cert. Tract.* Wks. I. 5 Zour merchandrice..quhay speikis not of it?

merchandry ('mɜːtʃəndrɪ). *Obs.* exc. *arch.* Forms: 5 **marchandrye,** 6 **marchaundrie, -drye, merchandrie,** 7, 9 **merchandry.** [prob. a. AF. ****marchanderie***, f. *marchand* MERCHANT *sb.*; see -ERY, -RY. Cf. the later MERCHANTRY.] Trade, commerce; the business of a merchant.

1436 *Libel Eng. Policy* in *Pol. Poems* (Rolls) II. 174 And alle this is colowred by marchandrye. **1550** LEVER *Serm.* (Arb.) 29 A myscheuouse marte of merchandrie is this. *a* **1663** SANDERSON *Cases of Consc.* (1678) 44 He may follow Husbandry, and Merchandry, upon his own choice. **1889** J. PAYNE *Alaeddin* 69 The Maugrabin talked with Alaeddin upon matters of merchandry and the like.

attrib. **1561** C. HINDILL in *Child-Marr.* (1897) 72 Stockfishe, red heringes and such marchaundrie wares.

†merchandy. *Obs.* Forms: 4 **marchaundye, -die, -chandie,** 5 **merchaundy,** 6 **merchandie.** [a. OF. *marchandie*, f. *marchand* MERCHANT. Cf. MERCHANTY.]

1. Trade, traffic, commerce.

1303 R. BRUNNE *Handl. Synne* 5792 Y rede þou bye A man to do þy marchaundye. **1390** GOWER *Conf.* I. 179 The greteste of Barbarie, Of hem whiche usen marchandie, Sche hath converted. **1599** MARSTON *Sco. Villanie* I. ii. 61 Heroes heires Are made much of: how much from merchandie?

b. ***to make merchandy of***: to traffic in.

1388 WYCLIF *2 Pet.* ii. 3 Thei schulen make marchaundie of ȝou.

2. Mercantile commodities.

c **1330** R. BRUNNE *Chron. Wace* (Rolls) 14878 Marchauntz come no childre to bye, Rather þan oþer marchaundie. **1388** WYCLIF *Ezek.* xxvii. 15 Many ilis [weren] the marchaundie of thin hond. **1439** *Rolls of Parlt.* V. 6/1 Every Ton of Wyne ..comyng by way of Merchaundy into youre seide Roialme. *Ibid.*, In the which the same Merchaundy was shipped.

merchant ('mɜːtʃənt), *sb.* and *a.* Forms: α. 3–6 **marchaund,** 3–7 **marchand,** 5 **merchaund,** 5–7 **merchand.** β. 3–6 **marchaunt(e,** 3–8 **marchant,** 4 **marchont, machaunt,** 5 **marzhaunt,** 5–6 **merchaunt,** 4– **merchant.** [a. OF. *marchand*, earlier *marchëant* (mod.F. *marchand*) = Pr. *mercadan-s*, It. *mercatante*:—popular L. **mercātant-em*, pr. pple. of **mercātāre*, freq. of *mercārī* to trade, f. *merc-, merx* merchandise.

It is possible that two popular Latin forms have coalesced in OF., viz. **mercātantem* and *mercantem* (whence It. *mercante* merchant), pr. pple. of *mercārī* (see above).]

A. *sb.*

1. a. One whose occupation is the purchase and sale of marketable commodities for profit; originally applied *gen.* to any trader in goods not manufactured or produced by himself; but from an early period restricted (exc. *Sc.* and *dial.*: see d) to wholesale traders, and *esp.* to those having dealings with foreign countries.

Often with defining word, indicating the class of goods dealt in, as in *coal-, corn-, spirit-, wine-merchant*, etc. (some of which combinations are frequently applied to retail traders), or the countries traded with, as *East India, Turkey merchant*.

c **1290** *S. Eng. Leg.* I. 53/2 Seint Fraunceys,..Marchaunt he was in his ȝonghede. *a* **1300** *Cursor M.* 28031 Þe fole marchand is eth to duell. *c* **1320** *Sir Tristrem* 1543 Marchaunt icham, y wis, Mi schip liþ here bi side. *c* **1400** MAUNDEV. (1839) xi. 122 Thidre comethe Marchauntes with Marchandise be See. *c* **1460** J. RUSSELL *Bk. Nurture* 1071 in *Babees Bk.*, Marchaundes & Franklonz..may be set semely at a squyers table. **1474** CAXTON *Chesse* 42 b, The marchans of cloth lynnen and wollen. **1513** MORE in Grafton *Chron.* (1568) II. 776 A wise Marchant neuer aduentureth all his goodes in one ship. **1596** DALRYMPLE tr. *Leslie's Hist. Scotl.* IX. 252 In the meine tyme our Marchantes quha feiret na Ill,..sayled (in haist) to France. **1631** WEEVER *Anc. Funeral Mon.* 341 He is properly called a Marchant, *qui mare trajicit*, who passeth ouer the Seas, *et merces inde avehit*, and from thence transports merchandise. **1644** EVELYN *Diary* 17 Oct., The marchands being very rich, have..no extent of ground to employ their estates in. **1711** ADDISON *Spect.* No. 21 ¶7 The Cockle-shell-Merchants and Spider-catchers. **1847** A. & H. MAYHEW *Greatest Plague of Life* xii. 183 If three barges and one wagon make a coalheaver, I should like to know what makes a merchant. **1875** JOWETT *Plato* (ed. 2) III. 242 The importers and exporters, who are called merchants. **1881** R. G. WHITE *Eng. Without & Within* xvi. 387 He was not a merchant. He had never been engaged in foreign trade.

¶ As a mistranslation of L. *mercenarius* 'hireling'.

1382 WYCLIF *John* x. 12, 13.

b. *transf.* and *fig.*

c **1532** LATIMER *Let. to Baynton* in Foxe *A. & M.* (1583) 1751 Maruphus,..an Italian, and in times past a marchaunt of dispensations. **1538** STARKEY *England* II. i. 164 We may by al thyng of God, who ys the only marchant of al thyng that ys gud. *a* **1626** BACON *New Atl.* (1900) 44 These wee call

Merchants of Light. **1818** SHELLEY *Marenghi* i. 4 Until the exchange Ruins the merchants of such thriftless trade. **1893** *Westm. Gaz.* 15 May 3/2 The gagging low comedian, ('low comedy merchant' is the crushing American phrase).

†**c.** Phrases. ***to play the merchant with***: to cheat, get the better of (a person). ***to have*** or ***put on merchant's ears***: to affect not to hear. *Obs.*

1593 NASHE *Christ's T.* 83 Is it not a common prouerbe.. when any man hath cosend.. vs, to say, Hee hath playde the Merchant with vs? **1593** G. HARVEY *Pierce's Super.* 166 The wisest Oeconomy maketh especiall account of three singular members, a marchants eare; a pigges mouth; and an Asses backe. **1595** LYLY *Woman in Moone* I. i. 169, I see that seruants must haue Marchants ears. **1622** MABBE tr. *Aleman's Guzman d'Alf.* II. 7, I put on Merchants Eares, not vouchsafing to give them the hearing. **1632** ROWLEY *Woman Never Vext* IV. i. 51, I doubt Sir, he will play the merchant with us.

d. A shopkeeper. Now only *Sc.*, *north. dial.*, and *U.S.*

1362 LANGL. *P. Pl.* A. II. 188 Bote Marchaundes Metten with him and maaden him to abyden, Bi-souȝten him in heore schoppes to sullen heore ware. **1609** in *North Riding Records* (1884) I. 15 Will. Foreste of Midleham [presented] for useinge the trade of a marchant, not having served, &c. **1704** S. KNIGHT *Jrnl.* (1825) 56 [The Indians] give the title of merchant to every trader. *c* **1730** BURT *Lett. N. Scotl.* (1818) I. 66 A pedling shopkeeper that sells a pennyworth of thread, is a merchant. **1784** J. F. D. SMYTH *Tour U.S.A.* I. 99 Linen-drapers, grocers, stationers, &c. are not known here; they are all comprehended in the single name and occupation of merchant, or store-keeper. **1798** *Monthly Mag.* VI. 437 In Scotland every little retail shop-keeper is dignified with the title of merchant. **1809** 'D. KNICKERBOCKER' *Hist. N.Y.* II. VII. x. 251 If peradventure some straggling merchant of the east, should stop at his door, with his cart load of tin ware or wooden bowls, [etc.]. **1818** in *Trans. Illinois State Hist. Soc. 1910* 162 Dry goods are geting very cheap, the country is full of them; we have more merchants than any thing else. **1837** LOCKHART *Scott* (1839) III. 117 A merchant (that is to say a dealer in everything from fine broadcloth to children's tops). **1845** DE QUINCEY *Autobiog.* Wks. 1889 I. 30 My father was a merchant; not in the sense of Scotland, where it means a retail dealer,.. but in the English sense. **1853** *Harper's Mag.* Aug. 425/1 The subject, we take it, is the 'merchant' of a country-store; quite a different variety from the big bugs of the trade in the Great Metropolis. **1859** BARTLETT *Dict. Amer.*, *Merchant*, a term often applied in the United States to any dealer in merchandise, whether at wholesale or retail; and hence sometimes equivalent to 'shopkeeper'. **1871** W. ALEXANDER *Johnny Gibb* xxxiii. 233 A lounge about the merchant's shop door.. is inexpressibly grateful. **1871** R. SOMERS *Southern States since War* 129 Few are able at the end of the year to square accounts with 'the merchant'. **1897** J. L. ALLEN *Choir Invisible* i. 5 A heavy roll of home-spun linen, which she was taking to town to her aunt's merchant as barter for queen's-ware pitchers. **1924** *Scots Mag.* Aug. 342 The merchan's in an awfu' ill teen the day, swearin' like a' that. **1961** *Buchan Observer* 6 June 5 (Advt.), For Sale, by Private Bargain, this well-sited General Merchant's Business, at the junction of the main Fraserburgh and Peterhead Roads. **1975** 'E. LATHEN' *By Hook or by Crook* xiii. 129 An ancient panama.. part of the summer uniform demanded of city merchants.

e. *Sc.* A buyer, purchaser; a customer. Also *fig.* Phrase, ***to have one's eye one's merchant***: to be one's own appraiser (of goods to be bought).

1673 FOUNTAINHALL in M. P. Brown *Suppl. Dict. Decis.* (1826) III. 34 *Esto* the horse had been insufficient, *sibi imputet*, his eye being his merchant. **1835** MONTEATH *Dunblane* (1887) 71 (E.D.D.) His aid and assistance in procuring merchants for the goods. **1884** D. GRANT *Lays & Leg. North* 83 There wis na want o' merchan's Eager for her hert an' han'.

f. merchant of death, one who makes a profession of war; *spec.*, a dealer in armaments; a mercenary soldier.

1934 ENGELBRECHT & HANIGHEN *Merchants of Death* xviii. 261 The business of the arms industry is steadily increasing.. and governments are everywhere drawing closer the ties which bind them in a virtual partnership with the merchants of death. **1956** C. W. MILLS *Power Elite* viii. 189 Top generals.. lived through the general anti-militarist peace of the 'twenties and 'thirties, begging for appropriations, denying the merchants-of-death charges. **1959** E. AMBLER *Passage of Arms* ix. 233 Nowadays.. we don't hear the phrase 'merchants of death' very much. **1963** *Guardian* 11 Jan. 8/1 A mist of superstition and loathing of the trade in arms, of the 'Merchants of Death'. **1974** D. SEAMAN *Bomb that could Lip-Read* xi. 98 Inflation would hit a merchant of death as much as any working man.

†**2.** A supercargo. *Obs.*

1614 RALEIGH *Hist. World* I. IV. ii. §18. 204 Hee.. pretending the death of his Marchant, besought the French .. that they might burie their Marchant in hallowed ground. **1681** R. KNOX *Hist. Relat. Ceylon* IV. i. 118 My Father the Captain ordered me with Mr. John Loveland, Merchant of the Ship, to go on shore.

3. A fellow, 'chap'. Now usu. with a qualifying word, as ***speed merchant***, denoting one who has an interest in or partiality for the thing specified. *slang.*

1549 COVERDALE, etc., *Erasm. Par. 2 Cor.* 60 Beare this muche with my foolyshenesse,.. that synce these marchauntes.. so much crake of themselues, that I may also somewhat glorye of my selfe. **1567** DRANT *Horace Ep.* I. viii. D vj, A giddie marchaunte I. **1573** G. HARVEY *Letter-bk.* (Camden) 52 Marchant and merchant were too quiet and soft words for them. **1573** *New Custom* I. i. A iij, I woulde so haue scourged my marchant that his breeche should ake. **1576** FLEMING *Panopl. Epist.* 155 You had flatterers and mealemouthed merchants in high estimation. **1606** CHAPMAN *Gent. Usher* Plays 1873 I. 281 Nay good unkle now, sbloud, what captious marchants you be. **1610** CARLETON *Jurisd.* vii. 172 The King to hold fast this slippery Merchant, required all the Bishops to set to their.. seales to those Lawes. **1886** *Referee* 17 Oct. 2/3 The success of 'Indiana' mainly depends upon the extravagant humours of the chief low-comedy merchant. **1909** J. R. WARE *Passing Eng.* 175/2 The theatre coming to be called the 'shop', actors dubbed themselves 'merchants', qualified by their line. **1914** *Automotor Jrnl.* 246/2 It may be that when the new road has been built the speed merchant and the road-hog.. may pay their money and betake themselves to their favourite seaside haunt at any speed they like. **1919** J. BUCHAN *Mr. Standfast* ix. 176 Some movie-merchant had got a graft with the Government, and troops had been turned out to make a war film. **1923** *Daily Mail* 15 Feb. 6 The chauffeur of a motor-car has a rain-blurred wind-screen, and the goggled 'speed-merchant' cannot see so well as usual. **1929** A. CONAN DOYLE *Maracot Deep* 244 Storr, the googlie merchant, had a better showing with four for ninety-six. **1933** D. L. SAYERS *Murder must Advertise* xviii. 316 He was now faced by the merchant with the off-break. The first two balls he treated carefully. **1957** *Railway Mag.* Nov. 752/2 One wonders how many drivers, other than the confirmed speed merchants, will even attempt to run the 8.20 a.m. from Kings Cross from Hitchin to Huntingdon in 24 min. **1963** *Pix* 28 Sept. 63 Being a good weather 'merchant' is one of the finest refinements in surfing. **1970** D. FRANCIS *Rat Race* vi. 83 Here is this bloody bomb merchant running around loose with no one knowing what he'll do next. **1971** *Guardian* 24 Sept. 13 Anthony Tucker on America's leading doom merchant Mister Catastrophe. **1971** G. SIMS *Deadhand* II. iii. 97 Sorry to be such a gloom merchant. But.. we're broke, you see.

4. A trading vessel, merchantman.

1585 T. WASHINGTON tr. *Nicholay's Voy.* I. iv, [The pirates] lye in wayte thereabouts to entrap.. merchauntes comming thyther too lade salte. **1586** MARLOWE *Tamburl.* I. ii, And Christian merchants that with Russian stems Plough up huge furrows in the Caspian sea. **1610** SHAKS. *Temp.* II. i. 5 Some Saylors wife, The Masters of some Merchant, and the Merchant Haue iust our Theame of woe. **1709** *Lond. Gaz.* No. 4533/2 The Enemy took 9 of the Merchants. **1740** JOHNSON *Blake* Wks. 1787 IV. 371 A fleet of merchants under his convoy. **1899** KIPLING *Five Nations* (1903) 8 The pot-bellied merchant foreboding no wrong With headlight and side-light he lieth along. **1905** J. MASEFIELD *Mainsail Haul* 65 There's a fat merchant on the coast... We're going out for her.

†**5.** A kind of plum. *Obs.*

1602 DEKKER *Satirom.* F 4 b, I am.. to desire you to fill your little pellies at a dinner of plums behinde noone; there be Suckets, and Marmilads, and Marchants, and other long white plummes.

6. *attrib.* and *Comb.* **a.** Obvious combinations, chiefly appositive, as ***merchant †appraiser***, ***buyer***, ***-charterer***, ***-duke***, ***-factor***, ***-jeweller***, ***-king***, ***† leech***, ***† mercer***, ***preacher***, ***shipper***, ***-sovereign***, ***-wine-tunner***, ***woman***; also ***merchant-marring*** adj.

1663 in Picton *L'pool Munic. Rec.* (1883) I. 240 Assessed by the *marchant apprizers. **1670** PETTUS *Fodinæ Reg.* 93 No *Merchant buyer of Oar shall touch the King's Dish. **1841** *Penny Cycl.* XXI. 403/1 The *merchant-charterer is thereby discharged. **1818** BYRON *Ch. Har.* IV. lx, All hues Of gem and marble, to encrust the bones Of *merchant-dukes. **1585** PARSONS *Chr. Exerc.* II. iii. 13 Consider attentiuely, as a good *marchantfactor is wont to do, when he is arriued in a strange country. **1853** LYNCH *Self-Improv.* 25 Barks as it were manned and laden of God's merchant-factors, the saints and sages. **1800** *Asiatic Ann. Reg.*, *Misc. Tracts* 41/2 His profession of *merchant-jeweller. *c* **1820** S. ROGERS *Italy* (1839) 55 Of old the residence of *merchant kings. **1402** *Rolls of Parlt.* III. 519/2 Wolmongers.. *Marchant Leche.. Taillours [etc.]. **1596** SHAKS. *Merch. V.* III. ii. 274 And not one vessell scape the dreadfull touch Of *Merchant-marring rocks? **1591** SYLVESTER *Du Bartas* I. iii 522 You *Marchant Mercers and Monopolites, Gain-greedy Chapmen [etc.]. **1531** ELYOT *Governor* I. xxi. (1557) 69 As fastidiouse or fulsome to the readers as suche *marchante preachers be nowe to their customers. **1912** *Pitman's Commercial Encycl. & Dict. Business* II. 822/1 We will take as an example an indent for cotton goods, such as a large firm of *merchant shippers would receive. **1919** *Brit. Manufacturer* Nov. 16/2 Orders may.. be distributed by the merchant shipper of this country. **1826** POUNDEN *France & Italy* 82 These *merchant-sovereigns.. importing in their galeons the precious relics of ancient literature. **1766** ENTICK *London* IV. 350 The vintners.. were known by the name of *Merchant-wine-tunners of Gascoyne. **1560** DAUS tr. *Sleidane's Comm.* 120 This whiche I have spoken here of marchauntmen, concerneth also *marchaunt women called nunnes.

b. Special combinations: **merchant-bar**, a bar of 'merchant' iron; †**merchant-booth** *Sc.*, a trader's stall; **merchant** (formerly †**merchant's**) **iron**, iron in finished bars, ready for the market; **merchant's mark** (†**merchant mark**), a rebus, emblem, or other distinctive figure or device adopted by a merchant to be placed on the goods sold by him; in the Middle Ages often used (e.g. on seals or monuments) as a quasi-heraldic cognizance (cf. 'merkes of marchauntes' quot. *c* 1394 under MARK *sb.*[1] 11 a); **merchant prince** (? suggested by Isaiah xxiii. 8), a merchant of princely wealth and munificence; hence **merchant-princely** *a.*; **merchant rolls** = next; **merchant-train** (see quot. 1881).

1861 FAIRBAIRN *Iron* vi. 109 The bars produced by this second process [of rolling] are called *merchant-bars. **1884** W. H. GREENWOOD *Steel & Iron* §379 The commercial classification of malleable iron into No. 1, No. 2, best or No. 3 best-best... No. 2 or merchant bars, which is the lowest quality of bar iron available for the general smith's use. **1618** in *Scott. Hist. Rev.* July (1905) 358 Wrangous.. away takyng .. fra Alexander Duff Johnsone.. furth of his *merchand builth in Inverness.. off.. the guids geir and merchandeice. **1645–52** BOATE *Irel. Nat. Hist.* (1860) 111 They had one tun of good Iron, such as is called *Merchants-Iron. **1795** *Repert. Arts*, etc. III. 366 All sorts of merchant iron. **1884** W. H. GREENWOOD *Steel & Iron* §559 The mill rolls.. for rolling merchant iron. **1887** *Pall Mall G.* 5 Sept. 11/2 A contract for a considerable tonnage of what is called 'merchant iron'. **1540** *Test. Ebor.* (Surtees) VI. 97 Whiche morter haith my *marchaunte marke sett upon it. **1557** *Bury Wills* (Camden) 146 My litle silver pott wt the cover havinge a *marchaunts marke. **1586** FERNE *Blaz. Gentrie* I. 238 What do you then say to the coate of Armes of Godfrey of Bulloigne.. was that but a Merchants marke in your estimation? **1888** *Antiquary* XVII. 73 Great respect was paid to merchant's marks in the fourteenth, fifteenth and sixteenth centuries. **1843** L. M. CHILD *Lett. from N.Y.* viii. 53, I sometimes ask whether the age of Commerce is better than the age of War? Whether our '*merchant princes' are a great advance upon feudal chieftains? **1847** L. HUNT *Jar Honey* Pref. 13 A noble-hearted merchant prince. **1888** BURGON *Lives 12 Gd. Men* II. x. 252 Magdalen Hall.. is now (through the munificence of a merchant-Prince) Hertford College. **1961** NEW ENG. BIBLE *Rev.* xviii. 23 Your traders were once the merchant princes of the world. **1967** *N.Y. Times* (Internat. ed.) 11–12 Feb. 4/1 Prince Philip, describing himself as a merchant prince working to increase British exports, told 500 businessmen yesterday that no matter where he traveled he was questioned about Britain's financial woes. **1874** TROLLOPE *Way we live Now* (1875) I. x. 59 He.. had twice dined.. amidst all the magnificence of *merchant-princely hospitality in Grosvenor Square. **1928** *Daily Express* 20 Dec. 6 Even the final figure, the three million dollar trade, is nothing breath-bereaving nor merchant-princely. **1875** KNIGHT *Dict. Mech.*, **Merchant-rolls*. **1888** *Lockwood's Dict. Mech. Engin.*, *Mill Rolls*, or *Merchant Rolls*, or *Mill Train*, the merchant rolls of a rolling mill. **1861** FAIRBAIRN *Iron* vi. 110 Rollers for the puddling, boiler-plate, and *merchant train. **1881** RAYMOND *Mining Gloss.*, *Merchant-train*, a train of rolls for reducing iron piles or steel ingots, blooms, or billets to bars of any of the various .. shapes, known as merchant iron or steel.

B. *adj.*

In *law merchant*, *statute merchant*, *guild merchant*, the position of the adj. is due to the imitation of med.L. or AF.

1. a. Having relation to merchandise; relating to trade or commerce, *esp.* in ***law-***, ***statute-merchant***. Phr. †***in*** (or ***a***) ***merchant fare***: on a trading journey.

c **1400** *Beryn* 3624 When wee out of Rome in marchant fare went to purchase buttirflyes was our most entent. **1425** *Rolls of Parlt.* IV. 276 His merchant lettre,.. wytnessyng the value of the saide merchandise. *a* **1436** in *Blk. Bk. Admir.* (Rolls) II. 27 That he begynne his pleynt.. or to the comoune lawe, or to the lawe marchaund, or to the lawe maryn. **1506** in *10th Rep. Hist. MSS. Comm.* App. v. 325 That no foraine.. passe not over the see from hensforward a marchant fare except fishers and seefaring men. **1592** WEST *1st Pt. Symbol.* §41 A franktenement by Statute is either by vertue of a statute Staple, or of a statute Marchant. **1641** ROBINSON *Trades Encrease* 4 All marchant and marchant-like Causes and differences. **1663** [see LAW-MERCHANT]. **1797** *Encycl. Brit.* (ed. 3) XI. 399/2 All nations.. show a particular regard to the law-merchant. **1855** MACAULAY *Hist. Eng.* xii. III. 211 How much money had proprietors borrowed on mortgage, on statute merchant, on statute staple?

†**b.** ***merchant good***(***s*** (*Sc.*): marketable commodities (cf. *merchant iron* in A. 6 b). ***merchant weight***: the weight in use among merchants. *Obs.*

1544 *Extracts Aberdeen Reg.* (1844) I. 200 Sufficient merchand guid. **1550** *Reg. Privy Council Scot.* I. 85 To sell certane merchant gudis within the burgh. **1704** *Lond. Gaz.* No. 4014/4 Three Pounds Sixteen Shillings per Hundred, Merchant Weight.

2. Of a ship: Serving for the transport of merchandise. Hence, of or pertaining to the mercantile marine, as in ***merchant service***, ***seaman***. (Often written with hyphen.)

1375 BARBOUR *Bruce* XIX. 193 Marchand-schippis that saland war Fra Scotland to Flandriss. **1598** SYLVESTER *Du Bartas* II. i. IV. *Handy-Crafts* 23 Lo, how our Merchant-vessels to and fro Freely about our tradefull waters go. **1709** STEELE *Tatler* No. 4 ¶7 A Fleet of Merchant Ships coming from Scotland. **1769** FALCONER *Dict. Marine* (1780) s.v. *Mate*, A frigate of 20 guns, and a small merchant-ship, have only one mate in each. **1851** H. MELVILLE *Whale* xvi, I'll take that leg away from thy stem, if ever thou talkest of the merchant service to me again. **1872** YEATS *Growth Comm.* 279 As soon as England was able to protect her merchant-shipping. **1874** THEARLE *Nav. Arch.* 94 A merchant ship is little other than a shell of iron plates stiffened by transverse ribs. **1899** F. T. BULLEN *Way Navy* 64 A humble merchant seaman.

3. Of a town: Occupied in commerce, commercial. Also, consisting of merchants, as in ***guild-merchant***, ***merchant-guild***.

1467 Yeld marchaunt [see GUILD 4]. **1596** DALRYMPLE tr. *Leslie's Hist. Scot.* I. 45 A famous merchand toun, quhais name is Elgin. **1611** BIBLE *Isa.* xxiii. 11 The Lord hath giuen a commandement against the merchant citie to destroy the strong holdes thereof. **1764** BURN *Poor Laws* 9 All workmen shall bring.. to the merchant towns their instruments. **1856** R. A. VAUGHAN *Mystics* (1860) I. 176 The merchant-league of the Rhineland. **1870** BRENTANO in Toulmin Smith *Eng. Gilds* p. xciii, The formerly-mentioned Gilds of Dover, of the Thanes at Canterbury, as well as perhaps the Gild-Merchant at London. *Ibid.* xciv, Such also were the Gild-Merchant of York [etc.]. **1874** STUBBS *Const. Hist.* I. xi. 417 The merchant-guild contained all the traders.

merchant (ˈmɜːtʃənt), *v.* Now *rare.* Also 4–5 **marchaund(e**, 5 **marchaunte**, 6 **marchant**, 7 **merchand**. [a. OF. *marcheander*, now *marchander*, f. *marchand* MERCHANT *sb.*]

1. *intr.* To trade as a merchant. Also, †to negotiate; in bad sense, to bargain, haggle.

1377 LANGL. *P. Pl.* B. XIII. 394 And if I sent ouer see my seruauntz to Bruges,.. To marchaunden with monoye and maken her eschaunges [etc.]. *c* **1430** *Pilgr. Lyf Man.* III.

xxvi. (1869) 150 To begile þilke þat ben symple,..or þat ben nyce to marchaunde. **1481** CAXTON *Godeffroy* 115 The turke ..wold not suffre them of nothyng, sauf..for to marchaunte to bye and selle. **1525** LD. BERNERS *Froiss.* II. cxxix. [cxxv.] 366 The duke of Lancastre and the duches his wyfe had rather marchant with you and with your sonne than with the duke of Berrey. **1614** CORNWALLIS in Gutch *Coll. Cur.* I. 162, I held it not fit, we should merchant with our Sovereign. **1622** BACON *Hen. VII* 99 Besides that, Ferdinando..merchanded at this time with France for the restoring of the Counties of Russignon and Perpignian. **1679** L. ADDISON *1st St. Mahumedism* 80 He died in the 63 year of his age, after he had Merchanted 38, been two years in the Cave [etc.]. **1866** CARLYLE *Remin., Irving* (1881) I. 170 Graham never merchanted more.

2. *trans.* To trade or deal in; to buy and sell.
1511 *Act 3 Hen. VIII*, c. 8 §1 No Minister in City or Borough, which..ought to keep Assises of Wines and Victuals..should merchant Wines and Victuals. **1541** *Act 33 Hen. VIII*, c. 2 The said fishermen..do marchant and bie the said french fishe. **1893** W. D. SPELMAN in *Voice* (N.Y.) 5 Oct., The rare, rich cutlery which he merchanted.

merchantability (ˌmɜːtʃəntəˈbɪlɪtɪ). [f. MERCHANTABLE *a.*: see -ITY.] The condition or state of being fit or prepared for market; the ability to be bought or sold.
1939 *Credit Manual of Commercial Laws* (Nat. Assoc. Credit Men) 31 *Merchantability.* Where goods are bought by description from a dealer in goods of that kind..there is an implied warranty that they shall be of a merchantable quality. **1961** *Listener* 21 Sept. 417/1 This condition, unlike the condition of merchantability, may be expressly excluded. **1972** *N.Y. Law Jrnl.* 31 Oct. 17/6 The findings on such issues..constitute a breach of the implied warranty of merchantability. **1973** *Ibid.* 1 Aug. 4/6 The issue is whether the pacemaker was fit for the ordinary purpose for which pacemakers were used (merchantability).

merchantable (ˈmɜːtʃəntəb(ə)l), *a.* Also 5 **merchand-**, 6 **mer-**, **marchaunt-**, 6–7 **marchand-**, 7–8 **merchandable**. [f. MERCHANT *v.* + -ABLE.]
1. Fit or prepared for market; that may or can be bought or sold; saleable; marketable.
c **1480** *Cokwolds Daunce* 109 in Hazl. *E.P.P.* I. 43 Ther wyves hath ben merchandabull, And of ther ware compenabull. *a* **1502** ARNOLDE *Chron.* 128 J. D...affermid ..that the sayd peper was as good as any in the worlde and marchauntable. **1587** HERIOT in *Hakluyt's Voy.* (1600) III. 267 Which commodities, for distinction sake, I call Merchantable. **1611** COTGR. s.v. *Emploicte*, Ware that sells well..marchandable ware. **1656** HEYLIN *Surv. France* 181 About the time of Clement the fifth..they [indulgences] began to be merchantable. **1713** *Grand Rebell.* II. 336 Came ..to relieve their wants By mustering up a Merchandable store. **1769** *De Foe's Tour Gt. Brit.* (ed. 7) IV. 80 They [White Fish] were very well cured, merchantable, and fit for Exportation. **1776** ADAM SMITH *W.N.* IV. v. (1869) II. 96 A barrel of good merchantable herrings. **1875** MAINE *Hist. Inst.* iii. 88 Land has become a merchantable commodity. **1894** *Jrnl. R. Agric. Soc.* June 322 Feeding stuffs guaranteed of the usual good and merchantable quality.
b. *spec.* The designation of the highest of the three grades of Newfoundland cod-fish.
1883 JONCAS *Fisheries Canada* 19 (Fish. Exhib. Publ.).
c. *transf.* and *fig.*
1701 *Argt. for War* 25 The Project may pass on the other side the water, but will never be Merchantable, I hope, in England. *a* **1734** NORTH *Exam.* I. ii. §57 (1740) 60 Who.. will make ample Returns in good and merchandable Party-Work. **1864** G. A. SALA in *Daily Tel.* 5 May, The lawyers and inferior judges..are..mere merchantable creatures, incurably venal.
†**2.** Of or pertaining to trade; commercial. *Obs.*
a **1603** T. CARTWRIGHT *Confut. Rhem. N.T.* (1618) 176 Satisfaction from us to God, and remission from God to vs, can no more stand together, than marchandable paiment with bankerupt. *Ibid.* 469 The most traffiqueable and Marchandable Citie of all Asia. *a* **1670** BP. HACKET *Abp. Williams* I. (1692) 90 Let every man coin what money he will and observe if ever we can make a marchandable payment.
Hence **ˈmerchantableness**.
1737 BAILEY vol. II. (ed. 3). **1885** *Law Times* LXXIX. 132/2 In a sale by sample there is an implied warranty of merchantableness.

ˈmerchant-adˈventurer. *Obs.* exc. *Hist.* (See also MERCHANT-VENTURER.) A merchant engaged in the organization and dispatch of trading expeditions over sea, and the establishment of factories and trading stations in foreign countries. Hence, a member of an association of such merchants incorporated by royal charter or other lawful authority.
1496–7 *Act 12 Hen. VII*, c. 6 The Marchauntes Adventurers inhabite and dwelling in divers parties of this Realme. **1540** ELYOT *Image Gov.* (1556) 59 b, He wolde not suffre any citesen to bee a Merchaunt adventurer. **1575** LANEHAM *Let.* (1871) 62 Mercer, Merchantauenturer, and Clark of the Councel-chamber door. **1608** in Gross *Gild Merch.* I. 148 The Lawes, Customes (&c.) of the Fellowshippe of Merchantes Adventurers. **1622** BACON *Hen. VII* 163 There passed a Law, at the Suit of the Merchant-Aduenturers of England, against the Merchant-Aduenturers of London, for Monopolizing and exacting vpon the Trade. **1766** ENTICK *London* IV. 130 Mr. Robert Rogers, leather-seller and merchant-adventurer. **1890** *Spectator* 19 Apr., The merchant-adventurers who, in Africa now, as formerly in India, represent the European peoples.
fig. **1711** SHAFTESB. *Charac.* (1737) I. 304 Certain merchant-adventurers in the letter-trade, who in correspondence with their factor-bookseller, are enter'd into a notable commerce with the world.

merchant bank (ˈmɜːtʃənt bæŋk). [MERCHANT *a.* 1 + BANK *sb.*[3] 7.] A bank whose main business is the providing of long-term credit and the support and financing of trading enterprises. So **merchant banker**, a member of such a bank (also *pl.*, the bank as a firm); **merchant banking** *vbl. sb.*, the activity undertaken by a merchant bank.
1904 H. T. EASTON *Hist. Banks* xxi. 215 The chairman of the London and Westminster Bank stated some time ago that 'acceptances drawn by mercantile firms abroad is [*sic*] part of the business that ought to be carried on by a merchant or merchant-banker'. **1924** L. LE M. MINTY *Eng. Banking Methods* ii. 51 The Merchant Bankers..are a class of large importing and exporting firms that, in addition to their regular business in trade, carry on an accepting business... Many firms referred to as 'merchant bankers' are merchants no longer. **1926** W. LEAF *Banking* vii. 184 Several of the great merchant banking houses of the Continent found it worth their while to transfer their international offices to London. **1928** *Daily Mail* 25 July 18/1 Dr. David Jochelman... Merchant Banker. **1930** S. E. THOMAS *Princ. Banking* ii. 18 In a sixth class [of banks] are the various concerns in the City which are known as 'merchant bankers' or 'merchant banks'. Most of these function mainly as 'accepting houses'. **1933** B. ELLINGER *This Money Business* ii. 16 Merchant Bankers or Accepting Houses, whose business it is to accept bills for other people and earn a commission by doing so. **1940** T. S. ELIOT *East Coker* iii. 10 They all go into the dark..The captains, merchant bankers, eminent men of letters. **1959** *Chambers's Encycl.* II. 100/2 Mention may also be made of the London merchant bankers. Their traditional function has been to facilitate the finance of international trade by 'accepting' (guaranteeing) bills of exchange. **1961** M. SPARK *Prime of Miss Jean Brodie* vi. 161 A successful business man who varied in his line of business from canned goods to merchant banking. **1965** J. L. HANSON *Dict. Econ.* 276/1 Many foreign merchant bankers found it convenient to transfer their headquarters to London—hence the number of merchant banks in England with foreign names. **1965** PERRY & RYDER *Thomson's Dict. Banking* (ed. 11) 375/1 Merchant bank. The great merchant banking houses of today have evolved from the merchants who, coming to this country in the early or middle years of the eighteenth century, built up their business by lending their names to bills financing particular transactions and by accepting such bills made them first-class bills freely discountable. **1966** *Times Rev. Industry* Oct. 99/1 When I became chairman of Lazards last year I was able to put down my occupation as 'merchant banker' instead of the less reputable 'company director'... I certainly was not a 'merchant' and not really a 'banker'. **1972** *Accountant* 19 Oct. 500/2 The work of an accountant in the field of merchant banking or taxation are [*sic*] worlds apart from the work in manufacturing industry or in practice.

merchanter, -teer (ˈmɜːtʃəntə(r), mɜːtʃənˈtɪə(r)). *U.S.* [f. MERCHANT *sb.* + -ER[1], -EER[1] (after *privateer*).] = MERCHANTMAN 2.
1829 MARRYAT *F. Mildmay* xiv, I'll fit out a privateer, and take some o' your merchanters. **1890** *Public Opinion* (Washington) 30 Aug., A departure from the merchanteer type [of ship] was the immediate result.

ˈmerchanthood. [f. MERCHANT *sb.* + -HOOD.] The quality or condition of being a merchant.
1866 CARLYLE *Remin., Irving* (1881) I. 171 Finding merchanthood in Glasgow ruinous to weak health. **1873** *Argosy* XV. 308 He had plodded diligently through clerkhood to merchanthood.

†**merchantical**, *a.* *Obs.* In 7 **mar-**. [f. MERCHANT *sb.* + -IC + -AL[1].] ? Mercenary.
a **1618** RALEIGH *Royal Navy* 7 The..true building of a Ship is not to be left barely to the fidelity of a Marchanticall Artificer.

merchantile, obs. form of MERCANTILE.

merchanting (ˈmɜːtʃəntɪŋ), *vbl. sb.* [f. MERCHANT *v.* + -ING[1].] The action or practice of trading as a merchant. Also *attrib.*
1894 SIR E. CLARKE in *Times* 19 Feb. 3/2 Did you know they had any 'merchanting' transactions? *Ibid.*, Supposing you knew they had made a loss on 'merchanting' every successive year? **1899** *Daily News* 27 Mar. 3/5 These firms are chiefly engaged in the manufacturing and merchanting of belts and strapping for the textile trades. **1957** *Listener* 28 Nov. 876/1 There is London as a merchanting centre... I have in mind the work done by the commodity markets and the large merchanting houses in buying and selling throughout the world. **1963** *Times* 16 Feb. 6/1 The merchanting trade has a considerable processing element, about a third of the 9m. tons of compound feed produced in the United Kingdom being manufactured by country compounders. **1967** *Economist* 28 Oct. 420/2 Lord Cromer, when still Governor of the Bank of England, put a figure of £200 million on the overseas earnings from all of Britain's insurance, merchanting, brokerage and banking services in 1965. **1971** *Timber Trades Jrnl.* 21 Aug. 13/1 The merchanting and retail side of the timber trade. **1973** *Daily Tel.* 31 July 17 (Advt.), More depots have been acquired in the merchanting and retailing section where we now have 87 outlets.

merchanting (ˈmɜːtʃəntɪŋ), *ppl. a.* [f. MERCHANT *v.* + -ING[2].] Engaged in trade as merchants.
1930 *Observer* 9 Feb. 18/1 The merchanting body itself is in no greatly better case. **1957** *Times* 23 Dec. 11/2 Two main divisions—the producing subsidiary companies with their mills and the merchanting subsidiaries in Manchester and London.

ˈmerchantish, *a.* *nonce-wd.* [f. MERCHANT *sb.* + -ISH[1].] After the manner of a merchant.
1848 CLOUGH *Poems*, etc. (1869) I. 120 It [the Assembly] is extremely shopkeeperish and merchantish in its feelings.

ˈmerchantlike, *a.* and *adv.* [f. MERCHANT *sb.* + -LIKE.] **a.** *adj.* Resembling or befitting a merchant; also, †pertaining to merchants or commerce, mercantile (*obs.*). **b.** *adv.* After the manner of a merchant.
1422–61 in *Cal. Proc. Chanc. Eliz.* I. (1827) Introd. 20 Johan Goldesmyth receyved the verray value marchantlick in wolles of the same Johan Kymburleys. **1585** T. WASHINGTON tr. *Nicholay's Voy.* I. viii. 7 b, This citie is very merchantlike, for that she is situated vpon the Sea. **1593** SHAKS. *2 Hen. VI*, IV. i. 41 When Merchant-like I sell reuenge, Broke be my sword. **1641** H. ROBINSON *Trades Encrease* 4 All merchant and marchantlike Causes and differences. **1656** EARL MONM. tr. *Boccalini's Advts. fr. Parnass.* I. xlvii. (1674) 63 Shepherds Arithmetick..differs ..from the Merchant-like Arithmetick used in other affairs. **1736** AINSWORTH *Lat. Dict.* I, Merchantly, or Merchant like, *mercatorius.* **1855** MACAULAY *Hist. Eng.* xxi. IV. 552 This transaction seemed merchantlike and fair.

†**ˈmerchantly**, *a.* *Obs.* [f. MERCHANT *sb.* + -LY[1].] **a.** Of or pertaining to a merchant. **b.** In disparaging sense: Huckstering, pettifogging.
1599 NASHE *Lenten Stuffe* 21 An eniuersal [*sic*] marchantly formallity, in habitte, speach, gestures. **1647** CLARENDON *Hist. Reb.* v. §324 Tho' it might have some influence upon Merchantly Men, yet it stirred up most Generous minds to an Indignation on the King's behalf. **1660** GAUDEN *Brownrig* 142 His Parents [were] of Merchantly condition, of worthy reputation, and of very Christian conversation. *a* **1674** CLARENDON *Hist. Reb.* x. §179 Their absurd and merchandly trafficking with him for the price of returning to their Allegiance. **1736** [see MERCHANTLIKE].

ˈmerchantman. [f. MERCHANT *a.* + MAN.]
1. = MERCHANT *sb.* 1. *arch.*
1449 *Aberdeen Reg.* (1844) I. 402 That na merchand man of this burgh opin his both dorr to do ony merchandise.. apon the Sondai. **1530** PALSGR. 737/1 He hath the best storyd house of good housholde stuffe of any marchant man that I knowe. **1550** COVERDALE *Spir. Perle* xxix. (1560) 289 A marchant man maketh far voiages and great iourneis, and ventureth body and goods. **1638** FORD *Fancies* v. iii, All men of severall conditions; Soldier, Gentry, foole, scholler, Merchant man, and Clowne. **1719** D'URFEY *Pills* III. 126 'Mongst Merchant-men, there's not one in ten, But what is a cunning Angler. **1882** OUIDA *Maremma* iii, The port dues and shipping taxes have..nearly destroyed all the commerce of the minor merchantmen of Italy. **1898** K. TYNAN in *Westm. Gaz.* 12 Oct. 1/3 Battering at Dublin gates till the comfortable merchantmen within were fairly distracted.
2. A vessel of the mercantile marine.
1627 CAPT. SMITH *Seaman's Gram.* xii. 56 Not manned like a Merchant-man. **1711** ADDISON *Spect.* No. 21 ¶9 Fleets of Merchantmen are so many Squadrons of floating Shops. **1818** MRS. SHELLEY *Frankenst.* iii. (1865) 19 This letter will reach England by a merchantman now on its homeward voyage. **1856** OLMSTED *Slave States* 148 Merchantmen were paying twenty-five dollars for common able seamen.

merchant mill. *U.S.* ? *Obs.* [f. MERCHANT *a.* 1.] A mill engaged in the grinding of grain for the purpose of trade.
1774 P. V. FITHIAN *Jrnl.* (1900) 111 Mr. Carter's Merchant Mill begins to run to-day—She is calculated to manufacture 25,000 Bushels of Wheat a Year. **1816** U. BROWN *Jrnl.* in *Maryland Hist. Mag.* (1915) X. 273 He has a Merchant Mill, a Saw Mill,..all on the Waters of Bath. **1837** W. JENKINS *Ohio Gazetteer* 68 The village contains.. 1 large merchant mill,..with four run of stones. **1851** C. CIST *Sk. Cincinnati in 1851* 194 It proposes to perform in a small compass..the work of a merchant mill. **1877** W. A. JOHNSON *Hist. Anderson County, Kansas* 252 In the spring of 1874 Chris. Bouch..commenced the construction of a first-class merchant mill.

merchant navy (ˌmɜːtʃənt ˈneɪvɪ). [MERCHANT *a.* 2 + NAVY[1].] A fleet or number of ships used in trade and not for purposes of war.
In 19th-cent. official sources called 'merchant shipping', 'merchant service', 'mercantile marine', 'mercantile navy', but not 'merchant navy'.
1875 T. FARRER in A. Hurd *Merchant Navy* (1921) I. 80 The actual increase of our Merchant Navy is a most remarkable fact. **1921** A. HURD *Merchant Navy* I. 2 Within a few months of the opening of hostilities, the King, in a message of appreciation of the services of the merchant seamen, referred to 'his Merchant Navy',..and the Prime Minister..described the Merchant Navy as 'the jugular vein of the nation'. **1928** *Times* 14 Feb. 14/6 The King has appointed the Prince of Wales Master of the Merchant Navy and Fishing Fleets. The announcement will appear in the *London Gazette* to-night. **1929** *Ann. Reg. 1928* I. 10 On February 13 the King paid a graceful compliment to the British seafaring population outside the ranks of the Royal Navy by creating the Prince of Wales 'Master of the Merchant Navy and the Fishing Fleets'—a new title for which there was no exact precedent in British history or usage. **1937** *Discovery* June 165/1 Seamen, whether of the Royal Navy, the Merchant Navy, or the Fishing Fleet. **1965** S. J. HARLAND (*title*) The dustless road: a career in the Merchant Navy.

merchantry (ˈmɜːtʃəntrɪ). [f. MERCHANT *sb.* + -RY. Cf. MERCHANDRY.]
1. The business of a merchant; trade, commercial dealings.
1789 H. WALPOLE *Let to Miss H. More* Sept., I wish human wit, which is really very considerable in mechanics and merchantry, could [etc.]. *a* **1800** S. PEGGE *Anecd. Eng. Lang.* 267 Most of the streets..have their titles from their

Merchantry. **1864** MAYHEW *German Life* I. 165 In England, ..where merchantry is something beyond that of mere pedlar's work.

2. The body of merchants collectively.

1862 CARLYLE *Fredk. Gt.* XIII. vi. (1872) V. 73 Our Town-Council, and whole Merchantry and Citizenry, safe under this Prussian Sceptre.

'merchantship. *rare.* [f. MERCHANT *sb.* + -SHIP.] The office or function of a merchant. Used with *possess. adj.* as a title for a merchant.

1622 FLETCHER *Beggar's Bush* v. ii, Your Merchantship May breake, for this was one of your best bottoms, I thinke.

'merchant-'stranger. *Obs.* exc. *Hist.* [f. MERCHANT *sb.* + STRANGER.] A merchant who comes from another country by sea; a foreign or alien trader.

1553 EDEN *Treat. New Ind.* (Arb.) 21 Therfore the marchaund straungers lodge not out of their shippes. **1557** MACHYN *Diary* (Camden) 140 The xxiiij day of June was goodly serves kept at the Frere Austens by the marchandes strangers as has bene sene. **1606** G. WOODCOCKE *Hist. Ivstine* XXXVI. 114 The elder brothers..secretly laid for him, and..sold him to a Marchant-stranger. **1641** EARL OF CORK *Diary* in *Lismore Papers* Ser. I. (1886) V. 200 Mr. Michaell casteel of London, merchant stranger. **1654** GODDARD *Introd. Burton's Diary* (1828) I. 125 Resolved, that the merchants, commonly calling themselves merchants of the intercourse,..shall pay..all such sum and sums of money as shall be assessed..upon them..as any merchant-strangers. **1766** BARRINGTON *Observ. Stat.* (ed. 2) 21 By an ancient law of the Wisigoths, merchant strangers are not only to be well treated, but tried by their own laws.

'merchant-'tailor. Also with archaic spelling in the names of the 'Company of Merchant Taylors' and the 'Merchant Taylors' School'. [f. MERCHANT *sb.* + TAILOR.] **a.** A tailor who supplies the materials of which his goods are made. Hence, a member of the company of ***Merchant-Taylors.***

1504 WRIOTHESLEY *Chron* (Camden) I. 5 This yeare the Taylors sued to the Kinge to be called Marchant taylors. **1533** CROMWELL in Merriman *Life & Lett.* I. 356 Nicholas Glossop, an olde Auncient of youre Felisship of merchaunt Taillours. **1556** *Chron. Gr. Friars* (Camden) 87 John Harres a merchant-taylor in Watlynge stret. **1653** *Rec. Early Hist. Boston* (1886) X. 1, I Robert Keayne, Cittizen and Merchant Taylor of London by freedome,..now dwelling at Boston. **1687** [see LINEN-ARMOURER]. **1707** E. CHAMBERLAYNE *Pres. St. Eng.* III. xi. 386 That eminent School [Merchant-Taylors'] near Cannon-street, built by Sir Tho. White, Alderman, and Merchant-Taylor of London. **1818** H. B. FEARON *Sk. Amer.* 33 Taylors are numerous: they are denominated, (in conformity with the accustomed vanity of the country), 'Merchant Taylors'. **1839** *Penny Cycl.* XIV. 118/2 The first twelve are called the Twelve Great Companies... 7. Merchant Tailors. **1889** *Kansas City* (Missouri) *Times & Star* 13 Nov., Call on Ed. Howe, the artistic merchant tailor. **1922** JOYCE *Ulysses* 717 The establishment of George Mesias, merchant tailor and outfitter. **1975** *Times* 5 July 14/7 The following were elected officers of the Merchant Taylors' Company for the year beginning July 14.

b. One educated at Merchant-Taylors' School.

1877 *N. & Q.* 3rd Ser. VII. 347 Sir Henry Ellis (himself a Merchant Taylor). *Ibid.*, Old Merchant Taylors..who take an interest in their school.

'merchant-'venturer. *Obs.* exc. *Hist.* = MERCHANT-ADVENTURER. Also *fig.*

1550 LEVER *Serm.* (Arb.) 131 The marchaunt venturer, which..caryeth furth suche thynges, as maye well be spared, and bryngeth home suche wares as muste needes be occupyed in thys realm. **1556** MACHYN *Diary* (Camd.) 116 Gressem..marchand of the [staple] of Callys and marchand venterer. **1592** G. HARVEY *Pierce's Super.* Wks. (Grosart) II. 45 This brave Columbus of tearmes, and this onely merchant venturer of quarrels. **1642** ROGERS *Naaman* 188 The cause of God losing exceedingly by such Merchant venturers. **1769** *De Foe's Tour Gt. Brit.* (ed. 7) II. 125 The Merchant-Venturers of the City of Bristol. **1890** GROSS *Gild Merch.* I. 152 Edward VI incorporated the 'merchant venturers' inhabiting the town of Newcastle-upon-Tyne.

†**merchanty.** *Obs.* In 5–6 **marchauntie.** [Altered form of MERCHANDY, after MERCHANT *sb.*] **a.** Merchandise, goods. **b.** The whole body of merchants.

c **1480** *Childe of Bristowe* 64 in Hazl. *E.P.P.* (1864) I. 113 That good getyn by marchantye..therwith wille y melle. *a* **1502** ARNOLDE *Chron.* (1811) 101 The marchauntie of Amyas of Neele and of Corby purchased a letter ensealed w[t] y[e] common seal of y[e] cite.

merchasy, -aulcy, obs. ff. MARSHALSEA.

merchaundise, obs. form of MERCHANDISE.

merchaunt(t, -tyse, obs. ff. MERCHANT, -DISE.

Merche, obs. form of MARCH, MARROW *sb.*[1]

merchet ('mɜːtʃɪt). *Obs.* exc. *Hist.* Also 6–8 **marchet.** [Anglo-Fr. *merchet* (whence med.L. *mercheta*) = ONF. *market* MARKET *sb.*] A fine paid by a tenant or bondsman to his overlord for liberty to give his daughter in marriage.

1228 in *Mem. Ripon* (Surtees) I. 52 Merchet. **1492** *Acta Dom. Conc.* (1839) 291/2 For þe wrangwis..awaytakin & withhaldin fra þaim of certane hereȝeldis, bludwetis & merchetis. **1552** LYNDESAY *Monarche* 5711 Ȝe Lordis and Baronis,..That ȝour pure Tennantis dois oppres..With merchetis of thare marriage. **1577** HOLINSHED *Hist. Scot.* 258 Halfe a marke of siluer to bee payde to the Lorde of the soyle, in redemption of the womans chastitie, which..is called the marchets of women. **1609** SKENE *Reg. Maj.* 73 And she be the dochter of ane frie man,..her marchet sall be ane kow, or sax schillings. *Ibid.*, The marchet of the dochter of ane Earle perteines to the Queene, and is twelue kye. **1628** COKE *On Litt.* 140 Euerie tenant..shall pay to the Lord, for the marriage of his daughter without licence, a Fine; and it is called Marchet. **1900** CHEYNEY in *Eng. Hist. Rev.* XV. 31 Merchet is a more steady test [of a man's villainage], but even this is not always trustworthy.

merchy, obs. Sc. form of MARROWY.

merci, obs. form of MERCY.

†**merciable,** *a. Obs.* Also 4 **mercyabil,** 4–5 **merciabul,** 4–6 **mercyable, -byl, merciabil(l,** 5 **marciable.** [OF. *merciable*, f. *merci*: see MERCY.] Merciful, compassionate.

a **1225** *Ancr. R.* 30 Merciable Louerd. *a* **1340** HAMPOLE *Psalter* lxxvii. 42 He sall be made mercyabil till þaire synnys. **1382** WYCLIF *Hebr.* ix. 5 (MS. Trin. Dubl.) The propiciatorie [*gloss*] or merciable place. **1421–2** HOCCLEVE *Dialog.* 368 Thankid be our lord Ihesu merciable. **1513** BRADSHAW *St. Werburge* I. 2751 Who-so wyll haue mercy Must be mercyable. **1579** SPENSER *Sheph. Cal.* Sept. 174 He is so meeke, wise, merciable, And with his word his worke is convenable.

absol. **1303** R. BRUNNE *Handl. Synne* 3793 Blessyd be al mercyable! þey shul se God. *c* **1395** *Plowman's T.* 96 Christ so gan us teche, And meke and merciable gan bless.

†**merciably,** *adv. Obs.* [f. MERCIABLE + -LY[2].] Mercifully.

1387–8 T. USK *Test. Love* III. ix. (Skeat) l. 73 So that goddes hand, whiche that merciably me hath scorged, herafter..merciably me kepe and defende. **1535** JOYE *Apol. Tindale* (Arb.) 25 Yea he is redye, yf I fall, merciably to lifte me vp agayn.

mercial(l, obs. forms of MARTIAL.

†**'merciament.** *Obs. rare.* Also 5 **merceament,** 6 **mercyament.** [Aphetic form of AMERCIAMENT.] Amercement.

1432–50 tr. *Higden* (Rolls) II. 95 Blodewitte, a merciamente for effusion of bloode. **1494** FABYAN *Chron.* (1811) 344 Baylyes..were conuycte..for takynge of merceamentys otherwyse then the lawe them commaundyd. **1521** *Maldon* (Essex) *Liber B.* 57 Truly affur and sett al maner of mercyaments made highe no man for no malice, lowe no man for no love.

Mercian ('mɜːsɪən, 'mɜːʃ(ɪ)ən), *a.* and *sb.* Also 6 **Mercyen, -tian.** [f. *Mercia* (latinized from OE. *Merce, Mierce*, pl., lit. 'people of the march, marchers, borderers', f. *mearc* MARK *sb.*[1]) + -AN.]

A. *adj.* Of or belonging to the Old English kingdom of Mercia or its language.

Although the political limits of Mercia were different at different periods, it may broadly be said to have occupied the middle of South Britain, between Deira on the north and Wessex on the south, and between Wales on the west and Lindsey and East Anglia on the east. The Mercian dialect of Old English belongs to the Anglian (as opposed to the Saxon) division, and is the dialect from which modern standard English mainly descends.

1655 FULLER *Ch. Hist.* II. 89 Wolphere, the Mercian King. **1797** *Encycl. Brit.* (ed. 3) XI. 400/2 The extent of the Mercian territories was so ample as to admit..the constituting subordinate rulers. **1842** WRIGHT *Lyric P.* Pref. 6 We have another Mercian legend in Latin, *De Martyrio Sancti Wistani.* **1887** SKEAT *Holy Gosp. in A.S.* Pref. 7 The Old Mercian dialect. *Ibid.*, The Old Mercian glosses in the Rushworth MS. are of peculiar interest.

B. *sb.*

1. A native or inhabitant of Mercia.

1513 BRADSHAW *St. Werburge* I. 121 Her fathers kyngedome the realme of Mercyens. **1590** SPENSER *F.Q.* III. iii. 30 It shall make The warlike Mertians for feare to quake. **1656** BLOUNT *Glossogr.* s.v. *Merchenlage*, The third [division of England] was possessed and governed by the Mercians. **1876** LUMBY *Introd. to Higden* (Rolls) VI. p. xxxv, Victory declared for the Mercians.

2. The dialect of Old English spoken in Mercia.

1887 SKEAT *Holy Gosp. in A.S.* Pref. 7 A man whose ordinary dialect was Mercian. **1889** *Ibid.* Introd., The present edition of the Four Gospels (in Latin, Anglo-Saxon, Northumbrian and Old Mercian) brings together [etc.].

†**merciere.** *Obs.* [a. OF. *merciere* adj., merciful, f. *merci* MERCY.] One who pities.

a **1340** HAMPOLE *Psalter* lxxxv. 14 þou lord merciere and merciful: suffrand and of mykil mercy and sothfast. *Ibid.*, Merciere, doand dede of mercy.

merciful ('mɜːsɪfʊl), *a.* [f. MERCY *sb.* + -FUL.] Of persons, their actions, attributes, etc.: Having or exercising mercy; characterized by mercy.

a **1300** *E.E. Psalter* cxliv. 8 Mercifulle and milde herted in lande Lauerd, and mikel milde-herted and tholand. **1382** WYCLIF *Matt.* v. 7 Blessed be mercyful men, for thei shuln gete mercye. *a* **1425** *Cursor M.* (Trin.) 18359 Lord..þi wille is merciful wiþynne So þou dost awey oure synne. **1509** FISHER *Funeral Serm. C'tess Richmond* Wks. (1876) 291 Mercyfull also & pyteous she was vnto suche as was greuyd & wrongfully troubled. **1531** TINDALE *Expos. 1 John* (1537) 2 Understandynge them [ye promises of mercye]..after the mercifullest fashion. **1552** ABP. HAMILTON *Catech.* (1884) 25 How gratious and mercifull he is to al trew penitent persones. **1610** SHAKS. *Temp.* v. i. 178 Though the Seas threaten they are merciful, I haue curs'd them without cause. **1662** STILLINGFL. *Orig. Sacr.* II. vi. §11 The mercifull nature of God. **1715** DE FOE *Fam. Instruct.* I. i. (1841) I. 19 But God is merciful too, child. **1851** DIXON *W. Penn* xxvii. (1872) 247 She had obeyed the merciful promptings of her heart in sheltering a fellow-creature. **1886** CONST. F. WOOLSON *East Angels* xxxvii. 577 Merciful Heaven!..do you care for him?—is that it?

absol. **138.** WYCLIF *Sel. Wks.* III. 328 Blissed be þe mercyful. *c* **1460** *Wisdom* 1136 in *Macro Plays* 72 þe ouer parte of yowur reasun, Be wyche ye haue lyknes of Gode mest, Ande of þat mercyfull very congnycion.

b. In sarcastic use.

1805 *Med. Jrnl.* XIV. 566 It was merciful not to add a thousand [facts] whilst he was about it.

mercifully ('mɜːsɪfʊlɪ), *adv.* [f. prec. + -LY[2].] In a merciful manner. Also *occas.* through God's mercy.

a **1340** HAMPOLE *Psalter* cxvi. 2 þe redempcioun of man mercyfully hight is confermyd on vs. *c* **1450** *Godstow Register* 4/13 Late us be neuer to hym vnkynde Mercyfully þat made vs to be men. **1548–9** (Mar.) *Bk. Com. Prayer, Litany*, Mercifully forgeue the synnes of thy people. **1779** J. DUCHÉ *Disc.* (1790) I. i. 20 This mortified, penitent, afflicted state is mercifully intended to bring us to a proper sense of our helplessness. **1836** LADY WILLOUGHBY DE ERESBY in C. K. Sharpe *Corr.* (1888) II. 495 Mrs. Villiers, in galloping to cover..was pitched off,..but mercifully escaped with life and limb. **1903** A. B. DAVIDSON *Old Test. Prophecy* xv. 251 The house of God was at last overthrown though its overthrow was mercifully postponed.

mercifulness ('mɜːsɪfʊlnɪs). [f. MERCIFUL + -NESS.] The quality of being merciful.

1526 TINDALE *Rom.* xii. 1, I beseche you therfore brethren by the mercifulnes of God, that ye make youre bodyes a quicke sacrifise. **1650** JER. TAYLOR *Holy Living* (1727) 258 The next enemy to mercifulness..is anger. *a* **1708** BEVERIDGE *Thes. Theol.* (1710) I. 193 The names given in Scripture to it [forgiveness]..Mercifulness to our sins. **1852** ROBERTSON *Lect.* ii. (1858) 198 A school of warfare where the razzias of Africa have not taught either scrupulosity or mercifulness.

†**'mercify,** *v. Obs. rare.* [f. MERCY + -(I)FY.] *trans.* To pity, compassionate; to extend mercy to.

1596 SPENSER *F.Q.* VI. vii. 32 Many did deride, Whilest she did weepe of no man mercifide. **1733** CRAWFORD *Infidelity* (1836) 210 We must not only be mercified but justified.

merciless ('mɜːsɪlɪs), *a.* [f. MERCY + -LESS.]

1. Of persons, their actions, attributes, etc.: Devoid of mercy; showing no mercy; pitiless, unrelenting.

13.. *E.E. Allit. P.* B. 250 þer was malys mercyles & mawgre much scheued. *c* **1420** LYDG. *Siege Thebes* 2206 So mercyles in his cruelte Thilke day he was vpon hem founde. **1550** CROWLEY *Epigr.* 1236 Iudgemente shall be geuen,..Wythoute all mercye to suche as be mercyles. **1631** GOUGE *God's Arrows* iii. §94. 360 They..plotted the matchlesse, mercilesse, devilish, and damnable gun-powder-treason. **1719** DE FOE *Crusoe* I. (Globe) 249, I had rather..be devour'd alive, than fall into the merciless Claws of the Priests. **1843** PRESCOTT *Mexico* (1850) I. 291 A stern prince, merciless in his exactions. **1900** MORLEY *Cromwell* vi. 94 The merciless suppression of the rising of the Ulster chieftains.

absol. **1592** DANIEL *Delia* Sonn. xi, I pray in vaine, a merciles to moue.

b. *transf.* of inanimate things.

1582 STANYHURST *Æneis* I. (Arb.) 21 The southwynd merciles eager Three gallant vessels on rocks gnawne craggye reposed. **1596** SPENSER *F.Q.* IV. viii. 51 All dismayd through mercilesse despaire. **1634** SIR T. HERBERT *Trav.* 185 The mercilesse fury of the Sea. **1714** POPE *Let. to Teresa Blount*, Whatever ravages a merciless distemper may commit,..she shall have one man as much her admirer as ever. **1880** L. STEPHEN *Pope* iv. 103 A doggrel epitaph..turned his fine phrases into merciless ridicule.

†**c.** As *sb.* Mercilessness. *Obs. rare.*

1584 C. ROBINSON *Handf. Delites* (Arb.) 25 The torments ..Which he..had suffered long Al through this Ladies mercilesse.

†**d.** As *adv. Obs.*

1556 LAUDER *Tractate* 470 O Lord..help the pure that ar in stres Oppreſt and hereit mercyles.

†**2.** Obtaining no mercy. *Obs.*

c **1560** A. SCOTT *Poems* (S.T.S.) xvii. 11 All vertew in hir visage dois remane, Bot merciles I go from ȝeir to ȝeir. **1567** *Gude & Godlie Ball.* (S.T.S.) 119 God hes left us mercyles.

mercilessly ('mɜːsɪlɪslɪ), *adv.* [f. prec. + -LY[2].] In a merciless manner.

1609 BP. HALL *Song of Songs Paraphr.* iv. 8 Cruell and bloudy persecutors, who like Lions and Leopards haue tyrannized over thee, and mercilesly torne thee in peeces. **1660** C. ELLIS *Gentile Sinner* 197 Whilest she has been mercilessly torne in pieces, by the cruel teeth of those ravenous beasts. **1755** in JOHNSON. **1833** H. COLERIDGE *Biog. Bor., Marvell* 26 So mercilessly had the Church of Scotland been stripped..that she could not afford an episcopal establishment. **1883** STEVENSON *Treas. Isl.* III. xiv, The sun still shining mercilessly on the steaming marsh.

mercilessness ('mɜːsɪlɪsnɪs). [f. MERCILESS *a.* + -NESS.] The quality or condition of being merciless.

1591 TURNBULL *St. James* 103 With crueltie to seeke the vttermost of them; is mercilesnes and crueltie. **1607** HIERON *Wks.* I. 270 Mercilesnesse, cruelty..these and the like..bee our sinnes to this day. **1876** GEO. ELIOT *Dan. Der.* vi, She turned her eyes on him with calm mercilessness.

merciment, obs. variant of MERCEMENT.

†**mercimony.** *Obs.* In 4–5 **mercymonye.** [ad. L. *mercimōni-um* merchandise, f. *merci-, merx*

merchandise; in med.L. also reward, from association with *mercēdem* (F. *merci*).]

1. Reward.

1377 LANGL. *P. Pl.* B. XIV. 126 Ac god is of a wonder-wille by þat kynde witte sheweth, To ȝiue many men his mercymonye ar he it haue deserued.

2. Merchandise.

a **1412** LYDG. *Two Merchants* 31 What mercymony that men list devise, Is ther ful reedy and ful copious. **1494** FABYAN *Chron.* VII. 339 They came with theyr mercymonyes vnto the fayre of Waltham. *a* **1550** *Image Ipocr.* ii. 257 in *Skelton's Wks.* (1843) II. 426 Making parsemonyes Of Peters patrimonyes But great mercymonyes Of his seremonyes.

mercurate (ˈmɜːkjʊəreɪt), *v. Chem.* [f. MERCUR(Y *sb.* + -ATE³.] *trans.* To convert into a mercury derivative, esp. by replacing a hydrogen atom in an aromatic ring by a group containing mercury.

1923 *Org. Syntheses* III. 14 Phenol has been mercurated in water solution. **1942** FUSON & SNYDER *Org. Chem.* xxxi. 430 Hydrocarbons are mercurated by treatment at 90–160° for one or more hours. **1967** I. L. FINAR *Org. Chem.* (ed. 5) I. xx. 583 Aromatic compounds containing almost all the common functional groups have been mercurated.

So **ˈmercurated** *ppl. a.*; **mercuˈration**, the process of mercurating or of becoming mercurated.

1921 *Jrnl. Amer. Chem. Soc.* XLIII. 621 The 3 mercurated phenols were boiled with aqueous potassium iodide. **1923** *Org. Syntheses* III. 100 p-Tolylmercuric chloride has been prepared..by the direct mercuration of toluene with mercuric acetate. **1965** PHILLIPS & WILLIAMS *Inorg. Chem.* I. xi. 420 Mercuration of aromatic systems occurs very rapidly, presumably through a similar intermediate. **1967** I. L. FINAR *Org. Chem.* (ed. 5) I. xx. 584 The position of the acetoxymercuri-group can be found by treating the mercurated compound with halogen.

Mercure, obs. form of MERCURY.

Mercurean (mɜːkjʊˈriːən). [f. MERCURY + -EAN.] An inhabitant of the planet MERCURY.

1855 J. NICHOL in *Mem.* (1896) II. 113, I wonder what view of creation the inhabitants of Jupiter, or the sunny Mercureans now illustrate and expound.

Mercurey (‖mɛrkyre, ˈmɜːkjʊərɪ). Also **mercurey**. [Fr., name of a vineyard of the Côte Chalonnaise.] A Burgundy wine produced in the Chalonnais district of France.

1907 A. BENNETT *Grim Smile of Five Towns* iii. 225 It was a bottle of mercurey, a wine which has given me many dreadful dawns, but which I have never known how to refuse. **1928** P. M. SHAND *Bk. French Wine* iv. 173 Mercurey is the only real 'name' of the Côte Chalonnaise. *Ibid.*, Mercurey owes its classical name to a former temple of Mercury. **1958** A. L. SIMON *Dict. Wines* 110/1 Most of the *Mercurey* wines are red, and they are also of better quality than the few white wines of that district. **1972** D. MCLACHLAN *No Case for Crown* xiii. 165 The wine was his favourite *Mercurey*, which he ordered himself from France.

mercurial (mɜːˈkjʊərɪəl), *a.* and *sb.* [a. F. *mercuriel* and (as sb., in the sense B 1) *mercurial*, ad. L. *mercuriāl-is*, f. *Mercuri-us* MERCURY: see -AL¹.] **A.** *adj.*

1. a. Of or pertaining to the god Mercury; resembling what pertains to Mercury. Now *rare*.

†*mercurial statue, stone*: cf. MERCURY 2.

1599 B. JONSON *Cynthia's Rev.*, 1st Masque, A Petasus or Mercurial hat. **1611** SHAKS. *Cymb.* IV. ii. 310, I know the shape of's Legge: this is his Hand, His Foote Mercuriall: his martiall Thigh, The brawns of Hercules. **1637** EARL STIRLING *Parænesis to the Prince* lxxv, O! how this (deare Prince) the people charmes,..To see thee yong, yet manage so thine Armes, Have a Mercuriall minde and Martiall hands. **1638** CHILLINGW. *Relig. Prot.* I. iii. §34. 146 As the Wisemen were led by the Starre, or as a traveller is directed by a Mercuriall statue. **1716** HEARNE *Collect.* (O.H.S.) V. 282, I take them to be old mile Stones, or Mercurial Stones. **1874** SYMONDS *Sk. Italy & Greece* (1898) I. xiii. 285 A mercurial poise upon the ankle.

b. *nonce-use.* Applied to the 'profession' of thieving.

1744 WHITEHEAD *Gymnasiad* I. 37 *note*, Tricking, lying, evasion,..are a sort of properties pertaining to the practice of the law, as well as to the mercurial profession.

2. Pertaining to the planet Mercury. †Also in *Astrology*, influenced by Mercury, proceeding from the influence of Mercury. ***mercurial finger***: the little finger. *Obs.*

1390 GOWER *Conf.* III. 130 The sexte..Canis minor is; The which sterre is Mercurial Be weie of kinde. **1610** B. JONSON *Alchemist* I. iii, *Svb.*..I knew't, by certaine spots too, in his teeth, And on the naile of his mercurial finger. *Fac.* Which finger's that? *Svb.* His little finger. **1625** HART *Anat. Ur.* II. x. 120 Wilt thou..maintaine, that all Mercuriall diseases are seated in the head onely? *a* **1668** SIR W. WALLER *Div. Medit.* (1839) 40 Generally men are like that mercurial planet, good or bad according to their conjunction with others. **1690** LEYBOURN *Curs. Math.* 451 b, I shall forbear to add those distinctions which some have given them [*sc.* Comets] in reference to the Planets, they making some Solar, others Lunar, Mercurial..and Saturnine. **1862** G. WILSON *Relig. Chem.* 59 The mercurial day being, like our own, twenty-four hours long. **1881** PROCTOR *Poetry Astron.* vii. 252 The Mercurial climate.

3. Of persons: Born under the planet Mercury; having the qualities supposed to proceed from such a nativity, as eloquence, ingenuity, aptitude for commerce.

These qualities are identical with those assigned by the ancients to the god Mercury, or supposed to be due to his inspiration. Hence in some of the following quots. the allusion may be rather mythological than astrological, or perh. a mixture of the two.

1593 G. HARVEY *Pierces Super.* Wks. (Grosart) II. 63 You that intende to be fine companionable gentlemen,..enure your Mercuriall fingers to frame semblable workes of Supererogation. **1647** LILLY *Chr. Astrol.* lxxix. 438 Mercuriall men, viz. Schollars, or Divines would be his enemies. **1652** URQUHART *Jewel* Wks. (1834) 240 He speaks too well to be valiant; he is certainly more Mercurial than military. **1691** WOOD *Ath. Oxon.* I. 287 His mind being more Martial than Mercurial, he [W. Monson] applied himself to Sea-service.

4. Volatile, sprightly, and ready-witted. Originally a specific use of sense 3; now commonly apprehended as alluding to the properties of the metal mercury.

1647 TRAPP *Comm. Jas.* i. 1 The most nimble and Mercuriall wits in the world, but light. **1655** FULLER *Ch. Hist.* v. i. §40 He none of the most Mercurial amongst the Conclave of Cardinals, but a good heavy man. **1709** STEELE *Tatler* No. 30 ¶3 One of them was a mercurial gay-humour'd Man. **1827** DISRAELI *Viv. Grey* v. ix, The gay, gallant, mercurial Frenchman. **1873** DIXON *Two Queens* I. II. iii. 84 The people were a quick, mercurial, and artistic race. **1903** *Contemp. Rev.* Sept. 327 That curious, monkeyish, mercurial person M. Guyot de Montpeyroux.

5. Of or pertaining to mercury or quicksilver; consisting of or containing mercury. Also, of certain diseases or symptoms (e.g. ***mercurial eczema, glossitis, rash***): Produced by the exhibition of mercury. Hence, occas., of an organ, etc.: Showing 'mercurial' symptoms.

mercurial ointment: the 'blue ointment' composed of metallic mercury triturated with lard. ***mercurial (pneumatic) trough***: a pneumatic trough filled with mercury.

1657 G. STARKEY *Helmont's Vind.* Epist. Rdr., I have..rejected all Mercurial and Antimonial Medicaments, either Vomitive, Purgative, or Salivative. **1660** BOYLE *New Exp. Phys. Mech.* xvii. 108 The height of the Mercurial Cylinder. **1693** HALLEY in *Phil. Trans.* XVII. 652 The precise nicety of the Mercurial Barometers. **1744** BERKELEY *Siris* §100 A mercurial salivation is looked on by many as the only cure. **1786** J. HUNTER *Venereal Dis.* (1810) VI. iii. 503 The gums, inside of the cheeks, and the breath, were truly mercurial. **1789** CULLEN *Mat. Med.* II. 306 Our common mercurial ointment. **1807** *Med. Jrnl.* XVII. 379 What the author calls the mercurial rash, or, as it is called by some others, the Lepra mercurialis. *a* **1823** M. BAILLIE *Wks.* (1825) I. 13 Mercurial frictions were also employed. **1825** J. NICHOLSON *Operat. Mechanic* 525 This [Graham's] pendulum, which is called the mercurial pendulum. **1836–41** BRANDE *Chem.* (ed. 5) 401 It may often be..collected in dry phials, without a mercurial trough. **1843** R. J. GRAVES *Syst. Clin. Med.* xxviii. 362 An eruption, to which the name mercurial eczema has been given. **1867** SMYTH *Sailor's Word-bk.* 477 *Mercurial Gauge*, a curved tube partly filled with mercury, to show the pressure of steam in an engine. **1873** W. F. CLARKE *Dis. Tongue* 105 But happily 'mercurial glossitis' is now seldom seen. **1878** HUXLEY *Physiogr.* 78 He obtained it from the red mercurial powder. **1884** F. J. BRITTEN *Watch & Clockm.* 189 In the mercurial pendulum the jar of mercury does not answer so quickly to a change of temperature as the steel rod.

†**6.** *Old Chem.* Pertaining to, or consisting of, 'mercury' as one of the five 'principles' of bodies (see MERCURY 8). *Obs.*

1605 TIMME *Quersit.* I. v. 20 Sal amoniac doth participate of the mercurial beginning. **1633** HART *Diet of Diseased* II. xvii. 206 The mercuriall or waterish part [of milk] called serum.

B. *sb.*

†**1.** The plant mercury. *Obs.* [= L. (*herba*) *mercurialis*, OF. *mercuriel*, mod.F. *mercuriale*.]

1607 TOPSELL *Four-f. Beasts* (1658) 536 Take as much Mercurial sodden, as one's hand can hold,..and drink the same. **1626** BACON *Sylva* §41 Medecines Emollient; Such as are Milk, Honey, Mallowes, Lettuce, Mercuriall [etc.].

†**2.** A person born under the influence of the planet Mercury, or having the qualities characteristic of such a nativity; a lively or sprightly person; also, one addicted to cheating and thieving. *Obs.*

1598 SYLVESTER *Du Bartas* II. i. II. *Imposture* 443 Who, for sustayning of unequall Scale, Dreads not the Doom of a Mercuriall. **1614** TOMKIS *Albumazar* I. i. (1615) B, Come braue Mercurials sublim'd in cheating,..fellow-souldiers I'th' watchfull exercise of Theevery. **1622** BACON *Hen. VII* 113 This Youth..was such a Mercuriall, as the like hath seldome beene knowne. **1650** GENTILIS *Considerat.* 156 The Mercurials with their swiftnesse run over all things. **1696** PHILLIPS, *Mercurial*, or *Mercurialist*, one born under the Planet Mercury.

3. A preparation of mercury used as a drug in the cure of certain diseases; also more widely, any compound that contains mercury.

1676 WISEMAN *Surg.* VII. iv. 40 By Mercurials we do more certainly resolve them [nodes] and in a less time. **1716** M. DAVIES *Athen. Brit.* II. 352 The great Pox, which can scarce ever be cur'd without Viperals or Mercurials. **1735** BRACKEN in *Burdon's Pocket-Farrier* 71 *note*, The Cure is perform'd by Mercurials outwardly and inwardly. **1829–32** CHRISTISON *Treat. Poisons* xiii. (ed. 2) 380 The blue ointment, which is made of running mercury, will act as a mercurial when rubbed upon the skin. **1899** *Allbutt's Syst. Med.* VI. 151 The judicious employment of mercurials might prove highly beneficial. **1971** *Sci. Amer.* May 18/3 Among other inorganic mercurials, some of the oxides, such as the red oxide used in antifouling paint for ship bottoms may be potentially hazardous. **1971** *Nature* 23 July 222/1 The build-up of alkyl mercurials in the environment and their toxicological properties was the subject of many of the contributions.

mercurialism (mɜːˈkjʊərɪəlɪz(ə)m). *Path.* [f. MERCURIAL *a.* + -ISM.] The pathological condition induced by the absorption of mercury into the body.

1829–32 CHRISTISON *Treat. Poisons* xiii. (ed. 2) 372 [He] had..all the symptoms of mercurialism eight years after he had ceased to take mercury. **1862** *New Syd. Soc. Year-bk. Med. & Surg.* 319 An investigation of Constitutional Mercurialism. **1897** *Allbutt's Syst. Med.* IV. 596 It [i.e. Mercurial inunction] must be used with caution so as to avoid any symptoms of mercurialism.

Mercurialist (mɜːˈkjʊərɪəlɪst). [f. MERCURIAL + -IST.]

†**1.** One under the influence of the planet Mercury. *Obs.*

1569 J. SANFORD tr. *Agrippa's Van. Artes* 50 b, She pronounceth..another a Venerean, Mercurialist or Lunist. **1621** BURTON *Anat. Mel.* I. iii. I. iii. (1628) 181 Mercurialists are solitary, much in contemplation, subtile, Poets, Philosophers. **1651** CULPEPPER *Astrol. Judgem. Dis.* (1658) 96 That's the reason Mercurialists (if Mercury be strong) are so swift in motions, so fluent of speech.

†**b.** One having the qualities attributed to persons born under Mercury; an eloquent or ingenious person; a trader; *occas.* in bad sense, a sharper, thief. *Obs.*

1566 DRANT *Horace, Sat.* II. iii. F vj b, My witte so deepe soe sore to deale, such lucke, to win or saue, That me a Mercurialiste to surname then they gaue. **1576** FLEMING *Panopl. Epist.* ¶v, I may rather shew my selfe a Mercurialist, then a Martialist. **1589** WARNER *Alb. Eng.* Pr. Add. 152 Æneas, for personage the Iouilist, for well-spoken the Mercurilist. **1591** GREENE *Farew. Follie* (1617) C 2, Hee that..with a deepe insight marketh the nature of our Mercurialistes shall find as fitte a harbour for Pride vnder a Schollers Cappe as vnder a Souldiers Helmet. **1608** J. KING *Serm.* 5 Nov. 26 Where the great Mercurialists of the world for wit & deuises..haue a finger in the menaging of al Christian states. **1644** BULWER *Chiron.* 134 For such Mercurialists who addresse themselves to filch. **1655** H. L'ESTRANGE *Chas. I* 169 A foul blemish it would have been to the Mercurialists, to the Society of Jesus, should they have sate out in a work so proper to their imployment (the incitation of Kingdomes and States to turbulent commotions) as these Scot'sh broyls.

†**2.** A guide, director. (Cf. MERCURY 2.) *Obs.*

1635 GELLIBRAND *Variation Magn. Needle* 5 By the Prosthaphaereticall application thereof, the true point of the compasse (which is his principall Mercurialist) may be rectified.

3. A medical man who makes free use of preparations of mercury in the treatment of certain diseases.

During the first half of the 19th c. the authorities on the treatment of syphilis were divided into 'mercurialists' and 'non-mercurialists'.

1835 *Mem. Sir J. Y. Simpson* iii. 48 He appears to be a great mercurialist and promoter of the business of the apothecary. **1843** R. J. GRAVES *Syst. Clin. Med.* xxix. 367 The rational practitioner is neither a mercurialist nor a non-mercurialist.

mercuriality (mɜːkjʊərɪˈælɪtɪ). [f. MERCURIAL + -ITY.]

1. The condition of being mercurial; sprightliness; also, an instance of this.

1653 R. SANDERS *Physiogn.* 68 A curious mind, given to travel..his subtilty..all relates to his Mercuriality. **1838** DE QUINCEY *Lamb* Wks. 1858 IX. 154 The mercurialities of Lamb were infinite. **1898** *Spectator* 23 Apr. 580 The mercuriality of the Celtic temperament.

†**2.** The mercurial part (of something). *Obs.*

1471 RIPLEY *Comp. Alch.* in Ashm. (1652) 192 A naturall Mercuryalyte which cost ryght nought, Out of hys myner by Arte yt must be brought. **1657** G. STARKEY *Helmont's Vind.* 316 The Sulphur of any metall or minerall (that may be separated from the Mercuriality..) may be made into the form of an essentiall Salt.

mercurialization (mɜːˌkjʊərɪəlaɪˈzeɪʃən). [f. next + -ATION.]

1. *Med.* The action of subjecting to mercurial treatment; the condition of being affected by mercury.

1843 R. J. GRAVES *Syst. Clin. Med.* vi. 78 By judicious mercurialization of the patient, the destructive progress of the disease is arrested. **1883** *Holmes & Hulke's Syst. Surg.* (ed. 3) II. 557 Other more marked proximate causes have been mercurialisation..and erysipelas. **1897** *Allbutt's Syst. Med.* IV. 812 General mercurialisation is avoided.

2. A mercurial process employed in the development of photographs.

1853 R. HUNT *Man. Photogr.* 93 After the daguerreotype processes in the camera, and of mercurialization, have been completed, a very perfect picture is found.

mercurialize (mɜːˈkjʊərɪəlaɪz), *v.* [f. MERCURIAL + -IZE.]

†**1.** *intr.* To play the part of a 'mercurial' person; also *to mercurialize it.* *Obs.*

1611 COTGR., *Mercurializer*, to mercurialize it; to be humorous, fantasticall, new-fangled. **1656** BLOUNT *Glossogr.*, *Mercurialize*, to be humorous or phantastical, to be light footed; to prattle or babble; Also to be eloquent.

2. *trans.* To render mercurial in temper.

1862 *Temple Bar* VI. 195 A variety of amusements which ..mercurialise the race that delights in them.

3. *Med.* To subject to the action of mercury.

1843 R. J. GRAVES *Syst. Clin. Med.* viii. 96 You may have fully mercurialized your patient. **1880** M. MACKENZIE *Dis.*

Throat & Nose I. 35 Those who have..been mercurialised are very subject to the affection [of pharyngeal catarrh].

4. *Photography*. To treat with mercury; to expose to the vapour of mercury.

1843 [W. H. T.] *Photogr. Manip.* 27 Mercurializing the Plate. **1856** MILLER *Elem. Chem., Inorg.* 1144.

Hence **mer'curialized** *ppl. a.*, **mer'curializing** *vbl. sb.*

1841 *Amer. Jrnl. Sci.* XL. 138 A..mercurializing apparatus. **1845** *Photogr. made easy* 29 The mercurializing process. *Ibid.*, The mercurializing box. **1855** GROVE *Corr. Phys. Forces* (ed. 3) 91 The mercurialised portions of a daguerreotype. **1897** *Allbutt's Syst. Med.* II. 933 Men are said to have become mercurialised by volatilisation of the metal.

mercurially (mɜː'kjʊərɪəlɪ), *adv.* [f. MERCURIAL *a.* + -LY[2].]

1. In a mercurial or lively manner. *rare.*

1652 URQUHART *Jewel* Wks. (1834) 229 He [Crichtoun] would keep in that miscelany discourse of his such a climacterical and mercurially digested method, that [etc.].

2. By a mercurial process.

1881 ABNEY *Photogr.* 36 The metal plate is by contrast dark when compared with the mercurially-developed image. **1893** *Westm. Gaz.* 23 June 4/2 Fitted into holders of solid silver, mercurially gilt.

mer'curialness. *rare.* [-NESS.] Liveliness, sprightliness.

1817 W. IRVING *Life & Lett.* (1864) I. 390 They will serve to..give a dash of spirit and mercurialness to his character.

Mercurian (mɜː'kjʊərɪən), *a.* and *sb.* [f. MERCURY + -AN.]

A. *adj.*

†1. = MERCURIAL *a.* 3; sometimes interpreted as alluding to the qualities of the god Mercury.

1596 NASHE *Saffron-Walden* Wks. (Grosart) III. 142 The Mercurian heauenly charme of hys Rhetorique. **1616** BULLOKAR *Eng. Expos.*, Mercurian, eloquent as Mercury was. **1620** MELTON *Astrolog.* 6 Some Mercurian and nimble-finger'd Pick-pocket. **1677** W. HUBBARD *Narrative* Pref., Where Poetry, in Prose, made I did see By a Mercurian Brain, which sure was Thee.

2. Of or belonging to the god Mercury.

1838 *Brit. Cycl. Biog.* II. 206/2 [Linus] is said to have added the string lichanos to the Mercurian lyre.

3. *Astr.* Of or belonging to the planet Mercury.

1885 AGNES CLERKE *Pop. Hist. Astron.* 121 The Mercurian mass is now estimated at about 1 ÷ 4,360,000 that of the Sun.

B. *sb.*

1. One born under the influence of the planet Mercury.

1640 SOMNER *Antiq. Canterb.* 267 A commendation of Archery; not my owne, nor yet any meere Mercurians. **1677** W. HUBBARD *Narrative* II. 87 If Mars and Minerva go hand in hand, they will effect more good in an hour than those Verbal Mercurians in their lives. **1892** *Pall Mall G.* 4 Oct. 7/1 The long finger of Mercury is very noticeable in his case ..and proves Mr. Grossmith a true Mercurian.

2. An inhabitant of the planet Mercury.

1868 W. WHITE *Swedenborg* xviii. (ed. 2) 290 When the Mercurians met Swedenborg, they instantly explored his memory in search of all he knew.

†**mer'curiate.** *Chem. Obs.* [f. MERCURY + -ATE[1].] A salt of the supposed mercuric acid.

1801 *Encycl. Brit.* (ed. 3) Suppl. I. 388/2 Mercuriat of lime... Mercuriat of ammonia. **1802** T. THOMSON *Chem.* I. 433 This compound may be called mercuriat [*ed.* 3, 1807, mercuriate] of lime.

mercuric (mɜː'kjʊərɪk), *a. Chem.* [f. MERCURY + -IC.] †**a.** ***mercuric acid***: see quot. 1828–32. **b.** The distinctive designation of salts in which mercury exists in its higher degree of valency, as ***mercuric chloride*** = CORROSIVE SUBLIMATE; ***mercuric sulphide*** = VERMILION.

1828–32 WEBSTER, *Mercuric acid*, a saturated combination of mercury and oxygen. **1865** WATTS *Dict. Chem.* III. 900 Normal mercuric salts..are colourless. **1874** GARROD & BAXTER *Mat. Med.* (1880) 103 Mercuric chloride and sulphate of soda are produced.

mercurico- (mɜː'kjʊərɪkəʊ), combining form of MERCURIC in the names of numerous compounds of mercury with various salts, as ***mercurico-barytic, -calcic, cupric, potassic***, etc. (See Mayne *Expos. Lex.* 1856, and *Syd. Soc. Lex.* 1890.)

mercurification (ˌmɜːkjʊrɪfɪ'keɪʃən). [f. MERCURIFY: see -FICATION.]

1. †**a.** *Alch.* The action or process of obtaining the 'mercury' of a metal (*obs.*). **b.** The conversion of the ore of mercury into the pure metal.

1680 BOYLE *Produc. Chem. Princ.* IV. 148 Wary men may be excus'd, if they do not think fit to beleeve other processes of mercurification. **1757** tr. *Henckel's Pyritologia* 100 In the mercurification and regulation of cinnabar. **1797** *Encycl. Brit.* (ed. 3) XI. 401/2 *Mercurification*..the obtaining the mercury from metallic minerals in its fluid state.

2. The act of mixing with mercury or quicksilver (Worcester 1860).

†**mer'curify**, *v. Obs.* [f. MERCURY + -FY.]

1. *trans.* **a.** *Alch.* To change (a portion of a metallic mass) into the form of mercury. **b.** To extract liquid mercury from (metallic ore).

1680 BOYLE *Produc. Chem. Princ.* IV. 188 A part only of the metall is Mercurified. **1797** [see below].

2. To combine, treat or mingle with mercury; to mercurialize (Worcester 1846).

Hence †**mer'curified** *ppl. a.*

1680 BOYLE *Produc. Chem. Princ.* IV. 186 The Mercurifi'd portion. **1797** *Encycl. Brit.* (ed. 3) XI. 401/2 But these mercurified metals..are a kind of philosophical mercury.

mer'curio-'syphilis. *Path. rare.* [f. *mercurio-* taken as combining form of MERCURY.] A diseased condition supposed to be caused in part by syphilis and in part by the mercury employed for its cure. Hence **mer'curio-syphi'litic** *a.*, affected by mercurio-syphilis.

1829 SIR R. CHRISTISON *Treat. Poisons* (1832) 369 An ulcerated sore-throat of the mercurio-syphilitic kind. *a* **1882** —— in *Life* I. vi. 141 Mercurio-syphilis and mercurial cachexy had no place in his nosology.

†**mercurious** (mɜː'kjʊərɪəs), *a. Obs. rare.* [f. MERCURY + -OUS.] Of a mercurial temperament.

1591 SPARRY tr. *Cattan's Geomancie* 233 People Saturnious and Mercurious.

Hence †**mer'curiousness**, the condition of being like Mercury (in celerity).

a **1661** FULLER *Worthies, Kent* (1662) II. 85 He had given him for the Crest of his Arms, a Chappeau with Wings, to denote the Mercuriousnesse of this Messenger.

†**mercurism.** *Obs. rare*[−1]. [f. MERCURY + -ISM.] A Mercurial message.

1672 SIR T. BROWNE *Let. to Friend* ¶2 Tracts (1822) 112 Your affection may cease to wonder that you had not some secret sense or intimation thereof [*sc.* of his death] by dreams, thoughtful whisperings, mercurisms [etc.].

†**'mercurist.** *Obs.* [f. MERCURY + -IST.]

1. = MERCURIALIST 1.

1602 R. T. *Five Godlie Serm.* 139 As being a Martialist, affecting armes, rather then a Mercurist giuen to the Artes. **1656** HEYLIN *Extran. Vapulans* 166 Keep yourself to plain Grammar learning, and leave my Lady Philology to more learned Mercurists.

2. A writer of 'Mercuries' or news-letters.

1693 *Humours Town* 78 Dedicators and Preface-makers.. Jurnalists, Mercurists.

mercurochrome (mɜː'kjʊərəʊkrəʊm). *Pharm.* Chiefly *U.S.* [f. MERCUR(Y *sb.* + -O + Gr. χρῶμ-α colour.]

A mercury derivative, $C_{20}H_8O_6Br_2HgNa_2$, of fluorescein which forms greenish iridescent scales, dissolves in water to give a red solution, and is used as a weak antiseptic. (Orig. given a wider meaning: see quot. 1919.)

1919 H. H. YOUNG et al. in *Jrnl. Amer. Med. Assoc.* 15 Nov. 1484/1 To the substance obtained by substituting one atom of mercury in the molecule of dibromfluorescein we have given the name 'mercurochrome-220'. [*Note*] The name 'mercurochrome' will be applied generally to all the mercury-bearing dyes that we are investigating, the individual being distinguished by the laboratory number following the name. **1942** W. SIMPSON *One of our Pilots is Safe* iii. 63 They left my face uncovered, painted with scarlet mercurochrome. **1951** R. BRADBURY *Illustr. Man* (1952) 178 He smelled the cutting odours of iodine, raw adhesive, and pink mercurochrome. **1960** O. NASH *Boy is Boy* (1961), It's easy to spot a boy... He smells of licorice, he smells of mice, Of Mercurochrome, and vanilla ice. **1960** E. GURR *Encycl. Microsc. Stains* I. 262 Mercurochrome is an excellent substitute for eosin, as unlike the latter it is extremely fast to light and preparations stained with it do not fade even when exposed to strong sunlight for a very considerable time. **1961** J. HELLER *Catch-22* (1962) xiv. 100 Give me a minute or two to put some mercurochrome on these cuts.

mercurous ('mɜːkjʊərəs), *a. Chem.* [f. MERCURY + -OUS.] The distinctive designation of compounds in which mercury occurs in its lower degree of valency, as ***mercurous oxide, sulphide***, etc.

1865 WATTS *Dict. Chem.* III. 903 Mercurous fluoride is partly dissolved by water, partly decomposed into mercurous oxide and hydrofluoric acid. **1866** ROSCOE *Chem.* 220 The black or mercurous oxide. **1897** *Allbutt's Syst. Med.* II. 926 A solution of mercurous and mercuric nitrate.

Mercury ('mɜːkjʊərɪ), *sb.* Forms: 4–5 **marcure**, 4–7 **mercurie**, 5 **mercurye**, 5–7 **mercure**, 6 **marcury**, 7 *dial.* **marcary**, **markry**, 5– **mercury**. [ad. (partly through OF. *Mercure, Marcure*) L. *Mercuri-us*, prob. f. *merc-*, *merx* merchandise.

The Roman deity was prob. originally the god of commerce only; but in Latin literature he appears as completely identified with the Greek Hermes.

The transferred application to the planet is found in classical Latin; like the other planetary names, *Mercurius* became in med. Latin the name of a metal. The astronomical and chemical uses are common to the mod. European langs.; the use as a plant-name is Eng. only, suggested by L. *mercuriālis* (see MERCURIAL B).]

I. The god (and derived senses).

1. A Roman divinity, identified from an early period with the Greek Hermes (son of Jupiter and Maia), the god of eloquence and feats of skill, the protector of traders and thieves, the presider over roads, the conductor of departed souls to the Lower World, and the messenger of the gods; represented in art as a young man with winged sandals and a winged hat, and bearing the caduceus.

1340–70 *Alex. & Dind.* 667 For mercurie miche spak to mentaine iangle, ȝe holden him..god of þe tounge. **1390** GOWER *Conf.* II. 158 An other god..Mercurie hihte..The god of Marchantz and of thieves. **1509** HAWES *Joyf. Med.* 20 Thou Mercury the god of eloquence. **1564** *Brief Exam.* B iiij b, Wyne was consecrated vnto Bacchus,..Letters vnto Mercury. **1595** LYLY *Woman in Moone* IV. i, I will make her false and full of slights, Theeuish, lying, suttle, eloquent; For these alone belong to Mercury. **1601** SHAKS. *Twel. N.* I. v. 105 Now Mercury indue thee with leasing. **1602** —— *Ham.* III. iv. 58. **1781** COWPER *Conversat.* 838 May Mercury once more embellish man.

2. A statue or image of Mercury; *spec.* = HERMA; hence, †a sign-post.

1644 EVELYN *Diary* 8 Nov., A noble fountaine govern'd by a Mercury of brasse. **1667** DRYDEN & DK. NEWCASTLE *Sir M. Mar-all* IV, I stand here, methinks, just like a wooden Mercury, to point her out the way to matrimony. **1693** G. STEPNY in *Dryden's Juvenal* viii. (1697) 194 Those rough Statues on the Road (Which we call Mercuries). *a* **1697** AUBREY *Surrey* (1719) II. 92 Here was formerly a Mercury, or Directory-Post for travellers, with Hands pointing to each Road. **1709** STEELE *Tatler* No. 89 ¶11 You may be sure this addition disfigured the statues much more than time had. I remember..a Mercury with a pair of legs that seemed very much swelled with a dropsy. **1760–72** H. BROOKE *Fool of Qual.* (1809) II. 42 Have you any more blocks, madam, for the hewing out of our mercuries?

3. Applied *transf.* to persons: **a.** A messenger or news-bearer.

1594 SHAKS. *Rich. III*, II. i. 88 But he (poore man) by your first order dyed, And that a winged Mercurie did beare. **1678** BALLER in Rigaud *Corr. Sci. Men* (1841) II. 31 Mr. Gibbons (the mercury of these) waits on horseback at the door. **1678** ABP. SANCROFT *Occas. Serm.* (1694) 131 We give the Winds Wings, and the Angels too; as being the swift Messengers of God, the nimble Mercuries of Heaven. **1864** *Athenæum* 7 May 637 These chicken-hearted Mercuries [post-boys] always pulled up in Hammersmith, and drank their pint before they faced the common.

b. One who passes to and fro with messages between parties, esp. in amorous affairs; a go-between.

1598 SHAKS. *Merry W.* II. ii. 82 But what saies shee to mee? be briefe my good shee-Mercurie. **1638** SIR T. HERBERT *Trav.* (ed. 2) 268 Elgaz-zuli a nimble mercurie undertakes it, and by miraculous conceits agrees them, and fills up the late made breach. **1749** SMOLLETT *Gil Blas* (1797) III. 138, I am on the eve of becoming Mercury to the heir of the Kingdom. **1803** *Censor* 1 Aug. 93 He should sound her maid, who..will prove herself a very Mercury in delivering the letters that may be entrusted to her on either side. **1817** BYRON *Beppo* xvi, A letter, Which flies on wings of light-heel'd Mercuries.

c. A guide or conductor upon the road.

1592 MORYSON *Lett.* in *Itin.* I. 25 The Mercury you gave to guide me, brought me meate plentifully. **1617** *Ibid.* III. 11 God for his onely begotten Sonnes sake (the true Mercury of Travellers) bring us that are here strangers safely into our true Countrey. **1641** J. W[ADSWORTH] (*title*) The European Mercury. Describing the Highwayes and Stages from place to place, through the most remarkable parts of Christendome. **1642** MILTON *Apol. Smect.* Wks. 1851 III. 284 Others, as the Stoicks, to account reason, which they call the Hegemonicon, to be the common Mercury conducting without error those that give themselves obediently to be led accordingly.

†**d.** A nimble person; also, a dexterous thief.

1599 B. JONSON *Ev. Man out of Hum.* I. ii, I would ha' those Mercuries follow me (I trow) should remember they had not their fingers for nothing. **1609** *Ev. Woman in Hum.* I. i. in Bullen *O. Pl.* IV, There again my little Mercuries, froath them up to the brimme, and fill as tis needeful.

†**e.** One who hawks pamphlets or news-books.

1648 *Commons' Jrnls.* V. 436 That thirty thousand of these petitions were to come forth in print this day, and delivered to the Mercuries that cry about books. **1655** FULLER *Hist. Camb.* 24 Circumforanean Pedlers (ancestors to our modern Mercuries and Hawkers) which secretly vend prohibited Pamphlets. **1721** *Lett. fr. Mist's Jrnl.* (1722) II. 256 The Croud of Coffee-Men, Mercuries, Pamphlet-Shop-Keepers, and Hawkers.

4. A title for a newspaper or journal. †Formerly also used *gen.* = newspaper.

[**1626** B. JONSON *Staple of News* I. v, But what sayes *Mercurius Britannicus* to this?] **1643** (*title*) The Scotch Mercury, communicating the affairs of Scotland and the Northern Parts. No. 1, Oct. 5. **1644** NICHOLAS in Carte *Ormond* (1735) III. 279 Whereof your Excellence will find exact relation in the mercuries adjoined. **1664** BUTLER *Hud.* II. i. 56 With letters hung like Eastern Pidgeons, And Mercuries of furthest Regions. **1691** (*title*) The Athenian Mercury. Numb. 2. **1725** *Stamp-Office Notice* 3 Apr. in *Lond. Gaz.* No. 6362/1 No Journal, Mercury or Newspaper. **1791** D'ISRAELI *Curios. Lit., Orig. Newspapers* §14 A Mercury was the prevailing title of these 'News-Books'. **1855** MACAULAY *Hist. Eng.* xxi. IV. 542 No allusion to it [the bill of 1695 for the regulation of the press] is to be found in the Monthly Mercuries. **1906** (*title*) The Leeds Mercury.

II. The planet.

5. *Astr.* The planet nearest to the sun, and the smallest of the major planets.

c **1386** CHAUCER *Wife's Prol.* 703 And thus, god woot! Mercurie is desolat In Pisces, wher Venus is exaltat. **1390** GOWER *Conf.* III. 110 Of the Planetes the secounde Above the Mone hath take his bounde, Mercurie. *c* **1440** *Promp. Parv.* 333/2 Mercurye, sterre, *mercurius*. **1509** HAWES *Past. Pleas.* xvi. (Percy Soc.) 74 Fayre golden Mercury, wyth hys bemes bryght. **1611** SHAKS. *Wint. T.* IV. iii. 25 My Father.. who being (as I am) lytter'd vnder Mercurie, was likewise a

snapper-vp of vnconsidered trifles. **1642** HOWELL *For. Trav.* v. (Arb.) 33 Mercury swayeth ore the one [a Frenchman], and Saturne ore the other [a Spaniard]. **1832** MACGILLIVRAY *Humboldt's Trav.* xxiii. 336 At..Callao, Humboldt had the satisfaction of observing the transit of Mercury. **1880** BALL *Elem. Astron.* 191 The time in which Mercury revolves round the sun is 87 days.

6. *Her.* The name for the tincture purpure in blazoning by the names of the heavenly bodies.

1562 LEIGH *Armorie* 18, I will speake of the Planet appropried therto [*sc.* to the tincture purpure] and that hyght Mercurye. **1572** BOSSEWELL *Armorie* II. 57 The fielde is Mercury, an Equicerve, of the Moone. **1725** J. COATS *Dict. Heraldry* (1739). **1828–40** BERRY *Encycl. Herald.* I.

III. (With lower-case initial.) The metal (and derived senses).

7. A well-known metal (otherwise called QUICKSILVER), of a silver-white colour and brilliant metallic lustre. It is liquid at ordinary temperatures, solidifying at about −40°. It has the peculiar property of absorbing other metals, forming amalgams. It is found native, but is more commonly obtained by sublimation from cinnabar, its most important ore. Chemical symbol Hg (*hydrargyrum*). By the alchemists it was represented by the same sign as the planet Mercury (☿).

c **1386** CHAUCER *Can. Yeom. Prol. & T.* 219, 221 And in amalgaming and calcening Of quik-silver, y-clept Mercurie crude... Our orpiment and sublymed Mercurie. *c* **1485** *Digby Myst.* (1882) III. 318 Gold perteynyng to þe sonne ..þe fegetyff mercury, on-to mercuryus. **1555** EDEN *Decades* (Arb.) 363 They..amalgame it..with Mercurie or quicksyluer. **1604** E. G[RIMSTONE] *D'Acosta's Hist. Indies* IV. x. 235 The fume of Mercurie is mortall. **1612** WOODALL *Surg. Mate* Wks. (1653) 226 Sublimed Mercury is called onely by the name of Mercury, and by the vulgar speech, some call it white Marcary and Markry. **1614** W. BARCLAY *Nepenthes* A 6 b, There is no vegetall in the world, hath such affinitie with any minerall, as hath Tabacco with Mercure, or quicke-siluer. **1758** [see JUPITER 2 b]. **1863** *Fownes' Chem.* (ed. 9) 392 Alloys of mercury with other metals are termed amalgams.

b. A preparation of the metal or of one of its compounds (esp. the protochloride or calomel, and the bichloride or corrosive sublimate), used in medicine.

1789 W. BUCHAN *Dom. Med.* (1790) 659 Bolus of Rhubarb and Mercury. Take of the best rhubarb..half a drachm; of calomel, from four to six grains. **1801** *Med. Jrnl.* V. 73 He took no mercury nor any other medicine. **1903** SLOAN *Carlyle Country* xv. 125 Dr. Bell gave him mercury and solemnly commanded him to abstain from tobacco.

c. The column of mercury in a barometer or thermometer. Also *fig.*

1704 *Phil. Trans.* XXIV. 1629 An Experiment, to show the cause of the descent of the Mercury in the Barometer in a Storm. **1729** CLARKE tr. *Rohault's Nat. Philos.* 72, I filled a Tube three Foot and a half long, with Quicksilver,..I.. observed exactly the Height of the Mercury. **1756** C. LUCAS *Ess. Waters* I. 44 The mercury falls below 33 degrees of Fahrenheit's thermometer. **1883** MRS. BISHOP in *Leis. Hour* 195/1 The mercury has not been above 83°. **1897** *Westm. Gaz.* 4 June 2/1 People would like to stand in front of the mercury of war and see it rise or fall.

d. ***vegetable mercury***: (*a*) a name for the Brazilian plant *Franciscea uniflora* (*Treas. Bot.* 1866); (*b*) see quot. 1887.

1887 *Standard* 16 Sept. 5/2 The tree tomato..on the Spanish Mainland is known as..the 'vegetable mercury', from its supposed beneficial effect on the liver.

8. *Old Chem.* **a.** One of the five elementary 'principles' of which all material substances were supposed to be compounded; also called *spirit*. **b.** ***mercury of metals***: see quot. 1727–52.

1471 RIPLEY *Comp. Alch.* IV. vi. in Ashm. (1652) 145 Mercury and Sulphure vive. **14..** *Pater Sapientiae* ibid. 197 Some say that of Sulphur and Mercury all Bodyes minerall are made. **1592–3** G. HARVEY *New Lett.* Wks. (Grosart) I. 294 Three drops of the Mercury of Brimstone will strengthen the brain. **1605** TIMME *Quersit.* Ded., The spirit of the world..moueth..in all creatures, giving them existence in three, to wit—salt, sulphure, and mercury. **1712** tr. *Pomet's Hist. Drugs* I. 177 The Mercury of the Manna being brought to the fluid Nature of a Spirit, becomes a Solutive for Minerals. **1727–52** CHAMBERS *Cycl.*, *Mercury of metals*, or *of the philosophers*, is a pure fluid substance in form of common running mercury, said to be found in all metals, and capable of being extracted from the same. **1729** CLARKE tr. *Rohault's Nat. Philos.* xx. 109 Hence they conclude, that these five Substances, viz. Mercury, Phlegm, Sulphur, Salt and Caput mortuum,..are the only and the true Elements of all.. Mixed Bodies. **1731** P. SHAW *Three Ess. Artif. Philos.* 36 Attempts for procuring the Mercuries of the several Metals, to profit.

†**9.** *fig.* as an emblem of sprightliness, liveliness, volatility of temperament, inconstancy, wittiness, etc. Often in phr. ***to fix the mercury*** (*of*). *Obs.*

1682 DRYDEN *Medal* 263 Religion thou hast none: thy mercury Has passed through every sect, or theirs through thee. **1693** CONGREVE *Old Bach.* I. iv, As able as yourself and as nimble too, though I mayn't have so much mercury in my limbs. *a* **1700** B. E. *Dict. Cant. Crew*, *Mercury*, Wit. **1704** SWIFT *Tale of a Tub* Pref. ¶4 The moderns have artfully fixed this mercury [*sc.* Wit] and reduced it to circumstances of time, place, and person. **1709** FELTON *Classics* (1718) 9 'Tis difficult to fix the Mercury, and settle a brisk, lively Temper in a laborious plodding Track of Learning. **1710** PALMER *Proverbs* 200 They are all mercury; and a piece of wit, a bottle, or a jest, is a comfort, and supports 'em. *a* **1715** BURNET *Own Time* (1724) I. 265 He [Buckingham] was so full of mercury that he could not fix long in any friendship or to any design. **1732** POPE *Ess. Man* II. 177 'Tis thus the Mercury of Man is fix'd. *a* **1797** WALPOLE *George II* (1847) II. vii. 218 He had too much mercury and too little ill-nature to continue a periodical war.

IV. As a plant-name. [After L. (*herba*) *mercurialis*, MERCURIAL B 1; cf. L. *Hermūpoa* (Pliny) a. Gr. *Ἑρμοῦ πόα.]

10. a. The pot-herb ALLGOOD, *Chenopodium Bonus-Henricus*. Also ***English, false mercury***.

a **1400–50** *Stockh. Med. MS.* p. 203 Mercurie or papwourtz or þe more smerewourt: *mercurialis*. *c* **1450** *ME. Med. Bk.* (Heinrich) 74 Take malues, & mercurye, & seþe hem wyþ a messe of porke. **1548** [see 10 b]. **1578** LYTE *Dodoens* V. xi. 561 In English, Good Henry and Algood: of some it is taken for Mercurie. **1584** COGAN *Haven of Health* xxix. 45 It is a common prouerbe among the people, Be thou sicke or whole, put Mercurie in thy coole. **1597** GERARDE *Herbal* II. xliv. 259 English Mercurie, or good Henrie. **1620** VENNER *Via Recta* vii. 144 Mercurie is much vsed among other pot-hearbes. **1731** *Gentl. Mag.* I. 314 Take Marsh Mallow Leaves the Herb Mercury, Saxifrage and Pellitory of the Wall of each..three handfulls. **1785** MARTYN *Rousseau's Bot.* xvii. (1794) 221 The English Mercury or Allgood. **1865** W. WHITE *East. Eng.* II. 12 One of the dishes contained Mercury, a vegetable which I had never seen before.

b. The euphorbiaceous poisonous plant *Mercurialis perennis*. Also ***dog's, wild mercury***.

1548 TURNER *Names Herbes* (E.D.S.) 53 Mercurialis is called..in englishe Mercury... The herbe whiche is communely called in englishe mercury hath nothyng to do wyth mercurialis. **1578** LYTE *Dodoens* I. lii. 77 In English wilde Mercury, and Dogges Call. **1597** GERARDE *Herbal* II. xlviii. 263 Of wilde Mercurie... Dogs Mercurie. **1607** TOPSELL *Four-f. Beasts* (1658) 390 If you take white Hellebor, and the rindes of wilde Mercury..and lay them in the Mole-hole..it will kill them. **1762** B. STILLINGFL. in *Misc. Tracts* 216 Dogs mercury has been given internally, for want of knowing the natural classes. **1853** JOHNSTON *Bot. E. Bord.* 175 *Mercurialis perennis*. Mercury. **1887** *Pall Mall G.* 27 June 5/2 The dog's mercury raises its fresh yellow suckers for the spring shoots. **1893** E. H. BARKER *Wand. South. Waters* 57, I stood amidst the poisonous dog-mercury.

c. The euphorbiaceous plant *Mercurialis annua*. Also ***baron's, boy's, French, garden, girl's, maiden mercury***.

According to Britten and Holland, the *baron's* or *boy's* is the female and the *girl's* the male mercury.

1578 LYTE *Dodoens* I. lii. 75 The male garden Mercury, or the French Mercury. *Ibid.* 78 Phyllon... The male is called ἀρρενογόνον, whiche may be Englished Barons Mercury or Phyllon, or Boyes Mercury or Phyllon. And the female is called in Greeke θηλυγόνον: and this kinde may be called in English Gyrles Phyllon or Mercury, Daughters Phyllon, or Mayden Mercury. **1601** R. CHESTER *Love's Mart.*, etc. (N. Shaks. Soc.) 82 Sweete Sugar Canes, Sinkefoile, and boies Mercurie.

d. ***Scotch mercury***, the snapdragon, *Digitalis purpurea*. ***three-seeded mercury***, the euphorbiaceous genus *Acalypha*.

1846–50 A. WOOD *Class-bk. Bot.* 488 *Acalypha Virginica*. Three-seeded Mercury. **1853** JOHNSTON *Bot. E. Bord.* 157 *Digitalis purpurea*..Fox-glove... Scotch Mercury. Wild Mercury.—Common.

V. 11. *attrib.* and *Comb.*, as (sense 7) ***mercury cup, pump***; **mercury arc lamp** (also *ellipt.* as *mercury arc*) = *mercury vapour lamp*; **mercury arc rectifier**, a rectifier consisting of one or more graphite or iron anodes and a mercury pool cathode enclosed in an envelope from which the air has been pumped out; **mercury fulminate**, fulminate of mercury; **mercury gilding** (see quot. 1960); **mercury goosefoot** = 10 a, above; **mercury lamp** = *mercury vapour lamp*; **mercury pool**, a mass of liquid mercury, esp. one used as an electrode; †**Mercury rod**, the caduceus; **mercury rust**, a fungus, *Uredo confluens*, on the leaves of Dog's Mercury; †**Mercury's finger**, (*a*) = HERMODACTYL 1; (*b*) a finger-post; †**mercury sublimate**, corrosive sublimate; **mercury vapour lamp**, a lamp in which light (rich in the ultra-violet) is produced by an electric discharge through mercury vapour, the envelope being often coated with a fluorescent substance so as to produce more visible light (cf. *fluorescent lamp*); **mercury vapour pump**, a pump for producing high vacua which works by entraining molecules of the gas to be evacuated in a jet of mercury vapour; **mercury vapour rectifier** = *mercury arc rectifier*; †**Mercury's violets**, Canterbury Bells, *Campanula Medium*; †**mercury-water**, (*a*) a preparation of aqua regia and corrosive sublimate (see *aqua mercurialis* in Chambers Suppl. 1753); also (see quot. 1799); (*b*) a wash for the skin prepared from mercury; †**mercury woman** (see quot. and cf. MERCURY 3 e).

1906 *Trans. Amer. Inst. Electr. Engin.* XXIV. 372 The constant current *mercury arc rectifier system, as used for operating..mercury arc lamps..is sketched diagrammatically. **1916** F. B. PIDDUCK *Treat. Electr.* ix. 363 The absence of strong lines in the red unfits the mercury arc for certain purposes. **1936** TEAGO & GILL *Mercury Arcs* ii. 13 Steel containers are used for demountable mercury arcs of large output. **1971** *New Scientist* 3 June 564/1 The conventional sources of infrared radiation are hot bodies (the globar or mercury arc lamp). **1906** *Mercury arc rectifier [see *mercury arc lamp* above]. **1930** *Engineering* 24 Jan. 109/3 A 650-volt direct-current supply from mercury arc rectifiers. **1966** G. F. ALLEN *Brit. Rail after Beeching* v. 133 In the Eastern Region's multiple-units..the resultant distortions in the electrical circuitry were aggravated by serious failures of the mercury-arc rectifiers. **1849** NOAD *Electricity* 403 Used to connect the *mercury cups of a small battery. **1904** *Kynoch Jrnl.* Oct.-Dec. 199 The flame from the *mercury fulminate..ignites the charge of explosive contained in..the case. **1973** L. RUSSELL *Everyday Life Colonial Canada* xii. 150 The hammer [of a gun] was reduced to a simple head, designed to strike the top of the copper [percussion] cap. Under this top was a pinch of mercury fulminate, a compound so unstable that a moderate impact causes it to explode. [**1910** R. L. HOBSON *Worcester Porc.* xii. 100 A radical change came over the ware about 1780, when the cheaper process of mercurial gilding came into use... This later gilding has a more metallic and brassy appearance.] **1957** MANKOWITZ & HAGGAR *Conc. Encycl. Eng. Pott. & Porc.* 95/2 *Mercury gilding was introduced about 1785. **1960** R. G. HAGGAR *Conc. Encycl. Cont. Pott. & Porc.* 207/1 s.v. *Gilding*, Mercury-gilding came in about 1780, and consisted of a mixture of gold with mercury which could be painted onto the ware, the mercury being driven off as a vapour during the firing process. **1971** *Country Life* 10 June 1419/2 This mercury gilding was harder, longer wearing and more brilliantly lustrous than honey gilding, but tended to display a brassy tinge. **185.** MISS PRATT *Flower. Pl.* IV. 276 *Mercury Goosefoot, or Good King Henry. **1904** *Trans. Amer. Inst. Electr. Engin.* XXII. 73 Hewitt's investigations..are..pioneer work in the field of the *mercury lamps. **1966** HEWITT & VAUSE *Lamps & Lighting* xviii. 276 Mercury lamps are used for street lighting and to a limited extent in industrial installations. **1907** FRANKLIN & ESTY *Elem. Electr. Engin.* II. ix. 172 The mercury-arc rectifier consists essentially of a highly exhausted glass bulb..with two iron or graphite electrodes ..and the *mercury-pool electrode. **1956** *Nature* 11 Feb. 267/2 Industrially, the polarograph is finding an ever-increasing application as a continuous service indicator. For such purposes, the mercury-pool anode is unsatisfactory. **1970** J. SHEPHERD et al. *Higher Electr. Engin.* (ed. 2) xxv. 799 The connexions apply equally to 3- and 6-anode mercury-arc rectifiers in which case all the 'cathodes' are common and are in fact the mercury pool. **1873** ATKINSON *Ganot's Physics* (ed. 6) 147 Morren's *mercury pump..a mercurial air pump. **1625** BACON *Ess., Unity in Relig.* (end), Therefore it is most necessary, that..all Learnings,..as by their *Mercury Rod, doe damne and send to Hell, for euer, those Facts and Opinions. **1864** COOKE in *Pop. Sci. Rev.* III. 336 *Mercury Rust (*Uredo confluens*) on leaf of *Mercurialis perennis*. **1589** RIDER *Bibl. Scholast.* 1748 An hearb called *Mercuries finger, *Hermodactylus*. **1607** TOPSELL *Four-f. Beasts* (1658) 431 The herb called Mercuries-fingers or Dogs bane. **1640** BP. REYNOLDS *Passions* xxiv. (1647) 245 Precedents having the same precedence to Reason in vulgar judgements, which a living and accompanying guide hast to a Mercuries finger in a Travellers conceit. **1707** LUTTRELL *Brief Rel.* (1857) VI. 186 A French party..took some medicaments from them, among which was *mercury sublimate. **1799** G. SMITH *Laboratory* I. 86 Mercury sublimate or corrosive sublimate. **1904** *Brit. Pat.* 3657 2 The light given out is similar to that which is given out by an ordinary *mercury vapour lamp. **1909** *Westm. Gaz.* 6 Mar. 3/2 A 'new' process of sterilising milk by exposing it to the ultra-violet rays of a mercury-vapour lamp. **1943** J. B. PRIESTLEY *Daylight on Saturday* i. 2 The factory inside is.. lit with innumerable mercury-vapour lamps that produce a queer greenish-white mistiness of light. **1955** E. B. FORD *Moths* i. 15 Owing to the high power and surface-brightness of a mercury-vapour lamp, such a source may provide a more efficient means of collecting than an ordinary light. **1972** *New Yorker* 26 Aug. 20/3 In the glare of mercury-vapor street lamps, the Bronx presents a silent, bland, greenish face. **1926** J. H. SMITH tr. *Dunoyer's Vacuum Practice* i. 42 In *mercury vapour pumps the size of the orifice through which the vapour is driven is..of secondary importance. **1966** ADAM & EDWARDS tr. *Diels & Jaeckel's Leybold Vacuum Handbk.* I. vi. 90 Special forms of cold traps with maximum practicable conductivity have been designed for large mercury vapour pumps. **1908** M. SOLOMON *Electr. Lamps* xi. 283 This property of the mercury-vapour arc has led to the invention and development of *mercury-vapour rectifiers. **1966** R. G. KLOEFFLER *Electron Tubes* ix. 194 The mercury-vapor rectifier diode uses a hot cathode and mercury vapor under a low pressure. **1597** GERARDE *Herbal* II. cix. 363 Couentrie bels are called..*Mercuries violets. **1634** SANDERSON *Serm.* II. 291 There is a secret poyson in it, which in time will..seize upon every part; and, like *mercury-water or aqua fortis, eat out all. **1676** SHADWELL *Virtuoso* iii. 55 All manner of Washes, Almond-water, and Mercury-water for the Complexion. **1799** G. SMITH *Laboratory* I. 131 *note*, Mercury-water, so called by the workmen, is thus prepared. Take plate-tin of Cornwall, calcine it, [etc.]. **1661** BLOUNT *Glossogr.* s.v. *Hawkers*, Those people which go up and down the streets crying News-books, and selling them by retail, are also called Hawkers. And those women that sell them by whole-sale from the Press, are called Mercury Women.

†'**mercury**, *v.* *Obs.* [f. prec. sb.] *trans.* To wash with mercury-water.

1599 B. JONSON *Cynthia's Rev.* I. i, Your palmes..are as tender as..a ladies face new mercuried, the'ile touch nothing.

mercy ('mɜːsɪ), *sb.* Forms: 2–5 **merci**, 4–6 **mersy, mercye**, 4–7 **mercie**, 5 **merce**, 6 **mersye**, *Sc.* **marcie**, 3– **mercy**. [a. F. *merci*, earlier *mercit* = Pr. *merce-s*, Sp. *merced*, Pg. *mercê*, It. *mercede*:—L. *mercēdem* (nom. *mercēs*) reward, fee, in Christian Latin from the 6th c. often used in the sense of *misericordia* (= 1 below) and in that of thanks.]

The post-classical uses of *mercēs* are developed from the specific application of the word to the reward in heaven which is earned by kindness to those who have no claim, and from whom no requital can be expected. The Eng. uses explained below represent OF. senses that for the most part have not survived in Fr., where the word has been in great part superseded by *miséricorde*. The chief uses of *merci* in

mod.Fr. are in the sense 'thanks' (cf. GRAMERCY), and in phrases corresponding to those in 5 below.

1. a. Forbearance and compassion shown by one person to another who is in his power and who has no claim to receive kindness; kind and compassionate treatment in a case where severity is merited or expected. Phr. ***to have mercy on, upon,*** † ***of***; also † ***to do mercy to, take mercy on, show mercy***, etc. ***in mercy (to)***, in the exercise of mercy. † ***of*** or ***for mercy***, from consideration of mercy.

a **1225** *Juliana* 49 Milce haue ant merci, wummon, of mi wrecchedom. **1297** R. GLOUC. (Rolls) 1338 Of þe king þat is min vncle he is al at þin wille. Haue merci of him ich þe bidde. **1390** GOWER *Conf.* I. 353 Who that lawe hath upon honde, And spareth forto do justice For merci, doth noght his office. *c* **1400** *Destr. Troy* 8498 If ye no mercy haue on me,..Haue pite on youre pure sonnes. **1470–85** MALORY *Arthur* IV. viii. 128 She byddeth yow..doo batail to the vttermest without ony mercy. **1500–20** DUNBAR *Poems* xxii. 52 Thairfoir of mercy, and nocht of richt, I ask ȝow, schir, ..Sum medecyne gife that ȝe micht. **1523** LD. BERNERS *Froiss.* I. clxvi. 176, I humbly requyre you..yᵗ ye woll take mercy of these sixe burgesses. *a* **1533** —— *Huon* xlix. 165 He wyll slee you without mercy. **1769** *Junius Lett.* v. (1820) 27 In mercy to him, let us drop the subject. **1781** GIBBON *Decl. & F.* xxvii. III. 49 The emperor confessed, that, if the exercise of justice is the most important duty, the indulgence of mercy is the most exquisite pleasure, of a sovereign. **1792** BURKE *Corr.* (1844) IV. 17 Their enemies will fall upon them..and show them no mercy. **1796** H. HUNTER tr. *St.-Pierre's Stud. Nat.* (1799) I. 429 He massacres without mercy every thing that breathes. **1841** LANE *Arab. Nts.* I. 110 Take my body, then, in mercy, to the place where you are laid.

b. *spec.* God's pitiful forbearance towards His creatures and forgiveness of their offences.

c **1175** *Lamb. Hom.* 43 Lauerd haue merci of us forðon þa pinen of helle we ham ne maȝen iðolien. *a* **1225** *St. Marher.* 22 Drihtin, do me merci of þis dede. *a* **1250** *Owl & Night.* 1092 Ihesus his soule do mercy. *c* **1380** WYCLIF *Sel. Wks.* III. 29 Trustynge to Goddis mersy. **1481** CAXTON *Reynard* (Arb.) 74 God receyueth alle them that desyre hys mercy. **1548–9** (Mar.) *Bk. Com. Prayer, Morn. Prayer*, Lorde haue mercie upon us. **1591** SHAKS. *1 Hen. VI*, IV. iii. 34 Then God take mercy on braue Talbots soule. **1607** HIERON *Wks.* I. 121 What can it be but mercie, that we shall bee admitted to an inheritance immortall and vndefiled? **1641** HINDE *J. Bruen* xxxiv. 107 Betwixt the Bridge and the Brook, the Knife and the Throat, the mercy of God may appeare. **1667** MILTON *P.L.* III. 401 Father of Mercie and Grace.

†**c.** ***to have mercy*** (cf. 1): to receive pardon (*of* an offence). *Obs.*

a **1300** *Cursor M.* 9594, I sal noght fine merci to cri Betuixand he haue þi merci. *c* **1340** HAMPOLE *Prose Tr.* 43 Aske mercy and hafe it. **1426** LYDG. *De Guil. Pilgr.* 4098 But thow graunte, off thy pyte, That I may al outterly Off my Gyltes ha mercy. **1513** BRADSHAW *St. Werburge* I. 2752 Who-so wyll haue mercy Must be mercyable..; Who is without mercy of mercy shall mys.

2. a. Disposition to forgive or show compassion; compassionateness, mercifulness. Phr. ***of*** (or †***for***) ***one's mercy***.

a **1225** *Juliana* 48 Nis na merci wið þe, for þi ne ahestu nan habben. *a* **1225** *Ancr. R.* 30 Þet God þurh his milce & for his merci hiȝe ham ut of pine. *a* **1325** *Prose Psalter* l. 1 Ha mercy on me, God, efter þy mychel mercy. **1500–20** DUNBAR *Poems* lxii. 21 The mersy of that sweit meik Rois, Suld soft ȝow, Thirsill, I suppois. **1523** in Ellis *Orig. Lett.* Ser. I. I. 222 God of his mercie sende his grace of suche facion that it maye bee all for the beste. **1531** ELYOT *Gov.* II. vii, In whome mercye lacketh..in hym all other vertues be drowned. **1588** PARKE tr. *Mendoza's Hist. China* 410 God for his infinite mercy conuert them. **1599** SHAKS. *Hen. V*, II. ii. 179 The taste whereof, God of his mercy giue You patience to indure. **1872** MORLEY *Voltaire* (1886) 2 The infinite mercy and loving-kindness of a supreme creator.

b. Personified.

a **1300** *Cursor M.* 9561 Quen merci sagh him suagat be Of him sco can haf pite. **1362** LANGL. *P. Pl.* A. VI. 123 Merci is a Mayden þer..Heo is sib to alle synful men. *c* **1430** LYDG. *Min. Poems* (Percy Soc.) 12 A lady Mercy satt on his righte side. **1621** HAKEWILL *David's Vow* 28 These bee..the severall notes..of Mercie's Song. **1814** BYRON *Lara* II. x, None sued, for Mercy knew her cry was vain.

†**3.** ***to cry (one) mercy***: to beg for pardon or forgiveness. Hence in weakened sense = 'to beg (one's) pardon'; often *colloq.* with ellipsis of 'I'.

The personal object is expressed by simple dative, or (occas.) *to, on, upon*. In ME. also *to ask, bid, beseech, crave, seek mercy*: see numerous examples in Mätzner.

a **1225**, *a* **1240**, *a* **1300** [see CRY *v.* 1 b, c]. *c* **1315** SHOREHAM I. 1181–2 To oure lorde Mercy he cryþ, and biddeþ hym Mercy and misericorde. **1393** (*bis*), **1483**, *a* **1533** [see CRY *v.* 1 b, c]. **1578** WHETSTONE *2nd Pt. Promos & Cass.* III. ii. I iij b, O I ken you nowe syr, chy crie you mercie. **1591** SHAKS. *Two Gent.* v. iv. 94 Oh, cry you mercy, sir, I haue mistooke. **1594** LYLY *Moth. Bomb.* IV. ii. 28, I crie you mercy, I tooke you for a ioynd stoole. **1672** [see CRY *v.* 1 b]. **1681** DRYDEN *Span. Friar* IV. i, I cry thee mercy with all my Heart, for suspecting a Fryar of the least good-nature. **1692** —— *Cleomenes* Epil. 24, I give my judgment, craving all your mercies, To those that leave good plays, for damned dull farces. **1795** [see CRY *v.* 1 c].

4. In elliptical and interjectional uses. *mercy* = 'may God have mercy!'; hence as a mere expression of surprise, fear, or the like. Also ***mercy on us!*** †***for mercy! for mercy's sake! lord-a-mercy!*** (and in corrupt forms of the two last: cf. LORD *sb.* 6 b).

a **1240** *Lofsong* in *Cott. Hom.* 211 Louerd, þi merci. *a* **1300** *Cursor M.* 841 Merci, lauerd! strang wickedhed Broght adam to suilk a ded. **1362** LANGL. *P. Pl.* A. I. 11 Ich was a-ferd of hire Face..And seide 'Merci, Ma dame, What is þis to mene?' **1595** SHAKS. *John* IV. i. 12 'Mercie on me. **1601** —— *All's Well* I. iii. 155 God's mercie, maiden. **1610** —— *Temp.* I. ii. 436 Alacke, for mercy. **1611** —— *Wint. T.* III. iii. 70 Mercy on's, a Barne? *Ibid.* 105 Name of mercy, when was this, boy? **1634** MILTON *Comus* 695 Mercy guard me! **1671** —— *Samson* 1509 Mercy of Heav'n what hideous noise was that! **1800** MRS. HERVEY *Mourtray Fam.* I. 90 A black seal! oh, mercy! it certainly is some bad news about Henry. **1840** MARRYAT *Poor Jack* xxiii, Mercy on us! what was that? **1849** JAMES *Woodman* iii, But, mercy have us, What is here? **1855** W. BROOKE *Eastford* vi. 60 Massy sakes alive John! where have you been all the morning..? What! a lady drownded!..Lord-a-massy! **1858** THACKERAY *Virgin.* I. xxxii. 250 'And whom a mercy's name have we here?' breaks in Mrs. Lambert. **1860** EMILY EDEN *Semi-attached Couple* II. 127 Are you hurt? tell me, Helen, for mercy's sake. **1878** MRS. STOWE *Poganuc P.* iii. 23 Lordy massy, deacon, says I, don't you worry.

5. a. The clemency or forbearance of a conqueror or absolute lord, which it is in his power to extend or withhold as he thinks fit. Chiefly in phrases, as † ***to come to (one's) mercy***, to submit to his authority; also, to come (to God) for forgiveness; also † ***to do*** or ***put oneself in*** or ***to*** (another's) ***mercy***. † ***to take to*** (or ***into***) ***mercy***: to extend pardon to (one who yields at discretion); to give quarter to, receive the submission of. † ***(to yield) to*** or ***upon mercy***, (to surrender) at discretion.

In early use *to take to mercy* implied the commutation of the death sentence for a fine: cf. sense 8.

1303 R. BRUNNE *Handl. Synne* 11788, 11790 Þus seyþ þe clerk, seynt Austyn, Þe prestes mercy Þou do þe ynne; Þe prest ys crystys vycarye; Do þe alle yn hys mercy. *c* **1330** —— *Chron.* (1810) 168 Þe mene folk..Com to his mercy, doand him seruise. *a* **1400–50** *Alexander* 816 Lordis & othire Come to þat conquerour & on knese fallis, And in [*v.r.* on] his mercy & meth mekely þaim put. **1420** in *E. E. Wills* (1882) 47, I bequethe my soule into the mercy off mythfull Ihesu. **1480** CAXTON *Chron. Eng.* lxiv, Otta a lytel while ageynst hym stode but afterward he put hym to his mercy. **1481** —— *Reynard* (Arb.) 74 Thaugh one falle ofte and at laste aryseth vp and cometh to mercy, he is not therof dampned. **1523** LD. BERNERS *Froiss.* I. ccccxvii. 730 The kynge was counsayled to take them to mercy, so that..they shulde gyue to the kyng lx. thousande frankes. **1550** J. COKE *Eng. & Fr. Heralds* §63 (1877) 77 Kyng Edwarde the .III. and his sone prynce Edwarde..favoryng the nacion of Brytayne..toke hym to theyr mercy. **1577–87** HOLINSHED *Chron.* III. 271/1 Vpon their submission, the king tooke them to mercie, vpon their fine, which was seized at twentie thousand marks. **1585** T. WASHINGTON tr. *Nicholay's Voy.* IV. xv. 130 [Pompey] hauing..taken them [the pirates] into mercie, sent them into certaine townes..farre from the Sea. **1593** SHAKS. *3 Hen. VI*, I. iv. 30 Yeeld to our mercy, proud Plantagenet. **1600** HOLLAND *Livy* IX. xxiv. 331 Those they tooke to mercie upon their submission. **1617** MORYSON *Itin.* I. 269 The Pyrates..did cast into the Sea many Marriners yeelding to mercy. *a* **1671** LD. FAIRFAX *Mem.* (1699) 122 Which [*sc.* surrender] after 4 months close siege they were compelled to, and that upon mercy;..delivering upon mercy, is to be understood that some are to suffer, the rest to go free. **1760–72** H. BROOKE *Fool of Qual.* (1809) IV. 98 Since it is so,..I think I must take you to mercy. **1849** MACAULAY *Hist. Eng.* v. I. 643 Mercy was offered to some prisoners on condition that they would bear evidence against Prideaux.

†**b.** ***at mercy***: (that has surrendered) at discretion; absolutely in the power of a victor or superior, at his disposal; liable to punishment or hurt at the hands of another; on sufferance, liable to interference. Also, ***(to hold) in mercy***. Obs.

1605 SHAKS. *Lear* I. iv. 350 That..He may..hold our liues in mercy. **1607** —— *Cor.* I. x. 7 What good Condition can a Treatie finde I' th' part that is at mercy? *a* **1671** LD. FAIRFAX *Mem.* (1699) 121 Lord Capel, Sir George Lucas, and Sir George Lisle, who were prisoners at mercy upon the rendring of Colchester. **1690** LOCKE *Govt.* II. xvi. §183 My Life, 'tis true, as forfeit, is at Mercy, but not my Wife's and Children's. *a* **1715** BURNET *Own Time* (1724) I. 347 A connivance, such as that the Jews lived under, by which they were still at mercy. **1727** SWIFT *State Irel.* Wks. 1755 V. II. 166 The linen of the North, a trade casual, corrupted, and at mercy. **1768–74** TUCKER *Lt. Nat.* (1834) I. 265 The inhabitants of a town exert all their efforts in defending the ramparts,..because when those are taken the town lies at mercy.

c. ***at the mercy of (a person)***: wholly in his power, at his discretion or disposal; liable to any treatment he may choose to employ; liable to danger or harm from him. Similarly †***in the mercy of***; ***(to leave*** or ***trust) to the mercy of***. Also *transf.* and *fig.* (with things as subj. or obj.).

c **1350** *Will. Palerne* 4411 To þis bestes mercy i bowe me at alle, to worche with me is wille as him-self likes. **1481** CAXTON *Reynard* (Arb.) 106 Thy lyf is now in my mercy. **1588** SHAKS. *L.L.L.* v. ii. 856 Floutes, Which you on all estates will execute, That lie within the mercie of your wit. **1593** —— *Lucr.* 364 Shee..Lies at the mercie of his mortall sting. **1593** —— *2 Hen. VI*, I. iii. 137 Thy Crueltie..hath exceeded Law, And left thee to the mercy of the Law. **1665** BOYLE *Occas. Refl.* II. xiii. 141 The Syrians..found themselves at the mercy of their enemies. **1698** FRYER *Acc. E. India & P.* 10 We lay wholly at the mercy of the two unruly Elements, Fire and Water. **1715** DE FOE *Fam. Instruct.* I. iv. (1841) I. 84 Your character is at every body's mercy. **1819** BYRON *Juan* II. xlii, A wreck complete she roll'd, At mercy of the waves. **1888** BRYCE *Amer. Commw.* II. li. 292 Leaving the civil service at the mercy of a partisan chief. **1893** EARL DUNMORE *Pamirs* II. 50 Too precious to trust to the tender mercies of a baggage pony. **1902** *Field* 25 Jan. 134/1 Shortly afterwards Smith had the goal at his mercy, but kicked over.

6. In particularized sense: An act of mercy; esp. one vouchsafed by God to His creatures; an event or circumstance calling for special thankfulness; a gift of God, a blessing. ***one's mercies***, the good things which one has received from God.

a **1300** *E. E. Psalter* lxxxviii. 1 (Egerton MS.) Mercis of lauerd ouer al In euer-mare singe I sal. **1535** COVERDALE *Ps.* xxiv. 6 Call to remembraunce, O Lorde, thy tender mercyes & thy louinge kyndnesses. **1603** SHAKS. *Meas. for M.* v. i. 489 Thou'rt condemn'd, But for those earthly faults, I quit them all, And pray thee take this mercie to prouide For better times to come. **1651** [see CROWNING *ppl. a.* 2]. **1662** GURNALL *Chr. in Arm.* III. 518 Thou must not onely praise God for some extraordinary mercy, which once in a year betides thee,..but also for ordinary, every-day mercies. *a* **1716** SOUTH *Serm.* (1727) VI. vii. 227 Deliverance out of Temptation is undoubtedly one of the greatest Mercies that God vouchsafes his People. **1824** SCOTT *Redgauntlet* Let. i, I know your good father would term this *sinning my mercies*. **1829** —— *Jrnl.* 16 July, May Heaven continue this great mercy, which I have so much reason to be thankful for! **1851** LONGF. *Gold. Leg.* VI, Death never takes one alone.. Perhaps it is a mercy of God, Lest the dead there under the sod..should be lonely! **1852** MRS. STOWE *Uncle Tom's C.* xii, There was even room to doubt whether Tom appreciated his mercies. *Mod.* It is a mercy that you were able to come when you did.

7. ***works of mercy*** (also †***deeds***, †***duties of mercy*** and simply †***mercies***): acts of compassion towards suffering fellow-creatures.

Mediæval theology enumerated seven spiritual and seven corporal works of mercy (*opera misericordiæ*: cf. Luke x. 37 Vulg. *qui fecit misericordiam in illum*). ***Sisters of Mercy***, title of a R.C. sisterhood founded at Dublin in 1827 (*Catholic Dict.*); popularly often applied to the members of any nursing sisterhood. ***House of Mercy***, a name for a penitentiary or house of refuge.

1340 HAMPOLE *Pr. Consc.* 5764 Werkes of mercy and of almus. *c* **1340** —— in *Prose Tr.* Pref. 11 In fulfillynge..of the seven dedis of mercy bodili and gostly to a manys euen cristen. *c* **1380** *Lay Folks Catech.* (Lamb.) 1158 As þe sowle is better þan þe body So þese gostly mercyes be better þan þe bodyly mercyes. **1390** GOWER *Conf.* III. 198 Here goode name may noght deie For Pite, which thei wolde obeie, To do the dedes of mercy. *c* **1412** HOCCLEVE *De Reg. Princ.* 919 God wille þat þe body be releeued; It is on of þe werkes of mercy. **1533** GAU *Richt Vay* (1888) 15 Thay that dois notht the dedis of marcie to thair nichtburs. **1647** *Conf. Faith Assemb. Div. Westm.* xxi. (1650) 46 In the duties of necessity, and mercy. **1647** *Larger Catechism* (1650) 112 Making it our whole delight to spend the whole time (except so much of it as is to be taken up in works of necessity and mercy) in the publick and private exercises of Gods worship. **1824** SCOTT *Redgauntlet* ch. xiii. [Trumbull *loq.*], A work of necessity and mercy. **1868** *Nat. Gazetteer* I. 595 *Clewer*, ..There is..a penitentiary, called the House of Mercy, founded in 1849.

†**8.** = AMERCEMENT. ***to do*** or ***put in the mercy***, to amerce; ***to be in mercy*** (= med.L. *in misericordia*), to be liable to a fine. *Obs.* exc. *arch.* or *Hist.*

(See the note under sense 5.)

[**1292** BRITTON I. v. §9 [Soint] trestouz es autres en la merci pur la fole suffraunce.] **1297** R. GLOUC. (Rolls) 11155 Hii clupede sir Ion giffard, þat siwte ssolde þer to, To come oþer he ssolde in þe merci be ido. **1303** [see MERCY *v.* 1]. *c* **1350** in *Eng. Gilds* (1870) 349 ȝif hii be þennes, by-þowte ryȝtful enchesoun, euerych by hym-selue be in mercy of one besaunt. *Ibid.* 356 He is in þe kynges mercy vpon þe quantyte of þat mysdede. *a* **1500** in Arnolde *Chron.* (1811) 217 Non of yᵉ forsaid mercyes shalbe put but be othe of sad and honest men. ?**15..** *Rules Court York* in Drake *Eboracum* (1736) I. vi. 191 If the defendant put him in the mercie, the sheriffs shall have amerciaments of the defendant. **1768** BLACKSTONE *Comm.* III. App. i. 5 That the same William and his pledges of prosecuting, to wit, John Doe and Richard Roe, be in mercy for his false complaint. **1890** W. P. BAILDON *Sel. Civil Pleas* I. 44 Let them have their seisin thereof, and James is in mercy for the unjust detention. **1895** POLLOCK & MAITLAND *Hist. Eng. Law* II. II. iv. 512 At first the declaration that a man is in the king's or the lord's mercy implies that the king or lord may, if he pleases, take all his goods. **1914** G. F. DEISER *Year Bks. of Richard II: 12 Richard II* 161 The judgment was that the plaintiffs take nothing by their writ, but be in the mercy for their false plaint.

†**9.** Thanks. *Obs. rare.* (Cf. GRAMERCY.)

1362 LANGL. *P. Pl.* A. I. 41 'A Madame, Merci!' quaþ I, 'me likeþ wel þi wordes'. **1377** —— B. XIX. 72 Kynges.. offred mirre & moche golde, with-outen mercy askynge, Or any kynnes catel. *c* **1500** *Melusine* 129 Right grete thankes & thousand mercys to the damoyselle tha so moche honour sheweth to me.

10. *attrib.* and *Comb.*, as ***mercy-angel***, †***-doing***, ***-gate***, †***-shewer***; ***mercy-greatening***, ***-guided***, ***-lacking***, ***-tempered***, ***-wanting***, ***-winged*** adjs.; also passing into *adj.* (orig. *U.S.*): administered or performed out of mercy or pity in order to terminate or relieve pain or distress (cf. *mercy-stroke*), as ***mercy flight***, ***mercy killing*** (so ***mercy killer***; ***mercy-kill*** v. nonce-wd.), ***mission***, ***murder***, etc. †***mercy-stock***, ***-stool***, ***-table*** = MERCY-SEAT (*fig.*); †***mercy-stroke***, a *coup de grâce*.

1849 ROCK *Ch. of Fathers* II. 468 To watch, as it were by the grave, and like a *mercy-angel, cry aloud on all Christians. **1927** *Daily Express* 24 Mar. 3/6 The '*mercy bullet'..contains a chemical which is released on striking the animal. The fluid in the blood will cause temporary unconsciousness. **1969** *Listener* 23 Jan. 111/3, I had representatives in touch with both sides to get the *mercy corridor working, to try and get flights in by day as well as by night. **1382** WYCLIF *Ps.* l. 3 After the multitude of thi grete *mercy doingus [Vulg. *miserationum*]. **1933** *Meccano Mag.* Mar. 195/2 Never a month passes without a '*mercy flight' being carried out. **1944** *Beaver* Dec. 40/2 The aeroplane..is proving of the greatest value as a means of

conveying medical assistance... Such 'mercy flights' are increasing annually. **1973** *Guardian* 14 Feb. 4/4 Two American prisoners of war freed by the Communists were making mercy flights home tonight to be with their families. *a* **1600** in Farr *S. P. Eliz.* (1845) II. 473 Lamenting sore his sinfull life Before thy *mercy-gate. **1675** BROOKS *Gold. Key* Wks. 1867 V. 559 It is a *mercy-greatening mercy. **1833** ROCK *Hierurg.* (1892) I. 322 That God..whose sway Is *mercy-guided. **1957** *Observer* 8 Dec. 14/3 This [melodrama], with its brilliant young scientist strangling his wife and volunteering for deep freeze and being *mercy-killed by his boss. **1935** *Amer. Speech* X. 120/2 On the trail of the..*mercy killer..the public follows day by day. **1951** J. D. SALINGER *Catcher in Rye* xxi. 194 He feels sorry for it [a child]..sticks this blanket over her face..and makes her suffocate... He was a mercy killer. **1935** A. A. BRILL in *Vital Speeches* 16 Dec. 165 (*title*) Is '*mercy killing' justified? **1952** J. CARY *Castle Corner* Pref. 6 Think of Oates' suicide in the Antarctic, or thousands of 'mercy killings', which are technically murder. **1974** *Times* 6 Feb. 6/1 A Long Island doctor who was accused of a 'mercy killing' of a dying cancer patient, was acquitted. **1595** SHAKS. *John* IV. i. 121 Fierce fire and Iron..Creatures of note for *mercy-lacking [*Fo.* mercy, lacking] vses. **1972** *Reader's Digest* Mar. 76/1 (*heading*) Their *mercy missions reach new heights of skill and ingenuity. **1974** *Times* 23 Apr. 4/6 An Army convoy of 20 four-ton lorries left Lyneham..yesterday on the start of a 3,000-mile mercy mission to Niger. **1930** *Commonweal* (N.Y.) 16 July 293 *Mercy murders once more: euthanasia. **1943** S. M. EMERY *Commander of Clouds* 7 He turned the nose of his own kite toward the *mercy ship and thrust on more power. *a* **1565** R. TURNAR in Marbeck *Bk. of Notes* 332 In the power of God & *mercie shewer. **1550** BECON *Gov. Virtue* Wks. 1564 I. 244 And he is a *mercy stocke for our sinnes [1 John ii. 2]. **1550** HUTCHINSON *Image of God* Ep. Ded., Our sauiour & mercie stock saieth ye this knowledge is eternal lyfe. *a* **1536** TINDALE *Pathw. Script.* Wks. (1573) 379 Christ..is called in Scripture Gods *mercy stole. **1549** COVERDALE, etc. *Erasm. Par. Rev.* 17 The euerlasting word of God, which is and euer hath bene ye Mercie-stoole of all the worlde. **1702** C. MATHER *Magn. Chr.* VII. 70 His Hatchet in his hand, ready to bestow a *Mercy-stroak of Death upon her. **1549** COVERDALE, etc. *Erasm. Par. Rom.* 7 Nowe hath God declared Christ to be vnto all people the very propiciatory, *mercie table, and sacrifice. **1822** WORDSW. *Eccles. Sonn.* I. xxvi, With *mercy-tempered frown. **1944** F. CLUNE *Red Heart* 8 On an average, Doctor John Grieve Woods travels over 17,000 miles annually by air on *mercy-trips. **1632** LITHGOW *Trav.* III. 111 Transported here and there, Led with the *mercy-wanting winds. **1819** SHELLEY *Cenci* III. ii. 4 If so, the shaft Of *mercy-wingèd lightning would not fall On stones and trees.

† '**mercy**, *v.* *Obs.* [ad. OF. *merci-er* to thank, amerce, etc., f. *merci* MERCY *sb.*]

1. *trans.* To amerce.

1303 R. BRUNNE *Handl. Synne* 5490 3yf þou haue be so coueytous To mercs [*v.r.* mercye] men ouer outraious, And pore men, specyaly, þat ferde þe wers for þat mercy. *c* **1330** —— *Chron.* (1810) 112 Who þat was gilty þorgh þe foresters sawe, Mercied was fulle hi. **1426** AUDELAY *Poems* 39 Thai mercyn hem with mone and med prevely.

2. To thank. Const. *of* (= for).

1362 LANGL. *P. Pl.* A. III. 21 Mildeliche þenne Meede Merciede hem alle Of heore grete goodnesse. **1483** CAXTON *G. de la Tour* cxlii, Al the people..thanked & mercyed God ..of the delyueraunce of Cathonet. *c* **1500** *Melusine* 71 Therof I mercy & thanke you. *Ibid.* 90 Raymondin.. humbly mercyed the king of his good justice that he had doon to hym.

3. To clothe with mercy. *nonce-use.*

1645 RUTHERFORD *Tryal & Tri. Faith.* (1845) 104 If all that a saint hath be blessed, and every thing (to speak so), mercied and christianed,..his inheritance must be blessed.

Hence †**mercying** *vbl. sb.*, pitying, having mercy; used by Hampole to render L. *miseratio*.

a **1340** HAMPOLE *Psalter* xxiv. 6 Vmthynke ye of þi mercyingis lord. *Ibid.* cii. 4 The whilke corouns þe in mercy and in merciyngis.

mercyabil, -ble, -bull, obs. ff. MERCIABLE.

mercyall, obs. form of MARTIAL.

'**Mercy-seat.** The golden covering placed upon the Ark of the Covenant and regarded as the resting-place of God. Hence applied to the throne of God in Heaven, and to Christ as 'the propitiation for our sins'.

Heb. *kappōreth*, LXX. ἱλαστήριον, Vulg. *propitiatorium*, Wyclif 'propiciatorie'. Tindale's first rendering (1526) was 'the seate off grace' (*Hebr.* ix. 5); in both this and his later rendering he followed Luther's *Gnadenstuhle*. Cf. also *mercy-stock, stool, table*, in MERCY *sb.* 10.

1530 TINDALE *Ex.* xxv. 17, 18 And thou shalt make a merciseate of pure golde..and make .ii. cherubyns off thicke golde on the .ii. endes of the merseate. **1581** MARBECK *Bk. of Notes* 18 Brethren, we haue Iesus Christ the righteous and aduocate with the Father, he is the mercie seate of our sinnes. **1667** MILTON *P.L.* XI. 2 From the Mercie-seat above Prevenient Grace descending. **1710** ADDISON *Tatler* No. 267 ¶6 We find him prostrating himself before the great Mercy-Seat. **1779** COWPER *Hymn*, Jesus! where'er thy people meet, There they behold thy mercy-seat. **1875** MANNING *Mission H. Ghost* i. 9 The infinite merits of the Redeemer of the world are before the Mercy-seat of our Heavenly Father.

transf. **1592** DAVIES *Immort. Soul* I. xix. (1714) 24 The Man whom Princes do advance, Upon their gracious Mercy-seat to sit.

merd (mɜːd), ‖ **merde** (mɛrd). Forms: 5–7, 20 merd, 5, 20 merde, 6–7 mard, 7 mird. [a. F. *merde*:—L. *merda* dung. Now usu. treated as unnaturalized (*merde*).]

a. Dung, excrement; a piece of excrement, a turd. Also as *adj.*

1477 NORTON *Ordin. Alch.* iii. in Ashm. (1652) 39 In Haire, in Eggs, in Merds, and Urine. **1486** *Bk. St. Albans* b viij, For this sekennese take merde of a dove. **1577** KENDALL *Flowers of Epigr.* 82 If after thou of Garlike strong, the sauour wilt expell: A Mard is sure the onely meane, to put away the smell. **1610** B. JONSON *Alch.* II. iii, Haire o' the head, burnt clouts, chalke, merds, and clay. **1621** BURTON *Anat. Mel.* II. iii. II. 391 To dispute of gentry without wealth, is..to discusse the originall of a Mard. **1669** COKAINE *Ovid* 63 Oyntments Made of the spawn of Snakes, Spittle of Jews, And Mird of Infants. [*a* **1733** NORTH *Exam.* III. viii. (1740) 644 He..deals forth his Merda by the Hirelings of the Times.] **1920** T. S. ELIOT *Ara Vos Prec* 11 The goat coughs at night in the field overhead; Rocks, moss, stonecrop, iron, merds. *a* **1930** D. H. LAWRENCE *Phoenix* (1936) 13 Don't you see, in his [*sc.* a rabbit's] very immobility, how the whole world is *merde* to him? **1960** 'A. BURGESS' *Doctor is Sick* xv. 111 Lurching from one delightful street-smell to another—merds, garlic, mutton-fat, urine, food-tins. **1962** *Listener* 26 July 141/1 It's still evasion to ignore the new tragedy of what might be called the *merde* world. **1968** J. UPDIKE *Couples* ii. 167 'Janet, you disgust me,' Harold said. 'How can you unload this *merde* on three people who adore you?' **1970** *New Yorker* 7 Mar. 36 We cannot have that kind of pornographic *merde* in this majestic and high-minded sentence.

b. As *int. coarse slang.*

1920 E. E. CUMMINGS *Let.* 14 Oct. (1969) 74, I am *not* self-sufficient do I hear you say? Merde! **1924** D. H. LAWRENCE *Let.* 9 Aug. (1932) 606 A great *merde!* to all latter-day Joan-of-Arcism. **1933** 'G. ORWELL' *Down & Out* iii. 25 '*Merde!*' he used to shout, '*you* here again?' **1961** I. JEFFERIES *It wasn't Me!* x. 132 'Oh, well, Merde!' He stuck out his hand and I shook it. 'Merde to you.' **1974** N. FREELING *Dressing of Diamond* 78 He never lost his temper or said merde.

†**merdaille.** *Obs. Sc.* Also 4 **merdale**. [Fr., f. *merde* (see prec.) with collective suffix, lit. 'heap of dung'.] A dirty crew, rabble, 'scum'.

c **1375** BARBOUR *Bruce* IX. 249 Behynd thame set thai thar merdale. *c* **1375** *Sc. Leg. Saints* xl. (*Ninian*) 921 Quheine eschapit, but merdale, þat for to tak ves nan awaile. **1687** CLEVELAND *Rust. Rampant* 467 This Merdaille, these Stinkards, throng before the Gates.

‖**merdeka** (mɜːˈdeɪkə). [Malay.] Freedom, independence; *spec.* independence for Indonesia or Malaya.

1954 N. EPTON *Islands of Sunbird* iii. 58 South-west of the capital to the distant cocoanut palms and freedom, 'Merdeka', at last! Merdeka... An Indonesian official once told me that Merdeka is still a rousing rallying cry for many Indonesians. **1955** *Times* 16 Aug. 6/7 A banner bearing the word merdeka ('liberty'). **1961** P. KEMP *Alms for Oblivion* ii. 85 The nationalists did not spare their prisoners, whom they usually put to death by hewing in pieces to the greater glory of *Merdeka*. **1969** *Guardian* 2 Sept. 10/3 Tunku Abdul Rahman's Alliance Party..the old guard who had 'won' Merdeka. **1972** 'G. BLACK' *Bitter Tea* iii. 36 *Merdeka*..is how the Malays label their national sovereignty. The word means freedom.

† **merˈdiferous**, *a.* *Obs.*—⁰ [f. L. *merde-a* MERD + -(I)FEROUS.] (See quot.)

1656 BLOUNT *Glossogr.*, *Merdiferous* (*merdifer*), that farmeth dung, a Gold finder.

merdivorous (məˈdɪvərəs), *a.* *rare*—⁰. [f. mod.L. *merdivor-us* (f. *merda* MERD + *-vorus* eating) + -OUS.] Feeding on dung (said of insects).

1856 in MAYNE *Expos. Lex.*; and in mod. Dicts.

† '**merdous**, *a.* *Obs.*—⁰ [f. MERD + -OUS.] 'Full of dung or ordure' (Bailey 1721). Also † **merdose** in same sense, whence † **merdosity** (both in Bailey vol. II, 1727).

† **merˈdurinous**, *a.* *Obs. rare.* [f. L. *merda* MERD + *ūrīna* URINE *sb.* + -OUS.] Composed of dung and urine. Also *fig.*

a **1616** B. JONSON *Epigr.*, *On famous Voy.* 65 Who shall discharge first his merd-vrinous load. **1630** J. TAYLOR (Water-P.) *Wks.* II. 99/2 If shee thriue and grow fat, it is with the merdurinous draffe of our imperfections.

mere (mɪə(r)), *sb.*¹ Forms: 1 meri, 2–3 mære, 4 marre, 5 mer, 5–7 meere, 6–8 meare, 7 mayre, 7–9 meer, 9 *dial.* mare, mar, marr, 1– mere. [OE. *mere* str. masc., corresp. to OS. *meri* fem., sea (MDu., MLG. *mere* fem., neut., Du. *meer* neut., sea, pool), OHG. *meri*, *marī* (MHG., mod.G. *meer*) neut., sea, ON. *mar-r* masc., sea (MSw. *mär*, MDa. *mær* are from MLG.), Goth. *mari-* (nom. **mar*) in *mari-saiws* sea (also the derivative *marei*:—OTeut. type **marîn-* wk. fem.):—OTeut. **mari-*:— WAryan **mori-* or **mǝri-*, represented in OSl. and Russ. *more*, OIrish *muir*, Welsh *mor*, L. *mare* neut. (It. *mare*, Pr., Sp., Pg. *mar*, F. *mer* fem.).

The word is often referred to the Indogermanic root **mer-* (: *mor-*, *mr-*) to die, and supposed to have originally designated the sea as 'lifeless' in contrast with the land as abounding in vegetable life; but this is very doubtful; Brugmann suggests that the *r* may belong to the suffix.

The form *mar(r* (14th c. *marre*), occurring in senses 2 and 4, is abnormal. Cf. ON. *marr* (which, however, is known only in the sense 'sea'), and F. *mare* pond (from 12th c.).]

† **1.** The sea. *Obs.*

Mere Mediterane in quot. *c* 1425 is prob. from French.

a **1000** *Andreas* 283, & þu wilnast nu ofer widne mere? *c* **1205** LAY. 21773 þer walleð of þan mæren a moniare siden. [*c* **1425** WYNTOUN *Cron.* IX. xii. 1332 The Lord wes of the Oryent, Of all Jude, and to Jordane And swa to the Mere Mediterane.] **1447** BOKENHAM *Seyntys* (Roxb.) 74 O lord.. Wych..pharoo..drynklyddyst in the salt mere.

2. A sheet of standing water; a lake, pond. Now chiefly *poet.* and *dial.*

Freq. used of Grendel's abode in the Old English poem *Beowulf*.

Beowulf 1362 Nis þæt feor heonon milʒemearces, þæt se mere standeð. *a* **700** *Epinal Gloss.* 962 *Stagnum*, staeg *vel* meri. *c* **1000** *Ags. Gosp.* John ix. 7 Ga & þweah þe on syloes mere. *c* **1205** LAY. 21739 þat is a seolcuð mere iset a middelærde mid fenne & mid ræode. **13..** *E.E. Allit. P.* A. 158, I seȝ by-ȝonde þat myry mere, A crystal clyffe ful relusaunt. *a* **1400–50** *Alexander* 4093 Sone was he dreuyn with his dukis in-to a dryi meere. **1548** UDALL, etc. *Erasm. Par. Matt.* xvi. 85 b, He came vnto a meere which is called the sea of Galile. **1581** MULCASTER *Positions* xxiii. (1887) 95 Swimming in lakes and standing meres. **1651–7** T. BARKER *Art of Angling* (1820) 23 Either in mayre, or pond. **1774** GOLDSM. *Nat. Hist.* (1776) VI. 40 The meres of Shropshire and Cheshire. **1823** SCOTT *Peveril* i, As a tempest influences the sluggish waters of the deadest meer. **1842** TENNYSON *Sir Gal.* iv, Sometimes on lonely mountain-meres I find a magic bark. **1849** A. D. WACKERBARTH tr. *Beowulf* 53 It is not far, —a Mile from here, Where stands the Monster's sluggish Meer. **1855** B. THORPE tr. *Beowulf* 107/2 Departed home thence the gold-friend of men,..and on the mere they gaz'd. **1888** ANNIE S. SWAN *Doris Cheyne* iii. 53 She loved to.. watch the lovely shadows in the silent depths of the placid mere. **1896** BLASHILL *Sutton-in-Holderness* 4 Dotted over with sedgy marrs, of which Hornsea Marr, a veritable lake, is practically the last survivor. **1898** G. SAINTSBURY *Short Hist. Eng. Lit.* I. i. 5 Beowulf..soon hears from the King that his adventure is not done, and determines to finish it in the mere itself. **1912** *PMLA* XXVII. 208 (*title*) The haunted mere in *Beowulf*. **1951** *Speculum* XXVI. 33 Grendel's mere has other attributes... The hart pursued by hounds chooses rather to give up its life than to hide its head in the grove surrounding the pool. **1957** *Rev. Eng. Stud.* VIII. 6 All this radiance is eclipsed when under cover of darkness Grendel's mother carries off Æschere to her retreat below the mere.

† **3.** An arm of the sea. *Obs.*

1573–80 BARET *Alv.* M 271 A Mere, or water whereunto an arme of the sea floweth. **1622** CALLIS *Stat. Sewers* (1824) 70, I take it that a Bay and a Creek be all one, and that a Mere and a Fleet be also of that nature. *a* **1676** HALE *De Jure Maris* I. v. in *Hargrave's Tracts* (1787) I. 21 The abbot..had ..the fishing, yea and the soil of an arm or creek of the sea called a meere or fleete.

4. A marsh, a fen. Now *dial.*

13.. *Childh. Jesus* 598 in *Archiv Stud. neu. Spr.* LXXIV. 335, I salle the gyffe bothe..Marre and mosse, bothe feldes and fene. **1609** HOLLAND *Amm. Marcell.* XXII. viii. 201 The seventh [mouth of the Danube] is a mightie great one, and in manner of a meere, blacke. **1629** MAXWELL tr. *Herodian* (1635) 360 Being come to a mighty great Meare or Marish, whither the Germanes had fled. **1670** EVELYN *Diary* 22 July We rod out to see the greate meere or levell of recover'd fen lande. **1706** PHILLIPS, *Meer* or *Mear*,..a low marshy Ground. **1876** *Mid-Yorksh. Gloss.*, *Mere*, heard, at times, applied to ground permanently under water.

5. *attrib.*, as † *mere-rush*.

1555 W. WATREMAN *Fardle Facions* I. v. 72 They feede them [children] with the rootes of mererusshes.

mere, mear (mɪə(r)), *sb.*² *arch.* and *dial.* Forms: 1 ʒemǽre, mǽre, 2 mære, 3 mær, mare, 3–4 mer, 4–9 meer(e, 5 merre, 5–6 meyre, 6–9 meare, 3– mere, 5– mear. [OE. *ʒemǽre*, *mǽre* str. neut. = MDu. (Flemish) *mere*, *meer*, ON. (*landa*)-*mǽri* (Sw. *landamäre*):—OTeut. *(*ga*)-*mairjo*^m, cogn. w. L. *mūrus* (:—**moiros*) wall.]

1. a. A boundary; also, an object indicating a boundary, a landmark.

c **825** *Vesp. Psalter* ii. 8, & mæhte ðine ʒemæru eorðan [*et possessionem tuam terminos terrae*]. *c* **950** *Lindisf. Gosp.* Mark vi. 56 In londum uel in mærum [*c* **975** ʒimæru, Vulg. *in uicos uel in uillas*]. *c* **1000** *Ags. Gosp.* Mark v. 17 Hi bædon þæt he of hyra ʒemærum [*c* **1160** *Hatton* of hire mæren] fore. *c* **1205** LAY. 2133 Locrines mær [*c* **1275** mer] eode suð & east forð. **1387** TREVISA *Higden* (Rolls) I. 137 þilke men destingeþ nouȝt noþer to sette her feeldes by boundes, noþer by meres. *a* **1400–50** *Alexander* 211 With-in þe merris of Messedoyn þar na man him knewe. **1488** *Cal. Anc. Rec. Dublin* (1889) I. 493 They ridde over a meare westward till thei came to Our Lady well, and so straight over the said mer. **1546** LANGLEY *Pol. Verg. De Invent.* I. xv. 28 The meeres and butrelles with whiche they desseuered theyr porcions of lande. **1600** HOLLAND *Livy* 1403 The god of Meeres and Bounds *Terminus*. **1672** PETTY *Pol. Anat.* (1691) 310 Planting 3 millions of timber-trees upon the bounds and mears of every denomination of land. **1787** in *N. W. Linc. Gloss.* s.v., Where a person knows his own land by meres or boundaries. **1849** JAMES *Woodman* xviii, Such things as have been done this night shall not happen within our meres and go unpunished.

fig. **1590** SPENSER *F.Q.* III. ix. 46 So huge a mind could not in lesser rest, Ne in small meares containe his glory great.

b. *spec.* A green 'balk', or a road, serving as a boundary.

1607 MARKHAM *Caval.* IV. (1617) 13 Either some faire Hie-way, or else some plaine green Meare. **1893** J. T. FOWLER *Let. to Editor*, To road dividing Winterton and Winteringham is commonly called 'The Mere' or 'Winteringham Mere'. **1956** G. E. EVANS *Ask Fellows who cut Hay* xxv. 227 Robert Savage recently used it [*sc.* the word *mere*] to indicate the division between the *yards* on the Common. 'They called them *meres*: they were usually made wide enough so that each man could have a load o' muck taken to his yard.' **1972** *Parl. Debates Commons: Rep. Standing Comm. D: Local Govt. Bill, 18th Sitting* 27 Jan. 1043 A 'mere' is, in fact, a boundary.

2. *Derbysh. Lead-mining.* A measure of land containing lead ore.

1653 MANLOVE *Lead Mines* 123 Such as orders, to observe refuse; Or work their meers beyond their length and Stake. **1670** PETTUS *Fodinæ Reg.* 92 If any Miners..find any new Rake or Vein, the first Finder shall have two Meers. **1829**

Glover's Hist. Derby I. 67 Marking out in a pipe, or rake-work, two meeres of ground, each containing twenty-nine yards. **1851** *Act 14 & 15 Vict.* c. 94 Sched. i. §18 Every Meer of Ground shall contain Thirty-two Yards in Length.

3. *attrib.*, as in ***mere-balk***, †***-bound***, ***-furrow***, †***-mark***, †***-staff***, ***-stake***, †***-thorn***, ***-tree***. Cf. MERESMAN, MERESTONE.

1630 in *N.W. Linc. Gloss.* s.v., Of Richard Welborne for plowing vp the kings *meere balk. **1667** *Providence (R. I.) Rec.* (1892) I. 37 Bounded with a Meere bauke betweene the land of Henry Browne & his running to Mosshossick river. **1840** SPURDENS *Suppl. Forby's Voc. E. Anglia*, *Mear-balk, Meare-balk*, a ridge left unploughed in a field, as a division of lands. **1600** DYMMOK *Ireland* (1843) 22 North Clanneboy is devided into two partes; the ryver of Kellis being the *meare bounde. **1896** BLASHILL *Sutton-in-Holderness* 17 These strips were called at a later time '*mere-furrows', or 'balks'. **1611** SPEED *Hist. Gt. Brit.* IX. ii. §32 Some ruines of which *Meere-marke are yet appearing. **1631** WEEVER *Anc. Funeral Mon.* 866 The meere-markes, limits, or bondaries. **1552** HULOET, Bowne, buttell, or *merestafe, or stone. **1629** *Brasenose Coll. Muniments* 27. 104 Removed the *meere-stakes and boundaries. *a* **1000** in Kemble *Cod. Dipl.* III. 168 Of ðæm pytte on ðone dic, ðæt on *mærðorne. **1241** in *Newminster Cartul.* (1878) 202 Usque ad Merethorne. **1585** HIGINS *Junius' Nomenclator* 139 A *meere tree: a tree which is for some bound or limit of land.

†**mere**, *sb.*³ *Obs. rare*⁻¹. [Shortened from *mereman* MERMAN.] A merman or mermaid.

c **1220** *Bestiary* 584 He hauen herd told of ðis mere .. half man and half fis.

†**mere**, *sb.*⁴ *Obs.* [a. OF. *mere*:—L. *mātrem* MOTHER.] A mother.

a **1250** *Five Joys Virg.* in *Rel. Ant.* I. 48 Seinte Marie, maydan ant mere. ?*c* **1400** *Minot's Poems* (1897) App. ii. 104/80 Þan sal þe land duel in were, Als a stepchild withouten þe mere. *c* **1460–70** *Pol. Rel. & L. Poems* 232/763 To-fore þi fadir, [&] mere maree, þou schewist þi woundis rent on roode.

†**mere**, *sb.*⁵ *Obs.* [subst. use of MERE *a.*²] (See quot. 1607.)

1544 tr. *Nat. Brevium* 2 Ioynynge the myses vpon the mere. [Cf. MERE *a.*² 3, quot. 1628.] **1607** COWEL *Interpr.*, *Meere*, though an adiectiue, yet is vsed for a substantive, signifiing meere right, *Owld nat. br.* fol. 2.

mere ('mɛrɪ), *sb.*⁶ Also marree, meri. [Maori.] A Maori war-club, from 12 to 18 inches long, made of hard wood, whalebone, or greenstone. Also, a miniature greenstone version.

1829 J. F. ATKINS in R. McNab *Hist. Rec. N.Z.* (1908) I. 692 The chief .. shot him through the head, and with his *maree* (a short stone club, with a sharp edge) he split his skull. **1830** J. D. LANG *Poems* (1873) 116 Beneath his shaggy flaxen mat The dreadful marree hangs concealed. **1833** in R. McNab *Old Whaling Days* (1913) 48 An instrument made of a beautiful blue or green marble stone, which they call a Mary. **1851** MRS. WILSON *New Zealand*, etc. 48 The old man has broken my head with his meri. **1859** [see GREENSTONE 2 *attrib.*]. **1874** A. BATHGATE *Colonial Experiences* xviii. 258 The Maories used them [*sc.* stone implements] to kill the Moriories rather than .. degrade their own meres. **1883** RENWICK *Betrayed* 36 Full half-revealed a greenstone mere swung Upon his hip. **1905** W. B. *Where White Man Treads* 134 He yearned to take the taiha and mere from his hand, and substitute the axe and spade. **1921** *Outward Bound* June 46/2 The valuable greenstone from which the Maoris fashion all their meres, their tikis, canoe-chisels, brooches and other articles. **1938** R. FINLAYSON *Brown Man's Burden* 10 In the clear space by the flagpole old Tamarua is delivering a speech of welcome, mere in hand. **1942** N. MARSH *Death & Dancing Footman* ix. 158 It hung on the wall there... It came from New Zealand. .. It's called a mere. **1956** M. DUGGAN *Immanuel's Land* 15 The chipped greenstone *mere*. **1957** *N.Z. Listener* 22 Nov. 4/2 We know what a 'mere' .. or a 'hangi' is, but they remain essentially Maori in idea. **1975** D. BAGLEY *Snow Tiger* iv. 53 The greenstone *mere*—the Maori war axe.

†**mere**, *a.*¹ *Obs.* Also 1 mǽre, mére, 2–3 mære, 2–4 mere, 3 (*Lay.*) mare, meare. [OE. *mǽre* = OS. *mâri*, OHG. *mâri*, *mâre* (MHG. *mære*), ON. *mǽrr* (:—older *mâri-r*, in Runic inscriptions), Goth. *-mêrs* (in *wailamêrs* εὔφημος):—OTeut. **mǽrjo-*.] Renowned, famous, illustrious; beautiful, noble. (Said of persons and things.)

Beowulf 103 Wæs se grimma gæst Grendel haten, mære mearcstapa, se þe moras heold. *a* **700** *Epinal Gloss.* 737 *Percrebuit*, mere ueeard. *c* **1000** ÆLFRIC *Saints Lives* II. 334 Crist ȝeswutelaþ mannum þurh his mæran halȝan þæt he is ælmihtiȝ god. *a* **1175** *Cott. Hom.* 221 Forði ðe god hi ȝeworhte to meren anglen. *c* **1200** ORMIN 806 Þatt child .. Shall ben biforenn Drihhtin Godd Full mahhtiȝ mann & mære. *c* **1205** LAY. 27877 He .. lette makien beren riche and swiðe maren [*c* **1275** meare]. *c* **1330** R. BRUNNE *Chron. Wace* (Rolls 7045) Constant was eldest & mere. **13..** *Gaw. & Gr. Knt.* 878 Þenne a mere mantyle was on þat mon cast.

mere (mɪə(r)), *a.*² and *adv.* Forms: 6 meare, mer, *Sc.* meir, 6–8 meer(e, (7 mear, myere). [ad. L. *merus* undiluted, unmixed, pure. Cf. OF. *mer*, *mier* (AF. *meer*, which is the source of the Eng. word in legal uses), It., Sp., Pg. *mero*.

In the OE. *mǽre peneȝas* (see B.-T.), app. = med.L. *meri denarii* (see Du Cange, the adj. may be viewed as an adaptation of L. *merus*, or better as a use of MERE *a.*¹ suggested by the similarity in sound to the Latin word.]

A. *adj.*

†**1. a.** Of wine: Not mixed with water. *Obs.*

1545 RAYNOLD *Byrth Mankynde* 133 Let not the nourse vse any watered wyne, or myxed but mere and in his owne kynde. **1601** HOLLAND *Pliny* II. 275 Three cyaths of meere wine ful of the grape. **1660** JER. TAYLOR *Worthy Commun.* I. i. 35 Our wine is here mingled with water and with myrrhe, there it is mere and unmixt.

†**b.** Of a people or their language: Pure, unmixed. Chiefly in *mere Irish* (see IRISH *sb.* 1 a), now often misunderstood as a term of disparagement, the adj. being apprehended as in sense 5.

1561 T. HOBY tr. *Castiglione's Courtyer* I. (1577) E vj, Though it were not the meere ancient Tuscane tong, yet should it be the Italian tongue. **1568** GRAFTON *Chron.* II. 286. I will repeople the towne againe wyth mere Englishe men. **1577–87** STANYHURST *Descr. Irel.* viii. 44/2 in *Holinshed*, The disposition and maners of the meere Irish, commonlie called the wild Irish. **1605** VERSTEGAN *Dec. Intell.* (1628) Pref. Ep. [They] doe rather seeme to vnderstand them for a kind of forraine people, then as their owne true and meere Ancestors. **1623** LISLE *Ælfric on O. & N. Test.* To Rdr. 17 The meere Saxon monuments of .. Sir H. Spelman. **1648** GAGE *West Ind.* 55 There may not be above two thousand Inhabitants of meer Indians. **1711** J. GREENWOOD *Eng. Gram.* 10 Cardinal Wolsey, in his Embassy into France, commanded all his servants to use no French, but meer English. **1732–33** WOGAN in *Swift's Wks.* (1824) XVII. 456 Scarce any people are taken for mere Irish, either in England, or on the continent, but the vulgar of the country, and the few unfortunate exiles. **1836** H. G. WARD *Sp. Ho. Comm.* 28 Mar., No man who is 'a mere Irishman' can exist without feeling deep gratitude to the Honourable and Learned Member for Dublin.

†**c.** Of other things material and immaterial: Pure, unmixed. *Obs.*

c **1400** MAUNDEV. (Roxb.) xxv. 116 Bringand cowpez of gold full of meere mylk. **1535** HEN. VIII in Strype *Eccl. Mem.* (1721) I. App. liv. 140 The true, mere, and sincere word of God. **1613** PURCHAS *Pilgrimage* (1614) 84 Earthly happinesse .. is neuer meere and vnmixed, but hath some sowre sauce to rellish it. **1665** NEEDHAM *Med. Medicinæ* 388 The vitious humor .. not sincere or mere [*at non sincerum*], but mingled with the .. profitable humor. **1703** *Art & Myst. Vintners* 43 Take about 8 or 10 ounces of meere Chalk.

†**d.** quasi-*adv.* in comb. ***mere-pure*** adj. *Obs.*

1650 W. BROUGH *Sacr. Princ.* (1659) 17 Mere-pure-papists holding and doing all things in opposition to us. *Ibid.* 207 A meer-pure-sin, without motive.

2. Done, performed, or exercised by a person or persons specified without the help of any one else; sole. Chiefly *Law*, in phrases ***mere motion***, etc.

1444 *Rolls of Parlt.* V. 87/1 Of his especial grace, mere motion, and singuler devotion. **1449** *Ibid.* 161/1 This devout Collage is of his mere foundation. **1527** *Rec. St. Mary at Hill* 342 But leue theym to the mer disposicion of the said parson & parisheners. **1558** in *10th Rep. Hist. MSS. Comm.* App. v. 388 Of our own meare gifte and volantary willis. **1650** EARL MONM. tr. *Senault's Man bec. Guilty* 55 His nature being the meer work of God had no defaults. *a* **1718** PENN *Tracts* Wks. 1726 I. 681 It is said to be out of his meer and free Will, as if it were his meer Favour. **1881** JOWETT *Thucyd.* I. 211 We were wrong if of our mere motion we .. fought with you, and ravaged your land.

3. *Law.* ***mere right*** [AF. *meer dreit*, law-Latin *jus merum*]: right as distinguished from possession.

[**1292** BRITTON IV. v. §4 Qe cesti pleintif, qi est dreit heir celi qi drein presenta, ad meer dreit par le title de successioun.] **1559–60** *Act 2 Eliz.* in Bolton *Stat. Irel.* (1621) 284 That your Majestie .. is, and in verie deed, and of most meere right ought to bee .. our most rightful .. soveraigne. **1628** COKE *On Litt.* III. viii. 279 If .. hee ioyne the mise vpon the meere right. **1766** BLACKSTONE *Comm.* II. 197 This is frequently spoken of in our books under the name of the mere right, *jus merum*; and the estate of the owner is in such cases said to be totally devested, and put to a right.

†**4.** That is what it is in the full sense of the term; nothing short of (what is expressed by the sb.); absolute, entire, sheer, perfect, downright. *Obs.*

Collocations such as 'mere lying', 'mere folly', are still possible, but the adj. no longer means 'nothing less than', but 'nothing more than' (sense 5).

1536 HEN. VIII in Ellis *Orig. Lett.* Ser. II. II. 86 We .. wyll se yf .. he wyll of hys awne mynde confesse the mere trawthe. **1551** ROBINSON tr. *More's Utopia* II. (1895) 244 Whyche thynge they doo of meere pytye and compassion. **1577** *F. de L'isle's Legendarie* B viij, A kinde of importunatenes not farre different from meere violence. **1594** HOOKER *Eccl. Pol.* I. ii. §2 Our God is One, or rather very Oneness, and meer Unity. **1600** HOLLAND *Livy* XXII. xliii. 459 Complaining first of the dearth of victuals, and in the end, of meere hunger and famine. **1600** in *10th Rep. Hist. MSS. Comm.* App. v. 458 Thobstinacie, willfull disobedience, myere lienge and disceite of the countrie gentlemen. **1604** SHAKS. *Oth.* II. ii. 3. **1607** HEYWOOD *Wom. Killed w. Kindn.* Wks. 1874 II. 115 Pride is grown to vs A meere meere stranger. **1625** BACON *Ess., Friendship* (Arb.) 165 That it is a meere, and miserable Solitude, to want true Friends. **1634** SIR T. HERBERT *Trav.* 214 [The rivulet] discends so violently, that it makes meere Cattaracts by its motion. **1668** M. CASAUBON *Credulity* (1670) 31 The Greek Grammarians .. (meer strangers to the Hebrew). **1719** D'URFEY *Pills* (1872) III. 306 It blows a mere Storm. **1719** DE FOE *Crusoe* (1840) I. 146, I .. became, in a little time, a mere pastry-cook, into the bargain. **1746** CHESTERF. *Lett.* (1792) I. cviii. 295 You are a mere Oedipus, and I do not believe a Sphynx could puzzle you. **1749** SMOLLETT *Gil Blas* (1797) III. 45 He was .. fair as Love himself, a mere pattern in shape. **1775** WESLEY *Wks.* (1872) IV. 50 He seems to think himself a mere Phenix.

5. a. Having no greater extent, range, value, power, or importance than the designation implies; that is barely or only what it is said to be.

1581 PETTIE tr. *Guazzo's Civ. Conv.* II. (1586) 49 b, If I speake rather lyke a meere Citizen, than a Philosopher. **1586** HOOKER *Disc. Justif.* §32 (1612) 54 Nestorius .. held, that the Virgin .. did not bring forth the sonne of God, but a sole and a mere man. **1594** T. B. *La Primaud. Fr. Acad.* II. 345 The throate .. being onely a meere way and place of passage, through which meates and drinkes passe to and fro. **1610** A. COOKE *Pope Joan* 104 A meere layman. **1650** BAXTER *Saints' R.* II. vii. §7 To the meer English Reader I commend especially these [books]. **1671** MILTON *P.R.* IV. 535 To the utmost of meer man both wise and good, Not more. **1720** OZELL *Vertot's Rom. Rep.* I. I. 9 This military Function became a meer Title of Honour. **1750** GRAY *Long Story* 137 Decorum's turn'd to mere civility. **1758** S. HAYWARD *Serm.* p. xiv, Our public performances are .. looked upon as a meer form. **1820** W. IRVING *Sketch Bk.* I. 3 Even when a mere child I began my travels. **1827** HARE *Guesses* (1859) 339 Mere art perverts taste; just as mere theology depraves religion. **1849** MACAULAY *Hist. Eng.* V. I. 532 Those who had pecuniary transactions with him soon found him to be a mere swindler. **1874** GREEN *Short Hist.* vi. §4. 300 Immersed as Archbishop Warham was in the business of the State, he was no mere politician. **1892** *Law Rep., Weekly Notes* 188 1 The defendant had been maliciously making noises for the mere purpose of .. annoying the plaintiffs.

b. Used in the superlative and comparative.

1642 MILTON *Apol. Smect.* Wks. 1851 III. 305, I rather deeme it the meerest, the falsest, the most unfortunate guift of fortune. **1841** MISS SEDGWICK *Lett. Abr.* I. 269*, I have never seen people that seemed merer animals. **1868** FARRAR *Seekers* II. i. (1875) 201, I shall live despised and the merest nobody.

c. Esp. in *predic.* use: insignificant, ordinary; foolish, inept.

1732 SWIFT *Let.* 19 Feb. in *Corr.* (1965) IV. 4, I .. am as meer a Monk as any in Spain. **1893** BEERBOHM *Lett. to R. Turner* (1964) 64 She is still very mere but not quite so mere —in the strict sense of the word—as she was four weeks ago. **1919** D. ASHFORD *Young Visiters* v. 46 Peaple who have got something funny in their family and who want to be less mere if you can comprehend. **1942** M. DICKENS *One Pair of Feet* ix. 191 Sissons, who didn't count, because she was the Junior and mere. **1955** T. H. PEAR *Eng. Social Differences* viii. 182 In such situations American and Dominion soldiers have always felt less 'mere' than the English.

†**B.** *adv.* = MERELY *adv.*² *Obs.*

1534 in W. H. Turner *Select. Rec. Oxford* (1880) 126 Lawes .. repugnante and meere contrarie to ye Kings statuts. **1577** HANMER *Anc. Eccl. Hist.* (1619) 259 All such crimes as Athanasius was charged with, were meere false. **1601** SHAKS. *All's Well* III. v. 58 *Dia.*.. Thinke you it is so? *Hel.* I surely meere the truth. **1618** WITHER *Motto, Nec Curo*, I hate to have a thought o're-serious spent In things meere triviall, or indifferent. **1635** PAGITT *Christianogr.* I. ii. (1636) 51 Authority over the Clergie and matters meere ecclesiasticall.

†**mere**, *v.*¹ *Obs.* [OE. *merian*; cf. the more frequent *á-merian*, of the same meaning.] *trans.* To purify. Hence †**mered** *ppl. a.*

a **1000** *Sal. & Sat.* 55 (Gr.) To begonganne ðam ðe his gast wile meltan wið morðre, merȝan [*MS. B.* merian] of sorȝe. *a* **1272** *Luue Ron* 115 in *O. E. Misc.* 96 Hwat spekestu of eny bolde þat wrouht þe wise salomon Of iaspe, of saphir, of merede golde. **1340** *Ayenb.* 94 Huanne he [God] nhesseþ þe herte and makeþ zuete and tretable ase wex ymered.

mere, mear (mɪə(r)), *v.*² Also 6 mere, meyre, 6–7 meare, 6–9 meer. [f. MERE, MEAR *sb.*² (ONorthumbrian had *ȝimǽra*).]

1. *trans.* To mark *out* (land) by means of 'meres' or boundaries. Also, to record the position of (a boundary) by specifying its relation *to* a visible feature on the ground.

a **950** *Rituale Eccles. Dunelm.* (Surtees) 164 *Diterminans* [glossed] ȝimaerende. **1507** in Willis & Clark *Cambridge* (1886) II. 190 A certeyn parcell of Grounde .. meryd and staked by the masters of both the said Collegges. **1577–87** HOLINSHED *Chron.* II. 22/1 The paroch was meared from the Crane castell, to the fish shambles. **1598** *Manchester Crt. Leet Rec.* (1885) II. 136 Wee .. haue sett downe certen stakes wᶜʰ meyre out ye saide landes. **1621** EARL OF CORK in *Lismore Papers* (1888) Ser. II. III. 18 This purchase will .. meare and bounde his owne [property]. **1725** in S. O. Addy *Hall of Waltheof* (1893) 155 A place there comonly called Campo Lane being the overend of the said croft, as the same is now meared and staked out. **1863** in Curwen *Kirbie-Kendall* (1900) 84 The Scotch Burial Ground .. never had any trustees for itself alone, being only meered or walled off and excluded from the title made in 1804. **1925** A. S. GREEN *Hist. Irish State to 1014* xiii. 241 On all sides fertile soil was reclaimed for tillage, partitioned, mered, and fenced. **1932** *Instructions to Field Revisers* (Ordnance Survey) App. A. 47 Revision of Boundaries... It often happens that detail is placed on the actual boundary and the original fence entirely obliterated. Before mereing the new detail it is usual to consult the owner or tenant, and not mere on the supposed custom of the district. *Ibid.* 48 Fences to woods .. are, as a rule, maintained by the owner or occupier of the wood, .. and are, therefore, mered accordingly on Ordnance maps. **1971** *House of Commons Bill 1971–2, No. 2: Local Govt.* Sched. I. III. 192 The boundaries of the new local government areas shall be mered by Ordnance Survey. *Ibid.* 193 Any such boundary defined on the map annexed to any order under .. the Local Government Act 1958 by reference to proposed works shall .. be mered as if the boundary had not been so defined. **1975** J. B. HARLEY *O.S. Maps* i. 12 The surveyor who completes the map detail also .. perambulates and meres administrative boundaries. *Ibid.* iii. 39 Because boundaries are invisible .. their precise location in relation to visible ground features is recorded by perambulating the boundary line and 'mereing' it to those features.

†**2.** *intr.* To abut *upon*; to be bounded *by*. *Obs.*

1577 STANYHURST *Descr. Irel.* in *Holinshed* (1808) VI. 2 Ireland is divided into foure regions .. and into a fift plot, defalked from everie fourth part, and yet mearing on each part. **1610** HOLLAND *Camden's Brit.* II. 99 The County of Gallway meereth South upon Clare—West upon the Ocean. **1713** *Conn. Col Rec.* (1870) V. 396 From the said ford of Cowissick River meering with the said Cowissick River, to

a great oak tree markt, . . and thence meering on the east or easterly by and with the said Quinebaug River.

mere: see MAR, MARE, MAYOR, MERRY, MYRRH.

‖**mère** (mɛr, mɛə(r)). [Fr., mother.] An identifying word appended to a name (usu. a surname) to distinguish her from others of the name.

1862 Q. VICTORIA *Let.* 12 Nov. in R. Fulford *Dearest Mama* (1968) 130 All you say about poor Marie Leiningen Mère interests me. **1881** TROLLOPE *Ayala's Angel* I. xviii. 222, I am told by Tringle mère that I am less acceptable than old Traffick. **1947** M. LOWRY *Under Volcano* i. 23 Taskerson mère had taken a fancy to the French boy. **1967** J. FLEMING *No Bones about It* 98, I have never known Borgan *père* and *mère* attend a point-to-point. **1968** J. HAYTHORNE *None of us cared for Kate* 15 Prentice *mère* has been bombarding the Secretary of State with letters. **1973** *Listener* 1 Nov. 607/3 The execution of Hugo *mère's* lover.

-mere (mɪə(r)), terminal element repr. Gr. μέρος part, occurring with the sense 'part', 'segment' in various biological terms, as *centromere*, *genomere*, *hyalomere*, *metamere*.

†**mered**, *ppl. a. Obs. rare*$^{-1}$. In 7 meered. Formation and sense doubtful; possibly a corrupt reading. By some referred to MERE *v.*^{2}; by others regarded as f. MERE *a.*^{2} + -ED^1, and explained as 'sole, entire' (Schmidt).

1606 SHAKS. *Ant. & Cl.* III. xiii. 10 The itch of his Affection should not then Haue nickt his Captain-ship, at such a point, When halfe to halfe the world oppos'd, he being The meered question?

Meredithian (mɛrɪˈdɪθɪən), *a.* and *sb.* Also **-ean**. [f. the proper name *Meredith* + -IAN.]

A. *adj.* Of, pertaining to, or characteristic of George Meredith (1828–1909), English novelist and poet, or his works. **B.** *sb.* An admirer of Meredith.

1889 E. DOWSON *Let.* 7 July (1967) 89 Excuse me for straining after the Meredithian but I have been reading 'Diana' until I am pink and my brain quavers. **1891** *Lit. World* 29 May 510/3 Even the girl-actress catches the infection, and swathes her thought in Meredithean phrase. **1892** *Review of Reviews* Jan. 95/2 Meredithians owe a debt of gratitude to the publishers. **1909** *Daily Chron.* 22 Jan. 3/4 The bookseller, an enthusiastic Meredithian. **1910** *Westm. Gaz.* 9 Apr. 13/2 Your crazy Meredithian will tell you that this is because it is the least worthy of the master's works. **1928** *Daily Tel.* 5 June 12/7, I was never initiated into the inner Meredithian cult, though I have always been a great admirer of his poetry. **1935** J. AGATE *More First Nights* (1937) 123 One or two of my colleagues have dismissed this piece as 'Meredithian', as though that were a term of disparagement. **1936** CHESTERTON *As I was Saying* xvi. 100 In a score of ways, the modern world has followed the Meredithean model for the world. **1968** *Listener* 18 July 91/3 Inevitably, little of the Meredithian style remains.

†ˈ**meregoutte**. *Obs.* Also **-gout**. [a. F. *mèregoutte*, ad. med.L. *mera gutta* 'pure drop'.] The first running of juice from grapes or oil from olives, before pressure is applied.

1601 HOLLAND *Pliny* II. 331 A little vnpressed wine of the first running, called Mere- goutte. *Ibid.* 381 The Mere-gout of the grape that runneth out first without pressing.

mereid, obs. form of MARRIED.

c **1485** in *Cal. Proc. Chanc. Q. Eliz.* (1830) II. Pref. 74 The which Alis is mereid and covertbaren.

mereit, obs. Sc. form of MERIT.

merel (ˈmɛrəl). Forms: *sing.* 4 **merel**, 9 **marl**; *pl.* 5 **mereles**, **merellis**, **-ys**, 5–7 **merelles**, 7 **merills**, 7–8 **merils**, 9 **merrels**, **merril(l)s**, **merls**, 5– **merels**. Also *corruptly* 7 **miracle**, **moral**; and see MORRIS. [a. OF. *merel*, *marel* (mod.F. *méreau*) masc., *merelle*, *marelle* (mod.F. *mérelle*, *marelle*) fem.; the word in OF. meant a token coin, metal ticket, or counter.

Cf. Sicilian *marrella*, in 1617 used for the game of draughts (Carrera *Il Giuoco degli Scacchi*).]

1. One of the counters or pieces used in the game of 'merels' (see 2). Also *fig.*

1390 GOWER *Conf.* I. 18 So that under the clerkes lawe Men sen the Merel al mysdrawe. *Ibid.* III. 201 Wherof ensamples ben ynowhe Of hem that thilke merel drowhe. **1611** [see 2].

2. Chiefly *pl.* **a.** A game played on a board between two players, each with an equal number of pebbles, disks of wood or metal, pegs, or 'pins'. Called also *fivepenny morris*, and *ninepenny* or *nine men's morris*, according to the number of pins or men used. Also *attrib.* †**b.** The game of FOX AND GEESE. *Obs.*

On the continent the name was applied also to a game nearly identical with draughts, and to 'hop-scotch'.

a. *c* **1400** *Beryn* 1250 Leve now al thy foly, and thy rebawdy As Tablis, & merellis & þe hazardry. *c* **1449** PECOCK *Repr.* I. xx. 120 Where is it also grondid in Holi Scripture that men . . schulden pleie . . bi sitting at the merels? **1611** COTGR., *Merelles. Le Ieu des merelles.* The boyish game called Merills, or fiue-pennie Morris; played here most commonly with stones, but in France with pawnes, or men made of purpose, and tearmed Merelles. **1688** R. HOLME *Armoury* (1905) II. 68/1 A 9 Hole Board . . some terme this a miracle board and the game Miracles. **1694** HYDE *Hist. Nerdiludii* Wks. (1767) 359 Alia habet nomina secundum numerum frustulorum quibus luditur . . : sicut est marlin: alias three men's Morals, & nine men's Morals, & nine penny miracle, . . alias three penny moris, aut five penny moris, aut nine penny moris [etc.]. . . Pro his autem omnibus verius & rectius dicendum est three pin merells aut nine pin merells. **1706** PHILLIPS (ed. Kersey), *Merils*, . . otherwise call'd Fivepenny Morris. **1826** in *Hone's Every-day Bk.* II. 983 There is an ancient game, played by the 'shepherds of Salisbury Plain', and 'village rustics' in that part of the country, called 'Ninepenny Marl'. **1867** B. BRIERLEY *Marlocks* 95 One [chair] in particular had supplied the material for a 'merril' board. **1877** *Holderness Gloss.*, *Merrils*, a game played on a square board with 18 pegs, nine on each side. Called in many parts nine men's morris. **1889** *Folk-Lore Jrnl.* VII. 233 The boys of a cottage near Dorchester had . . carved a 'marrel' pound on a block of stone by the house.

b. **1902** REDSTONE in *Trans. R. Hist. Soc.* XVI. 195 The Royal household [under Edw. IV] found delight in games of chess and 'merelles'. For the latter game '2 foxis and 46 hounds of silver overgilt' were purchased to form 2 sets.

†ˈ**merely**, *adv.*^{1} *Obs.* [f. MERE *a.*^{1} + -LY^2.] Wonderfully, beautifully.

c **1205** LAY. 2677 þe king . . ane neowe burh makede . . mærliche feier. *c* **1400** *Sc. Trojan War* I. 337 Ascendande up þe greces gray Rith merely maide of marble-stane.

merely (ˈmɪəlɪ), *adv.*^{2} [f. MERE *a.*^{2} + -LY^2.]

†**1.** Without admixture or qualification; purely.

1548 CRANMER in Strype *Eccl. Mem.* II. App. AA. 98 Soch other moral lernyngs as are merely deryved out of scripture. **1605** BACON *Adv. Learn.* II. i. §4 These Narrations . . not to be mingled with the Narrations which are meerely and sincerely naturall. **1637** GILLESPIE *Eng.-Pop. Cerem.* III. iv. 63 Such things as are not merely, but mixedly Divine. **1645** PAGITT *Heresiogr.* (1662) 125 The witnesse of the spirit is merely immediate.

†**b.** Without the help of others. *Obs.*

1608 D. T[UVIL] *Ess. Pol. & Mor.* 2 To deliuer it vnto them, as if it had proceeded meerly from himselfe.

†**2.** Absolutely, entirely; quite, altogether. *Obs.*

1546 in *Eng. Gilds* (1870) 197 What goodes, catalles, . . or other stuff, do merely belong . . to all the sayd promocions. **1597** HOOKER *Eccl. Pol.* v. lxii. §18 That therefore baptisme by heretiques is meerely voyde. **1601** R. JOHNSON *Kingd. & Commw.* (1603) 48 The government is meerely tyrannicall: for the great Turke is so absolute a lord [etc.]. **1602** SHAKS. *Ham.* I. ii. 137. **1613** FLETCHER, etc. *Honest Man's Fort* v. iii, I . . am as happy In my friends good, as it were meerly mine. *a* **1619** FOTHERBY *Atheom.* II. iii. §2 (1622) 214 It is meerely impossible, that any thing should be the cause of it selfe. **1633** BP. HALL *Hard Texts* 29, I have not meerly lied in saying, she is my sister . . but onely dissembled. **1728** MORGAN *Algiers* I. Pref. 2, I wished, nay merely languished for their Destruction. **1788** WESLEY *Wks.* (1872) VI. 283 Those countries that are merely Popish; as Italy, Spain, Portugal.

†**b.** As a matter of fact, actually. *Obs.*

c **1596** HARINGTON in *Metam. Ajax* (1813) Introd. 13 As I say merely in the booke, the 118 page. **1601** LD. MOUNTJOY in Moryson *Itin.* (1617) II. 204 Not onely have [I] taken all occasions by the death of Captaines to extinguish their entertainement, but also have meerely discharged above five thousand.

3. Without any other quality, reason, purpose, view, etc.; only (what is referred to) and nothing more. Often preceded by *not*.

c **1580** SIDNEY *Ps* XXXIX. iii, The greatest state we see, At best, is meerely vanity. **1597** HOOKER *Eccl. Pol.* v. liv. §4 The incarnation of the Sonne of God consisteth meerely in the vnion of natures. **1603** SHAKS. *Meas. for M.* v. i. 459 Thoughts are no subiects Intents, but meerely thoughts. **1622** PEACHAM *Compl. Gent.* x. 94 Diuers of his workes, are but meerely translations out of Latine and French. **1690** LOCKE *Govt.* I. ix. §88 Men are not Proprietors of what they have meerly for themselves. **1729** BUTLER *Serm.* Wks. 1874 II. Pref. 5 The multitudes who read merely for the sake of talking. **1841** MISS MITFORD in L'Estrange *Life* (1870) III. viii. 117 The hero must be young and interesting—must have to do, and not merely to suffer. **1856** SIR B. BRODIE *Psychol. Inq.* I. iv. 131 It is not very common for any one to die merely of old age. **1875** JOWETT *Plato* (ed. 2) I. 99 Perhaps Nicias is serious, and not merely talking for the sake of talking. **1888** F. HUME *Mme. Midas* I. iv, To many people Cowper is merely a name.

merely, obs. form of MERRILY.

meremaid, etc., obs. forms of MERMAID, etc.

‖**merenchyma** (məˈrɛŋkɪmə). *Bot.* Also anglicized **merenchym**. [mod.L., f. Gr. μέρος part + *-enchyma* in PARENCHYMA.] Tissue consisting of ellipsoidal and spheroidal cells. Also *attrib.*

1839 LINDLEY *Introd. Bot.* I. i. (ed. 3) 7 *note*, Professor Morren has proposed the following nomenclature of tissue, which has some advantages over that now more commonly in use. I. *Parenchyma*; 1. *merenchyma*, or *sphærenchyma*, spherical; 2. *conenchyma*, conical [etc.]. *Ibid.* 15 Meyen has *Merenchyma* [*ed.* 1848 *Merenchym*] for ellipsoidal and spheroidal cells. **1849** BALFOUR *Man. Bot.* §5. **1900** JACKSON *Gloss. Bot. Terms*, *Merenchyma cells*, unpitted cells in the pith of trees, with intercellular spaces, and much elongated radially.

Hence **merenˈchymatous** *a.*, of the character of merenchyma.

1840 *Ann. Nat. Hist.* IV. 392 A cuticle with merenchymatous cells, swollen up, like bladders.

‖**meˈrenda**. [Sp. *merienda* (cf. *merendar* vb., to eat one's 'merenda'):—L. *merenda*.] A light meal or collation. Also **merendar** [from the verb].

1622 MABBE tr. *Aleman's Guzman d'Alf.* II. (1630) 282 Now they were beginning to fall to their merendar or intermealary repast. **1740** C'TESS HARTFORD *Corr.* (1805) II. 81 At every one of these visits there is a merenda provided for the ladies that attend the princess.

ˈ**mereness**. [f. MERE *a.*^{2}] †**1.** Purity. *Obs.*$^{-0}$

1648–60 HEXHAM *Dutch Dict.*, *Louterheyat*, Purety, Meerenesse, or Cleanenesse.

2. The state or quality of being merely something or of being small or insignificant.

1960 *Times Lit. Suppl.* 25 Mar. 193/3 Your reviewer . . and others have made something of the fact that Bevin used to refer to Lord Attlee as the Little Man. Lloyd George's colleagues used exactly the same phrase about him: both Prime Ministers lacked inches. Is it wise to see a value judgment in this statement of physical mereness? **1966** W. V. QUINE in *Jrnl. Philos.* LXIII. 658 The word 'concept', which Russell applied to these nonexistents, connotes mereness.

merengue (məˈrɛŋgeɪ). Also **meringue** (məræŋ). [f. Haitian Creole *méringue* and Amer. Sp. *merengue* (Webster).] A dance popular in Dominica and Haiti. Also *attrib.*

1936 L. A. HUDSON tr. *Possendorf's Damballa Calls* iv. 48 Dancing a second Merinque with Diane. **1956** M. STEARNS *Story of Jazz* iii. 25 The Haitian *meringues* sometimes sound a little like our ragtime without the force and drive. **1957** *New Yorker* 26 Oct. 166/2 In the cafés and restaurants one hears everything from Vivaldi to Afro-Cuban merengues. **1964** W. G. RAFFÉ *Dict. Dance* 318/2 The *Merengue* folk dance is very popular in the Dominican Republic as a favourite example of Caribbean rhythm. **1965** *Evening Standard* 17 Sept. 8/6 The kid who danced was doing the merengue... The solo merengue kid was dervishing around. **1972** *New Yorker* 21 Oct. 34/2 They danced tangos, merengues . . to the strains of the Nagy Hungarian band. **1973** *Sunday Advocate-News* (Barbados) 18 Mar. 14/4 [Haiti] Now cruise ships are calling once more and holiday-makers from the United States, Canada and Europe come by the planeloads to a festive welcome by meringue bands at the airport.

mereology (mɛrɪˈɒlədʒɪ). *Logic.* [ad. F. *meréologie*, irreg. f. Gr. μέρος part + -OLOGY.] (See quots. 1946, 1962.)

[**1937** A. TARSKI in J. H. Woodger *Axiomatic Method in Biol.* App. E. 161 The general theory of the concept 'part of' has been developed by S. Leśniewski under the name of *Meréologie*.] **1946** *Mind* LV. 368 The attempt to provide a foundation for mathematics in logic led Lesniewski to formulate a system consisting of 'Protothetic' . . 'Ontology' and 'Mereology' (which is formally similar to the Boolean algebra except for the exclusion of the null class). **1956** J. H. WOODGER tr. *Tarski's Logic, Semantics, Metamath.* ii. 25 The geometry of solids is based upon mereology, in the sense that the relation between part and whole is included in the system of primitive notions of the geometry of solids. **1962** W. & M. KNEALE *Devel. of Logic* vi. 426 An extended system of Boolean algebra in which there are two operations of a non-finitary character, namely that of taking the logical sum or union of all the elements of some specified set . . and that of taking the logical product or intersection of all the elements of some specified set... This extended system is closely related to . . 'mereology'. In fact the difference is simply that Leśniewski's system excludes the possibility of a null element included in every other element. **1967** H. SKOLIMOWSKI *Polish Analytical Philos.* iv. 106 In mereology the word 'part' is given the meaning it has in every-day usage, i.e. by a 'part' is understood a section of a given object, and such a section as is not identical with the object itself.

†ˈ**meresauce**. *Obs.* Also 5 **mersaus(e**, **mire sauce**. [? repr. AF. **muiresauce*:—L. *muria salsa* salt pickle. Cf. the synonymous OF. *salmuire*, mod.F. *saumure*.] Brine used for pickling.

? *c* **1400** in *Househ. Ord.* (1790) 435 Take felittes of braune and let hom lye in mersaus an houre. **1483** *Cath. Angl.* 240/2 Mire sauce, *muria*. **1494** FABYAN *Chron.* VI. ccxiv. 230 He . . slewe the sayde seruauntes of his brother, and hacked theym in small pecys, and cast them after in mere-sawce or salte. **1530** PALSGR. 244/2 Mere sauce for flesshe, *savlmvre*. **1681** W. ROBERTSON *Phraseol. Gen.* (1693) 877 Meer sauce, or brine.

mereschaum, variant of MEERSCHAUM.

merese (məˈriːz). [Etym. unknown.] A rib, flange, or collar, on the stem of a glass vessel. Also *attrib.*

1923 H. J. POWELL *Glass-Making in Eng.* iii. 44 *Merese*, a sharp-edged button between bowl and leg of wine glass, or connecting sections of stem or in place of step. **1935** *Burlington Mag.* Oct. 150/1 The two mereses and the foot-stem cast are of kinds which occur repeatedly. **1949** W. A. THORPE *Eng. Glass* (ed. 2) vi. 170 Meantime . . the foot merese is moving up the stem, regardless of its use as camouflage and boundary mark. **1960** H. HAYWARD *Antique Coll.* 182/1 *Merese knop*, a knop or protuberance in the stem of a drinking glass or other glass vessel of sharp-edged, flattened form. **1968** O. N. WILKINSON *Old Glass* vi. 100 'Mereses' (flat discs) and knopping appear, more commonly at the top and bottom of stems to disguise welding than as a decorative feature.

meresman (ˈmɪəzmən). [f. *mere's*, genit. of MERE *sb.*^{2} + MAN.] A man appointed to find out the exact boundaries of a parish, etc.

1828 R. GRIFFITH *Let.* 26 Sept. in C. Close *Early Yrs. Ordnance Survey* (1969) 112 Any casualty among the meresmen or expense incurred by calling back the boundary surveyors from distant parts . . must be charged to the Ordnance. **1867** HT. PARR *Stone Edge* vii. in *Cornh. Mag.* XV. 737, I were a fool to promise thretty shillin' a year for't,

—the Meresmen said as how it werna much above three acre. **1875** PARISH *Sussex Gloss.*, *Meresman*, a parish officer who attends to the roads, bridges and water-courses. **1884** *Times* 29 May 8/4 The boundaries laid down..were pointed out to the Ordnance Surveyors by Meresmen, or persons appointed by Her Majesty's Justices of the Peace. **1895** *Edin. Rev.* July 55 Great trouble was taken to secure the most trustworthy meresmen in each barony. **1935** *Rep. Progress Ordnance Survey* 1. 6 In 1841..the Survey Act of that year authorized the appointment, by Justices of the Peace in England..and by Sheriffs in Scotland, of 'meresmen' to aid the surveyors in identifying and locating the parish boundaries. *Ibid.*, The legally appointed meresmen often disagreed. **1972** *House of Commons Rep. Standing Comm. D: Local Govt. Bill* 27 Jan. 1043 A 'meresman' is someone whose job it is to ascertain.. boundaries.

merestead: see MESESTEAD.

merestone ('mɪəstəʊn). *arch.* and *dial.* [f. MERE *sb.*² + STONE.] A stone set up as a landmark.

956 in Birch *Cartul. Sax.* III. 154 Ðis synton ða landʒemæro..On mærstan, of mærstane on ðone ealdan ʒaran. ?**1360** *Durham Halm. Rolls* (Surtees) 26 Amovit unum merstane. **1483** *Cath. Angl.* 232/2 A Meyre stane, *bifinium.* **1577** tr. *Bullinger's Decades* (1592) 395 Thou shalt not remoue thy neighbours merestone. **1679** *Coll. Conn. Hist. Soc.* (1897) VI. 190 The meere stones of the lot. **1782** *MS. Indenture Estate at Babworth, co. Nottingham.*, Closes ..lying East of the meerstones or boundaries set up by Robert Rogers. **1839** STONEHOUSE *Axholme* 384 A Mere Stone called God's Cross. **1879** JEFFERIES *Amateur Poacher* iii, By the pond stood a low three-sided merestone or landmark. **1970** H. BRAUN *Parish Churches* xx. 235 Let it [*sc.* the church] rise from the land untroubled by fencing. Its yard can be kept from the plough by mere-stones. **1972** *Parl. Debates Commons: Rep. Standing Comm. D: Local Govt. Bill, 18th Sitting* 27 Jan. 1044 A 'merestone' is a boundary stone.

fig. **1617** BACON *Sp. to Hutton* Resusc. (1657) 1. 94 That you contain the Jurisdiction of the Court within the ancient Meere-stones, without Removing the Mark. **1877** TRENCH *Lect. Med. Ch. Hist.* 15 The merestone to mark where one era terminated and another began.

†**'mereswine.** *Obs.* Forms: see MERE *sb.*¹ and SWINE; also 6 **marswyn,** *Sc.* **meir-, meyrswyne,** 8–9 **meer swine.** [OE. *mereswín*, lit. 'sea-swine', f. *mere* MERE *sb.*¹ + *swín* SWINE. Cf. the equivalent OHG. *meriswîn* (MHG. *mereswîn*, mod.G. *meerschwein*), whence F. *marsouin.* Cf. MARSOUIN.] A dolphin or porpoise.

c **725** *Corpus Gloss.* (Hessels) B. 166 *Bacarius*, meresuin. *c* **1000** *Sax. Leechd.* II. 334 Nim mere-swines fel. *c* **1325** *Metr. Hom.* 25 The thride dai mersuine and qualle, And other gret fises alle Sal yel. **1419** *Liber Albus* (Rolls) I. 343 Item, de mereswyn, quantum dabit. **1541** BELLENDEN *Descr. Alb.* ix. in *Cron. Scot.* B vj b, This Frith [of Forth] is rycht plentuus of coclis,..pellok, merswyne, and quhalis. **1710** SIBBALD *Hist. Fife & Kinross* 49 The bigger [sort] beareth the Name of Dolphin; and our Fishers call them Meer-swines. **1822** CARLYLE *Early Lett.* (1886) II. 70 Waugh fixed his eye on an enormous meerswine.

merete, meretorious, obs. ff. MERIT, MERITORIOUS.

†**meretric,** *a. Obs. rare*⁻¹. = MERETRICIOUS.

1545 JOYE *Exp. Dan.* xii. 215 b, Thei thinke it impossible to be any knauerye or errours in so holy fathers with their meretrik mother.

†**meretricate,** *v. Obs.*⁻⁰ [f. late L. *meretrīcāt-* (*-trīcārī*), f. *meretrīc-em* harlot.]

1623 COCKERAM, *Meretricate*, to play the whore.

†**mere'tricial,** *a. Obs.* [f. L. *meretrīci-us* (see MERETRICIOUS) + -AL¹.] = MERETRICIOUS 1.

1751 LAVINGTON *Enthus. Meth. & Papists* III. 335 He saw them..standing before a public Stew, in meretricial Habits.

†**mere'trician,** *a.* and *sb. Obs.* [Formed as prec. + -AN.] **a.** *adj.* = MERETRICIOUS 1. **b.** *sb.* A harlot.

1630 BRATHWAIT *Eng. Gentlem.* (1641) 403, A mercenarie meretrician. *a* **1704** T. BROWN *Declam. in Def. Gaming* Wks. 1709 III. 142 Take from human Commerce Meretrician Amours, you will find a horrid Confusion of all things, and incestuous Lusts disturb every Family.

meretricious (mɛrɪ'trɪʃəs), *a.* [f. L. *meretrīci-us* (f. *meretrīc-*, *meretrix* harlot, fem. agent-n. f. *merērī* to earn money, serve for hire: see MERIT *sb.*) + -OUS.]

1. Of, pertaining to, characteristic of, or befitting a harlot; having the character of a harlot.

a **1626** BACON *New Atl.* 27 The Delight in Meretricious Embracements (wher sinne is turned into Art) maketh Marriage a dull thing. **1664** H. MORE *Exp. 7 Epist.* (1669) 101 Jezebel,..for all her paintings and fine meretricious pranking her self up,..was to be thrown out at the window. **1765** BLACKSTONE *Comm.* I. 436 It is a meretricious, and not a matrimonial, union. **1809** MALKIN *Gil Blas* VII. vii, A young stagefinch who had evidently suffered himself to be caught in the birdlime of her professional or meretricious talents. **1814** SHELLEY *Prose Wks.* (1888) II. 394 The lying and meretricious prude.

2. Alluring by false show of beauty or richness; showily attractive. Now often applied to the style of a painter or a writer.

1633 P. FLETCHER *Purple Isl.* VIII. ix, Strip thou their meretricious seemlinesse. **1662** S. P. *Acc. Latitude-men* in *Phenix* II. 503 The meretricious Gaudiness of the Church of Rome, and the squallid Sluttery of Fanatick Conventicles. **1709–10** ADDISON *Tatler* No. 120 ⁋5 The Front of it was raised on Corinthian Pillars, with all the meretricious Ornaments that accompany that Order. **1790** BURKE *Fr. Rev.* 59 A lust of meretricious glory. **1843** PRESCOTT *Mexico* I. vi. (1864) 55 The meretricious ornaments..with which the minstrelsy of the East is usually attended. **1846** WRIGHT *Ess. Mid. Ages* I. v. 185 The style he aims at is gaudy and meretricious. **1879** SEGUIN *Black For.* vi. 85 The meretricious excitement of the gambling-room.

absol. **1838** LYTTON *Alice* 55 No critic ever more readily detected the meretricious and the false.

Hence **mere'triciously** *adv.*, **mere'triciousness.**

1727 BAILEY vol. II, *Meretriciousness.* **179.** BURKE *Tracts on Popery Laws* Wks. 1812 V. 258 And meretriciously to hunt abroad after foreign affections. **1850** L. HUNT *Autobiog.* xxi. (1860) 343 The face [of the Venus de Medici] has the very worst look of meretriciousness, which is want of feeling. **1859** GULLICK & TIMBS *Paint.* 118 Its generally dauby meretriciousness. **1892** LOUNSBURY *Stud. Chaucer* III. vii. 181 The outspokenness of the original has been generally..omitted. For it, however, there has been substituted a veiled coarseness and meretriciousness.

†**mere'triculate,** *v. nonce-wd.* [f. L. *meretrīc-*, parodying *matriculate.*] *trans.* To deceive as a harlot does.

1611 CHAPMAN *May Day* 32, I haue not beene matriculated in the Vniuersity, to be meretriculated by him.

‖**meretrix** ('mɛrɪtrɪks). Pl. **meretrices** (mɛrɪ'traɪsiːz). [L.] A prostitute, harlot.

1564 MARTIAL *Treat. Cross* 139 Yff she were blacke, browne, barren, or common to mo, as *Meretrix* is a common name to them all. **1605** B. JONSON *Volpone* I. i, From Pithagore, she went into a beautiful peece Hight Aspasia, the Meretrix.

mereuh, -ewe: see MARROW, MEROW.

merewi: see MARROWY.

merganser (mɜː'gænsə(r)). [mod.L. (Gesner 1555), f. *merg-us* diver (water-fowl) + *anser* goose. The name is given by Willughby (1676) and Albin (1731) as Latin, with the Eng. equivalent 'goosander.'] Any bird of the genus *Mergus* or subfamily *Merginæ*, fish-eating ducks of great diving powers, with long narrow serrated bill hooked at the tip, inhabiting the northern parts of the Old World and N. America; esp. *Mergus merganser*, the common merganser or GOOSANDER. *M. serrator* is the Red-breasted Merganser, *M. cucullatus* the Hooded Merganser of N. America, *M. albellus* the White Merganser or SMEW.

1752 J. HILL *Hist. Anim.* 437 Mergus crista dependente, capite nigro-cærulescente collari albo. The Merganser. **1759** B. STILLINGFL. tr. *Biberg's Econ. Nat.* in *Misc. Tracts* (1762) 103 In the autumn, when the fishes hide themselves in deep places, the merganser..supplies the gull with food. **1768** PENNANT *Zool.* (1776) II. 471 Red Breasted Merganser. **1840** *Cuvier's Anim. Kingd.* 266 The Bay-breasted M[erganser] (*M. serrator*). *Ibid.* 267 The Hooded M[erganser]. **1852** MACGILLIVRAY *Brit. Birds* V. 199 The Mergansers, although few in number, seem yet to form a very distinct family. **1856** F. O. MORRIS *Brit. Birds* V. 270 Smew... White Nun. White Merganser. **1879** C. NAPIER *Lakes & Rivers* iv. 117 The Red-breasted Merganser (*Mergus serrator*) is one of the most beautiful of our ducks.

merge (mɜːdʒ), *sb. rare.* [f. the vb.] An act or instance of merging.

1805 FOSTER *Ess.* I. vii. (1806) 101 In him it was no debility of reason, it was at the utmost but a merge of it. **1905** *Pall Mall G.* 24 Apr. 3/2 The first barony of Pelham..merged in the Dukedom of Newcastle... The 'merges' of the 1611 baronetcy, Pelham of Laughton, have been many.

merge (mɜːdʒ), *v.* [ad. L. *mergĕre* to dip, plunge. The surviving uses (senses 2 and 3) come through Law Fr. *merger*, earlier translated 'drown' (see DROWN *v.* 6 b).]

†**1. a.** *trans.* To plunge or sink *in* a (specified) activity, way of living, environment, etc.; to immerse. (In quots. *refl.* and *pass.*) *Obs.*

1636 PRYNNE *Unbish. Timothy* 134 [They] merge themselves in pleasures, idlenesse, or secular affaires. **1637** —— *Brev. Prelates* 64 Thomas Woolsie..wholly merged himselfe in secular offices and state affairs. **1751** HARRIS *Hermes* III. iv. (1765) 350 The Vulgar merged in Sense from their earliest Infancy,..imagine nothing to be real, but what may be tasted or touched.

¶**b.** rarely *lit.*: To plunge or dip *in* a liquid.

1866 J. M. NEALE *Hymns Paradise* (ed. 2) 30 All his spite the Tempter urges; Casts in fire, in water merges [L. *aquis mergit*]. **1866** J. B. ROSE tr. *Ovid's Fasti* v. 754 So Tiber said, And in his grotto merged his dripping head.

2. In *Law*: To sink or extinguish (a lesser estate, title, etc.) *in* one which is greater or superior. Hence *gen.*, to cause (something) to be absorbed into something else, so as to lose its own character or identity; to sink or make to disappear.

a. Const. *in*, occas. *into.*

1728 [see MERGER¹ 1]. **1729** JACOB *Law Dict.* s. v. *Merger*, An Estate-tail cannot be merged in an Estate in Fee. **1766** BLACKSTONE *Comm.* II. 177 Whenever a greater estate and a less coincide and meet in one and the same person, without any intermediate estate, the less is immediately annihilated; or, in the law phrase, is said to be *merged*, that is, sunk or drowned, in the greater. **1791** BURKE *Let. Memb. Nat. Assemb.* Wks. 1792 III. 346 Their object is to merge all natural and all social sentiment in inordinate vanity. **1842** H. ROGERS *Ess.* (1874) I. i. 36 He is content to merge his historic character in that of a retailer of amusing oddities. **1856** KANE *Arct. Expl.* II. vii. 81 These shelves, though sometimes merged into each other, presented distinct and recognisable embankments. **1863** GEO. ELIOT *Romola* xix, That..his library..should not be merged in another collection. **1866** CRUMP *Banking* i. 7 This business he merged into a banking-house. **1868** STANLEY *Westm. Abb.* vi. (ed. 2) 447 The diocese, after ten years, was merged in the See of London. **1874** GREEN *Short Hist.* ii. §3. 68 The same forces which merged the Dane in the Englishman.

b. Without const.

1729 JACOB *Law Dict.* s. v. *Merger*, Where a Man hath a Term in his own Right, and the Inheritance descends to his Wife, so as he hath a Freehold in her Right; the Term is not merged or drowned. **1809** PINKNEY *Trav. France* 202 The ornaments may..lose their own effect by being attached to a building which, by exciting stronger emotions, necessarily merges the less. **1818** CRUISE *Digest* (ed. 2) I. 380 The estate of the copyholder being only at will, becomes merged by the accession of any greater estate. **1832** COLERIDGE *Table-T.* 19 Aug., That is the most excellent state of society in which the patriotism of the citizen ennobles, but does not merge, the individual energy of the man. **1835** I. TAYLOR *Spir. Despot.* iii. 98 None would pretend that..individual fitness for the office..should be so merged as is implied in adapting the hereditary principle to the clerical order. **1845** STEPHEN *Comm. Laws Eng.* (1874) II. 58 The contract by specialty merges or extinguishes that by parol.

3. a. *intr.* In *Law*: To be extinguished by absorption in a greater title, estate, etc. Hence *gen.*, to sink and disappear, to be swallowed up and lost to view, lose character or identity by absorption into something else. Const. *in*, *into.*

1726 VERNON *Chanc. Cases* I. 22 If a Copyholder pays a Rent to the Lord, and the Lord grants or releases this Rent to his Tenant, this shall Merge in the Copyhold. **1766** BLACKSTONE *Comm.* II. xii. 186 If an estate is originally limited to two for life, and after to the heirs of one of them, the freehold shall remain in jointure, without merging in the inheritance. **1802** SIR WM. SCOTT *Sp. April* 27 He is to take care..that the ecclesiastic shall not merge in the farmer, but shall continue the presiding and predominating character. **1814** CHALMERS *Evid. Chr. Revel.* v. 128 The Jews..merge into the name and distinction of Christians. **1841** J. R. YOUNG *Math. Dissert.* ii. 37 These roots can never merge into one and coincide. **1856** FROUDE *Hist. Eng.* (1858) I. i. 13 Serfdom had merged or was rapidly merging into free servitude. **1858** LD. ST. LEONARDS *Handy-Bk. Prop. Law* ix. 62 The tax has merged, and does not remain as a charge of which you can avail yourself. **1859** MILL *Liberty* ii. (1865) 31 But this, though an important consideration,..merges in a more fundamental objection. **1894** *Times* 16 Apr. 3/3 That was..an indication that the cause of action had not merged.

b. Of firms or trading companies: to combine or amalgamate; to combine *with* another.

1926 *Office Appliances* Feb. 49/1 With regard to merger reports..two propositions had been received—one to sell out; the other to merge with another company. **1930** J. B. PRIESTLEY *Angel Pavement* ii. 54 That's the way things are going all the time now,..big combinations—merging away till you don't know where you are. **1965** NEWMAN & LOGAN *Business Policies & Cent. Managem.* (ed. 5) xiv. 353 Poor health or old age makes them [*sc.* large stockholders] willing to merge at an attractive price. **1965** J. F. BRADLEY *Administrative Financial Managem.* xxviii. 577 If Company A and Company B are to merge, Company A might take over Company B.

Hence **merged** *ppl. a.*; **'merging** *vbl. sb.*

1839 YEOWELL *Anc. Brit. Ch.* viii. (1847) 77 It was the merging the individual in the corporate character. **1880** J. CAIRD *Philos. Relig.* 278 This absolute merging of the individual in the universal life. **1965** NEWMAN & LOGAN *Business Policies & Cent. Managem.* (ed. 5) xiv. 356 The character and the operating policy of the merged firms may differ..sharply.

mergee (mɜː'dʒiː). [f. MERGE *v.* + -EE¹.] One who takes part in a merger.

1964 *Punch* 30 Dec. 989/2 Mergees are going to need twice the stuff. **1967** *Time* 24 Nov. 60 Royal Little, retired founder of Textron, Inc., counsels..students on the pitfalls of getting together [in mergers]. These include such dangers as whether the mergee's inventory is all he says it is. **1971** *Atlantic Monthly* Oct. 85 Elsewhere in the motel—we learn later—the rival corporation, Penta, has chosen a more ingenious method: they tell their mergees that it seems important only that the change be comfortable for everyone.

mergence ('mɜːdʒəns). [f. MERGE *v.* + -ENCE.] The action of merging or condition of being merged.

1865 *Intell. Observ.* No. 42. 411 The mergence of twilight into night. **1874** GEO. ELIOT *Coll. Breakf. P.* 573 Say, the small arc of Being we call man Is near its mergence, what seems growing life Nought but a hurrying change towards lower types. **1893** H. WALKER *Three Cent. Scott. Lit.* II. 81 The mergence of one character in another.

mergent(e, obs. forms of MARGENT.

merger¹ ('mɜːdʒə(r)). [Law Fr. *merger*: see MERGE *v.* and -ER⁴.]

1. *Law.* **a.** Extinguishment of a right, estate, contract, action, etc., by absorption in another.

1728 VERNON *Chanc. Cases* II. 90 The Plaintiff..insisted that the Term was merged in the Daughter, as being also Heir at Law. The Court upon the Hearing relieved against the Merger. **1729** JACOB *Law Dict.*, If a Lessor, who hath the Fee, marries with the Lessee for Years; this is no Merger, because [etc.] **1818** COLEBROOKE *Obligations* 216 Where there is a confusion of rights, where debtor and creditor become one,..an immediate merger takes place. **1839** *Penny Cycl.* XV. 109/1 Estates tail are not subject to merger. **1861** MAY *Const. Hist.* (1863) I. v. 240 This increase is exhibited by the existing peerage alone—notwithstanding the extinction or merger of numerous titles in the interval. **1894**

Times 16 Apr. 3/3 That depended upon whether the judgment did operate as a merger of the action on the guarantee.

b. orig. *U.S.* The combination or consolidation of one firm or trading company with another. Also *transf.*

1889 *Boston* (Mass.) *Jrnl.* 17 Apr. 4/3 Ample powers of consolidation and merger, transfer and absorption of stock and kindred franchises are given. **1902** *Westm. Gaz.* 7 May 5/1 The Attorney-General is watching the steamship merger closely. **1904** *Daily News* 7 Apr. 6 A week or two ago a merger between two railways was forcibly dissolved by the judges of the Supreme Court. **1915** E. WALLACE *Man who bought London* vi. 54 The Shearman Anti-Trust Law which..drove what is known on the other side of the Atlantic as the 'mergers' out of business. **1928** *Manch. Guardian Weekly* 10 Aug. 104/2 Washington..is shown by the dispatches to suspect something like an Anglo-French alliance or merger or pooling behind the text of the naval compromise. **1930** J. B. PRIESTLEY *Angel Pavement* ii. 55 Along comes a big merger—a bit of syndicate and trust work—and up they go. **1931** CHESTERTON in *London Mercury* Feb. 342 The great moral institutions of modern times, the Straddle, the Wheat Corner, the Merger, and the rest. **1949** I. DEUTSCHER *Stalin* iii. 79 A merger between Mensheviks and Bolsheviks was the main item. **1949** WODEHOUSE *Uncle Dynamite* ii. 24, I have always hoped that you and Sally would eventually form a merger. **1961** *Listener* 16 Nov. 834/3 Theology seems to have made a 'merger' with philosophy for three centuries. **1970** T. LUPTON *Managem. & Social Sci.* (ed. 2) iv. 103 If an organization is being created *de novo*, as the result, say, of a merger. **1971** *Farmer & Stockbreeder* 23 Feb. 18/3 The crunch comes when we look at the most important reason for industrial mergers—marketing. **1974** WODEHOUSE *Aunts aren't Gentlemen* ii. 10, I had once asked her to marry me... In due season I suggested a merger. But apparently I was not the type, and no business resulted.

2. *gen.* An act of merging; the fact of being merged.

1881 *Athenæum* No. 2791. 556 A very little additional lapse of time witnessed the merger of the diocesan in the statesman. **1883** M. D. CHALMERS *Local Govt.* iv. 55 This.. would be a practical merger of the smaller in the larger parish. **1886** POSNETT *Compar. Lit.* 90 This progressive merger underlies the development of institutions and language. **1898** RENTON *Encycl. Laws Eng.* X. 622 The two latter [officers] have ceased to exist, the former of the two upon merger of the duties with those of the Queen's Remembrancer.

3. *attrib.* and *Comb.*

1914 W. H. LOUGH *Corporation Finance* (rev. ed.) xiv. 231 The average merger bond should prove a safe investment. **1926** *Office Appliances* Feb. 49/1 With regard to merger reports..two propositions had been received. **1928** *Daily Mail* 3 Aug. 18/2 There is no compulsion on the Preference shareholders to accept an offer from the merger company. *Ibid.* 18/3 The merger shares issued to..shareholders may bring a bigger income than the..Preference shares. **1964** G. G. FISCH *Organization for Profit* x. 140 The merger-acquisition specialist is the official corporate professional 'wheeler-dealer'. **1967** H. B. MAYNARD *Handbk. Business Administration* IX. xi. 125 The SEC's financial statement requirements in 'merger proxies' are..similar to those of Form S-1. *Ibid.*, In the merger situation, the acquired company will attempt to obtain SEC approval to terminate its reporting requirements.

merger[2] ('mɜːdʒə(r)). *rare*—^{0}. [f. MERGE *v.* + -ER[1].] One who or something which merges.

1846 in WORCESTER; and in later Dicts.

mergery-prater, variant of MARGERY-PRATER.

mergh(e, obs. forms of MARROW.

mergin, obs. f. MARGIN; var. MURGEON *sb.*[1]

mergrave, obs. form of MARGRAVE.

†**meri.** *Anat. Obs.* Also 5 mary, 5–6 mery. [a. med.L. *meri*, OF. *meri*, a. Arab. *marī'*.] The gullet or œsophagus.

c **1400** *Lanfranc's Cirurg.* 148 Bitwene þe necke & gula wiþinneforþ þere is ordeyned mary [*v. r.* mery], þat is to seie þe wesant. **1541** R. COPLAND *Guydon's Quest. Chirurg.* F ij b, The Meri otherwyse called Ysophagus. **1547** BOORDE *Brev. Health* ccclxxx. 121 b, In Englyshe it is named Isofagon or the mery.

meri, merialtie, obs. ff. MERRY, MAYORALTY.

meribauk, variant of MERRIBOWK *Obs.*

mericarp ('mɛrɪkɑːp). *Bot.* [a. F. *méricarpe*, irreg. f. Gr. μέρος part + καρπός fruit.] A portion of a fruit which splits away as a perfect fruit; *esp.* each of the two one-seeded carpels which together constitute the fruit (or cremocarp) in umbelliferous plants.

1832 LINDLEY *Introd. Bot.* 179 M. De Candolle calls the half of the fruit of Umbelliferæ *mericarp*. **1864** OLIVER *Elem. Bot.* II. 176 The mericarps are popularly called 'seeds', as Caraway-seeds, &c. **1875** BENNETT & DYER *Sachs' Bot.* 841 The fruit of *Erodium gruinum* and other Geraniaceæ splits up into five mericarps. **1887** GARNSEY & BALFOUR tr. *Goebel's Classif. & Morphol. Plants* 427 Two or more parts each containing a seed, and appearing to be a separate fruit; each of these may be called a mericarp or partial fruit, and the whole is a schizocarp.

meridarch ('mɛrɪdɑːk). *Hist.* [ad. Gr. μεριδάρχης, f. μεριδ-, μερίς part + -αρχης ruler.] (See quot.)

1866 G. F. MACLEAR *N. T. Hist.* I. III. iv. (1877) 46 Jonathan..was..raised to the rank of *meridarch*, or ruler of a part of the empire [1 Macc. x. 65; in *Bible* 1611 partaker of his dominion; *margin*, gouernour of a prouince].

meridean, obs. form of MERIDIAN.

merides, pl. of MERIS.

†**meridial**, *a. Obs.* In 6 merydyal(l. [ad. L. *merīdiāl-is*, f. *merīdiēs* mid-day.] **a.** South (wind). **b.** Belonging to mid-day.

c **1540** BOORDE *The boke for to Lerne* B ij b, The merydyall wynde of all wyndes is the most worst. *Ibid.* C iv b, Whole men..shuld..eschew merydyall slepe.

meridian (məˈrɪdɪən), *sb.* Also 4–5 meridien, 5 merydien. [From various elliptical uses of MERIDIAN *a.*, chiefly adopted from OF. or med.L.

Cf. L. *merīdiānum* (sc. *tempus*), noon; *merīdiānum*, the south; med.L. *meridiāna* (OF. *méridiane*, earlier *meriene*; mod.F. *méridienne*), noon, midday rest, siesta; F. *méridien* = sense 4 below; *méridienne* (= *ligne m.*), a meridian line.]

†**1.** Mid-day, noon. *Obs.* exc. in humorously pedantic use.

a **1380** *St. Augustine* 1673 in Horstm. *Altengl. Leg.* (1878) 90 Vppon a day aftur þe meridien Austin apeered to him þen. *c* **1391** CHAUCER *Astrol.* II. §44 Adde hit [to-geder], and þat is thy mene mote, for the laste meridian of the december, for the same ȝere wyche þat þou [hast] purposid. **1637** HEYWOOD *Lond. Mirrour* Wks. 1874 IV. 311 The very day that doth afford him light, Is Morning, the Meridian, Evening, Night. **1871** G. MEREDITH *H. Richmond* xlii, If any thing fresh occurred between meridian and six o'clock, he should be glad, he said, to have word of it by messenger.

b. ***night's meridian***: 'the noon of night', midnight. *nonce-use.*

1826 CARRINGTON *Dartmoor* 62 A fearful gloom, deep'ning and deep'ning, till 'Twas dark as night's meridian.

c. *Hist.* A mid-day rest or siesta. [tr. med.L. *meridiana*; cf. F. *méridienne*, OF. *merien(n)e*.]

1798–1801 J. MILNER *Hist. Winchester* II. 101 There was now a vacant space of an hour or an hour and an half, during part of which those [monks] who were fatigued were at liberty to take their repose,..which was called from the time of day when it was taken, The Meridian. **1820** SCOTT *Monast.* xix [Abbot *loq.*], As we have..in the course of this our toilsome journey, lost our meridian, indulgence shall be given [etc.].

d. *Sc.* A mid-day dram. (See also E.D.D.)

1818 SCOTT *Hrt. Midl.* iv, Plumdamas joined the other two gentlemen in drinking their *meridian* (a bumper-dram of brandy). **1825** CHAMBERS *Trad. Edinb.* II. 243 It was then [18th c.] the custom of all the shop-keepers in Edinburgh to drink what they called their *meridian*. This was a very moderate debauch,—consisting only in a glass of usquebaugh and a draught of small ale.

2. The point at which the sun or a star attains its highest altitude.

c **1450** LYDG. *Secrees* 347 Phebus..In merydien fervent as the glede. **1647** CRASHAW *Poems* 130 Sharp-sighted as the eagle's eye, that can Outstare the broad-beam'd day's meridian. *a* **1667** COWLEY *Ess.*, *Greatness*, There is in truth no Rising or Meridian of the Sun, but only in respect to several places. **1728** POPE *Dunc.* III. 195 *note*, The device, A Star rising to the Meridian, with this Motto, Ad Summa. **1843** JAMES *Forest Days* viii, The sun had declined about two hours and a half from the meridian.

b. *fig.* The point or period of highest development or perfection, after which decline sets in; culmination, full splendour.

1613 SHAKS. *Hen. VIII*, III. ii. 224 And from that full Meridian of my Glory, I haste now to my Setting. **1638** SIR T. HERBERT *Trav.* (ed. 2) 93 Yet in the meridian of his hopes [he] is dejected by valiant Rustang. *c* **1645** HOWELL *Lett.* (1655) III. ix. 17 Naturall human knowledg is not yet mounted to its Meridian, and highest point of elevation. **1673** TEMPLE *United Prov.* Wks. 1731 I. 67, I am of Opinion, That Trade has, for some Years ago, pass'd its Meridian, and begun sensibly to decay among them. **1700** DRYDEN *Fables* Pref. *Bb, Ovid liv'd when the Roman Tongue was in its Meridian; Chaucer, in the Dawning of our Language. *a* **1761** CAWTHORN *Poems* (1771) 61 My merit in its full meridian shone. *a* **1859** MACAULAY *Hist. Eng.* xxiii. (1861) V. 67 This was the moment at which the fortunes of Montague reached the meridian. The decline was close at hand. **1893** GEORGIANA HILL *Hist. Eng. Dress* II, 268 Dress was in its meridian of ugliness.

c. The middle period of a man's life, when his powers are at the full.

c **1645** HOWELL *Lett.* I. vi. lx. (1655) 307 You seem to marvell I do not marry all this while, considering that I am past the Meridian of my age. **1703** E. WARD *Lond. Spy* XVII. (1706) 406 As for her Age, I believe she was near upon the Meridian. **1795** MASON *Ch. Mus.* ii. 133 When Purcel was in the meridian of his short life. **1864** H. AINSWORTH *John Law* Prol. iii. (1881) 19 Though long past his meridian, and derided as an antiquated beau by the fops of the day. **1873** HAMERTON *Intell. Life* IV. ii. (1875) 143 Any person who has passed the meridian of life.

†**3.** The south. *Obs.* [So L. *meridianum*.]

1430–40 LYDG. *Bochas* VI. i. (1494) t ij b, Nowe in the west, nowe in the oryent, To sech stories north and meredien Of worthy princes that here to fore haue ben. **1432–50** tr. *Higden* (Rolls) I. 47 Asia..whiche goenge from the meridien or sowthe by the este vn to the northe, is compassede on euery syde with the occean. *Ibid.* VI. 41 Machomete made an ydole..havynge the face of hit towarde the meridien. **1601** HOLLAND *Pliny* I. 34 With vs the stars about the North Pole neuer go downe, and those contrariwise about the Meridian neuer rise. *Ibid.* 48 From the Meridian or South-point to the North.

4. [Ellipt. for *meridian circle* or *line*.] **a.** *Astr.* (More explicitly ***celestial m.***) The great circle (of the celestial sphere) which passes through the celestial poles and the zenith of any place on the earth's surface. **b.** (More explicitly ***terrestrial m.***) The great circle (of the earth) which lies in the plane of the celestial meridian of a place, and which passes through the place and the poles; also often applied to that half of this circle that extends from pole to pole through the place.

So named because the sun crosses it at noon. A terrestrial globe, or a map of the earth or part of it, has usually a number of meridians drawn upon it at convenient distances, marked with figures indicating their respective longitude or angular distance on a parallel from the *first meridian*, i.e. the meridian (in British maps that of Greenwich) conventionally determined to be of longitude 0°.

c **1391** CHAUCER *Astrol.* II. §39 And [yf] so be þat two townes haue illike Meridian, or on Meridian, than is the distance of hem bothe ylike fer fro the Est. **1549** *Compl. Scot.* vi. 51 Quhen the sune rysis at our est orizon, than it ascendis quhil it cum til our meridian. **1555** EDEN *Decades* 243 And commaunded a line or meridian to bee drawen Northe and south. **1594** BLUNDEVIL *Exerc.* IV. xviii. (1636) 461 Whereas the Terrestriall Globe is traced with 12 Meridians,..The Celestiall Globe is only traced with 6 Meridians. **1669** STURMY *Mariner's Mag.* II. 93 You must wait..till the Sun is upon the Meridian. **1678** HOBBES *Decam.* viii. 101 It will turn it self till it lye in a Meridian, that is to say, with one and the same Line still North and South. **1698** KEILL *Exam. Th. Earth* (1734) 231 All those who live under the same Meridian have twelve of the Clock at the same time. **1715** tr. *Gregory's Astron.* I. 211 Any such Secondary Circle drawn thro' any Place upon the Earth, is called the Meridian of that Place. *Ibid.* 212 They feigned therefore a first Meridian passing thro' the most Western Place of the Earth, that was then known. **1839** *Penny Cycl.* XV. 110/1 The terrestrial meridian is the section of the earth made by the plane of the celestial meridian. **1841** ELPHINSTONE *Hist. Ind.* II. 177 These two rājas soon reduced the Mussulman frontier to the Kishna on the south, and the meridian of Heiderábád on the east.

c. *transf.* (*a*) *Geom.* Occasionally applied to any great circle of a sphere that passes through the poles, or to a line, on a surface of revolution, that is in a plane with its axis. (*b*) ***magnetic meridian***: the great circle of the earth that passes through any point on its surface and the magnetic poles.

1704 J. HARRIS *Lex. Techn.* I, *Meridian Magnetical*, is a Great Circle passing through or by the Magnetical Poles. *a* **1721** KEILL *Maupertuis' Diss.* (1734) 47 The Meridians of the Spheroids are continually Algebraic Curves. **1832** *Nat. Philos.* II. *Magnet.* iii. 23 (Usef. Knowl. Soc.), The magnetic meridian. **1837** BREWSTER *Magnet.* 11 He..made numerous experiments with bars of iron and steel placed in the magnetic meridian.

d. ***meridian of a globe*** or ***brass meridian***: a graduated ring (sometimes a semicircle only) of brass in which an artificial globe is suspended and revolves concentrically.

1633 G. HERBERT *Temple*, *Size* viii, An earthly globe, On whose meridian was engraven, These seas are tears, and heav'n the haven. **1727–51** CHAMBERS *Cycl.* s.v. *Globe*, The globe itself thus finished, they hang it in a brass meridian.

e. *attrib.* in **meridian circle** (see also MERIDIAN *a.* 3), an astronomical instrument consisting of a telescope carrying a large graduated circle, by which the right ascension and declination of a star may be determined; a transit-circle; **meridian-mark**, a mark fixed at some distance due north or south of an astronomical instrument, by pointing at which the instrument is set in the meridian.

1849 HERSCHEL *Outl. Astron.* §190. 114 Thus also a meridian line may be drawn and a meridian mark erected.

5. *transf.* and *fig.* A locality or situation, considered as separate and distinct from others, and as having its own particular character; the special character or circumstances by which one place, person, set of persons, etc. is distinguished from others. Chiefly in figurative uses of astronomical phrases such as ***calculated to*** or ***for the meridian of*** = 'suited to the tastes, habits, capacities, etc., of'.

1589 R. HARVEY *Pl. Perc.* Ded. 4. I will present you at the law day for a ryot, though I be neither side man for this Meridian, nor Warden. **1621** BURTON *Anat. Mel.* II. ii. I. i. (1651) 231 Which howsoever I treat of, as proper to the Meridian of Melancholy. **1625** B. JONSON *Staple of N.*, *Prol. Court*, A Worke..fitted for your Maiesties disport, And writ to the Meridian of your Court. **1647** CLARENDON *Hist. Reb.* VII. §73 He was, at his suit, brought to the House of Commons' bar; where..with such flattery as was most exactly calculated to that meridian [etc.]. *a* **1677** HALE *Prim. Orig. Man.* I. i. 7 All other knowledge meerly or principally serves the concerns of this Life, and is fitted to the meridian thereof. **1712** ARBUTHNOT *John Bull* III. Publisher's Pref., Though they had been calculated by him only for the meridian of Grub-street, yet they were taken notice of by the better sort. *a* **1718** PENN *Tracts* Wks. 1726 I. 471 His words of the Trinity are modest, neither highly Athanasian, nor yet Socinian,..but calculated to both Meridians. **1748** SMOLLETT *Rod Rand.* xxviii. (1804) 186 This suggestion.. had the desired effect upon the captain, being exactly calculated for the meridian of his intellects. **1751** EARL ORRERY *Remarks Swift* (1752) 141 As this pamphlet was written for the meridian of Ireland. **1816** *Sporting Mag.* XLVIII. 34 This..could not fail in exciting ludicrous ideas, in the minds of the illiterate vulgar, for whose meridian it was calculated. **1835** W. IRVING *Newstead Abbey* Crayon Misc. (1863) 306 A course of anecdotes..such as suited the meridian of the..servants' hall.

meridian (məˈrɪdɪən), *a.* [a. OF. *meridien* (mod.F. *méridien*), or ad. L. *merīdiānus*, f. *merīdiēs* mid-day, noon, dissimilated form of

older *medīdiēs* (Varro), f. *medii-*, *medius* middle + *diēs* day.]

1. Of or pertaining to mid-day or noon. Now *rare* (humorously pedantic) exc. as in 2.

1432–50 tr. *Higden* (Rolls) V. 373 The kynge Albinnus beynge in slepe in his meridien tyme. *c* **1450** LYDG. & BURGH *Secrees* 1601 Moche sleep wyl kepe the in hih Estat,.. Merydien Reste, mylk whight and Argentyne. **1602** *2nd Pt. Return fr. Parnass.* III. iii, Hang me if he hath any more mathematikes then wil..tell the meridian howre by rumbling of his panch. **1620** VENNER *Via Recta* viii. 191 The morning and euening cold, and meridian heate, is cheifely to be auoyded. **1678** R. L'ESTRANGE *Seneca's Mor.* (1702) 349 The Romans had their Morning, and their Meridian Spectacles. **1788** GIBBON *Decl. & F.* xlviii. (1869) III. 27 At the meridian hour he withdrew to his chamber. **1806–7** J. BERESFORD *Miseries Hum. Life* (1826) IV. xliii, The meridian midnight of a thick London fog. **1862** MERIVALE *Rom. Emp.* xli. (1871) V. 80 Every citizen..plunged into the dark recess of his sleeping chamber for the enjoyment of his meridian slumber. **1881** TROLLOPE *Dr. Wortle's School* v. ii, The writer has perhaps learned to regard two glasses of meridian wine as but a moderate amount of sustentation.

†**b.** ***meridian devil***: transl. of Vulg. *dæmonium meridianum* Ps. xc[i], for which the Eng. Bible has 'the destruction that wasteth at noonday'.

a **1550** *Image Ipoc.* II in *Skelton's Wks.* (1843) II. 429 Thou arte a wicked sprite,..A beestely bogorian, And devill meridian. **1550** BALE *Eng. Votaries* II. 118 O deuyls merydyane, as the Prophet doth call yow.

c. ***meridian ring***, a ring so marked within the hoop as to serve the purpose of a sun-dial.

1867 *N. & Q.* 3rd Ser. XI. 381 Some years since I became possessed of a brass ring, about an inch and a half in diameter, which I was told was a meridian ring, and that at some period they were used as a means of ascertaining the time. **1877** W. JONES *Finger-ring* 451 Among the singular uses to which rings have been applied, I may mention what were called 'meridian'.

2. *esp.* Pertaining to the station, aspect, or power of the sun at mid-day.

c **1391** CHAUCER *Astrol.* II. §39 Whan that the sonne.. cometh to his verrey meridian place, than is hit verrey Midday. **1500–20** DUNBAR *Poems* lxxxv. 70 Aue Maria, gratia plena! Haile, sterne meridiane! **1635** QUARLES *Embl.* II. x. (1718) 101 Thou may'st as well expect meridian light From shades of black-mouth'd night. **1664** H. MORE *Myst. Iniq.* xvii. 61 Do naturally vanish in this Meridian and Vertical Sun-shine of the Gospel. **1762–9** FALCONER *Shipwr.* II. 141 The sun his high meridian throne Had left. **1781** CRABBE *Library* 9 Care veils in clouds the sun's meridian beam. **1840** BARHAM *Ingol. Leg., Leech of Folkestone*, The sun rode high in the heavens, and its meridian blaze was powerfully felt. **1898** R. BRIDGES *Growth of Love* Sonn. xxii, Strutting on hot meridian banks.

b. *fig.* Pertaining to or characteristic of the period of greatest elevation or splendour (of a person, state, institution, etc.).

1672 (*title*) A Prophecie lately transcribed..of Doctor Barnaby Googe,..predicting the rising, meridian, and falling condition of the States of the United Provinces. **1751** EARL ORRERY *Remarks Swift* (1752) 69 The poem itself is dated in the year 1713, when Swift was in his meridian altitude. **1796** MORSE *Amer. Geog.* II. 275 It [Dantzic] seems to be somewhat past its meridian glory. **1818** HAZLITT *Eng. Poets* iii. (1870) 59 Those arts, which depend on individual genius,..have always leaped at once..from the first rude dawn of invention to their meridian height and dazzling lustre. **1903** MORLEY *Gladstone* I. 25, 'I was bred', said Mr. Gladstone when risen to meridian splendour, 'under the shadow of the great name of Canning'.

†**c.** Of supreme excellence, consummate; also in bad sense. *Obs.*

1662 GLANVILL *Lux Orient.* Pref. (1682) 3 They lay stress on few matters of opinion, but such as are..very meridian truths. **1728** YOUNG *Love Fame* vi. 47 But with a modern fair, meridian merit Is a fierce thing, they call a nymph of spirit. *a* **1734** NORTH *Exam.* (1740) 186 Was it not strange Usage of a Queen Consort, when such an Effrontery, out of the Mouth of a Meridian Villain, in Public..should be let pass without so much as a Reprehension.

3. Pertaining to a meridian. Chiefly in collocations orig. referable to sense 2. ***meridian circle*** = MERIDIAN *sb.* 4. ***meridian line***: in early use = MERIDIAN *sb.* 4; now usually, a line (on a map, etc.) representing a meridian; also, a line traced on the earth's surface, indicating the course of a portion of a meridian as ascertained by astronomical observations. ***meridian altitude***: the angular distance between the horizon and the sun at noon, or (in later use) any heavenly body when crossing the meridian.

[*Meridian circle* represents L. *circulus meridianus*, transl. of Gr. κύκλος μεσημβρινός (f. μεσημβρία mid-day).]

c **1391** CHAUCER *Astrol.* Prol., Tables..for to fynde the altitude Meridian. *Ibid.* II. §39 The arch meridian þat is contiened or intercept by-twixe the cenyth and the equinoxial. **1549** *Compl. Scot.* vi. 47 It sal declair the eleuatione of the polis, and the lynis parallelis, and the meridian circlis. **1559** W. CUNNINGHAM *Cosmogr. Glasse* 138 If there be no Angle of sighte, it hathe the same Longitude and meridiane Line, and is plaine North or South from you. **1668** MOXON *Mech. Dyall.* 11 If the Sun shine just at Noon, hold up a Plumb-line so as the shadow of it may fall upon your Plane, and that shaddow shall be a Meridian Line. **1669** STURMY *Mariner's Mag.* IV. vii. 168 The true Meridian-distance between Lundy and Barbadoes. *Ibid.* VI. iii. 128 The Meridian-Altitude of an unknown Star. **1719** DE FOE *Crusoe* II. (Globe) 487, I shall not pester my Account ..with..Latitudes, Meridian-Distances,..and the like. **1833** HERSCHEL *Treat. Astron.* (1839) 56 The plane of the meridian is the plane of this circle, and its intersection with the sensible horizon of the spectator is called a meridian line. **1882** FLOYER *Unexpl. Baluchistan* 216 After getting a meridian altitude at noon, we left..for..Jangdā.

b. Passing along a meridian. *nonce-use.*

1658 SIR T. BROWNE *Hydriot.* 1st Epist. Ded., These may seem to have wandered farre, who in a direct and Meridian Travell, have but a few miles of known Earth between your selfe and the Pole.

4. Southern, meridional. *rare.*

1432–50 tr. *Higden* (Rolls) II. 253 Therefore peple descendenge from Sem..hade in possession the londe meridien [L. *terram meridianam*]. **1819** BYRON *Stanzas to the Po*, A stranger..Born far beyond the mountains, but his blood Is all meridian, as if never fann'd By the black wind that chills the polar flood.

5. *Geol.* [fig. use of sense 1: cf. the second quot.] Applied by Professor Rogers to the middle stage of the American palæozoic period, and to the formations representing that stage.

1858 H. D. ROGERS *Geol. Pennsylv.* I. 351 Meridian Strata in Perry County... The Meridian sandstone..is never more than 20 feet thick. *Ibid.* II. II. 749 These periods, applicable only to the American Palæozoic day, are the Primal, Aural,..Pre-Meridian, Meridian, Post-Meridian, Cadent, Vergent [etc.].

meridianal, var. MERIDIONAL *a.*

†**meridiation.** *Obs.*$^{-0}$ [ad. L. *merīdiātiōn-em* f. *merīdi-ēs* noon.] A mid-day rest, siesta.

1623 COCKERAM, *Meridiation*, a sleeping at noone tide. **1658** in PHILLIPS.

†**meridie.** *Obs.* [ad. L. *merīdiēs*.] Noon.

c **1391** CHAUCER *Astrol.* II. §44 Consider thy rote furst..& entere hit in-to thy slate for the laste merydye of December. *Ibid.*, The residue þat lewyth is thy mene mote fro the laste mer[y]die of December.

meridien, obs. form of MERIDIAN.

‖**meridies** (məˈrɪdiːz). *rare*$^{-1}$. [L. *merīdiēs* noon, middle point.] In quot. humorously bombastic for: The middle point (of night).

a **1667** COWLEY *Ess., Country Mouse*, About the Hour that Cynthia's Silver Light Had touch'd the pale Meridies of the Night.

meridional (məˈrɪdɪənəl), *a.* and *sb.* Also **meridianal**. [a. F. *méridional*, ad. late L. *merīdiōnāl-is*, irreg. f. *merīdiēs* mid-day, south: see MERIDIAN *a.*]

A. *adj.*

1. Of or belonging to the south; situated in the south: southern, southerly.

c **1400** MAUNDEV. (1839) xiv. 156 The Est partie & the Meridionalle partie. *c* **1520** BARCLAY *Jugurth* (1557) 49b, The meridyonall parte of the countrey. **1549** *Compl. Scot.* vi. 48 The pole antartic austral or meridional. **1653** R. SANDERS *Physiogn.* 169 The Meridional people are, for the most part, black and curled. **1703** T. N. *City & C. Purchaser* 36 Kitchins..ought to be placed in the Meridional part of the Building. **1830** *Fraser's Mag.* I. 594 We must not forget that Adosinda and Roderick are meridional Europeans. **1880** HAUGHTON *Phys. Geog.* v. 208 The Meridional Chain ..extends along the Western Coast.

absol. **1604** E. G[RIMSTONE] *D'Acosta's Hist. Indies* III. ii. 120 The meridionall (which they of the Ocean call South, and those of the Mediterranean sea, *Mezo giorno*) commonly is raynie and boisterous.

b. Pertaining to or characteristic of the inhabitants of the south (of Europe).

1847 *Blackw. Mag.* LXII. 418 His voice..retained..'a slight meridional accent'. **1860** MOTLEY *Netherl.* v. I. 138 A dark, meridional physiognomy..such was the Prince of Parma. **1905** *Q. Rev.* July 11 That there is such a thing as Latin rhetoric, which corresponds now, as in every preceding age, to the temperament best summed up in the word 'meridional'.

†**2.** Pertaining to the noontide position of the sun. ***meridional line*** = MERIDIAN *sb.* 4. *Obs.*

c **1386** CHAUCER *Sqr.'s T.* 255 Phebus hath laft the Angle meridional. *c* **1391** —— *Astrol.* II. §3 Whan þat þe sonne is ney the Meridional lyne. **1432–50** tr. *Higden* (Rolls) VII. 75 The sonne beynge in the centre meridionalle. **1608** WILLET *Hexapla Exod.* 245 The sun ascendeth vnto the meridianall [*sic*] point. **1796** MORSE *Amer. Geog.* I. 590 Mr. Ellicott drew a true meridional line by celestial observation. **1834** *Nat. Philos.* III. *Astron.* i. 15 (Usef. Knowl. Soc.), They are called meridians, or meridional lines, and the equator bisects all the meridians.

3. Pertaining to or characteristic of noonday; chiefly *fig.* Now *rare* or *Obs.*

1624 DONNE *Serm.* xix. (1640) 192 Meridionall brightnesse, the glorious noon, and heighth, is to be a Christian. **1673** *Lady's Call.* I. v. §39 Are God's safeguards to be only meridional, to shine out only with the noon-day sun? **1762** tr. *Busching's Syst. Geog.* III. 273 So large were the demesnes of this abbey, when in its meridional glory. **1839** *Fraser's Mag.* XIX. 469 All my troubles, cares, anxieties, perplexities—matutinal, meridional, and vespertinal.

4. Of or pertaining to, aligned with, a meridian.

1555 EDEN *Decades* 247 We..sayled from thense .lxxxx. degrees in lengthe meridionale. **1669** STURMY *Mariner's Mag.* IV. vii. 166 This Table of Latitudes, or Meridional Parts. **1709** BERKELEY *Th. Vision* §74 When the moon is viewed..in the meridional position. **1812** WOODHOUSE *Astron.* vii. 47 The meridional altitudes of heavenly bodies. **1882** PROCTOR in *Knowledge* No. 19. 399/2 Stars whose places were already determined by the use of their great meridional instrument. **1900** *Geogr. Jrnl.* XV. 540 The great meridional systems, *e.g.* the Urals and the Rocky mountains. **1936** *Discovery* Mar. 69/2 The endeavour of the continents themselves to rotate is generally in a different direction from that of the poles of the earth, so setting up meridianal directed forces acting westward.

b. Applied to designate markings on a roundish body that lie in a plane with its axis. Cf. MERIDIAN *sb.* 4c.

1658 SIR T. BROWNE *Gard. Cyrus* iv. *Hydriot.* etc. 62 In the circinations and sphærical rounds of Onyons,..the circles of the Orbes are ofttimes larger, and the meridional lines stand wider upon one side then the other. **1881** CARPENTER *Microsc. & Rev.* §427 (ed. 6) 507 Along one side of this body is a meridional groove, resembling that of a peach. **1893** TUCKEY *Amphioxus* 46 This [furrow] is likewise a meridional one, and is at right angles to the first. **1899** *Allbutt's Syst. Med.* VI. 209 Those [anastomoses] between the anterior and the posterior interventricular branch near the apex of the heart, forming a vertical or meridional circle.

B. *sb.* An inhabitant of the south; now *spec.* an inhabitant of the south of France.

1591 SYLVESTER *Du Bartas* I. iii. 209 The Sea..flows again; and then again it falls When she doth light th' other Meridionals. **1621** MOLLE *Camerar. Liv. Libr.* III. xiii. 189 The Meridionalls or Southern inhabitants. **1675** G. R. tr. *Le Grand's Man without Passion* 165 The Meridionals who banish formal courts and reveling from their assemblies, despise not gay cloathing. **1898** BODLEY *France* III. ii. 126 The hero of the trial was..a characteristic Meridional. **1899** MISS V. M. CRAWFORD *Stud. For. Lit.* 50 Daudet was able to paint a real sober picture of the Meridional in *Numa Roumestan*.

meridionality (mə,rɪdɪəˈnælɪtɪ). [f. prec. + -ITY.] The state of being meridional or on the meridian; aspect towards the south; the state of having an alignment or direction along a meridian (i.e. north or south).

1664 POWER *Exp. Philos.* III. 166 So that in process of time it is very probable it [the magnetical needle] will come to an exact Meridionality. **1721** BAILEY, *Meridionality*, it's Scituation in Respect to the Meridian, or the Scituation of its meridian. **1755** JOHNSON, *Meridionality*, position in the South; aspect towards the South. **1973** *Nature* 30 Mar. 295/1 During the present period of meridional global circulation the specific tendency over the European Arctic and sub-Arctic seas has been towards northerly meridionality and climatic deterioration... The increased northerly airflow has been held responsible..for the extension of sea ice to the north Icelandic coast.

meridionally (məˈrɪdɪənəlɪ), *adv.* [f. prec. + -LY².] In the direction of the meridian; north and south. Also, in the direction of the poles (of a magnet).

1613 M. RIDLEY *Magn. Bodies* 33 Cut a part from a Magnet stone meridionally. **1646** SIR T. BROWNE *Pseud. Ep.* II. ii. 58 In this manner pendulous, they [wires] will conforme themselves Meridionally; directing one extreame unto the North, another to the South. **1705** DERHAM in *Phil. Trans.* XXV. 2140 They would exert the same effects that Magnets are said to do, when sawn in two Meridionally. **1886** A. WINCHELL *Walks Geol. Field* 267 Here this broad ocean was interrupted by the meridionally disposed Colorado, Medicine-Bow, and Park Ranges.

merie, merierum, obs. ff. MERRY, MARJORAM.

merigal variant of MERRYGALL.

merihedral, -hedric, -hedrism: incorrect forms (in recent Dicts.) of MEROHEDRAL, -IC, -ISM.

merillon, obs. f. MERLIN.

meril(l)s: see MEREL.

merily, obs. form of MERRILY.

mering, mearing (ˈmɪərɪŋ), *vbl. sb.* Also **mereing**. [f. MERE *v.*² + -ING¹.]

†**1.** The action of the verb MERE; fixing of boundaries. *Obs.*

1574 in *10th Rep. Hist. MSS. Comm.* App. v. 335 Foure Aldermen shalbe elected surveighours yearely..to determyne all mischaunces and variaunces of mearing betwixt thinhabitaunts. **1579–80** NORTH *Plutarch, Numa* (1595) 78 For bounding & mearing, to him that will keepe it iustly: is a bond that brideleth power & desire. *c* **1600** in Renaud *Prestbury* (Chetham Soc.) 44 The meeringe and devydynge of the Churchyarde.

2. *concr.* = MERE *sb.*² 1. (See also quot. 1975.) Also *fig.*

1616 BOYLE *Diary* (1886) I. 132, I had a mearing between Kynaltalloon and Condons Lands held by Mʳ Thomas ffitz John. **1756** C. LUCAS *Ess. Waters* II. 123 These are within the districts of Franchimont, Malmendy and Stavelot, or thereabouts. I can not pretend to distinguish meerings. **1843** BLACKER in *Jrnl. R. Agric. Soc.* IV. II. 445 The necessity for drainage..; the advantage of straight mearings. **1873** O'CURRY *Manners Anc. Irish* III. 4 The same name [*Dun*]..would apply to any boundary or mearing formed of a wet trench between two raised banks or walls of earth. **1900** *Century Mag.* Feb. 605 Billy starts up an' lifts the tether to lead the goat to the mearin' of the parishes. **1920** E. POUND *Umbra* 113 At midnight mirk, In secrecies I nurse My served make In heart; nor try My melodies At other's door nor mearing. **1925** W. B. YEATS *Early Poems & Stories* 449 Some world out of sight and misty, that has for its mearing the colours that are beyond all other colours. **1932** *Instructions to Field Revisers* (Ordnance Survey) App. A. 46 When boundaries have been surveyed, the initials of mereings are shown in ink along the surveyed features. *Ibid.* 48 Mereings on O.S. maps show to which field or inclosure the boundary fence..belongs, whether or not the land on both sides is owned or occupied by one and the same person. **1975** J. B. HARLEY *O.S. Maps* iii. 39 The term mereing has also been extended to apply to the written statement indicating the precise relationship of a boundary to the adjacent detail (for example, 4 ft RH = 4 ft from root of hedge)... Where space permits, mereings in this sense are

placed parallel to the boundary, and when the type of mereing changes (as from the edge of a curb to the face of a wall) a special symbol..indicates the point of change.

3. *attrib.* as in ***mering-balk, -drain, -fence, -hedge, -stone, -wall.***

1769 FRENCH in A. Young *Tour Irel.* (1780) I. 370 He also made a deep mearing drain. **1846** T. KEIGHTLEY *Notes Bucolics & Georgics of Virgil* 9 On this side is the meering or boundary-hedge of sallows between you and your next neighbour. **1865** W. WHITE *E. Eng.* II. 194 A strip of land a rod in width, called a..mereing balk. **1911** J. CAMPBELL (*title*) Mearing stones: leaves from my note-book on tramp in Donegal. **1928** R. A. S. MACALISTER *Archæol. of Ireland* i. 26 A mearing-wall (as boundary-walls are called in Ireland). **1933** *Irish Press* 10 Nov. 1/4 A huge earth bank which serves as a mearing fence between the lands.

meringue[1] (mə'ræŋ, ‖mərɛ̃g). Also 9 erron. **marang.** [a. F. *meringue* (1739 in Hatz.-Darm.), of obscure origin. Cf. Sp. *merengue*, G. *meringe*, *meringel*.] **a.** A delicate confection the chief ingredients of which are pounded sugar and whites of eggs. It is made up in small cakes, or spread as an 'icing' over fruit, tarts, etc. Also, a small cake made of this. Hence ‖**meringué** (mərɛ̃ge), a dish composed of fruit with meringue; **meringued** *ppl. a.*, iced with meringue (= F. *meringué*).

1706 PHILLIPS (ed. Kersey), *Meringues* (Fr. in *Cookery*), a sort of Confection made of the Whites of Eggs whipt; fine Sugar, and grated Lemmon-peel, of the bigness of a Walnut; being proper for the garnishing of several Dishes. **1725** BRADLEY *Fam. Dict.* II. s.v., Meringue; a small sugar work of great use. **1845** ELIZA ACTON *Mod. Cookery* 456 Meringué of Pears... Put the meringue immediately into a moderate oven, and bake it half an hour. **1859** *Eng. Cookery Bk.* 299 Meringued Apples. Pare and core some large pippin apples,..cover them all over with a meringue put on in tablespoonfuls. **1860** O. W. HOLMES *Elsie V.* (1887) 90 There were also *marangs*, and likewise custards. **1892** *Encycl. Cookery* I. 933 Meringue consists essentially of whites of eggs beaten with caster sugar to a froth, and then set in a quick oven. **1896** MRS. CAFFYN *Quaker Grandmother* 8 He..insisted on her partaking of a large glass of iced lemonade, and three meringues.

b. ***meringue (à la) Chantilly***: a meringue filled with Chantilly cream; also *fig.*

1901 C. H. SENN *New Cent. Cookery Bk.* xxvii. 561 *Meringues à la Chantilly*... Fill the shells with whipped cream sweetened with vanilla sugar. **1949** *New Statesman* 15 Oct. 422/2 The food in the cafeteria is excellent, but it is in the dining-room that you get the Meringues Chantilly. **1959** *Listener* 2 July 39/1 For the meringues Chantilly take 3 egg whites. **1962** K. O'HARA *Double Cross Purposes* i. 5 An incredible figure wearing fly-leg heels, a meringue-chantilly hat and a pint of perfume. **1970** SIMON & HOWE *Dict. Gastron.* 264/1 (*heading*) Meringue Chantilly.

meringue[2], var. MERENGUE.

merino (mə'riːnəʊ). [a. Sp. *merino* adj., the distinctive epithet of 'a breed of sheep which is pastured in winter in Estremadura and in summer in *la montaña*' (Sp. Acad.); also applied to the wool of these sheep. Hence F. *mérinos* adj. and sb.

Sp. *merino* adj. represents L. *mājōrīnus* (f. *mājor* greater), prob. in its early sense 'of a larger kind' (Pliny). Etymologists, however, have supposed it to be derived from *merino* sb., overseer of cattle pastures (also the title of certain judicial officers), which represents certain substantival uses of *mājōrīnus* in med. Latin.]

1. a. In full ***merino sheep***: A variety of sheep prized for the fineness of its wool, introduced from Spain to England at the close of the 18th c. and extensively used for the improvement by crossing of the fleece-bearing sheep of Britain and the Colonies. Also *attrib.* as ***merino breed, fleece, flock, stock, wool.***

1781 DILLON *Trav. Spain* 48 The Merino sheep, of which it is computed there are between four and five million in the kingdom. *Ibid.* 53 These Merino flocks. **1810** WELLINGTON in Gurw. *Desp.* (1838) VI. 558 Neither Americans nor English will ever derive any general advantage from the Merinos. **1812** E. SHEPPARD in *Nicholson's Jrnl.* (1813) XXXIV. 122 Having had the experience of more than ten years, both in the growth and manufacture of British Merino wools. **1813** JEFFERSON *Writ.* (1898) IX. 442 The Merino sheep are spreading over the continent and thrive well. **1837** YOUATT *Sheep* v. 146 The Merino flocks and the Merino wool have improved under the more careful management of other countries. *Ibid.* 154 The Merino fleece is in Spain sorted into four parcels. **1879** *Cassell's Techn. Educ.* IV. 260/1 Sheep sprung from the Merino stock.

b. *fig.* **pure merino** *Austral. slang*, an early immigrant to Australia with no convict origins; a member of a leading family in Australian society; a person of fine breeding or good character. Hence as *attrib. phr.*, first-class; well-bred; excellent.

1827 P. CUNNINGHAM *Two Yrs. New South Wales* II. xxiv. 116 The *legitimates*..such as have *legal* reasons for visiting the colony; and the *illegitimates*, or such as are free from that stigma. The *pure Merinos* are a variety of the latter species, who pride themselves on being of the *purest blood* in the colony. **1827** *Monitor* 13 Jan. 2 It operates greatly to the credit of the Pure Merino Bank. **1936** M. FRANKLIN *All that Swagger* vii. 69 It was too early to regard Delacy as a deserter,..he was a pure merino who would not abscond from a fine young wife. **1941** BAKER *Dict. Austral. Slang* 46 *Merino, pure*, originally, a free settler. Later, members of the alleged 'leading families'. Also (adj.) first-class, superlative in quality. **1954** T. RONAN *Vision Splendid* 113 'Old Mentmore,' he explained, 'is one of your pure merino sportsmen: member of all the big racing clubs down south.' **1966** G. W. TURNER *Eng. Lang. Austral. & N.Z.* i. 9 These sterling characters were also known as *pure merinos* when the sheep industry began to be based on imported merino sheep.

2. a. A soft woollen material resembling, but finer than, French cashmere, originally manufactured of merino wool, and later of a fine wool mixed with cotton. Also *attrib.*

1818 M. EDGEWORTH *Let.* 29 Oct. (1971) 130 Tell me which you prefer the Merino or the Queens cloth... The Merino looks much the best in the piece. **1820** G. KEATS *Let.* in Keats *Lett.* (1958) II. 357 We will send Miss Brawn an india Crape dress or merino shawl or something scarce with you, but cheap with us. **1823** *Repos. Arts*, etc. Ser. III. I. 120 Gowns for home-dress..are of velvet, Merino, and *gros de Naples*. **1831** *Lincoln Herald* 9 Sept. 3/6 Trowsers, a pale lavender Merino. **1842** BISCHOFF *Woollen Manuf.* II. 415 They..imitated the article of cotton jeans, in worsted,..to which they gave the name of plainbacks out of which has sprung that..valuable branch of merinos. **1869** E. A. PARKES *Pract. Hygiene* (ed. 3) 405 In merino and other fabrics it [cotton] is used with wool. **1898** G. B. SHAW *Plays* II. *Candida* 82 A black merino skirt.

b. A dress made of this. Also, a merino shawl.

1845 M. M. NOAH *Gleanings* 16 Thin kid shoes and gloves [are worn by the lady of fashion]; a fine merino over her arm. **1848** MRS. GASKELL *Mary Barton* I. iv. 44 She put on her pretty new blue merino, made tight to her throat. **1849** C. BRONTË *Shirley* II. ii. 46 These fine sunny days began to make me ashamed of my winter merino; so I have furbished up a lighter garment. **1873** 'SUSAN COOLIDGE' *What Katy Did at Sch.* ix. 148 She shook her head over the simple, untrimmed merinoes and thick cloth cloaks.

3. A fine woollen yarn used in the manufacture of hosiery. Also *attrib.*

1886 *Housewife* I. 109/1 Garments made of merino, stockingette [etc.]. *Ibid.*, Merino underclothing. *Ibid.*, The material used for darning is..merino. **1888** MAUDE BRADSHAW *Indian Outfits* 23 Gauze-flannel and gauze-merino vests are principally worn. **1903** *Longm. Mag.* June 130 A pair of ordinary merino socks.

4. A variety of potato.

1849 E. EMMONS *Agric. N.Y.* II. 41 Merino Potato... Not highly esteemed for the table. **1853** *Trans. Mich. Agric. Soc.* V. 208 A great many varieties of the potato are cultivated in Europe and America. Some of the more approved kinds are ..the Merino [etc.]. **1887** A. W. TOURGÉE *Button's Inn* 178 He picked up the potatoes,..—delicate white 'Kidneys',.. and coarse red 'Merinoes'.

meriolyne, obs. Sc. form of MARJORAM.

†**merion.** *Obs.* [a. OF. *meriane*, *meriene*:—L. *merīdiāna*: see MERIDIAN *sb.*] Mid-day.

a **1400** *Pistill of Susan* 51 Wiþ two Maidenes al on, Semelyche Suson, On dayes in þe merion, Of Murþes wol here.

‖**meris** ('mɛrɪs). *Biol.* Pl. **merides** ('mɛrɪdiːz). [mod.L., a. Gr. μερίς part (stem μεριδ-); after F. *méride* (Perrier).] A permanent colony of cells which may either remain isolated or multiply by germination to form demes.

[**1883** P. GEDDES in *Encycl. Brit.* XVI. 842/2 Starting from the cell or plastid, he [Perrier] terms a permanent colony a méride. *Ibid.* 843/1 Tissues and organs result from division of labour in the anatomical elements of the mérides, and so have only a secondary individuality.]

merise (mə'riːz). See also MERRY *sb.*[2] [a. F. *merise* (from 13th c.), of unknown origin.] A kind of small black cherry.

1706 PHILLIPS (ed. Kersey), *Merise*, a kind of small bitter Cherry. **1836** *Penny Cycl.* VI. 431/1 The Merise or Merisier, Morello, Kentish and All Saint or everflowering cherry. **1849** *Knife & Fork* 23 About sixty years ago, a fragrant and delightful brandy was distilled from a small tart cherry called merises, a fruit peculiar in the Black Forest.

merish, obs. form of MARISH.

merisis ('mɛrɪsɪs). *Biol.* [mod.L., f. Gr. μερίς part (cf. MERIS) + *-sis*, Gr. suff. of action.] (See quot. 1962.)

1940 [see AUXESIS 2]. **1962** R. RUGH *Exper. Embryol.* (ed. 3) 486/2 *Merisis*, growth by cell multiplication (in plants).

merism ('mɛrɪz(ə)m). *Biol.* [f. Gr. μέρ-ος part, member + -ISM. Cf. Gr. μερισμός division.] (See quot.)

1894 BATESON *Materials Study Variation* 20 This phenomenon of Repetition of Parts..comes near to being a universal character of the bodies of living things. It will..be ..convenient to employ a single term to denote this phenomenon... For this purpose the term Merism will be used.

merismatic (mɛrɪz'mætɪk), *a. Biol.* [f. mod.L. *merisma*, a. Gr. μέρισμα separated part, f. μερίζειν to divide into parts: see -ATIC. In Fr. *mérismatique*.] Of cells, tissues, etc.: Having the property of dividing into portions by the formation of internal partitions. Of processes: Involving this kind of division.

1849 *Rep. & Pap. Botany* (Ray Soc.) 283 On merismatic Formation of Cells in the Development of Pollen. **1861** H. MACMILLAN *Footn. Page Nat.* 185 Diatoms, which carry on the process of merismatic division. **1876** DUNGLISON *Med. Lex.* s.v., 'Merismatic multiplication or reproduction'; that which occurs by the splitting or division of cells or of whole beings.

merismoid (mə'rɪzmɔɪd), *a. Bot.* [f. mod.L. *merisma* (see prec.) + -OID.] Of sporophores, esp. agarics: Having the cap branched or laciniate.

1857 BERKELEY *Cryptog. Bot.* §393 *Odontia* makes way rapidly for *Hydnum* in all its varied forms, resupinate, apodous, lateral, merismoid, and mesopod. **1886** STEVENSON *Hymenomycetes Brit.* II. 325 Merismoid,..resembling a Merisma—i.e. having a branched or laciniate pileus.

merispore ('mɛrɪspɔə(r)). *Biol.* [irreg. f. Gr. μέρος part + σπόρος, σπορά sowing, seed.] One of the secondary cells of a pluricellular spore.

1875 BENNETT & DYER tr. *Sachs' Bot.* 241 Each separate secondary cell of a spore of this description is usually capable of germination, and may be termed a Merispore. **1887** GARNSEY & BALFOUR *De Bary's Fungi* 98 The number of members (merispores) in a compound spore is different in different cases.

‖**merissa** (mə'rɪsə). A fermented beverage made from maize by the natives of the Soudan.

1884 J. COLBORNE *Hicks Pasha* 72 Merissa, the 'national' beverage of the Soudan. **1899** *19th Cent.* Aug. 277 The boy forgot his work over a pot of merissa beer.

merist ('mɛrɪst). *rare*$^{-1}$. [ad. Gr. μεριστής, f. μερίζειν to divide.] A divider.

1872 RUSKIN *Munera P.* 117 *note*, The administrators of the three great divisions of law are severally Archons, Merists, and Dicasts.

meristele (mɛrɪ'stiːl, -'stiːliː). *Bot.* [f. Gr. μερίς part + STELE.] A strand of vascular tissue made up of xylem surrounded by phloem. Hence **meri'stelic** *a.*

1894 S. H. VINES *Student's Text-bk. Bot.* I. 153 When the stem is monostelic, each leaf receives a portion, termed a meristele, of the stele of the stem. **1902** A. G. TANSLEY in *Encycl. Brit.* XXV. 413/1 Such a leaf-bundle contains parts of all the tissues of the stele, and is hence called a meristele. *Ibid.* 414/2 (*caption*) Meristelic arc of collateral bundles, united by conjunctive. **1911** [see DICTYOSTELE]. **1956** *Nature* 4 Feb. 218/1 There is a reduction in the number of meristeles in the axis and in the leaves [of *Dryopteris aristata* under conditions of starvation]. **1964** A. J. BROOK *Living Plant* xxxv. 441 Each vascular strand or meristele, consists of a central core of xylem surrounded by a ring of phloem.

meristem ('mɛrɪstɛm). *Bot.* [irreg. f. Gr. μεριστός divided, divisible, f. μερίζειν to divide, f. μέρος part; with ending after PHLOEM, XYLEM.] The unformed growing cellular tissue of the younger parts of plants; merismatic tissue. Also *attrib.*

1874 *Q. Jrnl. Microsc. Sci.* XIV. 304 The three systems of meristem in the stem. **1882** VINES *Sachs' Bot.* 129 In *Calodracon* (*Cordyline*) *Jacquini*, the meristem-ring is derived immediately, according to Nägeli, from the primary meristem of the apex of the stem. **1908** W. R. FISHER *Schlich's Man. Forestry* (ed. 2) V. I. i. 9 The widening of the cells of the meristem, or primary growing tissue of the yearling shoot, is caused by the water taken from the plasmic contents of the nascent organs. **1954** *Biol. Rev.* XXIX. 62 If the development is delayed, the bud appears as a 'detached meristem' in the sense that it is separated from other meristematic tissues by enlarging vacuolating cells. **1961** F. A. L. CLOWES *Apical Meristems* xi. 110 The primary meristem mantle..is prominent in some monocotyledons. **1967** *Times* 15 Mar. 7/1 The revolutionary method of propagating orchids by 'meristem' cuttings aroused great interest yesterday... This new method consists of cutting a tiny piece from the centre of the stem of an orchid..and placing it in a tube of culture solution. In two months this meristem cutting proliferates, producing as many as 20 tiny plants. **1974** *Nature* 2 Aug. 382/2 All divisions within the apical meristems of the shoots give rise to daughter cells with different fates: some remain meristematic.

Hence **meriste'matic** *a.*, of or of the nature of meristem; **meriste'matically** *adv.*, after the manner of meristem (*Cent. Dict.* 1890).

1882 VINES *Sachs' Bot.* 18 The meristematic cells of Phanerogams. **1894** OLIVER tr. *Kerner's Nat. Hist. Plants* I. 582 The groups of constructive, dividing, and enlarging cells, the so-called meristematic tissue. **1954, 1974** [see above].

meristic (mə'rɪstɪk), *a. Biol.* [f. MERISM: see -ISTIC. Cf. Gr. μεριστικός pertaining to division.] Pertaining to the phenomena of merism. Hence **me'ristically** *adv.*, in a meristic manner.

1894 BATESON *Materials Study Variation* 22 These numerical and geometrical, or, as I propose to call them, meristic changes. *Ibid.* 24 The tarsus of a Cockroach..may, through meristic variation, be divided into only four joints. *Ibid.* 26 The Similar Variation of Parts which are repeated Meristically in Series.

me͵ristoge'netic, *a. Bot.* [f. Gr. μεριστό-ς (see MERISTEM) + -GENETIC.] Produced by a meristem.

1887 GARNSEY & BALFOUR *De Bary's Fungi* 497.

merit ('mɛrɪt), *sb.* Forms: 3–7 **merite**, 4 **meriȝt**, 4–5 **meryt**, 4–6 **meryte**, 5 **merote**, **-et**, **-yde**, **-ytte**, **merrette**, 6 **merete**, **merrit**, *Sc.* **mereit**, 6–7 **meritt(e**, 3– **merit**. [a. OF. *merite* (mod.F. *mérite*), ad. L. *merit-um*, neut. pa. pple. of *merēre*, *merērī* to obtain for one's share, earn as pay, deserve; perh. cogn. w. Gr. μείρεσθαι to receive a share, μέρος share, part.]

†**1.** That which is deserved or has been earned, whether good or evil; due reward or punishment.

a **1300** *Cursor M.* 12890 Ion!.. Hu þat a costes þou was clene, Thoru þi merite was it sene [i.e. *through his being allowed to baptize Jesus*]. **13..** *E. E. Allit. P.* B. 613 3yf euer þy mon vpon molde merit disserued. *c* **1386** CHAUCER *Doctor's T* 277 Heere men may seen how synne hath his merite! *a* **1400–50** *Alexander* 5226 With me pas to my praysid modire þat þou may merote haue & menske & mede for þi werkis. **1484** CAXTON *Curiall* I, Thou.. reputest them the more worthy for to haue rewardes and merites. **1593** SHAKS. *Rich. II*, I. iii. 156 A deerer merit, not so deepe a maime,.. Haue I deserued at your Highnesse hands. *a* **1598** ROLLOCK *Lect. Passion* xvii. (1616) 156 Lord, saue us from the merite of sinne. **1602** MARSTON *Antonio's Rev.* V. v, Now murder shall receive his ample merite. **1643** SIR T. BROWNE *Relig. Med.* I. §7 It is but the merits of our unworthy Natures, if wee sleep in darkness until the last Alarum. **1706** PRIOR *Ode to Queen* 85 Those laurel groves (the merits of thy youth), Which thou from Mahomet didst greatly gain.

2. a. The condition or fact of deserving; 'character with respect to desert of either good or evil' (T.). Also *pl.* in the same sense. Now *rare.*

c **1374** CHAUCER *Boeth.* IV Pr. vi. 109 (Camb. MS.) Alle men wenen þat they han wel deseruyd it [*i.e.* sorowful thinges], and þat they ben of wykkede meryte. *a* **1450** *Knt. de la Tour* (1868) 89 So had she rewarde of her merite in the ende. **1513** BRADSHAW *St. Werburge* Prol. 69 After our meryte we shalbe sure To be rewarded. **1548–9** (Mar.) *Bk. Com. Prayer, Communion*, Not waiyng our merites, but pardonyng our offences, through Christe our Lorde. **1580** SIDNEY *Ps.* XLI. v, Raise me up, that I may once have might, Their meritts to requite. **1594** T. BEDINGFIELD tr. *Machiavelli's Florentine Hist.* (1595) 222 Either of them with others guiltie of the treason, were rewarded with the paines of their merit. **1605** SHAKS. *Lear* V. iii. 44, I do require them of you so to vse them, As we shall find their merites, and our safety May equally determine. **1635** PAGITT *Christianogr.* III. (1636) sig. I 7, I set the Death of our Lord Jesus Christ betwixt me and my bad merit. **1687** A. LOVELL tr. *Thevenot's Trav.* 253 They must be presented according to the merit of the business, whether good or bad. **1722** WOLLASTON *Relig. Nat.* ix. 214 In the future state men shall be placed and treated according to their merit.

b. *the merits* or, rarely, † *the merit* (of a case, question, etc.): chiefly in *Law*, the intrinsic 'rights and wrongs' of the matter, in contradistinction to extraneous points such as the competence of the tribunal or the like. Hence, *to discuss, judge* (a proposal, etc.) *on its merits*, i.e. without regard to anything but its intrinsic excellences or defects. *to have the merits* (Law): of a party to a suit, to be in the right as to the question in dispute (said esp. when for technical reasons a favourable decision cannot be given).

1569 *Reg. Privy Council Scot.* I. 687 The saidis Provest.. and Counsale.. quha best knew the meritis of the saidis actionis. **1621** ELSING *Debates Ho. Lords* (Camden) 115 He humbly desyred a favourable hearing of the meritts of his cause. **1713** SWIFT *Cadenus & V.* 134 Which, if it sped, Wou'd shew the Merits of the Cause Far better, than consulting Laws. **1760** FOOTE *Minor* I. Wks. 1799 I. 235 It is always the rule, to administer a retaining fee before you enter upon the merits. **1813** TAUNTON *Comm. Pleas Cases* III. 170 Inasmuch as the merits were with the Plaintiff.. he [the judge] refused to nonsuit him. **1885** *Law Times* LXXX. 133/1 It did not appear from the affidavits that the defendant had the merits. **1885** *Manch. Exam.* 10 July 5/4 It is not easy to ascertain the exact merits of the dispute. **1887** *Times* (weekly ed.) 17 June 3/2 Men are everywhere examining his policy on its merits. **1898** A. LANG *Making Relig.* iv. 74 The 'merits' of stories of second sight need discussion.

3. a. The quality of deserving well, or of being entitled to reward or gratitude.

1362 LANGL. *P. Pl.* A. I. 157 3e naue no more merit In Masse ne In houres þen Malkyn of hire Maydenhod, þat no Mon desyreþ. *c* **1400** *Rom. Rose* 5909 Selling axeth no guerdoning; Here lyth no thank, ne no meryte. **1432–50** tr. *Higden* (Rolls) IV. 471 This man was utterly unprofitable,.. reioycenge the name of dignite withowte merytte. **1500–20** DUNBAR *Poems* xc. 69 Small merit is of synnes for to irke Quhen thow art ald. **1596** SHAKS. *Merch. V.* II. ix. 39 For who shall goe about To cosen Fortune, and be honourable Without the stampe of merrit, let none presume To weare an vndeserued dignitie. **1612** BACON *Ess., Marriage*, The best works, and of greatest merit for the publike, haue proceeded from the vnmarried or childlesse men. **1781** GIBBON *Decl. & F.* xxxvi. (1869) II. 311 His merit was rewarded by the favour of the prince. **1850** TENNYSON *In Mem.* Prol. 35 For merit lives from man to man, And not from man, O Lord, to thee. **1881** *Contemp. Rev.* XL. 646 The principle of promotion by merit.

b. *spec.* in *Theology*, the quality, in actions or persons, of being entitled to reward from God.

Merit of CONDIGNITY, *of* CONGRUITY: see those words.

a **1225** *Ancr. R.* 160 He biȝet þeos þreo biȝeaten—priuilege of prechur, merit of martirdom, & meidenes mede. *c* **1315** SHOREHAM i. 756 Takc hys deaþ in þy meende: Naut lyȝt[e]: þe more þou þenkest so on hys deaþ, þe more hys þy meryte. *c* **1386** CHAUCER *Sec. Nun's T.* 33 Do me endite Thy maydens deeth, that wan thurgh hire merite The eterneel lyf. *c* **1420** *Chron. Vilod.* 4380 þis meracle þus y-do þorow þe meryde of þis blessud virgyn seynt Ede. *c* **1449** PECOCK *Repr.* I. xx. 119 Bi no deede a man hath merit, saue bi a deede which is the seruice and the lawe of God. **1526** *Pilgr. Perf.* (W. de W. 1531) 4 b, Feyth hath no meryte, where naturall reason of it selfe may discerne.. yᵉ thynge. **1692** BP. PATRICK *Answ. Touchstone* 138 It is frivolous to alledg the word Merit, so often used by the Fathers; for they mean no more thereby, but obtaining that which they are said to merit. *a* **1716** SOUTH *Serm.* (1727) V. x. 387 Merit is an unpardonable Piece of Popery. **1825** CANNING *Sp.* 21 Apr. *Sp.* (1828) V. 394 The next objection.. is, that the Roman Catholics ascribe an overweening merit and efficacy to human actions. **1898** A. G. MORTIMER *Cath. Faith & Practice* II. xi. 311 Merit.. implies a proportion between the work done and the reward given.

c. Claim to gratitude as the cause of some favourable state of things; the honour or credit of bringing about (something).

1711 SWIFT *Jrnl. to Stella* 15 Aug., And if there be no breach, I ought to have the merit of it. **1844** LD. BROUGHAM *Brit. Const.* xii. (1862) 177 The whole merit of the great change.. belongs to the Barons.

4. a. Claim or title to commendation or esteem, excellence, worth.

c **1420** *Pallad. on Husb.* IV. 808 But thingis iiij in hem [stalons] is to biholde: fourme and colour, merite and beaute. *Ibid.* 831 And next hem in merit is dyuers hued: Black bay, & permixt gray, mousdon also, The fomy, spotty hu, and many mo. **1606** G. W[OODCOCKE] *Hist. Ivstine* xxv. 93 There was so much of merit in him, That whereas he had continual warres with Lysimachus [etc.],.. yet was never ouercome by any of them. **1606** SHAKS. *Tr. & Cr.* II. ii. 24 What merit's in that reason which denies The yeelding of her vp? **1709** POPE *Ess. Crit.* 728 To him [Roscommon] the wit of Greece and Rome was known, And ev'ry author's merit but his own. **1711** STEELE *Spect.* No. 178 ¶4 A Woman of Merit. **1713** SWIFT *Cadenus & V.* 342 Merit should be chiefly plac'd In Judgment, Knowledge, Wit, and Taste. **1797** GODWIN *Enquirer* I. vi. 41 The dramatic merit.. of Livy. **1889** D. HANNAY *Capt. Marryat* 147 It is a child's story of merit—nothing more.

†**b.** The condition of being valued or honoured; esteem. *Obs.*

1752 FOOTE *Taste* Pref., Wks. 1799 I. 4 A man, who had ever great merit with his friends.

5. a. Something that entitles to reward or gratitude. Chiefly *pl.*; *spec.* in *Theology*, good works viewed as entitling to reward from God; also, the righteousness and sacrifice (of Christ) as the ground on which God grants forgiveness to sinners.

In the 17th c. sometimes const. *towards* (the person obliged); cf. L. *merita erga aliquem*.

c **1380** WYCLIF *Sel. Wks.* III. 423 Bot merytes of men ben dedis or lyves, þat God of his grace acceptis to mede. *c* **1491** *Chast. Goddes Chyld.* 9 Some for uncunnynge of receyuing of.. al suche gostly comfortis mene that they receyue hem by her owne merites. ? *a* **1500** *Chester Pl.* (Shaks. Soc.) II. 73 To bringe the people to Saulvacion By mirrette of thy bitter passion. **1542–5** BRINKLOW *Lament.* (1874) 86 Manifestly ye cast Christes meretes asyde. *Ibid.* 87 For who soeuer will seke.. to be made righteouse by the lawe, he is gone quite from Christ, and hys merites profyte hym not. **1662** *Bk. Comm. Prayer*, Collect 13th Sund. Trin., That we fail not finally to attain thy heavenly promises, through the merits of Jesus Christ our Lord. **1667** MILTON *P. L.* III. 290 Thy merit Imputed shall absolve them who renounce Thir own both righteous and unrighteous deeds. **1675** tr. *Camden's Hist. Eliz.* IV. (1688) 586 The large Extent of the Spanish Empire, his Powerfulness,.. his great merits towards the Church of Rome, and his taking Place.. before the French King [etc.]. **1807** CRABBE *Par. Reg.* III. 57 His merits thus and not his sins confest, He speaks his hopes and leaves to Heav'n the rest. **1885** *Cath. Dict.* (ed. 3) 495/2 Protestants hold.. that a man really has been justified by faith, or, in other words, that the merits of Christ have been imputed to him. **1897** A. G. MORTIMER *Cath. Faith & Practice* I. v. 83 His superabundant merits, which are laid up as a rich treasure for His Church.

b. In Buddhism (and Jainism), the good actions in one of a person's successive states of existence which help determine his fate in the next; esp. in phr. *to acquire merit.*

1832 C. COLEMAN *Mythol. Hindus* xiii. 220 Like the Buddhas, they [*sc.* the Jains] believe that there is a plurality of heavens and hells; that our rewards and punishments in them depend upon our merit or demerit. **1834** *Jrnl. Asiatic Soc. Bengal* III. 383 These attributes appertain to persons subject to mortal births and deaths, of which the series is as little limited as is that scale of cumulative merits to which it expressly refers. **1853** R. S. HARDY *Man. Budhism* ix. 450 Let him who has the opportunity of acquiring merit, by being born when the precepts of Budha are taught, be careful not to let his privileges pass away without improvement. **1863** E. SCHLAGINTWEIT *Buddhism in Tibet* iv. 25 Emancipation takes place either instantaneously, on account of the merit accumulated in previous existences, or by assiduous attention to the various exercises prescribed. **1876** *Encycl. Brit.* IV. 433/1 This seed of existence Buddhism finds in 'Karma', the sum of merit and demerit. **1901** KIPLING *Kim* xiv. 380 'She has acquired merit beyond all others,' said the lama. 'For to set a man upon the way to Freedom is half as great as though she had herself found it.' 'Umm,' said Kim thoughtfully, considering the past. 'It may be that I have acquired merit also... At least she did not treat me like a child.' **1909** W. J. LOCKE *Septimus* xv. 225 I've done little enough in the world..! Give me this chance of—the Buddhists call it, 'acquiring merit'. **1920** —— *House of Baltazar* iv. 43 'A strong man keeps temptation at his elbow in order to defy it.' 'In that way, honourable master, is merit acquired.' **1935** *Chambers's Encycl.* II. 527/2 According to Buddhist belief, when a man dies he is immediately born again, or appears in a new shape; and that shape may, according to his merit or demerit, be any of the innumerable orders of being composing the Buddhist universe—from a clod to a divinity. **1967** D. T. KAUFFMAN *Dict. Relig. Terms* 309/2 Buddhism sees merit as the result of selfless love. **1972** 'E. PETERS' *Death to Landlords!* xi. 162 The easiest way to peace of mind is to give. It is a fairly cheap way to acquire merit. **1974** *Encycl. Brit. Micropædia* VIII. 303/2 Merit making involves *dāna* (giving, such as offering food and robes to monks or donating a temple or monastery); *sīla* (the keeping of the moral precepts); and *bhāvanā* (the practice of meditation).

6. A commendable quality, an excellence.

1700 DRYDEN *Fables* Pref. *A b, I soon resolv'd to put their Merits to the Trial, by turning some of the Canterbury Tales into our Language. **1774** GOLDSM. *Retal.* 49 Would you ask for his merits? Alas! he had none. **1874** MICKLETHWAITE *Mod. Par. Churches* 185 The other method has the merit of economy. **1897** R. LE GALLIENNE in *Westm. Gaz.* 19 May 2/1 Faults first, merits afterwards! Such is our uncomfortable critical habit.

7. Phr. *to make a merit of*: to account or represent (some action of one's own) as meritorious. † *to make merit with*: to establish a claim to the gratitude of (a person).

1682 DRYDEN & LEE *Duke of Guise* IV. iii. (1683) 47 Stay here, and make a merit of your Love. **1691** DRYDEN *K. Arthur* II. 20 You might have made a Merit of your Theft. **1741** RICHARDSON *Pamela* (1824) I. 220 It made her a great merit with me, that she kept it [the secret]. **1759** FRANKLIN *Ess.* Wks. 1840 III. 271 He makes a merit of having gone farther in his condescensions. **1780** BURKE *Sp. at Bristol* Wks. 1842 I. 261, I might not only secure my acquittal, but make merit with the opposers of the bill. **1832** HT. MARTINEAU *Homes Abr.* vii. 104 He had made a merit of remaining at his work. **1860** READE *Cloister & H.* lxxx, He.. made a merit of it to himself.

8. Short for *merit card* (see 9, quot. 1879).

9. *attrib.* and *Comb.*, chiefly in recent terms denoting rewards for proficiency in school work, or prizes for skill in some athletic pursuit, as *merit certificate, cup, grant, medal*; also *merit-conscious, -like* adjs.; **merit-card**, in English elementary schools (see quot.); **merit increase**, an increase in pay resulting from *merit rating*; † **merit-merchant** = MERIT-MONGER; **merit money**, the money awarded in a merit increase; also *attrib.*; **merit rating**, the assessment of an employee's ability to do his job; a measurement of this ability; also *attrib.*; hence *merit rate*; **merit system**, the system of giving promotion in the civil service according to the deserts of the candidates (in U.S. opposed to 'spoils system'); † **merit-works**, 'good works' done for the sake of acquiring merit; so † **merit-worker** = MERIT-MONGER.

1879 RICE-WIGGIN & GRAVES *Elem. Sch. Manager* 105 The '*merit-card' system. Under this system, a cheap coloured ticket.. is given.. to every scholar who has made the total number of attendances possible in the previous week. When a scholar has gained twelve of these 'merits' he receives a prize in exchange for them. **1901** *Westm. Gaz.* 13 Feb. 10/1 They refuse to give a *merit-certificate to any child known to be addicted to cigarette-smoking. **1757** MR. & MRS. GREVILLE *Maxims, Charac. & Refl.* 130 A determined *merit-conscious air. **1902** *Westm. Gaz.* 29 Oct. 12/2 The 42nd.. won the *merit cup in open competition in shooting. **1882** *New Educ. Code* (ed. J. Russell) 28 No *merit grant is made unless [etc.]. **1952** *Federal Register* (U.S.) 15 Feb. 1466/1 The type of increase (such as 'ten percent increase', '*merit or length of service increase', 'inter-plant inequity'). **1959** J. H. TAYLOR *Personnel Administration* vii. 146 The descending line of authority should have a systematic basis for consideration of merit increases. **1961** R. LIKERT *New Patterns Managem.* ii. 15 Motivational forces.. are involved in reactions to rating systems linked to merit increases. **1967** H. B. MAYNARD *Handbk. Business Administration* XI. x. 109 Generally, merit increases are granted for improved performance. **1973** *Daily Tel.* 10 Mar. 2/5 The inquiry found considerable support for general changes in salary levels to be clearly distinguished from individual 'merit' increases. **1645** RUTHERFORD *Tryal & Tri. Faith* (1845) 175 This would seem pharisaical, and *merit-like, if holiness did not relate to the free promise of the covenant of grace. **1902** *Daily Chron.* 27 Oct. 9/6 Mr. Robert Maxwell, who won the *merit medal last year,.. proved successful. **1647** TRAPP *Comm.* I *Cor.* ix. 17 God will cast all such *merit-merchants out of his Temple. **1947** O. DE R. FOENANDER *Industr. Regulation Austral.* ix. 84 '*Merit money', whether purely voluntary, or under pressure from the Court in profitable industries, had, too, expanded. **1963** *Times* 11 Feb. 7/2 On the question of 'merit money' a spokesman said the title was misleading, and though theoretically such payments were at the discretion of supervisory staff they were not always based on merit and were sometimes virtually automatic. **1964** *Daily Tel.* 16 Jan. 23/1 (*heading*) Teachers' merit money urged by Bow Group. **1967** *Economist* 15 Apr. 278/2 The company's previous merit-money system has proved both unfair and inflationary. **1946** F. H. JOHNSON et al. *Job Evaluation* xiii. 264 Experience has shown that *merit rating's principal effect is to control the flow of newer workers as they go up the ladder. **1947** GILBRETH & COOK *Foreman in Manpower Managem.* xiv. 183 Requests for detailed discussion of the foreman's merit-rating sheet with executives will furnish a series of points of view.. which should be invaluable. **1954** *Merit Rating* (Brit. Inst. Managem.) ii. 6 An employee's merit rating history is invaluable for promotion purposes. **1959** *Gloss. Terms Work Study* (*B.S.I.*) 26 *Merit rating*, the systematic assessment of the behaviour and/or ability of workers in their work... *Merit rate*, the wage increment for a worker's merit. **1967** COULTHARD & SMITH in Wills & Yearsley *Handbk. Managem. Technol.* 206 Regrettably, the merit-rating forms usually place the emphasis on personality traits rather than performance... A more limited group have taken the merit-rating report to the next logical stage and set up a system of annual feedback meetings at which the manager and the subordinate carry out a post-mortem on the past year's work. **1880** D. B. EATON *Civ. Service Gt. Brit.* 161 The *merit system of appointments and promotions. **1899** *Nation* (N.Y.) 1 June 414/3 Some of the characteristics of the merit system as exemplified in the consular and diplomatic service of Great Britain. **1635** PAGITT *Christianogr.* I. iii. (1636) 109 Workes of Supererogation and *Merit workes. **1577** tr. *Bullinger's Decades* III. ix. 467 The name of Merits is.. not vsed in the Scriptures. For in that signification wherein our *Merite woorkers vse it, to wit, for meritorious woorkes, [etc.].

merit ('mɛrɪt), *v.* [a. F. *mérite-r*, f. *mérite* MERIT *sb.* Latin had *meritāre* (frequentative of *merērī*) to earn (money), to serve as a soldier.]

†**1.** *trans.* To reward, recompense. *Obs. rare.*

1484 CAXTON *Fables of Æsop* II. xix, An almesse that is done for vayne glorye is not merited but dismeryted. *c* 1500 *Melusine* xxxvi 264, I thanke you of this lyberall offre to goo with me & I shall meryte you, therfore, yf it playse god. *c* 1611 CHAPMAN *Iliad* IX. 258 Which if thou wilt surcease, The king will merite it with gifts.

2. To be or become entitled to or worthy of (reward, punishment, good or evil fortune or estimation, etc.); = DESERVE *v.* 1 and 2.

1526 *Pilgr. Perf.* (W. de W. 1531) 11 b, Who may meryte or deserue Grace beynge in synne? 1596 SHAKS. *Tam. Shr.* IV. iii. 41, I am sure sweet Kate, this kindnesse merites thankes. 1601 ? MARSTON *Pasquil & Kath.* II. 313 Any that meriteth the name of man. 1671 MILTON *P. R.* II. 456 Extol not Riches then,..more apt To slacken Virtue,..Then prompt her to do aught may merit praise. 1718 *Free-thinker* No. 8. 54 This presumptuous Wretch highly merited the Sentence pronounced upon him by Law. 1746 W. HORSLEY *Fool* (1748) I. 203 To what End, but to merit being robbed again? 1775 HARRIS *Philos. Arrangem.* Wks. (1841) 357 Others that less merit, or at least that we esteem less to merit our regard and attention. 1805 tr. *Lafontaine's Hermann & Emilia* III. 249 God knows how I have merited..that my last days should pass with so much satisfaction. 1813 SHELLEY *Q. Mab* III. 85 She only knows How justly to proportion to the fault The punishment it merits. 1842 TENNYSON *St. Simeon* 132 Good people, you do ill to kneel to me. What is it I can have done to merit this? 1884 *Manch. Exam.* 14 May 5/2 They would richly merit the severest censure.

b. with *inf.* as *obj.* (In early use occas.: †To obtain as one's deserts.)

a 1533 LD. BERNERS *Gold. Bk. M. Aurel.* (1546) H viij b, He merited to lese his life with .xxiii. strokes of penknyues. 1621 LADY M. WROTH *Urania* 488 Shee was farre from being contemptible, though not meriting to be admired. 1709 MRS. MANLEY *Secret Mem.* (1736) I. 114 You merit to be beloved. 1719 DE FOE *Crusoe* (1840) II. vi. 123 He merited..to be trusted. 1805 tr. *Lafontaine's Hermann & Emilia* III. 123 His wife..who merited to be the intimate friend of Emilia. *a* 1814 *Theodora* I. i. in *New Brit. Theatre* I. 280 Have I not merited to be unhappy?

c. Said of things.

1601 SHAKS. *All's Well* II. iii. 291 France is a dog-hole, and it no more merits The tread of a mans foot. 1626 C. POTTER tr. *Sarpi's Hist. Quarrels* 182 His counsels merited to be followed. 1656 EARL MONM. *Boccalini's Advts. fr. Parnass.* I. xxxi. 55 It merits memory, that..Virgil..caused Servius to be bastinadoed by his servant Daretes. 1768–74 TUCKER *Lt. Nat.* (1834) II. 170 Should he add that the combatants had the dress and appearance of gentlemen, I should think, to use the newspaper phrase, the thing merited confirmation. 1769 E. BANCROFT *Guiana* 350 My knowledge..being too imperfect to merit a communication. 1792 *Gentl. Mag.* 9/2 The subject..merits the attention of ..discerning minds.

3. *absol.* or *intr.* To be deserving of good or evil. Chiefly in phrase ***to merit well*** (*of* a person), and in clauses with *as* or *than*, where there is ellipsis of an infinitive.

1599 SHAKS. *Much Ado* III. i. 19 When I doe name him, let it be thy part, To praise him more then euer man did merit. 1626 C. POTTER tr. *Sarpi's Hist. Quarrels* 147 It seemed vnto the Spaniards that they had well merited of the Holy See. 1647 CLARENDON *Hist. Reb.* II. §51 The Earl of Essex who had merited very well throughout the whole Affair..was discharged..without ordinary Ceremony. 1719 *Freethinker* III. 183 The late Mr. Savery..merited largely from Posterity by the Invention of an Engine. 1767 S. PATERSON *Another Trav.* I. 120 Those men have merited so well of the republic of letters. 1887 BOWEN *Virg. Æneid* IV. 549 Die! as thy frailties merit; let steel thy sufferings close.

4. *trans.* To earn by meritorious action; *spec.* in *Theology*, to become entitled to (reward) at the hands of God; also, of Christ, to obtain by his merits (spiritual blessings) for mankind.

1543 JOYE *Confut. Winchester's Articles* 1 Winchester wold proue that workes muste iustifye, that is to saye, with owr workes we muste merite the remission of owr synnes. 1586 HOOKER *Disc. Justif.* §21 (1612) 27 Did they think that men doe merit rewards in heauen by the workes they performe on earth? 1588 A. KING tr. *Canisius' Catech.* 153 Christ is..that Lamb of God..quha onelie culd meritt vnto ws remission of sinnes. 1654 FULLER *Two Serm.* 53 For whom Christ merited Faith, Repentance, and Perseverance. 1674 HICKMAN *Quinquart. Hist.* (ed. 2) 107 Christ by his death did merit some supernatural things for the wicked. 1697 DRYDEN *Æneid* v. 465 What Prize may Nisus from your Bounty claim, Who merited the first Rewards? 1748 BUTLER *Serm.* Wks. 1874 II. 304 By fervent charity he may even merit forgiveness of men. 1898 A. G. MORTIMER *Cath. Faith & Practice* II. xi. 316 No man..can merit the first grace, or justification, nor, if he fall into mortal sin, can he merit a recovery from that state. Nor can he merit final perseverance.

5. *intr.* To acquire merit; to become entitled to reward, gratitude, or commendation. *Obs.* exc. *Theol.*

1526 *Pilgr. Perf.* (W. de W. 1531) 160 b, I meryte not in so sayenge my duty. 1530 PALSGR. 635/1 Some man maye meryte as moche to drinke small wyne as some do whan they drinke water. 1577 FULKE *Confut. Purg.* 451 Euery man must merite for him selfe. 1648 H. GRESBY tr. *Balzac's Prince* 260 The Mahometans think they merit when they kill strangers. *a* 1715 BURNET *Own Time* II. (1724) I. 147 Scotland, that had merited eminently at the King's hands ever since the year 1648. *a* 1718 W. PENN *Tracts* Wks. 1726 I. 481 No Man can merit for another. 1724 SWIFT *Drapier's Humble Addr.* Wks. 1751 IX. 80, I..am resolved that none shall merit at my Expence. 1897 A. G. MORTIMER *Cath. Faith & Practice* I. xi. 166 While we are in a state of mortal sin we cannot merit.

meritable ('mɛrɪtəb(ə)l), *a.* [f. MERIT *sb.* + -ABLE.] = MERITORIOUS.

1415 in Visct. Tarbat *Vindic. Rob. III* (1695) 37 That is meritable thing to bere Witness to the suthfastness. 1420 in Tytler *Hist. Scot.* (1864) II. 380 It is needeful and meritabil to ber lele witness to suthfastness to your Universitie. 1513 DOUGLAS *Æneis* XI. Prol. 162 Haill thy meryt thou had tofor thi fall, That is to say, thy warkis meritable, Restorit ar agane. 1598–9 B. JONSON *Case is Altered* II. iv, The people generally are very acceptiue, and apt to applaud any meritable worke. 1708 CIBBER *Lady's Last Stake* v. 62 O! there is a meritable Goodness in those Fears that cannot fail to Conquer. 1791–1823 D'ISRAELI *Cur. Lit.* (1851) 158 Several pious persons have considered it as highly meritable to abstain from the reading of poetry. 1927 *Observer* 20 Feb. 13/1, I should still have some meritable pieces left over in case the visitor wished to go to a few matinées. 1928 *Ibid* 15 Apr. 8 What an odd yet meritable set of people.

merited ('mɛrɪtɪd), *ppl. a.* [f. MERIT *v.* + -ED¹.] Deserved; well-earned.

1603 SHAKS. *Meas. for M.* III i. 206, I doe make my selfe beleeue that you may most vprighteously do a poor wronged Lady a merited benefit. 1787 MME. D'ARBLAY *Diary* 19 Aug., Seeing me the only person punished by her merited resentment. 1800 *Proc. E. Ind. Ho.* in *Asiat. Ann. Reg.* 149/2 A well merited compliment to the abilities and integrity of Sir Thomas Strange. 1835 URE *Philos. Manuf.* 412 To secure to New Lanark mills a merited celebrity. 1887 *Athenæum* 19 Feb. 251/2 Mr. Hall has acquired a merited reputation.

Hence **'meritedly** *adv.*, deservedly.

1665 MANLEY *Grotius' Low C. Wars* 95 Meritedly therefore, they desire an equal share of Liberty. 1857 HOOPER *Chapman's Iliad* Introd. 8 Many of these were of mushroom growth, and have meritedly sunk into oblivion.

†'meriter. *Obs.* Also 7 meritour. [f. MERIT *v.* + -ER¹.] One who or something which merits.

1607 HIERON *Wks.* I. 423 God the Sonne reneweth, as being the mediator and meriter of this changed estate. 1617 [see MERITRESS]. *a* 1626 BACON *Confess. Faith* Resusc. (1657) II. 120 A Meriter of Glory and the Kingdom. 1651 BAXTER *Inf. Bapt.* 143 We smart by that sin for which we smart, so that it is the means as well as the meriter of our misery.

†'meritful, *a. Obs. rare*⁻¹. [f. MERIT *sb.* + -FUL.] Full of merit, meritorious.

1660 WATERHOUSE *Arms & Arm.* 91 Meritful instances of Vertue.

merithal ('mɛrɪθæl). *Bot.* Also in mod.L. form **meri'thallus** (pl. *-thalli*). [f. Gr. μέρο-ς part + θαλλός a young shoot, frond.] A name originally given by Du Petit-Thouars (1756–1831) to an internode, but later applied with qualifying word to each of the three parts of the plant leaf, and by Gaudichaud to each of the three parts of a compound plant, the *radicular, cauline* and *foliar merithal.*

1849 *Rep. & Pap. Botany* (Ray Soc.) 255 On Gaudichaud's Theory of the Merithals. 1849 BALFOUR *Man. Bot.* §139, §169, §639.

meriting ('mɛrɪtɪŋ), *vbl. sb.* [-ING¹.] The action of the verb MERIT in various senses.

1549 COVERDALE, etc, *Erasm. Par. Ephes.* Prol., Stickyng to olde heathenyshe idolatrous worshippinges,..masse meritinges,..popyshe customes [etc.]. 1671 WOODHEAD *St. Teresa* II. iii. 20 They must help each other both in suffering, and meriting. 1851 C. L. SMITH tr. *Tasso* v. xvi, The other was proud of his own meritings.

meriting ('mɛrɪtɪŋ), *ppl. a.* Now *rare.* [f. MERIT *v.* + -ING².] That merits (something indicated in the context); also in 17th c. often *gen.*, deserving, meritorious.

1603 B. JONSON *Sejanus* v. x, If I could loose All my humanity now, 'twere well to torture So meriting a Traytor. 1605 BACON *Adv. Learn.* I. i. §3 It hath rather a sounding and vnworthie glorie, than a meriting and substantiall vertue. 1633 ROGERS *Treat. Sacram.* I. 86 The Holy Ghost expresses the meriting causes diversly. 1656 S. HOLLAND *Zara* (1719) 87 The most merriting Madam in the world. 1732 SWIFT *Advantages repealing Sacram. Test.* Wks. 1761 III. 292 There may be another Seminary in View, more numerous and more needy, as well as more meriting. 1742 J. GLAS *Treat. Lord's Supper* III. v. 137 The infinite, atoning, meriting Virtue of the Sacrifice. 1747 RICHARDSON *Clarissa* (1811) I. 243 Punishments are of service to offenders; rewards should be only to the meriting.

†'meritist. *Obs. rare*⁻¹. [f. MERIT *v.* + -IST.] A believer in the merit of good works.

1612 R. SHELDON *Serm. St. Martin's* 58 Let Leo an Ancient Pope confront against these latter Pontificians all of them being meritists (*de condigno* or *de congruo*) out of condignitie or congruitie *Ibid.* 59 All yee Pontifician Meritists out of congruitie and *de congruo*.

meritless ('mɛrɪtlɪs), *a.* [f. MERIT *sb.* + -LESS.]

1. Without merit; undeserving; worthless.

1596 DRAYTON *Leg.* i. 769 Esteeming Titles meritlesse and nought. 1630 J. TAYLOR (Water P.) *Wks.* I. 40, I am altogether meritlesse of any good. 1786 *Francis the Philanthropist* I. 217 Titles, too often right honourable only in the herald's book and the meritless patent of creation. 1891 *Athenæum* 1 Aug. 154/3 The volume is, in fact, as meritless as such volumes often are.

†2. Unmerited, undeserved. *Obs. rare.*

1603 *Cont. Adv. Don Sebast.* in *Harl. Misc.* (1810) V. 468, I have been grieved for your meritless afflictions. 1621 BRATHWAIT *Nat. Embassie*, etc. 251 Will..your flatt'ring humour nere haue end, Of all other meritlesse?

'merit-,monger. *contemptuous.* One who trades in merits; one who seeks to merit salvation or eternal reward by good works. (Very common in 16–17th c.)

1552 LATIMER *Serm.* (1562) 92 b, These merites mongers [*marg.* Merite mongers] haue so many good workes, that they be able to sell them for money 1626 PRYNNE *Perpet. Regen. Man's Est.* 258 Such a one which is justified, meerely by his owne righteousnesse, as your Popish merit mongers seeke to be. 1696 LORIMER *Goodwin's Disc.* vii. 85 Augustin, the great Defender of the Freeness of God's Grace..against all Merit-Mongers. 1846 HARE *Mission Comf.* (1850) 243 When merit-mongers teach, they add one thirst to another, and spin one law out of another.

Hence **merit-mongering** *vbl. sb.*; **merit-mongery**, a dealing in merits; **merit-monging** *ppl. a.*

1611 W. SCLATER *Key* (1629) 28 Let all..merit-monging-Preachers, iudge how well they carie themselues in their ministerie, that by magnifying the power of nature, crosse the verie end of their ministerie. 1845 H. ROGERS *Ess.* (1874) I. iii. 139 Luther..asserted against that whole system of spiritual barter and merit-mongering..his counter principle of the perfect gratuitousness of salvation. 1856 SPURGEON *Serm. New Park Street Pulpit* II. 95 Even among Protestants meritmongery is not gone by.

meritocracy (mɛrɪ'tɒkrəsɪ). [f. MERIT *sb.* + -OCRACY.] Government by persons selected on the basis of merit in a competitive educational system; a society so governed; a ruling or influential class of educated people. Hence **'meritocrat** *sb.* and *a.*; **,merito'cratic** *a.*

1958 M. YOUNG *Rise of Meritocracy* iv. 71 Before the meritocracy was fully established, age-stratification as a substitute for the hereditary order may have been necessary for the sake of social stability. 1958 *Economist* 1 Nov. 407/1 Mr Young's meritocratic Britain, though described with ostensible enthusiasm, is an odious place. 1960 *Guardian* 28 Apr. 10/4 If it [*sc.* Oxbridge] adopts purely intellectual criteria it..is accused..of creating an isolated meritocracy. 1960 *20th Cent.* Apr. 358 They teach their future rulers, oligarchic or meritocrat, how to acquire and wield power. 1961 *Harper's Bazaar* Feb. 56/1 The grammar schools..have given birth to a new class, the meritocracy. 1961 D. JENKINS *Equality & Excellence* vi. 110 One of [Michael] Young's most unlikely prognostications is that the best public schools will be taken over by the meritocrats. 1964 M. ARGYLE *Psychol. & Social Probl.* xi. 146 Selection in Britain is not only producing a meritocracy, but is perpetuating a class system. 1966 *Guardian* 9 July 4/3 The lobby which says the independent schools produce 'insensitive meritocrats'. 1967 *New Scientist* 10 Aug. 308/1 Public subsidy of the future meritocrat elite is efficient, but inequitable. 1969 *Sci. Jrnl.* June 9 Pronouncements on the issue by scientists alone might appear to be the jabberings of a meritocracy. 1973 *Guardian* 21 Apr. 13/8 The monarchy ..is, perhaps, our last stronghold..against the relentless advance of the meritocracy. 1973 *New Statesman* 28 Sept. 410/3 On the surface his background was impeccable for a rising Labour politician in the meritocratic Forties and Fifties. 1975 *Times Lit. Suppl.* 2 May 471/2 Keynes..was a meritocrat—not a democrat.

meritoir(e, variants of MERITORY.

meritor, variant of MERITER, MERITORY.

†meri'torian. *Obs. rare*⁻¹. [f. L. *meritōri-us* (see MERITORIOUS) + -AN.] One who believes or teaches the saving efficacy of good works.

1689 T. PLUNKET *Char. Gd. Commander* 53 What Paul or Peter, what Boanerges can Reach Meritorians to the Son of Man?

†meritorily, *adv. Obs.* [f. MERITORY *a.* + -LY².] Meritoriously. Also, deservedly.

c 1400 *Apol. Loll.* 15 No creature mai do iustli, wele, meritorili,..ne perseuerantli ani þing, not but if God wirk þat þing bi him, & in him. *c* 1449 PECOCK *Repr.* I. xx. 120 Ech of these deedis mowe be doon..vertuoseli and merytorili. 1502 ARNOLDE *Chron.* (1811) 177 Worthi and merytoryly they fallen in this sentence of corsyng.

meritorious (mɛrɪ'tɔərɪəs), *a.* [f. L. *meritōri-us* pertaining to the earning of money, earning or serving to earn money (f. *merēre*, *-ērī* to earn, deserve: see MERIT *sb.* and -ORY²) + -OUS.]

1. Of actions: Serving to earn reward; esp. in *Theology*, said of good works, penance, etc., as entitling to reward from God; productive of merit (†const. *to* the agent).

1432–50 tr. *Higden* (Rolls) IV. 405 The pilgrimage made to thapostles was more meritorius to the sawle than the faste of ij. yere. *Ibid.* VII. 169 Noble men of the realme purchasede of the pope that iourney to be prohibite, and to be chaungede into oþer meritorious dedes. *a* 1539 in *Archæologia* XLVII. 56 Charyte..without whiche..noo vertue can..be acceptable to almighty god, nor merytoryous to the doer. 1665 SIR T. HERBERT *Trav.* (1677) 84 'Twixt Baroch and Amadavad is intombed Polly-Medina a Mahometan Saint, highly reputed by the people; who in a way of meretorious Pilgrimage repair thither. 1681–6 J. SCOTT *Chr. Life* (1747) III. 176 In the precious Blood of this our meritorious and accepted Sacrifice we openly behold the Mercy of God. 1851 PUSEY *Let. Bp. London* 130/1 That our due sufferings might be sanctified by His, the Atoning and Meritorious Sufferings. 1856 P. E. DOVE *Logic Chr. Faith* VI. §5. 363 Man could not observe the law in any sense of meritorious observance.

†2. Of an action or agent: That earns or deserves some specified good or evil. Const. *of*. *Obs.*

1561 T. NORTON *Calvin's Inst.* I. Pref., Workes meritorious of eternall saluation. 1567 FENTON *Trag. Disc.* 1 b, If he..seame justly meritorious of reproche, we maye worthely imparte treble prayse to a barbarous Turke. 1641 H. L'ESTRANGE *God's Sabbath* 136 Which abuse..is I think

condignly meritorious of severe punishment. **1641** J. SHUTE *Sarah & Hagar* (1649) 140 Shall we think the doing of our duty to be meritorious of that which God hath promised? **1679** PULLER *Moder. Ch. Eng.* xi. 318 The Penances in the Church of Rome, which..are counted Deletory of Sin, and Meritorious of Pardon, our Church doth account no otherwise than Superstitious. **1682** *2nd Plea Nonconf.* 63 He must really be persuaded..that all ways of Worship.. different..from the Church of England, is meritorious of personal Ruine. **1709** MRS. MANLEY *Secret Mem.* (1736) III. 181 Cataline..would do something meritorious of his Promotion. *a* **1716** SOUTH *Serm.* (1717) V. 130 These Practices were satisfactory for Sin, and meritorious of Heaven. *a* **1758** EDWARDS *Hist. Redemption* III. ii. (1793) 322 [He] made it meritorious of salvation to fight for Him.

b. ***meritorious cause***: an action or agent that causes by meriting (some good or evil result).

1526 *Pilgr. Perf.* (W. de W. 1531) 136 b, God is the werker of ye sycknes & payne,..though man of hymselfe or woman be the cause merytoryous. **1688** BUNYAN *Jerus. Sinner Saved* (1700) 138 His Blood..is the meritorious cause of mans redemption. *a* **1703** BURKITT *On N.T.* Luke v. 26 Sin is the meritorious cause of sickness. **1828** A. JOLLY *Observ. Sund. Serv.* (1848) 178 The death which He endured was the meritorious cause of our life.

3. Deserving of reward or gratitude. Also (now usually) in vaguer use: Well-deserving; meriting commendation; having merit.

In recent literary criticism the word tends to be a term of limited praise, applied, e.g., to work that is recognized as painstaking and useful, but does not call forth any special warmth of commendation.

1494 FABYAN *Chron.* VII. 482 Good and merytoryous dedys shulde be holden in memorye. **1596** SPENSER *State Irel.* (Globe) 612/2 Insteede of so great and meritorious a service as they bost they performed to the King,..they did great hurt unto his title. **1625** B. JONSON *Staple of N.* II. iv, My meritorious Captaine..Merit will keepe no house nor pay no house rent. **1651** HOBBES *Leviathan* II. xxvii. 153 What Marius makes a Crime, Sylla shall make meritorious. **1773** *Parl. Deb.* 21 May, Mr. Solicitor General then moved, That Robert Lord Clive did, at the same time, render great and meritorious services to this country. **1781** GIBBON *Decl. & F.* xxxviii. (1869) II. 399 Revenge was always honourable, and often meritorious. **1817** BROUGHAM in *Parl. Deb.* 1799 The more this transaction was sifted, the more blameless..would the conduct of that meritorious individual appear. **1832** HT. MARTINEAU *Ella of Gar.* vi. 67 His patience had been most meritorious. **1905** *Athenæum* 24 June 774/2 In regard to historical accuracy..the volume is on the whole meritorious.

absol. **1682** DRYDEN & LEE *Duke of Guise* II. ii. (1683) 18, I will have strict Examination made Betwixt the Meritorious and the Base. *a* **1704** T. BROWN *Praise of Wealth* Wks. 1730 I. 84 None but the meritorious shall be fortunate.

Comb. **1821** LAMB *Elia* Ser. I. *All Fools' Day*, A pair of so goodly-propertied and meritorious-equal damsels.

†**4.** Bestowed in accordance with merit; merited.

1597 MIDDLETON *Wisd. Solomon* i. 9 God's heavy wrath and meritorious blame. **1632** LITHGOW *Trav.* x. 456 The Heauens have reducted me to this meritorious reward, and truely deserued.

†**5.** In the sense of L. *meritorius*: That earns money (by prostitution). *Obs. rare*$^{-1}$.

1636 B. JONSON *Discov.*, *Mali Choragi fuere*, Some love any Strumpet (be shee never so shop-like or meritorious) in good clothes.

meri'toriously, *adv.* [f. prec. + -LY².]

1. In a meritorious manner; †so as to acquire merit (*obs.*); †as a 'meritorious cause' (*obs.*); so as to deserve commendation.

1502 *Ord. Crysten Men* (W. de W. 1506) II. i. 87 That man may shewe synne & them kepe entyerly & merytoryously. **1576** FLEMING *Panopl. Epist.* 24 What is there..whereof either you, or shee might meritoriously powre out your complaintes against..Fortune? **1609** DOWNAM *Chr. Liberty* 22 Christ..hath meritoriously wrought our freedome. *a* **1639** WOTTON *Reliq.* (1651) 182 Nani had carried himself meritoriously in forraign Imployments. **1695** HUMFREY *Mediocria* 34 Christs righteousness is the meritorious, indeed the only meritorious, or meritoriously procuring efficient..cause of mans justification. *a* **1716** SOUTH *Serm.* (1727) IV. iii. 122 They also faced down the World, that they did well and meritoriously in those very Things, in which their Hypocrisy..did consist. **1816** KIRBY & SP. *Entomol.* (1818) I. 47 Would not the humblest contributor to such an end be deemed most meritoriously engaged? **1856** W. COLLINS *Rogue's Life* ii. [She] was, at that very moment, meritoriously and heartily engaged in eating her breakfast.

†**2.** Deservedly; in accordance with its deserts.

1607 TOPSELL *Four-f. Beasts* (1658) 138 They are to their masters..a singular safeguard;..for which consideration they are meritoriously termed..Canes Defensores. *a* **1647** BOYLE in Birch *Life* B.'s Wks. (1772) I. p. xxvi. Nizza, a place..meritoriously famous for that strength, which nature and art have emulously given it. **1665** SIR T. HERBERT *Trav.* (1677) 13 That great Cape which meritoriously is now call'd of good Hope.

meri'toriousness. [f. MERITORIOUS *a.* + -NESS.] The state or quality of being meritorious.

1639 FULLER *Holy War* III. x. (1640) 125 These murderers being instantly put to death, gloried in the meritoriousnesse of their suffering. *a* **1708** BP. BEVERIDGE *Thes. Theol.* (1711) III. 244 The reality and meritoriousness of Christ's death and Passion. **1884** A. R. PENNINGTON *Wiclif* viii. 271 The study of the works of that holy man..led him..to oppose the meritoriousness of good works.

† **meritory**, *a. Obs.* Forms: 4–5 **meritoire, -orie, -orye,** 4–6 **meritory,** 6 **meritori, meretory, merytory(e, -torie** 6 **meritor, meretorie.** [a. OF. *meritoire*, ad. L. *meritōrius*: see MERITORIOUS.] = MERITORIOUS.

1. Of actions: Serving to earn reward; productive of merit to the agent. Also, possessing merit, deserving, praiseworthy.

13.. *S. Erkenwolde* 270 in Horstm. *Altengl. Leg.* (1881) 272 More he menskes mene for mynnynge of riȝtes þen for al þe meritorie medes þat men one molde vsene. **1390** GOWER *Conf.* I. 19 How meritoire is thilke dede Of charite. *c* **1400** *Apol. Loll.* 50 It semiþ good, spedi, & meritori, þat þe kirk be honorid. *c* **1412** HOCCLEVE *De Reg. Princ.* 351 Oure feiþ not were vnto vs meritorie If þat we myghten by reson it preue. **1485** CAXTON *Chas. Gt.* 24 So many other labours merytoryes adioyned in the seruyce of god. **15..** *Aberdeen Reg.* (Jam.), Sene meritor, is to beir leill & suchtfast witnessing. [Cf. quots. 1415, 1420 s.v. MERITABLE.]

2. Earned, merited; = MERITORIOUS 4.

1523 SKELTON *Garl. Laurel* 429 So am I preuentid of my brethern tweyne In rendrynge to you thankkis meritory.

†**meritot.** A supposed variant of MERRYTOTTER, occurring as a corrupt reading in Chaucer, and hence in Blount and later Dictionaries.

14.. *Chaucer's Miller's T.* (MS. Camb.) 584 Sum gay gerl god it wot Hath brouȝt ȝow þus vp on the merytot [*other texts* viritoot, vyritote, veritote, verytrot]. Hence **1602** *Speght's Chaucer's Works* (ed. 2) *ibid.* Merytote. **1656** BLOUNT *Glossogr.*, *Meritot*, a sport used by children by swinging themselves in Bel-ropes, or such like, till they be giddy ..*Chauc.*

meritour, variant of MERITER.

†'**meritress.** *Obs. nonce-wd.* [f. MERITER + -ESS.] A female meriter.

1617 COLLINS *Def. Bp. Ely* I. v. 206 Which is first very insolent,..that faith should be a meritour at Gods hands, or a meritresse, if you will haue it so.

meritt(e, merk(e: see MERIT, MARK, MIRK.

merkat(e, obs. forms of MARKET.

merket(e, -kett, obs. forms of MARKET.

merkin ('mɜːkɪn). Also 7 **mirkin.** [app. a variant of MALKIN; but it is doubtful whether the various applications belong to the same word.]

†**1. a.** The female pudendum. *Obs.*

[**1535** LYNDESAY *Satyre* 1920 Mawkine.] **1656** FLETCHER *Martial* 95 Why dost thou reach thy Merkin now half dust? Why dost provoke the ashes of thy lust? **1671** SKINNER *Etymol. Ling. Angl.*, Merkin, *Pubes mulieris.* **1714** A. SMITH *Lives Highwaymen* II. 151 This put a strange Whim in his Head; which was, to get the hairy circle of her Merkin... This he dry'd well, and then return'd to the Cardinall, telling him, he had brought St. Peter's Beard.

b. (See quot. 1796.) Also, an artificial vagina.

1617 J. TAYLOR (Water-P.) *Trav. Bohemia* Wks. 1630 III. 94/2 A thousand hogsheads then would haunt his firkin, And Mistris Minks recouer her lost mirkin. **1660** *Mercurius Fumig.* No. 7. 56 The last week was lost a Merkin in the Coven-Garden. *a* **1680** ROCHESTER *To Author Play 'Sodom'* 35 Or wear some stinking Merkin for a Beard. **1796** *Grose's Dict. Vulg. Tongue* (ed. 3), *Merkin*, counterfeit hair for women's privy parts. **1886** R. F. BURTON tr. *Arabian Nights' Entertainments* X. 239 For the use of men they have the 'merkin', a heart-shaped article of thin skin stuffed with cotton and slit with an artificial vagina. **1962** E. WILSON *Night Thoughts* 203 Said Philip Sydney, buttoning his jerkin 'Allow me, darling: you have dropped your merkin.' **1967** G. LEGMAN *Fake Revolt* 31 A sort of ice-cold dildo-and-merkin combination. **1972** *Variant* I. VI. 54 *Variant* reporters interviewed a French pubic wig maker, the head of one of the world's most important firms making merkens and other 'intimate wigs'.

2. = MALKIN 3 b.

1802 JAMES *Milit. Dict.*, *Merkin*, a mop to clean cannon. **1875** KNIGHT *Dict. Mech.*

merkit, obs. form of MARKET.

merkland, variant of MARKLAND.

merkyte, obs. form of MARKET.

merle (mɜːl), *sb.* Also 6 **mirle, meryll,** 7–8 **mearl(e.** [a. F. *merle* masc. (OF. also fem.):—L. *merulus, merula* blackbird or ousel (also, the sea-carp). Cf. Pr., Sp. *merla*, Pg. *merlo, melro*, It. *merla, merlo*; also (from Fr.) MDu., MLG., early mod.G. *merle*, Du. *meerle*.]

1. The blackbird, *Turdus merula. arch.*

Perhaps never in popular use, but constantly occurring in Scottish poetry from the 15th c. Drayton adopted from some Scottish poet the traditional association of 'mavis and merle', which he frequently repeats, and which in the 19th c. often appears in English and American poetry from imitation of Scott or Burns. As used by Caxton and perh. by Philemon Holland, the word is an independent adoption from French.

For quots. 1450, 1549, 1604, 1725, 1810, see MAVIS.

1483 CAXTON *Gold Leg.* 146 b/2 A blacke byrde that is called a merle came on atyme to saynt benet. *c* **1524** *Thomas of Erceld.* (Lansd. MS.) 29, I harde the Meryll and the Iay. **1593** DRAYTON *Eclogues* i. 11 The jocund Mirle perch'd on the highest spray. **1612** —— *Poly-olb.* xiii. 62 Upon his dulcet pype the Merle doth only play. **1601** HOLLAND *Pliny* II. 382 The Thrush or Mauis..is soueraigne for the dysenterie: so is the Merle or black-bird. **1617** SIR W. MURE *Misc. Poems* xxi. 100 Heir Mearle and Mavis sing melodious layes. **1684** E. CHAMBERLAYNE *Pres. St. Eng.* I. (ed. 15) 6 What abundance of..merles, fieldfares, ousles. **1736** AINSWORTH *Lat. Dict.* II, *Merula*,..a mearle, a blackbird. **1791** BURNS *Lam. Mary* ii, The merle, in his noontide bow'r, Makes woodland echoes ring. **1863** LONGF. *Wayside Inn* I. *Birds of Killingw.* 2 It was the season, when through all the land The merle and mavis..building sing Those lovely lyrics. **1884** W. C. SMITH *Kildrostan* 64 My old heart Goes pit-a-pat to hear it; like the merle That sees a gled o'erhead.

¶ **2.** Used to render L. *merula*, the sea-carp.

1745 tr. *Columella's Husb.* VIII. xvi, A rocky sea nourishes fishes of its own name,..as the merle, the sea-thrush, and the sea-bream.

¶ **3.** Used for: The merlin, *Falco æsalon*.

1838 LONGF. *Drift-Wood* Prose Wks. 1886 I. 382 He can no longer fly his hawks and merles in the open country.

merle (mɜːl), *a.* [f. dial. *mirlet, mirly* speckled.] Of a dog, especially a collie: having blue-grey fur speckled or streaked with black. Also as *sb.*, a dog coloured in this way. Cf. MARLED *ppl. a.*², MIRLED *ppl. a.*

1905 C. H. WHEELER in J. Watson *Dog Bk.* v. 351 The remainder of the litter [of collies] were blue merles. **1936** A. W. MEYER *Dogs* 262 Merle—Bluish-gray with some black, as seen in certain collies. **1948** C. L. B. HUBBARD *Dogs in Brit.* xviii. 193 The eyes [of collies] are medium in size, almond in shape, and coloured brown except in merle dogs when they are 'wall' (a blue-and-white or china shade). *Ibid.* 463 Merle.—The term applied to a blue-grey mixture flecked or streaked with black, uncommon except in working sheepdogs. **1968** J. F. GORDON *Beagle Guide* 240 *Merle*, bluish-grey color marbled with black, seen in working sheepdogs. **1971** F. HAMILTON *World Encycl. Dogs* 67 (*caption*) Blue merles provide an extra challenge for Collie breeders, because of the difficulty of producing correct markings and a good color. Silva Gale from Shiel was not only a lovely merle but certainly lost no points in head.

merle, obs. f. MARL; var. MEDLE *Obs.*, medlar.

merligo, variant of MIRLIGO.

merlin¹ ('mɜːlɪn). Forms: 4 **merlioun,** 4–5 **merlion, -youn,** 4–6 **merlyon,** 5 **merlyn, -yone, -lone,** *Sc.* **merlȝeon,** 5–6 **marlyon,** 6 **merline, meryllon, marleon, -ian, -yne, murleon,** *Sc.* **marlȝeon,** 6–7 **marlion,** 6–8 **marlin,** 7 **merling, marlyn,** 6– **merlin.** [a. AF. *merilun* (Stengel *Descr. MS. Digby* 86, p. 10), aphetic from OF. *esmerillon* (mod.F. *émerillon*) = Pr. *esmerilho*, Sp. *esmerejon*, Pg. *esmerilhão*, It. *smeriglione*; an augmentative f. Com. Rom. **smerillo*, whence med.L. *smerillus*, OF. *esmeril* merlin, Sp., Pg. *esmeril* a kind of cannon (for the sense cf. 'falconet'); the Pr. *esmirle*, It. *smerlo* merlin, are cognate, but do not correspond formally. The word appears also in Teut. as OHG., MHG., *smirl* (mod.G. *schmerl*), ON. *smyrill* (13th c.); also MHG. *smerlîn* (mod.G. *schmerlin*), Du. *smerlijn*. It is disputed whether the word was adopted from Rom. into Teut., or vice versa; Kluge regards it as originally Teut. The view of Diez, that it represents L. *merula* (see MERLE *sb.*) with prefixed *s*, is unlikely both on account of form and sense.

A few examples of forms without initial *s* occur outside Eng., e.g. med.L. *merillus* (Germany, 15th c.), G. *merle, mirle* (Nemnich), early mod.Flemish *merlijn, marlijn* (Kilian); their relation to the longer forms is obscure.]

A European species of falcon, *Falco æsalon* or *lithofalco*, one of the smallest, but one of the boldest, of European birds of prey; the male bird (distinguished as *jack-merlin*: see JACK *sb.*¹ 27, 38) is remarkable for the beauty of its plumage. In recent use sometimes in a wider sense, corresponding to the mod.L. *Æsalon*, as applied by some ornithologists to a subdivision of the genus *Falco* including the merlin proper and some closely allied species.

In the 17th c. some writers regarded the name as properly belonging to the female bird.

c **1325** *Song of Mercy* 9 in *E. E. P.* (1862) 119 A merlyon a brid hedde hent. *Ibid.* 172 For Merlions feet been colde. *c* **1381** CHAUCER *Parl Foules* 611 ȝe have the glotoun fild I-now his paunche, Thanne are we wel! sayde thanne a Merlioun. **1382** WYCLIF *Lev.* xi. 13 An egle and a griffyn and a merlyoun. **14..** *Voc.* in Wr.-Wülcker 563/25 *Ametus*, a merlyn. *c* **1450** HOLLAND *Howlat* 638 Than rerit thir Merlȝeonis that mountis so hie. *c* **1475** *Pict. Voc.* in Wr.-Wülcker 761/8 *Hic aluctor*, a merlone. **1517** *Acc. Ld. High Treas. Scot.* (1903) V. 128 My lord governouris halkis and marleȝonis. **1530** PALSGR. 910 Meryllons, *esmerillons.* **1557** *Tottel's Misc.* (Arb.) 132 Lyke as the lark within the marlians foote With piteous tunes doth chirp her ȝelden lay. **1567** R. EDWARDS *Damon & Pithias* (1571) F j b, Masse, cham well be set: heres a trimme caste of Murleons. *a* **1586** SIDNEY *Arcadia* II. (1590) 114 A cast of Merlins there was besides. ? *a* **1600** in *Lyly's Wks.* (1902) III. 491 The Marlyne cannot euer sore on high. **1613** FLETCHER, etc. *Honest Man's Fort.* v. i, Keep a four-nobles nag and a black [*mod. edd.* Jack-] Merling. **1613** BOYLE in *Lismore Papers* (1886) I. 29, I sent ..to my lo^d^ Carew a caste of marlyns and a goshawk. **1616** SURFL. & MARKH. *Country Farm* 712 Of all sorts of Merlins, the Irish Merlin is the best,..you shall know her by her pale greene legs, and the contrarie Merlin by her bright yellow legs. *Ibid.* [see JACK *sb.*¹ 38]. **1668** WILKINS *Real Char.* II. v. §4. 146 Being the least of all Hawks called F. Merlin, M. Jack-Merlin. **1710** *Acc. Last Distemper Tom Whigg* I. 3 A jolly marlin that sate pruning..himself. **1893** NEWTON *Dict. Birds* 235 The majority of the Falcons..may be separated into five very distinct groups: (1) the Falcons pure and simple (*Falco* proper);..(4) the Merlins (*Æsalon*, Kaup); and (5) the Hobbies (*Hypotriorchis*, Boie). **1904** *Longm.*

Mag. Apr. 533 The hen harrier and the little merlin are equally mischievous.
attrib. **1851** MAYNE REID *Scalp Hunt.* xii. 88 Noble dames watching the flight of the merlin hawks.

†**Merlin**². *Obs.* The name of the soothsayer of the Arthurian legend; used as the title of various prophetic almanacs and the like.
1644 LILLY (*title*) England's propheticall Merline, fortelling..the actions depending upon the influence of the conjunction of Saturn and Jupiter 164$\frac{2}{3}$. **1653** (*title*) The Madmerry Merlin, or the Black Almanack [for 1654]. **1654** (*title*) The Royal Merlin, or Great Britians Royal Observator. **1656–1838** (*title*) Rider's Brit[t]ish Merlin.

merlin³ (ˈmɜːlɪn). [Perh. from the name of *Merlin*, a celebrated racehorse, from which the Welsh breed of ponies is said to be descended (Youatt *The Horse* 58).] A small Welsh pony.
1883 *Encycl. Brit.* XVI. 789/1 [Montgomery] was long famous for its hardy breed of small horses called *merlins.*

merlin, obs. form of MARLINE.

Merlin-chair. An invalid wheel-chair (so called after its inventor J. J. Merlin 1735–1803).
1835 SMEDLEY *Let.* 4 May in *Poems* (1837) 429 A Merlin ..chair with many appendages and fashions of transformation. **1876** ALBEMARLE *Fifty Years of My Life* I. 242 He [C. J. Fox] used to wheel himself about in what was called a 'Merlin chair'. **1884** *Health Exhib. Catal.* 102/2 Self-propelling Merlin Chair.

†ˈ**merling.** *Obs.* Also 4–5 **marlynge**, 4–6 **merlinge**, 5 **marlyng**, 5–6 **merlyng(e**, 8 **merlin.** [ad. OF. *merlanke, merlanc, merlenc* (mod.F. *merlan*), f. *merle*:—L. *merula* some kind of fish (app. a transferred use of *merula* blackbird, MERLE *sb.*); the suffix is believed to be of Germanic origin, = -ING³.] The whiting, *Gadus merlangus.*
1307–8 *Durham Acc. Rolls* (Surtees) 3 Merlinges. *c* **1460** J. RUSSELL *Bk. Nurture* 834 Mustard is metest with.. makerelle, & also withe merlynge. **1513** *Bk. Keruynge* in *Babees Bk.* 167 Marlynge, makrell, and hake, with butter. **1525** in *Excerpta e libris domicilii Jacobi Quinti* (Bann. Cl.) 7, lxxxiiij merlingis,..perches,..fundolis. **1611** COTGR., *Merlan*, a whiting, a Merling. **1706** PHILLIPS (ed. Kersey), *Merlin* or *Merling*, a kind of Fish. **1736** AINSWORTH *Lat. Dict.* II, *Merula*..a fish called a merling, a whiting.

Merlin's grass. The aquatic plant *Isoetes lacustris* or QUILL-WORT.
[**17..** *S. Brewer's Bot. Journ. Wales in* 1726 (MS.) in Britten & Holland *Plant-n.*, The fish are larger there [at Llyn Ogwen, Carnarvonshire] than in any of the other lakes, which they attribute to the eating of [this plant], which they call *Gwair Merllyns*; *gwair* is hay, and *Merllyn* was a Welsh prophet.] **1837** G. W. FRANCIS *Analysis Brit. Ferns* 56 *Isoetes lacustris.* European Quillwort. Merlin's Grass.

merlion, marlion (ˈmɜː-, ˈmɑːlɪən). *Her.* [Perh. orig. a use of *merlion, marlion*, variants of MERLIN¹, but in the extant heraldic instances misapplied owing to association with F. *merlette*: see MARTLET, MARLET.] A heraldic bird, figured either as identical with the heraldic MARTLET 2, or with the *merlette* of French heraldry, which is depicted as having neither feet nor beak.
It is doubtful whether *merlyons* in the first quot. refers to embroidered figures of heraldic 'merlions' or of merlins, or whether it is not a wholly distinct word; in the latter case cf. med.L. *merlinus*, a hood worn by canons (Du Cange).
1553 *Inv. Ch. Surrey* (1869) 155 A sute of vestementes with merlyons solde for xx⁸. *Ibid.*, A cope of velvit with marlyons solde for xx⁸. **1610** GUILLIM *Heraldry* III. xvii. 159 He beareth Gules fiue Marlions wings in Saltire Argent. **1828–40** BERRY *Encycl. Herald.* I, *Merlette* or *Merlion*, an heraldic term used by French heralds for the martlet, but which they represent without beak, thighs, or legs. **1874** *Papworth's Ord. Brit. Armorials* 42/1 Sa. three marlions sinister wings displ. arg. **1889** ELVIN *Dict. Heraldry* s.v. *Marlions*, Two Marlions wings conjoined and expanded. *Merlet, Merlette* or *Merlion*, a Martlet.

merlio(u)n, variants of MERLIN¹.

merlon (ˈmɜːlən). *Fortification.* [F. *merlon* (= Sp. *merlon*, Pg. *merlão*), ad. It. *merlone*, augm. of *merlo, merla* battlement, perhaps a contraction of the synonymous *mergolo* (Florio), *mergola*, app. a dim. f. L. *mergæ* (pl.) pitchfork.] The part of an embattled parapet between two embrasures; †a similar structure on a battleship.
1704 J. HARRIS *Lex. Techn.* I, *Merlon*, in Fortification, is that Part of the Parapet which lies betwixt two Embrasures. **1757** W. SMITH *Hist. New York* 188 This Battery is built of Stone, and the Merlons consist of Cedar Joists, filled in with Earth. **1790** BEATSON *Nav. & Mil. Mem.* I. 101 Having her merlons filled with earth or sand, she [the Gallicia] drew full as much water as some of our eighty gun ships. **1833** STRAITH *Fortif.* 5 The solid portion of the parapet between two embrasures is called the merlon. **1894** R. S. FERGUSON *Hist. Westmorld.* 285 One of the merlons in the parapets is pierced for a small cannon.
Comb. *a* **1849** J. C. MANGAN *Poems* (1859) 238 He trained a horse to pace round narrow stones laid merlon-wise.

merlone, obs. form of MERLIN¹.

merls: see MEREL.

merlyng(e, obs. forms of MARLINE, MERLING.

merlyo(u)n, obs. forms of MERLIN *sb.*¹

mermaid (ˈmɜːmeɪd). Forms: 4–9 **mer-**, 5 **meer-**, 5–6 **mar-**, 5–7 **mere-**, 6 **meyr(e)-**, **mayr-**, 6–7 **mear(e)-**, 6–8 **mare-**, **mair-**, 7 **meir-** (see forms of MAID *sb.*); also 8 **mermade.** [f. MERE *sb.*¹ + MAID; cf. OE. *męrewīf* and MERMIN; also G. *meerjungfrau, meerfräulein.*]
1. a. An imaginary species of beings, more or less human in character, supposed to inhabit the sea, and to have the head and trunk of a woman, the lower limbs being replaced by the tail of a fish or cetacean. †In early use often identified with the SIREN of classical mythology.
c **1386** CHAUCER *Nun's Pr. T.* 450 Chauntecleer so free Soong murier than the Mermayde in the see. **1406** HOCCLEVE *La Male Regle* 236 It spekith of meermaides in the See. **1432–50** tr. *Higden* (Rolls) II. 369 Poetes feyne iij meremaydes [orig. *sirenes*] to be in parte virgines and in parte bryddes. *a* **1533** LD. BERNERS *Huon* lvi. 190 So swete a sownde that it semed to be the mermaydes of the see. **1592** DAVIES *Immort. Soul* II. vi. Did sense perswade Ulysses not to hear The Mermaids songs. **1601** HOLLAND *Pliny* I. 236 As for the Meremaids called Nereides, it is no fabulous tale that goes of them..onely their bodie is rough & skaled all ouer. *a* **1661** HOLYDAY *Juvenal* 265 Sea-monsters, such as mearmaids, and young tritons, half men, half fish. **1681** DRYDEN *Sp. Friar* IV. ii. 60 This Mermayd's melody Into an unseen whirl-pool draws you fast. **1762** GOLDSM. *Cit W.* lxxxi, They have laid their hoops aside, and are become as slim as mermaids. **1814** SCOTT *Ld. of Isles* III. xxviii, Mermaid's alabaster grot, Who bathes her limbs in sunless well. **1819** KEATS *Eve St. Agnes* xxvi, Half-hidden, like a mermaid in sea-weed. **1867** ROBY *Mermaid of Martin Meer* in *Trad. Lanc.* (ed. 4) II. 174 'Tis said a mermaid haunts yon water.
†**b.** Sometimes applied to the manatee or similar animals, whose form reminded observers of the mermaid of tradition. *Obs.*
1622 R. HAWKINS *Voy. S. Sea* xxxii. 78 These..are part terrestryall, and part aquatile, as the Mare-maide, Sea-horse, and other of that kind. **1756** NUGENT *Gr. Tour, Netherl.* I. 102 Among other things there is..the hand of a mermade..and several other curiosities.
2. a. A representation of this being, esp. *Her.*
Usually if not invariably depicted heraldically with long flowing golden locks, and holding in the right-hand a comb and in the left a mirror or hand-glass.
1464 *Will of Kent* (Somerset Ho.), Vnum meremayde de argento. **1533** *Visit. Lancs.* (Chetham Soc. No. 98) 55 A meyre mayd haire come & glasse or. **1631** HEYWOOD *London's Ius Hon.* Wks. 1874 IV. 276 Upon the top of the one stands a Sea Lyon vpon the other a Meare-maide or Sea-Nimphe. **1761** *Ann. Reg.* 238 The fishmongers pageants consisted of..two mairmaids [etc.]. **1874** *Papworth's Ord. Brit. Armorials* 983/1 Vert a mermaid arg. crined or holding a comb and glass of the third.
b. A favourite sign for a shop, inn, or tavern.
1428 in *E.E. Wills* (1882) 78 My mancion that is cleped the Mermaid in Bredstreet. **1463** *Mann. & Househ. Exp.* (Roxb.) 151 The dynnere at the Mermayde,..xiiij.s. vj.d. **1527** RASTALL *Abridg. Statutes* (Colophon), Enprynted in the chepe syde at the sygne of the mere mayde next to poulys gate. *a* **1616** BEAUMONT *Let. to B. Jonson* 44 What things have we seen Done at the Mermaid? **1639** MAYNE *City Match* III. iii. 30, I had made an Ordinary..at the Mermaid. **1678** DRYDEN *Kind Keeper* II. i. (1680) 13 How sits my *Chedreux*? *Ger.* O very finely! with the Locks comb'd down, like a Maremaids, on a Sign-post.
3. *transf.* †**a.** = SIREN; in 16–17th c. applied to a prostitute. *Obs.* **b.** *jocularly.* A woman who is at home in the water.
1590 SHAKS. *Com. Err.* III. ii. 45 Oh traine me not sweet Mermaide with thy note,..Sing Siren for thy selfe, and I will dote. **1595** MARKHAM *Sir R. Grinvile* lxxii, Honietongd Tullie, Mermaid of our eares. **16..** MASSINGER, etc. *Old Law* IV. i, *Gnotho.* I have Siren here already. *Agatha.* What? a mermaid? *Gnotho.* No, but a maid, horse-face! **1602** DEKKER *Satirom.* Wks. 1873 I. 234 A Gentleman..shall not ..sneake into a Tauerne with his Mermaid, but [etc.]. **1880** 'OUIDA' *Moths* I. 3 She had floated..semi-nude, with all the other mermaids *à la mode.*
4. The name of a country dance.
1701 *Newest Acad. Compliments* (N.), The Mermaid.— The leaders-up change sides, then turn each the other's partner [etc.]. **1716** *Playford's Dancing-Master* (ed. 16) I. 105 Maremaid [music and directions].
5. a. *false mermaid*, a plant of the North American genus *Flœrkea*, esp. *F. proserpinacoides.*
1845–50 MRS. LINCOLN *Lect. Bot.* App. v. 103/2 *Flœrkia palustris* (false mermaid). **1846–50** A. WOOD *Class-bk. Bot.* 200 *Flœrkea proserpinacoides*... False Mermaid. **1860** in A. GRAY *Man. Bot. North. U.S.* 74.
b. A vigorous climbing rose with single yellow flowers, produced by crossing *Rosa bracteata* (*Macartney rose*) with a yellow tea rose and introduced in 1918 by William Paul & Son.
1918 *Rose Annual* 148 The most sensational Rose among Climbers of the year was undoubtedly that fine Hybrid, Mermaid. The huge golden lemon single flowers charmed everyone who saw it. **1922** T. G. W. HENSLOW *Rose Encycl.* xix. 409/2 Mermaid..Wm Paul & Son 1918:—Flower sulphury yellow,..of great size, single, produced continuously from early summer till late in autumn. **1965** G. S. THOMAS *Climbing Roses* iv. 62 A few old roses.., and some newer varieties like 'Mermaid' and 'New Dawn', show that grace and recurrence of bloom can be combined. **1974** *Times* 26 Oct. 12/4 Plant a fast-growing rose like Mermaid or Albertine to cover the pergola.
6. *attrib.* and *Comb.*, as *mermaid-bride*; *mermaid-like* adv.: **mermaid-fish**, the monk-fish or angel-fish, *Rhina squatina*; **mermaid-pie**, a sucking pig baked whole in a crust; **mermaid-weed** *U.S.*, a name for aquatic plants of the genus *Proserpinaca*, having leaves toothed like a comb.
1823 BYRON *Island* IV. ix, Proud and exulting in his *mermaid bride. **1758** BORLASE *Nat. Hist. Cornw.* 265 The monk or angel-fish (otherwise termed the *Mermaid-fish, as Artedi says). **1602** SHAKS. *Ham.* IV. vii. 177 Her cloathes spred wide, And *Mermaid-like, a while they bore her vp. **1661** RABISHA *Cookery Dissected* 175 To bake a Pigg to be eaten cold, called a *Maremaid Pie. **1846–50** A. WOOD *Class-bk. Bot.* 267 *Proserpinaca palustris.* Spear-leaved *Mermaid-weed... *P. pectinacea*... Cat-leaved Mermaid-weed.
b. With possessive, as **mermaid's egg** = *mermaid's purse* (*Cent. Dict.* 1890); **mermaid's fishlines**, a common cord-like seaweed, *Chorda filum* (ibid.); **mermaid's glove**, (*a*) a British sponge, *Halichondria palmata*, somewhat resembling a glove; (*b*) *pl.* = DEAD-MAN'S FINGERS 2, *Alcyonium digitatum*; **mermaid's hair**, a dark green filamentous seaweed, *Lyngbya majuscula* (*Cent. Dict.*); **mermaid's head**, one of the small rounded sea-urchins, as *Spatangus cordatus*; **mermaid's lace**, (*a*) an alleged name for a kind of coralline; (*b*) applied to a kind of Venetian point lace whose pattern is said to have been imitated from this; **mermaid's purse**, the horny egg-case of a skate, ray, or shark (= SEA-PURSE); **mermaid's trumpet**, the shell of one of the Turbinacean gasteropods (? *Nerita*).
1808 FORSYTH *Beauties Scotl.* V. 138 The sponge called *mermaid's glove. **1865** GOSSE *Year at Shore* 74 The animal is sometimes, however, called cow's paps, and sometimes mermaid's gloves. **1863** WOOD *Nat. Hist.* III. 769 The Mermaid's Glove..is certainly the largest of the British Sponges. **1662** RAY *Three Itin.* III. 169 A pretty shell covered with prickles or bristles, which the Welch call *mermaid's heads. **1865** MRS. BURY PALLISER *Hist. Lace* 46 In the islands of the Lagune there still lingers a tale of the first origin of this most charming production. A sailor youth ..brought home to his betrothed a bunch of that pretty coralline known..as the *mermaid's lace. The girl.. imitated it with her needle, and..produced that delicate guipure which before long became the taste of all Europe. **1882** CAULFIELD & SAWARD *Dict. Needlework*, *Mermaids Lace*, a name sometimes given to fine Venetian Points, from the legend of a lace maker having copied the seaweed known as Mermaid—making of it one of the patterns in Venetian Point. **1836** YARRELL *Brit. Fishes* II. 368 These cases..are called *Mermaid's purses. **1668** CHARLETON *Onomasticon* 182 *Nerites*..the *Mere-maids Trumpet.

mermaiden (ˈmɜːmeɪd(ə)n). Now *rare.* Forms: see prec. and MAIDEN. [f. MERE *sb.*¹ + MAIDEN; cf. prec.] = MERMAID 1, 2.
? *a* **1366** CHAUCER *Rom. Rose* 680 But it was wondir lyk to be Song of meremaydens of the see. *c* **1440** *Jacob's Well* 150 A mermayden of þe se..hath a body as a womman, & a tayl as a fysch, & clawys as an eryn. **1538** *Acc. Ld. High Treas. Scot.* in Pitcairn *Crim. Trials* I. *293 Ane Terget of Gold, with ane Marmadyne in it of dyamontis. **1584** COGAN *Haven Health* (1636) 170 A Syren or Mermayden, that is, halfe fish and halfe flesh. **1848** E. FORBES *Naked-eyed Medusæ* 70 Sufficiently graceful to be the nightcap of the tiniest and prettiest of mermaidens. **1849** M. ARNOLD *Forsaken Merman* vi, The cold strange eyes of a little Mermaiden.

mermalade, obs. form of MARMALADE *sb.*

merman (ˈmɜːmən). Also 7 **mere-**, **mare-**, **mairman.** [f. MERE *sb.*¹ + MAN *sb.*, after MERMAID; cf. G. *meermann*, Du. *meerman.*]
1. The male of the mermaid; an imaginary marine creature with a man's head and trunk, and a fish's or cetacean's tail instead of the lower limbs.
In *Heraldry*, the merman (also called *triton* or *Neptune*) is depicted as holding in the right hand a trident, and in the left a conch-shell trumpet.
1601 HOLLAND *Pliny* I. 236 Knights of Rome..who testifie, that..they haue seen a Mere-man, in euery respect resembling a man. **1611** MUNDAY *Chryso-thriambos*, A Mare-man and a Mare-maid..do figure the long continued love and amity, which..hath been betweene the Goldsmiths and Fishmongers. **1678** *Lond. Gaz.* No. 1344/1 He and his Company, upon their crossing the Severne, saw a Mair-man appear a pretty while above water. **1711–12** SWIFT *Jrnl. to Stella* 12 Mar., Mermen are he-mermaids; Tritons, natives of the sea. **1823** BYRON *Island* IV. v, Did they with ocean's hidden sovereigns dwell, And sound with mermen the fantastic shell? **1893** CUSSANS *Handbk. Her.* (ed. 4) 101 A Triton is sometimes called a Merman or Neptune.
Comb. *a* **1845** HOOD *Sub-marine* ii, But (merman-like) he look'd marine All downward from the waist.
2. *merman's shaving brushes*, 'a name given in North America to different species of *Chamædoris* and *Penicillus*' (*Treas. Bot.* 1866).

mermayd, -en, obs. forms of MERMAID, -EN.

mermelade, obs. form of MARMALADE *sb.*

mermiden, -on, obs. forms of MYRMIDON.

†**mermin.** *Obs.* Forms: 1 meremenin, -en (gen. pl. meremenna, -mennena), 1, 3 meremen, 3 mereman, mer(e)minne, mermyn(n. [OE. *męremęnen*, app. f. *męre* sea, MERE *sb.*¹ + *męnen* neut., female slave:—prehistoric **manînom*; cf. ON. *man* neut., slave (male or female), girl.

Corresponding or cognate forms in other Teut. langs. are OHG. *meremanni*, *merimenni*, *mer(i)-min* neut., *meriminna* fem. (MHG. *mereminne*, *merminne* fem.), Du. *meermin* fem., mermaid or siren, ON. *marmennill*, *-mendill* masc., merman, triton (mod.Icel. corruptly *marbendill*; also ON. *margmelli*, mod.Norw. *marmæle*, prob. an etymologizing perversion, as if 'one who speaks much').

The 13th c. form *mereman* prob. belongs here rather than to MERMAN, which does not otherwise occur before 17th c.]

A mermaid or siren.

*c*725 *Corpus Gloss.* (Hessels) S 349 *Sirina*, meremenin. *c*1000 *Ags. Gloss.* in Wr.-Wülcker 506/5 *Sirenarum*, meremennena. *c*1050 *Ags. Voc.* ibid. 277/28 *Serina*, meremen. *c*1205 LAY. 1321 þer heo funden þe merminnen [Wace *seraines*] þ beoð deor of muchele ginnen. *c*1220 *Bestiary* 557 Ðe mereman is a meiden ilike on brest and on bodi. *a*1225 *Leg. Kath.* 1500 Ah ich drede þæt tis dream me dreie toward deaðe, as deð mereminnes. 1382 WYCLIF *Josh.* Prol., The deth berynge songis of mermynns [Jerome *mortiferos Sirenarum cantus*]. 1387 TREVISA *Higden* (Rolls) V. 397 þe oost of Rome siȝ mermyns in liknes of men and of wommen [Higd. *sirenæ in specie viri et mulieris*].

mermole, obs. variant of MORMAL.

mermoset, obs. form of MARMOSET.

†**mermoyse.** *Obs. rare*⁻¹. [a. MDu. *mermoeyse*, *marmoyse*, believed to be a shortening of F. *marmouset*: cf. MARMOSE.] = MARMOSET 1.

1481 CAXTON *Reynard* xxxiv. (Arb.) 98, I wende hit had be a mermoyse a baubyn or a mercatte for I sawe neuer fowler beest.

mermydon, obs. form of MYRMIDON.

‖**mero** ('mɛərəʊ). [Sp.] A name applied to the sea-perch (*Serranus*) and various other serranoid fishes, now esp. the genera *Epinephelus* and *Promicrops*, otherwise known as jew-fishes.

1763 W. ROBERTS *Nat. Hist. Florida* 18 There is very good fishery, where is plenty of meros and pardos. 1772–84 *Cook's Voy.* (1790) IV. 1225 Fishes are found in great quantities, particularly dolphins, sharks, meros, lobsters, mussels. 1883 *Fisheries Exhib. Catal.* 351 Two Tins of.. Mero in oil; two of Mero, pickled; one of Mero, with tomato sauce. 1884 *Health Exhib. Catal.* 159/2 Mero (*Terranus* [*read* Serranus]),.. Prepared Mero.

mero-¹ ('mɛrəʊ), before a vowel **mer-**, combining form of Gr. μέρος 'part, fraction', occurring in various scientific and technical terms; sometimes opposed to HOLO-. In terms of *Crystallography* (MEROHEDRAL, MEROSYMMETRY, etc.), it denotes that a crystal or crystalline form is deficient in the number of faces requisite to build up the geometrically complete form belonging to its system. **'merocrine** (-kraɪn) *a. Physiol.* [ad. F. *mérocrine* (L. Ranvier 1887, in *Jrnl. de Micrographie* XI. 9), f. Gr. κρίν-ειν to separate], of, pertaining to, or designating a gland in which secretion is unaccompanied by any substantial change in the secreting cells; **mero'cyanine** *Chem.* [so called from having part of the structure of cyanine dyes], any of a class of neutral dyes (many of which are used as sensitizers for photographic emulsions) in which a nitrogen atom (usu. part of a basic heterocycle) is linked to a carbonyl group (usu. part of an acidic heterocycle) by a conjugated chain of carbon atoms; freq. *attrib.* in *merocyanine dye*; **'merocyte** *Biol.* [Gr. κύτος hollow: see -CYTE], the segmenting nucleus of a meroblastic ovum (*Syd. Soc. Lex.* 1890); **mero'gastrula** *Biol.*, the gastrula of a meroblastic egg (*Cent. Dict.* 1890); **mero'genesis** *Biol.*, segmentation; hence **meroge'netic** *a.*, pertaining to or characterized by merogenesis (*Cent. Dict.*); **meroistic** (-'ɪstɪk) *a. Biol.* [Gr. ᾠόν egg], producing imperfect as well as fully developed ova; **mero'mictic** *a.* [ad. G. *meromiktisch* (I. Findenegg 1935, in *Internat. Rev. d. ges. Hydrobiol.* XXXII. 377), f. Gr. μικτός mixed], applied to a lake in which, when overturn occurs, water below a certain depth does not take part in it owing to its high density (usu. the result of a high salt concentration); so **mero'mixis** [Gr. μίξις mixing], the state of being meromictic; **'meromorph, mero'morphic** *adjs. Math.* [Gr. μορφή form], similar in nature to a rational fraction (*Cent. Dict.*); **mero'myosin** *Biochem.*, either of the two fractions obtained from myosin by the action of enzymes, of which the lighter fraction consists of long rod-shaped molecules from the 'tail' of the myosin molecule and the heavier one consists of molecules having a short rod-shaped portion attached to a globular 'head'; **meropa'ronymy** [PARONYMY], incomplete paronymy; **mero'plankton** *Biol.* [back-formation from the adj.], a collective term for aquatic organisms that are meroplanktonic; **meroplank'tonic** *a.* [ad. G. *meroplanktonisch* (E. Haeckel *Plankton-Studien* (1890) iii. 25)], passing only part of the life-cycle drifting or swimming weakly in water; **'merosome** *Zool.* [Gr. σῶμα body], a segment of the body of a segmented animal (*Syd. Soc. Lex.*); hence **mero'somal** *a.*, pertaining to or of the nature of a merosome; **mero'zoite** *Zool.* [ad. F. *mérozoïte* (P. L. Simond 1897, in *Ann. de l'Institut Pasteur* XI. 551): see -ZOITE], (in many sporozoa, esp. in the orders Coccidia and Hæmosporidia) any of the cells produced by multiple fission (schizogony) of a schizont.

1905 GOULD *New Med. Terms* 358/1 *Merocrine. 1928 E. V. COWDRY *Special Cytol.* I. ii. 36 The sweat, or sodoriferous glands, are of distinctly different nature... Ranvier speaks of these glands as 'merocrine'. 1958 *Gray's Anat.* (ed. 32) 1302 Most of the sweat glands are merocrine in nature, i.e. produce their thin watery secretion without demonstrable changes in the gland epithelium. 1965 LEE & KNOWLES *Animal Hormones* v. 91 [In the thyroid gland] the colloid is secreted from the surface of the epithelium into the lumen of the acinus (merocrine secretion). 1937 L. G. S. BOOKER *U.S. Pat. 2,078,233* 27 Apr. 6/1 It has recently been proposed to call the dyes of this new and very large class, *merocyanine dyes. 1955 D. GRAHAM in H. A. Lubs *Chem. Synthetic Dyes & Pigments* xii. 676 The λ max. of a strongly polar merocyanine dye shifts to a shorter wavelength with an increase in polarity of the solvent. The λ max. of a weakly polar merocyanine shifts to longer wavelengths. 1956 K. M. HORNSBY *Basic Photogr. Chem.* iii. 34 While these merocyanines are.. useful sensitisers, those containing a > C = S grouping.. can be converted to more complex dyes. 1973 *Nature* 21–28 Dec. 508/1 This was achieved in a giant axon using a merocyanine dye; in a stained axon a single action potential gave rise to a fluorescence increase which was detectable with a signal-to-noise ratio greater than 10:1. 1881 LANKESTER in *Encycl. Brit.* XII. 555/1 The *merogenesis (segmentation or bud-formation) can only show itself by.. compelling.. the organs or regions of the body of the primary unit to assume the form of new units. 1877 HUXLEY *Anat. Inv. Anim.* vii. 443 Dr. A. Brandt has proposed the term panoistic for ovaries of the first mode, and *meroistic for those of the second and third modes of development of the ova here described. 1888 [see PANOISTIC]. 1937 *Trans. Connecticut Acad. Arts & Sci.* XXXIII. 74 The lake is in fact *meromictic, to use Findenegg's (1935) useful term. 1970 *Limnol. & Oceanogr.* XV. 363 (*heading*) Physicochemical limnology and geology of a meromictic pond on the Red Sea shore. 1955 *Mem. Ist. Ital. Idrobiol. de Marchi* VIII. Suppl. 141 (*heading*) Längsee: a history of *meromixis. 1970 *Limnol. & Oceanogr.* XV. 363 The meromixis is described of a small (140 × 50 m) coastal pond on the Sinai shore of the Red Sea. 1952 A. G. SZENT-GYÖRGYI in *Federation Proc.* XI. 297/1 The fraction with the lower sedimentation constant (*meromyosin-L), has the peculiar solubility of myosin... The fraction with the higher S_{20} (meromyosin-H), is soluble at any KCl concentration at $_pH$ 7 and precipitates at $_pH$ 5·1. 1966 *McGraw-Hill Yearbk. Sci. & Technol.* 258/2 These experiments have shown that the myosin molecules aggregate in an antiparallel, overlapping fashion, the straight L-meromyosin forming the backbone of the filament and the H-meromyosin constituting the cross bridges. 1889 *Buck's Handbk. Med. Sci.* VIII. 519/2 The host of cases (easily found in any large English dictionary) in which two or more possible forms are wanting, may be accepted as illustrations of partial paronymy or *meroparonymy. 1909 GROOM & BALFOUR tr. *Warming's Oecol. Plants* xxxviii. 161 These terms 'neritic' and 'pelagic' or 'oceanic' plankton approximately correspond to Haeckel's '*meroplankton' [*printed* 'neroplankton'] and 'holoplankton'. 1942 H. U. SVERDRUP et al. *Oceans* xvii. 814 This temporary element, or meroplankton as it is sometimes called, is especially abundant in the neritic waters. 1967 *Oceanogr. & Marine Biol.* V. 241 The results are summarized and brought together in a voluminous thesis on the larvae of Crustacea Decapoda of the meroplankton of the Gulf of Marseilles. 1973 *Nature* 16 Feb. 475/2 There are few comparable estimates of growth efficiencies for meroplankton species. 1893 G. W. FIELD tr. *Hæckel's Planktonic Stud.* in *Rep. U.S. Comm. Fisheries 1889–91* 583 The *meroplanktonic organisms.. are found swimming in the sea only for a part of their lives, passing the other part vagrant or sessile in the benthos. 1903 *Amer. Naturalist* XXXVII. 516 The meroplanktonic stage.. was apparently suppressed even in the earliest species of Fulgur. 1963 J. E. G. RAYMONT *Plankton & Productivity in Oceans* xiv. 371 Even with coastal or neritic plankton it is not the meroplanktonic species which cause the main seasonal fluctuations. 1900 *Jrnl. R. Microsc. Soc.* 336 In the author's nomenclature this process of asexual multiplication is known as schizogony, the mother-cells are schizonts, and the daughter-cells *merozoites. 1940 L. H. HYMAN *Invertebrates* I. iii. 144 The growing vegetative parasite is called a trophozoite. When this.. undergoes multiple fission directly into agametes, it is called a schizont or agamont, the multiple fission is termed schizogony or agamogony, and the agametes are known as merozoites. 1967 J. H. WILMOTH *Biol. Invertebr.* ii. 40/2 Among the Coccidia, multiple division occurs during both asexual and sexual phases. *Eimeria schubergi* parasitizes the intestinal cells of the centipede, *Lithobius*. Infective sporozoites invade epithelial cells of the host. Schizogony produces many merozoites which are freed to invade new cells.

mero-² ('mɪərəʊ-, mɪə'rɒ-), combining form of Gr. μηρός 'thigh', occurring in certain mod. scientific terms. **'merocele** *Path.*, femoral hernia; hence **mero'celic** *a.*, of or belonging to merocele (*Syd. Soc. Lex.* 1890). **merocerite** (-'ɒsəraɪt) *Zool.* [Gr. κέρας horn], one of the joints in the antennæ in crustaceans, which rests upon the ischiocerite; hence **merocer'itic** (-sə'rɪtɪk) *a.*, of the nature of or pertaining to a merocerite. **merognathite** *Zool.* [Gr. γνάθος jaw: see -ITE], the fourth joint of a crustacean gnathite. **meropodite** (-'ɒpədaɪt) *Zool.* [Gr. ποδ-, πούς foot], that joint of an endopodite which is borne on the ischiopodite; **meropo'ditic** *a.*, pertaining to or of the nature of a meropodite (*Cassell's Encycl. Dict.* 1902).

1802 TURTON *Med. Gloss.*, *Merocele. 1835–6 *Todd's Cycl. Anat.* I. 396/1 Hernia of the bladder.. is developed at the same point as a merocele. 1877 HUXLEY *Anat. Inv. Anim.* vi. 314 To its inner portion an ischiocerite is connected, bearing a *merocerite and carpocerite. 1859 SALTER in *Brit. Org. Rem.*, *1st Monograph* 43 *Merognathite. 1870 ROLLESTON *Anim. Life* 94 The fourth, the longest of all the segments.. is known as the *meropodite.

†**merobibe.** *Obs.*⁻⁰ [ad. L. *merobib-us* (Plautus), f. *mero-*, *merum* unmixed wine + *bib-ĕre* to drink.] 'One who drinks pure Wine without a mixture of Water' (Bailey 1727 vol. II).

meroblast ('mɛrəʊblæst). *Biol.* [f. MERO-¹ + Gr. βλαστός germ, -BLAST.] An ovum which is only partly germinal. Hence **mero'blastic** *a.*, having only a partial power of germination. (Opposed to *holoblast*, *-ic.*)

1870 NICHOLSON *Man. Zool.* 193 The ovum is 'meroblastic', a portion only of the vitellus undergoing segmentation. 1884 CALDWELL in *Australasian* Suppl. 8 Nov. 3/3 Monotremes oviparous, meroblast ovum. 1888 ROLLESTON & JACKSON *Anim. Life* 371 *Monotremata*... The ova are large and meroblastic.

me'rocracy. *nonce-wd.* [f. Gr. μέρο-ς part: see -CRACY.] Government by a part.

1679 FILMER *Free-holder* xii. 173 Why must an Assembly of part be called an Aristocratie, and not a Merocratie?

merogony (mə'rɒgənɪ). *Biol.* [f. MERO-¹ + Gr. -γονία begetting.] The production of an embryo from a portion of an egg not containing a nucleus. Hence **mero'gonic** *a.*, pertaining to or effected by merogony.

1899 *Nature* 2 Nov. 24/1 On merogonic impregnation and its results, by M. Yves Delage. *Ibid.*, Since it [the fertilization of non-nucleated ovular cytoplasm].. is a process which may be generalised, the author [M. Yves Delage] proposes to give it the name of merogony.

merohedral (mɛrəʊ'hiːdrəl), *a. Cryst.* [f. MERO-¹ + Gr. ἕδρα seat, base + -AL¹.] Of a crystal: Having less than the full number of faces admitted by the type of symmetry to which it belongs. So **mero'hedric** *a.* in the same sense (Webster Suppl. 1902); **mero'hedrism**, the property of being merohedral.

1888 TEALL *Brit. Petrogr.* 438 *Merohedrism*, a crystallographic term embracing both *hemihedrism* and *tetartohedrism*. 1895 STORY-MASKELYNE *Crystallogr.* §137 The term merohedral will be reserved for certain cases in which a defalcation is met with in the faces of a crystal out of accord with any fixed law of symmetry; though sometimes such a merohedral crystal simulates the mode of grouping of a crystal belonging to a different type of symmetry from its own. 1899 W. J. LEWIS *Crystallogr.* 149 The forms of certain classes were regarded as merohedral divisions of a more symmetrical form. *Ibid.* 259 The views underlying the ideas of merohedrism lead to inconsistencies.

Meroitic (mɛrəʊ'ɪtɪk), *a.* and *sb.* [f. *Mero-ë*, the name of the capital of an ancient Nubian kingdom in north-east Africa, + *-itic.*]

A. *adj.* Of, belonging to, or pertaining to an ancient Nubian kingdom (see above), its language, or its inhabitants. **B.** *sb.* The language of this kingdom.

1852 tr. *C. R. Lepsius's Discoveries in Egypt* xx. 227 Three royal personages.. had built the principal temples in Naga, Ben Naga and in Wadi Temêd, and belonged.. to the most shining period of the Meroitic Empire. 1902 E. A. W. BUDGE *Hist. Egypt* VIII. 169 The Meroïtic inscriptions have not as yet been deciphered. 1911 F. L. GRIFFITH *Karanòg* vii. 83 It may be that, while Meroitic was the official language for writing, Nubian was the mother-tongue of Lower Nubia. 1911 A. H. SAYCE in J. Garstang et al. *Meroë* ix. 50 Whether *u*ᶜ was actually the word for 'land' in Meroitic is.. uncertain. *Ibid.* 51 The destruction is more complete even than that of the Meroitic temples at Kerma and Kawa. 1934 A. TOYNBEE *Study of Hist.* II. 117 This Meroitic Power lived on, as a politically independent embodiment of the Egyptiac Society, until the third century of the Christian Era. 1955 A. J. ARKELL *Hist. Sudan* vii. 160 The Meroitic hieroglyphic.. script seems to have been invented on the basis partly of the Meroitic cursive script, and partly of Egyptian hieroglyphs. 1967 P. L. SHINNIE *Meroe* v. 133 There is also just a hint that Meroitic may be related to the little-known group of languages known as Koman, now spoken in a limited area up the Blue Nile and around Jebel Gule. *Ibid.* vii. 156 The numerous finds of glass vessels imported as containers for oils and unguents as well as the mirrors show that Meroitic ladies, at least of the richer classes, took considerable trouble over their appearance.

merology (mə'rɒlədʒɪ). *Biol.* [f. Gr. μέρο-ς part, member + -LOGY.] That branch of anatomy which deals with the elementary tissues and fluids of the body (*Syd. Soc. Lex.* 1890).

1857 DUNGLISON *Med. Lex.*

meroola, var. MARULA.

meroon, obs. form of MAROON.

merop (ˈmɛrɒp), *a. nonce-wd.* [a Gr. μεροπ-, μέροψ speaking articulately.] Gifted with the power of speech. So **meˈropic** *a.* (in same sense).
1854 BADHAM *Halieut.* 224 Mute creatures [seem] as capable of jealousy and resentment as loud-tongued meropic man! **1864** BLACKMORE *Clara Vaughan* (1889) 172 He has no tongue, no merop tongue, I mean.

‖**meropia** (məˈrəʊpɪə). *Path.* [mod.L., f. MERO-[1] + Gr. -ωπία, f. ὠπ-, ὤψ eye: cf. *myopia, amblyopia.*] Dullness or obscuration of sight (Mayne *Expos. Lex.* 1856).

meropidan (məˈrɒpɪdən), *a.* and *sb. Ornith.* [f. mod.L. *Meropid-æ* + -AN.] **a.** *adj.* Of or pertaining to the picarian family *Meropidæ* (*Cassell's Encycl. Dict.* 1885). **b.** *sb.* A bird of the family *Meropidæ.*
1842 BRANDE *Dict. Sci.* etc., *Meropidans, Meropidæ*, the family of Insessorial birds of which the bee-eater (*Merops*) is the type.

†**meropie.** *Her. Obs.* [a. L. *merops*, a. Gr. μέροψ bee-eater.] = MEROPS.
1572 BOSSEWELL *Armorie* III. 26 b, On a torce d'Argente and Azure, a Meropie volante, Sable, membred Gules.

‖**merops** (ˈmɛrɒps). [L., a. Gr. μέροψ.] The bee-eater, *Merops apiaster.* (*Obs.* exc. *Ornith.* as the name of the genus.)
[**1678** RAY *Willughby's Ornith.* 148 Bellonius..writes thus concerning the Merops.] **1688** R. HOLME *Armoury* II. 262/1 The Merops, or Bee-eater, is like the Kings-Fisher in shape. **1706** in PHILLIPS (ed Kersey).

meroquin, meror, obs. ff. MAROQUIN, MIRROR.

meˈrorganize, *v. rare.* [f. MERO-[1] + ORGANIZE *v.*] *trans.* To bring into a partially organized state. Hence **merorganized, merorganizing,** *ppl. adjs.* Also **merorganiˈzation** (see quot. 1855).
1827 PROUT in *Phil. Trans.* CXVII. 375, I have provisionally adopted the term *merorganized*,..meaning to imply by it that bodies on passing into this state, become partly, or to a certain extent, organized. Thus starch I consider as *merorganized* sugar. *Ibid., note*, Any substance may be supposed capable of performing the part of a merorganizing body. **1855** OGILVIE *Suppl., Merorganization*, organization in part, or partial organization.

‖**meros** (ˈmɪərɒs). In Dicts. also **merus.** [mod.L., a. Gr. μηρός thigh.]
1. *Arch.* (See quots.)
1823 P. NICHOLSON *Pract. Build.* 588 Meros; the middle part of a triglyph. **1842–59** GWILT *Archit.* 1004 *Meros*, the plane face between the channels in the triglyphs of the Doric order.
2. *Anat.* The thigh.
1802 TURTON *Med. Gloss.* **1890** *Syd. Soc. Lex.*
3. One of the joints of a maxilliped.
1855 BATE in *Rep. Brit. Assoc.* 33 The third leaf-like plate consists of two joints, the fourth and the fifth, the meros and the carpus. **1857** —— in *Phil. Trans.* CXLVIII. 604 Fig 10 to 14. Pereiopoda:—*a*, Coxa; *b*, Basos; *c*, Ischium; *d*, Meros.

merostome (ˈmɛrəʊstəʊm). *Zool.* [ad. mod.L. *Merostomata* neut. pl., f. MERO-[1] + Gr. στόμα, στοματ- mouth; so called as having the mouth divided into separate parts.] Any arthropod of the order *Merostomata.* So **meroˈstomatous, meˈrostomous** *adjs.*, of or belonging to the *Merostomata.*
1881 GILL in *Smithson. Rep.* 431 The Merostomes, i.e. the Horseshoe Crabs of the present epoch.

merosymmetry (mɛrəʊˈsɪmɪtrɪ). *Cryst.* [f. MERO-[1] + SYMMETRY.] The condition or quality of being merohedral. So **merosyˈmmetrical** *a.* = MEROHEDRAL.
1875 *Chem. News* 19 Mar. 121 Such partially developed forms Mr. Maskelyne designated as mero-symmetrical forms. *Ibid.*, The varieties of mero-symmetry that a crystal may present. **1878** GURNEY *Crystallogr.* 55. **1895** STORY-MASKELYNE *Crystallogr.* §137 Mero-symmetrical forms may be hemi-symmetrical.

merosystematic (mɛrəʊsɪstɪˈmætɪk), *a. Cryst.* [f. MERO-[1] + SYSTEMATIC.] Having less than the number of normals by the law of symmetry.
1878 GURNEY *Crystallogr.* 39 Such forms are called merosystematic or merosymmetrical, or partially symmetrical forms. **1895** STORY-MASKELYNE *Crystallogr.* §139 Holo- and mero-systematic forms.

merour(e, obs. forms of MIRROR.

†**meroure.** *Obs. rare*[−1]. [a. L. *mæror*, f. *mærēre* to mourn.] Lamentation, sorrowing.
c **1450** *Mirour Saluacioun* 3770 In whas absence..eure sho contynuyd in weping and in meroure.

-merous, the ending of the adjs. *dimerous, trimerous, tetramerous, pentamerous*, etc., used *Bot.* in the sense of 'having (a specified number of) parts'. The numeral part of these words is often expressed in writing by an arabic figure, which is sometimes replaced by the English numeral word, as in *2-merous, five-merous.*
1870 HOOKER *Stud. Flora* p. x, Papaveraceæ. Flowers regular 2-merous. **1888** *Athenæum* 18 Aug. 228/2 A corolla of four petals could not have been provided with the same amount of nutritive material as a five-merous one.

Merovingian (mɛrəʊˈvɪndʒɪən), *a.* and *sb.* [a. F. *Merovingien*, f. med. L. *Merovingī* pl., the designation of Clovis and his descendants, repr. a Germanic word formed with patronymic suffix -ING[3] from the name (in L. form *Meroveus*) of the reputed ancestor of the family.] **A.** *adj.* Pertaining to the line of Frankish kings founded by Clovis (Chlodovech, in OHG. Hludwîg), and to the kingdoms reigned over by them in Gaul and Germany from about A.D. 500 to A.D. 751–2, when their rule was succeeded by that of the Carolingian dynasty. In *Palæogr.*, applied to the style of handwriting peculiar to the Merovingian period in the Frankish empire. **B.** *sb.* A king or other member of this royal line. In *Palæogr.* = Merovingian script.
1694 *Hist., Geogr. & Poet. Dict., Meroveans*, or *Merovingians*, a Name given to the Kings of France of the First Race. **1781** GIBBON *Decl. & F.* xxxv. III. 400 The Franks..had wisely established the right of hereditary succession in the noble family of the Merovingians. *Ibid.* xxxviii. III. 592 The wealth of the Merovingian princes consisted in their extensive domain. *Ibid.* 594 The..silent decay of the Merovingian line. **1867** J. B. DAVIS *Thesaur. Craniorum* 74 Merovingian Frank. *Ibid.*, Nos. 208 to 210 are from the Merovingian Cemetery at Envermeu, near Dieppe. *Ibid.* 75 Average Measurements of..Merovingian Skulls. **1892** E. M. THOMPSON *Gr. & Lat. Palaeogr.* xvi. 226 Merovingian Writing. *Ibid.* 231 The extravagances of the cursive Merovingian. **1900** EARL ROSEBERY *Napoleon* xii. 152 The ladies of his party..had to be conveyed in a Merovingian equipage drawn by several yoke of oxen.

merow, -owe, -owȝ, obs. ff. MARROW *sb.*[1]

meroxene (məˈrɒksiːn). *Min.* [ad. G. *meroxen* (W. Haidinger 1845), after A. Breithaupt's *Astrites meroxenus* (1841), 'probably from μέρος a part, and ξένος strange, because it is a part of what had been called uniaxial mica' (A. H. Chester).] A variety of biotite.
1854 DANA *Syst. Min.* (ed. 4) II. 226 The Vesuvian biotite occurs in brilliant crystals (Meroxene).

merpeople: see MER-.

†**merpyss.** *Obs. rare*[−1]. = PISMIRE.
1527 ANDREW *Brunswyke's Distyll. Waters* F iv, Than the merpysses shall..leve theyr egges behynde them.

merquisate, obs. form of MARCASITE.

merre, obs. form of MERE *sb.*[2], MYRRH.

merrels: see MEREL.

†**merribowk.** *Obs.* Also **meribauk, merry bauks.** [f. MERRY *a.* + BOWK. Cf. *sillibouk.*] A sillibub or posset.
1611 COTGR., *Laict aigre*, whay; also, a sillibub, or merribowke. **1613** BEAUM. & FL. *Coxcomb* III. iii. (1647) 108/2 And can you milke a Cow? and make a merrybowk [? *read*-buck *or* -bouk]? **1664** O. HEYWOOD *Diaries*, etc. (1883) III. 86 She had drunk six meribauk pots ful of ale. **1674** RAY *N.C. Words, Merry bauks*: a cold Posset, *Derb.*

†**ˈmerrify**, *v. Obs. nonce-wd.* [f. MERRY *sb.*[1] + -FY.] *trans.* To cause to be merry.
1780 MME. D'ARBLAY *Diary* (1904) I. 347 It merryfied us all.

merril(l)s: see MEREL.

merrily (ˈmɛrɪlɪ), *adv.* Forms: see MERRY *a.* and -LY[2]; also 4–6 **merely**, 4–7 **merily**, 5 **merelly**, 6 **merrellie, -ely, merelie, -ye**, 6– **merrily.** [f. MERRY *a.* + -LY[2].]
1. In early use: Pleasantly, agreeably, cheerfully, happily. In modern use: With exuberant gaiety, joyously, mirthfully, hilariously.
13.. *Gaw. & Gr. Knt.* 2295 Þen muryly efte con he mele, þe mon in þe grene. *c* **1386** CHAUCER *Manciple's T.* 34 No nyghtyngale Ne koude..Syngen so wonder myrily and weel. *a* **1400–50** *Alexander* 3862 Þe mone ouir þe montayns meryly it schynes. *c* **1440** *Gesta Rom.* xvi. 58 (Harl. MS.) The brid, þat sang so murely in the top of the tre, is þi conscience. **1552** in *Liturg. Serv. Q. Eliz.* (1847) 247 That I may.. even in the very pangs of death, cry boldly and merrily unto thee. **1553** BRENDE *Q. Curtius* x. 208 b, When he had spoken those wordes, he went merelye [orig. *alacriter*] into the fire. **1606** SHAKS. *Tr. & Cr.* v. x. 42 Full merrily the humble Bee doth sing. **1656** EARL MONM. tr. *Boccalini's Advts. fr. Parnass.* 126, I see the fire of Heresie.. breaks most forth there, where they drink merriliest. **17..** in Scott *Redgauntlet* ch. iv, Merrily danced the Quaker's wife, And merrily danced the Quaker. **1799** WORDSW. *Fountain* 22 No check, no stay, this Streamlet fears; How merrily it goes! **1848** DICKENS *Dombey* iv, 'Oh, very well, Uncle', said the boy, merrily. **1875** JOWETT *Plato* (ed. 2) I. 462, [I] would not go out of life less merrily than the swans.
†**2.** Jocularly, facetiously, wittily, in jest. *Obs.*
c **1386** CHAUCER *Wife's T.* 336 Iuuenal seith of pouerte myrily The poure man [etc.]. *a* **1548** HALL *Chron., Edw. V.* 21 This man merely..saied to his awne sonne that he would make him inheritor of ye croune meaning his awne house. **1568** GRAFTON *Chron.* II. 16 Philip the French king beyng merely disposed, sayde that william lay in Childebed, and norrisshed his fat belly. *a* **1626** BACON *New Atl.* 14 We knew he spake it but merrily. **1704** HEARNE *Duct. Hist.* (1714) I. 431 Treves..is..of no great Beauty of it self..and the Air generally so clouded..that it is by some called merrily *Cloaca Planetarum.*
Comb. **1767** S. PATERSON *Another Trav.* I. 129 The fleers of some of my merrily-disposed readers.
3. With alacrity; hence, with reference to inanimate things, briskly.
1530 PALSGR. 547/1 These beestes fede meryly towardes nyght. **1720** DE FOE *Capt. Singleton* v. (1840) 80 We went merrily up the river with the flood. **1899** *Times* 25 Oct. 5/3 The Mauser bullets rattled merrily, but impotently, on the armour [of a train]. **1912** G. B. SHAW *John Bull's Other Island* Pref. p. vi/2 He chalks up No Surrender merrily, and puts up one of the famous fights of history. **1926** W. R. INGE *Lay Thoughts* III. i. 185 The process [*sc.* increase of population] went on merrily at first because the new countries produced far more food than they needed for themselves. **1939** JOYCE *Finnegans Wake* III. 615 On the top of the longcar, as merrily we rolled along, we think of him looking at us yet. **1966** *Listener* 17 Feb. 247/1 Frontier wars ..continue as merrily in our own nuclear age as ever they did before 1914. **1972** R. ADAMS *Watership Down* xxxiii. 261 Why not a water-rabbit? I shall float merrily along—. **1974** *Observer* 3 Mar. 34/3 McKenzie merrily complained that the Battleground machine wasn't telling him anything.

merriment (ˈmɛrɪmənt). [f. MERRY *v.* + -MENT.]
†**1.** Something that contributes to mirth; a jest; 'a piece of fooling'; *spec.* a brief comic dramatic entertainment. *Obs.*
1576 FLEMING *Panopl. Epist.* 151 Your talke replenished with pleasant meriments. **1589** WARNER *Alb. Eng.* VI. xxx. (1612) 146 When they, indeed of merriments in Loue did theare conspire. *c* **1590** MARLOWE *Faustus* (1604) E 3, Beleeue me maister Doctor, this merriment hath much pleased me. **1592** NASHE *P. Penilesse* (ed. 2) 27 They shal not be brought vpon the Stage for any goodnes, but in a merriment of the Usurer and the Diuel. **1597** SHAKS. *2 Hen. IV*, II. iv. 324 Hee will..turne all to a merryment, if you take not the heat. **1632** LITHGOW *Trav.* VI. 292, I kept..the Germanes from langour, cherishing them with iouiall merriments.
†**b.** A humorous or scurrilous publication. *Obs.*
1697 BENTLEY *Diss. Epist.* etc., *Æsop* §9. 148 Not a bit better than our Penny-Merriments, printed at London-Bridge. **1824** DIBDIN *Libr. Comp.* 598 The rapid increase of cheap pamphlets (under the title of *Merriments*).
2. The action (or †an act) of merry-making, or of 'making merry' over something; hilarious enjoyment or jocularity; mirth, fun; †a festivity.
1588 SHAKS. *L.L.L.* v. ii. 139 They doe it but in mocking merriment. **1596** —— *Merch. V.* II. ii. 212 We haue friends That purpose merriment. **1602** —— *Ham.* v. i. 210 Your flashes of Merriment that were wont to set the Table on a Rore? **1663** BUTLER *Hud.* I. i. 674 [People] to crack'd Fiddle and hoarse Tabor, In Merriment did drudge and labour. **1674** PLAYFORD *Skill Mus.* I. 61 Feasts and other Merriments. **1699** BENTLEY *Phal.* 199 The Merriments in the Attic Villages. **1796** CRAUFURD in *Ld. Auckland's Corr.* (1862) III. 337 Beaulieu and his exploits were subjects of merriment in the army. **1869** FREEMAN *Norm. Conq.* III. xii. 162 And, mingled with all this, there is a certain element of grim merriment. **1903** *Edin. Rev.* Apr. 498 The old harvest or 'horkey' suppers with their feasting and merriment.. have too often been allowed to die out.
b. Used for: A subject for mirth.
1810 SCOTT *Lady of L.* I. xvi, A summer night, in greenwood spent, Were but to-morrow's merriment.
†**c.** Entertainment, amusement. *Obs.*
1590 SHAKS. *Mids. N.* III. ii. 146, I see you are all bent To set against me, for your merriment.

merriner, obs. form of MARINER.

merriness (ˈmɛrɪnɪs). Now *rare.* [f. MERRY *a.* + -NESS.] The quality or condition of being merry (in various senses of the adj.).
a **1300** *Cursor M.* 20510 Sittes stell now mar and lesse, And hers now þis mirines. *c* **1374** CHAUCER *Boeth.* III. Pr. ii. 52 (Camb. MS.) Wyf and chyldren þat men desyren for cause of delit and of merynesse. **1500–20** DUNBAR *Poems* xxiii. 31 Tak thow example and spend with mirriness. **1567** *Gude & Godlie Ball.* (S.T.S.) 76 The Angellis sang with merynes. **1599** JAS. I Βασιλ. Δωρον (1603) 115 Tempering it with grauitie, and quicknesse, or merrinesse, according to the subject, and occasion of the time. **1638** SIR T. HERBERT *Trav.* (ed. 2) 2 We vomited out a like eccho of thunder, plowing up the liquid seas in merrinesse. **1848** *Tait's Mag.* XV. 114 Joy and merriness are not for me. **1886** *Maneh. Exam.* 16 Nov. 5/5 The merriness which is supposed to be characteristic of the music of a peal of bells.

merring, variant of MARRING *vbl. sb.*

merro(u)r(e, obs. forms of MIRROR.

merrow (ˈmɛrəʊ). *Anglo-Irish.* [a. Irish *muirrúghach.*] A mermaid.
1828 T. C. CROKER *Fairy Leg.* II. 17 The Irish word Merrow..answers exactly to the English mermaid. **1889** FROUDE *Two Chiefs Dunboy* xxv, You slip through their hands like a merrow.

merrowre, obs. form of MIRROR.

merry (ˈmɛrɪ), *sb.* [altered form of MERISE, probably due to interpretation of the *s* as a plural ending.] A kind of black cherry. Also *attrib.*
1595 CHAPMAN *Ovid's Banq. Sence* B 2 b, White and red Iessamines, Merry, Melliphill. **1707** MORTIMER *Husb.*

(1721) II. 265 They [cherries] do best grafted on the Black-Cherry-stock, or the Merry-stock. **1757** COOPER *Distiller* III. lii. (1760) 221 The black cherry, the Merry or Honey Cherry. **1825** COBBETT *Rur. Rides* 86 There are not many of the merries, as they call them in Kent and Hampshire. **1899** *Longm. Mag.* Dec. 179 The wild cherry tree, or merry-tree, also known..as the 'Gean'.

merry ('mɛrı), *a.* and *adv.* Forms: 1 myiȝe, murȝe, myriȝe, miriȝe, merȝe, 1–3 meriȝe, 3 murȝe (*comparative* murgre, murgore, *superl.* murgost, -gust), 3–4 murye, muri, 3–5 murie, 4 murye (*compar.* murer), 4–5 mury; 3–4 miri(e, 4–5 myry, miry, 4–6 myrie, 4–5 myri, (5 *compar.* mirgurre), 5–6 *Sc.* mirrie, mirry, myrrie, 6 myrry, *Sc.* mirre; 3–6 meri, 4–5 merey, 4–6 merie, -y(e, 5 merrye, 5–6 mere, 6 *Sc.* meary, 6–7 merrie, 6– merry. [OE. *myr(i)ȝe* (:—OTeut, type **murgjo-*), whence *myrȝð* MIRTH; outside English the only cognate corresponding in sense is MDu. **merch*, whence *merchte* = MIRTH, *merchtocht* rejoicing, *mergelijc* joyful, *mergen* = MERRY *v.* It is, however, probable that the word is identical with the OTeut. **murgjo-* short, represented by OHG. *murg-fâri* lasting a short time, and by the Gothic derivative *ga-maurgjan* to shorten, and presumably descending, with Gr. βραχύς, from an Indogermanic *mr̥ghu-*.

The transition from the assumed original sense 'short' to the OE. sense 'pleasant' is somewhat difficult, but may have been brought about through the intervention of a derived factitive verb, meaning 'to shorten', and hence 'to shorten time', 'to cheer'; cf. ON. *skemta* to amuse, f. *skamt*, neut. of *skamm-r* short.]

A. *adj.*

1. Of things: Pleasing, agreeable.

†**a.** Of occupations, events, or conditions: Causing pleasure or happiness; pleasing, delightful. *Obs.*

a merry meal: see MEAL *sb.*² 2 f.

c **888** K. ÆLFRED *Boeth.* xxxi. §1 For þy ic nat hwæt þa woruldlustas myrȝes bringað [L. *quid habeat jucunditatis*] hiora lufiȝendum. *a* **1000** *Boeth. Metr.* xiii. 45 Him þa twigu þincað emne swa merȝe þat hi þæs metes ne recð. *c* **1000** ÆLFRIC *Hom.* (Th.) I. 154 Ðeos woruld, þeah ðe heo myriȝe hwiltidum ȝeþuht sy. *c* **1205** LAY. 10147 Þa þuhte Elæuðerie þat tiðende swiðe murie. *a* **1225** *Ancr. R.* 390 He..spek swuðe sweteliche & so murie wordes þet heo muhten þe deade arearen urom deaðe to liue. *c* **1290** *S. Eng. Leg.* I. 179/19 Guod it is and murie: breþren to wonie i-fere. *c* **1325** *Spec. Gy Warw.* 905 Hu murie hit were, to haue þe siht Off godes face, þat is so briht. **1435** MISYN *Fire of Love* 57 No þinge is meriar þen Ihesu to synge. **1502** ATKINSON tr. *De Imitatione* III. vi. 200 Nothynge is more swete than is loue, ..nothynge..meryer [L. *jucundius*]. **1567** TURBERV. *Epit.*, etc. 110 b, Let others then that feelen ioy Extole the merrie Month of May.

b. †Of a place or country: Pleasant, delightful in aspect or conditions (*obs.*). So originally in the designation ***Merry England***, in which the adj. was subsequently apprehended as in sense 3. Also ***Merrie England***, freq. in ironic or satirical use; so ***Merrie Englander***.

c **1205** LAY. 24964 For grið makeð godne mon gode workes wurchen,..þat lond bið þa murgre. *c* **1250** *Gen. & Ex.* 212 God bar him in-to paradis,..bi-taȝte him al ðat mirie stede. *a* **1300–1400** *Cursor M.* 8 (Gött.) Brut þat berne bolde of hand, First conqueror of meri ingland. **13..** *E. E. Allit. P.* A. 935 Now tech me to þat myry mote [Jerusalem]. **1398** TREVISA *Barth. De P. R.* XV. v. (Tollem. MS.), It [Armenia] is most mery londe with herbes, corne, wodes and frute. **1415** HOCCLEVE *To Sir J. Oldcastle* 487 Remember yow, heuene is a miry place And helle is ful of sharp aduersitee. **1436** *Siege Calais* in *Pol. Poems* (Rolls) II. 156 The crown of mery Yngland. **1500–20** DUNBAR *Poems* xxv. 21 Edinburgh the mirry toun. **1590** SPENSER *F. Q.* I. x. 61 Saint George of mery England, the signe of victoree. **1596** —— *Prothal.* 128 To merry London, my most kyndly Nurse. [**1782** COWPER *Gilpin* 125 Thus all through merry Islington These gambols he did play. **1828** SCOTT *F. M. Perth* i, Perthshire contains ..tracts, which may vie with the richness of merry England herself.] **1839** G. DANIEL in *Bentley's Misc.* V. 98 (*title*) Merrie England in the olden time. *c* **1882** (*title*) Merrie England its kings & queens..with pictures and stories from English history. **1893** *Ladies' Home Jrnl.* Feb. 13/1 The old Roman custom..was transplanted to merrie England. **1902** HOOD & GERMAN (*title*) Merrie England: a new and original comic opera in two acts. **1912** A. HUXLEY *Let.* 16 June (1969) 43 It [*sc.* a monument] is made of a peculiar grey stone, which looks just like that horrible papier-mâché stone of which ruined castles are made in exhibitions of Merrie England. **1930** E. WAUGH *Labels* 22 The Merrie-Englanders have so eloquently upheld the cause of freedom that a subdued but smouldering resentment is now one of our national characteristics. **1946** J. B. PRIESTLEY *Bright Day* x. 301 The war was over, democracy saved, and here was Merrie England. **1970** H. BRAUN *Parish Churches* xx. 236 The happy breed of the wool-rich yeomen followed in that Merrie England which was later to turn to mourning for Englishmen clubbed to death by neighbours in the Great Rebellion. **1971** B. INGLIS *Poverty & Industr. Revolution* iv. 197 Cobbett..was far from being a Merrie Englander, in the sense of seeing the past bathed in a romantic glow. **1973** *Radio Times* 13 Dec. 27 (*caption*), The redoubtable Dr Who returns..to fight *The Time Warrior* in not-so-merrie England: 5.10. **1974** *Punch* 23 Oct. 654/1 Mecca had planned to build a Merrie Englande entertainment complex to rival Disneyland.

Proverbial phrase. **1550** HUTCHINSON *Image of God* Epist. (1560) ☛iij, It was a mery world (quod yᵉ papist) before the Bible came forth in englysh, all thinges were good chepe and plentyful. **1593** SHAKS. *2 Hen. VI*, IV. ii. 9 It was neuer merrie worlde in England, since Gentlemen came vp. **1601** —— *Twel. N.* III. i. 109.

†**c.** Of sound or music: Pleasant, sweet. Hence of animals, esp. birds: Having a pleasant voice. *Obs.* (Cf. sense 3.)

c **1000** *Ags. Hymn* (Surtees) 141 Mid meriȝum..lofsange *dulci ymno.* *c* **1350** *Will. Palerne* 2192 Alle men þat mut herde of þe muri houndes. *c* **1385** CHAUCER *Nun's Pr. T.* 31 His voys was murier than the murie Orgon. **1387** TREVISA *Higden* (Rolls) IV. 307 Þe emperour bouȝt þat mery bridde. *c* **1400** LYDG. *Chorle & Bird* xv, Ryngyng of feters is no mery sowne. *c* **1420** *Chron. Vilod.* 2101 A merry masse þer was y-songe. **1500–20** DUNBAR *Poems* xlvi. 3, I hard a merle with mirry notis sing. *Ibid.* 26 This mirry gentil nychtingaill. **1535** COVERDALE *Ps.* lxxx[i]. 2 Brynge hither the tabret, the mery harpe & lute.

†**d.** Of weather, climate, atmospheric conditions, etc.: Pleasant, fine. Of a wind: Favourable.

1297 R. GLOUC. (Rolls) 5697 Þe erþe ȝeld betere & þet weder was murgore by is daye & lasse tempeste in þe se þan me er ysaye. **13..** *E.E. Allit. P.* B. 804 In þe myry mornyng ȝe may your waye take. **1390** GOWER *Conf.* II. 332 He telth ..hou ther schon a merye Sunne. *c* **1400** *Laud Troy Bk.* 14412 Seuen dayes fauȝt thei to gedre, And al that while was mury wedre. *c* **1410** LOVE *Bonavent. Mirr.* v. (1510) Cij, Our Lorde God after tempeste sendethe soft and mery wedder. *c* **1450** *Merlin* 384 The seson was myri and softe. **1576** FLEMING *Panopl. Epist.* 423 Euen as Gouernours of shippes..cut the waues as they are furthered with a merrie winde: euen so let us frame our studie and labour. **1590** SHAKS. *Com. Err.* IV. i. 90 The merrie winde Blowes faire from land. **1599** HAKLUYT *Voy* (1904) IV. 360 At the next mery wind tooke shipping. **1630** WINTHROP *New Eng.* (1853) I. 18 We tacked about..with a merry gale in all our sails. **1685** DRYDEN tr. *Hor. Ode* III. xxix. 101 In my small Pinnace I can sail,..And running with a merry gale,..my safety seek..Within some little winding Creek.

fig. **1402** *Repl. Friar D. Topias* in *Pol. Poems* (Rolls) II. 72 Whi with not thi cow make myry weder in thi dish?

†**e.** Of dress: Handsome, gay. *Obs.*

a **1400–50** *Alexander* 2864 A mery mantill of mervailous hewis.

†**f.** Of herbs, drugs, etc.: Pleasant to the taste or smell. *Obs.*

c **1386** CHAUCER *Nun's Pr. T.* 146 Ye shul haue digestyues ..Of herbe yue, growyng in oure yeerd, thir mery is. **1398** TREVISA *Barth. De P. R.* XVII. xxvii. (1495) 620 Cassia is swete and mery of smell.

†**g.** ***a merry mean***: a happy medium.

1399 LANGL. *Rich. Redeles* II. 139 But mesure is a meri mene þouȝ men moche yerne. *c* **1460** J. RUSSELL *Bk. Nurture* 107 Mesure is a mery meene whan God is not displesed. *a* **1575** GASCOIGNE *Posies, Flowers* 41 Thus learne I by my glasse, that merrie meane is best. **1616** SURFL. & MARKH. *Country Farm* 580 So greatly..is the merrie meane commended.

h. Of a saying, jest, etc.: Amusing, diverting, funny. *Obs.* or *arch.*, with mixture of sense 3.

c **1470** HENRY *Wallace* II. 36 Quhen Wallas herd spek of that mery saw, He likyt weill at that mercat to be. **1530** PALSGR. 244/2 Mery taunt, *lardon.* *Ibid.*, Mery jeste a ryddle, *sornette.* **1563** *Homilies* II. *Idolatry* III. (1859) 265 Seneca much commendeth Dionysius, for his merry robbing of such decked and jewelled puppets. **1588** SHAKS. *Tit. A.* V. ii. 175 Two of her Brothers were condemn'd to death, My hand cut off, and made a merry iest. **1595** DUNCAN *App. Etymol.* (E.D.S.) 68 *Facetiæ*, mirrie bourds. **1632** LITHGOW *Trav.* IX. 378 There is a merry secret heere concerning the women. **1728** MORGAN *Algiers* I. vi. 185 The Notions all the Mussulmans have of the Antichrist..are really merry. *Ibid.* 188, I had like to have left out the very merriest Passage in the whole Story. **1769** E. BANCROFT *Guiana* 328 A variety of fables which are merry. **1849** JAMES *Woodman* ii, He gave me the merry book [a copy of Chaucer].

2. Of looks or appearance: †Pleasant, agreeable, bright (*obs.*); hence, expressive of cheerfulness, mirthful, hilarious (in modern use merged in sense 3).

a **1225** *Leg. Kath.* 314 Þi leor is, meiden, lufsum, & ti muð murie. *c* **1250** *Gen. & Ex.* 2258 Her non hadden ðo loten miri. **13..** *Seuyn Sag.* (W.) 3357 The erl come with meri chere, Omang al that folk in fere. *c* **1440** *Promp. Parv.* 338/2 Myry yn chere, *letus.* **1559** *Passage Q. Eliz.* A ij, Her grace by holding vp her handes, and merie countenaunce to such as stode farre of,..did declare her selfe [etc.]. **1703** *Lond. Gaz.* No. 3948/4 A dun Gelding..with a round Barrel, longish Legg'd,..a merry Countenance. **1861** HUGHES *Tom Brown at Oxf.* iii, He was a pleasant-looking fellow,..with dark hair, and a merry brown eye.

3. a. Of persons and their attributes: Full of animated enjoyment (in early use chiefly with reference to feasting or sport); joyous, mirthful, hilarious. Also of permanent temper or disposition: Given to joyousness or mirth.

the Merry Monarch: a frequent designation for Charles II. †***merrymeinie*** (obs.), ***merrymen*** (see MERRY MAN 1): applied in ballad poetry to the followers of Robin Hood; hence sometimes used *allusively*.

c **1320** *Sir Tristr.* 1198 A miriman were he ȝif he o liue ware. *c* **1350** *Will. Palerne* 4926 As þei muriest at þe mete þat time seten, þer come menskful messageres. *c* **1375** *Cursor M.* 4812 (Fairf.) Quen þai saghe þer corne plente Murer [*earlier texts* gladder, bliþer] men miȝt neuer be. *a* **1380** *Min. Poems fr. Vernon MS.* 680 Whon men beoþ muryest at heor Mele: I rede ȝe þenke on ȝusterday. *c* **1400** *Destr. Troy* 4787 Mery was the menye & maden gret Ioye. *c* **1461** *E.E. Misc.* (Warton Cl.) 48 The boy was mery y-nowe. **1500–20** DUNBAR *Poems* xxv. 27 Bring ȝow sone to Edinburgh ioy, For to be mirry amang ws. *c* **1510** *Lytell Geste Robyn Hood* iv. in *Neuengl. Leseb.* (1895) I. 180/14 And he founde there Robyn hode And all hys mery meyne. *Ibid.* v. 180/115 Buske you my mery yonge men. **1513** MORE in Grafton *Chron.* (1568) II. 784 King Edward woulde say that he had three concubines,..one, the meriest, one the wyliest, the thirde the holyest harlot in the realme... But the meriest was Shores wife. **1606** SHAKS. *Tr. & Cr.* I. ii. 27 He is melancholy without cause, and merry against the haire. **1632** LITHGOW *Trav.* III. 90, I was exceeding merry with my old friends. ? *c* **1665** ROCHESTER *Sat. on King* 19 Restless he rolls about from Whore to Whore A merry Monarch, scandalous, and poor. **1712** STEELE *Spect.* No. 462 ¶5 This very Mayor afterwards erected a statue of his merry Monarch in Stocks-Market. **1794** MRS. RADCLIFFE *Myst. Udolpho* xxv, Poor Ludovico would be as merry as the best of them, if he was well. **1832** W. IRVING *Alhambra* II. 262 His memory was always cherished as that of a merry companion. **1849** JAMES *Woodman* ii, She was the merriest little abbess in the world.

†**b.** Happy. *Obs.*

a **1380** *S. Ambrosius* 426 in Horstm. *Altengl. Leg.* (1878) 15/1 He..wepte for holymen and murie þat passed weren vp to glorie. **1388** WYCLIF *Job* xxi. 23 This yuel man dieth ..riche and blesful, that is, myrie. **1513** MORE in Grafton *Chron.* (1568) II. 781 The true Lorde Hastinges..was neuer merier, nor thought his life in more suretie in all his dayes. **1529** MORE in *Four C. Eng. Lett.* (1880) 12, I pray you be with my..household mery in God.

transf. **1634** SIR T. HERBERT *Trav.* 184 [Silkworms] will be no where merry nor vsefull, but where are store of Mulbery Trees.

c. Pleasantly amused; hence, facetious, 'pleasant'. Const. *with, on, upon* (a person). *Obs.* or *arch.* (Cf. *make merry*, 3 e below.)

1607 SHAKS. *Timon* III. ii. 42, I know his Lordship is but merry with me. **1703** ROWE *Fair Penit.* Ded., There is hardly such a thing as being merry, but at another's Expence. **1694** ATTERBURY *On Prov.* xiv. 6, Serm. 1726 I. 195 They were Men who..took their Fill of all the Good Things of this World; and..were very merry, and very bitter upon those that did not. **1709** SWIFT *Merlin's Proph.* Wks. 1755 II. I. 179 Astrology..is by no means an art to be despised, whatever Mr. Bickerstaff, or other merry gentlemen are pleased to think. **1714** *Spectator* No. 573 (init.), You are pleased to be very merry, as you imagine, with us Widows. **1772** FOOTE *Nabob* I. 17 You are merry, Sir. **1831** LYTTON *Godolphin* 9 You are merry on me, I see.

d. Hilarious from drink; slightly tipsy. (Cf. *market merry.*)

1575–6 *Durham Depos.* (Surtees) 287 The said Sʳ Richerd, being mery with drinke, maid a quarrell to this examinate. *Ibid.* 288 The said Sʳ Richerd will be mery with drinke ther, but not dronken. **1681** LUTTRELL *Brief Rel.* (1857) I. 134 Mr. Verdon..returning home pretty merry, took occasion to murder a man on the road. **1719** D'URFEY *Pills* III. 7 Drunk, which the vulgar call merry. **1838** JAMES *Robber* vi, Doveton, who was beginning to get merry, and eke good-humoured in his cups.

e. Phrases. ***to make merry*** (refl. and intr.): to be festive or jovial; to indulge in feasting and jollity. ***to make merry (over,*** †***with)***: to make fun (of), to ridicule. ***merry hell***: see HELL *sb.* 10 q.

c **1320** *Sir Tristr* 3085 Boþe seiȝe he Wiþ too houndes mirie made. *c* **1350** *Will Palerne* 1880 Make we vs merie for mete haue we at wille. *c* **1440** *Cast. Persev.* 2709 Make us mery, & lete hym gone! he was a good felawe. **1500–20** DUNBAR *Poems* xiii. 32 Sum makis him mirry at the wynis. **1530** PALSGR. 625/2 Make mery, syrs, we shall go hence to morowe. **1628** EARLE *Microcosm.*, *Tavern* (Arb.) 33 Men come heere to make merry. **1761** HUME *Hist. Eng.* II. xxviii. 135 The people made merry with the Cardinal's ostentation. **1771** GOLDSM. *Hist. Eng.* II. 403 The people made merry with this absurd and brutal statute. **1791** *Gentl. Mag.* 19/1 My horse took fright at some hay-makers who were carouzing and making merry. **1832** TENNYSON *Pal. of Art* 3 Oh, soul, make merry and carouse. **1890** *Sat. Rev.* 25 Oct. 481/2 He makes merry over their deficiencies.

f. In proverbs and proverbial comparisons. ***the more the merrier.*** (See also CRICKET *sb.*¹ 1 d, GRIG *sb.*¹ 5.)

13.. *E.E. Allit. P.* A. 850 Bot vchon enle we wolde were fyf, þe mo þe myryer. **13..** *K. Alis.* 1163 Swithe mury hit is in halle, When the burdes wawen alle. **1546** J. HEYWOOD *Prov.* (1867) 65 It is mery in halle, when berds wag all. **1562** —— *Prov. & Epigr.* (1867) 433 Tis good to be mery and wyse: How shall fooles folow that aduyse? **1564** PILKINGTON *Let.* Wks. (Parker Soc.) Pref. 7 The bishop of Man liveth here at ease, and as merry as Pope Joan. **1595** SHAKS *John* IV. i. 18, I should be as merry as the day is long. **1614** JONSON *Barth. Fair* (1631) I. vi. 83, I, and Salomon too, Win, (the more the merrier) Win, we'll leaue Rabby Busy in a Booth. *a* **1643** W. CARTWRIGHT *Ordinary* III. iv, I'l be As merry as a Pismire. *a* **1745** SWIFT *Direct. Servants, Footman*, Live a short life and a merry one. **1768–74** TUCKER *Lt. Nat.* (1834) II. 337 He knew how to be merry and wise. **1792** BURNS '*Here's a health to them that's awa*'', It's gude to be merry and wise, It's gude to be honest and true. **1811** JANE AUSTEN *Sense & Sens.* II. iii. 38 The more the merrier say I, and I thought it would be more comfortable for them to be together. **1873** HAMERTON *Intell. Life* I. v. (1876) 29 Merry as a lark. **1874** TROLLOPE *Way we live Now* (1875) I. xxxiii. 208 The more the merrier. Ruby'll have enough for the two o' you, I'll go bail. **1922** E. O'NEILL *Hairy Ape* (1923) v. 47 De more de merrier when I gits started. **1928** A. HUXLEY *Point Counter Point* xi. 168 The more the merrier was her principle; or if 'merrier' were too strong a word, at least the noisier, the more tumultuously distracting. **1952** 'M. COST' *Hour Awaits* 28 The more the merrier,..for with her cousins also crowding the Hotel, additional 'cover' would be afforded. **1974** 'D. FLETCHER' *Lovable Man* II. 120, I moved over to features. More the merrier. I'm free-lance now.

4. Of times or seasons: Characterized by festivity or rejoicing.

1567 [see 1]. **1596** SHAKS. *2 Hen. IV*, v. iii. 38 Welcome merry Shrouetide. **1617** MORYSON *Itin.* II. 87 To keepe a merry Christmas. **1667** LD. SANDWICH *Let.* in *Sir W. Temple's Wks.* (1720) II. 136, I wish you a very merry Christmas. **1710** SWIFT *Jrnl. to Stella* 21 Dec., But first I will wish you a merry Christmas and a happy New Year. **1710–11** *Ibid.* 25 Mar., 25. Morning. I wish you a merry new year: this is the first day of the year, you know, with us. **1843** DICKENS *Christmas Carol* iii. They wished each other Merry Christmas in their can of grog.

5. Special collocations: †**merry-bout**, *slang*, an act of sexual intercourse; †**merry main** (see

MAIN *sb.*[3] 1), a game at dice; †**merry Monday**, the Monday before Shrove Tuesday; **merry night**, *north. dial.*, a night given up to festivities and sport. For *merry dancers*, *Greek*, *grig*, *pin*, see DANCER 5, GREEK *sb.* 5, GRIG *sb.*[1] 5, PIN *sb.* 11. See also MERRY-ANDREW, MERRY-MAN, etc.

1780 *Newgate Cal.* V. 314 Being asked..if she thought it proper for a woman of decency to ask another 'how she did after this *merry-bout', and 'whether she thought a rape was a merry-bout'. **1665** *Merry main [see MAIN *sb.*[3] 1]. **1667** DRYDEN *Secr. Love* IV. i, Come, gentlemen, let's lose no time: While they are talking, let's have one merry main before we die, for mortality sake. **1729** GAY *Polly* III. (1772) 198 Does not this drum-head here,..tempt you to fling a merry main or two? **1565** in Picton *L'pool Munic. Rec.* (1883) I. 35 Monday next before Fasten's eve or Shrovetide called *Merry Monday. **1803** R. ANDERSON *Cumbld. Ball.* 65 Aa, lad! sec a *murry-neet we've hed at Bleckell. **1819** WORDSW. *Waggoner* II. 30 'Tis the village Merry-Night! **1837** *Penny Cycl.* VIII. 223/2 Cumbrian peasantry have various festive meetings, called the *kirn*, or harvest-home, sheep-shearing, merry nights, and upshots.

6. *Comb.* **a.** parasynthetic, as ***merry-conceited***, ***-eyed***, ***-faced***, ***-hearted***, ***-lipped***, ***-minded***, ***-witted*** adjs.

1547-64 BAULDWIN *Mor. Philos.* (Palfr.) 6 Aristippus.. was a merry-witted fellow. **1548** SIR P. HOBY in Strype *Eccl. Mem.* (1721) II. App. Y. 79, I hear say he is a man somewhat aged and merry-conceited when he list. **1611** BIBLE *Isa.* xxiv. 7 All the merrie hearted doe sigh. **1625** K. LONG tr. *Barclay's Argenis* IV. xii. 277 He was..merry-conceited in words. **1648-60** HEXHAM, *Klucht-sinnigh*, Merrie-minded. **1684** OTWAY *Atheist* III. i, You Plump-cheek'd merry-ey'd Rogue. **1816** L. HUNT *To J. H.* 20 It [*sc.* a mouth] breaks into such sweetness, With merry-lipped completeness. **1838** DICKENS *Nich. Nick.* vi, The merry-faced gentleman sent round the punch. **1851** RUSKIN *Stones Ven.* (1874) I. xx. 220 Clear, crisp, ringing, merry-minded waves.

b. quasi-*adv.* with another adj.

a **1618** SYLVESTER *Auto-machia* 125 Sailing all my Life On merry-sorry Seas. **1865** KINGSLEY *Herew.* x, They are laughing and roaring now, merry-mad every one of them.

B. *adv.* **a.** = MERRILY.

c **1220** *Bestiary* 570 Mirie ȝe singeð ðis mere. *c* **1320** *Seuyn Sag.* (W.) 556 Foules songe therinne murie. *c* **1381** CHAUCER *Parl. Foules* 592 Daunsith he murye that is myrtheles? **14..** *Sir Beues* 107 (MS. E.) Bellys he herde merye rynge. **14..** *Arth. & Merl.* 2485 (Kölbing) He was grauen & layd full merrye In the towne of Glasenburye. **1546** *Supplic. Poore Commons* (E.E.T.S.) 87 They wedde and bury, and synge ful mery, but all for money. **1567** *Gude & Godlie Ball.* (S.T.S.) 68 We suld..Without ony dissemmillance Be blyith, and myrrie sing.

b. *Comb.*, as ***merry-running***, ***-singing***, ***-turned***; **merry-begot**, **-begotten** *dial.*, illegitimate; also *sb.*, a bastard.

1549 CHALONER *Erasm. on Folly* I j b, With suche taunts and meritourned answers they provoke men to laughter. **1593** NASHE *Christs T.* Wks. (Grosart) V. 109 The younger men in their merry-running Madrigals. **1606** SYLVESTER *Du Bartas* II. iv. II. *Magnif.* 1133 A willing Troup of merry-singing Swains. **1785** GROSE *Dict. Vulg. Tongue*, *Merry begotten*, a bastard. **1890** HALL CAINE *Bondman* I. vi, Maybe you think it nice to bring up your daughter with the merry-begot of any ragabash that comes prowling along.

†**merry**, *v.* *Obs.* [OE. *myrgan* (:—*murgjan), related to *myrge* MERRY *a.*]

1. *intr.* To be merry.

c **1000** *Ags. Ps.* (Th.) xlvi. 1 Fæȝniað and myrȝað Gode mid wynsumre stemne. *a* **1310** in Wright *Lyric P.* xiv. 45 In May hit murgeth when hit dawes. *c* **1460** *Towneley Myst.* xiii. 714 Lo, he merys; lo, he laghys, my swetyng.

2. *trans.* To make (a person, etc.) merry.

a **1310** in Wright *Lyric P.* xiii. 44 Wowes this wilde drakes, Miles murgeth huere makes. *c* **1400** *Pride of Life* (Brandl, 1898) 296 A ha, solas, now þou seist so þou miriest me in my mode. **1627-77** FELTHAM *Resolves* I. xxv. 44 Though pleasure merries the Senses for a while: yet horror after vulturs the unconsuming heart.

merry-andrew, **merry-Andrew** (ˌmɛrɪ ˈændruː). [app. f. MERRY *a.* + *Andrew* proper name (cf. ANDREW 2).

Hearne's statement, in the preface to his edition of Benedictus Abbas (1735) that 'Merry Andrew' was originally applied to Dr. Andrew Borde (died 1549) has neither evidence nor intrinsic probability, though Borde had a reputation for buffoonery, as is shown by the traditional attribution to him of various collections of jests. In 1668 (29 Aug.) Pepys says that he saw at Bartholomew Fair a ridiculous play called 'Marry Andrey', but that this title has any connexion with *merry-andrew* is very doubtful.]

1. One who entertains people by means of antics and buffoonery; a clown; properly (in early use), a mountebank's assistant.

1673 DRYDEN *Epil. to Univ. Oxford* 11 Th' Italian Merry-Andrews took their place, And quite Debauch'd the Stage with lewd Grimace. **1677** W. SHERLOCK *Answ. T. Danson* 69 As ridiculous..as it would be very gravely to confute Tom Thumb, or merry Andree, of a Town Lampoon. **1697** DRYDEN *Æneid* Ded., This is like Merry Andrew on the low rope, copying lubberly the same tricks which his master is so dexterously performing on the high. **1749** FIELDING *Tom Jones* XII. viii, He found the master of the puppet-show belabouring the back and ribs of his poor Merry-Andrew. **1851** BORROW *Lavengro* lii. (1893) 202 Listening to the jokes of the merry-andrews from the platforms in front of the temporary theatres.

b. *fig.*

1694 WOOD *Life* (O.H.S.) III. 458 *note*, To make your self the merry andrew of the company [you] did venter upon a person freely to expose him to scorne. **1772** NUGENT tr. *Hist. Fr. Gerund* I. 488 Those who are not sought out as the Merry-Andrews of the pulpit. **1827** CARLYLE *Misc.*, *Richter* (1857) I. 11 Richter is a man of mirth, but he seldom or never condescends to be a merryandrew.

c. *attrib.* or as *adj.*

1689 *Answ. Lords & Commoners Sp.* 25 A Reverend Prelate..whom he stiles, in a sort of a Merry-Andrew-vein, Church of England Apostle and Captain of her Life-Guard. **1798** *Lit. Mem. Living Authors* I. 119 The jokes and merriment of this merry-andrew philosopher. **1816** *Sporting Mag.* XLVII. 177 Scroggins made some merry-andrew tricks to save his wind. **1847** ALB. SMITH *Chr. Tadpole* xlix. (1879) 422 A poor fellow who went about the country in the merry-Andrew line.

d. *Comb.*, as ***merry-andrew-like*** adv.

1787 WOLCOT (P. Pindar) *Lousiad* II. Wks. I. 238 Turn it [thy wig] inside out, And wear it, Merry-Andrew like, about.

2. *pl.* Playing cards of the lowest quality.

1866 [see HARRY *sb.*[2] 3]. **1867** FRY *Playing-Card Terms* in *Philol. Soc. Trans.* 55 *Andrews, Merry Andrews*, Playing-cards of the fourth or lowest class or quality.

Hence **merry-'andrew**, **merry-'andrewize** *vbs. intr.*, to play the merry-andrew; **merry-'andrewism**, buffoonery, clownishness.

1836 *Fraser's Mag.* XIII. 37 Nothing is more distasteful ..than the undiscriminating Merryandrewism of an ingrained vulgarian. **1861** T. L. PEACOCK *Gryll Gr.* viii, Arch-quacks have taken to merry-andrewizing in a new arena. **1891** G. MEREDITH *One of our Conq.* III. iii. 40 He can, if imps are in him, merryandrew as much as he pleases.

merry-bauks, **-bush**: see MERRIBOWK.

†**merry-gall.** *Obs.* Also 6 **merrygald**, 7 **merigal.** [See GALL *sb.*[2]: the first element might so far as form is concerned be *mery* MARROW[1], but the sense of the combination is not obvious.] A sore produced by chafing.

1575 TURBERV. *Venerie* 139 (May be) he seekes to haue my Sewet for himselfe, Whiche sooner heales a merrygald then Pothecaries pelfe. **1597** GERARDE *Herbal* III. l. 1202 If such as iourney or trauell do carry with them a branch or rod of *Agnus castus* in their hand, it will keepe them from merry gals, and wearines. **1601** HOLLAND *Pliny* II. 101 It healeth all merry-gals and raw places where the flesh is rubbed off or chafed: it helpeth the rank rammish smel vnder the arm-holes [L. *intertriginum et alarum vitiis perfrictionibusque.. non dubie mederi*]. *Ibid.* 319 It is good to anoint merigals therwith, namely, when one part of the body is fretted & chafed against another [L. *prodest et confricatis membris*].

merryghe, obs. form of MARROW *sb.*[1]

†**'merry-go-down.** *slang. Obs.* Strong ale.

a **1500** *Songs & Carols* (Percy Soc.) 92 Where is the best wyn? tell yow me... I know a drawght off mery-go-downe, The best it is in all thys towne. **1577** HARRISON *England* II. xi. 86 A pot of hufcappe or mery go downe. **1599** NASHE *Lenten Stuffe* Ded. A 3 b, You..can do no lesse then present mee with the best mornings draught of merry-go-downe in your quarters.

merry-go-round.

1. A revolving machine carrying wooden horses or cars, on or in which persons ride round and round for amusement; a roundabout.

1729 *Daily Post* 23 Aug., Here's the merry-go-rounds: Come, who rides? **1806-7** J. BERESFORD *Miseries Hum. Life* (1826) xx. 252 May she fall to the ground From a merry-go-round. **1858** HAWTHORNE *Fr. & It. Note-Bks.* (1883) 26 There were merry-go-rounds, wooden horses, and other provision for children's amusements. **1896** E. A. KING *Ital. Highways* 76 It [*sc.* a steam organ] belonged to a travelling merry-go-round.

2. *fig.* A 'whirl'. Also **merry-go-rounder**, a cause of astonishment.

1838 DICKENS *O. Twist* II. xxv. 81 Oh, my eye! here's a merry-go-rounder!—Tommy Chitling's in love! **1856** R. W. PROCTER *Barber's Shop* xiii. (1883) 98 This elysium of a business, this merry-go-round of trade. **1890** H. G. DAKYNS *Xenophon* I. p. cxx, What a merry-go-round of soldierly adventure!

3. Used *attrib.* or as *adj.* of a railway system, whereby a train of coal hoppers runs perpetually on a circular route between consignor and consignee.

1963 *Mod. Railways* Jan. 23 Some of the desirable characteristics of the 'Merry-go-round' railway..are found in the Tyne Dock-Consett iron ore traffic of the N.E.R. **1966** G. F. ALLEN *Brit. Rail after Beeching* viii. 255 Inauguration of 'merry-go-round' coal supply by rail, one of the outstanding concepts of the Beeching era. **1970** *Railway Mag.* Oct. 552/1 Wagons, each capable of carrying up to 32 tons, are permanently coupled into 'Merry-go-round' trains, making 'non-stop' journeys between collieries and generating stations. *Ibid.*, The fully-automated 'Merry-go-round' system works efficiently. *Ibid.* 584/2 Merry-go-round workings in the Knottingley area have seen a variety of motive power recently. **1972** P. LEVY *Spotlight on Trains* 32 British Rail came up with the idea of the 'merry-go-round' train..a long train of coal hoppers running in a circular route between the coal mine and the power station. **1973** *North Berks Herald* 13 Dec. 1/2 Sixteen merry-go-round coal trains have been arriving at Didcot power station each week.

†**merry-go-sorry.** *Obs.* A mixture of joy and sorrow.

1599 BRETON *Mis. Mavillia* (Grosart) 49/2 Joying to see the kinde heart of this other olde gentleman, sorie to be an occasion of such anger to himselfe, and trouble to his house, betwixt a merrie, goe sorie, I fell to such weeping, as quite spilde mine eyes. **1600** —— *Fort. two Princes* 52. **1606** [? BRETON] *Choice, Chance*, etc. (1881) 76 Thou hast told me of such a Merry goesory, as I haue not often heard of: I am sorry for thy ill fortune, but am glad to see thee aliue.

†**merry land** = *Maryland*, the name of a district in N. America (now one of the United States), applied to a kind of tobacco. Cf. F. *maryland*.

1688 R. HOLME *Armoury* III. xxii. (Roxb.) 274/1 Sorts of Tobacco..Merry land, leafe Tobacco.

merrymaid, *dial.* variant of MERMAID.

1865 R. HUNT *Pop. Rom. W. Eng.* (1881) 149 The 'merrymaids' of the Cornish fishermen and sailors possess the well-recognised features of the mermaid.

merry-make (ˈmɛrɪmeɪk), *sb. arch.* [app. f. vbl. phr. *make merry*, with inversion as in the later MERRY-MAKING.] = MERRY-MAKING.

1579 SPENSER *Sheph. Cal.* Nov. 9 Now nis the time of merimake. *a* **1586** *Satir. Poems Reform.* xxxvii. 51 Gif ȝe lyk musik, mirthe, or myrrie mak. **1633** P. FLETCHER *Purple Isl.* I. xxviii, With fearless merry-make and piping. **1638-48** G. DANIEL *Eclog* iii. 29 The Simple Merrie-make of older Swains Was Innocent. **1822** W. TENNANT *Thane of Fife* VI. xlviii, The din of merry-make and boast! **1833** LONGF. *Outre-Mer* Prose Wks. 1886 I. 52 The rural sports and merrimakes of the village. **1844** MRS. BROWNING *Drama of Exile* Poems 1850 I. 5 We'll have feasts And funerals also, merrymakes and wars. **1893** KATH. L. BATES *Eng. Relig. Drama* 23 England was wonted to take her merry-makes as a gift from the hand of Religion.

'merry-make, *v. rare.* [Formed as prec.] *intr.* To make merry; to be festive.

1714 GAY *Sheph. Week* Tues. 50 Whilom with thee 'twas Marian's dear delight To moil all day and merry-make at night. **1853-8** HAWTHORNE *Eng. Note-Bks.* (1879) I. 240 Dancing and otherwise merrymaking. **1859** FITZGERALD tr. *Omar* xxxv, I think the Vessel, that with fugitive Articulation answer'd, once did live, And merry-make. **1894** DU MAURIER *Trilby* I. 220 Ye young who pawn each other's watches, and merrymake together on the proceeds.

merry-maker (ˈmɛrɪmeɪkə(r)). [f. MERRY *a.* + MAKER, after next.] One who makes merry or takes part in festivities.

1827 G. GRIFFIN *Holland-Tide* iii. 236 Music..was constantly in high request..among the merry-makers. **1843** *Zoologist* I. 35 A party of merry-makers, who resorted to this unwonted saloon to sip their wine. **1884** *Illustr. Lond. News* 13 Sept. 243/3 The merrymakers did not break up until a late hour.

'merry-making, *vbl. sb.* [f. MERRY *a.* + MAKING *vbl. sb.*] The action of making merry; conviviality; also, an occasion of festivity, a convivial entertainment.

1714 MANDEVILLE *Fab. Bees* (1725) I. 186 If a woman at a merry-making dresses in man's cloathes. **1779** MME. D'ARBLAY *Diary* 13 June, Her..gay, laughing face inspires an almost immediate wish of conversing and merry-making with her. **1819** *Sporting Mag.* IV. 209 A merry-making, on the death of a relation. **1830** TENNYSON *Poems* 93 See! our friends are all forsaking The wine and the merry-making. **1833** HT. MARTINEAU *Briery Creek* v. 107 The Irish betake themselves to rebellion when stopped in their merry-makings. **1876** GREEN *Stray Stud.* 55 The tedious length of an English merry-making would be unintelligible to him [*sc.* an Italian].

attrib. **1870** MORRIS *Earthly Par.* (1890) 310/1 We Twain Not oft again..Unto this merry-making place shall ride.

So **'merry-making** *ppl. a.*

1838 DICKENS *Nich. Nick.* vi, Such jolly, roystering, rollicking, merry-making blades. **1873** SYMONDS *Grk. Poets* iii. 94 First must merry-making men address the gods with holy songs.

merry man, **'merryman.**

1. *pl.* ***merry men***: the companions in arms or followers of a knight, an outlaw chief, etc. Also *colloq.* (somewhat jocular): followers, subordinates.

c **1386** CHAUCER *Sir Thopas* 128 His murie men comanded he To make hym bothe game and glee. *c* **1400** *Gamelyn* 774 Yong Gamelyn..fond his mery men under woode-bough. *c* **1510** *Lytell Geste of Robyn Hood* iv. in Child *Ballads* III. 66 And Robyn and his mery men Went to wode anone. *c* **1550** *Hunting of Cheviot* 37 *Ibid.* III. 309 Fyghte ye, my myrry men, whyllys ye may. **1600** SHAKS. *A. Y. L.* I. i. 121 They say he is already in the Forrest of Arden, and a many merry men with him. **1810** SCOTT *Lady of L.* v. xviii, Still at the gallop prick'd the Knight, His merry-men follow'd as they might. **1873** TROLLOPE *Phineas Redux* (1874) I. i. 2 Moderate Liberals had been glad to give Mr. Daubeny and his merry men a chance. **1921** *Daily Colonist* (Victoria, B.C.) 8 Apr. 4/3 The result of their round robin was equally effective;.. it took the place of the robber's mask so that no one could tell the leaders from their merrymen. **1932** D. L. SAYERS *Have his Carcase* xvi. 205 It's Umpelty and his merry men. Pass me the field-glasses, Bunter. **1939** JOYCE *Finnegans Wake* I. 48 *Hurleyquinn* the zitherer of the past with his merrymen all. **1960** N. MITFORD *Don't tell Alfred* ii. 24 He will keep Bouche-Bontemps and his merry men in a state of chronic perplexity. **1970** *Punch* 17 June 890/1 The Tories, according to Harold Wilson and his merry men, are dishonest, heartless, reckless and dangerous. **1973** *Times* 24 Nov. 11/4 Tomorrow night Miss Laine, Mr Dankworth and his three merry men will be in concert in Glasgow. **1973** R. PERRY *Ticket to Ride* iv. 61 Abbott and his merry men still weren't on my trail.

2. (As one word.) A jester or buffoon. ? *Obs.*

1785 GROSE *Dict. Vulgar Tongue*, *Merry Andrew*, or *Mr. Merryman*, the jack pudding, jester, or zany of a mountebank, usually dressed in a party coloured coat. **1838** THOMS in *Bentley's Misc.* III. 623 The equestrian clown at Astley's, as the Mister Merryman who attends the horsemanship at that theatre is professionally designated. **1858** DORAN *Ct. Fools* 58 In the fifteenth century, when the fashion of wearing bells was abandoned to the professional merry-men.

‖**3.** The surname Merriman has sometimes been used allusively.

1596 HARINGTON *Metam. Ajax* 84 *Hæc tria mens læta, requies, moderata dieta*, Doctor Diet, Doctor Quiet, and Doctor Meryman.

merry-meeting. A festive or convivial gathering.

a **1653** JER. TAYLOR *Serm. Gold. Grove, Winter* xv. 191 This..struck their fancy luckily, and maintained the merry meeting. **1699** SOUTH *Serm.* (1842) III. 51 He can..in those higher speculations forget all his merry-meetings and companions. **1723** DK. WHARTON *True Briton* No. 58. II. 505 If he has not that Zeal without Knowledge to improve a Merry-meeting into a Riot. **1847** L. HUNT *Men, Women, & B.* II. xi. 268 He had carried his merry-meetings to an unusual extent. **1890** 'R. BOLDREWOOD' *Col. Reformer* (1891) 293 He was..made free of all their small gatherings and merry-meetings.

merryment, -nes, obs. ff. MERRIMENT, -NESS.

merry-sole, var. *Mary-sole*: see MARY I c.

1880–4 F. DAY *Brit. Fishes* II. 22 *Arnoglossus megastoma*. .. Names.—*Whiff, merry sole*, a term applied due to its active movements when in the water.

merrythought (ˈmɛrɪθɔːt). [f. MERRY *a.* + THOUGHT *sb.*: see below.] The FURCULA or forked bone between the neck and breast of a bird; also, the portion of a bird when carved that includes this bone. Also *attrib.*

The name, like the synonym *wish-bone*, alludes to the playful custom of two persons pulling the furcula of a fowl until it breaks; according to the popular notion, the one who gets the longer (in some districts, the shorter) piece will either be married sooner than the other, or will gain the fulfilment of any wish he may form at the moment.

1607 DEKKER *Northw. Hoe* III. Wks. 1873 III. 42, I longd for the merry thought of a phesant. **1611** COTGR., *Lunette*, the merrie-thought; the forked craw-bone of a bird, which we vse, in sport, to put on our noses. **1711** ADDISON *Spect.* No. 7 ¶2, I..have seen a Man in Love grow pale and lose his Appetite, upon the plucking of a Merry-thought. **1716** R. WALLER in *Phil. Trans.* XXIX. 513 Under the Clavicula or Merry-thought-bone. *a* **1756** MRS. HAYWOOD *New Present* 269 Then cut up the merry-thought. **1843** LEVER *J. Hinton* ii, Simpering old maids cracked merry thoughts with gay bachelors. **1890** COUES *Field & Gen. Ornithol.* II. 136 The lower belly of the curve, convex forward, fitting in between the forks of the merrythought (Lat. *furculum*).

ˈ**merry-totter.** *dial.* Also 8–9 **-trotter**. [f. MERRY *a.* + TOTTER *sb.*] A see-saw; a swing.

c **1440** *Promp. Parv.* 338/2 Myry tottyr [*v.r.* miritotyr], chylderys game,..*oscillum*. **1483** *Cath. Angl.* 235/2 A Merytotyr, *oscillum, petaurus*. **1659** C. HOOLE tr. *Comenius' Orbis Sensualium* (1672) 277 Boyes..tossing and swinging themselves upon a Merry-totter [L. *super Petaurum*]. **1790** GROSE *Provinc. Gloss.*, *Merry-totter*, a see-saw. **1862** 'TOM TREDDLEHOYLE' *Bairnsla Foaks Ann.* 4 (E.D.D.) Merry-trotter.

Merry Widow. a. The English name of Franz Lehár's operetta *Die Lustige Witwe* (first produced (in German) in Vienna, 1905, and (in English) in London, 1907) used allusively, freq. joc., of an amorous or designing widow.

1907 *Times* 10 June 4/3 The fame of *Die Lustige Witwe* must have preceded the coming of the opera, for the appearance of the composer was greeted with thunders of applause... *The Merry Widow*..is a genuine light opera... Perhaps, in the original, Sonia..is a 'merry' widow. **1922** JOYCE *Ulysses* 209 Woos and wins her, a whoreson merry widow. **1942** H. C. BAILEY *Dead Man's Shoes* xxvii. 105 Randolph also found the marriage in the paper that morning... He burst out laughing..'Queen Caroline! The merry widow!' **1961** *Studies in Eng. Lit.* (Houston, Texas) I. IV. 23 (*heading*) *Lady Susan*: Jane Austen's character of the Merry Widow. **1965** J. M. CAIN *Magician's Wife* (1966) iv. 31 She'll be a Merry Widow, that we know for sure, but not with your help.

b. Used *attrib.* and *absol.* to designate a type of ornate, wide-brimmed hat.

1908 *Daily Chron.* 9 July 1/4 The women in the galleries took off their 'Merry Widow' hats, and waved them frantically. **1909** *Ibid.* 21 Jan. 7/3 A huge Merry Widow of the approved Occidental pattern from China. **1922** JOYCE *Ulysses* 554 Under the umbrella appears Mrs. Cunningham in Merry Widow hat and kimono gown. **1956** C. H. B. KITCHIN *Secret River* i. 61 Mrs. Ashworth in a Merry Widow hat, in which she thought she had looked ravishing. **1966** *Times* 15 June 15/5 When *The Merry Widow* music echoed across Europe, Lily Elsie wore *the* hat every night at Daly's. It caught on. From the opening night, June 8, 1907, everybody wore the Merry Widow hat.

ˈ**merry-wing.** [f. MERRY *a.* + WING *sb.*; app. with reference to the rapid beating of the wings.]

†**1.** A kind of gnat or mosquito found in the West Indies, esp. Jamaica and Barbados. *Obs.*

1671 OGILBY *Amer.* 340 In some parts of the Countrey [in Jamaica] there are also a sort of stinging Flies, call'd Muschilli and Merrywings. **1706** PHILLIPS (ed. Kersey), *Merry-wings*, a sort of Fly, very troublesome in the Night, in the Island of Barbadoes. **1750** G. HUGHES *Barbados* 87 The Merry-Wing..is a very minute Fly... They seem to be exactly of the same Species with the Gnat in England.

2. *U.S.* The golden-eye, *Clangula glaucion*.

1888 G. TRUMBULL *Names of Birds* 78.

†**mers.** *Sc. Obs.* Also 6 **merse**. [a. MDu. *merse* (mod.Du. *mars*) 'top' of a mast, literally 'basket'.] A round-top surrounding the lower masthead. Also *attrib.* in *mers clothes*, streamers and hangings suspended from the 'mers'.

1494 *Acc. Ld. High Treas. Scot.* (1877) I. 253 Item for ane gret mast, ane ra, ane swken, a pygy mast; and thir rais and the takling with ane mers,..and for ane pomp and other small graith, x *li.* **1504–6** *Ibid.* (1901) III. 89 Item xxvj elne carsay blew, rede, quhit and ȝallow to be ij mers clathis to the schip. **1505–6** *Ibid.* 183 Item..to the man that maid the mers of the schip, in drinksilvir xiiijs. **1506** *Ibid.* 189 Item.. to Alexander Chamir, payntour, quhilk payntit the mers of the Kingis schip x Franch crounis. **1508** DUNBAR *Gold. Targe* 52 A saill, als quhite as blossum vpon spray, Wyth merse of gold, brycht as the stern of day.

mersalyl (ˈmɜːsəlɪl). *Pharm.* [f. MER(CURY *sb.* + SAL(IC)YL.]

The sodium salt, $C_{13}H_{16}NO_6HgNa$, of *o*-[(3-hydroxymercuri-2-methoxypropyl)-carbamoyl]phenoxyacetic acid, which is a powerful diuretic formerly used in the treatment of œdema.

1936 *Brit. Pharmacopœia 1932* Add. I. 46 (*heading*) Mersalyl. **1940** *Jrnl. Amer. Med. Assoc.* 23 Nov. 1786/1 (*heading*) The effect of mersalyl (Salyrgan) on plasma volume. **1958** *Times* 23 Apr. 15/4 He had referred to ammonium chloride as a diuretic normally used in conjunction with mersalyl. **1972** *Nature* 7 Apr. 301/2 Mersalyl, a potent inhibitor of myofibrillar ATPase, was without effect on the contraction induced by calcium.

mersatorial (mɜːsəˈtɔərɪəl), *a. Ornith.* [f. mod.L. *mersātor* diver: see -IAL.] Belonging to Macgillivray's order *Mersatores*.

1852 MACGILLIVRAY *Brit. Birds* V. 424 They [*sc.* the Procellariinæ] are mersatorial birds.

mersaus(e, mersch, merschale: see MERESAUCE, MARCH *sb.*³, MARSH¹, MARSHAL.

merschaundrice, merschion: see MERCHANDISE, MARCHION.

merse (mɛrs), *sb. Sc.* [Sc. repr. OE. *męrsc*, MARSH¹.] Low flat land, usually beside a river or the sea; marsh. Also *attrib.*

The Merse is used as the proper name of the district of Berwickshire between the Lammermoors and the Tweed.

a **1810** in Cromek Rem. *Nithsdale Song* 234 There's a maid has sat o' the green merse side Thae ten lang years and mair. **1856** AIRD *Poet. Wks.* 188 Go the rooks Down to the sea..on the flat merse To tear up tufts of grass for grubs below. *a* **1856** in G. Henderson *Pop. Rhymes Berwick* 105 A Merse mist alang the Tweed In a harvest mornin's gude indeed. **1869** LANDRETH *Life Adam Thomson* I. 5 A bloody skirmish between Merse-men and Northumbrians. **1875** W. MCILWRAITH *Guide Wigtownshire* 78 A little bit of merse-land, detached by the windings of the River Luce, is called St. Helen's Island.

merse, mersement: see MERCE, MERCEMENT.

Mersenne (mɜː-, ‖mɛrˈsɛn). *Math.* The name of Marin *Mersenne* (1588–1648), French mathematician and musician, used *attrib.* and in the possessive to designate numbers of the form $2^p - 1$ (where *p* is a prime number).

1892 *Messenger of Math.* XXI. 40 The riddle as to how Mersenne's numbers were discovered remains unsolved. **1911** *Encycl. Brit.* XIX. 863/1 Similar difficulties are encountered when we examine Mersenne's numbers, which are those of the form $2^p - 1$, with *p* a prime; the known cases for which a Mersenne number is prime correspond to *p* = 2, 3, 5, 7, 13, 17, 19, 31, 61. **1939** USPENSKY & HEASLET *Elem. Number Theory* iv. 82 Numbers of the form $2^p - 1$ are called Mersenne's numbers because of a statement made concerning them in the preface to his 'Cogitata physico-mathematica', published in 1644. **1966** OGILVY & ANDERSON *Excursions in Number Theory* ii. 22 The Mersenne number $2^{11} - 1$ is composite (it equals 23 × 89). **1974** *Nature* 16 Aug. 610/3 The largest known Mersenne prime, by 1971, is $2^p - 1$ where *p* = 19937.

merser: see MERCER.

Mersey (ˈmɜːzɪ). The name of the river *Mersey*, on which stands the city of Liverpool, applied *attrib.* in **Mersey beat, Mersey sound**, to the kind of popular music associated with 'The Beatles' [BEATLE].

1963 *Meet the Beatles* 12/2 The Beatles, undoubted monarchs of the Mersey Beat scene. **1965** S. JEPSON *Third Possibility* v. 36 The Mersey sound banged and twanged into the night. *a* **1966** M. ALLINGHAM *Cargo of Eagles* (1968) iv. 60 The adenoidal moan of the Mersey beat: '*I wanna be your rave...*' **1969** C. BOOKER *Neophiliacs* viii. 203 The 'Liverpool phenomenon' and the 'Mersey Sound' were now [*sc.* in 1963] arousing interest far beyond circles normally interested in pop music.

Merseysider (ˈmɜːzɪsaɪdɛ(r)). [f. *Mersey side* (SIDE *sb.*¹ 7 a) + -ER¹.] A dweller on a bank of the river Mersey in England, *spec.* within the area of Liverpool. Cf. CLYDESIDER.

1943 *Bombers over Merseyside* (Liverpool Daily Post) 25 (*caption*) It was spectacles of destruction, such as this, that steeled the Merseysiders' resolution to defeat the Luftwaffe's brazen challenge. **1963** *Times* 17 Apr. 3/6 Everton took root in Birmingham territory, yet..the Birmingham defensive covering was such that there were serious doubts about the Merseysiders' ability to create the vital chink. **1966** 'L. LANE' *ABZ of Scouse* Foreword, A Scouser is a Merseysider who conducts his ordinary, everyday conversations in Scouse. **1971** N. FISHER *Rise at Dawn* vi. 95 This was driven by Lance-Corporal Simmonds ..a taciturn Merseysider. **1973** *Guardian* 4 June 16/4 The peculiar inspirational quality of the city..laughs at the rest of the world who has never known the magic of being..a Merseysider.

mersh, mershal(l: see MARCH *v.*², MARSHALL.

mersion (ˈmɜːʃən). ? *Obs.* [a. F. *mersion*, ad.L. *mersiōn-em*, n. of action f. *mers-*, *mergĕre* to dip: see MERGE *v.*] The action, or act, of dipping; *spec.* with reference to baptism.

1659 H. L'ESTRANGE *Alliance Div. Off.* 365 Mersion or dipping is not of the necessity of the Sacrament, sprinkling being in every way as operative. **1669** BARROW *Sacraments in Creed* etc. (1697) 444 The mersion also in Water, and the emersion thence, doth figure our death to the former, and receiving to a new life. **1691** W. NICHOLLS *Answ. Naked Gospel* 32 The custom of the trine mersion seems to be very ancient in the Church, if not Apostolical.

merss(h, mersery: see MARSH¹, MERCERY.

mersshall: see MARSHAL.

mersy(e, mersyment, merte, mertelage, mertenet(te: see MERCY, MERCEMENT, MART *sb.*², MARTILOGE, MARTINET.

merth(e: see MART *sb.*¹, MIRTH.

Merthiolate (mɜːˈθaɪəleɪt). *Pharm.* Also **merthiolate**. [f. *mercurithiosalicylate*, f. MERCURI(CO- + THIO- + SALICYLATE *sb.*] A proprietary name (in the U.S.) for thiomersal, sodium ethyl mercurithiosalicylate.

1928 *Official Gaz.* (U.S. Patent Office) 6 Nov. 14/2 Eli Lilly and Company... *Merthiolate* for medicine or pharmaceutical preparation—viz., sodium mercurithiosalicylate or organic mercury compound solution useful in antisepsis. **1931** *Amer. Jrnl. Hygiene* XIII. 310 Merthiolate is found to have certain unusual properties ..which makes it well adapted to tissue antisepsis. **1957** F. & R. LOCKRIDGE *Tangled Cord* (1959) xii. 150 Hilda Graham ..had found merthiolate in a medicine cabinet in the bathroom and poured it on Ferris's foot. **1973** *Nature* 21/28 Dec. 521/2 The supernatant was decanted, a sample removed for protein estimation by the method of Lowry, and stored at 4°C with the addition of 1/10,000 merthiolate as preservative.

mertilloge, mertinet, mertle, mertlete: see MARTILOGE, MARTINET, MYRTLE, MARTLET.

Mertonian (mɜːˈtəʊnɪən), *sb.* and *a.* [f. the name of *Merton* College (founded by Walter de Merton in 1264) + -IAN.] **A.** *sb.* A member of Merton College, Oxford.

1883 *Fortn. Rev.* XXXIX. 34 Another Mertonian, John Tatham,..was elected Rector of Lincoln College. **1899** B. W. HENDERSON *Merton College* 172 Not a few Mertonians have been appointed to University Chairs. **1954** *Postmaster* (Merton College, Oxf.) Sept. 13 The only other Mertonian to appear in New London was Louis MacNeice. **1961** D. KNOWLES *Eng. Mystical Trad.* iii. 41 In mathematics and kindred sciences the series of great Mertonians at Oxford, Thomas Bradwardine, Richard Swineshead, William Heytesbury and Ralph Strood were the masters of the academic world of their day. **1971** E. GRANT *Physical Sci. in Middle Ages* iv. 25 The Mertonians arrived at a precise definition of uniform acceleration.

B. *adj.* Of or pertaining to Merton College or its members; used *spec.* with reference to a school of mathematics and astronomy that existed there in the 14th century.

1899 B. W. HENDERSON *Merton College* 278 The society.. entertained a large Mertonian company at a dinner in Hall. **1947** G. SARTON *Introd. Hist. Sci.* III. i. 116 Our knowledge of the early Mertonian scientists is very insufficient, because a good part of the Merton library and archives was sold as waste paper about the middle of the sixteenth century. **1959** A. C. CROMBIE in M. Clagett *Critical Probl. Hist. Sci.* 91 In finding expressions for rates of change, they [*sc.* Oxford mathematicians] formulated sophisticated concepts like those of acceleration and instantaneous velocity..and reached important results like the Mertonian Mean Speed Law. **1974** A. J. POMERANS tr. *Clavelin's Nat. Philos. Galileo* ii. 80 This proof..remained indirect, as did all the Mertonian attempts to prove the mean-speed theorem.

mertri(c)k: see MARTRIX.

†**mertun.** *Obs. rare*$^{-1}$. [? From the name of *Merton* Abbey (Surrey).] A kind of church bell.

1536 *Nottingham Rec.* III. 198 Compositura sive factura cujusdam campanae mediocris Anglice 'a mertun'.

mertymas, -mes, obs. forms of MARTINMAS.

Meru (ˈmɛruː), *sb.* and *a.* Also **Mweru**. [f. the name of a town and district in central Kenya.] **A.** *sb.* **a.** A Bantu tribe inhabiting the Meru region of Kenya; also, a member of this tribe. **b.** The language of this people. **B.** *adj.* Of or pertaining to the Meru people or their language.

[**1883** R. N. CUST *Sk. Mod. Lang. Afr.* II. xii. 342 A little to the North of the Ma-Konde dwell the Wa-Mwera, not a large tribe, but..they have a separate language.] **1909** J. H. PATTERSON *In Grip of Nyika* xxviii. 350 They approached, decked out in all the finery of the Meru belles, and each with a broad smile..selected a favourite warrior. **1910** C. W. HOBLEY *Ethnol. of A-Kamba* vi. 156 Mweru is the name of a very large tribe living on the North and N.E. slopes of Kenia and on the Jombeni range. **1919** H. H. JOHNSTON *Compar. Study Bantu & Semi-Bantu Lang.* iii. 112 The Meru dialect..is said to be markedly distinct. It is spoken in the north-east portion of the Kikuyu area. **1942** *Man* XLII. 58/1 To the north of the Mwimbi and Tharaka, near

neighbours also of both the Kikuyu and Kamba peoples, are to be found the Meru-speaking peoples, numbering roughly some 150,000. *Ibid.* 59/1 The most significant feature of the Meru tribal organization is the intricate system of age grades which cuts across family and clan loyalties. **1944** W. H. LAUGHTON *Meru* 8 The Meru live in families in small groups of huts built on the numerous hillsides. **1953** J. MIDDLETON in *Ethnogr. Survey Afr.: E. Cent. Afr.* (Internat. Afr. Inst.) v. 40 The Meru have a system of age-sets based on circumcision. **1963** *Times* 25 May 8/7 Fighting broke out when..Somalis surrounded the polling station..intent on preventing Turkana and Meru tribes people from voting.

† **merul.** *Obs. rare*⁻¹. [ad. L. *merula*.] = MERLE *sb.*
1694 MOTTEUX *Rabelais* v. (1737) 230 The gay Merul and warbling Philomel.

merula, var. MARULA.

meruline (ˈmɛrjʊlɪn), *a. Zool.* [ad. mod.L. *merulīnus*, f. L. *merula* MERLE *sb.*] Of or pertaining to the genus *Merula* or to the subfamily *Merulinæ* (*Cent. Dict.* 1890). So **meruˈlinous** *a. Zool.* in the same sense (Mayne *Expos. Lex.* 1856).

† **merumsuratum** = *Marum Syriacum*: see MARUM.
c **1710** CELIA FIENNES *Diary* (1888) 190 Wᵗʰ..ffilleroy finely Cut, and ffirrs and merumsuratum wᶜʰ makes the fine snuff.

merur(e, obs. forms of MIRROR.

† **meruw**, *a. Obs.* Forms: 1 mearu, *Mercian* meru, 3 meruw, mereuh, 4 meruȝ. [OE. *mearu* (stem *mearw-*) = OHG. *marawi* (MHG. *mar*, *marw-*), ablaut var. of OHG. *mur(u)wi* (MHG. *mürwe*, *mür*, mod.G. *mürbe*) of the same meaning.] Soft, tender.
c **975** *Rushw. Gosp.* Matt. xxiv. 32 þonne telȝra his merwe biþ..ȝe witan þæt neh is sumer. *c* **1000** *Sax. Leechd.* I. 216 ȝyf þonne se lichoma mearu [*v.v.* mearuw] sy seoð on huniȝe leȝe to þam sare. *a* **1225** *Ancr. R.* 378 Ȝunge impen me bigurt mid þornes, leste bestes ureten ham þeo hwule þet heo beoð meruwe. *c* **1275** *Luue Ron* 44 in *O.E. Misc.* 94 Hwenne hit schal to-glide hit is fals and mereuh and frouh. *c* **1320** *Sir Beues* (A.) 2525 Ich was so lite & so meruȝ, Eueri man me clepede dweruȝ.

merv (mɜːv). [Short for F. (*satin*) *merveilleux*.] A silk material for ladies' dresses and dress-trimmings.
1887 *Daily News* 11 May 5/7 A skirt of black Merv, covered with tulle. **1890** *Ibid.* 10 June 7/5 Rich satin Mervs. All silk.

mervail(e, -veil(l(e, etc., obs. ff. MARVEL.

‖ **merveilleux, -euse** (mɛrvɛjø, -øz). [Fr.: see MARVELLOUS.] Contemporary names for the extravagantly dressed French fops and 'fine ladies' of the period of the Directory, who affected a revival of the classical costume of ancient Greece.
[**1819**: cf. MARVELLOUS B.] **1892** *Daily News* 19 Oct. 5/1 The 'merveilleuse' of the Directory in France. The 'merveilleuse', or 'ultra-fashionable', as the writer..rather inadequately translates her title, 'walked..half naked in the Champs Elysees'. **1898** LADY MARY LOYD tr. *O. Uzanne's Fashion in Paris* i. 8 The Ecrouelleux, the Inconcevables, the Merveilleux, with their chins sunk in their huge cravats. *Ibid.* 19 The Merveilleuses survived the Incroyables by a couple of years.

merviade: see MARAVEDI.

merwaal, -waill(e, etc., obs. ff. MARVEL.

merwe, merwe(i)ll: see MARROW *sb.*¹, MARVEL.

merwoman (ˈmɜːwʊmən). [See MER- and cf. G. *meerfrau*, *meerweib*.] A name for a MERMAID when older or wedded.
1809 *Chron.* in *Ann. Reg* 394/2 In a History of the Netherlands it is stated that in the year 1403, the dikes were broken near Campear by an inundation; and when the inundation had returned, a Merwoman was left in the Dermet Mere. **1884** F. J. CHILD *Eng. & Sc. Pop. Ball.* I. 366/1 The merman asks her the reason, and she answers, They all say that you are the merwoman's son.
transf. **1846** M. J. HIGGINS *Ess.* (1875) Mem. 26 It was really admirable to watch the good-humour, dexterity, and patience of the old merwoman.

mery, obs. form of MARROW *sb.*¹, MERRY.

merycism (ˈmɛrɪsɪz(ə)m). *Path.* [ad. mod.L. *mērycismus*, ad. Gr. μηρυκισμός rumination, f. μηρυκίζειν to ruminate, f. μηρυκ-, μηρυξ occurring as the name of a ruminating fish.] A rare disease of the stomach, in which the food, after having been swallowed some time, is returned into the mouth and remasticated.
1856 MAYNE *Expos. Lex.* s.v. *Merycismus*. **1860** *New Syd. Soc. Year-Bk. Med. & Surg.* 235 Abdominal Merycism (regurgitation of chyme) appearing as the symptom of a masked ague.

meryhed, meryly, merynes, meryt(e, etc.: see MARROWED, MERRILY, MERRINESS, MERIT, etc.

† **mes.** *Obs.* Also 4–5 messe, 5 measse. [a. AF. *mes* (see Skeat *Chaucer's Wks.* I. 429 and Du Cange *Glossarium Gallicum* s.v.), app.:—L. *missum*, neut. pa. pple. of *mittĕre* to send, put forth.] Proper distance or range for shooting. ***to mark*** (a person) ***at*** or ***with a mes***: to strike.
The use in the first quot. is obscure; the word may have been used in a strained sense for 'a blow', 'the force of a blow'. But the reading of the passage seems doubtful.
13.. *E.E. Allit. P.* B. 215 Dryȝtyn with his dere dom hym drof to þe abyme, In þe mesure of his mode, his mes neuer þe lasse Bot þer he tynt þe type dool of his tour ryche. ? *a* **1366** CHAUCER *Rom. Rose* 1453 To shete, at good mes, to the dere. *a* **1380** *Pistill Susan* 320 (Phillips MS.) An aungil ..haþ braundisshid his brond..To marke þi myddil at a messe in more þan in þre. *c* **1440** *York Myst.* xi. 162 Bot þe Jewes þat wonnes in Jessen Sall noȝt be merked with þat messe. [*c* **1460** *Towneley Myst* viii. 175 measse].

mes, obs. form of MASS *sb.*¹, MEASE, MESS.

mesa (ˈmeɪsə). [Sp. *mesa*, lit. 'table':—L. *mēnsa*.]
1. A high table-land. Also *attrib.*
1775 ROMANS *Florida* App. 57 This Table Land is called Mesa Maria. **1859** MARCY *Prairie Trav.* 314 The road.. ascends to a low mésa. **18..** *Reports on Pacific Railroad* I. 84 (Bartlett) The mesa, or table-land character, is exhibited only along the line of river-valleys. **1882** *Rep. to Ho. Repr. Prec. Met. U.S.* 636 The top sometimes several miles wide, mesa-like and comparatively level. **1948** C. A. COTTON *Landscape* (ed. 2) x. 139 (*caption*) The Schlern mesa, of dolomite, South Tyrol. **1951** WODEHOUSE *Old Reliable* v. 68 There he was..under the dressing-table, with his fanny sticking up like a mesa in the Mojave desert. **1963** A. LUBBOCK *Austral. Roundabout* 73 The descent on the northern side of the plateau winds down, between table-top mesas and rugged bluffs. **1970** R. J. SMALL *Study of Landforms* iii. 72 To the east of Lyme Regis..very broad valleys are separated in interfluves occasionally surmounted by butte-like hills..and mesa-like plateaus developed in the near horizontal Upper Liassic sandstones. **1974** H. MACINNES *Climb to Lost World* x. 163 Only the proud tops of the neighbouring mesas stood out above the swirling clouds. *Ibid.* xii. 217 We saw a magnificent panorama of mesas: a weird contorted skyline of grotesque sandstone figures towards the Venezuelan part of the summit.
fig. **1963** V. NABOKOV *Gift* iii. 150 Out of the total of five hundred copies printed, four hundred and twenty-nine still lay, dusty and uncut, forming a neat mesa in the distributor's warehouse.
2. *Electronics.* In some transistors and semiconductor diodes, a raised, flat-topped portion of *n*- or *p*-type semiconductor surrounded by an area from which the upper layer has been etched away to expose the underlying *p*- or *n*-type material (respectively). Usu. *attrib.*, as ***mesa diode, transistor***.
1958 C. H. KNOWLES in *Electronic Industries* (Philadelphia) Aug. 55 Recent developments at several locations have resulted in a new line of VHF-UHF Transistors... We will refer to this new line of transistors as Mesa Transistors. *Ibid.*, The Mesa Transistor gets its name from its physical configuration... A basic part of its structure is the 'Mesa', (Spanish name for ' table'), which is the active region of the transistor. **1962** SIMPSON & RICHARDS *Physical Princ. Junction Transistors* viii. 169 Following construction of the device the germanium surrounding the electrodes was etched away to form the table-like area or 'mesa'. **1966** *McGraw-Hill Encycl. Sci. & Technol.* VII. 316/1 Silicon mesa diodes are also used for high-speed, low-power applications. **1972** BOYLESTAD & NASHELSKY *Electronic Devices & Circuit Theory* iii. 137 The diffusion technique is employed in the production of mesa and planar transistors, each of which can be of the diffused or epitaxial type. **1973** *Nature* 12 Jan. 92/3 Improved cut-off frequency..and noise performance result in useful performance up to 4 GHz with promise of extending this to at least 8 GHz by reverting to an improved version of the old 'mesa' design.

mesaconic (mɛsəˈkɒnɪk), *a. Chem.* [f. Gr. μεσ-ός middle + (IT)ACONIC; intended to denote the intermediate position of this acid between the itaconic and citraconic acids.] ***mesaconic acid***: an acid, isomeric with itaconic acid, obtained by boiling a weak solution of citraconic acid with nitric acid. ***mesaconic ether***: see quot. 1865. Hence **meˈsaconate**, a salt of mesaconic acid.
1854 THOMSON *Cycl. Chem.*, *Mesaconic Acid*. **1856** WATTS tr. *Gmelin's Handbk. Chem.* X. 428 Mesaconate of Ammonia. **1865** WATTS *Dict. Chem.*, *Mesaconic Ether*, $C_9H_4O_4$... Obtained by distilling a mixture of mesaconic acid, sulphuric acid, and alcohol.

mesad (ˈmɛsæd), *adv.* [F. Gr. μέσ-ος middle + *-ad* as in DEXTRAD.] = MESIAD.
1882 WILDER & GAGE *Anat. Technol.* 27 Substituting *mesal* for *mesial*,..we have *mesad*. *Ibid.* 212 Lift the border near its middle, and trace it mesad. **1894** GOULD *Illustr. Med. Dic.*, *Mesad*, toward the mesial or mesal line or plane; towards the meson.

mesager, obs. form of MESSENGER.

mesail. *Antiq.* Also mursail, mezail. [a. F. *mésail*, *mézail*, *mursail*, app. repr. OF. *muçaille* concealment, f. *mucier* to hide.] (See quot.)
1869 BOUTELL *Arms & Arm.* viii. (1874) 127 This piece, called the *mesail*, or *mursail*..but more generally known in England as the *ventaile*, or visor, was pierced for both sight and breathing. **1870** C. C. BLACK tr. *Demmin's Weapons of War* 278 The armet is the most perfect form of helmet. It is composed of the crown with crest, the vizor, nose-piece and ventoyle (these latter three forming altogether the *mezail*), and the gorget.

mesairaick, obs. form of MESARAIC.

mesais, variant of MISEASE.

mesal (ˈmɛsəl), *a.* [f. Gr. μέσ-ος middle + -AL¹.] = MESIAL. Hence **ˈmesally** *adv.* = MESIALLY.
1882 [see MESAD *adv.*]. In recent Dicts.

mesallantoid (mɛsəˈlæntɔɪd), *a. rare.* [f. Gr. μέσ-ος middle + ALLANTOID.] Having an allantois of intermediate size. (Cf. MEGALLANTOID, MICRALLANTOID.)
1877 W. TURNER *Hum. Anat.* II. 869 M. H. Milne-Edwards..has placed the Carnivora and Pinnipedia..in a Mesallantoid legion of mammals.

‖ **mésalliance** (mezaljɑ̃s, mɪˈsælɪəns). [Fr., f. *més-* MIS- + *alliance* ALLIANCE. Cf. MISALLIANCE.] A marriage with a person of inferior social position.
1782 H. WALPOLE *Let. to Mason* 25 June, We are well off when from that mesalliance there spring some bastards called Episodes. **1827** CANNING *Sp. Ho. Com.* 12 June in *Hansard* (1828) XVII. 1255 An account of a union, or rather of what the French called a *mésalliance* between a man of colour and a white woman. **1840** THACKERAY *Paris Sk.-bk.* (1869) 39 In England..a grocer's daughter would think she made a mesalliance by marrying a painter. **1885** MABEL COLLINS *Prettiest Woman* x, It seems hardly likely that another prince will make a mésalliance for the sake of a Milovitch.

mesamœboid (mɛsəˈmiːbɔɪd), *a.* and *sb. Biol.* [f. Gr. μέσ-ος middle + AMŒBOID.] **a.** *adj.* In ***mesamœboid cell*** = **b.** **b.** *sb.* One of the amœba-like cells which are developed in the mesoderm.
1890 *Syd. Soc. Lex.*, *Mesamœboid cells*..*Mesamœboids*. **1905** *Brit. Med. Jrnl.* 25 Feb. 441 A special ingrowth of micronuclear cells derived from the pigmented group gave rise to the mesamœboid (mesoblastic) cells.

mesanger, obs. form of MESSENGER.

‖ **mesaræum** (mɛsəˈriːəm). *Anat.* ? *Obs.* Also 7 mezereum. Also after the Gr. form, 6 mesareon, 9 mesaraion. [med.L., a. Gr. μεσάραιον, f. μέσον middle + ἀραιά flank, belly.] = MESENTERY 1.
1594 T. B. *La Primaud. Fr. Acad.* II. 353 The mesentery ..is also called by some mesareon... Others take mesareon to be the highest part of the mesentery. **1661** LOVELL *Hist. Anim. & Min.* 517 The humour..which is in the ventricle, intestines, and mezereum. **1727–41** CHAMBERS *Cycl.*, Mesaræum, is also used in a more restrained sense for a part, or division of the mesentery; being that fastened to the small guts. **1890** *Syd. Soc. Lex.*, *Mesaraion*.

mesaraic (mɛsəˈreɪɪk), *a.* and *sb. Anat.* Forms: 5 miseraic, -ayke, -ak, 6 -aike, mes(s)erayke, 7 mesairaick, meserai(c)k, -aique, -iacke, miseraick, 7–8 mesaraick(e, 7–9 meseraic, (9 *erron.* mesaræic), 8– mesaraic. [ad. med.L. *mesaraïcus*, a. Gr. μεσαραϊκός, f. μεσάραιον MESARÆUM.]
A. *adj.* Of or pertaining to the mesentery; = MESENTERIC.
c **1400** *Lanfranc's Cirurg.* 27 Veynis miserak ben smale veynes þat comen out of þe veyne þat is clepid porta. **1541** R. COPLAND *Guydon's Quest. Chirurg.* H iij b, To brynge the Chilus to the lyuer by meanes of the veynes mescraykes [*sic*]. **1615** CROOKE *Body of Man* 104 Duodenum, Ieiunum, and Ileon,..are easily distinguished by their scituation, length, and by their Meseraick veines. **1651** BIGGS *New Disp.* ¶ 117 Scammony..and vitriol do equally liquate the mesaraick bloud. **1831** R. KNOX *Cloquet's Anat.* 786 Its veins [*sc.* of the pancreas] pour their contents..into the small mesaraic and splenic veins. **1869** HUXLEY *Introd. Classif. Anim.* 139 *Meseraic* = mesenteric. The omphalo-meseraic vessels pass from the intestine to the umbilical vesicle in the embryo.
B. *sb.* One of the mesaraic veins.
1528 PAYNEL *Salerne's Regim.* D ij b, Whiche departeth to the lyuer by þe veines called miseraikes. **1615** TOMKIS *Albumazar* I. i. B 1 b, And what they [*sc.* the guts] spare, The meseraicks filch, and lay't i'th liver. **1646** SIR T. BROWNE *Pseud. Ep.* II. v. §3. 85 At the mouthes of the miseraicks. **1836–9** *Todd's Cycl. Anat.* II. 43/1 The venous sinus gives out..the mesaraics to the under surface of the cæca.

† **mesaˈraical**, *a. Obs.* [f. MESARAIC + -AL¹.] = MESARAIC *a.*
1569 R. ANDROSE tr. *Alexis' Secr.* IV. III. 37 To heale..the obstruction of the Mesaraicall veynes. **1623** HART *Arraignm. Ur.* ii. 5 The naturall voluntary expulsion of that superfluous humour into the guts by the miseraicall veines.

mesarch (ˈmɛzɑːk), *a.* [f. MES(O- + Gr. ἀρχή beginning.] **1.** *Bot.* [a. G. (H. zu Solms-Laubach *Einleitung in die Paläophytologie* (1887) xi. 263).] Of the development of the primary xylem, spreading in two or more directions from the earliest parts formed.
1891 [see EXARCH *a.*]. **1902** A. G. TANSLEY in *Encycl. Brit.* XXV. 414/2 (*caption*) Typical siphonostele (represented as mesarch) with internal phloem. **1954** *Biol. Rev.* XXIX. 63 Such studies resulted in the recognition of the now well-known centripetal and centrifugal patterns of differentiation, the exarch, endarch, and mesarch types of xylem. **1965** K. ESAU *Plant Anat.* (ed. 2) xv. 378 In the third [type of xylem] the differentiation progresses in two or more directions from the first mature xylem elements. The resulting primary xylem is called mesarch.
2. *Ecology.* (See quot. 1923.)

1923 G. E. NICHOLS in *Ecology* IV. 171 A third type [of succession] is here suggested, *viz.*, mesarch... Mesarch series are those which originate in mesophytic habitats such as are afforded by moist, rich soils, and in which the vegetation likewise becomes progressively more and more advanced. **1960** [see HYDRARCH *a.*].

mesarteritis (mɛsɑːtəˈraɪtɪs). *Path.* [mod.L., f. Gr. μέσ-ος middle + ἀρτηρία artery + -ITIS.] Inflammation of the middle coat of an artery.

1875 JONES & SIEV. *Pathol. Anat.* 374 The outer and middle coats are chiefly or solely affected, and it is called by some periarteritis and mesarteritis.

Hence **mesarteritic** (mɛsɑːtəˈrɪtɪk) *a.*, relating to mesarteritis.

1890 *Syd. Soc. Lex.*, *Mesarteritic induration*, a form of granulation, or cicatricial, tissue found in the coats of an artery affected with chronic endarteritis.

mesaticephalic (ˈmɛsətɪsɪˈfælɪk) *a.* [f. Gr. μέσατ-ος midmost (superl. of μέσος middle) + κεφαλή head + -IC (after *cephalic*).] = MESOCEPHALIC.

1879 FLOWER *Catal. Mus. Coll. Surg.* I. 251 The indices of breadth..are:—Dolichocephalic..below 750. Mesaticephalic..750 to 800. Brachycephalic..above 800.

So ˌ**mesatiˈcephalism**, the condition of being mesaticephalic; ˌ**mesatiˈcephalous** *a.* = MESATICEPHALIC; ‖ˌ**mesatiˈcephalus**, (*a*) a skull to which is applied the term mesaticephalic; (*b*) a person with a mesaticephalic skull; ˌ**mesatiˈcephaly** = MESATICEPHALISM.

1863 THURNAM in *Mem. Anthrop. Soc.* (1865) I. 150 An intermediate ovoid form (mesati- or ortho-cephalism). **1880** A. H. KEANE in *Nature* XXI. 281 [Afghan] Type, long, oval face, arched nose, head mesaticephalous. **1896** *Nat. Science* Sept. 154 The mesaticephaly..may be due to a crossing between brachycephalous Negrillos and Negros.

mesatipellic (ˌmɛsətɪˈpɛlɪk), *a. Anthrop.* [f. Gr. μέσ(σ)ατ-ος midmost (superl. of μέσος middle) + -I- + πέλλ-α wooden bowl (taken in sense PELVIS) + -IC.] Characterized by an index of the pelvic brim between 90 and 95.

1886 W. TURNER *Rep. Crania* in *Rep. Sci. Results Voy. H.M.S. Challenger* XVI. 40 In the males the same index was at or about 91, so that they were mesatipellic. **1924** *Proc. Soc. Antiquaries Scotl.* LVIII. 34 An index of 93·22 is mesatipellic, and considerably higher than that of the average European male. **1966** B. J. ANSON *Morris's Human Anat.* (ed. 12) iv. 282/2 Pelves with an index below 90 are platypellic; from 90 to 95, mesatipellic; and above 95, dolichopellic.

mesauenteur, -ure, obs. ff. MISADVENTURE.

mesaxon (mɛˈsæksɒn). *Anat.* [f. MES(ENTERY (see quot. 1955) + AXON.] In a nerve fibre, a structure composed of a pair of parallel membranes contiguous with the plasma membrane of the Schwann cell, forming in an unmyelinated fibre a channel leading from the outside of the cell to the axon it surrounds and in a myelinated fibre a spiral round the axon that constitutes the myelin sheath.

1955 H. S. GASSER in *Jrnl. Gen. Physiol.* XXXVIII. 713 The membrane sharply visible on the outside of the Schwann tubes may be taken as the starting point. To this membrane..the axons are in continuous attachment. On account of the analogy with the mesentery the attachments have been designated mesaxons. **1961** *Lancet* 16 Sept. 656/1 H. F. de Webster..in a study on the demyelination which occurs in experimental diphtheritic neuritis found that the earliest changes amount to focal fragmentation of the mesaxons. **1970** J. PICK *Autonomic Nervous System* v. 127/1 According to Gasser.., an unmyelinated nerve fiber usually consists of several axons which are placed in the infoldings of their Schwann cell. The plasma membrane of this sheath cell doubles up and together with the intervening channel forms the mesaxon. Upon reaching the axon, the membranes of the mesaxon separate and surround the axolemma.

mesbyleue, obs. form of MISBELIEVE.

‖**mescal** (mɛˈskæl). Also 8 mescale, 8–9 mezcal, 9 mascal, mexcal, mexical, mixcal, muscal(e. [Sp. *mezcal*, a. Mexican *mexcalli*.]

1. A strong intoxicating spirit distilled from the fermented juice of the American aloe.

1828 SIR H. G. WARD *Mexico* I. 59 A strong kind of brandy called mexical, or Aguardiente de Maguey. **1833** B. LUNDY *Jrnl.* 16 Oct. in *Life B. Lundy* (1847) x. 61 They have a kind of whiskey here, called muscal, which is distilled from a plant called Maguey. **1850** W. R. RYAN *Personal Adventures Upper & Lower Calif.* I. 193 The usual beverages, besides water, are wine, *mascal*, and *aguardiente*. **1854** BARTLETT *Explor. Texas*, etc. I. 290 Mezcal, or aguardiente. **1854** in *Southwestern Hist. Q.* (1931–2) XXXV. 235 About one dozen men came over, bringing.. muscal liquor... This Liquor has a tast between whiskey and brandy, and considerable intoxicating power. **1887** F. FRANCIS *Saddle & Mocassin* iv. 68 The Mexican..reduced himself to a state of complete intoxication with *mascal*. **1888** FANNY C. GOOCH *Face to face w. Mexicans* 562 Mescal is made from a liquor obtained by pressing the leaves of the maguey in a mill. **1926** D. H. LAWRENCE *Plumed Serp.* iv. 80 The fiery white brandy distilled from the maguey: mescal, tequila. **1947** M. LOWRY *Under Volcano* x. 319 There had been until recently several drinks of mescal (why not?—the word did not intimidate him, eh?) waiting for him outside in a lemonade bottle. **1974** *Encycl. Brit. Macropædia* X. 972/2 The alcoholic liquor mescal is distilled from pulque.

2. a. Any of several plants of the genus *Agave* found in Mexico and the southwestern United States that are used as sources of fermented liquor, food, or fibre, esp. the American aloe or maguey, *A. americana*, a stemless plant having long spiny leaves.

1743 J. LOCKMAN tr. *Trav. Jesuits* I. 399 On the Mountains grew Mescales, a fruit peculiar to the Country, and is gathered all the year round. **1759** [see 2 b]. **1808** W. SHALER *Jrnl. Voy. between China & Amer.* (1935) 53 They also have a plant called the mixcal. **1848** W. H. EMORY *Notes Mil. Reconn.* 59 This afternoon I found the famous mezcal, (an agave,) about three feet in diameter, broad leaves, armed with teeth like a shark. **1851** MAYNE REID *Scalp Hunt.* i. 14 The agave, the far-famed mezcal-plant of Mexico. **1886** *Ann. Rep. Smithsonian Inst.* (1889) II. 652 Mescal fiber, Arizona. **1891** *Century Mag.* Mar. 653 Along deserts bristling with spines of the cactus, spanish bayonet, mescal and palo verde. **1914** C. F. SAUNDERS *With Flowers & Trees in Calif.* 139 The mescal buds are capable of making by distillation one of the fieriest intoxicants known. **1951** KEARNEY & PEEBLES *Arizona Flora* II. 192 The names century-plant and mescal are applied to the large, paniculate species, and some of the small species are known as lechuguilla and amole.

b. The cooked root of the mescal as an article of food.

1759 tr. *Venegas's Nat. & Civil Hist. Calif.* I. 44 The mountains and forests yield the mezcal,..the root of which boiled is a principal ingredient of the mexcalli. **1831** J. O. PATTIE *Personal Narr.* 63, I afterwards ascertained that it was a vegetable called by the Spanish mascal (probably maguey). **1844** J. GREGG *Commerce Prairies* I. 290 Those [Apaches] that are found east of the Rio del Norte are generally known as Mezcaleros, on account of an article of food in use among them, called mezcal. *Ibid.*, Mezcal is the baked root of the maguey. **1881** *Amer. Naturalist* XV. 875 The 'mescal' of the Arizona Apaches, that is, the baked head of the *Agave palmeri* and *Agave parryi*. **1951** KEARNEY & PEEBLES *Arizona Flora* II. 192 The name 'mescal' is applied also to the food obtained by roasting the caudex and emerging flower stalk. *Ibid.* 193 Even at the present time a small quantity of mescal is made by the Papagos.

3. a. A small desert cactus, *Lophophora williamsii* (formerly *Anhalonium lewinii*, etc.), found in northern Mexico and southern Texas and having a soft, segmented body a few inches high in the form of a flattened globe. Cf. PEYOTE.

1885 [see *mescal head* in 4]. **1895** *Therapeutic Gaz.* XI. 579/2 In connection with the physiological action of the mescal, its use by the Indians is of great interest. **1896** *Ibid.* XII. 8/1 The exercises open with a prayer by the leader, who then hands each man four mescals, which he takes and eats. **1911** *Encycl. Relig. & Ethics* IV. 736/1 The Nahuatl *peyotl* ..under the incorrect title of *mescal*..is well known to the whites. **1920** *Sci. Amer.* 14 Feb. 157 The peyote, often popularly miscalled 'mescal' through confusion with the maguey cactus from which a fiery intoxicant is prepared, is a species of small cactus widely used for both medicinal and ceremonial purposes by the Indian tribes of the southwestern U.S. **1937** J. BORG *Cacti* 209 Lophophora Williamsii (*Lem.*) *Coulter*... This is the famous mescal or peyotl of the ancient Mexicans.

b. A preparation of the cactus for ingestion.

1896 *Brit. Med. Jrnl.* 5 Dec. 1625/2 The history of the use of mescal by the Indians of New Mexico is very well known in the United States. **1899** *Jrnl. Physiol.* XXX. 83 'Mescal' never gives rise to merriment, but rather to a condition of ideal content, and produces wakefulness. **1937** J. BORG *Cacti* 209 The dried tops of the plant made into bunches or wreaths used to be sold as mescal.

4. *attrib.* and *Comb.*, as ***mescal-eater***, ***intoxication***; ***mescal-inspired*** adj.; **mescal button**, a dried disc-like top of the cactus *Lophophora williamsii*, eaten or drunk as a decoction for its intoxicating and hallucinogenic effects (cf. MESCALINE); also, the plant itself, = sense 3 a; **mescal head** = *mescal button*.

1888 *Therapeutic Gaz.* IV. 232/1, I undertook to experiment with a drug..which they had received from Mexico. In its own country the drug is said to be called 'Muscale Buttons', and is used as a narcotic, food, or relish. *Ibid.*, *Anhalonium Lewinii*, nov. spec., Mexico. Local name, 'Muscale Buttons'. **1896** *Brit. Med. Jrnl.* 5 Dec. 1625/2, I took fully $1\frac{1}{2}$ drachm of an extract of which each drachm represented one mescal button. **1913** *Jrnl. Nervous & Mental Dis.* XL. 427 We endeavoured further to extend knowledge of pathological mental states by producing mental conditions nearly allied to generally recognized types of insanity... For this purpose we used the Mexican drug [*printed* drag] pelotte—the mescal button. **1959** O. & M. LEESE *Desert Plants* iv. 41 There are too the Lophophoras or Anhaloniums, known as the Mescal Button or Peyote, which are devoid of spines and look somewhat like a denizen of the sea. **1934** R. HAMER in R. Skelton *Poetry of Thirties* (1964) 88 The mescal-eater's almost heard Omnipotent transcendental word. **1885** *Outing* Oct. 24/2 The old and young squaws..had brought down from the hillsides donkey-loads of mescal-heads. **1933** L. SPIER *Yuman Tribes* 55 The mescal heads were baked in a pit. **1946** in M. Lowry *Let.* 2 Jan. (1967) 61 The mescal-inspired phantasmagoria, or heebie-jeebies, to which Geoffrey has succumbed. **1897** *Lancet* 5 June 1541/2 It cannot be said (from my experience) that the pleasure of mescal intoxication lies in any resultant passive emotional state such as is produced by tea or alcohol, but strictly in enjoyment of the colour visions produced.

mescaline (ˈmɛskəlɪn, -iːn). Also **mescalin**, †**mezcaline**. [ad. G. *mezcalin* (now *mescalin*) (A. Heffter 1896, in *Ber. d. Deut. Chem. Ges.* XXIX. 222), f. Sp. *mezcal* MESCAL: see -IN[1], -INE[5].]

a. The alkaloid 3,4,5-trimethoxyphenethylamine, $(CH_3O)_3{\cdot}C_6H_2{\cdot}CH_2CH_2NH_2$, which is the chief active principle of mescal buttons, producing effects similar to those of LSD but much less strongly.

1896 *Jrnl. Chem. Soc.* LXX. I. 267 Alkaloïds of *Anhalonium Lewinii*, Hennings (*Lophophora Lewinii*, Rusby).—The dried 'discs' (Scheiben) of this cactus are used by the Indians of N. Mexico for the preparation of an intoxicant, and are brought into commerce under the name of 'Muscale buttons'... They were extracted with 70 per cent. alcohol, and the residue obtained by evaporating this extract was extracted with ether and then with chloroform. The chloroform dissolved an alkaloïd which was named mezcaline. **1899** *Jrnl. Physiol.* XXV. 82 Mezcaline, whilst agreeing precisely with the other alkaloids as regards cardiac and respiratory action, etc., appeared more effective in the production of colour visions. **1900** DORLAND *Med. Dict.* 384/1 Mescalin. **1936** *Mind* XLV. 68 My first experience of a similar kind was during an experiment with mescaline. **1956** A. HUXLEY *Heaven & Hell* i. 11 The soul is transported to its far-off destination by the aid of..mescalin. **1958** M. ARGYLE *Relig. Behaviour* ix. 112 A number of drugs produce quasi-mystical experiences, the best-known being mescaline. **1962** *Q. Rev.* XVI. 136 The outstanding result of mescaline ingestion is visual hallucination, but depersonalisation and time distortion frequently occur. **1966** T. PYNCHON *Crying of Lot 49* i. 17 The experiment he was helping the community hospital run on effects of LSD-25, mescaline, psilocybin, and related drugs on a large sample of suburban housewives. **1974** *Sci. Amer.* June 66/1 Other hallucinogenic agents such as mescaline and amphetamine, on the other hand, are related in structure to noradrenaline.

b. *attrib.*, as ***mescaline hallucination***, ***psychosis***.

1913 *Jrnl. Nervous & Mental Dis.* XL. 432 A mescalin hallucination is felt to be much more objective than a mere idea such as a visual image. **1941** *Arch. Neurol. & Psychiatry* (Chicago) XLV. 130 (*heading*) Mescaline hallucinations in artists. **1940** *Jrnl. Mental Sci.* LXXXVI. 36 The feeling of unreality, both as regards the self and the external world, so often found in schizophrenics, is one of the typical features of the mescaline psychosis. **1958** M. ARGYLE *Relig. Behaviour* ix. 114 It is acute schizophrenia which most resembles 'mescaline psychosis', and Andis has described a number of psychotic patients whose reported experiences resembled mescaline psychosis more than the classical type of psychosis.

mescalism (ˈmɛskəlɪz(ə)m). [f. MESCAL + -ISM.] **a.** The practice of taking mescal buttons. **b.** The state of intoxication produced by them.

1902 *Amer. Anthropologist* Oct.–Dec. 789/1 Through mescalism one seems almost to 'attain an objective knowledge of one's own personality'. **1936** *Mind* XLV. 70 Like the starry and bejewelled scenes observed in mescalism, spots of light or their relatives seen in hypnagogic images have also a retro-retinal origin.

mescel(l)in(e, obs. forms of MASLIN[2].

meschance, obs. form of MISCHANCE.

†**meschancie**. *Obs. rare*[−1]. In quot. mis- [f. MESCHANT: see -ANCY.] Wickedness.

1609 *Pitcairn's Crim. Trials* III. 5 For forder manifestatioun of ȝoure extreame and maist vnnaturall mischancie.

†**meschant**, *a.* and *sb. Obs.* Forms: 5 **meschaunt(e, mysch(e)aunt(e**, 5, 7 **mischaunt**, 6 **mischand, -eant, mechient, meschante, mysch(e)ant, mechant**, 6–7 **mischant, mishant, meschant**. [a. OF. *mescheant* unlucky, wicked (mod.F. *méchant* wicked), orig. pr. pple. of *mescheoir* to be unlucky + *mes-* MIS- + *cheoir* to fall:—popular L. **cadēre* for class. L. *cadĕre*. Frequent in Caxton; in the 16th c. mainly Sc.]

A. *adj.*

1. Wicked, bad, base.

a **1450** *Knt. de la Tour* 126 It is a myschaunt thinge for any gentille woman, other to striue or to chide in ani manere. *c* **1570** *Satir. Poems Reform.* xx. 146 All thay yat dois..With mischant mynde maling Aganis the treuth. **1629** *Reg. Privy Council Scot.* Ser. II. III. 4 The..purging of the land frome suche a mischaunt persoun. **1649** BP. GUTHRIE *Mem.* (1702) 6 This Meschant Business..gave the Ministers Affairs such a Blow, that..they were never able to make it up again.

2. Miserable, wretched.

1471 CAXTON *Recuyell* (Sommer) 48 Than he retorned poure and myschant vnto his fader Tytan. **1530** PALSGR. 318/2 Meschante myserable, *meschant*.

B. *sb.* A wretch, a villain.

c **1489** CAXTON *Sonnes of Aymon* iv. 125 Thenne he sayd to his children 'Myschaunt, your ledernes and slouth hath overcomen you'. **1570** in Spottiswood *Hist. Ch. Scot.* v. (1677) 238 They..had unworthily cut off his Uncle and Regent, by suborning a mischant to kill him treacherously. *a* **1585** POLWART *Flyting w. Montgomerie* 131 Mischiewous mishant. **1664** PEPYS *Diary* 6 Sept., Cromwell, notwithstanding the meschants in his time, which were the Cavaliers, did [etc.].

Hence †**meschantly** *adv.*, †**meschantness**.

1491 CAXTON *Vitas Patr.* (W. de W. 1495) II. 256/2 The tyme that he had lost & wasted in lyuyng myschauntly. **1573** *Satir. Poems Reform.* xl. 205 Upricht men ar murtherit mischantlie. **1623** in Pitcairn *Crim. Trials* III. 549 How mischantlie and barbaruslie the innocent Gentillman was murdreist. **1644** D. HUME *Hist. Doug.* 153 Which I confesse is so profound and deep a folly, and mischantnesse, that I can by no means sound it. **1661** R. BAILLIE *Lett. & Jrnls.* (1842) III. 468 Mr. Blair, Mr. Dickson, and Mr. Hutcheson, were, without all cause, mischantly abused by his pen.

† **meschantery.** *Obs. rare*⁻¹. [f. MESCHANT + -ERY.] A wicked deed.

1665 SIR T. HERBERT *Trav.* (1677) 337 The good man by that delusive spell is rendred a ridiculous spectator, and seemingly an assentor to their meschanteries.

meschaunce, -cheaunce, obs. ff. MISCHANCE.

meschef, -chief, etc., obs. ff. MISCHIEF.

meschit(e, -ito: see MESQUITA *Obs.*, mosque.

† **meschyne.** *Obs. rare*⁻¹. [? a. OF. *meschine*, fem. of *meschin*, *mesquin*: see MESQUIN. (But cf. MDu. *meskijn* girl, wench.)] A bad woman.

1490 CAXTON *Eneydos* xv. 58 This meschyne .. that Ioyeth her to recyte .. more lesyng than trouth.

mescita, variant of MESQUITA *Obs.*

mesclin, obs. form of MASLIN².

mescontent, -creance, etc.: see MIS-.

mescroyance. *quasi-arch. rare*⁻¹. [a. OF. *mescroyance*, f. *mescroyant*: see next.] Misbelief.

1876 RUSKIN *Fors Clav.* lxxii. 383 The elements of Croyance and Mescroyance are always chemically separable.

† **mescroyant.** *Obs. rare*⁻¹. [a. OF. *mescroyant*, var. of *mescreiant*, *mescreant*: see MISCREANT.] A misbeliever.

1711 HICKES *Two Treat. Chr. Priesth.* (1847) II. 365 The Church and clergy .. are every day .. insulted by every vile mescroyant, and every blaspheming tongue.

mescuite, variant of MESQUITA, MESQUIT *Obs.*

‖ **mesdames** (medam). [Fr., pl. of MADAME.]

1. The plural of MADAME.

c **1573** GASCOIGNE *Posies, Flowers* 43 And wherefore maruaile you Mez Dames, I praye you tell mee then. **1774** GIBBON *Let.* 24 May in *Life & Lett.* (1869) 233 The Mesdames, by attending their father, have both got the smallpox.

2. Used to supply the want of an Engl. pl. of 'Mrs.'

1792 WOLCOT (P. Pindar) *Ode to Margate Hoy* 37 My good friend Johnson—Mesdames Windsor, Kelly. **1879** *Illustr. Lond. News* 15 Mar. 258/2 Mesdames Down and Jamieson.

‖ **mesdemoiselles**, pl. of MADEMOISELLE.

1792 W. ROBERTS *Looker-on* No. 52 (1795) III. 27 The practice among fashionable mothers of committing their children to the care of French Mesdemoiselles.

mesdo, obs. form of MISDO.

mese (miːz), *sb.*¹ *Obs.* exc. *s.w. dial.* Also 7-9 meese, 9 meesh, mews, etc. [OE. *méos* = Flem. *mies* (cited Kilian as obsolete), OHG. *mios* (MHG., mod.G. dial. *mies*), ON. *mýr-r* (see MIRE *sb.*):—OTeut. types *'*meuso-z*, **meu'zo-z*, related by ablaut to **moson-*, ON. *mose* MOSS *sb.*] Moss.

a **900** tr. *Bæda's Hist.* III. ii. §2 þa brohte him sumne dæl ealdes meoses, þe on þam halȝan treo aweaxen wæs. **13..** *Sir Orfeo* 246 (Zielke 1880) 98 Þis king mote make his bed in mese. **14..** *Treat. Gardening* in *Archæologia* LIV. I. 161 Upon the clay thu schalt mese layne. *c* **1639** *Berkeley MS.* in *Glouc. Gloss.* (E.D.S.), Meese, meesy, i.e. mosse, mossy. **1886** ELWORTHY *W. Somerset Word-bk.*, *Mews* (mue·z), moss. **1886** *Dorset Gloss.*, *Meesh*, moss. **1893** *Wiltsh. Gloss.*, *Mesh* (*e* long), moss or lichen on an old apple-tree.

† **mese**, *sb.*² *Obs.* Forms: 4-7 mees, 5-6 mes, 5-7 messe, mese, 5-8 mease, meese, 6 meas, meis(s)e, myse, 7-8 mise. [a OF, *mes* masc., *mese* fem.:—late L. *mansum* (*-us*), *mansa*: see MANSE.] = MESSUAGE.

[**1321-2** *Rolls of Parlt.* I. 405/1 Un mees de iiijˣˣ acres de terre.] **1402** HOCCLEVE *Let. Cupid* 334 Ne men bereve hir landes ne hir Mees. **1467** *Godstow Reg.* 347 A dwellyng place (or a mese) with a plough-lond. **1527** in *Visit. Southwell* (Camden) 132 My capitall meas in Ragenhill. **1546** *Yorks. Chantry Surv.* (Surtees) I. 150, j myse buylded lying in Wodhouse. *a* **1604** HANMER *Chron. Irel.* (1633) 194 The eldest can demand no more than her sisters; but the chiefe mease by reason of her auncienty. **1720** STRYPE *Stow's Surv.* (1754) II. VI. iii. 634/1 In the Palace yard were anciently pales within which were two Messes, the one called Paradise and the other called the Constabulary. **1729** *MS. Indenture estate at Crich, co. Derby*, A messuage .. closes thereto belonging, called the meese, furlongs [etc.].

fig. **1591** SYLVESTER *Du Bartas* I. iv. 239 Thou [Aries] .. Doest hold the First house of Heav'n's spacious Meese [Fr. *possedant du Ciel la premiere maison*].

‖ **mese** ('mɛsiː), *sb.*³ [Gr. μέση (sc. χορδή string), fem. of μέσος middle.] In ancient Greek music, the middle string of the seven-stringed lyre, and its note; subsequently, the key-note of any of the scales in use.

1603 HOLLAND *Plutarch's Mor.* 796 The three termes or bounds which make the intervals in an octave or eight, of musicke harmonicall, to wit, *Nete*, *Mese*, and *Hypate*, that is to say, the Treble, the Meane, and the Base. *Ibid.* 1252 Thus may a man soone perceive .. who plaieth upon a pipe after the old maner: For by his good will, the Hemitone in the Mese, will be incompounded. **1760** *Phil. Trans.* LI. 700 The antients agree in their accounts of the relative pitch of the meses. **1905** *Athenæum* 22 July 122/3 The direct descendant of the *mese* in the old Greek music.

mese (miːz), *v. Sc.* and *north. dial.* Forms: 4-5 mes, 4-9 mease, 5 meese, 5, 9 mees, (6 maiss, meiss, meys, miess, mise), 6-7 meis(e, 4- mese. [Aphetic f. AMESE *v.*]

1. *trans.* To mitigate, assuage, appease, calm (a person's anger, sorrow, etc.); to settle (disputes).

13.. *E. E. Allit. P.* B. 764 Wylt þou mese þy mode & menddyng abyde? *c* **1440** *York Myst.* xliii. 238 Nowe might þer Jewes þare malise meese. *c* **1450** *St. Cuthbert* (Surtees) 1051 Þe childe with mylde wordes he meesyd. **1456** SIR G. HAYE *Law Arms* (S.T.S.) 21 To mes all thir debatis, it was ordanyt that Rome suld be .. soverane kirk. **1535** STEWART *Cron. Scot.* II. 104 The nobillis .. With fair wordis misit the multitude. *c* **1560** A. SCOTT *Poems* (S.T.S.) iv. 60 Sum luvis dance vp and doun, To meiss thair malancoly. **1629** SIR W. MURE *True Crucifixe* 596 Yet did not mease the causeless spight. **1721** KELLY *Scot. Prov.* 138 He should be sindle angry, that has few to mease him. **1862** HISLOP *Prov. Scot.* 107 If you be angry, sit laigh and mease you.

2. To calm (wind, tempest, etc.), quench (fire).

c **1375** *Sc. Leg. Saints* iii. (*St. Andreas*) 62 Swyth þe gret fyre can he mes. **1513** DOUGLAS *Æneis* III. ii. 2 The blastis mesit, and the fluidis stabill. **1533** BELLENDEN *Livy* II. xxiii. (S.T.S.) 227 Þe noyes .. was sum parte mesit.

mese: see MASS *sb.*¹, MEASE, MESS.

mese, var. MEZE.

mesease, obs. form of MISEASE.

meseems (miː'siːmz), *impers. v. arch.* Also meseemeth. *Pa.t.* meseemed. [Orig. two words, *me* (dative: see ME *pron.*¹ 2 a) and *seems* 3rd pers. sing. of SEEM *v.* Cf. METHINKS.] It seems to me. (Used with dependent clause or parenthetically.)

c **1400** MAUNDEV. (1839) v. 61, I seyde .. that thei diden synne, to hide Goddis Myracle, as me seemed. **1487** CAXTON *Bk. Gd. Manners* IV. v. (*c* 1515) I vj, And me semeth yᵗ the partye that forfayteth his maryage dooth agaynst the lawe of nature. **1564** HAWARD *Eutropius* To Rdr. 1 For which causes (me semes) I have taken upon mee .. a hard enterprize. **1586** A. DAY *Eng. Secretary* II. (1625) 68 It were a comfort vnto vs all to see you, hauing beene as me seemeth very long absent. **1627** W. SCLATER *Exp. 2 Thess.* (1629) 71 Mee seemes hee makes it something more excellent then Faith it selfe. **1850** CARLYLE *Latter-d. Pamph.* ii. (1872) 47 Meseems I could discover fitter objects of piety! **1859** TENNYSON *Elaine* 672 For they talk'd, Meseem'd, of what they knew not. **1876** MORRIS *Sigurd* (1877) 307 Meseemeth this is the hour when men array the dead.

meseise, obs. form of MISEASE.

† '**mesel**, *a.* and *sb. Obs.* Forms: 3-6 mesel, -el(l)e, (4 meosel, mesale, meseile, mezel, myssel(e, -ale, musel, mysale), 4, 7 messel(l, 4-6 mesell, mesyl(l, mysel, (6 messille, mesall, 7 mesill, mezill, meazel, 8 meazle). [a. OF. *mesel* leprous, leper:—L. *misellus* wretched, wretch, dim. of *miser* wretched.] **A.** *adj.* Leprous.

a **1300** *Cursor M.* 14446 And o ten men þat war mesell, .. he gaf til ilkan þair hele. **1340** *Ayenb.* 202 Naaman þet wes mesel. *c* **1450** *Mirour Saluacioun* 4628 Ane horrible seke mesel man. *a* **1550** *Image Ipocr.* IV. in *Skelton's Wks.* (1843) II. 444 Oh mesell Mendicantes, And mangy Obseruauntes. **1607** R. C[AREW] tr. *Estienne's World of Wonders* 357 Thou measell wretch.

b. Of fish. (So in OF.)

a **1400** *Chalm. Ayr* xx. in *Sc. Acts* (1814) I. 335 Quhen þai opyn fische þai luke nocht quheder þai be mesale fische or wane. **1536** BELLENDEN *Cron. Scot.* (1821) I. p. xliii, Utheris .. brekis thaimself be thair fall, and growis mesall.

c. Of swine: see MEASLE *a.*

B. *sb.*

1. A leper.

1297 R. GLOUC. (Rolls) 8963 [She] wess þe meseles [*v.rr*, mysseles, myseles] vet echone. *a* **1300** *Cursor M.* 8169 Thoru þe .. sal þis mesele, Be sauf and sund of al vnhele. **1362** LANGL. *P. Pl.* A. III. 128 As Comuyn as þe Cart-wei .. To Preostes, to Minstrals to Mesels in hegges. *c* **1422** HOCCLEVE *Min. Poems* xxiv. 469 He eet ther-of .. But he ther-thurgh becam a foul mesel. *c* **1550** BALE *K. Johan* (Camden) 82 Both crypple, halte, and blynde, Mad men and mesels.

b. *fig.* A foul person. (Used in 17th and 18th c. as a term of abuse.)

c **1422** HOCCLEVE *Jereslaus's Wife* 797 Woost thow nat weel thow art a foul mesel? Telle out, let see shryue thee cleene and wel. *c* **1520** *Wyse chylde & Emp. Adrian* (W. de W.) (1860) 14 Those that sellen them [*sc.* benefices] shall be mesellys in the soule as Jesse [*i.e.* Giezi, *Gehazi*]. **1605** *Lond. Prodigal* C 2 b. Chil be abaffeled vp and downe for a messell and a scoundrel. **1606** *Choice, Chance*, etc. (1881) 6 An old mezill will haue a misers tricke. **1746** *Exmoor Scolding* (E.D.S.) 30 What's me-an by that, ya long-hanjed Meazle?

2. Leprosy. Also *transf.*, an affliction.

c **1375** *Cursor M.* 11827 (Fairf.) Ouer alle he was with mesel playne [*earlier texts* was he mesel plain]. *c* **1400** *Prymer* in Maskell *Mon. Rit.* (1847) II. 104 That thou fouche suaf to .. releeue the meselis [*L. miserias*] of pore men and thrallis. **1470-85** MALORY *Arthur* XVII. xl. 705 Whanne she had layne a grete whyle she felle vnto a mesel. **1530** PALSGR. 244/2 Mesyll the sickenesse, *mesellerie*.

3. *attrib.*, as *mesel-cote*, *house*.

1402 *Will of Neve* (Somerset Ho.), Les meselcotes in Kent-strete. *c* **1330** R. BRUNNE *Chron.* (1810) 136 To meselle houses of þat same lond, þre þousand mark vnto þer spense he fond.

mesel, mesalade: see MEASLE, MALASADE.

† '**meseled**, *ppl. a. Obs.* Also 7 measel'd, meselled, mezel'd. [f. MESEL + -ED.] Leprous. Cf. MEASLED *a.*

1607 CHAPMAN *Bussy D'Ambois* Plays 1873 II. 126 Not a pezzants entrailes you shall finde More foule and mezel'd. **1611** COTGR., *Meseau*, a meselled, scuruie, leaporous, lazarous person. *a* **1616** BEAUM. & FL. *Scornf. Lady* II. iii, Steweard, you are an Asse, a measel'd mungrell.

Hence † '**meseledness**.

1611 COTGR. *Meseldnesse*, leprosie, scurvinesse.

meself, *Obs.*: see MYSELF.

† '**meseling**, *a. Obs.* [f. MESEL *a.* + -ING².] Leprous; full of disease.

c **1425** *Macro Plays* (E.E.T.S.) 144 In meselynge glotonye .. I norche my syster Lecherye.

meselle, -elled, obs. ff. MEASLE, MEASLED.

† '**meselness.** *Obs. rare*⁻¹. [f. MESEL *a.* + -NESS.] Leprosy.

c **1520** M. NISBET *New Test. in Scots* Luke v. 12 (S.T.S.) I. 207 A man full of meselnes [WYCLIF lepre].

† '**meselry.** *Obs.* Forms: see MESEL. [a. OF. *mesel(l)erie*, f. *mesel* MESEL: see -RY.] Leprosy.

a **1300** *Cursor M.* 29185 Þar was a woman hight mari, þat sumtime wat [? *read* smetyn was; *Cotton Galba has* was smetyn] wit meselri. *c* **1330** R. BRUNNE *Chron.* (1810) 140 For foule meselrie he comond with no man. **14..** *Nom.* in Wr.-Wülcker 707/24 *Hec lepra*, a mesylery. **1496** *Dives & Paup.* (W. de W.) IX. iv. 350 Giezi was smyten with foule myselrye. *c* **1500** *Rowlis Cursing* 45 in Laing *Anc. Poet. Scotl.*, Maigram, madness or missilry. *c* **1520** M. NISBET *New Test. in Scots* Luke v. 13 And anon the meselrie passit away fra him. **1623** tr. *Favine's Theat. Hon.* III. x. 447 Infected with Leaprosie, Meazelrie, and the like.

b. Measly condition (of swine).

1587 MASCALL *Govt. Cattle, Hogges* (1627) 265 The cause of measelry in a hog.

† '**mesely**, *a. Obs.* In 6 misly, 7 meezlie, mezely. [f. MESEL + -Y.] Leprous; in quots. a term of contempt; cf. MEASLY.

a **1585** MONTGOMERIE *Flyting w. Polwart* 754 Misly kyt! and thou flyt, Ile dryt in thy gob. *a* **1693** *Urquhart's Rabelais* III. xlviii. 386 There is no scurvy, mezely, leprous or pocky Ruffian [etc.].

absol. a **1640** DAY *Peregr. Schol.* Wks. 1881 I. 44 For Lerneing che could not abid un, the fowle meezlie wod Imake a game playe on un & send [etc.].

‖ **mesembryanthemum** (mɛˌsɛmbrɪ'ænθɪməm). *Bot.* [mod.L., miswritten for **mesēmbrianthemum*, ad. assumed Gr. type *μεσημβριάνθεμον, f. μεσημβρία noon + ἄνθεμον flower.

The name, rendered in Eng. as *Midday-flower* and in Ger. as *Mittagsblume*, refers to the fact that several species open their flowers only for a short time at mid-day.]

The typical genus of the N.O. *Mesembryaceæ*; a plant of this genus, a fig-marigold.

[**1753** CHAMBERS *Cycl. Supp.* s.v., Mesembryanthemum, in botany, the name by which Dillenius, Linnæus, and others, have called the plants usually named *Ficoides*.] **1825** *Greenhouse Comp.* I. 105 Mesembryanthemums require it [*sc.* water] chiefly when they are in flower. **1884** MRS. C. PRAED *Zéro* xxi, Grey walls were ablaze with mesembryanthemum.

mesen, obs. form of MIZEN.

mesencephal(e (mɛsən'sɛfəl). *Anat.* [a. F. *mésencéphale.*] = MESENCEPHALON.

1839-47 *Todd's Cycl. Anat.* III. 684/2 The mesocephale or mesencephale. The name was suggested by Chaussier. **1889** *Buck's Handbk. Med Sci.* VIII. 128/2 In early embryonic stages the mesencephal is the most conspicuous region of the entire brain.

mesencephalic (mɛsɛnsɪ'fælɪk), *a. Anat.* [f. MESENCEPHALON + -IC. Cf. *cephalic.*] Pertaining to or connected with the mesencephalon.

1854 OWEN *Skel. & Teeth* in *Circ. Sci* I. *Org. Nat.* 193 The mesencephalic vertebra. **1880** GUNTHER *Fishes* 86 Mesencephalic arch.

‖ **mesencephalon** (mɛsɛn'sɛfəlɒn). *Anat.* [mod.L., f. Gr. μέσ-ος middle + ἐγκέφαλον ENCEPHALON.] The mid-brain.

1846 OWEN *Vertebr. Anim.* II. 177 The next succeeding primary division of the brain, is called the 'mesencephalon'. **1875** HUXLEY in *Encycl. Brit.* I. 767/1 The mesencephalon is divided above .. into two optic lobes.

‖ **mesenchyma** (mɛ'sɛŋkɪmə). *Biol.* Also anglicized **mesenchyme** ('mɛsɛŋkaɪm). [mod.L. *mesenchyma*, f. Gr. μέσ-ος middle + ἔγχυμα infusion.] The cellular tissue which, arising from the hypoblast or the epiblast, constitutes, in some of the lower forms of animal life, the mesoblast. Also *attrib.* in *mesenchyme cell* = MESAMŒBOID.

1888 ROLLESTON & JACKSON *Anim. Life* Gen. Introd. 28 The cells arise as immigrants (mesenchyme cells) from the walls of the blastosphere. **1890** *Syd. Soc. Lex.* **1904** *Brit. Med. Jrnl.* 10 Sept. 584 The primary leucocytes, or wandering mesenchyme cells.

Hence **me'senchymal**, **mesen'chymatous** *adjs.*, pertaining to the mesenchyma.

1886 *Buck's Handbk. Med. Sci.* III. 194/1 The ordinary mesenchymal cells. **1886** *Jrnl. Roy. Microsc. Soc.* Feb. 54

The body-cavity [of the Polyzoa] contains 'mesenchymatous' (Hertwig) elements.

mesenterial (mɛsɛn'tɪərəl), *a.* [f. med.L. *mesenterium* MESENTERY + -AL[1].] = MESENTERIC.

1605 TIMME *Quersit.* Ded. 2 The anatomizing of every mesenteriall veine. **1880** GÜNTHER *Fishes* 128 The commencement and end of the intestinal tract are fixed by mesenterial folds. **1890** *Nature* 20 Mar. 457 The mesenterial filaments of the Alcyonarians.

mesenteric (mɛsɛn'tɛrɪk), *a.* [ad. mod.L. *mesentericus*, f. *mesenterium* MESENTERY: see -IC.] Pertaining to, connected with, or affecting the mesentery.

1656 BLOUNT *Glossogr.* s.v. *Artery*, Mesenterique Arteries, are two, an upper, which distributes it self among the small guts, and an under one, which goes to the lower part of the Mesentery. **1710** T. FULLER *Pharm. Extemp.* 129 The Bark..being the cause of..Mesenteric Obstructions. **1836** J. M. GULLY *Magendie's Formul.* (ed. 2) 105 M. Brera is not the only one who has given iodine in mesenteric disease.

So †**mesen'terical** *a.* Hence **mesen'terically** *adv.*, like the mesentery.

1664 POWER *Exp. Philos.* III. 191 The Mesenterical and Thoracical Lacteae. **1829** J. L. KNAPP *Jrnl. Nat.* 130 Bolton and Micheli represent the pileus as cellular, like a honeycomb. All that I have seen are mesenterically puckered.

mesen'teriform, *a. rare.* [f. MESENTERY + -(I)FORM.] Resembling the mesentery.

1846 DANA *Zooph.* (1848) 708 Mesenteriform, consisting of suberect plicately aggregated laminæ.

‖**mesenteritis** (mɛsɛntə'raɪtɪs). [mod.L., f. *mesenterium* MESENTERY: see -ITIS.] Inflammation of the mesentery.

1802 TURTON *Med. Gloss.* **1844** HOBLYN *Dict. Med.*

‖**mesenteron** (mɛ'sɛntərɒn). [mod.L., f. Gr. μέσ-ος middle + ἔντερον gut, bowel.] 'The digestive portion of the primitive alimentary canal or archenteron' (*Syd. Soc. Lex.*). Hence **mesente'ronic** *a.* (in recent Dicts.).

1877 RAY LANKESTER in *Q. Jrnl. Microsc. Sci.* 431 As archenteron divides into parentera and metenteron, so metenteron divides into *hepatentera* or hepatic cæca and *mesenteron*. **1893** A. E. SHIPLEY *Zool. Invert.* 312 Two long white tubes—the Malpighian tubules—open into the posterior end of the mesenteron.

mesentery ('mɛsəntərɪ). Also 6 mis-. [ad. med.L. *mesenterium*, a Gr. μεσεντέριον, f. μέσ-ος middle + ἔντερον intestine. Cf. F. *mésentère*.]

1. *Anat.* **a.** A fold of peritonæum which attaches some part of the intestinal canal (in restricted use, the jejunum and ileum only) to the posterior wall of the abdomen.

1547 BOORDE *Brev. Health* II. xlv. 14 The misentery whiche is a pellycle or a skyn the whiche doth tye the guttes together. **1663** BOYLE *Usef. Exp. Nat. Philos.* II. i. 10 The discoveries of the milky Vessels in the Mesentery by Asellius. **1718** J. CHAMBERLAYNE *Relig. Philos.* (1730) I. iv. §11 Notwithstanding all its Turnings, it [*sc.* the Bowels] is fastened in such a Manner to the Mesentery, that it is not possible for the Food to mistake its Way. **1872** MIVART *Elem. Anat.* ix. (1873) 403 Those folds of membrane, the mesenteries which suspend the viscera from the backbone.

‖*β.* In Latin and Greek forms **mesenterium**, **mesenterion**, (†**mezentereon**).

1541 R. COPLAND *Guydon's Quest. Chirurg.* H iv b, Howe may the Mezentereon be knowen by Anathomy? **1594** T. B. *La Primand. Fr. Acad.* II. 350 The manifolde knitting of it [*sc.* the ileum] to the mesenterium. **1631** WIDDOWES *Nat. Philos.* 63 The lesse principall parts of concoction, are the gutts and mesenterion. **1857** L. AGASSIZ *Contrib. Nat. Hist. U.S.A.* II. 601 To form a pendent double curtain, or support of the intestine, the mesenterium.

2. *Zool.* (*pl.*) The vertical plates which divide the body cavity in actinozoa.

1861 J. R. GREENE *Man. Anim. Kingd., Cœlent.* 172 In *Cerianthus* two of the mesenteries descend..almost to the orifice at the base of the general cavity. **1875** HUXLEY in *Encycl. Brit.* I. 129/2 Thin membranous lamellæ, the so-called mesenteries, which radiate from the oral disk and the lateral walls of the body to the parietes of the visceral tube.

3. *attrib.* and *Comb.*

1626 BACON *Sylva* §44 The Mesentery Veines. **1846** DANA *Zooph.* iv. (1848) 35 A thin and extensile membrane, which has a mesentery-like appearance.

†**mese-place.** *Obs.* Also 5 mesplace, 7 *corruptly* meest place, 7–8 mise-place. [f. MESE *sb.*[1] + PLACE *sb.*] = MESE *sb.*[1]

14.. *Voc.* in Wr.-Wülcker 596/6 *Messuagium*, a mesplace. **1441** in W. P. Baildon *Sel. Cases Chanc.* (1896) 131 To bye of hym a mees·place. **1523** FITZHERB. *Surv.* xx. (1539) 41 I. B. holdeth a mese place frely of the lord by charter. **1607** NORDEN *Surv. Dial.* II. 55 The parcell of the Land lately belonging to this heriotable meest place. **1672** *Cowell's Interpr., Mease*,..in some places called corruptly a *Mise* or *Miseplace*.

meseraic, -ai(c)k, etc., obs. ff. MESARAIC.

mesereon, obs. form of MEZEREON.

mesestead. Forms: *α.* 6 meastead, mestede, 6–7 meestead, 7–8 measestead, mested. *β.* 7 misted. *γ.* 7 meadstead, 7–9 midstead. *δ.* 7 meerstead, 9 merestead. [f. MESE *sb.*[2] + STEAD *sb.* The *γ* and *δ* forms are etymologizing perversions, due to association with MEAD *sb.* and MERE *sb.*[2] respectively.] A messuage.

α. **1546** *Yorks. Chantry Surv.* (Surtees) I. 179 One mestede in Exthorpe. **1590** *Crt. Rolls Manor of Dewsbury* in *N. & Q.* 9th Ser. V. 349/2 A messuage or tenement called meestead or the New Walles. **1622** *MS. Indenture Sir R. Swifte's Estate at Doncaster*, All those several meesteads as they now lie unbuilt upon and walled in from the street. *c* **1700** DE LA PRYME *Diary* (Surtees) 316 A larg map of yᵉ whole parish, having every field, ing, close, mested, croft, cavel, intack, &c...in it. **1714** *Lond. Gaz.* No. 5204/8 A Messuage or Measestead, where a House or Barn formerly stood.

β. **1633** *Plymouth Col. Rec.* (1855) I. 16 Richard Higgens hath bought of Thomas Little his now dwelling house and misted. *Ibid.* 18, 24, 45.

γ. **1637** *Plymouth Col. Rec.* (1855) I. 57 A midstead is graunted to George Russell in the towne of Plymouth. **1640** *Ibid.* 145 Willm Sherman is graunted a meadstead about the Stoney Brooke, in Duxborrow. **1896** S. O. ADDY in *N. & Q.* 8th Ser. X. 349 In the township of Royston, near Barnsley, there are eighteen freeholders..known as 'midstead owners'. *Ibid.*, For more than two centuries the 'midstead owners' have kept a book in which their rules and ordinances ..have been recorded. *Ibid.* 470 A certain number of houses were known as 'midstead houses'.

δ. *c* **1620** *Plymouth Col. Rec.* XII. 3 The meersteads and garden plotes of [those] which came first. **1858** LONGF. *M. Standish* viii. 4 Busy with hewing and building, with garden-plot and with mere-stead. [**1883** *New Eng. Hist. & Gen. Reg.* XXXVII. 277 Peter Brown, whose first house and 'meerstead' was on the south side of Leyden Street.]

‖**meseta** (me'seta). [Sp., dim. of *mesa* MESA, f. L. *mēnsa* a table.] A plateau; *spec.* the high plateau of central Spain. Also *attrib.*

1904 T. H. HOLDICH *Countries of King's Award* xiii. 366 The moraines streak the surface of the 'mesetas', which here represent the beds of ancient lakes and are disposed more or less in the form of terraces. **1905** *Spectator* 28 Jan. 112/2 The region of the Patagonian Andes..presents a jumble of mountains, rivers, 'mesetas', 'pampas', forests, and glaciers. **1958** FISHER & BOWEN-JONES *Spain* I. ii. 20 By far the largest proportion of Spain is occupied by the Meseta, which, however, is far from being a uniform mass. It is best regarded as comprising two enormous table-lands, or upland basins, which are separated by a diagonally-running fold mountain series. **1962** R. WAY *Geogr. Spain & Portugal* xiii. 257 The peasants..have long journeys to make by mule or ox before they begin their day's work, and then have to endure the vagaries of the meseta climate, particularly strong winds. **1963** *Guardian* 13 July 6/4 The regions of the high *meseta*—the Castiles, Aragon, Leon, and Estremadura. **1969** J. MANDER *Static Society* ii. 81 The landscape resembles..the *meseta* of Spain.

mesethmoid (mɛ'sɛθmɔɪd). *Anat.* [f. Gr. μέσ-ος middle + ETHMOID.] The middle ethmoid bone. Also *attrib.* in ***mesethmoid cartilage***.

1875 C. C. BLAKE *Zool.* 46 The ossified portion of the mesethmoid. **1875** HUXLEY & MARTIN *Elem. Biol.* (1877) 193 The Olfactory organs are two wide sacs which occupy all the space between the mesethmoid cartilage, the antorbital processes, and the premaxillæ and maxillæ.

So **meseth'moidal**
(in recent Dicts.).

meseyn, meseyse: see MIZEN, MISEASE.

mesfeat, variant of MISFAIT *Obs.*

mesh (mɛʃ), *sb.* Forms: 6–7 meishe, meash, 6–8 (9 *dial.*) mash, (8 marsh), 6– mesh. [Known only from the 16th c.; cogn. w. OE. *max* (? **mæsc*.) neut., net and ON. *mǫskve* (see MASK *sb.*[1]); but the precise nature of the relation is undetermined.

The Teut. langs. have words with this meaning representing two ablaut-types: (1) OTeut. **mask-* (OE. *max*, ? **mæsc* ? neut.; OHG. *masca*, MHG., mod.G. *masche* fem.; M.Du. *masche* fem.; ON. *mǫskve*, Norw. *moske* wk. masc.; Sw. *maska*, Da. *maske* fem. are from LG.); (2) OTeut. **mǣsk-* (OHG. *mâsca*, MHG. ? *mâsche*; MDu. *maesche*). The Eng. form *mash* would regularly represent an OE. **mæsc*, but the OE. word occurs only once in the metathetic form *max*, and in that instance means 'a net'. The 16th c. forms *meishe*, *meash*, indicate a pronunciation with long vowel, (mɛːʃ); for the shortening to *mesh* cf. *flesh*. On the whole, on account of the absence of the word in ME., its form-history in the 16th c., and the frequency with which fishing terms were adopted from Du., it seems not improbable that *meash* (shortened to *mesh*) and *mash* represent adoptions respectively of the MDu. forms *maesche* and *masche*. The resemblance between the Eng. form *marsh* (18th c.) and the Flemish *maersche* (Stallaert) is prob. accidental.

The Teut. **mǣsk-* (: **mask-*) is cognate with the Lithuanian *mezgù* I knit, *mazga-s* knot.]

1. a. One of the open spaces or interstices of a net, the size of which is determined by the distance of adjacent knots from one another. Also, the similar space in any network, as a sieve.

1558–9 *Act 1 Eliz.* c. 17 §3 Onely withe Nett or Tramell, wherof every Meshe or Maske shalbee twoo ynches and a half broade. **1586** FERNE *Blaz. Gentrie* II. 33 A Mascle in Armory, is a representation of the mash of a net. **1615** E. S. *Britain's Buss* in Arb. *Garner* III. 629 Netting (of sixty masks or mashes or holes deep). **1727** DE FOE *Hist. Appar.* iv. (1840) 44 They are like those foolish fish that are caught in large nets, that might get out at every square of the mesh. **1747** *Gentl. Mag.* 311 The mashes of the iron wire sieve were ..small. **1749** *Wealth Gt. Brit.* 49 The marshes of the nets ..are to be one inch square. **1839** URE *Dict. Arts* 577 The masses are..sifted through sieves having 20 meshes in the square inch. **1873** *Act 36 & 37 Vict.* c. 71 §39 (4), Such mesh shall not be less than one and a half inch from knot to knot. **1879** *Plain Knitting*, etc. 46 Pass the twine round the mesh-stick from above to form the mesh.

b. *pl.* The threads or cords which bound the interstices of a net; hence (also *collect. sing.*) network, netting.

1602 CAREW *Cornwall* 32 Square nets..thorow which the schoell of Pilchard passing, leaue many behind intangled in the meashes. **1685** DRYDEN *Horace* Epode ii. 52 To betray The Larkes that in the Meshes light. **1734** *Phil. Trans.* XXXVIII. 235 The Mashes, or Filaments of the Net are not very perceptible. **1860** PUSEY *Min. Proph.* 47 The net, with its thin light meshes. **1879** HARLAN *Eyesight* iii. 41 If we hold a veil between our eyes and a book, we can either read through it, or see its meshes distinctly, but we cannot do both at the same time.

c. *Electr.* A closed loop of windings or other impedances connected in series.

1881 J. C. MAXWELL *Treat. Electr. & Magnetism* (ed. 2) I. II. vi. 374 If the conducting wires form a simple network and if we suppose that a current circulates round each mesh, then the actual current in the wire which forms a thread of each of two neighbouring meshes will be the difference between the two currents circulating in the two meshes. **1892** S. P. THOMPSON *Dynamo-Electr. Machinery* (ed. 4) xxiv. 709 The three coils may be joined..in a closed mesh joined with the three lines at its corners. **1970** J. SHEPHERD et al. *Higher Electr. Engin.* (ed. 2) ii. 47 Circuits involving multiple meshes may be solved by considering either the meshes (mesh analysis) or the junctions (node analysis).

d. With prefixed numeral, e.g. *50 mesh*, designating a screen with that number of square openings per unit length (e.g. per inch), and applied to materials which will pass through such a screen (but, usually, not through the next finest screen).

1930 *Engineering* 22 Aug. 223/2 The dust cloud which it would encounter would consist..of particles ranging from 60 mesh to beyond 200 mesh. **1932** RILEY & JOHANNSEN *Med. Entomol.* xvii. 264 A 16-mesh screen is ordinarily employed. **1933** W. T. READ *Industr. Chem.* vii. 65 This relationship has been established by the United States Bureau of Standards for 200-mesh screens so that the wire has a diameter of $2{\cdot}1 \times 10^{-3}$ in. and each opening a width of $2{\cdot}9 \times 10^{-3}$ in., thus giving 200 openings per linear inch. **1948** PIERCE & HAENISCH *Quantitative Analysis* (ed. 3) v. 63 The usual sample for analysis should pass a screen of 80–100 mesh or smaller. **1971** *Nature* 25 June 524/2 Samples of powder were first ground to 400 mesh and then briquetted.

2. *fig.* chiefly with reference to entanglement in a snare.

1540–1 ELYOT *Image Gov.* 20 It shall be almost impossible for hym to escape, but that in one meishe or other he shall be tangled. **1596** SHAKS. *Merch. V.* III. ii. 122 Here in her haires The Painter plaies the Spider, and hath wouen A golden mesh t'intrap the hearts of men. **1613** FLETCHER, etc. *Captain* III. iv, I doubt mainly, I shall be i' the mash too. **1648** HERRICK *Hesper.*, *On Julia's Haire*, 'Tis I am wild, and more then haires Deserves these mashes and these snares. **1754** FIELDING *Jrnl. Voy. Lisbon* (1755) 204 While a fisherman can break through the strongest meshes of an act of parliament, we [etc.]. **1823** SCOTT *Peveril* xlvii, The strongest meshes that the laws of civil society ever wove to limit the natural dignity of man. **1897** GLADSTONE *E. Crisis* 15 Greece has extricated it from the meshes of diplomacy.

3. *transf.* Network, interlaced structure: **a.** in animal and vegetable bodies.

1712 BLACKMORE *Creation* VI. 380 The greatest Portion of th' Arterial Blood, By the close Structure of the Parts withstood, Whose narrow Meshes stop the grosser Flood By apt Canals [etc.]. **1834** MCMURTRIE *Cuvier's Anim. Kingd.* 259 The branchiæ usually consist of large lamellæ covered with vascular meshes. **1884** BOWER & SCOTT *De Bary's Phaner.* 285 Very elongated meshes are found in the runner-like branches of the rhizome of Struthiopteris.

b. in other things.

1818 KEATS *Endymion* II. 312 The ivy mesh, Shading its Ethiop berries. **1858** CARLYLE *Fredk. Gt.* x. i. (1872) III. 198 The loitering waters straggle, all over that region, into meshes of lakes. **1860** TYNDALL *Glac.* II. v. 250 Air which was originally entangled in the meshes of the fallen snow.

c. *Building.* A steel network used as reinforcement in concrete.

1904 C. F. MARSH *Reinforced Concrete* ii. 44 The ribs on the Cottançin system are considered as N-girders, of which the joints are absolutely fixed, the mesh forming the tension bracing and the concrete the compression bars. **1936** E. PROBST *Princ. Plain & Reinforced Concrete Construction* ii. 97 Ready-made reinforcements are often used for slabs and also for beams and columns. An example of this is the triangular mesh, made from interwoven round steel bars. **1948** L. J. MURDOCK *Concrete Materials & Pract.* xvii. 251 Expanded-metal (steel) reinforcement..is made by cutting slits in blank steel plate and sheets and then expanding them into diamond-shaped meshes. **1971** B. P. HUGHES *Limit State Theory for Reinforced Concrete* 397 The fabric in sections is indicated by heavy dashed lines—for oblong mesh, long or short dashes according to whether the section is parallel or at right angles to the main wires.

4. *Machinery.* [f. MESH *v.*] **a.** See quot.

1875 KNIGHT *Dict. Mech.*, *Mesh.* 1. (*Gearing.*) Or *mash.* The engagement of the teeth of wheels with each other or with an adjacent object, as the rack, in a rack and pinion movement.

b. *in*, or *out of*, *mesh.* Of gearwheels or their teeth: engaged, or not engaged, with each other. So *into mesh.*

1904 A. B. F. YOUNG *Compl. Motorist* 78 When the top gear is engaged, none of the other gears are in mesh, although they rotate. **1905** R. T. SLOSS *Bk. Automobile* 207 The gears must be thrown into mesh sharply or not at all. **1921** [see COASTING *vbl. sb.* 4 c]. **1948** *Motor Manual* (ed. 33) vii. 126 If one wheel has 20 teeth and another has 40, the two being in mesh, then the larger one will turn exactly half as fast as the smaller one. *Ibid.* 129 At one time it was common to slide one gear along splines on its shaft..so that its teeth came into mesh with those of its mate. **1972** 'J. & E. BONETT'

No Time to Kill xi. 143 The gears of his brain, he reflected, were not in mesh. A walk before breakfast might re-engage them.

5. Short for *mesh-stick*.

1882 CAULFEILD & SAWARD *Dict. Needlework*, s.v., Implements made of ivory, bone, or boxwood, and employed in Embroidery and Netting, are known as Meshes.

6. *attrib.* and *Comb.*, as **mesh-bag**, **-like** adj., **net**, **-pin**, **screen**; (sense 1 c) **mesh-connected** adj., **-connection**; **mesh-stick**, 'a flat slat with rounded ends, used to form the mesh of nets, the loops being made over it and knotted on its edge' (Knight *Dict. Mech.* 1875).

1911 *Daily Colonist* (Victoria, B.C.) 25 Apr. 6/4 (Advt.), Solid Gold *Mesh Bags, nothing more intrinsically beautiful in the category of Hand Bags. **1920** *Edin. Rev.* Oct. 349 The mesh-bag in which the Mexican hunters carried their arrow heads. **1960** L. HELLMAN *Toys in Attic* I. 27 Gives Anna a large gold mesh bag. **1896** D. C. & J. P. JACKSON *Alternating Currents* viii. 395 In a three-phase machine, if the armature is *mesh-connected, the pressure between any two collector rings is equal to the pressure developed in one coil. **1954** E. HUGHES *Fund. Electr. Engin.* vi. 221 (*caption*) Conventional representation of a mesh-connected winding. **1896** D. C. & J. P. JACKSON *Alternating Currents* xiii. 552 The arrangements are either of the star or *mesh connection. **1971** *Gloss. Electrotechnical, Power Terms (B.S.I.)* II. i. 7 *Mesh connection*, in a polyphase device or system of devices. The arrangement in which the end of each phase is connected to the beginning of the next in sequence so as to form a ring, each point of connection being connected to a terminal. **1845** J. F. SOUTH *Zool.* in *Encycl. Metrop.* VII. 262/2 The *mesh-like spaces of the cavernous bodies. **1883** SIR A. SHEA *Newfoundland Fisheries* 12 (Fish. Exhib. Publ.), Herrings are taken in *mesh nets and in seines. **1795** in *Abridgm. Specif. Patents, Needles*, etc. (1871) 2 [Bell, William.—Manufacturing] all sorts of needles, .. netting needles, *mesh pins, and sail needles. **1877** RAYMOND *Statist. Mines & Mining* 426 Dry ore, sized between 10 and 20 *mesh screens (to the linear inch). **1879** *Mesh-stick [see sense 1].

mesh (mɛʃ), *v.* Also 6 **meash, masshe**, 7 **meishe**, 6–9 **mash**. [f. MESH *sb.*, but found somewhat earlier in our quots.]

1. *trans.* To catch in the meshes of a net.

a **1547** SURREY in *Tottel's Misc.* (Arb.) 7, I know.. How smal a net may take and meash a hart of gentle kinde. **1843** LYTTON *Last Bar.* III. iii, And shew him how even the lion may be meshed. **1888** *Whitby Gaz.* 23 Nov. 3/1 The large ones cannot get meshed in the small meshes.

2. *transf.* and *fig.* or in figurative context: To entangle, involve inextricably.

1532 MORE *Confut. Tindale* Wks. 491/1 Luther was hymselfe also so meshed in thys matter, .. that [etc.]. **1583** STOCKER *Civ. Warres Lowe C.* II. 67 And so bee masht in the net, by fayre speeches. **1627** DRAYTON *Quest Cinthia* 121 The Flyes by chance mesht in her hayre. **1789** E. DARWIN *Bot. Gard.* II. (1791) 111 Fine hapless swains.. The harlot meshes in her deathful toils. **1836** LYTTON *Athens* (1837) II. 562 Headlong from the car Caught and all meshed within the reins he fell. **1848** KINGSLEY *Saint's Trag.* IV. iii. 141 Poor soul whose lot is fixed here Meshed down by custom.

3. a. *refl.* and *intr.* (for *refl.* or *pass.*). To become enmeshed or entangled.

1589 WARNER *Alb. Eng.* VI. xxix. (1602) 144 She pitched Tewe, he masshed. **1594** PLAT *Jewell-ho.* III. 54 [The fish] will run forwarde and mash themselues in the tramell. **1604** PARSONS *3rd Pt. Three Convers. Eng., Relation of Trial* 215 As a hare in the nett [he] mesheth himselfe more and more by struglinge. **1801** PENNANT *Journ. Lond. to Isle of Wight* 72 After which they [mackarel] will not mesh, but are caught with hooks. **1827** in J. G. Cumming *I. of Man* (1848) 312 In the summer fishery the herrings always mesh with their heads to the north. **1864** J. BRUCE in *Glasgow Daily Herald* 24 Sept., When the herring are very large they swim lazily, and do not mesh well.

b. *intr.* (*machinery.*) Of the teeth of a wheel, etc.: To be engaged *with* another piece of machinery. Also *trans.*, to cause (gears, esp. those of a motor vehicle) to become engaged; to put into mesh.

1850 *Rep. Comm. Patents 1849* (U.S.) 155 What I claim as new.. is.. the shaft H, with the pinions *i*, mashing into racks II. **1860** BARTLETT *Dict. Amer.* (ed. 3) 265 In machinery, one wheel is said to *mash* into or with another, i.e. to 'engage' with it. **1875** KNIGHT *Dict. Mech.* 1383/2 *Mangle-rack*, a rack having teeth on opposite sides, engaged by a pinion which meshes with the opposite sides alternately. **1890** *Cent. Dict.*, *Mesh*, to engage (the teeth of wheels or the teeth of a rack and pinion) with each other. **1895** *Outing* (U.S.) XXVII. 55/1 Wooden cogs, which meshed into a horizontal wheel. **1907** C. WHEELER *Bicycles in Making* 78 Small pinion wheels.. also mesh with what is called a fulcrum pinion. **1913** R. KENNEDY *Bk. Motor Car* II. 194 Then.. gear wheels which are revolving have to mesh with gear wheels which are stationary. **1926** J. A. MOYER *Gasoline Automobiles* (ed. 2) vii. 237 The rod *A*.. meshes the gear wheel *B* with the flywheel *C*. **1935** M. M. ATWATER *Murder in Midsummer* xx. 192 He meshed the gears and the old car moved slowly away. **1957** *Laboratory Investigations* VI. 562 Racks are mounted on the sides of the blades to mesh with the idling gear in each plate. **1961** L. GRIBBLE *Wantons die Hard* i. 15 He meshed the gears and the car headed out of.. Tyler Place. **1972** H. BUCKMASTER *Walking Trip* 58 Norman .. meshed the gears noisily as he watched for an entrance into the traffic.

†**c.** *intr.* To thread one's way *through*. *Obs.*

1665 HOOKE *Microgr.* 214, I.. have seen it [a Mite] very nimbly meshing through the thickets of mould.

d. *intr.* (occas. *trans.*). To fit in; combine. Also const. *with*. (Cf. sense 3 b.)

1944 H. G. WELLS *'42 to '44* 65 Such perplexities and failures to mesh are by no means confined to Anglo-Russian relationships. **1951** *Good Housek. Home Encycl.* 291/2 The units are generally designed to 'mesh' together. **1963** *New Society* 7 Nov. 19/1 Many young people are bewildered by school and unable to mesh with it. **1964** I. L. HOROWITZ *New Sociol.* 15 The general theory of action is really a general theory of how the parts mesh to form a whole. **1967** *Listener* 9 Nov. 609/3 What has always meshed best in his verse is precisely the neat machinery of ideas which he shared with half a dozen contemporaries, such as Mr Alvarez and Miss Jennings. **1968** *Economist* 17 Feb. 54/4 The difficulties of meshing management and staff at Holland's Amro bank, four years after that merger. **1971** *Nature* 12 Nov. 61/1 The TXE-4.. cannot mesh with the pulse code modulation digital transmission systems which the Post Office is installing.

4. *trans.* †**a.** To make meshes in. *Obs.*

1666 *Third Adv. Painter* 20 Our stiffe Sayls, Masht and Netted into Lace.

b. To construct the meshes of (a net). *rare*$^{-1}$.

[**1615**: see MESHING *vbl. sb.*] **1882** *Harper's Mag.* LXV. 5 Mending old nets and meshing new ones.

mesh: see MASH, MEASE, MEUSE.

meshed (mɛʃt), *a.* [f. MESH *sb.* + -ED^{2}.] Having the form or appearance of mesh-work; tangled, intricate. Also, intricately marked *with*.

1664 POWER *Exp. Philos.* I. 11 Her eyes are most neatly latticed or mashed like a net. **1776–96** WITHERING *Brit. Plants* (ed. 3) IV. 57 Wrinkled or meshed, with hollows on each side. **1878** H. M. STANLEY *Dark Cont.* I. x. 221 The tangle of meshed undergrowth. **1899** *Allbutt's Syst. Med.* IV. 119 It commonly shows several little pits on its surface, which give it a meshed appearance.

meshese, obs. form of MISEASE.

meshing ('mɛʃɪŋ), *vbl. sb.* [f. MESH *v.* + -ING^{1}.]

a. The making of meshes in a net; a meshed structure; mesh-work.

1615 CROOKE *Body of Man* 904 Their coniunction is like the Meishing of a net or Plashing of a hedge. **1884** PATON in *Encycl. Brit.* XVII. 359/1 A little practice in meshing is sufficient to develop wonderful dexterity of movement. **1907** *Daily Chron.* 25 Sept. 8/4 Splash! go the dredges, small scoops of steel meshing. **1926** *Brit. Weekly* 26 Aug. 430/2, I had a copper frame constructed with a panel of copper meshing to which the letters were fixed. **1968** J. ARNOLD *Shell Bk. Country Crafts* 300 While the Honiton makers worked the pattern first and then 'grounded' it with meshing, .. in the East Midlands pattern and ground were made in a single process.

b. *attrib.*: **meshing-knot**, a knot used in making meshes; **meshing-net** (also *mashing-*), a net in which fish are caught in the meshes by their gills.

1795 HUTTON *Math. Dict.* s.v. *Knot*, Fig. 10, a Meshing knot, for nets; and is to be drawn close. **1883** E. P. RAMSAY *Food-Fishes N.S. Wales* 5 (Fish. Exhib. Publ.), The ordinary drawing-seines and mashing-nets.

'meshing, *ppl. a.* [-ING^{2}.] Entangling.

1586 WARNER *Alb. Eng.* II. xi. 47 By any pleasant tale, Or dazeling toys of meshing loue.

meshuga, meshugga (mɪ'ʃʊgə), *a. slang.* Also **mash-, meshuggah, meshuger, mishugge**, etc. [ad. Yiddish *meshuge*, f. Heb. *mĕshuggā'* part. of *shāgag*, to go astray, wander; cf. G. *meschugge* crazy.] Mad, crazy; stupid. The adj. has the form **meshugener, meshugenah**, etc., when it precedes its noun. This form is also used as *sb.*

1892 I. ZANGWILL *Childr. Ghetto* I. 156 She's meshuggah —quite mad! **1900** *Atlantic Monthly* LXXXVI. 108/2 'Meschugener,' leered the banker. **1922** JOYCE *Ulysses* 157 Meshuggah. Off his chump. **1930** *Amer. Mercury* Dec. 455/1 Me broad gets caught in a snow-storm [= becomes drugged with cocaine] an' goes meshuga. **1952** V. GOLLANCZ *My Dear Timothy* xii. 110 My father probably murmured to my mother.., 'The boy's *meshuggah* (which means cracked).' **1959** B. KOPS *Hamlet of Stepney Green* II. ii. 44, I don't like saying this, Bessie, but your boy is meshuger. **1961** B. VAWTER *Conscience of Israel* i. 22 The 'son of *nabi*' sent by Elisha to anoint Jehu is called by Jehu's companions 'this madman'—*meshugga*. **1962** J. BALDWIN *Another Country* (1963) III. i. 377 We finally got that *meshugena* of a broken-down movie star in town. **1968** L. ROSTEN *Joys of Yiddish* 237 A crazy man is a *meshuggener*. A crazy woman is a *meshuggeneh*. That *meshuggener*! Has he gone yet? **1971** *Sunday Times* (Johannesburg) 28 Mar. 4/3 Going steady!.. What kind of a meshugenah idea is this? **1972** *Listener* 24 Aug. 243/3 My favourite speaker was known to us all as Meshuggener Moishe. *Ibid.* 244/1 That Moishe, bless him, is he a meshuggener! **1973** *Jewish Chron.* 19 Jan. 24/1 The kids at school call me meshugga. That means crazy.

meshugaas (mɪ'ʃʊgɑːs). *slang.* Also **mishugas**. [ad. Yiddish *meshugaas* f. Heb. *mĕshuggā'* (see prec.).] Madness, craziness; nonsense, foolishness.

1907 I. ZANGWILL *Ghetto Comedies* 59 'Hannah, will you explain to me what this *meshugaas* (madness) is?' cried S. Cohn, lapsing into a non-Anglicism. **1970** L. M. FEINSILVER *Taste of Yiddish* i. 59 Everyone has his own wackiness—often heard as 'We all have our own mishugas'. **1971** *Sunday Times* (Johannesburg) 28 Mar. 4/2 He is so well-acquainted and up-to-date with genes and other anthropological meshugaas.

meshumad, meshummad (mɪ'ʃʊmɑːd). Pl. **-im**. [Yiddish, f. Heb. *mĕshummādh*, lit. one who is destroyed.] An apostate from Judaism.

1892 I. ZANGWILL *Childr. Ghetto* I. 14 The new-fangled Jewish minister.. rigged out like the Christian clergyman, has been mistaken for.. a *Meshumad*, and pelted with gratuitous vegetables. **1903** R. T. HERFORD *Christianity in Talmud & Midrash* II. ii. 336 'Meshummadim' are those who wilfully transgress some part of the ceremonial law, and thereby proclaim their apostasy. **1938** *Vallentine's Jewish Encycl.* 45 The Heb. words for apostate are *min*, .. *mumar*, .. *meshumad* (one who has renounced his religion or, perhaps, one who has been baptized), and *apikoros*.. The terms *mumar* and *meshumad* are often used indiscriminately.. The *Meshumadim*, from early Middle Ages, developed a super-zeal for their new religion. **1962** *Stand. Jewish Encycl.* 1308 *Meshummad* (Heb.): a convert to Christianity; an apostate (used opprobriously). **1968** L. ROSTEN *Joys of Yiddish* 238 Jews distinguish forced converts, or *anusim*, from those who joined another faith of their own volition, *meshumadim*.

'mesh-work. Meshes collectively; structure consisting of meshes; network. *lit.* and *fig.*

1830 LINDLEY *Nat. Syst. Bot.* 263 A meshwork of cellular tissue. **1844** STEPHENS *Bk. Farm* II. 280 A riddle consists of open mesh-work forming its bottom.

attrib. **1854** J. SCOFFERN in *Orr's Circ. Sci., Chem.* 222 A mesh-work cage of wire gauze. **1899** *Allbutt's Syst. Med.* VII. 171 A porous meshwork structure.

meshy ('mɛʃɪ), *a.* [f. MESH *sb.* + -Y.] Consisting of meshes.

1602 CAREW *Cornwall*, *'Lines on Sammon'* 29 b, Some build his house but his thence issue barre. Some make his meashie bed, but reaue his rest. **1726** POPE *Odyss.* XXII. 427 And scarce the meshy toils the copious draught contain. **1869** TOZER *Highl. Turkey* II. 156 The net's meshy folds.

mesiad ('miːzɪæd, 'mɛsɪæd), *adv.* [f. MESI-AL + -AD: see DEXTRAD *adv.* Cf. MESAD.] Towards the median line of a body.

1803 J. BARCLAY *New Anat. Nomencl.* 166 In the head and trunk, Mesiad will signify towards the mesial aspect. **1857** GOODSIR in *Edinb. New Philos. Jrnl.* V. 150 Situated mesiad of any part of this bone.

mesial ('miːzɪəl, 'mɛsɪəl), *a.* [irreg. f. Gr. μέσ-ος middle + -IAL.] Pertaining to, situated in, or directed towards the middle line of a body; = MEDIAN *a.*^{1} 2. Also, situated mesially with respect *to*.

1803 J. BARCLAY *New Anat. Nomencl.* 144 Supposing the falx a mesial plane. **1808** —— *Muscular Motions* 374 Where clavicles are present, the heads of the scapulæ are removed farther from the mesial line. **1880** GÜNTHER *Fishes* 69 The hyoid consists generally of a pair of long and strong lateral pieces, and a single mesial piece. **1899** *Allbutt's Syst. Med.* VI. 786 Bechterew places the sensory fibres of the cranial nerves mesial to the fillet in the pons Varolii.

mesially ('miːzɪəlɪ, 'mɛsɪəlɪ), *adv.* [f. prec. + -LY^{2}.] In a mesial position or direction.

1849–52 *Todd's Cycl. Anat.* IV. 939/2 The chin is thrust forward mesially when both joints are affected. **1899** *Allbutt's Syst. Med.* VII. 274 The most mesially situated fibres of the crus.

mesian ('miːzɪən, 'mɛsɪən), *a.* [irreg. f. Gr. μέσ-ος middle + -IAN.] = MESIAL.

1837 W. STOKES *Diagn. & Treatm. Dis. Chest* I. ii. (N. Syd. Soc.) 164 The morbid signs extend across the mesian line. **1862** H. W. FULLER *Dis. Lungs* 7.

mesic ('mɛsɪk, 'miːsɪk), *a.*^{1} *Ecology.* [f. Gr. μέσ-ος middle + -IC.] Having, or characterized by, a moderate amount of moisture.

1926 [see HYDRIC *a.*^{2}]. **1967** M. E. HALE *Biol. Lichens* vii. 91 The curves of frequency show the relative abundance of lichens in oak-dominated woods and their rarity.. in mesic climax forests. **1974** *Environmental Conservation* I. 60/1 A small tracked vehicle.. was employed to establish a series of repetitive passes in a level mesic 'meadow'.

mesic ('miːzɪk, 'mɛzɪk), *a.*^{2} *Nuclear Physics.* [f. MES(ON^{3} + -IC.] Of, pertaining to, or being a meson; applied *spec.* to a system analogous to an atom in which a meson takes the place of either an orbital electron or the nucleus.

1939 *Physica* VI. 877 'Mesic' charges. **1952** R. E. MARSHAK *Meson Physics* iv. 153 There are also selection rules for radiative and mesic absorption. **1956** S. TOLANSKY *Introd. Atomic Physics* (ed. 4) xix. 328 Since mesons only exist virtually within unexcited nuclei and are only made free to exist alone by collision processes, there are no mesic atoms in normal unexcited materials. **1969** *Sci. Jrnl.* July 44/1 The pion can be used to prepare mesic atoms in which a π^- replaces an electron in the atom. **1972** *Physics Bull.* Mar. 148/2 The meson then cascades down first by Auger transitions and, as it reaches lower orbits, increasingly by radiative transitions, emitting mesic x rays.

mesidine ('mɛsɪdɪn). *Chem.* [f. MESI(TYL) + *-idine* as in *cumidine* (G. Maule 1849: see NITRO-MESIDINE).] An oily liquid obtained by boiling nitro-mesitylene with tin and hydrochloric acid.

1866 ODLING *Anim. Chem.* 60 Certain highly complex bodies procurable from vinegar, such as mesidine $C_9H_{13}N$, and nitro-mesidine $C_9H_{12}N_2O_2$.

'mesio-, used as combining form of MESIAL.

1803 J. BARCLAY *New Anat. Nomencl.* 174 The position of the heart in the thorax will be expressed by the two compounds *mesio-sinistral* and *atlanto-sacral*. **1872** HUMPHRY *Observ. Myology* 107 Especially is this the case.. in the 'mesio-dorsal' part of the lateral muscle.

mesion ('miːzɪən, 'mɛsɪən). *Anat.* [irreg. f. Gr. μέσ-ος middle.] = MESON^{1}.

1803 J. BARCLAY *Anat. Nomencl.* 121 Suppose a plane, to pass along the middle of the neck, the mediastinum, and linea alba, and to dividing [*sic*] the neck and the trunk into similar halves.. and let this plane be denominated Mesion.

mesistem (ˈmɛsɪstɛm). *Bot.* Shortened form of MESOMERISTEM.
1884 [see PERIMERISTEM].

mesite (ˈmiːsaɪt). *Chem.* Also **mesit**. [ad. mod.L. *mesita*, *mesitēs*, a. Gr. μεσίτης go-between, f. μέσ-ος middle. Cf. F. *mésite*.]
†**1.** A name given to acetic ether, 'because it holds a middle place between alcohol and ether' (*Syd. Soc. Lex.*). *Obs.*
1838 T. THOMSON *Chem. Org. Bodies* 366 Reichenbach considers mesite as identical with acetone.
2. (See quot. 1865.)
1842 T. GRAHAM *Elem. Chem.* 836 Mesite. **1849** KANE *Elem. Chem.* (ed. 2) 826 Mesit. **1865** WATTS *Dict. Chem.*, *Mesite*, an oxygenated oil..said to be obtained by distilling lignone with sulphuric acid. (Wiedemann and Schweizer.)

mesitene (ˈmɛsɪtiːn). *Chem.* [f. MESITE + -ENE. Cf. F. *mésitène*.] A volatile oil resembling mesite (sense 2).
1842 T. GRAHAM *Elem. Chem.* 836 Mesiten. **1855** WATTS tr. *Gmelin's Handbk. Chem.* IX. 52 Mesitene. Produced by distilling lignone, mesite, or xylitic naphtha with oil of vitriol. *a* **1864** GESNER *Coal, Petrol.*, etc. (1865) 89 Mesetine. **1865** WATTS *Dict. Chem.*

mesitic (mɪˈsɪtɪk), *a. Chem.* [f. MESITYL + -IC. Cf. F. *mésitique*.] Derived from mesityl: see quots.
1838 R. D. THOMSON *New Chem. Subst.* in *Brit. Ann.* 344 Mesitic ether. **1855** WATTS tr. *Gmelin's Handbk. Chem.* IX. 6, 27, etc. **1865** —— *Dict. Chem.*, *Mesitic Alcohol.* A name given to acetone, on the supposition that it is an alcohol containing the radicle mesityl, C^3H^5, isomeric with allyl... *Mesitic Ether.* Syn. with Oxide of Mesityl.

mesitine (ˈmɛsɪtɪn). *Min.* [ad. G. *mesitin* (*mesitinspath*, A. Breithaupt 1827), f. Gr. μεσίτης go-between, 'because its rhombohedron is intermediate in angle between magnesite and siderite' (A. H. Chester).] Carbonate of magnesium and iron, called also *mesitine-spar*. Also ˈ**mesitite**.
1828 *Edinb. Jrnl. Sci.* VIII. 181 Mesitine-spar. **1865** WATTS *Dict. Chem.*, *Mesitin-Spar*... Breunnerite, Pistomesite. This mineral occurs in rhombohedral crystals isomorphous with spathic iron ore and magnesite. **1868** DANA *Syst. Min.* (ed. 5) II. 687 Mesitite.

mesityl (ˈmɛsɪtɪl). *Chem.* Also **mesitule**. [Formed as MESITE + -YL.] The hypothetical radical of acetone. Hence **mesitylene** (mɪˈsɪtɪliːn), 'a hydrocarbon, isomeric with cumene, produced by the action of sulphuric acid upon acetone' (Watts); **mesityˈlenic** *a.*, derived from mesitylene; **mesiˈtylic** *a.*, derived from or containing mesityl; **mesitylol** (mɛˈsɪtɪlɒl) = MESITYLENE.
1838 R. D. THOMSON *New Chem. Subst.* in *Brit. Ann.* 332 Mesitylene. **1855** WATTS tr. *Gmelin's Handbk. Chem.* IX. 17 *Mesitylene* or *Mesitylol* C^6H^4. *Ibid.* 27 Chloride of Mesityl. **1859** *Fownes' Chem.* 397 It has received the name *mesitilole*. *Ibid.*, An organic salt-basyle, containing C_6H_5, to which the name of *mesityl* has been given. **1873** WILLIAMSON *Chem.* §289 The so-called mesitylic oxide ($C^6H_{10}O$), which has been considered as the ether of acetone. **1885** REMSEN *Org. Chem.* (1888) 246 Mesitylene..when boiled with dilute nitric acid,..yields mesitylenic acid, $C_9H_{10}O_2$.

meskal, variant of MISKAL.

mesked, -keeto, -kite, etc., var. ff. MESQUITA.

meskin(s, meslade: see MASKINS, MALASADE.

†**mesle.** *Her. Obs.* [Subst. use of OF. *meslé* pa. pple., see next.] A partition by an indented or irregular line.
1562 LEIGH *Armorie* 134 b, Nowe I will shewe you of nyne sondry mesles whiche are so called, because they enter meddell the one within the other, contrary to plaine particion. **1586** FERNE *Blaz. Gentrie* 204.

‖**meslé(e**, *a. Her. Obs.* [OF. *meslé* pa. pple. of *mesler* (mod.F. *mêler*) to mix.] (See quots.)
1632 GUILLIM *Heraldry* VI. vi. (ed. 2) betw. 420–1 The Marquesse his Coronet is Meslée, that is, part flowred and part pyramidall pearled. **1894** *Parker's Gloss. Her.*, *Meslé*: mingled. Used by a few old writers in describing a field of metal and colour in equal proportions, as gyronny, paly.

mesledine, meslen, etc.: see MASLIN[2].

mesmeˈree, 'the person on whom a mesmerist operates' (Ogilvie 1882).

mesmerian (mɛzˈmɪərɪən), *a.* and *sb. rare.* [f. *Mesmer* (see MESMERISM) + -IAN. Cf. F. *mesmérien*.] **a.** *adj.* Mesmeric. **b.** *sb.* A follower of Mesmer, a believer in mesmerism.
1802 ACERBI *Trav.* I. 271 The mesmerians..have their minds so heated by the extraordinary..aspect of those phenomena [etc.]. **1840** *Fraser's Mag.* XXI. 533 The knight did not try the Mesmerian process on himself.

mesmeric (mɛzˈmɛrɪk), *a.* [f. *Mesmer* (see MESMERISM) + -IC.] Pertaining to, characteristic of, producing, or produced by mesmerism. ***mesmeric passes***: see PASS *sb.*[2] 11.
1829 R. CHENEVIX in *Lond. Med. & Phys. Jrnl.* VI. 222 This day, after mesmerising her for nine minutes, she fell into mesmeric sleep. *Ibid.* VII. 117 Ireland having been thus put to sleep by my mesmeric action. **1847** DICKENS *Haunted M.* (C. D. ed.) 219 This example had a powerful, and apparently, mesmeric influence on him of the boots. **1876** C. M. DAVIES *Unorth. Lond.* (ed. 2) 55 She was making mesmeric passes.
So **mesˈmerical** *a.* (*rare*) in the same sense; **mesˈmerically** *adv.*, by means of mesmerism.
1840 C. H. TOWNSHEND *Facts in Mesmerism* II. ii. 115 A cousin of mine could not be influenced by me mesmerically. *Ibid.* iii. 204 While he was sleeping mesmerically. **1852** HAWTHORNE *Blithedale Rom.* I. vi. 102 Zenobia's sphere.. transformed me, during this period of my weakness, into something like a mesmerical clairvoyant. **1862** LYTTON *Str. Story* I. 90 Armed with a lock of Lilian's hair and a glove she had worn, as the media of mesmerical rapport.

mesmerism (ˈmɛzmərɪz(ə)m). [f. name of F.A. *Mesmer*, an Austrian physician (1734–1815) + -ISM. Cf. F. *mesmérisme*.] The doctrine or system, popularized by Mesmer, according to which a hypnotic state, usually accompanied by insensibility to pain and muscular rigidity, can be induced by an influence (at first known as 'animal magnetism') exercised by an operator over the will and nervous system of the patient. **b.** The process or practice of inducing such hypnotic state; the state so induced. **c.** The influence supposed to operate. Cf. *animal magnetism* (ANIMAL C. 1), MAGNETISM 3.
1802 ACERBI *Trav.* I. 89 One subject on which the Duke ..has been charged with weakness, namely, mesmerism, or animal magnetism. **1829** R. CHENEVIX in *Lond. Med. & Phys. Jrnl.* VI. 223 The touch of my finger..roused her from her state of mesmerism. **1844** E. FITZGERALD *Lett.* (1889) I. 142 And Miss Martineau has been cured of an illness of five years by Mesmerism! **1883** 'OUIDA' *Wanda* I. 300 You believe in mesmerism and disbelieve in God.

mesmerist (ˈmɛzmərɪst). [f. *Mesmer* (see prec.) + IST.] One who practises mesmerism. Also *occas.* a believer in mesmerism.
1840 C. H. TOWNSHEND *Facts in Mesmerism* I. 16 Perhaps the error has originated with the Mesmerists themselves. **1852** SMEDLEY *L. Arundel* i. 16, 'I made use of one of the secrets of the mesmerist', replied Lewis; 'I managed her by the power of a strong will over a weak one'. **1899** *Allbutt's Syst. Med.* VIII. 427 According to the mesmerists, offences against the person might be committed in hypnosis.

mesmerite (ˈmɛzməraɪt). *rare*[−1]. [f. *Mesmer* (see MESMERISM) + -ITE.] A believer in mesmerism.
1842 MISS MITFORD in L'Estrange *Life* (1870) III. ix. 156 He told me..that Mrs. Trollope is a thorough-going mesmerite, constantly at Dr. Elliotson's.

mesmerizable (ˈmɛzməˌraɪzəb(ə)l), *a.* Also **-ible**. [f. MESMERIZE *v.* + -ABLE.] Capable of being mesmerized. Hence ˌ**mesmerizaˈbility**.
1840 J. ELLIOTSON *Hum. Physiol.* 1180 A thing not directly mesmerisable, but mesmerisable by contact with a directly mesmerisable metal. **1840** C. H. TOWNSHEND *Facts in Mesmerism* II. iii. 134 An experiment..as to the mesmerisibility [*sic*] of mankind in general.

mesmerization (ˌmɛzməraɪˈzeɪʃən). [f. MESMERIZE *v.* + -ATION.] The action of mesmerizing.
1829 R. CHENEVIX in *Lond. Med. & Phys. Jrnl.* VII. 117 In two minutes' mesmerization, Ireland's eyes began to water. **1845** *Blackw. Mag.* LVII. 223 The mesmerisation of water.

mesmerize (ˈmɛzməraɪz), *v.* [f. *Mesmer* (see MESMERISM) + -IZE.] *trans.* **a.** To subject (a person) to the influence of mesmerism. Also *transf.* and *fig.*, to fascinate, spellbind.
1829 R. CHENEVIX in *Lond. Med. & Phys. Jrnl.* VI. 222, I mesmerised the patient through the door. **1863** MRS. A. E. CHALLICE *Heroes*, etc. *Time Louis XVI*, II. 77 Dr. Mesmer found it impossible to mesmerize Dr. Franklin.
transf. **1862** H. AÏDÉ *Carr of Carrl.* I. 137 Carr would almost have forgotten her existence, had it not been for those eyes which mesmerised him every now and then, in spite of himself. **1886–94** H. SPENCER *Autobiog.* II. xlvi. 188 The judicial faculty has been mesmerised by the confused halo of piety which surrounds them. **1936** G. B. SHAW *Simpleton* I. 50 *Vashti*... Would you not die for me? *Iddy*. (*mesmerized by her eyes*) Oh DEAR!!! Yes: your eyes make my heart melt. **1940** W. FAULKNER *Hamlet* II. i. 113 She seemed to be momentarily mesmerised by a complete inert soft surprise. **1955** *Economist* 26 Mar. 1068/1 Members seemed to be mesmerised by an uncouth demagogue sitting with his acolytes in the public gallery. **1975** *Times* 24 July 4/7 Sir G. Howe said..Labour ministers..had been mesmerized by their own verbal fantasies.
b. with inanimate object.
1840 C. H. TOWNSHEND *Facts in Mesmerism* II. iii. 224, I have..*mesmerised*, as it is called, a glass of water, half an hour before it was presented to the sleep-waker.
c. *absol.* or *intr.*
1829 R. CHENEVIX in *Lond. Med. & Phys. Jrnl.* VI. 227 Every one can mesmerise, though not all with equal effect. **1865** TENNYSON in Ld. Tennyson *Memoir* (1897) II. 21, I can't mesmerize, I never mesmerized anyone in my life.
Hence ˈ**mesmerized** *ppl. a.*, ˈ**mesmerizing** *vbl. sb.* and *ppl. a.*
1829 R. CHENEVIX in *Lond. Med. & Phys. Jrnl.* VI. 222 The use of mesmerised water..had entirely assuaged the thirst. *Ibid.* 223 The spasmodic contractions were entirely removed after the twelfth day of mesmerising. **1840** C. H. TOWNSHEND *Facts in Mesmerism* II. i. 80 Having heard it said that mesmerised persons could feel any injury that was inflicted on the mesmeriser. **1886** *Athenæum* 6 Mar. 323/3 Verena Tarrant, daughter of a vulgar mesmerizing quack.

mesmerizee (mɛzməraɪˈziː). [f. MESMERIZE *v.* + -EE.] One who is mesmerized.
1829 R. CHENEVIX in *Lond. Med. & Phys. Jrnl.* VI. 226 Here neither the mesmeriser nor the mesmerisee had the slightest conviction upon the subject.

mesmerizer (ˈmɛzməraɪzə(r)). [Formed as prec. + -ER[1].] One who mesmerizes.
1829 [See MESMERIZEE]. **1855** BROWNING *Lovers Quarrel* xi, When the mesmerizer Snow With his hand's first sweep Put the earth to sleep. **1859** DICKENS *Lett.* (1880) II. 100 The alleged mesmeriser.

mesmero- (ˈmɛzmərəʊ), taken as the combining form of MESMERISM, as in **mesmero-phrenology**, the application of mesmerism to the phrenological 'organs', in order to evoke or control their specific activities (cf. *phreno-mesmerism*); hence ***mesmero-phrenological*** adj. Also ˌ**mesmero-ˈmania**, a mania for mesmerism.
1842 *Medico-Chirurg. Rev.* XXXVII. 593 Mesmero-Phrenology. *Ibid.*, Various mesmero-phrenological experiments. **1843** *Ibid.* XXXVIII. 577 The Mesmero-mania has nearly dwindled, in the metropolis, into anile fatuity.

mesmoire, rare obs. variant of MEMOIR.

†**mesnage**, *sb. Obs.* [a. obs. F. *mesnage*, var. *ménage* (cf. MANAGE *sb.* and MÉNAGE).] Careful or economical management.
1664 JER. TAYLOR *Dissuas. Popery* II. Introd., Some [reasons] rely upon the state of exterior affairs, and introduced œconomics, or accidental mesnage of things.

†**mesnage**, *v. Obs.* [a. obs. F. *mesnager*, var. *ménager* (cf. MANAGE *v.*, etym. note).] *trans.*
a. To take advantage of, 'husband'. **b.** To control, manage.
1654 BRAMHALL *Just Vind.* iv. (1661) 56 With what a depth of prudence the Roman court hath mesnaged all occasions..to the advantage..of that See. **1695** LD. PRESTON *Boeth.* IV. 202 Whilst the World's Creator..ruling mesnageth the Reins of things.

†**mesnagery.** *Obs.* [a. obs. F. *mesnagerie*: cf. MENAGERIE.] Management; economy.
1652–3 BRAMHALL *Let.* 27 (17) Feb., Wks. 1842 I. p. xciii, The most ill mesnagery of those who were trusted by the other adventurers. *a* **1693** *Urquhart's Rabelais* III. ii, Many speak of..that Vertue of mesnagery that know not what belong to it.

†**mesnagier.** *Obs.* [a. obs. F. *mesnag(i)er*, f. *ménager* to control.] A manager.
a **1693** *Urquhart's Rabelais* III. ii, If he should..not become a better mesnagier it would prove..impossible for him..to make him rich.

mesnality (miːˈnælɪtɪ). *Law.* [Altered form of next: cf. COMMONALITY.] = next.
1643 PRYNNE *Sov. Power Parl.* I. (ed. 2) 100 As all Mesnalities..by the deaths of their Tenants without heire, returne..to those Lords..by whom they were originally created. **1848** in WHARTON *Law Lex.*

mesnalty (ˈmiːnəltɪ). *Law.* Also 6 **menalte, -tie**, 6–7 **-ty**, 7 **menealtie**. [a. Law F. *menalte*, *mesnalte*, f. OF. *mene*, *mesne* MESNE *a.*, after AF. *comunalte* COMMONALTY.] The estate of a mesne lord; the condition of being a mesne lord.
1542–3 *Act 34 & 35 Hen. VIII*, c. 5 §15 If any person.. shall..make by fraude..any estates, condicions, mesnalties, tenures, or coneuiaunces. **1577–87** HOLINSHED *Chron.* (1807–8) III. 27 A subsidie..of everie knights fee twentie shillings, whether the same were holden of him by menaltie, or otherwise. **1628** COKE *On Litt.* 152 b, If the lord confirm the tenant to hold of him..the mesnalty is extinct. **1642** tr. *Perkins' Prof. Bk.* v. §322. 142 If there be Lord, Mesne and Tenant..and the Mesne taketh a wife..and dyeth the wife shall be endowed of the menealtie. **1768** BLACKSTONE *Comm.* III. 234 If he [the mesne lord] makes default therein,..he shall be forejudged of his mesnalty, and the tenant shall hold immediately of the lord paramount himself.

mesne (miːn), *a.*, *sb.*, and *adv.* Also 5 **meosne**, 5–7 **measne**, 6 **mesn**, 7–8 **measn**. [a. Law F. *mesne*, altered spelling of AF. *meen* MEAN *a.*]
A. *adj.*
1. *Feudalism.* **a.** ***mesne lord***: a lord who holds an estate of a superior lord.
1614 SELDEN *Titles Hon.* II. v. §4 [The vavasour] either held of a mesne lord, and not immediately of the king, or at least of the king as of an honour or mannor, and not in chief. **1754** HUME *Hist. Eng.* I. App. ii. 251 Men..whose duty was immediately paid to the mesne lord that was interposed between them and the throne. **1869** W. S. ELLIS *Antiq. Her.* x. 236 The mesne lord did not, as a customary practice.., imitate the insignia of his feudal chief.
¶ **b.** ***mesne tenant***: inaccurately used to denote one who holds of a mesne lord.
1853 PARKER *Dom. Archit.* II. Introd. 24 The mesne tenants of the great barons. **1869** W. S. ELLIS *Antiq. Her.* x. 232 The theory of derivative coats having been adopted by mesne tenants from their feudal superiors.
†**c.** ***mesne land***: = MESNALTY. *Obs.*
a **1575** GASCOIGNE *Posies*, *Flowers* 41 He racketh vp our rentes and keepes the best in hand, He makes a wondrous deale of good out of his own measne land.

2. Occurring or performed at a time intermediate between two dates.

mesne encumbrance: an encumbrance the right of priority of which is intermediate between the dates of two other encumbrances. ***mesne profits***: the profits of an estate received by a tenant in wrongful possession between two dates.

1548 STAUNFORD *King's Prerog.* (1567) 84 b, Where the king is to be answered of the mesne issues and profits perceued and taken of any landes which [etc.]. **1648** MILTON *Observ. Art. Peace* Wks. 1738 I. 327 That no Man shall be question'd by reason hereof, for Measne Rates or Wastes, saving wilful Wastes. **1709** J. JOHNSON *Clergym. Vade M.* II. 137 That [where a bishop has died] the Mesne profits of the widow church be secured by the *Oeconomus*. **1883** SIR R. BAGGALLAY in *Law Times Rep.* L. 193/2 A mortgagee was prohibited from tacking so as to gain priority against a mesne registered incumbrance.

b. ***mesne process***: that part of the proceedings in a suit which intervenes between the primary and the final process.

a **1625** SIR H. FINCH *Law* (1636) 436 Mesne processe which is for any necessarie act to be done, not onely for the plaintife against the defendant, but for ether of them against any other. **1721** *Lond. Gaz.* No. 5953/1 He had been committed by Mesne Process. **1861** MAY *Const. Hist.* (1863) II. xi. 280 In the reign of George I arrests on mesne process, issuing out of superior courts, were limited to sums exceeding £10.

3. Intermediate, intervening: applied to persons.

1810 J. MARSHALL *Const. Opin.* (1839) 129 Neither James Greenleaf nor Peck nor any of the mesne vendors between Greenleaf and Peck, had any notice [etc.]. **1884** *Q. Rev.* Jan. 161 One or more of the middlemen or mesne lessees.

†**B.** *sb. Obs.*

1. = MEAN *sb.*[2] 1 and 10.

1447 *Rolls of Parlt.* V. 130/1 Execute by such processe and meosnes, as it shall seme hym resonable. **1472-3** *Ibid.* VI. 39/1 To aredye youre self by all measnes to you possible. **1822** C. BUTLER *Remin.* (ed. 3) 240 These are extreme cases, —the application of them to the mesne is not very difficult.

2. = *mesne lord* (see A. 1).

1531 *Dial. on Laws Eng.* I. xxx. G v b, Assyse may lye for the lorde.. agaynste the mesne onely. **1641** *Termes de la Ley* 202 s.v., He of whom the Mesne holdeth, is called chiefe Lord. **1642** [see b]. **1704** J. HARRIS *Lex. Techn.* I, *Mesn*, or *Measn*,.. signifying him that is Lord of a Manor.

b. ***writ of mesne***: 'an ancient and abolished writ, which lay when the lord paramount distrained on the tenant paravail; the latter had a writ of mesne against the mesne lord' (Wharton *Law Lex.*).

1602 FULBECKE *1st Pt. Parall.* 48 The writ of mesne, because it is in the realty, ought alwaies to suppose the husband and wife to be mesnes. **1642** tr. *Perkins' Prof. Bk.* v. §432 (1657) 161 If there be Lord, Mesne, and tenant,.. & the tenant bringeth a Writ of Mesne against the Mesne. **1818** CRUISE *Digest* (ed. 2) V. 75 A fine may be levied on every writ by which lands may be demanded,.. such as a writ of mesne.

C. *adv.* At a time intermediate (*between* two other times).

1439 *Rolls of Parlt.* V. 17/2 Mesne bitwene ye date of ye seide writte, and ye dai of ye retourne yereof. **1642** tr. *Perkins' Prof. Bk.* xi. §806 (1657) 311 As if the day of payment of the annuity bee incurred Mesne after his admission and his induction.

meso- (ˈmɛsəʊ, ˈmiːsəʊ, ˈmiːzəʊ), before a vowel sometimes **mes-**, combining form of Gr. μέσος middle, used in scientific terms of mod. formation, many of which have correlates with PRO-, or PROTO-, and META-[1]. The words of this formation that are specially important, or require detailed explanation, are treated in their alphabetical place. Of the others, which are almost innumerable, the following are examples:—ˌ**mesaorˈtitis** (also **mesoaortitis**) *Med.*, inflammation of the middle layer of the aorta. **mesaˈxonic** *a. Zool.* [Gr. ἄξων, ἀξον- axis], of the feet of certain ungulate mammals: having the axis in the central toe. **meˈsectoderm** *Embryol.* [ad. G. *mesektoderm* (J. B. Platt 1894, in *Archiv f. mikrosk. Anat.* XLIII. 913)], (*a*) that part of the mesenchyme which is derived from ectoderm rather than from mesoderm; (*b*) (see quot. 1956). **meˈsendoderm**, **meˈsentoderm** *Embryol.* [ad. and a. G. *mesentoderm* (J. B. Platt 1894, in *Archiv f. mikrosk. Anat.* XLIII. 913)], (*a*) that part of the mesenchyme which is derived from endoderm rather than from mesoderm; (*b*) (see quot. 1957). **Meso-Aˈmerica, Mesoamerica** [f. Sp. *Mesoamérica* (P. Kirchhoff in *Acta Americana* (1943) I. 92)], the central region of America, from northern Mexico to Nicaragua, which was civilized in pre-Spanish times. **Meso-Aˈmerican** *a.*, of or pertaining to Meso-America; also as *sb.*, an inhabitant of Meso-America. **mesoaortitis**, var. *mesaortitis* above. ˌ**meso-aˈppendix** *Anat.*, the fold of peritonæum attached to the vermiform appendix. ‖**mesoarium** (-ˈɛərɪəm) *Anat.* [Gr. ᾠάριον taken as = OVARIUM], the fold of peritonæum which suspends the ovary; hence **mesoarial** (-ˈɛərɪəl) *a.* **mesoˈbranchial** *a. Zool.*, applied to that lobe of the carapace of a crab which overlies the middle part of the branchial chambers. **mesocalˈcaneal** *a.*: see quot. and CALCANEAL. **mesoˈcambrian** *a.* and *sb.*, = Middle Cambrian (H. S. Williams *Journ. Geol.* 1894). **mesocamˈphoric** *a. Chem.*, the name of a dibasic acid formed by heating a mixture of dextrocamphoric acid and hydrochloric acid (Watts *Dict. Chem.* 2nd Suppl. 1875, 235). **mesochil** (ˈmɛsɒkɪl), ‖**mesochilium** (-ˈkɪlɪəm) *Bot.* [Gr. χεῖλος lip: see -IUM], the middle portion of the labellum of an orchid. ‖**mesocœle** (ˈmɛsəʊsiːl), **-cœlia** (-ˈsiːlɪə) *Anat.* [Gr. κοιλία cavity, ventricle], the ventricle of the mesencephalon of invertebrates; hence **mesocœlian** (-ˈsiːlɪən) *a.*, pertaining to this. ˈ**mesoconch** (-kɒŋk), **mesoconchic** (-ˈkɒŋkɪk), **-conchous** (-ˈkɒŋkəs) *adjs. Anthropol.* [Gr. κόγχ-ος eye-socket], having orbits of moderate height in relation to their width, as expressed by the orbital index (see quots.); so ˈ**mesoconchy** (-kɒŋkɪ), the property of being mesoconchic. **mesoˈcoracoid** *Ichthyol.* [see CORACOID], in some teleostean fishes, a bone situated between and bridging the HYPERCORACOID and HYPOCORACOID. **mesocuˈneiform** *Anat.* [see CUNEIFORM], the middle cuneiform bone of the tarsus; also **mesoˈcuniform** (in recent Dicts.). **mesocyst** (ˈmɛsəʊsɪst) *Anat.* [see CYST], 'the double layer of peritonæum attaching the gall-bladder to the liver when the former is completely surrounded by serous membrane' (*Syd. Soc. Lex.* 1890). **mesodesm** (ˈmɛsəʊdɛz(ə)m) *Bot.* [Gr. δεσμός band]: see quot. ˌ**meso-deˈvonian** *a.* and *sb.*, = Middle Devonian (H. S. Williams *Journ. Geol.* 1894). **meso-diaˈstolic** *a.*, occurring in the middle of the diastole. ˈ**mesodont** *a.* [Gr. ὀδοντ-, ὀδούς tooth], (*a*) *Anthropology*, having the teeth of medium size; (*b*) *Ent.* of Coleoptera, having the mandibles of medium size. **mesoˈdorsal** *a. Zool.*, situated on the middle of the back. ‖**mesoduoˈdenum** *Anat.*, the fold of peritonæum that supports the duodenum (*Cent. Dict.* 1890); hence **mesoduoˈdenal** *a.* ˈ**mesoform** *Physical Chem.* = *mesophase* below. **mesogenous** (mɛˈsɒdʒɪnəs) *a.* [see -GEN and -OUS], increasing by growth at or from the middle, as the spores of certain fungi (*Cent. Dict.*). ‖**mesoglœa** (-ˈgliːə) *Zool.* [Gr. γλοία glue], the mesodermal layer in sponges and other *Cœlenterata*; hence **mesoˈglœal** *a.* ‖**mesogluˈtæus**, the middle gluteal muscle, *glutæus medius* (*Cent. Dict.*); hence **mesoglu-tæal** (-gluːˈtiːəl) *a.* **mesognathic** (-ˈgnæθɪk), **mesognathous** (mɛˈsɒgnəθəs) *adjs. Anthropology* [Gr. γνάθος jaw], applied to those skulls the gnathic index of which ranges between 98 and 103. Hence **meˈsognathism** (*Syd. Soc. Lex.*), **meˈsognathy** (*Cent. Dict.*), the condition of being mesognathous. ‖**mesoˈhepar** [see HEPAR], 'a fold of peritonæum attached to the free edge of the right lobe of the liver in many animals' (*Syd. Soc. Lex.*). ‖**mesohepaticon** [Gr. ἡπατικός HEPATIC] = prec. ‖**mesohippus** (-ˈhɪpəs) *Palæont.* [Gr. ἵππος horse], one of the ancestral forms of the horse, the remains of which are found in the Lower Miocene. **mesoˈkurtic** *a. Statistics* [Gr. κύρτ-ος bulging], applied to (a graph of) a frequency distribution having the same kurtosis as the normal distribution; hence **mesokurˈtosis** [KURTOSIS], the property of being mesokurtic. **mesolobe** (ˈmɛsəʊləʊb) *Anat.* [LOBE], the corpus callosum of the brain; hence **mesolobar** (mɛsəʊˈləʊbə(r)) *a.* **mesomere** (ˈmɛsəʊmɪə(r)) *Zool.* [Gr. μέρος part], (*a*) a protovertebra (*Syd. Soc. Lex.*); (*b*) a blastomere of medium size (Webster *Suppl.* 1902). **mesomeristem** (-ˈmɛrɪstɛm) *Bot.* [see MERISTEM], the innermost layer of the exomeristem. ˌ**mesoˈmetatarse** *Anat.* [see METATARSUS], the middle metatarsal bone. ‖**mesometritis** (-mɪˈtraɪtɪs) *Path.* [see -ITIS], inflammation of the ‖**mesometrium** (-ˈmɛtrɪəm) or **mesometry** (mɛˈsɒmɪtrɪ) *Anat.* [Gr. μήτρα womb], the fold of peritonæum supporting the uterus or (in birds) the oviduct. **mesoˈnasal** *a. Anat.* [see NASAL], belonging or relating to the middle of the nose. **mesonemertine** (-nɪˈmɜːrtaɪn) *a.* [generic name *Nemertes*], belonging to the *Mesonemertini*, a division of the *Vermes* intermediate between the *Protonemertini* and *Metanemertini*. **mesonotum** (-ˈnəʊtəm) *Ent.* [Gr. νῶτον back], the dorsal portion of the mesothorax; hence **mesonotal** (-ˈnəʊtəl) *a.* **mesoˈparaffin** *Chem.*, one of a class of paraffins intermediate between the isoparaffins and the neoparaffins. ‖**mesopaˈrapteron** *Ent.* [see PARAPTERUM], the parapteron of the mesothorax; hence **mesopaˈrapteral** *a.* (*Cent. Dict.*). ˈ**mesopause**, the boundary between the mesosphere and the thermosphere, at an altitude of about 80 km. (50 miles), where the temperature stops decreasing with height and starts to increase. ˈ**mesophase** *Physical Chem.* [a. G. *mesophase* (Zocher & Birstein 1929, in *Zeitschr. f. physikal. Chem.* A. CXLI. 415)], a mesomorphic phase. **mesoˈphilic** *a. Biol.* [-PHILIC], (of an organism, esp. a bacterium) flourishing at moderate temperatures; so ˈ**mesophile**, a mesophilic organism. ‖ˌ**mesophleˈbitis** *Path.* [Gr. φλέψ, φλεβ- vein], inflammation of the middle coat of a vein. **mesopic** (mɛˈsɒpɪk) *a. Anthropology* [Gr. ὤψ, ὠπ- face], see quot. ‖**mesoˈplankton** *Biol.*, the PLANKTON living between about a hundred fathoms from the bottom and a hundred from the surface; hence **mesoplankˈtonic** *a.* **mesoplast** (ˈmɛsəʊplæst) *Biol.* [Gr. πλαστ-ός moulded], the nuclear matter of a cell (Ogilvie 1882); hence **mesoˈplastic** *a.*, relating to the mesoplast (*Cent. Dict.*). ‖**mesoplastron** (-ˈplæstrɒn) *Zool.* [see PLASTRON], an inclusive name for two parts of the plastron that are developed in certain tortoises; hence **mesoˈplastral** *a.* ‖**mesopleuron** (-ˈplʊərɒn), pl. **-pleura** *Ent.* [Gr. πλευρόν rib], one of the pleura of the mesothorax; hence **mesoˈpleural** *a.* ‖**mesorchium** (-ˈɔːkɪəm) *Anat.* [Gr. ὄρχις testicle], the fold of peritonæum which supports the genital gland in some animals; hence **meˈsorchial** *a.* ‖**mesoˈrectum** *Anat.*, the fold of peritonæum which supports the RECTUM; hence **mesoˈrectal** *a.* (in recent Dicts.). **mesoˈretina** *Anat.*, the mosaic layer of the RETINA. **mesorostral** (-ˈrɒstrəl) *a. Zool.* [ROSTRUM], in the cetaceous genus *Mesoplodon* or *Ziphius*: see quot. **mesoˈsalpinx** *Anat.* [SALPINX 2], an upper fold of each of the broad ligaments of the uterus which contains and supports the Fallopian tube. **mesoˈsaprobe, mesosaˈprobic** *adjs.* [ad. G. *mesosaprobe* (Kolkwitz & Marsson 1908, in *Ber. Deutsch. Bot. Ges.* XXVI. 507): see SAPROBE], of running water: partially polluted. ˈ**mesoscaph(e** [ad. F. *mésoscaphe* (J. Piccard): cf. BATHYSCAPH(E], a submersible vessel designed for exploration of the sea at moderate depths. ‖**mesoscapula** (-ˈskæpjʊlə) *Anat.*, the spine of the scapula; hence **mesoˈscapular** *a.* **mesoˈscopic** *a. Geol.* [after *micro-*, *macroscopic*], large enough for examination with the naked eye but small enough for examination as a single entity. ‖**mesoscuˈtellum** *Ent.* [SCUTELLUM], the smaller and posterior part of the notum of an insect; hence **mesoscuˈtellar** *a.* ‖**mesoˈscutum** *Ent.* [SCUTUM], the larger and anterior part of the notum of an insect. **mesoseismal** (-ˈsaɪzməl) *a.* [Gr. σεισμός earthquake], pertaining to the centre of intensity of an earthquake. ˈ**mesosphere**, the layer of the earth's atmosphere between the stratopause below and the mesopause above; hence **mesoˈspheric** *a.* **mesostaphyline** (-ˈstæfɪlaɪn) *a.* [Gr. σταφυλή uvula], having a palatal index of from 80 to 85 (*Syd. Soc. Lex.*). **mesostasis** (mɛˈsɒstəsɪs) *Min.* [Gr. στάσις placing], the interstitial substance of rocks that are partly amorphous and partly crystalline. **mesostate** (ˈmɛsəʊsteɪt): see quot. ‖**mesostethium** (-ˈstiːθɪəm) *Ent.* [Gr. στηθίον, στῆθος breast]: see quot. **mesostome** (ˈmɛsəʊstəʊm) *Zool.* [Gr. στόμα mouth], a planarian of the genus *Mesotoma*. **mesostylous** (-ˈstaɪləs) *a. Bot.* [STYLE], applied to flowers that have styles intermediate in length between the macrostylous and the microstylous. **mesosuchian** (-ˈsjuːkɪən) *a. Zool.* [Gr. σοῦχος crocodile], belonging to the extinct suborder *Mesosuchia* of crocodiles; *sb.* a crocodile of this suborder; also **mesoˈsuchious** *a.* (in recent Dicts.). **mesosyˈstolic** *a. Path.*, occurring in the middle of the systole. ‖**mesotarsus** *Ent.*, the tarsus of the middle leg of an insect; cf. *protarsus*, *metatarsus*: hence **mesoˈtarsal** *a.* (in recent Dicts.). **mesotarˈtaric** *a. Chem.*, inactive tartaric acid. **mesotheca** (-ˈθiːkə), **-theque** (-θiːk) *Zool.* [Gr. θήκη case], the middle one of the three laminæ of the perigonium in Hydrozoa. ‖**mesothecium** *Bot.* [THECIUM], (*a*) the intermediate layer of cells in an unripe anther (*Cassell's Encycl. Dict.*); (*b*) the thecium of lichens (Jackson *Gloss. Bot. Terms* 1900).

‖**Mesotherium** (-ˈθɪərɪəm) *Palæont.* [Gr. θηρίον wild beast], a genus of fossil rodents of South America; a rodent of this genus. **mesoˈthermal** *a. Petrol.*, of, pertaining to, or designating mineral and ore deposits formed by hydrothermal action at intermediate temperature and pressure. **mesotymˈpanic** *Ichthyol.* [TYMPANIC] = SYMPLECTIC. **meso-ˈuterine** *a. Anat.*, the epithet of the fold of peritonæum supporting the uterus. ‖**mesovarium** (mɛsəʊˈvɛərɪəm) *Anat.* [L. *ōvarium* OVARY] = MESOARIUM. ‖**mesovenˈtriculum** *Anat.*, 'the gastro-hepatic omentum' (*Syd. Soc. Lex.*).

1909 *Cent. Dict.* Suppl., *Mesaortitis. **1910** *Practitioner* Apr. 422 A large proportion of all cases of aneurysm in young and middle-aged men are due to a syphilitic mesaortitis. **1962** *Lancet* 28 Apr. 889/2 The response to the mesoaortitis of syphilis is primarily an endarteritis. **1898** A. S. WOODWARD *Outl. Vertebr. Palæont.* 319 They [*sc.* Perissodactyla] are all digitigrade quadrupeds, with the axis of both feet passing through the digit No. iii (hence *mesaxonic). **1933** A. S. ROMER *Vertebr. Paleont.* xvi. 300 In the majority of ungulates..the third toe was the longest, and the axis of symmetry of the foot lies through this digit (mesaxonic). **1974** *Nature* 8 Mar. 174/2 In the development of a mesaxonic foot perissodactyls have reduced the astragalo-cuboid contact. **1894** *Jrnl. R. Microsc. Soc.* 544 Miss J. B. Platt has studied the ontogenetic differentiation of the ectoderm in *Necturus*. The 'mesoderm' in the head is differentiated by the yolk spherules which it contains into two sharply separable layers—*mesectoderm and mesendoderm. **1921** *Jrnl. Compar. Neurol.* XXXIII. 4 In 1894 Miss Platt elaborated the idea..introducing the terms mesectoderm and mesentoderm for mesenchyme derived from the ectoderm and endoderm, respectively. **1938** *Nature* 23 Apr. 754/1 The mesectoderm..normally migrates ventrally over the mesentoderm. **1956** C. H. WADDINGTON *Princ. Embryol.* xii. 256 'Mesectoderm'..is also used for the epiblast of a blastoderm before the mesoderm has invaginated and thus become separated from the ectoderm. **1965** L. B. AREY *Developmental Anat.* (ed. 7) ii. 22 Mesenchyme is predominantly derived from the mesoderm,..but some of it comes from the ectoderm and this contribution is often called mesectoderm. **1894** *Mesendoderm [see *mesectoderm* above]. **1964** H. W. MANNER *Elem. Compar. Vertebr. Embryol.* v. 50 The morphological result of this invagination [of the blastula] is a cup-like structure, composed of two layers of cells, an outer ectoderm and an inner mesendoderm, so called because it contains the presumptive material for both the mesoderm and endoderm. **1921, 1938** *Mesentoderm [see *mesectoderm* above]. **1957** *Dorland's Med. Dict.* (ed. 23) 818/2 *Mesentoderm*, the inner layer of an amphibian gastrula not yet separated into mesoderm and entoderm. **1948** A. L. KROEBER *Anthropol.* (rev. ed.) xviii. 793 We have seen that native *Meso-America..consisted of most of what now is Mexico and of Guatemala and that it constituted the North American half of prehistoric Nuclear America. **1952** tr. *P. Kirchhoff's Mesoamerica* in S. Tax *Heritage of Conquest* 23 We include these tribes in Mesoamerica, because of the very considerable number of..Mesoamerican cultural traits. **1967** L. DEUEL *Conquistadors without Swords* xv. 189 The close parallels between the formative cultures of Mesoamerica and the Central Andes became evident. **1974** *Encycl. Brit. Macropædia* XI. 934/2 About half of Mexico; all of Guatemala, British Honduras, and El Salvador; and parts of Honduras and Costa Rica are included in Meso-America. **1948** A. L. KROEBER *Anthropol.* (rev. ed.) xviii. 786 The term 'South Mexican-Central American' would..be more accurate..but it is cumbersome; and **Meso-American* has been suggested and employed as a convenient coinage that runs no risk of being confused. **1956** R. REDFIELD *Peasant Society & Culture* 74 Those Meso-American peoples. **1965** *Canad. Jrnl. Ling.* Spring 101 Jicaque, a Mesoamerican language. **1967** L. DEUEL *Conquistadors without Swords* xv. 189 Its importance as a prototype of Mesoamerican architecture may well be compared to the step pyramid of Zoser in early dynastic Egypt. **1969** J. MANDER *Static Society* ii. 83 What is true of the Aztecs is true of the Meso-American and Andean civilisations. **1974** *Encycl. Brit. Macropædia* XI. 935/1 The only linguistic groups that played any great part in Meso-American civilization were the Mixtec and Zapotec. *Ibid.*, The Meso-Americans reached stages of development unknown away from those areas. **1897** *Allbutt's Syst. Med.* III. 880 The *meso-appendix. **1875** HUXLEY in *Encycl. Brit.* I. 768/2 The *mesoarial and mesorchial folds of the peritoneum. **1846** OWEN *Vertebr. Anim.* I. *Fishes* 288 In the young Lamprey the ovarium is a..membranous plate, suspended by a fold of the peritoneum (*mesoarium). **1877** HUXLEY *Anat. Inv. Anim.* vi. 343 The branchial region is sub-divided into epibranchial, *mesobranchial, and metabranchial lobes. **1854** OWEN *Skel. & Teeth* in *Circ. Sci.* I. *Org. Nat.* 225 There are three calcaneal processes; one, called the 'entocalcaneal',..a second, called the '*mesocalcaneal'. **1866** *Treas. Bot.*, **Mesochil, Mesochilium.* **1849** BALFOUR *Man. Bot.* §1058 This labellum [in *Orchidaceæ*]..is sometimes divided by contraction, so as to exhibit three distinct portions, the lowest being the hypochilium..the middle, *mesochilium..and the upper, epichilium. **1884** T. J. PARKER *Zootomy* 23 They contain a cavity, the aqueduct of Sylvius, or *mesocœle. **1887** WILDER in *Amer. Nat.* XXI. 914 Mammalia—Mesocœle tubular; *mesocœlian roof quadrilobate. **1909** *Cent. Dict.* Suppl., *Mesoconch. **1920** H. H. WILDER *Lab. Man. Anthropometry* i. 67 Chamaeconch..below 76. Mesoconch..76–85. **1960** M. F. A. MONTAGU *Introd. Physical Anthropol.* (ed. 3) 606 Mesoconch..[Orbital index of] 76·0–84·9. **1909** *Cent. Dict.* Suppl., *Mesoconchic. **1960** J. COMAS *Man. Physical Anthrop.* vii. 409 Mesoconchic..[an orbital index of] 83·0 to 88·9. **1885** *Jrnl. R. Anthrop. Inst.* XIV. 71 *Mesokonchous ..[orbital index of] 80·1 to 85·0. **1904** *Biometrika* III. 214 (*table*) *Mesoconchy. **1868** W. K. PARKER *Shoulder-girdle Vertebr.* 8 The middle bar, which underprops the middle glenoid facet, is the '*meso-coracoid'. *Ibid.* 152 A short curved meso-coracoid process. **1854** OWEN *Skel. & Teeth* in *Circ. Sci.* I. *Org. Nat.* 244 The small bone, called 'splint-bone'..articulated to the '*mesocuneiform'. **1898** *Allbutt's Syst. Med.* V. 1018 Mid-diastolic or *meso-diastolic murmur. **1884** FLOWER in *Jrnl. Anthrop. Inst.* XIV. 186 *Mesodont Races. Chinese, American Indians [etc.]. **1890** *Syd. Soc. Lex.*, *Mesodont*, a term applied to those skulls in which the product of the division of the length of the crowns of the molar and bicuspid teeth multiplied by 100, by the basin[as]al length, lies between 42 and 44. **1899** D. SHARP *Insects* II. (Camb. Nat. Hist.) 193 Mesodont. **1871** PHILLIPS *Geol. Oxford* 178 These are usually *mesodorsal spines. **1933** *Trans. Faraday Soc.* XXIX. 1008 For a *mesoform to appear, it is necessary for these [binding] forces to persist in either one or two dimensions after loosening of the third. **1946** *Thorpe's Dict. Appl. Chem.* (ed. 4) VII. 350/2 Some substances show only one of these mesophases; some show both, in which case the smectic is always the lower-temperature form. The matter is somewhat complicated, however, by the existence of substances which show three, four, and even five mesoforms. **1886** *Proc. Zool. Soc.* 574 Silicea with soft *mesoglœa or mesodermal ground substance. **1889** GEDDES & THOMSON *Evol. Sex* 90 The ova [of sponges] are highly nourished *mesoglœal cells. **1891** CUNNINGHAM in *Trans. R. Irish. Acad.* XXIX. 581 The *mesognathic class. **1878** FLOWER in *Proc. Roy. Inst.* VIII. 615 When the latter dimension [*sc.* basi-alveolar length] exceeds the former [*sc.* basi-nasal length], the face is said to be prognathous; when the reverse is the case, it is orthognathous; when the two dimensions are equal or thereabouts, it is *mesognathous. **1884** T. J. PARKER *Zootomy* 391 *Mesohepar. **1905** ROLLESTON *Dis. Liver* 24 The connective tissue uniting the right lobe of the liver to the diaphragm (the *mesohepaticon). **1877** LE CONTE *Elem. Geol.* II. (1879) 509 Next came [after Eohippus and Orohippus] in the Lower Miocene the *Mesohippus. **1905** *Mesokurtic [see LEPTOKURTIC *a.*]. **1972** R. B. CAIN *Elem. Statistical Concepts* xix. 159 Any curve which has the same degree of kurtosis as the standard normal curve is said to be mesokurtic. **1905** K. PEARSON in *Biometrika* IV. 173 The *mesokurtosis of the Gaussian curve is not a universal characteristic of frequency distributions. **1943** M. G. KENDALL *Adv. Theory Statistics* I. v. 129 [For the normal distribution] we also have $\beta_2 = 3, \gamma_2 = 0$, which accounts for the standard adopted for mesokurtosis. **1855** DUNGLISON *Med. Lex.*, **Mesolobar*, belonging to the *Mesolobe* or *Corpus callosum. Mesolobar Arteries*,..are the arteries of the corpus callosum. **Mesolobe*, corpus callosum. **1884** *Mesomeristem [see PERIMERISTEM]. **1890** *Syd. Soc. Lex.*, **Mesometritis.* **1835–6** *Todd's Cycl. Anat.* I. 357/2 The oviduct..is attached to and supported by a duplicature of peritoneum called the **mesometrium. Ibid.*, The *mesometry differs most from the mesentery when the female organs are in full sexual action. **1868** W. K. PARKER *Shoulder-girdle Vertebr.* 24 On the head may be seen the quasi-ethmoid or *meso-nasal; two nasals [etc.]. **1890** *Syd. Soc. Lex.*, *Mesonasal cavity*, a blind membranous pouch, situated in the diverging angle of the posterior forks of the internasal cartilage in the developing salmon. **1902** A. E. SHIPLEY in *Encycl. Brit.* XXXI. 120/2 The *Mesonemertine and one or two aberrant species. **1836** SHUCKARD tr. *Burmeister's Man. Entom.* 78 The *mesonotum. **1876** ODLING in *Lond.* etc. *Phil. Mag.* Mar. 206 *Mesoparaffins. **1950** S. CHAPMAN in *Jrnl. Atmospheric & Terrestrial Physics* I. 121 The..upper boundary..would be the stratopause, and the mesosphere would extend from this level to the *mesopause. **1963** *New Scientist* 25 July 169/2 At a height of some fifty miles there is a sudden drop in the temperature of the atmosphere from freezing point to about −80°C. It is here, in the 'mesopause', that the so-called 'noctilucent' clouds occur. **1972** *Nature* 28 Jan. 215/1 A sounding rocket was launched..chiefly to study the ion composition around the cold summer mesopause. **1929** *Brit. Chem. Abstr.* A. 870/1 *Mesophases occupy an intermediate position between crystals and purely amorphous substances. **1937** O. B. DARBISHIRE tr. *A. von Buzágh's Colloid Syst.* vii. 135 Mesophases only show a symmetrical arrangement in certain given directions, and not in all three directions of space. **1972** *Physics Bull.* May 279/1 The characteristic anisotropy of the mesophase is now known to result from the strong tendency of the constituent molecules to lie with their long axes parallel. **1928** P. H. FOSTER in C. M. Hilliard *Text-bk. Bacteriol.* viii. 95 *Mesophiles..may be further subdivided to distinguish organisms which have as their optimum temperature 37°C..and those growing best below this, usually between 20° and 30°C. **1969** *New Scientist* 27 Nov. 450/2 Mesophiles (organisms with a maximum temperature for growth of 37°C and a minimum less than 20°C) multiply rapidly. **1897** LEHMANN & NEUMANN *Atlas & Essent. Bacteriol.* 98 *Mesophilic bacteria: minimum at 10°–15°, best at 37°, maximum at about 45°. **1964** *New Scientist* 12 Nov. 445/2 The method of the Microalgae Research Institute is to separate its algal strains into high-temperature or 'thermophilic', normal temperature or 'mesophilic', and low-temperature or 'psychrophilic' varieties. **1875** JONES & SIEV. *Pathol. Anat.* 400 The *mesophlebitis and periphlebitis of Virchow. **1885** O. THOMAS in *Jrnl. Anthrop. Inst.* XIV. 334 Individual skulls or races having indices above 107·5 might be called platyopic or flat-faced; from 107·5 to 110·0, *mesopic. **1898** G. H. FOWLER in *Proc. Zool. Soc.* 575 Prof. Agassiz..refuses to accept the alleged existence of a *mesoplankton. *Ibid.* 1029 The supposition that *Globigerina pachyderma* is a *mesoplanktonic form. **1889** *Nature* 2 May 7/1 In the Pleurodira the first two families are distinguished from one another by the presence or absence of a *mesoplastral bone. **1848** MAUNDER *Treas. Nat. Hist.* 794 **Mesopleura*, the lateral surfaces of the *mesothorax*. **1875** *Mesorchial [see *Mesoarial* above]. **1855** DUNGLISON *Med. Lex.*, **Mesorchium.* **1875** HUXLEY & MARTIN *Elem. Biol.* (1877) 183 A sort of testicular mesentery or mesorchium. **1835–6** *Todd's Cycl. Anat.* I. 506/1 Along the posterior wall we find the rectum with its *mesorectum. **1889** J. LEIDY *Anat.* (ed. 2) 877 The processes of the pigment-cells of the ectoretina extend between the rods of the *meso-retina. **1872** SIR W. TURNER in *Trans. Roy. Soc. Edinb.* XXVI. 768, I have named the dense solid bar in the middle of the beak the *meso-rostral bone. **1890** *Syd. Soc. Lex.*, **Mesosalpinx*, the fine fold of peritonaeum which continues the mesovarium to the Fallopian tube in the foetus. **1901** *Gray's Anat.* (ed. 15) 1013 The Fallopian tube is contained in a special fold of the broad ligament, which is attached to the part of the ligament near the ovary, and is known by the name of the mesosalpinx. **1970** L. J. A. DIDIO *Synopsis Anat.* 297/2 The position of the ovarian ligaments divides each broad ligament into an upper mesosalpinx and a lower mesometrium. **1927** *Glasgow Herald* 11 June 4/2 Investigators distinguish a..*meso-saprobe zone which carp, tench, sticklebacks, and the like can endure. **1925** *Bull. Illinois Nat. Hist. Survey* XV. 441 The polluted or *mesosaprobic zone represents the next step towards purification of the waters. A variety of higher water-plants may exist..and there may be considerable amounts of dissolved oxygen present. **1970** tr. *J. Schwoerbel's Methods Hydrobiol.* 8 This self cleansing of running water..leads from the poly-saprobic zone through the meso-saprobic zone to the oligo-saprobic zone with only small residues of pollution. **1955** *Britannica Bk. of Year* 490/1 **Mesoscaphe*, an underwater helicopter designed by Auguste Piccard. **1963** *Observer* 13 Jan. 14/4 The mesoscaphe, a cylindrical steel shell sealed at each end, will be lighter than water even when fully loaded with passengers. **1969** *New Scientist* 19 June 626/1 The submersible..is a direct descendant of the *Auguste Piccard*—the 'mesoscaph' that, carrying 40 passengers at a time, gave thousands of visitors..a glimpse of the depths of Lake Geneva. **1973** *Times Lit. Suppl.* 13 July 815/4 Twenty years ago Auguste Piccard..conceived the idea of a mesoscaphe or exploratory vessel that could operate at intermediate depths. In 1964 his son Jacques.. launched the first mesoscaphe. **1868** W. K. PARKER *Shoulder-girdle Vertebr.* 11 The præ-scapula and *meso-scapula in one half-cleft ray. *Ibid.* 27 A scapular, a *meso-scapular, and a præ-scapular bar. **1957** WEISS & MCINTYRE in *Jrnl. Geol.* LXV. 577/2 The different kinds of *mesoscopic structures found in the area. [*Note*] The use of the terms 'microscopic', 'mesoscopic', and 'macroscopic' in this paper accords with the definitions suggested elsewhere by one of the writers (Weiss, 1957 [= 'at press': *published* 1958]), as follows:..2. *Mesoscopic*: This covers fields ranging in size from a single hand specimen to a single continuous exposure (generally, but not always, of small size) in which data can be measured with sufficient accuracy and continuity to allow determination of its over-all structural geometry. **1965** G. J. WILLIAMS *Econ. Geol. N.Z.* vi. 66/1 Grindley (1963) noted that post-metamorphic folding in southern Westland was accompanied by axial-plane cleavage on mesoscopic shear folds. **1969** *Nature* 22 Nov. 827/1 Attention is to be confined to structures on what is called the mesoscopic scale, that is, visible in anything between hand specimen and outcrop. **1899** D. SHARP *Insects* II. (Camb. Nat. Hist.) 312 In some of the higher forms this *meso-scutellar lobe is prominent. **1833** *Entomologist's Mag.* I. 28 The *meso-scutellum has a yellow margin, interrupted toward the base. **1883** JOHNSTON-LAVIS in *Nature* 6 Sept. 438/2 Most people not in the *mesoseismal area felt first the 'susultatorio' or vertical movement. **1950** S. CHAPMAN in *Jrnl. Atmospheric & Terrestrial Physics* I. 121, I propose the name **mesosphere* for the layer between the top of the stratosphere and the major minimum of temperature existing somewhere below 100 km. **1961** *New Scientist* 30 Nov. 568/3 Winds at heights of 80 to 100 km in the Earth's atmosphere—in the so-called mesosphere. **1973** *Physics Bull.* Dec. 727/1 The fifth experiment aboard Concorde concerned emission from the stratosphere and mesosphere arising from the electronic transition between the metastable $^1\Delta_g$ and the ground $^3\Sigma_g^-$ states of molecular oxygen. **1960** *Meteorol. & Geoastrophysical Abstr.* XI. 1535 *Mesospheric temperatures. **1972** *Nature* 28 Jan. 194/1 It is, perhaps, of interest to enquire whether the low mesospheric temperatures existing at the time of the flight render the weakly-bound cluster ions more stable. **1888** *Nature* 15 Mar. 459/2 The presence of a hypocrystalline interstitial substance (*mesostasis) wedged in between the felspars. **1885** M. FOSTER in *Encycl. Brit.* XIX. 19/1 The specific material of a secretion, such as the trypsin of pancreatic juice, comes from the protoplasm of the cell, through a number of intermediate substances, or *mesostates as they are called. **1826** KIRBY & SP. *Entomol.* III. xxxiii. 382 **Mesostethium*... A central piece between the intermediate and posterior legs, and bounded laterally in *Coleoptera* by the *Parapleuræ*—along the middle of which, where it exists, the *Metasternum* runs. **1876** *Beneden's Anim. Parasites* 161 In the autumn of 1871, nearly all the *mesostomes perished through the presence of those parasitical organisms. **1887** WARD tr. *Sachs' Physiol. Plants* 790 In addition to those with macrostylous and those with microstylous flowers, there is found also one with *mesostylous flowers. **1886** GÜNTHER in *Encycl. Brit.* XX. 466/1 The surviving *Mesosuchian Crocodiles of the Jurassic period. **1898** *Allbutt's Syst. Med.* V. 976 It [a cardiac murmur] is manifested only of the ventricular contraction, and is *meso-systolic. **1897** PARKER & HASWELL *Text-bk. Zool.* II. 366 The ankle-joint of the bird is a *meso-tarsal joint. **1865** WATTS *Dict. Chem.* III, *Mesotartaric Acid. **1859** ALLMAN in *Ann. Nat. Hist.* Ser. III. IV. 140 They [*sc.* tentacles] surround an orifice in the *mesotheque. **1871** —— *Gymnobl. Hydroids* Introd. 15 *Mesotheca.* **1876** ALSTON in *Proc. Zool. Soc.* 98 Fossil genus:—*Mesotherium. **1883** FLOWER in *Encycl. Brit.* XV. 372/2 The extinct South American *Mesotherium*, half Rodent and half Ungulate. **1922, 1969** *Mesothermal [see *hypothermal* adj. c s.v. HYPO- II]. **1846** OWEN *Vertebr. Anim.* I. *Fishes* v. 110 The stylo-hyoid being attached near the junction of the epi-tympanic with the *meso-tympanic. **1876** tr. *Wagner's Gen. Pathol.* 339 The..*meso-uterine folds of the peritoneum. **1890** *Syd. Soc. Lex.*, **Mesovarium.*

2. *Chem.* (Often italic.) **a.** [app. first used in *mesotartaric*.] As an inseparable formative element in chem. names denoting the meso isomer (see below), as ***meso-erythritol***, ***-inositol***; ***mesotartaric*** adj. (see above).

1936 *Chem. Abstr.* XXX. 7625 While *meso*-inositol can serve as a part of the bios complex, it has never been isolated from yeast. **1937** F. C. WHITMORE *Org. Chem.* 385 Since the liquid 1,4-dibromide gives *meso*-erythritol it must be the *cis* form of configuration (A). **1968** I. L. FINAR *Org. Chem.* (ed. 4) II. vii. 231 On oxidation, D-erythrose gives *meso*-tartaric, and on reduction gives *meso*-erythritol. **1971** *Biochim. & Biophys. Acta* CCXLI. 204 Pea chloroplasts are also impermeable to the six-carbon cyclic polyhydroxy alcohol, *meso*-inositol.

b. Used as quasi-*adj.* (either as a separate word, usu. *attrib.*, or joined by a hyphen to a following sb.) to denote an isomer which has one or more pairs of enantiomorphic structural units

so arranged that the molecule as a whole is optically inactive; as ***meso form, isomer***.

1896 *Jrnl. Chem. Soc.* LXX. I. 412 It is impossible to say which is the racemic acid and which the meso-form. **1907** J. B. COHEN *Org. Chem. Adv. Students* I. ii. 94 Ordinary inositol from beans and flesh is a meso compound. **1937** F. C. WHITMORE *Org. Chem.* 53 These are stereo-isomers of the same type as the tartaric acids, one being meso and the other racemic. *Ibid.* 371 Usually the meso-form can be separated from the *dl*-form by patient application of fractionation. **1956** *Nature* 11 Feb. 281/1 When it [*sc.* the filtrate] was acidified..the meso-isomer precipitated. **1968** R. O. C. NORMAN *Princ. Org. Synthesis* v. 154 As with other examples of diastereoisomers, the properties of *meso* forms are different from those of the isomeric mirror-image pairs.

mesoblast (ˈmɛsəʊblæst). *Biol.* [f. MESO- + -BLAST.] The middle layer of the BLASTODERM, between the EPIBLAST and the HYPOBLAST. Also *attrib.* Hence ˈ**mesoblasted** *a.*, having a mesoblast.

1857 AGASSIZ *Contrib. Nat. Hist. U.S.A.* II. 467 The mesoblast of the yolk cell. *Ibid.* II. 617 Some of the mesoblasted cells are united to those without mesoblasts. **1873** F. M. BALFOUR in *Q. Jrnl. Microsc. Sci.* XIII. 269 The mesoblast-cells.

mesoblastic (mɛsəʊˈblæstɪk), *a.* [f. MESOBLAST + -IC.] Of or pertaining to the mesoblast.

1874 F. M. BALFOUR in *Q. Jrnl. Microsc. Sci.* XIV. 342 Primitively a true hypoblastic structure which has only by adaptation become an apparently mesoblastic one. **1896** *Allbutt's Syst. Med.* I. 201 Histologically all new growths may be classed in two series, viz. those of mesoblastic and those of epithelial origin.

mesobranchial: see MESO-.

‖**mesocæcum** (mɛsəʊˈsiːkəm). *Anat.* A fold of peritonæum which sometimes supports the cæcum. Hence **mesoˈcæcal** *a.*, pertaining to the mesocæcum (in recent Dicts.).

1835–6 *Todd's Cycl. Anat.* I. 14/2 On the right side..it [the peritoneum] sometimes forms a fold termed *mesocæcum*. **1858** H. GRAY *Anat.* 602 The Meso-Cæcum.. serves to connect the back part of the cæcum with the right iliac fossa.

mesocalcaneal, -camphoric: see MESO-.

mesocarp (ˈmɛsəʊkɑːp). *Bot.* [ad. mod.L. *mesocarpium*, *-carpus*, f. Gr. μέσο-ς MESO- + καρπός fruit.] The middle layer of a PERICARP.

1849 BALFOUR *Man. Bot.* §524 The pericarp consists usually of three layers: the external, or epicarp.. ; the middle, or mesocarp.. ; and the internal, or endocarp. **1861** BENTLEY *Man. Bot.* 300.

mesocephal (mɛsəʊˈsɛfəl, miːzəʊ-). [f. MESOCEPHAL-I *sb. pl.*] One who has a mesocephalic skull.

1900 [see DOLICHOCEPHAL]. **1901** [see BRACHYCEPHAL]. **1935** HUXLEY & HADDON *We Europeans* vi. 185 In South Arabia..they [*sc.* the Jews] are preponderantly dolicocephals, and in North Africa dolicocephals or low mesocephals. **1957** C. G. SELIGMAN *Races Afr.* (ed. 3) iv. 78 They are essentially mesocephals, perhaps reaching the lower grades of brachycephaly.

†**mesocephale, mesocephalon,** = MESENCEPHAL(E, MESENCEPHALON.

1839–47 *Todd's Cycl. Anat.* III. 684/2 The mesocephale or mesencephale. **1853** CARPENTER *Hum. Phys.* (ed. 4) 734 The part of the encephalon known as the Tuber Annulare to which the name of Mesocephale has been given. **1890** *Syd. Soc. Lex.*, *Mesocephalon*, the *Mesencephalon*.

mesocephalic (ˌmɛsəʊsɪˈfælɪk), *a.* [f. Gr. μέσο-ς MESO- + κεφαλ-ή head + -IC: cf. CEPHALIC.]

1. *Craniometry.* Applied to skulls intermediate between *dolichocephalic* and *brachycephalic*; also to skulls having a capacity of from 1350 to 1450 cubic centimetres.

1866 MEIGS *Observ. Cran. Forms Amer. Aborigines* 13 Such deviations fall naturally into an intermediate or mesocephalic group. **1887** *Academy* 17 Sept. 188/1 The Tchuds are either mesocephalic or dolichocephalic.

2. Anat. ***mesocephalic flexure***: 'the angular bend of the floor of the craniospinal cavity'.

1858 HUXLEY in *Proc. Roy. Soc.* IX. 421.

So ‖**mesocephali** (-ˈsɛfəlaɪ) *sb. pl.* [mod.L.], persons having mesocephalic skulls; **mesoˈcephalism, mesoˈcephaly**, the condition or quality of being mesocephalic.

1866 MEIGS *Observ. Cran. Forms Amer. Aborigines* 24 The Huron crania belong partly to the Brachycephali, and partly to the Mesocephali. **1885** *Athenæum* 27 June 827/1 In the former locality there exists a taller, darker, and more brachycephalic race, whilst in the latter mesocephaly prevails. **1888** CLEVENGER in *Amer. Nat.* XXII. 614 Departures from a width of eight and length of ten (mesocephalism)..determine whether the skull shall be considered long [etc.].

mesocephalon: see MESOCEPHALE.

mesochil, -cœle, -cœlian: see MESO-.

‖**mesocolon** (mɛsəʊˈkəʊlɒn). *Anat.* [mod.L., a. Gr. μεσόκωλον, f. μεσο- MESO- + κῶλον COLON.] The fold of peritonæum which supports the colon.

1693 tr. *Blancard's Phys. Dict.* (ed. 2), *Mesocolon*, that part of the Mesentery which is continued to the great Guts. **1835–6** *Todd's Cycl. Anat.* I. 14/1 The folds respectively termed right and left *mesocolon*. **1858** H. GRAY *Anat.* 602 The ascending Meso-Colon.

Hence **mesocolic** (-ˈkɒlɪk) *a.*, relating to the mesocolon.

1831 R. KNOX *Cloquet's Anat.* 761 Mesocolic Ganglia. **1897** *Allbutt's Syst. Med.* III. 806 Mesocolic or mesenteric hernia.

mesocoracoid: see MESO-.

mesocracy (mɛˈsɒkrəsɪ). *rare*⁻⁰. [f. Gr. μέσο-ς middle + -κρατία: see -CRACY.] Government by the middle classes.

1895 *Funk's Stand. Dict.*, *Mesocracy.*

mesocratic (mɛsəʊˈkrætɪk), *a.* [f. as prec. + -IC.] **1.** Pertaining to the middle classes.

1857 *Q. Rev.* Oct. 331 Rugby, a local foundation of mere mesocratic origin.

2. *Petrol.* [after *leuco-*, *melanocratic*.] Of a rock: intermediate between a leucocratic and a melanocratic rock.

1904 *Amer. Geologist* XXXIV. 134 The main body of the boss is made up of a coarsely crystalline, mesocratic, hornblende gabbro. **1954** [see *leucocratic* adj. s.v. LEUCO-].

mesocuneiform to **mesocyst**: see MESO-.

mesode (ˈmɛsəʊd). *Gr. Prosody.* [ad. Gr. μεσῳδός, f. μεσο- MESO- + ᾠδή ODE.] A portion of a choral ode, coming between the strophe and antistrophe, without anything to correspond with it.

1850 MURE *Lit. Greece* III. 58. **1888** J. GOW. *Comp. to Classics* 285 We are told that mesodes and epodes were sung by the chorus standing.

mesoderm (ˈmɛsəʊdɜːm). [f. Gr. μέσο-ς middle + δέρμα skin.]

1. *Bot.* **a.** 'The middle layer of tissue in the shell of the spore-case of an urn-moss' (*Treas. Bot.* 1866). **b.** 'The middle layer of the bark' (*Syd. Soc. Lex.* 1890).

1874 *Q. Jrnl. Microsc. Sci.* XIV. 159 As soon as the two primary germ-lamellæ begin to differentiate and to develop between them a middle cell-layer (mesoderm).

2. *Biol.* = MESOBLAST.

1873 W. S. DALLAS (tr. Haeckel) in *Ann. Mag. Nat. Hist.* Ser. IV. XI. 257 The origin of the Mesoderm. **1877** RAY LANKESTER in *Q. Jrnl. Microsc. Sci.* XVII. 416 The contractile fibrous appendices of the ectoderm..formed a.. primitive mesoderm or mesoblast.

attrib. **1874** *Q. Jrnl. Microsc. Sci.* XIV. 159 The mesoderm-layer. **1884** *Ibid.* XXIV. 90 To determine the part played by wandering mesoderm cells immediately below the thin ectoderm.

Hence **mesoˈdermal, mesoˈdermic** *adjs.*, of, relating to, or derived from the mesoderm.

1877 HUXLEY *Anat. Inv. Anim.* iii. 143 The mesodermal layer. **1884** *Q. Jrnl. Microsc. Sci.* XXIV. 107 Mesodermal Plasmodia, are..found even in the higher animals, not excepting Man himself. **1884** W. PATTEN *ibid.* 590 The fusion of the edges of the mesodermic folds.

mesodesm, -diastolic: see MESO-.

mesodic (mɛˈsɒdɪk), *a. Gr. Prosody.* [ad. Gr. μεσῳδικός, f. μεσῳδός MESODE.] Relating to, or having the character of, a mesode.

1879 J. W. WHITE tr. *Schmidt's Rhythmic & Metric* 127 A mesodic period arises from the inverted arrangement of the sentences about an interlude. **1883** JEBB *Sophocles, Œdipus Tyr.* p. lxxxi, A mesodic stichic period.

mesodont, -duodenum: see MESO-.

‖**mesogaster** (mɛsəʊˈgæstə(r)). *Anat.* [mod.L., f. Gr. μέσο-ς middle + γαστήρ stomach.] A membrane, part of the mesentery, which attaches the stomach to the dorsal wall of the abdomen. Hence **mesoˈgastral** *a.*, pertaining to the mesogaster (in recent Dicts.).

1807 HOME in *Phil. Trans.* XCVII. 161 The pyloric [portion] is bent upwards and retained in that situation by the mesogaster. **1884** T. J. PARKER *Zootomy* 297 The mesogaster, or sheet of peritoneum connecting the stomach with the dorsal wall of the abdominal cavity.

mesogastric (mɛsəʊˈgæstrɪk), *a.* [f. mod.L. MESOGASTRIUM + -IC.]

1. *Anat.* Pertaining to the mesogastrium.

1843 OWEN *Invertebr. Anim.* Gloss., *Mesogastric.* The membrane which forms the medium of attachment of the stomach to the walls of the abdomen. **1897** *Allbutt's Syst. Med.* III. 806 Meso-gastric hernia.

2. *Zool.* In Crustacea, the middle lobe of the gastro-hepatic area of the carapace.

1877 HUXLEY *Anat. Inv. Anim.* vi. 343 A median mesogastric lobe.

‖**mesogastrium** (mɛsəʊˈgæstrɪəm). *Anat.* Also (anglicized) **mesogastry** (-gæstrɪ). [mod.L., f. Gr. μέσο-ς middle + γαστρ-, γαστήρ stomach.]

1. The umbilical region of the abdomen, between the EPIGASTRIUM and the HYPOGASTRIUM.

1855 in OGILVIE.

2. = MESOGASTER.

1846 OWEN *Vertebr. Anim.* I. *Fishes* ix. 241 There are two parallel mesogastries in the Eel. **1878** BELL tr. *Gegenbaur's Comp. Anat.* 565 The changes of the mesogastrium.

mesogenous to **mesognathy**: see MESO-.

†ˈ**mesograph.** *Obs.* [ad. Gr. μεσόγραφον mean proportional, neut. of μεσόγραφος, f. μέσο-ς middle + -γραφος written.] In quot. taken = MESOLABE.

1579–80 NORTH *Plutarch, Marcellus* (1595) 335 Certain instruments, called Mesolabes or Mesographes, which serue to find these meane lines proportionall.

mesohepar to **mesohippus**: see MESO-.

mesolabe (ˈmɛsəʊleɪb). [ad. L. *mesolabium* (Vitr.), f. Gr. μεσόλαβος (or -ον), f. μέσο-ς middle, mean + λαβ-, λαμβάνειν to take.] An instrument used for finding mean proportional lines.

1579–80 [see MESOGRAPH]. **1675** COLLINS in Rigaud *Corr. Sci. Men* (1841) I. 219 The spiral line, with M. Tschirnhaus's angular instrument, makes the mesolabe. **1789** BURNEY *Hist. Mus.* III. ii. 164 The Mesolabe..is said to have been invented either by Archytas of Tarentum or Eratosthenes for the purpose of halving an interval.

mesole (ˈmɛsəʊl). *Min.* [Named by Berzelius 1822 to indicate its close relation to *mesolite*.] A variety of THOMSONITE.

1822 BERZELIUS in *Edin. Philos. Jrnl.* VII. 6 These two minerals have a great relation with the Mesolite; and in order to distinguish them, I shall call the upper stratum Mesole, and the lower grained Mesoline. **1843** PORTLOCK *Geol.* 210 Augite occurs..in the cavities of the augitic rock at Portrush, coated by, and associated with, Mesole.

mesolect (ˈmɛsəʊlɛkt). *Linguistics.* [f. MESO- + -LECT.] In a post-creole community, a social dialect that has features in common with both the standard language and the creole; an intermediate form between the acrolect and the basilect. Also, an intermediate variety in any speech continuum.

1971 [see -LECT]. **1977** [see ACROLECT]. **1978** *Archivum Linguisticum* IX. 35 It is perhaps noteworthy that the mesolect is not a homogeneous variety. **1983** *English World-Wide* IV. 80 With respect to the continuum, sentence (3) is represented in the mesolect as well as in the polar nodes of the continuum. **1985** *Amer. Speech* LX. 34 The varieties he calls 'North Am. NE' correspond to the spectrum of mesolects in the black English of the southeastern United States.

Hence **mesoˈlectal** *a.*, of, pertaining to, or characteristic of a mesolect.

1977 *Language* LIII. 336 Casual speech is formed by switching to a basilectal variety, while careful speech is simply more mesolectal or acrolectal. **1982** [see BASILECTAL *a.*]. **1984** *English World-Wide* V. 230 Unlike true mesolectal varieties, the interlanguage pidgin is not the product of aspirations toward NSE usage from a Pidgin-proper point of departure.

mesoline (ˈmɛsəʊlaɪn). *Min.* [Named by Berzelius 1822: cf. MESOLE] A white granular mineral found in the Faroe Islands, 'now classed with levynite' (Chester *Names Min.* 1896).

1822 [see MESOLE].

mesolite (ˈmɛsəʊlaɪt). *Min.* [ad. G. *mesolith* (1816), f. Gr. μέσο-ς middle: see -LITE.] A hydrated silicate of aluminium, calcium, and sodium: so named because it is chemically intermediate between natrolite and scolecite.

1822 BERZELIUS in *Edin. Philos. Jrnl.* VII. 8 Mesolite or Needlestone from Faroe. **1883** M. F. HEDDLE in *Encycl. Brit.* XVI. 423/2 *Fargite*, consisting of two equivalents of natrolite and one of scolecite, and *Mesolite*, consisting of one of the former, and two of the latter.

mesolithic (mɛsəʊˈlɪθɪk), *a.* [f. Gr. μέσο-ς middle + λίθος stone + -IC.]

1. *Geol.* Used for MESOZOIC. *rare.*

1876 RAY LANKESTER tr. *Haeckel's Hist. Creat.* II. xv. 12 The mesolithic or mesozoic epoch.

2. *Archæol.* Belonging to a part of the prehistoric 'stone age' intermediate between the PALÆOLITHIC and the NEOLITHIC.

1866 *Jrnl. Anthropol. Soc.* IV. p. clxxxiv, The author [*sc.* H. M. Westropp] described in some detail the characteristic forms of the gravel drift, flint implements of Ireland, and polished stone implements. The following terms were proposed by the author to distinguish them—Palæolithic, Mesolithic, Kainolithic. **1888** *Pall Mall G.* 2 Apr. 10/1 Penka's attempt, in his 'Herkunft der Arier', to make out a mesolithic age. **1892** J. A. BROWN in *Jrnl. Anthrop. Inst.* XXII. 94, I venture to suggest the following four divisions. .. 1. Eolithic... 2. Palæolithic... 3. Mesolithic... 4. Neolithic. **1932** *Jrnl. R. Anthrop. Inst.* LXII. 257 Until recently the true Mesolithic was unknown in Palestine, although it was the custom among local archaeologists to describe as such the industry containing small unpolished axes or adzes which is found so abundantly on the surface all over the country. **1936, 1970** [see EPIPALÆOLITHIC *a.*]. **1975** *Guardian* 21 Jan. 6/3 The Mesolithic or Middle Stone Age. *Ibid.* 6/7 Mesolithic man achieved partial domestication of the red deer.

mesolobar, -lobe: see MESO-.

mesology (mɛˈsɒlədʒɪ). [f. Gr. μέσο-ν (neut. of μέσος middle, taken as = 'medium') + -LOGY.]
1. The science of means (of attaining happiness). Only in Bentham.

1811-31 BENTHAM *Logic* App., Wks. 1843 VIII. 283/2 Then so it is that with that portion of the field of eudæmonics which is occupied by mesology..is coincident.

2. The science of the relations between organisms and their environment.

1883 QUAIN *Dict. Med.* 973 *Mesology...* This term, recently introduced by Bertillon, conveniently expresses the investigation of the mutual relationship existing between living beings and their surroundings.

Hence **meso'logical** *a.*, pertaining to mesology; **me'sologist**, a student of mesology (*Funk's Stand. Dict.* 1895).

1886 *Buck's Handbk. Med. Sci.* III. 382/1 Grapes contain the mineral salts in variable quantity, the proportion depending on the variety of grape and on mesological conditions.

mesomere: see MESO-.

mesomerism (mɛˈsɒmərɪ(ə)m). *Chem.* [(in sense a) ad. F. *mésomérie* (A. Cornillot 1927, in *Ann. de Chim.* VIII. 267), f. *meso-* MESO- after *tautomérie* TAUTOMERISM.] †**a.** A kind of tautomerism (see quot.). *Obs.*

1928 *Chem. Abstr.* XXII. 2155 The term *mesomerism* is proposed to designate affinitive tautomerism and distinguish it from structural tautomerism (or desmotropism) and activation tautomerism (or tautomerism proper).

b. The property exhibited by certain molecules of having a structure which cannot adequately be represented by a single structural formula but can only be said to be intermediate between two or more graphical structures which differ in the distribution of electrons; resonance.

1934 *Nature* 23 June 947/1 Mesomerism and tautomerism are different concepts. **1951** I. L. FINAR *Org. Chem.* I. ii. 15 Heisenberg (1926), from quantum mechanics, supplied a theoretical background for mesomerism; he called it resonance, and this is the name which is widely used. **1973** B. J. HAZZARD tr. *Organicum* III. iv. 147 The capacity of a substituent for entering into mesomerism with a neighbouring double bond is defined as the mesomeric effect, and its sign is determined..by the polarization of the substituent accompanying the mesomerism.

So **meso'meric** *a.*, exhibiting or arising from mesomerism (sense b).

1933 C. K. INGOLD in *Jrnl. Chem. Soc.* 1124 The permanent polarisation associated with the tautomeric effect was originally distinguished by the name 'electronic strain', but this term has not proved convenient and, on account of considerations indicated later, the designation *mesomeric* effect is now substituted. **1956** E. DE B. BARNETT *Mechanism Org. Chem. Reactions* i. 5 Neither the double-bonded formula nor the dipolar formula is a true representation of the molecule, which must be regarded as a mesomeric hybrid to which both structures contribute. **1973** B. J. HAZZARD tr. *Organicum* III. iv. 146 A mesomeric system may involve not only double and triple bonds between the various bond partners but also free electron pairs conjugated with them.

mesomeristem to **mesometry:** see MESO-.

mesomorph (ˈmɛsəʊmɔːf, ˈmiːzəʊ-). [f. MESO- + Gr. μορφ-ή form.] **1.** *Anthropometry.* A person with a powerful, compact body-build in which the physical structures developed from the mesodermal layer of the embryo, i.e. the bones, muscles, and connective tissues, predominate: one of W. H. Sheldon's three constitutional types (cf. ECTOMORPH, ENDOMORPH 2).

1940 W. H. SHELDON *Varieties Human Physique* iii. 35 Bones, muscles, connective tissue..predominate overwhelmingly in the variants of type 2. We therefore call these variants mesomorphs. **1944** A. HUXLEY *Let.* 19 July (1969) 508 The football team entirely composed of big-boned, large-faced mesomorphs. **1951** AUDEN *Nones* (1952) 56 Behold the manly mesomorph Showing his splendid biceps off. **1971** J. Z. YOUNG *Introd. Study Man* xxxix. 573 In mesomorphs muscle and bone predominate, ..and they are adventurous, aggressive, extroverted, and dominating.

Hence **'mesomorphy**, the mesomorphic body-build; the quality of being mesomorphic.

1940 W. H. SHELDON *Varieties Human Physique* i. 5 Mesomorphy means relative predominance of muscle, bone, and connective tissue. **1944** [see ENDOMORPHY]. **1962** [see ECTOMORPH]. **1969** DOWNS & BLEIBTREU *Human Variation* vii. 248 A football player, for example, would be high in mesomorphy.

2. *Physical Chem.* = *mesophase* (s.v. MESO-). *rare.*

1969 [see MESOMORPHISM].

mesomorphic (mɛsəʊˈmɔːfɪk, ˈmiːzəʊ-), *a.* [f. MESO- + Gr. μορφ-ή form + -IC.] **1.** *Physical Chem.* [ad. F. *mésomorphe* (G. Friedel 1922, in *Ann. de Physique* XVIII. 273).] Existing in, pertaining to, or designating the state of a liquid crystal, intermediate between the ordered state of matter in crystals and the disordered state in ordinary liquids.

1923 *Chem. Abstr.* XVII. 3267 (*heading*) The mesomorphic states of matter. **1938** [see *liquid crystal* s.v. LIQUID *a.* 7]. **1940** GLASSTONE *Text-bk. Physical Chem.* vii.

506 Mesomorphic behavior is restricted to substances having long chains. **1962** [see *liquid crystal* s.v. LIQUID *a.* 7]. **2.** Characteristic of or resembling a mesomorph; of or pertaining to mesomorphy.

1940 W. H. SHELDON *Varieties Human Physique* i. 5 The mesomorphic physique is normally heavy, hard, and rectangular in outline. **1944** A. HUXLEY *Let.* 19 July (1969) 508 The ectomorph and his endomorphic wife in the museum, looking at the mesomorphic ideal of Greek sculpture. **1959** *Chambers's Encycl.* XI. 335/2 Correlation coefficients as high as 0·8 have been obtained..between the somatotonic component and extreme mesomorphic physique. **1963** *Punch* 25 Dec. 935/3 Mesomorphic McCarthies.

mesomorphism (mɛsəʊˈmɔːfɪz(ə)m, miːzəʊ-). *Physical Chem.* [f. MESOMORPH(IC *a.* + -ISM.] The state of being mesomorphic.

1933 [see LYOTROPIC *a.* 2]. **1969** J. S. DAVE et al. in G. H. Brown et al. *Liquid Crystals* 2 II. 229 The authors have investigated mixed mesomorphism in the binary mixtures wherein one of the components is a pure smectic mesomorph and the other a non-liquid crystalline Schiff's base.

mesomorphous (mɛsəʊˈmɔːfəs, miːzəʊ-), *a.* *Physical Chem.* [f. as prec. + -OUS.] = MESOMORPHIC *a.* 1.

1930 *Engineering* 7 Nov. 575/3 The so-called liquid crystals of Lehmann, which he regards as mesomorphous crystals. **1972** P. A. WINSOR in Brown & Labes *Liquid Crystals* 3 I. 66 An idealized phase diagram showing the relationships between the amorphous solution phase and the succession of fused mesomorphous solution phases found in binary amphiphile/water system[s] is shown.

mesomur, obs. form of MIDSUMMER.

mesomyodian (ˌmɛsəʊmaɪˈəʊdiən), *a.* *Ornith.* [f. mod.L. *Mesomyōdī* pl. (see below) + -AN. The mod.L. name was introduced by Garrod in 1876, and was f. MESO- + -*myōdī* after *Polymyōdī*, a name introduced by Joh. Müller 1847 for one of the three groups in his classification of Passerine birds; this name was intended to express 'having many song-muscles', being (irreg.) f. πολυ- (see POLY-) + μῦ-ς muscle + ᾠδή song.] Belonging to the *Mesomyodi*, a division of birds in which the intrinsic muscles of the syrinx are inserted at the middle of the upper bronchial half-ring.

1876 GARROD in *Proc. Zool. Soc.* 518 A large collection of Mesomyodian birds. **1884** COUES *Key N. Amer. Birds* (ed. 2) 239 The mesomyodian or clamatorial type of syrinx.

So **mesomy'odic**, **mesomy'odous** *adjs.*

1890 *Syd. Soc. Lex.*, *Mesomyodic*, having lateral muscles only, as the syrinx of the Suborder *Clamatores*, Order *Coracomorphæ*. **1890** *Century Dict.*, *Mesomyodous*.

‖**meson**[1] (ˈmɛsɒn). *Anat.*, etc. [mod.L., a. Gr. μέσον, neut. of μέσος middle.] The median plane, which divides a body into two symmetrical halves.

1883 WILDER & GAGE *Anat. Techn.* 33 The Meson..is a plane passing lengthwise of the body and dividing the whole into approximately equal and similar right and left halves. **1889** *Buck's Handbk. Med. Sci.* VIII. 536/1 The meson, mesal, or medial plane.

‖**meson**[2] (mɛˈsɒn). [a. Sp. *mesón* an inn.] A type of inn in Mexico (see quot. 1861).

1824 J. R. POINSETT *Notes on Mexico* iv. 32 We entered the town..and drove through it to the meson. **1847** G. A. F. RUXTON *Adventures Mexico & Rocky Mts.* viii. 52 The meson was better than usual, being the stopping place of the diligencia to Fresnillo. **1861** E. B. TYLOR *Anahuac* 209 The *meson* of Mexico is a lineal descendant of the Eastern Caravanserai... It consists of two courtyards, one surrounded by stabling and the other by miserable rooms for the travellers, who must cook their food themselves, or go elsewhere for it. **1910** A. SANTLEBEN *Texas Pioneer* 164 Meson means an inn or hostelry. **1955** *Amer. Speech* XXX. 258 *Meson*, an inn.

‖**meson**[3] (ˈmiːzɒn, ˈmɛzɒn). *Nuclear Physics.* [Alteration of the earlier name MESOTRON: see -ON[1].] **a.** Any of a group of unstable subatomic particles (first found in cosmic rays) that are intermediate in mass between an electron and a proton; the name is now commonly restricted to particles that are strongly interacting and have zero or integral spin (cf. MUON), certain of which occur in atomic nuclei as transmitters of the binding force between the nucleons.

1939 H. J. BHABHA in *Nature* 18 Feb. 276/2 The name 'mesotron' has been suggested by Anderson and Neddermeyer..for the new particle found in cosmic radiation with a mass intermediate between that of the electron and proton. It is felt that the 'tr' in this word is redundant, since it does not belong to the Greek root 'meso' for middle; the 'tr' in neutron and electron belong, of course, to the roots 'neutr' and 'electra'... It would therefore be more logical and also shorter to call the new particle a meson instead of a mesotron. **1942** POLLARD & DAVIDSON *Appl. Nucl. Physics* ii. 13 The positive and negative mesotrons or mesons should be mentioned here. **1947** *Sci. News* IV. 125 Mesons are the most penetrating component of cosmic rays. **1948** *Times* 10 Mar. 4/7 Other scientists spoke of mesons as the 'cosmic cement' which is believed to hold together the nucleus of the atom. **1963** S. TOLANSKY *Introd. Atomic Physics* (ed. 5) xxiii. 391 They [*sc.* muons] were once called mu-mesons but it was recognised that they were not in fact mesons since they had different spins. They are fermions, not bosons, and now the name meson is reserved for bosons only. **1971** *Sci. Amer.* Oct. 42/3 Such high-energy cosmic ray collisions produce a shower of secondary particles,

principally kaons (*K* mesons) and pions (pi mesons), which in turn decay spontaneously into muons. *Ibid.*, The detector, a 2,000-ton array of concrete water tanks, light-collecting tubes and gas-filled cylinders, was designed to record the arrival of muons, or mu mesons.

b. Special Comb.: **meson factory** *colloq.*, an establishment having a high-energy accelerator for producing an intense beam of mesons and the equipment for making experimental use of such a beam.

1966 *Physics Today* Dec. 21/1 Meson factories, which will produce beams of nucleons and mesons thousands of times more intense than those presently available, can be expected to take us to our next level of understanding of nuclear structure... By meson factory I mean a complete nuclear-physics installation based on an accelerator of 500–1000 MeV, which is capable of providing at least 100 microamperes of high quality external beam. All ancillary facilities for performing high precision experiments with the primary and secondary beams are included: targeting, beam transport, data-handling equipment and beam dumps for the residual beams. **1972** *Physics Bull.* Mar. 148/3 With the completion of high intensity proton accelerators, meson factories, around the world.., it will soon be possible to produce muonic atoms and molecules copiously.

meson, obs. form of MASON, MIZEN.

mesonasal: see MESO-.

†**mesonaut.** *Obs.*⁻⁰ [ad. L. *mesonauta*, one in the middle bench of rowers, f. Gr. μέσο-ς middle + ναύτης sailor.]

1623 COCKERAM, *Messonant* [sic], a gally-slaue.

mesondewe, -dieu, etc., obs. ff. MEASONDUE.

mesonemertine: see MESO-.

‖**mesonephron, -nephros** (mɛsəʊˈnɛfrɒn, -ˈnɛfrɒs). *Zool.* [mod.L., f. Gr. μέσο-ς middle + νεφρός kidney.] The Wolffian body. Hence **meso'nephric** *a.*, pertaining to the mesonephron.

1877 RAY LANKESTER in *Q. Jrnl. Microsc. Sci.* XVII. 429 The archinephric duct splits into two—one, the 'pronephric duct'..; the other, 'mesonephric duct', in connection with the posterior nephridia, forming the 'mesonephron'. **1887** *Amer. Nat.* XXI. 590 It is possible..that..an anterior section (pronephros) came to be developed earlier than the posterior portion (mesonephros). **1897** *Allbutt's Syst. Med.* IV. 340 A mesonephric fold of peritoneum.

mesonic (miː-, mɛˈzɒnɪk), *a.* *Nuclear Physics.* [f. MESON[3] + -IC.] = MESIC *a.*[2]

1939 *Nature* 8 July 78/1 The most important problem is the construction of a classical model of the heavy mass by means of a mesonic field in the same manner as the electronic mass is built up from an electromagnetic field. **1953** *Physical Rev.* XCII. 801/2 The use of the μ⁻ meson as a nuclear probe is possible because the mesonic orbits are much closer to the nucleus than the corresponding electron orbits. **1954** *Ibid.* XCVI. 1145 The effects of vacuum polarization on the energy levels of π and μ mesonic atoms are computed. **1959** *Chambers's Encycl.* XIII. 241/2 The measurement of mesonic mass is very difficult. **1968** M. S. LIVINGSTON *Particle Physics* vi. 122 The first estimate of the mass of the muon came from studies of the ionization density of the tracks of mesonic particles in cloud chamber photographs of cosmic rays.

mesonomic (mɛsəʊˈnɒmɪk, ˈmiːzəʊ-), *a.* *Law.* [f. MESO- + Gr. νόμ-ος law + -IC.] In the terminology of A. Kocourek: 'a jural relation which does not directly affect the natural physical freedom of a human being with the support of the law but yet has legal consequences in its evolution'. Opp. ZYGNOMIC *a.*

1927 A. KOCOUREK *Jural Relations* v. 69 Compared with zygnomic relations, mesonomic relations are inferior in legal potency. A zygnomic relation directly constrains the servus of the relation with the support of the law, but a mesonomic relation either does not constrain the servus directly or lacks the support of the law. **1930** —— *Introd. Sci. of Law* iv. 294 Put broadly, the function of mesonomic relations is to initiate or destroy zygnomic relations. *Ibid.*, Mesonomic relations have many different forms and functions... The power to commit a tort is mesonomic. The duty to pay damages for the tort is zygnomic. The power to violate a contract is mesonomic. The duty to pay damages is zygnomic... A duty owed by a subject to the sovereign not to commit a crime is mesonomic. The power of a prosecutor to prosecute a criminal offender is zygnomic. **1964** J. STONE *Legal Syst. & Lawyers' Reasonings* iv. 148 Kocourek's mesonomic-zygnomic distinction is no doubt a valuable one, even if we shrink back at the neologisms. *Ibid.* 149 For citizens' counsellors, as well as for citizens.., it is predominantly in the range of alternative courses left open by privileges and powers, the mesonomic relations, that attention and concern mainly moves.

mesonotal to **mesopause:** see MESO-.

mesopelagic (mɛsəʊpɪˈlædʒɪk, miːzəʊ-), *a.* *Biol.* [f. MESO- + PELAGIC *a.*] Of, pertaining to, or designating the intermediate depths of the sea, *spec.* those between 200 and a thousand metres down.

1951 ALLEE & SCHMIDT *Hesse's Ecol. Animal Geogr.* (ed. 2) xiv. 312 The eyes of many mesopelagic animals are especially large. **1957** *Mem. Geol. Soc. Amer.* LXVII. I. 643 Among the typical animals of the mesopelagic zone..are such well-known fishes as *Idiacanthus, Chauliodus, Stomias,* and the lantern fishes. **1964** *Oceanogr. & Marine Biol.* II.

367 The photophores of most mesopelagic animals shine downwards (if the creature swims with its ventral surface downwards), and the colour of the light they emit is approximately that of..transmitted sun- and sky-light. **1970** [see *dysphotic* adj. s.v. DYS-]. **1975** *Nature* 5 June 452/2 The mesopelagic migrants, spending the daytime at depths down to perhaps 1,000 m and rising to within 200 m or so of the surface at night, show an increased respiratory rate not only with increased temperature but also with increased pressure.

mesophase to **mesophlebitis**: see MESO-.

‖**mesophlœum** (mɛsəʊˈfliːəm). *Bot.* [mod.L., f. Gr. μέσο-ς middle + φλοιός bark.] The middle layer of the bark in exogens.

1839 LINDLEY *Introd. Bot.* I. ii. (ed. 3) 89 The Mesophlœum of Link, or cellular integument of others, composed of cells, usually green.

mesophragm (ˈmɛsəfræm). *Zool.* Also in Latin form. [ad. mod.L. *mesophragma*, f. Gr. μέσο-ς middle + φράγμα partition.] **a.** *Ent.* The partition that separates the mesothorax from the metathorax. **b.** In Crustacea (see quot. 1880).

1826 KIRBY & Sp. *Entomol.* III. 379 *Mesophragma* (the Mesophragm). **1880** HUXLEY *Crayfish* iv. 158 The inner prolongation of the capital [of an endosternite] is called the mesophragm. **1899** D. SHARP *Insects* II. (Camb. Nat. Hist.) 312 The great mesophragma.

Hence **mesophragmal** (mɛsəʊˈfrægməl) *a.*, pertaining to the mesophragm.

1877 HUXLEY *Anat. Inv. Anim.* vi. 310 The mesophragmal [apophysis].

mesophyll (ˈmɛsəʊfɪl). *Bot.* Also in Latin form. [ad. mod.L. *mesophyllum*, f. Gr. μέσο-ς middle + φύλλον leaf.]

1. The parenchyma of a leaf; the soft inner tissue of a leaf lying between the upper and lower layers of epidermis. (Cf. DIACHYMA, DIPLOE.)

1839 LINDLEY *Introd. Bot.* (ed. 3) 122 The cellular tissue of which the rest of the leaf is composed is parenchyma, which Link then calls *diachyma*, or that immediately beneath the two surfaces *cortex*, and the intermediate substance *diploe*. De Candolle calls these two, taken together, the *mesophyllum*. **1848** —— *Introd. Bot.* (ed. 4) I. 253 The cellular tissue of the bark, mesophyll or cortical integument.

attrib. **1881** DARWIN *Veg. Mould* 41 Some of the mesophyll cells contained nothing but broken down granular matter.

2. The line of demarcation between a leaf and the leaf-stalk. ? *Obs.*

1839 LINDLEY *Introd. Bot.* II. v. (ed. 3) 319 The line of demarcation between the internode and petiole is called the *mesophytum*; that between the lamina and petiole the *mesophyllum*.

mesophyllic (mɛsəʊˈfɪlɪk), *a. Bot.* [f. Gr. μέσο-ς + φύλλ-ον leaf + -IC.] Belonging to or situated in the middle of a leaf.

1882–4 COOKE *Brit. Freshw. Algæ* I. 202 A tube..which..proceeds as far as the mesophyllic parenchyma.

mesophyte (ˈmɛsəʊfaɪt). *Bot.* [f. Gr. μέσο-ς middle + φυτόν plant.]

1. A plant belonging to a class intermediate between hydrophytes and xerophytes, *i.e.* avoiding extremes of moisture and dryness.

1899 HALSTED in *Pop. Sci. Monthly* Nov. 110. **1902** J. M. COULTER *Plant Studies* 175 There is a great middle region of medium water supply, and plants which occupy it are known as mesophytes, the plants of medium conditions.

2. (See quot.)

1890 *Syd. Soc. Lex.*, *Mesophyte*, applied by Clarion to that which is commonly called the vital knot in plants, that is to say, the line of demarcation between the ascending and descending parts of the vegetable.

Hence **mesoˈphytic** *a.*, pertaining to or characterized by the class of plants called mesophytes.

1899 *Nat. Science* July 10 The mesophytic woods.

‖**mesophytum** (meˈsɒfɪtəm). *Bot.* [mod.L. form of MESOPHYTE.] **a.** The line of demarcation between the internode and the petiole. **b.** = MESOPHYTE 2.

1839 [see MESOPHYLL 2]. In mod. Dicts.

mesopic to **mesopleuron**: see MESO-.

mesopod, -pode (ˈmɛsəpɒd, -pəʊd), *sb. Zool.* Anglicized form of MESOPODIUM.

1877 RAY LANKESTER in *Q. Jrnl. Microsc. Sci.* XVII. 431 Development of a mesopod (molluscan foot). **1890** *Syd. Soc. Lex.*, *Mesopode*.

mesopod (ˈmɛsəpɒd), *a. Bot.* [ad. mod.L. *mesopod-us*, f. Gr. μέσο-ς (see MESO-) + ποδ-, πούς foot.] Having a short stalk centrally placed.

1857 BERKELEY *Cryptog. Bot.* §393 Hydnum in all its varied forms, resupinate, apodous, lateral, merismoid, and mesopod.

‖**mesopodium** (mɛsəʊˈpəʊdɪəm). [mod.L., f. Gr. μέσο-ς middle + ποδ-, πούς foot: see -IUM.]

1. *Zool.* The median region of the foot in mollusca.

1853 HUXLEY in *Phil. Trans.* CXLIII. I. 36 The posterior edge of the propodium carries a cup-shaped disk... This is commonly called the sucker... It may be called the mesopodium. **1883** RAY LANKESTER in *Encycl. Brit.* XVI. 653/1 The foot of the Azygobranchia..often divided into..a fore, middle, and hind lobe, pro-, meso-, and metapodium.

2. *Bot.* The intermediate portion of the phyllopodium.

1895 VINES *Bot.* ii. 45.

Hence **mesoˈpodial** *a.*, relating to the mesopodium.

In recent Dicts.

Mesopotamia (mɛsəpəˈteɪmɪə). [a. Gr. μεσοποταμία (sc. χωρά) country between two rivers (applied spec. as below), f. μέσο-ς middle + ποταμός river.] **1. a.** A proper name for the tract between the Tigris and the Euphrates. Sometimes used *allusively* in etymological sense for: A tract between two rivers.

1854 R. G. LATHAM *Native Races Russian Emp.* 177 The Doab, Entre Rios, or Mesopotamia, bounded by the rivers Obi and Irtish. **1886** *Pall Mall Gaz.* 23 June 13/2 Every Oxford man has known and loved the beauties of the walk called Mesopotamia. **1944** G. B. CRESSEY *Asia's Lands & Peoples* xxvi. 401/2 The land between the rivers, that is, the true 'Mesopotamia', is thus capable of easy irrigation from either side. **1963** A. R. WOOLLEY *Clarendon Guide Oxf.* 130 A path continues between the river and a mill-race and this is known as Mesopotamia.

b. = BELGRAVIA.

1864 E. YATES *Broken to Harness* (ed. 3) xv. 271 A house in Great Adullam Street, Macpelah Square, in that district of London whilom known as 'Mesopotamia'.

2. As the type of a word which is long, pleasant-sounding, and incomprehensible; used allusively for something which gives irrational or inexplicable comfort or satisfaction to the hearer (see quots.).

1827 SCOTT *Chron. Canongate* 1st Ser. I. v. 109 She resembled exactly in her criticism the devotee who pitched on the 'sweet word Mesopotamia', as the most edifying note which she could bring away from a sermon. **1870** *Brewer's Dict. Phr. & Fable* 572/1 *The true 'Mesopotamia' ring..i.e.*, something high-sounding and pleasing, but wholly past comprehension. The allusion is to the story of an old woman who told her pastor that she 'found great support in that comfortable word *Mesopotamia*'. **1886** 'M. GRAY' *Silence of Dean Maitland* III. III. iv. 94 It was said of the Bishop of Belminster that he could pronounce the mystic word 'Mesopotamia' in such a manner as to affect his auditors to tears; but of the dean it might be averred that his pronunciation of 'Mesopotamia' caused the listeners' hearts to vibrate with every sorrow and every joy they had ever known, all in the brief space of time occupied by the utterance of that affecting word. **1906** F. M. PARSONS *Garrick & his Circle* 245 Whitefield possessed the inborn gift of preaching to the nerves, and there is an edifying, though probably fallacious, report of Garrick's having remarked that he could pronounce 'Mesopotamia' in such a way as to move any audience to tears. **1908** G. B. SHAW *Platform & Pulpit* (1962) 47 There are people who will swallow as inspired revelation any sort of stuff that, so to speak, has the word Mesopotamia in it. **1924** L. PARIO *What is Modernism?* p. xviii, The reaction to words is a curious psychological—I suspect pathological— phenomenon. The oft-told tale of the good woman who found 'Mesopotamia' a soothing word is one example.

Mesopotamian (mɛsəpəˈteɪmɪən), *a.* and *sb.* [f. prec. + -AN.] **a.** *adj.* Pertaining to Mesopotamia. **b.** *sb.* A native or inhabitant of Mesopotamia (the larger part of which is now Iraq).

1616 T. CORYAT *Traveller for English Wits* 42 Your generosities most obliged Countreyman,..the Hierosolymitan - Syrian - Mesopotamian - Armenian - Median.., Thomas Coryate. **1673** A. WOODHEAD *Guide to Controversies Relig.* (ed. 2) III. viii. 283 The Assyrians, Persians, and Mesopotamians, are ranged also under a new Patriarch. **1880** R. S. POOLE in *Encycl. Brit.* XI. 808/2 Mesopotamian cuneiform. **1935** HUXLEY & HADDON *We Europeans* vi. 175 A North Syrian group which received accretions from Mesopotamian, Egyptian, Hittite, Amorite, and perhaps other sources. **1952** GERTH & MARTINDALE tr. *Weber's Anc. Judaism* I. i. 6 The rise to political prominence of Babylonian power at the end of the third millenium and the continuous ascendancy of Babylon..constituted later aspects of Mesopotamian influence. **1954** H. FRANKFORT *Art & Archit. Anc. Orient* p. xxv, The Mesopotamians congregated in cities. *Ibid.* 6 The Mesopotamian deeply felt the enormity of the presumption that man should offer residence to a deity. **1974** *Encycl. Brit. Micropædia* VI. 820/1 Because religion provided the only total view of existence in ancient Mesopotamian civilization, religious themes, attitudes, and presuppositions were frequently included in quasi-secular writings.

mesopotamic (mɛsəpəˈtæmɪk), *a. rare.* [Formed as prec. + -IC.] Of the nature of a 'Mesopotamia' or district between two rivers.

1895 *Archæol. Æliana* XVII. II. 283 French antiquaries assign the mesopotamic part of Belgium as the birth-place of Carausius.

‖**mesopterygium** (ˌmɛsəʊptəˈrɪdʒɪəm). *Ichthyol.* [mod.L., f. Gr. μέσο-ς middle + πτερύγιον fin, dim. of πτέρυξ wing.] The central flat cartilaginous portion of the fin in certain fishes.

1878 MIVART in *Nature* 18 July 309/2 Three basal cartilages..called respectively the *Propterygium*, the *Mesopterygium*, and the *Metapterygium*.

Hence **mesopteˈrygial** *a.*, pertaining to the mesopterygium.

In recent Dicts.

mesopterygoid (mɛsəʊˈptɛrɪgɔɪd). *Zool.* [f. MESO- + PTERYGOID.]

1. In full ***mesopterygoid process***: In birds, the part of the pterygoid which articulates with the palatine bone or the basipterygoid process of the splenoid, or with both.

1875 W. K. PARKER in *Encycl. Brit.* III. 706/2 'Mesopterygoid process'. *Ibid.* 711/1 All the *Schizognathæ*, except the Fowl tribe, have 'meso-pterygoids'.

b. ***mesopterygoid fossa***: see quot.

1881 MIVART *Cat* iii. 70 The very considerable space included between the two pterygoid plates is called the meso-pterygoid fossa, and that is single and median.

2. In teleostean fishes, a thin bony lamina in the skull, which fits against the upper edge of the pterygoid.

1890 in *Syd. Soc. Lex.*

mesorchium to **mesorostral**: see MESO-.

mesorrhine, mesorhine (ˈmɛsəʊraɪn), *a.* and *sb. Anthropology.* [f. Gr. μέσο-ς middle + ῥῖν-, ῥίν nose.]

A. *adj.* Applied by Broca to noses, skulls, or persons having a nasal index from 48 to 53 (intermediate between *leptorrhine* and *platyrrhine*).

1878 FLOWER in *Proc. Roy. Inst.* VIII. 616. **1896** A. H. KEANE *Ethnol.* 284 Narrower nose, often mesorrhine and prominent.

B. *sb.* A person or skull having a nasal index intermediate between leptorrhine and platyrrhine. Hence **ˈmesorrhiny**, the state or quality of being mesorrhine.

1904 *Biometrika* Mar.–July 214 Nasal Index. Mesorrhiny. **1953** BEALS & HOIJER *Introd. Anthropol.* iv. 98 Mesorrhines, like the Polynesians, who live in tropical regions.

mesorrhinian, mesorhinian (mɛsəʊˈrɪnɪən, mɛsəʊˈraɪnɪən), *a.* and *sb. Anthropology.* [f. prec. + -IAN.] **a.** *adj.* = MESORRHINE. **b.** *sb.* A person having a mesorrhine skull.

1878 BARTLEY tr. *Topinard's Anthrop.* II. ii. 257 The mesorrhinians, with the nasal skeleton moderate. **1887** *Nature* 10 Feb. 357/1 Including under the platyrhinian section all the black races, under the mesorhinian the yellow races.

‖**mesorrhinium, -inum** (mɛsəʊˈrɪnɪəm, -ˈaɪnəm). *Ornith.* [mod.L., f. Gr. μέσο-ς middle + ῥῖν-, ῥίν nose.] (See quots.)

1856 MAYNE *Expos. Lex.*, *Mesorhinium*... Term used by Illiger for the part of the beak which is comprised between the two nostrils. **1892** MIVART *Elem. Ornithol.* 147 The part of the bill between the nostrils is called the *mesorhinum*.

mesoscale (ˈmɛsəʊskeɪl, ˈmiːzəʊ-). *Meteorol.* Also meso-scale. [f. MESO- + SCALE *sb.*[3]] An intermediate scale, between that of high- and low-pressure systems on the one hand and that of microclimates on the other, on which such phenomena as storms occur. Freq. *attrib.*

1956 T. FUJITA *Mesoanalysis of the Illinois Tornado of Apr. 9, 1953* (Univ. of Chicago Dept. Meteorol. Technical Rep. to U.S. Weather Bureau, Contract No. Cwb 8613) 2 A method of analyzing mesoscale charts. **1959** *Modernizing the Aviation Weather Service* (U.S. Weather Bureau) 39 This meso-scale is considered a necessary link between the present synoptic scale and local weather events. **1969** *Britannica Bk. of Year* (U.S.) 518 Basic research continued into cyclonic storms and other aspects of the meso-scale or so-called secondary circulation of the atmosphere, including tropical cyclones (hurricanes and typhoons), mid- and high-latitude lows, and tornadoes. **1970** *Nature* 15 Aug. 646/2 Is there any sense in seeking to understand the effects of, say, major afforestation schemes on climate in the surrounding region without knowing much more about the behaviour of the atmosphere on the mesoscale? **1971** *Sci. News Let.* 30 Jan. 81 Dr. H. A. Panofsky..pointed to weaknesses in the knowledge of mesoscale meteorology, the meteorology of areas 10 to 20 miles in diameter. **1974** *Times Lit. Suppl.* 13 Sept. 982/3 Given the 3 to 5 kilometre photographic resolution, satellite data are most usefully applied to macroscale phenomena such as the major global wind patterns, or to mesoscale phenomena ranging in scale from 10 to 100 kilometres.

mesoscapula to **mesoseismal**: see MESO-.

mesoseme (ˈmɛsəʊsiːm). [a. F. *mésosème* (Broca), f. Gr. μέσο-ς middle + σῆμα sign, 'index'.] Of skulls: Having an orbital index from 84 to 89.

1878 FLOWER in *Proc. Roy. Inst.* VIII. 617 It is convenient to group them [orbital indices] into three—the high (*megaseme*), intermediate (*mesoseme*), and low (*microseme*). **1886** MACALISTER in *Jrnl. Anthrop. Inst.* XVI. 151 The average Fijian being platyrhine and mesoseme. **1896** *Nat. Science* Sept. 154 The skull is mesoseme (87·8).

mesosiderite (mɛsəʊˈsɪdəraɪt, -saɪˈdɪəraɪt, miːzəʊ-). *Geol.* [ad. G. *mesosiderit* (G. Rose 1865, in *Amtlicher Bericht 39. Versammlung deutscher Naturforscher und Ärzte, Giessen 1864* 111); see MESO- and SIDERITE[1].] Any of the stony-iron meteorites in which the silicates are principally present as pyroxene and plagioclase.

1868 *Geol. Mag.* V. 76 Meteorites have long since been arranged under two great divisions, the irons and the stones. .. In examining a certain number of these masses it has been

thought convenient by some to establish a third, or intermediate division, to which the names of *Mesosiderites*, *Lithosiderites*, or of *Siderolites*, have been given. *Ibid.* 78 For these meteorites M. Rose has proposed a special name, that of *mesosiderites*. **1918** G. T. PRIOR in *Mineral. Mag.* XVIII. 151 In the Rose-Tschermak-Brezina classification of meteorites the intermediate class of stony-irons, in which iron and stony matter occur in approximately equal amounts and to which Maskelyne gave the name siderolites, is divided into (1) siderolites proper..and (2) lithosiderites, comprising the groups of the mesosiderites, grahamites, and lodranites. Mesosiderites are defined as consisting of iron and crystalline olivine and bronzite... As seen in the following pages, chemical and microscopic examination of typical members of these two groups fails to reveal any real distinction between them based on the amount of felspar they contain. For the combined group, all the members of which contain abundant felspar, it is proposed to retain the earlier name of mesosiderite. **1962** B. MASON *Meteorites* viii. 120 The stony-irons are a minor group of meteorites... They are divided into two major groups according to the nature of the silicate minerals, the pallasites (olivine stony-irons) and mesosiderites (pyroxene-plagioclase stony-irons).

mesosome (mɛsəʊˈsəʊmə). Also **mesosoma**. [f. mod.L. *mesosoma*, f. Gr. μέσο-ς middle + σῶμα body.] **1.** *Zool.* **a.** In lamellibranchiate molluscs, the middle region of the body which gives rise to the foot. **b.** In Arachnids, the middle portion of the animal, between 'head' and 'tail'. **c.** The central part of the body of certain other invertebrates.

1877 HUXLEY *Anat. Inv. Anim.* viii. 475 From the sides of the mesosoma..the branchiae project into the pallial cavity. **1932** BORRADAILE & POTTS *Invertebrata* xv. 450 The lung books are found on segments 3–6 of the mesosoma. **1962** D. NICHOLS *Echinoderms* xiv. 174 The lophophore itself is borne by the mesosome, and there is a strong partition between this division of the body and the metasome.

2. *Bacteriology.* A cytoplasmic structure in many bacteria which is principally composed of membranes, probably being formed by invagination of the cell membrane, and may be a site of active respiratory activity and the place of attachment of the bacterial genome.

1960 P. C. FITZ-JAMES in *Jrnl. Biophysical & Biochem. Cytol.* VIII. 508/2 This [*sc.* 'dense body'] is probably an unsuitable name. Certainly they are not always electron dense... Since they appear to be attached to the surface membranes of the cell, one should adopt the suggestion of Robertson..for such membrane-attached cytoplasmic structures and use the term 'mesosomes'. Henceforth in this paper this term will be used. **1968** H. HARRIS *Nucleus & Cytoplasm* vi. 123 The loss of the ability to form the cell wall appears to be associated with the disappearance from the cytoplasm of the cell of specific membranous structures, known as 'mesosomes', which appear to be essential for the formation of the wall. **1974** *Nature* 1 Feb. 303/1 These properties together with the possession of fimbriae and the absence of mesosomes are commonly shared by Gram-negative, but generally absent in Gram-positive bacteria.

Hence **mesosoˈmatic** *a.*, pertaining to the mesosoma.

1893 SHIPLEY *Zool. Invertebr.* xx. 391 The seventh appendage, or the first mesosomatic, consists of a semi-circular plate-like structure hinged on to the body.

mesosperm (ˈmɛsəʊspɜːm). *Bot.* [ad. mod.L. *mesosperm-um*, f. Gr. μέσο-ς middle + σπέρμ-α seed.] The middle coat or covering of a seed.

1849 BALFOUR *Man. Bot.* §578 Sometimes the secundine remains distinct in the seed, forming what has been called a *mesosperm*. **1852** HENSLOW *Dict. Bot. Terms*, *Mesospermum*. Synonyme for Sarcodermis.

mesospore (ˈmɛsəʊspɔə(r)). *Bot.* Also in Latin form **mesosporium**. [ad. mod.L. *mesosporium*, f. Gr. μέσο-ς middle + σπόρ-ος seed.] The middle layer of a spore. Hence **mesoˈsporic** *a.*, pertaining to a mesospore (in recent Dicts.).

1882–4 COOKE *Brit. Fresh-w. Algæ* I. 109 The cell-contents surround themselves with a new layer of cellulose (mesosporium) within the original one (exosporium). *Ibid.* 311 Mesosporium, Mesospore.

mesostaphyline, -stasis: see MESO-.

mesosternal (mɛsəʊˈstɜːnəl), *a.* and *sb.* [f. MESOSTERNUM + -AL[1].]

A. *adj.* Pertaining to the mesosternum.

1816 KIRBY & SP. *Entomol.* vi. (1843) I. 162 *note* 1, Those tribes of *Melolontha* F., that have mesosternal prominence. **1868** W. K. PARKER *Shoulder-girdle Vertebr.* 119 The two additional meso-sternal segments of the Cyclodonts.

B. *sb.* A mesosternal part or element.

1854 OWEN *Skel. & Teeth* in *Circ. Sci.* I. *Org. Nat.* 216 In some extinct chelonia the number of these lateral elements of the plastron is increased by an intercalated pair, which I have called, 'mesosternals'. **1868** W. K. PARKER *Shoulder-girdle Vertebr.* 223 In Cercocebus there are five well-made meso-sternals.

‖**mesosternebra** (mɛsəʊˈstɜːnɪbrə). *Anat.* Also anglicized **-sterneber**. [mod.L., f. Gr. μέσο-ς middle + *sternebra*: see STERNEBRA.] Any of the sternebræ which intervene between the manubrium of the sternum and the ensiform appendage. Hence **mesoˈsternebral** *a.*

In recent Dicts.

mesosternite (mɛsəʊˈstɜːnaɪt). *Zool.* [f. MESO- + STERNITE.] A mesosternal sternite.

1888 ROLLESTON & JACKSON *Anim. Life* 303 [In the Geometrical Spider.] Mesosternite, surrounded by the basal joints of the four ambulatory limbs.

‖**mesosternum** (mɛsəʊˈstɜːnəm). [mod.L., f. MESO- + STERNUM.]

1. *Ent.* †**a.** In Kirby's use (see quot. 1826). **b.** By later writers applied to the middle 'sternum'.

1826 KIRBY & SP. *Entomol.* III. 566 The central part of the *medipectus*, or that which passes between the mid-legs when elevated, protruded, or otherwise remarkable, is called the *mesosternum* or mid-breast-bone. **1836** SHUCKARD tr. *Burmeister's Man. Entom.* 82 The *mesosternum* (*peristethium* of Kirby and Spence), is, as well as the scapulæ, divided into two parts.

2. *Anat.* That part of the breast-bone lying between the præsternum and the xiphisternum.

1868 W. K. PARKER *Shoulder-girdle Vertebr.* 71 The three great divisions into manubrium (præ-sternum), body (mesosternum), and xiphoid process (xiphisternum) are marked out. **1872** NICHOLSON *Palæont.* 399 All the other ribs are connected with the mesosternum.

mesostethium to **mesothecium**: see MESO-.

mesothelioma (ˌmɛsəʊθiːlɪˈəʊmə). *Path.* Pl. **-omas, -omata.** [f. next + -OMA.] A tumour of mesothelium; formerly, †a tumour composed of cells derived from the embryonic mesothelium.

1909 J. G. ADAMI *Princ. Path.* I. 647 Of mesothelial origin: Tumors (mesotheliomas) whose characteristic constituents are cells derived in direct descent from the persistent mesothelium of the embryo. (*a*) Typical.—Adenoma of kidney, testicle,..'mesothelioma' of pleuræ, peritoneum, etc. *Ibid.* 746 If a convenient term is required for all this order of tumors, the transitional adenocarcinomas of adrenal, kidney, ovary, and testis, we have, from embryogenetic considerations, suggested the term mesothelioma. **1921** *Lancet* 23 July 173/2 The true nature of these tumours has been the subject of much controversy as is seen by the variety of names given to them —e.g. endothelial cancer,..mesothelioma, and so on. **1966** WRIGHT & SYMMERS *Systemic Path.* I. i. 6/1 Primary tumours of the pericardium..are very rare: most of those that have been described appear to have arisen from mesothelial cells, and may in consequence be termed 'mesotheliomas'. **1971** *Brit. Med. Bull.* XXVII. 71/2 Wagner..discovered the first of a large group of pleural and peritoneal tumours—mesotheliomata—apparently related to exposure to crocidolite. **1973** *Nature* 8 June 352/2 Mesotheliomas of the pleura and peritoneum have been linked with the inhalation of asbestos fibres.

mesothelium (mɛsəʊ-, miːzəʊˈθiːlɪəm). *Embryol.* and *Histology.* Pl. **-thelia.** [f. MESO- + EPI)THELIUM.] In a vertebrate embryo, epithelium that forms the surface layer of the mesoderm and lines the body-cavity; in a post-natal organism, the tissue derived from this that forms the lining of the pleuræ, peritoneum, and pericardium (by some writers, esp. pathologists, not regarded as epithelium).

1886 C. S. MINOT in *Buck's Handbk. Med. Sci.* III. 176/1 The whole of the mesoderm..does not go through this metamorphosis, but..a part remains closely compacted; but ultimately it is only the single layer of cells immediately bounding the cœlom, and the cells constituting the myotomes.., which remain thus close together. These cells, therefore, have all the characteristics of an epithelium, so that the cœlom is limited by an epithelium of cuboidal cells, for which I have proposed the name *mesothelium*. *Ibid.* 176/2 Derivatives of the mesothelium (epithelial mesoderm). **1945** W. J. HAMILTON et al. *Human Embryol.* vi. 80 The mesoderm bounding the coelom [of the embryo] will persist throughout life as an epithelium (so-called mesothelium) which forms the visceral and parietal linings of the peritoneal, pleural and pericardial cavities. Parts of the peritoneal mesothelium become specialized to form the germinal epithelium, the paramesonephric ducts..and the cortex of the suprarenal gland. **1950** A. W. HAM *Histol.* xi. 140/1 Endothelium and mesothelium, structurally, are both typically epithelial... Nevertheless, pathologists usually prefer to consider endothelium and mesothelium as apart from ordinary epithelium because endothelial and mesothelial cells behave differently from ordinary epithelial cells. **1960** F. D. ALLAN *Essent. Human Embryol.* xvii. 165 The cells of the cortical primordium are derived from the coelomic mesothelium. **1968** PASSMORE & ROBSON *Compan. Med. Stud.* I. xvii. 3/2 Endothelia and mesothelia arise only from mesoderm.

Hence **mesoˈthelial** *a.*

1892 C. S. MINOT *Human Embryol.* (1897) vii. 159 Although the pancreas, ovary, and spinal cord all contain connective tissue, we do not call them mesenchymal, but respectively entodermal, mesothelial, and ectodermal. **1946** B. M. PATTEN *Human Embryol.* xv. 469 In the case of a part of the gut tract which lies within the body cavity, the corresponding connective-tissue layer will be supplemented by an epithelial layer derived from the mesoderm which lines the coelomic cavities... This mesothelial layer provides a smooth, moist surface which permits the viscera within the body cavity to change shape and position with a minimum amount of friction. **1950** [see above]. **1968** PASSMORE & ROBSON *Compan. Med. Stud.* I. xvi. 5/2 (*heading*) Mesothelial or serosal sac membranes.

mesotherium: see MESO-.

mesotherm (ˈmɛsəʊθɜːm). *Bot.* [f. Gr. μέσο-ς middle + θερμός hot. Cf. MEIOTHERM.] A plant requiring a moderately warm temperature. Hence **mesoˈthermic** *a.*

1875 J. G. BAKER *Bot. Geog.* 48 Mesotherm, characteristic of the subtropical or warm-temperature zone, and therefore needing to be entirely protected from frost. *Ibid.* 51 Mesotherm types. *Ibid.* 102 Geographical Range of the Mesotherms. **1903** W. R. FISHER tr. *Schimper's Plant-Geogr.* 236 The most important family of the north temperate zone among the *Polycarpicae*, that of the Ranunculaceæ, is mesothermic and microthermic. **1960** N. POLUNIN *Introd. Plant Geogr.* x. 201 Examples [of climatic relics] are the mesothermic plants to be found in some boreal areas that have cooled at least since the 'postglacial optimum' when such plants presumably migrated to these areas. *Ibid.* 285 The great world vegetational zones.. depend primarily on temperature, and we find it convenient to distinguish between megatherms (plants favouring warm habitats), microtherms (plants favouring cold habitats), and the intermediate mesotherms.

mesothesis (mɛˈsɒθɪsɪs). *rare.* [f. Gr. μέσο-ς middle + θέσις action of putting: see THESIS.] Something interposed, serving to connect or reconcile antagonistic agencies or principles.

1812–29 COLERIDGE in *Lit. Rem.* (1838) III. 93 Both alike have quenched the Holy Spirit, as the mesothesis of the two. **1849** FROUDE *Nemesis of Faith* 157 The final mesothesis for the reconciling the two great rivals, Science and Revelation.

mesothet (ˈmɛsəʊθɛt). *rare*[−1]. [f. Gr. μέσο-ς middle + θετόν neut. of θετός placed.] = prec. (In quot. humorously pedantic.)

1850 KINGSLEY *Alt. Locke* xxi, A curious pair of 'poles' the two made; the mesothet whereof, by no means a *punctum indifferens*, but a true connecting spiritual idea, stood on the table—in the whisky-bottle.

So **mesothetic** (mɛsəʊˈθɛtɪk), **mesoˈthetical** *adjs.*, occupying a middle position.

1837 *Fraser's Mag.* XVI. 97 Mr. Carlyle avoids the synthetical, as well as the analytical, and looks down upon both from the mesothetical. **1848** KINGSLEY *Yeast* xv, An honest development of the true idea of Protestantism, which is paving the way to the mesothetic art of the future. **1871** —— in *Devon. Assoc. Trans.* IV. 384 While the true philosopher sought for the mesothetic or middle truth.

‖**mesothorax** (mɛsəʊˈθɔəræks). *Ent.* [mod.L., f. MESO- + THORAX.] The middle ring or segment of the thorax of insects.

1826 KIRBY & SP. *Entomol.* xxxiii. III. 371. **1833** G. R. GRAY *Entom. Australia* 1. 18 The mesothorax [of *Trigonoderus Childrenii*] is somewhat triangular in form, and keeled down the centre. **1870** ROLLESTON *Anim. Life* 77 The dorsal part of the mesothorax.

Hence **mesothoracic** (-θəˈræsɪk) *a.*, pertaining to the mesothorax.

1839 WESTWOOD *Mod. Classif. Insects* I. 17 The mesothoracic and metathoracic segments. **1878** RILEY in *Amer. Nat.* XII. 215 The first pair of spiracles are distinctly mesothoracic and dorsal in the triungulin.

mesothorium (mɛsəʊˈθɔərɪəm, miːzəʊ-). *Chem.* [mod.L. (O. Hahn 1907, in *Ber. d. Deut. Chem. Ges.* XL. 1469): see MESO- and THORIUM.] Either of two radioactive nuclides in the thorium decay series: ***mesothorium I*** (symbol MsThI), the isotope of radium with mass number 228, produced by the alpha decay of thorium 232, or ***mesothorium II*** (symbol MsThII), the isotope of actinium with mass number 228, produced by the beta decay of mesothorium I.

1907 *Jrnl. Chem. Soc.* XCII. II. 359 The suggestion is made that thorium is not directly transformed into radiothorium, but into an intermediate product, 'Mesothorium', which then yields radiothorium. **1935** *Jrnl. R. Aeronaut. Soc.* XXXIX. 857 The mesothorium preparation produces a point source of gamma radiation suitable for the inspection of thick metal objects for which X-ray investigation becomes very expensive. **1937** *Nature* 21 Aug. 318/1 *Lemna* [duckweed] accumulates mesothorium I and concentrates it a hundredfold as compared with its content in the water. **1969** R. F. LANG tr. *Henglein's Chem. Technol.* 546 Mesothorium is present in monazite to the extent of 1 mg per t, and serves as a substitute for radium.

mesotonic (mɛsəʊˈtɒnɪk), *a. Mus.* [f. Gr. μέσο-ς middle + τόν-ος TONE + -IC.] = MEAN TONE *adj.*

1864 A. J. ELLIS in *Proc. Roy. Soc.* XIII. 408 This is known as the System of Mean Tones, or the *Mesotonic System*, as it will be here termed. **1896** A. J. HIPKINS *Pianoforte* 103 To extend Mesotonic or Mean tone tuning to the keys of E flat and A flat major.

‖**mesotrocha** (mɛˈsɒtrəkə), *sb. pl.* Also **-æ**. [mod.L., f. Gr. μέσο-ς middle + τροχός wheel, rim.] Ciliated larvæ of polychætous annelids in which one or more rows of cilia encircle the middle of the body. Hence **meˈsotrochal** *a.*, also **meˈsotrochous** *a.* (in recent Dicts.), having a ciliated ring round the middle.

1877 HUXLEY *Anat. Inv. Anim.* v. 243 Mesotrocha. *Ibid.* 248 A mesotrochal Annelidan larva. **1888** ROLLESTON & JACKSON *Anim. Life* 606 Mesotrochae.

mesotron (ˈmiː-, ˈmɛzəʊtrɒn, ˈmɛsəʊtrɒn). *Nuclear Physics.* Now *rare* or *Obs.* [f. MESO- + -TRON.] The name orig. given to the meson (MESON[3]).

1938 ANDERSON & NEDDERMEYER in *Nature* 12 Nov. 878/2 The existence of particles intermediate in mass between protons and electrons has been shown in experiments on the cosmic radiation... We should like to suggest..the word 'mesotron' (intermediate particle) as a name for the new particles. It appears quite likely that the appropriateness of this name will not be lost, whatever new facts concerning these particles may be learned in the future. **1939** *Ibid.* 13

May 796/2 The meson or mesotron was first introduced by Yukawa to serve as the connecting link between β -ray disintegration and the forces responsible for nuclear binding. **1942** *Endeavour* Jan. 22/2 Skobeltzyn.. has argued against the theory of Heisenberg and Euler that 'the spontaneous disintegration of mesotrons is the mechanism responsible for the formation of the electronic component observed in the lower layers of the atmosphere. **1949** Koestler *Insight & Outlook* x. 136 The so-called 'elementary particles'—electrons, photons, neutrons, mesotrons, and so forth.

mesotympanic: see MESO-.

† **'mesotype.** *Min. Obs.* [a. F. *mésotype* (Haüy 1801), f. Gr. μέσο-ς middle + τύπος TYPE.] A name including the minerals now called natrolite, scolecite, mesolite, and thomsonite.

(The form of the crystal is intermediate between those of analcite and stilbite; hence the name.)

1804 *Edin. Rev.* III. 311 The mezotype corresponds to the fibrous and acicular zeolytes. **1815** MacCulloch in *Trans. Geol. Soc.* III. 86 Mesotype.. is found in three states, a compact, a mealy, and a crystallized form. **1852** Th. Ross *Humboldt's Trav.* II. xvii. 79 Crystals of pyroxene and mesotype.

meso-uterine to **-ventriculum:** see MESO-.

mesoxalic (mɛsɒk'sælɪk), *a. Chem.* [f. MESO- + OXALIC *a.*] ***mesoxalic acid***: a dibasic acid obtained from alloxan. Hence **mesoxalate** (mɛ'sɒksəleɪt), a salt of mesoxalic acid. Also **mesoxalyl** (mɛ'sɒksəlɪl), the radical of alloxan (*Syd. Soc. Lex.* 1890); *attrib.* in **mesoxalyl-urea**, a synonym of alloxan (ibid.).

1838 R. D. Thomson in *British Ann. for* 1839, 381 Mesoxalic acid.. mesoxalate of barytes. **1878** Kingzett *Anim. Chem.* 203 Alloxan is resolved into urea and mesoxalic acid by the action of boiling baryta water. **1894** *Nature* 26 July 311/2 Bismuth mesoxalate. **1895** Thomson & Bloxam *Bloxam's Chem.* 749 Alloxan.. or mesoxalyl-urea.

mesozeugma: see MESO-.

‖**Mesozoa** (mɛsəʊ'zəʊə), *pl. Zool.* [mod.L., f. Gr. μέσο-ς middle + ζῷα pl. of ζῷον animal.] Van Beneden's name for forms intermediate in structure between the Protozoa and the Metazoa. (The Orthonectids and Dicyemids, which he placed in this division, are now recognized as Metazoa, but it is believed that true Mesozoa exist.) Also *sing.* **meso'zoon**, one of the mesozoa.

1877 *Q. Jrnl. Microsc. Sci.* XVII. 144 The 'Mesozoa'.. may be characterized as multicellular organisms, composed of two kinds of cells, one layer of which.. is a true ectoderm; whilst the second layer.. constitutes the endoderm. **1877** Huxley *Anat. Inv. Anim.* 676 The representatives of a distinct division, the Mesozoa, intermediate between the Protozoa and the Metazoa. **1892** *Ann. & Mag. Nat. Hist.* Ser. vi. IX. 79 The Mesozoon *Salinella*.

Mesozoic (mɛsəʊ'zəʊɪk), *a. Geol.* [f. Gr. μέσο-ς middle + ζῷον animal + -IC.] The name given by Phillips to the secondary period, intermediate between the PALÆOZOIC and the CAINOZOIC.

1840 J. Phillips in *Penny Cycl.* XVII. 154/1 Corresponding terms (as Palæozoic, Mesozoic, Kainozoic, &c.) may be made, nor will these necessarily require change upon every new discovery. **1861** J. R. Greene *Man. Anim. Kingd., Cœlent.* 239 Mesozoic, Cainozoic, and Recent Corals, which occur in more than one Geological Period. **1880** Haughton *Phys. Geog.* vi. 269 The Marsupials of the Mesozoic strata.

† **'mespile.** *Obs.* Also 6 mespy(l)le, myspylle. [ad. L. *mespilus, -um, -a*, a. Gr. μέσπιλον, μεσπίλη, whence (ultimately) MEDLAR.] A medlar.

1398 Trevisa *Barth. De P.R.* xvii. cxxxvi. (E. Mus. MS.), þe sauour þerof [the fruit of the rose] is bitinge and somdele soure as þe sauour [of] mespiles. **1500** Bollard tr. *Godfredi on Pallad.*, Of mespyles v. medlers. **1545** Raynold *Byrth Mankynde* 81 Wyld peres, medlers or myspylles.

‖**mespilus** ('mɛspɪləs). *Gardening.* [L.; see prec.] Applied to certain ornamental trees formerly included in the genus *Mespilus*, but now placed in the genus *Cratægus*.

1767 Abercrombie *Ev. Man his own Gard.* (1803) 606 Hardy kinds of flowering shrubs and trees.. such as.. mezereons, mespiluses. **1885** Lady Brassey *The Trades* 397 Planted.. with oranges, lemons, hibiscus, and mespilus.

‖**'mesplier.** *Obs.* [a. OF. *mesplier* (= *nesplier*, mod.F. *nèflier*), f. *mesple* (= *nesple*, mod.F. *nèfle*):—L. *mespilus*; see MESPILE.] A medlar-tree.

1480 Caxton *Ovid's Met.* x. iv. (Roxb. Club), To this assemblement came.. Lawrers, Mespliers [etc.].

Mespot ('mɛspɒt). Also **Mess-pot.** Slang abbrev. of MESOPOTAMIA.

1917 *To-Day* 6 Jan. 246/3 *Mesopotamia*.—So you call it the 'Mess-pot', do you? **1920** *Sat. Rev.* 3 July 4/1 The 'Messpot' madness. **1933** J. Buchan *Prince of Captivity* I. iii. 107 What front were you on—the Western, Palestine, Mespot? **1943** C. S. Forester *Ship* viii. 48 Mr. Whipple.. had gone off and joined the army and had done his bit in Mespot.

mespresion, mesprise, etc., obs. ff. MISPRISION, MISPRIZE.

‖**mesquin** (mɛskæ̃), *a.* [Fr.] Mean, sordid, shabby.

1706 Evelyn *Acc. Architects & Archit.* (ed. 2) 10 They [*sc.* the Moors] set up those Slender and Misquine [*sic*] Pillars.. and other incongruous Props. **1828** Marq. Normanby *Engl. in France* II. 102 It heightens the beauty of the picturesque, and slurs over the *mesquin* and the mean. **1871** Kingsley *At Last* ii, The mesquin and scrofulous visages, which crowd our alleys.

† **mesquita, mesquit**[1]. *Obs.* Forms: α. 6 meschita, -quito, moskyta, -quita, 6–7 mes-, mezquita, 7 mescita, -keeto, -keito, -kita, mosquetto, -quito. β. 6 muscot, 6–7 meskit, 7 machit, meschit(e, -cuite, mesked, mes-, mosquit(e, 7–8 meskite. [a. Sp. *mezquita* and It. *meschita*, ad. African Arab. *masgid*, dial. pronunciation of MASJID. Some of the β forms may come directly from Arab.] = MOSQUE.

α. **1576** Eden *Trav. W. & E. Indies* (1577) 365 b, A Temple or Meschita. **1598** W. Phillip *Linschoten* I. xliii. 79 The Moores like wise haue their Mesquitos. **1599** Hakluyt *Voy.* II. I. 208 This famous and sumptuous Mosquita hath 99. gates, and 5. steeples. **1627** R. Ashley *Almansor* 9 The Friday.. hee.. went in solemnitie to the great Mesquita. **1657** Howell *Londinop.* 384 The Gran Cairo in Egypt, a City.. having five and thirty thousand Meskeetos. **1661** Cowley *Cromwell* Verses & Ess. (1669) 73 They said he [*sc.* Cromwell].. would have sold.. St. Peters (even at his own Westminster) to the Turks for a Mosquito.

β. **1477** Caxton *Dictes* 58 b, Somme men saye that legmon is buried in a toun called karaualle bitwene the mesquitte & the marche. *c* **1564** A. Jenkinson in *Hakluyt's Voy.* (1598) I. 347 Prince Ismael lieth buried in a faire Meskit. **1590** Webbe *Trav.* (Arb.) 21 In the said Cittie [*sc.* Cairo], there is 12 thousand Churches, which they tearme Muscots. **1612** Brerewood *Lang. & Relig.* xxvi. 227 The publick service of the Jews and of the Mahumetans, in their synagogues and meskeds. **1613** Purchas *Pilgrimage* (1614) 229 There is also a Meschit there for the Arabians and Turkes. *Ibid.* v. xvii. 538 They neuer goe to their Watches before they haue prayed in the Mesquit. **1658** Phillips, *Meskite*, a Church, or Synagogue among the Turks and Moors. **1665** Sir T. Herbert *Trav.* (1677) 308 They.. lodge the Carcass not in the Machits or Churches but Church-yards.

mesquite, mesquit[2] ('mɛski:t, mɛ'ski:t). Also **mezquit(e, mezkeet, mesketis, muskeet, masketo, moscheto, musqueto, mus-, mesquito; musquet, -quit, -kit; muskeete.** [a. Mexican Sp. *mezquite*.]

1. a. Either of two leguminous trees growing in S.W. North America, *Prosopis juliflora* (honey mesquite), and *P. pubescens* (screw-pod mesquite).

1759 tr. *Venegas's Nat. & Civil Hist. Calif.* I. 100 Their most usual device was to hold up in their hands some little tablets of wood made with great labour, for want of iron tools of mesquite. **1806** M. Lewis in *Deb. Congress U.S.* (1852) 9th Congress 2 Sess., App. 1083 A bean that grows in great plenty on a small tree resembling a willow called masketo. **1838** 'Texian' *Mexico v. Texas* 70 Even where a tree appears it is sure to be a mesquite (*Mimosa nilotica*). **1838** C. Newell *Hist. Revolution Texas* 147 Live oak,.. black walnut, cypress, and musquit prevail. **1851** Mayne Reid *Scalp Hunt.* i. 14 Here and there are trees of acacia and mezquite, the denizens of the desert land. **1854** Bartlett *Mex. Boundary* I. iv. 75 The mezquit.. belongs to the same natural family as our locust. **1872** Schele de Vere *Americanisms* 121 The *Mesquite* or *Muskeet* (Algarobia glandulosa), a bastard-locust. **1909** 'O. Henry' *Roads of Destiny* viii. 129 Near the store, scattered among the mesquite and elms, stood the saddled horses of the customers. **1948** *Reader's Digest* Jan. 70/1 Anywhere in America has its particular hearth perfume—.. mesquite floating out of desert chimneys in the Southwest. **1969** T. H. Everett *Living Trees of World* 201/1 The mesquite.. [is] a native of the southwestern United States, Mexico, Central America and the West Indies.

b. A thicket of mesquite trees.

1834 A. Pike *Prose Sk. & Poems* 63 We emerged from the broken hills into the mesquito. **1910** W. M. Raine *Bucky O'Connor* 224 The Irishman.. kept his party in the mesquit till the headlight of an approaching train was visible. **1945** *New Yorker* 25 Aug. 26 A railroad bull came walking along the tops of the cars and kicked me into the mesquite. **1974** *Sci. Amer.* Apr. 104/1 The particular dung beetles concerned would colonize only pads dropped in open pastures, however, and not those dropped in the dense growth of mesquite, where the cattle sought shelter from the heat of the day.

2. In full ***mesquite-grass***: A general name for grasses growing in the neighbourhood of the mesquite tree, esp. the genera *Bouteloua* and *Buchloe*.

1823 W. B. Dewees *Lett. from Early Settler Texas* (1852) 35 The musquit grass grows very thick and about three feet high, and looks very much like a blue grass pasture. **1831** M. Holley *Texas* (1833) vi. 69 The pasturage here.. called Muskit grass, (pronounced Muskeet) bears a strong resemblance to the blue grass. **1851** Mayne Reid *Scalp Hunt.* xxvi. 187 A desert country, covered with wild sage and mezquite. **1857** Olmsted *Journ. Texas* 135 A great change occurred here in the prairie grass—we had reached the mesquit grass. **1904** *Blackw. Mag.* Nov. 649/2 A shimmering prairie of mesquite.

3. *attrib.* and *Comb.*, as ***mesquite bush, flour, leaf, tree, wood***; **mesquite bean**, the pod of the mesquite tree; **mesquite grass** (see 2).

1869 in *Daily News* Sept. (1892) 6/7 He ate a few green pods and leaves of a mezquit bush.. . A few *mezquit beans. **1806** M. Lewis in *Deb. Congress U.S.* (1852) 9th Congress 2 Sess., App. 1103 Some small cultivated fields, fenced round with small cedar and *moscheto brush. **1834** A. Pike *Prose Sk. & Poems* 56 The valley was.. full of small hills interspersed with *mezquito bushes. **1887** F. Francis Jun. *Saddle & Mocassin* 73 Wave after wave of rolling country sparsely covered with *mesketis*-bush. **1854** Bartlett *Explor. Texas*, etc. II. 217 The *mezquit flour, which is ground very fine, has a sickish sweetness. **1867** A. D. Richardson *Beyond Mississippi* xix. 226 Another waiting coach was soon rolling us forward among *mesquite groves. **1859** Marcy *Prairie Trav.* 291 There is but little grass here, but in the season the *mesquite leaves are a good substitute. **1905** A. Adams *Outlet* 16 The horses had run idle during the winter in a large *mesquit pasture. **1957** J. Kerouac *On Road* (1958) 166 Tucson is situated in beautiful *mesquite riverbed country. **1831** J. O. Pattie *Personal Narr.* 59 We found the river skirted with very wide bottoms, thick set with the *musquito trees. **1860** *Merc. Marine Mag.* VII. 212 A few.. *mesquit* trees are now and then met with. **1831** J. O. Pattie *Personal Narr.* 83 There is here little timber, beside *musqueto wood, which stands thick. **1846** J. A. Quitman *Diary* 13 Aug. in J. F. H. Claiborne *Life & Corr. J. A. Quitman* (1860) I. 239 The steamer purchases muskeet-wood at $2.50 per cord for dry, $2.25 green. **1891** C. Roberts *Adrift Amer.* 149, I used to hitch up a team and go out on the prairie and pick up mesquite wood.

† **me'squitical,** *a. Obs.* In 7 meschiticall. [f. MESQUITA + -ICAL.] Pertaining to a mosque.

1613 Purchas *Pilgrimage* (1614) 315 The multitudes of other Churches, as silly captiued Damsels, attending and following thee into this Meschiticall slauerie.

mesquito, variant of MESQUITA *Obs.*

mess (mɛs), *sb.* Forms: 3–6 mes, (3 meisse), 4–5 mees, 4–7 messe, 5–6 mese, *Sc.* mais, (6 *Sc.* meis, 7 *Sc.* meiss), 5–7 measse, 6 mease, meace (meesse, meece), 5– mess. [a. OF. *mes* = sense 1 below (mod.F. *mets* viand, dish) = It. *messo* course of a repast:—late L. *missum*, neut. pa. pple. of L. *mittĕre* to send (in Rom. use, to put).]

I. Portion of food (and transferred uses).

1. a. A serving of food; a course of dishes; a prepared dish (of a specified kind of food). Now only *arch.* exc. as in 2.

a **1300** *Cursor M.* 12559 Noþer durst þai.. brek þair brede, ne tast þair mes Til he.. wit beniscun þaim badd. *c* **1330** *King of Tars* 86 The Soudan sat at his des, Iserved of his furste mes. *c* **1400** Maundev. (Roxb.) xxxiv. 154 Þai bring him mete and euermare fyfe meesez togyder. *c* **1425** *Voc.* in Wr.-Wülcker 658/8 *Hoc frustrum*, mese, gobyt. **1577** Holinshed *Chron.* III. 920/1 The which [servants] togither kept also a continuall messe in the hall. **1604** Shaks. *Oth.* iv. i. 211, I will chop her into Messes: Cuckold me? **1631** Heywood *Eng. Eliz.* (1641) 175 Before the second messe came in, he fell sick at the table. **1751** Hume *A Dialogue* in *Enq. Princ. Morals* 228 My friend Alcheic form'd once a Party for my Entertainment,.. and each of us brought his Mess along with him. **1819** Byron *Juan* ii. xli, For want of water, and their solid mess Was scant enough. **1841** James *Brigand* xix, Here comes the old woman with my mess of food. **1888** Stevenson *Black Arrow* 144 Three or four men sat drinking ale and eating a hasty mess of eggs.

fig. **1563** Foxe *A. & M.* (1583) II. 1845/2 What an euill messe of handling this Whittle had, and how he was.. all to beaten.. manifestly may appeare. **1603** Dekker *Wonderfull Yeare* C j b, Most blisfull Monarch.. Seru'd with a messe of kingdomes. *a* **1764** Lloyd *Poet* Poet. Wks. 1774 II. 17 As colleges, who duly bring Their mess of verse to every king. **1770** N. Nicholls in *Corr. w. Gray* (1843) 117 In hopes of learning a little profane history to mix with my divine, which is really a bad mess by itself.

† **b.** ***worms' mess***, food for worms. *Obs.*

a **1300** *Sarmun* vi. in *E.E.P.* (1862) 2 Þi fleisse nis naȝte bot worme-is meisse. *c* **1460** *Towneley Myst.* xxxi. 118 Ne flesh he was wonte to fede, It shall be Wormes mese.

c. A quantity (of meat, fruit, etc.) sufficient to make a dish. (Now *dial.* and *U.S.*) Also, the quantity of milk given by a cow at one milking.

1513 More *Rich. III* (1883) 46 You haue very good strawberies at your gardayne in Holberne, I require you let vs haue a messe of them. *a* **1533** Frith *Agst. Rastell* 242 A shrewd cow, which, when she hath given a large mess of milk, turneth it down with her heel. **1597** Shaks. *2 Hen. IV*, ii. i. 103 Goodwife Keech.. comming in to borrow a messe of Vinegar. **1621** in *Black Bk. Taymouth* (Bannatyne Cl.) 313 Off new salt beiff i quarter iiii meiss. **1697** S. Sewall *Diary* (1878) I. 455 Betty gets her Mother a Mess of English Beans. **1775** B. Romans *Florida* 12 (Th.), He told me that his mother had an inclination to eat fish, and he was to come to get her a mess. **1842** *Knickerbocker* XIX. 557 Sally couldn't hardly bring in the pail, she gave such a mess. **1861** O. W. Norton *Army Lett.* (1903) 26 H. and I got enough [potatoes] for a mess, and some parsnips. **1870** Lowell *Study Wind.* 8 His is the earliest mess of green peas. **1872** *Rep. Vermont Board Agric.* I. 197, I tested their milk by weighing every mess for a month. **1877** *Ibid.* IV. 54 We took off what cream arose on the night's mess, and churned it. **1883** J. C. Harris *Nights with Uncle Remus* iii. 30 Brer Rabbit, he hop in, he did, en got 'im a mess er greens, en hop out ag'in.

d. *U.S.* A take or haul of fish.

1854 Thoreau *Walden, Spring* (1884) 338, I got a rare mess of golden and silver and bright cupreous fishes. **1901** R. D. Evans *Sailor's Log* vi. 59 The captain.. sent me a mess of the finest mackerel I ever saw.

e. *N. Amer.* A quantity or number *of* something. See also quot. 1970.

1830 *Mass. Spy* 23 June (Th.), We saw yesterday a large mess of early potatoes. **1834** C. A. Davis *Lett. J. Downing* 40 With that, he out with his wallet, and unrolled a mess on 'em. **1854** *Knickerbocker* XLI. 502 There was wolves in the Holler—an unaccountable mess of 'em. **1872** *Rep. Vermont Board Agric.* I. 634 They will dress a mess of ore to any required per cent. **1939** L. M. Montgomery *Anne of Ingleside* xxxviii. 300 Tell Susan Baker I'm much obliged for that mess of turnip greens she sent me. **1956** B. Holiday

Lady sings Blues (1973) xix. 154 Just before I was set to go on for the second set a big mess of gardenias arrived backstage. **1966** W. T. E. KIRKEBY *Ain't Misbehavin'* v. 51 This is Fats Waller, the baby who plays that mess of organ over at the Lincoln. **1970** C. MAJOR *Dict. Afro-Amer. Slang* 81 *Mess*, large quantity;..someone..[who] is remarkable or puzzling.

2. a. Applied (in early use only contextually, in later use *spec.*) to a 'made dish', or to a portion or a kind of liquid, partly liquid, or pulpy food, such as milk, broth, porridge, boiled vegetables, etc.

The expression ***a mess of pottage***, proverbially current in allusions to the story of Esau's sale of his birthright (Gen. xxv. 29–34), does not occur in the Bible of 1611, though found in this connexion as early as 1526 (see quot. below). It appears in the heading of ch. xxv. in the Bibles of 1537 and 1539, and in the Geneva Bible of 1560. Coverdale (1535) does not use it either in the text or heading of this chapter (his words being 'meace of meate', 'meace of ryse'), but he has it in 1 Chron. xvi. 3 and Prov. xv. 7.

14.. *Sir Beues* 83 (MS. C.), But onys yn a weke a symple messe Of sodyn barley was hart lees. *c* **1456** *How wise man taught his son* 99 in Hazl. *E.P.P.* I. 173 Bettyr it is..A mes of potage..Then for to have a M. mes, With great dysese and angyr sore. **1526** *Pilgr. Perf.* (W. de W. 1531) 1. xi. 30 Som for a messe of potage, with Esau, careth nat to sell the euerlastyng inheritaunce of heuen. *a* **1592** LODGE & GREENE *Looking Gl. Lond. & Eng.* (1881) 20, I want my mease of milke when I goe to my worke. **1595** DUNCAN *App. Etymol.* (E.D.S.) 70 *Iusculum*, a mease of brue. **1598** SHAKS. *Merry W.* III. i. 63, I had as lief you would tell me of a messe of porredge. **1632** MILTON *L'Allegro* 85 Hearbs, and other Country Messes. **1633** HEYWOOD & ROWLEY *Fortune by Land* III. i, Give..a word to the dayry maid for a mess of cream. **1669** WORLIDGE *Syst. Agric.* (1681) 41 The Meal makes..good Pottage, and several other Messes. **1711** SWIFT *Jrnl. to Stella* 23 Dec., I have..eaten only a mess of broth and a roll. **1772–84** COOK *Voy.* (1790) V. 1771 Having observed several messes of porpoise broth preparing. **1884** *Fortn. Rev.* Mar. 379 They are fond of farinaceous messes.

b. A quantity of liquid or mixed food for an animal; a kind of such food.

1738 POPE *Epil. to Sat.* ii. 176 If one [*sc.* hog]..Has what the frugal, dirty soil affords, From him the next receives it, thick or thin, As pure a mess almost as it came in. **1810** *Sporting Mag.* XXXVI. 251 The infernal mess alluded to.. being ordered for race-horses. **1841** BROWNING *Pippa Passes* ii, 'Tis only a page..Crumbling your hounds their messes! **1860** MISS YONGE *C'tss Kate* i, [He was] mixing a mess of warm milk for the young calves.

c. In contemptuous or disgusted use: A concoction, jumble, medley.

1828–32 WEBSTER, *Mess*, 2. A medley; a mixed mass. **1836** *Backwoods of Canada* 124 Rice, sugar, currants, pepper and mustard all jumbled into one mess. **1854** MISS BAKER *Northampt. Gloss.*, *Mess*, a hodge-podge, or dirty, disagreeable mixture. Any culinary preparation that is unpalatable would be called 'a nasty mess'.

3. a. A state of confusion or muddle; a condition of embarrassment or trouble; esp. in phr. ***to get into a mess. to make a mess of***: to bungle (an undertaking).

1834 MARRYAT *P. Simple* xxxiii, Here's a pretty mess! if I put on my great coat I shall be dead with sweating; if I put on no jacket I shall be roasted brown. **1862** DARWIN in *Life & Lett.* (1887) II. 392, I am rejoiced that I passed over the whole subject in the 'Origin', for I should have made a precious mess of it. **1875** RUSKIN *Fors Clav.* lv. 199 Their affair gets into a mess. **1891** S. C. SCRIVENER *Our Fields & Cities* 173 But never mind, Charlie boy, keep out of messes.

b. A dirty or untidy condition of things.

1851 MAYHEW *Lond. Labour* (1864) II. 193/1 They make it a rule when they receive neither beer nor money from a house to make as great a mess as possible the next time they come. **1867** SMYTH *Sailor's Word-bk.*, *Mess*,..the state of a ship in a sudden squall, when everything is let go and flying.

c. (See quot.)

1844 STEPHENS *Bk. Farm* II. 165 The London butcher.. will..reject such cattle or sheep as are what is termed in a *mess*; that is, depressed, after excitation by being overlaid or overdriven.

d. *colloq.* Excrement, esp. of an animal; usu. in phr. ***to make a mess***.

1903 in *Eng. Dial. Dict.* s.v. Mess, *sb.*[2] 4. **1928** KIPLING *Limits & Renewals* (1932) 50 It [*sc.* a dog]'s made a mess in the corner. **1937** V. WOOLF *Years* 245 The pigeons were a nuisance, he thought, making a mess on the steps. **1939** A. HUXLEY *After Many a Summer* I. x. 138 A lovely stinking little baby who still made messes in its bed. **1940** N. MITFORD *Pigeon Pie* ix. 144 Perhaps, she thought, the bird wants to go out... It made a mess on her skirt. **1960** *Woman's Own* 6 Aug. 49/2 It's the dog. It made a mess on the carpet. **1972** *New Yorker* 30 Sept. 44/2 Happy..had helped them unpack by..pulling one of Mrs. Webster's dresses from a hanger and then making a mess on it.

e. *slang.* An objectionable, ineffectual, or stupid person.

1936 M. MITCHELL *Gone with Wind* I. vi. 122 'Oh,' thought Scarlett... 'To have that mealy-mouthed little mess take up for me!' **1938** E. BOWEN *Death of Heart* I. ii. 40 From what you say, her mother was quite a mess. **1965** M. SPARK *Mandelbaum Gate* iv. 104 These were lapsed Jews, lapsed Arabs, lapsed citizens, runaway Englishmen, dancing prostitutes, international messes.

II. Company of persons eating together.

4. a. Originally, each of the small groups, normally of four persons (sitting together and helped from the same dishes), into which the company at a banquet was commonly divided. Now only in the Inns of Court, a party of four benchers or four students dining together. Hence, a company of persons (members of some official or professional body) who regularly take their meals together; e.g., the company of judge and barristers who dine together when on circuit (see also b).

c **1420** LYDG. *Assembly of Gods* 257 So he her set furst at hys owne messe. *c* **1460** J. RUSSELL *Bk. Nurture* 1050 in *Babees Bk.* 72 Bisshoppes, Merques, vicount, Erle goodly, May sytt at .ij. messez. *Ibid.* 1057 Of alle oþer estates to a messe iij. or iiij. *Ibid.* 1065 Of alle oþur estates to a messe ye may sette foure & foure. **1591** *Wills & Inv. N.C.* (Surtees) II. 199 For the charges of xij mease, that dyned at his owne house, 2[l] . 8[d] . **1607** BEAUMONT *Woman Hater* I. ii, Nor should there stand any..pyes, at the nether end, fill'd with mosse and stones, partly to make a shew with, and partly to keepe the lower messe from eating. **1654** GATAKER *Disc. Apol.* 40 His fellow-Benchers that were in the same Messe with him. **1671** H. M. tr. *Erasm. Colloq.* 395 To every mess of guests set three dishes. **1681** LUTTRELL *Brief Rel.* (1857) I. 99 An addresse..was moved by some in the hall [in Grayes Inn] that day at dinner, and being (as is usuall) sent to the barr messe to be by them recommended to the bench. **1821** in *N. Eng. Hist. & Gen. Reg.* (1876) XXX. 191 Here a number of members [of Congress], vulgarly called a 'Mess', put up, and have a separate table. **1866** MANSFIELD *School Life* (1870) 219 [Winchester], The Præfects' tables in Hall were called 'Tub, Middle, and Junior Mess' respectively. **1882** SERJ. BALLANTINE *Experiences* I. v. 65 *page heading*, Circuit mess. [Account of its usages, *c* 1834.] **1899** ATLAY *Famous Trials* 388 Dr. Kenealy's fellow-barristers on the Oxford Circuit called upon him to show cause before the mess on the allegation of having [etc.]... He declined to appear, and was duly expelled from the mess.

b. In the Army and Navy: Each of the several parties into which a regiment or ship's company is systematically divided, the members of each party taking their meals together. Phr. ***to lose the number of one's mess***: to die, be killed. Also, the place where food is served (see quot. 1886.

1536 *Ld. Treas. Acc. Scotl.* (1905) VI. 450 The expensis of xxxij meis of marineris, gunnaris, and utheris in the New Havin. **1599** E. WRIGHT *Voy. Azores* 17 They willingly agreed that every mease should bee allowed at one meale but halfe so much drinke as they were accustomed. **1769** FALCONER *Dict. Marine* (1780), *Mess*, a particular company of the officers or crew of a ship, who eat, drink, and associate together. **1807** in A. Paget *Paget Papers* (1896) II. 314 If we are going against Copenhagen many of us will lose the number of our mess. **1822** *Gen. Regul. & Orders Army* 123 Commanding Officers are enjoined, when practicable, to form a Serjeants' Mess, as the means of supporting their consequence and respectability in the Corps. **1834** MARRYAT *P. Simple* xxxiii, I have an idea that some of us will lose the number of our mess. **1840** ALISON *Hist. Europe* (1849–50) VIII. liii. §26. 421 The situation of privates who had risen to the officers' mess was not so comfortable. **1858** SIMMONDS *Dict. Trade*, *Mess*..a number of men who take their meals together; thus in vessels of war there are ward-room and gun-room messes, comprising commissioned and subordinate officers. The seamen and marines' messes consist of a dozen or more under the superintendence of a non-commissioned or petty officer. **1886** BARING-GOULD *Court Royal* iv, When one of H.M. vessels was put in commission, the mess was furnished with new linen, plate, china, glass. **1890** G. STABLES *For England*, etc. xvi. 234 The mess to which this man belonged is little more than a hot-bed of mutiny. **1911** C. E. W. BEAN *'Dreadnought' of Darling* xxx. 260 That meant a ride out to the blacks' camp and some of them losing the number of their mess. It did not matter who was shot. **1934** G. B. SHAW *Too True to be Good* II. 76 The conversation in the officers' mess doesnt suit me. *Ibid.* III. 81 *Sweetie.* Well, of course. Youre in the sergeants' mess. **1969** D. HAY *Man in Hot Seat* vi. 60 At the Aldershot end of the airfield..stood the long blue-carpeted Mess of the Empire Test Pilots' School.

c. Without article: The taking of such a meal.

1778 *Camp Guide* 7 I'm summon'd to mess. **1875** JOWETT *Plato* (ed. 2) III. 294 They will go to mess and live together like soldiers in a camp. **1876** BESANT & RICE *Gold. Butterfly* xiii, One evening after mess he told Colquhoun that [etc.].

d. *gen.* = 'Table' (in the senses 'company at an entertainment'; 'provision of food').

1861 G. F. BERKELEY *Sportsm. W. Prairies* xiv. 239 He never brought anything from my kitchen to the general mess. **1840** ARNOLD *Hist. Rome* II. 551 The members of the aristocracy [of Athens] had their clubs, where they habitually met at a common mess or public table. **1878** BOSW. SMITH *Carthage* 26 There were public messes, as they were called, but these were not..analogous to the Spartan Syssitia.

†5. *transf.* A company or group of four persons or things. *Obs.*

1526 SKELTON *Magnyf.* 1009 Let me se..Yf I can fynde out So semely a snowte Amonge this prese: Euen a hole mese. **1588** SHAKS. *L.L.L.* IV. iii. 207 You three fooles, lackt mee foole, to make vp the messe. **1593** —— *3 Hen. VI*, I. iv. 73 Where are your Messe of Sonnes, to back you now. *a* **1625** FLETCHER, etc. *Fair Maid Inn* III. i, The messe and halfe of suiters. *a* **1661** FULLER *Worthies* I. (1662) 13, I meet with a mess of English Natives advanced to that Honour... Yea, I assure you, four Popes was a very fair proportion for England.

punningly. **1617** (*title*) Ianva Lingvarvm Qvadrilingvis, or a Messe of Tongves: Latine, English, French, and Spanish. Neatly serued vp together, for a wholesome repast.

6. *U.S.* Short for *mess-beef* (see 7).

1859 *New York Herald* Market Report (Hoppe), Prime mess and beef ham. **1884** *Harper's Mag.* July 299/1 [Chicago.] The average weight of the class of animals used for 'mess' and 'canning' is 950 pounds... The division [of the carcasses] is made into..pieces..viz. loins, ribs, mess, plates, chucks, rolls, rumps, [etc.]... 'Extra mess' is composed of chucks, plates, rumps, and flanks.

III. 7. *attrib.* and *Comb.* (sense 3) ***mess-maker***; (sense 4), as ***mess-article***, ***-bag***, ***-basket***, ***-beef***, ***-berth***, ***-bill***, ***-bread***, ***-cabin***, ***-chest***, ***-cloth***, ***-deck***, ***-dinner***, ***-fire***, ***fund***, ***-gear***, ***-hall***, ***-kid*** (see KID *sb.*[4]), ***-list***, ***-making***, ***-man***, ***-meat***, ***-money***, ***-pan***, ***-pork***, ***-pot***, ***-room*** (also *attrib.*), ***-sergeant***, ***-table***, ***-tent***, ***-tin***, ***-traps***, ***-writer***; **mess-boy** *Naut.*, one who waits at table in a mess-room; **mess-jacket**, a short tailless jacket reaching just below the waist-line; **mess-kit**, (*a*) utensils for cooking or handling food; (*b*) (military) uniform designed to be worn at meals. Also MESSMATE.

1828 P. CUNNINGHAM *N.S. Wales* (ed. 3) II. 215 All the mess-berths and *mess articles numbered according to their corresponding messes. **1885** *Outing* VII. 55/1 From some dark corner of the *messbags, or petacas, he unearthed a handful of dried apples. **1839** *Knickerbocker* XIII. 211 Tell Margaret to prepare the *mess-basket. **1766** W. GORDON *Gen. Counting-ho.* 319, 45 barrels full bound *mess-beef. **1883** P. L. SIMMONDS *Useful Anim.*, *Mess Beef.* This is usually put up in pieces of 8 lbs., and sold in tierces of 304 lbs. **1828** *Mess berth [see *mess article* above]. **1916** F. M. FORD *Let.* 29 Nov. (1965) 78 Also I have found a considerable portion of my *Mess Bill out of Auction. **1917** W. OWEN *Let.* 24 May (1967) 464 There have been a number of Mess Bills, & other cheques drawn lately. **1934** E. BOWEN *Cat Jumps* 67 If mess-bills ran up..was John to blame? **1963** *Times* 24 May 14/7 Chits were signed, which sooner or later found their way to the Mess and appeared on one's mess-bill. **1818** 'A. BURTON' *Adventures J. Newcome* II. 74 The *Mess-boy to the Coppers dragged it [*sc.* a pudding]. **1955** C. S. FORESTER *Good Shepherd* 116 A big pot of coffee. And a sandwich. Tell the mess-boy I want one of my specials. **1964** O. E. MIDDLETON in C. K. Stead *N.Z. Short Stories* (1966) 210 The messboy's discreet ropesoles pad patiently to and fro. **1970** *Islander* (Victoria, B.C.) 22 Feb. 5/1 The American trading schooner Nanook arrived. Its messboy had hanged himself for some unknown reason. **1615** E. S. *Britain's Buss* in Arb. *Garner* III. 628 Baskets for *mess-bread. **1867** SMYTH *Sailor's Word-bk.*, *Ward-room*, the commissioned officers' *mess cabin. **1830** J. F. COOPER *Water Witch* III. ix. 258 The smaller booms with the *mess-chest and shot-boxes were all that lay between the group.. and the depths of the ocean. **1858** T. VIELÉ *Following Drum* 15 A camp-kettle, mess chest, bundle of canvas, and set of tent poles. **1888** *Century Mag.* 851/1 We have a stout four-horse wagon..; in its rear a mess-chest is rigged to hold the knives, forks, cans, etc. **1839** C. F. BRIGGS *Adventures H. Franco* I. xxiii. 250 Throwing down my knife..I leaped on to the *messcloth, and gave him a blow in the eye. **1855** OGILVIE Suppl., **Mess-deck*, the deck on which a ship's crew mess. **1803** SCOTT *Let.* 10 July (1932) I. 195, I can proceed no further being alarmed by the Bugle Call not indeed to summon to battle but to the less hazardous task of a *Mess Dinner where our Society tho' somewhat noisy is very good humoured. **1825** H. WILSON *Mem.* II. 116 The mess-dinner at Lewes..must more resemble a..private party than a mess-room, as they seldom mustered more than seven or eight persons together at table. **1885** A. EDWARDES *Girton Girl* I. xiv. 283 The usual guest-night at mess. Curious how precisely alike all mess dinners are. **1837** W. IRVING *Capt. Bonneville* (1895) I. 24 The various *mess-fires were surrounded by picturesque groups. **1850** L. H. GARRARD *Wah-to-Yah* xii. 180 He..walked to a messfire. **1850** J. J. HORT *Horse Guards* 70 He cannot act otherwise than by occasionally adding to the *mess and the band funds. **1876** VOYLE & STEVENSON *Mil. Dict.* (ed. 5) 254/1 Married men pay one half if they do not regularly attend the mess, but they pay all contributions to the mess fund. **1970** V. CANNING *Great Affair* xii. 216 Ex-pilot officer Robinson, cashiered for fiddling the mess funds. **1890** *Cent. Dict.*, *Mess-gear. **1918** L. E. RUGGLES *Navy Explained* 98 *Mess gear*, the tableware, plates, cups, saucers, food containers and implements used by mess cooks. **1862** G. C. STRONG *Cadet Life at West Point* 66 We were as unfortunate in the *mess-hall as out of it. **1958** *Listener* 6 Nov. 717/1 Food eaten at the communal mess-hall [in China]. **1891** E. KINGLAKE *Australian at. H.* 91 The *mess-jackets of one or two officers..may be seen, and some naval uniforms. **1905** A. M. BINSTEAD *Mop Fair* i. 10 A tall blonde in a heel-tipping skirt and mess-jacket of blue herring-bone. **1851** *Catal. Gt. Exhib.* 786 Ships'..*mess kid, brass hooped. *a* **1877** KNIGHT *Dict. Mech.* II. 1421/2 **Mess-kit*, that portion of camp equipage consisting of cooking utensils. **1953** J. MASTERS *Lotus & Wind* vii. 89 His mess-kit was grey and black with silver facings. **1954** W. FAULKNER *Fable* (1955) 343 Bottles, old messkits. **1828** P. CUNNINGHAM *N.S. Wales* (ed. 3) II. 215 On the *mess-list being arranged upon deck, they are..placed..in their respective messes. **1929** D. H. LAWRENCE *Pansies* 89 It is hard..to put up with the clever *mess-makers. *a* **1734** NORTH *Life Ld. Guilford* (1742) 35 This Friendship began by *Mess-making in the Temple-Hall. **1850** *Punch* 20 July 33/1 *Messman wanted for a Cavalry Regiment. **1920** *Chambers's Jrnl.* May 285/2 Understanding the messman to have come off from the Colon with plenty of oysters. **1903** *Daily Chron.* 29 Dec. 5/3 Russia has given..an urgent order for 1,000,000lb. of *mess meat. **1833** MARRYAT *P. Simple* vi, The three guineas which you received as *mess-money. **1813** *Niles' Reg.* III. 295/2 [List of Military Supplies] *Mess pans. **1846** R. B. SAGE *Scenes Rocky Mts.* xxvii. 227 A large tin mess-pan, and a tin-cup and plate for each of its number. **1861** O. W. NORTON *Army Lett.* (1903) 35 New knapsacks, canteens..mess pans and a complete outfit. **1832** *Louisville* (Kentucky) *Public Advertiser* 10 Mar., *Mess and Prime Pork in barrels and half barrels, for sale. **1848** *Rep. Comm. Patents 1848* (U.S.) 527 The finest and fattest [hogs] making clear and mess pork. **1874** C. GEIKIE *Life in Woods* i. 10 A piece or two of sailor's mess-pork. **1857** R. GLISAN *Jrnl. Army Life* (1874) viii. 86, I shall be able to say good bye to the *messpots of Uncle Sam. **1811** *Sporting Mag.* XXXVII. 152 No Officer was permitted to carry the newspapers out of the *messroom. **1855** THACKERAY *Newcomes* II. 298 Not disturbed by the mess-room raillery of the Campaigner. **1859** LANG *Wand. India* 361, I will introduce to you all the servants—the *mess-sergeant especially. **1819** J. A. QUITMAN *Diary* 15 Nov. in J. F. H. Claiborne *Life & Corr. J. A. Quitman* (1860) I. 42 Mrs. and Miss Griffith, charmed with our *mess-table, became our boarders. **1830** M. DONOVAN *Dom. Econ.* I. 45 An officer,..after getting intoxicated at the mess-table [etc.]. **1895** M. A. JACKSON *Mem. Stonewall Jackson* xi. 191, I took my meals with him and the staff at their mess-table. **1774** LD. HARRIS in *Life & Services* (1845) 34 She..passed close by our *mess-tent.

1916 in 'Contact' *Airman's Outings* (1917) 266 A great wind ..whines past the *mess-tent. **1879** *Cassell's Techn. Educ.* IV. 215 Our men carry a *mess-tin, and a water bottle. **1867** SMYTH *Sailor's Word-bk.*, **Mess-traps*, the kids, crockery, bowls, spoons, and other articles of mess service. **1893** FORBES-MITCHELL *Remin. Gt. Mutiny* 175 For many years [he] had filled the post of *mess-writer, keeping all the accounts of the mess.

mess (mɛs), *v.* [f. MESS *sb.*; the senses represent independent formations.]

1. a. *trans.* To serve up (food); to divide (food) into messes or portions. *Obs.* exc. *dial.*

?*c* **1390** *Form of Cury* lxii. (1780) 35 Take alkenet..and droppe above with a feþer, and messe it forth. *c* **1430** *Two Cookery-bks.* 30 Florche it a-bouyn with Pome-garned, & messe it; serue it forth. **1530** PALSGR. 635/1, I messe meate, I sorte it or order it in to messes, as cookes do whan they serve it. **1886** *Cheshire Gloss.*, Come an' tay th' cheilt, wheile aw mess th' dinner for th' men.

b. *intr.* To prepare messes for animals. *rare.*

1840 *Cottager's Man.* 36 in *Libr. Usef. Knowl., Husb.* III, There will be no necessity for messing every time the pig wants a meal.

†**2.** To divide (a ship's company) into messes. *Obs.*

1627 CAPT. SMITH *Seaman's Gram.* ix. 39 To messe them foure to a messe. **1690** STRUTTON *Relat. Cruelties of French* 10 We Mest our selves seven and seven together.

3. a. *intr.* To take one's meals, esp. as a member of a mess; also *rarely* to feed *upon* (a specified kind of food).

1701 FARQUHAR *Sir H. Wildair* III. ii, I shall find better mutton commons by messing with you, brother. **1743** BULKELEY & CUMMINS *Voy. S. Seas* 196 We never us'd to mess together. **1786** tr. *Beckford's Vathek* (1868) 82 It was his horrible look that sent us hither to listen to sermons and mess upon rice. **1833** MARRYAT *P. Simple* iv, Now that we are in harbour, I mess here. **1876** DAVIS *Polaris Exp.* vii. 176 The officers who had messed with him,..knew that the life of the expedition was gone.

b. *trans.* To supply with meals.

1811 WELLINGTON in Gurw. *Desp.* (1838) VIII. 295 The soldiers..were not at all times messed in the manner pointed out by your order. **1882** FLOYER *Unexpl. Baluchistan* 79 The Khan..was most hospitable, even to the extent of messing me at his own 'table'.

4. *intr.* **a.** To make a mess, put things into a disorderly or untidy state; to dabble in water, mud, etc. Also, to 'potter', busy oneself in an untidy way, or with no definite purpose or result (const. *about* or with advs. *about*, *around*, *away*). Phr. ***to mess about in boats.***

1853 MRS. LYNN LINTON in *Life* vii. 83, I mess about my flowers and read snatches of French. **1886** *Tip Cat* xix. 263 Messing about with sulphur and lime and all the rest of it. **1886** G. ALLEN *Maimie's Sake* xxi, Sydney was..messing away..at his nasty chemicals. **1894** K. GRAHAME *Pagan P.* 129 What boy has ever passed a bit of water without messing in it? **1908** K. GRAHAME *Wind in Willows* i. 7 There is *nothing*—absolutely nothing—half so much worth doing as simply messing about in boats. **1932** *Amer. Speech* VII. 334 Mess around, to 'kill time'; to interfere; to meddle. **1957** D. ROBINS *Noble One* iv. 41, I can't see the attraction of messing around with a lot of sick animals. **1962** J. CANNAN *All is Discovered* iv. 87 What he enjoyed was messing about in boats and sitting in the sun. **1964** *Evening Post* (Wellington, N.Z.) 4 Jan., A few audible reminders to himself to 'stop messing around' failed to help matters. **1970** H. E. ROBERTS *Third Ear* 10/1 Mess around, to engage in a great deal of purposeless activity. **1973** *Times* 18 Apr. 3/2 (Advt.), And if you ask the Chancellor of the Exchequer what a company like ours is doing 'messing about in boats' he'll tell you we're the world's largest manufacturer of quality inflatable leisure craft.

b. ***to mess with***: to interfere or get involved with; to make a mess of; to trouble or annoy. *U.S. colloq.* or *dial.* Cf. sense 7.

1903 *Dialect Notes* II. 299 *Mess with*, to meddle with; also, to make a mess of. 'Don't mess with your food.' **1913** *Ibid.* IV. 5 *Mess with*, to associate with. 'We don't mess with those people.' **1955** S. WHITMORE *Solo* 27 And what little lady is going to mess with you. **1955** SHAPIRO & HENTOFF *Hear me talkin' to Ya* 374 The really good musicians are too smart to mess with it. **1956** B. HOLIDAY *Lady sings Blues* (1973) iv. 46 This talk about a big tone messed with Lester for months. **1968** E. GAINES in A. Chapman *New Black Voices* (1972) 101, I never messed with a woman I didn't love. **1971** *Black World* Apr. 66 You hit her with a chair leg. You didn't have no right to mess with that poor girl.

c. ***to mess up***: to make a mess or muddle of a situation; to get into trouble; to become mixed up or involved. *U.S. colloq.*

1933 *Amer. Speech* VIII. III. 29/2 Boy, I ain't a-goin' t' mess up no more from now on. **1938** M. K. RAWLINGS *Yearling* xxiii. 290 If she's nothin' but one o' them leetle ol' chipperdales, why do he mess up with her? **1956** B. HOLIDAY *Lady sings Blues* (1973) iii. 33 When the time came to take those bills off the table, I was always messing up. **1969** H. KOHL in T. Kochman *Rappin' & Stylin' Out* (1972) 110 He wanted to learn badly, they told me, and was messing up by memorizing the signs in the neighborhood and thinking that's all there was to reading.

5. *trans.* To make a mess of; to disorder, make dirty, soil (a thing); to muddle (a business); to spoil, ruin. Also with *up*.

1854 W. COLLINS *Hide & Seek* III. iv. 108 That's the first pair of trousers I ever ventured to cut out for you..; and the long and short of it is, I've messed 'em. **1859** C. READE *Love me Little* i, It messes one's things so to pick them to pieces. **1862** H. MARRYAT *Year in Sweden* I. 165 The authorities,..convinced of the folly of messing matters, have caused a plan to be drawn out on a grand..scale. **1883** FREEMAN in W. R. W. Stephens *Life & Lett.* (1895) II. 275 The friars' churches at Gloucester..are utterly messed and made up into houses. **1901** *Scribner's Mag.* (U.S.) XXIX. 404/1 Lank told him that he had messed the whole business. **1909** *Dialect Notes* III. 349 The house is all messed up. **1919** G. B. SHAW *Heartbreak House* II. 85, I get my whole life messed up with people falling in love with me. **1959** I. FLEMING *Goldfinger* xiv. 194 Bond only prayed that she hadn't got some private plot involving him or Goldfinger that was going to mess up his own operation. **1966** *Word Study* Dec. 3/2 There's no real point in worrying anyhow. It just messes you up.

6. ***to mess about***: to handle roughly or too familiarly; to inconvenience or annoy. Also with *around*. *dial.* or *colloq.*

1874 *Slang Dict.*, *Mess*, to interfere unduly. Costermongers refer to police supervision as 'messing'. **1901** *Essex Weekly News* 8 Mar. 3/3 Defendant was 77 years old, and had never been messed about by policemen before. **1934** A. P. HERBERT *Holy Deadlock* 276 Why *should* our private lives be spied upon—and messed about in a Court like this? **1955** *Times* 20 May 14/6 If industry is once again going to be messed about by Government interference—more nationalization, more controls. **1957** M. SPARK *Comforters* v. 110 Her great desire to travel by train was dispersed by the obvious necessities of going to Mass, and of not messing Laurence around any further. **1973** *Time Out* 2–8 Mar. 14/1 My impression is that when the surge of violence was on—at its height, two years ago—quite a few teachers got messed about. It was somewhere beyond extreme rudeness, but short of your actual NAS physical assault.

7. *Sc.* To mix, associate *with*; only in phr. ***to mess or (and) mell.***

1821 GALT *Ann. Parish* xxiv. (1895) 159 She..would not let me..mess or mell wi' the lathron lasses of the clachan. **1822** —— *Steam-boat* iv. 88 This is an observe that I have made..since I began..to mess and mell more with the generality of mankind. **1887** J. SERVICE *Dr. Duguid* (ed. 3) 281 He would neither mess nor mell wi' ony o' the new reformers.

mess, obs. form of MASS *sb.*[1]

‖**messa di voce** (ˈmessa di ˈvotʃe). Pl. messe di voce. [It., lit. 'placing of the voice'.] In singing, a gradual crescendo and diminuendo on a long-held note.

1801 in BUSBY *Dict. Mus.* **1876** STAINER & BARRETT *Dict. Mus. Terms* 286/2 *Messa di Voce (It.)*, the swelling and diminishing of the sound of the voice upon a holding note. **1938** *Oxf. Compan. Mus.* 567/2 [In the eighteenth century] every long note (irrespective of the sense of the words) was expected to bear a *messa di voce*. **1958** *Listener* 14 Aug. 250/3 The tenor's wonderful *messa di voce* at the cadence leading to the reprise. **1964** *Conc. Oxf. Dict. Opera* 259/1 *Messa di voce*.., the art of swelling and diminishing tone on a single note.

message (ˈmɛsɪdʒ), *sb.*[1] Forms: 4–7 **massage**, 5 **masage**, (4 **messag**, **missage**, 5 **massache**, 6 **mesuage**, **messege**, 6, 8 **messuage**, 7 **meswage**), 3– **message**. [a. F. *message* = Pr. *messatge*, Sp. *mensaje*, Pg. *mensage(m*, It. *messagio*:—popular L. **missaticum* (a med.L. word of this form occurs in the 12th c.), f. L. *miss-*, *mittĕre* to send.]

1. a. A communication transmitted through a messenger or other agency; an oral or written communication sent from one person to another; also, †intelligence, tidings, news. *Obs.*

1297 R. GLOUC. (Rolls) 3645 To þe king com message þat þe scottes..dude him gret outrage. *c* **1330** R. BRUNNE *Chron.* (1810) 40 Þis was his message, his Danes wild he venge Ageyn him in bataile. **1382** WYCLIF *2 Kings* vii. 9 This is forsothe a day of good message. **1462** MARG. PASTON in *P. Lett.* II. 99, I have spoken with my modre and seide to here as ye desired me to doo, and sche seide sche knewe the massache weele inowe before. **1503–4** *Act 19 Hen. VII*, c. 34 *Preamble*, Dyvers messeges and writinges to hym sent. **1596** SHAKS. *Merch. V.* I. i. 164 Sometimes from her eyes I did receiue faire speechlesse messages. **1667** MILTON *P.L.* XI. 299 Gently hast thou tould Thy message. **1722** DE FOE *Relig. Courtsh.* I. i. (1840) 22 You cannot desire me to carry such a message. **1840** MISS MITFORD in L'Estrange *Life* (1870) III. vii. 107, I had a kind message from Captain Marryat once, when somebody whom he knew was coming here. **1902** T. M. LINDSAY *Church in Early Cent.* viii. 355 They [acolytes] were the servants of the Christian priests..carrying their messages or letters.

¶ Often applied to a communication sent by telegraph; hence *transf.*

1847 TENNYSON *Princess* Prol. 78 Thro' twenty posts of telegraph They flash'd a saucy message to and fro Between the mimic stations. **1884** J. TAIT *Mind in Matter* (1892) 71 Messages can pass through the brain and the nerves every moment.

b. In religious language: A divinely inspired communication by a prophet; tidings sent by God. Freq. *transf.*; esp., the broad meaning (of something); a view expressed in a piece of writing, etc., esp. one communicating a criticism of a social or political matter.

1546 BALE *Eng. Votaries* I. (1560) Ep. Ded., A ioyfull massage declaring full remission to be geuen frely in Christe. **1781** J. LOGAN in *Sc. Paraphr.* XXXIV. iv, His oracles of truth proclaim the message brought to man. **1892** WESTCOTT *Gospel of Life* p. xviii, If we are to deliver our message as Christians we must face the riddles of life. **1902** A. B. DAVIDSON *Called of God* vii. 201 Isaiah's message is twofold; first ruin and then redemption.

transf. **1828** CARLYLE *Misc.* (1857) I. 238 Byron and Burns ..had a message to deliver. **1895** ELLACOMBE *Glouc. Garden* xxv. 279 Every plant has its own separate message and lesson. **1936** *Time* 17 Feb. 46/2 In *Modern Times*, the 'message' has been underlined rather than, as in the old days, subconsciously implied. **1940** 'G. ORWELL' *Inside Whale* 156 It will be seen that once again I am speaking of these people as though they were not artists, as though they were merely propagandists putting a 'message' across. **1949** H. NICOLSON *Diary* 7 Sept. (1968) 174 T. S. Eliot..is off to lecture in Germany. He asked me whether they would expect a 'message'. I said the only thing to do was to treat them as ordinary members of cultured society. **1955** *Times* 12 May 13/4 Mr. Kauffmann resembles other talented American novelists in that his real gifts for story-telling and satirical observation are somewhat obscured by too heavy an insistence on the 'message' implicit in the plot. **1969** J. ARGENTI *Managem. Techniques* ix. 54 If the chairman of the company shows an informed interest in techniques just occasionally, this should be enough for the message to get through to all levels. **1970** *Guardian* 17 Aug. 6/2 David Halliwell is..the black sheep of the student militants...'Do you approve?' asked a nicely-dressed teenager, identifying the shock with the message. **1975** *Broadcast* 23 June 17/1 The medium may not be the message, but undeniably the characteristics of the medium shape the message.

c. An official communication from the Sovereign to Parliament; also, a communication from Parliament to members of the royal family, or between the two houses of Parliament themselves; *U.S.* a communication from a chief executive officer to a legislative body conveying instructions or information on matters of policy; *esp.* the Presidential address transmitted to Congress at the opening of the Session.

1566 *House of Commons Jrnl.* 30 Sept. (1742–62) I. 73/1 At which Thirtieth Day of September, 1566,..Mr. Comptroller..with a convenient Number, went up to the Lords with that Message. **1621** *Ibid.* 13 Feb. (1742–62) I. 520/1 Having faithfully discharged themselves in their Message to the King. **1625** WHITELOCK *Mem.* (1853) 3 The commons..voted to give the king two subsidies, for which the king thanks them by a message. **1701** *House of Commons Jrnl.* 20 June (1742–62) XIII. 638/1 A Message was sent to the House of Commons, by Mr. Baron Tracy and Mr. Baron Berry. **1711–12** SWIFT *Jrnl. to Stella* 17 Jan., The Queen's message was only to give them notice of the peace she is treating. **1758** *Mem. Last War* 35 The Governor thereupon moved the Assembly in two other Messages to resume the Consideration of this Enterprize. **1801** HAMILTON *Wks.* (1886) VII. 200 Instead of delivering a speech to the Houses of Congress,..the President has thought fit to transmit a Message. **1818** *House of Commons Jrnl.* 6 June LXXIII. 424/1 Resolved, *Nemine Contradicente*, That a Message be sent from this House to congratulate their Royal Highnesses the Duke and Duchess of Cambridge, on their happy nuptials. **1820** *House of Lords Jrnl.* 15 Aug. LIII. 367/2 Ordered, *Nemine Dissentiente*, That a Message of Condolence be sent from this House to His Royal Highness The Duke of York..and that The Duke of Wellington and The Earl Graham do attend His Royal Highness with the said Message. **1844** ERSKINE MAY *Law of Parl.* xvi. 249 A message is the most simple and frequent mode of communication; it is daily resorted to for sending bills from one house to another [etc.]. *Ibid.* xvii. 268 Messages are frequently sent by both houses to members of the royal family, to congratulate them upon their nuptials..or other auspicious events..or to condole with them on family bereavements. *a* **1859** MACAULAY *Hist. Eng.* xxiv. (1861) V. 177 William..sent down to the Commons a message,..written throughout with his own hand. **1862** J. M. LUDLOW *Hist. U.S.* 169 The President, in his message of the year.. referred in terms of sympathy with Texas to its struggle with Mexico. **1950** *Times* 21 Oct. 3/5 Before 1855..messages were always carried to the Lords by members of the Commons themselves, and from the Lords to the Commons by Masters in Chancery or judges.

2. a. The business entrusted to a messenger; the carrying of a communication; a mission, an errand.

c **1290** *S. Eng. Leg.* I. 24/26 Heo weoren Messagers: and from an heiȝ mon heo come To don to him a Message. *c* **1380** WYCLIF *Sel. Wks.* III. 272 Þat an angel of God schal not do Goddis massagis to save Cristene soulis. **1390** GOWER *Conf.* III. 300 His doghter..He bad to gon on his message. *c* **1440** *Alphabet of Tales* 72 Such men sulde be no baillays, nor go no messagies. **1470** *Gol. & Gaw.* 401 Our souerane Arthour ..Has maid ws thre as mediatour, His message to schaw. **1526** *Pilgr. Perf.* (W. de W. 1531) 32 b, Yf man shall haue sufficyent faculty to do the message of God. **1591** SHAKS. *1 Hen. VI*, IV. vii. 53 On what submissiue message art thou sent? **1667** MILTON *P.L.* v. 289 All the Bands Of Angels.. to his message high in honour rise; For on som message high they guessd him bound. **1720** PETRIE *Rules Deportm.* ii. Wks. (1877) 6 A Gentleman ought not to run or walk too fast in the Streets, lest he be suspected to be going a Message. **1840** MARRYAT *Poor Jack* iv, I..ran messages. **1849** THACKERAY *Pendennis* xvii, She bethought her..how he had gone on messages for her.

†**b.** Phrase. (To go, send, etc.) ***in*** (also ***of, on***) ***message***: on the business of carrying a communication or of doing an errand. *Obs.*

1297 R. GLOUC. (Rolls) 7405 A monek he sende him in message. **1382** WYCLIF *2 Cor.* v. 20 Therfore we ben sett in legacie, or message, for Crist. **1443** *Acts Privy Council* (1835) V. 238 To paie to Coler pursivant þe whiche goethe now in þe Kynges message beyonde þe see xl.s. **1456** SIR G. HAYE *Law Arms* (S.T.S.) 116 Quhen ony is send in message to the inymyes. **1548** HALL *Chron.*, *Hen. VII* 12 b, He sent on message Christopher Urswicke to Charles. **1557** F. SEAGER *Schoole of Vertue* 726 in *Babees Bk.*, How to order thy selfe being sente of message. **1593** SHAKS. *2 Hen. VI*, IV. i. 113, I go of Message from the Queene to France. **1622** BACON *Hen. VII* 142 The King..sent Sir Richard Gvilford into Kent in message.

c. Phr. ***to get the message***: to understand a position stated or implied.

1964 'C. E. MAINE' *Never let Up* xv. 149 'Let's go in and have a drink anyway.' 'Now you're getting the message,' he commented. 'Lead the way.' **1967** O. WYND *Walk Softly, Men Praying* viii. 134 They didn't ask me in for a drink... Richard..realized it would only be postponing the inevitable. He had got the message at last. **1972** D. LEES *Zodiac* 90 They don't seem able to make up their minds

whether to warn me off or knock me off but I do get the message loud and clear and..I'm going. **1974** *Times* 9 Jan. 14/8 (*heading*) Will Nato get the message?

†**3.** A person or body of persons conveying a communication; one or more messengers or envoys, an embassage. [So in OF.] *Obs.*

c **1330** R. BRUNNE *Chron.* (1810) 78 A message tille him nam vnto Normundie, Teld William eueridele of Malcolme robberie. *c* **1386** CHAUCER *Man of Law's T.* 235 The hooly lawes of oure Alkaron, Yeuen by goddes message Makomete. *a* **1450** *Le Morte Arth.* 2256 Then was A bischope at Rome, Off Rowchester,.. Tylle ynglande he, the message, Come. *c* **1470** HENRY *Wallace* VIII. 541 Wallace has herd the message say thair will. *c* **1475** *Rauf Coilȝear* 905 Fra the Chane of Tartarie, At him this message wald I be, To tell him [etc.].

4. *attrib.* and *Comb.*, as **message bag**; **message-carrying**; **message-boy** *Sc.*, an errand-boy; **message card**, a card on which a message may be written; in the 18th c. *spec.* a card of invitation to a reception or entertainment; **message-form**, a printed form for a telegraphic message; **message-lad** = *message-boy*; **message rate** *Hist.*, in the British Post Office, a fixed rate of payment per message sent by telephone (opposed to a subscription entitling to 'unlimited service'); **message-stick**, a stick or small block of wood carved with significant marks, used as a means of communication in Norway and among the Australian aborigines.

1917 'CONTACT' *Airman's Outings* vii. 184 The contact patrol buses..by means of *message bags dropped over brigade headquarters report progress to the staff. **1948** 'N. SHUTE' *No Highway* xi. 289 Stubbs came back with the message bag. **1896** CROCKETT *Cleg Kelly* (ed. 2) 56, I came ..to ask about the situation of a *message-boy. **1755** W. WHITEHEAD in Dodsley *Poems* II. 264 (*title*) On a *Message-Card in Verse, Sent by a Lady. **1804** *European Mag.* XLV. 418/2 His visits were admitted without the punctilios of message-cards. **1851** *Illustr. Catal. Exhib.* 102/2 Paper and Stationery... Message Cards, plain and ornamental. **1829** BENTHAM *Justice & Cod. Petit.* 179 The business of *message-carrying. **1900** *Post Office Guide* Jan. 518 Postage stamps are used for the payment of telegrams, and the public are required to affix them to the *message-forms. **1836** DICKENS *Sk. Boz* (1837) 2nd Ser. 101 The mother had got the boy a *message-lad's place in some office. **1901** *Daily Chron.* 30 Nov. 7/7 [Post Office Telephones.] Most of these [agreements] are at what is known as the *message rate. **1860** *Leisure Hour* 3 May 287/1 To this day the people in Norway are called together for the despatch of public business, in a somewhat similar manner. A bud-stick, or *message-stick.. is painted and stamped with the royal arms. **1881** *Academy* 24 Sept. 243 Three message-sticks from Australia which prove that even degraded savages may invent real written characters. **1898** in MORRIS *Austral Eng.*

†'**message**, *sb.*[2] *Obs. rare*$^{-1}$. [? f. *mess* MASS *sb.*[1] + -AGE.] ? The action of saying mass.

c **1440** *Alphabet of Tales* 58 He sente þurgh all his bisshoppryke, & garte do message & oders prayers & suffrage of halie kurk for hym.

message ('mɛsɪdʒ), *v.* [f. MESSAGE *sb.*[1]]

1. *trans.* To send as a message; to send by messenger; *spec.* to transmit (a sketch, plan, etc.) by means of signalling, telegraphing, etc.

1583 STANYHURST *Æneis* IV. (Arb.) 107 Hee did, in expressed commaund, to me message his erraund. **1636** W. DENNY in *Ann. Dubrensia* (1877) 14 Then by and by swift racing Naggs contend Who first, shall message Conquest to the end, Of their appointed course. **1886** *Longm. Mag.* VII. 416 The result obtained..is easier to message. **1887** *Pall Mall G.* 24 Mar. 11/1 A series of rules by which any drawing may be 'messaged' and signalled. **1896** *Columbus (Ohio) Dispatch* 18 Mar. 7/1 The bill was messaged over from the house last evening.

2. *intr.* To carry a message. *nonce-use.*

1840 DICKENS *Barn. Rudge* xxiv, Our people go backwards and forwards..lettering and messaging, and fetching and carrying.

Hence '**messaging** *vbl. sb.*

1865 CARLYLE *Fredk. Gt.* XV. iii. V. 289 We can get no free messaging from part to part of our own Army even. *Ibid.* XIX. ii. (1873) VIII. 127 Montalembert's watching, messaging about.

messageer, -er(e, obs. ff. of MESSENGER.

messageless ('mɛsɪdʒlɛs), *a.* [f. MESSAGE *sb.*[1] + -LESS.] Without a message; having no message to communicate.

1925 *Brit. Weekly* 18 June 268/2 He lost his faith in the Bible..and (to use his own significant words) 'I became a messageless man'. *a* **1930** D. H. LAWRENCE *Last Poems* (1932) 283 The dark and gleaming beauty of the messageless gods.

‖**messagerie** (mɛsaʒri). [Fr.: see MESSAGERY.] Usu. *pl.* The transportation or delivery of goods, messages, or people; a conveyance for these. Also *attrib.* So **messageries maritimes**, the transport of goods, etc., by sea; the name of a shipping-line.

1792 A. YOUNG *Trav. France* I. 11 In ten miles we met not one stage or diligence; only two messageries, and very few chaises. **1878** LADY C. SCHREIBER *Jrnl.* 29 June (1952) 150 We took our passage in the French Messageries boat. **1907** G. B. SHAW *John Bull's Other Island* p. x, Many Englishmen like Frenchmen better than Englishmen, and never go on board a Peninsular and Oriental steamer when one of the ships of the Messageries Maritimes is available. **1931** E. WAUGH *Remote People* 12 French colonial officials, their wives and disorderly children..make up the bulk of a normal Messageries Maritimes passenger list. **1934** A. CHRISTIE *Murder on Orient Express* II. xiv. 169 He saw me on board a French Messagerie boat for Smyrna. **1974** S. COULTER *Chateau* II. vi. 286 She had come down by the Messageries coach.

messagery ('mɛsɪdʒərɪ). *Obs.* or *arch.* Also 4 **messagerie**, 7 **-gry**. [a. F. *messagerie*, f. *messager*: see MESSENGER and -ERY.]

1. The office or function of a messenger; the performance of a message or errand. *Obs.* exc. *arch.*

c **1381** CHAUCER *Parl. Foules* xxxiii, I saw..Fool hardynesse & flatterye, & desyr, Messagerye & meede & oþer thre. **1658** PHILLIPS, *Messagry*, (old word) diligence in doing a message. **18..** CARLYLE *Hist. Sk.* (1898) 80 There are the country carriers [on a market day], packing, unpacking; swift diligence, thousandfold messagery looking through their eyes.

2. A body of messengers. *Obs. rare*$^{-1}$.

c **1500** *Melusine* 69 In this messagery or embassade were sent two wyse knightes.

messagier, -gre, -gy(e)r, obs. ff. MESSENGER.

messal, -ale, obs. ff. MISSAL *sb.*

Messalian (mɛ'seɪlɪən), **Massalian** (mæ'seɪlɪən), *sb.* and *a.* *Eccl. Hist.* Also 6–9 **Massilian**, 8 **Messallian**. [ad. late Gr. *Μεσσαλιανός* (Theodoret), *Μασσαλιανός* (Epiphanius), ad. Syr. *mᵉçalyânâ* given to prayer; the Greek writers render it by *εὐχίτης* (see EUCHITE) and *εὐχόμενος* one who prays. Some of the forms of the word are due to association with the place-name *Massalia*, *Massilia*, Marseilles.]

A. *sb.* A member of an ancient heretical sect, variously identified by early writers with the Euchites and with the Hesychasts.

a **1591** H. SMITH *Serm.* (1637) 380 If your lippes be not alwayes going, which was the heresie of the Messalians. **1708–22** BINGHAM *Orig. Eccl.* XX. iii. §5 The Massalians, or Euchites [kept Sunday as a fast]. **1833** MOORE *Trav. Irish Gentl. in Search Relig.* I. 262 The Messalians..imagined that the whole atmosphere was brimful of devils. **1880** *Encycl. Brit.* XI. 782/2 Hesychasts (..sometimes referred to as Euchites, Massalians, or Palamites), a quietistic sect.

B. *adj.* Of or pertaining to the Messalians.

1597 HOOKER *Eccl. Pol.* V. lxxiv. §1 We..should be like those Massilian heretiques which doe nothing else but pray. **1654** H. L'ESTRANGE *Chas. I* (1655) 127 He was..disrelisht by them who inclined to the Massilian and Arminian Tenets. **1882–3** SCHAFF *Encycl. Relig. Knowl.* III. 2152 The Massilian Monks are described as holding, that by faith and baptism any one can be saved, if he only will.

Messalina (mɛsə'liːnə). The name of Valeria *Messalina*, third wife of the Roman emperor Claudius, used allusively for a licentious and scheming woman.

1887 *Athenæum* 8 Oct. 467/1 His heroine is a New York Messalina who fastens herself upon a villain of the worst type. **1925** W. J. LOCKE *Great Pandolfo* xx. 257 I'm not either a Messalina, or one of the *grandes amoureuses*. **1931** G. J. RENIER *The English* iv. 85 Messalinas are exceptions. A woman needs only one partner. **1946** KOESTLER *Thieves in Night* 146 Particularly Gaby, our red-haired Viennese Messalina who, having a year ago left Max for Mendl, has now left Mendl too. **1975** 'J. LYMINGTON' *Spider in Bath* ii. 39 'Unfaithful bitch!' he cried. 'Messalina! Medusa! Gorgon!'

messaline ('mɛsəliːn). [Fr., = *Messalina* (see prec.).] A soft, lightweight, and lustrous twilled-silk fabric. Also *attrib.*

1909 *Public Ledger* (Philadelphia) 26 June 7/7 Sale of Pongee & Messaline Dresses (title). *Ibid.*, Beautifully made of extra fine natural pongee silk and messaline. **1920** *T. Eaton & Co. Catal.* Spring & Summer 1/2 This delightful Frock of Messaline Silk. **1921** *Daily Colonist* (Victoria, B.C.) 11 Oct. 5/3 (Advt.), Black Messaline Silk, a beautiful heavy quality for making skirts and dresses. *Ibid.* 23 Oct. 16/4, 36-Inch Black Messaline, in an exceptionally good dye. A well woven silk in which you will realize the best wear. **1968** J. IRONSIDE *Fashion Alphabet* 241 *Messaline*, named after the wife of the Emperor Claudius (Messalina) this is a lustrous..satin-weave silk fabric.

messan ('mɛsən). *Sc.* Forms: 6–8 **messen**, 8 **messon**, 9 **messin**, 5– **messan**. [? a. Gael. *measan* = Irish *measán*, M.Irish *mesán* (Macbain).] A lap-dog; also applied to a person as a term of abuse. Also *attrib.* as **messan-dog**, **-cur**, **-tyke**.

a **1500** *Bernard. de cura rei fam.* (E.E.T.S.) 13 Litile doggis and messanys with þar bellis. **1508** KENNEDIE *Flyting w. Dunbar* 495 A crabbit, scabbit, euill facit messan tyke. **1596** DALRYMPLE tr. *Leslie's Hist. Scotl.* I. 22 The varietie of Messen dogs, wᵗ quhilkes gentle women vses to recreate thame selfes. **1719** HAMILTON *Ep.* I. iii. in Ramsay *Poems* (1877) II. 232 To petty poets, or sic messens. **1786** BURNS *Twa Dogs* 18 Na pride had he, But wad hae spent an hour caressan, Ev'n wi' a Tinkler-gipsey's messan. **1828** SCOTT *F. M. Perth* xv, I met him..with a common minstrel wench, with her messan and her viol on his..arm. **1853** CARLYLE in *Atlantic Monthly* LXXXII. (1898) 685 The white mat on Jane's lap is her wretched little messin-dog.

messangier, -yer, -yre, obs. ff. MESSENGER.

Messapian (mə'seɪpɪən), *sb.* and *a.* Also **Me'ssapic**. [f. L. *Messāpi-us* + -AN.]

A. *sb.* **a.** A native or inhabitant of the ancient district of Messapia (now Apulia and Calabria) in southern Italy. **b.** The language of the Messapians. **B.** *adj.* Of or pertaining to the Messapians or their language.

1773 [see IAPYGIAN *a.* and *sb.*]. **1876** *Encycl. Brit.* IV. 650/2 The inhabitants [of Calabria] were Sallentines and Calabrians or Messapians, both probably of Pre-Hellenic or Pelasgic race. **1880, 1882** [see IAPYGIAN *a.* and *sb.*]. **1932** W. L. GRAFF *Lang.* 375 Venetic of Northeastern Italy and the South Italian Messapic. **1932** *Times Lit. Suppl.* 21 July 530/4 The three groups of Apulian vases, Messapian, Peucetian and Daunian. **1948** D. DIRINGER *Alphabet* II. viii. 471 The Messapic or Messapian was the earliest European offshoot of the Greek language. **1949** *Oxf. Class. Dict.* 560/2 The Apulian Peucetii..and Daunii..also spoke Messapic. **1966** M. S. BEELER in Birnbaum & Puhvel *Anc. Indo-European Dial.* 52 The undoubtedly Illyrian Messapic of the southeastern end of the peninsula.

messaye, obs. form of MISSAY *v.*

messchance, obs. form of MISCHANCE.

messe: see MASS *sb.*[1], *v.*[1], MEASE, MESSIAH.

messeger, obs. form of MESSENGER.

messeigneurs, pl. of MONSEIGNEUR.

messeline, -ling, obs. forms of MASLIN[2].

messelinge, -yne, -yng, obs. ff. MASLIN[1].

messell(e, variants of MEASLE *a. Obs.*

†**messellawny.** *Obs.* Also 7 **messelane**, **misselane**. Some textile fabric.

1612 *Sc. Bk. Customs* in *Halyburton's Ledger* (1867) 322 Missellanes the peice contening xxx elnis xxxvi li. *a* **1625** *Rates Merchandizes*, Misselanes the peece, containing thirtie yards. **1642** *Ibid*, Messelanes. **1640** in Entick *London* II. 178 Messellawny, the piece.

messelyng, obs. form of MASLIN[1].

messenger ('mɛsɪndʒə(r)). Forms: α. 3–6 **messager**, 3–5 **-ere**, (4 **mesager**, **messagyr**, **-gre**), 3–4 **messagyer**, **messeger**, (4 **messagere**, **masager**), 5 **massageer** (**messageer**), 4 **mas(s)eger**, 5 **-gere**, 5–6 **messagier**, (5 **massagier**, 6 **messurger**). β. 4–6 **messanger**, 4–5 **-ere**, **-ir**, 5–6 **-aunger**, (4 **mesanger**, 5 **messongere**, **myssanger**), 4–7 **messinger**, 5 **-ere**, 4–5 **messynger(e**, (4 **mensanger**, **-syngere**, **massingere**, 5 **masynger**, 6 **mesynger**), 4–5 **massenger**, 5 **massanger(e**, **messengere**, (**masenger**, **-yr**, **messengyr**), 5 **messangier**, **-yer**, **-yre**, 6 **messengier**, 4– **messenger**. [ME. *messager*, *-ier*, a. F. *messager* (OF. also *messagier*), f. *message*: see MESSAGE *sb.* Cf. Pr. *messatgier*, Sp. *mensajero*, Pg. *mensageiro*, It. *messaggiero*, *-ere*. For the insertion of *n* in the β forms, cf. PASSENGER, etc.]

1. a. One who carries a message or goes on an errand; †an envoy, ambassador (*obs.*). ***corbie messenger***: see CORBIE 2.

(***God's***) ***messenger***: (*a*) used for ANGEL *sb.*, as representing the etymological sense of that word, and as expressing the function assigned to angels in Scripture; (*b*) applied to a prophet, or to a clergyman, as charged with a message from God to mankind.

α. *a* **1225** *Ancr. R.* 190 Heie monnes messager, me schal heiliche underuongen. **1362** LANGL. *P.Pl.* A. IV. 115 Bote hit beo Marchaund..or Messager with lettres. **1481** CAXTON *Godeffroy* i. 18 Machomet..which was messager of the deuil. **1521–2** DOUGLAS in Ellis *Orig. Lett.* Ser. III. I. 295 For baith by messurger and write I declarit him playnlie I wald pass throᵗ this Realme. **1558** KNOX *First Blast* (Arb.) 6 The especiall dutie of Goddes messagers is to preache repentance. **1560** DAUS tr. *Sleidane's Comm.* 389 The next day..came messagers and letters that Auspurge was taken.

β. **13..** *K. Alis.* 7609 Ac, by special messangere, Y wol sende hire love-drewry. *c* **1450** HOLLAND *Howlat* 231 The Dow, Noyis messinger. **1460** *Lybeaus Disc.* 1747 (Kaluza) A maide, þat is her messengere..brouȝt me her. **1535** COVERDALE *1 Sam.* xix. 20 Saul sent his messaungers to Dauids house, that they shulde..kyll him. **1588** in *Harl. Misc.* (1809) II. 87 If he minded to revenge against any other nation, he would plead the cause by messengers. **1624** S. WARD in *Ussher's Lett.* (1686) 321 This Messenger bringeth the Book, and things from Mr. Crane. **1667** MILTON *P.L.* VII. 572 God..Thither will send his winged Messengers On errands of supernal Grace. **1719** DE FOE *Crusoe* (1840) II. xiv. 295 Messengers were sent express. **1859** W. COLLINS *Q. of Hearts* (1875) 14 [He] sent off a mounted messenger with the letter.

b. The bearer *of* (a specified message).

α. **1577** DEE *Relat. Spir.* I. (1659) 63 Those that are the Messagers and Angles of the Dignified and Triumphant Glory. **1583** GOLDING *Calvin on Deut.* cix. 672 Yet doth God appoint vs to be..messagers of his vnfallible trueth.

β. *a* **1340** HAMPOLE *Psalter* ciii. 5 When þou wol þou makis þaim [gostis] messangers of þi will. **1595** SHAKS. *John* II. i. 260 Messengers of Warre. *a* **1625** FLETCHER, etc. *Fair Maid Inn* III. ii, At next visit, Madam, I'll be a messenger of comfort. **1703** DE FOE in *15th Rep. Hist. MSS. Comm.* App. IV. 76 You must not refuse to be the messenger of my acknowledgments.

†**c.** In New England (17th c.), the representative of a Congregational church at a synod. *Obs.*

The title may have been suggested by ἄγγελος 'angel' (of a church) in Rev. i–iv.

1646 in *Rec. Massachussetts* (1853) II. 155 To assemble the churches, or their messengrs, upon occasion of counsell. *Ibid.*, A publike assembly of the elders and other messengers of the severall churches. **1665** J. ELIOT *Commun. of Churches* 4 The Intrinsecall and proper Efficients of a Council, are the Churches, who elect and send Messengers to that end. *Ibid.*, The Members Constituent of a Council, are Church-Messengers.

d. *fig.*

c **1400** *Rom. Rose* 2919 The eye is a good messangere, Which can to the herte..Tidyngis sende. **1490** CAXTON *Eneydos* xix. 71 [Mount Caucasus] sendeth doun her colde messagers as snowe, froste, heyle, & tempeste. **1591** SHAKS. *Two Gent.* II. ii. 77 His teares, pure messengers, sent from his heart. **1615** CROOKE *Body of Man* 535 The Sences..are the messengers and interpreters of the Soule. **1812** *Chron.* in *Ann. Reg.* 83 Casting these leaden messengers of death [*sc.* bullets]. **1832** W. IRVING *Alhambra* II. 39 Day after day he watched for the return of the messenger of love [*sc.* a bird]. **1860** RUSKIN *Mod. Paint* V. VI. vi. 43 It [the trunk] is rather a messenger to the roots.

e. Used as the name of a newspaper, periodical, etc.

1834 (*title*) Southern literary messenger. **1886** *Encycl. Brit.* XXI. 109/2 Many excellent literary journals and magazines..among these..the time-honoured *Viestnik Yevropî* ('Messenger of Europe'). **1922** JOYCE *Ulysses* 460 *Messenger of the Sacred Heart* and *Evening Telegraph* with Saint Patrick's Day Supplement. **1975** (*title*) Kent Messenger.

f. *Biol.* A molecule or substance that carries genetic information. Freq. *attrib.* (cf. *messenger RNA* in 7).

1961 BRENNER, JACOB & MESELSON in *Nature* 13 May 576 The paradox..can be resolved by the hypothesis, put forward by Jacob and Monod [in *J. Mol. Biol.* (in the press)], that..ribosomes are non-specialized structures which receive genetic information from the gene in the form of an unstable intermediate or 'messenger'. **1962** *Listener* 8 Mar. 413/2 'Messenger' molecules of RNA. **1969** A. M. CAMPBELL *Episomes* ix. 116 The genes of one operon are all transcribed onto the same messenger molecule. *Ibid.* 117 The rate of messenger synthesis. **1971** *Nature* 2 July 12/1 Where there are no operons messengers are evidently monocistronic.

†**2.** *esp.* **a.** A servant sent forward to prepare the way; a forerunner, precursor, harbinger. *Obs.*

c **1325** *Metr. Hom.* (1862) 44 He [St. John] was ryt Cristes messager. **1340** *Ayenb.* 195 Huanne a riche man ssel come to ane toune..he zent his messagyers be-uore uor to nime guod in. **1382** WYCLIF *Luke* ix. 52 And he sente messangeris bifore his siȝt. **1596** SHAKS. *Merch. V.* v. i. 117 There is come a Messenger before To signifie their comming. [**1884** BIBLE (R.V.) *Mal.* iii. 1 (as in earlier versions).]

b. *fig.*

a **1225** *Ancr. R.* 190 Ich am þe scheadewe, seið þis messager, þet is, worldes pine. *c* **1374** CHAUCER *Troylus* III. 1368 [1417] And lucifer, þe dayes messager, Gan for to ryse, and out here bemys þrow. *c* **1386** —— *Knt.'s T.* 633 The bisy larke, messager of day. —— *Man of Law's Prol.* 6 Of Aprill, that is messager to May. **1545** *Primer, Lauds* C iij b, The birde, of day messinger, Croweth and sheweth, that light is nere. **1601** SHAKS. *Jul. C.* II. i. 104 Yon grey Lines, That fret the Clouds, are Messengers of Day.

c. *cuckoo's messenger*: (see quot.).

1885 SWAINSON *Prov. Names Birds* 103 Wryneck... From its arrival the same time as, or a little before, the cuckoo, it has the names of..Cuckoo's messenger [etc.].

d. *pl.* Small clouds detached from the main mass.

1787 BEST *Angling* (ed. 2) 145 When..there are small black fragments of clouds like smoke, flying underneath, which some call messengers,..rain is not far off. **1880** JEFFERIES *Gr. Ferne F.* 133.

3. a. A government official employed to carry dispatches, and, formerly, to apprehend state prisoners; esp. one employed by the Secretaries of State. *Messenger of the Exchequer* (see quot. 1706). *King's* or *Queen's Messenger*, one who conveys dispatches to or from the Sovereign.

1535 *Act 27 Hen. VIII*, c. 27 §3 There shalbe..one other person, which shalbe called Messanger of the same Courte. **1694** WOOD *Life* 2 Aug. (O.H.S.) III, Most of the messingers are gone into the country to fetch up persons seised upon account of the plot. **1696** PHILLIPS, *Messenger*, one that attends upon the King and his Council to carry Dispatches, and waits upon the Sergeant at Arms to Apprehend Prisoners of State. **1706** —— (ed. Kersey), *Messengers of the Exchequer*, certain Officers in that Court, four in Number, who as Pursuivants, attend the Lord Treasurer, to carry his Letters and Orders. **1713** SWIFT *Jrnl. to Stella* 31 Mar., Mr. Noble..was..seized again by the Sheriff, and is now in a messenger's hands at the Black Swan in Holborn. **1732** BERKELEY *Alciphr.* I. §9 A man had better a thousand times be hunted by bailiffs or messengers. **1866** *Guide to Employm. in Civ. Serv.* 71 War Department... Messengers, Queen's Messengers, and Letter-carriers. **1874** *Act 37 & 38 Vict.* c. 81 §4 The office of messenger or pursuivant of the Great Seal shall as a separate office be abolished. **1879** C. MARVIN *Public Offices* 201 A Queen's Messenger who is about to set off in five minutes' time for Cairo.

b. *Sc.* **messenger(-at-arms)**: see quot. 1838.

1482 in Rymer *Foedera* (1711) 166/1 We..Constitute..the same Gartier and Northumberlond, our Ambassadours, Oratours, Procuratours, Factours, and Masseagers. **1587** *Sc. Acts. Jas. VI* (1814) III. 449/2 Of late ȝeiris þair is enterit in the office of armes sindry extraordinar maseris..and a verie greit nowmer of messingeris. **1753** R. THOMSON (*title*) A Treatise of the Office of Messenger. *Ibid.* 2 There ought only to be in all Scotland 200 Messengers, or Officers of Arms (including Heralds, Macers and Pursuivants, 17 in Number). **1812** TENNANT *Anster F.* II. xxxiii, Sheriffs learn'd..and messengers-at-arms, with brows of brass. **1838** BELL *Dict. Law Scot.*, *Messenger-at-arms*; an officer appointed by, and under the control of the Lyon King-at-Arms... They are employed in executing all summonses and letters of diligence, both in civil and criminal matters. Our signet letters..were constantly directed to messengers-at-arms, as sheriffs in that part. **1872** MICHIE *Deeside Tales* 17 (E.D.D.) A messenger-at-arms..the terror of evil doers far and wide.

†**c.** ***messenger of the press***, an officer appointed to search for unlicensed publications and presses.

1682 LUTTRELL *Brief Rel.* (1857) I. 226 The Stationers company..have called one Robert Stephens (a common messenger of the presse) on the livery. **1694** WOOD *Life* 16 Oct. (O.H.S.) III, Tomson the printer was seized on by Stephens the messenger of the press, in the act of printing a pamphlet reflecting on the Government. **1706** in PHILLIPS (ed. Kersey).

d. *Bankruptcy law.* (See quot. 1894.)

1732 *Act 5 Geo. II*, c. 30 §4 That every such Bankrupt..shall be..required..to deliver up.. all his..Bookes of Accounts..not seized by the Messenger of the said Commission. **1883** *Act 46 & 47 Vict.* c. 52 §153 The official solicitors and messengers in bankruptcy..shall be transferred to and become officers of the Board of Trade. **1894** G. Y. ROBSON *Law Bankruptcy* (ed. 7) 77 The messenger was a sort of sheriff's officer employed to execute the orders and warrants of the court. Originally..a messenger was attached to the court of each commissioner... In the Bankruptcy Act, 1883, the messenger and his staff are transferred to..the Board of Trade, and are to perform analogous duties to those previously discharged by them.

e. (See quot.)

1867 SMYTH *Sailor's Word-bk.*, *Messengers*, boys appointed to carry orders from the quarter-deck.

4. An endless rope or chain passing from the capstan to the cable to haul it in. Also, a similar contrivance for hauling-in a dredge. Also, 'any line sent ahead by which a larger line is run to a dock, buoy or similar use' (G. Bradford *Gloss. Sea Terms* 1927).

1633 T. JAMES *Voy.* 80 We..put our Cables ouer-boord, with Messengers vnto them. **1784** J. KING *Cook's Voy. Pacific* III. 475 Having, in our endeavours to heave the anchor out of the ground, twice broken the old messenger, and afterward a new one. **1882** NARES *Seamanship* (ed. 6) 159 The messenger is an endless chain passing round the capstan and two rollers in the manger.

5. a. (See quot.)

1746 CHESTERF. *Lett.* (1845) I. 53 My long and frequent letters..put me in mind of certain papers, which you have very lately, and I formerly, sent up to kites, along the string, which we called messengers; some of them the wind used to blow away,..and but few of them got up and stuck to the kite. **1864** *Every Little Boy's Bk.* 99 Some boys amuse themselves by sending messengers up to their kites when they have let out all their string. A messenger is formed of a piece of paper three or four inches square.

b. A device which may be sent down a line in order to trip some mechanism attached to it.

1929 *Jrnl. du Conseil* IV. 193 When a messenger is sent down the line it first hits the arm holding the stop. By the blow the stop is forced away, the messenger below is set free. **1959** H. BARNES *Oceanogr. & Marine Biol.* iii. 113 When the required depth has been reached, the bottle is allowed to remain there for 3 to 5 minutes, so that the thermometer may reach equilibrium and a 'messenger' is then sent down the wire. The hook is released and the springs contract closing the bottle. **1963** H. F. P. HERDMAN in M. N. Hill *Sea* II. vi. 124 When the messenger hits this catch, the lids are immediately closed and the bottle falls away through 180°.

6. The secretary-bird.

1793 *Buffon's Birds* VII. 316.

7. *attrib.* and *Comb.*, as ***messenger-authority***, ***-bird***, ***-boy***, ***-wind***; ***messenger-like*** adv.; **messenger cable**, a cable used to support a power cable or other conductor of electricity; a suspension cable or wire; **messenger RNA** *Biol.*, RNA which, after being synthesized in a cell nucleus in accordance with the genetic information carried by a gene ('transcription'), passes out of the nucleus and carries this information to a ribosome, where it determines which particular protein is synthesized there ('translation'); abbrev. *mRNA* (M 5); **messenger sword**, a sword-like implement, constituting a credential of the royal messengers of Ashantee (*Cent. Dict.* 1890); **messenger wire** = *messenger cable.*

1711 SHAFTESB. *Charac.* (1737) III. 337 There are further miracles remaining for 'em to perform, e'er they can in modesty plead the apostolick or messenger-authority. **1869** TOZER *Highl. Turkey* II. 327 A messenger-bird is described as issuing from the gloomy dungeon. **1876** J. S. INGRAM *Centenn. Exposition* 713 The messenger boys were seen everywhere conspicuous in their neat uniforms. **1886** *Pall Mall Gaz.* 26 Aug. 11/1 A Wall-street banker..sent a note by a district messenger boy to the office of his broker. **1922** JOYCE *Ulysses* 84 Messenger boys stealing to put on sixpence. **1959** N. MAILER *Advts. for Myself* (1961) 208, I was amateur agent for it, messenger boy, editorial consultant..and I made a hundred mistakes. **1916** *Stand. Rules Amer. Inst. Electr. Engin.* §778 A messenger wire or cable is a wire or cable running along with and supporting other wires, cables or contact conductors. **1948** *Building, Estimating & Contracting* (Amer. Techn. Soc.) IX. 48 A stranded steel messenger cable is strung over the chord of the trusses. **1594** G. ELLIS in *Buccleuch MSS.* (Hist. MSS. Comm.) 25 He is upon a journey, messenger like,..to apprehend..her Majesty's loving subjects. **1961** BRENNER, JACOB & MESELSON in *Nature* 13 May 577/1 Model III implies that a special type of RNA molecule, or 'messenger RNA', exists which brings genetic information from genes to non-specialized ribosomes. **1961** JACOB & MONOD in *Jrnl. Molecular Biol.* III. 350 A small fraction of RNA, first observed by Volkin & Astrachan (1957) in phage infected *E. coli* and recently found to exist also in normal yeasts..and coli.., does seem to meet all the qualifications listed above. This fraction (which we shall designate 'messenger RNA' or M-RNA) amounts to only about 3% of the total RNA. **1970** AMBROSE & EASTY *Cell Biol.* iii. 113 Three types of RNA are involved in protein synthesis in the cytoplasm—messenger, transfer, and ribosomal RNA. **1973** *Sci. Amer.* Aug. 21/1 Some of the RNA (messenger RNA) determines the structure of the proteins (primarily enzymes) that constitute or manufacture all the tissues of the organism. **1898** *Blackw. Mag.* Mar. 427 The messenger-wind that drives before the dawn. **1898** E. J. HOUSTON *Dict. Electr. Words* (ed. 4) 849/2 Messenger wire of aerial cable. **1916** Messenger wire [see *messenger cable* above]. **1948** *Man. Uniform Traffic Control Devices* (U.S. Pub. Roads Admin.) III. 117 All overhead cable shall be supported by a suitable aerial messenger wire whenever there is a span of more than 30 feet.

messengership ('mɛsɪndʒəʃɪp). [f. MESSENGER + -SHIP.] The office or function of a messenger.

1611 COTGR. s.v. *Messagerie*, A messengership; the estate, office, or function of a messenger. **1880** FAWCETT *Sp.* in *Ho. Comm.* 20 Aug., Candidates for messengerships—by which I presume is meant rural letter carrierships.

messengery. *Sc.* ? *Obs.* Also 6 **messingerie.** [f. MESSENGER + -ERY. Cf. MESSAGERY.] The office of messenger-at-arms.

1587 *Sc. Acts Jas. III* (1814) III. 449/2 He..commandis lioun king of armes That he onnawys ressaue ony maner of personis to the office of messingerie in tyme cuming except it be [etc.]. **1753** R. THOMSON *Office of Messenger* 17 That the said M, Messenger within the Sheriffdom of —— shall leilly, truly and honestly use and exerce the Office of Messengery.

Messenian (mɛ'siːnɪən), *sb.* and *a.* [f. L. *Messenius*, Gr. Μεσσήνιος Messenian + -AN.]

A. *sb.* **a.** A native or inhabitant of Messenia, a region in the south-west Peloponnese bordered on the east by Laconia. **b.** The dialect of this region. **B.** *adj.* Of or belonging to Messenia.

1579 NORTH tr. *Plutarch's Lives* 674 The Lacedæmonians brake of from this general peace, and..made warre, in hope to recouer the Messenians contrie. **1600** HOLLAND tr. *Livy's Romane Hist.* XXXVI. 936 But the Messenians..sent the embassadors away. **1794** T. TAYLOR tr. *Pausanias' Descr. Greece* I. IV. iv. 346 A disagreement, for the first time, took place between the Messenians and Lacedæmonians. **1826** *Kaleidoscope* 14 Feb. 261/2 Ephemerus, the Messenian, advanced this paradoxical opinion. **1830** W. M. LEAKE *Trav. Morea* I. 366 Andhrússa..is advantageously situated, overlooking the rich Messenian plain. **1910** C. D. BUCK *Introd. Study Gk. Dial.* 10 The Doric Group... 2. *Messenian.* There is scarcely any material until a late period, when the dialect is no longer pure. **1911** *Encycl. Brit.* XXV. 610/1 Under Alcamenes and Theopompus a war broke out between the Spartans and the Messenians, their neighbours on the west. **1958** R. LIDDELL *Morea* II. 95 Currants from the rich Messenian vineyards lay everywhere. **1960** A. R. BURN *Lyric Age Greece* ix. 182 A Messenian hero, Aristomenes..gained fame in song. **1968** V. EHRENBERG *From Solon to Socrates* ii. 33 The kings Polydorus and Theopompus, the contemporaries of the First Messenian War. *Ibid.* vii. 275 The place was held by Messenians from Naupactus. **1969** A. TOYNBEE *Some Probl. Greek Hist.* III. ii. 164 It is probable that the Laconians and Messenians..were of mixed origin. **1972** A. BARTONĚK *Classification West Gk. Dial.* 91 In principle..Messenian produces the impression of representing an archaic form of Laconian. **1974** *Encycl. Brit. Micropædia* VI. 822/3 Many modern historians believe that there were only two early Messenian wars; the first (*c.* 735–*c.* 715) was the Spartan conquest of Messenia; but a Messenian revolt precipitated a second war, in which the Spartans were ultimately successful.

messer[1] ('mɛsə(r)). ? *Obs.* [? f. MESS *v.* + -ER[1].] ? A purveyor of meat for ships.

1644–5 *Will W. Cruse* (Somerset Ho.), W. Cruse of co. Somerset, Messer. **1746** in W. Thompson *R. N. Advoc.* (1757) 24 Though strongly opposed by Messers and Salters, they were obliged to..salt them [*sc.* the hogs].

messer[2] ('mɛsə(r)). *colloq.* [f. MESS *v.* + -ER[1].] One who makes a mess; a muddler, bungler (see also quot. 1951).

1937 E. POUND *Let.* July (1971) 296 The respectable and the middle generation, illustrious punks and messers, fakes like Shaw, stew like Wells, nickle cash-register Bennett. **1949** F. SARGESON *I Saw in my Dream* xiii. 131 Though of course he's an old messer. **1951** PARTRIDGE *Dict. Slang* (ed. 4) 1108/2 *Messer*,..a 'near' prostitute; an amateur not above taking money or a present... A man, or a woman, that does not keep to one lover. **1966** 'J. HACKSTON' *Father clears Out* 69 Where money and accounts were concerned she was the greatest messer living.

messer, obs. form of MACER[1].

messerayke, obs. form of MESARAIC.

Messerschmitt ('mɛsəʃmɪt). Also (erron.) **Messerschmidt.** [f. the name of Willy *Messerschmitt* (b. 1898), German aircraft designer.] Any of several types (esp. fighters) of German military aircraft used in the 1939–45 war. Also as *adj.*

1940 I. HALSTEAD *Wings of Victory* I. ii. 52 The Messerschmitts attacked us from the rear. **1948** A. M. TAYLOR *Lang. World War II* (rev. ed.) 130 *Messerschmitt*, twin-engined German fighter monoplane, especially adapted to bomber escort work. **1955** E. M. HULL in G. Conklin *Sci.-Fiction Adventures in Dimension* 12 If a flight of Messerschmitts attack us in the next five minutes, our machine-guns won't be much good. **1957** L. G. S. PAYNE

Air Dates 276 Munich, where Messerschmitt 262 jet fighters were being built. **1969** *Listener* 1 May 595/3 A wartime Spitfire chasing about after Messerschmidts over Kent. **1971** L. DEIGHTON *Declarations of War* 155 Above them the Messerschmitts and Spitfires were now only a mile apart.

messet (ˈmɛsɪt). *dial.* Also 7 misset. [? Altered from Sc. MESSAN, after dim. ending -ET¹.] A lap-dog. Also *attrib.* (Cf. MESSAN.)

1631 BRATHWAITE *Whimzies, Pedler* 139 Would you have a true survey of his family..? You shall finde them subsist of three heads: himselfe, his truck, and her misset. **1640** —— *Lanc. Lovers* iv. c 3, Hee would..carry her Misset, open her pue [etc.]. **1646** J. HALL *Poems* 10 Suppose dame Julia's Messet thinkes it meet To droop or hold up one of 'ts hinder feet. *a* **1694** M. ROBINSON *Autobiog.* (1856) 51 A breed of messet spaniels, very little, beautiful, and of rare conceit. **1822** BEWICK *Mem.* 27 She kept a messet dog.

†**Meˈssiacal**, *a. Obs. rare*⁻¹. [f. MESSIAH + -ACAL.] = MESSIANIC.

1614 JACKSON *Creed* III. xviii. §3 Nor Propheticall, nor Apostolicall, nor Messiacall, much lesse could Papall authority make them belieue.

Messiah (mɪˈsaɪə). Forms: α. 4 **Messie**, 4–5 **Messye**, 5 **Messy, Messe, Myssye**; β. 3 **Messyas**, 4–8 **Messias**; γ. 7 **Messiah**. [The α forms are a. F. *Messie*, ad. L. (Vulg.) *Messīās*, a. Gr. Μεσσίας, ad. Aramaic *m'shīḥā*, Heb. *māshīᵃḥ* anointed (in the LXX rendered Χριστός, CHRIST), f. *māshaḥ* to anoint. These forms do not occur in any Eng. transl. of the Bible, though common in other literature down to the 15th c. The form *Messias* was used in John i. 41 and iv. 25 (the only passages in which the word is found in the Gr. or Latin N.T.) by Wyclif after the Vulgate, and by later translators from 1526 to 1611 directly after the Greek. The form *Messiah*, invented by the translators of the Geneva Bible of 1560, is an alteration of the traditional *Messias*, intended to give it a more Hebraic aspect (the translators having on principle eliminated the Græcized forms of proper names from the O.T., though retaining them in the N.T.). In the Bible of 1611 it was adopted in Dan. ix. 25, 26, and although it occurs in no other passage of the 'Authorized Version', it eventually became the only current form. The Revisers of 1880–84 have substituted it for *Messias* in the two N.T. passages, but on the other hand have removed it from its original place in Dan. ix, where they read 'the anointed'.] The Hebrew title (= 'anointed') applied in the O.T. prophetic writings to a promised deliverer of the Jewish nation, and hence applied to Jesus of Nazareth as the fulfilment of that promise. (Chiefly preceded by *the* or defining word, exc. in the three Bible passages and sometimes in poetry, where it is treated as a proper name.) Hence *transf.*, an expected liberator or saviour of an oppressed people or country. (Written with capital M.)

α. **13..** *Propr. Sanct.* (Vernon MS.) in *Archiv Stud. neu. Spr.* LXXXI. 87/152 Andrew þenne to Symound tolde: 'Messye we ha founde'. ? *a* **1400** *Morte Arth.* 3998 Here I make myn avowe,..To Messie, and to Marie. **1430–40** LYDG. *Bochas* IX. i. 20 b, Sayd openly that he was Messy. *c* **1500** *Cov. Corpus Chr. Plays* i. 425 Yt ys seyd..That of the lyne of Jude Schuld spryng a right Messe.

β. [*c* **1000** *Ags. Gosp.* John i. 41 We ȝemetton messiam þæt is ȝereht crist.] *c* **1275** *Woman of Samaria* 55 in *O.E. Misc.* 85 Louerd heo seyde nv quiddeþ men þat cumen is Messyas. **1382** WYCLIF *John* i. 41 We han founde Messias, that is interpretid Crist. [So all later versions down to **1611**.] **1595** B. BARNES *Spir. Sonn.* x, Heavenly Messias! sweete anointed King! **1644** HOWELL *Eng. Teares* (1645) 181 To beat Religion into brains with a Pole axe, is to make Moloch of the Messias. **1681–6** J. SCOTT *Chr. Life* (1747) III. 531 Therefore do the modern Jews say, that the Messias is not yet come.

γ. **1560** BIBLE (Genev.) *Dan.* ix. 25 From the going forthe of the commandement..to builde Ierusalem, vnto Messiah the prince...26 And after thre score & two wekes, shal Messiah be slayne. [So **1611**.] **1653** MILTON *Ps.* ii. 6 Against the Lord and his Messiah dear. **1666** DRYDEN *Ann. Mirab.* cxiv, The wily Dutch, who, like fallen angels, feared This new Messiah's coming. *a* **1716** SOUTH *Serm.* (ed. 6) III. 299 All pretended false Messiahs vanish'd upon the Appearance of Christ the true one. **1776** J. ADAMS in *Fam. Lett.* (1876) 158 We are waiting, it is said, for Commissioners; a messiah that will never come. **1821** SHELLEY *Hellas* notes 57 The Greeks expect a Saviour from the West. It is reported that this Messiah had arrived..in an American brig.

attrib. **1850** CARLYLE *Latter-d. Pamph.* IV. 5 A People whose bayonets were sacred, a kind of Messiah People, saving a blind world in its own despite.

Messiahship (mɪˈsaɪəʃɪp). [f. MESSIAH + -SHIP.] The character or office of the Messiah or of a Messiah.

1627 S. WARD *Happin. Practice* 23 By this, Christ demonstrated..his Messiasship. *a* **1716** SOUTH *Serm.* (ed. 6) III. 299 The Messiahship was pretended to by several Impostors. **1856** R. A. VAUGHAN *Mystics* (1860) II. 289 Hegel condescends to throw to Behmen some words of patronising praise, as a distant harbinger of his own philosophical Messiahship.

Messianic (mɛsɪˈænɪk), *a.* [ad. mod.L. *Messiānic-us*, f. *Messīās*: see MESSIAH and -IC. Cf. F. *messianique*, G. *messianisch*.] Of, pertaining to, or relating to the Messiah.

a **1834** COLERIDGE *Lit. Rem.* (1838) III. 15 It [Ps. lxxxvii] seems clearly Messianic. *Ibid.* 179 Doubts of his [Christ's] Messianic character and divinity. **1883** FARRAR *St. Paul* (1883) 107 In all ages the Messianic hope had been prominent in the minds of the most enlightened Jews.

Hence **Messiˈanically** *adv.*, as referring to the Messiah.

1896 *Academy* 18 July 52/1 This expression..was very soon after understood Messianically.

So **Meˈssianism**, belief in a coming Messiah; **Meˈssianize** *v.* (nonce-wd.) *trans.*, to imbue with a Messianic character.

1876 BP. ALEXANDER *Witness of Ps.* (1877) 23 It will be observed that any one Psalm, definitively Messianised, is pregnant with the Messianic principle. *Ibid.*, Messianism becomes at once the central scheme. **1904** *Contemp. Rev.* Aug. 198 Jesus Christ gets behind the formal Messianism of his time.

Messias, variant of MESSIAH.

‖**Messidor** (mesidɔr). [Fr.; f. L. *messi-s* harvest + Gr. δῶρον gift.] The tenth month of the French revolutionary calendar.

1838 NICOLAS *Chronol. Hist.* 182 Messidor (Harvest Month) June 19–July 18.

Messie, obs. form of MESSIAH.

†**Meˈssiess**. *Obs. nonce-wd.* [f. MESSIAH + -ESS.] A female Messiah.

1685 LOVELL *Gen. Hist. Relig.* 50 That the Messiah came into the world onely for Men, and that the Lady Iean was to be the Messiess of the Women.

messieurs (ˈmɛsjʊəz, ‖mesjø), *sb. pl.* [a. Fr., pl. of MONSIEUR.]

1. a. The plural of MONSIEUR, in its various uses. (When used as a prefixed title, now commonly represented, as in Fr., by the abbreviation *MM.*)

1624 MASSINGER *Parl. Love* I. v, My lord of Orleans.. assisted By the messieurs Philamour and Lafort. **1696** VANBRUGH *Relapse* I. iii, Hey, messieurs, entrez. **1731** FIELDING *Tom Thumb* I. iii, Let Rome her Cæsar's and her Scipio's show, Her Messieurs France, let Holland boast Mynheers. **1770** J. Z. HOLWELL *Orig. Princ. Anc. Bramins* viii. §102 (1779) 119 However Mess. Yvon and Bouillet refute the Cartesian hypothesis, by [etc.]. **1827** SCOTT *Napoleon* VIII. 83 The two Messrs. de Polignac were deeply engaged. **1841** EMERSON *Method Nat.* Wks. (1881) II. 225 Why should not then these messieurs of Versailles strut and plot for tabourets and ribbons?

b. *nonce-use.* Imitating the Fr. use of the title before a personal designation in the plural.

1809 BYRON *Bards & Rev.* ix. *note*, Messieurs the Spirits of Flood and Fell. **1854** THACKERAY *Newcomes* I. i. 8, I warrant Messieurs the landlords their interests would be better consulted by keeping their singers within bounds.

c. nonce-use. *the Messieurs* = the French.

1889 DOYLE *Micah Clarke* 162 Two campaigns with the Messieurs in the Palatinate.

2. a. Used to supply the want of an English plural of MR. (Commonly in the abbreviated form Messrs.)

1779 MME. D'ARBLAY *Diary* (1842) I. 211 Lord Mordaunt, Messieurs Murphy, Fisher, and Fitzgerald. **1793** SMEATON *Edystone L.* §131, I returned with Messrs. Jessop and Richardson to Plymouth. **1849** THACKERAY *Pendennis* I. xviii. 164 Lady Agnes..voted the two Messieurs Pendennis most agreeable men. **1888** MAPLESON *Mem.* (ed. 2) I. 215 Messrs. Steinway now..undertook to supply each leading member of the Company with pianos.

b. *nonce-use.* As a title of address (without reference to foreigners) = 'Gentlemen'; 'Sirs'.

1789 WOLCOT (P. Pindar) *Tithe Rencounter* Wks. 1792 III. 27 Messieurs! I've search'd our ancient *Modus* over.

messilling, obs. form of MASLIN¹.

messin, obs. form of MESSAN.

†**ˈmessing**, *sb. Obs.* [? a. Du. *messing* (see MASLIN¹).] = MASLIN¹.

1371 *Fabric Rolls York Minster* (Surtees) 10, xxj lb. de messyng emptis de Ricardo Kyng 3*s.* 6*d.* **1379** *Mem. Ripon* (Surtees) III. 99 In ij petr. ij lb. de messyng emp. 4*s.* 2*d.*

ˈmessing (ˈmɛsɪŋ), *vbl. sb.* [f. MESS *v.* + -ING¹.] The action of the verb MESS¹.

†**1.** Feasting, banqueting. *Obs. rare*⁻¹.

1340 *Ayenb.* 71 Gerlondes, robes, playinges, messinges, and alle goudes byeþ ous yfayled. [*Orig.* (ed. 1495) *has*: Chapeaux, deduis, et tous biens nous sont faillis.]

2. Participation in a mess or common meal.

1822 *Regul. & Ord. Army* 123 The Regularity of the Men's Messing is an object of primary Importance. **1864** *Athenæum* 5 Nov. 598/1 The introduction of the system of messing in our jails. **1898** *Folk-Lore* June 118 A right of free messing at the table of the Homeric king.

3. The providing of food to a (soldier's) mess; also *concr.* the food served out to a man; *rarely* payment for such food.

1811 WELLINGTON in Gurw. *Desp.* (1838) VIII. 295 By what you had seen of the messing of both regiments..it does appear that the soldiers..were not at all times messed in the manner pointed out by your order. **1884** SIR F. S. ROBERTS in *19th Cent.* June 1069 Rations should include what is now known as 'extra messing'. **1884** *Pall Mall G.* 9 Sept. 6/1 Out of the private's pay, after deducting 'messing'..he has to [etc.]. **1895** R. BLATCHFORD *Merrie England* vi. 48 His duty is to expend the messing money and superintend the messing.

4. *attrib.*, as *messing allowance, money.*

1892 *Pall Mall G.* 25 Feb. 6/2 The soldier..should receive a messing allowance of 3*d.* a day. **1889** *Daily News* 2 Jan. 2/4 Nor has the soldier been called on to pay a farthing more than the 3*d.* a day messing money he has always paid.

messinger(e, obs. forms of MESSENGER.

‖**messire** (mɛsir). Now only *Hist.* [Fr.; repr. the nom. (L. *meus senior*), while *monsieur* represents the accusative (L. *meum seniōrem*).] A title of honour (= Sir) prefixed to the name of a French noble of high rank, and later to the names of persons of quality, and members of the learned professions; also used as a form of address.

1477 EARL RIVERS (Caxton) *Dictes* 2 A worschipful man callid messire Jehan de Teonuille. *a* **1548** HALL *Chron., Hen. VIII* 206 Messire Pomoray the Frenche Ambassador. **1865** BARING-GOULD *Werewolves* xii. 215 Do you think then, messire, that your servants will accuse you?

Mess-John: see MAS *sb.*¹ 2.

messlyng, obs. form of MASLIN¹.

messmate (ˈmɛsmeɪt). [f. MESS *sb.* + MATE *sb.*]

1. A companion at meals; one of a mess, esp. of a ship's mess.

1746 *Brit. Mag.* 346, I..had him for a Mess-mate. **1771** SMOLLETT *Humph. Cl.* 10 June, At two in the afternoon, I found myself one of ten messmates seated at table. **1835** MARRYAT *Jac. Faithf.* x, He was..a good, quiet, honest messmate, as ever slung a hammock.

Proverbial. **1867** SMYTH *Sailor's Word-bk* s.v., Messmate before a shipmate, shipmate before a stranger [etc.].

2. *Biol.* = COMMENSAL B. 2.

1876 *Beneden's Anim. Parasites* i. 1 Animal messmates. *Ibid.* 3 There are some free messmates which never renounce their independence... The others, the fixed messmates, instal themselves with a neighbour, and live at their ease. *Ibid.* 48 We only know one Ophiurus which lives as a messmate on a comatula. **1879** [see COMMENSAL B. 2].

3. *Austral.* A name given to some species of Eucalyptus; esp. *E. amygdalina* and *E. obliqua*.

1889 J. H. MAIDEN *Usef. Plants* 429 Because it is allied to, or associated with, 'Stringybark', it [*Eucalyptus amygdalina*] is also known by the name of 'Messmate'. **1890** *Melbourne Argus* 7 June 13/4 Dead messmates and white gums rise like gaunt skeletons from..the underwood.

Hence **ˈmessmatism** *Biol.* = COMMENSALISM.

1886 *Lond. Q. Rev.* July 246 Marine Messmatism. One of the most interesting features of life in the waters is that which has been called 'Commensalism', or, if we may adopt a newly coined word, 'Messmatism'.

messon, messongere, obs. ff. MESSAN, MESSENGER.

‖**ˈmessor.** [a. L. *messor.*]

1. 'A reaper or mower' (Blount *Glossogr.* 1656). *Obs.*⁻⁰ Hence †**meˈssorious** *a.*, belonging to reaping (ibid.).

2. *Ent.* [mod.L. (A. Forel 1890, in *Ann. Soc. Ent. Belg. Bull.* p. lxviii).] A member of the genus of harvesting ants so called. Also *attrib.*

1924 J. A. THOMSON *Sci. Old & New* xii. 68 In the case of the Messor ants of the Sahara there are deep and spacious underground galleries, in which food is accumulated for the dry season.

messo-tinto, obs. form of MEZZOTINTO.

messour, obs. form of MACER¹.

1625 *Burgh Rec. Glasgow* (1876) I. 345 Ane presentatioune to be maid in favouris of Williame Fischer, sone to Matho Fischer, messour, of the first vacant place of ane brussour within the colledge of Glasgw.

messrs.: see MESSIEURS 2 a.

messuage (ˈmɛsweɪdʒ). Also 5–7 **mesuage**. [a. AF. *messuage, mesuage*, prob. orig. a graphic corruption of *mesnage*: see MENAGE.

The main difficulty in the way of this etymology is the existence of a continental OF. *masuage, masuiage, masowaige*, denoting a tenement of some kind, and a related *masuier, masuwier, masoier, mazowier*, tenant of a '*masuage*' (cf. Frankish Latin *mansuarius, mansoarius*). OF. had also *masurage* denoting a tenement, and *masurier* the corresponding term for the tenant, f. *masure*:—late L. type **mansūra* dwelling, f. *manēre* to dwell.]

Originally, the portion of land intended to be occupied, or actually occupied, as a site for a dwelling-house and its appurtenances. In modern legal language, a dwelling-house with its outbuildings and curtilage and the adjacent land assigned to its use. *capital messuage*: see CAPITAL *a.* 6 b.

[**1290** *Rolls of Parlt.* I. 53/2 De uno Messuagio cum pertin' ibidem.] *c* **1386** CHAUCER *Reeve's T.* 59 The person of the toun..In purpos was to maken hir his heir Bothe of his catel and his messuage. **1463** *Will J. Baret* in *Bury Wills* (Camden) 24, I beqwethe to William Baret,..myn hefd place, othir wyse callyd a mesuage, wiche I dwellyd in. **1577** in *Misc. Gen. & Her.* Ser. III. I. 83 The said William was also seised..of one messuage non edeficat. **1588** FRAUNCE *Lawiers Log.* I. vi. 31 b, A messuage is made of two partes, del terre et structure. **1609** SKENE *Reg. Maj.* 33 Reservand alwaies the chiefe messuage, to the eldest sonne. **1639** *MS.*

Indenture, estate at Knedlington, co. York, A sellion, being the fourth part of one messuage lying on the marsh. **1797** *Trans. Soc. Arts* XV. 120 John Sutton certifieth, that he is the occupier of a messuage and a farm. **1820** MISS MITFORD in L'Estrange *Life* (1870) II. v. 91 Our residence is a cottage ..—a messuage or tenement, such as a little farmer.. might retire to. **1837** LOCKHART *Scott* III. 69 The magnificent Castle of Drumlanrig in Nithsdale, the principal messuage of the dukedom of Queensberry. **1842** TENNYSON *Edwin Morris* 126 They wedded her to sixty thousand pounds, To lands in Kent and messuages in York.

b. *Comb.*: †**messuage-stead.**

1564 *Yorks. Chantry Surv.* (Surtees) 277, ij messuage steids, with one kilnehouse. *Ibid.* 334 One mesuage stede, not buylded upon.

messuage, obs. form of MESSAGE.

†**messuager.** *Obs. rare.* [f. MESSUAGE + -ER[1].] One who holds or possesses a messuage.

1666–7 *N. Riding Rec.* VI. 108 The cottagers, the husbandmen, and the messuagers of Melmerby. **1739** *Bewholm Inclos. Act* 6 Proprietors, messuagers, cottagers.

mess-up. *colloq.* [f. *to mess up* (MESS *v.* 5).] = MESS *sb.* 3.

1902 C. J. C. HYNE *Mr. Horrocks, Purser* 111, I should say he feels this mess-up more than any of us. **1920** W. J. LOCKE *House of Baltazar* xxii. 274 It is ruin to your career and a mess up of your whole life. **1929** *Star* 21 Aug. 12/3, I am afraid there has been a bit of a mess-up.

messurger, rare obs. form of MESSENGER.

messy (ˈmɛsɪ), *a.* [f. MESS *sb.*[2] + -Y[1].] **a.** Of the nature of a mess; attended with 'messes' or disorder; untidy.

1843 MRS. CARLYLE *Lett.* I. 235, I have had your letter, for consolation in my messy job [glazing and painting]. **1890** *Spectator* 15 Feb., The boy who holds the mirror.. is, for Velazquez, somewhat messy in execution. **1899** F. T. BULLEN *Log Sea-waif* 210 How we did hate the messy, fiddling abomination.

b. *colloq.* Immoral; unethical.

1924 LAWRENCE & SKINNER *Boy in Bush* xxi. 299, I can't bear to think of Monica messy with Easu. **1928** D. H. LAWRENCE *Woman who rode Away* 198 He was a perfectly decent boy, and there would never have been anything messy to fear from him. **1960** WENTWORTH & FLEXNER *Dict. Amer. Slang* 337/1 *Messy*,.. immoral; unethical.

Hence ˈ**messiness.**

1893 *Brit. Jrnl. Photogr.* 15 Dec. 793 Although there is no difficulty in making it, yet is there a certain amount of messiness.

mest(e, obs. ff. MOST.

mestang, var. MUSTANG.

mestee: see MUSTEE.

mestelyn, obs. form of MASLIN[2].

mesteque. ? *Obs.* Also mastique, mestica, mestique. [Of obscure origin.

Réaumur *Hist. des Insectes* (1738) IV. 90 says: 'Elle [la cochenille fine] est appelée cochenille Mesteque, parce qu'on en fait des recoltes à Meteque [*sic*] dans la province de Honduras'. No such place-name is known to have existed in Honduras; perh. what is meant is *Mixteca*, the name of the ancient Mexican province corresponding to the present Oaxaca. It is doubtful whether the word ever had any English currency: there is some ground for the suspicion that Réaumur is the source of all the later references to it.]

The finest kind of cochineal.

[**1600** *Hakluyt's Voy.* III. 455 [Voy. R. Tomson in N. Hisp. 1555.] There is a place called the Misteca, fiftie leagues to the Northwest [of Mexico], which doth yeeld great store of.. Cochinilla.] **1667** PETTY *Dycing* in Sprat *Hist. R. Soc.* (1722) 298 Cochineal is of several sorts, *viz.* Silvester and Mestequa. **1753** CHAMBERS *Cycl. Supp.* s.v. *Progall-insect*, There are two kinds of cochineal, the finer called *mestique*, the other termed wild cochineal. **1780** *Ann. Reg.* II. 104 [citing Réaumur] A much finer cochineal, known by the name of mestica. **1797** *Encycl. Brit.* (ed. 3) V. 109/2 In trade, four sorts [of cochineal] are distinguished, *Mastique, Campeschane, Tetraschale*, and *Sylvester*. **1839** URE *Dict. Arts* 303 Two sorts of cochineal are gathered—the wild.. and the cultivated, or the *grana fina*, termed also *mesteque*, from the name of a Mexican province.

mester, variant of MISTER *Obs.*

†ˈ**mestful**, *a. Obs. rare.* [f. L. *mæst-us* sad + -FUL.] = MESTIVE.

1577 T. KENDALL *Flowers of Epigrammes* F v, Emong all other birds, moste mestfull birde am I. **1598** TOFTE *Alba* (1880) 17 Vnto whom shall I (now) dedicate This mestfull verse, this mournfull Elegie?

mesti, variant form of MUSTEE.

mestica, variant form of MESTEQUE.

mesticall, variant form of MISKAL.

mestick, mestico, variant forms of MESTIZO.

mestier, variant form of MISTER *Obs.*, trade.

†**meˈstifical**, *a. Obs.*—[0] [f. L. *mæstific-us* (f. *mæstus* sad + *-ficus* making) + -AL[1].]

1656 BLOUNT *Glossogr.*, *Mestifical*, that maketh heavy or sad.

mestigo, mestilione: see MESTIZO, MASLIN[2].

[**mestino**, a spurious form of MESTIZO in Brande *Dict. Sci.* etc. (1842), and in later Dicts. (Webster *Suppl.* 1902 confounds it with the Sp. *mesteño* MUSTANG.)]

mestique, var. MESTEQUE, kind of cochineal.

mestisa, -ise, -iso, -ito, obs. ff. MESTIZO.

†ˈ**mestive**, *a. Obs.* Also 7 mæstive. [as if ad. L. type **mæstīvus*, f. *mæs-*, *mærēre* to mourn: see -IVE.] Mournful.

1578 T. PROCTOR *Gorg. Gallery* M ij b, A carking care, a mount of mestiue mone. **1609** J. DAVIES *Holy Roode* (Grosart) 6/2 This kinde Pellican in mæstiue moode.

‖**mestiza** (mɛˈstiːzə). Also 7 **mestisa, mus-, mostesa.** [Sp., fem. of *mestizo*.] A woman of the mestizo race. Also *attrib.*

c **1582** M. PHILIPS in *Hakluyt's Voy.* (1600) III. 482 Paul Horsewell is maried to a Mestisa, as they name those whose fathers were Spaniards, and their mothers Indians. **1697** DAMPIER *Voy.* (1729) I. 388 Mr. Fitz-Gerald had in this time gotten a Spanish Mustesa Woman to Wife. **1760–72** tr. *Juan & Ulloa's Voy.* (ed. 3) I. 121 The Mestiza, or Negro women, or the coloured women as they are called here [Panama]. **1851** MACMICKING *Recoll. Manilla* 61 The Mestiza girls being frequently good-looking. **1890** *Pall Mall G.* 5 Aug. 2/1 The olive-skinned mestizas.

‖**mestizo** (mɛˈstiːzəʊ). Forms: 6 **mastizo**, 6–7 **mestico**, 7 **mastiso, mestiso, -tisa, mostesa, musteese, -tezo, mestick**, 7–8 **mestise, mostese**, 7–9 **mestize**, 8 **mestigo, mestito, mustice, -tizo**, 6– **mestizo.** [Sp. *mestizo*, Pg. *mestiço*, = Pr. *mestis*, F. *métis*:—popular L. type *mixticius*, f. L. *mixt-us*, pa. pple. of *miscēre* to mix.] **a.** A Spanish or Portuguese half-caste; now chiefly, the offspring of a Spaniard and an American Indian. Also applied to other persons of mixed blood, or to a Central or South American Indian who has adopted European culture.

In the occasional application to a Portuguese half-caste, it should now have the Pg. spelling *mestiço*.

c **1588** PRETTY in *Hakluyt's Voy.* (1600) III. 814 A Mestizo is one which hath a Spaniard to his father and an Indian to his mother. **1613** PURCHAS *Pilgrimage* (1614) 486 The Portugalls many of them are married with Indian women, and their posteritie are called Mesticos. *a* **1616** HAKLUYT *Divers Voy.* App. (1850) 167 Worsted stockings knit which are worn of the mastizoes. **1678** in *Notes & Extracts Rec. Fort St. George* I. (1871) 88 (Y.) Europeans, Musteeses, and Topasees. **1698** FRYER *Acc. E. India & P.* 57 Beyond the Outworks live a few Portugals Mustezos or Misteradoes. **1704** *Collect. Voy. & Trav.* III. 76/1 The Mestito's or Mongrel Breed of a Spanish Man and Indian Woman. **1782** H. WALPOLE *To Mason* 8 July *Lett.* (1858) VIII. 251 Even demigods have intermarried till their race are become downright *mestises*. **1842** PRICHARD *Nat. Hist. Man* v. (1845) 21 What gives these Mestizos a peculiarly striking appearance is the excessively long hair of the head. **1875** JAGOR *Trav. Philippines* 290 Creoles and mestizes are for the most part too idle even to keep sheep. **1878** C. HALLOCK *Amer. Club List & Sportman's Gloss.* p. vii/2 *Mestizo* (Sp.), a cross between an Indian and a negro. **1909** WEBSTER *Mestizo*... In Spanish America and the Philippines, a person of mixed blood; esp., the offspring of a European or person of European stock and an (East) Indian, Negro, Malay, or other person of dark, non-European stock; often specif., *Phil. I.*, a person of Chinese and native blood. **1930** R. MACAULAY *Staying with Relations* vi. § 1. 75 They [*sc.* the Spaniards] go mestizo sooner or later, and are the better for it; a little Indian blood gingers them up. **1941** R. HUMPHREYS *Latin Amer.* 6 In Brazil.. half the population is white, but Indians predominate in the interior, mestizos in the north, and the negro element is strong in Bahia. **1959** [see CHOLO, CHOLO]. **1962** N. MAXWELL *Witch-Doctor's Apprentice* v. 52 Cholo means mestizo, half-breed. Seems it's more polite to call a man half-breed than an Indian. **1967** WEBSTER, *Mestizo*... 2: a completely acculturated Central or So. American Indian. **1969** *Time* 14 July 14/2 *Mestizo*, person of mixed Spanish and Indian blood, as are most Mexican Americans. **1973** *Nat. Geographic* May 642/1 Juan himself is a mestizo, part Indian, part Spanish. **1974** *Encycl. Brit. Micropædia* VI. 824/3 In some countries—*i.e.*, Ecuador—the word has acquired social and cultural connotations; a pure-blooded Indian who has adopted European dress and customs is called a mestizo (or cholo).

b. *attrib.*, as ***mestizo labourer, -lad, town***, etc.; **mestizo-wool**, South American wool from mixed breeds of sheep (*Funk's Stand. Dict.*).

1617 COCKS in *Lett. E. Ind. Comp.* (1901) V. 15 There came a Mestiza Indian to me. **1880** C. R. MARKHAM *Peruv. Bark* 136 Pablo Sevallos the mestizo lad. **1970** L. GREBLER et al. *Mexican-Amer. People* xiv. 322 A leisured 'Spanish' *hidalgia* and a mass of *mestizo* and Indian laborers. **1727** A. HAMILTON *New Acc. E. Ind.* II. xxxiii. 10 A poor Seaman had got a pretty Mustice Wife. **1887** L. OLIPHANT *Episodes* (ed. 4) vi. 118 There was absolutely nothing to see in the sleepy little *mestizo* town.

mestlen, -lin(g, -lyon, obs. ff. MASLIN[1, 2].

‖**mesto** (ˈmɛsto), *a. Mus.* [It., f. L. *maestus* sad.] As a direction in music: sad, mournful.

1811 in BUSBY *Dict. Mus.* (ed. 3). **1880** GROVE *Dict. Mus.* II. 315/2 *Mesto*, 'sadly'; a term used three times by Beethoven, in the pianoforte sonatas, op. 10, no. 3, and op. 59, and in the slow movement of Quartet op. 18, no. 7. The slow movement of the first of these is called Largo e mesto, and of the second and third Adagio molto e mesto. It is also used by Chopin in the Mazurkas, op. 33, nos. 1 and 4. **1938** *Oxf. Compan. Mus.* 568/1 *Mesto* (It.), 'mournful', sad. **1959** *Collins Mus. Encycl.* 424/1 *Mesto*.., sad.

mestome (ˈmɛstəʊm). *Bot.* [ad. Gr. *μέστωμα* (taken in the sense 'filling up'), f. *μεστοῦν* to fill up, f. *μεστός* full.] Schwendener's term for those parts of a fibro-vascular bundle which do not conduce to its strength.

1885 GOODALE *Physiol. Bot.* 191.

mestor, mestrall: see MISTER, MISTRAL.

mestranol (ˈmɛstrənɒl). *Pharm.* [f. ME(THYL + Œ)STRA(DIOL + *-n-* + -OL.] The 3-methyl ether, $C_{21}H_{26}O_2$, of ethinylœstradiol which has actions similar to, but more potent than, those of œstradiol and is used in treating disorders of menstruation, fertility, and pregnancy, and (together with a progestational agent) as a contraceptive.

1962 *Approved Names* (Brit. Pharmacopœia Comm.) 15 Mestranol. **1963** *Federation Proc.* XXII. 481 A 2-year.. test was conducted.. to determine the safety of Ortho-Novum, an oral contraceptive preparation containing norethindrone .. and mestranol.. in a ratio of 1,000 to 6. **1968** *Times* 21 Dec. 13/8 Most of the young quail fed on mestranol became sterile. **1971** *Brit. Med. Bull.* XXVII. 26/1 No difference could be detected between the risks associated with two different types of oestrogen (mestranol and ethynyloestradiol [*sic*]) when used in the same dose.

mestres(se, mestyer(e, mestyf, mestylyon, mesuage, mesure: see MISTRESS, MISTER, MASTIFF, MASLIN[2], MESSUAGE, MEASURE.

Mesvinian (mɛsˈvɪnɪən), *a.* and *sb. Archæol.* [ad. F. *mesvinien*, f. *Mesvin* in Belgium: see -IAN.] **A.** *adj.* Belonging to the middle palæolithic period or culture of Belgium. **B.** *sb.* The Mesvinian period.

1911 W. J. SOLLAS *Anc. Hunters* 109 The Mesvinian, now accepted as the oldest of the Palaeolithic horizons. *Ibid.* 111 The Mesvinian implements are ruder than the Chellean, and the characteristic boucher is lacking. **1922** *Proc. Prehist. Soc. E. Anglia* III. 602 The Mesvinian Industry.. might well be the precursor of the Mousterian Industry. **1948** [see EOLITHIC *a.*].

meswage, mesyl(le, mesyng, mesynge: see MESSAGE, MEASLE, MASSING *vbl. sb.*[1], MESSENGER.

met (mɛt), *sb.*[1] *Obs.* exc. *dial.* Forms: [1 ȝemet(t], 3– met, mett. Also 3, 5–6 mete, (7 meat). Also I-MET. [OE. *ȝemet* neut. = OS. *gimet* (Du. *gemet* acre), OHG. *gamez*, ON. *mét* neut. pl., weight of a balance:—OTeut. **ga-metom*, f. root **met-* to measure: see METE *v.*

The form I-MET survived only to the beginning of the 13th c. in the south; in other dialects the prefix was lost still earlier, according to the general rule with regard to sbs.] = MEASURE *sb.* in various senses.

†**1.** Size, dimension or quantity as determinable by measurement; = MEASURE *sb.* 2, b, c. Sometimes = distance. *Obs.*

[*c* **888** K. ÆLFRED *Boeth.* xviii. § 1 [Ptolomeus] se towrat ealles þises middanȝeardes ȝemet on anre bec. *c* **1050** *Laws Northumbr. Priests* lvi. (Liebermann), Betweonan Eferwic & six mila ȝemete.] **13..** *Cursor M.* 8123 (Gött.) And all pair schapp was turned new, Of man-kind had þai þe mett. *c* **1330** R. BRUNNE *Chron. Wace* (Rolls) 14978 Þe lengþe of þe Ilde of Tenet, Sex myle þen ys þe met. *c* **1420** *Pallad. on Husb.* III. 199 A xl foote of mette Vche elm away from other most be born. *a* **1529** SKELTON *E. Rummyng* 333 She.. bad Elynour.. fyll in good met.

2. The action of measuring. ***by*** or ***with met***: as determined by measuring.

a **1300** *Cursor M.* 8814 Þai lete it [þe tre] don wit-vten lett, And fand it merc inogh wit mett [*a* **1425** (Trin.) bi met]. *c* **1386** CHAUCER *Parson's T.* 725 To take þy neighebours catel agayns his wille.. be it by mette or by mesure. *c* **1400** *Laud Troy Bk.* 9480 Two hundred fet was it be met.

†**3.** A method or system of measuring; = MEASURE *sb.* 6. *Obs.*

c **1250** *Gen. & Ex.* 439 Met of corn, and wiȝte of se, And merke of felde, first fond he. **1580** *Reg. Privy Council Scot.* III. 300, xxxii bollis wattir mett. **1627** *Rep. Parishes Scotl.* (Bann.) 2 Four bollis otis rining mett.

4. A unit of measurement, esp. of capacity. Now *dial.* = a bushel or (in some parts) two bushels.

[*c* **1000** ÆLFRIC *Deut.* xxv. 15 Hæbbe ælc man.. rihte ȝemetu on ælcum þingum.] *c* **1250** *Gen. & Ex.* 3333 A met ðor was, it het Gomor. *a* **1300** *Cursor M.* 28437 Again þe lagh in land is sett, Haf i wysed fals weght and mette. **1513** DOUGLAS *Æneis* VIII. *Prol.* 40 The myllar mythis the multur wyth a met scant. **1624** A. HUNTAR (*title*) Treatise of Weights, Mets and Measures of Scotland; with their quantities, and true foundation. **1660** HEXHAM, *Een Gemeet Landes*, a Meat or Measure of Land. **1691** RAY *N.C. Words* 48 A *Met*: a Strike or four Pecks,.. in York-sh. two Strike. **1793** *Statist. Acc. Scot.* VII. 589 Herrings.. sell for 1d. per score, or 3s. per mett, nearly a barrel of fresh ungutted herrings. **1876** *Whitby Gloss.*, *Met*, two bushels.

5. An instrument for measuring = MEASURE *sb.* 4. *Obs.* exc. *dial.* (see E.D.D.).

[*c* **1030** *Laws of Cnut* II. ix. (Liebermann), ȝemeta & ȝewihta rihte man ȝeorne.] *a* **1300** *Cursor M.* 12398 Þe knaue þat þis timber fett Heild noght graithli his mett, Bot ouer scort he broght a tre. *c* **1440** *Alphabet of Tales* 330 Sho .. tuke hur mettis & hur mesurs at sho fillid ale with. *a* **1733** *Shetland Acts* 16 in *Proc. Soc. Ant. Scot.* (1892) XXVI. 199 The trying and adjusting of bismers with the stoups, cans, and other mets and measures.

6. a. A quantity measured out; *esp.* a quantity of anything as measured out according to a

certain unit of measurement, as a ***met of coals***. Now only *dial.*

[*c* **1000** *Ags. Gosp.* Matt. xiii. 33 On þrim ȝemetum melwes.] *c* **1200** ORMIN 14034, & twafald oþerr þrefald mett þa fetless alle tokenn. **13..** *E.E. Allit. P.* B. 625 þre mettez of mele menge & ma kakez. **1522** *Test. Ebor.* (Surtees) V. 145 To every of them oon mette of corne, scilicet, half of whete, and the other halfe malte. **1636** *Farington Papers* (Chetham Soc.) 12, 23 Metts Banberie Malte. **1765** *Lond. Chron.* 3 Jan. 16 The prisoners in Ouse-Bridge gaol received.. 10 mets of coals from his Grace the Archbishop. **1891** A. MATTHEWS *Poems & Songs* 19 A wab o' claith, a pirn wheel A met o' coals, a cheese, a neep.

fig. *c* **1230** *Hali Meid.* 273 [He] earneð him..met of heouenliche mede. **1572** *Satir. P. Reform.* xxxiii. 343 Quhilks for to out with dowbill met and mesure, The vther tway ȝe ludgeit at thair plesure.

b. In Matt. vii. 2 and echoes.

[*c* **975**, *c* **1175**: see I-MET.] *a* **1300** *Cursor M.* 25318 Wit sli mett als yee bi and sell, Wit þat ilk sal you be mett. *c* **1330** *Spec. Gy de Warewyke* 549 Alswich met as þu metest me, Alswich i wole mete to þe.

c. ***by*** or ***with large met***: in abundance.

c **1290** *St. Nicholas* 150 in *S. Eng. Leg.* 244 And hou heo hadden bi large met wel more corn i-brouȝt. *c* **1450** *Hymns Virg.* 118 Hytt [the rayne] schalle ouergo wyth large mett Alle that ys in erth I-sett.

†**7.** Extent not to be exceeded; limit, bounds; = MEASURE *sb.* 12. ***withute met***(*e*: beyond bounds. ***with met***: 'by measure'. *Obs.*

[*c* **888** K. ÆLFRED *Boeth.* xl. §1 þylæs hi cweþan þ wit sprecan ofer monnes ȝemet. *c* **1000** *Ags. Gosp.* Matt. xxiii. 32, & ȝefylle ȝe þ ȝemet eowra fædera.] *c* **1200** ORMIN 17986 Forr Godd ne ȝifeþþ nohht wiþþ mett Hiss Gastess Hallȝhe Frofre. *a* **1240** *Sawles Warde* in *Cott. Hom.* 251 Helle is wid wið ute met ant deop wið ute grunde. *Ibid.* 263 Ha luuieð god wið ute met.

†**8.** Moderation, temperance; = MEASURE *sb.* 13. Also, modesty. *Obs.*

[*a* **1000**: see I-MET.] *c* **1200** ORMIN 6116 Wiþþ mett & mæþ i mete & drinnch, & ec inn ȝure claþess. *a* **1240** *Sawles Warde* in *Cott. Hom.* 255 For ne mei na wunne ne na flesches licunge..bringe me ouer þe midel of mesure and of mete. *c* **1357** *Lay Folks Catech.* 445 Methe is mesur and met [*Lamb. MS.* mede] of al that we do.

9. *Comb.*, as **met-loom**, instrument for measuring; **met-poke**, a bag serving as a measure. (See also *met-line*, *-rod*, *-stick*, *-wand*, *-yard* s.vv. METELINE, METEROD, etc.)

1528 *Burgh Rec. Stirling* (1887) 33 The baillies sall caus all metloumis pyntis, quhartis and chopynnis, to cum to the tolbouit. **1641** BEST *Farm. Bks.* (Surtees) 100 When wee sende wheate [etc.]..to markette..wee putte it into mette-poakes.

met., **met**, *sb.*², colloq. abbrev. of METROPOLITAN *a.* (as in *Metropolitan Railway*, *Metropolitan Opera House*, *Metropolitan Police*, etc.). In *pl.*: stocks or shares in the London Metropolitan Railway.

1886 H. BAUMANN *Londinismen* 107/2 *Mets*, Aktien der unterirdischen (Metropolitan) Eisenbahn. **1896** FARMER & HENLEY *Slang* IV. 305/2 *Met.* 1. A member of the Metropolitan (or New York) Base-Ball Club. 2. in *pl.* (Stock Exchange), Metropolitan Railway Shares. 3. *The Met* (London), the Metropolitan music-hall. **1908** *Daily Report* 7 Feb. 1/4 Both 'Mets.' and 'Districts' have moved in contrast with the Railway market generally. **1926** [see METROLAND]. **1937** 'C. MCCABE' *Face on Cutting-Room Floor* iii. 18 Then I was suddenly in the crowd of clerks and typists rushing towards King's Cross Met station. **1944** 'D. HUME' *Toast to Corpse* ix. 91 You haven't had thirty years in the Mets for nothing, and you've been about a bit. **1946** L. BAKER *Out on Limb* viii. 85 She walked like a queen,..sang like head bird at the Met, and had a brilliant career. **1953** *Manch. Guardian Weekly* 1 Oct. 2/4 There is very little Wagner at the Met this year. **1968** 'M. UNDERWOOD' *Man who killed too Soon* xiv. 120 Inspector Drew's colleagues in other forces, especially those in the Met. **1971** [see FIRM *sb.*¹ 2 c]. **1972** P. MARKS *Collector's Choice* i. 15 The crowds came to ogle the Van Goghs and the multi-million-dollar Rembrandts—the Met had thirty-seven. **1973** *Radio Times* 26 Feb. 7 It is no longer cheap to travel to and from London on the Met. **1973** 'S. HARVESTER' *Corner of Playground* III. iv. 202 An operatic mezzo-soprano, who had sung at the Met, La Scala, Covent Garden. **1974** S. GULLIVER *Vulcan's Bulletins* 112 Something or other might be found to interest the Mets or the Home Office... Your trading days would be over. **1974** D. RAMSAY *No Cause to Kill* II. 147 The television set blared baseball. The New York Mets were playing the Los Angeles Dodgers.

met., **met**, *sb.*³, colloq. abbrev. of METEOROLOGICAL *a.* or of *Meteorological Office*(*r*). Freq. with capital initial.

1940 *War Illustr.* 26 Jan. 19/2 One of the 'Met. men' studying the big thermometer attached to one of the inter-plane struts of his 'Gladiator'. **1942** T. RATTIGAN *Flare Path* I. 113 What's the met. report like? **1943** L. CHESHIRE *Bomber Pilot* iii. 45 The latest 'met' forecast came in... Navigation should be easy. **1943** HUNT & PRINGLE *Service Slang* 45 *Met.* or *Mets.*, the Meteorological Officer. [R.A.F.] **1943** *R.A.F. Jrnl.* Aug. 32 The Met. Officer has sent his obs. through each hour. **1958** *New Scientist* 15 May 9/2 The met. observations become meaningful only when compared with the observations made by the other parties all over the continent. **1964** *Punch* 7 Oct. 527/1 Metmen ask each other. **1970** *New Scientist* 24 Dec. 569/1 It is almost inevitable.. that the Met Office will come in for derision over their latest idea. **1972** K. CAMPBELL *Thunder on Sunday* 9 He picked up the blue weather folder that the Met Officer at Keflavik had given him. **1973** W. M. DUNCAN *Big Timer* i. 14 The met men promise a hard winter. **1974** L. LAMB *Man in Mist* viii. 50 The Superintendent turned..to ask what the met. report had been.

†**met**, *ppl. a.* *Obs.* [See METE *v.*¹] Measured.

c **1375** *Sc. Leg. Saints* xl. (*Ninian*) 1406 Twa hundre myle of met way. *a* **1400** *Sir Perc.* 1708 The stede..Leppe up over an hille Fyve stryde mett. *c* **1460** *Towneley Myst.* xii. 484 This botell..It holdys a mett potell.

met: see METE.

‖**meta** ('miːtə), *sb.*¹ *Rom. Antiq.* Pl. **metæ** ('miːtiː). [L. *mēta*.] One of the conical columns set in the ground at each end of the Circus, to mark the turning-place in a race. Hence *transf.* A boundary.

1577 HARRISON *Descr. Brit.* i. 2 in *Holinshed*, So that the aforesaid line shall henceforth be their *Meta* and partition from such as be ascribed to America. **1662** RAY *Three Itin.* III. 183 In Somersetshire they have a way of setting their mows of corn on a frame..standing upon four stones cut with a shank, and upon that an head like a meta. **1845** *Athenæum* 1 Feb. 126 We have the cross erected between two 'metæ'.

'meta, Meta, *sb.*² Abbrevs. of METALDEHYDE. *Spec.* a block of metaldehyde used (*a*) as fuel for cooking and heating, (*b*) for killing slugs. Also *attrib.*

Registered as a proprietary term by Lonza Elektrizitätswerke, Switzerland, in 1924 *Trade Marks Jrnl.* 26 Mar. 717 (as a fuel) and in 1938 *Ibid.* 18 May 603 (slug-killer).

1925 E. F. NORTON *Fight for Everest 1924* v. 102 Our loads ..comprise one 10-lb. tent, two sleeping bags, food and 'meta' (solid spirit). *Ibid.* 706 The meta cooker doing its indifferent best to produce half a pot of warm water. **1938** *Times* 26 Nov. 15/6 Tablets of Meta crushed and used by itself or mixed with bran, may be put about among plants before dark and the victims collected in the morning. **1947** F. SMYTHE *Again Switzerland* vi. 120 He carries with him a packet of 'meta' fuel. **1952** E. R. JANES *Flower Garden* 119 Metaldehyde (Meta) is a very fine slug killer... Under some conditions in the dead of winter it is hardly possible to apply Meta. **1955** P. BAUER *Kanchenjunga Challenge* IV. iv. 196 We went on travelling light with perhaps the Zdarsky sack and a small meta-tablet cooker.

meta ('mɛtə), *a. Chem.* Now usu. italicized. [f. META- *prefix*.] Characterized by or relating to (substitution at) two carbon atoms separated by one other in a benzene ring; at a position next but one *to* some (specified) substituent in a benzene ring. Also as *adv.*

1876 *Jrnl. Chem. Soc.* XXIX. 237 The author places the sulpho-acids obtained by the action of sulphuric acid on.. iodobenzene in the meta (1:3) series. **1924** E. J. HOLMYARD *Outlines Org. Chem.* xix. 367 The *para* isomer $C_6H_4X_2$ can yield only *one* trisubstitution product $C_6H_3X_3$, while the *ortho* can give *two* and the *meta* can give *three*. **1938** L. F. FIESER in H. Gilman *Org. Chem.* I. ii. 146 There is..no such enormous difference in reaction rate..as there is between the ortho-para directing amines and the meta orienting ammonium salts. **1949** [see ORIENT *v.* 4 a]. **1968** R. O. C. NORMAN *Princ. Org. Synth.* xi. 357 Position *a*, which is *ortho* to acetamido and *meta* to methyl, is more reactive than position *b*, which is *meta* to acetamido and *ortho* to methyl.

meta- ('mɛtə), *prefix*, before a vowel normally **met-** (also before *h*, the resulting *meth-* being pronounced (mɛθ)), repr. Gr. μετα-, μετ- (μεθ-), which occurs separately as the prep. μετά with, after; etymologically corresponding to MID *prep.* In Gr. the prefix is joined chiefly to verbs and verbal derivatives; the principal notions which it expresses are: sharing, action in common; pursuit or quest; and, especially, change (of place, order, condition, or nature), corresponding to L. *trans-*. In some few formations μετα- represents the prep. μετά in syntactical combination, with the sense after or behind, as in μετάφρενον METAPHRENON.

The words derived from Gr. words containing the prefix, or from assumed Greek types normally constructed, are given in their alphabetical place. The words enumerated in this article are modern formations, in which the prefix is employed in ways not strictly in accordance with Greek analogies. The prefix is often hyphened, and the *a* remains unelided before a vowel or *h*.

1. a. The supposed analogy of METAPHYSICS (misapprehended as meaning 'the science of that which transcends the physical') has been followed in the practice of prefixing *meta-* to the name of a science, to form a designation for a higher science (actual or hypothetical) of the same nature but dealing with ulterior and more fundamental problems. **meta'chemistry** ? *nonce-wd.*, the chemistry of the supersensible. **meta-'ethics**, a name applied to the study of the foundations of ethics, esp. of the nature of ethical statements; hence **meta-'ethical** *a.* **meta-'history**, inquiry into the principles governing historical events; so **meta-hi'storic(al** *adjs.*, transcending history, controlling the course of history. **metaphi'losophy**, inquiry into the problems ulterior to philosophy or philosophical theories; so **metaphilo'sophical** *a.* **metaphysi'ology**, a name invented by G. H. Lewes for a doctrine of life and vital phenomena which should base itself on principles outside of and higher than those of physiology and the material organism; hence **metaphysio'logical** *a.*, **metaphysi'ologist**. **metasoci'ology** (see quot. 1970); so **metasocio'logical**, **meta-soci-olo'gistic** *adjs.* **meta-the'ology**, (*a*) *nonce-wd.*, a profounder theology than that recognized by divines; (*b*) the philosophical study of the nature of religious language or statements; hence **meta-theo'logian**, **meta-theo'logical** *a.* Similarly in **meta-'element**, **meta'gnostic** *a.*, [cf. GNOSTIC *a.*], **metaorganism** (see quots); **metaphe'nomenal** *a.*, existing behind phenomena. See also METAGEOMETRY, METEMPIRIC.

1856 EMERSON *Eng. Traits, Lit.* Wks. (Bohn) II. 106 It seems an affair of race, or of *metachemistry. **1888** W. CROOKES in *Jrnl. Chem. Soc.* LIII. 487 The possible existence of bodies which, though neither compounds nor mixtures, are not elements in the strictest sense of the word; —bodies which I venture to call '*meta-elements'. **1949** A. J. AYER *Philos. Ess.* (1954) x. 246 All moral theories..are neutral as regards actual conduct. To speak technically, they belong to the field of *meta-ethics, not ethics proper. *Ibid.*, Expounding my meta-ethical theory. **1957** D. M. MACKINNON *Study in Ethical Theory* i. 10 The moral philosopher is..preoccupied with..problems of meta-ethics, with the question of where ethical language belongs on the language-map. *Ibid.* 11 This problem of the relation of duty and good is in some sense meta-ethical. **1966** G. C. KERNER *Revolution in Ethical Theory* 1 The problems of ethical theory are thus..problems..of moral language;.. they are 'meta-ethical'. *Ibid.* ii. 70 Meta-ethics is conceived to be a purely theoretical and ethically neutral enterprise. **1973** *Nature* 26 Jan. 249/2 With someone who prefers an incoherent picture of nature, I have no idea how to proceed —just as in meta-ethics, one is powerless to proceed with someone who regards a universe without sentience as possessing greater intrinsic value than one with sentience. **1886** H. MAUDSLEY *Nat. Causes & Supern. Seemings* 122 Regions..that are beyond knowledge, not beyond nature; *metagnostic, not metaphysical. **1929** R. HUGHES tr. *Deissmann's New Testament in Light of Mod. Res.* vi. 172 The holy is pre-historic and *metahistoric. **1945** G. DIX *Shape of Liturgy* ix. 264 These *meta-historical facts of the resurrection and ascension. **1949** *Mind* LVIII. 411 The value of morals as 'meta-historical reason' controlling history and determining the future. **1969** P. A. ROBINSON *Freudian Left* 148 The typical practicing psychoanalyst carefully distinguished the discrete precepts and techniques of his therapeutic science from the ambitious meta-historical adventures in which Freud had indulged. **1957** *Times Lit. Suppl.* 27 Dec. 782/2 *Metahistory (which stands in much the same relation to history as metaphysics does to physics). **1964** C. S. LEWIS *Discarded Image* viii. 175 What Virgil puts forward in a mythical form is precisely meta-history. **1866** MYERS *Phantasms of Living* II. 278 That this body of ours..is interpenetrated with a '*meta-organism' of identical shape and structure, and capable sometimes of detaching itself from the solid flesh. **1844** TAPPAN *Elem. Logic* 12 Those objects which, by supposition, lie beyond immediate consciousness, are *metaphenomenal. **1882** G. S. MORRIS *Kant's Critique* vi. (1886) 189 No distinction of phenomena from the metaphenomenal, as objects of knowledge. **1942** *Mind* LI. 284 'Why are no philosophical disputes ever settled?' It is with this '*metaphilosophical' problem..that Professor Ducasse's book..is concerned. **1964** *Philos. Rev.* LXXIII. 554 Blakeley..proposes an original and provocative metaphilosophical thesis. **1970** M. LAZEROWITZ in *Metaphilosophy* I. 91 *Metaphilosophy is the investigation of the nature of philosophy, with the central aim of arriving at a satisfactory explanation of the absence of uncontested philosophical claims and arguments. **1876** LEWES in *Fortn. Rev.* Apr. 479–86 *Metaphysiology. *Metaphysiological. *Metaphysiologists. **1959** R. BIERSTEDT in L. Gross *Symposium Sociol. Theory* 137 The distinction between methodological (or *metasociological) theory on the one hand and substantive (or sociological) theory on the other. **1964** P. MEADOWS in I. L. Horowitz *New Sociol.* 448 Formulations which phrase a *meta-sociologistic model, that is, the theme that beyond the teeming and changing varieties of social life and differentiated functions there are social patterns generating and guiding the social work life. **1958** W. STARK *Sociol. of Knowl.* I. iv. 197 A *metasociology which would be..a study of man as he appears in all societies, of man *as such*. **1970** G. A. & A. G. THEODORSON *Mod. Dict. Sociol.* 254 *Metasociology*, the branch of sociological theory that is concerned with the methods and logic of sociological inquiry, rather than with propositions, principles, and generalizations about social life. **1967** *Philosophy* XLII. 197 The *meta-theologian..claimed that Christian discourse, as it stands, is incoherent. **1969** R. S. HEIMBECK *Theol. & Meaning* i. 20 Since 1955, the quantity of *metatheological literature has multiplied many times over. *a* **1615** DONNE *Ess.* (1651) 129 A *Meta-theology and a Superdivinity above that which serves our particular consciences. **1957** I. M. CROMBIE in B. Mitchell *Faith & Logic* ii. 77 It is from reading theology, not meta-theology, that one can come to understand how theological statements work. **1959** P. MUNZ *Probl. Relig. Knowl.* 12 The meta-theology which I have put forward neither stands nor falls with any one particular theological opinion which I have expressed or implied. **1967** *Philosophy* XLII. 195 One piece of meta-theology which has won wide acceptance..is that 'God' is not a substance-word.

b. Prefixed to various classificatory words to designate concern with the ulterior or underlying principles peculiar to that classification, as ***metacriterion***, ***metacriticism***, (hence ***metacritical*** adj., ***-ally*** adv.), ***metasystem***, ***metatheorem***, ***metatheory*** (so ***metatheoretic***, ***-ical*** adjs.).

1953 C. E. BAZELL *Ling. Form* v. 63 Universality of application is only one *meta-criterion for the choice of criteria. **1954** C. F. HOCKETT in *Word* X. 233 Neither any existing version of IA nor any existing version of IP meets

all the metacriteria. **1963** *Listener* 3 Jan. 21/1 They [*sc.* the techniques of modern criticism] could make exciting sense (if not in strictly critical terms, then in *metacritical ones) of works which would have seemed absurd if taken literally. **1970** A. RODWAY *Truths of Fiction* i. 9 Concentrate, metacritically, on what the text refers to... Study of form is purely critical, of content either critical or metacritical; of what the work leads to, whether in the way of causes or effects or general topics, purely metacritical. **1966** *Philosophy* XLI. 320 The aesthetician..is concerned (among other things) with *metacriticism. **1970** A. RODWAY *Truths of Fiction* i. 6 The logical primacy of intrinsic criticism suggests that extrinsic criticism might also be called *metacriticism*. **1956** J. H. WOODGER tr. *Tarski's Logic, Semantics, Metamath.* 116 It is possible to construct a particular science, namely the '*metasystem', in which the given system is subjected to investigation. **1964** P. MEADOWS in I. L. Horowitz *New Sociol.* 452 Metasystem or general systems theory. **1969** *New Scientist* 4 Sept. 461/1 What Professor Beer is asking for is that we approach the problem at a higher level—the level of the 'metasystem'. **1940** W. V. QUINE *Math. Logic* ii. 89 We establish theorems wholesale, by arguments which show that the appropriate sequences *could* be found for each particular case. Such principles, describing general circumstances under which statements are theorems, will be called *metatheorems. **1943** *Mind* LII. 267 Closely connected with the distinction between use and mention is that between a theorem and a metatheorem, the latter being, as the name suggests, a theorem *about* theorems, wherein symbols are mentioned and names of symbols used. **1971** G. HUNTER *Metalogic* p. xii, Complete proofs for metatheorems (theorems *about* a system) are..more laborious for natural deduction systems than for axiomatic ones. *Ibid.* I. 11 A theorem about a theorem (also called a metatheorem) is a true statement about the system expressed in the metalanguage. **1965** B. MATES *Elem. Logic* viii. 128 We are now in a position to.. give informal proofs of a number of *metatheoretic generalizations about the theorems of logic. **1953** *Mind* LXII. 557 The *meta-theoretical problems of logical calculi, such as independence of axioms, completeness, and decision methods. **1956** E. H. HUTTEN *Lang. Mod. Physics* iii. 81 When we want to explain how scientific theories are constructed..we must speak *about* them; and this requires a suitable terminology. This *meta-theory, or methodology, is as necessary to science as grammar is to ordinary language. **1963** *Language* XXXIX. 208 A metatheory for semantics must also exhibit the relations between semantics and other areas of linguistics. **1974** *Sci. Amer.* May 122/3 He outlines a metatheory in which the universe at every micromicroinstant branches into countless parallel worlds.

2. *Path.* Used to form adjs. applicable to diseases or symptoms, with the sense 'arising subsequently to' (that which is indicated in the body of the word). **meta-ar'thritic**, following or consequent on gout. **metapneu'monic**, following or consequent on pneumonia. **meta,splenome'galic** [Gr. σπλήν spleen, μεγαλο-, μέγας great], preceded by enlargement of the spleen.

1898 *Allbutt's Syst. Med.* V. 862 The *meta-arthritic endocarditis. *Ibid.* 164 *Metapneumonic pleurisy. **1905** H. D. ROLLESTON *Dis. Liver* 308 *Metasplenomegalic hypertrophic biliary cirrhosis.

3. *Anat. and Zool.* Used to express the notion of 'behind' (cf. METAPHRENON); also often that of 'hinder', 'hindmost', 'situated at the back'; sometimes correlated with PRO- and MESO-. **meta'branchial** *a.* [Gr. βράγχια gills], applied to a division of the carapace of a crab situated behind and to one side of the mesobranchial lobe. **meta'facial** *a.*, applied to the angle which the pterygoid processes make with the base of the cranium. ‖**metapa'rapteron** *Ent.*, the parapteron of the metathoracic segment; hence **metapa'rapteral** *a.* (*Cent. Dict.*). **metapneustic** (-'pnju:stɪk) *a. Ent.* [Gr. πνευστικ-ός relating to breathing], having a single pair of spiracles situated at the posterior end of the abdomen. **metapore** ('mɛtəpɔə(r)) [PORE], an orifice in the pia mater covering the fourth ventricle of the brain; the foramen of Magendie. ‖**metascu'tellum**, ‖**meta'scutum**, the scutellum and scutum (respectively) of the metathorax of an insect; hence **metascu'tellar**, **meta'scutal** *adjs.* (in recent Dicts). **metasthenic** (-'sθɛnɪk) *a. Ent.* [Gr. σθένος strength], having most strength in the hinder part of the body; *sb. pl.*, a division of insects characterized in this way.

1877 *Metabranchial [see *mesobranchial* s.v. MESO-]. **1878** BARTLEY tr. *Topinard's Anthrop.* II. iii. 291 The *meta-facial angle of Serres, which the pterygoid processes form with the base of the skull. **1891** BERNARD tr. *Lang's Comp. Anat.* I. 482 The tracheal system is then called *meta-pneustic. **1899** D. SHARP *Insects* II. 450 (Camb. Nat. Hist.) Some begin life in the metapneustic state, and afterwards become amphipneustic. **1889** *Buck's Handbk. Med. Sci.* VIII. 123/2 The orifice here called *metapore. **1899** D. SHARP *Insects* II. 313 (Camb. Nat. Hist.) The hind margin of the *metascutellum. **1863** DANA in *Amer. Jrnl. Sci.* Ser. II. XXXVI. 323 The condition may be described as ..*Metasthenic..if a posterior pair [of locomotive organs] is the more important and the anterior are weak or obsolete. *Ibid.* 335 The two highest divisions, Prosthenics and Metasthenics.

4. *Bot.* and *Zool.* Used with the sense 'later', 'subsequent', 'more developed'; sometimes indicating the latest of three stages, correlated with PROTO- and MESO-. **'metacneme** [Gr. κνήμη tibia; cf. CNEMIAL *a.*], a secondary mesentery which develops in some Zoantherians; so **metac'nemic** *a.* **metane'phridium** [a. G. *metanephridium* (B. Hatschek *Lehrbuch der Zoologie* (1889) II. 162): see NEPHRIDIUM], in certain invertebrates, a nephridium with a ciliated opening into the coelom; so **metane'phridial** *a.* **'metaphase**, [a. G. *metaphase* (E. Strasburger 1884, in *Arch. f. mikrosk. Anat.* XXIII. 260)], the stage in mitotic or meiotic nuclear division which follows prophase and precedes anaphase, during which the chromosomes become arranged with their centromeres on the equatorial plate; a dividing nucleus at this stage. **meta'phloem**, a constituent of primary phloem which is formed after the earliest development of the shoot. **'metaphyte**, ‖**me'taphyton**, a multicellular plant; hence **meta'phytic** *a.* (Jackson *Gloss. Bot. Terms* 1900). **meta'tracheal** *a. arch.*, usu. in phrase ***metatracheal parenchyma***, describing the structure of wood in which concentric bands of parenchyma independent of the vessels are formed. **meta'xylem**, a constituent of the primary xylem which is formed after the earliest development of the shoot.

1900 J. E. DUERDEN in *Johns Hopkins Univ. Circular* XIX. 47/2 The first six pairs of mesenteries are found to differ so essentially in their mode of origin and significance from the mesenteries appearing later that I find it convenient to have some word which will include them either as a whole or individually. I therefore propose for them the term 'Protocnemes', and shall refer to the mesenteries subsequently developed as '*Metacnemes'. **1902** *Ann. & Mag. Nat. Hist.* IX. 397 The different fundamental types of metacnemic sequence now known within the Actiniaria and Madreporaria. *Ibid.*, The metacnemes arise as unilateral pairs at one, three, seven, etc. regions within all the six primary exocoeles. **1940** L. H. HYMAN *Invertebrates* I. vii. 589 In most forms [of sea anemone] additional septa called metacnemes arise in pairs. **1940** L. H. HYMAN *Invertebrates* I. ii. 37 The nephridial system of the coelomate invertebrates is of the *metanephridial type, i.e., the nephridial tubules begin as coelomic openings. **1963** R. P. DALES *Annelids* v. 98 The metanephridial funnels or postnephridial solenocytes lie in the coelomic fluid. **1930** W. R. COE in *Biol. Bull.* LVIII. 208 This type of excretory organ may be designated a *metanephridium in order to distinguish it from the more usual type, protonephridium, found in nemerteans. **1967** E. J. W. BARRINGTON *Invertebr. Struct. & Function* xii. 236 The nephridium occurs in two main forms, the protonephridium and the metanephridium. **1890** *Syd. Soc. Lex.*, **Metaphase*,..the stage of the nuclear spindle in karyokinesis. **1887** tr. *Strasburger's Bot.* 363 Now begin the phases of separation and rearrangement of the daughter-segments, the *metaphases of division. **1924** E. W. MACBRIDE *Study of Heredity* ii. 42 The formation of the equatorial plate and of the spindle is known as the metaphase. **1961** *Lancet* 26 Aug. 489/1 Metaphases in freshly aspirated sternal and iliac crest marrow were analysed. **1962** *Ibid.* 26 May 1098/2 Rich crops of cells in metaphase were obtained twice. **1969** *Times* 20 June 7/3 Shortly before ovulation the oocyte goes through the process of cell division and then starts to divide a second time, a stage known as metaphase 2. **1973** *Nature* 1 June 290/2 Well-spread metaphases were photographed with a 95 × fluoride objective. **1902** *Encycl. Brit.* XXV. 413/1 In many cases external protophloem..can be distinguished from *metaphloem. **1965** K. ESAU *Plant Anat.* (ed. 2) xii. 292 The sieve elements of the metaphloem are commonly longer and wider than those of the protophloem. **1893** SHIPLEY *Zool. Invert.* 3 The *Metaphyta and Metazoa, or the multicellular plants and animals. **1897** HARTOG in *Nat. Science* Oct. 234 The higher animals and plants we term Metazoa and *Metaphytes respectively. **1908** BOODLE & FRITSCH tr. *Solereder's Systematic Anat. Dicotyledons* II. 1143 The wood parenchyma generally forms tangential bands (known as the '*metatracheal' parenchyma in contrast to the 'paratracheal' parenchyma, aggregated round about the vessels). **1933** *Tropical Woods* XXXVI. 9 *Metatracheal parenchyma*, aggregated wood parenchyma forming concentric laminae, mostly independent of the vessels and vascular tracheids. **1970** WILSON & WHITE *Jane's Struct. Wood* (ed. 2) vi. 116 Apotracheal parenchyma may occur as ..tangentially arranged sheets of cells..or in more extensive tangential bands... The two latter types are sometimes referred to as metatracheal parenchyma but this term is better avoided. **1902** *Encycl. Brit.* XXV. 415/1 Sometimes..the centre of a bulky root stele has strands of *metaxylem..scattered through it. **1965** K. ESAU *Plant Anat.* (ed. 2) xi. 243 The metaxylem, which appears after the protoxylem, is in the process of differentiation while the shoot is elongating.

5. *Geol.* **a.** In imitation of METAMORPHISM, the prefix has been used irregularly to form words referring to certain specific varieties of metamorphic processes, as **meta'chemic** *a.*, **meta'pepsis** (hence **meta'peptic** *a.*), **meta'taxis** (hence **meta'taxic** *a.*), **me'tatropy**: see quots.

1893 GEIKIE *Text-bk. Geol.* IV. VIII. 596 *note*, *Metasomatosis, metasomatic*..and **metachemic* applied to chemical metamorphism or alteration of constitution or substance. **1878** KINAHAN *Geol. Irel.* 175 One kind of Metamorphism is Regional, or extends over large areas. The rocks affected by it seem to have been under the influence of intensely heated water or steam, which, as it were, stewed them, from which the action may be called *metapepsis. *Ibid.* 177 *Metapeptic rocks. *Ibid.*, Metapeptic action. **1889** A. IRVING *Metamorph. Rocks* 65 *Metataxic work done by Solar and Lunar Tides. *Ibid.* 5 Slaty cleavage and its concomitant phenomena..will be considered under the term *Metataxis. *Footn.* This term is preferred to the cognate term Metastasis (Bonney). *Ibid.*, *Metatropy, or changes in the physical characters of rock-masses.

b. Prefixed to the names of rocks or of classes of rock to indicate that they have undergone metamorphism, as ***metadiorite***, ***metadolerite***, ***metagranite***, ***metasediment*** (hence ***metasedimentary*** adj.), ***metasyenite***, ***metavolcanic***; also ***metaigneous*** adj.

1876 J. D. DANA in *Amer. Jrnl. Sci. & Arts* XI. 121 The rocks are..*Metamorphic doleryte, metamorphic diabase*, and *metamorphic melaphyre*... To distinguish these metamorphic rocks from the igneous of the same composition, they are named, on my suggestion, *metadoleryte, metadiabase*, and *metamelaphyre*. The examples are part of a long series of rock species which have representatives both among igneous (or intrusive) and metamorphic rocks. Other kinds are *dioryte* and *metadioryte, syenyte* and *metasyenyte, felsyte* and *metafelsyte*, etc. **1920** A. HOLMES *Nomencl. Petrol.* 154 *Meta-*, a prefix used before the names of igneous rocks to signify that the mineral and chemical composition of the latter have been modified by alteration. **1942** M. P. BILLINGS *Struct. Geol.* xii. 215 Metasediments, metavolcanics, and meta-igneous rocks are metamorphic rocks derived, respectively, from sedimentary, volcanic, and igneous rocks. **1961** J. CHALLINOR *Dict. Geol.* 126/1 *Meta-(rock)*. A metamorphosed rock which was originally of the kind or type included in the name. Thus 'metasediment' or 'metasedimentary rock', 'meta-igneous rock', 'metadolerite', &c. **1973** *Nature* 21 Sept. 120/1 The metasediments occur in a (refolded) syncline among granitic gneisses. *Ibid.* 139/2 The lithology of some of these enclaves strongly suggests that they were originally supracrustal rocks similar to those that occur at Isua, including metasedimentary ironstones.

6. In *Chemistry*. **a.** *Meta-* is used to designate compounds derived from, metameric with, or resembling in composition those to the names of which it is prefixed, as *metachloral*, METALDEHYDE, etc. More systematically, it is used to distinguish one class of acids and their corresponding salts from another class (the ORTHO- acids) consisting of the same elements in different proportions, the *meta-* acids containing one, two, or three molecules of water less than the *ortho-* acids; the salts of these acids have names formed by replacing *-ic* by *-ate*. (A few of these compounds will be found in their alphabetical place; the most important of those remaining are placed below.)

The use of the prefix in chemistry was first introduced by Graham in 1833 (*Phil. Trans.* 253): see METAPHOSPHATE, METAPHOSPHORIC. The more definite use (correlated with *ortho-*) was introduced by Odling in 1859.

1861 ODLING *Man. Chem.* I. xiii. *Contents*, Phosphorus and Oxygen... Meta-compounds. **1892** MORLEY & MUIR *Watts' Dict. Chem.*, Meta-acids and meta-salts.

meta'boric acid, 'a white powder, obtained by heating ordinary boric acid or orthoboric acid to 100° C.' (*Syd. Soc. Lex.* 1890). **meta'cellulose**, the substance of which the cell-walls of fungi consist, differing from ordinary cellulose. **meta'chloral**, a white amorphous solid formed by the action of sulphuric acid on chloral. **meta'cresol**, one of the three modifications of cresol (*ortho-*, *meta-* and *paracresol*). **meta'gelatin**, a form of gelatin that remains fluid, used in photography, made by boiling and cooling a solution of gelatin several times. **meta'gummic** = METARABIC. **meta'lumina**, a name given to the soluble dihydrate of aluminium obtained by the action of heat on a solution of the acetate. **meta'morphia**, **meta'morphine**: see quots. **me'tamylene**, 'a compound polymeric with amylene, contained in the higher portion of the distillate produced by heating amylic alcohol with sulphuric acid' (Watts). **meta-o'leic** (also **meto'leic**) **acid**, an acid resulting from the action of sulphuric acid on oleic acid. **metaoxyben'zoic acid**, 'an isomeride of salicylic acid' (*Syd. Soc. Lex.*). **meta'pectic acid**, the final product of chemical action upon pectin. **meta'pectin**, an isomeric form of pectin produced by boiling with dilute acids. **meta'protein**, an intermediate product in the hydrolysis of a protein which is soluble in acids and alkalis but insoluble in water. **me'tarabic acid**, 'a substance, also called *Cerasin*, obtained by heating gum arabic to 100° C.' (*Syd. Soc. Lex.*). **me'tarsenic acid**: see quot. **metasi'licic acid**, a transparent vitreous substance obtained by drying silicic acid over anhydrous sulphuric acid. **metatar'taric acid**, a modification of tartaric acid obtained by melting it. **metati'tanic acid**: see quot. **meta'toluic acid**: see quot. **meta'tungstic acid**, a yellow solid used as a test for alkaloids.

1863 WATTS *Dict. Chem.* I. 639 Nearly all borates may be arranged in two classes, orthoborates and *metaborates (so called from their analogy with the ortho- and metaphosphates and silicates). **1885** GOODALE *Physiol. Bot.* (1892) 35 *note*, Cellulose dissolves at once in cuprammonia; paracellulose, only after the action of acids; *metacellulose, not even then. **1876** *Encycl. Brit.* V. 676/2 When kept for some days..chloral undergoes spontaneous change into the polymeride *metachloral,..a white porcelaneous body. **1881** WATTS *Dict. Chem.* VIII. 1286 *Metacresol. **1858**

SUTTON *Dict. Photogr.*, *Metagelatine. **1879** *Encycl. Brit.* X. 131/2 Gelatin so treated [with hot solutions of oxalic acid] has been called *metagelatin.* **1862** WATTS tr. *Gmelin's Handbk. Chem.* XV. 205 *Metagummic Acid. *Ibid.* 206 *Metagumate of lime. **1862** GRAHAM in *Jrnl. Chem. Soc.* XV. 247 Two soluble modifications of alumina appear to exist, alumina and *metalumina. **1890** *Syd. Soc. Lex.*, **Metamorphia*, one of the alkaloids separated from laudanum. **1865** WATTS *Dict. Chem.* III. 976 **Metamorphine*, an opium-base, the hydrochlorate of which is obtained, as a residue, in the preparation of opium-tincture by means of lime and sal-ammoniac. **1838** T. THOMSON *Chem. Org. Bodies* 124 M. Fremy was unable to obtain any of the *meta-oleates in a crystallized state. *Ibid.* 123 *Meta-oleic acid differs from it [*sc.* oleic acid] by containing two additional atoms of water. **1873** RALFE *Phys. Chem.* 132 The parapeptone being removed by filtration, the neutralized filtrate is again acidified when another precipitate, *metapeptone, is thrown down. **1909** *Cent. Dict.* Suppl., *Metaprotein. **1911** *Encycl. Brit.* XIX. 922/1 The first result of the action of this secretion on protein matter is to render it soluble—a metaprotein or acid albumin (syntonin) being formed. **1949** G. B. BACHMAN *Org. Chem.* xviii. 220 Primary derivatives: proteins, metaproteins, and coagulated proteins. **1861** ODLING *Man. Chem.* I. 338 *Metarsenates and pararsenates are converted respectively into monometallic and dimetallic common arsenates by the action of water. *Ibid.*, *Metarsenic acid $HAsO_3$, is formed by gradually heating common arsenic acid to a temperature of 200°–205°. **1859** *Meta-silicates [see ORTHO- 2]. **1872** WATTS *Dict. Chem.* VI. 825 *Metasilicic Acid. **1848** BRANDE *Chem.* (ed. 6) 1315 Saccharic Acid... Erdmann, who repeated Guérin Varry's experiments in 1837, regarded this acid as isomeric with tartaric acid, and called it *metartaric acid. **1856** WATTS tr. *Gmelin's Handbk. Chem.* X. 328 *Metatartrate. **1854** R. D. THOMSON *Cycl. Chem.*, **Metatitanic Acid*, Ti_3O_6. Small shining plates, separating when anhydrous bichloride of titanium is saturated with carbonate of barytes, adding water and boiling rapidly. **1873** *Jrnl. Chem. Soc.* XI. 276 Uvitic acid prepared by Finckh's process from pyrotartaric acid decomposes into *metatoluic acid when heated with lime. **1854** R. D. THOMSON *Cycl. Chem.*, **Metatungstic Acid.*

b. In the names of isomeric benzene di-derivatives, *meta-* denotes those compounds in which the two radicals that replace hydrogen in the benzene-ring are regarded as attached to alternate carbon atoms. (The use was introduced by Körner in 1867; cf. ORTHO- 2 b, PARA- 2 b.) So also ***metacoumaric acid, metacoumarate.***

As the number of these is unlimited, no list is given; a few examples are appended in the quots. below.

1873 *Jrnl. Chem. Soc.* XI. 1147 The metadiamidobenzene of Griess. **1875** *Ibid.* XIII. 156 When metachlorophenol is fused with potash, it is readily converted into pyrocatechin; the relation between metanitrophenol, metachlorophenol, and pyrocatechin being thus proved. *Ibid.*, Metanitrometachlorophenol appears to be converted into metanitrodichlorophenol by the action of chlorine. **1876** H. E. ARMSTRONG *ibid.* I. 212 The three Isomeric Dibromobenzenes... Paranitrobromobenzene,.. Metanitro-bromobenzene,.. Orthonitrobromobenzene. **1879** WATTS *Dict. Chem.* VIII. 210, *a*- or metapherylene-diamine. **1899** CAGNEY *Jaksch's Clin. Diagn.* vii. (ed. 4) 381 Metadiamido-benzol is coloured a deep yellow by nitrites. **1905** *Brit. Med. Jrnl.* 27 May 1144 They [i.e. benzenoid ortho- and para- compounds] both differ markedly from their isomerides of the meta-series... In the meta-compound these groups [i.e. ortho-coumaric and para-coumaric acids] are in apothetic positions with respect to each other so that the meta-acid might be expected to exhibit the dual properties of a phenol and a cinnamic acid. *Ibid.*, Sodium meta-coumarate... The meta-coumaric acid required for this preparation was produced synthetically from meta-nitrobenzaldehyde.

7. *Min.* Used to designate a mineral that is found along with another or is closely related to it, *spec.* denoting (partial) dehydration; as ***metabrushite*** (a calcium phosphate allied to brushite), ***metachlorite, metacinnabar(ite, metagadolinite, metalonchidite, metanocerite, metasericite, metastibnite, metavoltine*** (see A. H. Chester *Dict. Min.* 1896).

1854 DANA *Syst. Min.* (ed. 4) II. 297. **1865** JULIEN in *Amer. Jrnl. Sci.* Ser. II. XL. 371 Metabrushite. This new mineral has been observed to occur only with the guano as a matrix.

meta-acids, meta-arthritic: see META- 6, 2.

‖**metabasis** (mɛˈtæbəsɪs). [mod.L., a. Gr. μετάβασις, related to μεταβαίνειν to change one's place, f. μετα- META- + βαίνειν to go. (Cf. BASIS.)] A transition, *spec.* in *Rhetoric*, from one subject or point to another, in *Medicine*, from one remedy, etc. to another (= METABOLA).

1657 J. SMITH *Myst. Rhet.* 137 Metabasis... A figure whereby the parts of an oration or speech are knit together: and is, When we are briefly put in mind of what hath been said, and what remains further to be spoken. **1693** tr. *Blancard's Phys. Dict.* (ed. 2), *Metabasis*, the passing from one Indication to another, from one Remedy to another. **1882** *Sat. Rev.* LIV. 347 A somewhat dangerous metabasis which he strives to make from the genus of natural science into that of social philosophy.

metabatic (mɛtəˈbætɪk), *a.* [ad. Gr. μεταβατικός, f. μεταβαίνειν: see prec. and -IC.]

1. *Rhet.* Pertaining to metabasis.

1900 *Expositor* Nov. 391 Even if the δέ be genuine.. it is not adversative but metabatic.

2. *Thermodynamics.* In ***metabatic function*** (see quot.).

1855 RANKINE *Misc. Sci. Papers* (1881) 225 The function ..whose identity for the two substances expresses the condition of equilibrium of the actual energy between them, may be called the *metabatic* function for that kind of energy. In the science of thermodynamics the metabatic function is *absolute temperature.*

metabiˈology. Also **meta-biology.** [f. META- 1 + BIOLOGY.] A hypothetical or postulated science dealing with phenomena of living organisms beyond the scope of conventional biology, or treating them in a more fundamental way. Chiefly in non-scientific use, freq. with allusion to Shaw.

1921 G. B. SHAW *Back to Methuselah* Pref. p. lxxxv, As the conception of Creative Evolution developed I saw that we were at last within reach of a faith which complied with the first condition of all the religions that have ever taken hold of humanity: namely, that it must be, first and fundamentally, a science of metabiology. **1936** *Scrutiny* Mar. 377 And Keats's genius.. is not really illuminated by the procedure of *Keats und Shakespeare* or, except as another of Metabiology's cloudy trophies, exalted. **1945** K. R. POPPER *Open Society* I. v. 72 Plato's idealist historicism ultimately rests.. upon a kind of meta-biology of the race of men. **1962** A. HUXLEY *Let.* 1 Mar. (1969) 929 He would radiate a kind of religious enthusiasm—about Dostoevsky and his ideas, about 'metabiology', about Lawrence as 'The Son of Man', the 20th-century Messiah. **1968** *New Scientist* 21 Nov. 415/2 They will be searching for a new integral approach to biology, in which organisms will be described *as a whole*, rather than simply in the terms of the molecules from which the organisms are constructed... Monod offered to these members of a future biological avant-garde the term 'meta-biology'.

So ˌ**metabioˈlogical** *a.*

1921 G. B. SHAW (*title*) Back to Methuselah: a metabiological pentateuch. **1935** *Theology* XXX. 89 The metabiological reality which Mr. Murry would substitute for Deity. **1960** C. S. LEWIS *Four Loves* v. 125 A theory [of the love of lovers] more likely to be accepted in our own day is what we may call Shavian—Shaw himself might have said 'metabiological'—Romanticism. According to Shavian Romanticism the voice of Eros is the voice of the *élan vital* or Life Force. **1967** *Listener* 3 Aug. 141/2 Belonging to this period was the spirited exchange of letters between Bernard Shaw, Julian Huxley and others which lasted from the beginning of November 1942 to well into March 1943—referred to in the office as the metabiological marathon.

metabiosis (mɛtəbaɪˈəʊsɪs). *Biol.* [f. META- + Gr. βίωσις mode of life, but formed as back-formation from the adj.] A type of symbiosis in which one of the organisms modifies the environment before the second is able to live in it. So **metabiˈotic** *a.* [ad. G. *metabiotisch* (C. Garré 1887, in *Correspondenz-Blatt für Schweizer Aerzte* 1 July 390).]

1899 *Knowledge* July 151/2 It [*sc.* the yeast organism] is dependent upon its predecessor for its particular action—that is to say, we have here a condition of metabiosis. *Ibid.* 152/1 This implies nothing more or less than metabiotic relationships between the different kinds of the bacteria concerned. **1966** F. H. MEYER in S. M. Henry *Symbiosis* I. iv. 172 The nitrite bacteria are dependent on ammonia-producing organisms, while the nitrate bacteria are again dependent on the activity of the nitrite bacteria. For such direct living 'one after another', Garré gave [*sic*] the name metabiosis.

metaˈbletic, *a.* [ad. Gr. μεταβλητικός, f. μεταβάλλειν to exchange.] Of the nature of barter.

1754 FIELDING *Voy. Lisbon* (1755) 180 Merchants.. changed the Metabletic, the only kind of traffic allowed by Aristotle in his Politics, into the Chrematistic.

‖**Metabola** (mɛˈtæbələ), *sb. pl. Ent.* Formerly **Metabolia.** [mod.L. neut. pl., f. Gr. μετάβολος changeable.] A division of insects comprising those which undergo complete metamorphosis.

1817 LEACH *Zool. Misc.* III. 58 *Subclassis* 11, Metabolia. **1855** DALLAS *Nat. Hist.* I. 342 The suctorial *Metabola.* **1888** ROLLESTON & JACKSON *Anim. Life* 508 In the *Metabola*, three well marked stages are distinguishable.

‖**metabole** (mɛˈtæbəliː). *Med.* Also **-bola.** [late L., a. Gr. μεταβολή, related to μεταβάλλειν to change.] (See quots.)

1693 tr. *Blancard's Phys. Dict.* (ed. 2), *Metabole*, a change of Time, Air, or Diseases. **1722** QUINCY *Lex. Physico-Med.* (ed. 2), *Metabasis*, and *Metabole*, signifies any Change from one thing to another, either in the curative Indications, or the Symptoms of a Distemper. **1755** JOHNSON, *Metabola.*

metabolian (mɛtəˈbəʊlɪən). *Ent.* [f. mod.L. *metabolia* (see METABOLA) + -AN.] An insect of the division *Metabola.*

1835 KIRBY *Hab. & Inst. Anim.* II. 18 Dr. Leach.. subdivides.. Insects into *Ametabolians* and *Metabolians.*

metabolic (mɛtəˈbɒlɪk), *a.* [ad. Gr. μεταβολικ-ός changeable, or f. METABOLE + -IC.]

1. Pertaining to or involving transition.

(In quot. humorously pedantic.)

1743 FIELDING *Phil. Trans.* Wks. 1775 IX. 231 We are forced to proceed.. by the metabolic or mutative [method], not by the schystic or divisive.

2. *Biol.* and *Chem.* Pertaining to, involving, characterized or produced by, metabolism.

[An adaptation of G. *metabolisch*, first used in 1839 by Schwann (*Mikroskopische Untersuchungen* 229).]

1845 G. E. DAY tr. *Simon's Anim. Chem.* I. 140 A dialytic, catalytic, or, as Schwann terms it, a metabolic change on the plasma of the blood. **1902** D. N. PATON in *Encycl. Brit.* XXXI. 560/1 When such functional disturbances affect the general nutrition of the body they have been termed Metabolic Diseases (*Stoffwechselkrankheiten*).

3. *Ent.* = METABOLOUS.

1882 in OGILVIE.

4. *Zool.* (See quot.)

1882 SAVILLE-KENT *Infusoria* II. 870 *Metabolic*, changeable in form; applied by Cohn to the Infusoria in the same sense as polymorphic.

5. *Biol.* Of unicellular organisms, exhibiting metaboly.

1906 M. HARTOG in *Cambr. Nat. Hist.* I. v. 125 Such movements, permissible by the perfectly flexible but firm pellicle, are termed 'metabolic' or 'euglenoid'. **1926** G. N. CALKINS *Biol. Protozoa* vi. 254 In all cases of amoeboid and metabolic forms the cell symmetry is variable. **1955** *New Biol.* XIX. 116 Change in shape in unicellular organisms is referred to by the somewhat confusing term 'metaboly' and organisms which exhibit it are termed 'metabolic'.

So **metaˈbolical** *a.*, pertaining to METABOLISM 2. Hence **metaˈbolically** *adv.*, in, or as regards, metabolism.

1880 *Brit. Q. Rev.* Oct. 309 The next stage.. in the history of our doctrine was the.. elaboration of the *metabolical* theory. **1913** *Jrnl. Amer. Med. Assoc.* 18 Oct. 1465/1 The total metabolically active tissues of the body. **1928** *Biochem. Jrnl.* XXII. 1049 Patients, suffering from various complaints, though presumed to be metabolically sound. **1964** *Oceanogr. & Marine Biol.* II. 178 This classification is important metabolically. **1967** [see GUANASE].

metabolism (mɛˈtæbəlɪz(ə)m). [f. Gr. μεταβολή change + -ISM.]

1. *Biol.* and *Chem.* The process, in an organism or a single cell, by which nutritive material is built up into living matter (***constructive metabolism, anabolism***), or by which protoplasm is broken down into simpler substances to perform special functions (***destructive metabolism, catabolism***); the rate at which the body functions over all; the sum of the chemical changes undergone in the body by any particular substance.

1878 FOSTER *Phys.* Introd. 2 The protoplasm is continually undergoing chemical change (metabolism). **1896** *Allbutt's Syst. Med.* I. 154 In the accession of fever increased metabolism precedes rise of temperature. **1951** A. GROLLMAN *Pharmacol. & Therapeutics* iii. 77 Metabolism of alcohol.. proceeded at about the same rate irrespective of whether the subjective was at rest or engaged in muscular activity. **1962** A. PIRIE (*title*) Lens metabolism in relation to cataract. **1966** WRIGHT & SYMMERS *Systemic Path.* II. xxxi. 1098/1 Thyroid hormone stimulates metabolism, increases oxygen consumption, and causes a rise in heat production. **1968** PASSMORE & ROBSON *Compan. Med. Studies* I. xxxi. 1/1 The liver holds a key place in the metabolism of the body. **1969** J. H. GREEN *Basic Clin. Physiol.* xvii. 96/1 If the thyroid gland is underactive (hypothyroidism),.. there will be a reduction in the body's metabolism. **1971** B. N. LA DU et al. (*title*) Fundamentals of drug metabolism and drug disposition. **1972** *Internat. Jrnl. Biochem.* III. 294 (*heading*) An anti-anabolic role of adenosine 3′, 5′-cyclic monophosphate in the control of liver metabolism.

2. *Theol.* A term proposed to describe the views of some early fathers upon the Eucharist (see quot.).

1880 MᶜCLINTOCK & STRONG *Cycl. Bibl. Lit.*, *Metabolism* is a term coined by.. Rückert to describe the doctrinal views of.. Ignatius, Justin, and Irenæus on the Lord's Supper. They stand midway between strict transubstantiation and the merely symbolical view.

metabolite (mɛˈtæbəlaɪt). [f. prec. + -ITE.]

a. Any substance formed from another by metabolism. **b.** A substance necessary to metabolism or to a particular metabolic process.

1884 *Pop. Sci. Monthly* XXIV. 770 Urea being a nitrogenous metabolite. **1899** CAGNEY *Jaksch's Clin. Diagn.* vi. (ed. 4) 248 Certain colourless metabolites or chromogens of bilirubin. **1923** *Jrnl. Physiol.* LVII. 248 The increased combustion of sugar is immediately followed by the physiological oxidation of the accumulated fatty acid metabolites. **1946** P. H. MITCHELL *Textbk. Biochem.* xii. 322 The modern view of typical cases of biological oxidation is that enzymes catalyze the transfer of H_2 from a fuel food (the metabolite) to another substance. **1951** M. ABERCROMBIE et al. *Dict. Biol.* 159 Most metabolites are made by the organism in the course of metabolism; others must be taken in from the environment... Autotrophic organisms need to take in only inorganic metabolites, e.g. water, carbon dioxide, nitrates... Heterotrophic organisms need.. a wide range of organic metabolites from the environment. **1965** LEE & KNOWLES *Animal Hormones* iv. 76 Progesterone appears to be an intermediary metabolite in the formation of adrenal cortical hormones. **1967** [see FUSIDIC *a.*]. **1967** M. E. HALE *Biol. Lichens* iv. 58 Nitrogen is an essential metabolite for synthesizing proteins in both the alga and fungus. **1970** G. R. TAYLOR *Doomsday Bk.* vi. 130 In the body.. DDT tends to convert into similar substances known as DDE and DDD, the three being known.. as 'DDT and its metabolites'.

metabolizable (mɛˈtæbəlaɪzəb(ə)l), *a.* [f. METABOLIZ(E *v.* + -ABLE.] Capable of being metabolized: applied to (*a*) substances that can be utilized by the body, and (*b*) energy that can be made available or produced by metabolic processes.

1905 *Bull. Bureau Animal Industry, U.S. Dept. Agric.* No. 74. 7 The metabolizable, available and utilizable energy of the hay. **1957** G. E. HUTCHINSON *Treat. Limnol.* I. ix. 617 Metabolizable material derived from the mud. **1961** *Ann. Rev. Physiol.* XXIII. 17 The metabolizable energy supplied by a feed. **1968** *New Scientist* 28 Nov. 496/1 They have

investigated the possibility of obtaining metabolizable sugars from sawdust on a commercial basis.

Hence **me,taboliza'bility**, capability of being metabolized.

1929 MITCHELL & HAMILTON *Biochem. Amino Acids* vii. 360 The experiments..demonstrate the ready metabolizability of histidine, as compared..with..imidazole lactic acid. **1949** *Jrnl. Agric. Res.* LXXVIII. 487 The digestibility and metabolizability of two rations by sheep are reported.

metabolize (mɛ'tæbəlaɪz), *v. Biol.* [f. Gr. μεταβολή change + -IZE.]

1. *trans.* To affect by metabolism. Hence **me'tabolized** *ppl. a.*

1887 *Science* 18 Mar. 264/1 We doubt the value to a man of a mass of indefinite ill-digested text-book information. Occasionally an omnivore can take in everything, and digest and so metabolize it as to organize it into healthy mental tissue. **1900** *Lancet* 28 July 248/1 The removal of the incompletely metabolised end products. **1905** *Brit. Med. Jrnl.* 25 Feb. 444 His plain rational diet is digested—metabolized and assimilated.

2. *intr.* To perform metabolism.

1934 in WEBSTER. **1943** *Bacteriol. Rev.* VII. 139 The animal tissue cell is formed and metabolizes in an environment which is stabilized within narrow limits compared with the wide range of..conditions to which bacteria are subjected. **1971** *Sci. Amer.* Dec. 36/3 The anoxybiotic species does not stop metabolizing as soon as it encounters anaerobic conditions; it continues to metabolize for as long as six days, even though the new metabolic end product is unusual and potentially harmful.

†**metabolon** (mɛ'tæbəlɒn). *Physics. Obs.* [ad. Gr. μεταβόλον, neut. of μεταβόλος changeable, f. μεταβάλλειν to change.] A radioactive atom produced in the process of radioactive disintegration.

1903 RUTHERFORD & SODDY in *Phil Mag.* V. 586 At each stage [of disintegration] one or more α 'rays' are projected, until the last stages are reached, when the β 'ray' or electron is expelled. It seems advisable to possess a special name for these now numerous atom-fragments, or new atoms, which result from the original atom after the ray has been expelled, and which remain in existence only a limited time... We would..suggest the term *metabolon* for this purpose. **1904** E. RUTHERFORD *Radio-Activity* x. 324 The various metabolons from the radio-elements are distinguished from ordinary matter by their great instability and consequently rapid rate of change.

metabolous (mɛ'tæbələs), *a. Ent.* [f. Gr. μεταβόλ-ος changeable + -OUS.] Undergoing complete metamorphosis; belonging to the division METABOLA of insects.

1861 J. HOGG *Microsc.* (1867) 601 Some metabolous insects.

metaboly (mɛ'tæbəlɪ). *Biol.* [ad. G. *metabolie* (M. Perty *Zur Kenntnis kleinster Lebensformen* (1852) 127), f. Gr. μεταβολή change.] The changes of shape characteristic of certain unicellular organisms; euglenoid movement.

1890 in *Century Dict.* **1926** G. N. CALKINS *Biol. Protozoa* vi. 254 Metaboly may still be observed. **1969** F. E. ROUND *Introd. Lower Plants* ii. 13 A characteristic of *Euglena* is the spirally striate pellicle which is pliable and allows the cell to assume a variety of shapes—metaboly—an unfortunate term.

metaboric, metabranchial, metabrushite: see META- 6 a, 3, 7 a.

metacarp ('mɛtəkɑːp). *Anat.* Now *rare* or *Obs.* [ad. mod.L. METACARP-US. Cf. F. *métacarpe*.] = METACARPUS.

1683 A. SNAPE *Anat. Horse* IV. xix. (1686) 182 The Metacarp, or back of the hand in men. **1808** BARCLAY *Muscular Motions* 409 The two first, with the abductor indicis manus, which should have been added to this number, being inserted into the metacarp.

metacarpal (mɛtə'kɑːpəl), *a.* and *sb.* [f. METACARP-US + -AL[1].]

A. *adj.* Of or belonging to the metacarpus.

1739 S. SHARP *Surg.* 223 When you cut the Finger from the Metacarpal Bone. **1851** D. WILSON *Preh. Ann.* (1863) I. iv. 123 The metacarpal bone of a wolf.

B. *sb.* A metacarpal bone.

1854 OWEN *Skel. & Teeth* in *Circ. Sci.* I. *Org. Nat.* 212 The four normal metatarsals are much longer than the corresponding metacarpals. **1890** COUES *Field & Gen. Ornith.* II. 159 No bird now has free metacarpals in adult life.

b. *attrib.*

1875 KNIGHT *Dict. Mech.* 1421/2 *Metacarpal saw*, a narrow-bladed saw..used for dividing the bones of the fingers or middle hand or of the foot in amputation. **1895** *Arnold's Catal. Surg. Instr.* 26.

‖**meta'carpion, -ium.** *Anat.* ? *Obs.* [Gr. μετακάρπιον, mod.L. *metacarpium*, f. μετά META- + καρπός wrist.] = METACARPUS.

1597 A. M. tr. *Guillemeau's Fr. Chirurg.* 29 b/2 The first [hand vein] descendeth alongest the *Metacarpion* of the hande. **1693** tr. *Blancard's Phys. Dict.* (ed. 2), *Metacarpus* and *Metacarpium*, the back of the Hand, made of Four Oblong little Bones. **1704** J. HARRIS *Lex. Techn.* I. **1890** *Syd. Soc. Lex.*, *Metacarpion*.

meta'carpo-, used as comb. form of next in ***metacarpo-carpal, -metacarpal, -phalangeal*** adjs.; ***metacarpo-phalanges*** sb. pl.

1840 E. WILSON *Anat. Vade M.* (1842) 92 The..metacarpo-phalangeal and phalangeal joints. **1846** OWEN *Vertebr. Anim.* I. 160 Metacarpo-phalanges. **1890** *Syd. Soc. Lex.*, *Metacarpo-metacarpal articulations*, the four inner metacarpal bones are connected to each other at their carpal extremities by their arthrodial articulations, each provided with dorsal, palmar, and interosseous ligaments. **1899** *Allbutt's Syst. Med.* VII. 209 Flexion of the metacarpo-carpal joint cannot be performed by the long flexor alone.

‖**metacarpus** (mɛtə'kɑːpəs). *Anat.* [mod.L., altered from Gr. μετακάρπιον METACARPION.] That part of the hand which is situated between the wrist and the fingers: in vertebrates generally, that part of the manus which is situated betweeen the carpus and the phalanges.

1676 WISEMAN *Chirurg. Treat.* VII. ii. 479 Where the Conjunction is called Synarthrosis; as in the joyning of the Carpus to the Metacarpus. **1881** MIVART *Cat* 89 The middle solid part of the paw, called the metacarpus. **1896** NEWTON *Dict. Birds* 859 The *Metacarpus* is composed of three bones, the first, second, and third metacarpals, while trace of a fourth has been observed in embryos.

metacellulose: see META- 6 a.

metacentral (mɛtə'sɛntrəl), *a. rare.* [f. next + -AL[1].] = METACENTRIC.

1887 *Westm. Rev.* June 368 Signor Poli..believes it necessary in the case of armoured ships to take the areas of the several compartments into consideration in constructing the metacentral diagram.

metacentre ('mɛtəsɛntə(r)). [ad. F. *métacentre* (Bouguer 1746), f. *méta-* META- + *centre* CENTRE.]

1. *Hydrostatics* (and *Shipbuilding*). The limiting position of the point of intersection between the vertical line passing through the centre of gravity of a floating body when in equilibrium and the vertical line drawn through the centre of buoyancy when the body is slightly displaced; the *shifting centre*. To ensure stable equilibrium this point must be above the centre of gravity.

1794 *Rigging & Seamanship* II. 283 The metacenter..has been likewise called the *shifting center*. **1873** J. PEAKE *Nav. Archit.* (ed. 3) 47 The Height of the Metacentre above the Centre of Gravity of displacement.

2. *Biol.* (See quot.)

1902 MITCHELL in *Encycl. Brit.* XXVIII. 343/2 A new centre of modification..a metacentre.

metacentric (mɛtə'sɛntrɪk), *a.* [ad. F. *métacentrique*, f. *métacentre*: see prec. and -IC.]

1. Of or pertaining to a metacentre.

1798 *Phil. Trans.* LXXXVIII. 242 The curve..is termed the metacentric curve, being the line traced by the successive metacentres. **1881** *Times* 6 Jan. 11/2 The result of the inclination at Pembroke is shown in a metacentric diagram.

2. *Cytology.* [-CENTRIC 2.] Of a chromosome: having the centromere in or near the centre.

1939 C. D. DARLINGTON in *Jrnl. Genetics* XXXVII. 357 Two sister chromatids would become the concurrent arms of a new metacentric chromosome. **1945, 1946** [see ACROCENTRIC *a.*]. **1962** *Lancet* 2 June 1158/1 The 46 chromosomes..in the cultured cells of the blood of their patient included an unpaired metacentric chromosome. **1970** *Nature* 5 Dec. 938/2 Somatic mouse cells have forty acrocentric and telocentric and no metacentric chromosomes.

Hence as *sb.*, a metacentric chromosome.

1945 M. J. D. WHITE *Animal Cytol. & Evolution* iv. 56 Whether such a metacentric could pass through an indefinite number of mitoses without being frequently disrupted is open to doubt. **1961** *Lancet* 26 Aug. 463/2 The usual human Y..is normally about the same length as the smallest metacentric..or very slightly longer. **1971** *Nature* 15 Oct. 481/2 The karyotype presented as typical by Kao and Puck was interpreted by them as having three hamster telocentrics replaced by two human metacentrics.

metacetic (mɛtə'siːtɪk), *a. Chem.* [f. META- 2 + ACETIC.] = PROPIONIC.

1854 R. D. THOMSON *Cycl. Chem.*, *Metacetic Acid. Metacetonic acid.* A synonyme of Propionic acid.

metacetone (mɛ'tæsɪtəʊn). *Chem.* [a. F. *métacétone* (Fremy): see META- 2 and ACETONE.] A colourless oil obtained by the distillation of sugar or starch with quicklime.

1838 T. THOMSON *Chem. Org. Bodies* 364 M. Fremy discovered that when 1 part of sugar is intimately mixed with 8 parts of unslacked lime, and distilled, the product consists of two liquids, one of which is acetone, and to the other he has given the name of metacetone. **1844** FOWNES *Chem.* 409.

Hence **metacetonic** (-æsɪ'tɒnɪk) *a.* = METACETIC; **metacetonate**, a salt of metacetonic acid.

1848 BRANDE *Chem.* (ed. 6) 1733 Metacetonic Acid. Metacetylic Acid. *Ibid.*, Metacetonate of soda. **1862** [see METACETIC].

metacetyl (mɛ'tæsɪtɪl). *Chem.* [f. META- 2 + ACETYL.] = PROPIONYL. Hence **metace'tylic** = METACETONIC.

1848 BRANDE *Chem.* (ed. 6) 1732 Metacetone. Oxide of Metacetyle. *Ibid.* 1733 Metacetylic Acid. **1890** *Syd. Soc. Lex.*, *Metacetyl.*

metachemic, metachemistry, metachloral, metachlorite: see META- 5, 1, 6 a, 7 a.

metachromasia (mɛtəkrəʊ'meɪzɪə). *Biol.* Also in anglicized form **metachromasy** (-'krəʊməsɪ). [mod.L., f. META- + Gr. χρῶμα, χρωματ- colour: see -IA[1].] The property exhibited by certain biological materials and structures of staining a different colour from that of the stain used; also, the corresponding property of certain stains of changing colour in the presence of certain biological materials and structures.

1903 *Lancet* 18 July 177/1 The cells which contain granules contain also a store of ferment (zymogen), whilst the cells that are destitute of granules exhibit the reaction of mucin (metachromasy). **1956** *Nature* 3 Mar. 428/1 Anaphylactic shock brought out..degranulation and decrease of the metachromasia of the remaining granules in most of the cells. **1960** L. PICKEN *Organization of Cells* x. 481 The amoebae..are found to become metachromatic..in increasing numbers as aggregation approaches... The appearance of metachromasy seems, however, to precede sensitivity to acrasin. **1964** W. G. SMITH *Allergy & Tissue Metabolism* iii. 33 Both tissue and blood mast cells are characterised by a coarse granular cytoplasm possessing a strong affinity for basic dyes, some of which change colour (exhibit metachromasia) as staining occurs. **1967** *New Scientist* 2 Feb. 275/2 These fragments are then encapsulated by a high polymer (producing the green metachromasia) and enter some kind of 'spore' stage. **1971** E. GURR *Synthetic Dyes* I. ii. 63 The significance of the dimer spectra in terms of theories of metachromasy is discussed.

metachromatic (,mɛtəkrəʊ'mætɪk), *a.* [f. META- + Gr. χρῶμα, χρωματ- colour + -IC.]

1. Pertaining to metachromism.

1876 *Chem. News* 11 Feb. 60/2 From a study of the two classes [of metachromes] the following metachromatic scale was arrived at:—White, colourless, violet, indigo, blue [etc.].

2. *Biol.* Exhibiting or involving metachromasia.

1897 MUIR & RITCHIE *Man. Bacteriol.* i. 11 It is..very probable that the occurrence of metachromatic granules in a bacterium indicates the onset of degenerative changes. **1902** *Jrnl. R. Microsc. Soc.* 89 (*heading*) Metachromatic granules in sporiferous bacteria. **1925** C. H. BROWNING *Bacteriol.* ii. 29 Sometimes with methylene-blue these beads stain of a different tint from the rest of the bacillus (metachromatic staining). **1957** *New Biol.* XXIV. 52 Structures which change the colour of the stain in this way are said to be metachromatic. **1964** W. G. SMITH *Allergy & Tissue Metabolism* iii. 36 Metachromatic staining of the faded granules began.

Hence **metachro'matically** *adv.*

1908 *Anatomical Rec.* II. 106 Sections from such material stained in toluidene blue show the mucous secretion metachromatically stained, but no metachromatism is visible in the demilune cells. **1957** *New Biol.* XXIV. 54 Polysaccharides of high molecular weight other than heparin stain metachromatically. **1971** *Nature* 24 Sept. 264/2 The lipid mass was stained metachromatically pale orange-brown with cresyl violet..and thionin.

metachromatism (mɛtə'krəʊmətɪz(ə)m). [Formed as prec. + -ISM.] **a.** Change or variation of colour (see quots.).

1876 ACKROYD in *Chem. News* 25 Aug. 75/1 We venture, therefore, to propose for the phenomenon the name of Metachromatism. **1890** *Syd. Soc. Lex.*, *Metachromatism*, a change or alteration of colour, as in the hair or feathers, from advance of age.

b. *Biol.* = METACHROMASIA.

1893 *Jrnl. R. Microsc. Soc.* 563 (*heading*) Metachromatism of parasitic sporozoa and carcinoma cells. **1904** *Brit. Med. Jrnl.* 3 Dec. 1507 Under certain conditions of staining, different parts of the cell protoplasm possess different chemical affinities to the dye..(metachromatism). **1908** [see METACHROMATICALLY *adv.*]. **1917** C. E. MARSHALL *Microbiol.* (ed. 2) ii. 43 These bodies..are stained violet-red by most of the basic dyes, aniline blue or violet... By reason of this property of metachromatism, they have been called metachromatic granules.

metachrome ('mɛtəkrəʊm), *sb.* and *a.* [f. META-[1] + Gr. χρῶμα colour.]

A. *sb.* A body that changes colour.

1876 *Chem. News* 11 Feb. 60/2 The author..passed on to the classification of metachromes, which he [Ackroyd] arranges in two groups.

B. *adj. Dye Chem.* Designating mordant dyes and their mordants that may be applied simultaneously in the same bath, and the method of dyeing by this process.

1901 *Jrnl. Soc. Dyers & Colourists* XVII. 66/1 Metachrome Brown B Paste: This colour is the first of a new series of (metachrome) dyes which have the property of dyeing in the single bath with metallic salts. *Ibid.*, With less than 3 per cent. dyestuff, 3 per cent. metachrome mordant must be used, but with larger amounts of dyestuff an equal amount. **1927** HORSFALL & LAWRIE *Dyeing Textile Fibres* ix. 263 The meta-chrome process as originally introduced..was confined to a comparatively small number of dyestuffs derived from picramic acid. **1963** A. J. HALL *Textile Sci.* iv. 184 The third (metachrome) method enables both dye and bichromate to be applied at the same time and it depends on the fact that no appreciable combination occurs between the

bichromate and the wool or the dye under alkaline conditions, but this holds only for a limited number of dyes. **1971** R. L. M. ALLEN *Colour Chem.* iv. 45 In 1900 the Berlin Aniline Company devised the metachrome method whereby selected dyes can be applied simultaneously with a chroming agent.

metachromism (mɛtəˈkrəʊmɪz(ə)m). [Formed as prec. + -ISM.] Colour-change.
1876 *Chem. News* 11 Feb. 60/2 Metachromism, as he [Ackroyd] terms the changes of colour which various substances undergo when heated.

metachronism (mɛˈtækrənɪz(ə)m). [ad. med.L. *metachronism-us*, a. late Gr. type *μεταχρονισμός, f. μετα- META- + χρόνος time. Cf. F. *métachronisme*.
Normally the word should mean 'transposition of dates' (cf. quot. 1656 below); but it has been associated with Gr. μετάχρονος, μεταχρόνιος happening later, f. μετά after + χρόνος time; hence the sense explained below, which seems to be that of all the available instances.]
1. An error in chronology consisting in placing an event later than its real date. (Cf. PARACHRONISM.)
1617 HALES *Serm.* 36 There are in Scripture.. anachronismes, metachronismes, and the like, which bring infinite obscuritie to the text. **1656** BLOUNT *Glossogr.*, *Metachronism*, an error in the connexion of things or times, by reckoning or accounting short or beyond the truth. **1677** R. CARY *Chronology* II. i. I. xx. 157 Our Authour..is..guilty of a foul Metachronysm, in accomodating the 5th of Cambyses to his 4986 of the World.
2. *Biol.* The co-ordination of the movement of parts, esp. cilia, into a progressive wave.
1905 *Jrnl. Exper. Zool.* II. 408 It is the principal object of this paper to discuss the cause of metachronism in ciliary action. **1928** J. GRAY *Ciliary Movement* vii. 117 Any particular cilium is slightly in advance of the cilium behind it in the series and slightly behind the one just in front of it. This regular sequence is known as metachronism. **1972** M. S. GARDINER *Biol. Invertebr.* IV. xi. 189/1 In Metazoa, the cilia on adjacent cells may exhibit a similar coordination in metachronism.
So **metaˈchronal** *a.*, exhibiting or characteristic of metachronism (sense 2); **metaˈchronally** *adv.*
1905 *Jrnl. Exper. Zool.* II. 407 The cause of metachronal action is..to be sought..in the mechanical effect of one cilium on another. *Ibid.*, These swimming plates are arranged in rows and the members of each row, like ordinary cilia, beat metachronally, not synchronally. **1928** J. GRAY *Ciliary Movement* vii. 118 Although the direction of the metachronal wave..differs in different tissues, it is remarkably constant in each particular case. **1940** G. S. CARTER *Gen. Zool. Invertebr.* viii. 359 Metachronal rhythm is not confined to metazoan cilia; it can be well seen in such ciliate protistans as *Opalina*. **1962** D. NICHOLS *Echinoderms* viii. 99 In at least one urchin, *Diadema*, the spines show metachronal rhythm during locomotion, and they move the animal across the ocean floor with considerable speed. **1971** *Nature* 12 Feb. 491/1 The cilia of these last two cell types beat metachronally.

‖**metachrosis** (mɛtəˈkrəʊsɪs). [mod.L., f. Gr. μετα- META- + χρῶσις colouring.] Colour-change.
1887 E. D. COPE *Orig. Fittest* 211 The power of metachrosis, or of changing the color at will, by the expansion under nerve-influence of special pigment cells.

metacinnabar(ite: see META- 7 a.

metaˈcinnamein. *Chem.* Also **-ine.** [a. F. *métacinnaméine* (Fremy): see META- 6.] A substance isomeric with cinnamein, obtained by keeping cinnamein under water.
1848 FOWNES *Chem.* (ed. 2) 451. **1874** GARROD & BAXTER *Mat. Med.* 236 Metacinnamein.

metaˈcinnamene. *Chem.* [See META- 6 a.] (See quot. 1886.)
1857 MILLER *Elem. Chem.* III. vii. §1 (1862) 560 Metacinnamene, or styracin. **1886** *Athenæum* 30 Jan. 172/3 Metacinnamene, a highly refracting glass-like solid, obtained by the action of light or heat upon cinnamene.

metacism (ˈmɛtəsɪz(ə)m). [ad. late L. *metacismus*, corruptly ad. late Gr. μυτακισμός 'fondness for the letter μ' (L. & Sc.), f. μῦ the name of the letter. Cf. ITACISM.] The placing of a word with final *m* before a word beginning with a vowel; regarded as a fault in Latin prose composition.
This is the sense in the original of quot. 1844; but the grammarians explain *metacismus* or *myotacismus* as the fault of pronouncing a final *m* which ought to be elided before a following vowel.
[**1656** BLOUNT *Glossogr.*, *Metacism*, a fault in pronouncing.] **1844** tr. *St. Gregory's Morals on Job* I. Epist. 11, I do not escape the collisions of metacism.

metacœle (ˈmɛtəsiːl). *Biol.* [f. Gr. μετα- META- + κοῖλος hollow.] That type of cœlom which is of secondary development.
1884 BOURNE in *Q. Jrnl. Microsc. Sci.* XXIV. 477 An archaic enterocœle thus gradually undergoes diacœlosis, being replaced by a metacœle.

‖**metacœlia** (mɛtəˈsiːlɪə). [mod.L., f. Gr. μετα- META- + κοιλία ventricle.] The posterior part of the fourth ventricle of the brain.
1882 WILDER & GAGE *Anat. Techn.* 482 Metacœlia... Syn. Ventriculus quartus, caudal portion.

metacœlome (mɛtəˈsiːləʊm). *Biol.* Also **-om.** [f. META- + CŒLOME.] (See quot.)
1888 ROLLESTON & JACKSON *Anim. Life* 223 Nephridial funnels appear to be present in all Leeches... They are perforate in Nephelis and Trochaeta, and in these genera they open into special spaces developed in the botryoidal tissue, termed by Gibbs Bourne 'metacoelome'.
So ‖**metacœlosis** (-siːˈləʊsɪs): see quot.
1884 BOURNE in *Q. Jrnl. Microsc. Sci.* XXIV. 477 This development of new cœlomic space (botryoidal tissue) may be termed metacœlosis.

metacommuniˈcation. [META- 1.] Communication that takes place with, or underlies, a more obvious form of communication; principles or theories about communication derived from the study of communication. Hence **metacommuniˈcational, metacoˈmmunicative** *adjs.*
1951 RUESCH & BATESON *Communication* vi. 152 He is, also,..making implicit metacommunicative statements about his own position and stock of information. *Ibid.* vii. 203 (*heading*) Communication between two persons and metacommunication. **1963** T. A. SEBEOK in J. A. Fishman *Readings Sociol. of Lang.* (1968) 28 The metacommunicative messages used by rhesus monkeys, enabling them to distinguish between play and nonplay, have received particularly careful attention. **1967** J. A. MEERLOO in L. Thayer *Communication* 54 We cannot, of course, recover man's contemplations about himself from fossil remains, and data from living nonliterate men are lamentably deficient in metacommunicational material. **1967** P. WATZLAWICK et al. *Pragmatics Human Communication* i. 40 When we no longer use communication to communicate but to communicate *about* communication, as we inevitably must in communication research, then we use conceptualizations that are not part of but *about* communication. In analogy to metamathematics this is called metacommunication. **1974** *Publishers Weekly* 29 Apr. 47/3 The author is one of the students of 'metacommunications' or body language—Gregory Bateson and Raymond Birdwhistell are the two best-known names in this field, though their work derives from anthropologists such as Lorenz.

meta-compounds: see META- 6.

‖**metacondylus** (mɛtəˈkɒndɪləs). *Anat.* Also anglicized **metaˈcondyle.** [mod.L.: see META- and CONDYLE.] That phalanx of a finger that bears the nail.
1693 tr. *Blancard's Phys. Dict.* (ed. 2), *Metacondyli*, the utmost bones of the fingers. **1848** CRAIG, *Metacondyle.*

metacone (ˈmɛtəkəʊn). *Zool.* [f. META- + CONE *sb.*[1]] An external cusp on the outer back corner of a mammalian upper molar tooth. Hence **metaˈconal** *a.*
1888 H. F. OSBORN in *Amer. Naturalist* XXII. 1072 Proposed terms... Metacone. **1896** *Proc. Zool. Soc.* 570 The dental germ presenting the appearance of a high cone with a large posterior heel (metaconal region) and a slight internal extension. *Ibid.*, The posterior extension representing the metacone. **1933** A. S. ROMER *Vertebr. Paleont.* xii. 248 Inside the metacone [there is often] a smaller one [*sc.* cusp], the metaconule. **1971** P. HERSHKOVITZ in A. A. Dahlberg *Dental Morphol. & Evolution* viii. 103 In the first molar of *Potamogale*, the first indication of the metacone is a wedgelike indentation. *Ibid.* 129 In cercopithecoids, crista V is transverse and meets the buccal and metaconal portion of the plagiocrista.

metaconid (mɛtəˈkəʊnɪd). *Zool.* [f. METACON(E + -ID[5].] A cusp on a mammalian lower molar tooth corresponding to the metacone on an upper molar.
1888 H. F. OSBORN in *Amer. Naturalist* XXII. 1073 Only the paracone and metaconids and hypoconids [of *Amphitherium*] have been observed heretofore. **1904** *Ann. & Mag. Nat. Hist.* XIII. 409 The antero-internal cusp not or scarcely divided into its constituent paraconid and metaconid. **1919** [see HYPOCONID]. **1933** A. S. ROMER *Vertebr. Paleont.* xii. 248 The lower teeth tend also to square up..so that the four definitive cusps are the protoconid, metaconid, entoconid, and hypoconid. **1968** R. ZANGERL tr. *Peyer's Compar. Odontol.* 186 In the lower jaw..paraconid and metaconid are lingual. **1975** *Nature* 31 July 402/2 Paraconid and metaconid were clearly separated at their bases on the medial face of the tooth.

metacontrast (mɛtəˈkɒntrɑːst, -æ-). *Psychol.* [ad. G. *metakontrast* (R. Stigler 1910, in *Arch. f. ges. Physiol.* CXXXIV. 386), f. Gr. μετα- META- + *kontrast* CONTRAST *sb.*] A change, esp. a diminution, in the after-effect of a visual stimulus as a result of a second stimulus following shortly afterwards.
1950 *Jrnl. Optical Soc. Amer.* XL. 796/1 An investigation of the effect of variation of the luminance, exposure asynchrony, and spatial separation of the stimuli on the magnitude of metacontrast. **1971** *Jrnl. Gen. Psychol.* LXXXIV. 86 Masking and metacontrast studies do, however, demonstrate that a second stimulus may impair the perception of the first stimulus. **1972** *Science* 13 Oct. 179/3 They suggest that temporally backward and spatially lateral inhibition (metacontrast) occurs when the duration of the flash is long enough.

metaconule (mɛtəˈkəʊnjuːl). *Zool.* [f. METACON(E + *-ule*.] An intermediate cusp between the hypocone and the metacone of a mammalian upper molar tooth.
1888 H. F. OSBORN in *Amer. Naturalist* XXII. 1074 The Bunodont series are universally characterized by the initial or advanced development of the proto- and metaconules in the upper molars. **1905** *Amer. Geologist* XXXV. 244 The intermediate cusps (protoconule and metaconule) are both well-defined. **1968** R. ZANGERL tr. *Peyer's Compar. Odontol.* 187 Intermediate cusps occurred.., a metaconule between protocone and metacone. **1971** W. D. TURNBULL in A. A. Dahlberg *Dental Morphol. & Evolution* ix. 163 (*caption*) Specimen consists of the protocone and metaconules.

metacoumarate, -coumaric: see META- 6 b.

‖**metacrasis** (mɛtəˈkreɪsɪs). [f. META- + CRASIS.]
1. *Bot.* 'Kinetic metabolism, transmutation of energy' (Jackson *Gloss. Bot. Terms* 1900).
1884 BOWER & SCOTT *De Bary's Phaner.* 509 The process of metacrasis which produces the duramen.
2. *Geol.* (See quot.)
1886 BONNEY in *Proc. Geol. Soc.* 59 *Metacrasis* (recombination), denoting changes like the conversion of a mud into a mass of quartz with mica and other silicates. **1893** GEIKIE *Text-bk. Geol.* IV. VIII. 596 *note*, *Metacrasis*, denoting such transformations as the conversion of mud into a mass of mica, quartz, and other silicates.

metacresol: see META- 6 a.

‖**metacromion** (mɛtəˈkrəʊmɪɒn). *Zool.* [f. META- + ACROMION.] In some mammals, a process of the spine of the scapula behind the acromion. Hence **metaˈcromial** *a.*
1868 W. K. PARKER *Shoulder-girdle Vertebr.* 204 At its root this large acromion sends backwards a rudimentary 'metacromion'. *Ibid.* 207 The metacromial process.

metacryst (ˈmɛtəkrɪst). *Petrol.* [f. META- + *-cryst* after PHENOCRYST.] A large crystal formed in a metamorphic rock by recrystallization.
1913 W. LINDGREN *Mineral Deposits* xi. 158 An individual in another may be briefly called a metasome; if the metasome develops strongly with crystal outlines it may be called a metacryst. **1932** F. F. GROUT *Petrogr. & Petrol.* 365 Metacrysts commonly have abundant inclusions..and in some the inclusions are oriented so as to show that the metacrysts grew by replacement. **1963** D. W. & E. E. HUMPHRIES tr. *Termier's Erosion & Sedimentation* xvii. 339 Dolomite is present in limestones as rhombic 'metacrysts' which can cut across original structures (for example, oolites) and fossils.

metacyclic (mɛtəˈsɪklɪk), *a.* *Math.* [f. META- + CYCLE *sb.* + -IC.] Pertaining to the permutation of a set of elements in a cycle. (*Cent. Dict.* 1890.)

metadiorite, -dolerite: see META- 5 b.

metadore, obs. form of MATADOR.

metadyne (ˈmɛtədaɪn). *Electr.* [ad. F. *métadyne* (J. M. Pestarini 1930, in *Rev. gén. de l'Électr.* XXVII. 355/1), f. META- + Gr. δύναμις power.] A rotary direct-current generator in which the output voltage can be varied by a small signal applied to a control field perpendicular to the main field and which is used in position- or speed-control systems.
1930 *Sci. Abstr.* B. XXXIII. 376 The 'Métadyne' is a direct-current machine having more than two brush axes per pole-pair. **1945** [see AMPLIDYNE]. **1951** F. J. TEAGO in P. Kemp *Electr. Engin.* III. 89/1 One of the chief reasons for using metadyne control is that the alternating current may be kept constant. **1970** J. SHEPHERD et al. *Higher Electr. Engin.* (ed. 2) xiv. 496 Metadyne generators are uncompensated or undercompensated cross-field generators.

meta-element: see META- 1.

metafacial: see META- 3.

metafor, obs. form of METAPHOR.

metagadolinite: see META- 7 a.

metagalaxy (mɛtəˈgæləksɪ). *Astr.* [f. META- 1 + GALAXY *sb.*] The entire system of galaxies (see quot. 1930); also, a cluster or group of galaxies. So **metagaˈlactic** *a.*
1930 H. SHAPLEY *Flights from Chaos* xiii. 141 Corresponding to individual stars, multiples, and star clusters we have galaxies, multiple galaxies, and clusters of galaxies... To designate the system including all of these I propose to use Lundmark's term, the Metagalactic system —or, more briefly, the Metagalaxy. **1951** *Astron. Jrnl.* Apr. 47/2 (*heading*) Differential rotation of the inner metagalaxy. **1957** H. SHAPLEY *Inner Metagalaxy* p.v, The terms 'Metagalaxy' and 'metagalactic' refer to the total recognized assemblage of galaxies. The Metagalaxy includes also whatever there may be in the way of gas, particles, planets, stars, and star clusters in the spaces between the galaxies. It is essentially the measurable material universe. **1965** *Rev. Mod. Physics* XXXVII. 654/1 In principle there may be several condensations of the initial plasma so that there may be other metagalactic systems in the universe. *Ibid.* 663/2 According to Klein there may be other metagalaxies in the universe. **1965** J. D. NORTH *Measure of Universe* ii. 20 His prediction of a high collision rate between the nebulae of a single metagalaxy. *Ibid.* App. 408 The galaxies assigned to the Local Group increased in number and the 'local metagalaxy' took its place with the other known clusters. **1970** *Nature* 12 Dec. 1069/1 According to this scheme, an initial contraction of the metagalaxy (containing equal amounts of matter and antimatter) resulting from its self-gravitation was turned into an expansion by the pressure of radiation produced by annihilation reactions. *Ibid.*, Although the gravitational and radiation fields in this case are metagalactic, the scale of the matter-antimatter

separation is determined by the magnetic field and is likely to be much more local.

metagallic (mɛtəˈgælɪk), *a. Chem.* [f. META- + GALLIC *a.*[2]] ***metagallic acid***: an acid obtained by heating gallic acid. Hence **metaˈgallate**, a salt of metagallic acid.

1835 *Amer. Jrnl. Sci.* XXVIII. 126 Metagallic acid. **1836** BRANDE *Chem.* (ed. 4) 933. *Ibid.*, Metagallate of potassa. **1865** WATTS tr. *Gmelin's Handbk. Chem.* XV. 458 Metagallic acid (Mulder's melangallic, Gerhardt's gallulmic acid).

‖**metagaster** (mɛtəˈgæstə(r)). *Biol.* [mod.L.: see META- and GASTER.] Haeckel's phylogenetic term for the later, more highly differentiated stomach of the Craniota, as distinguished from the primitive intestine or protogaster. Hence **metaˈgastral** *a.* (in recent Dicts.).

1879 tr. *Haeckel's Evol. Man* II 321 The differentiated or secondary intestine ('after intestine or metagaster').

metagastric (mɛtəˈgæstrɪk), *a. Zool.* [f. META- + Gr. γαστήρ belly + -IC.] Applied to portions of the carapace in brachyurous crustaceans situated towards the hinder part of the gastro-hepatic area.

1877 HUXLEY *Anat. Inv. Anim.* vi. 343 The latter [gastric lobe area] is again subdivided into two epigastric lobes, two protogastric lobes, a median mesogastric lobe, two metagastric lobes, and two urogastric lobes.

‖**metagastrula** (mɛtəˈgæstrʊlə). *Biol.* [mod.L.: see META- and GASTRULA.] Haeckel's term for a secondary modified gastrula (see quot.).

1879 tr. *Haeckel's Evol. Man* I. 199 The more or less varying Gastrula-form, which results from this kenogenetic egg-cleavage, may be called, generally, the secondary, modified Gastrula, or Metagastrula.

metage (ˈmiːtɪdʒ). Also 6 *Sc.* **mettage, mettege,** 7 **meatage.** [f. METE *v.* + -AGE.]

1. The action of measuring officially the content or weight of a load of grain, coal, etc.

15.. *Aberd. Reg.* XXIV. (Jam.), The mettege of colis, salt, lym, corne, fruit, and sic mensturable [*sic*] gudis. **1576** *Reg. Privy Council Scot.* II. 578 To pay thre penneis for the mettage of every laid [of malt] quhilk sal happin to be presentit. **1636** *Maldon, Essex, Borough Deeds* (Bundle 110) I For the meatage of 10 quarter of barly, 5*d.* **1753** *De Foe's Tour Gt. Brit.* (ed. 5) II. 137 Acts have very lately passed in relation to the Admeasurement or Metage of Coals for the City of Westminster. **1872** *Daily News* 15 Apr. 5/2 The arrangements with respect to the metage of grain in the port of London.

2. The duty paid for such measuring. (Cf. MEASURAGE.)

1527 *Burgh Rec. Edin.* (1869) I. 232 Togidder with the mettage, viz. viijd. for ilk chalder. **1854** *Fraser's Mag.* XLIX. 564 The right of the Corporation to the metage of corn, fruit, and other articles, is recognised and confirmed in the first charter of James I. **1887** *Times* 27 Aug. 11/4 The ordinary fruit metage produced £654.

3. *attrib.*

1546-7 *Burgh Rec. Stirling* (1887) 46 Thai sall pay tharfor iiijd. of the chalder of mettage silveir. **1746** *Act* 19 *Geo. II*, c. 35 §10 The Amount of the Metage Charge [of Coals]. **1800** COLQUHOUN *Comm. Thames* xv. 456 On payment of the Metage Duty. **1865** *Daily Tel.* 16 Nov. 8/1 Merchants .. interested in the question of the metage dues.

metagelatin: see META- 6 a.

metagenesis (mɛtəˈdʒɛnɪsɪs). *Biol.* [mod.L.: see META- and GENESIS.]

†**1.** Used by Owen (*parthenogenesis*, 1849) for: Alternation of generations (see ALTERNATION 1 b).

Owen, however, included under this designation certain metamorphoses not now recognized as instances of alternation of generations.

2. Now used in more restricted sense (see quot.).

1889 GEDDES & THOMSON *Evol. Sex* xv. 207 Simple alternation between sexual and asexual reproduction .. is called .. metagenesis.

ˌ**metageˈnetic**, *a.* [f. META- + GENETIC.]

1. *Zool.* Pertaining to, characterized by, or involving metagenesis.

1849 OWEN *Parthenogenesis* 17 The successive generations, which .. complete the metagenetic cycle. **1877** BALFOUR in *Encycl. Brit.* VII. 629/1 The peculiar metagenetic mode of development.

2. *Cryst.* Applied to certain twin crystals (see quot.).

1883 HEDDLE in *Encycl. Brit.* XVI. 367/1 In metagenetic twins the crystal was at first simple, but afterwards, through some change in the material furnished for its increase or possibly induced in itself, it received new layers, or an extension *in a reversed position*.

Hence **metageˈnetically** *adv.*, by metagenesis.

1868 DARWIN *Anim. & Pl.* II. 367 If, instead of a single individual, several were to be thus developed metagenetically within a pre-existing form.

metageˈometry. [See META-.] The geometry of non-Euclidean space. So **metageˈometer**, one who studies metageometry. **metageoˈmetrical** *a.*, pertaining to metageometry. ˌ**metageomeˈtrician** = METAGEOMETER.

1882 STALLO *Concepts Mod. Physics* 258 'Space in general' (as distinguished from 'flat space', in the metageometrical sense). **1897** B. A. W. RUSSELL *Found. Geom.* Cont. p. vii, Metageometry began by rejecting the axiom of parallels. *Ibid.* 56 To urge, with the Metageometers, that non-Euclidean systems are logically self-consistent. **1898** CAYLEY *Coll. Math. Papers* (Suppl. Vol.) Index, Metageometry. **1903** *Science* 16 Jan. 106/2 Our metageometricians tried to derive the basic geometrical principles from pure reason but failed.

metagnathous (mɛˈtægnəθəs), *a.* [f. Gr. μετά META- + γνάθος jaw + -OUS.] Having the tips of the mandibles crossed. Hence **meˈtagnathism**, the condition of being metagnathous.

1872 COUES *Key N. Amer. Birds* 24 The metagnathous [class], in which the points of the mandibles cross each other. **1890** —— *Field & Gen. Ornithol.* II. 150 Each mandible may be oppositely falcate, as in the crossbill, constituting metagnathism.

metagnomy (mɛˈtægnəmɪ). *Psychics.* [ad. F. *métagnomie* (Boirac, 1917), f. META- + Gr. γνώμη thought.] The acquisition of information by supernormal means; divination. So ˈ**metagnome**, one who has the power of metagnomy; a medium; **metagˈnomic** *a.*, of or pertaining to metagnomy.

1919 W. DE KERLOR tr. *Boirac's Psychol. of Future* xi. 232 Clairvoyance, or 'metagnomy'. *Ibid.* 256 It is especially in the somnambulistic state, natural or provoked, that metagnomic manifestations occur. *Ibid.* 257 The mesmerist or hypnotist .. evokes the metagnomic faculty. **1933** T. BESTERMAN tr. *Driesch's Psychical Res.* I. i. 2 The subject of the investigation, the sensitive, the medium, the metagnome, or whatever one likes to call him. **1960** *New Scientist* 28 July 306/2 Prosopopesis, metagnomy, telergy and teleplasty: if these are accepted, what remains of the 'laws' of physics, chemistry, biology and psychology? **1965** *Listener* 29 Apr. 639/3 With the existence of such phenomena as telepathy, metagnomy, precognition, etc., now well established, .. there is surely a possibility that some astrologers may be psychically gifted individuals.

metagon (ˈmɛtəgɒn). *Biol.* [f. META- + Gr. γόνος offspring.] (See quot. 1968.)

1962 GIBSON & BEALE in *Genetical Res.* III. 25 As a provisional hypothesis .. we proposed that the cytoplasm of mate-killer paramecia contained, in addition to the visible mu particles, certain other factors, here denoted 'metagons', which are assumed to be formed only in the presence of one or other of the genes M_1 and M_2. **1964** *New Scientist* 6 Aug. 322/2 Particles of RNA called 'metagons'. **1968** R. RIEGER *Gloss. Genetics & Cytogenetics* 285 *Metagon*, presumably, a primary, gene-initiated product in *Paramecium* which is RNA (complementary to the DNA of a specific gene) in nature, conditionally stable, infectious (capable of transmission from one *Paramecium* to another through the cytoplasm and the external medium), and capable of replication under certain conditions.

metagram (ˈmɛtəgræm). [f. Gr. μετα- META- + γράμμα letter, after *anagram*.] A kind of puzzle turning on the alteration of a word by removing some of its letters and substituting others.

1867 *London Society* XII. 307 We therefore welcome a new sort of 'gram... Its name, metagram, is derived from two Greek words, signifying a 'change of letters'. It is on this change that the whole thing turns. **1882** GROSART in *Spenser's Wks.* III. p. lxxxii, An anagram or metagram.

†**metaˈgrammatism.** *Obs.* [ad. Gr. μεταγραμματισμός (Galen), f. μετα- META- + γραμματ-, γράμμα letter: see -ISM.] The transposition of letters in a word or phrase; anagrammatism. So **metaˈgrammatize** *v.* [Gr. μεταγραμματίζειν (Tzetzes)], 'to alter the letters' (L. & Sc.).

1605 CAMDEN *Rem.*, *Anagr.* 150 Anagrammatisme, or Metagrammatisme. **1702** C. MATHER *Magn. Chr.* III. I. iii. (1852) 319 Mr. Ward, .. observing the great hospitality of Mr. Wilson, in conjunction with his metagrammatising temper, said, 'That the anagram of John Wilson was, I pray, come in: you are heartily welcome'.

metagranite: see META- 5 b.

metagraphy (mɛˈtægrəfɪ). [f. Gr. μετα- META- + -γραφία writing, -GRAPHY.] Transliteration. Hence **metaˈgraphic** *a.*

1872 LATHAM *Dict.*, *Transliteration*, translation or rendering of the letter of one alphabet by its equivalent in another; metagraphy: (this latter word giving *metagraphic* as its adjective, a more convenient one than *transliterative* or *transliterational*). **1888** T. WATTS in *Athenæum* 17 Mar. 340/2 It was his [Latham's] belief in the system of metagraphy as applied to non-European alphabets that made him a very early advocate of phonetic spelling.

metagrobolize (mɛtəˈgrɒbəlaɪz), *v. humorous.* Also 7–8 **-grabolise, -ize.** [ad. obs. F. *metagraboulizer* (Rabelais) 'to dunce vpon, to puzzle, or (too much) beate the braines about' (Cotgr.).] *trans.* **a.** To puzzle, mystify. **b.** To puzzle out. So **metaˈgrobolism**, mystification.

1653 URQUHART *Rabelais* I. xix, I have been these eighteen dayes in metagrabolising this brave speech. *a* **1693** *Ibid.* III. xxii, The Autonomatick Metagrobolism of the Romish Church. *Ibid.* xxvi. 212, I find my Brains .. metagrobolized and confounded. **1788** H. CLARKE *Sch. Candidates* (1877) 10 My prolegomena to a public speech which I had been a whole synodical month in matagrabolizing [*sic*]. **1899** KIPLING *Stalky* 119 Come to think of it, we have metagrobolised 'em.

metagummic: see META- 6 a.

‖**métairie** (metɛri). [Fr., f. *métayer*.] A farm held on the MÉTAYER system.

1817 C. CLAIRMONT in Dowden *Shelley* (1887) II. 115, I should choose .. to cultivate a little *métairie* among the mountains. **1848** MILL *Pol. Econ.* II. viii. §3 (1876) 190 In the other parts of Tuscany, where the metairies are larger.

metake (ˈmetake). [Japanese.] A tall slender Japanese bamboo, *Pseudosasa* (or *Arundinaria*) *japonica*.

1896 A. B. FREEMAN-MITFORD *Bamboo Garden* 69 *Arundinaria japonica* or Métaké... The word Métaké, or, more correctly, Médaké, means in Japanese 'female Bamboo', but there is no scientific reason for using the word 'female' in connection with this species. *Ibid.* 72 The Japanese gardeners consider Ya-daké and Mé-také to be two different plants. **1966** F. A. MCCLURE *Bamboos* 293 *Pseudosasa japonica* (*Arundinaria japonica*; *Sasa japonica*). Metake; Yadake; arrow bamboo. **1971** *Country Life* 18 Nov. 1371/1 The common Metake, *Arundinaria* or *Pseudosasa japonica* .. [is] a particularly fine species [of bamboo] with slender canes quite 10 ft. high and glossy green leaves that are glaucous beneath.

metakinesis (mɛtəkaɪˈniːsɪs). Now *rare*. Pl. **-kineses.** [mod.L., f. META- + Gr. κίνησις motion.] **1.** *Cytology.* [coined (in Ger.) by W. Flemming in *Zellsubstanz, Kern und Zelltheilung* (1882) xx. 268.] **a.** (See quot. 1968.)

1888 [see *homœotypical* adj. (HOMŒO-)]. **1899** *Jrnl. R. Microsc. Soc.* Apr. 168 Karyokinesis in the Root-tips of Allium... Anaphase. (5) After the longitudinal segmentation of the chromosomes, which, as a general rule, does not begin until the chromosomes are in the equatorial plane, the daughter chromosomes are gradually pulled apart... This stage is known as metakinesis. **1903** *Bot. Gaz.* XXXV. 251 Heuser ('84) seems to have been the first to call attention to the double character of the daughter chromosomes in the diaster stage of *Tradescantia virginica*, but he interpreted the separation of the daughter segments during metakinesis of the first mitosis as a transverse division. **1968** R. RIEGER *Gloss. Genetics & Cytogenetics* 286 *Metakinesis*, the separation of the two chromatids of each chromosome and their movement to opposite spindle poles during anaphase of mitosis.

b. [given this sense by F. Wassermann 1926, in *Zeitschr. f. Anat. u. Entwicklungsges.* LXXX. 399.] (See quot. 1968.)

1948 W. ANDREW tr. *E.D.P. de Robertis's Gen. Cytol.* viii. 182 The prometaphase generally begins with the disintegration of the nuclear membrane... When the nuclear membrane has disintegrated, a more fluid zone is noted in the center of the cell in which the chromosomes .. begin to be displaced in apparent disorder toward the equator. This mechanism of equatorial arrangement was called metakinesis (Wassermann). **1968** R. RIEGER *Gloss. Genetics & Cytogenetics* 286 *Metakinesis*, .. chromosome congression to the spindle equator.

2. A manifestation of consciousness or mental phenomena.

1890 C. L. MORGAN *Animal Life* xii. 467 We call manifestations of energy 'kinetic' manifestations, and we use the term 'kinesis' for physical manifestations of this order. Similarly, we may call concomitant manifestations of the mental or conscious order 'metakinetic', and may use the term 'metakinesis' for all manifestations belonging to this phenomenal order. *Ibid.* 488 When, in man, the metakineses associated with these neural kineses assume the form of hypotheses, theories, interpretations of nature, moral ideals, and religious conceptions, these are .. no longer subject to the law of natural selection. **1892** K. PEARSON *Gram. Sci.* ix. 401 This metakinesis does not appear to be more than a metaphysical name for non-conscious life, for there is no sense-impression that we have of such life that we can describe as metakinetic. **1903** L. F. WARD *Pure Sociol.* 156 Morgan's metakinetic energy is therefore the same as my conative energy or form of causation, and the difference between kinesis and metakinesis is the difference between motion produced by physical or ordinary efficient causes and motion produced by psychic or conative causes.

Hence **metakiˈnetic** *a.*

1890, etc. [see 2 above]. **1925** *Glasgow Herald* 11 July 4 Who can be sure that there is not a psychical or metakinetic side to the mountain and the precious stone, the waterfall and the great sea?

metal (ˈmɛt(ə)l), *sb.* (and *a.*) Forms: 4 **matalle, matel, metail(le, -tayl,** 4–6 **metel(l,** 4–7 **metall(e,** 4–8 **mettal,** 5 **metelle, mettaill,** 6 **meatall(e, metale, metle, mettel(l,** 6–9 **mettle,** 7 **mattell,** 3– **metal.** [a. OF. *metal*, *metail* (mod.F. *métal*), ad. L. *metallum* mine, quarry, substance obtained by mining, metal, ad. Gr. μέταλλον mine; app. related in some way to μεταλλᾶν to seek after, explore. The word has passed (directly or indirectly) from Latin into all the Rom. and Teut. langs.: cf. Pr. *metalh*, Sp., Pg. *metal*, It. *metallo*; G. *metall*, Du. *metaal*, Sw. *metall*, Da. *metal*.]

1. a. Any member of the class of substances represented by gold, silver, copper, iron, lead, and tin. Originally this class was regarded as including only these bodies together with certain alloys (as brass and bronze), and hence as definable by their common properties, viz. high specific gravity and density, fusibility, malleability, opacity, and a peculiar lustre (known specifically as 'metallic'). In process of time other substances were discovered to have most but not all of these properties; the class was thus gradually extended, the properties viewed

as essential to its definition becoming fewer. From the point of view of modern Chemistry, the 'metals' are a division (including by far the greater number) of the 'elements' or simple substances. Among them are all the original (simple) 'metals'; of the later additions to the list some possess all the properties formerly viewed as characteristic of a metal, while others possess hardly any of them; the 'metallic lustre' is perhaps the most constant. By some chemists the radical ammonium (NH_4) and derivatives thereof have been designated as 'metals', on account of the analogy of their compounds with those of the metals potassium and sodium.

In popular language the term is not applied to a metallic element when in such a state of combination that its identity is disguised. (Cf. METALLIC *a.* 2.)

† ***noble*** or ***perfect metals***: gold and silver, as being the only metals that were known to be capable of enduring any ordinary fire without being 'destroyed'; opposed to ***base*** or ***imperfect metals***.

a **1300–1400** *Cursor M.* 2298 (Gött.) Þai made ymagis of meteles sere. **1340** *Ayenb.* 167 Be þise uirtue is strang þe man ase þet ysen þet alle metals a-dauntep. **1474** CAXTON *Chesse* III. ii, Vnto the goldsmythes behoueth golde and siluer and alle other metallys, yren and steel to other. **1588** SHAKS. *L.L.L.* III. i. 60 Is not Lead a mettall heauie, dull, and slow? **1661** J. CHILDREY *Brit. Bacon.* 112, I should think Lead were the easiest of all metalls to melt. **1751** J. HILL *Mat. Med.* 4 The Class of the Metals..includes only six Bodies, which are, 1. Gold. 2. Silver. 3. Copper. 4. Tin. 5. Iron. And 6. Lead... The Chemists have divided the Metals into two Classes, the perfect and the imperfect. **1797** *Encycl. Brit.* (ed. 3) XI. 443/2 To free the noble metals from the stony matter which surrounds them, and to reduce the baser ones from their calciform to a metallic state. **1874** ROSCOE *Elem. Chem.* xiv. 142 The metals of the alkalies and alkaline earths. *Ibid.* xvii. 186 [Hydrogenium] has..been shown to conduct heat and electricity, and to be magnetic, in these respects acting as a metal.

b. The constituent matter of a metal or of metals collectively; metallic substance.

1297 R. GLOUC. (Rolls) 144 Ire at gloucestre, Metal, as led and tyn, in þe contreie of eccestre. **13..** *K. Alis.* 6242 Pilers of matel strong. **13..** *Gaw. & Gr. Knt.* 169 Alle þe metail anamayld was þenne. *c* **1440** *Jacob's Well* 10 He made hym drynke reed brennying metal moltyn. **1551** ROBINSON tr. *More's Utop.* I. (1895) 64 Them they condempned into ston quarris, and in to myenes to dygge mettalle. **1649** BP. REYNOLDS *Serm. Hosea* i. 12 The hammer breaks mettall, and the fire melts it. *a* **1725** WHITWORTH *Acc. Russia* (1758) 108 Every battalion having two long three pounders of mettle. **1820** COMBE *Dr. Syntax, Consol.* IV. 361 If they had nought but polished mettle, Or the bright cover of a kettle. **1880** *Expositor* XI. 291 Like a mirror of polished metal.

c. As the material of arms and armour.

c **1400** *Destr. Troy.* 9520 Mallyng þurgh metall maynly with hondes,..knockyng þurgh helmys. *c* **1470** HENRY *Wallace* V. 190 His suerd he drew of nobill metall keyne. **1595** SHAKS. *K. John* v. ii. 16 That I must draw this mettle from my side To be a widdow-maker. **1663** BUTLER *Hud.* I. ii. 83 Both kinds of metal he prepar'd, Either to give blows or to ward. *c* **1672** *Sir H. of Grime* xxiii. in Child *Ballads* IV. 11/2 My sword, That is made of the mettle so fine.

d. *pregnantly* for: Precious metal, gold.

1590 SHAKS. *Com. Err.* IV. i. 82 But sirrah, you shall buy this sport as deere, As all the mettall in your shop will answer. **1594** —— *Rich. III*, IV. iv. 382. **1596** —— *Merch. V.* I. iii. 135. **1601** —— *Twel. N.* II. v. 17 Heere comes the little villaine: How now my Mettle of India?

e. *spec.* = CAST-IRON. (More fully ***cast-metal***: see CAST *ppl. a.* 8.)

Other specific uses (besides those referred to under 5) are current in particular trades: e.g. as applied to the fittings of pocket knives *metal* denotes brass as opposed to German silver.

1794 [see CAST *ppl. a.* 8]. **1862** *Catal. Internat. Exhib.* No. 6057 Kitchener..the back and sides fitted with metal covings or plates. **1875** KNIGHT *Dict. Mech.* 1423/1 *Metal*, the workman's term for cast-iron.

f. *fig.* (In 16–17th c. often = the 'stuff' of which a man is made, with reference to character: cf. METTLE.)

1552 LATIMER *Serm. Lord's Prayer* v. (1562) 34 b, What? (say they) they be made of such metall as we be made of. **1588** SHAKS. *Tit. A.* IV. iii. 47 Marcus, we are..No big-bon'd men,..But Mettall, Marcus, steele to the very backe. **1589** PUTTENHAM *Eng. Poesie* III. v. (Arb.) 161 Men doo chuse their subiects according to the mettal of their minds. **1642** ROGERS *Naaman* To Rdr. II. iii, Then she shewes the metall she is made of. **1681** DRYDEN *Abs. & Achit.* 310 Too full of Angels Metal in his Frame. **1687** T. BROWN *Saints in Uproar* Wks. 1730 I. 73 A notable fellow of his inches, and metal to the back. **1887** *Athenæum* 8 Oct. 461/3 Defoe wrought no base metal into the fine gold of his mother-tongue. **1895** *Harper's Weekly* Feb. 340/2 It seems to me that there was lighter metal in the crews.

2. *Her.* Either of the tinctures or and argent.

c **1450** HOLLAND *Howlat* 420 Signess..Off metallis and colouris in tentfull atyr. **1562** LEIGH *Armory* 1 There are nine soondrye fieldes, of the whiche, seuen of them be termed Colours, & two, Mettalles... The two metalles, are Goulde and siluer. **1610** GUILLIM *Heraldry* II. ii. 41 In Blazoning of any Armes, you must first express the Metall, Colour or Furre of the Field. **1625** MARKHAM *Souldiers Accid.* 31 Mettall may not be carried on mettall. *a* **1659** CLEVELAND *On Sir T. Martin* 24 Metal on Metal is false Heraldry. **1881** A. MACGEORGE *Flags* 109 The Dutch and Russian ensigns have the same tincture as those of the present French flag... The latter has the metal, the white, uppermost, and the two colours, the blue and the red.. placed together below.

3. = ORE (after Spanish).

1604 E. G[RIMSTONE] *D'Acosta's Hist. Indies* IV. vi. 223 They say..that the metall lay above the ground the height of a launce, like unto rockes. **1881** RAYMOND *Mining Gloss.*, *Metal*, Sp. 1. This term is applied both to the ore and to the metal extracted from it.

†**4.** A mine; in phr. ***to condemn to metals*** [L. *condemnare ad metalla*]. *Obs. rare*$^{-1}$.

1660 JER. TAYLOR *Duct. Dubit.* I. Ep. Ded., As Slaves live, that is, such who are civilly dead, and persons condemn'd to metals.

5. With qualification (see below): A specific alloy of two or more metals used in an art or trade. Also used, without qualification, as short for any of these (see quots.).

Bath, Britannia, composition, Dutch, fusible, organ, pipe, plate, prince's, queen's, red, refined, type, white, yellow metal: see these words. Also BELL-METAL, GUN-METAL. A certain number of alloys are named after their inventors, as *Aich's, Gedge's, Kier's, Muntz's, Newton's, Rose's, White's metal.*

1729 *Extracts Burgh Rec. Stirling* (1889) 205 One McLaren, who was..incarcerat in the tolbooth..for offering to sell hard mettle instead of silver to some people in this burgh. **1825** J. NICHOLSON *Operat. Mechanic* App. 711 Metal for Flute-key Valves 4 oz. lead and 2 oz. antimony. **1845** *Encycl. Metrop.* VIII. 655/2 The tin is first converted into what is called hard metal or alloy, 75 parts copper and 25 parts tin. **1868** JOYNSON *Metals* 97 The metal [is] run into pigs, in the state known technically as coarse metal, or more generally 'regulus'. **1876** HILES *Catech. Organ* iv. (1878) 22 Metal is a technical name applied by Organ builders to a mixture of tin and lead, and generally should mean half tin, and half lead.

6. An object made of metal.

†**a.** A medal or coin. (Cf. METALLIC *a.* 6.) *Obs.*

1574 HELLOWES *Gueuara's Fam. Ep.* (1577) 21 Hence it proceedeth, that the true and moste auncient metalls be not of golde but of iron.

†**b.** A speculum or reflector of a telescope. *Obs.*

1693 *Lond. Gaz.* No. 2909/4 Concave Metals, Concave Burning, and Reading Glasses, of all sizes. **1777** MUDGE in *Phil. Trans.* LXVII. 324 A very distinct and perfect two-foot metal.

c. *pl.* The rails of a railway, tramway, etc.

1841 *Ann. Reg.* 119 He found the deceased lying on the road, between the 'metals'. **1894** *Times* 12 Jan. 11/6 The trunk of a tree over 50ft. long fell upon the metals, and the express..cut right through it.

d. *Electr.*

1881 SIR W. THOMSON in *Nature* No. 619. 435 Imagine a domestic servant going to dust an electric lamp with 80,000 volts on one of its metals.

7. *Gunnery.* **a.** The metal composing the barrel of a gun. Also (= ***line of metal***, quot. 1859) in phr. ***over metal***, etc. (see quots. 1688, 1704).

1644 NYE *Gunnery* (1670) 40 If the Piece lye point-blank, or under metall. **1669** STURMY *Mariner's Mag.* v. xi. 46 A Gunner ought..to proportion his Charge according to the thinnest side of the Metal. *Ibid.* xii. 68 The difference of Shooting by the Metal, and by a Dispert. **1688** R. HOLME *Armoury* III. xviii. (Roxb.) 140/2 She lies ouer mettle, when the mouth is higher then the breech. She lies right with her mettle, that is she lies point blank, or streight. **1704** J. HARRIS *Lex. Techn.*, *Metal*, a word frequently used about a Piece of Ordnance, or Great Gun: The Outside or Surface of her is called, the Superficies of her Metals: When the Mouth of a Great Gun lies lower than her Breech, they say, She lies under Metal. **1859** F. A. GRIFFITHS *Artil. Man.* (1862) 52 *The Line of metal* is an imaginary line drawn along the surface of the metal between the two sights.

b. The aggregate number, whole mass or effective power of the guns on a ship of war. ***heavy metal***: see HEAVY *a.*[1] 6.

1757 CHESTERF. *Lett.* cccxx. (1792) IV. 91 They had eighteen [ships] and a greater weight of metal, according to the new sea phrase. **1762** FALCONER *Shipwr.* II. 495 From the torn ship her metal must be thrown.

fig. **1871** R. W. B. VAUGHAN *Life St. T. Aquin* I. 773 He possessed all the qualities necessary for success—weight of metal, as well as precision of aim.

8. Material, matter, substance, *esp.* earthy matter.

c **1570** *Durham Depos.* (Surtees) 197 Two skepfull of sande; no other mettell, stone, clay, or rubbish. **1593** *Rites of Durham* (Surtees 1903) 3 Cressetts of Earthen mettall. **1599** MINSHEU *Sp. Dial.* 12/2 With glasse, or China mettall, or earth. **1684** T. BURNET *Theory Earth* II. 46 Clayey soils, and such like, may by the strength of fire be converted into brick, or stone, or earthen metal. **1689** SHADWELL *Bury F.* II. 19 There's a pair of Gloves of the same mettle.

9. The material used for making glass, in a mólten state.

1589 *Pappe w. Hatchet* D iv, A settled raigne is not like glasse mettal, to be blowne in..fashion of euerie mans breath. **1660** BOYLE *New Exp. Phys.-Mech.* ix. 71 The Vessels..being made of much purer and clearer metall, as the Glass-men speak. **1845** G. DODD *Brit. Manuf.* IV. 49 The pots are full of 'metal' looking like liquid fire. **1890** W. J. GORDON *Foundry* 132 One of the men rolls up on its end just enough 'metal' to make the bottle.

10. a. Hardened clay, shale.

1708 J. C. *Compl. Collier* (1845) 15 To keep the Earth, or some times soft Mettle, or Minerals,..from falling into the Pit. **1799** J. ROBERTSON *Agric. Perth* 34 The azure [slates] are the best metal. **1808** H. HOLLAND *Surv. Cheshire* 28 The workmen distinguish the clay by the appellation of *metal*, giving it the name of red, brown, or blue metal, according to its colour. **1883** GRESLEY *Coal-mining Gloss.*, *Metals*, marl beds more or less indurated.

b. *Sc.* 'All the rocks met with in mining ore' (Raymond *Mining Gloss.* 1881).

1807 HEADRICK *Arran* 78 This must be a trouble in the metals, not a vein.

11. Broken stone used in macadamizing roads or as ballast for a railway. Also *road metal.*

1782 in *Sc. Nat. Dict.* (1965) VI. 259/3 The mettle for the road is not to be got but at the south end of the road. **1815** T. TELFORD *Life T. Telford* (1838) 483 The metal to be of the best blue or red whin. **1838** *Civ. Eng. & Arch. Jrnl.* I. 275/1 The quantity of the metal deposited would have formed, on ordinary ground, an embankment twenty-four or twenty-five feet high. **1845** ATKINSON in *Proc. Berw. Nat. Cl.* II. No. 13. 132 The roads of Hutton..with their wayside heaps of greenstone 'metal'. **1879** LUBBOCK *Addr. Pol. & Educ.* ix. 155 The Sarsen stone is unsurpassed for road metal. *c* **1906** P. C. COWAN *Making & Maintenance Roads* 17 The old macadam surface was first carefully levelled up and solidly rolled with any necessary amount of new metal. **1970** *N.Z. Listener* 21 Sept. 14/3 The lush pastures gave way to upland scrub country; the road metal became pumice and then clay merely.

†**12.** (See quot.) *Obs.*

1611 FLORIO *Souátta*, a strap or leather of a whip, our boyes call it mettall.

13. *attrib.* and *Comb.* **a.** simple attrib., as †***metal-matter***, †***-ore***, ***-yield***. This passes into an adj. = 'consisting or made of metal'.

c **1380** WYCLIF *Sel. Wks.* III. 67 It is a knowen þing þat hillis holden stoones and metal-oor. **1612** STURTEVANT (*title*) Metallica,..comprehending the doctrine of diverse new Metallical Inventions, but especially how to..work all kinde of mettle-oares. *Ibid.* 107 Mettle matter [see METALLAR]. **1636** JAMES *Iter Lanc.* (Chetham Soc.) 236 This faire cleere springe which courses through ye hills Conveys summe mettall tincture in hir rills. **1724** *Lond. Gaz.* No. 6260/3 A ..Coat, with..white Mettal Buttons. **1845** P. BARLOW in *Encycl. Metrop.* VIII. 489/1 Enamels, as before stated, are usually laid upon a metal ground. **1858** SIMMONDS *Dict. Trade*, *Pegged boots*, boots with wooden pegs in the soles, instead of metal nails or brads. **1877** RAYMOND *Statist. Mines & Mining* 284 The total metal-yield for that year amounted to $5,362,383. **1879** McCARTHY *Own Times* II. xxvii. 317 The intensity of the cold was so great that no one might dare to touch any metal substance in the open air.

b. objective and obj. gen., as ***metal-broker***, ***-detector***, ***-grinder***, ***-melter***, ***-mining***, †***-monger***, †***-monging***, ***-roller***, ***-turner***, ***-worker***, ***-working***; ***metal-bearing***, ***-clattering***, ***-cutting***, ***-using*** adjs. **c.** parasynthetic and instrumental, as ***metal-bound***, ***-bushed***, ***-clad***, ***-clasped***, ***-faced***, ***-lined***, ***-lustred***, ***-rimmed***, ***-sheathed***, ***-studded*** adjs. **d.** similative, as ***metal-blue***, ***-cold*** adjs.

1882 *Rep. to Ho. Repr. Prec. Met. U.S.* 12 Where there has been no *metal-bearing ore to defray expenses, assessments have been levied. **1930** BLUNDEN *Poems* 309 The *metal-blue cucumber slices. **1869** TOZER *Highl. Turkey* I. 200 The long *metal-bound guns without one of which an Albanian rarely moves. **1858** SIMMONDS *Dict. Trade*, **Metal-broker*, a dealer in metals or minerals. **1883** *Man. Seamanship for Boys' Training Ships R. Navy* (Admiralty) (1886) 14 *Spindle* ..passes through a *metal bushed hole in the partners, up through the centre of the barrel. **1926** *Gloss. Terms Electr. Engin.* (*B.S.I.*) 87 **Metal-clad*, a qualifying term applied to apparatus to denote that the conducting parts are entirely enclosed in a metal casing. **1931** *Flight* 22 May 461/1 So gradually..the general theory of the metalclad airship was mathematically and experimentally proved. **1956** *Proc. Inst. Electr. Engin.* CIII. A. 82/1 When closing a metalclad switch I have observed..sparks jumping from one metal part to another. **1899** KIPLING, *Stalky* 203 A red-bound *metal-clasped book. **1932** D. GASCOYNE *Roman Balcony* 12 A *metal-clattering cavalcade Advanced Across the beach. **1918** D. H. LAWRENCE *New Poems* 47 Is it all nought? Cold, *metal-cold? **1934** WEBSTER, *Metal-cutting *adj.* **1961** *Times* 29 Dec. 12/4 Metalcutting machines. **1971** B. ST. J. WILKES *Nautical Archaeol.* vi. 120 *Metal detectors are sold quite extensively in the US and Canada to amateur 'prospectors' to aid their hunt for gold. **1975** *Guardian* 1 Oct. 2/1 Chicago police will be using hand-held metal detectors on all crowds who come near President Ford. **1934** *Archit. Rev.* LXXV. 34/1 There are various *metal-faced papers on the market. **1967** *Jane's Surface Skimmer Systems 1967–68* 60/2 The float table's conveying surface is of metal-faced plywood construction. **1898** *Allbutt's Syst. Med.* V. 253 The pulmonary fibrosis of *metal-grinders, of stone-workers, of potters. **1876** VOYLE & STEVENSON *Milit. Dict.* 254 *Metal-lined cases are used as portable magazines. **1862** G. M. HOPKINS *Vision of Mermaids* (1929), Others small braids enclustered Of glassy-clear Aeolis, *metal-lustred With growths of myriad feelers. **1626** JACKSON *Creed* VIII. xxvii. §2 Cast them into the furnace, or to the *metal-melter. **1855** J. R. L[EIFCHILD] *Cornwall Mines* 284 The great advantage..of *metal-mining over coal-mining is [etc.]. **1576** FLEMING *Panopl. Epist.* 283 They dig the ground like greedie *metal mongers. **1631** J. DONE *Polydoron* 85 A *Metall-monging Alchimist is but a hors-keeper to a Coyner however he curries his tromperie. **1932** C. ISHERWOOD *Memorial* I. iii. 36 Eric's tall bony figure, with his *metal-rimmed glasses and the odd pauses in his speech. **1900** *B'ham Weekly Post* 4 Aug. 16/3 *Metal-rollers not only worked themselves, but had men under them. **1909** *Q. Rev.* Jan. 148 Motor-cars,..having armoured or *metal-studded tires damage the surface. **1858** SIMMONDS *Dict. Trade*, **Metal-turner*. **1898** *Allbutt's Syst. Med.* V. 24 Knife-grinders, metal-turners, and needle-pointers. **1928** C. DAWSON *Age of Gods* iii. 50 What we term the neolithic age in Europe was really the first stage in the diffusion of the higher *metal-using culture of the Near East. **1964** T. L. KINSEY *Audio-Typing & Electr. Typewriters* vii. 77 A large proportion of the remainder are at work in the engineering and other metal-using industries. **1860** PIESSE *Lab. Chem. Wonders* 69 *Metal-workers find it of great service. **1882** *Rep. to Ho. Repr. Prec. Met. U.S.* 598 *Metal-working tools, that is, tools for cold processes, such as turning, planing [etc.].

14. Special comb.: **metal age** *Archæol.*, the period or stage of development in the human race in which copper and bronze were used for making weapons and tools; **metal arc welding**, arc welding in which the melting of a metal electrode provides the joining material; **metal**

bath, a bath (of mercury, lead, fusible alloys, etc.) used in chemical operations requiring a higher temperature than can be produced by means of a water bath; **metal bed**, the bed of 'metal' or broken stone laid down in the process of macadamizing a road; **metal carrier** (see quot.); **metal drift**, 'a heading driven in stone' (Gresley *Coal-mining Gloss.* 1883); **metal-edge** *Coal-mining* (see quot.); **metal fatigue**, fatigue (sense 1 b,) of metal; **metal gauge**, a gauge for determining the thickness of sheet-metal (Knight *Dict. Mech.* 1875); †**metal ȝeter**, one who casts metal, a founder; **metal leaf**, a name commonly applied to the Dutch leaf to distinguish it from gold-leaf (*Ure's Dict. Arts* 1875); **metal maw**, a stomach strong enough to digest anything; **metal Mike** *Naut. colloq.* (see quot. 1961); **metal paper** (see quot.); †**metal pit**, a mine containing metal; **metal polish**, a polish used for brightening metals; **metal proof**, ? bullet-proof; **metal rectifier** *Electr.*, a rectifier in which rectification takes place at the junction of a metal and another solid substance (such as copper oxide or selenium); **metal ridge, rig** *Coal-mining* (see quots.); †**metal smith**, one who forges metal, a metal-worker; **metal stone**, †(*a*) the ore of a metal; (*b*) (see quot. 1851); **metal thread, yarn** = *metallic thread, yarn* (METALLIC *a.* 1 f); **metal-to-metal** *a.*, used of a contact or connection; **metal value**, value (of coin) considered merely as metal; **metal-visaged** *a.*, having a hard immobile countenance; **metal-work**, work, esp. artistic work, in metal; **metal-works**, a factory where metal is produced.

1927 PEAKE & FLEURE *Hunters & Artists* vii. 112 The dawn of the *Metal Age. **1951** *Proc. Prehist. Soc.* XVII. 1 The beginnings of a Metal Age in the Middle East are known to go back before the earliest written documents. **1963** H. N. SAVORY in Foster & Alcock *Culture & Environment* iii. 33 We can no longer think of a Secondary Neolithic element in south Wales as something introduced only a short while before the dawn of the Metal Age. **1926** *Jrnl. Iron & Steel Inst.* CXIV. 611 *Metal arc welding can also be used for this purpose. **1952** FUCHS & BRADLEY *Welding Pract.* II. v. 107 One of the characteristic features of metal arc welding..is the highly localised intensity of heat input. **1968** J. GIACHINO et al. *Welding Technol.* iv. 70 Gas metal-arc welding was considered a high current density, small diameter filler wire process. **1861** SMILES *Engineers* II. 429 He specified that the *metal bed was to be formed in two layers. **1892** *Labour Commission* Gloss., **Metal Carriers*, those who take the pig-iron out of the troughs of sand into which it has been placed to cool, and stack it on the trucks used in conveying it away for sale. **1845** *Encycl. Metrop.* VIII. 215/1 In the third stage, the crack is completed, and the edges assume a sharp distinct form called *metal edges. **1954** *This Week's Listening* 30 Dec. 18 *No Highway* is about *metal fatigue, which one of the characters describes as 'a disease of the metal'. **1958** *Economist* 11 Oct. 169/2 The Comet should, by rights, have been in service on the North Atlantic four years ago: the lapse of time is a measure of the work needed to stiffen its skin against metal fatigue that sent two of the original Comets in quick succession to the bottom of the Mediterranean. **1973** P. DICKINSON *Green Gene* ix. 180 It's like metal fatigue. You stand the stresses OK for years, so you think you'll stand them for ever. Then you snap, under no load at all. **13..** *K. Alis.* 6735 A queynte mon, a *metal geoter, That couthe caste in alle thyng. **1613** PURCHAS *Pilgrimage* (1614) 92 It is not to bee doubted but the *metall-mawes of those Ostriges could also digest the other. **1929** *Yachting* June 41/2 While in the act of setting 'Metal Mike' on the new course, we sighted a small ship's boat a point on the starboard bow. **1961** F. H. BURGESS *Dict. Sailing* 145 *Metal Mike*, the 'automatic helmsman'. **1901** *J. Black's Carp. & Build., Home Handicr.* 39 If the paste is not to be used for gilt papers (sometimes called '*metal' or 'gold' papers), add 2 oz. of powdered alum. *a* **1603** T. CARTWRIGHT *Confut. Rhem. N.T.* (1618) 656 He is verily worthy to be condemned to dig in the *metall pits. **1927** *Wireless World* 30 Nov. 733/1 (*heading*) Battery charging rectifier incorporating the new dry '*metal' rectifier. **1971** B. SCHARF *Engin. & its Lang.* xx. 276 Three important types of rectifier are diode rectifiers, mercury arc rectifiers and metal rectifiers. **1851** GREENWELL *Coaltrade Terms, Northumbld. & Durham* 36 *Metal Ridge. **1883** GRESLEY *Coal-mining Gloss.*, *Metal ridges*, pillars forming themselves into supports to the roof, formed by the creep in the boards. **1860** *Eng. & For. Min. Gloss., Newc. Terms*, **Metal rig*, the strata forced up by a creep. **1382** WYCLIF *Isa.* xli. 7 The *metal smyth [1388 A smyth of metal; L. *faber ærarius*] smytende hym with an hamer. **1612** S. STURTEVANT *Metallica* 35 Prepared or roasted oares, Mine-stones, or *Mettle-stones beeing the fitt matter of Metallique liquours. **1851** GREENWELL *Coal-trade Terms, Northumbld. & Durh.* 36 *Metal stone*, a mixture of shale with sandstone. **1959** *Times* 28 Apr. 20/6 A Chinese silk and *metal-thread carpet. **1967** E. SHORT *Embroidery & Fabric Collage* ii. 49 Gold and silver threads couched by hand, or synthetic metal threads (Lurex) used on the machine. **1906** *Metal-to-metal [see *leather-faced* adj. s.v. LEATHER *sb.* 5 c]. **1910** *Daily Chron.* 2 Feb. 5/1 The surface where the wheel had been on the axle showing a bright metal-to-metal contact. **1922** *Encycl. Brit.* XXX. 36/2 The head of steel being secured to the liner with a plain metal-to-metal joint by bolts from the head to the crank-case. **1971** *Flying* Apr. 5/1 Aluminium honeycomb panel construction and metal-to-metal bonding. **1901** *Munsey's Mag.* (U.S.) XXIV. 772/1 A deposit of coins was found on Richmond's Island, near Portland, Maine, which, though of the *metal value of only a hundred dollars, was of great interest because [etc.]. **1837** DICKENS *Pickw.* xlviii, Even the *metal-visaged Mr. Martin condescended to smile. **1850** *Parker's Gloss. Archit.* (ed. 5) I. 302 **Metal-work.* **1872** YEATS *Growth Comm.* 52 [Corinth] being especially celebrated for metal-work and porcelain. **1908** *Westm. Gaz.* 3 Oct. 10/1 On the hours of work in foundries and *metal-works generally the Committee felt itself still imperfectly informed. **1913** J. M. MATTHEWS *Textile Fibres* (ed. 3) i. 12 Bayko *metal yarn is a textile product recently introduced.

metal, *v.* [f. METAL *sb.*]

1. *trans.* To furnish or fit with metal.

1617 CAPT. PEPWELL in *Lett. E. Ind. Comp.* (1901) V. 155 The muskets are generally naught, being not well metalled. **1876** PREECE & SIVEWRIGHT *Telegraphy* 230 Where the pipes run side by side with gas-pipes, it is desirable to metal the joints.

†**2.** To provide the 'metal' or material of. *Obs.*

1610 HEYWOOD *Gold. Age* III. i. Wks. 1874 III. 38 Oh you crownes, Why are you made, and mettald out of cares?

3. To make or mend (a road) with 'metal'.

1806 FORSYTH *Beauties Scotl.* IV. 269 [The stone] is soft, and..has been found totally unfit for metalling roads. **1890** *Spectator* 6 Sept., Roads..so well metalled with granite that they are hardly ever dusty.

metalanguage (mɛtəˈlæŋgwɪdʒ, ˈmɛtə-). [See META- 1, 1 b.] A language which supplies terms for the analysis of an 'object' language; a system of propositions about other propositions.

[**1935** A. TARSKI in *Studia Philosophica* I. 282 Die Namen der Ausdrücke der ersten Sprache und der zwischen ihnen bestehenden Relationen gehören schon zu der zweiten Sprache, der sog. Metasprache (welche übrigens die Grundsprache als Fragment enthalten kann).] **1936** *Mind* XLV. 486 The concepts *analytic* and *contradictory* in the language *L*, for instance, cannot be defined in *L*, as Carnap has shown. In order to escape from these restrictions one must build up a new language (a so-called *meta-language*) disposing of more means of expressing thoughts than the former. **1947** H. REICHENBACH *Elem. Symbolic Logic* i. 9 We say that signs of signs constitute a language of a higher level, which we call *metalanguage*. **1948** L. HJELMSLEV in *Studia Linguistica* I. 75 This would mean, in logistic terms, that linguistics is a metalanguage of the first degree, whereas phonetics and semantics are metalanguages of the second degree. **1954** A. J. AYER *Philos. Ess.* 12 Particulars, considered as occasions, would be referred to only at the level of the meta-language; when it was a question not of using the language, but of talking about its use. **1959** *Listener* 1 Oct. 520/1 We can then avoid the clumsy term 'meta-language'—the name for the language in which we talk about the terms of any formalized language. **1960** E. DELAVENAY *Introd. Machine Transl.* vii. 110 Between metalanguage and pure poetry, from the clear and distinct expression of a scientific representation to the synthetic expression of the vibrations of the poet's ego at the centre of his individual universe, there exists a whole vast range of untranslatables. **1962** *Times Lit. Suppl.* 13 Apr. 252/5 Machine translation research may be of value..in that, because one of its basic techniques is the establishment of a meta-language or intermediate language of ideas, it is in principle capable of constructing automatically an abstract. **1964** C. CHERRY in *Endeavour* Jan. 13/2 A meta-language is a formal language-system for describing language or a linguistic source. Strictly, a book of grammar is written in a meta-language—it defines a syntax but is itself not literature. **1973** *Computers & Humanities* VII. 223 Each segment is analyzed as to content and translated into a 'meta-language', which allows unambiguous comparisons among the variant readings.

Hence ˈ**meta-**ˈ**meta,language**, a language used in the description of another language which is itself a meta-language; the universal linguistic or symbolic system from which a particular metalanguage derives.

1954 I. M. COPI *Symbolic Logic* App. B. 341 The first of these is the meta-metalanguage's synonym for the name relation in the metalanguage. **1957** N. CHOMSKY *Syntactic Struct.* vi. 54 Linguistic theory will thus be formulated in a metalanguage to the language in which grammars are written—a metametalanguage to any language for which a grammar is constructed. **1963** H. B. CURRY *Found. Math. Logic* ii. 31 In that case we use a third language, L_3, customarily called the metametalanguage. **1967** *Encycl. Philos.* VII. 352/2 A proof of adequacy..requires an inductive argument of the meta-metalanguage.

metalation (mɛtəˈleɪʃən). *Chem.* [f. METAL *sb.* + -ATION.] The introduction into an organic compound of an atom of a metal in place of one of hydrogen (usu. one attached to an aromatic ring).

1934 GILMAN & YOUNG in *Jrnl. Amer. Chem. Soc.* LVI. 1415/1 The term metalation is proposed for reactions involving replacement of hydrogen by a metal to give a true organometallic compound. *Ibid.*, Metalations were effected by metals, organometallic compounds and salts. **1937** F. C WHITMORE *Org. Chem.* 724 The aniline sulfate solution contains the strongly positive group $-NH_3$ and consequently gives *m*-substitution. The 'metalation' of benzine apparently offers an exception to this generalization. **1957** E. G. ROCHOW et al. *Chem. Organometallic Compounds* iii. 54 Metalation reactions occur only with the derivatives of the strongly electropositive alkali and alkaline earth metals and, rarely, magnesium. **1968** R. O. C. NORMAN *Princ. Org. Synthesis* xi. 392 Electrophilic metalations by metal salts should not be confused with the metalation of aromatic compounds with metal.

Hence (as a back-formation) ˈ**metalate** *v. trans.*, to bring about metalation in; ˈ**metalated,** ˈ**metalating** *ppl. adjs.*

1939 *Jrn. Amer. Chem. Soc.* LXI. 109/2 Phenyl ether was not metalated by triphenylmethylsodium. **1954** *Organic Reactions* VIII. vi. 260, *n*-Butyllithium metalates thiophene in the 2 position. *Ibid.* 261 The usual metalating agents..yield volatile acids which are easily separated from the acids of higher molecular weight obtained from the metalated products themselves. **1966** *McGraw-Hill Encycl. Sci. & Technol.* IX. 402/2 The most commonly used 'metalating agent'..is *n*-butyllithium in ether solution.

metalaw (ˈmɛtəlɔː). [f. META- 1 + LAW *sb.*[1]] A hypothetical legal code based on the principles underlying existing legal codes and designed to provide a framework of agreement between diverse legal systems (orig. conceived as between terrestrial and possible extra-terrestrial beings); so **metaˈlegal** *a.*, of questions, etc.: pertaining to the basic principles underlying legal systems or upon which laws are formulated.

1956 *N.Y. Times* 20 Sept. 12/3 Andrew G. Haley..sought to codify some general principles of space law or 'metalaw' as he called it, by analogy to metaphysics. **1956** A. G. HALEY (*title*) The present day developments in space law and the beginnings of metalaw. **1957** *Observer* 20 Oct. 14/4 Still more tricky are the laws which should govern our relations with any extra-terrestrial intelligent beings we may meet. Here, something which Mr. Haley [an American lawyer] calls 'Metalaw' must prevail. **1959** BENN & PETERS *Social Princ. & Democratic State* iii. 58 What criteria must a rule satisfy to be a valid law?.. How are legal rules related to particular decisions..? These questions..involve analysis of the formal structure of a legal system, and of the relation between norms of different levels of generality; they might be termed metalegal questions. **1969** *New Scientist* 2 Jan. 36/3 The legal aspects of space—what is now called 'metalaw'—a subject that has an interest of its own. **1971** G. SCHWARZENBERGER *Internat. Law & Order* iv. 29 Alleged rules of international *jus cogens* which are based on no other evidence than postulates of natural law or other metalegal norms must be ignored on the level of *lex lata*.

metalˈbumin. *Chem.* [f. META- + ALBUMIN.] A form of albumin found in dropsical fluids, etc. Also **metalˈbumen** [see ALBUMEN].

1854 R. D. THOMSON *Cycl. Chem.* **1875** tr. *von Ziemssen's Cycl. Med.* X. 369 Paralbumen and metalbumen are, however, not fixed bodies. **1878** KINGZETT *Anim. Chem.* 381 Metalbumin is met with in dropsical fluids. **1885** [see *paralbumin*, PARA-[1] 2 a]. **1899** CAGNEY *Jaksch's Clin. Diagn.* viii. (ed. 4) 422 Metalbumin.

metal'd, obs. form of METTLED.

meˈtaldehyde. *Chem.* [f. META- 2 a + ALDEHYDE.] A solid isomeric with aldehyde. Cf. META *sb.*[2]

1841 BRANDE *Chem.* 1330 By long keeping, aldehyd spontaneously changes into two isomeric compounds, *metaldehyd*, and *elaldehyd*; the former solid, the latter liquid. **1885** REMSEN *Org. Chem.* (1888) 49 Metaldehyde. **1949** *New Biol.* VI. 29 The most usual and one of the most successful methods of killing large numbers is to put out heaps of bran mixed with metaldehyde—the bran attracts the slugs which feed on the mixture, while the metaldehyde causes them to slime so profusely that they remain on the surface of the soil in close proximity to the bait. Here they die partly as the result of the metaldehyde acting as a stomach poison and partly owing to desiccation. **1963** *Which?* Mar. 88/2 A comparatively 'safe' poison is metaldehyde, now the most generally used for killing slugs. **1974** *Country Life* 24 Oct. 1228/1 Work at the Terrington EHF has compared metaldehyde and methiocarb [slug] pellet baits.

‖**metalepsis** (mɛtəˈlɛpsɪs). *Rhet.* [a. L. *metalēpsis*, Gr. μετάληψις, n. of action to μεταλαμβάνειν to substitute, to change the sense of (words), f. μετα- META- + λαμβάνειν to take.] A rhetorical figure mentioned by Quintilian, consisting in the metonymical substitution of one word for another which is itself figurative. (In many English examples the use appears to be vague or incorrect.)

1586 A. DAY *Eng. Secretary* II. (1625) 79 *Metalepsis*, or *Transumptio*, when by a certaine number of degrees we goe beyond that we intend in troth, and haue meaning to speake of, as to say Accursed soyle that bred my cause of woe. **1657** J. SMITH *Myst. Rhet.* 3 Metalepsis, which is when divers Tropes are shut up in one word: as, 2 King. 2. 9. I pray thee let me have a double portion of thy spirit. **1783** BLAIR *Rhet.* xiv. (1812) I. 339 When the Trope is founded on the relation between an antecedent and a consequent, or what goes before, and immediately follows, it is then called a Metalepsis.

metalepsy (ˈmɛtəlɛpsɪ). *Chem.* [ad. F. *métalepsie*, f. Gr. μετάληψις: see prec.] Dumas' term for the substitution theory in Chemistry.

1852 WATTS *Gmelin's Hand-bk. Chem.* VII. 71.

metaleptic (mɛtəˈlɛptɪk), *a.* [ad. mod.L. *metalēpticus*, a. Gr. μεταληπτικός, f. μεταλαμβάνειν: see METALEPSIS.] **a.** Participating or acting with: *spec.* applied to muscles. **b.** Pertaining to metalepsis or to metalepsy.

1656 BLOUNT *Glossogr.*, *Metaleptick*..that hath the power of participating, or pertains to the figure *Metalepsis*. **1693** tr. *Blancard's Phys. Dict.* (ed. 2), *Metalepticus*, a Metaleptick Motion of the Muscles. **1890** *Syd. Soc. Lex.*

So **metaˈleptical** *a.*

1850 in OGILVIE.

metaˈleptically, *adv.* ? *Obs.* [f. METALEPTIC *a.* + -AL[1] + -LY[2].] By metalepsis.

1655 tr. *Sanderson's Promiss. Oaths* i. §9. 19 The name of Promises may Metaleptically be extended to Comminations. **1672** W. PENN *Spir. Truth Vind.* 46 The Holy Spirit is properly given unto men, and not Metonymically nor

Metolepsically [*sic*]. **1674** OWEN *Holy Spirit* Wks. 1852 III. 85 One or other of these things is or may be metaphorically or metaleptically ascribed unto this or that thing which are not persons when [etc.].

‖**metalik** (mɛˈtælɪk). Also **metallic, metalick.** [Turkish, prob. f. mod. Gr. μέταλλον METAL + *-lik* suffix as in *beshlik* five-piastre piece.] A former Turkish coin worth 10 paras or about a halfpenny.

1895 CALLAN *From Clyde to Jordan* xx. 222 Each cup costs a *metallic* (value ½*d.*), and there are usually four metallics in a piastre. **1897** MRS. W. M. RAMSAY *Every Day Life in Turkey* ii. 60 On the babies I generally bestowed a *metalik* (value a halfpenny) 'for luck'.

metalimnion (mɛtəˈlɪmnɪən). Pl. **-limnia.** [f. META- + Gr. λιμνίον, dim. of λίμνη lake.] The layer of water in a stratified lake which lies beneath the epilimnion and above the hypolimnion and in which the temperature decreases rapidly with depth. So **metalimˈnetic** *a.* [cf. Gr. λιμνήτης living in marshes], of or within the metalimnion.

1935 P. S. WELCH *Limnol.* II. iv. 54 The term *thermocline* was first used by Birge in 1897... Since then, the terms *transition zone, mesolimnion,* and *metalimnion* have been proposed. **1957** G. E. HUTCHINSON *Treat. Limnol.* I. vii. 428 It is convenient to define the widely used term *metalimnion* to designate the whole of the region in which the temperature gradient is steep. *Ibid.* 464 In general, the smaller lakes.. showed very striking metalimnia at depths of between 3 and 10 m. **1957** Metalimnetic [see EPILIMNION]. **1960** *Limnology & Oceanogr.* V. 216 (*heading*) The cause of a metalimnetic minimum of dissolved oxygen. **1974** *Nature* 8 Feb. 393/2 During the summer, in the metalimnion of Lake Kinneret, the photosynthetic, green sulphur bacterium, *Chlorobium phaeobacteroides* can reach concentrations as high as 10^7 cells ml^{-1}.

metaline (ˈmɛtəliːn). [f. METAL *sb.* + -INE[4].] **1.** (See quot. 1875.)

1870 S. GWYNNE *Patent* No. 190 Metaline. **1875** KNIGHT *Dict. Mech.* 1220/2 *Metaline* is a material formed of metals, oxides of metals, and organic matter, reduced to powder, compounded with wax, gum, or fatty matters, and subjected to heavy pressure, so as to form solids of proper shape to form boxes and bearings for shafts or axles. **1883** *Fisheries Exhib. Catal.* (ed. 4) 80.

2. A kind of thread for sewing leather, made of twisted strands of linen and brass, copper, or steel wire. (*Cent. Dict.* 1890.)

Hence **ˈmetalined** *a.*, lined with metaline (see 1).

1878 *Eng. Mechanic* 23 Aug. 254 Metalined Bearings.

metalingual (mɛtəˈlɪŋgwəl), *a.* [f. META- + LINGUAL *a.*] = METALINGUISTIC *a.*

1950 *Mind* LIX. 490 Due.. to the common confusion of words and things its metalingual character has been overlooked. **1961** *Word* XVII. ii. 128 To these R. Jakobson has recently added three more functions—the poetic, phatic and metalingual. **1964** E. A. NIDA *Toward Sci. Transl.* iii. 45 In this volume the words *metalanguage* and *metalingual* refer to that part of language which is used in speaking about language itself, namely, the terms designating all the various features of language and the way these are used in describing and talking about languages.

metalinguistic (mɛtəlɪŋˈgwɪstɪk), *a.* and *sb.* [f. META- + LINGUISTIC *a.* (cf. METALANGUAGE).]

A. *adj.* Of or pertaining to a metalanguage, or to metalinguistics (see B). **B.** *sb. pl.* Trager's term for that branch of linguistics which is concerned with the relation of language to the other elements of a culture (see also quot. 1974). Hence **metaˈlinguist** *sb.*, **metalinˈguistically** *adv.*

1944 *Mind* LIII. 26 It cannot occur at the zero-level (it is a metalinguistic statement). **1944** H. REICHENBACH in P. A. Schilpp *Philos. B. Russell* 53 The use of a metalinguistic vocabulary is not a sufficient criterion for a more advanced state of logical analysis. **1949** G. L. TRAGER in *Studies in Ling.: Occasional Papers* I. 7 The full statement of the.. relations between the language and any of the other cultural systems will contain all the 'meanings' of the linguistic forms, and will constitute the metalinguistics of that culture. **1951** TRAGER & SMITH *Outl. Eng. Struct.* 83 The metalinguist can turn it [*sc.* a datum] into a conclusion by clearly identifying out the microlinguistic characteristics of the speech. **1951** *Language* XXVII. III. 212 The discussion of linguistic research techniques is not a linguistics as we have known it, but rather a metalinguistics. **1952** R. M. HARE *Lang. Morals* I. iii. 38 A metalinguistic analysis is tempting. *Ibid.*, Some hypothetical imperatives might be analysed metalinguistically. **1953** C. E. BAZELL *Ling. Form* viii. 98 The study of micro-criteria, whether phonetic or semantic, belongs to metalinguistics. **1966** J. J. KATZ *Philos. of Lang.* v. 222 S is metalinguistically true if, and only if, the semantically interpreted underlying phrase marker for its constituent sentence satisfies the condition in the reading for its metalinguistic predicate. **1967** C. L. WRENN *Word & Symbol* 4 The rather programmatic 'science' of metalinguistics recognises the need to study language and culture in intimate relationship. **1972** G. H. FISHER *Public Diplomacy* v. 119 This aspect of comparative linguistics is in its infancy. Anthropologists and linguistic scientists.. call it 'metalinguistics'. **1974** *Encycl. Brit. Micropædia* VI. 827/3 Some linguists use the term metalinguistics in reference to the study of metalanguages, languages or codes used to discuss or describe other languages.

†**ˈmetallar,** *a.* and *sb.* *Obs. rare*[−1]. In quot. **mettellar.** [f. METAL *sb.* + -AR.] **a.** *adj.* Metallic. **b.** *sb.* A metallic substance.

1612 STURTEVANT *Metallica* 107 The mettle-matter is that Mettellar substance which is put into the Furnace to be baked, boyled, or nealed, which in one word may be called Mettellar... There are three sorts of Mettellars.

†**ˈmetallary.** *Obs.* [ad. L. *metallārius* miner, f. *metallum* METAL *sb.*: see -ARY. Cf. OF. *metallaire.*]

a. A miner or worker in metals. **b.** One skilled in the nature and kinds of metals.

1641 J. TRAPPE *Theol. Theol.* iii. 135 Do herein as the Wise Merchant or Metallary, who.. digs deeper and deeper till he be owner of the whole treasure. **1657** TRAPP *Comm. Ps.* xvii. 611 Thou hast tryed mee, as Metallaries do their gold and silver. **1686** HORNECK *Crucif. Jesus* 793 Metallaries, and Lapidists,.. that make a very strict examination, whether the precious stone be truly oriental or no.

metall'd, obs. form of METTLED.

metalled (ˈmɛt(ə)ld), *ppl. a.* [f. METAL *sb.* or *v.* + -ED.]

1. †**a.** Consisting or made of metal; containing metal. Also in comb., as ***pure metalled.*** *Obs.*

1591 JAS. I *Poet. Exerc., Lepanto*, Sonet, The mettal'd minds [= mines]. **1609** DAVIES *Holy Roode* F 3 b, Looke on this Crosse.. It cures forth-with, like Moises metl'd Snake. *a* **1638** MEDE *Wks.* III. (1672) 587 The four metalled parts thereof [*sc.* The Monarchical Image in Daniel] were Types of four.. Kingdoms. **1655** GURNALL *Chr. In Arm.* verse xv. § 1 (1669) 358/2 That is the pure metall'd Sword or Knife, which bends this way, and that way, but returns to its straitness again.

†**b.** *transf.* Composed of material (of a certain kind). *Obs.*

1575 LANEHAM *Let.* (Ballad Soc.) 20, I cannot tell what too make of him, saue that I may gesse hiz bak be metalld like a Lamprey.

c. Having a covering or fittings of metal.

1821 W. C. WELLS *Ess. on Dew* (1866) 36 These differences were caused by the metalled case obstructing the transmission of the temperature of the air to the enclosed instrument. **1876** DIXON *White Conq.* I. xvi. 155 A stream of sunshine lies on painted wall and metalled roof. **1885** *Pall Mall G.* 14 Feb. 7/2 The expediency of replacing the heavily metalled lamps at the Guards' Memorial with globes of modern construction.

2. Of roads: Made with 'metal'.

1825 J. C. LOUDON *Encycl. Agric.* 511 In a road from a highway to a farmery, it may often be advisable to place the metalled road in the middle. **1839** *Penny Cycl.* XX. 31/1 The formation of metalled roads. **1878** *N. Amer. Rev.* CXXVII. 154 Railways and good metaled roads. **1955** *Times* 25 June 7/6 They live in this far-away valley at the end of a good metalled road that accompanied by power and telephone lines winds over the pass from Malakand. **1969** *Jane's Freight Containers 1968–69* 139/2 It has its own drinking water system, sewage, drains, metalled roads and mains.

†**3.** In ***well-metalled***: well paid, remunerative.

a **1734** NORTH *Lives* (1826) I. 249 The traverses of these indictments, tried at the assizes,.. are.. beyond what are had in most of the circuit beside, and well-metalled causes.

metalleity (mɛtəˈliːɪtɪ). [ad. F. *métalléité*, as if ad. L. **metalleitās*, f. *metalleus* of the nature of metal, f. *metallum* METAL *sb.*] The quality of being metallic; metallic qualities in the aggregate.

1754 HUXHAM in *Phil. Trans.* XLVIII. 859 The most perfect metallic bodies, which loose their metalleity, as Becher calls it, as malleability, and other metallic properties. *a* **1834** COLERIDGE *Hints Theory of Life* (1848) 69 The metalleity, as the universal base of the planet.

†**ˈmetaller.** *Obs.* In 7 **mateller.** [f. METAL *sb.* + -ER[1].] One who works in metal.

1658 *Rec. Elgin* (New Spald. Club) I. 305 Matellers of all sortes, such as pewterars [etc.].

metallescent (mɛtəˈlɛsənt), *a.* *rare*[−0]. [ad. F. *métallescent*, f. L. *metallum* METAL *sb.*: see -ESCENT.] 'Applied to a body of which the surface exhibits metallic colours' (*Syd. Soc. Lex.* 1890).

metallic (mɪˈtælɪk), *a.* and *sb.* [ad. L. *metallic-us* (or the derived F. *métallique*), a. Gr. μεταλλικός, f. μέταλλον METAL *sb.*] **A.** *adj.*

1. a. Of or pertaining to, consisting of or containing, a metal or metals; of the nature of or resembling a metal.

metallic beds, 'beds consisting of iron ore' (Ogilvie 1850). ***metallic glasses*** (see quot. 1807).

1567 MAPLET *Gr. Forest* A vij b, Ye Mettals Roote is eyther Mettal, or some thing Metallick. **1654** WHITLOCK *Zootomia* 566 Metallick Transmutation. **1667** MILTON *P.L.* I. 673 Metallic Ore. **1670** PETTUS *Fodinæ Reg.* Introd., The true Electrum, or Metallick Amber, or seventh Metal. **1756** C. LUCAS *Ess. Waters* III. 237 Many metallic minerals are likewise found. **1800** tr. *Lagrange's Chem.* I. 102 The phosphoric acid unites itself to metallic oxides, and forms salts. **1806** *Med. Jrnl.* XV. 564, I did not imagine, that, on the former supposition, any of the metallic medicines could be of material service. **1807** AIKIN *Dict. Chem. & Min.* II. 97/2 At a high heat they [metals] become more or less transparent, assume the vitreous texture, and are called metallic glasses. **1874** ROSCOE *Elem. Chem.* xvii. 185 The chemical composition of the alloys is not so definite.. as that of the other metallic compounds. **1890** *Syd. Soc. Lex.*, *Metallic sulphide*, a combination of a metal with sulphur.

b. Involving coin as distinguished from paper money. ***metallic currency***: the gold, silver, and copper in use as money; opposed to ***paper currency***.

1790 BURKE *Fr. Rev.* Wks. 1808 V. 426 They made a sort of swaggering declaration,.. that there is no difference in value between metallick money and their assignats. **1833** HT. MARTINEAU *Charmed Sea* vii. 109 Day by day, did he look with jealous eyes on the heaps of silver which he must not touch, and long for the security of metallic currency. **1895** *Daily News* 2 Jan. 5/7 No transactions except on a metallic basis were possible.

c. Made of metal. *rare.*

1711 W. KING *Rufinus, or Favourite* 195 A palace.. With Parian pillars and metallic beams.

d. ***metallic pencil***: a pencil with a tip made of lead or alloy, for writing indelibly on paper with a prepared surface, used for note-books. (? Hence) ***metallic book, paper.***

1855 OGILVIE *Suppl.*, *Metallic paper*, paper, the surface of which is washed over with a solution of whiting, lime, and size. Writing done with a pewter pencil upon paper prepared in this manner is almost indelible. **1862** *Catal. Internat. Exhib.* No. 5150 Metallic betting books. **1866** LIVINGSTONE *Last Jrnls.* (1873) I. Introd. 4 The doctor always had metallic note books in use. **1874** [see METALLICIAN I].

e. ***metallic circuit*** (Telegr.), a circuit composed entirely of metal conductors, as opposed to one in which the return path of the current is through the earth; similarly ***metallic return.***

1854 W. F. COOKE *Electr. Telegr.* 25 If, from the copper at one end, a piece of wire, or metallic circuit is carried.. round to the zinc.. a current of electricity immediately passes through the wire. **1928** A. WILLIAMS *Telegr. & Telephony* ix. 131 The first telephone companies had a hard fight to interest the public in their services, and to keep down costs —which would have been nearly doubled by a metallic return—only one wire was used for each subscriber. *Ibid.*, The result was that lines with earth-return lines had to be converted into metallic circuits.

f. ***metallic thread, yarn***: thread made from metal, or a synthetic material resembling metal.

1904 J. M. MATTHEWS *Textile Fibres* i. 4 Metallic threads are largely imitated by coating linen yarns with a thin film of gold or silver. **1963** A. J. HALL *Textile Sci.* ii. 105 Metallic yarns are made by various methods which include bonding metal. **1968** J. IRONSIDE *Fashion Alphabet* 211 Today, aluminium or plastic has been substituted for the rather heavy metals and 'metallic' yarns are now light, soft and non-tarnishing.

g. ***metallic soap***: any of a class of soaps that are salts of carboxylic acids with an alkaline-earth metal or a heavy metal (instead of with an alkali metal as in ordinary soap) and are soluble in organic solvents but not in water, some of which are used in waterproofing materials, finishing textiles, and making anti-oxidants, lubricants, and fungicides.

1918 H. SEYMOUR *Reproduction of Sound* ii. 44 The metallic soaps so long in use [for the moulding and shaping of disc record blanks] have been superseded on the score of efficiency.. but the [new] substance is more difficult to handle than the metallic soaps. **1940** A. WOOD *Acoustics* xviii. 504 The recording wax is a circular slab.. which is composed of a metallic soap and has a highly polished plane surface. **1952** R. A. PINGREE in H. C. Speel *Textile Chem. & Auxiliaries* xx. 404 Air permeable water-resistant treatments were first obtained by depositing a metallic soap in and upon the fibers of the fabric. **1971** *Materials & Technol.* IV. ii. 70 Metallic soaps of long chain fatty acids will gel lubricating oil fractions and the properties of the grease will be governed mainly by the metallic radical.

h. ***metallic arc welding*** = *metal arc welding* s.v. METAL *sb.* 14.

1927 *Jrnl. Iron & Steel Inst.* CXV. 909 The welding processes considered by the author are thermit welding, resistance welding.. and metallic arc welding. **1948** F. KOENIGSBERGER in H. W. Baker *Mod. Workshop Technol.* I. ix. 181 Metallic-arc welding is the arc-welding process most frequently used in general engineering.

2. Having the form or outward characters of a metal; *esp.* said of a metal when occurring uncombined with other substances.

1797 *Encycl. Brit.* (ed. 3) XI. 433/2 The platina is found native like the gold, and in its metallic state. **1831** [see METALLICITY]. **1874** ROSCOE *Elem. Chem.* xx. 222 Metallic aluminium is obtained by passing the vapour of aluminium chloride over metallic sodium. **1877** RAYMOND *Statist. Mines & Mining* 240 The ore is.. free from base metals, and carries metallic silver.

3. Of a quality: Such as is characteristic of metals. **a.** Of colour or appearance, esp. in ***metallic lustre***, the peculiar sheen characteristic of metals. Hence, of things, having a lustre of this kind.

1794 KIRWIN *Elem. Min.* (ed. 2) I. 333 The external lustre is casual, but the internal is strong and inclining to the metallic. **1797** *Encycl. Brit.* (ed. 3) XI. 450/2 A shining metallic colour. **1822** LATHAM *Gen. Hist. Birds* III. 274 Metallic Cuckow... Inhabits Sierra Leone. **1854** MEALL *Moubray's Dom. Poultry* 64 *Metallic*—the indescribable rainbow hues and tints seen on live fish, on some minerals and ores, and on bright steel when placed in the fire. **187.** *Cassell's Nat. Hist.* IV. 31 Some peculiar metallic-plumaged birds, known as the Metallic Cuckoo Shrikes (*Campophaga*). **1882** *Garden* 17 June 433/1 The sepals are a sort of metallic green. **1890** 'R. BOLDREWOOD' *Col. Reformer* (1891) 214 The long lagoon lay darkly metallic. **1893** NEWTON *Dict. Birds* 97 Subjective structural, prismatic, or metallic colours... The metallic portions of the radii are composed of [etc.]. **1936** *Discovery* Dec. 367/2 The marvellous, metallic blue

Morphos are eminently characteristic of Tropical America. **1968** *Motor* 21 Dec. 66/3 (Advt.), Lotus Elan..metallic blue with matching interior. **1975** G. V. HIGGINS *City on Hill* xi. 233 A metallic blue Opel.

b. Of sound: Resembling that produced by metal when struck; often applied to a voice or tone of a harsh unmusical timbre.

Used in Pathology to describe auscultatory sounds, as ***metallic breathing, echo, heart-sounds, jingling, resonance, ring, tremor*** (Syd. Soc. Lex.).

1834 J. FORBES *Laennec's Dis. Chest* (ed. 4) 313 The cavernous respiration and metallic tinkling. **1839–40** W. IRVING *Wolfert's R.* (1855) 253 Their deep metallic voices. **1872** J. C. JEAFFRESON *Brides & Bridals* I. x. 151 It is strange that..a singularly hard and harsh voice should be stigmatized as 'metallic'. **1883** E. INGERSOLL in *Harper's Mag.* Jan. 204/2 A finch..chirping in a metallic manner.

c. Of taste: 'Coppery'. Also, of the taste of tea made in a metal tea-pot.

1803 *Med. Jrnl.* X. 39 Metallic taste, fetid breath [etc.]. **1909** *Chambers's Jrnl.* Nov. 693/1 The objection to metal is simply that there is a danger of giving the tea what is known as a 'metallic' taste.

d. *fig.*

1828 CARLYLE *Misc.* (1857) I. 161 Among clear metallic heroes, and white, high stainless beauties. **1848** CLOUGH *Amours de Voy.* I. 110 With metallic beliefs and regimental devotions. **1875** KINGLAKE *Crimea* (1877) V. i. 364 A courage so rigid, that almost one might call it metallic. **1882** *Society* 14 Oct. 18/2 Your style is somewhat metallic and unsympathetic.

4. Yielding or producing metal; metalliferous.

1689 PACKE tr. *Glauber's Wks.* (title-p.), Choice secrets in Medicine and Alchemy, working of Metallic Mines. **1758** JOHNSON *Idler* No. 55 ¶4 The black inhabitants of metallic caverns. **1796** KIRWAN *Elem. Min.* (ed. 2) I. 421 Metallic veins are never found in beds of lava. **1870** YEATS *Nat. Hist. Comm.* 112 In the small islands of volcanic origin, metallic lodes, or ores are rare.

†**5.** Connected with mining or metallurgy. *Obs.*

1670 PETTUS *Fodinæ Reg.* Introd., A Dictionary of such words as concern the Metallick and Chemick Arts. **1762** tr. *Busching's Syst. Geol.* III. 580 All metallic attempts there, a few iron mines excepted, have turned out to the disadvantage of the undertakers. **1834** W. GODWIN *Lives Necromancers* 359 He visited the mines of Bohemia, Sweden and the East to perfect himself in metallic knowledge.

†**6.** ***metallic history*** [F. *histoire métallique*]: history as shown by coins struck during the period dealt with. Cf. MEDALLIC *a.*[1] *Obs.*

1727–41 CHAMBERS *Cycl.* s.v. *Metallic*, F. Romani has published a metallic history of the popes.

7. *Comb.*, as ***metallic-coloured, -looking*** adjs.

1839 WESTWOOD *Classif. Insects* I. 12 Body subquadrate, metallic coloured. **1874** GARROD & BAXTER *Mat. Med.* 56 It occurs in crystalline metallic-looking powder of a steel-grey colour.

B. *sb. pl.* **a.** Articles or substances made of or containing metal.

1612 STURTEVANT *Metallica* 35 Metallica is an Ignick inuention, for the cheaper making of all kindes of mettles or Metalique concoctures,..wherevpon the materials and things made by this Arte, are called Metaliques. **1796** MORSE *Amer. Geog.* II. 425 Bituminous particles, mixed with..minerals, metallics, and vitrified sandy substances. **1880** J. PERCY *Metallurgy, Silver & Gold* I. 248 The 'metallics' or unpulverizable metallic residue may be assayed by cupellation direct, or by [etc.].

b. *U.S.* (*Mech.*) Powdered metal for lining the bearings of machine shafts.

1894 *U.S. Tariff* §180 in *Times* 16 Aug. 6/4 Bronze powder, metallics or fitters, bronze or Dutch metal, or aluminium, in leaf.

metallical (mɪˈtælɪkəl), *a.* ? *Obs.* [f. METALLIC *a.* + -AL[1].] = METALLIC.

1577 HARRISON *Descr. Brit.* III. xi. 238 in *Holinshed*, Whose mixture would induce a metallicall toughnesse vnto it, whereby it should abide the hammer. **1650** SIR T. BROWNE *Pseud. Ep.* VI. xii. (ed. 2) 285 Whether black tinctures from metallicall bodies be not from vitriolous parts contained in their sulphur.

metallically (mɪˈtælɪkəlɪ), *adv.* [f. METALLICAL *a.* + -LY[2].]

1. By means of a metal or metals.

1839 NOAD *Lect. Electricity* 190 One [of the plates] was insulated, and the other metallically fixed by its extremity to a plate of platinum. **1909** *Physical Rev.* XXVIII. 159 The clamp *K* containing the molybdenite is metallically connected with the binding post *H*. **1913** V. B. LEWES *Oil Fuel* vi. 173 A second platinum rod also passes through the cover, being metallically connected with it.

2. With regard to (the constituent) metal.

1889 *Pop. Sci. Monthly* Jan. 299 A metallically pure cylinder of wrought or cast iron.

3. With a metallic voice.

1872 HOWELLS *Wedd. Journ.* (1884) 129 The tram-boy came back, and metallically, like a part of the machinery, demanded 'Ten Cents!'

4. In the manner of a metal or metals.

1944 *Physical Rev.* LXVI. 326/1 There are some substances such as the aniline dyes and $KMnO_4$ which reflect metallically in narrow wave-length regions.

metallician (mɛtəˈlɪʃən). [f. METALLIC: see -ICIAN.]

1. *Racing slang.* A bookmaker (see quot. 1874).

1874 *Hotten's Slang Dict.*, *Metallician*, a racing bookmaker. Bookmakers use metallic books and pencils. **1887** *Daily Tel.* 12 Mar. 5/2 In Australia the bookmaker has to pay dearly... As for the long-suffering Australian public, they are mulcted..as heavily as the much-taxed metallician.

2. A stone-breaker. ? *nonce-use.*

1890 'R. BOLDREWOOD' *Col. Reformer* (1891) 55 'This entertainment, which is given by me', continued the metallician.

metallicity (mɛtəˈlɪsɪtɪ). *rare.* [f. METALLIC *a.* + -ITY.] The quality of being metallic.

1831 *Amer. Jrnl. Sci.* XIX. 188 The..method which Dr. Wollaston employed to discover metallic titanium in the scoria of iron, and to prove the metallicity of the small crystals of titanium. **1883** *Encycl. Brit.* XVI. 32/1 The alchemists..held that mercury..enters into the composition of all metals, and is the very cause of their metallicity.

metallicly (mɪˈtælɪklɪ), *adv.* [f. METALLIC *a.* + -LY[2].] = METALLICALLY.

1897 in WEBSTER. **1901** WATERHOUSE *Conduit Wiring* 14 The galvanizing practically closing and metallicly uniting the edges of the Conduit.

†**meta'llicolous**, *a.* [f. L. *metallum* METAL + *col-ĕre* to worship + -OUS.] Worshipping metals.

1657 TOMLINSON *Renou's Disp.* 400* Which the metallicolous alchymists say, is produced by their sulphur.

metallifacture (mɪˈtælɪfæktjʊə(r)). *rare*⁻¹. [f. L. *metallum* METAL *sb.* + *factūra* making, FACTURE.] The manufacture of metal articles.

1847 R. PARK *Pantalogy* (ed. 4) 478 Under the head of Metallifactures, we include the manufacture of hardware, brassware and jewelry.

metalliferous (mɛtəˈlɪfərəs), *a.* [f. L. *metallifer* (f. *metallum* METAL *sb.* + *-fer* bearing): see -FEROUS.] Bearing or producing metal.

1656 BLOUNT *Glossogr.*, *Metalliferous*, that brings forth metals. **1796** KIRWAN *Elem. Min.* (ed. 2) I. 455 The metalliferous stone of Born. **1869** E. A. PARKES *Pract. Hygiene* (ed. 3) 95 In the metalliferous mines the air..is poor in oxygen.

†**metallifi'cation.** *Obs.* [f. L. *metallum* METAL *sb.* + -FICATION.] The process of becoming a metal.

1669 W. SIMPSON *Hydrol. Chym.* 221 Each Metal possesseth the predominancy of..one of the Planetary Orders..by the cooperation of the septenary properties at Metallification.

metalliform (mɪˈtælɪfɔːm), *a.* [f. L. *metallum* METAL *sb.* + -(I)FORM.] Having the form of a metal, resembling metal.

1796 KIRWAN *Elem. Min.* (ed. 2) I. 167 Metalliform asbestoid.

metallify (mɪˈtælɪfaɪ), *v.* [Formed as prec.: see -IFY.] *trans.* To extract the metal from (ore).

1887 *Encycl. Brit.* XXII. 70/1 The Augustin process of silver extraction is only a peculiar mode of metallifying and collecting the silver of an ore after it has been by some preliminary operation converted into chloride or sulphate.

metalline (ˈmɛtəlaɪn), *a.* Also 6 **mettalline, mettalyne, metallyen,** 6–7 **mettaline,** 6–8 **metaline,** 7 **metallin.** [ad. F. *métallin*, f. *métal* METAL *sb.*: see -INE[1].]

1. = METALLIC 1.

1471 RIPLEY *Comp. Alch.* Ep. iii. in Ashm. *Theat. Chem. Brit.* (1652) 111 Bodies..Minerall and Mettaline. **1555** EDEN *Decades* 334 This metalline body that we caule golde. **1563** T. GALE *Antidot.* II. 7 b, Emplasters be medicynes whyche take into their composition, dyuers kyndes of symples, but chefelye metallyen bodyes and these are..to be boyled together. **1592** CHETTLE *Kinde-harts Dr.* (1841) 25, I muse not a little what wonderfull mettaline preparatiue it is ye boast on. **1622** MALYNES *Anc. Law-Merch.* 272 Mines, Mettaline and Minerall. **1634** T. JOHNSON *Parey's Chirurg.* XII. ix. (1678) 298 Adding to the former Ointments Metalline Powders. **1781** HORNBLOWER in J. Nicholson *Operat. Mechanic* (1825) 182, I condense the steam, by causing it to pass in contact with metalline surfaces. **1804** *Edin. Rev.* IV. 139 The metalline salts. **1822–34** *Good's Study Med.* (ed. 4) I. 132 Various metalline emetics. **1855** BREWSTER *Newton* I. iii. 49 Without separating the sulphureous from the metalline part of that mixture.

b. Impregnated with metallic substances. Also, of vapours, arising from or produced by metals.

1626 BACON *Sylva* §84 Smiths water or other Metalline water. *Ibid.* §918 Those that deale much in Refining..have their Braines Hurt and Stupefied by the Metalline Vapours. **1633** T. ADAMS *Exp. 2 Peter* ii. 3. (1865) 270 Physicians..send them to the mineral or metalline baths. **1719** HAUKSBEE *Phys.-Mech. Exp.* (ed. 2) Supp. 285 Damps, or Steems..impregnated with Metalline Effluvia. **1890** *Syd. Soc. Lex.*, *Metalline waters* = mineral waters.

c. Made of metal.

1575 BANISTER *Chyrurg.* II. (1585) 275 By mettalline instrumentes, and manuall operation. **1665** G. HAVERS *P. della Valle's Trav. E. India* 111 A combustible liquor, which the man..carries..in a metalline bottle. **1731** P. SHAW *Three Ess. Artif. Philos.* 41 The Art of Printing on Paper, with Metalline Types. **1778** BP. LOWTH *Isaiah* Notes 68 A metalline mirror.

2. Resembling metal in appearance, lustre, etc.

1596 RALEIGH *Discov. Guiana* 58 The rocks of a blew metalline colour, like vnto the best steele ore. **1664** EVELYN *Sylva* (1679) 25 [A kind of oak] seeming to partake of a ferruginous, and metallin shining nature. **1822** LATHAM *Gen. Hist. Birds* III. 301 Metalline Cuckow... Inhabits Africa. [Cf. METALLIC *a.* 3.] **1831** BREWSTER *Optics* xx. 179 A plate of a highly refractive metalline glass.

3. Yielding or producing metals, metalliferous. Cf. METALLIC *a.* 4.

1620 VENNER *Via Recta* 8 [Springs] which rise from sulphurous, bituminous, or metalline places. **1727–41** CHAMBERS *Cycl.* s.v. *Gold*, They first break the metalline stone with iron mallets.

metalling (ˈmɛtəlɪŋ), *vbl. sb.* [f. METAL *v.* (or *sb.*) + -ING[1].]

1. The process of making or mending roads with 'metal'. Also *concr.* = METAL *sb.* 11.

1819 TELFORD in McAdam *Rem. Road Making* (1823) 193 We..make use of metalling, or broken stones, on the middle part of the road. **1885** SIR N. LINDLEY in *Law Rep.* 15 Q.B.D. 4 The metalling of the roads is better and more quickly consolidated by steam rollers.

2. Metal-work. *rare*⁻¹.

1878 C. T. NEWTON in *Academy* 19 Jan. 59/1 The bowl seems like a local imitation of Phoenician metalling.

†**'metallish,** *a.* *Obs.* [f. METAL *sb.* + -ISH.] Resembling or of the nature of metal, metallic.

1530 PALSGR. 318/2 Metallysshe belongynge to metall, *metallicque.* **1581** MULCASTER *Positions* xxxvii. (1887) 158 If any metall be to massie,..or if any metallish meane, where money will scale, do enter that fort. **1683** PETTUS *Fleta Min.* II. xlvii. 218 Both these species are Metallish and go in the Gold.

metallist (ˈmɛtəlɪst). Also **metalist.** [f. METAL *sb.* + -IST.]

1. One who is skilled in or works in metals. Now *rare.*

1646 SIR T. BROWNE *Pseud. Ep.* VI. xii. 336 Iron (as Metallists express it) consisting of impure Mercury and combust sulphur, becomes of a darke and sad complexion. **1703** MOXON *Mech. Exerc.* 243 Metalists use a kind of Tarrace in their vessels for fining of Mettals. **1834** *Oxf. Univ. Mag.* I. 411 A cautious metallist from Cornwall demanded fiercely what a stratum was.

2. An advocate of the use of a particular metal as currency. (Cf. BIMETALLIST, MONO-METALLIST.)

1886 *Science* 23 July 75/1 He has recently reaped a golden harvest by carrying out the principles of the silver metallists.

metallity (mɪˈtælɪtɪ). *rare*⁻¹. [f. METAL *sb.* + -ITY. Cf. METALLEITY.] The quality or condition of being a metal.

1884 tr. *Lotze's Logic* 37 Only metallity explains their degree of specific gravity.

metallization (mɛtəlaɪˈzeɪʃən). [f. next + -ATION.] The process of metallizing or condition of being metallized; conversion into a metallic state; the process of coating or covering with metal. Also, the result of such a process.

1669 W. SIMPSON *Hydrol. Chym.* 57 Middle minerals, which are in the road to metalization. **1796** KIRWAN *Elem. Min.* (ed. 2) II. 90 Susceptible of metallization. **1808** DAVY in *Phil. Trans.* XCVIII. 362, I have heated the amalgam of potassium, in contact with both hydrogene and nitrogene, but without attaining their metallization. **1811** PINKERTON *Petral.* II. 556 Some substances collected in tolerably large heaps, boiled up having the appearance of a brilliant metallisation. **1819** BRANDE *Chem.* 307 *note*, When mercury is negatively electrized in a solution of ammonia..the metal ..becomes of the consistency of butter, an appearance which has sometimes been called the *metallization of ammonia*. **1876** *Chem. News* 7 July 9/2 (*heading*) Metallisation of organic bodies to render them fit to receive galvanic deposits. **1934** *Archit. Rev.* LXXV. 33/3 Metal surfaces may now be obtained by a new process called metallization, which enables any dry non-greasy surface to be sprayed with metal. **1952** J. DELMONTE *Plastics Molding* xiv. 430 In vacuum metallization, the art has been successfully developed for coating molded plastic parts. **1967** *Electronics* 6 Mar. 25 Litton engineers haven't decided whether to use a single or two-layer metalization to interconnect the circuits within the wafers.

metallize (ˈmɛtəlaɪz), *v.* Also **metalize.** [f. METAL *sb.* + -IZE.]

1. a. *trans.* To render metallic; to impart a metallic form or appearance to.

1594 PLAT *Jewell-Ho.* I. 22 By wood that is both metalized and petrified in clay groundes. **1782** KIRWAN in *Phil. Trans.* LXXII. 200 Inflammable air is then the principle that metallizes metallic earth. **1800** HENRY *Epit. Chem.* (1808) 213 The lead is again metallized. **1825** J. NICHOLSON *Operat. Mechanic* 769 The surface of the iron thus becomes perfectly metallized. **1912** G. B. BARHAM *Devel. Incandescent Electr. Lamp* iv. 37 When the untreated carbon filament, used as a base, is metallized, its weight is reduced by about 8 per cent.

fig. **1849** CLOUGH *Poems*, etc. (1869) I. 298 Better far that this precious imponderable lie crystallised or metallized within us, than be..let free to escape.

b. To coat or cover with metal.

1911 *Engin. & Mining Jrnl.* XCI. 532/1 It [*sc.* the process] mainly consists of throwing finely distributed liquid metal ..against the surface to be metallized. **1929** *Daily News* 16 Jan., Doors, window sashes, wainscotings, panel boards and panelling can be artistically metalized with one metal or another. **1952** J. DELMONTE *Plastics Molding* xiv. 431 Another technique of metallizing plastic parts..is the chemical deposition of a silver film upon a carefully cleaned plastic surface. **1973** M. I. KOHAN *Nylon Plastics* xvii. 585 Small nylon parts can often be vacuum metallized without predrying.

2. To treat with sulphur and heat, as india-rubber; to vulcanize. (*Funk's Stand. Dict.* 1895.)

Hence **'metallized, 'metallizing** *ppl. adjs.* **'metallizer,** (*a*) a machine or plant for

metallizing; (*b*) a person or organization involved in metallizing; **'metallizing** *vbl. sb.*

1754 HUXHAM in *Phil. Trans.* XLVIII. 839 It appears then, that some internal metallizing sulphur . . is absolutely necessary to combine the metallic earth together. **1882** E. O'DONOVAN *Merv Oasis* II. xliv. 246 Had I not been told of the origin of the metallized appearance, I should have decidedly said that it was some lacquered surface, developed in the process of baking the brick itself. **1905** J. C. HOWELL in *Electrician* 28 July 590/1 On account of the positive-resistance curve and physical characteristics of these filaments, they have been given the name 'metallised filaments'. **1911** *Engin. & Mining Jrnl.* XCI. 532/1 The metallizing process invented by M. U. Schoop, of Zurich, is . . different from any process so far known. **1912** G. B. BARHAM *Devel. Incandescent Electr. Lamp* iv. 37 It is said that the intense temperature of the metallizing process changes the composition of the carbon filament by removal of the ash residue and by the volatilization of the hydrocarbon contained in the filament. **1952** J. DELMONTE *Plastics Molding* xiv. 429 The metallizing of plastics parts has become a popular procedure for some molded parts. **1955** *Sci. News Let.* 21 May 336/3 Game includes five metalized, full-color replicas of regulation traffic signs. **1969** W. R. R. PARK *Plastics Film Technol.* viii. 195 As the applications for metallized film continued to grow, more sophisticated continuous metallizers have been evolved. **1969** R. F. LANG tr. *Henglein's Chem. Technol.* 807 Metallizing of fabrics increases their value. **1973** M. I. KOHAN *Nylon Plastics* xvii. 585 The composition of these lacquers is proprietary with metallizers. **1974** *Sci. Amer.* Mar. 112/2 A simple measurement of the focal length can be made by standing the mirror on edge, directing a flashlight toward the metallized surface [etc.].

metallo-, before a vowel **metall-**, comb. form of Gr. *μέταλλον* METAL *sb.*, used in a number of technical terms, as **metallochrome** ('mɛtələʊkrəʊm) [Gr. *χρῶμα* colour], a prismatic tinting imparted to polished steel plates by depositing on them a film of lead oxide. **metallochromy**, the art or process of colouring metals (1860 in Worcester citing Nobili). **me'talloenzyme** *Biochem.*, an enzyme which is a metalloprotein. **ˌmetalloge'netic** *a.*, of or pertaining to metallogeny; hence **ˌmetalloge'netically** *adv.* **metallo'genic** *a.*, (*a*) (of an element) occurring in ores or as the native metal, rather than in rocks; (*b*) = *metallogenetic* adj. **meta'llogeny** *Geol.* [ad. F. *métallogénie* (L. de Launay *Sci. Géol.* (1905) ix. 263): see -GENY], (the study of) the origin of mineral deposits, esp. as related to petrographic and tectonic features. †**meta'llognomy** [after PHYSIOGNOMY], the art of discovering hidden metals. **ˌmetallo-or'ganic** *a. Chem.* = *organometallic* adj. s.v. ORGANO-; also (*rare*) **ˌmetal(l)or'ganic** *a.* **me'tallophone** [Gr. *φωνή* sound], (*a*) a keyed instrument with outside resemblance to a piano, but having metallic bars instead of strings (Knight *Dict. Mech.* IV. 1884); (*b*) see quot. 1887. **metallo'plastic** *a.*, pertaining to the arts of depositing metals or obtaining metal casts by either electric or chemical methods (*Cent. Dict.* 1890). **me'talloprotein** *Biochem.* (see quot. 1964). **metalloscopy** (mɛtə'lɒskəpɪ) [-SCOPY]: see quot.; hence **metallo'scopic** *a.* †**metallostatics** *sb. pl.*, the art of discovering the composition of metals and minerals. **me'tallotechny** (-'tɛknɪ) [Gr. *τέχνη* art], the art of working in metals. **metallo'therapy** [Gr. *θεραπεία* healing], the use of metals in healing or preventing diseases. So **metallothera'peutic** *a.*

1841 BRANDE *Chem.* (ed. 5) 836 *Metallo-chromes.— . . Those beautiful prismatic tints which Nobili originally described under the above name. **1860** TYNDALL *Glac.* 237 The colours of tempered metals and the beautiful metallochrome of Nobili are . . due to a similar cause. **1884** W. H. WAHL *Galvanoplastic Manip.* 407 (Cent.) *Metallochromy is used to produce decorative effects upon objects of copper, tombac, and brass, previously treated to a thin electro-gilding. **1955** *Adv. Protein Chem.* X. 321 The *metalloenzyme can be isolated from its matrix, retaining all of its metal complement in the 'natural' state. **1971** WISEMAN & GOULD *Enzymes* iii. 43 It is mainly this involvement in metalloenzymes and metal-activated enzymes which is responsible for the requirement for these metal ions . . in the food of animals. **1972** *Nature* 15 Dec. 417/1 Nitrogenase is a metalloenzyme containing iron and molybdenum both of which are essential for catalytic activity. **1909** *Cent. Dict.* Suppl., *Metallogenetic province. **1910** *Q. Jrnl. Geol. Soc.* LXVI. 281 His [*sc.* de Launay's] object is to delineate the various regional types of ores . . , the regional types being termed 'metallogenetic provinces'. **1965** G. J. WILLIAMS *Econ. Geol. N.Z.* vi. 61/2 The interplay of opinion reflecting metallogenetic fashions current from time to time. **1926** *Mineral. Abstr.* III. 133 Igneous activity was subordinate in Palaeozoic times, but very extensive and of much significance *metallogenetically during the late Mesozoic in both Japan and Korea. **1920** H. S. WASHINGTON in *Jrnl. Franklin Inst.* CXC. 782 It may be as well to suggest here, and to use henceforward, two terms. . . We may call the 'rock elements' petrogenic and the 'ore elements' *metallogenic. **1959** *Nature* 28 Nov. 1693/1 During the past few decades the problem of construction of metallogenic maps of various countries . . has been discussed. **1974** *Encycl. Brit. Micropædia* VI. 828/2 Among the excellent examples of metallogenic provinces in North America are the gold province on the Canadian Shield [etc.]. **1905** *Nature* 13 Apr. 576/1 On the possible *rôle* of slipping in *metallogeny. **1908** O. C. WILLIAMS tr. *L. de Launay's World's Gold* p. xiv, Those who . . are interested in the manner of the concentration of metals in the earth or in what I call their 'Metallogeny'. **1959** *Nature* 28 Nov. 1693/1 Valuable contributions to the metallogeny of various ores were recently made by N. S. Shatsky. **1971** *Mineralium Deposita* VI. 404/1 This note is only intended to link some past ideas of the authors with what may emerge in the future as a key model of metallogeny. **1665** *Phil. Trans.* I. 112 Of *Metallognomy or the signs of latent Metals, and by what art they may be discovered. **1886** E. F. SMITH tr. *V. von Richter's Chem. Carbon Compounds* 141 Most of the *metallo-organic compounds can be prepared by the direct action of the metals or their sodium amalgams upon the bromides and iodides of the alkyls. **1946** *Nature* 30 Nov. 791/1 This suggests that some of the polyvalent metal in soil exists as an insoluble metallo-organic complex with some of the organic matter. **1974** *Sci. Amer.* Oct. 75 (*caption*) Metallo-organic complexes, such as titanium diisopropoxide [$Ti(OR)_2$], also fix nitrogen under ambient conditions. **1887** *Sci. Amer.* 19 Feb. 120/2 The *metalophone is similar in form to the zylophone, but as its name suggests, the vibrating bars are made of metal—hardened steel. **1961** K. P. WACHSMANN in A. Baines *Mus. Instruments* i. 31 Whereas the metallophones can be dated —the saron to not much before A.D. 900 and the gender to not later than A.D. 1157—the ancestry of the xylophone is quite obscure. **1961** P. KEMP *Alms for Oblivion* vi. 102 A *gamelan* of musicians invited by Le Mayeur to play us Balinese music. . . There were metallophones with polished bronze keys of different pitch. **1969** *Listener* 10 July 58/1 One has read a lot about the exotic Balinese gamelan orchestra with its myriad metallophones. **1972** *Where* Sept. 252/2, I was . . unprepared, and unfortunately quite inequipped, for the spate of song books now also coping for xylophones, chime bars, guitars, tuned percussion, autoharps, Indian bells, metallophones, wood blocks, glockenspiels and maracas. **1940** *Biochem. Jrnl.* XXXIV. 1163 The *metallo-protein compounds present in the red blood corpuscles. **1964** *Ann. Rev. Biochem.* XXXIII. 331 The term metalloprotein is used to designate those types of metal-protein complexes in which the strength of the binding is so great that a metal atom can be considered an integral part of the structure of the protein. **1971** *Nature* 10 Sept. 136/2 The ferredoxins are members of a class of metalloproteins known as iron-sulphur proteins. **1890** WEBSTER, **Metalorganic*. . . Written also *metallorganic*. **1965** *Polymer Rev.* VIII. p. v, The Editors invited Professor Andrianov to write a monograph on his pioneering work on metalorganic polymers—or 'elemento-organic polymers', as they are called in the Soviet Union. **1974** *Nature* 27 Sept. 307/1 The surfaces were covered with a monolayer of metallorganic soap. **1888** *Amer. Jrnl. Psychol.* I. 503 *Metaloscopic phenomena are most analogous to those here described. **1887** *Buck's Handbk. Med. Sci.* IV. 749 *Metalloscopy . . is the art of determining by external application what metals or metallic substances act most easily and favorably upon a given person. **1890** *Syd. Soc. Lex.*, *Metalloscopy*, a term applied to the phenomena observed in cases of hysterical anæsthesia after the application of a metallic plate or plates to the skin of the affected part which recovers its sensibility, while the corresponding point of the other and unaffected limb loses its sensibility. **1665** *Phil. Trans.* I. 113 Fifthly, of *Metallostaticks, whereby the mixture of Mettals and Minerals may be certainly known. **1881** T. E. BRIDGETT *Hist. Holy Eucharist* I. 8 It will be sufficient for my purpose to touch on architecture, *metallotechny, embroidery, just so far as they served devotion. **1877** *Eng. Mechanic* 8 June 299/1 *Metallotherapy.

metallograph (mɪ'tæləʊgrɑːf, -æ-). [Back-formation from METALLOGRAPHY: see -GRAPH.] A print produced by the process of metallography.

In recent Dicts.

metallographer (mɛtə'lɒgrəfə(r)). [f. METALLOGRAPH-Y + -ER.] A student of metallography.

1902 *Jrnl. Iron & Steel Inst.* LX. 242 Samples cut from . . test bars have already been . . microscopically examined by an eminent metallographer. **1904** [see METALLOGRAPHIC 2]. **1961** *Evening Standard* 17 July 14/5 Metallographer required . . for examination of ferrous and non-ferrous materials. **1966** D. G. BRANDON *Mod. Techniques Metallogr.* 3 The successful metallographer combines an understanding of the effects of specimen preparation with a knowledge of the optics of image formation.

metallographic (mɪˌtæləʊ'græfɪk), *a.* [f. METALLOGRAPHY + -IC. Cf. F. *métallographique.*]

1. Relating to the description of coins.

1838 B. CORNEY *Ideas on Controversy* xix. 19 You have been censured for some metallographic absurdity.

2. Relating to metallography (sense 2).

1904 J. E. STEAD *Osmond's Microsc. Anal. Metals* Pref. 5 The accuracy of Mons. Osmond's metallographic work has received universal recognition, as is amply proved by the writings of metallographers in Europe and America.

3. Pertaining to or produced by metallography.

1888 *Times* 3 Oct. 5/3 If Kaiser Friedrich really confided metallographic copies of his diary to . . such persons as Dr. Geffken.

metallographical (mɛtələʊ'græfɪkəl), *a.* [f. METALLOGRAPHIC *a.* + -AL[1].]

= METALLOGRAPHIC *a.*

1902 *Jrnl. Iron & Steel Inst.* LX. 242 No regard has been paid to the chemical or purely metallographical alterations . . connected with the process of heating or annealing any iron material with subsequent slow or sudden cooling. **1950** *Engineering* 10 Nov. 341/2 However carefully determined the mechanical and metallographical factors might be [etc.].

Hence **metallographically** *adv.*, by metallographic methods.

1936 L. R. VAN WERT *Introd. Physical Metallurgy* ii. 23 Crystallographers distinguish six distinct crystal types. Only three of these are of any interest metallographically. **1967** A. H. COTTRELL *Introd. Metall.* xx. 373 Determining the extent of the isothermal transformation metallographically. **1969** J. A. SCOTT in A. F. Madayag *Metal Fatigue* iii. 92 Microscopic examination of a metallographically prepared sample is the usual method of inspection for inclusions.

metallographist (mɛtə'lɒgrəfɪst). *rare*$^{-0}$. [f. METALLOGRAPHY + -IST.] 'A writer concerning metals' (Bailey, folio, 1736).

metallography (mɛtə'lɒgrəfɪ). [ad. mod.L. *metallographia*, a. Gr. *μεταλλογραφία*, f. *μέταλλον* METAL *sb.* + *-γραφία* -GRAPHY. Cf. F. *métallographie.*]

1. 'A treatise or description of metals' (Bailey 1721). *rare*$^{-0}$.

2. The descriptive science relating to the internal structure of metals.

1871 T. A. BLYTH (*title*) Metallography as a separate Science, or the Student's Handbook of Metals, etc., etc. **1901** *Engineering Mag.* XIX. 751/1 We have long been accustomed to ascribe all mechanical changes in metals directly to molecular displacements, but metallography has thrown a new light on this subject.

3. A printing-process akin to lithography, in which metal plates are used instead of stones.

1875 in KNIGHT *Dict. Mech.*

†**me'tallogy.** *Obs. rare*$^{-1}$. [Badly f. METAL *sb.* + -LOGY.] The science of metals.

1811 PINKERTON *Petral.* Introd. 4, I would propose . . that the mineral kingdom be considered as divided into three provinces: 1. Petralogy . . 2. Lithology . . 3. Metallogy, or the knowledge of metals.

metalloid ('mɛtəlɔɪd), *a.* and *sb.* [f. METAL *sb.* + -OID. Cf. F. *métalloïde.*]

A. *adj.* Having the form or appearance of a metal. Also, of or pertaining to metalloids.

1836 BUCKLAND *Geol. & Min.* (1837) I. 41 The metalloid bases of the earths and alkalies. **1855** in OGILVIE *Suppl.*

B. *sb. Chem.* †**a.** The metallic base of a fixed alkali or alkaline earth. *Obs.*

1832 in WEBSTER. **1837** PHILLIPS *Geol.* 27 The remaining substances are metallic or metalloidal. Seven of them are earthy metals or metalloids.

b. Formerly, a non-metallic element. Now usu., an element intermediate in its properties between a typical metal and a typical non-metal.

1832 *Amer. Jrnl. Sci.* XXII. 250 *note*, [Berzelius remarks] Hence the division into *metallic* and *non-metallic* bodies; the latter class I call by the name of *metalloids*. **1836** W. T. BRANDE *Man. Chem.* (ed. 4) v. 318 And then, adverting particularly to the unmetallic substances, he [*sc.* Berzelius] subdivides them into three classes, namely,—1. Permanently elastic or gaseous bodies (Gazolyta). . . 2ndly. Metalloids: sulphur, phosphorus, carbon, boron, and silicon. 3rdly. Salifying substances (Halogenia). **1869** ROSCOE *Elem. Chem.* 185 In the compounds with the metalloids the physical properties of the metals as a rule disappear. **1876** *Encycl. Brit.* V. 476/1 The non-metallic elements are also sometimes termed metalloids, but this appellation . . strictly belongs to certain elements which do not possess the properties of the true metals although they more closely resemble them than the non-metals in many respects. **1894** G. S. NEWTH *Text-bk. Inorg. Chem.* I. ii. 8 The element arsenic possesses many of the physical properties of a metal, but in its chemical relations it is more allied to the non-metals; such elements as these are often distinguished by the name *metalloids*. **1959** *Nomencl. Inorg. Chem.* (I.U.P.A.C.) 10 The word metalloid should not be used to denote non-metals. **1959** B. CHALMERS *Physical Metall.* ii. 72 In these structures, the anion is a 'metalloid', such as sulfur, selenium, tellurium, tin, or antimony, and the cation is a transitional metal, such as chromium, nickel, iron, etc. **1964** E. G. ROCHOW *Organometallic Chem.* (1965) ii. 10 There also are some elements which look like metals but are brittle and have the electrical properties of semiconductors; these are commonly called the metalloids.

metalloidal (mɛtə'lɔɪdəl), *a.* [f. METALLOID *sb.* + -AL[1].] = METALLOID *a.* ***metalloidal diallage***, an obsolete synonym of hypersthene (Chester *Dict. Names Min.*).

1837 [see METALLOID]. *a* **1864** GESNER *Treat. Oils* (1865) 118 The metalloidal elements. **1880** PROCTOR *Rough Ways made Smooth* 86 The matter forming the solid centre of the earth consists probably of metallic and metalloidal compounds.

metallurgic (mɛtə'lɜːdʒɪk), *a.* [f. METALLURGY + -IC. Cf. F. *métallurgique.*] = next.

1778 J. C. LETTSOM *Hist. Orig. Med.* vi. 98 Metallurgic chemistry was one of the most remote inventions. *a* **1797** H. WALPOLE *Mem. Geo. II* (1847) II. iv. 130 The metallurgic artist loses gold; the State artist gets it. **1860** R. H. LAMBORN *Metall. Copper* 105 The metallurgic processes of copper smelting. **1871** CARLYLE in *Mrs. Carlyle's Lett.* II. 362 Partner in some prosperous metallurgic or engineering business.

metallurgical (mɛtə'lɜːdʒɪkəl), *a.* [Formed as prec. + -AL[1].] Pertaining to the working of metals; of, pertaining to, or connected with metallurgy.

1812 SIR H. DAVY *Chem. Philos.* 20 A metallurgical school had before this time been founded in Germany. **1827** FARADAY *Chem. Manip.* i. 11 Metallurgical processes. **1868** GLADSTONE *Juv. Mundi* xv. §4 (1869) 530, I have high metallurgical authority for stating, that the sheathing of

Chalcos on walls..must..have been some material other than bronze.

metallurgically (mɛtəˈlɜːdʒɪkəlɪ), *adv.* [f. METALLURGIC, -ICAL *adjs.*: see -ICALLY.] From a metallurgical point of view; as regards metallurgy.

1890 in *Cent. Dict.* **1911** F. W. HARBORD in Harbord & Hall *Metall. Steel* (ed. 4) I. viii. 199 What is to all intents and purposes metallurgically the Bertrand–Thiel process is at work in the Hoesch Works in Germany. **1968** *Physics Bull.* Dec. 411/2 A metallurgically good type II superconductor shows electrical resistance in the vortex state.

metallurgist (ˈmɛtəlɜːdʒɪst, mɪˈtælɜːdʒɪst). [f. METALLURGY + -IST. Cf. F. *métallurgiste.*] One who is skilled in metallurgy; a worker in metal.

1670 W. SIMPSON *Hydrol. Ess.* 22 If you be a good metallurgist and skilful mechanick. **1796** KIRWAN *Elem. Min.* (ed. 2) II. 245 That eminent Metallurgist Dr. Swab. **1871** *Athenæum* 3 June 690 The miners and metallurgists of the United States are trying to form an organization on the model of our Iron and Steel Institute.

metallurgy (ˈmɛtəlɜːdʒɪ, mɪˈtælədʒɪ). [ad. mod.L. *metallurgia*, a. Gr. *μεταλλουργία, f. μεταλλουργός, f. μέταλλον METAL *sb.* + -εργος working, worker. Cf. F. *métallurgie* (1741 in Hatz.-Darm.).] The art of working metals, comprising the separation of them from other matters in the ore, smelting, and refining; often, in a narrower sense, the process of extracting metals from their ores. Now understood as including the scientific study of the structure, properties, and behaviour of metals.

1704 J. HARRIS *Lex. Techn.* I., *Metallurgy*, is the Working or Operation upon Metals, in order to render them most fine, hard, bright, beautiful, serviceable or useful to Mankind. **1785** WARTON *Milton's Poems* 188 *note*, Drayton personifies the Peak in Derbyshire, which he makes a witch skilful in metallurgy. **1797** *Encycl. Brit.* (ed. 3) XI. 422/1 With others, therefore, we have chosen to restrain *Metallurgy* to those operations required to separate metals from their ores for the uses of life. **1868** H. BAUERMAN (*title*) A treatise on the metallurgy of iron. **1914** W. ROSENHAIN *Introd. Study Physical Metall.* i. 1 The scope of Physical Metallurgy..brings it well over the border-land of several sister-sciences— such as chemistry.., physics.., and that branch of knowledge generally known as 'strength of materials'. **1948** R. H. HARRINGTON *Mod. Metall. Alloys* p. ix, The House of Metallurgy has, today, many rooms filled with stacks of measured data concerning heat treatments, physical properties, micro-structures, and crystal lattice measurements. **1950** *Sci. News* XV. 138 Modern metallurgy borders also on physics and chemistry, mining and mineral dressing, applied mechanics and physical chemistry. **1967** A. H. COTTRELL *Introd. Metall.* i. 1 Metallurgy is now a disciplined applied science based on a clear understanding of the structures and properties of metals and alloys.

metally (ˈmɛtəlɪ), *a.* [f. METAL *sb.* + -Y[1].]

1. Metallic, metalline. *Obs.* exc. *poet.*

1398 TREVISA *Barth. De P. R.* VI. xxi. (1495) 210 Metally water [L. *aqua metallina*] folowyth the doynge of & kinde of metall. **1559** MORWYNG *Evonym.* 61 Certaine metallye thynges as requyre to be destilled with a greate and continuall fyre. **1898** G. MEREDITH *Empty Purse* in *Poems* II. 202, I can hear a faint crow Of the cock..As down the new shafting of mines, A cry of the metally gnome.

2. *dial.* Mixed with shale (see E.D.D.).

ˈmetally, *adv. Obs. rare.* [f. METAL *sb.* + -LY[2].] With a metallic sound or ring.

1661 *Sir A. Hasleriġ's Last Will & Test.* 3 A Fift-Monarchy-Man I was cordially, whose Spirits now when I am dying sound in mine ears mettally stirring.

metal-man.

1. A worker or dealer in metal; also, a miner.

1566 *Eng. Ch. Furniture* (Peacock) 71 Sensors ij crewetes and ij handbells—Robt Warren..being then churchwarden had who sold theim to a metle man. **1621** BURTON *Anat. Mel.* I. ii. III. x. (1651) 111 A Smith, or a Metalman, the pot's never from's nose. **1658** BROMHALL *Treat. Specters* I. 30 Drowsy dotards, habited like the mettal-men.

2. A man made of metal.

1591 SYLVESTER *Ivry* 344 Whence coms this iron spawn? These metal-men?

3. 'One who repairs underground roads' (Gresley *Gloss. Terms Coal-mining* 1883).

metalogic (mɛtəˈlɒdʒɪk). [f. META- + LOGIC.] The part of metaphysics which relates to the foundations of logic. See also quots. 1936, 1937.

1842 THOMSON *Outl. Laws Th.* Introd. 23 Only according to our view it is not Logic. Let it be called by an old name, Metalogic, or what its constructors will. **1878** S. H. HODGSON *Philos. Refl.* I. 358 The logical branch of metaphysic,..which we may fitly call Metalogic. **1902** R. R. MARETT in H. Sturt *Personal Idealism* v. 232 The no-man's-land of dogmatic 'Metalogic'. **1936** *Mind* XLV. 482 If a contradiction appears at the end of a chain of inferences one at least of two cases must be realised according to a very evident theorem of metalogic: (1) either there is a fallacy in the chain..or (2) the premises are contradictory. *Ibid.* 485 Lukasiewicz, the great Polish logician, has generalised that idea by introducing what he calls *metalogic*, which has to ordinary logic the same relation as metamathematics to mathematics. **1937** A. SMEATON tr. *Carnap's Logical Syntax of Lang.* 9 The Warsaw logicians..have spoken of ..*metalogic*... The word 'metalogic' is a suitable designation for the sub-domain of syntax which deals with logical sentences in the narrower sense. **1955** A. N. PRIOR *Formal Logic* 64 The consideration of these deductions from outside may be called 'metalogic', and that is in fact the name now commonly applied to it. **1963** R. CARNAP in P. A. Schilpp *Philos. R. Carnap* 54 At that time I defined the term 'metalogic' as the theory of the forms of the expressions of a language. Later I used the term 'syntax' instead.

metalogical (mɛtəˈlɒdʒɪkəl), *a.* [f. META- + LOGICAL.] Belonging to metalogic. Also, beyond or outside the province of logic. Cf. prec.

1865 S. H. HODGSON *Time & Space* 345 Chapter vii, Metalogical. **1873** *Contemp. Rev.* XXI. 446 Certain logical, metalogical, empirical and transcendental truths. *a* **1881** A. BARRATT *Phys. Metempiric* (1883) 193 From the nature of the other metalogical assumptions. **1951** J. ŁUKASIEWICZ *Aristotle's Syllogistic* 103 The..metalogical principle of traditional logic: 'utraque si praemissa neget, nil inde sequetur'. **1955** A. N. PRIOR *Formal Logic* 65 'Metalogical' demonstrations ought..to be themselves 'logical' in the sense of being cogent.

Hence **metaˈlogically** *adv.*

1946 C. I. LEWIS *Analysis of Knowledge* v. 129 Analytic statements in non-logical terminology, like 'All birds are bipeds', will not be metalogically derivable from its postulates. **1955** A. N. PRIOR *Formal Logic* 132 This rule is metalogically derivable.

metaloˈgician. [f. METALOGIC: see -ICIAN.] One who is versed in metalogic.

1902 R. R. MARETT in H. Sturt *Personal Idealism* v. 237 A condition of existence which even the 'metalogician' finds it difficult to conceive. **1964** *Amer. Philos. Q.* I. 236/2 As used by grammarians, metalogicians, etc., they mention a type.

metalogue (ˈmɛtəlɒg). *rare*[−1]. [f. META-, on model of *prologue* and *epilogue*.] A speech delivered between the acts or scenes of a play.

1956 AUDEN & KALLMAN *Magic Flute* [at end of Act I] 57 Metalogue (To be spoken by the singer taking the role of *Sarastro*.)

metalonchidite: see META- 7 a.

metals, variant of METELS *Obs.*, a dream.

metalumina: see META- 6 a.

metamathematical (ˌmɛtəmæθɪˈmætɪkəl), *a.* [f. as next, after *mathematics, mathematical.*]

a. Beyond the scope of mathematics. *rare.*

1833 SIR W. R. HAMILTON in R. P. Graves *Life* II. 68 In the application of the mathematics themselves there must (if I may venture on the word) be something metamathematical.

b. Of or pertaining to metamathematics.

1926 F. P. RAMSEY in *Mathematical Gaz.* XIII. 188 It is contended that the principles used in the metamathematical proof that the axioms of mathematics do not lead to contradiction, are so obviously true that not even the sceptics can doubt them. **1933** M. BLACK *Nature of Math.* 150 It is extremely probable that a metamathematical proof of the consistency of the whole of pure mathematics is impossible. **1952** S. C. KLEENE *Introd. Metamath.* vi. 140 In either case, the rules of inference must have the character of schemata, i.e. they must employ metamathematical variables, since infinitely many applications have to be provided for. **1971** *Nature* 8 Jan. 104/2 Hilbert's programme for demonstrating the consistency of arithmetic by metamathematical methods resulted in a new outburst of activity which culminated..with Gödel's incompleteness theorem.

Hence **ˌmetamatheˈmatically** *adv.*, by means of, or from the point of view of, metamathematics.

1937 *Philos. of Sci.* IV. 329 Gödel has proved metamathematically that there are surely theorems and problems about the natural numbers which cannot be proved or solved by elementary means. **1956** J. H. WOODGER tr. *Tarski's Logic, Semantics, Metamath.* 116 Let us now consider the situation metamathematically. **1967** S. C. KLEENE *Math. Logic* § 39. 214 Ackermann in 1924–5 thought he had proved metamathematically the consistency of N.

metamathematician (ˌmɛtəmæθɪməˈtɪʃən). [f. next, after *mathematics, mathematician.*] An expert in metamathematics.

1935 *Mind* XLIV. 394 The metamathematician may use mathematical induction for the recursive definition of simple functions. **1952** S. C. KLEENE *Introd. Metamath.* iii. 64 The interpretation motivates the metamathematician in his choice of the particular formal system which he introduces by his definitions.

metamathematics (ˌmɛtəmæθɪˈmætɪks), *sb. pl.* (*const. as sing.*). [f. META- 1 + MATHEMATICS *sb. pl.*, after G. *metamathematik* (D. Hilbert 1923, in *Math. Ann.* LXXXVIII. 153).] The field of study concerned with the structure and formal properties of mathematics and similar formal systems.

1890 in *Cent. Dict.* **1926** *Encycl. Brit.* II. 831/1 The science on which Hilbert is now (1926) engaged, which takes for its subject matter the meaningless formulae of mathematics, he calls metamathematics, and believes it to be capable of establishing many important results relating to the multiplicative axiom or axiom of selections, and to the continuum problem. **1940** *Mind* XLIX. 242 The investigation of calculi, in this light, independently of all regard for the 'meaning' of the component complex marks, was christened metamathematics. **1952** S. C. KLEENE *Introd. Metamath.* iii. 63 The formal systems which are studied in metamathematics are (usually) so chosen that they serve as models for parts of informal mathematics and logic with which we are already more or less familiar, and from which they arose by formalization. **1956** E. H. HUTTEN *Lang. Mod. Physics* ii. 35 That we require a meta-mathematics in order to prove the consistency and completeness of mathematics..does not mean that we are confronted with the final break-down of logic and mathematics. **1963** G. T. KNEEBONE *Math. Logic* 381 Metamathematics began as a study of particular formal systems, and it was initially concerned with questions of consistency and completeness of given sets of axioms. But it now embraces investigations of altogether wider scope, designed to yield fundamental information about entire classes of formal systems of some particular kind. **1966** J. J. KATZ *Philos. of Lang.* iii. 27 Metamathematics, as the general theory of the formal structure of the language of mathematics, was closely parallel to Carnap's idea of logical syntax, as the general theory of the formal structure of scientific and factual discourse. No wonder, then, that metamathematics appealed to Carnap as a model for his theory of logical syntax.

ˌmetameˈconic, *a. Chem.* [META- 2 a.] = COMENIC. Hence **ˌmetaˈmeconate,** a salt of metameconic acid.

1836 BRANDE *Chem.* (ed. 4) 1021 [If the crystals of meconic acid are] boiled in water, carbonic acid is evolved, the solution becomes brown, and metameconic acid is formed. *Ibid.* 1022 The neutral metameconates of ammonia and potassa.

metamer (ˈmɛtəmɜː(r)). *Chem.* Also **-mere.** [Back-formation from METAMERIC.] A compound which exhibits the phenomena of metamerism; a compound which is metameric with something else.

1882 *Nature* 11 May 43 Ammonium sulphocyanite, and its metamer theocarbamide.

metameral (mɛˈtæmərəl), *a.* [f. next + -AL[1].] = METAMERIC.

1890 in *Century Dict.*

metamere (ˈmɛtəmɪə(r)). *Zool.* Also **meˈtameron,** pl. **-mera.** [f. Gr. μετα- META- + μέρος part.] One of the several similar segments of which certain bodies consist.

'Thus, in the crayfish a metamere consists of a central part termed the somite, with two appendages; each segment of the body can be reduced to this common type; the whole structure being capable of resolution into the skeletons of twenty separate metameres' (*Syd. Soc. Lex.*).

1877 HUXLEY *Anat. Inv. Anim.* i. 53 The middle line of each of the ambulacral metameres. **1879** tr. *Haeckel's Evol. Man* I. ix. 268 In Man the number of these like segments or metamera is about forty.

metameric (mɛtəˈmɛrɪk), *a.* [f. Gr. μετα- META- + μέρος part + -IC.]

1. *Chem.* Characterized by metamerism.

1847 *Turner's Elem. Chem.* (ed. 8) I. 176. **1885** REMSEN *Org. Chem.* 31 Bodies may have the same per centage composition and the same molecular weights. Such bodies are said to be metameric.

2. *Zool.* Of or pertaining to metameres.

1875 tr. *Schmidt's Desc. & Darw.* 54 The metameric formation, as it is termed by Haeckel,—is totally foreign to the Molluscs. **1877** RAY LANKESTER in *Q. Jrnl. Microsc. Sci.* XVII. 427 This transient metameric segmentation of the Holothurian.

Hence **metaˈmerically** *adv.*, with metameric segmentation.

1878 BELL tr. *Gegenbaur's Comp. Anat.* 602 A dilatation of these metamerically arranged canals. **1888** BEDDARD in *Q. Jrnl. Microsc. Sci.* XXIX. 278 Metamerically disposed tufts of tubules.

metameride (mɛˈtæməraɪd). *Chem.* [f. METAMER-IC + -IDE.] = METAMER.

1857 MILLER *Elem. Chem., Org.* i. Introd. 5 The formation of isomerides, metamerides, and polymerides, as bodies which possess the same percentage composition may be termed.

metamerism (mɛˈtæmərɪz(ə)m). [Formed as METAMERIC: see -ISM.]

1. *Chem.* The condition of those isomeric compounds, which, although they have the same composition and molecular weight, have different chemical properties.

1848 WATTS tr. *Gmelin's Handbk. Chem.* I. 110 Metamerism. This term is applied by Berzelius to the case in which the compound atoms of two chemical compounds containing the same elementary atoms, and for the most part in the same proportions, are nevertheless made up of different proximate elements. **1885** REMSEN *Org. Chem.* Index.

2. *Zool.* The condition of consisting of metameric sections; metameric segmentation; also, an instance of this.

1877 RAY LANKESTER in *Q. Jrnl. Microsc. Sci.* XVII. 427 This latter..breaks up into four circlets by development of cross-pieces in correspondence with a metamerism.

metamerized (mɛˈtæməraɪzd), *a.* [Formed as prec.: see -IZE.] Divided into metameric segments. Similarly **metameriˈzation**, the condition of being metamerized.

1878 BELL tr. *Gegenbaur's Comp. Anat.* 602 Although the vertebrate body is a metameric one, this archinephric duct is not a metamerised organ. **1880** *Q. Jrnl. Microsc. Sci.* XX. 232 The metamerisation is less distinct than in Rhopalura.

metamerous (mɛˈtæmərəs), *a. Zool.* [See METAMERIC and -OUS.] = METAMERIC 2. Hence **meˈtamery** = METAMERISM.

1887 HUBRECHT in *Q. Jrnl. Microsc. Sci.* XXVII. 610 All those cases of metamery in the animal kingdom which do not fall under the head of strobilation... Incipient metamery.. may further differentiate in the most diverse directions. *Ibid.* 613 A regular, rigorously metamerous arrangement of this multiple material. *Ibid.* 618 The metamerous gill-slits.

meta-metalanguage: see METALANGUAGE.

metamict (ˈmɛtəmɪkt), *a. Min.* [ad. Da. *metamikt* (W. C. Broegger 1893, in *Salmonsens Konversationsleksikon* I. 743/2), f. Gr. μετα- META- + μικτ-ός mixed, blended.] Of a mineral: converted into an amorphous state as a result of the radioactive decay of atoms contained in it. Also applied to the state itself.

1927 *Phil. Mag.* IV. 525 Metamict substances like xenotime and thorite have probably been formed under very high pressure. **1950** *Science* 24 Mar. 312/2 For materials which are completely metamict, it would be possible to determine only a minimum age. **1965** G. J. WILLIAMS *Econ. Geol. N.Z.* xiii. 203/2 He suggested the red colouration occurs only in pegmatites sufficiently old for the transformation of the radioactive mineral to the metamict state. **1970** *Nature* 11 Apr. 147/2 Quartz is thus a 'metamict' mineral, like zircon.

Hence **ˌmetamictiˈzation**, the process of becoming, or state of being, metamict; **ˈmetamictness**, metamict character.

1952 *Amer. Mineralogist* XXXVII. 142 There has been some speculation as to the reasons for variations in degree of metamictness of different samples of the same mineral. *Ibid.* 154 More powerful sources of radiation..might prove useful in the study of metamictization. **1966** *McGraw-Hill Encycl. Sci. & Technol.* VIII. 296*a*/1 X-ray methods do not permit a close estimate of the degree of metamictness. **1970** *Science* 30 Jan. 617/1 The U and Th contents of baddeleyite are quite low, which explains the high transparency and the lack of metamictization.

metamorphia: see META- 6 a.

metamorphic (mɛtəˈmɔːfɪk), *a.* [irreg. f. Gr. μετα- META- + μορφή form + -IC: suggested by *metamorphosis*. Cf. F. *métamorphique*.]

1. a. Characterized by or exhibiting metamorphosis or change of form.

1816 G. S. FABER *Orig. Pagan Idol.* III. 114 The more complex metamorphic transmigration, by which the same human soul was thought to pass successively through the bodies of animals. **1870** LOWELL *Among my Bks.* Ser. I. (1873) 195 How futile is any attempt at a cast-iron definition of those perpetually metamorphic impressions of the beautiful.

b. in scientific uses (cf. METAMORPHOSIS 3).

1850 *Fraser's Mag.* XLI. 656 The first sight of it suggests the presence of a salamander in a metamorphic stage. **1876** tr. *H. von Ziemssen's Cycl. Med.* V. 542 When the cavities have become larger,..we not infrequently hear also, what has been described by Seitz as metamorphic respiration. **1882** SAVILLE-KENT *Infusoria* II. 870 *Metamorphic*, changeable in form.

2. *Geol.* Pertaining to, characterized by or formed by metamorphism. Of a rock or rock-formation: That has undergone transformation by means of heat, pressure, or natural agencies. Also as *sb.* (usu. *pl.*), a metamorphic rock.

1833 LYELL *Princ. Geol.* III. 375 For these last [*sc.* altered stratified rocks] the term 'metamorphic' (from μετα, *trans*, and μορφη, *form*) may be used. **1862** WHEWELL in *Life* (1881) 528, I was not much in the Geological Section [of the Brit. Assoc.], and do not know if they had there any discussion of metamorphic doctrines. **1865** PAGE *Geol. Terms* s.v., It is usual to restrict the term 'Metamorphic System' to those crystalline schists—Gneiss, Quartz-rock, Mica-schist, and Clay-slate—which underlie all the fossiliferous strata. **1881** KING & ROWNEY *Old Chapter Geol. Rec.* 49 The rocks of the locality are well-bedded metamorphics. **1923** *Univ. of Toronto Studies, Geol. Ser.* XVI. 7 A few blocks of the same granite were observed along with metamorphics like those seen in the till. **1970** *N.Z. Jrnl. Geol. & Geophysics* XIII. 72 Piroutet..regarded all the metamorphics as pre-Cambrian rocks.

transf. **1845** DARWIN *Voy. Nat.* xv. (1873) 325 In frozen snow the columnar structure must be owing to a 'metamorphic' action, not to a process during deposition. **1861** MAX MÜLLER *Sci. Lang.* 42 In Sanskrit..what remains is a kind of metamorphic agglomerate which cannot be understood without a most minute microscopic analysis.

3. That causes metamorphism or metamorphosis.

1853 CARPENTER *Hum. Physiol.* (ed. 4) 48 This metamorphic action of the liver would seem to be influenced by conditions of the nervous system. **1882** GEIKIE *Text-bk. Geol.* IV. viii. 571 Rocks..altered by the action of percolating water or other daily acting metamorphic agent. **1892** LD. LYTTON *King Poppy* Epil. 132 Nor all your metamorphic philtres.

metamorphine: see META- 6 a.

metamorphism (mɛtəˈmɔːfɪz(ə)m). [Formed as METAMORPHIC + -ISM.]

1. *Geol.* The process of change of form or structure produced in a rock by various natural agencies; the quality of being metamorphic.

1845 *Encycl. Metrop.* VI. 564/1 By the metamorphism of the chalk into the characters of primary limestone. **1854** WOODWARD *Mollusca* II. 223 Shell impunctate: Profr. King attributes this to metamorphism. **1865** PAGE *Geol. Terms* s.v., This change, or metamorphism, whether produced by heat, pressure, or chemical agency, has conferred upon them [*sc.* the crystalline schists] the term of Metamorphic rocks.

2. The process of metamorphosis (of an insect).

1866 TATE *Brit. Mollusks* iv. 153 An insect in its second stage of metamorphism.

metamorphist (mɛtəˈmɔːfɪst). [f. METAMORPH-OSIS + -IST.]

†**1.** (See quot.) *Obs.*

1694 *Hist., Geogr. & Poet. Dict.*, *Metamorphists*, or Transformers, a Name given in the XVIth Century to those Sacramentarians, who affirmed, That the Body of Jesus Christ ascended into Heaven, is wholy Deified. **1752** in CHAMBERS *Cycl.*

2. One who holds the theory of metamorphism.

1889 A. IRVING *Metamorph. Rocks* 65 A general *laissez-faire* sort of acceptance of the views of the more advanced metamorphists.

metamorphize, *v.* Also -ise. [f. Gr. μετα- META- + μορφή form + -IZE; after *metamorphosis*.] = METAMORPHOSE *v.*

1591 SHAKS. *Two Gent.* II. i. 32 And now you are Metamorphis'd with a Mistris, that when I looke on you, I can hardly thinke you my Master. **1596** HARINGTON *Metam. Ajax* 45 Masselyna..was worthie..to have bin metamorphized into Ajax. **1656** S. HOLLAND *Zara* (1719) 52 Metamorphize Men into Beasts, and Beasts into Men. **1748** *Anson's Voy.* III. viii. 383 The greatest part of them were strangely metamorphised by the heat of the hold. **1943** W. STEVENS *Let.* 29 Mar. (1967) 444 It would not help to change them to something else, any more than it would help to metamorphize this, that or the other (clouds into foam, living blossoms to blossoms without life, heat to a form of heat).

Hence **metaˈmorphized** *ppl. a.*, **metamorphizing** *vbl. sb.*

1613 F. ROBARTS *Revenue of Gosp.* 96 They are not men of reason..but metamorphised wolues, dogs, and tygres. **1609** J. RAWLINSON *Fishermen*, etc. 8 The metamorphising of men into fishes.

metamorphology (mɛtəmɔːˈfɒlədʒɪ). [f. METAMORPHO-SIS + -LOGY.] The scientific study of the post-embryonic metamorphosis of animals.

1879 tr. *Haeckel's Evol. Man.* II. 460 Later [i.e. post-embryonic] changes form the subject of the science of Metamorphoses, or Metamorphology.

‖**metamorphopsia** (mɛtəmɔːˈfɒpsɪə). [mod.L., irreg. f. *metamorph-ōsis* + Gr. -οψία kind of sight, f. root ὀπ- to see (in ὄψομαι fut. of ὁρᾶν).] An affection of the sight characterized by distortion of things seen.

1823 in CRABB *Technol. Dict.* **1855** in MAYNE *Expos. Lex.* **1894** G. MACKAY *Blinding of Retina* 36 He [the patient] had noticed some metamorphopsia, for in walking along a street the area railings at a certain distance appeared to have an upward bend.

metamorphosable (mɛtəˈmɔːfəsəbl), *a. rare*$^{-1}$. [f. METAMORPHOSE *v.* + -ABLE.] Capable of change of form.

1887 M. ARNOLD *Ess. Crit.* Ser. II. (1895) 310 Amiel tells us of his 'protean nature essentially metamorphosable, polarisable, and virtual'.

metamorphoscope (mɛtəˈmɔːfəʊskəʊp). [f. METAMORPHOSIS + -SCOPE.] (See quot.)

1875 KNIGHT *Dict. Mech.* 1426/2 *Metamorphoscope*, a toy having an opening at which the pictures on several belts are presented, the respective belts having head, body, and leg portions of figures. The belts are of different lengths, so as to mismatch the sections as they are revolved.

metamorphose (mɛtəˈmɔːfəʊs, -fəs), *sb.* Also 7 -os. [Anglicized form of METAMORPHOSIS. Cf. F. *métamorphose*.]

1. = METAMORPHOSIS. Now *rare*.

1608 MIDDLETON *Fam. Love* IV. ii, My Metamorphos is not held vnfit. *a* **1649** DRUMM. OF HAWTH. *Poems* Wks. (1711) 1 What metamorphose strange is this I prove? My self now scarce I find my self to be. **1732** SIR C. WOGAN in *Swift's Wks.* (1841) II. 671 This wonderful metamorphose of mere animals into smart and dexterous fellows, by the change of air. **1810** *Splendid Follies* II. 116 The evident improvement, and elegant metamorphose the room had undergone. **1865** MOZLEY *Mirac.* ii. 47 But thus transmuted, the inductive principle issues out of this metamorphose, a fiction not a truth. **1870** *Eng. Mech.* 28 Jan. 484/1 The same metamorphose takes place in animals.

2. A kind of firework.

1818 in *Pall Mall G.* (1885) 5 Nov. 4/2 Superior Fireworks... A metamorphose, with alternate change.

metamorphose (mɛtəˈmɔːfəʊz, -fəs), *v.* Also 6–7 -oze. [a. F. *métamorphoser* (1553 in Hatz-Darm.), f. *métamorphose* sb.: see METAMORPHOSIS.]

1. a. *trans.* To change in form; to turn *to* or *into* something else by enchantment or other supernatural means.

1576 GASCOIGNE *Del. Diet for Drunkards* (1792) 15 They feigned that Medea, Circe, and such other coulde Metamorphose & transforme men into Beastes, Byrdes, Plantes, and Flowres. **1589** GREENE *Menaphon* (Arb.) 40 This..draue Menaphon into such an extasie for ioy, that he stood as a man metamorphozed. **1642** W. PRICE *Serm.* 14 Remember Lots wife: she was metamorphoz'd to a pillar of salt. **1709** STEELE *Tatler* No. 21 ¶9 Many of the said Men were by the Force of that Herb metamorphosed into Swine. **1859** GEO. ELIOT *A. Bede* xii, Perhaps they metamorphose themselves into a tawny squirrel. **1874** LADY HERBERT tr. *Hübner's Ramble* (1878) II. iii. 530 A god metamorphosed into a dragon.

b. *intr.* with *into*.

1927 HALDANE & HUXLEY *Animal Biol.* ix. 180 When the tadpole metamorphoses into the frog, some of its tissues start to dedifferentiate.

2. (Chiefly *transf.* and *fig.* of 1; also *gen.*) *trans.* To change the form or character of; to alter the nature or disposition of; to transform. Const. *to*, *into*.

1576 GASCOIGNE *Del. Diet for Drunkards* (1792) 12 For was not Noah..through this beastly vice, so Metamorphosed, that he lay in his Tent uncovered. **1598** BARRET *Theor. Warres* I. i. 2 Long peace, and neglect of Martiall discipline hath metamorphosed manly mindes. **1621** LADY M. WROTH *Urania* 12, I was at that instant metamorphosed into miserie it selfe. **1741** W. OLDYS *Eng. Stage* vi. 93 They formed a Select Company, and Metamorphosing the Tennis-Court..opened their new Theatre. **1777** BURKE *Corr.* (1844) II. 152 Never were a people so metamorphosed. The plain farmer and even the plain quaker is become a soldier. **1820** W. IRVING *Sketch Bk.* I. 80 He recognised on the sign, the ruby face of King George..but even this was singularly metamorphosed. **1866** LIDDON *Bampt. Lect.* vi. (1875) 344 The regenerate man has been metamorphosed, his moral being is reconstructed. **1876** GEO. ELIOT *Dan. Der.* I. viii, This patient..from being the brightest..spirit in the household was metamorphosed into an irresponsive dull-eyed creature.

3. In scientific applications: To subject to METAMORPHOSIS or METAMORPHISM.

1664 POWER *Exp. Philos.* I. 27 When she was metamorphos'd into a Locust, I could discern no Mouth in the Microscope. **1665** SIR T. HERBERT *Trav.* (1677) 184 The Worm is metamorphosed into a Butter-Fly. **1839–47** CARPENTER in *Todd's Cycl. Anat.* III. 742/2 The wonderful processes of chemical and vital transformation, which take place during the period of incubation [of an egg], the albumen which it contained at first is metamorphosed into bone, cartilage, nerve,..feathers, &c., &c. **1851** OWEN in *Edin. New Philos. Jrnl.* Apr. 271 Before the individual has finally metamorphosed itself into the winged male or winged oviparous female. *Ibid.* 273 They..become circular flattened pupæ: and are finally metamorphosed into monostomes. **1858** GEIKIE *Hist. Boulder* xii. 246 A portion of the shale..has become in consequence highly metamorphosed. **1882** —— *Text-bk. Geol.* IV. viii. §1. 571 Nearly all rocks..have been metamorphosed.

metamorphosed (mɛtəˈmɔːfəʊzd, -fəst), *ppl. a.* [f. METAMORPHOSE *v.* + -ED[1].] In senses of the verb.

1603 KNOLLES *Hist. Turks* (1621) 1117 Yet..would not these metamorphosed monsters yeeld the towne vnto the Turkes. **1656** S. HOLLAND *Zara* (1719) 76 A number of Metamorphosed Men turned into Beasts by the Inchantments of this wicked Sorceress. **1703** MAUNDRELL *Journ. Jerus.* (1732) 85 The Monument of Lot's Metamorphos'd Wife. **1729** FIELDING *Temple Beau* (1775) I. 102 These cloaths! these looks! these airs! give me reason to wonder how I recollected my metamorphosed friend. **1859** DARWIN *Orig. Spec.* xiii. (1903) 175 Naturalists frequently speak of the skull as formed of metamorphosed vertebræ; the jaws of crabs as metamorphosed legs; the stamens and pistils of flowers as metamorphosed leaves. **1878** A. H. GREEN *Coal* ii. 43 The rocks..are highly metamorphosed Lower Silurian beds. **1899** *Allbutt's Syst. Med.* VI. 160 These old, metamorphosed thrombi.

metamorphoser (mɛtəˈmɔːfəʊzə(r), -fəsə(r)). [f. METAMORPHOSE *v.* + -ER[1].] One who or that which metamorphoses.

1576 GASCOIGNE *Del. Diet. for Drunkards* (1792) 14 What shall I name this man, but a beastly Metamorphoser, both of himself & of others? **1769** B. ALEXANDER in *Monthly Rev.* XLII. 102 The impositions of a crafty metamorphoser. **1839** LADY LYTTON *Cheveley* (ed. 2) III. i. 23 He was as good a metamorphoser of bipeds as the Yorkshire ostler was of quadrupeds.

metamorphosic (mɛtəˈmɔːfəsɪk), *a.* [f. METAMORPHOS-IS + -IC. Cf. F. *métamorphosique*.]

Of or pertaining to metamorphosis.

1782 POWNALL *Treat. Antiq.* 69 All the metamorphosic fables of the Ancients, turning policied and commercial people into horrid and savage monsters, will..evaporate before the light of truth. **1890** *Syd. Soc. Lex.*, *Metamorphosic breathing*, Gerhard's term for a respiratory sound, which begins as a puerile breathing, but during the course of the inspirations assumes another character..; he believes it to be a reliable sign of a pulmonary cavity.

metamorphosical (mɛtəmɔːˈfəʊzɪkəl), *a. nonce-wd.* [Formed as prec. + -AL[1].] Changeable.

1811 *Sporting Mag.* XXXVIII. 28 It was me lot to be in a metamorphosical humour.

metamorphosing (mɛtəˈmɔːfəʊzɪŋ, -fəsɪŋ), *vbl. sb.* [f. METAMORPHOSE *v.* + -ING[1].] The action of the verb METAMORPHOSE.

1608 TOPSELL *Serpents* (1658) 596 From this changing of rods into Serpents, came the several metamorphosing of sundry other things into Serpents also. **1878** T. SINCLAIR *Mount* 253 None has been nearer to seeing the Shakespearean metamorphosing here than Macdonald.

attrib. ?**1730** *Royal Remarks* 21 We were soon hurried away to a Metamorphosing House in the Hay-Market.

metaˈmorphosing, *ppl. a.* [f. METAMORPHOSE *v.* + -ING[2].] That metamorphoses or causes metamorphosis.

1620 T. GRANGER *Div. Logike* 32 All things are become new, spirituall, faithfull,..by the metamorphosing Spirit. **1878** BELL tr. *Gegenbaur's Comp. Anat.* 8 [It] in effect operates as a modifying and even metamorphosing agent. **1888** *Pall Mall G.* 15 June 13/2 That..current of civilization from whose metamorphosing waves a woman inevitably emerges either a Vera or a Princess Napraxine.

b. That undergoes metamorphosis.

1822–34 *Good's Study Med.* (ed. 4) IV. 507 The flea undergoes all the changes of the metamorphosing tribes of insects. **1898** *Allbutt's Syst. Med.* V. 205 The 'metamorphosing' breathing of Seitz consists of an

inspiratory sound harsh or rough at its commencement, becoming hollow or tubular towards the end of the act of inspiration.

metamorphosis (mɛtəˈmɔːfəsɪs). Pl. **metamorphoses** (-siːz). [a. L. *metamorphōsis*, a. Gr. μεταμόρφωσις, n. of action f. μεταμορφοῦν to transform, f. μετα- META- + μορφή form. Cf. METAMORPHOSE *sb.*]

1. The action or process of changing in form, shape or substance; *esp.* transformation by magic or witchcraft.

1533 MORE *Debell. Salem* Wks. 929/1 Salem & Bizans sometime two great townes..were.. with a meruailouse metamorphosis, enchaunted and turned into twoo englishe men. **1618** BOLTON *Florus* (1636) 77 As if by a kind of metamorphosis, the gods had..changed trees to Vessels. **1674** *Govt. Tongue* xii. 204 One would think we were fallen into an Age of Metamorphosis, and that the Brutes did (not only Poetically and in fiction) but really speak. For the talk of many is so bestial, that [etc.]. **1794** SULLIVAN *View Nat.* IV. 179 From the metempsychosis, however, arose the doctrine of the metamorphosis. **1856** RUSKIN *Mod. Paint.* III. IV. xvii. §6 A fourth..will begin to change them in his fancy into dragons and monsters, and lose his grasp of the scene in fantastic metamorphosis. **1869** TOZER *Highl. Turkey* II. 264 The points..on which the stories turn are transformations and metamorphoses of various kinds.

b. A metamorphosed form.

1589 GREENE *Menaphon* (Arb.) 73 Samela..stoode amazed like Medusaes Metamorphosis. **1638** RANDOLPH *Hey for Honesty* II. i, But come you pig-hogs, let us leave jesting. I restore you to your old metamorphosis, as you may see in the first leaf of Virgil's *Bucolics*. **1859** GEO. ELIOT *A. Bede* vi, An amount of fat on the nape of her neck, which made her look like the metamorphosis of a white sucking-pig.

2. *transf.* A complete change in the appearance, circumstances, condition, character of a person, of affairs, etc.

a **1548** HALL *Chron., Hen. VI* 161 Ihon Cade..departed secretly in habite disguysed, into Sussex: but all his metamorphosis or transfiguracion litle prevailed. **1598** BARCKLEY *Felic. Man* (1631) 195 The Hermit..asked him how it chanced that he was fallen into such a metamorphosis? **1656** EARL MONM. tr. *Boccalini's Advts. fr. Parnass.* I. xxix. (1674) 32 The Metamorphosis is too great, when from being a private man, one becomes a Prince. **1691** WOOD *Ath. Oxon.* I. 825 News was brought him of a metamorphosis in the State at home. **1791** BOSWELL *Johnson* an. 1753 (1816) I. 233 Whatever agreement a Chief might make with any of his clan, the Heralds-Office could not admit of the metamorphosis. **1820** W. SCORESBY *Acc. Arctic Reg.* I. 386 The mountains along the whole coast, assumed the most fantastic forms... These varied and sometimes beautiful metamorphoses..suggested the reality of fairy descriptions. **1853** C. BRONTE *Villette* xxvii, His visage changed as from a mask to a face:..I know not that I have ever seen in any other human face an equal metamorphosis. **1857** BUCKLE *Civiliz.* viii. 519 By a singular metamorphosis, the secular principle was now represented by the Catholics, and the theological principle by the Protestants. **1867** LYDIA M. CHILD *Rom. Repub.* v. 64 The disguises were quickly assumed, and the metamorphosis made Rosa both blush and smile.

3. In scientific uses.

a. *Physiology.* Change of form in animals and plants, or their parts, during life; *esp.* in *Ent.*, a change or one of a series of changes which a metabolous insect undergoes, resulting in complete alteration of form and habit. ***coarctate metamorphosis*** (Ent.): see COARCTATE b.

1665 *Phil. Trans.* I. 88 Their [silkworms] metamorphoses are four. **1722** QUINCY *Phys. Dict.* (ed. 2), *Metamorphosis*, is applied by Harvey to the Changes an Animal undergoes both in its Formation and Growth; and by several to the various Shapes some Insects in particular pass through, as the Silk Worm and the like. **1797** *Encycl. Brit.* (ed. 3) XIV. 712/1 A new form or change of appearance is always implied in metamorphosis or transformation..; as when the lobes of a seed are converted into seminal leaves. **1828** STARK *Elem. Nat. Hist.* II. 232 The transformations or metamorphoses of insects embrace three states. **1835-6** *Todd's Cycl. Anat.* I. 106/1 We find that the whole of its [*sc.* the terrestrial salamander's] metamorphosis takes place whilst in the oviduct. **1881** F. M. BALFOUR *Comp. Embryol* II. 113 The change undergone by the Tadpole in its passage into the Frog is so considerable as to deserve the name of a metamorphosis. **1888** ROLLESTON & JACKSON *Anim. Life* 161 A perfect metamorphosis, such as that of Sphinx, with three well-marked stages, larva, pupa, and imago. **1897** PARKER & HASWELL *Zool.* II. XIII. 32 It [the Ascidian]..soon begins to undergo the *retrogressive metamorphosis* by which it attains the adult condition.

b. *Morphology.* The modification of organs or structures in form or function (including teratology).

1839 *Penny Cycl.* XV. 131/2 Metamorphosis of organs, in the Vegetable Kingdom, consists in an adaptation of one and the same organ to several different purposes. **1849** BALFOUR *Man. Bot.* §641. 307 The different parts of the flower may be changed into each other, or into true leaves... These changes may take place from without inwards, by an ascending or direct metamorphosis, as in the case of petals becoming stamens; or from within outwards, by descending or retrograde metamorphosis, as when stamens become petals.

c. *Evolution.* Secular change of form.

1847-9 *Todd's Cycl. Anat.* IV. 623/2 A unity which has undergone such an infinitely graduated metamorphosis of its parts as to yield these unequal skeletal forms. **1876** RAY LANKESTER tr. *Haeckel's Hist. Creat.* I. 90 His [Goethe's] idea of metamorphosis is almost synonymous with the theory of development. **1903** tr. *Strasburger's Bot.* (ed. 2) I. 10 The various modifications which the primitive form has passed through constitute its metamorphosis.

d. *Histol.* The change of form which goes on in the elements of living organic structures; *e.g.* in blood-corpuscles, animal or vegetable tissue, etc. *Path.* 'The morbid change of the elements of tissues into another form of structure' (*Funk's Stand. Dict.*).

1839-47 CARPENTER in *Todd's Cycl. Anat.* III. 750/1 The production of the simple structureless membranes..must be attributed, we think, to the consolidation of a thin layer of blastema, rather than to any metamorphosis of cells. **1845-6** G. E. DAY tr. *Simon's Anim. Chem.* I. 133 The metamorphosis [of blood-corpuscles] occurs in the peripheral system. **1857** *G. Bird's Urin. Deposits* (ed. 5) 440 Every animal developes,..during the process of metamorphosis of tissue, a series of nitrogenized substances. **1869** E. A. PARKES *Pract. Hygiene* (ed. 3) 184 There is a much more rapid metamorphosis of tissue in carnivorous animals. **1882** VINES *Sachs' Bot.* 708 These reserve-materials [in dormant seeds, bulbs, tubers] must undergo repeated Metamorphosis while they are being conveyed to the growing organs.

e. *Chem.* The change of a compound to a new form; *esp.* 'the chemical change occurring in a compound substance under the influence of some other body which itself does not change' (*Syd. Soc. Lex.* 1890).

1853 CARPENTER *Hum. Physiol.* (ed. 4) 47 When there is a deficiency of fatty matters in the food, these may be formed by a metamorphosis of its saccharine constituents. *Ibid.* 52 The chemical metamorphoses which take place in the economy. *Ibid.* 90 The lactic acid, chiefly generated in the substance of the muscles (probably by the metamorphosis of a saccharine compound). **1862** MILLER *Elem. Chem.* III. 58, 61 Production of Chemical Metamorphoses... 1. Oxidation. ..2. Metamorphoses by Reduction...3. Metamorphoses by Substitution. **1843** R. J. GRAVES *Syst. Clin. Med.* Introd. Lect. 34 Professor Liebig applied the name of metamorphosis to those chemical actions in which a given compound by the presence of a peculiar substance, is made to resolve itself into two or more compounds.

metaˈmorphosist. *rare*—⁰. [f. METAMORPHOS-IS + -IST.] = METAMORPHIST.

1848 in CRAIG.

metamorphosize (mɛtəˈmɔːfəsaɪz), *v.* [f. METAMORPHOS(IS + -IZE.] *trans.* and *intr.* = METAMORPHOSE *v.* Hence **metaˈmorphosized** *ppl. a.*

1908 *Dict. Nat. Biogr.* V. 1312/1 Dowsing's acquaintance with 'Lating'..led him to metamorphosise Dr. Billingford into a maid recommending her daughter's soul to the Virgin Mary. **1928** *Observer* 29 Jan. 9/3 It may well be found that Unwin and his biographer between them have metamorphosised the study of economic history in this country. **1969** *Daily Tel.* 4 Aug. 15/1 It [*sc.* Shaw's *As Far as Thought Can Reach*] envisages the world in A.D. 30,000, when children of 17 are hatched from eggs to spend a few years on adolescent pursuits—love, mating, music, the dance—before metamorphosising into Ancients. **1972** *Ibid.* 17 May 12/6 The parable of metamorphosised man is beautifully photographed by Walter Lassally.

†**metamorphostical,** *a. Obs. rare.* [irreg. f. METAMORPHOS-IS. Cf. *metamorphosical.*] Of or pertaining to metamorphosis.

1722 ARBUTHNOT, etc. *Ann. Mirab.* in *Miscell.* 1732 III. 86 The *Annus Mirabilis*, or the Metamorphostical Conjunction: a Word which denotes the mutual Transformation of Sexes. **1895** WOOD MARTIN *Pagan Ireland* 84 The soul of a man might pass into a deer, a boar ..&c,..a continuous metamorphostical existence.

†**metaˈmorphosy.** *Obs.* Anglicized form of METAMORPHOSIS.

c **1530** L. COX *Rhet.* (1899) 71 And so dothe Ulysses conclude his oracyon in the .xiii. boke of Ouide Metamorphosy. **1606** WARNER *Alb. Eng.* XIV. lxxxix. (1612) 363 Like tales and Metamorphosies passe many in this Chat. *a* **1698** TEMPLE *Poems* 46 If ever any reasonable Soul Harbor'd in shape of either brute or fowl, This was the Mansion: Metamorphosie Gain'd here the credit lost in Poetrie.

metamorphotic (mɛtəmɔːˈfɒtɪk), *a.* [f. METAMORPHOSIS: see -OTIC.] Pertaining to or based on metamorphosis; causing metamorphosis.

1816 BENTHAM *Chrestomathia* Wks. 1843 VIII. 145 *Metamorphotic*, is the appellation by which these several branches of the Psychico-physical division of the aggregate system of sources of motion may be designated. **1826** KIRBY & SP. *Entomol.* IV. 420 The Era of Swammerdam and Ray, or of the Metamorphotic System. **1827** CARLYLE *Germ. Rom., Quintus Fixlein* III. 282 To his eyes, this birth-day, in the metamorphotic mirror of his superstitious imagination ..would burn forth like a red death-warrant.

metamorphy (mɛtəˈmɔːfɪ). [Formed as METAMORPHIC: see -Y.] = METAMORPHOSIS.

1869 MASTERS *Veget. Terat.* 241 In the present work the term metamorphy is employed to distinguish cases where the ordinary course of development has been perverted or changed. **1879** STORMONTH *Man. Sci. Terms*, *Metamorphosis*..bot...sometimes called *metamorphy*.

metamylene: see META- 6 a.

metanalysis (mɛtəˈnælɪsɪs). *Philol.* [f. MET(A- + ANALYSIS.] Reinterpretation of the division between words or syntactic units: as *adder* < OE. *nædre* by analysis in ME. of *a naddre* as *an addre*. Hence **meˈtanalyse** *v. trans.*

1914 O. JESPERSEN *Mod. Eng. Gram.* II. v. 141, I have ventured to coin the word 'metanalysis' for the phenomenon frequent in all languages that words or word-groups are by a new generation analyzed differently from the analysis of a former age. **1940** —— *Ibid.* V. xix. 308 A good many sentences of this type are double-barrelled and present the possibility of a 'metanalysis', by which 'It is good for a man/not to touch a woman' may come to be apprehended 'It is good/for a man not to touch a woman'. **1957** G. V. SMITHERS *Kyng Alisaunder* II. 138 *jker* < OE. *nicor* by a process of metanalysis in which an initial consonant is treated as the final consonant of the preceding word, or a final consonant is attracted into the beginning of the next word. **1962** R. QUIRK *Use of English* viii. 127 When the French word *crevice*..was introduced into Middle English, its connexion with 'sea food' caused people to *metanalyse* the final syllable as *-fish* ('crayfish'). **1970** B. M. H. STRANG *Hist. English* iv. 250 Assimilations account for the /m/ (earlier /n/) in such words as *comfort, noumpire* (later metanalysed as *umpire*). *Ibid.* 268 *For then ones* metanalysed as *for the nonce*. **1972** J. L. DILLARD *Black English* iv. 162 *Metanalysis* describes the analysis of words or groups of words into new elements...*a napron* was metanalyzed to *an apron*.

‖**metanephron, -nephros** (mɛtəˈnɛfrɒn, -ˈnɛfrɒs). *Zool.* [mod.L., f. Gr. μετα- META- + νεφρός kidney.] The hinder division of the typical segmental organ in vertebrates, from which are developed the kidney and the ureter. Hence **metaˈnephric** *a.*

1877 RAY LANKESTER in *Q. Jrnl. Microsc. Sci.* XVII. 430 A metanephron with metanephric duct distinct from the Wolffian or mesonephric duct. **1884** A. SEDGWICK *ibid.* XXIV. 79 The metanephros persists as the functional kidney.

metanocerite: see META- 7 a.

metanoia (mɛtəˈnɔɪə). [Gr. μετάνοια, f. μετανοεῖν to change one's mind, to repent.] Penitence, repentance; reorientation of one's way of life, spiritual conversion.

1873 M. ARNOLD *Lit. & Dogma* vii. 196 Of 'metanoia', as Jesus used the word, the lamenting one's sins was a small part; the main part was something more active and fruitful, the setting up an immense new inward movement for obtaining the rule of life. And 'metanoia', accordingly, is: *a change of the inner man.* **1881** *Amer. Church Rev.* July 167 What a Metanoia was there, to both Jesus and John!.. And what a Metanoia had come also upon the disciples of John and upon Israel! **1918** *Encycl. Relig. & Ethics* X. 733/2 'Repentance' has an emotional tone; μετάνοια is ethical and intellectual; the former is negative—a turning away from sin; the latter is positive—an enthusiasm for righteousness. **1939** V. A. DEMANT *Relig. Prospect* ix. 237 If we understand St. Paul's use of the word 'spiritual', not in our misleading sense of 'non-material' but as the nature of a creature turned to God, we see how this *metanoia*, this turning about, brings a restored understanding of the order of human powers and faculties. **1945** A. HUXLEY *Let.* 10 Apr. (1969) 520 Virgil's *metanoia* was in the nature of a death-bed repentance. **1969** F. DE GRAEVE in J. Kerkhofs *Mod. Mission Dialogue* p. xvi, It must reveal the Church..as the community in which the religious intentionality of all people can blossom into that newness of life that is the real metanoia. **1973** E. POWELL *No Easy Answers* xii. 123 To entertain this idea and to be penetrated with it is the change of mind, repentance, *metanoia*, of which the baptist was not the announcer but the forerunner.

‖**metanotum** (mɛtəˈnəʊtəm). *Ent.* [mod.L., f. Gr. μετα- META- + νῶτον back.] The dorsal part of the metathorax in insects. Hence **metaˈnotal** *a.* (in recent Dicts.).

1860 J. DUNCAN *Introd. Entom.* I. 109 The dorsal portion [of the metathorax] is the *metanotum*, commonly quadrangular. **1877** HUXLEY *Anat. Inv. Anim.* vii. 400 The metanotum, or tergal portion of the metathorax.

metantimonic (mɛtæntɪˈmɒnɪk), *a. Chem.* [ad. F. *métantimonique* (Fremy): see META- and ANTIMONIC.] ***metantimonic acid***: the hydrate produced when pentachloride of antimony is treated with water.

1854 R. D. THOMSON *Cycl. Chem.* **1869** ROSCOE *Elem. Chem.* 256.

Hence **metantiˈmon(i)ate**, a salt of metantimonic acid.

1863 *Fownes' Chem.* (ed. 9) 368 Metantimonate of potassa. **1863** BRANDE & TAYLOR *Chem.* Index, Metantimoniates.

meta-oleic to **metaphenomenal:** see META-.

metaphery (məˈtæfərɪ). *Bot.* [f. Gr. μετα- META- + -φερεια (cf. PERIPHERY), φέρειν to carry.] 'The displacement of organs, as when alternate become opposite' (Jackson *Gloss. Bot. Terms*).

1869 M. T. MASTERS *Veget. Terat.* 91 Morren..speaks of this transposition as metaphery. **1879** in STORMONTH *Man. Sci. Terms.*

metaphone (ˈmɛtəfəʊn). *Phonetics.* [f. META- + PHONE *sb.*[1]] (See quots.)

1930 H. E. PALMER *Princ. Romanization* II. 52 Contrasted with *monophones* we have *metaphones*, which we may define as two or more phones which serve jointly as units of meaning within the limits of a given linguistic community. **1934** YUEN-REN CHAO in M. Joos *Readings in Linguistics* (1958) 38/2 A dynamophone is a metaphone which contains two or more phones differing..in quality. **1966** M. PEI *Gloss. Ling. Terminol.* 161 *Metaphone*, a free allophonic variant chosen in preference to another because regarded as more suitable to the type of speech used (*tomahto, eyether*, used in a given situation instead of the more customary pronunciations of *tomato, either*). **1972** HARTMANN & STORK *Dict. Lang. & Ling.* 140 *Metaphone*, a free variant of a phoneme, e.g. [-ai] or [iː] in *neither*.

metaphony (mɛˈtæfənɪ). *Philol.* [a. F. *métaphonie*, f. Gr. μετα- META- + φωνή sound.] A term proposed to take the place of UMLAUT. Hence **metaˈphonic** *a.*; **metaˈphonical** *a.*, **metaˈphonized** *ppl. a.*

1894 V. HENRY *Comp. Gram. Eng. & Germ.* II. i. §4. **1950** *Trans. Philol. Soc.* *1949* 23 The name *apophony* may be retained for the quantitative alternations, and..the qualitative alternations may be distinguished as *metaphony.* **1953** K. JACKSON *Lang. & Hist. Early Brit.* 371, -āu̯i- > eu appears to be due to metaphony rather than to palatalisation. **1957** *Archivum Linguisticum* IX. 107 Metaphonic Spanish and Portuguese verbs. **1970** *Ibid.* I. 22 Moreover, in Lena all adjectives of the type *blanco* have three forms: one ending in -u which undergoes metaphony and is used in agreement with masc. nouns. **1973** A. H. SOMMERSTEIN *Sound Pattern Anc. Greek* ii. 76 There are three main ablaut rules—Vṛddhi, Vowel Weakening and *e/o* ablaut or metaphony.

metaphor (ˈmɛtəfə(r)). Forms: α. 6–7 **metaphore**, (6 **metafor**), 6– **metaphor**. β. 6–7 **metaphora**. [a. F. *métaphore*, ad. L. *metaphora*, a. Gr. μεταφορά, f. μεταφέρειν to transfer, f. μετα- META- + φέρειν (root φερ-: φορ-) to bear, carry.] The figure of speech in which a name or descriptive term is transferred to some object different from, but analogous to, that to which it is properly applicable; an instance of this, a metaphorical expression. ***mixed metaphor***: see quot. 1824.

α. **1533** HEN. VIII in Wotton *Lett.* (1654) Suppl. 8 And rather then men would note a lye when they know what is meant, they will sooner by allegory or metaphor draw the word to the truth. **1553** T. WILSON *Rhet.* 91 b, A metaphor is an alteration of a woorde from the proper and naturall meanynge, to that whiche is not proper, and yet agreeth therunto, by some lykenes that appeareth to be in it. **1555** BONNER *Homilies* 71* Chryste alwayes in hys speakynge dyd vse fygures, metaphores and tropes. **1563** *Mirr. for Mag., Collingbourne* xxxvii, These metafors I vse with other more. **1646** SIR T. BROWNE *Pseud. Ep.* v. ix. 247 An horn is the hieroglyphick of authority, power, & dignity, and in this Metaphor is often used in Scripture. **1712** ADDISON *Spect.* No 289 ¶8 Those beautiful Metaphors in Scripture, where Life is termed a Pilgrimage. **1821** LAMB *Elia* Ser. I. *Imperf. Sympathies*, He stops a metaphor like a suspected person in an enemy's country. 'A healthy book!'..'Did I catch rightly what you said?' **1824** L. MURRAY *Eng. Gram.* (ed. 5) I. 493 We should avoid making two inconsistent metaphors meet on one object. This is what is called mixed metaphor. **1841** TRENCH *Parables* i. (1877) 9 The allegory stands to the metaphor,..in the same relation that the parable does to the ..simile. **1876** MOZLEY *Univ. Serm.* xvi. (1877) 265 The metaphor of the poet is perfectly true in fact, for life *is* a stage.

β. **1586** A. DAY *Eng. Secretary* II. (1625) 77 *Metaphora*, which is, when a word from the proper or right signification is transferred to another neere vnto the meaning. **1598** SYLVESTER *Du Bartas* II. ii. II. *Babylon* 369 Better then Greek with her..Fit Epithets, and fine Metaphora's. **1650** EARL MONM. tr. *Senault's Man bec. Guilty* 175 The Metaphora, which is so frequent with them,..is it not an imposture?

b. *Comb.*, as ***metaphor-making***, ***-monger***.

1670 EACHARD *Cont. Clergy* 46 These indiscreet and horrid metaphor-mongers. **1889** MIVART *Orig. Hum. Reason* 273 This power of metaphor-making.

† **metaphorally**, *adv.* *Obs.* *rare*⁻¹. [f. METAPHOR + -AL¹ + -LY².] Metaphorically.

1548–50 THOMAS *Ital. Dict.*, *Chimera*, a proper name, but *metaphorollie* [sic], it is many times taken for an harde or subtill imaginacion.

metaphoric (mɛtəˈfɒrɪk), *a.* [f. METAPHOR + -IC.] = METAPHORICAL.

1597 in Farr *S. P. Eliz.* (1845) II. 447 Restraine your haughtie metaphoricke lines. **1669** GALE *Crt. Gentiles* I. I. ii. 11 Traditions; which he wraps up in..metaphoric, and Allegoric notions. **1726** SWIFT *To a Lady in Heroic Style* 119 Metaphoric Meat and Drink Is to understand and think. **1875** M. & FR. COLLINS *Sweet & Twenty* I. xvi, Sarah..did not understand Miss Litton's metaphoric language.

metaphorical (mɛtəˈfɒrɪkəl), *a.* [f. METAPHOR + -IC + -AL¹.] Of or characterized by the use of metaphor; of the nature of metaphor; used metaphorically; not literal; figurative.

a **1555** LATIMER in Foxe *A. & M.* (1563) 1312/2 They thinke not that it is a corporal worme, but a spiritual & a Metaphorical worme. **1665** BUNYAN *Holy Citie* (1669) 251 For both the word Water, and that of Life, they are but metaphorical Sayings. **1741** RICHARDSON *Pamela* (1824) I. cii. 490 [She] delights..in..metaphorical flourishes. **1825** COLERIDGE *Aids Refl.* 2 A man without reflection is but a metaphorical phrase for the instinct of a beast. **1883** H. DRUMMOND *Nat. Law in Spir. W.* vii. (1884) 235 To impose a metaphorical meaning on the commonest word of the New Testament is to violate every canon of interpretation.

Hence **metaˈphoricalness**.

1882 in OGILVIE.

metaphorically (mɛtəˈfɒrɪkəlɪ), *adv.* [f. METAPHORICAL + -LY².] In a metaphorical sense; by the use of metaphor.

1571 GOLDING *Calvin on Ps.* ii. 3 By terming his government metaphorically by the name of 'Bondes and yoke'. **1660** T. GOUGE *Chr. Directions* ix. (1831) 56 Which words, 'If thy right hand offend thee, cut it off' &c., are not literally to be taken, but metaphorically. **1756** BURKE *Subl. & B.* III. xxvi, We metaphorically apply the idea of sweetness to sights and sounds. **1844** STANLEY *Arnold* (1858) I. vi. 244 Literally as well as metaphorically blind. **1885** *Manch. Exam.* 2 May 6/2 Mr. Broadhurst metaphorically fell upon Mr. Bentinck's neck.

metaphorist (ˈmɛtəfərɪst). *rare.* [f. METAPHOR + -IST.] One who deals in metaphors.

1727 POPE, etc. *Art of Sinking* 115 A poet or orator would have no more to do but to send to the particular traders in each kind, to the metaphorist for his allegories, to the simile-maker for his comparisons. **1891** HANNAH LYNCH *G. Meredith* 33 The marvellous performance of a juggling metaphorist.

metaphorize (ˈmɛtəfəraɪz), *v.* [f. METAPHOR + -IZE. Cf. F. *métaphoriser.*] *trans.* **a.** To change metaphorically *into*. **b.** To ply with metaphor.

1731 J. CONSTABLE *Reflections Accuracy of Style* 100, I wish too, that..the vanity of metaphorizing did not put several upon a greater stretch of thoughts than their wit will bear. **1789** T. TWINING *Aristotle's Treat. Poetry* (1812) II. 292 Every reader will recollect Milton's beautiful application of this metaphor..to the dew-drops, metaphorized into pearls. **1801** SOUTHEY *Let.* 25 July in *Life* (1850) II. 153 Every character [in the play] reasoning, and metaphorising, and metaphysicking the reader most nauseously. **1909** *N.Y. Even. Post* 27 Nov. 5 However agitated or depressed they may be, they must go on metaphorising. **1949** WELLEK & WARREN *Theory of Lit.* xv. 202 We metaphorize also what we love, what we want to linger over, and contemplate.

† **metaphorous**, *a.* *Obs.* *rare*⁻¹. [f. METAPHOR + -OUS.] Full of or characterized by metaphor.

1658 BROMHALL *Treat. Specters* VII. 362 Metaphorous speeches.

metaphosphate (mɛtəˈfɒsfət). *Chem.* [META- 2 a.] A salt of metaphosphoric acid.

1833 [see next]. **1869** ROSCOE *Elem. Chem.* 160 Sodium metaphosphate.

metaphosphoric (mɛtəfɒsˈfɒrɪk), *a.* *Chem.* [META- 2 a.] ***metaphosphoric acid*** (HPO_3): an acid containing a molecule of water less than orthophosphoric acid.

1833 T. GRAHAM in *Phil. Trans.* 277, I shall take the liberty to designate provisionally the acid of the fused biphosphate of soda, the Metaphosphoric acid..; and the fused salt itself, the Metaphosphate of soda. **1899** tr. *R. von Jaksch's Clin. Diagn.* vii (ed. 4) 299 If to urine which contains albumin a little solid metaphosphoric acid be added, a precipitate or turbidity forms.

metaphragm (ˈmɛtəfræm). *Ent.* Also in Latin form. [ad. mod.L. *metaphragma*, f. Gr. μετα- META- + φράγμα partition.] The wall that separates the abdomen from the thorax in insects.

1826 KIRBY & SP. *Entomol.* III. 382 Metaphragma (the Metaphragm). *Ibid.* IV. 591 The cavity of the chest.. between the mesophragm and metaphragm.

metaphrase (ˈmɛtəfreɪz), *sb.* [ad. mod.L. *metaphrasis*, ad. Gr. μετάφρασις, n. of action from μεταφράζειν to translate, paraphrase: see META- and PHRASE *sb.* Cf. F. *métaphrase.*]

† **1.** A metrical translation. *Obs.*

1627 BP. HALL *Dauids Ps. Metaphr.* Ded., Apollinarius.. wrote..all the Hebrew scriptures in Heroicks;..his metaphrase of the Psalmes is still in our hands. **1631** in *Bannatyne Club Misc.* I. 245 The receaving of this new metaphrase, and rejecting of the old, sall geve occasion to foranners to call us light headed Scots. **1767** HARTE *Amaranth* Pref., A paraphrase (or metaphrase rather) of the xxviiith chapter of Deuteronomy; which, I believe, hath never yet been turned into English verse.

2. A rendering into other words; a translation; in later use, a word-for-word translation in contradistinction to a paraphrase.

1640 SHIRLEY *Hum. Courtier* IV. i. G 1 b, *Orseolo.* What does she thinke? *Lau.* Y'are insufficient. *Or.* How? a metophrase [*sic*] upon that word. *a* **1646** J. GREGORY *Posthuma* (1650) 224 Where the English Metaphrase readeth, Thou shalt accept [etc.]... The Hebrew saith, Thou shalt consume, &c. **1680** DRYDEN tr. *Ovid's Ep.* Pref., Ess. (ed. Ker) I. 237 Metaphrase, or turning an author word by word, and line by line, from one language into another. **1697** — tr. *Virg. Æneid* Ded. (e) 4 b, The way I have taken is not so streight as Metaphrase, nor so loose as Paraphrase. **1823** DE QUINCEY *Lett. to Yng. Man* Wks. XIV. 84 *note*, It is too much of a mere metaphrase of Kant. **1903** W. R. ROBERTS in *Class. Rev.* XVII. 131/2 Metaphrase can hardly be made to do duty for paraphrase.

fig. **1822** LAMB *Elia* Ser. I. *Some Old Actors*, Such playful selections and specious combinations rather than strict metaphrases of nature.

metaphrase (ˈmɛtəfreɪz), *v.* [f. prec. sb.: but cf. Gr. μεταφράζειν.]

† **1.** *trans.* To translate, esp. in verse. *Obs.*

1608 BP. HALL in *Sylvester's Du Bartas* To Author, To Mr Iosuah Sylvester, of his Bartas Metaphrased. **1633** FLETCHER *Poet. Misc.* 86 Certain of the royal Prophets Psalmes metaphrased. **1649** T. W[EAVER] (*title*) Plantagenets Tragicall Story: or the Death of King Edward the Fourth... Metaphrased by T. W. gent.

2. To alter the phrasing or language of; to render into other words.

1868 *Contemp. Rev.* IX. 294 He [Simeon Metaphrastes] did not in all cases assemble materials in their original shape, but often 'metaphrased' or manipulated them in such a way as to deprive the mass of all value. **1883** SCRIVENER *Introd. Crit. N.T.* 508 He too [Clement of Alexandria] complains of those who tamper with (or metaphrase) the Gospels for their own sinister ends.

Hence **ˈmetaphrasing** *vbl. sb.*

1631 in *Bannatyne Club Misc.* I. 237, I have not as zit.. considdered what libertie they have takin in the metaphrasing to add, insert, or degresse.

‖ **metaphrasis** (mɛˈtæfrəsɪs). *Obs.* [mod.L.: see prec.] = METAPHRASE.

a **1568** ASCHAM *Scholem.* II. (Arb.) 104 *Metaphrasis*..is all one with *Paraphrasis*, saue it is out of verse, either into prose, or into some other kinde of meter: or els, out of prose into verse. **1603** HOLLAND *Plutarch's Mor.* 984 Some rhetoricall figures, catachreses and metaphrases. **1706** PHILLIPS (ed. Kersey), *Metaphrasis*, a bare Translation out of one Language into another.

metaphrast (ˈmɛtəfræst). [ad. Gr. μεταφράστης, f. μεταφράζειν to translate, f. μετα- META- + φράζειν to speak.] One who renders a composition into a different literary form, e.g. by turning prose into verse, or one metre into another; also, †a translator.

1610 HOLLAND *Camden's Brit.* I. 68 Simeon that great Metaphrast. **1642** CUDWORTH *Lord's Supper* 13 For so both the Syriack Metaphrast expounds it..and the Arabick. *a* **1695** WOOD *Fasti Oxon.* (1815) 516 George Sandys, esq.; the famous traveller and excellent poetical metaphrast. **1778** WARTON *Hist. Eng. Poetry* II. 190 He [Symeon] obtained the distinguishing appellation of the Metaphrast, because..he modernised the more antient narratives of the miracles and martyrdoms..for the use of the Greek church. **1896** J. W. MACKAIL *Lat. Lit.* (ed. 2) 128 The later metaphrasts, who occupied themselves with turning heroic into elegiac poems by inserting a pentameter between each two lines.

metaphrastic (mɛtəˈfræstɪk), *a.* and *sb.* [ad. Gr. μεταφραστικός, f. μεταφράστης: see prec.]

A. *adj.*

1. Of the nature of metaphrase.

1778 WARTON *Hist. Eng. Poetry* II. 169 Maximus Planudes..has the merit of having familiarised to his countrymen many Latin classics..by metaphrastic versions.

2. *Gram.* (See quot.) *rare*⁻¹.

1861 MAX MÜLLER *Sci. Lang.* Ser. I. viii. (1864) 338 The formation of such phrases as the French *j'aimerai*, for *j'ai à aimer*..may be called analytical or metaphrastic.

B. *sb. pl.* The art of translation or interpretation.

1895 *Q. Rev.* Oct. 328 There is no lost work on Hermeneutics or Metaphrastics to be recovered from an Egyptian grave.

So **metaˈphrastical** *a.* = METAPHRASTIC.

1860 in WORCESTER.

metaˈphrastically, *adv.* [Formed as prec. + -LY².] By way of metaphrase.

1577 HANMER *Anc. Eccl. Hist.* (1663) 73 Some report that he presumed metaphrastically to alter the words of the Apostle, correcting as it were the order of the phrase. **1652** T. MANLEY *Afflict. Saints* title-p., The whole Booke of Job, composed into English Heroicall Verse, metaphrastically. **1894** R. FENTON in W. W. Lloyd *E. Fenton* 121 Which we may metaphrastically translate:—Milton, now, a disappointed, blind, distressed old man.

‖ **metaphrenon**, **-phrenum** (mɛˈtæfrɪnɒn, -frɪnəm). Also 7 *anglicized* **metaphren(e.** [Late L., a. Gr. μετάφρενον, f. μετά after + φρήν midriff.] The part of the back that is behind the diaphragm.

1621 BURTON *Anat. Mel.* I. v. III. i. (1651) 401 The metaphrene, or part of the back which is over against the heart. **1661** LOVELL *Hist. Anim. & Min.* 90 Brest strong, metaphren broad. **1693** tr. *Blancard's Phys. Dict.* (ed. 2), *Metaphrenum.* **1706** PHILLIPS (ed. Kersey), *Metaphrenum*, that part of the Back which comes after the Diaphragm, or Midriff. **1856** MAYNE *Expos. Lex.*, *Metaphrenon, Metaphrenum.*

metaphyseal, **metaphysial**: see METAPHYSIS.

metaphysic (mɛtəˈfɪzɪk), *sb.*¹ In 4 **methaphesik**, 5 **metaphesyk**, **methephisike**, 6 **methaphisick**, 6–7 **metaphisi(c)k(e**, **-physi(c)ke**, (7 **-phisique**), 7–8 **-physick**, (9 **-physique**). [ad. scholastic L. *metaphysica* fem. sing., substituted (on the analogy of other names of sciences: cf. *physic*) for the older *metaphysica* neut. pl.; see METAPHYSICS. Cf. F. *métaphysique*, G. *metaphisik.*

The sing. form alone appears in Eng. before the 16th c. In the 17th and 18th c. it was almost superseded by METAPHYSICS; in the 19th c., owing to German influences it began to be preferred by many philosophical writers.]

1. a. = METAPHYSICS 1 a.

1387 TREVISA *Higden* (Rolls) III. 365 He [Aristotle] made ..problemys of perspective and of methaphesik [1432–50 problemes perspective and metaphisicalle, orig. *et perspectiva problemata et metaphysicam*]. *c* **1450** *Cov. Myst., Doctors in Temple* 189 Ageyn oure argemente is no recystence In metaphesyk ne astronomye. **1527** TINDALE *Par. Wicked Mammon* Wks. (1573) 88/1 How shoulde he vnderstand the scripture, seing he is no Philosopher, neyther hath sene his metaphisike? **1586** T. B[EARD] *La Primaud. Fr. Acad.* I. 72 Physike, which is the studie of naturall things: Metaphysike, which is of supernaturall things. **1605** BACON *Adv. Learn.* II. vii. §3 The one part which is Phisicke enquireth and handleth the Materiall & Efficient Cavses, & the other which is Metaphisicke handleth the Formal and Final Cavses. **1742** POPE *Dunc.* IV. 645 Physic of Metaphysic begs defence, And Metaphysic calls for aid on Sense. **1775** HORSLEY in *Phil. Trans.* LXV. 182 The uncertain conclusions of an ill-conducted analogy, and a false metaphysic, were mixed with the few simple precepts derived from observation. **1817** COLERIDGE *Biog. Lit.* ix. (1882) 71 [Fichte] supplied the idea of a system truly metaphysical, and of a metaphysique truly systematic. **1873** M. ARNOLD *Lit. & Dogma* (1876) 399 The mis-attribution

to the Bible.. of a science and an abstruse metaphysic which is not there. **1883** E. CAIRD in *Encycl. Brit.* XVI. 79 For Aristotle, metaphysic is the science which has to do with Being as such, Being in general. **1918** B. RUSSELL in *Monist* XXVIII. 496 In the present lectures, I shall try to set forth .. a kind of logical doctrine which seems to .. result from the philosophy of mathematics..: a certain kind of logical doctrine, and on the basis of this a certain kind of metaphysic. **1968** J. M. ZIMAN *Public Knowl.* iii. 38 One further condition may be necessary for consensible knowledge—a common metaphysic. Those who participate in the consensus must already share many beliefs. **1969** *N.Y. Rev. Bks.* 16 Jan. 15/1 The United States, whose metaphysic, according to Lionel Trilling, is always material and practical, has much more closely fulfilled the nineteenth-century Comtean vision of the future. **1972** D. BELL in Cox & Dyson *20th-Cent. Mind* I. vi. 211 On this central point Bosanquet's metaphysic remains impenetrably obscure, sustained by a combination of piety and metaphor.

b. = METAPHYSICS 1 b.

1865 J. H. STIRLING *Sir W. Hamilton* 41 The true metaphysic of the subject nowhere finds itself represented in the preceding discussion. **1874** LEWES *Probl. Life & Mind* Ser. I. I. Introd. I. iv. 67 Every science has its metaphysic.

¶ **2.** Something visionary.

1606 WARNER *Alb. Eng.* XIV. lxxxi. (1612) 341 Or for a Metaphysick hold the Proiect of her prayse.

metaphysic (mɛtəˈfɪzɪk), *a.* and *sb.*² [ad. scholastic L. *metaphysicus* adj., developed from *metaphysica* sb. pl.: see METAPHYSICS. Cf. F. *metaphysique*, Sp. *metafísico*, It. *metafisico*.]

A. *adj.* = METAPHYSICAL. Now *rare*.

1528 TINDALE *Obed. Chr. Man* To Rdr. 18 Alleginge vnto them textes of logycke, of naturall philautia, of methaphisick and morall philosophy. **1569** J. SANFORD tr. *Agrippa's Van. Artes* liii. 70 The whiche because they be not in the nature of thinges, but are supposed to be aboue nature, therefore they call them transnaturall or Metaphisicke. *a* **1631** DONNE *Paradoxes* (1652) 25 And that poore knowledg.. we call Metaphysicke, supernaturall. **1663** BUTLER *Hud.* I. i. 150 He knew what's what, and that's as high As metaphysic wit can fly. **1683** E. HOOKER *Pref. Pordage's Mystic Div.* 102 Even the most Metaphysic subtilissimoes after that thei haue fatigated.. themselves with their Divisions and Subdivisions. **1750** WALPOLE *Let. to Mann* 2 Aug., The Bishop of Durham [Chandler].. is succeeded by Butler of Bristol, a metaphysic author. **1779** JOHNSON *L.P.*, *Cowley* Wks. II. 26 Milton tried the metaphysick style only in his lines upon Hobson the Carrier. **1790** BURKE *Fr. Rev.* 8 The metaphysic knight of the sorrowful countenance. **1793** W. F. MAVOR *Chr. Politics* 18 A metaphysic liberty and equality intoxicated the mad multitude. **1873** BROWNING *Red Cott. Nt.-cap* 1178 What foe would dare approach? Historic Doubt?.. Acumen metaphysic?

† **B.** *sb.*² A metaphysician. *Obs.*

a **1586** SIDNEY *Apol. Poetrie* (Arb.) 25 And the Metaphisick, though it be in the seconde and abstract notions, and therefore be counted supernaturall: yet doth hee indeede builde vpon the depth of Nature. **1589** PUTTENHAM *Eng. Poesie* I. iv. (Arb.) 25 They [poets] were the first Astronomers and Philosophists and Metaphisicks. **1623** COCKERAM, *Metaphisicks*, one skild in these Artes. *Metaphysicke*.

meta'physic, *v. rare.* [f. prec. sb. Cf. F. *métaphysiquer*.] *trans.*

a. To treat metaphysically. **b.** To ply with metaphysics.

1782 H. WALPOLE *Lett. to G. Hardinge* Priv. Corr. (1820) IV. 306 A piece of genuine French, not metaphysicked by La Harpe, by Thomas, &c. **1801** [see METAPHORIZE *v.*].

metaphysical (mɛtəˈfɪzɪkəl), *a.* [f. METAPHYSIC + -AL¹.]

1. a. Of or belonging to, or of the nature of, metaphysics; such as is recognized by metaphysics.

1432-50 [see METAPHYSIC *sb.*¹ 1]. **1532** MORE *Confut. Tindale* Wks. 386/1 Argumentes grounded vpon philosophy & metaphisicall reasons. **1550** NICOLLS *Thucyd.* v b, The sciences that he calleth speculatiue, be the metaphisicals. **1646** SIR T. BROWNE *Pseud. Ep.* VII. iii. 345 A popular expression, which will not stand a Metaphysicall and strict examination. **1660** JER. TAYLOR *Duct. Dubit.* I. v. Rule i. §6 Negative doubt is either Metaphysical or Moral. **1690** LOCKE *Hum. Und.* IV. vi. (1695) 333, 1. Moral Truth... 2. Metaphysical Truth, which is nothing but the real Existence of Things, conformable to the Ideas to which we have annexed their Names. **1792** D. STEWART *Philos. Hum. Mind* I. 72 The word *cause* expresses something which is supposed to be necessarily connected with the change; and without which it could not have happened. This may be called the *metaphysical* meaning of the word; and such causes may be called *metaphysical* or *efficient causes*. **1867** BP. FORBES *Explanation 39 Articles* i. (1881) 14 The triple distinction of God's attributes into metaphysical, intellectual, and moral. **1884** tr. *Lotze's Metaph.* II. v. 301 Instead of a metaphysical theory, what he gives is scarcely more than a logical classification.

b. Applied with more or less of reproach to reasoning, ideas, etc. which are considered over-subtle, or too abstract.

1646 BP. MAXWELL *Burd. Issachar* 31, I confesse, this Divinitie is so transcendent and Metaphysicall, that it exceeds my capacitie. **1720** SWIFT *To Yng. Clergyman* Wks. 1751 V. 24 Some Gentlemen.. are apt to fill their Sermons with Philosophical Terms and Notions of the metaphysical or abstracted Kind. **1727-41** CHAMBERS *Cycl.* s.v., The word is also used to denote something subtile, abstract, and refined. In which sense we say, such a reasoning, such a proof, is too *metaphysical*, &c.

quasi-*sb.* **1935** E. R. EDDISON *Mistress of Mistresses* x. 192 You may have a nose for metaphysicals.. but here you cry out upon no trail. I know nothing. Only, I am.

c. Applied to concepts or propositions which, by relying on abstract principles, are not considered verifiable in terms acceptable to some logical positivist or linguistic philosophers. Cf. METAPHYSICS *sb. pl.* 1 c.

1865 MILL in *Westm. Rev.* XXVII. 344 The mode of thought which M. Comte terms Metaphysical, accounts for phænomena by ascribing them, not to volitions either sublunary or celestial, but to realized abstractions. **1922** tr. *Wittgenstein's Tractatus* 151 *Where in* the world is a metaphysical subject to be noted? **1936** A. J. AYER *Lang., Truth & Logic* i. 31 We may accordingly define a metaphysical sentence as a sentence which purports to express a genuine proposition, but does, in fact, express neither a tautology nor an empirical hypothesis. **1950** R. CARNAP *Logical Found. Probability* ii. 38, I hope that nobody will misinterpret my statement of the objectivity of logical relations as a metaphysical statement of the 'subsistence' of these relations in a Platonic heaven. **1953** G. E. M. ANSCOMBE tr. *Wittgenstein's Philos. Investigations* §116 What *we* do is to bring words back from their metaphysical to their everyday use.

2. Based on abstract general reasoning; determined on theoretic or *a priori* principles.

1647 CLARENDON *Hist. Reb.* v. §361 When they saw.. that, from metaphysical considerations what might be done in case of necessity, the militia of the kingdom was actually seized on. **1773** JOHNSON in *Boswell* 8 May, There seems (said he), to be in authours a stronger right of property than that by occupancy; a metaphysical right, a right, as it were, of creation, which should from its nature be perpetual. **1826** SCOTT *Woodst.* vi, In many a case, where wars have been waged for points of metaphysical right, they have been at last gladly terminated, upon the mere hope of obtaining general tranquillity.

3. [Partly in a pseudo-etymological sense = 'beyond what is physical'.] **a.** Applied, esp. in explicit contrast to *physical*, to what is immaterial, incorporeal, and supersensible.

1577 G. HARVEY *Letter-bk.* (Camden) 56 And all that glorious company Of parsonages heroicall To greete with salutations Divine and metaphysicall. **1608** TOPSELL *Serpents* (1658) 591 The blessed Trinity.. framed both the beneficial and hurtful Creatures, either for a Physical or Metaphysical end. **1668** H. MORE *Div. Dial.* I. xxviii. (1713) 58 *Hyl.*... There is also a Substance distinct from Matter, which therefore must be immaterial, and consequently Metaphysical. **1775** HARRIS *Philos. Arrangem.* (1841) 377 Thus, having before considered physical motion, have we now considered what may be called metaphysical, or.. causative motion. **1864** LOWELL *Fireside Trav.* 316 Beautiful as fire is in itself, I suspect that part of the pleasure is metaphysical, and that the sense of playing with an element which can be so terrible adds to the zest of the spectacle. **1877** S. COX *Salv. Mundi* iv. 56 That.. the wicked will be turned into a place of.. torment physical or metaphysical.

b. That is above or goes beyond the laws of nature; belonging to an operation or agency which is more than physical or natural; supernatural.

1590 MARLOWE *2nd Pt. Tamberl.* IV. ii, The essentiall fourme of Marble stone, Tempered by science metaphisicall, And Spels of magicke from the mouthes of spirits. **1605** SHAKS. *Macb.* I. v. 30 The Golden Round, Which Fate and Metaphysicall ayde doth seeme To haue thee crown'd withall. **1628** WITHER *Brit. Rememb.* II. 1059 The Pestilence.. partly metaphysicall appears, And partly naturall. **17..** WARBURTON *Note on Rape of Lock* I. 20 As the subject of the epic consists of two parts, the metaphysical and the civil. **1822** SCOTT *Pirate* xxxviii, In these plain words there is no metaphysical delusion. **1847** EMERSON *Repr. Men, Goethe* Wks. (Bohn) I. 392 The lurking dæmons sat to him,.. and the metaphysical elements took form.

† **c.** Surpassing what is natural or ordinary; extraordinary, transcendent. *Obs.*

1589 GREENE *Menaphon* (Arb.) 75 The excellence of such a Metaphysicall vertue, I meane (shepheards) the fame of your faire Samela, houering in the eares of euerie man as a miracle of nature.

d. *Christian Science.* Applied to that which transcends matter or the physical; ***metaphysical healer***, one who heals physical ills through metaphysics; so ***metaphysical healing***.

1876 A. B. ALCOTT *Jrnls.* (1938) 466 A wider acquaintance with idealism in its various phases will be serviceable to these 'Metaphysical Healers' and 'Christian Scientists' as they call their school. **1884** M. B. EDDY in *Christian Sci. Jrnl.* 2 Feb. 2 Metaphysical healing, or Christian Science, is a demand of the times. **1907** 'MARK TWAIN' *Christian Sci.* I. 70 Mrs. Eddy is president of the Trust's Metaphysical College in Boston, where the student of C.S. healing learns the game by a three weeks' course. **1939** M. GREGORY *Psychotherapy* iv. 178 Students, intoxicated with her doctrines, came there for instruction in metaphysical 'obstetrics' and moral science. **1958** T. L. LEISHMAN *Why I am Christian Scientist* viii. 116 Now, as then, signs and wonders are wrought in the metaphysical healing of physical disease. **1972** *Pioneers in Christian Sci.* (Mary Baker Eddy Mus., Longyear Hist. Soc.), Asa Gilbert Eddy.. studied with her and began the practice of metaphysical healing.

4. Of persons, their minds, etc.: Addicted to or fitted for the study of metaphysics.

a **1628** F. GREVILLE *Sidney* (1652) 175 Many Metaphysicall Phormio's before me, who had lost themselves in teaching Kings, and Princes, how to govern their People. *a* **1652** J. SMITH *Sel. Disc.* i. 24 The fourth is ἄνθρωπος θεωρητικος, the true metaphysical and contemplative man. **1683** PETTUS *Fleta Min.* II. 3 Majerus and Spagnetus .. being a sort of Metaphisical Chimists, who do make it a chief Principle of that Science to be strict in their Devotion towards God. **1853** KINGSLEY *Hypatia* I. Pref. 12 In the more metaphysical and contemplative East. **1856** MRS. STOWE *Dred* I. xv. 203 His metaphysical talent.

Comb. **1654** GAYTON *Pleas. Notes* 117 A Metaphysicall pated Disputant.

5. Adopted by Johnson as the designation of certain 17th cent. poets (chief of whom were Donne and Cowley) addicted to 'witty conceits' and far-fetched imagery. In more recent use, of poetry which expresses emotion within an intellectual context; also *ellipt.* as *sb.*, a metaphysical poet. Hence **metaphysi'cality**, the quality of being metaphysical.

[**1693** DRYDEN *Orig. & Progr. Satire* Ess. (ed. Ker) II. 19 He [Donne] affects the metaphysics, not only in his satires, but in his amorous verses, where nature only should reign; and perplexes the minds of the fair sex with nice speculations of philosophy, when he should engage their hearts... In this.. Mr. Cowley has copied him to a fault.] *a* **1744** POPE in J. Spence *Anecd.* (1820) 173 Cowley.. as well as Davenant borrowed his metaphysical style from Donne. **1779** JOHNSON *L.P.*, *Cowley* Wks. II. 22 About the beginning of the seventeenth century appeared a race of writers that may be termed the metaphysical poets... The metaphysical poets were men of learning, and to shew their learning was their whole endeavour. **1785** T. WARTON *Milton's Poems* Pref. 15 But what are these conceptions [of Cowley's]? Metaphysical conceits, all the unnatural extravagancies of his English poetry. **1814** SOUTHEY in *Q. Rev.* XII. 82 The metaphysical school, which marred a good poet in Cowley, and found its proper direction in Butler, expired in Norris of Bemerton. **1898** G. SAINTSBURY *Short Hist. Eng. Lit.* VII. ii. 412 Crashaw is perhaps the chief metaphysical, the type of the whole class. **1906** H. J. C. GRIERSON *First Half 17th Cent.* ix. 374 In Donne's love-poetry there is a real metaphysical strain, while the range of erudition from which he draws his imagery was something altogether new. **1921** G. SAINTSBURY in *Times Lit. Suppl.* 27 Oct. 698/2 [Dryden] might.. so use 'metaphysics' as equivalent to 'second thoughts', things that come *after* the natural first; and, once more, this definition would, I think, fit all the poetry commonly called 'metaphysical'. *Ibid.*, I only hope that in a second edition he will add a few more 'specimens' of the lighter metaphysicality. **1936** *Essays & Stud.* XXI. 137, I use 'metaphysical' not in the Johnsonian sense of 'conceited', but as implying a certain refinement and complexity of thought—a kind of ecstasy of intellectual parturition as we find it in Shakespeare and Donne. **1947** C. DAY LEWIS *Colloq. Element Eng. Poetry* 21 The poets of the Romantic Movement gave an outlet to new ideas.. beneath the crust of their age, just as the Metaphysicals had done for the new ideas of their time. **1955** R. GRAVES *Crowning Privilege* ii. 27 Dryden's conversion from metaphysicality was not to the poetic faith of his English predecessors, but to current French theory. **1960** D. DAICHES *Crit. Hist. Eng. Lit.* II. xiv. 1114 The insistence that intellect and emotion should work together in poetry and that one should seek to recover the 'unified sensibility' of the metaphysical poets. *Ibid.* 1116 But the poets who began to write in the late 1920's and 1930's saw both Hopkins and Eliot as their masters, as well as the metaphysicals.. and the popular singers of the English music hall.

6. Used for: Fanciful, fantastic, imaginary.

1727-41 CHAMBERS *Cycl.* s.v., A *metaphysical* case, is an imaginary or chimerical case, which can scarce ever happen, or not without much difficulty; and which ought not to be laid down as a rule for common occasions. **1809** J. LAWRENCE *Hist. Horse* 125 The colours of horses, notwithstanding the metaphysical notions of former days, are of very little consequence in relation to their goodness. **1827** SCOTT *Chron. Canongate* Introd. i, Those metaphysical persons whom the law of the neighbouring country terms John Doe and Richard Roe.

7. in appos. use, as ***metaphysical-aesthetical***, ***metaphysical-epistemic*** adjs.

1963 *Times Lit. Suppl.* 4 Jan. 4/4 Dr. Kramrisch does not disdain any of the resources of jargon, metaphysical-aesthetical, aesthetical-theosophical. **1971** *Hist. of Sci.* X. 111 A consistent and effective metaphysical-epistemic understanding of science.

metaphysically (mɛtəˈfɪzɪkəlɪ), *adv.* [f. prec. + -LY².] In a metaphysical manner or sense; according to the principles of metaphysics; from a metaphysical point of view.

1579 J. JONES *Preserv. Bodie & Soule* I. lx. 90 Whether they be Mathematically measured, or Metaphisically pondered. **1616** CHAMPNEY *Voc. Bps.* 13 To haue true authoritie or calling; and to haue true and sufficient proofe of the same, are not heere nicely or metaphysically distinguished. **1748** HARTLEY *Observ. Man* I. iv. §3 The same Conclusion follows, tho' we should suppose the Punishments of a future State not to be absolutely and metaphysically infinite. **1790** BURKE *Fr. Rev.* Wks. 1808 V. 126 The pretended rights of these theorists are all extremes; and in proportion as they are metaphysically true, they are morally and politically false. **1897** B. A. W. RUSSELL *Found. Geom.* 68 Metaphysically, space has no elements.

† **b.** Supernaturally; preternaturally. *Obs.*

1580 G. HARVEY *Three Proper Lett.* 20 The Eclipse of the Sunne that darkened all the Earth.. at Christes Passion, happening altogether prodigiously and Metaphysically in *Plenilunio*. **1607** TOPSELL *Four-f. Beasts* (1658) 384 The proverb.. may as well be applyed metaphysically to the Beast Linx, as Poetically to the man Lynceus.

metaphysician (mɛtəfɪˈzɪʃən). [a. F. *métaphysicien* (14th c.), f. METAPHYSIC: see -ICIAN.]

1. One who is versed in metaphysics.

1597 G. HARVEY *Trimm. Nashe* Wks. (Grosart) III. 22 Thoughe (as I am a Cirurgeon) I coulde picke your teeth, for the other stinkinge breath, yet this I durst not meddle with, this hath neede of a metaphisition. **1654** WHITLOCK *Zootomia* 160 The very essence of them, or *immediatè consequens Essentiam* (as the Metaphysitians word it), that which is but one degree from their Essence. **1677** HORNECK *Gt. Law Consid.* iv. (1704) 239 The Metaphysician, that speculates things above sense and nature. **1796** BURKE *Let. Noble Ld.* Wks. 1808 VIII. 57 Nothing can be conceived more hard than the heart of a thoroughbred metaphysician. **1818** BYRON *Juan* I. xci, He.. turn'd, without perceiving his condition, Like Coleridge, into a metaphysician. **1877** E. R. CONDER *Bas. Faith* iv. 145 Metaphysicians, it seems, have always been trying to get at the back of knowledge. **1936** A.

J. AYER *Lang., Truth & Logic* i. 33 The metaphysician fails to see this [*sc.* 'substance' fallacy] because he is misled by a superficial grammatical feature of his language. **1956** J. O. URMSON *Philos. Analysis* vii. 110 But let us now suppose that the technical statements we are brought up against are the technical statements of metaphysicians. **1958** G. J. WARNOCK *Eng. Philos. since 1900* ix. 121 Even if..the conclusion could really be drawn that the metaphysician's employment of language was without significance.

2. One who practises metaphysical healing. Cf. METAPHYSICAL *a.* 3 d.

1881 M. B. EDDY *Sci. & Health* (ed. 3) iii. 151 Metaphysicians can heal the sick, absent from them: space is no obstacle to mind.

Hence **metaphy'sicianism** *nonce-wd.*, metaphysical philosophizing.

a **1849** POE *Imp of Perverse* Wks. 1865 I. 353 Phrenology, and in great measure, metaphysicianism have been concocted *à priori.* —— *E. B. Browning* ibid. III. 423 The preposterously anomalous metaphysicianism of Coleridge.

metaphysicize (mɛtəˈfɪzɪsaɪz), *v.* [f. METAPHYSIC + -IZE.]

1. *intr.* To indulge in metaphysical speculation; to think, talk or write metaphysically. Also quasi-*trans.* with *away*: To get rid of by such studies. Hence **meta'physicizing** *vbl. sb.*

1793 SOUTHEY *Let. to G. C. Bedford* 26 Oct. in *Life* (1849) I. 185, I have been reading the history of philosophy..till I have metaphysicized away all my senses. ?**1796** COLERIDGE *Unpubl. Lett. to J. P. Estlin* (1884) 18, I would write Odes and Sonnets morning and evening, and metaphysicize at noon. **1823** DE QUINCEY *Walking Stewart* Wks. 1858 VIII. 3 He was everlastingly metaphysicizing against metaphysics. **1889** J. M. ROBERTSON *Ess. Crit. Method* 164 We are either witnessing a confusion of thought or a very subtle piece of metaphysicizing.

2. *trans.* To treat or expound metaphysically.

1830 WILSON in *Blackw. Mag.* XXVII. 943 Boscovich has metaphysicized matter, and shewn that there need be none. .. Others have metaphysicized vision.

metaphysico- (mɛtəˈfɪzɪkəʊ), used as combining form of METAPHYSIC *a.*, in the sense 'partly metaphysical, partly...'

1757 WARBURTON in W. & Hurd *Lett.* (1809) 229 Pray ask our friend..whether my metaphysico-ethical philosophy be right. **1848** D. G. ROSSETTI *Let.* 20 Aug. (1965) I. 40 Hunt's stanzas..partook of the metaphysico-mysterioso-obscure. **1850** H. L. MANSEL *Lett., Lect. & Rev.* (1873) 12 Another metaphysico-grammatical theory. **1904** *Q. Rev.* July 266 The absence of the metaphysico-religious element in his constitution. **1904** *Brit. Med. Jrnl.* 15 Oct. 961 'Responsibility' was not a medical conception: it was a metaphysico-legal conception. **1905** *Spectator* Suppl. 28 Jan. 119/1 One of those extremely clever and almost painfully 'up-to-date' metaphysico-theological books which America produces in such abundance. **1930** D. B. W. LEWIS *Stuffed Owl* p. xx, Verse which..crystallises the metaphysico-theologo-cosmologo-nigology to which the best modern thought..inclines. **1936** L. S. STEBBING in Day Lewis & Stebbing *Imagination & Thinking* 15 The truth of this statement is logically independent of any metaphysico-psychologist's *-ism.* **1955** H. B. ACTON *Illusion of Epoch* 3 The criticisms that apply no more to it than they do to other metaphysico-ethical systems.

†**metaphy'sicous**, *a. Obs. rare*$^{-1}$. [f. METAPHYSIC + -OUS.] Versed in metaphysics, metaphysical.

1683 E. HOOKER *Pref. Pordage's Mystic Div.* 95 Let men boast of..their elaborate Demonstrations, made out by the most Metaphysicous Divines, in Religion.

metaphysics (mɛtəˈfɪzɪks), *sb. pl.* [pl. of METAPHYSIC *sb.*, repr. med.L. *metaphysica* (neut. pl.), med.Gr. (τὰ) μεταφυσικά (neut. pl.), an alteration of the older τὰ μετὰ τὰ φυσικά, 'the (works) after the Physics' (cf. META- and PHYSICS), the title applied, at least from the 1st century A.D., to the 13 books of Aristotle dealing with questions of 'first philosophy' or ontology.

This title doubtless originally referred (as some of the early commentators state) to the position which the books so designated occupied in the received arrangement of Aristotle's writings (τὰ φυσικά being used to signify, not the particular treatise so called, but the whole collection of treatises relating to matters of natural science). It was, however, from an early period used as a name for the branch of study treated in these books, and hence came to be misinterpreted as meaning 'the science of things transcending what is physical or natural'. This misinterpretation is found, though rarely, in Greek writers, notwithstanding the fact that μετά does not admit of any such sense as 'beyond' or 'transcending'. In scholastic Latin writers the error was general (being helped, perhaps, by the known equivalence of the prefixes *meta-* and *trans-* in various compounds); and in English its influence is seen in the custom, frequent down to the 17th c., of explaining *metaphysical* by words like 'supernatural', 'transnatural', etc.]

1. a. That branch of speculative inquiry which treats of the first principles of things, including such concepts as being, substance, essence, time, space, cause, identity, etc.; theoretical philosophy as the ultimate science of Being and Knowing.

Formerly often preceded by *the* (cf. 'the mathematics'). Now usually construed as singular.

1569 J. SANFORD tr. *Agrippa's Van. Artes* liii. 70 Of the Metaphisickes, that is, thinges supernaturall and the Science of them. **1596** SHAKS. *Tam. Shr.* I. i. 37 The Mathematickes, and the Metaphysickes, Fall to them as you finde your stomacke serues you. *a* **1619** FOTHERBY *Atheom.* II. xiv. §2 (1622) 356 The Metaphysickes, considering the pure essence of things. **1651** HOBBES *Leviath.* IV. xlvi. 376 If such Metaphysiques..be not Vain Philosophy, there was never any. **1677** GALE *Crt. Gentiles* II. IV. 211 May we not take it for granted that nothing properly belongs to Metaphysics but what is Supernatural, as the name importes. **1697** J. SERGEANT *Solid Philos.* 459 Hence is demonstrated, that Metaphysicks is absolutely the Highest Science. **1718** J. CHAMBERLAYNE *Relig. Philos.* Pref. (1730) 1, I have not made use of the Metaphysicks. **1775** HARRIS *Philos. Arrangem.* (1841) 368 Metaphysics are properly conversant about primary and internal causes. **1845** MAURICE *Mor. & Met. Philos.* in *Encycl. Metrop.* II. 545/1 It is impossible to follow the track of any great moral question without entering into the region of pure Metaphysics. **1847** TENNYSON *Princess* III. 283 'How', she cried, 'you love The metaphysics!' *a* **1862** BUCKLE *Misc. Wks.* (1872) I. 506 Metaphysics, as it must be the end of all Knowledge, so it was the beginning of all Knowledge. **1951** G. J. WARNOCK in Edwards & Pap *Mod. Introd. Philos.* (1973) 781, I do not know..how the term 'metaphysics' really ought to be defined. I suspect..that it is useless to try to divide philosophy into compartments. **1959** P. F. STRAWSON *Individuals* viii. 247 If metaphysics is the finding of reasons, good, bad or indifferent, for what we believe on instinct, then this has been metaphysics. **1960** C. C. GILLISPIE *Edge of Objectivity* xi. 496 Comte had to..repudiate not only metaphysics but also ontology. Thus would he deprive science of any and every claim to deal with objective reality or with any truth deeper than consistency or efficacy. **1967** J. W. YOLTON *Metaphysical Analysis* (1968) xi. 189 The typical double level of metaphysics: the level of exposition, which is always external to the system being developed, and the level of participation in the system.

fig. *a* **1658** CLEVELAND *Gen. Poems* (1677) 13 Call her the Metaphysicks of her Sex, And say she tortures Wits, as Quartans vex Physicians.

b. With *of*: The theoretical principles or higher philosophical *rationale* of some particular branch of knowledge. Occas. construed as *sing.*

1845 CRAIK *Hist. Lit. Eng.* V. 200 Burke was our first..writer on the philosophy of practical politics. The mere metaphysics of that science..he held..in..contempt. **1859** MILL in *Fraser's Mag.* LIX. 489/2 His [*sc.* Austin's] book on the *Province of Jurisprudence* stepped at once into the very highest authority on what may be termed the metaphysics of law. **1872** O. W. HOLMES *Poet Breakf.-t.* iv. 125 The metaphysics of attention have hardly been sounded to their depths. **1958** W. STARK *Sociol. of Knowl.* I. iv. 197 A metasociology which would be, not a metaphysics, in so far as metaphysics is divorced from the empirical, but a study of man as he appears in all societies. **1964** A. W. GOULDNER in I. L. Horowitz *New Sociol.* 209 This..is a metaphysics of the underworld, in which conventional society is seen from the standpoint of a group outside of its own respectable structures.

c. In various inaccurate or extended uses (partly based on the erroneous etymology mentioned above): see quots. Used by some followers of positivist, linguistic, or logical philosophy: concepts of an abstract or speculative nature which are not verifiable by logical or linguistic methods.

1727–41 CHAMBERS *Cycl.* s.v., Some define metaphysics, that part of science which considers spirits, and immaterial beings. **1776** ADAM SMITH *W. N.* v. i. (1869) II. 355 What are called metaphysics or pneumatics were set in opposition to physics **1836–7** SIR W. HAMILTON *Metaph.* vii. (1859) I. 121 The Philosophy of Mind,—Psychology or Metaphysics, in the widest signification of the terms,—is three-fold. **1857** BUCKLE *Civiliz.* iii. 149, I mean by metaphysics, that vast body of literature which is constructed on the supposition that the laws of the human mind can be generalized solely from the facts of individual consciousness. **1865** MILL in *Westm. Rev.* XXVII. 347 In repudiating metaphysics, M. Comte did not interdict himself from analysing or criticising any of the abstract conceptions of the mind. **1936** A. J. AYER *Lang., Truth & Logic* 30 Philosophy, as a genuine branch of knowledge, must be distinguished from metaphysics. **1937** A. SMEATON tr. *Carnap's Logical Syntax of Lang.* 8 The sentences of metaphysics are pseudo-sentences which on logical analysis are proved to be either empty phrases or phrases which violate the rules of syntax. **1956** J. O. URMSON *Philos. Analysis* vii. 106 The view of Wittgenstein that metaphysics was not merely outdated as the old positivism had it, but was a logically impossible enterprise, being excluded by the essential nature of language. **1957** S. KÖRNER in C. A. Mace *Brit. Philos. in Mid-Cent.* 126 This principle [of verification]..has dominated European thought for at least three centuries..and its acceptance does not mean, therefore, the end of metaphysics as had been believed by some logical positivists. **1966** R. STERNFELD *Frege's Logical Theory* II. iii. 55 Thus, the general problem of existence is simply replaced by arithmetical attribution, plus Frege's philosophic superstructure. And this portion of metaphysics is replaced by arithmetic.

†**2.** Used by Marlowe for: Occult or magical lore. (Cf. METAPHYSICAL *a.* 3 b.) *Obs.*

c **1590** MARLOWE *Faust.* i. (1604) A3 These Metaphysickes of Magicians, And Negromantike bookes are heauenly.

metaphysiology, etc.: see META- 1.

metaphysis (mɛˈtæfɪsɪs). [mod.L., ad. assumed Gr. *μετάφυσις, f. μεταφύεσθαι to become by change, f. μετα- META- + φυ- to grow.]

1. Transformation; metamorphosis. *rare*$^{-0}$.

1755 in JOHNSON (citing *Dict.*).

2. *Anat.* [after DIAPHYSIS, EPIPHYSIS.] The region either at one or at both ends of a growing long bone which lies between the diaphysis and the epiphysial cartilage and which is the site of advancing ossification.

1913 DORLAND *Med. Dict.* (ed. 7) 560/2 *Metaphysis*, the end of the diaphysis of a long bone where it joins the epiphysis. **1926** *Biochem. Jrnl.* XX. 380 The upper end of the tibia was isolated and slices..containing the epiphyseal cartilage, the metaphysis and a little of the shaft were made. **1947** *Radiology* XLIX. 347/1 In the rat the isotopes that seek bone come down not only in old bone but predominantly in the zone of new bone growth in the metaphysis. **1966** *Lancet* 31 Dec. 1430/1 The proximal metaphysis contained less bone than the distal metaphysis in both control and treated animals.

Hence **metaphyseal**, **-physial** *adjs.* (mɛtəˈfɪzɪəl, -fɪˈsiːəl), of or pertaining to a metaphysis.

1913 DORLAND *Med. Dict.* (ed. 7) 560/2 *Metaphyseal*, pertaining to a metaphysis. **1931** D. M. GREIG *Clin. Observations Surg. Path. Bone* vii. 190 This slim exostosis has doubtless been one of the earliest manifestations of the metaphysial growth disturbance. **1961** *Lancet* 30 Sept. 744/2 Vertebral osteomyelitis commences in the metaphyseal region of the vertebral body. **1966** *Ibid.* 31 Dec. 1430/1 This appearance resembled the metaphysial sclerosis sometimes seen in vertebræ of patients with secondary hyperparathyroidism.

metaphyte, **-phytic**, **-phyton**: see META- 4.

‖**metaplasia** (mɛtəˈpleɪzɪə). *Phys.* and *Path.* [mod.L., as if a. Gr. *μεταπλασία, f. μεταπλάσσειν to mould into a new form, f. μετα- META- + πλάσσειν to mould.] Transformation of one kind of adult tissue into another.

1890 *Syd. Soc. Lex*, s.v., Cartilage is transformed into mucoid or areolar tissue, or into bone, by undergoing metaplasia. **1896** *Allbutt's Syst. Med.* I. 202 Among normal tissues a transformation of one variety into another..has received from Virchow the distinctive name of metaplasia.

‖**metaplasis** (mɛˈtæpləsɪs). *Biol.* [mod.L., after G. *metaplase* (Haeckel 1866), a. Gr. μετάπλασις, n. of action f. μεταπλάσσειν: see prec.] Haeckel's term for the middle or adult period of ontogenetic development: correlated with *anaplasis* and *cataplasis.*

1888 HYATT in *Proc. Boston Soc. Nat. Hist.* XXIII. 405.

metaplasm[1] (ˈmɛtəplæz(ə)m). [ad. L. *metaplasmus* (app. used by Quintilian in the sense of rhetorical figure), Gr. μεταπλασμ-ός (explained by L. & Sc. as the formation of cases or tenses from a stem different from that of the nom. or pres.), f. μεταπλάσσειν: see prec.] **a.** *Rhet.* The transposition of words from their usual or natural order. **b.** *Gram.* The alteration of a word by addition, removal or transposition of letters or syllables. Also, the formation of oblique cases from a stem other than that of the nominative.

[**1432–50** tr. *Higden* (Rolls) VI. 183 Of the rewles of feete metricalle, of metaplasmus, of dialog metricalle.] **1617** COLLINS *Def. Bp. Ely* II. x. 475 So fares it in this Metaplasme of names many times: *Dignos et indignos non iam discernit dignitas, sed confundit.* **1758** NUGENT tr. *Port Royal's Method Lat. Tongue* I. 327 This Metaplasm or transformation is made by adding, taking away, or changing, either a letter, or a syllable. **1889** HANSSEN in *Amer. Jrnl. Philol.* X. 39 *Intercalarius* (but it is possible that this latter is simply a metaplasm for *intercalaris*).

metaplasm[2] (ˈmɛtəplæz(ə)m). *Biol.* [f. META- + *-plasm* as in *protoplasm.*] That part of protoplasm which contains the formative material.

1875 BENNETT & DYER tr. *Sachs' Bot.* 41 *note*, J. Hanstein gives to the substances mingled with the true protoplasm and which undergo many transformations, the collective name of 'Metaplasm'. **1877** RAY LANKESTER in *Q. Jrnl. Microsc. Sci.* XVII. 403 Granular matter, which as metaplasm is distinguished from the hyaline protoplasm in which such granules float.

metaplast (ˈmɛtəplæst). *Gram.* [as if ad. Gr. *μεταπλαστόν neut. vbl. adj., f. μεταπλάσσειν: cf. METAPLASM[1].] A noun of which the cases are formed from different stems.

1864 in WEBSTER. **1877** MARCH *Comp. Ags. Gram.* §100. 52 Irregular Nouns. Such are without case-endings (Indeclinable),..or they vary..in stem (Metaplasts), [etc.].

metaplastic (mɛtəˈplæstɪk), *a.* [ad. assumed Gr. *μεταπλαστικός, f. μεταπλάσσειν: see METAPLASIA.]

1. *Gram.* Characterized by METAPLASM (1 b).

1877 MARCH *Comp. Ags. Gram.* §100. 52 Many conforming regulars, and heteroclites, are metaplastic.

2. *Biol.* Relating to metaplasis.

1888 HYATT in *Proc. Boston Soc. Nat. Hist.* XXIII. 405 Metaplastic relations.

3. *Phys.* Relating to metaplasia.

1890 in *Syd. Soc. Lex.*

metaplastology (mɛtəplæˈstɒlədʒɪ). *Biol.* [f. METAPLAST-IC + -(O)LOGY.] Haeckel's term for the relationship of the phenomena of metaplasis to those of the acme in phylogeny.

1888 HYATT [see METAPLASTIC 2].

‖**metapleuron** (ˈmɛtəplʊərɒn). Pl. **metapleura** (-ˈplʊərə). Also in anglicized forms **metapleur(e).** [mod.L., f. Gr. μετα- META- + πλευρά rib.] See quot. 1875. **a.** *Ent.* (see quot. 1848). **b.** *Zool.* In

the Amphioxus (see quot.). Hence **meta'pleural** *a.*, relating to the metapleura.

1848 MAUNDER *Treas. Nat. Hist.* 794 *Metapleura*, the lateral surfaces of the metathorax. **1875** RAY LANKESTER in *Q. Jrnl. Microsc. Sci.* XV. 267 Metapleura, the upstanding hollow ridges or latero-ventral folds which, in Amphioxus, form the lateral margins of the ventral surface. *Ibid.* 262 The latero-ventral (metapleural) lymph space. *Ibid.* 263 The lumen of the metapleur of Amphioxus. **1888** ROLLESTON & JACKSON *Anim. Life* 439 The epipleures form two prominent longitudinal folds—the metapleures.

metapneumonic, -pneustic: see META- 2, 3.

metapodial (mɛtə'pəʊdɪəl), *a.* and *sb.* [ad. mod.L. *metapodiālis* (neut. pl. *metapodiālia*: see B), f. *metapodium*: see next and -AL[1].]

A. *adj.* (In recent Dicts.)

1. Pertaining to the metapodium of molluscs.

2. Pertaining to the metapodialia (see B).

B. *sb.* One of the ‖**metapodi'alia** *sb. pl.*, the bones of the metacarpus and metatarsus taken together.

1882 WILDER & GAGE *Anat. Techn.* 42 The metapodials are comparatively simple elements. **1896** MARSH in *16th Rep. U.S. Geol. Survey* I. 185 The metapodials are much more slender and the phalanges are less robust than in the other members of the order.

‖**metapodium** (mɛtə'pəʊdɪəm). [mod.L., f. Gr. μετα- META- + ποδ-, πούς foot.]

1. *Anat.* = METATARSUS.

1856 in MAYNE *Expos. Lex.*

2. The posterior lobe of the foot in molluscs. Also anglicized **metapode** ('mɛtəpəʊd).

1853 HUXLEY in *Phil. Trans.* CXLIII. I. 36 The tail or metapodium is subcylindrical at its base. **1875** NICHOLSON *Man. Zool.* xlvii. (ed. 4) 342 In the *Heteropoda*..and in the Wingshells (*Strombidæ*), the foot exhibits a division into three portions—an anterior, the 'propodium'; a middle, the 'mesopodium'; and a posterior lobe, or 'metapodium'.

metapolitical (ˌmɛtəpə'lɪtɪkəl), *a.* [See META- I. Cf. G. *metapolitisch* (Stein, 1817).]

1. Lying outside the sphere of politics.

1647 M. HUDSON *Div. Right Govt.* II. x. 156 The limitation of the Kings power, in order to Evangelicall duties, which are *extra-regalia*, and Metapoliticall matters. **1937** J. M. MURRY *Necessity of Pacifism* ii. 38 The deep-seated social urge towards life becomes necessarily anti-political in its manifestation. Perhaps meta-political would be a better word. It points and thrusts *beyond* politics.

2. Relating to metapolitics; given to the study of metapolitics.

1809-10 COLERIDGE *Friend* (1818) II. 82 The metaphysical (or as I have proposed to call them, *metapolitical*) reasonings hitherto discussed, belong to Government in the abstract. **1878** SEELEY *Stein* III. 391 Fries, as Professor, taught a new political creed founded on the philosophy of Kant. Stein was assuredly not wrong in calling the new school *metapolitical*. **1889** CAMPION in *Lux Mundi* XI. 461 If man is 'metaphysical *nolens volens*', it is equally true that he is metapolitical, to use Martensen's happy word, *nolens volens*.

metapolitician (ˌmɛtəpɒlɪ'tɪʃən). [f. next, after *politician*.] One who holds or advocates metapolitical theories.

1809-10 [see METAPOLITICS]. **1816** SOUTHEY *Ess.* (1832) I. 390 The meta-politicians, as they have aptly been called, who bewilder themselves with abstractions. **1878** SEELEY *Stein* I. 30 Lest..the management of affairs should..pass into the hands of those whom he calls, with strong contempt, *metapoliticians*.

metapolitics (mɛtə'pɒlɪtɪks), *sb. pl.* Also *occas.* sing. **metapolitic**. [See META- I.] Abstract political science; the investigation of the speculative basis of political doctrines; *contemptuously*, unpractical political theorizing.

1784 DE LOLME *Eng. Const.* II. xvii. (ed. 4) 419 *note*, It may, if the reader pleases, belong to the Science of *Metapolitics*, in the same sense as we say *Metaphysics*. **1809-10** COLERIDGE *Friend* (1818) I. 309 *note*, As 'Metaphysics' are the science which determines what can, and what can not, be known of Being..so might the philosophy of Rousseau and his followers not inaptly be entitled, *Metapolitics*, and the Doctors of this School, Metapoliticians. **1889** CAMPION in *Lux Mundi* XI. 461 Every statesman..has consciously or unconsciously such a metapolitic.

‖**metapophysis** (mɛtə'pɒfɪsɪs). *Anat.* Pl. -ses. [mod.L., f. META- + APOPHYSIS.] A small vertebral prominence.

1866 in BRANDE & COX *Dict. Sci.*, etc. **1897** PARKER & HASWELL *Zool.* II. XXII. 420 Metapophyses and anapophyses.

metapsychic (mɛtə'saɪkɪk), *a.* [ad. F. *métapsychique*; cf. METAPSYCHICS *sb. pl.*] = next.

1905 *Westm. Gaz.* 25 Feb. 10/3 The new President [*sc.* M. Richet]..suggested the term 'metapsychic sciences' as a substitute for 'modern miracle'. **1923** S. DE BRATH tr. *Richet's 30 Yrs. Psychical Res.* 4 The terms 'supernatural' and 'supernormal' must therefore be rejected along with 'the occult'.. I proposed the term Metapsychic.

metapsychical (mɛtə'saɪkɪkəl), *a.* [f. META- + PSYCHICAL *a.*, after METAPHYSICAL *a.*] That is beyond the sphere of ordinary psychology; pertaining to METAPSYCHICS.

1905 L. I. FINCH tr. J. Maxwell (*title*) Metapsychical phenomena. **1914** A. L. TEIXEIRA DE MATTOS tr. *Maeterlinck's Unknown Guest* 50 Nevertheless it may be said that these regions quite lately annexed by metapsychical science are as yet hardly explored. **1927** *Glasgow Herald* 19 Apr. 12 The author of this book was the director of the Metapsychical Institute of Paris.

metapsychics (mɛtə'saɪkɪks), *sb. pl.* [ad. F. *métapsychique* (C. Richet 1905, in *Proc. Soc. Psychical Research* XIX. 2), f. Pol. *metapsychika* (W. Lutosławski 1902, in *Wykłady Jagiellońskie* II), after METAPHYSICS *sb. pl.*] A name applied to a science or study of certain phenomena which are 'beyond the scheme of orthodox psychology'. Cf. PARAPSYCHOLOGY.

1905 O. LODGE in L. I. Finch tr. *Maxwell's Metapsychical Phenomena* p. xi, To emphasise the fact that these occurrences are at present beyond the scheme of orthodox psychology..Professor Richet has suggested that they be styled 'meta-psychical phenomena', and that the nascent branch of science..be called for the present 'Metapsychics'. **1922** B. MIALL tr. *Maeterlinck's Gt. Secret* xi. 249 The recent researches of Dr. W. Crawford which have made a sensation in the world of metapsychics. **1957** *Encycl. Brit.* XXI. 245/1 A group of investigators..are not prepared to accept the explanation in terms of human survival and.. therefore dislike the term spiritualism, preferring to employ some noncommittal term such as metapsychics or parapsychology.

Hence **meta'psychism**; **meta'psychist**, a student of metapsychics.

1922 *Glasgow Herald* 27 Oct. 4 Modern spiritualism, under the term Metapsychism, is favourably viewed. **1922** B. MIALL tr. *Maeterlinck's Gt. Secret* xi. 216 Our occultists, who are now assuming the name of metapsychists. **1927** *Brit. Jrnl. Psychical Res.* I. VII. 207 It was said that the English spiritualists did not understand the French metapsychists. **1928** *Daily Express* 27 June 6/4 What a palpitating problem for the psychologists and the metapsychists!

metapsychological (mɛtəsaɪkəʊ'lɒdʒɪkəl), *a.* [f. next.] Of or pertaining to metapsychology.

1922 J. STRACHEY tr. *Freud's Group Psychol.* 63 It is much more difficult to give a clear metapsychological representation of the distinction. **1924** W. B. SELBIE *Psychol. Relig.* 295 These questions..cannot be settled on psychological or even on metapsychological grounds. **1944** *Scrutiny* XII. 137 The metapsychological stage for the poet is..an attempt..to achieve some sort of compromise between a desire for ultimate belief..and the many confused modern influences which have moulded his sensibility. **1952** E. WEISS in Alexander & Ross *Dynamic Psychiatry* 61 The history of metapsychological concepts, as they developed in the study of psychoanalysis. **1972** M. SCHUR *Freud: Living & Dying* III. xiv. 375 All these metapsychological explanations can be applied to neurotic anxiety.

metapsychology (mɛtəsaɪ'kɒlədʒɪ). [f. META- I + PSYCHOLOGY.] A name given to speculative inquiry regarding the ultimate nature of the mind and its functions which cannot be studied experimentally.

1909 in *Cent. Dict.* Suppl. **1914** A. A. BRILL tr. *Freud's Psychopathol. Everyday Life* 309 We venture to explain in this way the myths of paradise and the fall of man, of God, of good and evil, of immortality and the like—that is, to transform *metaphysics* into *meta-psychology*. **1946** J. H. MASSERMAN *Princ. Dynamic Psychiatry* 285/1 *Metapsychology*, a psychological theory that cannot be verified or disproved by observation or reasoning. **1970** *Jrnl. Gen. Psychol.* LXXXIII. 71 Those who like to conceptualize their data from the point of view of psychoanalytic metapsychology. **1970** H. F. ELLENBERGER *Discovery of Unconscious* x. 754 He [*sc.* L. Daudet] also wrote nonfiction about daydreams and human personality, notably on the ego and the Self, and he called his own psychological system a metapsychology.

metapsychosis (mɛtəsaɪ'kəʊsɪs). *rare.* Pl. -oses. [f. META- + PSYCHOSIS 2.] The supposed psychic action of one mind upon another.

1885 *Proc. Soc. Psychical Res.* III. 422 It would be a grave retardation of science were it assumed that this strange metapsychosis was a medical curiosity alone. **1902** J. M. BALDWIN *Dict. Philos. & Psychol.* II. 668/2 The term metapsychosis has been suggested to designate mental stata especially of the percipient under telepathic conditions. **1945** C. WILLIAMS *All Hallows' Eve* vii. 112 The terrible metapsychosis gnawed at him.

‖**metapterygium** (ˌmɛtəptə'rɪdʒɪəm). *Ichth.* [See META-.] The hindmost section of the pterygium in certain fishes.

1878 BELL tr. *Gegenbaur's Comp. Anat.* 478 The metapterygium represents the stem of the archipterygium and the rays on it. **1880** GÜNTHER *Fishes* iv. 80 The pectoral fin is supported by three bones, pro-, meso-, and metapterygium.

Hence **metapte'rygial** *a.* (in recent Dicts.), **metapte'rygian** *a.* (*Syd. Soc. Lex.*), belonging or relating to the metapterygium.

metapterygoid (mɛtəp'tɛrɪgɔɪd). *Ichth.* [f. META- + PTERYGOID.] In full *metapterygoid bone*: A bone in the skull of a teleostean fish, which fits against the anterior border of the hyomandibular and symplectic bones.

1872 MIVART *Elem. Anat.* 395 In osseous Fishes a yet further segmentation occurs, as we find in addition a third bone, called the meta-pterygoid.

‖**metaptosis** (mɛtəp'təʊsɪs). [mod.L., a. Gr. μετάπτωσις, n. of action of μεταπίπτειν to undergo a change, f. μετα- META- + πίπτειν (πτω-) to fall.]

1. *Med.* Change in the nature or the seat of a disease. ? *Obs.*

1693 tr. *Blancard's Phys. Dict.* (ed. 2), *Metaptosis*, the degenerating of one Disease into another, as of a Quartane Ague into a Tertian; and on the contrary, of an Apoplexy into a Palsie.

2. *Logic.* 'The change of a proposition from being false to being true, or the reverse' (*Cent. Dict.* 1890).

metar, obs. form of METER *sb.*[1]

metarabic: see META- 6 a.

metargon (mɛ'tɑːgɒn). *Chem.* [f. META- + *argon*.] The name given by Sir W. Ramsay to an elementary substance obtained by him from the volatilization of the white solid which remained after the evaporation of liquid argon.

1898 *Westm. Gaz.* 17 June 7/2 Professor Ramsay, F.R.S., in continuation of his recent research on a new gas in atmospheric air, has this week gone still further... Argon, it now seems, has companion gases, their names, using the professor's nomenclature, being 'neon' (new) and 'metargon'.

metarhodopsin (ˌmɛtərəʊ'dɒpsɪn). *Biochem.* Also **meta-rhodopsin**. [f. META- + RHODOPSIN.] Either of two interconvertible intermediates (the orange metarhodopsin I and the yellow metarhodopsin II) that are formed when rhodopsin is bleached by light, being produced from lumirhodopsin and undergoing spontaneous hydrolysis to retinal and opsin.

1950 G. WALD et al. in *Science* 17 Feb. 180/1 If the solution of lumi-rhodopsin is warmed to about −20°C, a further change occurs in darkness. The absorption band shifts another 7–9 mμ toward the blue, with little further change in height or shape... We shall call this second product meta-rhodopsin. **1970** G. S. BRINDLEY *Physiol. Retina* (ed. 2) i. 11 Figure 1.4 shows the effect of pH on the absorption spectrum of metarhodopsin at 3·2°C. Increase of temperature favours the acid form ('metarhodopsin II'). *Ibid.*, It seems that when rhodopsin is bleached by light the alkaline form ('metarhodopsin I') is always formed first, and this passes quickly into the equilibrium mixture appropriate to the pH and temperature. **1975** [see LUMIRHODOPSIN].

metarsenic, meta-salts: see META- 6 a.

metarule ('mɛtəruːl). [f. META- I + RULE *sb.*] A convention or universal rule in a symbolic system, esp. a linguistic system.

1957 *Encycl. Brit.* XIV. 319/1 The inference schemas which make up the calculus are never confused with the meta-rules for their reduction to one another. **1966** J. R. ROSS in Reibel & Schane *Mod. Stud. in English: Readings in Transformational Gram.* (1969) 289, I propose that the following metarule, or convention, be added to the theory of grammar. **1970** *Language* XLVI. 28 Then objective guidelines are needed, meta-rules, to decide on the priority of application. **1972** W. LABOV in Stockwell & Macaulay *Ling. Change & Generative Theory* 160 We can then argue for an alpha-switching meta-rule which reverses the direction of the nasality constraint.

metaschematism (mɛtə'skiːmətɪz(ə)m). [ad. mod.L. *metaschēmatismus*, a. Gr. μετασχηματισμός, vbl. sb. of μετασχηματίζειν to change the form of, f. μετα- META- + σχηματ-, σχῆμα form: see -ISM.]

1. *Path.* 'A change of the form of a disease, as when hæmoptysis follows suppression of the menses' (*Syd. Soc. Lex.*, s.v. *Metaschematismus*).

1847 tr. *Von Feuchtersleben's Med. Psychol.* (Syd. Soc.) 266 *note*, Perhaps every metastasis is only a metaschematism. **1876** tr. *Wagner's Gen. Pathol.* 320 At other times they [*sc.* calculi] are transformed into other substances: Metaschematism.

2. *gen.* A fresh arrangement.

1888 *Athenæum* 18 Aug. 214/2 A new arrangement or metaschematism of atoms.

metascience ('mɛtəsaɪəns). [f. META- I + SCIENCE.] (See quot. 1938.) So **metascien'tific** *a.*, of or pertaining to metascience; **meta-scien'tifically** *adv.*

1938 C. W. MORRIS in *Internat. Encycl. Unified Sci.* I. I. 69 We may introduce the term 'metascience' as a synonym for 'the science of science'. **1953** *Brit. Jrnl. Psychol.* XLIV. 52 [Scientific] problems are periodically discarded.. because they are intrusions from 'meta-science' and depend, therefore, upon emotional bias for working solution. **1954** J. G. KEMENY in P. A. Schilpp *Philos. R. Carnap* (1963) 712 Degree of confirmation..is used meta-scientifically, it is applied to theories. **1965** P. CAWS *Philos. of Sci.* iv. 28 The clarification and refinement of concepts..is a metascientific activity. **1971** J. WIATR in R. Klibansky *Contemp. Philos.* IV. 308 Historical materialism, defined as philosophical meta-scientific reflection of the greatest importance for all the social sciences.

metascutellum, -scutum: see META- 3.

metasequoia (mɛtəsɪ'kwɔɪə, -sɪ'kɔɪə). [mod. L. (S. Miki 1941, in *Jap. Jrnl. Bot.* XI. 261), f. META- + SEQUOIA.] A deciduous, coniferous tree of the genus so called, belonging to the family

Pinaceæ and known only from fossil remains until the single living species, *Metasequoia glyptostroboides*, was discovered in the Szechuan province of China in 1941; also called dawn redwood or water fir. Also *attrib.*

1948 *Science* 6 Feb. 140/2 This living *Metasequoia* is a large tree... It is deciduous, the trees being leafless in the winter months. **1948** *Jrnl. N.Y. Bot. Garden* XLIX. 204 (*caption*) The landlord of the property where the second lot of *Metasequoia* trees was discovered. **1950** *Ecology* XXXI. 262/2 The general region within which lies the home of Metasequoia is a mountainous tableland cut by deep valleys, southeast of the Yangtze River. **1960** *Times* 19 Sept. 5/3 The 'living fossil' tree, *Metasequoia*. **1971** *Country Life* 2 Sept. 553/3 This border has a backing of large shrubs that include bamboos..and is dominated by the metasequoia.

metasericite, metasilicic: see META- 7 a, 6 a.

‖**metasoma** (mɛtəˈsəʊmə). *Zool.* Also anglicized **metasome** (ˈmɛtəsəʊm). [mod.L., f. Gr. μετα- META- + σῶμα body.]

1. In Cephalopods, the posterior portion of the body, enveloped in the mantle.

1872 NICHOLSON *Palæont.* 272 A posterior portion, enveloped in the mantle, and containing the viscera (metasoma). **1882** OGILVIE, *Metasome, Metasoma.*

2. In Lamellibranchs, the part of the body which lies behind the foot.

1877 HUXLEY *Anat. Inv. Anim.* 475 The part which.. contains the posterior adductor may be termed the metasoma.

3. In Arthropods and Arachnids, the hinder portion of the animal, into which the abdomen is continued; the hinder part of the abdomen.

1893 SHIPLEY *Zool. Invert.* 398 The heart..is continued backward in the scorpion as a posterior aorta which traverses the metasoma.

metasomatic (ˌmɛtəsəʊˈmætɪk), *a.* [f. prec. or next: see -IC.]

1. *Zool.* Pertaining to the metasoma.

1890 in *Century Dict.* **1893** SHIPLEY *Zool. Invert.* 398 Extends into the narrow metasomatic segments.

2. *Geol.* Pertaining to or of the nature of METASOMATISM.

1886 T. S. HUNT *Min. Physiol. & Physiogr.* 84 A metasomatic hypothesis of the origin of crystalline rocks. **1896** VAN HISE in *16th Rep. U.S. Geol. Surv.* I. 690 Minerals ..produced from other minerals by metasomatic processes.

Hence **metasoˈmatically** *adv.*

1921 *Geol. Mag.* LVIII. 553 The great eastern mass of rauhaugite is metasomatically derived from sövite. **1965** *Amer. Mineralogist* L. 1485 Hibschite or hydrogrossular.. has long been known from..metasomatically altered anorthosites and pyroxenites.

metasomatism (mɛtəˈsəʊmətɪz(ə)m). *Geol.* [f. META- + Gr. σωματ-, σῶμα body + -ISM.] = METASOMATOSIS.

1886 T. S. HUNT *Min. Physiol. & Physiogr.* 83 Constituting what has been appropriately designated metasomatism. **1896** VAN HISE in *16th Rep. U.S. Geol. Surv.* I. 689 Metasomatism may be defined as the process of metamorphism by which original minerals are partly or wholly altered into other minerals, or are replaced by other minerals, or are recrystallized without chemical changes.

Hence **metaˈsomatist**, one who holds the geological theory of metasomatosis (*Funk's Stand. Dict.* 1895).

metasomatize (mɛtəˈsəʊmətaɪz), *v.* *Geol.* [f. METASOMAT(ISM + -IZE.] *trans.* To change as a result of metasomatism. So **metaˈsomatized** *ppl. a.*

1942 *Mineral. Abstr.* VIII. 242 Xenoliths of siltstone or sandstone country-rock are metasomatized to granophyre. **1955** *Mineral. Mag.* XXX. 681 The carbonatite contains abundant fragments of fine-grained phlogopite-rock, which can be shown to represent metasomatized fragments of brecciated gneiss. **1963** Metasomatized [see JOHANNSENITE].

metasomatome (mɛtəˈsəʊmətəʊm). *Anat.* [f. META- (app. used unjustifiably in the sense 'between') + SOMATOME.] (See quot.) Hence **metasomaˈtomic** *a.*

1857 GOODSIR in *Edin. New Philos. Jrnl.* V. 122 As the mouth is only one of a number of openings situated between somatomes, I find such openings conveniently distinguished as metasomatomic. **1858** HUXLEY in *Proc. Roy. Soc.* (1859) IX. 426 Professor Goodsir's terms of *Somatomes* for the segments and *Metasomatomes* for their interspaces. *Ibid.* 427 The intervals between every pair of metasomatomes.

‖**metasomatosis** (ˌmɛtəsəʊməˈtəʊsɪs). *Geol.* [mod.L., f. META- + Gr. σωματ-, σῶμα body + -OSIS.] The transformation of one rock into another of an entirely different kind.

1886 T. S. HUNT *Min. Physiol. & Physiogr.* 105 Although the crystalline rocks..have been supposed to be..the subject of wide-spread metasomatosis. **1888** TEALL *Brit. Petrogr.* 438 *Metasomatosis*, the change of material due to chemical agencies, undergone by rocks subsequent to their formation.

metasome: see METASOMA.

metasperm (ˈmɛtəspɜːm). *Bot.* [f. META- + Gr. σπέρμα seed.] = ANGIOSPERM.

1878 MACNAB *Bot.* ix. (1883) 160 Phanerogamia. A. Archisperms or Gymnosperms... B. Metasperms or Angiosperms. **1890** *Syd. Soc. Lex.*

metasplenomegalic: see META-[1] 2.

metastability (mɛtəstəˈbɪlɪtɪ). [f. next, after *stable, stability*.] The property or state of being metastable.

1901 *Jrnl. Physical Chem.* V. 270 (*heading*) The metastability of the Weston cadmium cell. **1914** W. ROSENHAIN *Introd. Study Physical Metall.* xiv. 328 The metallic state, in the conditions which prevail at the surface of the earth, is for the majority of metals a state of chemical meta-stability. **1924** *Nature* 13 Dec. 859/2 Atomic theory would suggest that these lines were connected with a faint metastability of certain possible quantum states of the atoms. **1950** *Engineering* 3 Feb. 137/3 This type of under-cooling is made possible only by the metastability of iron carbide. **1968** C. G. KUPER *Introd. Theory Superconductivity* i. 4 The latter is a small and very simple device which exploits the metastability of superconducting persistent currents.

metastable (mɛtəˈsteɪb(ə)l), *a.* [Irreg. f. META- + STABLE *a.*, as tr. of G. *metastabil* (coined in sense 1 by W. Ostwald, in *Lehrb. d. allgemeinen Chem.* (1893) II. I. 517).] **1.** Of a physical system: persisting (in its existing state) when undisturbed or subject to disturbances smaller than some small or infinitesimal amount, but passing to a more stable state when subject to greater disturbances.

1897 *Jrnl. Chem. Soc.* LXXII. II. 309 The author gives to the above form of instability, where the change to solid can only be caused by the presence of the solid itself, the name of 'metastabile' [*sic*]. *Ibid.* 777/1 (Index), Equilibrium, metastable and labile. **1899** J. WALKER *Introd. Physical Chem.* xi. 101 A supercooled liquid may be kept for a very long time without any solid appearing, but as soon as the smallest particle of the substance in the more stable solid phase is introduced, the less stable, or, as it has been called, the metastable phase is transformed into it. **1940** GLASSTONE *Text-bk. Physical Chem.* vi. 459 The term metastable is used to describe a definite equilibrium, which is nevertheless not the most stable equilibrium at the given temperature; a metastable system undergoes spontaneous change on the addition of the stable phase. **1941** J. H. KEENAN *Thermodynamics* xxiii. 404 A system is in a state of metastable equilibrium if for all infinitesimal possible variations $\Delta S)_E < 0$, that is, $\Delta E)_S > 0$, while for some finite possible variations $\Delta S)_E > 0$, that is, $\Delta E)_S < 0$. A marble at rest at the bottom of the higher of two depressions in a continuous surface is an example of metastable equilibrium. **1954** *Electronic Engin.* XXVI. 60/1 The 11 points *a, c, e,... t, u* are the stable positions corresponding to the digits 0, 1, 2,...9 and the reset point [of the counting tube], whereas the 10 points *b, d, f,...* are metastable. Suppose the anode current is at the point corresponding to *b* and a small disturbance shifts the beam to the left... The beam will then move farther away..and soon reach the point corresponding to *c* at which it will remain despite any small disturbances. **1968** C. G. KUPER *Introd. Theory Superconductivity* i. 11 Long-lived metastable states cannot be rejected *a priori* as impossible. Diamond at room temperature shows no tendency to graphitize, nor glass to crystallize. But in all cases like these the excess entropy is frozen in by the *immobility* of the atoms at low temperatures.

2. *Physics.* Of an excited state of an atom, nucleus, or other quantum-mechanical system: having an exceptionally long lifetime because the transitions to states of lower energy are forbidden transitions. [Introduced in this sense (in Ger.) by Franck & Knipping 1919, in *Physik Zeitschr.* XX. 485/2.]

1922 A. D. UDDEN tr. *Bohr's Theory of Spectra* III. 86 These experiments showed that the impact of electrons could bring helium into a 'metastable' state from which the atom cannot return to its normal state by means of a simple transition. **1942** J. D. STRANATHAN *'Particles' of Mod. Physics* xi. 455 It seems that certain nuclei can exist for considerable time in an excited state, known as a metastable state. **1961** POWELL & CRASEMANN *Quantum Mech.* xii. 458 The ground state of the orthohelium system..is therefore stable with respect to optical transitions of the usual kind, and has a correspondingly long lifetime. For this reason, it is frequently referred to as a metastable state. **1973** *Sci. Amer.* Feb. 93/2 The singlet and triplet metastable states have long lifetimes because they have no means of radiating their energy.

metastably (mɛtəˈsteɪblɪ), *adv.* [f. prec. + -LY[2].] In a metastable state.

1938 A. JOHANNSEN *Descr. Petrogr. Ign. Rocks* IV. 401 Clinopyroxenes..may form metastably at lower temperatures. **1963** W. A. DEER et al. *Rock-Forming Min.* IV. 181 The higher temperature forms..can exist metastably below their inversion temperatures. **1973** A. D. EDGAR *Exper. Petrol.* iii. 61 For some compositions it may be necessary to avoid certain very reactive components, e.g. α-cristobalite, which is known to persist metastably well below its equilibrium stability field.

Metastasian (mɛtəˈsteɪsɪən, -zɪən), *a.* [f. the name of Pietro *Metastasio* (1698–1782), Italian poet and librettist + -AN.] Of or pertaining to P. Metastasio or characteristic of his works.

1947 A. EINSTEIN *Mus. Romantic Era* ix. 89 Canzonets on Metastasian texts. **1961** *Times* 16 Feb. 16/7 The Metastasian masterpiece, *Il Zio.* **1963** *Listener* 14 Feb. 313/2 Dissatisfied with the Metastasian libretto, he looked to Paris for an alternative. **1964** *Conc. Oxf. Dict. Opera* 259/2 It was against the abuses to which Metastasian opera lent itself—above all the halting dramatic progress, with the plot continually arrested to make way for demonstrations of vocal skill—that Gluck rebelled.

‖**metastasis** (mɛˈtæstəsɪs). Pl. **metastases** (mɛˈtæstəsiːz). [late L., a. Gr. μετάστασις removal, change, n. of action of μεθιστάναι to remove, change: see META- and STASIS.]

1. *Rhet.* A rapid transition from one point to another.

1586 A. DAY *Eng. Secretary* II. (1625) 96 *Metastasis* or *Transitio*, when in briefe words we passe from one thing to another. **1589** PUTTENHAM *Eng. Poesie* III. xix. (Arb.) 240 *margin, Metastasis*, or the flitting figure, or the Remoue. **1696** PHILLIPS (ed. 5).

2. In various scientific uses.

a. *Phys.* and *Path.* The transference of a bodily function, of a pain or a disease, of morbific matter, etc. from one part or organ to another.

1663 BOYLE *Usef. Exp. Nat. Philos.* II. xx. 294 What not unfrequently happens in distempered Bodies by the *Metastasis* of the Morbifique matter. **1747** tr. *Astruc's Fevers* 354 The milk..is very often thrown on other parts, where it creates *metastases* the most incorrigible and obstinate. **1842** *Medico-Chirurg. Rev.* XXXVII. 557 Hysteria; Catalepsy; Metastasis of Hearing, &c. **1898** P. MANSON *Trop. Diseases* ix. 175 The metastasis of the pains. **1903** MYERS *Hum. Personality* I. Gloss. 19 *Metastasis*, change of the seat of a bodily function from one place..to another.

b. *Biol.* The transformation of chemical compounds into other compounds in the process of assimilation by an organism.

By some writers restricted to signify the change of non-living into other non-living matter; by others treated as synonymous with METABOLISM.

1875 BENNETT & DYER tr. *Sachs' Bot.* 626 Assimilation and Metastasis (Stoffwechsel). **1878** BELL tr. *Gegenbaur's Comp. Anat.* 13 Metastasis, or change in the arrangement of chemical elements. The body nourishes itself by replacing the material used up in metastasis by fresh matter, which is received from without.

c. *Geol.* (See quot.)

1886 BONNEY in *Proc. Geol. Soc.* 59 Metastasis (change of order), denoting changes rather of a paramorphic character, such, for example, as the crystallization of a limestone, the devitrification of a glassy rock.

3. *gen.* Transformation; change from one condition to another. *rare.*

1831 SIR W. HAMILTON *Discuss.* (1852) 21 *note*, The Infinite and Absolute are only the names of..two subjective negations, converted into objective affirmations... Some, more reasonably, call the thing unfinishable—infinite; others, less rationally, call it finished—absolute. But in both cases, the metastasis is in itself irrational. **1887** STEVENSON *Mem. & Portraits* vii. 116 The lamp and oil man, just then beginning, by a not unnatural metastasis, to bloom into a lighthouse-engineer.

metastasize (mɛˈtæstəsaɪz), *v.* *Path.* [f. METASTAS(IS + -IZE.] *intr.* Of a disease, esp. a tumour: to pass from one part or organ to another; to undergo metastasis (sense 2 a).

1907 *Jrnl. Med. Res.* XVII. 187 As might be expected the tendency to metastasize is much greater in certain tumours than in others. **1947** *Nature* 4 Jan. 15/1 Many prostatic cancers which have metastasized stand still or disappear after the removal of the patients' testicles. **1974** PASSMORE & ROBSON *Compan. Med. Stud.* III. xix. 14/2 This tumour invades neighbouring structures, advances along nerves and often recurs after local removal. It may eventually metastasize to distant organs.

metastatic (mɛtəˈstætɪk), *a.* [f. METASTASIS: cf. STATIC and rare Gr. μεταστατικός.]

1. *Min.* (See quot.)

1816 R. JAMESON *Char. Min.* (ed. 2) 218 A crystal is named ..Metastatic (metastatique), that is to say, transferred, when its plane angles and solid angles are the same as those of the nucleus, and are thus transported to the secondary form. Example, Metastatic calcareous-spar.

2. Pertaining to, characterized or produced by metastasis.

a. *Path.* **1822–34** *Good's Study Med.* (ed. 4) IV. 316 As sometimes happens in metastatic dropsy from repelled gout. **1841** *Medico-Chirurg. Rev.* XXXV. 563 Metastatic Abscess. **1892** *Tuke's Dict. Psychol. Med.* II. 697 *Metastatic Insanity*, any form of insanity which appears and disappears with the disappearance or appearance of certain physical affections, *e.g.* asthma, gout, erysipelas, &c.

b. *Biol.* **1880** BESSEY *Bot.* 186 Those metastatic changes which take place in the ordinary growth of plants.

So **metaˈstatical** *a.* = METASTATIC 1. **metaˈstatically** *adv.*, by metastasis (in recent Dicts.).

1817 R. JAMESON *Char. Min.* (ed. 3) 224 The metastatical variety of calcareous spar.

‖**metasternum** (mɛtəˈstɜːnəm). [mod.L., f. META- + STERNUM.]

1. *Ent.* The median ventral piece of the metathorax in insects.

1826 KIRBY & SP. *Entomol.* III. xxxv. 579 The central part of the *mesostethium* when elevated or porrected, or otherwise remarkable, is called the *metasternum*. **1838** WESTWOOD *Entom. Text-bk.* 272 The under surface of..the metasternum is generally a horny covering.

2. *Anat.* The xiphisternum or ensiform appendage.

1868 W. K. PARKER *Shoulder-girdle Vertebr.* 123 A supplementary sternal plate ('metasternum'). **1884** DISTANT in *Proc. Zool. Soc.* 460 Disks of meso- and metasternums pitchy. **1890** in *Syd. Soc. Lex.*

Hence **metaˈsternal** *a.*, pertaining to the metasternum; *sb.* a metasternal plate.

1826 KIRBY & SP. *Entomol.* III. xxxv. 579 The *Tettigoniæ* F. have usually a distinct metasternal point between their hind-legs. **1868** W. K. PARKER *Shoulder-girdle Vertebr.* 121

These plates are rudimentary 'meta-sternals'. **1873** LE CONTE *Classif. Lepidoptera N. Amer.* II. 312 Metasternal pores distinct.

metasthenic, metastibnite: see META- 3, 7 a.

‖**metastoma** (mɛ'tæstəmə). *Zool.* Also anglicized **metastome** ('mɛtəstəʊm). [mod.L., f. Gr. μετα- META- + στόμα mouth.]

1. The LABIUM or lower lip of crustaceans.

1859 HUXLEY in *Brit. Org. Rem., 1st Monograph* 16 The Metastoma [in Pterygotus]..is an oval plate with margins much thinner than the centre. **1876** PAGE *Adv. Text-bk. Geol.* xii. 210 A broad heart-shaped metastome or mouthpiece.

2. Haeckel's term (1872) for the secondary (*i.e.* permanent) mouth in the vertebrata.

1879 tr. *Haeckel's Evol. Man* II. 469.

‖**metastomium** (mɛtə'stəʊmɪəm). *Zool.* [Formed as prec.] Lankester's term for the whole hinder (*i.e.* the mouthed) portion of a simple metazoan soma. Hence **meta'stomial** *a.*

1877 RAY LANKESTER in *Q. Jrnl. Microsc. Sci.* XVII. 427.

metastrophe (mɛ'tæstrəfiː). [a. Gr. μεταστροφή change from one thing to another; related to μεταστρέφειν to turn round, f. μετα-, META- + στρέφειν to turn.]

†**1.** ? *nonce-use.* (See quot.)

1654 H. L'ESTRANGE *Chas. I* (1655) 93 The Town suffering a metastrophe, change of name as well as nature, was ordered to be called..Borgo Maria.

2. *Cryst.* (See quot.) Hence **meta'strophic** *a.*

1895 STORY-MASKELYNE *Crystallogr.* 99 A solid figure is symmetrical to an axis when every *radius vector* moving in a plane perpendicular to the axis and meeting a point of the figure would also meet corresponding points at the same distances from the axis at each revolution through an arc-angle of 2 π/n. The aspect of such a solid figure will not therefore be changed by a revolution of the solid round this axis through the angle 2 π/n, and any portion of its surface so revolving will move into a position in which it will be congruent with another portion of the surface entirely corresponding to it. DEF.—Congruence of this kind will be termed *metastrophe*, and such corresponding parts will be said to be *metastrophic* to each other. **1899** W. J. LEWIS *Crystallogr.* 18 We shall generally express the relation by saying that the like faces, edges and coigns disposed about an axis of symmetry are interchangeable or *metastrophic.*

metasyenite: see META- 5 b.

‖**metasyncrisis** (mɛtə'sɪnkrɪsɪs). *Path.* [mod.L., a. Gr. μετασύγκρισις, f. μετασυγκρίνειν to use diaphoretics: see META- and SYNCRISIS.]

a. The evacuation of morbid matter, esp. through the pores of the skin. **b.** (See quot. 1706.)

1541 R. COPLAND *Galyen's Terap.* 2 E j b, Metasyncresis, which may sygnyfy as moche as Metaporopoesis in Greke. That is to say, mutacyon of the state of pores & smal conduytes. **1693** tr. *Blancard's Phys. Dict.* (ed. 2), *Metasyncrisis*, the Operation of a Medicine externally applied, which fetches out the Humours from their closest Recesses. **1706** PHILLIPS (ed. Kersey), *Metasyncrisis*, a restoring of the Parts or Passages of the Body to their natural State. **1847** tr. *Feuchtersleben's Med. Psychol.* (Syd. Soc.) 38 The Methodist, Thessalus..the inventor of Metasyncrisis (μετασύγκρισις) (*recorporatio*), a method which still forms our principal..corporeal means in the treatment of insanity.

metasyncritic, -ical (mɛtəsɪn'krɪtɪk, -ɪkəl). [f. Gr. μετασυγκριτικ-ός, f. μετασύγκρισις: see prec.] Of the nature of, pertaining to, or producing metasyncrisis.

metasyncritic(al circle, cycle: 'the methodical use of metasyncritic remedies' (*Syd. Soc. Lex.* 1890).

1651 WITTIE tr. *Primrose's Pop. Err.* IV. xxxii. 329 A very strong metasyncriticall plaister. **1725** FREIND *Hist. Physick* I. 124 The Resumptive or Metasyncritical Circle. **1847** tr. *Feuchtersleben's Med. Psychol.* (Syd. Soc.) 332 The metasyncritic method. *Ibid.* 338 To excite, through the nervous system, a salutary (metasyncritical) action.

metatarsal (mɛtə'tɑːsəl), *a.* and *sb. Anat.* [f. METATARS-US + -AL[1].]

A. *adj.* Of or belonging to the metatarsus.

1739 S. SHARP *Surg.* 223 It may happen that the Bones of the Toes, and part only of the Metatarsal Bones are carious. **1899** A. H. EVANS *Birds* 10 A fusion of the second, third, and fourth metatarsal bones.

B. *sb.* Any bone of the metatarsus.

1854 OWEN *Skel. & Teeth* in *Circ. Sci.* I. *Org. Nat.* 212 The second metatarsal supports three phalanges. **1899** *Allbutt's Syst. Med.* VI. 666 Tight or badly fitting shoes exerting pressure on the head of the metatarsal.

‖**metatarsalgia** (ˌmɛtətɑː'sældʒɪə). *Path.* [f. METATARSUS + Gr. -αλγία pain.] Pain in the metatarsus.

1889 *Lancet* 6 Apr. 707/1.

'metatarse. Anglicization of METATARSUS.

1890 in *Century Dict.* **1894** NEWTON *Dict. Birds* 616 Their tendons unite about the middle of the metatarse.

metatarso- (mɛtə'tɑːsəʊ), comb. form of next used to denote 'belonging to the metatarsus and ..'; in **metatarso-phalangeal** *a.*, belonging to the metatarsus and the phalanges; *sb.* a metatarso-phalangeal joint; also **metatarso-digital** in the same sense.

1831 R. KNOX *Cloquet's Anat.* 390 The last four metatarso-phalangeal articulations. **1876** *Quain's Anat.* (ed. 8) I. 181 In the first metatarso-digital articulation. **1879** *St. George's Hosp. Rep.* IX. 331 The ankle, elbow, and first metatarso-phalangeal. **1887** *Brit. Med. Jrnl.* 2 Apr. 728/1 The Metatarso-Phalangeal Joint of the Great Toe.

‖**metatarsus** (mɛtə'tɑːsəs). *Anat.* Pl. **metatarsi** (-aɪ). [mod.L.: see META- and TARSUS.] The group of five long bones of the foot lying between the tarsus and the toes. In birds, the bone which corresponds to tarsus and metatarsus together.

1676 WISEMAN *Surg.* VII. ii. 479 The joyning of..the Tarsus to the Metatarsus. **1682** in *Phil. Collect.* No. 5. 147 Sixty three large Scales, reaching up all along his [*sc.* the Oestridge's] Foot before, or before those Bones which answer to the Metatarsus. **1879** WRIGHT *Anim. Life* 7 In the Jerboa, among the rodents, the three middle metatarsi form but a single bone. **1899** A. H. EVANS *Birds* 10 The covering of the metatarsus is usually 'scutellated'.

b. *Ent.* (*a*) The proximal joint of the tarsus, esp. when much developed. (*b*) The entire tarsus of the hind foot.

1816 KIRBY & SP. *Entomol.* xv. (ed. 2) I. 494 [The bee] next seizes one of the laminæ of wax with a pincer formed by the posterior metatarsus and tibia.

metatartaric: see META- 6 a.

metataxis, meta-theology: see META- 5, 1.

‖**metate** (mə'tɑːteɪ). [Aztec *metatl.*] A flat or somewhat hollowed oblong stone, upon which grain, cocoa, etc. is ground by means of a smaller stone. Also *metate-stone* (Funk's *Stand. Dict.*).

1834 in *Southwestern Hist. Q.* (1942) XLV. 330 Mrs. Roark had a Mexican utensil for grinding corn, called a *metate*. It was a large rock which had a place scooped out of the center that would hold a peck of corn. **1847** W. S. HENRY *Campaign Sk. War with Mexico* 134 The eldest was on her knees at the medatstone, grinding corn. **1854** BARTLETT *Explor. Texas*, etc. II. 245 Several broken metates, or corn-grinders, lie about the pile. *Ibid.* 276. **1932** E. WILSON *Devil take Hindmost* xviii. 199 In the caves there are only the metates left—the big stones on which they [*sc.* the Indians] ground their meal. **1972** *Sci. Amer.* May 89/3 The *manos*, or stone rollers, and *metates*, or shallow stone troughs, that are used together to grind maize. **1975** *Ibid.* Jan. 100/3 Other fragments showed evidence of splitting, indicating that the grain had been prepared not by pounding but by being rolled back and forth on a stone *metate.*

‖**Metatheria** (mɛtə'θɪərɪə), *sb. pl. Zool.* [mod.L., f. Gr. μετα- META- + θηρίον animal.] Huxley's term (correlative with *Prototheria* and *Eutheria*) for the Marsupials. Hence **meta'therian** *a.*, belonging to the *Metatheria*; *sb.*, an animal of this division.

1880 HUXLEY in *Proc. Zool. Soc.* 654 An intermediate type between that of the Prototheria and that of the higher mammals, which may be termed that of the Metatheria. *Ibid.* 657 There is no known..Marsupial which has not far more widely departed from the Metatherian type. **1894–5** *Roy. Nat. Hist.* (ed. Lydekker) III. 283 Mammals are divided into three primary groups or subclasses, viz.: 1. Eutherians, or Placentals... 2. Metatherians, or Implacentals, including the Pouched Mammals. 3. Prototherians, represented only by the Egg-laying Mammals.

metathesis (mɛ'tæθɪsɪs). Pl. **metatheses** (mɛ'tæθɪsiːz). [a. late L. *metathesis* (in sense 1), a. Gr. μετάθεσις, n. of action of μετατιθέναι to transpose, change: see META- and THESIS. Cf. F. *métathèse.*]

1. † **a.** *Rhet.* The transposition of words (*obs.*). **b.** *Gram.* The interchange of position between sounds or letters in a word; the result of such a transposition. Also, ***quantitative metathesis***, ***metathesis of quantity***, a change of sequence *long vowel + short vowel* to *short vowel + long vowel.*

1608 HIERON *2nd Pt. Def. Ministers' Reasons for Refusal Subscript.* 114 By a metathesis or transposition [he] hath misplaced some of their words. **1660** JER. TAYLOR *Duct. Dubit.* IV. i. rule 2 §36 *Tahur*, which is the Metathesis of *Hurta*, a thief. **1796** PEGGE *Anonym.* (1809) 347 It is necessary sometimes to attend to the metathesis, or transposition of letters. I make no doubt but Sir John Falstaff is formed from Sir John Fastolph. **1862** RAWLINSON *Anc. Mon., Chald.* I. viii. 196 The Assyrian Nipur, which is Nipru, with a mere metathesis of the two final letters. **1890** *Athenæum* 15 Feb. 208/2 The suggested metathesis *kiriyka* to *kikirya* does not recommend itself strongly. **1891** D. B. MONRO *Gram. Homeric Dial.* (ed. 2) 15 *Metathesis.* This term has been employed to explain a number of forms in which a short vowel is lost before a liquid, and the corresponding long vowel follows the two consonants thus brought together: as ξυμ-βλή-την *met*, Mid. βλῆ-το *was struck* (βάλ-, βέλ-ος). *Ibid.* 51 G. Curtius..made the counter-supposition that..the successive steps might be ὁράοντες, ὁρώοντες and (by metathesis of quantity) ὁρόωντες. **1901** H. OERTEL *Lect. Study Lang.* 227 What goes under the name of 'quantitative metathesis' in Greek hardly belongs here. The 'metathesis' is confined to adjacent vowels, and the quantitative increase of the second vowel is probably compensative in its nature, going parallel with a quantitative reduction of the first. **1931** B. F. C. ATKINSON *Gr. Lang.* 206 Another curious phenomenon of the metre is the metathesis of quantities or shortening of a long vowel or diphthong before hiatus. **1933** C. D. BUCK *Compar. Gram. Gr. & Lat.* 93 Long vowels are shortened before other vowels in various dialects... When the second vowel is short it may be lengthened, resulting in what is known as 'quantitative metathesis'. **1959** A. CAMPBELL *Old Eng. Gram.* 184 By full metathesis a consonant moves from immediately before a vowel to immediately after it, or the reverse. *Ibid.* 185 More usual than full metathesis is reversal of order in consonant groups, so that e.g. *sk* > *ks*, *sp* > *ps*. **1973** A. H. SOMMERSTEIN *Sound Pattern Anc. Gr.* 70 Another non-occurring vowel sequence is [ēǭ]. Quantitative Metathesis can be extended without difficulty to modify this sequence by shortening the first vowel (there is no need to lengthen the second, it being already long).

erroneous use. **1751–2** FIELDING *Covent Gard. Jrnl.* 9 Nov., The first syllable is Bob, change o into a, which is only a metathesis of one vowel for another, and you have Bab.

†**2.** *Path.* **a.** = METASTASIS. **b.** The transposition of a solid morbific substance (that cannot be evacuated) from one part to another where it will be less injurious.

1696 PHILLIPS (ed. 5), *Metathesis*... In Physick it is when a Disease goes from one part to another. **1753** CHAMBERS *Cycl.* Suppl., *Metathesis*,..a change of place in such humours, or other diseased parts, as cannot be absolutely removed or sent off. Thus a *Metathesis* of a cataract is a depression thereof, so that it no longer shuts out the light. **1832** WEBSTER (citing *Coxe*), *Metathesis* in medicine, a change or removal of a morbid cause, without expulsion.

3. *gen.* Change or reversal of condition.

1705 GREENHILL *Art Embalm.* 105 What a Metathesis is this! that he who perhaps was born of Royal Blood..shall now cry out with Job 17. 14, To Corruption, thou art my Father. **1873** H. ROGERS *Orig. Bible* v. (1878) 153 *note*, The slow processes, the abrupt transitions, the sudden metatheses, which history so often reveals.

4. *Chem.* (See quots.)

1872 J. P. COOKE *New Chem.* (1874) 245 Metathesis consists in the interchange of atoms or groups of atoms between two molecules, and implies that the structure of these molecules is not otherwise altered. **1887** REMSEN *Elem. Chem.* 11 Double decomposition or metathesis... In double decomposition two or more substances act upon one another and give rise to the formation of two or more new ones. Thus when hydrochloric acid acts upon marble two substances, calcium chloride and carbonic acid, are formed.

metathesize (mɛ'tæθɪsaɪz), *v.* [f. METATHESIS 1 b + -IZE.]

a. *intr.* To undergo metathesis. **b.** *trans.* To transpose (sounds, etc.) by metathesis; to subject (a word, etc.) to metathesis of some of its constituent sounds. Hence **me'tathesized** *ppl. adj.*

1920 H. C. WYLD *Hist. Mod. Colloq. Eng.* 300 In Received Standard we use many metathesized forms, such as *wright* O.E. *wyrhta*. **1946** E. A. NIDA *Morphol.* ix. 180 A preconsonantal *y* metathesizes with the following consonant. **1951** *Traditio* VII. 411 About the second theme, *-ferth*, there can be little room for disagreement. It is obviously a metathesized form of *frith* (peace) which occurs in many Germanic names. **1959** M. SCHLAUCH *Eng. Lang. in Mod. Times* vi. 161 There are instances [in Northern dialects] of metathesised *r*, as in *gert* for *great*. **1968** F. G. LOUNSBURY in J. A. Fishman *Readings Sociol. of Lang.* (1968) 52 Cayuga has many metathesized pairs [of syllables] in similar alternation, where the metatheses affect the relative order of vowels and the glottal stop. **1971** *Canad. Jrnl. Ling.* Fall 5 The only way to save the hypothesis of sibilant dissimilation would be to posit some rule metathesizing /z/ and /s/, and there appears to be no real evidence for voicing metathesis in modern Greek dialects. **1973** A. H. SOMMERSTEIN *Sound Pattern Anc. Greek* ii. 30 Send them first to /dz/; then we will need to metathesize this to [zd].

metathetic (mɛtə'θɛtɪk), *a.* [ad. Gr. μεταθετικός, f. μετατιθέναι (see METATHESIS).] Characterized by or involving metathesis. So **meta'thetical** *a.*

1855 both in OGILVIE *Suppl.* **1872** J. P. COOKE *New Chem.* (1874) Index 324 Metathetical reactions.

metathoracic (ˌmɛtəθə'ræsɪk), *a.* [f. next: cf. THORACIC.] Of or belonging to the metathorax.

1836–9 *Todd's Cycl. Anat.* II. 972/2 The metathoracic segment. **1877** HUXLEY *Anat. Inv. Anim.* vii. 425 The metathoracic wings.

‖**metathorax** (mɛtə'θɔəræks). *Ent.* [mod.L.; see META- and THORAX.] The hindmost segment of the thorax in insects.

1816 KIRBY & SP. *Entomol.* xxiii. (1818) II. 318 The..abdomen and metathorax. **1877** HUXLEY *Anat. Inv. Anim.* vii. 400 The..tergal portion of the metathorax.

†**me'tation.** *Obs.*[−0] [ad. L. *mētātiōn-em*, n. of action f. *mētārī* to mark or lay out (a camp).] (See quot.) Also **me'tator** [agent-n.].

1623 COCKERAM, *Metation*, a setting in order. *Ibid.*, *Metator*, hee which setteth in order. **1661** BLOUNT *Glossogr.* (ed. 2), *Metator* (Lat.), a planter or setter in order, a measurer out of the place for a Camp to pitch in, a measurer of Land.

metatitanic, metatoluic: see META- 6 a.

metatome ('mɛtətəʊm). *Arch.* [f. Gr. μετα- META- + -τομή cutting (τέμνειν to cut).] The space or interval between two dentels.

1842 GWILT *Archit.*

metatony (mɛ'tætənɪ). *Linguistics.* Also **metatonie.** [ad. F. *métatonie* (F. de Saussure 1894, in *Mémoires de la Société de Linguistique de Paris* VIII. 429), f. META- + TONE *sb.* + -Y[3].] In

Baltic and Slavonic languages, one of certain kinds of substitution of one distinctive intonation for another in a given syllable; these substitutions collectively. Hence **meta'tonic** *a.*

1936 *Trans. Philol. Soc.* 17 The long monophthongs, which have now a rising intonation, are abnormal. Except in loan words, they are due to various obscure causes, known collectively as *metatonie. Ibid.* 29 But *metatonie* in the Slavonic period (i.e. *nowocyrkumfleksowa*) may be present in some of these cases. **1949** ENTWISTLE & MORISON *Russian & Slavonic Languages* iv. 74 The process by which acutes change to circumflexes and *vice versa* is known as metatony. **1957** C. S. STANG *Slavonic Accentuation* 21 Thus neo-acute does not arise as a result of metatony, if by this term is implied a change of intonation within one and the same stressed syllable. *Ibid.* 23 An assumption based on the behaviour of metatonic circumflex. **1960** W. K. MATTHEWS *Russ. Hist. Gram.* ii. 42 The Russian form *voróna*.. illustrates a shift of stress forward in the word, which is known as progressive metatony and is the outcome here of the greater energy of the acute accent as compared with that of the circumflex. *Ibid.* vi. 99 The modern instances of metatony or shift of stress..have parallels in the fourteenth century. **1965** G. Y. SHEVELOV *Prehist. of Slavic* xxxiii. 532 He [*sc.* Rozwadowski] called [the] whole phenomenon of their rise and all the changes associated with it metatony... The original idea of metatony as a pitch mutation resulting in the appearance of the two new intonations was a typical product of the Neogrammarian approach. *Ibid.* 533 Metatonic changes are most marked in those Sl[avic] languages or dialects which preserve distinctive (phonemic) pitch. **1973** T. MATHIASSEN in A. Ziedonis et al. *Baltic Lit. & Linguistics* 165, I am inclined to assume for such cases.. only the working of metatony, which involves merely a shift of *intonation* from circumflex to acute.

Metatron (mə'tætrən). [Etym. uncertain.] In Jewish theology, a supreme angelic being, usually identified with either Michael or Enoch.

1865 C. D. GINSBURG *Kabbalah* 27 The Kabbalistic description of *Metatron* is taken from the Jewish angelology of a much older date than this theosophy... Metatron..is the Presence Angel..the visible manifestation of the deity. **1904** *Jewish Encycl.* VIII. 519 *Meṭaṭron*,..name of an angel found only in Jewish literature... Meṭaṭron combines various traits derived from different systems of thought. **1914** *Encycl. Relig. & Ethics* VII. 625/1 This mediator is usually known as Meṭaṭron... Meṭaṭron appears in a praiseworthy capacity in his relations with Moses... Michael and Meṭaṭron are sometimes interchanged. **1941** G. G. SCHOLEM *Major Trends Jewish Mysticism* ii. 66 The Metatron mysticism which revolves round the person of Enoch..who..was raised..to the rank of first of the angels. **1959** D. D. RUNES *Conc. Dict. Judaism* 168/2 *Metatron*, the highest angel, identified with the archangel Michael, or with Enoch who was transformed into a heavenly being; a mystic figure. **1967** D. T. KAUFMAN *Dict. Relig. Terms* 310 *Metatron*, in Jewish belief, a supreme angelic being.

metatrophic (mɛtə'trəʊfɪk), *a. Biol.* [ad. G. *metatroph* (A. Fischer *Vorlesungen über Bakterien* (1897) v. 47), f. META-: see TROPHIC *a.*] Needing the presence of organic substances for nutrition.

1900 A. C. JONES tr. *Fischer's Struct. & Functions Bacteria* v. 48 The metatrophic bacteria..cannot live unless they have organic substances at their disposal. **1902** *Encycl. Brit.* XXV. 439/1 Some Angiosperms are persistently heterotrophic, either as saprophytes (metatrophic) or as parasites (paratrophic), and this manner of life involves some kind of symbiosis. **1930** S. THOMAS *Bacteriol.* (ed. 2) v. 75 Metatrophic bacteria..include the bacteria causing fermentation, decay, and the decomposition of fatty substances.

metatropy, metatungstic: see META- 5, 6a.

metatype ('mɛtətaɪp). [f. META- + TYPE *sb.*]

†**1.** = ANTITYPE 1. *Obs.*

1658 T. WALL *Charac. Enemies Ch.* 37 Amaleck is a true Metatype of the divel.

2. *Zool.* (See quot.)

1893 O. THOMAS in *Proc. Zool. Soc.* 242 A metatype is a specimen received from the original locality after the description has been published, but determined as belonging to his own species by the original describer himself.

metavoltine: see META- 7a.

Metawileh (mɛ'tɑːwɪleɪ). Also **Matawila, Metawaileh, Metawala,** etc. [ad. Arab. *matāwila*, pl. of *mutawālī* one who professes to love 'Alī.] Name of a sect of the followers of 'Alī who live in Lebanon and Syria.

1799 W. G. BROWNE *Travels* 406 Some precaution was necessary against the *Metaweli*, Mohammedans of the sect of Ali, who once formed a powerful and ferocious tribe. **1845** *Encycl. Metrop.* XXV. 395/1 'Alí, whose followers, here called Motewális, or Mutewellís, are persecuted by the Sunnís. *Ibid.*, This word..has been variously spelt Metwalí, Motwâli, &c. **1860** D. URQUHART *Lebanon* I. xi. 94 The Metuali race... In religion..are Shiites, in race Arabs. *Ibid.* 96 The Metuali..do not exceed 60,000. **1875** *Encycl. Brit.* III. 177/1 In 1400 it [*sc.* Baalbec] was pillaged by Timur..and afterwards it fell into the hands of the Metaweli, a barbarous predatory tribe. **1888** *Ibid.* XXIII. 711/1 The present town [of Tyre] has arisen since the Metâwila occupied the district in 1766. **1900** G. BELL *Let.* 8 June (1927) I. 119 The Metawaileh (he belonged to that peculiar Muhammadan sect—please note that in the plural the accent is on the second syllable—Metâwaileh). **1909** T. E. LAWRENCE *Let.* 2 Aug. (1938) 68 Nabatiyeh, the Metawileh (Xtian) Headquarters in the hills. **1917** —— *Let.* 10 July (1938) 231 The Metowala [*sic*] of the Jebel Amr. **1926** —— *Seven Pillars* (1935) v. lviii. 331 On the higher slopes of the hills clustered settlements of Metawala, Shia Mohammedans from Persia generations ago. **1969** H. Z. HIRSCHBERG in A. J. Arberry *Relig. Middle East* II. xviii. 340 A harsh judgement awaits the Mutāwila (the adherents of 'Alī).

Metaxa (mɛ'tæksə). Also **metaxa, -as**. In full, ***Metaxa brandy***. A proprietary name for a dark Greek brandy; a drink or glass of this brandy.

1940 H. J. GROSSMAN *Guide to Wines, Spirits & Beers* xviii. 184 A great deal of brandy is distilled in Greece... A sweet, dark, resinous brandy, which is quite popular and sells in fair quantities, is Metaxa. **1948** S. ELLIN *Dreadful Summit* (1958) ix. 91 Dr. Cooper said to the bartender, '..Make it two Metaxas.' **1962** K. ROYCE *Night Seekers* v. 69 Spurling ordered Turkish coffee..and a bottle of Metaxa. **1966** 'A. HALL' *9th Directive* xxiii. 213, I went into the bar and drank a Greek Metaxa brandy. **1967** E. AMBLER *Dirty Story* I. iii. 25, I sipped Metaxa. **1974** C. SPENCER *How Greeks kidnapped Mrs Nixon* x. 68 Kalvos gave them a bottle of Metaxas brandy. **1975** *Times* 6 Sept. 5/4 Metaxas is the big name in Greek brandy.

metaxenia (mɛtə'ziːnɪə). *Bot.* [f. META- + XENIA.] (See quots.)

1928 W. T. SWINGLE in *Jrnl. Heredity* XIX. 263/1 In order to be able to refer to this newly discovered action of pollen on the ovarial tissues of the mother plant..I proposed at Phoenix, Arizona, in February, 1926, the term metaxenia to designate the action of the male parent on tissues of the mother plant outside of the embryo and endosperm. The term metaxenia is formed..by analogy with the term xenia which denotes the influence exerted by the male parent on the endosperm of the seed. **1949** DARLINGTON & MATHER *Elem. Genetics* 426 Xenia, the effect of more distantly related, as contrasted with more closely related, pollen on the maternal tissue of a fruit... Metaxenia has been used for true xenia. **1973** PROCTOR & YEO *Pollination of Flowers* xi. 351 The pollinations which produce larger seeds yield dates with more flesh (i.e. maternal tissue), the pollen having influenced the flesh indirectly ('metaxenia') through its direct genetic effect (xenia) on the seed.

metaxin (mɛ'tæksɪn). [f. Gr. μεταξύ between + -IN.] A proteid forming the material of the fibrils of plastids.

1890 in *Century Dict.* **1900** in Jackson *Gloss. Bot. Terms.*

metaxite (mɛ'tæksaɪt). *Min.* [Named (*metaxit*) by A. Breithaupt in 1832, f. Gr. μέταξα silk, in allusion to its lustre.] A name for some fibrous varieties of serpentine.

1836 T. THOMSON *Min. Geol.*, etc. I. 171 The metaxite of Breithaupt is also a variety of serpentine. **1866** *Reader* 10 Feb. 156/1 Tufts of Metaxite.

‖**métayage** (metɛjaʒ). [Fr., irreg. f. *métayer*: see next.] A system of land tenure in Western Europe and also in the United States, in which the farmer pays a certain proportion (generally half) of the produce to the owner (as rent), the owner generally furnishing the stock and seed or a part thereof. Also *attrib.* in ***métayage system***.

1877 D. M. WALLACE *Russia* xxi. 336 They..farmed part of their land on the *métayage* system. *Ibid.* xxxi. 519 The third solution was the system commonly known as *métayage*. **1898** *Nat. Rev.* Aug. 907 The system of 'métayage' is not used in Southern Italy.

‖**métayer** (metɛje). Also 9 **metayar**. [F. *métayer*:—med.L. *medietārius*, f. *medietās* half: see MEDIETY, MOIETY.] A farmer who holds land on the métayage system. Also *attrib.* as in ***métayer system, tenancy***.

1776 ADAM SMITH *W. N.* III. ii. I. 473 A species of farmers known at present in France by the name of Metayers. **1804** *Edin. Rev.* IV. 321 The system of rural economy in Hindustan, closely resembles..the metayer system. **1856** CRAUFORD in *Encycl. Brit.* XII. 691/1 Rural labourers [in Japan] were occupants or at best metayers. **1875** MAINE *Hist. Inst.* vi. 163 Metayer tenancy. **1886** A. WEIR *Hist. Basis Mod. Europe* (1889) 110 Dauphiny, where the worst kinds of metayer farming obtained.

†**me'taying.** *Obs. rare.* [irreg. f. MÉTAYER: see -ING[1].] Farming on the métayage system. Also *attrib.*

1792 A. YOUNG *Trav. France* 399 The metaying system. *Ibid.* 401 The evils of metaying.

metayl, metayn, obs. ff. METAL, MITTEN *sb.*

‖**Metazoa** (mɛtə'zəʊə), *sb. pl.* [f. Gr. μετα- META- 4 + ζῷα pl. of ζῷον animal. (E. Haeckel 1874, in *Jenaische Zeitschr. Naturw.* VIII. 10).] Haeckel's term for one of the two great divisions (the other being PROTOZOA) of the animal kingdom, comprising those animals whose bodies consist of many cells. Also sing. **meta'zoon**, one of the Metazoa.

1874 HUXLEY in *Jrnl. Linn. Soc., Zool.* XII. 202 The Metazoa of Haeckel. *Ibid.* 205 The next stage in the development of the embryo of a Metazoon consists [etc.]. **1878** BELL tr. *Gegenbaur's Comp. Anat.* 89 This division is the first of the Metazoa, or organisms which are undoubtedly animals. **1940** L. H. HYMAN *Invertebrates* I. v. 249 Even the simplest Metazoa are two-layered or diploblastic. **1963** A. REMANE in E. C. Dougherty et al. *Lower Metazoa* ii. 26 No biologist regards *Protohydra* as the most primitive metazoön.

metazoan (mɛtə'zəʊən), *a.* and *sb.* [f. prec. + -AN.] **a.** *adj.* Belonging to or characteristic of the Metazoa. **b.** *sb.* One of the Metazoa.

1884 HYATT in *Proc. Boston Soc. Nat. Hist.* XXIII. 140 The adult ascon, the lowest Metazoan. **1886** GEDDES in *Encycl. Brit.* XX. 419/1 The Metazoan segmentation of the ovum. **1904** *Brit. Med. Jrnl.* 15 Oct. 971 For every character presented by a Metazoan individual, a man for example, there is always a second character latent or dormant in his germ-cells. **1940** L. H. HYMAN *Invertebrates* I. v. 250 The ancestral metazoan would not have required a digestive sac or mouth. *Ibid.* 252 The three lowest metazoan phyla, the Porifera, the Cnidaria, and the Ctenophora, are commonly stated to have remained at the gastrular level of construction. **1965** B. E. FREEMAN tr. *Vandel's Biospeleol.* vii. 64 Those Metazoan groups which are almost exclusively marine are represented underground by very few species. **1971** *Nature* 28 May 260/1 Gravity corers are widely used for the collection of the smallest marine metazoans (meiofauna) from subtidal grounds.

So **meta'zoic** *a.* = METAZOAN *a.*

1877 HUXLEY *Anat. Inv. Anim.* i. 47 What distinguishes the metazoic aggregate is that [etc.].

metbord, -buird, metch(e, metcorn: see MEAT-BOARD, MATCH, METECORN.

mete (miːt), *sb.*[1] Also 5 mette, 6 met, 6–7 mett, 7 meate, 7–8 meet. [a. OF. *mete, mette*, ad. L. *mēta* goal, boundary.]

†**1.** A goal. *Obs.*

1402 *Repl. Friar Daw Topias* in *Pol. Poems* (Rolls) II. 86 Thou concludist thi silf, and bryngest thee to the mete there I wolde have thee. **1480** CAXTON *Ovid's Met.* x. viii, He passed her and cam to the mette to fore her.

2. A boundary or limit (material or immaterial); a boundary stone or mark; *esp.* in phrase ***metes and bounds*** [= AF. *metes et boundes* (1325 in *Rolls Parlt.* I. 434/2)], common in legal use; also *fig.*

1471 CAXTON *Recuyell* (Sommer) 363 And fynably they were brought to so strayte metes and boundes that [etc.]. **1525** LD. BERNERS *Froiss.* II. cci. [cxcvii.] 615 The kynge hathe clerely gyuen to hym..the hole duchy of Acquytayne, so as it extendeth in metes and lymytacyons. **1563** J. DOLMAN in *Mirr. Mag., Ld. Hastings* xcii, Untimely neuer comes the liues last mett. **1607** NORDEN *Surv. Dial.* I. 19 If the ditches, which are the ordinary meeres, meates and bounds betweene seueral mens lands, be confounded. **1768** *Conn. Col. Rec.* (1885) XIII. 52 To ascertain by meets and bounds the width of said cart-road thro said meadow. **1818** CRUISE *Digest* (ed. 2) I. 197 Dower was assigned by metes and bounds, because it was a tenancy of the heir. **1878** LANIER *Marshes of Glynn* 39 As a belt of the dawn, For a mete and a mark To the forest-dark. **1894** *Q. Rev.* Jan. 30 The introspective genius knows his metes and bounds.

†**mete**, *sb.*[2], anglicized form of MEATUS.

1460–70 *Bk. Quintessence* 16 þe palesye vniuersel comeþ of haboundaunce of viscous humouris closynge þe metis of vertu animale, sensityue, and motyue.

mete (miːt), *sb.*[3] [f. METE *v.*[1]; cf. MET *sb.*[1]] Measure.

1768 J. ROSS *Ode loss Friend* Wks. 224 (MS.) The pow'r Of solemn Young or softer Thomson's mete! **1834** HOGG *Mora Campbell* 30 Noted for heroes tall and fair Of manly mete and noble mien. *a* **1871** MISS CARY *Nobility* ii. (Funk), We get back our mete as we measure.

mete (miːt), *v.*[1] Inflected **meted, meting**. Forms: *Inf.* 1 metan, (meotan), 3, 6 mette, 4–6 meet(e, 6–7 meat(e, mett, 8 met, 3– mete. *Pa. t.* 1 mæt, 4–6 mett(e, 4–7 met, (4 mat(te, maat, mete, me(e)tid, 4–5 metede, 6 mott), 7– meted. *Pa. ppl.* 1–2 ȝemeten, 1–6 meten, 2–3 imeten, 3– 6 mett(e, (4 ymeten, metun, 5 metyn, 6 metten, -on, mottun, meated, 7 mete, *dial.* 9 metit), 4–6 moten, metid, 4–8 (9 *dial.*) met, 7– meted. [A Com. Teut. originally str. vb.: OE. *metan* (*mæt, mǣton, ȝemeten*) corresponds to OFris. *meta*, OS. *metan* (Du. *meten*), OHG. *mezzan* (MHG. *mezzen*, mod.G. *messen*), ON. *meta* to value (Sw. *mäta* to measure), Goth. *mitan*:—OTeut. **met-* (:*mat-*: *mǣt-*):—pre-Teut. **med-* (:*mod-*: *mēd-*) cogn. w. Gr. μέδιμνος MEDIMN, L. *modius* bushel; other cognates are L. *meditārī* and the words cited s.v. MEDITATE.

The Teut. **met-* has no direct connexion with the synonymous L. *mētīrī*; but many scholars regard the W. Indogermanic **mēd-* and *mēt-* as parallel extensions of *mē-*.

The verb was frequently conjugated weak as early as the 14th c.; the original strong inflexions did not entirely disappear until late in the 16th c.]

1. *trans.* To ascertain or determine the dimensions or quantity of; = MEASURE *v.* 2. Also with dimensions as obj. Now only *poet.* and *dial.*, exc. in allusions to Matt. vii. 2.

c **975** *Rushw. Gosp.* Matt. vii. 2 In ðæm ȝemete þe ȝe metaþ bið eow meten. *c* **1000** ÆLFRIC *Gram.* xiii. (Z.) 84 Ælc þæra ðinga, þe man wihð on wæȝan oððe met on fate. *c* **1200** *Trin. Coll. Hom.* 213 Gif hit chepinge be þe me shule meten oðer weien þe [etc.]. *c* **1290** *S. Eng. Leg.* I. 244/142 þe schipmen ..token þe bischope wel i-metene Ane houndred quarteres ȝwete. **1382** WYCLIF *Ezek.* xl. 5 He metid [**1388** mat] the breede of the beeldyng with oo ȝerd. **1388** —— *Ruth* iii. 15 He mete [**1535** COVERDALE meet] sixe buyschels of barly. *c* **1420** *Chron. Vilod.* 4620 And wᵗ hurre fote he metede þe lengthe of þat space. *c* **1483** CAXTON *Dialogues* 44 Paulyn.. Hath so moche moten Of corne..That he may no more for age. **1556** J. HEYWOOD *Spider & F.* xcii. 49 Our mesurs mette to other, shal to vs be mottun. **1607** TOURNEUR *Rev.*

Trag. II. i, Lands that were mete by the Rod. **1781** CRABBE *Library* 302 She..Metes the thin air and weighs the flying sound. **1805** in Chambers *Pop. Poems Scot.* (1862) 152 Says Tam, 'We'll hae them met;' They measured just eight score o' pecks. **1865** SWINBURNE *Lament.* 23 No hand has meted his path.

with clause. a **1225** *Ancr. R.* 232 He þet meteð hu heih is þe heouene & hu deope is þe eorðe. c **1391** CHAUCER *Astrol.* II. §42 a, Mete how many foot ben be-twen þe too prikkis.

fig. a **1556** LD. VAUX in *Parad. Dainty Dev.* (1578) 7 b, When I..mette in mind eache steppe youth strayed a wry. **1876** BLACKIE *Songs Relig. & Life* 48 All men Who..mete with kingly ken The starry-peopled sky.

b. To be the 'measure' of. *poet. rare.*

1844 MRS. BROWNING *Drama of Exile* Poems 1850 I. 52 Cast out, cast down—What word metes absolute loss?

†**c.** To complete the full 'measure' or amount of. Also with *forth, out. Obs.*

1600 FAIRFAX *Tasso* XV. xxxix. 274 Nor yet the time hath Titans gliding fire Met forth. **1698** FRYER *Acc. E. India & P.* 12 Their Wings..mete out twice their length. *Ibid.* 240 To Bury metes out Twelve Miles more. **1791** BURNS *To Mr. Maxwell of Terraughty on his Birthday* ii, This day thou metes threescore eleven.

†**2.** *absol.* or *intr.* To take measurements; = MEASURE *v.* 1 h. *Obs.*

1388 WYCLIF *Exod.* xvi. 18 Thei metiden [1382 mesurden] at the mesure gomor. c **1483** CAXTON *Dialogues* 16 Dame, mete well. **1530** PALSGR. 635/2, I wyll nat mete by your busshell. **1649** R. HODGES *Plain Direct.* 13 A yard to mete withal.

†**b.** To measure distances *for* shooting at a mark; hence, to aim *at*. *Obs.*

1534 MORE *Comf. agst. Trib.* I. Wks. 1157/2 We shal nowe meate for the shoote and consider..how farre of your arrowes are from the prik. **1588** SHAKS. *L.L.L.* IV. i. 134 Let the mark haue a pricke in 't to meat at.

†**3.** *trans.* To mark (*out*) the boundary or course of; = MEASURE *v.* 3. *Obs.*

In late use prob. regarded as a derivative of METE *sb.*[1]

c **825** *Vesp. Psalter* lix. 9, & ʒemære ʒetelda ic meotu [Vulg. *metibor*]. a **1000** *Cædmon's Exod.* 92 (Gr.) Wicsteal metan. **1382** WYCLIF *Deut.* xxi. 2 The spacis of alle the cytees bi enuyroun shal be meetid from the place of the careyn. c **1440** *Promp. Parv.* 336/1 Meete londe, or set bowndys, *meto.* **1513** [see MEASURE *v.* 3]. **1535** COVERDALE *Ps.* lix. [lx.] 6, I wil deuyde Sichem, & mete out the valley of Suchoth. **1567** DRANT *Horace, Ep.* I. xvi. E vij, Hebrus that meteth Thracia. **1568** GRAFTON *Chron.* I. 96 He met out a large and great circuit of ground. **1609** SKENE *Reg. Maj.* 29 Command sall be giuen to the Schiref, to cause mett, and measure the samine [*sc.* a dowry]. **1632** HEYWOOD *1st Pt. Iron Age* I. i. Wks. 1874 III. 267 Of all your flourishing line ..Not one shal liue to meate your Sepulchre. a **1637** B. JONSON *Sad Shepherd* I. ii, And a fair dial to mete out the day. **1819** W. TENNANT *Papistry Storm'd* (1827) 137 The heralds had the rink-room metit, The barriers set, and lists completit.

4. To estimate the greatness or value of; to appraise; = MEASURE *v.* 6. *arch.*

In *OE.* also = to compare (const. *wið, be*).

c **888** K. ÆLFRED *Boeth.* xiii. §1 Ne sint hi no wið eow to metanne. **971** *Blickl. Hom.* 133 Se sweʒ wæs þæs Halʒan Gastes be winde meten. **1382** WYCLIF *2 Cor.* x. 12 We metinge, or mesuringe, vs in vs silf, and comparisownynge vs silf to vs. **1398** TREVISA *Barth. De P. R.* II. iv. (1495) 31 They [aungels] deuyde mete and waye all mennes werkes good and euyll. c **1440** *York Myst.* xxiii. 116 þat goddis sone is þis, Euyn with hym mette and all myghty. **1595** SPENSER *Col. Clout* 365 For not by measure of her owne great mynd, And wondrous worth, she mott my simple song. **1597** SHAKS. *2 Hen. IV*, IV. iv. 77 A Patterne, or a Measure..By which his Grace must mete the liues of others. **1702** JEFFERSON *Writ.* (1830) III. 489 A simple measure by which every one could mete their merit. **1866** J. H. NEWMAN *Gerontius* §3 Spirits and men by different standards mete The less and greater in the flow of time.

†**5.** To traverse (a distance); = MEASURE *v.* 11. Also *absol.* or *intr.* (and *refl.*). To go, proceed. *Obs.*

Beowulf 1633 Ferdon forð..foldweʒ mæton. **1340** HAMPOLE *Pr. Consc.* 7695 Himself fra erth, upward met þat way, When he stey tylle heven. a **1400-50** *Alexander* 455 þan metis he him to Messadone. *Ibid.* 4803 þan metis he doun of þe mounte in-to a mirk vale. **1621** QUARLES *Feast for Worms* viii. G 3, A Citty..whose ample wall, Who vndertakes to mete with paces, shall [etc.]. **1697** CREECH tr. *Manilius* III. 107 Take all that space the Sun Meets out, when every daily Round is Run.

impers. pass. a **1400-50** *Alexander* 374 Qwen it was metyn to þe merke þat men ware to ryst. *Ibid.* 564 Fra þe none tyme Till it to myddav was meten on þe morne efter.

6. (Often with *out.*) To apportion by measure; to assign in portions; to portion or deal out; *esp.* to allot (punishment, praise, reward, etc.).

Uncommon till the 19th c.; now the chief current sense, but only in literary use.

a **1300** *Cursor M.* 26529 [Christ] þat metes ilk man his mede. a **1600** MONTGOMERIE *Misc. Poems* ii. 23 Thou..mett thame moonshyn ay for meill. **1676** TOWERSON *Decalogue* 463 Our recreations should be meted by smaller portions. **1721** RAMSAY *Tartana* 263 When beauty's to be judg'd without a vail, And not its powers met out as by retail, But wholesale. **1798** MALTHUS *Popul.* (1817) I. 278 The food of the country would be meted out..in the smallest shares that could support life. **1842** TENNYSON *Ulysses* 3, I mete and dole Unequal laws unto a savage race. **1858** CARLYLE *Fredk. Gt.* IV. viii. (1872) II. 17 His very sleep was stingily meted out to him. **1878** H. M. STANLEY *Dark Cont.* II. xiii. 382 What punishment shall I mete to this thief?

†**mete,** *v.*[2] *Obs.* Forms: *Inf.* 1 mǽtan, 3-6 mete, 4 meete(n, 6 meit. *Pa. t.* 1 mǽtte, 1-5 mete, 3 matte, 3-5 mette, 3-6 mett, 3-7 met. *Pa. pple.* 3 imet, 3-4 met, 4 mete, 4-5 ymet. [OE. *mǽtan* wk. vb.; not found outside English.]

1. *impers.* **me mette**: it occurred to me in a dream; I dreamt. Also with *sb.*, as ***me mette sweven***, I dreamt a dream.

The analogy of ON, *draum dreymdi mik* (see DREAM *v.*[2] 3) suggests taking *sveven* (or equivalent sb.) as accus. and the vb. as impers.; on the other hand, the sb. may be the nom. and the vb. may have the meaning 'to occur to (a person) in a dream'.

c **1000** ÆLFRIC *Gen.* xxxvii. 5 Witodlice hit ʒelamp þæt hine mætte. c **1000** —— *Deut.* xiii. 1 Gif æniʒ witeʒa..secʒe þæt him mætte swefen. **1297** R. GLOUC. (Rolls) 4140 At tyme of midniʒt of þe niʒt him mette a greuous cas. ? a **1366** CHAUCER *Rom. Rose* 26 Me mette swiche a swevening, That lykede me wonders wel. c **1385** —— *L.G.W.* Prol. 210 Me mette how I lay in the medewe thoo. **1393** LANGL. *P. Pl.* C. VI. 109 Thenne mette [*v.r.* mete] me moche more þan ich byfore tolde Of þe mater þat ich mette fyrst on maluerne hulles. a **1400-50** *Alexander* 422 Quen he wroʒt had his will þen witrely him metis, þat he bowes to hire belechiste. a **1643** W. CARTWRIGHT *Ordinary* II. ii. (1651) 26 All night me met eke that I was at Kirke. [The speaker is 'Robert Moth, an Antiquary'.]

2. *trans.* To dream (a dream, *that* something happened, etc.).

c **1000** *Sax. Leechd.* III. 176 Gyf man mete þæt he fela gosa hæbbe. c **1290** *S. Eng. Leg.* I. 281/104 Seint Domenic matte..þat seint petur him bi-tok Ane staf. **13..** *Seuyn Sag.* (W.) 2063 Ich mot mete a sweuen to-night. c **1381** CHAUCER *Parl. Foules* 104 The louere met he hath his lady wonne. c **1430** *Hymns Virg.* 81 Al þat we haue lyued heere, It is but as a dreem y-met. **1513** DOUGLAS *Æneis* II. v. 36 The first quiet Of naturale sleip..Stelis on fordoverit mortale creaturis, And in thair swewynnis metis quent figuris. c **1570** *Pride & Lowl.* (1841) 65, I..mused of these matters that I mett.

3. *intr.* To dream (*of*).

a **1300** *K. Horn* 1522 (Camb. MS.) þat niʒt horn gan swete, And heuie for to mete Of Rymenhild his make. **1393** LANGL. *P. Pl.* C. XII. 167 In a wynkynge ich worth and wonderliche ich mette. c **1430** *Syr Gener.* (Roxb.) 6567 Al night I haue of him met.

Hence **i-met** *ppl. a.*

a **1225** *Juliana* 74 Ant as imet sweuen aswindeð hire murhðen.

†**mete,** *v.*[3] *Obs.* [OE. *métan*; not found outside Eng.] *trans.* and *intr.* To paint, design.

c **1000** ÆLFRIC *Gram.* xxviii. (Z.) 174 *Pingo* ic mete. c **1200** ORMIN 1047 þeʒʒ haffdenn liccness metedd Off Cherubyn. c **1250** *Gen. & Ex.* 2701 He carf..Two likenesses, so grauen & meten [etc.].

mete: see MATE *a.*, MEAT, MEET, MET.

†**metecorn.** *Obs.* Also 4 mette-, 5 met-. [OE., f. *mete* MEAT *sb.* + CORN[1].] An allowance (properly, of corn) made to servants, to inmates of a hospital, etc.

1050 in Thorpe *Charters* (1865) 580 Ilk habbe his.. metecu & his metecorn. **1320** *Rolls of Parlt.* I. 367/1 Stipendia & metecorn, ac cetera debita servientum in monasterio predicto. **1385-6** *Durham Acc. Rolls* (Surtees) 391 Tribus servientibus apud le Hough pro le mettecorn. **1402-3** *Ibid.* 218 Pro frumento et pecunia datis pro metkorn hominibus de hospitalibus de Witton et de Maudelens. c **1440** *Promp. Parv.* 335/2 Mete corne, *panicium.* **1522-3** *Durham Acc. Rolls* (Surtees) 255 Pro le metcorn sowlsilver et aliis necessariis. [**1706** PHILLIPS (ed. Kersey).]

†**mete-custi,** *a. Obs.* Also -cousti. [f. MEAT *sb.* + CUSTI *a.*, liberal.] Liberal with food, hospitable.

c **1205** LAY. 19932 He wes mete-custi [c **1275** mete-cousti]. *Ibid.* 23257.

meted ('miːtɪd), *ppl. a.* [f. METE *v.*[1] + -ED[1].] Measured; apportioned.

1775 ASH, *Meted*, measured, reduced to a measure. **1887** MORRIS *Odyss.* XI. 185 In peace Telemachus dwelleth, and meted feasts doth he share.

meteer, obs. form of METRE.

†**metefetill.** *Obs.* [OE. *meteféte ls*: see MEAT *sb.* and FETLES.] A cupboard for food.

c **1000** ÆLFRIC *Gloss.* in Wr.-Wülcker 107/5 *Sitarchia*, metefætels, *uel* sceatcod. c **1440** *Promp. Parv.* 335/2 Metefytel [*printed* metesytel], to keep in mete [*Pynson* mete fetyll or almery], *cibulum.*

†**metegift,** *a. Obs.* [f. *mete* MEAT *sb.* + ? GIFT. (The formation of the second element is obscure.) Cf. MEAT-GIVER.] Hospitable.

a **1400** *R. Brunne's Chron. Wace* (Rolls) 4076 (Petyt MS.), & metegift man viandoure [*Lamb. MS.* & lyberal man, & vyaundour].

†**metekin.** *Obs.* Also 3 mætecun. [f. *mete* MEAT *sb.* + KIN *sb.*[1]] Kind of food; provision.

c **1200** ORMIN 8645 þin Laferrd Godd Allmahhtiʒ wat ..þatt nafe icc nohht off metekinn Till me. c **1205** LAY. 941 þat..he us ʒeue..al his beste mæte cun.

metel ('miːtəl). Also 6 methel. [a. mod.L. *methel*, a. Arab. *jauz māþil* (where *jauz* means 'nut'). Cf. F. *noix met(h)elle* 'thorn-apple' (Cotgr.), *métel* = sense b (Littré).] †**a.** ***methel nut, nut methel***: a narcotic fruit or seed described by Avicenna as resembling a nut covered with small spines, and also as similar to nux vomica; probably the Thorn-apple, *Datura Stramonium. Obs.* **b.** In the form ***metel***, applied by Linnæus as the specific name of the Hairy Thorn-apple, *Datura Metel*, and hence sometimes used as the Eng. name of that plant.

1528 PAYNEL *Salerne's Regim.* (1541) 63 The nutte methel which, as Auicen saythe, is venomous, wherfore hit sleeth. **1568** TURNER *Herbal* III. 49 Of the nutte called the vomitinge nutt, and of the nut of Methel. The vomitinge nut and the Methel are not in al poyntes vnlyke... Matthiolus writeth that the flat nuttes like litle cheses which haue ben solde hytherto: for vomitinge nuttes are nuttes methel, and they that haue bene hytherto vsed for methel nuttes are the righte *nuces vomicæ.* **1597** GERARDE *Herbal* II. lvii. 278 The first of these Thorne apples may be called in Latin *Stramonia*, and *Pomum* or *Malum spinosum*..of Serapio and others it is thought to be *Nux methel*: Serapio in his 375. chapter saith, that *Nux methel* is like vnto *Nux voxima.* **1753** CHAMBERS *Cycl. Supp.*, *Metel*,..the name of a sort of *nux vomica*, of the same shape with the common kind, but somewhat larger. **1887** MOLONEY *Forestry W. Afr.* 395 Metel or Hairy Thorn Apple.

meteles: see METELS and MEATLESS.

†**meteline.** *Obs.* [f. METE *v.*[1] + LINE *sb.*[1] Cf. Du. *meetlijn.*] A measuring line.

1535 COVERDALE *2 Chron.* iv. 2 A metelyne of thirtie cubites. **1583** GOLDING *Calvin on Deut.* xi. 63 Hee..hath stretched out his meeteline to appoint euery people their countrey to dwell in.

†**metels.** *Obs.* Also meteles, -is, -us, meetel(e)s, metals. [f. METE *v.*[2] + -ELS.] A dream.

1340 *Ayenb.* 165 Ydelnesse be bysihede. Vor þise bysyhedes byeþ ase meteles. **1362** LANGL. *P. Pl.* A. VIII. 131 Musyng on þis Meteeles [*v.r.* metelis, **1393** C. X. 297 meteles] A myle wei Ich ʒeode. **1382** WYCLIF *Acts* ii. 17 ʒoure eldris schulen dreme meetels.

metely, obs. form of MEETLY *a.* and *adv.*

metembryo (mɛ'tɛmbrɪəʊ). [f. META- + EMBRYO.] The gastrula stage of a metazoon.

1887 HYATT in *Proc. Boston Soc. Nat. Hist.* 397 The proper name for these stages would..be Metembryo, in allusion to the fact that the ovum at this stage is probably essentially a Metazoon.

Hence **metembry'onic** *a.*, 'of or pertaining to a metembryo' (*Cent. Dict.* 1890).

metempiric (mɛtɛm'pɪrɪk). [f. META- + EMPIRIC.

Introduced, together with the related words, by G. H. Lewes in 1874.]

1. (Also **metempirics** with sing. construction: cf. *metaphysic, metaphysics.*) The philosophy of things that lie outside the sphere of knowledge derived from experience.

The writers quoted differ greatly in their application of the term, but the question between them is what is meant by 'experience'; the definition given above would be accepted on both sides.

1874 LEWES *Probl. Life & Mind* Ser. I. I. 18 Metempirics sweeps out of this region in search of the *otherness* of things. a **1881** A. BARRATT *Phys. Metempiric* xi. (1883) 130 Any metempiric which does more than numerically multiply, or vary in degree, existence such as we have it in experience, or which postulates beings whose qualities bear no resemblance to those of experience, must be at once rejected.

2. One who believes in or supports metempirical philosophy; a metempiricist.

a **1881** A. BARRATT *Phys. Metempiric* iii. (1883) 19 Every man who believes in the consciousness of his fellows—every man who uses the word 'we'—is a Metempiric.. **1882** in OGILVIE, and in later Dicts.

metempirical (mɛtɛm'pɪrɪkəl), *a.* [f. META- + EMPIRICAL.] Pertaining to matters outside the range of knowledge derived from experience. Also, of opinions and their advocates: Maintaining the validity of concepts and beliefs based otherwise than on experience.

1874 LEWES *Probl. Life & Mind* Ser. I. I. 17 If then the Empirical designates the province we include within the range of Science, the province we exclude may fitly be styled the Metempirical. a **1881** A. BARRATT *Phys. Metempiric* ii. (1883) 17 The simplest Metempirical assumption, and one made by every man, is that there *is* a Metempirical existence, that he and his own experience are not all that has ever existed. **1888** *Athenæum* 11 Feb. 184 It appropriated for empiricism doctrines hitherto the special property of metempirical schools.

Hence **metem'pirically** *adv.*, in a metempirical sense or manner.

1884 *Spectator* 2 Feb. 161 Every atom..is ..'metempirically', as he [*sc.* Barratt] calls it—a centre of consciousness.

metempiricism (mɛtɛm'pɪrɪsɪz(ə)m). [f. METEMPIRIC + -ISM.] Metempirical philosophy.

1882 in OGILVIE.

metempiricist (mɛtɛm'pɪrɪsɪst). [Formed as prec. + -IST.] = METEMPIRIC *sb.* 2.

1874 LEWES *Probl. Life & Mind* Ser. I. I. 28 *note*, The distinction between the empiricist and metempiricist. **1874** —— in *Contemp. Rev.* XXIV. 689 This is the empirical standpoint. It is of course disputed by metempiricists.

ˌmetem'psychic, *a. rare.* [f. METEMPSYCHOSIS after *psychic.*] Pertaining to metempsychosis.

1886 LADY BURTON *Arab. Nts.* (Abr. ed.) I. Foreword 7 A reminiscence of some by-gone metempsychic life in the distant Past.

†**metempsychize**, *v. Obs.* [f. METEMPSYCHOSIS + -IZE.] = METEMPSYCHOSE *v.*

1618 *Barnevelt's Apol.* Ded. A iv, Lest I also..bee commanded..to metempsychize and turne my selfe into a Swine.

metempsy'chosal, *a.* [f. METEMPSYCHOS-IS + -AL[1].] Of the nature of metempsychosis.

1848 *Tait's Mag.* XV. 704 Composed, or metempsycosal immortality, is one of the pivots of the system of harmony.

†**metempsychose**, *sb. Obs.* [a. F. *métempsycose* (Charron, 16th c.), ad. late L. *metempsychōsis*.] = METEMPSYCHOSIS.

1630 LENNARD tr. *Charron's Wisd.* (1658) 32 The Metempsychose and transanimation of Pythagoras. **1786** HAN. MORE *Bas Bleu* 161 And he, who wilder studies chose [might] Find here a new metempsychose.

metempsychose (mɛtɛmpsɪ'kəʊs), *v.* Also 7 **metempseuc(h)ose**, **-psuchose**. [f. METEMPSYCHOS-IS.] *trans.* To transfer or translate (a soul) from one body to another. Also *transf.* and *fig.* Hence **metempsy'chosed** *ppl. a.*

1594 W. PERCY *Coelia* (1877) 15 To other bodies of like simpathie, Thou art the last of these Metemps'chosed. *a* **1634** RANDOLPH *To Mr. Feltham* 10 When minds change oftner then the Greek could dream, That made the Metempseucos'd soule his theame. **1651** BIGGS *New Disp.* Pref. 5 It is great pity she [*sc.* England] should..thereby have her metempseuchos'd Genius transmigrate into another People. *a* **1678** MARVELL *Loyal Scot* 167 Wks. (Grosart) I. 222 Lest in time he were Metempsychos'd to some Scotch Presbyter. **1843** *Fraser's Mag.* XXVIII. 277 Their passion..having, in the meantime, metempsychosed itself into a platonisation.

†**metempsychosical**, *a. Obs.* [Formed as prec. + -ICAL.] Relating to metempsychosis.

1622 'JACK DAWE' *Vox Graculi* 38 All Metempsichosicall coniectures. **1905** W. J. LOCKE *Morals M. Ordeyne* xviii. 217, I have bemused myself with gnostic and metempsychosic speculations.

metempsychosis (mɛˌtɛmpsaɪ'kəʊsɪs). Pl. -oses (-'əʊsiːz). Also 6 **metempsichosis**, 7 **metempsuchosis, metemsychosis, metampsycosis**, 7–8 **metempsycosis**. [Late L. *metempsychōsis*, a. Gr. μετεμψύχωσις, formed on the analogy of other nouns of action from μετα- META- + ἐν in + ψῡχή soul. Cf. F. *métempsychose*.

Formerly often stressed *metem'psychosis*: cf. *metamorphosis*.]

Transmigration of the soul; passage of the soul from one body to another; *chiefly*, the transmigration of the soul of a human being or animal at or after death into a new body (whether of the same or a different species), a tenet of the Pythagoreans and certain Eastern religions, esp. Buddhism.

c **1590** MARLOWE *Faust.* (1604) F 2 b, Ah Pythagoras metem su cossis [sic] were that true, This soule should flie from me, and I be changde Vnto some brutish beast. **1591** JAS. I *Furies* 1059, *Poet. Exerc.* E 3 b, The Fond Metempsichosis straunge. **1606** DEKKER *Newes from Hell* Non-Dram. Wks. (Grosart) II. 103 Into whose soule (if euer there were a Pithagorean Metempsuchosis). **1659** T. PECKE *Parnassi Puerp.* 2 Suppose Pythagoras the white did kiss, When he talkt of a Metemsychosis. **1661** A. BROME *To Mr. J. B.* Poems 111 How great a joy 'twould be, how great a bliss, If we could have a *Metampsycosis*! **1682** SIR T. BROWNE *Chr. Mor.* III. §23 Dream not of any kind of Metempsychosis or transanimation, but into thine own body, and that after a long time, and then also unto wail or bliss, according to thy first and fundamental Life. **1757** J. H. GROSE *Voy. E. Indies* 297 Their belief of the Metempsychosis makes them [Gentoos] extend it to every animated creature. *a* **1862** BUCKLE *Misc. Wks.* (1872) I. 330 In the oldest Hindoo book we find the metempsychosis into animals.

b. *transf.* and *fig.*

1619 PURCHAS *Microcosmus* lix. 593 If..it [Athens] be there sunke into the ground, and be by some Metempsychosis reuiued in England. *a* **1834** COLERIDGE *Shaks. Notes* (1849) 25 Follow the wandering spirit of poetry through its various metempsychoses, and consequent metamorphoses. **1864** LOWELL *Fireside Trav.* 298 Departed empire has a metempsychosis, if nothing else has.

metempsychosist (mɛtɛmpsaɪ'kəʊsɪst). [f. METEMPSYCHOS-IS + -IST. Cf. F. *métempsychosiste*.] One who believes in metempsychosis.

1834 J. WHITE *Let.* in Mrs. Gordon *'Chr. North'* xiv. (1879) 390 Have you ever thought of making Hogg a metempsychosist? what a famous description he would give of his feelings when he was a whale..or a tiger [etc.]. **1885** MRS. LYNN LINTON *C. Kirkland* I. vii. 198 She was..in a sense a metempsychosist, and believed that we had all known each other in another life—all of us who loved in this.

metempsychosize (mɛtɛmpsaɪ'kəʊsaɪz), *v.* [f. as prec. + -IZE.] *trans.* = METEMPSYCHOSE *v.*

a **1843** SOUTHEY *Doctor* ccxii. (1847) VII. 135 If Rhadamanthus and his colleagues..had..sewed him [Izaak Walton] metempsychosized into a frog, to the arming iron, with a fine needle and silk, with only one stitch.

‖**metemptosis** (mɛtɛmp'təʊsɪs). [mod.L., f. Gr. μετά after + ἔμπτωσις, n. of action of ἐμπίπτειν to fall in or upon. In F. *métemptose*.] The solar equation necessary to prevent the calendar new moon from happening a day too late. (The opposite of *proemptosis*.)

1727–41 CHAMBERS *Cycl.* s.v., By the metemptosis, a bissextile is suppressed each one hundred thirty four years, that is, three times in four hundred years.

†'**meten**, *ppl. a.* Also **meeten**. [Strong pa. pple. of METE *v.*[1]] Measured.

c **1375** *Cursor M.* 7332 (Fairf.) He [Saul] was heyer þen any man large bi a meten span. **16..** *Will Stewart & John* xvii. in Child *Ballads* II. 434/1 And as they did come home againe—I-wis itt was a meeten mile.

metencephalon (mɛtɛn'sɛfəlɒn). *Anat.* Also **me'tencephal**. [mod.L., f. Gr. μετά after + ἐγκέφαλ-ος brain, f. ἐν in + κεφαλ-ή head.] **a.** In Huxley's use: The cerebellum with the pons Varolii. **b.** 'The posterior division of the third, or posterior primary, cerebral vesicle. It corresponds with the medulla oblongata, the fourth ventricle, and the auditory nerve' (*Syd. Soc. Lex.* 1890).

1871 HUXLEY *Anat. Vert.* 57. **1876** *Quain's Anat.* (ed. 8) II. 755 Metencephalon. Medulla Oblongata, Fourth Ventricle, Auditory nerve..afterbrain. **1882** WILDER & GAGE *Anat. Techn.* 419 Note the lateral expansion of the myelon to form the metencephalon (medulla). **1889** *Buck's Handbk. Med. Sci.* VIII. 123/2 Metencephal.

Hence **metence'phalic** *a.*, of or pertaining to the metencephalon.

1890 *Century Dict.* **1899** *Proc. Zool. Soc.* 1024 The metencephalic fossa of the Pygopodes.

‖**metensarcosis** (mɛtɛnsɑː'kəʊsɪs). [f. Gr. μετα- (denoting change) + ἐνσάρκωσις (f. ἐν in + σάρξ flesh), after *metensomatosis*: see -OSIS.] The transference of the flesh of one body to another.

1875 A. W. WARD *Hist. Dram. Lit.* II. 589 *note*, Almeria's offer to clothe the rotten bones of her (supposedly) dead lover with her own flesh—a species of metensarcosis altogether original.

‖**metensomatosis** (ˌmɛtɛnsəʊmə'təʊsɪs). Also 7 **metempsomatosis**. [mod.L., a. Gr. μετενσωμάτωσις (Clement of Alexandria), f. μετα- (denoting change) + ἐνσωμάτωσις (f. ἐν in + σωματ-, σῶμα body): see -OSIS.]

a. Re-embodiment (of the soul). **b.** 'The transference of the elements of one body into another body and their conversion into its substance, as by decomposition and assimilation' (Ogilvie 1882).

1630 LORD *Banians* 51 Plato and Pythagoras that haue name for defending this Metempsychosis or Metempsomatosis. **1865** FARRAR *Chap. Lang.* iv. 50 Man's body..is composed of the very same materials..which constitute the inorganic world..and which may serve in endless metensomatosis for we know not what organisms yet to come. **1890** *Contemp. Rev.* LVII. 262 The leading doctrine of Buddhism is the theory of metensomatosis.

‖**metenteron** (mɛ'tɛntərən). *Biol.* [mod.L., f. Gr. μετά after + ENTERON.] The enteron (or alimentary canal) in any modification of its primitive form. Hence **metente'ronic** *a.* (in recent Dicts.).

1877 RAY LANKESTER in *Q. Jrnl. Microsc. Sci.* XVII. 419 Digestive Sac or Metenteron. *Ibid.* 428 When once the cælom is accomplished as a cavity definitely shut off from the 'metenteron'—the name we now give to what remains of the archenteron.

meteor ('miːtɪə(r)). Also 6 metior, 6–7 meteore, 7 meator, meatu(a)re, meteour. [ad. mod.L. *meteōrum*, a. Gr. μετέωρον in pl. = atmospheric phenomena, subst. use of μετέωρος raised, lofty, 'sublimis', f. μετα- META- + ἑωρ- ablaut-var. of the root of ἀείρειν to lift up. Cf. F. *météore* (13–14th c.), It. *meteora*, Sp., Pg. *meteoro*.]

1. Any atmospheric phenomenon. Now chiefly confined to technical use.

Atmospheric phenomena were formerly often classed as ***aerial*** or ***airy meteors*** (winds), ***aqueous*** or ***watery meteors*** (rain, snow, hail, dew, etc.), ***luminous meteors*** (the aurora, rainbow, halo, etc.), and ***igneous*** or ***fiery meteors*** (lightning, shooting stars, etc.).

1471 RIPLEY *Comp. Alch.* Ep. iii. in Ashm. *Theat. Chem. Brit.* (1652) 111 In the boke of Meteors. **1576** FLEMING *Panopl. Epist.* 352 Hoare frostes,..and such like colde meteors. **1602** ROWLANDS *Tis Merrie when Gossips meete* 13 A vicious man is like a fyrie Meature, Which shewes farre off a terror to the eye. **1604** JAS. I *Counterbl.* (Arb.) 104 Vapours ..are..turned into raine and such other watery Meteors. **1659** STANLEY *Hist. Philos.*, *Epicurus* (1687) 902/1 These are the aerial Meteors... We shall begin with the Clouds. **1857** S. P. HALL in *Merc. Marine Mag.* (1858) V. 10 The centre of the meteor [a cyclone] passing to the southward of the island. **1866** WHITTIER *Snow-Bound* 46 In starry flake, and pellicle, All day the hoary meteor fell. **1905** *Edin. Rev.* Jan. 220 It is therefore incumbent on him to study the nature of these meteors [typhoons].

2. *spec.* **a.** A luminous body seen temporarily in the sky, and supposed to belong to a lower region than that of the heavenly bodies; a fireball or shooting star (in the 17th c. also †a comet).

In its modern restricted use, the term may be scientifically defined to mean: A small mass of matter from celestial space, rendered luminous by the heat engendered by collision with the earth's atmosphere.

1593 SHAKS. *Rich. II*, II. iv. 9 And Meteors fright the fixed Starres of Heauen. **1608** D. T[UVIL] *Ess. Pol. & Mor.* 90 The difference betweene a starre, and a Meteor. **1609** ARMIN *Maids of More-Cl.* (1880) 96 Pine let me in them, if the Sonne of hope Shine as a troubled meatuare in the sky. *a* **1625** FLETCHER *Hum. Lieut.* IV. viii, I am above your hate, as far above it,..As the pure Stars are from the muddy meators. **1667** MILTON *P.L.* I. 537 Th' Imperial Ensign.. Shon like a Meteor streaming to the Wind. **1680** EVELYN *Diary* 12 Dec., I saw a meteor of an obscure bright colour, very much in shape like the blade of a sword. **1695** PRIOR *Eng. Ballad on Taking Namur* xii, If thou hadst dubb'd thy star a meteor, That did but blaze, and rove, and die. **1750** *Phil. Trans.* XLVII. 3 A meteor was seen at Norwich by thousands of people. **1819** S. ROGERS *Hum. Life* 35 And such is Human Life;..It glimmers like a meteor and is gone. **1878** NEWCOMB *Pop. Astron.* III. v. 388 The varied phenomena of aërolites, meteors, shooting-stars.

b. Applied to other luminous appearances, as the aurora borealis, the ignis fatuus, etc.

1592 SHAKS. *Rom. & Jul.* III. v. 13 Yond light is not daylight,..It is some Meteor that the Sun exhales. **1783** HEY in *Phil. Trans.* LXXX. 39 A species of that kind of meteor called aurora borealis. **1786** tr. *Beckford's Vathek* 176 Those phosphoric meteors that glimmer by night in places of interment. **1847** LYTTON *Lucretia* II. Epil. III. 295 You may enlighten the clod, but the meteor still must feed on the marsh. **1868** FARRAR *Silence & V.* ii. (1875) 4 That he may plunge after the delusive meteor which flickers hither and thither over the marsh of death.

†**c.** ***next the meteors***: high up. *Obs. rare*$^{-1}$.

1638 BAKER tr. *Balzac's Lett.* (vol. III.) 49, I always find you in the chamber next to the Meteors; which high region I conceive you have chosen, that you may be the nearer to take the inspirations of heaven.

d. *loosely.* A meteoroid.

1884 *Leisure Hour* Nov. 681/1 To the meteors which thus move in streams the appropriate designation meteoroids has recently been given. **1903** A. R. WALLACE *Man's Place in Universe* vi. 119 Collisions of meteors within each swarm or cloud would produce luminous nebulosity.

3. *transf.* and *fig.* (from sense 2 a).

1590 SHAKS. *Com. Err.* IV. ii. 6 His hearts Meteors tilting in his face. **1643** SIR T. BROWNE *Relig. Med.* I. §13 The Devils do know Thee, but those damnèd meteors Build not Thy Glory, but confound Thy Creatures. **1752** JOHNSON *Rambler* No. 208 ¶3, I have seen the Meteors of fashion rise and fall. **1769** G. WHITE *Selborne* (1789) 70 Th' impatient damsel hung her lamp on high: True to the signal, by love's meteor led, Leander hasten'd to his Hero's bed.

†**4.** *pl.* A study of or a treatise on meteors. *Obs.*

1594 PLAT *Jewell-ho.* II. 40 Neither out of Aristotles physicks..nor Garsceus meteors, nor out of any of the olde philosophicall Fathers, &c. **1604** E. G[RIMSTONE] *D'Acosta's Hist. Indies* III. xiv. 162 This second opinion is true..not so much for the reasons which the Philosophers give in their Meteors, as [etc.]. **1656** EARL MONM. tr. *Boccalini's Advts. fr. Parnass.* 257 Apollo some months ago ..made Ptolemy, that prince of cosmographers, the chairman..to whom he gave Aristotle for his companion in Meteors, Euclid in the Mathematicks [etc.].

5. A name for a confection (see quot.).

1827 G. A. JARRIN *Ital. Confectioner* (ed. 3) 195 Meteors. Three whites of Eggs, 1lb. Sugar, made into Syrup, and any Essence you please.

6. *attrib.* and *Comb.* **a.** Simple attrib., as ***meteor-field***, ***-fire***, ***-light***, ***-shower***; ***meteor-like*** adj. and adv. **b.** obj., as ***meteor-breathing***, ***-eclipsing*** adjs. **c.** instrumental, as ***meteor-blazoned***, ***-lighted*** adjs. **d.** Special combs.: **meteor bumper** *Astronautics*, a structure on the outside of a spacecraft that serves to protect it from the impacts of meteoroids; **meteor-cloud**, 'a cloud-like train left by a meteor in the upper air' (*Cent. Dict.* 1890), also 'an expanse of space thickly studded with meteors or meteoric particles' (*Cassell's Encycl. Dict.* 1885); **meteor-current**, 'the current or stream of meteors moving together in the same orbit' (*Ibid.*); **meteor-dust**, matter in a state of fine division, supposed to be diffused through interstellar space; **meteor-powder**, a powdered-up alloy which is mixed with steel to form *meteor-steel*; **meteor-spectroscopy**, the spectroscopic observation of meteors; **meteor-spectrum**, the spectrum produced by the light from a meteor; **meteor-steel**, an alloyed steel with a wavy appearance, resembling Damascus steel; **meteor-stone** = *meteoric stone* (see METEORIC 3); also *fig.*; **meteor-streak**, a streak of light left behind by a meteor after it has disappeared; **meteor-stream** = *meteor-current*; **meteor-swarm**, **-system**, an aggregation of meteoroids pursuing the same orbit; **meteor trail**, a bright streak of ionized gas formed by a meteor passing through the upper atmosphere, which can provide a reflector for radio communication.

1813 SCOTT *Trierm.* III. xiv, No misty phantom of the air, No *meteor-blazon'd show was there. **1819** SHELLEY *Prometh. Unb.* II. iii. 3 The mighty portal, Like a volcano's *meteor-breathing chasm. **1951** *Jrnl. Brit. Interplanetary Soc.* X. 275 For space station lifetimes of more than one year, it is concluded that either a heavily-armoured hull or a '*meteor bumper' will be required. **1960** *Aeroplane* XCVIII. 680/2 Dorsey described the space-laboratory as a double shell, three compartment, cylinder with convex end domes. The outer shell, made of beryllium, would serve as a 'meteor bumper' and thermal shield. **1962** F. I. ORDWAY et al. *Basic Astronautics* xi. 450 A double-wall meteor bumper in which the outer wall serves to break up the impacting meteor. **1870** *Rep. Brit. Assoc.* 76 The *meteor-currents..will shortly be supplemented [etc.]. **1869** HUXLEY *Lay Serm.* xi. (1870) 273 Sir W. Thomson..shows

that *meteor-dust..would account for the remainder of retardation. **1819** SHELLEY *Prometh. Unb.* IV. 5 For the sun ..Hastes, in *meteor-eclipsing array. **1718** BLACKMORE *Alfred* x. (1723) 343 Their peaks survey the *Meteor-Fields below. **1753** MASON *Elegy to Yng. Noblem.* 23 The Muse full oft pursues a *meteor fire. **1804** CHARLOTTE SMITH *Conversations*, etc. I. 178 False *meteor-lights their steps entice. **1795** SOUTHEY *Joan of Arc* II. 149 Upon the topmost height the Maiden saw A *meteor-lighted dome. *a* **1631** DONNE *Calme* 22 We can nor lost friends, nor sought foes recover, But *meteorlike, save that wee move not, hover. **1646** CRASHAW *Musick's Duel* 137 The lute..Whose flourish (meteor-like) doth curle the aire With flash of high-borne fancyes. **1813** BYRON *Giaour* vii, As meteor-like thou glidest by. **1827** *Repert. Patent Invent.* III. 206 The mixture..we call *meteor powder. **1877** G. F. CHAMBERS *Astron.* IX. iii. (ed. 3) 798 Another *meteor shower of great importance occurs annually on August 10. **1881** HERSCHEL in *Nature* XXIV. 507 Some *meteor-spectrum observations, which.. unfold some of the most important results arrived at in *meteor-spectroscopy since its commencement in the year 1866. **1827** *Repert. Patent Invent.* III. 205 This said alloyed steel we [the patentees] call *meteor steel. **1822** MOORE *Mem.* (1853) IV. 153 One of those *meteor-stones which generate themselves so unaccountably in the high atmosphere of his fancy. **1869** *Rep. Brit. Assoc.* 216 Certain persistent *meteor-streaks determined by Professor Newton in the United States, on the 14th of November last. **1877** G. F. CHAMBERS *Astron.* x. ii. (ed. 3) 835 The incalculable number of *meteor-streams that must exist in the solar system. *Ibid.*, The only *meteor-systems whose orbits have been determined travel on the same orbits with well-known comets. **1930** R. H. BAKER *Astron.* vi. 246 (*caption*) *Meteor trail. **1935** —— *Introd. Astron.* ix. 195 It is estimated that a single observer can see an average of ten meteor trails in the course of an hour on clear, moonless nights. **1958** *Jrnl. Atmospheric & Terrestrial Physics* XII. 329 At an early stage it became apparent that reflections from meteor trails play an important part in v.h.f. ionospheric forward scattering. **1968** *Radio Communication Handbk.* (ed. 4) xii. 17/2 There are times when the more orthodox modes of propagation fail to provide a satisfactory means of communication and one or other of the various forms of propagation by scatter may then offer a useful alternative: these include tropospheric scatter, ionospheric scatter..and meteor-trail scatter.

7. Passing into *adj.* = **a.** Blazing or flashing like a meteor.

a **1711** KEN *Hymns Evang.* Poet. Wks. 1721 I. 88 A Crown of meteor-stars adorn'd his Head, All calculated for exciting Dread. **1765** BEATTIE *Judgm. Paris* xlix, Fate scatters lightning from thy meteor-shield. **1786** BURNS *Vision* II. xviii, Misled by Fancy's meteor-ray. **1799** CAMPBELL *Pleas. Hope* I. 59 With meteor-standard to the winds unfurl'd. **1801** —— *Ye Mariners* iv, The meteor flag of England Shall yet terrific burn. **1810** *Associate Minstrels* 88 For thee his glowing torch did Genius fire:— Who now its meteor-brightness shall recal? **1864** BROWNING *Abt Vogler* iv, Meteor-moons, balls of blaze.

b. Of short duration, passing rapidly, transient.

1803 BEDDOES *Hygëia* x. 49 With the help of this scaffolding, his castles run up into the air with meteor rapidity. **1811** W. R. SPENCER *Poems* 49 Can bid the meteor-forms of mem'ry last. **1813** SHELLEY *Q. Mab* IV. 101 The meteor-happiness, that shuns his grasp. **1902** A. LANG *Hist. Scot.* II. xiii. 394 Bothwell's meteor course was run.

meteorette (ˌmiːtɪəˈrɛt). [f. METEOR + -ETTE.] A small meteor.

1876 *Gentl. Mag.* XVI. 552 Specks flitting like meteorettes over the crests of the billows.

meteoric (miːtɪˈɒrɪk), *a.* [Partly ad. med.L. *meteōric-us* ('elevatus, attentus', Du Cange), f. Gr. μετέωρος (see METEOR); partly f. METEOR + -IC. Cf. F. *météorique*.]

†**1. a.** Pertaining to the region of mid-air. **b.** *nonce-use.* Elevated, lofty. *Obs.*

a **1631** DONNE *Lett.* (1651) 46 Our nature is Meteorique, we respect (because we partake so) both earth and heaven. **1832** S. TURNER *Sacr. Hist.* I. i. 14 *note* (tr. Diodorus Siculus), The fiery particles ascended to the most meteoric or highest regions [Gr. πρὸς τοὺς μετεωροτάτους τόπους].

2. a. Of or pertaining to the atmosphere or its phenomena; meteorological, atmospherical.

1830 HERSCHEL *Stud. Nat. Phil.* III. iii. (1851) 286 The action of meteoric agents, rain, wind, frost, &c. **1834** MRS. SOMERVILLE *Connex. Phys. Sci.* xxvi. (1849) 299 Wind, rain, snow, fog, and the other meteoric phenomena. **1856–64** THOMAS *Med. Dict.*, *Meteoric*... Applied..to waters which accrue from condensation of the vapours suspended in the atmosphere. **1965** G. J. WILLIAMS *Econ. Geol. N.Z.* viii. 94/2 Morgan (1924) had difficulty in visualizing how meteoric solutions could descend to the depth at which veins have been found. **1969** C. OLLIER *Volcanoes* ii. 17 The water emitted by hot springs is usually of meteoric origin, that is derived from rain, and only a very minor part is likely to be derived from magma.

b. *Bot.* Dependent upon atmospheric conditions (see quots.).

1789 E. DARWIN *Bot. Gard.* II. 62 *note*, Linneus..divides them first into *meteoric* flowers, which..are expanded sooner or later, according to the cloudiness, moisture, or pressure of the atmosphere. 2d, *Tropical* flowers..3d, *Æquinoctial* flowers. **1849** J. H. BALFOUR *Man. Bot.* §484 Many flowers, or heads of flowers, do not open during cloudy or rainy weather, and have been called *meteoric*. **1857** BERKELEY *Cryptog. Bot.* §226 That a large portion of them [*sc.* fungi] are dependent entirely on matters contained in the air, and in consequence that many are essentially meteoric.

3. a. Of, pertaining to, or derived from meteors; consisting of meteors. ***meteoric stone*** = METEORITE.

1812 SIR H. DAVY *Chem. Philos.* 424 In all the meteoric stones that have been examined it is remarkable that the iron is alloyed by from 1·5 to 17 per cent. of nickel. **1822** FARADAY *Exp. Res.* xvi. (1859) 70 Specimens of meteoric iron. **1835** OLMSTED in *Jrnl. Franklin Instit.* XVI. 374 On the morning of the 13th of November, there was a slight repetition of the *Meteoric Shower*, which presented so remarkable a spectacle on the corresponding morning of 1833. **1842** DICKENS *Amer. Notes* viii, Like something meteoric that has fallen down from the moon. **1856** KANE *Arct. Expl.* I. xxxi. 428 The annual meteoric shower. **1869** *Rep. Brit. Assoc.* 217 These meteoric epochs of the 10th, 20th, and 30th of April. **1870** *Ibid.* 78 Each of these meteoric dates in the coming year. **1897** W. F. DENNING in *Observatory* Mar. 123 Meteoric observers..are extremely fortunate as regards their prospects in the immediate future.

b. ***meteoric paper*** = natural flannel (FLANNEL *sb.* 4). ***meteoric steel*** = meteor steel (METEOR 6).

1831 J. HOLLAND *Manuf. Metal* I. 249 Meteoric steel. **1856** GRIFFITH & HENFREY *Microgr. Dict.* 424 Meteoric Paper.

4. *fig.* Transiently or irregularly brilliant, flashing or dazzling like a meteor; also rapid, swift.

1836 H. F. CHORLEY *Mrs. Hemans* (1837) I. 76 To his [Kean's] splendid meteoric talent she did full justice. **1861** CRAIK *Hist. Eng. Lit.* II. 235 The first Earl [of Shaftesbury], the famous meteoric politician of the reign of Charles II. **1895** *Daily Chron.* 16 Jan. 5/7 We had occasion to undertake a somewhat meteoric flight from Balmoral.

†**meteˈorical**, *a. Obs. rare.* [Formed as prec.: see -ICAL.] = METEORIC *a.*

1651 BP. HALL *Soliloq.* xii. 42 The meteoricall light which appears in Moorish places. **1662** J. CHANDLER *Van Helmont's Oriat.* 119 Thus far the Church admitteth of Meteorical Predictions, the barrennesses of years, and their fruitfulnesses,..Plagues, inundations [etc.].

meteorically (miːtɪˈɒrɪkəlɪ), *adv.* [f. METEORIC: see -ICALLY.] **a.** In accordance with atmospheric conditions.

1882 VINES tr. *Sachs' Bot.* 875 A rise of temperature at 3 a.m. distinctly accelerated the assumption of the diurnal position by the leaves of *Impatiens*, but it seemed to have little or no effect upon other meteorically sensitive leaves.

b. With the suddenness and speed of a meteor.

1916 A. S. NEILL *Dominie's Log* xiv. 154 She dons the bridal white, and at once she rises meteorically in the social scale. **1955** *Sci. Amer.* Apr. 38/3 Meanwhile they also spread through the Straits of Mackinac into Lake Michigan and increased meteorically there. **1973** *Current Hist.* May 204/1 Born in 1926, he had joined the Communist party in 1943, fought with the Partisans, and risen meteorically in the Croatian Communist party.

meteorism (ˈmiːtɪərɪz(ə)m). *Path.* [ad. medical L. *meteōrism-us*, a. Gr. μετεωρισμ-ός elevation, f. μετεωρίζειν (see METEORIZE). Cf. F. *météorisme* (16th c., Paré).] Flatulent distention of the abdomen with gas in the alimentary canal.

1843 R. J. GRAVES *Syst. Clin. Med.* x. 109 Tenderness of the belly, meteorism and exhausting diarrhœa. **1899** *Allbutt's Syst. Med.* VIII. 576 Diarrhœa..with meteorism.

‖**meteorismus** (ˌmiːtɪəˈrɪzməs). [See prec.]

1. *Path.* = METEORISM.

1879 *St. George's Hosp. Rep.* IX. 735 Meteorismus is an early symptom in intussusception. *Ibid.*, Meteorismus is restrained somewhat by the external application of ice.

2. = SUBLIMATION.

1890 in *Syd. Soc. Lex.*

meteorist (ˈmiːtɪərɪst). [f. METEOR + -IST.] One versed in the study of meteors.

1898 *Westm. Gaz.* 19 Jan. 8/1 Our Leading Meteorist.

meteoristic (miːtɪəˈrɪstɪk), *a.* *Path.* [f. METEORISM: see -ISTIC.] Pertaining to or affected by meteorism.

1877 tr. *von Ziemssen's Cycl. Med.* VII. 609 These overloaded and meteoristic loops [of intestine]. **1897** *Allbutt's Syst. Med.* III. 872 The abdomen soon becomes retracted in cholera, but meteoristic in acute strangulation.

meteorite (ˈmiːtɪəˌraɪt). [f. METEOR + -ITE[1].] A fallen meteor; a mass of stone or iron, that has fallen from the sky upon the earth; a meteoric stone. Also (*loosely*), a meteor or meteoroid.

1824 *Phil. Mag.* LXIV. 113, I shall..pass in review..the principal new facts..respecting igneous meteors and meteorites, which have been made known..during the year 1823. **1834** OLMSTED in *Amer. Jrnl. Sci.* XXVI. 132 Although bodies of this class, or *Meteorites*, may occasionally present the same appearance as a 'shooting star', yet [etc.]. **1853** PHILLIPS *Rivers Yorks.* iii. 106 A great meteorite or mass of iron 56 lbs. in weight fell from the sky. **1874** TAIT *Rec. Adv. Phys. Sci.* x. (1876) 254 Meteorites, the so-called falling stars,..follow a perfectly definite track in space.

attrib. **1880** AGNES GIBERNE *Sun, Moon & Stars* 216 Among the many different Meteorite-rings which are known, two of the most important are the so-called August and November systems. *Ibid.*, A certain number of meteorite-systems are now pretty well known to astronomers.

Hence **'meteoˌrital, meteo'ritic, meteo'ritical** *adjs.*, of, pertaining to, or relating to meteorites; **meteo'ritically** *adv.*

1867–77 G. F. CHAMBERS *Astron.* 781 The produce of a meteoritic shower may be divided into meteoric iron and meteoric stone. **1889** A. WINCHELL in J. C. Irons *J. Croll* (1896) 466 The theory of meteorital aggregation. **1919** BEERBOHM *Seven Men* 5 At the end of Term he settled in —or rather, meteoritically into—London. **1939** *Pop. Astron.* XLVII. 328 The Editor ventures the following suggestions relative to three..meteoritical terms. **1946** *Ibid.* LIV. 430 These amendments went into effect at the adjournment of the meeting on September 10; whereupon the name of the Society was officially changed from 'The Society for Research on Meteorites'..to 'The Meteoritical Society'. (It is hardly necessary to add that *meteoritical* is merely the adjective of *meteoritics*, defined as 'the science of meteorites and meteors'.) **1950** *New Mexico Q.* Autumn 270 The Institute of Meteoritics, the first scientific organization, at least in the English-speaking world, devoted to meteoritical research. **1974** *Geotimes* Mar. 8, Aug. 7–9 Meteoritical Society, ann. mtg, Los Angeles.

meteoritics (ˌmiːtɪəˈrɪtɪks), *sb. pl.* (const. as sing.). [f. METEORIT(E + -ICS, as ad. Russ. *meteoritika* (Yu. I. Simashko 1889, in *Niva* XX. 82/2).] The scientific study of meteors and meteorites.

1934 in WEBSTER. **1946**, **1950** [see METEORITICAL *a.*]. **1952** *Jrnl. Brit. Interplanetary Soc.* XI. 243 The astronomer in particular is interested in the composition of meteorites as chemical samples of the universe... The techniques of investigation are, however, not astrophysical but rather mineralogical and metallurgical, and it is hoped that the coining of the new term 'meteoritics' for the subject..may signify an increased co-operation between astronomers and the laboratory investigators. **1960** I. VIDZIUNAS tr. *Krinov's Princ. Meteoritics* i. 29 One of the most important areas of meteoritics is the study of the motion of meteoric bodies in the Earth's atmosphere and the observation of bolides. **1963** *Nature* 5 Jan. 38/1 Meteoritics is a young science. Only since around 1945 has extensive research been undertaken. **1975** *Sci. Amer.* Jan. 29/1 In recent years the discipline of meteoritics has moved beyond the taxonomic stage, and sound geochemical and physical reasoning has been applied in interpreting the masses of data.

Hence **meteo'riticist**, an expert in meteoritics.

1952 *Jrnl. Brit. Interplanetary Soc.* XI. 243 The first problems that meteoriticists (!) must tackle are the location and classification of falls, and a statistical analysis of the information so obtained. **1971** *New Scientist* 3 June 556/1 From studies of the amount of xenon present in various meteorites, meteoriticists had speculated that Pu-244 once existed in achondritic meteorites. **1975** *Sci. Amer.* Jan. 29/2 Some meteoriticists boldly construct multistage scenarios of condensation, agglomeration, accretion, heating, metamorphism and differentiation to explain the accumulated facts.

meteorization (ˌmiːtɪəraɪˈzeɪʃən). *Path.* [f. next + -ATION.] 'The state or process of generating gas in the abdomen' (*Syd. Soc. Lex.* 1890).

1856 in MAYNE *Expos. Lex.*

†**meteorize**, *v. Obs.* or *arch.* [ad. Gr. μετεωρίζειν to elevate (μετεωριζόμενος suffering from flatulency), f. μετέωρο-ς raised, lofty: see METEOR and -IZE. Cf. F. *météoriser*.]

1. *trans.* To vaporize, convert into vapour. Also *intr.* to become vaporized, pass into the air in vapour. Only in Evelyn, who uses it frequently.

1657–83 EVELYN *Hist. Relig.* (1850) I. 27 The grosser exhalations are meteorized, circulated, and condensed into clouds. **1664** —— *Sylva* (1679) 29 The dew that impearls the leaves [of oaks] in May, insolated, meteorizes and sends up a liquor, which is of admirable effect in ruptures. **1675** —— *Terra* (1676) 173 Of all Waters, that which descends from Heaven, we find to be the richest.., as having been already meteoriz'd, and circulated in that great digestory.

2. *intr.* To resemble a meteor; to flash, sparkle.

1828 *Blackw. Mag.* XXIV. 268 It was imperative upon them to scintillate—to coruscate—to meteorize—to make the natives..believe that 'a new sun had risen on mid-day'.

3. *trans.* To affect with meteorism.

1826 [see next].

'meteorized, *ppl. a. Path.* [f. prec. + -ED[1].] Characterized by meteorism.

1826 H. BEST *Four Yrs. France* 347 This proceeded from a meteorized state of the bowels.

meteorogram (ˈmiːtɪərəgræm). [f. METEORO(GRAPH + -GRAM.] A record furnished by a meteorograph.

1904 *U.S. Dept. Agric. Monthly Weather Rev.* XXXII. 121/2, (1) instrumental errors, (2) errors in exposure of instruments when comparing with standards, (3) errors in reading from meteorograms. **1923** N. SHAW *Forecasting Weather* (ed. 2) v. 144 The trace given by a barometer is called a 'barogram', that by a thermometer a 'thermogram', while a trace of either the direction or force of wind is called an 'anemogram'. When two or more of these traces are all combined in one picture..the whole is called a 'meteorogram'. **1955** W. J. SAUCIER *Princ. Meteorol. Analysis* xii. 386 (*heading*) 'Meteorograms' of surface weather elements for 27 February through 3 March 1950.

meteorograph (ˈmiːtɪərəgrɑːf, -æ-). [a. F. *météorographe*, f. Gr. μετεωρο- METEOR + -γράφος -GRAPH.] An apparatus for automatically recording several different kinds of meteorological phenomena at the same time.

1780 *Monthly Rev.* LXIII. 499 A piece of mechanism, which he [Magellan] calls a *perpetual meteorograph*. **1879** *Smithsonian Rep.* (1880) 519 A universal meteorograph, designed for detached observatories. **1900** *Standard* 21 July 3/1 A Richard meteorograph..by which traces of the barometric pressure, temperature, and humidity are continuously and automatically recorded on rotating papered cylinders.

meteorography (ˌmiːtɪəˈrɒgrəfɪ). [f. Gr. μετεωρο- METEOR + -γραφία -GRAPHY.] The

descriptive science of meteors, or of meteorological phenomena.

1736 BAILEY (folio) Pref., *Meteorography*..a Treatise or Description of Meteors. **1776** B. MARTIN *Bibl. Technol.* (ed. 4) 330 Meteorography is a description of the meteors of the air; as vapours, clouds, rain, thunder, &c.

Hence **meteoro'graphic, -'graphical** *adjs.*, of or pertaining to meteorography.

1867 *Every Saturday* IV. 472 (Poole's Index), Meteorographical Apparatus. **1882** OGILVIE, *Meteorographic*; and in recent Dicts.

meteoroid ('miːtɪərɔɪd), *a.* and *sb.* [f. METEOR + -OID.] **a.** *sb.* A body moving through space, of the same nature as those which when passing through the atmosphere become visible as meteors. **b.** *adj.* Of the nature of a meteoroid.

1865 H. A. NEWTON in *Amer. Jrnl. Sci.* Ser. II. XXXIX. 198 The term *meteoroid* will be used to designate such a body before it enters the earth's atmosphere. **1867** PHIPSON *Meteors*, etc. xvi. 176 The perturbations of meteoroid masses circulating in space..must be considerable. *Ibid.* 178 The satellite and planetary theories of meteoroids. **1871** *Rep. Brit. Assoc.* 45 A very small nebular mass of meteoroids or of cometoids having been deflected [etc.].

Hence **meteo'roidal** *a.*, of or pertaining to meteoroids.

1881 *Smithsonian Rep.* 29 This remarkable group of planetoidal or meteoroidal bodies forms a tolerably wide zone or ring between the orbits of Mars and Jupiter. **1883** *American* VII. 152 The meteoroidal or cosmical dust of the realms of space.

meteorolite ('miːtɪərəlaɪt). Also 9 **meteorolithe.** [ad. F. *météorolithe*, f. Gr. μετεωρο- METEOR + λίθος stone: see -LITE.] = METEORITE.

1812 SOUTHEY *Omniana* II. 204 [*heading of paragraph*] Meteorolithes. **1821** URE *Dict. Chem.*, *Meteorolites*, or *Meteoric Stones.* **1822** P. CLEAVELAND *Min. & Geol.* (ed. 2) II. 772 Meteorolite. *a* **1835** MᶜCULLOCH *Attributes* (1837) II. 412 If the meteorolites should ever be proved to be fragments of the presumed planet. **1866** HERSCHEL *Fam. Lect. Sci.* ii. 73 Meteorolites which..have come to the earth from very remote regions of the Planetary spaces.

Hence **meteoro'litic** *a.*

1824 MACCULLOCH *Highl. Scot.* IV. 159 It is more ingenious to imagine the fashion derived from some similar respect paid to a meteorolitic Palladium in former days.

†**meteo'rologer.** *Obs.* [f. Gr. μετεωρολόγ-ος: see METEOR and -LOGER.] = METEOROLOGIST.

1683 J. GADBURY in *Wharton's Wks.* Pref. 15 The watchful and industrious Meteorologer, who makes it his Work to attend the Motions of Winds, Rains, Thunders. **1686** GOAD *Celest. Bodies* II. i. 147 The Trajections and shooting of the Stars..of which Meteorologers write.

†**meteoro'logian.** *Obs.* [Formed as prec.: see -LOGIAN.] = METEOROLOGIST.

1614 PURCHAS *Pilgrimage* (ed. 2) 537 The Athenians persecuted Naturall Philosophers, and Meteorlogians [*sic*], as aduersaries to Diuinitie. **1635** PERSON *Varieties* I. 18 These our meteorologians call *Ignes fatui*,..wildefires. *Ibid.* II. 55.

meteorologic (miːtɪərə'lɒdʒɪk), *a.* [Formed as next: see -LOGIC.] = next.

1760 WINTHROP in *Phil. Trans.* LII. 7 But no such thing occurs at present; unless you should be of opinion, that the two following accounts, in the meteorologic way, are so in some degree. **1857** H. SPENCER in *Westm. Rev.* Apr. 447 Not only has every extensive region its own meteorologic conditions, but [etc.]. **1873** *Nature* 11 Dec. 103/2 Meteorologic sections of the atmosphere.

meteorological (ˌmiːtɪərə'lɒdʒɪkəl), *a.* (*sb.*) [f. Gr. μετεωρολογικ-ός, f. μετεωρο- METEOR: see -LOGIC and cf. F. *météorologique.*] **a.** Pertaining to or connected with the science of meteorology. Also, pertaining to atmospheric phenomena.

1570 DEE *Math. Pref.* b iij b, His [Aristotle's] Meteorologicall bookes, are full of..demonstrations of the ..power of the heauenly bodies. **1572** R. T. *Discourse* Ep., The generation and causes of Raine, Winde, Snowe, and such Meteorologicall things. **1674** BOYLE *Excell. Theol.* I. iii. 93 His Meteorological Epistle to Pythocles. **1791** BOSWELL *Johnson* (1831) I. 307 A very curious meteorological instrument. **1803** *Med. Jrnl.* X. 313 As I kept no meteorological diary, the facts relative to the weather are deduced from my memory. **1840** *Abstr. Papers* in *Phil. Trans.* (1843) IV. 200 Meteorological Register kept at Port Arthur, Van Diemen's Land, during the year 1838.

b. ***Meteorological Office, officer.***

1930 *Daily Express* 6 Oct. 2/4 Mr. M. A. Giblett, M.Sc., meteorological officer, R 101..organised the necessary meteorological services for airship flights to Canada. **1937** *Discovery* Jan. 5/1 For this a Benndorf self-registering electrometer was kindly lent by the Meteorological Office. **1967** *Ships' Code & Decode Bk.* (Meteorol. Office) (ed. 7) 66 Meteorological Officers. **1968** *Measurement Upper Winds by Pilot Balloons* (Meteorol. Office) (ed. 4) 37 The Meteorological Office has produced electric torches for use with pilot balloons. **1975** *Times* 12 Aug. 3/4 The Meteorological Office held a competition..for the best ideas for a new television presentation of weather.

meteorologically (ˌmiːtɪərə'lɒdʒɪkəlɪ), *adv.* [f. prec. + -LY².] According to or by means of the science of meteorology; with regard to meteorological facts.

a **1673** JOS. CARYL in Spurgeon *Treas. Dav.* Ps. xxix. 2 David answereth meteorologically as well as theologically. **1794** SULLIVAN *View Nat.* I. 336 This vapour..or as it is meteorologically explained, this thin vesicle of water, or other humid matter. **1894** *Naturalist* 13 The season..will long be remembered meteorologically on account of the marvellous weather experienced.

†**meteorolo'gician.** *Obs. rare.* [f. Gr. μετεωρολόγος: see METEOROLOGER and -ICIAN.] = METEOROLOGIST.

1580 G. HARVEY in *Three Proper Lett.* 21 Aristotle, Plinie, and other Meteorologicians. **1588** J. HARVEY *Disc. Probl.* 91 A cunning Astronomer, and expert Meteorologician.

†**meteorologics,** *sb. pl. Obs.* [repr. Gr. τὰ μετεωρολογικά, neut. pl. of μετεωρολογικός METEOROLOGIC: see -ICS.] = METEOROLOGY.

(In quots. representing the title of Aristotle's treatise.)

1700 S. PARKER *Six Philos. Ess.* 45 Aristotle..in his Second Book of Meteorologicks. **1837** WHEWELL *Hist. Induct. Sci.* I. 41 The 'Meteorologics' [of Aristotle]..does not exhibit the doctrines..of the school in so general a form.

meteorologist (ˌmiːtɪə'rɒlədʒɪst). [f. Gr. μετεωρολόγος (see METEOROLOGER): see -LOGIST and cf. F. *météorologiste.*] One who is skilled in meteorology.

1621 BURTON *Anat. Mel.* I. ii. I. ii. (1651) 46 Whirlewindes ..and..stormes; which..our Meteorologists generally refer to natural causes. **1685** BOYLE *Effects of Mot.* ii. 14 The wonderful effects Lightning has produced: of which effects ..the Writings of Meteorologists afford good store. **1820** SCORESBY *Acc. Arctic Reg.* I. 348 Professor Leslie..in his invention of a correct hygrometer..has presented the meteorologist with a gift which [etc.]. **1878** JEVONS *Prim. Pol. Econ.* iii. 32 Meteorologists have now prepared maps of the oceans showing the sea-captain where he will find winds and currents most favourable to a rapid voyage.

meteorology (ˌmiːtɪə'rɒlədʒɪ). [ad. Gr. μετεωρολογία, f. μετεωρο- METEOR + -λογία -LOGY. Cf. F. *météorologie.*]

1. The study of, or the science that treats of, the motions and phenomena of the atmosphere, *esp.* with a view to forecasting the weather.

1620 T. GRANGER *Div. Logike* 301 In the first Booke hee prosecuteth more common, and generall things; as, Astrologie, Meteorology. **1650** SIR T. BROWNE *Pseud. Ep.* III. x. (1658) 161 In sundry Animals we deny not a kind of natural Meteorology, or innate presention both of wind and weather. **1768–74** TUCKER *Lt. Nat.* (1834) II. 466 Zoology [is] the knowledge of animals;..meteorology and mineralogy, that of vapours and fossils. **1816** T. L. PEACOCK *Headlong Hall* i, The various knotty points of meteorology, which usually form the exordium of an English conversation. **1862** SIR H. HOLLAND *Ess.*, *Atlantic Ocean* 208 Meteorology cannot yet take its place among the exact sciences.

2. The character, as regards weather, atmospheric changes, etc., *of* a particular region.

1684 T. BURNET *Th. Earth* II. v. 224, I easily discover'd, that..the Meteorology of that World was of another sort from that of the present. *a* **1850** J. A. MASON (*title*) A Treatise on the Climate and Meteorology of Madeira. **1879** A. R. WALLACE *Australasia* ii. 31 The hot winds, which are another remarkable feature of the meteorology of Australia, occur in [etc.].

meteoromancy ('miːtɪərəmænsɪ). [fr. Gr. μετεωρο- METEOR + μαντεία divination, -MANCY. Cf. F. *météoromancie.*] Divination by the observation of meteors.

1797 *Encycl. Brit.* (ed. 3) XI. 622/1. **1845** SMEDLEY in *Encycl. Metrop.* XVIII. 174/2 In Etruria, the frequency of sacrifice and the temperament of the air, gave popularity to Extispicy and Meteoromancy.

meteorometer (ˌmiːtɪə'rɒmɪtə(r)). [f. Gr. μετεωρο- METEOR + -METER.] An apparatus for receiving and transmitting records of atmospherical conditions and changes.

1862 in KNIGHT *Dict. Mech.* (1875) s.v.

meteoroscope ('miːtɪərəˌskəʊp). [In sense 1, ad. Gr. μετεωροσκόπιον; in sense 2, f. μετεωρο- METEOR + -SCOPE.]

†**1.** An instrument for taking observations of heavenly bodies. *Obs.*

1614 TOMKIS *Albumazar* II. v. (1615) E I b, With Astralobe [*sic*] and Meteoroscope I'le find the Cuspe [etc.].

2. 'An instrument for measuring the apparent path of a meteor' (*Funk's Stand. Dict.* 1895).

†**meteoroscopics,** *sb. pl. Obs. rare.* [ad. Gr. μετεωροσκοπικ-ά neut. pl.: see METEOR, -SCOPIC, and -ICS.] The science of observing the stars.

1788 T. TAYLOR *Proclus* I. 79 The other is metheoroscopics [*sic*], which finds out the differences of elevations, and the distances of the stars [etc.].

meteoroscopy (ˌmiːtɪə'rɒskəpɪ). *rare.* [f. Gr. μετεωρο- METEOR + -σκοπία -SCOPY. Cf. F. *météoroscopie.*] Observation of the stars.

1658 PHILLIPS, *Meteoroscopie*, that part of Astrology, which handleth the difference of Sublimities, and distance of Stars. **1686** GOAD *Celest. Bodies* III. iii. 455 A Gentleman given to Metoroscopy [*sic*], looking on the two Stars in ♂ saw three. **1829** T. L. PEACOCK *Misfort. Elphin* xiii. 180 The topographers..had not the advantage of this piece of meteoroscopy.

Hence **meteo'roscopist** *rare*⁻⁰, an observer of the stars.

1727 in BAILEY vol. II.

meteoroso'phistical, *a. rare*⁻¹. [f. Gr. μετεωροσοφιστ-ής 'astrological sophist' + -ICAL.]

1814 T. L. PEACOCK *Wks.* (1875) III. 121 A delectable treat to the observer of phenomena, who may be desirous of contemplating a meteorosophistical spider completely entangled in his own cobweb.

meteorous ('miːtɪərəs, also *poet.* miː'tiːərəs), *a.* [f. Gr. μετέωρ-ος raised on high, μετέωρ-α neut. pl. METEOR + -OUS.] = METEORIC.

1667 MILTON *P.L.* XII. 629 Gliding meteorous, as Ev'ning Mist..o're the marish glides. **1720** POPE *Iliad* XXIV. 101 Iris ..Meteorous the face of ocean sweeps. **1750** JOHNSON *Rambler* No. 68 ¶3 Meteorous pleasures which dance before us and are dissipated. **1807** WRANGHAM *Serm. Transl. Script.* I The wavering and meteorous glare of the Eighth Henry. **1841** D'ISRAELI *Amen. Lit.* (1859) II. 343 We must conclude that there are meteorous beings, whose eccentric orbits we know not how to describe. **1882** SUTTON in *Society* 7 Oct. 16/1 Thy wavering, meteorous, quixotic indulgence [said of a comet].

†**meteory.** *Obs. rare*⁻¹. [f. METEOR + -Y.] Condition of atmosphere.

1600 TOURNEUR *Transf. Metam.* xlii. Plays & P. 1878 II. 204 And chaoiz'd Ideas of conceit Doth make his gesture seem a troubled skie: And fills his count'nance with sad meteorie.

metepencephalon (ˌmɛtɛpɛn'sɛfələn). *Anat.* Also anglicized **metepencephal** (-'sɛfəl). Pl. **metepencephala.** [mod.L., f. META- + EPENCEPHALON.] In Wilder's nomenclature, the metencephalon and epencephalon taken together and considered as one segment.

1885 WILDER in *N.Y. Med. Jrnl.* 21 Mar. 326 It is elsewhere suggested that those who admit only one segment between the mesencephalon and the myelon may apply thereto the comprehensive name *metepencephalon*, and to its cavity *metepicœle.* **1889** —— in *Buck's Handbk. Med. Sci.* VIII. 130/2 The compacted motor and sensory conductors between the prosodiencephal and metepencephal.

Hence **metepence'phalic** *a.*, of, pertaining to, or connected with the metepencephalon.

1890 in *Century Dict.*; and in later Dicts.

metepicœle (mɛ'tɛpɪsiːl). *Anat.* [f. META- + EPICŒLE.] The fourth ventricle of the brain.

1885 [see METEPENCEPHALON]. **1889** WILDER in *Buck's Handbk. Med. Sci.* VIII. 130/1 There is no evidence of the lines of division of the endyma in exposing the metepicœle ('fourth ventricle').

†**'metepole.** *Obs.* [f. METE *v.*¹ + POLE.] A measuring rod.

1571 GOLDING *Calvin on Ps.* lxxiv. 2 They wer wont to butte out grounds with metepoles as with lynes.

meter ('miːtə(r)), *sb.*¹ Also 5 **metere, metar,** 6 **meater,** 6–7 **metter,** 8 **meeter.** [f. METE *v.*¹ + -ER¹.] One who measures; a measurer; *esp.* one whose duty or office is to see that commodities are of the proper measure, as ***coal-meter, land-meter***: see these words.

1382 WYCLIF *Zech.* ii. 1 In his hond a litil covrde of meters [**1388** meteris, Vulg. *funiculus mensorum*]. **1468** *Maldon, Essex* Liber B. lf. 15 (MS.) And the metere shall stryke the busshell & make the hepe trewely betwixe party and party. And the comounn meter shall mete trewely the corne to be delyuered atte hythe. *c* **1483** CAXTON *Dialogues* 44 Paulyn the metar of corne. **1519** *Burgh Rec. Edin.* (1869) I. 190 And at na metter mett the said meill bot the bringare thairof to the merkat vnder the payne of banesing. **1542–3** *Act 34 & 35 Hen. VIII*, c. 9 §5 The said common meater to haue for the measuring of euery way of corne .ii.d. **1577** HARRISON *England* II. v. (1877) I. 127 A verie sharpe imprecation.. promiseth like measure to the meter, as he dooth mete to others. **1666** *Act 18 & 19 Chas. II*, c. 8 §34 Before they shall breake Bulke or have a Meter assigned for the measureing or weighing of any Coales..to be delivered from on board any such Shipp. **1681** *MS. Indenture Finkill Street, Hull*, William Haward metter. **1796** BURKE *Let. Noble Ld.* Wks. VIII. 38 But the aulnager, the weigher, the meter of grants, will not suffer us to acquiesce in the judgement of the prince reigning at the time when they were made. **1800** COLQUHOUN *Comm. Thames* xi. 331 To appoint sworn Meters, for measuring Coals in the Port of London. **1861** MAYHEW *Lond. Labour* III. 260 After the ship is sold she is admitted from the Section into the Pool, and a meter is appointed to her from the coalmeter's office. **1881** *Times* 11 Apr. 4/5 When a barge with the plaintiff's corn in it arrived in the creek..the creek men were to hand over the meter's ticket of the corn to the plaintiff's foreman.

fig. **1825** HAZLITT *Spirit of Age* 44 Reason is the meter and alnager in civil intercourse, by which each person's.. pretensions are weighed.

†**'meter,** *sb.*² *Obs. rare*⁻¹. [f. METE *v.*² + -ER¹.] A dreamer.

1340 *Ayenb.* 32 Þe meteres þet habbeþ drede of hare metinges.

meter ('miːtə(r)), *sb.*³ Also 9 (*rarely*) **metre.** [First used in *gas-meter*; probably an application of METER¹, suggested by the earlier GASOMETER or by the other words with the ending -METER.]

1. a. (In full ***gas-meter.***) An apparatus for automatically measuring and recording the volume of gas supplied for lighting or other purposes.

In the ordinary forms, the gas is made to pass through receptacles of known capacity, each filling and discharge of one of these being registered by the movement of an index on a dial. ***dry meter***: a meter in which no water is used; the

earlier and still commonly used form being called for distinction *wet meter*.

1815 [see GAS *sb.*[1] 7]. **1830** in *Fifesh. Advert.* 21 Sept. (1888) 4/3 To limit the price of gas by meter to 12*s.* nett per 1000 cubic feet. **1874** MICKLETHWAITE *Mod. Par. Churches* 195 After turning all off at the meter.

b. In extended sense: Any apparatus for automatically measuring and recording the quantity of a fluid or the like flowing through it. Used with prefixed word, as ***water-meter***, ***electric light meter***, etc., exc. where the purpose is sufficiently indicated by the context.

Also, with prefixed attributive word, in the names of instruments for measuring electrical quantities of various kinds, as *ampere-meter*, *coulomb-meter*, *farad-meter*, *ohm-meter*, *voltmeter*, *watt-meter*, which see under their respective first elements. See the remarks on these under -METER.

1832 BABBAGE *Econ. Manuf.* viii. (ed. 3) 57 The sale of water by the different companies in London, might also, with advantage, be regulated by a meter. **1858** GREENER *Gunnery* 52 This machine I termed an explosion metre;.. In each of these experiments the greatest accuracy was observed, in preparing the metre as well as in weighing the charge.

c. *fig.* A 'gauge', self-acting measure of the fluctuations of something.

1860 EMERSON *Cond. Life, Wealth* Wks. (Bohn) II. 351 The coin is a delicate meter of civil, social, and moral changes. **1870** —— *Soc. & Solit., Eloq.* ibid. III. 26 The audience is a constant meter of the orator.

d. = *exposure meter*.

1920 *Sat. Westm. Gaz.* 22 May 16/2 The golden rule is to expose by meter on the holiday, and leave all else to the return home.

e. *U.S. slang.* (See quots.)

1940 *Music Makers* May 37/2 *Meter*, quarter, twenty-five cents. **1960** WENTWORTH & FLEXNER *Dict. Amer. Slang* 337/2 *Meter*, a quarter... From the coin which often is needed to operate a gas meter. Orig. Negro use. Never common. **1970** C. MAJOR *Dict. Afro-Amer. Slang* 81 *Meter*, twenty-five cent coin.

f. = *parking meter*.

1960 *Daily Tel.* 31 Mar. 15/1 What promises to be the most important experiment in traffic control starts next Monday, when car parking over the whole of Mayfair becomes subject to meters. **1973** *Weekly News* (Glasgow) 11 Aug. 2/2 After a search, I found a parking place in Glasgow on a Saturday afternoon. I was standing next to the meter.. when a man who'd been standing on the opposite pavement came over. **1974** *Times* 21 Jan. 12/8 Since many meters in the Whitehall area have been suspended because of bomb threats, the wardens had a field day.

2. a. *attrib.*, as ***meter box***, ***chamber***, ***house***, ***inspector***, ***rent***, ***-wheel***.

1882 *Worcester Exhib. Catal.* iii. 16 Mr. Palmer's Patent *Meter Boxes. **1889** *Pall Mall Gaz.* 1 July 6/3 The pumps discharge into a *meter chamber, where the sewage is measured. **1897** *Daily News* 1 June 3/3 Land for *meter houses and other works. **1895** *Ibid.* 10 Oct. 6/4 The *meter inspectors. **1895** *Westm. Gaz.* 17 Apr. 3/3 It is fairer to charge a *meter rent than to charge a higher price for the gas. **1875** KNIGHT *Dict. Mech.*, **Meter-wheel*, one used in connection with gas and liquid meters and air-carbureting machines.

b. Special Combs.: **meter-feeder**, a motorist who illicitly extends his parking time by putting more money in the meter instead of moving away; so **meter-feeding** *vbl. sb.*; **meter maid** orig. *U.S.* (see quot. 1958); **meter-park** *v. trans.*, to park a vehicle at a parking meter; **meter-parking**, the use of parking meters; a place at a parking meter; **meter-reader**, a person responsible for reading gas or electricity meters; **meter-reading**, the reading of a meter or meters; **meter zone**, a limited area where the parking of vehicles is controlled by meters.

1965 *Guardian* 5 Apr. 8/2 The would-be meter feeder is tipped off if a hostile scout appears. **1972** *Ibid.* 8 May 9/6 Scotland Yard.. was setting up a special vigilante squad whose job was to keep tabs on meter feeders in Central London. **1966** *Punch* 5 Jan. 15/1 Driving dangerously, you may think, is obviously much more criminal than meter-feeding. But meter-feeding is a deliberately calculated breach of the law, whereas dangerous driving may be accidental. **1969** *Guardian* 28 Mar. 22/4 We realize councils must do something to stop meter feeding. **1957** in *Amer. Speech* (1961) XXXVI. 282 Surveys conducted in cities using 'meter maids' have found that their meter revenue increased. **1958** *Britannica Bk. of Year* 519/2 *Meter maid*, .. a woman police official with the task of patrolling metered parking-sites and reporting parking offences. **1968** *Harper's Mag.* Feb. 41 A Meter Maid was soon watching me censoriously. **1970** S. ELLIN *Man from Nowhere* xxx. 150 Some meter maid found him when she looked in the car where it was parked uptown. **1970** *Sunday Times* 3 May 28/7 Why do meter maids.. never look glamorous at all? **1971** H. C. RAE *Marksman* III. 212 The Mark 10 was meter-parked close to the side entrance. **1959** *Daily Tel.* 15 Dec. 1/7 In the past month, 81 motorists were convicted of contravening the existing meter parking scheme. **1963** D. B. HUGHES *Expendable Man* (1964) iv. 109 There were no meter parkings open near the courthouse. **1963** *Times* 8 Jan. 9/3 In an ideal world, everyone in uniform, from guardsmen to meter readers, would be immaculately turned out and dressed in strict conformity with the rules of their service. **1971** A. PRICE *Alamut Ambush* x. 123 A duty caller like the meter reader and the postman. **1974** *Times* 18 Apr. 14 Where the occupiers are out when he calls, the meter-reader leaves a card, inviting them to be at home next day. **1957** V. J. KEHOE *Technique Film & Television Make-Up* viii. 96 The middle of the ratio scale on a meter reading. **1959** *Daily Tel.* 15 Dec. 1/7 Larger meter zone by April. **1963** *Sunday Express* 3 Mar. 4/4, I had paid out over £220 in parking fines in the past 21 months because I lived in a 'meter zone'.

meter ('miːtə(r)), *sb.*[4] ? *U.S.* Either of two strengthening lines of a seine or gill net.

1884 KNIGHT *Dict. Mech.* Suppl. [In later Dicts.]

†**meter**, *sb.*[5] *Obs. rare*[−1]. [? a. F. *métier*: see MESTIER.] ? Office.

c **1510** BARCLAY *Mirr. Gd. Manners* (1570) F ij, O Priest.. Howe muche more thou passest in great aucthoritie, In meter or order, in office or prebende, So muche loke in vertue and maners to ascende. [Orig. *Aspice quam differs alijs in veste sacerdos, Tantum differre moribus ipse velis.*]

'**meter**, *v.* [METER *sb.*[3]]

1. a. To measure by means of a meter. Also, to supply through a meter.

1884 *Science* III. 497 The real proportions of air and gas were not determinable, except by metering both. **1894** *Times* 14 Aug. 11/4 The oil, waste, water, and general engine-room stores work out to ·0657 penny per unit metered. **1968** *Brit. Med. Bull.* 192/2 It is meaningful to envisage computer power being metered to separate offices.

b. *trans.* To regulate the flow of; to deliver (fluid) in regulated amounts *to*.

1932 *Compression Ignition Engines* xi. 132 Injection Pump.—A mechanical device which meters the liquid fuel in controllable quantities and delivers it at a set pressure to the working cylinders. **1963** *Adv. Space Sci. & Technol.* Suppl. I. 173 In addition to atomizing and mixing the liquids, it meters the flow to the combustion chamber. **1972** *Sci. Amer.* Aug. 21/2 Oil could also be metered to the critical contact region.

2. To measure (the parking-time) of motorists, etc., by means of parking meters; to provide with parking meters.

1957, etc. [implied in METERED *ppl. a.* below]. **1962** *Times* 16 Apr. 11/3 Brighton has proposed to meter the sea-front motorists' parking-time. **1963** 'W. HAGGARD' *High Wire* iii. 24 The comfortable little street.. had recently been metered.

So '**metered** *ppl. a.*

1928 M. RITTENBERG *Mail-Order made Easy* xiv. 177 'Metered' mail—where a printed impression is put on the envelope instead of an adhesive stamp. **1957** *New Yorker* 26 Oct. 36/1 You can park scooters almost anywhere without getting a ticket. In a metered area, the usual thing is to park them sidewise, between two parked cars. **1960** *Guardian* 13 Jan. 6/7 When all Mayfair becomes metered.. the position of the motorists will be worse than ever. **1961** *Ibid.* 27 June 5/6 A motorist.. may only park his car in a metered parking place. **1963** 'W. HAGGARD' *High Wire* iii. 24 This was a metered parking ground. **1968** *Listener* 27 June 851/1 The trouble is that in this country taxi-drivers who work for garages and not for themselves are commonly paid no set wages, but instead a proportion of the metered fare—say, 40 per cent.

meter: see METRE *sb.*[1] and [2].

-meter, in actual use commonly -'*ometer*, and in some later formations -'*imeter*, a terminal element in words denoting scientific instruments for automatically measuring something. Many words with this ending, as *barometer*, *hydrometer*, *hygrometer*, *thermometer*, were formed in the 17th c., and represent mod.L. forms in *-metrum* (F. *-mètre*, It. *-metro*). In these early examples the ending is always appended to Gr. noun-stems, or combining forms in *-o*, and the mod.L. form shows that it was intended to represent the Gr. *μέτρον* measure (see METRE *sb.*[1]); the formation is irregular, as the Gr. word does not occur in combination with sbs., and would not correctly express the required notion of 'instrument that measures'. In the 18th and 19th c. many additional words were formed with this ending on Greek bases, as *actinometer*, *anemometer*, *chronometer*, *eudiometer*, etc. Near the end of the 18th c. hybrid formations began to be introduced (many of them first occurring in Fr.). In some of these the form of Greek compounds is imitated, as in *gasometer*, *galvanometer*, *alcoholometer*, *lactometer*, *pedometer*; in others the combining-vowel *i* of the Latin first element is retained, as in *calorimeter*, *gravimeter*, *densimeter*, *velocimeter*. In some late formations *-meter* is appended to modern words without any attempt to assimilate the form of the first element to that of a Gr. or Latin combining form, as in *voltameter*, *ammeter*. Cf. also the names of electrical measuring instruments mentioned under METER *sb.*[3] 1 b, which might perhaps be more correctly viewed as examples of the suffixed *-meter* than as examples of the sb. with defining word.

Jocular nonce-words in *-ometer* have been frequently formed; chiefly in imitation of Sydney Smith's FOOLOMETER, with the sense 'a means of measuring or ascertaining the opinion or prevalent character of some class of people'; also occasionally in names of imaginary instruments for measuring the amount or degree of something, as in *obscenometer*. Similar hybrid formations have sometimes been adopted as trade names for certain instruments, e.g. ***comptometer*** [F. *compte* account], a kind of calculating machine, ***distance-ometer***.

1828 *Athenæum* 16 Jan. 44/1 We shall be obliged by an account, for our Scientific Report, of the obscenometer by which the 'Stock Board' of the Company are enabled so curiously to apportion the measures of indecency. **1859** *Sat. Rev.* VII. 141/2 The member for Birmingham has supplied Parliament with an admirable democratometer, without which it might have been hurried into violent and uncalled-for changes, through a total misapprehension of the real state of public feeling. **1864** *Daily Tel.* 29 Oct., Archdeacon Denison.. may be.. taken as a kind of clericometer for what is most violent and least sensible in the ecclesiastical world. **1883** *Eng. Mech.* 6 Apr. p. vii, The New Distanceometer. **1894** *Times* 19 Mar. 13/5 The comptometer.. is a machine specially adapted for subtraction, multiplication and division.

meterage ('miːtərɪdʒ). [f. METER *sb.*[1] + -AGE.]

a. 'The act of measuring' (Ogilvie 1882). **b.** 'The measurement itself'. **c.** 'The price paid for measurement' (Cassell's *Encycl. Dict.* 1885).

metereza: see METREZA.

metering ('miːtərɪŋ), *vbl. sb.* [f. METER *v.* + -ING[1].] Measuring; freq. *attrib.* as ***metering-point***, ***pump***, ***station***, etc. Also in other senses of METER *v.*

1913 *Wireless World* May 93/2 We must take a point just behind the metering-point.. as the beginning of the plant essential to the particular system under consideration. **1935** *Geogr. Jrnl.* LXXXV. 538 At each metering station a sufficient number of discharge measurements is taken. **1935** *Economist* 7 Dec. 1143/1 The development of the hand-operated metering pump affixed to an underground tank at garages.. revolutionised the service of distribution. **1959** *Daily Tel.* 24 Dec. 6/2 To improve off-street parking by general metering of the kerbs. **1962** *Rep. Comm. Broadcasting 1960* 264 in *Parl. Papers 1961–2* (Cmnd. 1753) IX. 259 Metering and access-barring apparatus. **1963** *Lancet* 5 Jan. 17/1 In order to do this, a multi-channel metering pump was made which consists of laminæ massaging silicone-rubber or plastic tubes. **1973** *Country Life* 20 Sept. 826/1 Full aperture metering gives you a bright clear image of the subject... The FD range consists of fully automatic metering lenses.

†'**meterod**. *Obs.* Also **metrod**. [f. METE *v.*[1] or MET *sb.*[1] + ROD *sb.* Cf. MDu. *meteroede*, Du. *meetroede*.] A measuring rod. Also *fig.*

1535 COVERDALE *Ezek.* xl. 5 The meterodde that he had in his honde, was six cubites longe and a spanne. **1556** WITHALS *Dict.* (1568) 14/1 A metrod, to measure the land with. **1579** J. JONES *Preserv. Bodie & Soule* I. xli. 92 Measured by the meterod of affection.

†'**metership**. *Obs.* [f. METER *sb.*[1] + -SHIP.] The office of meter or measurer.

1536 HENRY VIII in Ellis *Orig. Lett.* Ser. II. II. 90 The office of metershippe of lynyn clothe and canvas within our Cytie of London. **1541** WRIOTHESLEY *Chron.* (Camden) I. 129 The metershippe of cloth of gould, velvett, silkes, and lynnen cloath.

†'**metesel**. *Obs.* [f. *mete* MEAT *sb.* + *sel* SEEL, fitting time.] Meal-time.

c **1330** R. BRUNNE *Chron.* (1810) 334 It neghed nere metesel.

†'**meteship**. *Obs.* Forms: 1 **metscype**, 3 **metisupe**, 4 **metscip**, 4–5 **mets(c)hip**, **meteship(e**, **-shep**, **meetship**. [OE. *mętscipe*, f. *męte* MEAT *sb.*: see -SHIP.] The action of taking food; a repast.

a **1000** *Laws Athelstan* VI. c. 8 § 1 (Schmid) Habban þa xii menn heora metscype togædere. *c* **1200** *Trin. Coll. Hom.* 11 At ferme and at feste masthwat at ilche laðeð metisupe. *a* **1300** *Cursor M.* 7453 Of his metscip was mesur nan, He wald ete seuen sccp him an. *a* **1300–1400** *Ibid.* 12565 (Gött.) Quen he suld to metschip ga. **1398** TREVISA *Barth. De P.R.* VI. xxiii. (Tollem. MS.), Mete and drynke han ordinaunce and respecte to meteshep and to festis.

†'**metesome**, *a. Obs. rare*[−1]. [f. METE *v.*[1] + -SOME.] Measurable.

1674 N. FAIRFAX *Bulk & Selv.* 107 It [the atom] may be metesom by Mathematical measures of the minds making.

†**metessing**. *Obs.* Dung (of a hawk).

1486 *Bk. St. Albans* c iiij b, Hir metessing will defowle hir foundement.

'**metestick**, '**metstick**. [f. METE *v.*[1] or MET *sb.*[1] + STICK *sb.*] A stick or staff for measuring.

a. *Naut.* (See quot. 1815.) **b.** *Sc.* 'A wooden instrument or bit of wood used for taking the measure of the foot' (Jam.).

1815 *Falconer's Dict. Marine* (ed. Burney), *Mete-stick*, a staff of a certain length, fixed on a broad board at right angles, in order to.. determine the necessary height of a hold, and to level the ballast. **1821** *Blackw. Mag.* VIII. 432 The 'met-stick' pair'd away to suit the size.

metestrus, -um, varr. METŒSTRUS.

metethereal (mɛtɪ'θɪərɪəl), *a.* Also **metetherial**. [f. META- + ETHEREAL.] (See quot. 1903.)

1903 F. W. H. MYERS *Hum. Personality* I. Gloss. 19 *Metetherial*, that which appears to lie after or beyond the ether; the metetherial environment denotes the spiritual or transcendental world in which the soul exists. **1911** T. FLOURNOY *Spiritism & Psychol.* ii. 57 We participate.. in a higher order of phenomena—of a metethereal world, as Myers called it. **1924** T. H. Y. TROTTER *Mus. & Mind* I. ii. 28 A metethereal world,.. transcendental and spiritual.

1963 *Listener* 24 Jan. 175/3 Esoteric volumes on astral projection, crammed with words like 'metethereal'.

metewand ('mi:twɒnd). Also 6–7 meat-, 5–7, 9 *dial.* met-, 7 meet-. [f. METE *v.*[1] or MET *sb.*[1] + WAND *sb.*] A measuring rod. Now *dial.*

c **1440** *Promp. Parv.* 336/1 Metwande, *idem quod* ȝerde. **1549** ALLEN *Jude's Par. Rev.* 36 The golden reed is as it were a golden met wonde. **1624** F. WHITE *Repl. Fisher* 318 A measure containing the length of a man, which was the meat-wand, or measure which the Angell held. **1668** CULPEPPER & COLE *Barthol. Anat.* Man. IV. xx. 355 The Drapers Metwand termed an Ell. **1876** *Whitby Gloss., Metwand, Met-wood,* or *Met-yard,* a measuring-rod. A draper's yard-stick.

b. *fig.* A standard of measurement or estimation. *literary.*

a **1568** ASCHAM *Scholem.* II. (Arb.) 101 A true tochstone, a sure metwand lieth before both their eyes. *a* **1656** BP. HALL *Rem. Wks.* (1660) 205 Time is the common measure of all things, the universal met-wand of the Almighty. **1700** C. NESS *Antid. agst. Armin.* (1827) 8 Measuring supernatural mysteries with the crooked metewand of degenerate reason. **1809–10** COLERIDGE *Friend* xiii. (1887) 53 The degree of his moral guilt is not the mete-wand of his condemnation. **1866** LOWELL *Lessing* Prose Wks. 1890 II. 223 He continually trips and falls flat over his metewand of classical propriety.

meteyard ('mi:tjɑ:d). Also 6 mette-, 6–7 meat(e-, 5, 9 *dial.* met-. [f. METE *v.*[1] or MET *sb.*[1] + YARD *sb.*] = METEWAND. Now *dial.*

c **1430** *Pilgr. Lyf Manhode* III. xxvi. (1869) 150 With þe grete met yerde she wole mesure þat þat she biggeth. **1535** COVERDALE *Lev.* xix. 33 Ye shal not deale wrongeously in iudgment, with meteyarde, with weight, with measure. **1553** T. WILSON *Rhet.* 83 b, The tailor hath his mette yarde and his measure. **1611** BIBLE *Transl. Pref.* ¶9 Neither is it the plaine dealing Merchant that is vnwilling to haue the waights, or the meteyard brought in place, but he that vseth deceit. **1876** [see METEWAND].

b. *fig.* (Cf. METEWAND b.)

a **1533** FRITH *Disput. Purgat.* Pref. A iij b, The verye worde of god.. whiche is the sure metyarde and perfeyte touchstone that iudgeth and examineth all thynges. **1658** ROWLAND *Moufet's Theat. Ins.* Pref., It shall suffice us to have measured the causes by humane capacity and mete-yard. **1898** R. F. HORTON *Commandm. Jesus* xii. 201 It is what this regenerate Ego desires that becomes the mete-yard of what we should do to others.

meteyne, meth, obs. ff. MITTEN *sb.*, MEAD[1].

meth (mɛθ), colloq. abbrev. METHEDRINE; also, a Methedrine tablet.

1967 *N.Y. Times* 16 Oct. 53 She was a good kid, if she hadn't been so freaked out on meth. **1968** *Guardian* 21 Nov. 20/3 The pushers passing out bombers, meths, dexes, and blues. **1972** M. J. BOSSE *Incident at Naha* i. 38 She snorted Methedrine... The Feeler offered me a snort of Meth, but I never use Speed. **1972** J. WAMBAUGH *Blue Knight* (1973) v. 74 She's a meth head and an ex-con.

meth, var. METHS.

meth- (mɛθ), used as comb. form of METHYL before a vowel in a few chemical names, as **'methacrylic acid,** 1-methylacrylic acid, $CH_2{:}C(CH_3)COOH$, a colourless compound melting at 15°C, which polymerizes when distilled and which is used in the manufacture of methacrylate resins; so **me'thacrylate,** (*a*) a salt of methacrylic acid; (*b*) any of the esters of methacrylic acid, some of which are used in making resins by polymerization (see *methyl methacrylate* s.v. METHYL c); **me'thoxide,** (a salt of) the anion CH_3O^-, derived from methanol.

1865 *Jrnl. Chem. Soc.* XVIII. 142 Ethylic methacrylate is readily decomposed by boiling alcoholic potash. *Ibid.*, Silver methacrylate is best obtained pure by precipitating ammonium methacrylate with nitrate of silver. **1936** *Industr. & Engin. Chem.* Mar. 269/1 The monomeric methacrylates cannot be stored or transported with safety. **1962** *Economist* 6 Oct. 74/3 An airdrying paint (based on methacrylates) has been used.. for several years. **1964** G. H. HAGGIS et al. *Introd. Molecular Biol.* iv. 91 (*caption*) A thin section preparation showing T_2 bacteriophage infection of *E. coli* bacteria (osmium tetroxide fixation and methacrylate embedding technique..). **1865** *Jrnl. Chem. Soc.* XVIII. 142 Methacrylic acid is a colourless oil, which.. possesses a faint odour, like pyrogallic acid. **1889** G. M'GOWAN tr. *Bernthsen's Text-bk. Org. Chem.* 166 Meth-acrylic acid.. is found in small quantity in Roman camomile oil, and smells like decaying mushrooms. **1972** *Materials & Technol.* IV. xii. 428 Technical production of methacrylic acid employs the oxidation of isobutene by a mixture of nitric acid and nitrogen dioxide to hydroxyisobutyric acid, which is then dehydrated. **1885** *Jrnl. Chem. Soc.* XLVIII. 1031 Anhydrous sodium methoxide, NaOMe, was prepared by heating the solution [of sodium in methyl alcohol] at 180–200° in a current of dry hydrogen. **1934** *Ibid.* 1204 The agreement between the values for the mobility of the methoxide ion is fair. **1965** *New Scientist* 26 Aug. 513/3 Ordinary methyl alcohol is sufficiently acidic to form salts with alkali metals like sodium and potassium, the 'methoxides', whose general formula is $CH_3O^-M^+$ (where M^+ is any metal ion).

metha: see METHO[1].

methadone ('mɛθədəʊn). *Pharm.* orig. *U.S.* Also -on (-ɒn). [f. METH(YL + A(MINO- + D(I-[2] + -ONE in 6-dimethylamino-4, 4-diphenyl-3-heptanone, the systematic chemical name.] A powerful synthetic analgesic, $(CH_3)_2N{\cdot}CH(CH_3){\cdot}CH_2{\cdot}C(C_6H_5)_2{\cdot}CO{\cdot}CH_2{\cdot}CH_3$, which is similar to morphine in its effects but less sedative and is used (usu. as the hydrochloride) as a substitute drug in the treatment of addiction to morphine or heroin.

1947 *Jrnl. Amer. Med. Assoc.* 23 Aug. 1483 The Council voted to recognise the word Methadon as the generic designation for 6-dimethylamino-4,4-diphenyl-3-heptanone. **1948** *Ann. N.Y. Acad. Sci.* LI. 17 It is not certain whether the Germans succeeded in the complete resolution of *dl*-methadone. **1952** W. T. SALTER *Textbk. Pharmacol.* vi. 81/1 The danger of addiction of racemic methadon and levo-methadon is about equal to that of morphine. **1962** K. ORVIS *Damned & Destroyed* xxiii. 174 A new drug, methadon, is being used successfully as a reduction treatment... The patient starts regaining strength—moral and physical strength—almost at once. **1967** *Martindale's Extra Pharmacopoeia* (ed. 25) 783/1 Symptoms of morphine withdrawal in addicts may also be mitigated by methadone substitution; addiction to methadone is easier to treat than addiction to morphine. *Ibid.* 800/2 Methadone hydrochloride may be used for the relief of severe pain of all types. **1970** *Sunday Times* 8 Mar. 1/2 She was taking big doses of heroin three times a day, together with the morphine-antagonist, methadone,.. every four hours. **1971** *Guardian* 4 June 3/3 The aim of the methadone programme is to switch the mainliner's addiction from heroin to methadone, an addictive drug.. which allows its addicts to lead a normal life... The methadone programme was begun in New York in 1965 by the Beth Israel Medical Centre. **1972** *Science* 26 May 882/2 Methadone not only reduces the hunger for heroin, it affects respiration, digestion, and sexual behavior; it also, as does any opiate, affects social and psychological behavior.

methæmoglobin (mɛθi:məʊ'gləʊbɪn). *Chem.* [See META- and HÆMOGLOBIN.] A derivative of hæmoglobin obtained by the exposure of an aqueous solution of oxyhæmoglobin to the air; called also **methæmo'globulin.** Hence **methæmoglobi'nemia** *Path.* [Gr. αἷμα blood], presence of methæmoglobin in the blood. **methæmoglobi'nuria** *Path.* [Gr. οὖρον urine], presence of methæmoglobin in the urine.

1870 SORBY in *Q. Jrnl. Microsc. Sci.* X. 400 Hoppe-Seyler's and Preyer's 'methæmoglobin'. **1888** *Med. News* LIII. 240 The author, in two cases, observed cyanosis, depending upon methemoglobinemia. **1890** BILLINGS *Nat. Med. Dict.*, *Methæmoglobinuria,.. Methæmoglobulin.* **1897** *Allbutt's Syst. Med.* IV. 288 The latter [i.e. hæmoglobinuria] is frequently a mixture of hæmoglobin with various derivatives such as methæmoglobinuria. **1899** CAGNEY tr. *Jaksch's Clin. Diagn.* i. (ed. 4) 73 The methæmoglobin acid solution.

methamatic, obs. form of MATHEMATIC.

methamphetamine (mɛθæm'fɛtəmi:n, -ɪn). *Pharm.* [f. METH- + AMPHETAMINE.] A methyl derivative, $C_6H_5{\cdot}CH_2{\cdot}CH(CH_3){\cdot}NH(CH_3)$, of amphetamine, used in the form of the hydrochloride, a white crystalline compound, as a stimulant of the central nervous system; its effects resemble those of amphetamine but are more rapid in onset and longer lasting.

1949 *Jrnl. Amer. Med. Assoc.* 22 Jan. 228 New and non-official remedies. Methamphetamine hydrochloride. ..*d*-Desoxyephedrine hydrochloride. **1951** A. GROLLMAN *Pharmacol. & Therapeutics* xi. 212 Methamphetamine hydrochloride.. may be considered as the methyl derivative of amphetamine. It is a potent analeptic and, like amphetamine, has been used in the treatment of narcolepsy, postencephalitic parkinsonism, alcoholism, and in certain depressive states.. and in the treatment of obesity. **1960** J. J. LEWIS *Introd. Pharmacol.* viii. 287 Amphetamine, dexamphetamine and methamphetamine have qualitatively similar properties but vary in potency. Methamphetamine is more potent than dexamphetamine which is in turn more potent than its racemate amphetamine. **1970** C. M. B. PARE in C. W. H. Harvard *Current Med. Treatm.* (ed. 3) xv. 479 Following injection of the methamphetamine the doctor directs the interview towards topics which he thinks may be particularly stressful.

methanation (mɛθə'neɪʃən). [f. METHAN(E + -ATION.] Conversion (esp. of carbon monoxide and hydrogen) into methane.

1956 M. GREYSON in P. H. Emmett *Catalysis* IV. vi. 506 The development of commercial methanation procedures is normally undertaken on the assumption that means exist, or will exist, for the conversion of coal to mixtures of hydrogen and carbon monoxide. **1969** R. F. LANG tr. *Henglein's Chem. Technol.* 425 This reaction is used for the production of especially high-grade fuel gases from water gas ($CO + 3H_2 - 48{\cdot}87$ kcal $= CH_4 + H_2O$) (methanation) ($CO_2 + 4H_2 - 39{\cdot}1$ kcal $= CH_4 + 2H_2O$). **1973** *Nature* 7 Dec. 326/2 It is the catalytic enrichment (a methanation) which is the key to the production of SNG [*sc.* substitute natural gas] and the Gas Board is loath to reveal the full details of its operation.

Hence (as a back-formation) **'methanate** *v. trans.*, to convert into methane, to subject to methanation.

1963 DIRKSEN & LINDEN *Pipeline Gas from Coal by Methanation of Synthesis Gas* (U.S. Inst. Gas Technol. Res. Bull. No. 31) p. iii, This program established that a variety of nickel catalysts were capable of methanating synthesis gas to 900 Btu/SCF pipeline gas. **1974** *Sci. Amer.* Apr. 9/3 Methanating animal wastes from feed-lots in the Middle West is probably the best application of this idea.

methane ('mɛθeɪn, 'mi:θeɪn, 'mi:-). *Chem.* Also -an. [f. METH(YL) + -ANE.] Light carburetted hydrogen, methyl hydride or marsh-gas (CH_4), a colourless odourless gas emanating from stagnant pools, volcanoes, petroleum wells, and esp. from coal-seams, in which, mixed with seven or eight parts of air, it forms a violent explosive (cf. FIRE-DAMP).

1868 *Fownes' Chem.* (ed. 10) 178 Methane or Marsh Gas; ..Fire-damp.—This gas is but too often found to be abundantly disengaged in coal-mines. **1893** *Brit. Jrnl. Photogr.* XL. 812 The mean temperatures of explosions with methane, ethane and propane were 667°, 616°, and 547° respectively. **1899** CAGNEY tr. *Jaksch's Clin. Diagn.* vii. (ed. 4) 383 The urine held hydrogen, nitrogen,.. and probably methan.

methaniline (mɛ'θænɪlaɪn). *Chem.* [f. METH(YL) + ANILINE.] = *methylaniline*: see METHYL.

1857 WATTS tr. *Gmelin's Handbk. Chem.* XI. 300. **1881** *Athenæum* 17 Dec. 819/2 The chlorhydrates of methaniline and other aniline products.

methanol ('mɛθənɒl). *Chem.* [f. METHAN(E + -OL.] Methyl alcohol. CH_3OH, a colourless, volatile, poisonous liquid with a pungent odour which is produced mainly by the high-pressure reduction of carbon monoxide or dioxide with hydrogen and is used as an intermediate in the synthesis of formaldehyde, as a solvent, and as a denaturant for ethyl alcohol.

The adoption of *methanol* as the systematic name of methyl alcohol was a consequence of Resolution 15 (on alcohols and phenols) of the report of 1892 of the International Conference on Chemical Nomenclature (see *Nature* (1892) 19 May 58–9).

1894 G. M'GOWAN tr. *Bernthsen's Text-bk. Org. Chem.* (ed. 2) 87 Methyl alcohol. [*Note*] 'O[fficial] N[ame]' Methanol. **1932** *Discovery* May 165/2 Besides its important use as a methylating agent, methanol is the raw material for formaldehyde. **1958** *Times Rev. Industry* Dec. 57/2 Refueller.. designed for replenishing aircraft with.. methanol. **1973** *Daily Tel.* 27 July 2/7 Hawkshaw.. knew that methanol was an anti-freeze substance used on buses and for stripping paint and cleaning paintbrushes.

Hence **metha'nolic** *a.*, in or of methanol.

1953 *Jrnl. Polymer Sci.* X. 375 The results of viscosity and molecular weight determination obtained in methanolic solution are presented in Figure 2. **1975** *Nature* 3 Jan. 8/1 Solvolysis of $[\{(C_5H_5)_2Ti\}_2N_2]$ with methanolic HCl yields mainly nitrogen.

methanometer (mɛθə'nɒmɪtə(r)). *Mining.* [f. METHANE + -(O)METER.] An instrument invented by Monnier (see quot.).

1881 *Nature* XXIV. 94 Automatic methanometer, or automatic analyser of fire-damp. [Also, in recent Dicts.]

methaphesik, -physick, obs. ff. METAPHYSIC.

methaqualone (mɛ'θækwələʊn). *Pharm.* [f. *2-methyl-3-o-tolyl-4(3H)-quinazolinone*, the systematic chemical name (with inserted *a*), f. METHYL + TOLYL + *quinazolin(e* (f. QUIN(OLINE + *azol(e* (f. AZ(O- + -OLE) + -INE[5]) + -ONE.]

A hypnotic and sedative drug used generally in the form of its hydrochloride, $C_{16}H_{14}N_2O{\cdot}HCl$, a white crystalline powder with a bitter taste.

1961 *Brit. Med. Jrnl.* 21 Jan. 173/1 Methaqualone in a single dose of 150 mg. is a reliable hypnotic. **1969** *Daily Tel.* 17 Dec. 13/1 Methaqualone, a drug used by thousands of people in sleeping tablets and slimming capsules, is to be referred to the Committee on Safety of Drugs. **1973** *N.Y. Times* 10 June I. 59/1 Nonmedical use quickly spread when users found that methaqualone can produce a tingly, relaxed, uncoordinated drunken euphoria. It also developed a reputation—some say unfounded—as a powerful aphrodisiac. **1973** *Daily Tel.* 11 July 2/8 Mandrax is the trade name for a sleeping tablet otherwise known as methaqualone and has been controlled as a potentially dangerous drug since 1971 following cases of abuse by drug addicts.

†**methe,** *sb. Obs.* Forms: 1 **mǽþ**, 3 **maþe, mæþ, meaþ**, 3–5 **meþ**, 4–5 **methe**, 5 **meeþ**. [OE. *mǽþ* fem.:—OTeut. type **mǣþi-z* (not found outside Eng.) = Gr. μῆτι-ς counsel, Skr. *māti* measure:—Indogermanic **mēti-s* whence L. *mētīri* to measure; f. root **mē-* (Teut. **mǣ-*) to measure, whence OTeut. **mǣlo*ᵐ MEAL *sb.*[2]]

1. Measure, proportion, fixed quantity.

c **1000** ÆLFRIC *Exod.* xxii. 17 ȝif se fæder hiȝ him syllan nelle, ȝilde be þære ȝiftan mæðe. *c* **1205** LAY. 977 Ȝif we sceoteð to heora mæðe [*c* **1275** meþe] þat bið ure imone deað. *a* **1300** *E.E. Psalter* lxxix. 6 þou salt.. gif vs drink in teres in meth [Vulg. *in mensura*].

2. Moderation, temperance.

c **1200** *Trin. Coll. Hom.* 29 Cune sume meðe þenne þu almesse makest. *a* **1240** *Sawles Warde* in *Cott. Hom.* 257 Mi þridde suster meað spekeð of þe middel sti bituhhe riht. *c* **1357** *Lay Folks Catech.* (MS.T.) 440 The seuent vertu and the laste is methe or methefulnesse,—*Temperancia.*

3. Respect, consideration; kindness.

c **1000** *Inst. Polity* c. 25 in Thorpe *Laws* II. 338 Ælc cristen man ah mycele þearfe þæt he on þam gride mycle mæþe wite. *c* **1250** *Gen. & Ex.* 2498 Alle he fellen him ðor to fot, To beðen meðe and bedden oc. *a* **1310** in Wright *Lyric P.* 103 Ȝef ich the buere to muche meth, Thou wolt me bringe to helle deth. *c* **1320** *Cast. Love* 318 Heo him duden in prisun of deþ, And pynede him sore wiþ-outen meþ. **13..** *Propr. Sanct.* (Vernon MS.) in *Archiv Stud. neu. Spr.* LXXXI. 102/315 But þer as God, ful of meþ, ffleih to Egipte from his deþ [etc.]. *a* **1400–50** *Alexander* 816 All.. on knese fallis, And in his mercy & meth mekely þaim put.

4. Modesty, gentleness.

*c*1325 *Know Thyself* 35 in *E.E.P.* (1862) 131 With þi maistrie medel þi meþ For vche mon ouȝt hym self to knowe. *c*1325 *Metr. Hom.* 107 And Mari ledd hir lif with methe, In a toun that hiht Nazarethe. 13.. *Metr. Hom.* (Vernon MS.) in *Archiv Stud. neu. Spr.* LVII. 269 But heo hedde Meth, as worschipful wyf, ffor heo nas nout to hastyf. *c*1375 *Cursor M.* 7858 (Fairf.) Of him come Iesse meke of meth. *c*1450 *Cov. Myst.* (Shaks. Soc.) 157 Amos spak with mylde methe.

† **methe**, *a. Obs.* Cf. MYTH *a.* [? From the attrib. use of prec.] Gentle, courteous.

*a*1300 *Cursor M.* 10152 Elizabeth, An hali leuedi mild and meth, þat spused was to zachari. *a*1440 *St. John Evang.* (Thornton MS.) 57 Thou was methe and meke as maydene for mylde.

† **methe**, *v. Obs.* [OE. *mǽðian*, f. METHE *sb.*]

1. *trans.* To spare, have mercy upon. (In OE. with dative.)

*c*1000 WULFSTAN *Hom.* 59/17 He sylð arleasnysse þæt he ne ariȝe ne eac ne mæðiȝe his underþeoddum ne his ȝelicum. *c*1250 *Gen. & Ex.* 1046 Quad god, 'find ic ðor ten or mo, Ic sal meðen ðe stede for ðo'.

2. To moderate, regulate, temper.

*c*1200 *Trin. Coll. Hom.* 13 Ðet foremeste is riht medeme mel þe man þe hit meðeð riht þe suneð aleð gestninge [etc.]. *Ibid.* 139 He..meðede þo his liflode swo þat he was bicumelich to swiche wike. *c*1330 R. BRUNNE *Chron. Wace* (Rolls) 13615 Ȝyf þey hem self couþe haue meþed & als þer strokes couþe haue leþed..Gret prowesse of þem had ben told.

methe, variant of MATHE, MEAD *sb.*[1]

Methedrine (ˈmɛθədrɪn, -iːn). *Pharm.* [f. METH(YL + BENZ)EDRINE.] A proprietary name for methamphetamine.

1939 *Trade Marks Jrnl.* 11 Jan. 46/2 Methedrine... Pharmaceutical and veterinary preparations. The Wellcome Foundation Ltd.,..London,..manufacturing chemists. 1943 *Brit. Med. Jrnl.* 20 Mar. 348/2 Methedrine has been found to be an effective blood-pressure-raising drug. 1965 J. POLLITT *Depression & its Treatment* iv. 47 Methedrine produces euphoria, mental alertness and pressure of talk. 1967 *Economist* 11 Nov. 628/2 Their deaths were just one instance of the violent crime that is being associated with the increasing use of an amphetamine with the trade name of Methedrine and the nick-name of 'speed'. 1975 *Harpers & Queen* May 126/2 Out come..a half-dozen bottles of Methedrine.

† **ˈmetheful**, *a.*[1] *Obs.* [OE. *mǽþfull*: see METHE *sb.* and -FUL.] Moderate; gentle.

*c*1000 ÆLFRIC *Gram.* xxxviii. (Z.) 236 *Humanus* mæðfull oððe mennisclic. *a*1225 *Ancr. R.* 430 Inouh meðful ich am, þet bidde so lutel. *a*1240 *Sawles Warde* in *Cott. Hom.* 257 Meaðful in alles cunnes estes. *a*1310 in Wright *Lyric P.* 32 A mihti methful mai, that ous hath cast from cares colde. 13.. *Minor Poems fr. Vernon MS.* l. 557 Drink þat þou beo meþful, And lyue in hele good. *c*1425 *Eng. Conq. Irel.* 112 He was a man methefull, suttell, & stalwarth.

Hence † **methefully** *a.* and *adv.*, moderate(ly); † **methefulness**, moderation.

*a*1225 *Ancr. R.* 414 Non ancre ne ouh forto nimen bute gnedeliche [*MS. C.* meðfulliche] þet hire to neodeð. *a*1300 *E.E. Psalter* xxxviii. 7 Lokc, methfullike [*mensurabiles*] mi daies set þou. 1357 Methefulnesse [see METHE *sb.* 2].

† **ˈmetheful**, *a.*[2] *Obs.* In 3 methful. [f. OE. *méðe* weary + -FUL.] Weary.

*a*1300 *E.E. Psalter* iii. 5, I am methful, for i slepe.

metheglin (mɪˈθɛglɪn). *Obs.* exc. *Hist.* and *dial.* Forms: 6 **methglen, -eghelen, -line, -lem,** 6–7 **metheglen, -lyn,** 7 **mathiglin, metheglings,** (**methæglen**); 6– **metheglin.** [a. Welsh *meddyglyn*, f. *meddyg* healing, medicinal (ad. L. *medicus*) + *llyn* liquor.] A spiced or medicated variety of mead, originally peculiar to Wales.

1533 ELYOT *Cast. Helthe* (1541) 36 Metheglyn, whiche is moste used in Wales, by reason of hotte herbes boyled with hony, is hotter than meade. 1550 J. COKE *Eng. & Fr. Heralds* §207 (1877) 117 We have good-ale, bere, metheghelen, sydre, and pirry. 1568–70 in H. Hall *Soc. Eliz. Age* (1887) 245 A Cupp of methglen. 1620 VENNER *Via Recta* ii. 41 If Rosemary, Hyssop, Time, Orgaine, and Sage, be first well boyled in the water, wherof you make the Metheglin, it will be the better. 1623 C. BUTLER *Fem. Mon.* x. Xij, Methæglen is the more generous or stronger Hydromel, being vnto Mede as Vinum to Lora. 1633 ROWLEY *Match at Midnight* II. i, Some metheglings, the wine of Wales. 1666 PEPYS *Diary* 25 July, I drinking no wine, had metheglin for the King's own drinking. 1731 P. SHAW *Three Ess. Artif. Philos.* 49 The Method of Brewing with Honey, for Mead, Metheglin [etc.]. 1789 J. MORSE *Amer. Geogr.* 197 The perry..is an agreeable liquor, having something of the harshness of claret wine, joined with the sweetness of metheglin. 1839 J. K. TOWNSEND *Narr. Rocky Mts.* v. 203 Among the rest, was some *metheglen* or diluted alcohol sweetened with honey. 1855 T. C. HALIBURTON *Nat. & Hum. Nat.* II. ix. 267 All the friends of the new married couple..did nothing for a whole month, but smoke, drink metheglin, [etc.]. 1971 J. DOXAT *Drinks & Drinking* 152 *Metheglin*, old name for mead, but probably, from its derivation, from an ancient Welsh word for 'spicey potion'.

attrib. 1887 G. MEREDITH *Ballads & P.* 105 Cambria's old metheglin demon Breathed against our rushing tide.

Hence **meˈtheglinist** *nonce-wd.*, a brewer of metheglin.

1655 SIR J. MENNIS *Musarum Del.* 29 While there's a Cider-Man Or a Metheglenist,..I do forswear to sup Of wicked Sack.

methel: see METEL.

† **ˈmetheless**, *a. Obs.* [OE. *mǽþléas*: see METHE *sb.* and -LESS.] Immoderate.

*c*1000 ÆLFRIC *Hom.* (Th.) II. 516 Ða het Martinus ða mæðleasan fuȝelas ðæs fixnoðes ȝeswican. *a*1225 *Ancr. R.* 96 Ȝif he is meðleas, ileueð him þe wurse. 13.. *E.E. Allit. P.* B. 273 Þose wern men meþelez & maȝty on vrþe.

† **ˈmethely**, *a. Obs.* [OE. *mǽþlic*: see METHE *sb.* and -LY[1].] Moderate, proper, suitable.

958 *Will* in Thorpe *Charters* 509 ȝif hwilc forwyrht man hiowan ȝesæce, bio se þingad swa hit medlic sio be þæs geltes meðe. *a*1035 *Cnut's Secular Laws* c. 71 (Lieberm.) Beon þa hereȝeata..swa hit mæðlic si. *c*1200 *Trin. Coll. Hom.* 63 Meðeliche eting and drinking aȝen to temien þe lichames orguil.

b. Of medium stature. (Cf. MEETLY *a.*)

*c*1425 *Eng. Conq. Irel.* 98 Meyler was a man..of body, somdel more than methlych, ful stalwarth, wel I-brested.

† **ˈmethely**, *adv. Obs.* [OE. *mǽþlíce*, f. prec.: see -LY[2].] Moderately, temperately; meekly.

*c*1000 ÆLFRIC *Gram.* xxxviii. (Z.) 236 *Humane* and *humaniter* mæðlice oððe mennisclice. *c*1250 *Gen. & Ex.* 1758 Ðus meðelike spac ðis em. *c*1425 *Eng. Conq. Irel.* 76 His maner was euer-more to hold hym methelyche.

methenamine (mɛˈθiːn-, məˈθɛnəmiːn). *Pharm.* [f. METHEN(E + AMINE.] The name given to *hexamethylenetetramine* (s.v. HEXA-) in the *Pharmacopeia of the U.S.A.*

1926 *Pharmacopeia U.S.* 238 Methenamine. 1926 *Dispensatory U.S.A.* (ed. 21) 695/2 Not only are there a large number of compounds of methenamine upon the market, but the official drug is sold under an almost innumerable number of trade names. 1948 E. POUND *Pisan Cantos* (1949) lxxiv. 17 Methenamine eases the urine. 1951 A. Grollman *Pharmacol. & Therapeutics* xxv. 526 Hexamethylenetetramine (($(CH_2)_6N_4$), official as methenamine (U.S.P.) and hexamine (B.P.)..is of interest from its liberating formaldehyde in the course of its excretion in the urine. 1969 J. H. THOMPSON in J. A. Bevan *Essent. Pharmacol.* xlix. 511 Methenamine mandelate is a mixture of methenamine and mandelic acid.., two old urinary antiseptic agents which today are rarely given separately.

methene (ˈmɛθiːn). *Chem.* [f. METH-YL + -ENE.] = METHYLENE.

1885 in *Cassell's Encycl. Dict.*

methenyl (ˈmɛθɪnɪl). *Chem.* [f. METHENE + -YL.] The hypothetical hydrocarbon radical CH; usually *attrib.*

1868 *Fownes' Chem.* (ed. 10) 557 Methenyl chloride (chloroform).

methephisike, obs. form of METAPHYSIC.

mether, variant of MADDER *sb.*[2], *Anglo-Irish.*

1841 S. C. HALL *Ireland* III. 297 The mether was square, and not round..and to drink out of it was no easy task.

metherinx, variant of MEDRINACKS *Obs.*

methicillin (mɛθɪˈsɪlɪn). *Pharm.* [f. METH- + PEN)ICILLIN.] A penicillin, $C_{17}H_{19}N_2O_6NaS{\cdot}H_2O$, which is especially useful for its activity against staphylococci which produce penicillinase. Also called ***methicillin sodium*** or ***sodium methicillin.***

1961 *Brit. Med. Jrnl.* 25 Mar. 865/1 During a period of 12 weeks one ward was sprayed at regular intervals daily with 4g. of methicillin. 1963 *Brit. Pharmacopœia* 486 Methicillin Sodium is the monohydrate of sodium 6-(2,6-dimethoxybenzamido)penicillinate. 1968 *New Scientist* 18 Jan. 118/3 There were signs of bacterial infection in the lungs, and the doctors prescribed methicillin. 1970 *Daily Tel.* 23 Oct. 13/3 The second [semi-synthetic penicillin], methicillin, was active against the resistant staphylococci and was soon accepted as a major life-saving antibiotic.

methide (ˈmɛθaɪd). *Chem.* [f. METH-YL + -IDE.] A combination of methyl with a metal.

1868 *Fownes' Chem.* (ed. 10) 596 Zinc methide. 1897 *Allbutt's Syst. Med.* II. 933 Mercuric methide.

methinks (miːˈθɪŋks), *impers. v.* Now *arch.* and *poet.* Pa. t. **methought** (miːˈθɔːt). Forms: see below and cf. THINK *v.*[1] [OE. *mé þyncþ* (pa. t. *mé þúhte*), where *mé* is dative, and *þyncþ* the 3 pers. sing of *þyncean* to seem: see THINK *v.*[1]

As THINK *v.*[1] did not, exc. in this phrase, survive beyond the 14th c., and had no very wide currency after 1250, the syntax of *methinks* became obscure. Hence it underwent various alterations of form. The verb being supposed to be THINK *v.*[2], it followed that it ought to be in the first person; hence the form *me think*, in which probably the pronoun was still correctly apprehended as a dative. In the 16–17th c. there occur the forms *my think, my thought(s*, which are attempts to obtain a normal syntax by taking *think, thought*, as sbs. The curious form *methoughts*, used in the 17th and the first half of the 18th c., prob. owes its *s* to the analogy of the present tense *methinks*.]

It seems to me. (Used with dependent clause or parenthetically.)

1. *Present tense.* † *α.* **methinketh.**

*c*888 K. ÆLFRED *Boeth.* xxiv. §3 Me þincð þæt hit hæbbe ȝeboht sume swiðe leaslice mærðe. *a*1200 *Moral Ode* 5 Vnnet lif ich habbe iled, and ȝet me þingþ ilede. 1390 GOWER *Conf.* II. 95 With such gladnesse I daunce and skippe, Me thenkth I touche noght the flor. 1447 BOKENHAM *Seyntys* (Roxb.) 2 And yet methinkyth it were pete That my werk were hatyd for me. 1577 B. GOOGE *Heresbach's Husb.* I. (1586) 10 There is a Hopper (mee thinketh) ouer the toppe of the Oast. 1607 HIERON *Wks.* I. 439 Me thinketh this motiue should not be without effect.

¶ *Substantive use.* 1594 HOOKER *Eccl. Pol.* IV. iv. §2 When they opposed their *Me thinketh* vnto the orders of the Church of England.

β. **methinks.**

1560 WHITEHORNE *Arte Warre* (1573) 103 b, Nor me thinkes that there resteth other to tell you then certaine general rules. 1599 SHAKS. *Much Ado* III. ii. 16 Methinkes you are sadder. 1661 MARVELL *Corr.* Wks. (Grosart) II. 76 'Tis methinks an unpleasant business. 1711 STEELE *Spect.* No. 6 ⁋5 Respect to all kind of Superiours is founded methinks upon Instinct. 1762–71 H. WALPOLE *Vertue's Anecd. Paint.* (1786) IV. 281 Methinks a strait canal is as rational at least as a mæandring bridge. 1863 HAWTHORNE *Our Old Home* (1879) 119 Methinks a person of delicate individuality..could never endure to lie buried near Shakespeare. 1871 R. ELLIS tr. *Catullus* xciii. 1 Lightly methinks I reck if Caesar smile not upon me.

† *γ.* **methink.**

*a*1300 *Cursor M.* 16332 (Cott.) Me thinc it es noght sua. 13.. *Guy Warw.* (A.) 616, & he wald me so o loue ȝerne, Me þenke y no myȝt it him nouȝt werne. *c*1470 HENRY *Wallace* I. 385 It war resone, me think, yhe suld haif part. 1564–78 BULLEYN *Dial. agst. Pest.* (1888) 19 Me thinke I see twoo men in long gounes with short beardes at the gates. 1659 *Gentl. Calling* v. x, So dismal a consequent, as, methink, should like Lot's wife, remain a perpetual monument to deter others.

† *δ.* **my think(s.**

1530 CROME in Strype *Eccl. Mem.* III. App. x. 20 And my think that this manner of praying dooth not dysanull.. purgatorye. *a*1619 FLETCHER *Mad Lover* II. iii, My thinks a gentleman should keepe his word.

2. *Past tense.* *α.* **methought.**

*c*1200 *Vices & Virtues* 13 And ȝif ic nadde, me ðuhte þat hit nas naht wel betowen, ðar ic hit idon hadde. *a*1300–1400 *Cursor M.* 8171 (Gött.) Me thoght [*Cotton* me thoght] to night on þis-kyn wise, þat we war bath in paradise. *c*1420 LYDG. *Assembly of Gods* 343 Me thought he was gayly dysgysyd at that fest. 1535 COVERDALE *Judg.* vii. 13 Me thoughte a baken barlye lofe came rollinge downe to yᵉ hoost of yᵉ Madianites. 1651 H. MORE *Enthus. Tri.*, etc. (1656) 309, I dream'd thus. Methought I was at a friends house in the rode betwixt London and Scotland. 1711 POPE *Temp. Fame* 498 While thus I stood..One came, methought, and whisper'd in my ear. 1832 TENNYSON *Dream Fair Wom.* xiv, At last methought that I had wander'd far In an old wood. 1878 H. PHILLIPS *Poems fr. Spanish & Germ.* 48 Methought my days were ended.

† *β.* **methoughts.**

1594 SHAKS. *Rich. III*, I. iv. 9 Me thoughts that I had broken from the Tower. 1620 WOTTON *Let. to Bacon* in *Reliq.* (1651) 413 The draught of a Landskip on a piece of paper, me thoughts masterly done. 1711 ADDISON *Spect.* No. 63 ⁋3 Methoughts I was transported into a Country that was filled with Prodigies. 1751 *Female Foundling* I. 30 The inward Satisfaction which I felt, had spread in my Eyes I know not what of melting and passionate, which methoughts I had never before observed.

† *γ.* **my thought.**

*a*1300 [see *a*]. 1503 HAWES *Examp. Virt.* iv. 3 My thought it was an heuenly syght. 1621 LADY M. WROTH *Urania* 435 Then my thought I saw he had commission.

methionic (mɛθɪˈɒnɪk), *a. Chem.* [f. ME(THYL) + Gr. θεῖον sulphur: see -IC.] ***methionic acid***, a disulpho-acid obtained from aniline. Hence **methionate** (meˈθaɪəneɪt), a salt of methionic acid.

1842 T. GRAHAM *Elem. Chem.* 779 Two other acids of this class have been obtained, methionic acid..and althionic acid. 1853 WATTS tr. *Gmelin's Handbk. Chem.* VIII. 435 Evaporating the filtrate till it begins to deposit needles of methionate of baryta. 1862 MILLER *Elem. Chem., Org.* v. §2 (ed. 2) 310 The first compound upon this list [disulphometholic acid] is identical with Liebig's methionic acid.

methionine (mɛˈθaɪəniːn). *Chem.* [Blend of METH- + THION: see -INE[5].] A sulphur-containing amino-acid, $CH_3{\cdot}S{\cdot}CH_2{\cdot}CH_2{\cdot}CH(NH_2){\cdot}COOH$, which is probably a constituent of all proteins.

1928 BARGER & COYNE in *Biochem. Jrnl.* XXII. 1418 Since the amino-acid has a good title to be regarded as a constituent of protein, a shorter name than γ-methylthiol-α-aminobutyric acid seems desirable, and.. we suggest for it the name *methionine*, in allusion to the characteristic grouping. 1956 *Nature* 11 Feb. 280/1 The amino-acid requirement of this organism [*sc.* a trypanosomid flagellate] could be satisfied by methionine alone. 1962 [see ISOLEUCINE]. 1971 J. Z. YOUNG *Introd. Study Man* xxiii. 315 Old people are said to require more methionine than young. 1972 *McGraw-Hill Yearbk. Sci. & Technol.* 123/1 Since methionine is the only metabolic precursor of homocysteine in the human diet, deliberate reduction in the amount of dietary animal protein, which contains more methionine than plant protein, may prove to be effective in preventing arteriosclerosis.

methisazone (mɛˈθɪsæzəʊn). *Pharm.* [f. METH(YL + IS(ATIN + THIOSEMICARB)AZONE (cf. the chemical name given in def.).] A fine orange-yellow powder that has prophylactic activity against smallpox; *N*-methylisatin β-thiosemicarbazone, $C_{10}H_{10}N_4OS$.

1964 *Brit. Med. Jrnl.* 5 Sept. 621/1 Methisazone breaks new ground in the rational therapy of virus infections. 1966 *New Scientist* 17 Nov. 336/3 Dr D. J. Bauer and Dr K. Apostolov..had shown methisazone ('Marboran') to be active against certain adenoviruses growing in tissue culture. 1970 PASSMORE & ROBSON *Compan. Med. Stud.* II. xx. 36/1 In man, methisazone has been shown to be effective in preventing disease in contacts of patients suffering from smallpox... Methisazone has not been shown to be effective in treating established infections.

†**methium.** *Obs.* Some kind of drug.
1610 [see KERMES 1].

metho[1] ('mɛθəʊ). *Austral.* and *N.Z. colloq.* Also **metha** (*rare*). [f. *meth(ylated spirit* + -O.]

1. Methylated spirit. Also *attrib.*

1933 *Bulletin* (Sydney) 18 Oct. 10/2 A metho. drinker—a regular visitor—came into the pharmacy the other day. *Ibid.* 1 Nov. 11/1 Charged in a Melbourne court with having drunk metho., an elderly gent. at first declared [etc.]. **1935** K. TENNANT *Tiburon* ii. 23 The two metho-drinkers were escorted out firmly. **1938** 'R. HYDE' *Nor Years Condemn* x. 190 They drink a lot of metha, don't they? Great names they've got for it—Phar Lap, and Johnny Gee, and White Light. **1944** W. E. HARNEY *Taboo* (ed. 3) 33 She is a 'metho' addict and, as a result, is blind and half paralysed. **1945** O. E. BURTON *In Prison* 116 A half-crazed sponge for absorbing 'metho'. **1953** A. UPFIELD *Murder must Wait* xvii. 153 The straight-out metho drinkers and city crooks. **1973** *Sunday Mail* (Brisbane) 18 Mar. 25/5 The oldtimer who'd tried to smuggle it through, by carrying it nonchalantly in his hand, surrendered it sadly. When it comes to metho spotting, Envoy Smith has the nose of a connoisseur.

2. A person who is addicted to drinking methylated spirit. See also METHS.

1933 *Bulletin* (Sydney) 1 Nov. 11/1 A John Hop who has helped to deal with many 'methos.' tells me not a few prefer petrol. **1945** BAKER *Austral. Lang.* 166 Addicts of these noxious drinks are known as *meths, methos,* [and] *metho artists.* **1966** G. W. TURNER *Eng. Lang. Austral. & N.Z.* vi. 118 Words in *-o* are more specifically Australian, though ..*metho* (a drinker of methylated spirits) and *smoko* (with the sense 'morning or afternoon tea'..) are current in New Zealand. **1973** *Brisbane City Mission* Sept. 17/2 The methos... When a man takes to drinking methylated spirits, you know..that he has no thought for betterment of his lot.

Metho[2] ('mɛθəʊ). *Austral.* Colloq. abbrev. of METHODIST 4.

1941 in BAKER *Dict. Austral. Slang* 46. **1961** P. WHITE *Riders in Chariot* viii. 232 Only the civil servants are Roman Catholics here... Arch and me are Methoes, except we don't go; life is too short.

method ('mɛθəd), *sb.* [a. F. *méthode* (Rabelais) or ad. L. *method-us*, a. Gr. μέθοδος pursuit of knowledge, mode of investigation, also as a term in Medicine (see below); f. μετα- META- + ὁδός way.

The word is now common to all Rom. and Teut. langs. (It. *metodo*, Sp. *método*, G. *methode*, etc.) with approximately the same senses as in Eng. The sense of 'systematic arrangement' (branch II below) is foreign to Greek: it was developed through the special application of L. *methodus* by some logicians of the 16th c. (see sense 4).]

I. Procedure for attaining an object.

†**1.** *Med.* **a.** The regular, systematic treatment proper for the cure of a specific disease. *Obs.*

(Now merged in sense 3, where see quots. 1725, 1800, 1887.)

1541 R. COPLAND *Galyen's Terap.* 2 A iij, Euery kynde of dysease hath his owne Methode. **1563** T. GALE *Inst. Chirurg.* 21 b, The Methode of curyng compounde tumors against nature. **1578** BANISTER *Hist. Man* Epist. A iv, Then did I clearely see, how that to write Methodes or means to cure the affected partes of the body..might [etc.]. **1696** PHILLIPS, *Method*,..that part of Physick whereby, remedies are found out by the Indications for the Restoration of Health.

fig. **1597** HOOKER *Eccl. Pol.* v. i. §1 To see wherein the harm which they feel consisteth,..and the method of curing it. *a* **1716** SOUTH *Serm.* (1744) IX. 38 Let such persons..not quarrel with the great physician of souls for having cured them by easy and gentle methods.

b. *Hist.* The system of medicine practised by the 'methodics' or 'methodists'.

1541 R. COPLAND *Galyen's Terap.* 2 D iv, That is the maner to heale by Methode..yf it so be that Methode is an vnyuersall way. **1601** HOLLAND *Pliny* II. 344 Thessalus [*marg.*] He reduced Physicke into a Method: and from him descended the sect called Methodici. *a* **1790** W. CULLEN *Lect. Hist. Med.* Wks. 1828 I. 383 This easy plan was, by way of eminence called the Method, and the persons who followed it the Methodics.

2. a. A special form of procedure adopted in any branch of mental activity, whether for the purpose of teaching and exposition, or for that of investigation and inquiry.

1586 SIR E. HOBY *Pol. Disc. Truth* iv. 8 And Plato called a Methode, a fire sent from heauen, which giueth the light that maketh the trueth knowen. **1604** R. CAWDREY *Table Alph.*, *Method*, an order, or readie way to teach, or doo any thing. **1605** BACON *Adv. Learn.* II. xvii. §4 Knowledge.. ought to be delivered and intimated, if it were possible, in the same method wherein it was invented. **1644** MILTON *Educ.* 2 The same method is necessarily to be follow'd in all discreet teaching. *a* **1711** KEN *Hymnotheo* Poet. Wks. 1721 III. 254 He has of Knowledge the true Method shewn, To rise Truths abstruse, from Truths well-known. **1780** BENTHAM *Princ. Legisl.* xviii. §56 The method of division here pursued. **1852** J. CURWEN (*title*) The Pupil's Manual of the Tonic Sol-Fa Method of teaching to sing. **1869** J. MARTINEAU *Ess.* II. 55 Mental science does not differ from physical in its methods. **1875** JOWETT *Plato* (ed. 2) IV. 136 The theses of Parmenides are expressly said to follow the method of Zeno. **1875** MAINE *Hist. Inst.* i. 18 It is a distinct property of the Comparative Method of investigation to abate national prejudices. **1876** L. STEPHEN *Eng. Th. 18th C.* i. §30 I. 30 Hume..agrees with Descartes..in pursuing the simple introspective method. **1879** LUBBOCK *Sci. Lect.* v. 139 The methods of archæological investigation are as trustworthy as those of any natural science.

†**b.** The rules and practice proper to a particular art. *Obs.*

1662 EVELYN *Diary* 22 Aug., The intention being to reduce that art [*sc.* ship-building] to as certaine a method as any other part of architecture.

c. in the names of certain specific procedures in mathematics and experimental science.

1685 WALLIS *Algebra* lxxiii. 280 The Method of Exhaustions. *Ibid.* lxxxv. 318 Another Method of Approximation, by Mr. Isaac Newton. **1718–19** *Phil. Trans.* XXX. 923 A letter of M. l'Abbé Conti..concerning the dispute about the Invention of the Method of Fluxions, or Differential Method. **1727–41** CHAMBERS *Cycl.*, *Method*, *methodus*, is more peculiarly used in mathematics for divers particular processes for solving problems.—In this sense we say *Method of exhaustions..Method of fluxions..Method of tangents.* **1838** DE MORGAN *Th. Probab.* in *Encycl. Metrop.* (1845) II. 451 The method of correction known by the name of that of *least squares*..was proposed by Legendre in 1806. **1843** MILL *Logic* III. viii, Of the Four Methods of Experimental Inquiry. *Ibid.* III. xi, Of the Deductive Method. **1843** MILL *Logic* I. III. viii. 450 These two methods may be respectively denominated the Method of Agreement, and the Method of Difference. *Ibid.* 462 This method may be called the Indirect Method of Difference, or the Joint Method of Agreement and Difference. *Ibid.* 465 The Method of Residues is one of the most important among our instruments of discovery. *Ibid.* 470 The method by which these results were obtained, may be termed the Method of Concomitant Variations. **1916** H. W. B. JOSEPH *Introd. Logic* (ed. 2) xx. 434 So obvious is the difficulty of finding such instances as these canons require, that Mill, having begun by mentioning four methods (of Agreement, of Difference, of Residues, and of Concomitant Variations), adds a fifth, which he calls the Joint Method of Agreement and Difference. **1929** A. N. WHITEHEAD *Process & Reality* 6 When the method of difference fails, factors which are constantly present may yet be observed under the influence of imaginative thought. **1953** I. M. COPI *Introd. Logic* xii. 365 We may begin with an example or two in which the scrupulous use of the Methods results in a more or less conspicuous failure to discover the cause of a given phenomenon. **1965** S. F. BARKER *Elem. Logic* vii. 237 When we infer from these data that the hamburgers caused the ptomaine, we are employing what Mill called the method of concomitant variation.

d. in the title of treatises of instruction in an art or science.

1686 (*title*) A new and easie Method to learn to sing by book, etc. **1758** NUGENT (*title*) A new Method of learning with Facility the Latin Tongue. **1842** TENNYSON *Amphion* 79 They read Botanic Treatises, And Works on Gardening thro' there, And Methods of transplanting trees To look as if they grew there.

e. *Theatr.* A theory and practice of acting associated with the Russian actor and director Konstantin Stanislavsky (1863–1938), in which the actor seeks the complete illusion of reality by identifying himself as closely as possible with the part he plays. Often *attrib.*, as ***method-acting***, ***actor***, ***school***, etc. Also ***method-act*** vb., ***method-acted*** ppl. adj. Hence (not in common use) ***methodic***, ***methody*** adjs.; ***methodism***, ***methodist*** sbs.

1923 O. M. SAYLER *Russian Theatre* 254 'My method, though imperfect,' he [*sc.* Stanislavsky] says, 'I consider psychologically natural.' **1925** H. CARTER *New Spirit European Theatre* xviii. 225 The third movement also was a form of protest by theatrical reformers, who were sick of M. Stanislavsky's hair-for-hair actualistic method. *Ibid.* 230 Stanislavsky was unable to change his method of production and style, which were suited to a particular species of bourgeoisie play. **1954** F. M. WHITING *Introd. Theatre* vi. 136 The actor, if sufficiently sensitive to the drives and motives of the character he portrays, will 'instinctively' sense what the basic responses should be. To achieve this goal, Stanislavski devised his method. **1956** K. TYNAN in *Harper's Mag.* Mar. 63/2 This is Stanislavsky without Freud, physiological acting without the psychiatric glosses beloved of American 'method' actors. **1957** *Observer* 15 Dec. 10/4 Eli Wallach, the American disciple of the Method .., was admirably solid, but not noticeably more absorbed in his role than some of our own best actors look to be in theirs. **1958** E. DUNDY *Dud Avocado* I. vii. 114 The Method ..the Stanislavsky Method: working for realism through improvisations and sense memory, and emotional recall. **1958** *Times* 11 Nov. 4/5 It was surely not for nothing that [Jackson] Pollock himself belonged to the country that has promulgated the cult of 'method' acting. **1959** *Times Lit. Suppl.* 27 Mar. 172/1 The whole 'Method' school about which so much pedantic and often absurd controversy has raged are dealt with mordantly. **1959** *Spectator* 29 May 765/1 This was a Method *Don Giovanni*, with real people caught up in a real drama. **1959** *Guardian* 15 Oct. 8/3 What emotional exercises had he done in preparation for Romeo? The real Methodist is not so much different in kind as different in degree. **1960** R. LEWIS *Method—or Madness?* i. 4 One hears that Method actors are 'mumblers'. *Ibid.* iv. 75 Another reason that some actors..seem 'Methody', or inexplicably involved, is that their approach is *too* analytical. **1960** *New Left Rev.* Sept.–Oct. 65/1 The method-acted *Tomorrow With Pictures.* **1961** *20th Cent.* Feb. 134 Other factors include the impact of Method-ism in the theatre. **1962** *New Statesman* 19 Jan. 97/1 This long film forfeits seriousness..by being..too thunderously repetitious, too Methodic, strenuous and symbolic. **1963** *Times* 17 Jan. 4/6 Even the Method groups that were flourishing in London a few years ago have now mainly vanished. **1967** *Spectator* 7 July 22/2 His method acting is not merely an attack on their academic ennui, but a mask for his own profound frustrations. **1970** J. QUARTERMAIN *Man who walked on Diamonds* xvii. 90 Method-act yourself into a super-sleuth. **1971** J. WILLETT in A. Bullock *20th Cent.* 243/1 In America ..the Group Theater..applied the realistic Stanislavsky 'method' for social ends. **1972** *Daily Colonist* (Victoria, B.C.) 24 Feb. 44/1 A method actor will use his own memory to simulate an emotion for the cameras. **1973** H. MCCLOY *Change of Heart* xii. 146 If she could feel like that, maybe she would look like that. 'Method' acting. Stanislavsky.

3. a. In wider sense: A way of doing anything, esp. according to a defined and regular plan; a mode of procedure in any activity, business, etc.

1590 SHAKS. *Com. Err.* II. ii. 34 If you will iest with me, know my aspect, And fashion your demeanor to my lookes, Or I will beat this method in your sconce. **1606** —— *Ant. & Cl.* I. iii. 7 Madam, me thinkes if you did loue him deerly, You do not hold the method, to enforce The like from him. **1602** [? COOKE] *How a man may choose good wife* B 3 b, I will prescribe a methode How thou shalt win hir without al peraduenture. **1660** BARROW *Euclid* I. ix. *Coroll.*, The method of cutting angles. **1684** BUNYAN *Pilgr.* II. 42 The Hen did walk in a fourfold Method towards her Chickens. *a* **1715** BURNET *Own Time* (1724) I. 359 He did very often assure me he was against all violent methods, and all persecution for conscience sake. **1719** DE FOE *Crusoe* I. 336 The old Man began to ask me, if he should put me in a Method to make my Claim to my Plantation. **1725** N. ROBINSON *Th. Physick* 262 This is the only Method to be continued while the Symptoms are not extremely dangerous. **1761** GRAY *Sketch* 2 Too poor for a bribe, and too proud to importune, He had not the method of making a fortune. **1793** SMEATON *Edystone L.* §274 In our work, it was performed in the following method. **1800** *Med. Jrnl.* IV. 494 Mr. P. was delighted to hear that I thought a cure was not impracticable, and laboured ardently to persuade me to inform him of the method I should use. **1800** tr. *Lagrange's Chem.* I. 365 Scheele has given two methods for obtaining this acid. **1819** BYRON *Juan* I. vii, This is the usual method, but not mine—My way is to begin with the beginning. **1868** LOCKYER *Elem. Astron.* vii. (1879) 256 There are two methods of observing the time of transit over a wire, one called the eye and ear method, the other the galvanic method. **1874** MICKLETHWAITE *Mod. Par. Churches* 200 A perfect method of warming churches has yet to be invented. **1887** *Brit. Med. Jrnl.* 26 Feb. 448/2 Benefit from this line of treatment must not be expected immediately, and the method should be persevered with for at least some months.

†**b.** A scheme, plan of action. *Obs.*

1704 J. TRAPP *Abra-Mulé* I. i. 319 All my Designs and Methods still were cross'd.

†**c.** A mode (of employment). *Obs.*

1712 STEELE *Spect.* No. 294 ¶1 Sixteen hundred Children, including Males and Females, put out to Methods of Industry.

d. In generalized use: The methods of procedure in any department, considered as the object of a branch of study; *esp.* with reference to teaching. Cf. sense 6.

1848 W. ROSS (*title*) The Teacher's Manual of Method; or general principles of teaching and school-keeping. **1879** A. PARK (*title*) A Manual of Method for Pupil-Teachers and Assistant Masters.

e. *Campanology.* (See quot. 1901.)

1668 'CAMPANISTA' *Tintinnalogia* 2 Before I Treat of the method and diversity of Peals, I think it not impertinent to speak something of the Properties wherewith a Young Ringer ought to be qualified. **1852** B. THACKRAH *Art Change Ringing* 14 These twenty-four changes may be rung in several other methods. **1879** W. BANISTER *Art & Sci. Change Ringing* (ed. 2) 14 The Plain Bob Method—is applicable to any number of bells, but is properly an even bell method. **1901** H. E. BULWER *Gloss. Technical Terms Bells* 10 *Method*, any special way in which continuous 'changes' on five or more bells are produced by the regular and orderly movement of all, without repetition of any one 'change'. **1901, 1928** [see EXTENT *sb.* 7]. **1962** G. E. EVANS *Ask Fellows who cut Hay* (ed. 2) xviii. 147 The old ringer answered.., 'No tunes. We allus rang the *method*, the same as we did in the steeples.' **1965** W. G. WILSON *Change Ringing* xviii. 149 We showed how variations in a method could be made in the Plain Bob type of method by means of second place.

II. Systematic arrangement, order.

4. A branch of Logic or Rhetoric which teaches how to arrange thoughts and topics for investigation, exposition, or literary composition.

1551 T. WILSON *Logike* E iv b, The maner of handeling a single Question, and the readie waie howe to teache and sette forth any thyng plainlie, and in order, as it should be, in latine Methodus. *Ibid.* K ij, We spake before of a methode, or directe order to be vsed in all our doinges. **1588** FRAUNCE *Lawiers Log.* I. i. 7 Methode hath only to deale with the ordering and setling of many axioms. **1605** BACON *Adv. Learn.* II. xvii. §2 Methode hath beene placed, and that not amisse in Logicke, as a part of Iudgement; For as the Doctrine of Syllogismes comprehendeth the rules of Iudgement vppon that which is inuented. So the Doctrine of Methode contayneth the rules of Iudgement vppon that which is to bee deliuered. **1627** HAKEWILL *Apol.* (1630) 261 To this body [the art of Logic] have they not improperly added the doctrine of Methods as a necessary limbe thereof. *a* **1679** HOBBES *Rhet.* (1681) 1 We see that all men naturally are able in some sort to accuse and excuse: Some by chance; but some by method. This method may be discovered: and to discover Method is all one with teaching an Art. **1713** STEELE *Englishm.* No. 7. 46 Their Children were instructed early in the Rules of Method. **1725** WATTS *Logic* IV. i, In logic..Method is the disposition of a variety of thoughts on any subject, in such order as may best serve to find out unknown truths. **1780** BENTHAM *Princ. Legisl.* xvi. §1 *note*, The particular uses of method are various: but the general one is, to enable men to understand the things that are the subjects of it. **1827** HUTTON *Course Math.* I. 3 Method is the art of disposing a train of arguments in a proper order, to investigate either the truth or falsity of a proposition, or to demonstrate it to others when it has been found out. **1849** ABP. THOMSON *Laws Th.* (ed. 2) 95 *Method*, which is usually described as the fourth part of Logic, is rather a complete practical Logic. **1870** JEVONS *Elem. Logic* xxiv. 201 Method is..defined as consisting in such a disposition of the parts of a discourse that the whole may be most easily intelligible.

5. Orderly arrangement of ideas and topics in thinking or writing; orderliness and sequence of thought or expression. Phr. ***method in one's***

madness (also varr. of this expression, normally with allusion to quot. 1602): reason, orderliness, or sense lying behind one's apparent insanity or stupidity.

1559 W. Cunningham *Cosmogr. Glasse* 3 They [certain writers] obserue no order or Methode in their teaching. **1581** Lambard *Eiren.* ii. vii. (1588) 223 To me, that am desirous to follow some order, and methode of discourse, the generall must alwayes go before the particular. **1592** Warner *Alb. Eng.* vii. xxxv. (1612) 171 Though his words lackt methode, yeat they moued. **1602** Shaks. *Ham.* ii. ii. 208 Though this be madnesse, Yet there is Method in't. **1649** Roberts *Clavis Bibl.* Introd. iii. 39 Method and order, as it is the mother of memory, so it is a singular friend to a cleare understanding. **1651** Hobbes *Leviath.* ii. xxx. 184 Unlesse we shall think there needs no method in the study of the Politiques. **1709** Pope *Ess. Crit.* 654 Horace still charms with graceful negligence, And without method talks us into sense. **1753** Johnson *Adventurer* No. 85 ⁋17 Method is the excellence of writing, and unconstraint the grace of conversation. *a* **1834** Coleridge *On Method* in *Encycl. Metrop.* I. Introd. 2 The total absence of Method renders thinking impracticable. **1842** H. Rogers *Ess.* (1874) I. i. 33 His very method..consists in a contempt of all method. **1843** Poe *Gold-Bug* in *Dollar Newspaper* (Philadelphia) 21 June 1/7 My friend, about whose madness I now saw, or fancied that I saw, certain indications of method. **1850** F. E. Smedley *Frank Fairleigh* xxix. 241 A fear of completely knocking up..induced me to preserve some little method in my madness. **1880** W. Sanday in *Expositor* XI. 362 He sought to give to the allegorical interpretation a greater method. **1894** A. Conan Doyle *Mem. Sherlock Holmes* 128, I have usually found that there was method in his madness. **1911** Brereton & Rothwell tr. *Bergson's Laughter* i. 2 The comic spirit has a logic of its own, even in its wildest eccentricities. It has a method in its madness. **1922** Chesterton *Man who knew too Much* 110 He may be mad, but there's method in his madness. There nearly always is method in madness. It's what drives men mad being methodical. **1953** A. Huxley *Let.* 21 July (1969) 680 There is, in the long run (at least I hope so), some kind of method in my madness.

6. a. The order and arrangement observed in framing a particular discourse or literary composition; an author's design or plan.

1591 Shaks. *1 Hen. VI*, iii. i. 13 *Verbatim* to rehearse the Methode of my Penne. **1594** —— *Rich. III*, i. ii. 116 To leaue this keene encounter of our wittes, And fall something into a slower method. **1596** Spenser *State Irel.* Wks. (Globe) 609/2 Tell them then, I pray you, in the same order that you have now rehearsed them; for there can be noe better methode then this which the very matter it self offereth. **1597** Morley *Introd. Mus.* Pref., As for the methode of the booke, although it be not such as may in euery point satisfie the curiositie of Dichotomists: yet is it such as I thought most conuenient for the capacitie of the learner. **1622** Wither *Fair Virtue* C 2 b, If my Methode they deride, Let them know, Loue is not tide In his free Discourse, to chuse Such strict rules as Arts-men vse. **1653** H. More *Antid. Ath.* iii. xii. (1712) 126, I had here ended all my Stories, were I not tempted by that remarkable one in Bodinus to outrun my method. **1706** London & Wise *Retir'd Gard'ner* I. Pref. A j b, The first of these Books was ..perus'd by several ingenious Gentlemen, who liking the Method of it, were desirous to have it translated. **1784** Cowper *Task* iii. 279 What's that which brings contempt upon a book, And him who writes it, though the style be neat, The method clear, and argument exact?

†**b.** A regular, systematic arrangement of literary materials; a methodical exposition. *Obs.*

1589 Puttenham *Eng. Poesie* i. ii. (Arb.) 21 If Poesie be now an Art,..and yet were none, vntill by studious persons fashioned and reduced into a method of rules and precepts. **1605** Bacon *Adv. Learn.* ii. xvii. §6 The deliuerie of knowledge in Aphorismes, or in Methodes; wherein wee may obserue that it hath beene too much taken into Custome, out of a fewe Axiomes or Obseruations, vppon any Subiecte, to make a solemne, and formall Art; filling it with some Discourses, and illustratinge it with Examples; and digesting it into a sensible Methode. But the writinge in Aphorismes hath manye excellent vertues, whereto the writinge in Methode doth not approach. *Ibid.* §7. **1611** Bible *Transl. Pref.* ⁋3 Cutting off the superfluities of the lawes, and digesting them into some order and method. **1680** (*title*) A brief Method of the Law. Being an exact alphabetical disposition of all the heads necessary for a perfect Commonplace. **1706** London & Wise *Retir'd Gard'ner* I. Pref. A ij, Several gentlemen would often have ask'd us Questions relating to our Profession, but were at a Loss how to form them into a Method, and word them so that we might rightly understand what they meant. **1829** Bentham *Justice & Cod. Petit.* Prelim. Expl. p.v, In the disposition made of the matter of the original draft..a method..has been given to it.

†**c.** The scheme or summary of the contents of a book, set forth in a table. *Obs.*

1601 Shaks. *Twel. N.* i. v. 244 *Ol.* In his bosome, In what chapter of his bosome? *Vio.* To answer by the method in the first of his hart. *a* **1613** Overbury *A Wife* (1614) B, The Method. First of Mariage, and the effect thereof, children. Then of his contrarie, Lust; then [etc.]. **1652** Needham tr. *Selden's Mare Cl.* 3 And with these wee shall now begin; for the Method of the second Book is more conveniently put there before it.

7. In wider sense: Orderliness and regularity in doing anything; the habit of acting according to plan and order.

1611 Beaum. & Fl. *King & no K.* v. iv, There is a method in mans wickednesse, It growes vp by degrees. **1647** Clarendon *Hist. Reb.* i. §33 That so putting the Houses into some method and order of their future debate, they would be more easily regulated than if they were in the beginning left to that liberty which they naturally affected. **1714** Swift *Pres. St. Affairs* ⁋2 After which I know no Talents necessary besides Method and Skill in the common forms of business. **1754** Richardson *Grandison* (1811) V. xiv. (cont.) 125 But early hours, and method, and ease, without hurry, will do every thing. **1843** *Penny Cycl.* XXVII. 231/2 No man ever gave himself up more entirely to any object, or prosecuted it..with..more method and skilful management.

†**8.** A particular state of orderly arrangement; a disposition of things according to a regular plan or design. *Obs.*

1635 Shirley *Coronat.* i. (1640) C, A small wound Ith' head, may spoyle the method of his haire. **1677** Marvell *Corr.* Wks. (Grosart) II. 561, I am frequent with Mr. Fisher and our Counsell, having put all things into the best method for an hearing. *a* **1715** Burnet *Own Time* (1724) I. 207 The king was beginning to put things in great method, in his revenue, in his troops [etc.]. **1716** Addison *Drummer* iv. i, I would have all the knives and forks..laid in a method. **1754** Richardson *Grandison* (1811) V. xiv. (cont.) 125 All is in such a method, that it seems impossible for the meanest servants to mistake their duty.

9. *Nat. Hist.* A system; scheme of classification.

Now most naturally interpreted as short for 'method of classification', which would commonly be apprehended as an instance of sense 2 or 3. Of the difference between 'system' and 'method', contradictory accounts were formerly given: see quots.

1826 Kirby & Sp. *Entomol.* IV. 355 *Method* and *System* ..have often been..used indifferently to signify the same thing... But if we consider their real meaning,— a *Method* should signify an *Artificial*, and a *System* a *Natural* arrangement of objects. **1828–32** Webster, *Method*...3. Classification;..as,..the method of Ray; the Linnean method... A distinction is sometimes made between *method* and *system*. *System* is an arrangement founded, throughout all its parts, on some one principle. *Method* is an arrangement less fixed and determinate... Thus we say, the *natural method*, and the *artificial* or *sexual system* of Linnæus. **1834** McMurtrie *Cuvier's Anim. Kingd.* 4 This scaffolding of divisions, the superior of which contain the inferior, is called a *method*.

III. 10. *Comb.*: †*method-monger*, a contemptuous term for one who deals in logical 'method'; in quot. 1647 with a play on Gr. μεθοδεία (rendered 'wiles' in the Revised Version of 1881); **methods engineer**, a person concerned with method study and methods engineering in a business; **methods engineering**, the organization of business methods through method study; **method(s) study**, the use of time-and-motion study and other systems to determine the most efficient methods to use in business activities.

1617 Donne *Serm.* Luke xxiii. 40 (1661) III. 5 We steal our Learning if we..deale upon Rhapsoders, and Common placers, and Method-mongers. **1647** Trapp *Comm. Eph.* iv. 14 The devil and his disciples are notable method-mongers, so as to deceive, if it were possible, the very elect. **1676** R. Dixon *Two Test.* To Rdr. 12 Such are our systematical Method-mongers, blundering in their Dichotomies after the way of Ramus or Keckerman. [**1928** R. C. Davis *Princ. Factory Organization & Managem.* vi. 72 The methods manager or industrial engineer is concerned primarily with the efficient application of the human forces of the organization.] **1939** Maynard & Stegemerten *Operation Analysis* i. 5 Time formulas are useful mathematical devices that the methods engineer employs. **1944** —— *Guide to Methods Improvement* ii. 9 A methods engineer secured a position in a textile mill in the South. **1953** J. R. Immer *Materials Handling* iii. 30 This part of materials movement is..more often the concern of the methods engineer than of the materials-handling engineer. **1960** *News Chron.* 28 July 8/8 (Advt.), Methods Engineer..experience of Time and Methods Study and Ratefixing. **1939** Maynard & Stegemerten *Operation Analysis* i. 1 Before discussing the methods-engineering procedure in detail, it will be advisable to formulate a clear statement of what the term covers... Methods engineering is the industrial science which is chiefly concerned with increasing labor effectiveness. **1944** —— *Guide to Methods Improvement* i. 5 In order to continue to make improvements in methods, a procedure known as 'method engineering' has been developed. **1953** J. R. Immer *Materials Handling* iv. 41 The methods-engineering department has the responsibility for 'planning the manual part of the operation'. **1932** A. H. Mogenson *Common Sense appl. to Motion & Time Study* i. 11 More attention is being given to this phase of methods study at present. **1939** Maynard & Stegemerten *Operation Analysis* i. 2 A methods study always begins with a careful primary analysis of existing conditions. **1955** *Furniture Devel. Council Newslet.* June 3/2 Efficient method study cannot be put into practice without a sound knowledge of the work in hand. **1959** *Gloss. Terms Work Study* (*B.S.I.*) 6 *Method study*, the systematic recording and critical examination of existing and proposed ways of doing work, as a means of developing and applying easier and more effective methods and reducing costs. **1969** J. Argenti *Managem. Techniques* i. 2 One glance round the factory is enough to reveal to an expert whether the manager there has been using Method Study, for example. *Ibid.* 167 The Method Study Officer..analyses the purpose and function of each step in the process.

†'**method**, *v.* *Obs.* *rare*$^{-1}$. [f. method *sb.*] *trans.* To methodize, arrange.

1640 Bp. Reynolds *Passions* xlii. 547 He [the Devil] is able..so to method and contrive his devices, that [etc.].

Methodee, var. Methody.

‖**Methodenstreit** (mɛ'todənʃtraɪt). [G., lit. 'methods struggle'.] Discussion or dispute of opinions concerning the methodology of a field of study.

1958 *Spectator* 7 Feb. 173/2 In history, since the *Methodenstreit* of sixty years ago, the flood of 'scientific' research [etc.]. **1968** *Explorations in Entrepreneurial Hist.* VI. 75, I would like to narrow my comments on this twentieth-century *Methodenstreit* to three questions. **1970** *Computers & Humanities* V. 2 A literature of criticism is just beginning to emerge, but it has not yet created the type of *Methodenstreit* that has apparently debilitated scholarship in economic history.

†**me'thodian.** *Obs.* *rare*$^{-1}$. [f. method *sb.* + -ian.] = methodist 1.

1612 Cotta *Disc. Dang. Pract. Phys.* i. ii. 10 The Empericke trusting to experience alone without reason, and the methodian unto the abuse of right reason.

methodic (mɪ'θɒdɪk), *a.* and *sb.* *Obs.* exc. *Hist.* Also 6 **-yke**. [ad. late L. *methodic-us*, a. Gr. μεθοδικ-ός, f. μέθοδος method: see -ic and cf. F. *méthodique* (16th c.).] **A.** *adj.*

†**1.** The distinctive epithet of one of the three ancient schools of physicians, holding views intermediate between those of the Dogmatic and the Empiric school.

1541 R. Copland *Galyen's Terap.* 2 B iv, After the sentence of the Methodyke secte. **1701** Grew *Cosm. Sacra* iv. viii. 266 Thessalus, the Head of the Methodick Sect in the Reign of Nero. **1751** Johnson *Rambler* No. 156 ⁋1 Every animal body, according to the methodick physicians, is, by the predominance of some exuberant quality, continually declining towards disease and death.

2. = methodical *a.* in various senses: pertaining to method; constructed, performed, or carried on in accordance with method; *rarely* of persons, observant of method, characterized by regularity of procedure.

1620 K. James *Let. to Bacon* 16 Oct. in *Resuscitatio* (1657) ii. 83 You could not have made choice of a Subject more befitting..your universal, and Methodick, Knowledge. **1663** J. Spenser *Prodigies* (1665) 137 Some native and methodick powers, and springs of motion in things. **1669** Gale *Crt. Gentiles* i. iii. x. 104 There is no piece of Pagan Oratorie so methodic and harmonious, as sacred Scriptures. **1729** T. Cooke *Tales*, etc. 120 When was I known basely to court the Schools, Or not to rail at dull Methodic Fools..? **1869** Seeley *Lect. & Ess.* i. 17 The nation which..by methodic study and science of destruction, had crushed all the surrounding nationalities. **1886** Mrs. Burnett *Little Ld. Fauntleroy* x, It was as unlike the methodic old lawyer to be agitated..as it was to be late.

3. *Theatr.* (See method *sb.* 2 e.) *rare.*

B. *sb.*

1. *Hist.* A physician of the 'methodic' school; = methodist 1.

1541 R. Copland *Galyen's Terap.* 2 G j, That is to wyt the indycacyon y^t is taken of the myghtynes of the dysease, which the Methodykes onely haue nat left..but also dyuers of the racyonalles, & Emperykes. **1659** Macallo *Can. Physick* i. 1 The Methodick practizing in Physick hath, First, a knowledge of the Disease: next, foretelleth the event of it: and last, goeth about to cure the same. **1771** T. Percival *Ess.* (1777) I. 25 Themison..founded a new sect called the Methodics. *a* **1790** W. Cullen *Hist. Med.* Wks. 1828 I. 383 This easy plan was..called the Method, and the persons who followed it the Methodics. **1864** *Chambers's Encycl.* VI. 385/2 During the greater part of the first two centuries of our era, the Methodics were the preponderating medical sect.

2. *pl.* **a.** The science of method; methodology. (Ogilvie 1882, and later Dicts.)

Webster 1864 has the sing. in this sense.

b. esp. in the teaching of languages.

1962 P. Strevens *Papers in Lang.* (1965) v. 70 This organizational framework for arranging linguistic terms into a teachable pattern is known in Britain as *Methodics*. **1964** *New Statesman* 6 Mar. 378/1 (Advt.), Applications are invited for a post as Lecturer in the methodics of language teaching. **1964** M. A. K. Halliday et al. *Ling. Sci.* x. 200 Methodics is a framework of organization for practical language teaching, in which pedagogical techniques and linguistic theory cross-fertilize each other.

methodical (mɪ'θɒdɪkəl), *a.* [f. late L. *methodicus*: see prec. and -ical.]

1. *Hist.* = methodic *a.* 1.

1597 A. M. tr. *Guillemeau's Fr. Chirurg.* 49 b/1 The Empiricke medicamentes which the Methodicall Physicianes doe so disdayne. **1650** Gentilis *Considerations* 50 Though a great wise man compared a man that wanted Science, and had Experience, to an Empyrick Physitian, and the learned man to the Methodicall; yet hee was deceived in the comparison. **1727–41** Chambers *Cycl.* s.v. *Methodists*, Galen..scrupled not to assert, that the *methodical heresy* ruined every thing that was good in the art [of medicine]. **1837** Whewell *Hist. Induct. Sci.* (1857) I. 192 That.. medical sect which was termed the empirical, in contradistinction to the rational and methodical sects.

2. Characterized by method or order; constructed, performed, or carried on in accordance with method; arranged or disposed with order or regularity.

1570 Dee *Math. Pref.* b j, There are other (very many) Methodicall Artes. **1645** Milton *Tetrach.* 23 Yet Moses.. condescends in this place to such a methodical and School-like way of defining, and consequencing, as in no place of the whole Law more. **1698** Farquhar *Love & Bottle* iv. ii, Then they hate to hear a fellow in Church preach methodical Nonsense, with a Firstly, Secondly, and Thirdly. **1711** Addison *Spect.* No. 3 ⁋2, I fell insensibly into a kind of Methodical Dream, which disposed all my Contemplations into a Vision or Allegory. **1862** Burton *Bk. Hunter* (1863) 99 This is to be a methodical discourse. **1903** *Expositor* May 390 Methodical directions for the management of missions were not bequeathed by the Lord to his disciples.

b. Of material things: Arranged in a neat or orderly manner. *rare.*

1650 Fuller *Pisgah* ii. Gad §15. 79 No methodicall monument but this hurdle of stones was fittest for such a causer of confusion [Absalom]. **1904** *Union Mag.* Jan. 5/2

He always wore a tightly buttoned up frock-coat..and a methodical black neck-tie.

3. Of persons, their actions, etc.: Acting with or observant of method or order.

1664 PEPYS *Diary* 29 Feb., I find him a most exact and methodicall man. **1706** ADDISON *Rosamond* I. ii, Let me appear, Great sir, I pray Methodical in what I say. **1820** W. IRVING *Sketch Bk., Angler* ¶13 The English are methodical even in their recreations. **1865** DICKENS *Mut. Fr.* II. i, Small, ..neat, methodical, and buxom was Miss Peecher. **1875** *Lyell's Princ. Geol.* II. III. xxxvi. 289 Unconscious selection acts more powerfully than methodical selection.

Hence **methodi'cality**, *rare*, the property of being methodical.

1861 *Temple Bar* II. 549 You can see the methodicality of these folks in every thread of their clothes.

methodically (mɪ'θɒdɪkəlɪ), *adv.* [f. METHODICAL *a.* + -LY².] In a methodical manner; in accordance with a prescribed method; with method or regularity.

1570 DEE *Math. Pref.* c iv, You may Methodically register the whole. **1668** HALE *Pref. Rolle's Abridgm.* c, A Stock of learning, methodically digested and fitted to his use. **1756** C. LUCAS *Ess. Waters* II. 3 Great pains have been taken to class mineral waters methodically. **1758** J. S. *Le Dran's Observ. Surg.* (1771) 61, I dressed the Patient methodically. **1859** C. BARKER *Assoc. Princ.* i. 26 An apartment..fitted up with forms and desks methodically arranged. **1890** BOWEN in *Law Times Rep.* LXIII. 690/1 The Lord Chancellor or some other authority should methodically inquire into these differences.

me'thodicalness. [f. METHODICAL *a.* + -NESS.] The quality of being methodical.

1678 CUDWORTH *Intell. Syst.* I. iii. 139 A mere fortuitous and temerarious nature, devoid of all order and methodicalness. **1706** tr. *Dupin's Eccl. Hist. 16th C.* II. v. 27 Tapper writes with great Methodicalness and Easiness.

methodism ('mɛθədɪz(ə)m). In senses 1, 3 with capital initial. [f. METHOD *sb.* + -ISM, after next.]

1. The system of religious doctrine, practice, and organization characteristic of Methodists.

1739 WESLEY *Wks.* (1872) I. 225 The true old Christianity, which, under the new name of Methodism, is now also everywhere spoken against. **1768** WHITEFIELD *Let. to Dr. Durell* Wks. 1771 IV. 328 If you should desire..a definition of Methodism itself..you may easily be gratified. It is no more nor less than 'faith working by love'. 'A holy method of living and dying to the glory of God'. **1851** CARLYLE *Sterling* III. iii. (1872) 190 An honest, ignorant good man, entirely given-up to Methodism.

2. Adherence to fixed methods; excessive regard for methods.

1856 *Chamb. Jrnl.* V. 178 The Somerset House gentlemen usually introduce their official methodism at home. **1874** BLACKIE *Self-Cult.* 67 Such a formal methodism of conduct springs from narrowness. **1881** LIDDON in *Chr. World Pulpit* XX. 98/1 When..habit is merely the surviving methodism or the skeleton of a life which is no more. **1885** T. P. O'CONNOR *Gladstone's Ho. Comm.* 59 Sir Stafford Northcote's dull..methodism of words and thought.

3. The doctrines and practice of the 'methodic' school of physicians.

1896 T. C. ALLBUTT in *Classical Rev.* X. 346/2 A second school was Methodism, which was satisfied to refer all symptoms and all disease to the variations of the 'strictum' and the 'laxum'; that is, to the restriction or laxity of the secretions and other fluids of the body. **1958** D. GUTHRIE *Hist. Med.* (rev. ed.) v. 67 This theory, known as 'Methodism', was elaborated by Themison (123–43 B.C.), the pupil of Asclepiades.

4. *Theatr.* (See METHOD *sb.* 2 e.) *rare.*

methodist ('mɛθədɪst). With capital initial in specific uses. [ad. mod.L. *methodista*: see METHOD *sb.* and -IST. Cf. F. *méthodiste*.]

1. *Hist.* A physician of the 'methodic' school. (See METHODIC *a.* 1.) In the 17th c. sometimes applied to the regular or orthodox medical practitioners of the day, in contradistinction to those who favoured the use of new remedies.

According to Celsus, the members of this school (called in Latin *methodici*, in Gr. *μεθοδικοί*) differed from the Dogmatic school in basing their treatment not on principles deduced from a classification of diseases according to their origin, but on the theory that morbid conditions consisted either in 'looseness', 'tightness', or a mixture between the two (*fluens, strictum, mixtum*), each of the three states having its appropriate set of remedies. The founder of the school was Themison, about A.D. 100.

1598 MARSTON *Sco. Villanie* I. i, As many more, As methodist Musus kild with Hellebore. **1607** WALKINGTON *Opt. Glass* 44 The inexpert phisician, I meane Empyricall, as also the methodist or dogmatist. **1733** CHEYNE *Eng. Malady* II. (1734) 227 The true Foundation of the Distinction between..the strait and loose of the ancient Methodists. **1845** F. ADAMS tr. *Ægineta* II. xxxix. Comm. I. 293 Soranus, the great master of the Methodists.

fig. **1615** JACKSON *Creed* IV. III. v. §2 All of us have some or other tender part of our souls which we cannot endure should be ungently touched; Every man must be his own methodist to find them out.

2. One who is skilled in, or attaches importance to, method; one who follows a (specified) method. Now *rare.*

1593 G. HARVEY *Pierces Super.* 110 The finest Methodists, according to Aristotles golden rule of artificiall Boundes, condemne Geometricall precepts in Arithmetique, or Arithmeticall precepts in Geometrie, as irregular, and abusiue. **1621** BP. MOUNTAGU *Diatribæ* 79 Aristotle..was too good a Methodist, and Logician to confound the limits and boundaries of Arts. **1647** FARINDON *Serm.* xx. (1672) I. 394 He teacheth us how we shall fear *rectâ methodo*, to be perfect Methodists in Fear, and that we misplace not our fear. **1658** J. SPENCER *Things New & Old* 161 Our..plain pack-staffe Methodists, who esteem of all flowers of Rhetorick in Sermons, no better then stinking weeds. **1706** PHILLIPS (ed. Kersey), *Methodist*, one that treats of a Method, or affects to be methodical. **1802** BEDDOES *Hygëia* I. 87 What are these methodists in meat and drink, whom we are all so justly averse to the idea of resembling? **1824** J. JOHNSON *Typogr.* II. lxv. 95 But some, who are still better methodists..divide each side of the paper into two columns. **1886** *Cycl. Tour. Club Gaz.* IV. 121 They..despise the cut-and-dried programme of the methodist..and prefer to wander of their own free will.

b. *Nat. Hist.* One who classifies or arranges according to a particular method or scheme. Also, in Kirby's use, an advocate of an artificial in preference to a natural method of classification.

1753 CHAMBERS *Cycl. Supp., Methodists*,..persons who have..bestowed their labours upon the disposition and arrangement of plants. **1774** GOLDSM. *Nat. Hist.* (1824) I. xxxvi. 291 The methodists in natural history. **1826** KIRBY & SP. *Entomol.* IV. 356 Under this view system-makers would be divided into two classes—the Methodists and Systematists. **1893** NEWTON *Dict. Birds* 276 Several systematists referring it [the genus *Henicurus*] to the *Motacillidæ*,..while other methodists..placed it next to *Cinclus*.

c. *Theatr.* (See METHOD *sb.* 2 e.) *rare.*

3. *Eccl.* †**a.** One who advocates a particular 'method' or system of theological belief; applied esp. to the Amyraldists or Semi-Arminians. *Obs.*

1692 R. TRAILL *Sel. Writ.* (1845) 167 The new methodists about the grace of God had too great an increase in the French churches. [**1702** I. MATHER in C. Mather *Magn. Chr.* (1702) IV. 132 Parum aut nihil asserunt Amyraldistæ, quos Novatores & Methodistas vocant.]

b. The name given in the 17th c. to a class of Roman Catholic apologists.

1686 WAKE *Def. Exposition* 85, I was willing to hope, that ..such a peaceable Exposition of the Doctrine of the Church of England might.. have been received with the same civility by them, as that of the Church of Rome was by us; and that our new Methodists had not so wholly studied the palliating part of their Master, as not [etc.]. **1765** MACLAINE tr. *Mosheim's Eccl. Hist.* XVII. II. I. xv, This new species of polemic doctors were called Methodists, and the most eminent of them arose in France. **1882–3** *Schaff's Encycl. Relig. Knowl.* III. 1863 The Jesuits were the first to give systematic representations of the method of polemics; hence they were called 'Methodists'.

4. a. Originally, a term applied to the members of a religious society (nicknamed 'the Holy Club'), established at Oxford in 1729 by John and Charles Wesley and other members of the University, having for its object the promotion of piety and morality; subsequently applied to those who took part in or sympathized with the evangelistic movement led by the Wesleys and George Whitefield. **b.** In later use, a member or adherent of any one of a number of religious bodies or denominations which originated directly or indirectly from the labours of the Wesleys and Whitefield, and which came together in 1932 to form the Methodist Church of Gt. Britain and Ireland.

In England, during the nineteenth century, the designation belonged especially to the members and adherents of the Wesleyan-Methodist Society founded by John Wesley, and of the various other bodies that proceeded from it or from each other by succession, as the New Connexion Methodists, the Primitive Methodists, the United Methodist Free Church, and others. All these bodies accepted in the main the Arminian theology of Wesley, and in nearly all of them the ministers (called 'travelling preachers') changed their place of abode after a certain period (usually three years). In the U.S. the most influential body of Methodists is the Methodist Episcopal Church, which is in full communion with the Methodist Church in Great Britain. There are also several other bodies in the U.S. that adopt the name as a part of their official designation. In Wales the name 'Methodists' was formerly used to denote the body more fully known as 'Calvinistic Methodists', which was founded by Welshmen influenced by the teaching of Whitefield.

The origin of the name, as applied to the associates of the Wesleys at Oxford, is somewhat obscure. Cf., however, sense 3 a, and the 17th c. use in examples like quots. 1647, 1658, in sense 2.

1733 (*title*) The Oxford Methodists, some account of a Society of Young Gentlemen in that City. **1741–3** WESLEY *Extract of Jrnl.* (1749) 68, I know no principles of the Methodists (so called) which are contrary to the word of God. **1770** *Junius Lett.* xxxvi. *To Dk. Grafton* 14 Feb., You gave us nothing but the..whining piety of a Methodist. **1771** SMOLLETT *Humph. Cl.* 10 Aug., Nobody reads sermons but Methodists and Dissenters. **1846** MCCULLOCH *Acc. Brit. Empire* (1854) II. 279 The principal classes of dissenters are denominated methodists, independents, baptists, presbyterians,..&c. **1858** T. MCCOMBIE *Hist. Victoria* xxii. 317 It is but justice to the Wesleyan Methodists to say, that their church seems well adapted for propagating Christianity in new countries. **1864** *Chambers's Encycl.* VI. 427/1 The Welsh Calvinistic Methodists..are not a secession from the followers of Wesley, but originated partly in the preaching of..Whitefield, and partly in that of Howel Harris, a Welsh clergyman of the Church of England. **1887** W. S. GILBERT *Ruddigore* I. Plays, Ser. III. (1895) 222 He combines the manners of a Marquis with the morals of a Methodist.

c. *transf.* Applied contemptuously to a person of strict religious views.

1758 MRS. DELANY in *Life & Corr.* 523 We met with an archdeacon Golden..in his appearance a jolly, open, cheerful countenance,..he thinks it his duty to uphold any orthodox point; and that, I suppose, has gained him the title of methodist. *c* **1813** MRS. SHERWOOD *Stories Ch. Catech.* xxxiii. 353 The women of the regiment soon gave her the name of a methodist. [*Footnote*] This term, as used in India, ..is a name of reproach given to those..who are more serious than their neighbours. **1834** *Tait's Mag.* I. 387/2 For this hardship his remedy was, that the Methodists, his general term for all dissenters, should be made to contribute double, to relieve churchmen of such burdens.

5. *attrib.* (sense 4), passing into *adj.* with the sense: Pertaining to Methodists or Methodism. Also comb. ***Methodist-like, -mad*** adjs.

1751 LAVINGTON *Enthus. Meth. & Papists* III. 317 How horrible the Process was in these Methodist-like Initiations will appear [etc.]. **1766** WESLEY *Jrnl.* 5 Sept., A Methodist Preacher. **1768–74** TUCKER *Lt. Nat.* (1834) I. 493 Had I run opera-mad..or methodist-mad..I might have found companions enow. **1771** SMOLLETT *Humph. Cl.* 18 July, He attended Mrs. Tabby to the methodist meeting. **1850** LYELL *2nd Visit U.S.* II. 18 Four neat and substantial wooden churches,..the Presbyterian, Baptist, Methodist, and Episcopalian. **1840** B. E. HILL *Pinch—of Snuff* 102 A good woman..was driven Methodist-mad. **1859** [see CONNEXION 8]. **1874** GREEN *Short Hist.* x. (1880) 720 But the Methodists themselves were the least result of the Methodist revival. **1903** COURTHOPE *Hist. Eng. Poetry* xi, *heading*, The Methodist movement in poetry.

Methodistic (mɛθə'dɪstɪk), *a.* [f. prec. + -IC.]

1. Of or pertaining to the doctrines, beliefs, methods or appearance of the Methodists; characteristic of or pertaining to the Methodists.

1791 HAMPSON *Mem. Wesley* II. 3 His first labours in the methodistic vineyard. **1811** BYRON *Hints fr. Horace* 31 Then spare our stage, ye methodistic men! **1820** POLWHELE in *Lavington's Enthus. Meth. & Papists* Introd. 203 A further specimen of methodistic cant on the subject of inspiration. **1839** *Penny Cycl.* XV. 142/2 [The candidate for admission as a minister] undergoes an examination as to his personal acquaintance with Christianity, his Methodistic orthodoxy, and attachment to its discipline. **1849** CLOUGH *Dipsychus* I. iv. 124, I recognise, and kiss the rod—The methodistic 'voice of God'.

Methodistical (mɛθə'dɪstɪkəl), *a.* [Formed as prec.: see -ICAL.] Of or pertaining to the Methodists or Methodism; resembling a Methodist; usually with disparaging implication.

1749 FIELDING *Tom Jones* VIII. viii, She is at present..free from any methodistical notions. **1820** SOUTHEY *Wesley* II. 462 Meeting a man there one day, he asked him, in a methodistical manner, if he knew Jesus Christ. **1889** D. HANNAY *Capt. Marryat* 38 What was called in the navy a 'blue light', that is a pious man of a somewhat Methodistical turn.

Hence **Metho'distically** *adv.*, in accordance with the principles of Methodism or the practice of Methodists.

1787 ANNA SEWARD *Lett.* (1811) I. 301 And so Mr. — talks methodistically. **1820** POLWHELE in *Lavington's Enthus. Meth. & Papists* Introd. 26 We..term those Methodists who (whether Clergymen or Laymen) are Methodistically religious. **1884** *American* VIII. 84 The whole course of the Christian life, as conceived Methodistically, seems to us to labor under this defect.

†**Metho'distico-**, used as combining form of METHODISTIC.

1751 LAVINGTON *Enthus. Meth. & Papists* III. 350 Thus endeth this Methodistico-Monkish Story. **1805** T. HARRAL *Scenes of Life* II. 193 Methodistico-jacobincial rant.

'methodisty, *a. rare*⁻¹. [f. METHODIST + -Y.] Of a Methodist appearance or character.

1837 MARRYAT *Dog Fiend* liv, It would have made you laugh to see his methodisty face.

methodization (mɛθədaɪ'zeɪʃɛn). [f. next + -ATION.] The action or process of methodizing; the state of being methodized, esp. in *Logic*.

1802–12 BENTHAM *Ration. Judic. Evid.* (1827) II. 231 When, in order to allow the necessary time..for research and methodization, depositions in the form of ready-written answers have been allowed. *a* **1866** J. GROTE *Exam. Utilit. Philos.* (1870) 104 No greater results have flowed..from the theoretical methodization..of the object, which utilitarianism teaches.

methodize ('mɛθədaɪz), *v.* Also -ise. [f. METHOD *sb.* + -IZE.]

1. a. *trans.* To reduce to method or order; to arrange (thoughts, ideas, expression, etc.) in an orderly manner.

1589 NASHE *Anat. Absurd.* Ep. Ded. 2, I..coulde not but methodize this admiration in this digression. **1671** BAXTER *Holiness Design Chr.* lxiv. 18 They have not the skil to word and methodize their notions rightly. **1700** DRYDEN *Sigism. & Guisc.* 258 The royal spy..retired unseen, To.. methodize revenge. **1713** BERKELEY *Guardian* No. 39 ¶8 He should be taught..to order and methodise his ideas. **1881** SHORTHOUSE *J. Inglesant* (1882) II. 371 That art of reasoning..which methodizes and facilitates our discourse.

absol. **1707** POPE *Let. to Wycherley* 29 Nov., To methodize in your Case, is full as necessary as to strike out. *a* **1834** COLERIDGE *On Method* in *Encycl. Metrop.* I. Introd. 5 The mind..is disposed to generalize and methodize to excess.

b. To render (a person) orderly or methodical.

1814 MME. D'ARBLAY *Let.* 3 Apr., I have given him..to soberise and methodize him a little, a private tutor.

c. To convert into Methodists.

1846 A. Wiley in *Indiana Mag. Hist.* (1927) XXIII. 428 Some disciples who are hard cases, will be hard to methodize.

2. *intr.* To talk methodistically.

1771 Smollett *Humph. Cl.* 12 Sept., She was grave and gay by turns. She moralized and Methodized; she laughed, and romped [etc.].

3. *Theatr.* = *method-act* vb. (see method *sb.* 2 e).

1958 *Spectator* 31 Jan. 136/3 The pouting and posturing and methodising. **1960** *Ibid.* 18 Nov. 782/3 John Dexter's production has been much condemned.. Perhaps he should have varied the pace, Methodised the delivery.

Hence **'methodized** *ppl. a.*; **'methodizing** *vbl. sb.* Also **'methodizer**, one who methodizes.

a **1586** Sidney *Arcadia* iii. (1598) 312 All her long methodized oration was inherited onely by such kinde of speeches. **1646** R. Baillie *Lett. & Jrnls.* (Bannatyne Club) II. 401 Yet, in the review, the alteration of words, and the methodizeing, takes up so much time, that we know not when we shall end. **1655** Fuller *Ch. Hist.* vi. ii. 294 Their methodizing was meerly managed by the will of the Clerk of the Writs. **1678** Cudworth *Intell. Syst.* i. iv. §13 God was only the Orderer, or the Methodizer and Harmonizer thereof. **1796** Burke *Regic. Peace* ii. Wks. VIII. 235 The methodized reasonings of the great publicists and jurists. **1841** D'Israeli *Amen. Lit.* (1867) 158 This methodiser of commonplaces. **1886** A. Weir *Hist. Basis Mod. Europe* (1889) 113 The methodised frivolity of their lives.

methodizing ('mɛθədaɪzɪŋ), *ppl. a.* [-ing².]

1. That methodizes.

1832 Carlyle in *Fraser's Mag.* V. 412 Hume has the widest, methodising, comprehensive eye. **1902** J. H. Rose *Napoleon I*, I. xii. 284 This methodizing genius.

2. Inclined to Methodism.

1820 Southey *Wesley* II. 396 The greater part of the methodizing clergy adhered to Lady Huntingdon's party in the dispute. **1842** Whately *Let.* in *Life* (1866) II. 6 A Methodising sailor might call it the log-book of a voyage to heaven.

methodless ('mɛθədlɪs), *a.* [f. method *sb.* + -less.] Devoid of method, order or regularity; lacking the habit of order.

1609 A. Craig *Poet. Recreat.* To Rdr. 5 Excuse me (good Reader) for the methodlesse placing of these Passions. **1849** Rock *Ch. of Fathers* II. 373 Hearne, that untiring, but methodless antiquary. **1887** Saintsbury *Hist. Eliz. Lit.* x. (1895) 369 The very maddest, most methodless, of the 'Metaphysicals' cannot touch Crashaw in his tasteless use of conceits.

methodology (mɛθə'dɒlədʒɪ). [ad. mod.L. *methodologia* (J. F. Buddeus *Isagoge*, 1727) or F. *méthodologie*: see method *sb.* and -logy.] The science of method, 'methodics'; a treatise or dissertation on method; *Nat. Hist.*, systematic classification. Also, the study of the direction and implications of empirical research, or of the suitability of the techniques employed in it; also *attrib.*

In some contexts weakened to mean little more than 'method'.

1800 *Med. Jrnl.* III. 579 The first treats..of the methodology of medicine. **1809–10** Coleridge *Friend* (1818) III. 181 A very different school of methodology and philosophy than Paris could have afforded. **1835** *R. D. Thomson's Rec. Gen. Sci.* II. 65 These divisions [*sc.* De Candolle's divisions of botanical science] are Organography ..; Physiology..; Methodology [etc.]. **1837–8** Sir W. Hamilton *Logic* (1866) III. iii. 56 Such treatises are..only methodologies of the art or science to which they relate. **1902** *Dial* (Chicago) XXXII. 79/1 Bibliographical methodology (*i.e.* methods of compilation and recording). **1932** W. E. D. Allen *Hist. Georgian People* vii. 91 Alp-Arslan and his commanders were tacticians who evolved a new methodology in mediæval Asiatic war. **1937** T. Parsons *Struct. Social Action* ii. v. 178 (*heading*) The methodology and main analytical scheme. **1944** F. Kaufmann *Methodology of Social Sci.* p. vii, A reconsideration of the problem how the logical analysis of scientific procedure (methodology) is related to deductive logic. **1949** Shils & Finch tr. *Weber's Methodology of Social Sci.* iii. 114 The most significant achievements of specialist methodology use 'ideal-typically' constructed conceptions of the objectives. **1960** *Amer. Speech* XXXV. 212 The authors tell too little about their methodology. **1970** O. Dopping *Computers & Data Processing* xxii. 343 So far, what we have considered is a straight simulation which does not give rise to any methodology difficulties. **1971** *World Archaeol.* III. 210 The main challenge appears to be in establishing connections that bridge the methodologies of different fields of study. **1972** *Jrnl. Social Psychol.* LXXXVII. 127 None of these methodologies have been extended into the realm of applied psychology. **1974** *Nature* 22 Mar. 294/3 The interfacing of the two techniques..is discussed in depth together with the methodology of operating them together.

Hence **methodo'logical** *a.* [cf. mod.L. *methodologicus* (A. H. Francke, *c* 1720)], of or pertaining to methodology. **methodo'logically** *adv.*, in a methodological manner or respect. **metho'dologist**, one who treats method as a science.

1849 Lankester tr. *Schleiden's Sci. Bot.* Pref., A Methodological Introduction. **1865** *Fraser's Mag.* May 609 The French are miraculous methodologists. **1883** *American* VI. 10 Lord Bacon was the first to call in question the doctrine of final causes. He did so only as a methodologist. **1895** G. F. Moore *Crit. & Exeget. Comm. Judges* Introd. 26 It is methodologically an unreasonable demand [etc.]. **1897** F. C. S. Schiller in *Contemp. Rev.* June 872 As a methodological device this was quite justifiable; every inquiry must begin somewhere, and Darwin chose to begin here. **1914** B. Russell *Our Knowl. External World* viii. 238 It is necessary to practise methodological doubt, like Descartes, in order to loosen the hold of mental habits. **1937** T. Parsons *Struct. Social Action* i. i. 23 These [assumptions] may lie in a number of different directions. But the ones to which special attention should now be called are the 'methodological'. **1941** J. C. Ransom *New Crit.* ii. 208 In my mind Dante's beliefs are very bold speculations at which the accusing finger has pointed steadily for a long time now, but substantively are better grounded, and methodologically far more consistent, than Shelley's beliefs. **1942** *Economica* IX. 286 That he [*sc.* the social scientist] systematically starts from the concepts which guide individuals in their actions, is the characteristic feature of that methodological individualism which is closely connected with the subjectivism of the social sciences. **1949** Shils & Finch tr. *Weber's Methodology of Social Sci.* iii. 113 The professional methodologist will take umbrage at many of Meyer's formulations. **1952** K. R. Popper *Open Society* (ed. 2) I. iii. 31, I use the name methodological essentialism to characterize the view..that it is the task of pure knowledge or 'science' to discover and to describe the true nature of things, i.e. their hidden reality or essence. **1962** F. Williams tr. *Sartre's Imagination* p. vi, This truism has some far-reaching methodological implications, however. **1964** Gould & Kolb *Dict. Social Sci.* 425/2 The methodologist examines systematically and logically the aptness of all research tools, varying from basic assumptions to special research techniques, for the scientific purpose. *Ibid.* 471/1 Methodologically the term [*sc.* non-empirical] is used to describe all methods of acquiring belief other than those of positive science. **1965** B. B. Wolman *Scientific Psychol.* 18 One form of this practice is an extreme and radical methodological reductionism. Instead of developing methods and concepts derived from human life, they imitate ..physical science. **1969** R. Blackburn in Cockburn & Blackburn *Student Power* 203 What is sometimes called 'methodological individualism' (the bourgeois doctrine that all statements about society can be reduced to statements about individuals) is a device for evading such facts as these. **1972** *Computers & Humanities* VII. 86 When one kind of analysis is conveniently included in the package but a more methodologically sound analysis is not, inappropriate analysis may result. **1973** *Amer. Speech 1970* XLV. 124 Labov has led something of a methodological revolution.

methods-time. [f. pl. of method *sb.* + time *sb.*] Used *attrib.*, esp. in phr. ***methods-time measurement*** (also with capital initials): see quots. 1948², 1968. Abbrev. *MTM*.

1948 H. B. Maynard et al. *Methods-Time Measurement* p. v, The methods-time measurement procedure eliminates the necessity for judging the performance level at which an operator works while being observed. *Ibid.* ii. 12 Methods-time measurement is a procedure which analyzes any manual operation or method into the basic motions required to perform it and assigns to each motion a predetermined time standard which is determined by the nature of the motion and the conditions under which it is made. *Ibid.* iii. 25 The desirability of having accurate methods-time data available has long been recognized by methods engineers. *Ibid.* xv. 129 A question which was uppermost all during the period when the methods-time standards were being developed. **1952** A. G. Shaw *Purpose & Pract. Motion Study* iii. 60 The Methods-Time Measurement technique analyses a movement cycle into elements. **1959** V. H. Rotroff *Work Measurement* iii. 30 Applying the MTM technique, the analyst summarizes all motions required to perform the job properly. **1968** Johannsen & Robertson *Managem. Gloss.* 87 *Methods Time Measurement*, a predetermined motion time work measurement technique devised by the Methods Engineering Council (USA) which analyses manual operations and methods into basic motions required to perform them... There are nine basic MTM motions.

Methody ('mɛθɒdɪ). Also 8–9 **-dee**. Vulgar or dialectical perversion of Methodist. Also *attrib.*

1753 J. Wesley *Jrnl.* 8 Aug. (1913) IV. 78 As soon as we entered the town [*sc.* Mevagissey] many ran together, crying, 'See, the Methodees are come.' **1794** W. B. Stevens *Jrnl.* 19 Mar. (1965) 140 A mighty good Methody Parson comes every day. **1834** [see battleship c]. **1847** W. E. Forster in Reid *Life* (1888) I. vii. 207 Last evening I deluded them into a Methody meeting-house. *Ibid.* 208 Said rotten blanket being the Methody garment of the religious idea. **1848** Mrs. Gaskell *Mary Barton* vi, A good fellow, though too much of the Methodee. **1907** T. E. Kebbel *Lord Beaconsfield* xvi. 259 Do I not remember many a sturdy villager who was always ready with a gibe at 'the Methodies', as they were called. **1933** *Bulletin* (Sydney) 25 Oct. 20/1 You should have told him Methodies don't dance. **1962** G. Lawton *John Wesley's English* ix. 211 Three other nicknames for 'Methodist'—'Culamite', 'Macabee' and 'Methodee' may..be considered here.

methody, *a.*: see method *sb.* 2 e.

methol ('mɛθɒl). *Chem.* [ad. F. *méthol*, f. *méthyle* methyl: see -ol i.] A colourless liquid, produced in the distillation of wood.

1842 T. Graham *Elem. Chem.* 837. *a* **1864** Gesner *Coal, Petr.*, etc. (1865) 89.

methologie, -y, obs. forms of mythology.

methomania (mɛθəʊ'meɪnɪə). *Path.* [f. Gr. μέθη strong drink, drunkenness + -mania. Cf. F. *méthomanie*.] Periodic or intermittent drunkenness.

1856 in Mayne *Expos. Lex.* **1876** Fiske *Unseen World* xiv. 334 We have an increased amount of insanity, methomania, consumption [etc.]. **1887** *Buck's Handbk. Med. Sci.* IV. 120/2 Dipsomania, Methomania, Oinomania.

methonium (mɪ'θəʊnɪəm). *Pharm.* [f. meth- + -onium.] Any of various polymethylene bistrimethylammonium cations, $[(CH_3)_3N(CH_2)_xN(CH_3)_3]^{2+}$ (where *x* is an integer), or salts of these ions, some of which are used as ganglionic blocking agents in the treatment of hypertension.

[**1949**: cf. decamethonium, *hexamethonium* (s.v. hexa-).] **1950** *Lancet* 26 Aug. 353/1 (*heading*) 'Medical sympathectomy' in hypertension. A clinical study of methonium compounds. **1952** *Pharmacol. Rev.* IV. 220 The name of 'methonium' compounds for the members of the polymethylene bistrimethylammonium series has been approved by the British Pharmacopoeia Commission, and it is under this name, preceded by the appropriate numerical prefix, that they are now known. **1969** *Jrnl. Neurochem.* XVI. 1173 Some members of the methonium series are.. taken up by a saturable mechanism and..the uptakes can be described quantitatively by Michaelis-Menten type kinetics.

methopa, obs. form of metope.

methotrexate (mɛθəʊ-, mi:θəʊ'trɛkseɪt). *Pharm.* [Origin unknown.] 4-Amino-10-methylfolic acid, $C_{20}H_{22}N_8O_5$, an orange-brown powder which is a folic acid antagonist and is used in the treatment of tumours, esp. cancer and leukæmia.

1955 *Sci. News Let.* 5 Feb. 88/2 The new drug is an anti-folic acid compound very similar to Aminopterin. It is called Methotrexate by its manufacturers, Lederle Laboratories, Pearl River, N.Y. **1961** [see *mercapto-purine* s.v. mercapto(-)]. **1970** *Times Lit. Suppl.* 26 Mar. 332/4 Burkett's [*read* Burkitt's] tumour..can be treated easily and successfully by dosing with methotrexate. **1971** *Nature* 22 Oct. 518/3 The Food and Drug Administration has decided to allow the controversial drug methotrexate to be used for severe cases of psoriasis. **1973** *Brit. Pharmacopœia* 300/1 Methotrexate.

methought, pa. t. of methinks.

methoxy(-) (mɛ'θɒksɪ). *Chem.* [f. methoxy(l (cf. hydroxy-).] **a.** As an inseparable formative element in chem. names, indicating the presence of a methoxyl group, as ***methoxy-acetophenone***, ***-benzoic*** adj., ***-pyridine***, ***-succinic*** adj.; **me'thoxychlor**, a crystalline compound, $(C_6H_4OCH_3)_2CHCCl_3$, of similar chemical structure to DDT, which is used as an insecticide, esp. for veterinary hygiene.

1942 Fuson & Snyder *Org. Chem.* xxi. 288 A remarkable instance of catalysis has been observed in the formation of *p*-methoxyacetophenone from anisole by treatment with acetic anhydride **1964** N. G. Clark *Mod. Org. Chem.* xxiii. 479 Like the aromatic aldehydes, the ketones are frequently employed as synthetic intermediates, and as ingredients in perfumery. Some simple derivatives possess quite delightful odours, for example, *p*-methylacetophenone (hawthorn), *p*-methoxyacetophenone (heliotrope). **1895** Perkin & Kipping *Org. Chem.* II. xxvi. 397 The methylcresols..are oxidised by chromic acid, yielding the corresponding methoxybenzoic acids, $C_6H_4(OCH_3)\cdot COOH$. **1949** *Jrnl. Econ. Entomol.* XLII. 845/1 Ellenville line flies exhibited resistance to residues of both DDT and methoxychlor. **1959** H. Martin *Sci. Princ. Crop Protection* (ed. 4) x. 203 When methoxychlor was used instead [of DDT], Carter *et al.* were unable to detect the insecticide in the milk. **1969** K. A. Hassall *World Crop Protection* II. iv. 88 Methoxychlor..shows a lower tendency than DDT to dissolve in animal fats and also possesses a much lower acute oral toxicity to higher animals. It is therefore used on and near livestock. **1973** *Globe & Mail* (Toronto) 8 Sept. 8/3 City golf courses and cemeteries were relatively mosquito-free, having been fogged all along with methoxychlor, a new insecticide that doesn't have the harmful properties of DDT. **1889** G. M'Gowan tr. *Bernthsen's Text-bk. Org. Chem.* 486 Methoxy-pyridine and methyl-pyridone, which result from these two forms by exchange of H..for CH_3, are known. **1893** *Jrnl. Chem. Soc.* LXIII. 229 Inactive methoxy-succinic acid may be resolved into two active acids, of equal and opposite rotatory powers.

b. As an independent word, usu. *attrib.* and sometimes joined by a hyphen to the second element: = methoxyl.

1900 Perkin & Kipping *Org. Chem.* (rev. ed.) xxxiii. 485 By far the greater number of alkaloids contain one or two, sometimes three or more, methoxy-groups.., united with a benzene nucleus. **1946** *Jrnl. Pharmacol. & Exper. Therap.* LXXXVIII. 413 Substitution of chlorine by a..methoxy, butoxy or amyloxy group yields ineffective compounds. **1969** *Times* 10 Feb. 10/8 Dr. Shulgin..prepared many derivatives of mescalin, differing from the parent compound in their pattern of methoxy substitution on the phenyl ring. **1971** *Nomencl. Org. Chem.* (I.U.P.A.C.) (ed. 2) C. 154 The following contractions for oxygen-containing radical names are recommended... Methoxy CH_3-O-.

methoxyl (mɛ'θɒksɪl). *Chem.* [f. meth(yl) + ox(ygen) + -yl.] A hypothetical radical, CH_3O, analogous to hydroxyl.

1866 Frankland in *Jrnl. Chem. Soc.* XIX. 376 These radicals may be named *hydroxyl*, *methoxyl*, *ethoxyl*, &c.

methranee, variant form of matranee.

1845 Stocqueler *Handbk. Brit. India* (1854) 223 A methranee, or female sweeper.

methredate, -ridat(e, var. ff. of mithridate.

meths (mɛθs). Also **meth.** Colloq. abbrev. of *methylated spirit(s)*. Also *attrib.*, freq. as **meth(s)-drinker**, one who is addicted to drinking methylated spirits. (See also metho¹.)

1933 M. Marshall *Tramp-Royal on Toby* 367/1 *Meth*, methylated spirit. **1935** [see jake *sb.*²]. **1939** 'N. Shute' *What happened to Corbetts* i. 18 A Primus stove..and paraffin and meths. **1947** [see hottie, hotty *sb.*]. **1959** *Listener* 21 May 893/3 A lovely copper kettle with a meths-

burner underneath. **1961** *Times* 15 Aug. 11/3 The surly greetings of the meth-drinkers. **1966** J. Bingham *Double Agent* x. 149 It sounds like a meth-drinkers' camp. **1968** *Daily Tel.* 12 Nov. 16/2 Young people who work at clearing slag heaps, helping meths-drinkers or cleaning canals to make them navigable. **1970** M. Tripp *Man without Friends* i. 7 I'd seen a meths drinker spewing blood the night before. **1973** D. Jordan *Nile Green* xxxiv. 167, I shook my head like a meths drinker.

†'**Methuen.** *Obs.* A name jocularly applied to Portuguese wines imported under a preferential duty in accordance with the provisions of the commercial treaty of 1703 between England and Portugal, negotiated by Paul Methuen, the English minister at Lisbon.

1753 Armstrong *Taste* 53 The Man to genuine Burgundy bred up Soon starts the dash of Methuen in his Cup. **1754** Fielding *Voy. Lisbon* (1755) 205 That generous liquor which all humble companions are taught to postpone to the flavour of Methuen, or honest Port.

methule, obs. form of methyl.

Methuselah (mɪ'θju:zələ). Also 4–5 **Matus(s)ale, Matusalem,** 6 **Mathusalah,** 7–8 **Methusaleh, -salem.** [Heb. *mᵉthū'shelah.*

The corruption *Methusalem* (after *Jerusalem*) still survives in vulgar use. Purvey 1388 has *Matusalem* beside *Matusale*, perhaps from the accusative form *Matusalam* in the Vulgate.]

1. The name of one of the pre-Noachian patriarchs, stated to have lived 969 years (*Gen.* v. 27); hence used as a type of extreme longevity.

a **1380** *Minor Poems fr. Vernon MS.* xxxix. 186 3if a Mon may libben heer As longe as dude Matussale. **1647** Cowley *Mistr., Love & Life* i, So though my Life be short, yet may I prove The great Methusalem of Love. **1711** tr. *Werenfelsius' Meteors of Stile* 225 The Heliotrope is the Methusalem of Flowers. **1756** H. Walpole *Let. to Conway* 4 Mar., It is impossible not to laugh at him as if he was a Methusaleh! **1849** H. Rogers *Ess.* II. vi. 316 A good book is the Methuselah of these latter ages. **1888** J. B. Bailey (*title*) Modern Methuselahs, or Short Biographical Sketches of a few Advanced Nonagenarians, or actual Centenarians.

2. *transf.* A very large wine-bottle (see quots.).

1935 A. L. Simon *Dict. Wine* 172 *Methuselah*, double Jeroboam, holding 8 reputed quarts or 6·40 litres, equal to 225·350 fluid ounces. **1951** *Bohemian Life* (Bohemian Distrib. Co., Los Angeles, U.S.A.) Apr., Out-size bottles include the.. Methuselah.. 8 bottles or 213·30 ounces. **1959** *Gloss. Packaging Terms* (*B.S.I.*) 28 *Methuselah*, a wine bottle —capacity 9 reputed quarts. **1962** [see Balthazar]. **1972** E. Meigh *Story Glass Bottle* 73 Wine bottlers ransacked the Old Testament for names of kings and captains to name the bottles in which their valuable liquids were confined: thus, in ascending order of magnitude are jeroboams, rehoboams, methuselahs.

Hence **Me'thusalemess**, a female 'Methuselah'.

1790 H. Walpole *Let. to Miss A. Berry* 29 Nov., Madame Grifoni.. would now be a Methusalemess.

‖'**methy.** ? *Obs.* In 8 (? *erron.*) **marthy.** [Cree *methai* (in other dialects *menai, melai, meyai*).] (See quot. 1772.)

1772 Forster in *Phil. Trans.* LXIII. 152 The second of the Hudson's Bay fish, is called, by the wild natives of that country, *Marthy*, and is nothing else than our common Burbot, *Gadus Lota*, Linn. only vastly superior in size. **1836** J. Richardson *Fauna Bor.-Amer.* III. 248 *Gadus* (*Lota*) *maculosus* (Cuvier). The Methy.

methyl ('mɛθɪl). *Chem.* Formerly also **methule, -yle.** [a. F. *méthyle*, G. *methyl*, a back-formation from F. *méthylène*, G. *methylen*, methylene.

The G. *methyl* occurs in papers by Regnault in *Ann. der Pharmacie* XXXIII. 328 and XXXIV. 28 (1840). The back-formation was suggested by the fact that *-yl* (which Berzelius preferred to spell *-ule*), from the Gr. ὕλη in the sense of 'matter', had already been used in names of organic radicals (*benzoyl*, Wöhler & Liebig 1832; *ethyl*, Liebig 1834). The analysis of *methylene* into *methyl* + *-ene* gave rise to the use of -ene as a chemical suffix, as in *ethylene, benzene*, etc., and the identification of the last syllable of *methyl* with the suffix *-yl* led to the use of *meth-* as an element in the names of substances connected with or derived from wood spirit.]

a. The hypothetical radical of the monocarbon series (CH_3), the base of pyroxylic or wood spirit or pyroligneous naphtha, of formic acid and of a large series of organic compounds.

1844 Hoblyn *Dict. Med., Methyl*, the newly-discovered radical, or basyle, of wood spirit. **1847** Horsford in *Amer. Jrnl. Sci.* Ser. ii. IV. 333 The same is true of.. oxyd of methyle and alcohol. **1848** Craig, *Methule*, the name given to the hypothetical radical of pyroxylic acid. **1850** Daubeny *Atom. Theory* vii. (ed. 2) 226 A then hypothetical principle, composed of C_2H_3, which he [*sc.* Liebig] called methyle. **1871** Tyndall *Fragm. Sci.* (1879) I. xvii. 449 The positions of chloroform and iodide of methyl are inverted.

b. *attrib.* and *Comb.*, as *methyl compound, radical*, etc.; esp. in names of salts of methyl, e.g. *methyl bromide, chloride, hydride*. Also prefixed (often without hyphen) to the name of an organic compound to express the addition of methyl to its composition, or the replacement of hydrogen atoms by equivalents of methyl, as in *methylacetonamine, methylaniline, methylcarbonic* (*acid*), *methyl-codeia, methyl-uramine*, etc.

1844 Fownes *Chem.* Index, Methyle-compounds. **1866** Odling *Anim. Chem.* 45 Leave the urea and methylamine residues combined with one another in the form of methyl-uramine or methyl-guanidine. **1866** Roscoe *Elem. Chem.* 81 Methyl Hydride.. is a colourless, tasteless, inodorous gas. **1868** F. Guthrie in *Rep. Brit. Assoc., Sections* 38 Iodide of methylacetonamine. **1874** Garrod & Baxter *Mat. Med.* 201 The hypnotic effect of codeia is wholly destroyed by its conversion into methyl-codeia. **1878** *Nature* 25 July 337/1 Use of Methyl Chloride for the Production of Low Temperatures. **1885** Remsen *Org. Chem.* (1888) 357 Methyl-sulphonic acid.. methyl-carbonic or acetic acid. **1896** *Allbutt's Syst. Med.* I. 225 The methyl compound depresses the spinal cord. **1899** *Ibid.* VIII. 577 [Cacodylic acid] is a combination of arsenic with methyl radicals.

c. Special combinations: **methyl alcohol**, pyroxylic spirit; = methanol; **methylcellulose**, any of a range of white, tasteless compounds which are produced by etherifying cellulose with various proportions of methyl chloride or sulphate and are used as thickening, emulsifying, and stabilizing agents, esp. in the food industry, as laxatives, and in adhesives; **methyl'dopa** *Pharm.*, a whitish powder, $C_{10}H_{13}NO_4$, which is used as a hypotensive agent; **methyl ethyl ketone**, a colourless volatile liquid, $CH_3COCH_2CH_3$, which is widely used as a solvent for organic materials; butanone; **methylgly'oxal**, a yellow liquid aldehyde, CH_3COCHO, with a pungent odour, which readily polymerizes and is an intermediate in carbohydrate metabolism; **methyl green**, a green dye obtained by heating Paris violet with methyl chloride, much used in microscopical preparations; **methyl isobutyl ketone**, a liquid ketone, $(CH_3)_2CHCH_2COCH_3$, which is manufactured by the hydrogenation of mesityl oxide and widely used as a solvent; hexone; **methyl mercaptan**, methyl hydrosulphide, CH_3HS; **methyl methacrylate**, (*a*) the methyl ester of methacrylic acid, a volatile colourless liquid that readily polymerizes to resinous glass-like materials that are sold under trade-names such as *Lucite, Perspex*, and *Plexiglas*; (*b*) polymerized methyl methacrylate; **methyl orange**, an orange crystalline compound, $(CH_3)_2N{\cdot}C_6H_4{\cdot}N{:}N{\cdot}C_6H_4{\cdot}SO_3Na$, which is the sodium salt of an azo-dye made by coupling diazotized sulphanilic acid with dimethylaniline and is chiefly used (in dilute aqueous solution) as an acid-base indicator in volumetric analysis, giving a pink colour at a pH of 3 and a yellow colour at a pH of 4·4; **(6α-)methylpred'nisolone**, a synthetic compound, $C_{22}H_{30}O_5$, which functions as a glucorticoid and is used mainly in treating rheumatoid arthritis and rheumatic fever; **methyl red** [tr. G. *methylrot* (Rupp & Loose 1909, in *Ber. d. Deut. Chem. Ges.* XLI. 3905)], a red crystalline compound, $(CH_3)_2N{\cdot}C_6H_4{\cdot}N{:}N{\cdot}C_6H_4{\cdot}COOH$, that is analogous to methyl orange (anthranilic acid being used in its preparation in place of sulphanilic acid) and is used similarly, the colour of an alcoholic solution being red at a pH of 4·4 and yellow at a pH of 6; **methyl rubber**, an early synthetic rubber made by polymerization of dimethylbutadiene; **methyl salicylate**, a colourless or pale-yellow liquid, $C_6H_4(OH)CO{\cdot}OCH_3$, which is the chief constituent of oil of wintergreen and sweet birch oil and is used as a flavouring material, in perfumery, and in liniments and ointments; **methylte'stosterone** *Pharm.*, any of the methyl derivatives, $C_{20}H_{30}O_2$, of testosterone; *spec.* 17-methyltestosterone, a white crystalline powder with similar actions and uses to those of testosterone; ,**methylthi'ouracil**, any compound which is a methyl and a thio derivative of uracil; *spec.* 6-methyl-2-thiouracil, $C_5H_6N_2OS$, an antithyroid substance used to control thyrotoxicosis; **methyl violet**, Paris violet, a reddish-blue coal-tar dye obtained from dimethylaniline.

1847 Horsford in *Amer. Jrnl. Sci.* Ser. ii. IV. 333 *Methyl alcohol. **1850** Daubeny *Atom. Theory* viii. (ed. 2) 240 *Methylaniline, where the second atom is replaced by methyle instead of ethyle. **1899** Cagney tr. *Jaksch's Clin. Diagn.* v. (ed. 4) 156 A violet coloured watery solution of *methyl-aniline-violet. **1921** *Jrnl. Chem. Soc.* CXIX. i. 79 A *methyl cellulose of this limiting methoxyl content can be prepared which is representative of the whole of the original cellulose. **1947** Winding & Hasche *Plastics* iii. 119 Water solubility plus the ability to produce viscous solutions has made methyl cellulose useful as a thickening agent in the textile, food, and adhesive industries. Since it is edible, it can be used as a base for salad dressings. **1954** *Jrnl. Pharmacy & Pharmacol.* VI. 731 Methylcellulose eye-drops .. are liable to contamination by moulds. **1966** *Punch* 5 Jan. 11/1 In its survey of strawberry jam it [sc. *Which?*] found two specimens in which the composers had succeeded in soaring far above the sordid world of methyl cellulose and lecithin. **1954** *Arch. Biochem. & Biophysics* LI. 456 Two compounds, *α-methyl-3,4-dopa (α-MD) and α-methyl-3-hydroxyphenylalanine, respectively, added in a low range of concentrations, accelerated, and at higher concentrations, inhibited, kidney dopa decarboxylase. **1961** *New Zealand Med. Jrnl.* LX. 569/2 Methyl dopa, like other potent hypotensive agents, produces side-effects including fatigue. **1972** *Materials & Technol.* V. xxi. 792 Methyldopa and pargyline cause the replacement of noradrenaline by a weaker transmitter. **1876** *Jrnl. Chem. Soc.* XXIX. 897 By the reduction of *methyl-ethyl ketone, pinacone $C_8H_{18}O$ is obtained. **1938** H. P. Starck *Princ. Org. Chem.* vii. 186 Methyl ethyl ketone was formerly used as a solvent in the preparation of cordite from gun cotton and nitroglycerine. **1959** *Times Rev. Industry* Aug. 98/1 Methylethylketone for removing waxy materials. **1898** *Jrnl. Chem. Soc.* LXXIV. i. 224 *Methylglyoxal is formed from dihydroxyacetone.. when the latter is distilled with dilute sulphuric acid. **1913, 1951** Methylglyoxal [see glyoxalase]. **1962** A. Pirie *Lens Metabolism Rel. Cataract* 431 Experiments were done in the hope of detecting methylglyoxal which Salem and Crooke (1950) stated was formed from hexosediphosphate by liver. **1880** Friswell in *Jrnl. Soc. Arts* 445 By the action of methyl chloride, the well-known *methyl green was produced. **1888** *Jrnl. Chem. Soc.* LIV. 125 Its ketone.. is therefore identical with *methyl isobutyl ketone. **1960** *Times Rev. Industry* Dec. 16/3 The chloride is dissolved in water, and then treated with an organic solvent called methylisobutyl ketone (MIBK) which extracts the iron. **1973** H. M. Stanley in E. G. Hancock *Propylene* i. 9 The Shell Oil Company.. in 1937–8 commenced the manufacture of acetone derivatives, including diacetone alcohol, mesityl oxide and methylisobutyl ketone. **1844** Fownes *Chem.* 420 *Methyl-mercaptan.. is a colourless liquid, of powerful alliaceous odour. **1933** *Chem. Abstr.* XXVII. 4363 Thermoplastic products are obtained by polymerizing *methyl methacrylate.. by exposure to light or heat. **1936** *Industr. & Engin. Chem.* Oct. 1161/2 These properties make methyl methacrylate an outstanding plastic. **1964** N. G. Clark *Mod. Org. Chem.* x. 194 Acetone cyanohydrin.. is an important intermediate in the manufacture of methyl methacrylate, the material used for making the polymer 'Perspex'. **1967** *Times Rev. Industry* June 74/3 Methyl methacrylate and/or polyester reinforced glass fibre are used for hand basins, baths, complete bath room heat units, heating ducts, roof lights, &c. **1881** G. Lunge in *Chem. News* 16 Dec. 288/1 It is in reality a salt of sulpho-benzene-azo-dimethylamin, for which long name I propose the short and sufficiently clear name '*Methyl-orange'. **1930** Field & Weill *Electro-Plating* 56 The ordinary indicators used by the chemist such as litmus, methyl orange and phenolphthalein. **1969** H. A. Flaschka et al. *Quantitative Analytical Chem.* II. ix. 110 Methyl orange is therefore unsuited to the titration of a weak acid. **1957** *Ann. Rheumatic Dis.* XVI. 298/2 *6-Methyl-prednisolone was administered under various conditions to 41 patients with active peripheral rheumatoid arthritis. **1960** *Antibiotic Med.* VII. 704 The subcutaneous injection of depot methyl prednisolone has demonstrated significant permanent relief of refractory anal pruritus in 14 patients. **1973** *Jrnl. Amer. Med. Assoc.* 19 Feb. 896/1 Large doses of methylprednisolone were used intravenously as the sole steroid agent in 44 transplants in 43 renal allografted patients for the first two to three weeks after operation. **1910** *Jrnl. Chem. Soc.* XCVII. 2490 As a means of measuring colorimetrically the concentration of hydrogen ions in a solution, *methyl-red would probably be found valuable when such concentration lies between 10^{-5} and 10^{-6}. **1951** Whitby & Hynes *Med. Bacteriol.* (ed. 5) xii. 193 When *Bact. coli* is grown for 5 days at 30° C. in the glucose phosphate medium described above an acid reaction is maintained which is sufficient to give a red colouration on the addition of 0·04 per cent aqueous methyl red as indicator. **1969** Fischer & Peters *Brief Introd. Quantitative Chem. Analysis* viii. 212 At pH 4·2 (and below).. methyl red is present as the red acid form and.. it exists as the yellow base form if the pH becomes 6·2 (and above). **1919** *India-Rubber Jrnl.* 16 Aug. 18/2 The dye works laid themselves out for the manufacture of large quantities of *methyl-rubber hot polymerisation products. **1936** *Trans. Faraday Soc.* XXXII. 91 The sharpness of the fibre pattern depends on the sample of methyl rubber investigated. **1972** *Materials & Technol.* V. xiv. 456 During the first World War the Germans worked out.. the first factory-scale synthetic rubber plant which produced the so-called methyl rubber. .. The quality of this rubber was poor; it was only useful for the preparation of hard rubber battery boxes for submarines. **1876** *Encycl. Brit.* V. 572/2 Oil of wintergreen .. contains *methyl salicylate. **1948** *Jrnl. Amer. Med. Assoc.* 28 Feb. 651/2 Methyl salicylate is a potent and fairly rapidly acting poison. **1972** *Materials & Technol.* IV. xii. 448 Methyl salicylate, which is a known anti-rheumaticum, is made by the Fischer esterification of salicylic acid. **1936** *Biochem. Jrnl.* XXX. 292 Various.. derivatives methylated at position 17, including *methyltestosterone. **1955** W. Gaddis *Recognitions* ii. v. 526 Crossing the Atlantic Ocean to get laid. He can't even get it up without a dose of methyltestosterone. **1959** *Brit. Med. Jrnl.* 31 Jan. 259/2 Methyltestosterone was introduced to clinical medicine.. in 1939, and since that time must have been used for its androgenic and protein anabolic effects in thousands of cases. **1970** Passmore & Robson *Compan. Med. Stud.* II. xii. 11/2, 17α-Methyltestosterone is active by oral administration. **1974** *Nature* 13 Dec. 585/2 We have induced reversible infertility, with little effect on libido, in five healthy young men by giving them tablets containing methyltestosterone and ethynyloestradiol. **1944** *Q. Jrnl. Pharmacy & Pharmacol.* XVII. 318 *Methylthiouracil produces hyperplasia of the thyroid gland of the rat. **1960** *Lancet* 19 Mar. 653/2 Professor Wayne's references.. to methylthiouracil prompt me to record the long-term follow-up of 100 consecutive cases of thyrotoxicoses. **1968** *Listener* 18 July 70/1, I had recently been diagnosed as hyperthyroidic and had with remarkable benefit embarked on a course of methylthiouracil tablets.

methylal ('mɛθɪlæl). *Chem.* [ad. F. *méthylal*, f. *méthyle* methyl + *al*(*cool*) alcohol.] A mobile aromatic liquid obtained by heating methyl alcohol with manganese dioxide and sulphuric acid; occasionally employed as an anæsthetic.

1838 R. D. Thomson in *British Ann. for* 1839, 363 Methylal.. is contained in the formomethylal discovered by Dr. Gregory. **1881** B. W. Richardson in *Med. Temp. Jrnl.* XLVI. 81 Methylic alcohol, or methylal.

methylamine (ˈmɛθɪləmaɪn). *Chem.* Also **-min.** [f. METHYL + AMINE.] A compound in which one atom of the hydrogen in ammonia has been replaced by methyl. Also *attrib.*

1850 DAUBENY *Atom. Theory* viii. (ed. 2) 239 Methylamine. **1873** WATTS *Fownes' Chem.* (ed. 11) 569 Methylamine nitrate. **1897** *Allbutt's Syst. Med.* II. 788 From decomposing fish..methylamine..cadaverine and putrescine were extracted. **1898** *Ibid.* V. 35 Methylamin, ammonia and sulphuretted hydrogen are also found [in the sputum of fetid bronchitis].

methylate (ˈmɛθɪleɪt), *sb. Chem.* [Formed as METHYLIC: see -ATE[1].] A salt formed by the union of methyl with oxygen and a metallic base.

1835 KANE in *Rep. Brit. Assoc., Sections* 42 The sulphomethylate of potash. **1865** WATTS *Dict. Chem.* III. 1002 Methylate of ethylene. **1880** *Athenæum* 27 Nov. 713/1 Aluminic methylate.

methylate (ˈmɛθɪleɪt), *v. Chem.* [f. METHYL + -ATE.] *trans.* To introduce one or more methyl groups into (a compound or group); usually, to mix (spirit of wine) with such a quantity of pyroxylic spirit or some other substance as will render it unfit for drinking, so as to exempt it from the duties imposed in Great Britain and other countries upon alcohol. Hence **ˈmethylated** *ppl. a.*; **methyˈlation**, the process of methylating; **ˈmethylator**, one who methylates.

methylated spirit, containing about ten per cent. of pyroxylic spirit, is the form in which alcohol is most commonly employed for industrial purposes; also *ellipt.*

1861 *Jrnl. Chem. Soc.* XIII. 324 These crystals were not analysed, but there can be no doubt that they were the methylated phosphorus-urea of the allyl-series. *c* **1865** J. WYLDE in *Circ. Sci.* I. 63/2 Each lens should..be..washed ..with spirits of wine (not methylated spirits, because these contain a resin in solution). **1866** ROSCOE *Elem. Chem.* 334 Each of these methylated benzols yields an important series of derivatives. **1880** *Act 43 & 44 Vict.* c. 24 §3 'Methylate' means to mix spirits with some substance in such manner as to render the mixture unfit for use as a beverage. *Ibid.* §83 Spirits warehoused may..be delivered out, without payment of duty, for methylation. *Ibid.* §126 A retailer.. must not receive methylated spirits except from an authorised methylator. **1880** FRISWELL in *Jrnl. Soc. Arts* 444 This inference, was that the methylated derivatives of roseine could be obtained by the oxidation of the methylated derivatives of aniline. *Ibid.* 445 The violets obtained by the methylation of rosaniline. **1888** *Jrnl. Chem. Soc.* LIII. 778 An attempt was made to methylate acetyl-metanitranilide by the action of sodium ethylate and methyl iodide. **1912** D. H. LAWRENCE *Let.* 2 Sept. (1962) I. 142 We take rucksacks ..with food and methylated, cook our meals by some stream. **1917** *Jrnl. Chem. Soc.* CXI. 848 Experiments have proved the wide scope of the use of formaldehyde for methylating amino-compounds. **1929** *Jrnl. Amer. Chem. Soc.* LI. 2535 We have found methyl bromide to be a satisfactory methylating agent with both malonic ester and acetoacetic ester. **1938** MRS. BELLOC LOWNDES *Let.* 29 Sept. (1971) 165, I also got..rather more methylated, rice and matches than usual. **1967** I. L. FINAR *Org. Chem.* (ed. 5) I. xxvi. 683 Veratrole..may be prepared by methylating catechol with methyl sulphate in alkaline solution.

methylene (ˈmɛθɪliːn). *Chem.* [ad. F. *méthylène* (Dumas & Peligot, *Ann de Chimie et de physique* LVIII. 9), irregularly f. Gr. μέθυ wine + ὕλη wood; the inventors of the name explain its etymological meaning as 'vin ou liqueur spiritueuse du bois'.] A hypothetical radical of the hydrocarbons (CH_2); unknown in the free state, but occurring in many compounds, as ***methylene hydrate***, etc. **methylene-azure**, an oxidation product of methylene blue; **methylene-blue**, a coal-tar colour used in dyeing, and as a bacterioscopic reagent; **methylene chloride**, dichloromethane, CH_2Cl_2, a volatile liquid used as a solvent, esp. in paint-removers and for extractions in pharmacy, and as a refrigerant; **methylene-violet** = *methyl-violet.*

1835 *R. D. Thomson's Rec. Gen. Sci.* II. 375 Dumas has.. coined a new name to distinguish this base, viz. Methylene. **1838** T. THOMSON *Chem. Org. Bodies* 180 This is the compound to which Dumas and Peligot have given the name of hydrate of methylene, and which I have considered as methylene. **1874** GARROD & BAXTER *Mat. Med.* 167 Bichloride of Methylene has been recommended by Dr. Richardson as a safer anæsthetic than chloroform. **1880** *Jrnl. Chem. Soc.* XXXVIII. 307 Methylene chloride, CH_2Cl_2, is best obtained by cautiously adding hydrochloric acid to a mixture of alcohol, chloroform, and metallic zinc. **1890** *Syd. Soc. Lex.* s.v., *Methylene azure, M. blue.* **1898** *Allbutt's Syst. Med.* V. 412 Another most useful basic stain is methylene blue. **1904** *Brit. Med. Jrnl.* 10 Sept. 583 Methylene-azure. **1953** O. E. ANDERSON *Refrigeration in Amer.* xii. 193 Other absorption machines were brought out for air-conditioning work. One of these used methylene chloride as the refrigerant. **1957** H. R. SHEPHERD in E. Sagarin *Cosmetics* xxxvi. 803 Ethyl chloride, methylene chloride, and others..among the earliest aerosol propellents, are not presently being used for cosmetic purposes. **1973** *Oxf. Univ. Gaz.* CIII. Suppl. 5. 10 The goddess has now been degreased with lustrations of methylene chloride and acetone.

methylic (mɪˈθɪlɪk), *a. Chem.* [Orig. f. METHYL(ENE) + -IC; the term METHYL, to which the adj. was afterwards more normally referred, was introduced somewhat later. Cf. F. *méthylique.*] Of or pertaining to methyl. Chiefly in names of compounds, in which *methyl* is more commonly used attributively.

1835 KANE in *Rep. Brit. Assoc., Sections* 43 Methylic æther. **1849** —— *Elem. Chem.* (ed. 2) 826 In its action upon other bodies this substance ranges itself completely with wine-alcohol, and it is hence frequently termed methylic alcohol. **1849** R. V. DIXON *Heat* I. 75 Amylic, ethylic, and methylic alcohol follow sensibly the same law of contraction. **1873** WATTS *Fownes' Chem.* (ed. 11) 705 Methylic diethoxalate is easily decomposed by baryta-water.

methylol (ˈmɛθɪlɒl). *Chem.* [f. METHYL + -OL.] = *hydroxymethyl* s.v. HYDROXY- 3.

1898 *Jrnl. Chem. Soc.* LXXIV. I. 506 Nitrobutylic alcohol ..readily condenses with formaldehyde (1 mol.) to form a glycol (2-methylol-2-nitro-1-butanol). **1937** F. C. WHITMORE *Org. Chem.* 521 Formaldehyde condenses with urea to give methylol ureas, $NH_2CONHCH_2OH$ etc. The methylol groups can combine with more urea to form more and more complex molecules until a resin is formed. **1962** J. T. MARSH *Self-Smoothing Fabrics* i. 3 The fundamental basis of the process remains unchanged and depends on the application of methylol compounds within the fibre of the fabric followed by their further condensation.

methylosis (mɛθɪˈləʊsɪs). *Geol.* [f. Gr. μετα- META- + ὕλη matter: see -OSIS.] Change of matter or composition. Hence **methyˈlotic** *a.*, pertaining to or produced by methylosis.

1878 KINAHAN *Geol. Irel.* 177 A third class of Metamorphism..is due to the introduction and action of chemical substances from without; it has been called Methylosis. *Ibid.* 188 Some of the beds have been subjected to methylotic action... Some of which seem to be methylotic rocks. **1893** GEIKIE *Text-bk. Geol.* IV. VIII. 596 *note, Methylosis, methylotic,*..applied to chemical metamorphism or alteration of constitution or substance.

methysergide (mɛθɪˈsɜːdʒaɪd). *Pharm.* [f. METH- + L)YSERG(IC *a.* + AM)IDE.] 1-Methyl-D-lysergic acid butanolamide, $C_{21}H_{28}N_3O_2$, a serotonin antagonist that is administered, usu. in the form of its maleate, in the prophylaxis of recurrent migraine.

1962 *Amer. Jrnl. Med. Sci.* CCXLIII. 152/1 Fifty-seven patients..were treated with antiserotonin agent, methysergide (UML-491). **1962** *Daily Tel.* 30 July 11/6 Methysergide (Deseril), is being tested as a preventive against chronic forms of migraine. **1968** J. H. BURN *Lect. Notes Pharmacol.* (ed. 9) 30 In some patients methysergide causes dizziness and nausea and produces aching in the legs.

‖**methysis** (ˈmɛθɪsɪs). *Path.* [mod.L., a. Gr. μέθυσις drunkenness, f. μεθύειν to be drunk, f. μέθυ strong drink.] The state of being addicted to the excessive use of intoxicants (*Syd. Soc. Lex.* 1890).

1856 in MAYNE *Expos. Lex.* In mod. Dicts.

methystic (mɪˈθɪstɪk), *a. Med.* [ad. Gr. μεθυστικός, f. μεθύειν: see prec.] Of or belonging to drunkenness; intoxicating.

1856 in MAYNE *Expos. Lex.*

metic (ˈmɛtɪk). *Gr. Antiq.* [irreg. ad. Gr. μέτοικος (late L. *metœcus, metycus*), f. μετα- (denoting change) + -οικος dwelling, οἰκεῖν to dwell.] A resident alien in a Greek city, having some of the privileges of citizenship.

1808 W. MITFORD *Hist. Greece* xxi. III. 12 An imposition, in the manner of a poll-tax, on the metics, those numerous free residents in Attica who were not Athenian citizens. **1881** JOWETT *Thucyd.* I. 114 The entire Athenian force, including the metics, invaded the territory of Megara. **1974** *Sci. Amer.* Sept. 95/1 In Athens the free immigrants called *metics*, who were permanent residents rather than passing traders, may have outnumbered the slaves.

transf. **1904** *Speaker* 23 Jan. 401/1 The British Imperialists..have found that the rich metics are their Masters. **1921** *Times Lit. Suppl.* 10 Nov. 731/2 The proportion of the horrific in Poe's poetry..is entirely different; he is a metic in the land of shadows. **1936** *Ibid.* 14 Nov. 918/4 Sir Harry Preston was not Brightonian by birth —but then most of the town's great men have been metics.

attrib. **1850** GROTE *Greece* II. lxv. (1862) V. 592 Exempt from the metic-tax and other special burthens.

metical(le: see MISKAL.

meticuˈlosity. [f. L. *meticulōsus* METICULOUS + -ITY. Cf. F. *méticulosité.*] The quality of being meticulous; †timorousness (*obs.*); excessive scrupulousness.

1654 H. L'ESTRANGE *Chas. I* (1655) 60 So that such Leagues may more properly be called Leagues of meticulosity and fear, then of amity. **1656** in BLOUNT *Glossogr.* **1906** *Daily News* 20 Feb. 9/1 Meticulosity of detail. **1972** *Country Life* 16 Mar. 657/2 The meticulosity of manners was necessary inside or outside the novels, in the villainy of a manor house character or at the tea-table.

meticulous (mɪˈtɪkjʊləs), *a.* [ad. L. *meticulōsus* (or the derived F. *méticuleux*), f. *metus* fear.]

†**1.** Fearful, timid. *Obs.*

1535 STEWART *Cron. Scot.* II. 649 Gif thow be.. Meticulos, and dar nocht se blude drawin. *a* **1550** *Image Hypocr.* IV. 544 in *Skelton's Wks.* (1843) II. 445 Madd and meticulous. **1646** SIR T. BROWNE *Pseud. Ep.* II. vii. (1686) 78 Melancholy and meticulous heads. **1674** [Z. CAWDREY] *Catholicon* 16 They strive not so much in ingage Meticulous Scrupulous Women and Mechanicks.

2. Over-careful about minute details, over-scrupulous. In present usage: careful, punctilious, scrupulous, precise.

1827 *Blackw. Mag.* XXII. 489 He does many things which we ourselves, and we do not hold ourselves peculiarly meticulous, will not venture upon. **1877** SYMONDS *Renaiss. in It., Rev. Learn.* II. vii. 300 The decadence of Italian prose composition into laboured mannerism and meticulous propriety. **1904** MAJ. A. GRIFFITHS *50 Yrs. Public Service* xii. 162 The rule was enforced by a stringent and meticulous discipline. **1952** W. D. JACOBS *William Barnes, Linguist* i. 9 They [*sc.* Barnes's linguistic studies] present a possible solution to mongrelized English and an alternate program of greater scale and with more meticulous plan than any previous to Barnes. **1964** *New Statesman* 8 May 710/1 Wilson is far too meticulous a constitutionalist not to appreciate the impropriety—not to mention the impossibility—of an opposition's seeking to govern a country in advance. **1973** *Times* 4 May 2/7 Dr Ramsey said in a meticulous English accent: 'Can I just say [etc.].'

meticulously (mɪˈtɪkjʊləslɪ), *adv.* [f. prec. + -LY[2].] In a meticulous manner; †timidly (*obs.*); with excessive care about minute details, over-scrupulously. In present usage: in a careful or punctilious manner. (Cf. METICULOUS *a.* 2.)

1682 SIR T. BROWNE *Chr. Mor.* I. §33 (1716) 39 Move circumspectly not meticulously, and rather carefully sollicitous than anxiously sollicitudinous. **1900** *Academy* 31 Mar. 275/1 A dish meticulously concocted upon a recipe. **1961** 'J. WYNDHAM' *Consider her Ways* 90 He had..a black felt hat meticulously brushed. **1971** *Nature* 4 June 334/3 It is essentially a reference book, meticulously cross-referenced, with a huge bibliography and a good index. **1974** *Physics Bull.* Mar. 104/2 With the aid of a meticulously detailed account of the formal basis of quantum mechanics, Professor Scheibe has provided a precise characterization of the orthodox interpretation of the theory.

meˈticulousness. [-NESS.] The quality of being meticulous; meticulosity.

1923 *Sunday at Home* Mar. 382/2 He was measured and cautious in his statements to the point of meticulousness. **1927** *Daily Tel.* 2 Mar. 5/5 Examples..handed down to posterity in paint with a meticulousness that..never fails to charm us. **1928** *Observer* 1 July 15/6 The paragraph of last Sunday did not do justice to the meticulousness of the index to Mr. Shaw's 'Intelligent Woman's Guide to Socialism'. **1937** *Discovery* Jan. 32/2 The pleasing meticulousness of a Chinese drawing.

†**ˈmetient,** *a. Obs.*$^{-0}$ [ad. L. *mētient-em*, pres. pple. of *mētīrī* to measure.]

1656 BLOUNT *Glossogr.*, *Metient*, measuring, esteeming.

‖**métier** (metje). [Fr.:—popular L. **misterium*, alteration of L. *ministerium* (see MINISTRY), prob. influenced by *mystērium* MYSTERY.]

A trade or profession: in Eng. use chiefly *transf.*, a person's 'line', that in which one is specially skilled.

1792 CHARLOTTE SMITH *Desmond* I. xiii. 253 They wanted, indeed, to make me a monk; but I had a mortal aversion to that *métier*. **1842** BARHAM *Ingol. Leg.* Ser. II. *Auto-da-fé*, Heretic-burning—in fact, 'tis his *métier*. **1895** ZANGWILL *Master* II. vii. 211 Black-and-white was no more his *métier* than humour. **1950** T. S. ELIOT *Cocktail Party* III. 157 You understand your *metier*, Mr. Quilpe—Which is the most that any of us can ask for. **1958** *Listener* 27 Nov. 874/1 It is fashionable to regard technical and physical craft [in the theatre] as adventitious and to have no sense whatever of what the French call *métier*. **1975** *Times* 18 Sept. 36/2 The parallels started to extend from the man to the *métier*.

‖**metif** (ˈmeɪtɪf, ˈmiːtɪf, ‖metif). Also **-iff.** [F. *métif*, OF. *mestif* mongrel, ? derived from *métis* (see METIS) with substitution of suffix.] The offspring of a white and a quadroon. Also *attrib.*

1808 PIKE *Sources Mississ.* (1895) II. 510 The hospitality and goodness of the Creoles and Metifs began to manifest itself. **1827** J. F. COOPER *Prairie* I. x. 281 The metiffs or half-breeds, who claimed to be ranked in the class of white men. **1864** E. SARGENT *Peculiar* I. 42 A certain metif girl. **1859** BARTLETT *Dict. Amer.*, *Metif*, the offspring of a white person and a..quadroon. **1884** G. P. LATHROP *True* ii. 14 She was not of octoroon or metif parentage.

metigat(e, meting, obs. ff. MITIGATE, MITTEN *sb.*

meting (ˈmiːtɪŋ), *vbl. sb.*[1] Forms: see METE *v.*[1] [f. METE *v.*[1] + -ING[1].] The action of METE *v.*[1]; measuring; portioning *out*; etc.

c **1380** WYCLIF *Serm.* Sel. Wks. I. 11 Siche metyng of corn, of mele, or oþer þing. *c* **1440** *Promp. Parv.* 336/1 Metynge wythe mesurys, *mensuracio.* **1543** *Act 35 Hen. VIII*, c. 17 §7 The..meting and bounding of the said fourth Part of the said Woods. **1548** PATTEN *Exped. Scot.* Pref. ¶1 Although it bee not allways the truest meanes of meting to measure all mens appetites by one mans affeccion. **1624** A. HUNTER (*title*) Treatise of Weights, Mets and Measures of Scotland... Together with the Art of Metting, measuring and compting all sort of Land. **1644** BULWER *Chiron.* 122 The meeting and scanning of verses upon the Fingers. **1829** R. STORY *Mem. Isab. Campbell* vii. (1854) 104 She was in the habit also of acknowledging in every feeling or personal application of the words [of Scripture] the metings out of his sovereign love. **1867** SMYTH *Sailor's Word-bk.*, *Meteings*, the measurement and estimate of timber.

†**b.** *pl.* Dimensions. *Obs. rare*$^{-1}$.

1674 N. FAIRFAX *Bulk & Selv.* 110 The three meteings or dimensions of a body.

c. *Comb.*: **meting-pole, -rod** = METE-POLE, METE-ROD.

1606 HOLLAND *Sueton.* 4 With ten foote perches [*marg.* Or meeting poles] in their hands. **1881** ROSSETTI *Ballads &*

Sonn. (1882) 275 To take the meting-rod In turn, and so approve on God Thy science of Theometry.

†**meting**, *vbl. sb.*² *Obs.* Forms: see METE *v.*²; also 4 **matyng**. [f. METE *v.*² + -ING¹.] The action of METE *v.*²; dreaming; a dream.

c **1000** *Sax. Leechd.* III. 156 Seo mætingc. *c* **1250** *Kent. Serm.* in *O.E. Misc.* 27 þo nicht efter þet aperede an ongel of heuene in here slepe ine metinge. **13..** *K. Alis.* 261 By theo planetis, and by the steorres, Y can jugge alle weorres, Alle plaies, in alle matynges, And on alle othir thynges. *c* **1369** CHAUCER *Dethe Blaunche* 282 Ioseph..that red so The kynges metynge pharao. *c* **1430** *Pilgr. Lyf Manhode* II. xxxiii. (1869) 87, I wolde weene al were lesinge, or elles that it were meetinge.

metior, metir(e, obs. forms of METEOR, METRE.

metis (ˈmeɪtɪs). Also fem. **métisse**. [a. F. *métis*:—late L. *misticius*, whence also MESTIZO.] The offspring of a white and an American Indian, esp. in Canada. Also applied to other persons of mixed blood and *transf.* to animals and plants.

1816 C. ROBERTSON in *Publ. Hudson's Bay Rec. Soc.* (1939) II. 248 Your European Servants and Metiss are in many places deserting over to the North West Company. **1839** *Penny Cycl.* XV. 158/2 The mixed race [in Mexico] is mostly composed of the descendants of the Europeans and the aboriginal tribes: these are called *Metis* or *Mestizos*. **1883** *Encycl. Brit.* XV. 491/2 Of the latter [Indian half-breeds] one half are of English-speaking parentage..the remainder are known as Metis or Bois-brûlés. **1895** in *Funk's Stand. Dict.*, Métisse. **1902** *Encycl. Brit.* XXVI. 531/1 Then Manitoba was principally inhabited by English and French half-breeds (or Metis). **1949** *Amer. Speech* XXIV. 95 A common term to indicate a crossbreed between Persian lamb and other Asiatic species of lamb is *metis*, derived from the French for 'half-breed'. **1955** G. GREENE *Quiet Amer.* III. i. 196 Across the way a *métisse* with long and lovely legs lay..reading a glossy woman's paper. **1961** E. BRUTON *King Diamond* vi. 87 'She's not African. Not entirely anyway... She's a metisse.'..'I know he wouldn't have gone for an African.' 'He didn't exactly. She's half and half.' **1966** *Kingston* (Ontario) *Whig-Standard* 29 July 6/3 A settlement of about 1500 Cree Indians and 300 Metis. **1972** *Guardian* 4 July 16/2 The estimated 15,000 to 50,000 *métis* children in South Vietnam—children of American soldiers, either half-black or half-white. **1972** D. BLOODWORTH *Any Number can Play* v. 37 He nodded towards a plump Eurasian... 'Bonjour, les gars,' murmured the métis. **1974** *Sci. Amer.* June 115/1 In California the work has taken mainly the direction of producing new *métis* (crosses within species) by crossing Europe's temperate-climate and Mediterranean vines with a view to obtaining better grapes for the fertile but desertlike Central Valley. **1975** *Time* 3 Feb. 8/3 The oppression and mistreatment of the Indians and Métis..never become anything more than a rhetorical device.

‖**métissage** (metisaʒ). [Fr.: cf. METIS.] Cross-breeding. Also *fig.*

1895 in *Funk's Stand. Dict.* **1959** *Times* 13 Aug. 9/7 He is, too, on historical grounds, a firm believer in the value of *métissage*—the cross-fertilization of civilizations. **1972** *Guardian* 8 July 9/1 Léopold Senghor, President of Sénégal, ..is a great believer in the virtues of *métissage*, or racial mixture.

metisupe, metkorn: see METESHIP, METECORN.

metle, obs. form of METAL, METTLE.

†ˈ**metleyship**. *Obs.* [f. MET *sb.*¹ + *-ley* (of uncertain origin) + -SHIP.] The office of 'meter'.

1587 LD. BURGHLEY in *12th Rep. Hist. MSS. Comm.* App. VII. (1890) 12 [Concerning the office of the] weyleyship and metleyship [in Penrith].

metly, obs. form of MEETLY *a.* and *adv.*

metochy. *Obs. rare*⁻¹. [ad. Eccl. Gr. μετόχιον.] A grange belonging to a monastery.

1682 WHELER *Journ. Greece* IV. 325 Near this Harbour the Convent hath a Metochy, or Farm.

metœcious (mɪˈtiːʃəs), *a. Bot.* [f. Gr. μετα- (denoting change) + οἰκία house: see -IOUS.] = HETERŒCIOUS.

1882 VINES *Sachs' Bot.* 332 Such forms as these are said to be heterœcious (metœcious), to distinguish them from those above-mentioned which inhabit the same host throughout their whole life (autœcious).

Hence **metœcism** (mɪˈtiːsɪz(ə)m) = HETERŒCISM.

1887 GARNSEY & BALFOUR *De Bary's Fungi* 388 Metoecism, that is, enforced change of the living host, is not known outside the group of the Uredineae.

metœstrus (mɛˈtiːstrəs). *Biol.* Also -um, (*U.S.*) **metestrus** (-ˈɛstrəs, -iːstrəs) -um. [f. MET(A- + ŒSTRUS, ŒSTRUM.] The short period following œstrus in many mammals during which sexual activity subsides.

1900 W. HEAPE in *Q. Jrnl. Microsc. Sci.* XLIV. 8 Metœstrum or the Metœstrous Period.—If conception does not take place during œstrus the activity of the generative organs gradually subsides during a definite period, which I have called the metœstrum; and this is followed..by a long period of rest. **1923** *Amer. Jrnl. Anat.* XXXII. 340 Follicular phase [of the sexual cycle]: *a*, proestrus. *b*, oestrus. *c*, metoestrus (in certain species where ovulation is separated from oestrus by an interval). **1966** *McGraw-Hill Encycl. Sci. & Technol.* XI. 476/1 After metestrus a relatively longer period of diestrus occurs before proestrus recurs... All these phases can be demonstrated in the guinea pig and rat. **1973** *Nature* 12 Jan. 129/2 When the drug was administered on other days of the cycle, metoestrus, dioestrus or pro-oestrus, it failed to increase ovulation rate.

Hence **meˈtœstrous** *a.*

1900 [see above]. **1956** *Nature* 4 Feb. 235/1 These groups were of pro-œstrous, œstrous, metœstrous and diœstrous rats.

metol (ˈmɛtɒl). *Photogr.* [a. G. *metol*: arbitrarily named by the inventor.] The name of a developer (see quot. 1893). Also *attrib.*

1893 *Photogr. Ann.* 90 Metol, according to the statement of the maker (Hauff, of Feuerbach), is the sulphate of methylparamidometacresol. It is a white powder, soluble in water. *Ibid.* 92 Metol solutions harden gelatine. **1902** ABNEY in *Encycl. Brit.* XXXI. 687/1 Metol Developer.

metoleate, -oleic: see META- 6 a.

Metonic (mɪˈtɒnɪk), *a.* [ad. mod.L. *Metōnic-us*, f. *Metōn*, Gr. Μέτων, the name of the Athenian astronomer by whom the cycle was discovered.] ***Metonic cycle, period,*** †***year***: the cycle of 19 Julian years (closely approximating to 235 lunations) in which the moon returns (nearly) to the same apparent position with regard to the sun, so that the new and full moons occur at the same dates in the corresponding year of each cycle.

1696 PHILLIPS, *Metonic-Year*, is the Space of 19 years, in which space of Time, the Lunations return and happen as they were before. **1704** J. HARRIS *Lex. Techn.* I, *Metonick Year*, or *Period*..'tis sometimes called *The Great Metonic Year*, and is the same with the *Cycle of the Moon*. **1839** *Penny Cycl.* XV. 144/1 The first year of the first Metonic period commenced with the summer solstice of the year 432 B.C. **1881** ROUTLEDGE *Science* i. 12 The golden number being simply the ordinal position of the year in the Metonic cycle of nineteen years.

metonimical, -my: see METONYMICAL, -MY.

†**metoˈnomasy**. *Obs.* [ad. Gr. μετονομασία, n. of action of μετονομάζειν to change in name, f. μετα- (denoting change) + ὄνομα name.] A change (or translation) of name.

1609 BP. W. BARLOW *Answ. Nameless Cath.* 32 Hee is by his Metamorphosis, or Metonomasie translated into Mathæus Tortus.

metonomatosis (mɛˌtɒnəməˈtəʊsɪs). *nonce-wd.* [f. Gr. μετα- (denoting change) + ὀνοματ-, ὄνομα name + -OSIS.] A change of name.

1827 HARE *Guesses* Ser. I. (1873) 132 The Jacobinical metonomatosis of the months, and of the days of the week, might be lookt upon as a parody of the Quakerian.

metonym (ˈmɛtənɪm). [ad. assumed Gr. *μετώνυμον: see METONYMY and cf. *paronym*.] A word used in a transferred sense.

In quot. 1837–8 misused (? misprinted) for *metonymy*.

1837-8 SIR W. HAMILTON *Logic* xxxiii. (1860) II. 177 The term *testimony*, I may notice, is sometimes, by an abusive metonym employed for *witness*. **1862** MERIVALE *Rom. Emp.* liv. (1865) VI. 434 Tertullian and Lactantius explain this word as a metonym for Christ, signifying just or good.

metonymic (mɛtəʊˈnɪmɪk), *a.* [Formed as next + -IC.] = next.

1775 in ASH; and in later Dicts. **1952** M. MCCARTHY *Groves of Academe* (1953) v. 85 As he had paused in the hall outside Domnar's door..he had not yet..felt the metonymic urge that would prompt him..to substitute the effect for the cause. **1969** P. ANDERSON in Cockburn & Blackburn *Student Power* 261 'I' is no longer I in the opaque, metonymic *double-entendre* of Freud's patients.

metonymical (mɛtəʊˈnɪmɪkəl), *a. Rhet.* Also 6–7 **metonimical(l**. [(f. Gr. μετωνυμικ-ός, f. μετωνυμία METONYMY: see -ICAL.] Pertaining to or involving metonymy. Of words: Used in a transferred sense.

1579 FULKE *Heskins' Parl.* 210 The whole speache being figuratiue, both allegoricall, and metonymicall. **1610** J. DOVE *Advt. Seminaries* 9 The meaning of Saint Chrysostome is metonimicall, and not proper. **1674** OWEN *Holy Spirit* Wks. 1852 III. 115 This expression is metonymical, that being spoken of the cause which is proper to the effect. **1711** HICKES *Two Treat. Chr. Priesth.* (1847) II. 71 Learned men have taken altar here in the metonymical sense for the altar-offering. **1811** A. MᶜLEAN *Comm. Hebr.* vi. (1847) I. 245 The apostle continues the metonymical use of the word *hope*, by which it is put for the object or ground of it.

metonymically (mɛtəʊˈnɪmɪkəlɪ), *adv.* [f. prec. + -LY².] By metonymy.

1574 WHITGIFT *Def. Answ.* 152 But be it that they [*sc.* the words of the text] may be taken there metonimically (whiche is but a coniecture) that can not excuse [etc.]. **1671** FLAVEL *Fount. Life* xxx. 92 Hence sins are metonimically called Debts. **1708** *Brit. Apollo* No. 113. 1/1 *Anathema*..signifies ..Metonymically, a Person Devoted, or Accurs'd. **1884** J. PAYNE *Tales fr. Arabic* I. 46 *note*, The word *bilal* signifies 'moisture' or (metonymically) 'beneficence'.

metonymy (mɪˈtɒnɪmɪ). *Rhet.* Also 6–7 **metonymie, -imie, -imy**, 9 **metonomy**. Also 6–7 in Lat. form. [ad. late L. *metōnymi-a*, a. Gr. μετωνυμία, lit. 'change of name', f. μετ(α)- META- + ὄνομα, Aeol. ὄνυμα name.] A figure of speech which consists in substituting for the name of a thing the name of an attribute of it or of something closely related.

In quot. 1547 *metonomian* = μετωνυμίαν (accus.).

[**1547** HOOPER *Answ. Winchester's Bk.* D i b, Men seyth that they admyt metonomian, and say under the forme of breade is the trew bodye of Christ.] **1562** COOPER *Answ. Def. Truth* 106 b, The figure is named Metonymia: when the name of the thynge is geuen vnto the signe. **1573** CARTWRIGHT *Reply to Whitgift* 14 The Apostle by a metonimie *Subiecti pro adiuncto*, dothe giue to vnderstand from whence yᵉ assured persuasion doth spring. **1625** GILL *Sacr. Philos.* II. 156 *Shebet* signifies either a staffe, a truncheon, or Scepter,..and so by a metonymia it may signifie authority. **1657** J. SMITH *Myst. Rhet.* 15 A metonymie of the effect, is when the effect or thing caused, is put for its cause. **1668** H. MORE *Div. Dial.*, *Schol.* 575 Here is a double Metonymie, Christ is put for the Doctrine of Christ, and Hope for the Cause of Hope. **1676** W. HUBBARD *Happin. People* 4 By times we are to understand things done in those times, by a metonimy of the adjunct. **1868** BAIN *Ment. & Mor. Sci.* IV. xi. 403 By what is called 'metonymy', the fact intended to be expressed is denoted by one of the adjuncts.

me too (miː tuː). Phr. used alone or in various collocations (see quots.) of a person who, or a course of action which, adopts or acquiesces in the views, policies, etc., of someone else, often *spec.* those of one's political or other opponents. Freq. in a derogatory sense. orig. *U.S.* Also (with hyphen) as *vb.* Hence **me-ˈtooer, me-ˈtooism**.

The colloq. ejaculation 'Me too!' signifying either that the speaker shares another person's view or experience or that the speaker wants the same share as another is getting, is the basis of the modern use.

1745 CHESTERFIELD *Let.* 13 Apr. (1932) II. 596 You must mark out Lord Granville by exterminating without quarter all who belong to him... If you take this resolution,..I empower you to make what use you please of my name as quitting with you; and I say as Will Seymour did, *And me, too, sweet Jesus*. **1851** H. MELVILLE *Moby Dick* I. xxxix. 275 Me too; where's your girls? **1873** L. M. ALCOTT *Work* II. xi. 336 'Me too!' cried little Ruth, and spread her chubby hand above the rest. **1921** H. WILLIAMSON *Beautiful Yrs.* 128 'Where are you going?' 'Out.' 'Where to man?' 'Mr. Norman's.'..'Norman's, you said? Right-o. Me, too!' **1922** JOYCE *Ulysses* 459 *Mrs. Mervyn Talboys*... He implored me ..to give him a most vicious horsewhipping. *Mrs. Bellingham.* Me too. *Mrs. Yelverton Barry.* Me too. **1924** A. S. NEILL *Dominie's Five* xii. 245 'I'm going to start to-day to learn to read.' 'Me too,' said Donald. **1940** H. L. ICKES *Diary* (1954) III. 312, I think that Willkie overlooked the best chance that he had by being content merely to 'me too' the President on his foreign policies and most of his domestic ones instead of striking out for himself in a bold and positive way. **1949** *Time* 7 Feb. 10/3 We [*sc.* the Republicans] suffered because we tried to me-too the New Deal. **1949** *Sun* (Baltimore) 14 Dec. 2/1 A recommendation that..the Republican party..divest itself of 'me-tooism' and go to the people with a program clearly and unmistakably in opposition to that now offered by our opponents. **1951** *Economist* 10 Nov. 1109/1 He is against any 'Me Too' procedures, by which he means opposition acceptance of Administration policy at home or abroad. **1952** *Manch. Guardian Weekly* 1 May 3 If General Eisenhower gets the Republican nomination he will have to risk the shame of me-tooing the Truman policy. **1958** *Spectator* 1 Aug. 156/3 With the collapse of doctrinaire Socialism, and the adoption instead of a modified me-tooism, the range of controversy is being still further reduced. **1959** *Guardian* 28 Dec. 6/1 Wendell Willkie, Governor Dewey, and General Eisenhower were all..'me-tooers'—men whose chief appeal was to the vague, uncontroversial idealism of the non-partisan. **1960** *New Left Rev.* Jan./Feb. 1/2 The champions of 'me-too' advance into ..an 'American' future. **1960** J. R. ACKERLEY *We think the World of You* 82 The almost mad stare with which her starting eyes pierced and searched my own for the answer to the only question in the world: 'Me too?' **1962** *Sunday Times* 19 Aug. 18 'I'm a rugged individualist: I think for myself.' 'Me too.' 'Same here.' **1965** *Economist* 14 Aug. 607/2 The unions have few independent ideas to contribute to this design for a better America; they were 'me tooers' in Roosevelt's New Deal, Truman's Fair Deal and Kennedy's New Frontier. **1967** *Spectator* 13 Oct. 419/2 The usefulness of 'me-tooism' in capturing the floating voter should not be underestimated. **1975** G. V. HIGGINS *City on Hill* i. 18 Sam gets round to saying it on the floor a week later, and he's me-tooing.

metope¹ (ˈmɛtəpiː). *Arch.* Forms: 6 **methopa**, 7–8 **metop, metops**, 8–9 **metopa**, 7– **metope**. [ad. L. *metopa* (Vitruvius), a. Gr. μετόπη, f. μετά between + ὀπαί holes in a frieze to receive the beam-ends. Cf. F. *métope*, OF. *methope*.] One of the square spaces, either plain or sculptured, between the triglyphs in the Doric frieze. ***demi-, semi-metope***, the half-space between the corner and the triglyph next the corner.

1563 SHUTE *Archit.* C iij b, Bitwixte the .2. Triglyphos, you shall set Methopa. **1624** WOTTON *Archit.* in *Reliq.* (1651) 230 A sober garnishment now and then..of Triglyphs and Metopes alwayes in the Frize. **1665** MOXON tr. *Vignola* (1702) 34 The square place of the Friese between the Triglyphs is called a Metops. **1703** BOYER tr. *Perrault's Vitruvius* 32 Towards the Corners must be placed the Demi-Metops. **1727-41** CHAMBERS *Cycl.* s.v. *Metope*, Semi-Metope is a space somewhat less than half a metope, in the corner of a Doric frieze. **1776** R. CHANDLER *Trav. Greece* (1825) II. 62 All the metopes were decorated with large figures in *alto relievo*. **1876** HUMPHREYS *Coin-coll. Man.* vi. 58 A metope of the Parthenon.

metope² (ˈmɛtəʊp). *Zool.* [a. Gr. μέτωπ-ον forehead.] Applied by Huxley to the face of a crab.

1880 HUXLEY *Crayfish* 283 The fore part of the head is modified so as to bring about the formation of the characteristic metope.

metopic (mɪˈtɒpɪk), *a.* [f. Gr. μέτωπ-ον forehead + -IC.] **a.** Of or pertaining to the forehead; frontal. **b.** Of a skull: Having the metopic suture persisting.

1878 BARTLEY tr. *Topinard's Anthrop.* II. ii. 234 Metopic point.., a point situate in the median line between the two frontal eminences. **1879** FLOWER *Catal. Mus. Coll. Surg.* I. 14 A metopic cranium of a European. **1889** *Brit. Med. Jrnl.* 28 Sept. 736/2 The presence of the metopic suture is considered as an indication of criminality.

Metopirone (mɛtəʊˈpɪrəʊn). *Pharm.* Also **metopirone.** [f. 2-*met*hyl-1,2-di(*pyr*id-3-yl) propan-1-*one*, the chemical name (see METYRAPONE), with alteration of *y* to *i* and insertion of *o*.]

A proprietary name for metyrapone.

1960 *Lancet* 17 Dec. 1332/2 Metopirone is an 11 β-hydroxylase inhibitor which presumably prevents the production of aldosterone by the adrenal gland. **1961** *Trade Marks Jrnl.* 8 Feb. 172/1 Metopirone... Pharmaceutical preparations and substances for human use and for veterinary use. CIBA Limited.., Basle, Switzerland. **1962** *Lancet* 19 May 1041/2 The duration of the action of metopirone was investigated, in order to determine the best dosage schedule in tests of pituitary function. **1973** *Arch. Internat. de Pharmacodynamie et de Thérapie* CCII. 93 Metopirone was found to provoke in normal, but not in adrenalectomized rats, a three-fold increase in blood sugar and a four-fold increase in plasma adrenaline.

metopism (ˈmɛtəpɪz(ə)m). [f. Gr. μέτωπον forehead + -ISM.] (See quot.)

1879 FLOWER *Catal. Mus. Coll. Surg.* I. 14 Crania showing Metopism, or persistence of the frontal suture.

†**metopomancy.** *Obs.* [f. Gr. μέτωπο-ν forehead + μαντεία divination: see -MANCY.] Divination by the forehead or face.

1656 BLOUNT *Glossogr.* a **1693** *Urquhart's Rabelais* III. xxv, Ye know how by the Arts of Astrology,.. Chiromancy, Metopomancy,.. he foretelleth all things to come.

†**meto'poscoper.** *Obs.* [Formed as METOPOSCOPIST + -ER¹.] = METOPOSCOPIST.

1569 J. SANFORD tr. *Agrippa's Van. Artes* 50 b, A certaine man.. did so passingly depainte the likenesses of Images that by them the Metoposcoper hath tolde the yeares of death paste or to come. **1649** BULWER *Pathomyot.* II. iii. 146 Whatsoever inward.. affection of the mind is.. observed by Metoposcopers and others to appeare in the Forehead.

metoposcopic (mɛtəpəʊˈskɒpɪk), *a.* [ad. mod.L. *metōposcopic-us*, f. *metōposcopia* METOPOSCOPY. Cf. F. *métoposcopique.*] = next.

1864 in WEBSTER.

metoposcopical (mɛtəpəʊˈskɒpɪkəl), *a. rare*⁻¹. [Formed as prec. + -ICAL.] Pertaining or relating to metoposcopy.

1820 SCOTT *Abbot* xxxii, His learned face stooping until a physiognomist might have practised the metoposcopical science upon it, as seen from behind betwixt his gambadoes.

metoposcopist (mɛtəʊˈpɒskəpɪst). [f. late L. *metōposcop-us*, a. Gr. μετωποσκόπ-ος, f. μέτωπο-ν forehead + -σκόπ-ος observer: see -IST.] One who is versed in metoposcopy.

1570 DEE *Math. Pref.* c iv, The Anatomistes will restore to you, some part:.. The Metaposcopistes some. **1652** GAULE *Magastrom.* 188 Which way go the physiognomists, metoposcopists, and chiromantists to work? **1885** MACALISTER in *Encycl. Brit.* XIX. 4/1 Apion speaks of the metoposcopists who judge by the appearance of the face.

metoposcopy (mɛtəʊˈpɒskəpɪ). Also 7 erron. **metap-.** [ad. mod.L. *metōposcopi-a*, f. *metōposcopus* (see METOPOSCOPIST).]

1. The art of judging a person's character or of telling his fortune from his forehead or face.

1569 J. SANFORD tr. *Agrippa's Van. Artes* 50 b, Metoposcopie.. doth auaunte that she can foretel al mens beginninges, proceedinges, and endinges.. by the onely beholding of the foreheade. **1610** B. JONSON *Alch.* I. iii. A rule.. In metaposcopie, which I doe worke by. **1696** AUBREY *Misc.* 38 There was a Seam in the middle of his Fore head (downwards) which is a very ill sign in Metoposcopie. **1746** PARSONS in *Phil. Trans.* XLIV. 47 The Art of Physiognomy, especially the Metoposcopy, or what relates to the Face. **1893** LELAND *Mem.* II. 248 Interested.. as he always was in anything like chiromancy or metoscopy [*sic*].

2. The physiognomical characters of a man's forehead.

1653 R. SANDERS *Physiogn.* 200 This is the Metoposcopy of an excellent man. a **1693** *Urquhart's Rabelais* III. xxv. 203 Thou hast the Metoposcopy, and Physiognomy of a Cuckold. c **1886** L. HEARN in G. M. Gould *Concerning L. Hearn* (1908) 87 'Are you not a Greek?' I asked, for there was no mistaking the metoposcopy of that head. Yes; he was from Zante.

metops, obs. form of METOPE¹.

metoroscopy: see METEOROSCOPY.

‖**metosteon** (mɛˈtɒstɪɒn). *Ornith.* [mod.L., f. Gr. μετά behind + ὀστέον bone.] The centre of ossification for the posterior lateral processes of the sternum, behind the pleurosteon. Hence **me'tosteal** *a.*, pertaining to the metosteon.

1868 W. K. PARKER *Shoulder-Girdle Vetebr.* 100 The bony patches.. keep very clear of the metosteal 'interclavicle'. *Ibid.* 144 Behind each 'pleurosteon' there is, in the Gallinaceæ, and a few other types, in the Crows, for instance, another bony centre, the 'metosteon'. **1896** NEWTON *Dict. Birds* IV. 910.

‖**metovum** (mɛˈtəʊvəm). [mod.L., f. μετα- META- + OVUM.] An ovum in its second stage, e.g. a meroblastic ovum after formation of the food-yolk; also called *deutovum* (DEUTO- 2).

1879 tr. *Haeckel's Evol. Man* I. 223 The *protovum* is thus transformed into the *metovum* (after-egg) which is many times larger.. but.. is only a single.. cell.

metoxenous (mɛˈtɒksɪnəs), *a.* [Badly f. META- + Gr. ξένος stranger, guest.] = METŒCIOUS.

1887 GARNSEY & BALFOUR *De Bary's Fungi* 387 They [these Uredineae] are accordingly termed *heteroecious*, or still better *metoecious* or *metoxenous* as changing their place of habitation or host.

‖**Metran** (ˈmɛtræn). [Ethiopic.] The abuna, or head of the Abyssinian Church. Hence **'Metranate**, the office or the province of the metran.

1850 NEALE *East. Ch.* I. Introd. 24 The Catholicate of Ethiopia, under the Metran of Axum, had no Metropolitans. *Ibid.* 111. The Patriarchate of Alexandria, and Metranate of Ethiopia.

Metrazol (ˈmɛtrəzɒl). *Pharm.* Also **metrazol.** [f. *penta)me(thylenete)trazol*, its chemical name, f. PENTA- + METHYLENE + TETRA- + AZO- + -OL.] A proprietary name of LEPTAZOL.

1928 *Official Gaz.* (U.S. Patent Office) 11 Sept. 265/1 E. Bilhuber, Inc.... *Metrazol* for medicine for the heart and the vascular system. **1932** *Arch. Internat. de Pharmaco-dynamie et de Thérapie* XLII. 200 Cardiazol (metrazol) is pentamethylenetetrazol. **1950** *Brit. Jrnl. Psychol.* Dec. 104 Metrazol was used to induce convulsions in another unsuccessful attempt to apply therapy at a physiological level. **1973** *Physiol. & Behaviour* X. 94/2 Convulsive doses of Metrazol.. may not actually prevent memory storage but rather modify the conditions under which these processes take place.

metre (ˈmiːtə(r)), *sb.*¹ Forms: 1 **meter**, 4 **metur**, 4–5 **metir(e**, 5–6 **meetre**, **metyr**, 5–8 **meeter**, 6 **myter**, **mytre**, 6–7 **miter**, 7 **metar**, 8 **meteer**, 6–8 (9 *U.S.*) **meter**, 4– **metre**. [OE. *meter* (? *méter*) was ad. L. *metrum*, a. Gr. μέτρον, f. Indogermanic root **mē-* to measure; in the 14th c. the word was adopted afresh from OF. *metre* (mod.F. *mètre*); cf. Sp., Pg., It. *metro*, G. *meter*.]

1. Any specific form of poetic rhythm, its kind being determined by the character and number of the feet or groups of syllables of which it consists.

a **900** tr. *Bæda's Hist.* v. Concl., Ymenbec misenlice metre [*v.r.* metere]. Boc epigrammatum eroico metre [*v.r.* metere]. c **1050** *Byrhtferth's Handboc* in *Anglia* (1885) VIII. 314 þæt þæt riht meter vers sceal habban. c **1386** CHAUCER *Man of Law's Prol.* 48 Chaucer thogh he kan but lewedly On metres and on rymyng craftily. **1450–1530** *Myrr. our Ladye* 91 Whyche thre [verses] ar of dyuerse meter from the tother. a **1568** ASCHAM *Scholem.* II. (Arb.) 144 For the meter sake, some wordes in him [Terence], somtyme, be driuen awrie. **1599** THYNNE *Animadv.* 6 Bothe in matter, myter, and meaninge, yt must neede gather corruptione, passinge throughe so manye handes. **1657** SPARROW *Bk. Com. Prayer* (1661) 361 They used all decent and grave variety of rhymes and Meeters in their Hymns and Psalms. **1749** *Power Pros. Numbers* 74 To one or other of which [three Measures] (however various be the Metre) almost all kinds of English Verse may be reduced. **1864** TENNYSON *Hendecasyllabics* 4 All composed in a metre of Catullus. **1874** SYMONDS *Sk. Italy & Greece* (1898) I. xii. 250 Poetry employs words in fixed rhythms, which we call metres.

b. In the names of certain forms of verse used in English hymns, as ***common, long, particular, short metre***: see these words. Also, ***peculiar metre, proper metre*** (abbreviated P.M.): a metre used only in a particular hymn, or at least not identical with any of the metres having recognized names.

1798 *Select. Psalms & Hymns*, Hymn vii. Pec. M. *Ibid.*, Hymn x. Prop. M. *Ibid.*, Hymn xxii. Pecul. Metre. *Ibid.*, Hymn xxxvi. P.M.

2. Metrical arrangement or method.

c **1330** R. BRUNNE *Chron. Wace* (Rolls) 196 After þe Inglis kynges he [Langtoft] says þer pris þat all in metir fulle wele lys. c **1386** CHAUCER *Monk's Prol.* 93 In prose eek been endyted many oon, And eek in metre, in many a sondry wyse. c **1450** HOLLAND *Howlat* 35, I haue mekle matir in metir to gloss Of ane nothir sentence. a **1568** ASCHAM *Scholem.* I. (Arb.) 77, I will recite the very wordes of Homere and also turne them into rude English metre. **1667** MILTON *P.L.* Pref., Rime being.. the Invention of a barbarous Age, to set off wretched matter and lame Meeter. **1779–81** JOHNSON *L.P., Milton* Wks. II. 174 It is.. by the musick of metre that poetry has been discriminated in all languages. **1828** WHATELY *Rhet.* in *Encycl. Metrop.* I. 290 Then arrange this [prose] again into metre. **1858** MARSH *Eng. Lang.* xxv. 544 Metre may be defined to be a succession of poetical feet arranged in regular order, according to certain types recognized as standards, in verses of a determinate length. **1905** W. H. COBB (*title*) A Criticism of Systems of Hebrew Metre.

3. a. Composition 'in metre'; verse. †**b.** In particularized sense: A piece of metrical composition; a verse or poem; *occas.* a metrical version.

1340 HAMPOLE *Pr. Consc.* 489 Þis vers of metre þat es wreten here: *Dicentes E. vel A. quot-quot nascuntur ab Eva.* c **1350** *Will. Palerne* 5524 Þouȝh þe metur be nouȝt mad at eche mannes paye. c **1385** CHAUCER *L.G.W.* Prol. 562 Here byn twenty thousand mo [ladies] syttyng.. Make the metres of theym as the lest. **1423** JAS. I *Kingis Q.* iv, His metir suete, full of moralitee. **1475** *Bk. Noblesse* (Roxb.) 21 The vij^the metre of the .v. booke of Boecius. a **1533** LD. BERNERS *Gold. Bk. M. Aurel.* (1546) I ij, To wryte workes, to make metres, to studie antiquitees. **1556** ROBINSON tr. *More's Utop.* (1895) p. xciv, A meter of iiii verses in the Utopian tongue. **1577** HELLOWES *Gueuara's Chron.* 31 Traiane.. persuaded the Oratours to compounde many meetres to his praise. **1584** COGAN *Haven Health* (1636) 195 According to that old meeter, *Distentus venter vellet dormire libenter.* **1631** WEEVER *Anc. Funeral Mon.* 140 A certaine Lollard.. composed certaine virulent meeters against this and other of the Religious orders. **1662** PLAYFORD *Skill Mus.* I. i. (1674) 5 There is an old Metre.. it contains a true Rule of the Theorick part of Musick—, It begins thus, 'To attain the Skill of Musicks Art Learn Gam-Ut up and down by heart.' **1679** PULLER *Moder. Ch. Eng.* (1843) 43 The english metre of the Psalms. **1794** BLAKE *Songs Exper., Clod & Pebble* 8 A pebble of the brook Warbled out these metres meet. a **1800** COWPER *Ode to Apollo* 3 Those luckless brains That.. Indite much metre with much pains.

4. A metrical group or 'measure'; *spec.* a dipody in iambic, trochaic, and anapæstic rhythms.

1880 W. S. ROCKSTRO in Grove *Dict. Mus.* II. 317/1 Two feet usually constitute a Metre (or *Dipodia*). But in Dactylic Verse, each foot is regarded as a complete Metre in itself. **1903** W. R. HARDIE *Lect.* 210 Metres.. are 'lengths' or 'sections' of rhythm, beginning in a certain way, either with ἄρσις or θέσις, and of a fixed length.

5. *Gr. Mus.* = METRIC *sb. rare*⁻⁰.

1811 BUSBY *Mus. Dict.*, *Metre*, that part of the ancient music which consulted the measure of the verses.

6. *attrib.*, as ***metre ballad, -maker, -making*** (sb. and adj.), ***-monger***; **metre psalm**, a Bible psalm translated in verse.

1596 SHAKS. *1 Hen. IV*, III. i. 130, I had rather be a Kitten, and cry mew, Then one of these same *Meeter Ballad-mongers. **1611** COTGR., *Rimoyeur*, a rimer, a *meeter-maker. **1789** T. TWINING *Aristotle's Treat. Poetry* (1812) I. 253 A versifier—a meter-maker. **1841–4** EMERSON *Ess., Poet* Wks (Bohn) I. 157 It is not metres, but a *metre-making argument, that makes a poem. **1880** SWINBURNE *Stud. Shaks.* i. (ed. 2) 9 The guidance which can be given by no *metre-monger or colour-grinder. **1655** SANDERSON *Serm.* (1681) II. Pref. 7 Where your *metre-psalms? **1863** J. L. W. *By-gone Days* 102 Those beautiful Metre Psalms first versified by Francis Rous, an Englishman.

metre (ˈmiːtə(r)), *sb.*² Also *U.S.* **meter**, 9 **mètre.** [ad. F. *mètre* (mɛtr), ad. Gr. μέτρον measure.]

a. The fundamental unit of length of the metric system, approximately equal to 39·37 English inches. Now one of the base units of the International System of Units, and redefined in terms of the wavelength of a spectral line (at 605·8 nanometres) of an isotope of krypton (see quot. 1970).

It was intended to represent one ten-millionth of the length of a quadrant of the meridian; the standard metre kept at Paris nearly corresponds to this theoretical value.

1797 *Monthly Mag.* III. 434 The measures of length above the metre are ten times [etc.].. greater than the metre. **1831** *Jrnl. Roy. Instit.* I. 599 M. Francœur.. has found that the mètre is equal to 39·37079 English inches. **1869** ROSCOE *Elem. Chem.* (1871) 24 This metre, like all other standards of length, is an arbitrary length. **1877** RAYMOND *Statist. Mines & Mining* 442 We may assume.. that it would fall through 10 meters in .3·63 seconds. **1885** *Times* (weekly ed.) 2 Oct. 17/7 Houses, costing.. only £10 per cubic mètre. **1961** *Nature* 21 Jan. 195/1 The eleventh General Conference of Weights and Measures was held in Paris during October 11–20... One epoch-making scientific decision was taken, namely, to redefine the metre in terms of a natural atomic standard, the wave-length of light, thus deposing the platinum-iridium bar—the International Prototype Metre—from the supremacy it has held in the field of length measurements since 1889. *Ibid.* 196/2 The specification of the conditions of excitation and observation [of the radiation] ensures a reproducibility of the new optical metre to about 1 part in 100 millions. **1970** *Internat. System of Units* (*B.S.I.*) 5 The metre is the length equal to 1 650 763·73 wavelengths in vacuum of the radiation corresponding to the transition between the levels $2p_{10}$ and $5d_5$ of the krypton-86 atom. (11th CGPM (1960), Resolution 6). **1971** *Physics Bull.* July 397/1 The definition of the metre in terms of the wave-length of the orange spectral line of a krypton discharge was internationally accepted in 1960 and brought about a new interest in interferometry for length measurement.

b. *attrib.*, as ***metre gauge***; **metre-angle** *Ophthalm.* [tr. G. *meter-winkel* (A. Nagel, in Graefe & Saemisch *Handbuch der gesammten Augenheilkunde* (1880) VI. x. 479)], a unit of convergence equal to the angle between the line of sight of either eye and the median line passing between them when the eyes are fixating a point on that line one metre away; **metre-candle** = LUX *sb.*; **metre-gram(me), -ton**, etc., the amount of work required to raise a gramme, a ton, etc. one metre in one second; **metre-kilogram(me)-second**, used *attrib.* to designate a system of units in which the basic units of length, mass, and time are respectively the

metre, the kilogram, and the second, and which was taken as the basis of the International System of Units; commonly abbreviated *M.K.S.*, *m.k.s*; **metre-seven**, the name recommended by a committee of the British Association for the quantity 10^7 (ten million) metres.

1886 C. M. CULVER tr. *Landolt's Refraction & Accommodation of Eye* ii. 187 We are indebted to Nagel for the ingenious idea of rendering the mensuration of convergence so simple and..so practical. He calls this unit-angle the 'Meterwinkel' **metre-angle.* **1949** H. C. WESTON *Sight, Light & Efficiency* i. 27 The value of the metre-angle depends on the distance apart of the two eyes, but is commonly equal to about 1·75°. **1964** S. DUKE-ELDER *Parsons' Dis. Eye* (ed. 14) xxviii. 455 With an emmetropic person the amount of convergence, reckoned in metre angles, is the same as the amount of accommodation reckoned in dioptres. **1909** *Cent. Dict.* Suppl., *Meter-candle. **1915** R. A. HOUSTON *Treat. Light* xx. 362 It is often necessary to measure in foot-candles or metre-candles the degree of illumination of a surface. **1939** A. W. BARTON *Text Bk. Light* ix. 197 A metre-candle is equal to a lumen per square metre,..so that there are 10,000 metre-candles in a phot. **1970** M. V. KLEIN *Optics* iv. 126 Lux are also called meter-candles. **1885** *Pall Mall G.* 20 Mar. 6/1 The Government of India has adopted the *metre gauge for all the new branches of the various State railways. **1891** KIPLING *City Dreadf. Nt.* 78 The trucks were unloaded into the waggons of the metre-gauge colliery line in this wise. **1868** L. CLARK *Electr. Meas.* 45 The conventional unit of work *W* ordinarily employed in metrical measure is..that which will raise a weight of one gramme one metre in one second, and is called the *metre-gramme unit. **1940** *Chambers's Techn. Dict.* 544/1 *Metre-kilogramme-second (M-K-S) system of units. **1943** LEMON & FERENCE *Analytical Exper. Physics* ii. 38/1 Recently adopted by an international congress as the official system of metric units is the meter-kilogram-second (MKS) system. **1963** *Listener* 24 Jan. 156/1 The metre-kilogram-second system has been preferred by the Institute of Electrical Engineers. **1873** *Rep. Brit. Assoc.* 224 The approximate length of a quadrant of one of the earth's meridians is a *metre-seven or a centimetre-nine. **1881** SIR W. THOMSON in *Nature* No. 619. 434 Ideal water-wheels..would give just one *metre-ton per square metre of area.

metre ('miːtə(r)), *v.* Also 5 **meetre**, 6 **metyr, mitre**, 7 **meeter**. [f. METRE *sb.*[1]]

1. *trans.* To compose in or put into metre. ? *Obs.*

1447 BOKENHAM *Seyntys* (Roxb.) 58 The weddynge dytees metryd coryously. **1563** *Mirr. Mag., Collingbourne* x, They murdred me for metryng thinges amys. **1577–87** HOLINSHED *Chron. Scot.* 214/1 One Henrie, who was blind from his birth,..composed a whole booke in vulgar verse, in which he mitred all those things vulgarlie spoken of this Wallase. **1841** CATLIN *N. Amer. Ind.* (1844) I. xviii. 126 Perfectly metred but without rhyme. **1858** RAMSAY *Remin.* Ser. I. (ed. 7) 174 Jean said she thought David hadna taen much pains when he metred the Psalms.

2. *intr.* To compose verses; to versify.

c **1430** *Freemasonry* 569 Rethoryk metryth with oone speche amonge. *c* **1448** HOCCLEVE *Balade Dk. York* 48 If þat I in my wrytynge foleye..Meetrynge amis, or speke vnfittyngly. **1530** PALSGR. 635/2 Many a man can ryme well, but it is harde to metyr well. **1614** W. B. *Philosopher's Banquet* (ed. 2) 117 He..thus merrily Meeterd.

Hence †'**metring** *vbl. sb.*, versification.

1644 DIGBY *Nat. Bodies* xxviii. 250 Such of the liberall artes are employed, which belong to the cultiuating mans voyce; as Rhetorike, meetering, and singing.

metred ('miːtəd), *ppl. a.* [f. METRE *v.* + -ED[1].] Composed in metre; metrical. Also *loosely*, rhythmical.

1711 SHAFTESB. *Charac.* (1737) III. Misc. v. i. 264 In their elegant Stile and metred Prose. **1851** TAPPING *Manlove's Lead Mines* Pref., Manlove within the compass of 300 metred lines has produced a perfect and accurate digest of the voluminous mass of intricate mining customs. **1863** COWDEN CLARKE *Shaks. Char.* ix. 228 With what metred decorum the triumvirate would have bandied the festal amenities!

†'**metrede.** *Obs.* [f. METE *v.*[2] + *-rēde*, -RED.] A dream.

1390 GOWER *Conf.* III. 68 Nectanabus which causeth al Of this metrede the substaunce. *Ibid.* 69.

metreless ('miːtəlɪs), *a.* [f. METRE *sb.*[1] + -LESS.] Without metre.

1895 *Athenæum* 2 Mar. 273/1 If the name 'metreless poem' can properly be given to any form of imaginative literature. **1904** *Daily Chron.* 17 Sept. 3/2 There is the throb of metreless song in that passage.

†'**metrely,** *adv.* [f. METRE *sb.*[1] + -LY[2].] In metre, metrically.

c **1475** *Partenay* 6566 Ho it metre will..He most torn and wend, metrely to close.

†**metrenchyte.** *Obs. rare*[−1]. [ad. Gr. μητρεγχύτης (mod.L. *mētrenchyta*, *-tes*), f. μήτρα womb + ἐγχεῖν to pour in.] An instrument used for injections into the womb.

1601 HOLLAND *Pliny* II. 207 By infusion or injection with the metrenchyte. [**1693** tr. *Blancard's Phys. Dict.* (ed. 2), *Metrenchyta.* **1753** CHAMBERS *Cycl. Supp.*, *Metrenchytes.*]

†'**metrer.** *Obs.* In 4 **metrere, metriour**, 7 **meterer.** [f. METRE *sb.* + -ER[1].] One who writes in metre, a versifier.

1387 TREVISA *Higden* (Rolls) II. 81 A metrere brekeþ out in þis manere in preisynge of þis citee. *Ibid.* VIII. 169 Another metriour seide in þis manere [etc.]. **1627** DRAYTON *Agincourt*, etc. 205 Gascoine and Churchyard.. Accoumpted were great Meterers many a day.

metrete (mɪ'triːt). *Antiq.* Also 7 **mettret.** [ad. L. *metrēta*, ad. Gr. μετρητής, f. μετρεῖν to measure, f. μέτρον: see METRE *sb.*[1]] An ancient Greek liquid measure, equivalent to about 9 gallons.

1388 WYCLIF *John* ii. 6 There weren set sixe stonun cannes,..holdynge ech tweyne ether thre metretis. *c* **1420** *Pallad. on Husb.* XI. 443 Of fynest must in oon metrete. **1633** J. DONE *Hist. Septuagint* 56 These cups..helde more then two mettrets. **1890** *Century Dict.* s.v., The Attic, Macedonian, and Spanish metrete was about 40 liters... In Egypt the artaba was sometimes called a metrete.

†**me'treza.** *Obs.* Also **metereza.** [Pseudo-Italian alteration of F. *maîtresse.*] = MISTRESS.

1604 MARSTON & WEBSTER *Malcontent* I. iii, Me thinkes I see that Signior pawn his foot-cloth: that Metreza her Plate. *a* **1627** MIDDLETON *More Dissemblers* v. i. 92 Metereza Celia. *Ibid.* 107 Come, metereza.

metric ('mɛtrɪk), *a.*[1] and *sb.*[1] [ad. L. *metric-us* (Quintilian), a. Gr. μετρικ-ός, f. μέτρον METRE *sb.*[1] Cf. F. *métrique.*] **A.** *adj.*

1. = METRICAL *a.*[1] 1. *rare.*

18.. BLACKIE (Ogilvie), Hesiod with his metric fragments of rustic wisdom.

2. = METRICAL *a.*[1] 2. *esp.* relating to, involving, or defining distance; ***metric geometry*** = *metrical geometry* s.v. METRICAL *a.*[1] 2; ***metric space*** [tr. Ger. *metrischer raum* (F. Hausdorff *Grundzüge der Mengenlehre* (1914) vii. 211)], a set together with a metric defined for all pairs of elements of the set.

1866 *Q. Jrnl. Pure & Appl. Math.* VII. 54 Euclid I. 47 is an example of..metric geometry. **1873** *Proc. Lond. Math. Soc.* IV. 387 This metric geometry is due to Prof. Cayley. **1885** in *Cassell's Encycl. Dict.* **1910** VEBLEN & YOUNG *Projective Geom.* i. 12 The difference between projective and the ordinary Euclidean metric geometry. **1916** *Monthly Notices R. Astron. Soc.* LXXVI. 701 The line-element *ds* must be invariant for all transformations, and it entirely characterises the metric properties of the four-dimensional time-space. **1923** J. RICE *Relativity* xiii. 312 Space-time is a metric four-dimensional manifold. **1927** *Bull. Amer. Math. Soc.* XXXIII. 14 The following illustrations convey some notion of the scope of the concept metric space. If the aggregate P denotes the linear continuum of all real numbers and $(p, q) = |p - q|$, the resulting space is metric. Similarly euclidean space is also metric. **1963** R. A. ROSENBAUM *Introd. Projective Geom. & Mod. Algebra* i. 12 Note that all the items of this list of non-projective properties involve magnitudes of lengths and angles. Such 'metric' properties are the concern of traditional elementary geometry. The situation may be loosely described by stating that metric geometry treats of more highly restricted properties than those of projective geometry. **1968** E. T. COPSON *Metric Spaces* i. 3 The study of the properties of sets of 'points' in a 'space' whose only geometrical property is the existence of a 'distance' between each pair of 'points' is called metric space topology. *Ibid.* ii. 21 Different choices of metric on a given set E give rise to different metric spaces. **1971** *Nature* 5 Nov. 35/1 It has the properties of a metric function in a space, the elements of which are finite non-empty sets.

B. *sb. sing.* and *pl.*

1. The science or art that deals with metre, esp. with the laws of versification in Greek and Latin. (Cf. G. *die metrik*, F. *la métrique*, Gr. ἡ μετρική, τὰ μετρικά.)

1760 STILES *Grk. Music* in *Phil. Trans.* LI. 730 To harmonic, rhythmic and metric, in the theoretic, respectively answered melopœia, rhythmopœia, and poetic, in the practic. **1884** MAHAFFY in *Contemp. Rev.* June 904 Is the study of metric really banished from English classics? **1892** *Mod. Lang. Notes* VII. 100 Metrics and æsthetics go hand in hand. **1898** KEEP in *Amer. Jrnl. Philol.* XIX. 123 They were able to lecture on grammar, epigraphy, numismatics,..mythology, metrics, art, archaeology. **1905** *Athenæum* 29 July 140/2 The great Orientalist..attempted ..to connect the laws of Hebrew metrics with Oriental poetry in general. **1952** G. SARTON *Hist. Sci.* I. xx. 521 Ancient music included not only music as we understand it but also metrics, poetry. **1970** *Jrnl. Eng. & Gmc. Philol.* LXIX. 81 Rules for syntax and metrics in *Beowulf.*

2. *Math.* and *Physics.* A metric function, i.e. one defining a distance or an abstract quantity analogous to distance (see quot. 1962).

1921 *Proc. R. Soc.* A. XCIX. 104 In the non-Euclidean geometry of Riemann, the metric is defined by certain quantities, $g_{\mu\nu}$, which are identified by Einstein with the potentials of the gravitational field. **1934** C. C. KRIEGER tr. *Sierpiński's Introd. Gen. Topology* vi. 90 In every metric space M a metric, which is equivalent to the given one, can be established,..such that the new distances between the elements of M are all $\leqslant 1$. **1956** E. H. HUTTEN *Lang. Mod. Physics* iii. 114 Riemann gave a better representation for the multiplicity of geometries by taking space to be a three-dimensional manifold, and it is the metric given by a mathematical expression referring to distance that decides the type of geometry. **1962** B. H. ARNOLD *Intuitive Concepts Elem. Topology* viii. 138 The function of d is a metric in X if and only if the following conditions are satisfied for all points x, y, and z of X.(1) $d(x, y) \geqslant 0$. (2) $d(x, y) = 0$ iff $x = y$. (3) $d(x, y) = d(y, x)$. (4) $d(x, y) + d(y, z) \geqslant d(x, z)$. **1965** J. D. NORTH *Measure of Universe* iv. 63 In 1908 Minkowski introduced into the context of the Special Theory of Relativity the metric now known by his name: $ds^2 = dt^2 - (1/c^2)(dx^2 + dy^2 + dz^2)$. The null geodesics of Minkowski space-time represent the paths followed by light.

3. = METRE *sb.*[1] 1 a.

1933 T. S. ELIOT *Use of Poetry* ii. 38, I do not even believe that the metric of *The Testament of Beauty* is successful. **1941** R. GIRVAN in *Proc. Brit. Acad.* 1940 331 The metric is astonishing and cannot be paralleled in Anglo-Saxon poetry. **1951** T. S. ELIOT *Poetry & Drama* ii. 20 He [*sc.* Yeats] wrote plays in verse..in a metric which..is not really a form of speech quite suitable for anybody except mythical kings and queens.

4. (See quot. 1934.)

1934 H. C. WARREN *Dict. Psychol.* 166/2 *Metric*, a system or standard of measurement in terms of which the conclusions stated hold. **1968** *Language* XLIV. 715 The simplicity metric demands that one choose the unmarked segment as the underlying one, since its choice leads to less complexity in the phonological representation. **1973** A. H. SOMMERSTEIN *Sound Pattern Anc. Greek* iii. 94 This statement does not depend on the acceptance of a feature-counting simplicity metric. P. H. Matthews, in a seminar at Cambridge, has criticized the assumption that such a metric is the appropriate evaluation measure for grammars.

metric ('mɛtrɪk), *a.*[2] and *sb.*[2] [ad. F. *métrique*, f. *mètre* METRE *sb.*[2]] **A.** *adj.* **a.** Pertaining to that system of weights and measures of which the metre is the fundamental unit. ***metric ton***, 1000 kilogrammes (2204·6 lb. avoirdupois, or 0·9842 ton); = TONNE.

The system is decimal throughout, and the unit in each of its branches has a definite relation to the metre; for instance, the gramme, the unit of weight, represents the weight of a cubic centimetre of water.

1864 *Act 27 & 28 Vict.* c. 117 An Act to render permissive the Use of the Metric System of Weights and Measures... This Act may be cited as the 'Metric Weights and Measures Act, 1864'. **1873** MAXWELL *Electr. & Magn.* (1881) I. 2 In France, and other countries which have adopted the metric system. **1873** I. GREGORY *Brit. Metric Syst.* 47 How many metric pints are there in 20 thousand 'reputed pint' bottles? **1898** *Daily News* 27 May 7/3 That the government be urged to adopt the metric weights and measures. **1924** *Times Trade & Engin. Suppl.* 29 Nov. 238/3 The output of certain important goods has considerably increased:..sugar to 318,987 metric tons, against 270,279. **1957** G. E. HUTCHINSON *Treat. Limnol.* I. viii. 546 A quantity of salt of the order of 100,000 metric tons per year is transported. **1973** *Guardian* 25 Jan. 7/5 The Government yesterday took a hard line with newsprint manufacturers by allowing increases of only £2 a metric ton (tonne).

b. Having the metric system as the principal system of weights and measures.

1919 [see NEWTON, 2]. **1960** *Nature* 2 July 30/2 There is no strong feeling in industry or commerce that Britain is being adversely affected..in exports to metric countries by the retention of the Imperial system. **1961** *B.S.I. News* Apr. 16/1 The controversial issue of whether this country should 'go metric'. **1971** *Sci. Amer.* Sept. 76/2 A metric America.. would seem to be desirable in terms of our stake in world trade. **1974** *Times* 22 May 6 Virtually every country in the world is metric.

B. *sb.*[2] Metric measurement; metric weights and measures collectively.

1969 *Times* 21 July p. vii/5 Metric is so much easier to teach and to learn. **1970** *Daily Tel.* 21 May 10/5 Metric was so simple that a toddler could learn it, he said. And the litre was not strange to car-buyers. **1971** *Nature* 13 Aug. 439/1 The deliberate encouragement of the tendency towards metric could quite quickly create a situation in which the metric system was as widely used as the conventional system in the United States. **1973** *Country Life* 27 Dec. 2186/1 Once we get used to metric, things should be simpler for all of us.

-metric ('mɛtrɪk), a terminal element of adjs. corresponding to sbs. ending in -METER or -METRY.

metrical ('mɛtrɪkəl), *a.*[1] [f. late L. *metricus* relating (1) to measuring, (2) to metre: see METRIC *a.*[1] and -ICAL. Cf. OF. *metrical.*]

I. 1. Pertaining or relating to metre or versification; consisting of or composed in metre; having the characteristics of metre. *spec.* applied to Old or Middle English verse.

1432–50 tr. *Higden* (Rolls) VI. 183 Of..the rewles of feete metricalle,..of dialog metricalle. **1570–6** LAMBARDE *Peramb. Kent* (1826) 173 She uttered sundry metricall and ryming speeches. **1612** DRAYTON *Poly-olb.* iv. 186 Their Quantities, their Rests, their Ceasures metricall. **1774** WARTON *Hist. Eng. Poetry* v. (1840) I. 181 The old metrical romances. **1802** J. RITSON (*title*) Ancient Engleish metrical romanceës. **1807** S. TURNER *Hist. Anglo-Saxons* (ed. 2) II. 294 This poem [sc. *Beowulf*] is certainly a metrical romance in the Anglo-Saxon language. **1810** SCOTT *Lady of L.* II. vi. *note*, Graham (which, for metrical reasons, is here spelt after the Scottish pronunciation). **1815** W. H. IRELAND *Scribbleomania* 73 *note*, The productions of Lord Thurlow indicate a considerable share of metrical energy. **1830** B. THORPE tr. *Rask's Gram. Anglo-Saxon Tongue* 150 The Anglo-Saxons..in many M.S.S., carefully separate the verse by metrical points. **1855** KINGSLEY *Lett.* (1878) I. 456, I have adopted a sort of simple, ballad tone, and tried to make my prose as metrical as possible. **1897** *Mod. Lang. Notes* XII. 79 This regularity of arrangement holds only for the half line, the metrical unit. **1923** G. SAINTSBURY *Hist. Eng. Prosody* (ed. 2) I. II. i. 90 The metrical romances present by far the largest section..of earlier fourteenth-century verse-literature. **1930** FRENCH & HALE *M.E. Metrical Romances* p. v, The metrical romances are the first large body of English fiction. **1946** *Trans. Philol. Soc.* 1943–6 59 What neither Sievers nor any other writers..have ever pointed out, is that the 'five types' are language patterns not metrical patterns. **1953** *Speculum* XXVIII. 449 The discovery of..the non-existence of metrical formulas in the poetry of lettered authors. **1963** R. QUIRK in Brown & Foote *Early Eng. & Norse Stud.* 159 Metrical units in variation.

II. 2. Relating to, involving, used in, or determined by measurement. ***metrical geometry***: see quot. 1897 (opposed to 'descriptive geometry').

1650 J. WYBARD *Tactometria* 6 These kinde of metricall lines (or linear numbers). **1690** LEYBOURN *Curs. Math.* 192 All kind of Arithmetical and Metrical Operations. **1830** R. KNOX *Béclard's Anat.* 70 Its metrical extent, or its extent as compared with that of the body or with some of its parts. **1858** CAYLEY in *Math. Pap.* (1889) II. 592 We are then in the region of pure descriptive geometry: we pass out of it into metrical geometry by fixing upon a conic of the figure as a standard of reference and calling it the Absolute. **1878** PETRIE in *Jrnl. Anthrop. Inst.* (1879) VIII. 111 As an illustration of the metrical character of earthworks, we may refer to the East Everley works in Wiltshire. **1885** LEUDESDORF *Cremona's Proj. Geom.* ix. 50 Most of the propositions in Euclid's *Elements* are metrical, and it is not easy to find among them an example of a purely descriptive theorem. **1897** B. A. W. RUSSELL *Found. Geom.* 149 Metrical Geometry..may be defined as the science which deals with the comparison and relations of spatial magnitudes.

Hence **ˈmetrically** *adv.*[1], with regard to metre; (translated) into metre.

1789 *Elegant Extracts, Poetry* Pref. (1816) 7 Explaining every thing grammatically, historically, metrically, and critically. **1819** CAMPBELL *Ess. Eng. Poetry* II. *Specim.* I. 113 The heroic measure of Chaucer will be found in general..to be metrically correct. **1855** NEIL *Z. Boyd's Zion's Flowers* Introd. 16 Metrically translated books of the Bible.

metrical (ˈmɛtrɪkəl), *a.*[2] [f. F. *métrique* METRIC *a.*[2]: see -ICAL.]

1. = METRIC *a.*[2] (which is now more usual).

1797 *Monthly Mag.* III. 209/1 The ensuing year; when the French republic will have immortalized the first years of its establishment, by the adoption of a Metrical System. **1816** P. KELLY *Metrol.* Introd. 16 It was computed in France, that in three generations, their metrical system would be fully established. **1869** ROSCOE *Elem. Chem.* (1874) 444 Comparison of the Metrical with the Common Measures.

2. 'Having the dimensions of a French meter; as metrical blocks' (Webster 1847–54).

b. Of lenses or their measurement: Pertaining to the system of which the unit is the 'dioptric', i.e. a focal length of one metre.

1879 BRYANT *Pract. Surg.* (ed. 3) I. 301 The trial glasses ..are arranged according to what is known as the 'metrical system'. *Ibid., margin,* Metrical lenses.

metricalization. [-IZATION.] A making metrical in character.

1924 *Glasgow Herald* 13 Nov. 10 The question of the metricalisation of our coinage.

metrically, *adv.*[1]: see METRICAL *a.*[1]

ˈmetrically, *adv.*[2] [f. METRICAL *a.*[2] + -LY[2].] In or with the metric system.

1969 *Daily Tel.* 5 Sept. 25/2 A builder of iron and steel plants has found his design time reduced by 15 per cent. when working metrically.

metricate (ˈmɛtrɪkeɪt), *v.* [Back-formation from next: see -ATE[3].] **a.** *intr.* To change to or adopt the metric system of weights and measures.

1965 [see METRICATION]. **1968** *Guardian* 27 July 3 It may not be practicable to metricate, except possibly over a far longer period than that suggested. **1970** *Daily Tel.* 14 May 18 Current Admiralty Tide Tables, now beginning to metricate in earnest, propose to use decimetres. **1972** *B.S.I. News* June 17/2 Did it not take..nearly a century for Britain to decide to metricate?

b. *trans.* To convert or adapt to the metric system.

1970 *Times* 28 Oct. 7 The cost of metricating road signs.. would eventually have to be considered. **1972** *Daily Tel.* 13 Oct. 19/3 The Royal Navy..started to metricate Admiralty charts in 1970.

Hence **ˈmetricated** *ppl. a.*, made or sold in accordance with metric measurements; converted to or using the metric system.

1970 *Daily Tel.* 14 May 18 Your metricated cook cannot have, standing alongside the kitchen scales, a set of SI weights... There will be no SI weights. *Ibid.* 1 Dec. 3/2 When clothes are fully metricated, at least two things will still be recognisable in the old shapes, brassieres and shoes. **1971** *Timber Trades Jrnl.* 14 Aug. 54/3 This is the second season of metricated wood and the system is now accepted as normal practice among the merchants. **1972** *Bookseller* 18 Mar. 1642/3 Publishers have already invested hundreds of thousands of pounds in metricated editions of educational works. **1972** *B.S.I. News* June 12/1 The encouragement of the use of 'metricated' products.

metrication (mɛtrɪˈkeɪʃən). [f. METRIC *a.*[2] + -ATION.] The process of converting to the metric system of weights and measures; the adoption of the metric system.

1965 J. V. DUNWORTH (Director, Nat. Physical Lab.) in *Times* 29 Nov. 11/5 Earlier this year the National Physical Laboratory sought the guidance of the editor [*sc.* E. McIntosh] of the *Concise Oxford Dictionary* on this matter. .. His reply was as follows:—'Consider the following: Carbon(ize); decimal(ize);..methyl(ate); oxygen(ate). The modern tendency is to use -ize, -ization in forming new words rather than -ate, -ation. It seems to me that either *metrication* or *metricization* could be used.' In the light of these comments the N.P.L. and the Ministry of Technology chose 'metrication' on the grounds of brevity and euphony. The corresponding verb 'metricate' seems very satisfactory. **1966** *New Scientist* 6 Jan. 32/1 Some British scientists who have worked for years with dynes and oersteds, calories and millimetres of mercury, may think they need not share the worries of their fellow citizens about metrication. **1968** *Observer* 21 Apr. 7/1 The Board of Trade has refused to announce a programme for metrication. **1969** *Guardian* 27 Jan. 3/4 The metrication of large sections of British industry will soon be an accomplished fact. **1971** *Daily Colonist* (Victoria, B.C.) 25 Nov. 26/2 Creeping metrication is upon us and the CFL [*sc.* Canadian Football League] has taken official cognizance of the fact.

metrician (mɪˈtrɪʃən). Also 4 -cion, 6 -cien. [f. L. *metric-us* METRIC *a.*[1], after *physician.*]

†**1.** One who writes in metre. *Obs.*

1432–50 tr. *Higden* (Rolls) II. 19 To the lawde of whom a metricion [L. *metricus*] seithe [etc.]. **1494** FABYAN *Chron.* VII. 322 A metrician made theyse baladis of them. *c* **1530** *Crt. Love* v, Ye that ben metriciens me excuse. *a* **1548** HALL *Chron., Rich. III* 42 Because the fyrste lyne ended in dogge, the metrician coulde not..ende the seconde verse in Bore, but called the bore an hogge.

2. One who studies or is learned in metre.

1835–8 S. R. MAITLAND *Dark Ages* (1844) 445 Why..are you..trifling with the metricians, deceiving with the poets, and deceived with the philosophers? **1864** J. HADLEY *Ess.* (1873) 97 These Latin metricians..seem in their scanning of poetry to have beat time in the same way. **1892** W. R. HARDIE in *Class. Rev.* June 249/2 The most advanced metrician probably falls short of being able to..reconstruct the exact scheme which Æschylus or Pindar intended.

metricist (ˈmɛtrɪsɪst). [f. METRIC *a.*[1] + -IST.] One who is skilled in handling metre.

1881 *Athenæum* 7 May 618/2 But even if the poet were a sufficiently skilled metricist to [etc.].

metricize (ˈmɛtrɪsaɪz), *v.*[1] *rare.* [f. METRIC *a.*[1] + -IZE.] *trans.* To analyse the metre of.

1831 T. L. PEACOCK *Crotchet Castle* vi, She who can construe and metricise a chorus shall..pass in by herself.

metricize (ˈmɛtrɪsaɪz), *v.*[2] [f. METRIC *a.*[2] + -IZE.] *trans.* To adapt to the metric system. Hence **ˈmetricized** *ppl. a.*

1873 *Brit. Q. Rev.* LVII. 547 A graphic representation of the size of the different metricized measures as compared with the old ones is given in a chart at the end of the volume.

metricks, occas. var. MARTRIX *Obs.*, marten.

1769 *De Foe's Tour Gt. Brit.* IV. 316 Metricks, a four-footed creature, about the size of a large cat.

metridate, obs. form of MITHRIDATE.

†**ˈmetrificate**, *v. Obs. rare.*[−1] [f. ppl. stem of med.L. *metrificāre*, f. *metrum* METRE *sb.*[1]: see -FICATE.] *trans.* To write in metre.

1432–50 tr. *Higden* (Rolls) V. 321 His wife..metrificate her owne epitaphy in this wise.

metrification (ˌmɛtrɪfɪˈkeɪʃən). [ad. L. type **metrificātio*, n. of action f. *metrificāre* (see prec.).]

1. The construction of a metrical composition; also, metrical structure.

1861 WRIGHT *Ess. Archæol.* II. xx. 153 As..these final rhymes came..into use, the old system of metrification was ..abandoned. **1864** TENNYSON *Hendecasyllabics* 10 Should I flounder awhile without a tumble Thro' this metrification of Catullus. **1875** A. W. WARD *Hist. Eng. Dram. Lit.* (1899) I. 326 The metrification of *Tamburlaine* still shows some signs of uncertainty.

2. = METRICATION.

1965 *Observer* 5 Dec. 40/5 If of old measures we're forsakers..How describe it? There are cries For Metrification, Metricize. **1970** *Times* 17 Apr. 6 Now there was a threat of metrification of weights and measures. **1973** *Daily Tel.* 27 July 16 What angers us is the manner in which the Government has tried to persuade us that VAT..was to our benefit, like decimalisation, two-tier postal systems and now metrification. **1974** *Publishers Weekly* 25 Nov. 12/3 [*heading* 1980: Target Date for Metric Conversion in U.S.] Metrification has been called the non-issue of the century.

metrify (ˈmɛtrɪfaɪ), *v.* Also 6 metrefy. [ad. F. *métrifier* (14th c.), ad. L. *metrificāre*: see METRIFICATE and -FY.]

1. *trans.* To put into metre, make a metrical version of. Also *intr.*, to make verses.

1523 SKELTON *Garl. Laurel* 1382 Also a deuoute Prayer to Moses hornis, Metrifyde merely, medelyd with scornis. *Ibid.* 1464 Wherevpon he metrefyde after his mynde. **1589** PUTTENHAM *Eng. Poesie* II. xi[i]. (Arb.) 109 It [an obelisk] holdeth the altitude of six ordinary triangles, and in metrifying his base can not well be larger then a meetre of six. *a* **1693** *Urquhart's Rabelais* III. xvii. 143 It is metrified in this Octastick. **1861** IRVING *Hist. Scot. Poetry* 392 Twenty psalms were metrified by two individuals.

2. *intr.* = METRICATE *v.* a. *rare.*

1968 *Sunday Times* 31 Mar. 10 The Confederation of British Industry hopes that 75 per cent. of Britain's industries will have metrified by 1975.

Hence **ˈmetrified** *ppl. a.*, **ˈmetrifying** *vbl. sb.* Also **ˈmetrifier** (in quot., one who adopts classic metres in English verse).

1836 SOUTHEY *Life Cowper* C.'s Wks. II. 129 The license which the metrifiers took in this respect, infected other poets. **1887** *Sat. Rev.* 16 Apr. 552 The grimly metrified psalter.

metriour, variant of METRER *Obs.*

metrist (ˈmɛtrɪst). [ad. med.L. *metrista*, f. *metrum* METRE *sb.*[1]: see -IST.] **a.** A metrical writer. **b.** One who is skilled in metrical composition; an adept in the handling of metre.

1535 STEWART *Cron. Scot.* III. 223 In Lating toung ane metrost [*sic*] wes he. **1550** BALE *Image Both Ch.* II. hj b, Thomas smith..wyth such other blind Popish poetes and dirtye metristes. **1819** COLERIDGE in *Lit. Rem.* (1836) II. 378 There are not five metrists in the kingdom to whom I could ..have spoken so plainly. **1864** KNIGHT *Passages Work. Life* I. viii. 289 A very singular..poet, quite set apart from the troop of every-day metrists. **1875** LOWELL *Spenser* Prose Wks. 1890 IV. 328 Spenser was no mere metrist, but a great composer. **1894** R. C. JEBB in A. W. Ward *Eng. Poets* IV. 763 As a metrist he [Tennyson] is the creator of a new blank verse, different both from the Elizabethan and the Miltonic.

‖**metritis** (miːˈtraɪtɪs). *Path.* [mod.L., f. Gr. μήτρα womb: see -ITIS. Cf. F. *métrite.*] Inflammation of the uterus.

1843 R. J. GRAVES *Syst. Clin. Med.* vii. 80, I lately attended a fatal case of metritis after delivery. **1876** tr. *Wagner's Gen. Pathol.* 592 Diffused metritis originates most frequently in lacerations of the vagina.

Hence **metritic** (miːˈtrɪtɪk) *a.*, of or pertaining to metritis.

1856 in MAYNE *Expos. Lex.*

metrizable (mɛˈtraɪzəb(ə)l), *a. Math.* [f. as next + -ABLE, tr. G. *metrisierbar* (P. Urysohn 1924, in *Math. Ann.* XCII. 275).] Of a topological space: capable of being assigned a metric which makes it a metric space identical to the original space.

1927 *Bull. Amer. Math. Soc.* XXXIII. 25 It is therefore of interest to formulate the conditions that a space be metrizable in terms of continuous functions. **1968** E. T. COPSON *Metric Spaces* ix. 142 General topology is a generalization of the theory of metric spaces since there are topological spaces which are not metrizable.

So **metrizaˈbility**, the property of being metrizable.

1927 *Bull. Amer. Math. Soc.* XXXIII. 23 Axiom 1 is a sufficient condition for metrizability. **1964** W. J. PERVIN *Found. Gen. Topology* x. 158 In the case of separable metric spaces, Urysohn..found necessary and sufficient conditions for metrizability.

metrization (mɛtraɪˈzeɪʃən). *Math.* [ad. G. *metrisation* (P. Urysohn 1924, in *Math. Ann.* XCII. 275): see prec. and -ATION.] The process of assigning a metric to a metrizable topological space.

1927 *Bull. Amer. Math. Soc.* XXXIII. 14 The Metrization Problem. The problem is to state in terms of the concepts point, and point of accumulation the conditions that a topological space be metric. **1937** *Ibid.* XLIII. 141 This theorem gives conditions for the metrization of neighbourhood spaces and a comparatively simple method of introducing the metric. **1964** W. J. PERVIN *Found. Gen. Topology* x. 158 The metrization theorem.

†**ˈmetrize**, *v. Obs. rare*[−1]. [f. METRE *sb.*[1] + -IZE.] *trans.* To put into metre.

1572 BOSSEWELL *Armorie* 12 b, The whiche verses I haue thus metrized in Englishe.

†**metro**[1]. *Obs.* [It. or Sp.] = METRE *sb.*[1]

1619 H. HUTTON *Follies Anat.* Ep. Ded., Peruse my writ, And vse these Metroes of true meaning wit. *Ibid.* A 6 b, Nor in a Metro shew my Cupide's fire.

metro[2] (ˈmeɪtrəʊ). *colloq.* [Fr., abbrev. of (*Chemin de Fer*) *Métropolitain* Metropolitan Railway.] The Metropolitan Underground Railway of Paris (usu. in form **métro**). Hence applied to the underground railway in other countries. (Applied to London trains *metro* (ˈmɛtrəʊ) is an abbreviation of METROPOLITAN *a.* rather than a use in English of F. *métro.*)

1904 A. BENNETT *Jrnl.* (1932) I. 202 Wandering down through the Palais Royal and then taking the Métro. **1919** MENCKEN *Amer. Lang.* 110 In England..a subway is always a *tube*, or the *underground*, or the *Metro.* **1924** S. STORY *Dining in Paris* 12 Business men, clerks, stockbrokers..have lit the eternal cigarette..before going to a restaurant for dinner or taking omnibus or 'metro' to their distant homes. **1927** W. E. COLLINSON *Contemp. Eng.* 66 Recently attempts have been made to put the short form metro [for the Underground railway in London] before the public. **1953** X. FIELDING *Stronghold* IV. ii. 263, I realized why the ibex.. smelt so strongly of the Paris *métro.* **1963** *Listener* 7 Mar. 418/1 It was in the way of a roundabout and the new metro [in Rotterdam]. **1966** *Ibid.* 1 Dec. 801/1 The underground system..is called the *métro*, but, typical of bilingual Montreal, is more often referred to as the subway. **1973** *Nat. Geographic* May 658/1 The Metro, Mexico's new subway system, is one of the wonders of the city.

Metro[3] (ˈmɛtrəʊ). *Canad.* [Abbrev. of METROPOLITAN *a.* 2.] The Metropolitan area of Toronto and other Canadian cities. Also *attrib.* or as *adj.*

1957 *Maclean's Mag.* 17 Aug. 3/3 Metro chairman..said a Bloor Street subway would be a mistake; Metro would study others. **1962** *Time* (Canad. ed.) 26 Jan. 10/2 Canada's second experiment with metropolitan government... The Metro [of Winnipeg] did not follow Toronto Metro's example. **1963** J. N. HARRIS *Weird World Wes Beattie* (1964) xi. 138 The threat that the Metro Police would try it if the provincials didn't was sufficient to settle the matter. **1966** *Globe & Mail* (Toronto) 25 June 3/4 [He] faced an indirect challenge during the election campaign from a ginger group of eight Liberal in metro Winnipeg ridings. **1968** *Ibid.* 5 Feb. 1/9 There were 25,000 [drunks] charged in Metro Toronto last year. **1970** *Toronto Daily Star* 24 Sept. 35/2 (Advt.), This outstanding offer is good in Metro Toronto only. *Ibid.* 35/3 Metro-area delegates. **1975** *Globe & Mail* (Toronto) 11 June 3/4 A Toronto criminal lawyer says Metro police have told him some members of the Rastafarian Brethren are walking time bombs as far as violent crime in Metro is concerned.

metrochrome (ˈmɛtrəʊkrəʊm). [f. Gr. μέτρο-ν measure + χρῶμα colour.] An instrument for measuring colours.
1817 G. FIELD *Chromatics* (1845) 223 Thus used in conjunction the three gauges constituted a Metrochrome, or general measure and standard of colours.

metrocracy (miːˈtrɒkrəsɪ). [f. Gr. μητρ-, μήτηρ mother + -(O)CRACY.] = MATRIARCHY.
1891 E. WESTERMARCK *Hist. Hum. Marriage* (1894) 98 North America which is acknowledged.. to have been one of the chief centres of 'mother-right', or metrocracy.

metrod, variant of METEROD *Obs.*

metrograph (ˈmɛtrəʊgrɑːf, -æ-). [f. Gr. μέτρο-ν measure: see -GRAPH.] An apparatus for indicating the speed of a railway-train, and the hour of arrival and departure at each station.
1858 in SIMMONDS *Dict. Trade.*

metrographer (mɛˈtrɒgrəfə(r)). [f. Gr. μέτρο-ν METRE *sb.*¹ + -GRAPHER.] ? A writer on metre.
1821 *Blackw. Mag.* X. 388 Our worthy metrographer has been so unfortunate as to scan him wrong.

metroland (ˈmɛtrəʊlænd). [f. METRO(POLITAN *a.* + LAND *sb.* 3.] The area surrounding a metropolis; *spec.* the district around London served by the (Metropolitan) underground railway. Also, *collect.* the people inhabiting these areas. Hence **ˈmetrolander** *sb.*
1926 R. MACAULAY *Crewe Train* III. v. 295 That house at Great Missenden.. will suit them exactly. In metro-land, and such nice people all about... They *must* have a car, though; relying entirely on the Met. is too awkward, with so many strikes and so few late trains... After all, it's not London; metro-land can't be London. *Ibid.* vi. 298 Metro-landers have *pieds-à-terre* in London. **1938** J. BETJEMAN *Oxf. Univ. Chest* v. 102 The houses of Metroland and beechy Bucks dot the landscape. **1940** GRAVES & HODGE *Long Week-End* viii. 114 In 1923 the London Underground, wishing to popularize 'Metroland'.. published two guide-books. **1951** R. HOGGART *Auden* v. 137 The appropriate isolation for Auden is.. isolation in a vast anonymous metroland such as New York. **1963** *Times* 24 May p. iii/3 Under that great general manager Mr. R. H. Selbie, the Metropolitan invented Metroland. **1973** *Radio Times* 26 Feb. 7 The Metro-landers who bought houses took a great pride in their gardens.

Metroliner, metro-liner (ˈmɛtrəʊˌlaɪnə(r)). [f. METRO(POLITAN *a.* 2 + LINER² 8.] A high-speed inter-city train in the United States.
1969 'O. BLEECK' *Brass Go-Between* xiv. 156 Between Washington and New York they finally got one new high-speed Metroliner running. **1970** *Guardian* 19 Jan. 4/1 The metroliner, a Government-supported experiment in fast inter-city transport.. has cut the travelling time from Washington to New York.. by nearly ninety minutes. **1972** *Daily Tel.* 23 Nov. 9/2 The official said that the trains at present operating as metro-liners between the three [American] cities were capable of 150 mph. **1973** J. DI MONA *Last Man at Arlington* (1974) 57 The Metro-liner to Washington waited in the station.

metrology (mɛˈtrɒlədʒɪ). [f. Gr. μέτρο-ν measure + -LOGY. Cf. F. *métrologie.*]
1. a. A system or series of measures. **b.** The science of weights and measures.
1816 P. KELLY (*title*) Metrology; or an exposition of weights and measures. **1821** J. Q. ADAMS *Rep. Weights & Meas.* 84 The principle of decimal divisions can be applied only with many qualifications to any general system of metrology. *Ibid.* 85 The French metrology. **1846** GROTE *Greece* II. iv. II. 425 M. Boeckh's recent publication on Metrology. **1878** *Nature* 23 May 110/2 Mr. W. M. Flinders Petrie read a paper on inductive metrology, the purpose of which.. is to deduce the units of measure employed by ancient peoples from the dimensions of existing remains. **1969** *Physics Bull.* Sept. 365/2 A large proportion of conference participants deprecated the term 'measurement science' and the use of the term 'metrology' appeared to have a large measure of support. **1971** *Inside Kenya Today* Mar. 29/2 We might have weights manufactured to International Specifications, i.e. to specification of Legal Metrology.
2. The science of poetic metres. *rare*⁻¹.
1889 A. SIDGWICK in *Jrnl. Educ.* Feb. 116.
Hence **metroˈlogical** *a.*, pertaining or relating to metrology; **meˈtrologist, ˈmetrologue**, a writer on weights and measures.
1843 *Penny Cycl.* XXVII. 206/2 No metrologist has given the Romans credit for seeing that water would do just as well to.. adjust standards by, as wine. **1843** GROTE in *Class. Museum* (1844) I. 2 The cardinal principle of his metrological reasonings. *Ibid.* 7 'Great Attic talents', as they are called by Dardanus the ancient Metrologue. **1856** *Sat. Rev.* 8 Nov. 617/1 All sorts of weights and measures, from the cubit of Noah to the metrological standard of John Quincy Adams. **1883** *Jrnl. Hellenic Studies* IV. 340 The metrological analysis of the fathom must consequently entirely exclude the Attic foot. **1889** *Yale Coll. Obit. Record* 491 The American Metrological Society. **1969** *Physics Bull.* Sept. 365/2 A number of speakers considered that would-be metrologists would be better advised to make a broad study in science or engineering at the undergraduate level and specialize in metrology by spending a further year taking a MSc course in this discipline. **1970** *Daily Tel.* 14 May 18 For heaven's sake, exasperated metrologists explain, do try to remember that shop scales do not show the weight of apples; they show the force exercised by the apples in that particular gravitational environment.

metromania (mɛtrəʊˈmeɪnɪə). [f. Gr. μέτρο-ν METRE *sb.*¹ + -MANIA; after F. *métromanie.*] A mania for writing poetry. Hence **metroˈmaniac**, one affected with metromania; also *attrib.* or as *adj.*; **metromaˈniacal** *a.*, pertaining to or affected with metromania (Mayne *Expos. Lex.* 1856).
1794 GIFFORD *Baviad* (1811) 46 This pernicious pest, This metromania, creeps thro' every breast. [**1818** *Blackw. Mag.* III. 519 Of all the manias of this mad age, the most incurable.. seems to be no other than the *metromanie.*] **1830** W. TAYLOR *Hist. Surv. Germ. Poetry* I. 183 On a sudden [Bodmer] seemed to have acquired the facility of versification, and to display it with almost metromaniac eagerness. **1884** HUNTER & WHYTE *My Ducats & My Dau.* xiii. (1885) 179 No one knows what I have had to endure from the metromaniacs.

metrometer¹ (mɛˈtrɒmɪtə(r)). *rare*⁻⁰. [ad. F. *métromètre* (1780 in Hatz.-Darm.), f. Gr. μέτρο-ν METRE *sb.*¹ + *-mètre* -METER.] = METRONOME.
1876 in STAINER & BARRETT *Dict. Mus. Terms.*

metrometer² (miːˈtrɒmɪtə(r)). *rare*⁻⁰. [ad. mod.L. *mētrometr-um*, f. Gr. μήτρα- womb: see -METER.] = HYSTEROMETER.
1875 KNIGHT *Dict. Mech.*

metronome (ˈmɛtrənəʊm). [f. Gr. μέτρο-ν METRE *sb.*¹ + νόμος law, rule. Cf. F. *métronome.*]
a. An instrument used in music for marking the time by means of a graduated inverted pendulum with a sliding weight which can be regulated to make the required number of beats in a minute.
1816 *Repert. Arts, Manuf.*, etc. XXVIII. 128 [Patents] John Malzl, of Poland-street, Middlesex, Machinist; for an instrument or instruments.. for the improvement of musical performance, which he denominates a Metronome, or musical time-keeper. Dated December 5, 1815. *a* **1845** HOOD *To Kitchener* i, Or boiling eggs—timed to a metronome. **1889** *Infantry Drill* 504, ♩ = 108 Maelzel's Metronome. **1904** *Athenæum* 5 Nov. 626/1 The seconds of exposure [were] counted by a metronome.
attrib. **1857** *Encycl. Brit.* (ed. 8) XIV. 695/2 It is very desirable that composers should always affix *metronome* numbers to their compositions. **1880** W. S. ROCKSTRO in Grove *Dict. Mus.* II. 319/2 Maelzel.. in 1816 set up the first Metronome Manufactory on record.
b. *fig.* (In the first quot. app. used for: A conventional rule for metrical quantity.)
1822 TILLBROOK *Rem. Mod. Hexametrists* 73 Why leave the public without a guide to the accents and divisions of the Georgian hexameter? This should have been done either by—borrowing from the Latin rules,—adopting those of the early prosodians,—or by inventing a new *metronome.* **1858** O. W. HOLMES *Aut. Breakf.-t.* xi. (1891) 265, I should love to.. listen to the great liquid metronome as it beats its solemn measure. **1865** G. MACDONALD *A. Forbes* 11 And listen to the unfailing metronome of the flails.
Also as *v. intr.* (In quots. *fig.*)
1959 *Listener* 2 Apr. 600/2 They.. listened to the stillness of the white moonlight metronomed to the trot, trot, trot of the horse's hooves. **1962** L. DEIGHTON *Ipcress File* ii. 21 Pin-tables metronoming away the sunny afternoon.

metronomic (mɛtrəʊˈnɒmɪk), *a.* [f. METRONOME + -IC.] **a.** Of or pertaining to a metronome.
metronomic mark, the indication, placed at the head of a piece of music, of the pace at which it is to be performed.
1881 *Chicago Advance* 29 Dec. 832 The metronomic mark of most of the tunes is too fast. **1896** *Daily News* 17 Apr. 8/5 Mr. Edwards reprints the facsimile of the metronomic times for each number from a Mendelssohn MS.
b. *fig.* Resembling the action of a metronome.
1959 *Times* 30 May 3/1 The Hungarian.. is metronomic as she unwinds the rallies. **1963** *Listener* 3 Jan. 45/2 The metronomic dance music rhythm of our time. **1975** 'E. LATHEN' *By Hook or by Crook* xi. 107 Miss Martineau sobbed with metronomic regularity.
So **metroˈnomical** *a.*, **metroˈnomically** *adv.*, according to the metronome.
1822 *Repository* No. 80. 100 The vague directions as to tempo—'slow', 'very slow', &c. should be avoided.. when it is in our power to mark the time metronomically. **1866** ENGEL *Nat. Mus.* v. 177 The published collections of tunes seldom possess metronomical signs. **1970** R. P. WARREN *Incantations* 49 The disturbance you are so metronomically creating. **1974** *Daily Tel.* 14 Sept. 11/8 Both in the opening of the symphony and in the Adagio Mr Davis adopted and almost metronomically maintained tempi as fast as Beethoven has presumably imagined them.

ˌmetronomiˈzation. [f. METRONOME + -IZATION.] The determining or indicating of the rate at which music should be played.
1923 A. BETTI in *Music & Lett.* Jan. 3 Can the metronomisation of a piece be absolutely exact?

metronomy (mɛˈtrɒnəmɪ). [f. METRONOME + -Y.] The measuring of time by a metronome.
1850 in OGILVIE.

metronym (ˈmiːtrəʊnɪm). [f. Gr. μητρ-, μήτηρ mother + ὄνομα, Doric ὄνυμα name.] A metronymic name.
1904 *Nature* 5 May Suppl. p. xiii/2 The acceptance of metronyms in the genealogies as proofs of female kinship, while patronyms are rejected.

metronymic (miːtrəʊˈnɪmɪk), *a.* and *sb.* [ad. Gr. μητρωνυμικ-ός, f. μητρ-, μήτηρ mother + ὄνυμα, ὄνομα name. Cf. the earlier *matronymic(al).*]
a. *adj.* Derived from the name of a mother or other female ancestor, esp. by addition of a suffix or prefix indicating descent. Also said of such a suffix or prefix. (In recent Dicts.) Also applied to a people or state of society where such a system of naming prevails. **b.** *sb.* A metronymic name; a name derived from that of a mother or maternal ancestor.
1868 LIGHTFOOT *Comm. Philippians* (1873) 55 In not a few instances a metronymic takes the place of the usual patronymic. **1896** F. H. GIDDINGS *Princ. Sociol.* 158 In a metronymic group all relationships are traced through mothers; paternal relationships are ignored. **1903** L. F. WARD *Pure Sociol.* 339 The metronymic family. **1904** J. A. NAIRN *Herodas* 9 It is noticeable that Gryllos has a metronymic, not a patronymic. **1944** H. P. FAIRCHILD *Dict. Sociol.* 192/2 *Metronymic*, deriving the personal or family name from the mother or other matrilineal relative. **1960** C. WINICK *Dict. Anthropol.* 521/2 *System, metronymic*, tracing kinship exclusively through the mother.
So **metronymy** (miːˈtrɒnɪmɪ), the practice of using metronymics.
1891 *Sat. Rev.* 31 Jan. 140/1 M. Reclus finds what he calls 'metronymy' in Egypt under the Ptolemies. 'The newly-married man even dropped his own name to take that of his wife'.

metrop (mɪˈtrɒp). Colloq. abbrev. of METROPOLIS 2.
1888 [see KILO²]. **1919** WODEHOUSE *My Man Jeeves* 216, I think we've had about enough of the metrop. for the time being. **1925** —— *Carry on, Jeeves!* v. 105 Dear old Rocky made him look like a publicity agent for the old metrop! **1974** 'A. GILBERT' *Nice Little Killing* i. 13 'Know the Metrop?' She shook her head. 'You want to be a bit careful.'

‖**metroperitonitis** (ˌmiːtrəʊpɛrɪtəʊˈnaɪtɪs). *Path.* [mod.L., f. Gr. μήτρα womb + PERITONITIS.] Inflammation of the uterus and the peritoneum.
1845 DAY tr. *Simon's Anim. Chem.* I. 270. **1859** *Todd's Cycl. Anat.* V. 688/1 The pathological conditions of the serous coat are chiefly those of.. metroperitonitis.

‖**metrophlebitis** (ˌmiːtrəʊflɪˈbaɪtɪs). *Path.* [mod.L., f. Gr. μήτρα womb + PHLEBITIS.] Inflammation of the veins of the uterus.
[**1845** DAY tr. *Simon's Anim. Chem.* I. 252 Metrophlebitis puerperalis.] **1859** *Todd's Cycl. Anat.* V. 704/1 The introduction of.. venous pus.. in metrophlebitis.

metropole (ˈmɛtrəpəʊl). [a. OF. *metropole*, ad. L. *mētropolis*: see METROPOLIS.]
1. A chief town; = METROPOLIS.
13.. *S. Erkenwolde* 26 in Horstm. *Altengl. Leg.* (1881) 266 Londone.. þe metropol & þe mayster-tone. **1586** J. HOOKER *Hist. Irel.* in *Holinshed* II. 4/1 Bath, which was the metropole of Summersetshire. *Ibid.* 151/2 Dublin.. being the metropole and chiefe citie of the whole land. **1685** STILLINGFL. *Orig. Brit.* iv. 196 Those Cities which had the Title of *Augusta* conferred upon them, were.. chief Metropoles of the Provinces.
1937 A. HUXLEY *Let.* 3 June (1969) 422 Our nearest railway is Santa Fe, 70 miles away, and our metropole is Denver at 350 miles. **1970** *Financial Times* 23 Mar. 19/1 What Algeria lacked could easily come from the metropole. **1973** *Caribbean Contact* Jan. 10/2 The ill-defined.. countries of the Caribbean Sea are becoming states in their own right, and are slowly.. severing their traditional ties with their respective European metropoles.
2. *Eccl.* The see of a metropolitan; = METROPOLIS 1.
1862 NEALE *Ess. Liturgiol.* (1867) 300 That was a remarkable erection of metropoles which occurred just before the outbreak. **1888** *Ch. Times* 27 Apr. 364/3 York was designated as a metropole by St. Gregory, and did exercise some undefined jurisdiction over other sees in the North.
3. A luxury hotel.
1890 W. BOOTH *In Darkest Eng.* II. vi. 209 A superior lodging-house, a sort of poor man's Metropole. **1925** E. SITWELL *Troy Park* 74 That child is the small wicked ghost Of Metropoles and oyster bars.

†**metropolic**, *a. Obs.* [f. METROPOL-IS + -IC.] = METROPOLITAN, METROPOLITICAL.
1574 HELLOWES *Gueuara's Fam. Ep.* (1577) 326 Paphlagonia, whose Capital or Metropolike towne is Gernapolis. **1681-6** J. SCOTT *Chr. Life* (1747) III. vii. 445 Rogatianus, a Bishop of his [St. Cyprian's] metropolick Church.
So **metroˈpolical** *a.*, in the same sense; hence **ˌmetropoliˈcality**.
1550 BALE *Eng. Votaries* II. 50 b, Bryngyng with hym the metropolycall mantell of Anselme. **1637** BASTWICK *Litany* I. 21, I will.. so plauge [*sic*] the Metropolicallity of Yorke and Canterbury.. as I will neuer leaue them.

†**metropolie**. *Obs.* [? irreg. ad. L. *mētropolis*; some writers may have intended *metropolies* for a Latin plural.] = METROPOLIS.
1633 P. FLETCHER *Purple Isl.* II. xiv, The whole Isle, parted in three regiments, By three Metropolies is joyntly sway'd. *Ibid.* II. xxiii, This low regions Metropolie. **1635** PAGITT *Christianogr.* II. v. (1636) 19 The Metropolies and Arch-bishopricks.. belonging to the Patriarch of Constantinople. **1665** J. WEBB *Stone-Heng* (1725) 184 The Towns.. were Metropolies of Kingdoms, not Country Towns.

metropolis (mɪˈtrɒpəlɪs). Also 6- polus; *pl.*, 7 -polisses, 8 -polis's, 9 -polises. [a. L. *mētropolis*, a.

Gr. μητρόπολις, f. μητρο-, μήτηρ mother + πόλις city.]

1. The seat or see of a metropolitan bishop.

1535 STEWART *Cron. Scot.* II. 425 The bischopis sait.. Fra Abirnethie translatit hes he.. To Sanct Androis.. Metropolus of all Scotland to be. **1542** UDALL *Erasm. Apoph.* 117 And therof is metropolis called the chief citee where the archebishop of any prouince hath his see. **1595** SHAKS. *John* v. ii. 72 The great Metropolis and Sea of Rome. **1612** DRAYTON *Poly-olb.* xviii. 740 Let this Town [Canterbury].. Of all the British Sees be still Metropolis. **1727–41** CHAMBERS *Cycl.* s.v., In Asia, there were metropolis's merely nominal, that is, which had no suffragan, nor any rights of metropolitans. **1760–72** tr. *Juan & Ulloa's Voy.* (ed. 3) II. 145 Plata was erected into a bishopric in 1551,.. and in the year 1608 was raised to a metropolis. **1844** LINGARD *Anglo-Sax. Ch.* (1858) I. App. E. 342 Irenaeus was the bishop of Lyons, the metropolis of Gaul. **1850** NEALE *East. Ch.* I. Introd. 44 Marcianopolis lost its metropolitical rights, though it still continued a See; and Debeltus or Zagara became the Metropolis of the province.

2. The chief town or city of a country (*occas.* of a province or district), esp. the one in which the government of a country is carried on; a capital.

The metropolis, often somewhat pompously used for 'London'. Also, in recent use, occasionally applied to London as a whole, in contradistinction to *the City*.

1590 MARLOWE *2nd Pt. Tamburl.* III. v. 36 That sweet land, whose braue Metropolis Reedified the faire Semyramis. **1636** DAVENANT *Wits* IV. i, O, to live here i' th' fair metropolis Of our great isle. **1666** DRYDEN *Ann. Mirab. (heading)*, To the Metropolis of Great Britain, the most renowned.. City of London. **1695** ECHARD *Gazetteer* Pref., All the metropolisses of provinces. **1726** FRANKLIN *Jrnl.* Wks. 1887 I. 104 Newport.. is the metropolis of the island [Isle of Wight]. **1805** W. IRVING in *Life & Lett.* (1864) I. 149, I have not taken a single note since I have been in this metropolis [Paris]. **1807** SOUTHEY *Espriella's Lett.* I. 291 London is now so often visited, that the manners of the metropolis are to be found in every country gentleman's house. **1838** *Athenæum* 31 Mar. 233/2 Liverpool, New York, and the 'Great Metropolis'. **1862** P. M. IRVING *Life & Lett. W. Irving* (1864) I. i. 17 Kirkwall, the metropolis of the island group [Orkneys]. **1892** *Nation* (N.Y.) 21 July 44/1 She [Trinity College, Dublin] lives in a workaday world, because she lies at the heart of a metropolis.

fig. **1806** *Med. Jrnl.* XV. 195 The stomach is the metropolis, and all the other parts and provinces of the frame are dependent upon the proportion of its vigour or decay. **1863** HAWTHORNE *Our Old Home, Civic Banq.* II. 255 His stomach [appearing] to assume the dignified prominence which justly belongs to that metropolis of his system.

b. A chief centre or seat of some form of activity.

1675 TRAHERNE *Chr. Ethics* 517 Heaven is the metropolis of all perfection. **1743** J. MORRIS *Serm.* vii. 198 Their city was the fountain and metropolis of idolatry. **1783** BURKE *Sp. East-India Bill* Wks. IV. 78 This center and metropolis of abuse [the Carnatic], whence all the rest in India and England diverge, from whence they are fed and methodized. **1816** SCOTT *Tales of My Landl.* Ser. I. Introd., Our metropolis of law, by which I mean Edinburgh, or.. our metropolis and mart of gain, whereby I insinuate Glasgow. **1864** BRYCE *Holy Rom. Emp.* xvi. (1875) 272 To half the Christian nations Rome is the metropolis of religion, to all the metropolis of art.

c. *Nat. Hist.* The district in which a species, group, etc., is most represented.

1826 KIRBY & SP. *Entomol.* IV. 489 The metropolis of the group [*Petalocera*] is within the temperate zone. **1859** DARWIN *Orig. Spec.* vi. (1873) 135 Almost every species, even in its metropolis, would increase immensely in numbers, were it not for other competing species.

3. *Greek Hist.* The mother-city or parent-state of a colony. Hence occas. applied to the parent-state of a modern colony.

a **1568** ASCHAM *Scholem.* II. (Arb.) 135 Doing the dewtie of a good Colonia to her Metropolis. **1651** HOBBES *Leviath.* II. xxiv. 131 The Common-wealth from which they [*sc.* the colonists] went, was called their Metropolis, or Mother. **1837** *Penny Cycl.* VII. 359/1 If a colony wished to send out a new colony, this was properly done with the sanction of the metropolis. **1852** J. A. ROEBUCK *Hist. Whig Ministry* II. 197 The best means of making the wants of the colonies known to.. the metropolis which founds them.

metropolitan (mɛtrəˈpɒlɪtən), *a.* and *sb.* Also 6–7 **metra-**. [ad. late L. *metropolītānus*, f. Gr. μητροπολίτ-ης (see METROPOLITE).]

A. *adj.*

1. a. Belonging to an ecclesiastical metropolis; ***metropolitan bishop*** = B. 1. Also, pertaining to or characteristic of a metropolitan.

a **1548** HALL *Chron., Hen. VIII* 247 The metrapolitan Churche of Saint Andrewes. *a* **1600** HOOKER *Eccl. Pol.* VII. viii. §12 Archiepiscopal or Metropolitan prerogatives are those mentioned in old Imperial constitutions, to convocate the holy Bishops under them within the compass of their own Provinces. **1647** N. BACON *Disc. Govt. Eng.* I. xii. (1739) 22 London had the Metropolitan See, or was the chiefest in precedency. **1726** AYLIFFE *Parergon* 91 An Archbishop.. was elected by Provincial Bishops meeting together in the Metropolitan Church. **1902** A. M. FAIRBAIRN *Philos. Chr. Relig.* II. II. iii. 487 The Synagogue was provincial and sectarian, but the Temple was metropolitan and collective.

†**b.** ***metropolitan toe.*** (The allusion is obscure.)

1642 MILTON *Apol. Smect.* 19 A Bishops foot that hath all his Toes.. and a linnen Sock over it, is the aptest emblem of the Prelate himselfe. Who being a pluralist, may under one Surplice which is also linnen, hide foure benefices besides the metropolitan toe. **1673** [R. LEIGH] *Transp. Reh.* 127 When Arch-bishop Abbot was suspended we might say his metropolitan toe was cut off.

2. a. Of, pertaining to, or constituting a metropolis; ***metropolitan city*** or ***town*** = METROPOLIS. Also, belonging to or characteristic of 'the metropolis' (London).

In recent use occas. applied to designate institutions, etc. pertaining to London as a whole, in contradistinction to those that pertain to 'the City', as in ***metropolitan police***.

1555 EDEN *Decades* 259 The metrapolitane citie of Muscouia called Mosca. **1739** CIBBER *Apol.* (1756) II. 17 A great deal of that false flashy wit and forc'd humour which had been the delight of our metropolitan multitude. **1784** COWPER *Task* III. 737 Are not wholesome airs.. To be preferred to smoke, to the eclipse That metropolitan volcanoes make? **1864** *Act 27 & 28 Vict.* c. 116 §8 This Act may be cited.. as the 'Metropolitan Houseless Poor Act, 1864'. **1886** BYNNER *A. Surriage* xv. 173 How fast he was losing metropolitan tone and polish in the wilds of America. **1887** DOWDEN *Shelley* I. vi. 236 Dublin had sunk from a metropolitan to a provincial city. **1930** H. CRANE *Let.* 29 Nov. (1965) 359 In one of the many Doubleday-Doran shops in the metropolitan area. **1936** [see HINTERLAND]. **1958** *Listener* 11 Dec. 981/2 Black cities; white suburbs—that is how the current trend is often summarized... The pattern of 'metropolitan segregation' (as it has been called) has opened a new, and a frightening, chapter of the 'American Dilemma'. **1961** E. A. POWDRILL *Vocab. Land Planning* v. 89 The 'metropolitan region' is a giant urban regional system, different less in kind than in size from that of any urban region. **1963** *Times* 7 June 3/7 It contains a detailed breakdown of the rates levied by the 83 county boroughs and 28 metropolitan boroughs. **1969** *Daily Tel.* 12 June 23/2 Three areas—Manchester, Birmingham and Liverpool—will become Metropolitan authorities, with the key functions of planning, transportation and development... These three will have below them metropolitan district authorities running education, the personal social services, health and housing. **1971** *Ibid.* 17 Feb. 9 Six new metropolitan county councils are proposed by the Government in its plans for reorganisation of local government published today. **1972** *Times* 12 Feb. 14/8 His Lordship had not failed to observe the practice in some metropolitan courts. **1973** *Times* 12 May 1/1 The 36 metropolitan district councils in England and 37 district councils in Wales created under the Local Government Act 1972, will take over in 12 months' time the statutory powers of the present bodies which they will replace. **1974** *Daily Tel.* 1 Apr. 6/4 The 45 new counties will contain 332 districts, including 36 metropolitan districts covering towns in the six metropolitan counties.

b. Of or pertaining to an underground railway serving a large city; *spec.* of the London Underground Railway, now extended overground to serve an extensive suburban area. Also *ellipt.*

1867 TROLLOPE *Claverings* II. xix. 233 He was very keen at the present moment about Metropolitan railways. *c* **1875** 'BRENDA' *Froggy's Little Brother* (new ed.) iii. 33 A Metropolitan train was just in, and a crowd of passengers, as usual, came swarming up the steps into the street. **1883** E. W. HAMILTON *Diary* 13 Nov. (1972) II. 505 The proposal of the Metropolitan Railway to run an underground line from the back of the India Office to Knightsbridge, and thence across the Park to the Marble Arch and up the Edgeware Road. **1909** CHESTERTON *Tremendous Trifles* 244 A Metropolitan station, where I took a train home. **1934** H. G. WELLS *Exper. Autobiogr.* II. ix. 817 Moscow also is making an imitative tube system... It will be the least stable 'Metropolitan' in the world. *Ibid.* 819 The constructors of the new Metropolitan. **1959** [see DISTRICT *sb.* 3 g]. **1974** M. BIRMINGHAM *You can help Me* ii. 38 The Metropolitan train from Euston Square.. [to] Aldgate East.

c. Of a type of early English pottery found in or near London: (see quots.).

1891 J. E. & E. HODGKIN *Examples Early Eng. Pott.* 6 Of a less decorative character than most of the slip-decorated pieces is the ware which we have classed.. as *Metropolitan Slip*, the pieces in this group having been mainly found in or near London. *Ibid.* 9 Metropolitan Slip... A Jar of elegant shape, recently dug up.. near Bishopsgate Street. **1903** R. L. HOBSON *Catal. Eng. Pott. Brit. Mus.* 108 Examples of Metropolitan Slip ware, made of red clay, with ornament in white slip and a transparent yellowish lead glaze. **1924** RACKHAM & READ *Eng. Pott.* iii. 28 Another type of ware, showing the same technical methods as the Staffordshire slipwares, has been given the name of 'Metropolitan', because it has usually been found in or near London. *Ibid.*, The earliest date on a piece of Metropolitan ware is on a jug.., inscribed.. 1638. **1957** MANKOWITZ & HAGGAR *Conc. Encycl. Eng. Pott. & Porc.* 149/1 *Metropolitan slipware*, the name given to a class of red earthenware decorated with white trailed slip... Examples dated from 1638 to 1659 are recorded. *Ibid.* Plate 66 (caption) Metropolitan jug. **1967** *Times* 14 Mar. 21/7 (Advt.), A Metropolitan ware silver-mounted jug.

3. Belonging to or constituting the mother-country. Freq. with reference to France: of or pertaining to the home country (as distinct from colonial territories).

1806 JEFFERSON *Writ.* (1830) IV. 60 A safe carriage of all her productions, metropolitan or colonial. **1810** BENTHAM *Offic. Apt. Maximized* (1830) Pref. 21 On the question—by the metropolitan country shall this or that distant dependency be kept up,—there are two sides. **1910** *Encycl. Brit.* X. 795/2 The organization of the 'metropolitan troops' [in France] by regiments. **1943** H. NICOLSON *Diary* 4 Feb. (1967) 278 In Metropolitan France de Gaulle is the great symbol. **1958** *Optima* Mar. 22/1 Were peace to be restored, metropolitan France would have, within the following few years, to devote 2½ per cent. of her national revenue to raising the Algerian standard of living. **1959** B. & R. NORTH tr. *Duverger's Pol. Parties* (ed. 2) II. ii. 330 The practice of alliances.. made it possible for the Centre parties to gain 61% of the seats in metropolitan France with 51·4% of the votes. **1972** *Sci. Amer.* Apr. 19/3 Back in colonial times the metropolitan countries certainly maintained peace in and among their colonies.

†**4.** *fig.* (from 1 and 2). Principal, chief. *Obs.*

1626 JACKSON *Creed* VIII. xxi. §1 Of which [feasts] the passeover was the principal, or (as Chrysostome with some other of the ancients instile it) Metropolitan. **1632** BROME *Crt. Beggar* II. i. Wks. 1873 I. 201 Some call him the metrapolitane wit of Court. **1645** MILTON *Tetrach.* Wks. 1851 IV. 237 To acknowledge Gods ancient people their betters, and that language the Metropolitan language. **1651** BIGGS *New Disp.* ¶ 198 The Ascendand and first house, the metrapolitane place in the systeme of indications. **1686** J. DUNTON *Lett. fr. New-Eng.* (1867) 74 Mr. Increase Mather: .. He is deservedly called, The Metropolitan Clergy-Man of the Kingdom.

B. *sb.*

1. *Eccl.* **a.** [In Gr. μητροπολίτης, in L. *mētropolītānus*.] A bishop having the oversight of the bishops of a province; in the early church his see was in the metropolis of the province. In the West the term is now approximately co-extensive with *archbishop*; in the Greek church the metropolitan ranks above an archbishop and below a patriarch.

1432–50 tr. *Higden* (Rolls) II. 111 And to the metropolitan of London alle the cuntre of Cornewaile and alle Englonde was subiecte vn to the floode of Humbre. **1530–1** *Act 22 Hen. VIII*, c. 15 Wyllyam Archebysshoppe of Canturburye metropolytane and primate of all Englande. *a* **1643** LD. FALKLAND, etc. *Infallibility* (1646) 26 It hath beene agreed on, that all that are under the Metropolitan of Canterbury, should be called the Province of Canterbury. *a* **1674** MILTON *Hist. Mosc.* i. Wks. 1851 VIII. 480 The Emperor esteemeth the Metropolitan next to God, after our Lady and Saint Nicholas, as being his spiritual Officer. **1710** PRIDEAUX *Orig. Tithes* iii. 149 All the Metropolitans and Bishops of King Gontrans Kingdom. **1814** SOUTHEY *Roderick* xx. 318 If thou wert still The mitred metropolitan. **1833** R. PINKERTON *Russia* 189 The Council of Moscow.. was attended by.. five metropolitans, five archbishops [etc.]. **1897** *Catholic Dict.* (ed. 5) 50/2 At present the terms 'archbishop' and 'metropolitan' have the same meaning, except that the latter implies the existence of suffragans, whereas there may be archbishops without suffragans, as in the case of Glasgow.

transf. **1686** tr. *Chardin's Coronat. Solyman* 59 A new Sadre, or Mahometan Pontiff, or Metropolitan of the whole Empire.

b. *fig.* (in jocular or sarcastic use).

1630 RANDOLPH *Aristippus* Wks. (1875) 32 The Catholic Bishop of Barbers, the very Metropolitan of Surgeons. **1780** COWPER *Progr. Error* 186 Let Comus rise Archbishop of the land; Let him your rubric and your feasts prescribe, Grand Metropolitan of all the tribe.

2. A chief town or metropolis.

1549 *Compl. Scot.* xiii. 110 The toune of tribie, quhilk is the metropolitane & capital cite of that cuntre. **1585** T. WASHINGTON tr. *Nicholay's Voy.* II. ix. 72 b, Mytilene.. metropolitane of al the townes of Eolea. **1628** GAULE *Pract. Theory* (1629) 104 Christ could haue chosen Rome..; or Athens..; or Jerusalem..; And yet poore Nazareth, and little Bethlehem.. are.. preferred to those renowned Metropolitans. **1692** LUTTRELL *Brief Rel.* (1857) II. 531 Grenoble, the metropolitane of Dauphigny. **1874** SPURGEON *Treas. Dav.* Ps. lxxxvii. 3 The true 'eternal city', the metropolitan, the mother of us all.

†**3.** *fig.* = METROPOLIS 2 b. *Obs.*

a **1619** FOTHERBY *Atheom.* II. ix. § 2 (1622) 296 The prime and Metropolitan of the Mathematicall Sciences. **1704** N. N. tr. *Boccalini's Advts. fr. Parnass.* II. 204 That Naples should be allow'd the Title of Metropolitan of all Cities whatever for breaking of Colts, and Rome for managing of Men.

4. One who lives in a metropolis; one who has metropolitan ideas or manners.

1795 *Jemima* I. 83 You are a Paisley by nature as well as by birth, and incapable of becoming a worthy metropolitan. **1815** J. JEKYLL in *Bentham's Wks.* (1843) X. 486 To so inveterate a metropolitan as myself this is no grievance. **1882** O'DONOVAN *Merv. Oasis* II. liv. 407 The people at Merv considered themselves altogether as metropolitans.

5. A citizen of the mother-city or parent-state of a colony.

1846 GROTE *Greece* II. ii. II. 311 Both metropolitans and colonists styled themselves Hellens, and were recognised as such by each other.

metropolitanate (mɛtrəʊˈpɒlɪtəneɪt). [f. METROPOLITAN + -ATE¹.] The office or see of a metropolitan bishop.

1854 MILMAN *Lat. Chr.* III. 363 That ascending ladder of ecclesiastical honours, the priorate, the abbacy, the bishopric, the metropolitanate. **1895** W. H. HUTTON *Laud* iii. 120 He.. claimed the right to visit the Universities as inherent in the metropolitanate.

metroˈpolitancy. *rare*⁻¹. [f. METROPOLITAN *a.* + -CY.] The position of metropolis.

1889 WESTGARTH *Austral. Progr.* 45 Melbourne.. the.. rival of.. Sydney for the metropolitancy of the Australasian section of our Empire.

metropoliˈtaneously, *adv.* [f. METROPOLITAN + -EOUS + -LY².] In metropolitan fashion.

1852 DICKENS *Let.* 19 Oct., Are you never coming to town any more? Never going to drink port again, metropolitaneously, but always with Fielden?

metropolitanism (mɛtrəˈpɒlɪtənɪz(ə)m). [f. METROPOLITAN + -ISM.] Metropolitan spirit, ideas, or institutions.

1855 R. R. MADDEN *C'tess Blessington* II. 174 In the exuberance of his metropolitanism, he had a sort of reverential feeling even for the stones of London. **1861** J. S. BREWER *Giraldi Cambrensis Op.* (Rolls) I. Pref., The name Giraldus was bandied about from mouth to mouth, as the undoubted successor to the see of St. David's... The golden era of Metropolitanism had dawned on benighted..

Cambria. **1883** *Century Mag.* XXVI. 824 The architectural manifestations of metropolitanism.

metropolitanize (mɛtrəˈpɒlɪtənaɪz), *v.* [f. METROPOLITAN + -IZE.] *trans.* To make metropolitan in position, manners, ideas, etc.

1855 *Fraser's Mag.* LI. 630 Poor little Kirkwall.. seemed a mere village to the metropolitanized apprentice. **1897** *Spectator* 25 Dec. 919 He was himself not sufficiently metropolitanised for these efforts.

metropolitanship (mɛtrəˈpɒlɪtənʃɪp). [f. METROPOLITAN *sb.* + -SHIP.] The office, position, or see of a metropolitan bishop. In first quot. *fig.*

a **1638** MEDE *Wks.* (1672) III. 60 The Apocalyptical Babylon is not Babylon in Chaldæa, but a Counter-type thereof, most like for Universal Ambition and Metropolitanship of Spiritual Fornication. **1640** BASTWICK *Lord Bps.* ii. Biij, What a hot stirre was.. heretofore between the Prelates of Canterbury and Yorke for the universall Metropolitanship over all England? **1838** G. S. FABER *Inquiry* 267 Some further divisions produced another metropolitanship in Slavonia. *a* **1878** MOZLEY *Lect.* xvi. (1883) 261 The metropolitanship stood upon the Letters Patent.

metropolite (mɪˈtrɒpəlaɪt). [ad. late L. *mētropolīta*, a. Gr. μητροπολίτης, f. μητρόπολις METROPOLIS. Cf. F. *métropolite.*]

1. A metropolitan bishop; = METROPOLITAN B. 1.

1578 *Chr. Prayers* Yiij b *marg.*, Archb. & Metropolite. **1591** G. FLETCHER *Russe Commw.* xxi. 82 b, The Metropolite of Mosko. **1679** RYCAUT *Pres. St. Grk. Armen. Ch.* 95 The Patriarch of Constantinople is elected by the Metropolites, or Bishops. **1882–3** SCHAFF *Encycl. Relig. Knowl.* I. 595 With reservation of the right of the Bishop of Caesarea as metropolite.

†**2.** A metropolis. *Obs.*

1591 G. FLETCHER *Russe Commw.* i. 1 b, Nouograd velica was the Metropolite or chiefe cittie. **1635** PAGITT *Christianogr.* 34 These sixe Sees, the chiefe of Provinces and Metropolites.

3. *attrib.* or as *adj.* = METROPOLITAN.

1591 G. FLETCHER *Russe Commw.* iv. 12 b, The whole countrey of Russia is tearmed by some by the name of Moscouia the Metropolite citie.

†**metropolitic**, *a.* *Obs.* [ad. med.L. *mētropolīticus*, f. *mētropolīta* (see METROPOLITE).] = next.

1555 RIDLEY in Coverdale *Lett. Martyrs* (1564) 93 Farewell the cathedrall churche of Caunterburye, the Metropoliticke sea. **1612** SELDEN *Illustr. Drayton's Poly-olb.* xviii. 303 Canterbury [was] then honor'd with the Metropolitique See.

metropolitical (mɛtrəpəˈlɪtɪkəl), *a.* [Formed as prec. + -AL[1].]

1. *Eccl.* Of, pertaining to, or constituting a metropolitan bishop or see; = METROPOLITAN A. 1.

1541 *Act 33 Hen. VIII*, c. 31 The.. diocese.. to be of the prouince of the Archebyshoppe of Caunturburie, and vnder the iurisdiction metropolitical of the same. **1621** BP. MOUNTAGU *Diatribæ* 58 The new made Patriarch of Constantinople, sometime but a Suffragane to the Metropoliticall Sea of Heraclea. **1765** *Act 5 Geo. III*, c. 26 Preamble, The Bishoprick.. [was] united to the Prouince and Metropolitical Iurisdiction of York. **1901** *Standard* 9 Sept. 3/6 Preaching in York minster yesterday, Canon Fleming said: —Speaking to-day in this metropolitical Church [etc.].

fig. **1655** OWEN *Vind. Evang.* Ep. Ded., Affirming, that that Heresy hath fixed its Metropolitical seat here in England.

2. Of, pertaining to, or constituting a metropolis (capital or mother-city); = METROPOLITAN A. 2.

1603 KNOLLES *Hist. Turks* I. (1621) 1 The metropoliticall citie of Riga. **1667** WATERHOUSE *Fire Lond.* 90 The River of Thames.. will I trust in God for ever keep her in her Metropolitical station. **1710** STRYPE *Life Grindal* I. vii. 70 They.. proceeded as far as the Metropolitical City. **1726** AYLIFFE *Parergon* 91 A Metropolis or Metropolitical City is in respect to a Colony, what a Mother is to a Daughter.

metropolitically (mɛtrəpɒˈlɪtɪkəlɪ), *adv.* [f. prec. + -LY[2].]

1. As a metropolitan.

1637 BASTWICK *Litany* I. 13 If Father William of Canterbury think that I am affraid of him, he is metropolitically mistaken. **1644** LAUD in Neal *Hist. Purit.* (1736) III. 205 In all churches, and in all other places where you visit metropolitically. **1834** *Edin. Rev.* LVIII. 479 Visiting metropolitically the body of both universities.

†**2.** As in a mother-state. *Obs.*

1723 H. ROWLANDS *Mona Antiq. Restaurata* 78 That the Druids resided Originally and Metropolitically in the Isle of Mona.

metropolize (mɪˈtrɒpəlaɪz), *v.* [f. METROPOLIS + -IZE.]

1. *trans.* (*nonce-use*) ? To concentrate in one place.

a **1658** CLEVELAND *Obsequies* 79 Wks. (1687) 235 To beg a Neck with Claudius, metropolize all Worth.

2. *intr.* To visit 'the metropolis'. *nonce-use.*

1815 BYRON in J. Paget *Paradoxes & Puzzles* (1874), We mean to metropolise to-morrow, and you will address your next to Piccadilly.

metrorrhagia (miːtrəʊˈreɪdʒɪə). *Path.* Also anglicized **meˈtrorrhagy.** [mod.L., f. Gr. μήτρα womb + -ραγία breaking forth.] Uterine hæmorrhage. Hence **metroˈrrhagic** *a.*

[**1776–84** CULLEN *First Lines Pract. Physic* (1808) II. 1 Which discharges alone, are those properly comprehended under the present title [*sc.* menorrhagia]. The title of *Metrorrhagia* or *hæmorrhagia uteri*, might comprehend a great deal more.] **1856** MAYNE *Expos. Lex.*, *Metrorrhagicus* .. metrorrhagic... *Metrorrhagy.* **1879** *St. George's Hosp. Rept.* IX. 455 Abdominal pain and metrorrhagia. **1889** J. M. DUNCAN *Clin. Lect. Dis. Wom.* x. (ed. 4) 64 For there may be profuse menorrhagia with more irregular and less severe metrorrhagic loss.

metroscope[1] (ˈmiːtrəskəʊp). [ad. F. *métroscope*, f. Gr. μήτρα womb: see -SCOPE.] **a.** An instrument for examining the uterus. **b.** An instrument for listening to the sounds of the heart of the fœtus during gestation.

1855 DUNGLISON *Med. Lex.*, *Metroscope*, an instrument invented by M. Nauche, for listening to the sounds of the heart of the fœtus in utero-gestation, when the sounds.. are imperceptible through the parietes of the abdomen.

Hence **meˈtroscopy**, examination of the womb (Mayne *Expos. Lex.* 1856).

metroscope[2] (ˈmɛtrəskəʊp). [f. Gr. μέτρο-ν measure + -SCOPE.] An instrument for determining dimensions.

Snellen's metroscope, an instrument for ophthalmostatometric research (*Syd. Soc. Lex.* 1890).

1845 in C. Cist *Cincinnati Misc.* 270 A very ingenious instrument, called a Metroscope, which has been lately invented for the purpose of taking the measure of the human head so as to furnish an exact fit of hats. **1876** *Catal. Sci. App. S. Kens.* 38 Metroscope. For the determination of dimensions of distant bodies.

‖**metrostaxis** (miːtrəʊˈstæksɪs). [mod.L., f. Gr. μήτρα womb + στάξις dropping, falling in drops: cf. *epistaxis.*] Uterine hæmorrhage.

1889 J. M. DUNCAN *Clin. Lect. Dis. Wom.* xvii. (ed. 4) 134 Metrostaxis or bloody flow from the womb.

metrostyle (ˈmɛtrəstaɪl). [f. Gr. μέτρον measure + STYLE *sb.*] A device for regulating the speed of a mechanical piano. (Now disused.)

1904 E. NEWLANDSMITH *Temple of Art* 152 A totally wrong rendering of the work.. is obviated in the Pianola by an apparatus called the 'metrostyle'. By means of following with the metrostyle pointer a certain line drawn on the paper music-roll [etc.]. **1907** *World* 16 July 140/2 The Model 'K' is a pianola equipped with the Metrostyle. **1909** H. G. WELLS *Tono-Bungay* I. ii. 76 There was a different grand piano with a painted lid and a metrostyle pianola.

Hence **ˈmetrostyle** *v. trans.* and *intr.*, to regulate the speed of (a mechanical piano roll) by a metrostyle; to employ a metrostyle.

1908 G. KOBBÉ *Pianolist* ii. 31 Grieg—here are a couple of rolls from his 'Peer Gynt' suite metrostyled by himself. **1920** E. NEWMAN *Piano-Player* 147 The roll [of the piano-player] should be metrostyled by some artist who knows the work thoroughly. *Ibid.* 148 Careful metrostyling would no doubt do away with the necessity for most of the time signs.

metrotome (ˈmɛtrətəʊm). [f. Gr. μήτρα womb + -τόμος cutter, τέμνειν to cut.] A cutting instrument used in operating on the womb.

1856 in MAYNE *Expos. Lex.* **1861** *Med. Times* June 573 Front and Profile View of Dr. Coghlan's Probe-pointed Metratome [*sic*].

-metry (repr. Gr. -μετρία action or process of measuring, f. -μέτρης measurer, μέτρον measure), a terminal element of sbs. with the general sense 'action, process, or art of measuring (something specified by the initial element)'. A few of the words with this ending represent actual Greek words, as *geometry*, *stichometry*; many have been formed in modern times on assumed Gr. types, as *aerometry*, *anthropometry*, etc.; in the 19th c. there were many hybrid formations in which the initial element is a Latin or a modern word, as *alkalimetry*, *calorimetry*. Most of the sbs. in -METER have correlative words in *-metry*, denoting specifically the process of measuring by the instrument called '—meter'.

metsc(h)ip, -ship, variants of METESHIP *Obs.*

metstick, variant of METESTICK.

mett: see MEAT, MET, METE.

†**mettadel.** *Obs.* [ad. It. *metadella*, f. *metade*, *metà* half.] In Italy: 'A Measure of Wine, containing one Quart and near half a Pint, two whereof make a flask'.

1731 in BAILEY (ed. 5). **1833** J. BENNETT *Artificer's Compl. Lex.*

mettaill, -al, obs. forms of METAL.

†**mette.** *Obs.* [OE. *ȝemętta*:—OTeut. type **ga-matjon-*, f. **ga-* (synon. with L. *com-*) + **mat-* MEAT *sb.*] A companion at meat.

c **1000** ÆLFRIC *Hom.* (Th.) II. 282 Þa ȝemettan ne moston þæs lambes ban scænan. **1393** LANGL. *P. Pl.* C. XVI. 41 Pacience and ich weren yput to be mettes, And seten by our selue at a syd-table.

mette: see MEET, MET, METE.

mettege, mettel(l, obs. ff. METAGE, METAL.

metter, obs. form of METER *sb.*[1]

‖**metteur en scène** (mɛtœr ɑ̃ sɛn). [Fr., lit. 'one who puts on the stage'.] A producer of a play; a director of a film.

1911 *Proc. Musical Assoc.* Mar. 94 The producer or '*metteur en scène*' of a play draws up a plan of the whole action in every detail. **1921** CONRAD *Let.* 23 Oct. in G. Jean-Aubry *J. Conrad: Life & Lett.* (1927) II. 262 One of our most clever producers (*metteurs en scène*). **1930** *Times Lit. Suppl.* 17 Apr. 333/2 Mr Jacques Arnavon is a great *metteur-en-scène.* **1963** *Movie* Feb. 36/2 To treat *The Barber of Stamford Hill* as a tentative work is to predict that Wrede could become a notable *metteur en scene.* **1968** *Times Lit. Suppl.* 26 Sept. 1079/1 For Clair's *écriture*, as he readily admits, is primarily a matter of words on paper; from then on he is literally a *metteur en scène.* **1968** L. DURRELL *Tunc* iv. 196 But she is being directed and rehearsed by the *metteur-en-scène.* **1974** *Times* 4 Jan. 8/7 Murnau's greatness as *metteur-en-scène* is unimpaired by time.

mettle (ˈmɛt(ə)l), *sb.* (and *a.*) Also 6–7 **mettal(l**, 6–9 **metal.** [Originally the same word as METAL *sb.*, of which *mettle* was a variant spelling used indiscriminately in all senses. The senses explained below are in origin figurative uses of METAL *sb.* and developments of these, but they are so remote from the literal sense that the consciousness of the identity of the word has long been lost. The graphical differentiation is recognized in Kersey's Phillips, 1706, and in all succeeding Dicts., but was not always observed by writers of the 18th and early 19th c.]

1. Quality of disposition or temperament. (See METAL *sb.* 1 f.)

1584 LYLY *Campaspe* IV. i. 41 Swearing commeth of a hot mettal. **1601** SHAKS. *Twel. N.* III. iv. 300, I am one, that had rather go with sir Priest, then sir knight: I care not who knowes so much of my mettle. **1642** ROGERS *Naaman* 19 To try the spirit of men, of what mettle they are made of. **1789** WOLCOT (P. Pindar) *Subj. for Painters* Wks. 1792 III. 104 Showing the mettle of an arrant Quean. **1828** SCOTT *F. M. Perth* iii, Thou ken'st not the mettle that women are made of. **1897** GEN. H. PORTER in *Cent. Mag.* June 206 It showed the mettle of which he was made.

2. Of a horse, and occas. of other animals: Natural vigour and ardour; spirit.

1596 SHAKS. *1 Hen. IV*, IV. iii. 22 Your Vnckle Worcesters Horse came but to day, And now their pride and mettall is asleepe. **1662** J. DAVIES tr. *Olearius' Voy. Ambass.* 323 The taking away of the excess of Metal, which Stone-Horses are guilty of. **1655** WALTON *Angler* i. (1661) 8 Her [a falcon's] mettle makes her careless of danger. **1697** DRYDEN *Virg. Georg.* III. 209 As for the Females,.. Take down their Mettle, keep 'em lean and bare. **1709** POPE *Ess. Crit.* 87 The winged courser, like a generous horse, Shows most true mettle when you check his course. **1867** J. MARTINEAU *Ess.* II. 394 They have.. horses of best descent and mettle.

3. Of persons: Ardent or spirited temperament; spirit, courage.

1581 PETTIE tr. *Guazzo's Civ. Conv.* III. (1586) 149 It dulleth their wittes, and represseth their natural vigour, in such sorte, that there is no mettall left in them. **1596** SHAKS. *1 Hen. IV*, II. iv. 13 A Corinthian, a lad of mettle. *a* **1655** VINES *Lord's Supp.* (1677) 368 When Jacob had seen the sweet vision in Bethel.. it put mettle into him. **1706** PHILLIPS (ed. Kersey), *Mettle*, Vigour, Fire, Life, Sprightliness, Briskness; as *the Mettle of Youth.* **1718** *Free-thinker* No. 103. 346, I like the Lady's Wit and Mettle. **1866** G. MACDONALD *Ann. Q. Neighb.* xxxiv. (1878) 575, I found this only brought out his mettle.

punningly. **1604** DEKKER *Honest Wh.* I. i. Wks. 1873 II. 6 If the Duke had but so much mettle in him, as in a coblers awle. **1614** RALEIGH *Hist. World* V. i. 312 What other worldly help than the golden metall of their Souldiers, had our English Kings against the French?

4. Phrases. †**a.** *to give mettle to*: to encourage. **b.** *to be on* or *upon one's mettle*: to be incited to do one's best. **c.** *to put* or *set* (a person) *on* or *upon his mettle*, *to put to* (occas. *up to*) *his mettle*: to test his powers of endurance or resistance. **d.** † *to put* (a person) *off his mettle*: to daunt his courage. **e.** *to try* (a person's) *mettle* = c.

a. 1689 *Andros Tracts* II. 191 Our Conscience was that which gave metal to our Patience.

b. 1756 MITCHELL in Ellis *Orig. Lett.* Ser. II. IV. 374, I think it hardly possible he can escape, as everybody here are upon their mettle. **1887** *Times* 9 Apr. 5/5 They would have to contend against cavalry, who would be upon their mettle to show their superiority over the cyclists.

c. 1733 *Portland Papers* VI. (Hist. MSS. Comm.) 47 In such a manner as has put the gentlemen pretty much upon their mettle. **1800** WEEMS *Washington* i. (1877) 6 Even the common passions.. will put him up to his mettle, and call forth his best and bravest doings. **1859** LEVER *Dav. Dunn* xiii. 14 It puts us on our mettle, too, to see our old enemies the French taking the work with us. **1895** SNAITH *Mistr. D. Marvin* xlii, His.. sarcasm set me on my mettle. **1900** W. BAIRD *Gen. Wauchope* iii. 44 The soldiers were put to their mettle.

d. *a* **1745** SWIFT *Direct. Serv.* ¶ 2 Wks. 1751 XIV. 3 When you have done a Fault,.. behave yourself as if you were the injured Person; this will immediately put your Master or Lady off their Mettle.

e. 1786 *Har'st Rig* ii. (1794) 5 Let nane tyne heart, nor hand refrain, But try their mettle. **1882** FROUDE in *Longm. Mag.* Dec. 210 Romsdal's Horn.. will try the mettle of the Alpine Club when they have conquered Switzerland.

5. *attrib.* passing into *adj.* Spirited, mettlesome, 'game'. Now *arch.* and *Sc.*
1592 *Nobody & Someb.* A4b, *Arch.* Is not this Lasse a pretty Neat browne Wench? *Sicoph.* She is my liege, and mettell I dare warrant. **1651** FULLER *Abel Rediv.* 487 Where mettle Colts or restie jades are to be broken. **1818** SCOTT *Hrt. Midl.* xxxii, Thou wouldst be a mettle lass enow, an thou wert snog and snod a bit better. **1886** STEVENSON *Kidnapped* xxiii, He is an honest and a mettle gentleman. *Ibid.* xxviii, As he went by upon a mettle horse.

mettle, obs. form of METAL.

†ˈ**mettleable**, *a. Obs. rare*$^{-1}$. In 6 mettelable. [f. METTLE *sb.* + -ABLE.] Mettlesome.
1557–75 *Diurn. Occurr.* (Bannatyne Cl.) 58 The watch of the Ingliss horsemen..brak vpone the said Frenchemen with mettelable audacitie.

mettled (ˈmɛt(ə)ld), *a.* Also 6 mettald, 6–7 metled, 7 metal'd, metteld, 7–8 metall'd. [f. METTLE *sb.* + -ED^2.]
1. Full of mettle; mettlesome. Also in comb. ***high-mettled***, etc. **a.** of horses, etc.
1615 LATHAM *Falconry* (1633) 21 Such great metteld and selfe wilde hawkes. **1638** JUNIUS *Paint. Ancients* 267 He shall wonder that there is such a mettled fervencie in horses, as [etc.]. *a* **1764** R. LLOYD *Poetry Prof.* 22 Fine-bred things of mettled blood, Pick'd from Apollo's royal stud. **1870** EDGAR *Runnymede* xiv, Their mettled palfreys.
b. of persons.
1599 SANDYS *Europæ Spec.* (1632) 35 What great imployment with stirring and mettald spirits. **1668** ETHEREDGE *She wou'd if she cou'd* III. iii, They are mettled girls, I warrant them, Sir Joslin, let 'em be what they will. **1672** EARL ORRERY *Tryphon* Prol., As metled School-boys set to cuff. **1748** RICHARDSON *Clarissa* (1811) V. xii. 152 The sex love us mettled fellows at their hearts.
c. of actions.
1633 B. JONSON *Love's Welcome, Welbeck*, Such a light and metall'd Dance Saw you never yet in France. **1682** T. FLATMAN *Heraclitus Ridens* No. 74 (1713) II. 206 'Twas a mettled Speech, seasonable and successful. **1701** CIBBER *Love Makes Man* v. iii, I find thou hast done a mettled Thing. **1768** *Woman of Honor* II. 54 Not having a heart for such a mettled enterprize.
†**2.** Half-drunk. *Obs. rare*$^{-0}$.
1678 LITTLETON *Eng.-Lat. Dict.*, Mettled or fudled, *madulsa, semiebrius.*
3. With prefixed word: Having a 'mettle' or temperament of a specified kind.
1598 Heauie metled [see HEAVY *a.*^{1} 31]. **1660** H. MORE *Myst. Godl.* II. xii. 55 Where their minds are enraged and heightned by the sound of the Drum and the Trumpet, (which are able to put but an ordinarily-metall'd man out of his wits). **1828** SIR J. S. SEBRIGHT *Hawking* 52 The goshawk is so slack mettled, that it requires the most skilful management to make him fly at all.

mettlesome (ˈmɛt(ə)lsəm), *a.* [f. METTLE + -SOME.] Full of mettle; spirited. **a.** of horses, etc.
1662 J. DAVIES tr. *Mandelslo's Trav.* 29 *marg.*, The Indian Oxen as metalsome as the Horses in Germany. **1749** FIELDING *Tom Jones* IV. xiii, Her horse, whose mettlesome spirit required a better rider. **1852** MRS. STOWE *Uncle Tom's C.* vi. 39 The instant Haley touched the saddle, the mettlesome creature bounded from the earth with a sudden spring.
b. of a person.
1710 PALMER *Proverbs* 229 Imagination..'tis..increas'd by that love men have to themselves, which at once makes 'em blind and mettlesome. **1859** THACKERAY *Virgin.* lxii, A powerful mettlesome young Achilles.
†**c.** Of an organ of the body: Vigorous. *Obs.*
1668 CULPEPPER & COLE *Barthol. Anat.* II. vi. 104 In the Systole the Heart is vigorated and mettlesome, not in the Diastole.
†**d.** of actions. *Obs.*
1681 NEVILE *Plato Rediv.* 267 Some smart mettlesome Debates.
Hence ˈ**mettlesomely** *adv.* (1755 in Johnson), ˈ**mettlesomeness** (1727 in Bailey, vol. II).

‖**mettwurst** (ˈmɛtvuːrst). [G.] A type of smoked German sausage.
1895 *Army & Navy Co-op. Soc. Price List* 104/2 Mettwurst. **1911** [see BLUTWURST]. **1966** W. S. RAMSON *Austral. Eng.* 161 Some unrecorded borrowings from German may be in local use in parts of South Australia. Price noted that..*mettwurst*,..'sausage',..had 'penetrated to the English colonists'. **1971** *Sunday Times* (Colour Suppl.) 27 June 50/1 Mettwurst can be found in the form of a small sausage ('ends') or a horseshoe-shaped 'Westphalian' ring. Very heavily smoked; lightly spiced, no garlic. Mettwurst is eaten cold, sliced, but is also very good poached, sliced fairly thickly and served with boiled potatoes and cabbage.

mettzotinto, obs. form of MEZZOTINTO.

metuloid (ˈmɛtjuːlɔɪd). *Bot.* [f. L. *mētula* a small pyramid (dim. of META *sb.*^{1}) + -OID.] (See quot.)
1900 JACKSON *Gloss. Bot. Terms, Metuloids*, modified cystidia, encrusted with lime, which project from the hymenium of *Peniophora*, giving it a velvety appearance.

metump (line). *N. Amer.* = TUMP-LINE.
1754 in *Coll. New Hampsh. Hist. Soc.* (1824) I. 279 The deponent sold the said Indians two shirts, ..and there was next to their skin tied a number of small metump lines, not such as are usually made for tying packs. **1963** W. S. AVIS et al. *Dict. Canad. Eng., Intermediate Dict.* 561/1 *Metump*, a broad strap or headband that is passed around the forehead and attached to a load carried on the back.

metur, obs. form of METRE.

‖**meturgeman** (mɪˈtɜːrgɪmən). [Late Heb. *meʰthurgeʰmān*, f. Aram. *meʰthurgām*, pa. pple. of *targēm* to interpret. Cognate with TARGUM, DRAGOMAN.] (See quots.)
1865 DIXON *Holy Land* II. 146 The Meturgeman, an interpreter of the Law, whose duty it was to stand near the reader for the day, and translate the sacred verses, one by one, from the Hebrew into the vulgar tongue. **1881** *Ch. Rev.* Apr. 49 Persons were appointed to translate the Hebrew into Chaldee, and explain the sense as the reader proceeded. This was the office of meturgeman, or interpreter, which.. came to be recognized in every synagogue.

metus, obs. pl. form of MEAT.

†**Meˈtusiast**. *Obs. rare*$^{-1}$. [ad. Eccl. Gr. μετουσιαστής, agent-n. f. *μετουσιάζειν to change the substance of, f. μετα- META- + οὐσία substance, essence.] A believer in transubstantiation.
1607 T. ROGERS 39 *Art.* xxviii. (1633) 176 The Metusiastes and Papists..beleeue the substance of Bread and Wine is so changed into the substance of Christ his Body, as nothing remaineth but the reall Body of Christ, besides the accidents of Bread and Wine.

metwand, -yard: see METEWAND, METEYARD.

metyr, obs. form of METRE.

metyrapone (mɛˈtɪ-, mɛˈtaɪərəpəʊn). *Pharm.* [f. 2-*met*hyl-1,2-di(p*yr*id-3-yl)*p*ropan-1-*one*, the chemical name (f. METHYL + DI-^{2} + PYRIDYL + PROPAN(E + -ONE), with insertion of *a*.] A whitish crystalline compound, $C_5H_4N\cdot CO\cdot C(CH_3)_2\cdot C_5H_4N$, which inhibits the synthesis of cortisone and hydrocortisone and is used for testing the function of the anterior pituitary.
1962 *Lancet* 8 Dec. 1199/1 This paper reports the prevention of massive adrenal necrosis due to D.M.B.A. by the concurrent administration of metyrapone. **1970** PASSMORE & ROBSON *Compan. Med. Stud.* II. vi. 14/2 The metyrapone test depends upon the fact that the feedback control mechanism between the adrenal cortex and the hypothalamo-pituitary axis is mediated by the circulating concentration of unbound cortisol. **1973** *Clin. Pharmacol. & Therapeutics* XIV. 455 After 1 year of treatment urinary steroids and their responses to oral metyrapone were unchanged.

metzotin(c)to, obs. forms of MEZZOTINTO.

meu (mjuː). Also 6 mewe, 6- mew. [irregularly ad. L. *mēum*.] = MEUM^2.
1548 TURNER *Names Herbes* (1881) 53 Meum..is called of the Poticaries Meu. *Ibid.*, It may be called in englishe mewe or duche Dyl. **1578** LYTE *Dodoens* III. xv. 337 Mew groweth plenteously in Macedonia and Spayne. **1706** PHILLIPS (ed. Kersey), *Meu* or *Meum*, (Gr.) Mew, Spiknel, wild Dill, an Herb with a Stalk and Leaves like *Anis.* **1828** J. E. SMITH *Eng. Flora* II. 84 Spignel, Meu, or Bald-money. **1866** *Treas. Bot.* 740/2 Mew, *Meum athamanticum.*

‖**meubles** (mœbl), *sb. pl.* [Fr.: see MOBLE *sb.*] Household furniture.
1786 COWPER *Let. to Lady Hesketh* 26 Nov., This house, ..since it has been occupied by us and our *Meubles*, is [etc.]. **1835** H. GREVILLE *Diary* (1883) 78 The apartments of Louis XIV..are filled with many of the old *meubles* originally taken from the old palace.

†ˈ**meubling**, *vbl. sb. Obs.* [f. F. *meubler* to furnish, f. *meuble* (see MOBLE *sb.*).] Furnishing.
1621 JAS. I in Ellis *Orig. Lett.* Ser. I. III. 169 These provisions for her lying in and meubling are lyke to coste tenne thowsande.

meuer, variant of MURE *a. Obs.*

meule, obs. form of MULE.

‖**meum**^{1} (ˈmiːəm). [Latin, neut. of *meus* mine.] 'Mine', 'that which is mine', in the phr. **meum and tuum**: 'mine and thine'; what is one's own and what is another's. A popular phrase to express the rights of property. Also ***meum, tuum***; ***meum or tuum.***
1594 GREENE & LODGE *Looking-gl.* (1598) C iij, *Rasni.* What, wooe my subiects wife that honoureth me? *Radag.* Tut, Kings this *meum, tuum* should not know. **1612** BACON *Ess., Judicature* (Arb.) 458 For many times the thing deduced to Iudgement, may bee *meum et tuum*, when the reason and consequence thereof may trench to point of estate. **1627** ABBOT in Rushw. *Hist. Collect.* (1659) I. 448 You have allowed a strange Book yonder; which if it be true, there is no *Meum* or *Tuum*, no man in England hath any thing of his own. **1681–6** J. SCOTT *Chr. Life* III. (1696) 67 That which is the one's is the other's: their *Meums* and *Tuums* are confounded together. **1772** JOHNSON in *Phil. Trans.* LXIII. 146 They [N. Amer. Indians] are strict observers of *meum* and *tuum.* **1847** RUXTON *Adv. Mexico* 242 Regardless of the laws of *meum* and *tuum.* **1887** MOLONEY *Forestry W. Afr.* 82 The distinction between 'meum' and 'tuum' having been temporarily overlooked.

‖**meum**^{2} (ˈmiːəm). Also anglicized MEU, and in Gr. form MEON. [L., a. Gr. μῆον.] A genus of umbelliferous plants of the N.O. *Selelineæ*, containing only one species, *Meum athamanticum*, usually called spignel.
1548 TURNER *Names Herbes* (1881) 53 Meum called of the grecians Meon and Meion. **1727** BAILEY vol. II, *Meum*, the Herb Mew, wild Dill or Spikenel. **1854** S. THOMSON *Wild Fl.* III. (ed. 4) 296 The root[s] of the gout-weed.., of the meum or spignel,..have..been held in esteem.

‖**meunière** (mønjɛr), *a.* and *adv. Cookery.* [a. F. (*à la*) *meunière*, lit. 'in the manner of a miller's wife'.] Cooked in or served with hot butter (see quots.).
Usu. following the sb. qualified, as ***trout*** (*à la*) ***meunière***, etc.
1846 A. SOYER *Gastronomic Regenerator* 102 Brill à la Meûnière. **1895** G. A. SALA *Thorough Good Cook* 155 Sole à la Meunière. **1903** C. H. SENN *Pract. Gastron.* 74 (Truite) à la Meunière (Trout, Meunière Style).—Braised trout served with burnt butter, breadcrumbs, and chopped parsley. **1958** J. GROSSINGER *Art Jewish Cooking* (1962) 34 Baked stuffed brook trout meunière. **1959** *Good Food Guide* 145 Good filleted haddock meunière. *Ibid.* 161 Rainbow trout meunière. **1974** *Times* 1 June 13/3 We..opted for a well-known Mexican delicacy, *crialladas*... Served meunière, they tasted delicious.

meure, -ely: see MURE *a. Obs.*, MURELY *adv. Obs.*

Meursault (mœrso). [Name of a commune in the department of Côte d'Or, France.] A white wine of Burgundy, produced near Beaune.
1833 C. REDDING *Hist. Mod. Wines* v. 99 Between Volnay and Meursault the vineyard of Santenot is situated; it.. produces a celebrated white wine, called Meursault. **1907** *Yesterday's Shopping* (1969) 97/2 White Burgundy.. Meursault. **1928** E. WAUGH *Decline & Fall* II. vi. 198 He dined at Basso's..off bouillabaisse and Meursault. **1963** *Sunday Times* (Colour Suppl.) 27 Oct. 51/1 Just before serving, poach stuffed trout in fish stock and Meursault. **1967** A. LICHINE *Encycl. Wines* 354/1 Most Meursault is white and the wines are soft, round and feminine in texture, with a bouquet that eludes description, bordering now on the scent of violets, now on the aroma of almonds.

†ˈ**meurte**. *Obs. rare*$^{-1}$. [a. OF. *meurté*, f. *meür* ripe: see MURE *a.* and -TY.] Maturity, finished excellence.
1474 CAXTON *Chesse* III. v. G vj b, In al thyse maner of people ther oughte to be meurte of good maners [etc.].

‖**meurtrière** (mœrtrijɛr). [Fr.; fem. of *meurtrier* murderer, murderous, f. *meurtre* MURDER.] (See quot. 1802.)
1802 C. JAMES *Milit. Dict.*, *Meutriéres*, small loop holes, sufficiently large to admit the barrel of a rifle, gun or musquet, through which soldiers may fire, under cover, against an enemy. They likewise mean the cavities that are made in the walls of a fortified town or place. **1843** THACKERAY *Irish Sk. Bk.* I. xiv. 266 The points of whose weapons may be seen lying upon the ledge of the little narrow *meurtriere* on each side of the gate.

meuse, muse (mjuːs, mjuːz), *sb.* Now *dial.* Forms: 6- **muce, muse,** 8 **mewse,** 8–9 **mews,** 7- **meuse;** also 6 **mows, meuze,** 7 **muise,** 8 **muish,** 9 **muese, meesh.** [a. OF. *muce, musse, mouce*, mod. dial. *muche* hiding-place, hole in a hedge, f. *musser, muchier* to hide (whence MITCH *v.*). Cf. the synonymous MUSET.]
1. An opening or gap in a fence or hedge through which game, *esp.* hares, habitually pass, and through which they run, when hunted, for 'relief'.
1523 SKELTON *Garl. Laurel* 1384 He wrate of a muse [*ed.* **1568** mows] throw a mud wall; How a do cam trippyng in at the rere warde. **1575** TURBERV. *Venerie* 164 She..will all the daye long holde the same wayes..and passe through the same muses untill hir death or escape. **1578** LYTE *Dodoens* v. xlviii. 612 This herbe is founde in this Countrie in the Meuze of Corne feeldes. **1599** HARSNET *Agst. Darell* 140 But the Fox was neare driuen when he took this muce and hee ferreted out of it by verie pregnant depositions. **1623** SCOT *Highw. God* 55 A Hare started before Greyhounds will haue her accustomed way and muse, or die for it. **1754** COWPER *Ep. to R. Lloyd* 52 The virtuoso..The gilded butterfly pursues O'er hedge and ditch, through gaps and mews. **1756** *Gentl. Mag.* XXVI. 180 The most effectual method of destroying hares is by laying snares..in the muishes of hedges, dykes, and other fences. **1805** R. W. DICKSON *Pract. Agric.* II. 1206 A sort of small trap door, to which they are led by a narrow track or meuse. The rabbits, being thus taken [etc.]. **1821** *Blackw. Mag.* VIII. 531 It is doubted whether the stoutest March hare will have sufficient vivacity to carry him to his muese. **1884** *Upton-on-Severn Gloss.* s.v. *Muse*, Them Welshmen [Welsh sheep]'d go through a rabbit run or a har' muce. **1886** BARNES *Dorset Gloss.*, *Meesh*, the run or lair of a hare. **1895** *Athenæum* 2 Mar. 285/3 In a stone-wall country you will not find a hare close to the lee side..because of the concentrated wind which whistles through every 'meuse'.
b. *transf.* and *fig.* A loophole or means of escape; a device for, or way of, getting out of a difficulty.
a **1529** SKELTON *Replyc.* 212 How..ye had.. deuyllysshely deuysed The people to seduce, And chace them thorowe the muse Of your noughty counsell. **1606** WARNER *Alb. Eng.* XVI. cii. (1612) 404 When desprate Ruffins fraught with faults finde readily a Meuse. **1647** N. BACON *Disc. Govt. Eng.* I. lix. (1739) 115 In this Tragedy the Pope observing how the English Bishops had forsaken their Archbishops, espied a muse through which all the game of the Popedom might soon escape. **1655** R. FANSHAWE tr. *Camoens' Lusiad* III. lxxix, Stopt is each Meuse, and guarded in each part. **1858** R. S. SURTEES *Ask Mamma* xxix. 116 The

Major, after trying every meuse, and every twist, and every turn..was at length obliged to whip off.

2. The 'form' of a hare.

[**1597**: see MEAZE.] **1611** SPEED *Hist. Gt. Brit.* VI. vii. (1623) 69 Like to fearfull Hares.. who no sooner shall heare the cry of their pursuit, but their Muise or Fortresse will be left. **1890** *Gloucestersh. Gloss.*, *Mews*, a hare's form.

Hence **meuse** *v. intr.*, to go through a 'meuse'; **meusing** (*meshing*) *vbl. sb.* (also *attrib.*).

1666 *Voy. Emp. China* in *Misc. Cur.* (1708) III. 196 They Locked themselves together so closely, that they left no meshing Place for them to make their Escape by. **1681** *Relig. Clerici* 55 Their [the Romanists'] boldest champions, to avoid the danger of a close pursuit, muce nimbly, and sculk in the subterfuges of this thorny wilderness. **1706** PHILLIPS (ed. Kersey), *Musing*..among Hunters, the passing of a Hare thro' a Hedge. **1827** *Sporting Mag.* XX. 201 *note*, In counties so close as Yorkshire, hounds must occasionally meuse, when smaller hounds have advantage.

meuse, meute, obs. forms of MEWS, MUTE *sb.*

meuve, obs. form of MOVE.

meuwe, meuze, obs. ff. MEW *sb.*[1], MEUSE.

mevalonic (mɛvəˈlɒnɪk), *a. Chem.* [f. ME(THYL + VAL(ERIC *a.* + LACT)ON(E + -IC.] ***mevalonic acid***: 3,5-dihydroxy-3-methylvaleric acid, $C_6H_{12}O_4$, a crystalline compound which is a growth factor for some lactobacilli and is a precursor of cholesterol in animals and of carotenoids in plants.

1957 D. E. WOLF et al. in *Jrnl. Amer. Chem. Soc.* LXXIX. 1486/1 The name 'mevalonic acid' is now being used to designate β,δ-dihydroxy-β-methylvaleric acid. **1962** H. A. KREBS in A. Pirie *Lens Metabolism Rel. Cataract* 351 The reaction sequence is inhibited by cholesterol itself and some of its immediate precursors by stopping an early stage, probably that giving rise to mevalonic acid. **1973** *Plant Physiol.* LI. 110/1 Mevalonic acid-2-^{14}C was readily incorporated into the free, esterified, and glycosidic sterol fractions of tobacco..seedlings.

Hence **me'valonate**, the anion of mevalonic acid.

1959 A. WHITE et al. *Princ. Biochem.* (ed. 2) xix. 488 Mevalonic kinase..catalyzes the formation of phosphomevalonic acid and ADP from mevalonate and ATP. **1971** HUNTER & ROSE in Rose & Harrison *Yeasts* II. vi. 243 Brewer's solubles were shown to contain a compound which could replace acetate in sterol biosynthesis, and this compound was shown to be mevalonate.

meve, obs. form of MEW, MOVE.

mev(e)able, obs. forms of MOVABLE.

‖**mevy**. *Obs. rare*[−1]. [Related in some way to MEW *sb.*[1]] A sea-mew.

1613–16 W. BROWNE *Brit. Past.* II. i. 17 About his sides a thousand Seaguls bred, The Meuy, and the Halcyon.

mevyng(e, obs. forms of MOVING *vbl. sb.*

mew (mjuː), *sb.*[1] Forms: 1 mǽw (méau, méu, méȝ), 5 mewe, 7 meaw(e, 6– mew. [OE. *mǽw* str. masc. corresponds to OS. *mêu* (MDu., MLG. *mêwe* fem., whence mod.Ger. *möwe*; Du. *meeuw* fem.):—OTeut. type **maigwi-z*; related by consonant-ablaut to the synon. **maihwo-z*, whence OHG. *mêh*, ON. *má-r* (pl. *mávar*, *máfar*); the pre-Teut. forms would be *'*moiqo-s*, *moiqi-s*.] A gull, esp. the common gull, *Larus canus*; a sea-mew.

c **725** *Corpus Gloss.* (Hessels) A. 478 *Alcido*, meau. *a* **900** *Gloss.* in Cockayne *Shrine* 29/2 Larum, meu *vel* meȝ. *a* **1000** *Andreas* 371 (Gr.) Se ȝræȝa mæw. *c* **1440** *Promp. Parv.* 346/1 Mowe, byrd, or semewe, *aspergo*. *a* **1490** BOTONER *Itin.* (Nasmith 1778) 147 Aves vocatæ mewys. **1558** PHAER *Æneid* v. M ij b, A pleasant playne of feeld, where often Mewes and birds of seas doth kepe their haunting walke. **1624** CAPT. SMITH *Virginia* VI. 216 Meawes, Gulls,..and many other sorts [of birds]. **1693** DRYDEN *Persius' Sat.* vi. (1726) 292 And on her shatter'd Masts the Mews in Triumph ride. **1814** SCOTT *Ld. of Isles* III. xxvii, And clamour'd shrill the wakening mew. **1867** JEAN INGELOW *Poems, Sea Mews* iv, A rock, Where many mews made twittering sweet.

mew (mjuː), *sb.*[2] Forms: 4–5 muwe, meuwe, 5 mu, mwe, 4–7 mewe, 4–8 mue, (7 miew), 5– mew. [a. F. *mue* fem., vbl. sb. f. *muer* MEW *v.*[1] Cf. the equivalent Pr., Sp., It. *muda*.]

1. A cage for hawks, *esp.* while 'mewing' or moulting.

13.. *Guy Warw.* (Caius) 77 As demure [she was] As girfauk, or fawkon to lure, That oute of muwe were drawe. *c* **1386** CHAUCER *Sqr.'s T.* 635 And by hire beddes heed she made a Mewe [for a hawk]. *c* **1440** *Promp. Parv.* 347/2 Mv, of hawkys, *falconarium*. **1509** BARCLAY *Shyp of Folys* (1874) I. 222 They make of the churche, for theyre hawkes a mewe. **1623** SIR T. STAFFORD in *Lismore Papers* Ser. II. (1888) III. 79 The faulcon your Lordship sent was so brused and ragged..[that I] haue put her into a mieu. **1678** RAY *Willughby's Ornith.* 430 So leave them [*sc.* sparrow-hawks] in the Mew till they are clean mewed. **1783** BURKE *Sp. East-India Bill* Wks. IV. 67 A notorious robber and villain,..kept as a hawk in a mew, to fly upon this nation. **1820** SCOTT *Abbot* iv, He chanced..to descend to the mew in which Sir Halbert Glendinning kept his hawks.

fig. **1628** *Private Mem. Sir K. Digby* (1827) 64, I beseech you give me leave..to please myself awhile with flying abroad before I be put into the mewe. **1635** [GLAPTHORNE] *Lady Mother* IV. i. in Bullen *O. Pl.* II. 175 Were my soule Drawn from this mew of flesh twould quickly streatch Like a swift Falcon her aspiring wings.

b. ***in mew*** (rarely ***in the mew***): in process of moulting; also *fig.* in process of transformation.

1390 GOWER *Conf.* I. 326 As a bridd which were in Mue Withinne a buissh sche kepte hire clos. **1486** [see MEW *v.*[1] 1 a]. **1708** T. WARD *Eng. Ref.* (1716) 1 When Old King Harry youthful grew, As Eagles do, or Hawks in Mew. **1813** JEFFERSON *Writ.* (1830) IV. 202 Our present government was in the mew, passing from Confederation to Union.

2. †**a.** A coop or cage in which animals, *esp.* fowls, were confined for fattening. Also without article in phr. ***in mew***, cooped up. *Obs.* **b.** Now *dial.* a breeding-cage.

c **1386** CHAUCER *Prol.* 349 Ful many a fat partrich hadde he in Muwe. *c* **1440** *Promp. Parv.* 350/1 Mwe, or cowle (*MS. K.* mv), *saginarium*. **1556** WITHALS *Dict.* (1568) 38/2 A coupe or mewe for capons or other birdes to be kepte in, *auiarium*. **1566** ADLINGTON *Apuleius* IX. xli. 96 She thrust him into a mew made with twigges [L. *viminea cauea*]. **1601** HOLLAND *Pliny* I. 297 A Barton and Mue to keepe foule. **1749** FIELDING *Tom Jones* IV. iv, I must take care of my partridge mew. **1861, 1892** [see *Eng. Dial. Dict.*].

¶**c.** Misused to render med.L. *muta* MUTE *sb.*

1766 BLACKSTONE *Comm.* II. xxviii. 427 The king, according to the record vouched by sir Edward Coke, is entitled to six things; the bishop's best horse,..his cloak, or gown [etc.]: and, lastly, his *muta canum*, his mew or kennel of hounds.

3. †**a.** phr. ***in mew***: in hiding or confinement, cooped up. *Obs.*

c **1350** *Will. Palerne* 3336 But couwardli as caitifs couren [ȝe] here in meuwe. *c* **1374** CHAUCER *Troylus* I. 381 To hiden his desir in muwe From every wight y-born. *a* **1450** *Knt. de la Tour* (1868) 85 The quene was gretly ashamed, whanne she saye she most be in mue. *c* **1450** LYDG. & BURGH *Secrees* 2063 Keep tonge in mewe. **1471** J. PASTON in *P. Lett.* III. 12, I wold fayne my gray horse wer kept in mewe for gnattys. *c* **1530** LD. BERNERS *Arth. Lyt. Bryt.* (1814) 503 The dolphin said:..it anoyeth me greatly thus long to be closed in mewe! **1594** SPENSER *Amoretti* lxxx, Give leave to me, in pleasant mew To sport my muse and sing my loves sweet praise. **1600** FAIRFAX *Tasso* v. xliii, If my good seruice reape this recompence, To be clapt vp in close and secret mew.

†**b.** A place of confinement. *Obs.*

c **1400** *Rom. Rose* 4778 To escape out of his [Love's] mewe. **1526** SKELTON *Magnyf.* 35 Yet Lyberte hath ben lockyd vp and kept in the mew. **1590** SPENSER *F.Q.* II. v. 27 Captiv'd eternally in yron mewes And darksom dens. **1615** BRATHWAIT *Strappado* (1878) 120 Her husband..kept her in a Mew. **1622** J. REYNOLDS *God's Revenge* II. vii. 94 Vnaccustomed to bee pent up in so strait and darke a mew.

c. A secret place, a place of concealment or retirement; a den. Sometimes without article in †*to mew*. Now *rare*.

c **1430** LYDG. *Min. Poems* (Percy Soc.) 251 Skore that place [*sc.* the soul] from al goostly felthe..Thyn Hooly Goost close in that litil mwe. **1436** *Libel Eng. Policy* in *Pol. Poems* (Rolls) II. 170 Oure enmyse..flede to mewe, they durste no more appere. **1601** WEEVER *Mirr. Mart.* F ij, Some watchfull Poets secret mew. **1625** W. PEMBLE *Justification* (1629) 83 An Anchorites Mue. **1855** BROWNING *Fra Lippo* 47 I've been three weeks shut within my mew, A-painting for the great man, saints and saints. **1898** T. HARDY *Wessex Poems* 109 To shun his view By her hallowed mew I went from the tombs among To the cirque of the Gladiators.

4. *Comb.* †**mew-house** = sense 1.

c **1470** HARDING *Chron.* CLXXXIX. v, Maister of the Mew-house & his haukes fayre.

mew, *sb.*[3]: see MEW *int.*

mew (mjuː), *v.*[1] Forms: 4 muwe, 4–7 mewe, 5 mwe, 6–7 (9) mue, 6– mew. [a. F. *muer* to moult, also to shed horns (OF. also in wider sense, to change) = Pr., Sp., Pg. *mudar*, It. *mutare* to moult, change:—L. *mūtāre* to change, whence MUTABLE, MUTATION.]

1. a. *trans.* Of a hawk: To moult, shed, or change (its feathers); also of other birds. Also in *passive* with the bird as subject. Often in figurative context. Now only *arch.*

c **1380** *Sir Ferumb.* 1738 An .C. of gyrfacouns y asky to y-muwed ouer ȝere. **1486** *Bk. St. Albans* b j, Iff an hawke be in mewe yt same sercell feder shall be the last feder that she will cast, and tyll that be cast, she is neuer mewed. **1606** DRAYTON *Odes, To Cupid* 17 He [Cupid]..in the air hovers; Which when it him deweth, His feathers he meweth. *a* **1613** OVERBURY *A Wife*, etc. (1638) H iv b, Now she has mewed three coats, now shee growes weary [etc.]. *Ibid.*, She mewes her pounces, at all these yeares she flies at fooles and kils too. **1616** SURFL. & MARKH. *Country Farm* 716 For how much the earlier bird she [*sc.* a nightingale] is, by so much will she become the more perfect,..because that comming..to mue her feathers, if she [etc.]. **1639** T. DE GRAY *Compl. Horsem.* 167 Foules..in the summer season mowting and mewing their feathers. *a* **1682** SIR T. BROWNE *Tracts* iv. (1683) 106 Considering..his [the Hoopebird's] latitancy, and mewing this handsome outside in the Winter; they [*i.e.* the old Ægyptians] made it an Emblem [etc.]. **1869** BROWNING *Ring & Bk.* IX. 1233 Proud that his dove which lay among the pots Hath mued those dingy feathers.

¶**b.** Peculiarly used by Milton.

The precise sense intended is difficult to determine: perhaps 'to renew by the process of moulting'; some would render 'exchanging her mighty youth for the still mightier strength of full age'.

1644 MILTON *Areop.* 34 Methinks I see in my mind a noble and puissant Nation rousing herself like a strong man after sleep..: Methinks I see her as an Eagle muing her mighty youth, and kindling her undazl'd eyes at the full midday beam.

†**c.** *transf.* and *fig.* To shed or change (anything comparable to plumage, e.g. hair, clothes); to change (colour). Also in *passive*. *Obs.*

c **1374** CHAUCER *Troylus* II. 1209 (1258) With þat he gan hire humbly to saluwe With dredful chere and ofte his heweis muwe. **1614** TOMKIS *Albumazar* III. iv. (1615) F 3, Stand forth transform'd Antonio fully mued From browne soare feathers of dull yeomanry To th' glorious bloome of gentry. **1620** QUARLES *Jonah* (1638) 42 Their nakednesse with sackcloth let them hide And mue the vestments of their silken pride. *c* **1620** FLETCHER & MASS. *Lit. Fr. Lawyer* III. ii, 'Tis true, I was a Lawyer, But I have mewd that coat, I hate a Lawyer. **1633** FORD *Broken H.* II. i, The King has mew'd All his gray beard, in stead of which is budded Another of a pure Carnation colour. *a* **1658** CLEVELAND *Gen. Poems*, etc. (1677) 58 The Sun hath mew'd his Beams from off his Lamp.

causatively. *c* **1620** FLETCHER & MASS. *Double Marriage* III. ii, How he has mew'd your head, has rub'd the snow off, And run your beard into a peak of twenty.

d. *absol.* and *intr.* To moult. †Also *transf.* and *fig.* to change or lose one's covering; to assume a new aspect.

c **1532** DU WES *Introd. Fr.* in *Palsgr.* 950/3 To mue as a hawke, *muer*. **1567** TURBERV. tr. *Spagnuoli's Eclogues* ii. C iij, Euerything doth mewe, And shiftes his rustie winter robe. **1613** FLETCHER, etc. *Hon. Man's Fort.* v. i, One only suit to his backe which now is mewing. **1616** SURFL. & MARKH. *Country Farm* 721 Those [finches] which are taken in the neast, doe mue within a moneth that they are put in [the cage]. **1725** BRADLEY *Fam. Dict.* s.v. *Mewing*, Those.. which mew about the End of July, do it with Success. **1828** SIR J. S. SEBRIGHT *Hawking* 62 Hawks must be fed very high, and kept very quiet when they mew.

†**2.** *trans.* Of a stag: To cast or shed (his horns). Also *to mew his head*. *Obs.*

c **1410** *Master of Game* (MS. Digby 182) ii, þei [harts] mewe [*MS. Douce* meve] þer hornes. *Ibid.*, þenn þei meweþ hir heedes. *Ibid.* (MS. Bodley 546), And whanne þei haue meved [*v.r.* mwed] hure heedes. **1577** [see 2 b]. **1674** N. COX *Gentl. Recreat.* (1677) 65 The time of Harts Mewing, or Casting the Head.

fig. **1700** DRYDEN *Cinyras & Myrrha* 320 Nine times the Moon had mew'd her horns.

b. *intr.*

1577 HARRISON *England* III. iv. (1878) II. 26 It is also much to be maruelled at, that whereas they [deer] do yeerelie mew and cast their horns: yet in fighting they neuer breake off where they doo gripe or mew. **1774** GOLDSM. *Nat. Hist.* (1824) I. 384 When they [deer] cast their heads, they are said to *mew*.

†**3.** In gen. sense: To change, transmute. *Obs.*

15.. *Helyas* in Thoms *Prose Rom.* III. 76 They found but vi. children, to whome they did nothing but tooke away theyr chaines that was about their neckes wherby incontinent thei were mued in white swannes.

mew (mjuː), *v.*[2] Forms: 5–7 mewe, 5–8 mue, 6– mew. [f. MEW *sb.*[2]]

1. *trans.* To put a hawk in a 'mew', or cage, at moulting time; to keep up. ***to mew at large, at the stock*** or ***stone***: see quot. 1611.

a **1533** LD. BERNERS *Huon* lii. 177, I can mew a sparhawke. **1575** TURBERV. *Falconrie* 173 The place wherin you shoulde mew a hawke at the stocke should be a lowe parler or chamber upon the grounde. **1611** MARKHAM *Country Contentm.* I. viii. (1615) 95–6 Mewing at the stone or stocke.. If you mewe at the stocke, you shal haue a broad Table ..on which you must place..a free-stone or blocke of two foote hie, to which you shal fasten your hawke... If you mewe your hawke at large you shall put her loose into the mewe. *c* **1640** J. SMYTH *Lives Berkeleys* (1883) II. 285 Merlins, which sometimes she mewed in her own chamber. **1828** SIR J. S. SEBRIGHT *Hawking* 62 They [hawks] are sometimes kept loose in a room; but it is, in my opinion, much better to mew them on perches or on blocks. *Ibid.* 63 As it is difficult to procure Icelanders and gyrfalcons, these valuable birds are well worth mewing.

†**2.** To coop or shut *up* (poultry, etc.) in a coop for fattening. *Obs. rare.*

c **1430** LYDG. *Min. Poems* (Percy Soc.) 169 Fat Capons up mewed to the fulle. **1522** SKELTON *Why not to Court?* 219 He eateth capons stewed, Fesaunt and partriche mewed. **1639** HORN & ROB. *Gate Lang.* xiv. §147 Poultry shut up [*marg.* Coopt or mued up in a mue].

b. *transf.*

1594 SHAKS. *Rich. III*, I. i. 132 More pitty, that the Eagles should be mew'd, Whiles Kites and Buzards play at liberty.

3. To shut up, confine, enclose; to hide, conceal.

a **1450** *Knt. de la Tour* (1868) 85 Euery woman that disobeyed..her husbonde..shulde be mued alle a year. **1577–87** STANYHURST in Holinshed I. Ded. 8 The little paine I tooke therein was not so secretlie mewed within my closet, but [etc.]. **1590** SPENSER *F.Q.* II. iii. 34 The bush.. In which vaine Braggadocchio was mewd. *a* **1625** FLETCHER *Hum. Lieut.* IV. iv, They keep me mew'd up here as they mew mad folkes. **1634** SIR T. HERBERT *Trav.* 109 [He] mewes himselfe, his Wife, two sonnes and ten thousand men in this..Castle. **1693** DRYDEN *Juvenal* i. 186 Close mew'd in their Sedans, for fear of air. **1719** D'URFEY *Pills* (1872) I. 250 I'm mew'd in a smoky house. **1810** SCOTT *Lady of L.* v. vi, The young King mew'd in Stirling tower, Was stranger to respect and power. **1882** 'OUIDA' *Maremma* I. 72 There, galley-slaves are mewed in a bitter company.

fig. **1817** SHELLEY *Rev. Islam* II. xxxvi, The servitude In which the half of humankind were mewed Victims of lust.

b. ***to mew up***, in the same sense. (Now more usual.)

1581 PETTIE tr. *Guazzo's Civ. Conv.* I. (1586) 8 You cannot goe to visite the sicke..if you remaine alwaies mewed vp. **1617** HALES *Gold. Rem.* I. (1673) 11 Not to suffer your labours to be copst and mued up within the poverty of some pretended method. **1628** PRYNNE *Cens. Cozens* 39 Those Munkes and Nunnes, which..are mued vp in Forraine Cells and Cloisters. **1703** FARQUHAR *Inconstant* II. i, What does the old Fellow mean by mewing me up here with a couple of green girls? **1791–1823** D'ISRAELI *Cur. Lit.* (1858)

I. 8 Heinsius was mewed up in the library of Leyden all the year long. **1821** Scott *Kenilw.* xxix, Amy was no longer mewed up in a distant and solitary retreat. **1880** Mrs. Riddell *Myst. Pal. Gard.* xxvi, I have been kept mewed up, seeing nothing, knowing no one, going nowhere.

refl. **1581** Riche *Farew.* (Shaks. Soc.) 95 What moves thy mynde to mewe thee up so close. **1605** *Hist. Stukeley* E iij, We make them proud by mewing vp our selues In walled towns. **1622** Mabbe tr. *Aleman's Guzman D'Alf.* (1623) 139 [He] mewes himselfe up in a corner and dares not be seene. **1669** Penn *No Cross* I. v. §12 If every Body..should mew himself up within Four Walls. **1695** Congreve *Love for L.* I. i, 'Slife, Sir, what do you mean, to mew your self up hear with Three or Four musty Books? **1736** Ainsworth *Lat. Dict.*, To mew up one's self from the world, *ab hominum consortio secedere.*

†**4.** ? To restrain (speech, the tongue). *Obs.*

c **1530** *Interl. Beauty & Gd. Prop. Women* A iij b, It is a wonder to se theyre dyssemblyng,..Theyre folyshnes, theyre Ianglyng not mewde. **1594** Lyly *Moth. Bombie* II. i. 113 Mew thy tongue, or weele cut it out.

mew (mjuː), *v.*³ [Echoic: see MEW *int.* Cf. MAW, MIAOUW *vbs.*] *intr.* Of a cat (*occas.* of other animals): To utter the sound represented by 'mew'. Also of sea-birds.

c **1325** [see MEWT *v.*]. **14..** *Voc.* in Wr.-Wülcker 571/23 *Catello*, to mewe. **1562** J. Heywood *Prov. & Epigr.* (1867) 100, I neuer herd thy catte once mew. **1605** Shaks. *Macb.* IV. i. 1. **1711** *Acc. Sev. Late Voy.* II. 111 Of the Sea-dogs... Their little or young ones mew like Cats. **1747** Gray *Death Cat* 32 Eight times emerging from the flood She mew'd to ev'ry wat'ry God, Some speedy aid to send. **1843** Marryat *M. Violet* xiii, The cub [of a bear]..hurt itself, and mewed. **1877** L. Morris *Epic Hades* II. 102 The sea birds mewed Around me. **1884** Pae *Eustace* 129 The cat mews very little in the Hector. **1902** R. W. Chambers *Maids of Paradise* ix. 167, I heard the white-winged gulls mewing.

b. *transf.* Of a person: To utter this sound derisively. Cf. MEW *int.* 2.

1606 Dekker *Sev. Deadly Sins* To Rdr. (Arb.) 3 You stand somtimes at a Stationers stal, looking scuruily (like Mules champing vpon Thistles) on the face of a new Booke bee it neuer so worthy: and goe (as il fauouredly) mewing away. **1611** Middleton & Dekker *Roaring Girl* Prol. 6 Each one comes And brings a play in's head with him; vp he summes What he would of a Roaring Girle haue writ; If that he findes not here, he mewes at it.

c. *trans.* To express by mewing.

1900 Aflalo in *Cornh. Mag.* Nov. 628 The gulls were still mewing their plaintive dirge over the fishy harbour.

mew (mjuː), *int.* and *sb.*³ [Echoic: cf. MIAOW.]

1. *int.* Used to represent the cry of a cat. Also *sb.* as a name for this sound.

1596 Shaks. *1 Hen. IV*, III. i. 129, I had rather be a Kitten, and cry mew, Then [etc.]. **1718** Bp. Hutchinson *Witchcraft* 37 Whereupon the Cat whin'd and cried Mew. **1791** Cowper *Retired Cat* 88 A long and melancholy mew,.. Consoled him. **1851** Borrow *Lavengro* xcix, The silent mew of my mother's sandy-red cat.

†**2.** Used as a derisive exclamation. *Obs.*

1606 Day *Ile of Guls* Prol. (1881) 7 The rest thinking it in dislike of the play,..cry 'Mew! by Jesus, vilde!' *Ibid.* IV. iv. 91 Let their desarts be crowned with mewes and hisses. **1607** Dekker & Webster *Northward Ho* I. ii. Dekker's Plays 1873 III. 11 Pox a your gutts, your kidneys; mew: hang yee, rooke. **1633** Ford *Love's Sacr.* I. ii, And how does my owne Julia, mew vpon this sadnesse? What's the matter you are melancholly?

mew, variant of MAUGH.

c **1598** D. Ferguson *Sc. Prov.* (1785) 24 Make na twa mews of ae daughter.

mew: see MEU; obs. f. MOVE *v.*; obs. and dial. pa. t. of MOW *v.*¹; obs. var. MUID.

me-ward(s, orig. *to me ward(s* = towards me: see -WARD and TOWARD, TOWARDS.

1849 Mrs. Carlyle *Lett.* II. 74 The eyes starting out of them me-ward. **1882** Swinburne *Tristr. of Lyonesse*, etc. 87 Alas! to these men only grace, to these, Lord, whom thy love draws Godward, to thy knees—I, can I draw thee me-ward, can I seek, Who love thee not, to love me?

Mewari (mɛˈwɑːrɪ), *sb.* and *a.* [f. *Mewar*, a former native state of India, also known as Udaipur, now part of the state of Rajasthan.]

A. *sb.* The language spoken in Mewar. **B.** *adj.* Of or pertaining to Mewar or its inhabitants.

1888 Kipling *From Sea to Sea* (1899) I. 48 The Thakur ..spoke shrilly in Mewari. The Englishman replied in English-Urdu. *Ibid.* 51 Mewari [Mewarri, 1888 newspaper publ.]..is a heathenish dialect, something like Multani to listen to. **1925** A. Huxley *Let.* 21 Dec. (1969) 262 Bikaner [is]..inhabited..by a community which counts more millionaires to the thousand than any other population in India, perhaps in the world. These are the Mewari merchants, the Jews of India. **1958** [see MEWATI *sb.* and *a.*].

Mewati (mɛˈwɑːtɪ), *sb.* and *a.* Also **Mewatti**. [Native name (see def.).]

A. *sb.* **1.** An Indian people native to Mewat, a region south of Delhi and now part of Rajasthan; a member of this people, *spec.* one professing Islam. Cf. MEO. **2.** The language of this people, a dialect of Rajasthani. **B.** *adj.* Of or pertaining to this people or their language.

1788 J. Rennell *Mem. Map Hindoostan* p. xlix, Of the state of the internal government of Hindoostan, a judgment may be formed, by the punishment inflicted on the Mewatti, or the Banditti tribe, which inhabit the hilly tract, within 25 miles of Delhi. **1824** J. Malcolm *Mem. Cent. India* (ed. 2) II. xiv. 174 The Mewatties, a well-known Mahomedan tribe in Hindustan, have long resorted to Central India. **1832** J. Tod *Ann. Rajast'han* II. 393 Girdhur..with a small but select band hunted the Mewatti leader down, and..slew him in single combat. **1855** H. H. Wilson *Gloss. Judicial & Revenue Terms* 340/2 *Mewáti*,..a tribe of Rajputs inhabiting the province of *Mewat*, now known as *Mucheri*, and formerly notorious for their turbulent and predatory character. **1880** P. W. Powlett *Rajputana Gazetteer* III. 170 These repeated expeditions against the Mewáttis did not render them quiet. *Ibid.* 171 Rewári is referred to as being in the hands of a Mewátti chief. *Ibid.* 174 Humayun ..conciliated them..by causing his minister Bairám Khan to marry a younger daughter of the same Mewátti. **1896** W. Crooke *Tribes & Castes N.-W. Provinces & Oudh* III. 493 Common proverbs..mean that, in dealing with a Mewâti, you had better kick or abuse him before you do business with him. **1901** [see JAIPUR]. **1908** G. A. Grierson *Ling. Survey India* IX. II. 44 Mēwātī is, properly speaking, the language of Mewat, the country of the Mēōs, but it covers a larger tract than this. It is the language of the whole of the State of Alwar, of which only a portion is Mewat. *Ibid.* 45, I am not acquainted with any literary work in the Mēwātī dialect. **1908** *Imperial Gazetteer India* XVII. 313 The Muhammadan Meos call themselves Mewātīs. **1914** H. A. Rose *Gloss. Tribes & Castes Punjab & N.-W. Frontier Province* III. 80 In the Muhammadan historians the Meos appear to be unknown by that name, but the Mewátis were notorious throughout the Muhammadan period. **1957** [see JAIPUR]. **1958** B. N. Prasad in V. K. Narasimhan et al. *Lang. India* 90 The New or Modern Indo-Aryan languages... Rājasthānī (Mārwarī, Mewārī, Mālawi, Jaipuri and Mewatī). **1974** *Encycl. Brit. Micropædia* VIII. 395/1 Rajasthani's 20 dialects are classified into four main groups: the northeastern Mewati [etc.].

mewe, obs. f. MEW, pa. t. MOW *v.*, obs. var. MUID.

mewed (mjuːd), *ppl. a.*¹ [f. MEW *v.*¹ + -ED¹.] Of a bird: That has moulted (once or more).

c **1380** *Sir Ferumb.* 1750 Gyrfacouns y-muwed & white stedes & hertes of gresse y wene. **1486** *Bk. St. Albans* a viij b, And iff she be a mewed hawke. **1621** Sir R. Boyle in *Lismore Papers* (1886) II. 20, I..am to send my mewed goshawk to thearle of Bath. **1674** N. Cox *Gentl. Recreat.* (1677) 233 Mew'd-hawks, are such which have once or more shifted the Feather. **1727-41** Chambers *Cycl.* s.v. *Hawk.*

mewed (mjuːd), *ppl. a.*² [f. MEW *v.*² + -ED¹.] In senses of the vb.: Confined in a mew; shut up, concealed. Also with *up*.

1610 W. Folkingham *Art of Survey* I. x. 29 The dung found in the Bartons of mewed Blacke-birdes. **1638** Rawley tr. *Bacon's Life & Death* (1651) 10 Amongst Mewed Hawkes, some have been found to have lived thirty years. And amongst Wild Hawkes forty years.

†**ˈmewer**¹. *Obs. rare.* [f. MEW *v.*¹ + -ER¹.] See quot. 1688.

c **1450** *Bk. Hawking* in *Rel. Ant.* I. 305 If it [thi hawke] be a mewer put her [in mewe] in the month of January. **1688** R. Holme *Armoury* II. 236/2 A Mewer, or Mewed Hawk..are so called from December to the middle of May.

†**ˈmewer**². *Obs.* [f. MEW *v.*² + -ER¹.] One who mews, shuts *up*, or confines (another).

1626 Purchas *Pilgrims* II. 1270 They were..jealous mewers up of their wives.

†**ˈmewer**³. *Obs.* [f. MEW *v.*³ + -ER¹.] One who mews; a cat. Also, one who catcalls.

1611 Cotgr., *Miauleur*, a mewler, or mewer. **1649** W. M. *Wandering Jew* (1857) 54 Jew, I would have thee know, I am ..a mewer of Playes, a jeerer of Poets [etc.].

mewet, obs. form of MUTE *a.*

mewing (ˈmjuːɪŋ), *vbl. sb.*¹ [f. MEW *v.*¹ + -ING¹.] The action of MEW *v.*¹

1611 Cotgr., *Mue*,..the muing of a Hawke. **1655** Walton *Angler* I. i. (1661) 14 If I should..treat of their several Ayries, their Mewings,..and the renovation of their Feathers. **1797** *Encycl. Brit.* (ed. 3) XI. 633/2 *Mewing*, the falling off or change of hair, feathers, skin, horns, or other parts of animals.

b. *attrib.*, as ***mewing time***.

1651 N. Bacon *Disc. Govt. Eng.* II. vi. (1739) 35 Thus began the Mewing time of Prelacy, and the principal Feather of their wings to fall away. *a* **1653** G. Daniel *Idyll* iv. 27 'Tis but a mewing Time; what matter if Cold Gorges crampe the feet?

mewing (ˈmjuːɪŋ), *vbl. sb.*² [f. MEW *v.*²] The action of shutting up in a mew.

1575 Turberv. *Falconrie* 177 Martins are also woorth the mewyng if they be hardie. **1611** Markham *Country Contentm.* I. viii. (1615) 95 The mewing of long winged hawks.

mewing (ˈmjuːɪŋ), *vbl. sb.*³ [f. MEW *v.*³ + -ING¹.] The act of uttering mews.

1611 Cotgr., *Miaulement*, a mewling, or mewing. **1849** James *Woodman* xviii, Pshaw, I am sick of their mewing. **1881** Mivart *Cat* 226 All forms of mewing, howling, and other vocal manifestations, are modified expiratory actions.

mewing (ˈmjuːɪŋ), *ppl. a.* [f. MEW *v.*³ + -ING².] Uttering mews.

1871 G. Meredith *H. Richmond* xiii, No mewing sanctimoniousness. **1898** *Allbutt's Syst. Med.* V. 944 A piping or mewing sound.

mewl (mjuːl), *sb.* [f. MEWL *v.*] = MEW *sb.*³

1857 Mrs. Marsh *Rose of Ashurst* I. iii. 95 A woman's voice and a baby's mewl were heard.

mewl (mjuːl), *v.* Also 9 **mule**. [Echoic; cf. MIAUL *v.*] *intr.* **a.** To cry feebly, whimper, like an infant; to make a whining noise. Also *trans.* with *out*. **b.** To mew like a cat.

1600 Shaks. *A.Y.L.* II. vii. 144 The Infant, Mewling, and puking in the Nurses armes. **1611** Cotgr., *Miauler*, to mewle, or mew, like a cat. **1818** Hazlitt *Eng. Poets* vi. (1870) 151 Gargantua mewls, and pules, and slabbers his nurse. **1819** Moore *Mem.* (1853) III. 91 It [the music] was squalled and mewled out by Madames Branchia and Albert. **1861** *Crt. Life at Naples* II. 204 He would bid her dry her eyes, and not be puling and muling like a baby. **1882** P. Fitzgerald *Recreat. Lit. Man* II. xvii. 95 [A dog] growling, snarling, and even mewling with rage.

Hence **ˈmewling** *vbl. sb.* and *ppl. a.* Also **ˈmewler**.

1611 Cotgr., *Miaulement*, a mewling, or mewing. *Ibid. Miauleur*, a mewler, or mewer. **1755** Smollett *Quix.* (1803) IV. 67 The mewling of the cats. **1831** Moore *Mem.* (1854) VI. 210 His enharmonics like the mewlings of an expiring cat. **1844** Dickens *Mart. Chuz.* xxviii, You mewling, white-faced cat!

mewle, mewlyter, obs. ff. MULE, MULETEER.

Mewoh, var. MEO.

mewre, obs. form of MURE.

mews (mjuːz). Forms: 4 **muwes**, 4-7 **mewes**, 6 **mewys, mowse**, 7 **mues, muze, muse, mewse**, 8 **meuse**, 7- **mews**. [Plural of MEW *sb.*²; now construed as sing. in the senses below.]

1. The royal stables at Charing Cross in London, so called because built on the site where the royal hawks were formerly mewed. Now *Hist.*

c **1394** J. Malverne *Contn. Higden's Polychron.* an. 1387 (Rolls) IX. 104 Le Muwes apud Charryngg. **1529** Rastell *Pastyme* (1811) 280 At the Mewys, at Charynge Crosse. *a* **1548** Hall *Chron., Hen. VIII* 225 b, The kynges stable at Charyng crosse otherwise called the Mowse. **1667** *Lond. Gaz.* No. 132/4 A Bay brown Horse..taken out of the Muse on Thursday night. **1668** *Ibid.* No. 272/4 There was stoln out of His Majesties Stables at the Mews, a Baye Mare. *a* **1674** Clarendon *Hist. Reb.* XI. §204 The other Officers, with their Troops [quarter] in Durham House, the Mues, Covent Garden [etc.]. **1691** Wood *Ath. Oxon.* II. 711 He was hurried away in a Coach from the Mewse..to the Exchange in Cornhill. **1720** Gay *Trivia* Poems II. 215 His treble voice resounds along the Meuse, And Whitehall echoes—Clean your Honour's shoes. **1765** *Chron.* in *Ann. Reg.* 152/2 Eleven fine barbs arrived at the royal meuse, Charing-cross. **1820** Greville *Mem.* 16 June (1874) I. 30 There was some disturbance last night in consequence of the mob assembling round the King's mews.

2. a. A set of stabling grouped round an open space, yard, or alley, and serving for the accommodation of carriage-horses and carriages.

a **1631** Donne *Sat.* iv. 175 All whom the Mues, Baloune, Tennis, Dyet, or the stewes, Had all the morning held. **1632** Quarles *Div. Fancies* II. l. (1660) 77 The other Steed did stand In Persia's Mues. **1639** T. de Gray *Compl. Horsem.* 26 Others..by sometimes frequenting the muze and other places where riders use to menage. **1785** Trusler *Mod. Times* II. 20, I..made my escape into the Meuse, in which our stables stood. **1852** Dickens *Bleak Ho.* xiv, We went.. into Mr. Turveydrop's great room, which was built into a mews at the back. **1894** G. Moore *Esther Waters* 109 She.. saw the black dot [*sc.* a sparrow] pass down a mews and disappear under the eaves.

b. as *plural*.

1848 Dickens *Dombey* vii, Miss Tox's bedroom (which was at the back) commanded a vista of Mews. **1851** Mayhew *Lond. Labour* II. 207/2 The mews of London.. constitute a world of their own. **1872** Black *Adv. Phaeton* xviii, The large hotels in Liverpool have no mews attached to them.

c. A mews converted into accommodation for people.

1805 *Med. Jrnl.* XIV. 146 Mrs. Cottis, of Great York Mews, Baker Street. **1848** Thackeray *Vanity Fair* xxxiv. 305 Come down with me to Tom Corduroy's, in Castle Street Mews, and I'll show you such a bull-terrier. **1885** *List of Subscribers, Brighton* (South of Eng. Telephone Co.) 4 Nye, Sons & Silverthorne—Regency-mews. **1954** T. S. Eliot *Confid. Clerk* I. 9 And the flat in the mews? How soon will that be ready for him?

3. *attrib.*

1707 E. Chamberlayne *Pres. St. Eng.* III. (ed. 22) 552 Meuse keeper, James Lewis. **1817** W. Bray *Evelyn's Diary* 23 Feb. an. 1684 *note*, In Castle-street, near the Mews gate. **1932** *Times Lit. Suppl.* 10 Nov. 841/1 Elizabeth..lived in the inevitable mews flat. **1958** *Observer* 18 May 16/4 Those saucy, disreputable mews dwellings. **1964** D. Francis *Nerve* ii. 21 The big converted mews garage which served her as sitting-room, bedroom and rehearsal room. **1974** M. Babson *Stalking Lamb* xvii. 127 He intended to make the mews house his operational headquarters.

mews(e, var. ff. MEUSE; obs. form of MUSE *v.*

mewstead, obs. variant of MOWSTEAD *dial.*

mewt (mjuːt), *v. Obs.* exc. *dial.* Forms: 4 **meut**, 5 **mewte**, 8- **mewt**. [Echoic.] = MEW *v.*³

c **1325** *Gloss. W. de Bibbesw.* in Wright *Voc.* 152 *Chat mynowe*, meutet [*MS. Camb. Univ. Gg. I.* I. mewith]. **1483** *Cath. Angl.* 238/2 To Mewte as a catte, *catellare*. **1737** Ramsay *Sc. Prov.* (1797) 86 Wae's them that ha'e the cat's dish, and she ay mewting.

mewys, obs. form of MEWS.

Mex (mɛks), *a.* and *sb.* **a.** *U.S.* Colloq. abbrev. of MEXICAN *a.* and *sb.*

In quot. 1913, 'Mexican money'.

1854 G. D. Brewerton in *Harper's Mag.* Apr. 584/2, I thought it proper to consult with one of the Quartermaster's agents..which resulted in my receiving the information that the 'United States Hotel' upon the 'Plaza' provided 'chicken fixins and corn doins'—or, if a 'stranger' wanted 'Mex livin', *frijoles* and *tortillas* to boot—in better style than any other establishment in Santa Fé. **1906** *McClure's Mag.* June 121/1 'Where'd you get the coat?' I asked the Mex. **1913** *Ibid.* Mar. 119 Is that gold or Mex, dear? **1929** J. Parker *Old Army* 246 He was evidently not one of those who looked with pleasure upon 'Mex' officers. **1934** J. M. Cain *Postman always rings Twice* 97 Ensenada is all Mex. **1970** G. Jackson *Let.* 22 Mar. in *Soledad Brother* (1971) 187 An Italian..killed a Mexican in Folsom because the Mex suddenly started telling everyone not to trust someone. **1974** *Times* 21 Feb. 11/6 John Wayne's *The Alamo* ('better Tex than Mex') is a Goldwater Western.

b. *U.S. Forces' slang.* Foreign currency, esp. that of the Philippine Islands.

1898 *Amer. Soldier* (Manila, Philippine Islands) I. x. 8/1 We will send a set..to any address in America for 25 cents (mex). **1907** *Army & Navy Life* (U.S.) June 679 M stands for money, which is mostly in 'Mex'. **1926** Anderson & Stallings *What Price Glory?* in *Three Amer. Plays* II. 67, I wouldn't take a hundred dollars Mex. for that. **1941** T. Cruse *Apache Days & After* 287 The rent was $100 a month 'Mex', which translated as $50 in gold.

mex, mexen: see MIX *sb.*, MIXEN.

†**'Mexic**, *a. poet. Obs.* = MEXICAN *a.*

a **1678** Marvell *Bermudas* 36 Which, thence (perhaps) rebounding, may Eccho beyond the Mexique Bay. **1806** Fessenden *Orig. Poems* 153 Mexick gulphs of brighter rays.

mexical, variant of MESCAL.

Mexican ('mɛksɪkən), *a.* and *sb.* Also 7 **Mexicaine.** [ad. Sp. *Mexicano* (now written *Mejicano*), f. *Mexico*: see -AN.] **A.** *adj.* **a.** Of or pertaining to Mexico, a tract of country (now a republic) in the south-west of North America.

1696 Phillips, *Mexico*, a great and famous City of the Mexican Province of *Nova Hispania*. *a* **1846** J. H. Frere tr. *Aristoph., Birds* Introd. (1886) 178 War is not immediately declared against the gods, but a sort of Mexican blockade is established by proclamation. **1903** *Blackw. Mag.* Apr. 506/1 The parson lopes by sitting loose in his Mexican saddle.

b. In various names of natural and artificial products, etc.; as ***Mexican blanket, cotton, eagle, flycatcher, saddle, trader, wagon***; **Mexican allspice**, the fruit of *Eugenia Pimenta* (*Syd. Soc. Lex.* 1890); **Mexican banana**, a name sometimes given to a species of *Yucca*; **Mexican bird cherry, bit, blue-jay** (see quots.); **Mexican cloth**, 'a silk and wool French goods' (Knight *Dict. Mech.* Suppl. 1884); **Mexican clover** = next (*Cent. Dict.* 1890); **Mexican coca**, an American herb, *Richardsonia scabra*, yielding a nutritious fodder (Webster 1897); **Mexican embroidery**, a kind of embroidery, the patterns of which resemble the grotesque designs of ancient Mexican carving; **Mexican fruit fly**, a central American insect pest, *Anastrepha ludens*; **Mexican gamboge**, 'a gum-resin like gamboge obtained from *Vismia guttifera* and other species' (*Syd. Soc. Lex.*); **Mexican goose**, the snow-goose (G. Trumbull *Names Birds* 1888, p. 9); **Mexican goosefoot**, 'the *Chenopodium ambrosioides*' (*Syd. Soc. Lex.*); **Mexican gum**, 'the gum-resin obtained from *Chrysophyllum glycyphlœum*' (*ibid.*); **Mexican hairless (dog)**, a small dog of the breed so called, lacking hair except for tufts on the head and tail; **Mexican hog**, the peccary; **Mexican lily**, a plant with scarlet flowers, *Amaryllis reginæ*; **Mexican mulberry** (see quot.); **Mexican onyx**, a stalactitic variety of calcite; **Mexican orange (-blossom, -flower)** = CHOISYA; **Mexican overdrive** *U.S. slang* (see quots.); **Mexican persimmon** (see PERSIMMON 2); **Mexican poppy**, *Argemone mexicana*; **Mexican sarsaparilla** (see quot.); **Mexican shilling**, a silver coin of the value of $12\frac{1}{2}$ cents formerly current in some of the United States (*Cent. Dict.* s.v. *Bit*² 7); **Mexican snake-root** (see quot.); **Mexican tea**, (*a*) = *M. goosefoot*; (*b*) = *Jesuit's tea*, see JESUIT *sb.* 4c; **Mexican thistle**, *Cnicus* (*Erythrolæna*) *conspicuus*; also = *M. poppy*; **Mexican tiger-flower**, *Tigridia pavonia*; **Mexican War**, the war of 1846–8 between the U.S.A. and Mexico in which the allegiance of Texas was the most important issue; **Mexican weasel** = KINKAJOU (*Cent. Dict.*).

1884 Sargent *Forests N. Amer.* (Final Rep. 10th Census IX.) 219 *Yucca baccata* Torrey... Spanish Bayonet. *Mexican Banana. **1836** *Penny Cycl.* VI. 432/2 *Cerasus Capollim*, *Mexican bird cherry. **1884** Knight *Dict. Mech.* Suppl., **Mexican Bit*, a stiff cheek bit, having a high port, to which is attached a large ring, which, when the bit is in the horse's mouth, encircles the jaw. **1834** A. Pike *Prose Sk. & Poems* 74 We gave him a red and gaudy *Mexican blanket. **1894** *Harper's Mag.* Jan. 299/1 He had parted with Pedro for forty dollars, a striped Mexican blanket, and a pair of spurs. **187.** *Cassell's Nat. Hist.* IV. 16 The two *Mexican Blue Jays (*Cyanocitta coronata* and *C. diademata*). **1827** *Western Monthly Rev.* I. 82 The kinds of cotton which are chiefly cultivated are Louisiana, green seed, or Tennessee, and recently *Mexican. **1834** R. Baird *View of Valley of Mississippi* xxiv. 304 Cotton is the chief staple. Three kinds are cultivated,—sea island, Mexican, and green seed. **1835** in *Southwestern Hist. Q.* (1925) XXVIII. 190 The most common birds and fowls found [in Texas] are the *Mexican eagle, the hawk, [etc.]. **1836** M. Holley *Texas* v. 100 The Mexican eagle, which is among the smallest of the aquiline tribe. **1882** Caulfeild & Saward *Dict. Needlework*, **Mexican Embroidery*. **1870** *Amer. Naturalist* III. 473 A solitary *Mexican Fly Catcher..gave a specimen of the summer group of migrants. **1924** *Monthly Bull. Calif. Dept. Agric.* XIII. 55 The Federal Horticultural Board placed a quarantine against the *Mexican fruit fly in Mexico. **1947** *Jrnl. Econ. Entomol.* XL. 483/1 Neither four applications of a DDT spray nor three applications of DDT dust gave significant reductions in populations of the Mexican fruit fly, *Anastrepha ludens*. **1972** Swan & Papp *Common Insects N. Amer.* 627 The Mexican Fruit Fly, *Anastrepha ludens*, occurs in Central America, Mexico, and southern Texas, attacks citrus and mangoes chiefly; it is conspicuous—considerably larger than a house fly, brightly colored with attractive wing pattern. **1884** *Health Exhib. Catal.* 90/1 *Mexican Grass Hammocks. **1899** R. B. Lee *Hist. & Descr. Mod. Dogs Gt. Brit. & Ireland* (*Non-Sporting Division*) (new ed.) xix. 410 A peculiar looking object, and one which requires a great stretch of the imagination to call handsome, is the hairless, or, rather, the crested dog... He is mostly known as the *Mexican hairless dog. **1948** C. L. B. Hubbard *Dogs in Brit.* 296 The Mexican Hairless Dog..is recognised by the American Kennel Club and classified as a Toy Dog. **1970** *New Yorker* 28 Feb. 31/1 Larry Wolf..totally bald..plays a Mexican hairless. **1971** F. Hamilton *World Encycl. Dogs* 537 Although not recognized by the British or the American Kennel Clubs, the Xoloizcuintli (pronounced Shollosquintly) or Mexican Hairless Dog, is one of the oldest breeds, now almost extinct. **1821** T. Nuttall *Jrnl. Trav. Arkansa* ix. 216 The *Sus tajassu* or *Mexican hog is not uncommon some distance higher up Red river. **1836** M. Holley *Texas* v. 95 The Pecari or Mexican hog is even yet occasionally met with on the frontiers, in considerable gangs. **1760** J. Lee *Introd. Bot.* App. 317 Lily, *Mexican, *Amaryllis*. **1884** Sargent *Forests N. Amer.* (Final Rep. 10th Census IX.) 128 *Morus microphylla* Buckley... *Mexican Mulberry. **1895** Rider Haggard *Heart of World* xix, Polished blocks of the beautiful stone known as *Mexican Onyx. **1899** G. Jekyll *Wood & Garden* vi. 71 On the southern sides of the same gateway are two large bushes of the *Mexican orange-flower (*Choisya ternata*), loaded with its orange-like blooms. **1951** *Good Housek. Home Encycl.* 115/2 Mexican Orange, a bright-leaved, white-flowering shrub. **1971** H. L. V. Fletcher *Pop. Flowering Shrubs* viii. 176 *Choisya ternata*, an evergreen, is called the Mexican Orange Blossom. It has white scented flowers all spring and summer. It is easy in some gardens but of doubtful hardiness. **1975** *Times* 5 July 10/5 (*caption*) The Mexican orange..and *Senecio laxifolius*..both respond well to hand trimming. **1961** *Amer. Speech* XXXVI. 272 *Mexican overdrive... Coasting down hill with gears disengaged. **1971** M. Tak *Truck Talk* 105 *Mexican overdrive*, the 'gear' a trucker uses when, in going downhill, he throws the transmission out of gear and lets the truck coast down in neutral. **1884** Sargent *Forests N. Amer.* (Final Rep. 10th Census IX.) 105 *Diospyros Texana*, Scheele... Black Persimmon. *Mexican Persimmon. Chapote. **1848** W. H. Emory *Notes Mil. Reconn.* 13 We find in the bottoms *Mexican poppy. **1860** Gray *Man. Bot.* 25 *Argemone Mexicana*, Mexican Prickly Poppy [**1874** (ed. 5) M. Poppy]. **1936** F. Clune *Roaming round Darling* xxi. 211 We crossed a score of creeks in ten miles, fringed by tobacco-bush with privetlike leaves, and Mexican poppy simulating a Scotch thistle. **1965** *Austral. Encycl.* VII. 188/2 Most widespread and troublesome of introductions among the Papaveraceae is the Mexican poppy (*Argemone mexicana* and its variety *ochroleuca*), which was naturalized about Sydney more than a century ago. **1846** in *Calif. Hist. Soc. Q.* (1942) XXI. 203 Many of them [*sc.* Indians] had *Mexican saddles, cartridge boxes, and different parts of the Mexican dress. **1848** *Knickerbocker* XXXI. 328 Their strong, gaunt horses were equipped with rusty Spanish bits, and rude Mexican saddles. **1865** *Atlantic Monthly* Jan. 59/2 A Mexican saddle,—out of which you can scarcely fall. **1910** J. Hart *Vigilante Girl* 345 She galloped on in her high-peaked Mexican saddle. **1866** *Treas. Bot.* 1066/1 *Mexican Sarsaparilla is yielded by *Smilax medica*. **1890** Billings *Nat. Med. Dict.*, *Mexican snakeroot, *Asclepiodora decumbens* Gray; plant used as a specific for snake-bite. **1829** Loudon *Encycl. Plants* 638 *Psoralea glandulosa*, *Mexican tea. **1837** J. Macfadyen *Flora Jamaica* I. 20 *Argemone Mexicana*. *Mexican or Gamboge Thistle. **1906** F. Blersch *Handbk. Agric. S. Afr.* 144 Mexican poppy or yellow poppy, usually called Mexican thistle at the cape. **1829** Loudon *Encycl. Plants* 562 *Tigridia Pavonia*. *Mexican Tiger Flower. **1826** H. G. Rogers in H. C. Dale *Ashley-Smith Explor.* (1918) 208 He is what they term here [*sc.* in the Los Angeles area] a *Mexican trader. **1862** M. D. Colt *Went to Kansas* 30 So here may be seen the hugh *Mexican wagon, stubborn mule, swarthy driver. **1846** *Dollar Newspaper* (Philadelphia) 27 May 3/1 (*heading*) The *Mexican War. **1881** *Harper's Mag.* Jan. 258/2 The Mexican War..the Abolitionists declared..was waged to obtain new territory for the extension of slavery. **1931** E. O'Neill *Mourning becomes Electra* (1932) I. 19 He went to the Mexican War and come out a major.

c. *Comb.*, as **Mexican-American**, of or pertaining to Mexican settlers or their descendants in the U.S.A.; also as *sb.*

1953 *Jrnl. Social Issues* IX. I. 26 Another fortunate situation has been the fact that our Mexican-American membership has been the most insistent and aggressive in the fight against the illegal alien from Mexico, popularly called the wetback. **1964** S. M. Miller in I. L. Horowitz *New Sociol.* 293 This urban poor is composed of many strands:..Puerto Ricans and Mexican-Americans. **1972** *Jrnl. Social Psychol.* LXXXVII. 3 Mexican-Americans comprise one of the largest minority groups in the United States. **1973** D. Barnes *See Woman* (1974) p. i, To the north, Hollywood's own unique night life seethed... In the east, the Mexican-American community slept. **1973** *Black Panther* 21 July 14/1 The Mexican-American workers in the canneries.

B. *sb.*

1. A native or inhabitant of Mexico.

1604 E. G[rimstone] *D'Acosta's Hist. Indies* v. iv. 337 Heere the Mexicaines Idolatry hath bin more pernicious and hurtfull then that of the Inguas. **1776** Mickle tr. *Camoens' Lusiad* Introd. 30 *note*, These authors..have..greatly softened the horrid features of the Mexicans. **1837** W. Irving *Capt. Bonneville* I. 195 The young Mexican saw her struggles and her agony. **1876** Besant & Rice *Gold. Butterfly* Prol. i, The Mexicans rode in silence.

2. = *Mexican dollar*: see DOLLAR 4.

1827 J. F. Cooper *Prairie* I. v. 149 A foal that is worth thirty of the brightest Mexicans that bear the face of the King of Spain. **1836** *Knickerbocker* VIII. 580 The lad could not change the Mexican which I gave him. **1845** J. J. Hooper *Some Adventures Simon Suggs* 76 There's an old friend of mine..that's got three or four hamper baskets-full o' Mexicans. *c* **1890** A. Murdoch *Yoshiwara Episode* iv. 36 Two thousand seven hundred and thirty-six Mexicans!..Only about £450.

3. A variety of sheep.

1878 I. L. Bird *Lady's Life Rocky Mts.* (1879) x. 173 The flocks are made up mostly of pure and graded Mexicans. **1887** *Scribner's Mag.* II. 511/1 The season comes for the shearing of Southdowns or rough-fleeced Mexicans.

Hence **'Mexicanize** *v. trans.*, 'to cause to become like the Mexicans or Mexico, especially in respect to frequent revolutions' (*Funk's Stand. Dict.* 1895); to subject to the influence or domination of Mexicans. *intr.* 'to become like Mexico or the Mexicans' (*ibid.*); hence **'Mexicanized** *ppl. a.* So **,Mexicani'zation.**

1844 J. Gregg *Commerce Prairies* II. 119 To this great ball, however, no Americans were invited, with the exception of a Mexicanized denizen or two. **1872** 'Mark Twain' *Roughing It* 178, I had never seen such wild, free, magnificent horsemanship..as those picturesquely clad Mexicans, Californians, and Mexicanized Americans displayed. **1878** *Detroit Free Press* 2 June 4/1 'Mexicanization'—Taking evidence to see whether election protests were forged, and, if so, who forged them, who connived at the forgery, or were aware of it. **1887** C. F. Thwing *Serm., Foes Chr. Civ.* 8 The Mexicanized Spaniard is here, too proud to work. *Ibid.* 10. **1890** *Congress. Rec.* 5 June 5655/1 Gentlemen, do you know what a single silver standard means in this country? It means Mexicanization. **1900** *19th Ann. Rep. U.S. Bureau Amer. Ethnol. 1897–98* p. xvi, These Indians, now practically Mexicanized. **1904** *Baltimore American* 15 June 6 With the prospective passing of President Diaz, of Mexico, all the world will hope that his country will not revert to that condition which once led to the invention of the word Mexicanized. **1910** *N.Y. Even. Post* 13 Oct. 8 Some object to describing the Roosevelt plan as one to Mexicanize our government. But that is precisely what it is. **1938** *Newsweek* 28 Mar. 20/3 Cárdenas' swift action caught the British and American Governments off guard. Following developments in anxious silence, they feared the 'Mexicanization' campaign might next strike their mining interests. **1941** R. Humphreys *Latin Amer.* 23 To Mexicanize the Indian and to make the Mexican master in his own country. **1963** *Times* 6 July 18/5 After many months of negotiation..one of the major obstacles to the company's Mexicanisation proposals has now been cleared. **1973** *Nature* 13 July 66/3 Mexico recently passed two laws, one to regulate transfer of technology into the country in an attempt to make sure that the imported technology is suited to Mexico's needs, and the other to limit foreign investment, with the long-term goal of Mexicanizing industry.

†**Mexi'conian**, *a. Obs.* [irreg. f. MEXICO + -IAN.] = MEXICAN *a.*

1727 Ramsay *To Critic* 28 In Mexiconian forests fly Thousands [of creatures] that never wing'd our sky.

mey, obs. f. MAY.

meycock, var. MEACOCK *Obs.*

meyde, -en, obs. ff. MEAD, MAIDEN.

meydine, var. MEDINE.

meydles, var. MEEDLESS *a. Obs.*

meyd vyf, obs. f. MIDWIFE.

meyer, obs. f. MAYOR.

Meyerbeerian (maɪə'bɪərɪən), *a.* [f. the name of the German operatic composer Giacomo *Meyerbeer* (1791–1864) + -IAN.] Of, resembling, or characteristic of the style or work of Meyerbeer.

1890 G. B. Shaw *London Music 1888–89* (1937) 359 Mr Goossens seemed to me to be imperfectly in sympathy with the electrical Meyerbeerian atmosphere. **1955** E. Dent in H. van Thal *Fanfare for E. Newman* 103 Balthazar is a typically Meyerbeerian character, and his music is more like Meyerbeer than Donizetti.

Hence **Meyer'beeriad**, something resembling the style or work of Meyerbeer; **Meyer'beerianism** *sb.*; **'Meyerbeerish** *a.*

1947 A. Einstein *Mus. Romantic Era* xvii. 308 Serov..wrote a Biblical drama *Judith* and a grand opera *Rogneda*—both of which might be characterized as merely gaudy Meyerbeeriads. **1955** F. Toye in H. van Thal *Fanfare for E. Newman* 163 *Don Carlos* is permeated with Meyerbeerianism from beginning to end. **1962** *John o' London's* 8 Mar. 233/3 A certain amount of Meyerbeerish trafficking with 'grand opera'.

meyerhofferite (maɪə'hɒfəraɪt). *Min.* [f. the name of Wilhelm *Meyerhoff* (1864–1906), German chemist + -ITE¹.] A colourless to white

hydrated calcium borate that is found chiefly as an alteration product of inyoite.

1914 [see INYOITE]. **1951** C. PALACHE et al. *Dana's Syst. Min.* (ed. 7) II. 357 The meyerhofferite occurs as pseudomorphs after inyoite with a fibrous internal structure, as small transparent colorless crystals on the surface of these pseudomorphs, and as masses of interlaced glassy crystals or fibrous aggregates embedded in clay. **1967** [see INDERBORITE].

meygnall, obs. f. MENIAL.

meygne, meyheme, obs. ff. MAIM *v.*

meyk, obs. f. MEEK *a.*

meyle, obs. f. MEAL.

meyme, -pryse, obs. ff. MAIM *v.*, MAINPRISE *v.*

meyn, obs. f. MAIN, MEAN.

meynal(l, obs. ff. MENIAL.

meynchen(e, -yn, var. ff. MINCHEN *Obs.*

meynd(e, obs. pa. pple. of MENG *v.*

meyne, obs. f. MANY, MEAN, MEINIE, MIEN; var. MAYNE *v. Obs.*

meyneal, obs. f. MENIAL.

meynee, obs. f. MEINIE.

meynel, obs. f. MENIAL.

meynete(y)ne, obs. ff. MAINTAIN.

meyney, obs. f. MANY, MEINIE.

meyneyall, obs. f. MENIAL.

meynge, var. MENG *v.*

meyni(e, meynne, obs. ff. MEINIE.

meynpernour, -prise, -prize, obs. ff. MAINPERNOR, MAINPRISE.

meynt, obs. pa. t. of MENG *v.*

meynteine, etc.: see MAINTAIN, etc.

meynyal, meynye, obs. ff. MENIAL, MEINIE.

meyr(e, obs. ff. MAYOR.

meyre, obs. f. MEAR, MERE[2].

meyser, obs. f. MAZER.

meyt(e, obs. ff. MEAT.

mezail, var. MESAIL.

‖**mézair** (mezɛr). [Fr., f. It. *mezzaria* middle gait.] (See quot. 1960.)

1754 R. BERENGER tr. *Bourgelat's New Syst. Horsemanship* xvii. 115 The Mezair is higher than the Action of *Terre-a-Terre*, and lower than that of *Curvets*; we may therefore conclude, that the *Terre-a-Terre* is the Foundation of the Mezair, as well as of *Curvets*. **1928** *Daily Express* 22 June 11/3 There is the 'piaffe' in which the horses keep time without advancing, and the 'mezair', that sets them mincing forward, balancing on their hind legs. **1956** L. MINS tr. *Seunig's Horsemanship* (1958) iii. 313 The *mézair* is performed by having the horse fall back on its haunches after a gallopade. **1960** A. PODHAJSKY *Spanish Riding School Vienna* 36 The Mézair is a series of Levades following upon each other at short intervals, after each of which the forelegs always touch the ground for an instant, the hind-legs following in a jump and then the Levade is repeated, so that a small increase of space forward occurs.

mezanine, -i, -o, obs. ff. and pl. of MEZZANINE.

mezcal, var. MESCAL.

mezcaline, obs. var. MESCALINE.

‖**meze** (ˈmeɪzeɪ). Also **mese, mezée, mezze, mezzeh.** [Turk. *meze* snack, appetizer.] A type of hors-d'œuvre served esp. with an aperitif in Greece and the Near East. Also *attrib.*

1926 *Manch. Guardian Weekly* 19 Feb. 151/2 It is taken as a habit with the dried fish and *mézés* that accompany a summer beer. **1950** E. DAVID *Bk. Mediterranean Food* 146 Tarama is the name given to the dried eggs of grey mullet pressed and sold out of a barrel—a favourite mézé in Greece and Turkey. **1955** *Times* 16 July 1/5 It is customary, throughout Greece and the Near East, to serve Mezedes with your aperitif. **1957** L. DURRELL *Bitter Lemons* 25 We.. shared a stirrup-cup and a *meze*. **1958** R. LIDDELL *Morea* II. ii. 58 The bit of cheese or the meat ball, brought to me with a slice of tomato by way of *mézé*, when I drank my ouzo. **1966** J. ALDRIDGE *Statesman's Game* ix. 67 He drained his martini and said 'Louise! Bring in that mezée trolley will you?' **1968** J. CLEARY *Season of Doubt* xii. 216 Lucille.. passed around a tray of *mezzeh*, the traditional Lebanese hors-d'oeuvre. **1974** *Times* 16 Feb. 15/2 *Mezes*—a distinctive form of eating throughout the Middle East, where the concept of hors d'oeuvres is Lucullan.

mezeled, obs. f. MEASLED *ppl. a.*

Mezentian (mɪˈzɛnʃən), *a.* [f. *Mezent-ius* + -AN.] Comparable to the cruel action of Mezentius, a mythical Etruscan king, who caused living men to be bound face to face with corpses, and left to die of starvation (Virg. *Æn.* VIII. 485–8). So † **Mezentism**, action resembling that of Mezentius.

1659 FULLER *App. Inj. Innoc.* III. 81 A piece of Mezentism in his joyning of the Dead and Living together. **1837** SYD. SMITH *Let. to Archd. Singleton* Wks. 1859 II. 259/2 That fatal and Mezentian oath which binds the Irish to the English Church. **1874** STUBBS *Const. Hist.* i. I. 6 England.. spared from the curse of the.. Mezentian union with Italy, .. developed its own common law.

mezereon (mɪˈzɪərɪːən). Forms: 5 **mizerion,** 7–8 **mezerion,** 8 **mesereon,** 6– **mezereon.** [a. med.L. *mezereon*, ad. Arab. *māzaryūn* (Avicenna).]

1. The low shrub *Daphne Mezereon* of Europe and Asia, having purplish or rose-coloured flowers and red berries; also called † ***Dutch mezereon***.

1477 NORTON *Ord. Alch.* iii. in Ashm. (1652) 39 Celondine and Mizerion. **1578** LYTE *Dodoens* III. xxxvii. 368 Mezereon, as Auicenne, Mesne, and Serapio do write, is of two sortes. **1597** GERARDE *Herbal* III. lix. 1216 Apothecaries of our countrie name it Mezereon, but we had rather call it *Chemelæa Germanica*: in English Dutch Mezereon. **1626** BACON *Sylva* §577 Mezerions. **1664** EVELYN *Kal. Hort., Mar.* (1679) 13 Dutch Mezereon. **1706** J. GARDINER tr. *Rapin Of Gardens* (1728) 59 Lib'ral of Boughs and Leaves Mezerions bold,.. defy the sharpest Cold. **1789** MRS. PIOZZI *Journ. France* II. 376 Pots of Mazerion [*sic*] in flower at the windows. **1862** CHR. G. ROSSETTI *Goblin Market*, etc. 85 My leafless pink mezereons. **1872** OLIVER *Elem. Bot.* II. 126 The berries of Mezereon.. are poisonous.

2. *Pharm.* The dried bark of the root of the plant described above, used in liniments.

1789 W. BUCHAN *Dom. Med.* (1790) 513 Those who chuse to use the mezereon by itself, may boil an ounce of the fresh bark [etc.]. **1807** *Med. Jrnl.* XVII. 255 Decoctions of elm bark, mesereon, sassafras. **1874** GARROD & BAXTER *Mat. Med.* 346 Mezereon is a powerful local irritant.

3. *attrib.* and *Comb.*, as ***mezereon bark, berry, ointment, root, tree.***

1837 *Penny Cycl.* VIII. 308/2 A decoction of *mezereon bark. **1874** GARROD & BAXTER *Mat. Med.* 346 Mezereon Bark. The dried bark of Daphne Mezereum, or Mezereon; or of Daphne Laureola. **1837** *Penny Cycl.* VIII. 307/2 Linnæus speaks of a person having been killed by a dozen *mezereon berries. **1890** *Syd. Soc. Lex.*, **Mezereon ointment*. **1789** W. BUCHAN *Dom. Med.* (1790) 513 The *mezereon-root is.. found to be a powerful assistant to the sublimate. **1626** BACON *Sylva* §592 A *Mezerion-Tree. **1851** MRS. MARSH *Ravenscliffe* xiii, A few mezereon-trees were putting forth their blossoms.

‖**mezereum** (mɪˈzɪərɪəm). [mod.L., alteration of MEZEREON.] = prec.

a **1819** G. PEARSON in *Pantologia* VII. s.v., The mezereum has not the power of curing the venereal disease in any one stage. *Ibid.*, No mezereum had been taken. **1846** LINDLEY *Veget. Kingd.* 531 Mezereum bark. **1860** GRAY *Man. Bot.* 380 *Thymeleaceæ.* (Mezereum Family.)

mezle, mezlings, obs. ff. MEASLE *v.*, MEASLINGS.

mezquita, -e, var. ff. MESQUITA, MESQUITE.

‖**mezuza(h** (məˈzuːzə). Pl. **mezuzoth** (məˈzuːzəʊθ). [Heb. *mᵉzūzāʰ* door-post (Deut. vi. 9, etc.); in Rabbinic Heb. used as below.] Among the Jews, a piece of parchment inscribed on one side with the texts Deut. vi. 4–9 and xi. 13–21 and on the other with the divine name Shaddai, enclosed in a case which is attached to the door-post of the house, in fulfilment of the injunction in Deut. vi. 9.

The case is a glass tube, or has an opening covered with glass, talc, or horn, through which the name Shaddai is seen. On leaving or entering the house, a pious Jew touches the mezuza with his finger and puts the finger to his lips, repeating the words of Ps. cxxi. 8.

1650 CHILMEAD tr. *Leo of Modena's Rites, Customs* etc. *Jews* I. ii. 6 As often as they go in and out, they make it a part of their devotion to touch this Parchment, and kisse it: and this they call.. *Me-Zuzah*, that is, *The Post.* **1707** OCKLEY tr. *Leo of Modena's Hist. Jews* I. ii. 7 And this they call *Mezuza*. **1732** D'OYLY & COLSON tr. *Calmet's Dict. Bible* II. 194 *Mezuzoth.* **1855** SMEDLEY, etc. *Occult Sci.* 342 The mezuzoth or schedules for door-posts. **1892** ZANGWILL *Childr. Ghetto* II. 3 They don't kiss the Mezuzahs often in that house—the impious crew.

mezz (mɛz). *slang.* [f. the name of *Mezz* Mezzrow (1899–1972), a jazz clarinettist and drug addict.] Marijuana; **'mezzroll**, a marijuana cigarette.

1938 *Amer. Speech* XIII. 188/1 *Mezz*, marijuana. **1946** MEZZROW & WOLFE *Really Blues* (1957) 215 New words came into being.. *mezzroll*, to describe the kind of fat, well-packed and clean cigarette I need to roll. **1960** *Time* 25 Jan. 87/2 In U.S. slang marijuana is called.. mezz. **1972** *Sunday Sun* (Brisbane) 2 July 14/2 Detectives from the CIB Drug Squad in Brisbane are becoming quite familiar now with words like.. mezz, Mary Jane.

‖**mezza** (ˈmɛdzə), *a. Mus.* [Fem. of MEZZO *a.*] In various Italian combinations, as ***mezza-bravura, -manica, orchestra*** (see quots.); also MEZZA VOCE.

1811 BUSBY *Dict. Mus.* (ed. 3), *Mezza Bravura*, an expression used by the Italians to signify an air of moderate passion and execution. **1876** STAINER & BARRETT *Dict. Mus. Terms, Mezza manica*, half shift [in violin-playing]. *Mezza orchestra*, with half the orchestra.

‖**mezzadria** (mɛdzəˈdriːə). Also **mezzeria.** [It.] A system of land tenure in Italy whereby the farmer pays a proportion (orig. half) of the produce to the landowner as rent, the landowner usually supplying the stock, seeds, etc. Also *attrib.*, as ***mezzadria district, system***, etc. So **'mezzadro** (pl. -i), the tenant farmer of this system.

1875 *Encycl. Brit.* I. 415/1 A system.. in certain provinces of Italy.. called mezzeria.. the halving, that is, of the produce of the soil between landowner and landholder. **1909** KING & OKEY *Italy Today* (new ed.) viii. 171 In the *mezzadria* districts there are comparatively few agricultural labourers and therefore less pauperism. *Ibid.*, Occasionally, .. the rent is proportioned to the crop, and thus the system slides imperceptibly into *mezzadria*. **1928** L. B. REGISTER tr. *Calisse's Hist. Italian Law* III. xx. 727 In the years following .. the Germanic invasions land was not as yet capable of returning an adequate compensation for the labor required for cultivation... It was preferable to fix the return as a proportion of the profits,.. sometimes it was a proportion of the harvest, a half for example, as in the 'mezzeria'. **1949** L. OLSCHKI *Genius of Italy* (1950) i. 10 *Mezzadria* imposes hard penalties on the peasant. **1962** *Listener* 30 Aug. 309/2 He has always worked on the share-cropping system known as the *mezzadria*. **1964** *Economist* 4 July 55/2 The *mezzadri* strike, vote communist.., or leave for the cities. **1967** C. SETON-WATSON *Italy from Liberalism to Fascism* viii. 303 The *bracciante* resented the *mezzadro's* reliance upon his own family and his reluctance to employ paid labour. **1970** I. ORIGO *Images & Shadows* ix. 212 Our land was worked on the system which had been almost universal in Tuscany for nearly six centuries, the *mezzadria*,.. the tenant—called *mezzadro*,.. contributed the.. labour. **1973** *Daily Tel.* 23 Jan. 17/3 Mrs Doxat has plans for her vineyards, which are run under the *mezzadria* system, whereby the Italian tenant works them and takes 52 per cent. of the profits, while all capital investment is the owner's responsibility.

‖**mezza-majolica** (ˈmɛdzəməˈjɒlɪkə). [It.: lit. 'half-majolica' (see MEZZO).] Italian decorative pottery of the 15th, 16th, and 17th centuries; less ornamental and elaborate than true majolica.

1868 J. MARRYATT *Pottery & Porcelain* (ed. 3) 25 The outlines of the figures in mezza majolica are traced in black or blue. **1873** FORTNUM *Catal. Maiolica S. Kens. Mus.* 212 Circular Dish. 'Bacile.'.. 'Mezza Majolica.'

mezzani (mɛdˈzɑːnɪ). [It., pl. of *mezzano* middle, medium.] A type of medium-sized macaroni.

1895 'M. RONALD' *Century Cook Bk.* II. vii. 225 The macaroni called 'Mezzani', which is a name designating size, not quality, is the preferable kind for macaroni dishes made with cheese. **1958** *Catal. County Stores, Taunton* June 17 *Naples Macaroni.* Long—Mezzani, Tagliatelle, Linguine. **1964** M. WALDO *Art Spaghetti Cookery* (1965) 9 There are larger types [of pasta] such as *mezzani*, so large that merely one, stuffed with a filling, makes a portion.

mezzanine (ˈmɛzəniːn). Also 8 **mezanine,** (9 **mezzonine**); *Italian* 8 **mezanino,** 8–9 **mezzanino,** *pl.* 8 **mez(z)anini, mezaninis.** [a. F. *mezzanine*, ad. It. *mezzanino*, dim. of *mezzano* middle:—L. *mediānus* MEDIAN.]

1. a. A low story between two higher ones; *esp.* a low story between the ground floor and the story above, occas. between the ground floor and the basement. Cf. ENTRESOL. Also *attrib.* (quasi-adj.), *esp.* in ***mezzanine floor, story.***

1711 [see ENTRESOL]. **1715** LEONI *Palladio's Archit.* (1742) I. 46 The Closets.. have Mezzanino's or half Stories above them. *Ibid.* 59 On the Closets are Mezanini. **1726** —— *Designs* 1/2 The smaller stairs.. ascend to the Mezzanines. **1741** *Corr. betw. C'tess Hartford & C'tess Pomfret* (1805) III. 80 The princess di Forano,.. took us into the mezzanini, where the family live. **1754** POCOCKE *Trav.* (Camden) II. 140 To the saloon and hall there are as mezaninis above the windows. **1837** *Civ. Eng. & Arch. Jrnl.* I. 59/2 The domestic offices are admirably arranged in the basement and mezzanine stories. **1870** *2nd Rep. Dep. Kpr. Irel.* 11 The ground-floor and mezzanine story of this part of the building are arched constructions. **1876** B. CHAMPNEYS in Willis & Clark *Cambridge* (1886) III. 237 A large cupboard for stowage on a mezzanine. *Ibid.*, The stowage room on the mezzanine floor.

b. A platform or flooring laid over a floor to bring its height up to some required level.

1715 LEONI *Palladio's Archit.* (1742) I. 27 If any little Room or Closet should happen to be lower than the rest, what is wanting must be supplied by a Mezanine, or false Floor-Cieling.

c. *Theatr.* A floor beneath the stage, from which the short scenes and traps are worked. Also ***mezzanine floor.***

1859 SALA *Gas-light & D.* ii. 31 Work underneath the stage, on the umbrageous mezzonine floor. **1881** P. FITZGERALD *World Behind Scenes* 46 Below the stage on the mezzanine floor. **1886** *Stage Gossip* 69 The 'mezzanine' is the name of the lower stage—the one immediately below the 'boards' proper—and it is from here that all 'rises', 'sinks' and 'traps' are worked.

d. In a theatre or cinema: see quot. 1961. *U.S.*

1927 SEXTON & BETTS *Amer. Theatres of Today* 3/2 If.. the site is unusually small, or if, due to its location or to the high cost of land, the maximum number of seats are required, balconies and mezzanines are necessitated. *Ibid.* 4/2 Seats lost by reducing the length of the main balcony are obtained in a mezzanine balcony. **1933** *Radio City News* 1 May 1/3 It is now possible for patrons to reserve seats in the first smoking mezzanine for any performance of the week. **1957** *New Yorker* 29 June 22/1, I was in a movie house, fairly plush, in a sort of mezzanine, or balcony. **1961** BOWMAN &

BALL *Theatre Lang.* 219 *Mezzanine*, a seating area just above the orchestra, or the forward part of such an area; the first balcony.

2. A small window, less in height than breadth, occurring in entresols and attics, etc. Also ***mezzanine window***.

1731 BAILEY vol. II, *Mezzanine*, an Entresole, or little window, less in height than breadth, serving to illuminate an Attic, &c. **1837** *Foreign Q. Rev.* XIX. 78 There are mezzanine windows behind the entablature.

‖**mezza voce** ('mɛddza 'votʃe), *adv. Mus.* [It. *mezza* (see MEZZA) + *voce* VOICE.] With but half the voice; not loud, with a medium fullness of sound. Also more correctly ***a mezza voce***. Also as *sb.* and *adj.*

1775 *Ann. Reg.* II. 64/2 Instead of singing her airs as other actresses do, for the most part she only hums them over, a mezza voce. **1792** CHARLOTTE SMITH *Desmond* I. v. 60 Interrupting a tune he had been humming, *a mezza voce*. **1811** in BUSBY *Dict. Mus.* (ed. 3), *Mezza Voce*. **1877** G. B. SHAW *How to become Mus. Critic* (1960) 29 The critics will fall into raptures over his exquisite management of the *mezza voce*. **1927** *Sunday Times* 6 Mar. 7/3 Though he can achieve an extraordinary *mezza voce* at times, his voice is really far too big for a small hall. **1954** C. K. SCOTT *Fund. Singing* iii. 163 This is the principle of *mezza voce* which gives perhaps the most appealing sound that can be made. **1955** *Times* 29 June 3/1 He does not suffer from the common fault of Italian tenors of yelling continuously; his *mezza voce* is pleasing. **1958** *Times* 10 Nov. 14/3 She..impressed upon her excellent accompanist..a similar *mezza voce* treatment. **1973** *Guardian* 12 Mar. 8/3 A clear, *mezza voce* climax.

mezze(h, varr. MEZE.

mezzeria: see MEZZADRIA.

mezzin, obs. form of MUEZZIN.

‖**mezzo** ('mɛdzəʊ), *sb.*[1] Short for MEZZO-SOPRANO, also *attrib.* as ***mezzo voice***.

1832 *Westm. Rev.* XVII. 357 The distinct soprano, mezzo, contr'alto, and tenor voices. **1892** GUNTER *Miss Dividends* (1893) 78 This young lady..has a brilliant mezzo voice.

mezzo ('mɛdzəʊ), *sb.*[2] Short for MEZZOTINT.

1886 *Athenæum* 3 July 18/1 He was offered 240*l.* for a lot of early mezzos... One of these early mezzotints was worth a thousand pounds.

‖**mezzo** ('mɛddzo, 'mɛdzəʊ), *a. Mus.* [It. *mezzo* middle, half:—L. *medius*: see MEDIUM.] In various Italian combinations, as ***mezzo carattere***, ***forte*** (also as *sb.*), ***piano***, ***staccato*** (see quots.); **mezzo tenore** 'a voice of tenor quality and baritone range' (Stainer & Barrett 1876). See also MEZZO-SOPRANO, and the feminine MEZZA.

1811 BUSBY *Dict. Mus.* (ed. 3), *Mezzo Carattere*, an expression applied to airs of a moderate cast in point of execution. *Ibid.* Introd. 30 The Mezzo Forte, or rather loud. *Ibid.*, The Mezzo Piano, or rather soft. *Ibid.*, The Mezzo Staccato..or extremely smooth and distinct. **1878** T. HELMORE *Catech. Mus.* xxxiii. 68 Mezzo-staccato marks. **1955** *Times* 30 May 3/5 It seems a pity not to take advantage of it in place of the unblinking mezzo-forte adopted by Mr. Jones. **1967** *Times* 23 Nov. 8/8 She scarcely ever spoke at less than a shout and needs to find the occasional mezzo forte.

mezzo-brow, *sb.* and *a. colloq.* Now *rare*. [f. It. *mezzo* middle + BROW *sb.*[1]] = *middle-brow* (see MIDDLE *a.* 6).

1925 N. PLAYFAIR *Story Lyric Theatre* i. 6, I am not a 'high-brow', but what I believe is now called in America a 'mezzo-brow', an Uncompromising Mezzo-brow! And if you imagine that to be a 'mezzo-brow' means that one has no positive opinions..I give you the lie. **1925** *Times Lit. Suppl.* 12 Nov. 751/2 (*heading*) A mezzo-brow manager: the story of the Lyric Theatre, Hammersmith. **1935** *Punch* 19 June 734/2 He deplores..the red rash of rural villadom. But, resolutely mezzo-brow, he has a good word for Blackpool beach and the roadside Lido. **1940** [see BOOK *sb.* 14]. **1945** MENCKEN *Amer. Lang.* Suppl. I. 325 The search for a term to designate persons neither *high-brows* nor *low-brows* has led to the suggestion of *mizzen-brow* and *mezzo-brow*..but they have not caught on.

Mezzofanti (mɛdzəʊ'fæntɪ). The name of Giuseppe *Mezzofanti* (1774–1849), an Italian cardinal who was master of more than fifty languages, used to denote a person of exceptional linguistic ability. Hence **mezzo'fantic** *a.*

1872 G. M. HOPKINS *Let.* 3 Dec. (1956) 238 We have a half-English half-Italian young sucking Mezzofanti among us who could have written in seven languages to my knowledge. **1904** A. VAMBÉRY *Story my Struggles* I. i. 88 The high-flown announcements of my mezzofantic perfections remained without the slightest result. **1939** JOYCE *Finnegans Wake* II. 260 Long Livius Lane, mid Mezzofanti Mall. **1972** *Times Lit. Suppl.* 30 June 752/5 Misspellings are legion and mezzofantic in scope.

‖**Mezzogiorno** (meddzo'dʒɔrno). [It.] The southern part of Italy, including Sicily and Sardinia.

1932 JOYCE *Let.* 13 May (1966) III. 245 You seem to be cruising in the mezzogiorno. **1952** P. H. BONNER *SPQR* (1953) vi. 54 The cities of the Mezzogiorno, like Naples and Salerno and Bari. **1960** E. & R. CHEVALLIER *Mezzogiorno* 7 Magic is by no means a thing of the past in the Mezzogiorno. There are still witches in the land, and the people still fear the 'evil eye'. **1963** 'W. HAGGARD' *High Wire* viii. 92 He had ..a loving little wife in Naples, but he hadn't seen her for a year. That was a long time to leave a woman in the mezzogiorno. **1972** A. THORNE *Rome & S. Italy* ii. 45 The houses of the Mezzogiorno have far more in common architecturally with those of Byzantium and the islands of the Aegean. **1973** A. B. MOUNTJOY *Mezzogiorno* i. 10 An abundance of children characterized the villages and towns of the Mezzogiorno.

mezzograph ('mɛdzəʊgrɑːf, -æ-). [f. MEZZO *sb.*[2] + -GRAPH.] A photographic print imitating the effect of mezzotint.

1890 *Pall Mall G.* 1 Sept. 3/3 Meritorious mezzographs after Messrs. Burgess and Normand.

‖**mezzo-rilievo** (ˌmɛddzorili'evo). Pl. -os. Also 7 mezo-, 7–9 -relievo. [It. *mezzo* half + *rilievo* RELIEF *sb.*]

1. Half-relief; relief in which the figures project half their true proportions from the surface on which they are carved.

1598 R. HAYDOCKE tr. *Lomazzo* v. iii. 189 Imbossing halfe rounde called *mezzo relievo*. **1673** RAY *Journ. Low C.* 330 Having three pair of brass doors artificially cast or engraven with curious figures in *mezo relievo*. **1703** MAUNDRELL *Journ. Jerus.* (1810) 49 We saw..figures of men, carv'd in the natural rock, in mezzo relievo. **1820** T. S. HUGHES *Trav. Sicily*, etc. I. vii. 227 A piece of sculpture in mezzo-relievo representing a Jupiter and a Leda. **1860** J. NEWLANDS *Carp. & Joiner's Assist.* Gloss., *Demi-relievo*... It is also called mezzo-rilievo.

2. *concr.* A sculpture or carving in half-relief.

1665–6 EVELYN *Diary* 3 Jan., There are some mezzo-relievos as big as the life. **1821** WHITAKER *Richmondsh.* I. 155 A mezzo relievo by Westmacott, very finely wrought.

Hence †**mezzo-relievo** *v.*

1644 EVELYN *Diary* 27 Feb., In the Court is a Volary, and the statues of Charles IX, Hen. III, IV, and Lewis XIII, on horseback, mezzo-relievod in plaster.

‖**mezzo-soprano** (ˌmɛdzəʊsə'prɑːnəʊ, -ts-), *sb.* and *a. Mus.* [It.: see MEZZO *a.* and SOPRANO.]

a. The part intermediate in compass between the soprano and contralto; **b.** a voice of this pitch or compass; **c.** a person having such a voice.

1753 CHAMBERS *Cycl. Supp.*, *Mezzo Soprano*, in the Italian music, is the high tenor, which has the cleff C on the second line. **1878** T. HELMORE *Catech. Mus.* xliii. 84 The contraltos and mezzo-sopranos may sing the bass an octave higher in the exercises.

d. *attrib.* or *adj.*

1811 BUSBY *Dict. Mus.* (ed. 3), *Mezzo Soprano Cliff*, the name given to the Cliff when placed on the first line of the stave, in order to accommodate the Mezzo Soprano voice. **1885** MISS BRADDON *Wyllard's Weird* I. iii. 94 Hilda had a superb mezzo-soprano voice.

‖**mezzo termine** ('mɛddzo 'termine). *Pl.* -i. [It.: *mezzo* middle, *termine* term.] A middle term, measure, or period.

1768 H. WALPOLE *Let. to G. Montagu* 13 Aug., He only takes the title of *altesse*, an absurd mezzotermine, but acts King exceedingly. **1827** SCOTT *Chron. Canong.* Introd. i, I have all my life hated those treacherous expedients called *mezzo-termini*. **1841** LADY BLESSINGTON *Idler in France* II. iv. 84 Oh, the misery of the *mezzo termini* in the journey of life, when time robs the eyes of their lustre [etc.].

mezzotint ('mɛdzəʊ-, -ts-, 'mɛzəʊtɪnt), *sb.* [Anglicized form of MEZZOTINTO.]

1. = MEZZOTINTO 1. *Obs.* or *arch.*

1738 FRITSCH tr. *Lairesse's Art Paint.* 11 The half Tint which is laid next to the Extremity on the light Side and called Mezzo-tint. **1774** 'J. COLLIER' *Mus. Trav.* 28 Her back-ground; her mezzo-tints; and her clare-obscure were charming. **1880** SHORTHOUSE *J. Inglesant* (1882) II. vii. 162 Born in the dull twilight of the north, and having most of his mature years among the green mezzotints of Germany, he was now transplanted into a land of light and colour.

2. (= MEZZOTINTO 2.) A method of engraving copper or steel plates for printing, in which the surface of the plate is first roughened uniformly, the 'nap' thus produced being afterwards completely or partially scraped away in order to produce the lights and half-lights of the picture, while the untouched parts of the plate give the deepest shadows. Also, a print produced by this process.

The invention has often been ascribed to Prince Rupert, who certainly practised the method, and made it known in England; but it is now established that he learned it from a Hessian colonel, Ludwig von Siegen, of whom an example is extant dated 1642.

1800 J. DALLAWAY *Anecd. Arts Eng.* 474 *note*, There is a mezzotint taken from it by Faber. **1850** W. IRVING *Goldsmith* xxvii. 272 His portrait is to be engraved in mezzotint. **1886** SWINBURNE *Misc.* 86 Aurora Raby is a graceful sketch in sentimental mezzotint.

b. *attrib.*

1753 HOGARTH *Anal. Beauty* xii. 94 Could mezzo-tint prints be wrought as accurately as those with the graver, they would come nearest to nature, as they are done without strokes or lines. **1839** *Penny Cycl.* XV. 169/1 Previous to the mezzotint ground having been laid. **1870** RUSKIN *Lect. Art* v. 129 The arts of etching and mezzotint engraving.

c. *Photogr.* (See quot.)

18.. LEA *Photogr.* 194 (Cent.) Others modify the effects and soften their paper prints by interposing a sheet of glass, of gelatin, of mica, or of tissue paper between the negative and the paper; in this way are made the so-called Mezzotint Prints.

'**mezzotint**, *v.* [f. MEZZOTINT *sb.*] *trans.* To engrave in mezzotint.

1827 *Gentl. Mag.* XCVII. II. 3 Mezzotinting those on the motto. **1829** *Ibid.* XCIX. I. 347 By this discovery the lithographer acquires a very valuable process for mezzotinting. **1881** *Blackw. Mag.* Nov. 601 The picture was ..afterwards mezzotinted very indifferently.

b. *transf.* and *fig.* To represent as if in mezzotint.

1854 LOWELL *Jrnl. Italy* Pr. Wks. 1890 I. 168 The.. passengers..crawled out again,..their vealy faces mezzotinted with soot. **1870** —— *Study Wind.* (1871) 42 How many times I had lingered to study the shadows of the leaves mezzotinted upon the turf.

Hence '**mezzotinted** *ppl. a.*, '**mezzotinting** *vbl. sb.*

1877 'RITA' *Vivienne* VI. ii, The room was furnished with quaint mezzo-tinted cinque-cento furniture. **1884** *Pall Mall G.* 13 Mar. 3/2 For the mezzotinting the authorities have allowed Mr. Seymour Haden to remove the picture.

mezzotinter ('mɛdzəʊ-, -ts-, 'mɛzəʊtɪntə(r)). [f. MEZZOTINT *sb.* + -ER[1].] One who engraves or is skilled in mezzotint.

1763 H. WALPOLE *Catal. Engravers* (1765) 116 Mr. John Smith 1700. The best mezzotinter that has appeared, who united softness with strength, and finishing with freedom. *Ibid.* 130 John Faber junr...was the next mezzotinter in merit to Smith. **1895** *Daily News* 25 Nov. 3/6 Such an etcher or mezzotinter as Mr. Frank Short. **1902** A. WHITMAN (*title*) British Mezzotinters, Valentine Green.

‖**mezzotinto** (meddzo'tinto), *sb.* and *a.* Also 7 **metzo-tincto, mezo tinto, mascy tinter**, 8 **met(t)zotinto, messo-tinto**. [It.: *mezzo* half, *tinto* tint.]

†**1.** In the Italian sense: A half-tint. *Obs.*

1660 *A. Durer Revived* 18 Take a print done in *Metzo-Tincto*. **1739** ELIZ. CARTER tr. *Algarotti on Newton's Theory* (1742) II. 25 Neither Correggio, Titian, nor his rival Rosalba, did ever unite and shade their *Metzo Tintoes* with so much Exactness to form the Oval of a Face. **1787** P. BECKFORD *Let. Italy* (1805) I. 437 The Mosaic of the floor.. was improved and finished by Beccafumi in 1500, who made use of yellow marble as a mezzotinto. **1788** BURKE *Sp. agst. W. Hastings* Wks. XVI. 224 You will see, by this letter, that he [Hastings] kept his accounts in all colours, black, white, and mezzotinto: that he kept them in all languages, in Persian, in Bengallee, [etc.].

2. = MEZZOTINT *sb.* 2.

1661 EVELYN *Diary* 21 Feb., Prince Rupert first shewed me how to grave in Mezzo Tinto. **1665** PEPYS *Diary* 5 Nov., Mr. Evelyn..showed me..the whole secret of mezzo-tinto. **1669** A. BROWNE *Ars Pictoria* 110 The Manner or Way of Mezo Tinto. **1688** R. HOLME *Armoury* III. 156/1 Mascy Tinter..is a New and Late Invention of taking from a Plate any form or shape..by smooty shadows. **1715** HEARNE *Collect.* (O.H.S.) V. 104 The picture that is done in Mezzotinto of him. **1727** SWIFT *Let. to Gay* 23 Nov., Get me likewise Polly's Messo-tinto. **1780** *Newgate Cal.* V. 204 The prisoner..was indicted for causing to be engraved and cut in mezzo-tinto, on a plate of copper, a blank promissory note, containing the word *twenty* in white letters, on a black ground. **1883** S. C. HALL *Retrospect* II. 226 Martin 'scraped' in mezzo-tinto the major part of the many engraved plates he produced.

b. *attrib.* and *Comb.*

1688 G. PARKER & J. STALKER *Treat. Japanning*, etc. (title-p.), The Method of Guilding.., with the Art..of Painting Mezzo-tinto-Prints. **1697** Mezzo-Tinto Graving [see MELANOCHALCOGRAPHER]. **1745** *Daily Advertiser* 1 Oct. 3/3 A Metzotinto Print of that worthy Prelate Dr. Hough, late Bishop of Worcester. **1797** *Encycl. Brit.* (ed. 3) XI. 687/2 Edial..became a mezzotinto painter. **1812** R. H. in *Examiner* 28 Dec. 828/1 Mr. Meyer's ability in mezzotinto scraping..ranks with the most eminent. **1825** C. TURNER in *Phil. Mag.* LXV. 427 The deficiencies..in mezzotinto engraving. **1839** *Penny Cycl.* XV. 169/1 The mezzotinto ground being thus laid. **1845** DARWIN *Voy. Nat.* xv. (1873) 329 The sky..appeared like a mezzotinto engraving.

fig. *a* **1788** N. COTTON *A Fable* 34 Baxter, with apostolic grace, Display'd his mezzotinto face; While here and there some luckier saint Attain'd to dignity of paint.

Hence '**mezzotinto** *v.* = MEZZOTINT *v.*

a **1846** *Gentl. Mag.* cited in Worcester (1846).

mezzotype ('mɛdzəʊtaɪp). *Photogr.* [f. MEZZO *sb.*[2] + -TYPE. Cf. *photo-mezzotype*.] A kind of paper for photographic printing.

1894 *Brit. Jrnl. Photogr.* XLI. 56 With plain salted papers, or at any rate, with mezzotype, the only chemicals used are the necessary chloride of silver and a little acid. *Ibid.* 57 We believe that mezzotype is as perfect a paper of its class as it is possible to make.

Mganda, var. MUGANDA.

‖**mganga** (m'gaŋgə). Also **m'ganga, nganga**. Pl. **mgangas, waganga**. [Swahili *mganga*, pl. *waganga* medicine man.] In Tanzania and other parts of East Africa, the name given to a native doctor or witch-doctor. (In quots. 1864, 'an object used in magic rites, a charm'.)

1864 J. A. GRANT *Walk Across Afr.* p. xvi, M'ganga or Onganga; a general term for a charm, or for a man who divines events. *Ibid.* iii. 39 The only superstitious observance we noticed was in a field at the foot of a tree; a grass model of a hut was erected for the rain-god..and called, as usual, a 'M'ganga'. **1895** H. H. JOHNSTON *River Congo* (ed. 4) xvi. 273 Somebody is suspected of having caused the death by supernatural means, and the horrid old *nganga* or 'medicine man' who holds the inquest..is called upon to detect the guilty person. **1930** *Discovery* Aug. 265/1 The mganga (as the native calls his medicine-man) is the surgeon, physician, neurological expert, herbalist expert, toxicologist, and veterinarian. **1947** *E. Afr. Ann.* 1946–7

55/1 The 'mgangas', or general practitioners..prescribe or apply remedies, and in some cases even set fractures and do simple operations. **1965** J. Listowel *Making of Tanganyika* iv. 35 For thousands of years, the relationship between chiefs and witch doctors, in Swahili called *waganga*, had been a close one. **1971** N. Q. King *Christian & Muslim in Afr.* 67 The *mganga*, wrongly but regularly translated as 'witch-doctor', is a healer and 'putter-together', with knowledge of herbal and spirit powers.

Mgr. *R.C. Ch.* Abbrev. of MONSIGNOR, -NORE. Also **Msgr.**

1853 J. R. Logan in *Jrnl. Indian Archipelago* VII. 53, I have received valuable assistance..from Mgr. Pallegoix, Mgr. Le Fevre and several other learned missionaries. **1858** N. P. S. Wiseman *Let.* in M. F. Roskell *Mem. F. K. Amherst* (1903) v. 217 Mgr Searle joins me in these feelings. **1897** Addis & Arnold *Cath. Dict.* (ed. 5) 425/1 Mgr. Pap-Szilagyi has made a methodical compendium of these documents. **1922** Joyce *Ulysses* 312 The rt rev. Mgr M'Manus. **1959** E. Waugh *Life R. Knox* III. ii. 244 'Father Knox', a name prominent in letters since 1912 gave place to the less familiar 'Mgr Knox'. **1965** W. Mitchell tr. *Huyghe's Relig. Orders Mod. World* p. v, Contents... What do we mean by Religious? Mgr. Gerard Huyghe... The call to holiness in the Church Mgr. Charue.

mhendee, variant of MENDEE.

mho (məʊ). *Electr.* [Proposed by Sir W. Thomson (now Lord Kelvin): reversed spelling of OHM.] The unit of conductivity, being the conductivity of a body whose resistance is one ohm.

1883 Sir W. Thomson *Pop. Lect.* (1889) I. 130 Such an instrument at once gives conductivity, and you want a name (suppose you adopt *mho*) for the unit of conductivity, and call the instrument a *mhometer*..The number of *mhos*, or of *millimhos* will..measure the number of lamps in circuit. **1892** *Gloss. Electr. Terms* 12 in *Lightning* 3 Mar. Supp., *Mho.* The *mho* is the conductivity of a column of mercury of a constant cross section of one square millimetre, and of a length of 106·3 centimetres at the temperature of melting ice. (*Note.*—The conductivity of a conductor is the reciprocal of its resistance.)

So **mhometer** ('mɒmɪtə(r)), an instrument for measuring electrical conductivities.

1883 [see above].

mhorr (mɔː(r)). Also **m'horr, moh(o)r.** [Morocco Arabic.] A West African gazelle named by E. T. Bennett *Gazella mhorr*, having horns annulated with ten or twelve prominent rings.

'The animal is much sought after by the Arabs on account of producing the bezoar stones so highly valued in eastern medicine. These stones are commonly called in Marocco, Baid-el-Mhorr, mhorr's eggs' (*Penny Cycl.* 1834 II. 86).

1831 Trelawny *Adv. Younger Son* III. 39 Presently a mohr of the elk-kind burst cover. **1833** E. T. Bennett in *Trans. Zool. Soc.* (1835) I. 1 The M'horr Antelope. **1834** *Penny Cycl.* II. 85/2 The Mhorr..is four feet two inches long from nose to the origin of the tail. **1852** J. E. Gray *Catal. Mammalia Brit. Mus.* III. 59 *Gazella Sœmmeringii.* The Abyssinian Mohr.

mi (miː), *sb. Mus.* Also 6 **my**, 7, 9 **me.** [Orig. the first syllable of L. *mīra*: see GAMUT.] The name given by Guido to the third note in his hexachords, and since retained in solmization as the third note of the octave; also used (as in Fr. and It.) as a name for the note E natural, the third note in the scale of C major. (In Tonic Sol-fa often written *me.*)

a **1529** Skelton *Bowge Courte* 258 Lerne me to synge, Re, my, fa, sol. **1588** Shaks. *L.L.L.* IV. ii. 102 Old *Mantuan.* Who vnderstandeth thee not, *vt re sol la mi fa.* *c* **1645** Howell *Lett.* (1650) II. 77 The other [a German]..will drink often musically a health to every one of these 6 notes, Ut, Re, Mi, Fa, Sol, La. **1727–41** Chambers *Cycl.* s.v. *Gammut*, We may begin at *ut* in *c*, and pass into the first series at *mi.* **1811** Busby *Dict. Mus.* (ed. 3) s.v. *Scale*, The denomination first given to the arrangement made by Guido, of the six syllables *ut, re, mi, fa, sol, la.*

mi (maɪ), *a.* Colloq. abbrev. of MINOR *a.* 7.

1791 in *Eton School Lists* 1791–1850 (1863) 2 Mr. Douglas *ma.* Mr. Douglas *mi.* **1867** J. A. Symonds *Let.* Mar. (1967) I. 703 Our tutor lists will need to be filled up next term... I claim B mi as my own. **1932** Wodehouse *Louder & Funnier* 12 Faber *mi* got hold of the manuscript and refused to give it up, and Faber *ma*..hit him over the head. **1963** *Times* 5 June 14/3 Frost mi..was only allowed to shake his head.

mi, obs. form of MY.

miacid ('maɪəsɪd). *Palæont.* [f. mod.L. family name *Miacidæ*, f. the generic name *Miacis* (E. D. Cope 1872, in *Proc. Amer. Philos. Soc.* XII. 470): see -ID³.] A small, carnivorous mammal of the family Miacidæ, known from North American fossil remains of the Palæocene and Eocene epochs. Also as *adj.*

1966 R. & D. Morris *Men & Pandas* viii. 191 About thirty million years ago the ancestors of all the modern carnivores appeared on the scene. These were the miacids and they were small creatures rather like present-day civets. **1972** T. A. Vaughan *Mammalogy* xii. 194/2 Miacids were small and perhaps mostly arboreal carnivores. **1973** R. F. Ewer *Carnivores* v. 225 It is impossible to believe that any carnivore could have evolved a dentition of miacid type without some corresponding behavioural adaptations. **1973** *Nature* 14 Dec. 391/1 The earliest carnivora are the miacids *Protictis* and *Ictidopappus.*

† **'miagite.** *Min. Obs.* [f. *Miage* the name of a glacier near Mont Blanc + -ITE.] (See quot.)

1811 Pinkerton *Petralogy* II. 63 *Miagite.* The rock is generally considered as the most beautiful which has yet been discovered..it consists of concentric but irregular circles of white felspar and black siderite, disposed in broad or narrow lines. *Ibid.* 68 It was thought advisable..to term it Miagite, from the place where it was discovered by Saussure.

‖ **miai** ('miai). [Jap., f. *mi* seeing + *ai* mutually.] The first step in a Japanese arranged marriage whereby the prospective partners meet briefly in company with their families to decide if they are mutually acceptable.

1890 B. H. Chamberlain *Things Japanese* 221 The middleman arranges for what is termed the *mi-ai*, literally, the 'mutual seeing'—a meeting at which the lovers (if persons unknown to each other may be so styled) are allowed to see, sometimes even to speak to each other. **1902** L. Hearn *Kottō* x. 90 To arrange for the *miai* ('see-meeting') tomorrow. **1966** P. S. Buck *People of Japan* (1968) v. 62, I have a young friend who was married several months ago, who saw his wife for the first time at the miai seven weeks before the wedding.

mia-mia (maɪmaɪ). Also **miam, miami, mi-mi, mia-mie.** The Western Australian and Victorian native name for: A hut, a rude shelter.

1845 R. Howitt *Australia* 103 There she stood, in a perfect state of nudity, a little way from the road, by her miam. **1852** Mrs. Perry in Goodman *Ch. in Victoria* (1892) 167 One of the mia mias..was as large as an ordinary-sized circular summer-house. **1861** T. McCombie *Austral. Sk.* 15 Many diggers resided under branches of trees made into miamis or wigwams. **1868** Carleton *Austral. Nts.* 2 The mia-mia that the native dark Had formed from sheets of stringy bark. **1870** Tucker *Mute* 85 He yells the war-cry of his tribe around That makes the warriors from their mi-mis bound.

Miana-bug (mɪ'ɑːnəbʌg). [*Miana* the name of a town in Persia + BUG.] A species of tick, *Argas persicus*, whose bite is said to be occasionally fatal.

[**1821** Porter *Trav. Georgia*, etc. I. 265 Mianna..is a poor place, being best known by the ill name of its bugs.] **1862** *Chambers's Encycl.* IV. 100/2 The Miana Bug, or *Argas persicus.*

Miao (mɪ'aʊ), *sb.* and *a.* Also **Meo.** [Native name.] **A.** *sb.* **a.** A member of the Miao, a mountain-dwelling people of China and Indo-China; the Miao people. **b.** The language spoken by the Miao. **B.** *adj.* Of or pertaining to the Miao people or their language.

1917 S. Couling *Encycl. Sinica* 4/2 There have been frequent revolts of the Miao, the last great one being during the T'ai P'ing rebellion. The Miao women wear wonderfully embroidered clothes and short, white kilted skirts. **1937** E. Snow *Red Star over China* v. iii. 195 The Reds had a method. They had already safely passed through the tribal districts of the Miao and the Shan peoples, aborigines of Kweichow and Yunnan, and had won their friendship. **1939** L. H. Gray *Foundations of Lang.* 390 Miao, Yao, Khāmtī, the extinct Āhom, etc. **1948** D. Diringer *Alphabet* 418 Miao spoken on the borders of northern Siam. **1948** R. A. D. Forrest *Chinese Lang.* i. 33 Miao..has indeed close relationship with Chinese; but it is a relationship of influence and not of kinship. **1955** *Times* 9 May 8/4 The Meos, or Miaos as they are more commonly known in China, are more recent emigrants from Kweichow and Yunnan provinces. **1963** *Times* 24 Apr. 10/3 According to Prince Souvanna Phouma, the Pathet Lao has also demanded the withdrawal of trained Meo tribesmen, and it is not clear whether the rightist troops mentioned are Meo, or, for that matter, whether the latter have descended from their hills. **1970** *Daily Tel.* 4 Mar. 16/4 The Meo general and his predominantly Meo hill-tribe force..form the Government's only credible shield against the North Vietnamese. **1972** *Nat. Geographic* Feb. 275 Soon Meo harvesters will scrape off the sticky sap, boil it, and sell the crude narcotic for at least $25 a pound. **1972** *Times* 4 July 16/1 Some of the Meo have succeeded in preserving themselves and their cultural identity by not taking sides in the war. **1974** R. Butler *Buffalo Hook* xii. 105 They're an odd bunch, the Hainanese... The island's aboriginal people are called, of all things, Miao.

Miaotse (mɪ'aʊtsiː). Also **Miao-chia, Meaoutse, Miautsz', Miaotsze,** etc. = prec., sense A.

1836 J. F. Davis *Chinese* I. vii. 287 The Chinese law prohibits all marriages between subjects and foreigners, and even forbids any alliances between the unsubdued mountaineers, called Meaou-tse, in the interior of the empire, and its own people in the neighbouring plains. **1848** S. W. Williams *Middle Kingdom* I. iii. 147 The unsubdued Miautsz'..occupy the north-east portion of the [Western] province, in the mountain fastnesses between it and Kweichau. **1883** *Encycl. Brit.* XVI. 223/2 In figure the Miautse, both men and women, are shorter and darker-complexioned than the Chinese. **1911** *Ibid.* XVIII. 354/2 The emperor K'ien-lung..attacked the Miaotsze, who suffered a crushing defeat, and were compelled to purchase peace by swearing allegiance to their conquerors. **1917** S. Couling *Encycl. Sinica* 4/2 *Miao-chia*,..or *Miaotzu*..is the name given by Chinese to tribes calling themselves Mhong, whose head-quarters are in Kueichou, but who are also found in south Yünnan, Ssŭch'uan and Hunan. **1932** W. L. Graff *Lang.* 421 The Miaotse or Mautzy group, probably related to Tai.

miaow (mɪ'aʊ), *int.* and *sb.* Forms: 7 **miau**, 7–8 **meaw**, 9– **miaw, mieaou, meaow, miauw, miao(u)w, miow, mi-owe, me(e)ow.** [Echoic: the spelling is partly influenced by F. *miaou.* Cf. MEW *int.* and *sb.*³] The cry of a cat. Also, the name of this cry. Often used to imply that the person addressed is a 'cat' (see CAT *sb.*¹ 2 a).

1634 T. Johnson *Parey's Chirurg.* 151 They..cryed with the Cats miau, miau. **1833** *Penny Cycl.* I. 372/2 The word *mew* would be more expressively written *mieaou.* **1840** Marryat *Poor Jack* xxiii, '*Miaw!*' was the reply. They had heard the loud *miaw.* **1862** H. Kingsley in *Macm. Mag.* June 112 'Pussey, pussey!' she [Mrs. O'Neil] began, 'kitty, kitty, kitty! *Miaow, miaow!*' (Mr. Malone had accumulated property in the cats' meat business.) **1866** Miss Braddon *Trail Serpent* IV. v, The feeble miauw of an invalid member of the feline species. **1873** *Young Englishwoman* May 217/2 'Meow!' And an enormous cat came out. **1879** E. Garrett *Ho. by Works* I. 80 He [a cat] rose with a lazy *mi-owe.* **1937** M. Irwin *Stranger Prince* 321 'Congratulations, sweetheart! I did not know you had secured him...' 'Miaow!' **1947** M. Lowry *Under Volcano* vi. 166 Provocative nocturnal meows. **1948** 'E. Crispin' *Love lies Bleeding* xii. 134 'I sometimes wonder if she has any *deep* emotions at all.' 'Miaouw,' said Fen gently. Elspeth grinned. 'All right, I *am* being catty.' **1956** H. G. de Lisser *Cup & Lip* vii. 81 'What you really mean is that but for the help of the coolie..you couldn't have had Miss Ludford over here.' 'Meow, meow,' laughed Arthur. **1962** E. Bradford *Touchstone* xi. 91 'He's always..where the bar is.' She leaned forward. 'Miaouw!' **1965** L. Brain *It's Free Country* xv. 146 'P'raps she just likes men,' said Howard. 'Men with money,' said Susan. 'Miaow!' **1967** 'S. Woods' *And shame Devil* 89 'He probably has some money of his own. Otherwise, why should she have married him?' 'Miaow,' said Antony.

Hence **miaow** *v. intr.*, to make or counterfeit the cry of a cat (cf. MAW, MEW *vbs.*); **mi'aowing** *vbl. sb.*, the crying of a cat; **mi'aowing** *ppl. a.*, calling like a cat. Also **mi'aower.**

1632 Sherwood, To meaw, or meawle (as a cat), *miauler*... A meawing, or meawling, *miaulement*... A meawer, or meawler, *miauleur.* Meawing, or meawling, *miauleux.* **1731** Bailey vol. II, *Meawing*, the crying of a cat. **1825–80** Jamieson, To *Miauve*, to mew as a cat, Buchan. **1894** Baring-Gould *Kitty Alone* III. 167 A stray cat came..and meeowed. **1975** J. Symons *Three Pipe Problem* xvii. 174 It miaowed in faint protest, arched its back.

miargyrite (maɪ'ɑːdʒɪraɪt). *Min.* [ad. G. *miargyrit* (H. Rose 1829), f. Gr. μείων less + ἄργυρ-ος silver + -ITE.] A black sulph-antimonide of silver, which contains a smaller quantity of silver than red silver ore.

1836 T. Thomson *Min. Geol.*, etc. I. 650 The constitution of miargirite must be 11 atoms sesquisulphite of antimony, 6 atoms sesquisulphuret of silver. **1845** *Encycl. Metrop.* VI. 514/1 *Miargyrite*... Occurs in attached crystals. **1872** Raymond *Statist. Mines & Mining* 52 Our ores are chiefly antimonial sulphides, miargyrite, dark red silver ore, and light red silver ore.

miarolitic (miːərəʊ'lɪtɪk), *a. Petrol.* [ad. Ger. *miarolitisch* (H. Rosenbusch *Mikrosk. Physiogr.* (ed. 2, 1887) II. 39), f. It. dial. *miarolo*, name of a kind of granite containing cavities + *-lit* -LITE: see -IC.] Characterized by irregular cavities into which well-formed crystals project; also applied to the cavities themselves.

1895 A. Harker *Petrol.* ii. 31 Vacant spaces are apt to occur, into which project the sharp angles of well-formed crystals. This miarolitic or drusy structure is more or less marked in some granites (e.g. the Mourne Mts in Ireland). **1931** A. Johannsen *Descr. Petrogr. Igneous Rocks* I. iii. 36 Miarolitic cavities are generally irregular and angular in form, and are seldom more than a few inches in diameter. **1970** *Nature* 28 Nov. 850/2 The nepheline gabbro..is a subangular block coated by a thin crust of MnO_2... The texture is ophitic and miarolitic.

‖ **mias** ('maɪəs). *sing.* and *pl.* Also 9 **maias.** [Dayak *maias* (Howell & Baily *Sea-Dyak Dict.* 1900).] The orang-utan, *Simia satyrus.*

1840 J. Brooke *Jrnl.* in Mundy *Narr. in Borneo*, etc. (1848) I. 220 While lazily waiting the report of our Dyaks who were detached in search of the mias, we fell in with a party of Balows. *Ibid.* 221 After our interview with the Balow other mias were discovered. *Ibid.* 226 The mias, both pappan and rembi..have nests or houses in the trees. **1866** C. Brooke *Sarawak* I. 63 The Maias, or Orang-utan,..is very common in some parts [of Sarawak]. **1869** A. R. Wallace *Malay Archip.* I. iv. 62 Just a week after my arrival at the mines, I first saw a Mias.

miascite ('maɪəskaɪt). *Petrology.* Also **miascyte** and (in Dicts.) **miaskite.** [ad. G. *miaszit* (Wuttig 1814), f. *Miask* the name of a town in the Ural Mountains where the mineral was obtained: see -ITE.] (See quot. 1888.)

1854 Dana *Syst. Min.* (ed. 4) II. 246 *Miascite*, a granular slaty rock consisting of orthoclase, mica, and elæolite, with sometimes quartz, albite, and hornblende. **1868** *Ibid.* (ed. 5) II. 359 *Miascyte.* **1888** Teall *Brit. Petrogr.* 359 *Miascite*, term introduced by G. Rose for a rock occurring in the Ilmen Mountains in Russia, essentially composed of orthoclase, elæolite, and dark mica.

miasm ('maɪæz(ə)m). Also 7–8 **miasme.** [a. F. *miasme*: see next.] = MIASMA.

1650 Charleton *Paradoxes* Proleg. B 4, Upon every Solution of Continuity there is impressed an exotick Miasm, or putrefactive acidity. **1669** W. Simpson *Hydrol. Chym.* 71 It carrys of..the very seminal miasmes. **1799** Underwood *Dis. Children* (ed. 4) I. 288 Children born in an air, saturated as it were with the miasm of this disease [*i.e.* smallpox]..have nevertheless escaped the disease. **1822–34** *Good's Study Med.* (ed. 4) II. 423 The miasm of gaol fever. **1876** Bristowe *Theory & Pract. Med.* (1878) 282 The miasm may be carried by the wind and atmospheric currents beyond the limits of the area in which it is produced.

‖**miasma** (maɪˈæzmə). *Pl.* **miasmata** (maɪˈæzmətə), **miasmas**. [mod.L., a. Gr. *μίασμα* pollution, related to *μιαίνειν* to pollute. Cf. F. *miasme*.] Infectious or noxious exhalations from putrescent organic matter; poisonous particles or germs floating in and polluting the atmosphere; noxious emanations, esp. malaria.

1665 NEEDHAM *Med. Medicinæ* 395 The Miasma or Malign Inquination of blood and humors. **1720** QUINCY tr. *Hodges' Loimologia* 54 The pestilential Miasmata may be destroyed by the occursion of others. **1827** MACCULLOCH *Malaria* i. 1 It has long been familiar to physicians that there was produced by.. marshes and swamps, a poisonous and æriform substance, the cause, not only of ordinary fevers, but of intermittents; and to this unknown agent of disease the term marsh miasma has been applied. **1844** H. H. WILSON *Brit. India* II. 20 The deadly miasmata which render the forests on the skirts of the hills utterly impassable. **1862** MERIVALE *Rom. Emp.* xxxiv. (1865) IV. 181 Sardinia.. was afflicted by a pestilential miasma. **1882** 'OUIDA' *Maremma* I. 35 It was full of miasma and fever in the hot season.

fig. **1836** HOR. SMITH *Tin Trump., Mor. Cholera*, It seems to be the object of these institutions to propagate and disseminate the miasmata of vice instead of preventing their circulation. **1878** SMILES *Robt. Dick* ii. 13 The noxious miasmas that poison the whole human heart.

miasmal (maɪˈæzməl), *a.* [f. prec. + -AL¹.] Containing miasmatic effluvia or germs.

1853 *Fraser's Mag.* XLVIII. 267 You wittingly expose your innocent wife To this miasmal atmosphere of death. **1856** MRS. BROWNING *Aur. Leigh* VII. 300 We respond with our miasmal fog. **1895** R. F. HORTON *Teaching of Jesus* II. 175 Like a sunbeam on some forlorn and miasmal place, sterilising the germs of evil. **1919** T. S. ELIOT *Hippopotamus* in *Poems*, The True Church remains below Wrapt in the old miasmal mist.

miasmatic (maɪæzˈmætɪk), *a.* [f. Gr. *μιασματ-*, *μίασμα* MIASMA + -IC.] Pertaining to or having the nature of miasma; caused by noxious or infectious exhalations; malarial. Also *fig.*

1835 *Cycl. Pract. Med.* IV. 57/1 The softening in intermittents is owing to the miasmatic poison altering the qualities of the blood. **1857** R. TOMES *Amer. in Japan* ix. 194 The entire absence of marshes.. must exempt it from all miasmatic disease. **1881** DU CHAILLU *Land of Midnt. Sun* II. 60 The miasmatic equatorial African jungle. **1938** M. BRINIG *May Flavin* iv. 396 An incomparable California sun pushing the miasmatic mists back into the sea. **1968** 'HAN SUYIN' *Birdless Summer* I. vi. 132 Pao and his benevolent brothers bemoaned the miasmatic disorder in which they were involved.

Hence **miasˈmatical** *a.*, in the same sense; **miasˈmatically** *adv.*, after the manner of miasma.

1855 OGILVIE *Suppl., Miasmatical.* **1876** tr. *Wagner's Gen. Pathol.* 132 The infectious material may.. increase also outside of the organism, in the substrata of the surrounding soil, i.e. miasmatically.

miasmatist (maɪˈæzmətɪst). [f. *miasmat-*, MIASMA + -IST.] One versed in the phenomena of miasmatic exhalations; one who makes a special study of malarial diseases.

1890 in *Syd. Soc. Lex.*

miasmatize (maɪˈæzmətaɪz), *v.* [Formed as prec.: see -IZE.] *trans.* To affect by miasma.

1831 T. L. PEACOCK *Crotchet Castle* xi. (*init.*), The Captain was neither drowned nor poisoned, neither miasmatised nor anatomised.

miasmatology (maɪˈæzmətɒlədʒɪ). *Med.* [f. *miasmat-*, MIASMA + -(O)LOGY.] The study of miasmata; miasmology (Webster 1902).

miasmatous (maɪˈæzmətəs), *a.* [Formed as prec. + -OUS.] Generating miasma.

1864 *Sat. Rev.* 9 July 67/2 Cambodia.. is overspread with miasmatous forests.

miasmic (maɪˈæzmɪk), *a.* [f. MIASM + -IC.] = MIASMATIC. Hence **miˈasmically** *adv.*

1822–34 *Good's Study Med.* (ed. 4) I. 588 In a pure atmosphere, the miasmic materials easily become dissolved or decomposed. **1895** G. PARKER *When Valmond came to Pontiac* vi. (1896) 97 Beyond the mountain were unexplored regions,.. lost in a miasmic haze. **1938** E. WAUGH *Scoop* I. v. 81 Suddenly, miasmically, in the fiery wilderness, there came an apparition. **1961** B. FERGUSSON *Watery Maze* iii. 80 The Pantellaria project and another miasmic one were abandoned.

miasmifuge (maɪˈæzmɪfjuːdʒ). [f. MIASMA + -(I)FUGE.] That which destroys or disperses miasmata (*Syd. Soc. Lex.* 1890).

miasmology (maɪæzˈmɒlədʒɪ). [f. Gr. *μίασμ-α* miasma + -(O)LOGY.] A treatise on miasma; the science that treats of miasmata (Ogilvie 1882).

miasmous (maɪˈæzməs), *a.* [f. MIASM + -OUS.] Miasmatic, miasmal.

1884 J. P. MAHAFFY in *Harper's Mag.* May 903/1 A fertile but miasmous desert. [Also in mod. Dicts.]

miau, obs. form of MIAOW.

miaul (mɪˈɔːl), *v.* Forms: 7 **meawle**, **miol**, 8 **meaul**, 9 **mioul**, **miaul**. [ad. F. *miauler*, of echoic origin. (The form *meawle* perh. belongs to MEWL.)]

1. *intr.* To call or cry as a cat; to mew.

1632 SHERWOOD, To meaw, or meawle (as a cat), *miauler*. **1771** SMOLLETT *Humph. Cl.* 8 Nov., The poor animal [a cat] .. meauled. **1824** SCOTT *St. Ronan's* xxii, Lady Penelope is miauling like a starved cat. **1859** H. KINGSLEY *G. Hamlyn* II. 71 Domestic cats may mioul in the garden at night. **1886** R. F. BURTON *Arab. Nts.* I. 134 A black tom-cat, which miauled and grinned and spat.

2. *trans.* To sing with a voice like that of a cat.

1862 WRAXALL *Hugo's Misérables* III. xxii. (1877) 11 Her tom-cat, who might have miauled the Allegri Miserere. **1866** G. MEREDITH *Vittoria* xii, The boy.. concluded by miauling 'Amalia' in the triumph of contempt.

Hence **miˈauling** *vbl. sb.* and *ppl. a.* Also **miˈauler**, a cat.

1632 Meawler, meawling [see MIAOWER, MIAOWING]. *a* **1693** *Urquhart's Rabelais* III. xiii. 107 The.. mumbling of Rabets,.. humming of Wasps, mioling of Tygers, bruzzing of Bears. **1821** SCOTT *Kenilw.* xxxiii, I mind a squalling woman no more than a miauling kitten. **1884** *Graphic* Christmas No. 4/1 He.. sang in a shrill miawling treble. **1885** *Ibid.* 3 Jan. 7/1 While Bully is asleep the marauding miaulers come and appropriate his bone. **1885** *Punch* 13 June 280/1 Hark the.. miauling of Cats.

miauw, variant form of MIAOW.

mic, **mic.** (maɪk). Colloq. abbrev. of MICROPHONE. (Cf. MIKE *sb.*⁵)

1961 A. BERKMAN *Singers' Gloss. Show Business* 58 Microphone: (Abbr. mike or mic). **1973** *Sci. Amer.* Apr. 2/1 (Advt.), Eight input controls for complete mic/line mixing. **1974** *Some Technical Terms & Slang* (Granada Television), *Mic.*, microphone.

mica (ˈmaɪkə). *Min.* [a. L. *mīca* grain, crumb. The mod.L. use in Mineralogy was prob. originally contextual; the development of the specialized meaning may have been due to erroneous association with *micāre* to shine.]

†**1.** A small plate of talc, selenite, or other glistening crystalline substance found in the structure of a rock. In pl. *micæ*. *Obs.*

1706 PHILLIPS (ed. Kersey), *Mica*,.. Glimmer, or Cat-silver; a Mettallick Body like Silver, which shines in Marble, and other Stones, but cannot be separated from them. *a* **1728** WOODWARD *Nat. Hist. Fossils* (1729) I. I. viii. 170 A pale brown Earth, with very small Micæ in it. **1748** J. HILL *Hist. Fossils* 556 Dr. Woodward imagin'd the white parts of this as of the other Micæ in general to be Spar. **1803** SARRETT *New Pict. Lond.* 114 A great variety of Micæ or spangle stones.

2. Any one of a group of similar minerals composed essentially of silicate of aluminium variously combined with the silicates of other bases, such as soda, potash and magnesia, and occurring either in minute glittering plates or scales in granite and other rocks, or in crystals characterized by their perfect basal cleavage and their consequent separability into thin, transparent and usually flexible laminæ. ***water mica***, a trade name for clear, colourless mica.

1778 WOULFE in *Phil. Trans.* LXIX. 29 Mica or Glimmer. This.. is composed of very thin flexible flakes, more or less large. **1835** *R. D. & T. Thomson's Rec. Gen. Sci.* II. 445 Pinchbeck mica, iron pyrites, and titaniate of iron occur as accidental constituents. **1860** TYNDALL *Glac.* 3 Mica is a crystal which cleaves very readily in one direction. **1903** *Edin. Rev.* Oct. 390 A film of mica. **1905** *Jrnl. Franklin Inst.* Sept. 200 The clear kind is known to the trade as 'water mica'.

3. *attrib.* and *Comb.*, as ***mica battery***, ***goggles***, ***insulation***, ***plate***; ***mica-packed***, ***-scaled***, ***-topped*** adjs.; **mica flap**, the flap of a mica valve; **mica-powder**, a form of dynamite in which the siliceous earth is replaced by mica in fine scales; **mica-schist**, **-slate**, a slaty metamorphic rock composed of quartz and mica; **mica valve**, a device consisting of a flap of mica hinged at the top which is used to allow air to flow in one direction only.

1849 NOAD *Electricity* (ed. 3) 148 The lacquered knob of the *mica battery. **1906** J. W. THOMAS *Ventilation, Heating & Lighting of Dwellings* ii. 27 There are many chimney ventilators on the market, some having *mica flaps.. to shut against a down current. **1934** E. L. JOSELIN *Ventilation* iii. 44 Outlets with mica flaps are frequently fitted into chimney breasts near the ceiling. **1964** J. S. SCOTT *Dict. Building* 207 Mica-flap valve. **1905** *Daily Chron.* 10 Aug. 5/6 A polo cap, *mica goggles,.. and the usual.. allowance of lard constituted Burgess's costume. **1897** *Daily News* 20 July 6/2 It fused the *mica insulation of wires. **1909** *Westm. Gaz.* 9 Mar. 4/3 A new three-point sparking-plug.. which has no asbestos or *mica-packed joints. *a* **1963** S. PLATH *Crossing Water* (1971) 44, I shone, mica-scaled, and unfolded To pour myself out like a fluid. **1837** BREWSTER *Magnet.* 312 The successive thicknesses of the *mica plates. **1881** RAYMOND *Mining Gloss.*, *Mica-powder. **1833** LYELL *Princ. Geol.* III. 237 The sterile *mica-schist is barely covered with vegetation. **1878** LAWRENCE tr. *Cotta's Rocks Class.* 234 A complete series of transitions from.. gneiss through mica-schist into clay-slate. **1819** BAKEWELL *Introd. Mineral.* 477 *Mica-slate, or micaceous schistus. **1877** RAYMOND *Statist. Mines & Mining* 229 A large number of fine lodes, all occurring in limestone and mica-slate. **1958** A. WILSON *Middle Age of Mrs Eliot* III. 381 David banged his fist on the *mica-topped table in front of him so that its little contemporary steel-tube legs rattled. **1880** S. S. HELLYER *Plumber & Sanitary Houses* (ed. 2) xxii. 262 When no convenient place can be found for leaving the mouth of the induct-pipe open to the atmosphere, a *mica-valve can be fixed over it. **1909** G. B. SHAW in *Trans. Medico-Legal Soc.* VI. 217 One day on the Health Committee a question came up with regard to a mica valve not being in order.

miˈcaceo-calˈcareous, *a.* *Geol.* [f. *micaceo-* taken as comb. form of next + CALCAREOUS.] Containing mica and lime (*Cent. Dict.* 1890).

micaceous (maɪˈkeɪʃɪəs), *a.* *Min.* [f. MICA + -ACEOUS.] Containing or resembling mica; pertaining to or of the nature of mica, esp. in Combs. forming the descriptive names of various rocks, as ***micaceous lava***, ***sandstone***, ***schist***, ***shale***, ***slate***.

1774 PENNANT *Tour Scotl. in 1772*, 153 A micaceous slate, mixed with quartz. **1813** SIR H. DAVY *Agric. Chem.* (1814) 193 Micaceous schistus, which is composed of quartz and mica arranged in layers. **1849** DANA *Geol.* ix. (1850) 463 Blue micaceous shale. **1882** GEIKIE *Text-bk. Geol.* II. II. iii, As this silvery lustre is.. due to the presence of mica, it is commonly called distinctively micaceous.

micaceously (maɪˈkeɪʃəslɪ), *adv.* [f. MICACEOUS *a.* + -LY².] Like mica.

1933 H. G. WELLS *Bulpington of Blup* i. 18 It had walls and pinnacles of a creamy sort of rock that glittered micaceously.

micacious (maɪˈkeɪʃəs), *a.* [as if f. L. **micāc-em* (f. *micāre* to shine, sparkle) + -IOUS.] Sparkling.

1836 LOUDON *Encycl. Plants* 42 *Watsonia brevifolia* has its blossoms of a micacious hue, glittering in the sun. *a* **1843** SOUTHEY *Doctor* Interch. xxii. (1848) 537 There is the Cyclopean stile, of which Johnson is the great example; the sparkling, or micacious, possessed by Hazlitt.

micanite (ˈmaɪkənaɪt). *Telegraphy.* [f. MICA, after *vulcanite*.] A prepared form of mica used as an insulator.

1900 *Engineering Mag.* XIX. 709 The micanite used for the commutator sleeve.

†ˈ**micant**, *a.* *Obs.* [ad. L. *micant-em*, pres. pple. of *micāre* shine.] Shining, glittering.

1657 TOMLINSON *Renou's Disp.* 435 When micant sparks ascend from the metal.

micarelle (ˈmaɪkərɛl). *Min.* Also **-el**. [App. irreg. f. MICA.]

1. A micaceous mineral pseudomorphous after scapolite.

1794 KIRWAN *Elem. Min.* (ed. 2) I. 213 Hence the presence of magnesia is merely casual; therefore it must be regarded as a distinct species from mica, and hence I have given it the name of micarelle. **1811** PINKERTON *Petral.* I. 123 The white mica, which might be called micarel. **1836** T. THOMSON *Min. Geol.*, etc. I. 271 *Meionite*, or *Scapolite*. Paranthine,.. micarelle [etc.]. **1896** CHESTER *Dict. Min.*

2. A name used to designate an unknown mineral from which the pinite of Stolpen was derived.

1836 T. THOMSON *Min. Geol.*, etc. I. 386 *Pinite*. Micarell. **1845** *Encycl. Metrop.* VI. 525/1 *Micarelle*. Pinite or Scapolite.

So **micaˈrellite** in the same senses (*Cassell's Encycl. Dict.* 1885).

Micarta (maɪˈkɑːtə). Also **micarta**. [perh. f. MICA + It. *carta* paper.] A laminated electrical insulating material, originally consisting of paper, mica, and enamel: now a proprietary term for one composed of layers of paper or fabrics bound by a resin and used esp. in the form of sheets and tubes.

1912 *Sci. Abstr.* B. XV. 230 The coil is wrapped with several layers of a foil termed 'Micarta Folium', consisting of paper, mica, and enamel; the whole coil is then.. compressed. **1914** *Official Gaz.* (U.S. Patent Office) 10 Feb. 585/2 Westinghouse Electric & Manufacturing Co. .. *Micarta*.. Electrical insulating sheets and tubes. Claims use since Apr. 4, 1912. **1921** *Raw Material* IV. 449/2 The method of manufacturing *micarta*.. consists of impregnating the base material with a solution of the binder, evaporating the solvent and then fusing together laminations of impregnated base material by the action of heat under pressure. **1923** *Trade Marks Jrnl.* 3 Jan. 42 Micarta... Electrical insulating sheets and tubes... Westinghouse Electric and Manufacturing Company. **1938** *Jrnl. R. Aeronaut. Soc.* XLII. 9 For those engineers dealing with wooden or micarta airscrews or metal airscrews of less usual form. **1966** *Sci. & Technical Aerospace Rep.* IV. 667/1 The ablation rate of contoured Micarta (laminated plastics) specimens immersed in solid propellant exhaust gases was measured under closely controlled conditions.

micasiˈzation, **micatiˈzation**. *Geol.* [irreg. f. MICA + -IZE + -ATION.] (See quot. 1893.)

1893 GEIKIE *Text-bk. Geol.* (ed. 3) 617 Micasization—the production of mica as a secondary mineral from felspars or other original constituents. **1896** VAN HISE in *16th Rep. U.S. Geol. Surv.* I. 691 Some of the more important of these processes are micatization, feldsparization [etc.].

†**miˈcation**. *Obs.* [ad. L. *micātiōn-em*, n. of action f. *micāre* to move swiftly, *micāre digitīs* to play at mora ('How many fingers do I hold up?').] **a.** The action used in playing at mora. **b.** A beat of the pulse.

c **1645** *Vox Turturis* 8 Hence Causabonus saith *dimicare* to duell or fight is derived, which is properly by Lot or mication to put an end to controversie. **1656** STANLEY *Hist. Philos.* VIII. (1687) 466/2 By Lot, or Mication with the Fingers (*giuoco della mora*). **1725** BRADLEY *Fam. Dict.* s.v. *Pulse*, This Strength is made up with the Multiplicity and

Frequency of less Mications [*sc.* of the pulse] as in the Heights of Fevers.

Micawber (mɪˈkɔːbər). The name of Wilkins *Micawber*, a character in Dickens's novel 'David Copperfield', applied *gen.* to a feckless optimist with a habit of 'waiting for something to turn up'. Also *attrib.* and *Comb.*, as **Micawber-like** *a.*; **Mi'cawber** *v. intr.*, to behave like Micawber; **Micawberish** (mɪˈkɔːbərɪʃ) *a.*, characteristic of a Micawber, irresponsible; **Mi'cawberishly** *adv.*; so **Mi'cawberism**; **Mi'cawberite** = Micawber.

1852 GEO. ELIOT *Let.* 2 June (1954) II. 31 No good news yet, but I have a Micawber-faith that something will turn up. **1880** J. HOLLINGSHEAD *Plain Eng.* 2 Undeceived by the Micawberism of one class, or the dazzling brilliancy of the other. **1882** W. D. HAY *Brighter Britain!* I. vi. 143 A Micawber-like roll of his voice. **1920** *Glasgow Herald* 19 June 6 He was in a state of what may be described as 'Micawberish embarrassment'. **1927** *Observer* 22 May 8 Nancy's father, a sort of Micawberish Costigan. **1939** *Times Lit. Suppl.* 18 Mar. 162/3 We find a grand collection of literary people who have become household words, like.. Micawber. **1948** E. GOWERS *Plain Words* 48 The present inclination of the official is in the opposite direction. He is a Johnsonian rather than a Micawberite. **1949** I. DEUTSCHER *Stalin* iii. 70 Lenin treated such Socialists contemptuously as the romantic Micawbers of revolution. **1950** *Mind* LIX. 84 An opportunistic, capricious, or Micawberish policy. **1961** *Times* 5 June 15/3 The British Government can hardly be blamed for being somewhat Micawber-like in their approach to this problem. **1963** *Punch* 24 July 126/1 Every author must spend half his life Micawbering, waiting for something to turn up. **1969** *Times* 2 May (Suppl.) p. viii/3 History has been on the side of the Micawbers. **1971** *Guardian* 16 July 10/2 Mr Wilson's social contract.. will.. look remarkably like the 1964 or 1966 vintage, with a dash of Micawberism added. **1972** *Ibid.* 11 Oct. 12/2 The Green Paper's hope that growth will provide comes dangerously near the Micawber tradition. **1972** 'J. & E. BONETT' *No time to Kill* x. 138 Idle men who take a job in the sunshine that leads nowhere... today's Micawbers, aimlessly awaiting what will never turn up. **1973** *Nation Rev.* (Melbourne) 31 Aug. 1463/3 Despite portraying a Micawberlike optimism, Plorn died destitute. **1974** *Times* 7 Jan. 5/5 The Micawberish disasters that threatened them so long as the father—that sad barrister without briefs—was still alive. **1974** *Times* 4 Mar. 15/3 The Liberal Party.. has always Micawberishly hoped that some rich sympathizer would turn up.

†**mice-eyed**, *a. Obs. rare*⁻¹. [f. *mice*, pl. of MOUSE + EYED.] Having the keen eyes of mice.

1599 NASHE *Lenten Stuffe* 67 O for a Legion of mice eyed decipherers and calculaters vppon characters, now to augurate what I meane by this.

micelium, obs. variant of MYCELIUM.

micelle (mɪˈsɛl). *Biol.* Also **micella** (pl. **micellæ** (-iː)), **micell.** [ad. G. *micell* (C. Nägeli *Mikrophysik* (1877) 424.)] **a.** Each of the minute ordered aggregates of macromolecules from which the microfibrils of many natural and artificial fibrous materials are made up.

1881 *Encycl. Brit.* XII. 12/1 Nägeli concluded that these structures were made up of crystalline doubly refracting particles or micellæ, each consisting of numerous atoms and impermeable by water. **1882** VINES tr. *Sachs' Bot.* 664 *note* 1. **1885** GOODALE *Physiol. Bot.* (1892) 218 In the adherent film of water around each micella new micellæ of cellulose are supposed to be produced. **1937** O. B. DARBISHIRE tr. *A. von Buzágh's Colloid Syst.* vii. 133 The above structural picture of the cellulose micelle is in agreement with a number of physical and physico-chemical properties of cellulose. Chief among them is the well-known great stability of the cellulose micelle, as shown, for instance, by the insolubility of cellulose in water. **1946** *Nature* 10 Aug. 199/2 The main component of starch.. is considered to be a network of primary valency chains, which are linked in crystalline micells in which water is bound in the lattice. **1959** *Chambers's Encycl.* III. 222/1 Later evidence suggests rather that the micelles are areas in which the molecular chains are regularly arranged and crystalline; these merge into amorphous areas with possibly some of the long chains extending from one micelle to another. **1965** Micella [see CRYSTALLITE 4].

b. An ultramicroscopic aggregate in a colloid consisting of some tens or hundreds of ions or molecules.

1901 *Jrnl. Chem. Soc.* LXXX. II. 231 A 'micelle' is used to denote the smallest quantity of a colloid which possesses all the physical properties of the colloid and is formed by the association of molecules of large size. **1926** H. S. HATFIELD tr. *Freundlich's Colloid & Capillary Chem.* 371 For the micella of the gold sol we must take into account the fact that foreign substances enter into its structure, which largely determine its chemical properties. **1927** H. S. VAN KLOOSTER tr. *Kruyt's Colloids* vi. 102 The micell is the particle plus the entire double layer. **1949** ALEXANDER & JOHNSON *Colloid Sci.* I. ii. 31 It is generally agreed that the physical properties of soap solutions, such as surface activity, conductivity, osmotic coefficients, solubilization of organic compounds, the Krafft phenomenon, etc., are due.. to the occurrence of micelles. **1969** *New Scientist* 21 Aug. 379/1 The granules correspond to what are generally referred to as casein micelles, being formed by the denaturation and aggregation of the milk proteins during the manufacture of cheese. **1971** *Nature* 9 July 118/1 The bulk of DDT carried in contaminated water is probably in an organic environment, dissolved in suspended liquid fats, in soap and in detergent micelles.

Hence **mi'cellar** *a.*, pertaining to or composed of micellæ.

1893 W. N. PARKER tr. *Weismann's Germ-Plasm* 474 (Index) Micellar theory.

micellization (mɪˌsɛlaɪˈzeɪʃən). *Chem.* [f. MICELL(A + -IZATION.] The formation of micelles.

1966 *Jrnl. Amer. Chem. Soc.* LXXXVIII. 247/1 DPI [*sc.* dodecylpyridinium iodide] was chosen because a large spectral change accompanies its micellization and thus provides a self-indicator of the micellization process. **1972** *Nature* 3 Mar. 32/2 The results further suggest that at concentrations of ganglioside above 30% the formation of membranous structures would be inhibited by lipid micellization.

mich: see MITCH *v.*, MUCH *a.* and *adv.*

Michael (ˈmaɪkəl). Forms: α. 1 **Micha(h)el**, 3 (*Ormin*) **Michaæl**, 4 **Mychael**, 4, 6- **Michael**. β. 3 **Missel**, 4-5 **Michel**, 5 **Mychel**, 6 **Mychell**. γ. 3 **Mihael**, **Miȝhel**, 4 **Mihel**, **Myȝhell**, 5 **Myghell**, **Myghele**, 7 (in Comb.) **Mighill-**. [repr. Heb. *Mīkhāēl*, lit. 'who is like God?' Gr. Μιχαήλ, L. *Michael*, whence OF. *Michiel*, F. *Michel*, It. *Michele*, Sp. *Miguel*, Pg. *Miguel*, G. *Michael* (the archangel), *Michel* (in popular uses).

The γ forms, implying a pronunciation (mɪjɛl), are difficult to account for. They occur only in application to the archangel or his feast; for the baptismal name the β forms only were used down to the 17th c.]

1. a. The name of one of the archangels. ***the feast of St. Michael, St. Michael's day***: Michaelmas.

c **1000** ÆLFRIC *Hom.* I. 518 Michahel. *a* **1225** *Ancr. R.* 412 Seinte Mihaeles dei. **1297** R. GLOUC. (Rolls) 11032 A sein Misseles [*v.r.* Myhelles] dai. **1340** *Ayenb.* 1 Holy archanle Michael. **1362** LANGL. *P. Pl.* A. VIII. 36, I schal sende ow my-self seint Mihel myn Aungel. **1382** WYCLIF *Dan.* x. 13 Mychael [**1388** Myȝhel]. **14..** *Customs of Malton* in *Surtees Misc.* (1888) 59 Eftyr þe fest of Sayntt Myghell. **1667** MILTON *P.L.* II. 294 So much the fear Of Thunder and the Sword of *Michael* Wrought still within them.

b. ***St. Michael's pear*** [= F. *poire de St.-Michel*, G. *Michaelisbirne*]: a kind of pear that is ripe at Michaelmas.

1837 HAWTHORNE *Twice-told T.* viii, They strung him up to the branch of a St. Michael's pear-tree.

c. ***Order of St. Michael***: an old French military order instituted by Louis XI in 1462. ***Order of St. Michael and St. George***: an English civil order of knighthood instituted in 1818, shortly after the acquisition by Great Britain of Malta and the Ionian Islands, for the purpose of affording a special decoration to the natives of those islands; now granted as a reward for distinguished services as a diplomat, etc.

1530, 1591 [see ORDER *sb.* 8]. **1839** *Penny Cycl.* XIII. 246/2 There are also.. knights of the Ionian order of Saint Michael and Saint George.

†**2.** = MICHAELMAS. Also *attrib.* in ***Michael-cry, day, term***; **Michael('s)-tide**, Michaelmas-tide.

1406 HOCCLEVE *Misrule* 422 For Michel terme þat was last. **1426** in *Catal. Anc. Deeds in P.R.O.* IV. 547 That the said Richard be at Chestir the next Seterday after Myghelday in presens of the Chaumberlayn. **1573** TUSSER *Husb.* (1878) 28 Fresh herring plentie, Mihell brings. *Ibid.* 74 No danger at all to geld as they fall. Yet Michel cries please butchers eies. **1611** SPEED *Hist. Gt. Brit.* IX. xv. (1623) 802 From the next Michaels-tide vnto Easter. **1615** W. LAWSON *Country Housew. Gard.* (1626) 12 At Mighill-tide it will be good to sow Wall-flowers. *Ibid.* 51 Generally no keeping fruit [*sc.* will be ready] before Michael-tide. **1622** S. WARD *Life Faith in Death* (1627) 87 To be haunted with a Quartan from Michael to Ester. **1622** in *Buccleuch MSS.* (Hist. MSS. Comm.) I. 210 By Michael next my Lord.. makes accompt to bring her over.

3. As a common Christian name of men. Also in proverbial phrases.

1340 *Ayenb.* 1 Þis boc is dan Michelis of Northgate, y-write an englis of his owene hand. **1500–20** DUNBAR *Poems* xxii. 71 Twa curis or thre hes vpolandis Michell [*rimes* knitchell and nichell (= L. *nihil*)]. *a* **1625** FLETCHER *Woman's Prize* I. iii, *Petru.* Well there are more Maides then Maudlin, that's my comfort. *Mar.* Yes, and more men then Michael. **1785** GROSE *Dict. Vulg. T.*, *Michael.* Hip, Michael, your head's on fire.

4. = MICKEY FINN. *U.S. slang.*

1942 BERREY & VAN DEN BARK *Amer. Thes. Slang* §509/9 Opiate; 'knockout drops'... *Michael.* **1957** B. BUCKINGHAM *Boiled Alive* xxiv. 178 He only pretended to trust me and just slipped me a Michael in my drink. I passed out in the car a few minutes after leaving the bar.

5. Slang phr. ***to take the Michael*** (***out of***) = ***to take the micky*** (***out of***) (see MICKEY[1] 6).

1959 H. PINTER *Birthday Party* I. 9 They won't come. Someone's taking the Michael... It's a false alarm. **1962** *Spectator* 23 Feb. 242/2 Like many satirists Mayakovsky takes the michael out of both sides. **1966** L. DAVIDSON *Long Way to Shiloh* xi. 157 Jesus, did we take the Michael! We used to chat 'em up, these old bats out looking for prospects.

Michaelangelesque, var. MICHELANGELESQUE *a.*

michaelite (ˈmaɪkɪlaɪt). *Min.* [f. name of *St. Michaels*, in the Azores: see -ITE.] = FIORITE.

1821 WEBSTER in *Amer. Jrnl. Sci.* III. 391 From the island where this variety [*sc.* of siliceous sinter] occurs (St. Michaels) it might perhaps be distinguished by the term *Michaelite.*

Michaelmas (ˈmɪkəlməs). Forms: 1 **Sanct Michaeles mæsse**, 3 **Miȝheles-masse**; 3 **miel-**, **missel-**, 3, 5 **miȝhel**, 3-5 **mychel**, 4 **myel-**, **mihele-**, **misschel**, 4-5 **myhel**, 5 **myhil**, **myhell**, **michel-**, **miȝele-**, **mighell-**, **meghel-**, **mykel-**, **mykyl**, **myȝhel-**, 5-6 **myghel(l-**, **mighel-**, 6 **myell-**, **myhyl-**, **mihel-**, **michall-**, 7 **michal-**; 3- **masse**, etc. (see MASS *sb.*[1]); 4 **mykames**; 7- **Michaelmas.** Also 9 *dial.* **Mihil-**, **Mile-**, **Mildmas.** [f. the name of St. *Michael* the Archangel: see MASS *sb.*[1]] The feast of St. Michael, 29 Sept., one of the four quarter-days of the English business year.

[*a* **1123** *O.E. Chron.* an. 1101 Se eorl syððan oð ðet ofer sc̄e Michaeles mæsse her on lande wunode.] *c* **1290** *S. Eng. Leg.* I. 53/229 Op-on Miȝhel-masse fourtene-nyȝht. **1297** R. GLOUC. (Rolls) 9508 Þ e kinges poer & is ost.. wende vorþ to oxenford aboute mielmasse. **1377** LANGL. *P. Pl.* B. XII. 240 Fro mychelmesse to mychelmesse I fynde hem with wafres. **1389** in *Eng. Gilds* (1870) 35 Be-twixen þe feste of the natiuite of oure lady & Misschelmasse. **1435** *Nottingham Rec.* II. 361 At ye Anounsiacion of oure Lady and Meghelmes. **1452** in *Berks, Bucks & Oxon Archæol. Jrnl.* Oct. (1903) 78 For ij lb wex candells a ghens myhellmas xij.d. **1469** M. PASTON in *P. Lett.* II. 365 Wednsday or Thursday aftyr Mykylmes. **1475** *Presentm. Juries* in *Surtees Misc.* (1888) 26 At the gret cowrtes at Mykelmes, þe yer [etc.]. **1530** PALSGR. 804/2 At Mychelmesse, *a la saynt Michel* or *le jour de saint Michel.* **1536** *Anc. Cal. Rec. Dublin* (1889) I. 497 The wyche off trewythe was grawnttyd att myellmas last past. **1539** in W. A. J. Archbold *Somerset Relig. Ho.* (1892) 117 We intende.. to letowte the pastures and demeynes now from mighelmas forthe quarterly. **1598** SHAKS. *Merry W.* I. i. 212 Alhallowmas last, a fortnight a-fore Michaelmas. **1609** SKENE *Reg. Maj.*, *Burrow Lawes* c. 43. 124 The first [*sc.* head-court] is after the feast of Michalmes. **1661** MARVELL *Corr.* Wks. (Grosart) II. 70 Which sum.. shall be collected.. at Michal masse and Lady day. **1712** STEELE *Spect.* No. 424 ⁋5 By Michaelmas 'tis odds but we come to down-right squabbling. **1819** *Sport. Mag.* 274 He will blow upon his fingers before Mildmas [*footnote*, Michaelmas]. **1864** TENNYSON *North. Farmer, Old Style* xii, And I'd managed for Squoire coom Michaelmas thutty year.

b. *attrib.* and *Comb.*, as ***Michaelmas goose, onion, rent***; **Michaelmas blackbird**, the ring ouzel (*Turdus torquatus*); **Michaelmas crocus**, the autumn crocus (*Colchicum autumnale*); **Michaelmas daisy**, a sea-starwort, (*a*) wild aster (*Aster Tripolium*); (*b*) one of several garden asters of a shrubby habit and bearing masses of small purplish flowers; **Michaelmas day** = sense 1; **Michaelmas eve**, the evening before Michaelmas; †**Michaelmas moon** = HARVEST MOON; †**Michaelmas pardon** (see PARDON *sb.*[1] 3 b); **Michaelmas spring**, an autumnal spring; also *fig.*; **Michaelmas term**, a term or session (beginning soon after Michaelmas) of the High Court of Justice in England; and also of Oxford, Cambridge, and various other universities; **Michaelmas tide**, the season of Michaelmas.

Old Michaelmas day: the day that would have been called 29 Sept. if the Old Style had been retained without correction: from 1900 onwards this has been 12 Oct.

1822 LATHAM *Hist. Birds* V. 39 *note*, Ring Ouzel.. a British Species, only seen in spring and autumn. By some called the *Michaelmas Blackbird. **1785** MARTYN *Rousseau's Bot.* xxvi. (1794) 391 Many [Asters] as confounded under the Vulgar title of *Michaelmas Daisies. **1882** *Garden* 24 June 437/2 A brown-centred small Michaelmas Daisy. [*c* **1290** *S. Eng. Leg.* I. 304/165 Men synguez a-*Miȝheles-masse-day In holie church also Of one bataile þat seint Miȝhel with a dragun scholde do.] **1359** in *Eng. Gilds* (1870) 97 And yis gilde schal haue, by ȝere, foure mornspeches.. ye ferthe schal be on mykames day. **1463** *Mann. & Househ. Exp.* (Roxb.) 154 The fryday next afftyr Myhelmesse day my mastyr delyveryd to my sayd lord.. vj.s. viij.d. **1864** *Chambers' Bk. Days* II. 387/2 Michaelmas Day, the 29th of September, properly named the day of St. Michael and All Angels. **1297** R. GLOUC. (Rolls) 8793 So þat a *Missel-masse eue mid hor ost hii come. **1792** *Statist. Acc. Scot.* II. 438 *note*, The son-in-law binds himself to give him [the father-in-law] the profits of the first *Michaelmas moon. **1763** MILLS *Syst. Pract. Husb.* IV. 34 One of these crops, known by the name of *Michaelmas onions, is sown in August. **1624** CAPT. SMITH *Virginia* IV. (Arb.) 619 Thus they spend *Michaelmas rent in Mid-summer Moone, and would gather their Haruest before they haue planted their Corne. **1763** *Museum Rust.* (ed. 2) I. 75 If the markets are low, they fail in the payment of their Michaelmas rent. **1573** TUSSER *Husb.* (1878) 135 Be mindfull abrode of *Mihelmas spring. **1658** GURNALL *Chr. In Arm.* Verse 16. x. (1669) 210/1 God promised him a Michaelmas spring (I may so say) a son in his old age. **1721** AMHERST *Terræ Fil.* App. (1754) 281 He was, in *michael-mas-term following, admitted commoner in Oriel college. **1765** BLACKSTONE *Comm.* I. ix. 329 The morrow of All Souls..(which day is now altered to the morrow of St. Martin by the last act for abbreviating Michaelmas term). **1903** *Oxf. Univ. Cal.* p. xiii, Oct. 10. Oxford Michaelmas Term begins. **1903** *Longm. Mag.* Oct. 516 At *Michaelmas-tide heavy waggons lumber through the villages.

michaelsonite (ˈmɪkəlsənaɪt). *Min.* [f. the name of A. *Michaelson* (1868), who first analysed it: see -ITE.] = ERDMANNITE.

1868 DANA *Min.* (ed. 5) II. 289 Michaelsonite *Dana.* An orthite-like mineral occurring near Brevig.., containing, like muromontite, little alumina and some glucina.

michall, variant of MECHAL *Obs.*

Michal(l)mas, -mes, obs. ff. MICHAELMAS.

michare, obs. form of MICHER.

†**miche**, *sb.*[1] *Obs.* [a. OF. *miche*, of obscure origin; it does not regularly represent L. *mīca* crumb.

The same word appears in MDu., MLG. *micke* (mod.Du. *mik*), but it is uncertain whether it was adopted from Du. into Fr. or vice versa.]

A loaf of bread.

c **1290** *St. Brandan* 296 in *S. Eng. Leg.* I. 227 Twelf ȝwite Miches [*v.r.* suche loues] men brynguth us. *a* **1300** *Rel. Ant.* II. 192 He sal sitte in helle flitte with-oute wyn and miche. *c* **1400** *Rom. Rose* 5585 He that hath miches tweyne,.. Liveth more at ese,.. Than [etc.]. **1523** LD. BERNERS *Froiss.* I. cccixvi. 598 The lorde of Verby sent hym wyne largely, and thretie myches therwith. *c* **1640** J. SMYTH *Lives Berkeleys* (1883) I. 40 Fifty loafes called miches.

Hence †**michekin**, a little cake.

c **1440** *Promp. Parv.* 336/2 Mychekyne, *pastilla.*

†**miche**, *sb.*[2] *Naut. Obs.* Also 6 **meche**, 5–6 *Sc. pl.* **mykkis**. [Cf. G. *micke* in the senses below; also Du. *mik* forked stick. Cf. Sc. dial. *mitch*, a support for a mast when lowered (E.D.D.).]

a. A forked shaft for a pump. **b.** A wedge for sighting a cannon.

1495 *Naval Acc. Hen. VII* (1896) 157 Miches with a swivell a bolte & Ryng belongyng to the Ingyn to draw water owte of the seid dokke. *Ibid.* 194 Serpentynes of yron.. yche of them with his miches & forloke of yron.. Stone gonnes of yron.. with miches & forlokkes to the same.. Serpentynes of Brasse with his miche & forloke. *Ibid.* 261 Yron worke for xx of the seid gonnes that is to say xx miches xx boltes & xx forelokes. **1497** *Ibid.* 209 Michies with a swevell a bolt & a ryng of yron belongyng to the Ingynne to draw water at the Dokke. **1496** *Ld. Treas. Acc. Scotl.* (1877) I. 292 For mykkis and bandis to the gunnys. **1513** *Ibid.* (1902) IV. 485. **1514** *Lett. & Papers of Hen. VIII*, I. 4968 (MS.) Every chamber having one meche and one forlock.

miche, michel, obs. ff. MUCH, MICKLE.

miche: see MITCH *v.*

Michelangelesque (ˌmaɪkɪlændʒəˈlɛsk), *a.* Also **Michaelangelesque**. [f. the name of *Michelangelo* Buonarroti (1475–1564), a famous Italian artist: see -ESQUE.] Pertaining to or after the manner of Michelangelo.

1784 J. BARRY in *Lect. Paint.* iii. (1848) 133 The arm is a little too square and michelangelesque. **1845** R. FORD *Handbk. for Travellers Spain* II. viii. 635/2 Two grand subjects in *chiaro oscuro* on a gilded ground.. are quite Michael-Angelesque. **1856** M. D. WYATT in O. Jones *Gram. Ornament* xix. 4 Primaticcio, a master whose style of drawing was founded upon the Michael-Angelesque system of proportion. **1864** LOWELL *Fireside Trav.* 220 The Michael Angelesque olive-trunks. **1874** E. EASTLAKE tr. *Kugler's Handbk. Painting: Italian Schools* (ed. 4) I. IV. i. 251 In addition to his larger Michael-Angelesque peculiarities *Luca* may be known by the squareness of his forms in joints and extremities. **1886** RUSKIN *Præterita* II. 50, I.. progressed greatly and vitally in Michael-Angelesque directions. **1887** DOWDEN *Shelley* II. v. 239 Visions.. of Michelangelesque sublimity. **1903** [see CONTRAPPOSTO]. **1932** R. FRY *Let.* 10 Mar. (1972) II. 666 The cubico-Michelangelesque affair may best express the spirit of your house. **1934** R. CAMPBELL *Broken Record* iv. 84 He looked very Mosaic in the Michaelangelesque sense of the word. **1935** *Burlington Mag.* June 278 Some Michaelangelesque drawings by Maurice Delacre. **1956** K. CLARK *Nude* iv. 134 The same Michelangelesque motive is used. **1963** A. E. ELSEN *Rodin* 55 The Michelangelesque motive of the right elbow crossed over to the left thigh.. pleased the artist. **1970** T. HILTON *Pre-Raphaelites* viii. 196 In such Michelangelesque subjects as *The Wheel of Fortune*, Burne-Jones's relations with the Italian masters were always to be uneasy.

So **Micheˈlangelism**, the manner or tendencies in art of Michelangelo.

1883 C. C. PERKINS *Ital. Sculpture* III. iv. 350 The greater part of the sculpture.. shuns the Scylla of nullity and bad taste only to fall into the Charybdis of Michelangelism.

Michelin (ˈmɪtʃəlɪn, ‖miʃlɛ̃). The name of André *Michelin* (1853–1931) and Édouard *Michelin* (1859–1940), French manufacturers of motor vehicles, used to designate motor-vehicle tyres produced by the company they founded; freq. with allusion to the symbols included in its advertising, or to the gastronomic and touring guides produced by the company.

1902 C. L. FREESTON in A. C. Harmsworth et al. *Motors* 226 The tyre which was most favourably known abroad, i.e. the Michelin. *Ibid.*, The Michelin tyre is made in various sizes. **1921** W. J. LOCKE *Mountebank* iv. 45 The avocations that had led him to know the Inns of France with the accuracy of a Michelin guide. **1933** A. G. MACDONELL *England, their England* vii. 99 A blazer of purple-and-yellow stripes.. surmounted by a purple-and-yellow cap that made him somehow reminiscent of the Michelin twins. **1934** H. MILLER *Tropic of Cancer* 18 A caricature of a man.. Thyroid eyes, Michelin lips. **1951** G. GREENE *End of Affair* III. vii. 145, I can't stand twenty-four hours of maps and Michelin guides. **1954** *Observer* 18 July 10/3 The Michelin man (whose name is.. Bibendum) is.. evocative of such delights as foreign travel, luscious food, the best maps in the world. **1958** E. DUNDY *Dud Avocado* I. i. 11 Baedekers and Michelins and museum catalogues.. discarded as too boring and corny. **1959** *Motor Manual* (ed. 36) v. 130 The unusual Michelin X, in which three layers of steel cords are built into the cover between the casing and the tread. **1962** L. DEIGHTON *Ipcress File* 221 Joigny a Michelin-starred town a hundred kilometres south of Paris. **1968** A. DIMENT *Gt. Spy Race* viii. 125 The old charlatan has got a Michelin star to his name. **1971** C. BONINGTON *Annapurna South Face* App. B. 244 They [*sc.* down jackets] had the advantage of being quite close-fitting and did not make one feel like the Michelin tyre man. **1972** *Guardian* 20 Oct. 13/2 The spirit of the French Michelin man is quietly pacing the British byways. Michelin will bring out their first guide to British hotels and restaurants in March 1974. **1975** R. HILL *Jackdaw* 147 He opened his Michelin.. and studied the list of hotels.

Michelmasse, obs. form of MICHAELMAS.

Michelsberg (ˈmɪxəlzbɛrk). [Place-name in Baden, Germany.] A Neolithic Belgo-Germanic culture illustrated by remains (esp. pottery) found at Michelsberg. Also *attrib.* Cf. CORTAILLOD.

1929 PEAKE & FLEURE *Way of Sea* i. 12 The Michelsberg culture occurs at many sites near the Rhine between Lake Constance and Cologne. *Ibid.* ii. 21 The pottery.. was introduced from France into Switzerland.. about 2200 B.C., and here this culture developed into that known as Michelsberg, with its tulip-shaped vases, about a century later. **1954** S. PIGGOTT *Neolithic Cultures* ii. 32 A similar mingling of agricultural and hunter-fisher strains is probably perceptible in the Michelsberg culture in Belgium and the Rhineland. **1970** BRAY & TRUMP *Dict. Archaeol.* 146/2 *Michelsberg*, a Neolithic culture of Belgium, north France, the Rhineland and parts of Switzerland... There are many regional sub-groups. The Belgian one has leaf-shaped arrows, antler combs, flint mines, and enclosures similar in construction to causewayed camps, and may have links with the Windmill Hill culture.

Michelson (ˈmaɪkəlsən). *Physics.* The name of A. A. *Michelson* (1852–1931), German-born U.S. physicist, used *attrib.* and in the possessive to designate (*a*) the Michelson-Morley experiment (see next); (*b*) the type of interferometer that was used in this experiment (invented earlier by Michelson).

1902 *Encycl. Brit.* XXX. 250/1 Lodge.. studied the behavior of a beam of light which was divided into two portions by a semi-transparent mirror as in Michelson's interferometer. **1956** E. H. HUTTEN *Lang. Mod. Physics* iii. 99 The theory of *special* relativity rests mainly on the Michelson experiment. **1966** Michelson interferometer [see MICHELSON-MORLEY]. **1965** M. GARBUNY *Optical Physics* vi. 308 That such a wavetrain moving through space with a finite length has actually a physical significance.. can be demonstrated by the Michelson experiment. **1972** C. MØLLER *Theory of Relativity* (ed. 2) i. 28 Michelson's experiment was only the first of a long series of attempts to determine the motion of the earth relative to the ether.

Michelson-Morley (ˌmaɪkəlsən ˈmɔəlɪ). *Physics.* The names of A. A. *Michelson* (see prec.) and E. W. *Morley* (1838–1923), U.S. chemist and physicist, used *attrib.* to designate an experiment first performed by them in 1887 in which a beam of light is divided into two parts which are made to travel over paths at right angles to one another before being reunited, the behaviour of the resulting interference fringes (e.g. when the whole apparatus is rotated through 90 degrees) showing that the speed of light is the same in both directions, in contrast to what would be expected if the earth were in motion through an 'ether'; so ***Michelson-Morley apparatus***.

1913 O. LODGE *Continuity* 20 Many forms of statement of the famous Michelson-Morley experiment are misleading. **1925** I. A. RICHARDS *Princ. Lit. Crit.* x. 71 No new facts nor any new hypotheses—no Michelson-Morley experiment, nor any widened purview—led up to the separate value theory of art. **1965** D. BOHM *Special Theory of Relativity* xxii. 107 The Michelson-Morley experiment may be regarded as an excellent confirmation of the Lorentz contraction. **1966** *McGraw-Hill Encycl. Sci. & Technol.* VII. 505/1 The Michelson-Morley apparatus.. consists of a horizontal Michelson interferometer with its two arms at right angles.

michenerite (ˈmɪtʃənəraɪt). *Min.* [f. the name of C. E. *Michener*, 20th-cent. Canadian mineralogist + -ITE[1].] A palladium bismuthide, $PdBi_2$, or perhaps a telluride and bismuthide of palladium and platinum (see quot. 1963), which is found as greyish-white isometric crystals.

1958 HAWLEY & BERRY in *Canad. Mineralogist* VI. 200 Two palladium bismuthides from nickeliferous ores of the Frood Mine, Sudbury, Ontario, detected and described by C. E. Michener some years ago, are re-described and named michenerite and froodite. **1963** *Mineral. Abstr.* XVI. 283/1 Michenerite associated with the moncheite and kotulskite is shown to have a composition approximating to $Pd_{0.75}Pt_{0.25}BiTe$ rather than $PdBi_2$. **1972** *Ibid.* XXIII. 316/1 Moncheite and michenerite occur as disseminations between sulphides and rock-forming silicates and as idiomorphic grains.

micher (ˈmɪtʃə(r)), *sb.* Now *dial.* Forms: 3 **muchare**, 4–5 **mycher**, 4–6 **michare**, 6 **moicher**, **mychare**, 4, 6 **michir**, 7 **meecher**, **mitcher**, 4– **micher**. [Early ME. *muchare*, app. a. OF. **muchere*, *muchëor*, agent.-n. f. *mucher* MITCH *v.* (which is not recorded in Eng. till much later).]

1. A secret or petty thief. *Obs.*

a **1225** *Ancr. R.* 150 Þis world.. is al biset of helle muchares þet robbeð al þe gold-hordes þet heo muwen under-ȝiten. *c* **1357** *Lay Folks Catech.* (L.) 825 Who brekys þe seuynt comaundement, Mechers, Robbers and extorcioners. *a* **1400–50** *Alexander* 3541 To þis michare out of Messe-done þis mandment I write. *c* **1440** *Gesta Rom.* xxvii. 107 (Harl. MS.) To slepe, when oþere men wakithe, as dothe thevis and mychers. **1530** PALSGR. 244/1 Mecher a lytell thefe, *laronceav.* *c* **1555** HARPSFIELD *Divorce Hen. VIII* (Camden) 204 Where is Miser and Micher Micheas? where doth he now micher? **1563–83** FOXE *A. & M.* II. 804/2 Callyng him [*sc.* Becket] micher and theefe, for that hee wrought by craftes and imaginations. **1669** WORLIDGE *Syst. Agric.* (1681) 102 This [Fence] makes a speedy shelter for a Garden from Winds, Beasts, or such like injuries, rather than from rude Michers. **1787** GROSE *Provinc. Gloss.*, *Michers*, thieves, pilferers. Norf. **1823** SCOTT *Peveril* xxvii, Thou art turned micher as well as padder—Canst both rob a man and kidnap him!

†**2.** One who goes 'sneaking about' for dishonest or improper purposes; esp. in 16–17th c., a pander or go-between. *Obs.*

14.. *Nom.* in Wr.-Wülcker 687/1 *Hic circumforarius*, a mycher. *c* **1530** *Hyckescorner* 378 (Manly) Wanton wenches, and also mychers, With many other of the devylles offycers. **1547–64** BAULDWIN *Mor. Philos.* (Palfr.) 128 Hee detesteth & vtterly abhorreth the whole brood of priuie michers, secret vnderminers, hypocrites, & double dealers. *a* **1550** *Image Ipocr.* I. in *Skelton's Wks.* (1843) II. 419 Oh ye kynde of vipers,.. That haue so many miters! And yett ye be but mychers. *a* **1619** FLETCHER *Bonduca* I. ii, It may be a whore too; say it be: come, meecher, Thou shalt have both [drink and whore]. **1630** J. TAYLOR (Water P.) *Agst. Cursing & Swearing* Wks. I. 48/2 He is altogether ashamed, and like a Micher muffles his face in his hat.

†**b.** One who pretends poverty. *Obs.*

1611 COTGR., *Senaud*.. a rich micher, a rich man that pretends himselfe to be verie poore. **1696** PHILLIPS, A *Micher*, a covetous Person, a niggardly Pinch-penny.

3. A truant; one who improperly absents himself.

1530 PALSGR. 245/1 Michar, *bvissonnier.* **1532** MORE *Confut. Tindale* Wks. 577/1 He like a mycher and a trewant, played at buckle pitte by the way. **1562** COOPER *Answ. Def. Truth* 122 They be self will moichers, they be not diligent scholers, that leauyng their maisters teachyng will folow their owne interpretacions. **1594** LYLY *Moth. Bomb.* I. iii. 191 How like a micher he standes, as though he had trewanted from honestie! **1596** SHAKS. *1 Hen. IV*, II. iv. 450 Shall the blessed Sonne of Heauen proue a Micher, and eate Black-berryes? **1775** ASH, *Micher*, a lazy loitering fellow, one who keeps out of sight to avoid working. **1840** HOOD *Friend in Need* Wks. 1862 V. 275 When a young micher plays truant, it is not for a lounge about the homestead. **1891** S. MOSTYN *Curatica* 67 My schoolmaster.. who had gained a high reputation for his skill in dealing with the 'micher'.

4. Comb., as ***micher-like*** adv.

1586 B. YOUNG *Guazzo's Civ. Conv.* IV. 194 Hee hath dronke so micherlike [It. *furtivamente*], as though he were none of this companie.

†ˈ**micher**, *v. Obs. rare*−1. [f. MICHER *sb.*] *intr.* To sneak. Hence †ˈ**michering** *ppl. a.*

c **1555** [see MICHER *sb.* 1]. **1615** W. HULL *Mirr. Maiestie* 6 One meechering hypocrite crept into the marriage feast, with-out his wedding garment.

†ˈ**michery**. *Obs.* Also 4–5 **micherie**, **mecherie**, 5 **mychery(e**. [f. MICHER *sb.* + -Y.] Pilfering, thievishness; cheating.

1390 GOWER *Conf.* II. 346 With Covoitise yit I finde A Servant of the same kinde, Which Stelthe is hote, and Mecherie With him is evere in compainie. *Ibid.* 355 For Venus, which was enemie Of thilke loves micherie, Discovereth al the pleine cas To Clymene. *c* **1440** *Jacob's Well* 196 Þou hast get good in raueyn, thefte, & mycherye. *c* **1440** *Promp. Parv.* 337/1 Mychery, *capacitas, manticulatus, furtulum.* **1496** *Dives & Pauper* (W. de W.) VII. iv. 279/2 Somtyme a thynge is stolen preuely without wetynge of the lorde or of the keper and ayenst ther wyll, & it is called mycherye. **1565–73** *Durham Depos.* (Surtees) 251 He was suspect of michery and untreweth.

Michigan (ˈmɪʃɪgən). **a.** The name of the State on the Great Lakes of North America, used *attrib.* to denote a thing or type found in, peculiar to, or characteristic of Michigan.

1835 C. BRADLEY in *Ohio Archaeol. & Hist. Soc. Publ.* (1966) XV. 257 My conquered enemy was the massassagua, the Michigan rattlesnake. **1838** *State of Indiana Delineated* (J. H. Colton & Co.) 26 A rail road is located from Madison to Indianapolis, and the great Michigan road through the state commences here. **1855** 'Q. K. P. DOESTICKS' *Doesticks, what he Says* xii. 97 One was afflicted with the measles, and the other had the Michigan itch. **1857** *Trans. Illinois Agric. Soc.* III. 496 For this purpose [*sc.* subsoiling] the Michigan double or subsoil plow is used. **1884** G. B. GOODE *Fisheries U.S.: Nat. Hist. Aquatic Animals* 505 The Michigan Grayling.. is at present most interesting to the angler. **1900** *Atlantic Monthly* LXXXV. 102/2 Heavy horses or oxen draw a brace of huge wheels for hauling. (This is the Michigan buggy.) **1922** H. TITUS *Timber* 12 Didn't Michigan Pine build th' corn belt? **1932** *Evening Sun* (Baltimore) 9 Dec. 31/5 *Michigan roll*, a bankroll.. of stage money with a genuine banknote.. outside. **1955** *Publ. Amer. Dial. Soc.* XXIV. 116 If the *bundle* consists largely of small bills, it is called a *michigan bankroll*, or a *mish.* **1962** E. LUCIA *Klondike Kate* ix. 195 It proved to be a Michigan bank roll, for the only ten[-dollar bill] was on the outside, all the others being ones. **1971** M. TAK *Truck Talk* 105 *Michigan rig*, a double-bottom rig out of Michigan, where such combinations are legal.

b. *U.S.* A card game similar to Newmarket.

1944 A. H. MOREHEAD *Pocket Bk. Games* 80 Michigan is a simple game, yet rewards careful attention. **1946** 'L. FORD' *Honolulu Story* 176 'I want to play hearts. On the floor.' 'Michigan,' Mary said. 'Michigan it is.' **1952** E. KEMPSON et al. *Hoyle Up-to-Date* 215 (*heading*) Stops family. Newmarket (Boodle, Newmarket, Chicago, Saratoga, Michigan, Stops). **1972** R. HARBIN *Waddingtons Family Card Games* 110 In the USA, Newmarket is known as Michigan, or Chicago, or Boodle, or Stops; and they play it slightly differently. But I think that our name, and our rules, are better. **1974** W. B. GIBSON *Hoyle's Mod. Encycl. Card Games* 161 *Michigan*, a modern game of the 'stops' type,

played with a standard fifty-two-card pack, with cards running in ascending value. *Ibid.* 164 *New Market*, the English counterpart of *Michigan*.., the only difference being that the extra hand, or 'widow', is never taken up for play but is 'dead' from start to finish.

Michigander (mɪʃɪˈgændə(r)). [f. prec.] A native or inhabitant of the State of Michigan.

1848 A. Lincoln *Coll. Works* (1953) I. 509, I mean the military tail you Democrats are now engaged in dove-tailing on to the great Michigander. **1865** *Harper's Mag.* May 814/1 One of the Michiganders uses the goose-quill to some purpose. **1897** *Outing* XXX. 293/1 (*heading*) Michi-gander lawmakers. **1952** *Manch. Guardian Weekly* 8 May 4/2 Jackson would like to have been known thereafter as 'The Republican City' and several boosters and patriotic Michiganders did their best to make that name take.

Michiganian (mɪʃɪˈgeɪnɪən). [f. Michigan + -ian.] = prec.

1813 *Niles' Reg.* V. 185 The Michiganians. **1835** [see wolverene, -ine 3]. **1837** H. Martineau *Society in Amer.* I. 65 The Michiganians were in the singular position of having a state government in full operation, while they were excluded from the Union.

michil, variant of mickle.

miching: see mitching *vbl. sb.* and *ppl. a.*

† **miching malicho.** Occurs only in the Shaks. passage quoted, and echoes of it; of uncertain form, origin, and meaning.

It is probable, though hardly certain, that the first word is mitching *ppl. a.* The conjecture that the second word represents Sp. *malhecho* misdeed (whence Malone and subsequent editors print *mallecho*) yields a fairly satisfactory sense; but there is no evidence that the Sp. word was familiar in English, and its pronunciation (malˈetʃo) does not account for the forms in the early editions.

1602 Shaks. *Ham.* iii. ii. 146 Marry this is Miching Malicho [*sic* Fol. 1 (1623): Q 1 (1603) myching Mallico; Q 2 (1604) munching Mallico], that meanes Mischeefe. **1836** E. Howard *R. Reefer* xliii, There was no 'minching malicho', or anything like mischief. **1882** Stevenson in *Longm. Mag.* I. 71 Other spots again seem to abide their destiny, suggestive and impenetrable, 'miching mallecho'.

Michler (ˈmɪxlə(r), ˈmɪk-). The name of Wilhelm *Michler* (d. 1889), German chemist, used in the possessive to denote certain compounds first studied by him, as **Michler's hydrol**, 4,4′-bis(dimethylamino)benzhydrol, $[C_6H_4N(CH_3)_2]_2CHOH$, a crystalline compound which is made by the condensation of dimethylaniline and formaldehyde or by reduction of Michler's ketone and is an important intermediate for the synthesis of triphenylmethane dyes; **Michler's ketone**, the ketone $[C_6H_4N(CH_3)_2]_2CO$ corresponding to Michler's hydrol, which is made by treating phosgene or carbon tetrachloride with dimethylaniline.

1910 *Jrnl. Chem. Soc.* XCVIII. i. 451 Tetramethyldiaminobenzhydrylphosphinous acid.., prepared from Michler's hydrol, occurs in colourless crystals. **1971** R. L. M. Allen *Colour Chem.* viii. 110 Michler's hydrol..condenses with bases such as dimethylaniline to give triphenylmethanes which by oxidation and treatment with acids yield rosanilines. **1897** *Jrnl. Chem. Soc.* LXXII. i. 157 The author obtained crystalline leuco-bases of dyes by the condensation of Michler's ketone with various phenols. **1949** P. W. Vittum tr. *Fierz-David & Blangey's Fund. Processes Dye Chem.* i. 140 Michler's ketone and its homologs are important starting materials for the preparation of valuable triphenylmethane dyes such as Victoria blue B and Victoria pure blue BO.

micht, obs. Sc. form of might.

Michurinism (mɪˈtʃʊərɪnɪz(ə)m). Also **michurinism.** [f. the name *Michurin* + -ism.] Belief in or advocacy of the views of the Russian horticulturalist I. V. Michurin (1855–1935): = Lysenkoism.

1949 J. S. Huxley *Soviet Genetics & World Sci.* i. 23 Michurinism is..an essentially non-scientific or pre-scientific doctrine. **1955** *Bull. Atomic Sci.* June 210/1 Genetics seems to be the field of 'natural' science which is most abused with political and other special interests, in their attempts to fabricate theoretical bases for their practices, as in the case of Hitler's racist obsessions and Stalin's Michurinism. **1974** *Encycl. Brit. Micropædia* VI. 862/2 Michurin's theories of hybridization, labelled michurinism, which accepted completely the inheritance of acquired characteristics, were adopted as the official science of genetics by the Soviet regime.

Hence **Miˈchurinist**, one who believes in or advocates Michurinism; also as *adj.*

1949 *Ann. Reg. 1948* 210 The Michurinists, who regarded environment as the chief determinant of heredity. **1949** C. Zirkle *Death of a Science in Russ.* vii. 174 The most advanced, materialistic, biological science is the Michurinist trend in the Soviet agrobiology. **1957** C. Hunt *Guide to Communist Jargon* xxviii. 100 In 1948 it was the turn of the biologists, and a number of them were deprived of their posts for supporting Weissmann-Morganist as opposed to Michurinist genetics.

Mick¹ (mɪk). Also **mick.** Shortened form of proper name *Michael*, applied jocularly to an Irishman. Also sometimes applied derogatorily. Also *attrib.* or as *adj.*

1856 *Butte Record* (Oroville, Calif.) 20 Sept. 3/3 One of the 'bucks' jerked something from his belt..and made for a Mick. **1882** 'Mark Twain' *Innoc. at Home* ii, When the Micks got to throwing stones through the Methodis' Sunday-school windows. **1893** A. Fuller *Lit. Courtship* x. 93 If once she gets hold of that fact, you will wish you had been born a 'mick'. **1894** P. L. Ford *Hon. Peter Stirling* lvii. 369 Fortunately it's a Mick regiment, so we needn't worry over who was killed. **1913** J. London *Valley of Moon* 27 They's been too much drink, an' you know what the Micks are for a rough house. **1932** E. Wilson *Devil take Hindmost* vii. 38 The Communists..have..recruited..a considerable number of seedy unemployed—niggers, micks. **1943** [see Geordie 2]. **1961** *Spectator* 12 Aug. 254 Labels such as Wop, Polack and Mick. **1970** M. Kenyon *100,000 Welcomes* iv. 32 Where's Ireland, huh? Who needs Micks?

b. A Roman Catholic. Also **Mickey.** Freq. derogatory. Also *attrib.* or as *adj.*

1924 P. Marks *Plastic Age* 201, I suppose you refer to..my one mick friend, although he isn't Irish. **1948** P. White *Aunt's Story* 258 He says that Mother is wrong to send a girl to a convent with a lot of micks. **1956** 'N. Shute' *Beyond Black Stump* ii. 57 Stanley and Phyllis went to Church of England schools..but all the rest of us are Micks. **1960** *Times* 28 Jan. 15/5 Religious rivalries from Salvationists to Plymouth Brethren—united in hatred of the 'Mickeys' or Catholics. **1971** *Guardian* 27 May 13/7 Curiously, in the circumstances of the Australian fondness for the 'o' suffix, a Roman Catholic is apparently never a Catho, but remains, in lower-level Protto usage, a Mick. **1973** *Times* 31 July 12/7 On this theory the Council of Ireland can be presented as a second inter-Parliamentary tier—'a place where the Micks and Prods can get together occasionally' as one Assembly member put it—built on a structure that already exists.

c. Examples of various *slang* (usu. derogatory) extended uses.

1928 F. Scott Fitzgerald in *Sat. Even. Post* 28 Apr. 4/2 In sordid poverty, below the bluff two hundred feet away, lived the 'micks'—they had merely inherited the name, for they were now largely of Scandinavian descent. **1937** in Partridge *Dict. Underworld* (1949) 437/2 *Mick*, a road mechanic. **1941** J. Smiley *Hash House Lingo* 37 *Mick*, Englishman. **1958** L. A. G. Strong *Light above Lake* 94 He's a dismal ould mick of a God. **1974** *Amer. Speech 1971* XLVI. 81 *Mexican*: greaser, spick, wetback, mick, halfbreed.

d. ***mad mick***: a pick. *slang.*

1924 *Truth* (Sydney) 27 Apr. 6 *Mad mick*, a pick. **1935** A. J. Pollock *Underworld Speaks* 74/1 *Mad mick*, a pick (prison) **1973** F. Huelin *Keep Moving* 78 Well, I won't buy drinks f'r any bloody ganger, just f'r a chance to swing a mad mick.

mick² (mɪk). *Austral. slang.* [Origin unknown.] The head, or sometimes the reverse, of a penny (see also quot. 1919).

1919 W. H. Downing *Digger Dial.* 33 *Mick*, (1) the Queen's head on a coin... (2) a queen in a pack of cards. **1938** J. Robertson *With Cameliers in Palestine* xx. 198 'A pair of Micks', which means that the offerings [in the game of two-up] are not accepted. **1941** Baker *Dict. Austral. Slang* 46 *Mick*, the 'head' of a penny. **1953** T. A. G. Hungerford *Riverslake* 126 'Ten bob he tails 'em!' he intoned,..'I got ten bob to say he tails 'em—ten bob the micks!'

mick³ (mɪk). *slang.* Also **mickey, micky.** [var. of mike *sb.*³ reinterpreted as a proper name.] ***to do a mick***, etc., to go away, to clear off (see mike *sb.*³).

1937 Partridge *Dict. Slang* 519/1 *Mick, do a* [equated with *do a mike*]. **1959** I. & P. Opie *Lore & Lang. Schoolch.* x. 192 *Sending away*,..do a mickey. **1961** S. Chaplin *Day of Sardine* xi. 225, I laid the ring on the notepaper and did a mickey as soon as I heard the front doorbell go.

mick⁴ (mɪk). *slang.* [Origin unknown.] A seaman's hammock.

1929 *Papers Mich. Acad. Sci., Arts & Lett.* X. 308/1 *Mick*, an abridgement of 'face like a scrubbed hammock'. **1946** J. Irving *Royal Navalese* 115 *Mick*, hammock. **1961** Partridge *Dict. Slang* Suppl. 1183/1 *Mick*,..a seaman's hammock.

mick⁵ (mɪk). *dial.* Also **mickey, micky.** [Origin unknown.] A pigeon.

1940 *N. & Q.* 3 Aug. 79/1 Mick was the usual word for a pigeon, especially the domesticated kind [in Cheshire]. **1965** *Jrnl. Lancs. Dial. Soc.* Jan. 7 Woodpigeon..Mick, Micky: Southport, Liverpool. **1966** F. Shaw et al. *Lern Yerself Scouse* 23 *De mickeys are lettin on de roof*, the pigeons are alighting on the roof. **1966** 'L. Lane' *ABZ of Scouse* 68 *Mickey-snatcher*, a person who steals municipal pigeons.

mickel(l, mickeson, obs. ff. mickle, mixen.

mickery (ˈmɪkərɪ). *Austral.* Also **mickerie.** [Origin unknown.] **a.** A type of well (see quot. 1934). **b.** Marshy ground; = soak *sb.* 2 d. Also *attrib.*

1934 *Bulletin* (Sydney) 6 June 20/2 A mickery was a timbered well-shaft sunk into the sandy bed of a creek; it was worked by means of a pole placed across a forked stick, the pole having a bucket attached to one end and a weight to the other. **1935** H. H. Finlayson *Red Centre* x. 98 The Wonkonguroos, themselves an offshoot of the Aruntas, occupying until recently what is known as the mickerie country, a desolation to the north-west of the Yalliyandas. **1945** Baker *Austral. Lang.* iii. 58 *Mickery country*, country which holds moisture after rain or which is of swampy 'soak' type.

Mickey (ˈmɪkɪ). *U.S. slang.* [f. Mickey Mouse.] A type of radar-assisted bombsight. Also *attrib.*

1944 *News* (San Francisco) 28 Nov. 7/3 'Mickey', a sensational radar device which 'sees' through darkness, clouds and artificial smoke. **1944** *Time* 11 Dec. 24 Mickey was a British invention, freely given to the U.S. U.S. scientists later developed an improved model. It was first used by U.S. bombers just over a year ago; today every fleet of heavy bombers over Europe presumably is or will be equipped with it, on day or night raids. **1945** *News* (San Francisco) 15 Aug. 10 (Advt.), Mickey radar sends out super-high frequency radio waves which bounce back from solid targets and are picked up by the radar receiver and transformed into a radar picture on a screen like the one in a home television receiver. **1954** Berrey & Van den Bark *Amer. Thes. Slang* §819 *Mickey*, the improved American airborne radar. **1955** M. Reifer *Dict. New Words* 131/2 *Mickey*.., a radar-type bomb-sight that permits air navigation in zero visibility and pinpoint strategic bombing despite overcast or darkness. Named for the cartoon figure, Mickey Mouse, created by Walt Disney.

Mickey, var. Mick¹ b, Mickey Finn, Mickey Mouse.

mickey: see mick³, mick⁵, micky¹.

Mickey Finn (ˌmɪkɪˈfɪn). *slang* (orig. *U.S.*). Also **Mickey Flynn** and ellipt. **Mickey.** [Origin uncertain.] A strong alcoholic drink; a drink adulterated with a narcotic or purgative substance, usu. administered to a person with the deliberate intention of stupefying or greatly discomforting him; the adulterant itself; also *transf.* and *fig.* (Cf. *knock-out drops.*) Hence **mickey-ˈfinn** *v. trans.*, to adulterate with a Mickey Finn; to stupefy with a Mickey Finn; also *ellipt.*

1928 M. C. Sharpe *Chicago May* xii. 99, I got a bottle of brandy... He was lit up..but I shot a few more Mickey Finns (double drinks) into him. **1931** *Amer. Mercury* Mar. 316/1 But he never slipped an obstreperous customer the croton oil Mickey Finn of the modern night club. **1934** *Cosmopolitan* Apr. 131/1 She had been mickey-finned. **1934** J. O'Hara *Appointment in Samarra* (1935) iii. 86 The cheap bastard... I'd like to give him a Mickey Finn. **1935** N. Ersine *Underworld & Prison Slang* 53 *Mickey Finn*, a drink spiked with knockout drops. **1936** *Amer. Speech* XI. 124/1 *Mickey Flynn* or *Mickey Finn*, a knockout dose (often cigar ashes in a carbonated drink) administered to an addict or a sucker. **1938** A. J. Liebling *Back where I came From* 88 Mickeys..act so drastically that one may kill a drunk with a weak heart. **1951** Wodehouse *Old Reliable* v. 71 She had been about to suggest that the butler might slip into Adela's bedtime Ovaltine what is known as a knockout drop or Mickey Finn. **1957** P. Frank *Seven Days to Never* iv. 118 This was no ordinary hangover... He had been expertly mickey-finned. **1960** *Guardian* 17 June 7/4 The reader cannot be sure when Mr. Colquhoun is about to slip him a Bible..and when a Mickey Finn. **1962** E. Lucia *Klondike Kate* iv. 107 However, the dames seldom rolled the miners or slipped them a Mickey. **1966** R. W. Taylor *Doomsday Square* (1967) xiii. 144, I Mickey-Finned him with my little pressure syringe. Let him sleep. **1971** 'C. Franklin' *Home Secretary Affair* vii. 99 Two men..had mickey-finned his drink. **1972** M. Pugh *Murmur of Mutiny* xix. 144 I'd a couple or so in the sergeants' mess... They mustaf been mickied. **1973** D. Bagley *Tightrope Men* xii. 93 Meyrick was probably knocked out by a Mickey Finn in his nightly Ovaltine.

Mickey Mouse (ˈmɪkɪ maʊs). **1.** The name of a mouse-like character in a series of animated cartoons designed by the American cartoonist Walter Elias ('Walt') Disney (1901–66), used with direct or indirect reference to the character in these cartoons. Also *ellipt.* **Mickey**, a Mickey Mouse cartoon. Also *attrib.* or as *adj.*, characteristic of, resembling, or featuring Mickey Mouse. Frequently (esp. in *U.S.*) designating something small, insignificant, or worthless.

1934 R. Stout *Fer-de-Lance* v. 66 Everybody..would be ..laughing at us instead of going to a movie to see Micky Mouse. **1935** S. Lewis *It can't happen Here* ix. 84 Dr. Goebbels..is privily known throughout Germany as 'Wotan's Mickey Mouse'. **1936** N. Coward *To-night at 8.30* II. 49 We'll miss the Mickey. **1936** 'G. Orwell' *Let.* 26 Aug. in *Coll. Ess.* (1968) i. 228 You have moved too much away from the ordinary world into a sort of Mickey Mouse universe where things and people don't have to obey the rules of space and time. **1937** *Cinema Arts* July 24 The light which the electrician is aiming at Mr. Gable's head is the smallest 'spot' used in the studio, and is therefore known as a Mickey Mouse. **1939** *War Illustr.* 18 Nov. 310/3 Special 'Mickey Mouse' gas-masks in various colours and having separate eye-pieces and a little nose are being made for small children who are repelled by the ordinary ones. **1941** *San Francisco Examiner* 2 Mar. Pict. Rev. 7/1 George Graham, a timid, middle-aged mickey mouse who was afraid of crowds, people, anything. **1942** N. Streatfeild *I ordered Table for Six* 20 That little bit of the room at the top must have been a nursery once, there's some Mickie Mouses on that wallpaper. **1951** *San Francisco Examiner* 3 Feb. 1/3 (*heading*) 40th Division. Troops Lack Equipment. Woes of 'Mickey Mouse Army'. **1957** T. Gunn *Sense of Movement* 54 Bent keys, Italian grammars, Mickey Mouse caps. **1958** *Amer. Speech* XXXIII. 226 A 'Mickey Mouse course' means a *snap* course. **1962** *New Statesman* 19 Jan. 96/2 A Mickey Mouse clock ticks beside the marital bed. **1963** *Amer. Speech* XXXVIII. 176 [Kansas University slang] An assignment which is regarded as foolish and a waste of time is a *Mickey Mouse.* **1966** Mrs. L. B. Johnson *White House Diary* 4 June (1970) 387 It [*sc.* the graduation ceremony] is

such a mass production affair—'Mickey Mouse', as she calls it—not quite the sophisticated thing to do anymore. **1968** *Sunday Times* 20 Oct. 8/4 Cunningham referred to 'Micky Mouse' (unnecessary and childish) operations. **1969** C. Davidson in Cockburn & Blackburn *Student Power* 329 The forms given us for our self-government are of the Mickey Mouse, sand-box variety. **1972** J. Mosedale *Football* ii. 25 One reason for the AFL's reputation as a Mickey Mouse league is that it gave new life to NFL rejects. **1973** R. Ludlum *Matlock Paper* xix. 161 The average purchase of chips was $200 to $300. Hardly 'Micky Mouse'. **1974** *Globe & Mail* (Toronto) 13 Nov. 1/2 The titles kept the press and broadcast media from thinking 'it was such a Mickey Mouse operation'. **1975** *Amer. Speech* 1972 XLVII. 152 You getting flew coy with the gray boys, Mickey Mouse? *Ibid.* 153 *Mickey mouse n*, white; black who 'puts on a white face'.

2. *Mus.* Inferior dance-band music, similar to that played as a background to a cartoon film; usu. *attrib.*

1938 *Down Beat* Apr. 25/2 A strictly 'mickey mouse' band is still box office. **1945** *Ibid.* 1 Sept. 15/1 Strictly mickey mouse is what they [*sc.* night clubs] advocate, and many of the truly good musicians are forced to play the tripe in order to get work. **1954** *San Francisco Chron.* 17 June 17 (*heading*) Glenn Miller's music was all Mickey Mouse. **1958** *Amer. Speech* XXXIII. 225 A mickey or Mickey Mouse band is not merely a 'pop tune' band,.. but the kind of pop band that sounds as if it is playing background for an animated cartoon. **1966** *Crescendo* May 4/2 The jazzman's struggle for self-expression in a world of commercial Mickey Mouse bands. **1970** C. Major *Dict. Afro-Amer. Slang* 81 *Micky Mouse* (*music*), popular, commercialized music.

3. *Air Force slang.* A name applied to an electrical device which releases bombs from aircraft.

1941 *N.Y. Times* 6 Apr. 30/5 This war is producing a new batch of army slang... Many of the words are peculiar to certain units, and very few are yet in general use... An R.A.F. pilot calls his cockpit the 'pulpit'... The instrument releasing the bombs, an electrical distributor, is called a 'Mickey Mouse'. **1943** Hunt & Pringle *Service Slang* 46 *Mickey Mouse*, The bomb-dropping mechanism on some types of bomber aircraft is so called because it strongly resembles the intricate machinery portrayed in Walt Disney's cartoons. **1943** L. Cheshire *Bomber Pilot* i. 8 If I knew how to use 'Mickey Mouse', to open and shut bomb doors, or use a bomb-sight.

Hence **Mickey-mousing** (see quots.).

1957 Manvell & Huntley *Technique Film Music* ii. 38 'Mickey-Mousing' in film musical terminology.. means the exact, calculated dove-tailing of music and action. **1960** *Times* 1 Dec. 7/3 Odds and ends of Albeniz.. treated to what film composers would call 'mickey-mousing', with every detail of the music mirrored with stupefying literalness in the dancing. **1973** *New Society* 2 Aug. 288/1 What is known in the film-music trade as 'Mickey-Mousing'—the action of the film gets a simultaneous musical parody. When Tarzan swings down on his rope, a harp plays a descending glissando.

mickle ('mɪk(ə)l), **muckle** ('mʌk(ə)l), *a.*, *sb.*, and *adv.* *Obs.* exc. *dial.* and *arch.* Forms: α. 1–2 micel, mycel, 3 michil, 3–5 michel, mychel, 4–5 mychell, mechil, mechel, mychil. β. 2–3 muchele, 2–5 muchel, 3 mucchel, 3–5 mochil, 4 muchil, mochill, 4–5 mochel, 4–6 mochell, 5 mochyll, 6 (*arch.*) muchell. γ. [1–2 micl-], 3 mikel(l, -ul, mickel, 3–4 mikil, mykil, 3–6 mykel(l(e, mykyll, 4–5 mykill, -yl, 4–6 mykle, 5 mikille, mycul(le, 5–7 micle, mycle, 6 mykkylle, mickell, myckil, 5– mickle. δ. 3–5 mekyll, 3–6 mekil(l, 4 *Sc.* meekle, 4–5 mekille, -yl, 4–6 mekile, 5 mekel(l, -ul(l, mecul(le, 6 meakle, 6–7 *Sc.* meikill, 5–8 mekle, 9 *Sc.* meickle, 6– *Sc.* meikle. ε. 3 mucle, 4, 6 mokel(l, 8 mukel, 8– muckle. [Com. Teut.: OE. *micel* (also *mycel*) = OS. *mikil* (MLG *michel*), OHG. *mihhil* (MHG. *michel*), ON. *mikell*, also *mykell* (nom. and acc. neut. *miket*, *myket*, acc. masc. *mikenn*, *mykenn*; Sw. *mycken*, neut. *mycket*; Norw. dial *myken*, neut. *myket*; Da. *meget* neut.), Goth. *mikils*:—OTeut. **mikilo-*, corresponding to Gr. *μεγαλο-*, lengthened stem of *μέγας* great; the shorter form of the adj. is represented in Teut. only by ON. *miǫk* adv., very, which formally corresponds to Gr. *μέγα* neut. The root **meg-* (represented also in Armenian *mets* great, and perh. in L. *magnus*) appears to be allied to the Aryan root **magh-* of Skr. *mah*, *maha*, *mahan* great.

The OE. form *mycel* (which is not a mere graphic variant of *micel*, but stands for an actual pronunciation) is difficult to explain; it is commonly supposed to be due to association with *lȳtel* little *a.* The similar change of *i* into *y* in ON. *mykell*, *mykl-*, is believed to proceed from the influence of the *u* in the inflected forms *miklu*, *miklum*; but this explanation is not applicable to OE.

The phonology of the ME. and modern forms is in many points obscure. Normally, OE. *y* would become in the S.W. *u*, pronounced (ʏ), and elsewhere *i*; the abnormal *u* (in ME. also written *o*) of the β and ε forms has not yet been satisfactorily explained. The forms with *k* are northern and north-midland; the regular southern forms with *ch* are obsolete, having given place to the shortened *mich*, much.

In present dialectal use the prevailing form is *muckle*; but *mickle* and *meikle* are often used by modern Scottish writers even when their own colloquial dialect has only *muckle*. The archaistic use in non-dialectal poetry is rare, and almost confined to the form *mickle*.]

A. *adj.*

1. = great *a.*, in various applications.

a. with reference to size, bulk, stature.

α. **825** in Birch *Cartul. Sax.* I. 542 þonon on anne micelne stan. *c* **1000** Ælfric *Gen.* i. 16 And god ʒeworhte twa micele leoht. *c* **1425** *Cursor M.* 1320 (Trin.) A mychel tre.

γ. *a* **1300** *Cursor M.* 1320 Out-ouer þat well þan lokes he, And sagh þar stand a mikel tre. *c* **1330** R. Brunne *Chron. Wace* (Rolls) 12341 By a mykel fir he sat. *c* **1375** *Sc. Leg. Saints* xxvii. (*Machor*) 874 A man þat mykill vas. **1560** *Burgh Rec. Stirling* (1887) 72 Ane mykle pot, ane les pot, ane tyn pynt [etc.]. *a* **1657** Mure *Wks.* (S.T.S.) II. 254 She bure vnto him.. Ard. called mickle Archibald. **1789** Burns *Toothache* iii, I throw the wee stools o'er the mickle.

δ. *c* **1375** *Sc. Leg. Saints* x. (*Mathou*) 43 A citte, þat mekile wes & of gret fame. **1375** Barbour *Bruce* xviii. 308 His mekill hude helit haly The armyng that he on hym had. *c* **1440** *Alphabet of Tales* 62 þis Assenech was a mekull large womman as Sarra was. **1500–20** Dunbar *Poems* liv. 5 My ladye with the mekle lippis. **1596** Dalrymple tr. *Leslie's Hist. Scot.* I. 14 Thay mekle gret horse quhilkes.. beiris armed men of weir. **1725** Ramsay *Gentle Sheph.* ii. i, Set the meiklest peat-stack in a low. **1863** R. Quinn *Heather Lintie* 249 Glib cantin' Bauldy S—— now lies 'Neath this rouch meickle stane.

ε. **13..** *E.E. Allit. P.* B. 366 Was no brymme þat abod vnbrosten bylyue, þe mukel lauande loghe to þe lyfte rered. **15..** *Wyf Auchtirmwchty* 113 in *Bannatyne MS.* (Hunter. Club) 345 Vp scho gat ane muckle rung. **1748** Thomson *Cast. Indol.* ii. vii, [He] grew at last a knight of muckel frame. **1814** Scott *Wav.* xlii, Mr. Waverley's wearied wi' majoring yonder afore the muckle pier-glass. **1866** J. B. Rose tr. *Ovid's Met.* 337 The cormorant short-legged, with muckle throat. **1889** Barrie *Window in Thrums* xi, He was a terrible invalid, an' for the hinmost years o' his life he sat in a muckle chair nicht an' day.

†**b.** as a distinctive epithet for a place, building, etc. *Obs.*

1379 *Rolls of Parlt.* III. 69/1 Son College appellez Mokel Universite Hall en Oxenford. *c* **1400** *Brut* lvi. 50 Aurilambros & Vter.. assemblede a grete hoste forto come into michel Britaigne. **1459** *Paston Lett.* I. 462 Castre faste by Mikel Yermuth, in the shire of Norffolk.

c. said of a numerical aggregate, proportion, etc.

c **1200** Ormin 169, & he shall turrnenn mikell flocc Of þiss Judisskenn þeode Till Goddes Sune Jesu Crist. *c* **1205** Lay. 1746 þa Corineus of wode com mid michelene ferde. *Ibid.* 31435 Mucchel del heo sloȝen of þan monweorede. **1375** Barbour *Bruce* xvii. 183 He had A mekill rout of worthy men. *a* **1400–50** *Alexander* 69 Slik was þe multitude of mast so mekil & so thike, þat all him þoȝt þat he treis a hare wod it semyd. *Ibid.* 927 þe multitude sa mekill of men.

d. with reference to amount or degree. Now *rare* or *Obs.*; merged in sense 2, from which, when the sb. has no article, it is often hardly to be distinguished.

α. *c* **888** K. Ælfred *Boeth.* xxxviii. §2 Swiðe oft se micla anwald ðara yflena ʒehrist swiðe færlice. *a* **900** *O.E. Chron.* an. 664 (MS. A.), þy ilcan ʒeare wæs micel mancuealm. *c* **1250** *Gen. & Ex.* 1208 Michel gestninge made abraham. *c* **1374** Chaucer *Anel. & Arc.* 99 But natheles ful mychell besynesse Had he or þat he myght his lady wynne. **1390** Gower *Conf.* III. 381 Mechil grace ther uppon Unto the Citees schulde falle. *a* **1425** *Cursor M.* 18123 (Trin.) þer coom a mechel steuen. *c* **1430** *Syr Gener.* (Roxb.) 8445 Than had the Soudon michel care.

β. *a* **1200** *Moral Ode* 211 Godes wisdom is wel muchel and alswa is his mihte. *c* **1200** *Vices & Virtues* 47 Hit is me to muchel iswinch ðar embe to þenken. *c* **1330** *Assump. Virg.* (B.M. MS.) 747 And ihesu, þorw his mochil myȝt, Here feet and handes gan to ryȝt. ? *a* **1366** Chaucer *Rom. Rose* 45 And that is she that hath, y-wis, So mochel prys. *c* **1386** —— *Knt.'s T.* 1494 Thou shalt ben wedded vn to oon of tho That han for thee so muchel care and wo. **1413** *Pilgr. Sowle* (Caxton 1483) v. xiv. 110, I was ful sory that I was so soone departid fro so mochel ioye. *c* **1460** *Launfal* 282 A man of mochell myghte.

γ. *c* **1200** Ormin 788 Forr þatt wass to þatt gode preost Well swiþe mikell blisse. *c* **1220** *Bestiary* 319 He lepeð ðanne wið mikel list, Of swet water he haueð ðrist. *a* **1300** *Cursor M.* 18123 And eft þar come a mikel steuen, Als it a thoner war of heuen. *c* **1330** R. Brunne *Chron.* (1810) 2 þe Bretons, men of mykelle myght. *c* **1420** *Anturs of Arth.* xliii. (Ireland MS.), He wulle stond the in stoure, in-toe so mycul styd. **1522** *World & Child* (Roxb.) A iv, Mykyll is my myght. **1590** Spenser *F.Q.* ii. iv. 7 He was a man of mickle might. *Ibid.* iii. iv. 20 He.. mickle fame Did get through great adventures by him donne. **1591** Shaks. *1 Hen. VI*, iv. vi. 35 To morrow I shall dye with mickle Age. **1627** Drayton *Nimphidia* lxxxviii, To the Fayrie Court they went, With mickle ioy and merriment. **1819** Keats *Eve St. Agnes* xiv, But let me laugh awhile, I've mickle time to grieve. **1850** Blackie *Æschylus* II. 269 The riches stored by me with mickle care. **1887** W. S. Gilbert *Ruddigore* ii. 44 His gallantries were mickle. **1891** E. Field *Western Verse, Death Robin Hood* 24 With mickle woe His heart was like to break.

δ. *c* **1375** *Sc. Leg. Saints* i. (*Petrus*) 537 He had þerof rycht mekil wondir. *c* **1400** *Rowland & O.* 484 þᵉ Sarazene cryed with mekill myghte. *c* **1420** *Anturs of Arth.* xxxviii. (Ireland MS.), The kinge commawundet kindeli the Erle of Kente, For his meculle curtasy, to kepe the tother knyȝte. *c* **1420** *Sir Amadace* (Camden) xlv, Ther he wanne fulle mecul honoure. **1616** *Barbour's Bruce* (ed. Hart) ii. 245* Men of meekle might.

ε. **1205** Lay. 29752 And mid wurðscipe mucle haldeð his wike. **13..** *E.E. Allit. P.* B. 1164, & he hem halȝed for his & help at her nede In mukel meschefes mony, þat meruayl is to here.

e. with reference to power or importance. Now somewhat *rare*.

α. *a* **900** *O.E. Martyrol.* 28 Apr. 66 On þone ylcan dæg bið sancte Cristofores þrowung þæs miclan martyres. *a* **1325** *Prose Psalter* xlvii[i]. 1 Our Lord is michel & worþi to be praysed.

β. *a* **1200** *Moral Ode* 92 Hwet scule we seggen oðer don et þe muchele dome. *c* **1374** Chaucer *Boeth.* iv. Pr. i. 86 (Camb. MS.) The rith ordenee hows of so mochel a fader.

γ. *a* **1300** *Cursor M.* 17827 And thoru þair godd adonai, þair mikel godd of israel, þai coniurd þam na soth to hel. **15..** *Peebles to Play* xxiii, The meikill devill gang wi you.

δ. **1572** *Satir. Poems Reform.* xxxviii. 39 Solyman, Tamerlan, nor yit the mekle Deill.. was neuer sa wickit. **1796** Burns *To Mitchell* 3 Alake! alake! the meikle deil Wi' a' his witches Are at it. **1800** Tannahill *Poems* (1900) 120 Yon meikle folk Think siller stands for sense.

ε. **1600** W. Watson *Decacordon* (1602) 144 Great rich farmers or muckle carles of the countrey. **1819** W. Tennant *Papistry Storm'd* iii. (1827) 97 Our anchor's lost,.. We're perish'd a', baith sma' and muckle! **1896** 'L. Keith' *Indian Uncle* i. 4 There's nae gainsaying that oor Adam's the muckle man o' the family noo.

f. Const. *of*, *at*.

γ. *a* **1300** *Cursor M.* 283 þis lauerd þat is so mikul o might. *Ibid.* 15124 O þis iesu þat es sa wis Sa mikel alsua o lare. *Ibid.* 17969 þat goddes sone so mychel of myȝt, Among monkynde shal he liȝt.

δ. *c* **1375** *Cursor M.* 17969 (Gött.) þat goddes sun, sua mekil of might. **1500–20** Dunbar *Poems* xxxiv. 11 Than swoir ane courtyour mekle of pryd. ? *a* **1550** *Droichis part of play* 42 in *Dunbar's Poems* (S.T.S.) 315 Bot eftir he grew mekle at fowth.

2. a. A great quantity or amount of; = much *a.* (In Sc. now chiefly in negative and interrogative context.)

α. *c* **1000** *Sax. Leechd.* I. 76 ʒif mon on mycelre rade.. weorðe ʒeteorad [etc.]. **1154** *O.E. Chron.* an. 1137 Micel hadde Henri King gadered gold & syluer.

β. *c* **1205** Lay. 7283 Heo nomen of Romanisce londe muchel seoluer & gold. *c* **1380** Wyclif *Wks.* (1880) 92 Prelatis ouere þis robben oure lond of mochil tresour. **1579** Spenser *Sheph. Cal.* Feb. 109 A goodly Oake sometime had it bene.. And mochell mast to the husband did yielde.

γ. *c* **1400** Maundev. (Roxb.) i. 4 þe kyng.. haldes grete and mykill land. *Ibid.* iv. 13 Scho had mykill tresoure. *c* **1450** *Mirour Saluacioun* 3417 The Jewes.. gaf thaym mykel monee als. *c* **1450** *M.E. Med. Bk.* (Heinrich) 68 Take as mykel salt, as þow hast pouder. **1526** Skelton *Magnyf.* 1356 By me is conueyed mykyll praty ware.

δ. *c* **1375** *Sc. Leg. Saints* x. (*Mathou*) 464 He gert Inwirone al hyre In with mekil fuel, It to bryne. **1508** Dunbar *Flyting w. Kennedie* 189 Thow purehippit, vgly averill,.. Quhilk brewis mekle barret to thy bryd. **1596** Dalrymple tr. *Leslie's Hist. Scot.* I. 26 He gathiris mekle money. **1676** W. Row *Contn. Blair's Autobiog.* xii. (1848) 439 The honest Earl of Crawford feared mickle evil from this Session of Parliament. **1786** *Har'st Rig* xii, Duncan brags how meikle meal She's eaten here. **1823** Scott *Quentin D.* xxxi, You have had as meikle good fortune as if you had been born with a lucky-hood on your head.

ε. **1720** Ramsay *Edinb.'s Salut. to Ld. Carnarvon* iv, I'll no make muckle vaunting. **1816** Scott *Old Mort.* xiv, Neither of our sorrows will do muckle gude, that I can see. *a* **1859** in J. Watson *Living Bards of Border* 8 They were nae folk o' muckle gear. **1872** C. Gibbon *For the King* xxii, Madam, your father has not brought you muckle comfort.

†**b.** Qualifying *folk*, *people*: A great number of, many. *Obs.*

β. *c* **1275** *Passion of our Lord* 49 in *O.E. Misc.* 38 Mochel volk hym vulede.

γ. *c* **1200** Ormin 15748 He full wel wisste þatt tær wass sammnedd mikell follc þatt heȝhe daȝȝ to frellsenn.

δ. *c* **1440** *Alphabet of Tales* 60 Mekle peple þat was in þe kurk war sparrid in with þe watir.

3. Comb.: **mickle-hammer** (see quot.); **mickle-mouthed**, **muckle-mouthed** *a.*, applied proverbially to one whose face is rather disfigured by the disproportionate size of the mouth; **micklewame**, the stomach, esp. that of the ox used for culinary purposes; †**mickle-what** (cf. little-what), a great deal, something of many kinds; **mickle wheel**, the great wheel of a spinning wheel.

1843 Holtzapffel *Turning* I. 171 The spallers employ heavy axe-formed or *muckle-hammers, for spalling or scaling off smaller flakes [of granite]. **1721** Kelly *Sc. Proverbs* 253 *Mickle mouth'd Folk are happy to their Meat. **1951** J. D. Salinger *Catcher in Rye* xi. 93 She was sort of muckle-mouthed... When she was talking and got excited, ..her mouth sort of went in about fifty directions. **1596** Dalrymple tr. *Leslie's Hist. Scot.* i. 94 Thay take the hail *mekilwame of ane slain ox [etc.]. **1390** Gower *Conf.* I. 320 As he which cowthe *mochel what. *a* **1400–50** *Alexander* 130 Quadrentis coruen all of quyte siluyre full quaynte, Mustours & mekil quat mare þen a littill. *Ibid.* 5468. **1821** Galt *Ann. Parish* xii, Both little wheel and *meikle wheel. **1824** Scott *St. Ronan's* xvi, She.. talked something of matrimony, and the mysteries of the muckle wheel.

B. *absol.* and *sb.*

I. The adj. used *absol.*

1. a. A great quantity or amount; much. *to make mickle of*: to make much of, cherish.

α. *a* **1123** *O.E. Chron.* an. 1101 His men mycel to hearme æfre ʒedydon.

γ. *c* **1375** *Sc. Leg. Saints* xxx. (*Theodera*) 350 Hyme þat mykil of hyre mad. *c* **1400** *Sowdone Bab.* 1016 Mikille of my people have thay slayn. *a* **1529** Skelton *Col. Cloute* 559 The Church hath to mykel, And they haue to lytell. *a* **1701** Sedley *Poet. Pieces* Wks. 1722 II. 9 Hold, there's enough; nay, 'tis o'er mickle.

δ. *c* **1375** *Sc. Leg. Saints* xiii. (*Marcus*) 10 Sanct Ione þe ewangeliste, þat of cristis priwete mekil wyste. *a* **1400–50** *Alexander* 4397 Bot ay mekill wald haue mare as many man spellis. **1508** Dunbar *Tua Mariit Wemen* 60 Birdis hes ane better law na bernis be meikill.

ε. **1865** G. Macdonald *A. Forbes* 2 There'll be no muckle o' him to rise again. **1871** C. Gibbon *Lack of Gold* i, How muckle will this be worth, think ye.

†**b.** Most, the greatest part (*of* something). *Obs.*

a **1578** Lindesay (Pitscottie) *Chron. Scot.* (S.T.S.) I. 324 Quhene George Douglas come to Sanctandrois and remanitt thair mekill of ane day in dressing of his bussieness.

c. *so mickle* (in 17th c. Sc. written *sameikill*) = so much.

1437 *Rolls of Parlt.* IV. 503/2 Yef so mekill be necessarie yerto. *c* **1440** *Generydes* 6451 Ye will doo so mekill as take yᵉ

payn, To come so ferre. **1609** SKENE *Reg. Maj.* I. 39 b, Ilke ane of them sall haue sameikill, as is within his awin lordship and dominion. *Ibid., Stat. Alex. II*, 15 b, Quhat he hes taken fra anie man, he sall restore sameikill to him.

d. In certain adverbial phrases: ***for as mickle as***, forasmuch as; ***in as*** (†*sa*) ***mickle as***, in so far as, inasmuch as; †***unto so mickle***, so much that; †***as mickle to say as*** = 'as much as to say'.

a **1300** *Cursor M.* 19596 Sua aght all preistes.. In als mikel als in þaim es. *c* **1400** MAUNDEV. (Roxb.) Pref. 2 For als mykill as it es lang tyme passed sen þare was any general passage ouer þe see in to þe haly land [etc.]. *c* **1420** LYDG. *Assembly of Gods* 92 In as mekyll as hit ys now soo That ye hym here haue as your prysonere, I shall you shew my compleynt loo. *c* **1440** *Alphabet of Tales* 145 Hur moder.. blamyd hur & reprovid hur þerfor, vnto so mekle, sho slew hur moder. *c* **1550** *Exam. W. Thorpe* in Foxe *A. & M.* (1583) I. 534 For as mikle as your asking passeth my vnderstanding, I dare neither deny it nor graunt it. **1563** J. DAVIDSON in *Wodrow Misc.* (1844) I. 192 For that war als mekle to say as God had appointit the Kirk to be judge betuix the thing that is and is not. *a* **1572** KNOX *Hist. Ref.* Wks. 1846 I. 283 Never twa of thame universallie aggreing in all pointis, in samekle as thei ar of men.

†**2.** (*the*) ***mickle***: those who are great. *Obs.*

c **1220** *Bestiary* 548 Ðo arn ðe little in leue laȝe, Ðe mikle ne maiȝ he to him draȝen. *a* **1400** *Octavian* 1 Lytyll and mykyll, olde and yonge, Lystenyth now to my talkynge.

II. *sb.*

†**3.** Size, stature; bigness. *Obs.*

c **1369** CHAUCER *Dethe Blaunche* 454 A wonder wel farynge knyght.. Of good mochel [*v.r.* mykil] and right yong therto. **13..** *Gaw. & Gr. Knt.* 142 Bot mon most I algate mynn hym to bene, & þat þe myriest in his muckel þat myȝt ride. **1377** LANGL. *P. Pl.* B. XVI. 182 Þre leodes in o lith non lenger þan other, Of one mochel & myȝte in mesure and in lengthe. *c* **1400** *Destr. Troy* 6246 Ector.. Of whose mykill, & might, & mayn strenght, Dares.. duly me tellus. *c* **1400** MAUNDEV. (Roxb.) xxi. 96 Þe mykill of a mannes thee. *Ibid.* xxii. 103 Þai er riȝt faire and wele proporciound of þaire mykill. **1622** DRAYTON *Poly-olb.* xxviii. 335 Stones of a Spherick forme of sundry Mickles fram'd.

4. A large sum or amount. Chiefly in proverb, ***many a little*** (or ***pickle***) ***makes a mickle***.

1599 MIDDLETON *Micro-Cynicon* Wks. (Bullen) VIII. 126 Some little dirty spot.. Nothing in many's view, in her's a mickle. **1605** CAMDEN *Rem., Prov.* (1614) 310 Many a little makes a micle. **1712** STEELE *Spect.* No. 509 ¶6 But, I think, a Speculation upon Many a Little makes a Mickle.. would be very useful to the World. **1905** *Westm. Gaz.* 29 Apr. 3/1 Mony a pickle maks a muckle.

C. *adv.* [OE. has in advb. use several cases of the adj.: accus. neut. *micel*, genit. *micles* (early ME. *mucheles*), dat. pl. *miclum*, instrumental *micle*.]

1. To a great extent or degree; greatly; by far. Also in relative sense with *as*, *how*, *so* (see the corresponding use of MUCH *adv.*).

In Sc. *so mickle* was in 16–17th c. often written *sameikill*.

α. *c* **897** K. ÆLFRED *Gregory's Past. C.* ix. 60 Se læce bið micles to bald.. þe [etc.]. *a* **1000** *Cædmon's Gen.* 2713 Ic þegnum þinum dyrnde & sylfum þe swiðost micle. *c* **1250** *Kent. Serm.* in *O.E. Misc.* 26 Herodes i-herde þet o king was i-bore þet solde bi king of geus, swo was michel anud. *a* **1325** *Prose Psalter* li[i]. 7 He was michel worþ in his vanite. *c* **1420** *Chron. Vilod.* 841 Kynge Edgar was so mechel adredde. *a* **1425** *Cursor M.* 451 (Trin.) To god hym self wolde he be pere Not pere alone but mychel more.

β. *a* **1200** *Moral Ode* 258 Þo þe sungede muchel a drunke and an ete. *c* **1205** LAY. 3201 He mochul a þa wodeloker wilnede þeos mæidenes. *a* **1225** *Ancr. R.* 292 Muchel luuede he us. *c* **1275** *Wom. Samaria* 74 in *O.E. Misc.* 86 Þo byleuede þat folk mucheles þe more. **1340** *Ayenb.* 57 Mochel hi wolden ham wreþi. *c* **1374** CHAUCER *Troylus* I. 386 And ouer al þis ȝet muchel more he þouȝt what for to speke. *c* **1400** *Rom. Rose* 3442 Thy request Is not to mochel dis-honest. *a* **1425** *Cursor M.* 10981 (Trin.) Muchel for riȝte shal he swynke.

γ. *c* **1220** *Bestiary* 235 Ðe mire is maȝti, mikel ȝe swinkeð In sumer and in softe weder. *a* **1300** *Cursor M.* 4082 It bitidd mikel in þaa dauus. *c* **1330** R. BRUNNE *Chron. Wace* (Rolls) 1697 He triste to mykel on his myght. *a* **1340** HAMPOLE *Psalter* Prol., In þe translacioun i folow þe lettre als mykyll as i may. *c* **1400** *Rule St. Benet* 11 Mikyl walde he fle pride, þe prophete, als hali writ sais. *c* **1420** *Sir Amadace* (Camden) xx, On the dede cors.. Ful myculle his thoȝte was on! **1470–85** MALORY *Arthur* X. xiii. 434 Kynge Marke rode after hym praysynge hym mykel. **1526** SKELTON *Magnyf.* 1289 He wyll make it mykyll worse than it is. *c* **1620** A. HUME *Brit. Tongue* (1865) 13 They usurped y, a voual not mikle different from i. **1859** T. MOORE *Song. Sol., Durham Dial.* iv. 10 How mickle better's the luv then weyne!

δ. *a* **1300–1400** *Cursor M.* 6565 (Gött.) Mekil haue i trauayled for ȝou. *c* **1400** *Destr. Troy* 213 Mekyll comfordes me the crowne of this kyde realme. *a* **1400–50** *Alexander* 897 Þen merualid þam þe messangirs mekill of his speche. **1533** GAU *Richt Vay* (1888) 4, I traistit mekil of siclik orisons. **1573** TYRIE *Refut. Knox* To Rdr. 1 Thair is within his buke.. sum thinges nocht meakle appertenand to the caus. **1588** A. KING tr. *Canisius' Catech.* 66 Thay ar mair.. to be lamentit, yat thay traist samekle in yair auin blinde iudgment. *a* **1600** MONTGOMERIE *Misc. Poems* iii. 10 Sho is mair mobile mekle nor the mone. **1616** J. MAITLAND *Apol. W. Maitland* in *Scot. Hist. Soc. Misc.* (1904) II. 166 Abot of Londores he never wes, nor zit President of the Session, mekle les of the Privie Councell. **1813** E. PICKEN *Misc. Poems* II. 80 He reek'dna meikle on their trim. **1839** W. M'DOWALL *Poems* 39 (E.D.D.) Meikle wish'd the coming light Might be fu' clear an' sinny.

ε. **1786** BURNS *Brigs of Ayr* 175 Ye've said enough, And muckle mair than ye can mak to through. **1818** SCOTT *Br. Lamm.* viii, I think it may do—I think it might pass, if they winna bring it ower muckle in the light o' the window! **1893** CROCKETT *Stickit Minister*, etc. viii. 104, I would be muckle the better o't.

2. *Comb.*, as †***micklewise*** adj., greatly wise.

1650 BULWER *Anthropomet.* viii. 102 All which commodities our micklewise mothers defraud us of.

†**'mickle**, *v. Obs. rare.* [OE. *miclian*, *mycclian*, f. *micel* MICKLE *a.*] *trans.* To magnify. (In OE. also *intr.* to increase.)

971 *Blickl. Hom.* 13 Lufian we hine nu & his noman mycclian. *a* **1000** *Andreas* 1526 Myclade mereflod. *a* **1225** *Ancr. R.* 182 Sicnesse.. halt ine edmodnesse & mucheleð þe mede. *a* **1300** *E.E. Psalter* lxxi. 17 Alle genge mykel him þai salle.

†**'mickledom, 'muckledom.** *Obs. rare.* [f. MICKLE *a.* + -DOM.] Size, magnitude, greatness.

1596 DALRYMPLE tr. *Leslie's Hist. Scotl.* I. 31 Almaist of that same mekledome. **1665** SIR J. LAUDER *Jrnls.* (Scot. Hist. Soc.) 28 In the wery center.. of the table is planted about the meikledoom of a truncher a beautifull green smaradyes. **1686** G. STUART *Joco-ser. Disc.* 60 The muckledom of half a crown. **1681** W. ROBERTSON *Phraseol. Gen.* (1693) 684 For the michel-dome or greatness of it.

†**'micklehead, -hood.** *Obs.* Forms: *α.* 3 **mikelhode, mikelhade, mykelhede,** 4 **mikelhed**; *β.* 4 **moch-, mechelhede.** [f. MICKLE + -HEAD, -HOOD.] Greatness; fullness, abundance.

α. *a* **1300** *E.E. Psalter* viii. 2 For vpehouen es þi mykelhede [*v.r.* mikelhade, mikelhode; *Ags. Ps.* micelnis; *Vulg.* magnificentia] Ouer heuens þat ere brade. *Ibid.* xxviii. 3 God of masthede [*v.r.* mosthed, mikelhed] þonnered he Ouer watres fele þat be. *c* **1330** R. BRUNNE *Chron. Wace* (Rolls) 13324 Vnder an hil he [Arthur] set þem þere.. Þat when þe Romayns on þem had sight, Þe mikelhed schuld make þem aflight.

β. *a* **1300** *Floriz & Bl.* (Camb. MS.) 51 Þu art hire ilich of alle þinge, Boþe of semblaunt and of murninge, Of fairnesse and of muchelhede. **1340** *Ayenb.* 93 O god hou is nou grat þe mochelhede of þine zuetnesse. *Ibid.* 204 Vor be þe mochelhede of þe herte þe mouþ spekþ þet zayþ our lhord ine his spelle. *Ibid.* 218 Hy.. makeþ þe greate to mochelhedes and eteþ þe blodi snoden. *a* **1400** *Prymer* (1891) 26 Prayse ȝe hym aftir the mechelhede of his gretehed. *c* **1400** *Lay Folks Mass Bk.* App. iii. 125 For whi lord in helynge of my deedly sykenesse schal wel be schewyd and commendyd þe michilheed of þi goodnesse.

micklemote, micklegemote ('mɪk(ə)lməʊt, -gɪməʊt). *OE. Hist.* (Now *rare* or *Obs.*) [ad. OE. *micel ȝemót* great meeting: see MICKLE *a.* and MOOT *sb.*] The great council or parliamentary assembly under the Anglo-Saxon kings.

[*a* **1050** *OE. Chron.* an. 977 (MS. C.) Her wæs þæt myccle ȝemot æt Kyrtlingtune.] **1647** N. BACON *Disc. Govt. Eng.* I. xx. (1739) 36 Unto the Kings, Lords, and Clergy, must be added, as I said, the Freemen, to make up the Micklemote compleat. **1672–5** COMBER *Comp. Temple* (1702) 560 A Micelgemot or Great Council (now called a Parliament). *a* **1683** SIDNEY *Disc. Govt.* III. xxviii. (1704) 349 Sometimes meeting personally in the Micklegemots. **1832** AUSTIN *Jurispr.* (1879) II. xxviii. 536 The Mickle-mote or Wittenage-mote of the Anglo-Saxons was both the legislature and a court of justice. **1844** LD. BROUGHAM *Brit. Const.* x. (1862) 131 Whether a Great Council or a Witenagemote, or a Michelgemote, or a Colloquium, or a Parliament.

mickleness ('mɪk(ə)lnɪs). *Obs. exc. dial.* Forms: see MICKLE *a.* [f. MICKLE *a.* + -NESS.] Greatness, 'bigness' (in any sense); largeness; size.

α. *a* **1300** *E.E. Psalter* xxviii. 4 Steuen ofe lauerd in mikelnes [*v.r.* micelnisse, *Vulg.* magnificentia]. *Ibid.* l. 2 And after of þi reuthes þe mikelnes þou do awai mi wickednes. *a* **1325** *Prose Psalter* v. 7 Ich am, Lord, in þe miclenes of þy mercy. **1382** WYCLIF *Baruch* ii. 18 The soule that is sori vp on the mykilnesse of euel,.. ȝyueth to thee glorie. *c* **1400** MAUNDEV. (Roxb.) xvii. 79 Men fyndez dyamaundes.. of þe mykilnes of hesill nuttes. **14..** *MS. Lincoln* A. i. 17, lf. 28 (Halliw.) A grete multitude of swyne, that ware alle of a wonderfulle mekilnesse. **1868** ATKINSON *Cleveld. Gloss.*, *Micklish*, pretty large; of something in which the quality of 'mickleness' exists.

β. *c* **1200** *Trin. Coll. Hom.* 135 Þe childes michelnesse shende þe engel on fuwer þingen. *a* **1325** *Prose Psalter* l[i]. 2 And efter þe mychelnes of þy pites do way my wickednes. *c* **1380** WYCLIF *Sel. Wks.* III. 19 In mychilnes of þi glorie þou didist doun alle myn adversaries. **1388** —— *Gen.* xxxii. 12 The grauel of the see, that mai not be noumbrid for mychilnesse. —— *Exod.* ix. 24 It was of so greet mychelnes.. sith that folk was maad.

mickson, obs. form of MIXEN.

micky[1] ('mɪkɪ). [Applications of *Micky*, familiarly used for *Michael*. Cf. MICK[1], MIKE *sb.*[4]]

1. *Australian slang.* A young wild bull. Also **mick.**

1881 A. C. GRANT *Bush-life in Queensland* xvi. (1882) 165 There are three or four Mickies and wild heifers. **1890** 'R. BOLDREWOOD' *Col. Reformer* xviii. II. 98 The wary.. 'Micky', a two-year-old bull. **1934** *Bulletin* (Sydney) 1 Aug. 46/3, I lifted nearly two hundred Poolpee micks on my way back and took 'em home with me. **1958** *Amer. Speech* XXXIII. 167 *Mickey, maverick*, a wild young bull. **1966** BAKER *Austral. Lang.* (ed. 2) iii. 63 *Micky* or *mick*, an unbranded steer, perhaps from the Aboriginal *micky*, quick.

2. *U.S. slang.* An Irishman.

1858 J. D. LOVETT in *Harvard Mag.* July 267 While Mickey there stands, A-wringin' his hands, And Biddy is wipin' her eyes on her slave. **1890** BARRÈRE & LELAND *Dict. Slang*, *Mickey*.

3. *Austral.* A honeyeater, *Myzantha melanocephala*.

1911 J. A. LEACH *Austral. Bird Bk.* 173 Noisy Miner, Garrulous Honeyeater, Snake-Bird, Cherry-eater, Soldier, Micky, Squeaker, *Myzantha garrula*. **1931** N. W. CAYLEY *What Bird is That?* 81 Noisy Miner *Myzantha melanocephala*... Also called.. Soldier-bird, Micky, and Squeaker. In small parties, frequenting open forest country and partly cleared lands. **1971** *Courier-Mail* (Brisbane) 24 July 12/8 Mickeys, or Soldier Birds, or Noisy Miners, are great little fighters and battle the hawks, crows and goannas quite fearlessly.

4. Chiefly *Canad. colloq.* A flask of liquor.

1914 JACKSON & HELLYER *Vocab. Criminal Slang* 58 *Micky*, current amongst bottle drinkers. A corruption of Michael.. a flask of liquor. **1926** J. BLACK *You can't Win* vi. 66 A four-bit micky, a fifty-cent bottle of alcohol. **1935** A. J. POLLOCK *Underworld Speaks* 76/1 *Mickey*, half pint of bootleg whiskey. **1950** H. SUTTON *Footloose in Canada* 5 An American pint holds 16 ounces, a Canadian 'mickey', 12 ounces of rye, or 13 ounces of Scotch. **1971** *Islander* (Victoria, B.C.) 21 Mar. 16/2 Mark, the public nuisance that he was, bought his liquor in mickeys that he hid in the woodpile around the cannery. **1972** *Regional Lang. Stud.—Newfoundland* IV. 11 *Flask* is used in the Atlantic provinces only. In central and western Canada this would be a *micky*.

5. *slang.* The penis. *rare.*

1922 JOYCE *Ulysses* 765 Ill put on my best shift and drawers let him have a good eyeful out of that to make his micky stand for him.

6. Colloq. phr. ***to take the micky*** (***out of***) (someone): to act in a satirical, disrespectful, or teasing manner (towards). Cf. MIKE *sb.*[6] Hence **micky-take** *v.* and *sb.*, **micky-taking** *ppl. a.* and *vbl. sb.*

The more usual spelling of this sense is 'mickey'.

1952 'J. HENRY' *Who lie in Gaol* iv. 66 She's a terror. I expect she'll try and take the mickey out of you all right. Don't you stand for nothin'. **1954** A. HECKSTALL-SMITH *Eighteen Months* xi. 136 For a while everyone tried to take 'the Micky' out of Bobbie, but they soon gave up trying after the first foolish failure. Then their ridicule turned to admiration. **1956** A. WILSON *Anglo-Saxon Att.* II. i. 206 'You're not going to take the mickey out of me, Vin Salad, I'll spatter you,' he cried. **1957** L. P. HARTLEY *Hireling* 134 He had no great regard for Constance, except in so far as she sometimes took the mickey out of Hughie. **1958** *Observer* 28 Dec. 3/1 'Tonight' is not only a tough and irreverent programme, but glib and smart and anxious to take the mickey. **1959** R. STOREY *Touch it Light* in *Plays of Year* XVIII. 419 You don't stop at nothing, do you? As long as you can take the mickey. Mr. Funnyman, that's you. At any price. **1959** *Oxford Mail* 13 June 6/3 This modern dress, mickey-taking version of Aristophanes. **1959** *Vogue* Dec. 101 They'd think you were a nutter and laugh and mickey-take. **1960** E. W. HILDICK *Jim Starling & Colonel* ix. 76 The servers must have thought that no boy would dare to take the mickey in such circumstances. **1962** *Times* 20 July 10/6 The micky-taking ways of their own brand of insolent wise-cracking. **1965** *Listener* 25 Mar. 451/2 Those 'fruits' don't like people trying to, how do you say, take the mickey. **1967** *Spectator* 3 Nov. 535/2 One looks forward after reading this brilliant exercise in mickey-taking to Miss Tracy's next novel. **1968** J. LOCK *Lady Policeman* ix. 85 He keeps up a barrage of mickey taking. **1968** *Listener* 7 Nov. 622/3 He parried Kenneth Allsop's micky-take. **1971** B. W. ALDISS *Soldier Erect* 101 Geordie looked anxiously at me, in case I thought he was taking the micky too hard. **1973** 'J. PATRICK' *Glasgow Gang Observed* xiv. 127 Big Sheila indulged in the same sort of 'mickey-taking'.

micky[2] ('mɪkɪ). *N.Z.* Also **micky-mick, miki-miki,** etc. Representing a dialectal variant (within the Maori language) of MINGIMINGI.

1898 MORRIS *Austral Eng.* 294/2 Mingi.. in south New Zealand.. is often called Micky. **1907** 'G. B. LANCASTER' *Tracks we Tread* Gloss., *Mic-a-mic*, scrub. **1933** *Press* (Christchurch, N.Z.) 25 Nov. 15/7 *Scrub*.. The best known components in Canterbury are Manuka, Wild Irishman Miki-miki (of which the shepherds make walking sticks), and Mountain pine. **1944** *Mod. Jun. Dict.* (Whitcombe & Tombs) 258 *Micky-mick*, a corrupt form of mingi-mingi, the Maori name of a class of shrubs, one of which makes a good walking-stick. **1949** F. SARGESON *I saw in My Dream* xiv. 229 I'll make a garland for her hair. Out of micky-mick. **1963** B. PEARSON *Coal Flat* vii. 122 Willows and the trees they called.. mickeymick, mockamock, whiteywood, birch.

micky, var. MICK[3], MICK[5].

micle, -nes, obs. forms of MICKLE, -NESS.

Micmac ('mɪkmæk), *sb.* and *a.* [Native name, lit. 'allies'.] **A.** *sb.* **a.** An Indian people of the Maritime Provinces and Newfoundland in Canada; a member of this people. **b.** The Algonquian language of this people. **B.** *adj.* Of, pertaining to, or designating the Micmacs or their language.

1830 W. S. MOORSOM *Lett. from Nova Scotia* 110 The tribe to which the Indians of Nova Scotia belong is called the Micmac. *Ibid.* 112, I am not aware that any one Indian claims authority over the whole Micmac tribe. **1877** L. H. MORGAN *Anc. Society* II. vi. 174 They affiliate more closely with the Micmacs than with the New England Indians south of the Kennebeck. **1891** [see INDIAN *sb.* 2 b]. **1911** A. L. PRINGLE *Home of Evangeline* iv. 139 He taught her the Micmac, and proud she was in his absence to be catechist to the Indians. **1933** [see CREE *sb.* and *a.*]. **1964** P. K. BOCK in J. A. Fishman *Readings Sociol. of Lang.* (1968) 217 A recurrent situation on the Micmac Indian Reserve studied by the author in 1961 will be used to illustrate how the method of structural description.. may be applied. **1969** *Canad. Jrnl. Ling.* XV. 78 Micmac morphophonemics. **1969** *Observer* (Colour Suppl.) 18 May 25/1 The French.. offered the Micmac Indians a bounty for every scalp they took from the Beothuk of Newfoundland. **1972** G. V. HIGGINS *Friends of Eddie Coyle* vi. 35, I get five of these Micmacs come in, real Indians, for a change.

‖**mico** ('miːkəʊ). *Obs.* [Sp. *mico*, a. Tupi *micó*, = Carib *mecou*, applied to various species of

monkey.] A small South American marmoset of the genus *Hapale*.

1760–72 tr. *Juan & Ulloa's Voy.* (ed. 3) I. 55 Among the monkies of this country [Carthagena], the most common are the micos, which are also the smallest. **1774** GOLDSM. *Nat. Hist.* (1824) II. 158 The last, least, and most beautiful of all [the sagoins], is the Mico. **1867–8** *Nat. Encycl.* IX. 36 *Mico*, a beautiful species of monkey.

Micoquian (mɪˈkəʊkɪən), *a.* and *sb. Archæol.* Also **Micoquean.** [ad. F. *Micoquien* (O. Hauser *La Micoque* (1916) 55), f. La *Micoque* (see below).] **A.** *adj.* Of or pertaining to a late Acheulian culture (earlier called *Moustérien supérieur*) of southern France and England, represented by the remains found at La Micoque, near Les Eyzies (Dordogne) in S.W. France. **B.** *sb.* The Micoquian culture.

1937 GARROD & BATE *Stone Age Mt. Carmel* I. 120 By far the most instructive site for comparison..is La Micoque, type-station of the Tayacian and the Micoquian. *Ibid.*, Well-made Micoquian hand-axes. **1945** *Proc. Prehist. Soc.* XI. 21 The Summertown terrace gravels were deposited contemporaneously with the Upper Acheulian or Micoquian culture stage. **1946** F. E. ZEUNER *Dating Past* vi. 173 From the *base* of the Younger Loess I, a Micoquian handaxe was recovered. *Ibid.* 195 A new stage of the Acheulian cannot be recognized clearly before the advent of the Micoquian. **1957** *Encycl. Brit.* II. 238/2 The Micoquian, or Final Acheulean, is characterized by elongated hand axes. *Ibid.* 539/2 Some pieces belonging to the Micoquian..industry were excavated in 1937 in the terraces of the stream of Cubuksuyu at Etiyokusu near Ankara.

micracoustic (maɪkrəˈkaʊstɪk), *a.* and *sb.* Also erron. 8–9 **micrcoustic**. [a. F. *micracoustique*, f. Gr. μῑκρό-ς small + ἀκουστικός ACOUSTIC *a.*]

A. *adj.* Epithet of an instrument which makes weak sounds audible.

1855 DUNGLISON *Med. Lex.*, *Microcoustic.* *a* **1874** J. CHALMERS tr. *Erckmann-Chatrian* in *Casq. Lit.* V. 304/2 My micracoustic cornet. **1890** in *Syd. Soc. Lex.*

†**B.** *sb.* An instrument contrived to magnify small sounds (Chambers *Cycl. Supp.* 1753). *Obs.*

1683 *Phil. Trans.* XIV. 482 Microphones or Micracousticks that is Magnifying ear instruments. **1704** in J. HARRIS *Lex. Techn.* I.

micræsthete (maɪˈkrɛsθiːt). *Biol.* [f. Gr. μῑκρό-ς small + αἰσθητής 'one who perceives' (here used for 'organ of sense').] One of the numerous supposed tactile organs occupying the small pores (micropores) in the dorsal plates of certain chitons.

1884 MOSELEY in *Rep. Brit. Assoc.* (1885) 781 These megalæsthetes and micræsthetes. **1885** —— in *Q. Jrnl. Microsc. Sci.* XXV. 45 To the organs contained within the micropores I shall give the name micræsthetes.

micrallantoid (maɪkrəˈlæntɔɪd), *a. rare.* [f. MICR(O)- + ALLANTOID.] Having a small allantois. (Cf. MEGALLANTOID, MESALLANTOID.)

1877 W. TURNER *Hum. Anat.* II. 869 Milne Edwards has grouped them [the Rodentia, Insectivora, Cheiroptera, Quadrumana, and Man] together in a Micrallantoid legion.

micrander (maɪˈkrændə(r)). *Bot.* Also **-dre.** [f. Gr. μῑκρό-ς small + ἀνδρ-, ἀνήρ male.] A dwarf male plant produced by certain confervoid algæ.

1890 in *Century Dict.* **1900** JACKSON *Gloss. Bot.*

Hence **miˈcrandrous** *adj.*, pertaining to or connected with the dwarf males of fresh-water algæ (*Cassell's Encycl. Dict.* Suppl. 1902).

‖**micranˈthropos.** *nonce-wd.* [Assumed Gr., f. μῑκρ-ός small + ἄνθρωπος man, after MICROCOSM.] That which represents the whole man in little.

1825 COLERIDGE *Aids Refl.* Concl. 389.

micrencephaly (maɪkrɛnˈsɛfəlɪ). *Path.* [f. Gr. μῑκρό-ς small + ἐγκέφαλος brain.] General smallness of the brain, sometimes, but not necessarily accompanied by microcephaly (*Syd. Soc. Lex.* 1890). Hence **micrenceˈphalic** *a.*, of or belonging to micrencephaly (*Ibid.*). **micrenˈcephalous** *a.*, small-brained; having a small brain (*Cent. Dict.* 1890).

micrergate (maɪˈkrɜːgeɪt). *Zool.* [f. Gr. μικρ-ός small + ἐργάτης worker.] A small worker ant.

1907 W. M. WHEELER in *Bull. Amer. Mus. Nat. Hist.* XXIII. 56 The micrergate, or dwarf worker, is a worker of unusually small stature. It appears as a normal or constant form in the first brood of all colonies that are founded by isolated females. **1915** H. ST. J. K. DONISTHORPE *Brit. Ants* 41 The micrergate is a worker of unusually small size.

micrify (ˈmaɪkrɪfaɪ), *v.* [Irregularly f. Gr. μῑκρό-ς small, after *magnify*.] *trans.* To make small; to render insignificant.

1836 EMERSON *Nature* 67 This power which he [the poet] exerts..to magnify the small, to micrify the great. **1862** TYNDALL *Mountaineer.* viii. 71, I should look less cheerily into the future did I not hope to micrify, by nobler work, my episodes upon the glaciers.

micristology (maɪkrɪˈstɒlədʒɪ). *Biol.* [Irregularly f. MICRO- + HISTOLOGY.] (See quot.)

1864 THOMAS *Med. Dict.*, *Micristology*, the science which treats of the minutest organic fibres.

micrite (ˈmɪkraɪt). *Geol.* [f. MICR(OCRYSTALLINE *a.* + -ITE[1].] Microcrystalline calcite present as an interstitial constituent or matrix material in some kinds of limestone; a limestone consisting chiefly of this.

1959 R. L. FOLK in *Bull. Amer. Assoc. Petroleum Geologists* XLIII. 17 Finally, it was decided to use a composite word, the first part of which refers to the allochem composition... Whether the rock is type I or type II is shown by the second part of the name '-sparite' for those with sparry calcite cement and '-micrite' (pronounced 'mick-rite') for those with microcrystalline ooze matrix... Type III limestones, almost entirely ooze, are designated simply as 'micrite' without any allochem prefix. **1970** K. C. JACKSON *Textbk. Lithology* vi. 401 The proportion of micrite in limestone varies from a minor interstitial filling between allochems to the entire rock. **1973** *Nature* 2 Mar. 41/2 The patch reef, 13 m long and over 2 m high, tongues out to the west into 2 m of thinly bedded calcitic micrites of quiet water origin.

Hence **miˈcritic** *a.*, containing a high proportion of micrite.

1962 LEIGHTON & PENDEXTER in *Mem. Amer. Assoc. Petroleum Geologists* I. 37/2 Photographs *A* and *B* ..illustrate limestones composed of 90 per cent, or more, micrite. Two subtypes of these micritic limestones are recognized. **1973** *Nature* 20 July 145/2 The deep water Alpine Triassic is represented by cherty, micritic, radiolarian limestones with thin-shelled pelecypods.

micro (ˈmaɪkrəʊ). *Ent.* [Subst. use of MICRO-.]

1. Abbrev. of MICROLEPIDOPTERA *sb. pl.*, used to refer to a moth belonging to any of several families whose members are mostly smaller than those of interest to collectors, the Macrolepidoptera.

1869 *Rep. Comm. Agric. 1868* (U.S. Dept. Agric.) 313 The presence of 'micros' is indicated by discolored lines... It may be ascertained whether the 'micro' is at home by holding the leaf up to the light. **1890** in *Century Dict.* **1907** R. SOUTH *Moths Brit. Isles* 1st Ser. 6 Possibly, when this new order of things is more generally understood the so-called 'Micros' will receive their proper share of attention. **1972** L. E. CHADWICK tr. *Linsenmaier's Insects of World* 172/2 As for the 'micros', they are neither a uniform grouping nor properly to be separated from the rest of the moths.

2. *Fashion.* Short for *micro-skirt* (MICRO- 1 c).

1968 *N.Y. Times* 22 Jan. 36 Hemlines go to all lengths. In extremes, there are micros, which barely cover the buttocks; minis, maxis and the nineteen-thirties length. **1969** D. CLARK *Death after Evensong* ii. 40 She's some bird... Legs just a bit skinny for a micro, but still a good shape.

3. *Computing.* **a.** Abbrev. of MICROCOMPUTER.

1971 *Proc. Digital Equipment Computer Users Soc.* Fall 99 (*heading*) Seven 'micros' equal one mini. **1982** *Observer* 9 May 17/2 Digital, which claims world market leadership in the mini computer sector, will launch a highly competitive range of desk top micros aimed at business users. **1983** *Listener* 10 Feb. 33/2 The primary school kids have the opportunity of working with micros in their normal classroom activities. **1985** *Which Computer?* Apr. 52 (Advt.), Perfect Link II is a datacommunications program that links your micro to information services and other computers.

b. Abbrev. of *microprocessor* s.v. MICRO- 1.

1978 *Times* 9 Nov. 22/6 It is not certain that the use of micros will cause unemployment... Britain cannot control the pace of micro usage. **1980** *Univ. Coll. London Bull.* Dec. 9/2 These micros are among the most widely used chips. **1982** *Nature* 30 Sept. 408/3 Another function of the course is to help researchers interface their own micros to computerized instruments.

4. Abbrev. of 'microwave (oven)' (MICROWAVE 2, 3). Freq. *attrib.* orig. and chiefly *U.S.*

1973 *Weight Watchers* May 19/1 Sanyo's 'mini micro' (Model EM 8200) is a countertop oven. **1978** *Good Housekeeping* (U.S.) Dec. 286/3 Typical comments: ..'My micro is the easiest of all my appliances to clean, and I have many.' **1979** *Cuisine* Sept. 91/1 Two more micro tips: to get more juice from a lemon or orange, microwave the fruit for 30 seconds before squeezing it. **1980** *Christian Science Monitor* 21 Feb. 14 (*heading*) Micro dishes good for conventional cooking too. *Ibid.* (*caption*) New pots useable for micro. **1984** *Sears Catal.* 1985 Spring/Summer 852/1 Our micro/convection ovens..let you choose from microwave.., convection.., or micro/convection.

micro- (ˈmaɪkrəʊ, (esp. in *Med.*) ˈmɪkrəʊ), before a vowel micr-, repr. Gr. μῑκρο-, comb. form of μῑκρός small, used chiefly in scientific terms.

1. a. Prefixed to a sb. to indicate that the entity denoted by it is of relatively small size or extent, as ***microabscess, -aneurysm, bacillus, -bacterium, -biota, -chromosome, -conidium, -constituent, -crater, -earthquake, -environment*** (hence ***-environmental*** adj.), ***-event, -explosion*** (hence ***-explosive*** adj.), ***-ferment, -fossil, -fracture*** (so ***-fracturing*** vbl. sb.), ***-fungus, -gamete, -gonidium***, rarely in anglicized form ***-gonid*** (hence ***-gonidial*** adj.), ***-graver, -instability, -lens, -metazoan, -metazoon, -parasite*** (hence ***-parasitic*** adj.), ***-particle, -phenocryst, -plankton*** (hence ***-planktonic*** adj.), ***-population, -pore*** (hence ***-porous*** adj., ***-porosity***), ***-powder, -quantity, -sporophyll*** (hence ***-phyllary*** adj.), ***-state*** [STATE *sb.* 30], ***-system, -tektite, -vegetation, -zone; -zoogonidium.*** **ˈmicroatoll**, a circular growth of coral a few metres in diameter and with a central depression, such as is found in intertidal areas in warm seas and on the flats inside a coral reef. **ˈmicrobeam**, a very narrow beam of radiation. **ˈmicroblade** *Archæol.*, a flake chipped from a prepared flint core; **ˈmicroblast** *Biol.* = MICROCYTE. **ˈmicrobody** *Cytology*, one of the round or egg-shaped microscopic particles occurring in cytoplasm which are surrounded by a membrane and contain oxidases. **ˈmicrocapsule**, a minute capsule used to contain, and render temporarily inactive, drugs, dyes, etc. **ˈmicrocirculation** *Physiol.*, circulation of the blood in the smallest blood vessels. **ˈmicrocolony** *Biol.*, a group of animals or plants, esp. bacteria, found in a microhabitat; a very small group of cells in culture. **ˈmicrocontinent** *Geol.*, an oceanic, often submarine, plateau that is thought to be an isolated fragment of continental material; so **ˌmicrocontiˈnental** *a.* **ˈmicrocrack**, a microscopic crack; hence **ˈmicrocracked** *ppl. a.*, **ˈmicrocracking** *vbl. sb.* **ˈmicroculture** *Biol.*, (a) culture (of tissue, micro-organisms, etc.) on a small scale. **ˈmicroeˌlectrode**, an electrode with a very fine tip, such as one suitable for investigating the electrical properties of individual cells. **microˈfibril** *Biol.*, a small fibril in living tissue that is visible only under the electron microscope, esp. one of a group that together make up a fibril (such as a cellulose fibril in the wall of a plant cell); hence **microˈfibrillar** *a.* **microfiˈlaria** *Zool.*, the minute larval form of a filaria. **microgaˈmetocyte** *Biol.*, a cell containing microgametes. **ˌmicroˈhabitat** *Ecol.*, a habitat which is of small or limited extent and which differs in character from some surrounding more extensive habitat. **ˈmicrologic**, micro-electronic logic (LOGIC *sb.* 4); freq. *attrib.* **ˈmicromodule** *Electronics*, a miniaturized module, consisting of a stack of interconnected micro-elements. **micromuˈtation** *Biol.*, (an instance of) mutation that has a superficially small or trivial effect on the phenotype. **ˈmicro-operation** *Computers*, a simple operation carried out in response to a microinstruction (see also sense 2 a). **ˈmicro-order** *Computers*, a micro-instruction produced by a microprogram. **ˈmicroplate** *Geol.*, a relatively small lithospheric plate. **ˈmicro-process**, a process that occurs on a minute scale. **microˈprocessor** *Computers*, a processor small enough to be accommodated on a single chip, or just a few chips, and capable of serving as the central processing unit of a computer of comparable size. **ˈmicropulˌsation**, a small oscillation in the strength of the earth's magnetic field. †**microray** = MICROWAVE *sb.* (*obs.*); **ˈmicror(h)abd** *Zool.*, a name given by Sollas to certain minute flesh-spicules in the form of a 'rhabdus' found in some sponges. **ˈmicrosclere** *Zool.*, a minute or flesh spicule of a sponge, which supports only a single cell; hence **microˈsclerous** *a.*, having the character of a microsclere (*Cent. Dict.* 1890). **microˈseptum** *Zool.*, a small imperfect or sterile septum or mesentery of an actinozoan (*Ibid.*). **ˈmicrosphere**, ‖**microspˈhæra** *Biol.*, (*a*) epithet applied by Cohn to the micrococci found in vaccine lymph and in small-pox pustules; (*b*) the small initial chamber of a foraminifer in which there are a number of small nuclei; (*c*) any minute spherical object; *spec.* one of those obtained by the cooling of a solution of proteinoid; hence **microspheric** *a.* **ˈmicrostome** [Gr. στόμα mouth] *Bot.*, a small mouth or orifice, as that belonging to the capsule of certain mosses (*Cent. Dict.*). **ˌmicrostratifiˈcation**, a small-scale horizontal stratification of the water of a pond or lake. **ˈmicroswitch**, a switch which can be operated rapidly by a small movement. **microˈtrichium** *Ent.* [Gr. θρίξ, τριχ- hair], usu. in pl. **microˈtrichia**, minute hair-like structures found on the wings of certain insects, esp. those of the order Diptera. **microˈtubule** *Biol.*, any of the small, relatively rigid tubules, typically about 25 nanometres in diameter, that are present in the cytoplasm of many plant and animal cells and are thought to have a structural function and to be involved with cell motility; so **microˈtubular** *a.* **microtylote** *Zool.*, a small

TYLOTE. **micro'villus** *Biol.* (*pl.* -'villi), one of a number of minute projections from the surface of some cells; any process similar to a villus but smaller. **'microwire**, very fine glass-coated wire. **'microworld**, a realm or world (WORLD *sb.* 13) very restricted in its dimensions or variety. **microxea** *Zool.* [Gr. ὀξέα, var. ὀξύα spear], a minute spear-shaped sponge spicule. **microzoogo'nidium** (*pl.* -ia) *Bot.*, a zoogonidium of minute size. **microzoospore** *Bot.*, a minute motile spore.

1946 *Nature* 5 Oct. 487/2 Thrombo-angiitis, phlebitis and lymphangiitis with *micro-abscess formation can be found on study of sections of these structures. **1962** *Lancet* 1 Dec. 1134 The kidneys showed the changes of acute and chronic pyelonephritis, with microabscesses and gross fibrosis. **1948** PARSONS & DUKE-ELDER *Dis. Eye* (ed. 11) xvii. 371 These droplets..tend to obscure the lumen of the vessel, forming a small *micro-aneurysm. **1962** H. HEATH in A. Pirie *Lens Metabolism Rel. Cataract* 366 The fact that microaneurisms [*sic*] develop only in some cases of long-standing diabetes would seem to indicate a derangement in some slow metabolic process. **1933** P. H. KUENEN in *Snellius-Expedition* V. II. iii. 64 Conditions unfavourable to coral growth above low tide level certainly favour the formation of the *micro-atolls. **1963** D. W. & E. E. HUMPHRIES tr. *Termier's Erosion & Sedimentation* xiii. 286 Pools are frequently observed on the surface of the reef-flats... These pools contain micro-atolls which have overhanging margins, indicating a reaction against choking muds. **1967** *Oceanogr. & Marine Biol.* V. 488 Sometimes this calcareous worm produces small reefs fringing the piers, or even micro-atolls. **1899** *Allbutt's Syst. Med.* VIII. 904 The *microbacillus of Unna. **1875** tr. *von Ziemssen's Cycl. Med.* I. 588 *Micro-bacteria (rod-like bacteria); bacterium termo. **1890** *Syd. Soc. Lex.*, Microblast. **1950** *Engineering* 5 May 498/3 The Cambridge work on *micro-beams was most promising. It was nearing the stage when an investigator could look down a microscope, see a particle which he had etched, and direct X-rays on to that one particle, thus obtaining its diffraction pattern and identify it. **1962** *Times* 17 May 14/4 Investigate the effects of irradiation with a microbeam of ultraviolet light. **1972** *Science* 3 Nov. 461/2 Sea urchin sperm flagella are irradiated near their base with a laser microbeam. **1968** *New Scientist* 1 Aug. 223/1 Professor James B. Lackey..has been looking at..esturine [*sic*] habitats, concentrating on the *microbiota, especially the growth and decline of algae and protozoa. **1974** *Nature* 8 Feb. 361/2 Only a selection of the diverse Bungle Bungle microbiota [from Western Australia] is presented here. **1969** *Britannica Bk. of Year* (U.S.) 101 Late in the Upper Paleolithic and during the ensuing Mesolithic, it became the fashion to make smaller and smaller bladelettes. Commonly inserted as 'side blades' into lateral grooves in antler and bone projectile points, such '*microblades' lacerated the flesh of wounded game animals and thus promoted free bleeding and rapid death. **1972** *Sci. Amer.* Jan. 51/1 Working near Telegraph Creek in northwestern British Columbia in 1969 and 1970, Jason W. Smith and his colleagues from the University of Calgary unearthed several hundred delicate obsidian 'microblades', flakes seldom more than an inch long or a fifth of an inch wide, along with eight of the 'cores' that yield such blades. **1898** *Allbutt's Syst. Med.* V. 528 These [corpuscles] according to their sizes have been named normoblasts, megaloblasts, and *microblasts. **1954** J. RHODIN *Correlation Ultrastruct. Organization & Function in Tubule Cells Mouse Kidney* ii. 21 The number, size and shape of the *microbodies varies from cell to cell with a mean of about 10 in each cell. **1973** *Plant Physiol.* LI. 905/2 Electron micrographs frequently show association of microbodies with the rough endoplasmic reticulum. **1961** *New Scientist* 20 Apr. 115/3 The National Cash Register Company first developed *microcapsules of a dye in a colourless form, which were spread on paper. **1967** *Britannica Bk. of Year* (U.S.) 803/2 *Microcapsule*, a tiny capsule containing a liquid or solid substance (as a chemical or medicine) that is released when the capsule is broken, melted, or dissolved. **1969** *New Scientist* 3 Apr. 18 Microcapsules—tiny bags made of synthetic membrane containing enzymes or other active materials—show promise as a means of treating kidney failure. **1972** *Chem. Processing* Apr. 21/2 Wass, Pritchard have developed a dry system for the application of fragrance or flavour microcapsules during the printing process. **1905** E. B. WILSON in *Jrnl. Exper. Zool.* II. 375 Especially large or small chromosomes may be designated as 'macrochromosomes' or '*microchromosomes', irrespective of their behavior. **1958** C. P. SWANSON *Cytol. & Cytogenetics* xiii. 459 Apart from accessory chromosomes, which are generally..smaller than the usual chromosomes, microchromosomes are found throughout the plant and animal kingdom. **1969** BROWN & BERTKE *Textbk. Cytol.* 755/1 *Microchromosome*, very small metaphase chromosome of a karyotype possessing only two sizes of chromosomes, very small ones and quite large ones; the latter are called macrochromosomes. **1959** *Angiology* X. 241/1 Pressure differences in the vessels of the *microcirculation are small. **1969** *Sci. Jrnl.* Apr. 20/2 To increase an impaired microcirculation patients are commonly treated with histamine which is a strong vasodilator and rapidly relaxes the walls of capillaries. **1959** *New Biol.* XXX. 53 The fact that a large number of nests are collected each year may be attributed to birds successfully breeding in the inaccessible parts of the caves. These *micro-colonies form reservoirs from which the caves are restocked annually. **1968** *Brit. Med. Bull.* XXIV. 246/1 It is often found that cells grown in culture after irradiation show a spread of colony size;..there are often micro-colonies notably smaller than those growing from unirradiated controls. **1968** L. E. CASIDA in Gray & Parkinson *Ecol. Soil Bacteria* 100 Many soil bacteria grow as microcolonies within the larger pores of soil aggregates. **1973** R. G. KRUEGER *Introd. Microbiol.* iii. 31/2 Microcolonies are formed by some photosynthetic bacteria that produce buds from the ends of filamentous outgrowths of the cell. **1871** COOKE *Handbk. Brit. Fungi* II. 776 Hypomycetes... *Microconidia or Conidia proper very copious. **1901** TAYLOR & WHITE *U.S. Pat. 668,269* 19 Feb., When treated with higher heats..the steel of the tools show under the microscope a distinctly larger grained structure in many cases interspersed with austenite, a *micro-constituent of steel discovered by Osmond. **1930** *Times* 29 Mar. 17/1 The metallurgy of steel castings, and the discovery of about 25 micro-constituents of steel. **1966** D. G. BRANDON *Mod. Techniques Metallogr.* i. 1 Micro-constituents were successfully identified. **1965** HEEZEN & THARP in *Phil. Trans. R. Soc.* A. CCLVIII. 98 We may, of course, in referring to these aseismic ridges as *micro-continents, infer that they are either (1) fragments of former continents, or (2) nuclei of growing continents. **1966** R. W. FAIRBRIDGE *Encycl. Oceanogr.* 373/2 Madagascar is clearly a microcontinent. *Ibid.* 874/1 In the mid-ocean there have been identified..(3) true mid-ocean plateaus, to which Heezen has applied the genetic connotation 'microcontinent'. **1970** *Nature* 13 June 1044/2 We suggest that the East Canaries block is a microcontinent or sialic continental fragment detached from the African margin. **1966** R. W. FAIRBRIDGE *Encycl. Oceanogr.* 964/2 Submarine ridges and rises in other oceans..often have foundations of '*microcontinental' blocks. **1974** *Nature* 14 Mar. 204/2 This suggests that the Rockall-Faeroe Plateau as a whole may form a single *microcontinental fragment. **1950** *Welding Res.* Suppl. Sept. 473-s/2 The *microcracks have produced ..highly localized strain. **1960** W. D. BIGGS *Brittle Fracture of Steel* v. 154 Ingot irons and spectrographically pure irons do contain quantities of iron oxide in the form of inclusions in which micro-cracks may be nucleated. **1972** *Science* 2 June 1015/1 This can be attributed to the absence of water in the lunar rocks combined with the effects of porosity and microcracks. **1970** *Times* 22 May 27 At low thicknesses the deposits of chrome thrown by the new method are *microporous, while thicker coatings are *microcracked. **1956** *Welding Res.* Suppl. Feb. 78-s/3 The pearlite area.. showed no evidence of *microcracking. **1972** *Sci. Amer.* Nov. 92/2 Concrete is an inhomogeneous mixture of materials and is subject to local microcracking. **1965** *Jrnl. Appl. Physics* XXXVI. 3701/1 From the crater fields observed at low power density irradiation it can be concluded that the formation of *microcraters is an early stage in the development of laser-induced radiation damage of metal surfaces. **1970** *Daily Tel.* 7 Jan. 3 (*caption*) A grain of lunar soil highly magnified to reveal a microcrater. **1892** *Phil. Trans. R. Soc.* B. CLXXXIII. 132 (*caption*) Glass *micro-culture chamber in use with gas generators. **1973** *Nature* 5 Oct. 263/2 We analysed microcultures containing small numbers of cells (10^4 to 10^5) and the antibody response could be followed for up to 40 d. **1967** *N.Y. Times* 23 May 29 Before a volcano erupts it generates *micro-earthquakes, which we are able to detect on our seismographs. **1974** *Nature* 24 May 308/1 [They] used sonobuoys in an attempt..to see if, notwithstanding the lack of large earthquakes, they could detect microearthquake (magnitude less than 4·0) or earthquake swarm activity. **1917** *Amer. Jrnl. Physiol.* XLIV. 521 The electrodes were of copper or platinum, the muscle resting on an indifferent plate and subject above to the light contact of an active needle, microscopically sharpened—the *micro-electrode. **1946** *Nature* 20 July 97/2 As soon as the results of Granit's micro-electrode experiments on the retinæ of animals were published, it was clear that a method was wanted for obtaining similar information with regard to the colour vision of man. **1955** C. R. N. STROUTS et al. *Analytical Chem.* II. xviii. 576 A microelectrode usually consists of a platinum wire about 0·5 mm. in diameter, sealed into the side of a glass tube. **1966** T. PYNCHON *Crying of Lot 49* iii. 55 Something tidal began to reach feelers in past eyes and eardrums, perhaps to arouse fractions of brain current your most gossamer microelectrode is yet too gross for finding. **1954** *New Biol.* XVII. 7 Dr. Edney's account of the water relations of woodlice is a study in comparative physiology, within a single order, linked closely to the differences in environments—and indeed *micro-environments—of the species concerned. **1962** F. I. ORDWAY et al. *Basic Astronautics* xiii. 515 The apparent simplicity of the concept of a microenvironment within the spaceship leaves one serious gap. **1973** *Nature* 2 Mar. 20/2 Commitment may not occur until stem cells enter the microenvironment of the thymus or bursa (or bursa equivalent). **1971** *World Archaeol.* III. 128 A village..in a different *micro-environmental zone. **1974** *Nature* 27 Sept. 317/2 Oscillations of microenvironmental pO_2 in the medium overlaying attached cultures of 10^7 cells per 50 mm Petri plate were measured amperometrically with calibrated Pt/Ir micro-oxygen cathodes polarised between 0·6 and 0·8 V. **1949** A. PAP *Elem. Analytic Philos.* vii. 137 The belief in *micro-events involving micro-objects which are the hidden causes of observable events. **1957** C. DAY LEWIS *Poet's Way of Knowledge* 14 During the last half-century, physical scientists have moved towards the study of the micro-event. **1959** K. R. POPPER *Logic Sci. Discovery* viii. 196 Hypothetical and not directly observable 'micro events'. **1968** *Sci. Jrnl.* Nov. 44/2 The rate of current growth must be increased and the plasma contained in a special non-cylindrical shape—the so-called plasma focus. However, the process itself will be so brief as to resemble a strong explosion. If the dimensions of the system are not too large this can be manifested as a '*micro-explosion' which will be a good source of both fast neutrons and hard x-rays. **1971** *Jrnl. Physics D* IV. 1941 Joule heating immediately underneath an operating site raises the local temperature of the metal above its boiling point... The resulting micro-explosion..gives rise to a crater with a surrounding lip of electrode debris. **1974** *Sci. Amer.* June 24/1 Calculations were undertaken..to try to find out what would happen when tiny deuterium-tritium pellets were imploded to thermonuclear conditions by intense beams of laser light. It was also proposed that the fusion microexplosions could be applied to the generation of power. **1971** *Jrnl. Physics D* IV. 1945 The *micro-explosive disruption of the layer following Joule heating of the underlying metal causes collapse of the high trapped-ion field and the quenching of local emission. **1883** H. I. SLACK in *Knowledge* 1 June 323/1 Former articles upon *micro-ferments afford some information concerning ..the bacillus. **1938** *Nature* 19 Nov. 902/1 It may be observed..that the micelles themselves are aggregated into '*micro-fibrils', separated by spaces rather larger than the usual intermicellar spaces. **1962** J. T. MARSH *Self-Smoothing Fabrics* xx. 351 It is also probable that with cotton, there is some binding or entanglement of the microfibrils and even of the growth layers. **1970** T. S. & C. R. LEESON *Histol.* (ed. 2) ii. 37/1 In many cells cytoplasmic micro-fibrils are present, probably consisting of elongated protein molecules. **1971** *Sci. Amer.* June 44/3 Using the electron microscope to inspect the formation of ligament and tendon during the very first stages, we found no sign of the amorphous component in the embryonic elastic fibers. At this time the fibers appeared to consist only of the 110-angstrom microfibrils. **1956** *Nature* 18 Feb. 319/1 Sikorski and Woods pointed out the difficulty of reconciling the macrofibrillar type of structure observed in the follicle of a wool fibre with the occurrence of extended *microfibrillar sheets in disintegrated fibres. **1972** *Canad. Jrnl. Bot.* L. 479 The microfibrillar material transports sucrose in pulses at about 400 cm h^{-1}. **1878** *Lancet* 23 Mar. 440/2 *Micro-filariae in chylous urine. **1946** *Nature* 21 Dec. 913/1 The disease [*sc.* equine dermal filariasis] is associated with the presence of microfilariæ in the skin lesions. **1966** *New Scientist* 1 Sept. 482/3 Adult worms spawn progeny called microfilariae. They are ingested by, and develop in, several varieties of mosquito. **1924** *Bull. Amer. Assoc. Petroleum Geologists* VIII. 539 (*heading*) The value of *micro-fossils in petroleum exploration. **1961** J. CHALLINOR *Dict. Geol.* 127/2 There is no definite size limit for the category of microfossil, but one recent worker..has taken 2 mm. **1969** *Times* 11 Jan. 15/8 It is..possible that the rocks may have been contaminated by chemical fossils and microfossils after they were laid down. **1939** *Amer. Mineralogist* XXIV. 73 The streaks, patches, and veinlets of coarsely crystalline kaolinite and halloysite are sedimentary in origin and appear to be related to recrystallization along the *micro-fractures in the clay. **1973** *Jrnl. Biomech.* VI. 5/2 Preliminary results from our study of human materials have demonstrated evidence of healing or healed microfractures in the subchondral bone taken at autopsy from patients with early signs of degenerative joint disease. **1969** *Nature* 27 Sept. 1306/1 All the rock samples are characterized by small surface pits lined with glass, areas of spattered glass and whitish markings which are small areas of *microfracturing. **1874** *Hardwicke's Sci.-Gossip* 256 That rare and interesting *Micro-fungus *Xenodochus carbonarius*. **1920** Microfungus [see ENCROACH *sb.*]. **1971** N. E. HICKIN *Wood Preservation* 66 Micro-fungi... An imprecise term of no taxonomic significance, usually used to include those fungi whose classification is in doubt as no sexual process has been observed, the *fungi imperfecti*, and including also the smaller *Ascomycetes* with small sporophores. **1891** HARTOG in *Nature* 17 Sept. 484 *Microgamete. **1905** *Brit. Med. Jrnl.* 25 Feb. 442 After entering the stomach of the gnat, the *microgametocytes..produce microgametes. **1857** BERKELEY *Cryptog. Bot.* §123, The *micro-gonidia, which are supposed to be true antheridia, have..been described. **1884** HYATT in *Proc. Boston Soc. Nat. Hist.* XXIII. 67 Thesezoons..assume characteristics of true males or *microgonids. **1890** *Century Dict.*, *Microgonidial. **1926** *Guide Antiquities Stone Age Dept. Brit. & Mediaeval Antiquities Brit. Mus.* (ed. 3) 90 The early sites with the angle-graver or true graver, and the later with the *micro-graver as the typical implement. **1939** V. G. CHILDE *Dawn European Civilization* (ed. 3) i. 6 Pigmy flints or microliths, ingeniously worked into regular geometrical shapes..or into micrograyers. **1933** *Ecol. Monogr.* III. 169 Niche—the *microhabitat or ultimate division of the habitat including recognition of its modifying factors. **1970** *Watsonia* VIII. 93 Like several other British ferns, it shows a partiality for railway platforms, which often supply a very special moist and calcareous microhabitat. **1971** *Sci. Amer.* Sept. 105/3 All habitats—from the expanses of sea ice and open water to the microhabitats of tidal flats, leeward waters and protected valleys—are utilized [by Eskimos]. **1962** W. B. THOMPSON *Introd. Plasma Physics* viii. 235 Since the wavelength is so small, this instability is almost independent of the macroscopic geometry, and represents one of the '*micro-instabilities'. **1971** *Science Year 1972* 222 Fusion researchers have been trying to find magnetic-bottle configurations that will be able to reduce the microinstabilities to acceptable proportions. **1964** S. DUKE-ELDER *Parsons' Dis. Eye* (ed. 14) vii. 82 *Micro-lenses resting on the cornea are easier to fit and to wear. **1971** *Time* 19 July 48 Walon Green..used microlenses and extreme slow motion to get awesome footage of mayflies living out their brief lives. **1960** *Electronics* 25 Nov. 107/1 (*heading*) *Micrologic computer. **1965** *New Scientist* 25 Mar. 769/1 Marconi..has a pilot 'micro-logic' circuit manufacturing plant at its laboratories. **1971** J. H. SMITH *Digital Logic* i. 4 The Integrated Circuit. This is often referred to as micro logic. **1972** *Sci. Amer.* Sept. 2/1 (Advt.), This revolutionary small computer lets your people use the languages which best express the problems you need to solve. Its variable micrologic processor operates efficiently with each language by instantly restructuring itself as it shifts from one program or program segment to the next. **1964** *Oceanogr. & Marine Biol.* II. 382 This remarkable interstitial fauna..consisting of protozoans and *micrometazoans..has been eagerly studied since the twenties by Kiel zoologists. **1969** *New Scientist* 3 Apr. 34/2 The dozen or so *micrometazoa with which they are working. **1959** *Times* 19 Mar. 10/5 New miniature military radios, radar controls and other products of a revolutionary programme of *micro-module electronics. **1965** *Listener* 1 July 6/1 I.B.M. already has 80 per cent. of the world computer market. With its micro-modules it looks like keeping it. **1940** R. GOLDSCHMIDT *Material Basis of Evolution* 324 Among these evolutionary steps there are many of a type which preclude an evolution by slow accumulation of *micro-mutations. **1972** *Science* 12 May 623/3 In the 1930's population geneticists recognized micromutation as the raw material of evolutionary change. **1953** *Micro-operation [see MICROPROGRAM]. **1970** O. DOPPING *Computers & Data Processing* xii. 197 A program step, i.e. the execution of an instruction in a computer, consists of a number of program steps, or micro operations. **1953** *Micro-order [see MICROPROGRAM]. **1972** D. LEWIN *Theory & Design Digital Computers* iv. 71 The main function of the control unit is to decode the order digits of an instruction word, thereby generating the necessary sequence of control waveforms (micro-orders) to allow the instruction to be executed. **1884** *Science* 1 Feb. 130/1 The number of substances which are less injurious to man than to *micro-parasites is very small. **1899** *Allbutt's Syst. Med.* VIII. 196 Febrile *micro-parasitic type. **1969** *Encycl. Sci. Suppl.* (*Grolier*) 78 The search continues for facts about the similarities and differences between 'organized elements', microfossils, and *microparticles formed from amino acid polymers. **1926** G. W. TYRRELL *Princ. Petrol.* v. 86 The terms *microporphyritic* and **microphenocrysts* may be used when the texture can only be made out with the use of a microscope. **1946** *Jrnl. Geol.* LIV. 27/2 Microphenocrysts of augite are set in a microcrystalline to cryptocrystalline

and hyaline groundmass. **1973** *Nature* 9 Feb. 374/1 It occurs as inclusions in both the other minerals, and forms skeletal microphenocrysts about 0·05 mm across. **1903** *Jrnl. R. Microsc. Soc.* 638 Spinelli publishes a first contribution to the marine flora of Sicily... The *micro-plankton of the Sicilian coast has not been included. **1969** BENNISON & WRIGHT *Geol. Hist. Brit. Isles* xiv. 319 Marine microplankton has also been found [in the Wealden area]. **1971** *Nature* 30 Apr. 562/1 Cita and Blow compared the *microplanktonic succession in these stratotypes with that of the tropical zonation scheme. **1972** *Ibid.* 4 Feb. 253/2 From the point of view of plate tectonics the Mediterranean is a complicated part of the world, being a region of numerous small interacting plates (*microplates) rather than a part of one large one. **1967** *Oceanogr. & Marine Biol.* V. 543 There is a highly detailed zoning of ecological conditions and *micro-populations in the supra- and the mediolittoral zone. **1884** MOSELEY in *Rep. Brit. Assoc.* (1885) 781 A series of smaller pores ('*micro-pores'). **1885** —— in *Q. Jrnl. Microsc. Sci.* XXV. 40, I shall call them megalopores and micropores. **1956** *Nature* 17 Mar. 502/1 The same type of micro-pore structure as occurs in the coking coals. **1967** M. CHANDLER *Ceramics in Mod. World* iv. 133 Translucent alumina ceramics that contain no micropores. **1939** *Chem. Abstr.* XXXIII. 4099 With increasing percentages this reduction continues until with 5% of Cu_2O there is no change in vol. However, this is in part only apparent, since Cu_2O causes *microporosity. **1961** A. TAYLOR *X-ray Metallogr.* iii. 32 For the more subtle flaws and fine detail, such as hairline cracks or microporosity, the much more sensitive photographic method must be employed. **1963** J. OSBORNE *Dental Mech.* (ed. 5) xiv. 325 A shrinkage develops causing a microporosity throughout the entire casting. **1890** *Syd. Soc. Lex.*, *Microporous. **1955** *Sci. News Let.* 29 Jan. 67/1 Oxygen.. diffuses through a micro-porous filter disk made of porcelain and having 800,000,000 holes to the square inch. **1970** *Times* 22 May 27 At low thicknesses the deposits of chrome thrown by the new method are microporous. **1953** *Electronic Engin.* XXV. 233/1 *Micropowder magnets can be made—after the powder has been produced—in a great variety of shapes. **1965** *New Scientist* 6 May 368/1 This metal could be either in very finely divided state (micropowder) or else as a sintered iron oxide compound. **1936** *Mind* XLV. 275 Jordan's attempt to account for it in terms of an intensification of acausal *micro-processes is not supported by the facts. **1962** *Times* 13 Apr. 19/7 A higher resolution.. is still more attractive on account of the prospects it affords of exploring those structural details and micro-processes upon which the functioning of living matter depends. **1970** *IEEE Trans. Computers* XIX. 710 LX-1 is an integrated circuit prototype of a *microprocessor which is being used as a design vehicle to study the problems associated with the design and implementation of a similar computer constructed with large-scale integrated circuits. **1974** *Computer* July 22/2 There are at least four major classifications of systems that can be designed using microprocessors: calculators, controllers, data processors, and general-purpose computers. Controllers and calculators are the most likely candidates for single-chip CPUs. **1974** *Ibid.* Aug. 34/1 The present system uses a microprocessor and a small number of other custom LSI devices to control the spark ignition timing and EGR valve position based on a number of input engine variables. **1975** *Sci. Amer.* May 34/2 In 1971.. the Intel Corporation, which had undertaken to develop a calculator chip, chose to design it as a more versatile programmable, single-chip microprocessor. **1949** *Proc. Japan Acad.* XXV. ix. 24 A remarkable *micropulsation of *dH/dt* at the sudden commencement [of the magnetic storm] frequently took places [*sic*] during the summer and equinox, while it is weak during the winter. **1960** *Jrnl. Geophysical Res.* LXV. 1843/1 Micropulsations belong to the family of disturbances that have been related to the arrival of solar terrestrial particles. **1968** *McGraw-Hill Yearbk. Sci. & Technol.* 241/1 The instability also generates geomagnetic micropulsations and .. very low frequency radio emissions. (Micropulsations are small quasi-sinusoidal oscillations of the Earth's field having periods ranging from about 1/5 sec to several hundred seconds.) **1946** F. SCHNEIDER *Qualitative Organic Microanalysis* vi. 164 The method can be readily adapted to the use of *microquantities by the use of a reflux tube. **1971** *Nature* 7 May 11/2 The micro-quantities of compounds or isotopes which have now become detectable can serve as tracers to distinguish between, say, older and more recent material on the surface. **1887** SOLLAS in *Encycl. Brit.* XXII. 423/1 The flesh spicules when present are usually *microrabds or spirasters. **1931** *Electrician* 3 Apr. 509/2 The great advance made.. has opened up the range of wave-lengths between 10 cm. and 1 m. for practical use... These short wave-lengths have been designated '*micro-rays'. **1934** *Discovery* Sept. 242/2 The micro-rays used have the great advantage of freedom from disturbance by other wireless transmissions. **1937** *Jrnl. R. Aeronaut. Soc.* XLI. 47 The micro-ray equipments used on the commercial Lympne-St. Inglevert and the experimental Escalles-St. Margaret's [radio] links. **1887** SOLLAS in *Encycl. Brit.* XXII. 417/2 It is doubtful whether a distinction between megascleres and *microscleres can be maintained in the calcareous sponges. **1875** tr. *von Ziemssen's Cycl. Med.* II. 381 In the blood.. he has demonstrated the *micro-spheres. **1891** DALLINGER *Carpenter's Microsc.* xiv. 727 The 'microsphere' is followed by a larger number of chambers. **1960** *Science* 22 July 204/2 A tendency to yield microspheres having diameters in a bacterial range is illustrated. *Ibid.*, Another property of the microspheres is the tendency to shrink in sodium chloride solution hypertonic to that in which they are produced. **1965** R. S. YOUNG in S. W. Fox *Orig. Prebiological Syst.* iv. 349 It is difficult to imagine that this phenomenon of microsphere formation, so easily demonstrable in the laboratory, did not occur in nature if there were a suitable accumulation of building blocks. Whether this had anything to do with the origin of the cell is purely speculative at this stage, but it is certainly suggestive. *Ibid.* 354 The microsphere is a remarkably stable structure. **1974** *Nature* 10 May 177/1 About 100,000 microspheres 25 μm in diameter labelled with ^{46}Sc were injected into the left ventricle over 30 s. **1894** LISTER in *Phil. Trans.* CLXXXVI. 437 The microspheres in the two *microspheric examples measure 15 × 12·5μ and 13 × 11 μ. **1897** *Allbutt's Syst. Med.* I. 83 The microsphæræ previously referred to as infesting the amœba. **1898** SEDGWICK *Text-bk. Zool.* I. 9 The intervening stages between the zoospore, produced by the megalospheric form, and the microsphere. **1895** VINES *Textbk. Bot.* I. 432 In.. Phanerogams.. the *microsporophylls are morphologically simpler. *Ibid.* 78 When.. the flower includes only microsporophylls, it is called *microsporophyllary. **1962** *Economist* 20 Jan. 204/1 The *micro-states left behind by France—Niger, Chad, Dahomey, Togo. **1970** *Britannica Bk. of Year* (U.S.) 463 Other events included.. proposals that a special UN membership category be created for 'microstates'. **1974** *Austral. Outlook* XXVIII. I. 24 No clear and universally acceptable definition of a microstate has yet emerged. **1937** *Science* 26 Feb. 224/1 (*heading*) *Microstratification of the waters of inland lakes in summer. **1956** *Nature* 17 Mar. 520/1 With a small amount of plankton in such a large body of water [as Lake Tanganyika], it is possible that its distribution is uneven due to currents and microstratifications. **1957** G. E. HUTCHINSON *Treat. Limnol.* I. vi. 396 In very many lakes.. elaborate microstratification occurred throughout the hypolimnion. **1958** *Jrnl. Exper. Analysis of Behaviour* I. 173 The *S* read from loose printed pages; every time he stuttered, *E* pressed a *microswitch which activated an Esterline-Angus recorder. **1961** *New Scientist* 13 Apr. 16/1 Carbon dioxide is used for inflation, its flow being controlled.. for patients with very slight residual power, by an electrical system using micro-switches. **1967** E. CHAMBERS *Photolitho-Offset* ix. 128 The exposed film enters the processor at the film feeding station, the film activating a microswitch that starts a metering pump. **1940** *Ann. Rev. Biochem.* IX. 609 Since this is exactly the field served by the widely used Warburg manometric apparatus, and since the sensitivity of the diver method is about 1500 times as great as that apparatus, many possibilities of application to the *microsystem exist. **1969** *New Scientist* 27 Feb. 452 One early form of life could have been a thermodynamically open, self-assembled, proteinaceous microsystem, capable of propagating its own kind through the use of preformed poly-amino acids. **1967** *Nature* 22 Apr. 374/1 It is concluded that the glassy objects [in deep-sea sediments] discussed in this report are *microtektites, and that they constitute a portion of the Australasian strewn field which extends from Thailand to Tasmania. **1973** *Ibid.* 16 Feb. 431/2 Microtektites (diameters < 1 mm) are also associated with the two most recent strewn fields. **1934** C. H. CURRAN *Families & Genera N. Amer. Diptera* 488 *Microtrichia—The smaller abundant hairs of the wing. When these are present the wing is said to be villous. **1957** RICHARDS & DAVIES *Imms's Gen. Textbk. Entomol.* (ed. 9) I. 13 Microtrichia.. are minute hair-like structures, found, for example, on the wings of the Mecoptera and certain Diptera. They resemble very small covering hairs. **1963** D. B. SLAUTTERBACH in *Jrnl. Cell Biol.* XVIII. 384/2 It may be generally recognized that cells possess a '*microtubular system'. **1971** *Sci. Amer.* Aug. 52/3 At the base of every eukaryotic flagellum and cilium is a distinct microtubular structure: the basal body. **1963** D. B. SLAUTTERBACH in *Jrnl. Cell Biol.* XVIII. 367 Small cytoplasmic tubules are present in the interstitial cells and cnidoblasts of hydra. They are referred to here as '*microtubules'. **1974** *McGraw-Hill Yearbk. Sci. & Technol.* 124/2 Microtubules are hollow cylinders about 250 A.. in diameter which are present in a wide variety of cellular structures, including the mitotic spindle, cilia and flagella, and neural axons... They probably provide an internal 'cytoskeleton' that produces or maintains asymmetric cell structure, and they appear to be involved in the production of certain types of cell motility. **1887** SOLLAS in *Encycl. Brit.* XXII. 417 (Fig. 17), *Microscleres.. r*, *microtylote. **1956** *Nature* 4 Feb. 221/2 It seems quite plausible.. that the stream of nutrient salts and metabolites excreted by the cuticle serves as the nutrient medium of the epiphyllic *micro-vegetation. **1958** *Blumea* IX. 206 Barnacles were collected in order to get an impression of the algal microvegetation.. growing on them. **1953** BORYSKO & BANG in *Bull. Johns Hopkins Hosp.* XCII. 259 The cell surface in contact with the allantoic fluid was consistently characterized by the presence of variable numbers of small projections.. which we have named '*microvilli' to distinguish them from other types of surface projections (cilia, pseudopods, brush borders, blebs, etc.). These microvilli appeared as club-shaped projections extending into the allantoic sac. They were approximately 0·1 micron in width, ranging from 0·1 to 1·0 micron in length. **1968** *New Scientist* 28 Nov. 513/1 The skin of many tapeworms possesses a number of very small, finger-like projections. They are known as microvilli, from their resemblance to the larger, but similar, projections called villi found in the small intestine of most types of vertebrate. **1969** *Nature* 11 Oct. 116/2 (*caption*) This normal baby hamster kidney (BHK) cell is magnified about 3,300 times. The tendril-like processes are microvilli which appear at particular phases of the cell cycle, noticeably when the cell rounds up before division. **1963** *Times* 21 May 20/2 World scientists are taking their turn in a growing queue for Britain's newest export—glass-sheathed copper *microwire 50 times thinner than a human hair. **1970** *New Scientist* 30 Apr. 228/3, 100 grammes of micro-wire, about 100 km long, would cost £1000. **1955** O. KLEIN in W. Pauli *Niels Bohr* 117 Einstein .. may have felt that on the side of the quantum physicists the importance of the general relativity claim in the search for the laws of the *microworld was usually underestimated. **1967** *New Scientist* 18 May 383/2 The pavilion [at London Zoo] is an assemblage of micro-worlds in which the jumpers can jump, the climbers climb, the burrowers burrow and the nocturnal sleepers sleep. **1973** C. BONINGTON *Next Horizon* ii. 46 In the micro-world of an expedition the pettiest details, like an unwashed pan or an irritating mannerism, are blown up out of all proportion. **1887** SOLLAS in *Encycl. Brit.* XXII. 417 (Fig. 17), *Microscleres.. n*, oxyaster; .. *q*, the same, with two actines (a centrotylote *microxea). **1957** G. E. HUTCHINSON *Treat. Limnol.* I. ix. 609 By covering lake mud in the laboratory with oxygenated water, he was able to show that a *microzone of oxygen-poor water was rapidly produced above the mud. **1964** *Oceanogr. & Marine Biol.* II. 137 Cores often exhibit a well marked horizontal stratification into the microzones of Perfiljew. **1882** VINES tr. *Sachs' Bot.* 257 Other of the cells.. give birth to 16 or 32, *micro-zoogonidia. **1875** *Q. Jrnl. Microsc. Sci.* XV. 396 *Micro-zoospores (which conjugate, but otherwise in most cases appear incapable of germination).

b. Other terms in which *micro-* indicates reduced size or scale, but not of what is denoted by a following sb., as ***micro-distribution***; **ˈmicrobreccia** *Geol.* (see quot. 1972); **ˈmicrocamera**, a camera used in photomicrography; **ˌmicrocosmoˈpolitan**, one who regards himself as a citizen of every part of a particular society; a citizen of a defined and limited world; **ˈmicro-evoˌlution**, evolutionary change within a species or smaller group of plants or animals, taking a relatively short time; hence **ˌmicro-evoˈlutionary** *a.*; **ˈmicroglossary**, a glossary or dictionary of terms in a particular subject; **microplaˈsticity**, plastic flow which occurs in small areas of a material at stresses below the elastic limit of the bulk material; so **microˈplastic** *a.*; **ˈmicrorelief** *Physical Geogr.*, small-scale relief (RELIEF[3] 3 b); **ˌmicro-stimuˈlation** *Physiol.*, stimulation applied to a very small area; **ˈmicrotheory**, a theory about one particular aspect or part of some subject or phenomenon.

1948 *Jrnl. Geol.* LVI. 149 (in facing Table 3), Siltstone (gritty). a. siltstone proper. b. Micro-conglomerate or micro-breccia. **1951** E. B. KNOPF tr. *B. Sander's Contrib. Study of Depositional Fabric* 28 The fragments in this deformation breccia are calcitized crinkled dolomite and various sedimentary microbreccias. *Ibid.* 29 Some fragments in the microbreccia are themselves fragments of breccia. **1963** D. W. & E. E. HUMPHRIES tr. *Termier's Erosion & Sedimentation* xiii. 294 The true reefs contain several facies:.. breccias and microbreccias formed of fragments of calcareous organisms; oyster limestones; [etc.]. **1972** *Gloss. Geol.* (Amer. Geol. Inst.) 449/2 *Microbreccia*, (*a*) A poorly sorted sandstone containing relatively large and sharply angular particles of sand set in a very fine silty or clayey matrix; e.g. a graywacke. It is somewhat less micaceous than a siltstone. (*b*) A breccia within fragments of a coarser breccia (Sander, 1951, p. 28). **1973** *Nature* 23 Mar. 252/2 A feldspathic microbreccia from the Descartes region of the lunar highlands contains an unusual assemblage of pyroxene fragments. **1928** *Daily Express* 21 June 12 Modern science has at its disposal, 'doctors, chemists, biologists, ultra-violet lamps, micro-cameras, and spectroscopes'. **1958** *Newnes Compl. Amat. Photogr.* xxv. 219 Apart from the micro-camera, a plate camera is perhaps the next best. **1961** A. TAYLOR *X-ray Metallogr.* vi. 163 Equally good resolution may be obtained with quite small cameras provided the focus of the X-ray tube is restricted and the geometry of the camera and the specimen is suitably modified, as, for example, in certain microcameras. **1938** S. BECKETT *Murphy* xi. 240 It was as though the microcosmopolitans had locked him out. **1966** *Punch* 12 Jan. 50/1 Liberal Jewish New Yorkers.. are cosmopolitans, but New York is their cosmos. They are really microcosmopolitans. **1964** *Oceanogr. & Marine Biol.* II. 111 The study of.. micro-distribution with reference to mixing processes in the sea. **1971** *Nature* 25 June 524/2 So far it has not been possible to study the micro-distribution of lead in materials, except by using electron microprobes or rather crude microchemical techniques which are only really valid if the lead concentration is high. **1940** R. GOLDSCHMIDT *Material Basis of Evolution* 199 Microevolution by means of micromutation leads only to diversification within the species. **1963** DAVIS & HEYWOOD *Princ. Angiosperm Taxon.* ii. 72 They [*sc.* biosystematists] have gone a long way in elucidating the processes of evolution at and below the species level (micro-evolution). *Ibid.* xii. 405 The significance of ecological modifications in a micro-evolutionary context has probably been underestimated. **1974** T. HEYERDAHL *Fatu-Hiva* ii. 86, I was on constant look-out for animals to save in bottles and tubes for the study of trans-oceanic migration and micro-evolution. **1955** LOCKE & BOOTH *Machine Translation Lang.* 11 The main deficiency at the present time is the absence of adequate field dictionaries for various technical fields and for all relevant languages. Preparation of these *microglossaries*.. is important, though tedious work. **1956** *Nature* 7 Jan. 1/1 To solve the problem of word-order, the grammatical structure of the language must be investigated in detail and micro-glossaries—stem-ending dictionaries in the specified subject—must be compiled and coded. **1960** E. DELAVENAY *Introd. Machine Transl.* vi. 91 Research since 1949 has led to the provisional conclusion that in scientific texts non-grammatical poly-semantic nouns and verbs do not present any great difficulty within the limits of the restricted vocabulary of any given science or technical subject. Thus special restricted dictionaries—microglossaries—should be constituted. **1960** *Mech. Engin.* July 71/3 Future investigations should be extended to a variety of materials to investigate further the validity of microplastic-strain hysteresis energy as a criterion for fatigue fracture. **1966** *Jrnl. Strain Analysis* I. 415/2 It is.. a fact that plastic flow occurs in some parts of the cross-section even if the material is within the nominal elastic limit. This plastic deformation, which is of the same order of magnitude as the elastic strains, will be termed as [*sic*] micro-plastic throughout the paper. *Ibid.*, It is believed that micro-plasticity constitutes an important source of failure in the case of metal fatigue. **1972** T. IMURA in G. Thomas *Electron Microsc. & Struct. Materials* 129 The microplasticity can be attributed solely to the motion of edge dislocations. **1932** FULLER & CONARD tr. *Braun-Blanquet's Plant Sociol.* xi. 272 Causes of injury are.. direct effect upon soil formation by stirring of the fine earth and changing the microrelief (hummocks and paths). **1938** *Geogr. Jrnl.* XCII. 271 [Articles] deal with glaciation, with melting and formation of micro-relief, and with run-off and thawing of glaciers. **1968** R. W. FAIRBRIDGE *Encycl. Geomorphol.* 795 Relief refers to relative height, while microrelief refers to small-scale differences in relief. Microrelief consists of any minor undulations on the surface of the land, usually of a scale which would not show on a normal topographic map. **1946** *Nature* 28 Dec. 947/1 Two point sources of light of about the same brightness were presented to an observer by means of the micro-stimulation apparatus. **1972** *Jap. Jrnl. Pharmacol.* XXII. 635 (*heading*) Re-examination of a centrally-induced cough in cats using a micro-stimulation technique. **1956** W. H. WHYTE *Organization Man* (1957) 28 Perhaps an overall theory of behavior is.. a will-o'-the-wisp. If so, our efforts may still be rewarded by the salvage of

microtheories about limited areas. **1971** *Jrnl. Gen. Psychol.* LXXXIV. 155 Almost all of them have been extremely cautious about extending their data to explanatory microtheories of the perceptual phenomena.

c. *Fashion.* Denoting extreme shortness of a woman's garment, as in ***micromini***, ***-shift***, ***-skirt*** (hence ***-skirted*** adj.).

1967 *Word Study* Dec. 3/2 *Mini*.. has undergone further compounding in the formation *micromini* denoting an exceptionally short miniskirt. **1971** 'V. X. Scott' *Surrogate Wife* 40 She wore micro-minis to show lots of leg. **1967** *Punch* 1 Mar. 308/2 The latest collection included a transparent micro-shift worn over an emaciated G-string. **1966** *Courier-Mail* (Brisbane) 29 Aug. 11 Mini-skirts, Micro-skirts, Maxi-skirts—the fashion battle rages on in London. **1967** *Punch* 21 June 893/2 Micro-skirts are designed to keep elders in their place, for no woman over forty can wear them without looking idiotic. **1969** *Guardian* 27 May 2/4 Women students of Pretoria University turned up.. in ankle-length and calf-length dresses, in a campaign against 'micro-skirts'. **1973** J. Di Mona *Last Man at Arlington* (1974) viii. 73 A young blonde.. in a microskirt. **1967** *Times Educ. Suppl.* 13 Oct. 763 (*caption*) Mortar-boarded candidate.. for student office at Boston's North-eastern University and his mortar-boarded micro-skirted assistant.

2. Prefixed to sbs. and derived adjs. to denote 'microscopic' in the sense 'with the microscope', 'revealed by the microscope'.

a. Originally, denoting operations or branches of research carried on by means of microscopic examination; now often implying simply the smallness of scale of the subject, rather than any use of microscopy, and so passing into 6 (cf. MACRO- 1 e), as ***microanatomy*** (hence ***-anatomist***), ***-cautery***, ***-chemistry*** (hence ***-chemic***, ***-chemical***, adjs., ***chemically*** adv.), ***-cinematography*** (so ***-cinematographic*** adj.), ***-crystallogeny***, ***-crystallography***, ***-dissection*** (hence ***-dissect*** vb.), ***-ecology***, ***-geology*** (hence ***-geological*** adj., ***-geologist*** sb.), ***-injection***, ***-metallography*** (hence ***-metallographer***), ***-metallurgy***, ***-mineralogy*** (hence ***-mineralogical*** adj.), ***-operation*** (see also sense 1) (so ***-operative*** adj.), ***-palæontology*** (hence ***-palæontologic***, ***-logical*** adjs., ***-palæontologist***), ***-pathology*** (hence ***-pathological*** adj., ***-pathologist*** sb.), ***-petrology*** (hence ***-petrologist***), ***-physiography***, ***-physiology*** (hence ***-physiologist***), ***-sociology*** (hence ***-sociological*** adj.); ***-zoology***. **ˌmicroma'chining**, the process or technique of shaping objects on a very small scale by non-mechanical means; **ˌmicropinocy'tosis** *Biol.*, a submicroscopic form of pinocytosis in which material is taken into a cell as a result of the invagination and pinching off of the cell surface; hence **ˌmicropinocy'totic** *a.*

1964 G. H. Haggis et al. *Introd. Molecular Biol.* i. 1 The concentration of anatomists and *microanatomists on finer and finer detail may be illustrated by four centuries of work on the structure of the vascular system and the blood. **1935** *Times Lit. Suppl.* 24 Oct. 662 What he has done is to present in a lively—almost exciting—way the more significant facts of human physiology and *micro-anatomy as far as they have yet been discovered. **1946** *Nature* 26 Oct. 578/1 His researches have been mainly in the fields of micro-anatomy, embryology and the more physiological side of zoology. **1962** *Science Survey* III. 252 Her main interests have been in the micro-anatomy of the retina and its relationship to visual function in different animals. **1899** *Allbutt's Syst. Med.* VIII. 835 The *micro-cautery has been used also with fair results. **1890** *Syd. Soc. Lex.* s.v., **Micro-chemic a.*, of or pertaining to micro-chemistry. **1856** Highley in *Q. Jrnl. Microsc. Sci.* IV. 221 An instrument of structural, physical, *micro-chemical, and crystallological research. **1847–9** *Todd's Cycl. Anat.* IV. 137/2 *Micro-chemically the cells of cancer are insoluble in cold and boiling water. **1940** *Ann. Rev. Biochem.* IX. 610 Little used by biochemists or *microchemists. **1971** *Nature* 7 May 11/1 There is also methane.. in the indigenous rocks on the surface of the Moon. Is this.. the remnant of the primordial gas from which the Moon was formed? That, no doubt, is a question that will preoccupy lunar micro-chemists for a long time to come. **1890** *Syd. Soc. Lex.* s.v., **Micro-chemistry*, the chemical examination of minute bodies under the microscope. **1940** *Chem. Abstr.* XXXIV. 289 (*heading*) Micro tearing machine for the photomicrographic and *microcinematographic examination of materials. **1962** *Lancet* 1 Dec. 1172/1 The misshapen lymphocytes may reasonably be regarded as dying cells; this view is supported by the microcinematographic studies of human blood-cells by Bessis. **1952** *Chem. Abstr.* XLVI. 13336/3 *Microcinematography. **1971** *Nature* 10 Dec. 352/1 We are continuing to use single smooth muscle cells in dynamic studies of contraction recorded with microcinematography. **1856** Highley in *Q. Jrnl. Microsc. Sci.* IV. 124 *Micro-Crystallogeny. *Ibid.* 223 *Micro-Crystallography. **1973** *Ibid.* 2 Mar. 52/1 Cytoplasm was *micro-dissected from salivary glands of larvae. **1915** *Science* 19 Feb. 291/1 The cells were isolated and studied by means of *microdissection and vital staining in a hanging drop of the insect body fluid. **1972** *Sci. Amer.* June 95/1 A small bundle of fibers from a single receptor is separated by microdissection from the main trunk of the optic nerve and placed on an electrode. **1963** *New Society* 3 Oct. 26/1 A pioneering work in the *micro-ecology of housing estates. **1969** *Nature* 29 Nov. 846/1 The microecology of the blowfly's gut has not been well explored. **1875** Dawson *Dawn of Life* v. 104 The *micro-geologist well knows how.. mineral matter in solution can penetrate the smallest openings that the microscope can detect. **1857** *Amer. Jrnl. Sci.* Ser. ii. XXIV. 434 *Micro-geology of Ehrenberg. **1862** Stoddart in *Q. Jrnl. Microsc. Sci.* II. 147 On Micro-Geology. **1921** *Science* 28 Oct. 411/2 The microdissection and *microinjection of marine ova and of animal and plant cells. **1970** *Nature* 22 Aug. 857/2 For micro-injection we used a hydraulic system of mineral oil with the micro-pipette tip filled with tracer solution. **1960** K. R. Shoulders in *Proc. Western Joint Computer Conf.* 251/2 The most highly resolved construction process that we have any control over is what we call electron beam activated *micromachining. *Ibid.* 256/1 Electron-beam micromachining is the combination of certain methods of deposition, resist production, and etching. **1970** *New Scientist* 16 Apr. 101/1 Micromachining has received much publicity in the past, and forms the mainstay of Laser Associates' range of systems. **1895** *Nature* 15 Aug. 367/2 It may be that the *micro-metallographer has much to learn from the Japanese. *Ibid.* 367/1 The progress which has been made in *micro-metallography during the past ten years. **1899** *Proc. R. Soc.* LXV. 85 (*heading*) Experiments in *micro-metallurgy:—Effects of strain. **1958** *Engineering* 11 Apr. 458/1 The accomplishments in micrometallurgy at the laboratory soon led to the determination of some of the properties of the new metal. **1856** Highley in *Q. Jrnl. Microsc. Sci.* IV. 223 The instruments of *Micro-Mineralogical research. **1887** Bonney in *Q. Jrnl. Geol. Soc.* XLIV. 44 The result is micro-mineralogical change only. **1856** Highley in *Q. Jrnl. Microsc. Sci.* IV. 220 (*title*) Contributions to *Micro-Mineralogy. **1913** *Jrnl. R. Microsc. Soc.* 207 (*heading*) Apparatus for *micro-operations. **1968** *Sci. Jrnl.* Nov. 54/1 Micro-operations such as removing parts of the embryo or grafting tissues from one embryo to another. **1922** *Anatomical Rec.* XXIV. 18 Instruments for *micro-operative work. **1941** *Bull. Amer. Assoc. Petroleum Geologists* XXV. 1208 The progressive multiplication of the *micropaleontologic groups studied is considered. *Ibid.* 1219 These micropaleontologic objects he called 'microzoa'. **1972** *Biol. Abstr.* LIII. 3865/2 (*heading*) Lithologic and micropaleontologic study of the Lias.. of Mayorca. **1929** *Jrnl. Paleont.* III. 229 (*heading*) *Micropaleontological activities. **1973** *Nature* 13 July 74/2 Theyer presented palaeomagnetic and micropalaeontological data which seemed to invalidate the timing of what was thought to be one of palaeontology's most reliable datum planes. **1928** *Jrnl. Paleont.* II. 159 This is no reflection upon the *micropaleontologist. **1972** *Daily Tel.* 31 Aug. 21 (Advt.), The palynologist should preferably have experience in the Mesozoic/Tertiary, the micropalaeontologist preferably on Mesozoic/Tertiary Foraminifera. **1883** A. H. Foord (*title*) Contributions to the *micropalæontology of the Cambro-Silurian rocks of Canada. Part 1. **1928** *Jrnl. Paleont.* II. 158 Micropaleontology should, in no way, radically depart from the general field and fundamental principles of paleontology. It is merely a study of the smaller fossils whose characteristic features are studied by the aid of a microscope. **1957** *New Biol.* XXIV. 11 Micro-palaeontology, which is mainly the study of fossil foraminifera, has become an important and highly specialized profession and practically the whole of current research on these animals is devoted to this aspect of the matter. **1879** Rutley *Stud. Rocks* vii. 47 The special study of *micro-petrology. *Ibid.* xiii. 268 A determination of their precise origin is a difficult exercise for *micro-petrologists. **1974** *Sci. Amer.* May 136/3 Two clever *micro-physiologists have measured the power involved, and they conclude that one gliding algal filament.. used about 7,300 molecules of ATP per second to move. **1954** *New Biol.* XVI. 37 We cannot expect to close the evolutionary gap preceding the establishment of cellular organisms until we know far more of intracellular histology and *microphysiology. **1956** *Jrnl. Biophysical & Biochem. Cytol.* II. Suppl. 107 The particles, possibly coated with protein, become attached to the plasma membrane. Minute invaginations of the membrane, with the adherent granules, develop. The invaginated membrane is pinched off, resulting in the formation of an intracellular vacuole. Possibly a type of *micropinocytosis takes place. **1973** *Nature* 2 Mar. 57/1 Electron microscopic studies.. suggest that some synaptic vesicles form by a process of micropinocytosis at the presynaptic terminal membrane. *Ibid.* 57/2 A micropinocytotic origin of synaptic vesicles remains uncertain. **1942** *Jrnl. Legal & Pol. Sociol.* I. 55 We will forego here any prolonged analysis of this '*micro-sociological aspect', and will concentrate all our attention on the functional relationship between democracy and types of particular groups and all-inclusive societies. **1944** *Man* XLIV. 21/1 The most valuable contribution of the social anthropologist may well still lie in this micro-sociological field. **1972** P. Sheriff tr. *Rocher's Gen. Introd. Sociol.* I. i. 4 The microsociological plane of different types of social links. **1941** *Jrnl. Philos.* XXXVIII. 486 The problems of mass, community, and communion arise in '*microsociology'. **1944** *Man* XLIV. 21/1 Much of the anthropologist's work has lain hitherto in what may be called micro-sociology—the study of small groups or of small units in larger groups. **1959** G. D. Mitchell *Sociol.* i. 23 These two traditions may be said to be the forerunners of the modern tendency for sociology to bifurcate into what may be called macro- and micro-sociology. **1966** P. A. Sorokin *Sociol. Theories Today* IV. xiv. 470 Micro-sociology studies the simplest manifestation of social reality—sociability, that is, 'the multifarious ways of being bound by a whole and in a whole'. **1974** *Times Lit. Suppl.* 22 Nov. 1304/1 Micro-sociology, indeed any serious sociology of an analytic kind, has to begin with a study of the most elementary social relations. **1872** *Q. Jrnl. Microsc. Sci.* XII. 409 *Microzoology.

b. Denoting properties revealed by microscopic examination, as ***micro-character***, ***foliation***, ***-texture***.

1890 *Century Dict.*, **Microcharacter*, any zoological character derived from microscopic or other minute examination. **1887** Bonney in *Q. Jrnl. Geol. Soc.* XLIV. 44 A *microfoliation only is produced, which.. appears to be parallel to the original stratification. **1965** G. J. Williams *Econ. Geol. N.Z.* x. 157/2 The hardness and toughness of greenstone depends partly on its mineral composition, these qualities resulting from a *micro-texture of very closely felted and interwoven minute fibres. **1971** *Good Motoring* Sept. 9/2 A road surface which gives grip at low vehicle speeds must incorporate roadstone of a harsh rather than a polished micro-texture.

c. Denoting objects prepared for microscopic examination, as ***micro-section***, ***-slide***.

1890 *Century Dict.*, *Microsection*, a slice, as of rock, cut so thin as to be more or less transparent, and mounted on a glass in convenient form to be studied with the aid of the microscope. **1909** in *Cent. Dict.* Suppl. **1951** *Electronic Engin.* XXIII. 8/1 The combination of a television camera with a microscope makes it possible for a large group of students to watch simultaneously the events taking place on a microslide. **1971** *McGraw-Hill Yearbk. Sci. & Technol.* 359/2 A rapid detection method for the major components of cannabis.. involves the use of microslides for thin-layer chromatography.

3. *Phys.* and *Path.*, in sbs. of mod.L. form in *-ia*, compounded with Gr. names for different parts or functions of the body, and signifying arrested development of the part or function in question, as **microce'phalia** (see MICROCEPHALY). **micro'glossia**, congenital smallness of the tongue (Mayne *Expos. Lex.* 1856). **micro'gyria**, abnormal smallness of the gyri of the brain. **micro'mastia** [Gr. μαστ-ός breast], the condition in a post-pubertal woman of having an abnormally small breast. **micro'mazia** [Gr. μαζ-ός breast] = prec. **microph'thalmia** (also anglicized **'microphthalmy**) [Gr. ὀφθαλμός eye], 'a Disease in the Eyes, the having little Eyes' (Bailey, 1731); hence **microph'thalmic** *a.*; also **microph'thalmos**, abnormal smallness of the eye. **mi'cropsia** (also **'micropsy**) [Gr. -οψία kind of vision], term for the state of vision in which objects appear smaller than natural (Mayne).

1840 Billings *Med. Dict.* II. 154/1 *Microgyria. **1905** *Brit. Med. Jrnl.* 28 Oct. 1100/1 In this case of microgyria the right side of the brain was less than two-thirds the size of the left. **1920** *Brain* XLIII. 26 Microgyria, which has hitherto been usually known under the name of hemiatrophy of the brain or arrested development of the nervous system, has been comparatively rarely described, and merits further study. **1961** *Lancet* 2 Sept. 513/2 Microgyria was apparent in the posterior part of both lobes. **1918** Deaver & McFarland *Breast* iii. 45 These terms are applied to conditions in which there is congenital total absence of one or both of the mammary glands, or in which one or both glands are undeveloped or rudimentary in development. To the latter condition the term '*micromastia' might more correctly be applied. **1953** *New Statesman* 5 Sept. 254/3 About 4,000,000 young American women suffer in some degree from micromastia (immature breasts). **1965** L. B. Arey *Developmental Anat.* (ed. 7) xxiii. 452 Retention of the prepubertal condition (micromastia). **1890** *Syd. Soc. Lex.*, *Micromazia. **1894** W. R. Williams *Monogr. Dis. Breast* iii. 33 When the defect is less complete than in the above cases, we get a very small imperfectly-developed gland, like the normal male breast, or smaller—micromazia. **1928** F. Z. Snoop *From Monotremes to Madonna* 22 The breast may be absent, amazia; or very small, micromazia. **1856** Mayne *Expos. Lex.*, **Microphthalmia*, term for a morbid shrinking or wasting of the eye-balls; microphthalmy. [**1845** *Dublin Jrnl. Med. Sci.* XXVII. 29 Microphthalmus is the term applied by continental writers to that peculiar condition of the eye, when there appears to be an arrest of development of this organ at some particular period of its growth, without either atrophy or disease.] **1850** *Boston Med. & Surg. Jrnl.* XLII. 421 (*heading*) *Microphthalmos, complicated with congenital cataract in both eyes. **1934** *Arch. Ophthalm.* XI. 516 It is justifiable to consider the two forms of microphthalmos as one genetic entity with the morphologic distinction between microphthalmos with external, or orbital, cysts and microphthalmos with intraocular cysts. **1971** *Amer. Jrnl. Ophthalm.* LXXI. 1128/1 In colobomatous microphthalmos, the pathogenesis of the small eye is related to faulty closure of the embryonic fissure. **1849** Craig, **Microphthalmy*, a preternatural or morbid smallness of the eyes. **1868** Darwin *Anim. & Pl.* II. 24 Two sons were *microphthalmic. **1899** *Allbutt's Syst. Med.* VIII. 107 *Micropsia, or macropsia may be associated with the monocular diplopia. **1890** W. James *Princ. Psychol.* II. xix. 93 In consequence of this so-called *micropsy, Aubert relates that he saw a man apparently no larger than a photograph.

4. Prefixed to an adj. with the sense 'containing or possessed of some object or constituent in minute form, quantity or degree', as **micro'aerophil(e** = *microaërophilous*; also as *sb.*, a microaerophile organism. **ˌmicroaero'philic** = *microaërophilous*. **microaë'rophilous** [Gr. ἀερ-, ἀήρ air, φίλ-ος friend: see -OUS] *Bot.*, needing but little free oxygen (Jackson *Gloss. Bot.* 1900). **micro'carpous** [Gr. καρπός fruit] *Bot.*, having small fruit; also applied to mosses, having small urns (Mayne *Expos. Lex.* 1856). **micro'cellular**, containing or characterized by minute cells. **micro'ceratous, -cerous** [Gr. κέρας horn] *Ent.*, having small antennæ (*Ibid.*). **micro-'clastic** [CLASTIC] *Geol.*, minutely clastic. **micro'dactylous** *Path.* [Gr. δάκτυλος digit], having small digits (*Syd. Soc. Lex.* 1890). **'microdont** *Anat.* [Gr. ὀδοντ-, ὀδούς tooth], having small or short teeth. **micro'dontous** [f. prec.], in the same sense (*Syd. Soc. Lex.*). **micro-e'lectric**, having electric properties in a very small degree (*Cent. Dict.*). **'microform** *Bot.*, epithet of a heterœcious fungus with teleutospores only, which require a period of rest before germinating (Jackson *Gloss. Bot.*). **microgranu'litic** *Geol.* (see quot.). **microlepi'dotous** *Zool.* [Gr. λεπιδωτός scaly, f.

λεπιδ-, λεπίς scale], having very small scales (Mayne). **micro'petalous** *Bot.* [Gr. πέταλος a petal], having very small petals (Craig 1849). **mi'crophagous** *Zool.* [-PHAGOUS], feeding on minute particles. **micro'phyllous** *Bot.* [Gr. φύλλον leaf], having small leaves (Smart 1840). **microporphy'ritic** *Geol.*, consisting of porphyritic rock in which the felspar or other crystals are of microscopic size. **micropte'rygious** *Zool.* [Gr. πτέρυξ fin], having small fins (Mayne). **micro'spermous** *Bot.* [Gr. σπέρμα seed], having very small seeds or grains (Mayne). **microspheru'litic** *Geol.*, characterized by the presence of microscopic spherulites. **'microspined**, furnished with minute spines or spicules. **micro'splenic** *Path.*, not accompanied by enlargement of the spleen. **micro'stomatous, mi'crostomous** [Gr. στοματ-, στόμα mouth], having a small mouth (Mayne). **micro'stylar** *Arch.*, having a small style or column, epithet applied to a form of architecture in which there is a separate small order to each floor (Ogilvie, 1882). **micro'vascular**, of or pertaining to the smallest blood-vessels.

1903 *Science* 6 Mar. 371/1 The *microaerophiles will grow luxuriantly under normal conditions under diminished oxygen pressure. **1909** *Cent. Dict.* Suppl., Micro-aërophile *a.* **1957** G. E. HUTCHINSON *Treat. Limnol.* I. xiii. 757 It would seem that the limnetic purple bacteria are microaerophil rather than anaerobic. **1970** PASSMORE & ROBSON *Compan. Med. Stud.* II. xviii. 46/2 These micro-aerophiles often prefer a concentration of CO_2 that is higher than normal, e.g. 5–10 per cent. **1903** *Science* 6 Mar. 371 *Clostridium Pasteurianum*.. is an anaerobe, but it also grows in symbiosis with aerobic forms; it is, therefore, *microaerophilic. **1971** *Nature* 9 July 132/2 *Campylobacter*, a genus of microaerophilic bacteria including the organism formerly called *Vibrio fetus*. **1909** WEBSTER, *Microcellular. **1958** *Punch* 8 Oct. 476/3 Bottines have micro-cellular rubber soles and are very neat and light. **1965** *Biol. Abstr.* XLVI. 5347/1 (*heading*) Complex treatment of the microcellular bronchial carcinoma by means of the nitrogen mustard and X-rays. **1971** D. G. JONES in C. M. Blow *Rubber Technol. & Manuf.* x. 397 Microcellular soling containing minute discrete air cells and having a specific gravity as low as 0·3 is also used extensively. **1888** TEALL *Brit. Petrogr.* 439 **Microclastic*, an epithet applied by Naumann to such clastic rocks as are composed of small fragments. **1884** FLOWER in *Jrnl. Anthrop. Inst.* XIV. 185 The *Microdont section, containing all the so-called Caucasian or white races. *Ibid.*, Microdont Races. **1885** GEIKIE *Text-bk. Geol.* (ed. 2) 109 Where the minerals are grouped in small isolated grain-like individuals,.. the structure has been named by French petrographers *granulitic*, or where only discernible by the aid of the microscope, **micro-granulitic*. **1923** J. W. FOLSOM *Entomol.* (ed. 3) xiii. 373 According to the nature of their food, most insects may be classified as follows:.. **microphagous* ([feeding] on micro-organisms, as bacteria, yeasts, etc.). **1950** Microphagous [see CHEMOTAXIS]. **1963** R. P. DALES *Annelids* iii. 76 The evolution of the Polychaeta is thus mirrored by the evolution of feeding methods; a transition in one direction towards burrowing, tube building, sedentary life and microphagous feeding; and in the other to a more active scavenging or predatory existence. **1878** LAWRENCE tr. *Cotta's Rocks Class.* 67 *Micro-porphyritic textures or structures of rock. **1879** RUTLEY *Stud. Rocks* xi. 185 Rocks in which very small isolated crystals occur only being spoken of as micro-porphyritic. **1885** GEIKIE *Text-bk. Geol.* (ed. 2) 111 In many cases spherulites are only recognisable with the microscope, when they each present a black cross between crossed Nicol-prisms, and thereby characteristically reveal the *micro-spherulitic structure. **1881** P. M. DUNCAN in *Jrnl. Linn. Soc.* XV. 324 These.. have flesh-spicula acerate, fusiform, curved and *microspined. **1905** H. D. ROLLESTON *Dis. Liver* 318 Gilbert.. speaks of this as the *microsplenic or asplenomegalic form of biliary cirrhosis. **1959** *Ann. N.Y. Acad. Sci.* LXXXII. 236 Can anything be learned about the mechanism that damages blood vessels in diabetes mellitus by studying the dynamic morphology of the superficial *microvascular system in man? **1967** *Sci. News Let.* 9 Sept. 262 Precise formations of the *microvascular system and other spaces in organs of dead animals are revealed in detail when this liquid silicone compound is injected.

5. a. *Physics.* Prefixed to the name of a unit to form a name for one-millionth part of that unit, as ***micro-ampere, bar*** [BAR *sb.*[6] 1, 2], ***-calorie, -coulomb, -curie, -farad, -gramme*** (Webster 1902), ***-henry*** [HENRY[3]], ***-inch, -litre*** (*Cent. Dict.* 1890), ***-mho, -millimetre*** (see also below), ***-ohm, -poise, -rad, -second, -volt, -watt, -weber***. **'microdegree**, one millionth of a degree centigrade (kelvin). Also duplicated to denote division by a million million (corresponding to the single prefix PICO-), as in ***micromicrocurie, -farad***. **b.** In microscopic botany, ***micro-millimetre*** has by some been used for one-thousandth of a millimetre.

[**1873** *Rep. Brit. Assoc.* 224 For multiplication or division by a million, the prefixes *mega* and *micro* may conveniently be employed.]

1904 *Westm. Gaz.* 16 July 10/3 A *micro-ampere is the millionth part of an ampere. **1918** *Microbar [see BAR *sb.*[6] 2]. **1963** JERRARD & MCNEILL *Dict. Sci. Units* 22 Acoustic pressure of the order of one dyne cm^{-2} is now described by the microbar. **1971** *Nature* 1 Jan. 15/3 The figures.. indicate that a pressure wave moving at 330 m s^{-1} generates a displacement of the Earth's surface of 10 to 15 nanometres per microbar with periods between 20 and 100 s. **1969** *Sci. Jrnl.* Aug. 42 Heat flow through the ocean crust is on average 1·2 *microcalories/cm^2/s except in active regions such as mid-ocean ridges. **1892** *Gloss. Electr. Terms* 12 in *Lightning* 3 Mar. Supp., *Microcoulomb. **1911** *Sci. Amer.* 29 Apr. 429 The 'optimum' or most favorable dose of radiation, which developed the mold in four days, was found to be ½ *microcurie per cubic centimeter of air. **1958** *Immunology* I. 29 The status of the grafts was assessed at monthly intervals after grafting by administering 5 microcuries of ^{131}I intraperitoneally. **1970** PASSMORE & ROBSON *Compan. Med. Stud.* II. vi. 8/2 When used for diagnostic purposes, radioiodine is usually given by mouth in a dose of 5–15 microcuries. **1957** *Science Progress* XLV. 415 Another.. task would be the study of lattice specific heats at *microdegree temperatures. **1971** *Physics Bull.* Dec. 713/1 Recent work, such as the specific heat measurement by Ahlers (1971) is characterized by temperature resolution as small as a microdegree. **1873** *Rep. Brit. Assoc.* 224 The *microfarad is the millionth part of a farad. **1890** *Syd. Soc. Lex.*, **Micro-gramme*. A measure of weight.. it is equivalent to the one thousandth of a milligramme. **1868** L. CLARK *Electr. Meas.* 43 One millionth part of an ohm = 1 *microhm. **1909** *Cent. Dict.* Suppl., *Microhenry. **1911** *Physical Rev.* XXXII. 612 (*heading*) Inductance in microhenrys. **1964** R. F. FICCHI *Electr. Interference* iv. 39 Experience has shown that as the L exceeds 0·025 microhenries in magnitude, the effectiveness of the bond diminishes rapidly. **1941** OBERG & JONES *Machinery's Handbk.* (ed. 11) 1776 Assume that the quantities *a*, *b*, *c*, etc., equal the various profile measurements in *micro-inches. **1962** *B.S.I. News* June 24/2 Another firm.. even specified surface finished [? *read* finishes] in micro-inches on their drawings. **1970** *Sci. Amer.* Mar. 142/3 The rotor is driven magnetically on a superb ball-bearing axis. (The tolerances are specified to five or 10 microinches.) **1919** *Electric Jrnl.* XVI. 322 *Micromhos per mile of each conductor. **1940** *Bell System Technical Publ. Monograph B-1268* 7 One interesting commercial tube in which one stage of secondary electron multiplication is added to an ordinary tetrode, has a transconductance of 14,000 micromhos. **1962** SIMPSON & RICHARDS *Physical Princ. Junction Transistors* viii. 175 Present values of its mutual conductance are small (~100 micromhos). **1961** *Daily Tel.* 10 Oct. 18/3 In the past 23 days, the average amount of radioactivity in every kilogram of air has been 3·42 *micro-microcuries. **1909** *Cent. Dict.* Suppl., *Micro-microfarad. **1921** *Physical Rev.* XVIII. 143 This plate had coatings so small that its normal capacity was only about 0·67 micro-micro-farads. **1962** CORSON & LORRAIN *Introd. Electromagn. Fields* ii. 60 A sphere one meter in radius has a capacitance of about 100 micro-microfarads. **1884** FLINT *Princ. & Pract. Med.* (ed. 5) 62 Whose size is between two and six *micromillimetres. **1887** tr. *Nägeli & Schwendener's Microscope* 293 Harting's proposal to use the micromillimetre (= ·001 mm.) as the standard of unity deserves general acceptance. **1941** *Ann. Reg. 1940* 353 For hydrogen vapour it [*sc.* the viscosity] is *c.* 10 *micropoise at 14·5° K. **1963** JERRARD & MCNEILL *Dict. Sci. Units* 107 The viscosity of gases is frequently given in micropoises (μP); (air 181 μP at 20° C). **1969** *Times* 2 Sept. 10/4 On some of the islands of the atoll.. the intensity of fall-out radiation range[s] from three to seven *microrads an hour. **1906** A. E. KENNELLY *Wireless Telegr.* ix. 99 If we call the one millionth part of a second one *microsecond for convenience of description, then one complete wave would pass off in 1/2·5 microsecond. **1942** J. D. STRANATHAN *'Particles' of Mod. Physics* xii. 481 These particles are radioactive with a half life of a few microseconds. **1966** T. PYNCHON *Crying of Lot 49* v. 114 'Nearly three weeks it takes him,' marvelled the efficiency expert, 'to decide. You know how long it would've taken the IBM 7094? Twelve micro-seconds.' **1868** L. CLARK *Electr. Meas.* 43 One millionth of a volt = 1 *microvolt. **1909** *Cent. Dict.* Suppl., *Micro-watt. **1914** R. STANLEY *Text-bk. Wireless Telegr.* xvii. 261 Duddell carried out experiments to find the minimum power required to produce audible signals in a telephone receiver at different frequencies, and found that, while 430 microwatts were required at 300 frequency, only 7·7 microwatts were required at 900 frequency. **1970** *Physics Bull.* Sept. 403/2 Sound power of the order of a microwatt from a dripping tap. **1896** *Jrnl. Soc. Arts* 10 July 701/1 *Microwebers × linkages = microcoulombs × ohms.

6. Prefixed to the names of instruments and techniques with the sense 'specially designed for dealing with or measuring small effects or small quantities of material'. (In the names of techniques this use passes into 2 a.) ***microammeter, -balance, -burette*** (U.S. ***-buret***), ***-calorimeter*** (hence ***-calorimetric*** adj., ***-calorimetry***), ***-densitometer*** (hence ***-densitometric*** adj., ***-densitometry***), ***-determination, -electrophoresis*** (hence ***-electrophoretic*** adj., ***-electrophoretically*** adv.), ***-estimation, -gasometer*** (hence ***-gasometric*** adj., ***-gasometrically*** adv., ***-gasometry***), ***-gravimetric*** adj., ***-Kjeldahl*** (used *attrib.* or *absol.*: cf. KJELDAHL), ***-manometer*** (hence ***-manometric*** adj., ***-manometrically*** adv.), ***-method, -photometer*** (hence ***-photometric*** adj., ***-photometry***), ***-pipette, -respirometer*** [ad. G. *mikrorespirometer* (T. Thunberg 1904, in *Zentralbl. f. Physiol.* 3 Dec. 553)] (hence ***-respirometric*** adj., ***-respirometry***), ***-spectrograph*** (hence ***-spectrographic*** adj., ***-spectrography***), ***-spectrophotometer*** (so ***-spectrophotometric*** adj., ***-spectrophotometrically*** adv., ***-spectrophotometry***), ***-syringe, -technique***; **micro-audiphone**, an instrument for reinforcing or augmenting very feeble sounds (*Cent. Dict.* 1890). **micro-barograph**, an instrument designed to magnify the minor fluctuations of atmospheric pressure. **micro-battery**, a very small galvanic battery (Knight *Dict. Mech.* Suppl. 1884). **'microburner**, a small Bunsen burner for giving a single small flame. **micro-detector**, a sensitive galvanoscope (*Cent. Dict.*). **microdi'ffusion** *Chem.*, diffusion of the vapour of a substance in an open container into an adjacent container in which there is a second substance, by which the first may be detected; usu. *attrib.* **'microfilter**, a filter for separating out small quantities of material or very fine particles. **,micro-incine'ration**, a process by which tissue sections are heated to a high temperature so as to remove organic matter and facilitate chemical analysis *in situ* of the inorganic constituents left behind. **'microneedle**, a very fine needle used in micromanipulation. **micropantograph**, an instrument invented by Mr. Peters in 1852 for the production of microscopically small writing (Knight *Dict. Mech.* 1875). **micro-polariscope**, a polariscope for the analysis of microscopic objects. **'microprobe** = MICROANALYSER; also as *v. trans.*, to analyse with a microanalyser. **micro-refractometer**, a refractometer specially constructed for the detection of differences in the minute structure of blood corpuscles. **microrheometer**, an instrument for measuring the rate of flow of liquids through a capillary tube; hence **microrheo'metrical** *a.*, pertaining to or indicated by a microrheometer (*Cassell's Encycl. Dict.* 1885). **micro-tasimeter**, an instrument invented in 1878 by T. A. Edison for measuring infinitesimal pressure. **micro-telephone**, a telephone constructed to render audible very weak sounds; hence **micro-tele'phonic** *a.* (*Cent. Dict.*).

1930 *Telegraph & Telephone Jrnl.* Dec. 47/2 The deflection on the *microammeter is proportional to the speed at which the tongue of the standard relay is oscillating, and a direct speed reading is given on the microammeter scale in terms of words per minute or cycles per second. **1964** R. F. FICCHI *Electr. Interference* vii. 127 A useful indicating device for locating leaks can easily be constructed using a tuned circuit consisting of a coil and variable condenser together with a 0–100 microammeter and crystal diode detector (1N34). **1903** *Jrnl. Chem. Soc.* LXXXIV. II. 571 A *micro-balance with torsional control is described, having a sensitiveness of 0·0380 mg. per scale division. **1966** *McGraw-Hill Encycl. Sci. & Technol.* II. 74/1 Micro-balances, used to weigh masses of a fraction of a gram, may be of the beam or the torsion type. **1904** *Athenæum* 31 Dec. 911/3 The authors described an apparatus called the '*micro-barograph'. **1878** *Eng. Mechanic* 23 Aug. 602 A *Micro-battery for the Microphone. **1926** *Chem. Abstr.* XX. 2543 A *microburet for measuring minute drops is described. **1946** *Nature* 19 Oct. 556/2 The apparatus is completed by a microburette mounted on a movable arm. **1964** Micro buret [see BURETTE 2]. **1911** *Jrnl. Infectious Dis.* VIII. 351 Natural gas for the *microburner may be improved by causing it to pass through alcohol or benzine. **1938** *Jrnl. Laboratory & Clin. Med.* XXIV. 310 Two cubic centimeter samples of unhemolyzed serum are digested in pyrex test tubes.. with 1·5 c.c. of concentrated sulfuric acid... The digestion may be carried out.. rapidly by the direct flame of a microburner. **1962** *B.S.I. News* July 28 Specifies the following items of apparatus for use in micro-chemical analysis: (i) Crucible holder... (ii) Micro-burner jet for use with coal gas, giving a non-luminous flame up to about 5 cm in height. **1911** *Jrnl. Physiol.* XLIII. 261 (*heading*) A new form of differential *micro-calorimeter, for the estimation of heat production in physiological, bacteriological, or ferment actions. **1959** DAWSON & LONG *Chem. of Nucl. Power* i. 9 A microcalorimeter has been developed at Harwell for the rapid estimation of small amounts of polonium. **1924** *Chem. Abstr.* XVIII. 2723 (*heading*) Utilization in biology of the *micro-calorimetric method. **1971** *Nature* 22 Oct. 560/2 Micro-calorimetric studies of sperm whale ferri-MbCN have demonstrated a change in heat capacity (C_p) in the range 35° ± 18° C. **1924** *Chem. Abstr.* XVIII. 4483 *Microcalorimetry. **1973** *Nature* 16 Feb. 473/1 For research purposes, microcalorimetry provides highly informative data regarding microbial metabolism. **1935** *Discovery* Nov. 324 *Micro-densitometer for analysing sound track. **1966** *Aviation Week & Space Technol.* 5 Dec. 99/3 The CRT system will be used.. as a flying spot scanner and will scan through a precision optical chain providing a high-resolution microdensitometer. **1959** *Listener* 12 Mar. 451/2 *Micro-densitometric tracing of the profile of the crater. **1973** H. L. SNYDER in L. M. Bibermann *Perception of Displayed Information* iii. 89 The *X-Y* luminance patterns of any given object or area of a scene can then be determined by scanning microdensitometric measurements for a film transparency input to the television system. **1957** A. ENGSTRÖM in V. E. Cosslett et al. *X-Ray Microsc. & Microradiogr.* 32 *Microdensitometry of the fine-grained photographic emulsion presents the same type of problems as does direct microspectrography of biological material. **1973** *Nature* 17 Aug. 413/1 More has been achieved from a digitized array of optical densities of the image obtained by microdensitometry. **1925** *Analyst* L. 302 (*heading*) *Micro-determination of methoxyl. **1947** CHERONIS & ENTRIKIN *Semimicro Qualitative Org. Analysis* ii. 72 The Alber specific-gravity pipettes that are commercially available may be used for the microdetermination of densities. **1967** *Oceanogr. & Marine Biol.* V. 173 A colorimetric method has recently been described for micro-determination of lipids. **1939** E. J. CONWAY *Micro-Diffusion Analysis & Volumetric Error* i. 4 (*heading*) Scale and accuracy of the *micro-diffusion methods described. *Ibid.* ii. 7 (heading) A standard micro-diffusion apparatus or unit. **1956** *Nature* 31 Mar. 623/2 The asparaginase activity of the extract was estimated from the ammonia formed (by the Conway microdiffusion method). **1959** *Times* 14 Oct. 14/5 Ultracentrifuge and *micro-electrophoresis equipment. **1971** *Nature* 22 Oct. 567/1 Cell electrophoresis was performed with a thin walled cylindrical cell in a particle micro-electrophoresis

apparatus. **1961** *Lancet* 16 Sept. 656/2 *Microelectrophoretic analyses of the ribosenucleic acid formed in the neurone and in the glia. **1973** *Neuropharmacology* XII. 77 A technique has been described for stereotaxically performing microelectrophoretic studies on single brain cells in awake, non-paralyzed cats. **1963** *Federation Proc.* XXII. 625/2 Responses of neurones to *microelectrophoretically applied Acetylcholine (ACh).. have been obtained. **1973** *Jrnl. Pharmacy & Pharmacol.* XXV. 309 Responses of single cortical neurons to microelectrophoretically applied noradrenaline at pH 3·1 and 5·0 and to hydrogen ions were compared in the halothane-anaesthetized cat. **1922** *Analyst* XLVII. 80 (*heading*) *Micro-estimation of nitrogen and its biological applications. **1972** *Analytical Chem.* XLIV. 1879 (*heading*) Simultaneous microestimation of choline and acetylcholine by gas chromatography. **1911** *Jrnl. Chem. Soc.* C. II. 225 (*heading*) A *micro-filter for the treatment of small quantities of precipitate. **1958** *Ann. Rep. Chief Inspector of Factories on Industr. Health 1957* 23 in *Parl. Papers 1958–9* (Cmnd. 558) XIII. 183 He wore a micro-filter respirator. **1972** *Physics Bull.* Aug. 455/1 The difference is due to the use of a microfilter in an aircraft fuelling system. **1951** *Amer. Jrnl. Clin. Path.* XXI. 1153 (*heading*) A practical *microgasometer for estimation of carbon dioxide. **1972** *Analytical Biochem.* XLV. 112 The magnetic diver microgasometer is operated at a constant pressure so that the enclosed gas bubble can contract or expand freely. **1956** *Nature* 28 Jan. 185/2 In 1937, Linderstrøm-Lang introduced a *microgasometric method based on the principle of the Cartesian diver. **1967** *Internat. Jrnl. Neuropharmacol.* VI. 266 The electron microscopic-cytochemical technique has been applied directly to unfixed isolated neurons following microgasometric analysis. **1968** *Progress Brain Res.* XXIX. 41 Ultracytochemistry was then applied to individual neurons, which had been analyzed *microgasometrically. **1957** G. E. Hutchinson *Treat. Limnol.* I. xvii. 879 A technique involving characteristically ingenious *microgasometry.. has been used by Krogh and Lange. **1972** *Analytical Biochem.* XLV. 115 The dimensions of the ampullas most frequently used for magnetic microgasometry. **1931** *Industr. & Engin. Chem.* (*Analytical Ed.*) III. 345 An apparatus is described for *microgravimetric analyses, such as sulfate, halide, and phosphate determinations. **1966** *McGraw-Hill Encycl. Sci. & Technol.* II. 199/2 Microgravimetric analyses, in which weighings are made to ±0·002 mg on a Kuhlman beam balance. **1924** *Analyst* XLIX. 52 (*heading*) *Micro-incineration applicable to histochemical investigation. **1969** Brown & Bertke *Textbk. Cytol.* iii. 23/1 Micro-incineration involves the ashing of tissue sections at a temperature of about 600°C. This method can provide information regarding general distribution of certain minerals. **1923** *Jrnl. Amer. Chem. Soc.* XLVI. 2069 A new *micro-Kjeldahl method.. has been devised. **1946** *Nature* 30 Nov. 791/1 The extract was then filtered and its nitrogen content determined by micro-Kjeldahl. **1973** *Analytical Biochem.* LIII. 36 We have developed two simple modifications which minimize, if not eliminate, the excessive foaming encountered during micro Kjeldahl digestion of biological materials. **1897** *Jrnl. Physical Chem.* I. 596 The author's *micromanometer (l.c., 1895), giving measurements accurate to 0·0033 mm water or 0·00024 mm mercury was used. **1949** O. G. Sutton *Sci. of Flight* 201 The most sensitive micromanometer in general use, the Chattock-Fry gauge, is simply a glorified U-tube. **1972** *Physics Bull.* Aug. 491/2 The new vacuum micromanometer has been designed for applications requiring sensitive differential pressure measurements at high vacuum levels. **1937** *Discovery* July 224/2 We have new *micromanometric techniques which can be applied directly to small-celled animals or plants in life. **1956** *Jrnl. Laboratory & Clin. Med.* XLVII. 642 The development of the micromanometric methods described herein was undertaken because of the need for a precise but rapid method for detecting sudden alterations in acid-base balance. **1973** *Jrnl. Neurochem.* XX. 1029 The rate of oxygen consumption has been measured *micromanometrically in fresh mouse neuroblastoma cells. **1920** *Jrnl. Soc. Chem. Industry* 15 Mar. 206A/1 A *micro-method in which 1–2 c.c of urine and 1·5–3 c.c. of alkali need only be used. **1946** *Nature* 10 Aug. 199/2 We have developed a new micro-method for X-ray diffraction investigation of biological objects. **1967** *Oceanogr. & Marine Biol.* V. 171 A micro-method for determination of protein in extremely small quantities by the quenching of dye fluorescence has also been described. **1974** *Nature* 3 May 37/2 Studies of lymphocyte transformation *in vitro* were carried out by our micromethod. **1921** *Science* 28 Oct. 411/2 The method of making the glass *micro-needles and pipettes. **1940** C. Sherrington *Man on his Nature* iv. 116 The protein coat of the fertilized egg-cell.. can be cut by the 'microneedle' without loss of its rigidity. **1971** *Nature* 2 July 28/2 The microneedles are made from 1 mm 'Pyrex' or borosilicate glass rod drawn out to form a thin (~0·3 mm) shaft, ~50 mm long. **1899** J. Hartmann in *Astrophysical Jrnl.* X. 325 The apparatus.. may be designated as a *microphotometer, since it is a combination of microscope and photometer. **1947** *Jrnl. Brit. Interplanetary Soc.* VI. 162 Meteor light-curves, which must be examined photographically, with the help of a recording microphotometer. **1971** *Tsitologiya* XIII. 1530 The scanning and integrating microphotometer permits to define the quantity of substance, area and the linear dimension of micro-objects. **1952** *Chromosoma* V. 341 The *microphotometric evaluation of cytochemical color reactions, such as the Feulgen-reaction on desoxyribose nucleic acid (DNA), has in recent years attained increasing importance. **1960** *Jrnl. Histochem. & Cytochem.* VIII. 4/1 It is of importance in some microphotometric studies of cells and tissues to determine the protein content of a single cell, nucleus, or nucleolus. **1937** *Monthly Notices R. Astr. Soc.* XCVIII. 113 A slit ·025 mm. wide and <0·4 mm. high was used in all the *microphotometry. **1973** *Acta Cytol.* XVII. 94 It is the objective of this paper to examine the feasibility of using automated scanning microphotometry with computer analysis of the cell images for the purpose of differentiating nonmalignant from malignant cells in pleural fluid. **1918** *Biol. Bull.* XXXIV. 134 The capillary attraction in the lumen of a *micropipette.. is quite sufficient for the purpose. **1922** *Anatomical Rec.* XXIV. 2 With the micro-pipette.. one can.. inject substances into.. a cell. **1955** *Sci. Amer.* Aug. 98/2 Deposit five thousandths of a milliliter of serum on the ruled strip with a calibrated micro-pipette. **1968** *Times* 14 Nov. 8/7 A few of the cells, typically about three, are sucked up into a micropipette and injected through the slit in the first embryo. **1867** J. Hogg *Microsc.* I. ii. 147 The powers of the *micro-polariscope cannot be better displayed than in the exhibition of the foregoing phenomena. **1960** *Oxf. Univ. Gaz.* 19 Feb. 743/2 X-ray Fluorescent *Micro-probe. A study is being made of the possible archaeological applications of this very new technique. **1969** *Awake!* 22 Oct. 19/2 A painting that was supposedly done by a sixteenth-century painter was exposed as a forgery by this laser device, which is called a microprobe. **1973** *Nature* 12 Jan. 87/1 Six olivines (three from Venezuela and three from Ghana) microprobed at the Geophysical Laboratory in Washington showed.. an extremely constant Ni content. **1974** *McGraw-Hill Yearbk. Sci. & Technol.* 291/2 The ion microprobe mass spectrometer uses primary ions of argon or oxygen.. that are focused to a 1–2-μm spot before the sample is bombarded. **1886** *Athenæum* 27 Mar. 427/1 Mr. Crisp exhibited.. Prof. Exner's new *micro-refractometer. **1905** *Jrnl. Chem. Soc.* LXXXVIII. II. 44 By means of an apparatus termed the '*micro-respirometer'.. the respiratory exchanges in small objects like nerves can actually be measured. **1946** *Nature* 27 July 126/2 A Cartesian diver micro-respirometer. **1965** B. E. Freeman tr. *Vandel's Biospeleol.* xx. 342 The measurement of respiration is carried out in respiratory chambers or micro-respirometers. **1905** *Jrnl. Chem. Soc.* LXXXVIII. II. 44 *Micro-respirometric investigations. **1970** *Acta Soc. Bot. Poloniae* XXXIX. 497 The micro-respirometric technique has been used for many research works on leaves and leaf segments. **1960** E. J. Boell in Sasser & Jenkins *Nematology* viii. 109 (*heading*) The Cartesian diver technique in *microrespirometry and enzyme assay. **1973** *Soil Biol. & Biochem.* V. 271 A new method has been developed for microrespirometry utilizing gas chromatography. **1879** *Proc. Roy. Soc.* XXVIII. 280 The author [J. B. Hannay] proposes to use for liquids the term 'Microrheosis',.. the instrument being called the *microrheometer. **1934** *Photogr. Jrnl.* LXXIV. 518/2 The application of the *microspectrograph to the identification of organic compounds. **1953** *Experientia* IX. 422/2 The transmission curves obtained with the microspectrograph were transformed into extinction curves. **1950** T. Caspersson *Cell Growth & Cell Function* iii. 61 There are two groups of cell substances that are more easily studied by *microspectrographic procedures than any others. These are the proteins.. and the polynucleotides. **1947** *Acta Path. & Microbiol. Scand.* XXIV. 417 (*heading*) Ultraviolet *microspectrography as an aid in the study of the nucleotide content of bacteria. **1957** Microspectrography [see *microdensitometry* above]. **1951** *Rev. Sci. Instruments* XXII. 866/2 The electronic part of the *microspectrophotometer consists of the two photocells, one above the other. **1966** *McGraw-Hill Encycl. Sci. & Technol.* II. 595/1 Such microspectrophotometers, capable of carrying out spectral analyses within the dimensions of a single cell, will play an increasingly powerful role in furthering our knowledge of cell biology. **1950** T. Caspersson *Cell Growth & Cell Function* ii. 45 This is a further reason for the use of high-aperture lenses in *microspectrophotometric work. **1970** *Nature* 17 Oct. 255/2 Microspectrophotometric analyses of the salic particles in the visible and near ultraviolet show a continuous absorption spectrum increasing towards the ultraviolet. **1951** *Exper. Cell Res.* II. 301 In order to obtain significant data on the content of a certain absorbing substance of a whole cell the only as yet available way is to work *microspectrophotometrically with photographic procedures. **1971** J. M. Paulus *Platelet Kinetics* 330 Ploidy measurements of megakaryocytes have usually been obtained by determining microspectrophotometrically the total relative extinction of megakaryocyte nuclei. **1935** *Chem. Abstr.* XXIX. 1117 (*heading*) Ultraviolet absorption spectrum of sea-urchin eggs. Technic of *microspectrophotometry. **1972** *Amer. Jrnl. Bot.* LIX. 829/1 The two-wavelength method of microspectrophotometry.. was employed in the Feulgen-DNA studies. **1958** *Listener* 9 Oct. 563/1 The bacterial virus is really a tiny syringe—a *microsyringe. **1973** *Internat. Jrnl. Peptide & Protein Res.* V. 208/1 All dilutions and sampling by volume were performed with a microsyringe.. that delivered volumes accurate to $10^{-3} \pm 5 \times 10^{-4}$ ml. **1878** *Jrnl. Franklin Inst.* CVI. 173 Edison's *Micro-tasimeter. **1892** *Jrnl. R. Microsc. Soc.* 555 (*heading*) Zimmermann's botanical *microtechnique. **1956** *Nature* 28 Jan. 153/1 The general climate of micro-chemistry has changed greatly in the interval. In 1949 the applications of micro-techniques were few and not very widely used, but at the present day they are ubiquitous. **1964** *Oceanogr. & Marine Biol.* II. 111 The micro-techniques described here are primarily those for small or micro-amounts of sea water. **1881** *Athenæum* 12 Feb. 238/2 Father Deuza, the Italian astronomer, has been making some experiments with the *micro-telephone.

7. Prefixed to a sb. (or used *attrib.* without a hyphen) to indicate that the object designated has been reduced in size by the use of microphotography, or is used in connection with such an object, as ***micro book***, ***edition***, ***-record***, ***-recording***, ***-reproduction***, ***-text***; **'micro-reader**, **-viewer**, an apparatus that produces from microfilm or microprint an image enlarged sufficiently to be readable.

1970 *New Scientist* 31 Dec. 601/1 The micro book.. opens up the prospect of vast reductions in the world's consumption of paper. **1971** *Brit. Printer* Jan. 80/1 An inventor, who has been working for two years to develop a practicable 'micro book', has come up with a solution. *Ibid.*, Microfilming was not the simplest or most economical way of producing a micro book. **1970** *New Scientist* 31 Dec. 601/2 Publishers of technical journals.. could put out in micro editions some of the.. specialised research material that cannot be included in their normal issues. **1971** *Brit. Printer* Jan. 80/2 PVC paper also has the advantage, for micro editions, of being durable, difficult to tear and waterproof. **1949** M. C. Keeleyside in *Summary Proc. 3rd Ann. Conf. Amer. Theol. Library Assoc.* 11 The reading machines are new on the market. I am proud to say that our library has the first microreader that any library in the world ever possessed. **1970** *Publishers' Weekly* 8 June 152/1 Obviously it is not possible for people to read microfilmed material without some magnification device, hence the microreader which you can see in most libraries. **1948** *Sci. News* VII. 90 The Airgraph scheme.. made one advantage of such micro-records obvious to the general public. **1957** J. Burkett *Microrecording in Libraries* i. 8 Microrecording was first put on a business-like footing in 1928 when Eastman Kodak introduced its Recordak Division. *Ibid.* ii. 13 An opaque microrecord is.. a positive print made from a photographic negative. **1971** *Brit. Printer* Jan. 80/1 Davies started on the project mainly as a result of an inquiry from the American Council for Library Resources, which was interested in obtaining a small, cheap and portable method of retrieving micro-records. **1938** G. van Iterson in *Trans. 14th Conf. Fédération Internat. de Documentation* I. 149 (*heading*) The preparation and reading of micro-reproductions of treatises. **1958** *Engineering* 4 Apr. 443/3 To this [*sc.* the decrease in library accommodation] there is one reasonable solution and that is micro-reproduction. **1944** F. Rider *Scholar & Future of Research Library* II. i. 99 Why might we not combine the micro-texts of our books, and the catalog cards for these same books, in one single entity? *Ibid.* 100 A fair amount of micro-text can be put on the back of a standard-size catalog card. **1958** *Times Rev. Industry* Mar. 61/3 The United States has been a fertile ground for the spread of microtexts. **1973** *Computers & Humanities* VII. 163 Anyone who uses the subject part of an ordinary library catalog, whether in card, book, or microtext form, would benefit from this explanation. **1972** M. J. Bosse *Incident at Naha* iii. 153, I feel I'm turning into a library. I'll start dreaming I'm a card catalog or a microviewer.

8. *micro* is now freely prefixed to sbs., often resulting in trivial or nonce words; from being used as an independent word without a hyphen it passes into a quasi-*adj.* with the meanings:

a. Microscopic, minute; small-scale, small.

The examples are arranged in chronological order.

1922 *Encycl. Brit.* XXX. 34/2 Micro-investigation of glued joints proved the value of carefully preparing the timber and glue. **1926** R. W. Lawson tr. *Hevesy & Paneth's Man. Radioactivity* i. 2 Very small quantities of two different gases.. gradually accumulate within the tube, and can be detected by the methods of micro-gas analysis. **1931** *Boys' Mag.* XLV. 157/1 Any good crystal detector will do. One with fine or micro adjustment is to be preferred. **1935** *Discovery* Nov. 320/1 Whenever it finds a patch of.. dry, dusty ground, there it arrives... Such patches, for the purposes of that *Acrotylus*, are deserts. They are, in fact, micro-deserts. **1946** Koestler *Thieves in Night* 279 Pen-holders of olivewood with a tiny inlaid lens through which one could see a micro-panorama of Jerusalem. **1958** *Spectator* 15 Aug. 236/2 Micro, corneal and contact lenses. **1967** G. Wills in Wills & Yearsley *Handbk. Managem. Technol.* x. 176 At the macro level, marketing management became concerned with understanding its social environment; at the micro level, the concept of the marketing mix postulated a co-ordinative and integrative activity for product distribution and communication. **1969** *Jane's Freight Containers 1968–69* 552/2 Ten models of these 1-ton micro-fork lift trucks are available for loading and unloading containers. **1970** *Globe & Mail* (Toronto) 26 Sept. 9/5 More attention will be given to the ubiquitous 'micro' problems in non-sugar sectors of the [Cuban] economy. **1973** *Physics Bull.* Oct. 626/1 Finally, going lower than micro, we might mention the HP-45, Hewlett-Packard's new pocket 'scientific' calculator, said to be the most powerful of its size and price. **1974** *Sci. Amer.* July 134/2 A computer patiently runs the long repetitive scans looking for tiny needles in microhaystacks.

b. *Chem.* Of or pertaining to microanalysis. Cf. *micromethod* in 6, MICRO-SCALE.

1931 J. W. Brown in C. A. Mitchell *Recent Adv. Analytical Chem.* II. xv. 306 The work of Emich inspired Fritz Pregl.. to attempt to carry out organic determinations on a micro scale. **1937** *Ann. Rev. Biochem.* VI. 85 While many important studies have been made on reducing sugars in recent years, most of these have not involved the use of methods which are strictly micro. **1946** Belcher & Wilson *Qualitative Inorg. Microanalysis* i. 1 Micro methods handle solid samples over the range of 0·1 to 1 mg., and volumes of solution ranging from 0·02 to 0·2 ml. **1955** C. R. N. Strouts et al. *Analytical Chem.* I. xiv. 314 The economy of time afforded by many micro procedures favours their adoption even when the amount of sample available is sufficient for macroanalysis. **1971** *Nature* 19 Mar. 194/2 Any laboratory where the analysis of metals is practised at macro, micro or trace levels. **1974** *Encycl. Brit. Macropædia* IV. 79/2 Samples.. can be classified as macro (10^{-1} g), semi-micro ($10^{-1} - 10^{-3}$ g), micro ($10^{-3} - 10^{-6}$ g), sub-micro ($10^{-6} - 10^{-8}$ g), nanogram (10^{-9} g), or picogram (10^{-12} g).

microabscess, **-aerophil(e**, **-aerophilic**, **-aërophilous**, **-ammeter**, **-ampere**: see MICRO- 1, 4, 4, 4, 6, 5.

microanalyser (maɪkrəʊ'ænəlaɪzə(r)). Also (chiefly *U.S.*) **-analyzer**. [f. MICRO- 6 + ANALYSER, -ZER.] An instrument in which a beam of radiation (usu. electrons) is focused on to a minute area of a sample and the resulting secondary radiation (usu. X-ray fluorescence) is analysed to yield chemical information about the area.

1944 Hillier & Baker in *Jrnl. Appl. Physics* XV. 665/1 Figure 1 is a photograph of the first experimental model of an electron microanalyzer. **1959** *Electronic Engin.* XXXI. 680/1 In the Hinxton Hall microanalyser the specimen surface is scanned at slow speed by an electron beam focused to a diameter of less than one micron. **1960** *Archaeometry* III. 36 During the past eighteen months the Laboratory has been engaged upon the construction of an X-ray microanalyser for archaeological applications. **1966** D. G. Brandon *Mod. Techniques Metallogr.* 173 (*caption*) Secondary-ion emission microanalyser. **1973** *Histochem. Jrnl.* V. 176 EMMA-4 combines the full facilities of a conventional transmission electron microscope and an electron probe X-ray microanalyser.

microanalysis (maɪkrəʊə'nælɪsɪs). [f. MICRO- 2 a + ANALYSIS.] The analysis for chemical

information of very small samples, or very small areas of an object; now *spec.* the quantitative analysis of samples weighing only a few milligrammes (contrasted with semimicroanalysis and ultramicroanalysis). Cf. MICRO- 8 b.

1856 HIGHLEY in *Q. Jrnl. Microsc. Sci.* IV. 224 Micro-Analysis. **1904** tr. *Osmond's Microsc. Anal. Metals* 65 (*heading*) Micro-analysis of carbon steels. **1937** *Discovery* Aug. 227/2 The addition .. of the delicate weapon of micro-analysis to the analyst's armoury. **1966** D. G. BRANDON *Mod. Techniques Metallogr.* iii. 172 In all the methods of microanalysis discussed so far, a point-by-point determination of the x-ray emission or absorption spectrum is related to the chemical composition in order to find the spatial distribution of the components.

Hence **micro'analyst**, one who performs or is skilled in microanalysis; ˌ**microana'lytical** *a.*, of or using microanalysis.

1924 E. FYLEMAN tr. *Pregl's Quantitative Org. Microanalysis* i. 4 He has worked out a microanalytical method for the determination of glycerine. *Ibid.* ii. 13 A watch-maker's lens .. should always be in the pocket of the microanalyst. **1938** *Ann. Reg. 1937* 354 Paneth and Glückauf showed, by microanalytical methods, that when neutrons are produced by bombarding beryllium with gamma-rays the beryllium .. breaks down into helium. **1964** N. G. CLARK *Mod. Org. Chem.* xxiv. 496 He later returned to Graz, where he established an international reputation as a micro-analyst.

microanatomist, -anatomy, -aneurysm, -atoll, -audiphone, -bacillus, -bacterium: see MICRO- 2 a, 2 a, 1, 1, 6, 1, 1.

microbal (maɪ'krəʊbəl), *a. Biol.* [f. MICROBE + -AL¹.] = MICROBIAL.

1888 *Med. News* 12 May 506 Careful covering of the wound to guard against microbal invasion.

microbalance, -bar, -barograph: see MICRO- 6, 5 a, 6.

microbarom (maɪkrəʊ'bærəm). *Meteorol.* [f. MICRO- + BAROM(ETER.] A minute oscillation of atmospheric pressure with a period of the order of 5 seconds.

1939 BENIOFF & GUTENBERG in *Bull. Amer. Meteorol. Soc.* XX. 424/1 The waves .. exhibit no relation to microseisms nor to the barometric conditions in this region. No hypothesis as to their origin has yet been suggested. We designate them microbaroms. **1953** *Jrnl. Acoustical Soc. Amer.* XXV. 796/1 Microbaroms apparently originate in ocean storms associated with low pressure areas. **1967** *Times* 21 Nov. 3/5 The detection of microbaroms depends very much on the availability of sensitive equipment.

micro-battery: see MICRO- 6.

microbe ('maɪkrəʊb). *Biol.* [a. F. *microbe* (Sédillot 7 March 1878 in *Comptes rendus Acad. Sci.* LXXXVI. 634), f. Gr. μῑκρό-ς small + βίος life.

The Gr. βίος is here, as in mod. scientific formations generally, used in an incorrect sense: see BIO-. The sense of Gr. *μῑκρόβιος would be 'short lived'.]

An extremely minute living being, whether plant or animal; chiefly applied to the bacteria concerned in causing diseases and fermentation. Also *fig.*

1881 *Times* 1 Feb. 5/6 A small organism, or microbe, which .. he finds good reason to regard as the agent of the malady. **1890** in J. R. Ware *Passing Eng.* (1900) 175/2 The abdication by the Radical party of its proper functions has an unfortunate tendency to foster .. the microbe of sectionalism. **1893** *Brit. Med. Jrnl.* 20 May 1084 Ice .. has been found to contain dangerous microbes. **1899** *Allbutt's Syst. Med.* VII. 546 The meningitis may be produced by a growth of microbes.

microbeam: see MICRO- 1.

microbia, pl. of MICROBION.

microbial (maɪ'krəʊbɪəl), *a. Biol.* [f. MICROBI-ON + -AL¹.] Of or pertaining to microbes; due to or produced by microbes. Also **mi'crobially** *adv.*, by or with microbes.

1887 *19th Cent.* Aug. 244 There is a considerable difference found in the microbial richness of the air in different places. **1898** *Nature* 10 Feb. 355/2 Alcohol in relation to microbial diseases. **1899** *Allbutt's Syst. Med.* VIII. 471 Rheumatism is .. due to an infection .. by an agent of microbial nature. **1971** *Flying* Apr. 88 (Advt.), Microbially induced corrosion of fuel tanks. **1974** *Nature* 27 Sept. 316/2 Plants in the three microbially contaminated pots produced proteid roots.

So **mi'crobian** *a.*, in the same sense.

1883 *American* XVI. 318 Positively alive with microbian organisms. **1898** *Allbutt's Syst. Med.* V. 34 The bronchitis is secondary to the microbian invasion.

microbic (maɪ'krəʊbɪk), *a. Biol.* [f. MICROBE + -IC.] = prec.

1881 *Lancet* Apr. 553/1 M. Pasteur did not assert that this was the special microbic organism of rabies. **1905** H. D. ROLLESTON *Dis. Liver* 329 It is .. remarkable that .. microbic infection does not more often occur.

microbicide (maɪ'krəʊbɪsaɪd), *sb.* and *a. Biol.* [f. MICROBE + -(I)CIDE¹.]

A. *sb.* Something that kills microbes.

1887 *Brit. Med. Jrnl.* 12 Mar. 588 Many microbicides .. may therefore be employed subcutaneously.

B. *adj.* Microbicidal.

1885 *Brit. Med. Jrnl.* II. 1097/1 The sulphates of copper and zinc .. have an effective microbicide power. **1890** *Fortn. Rev.* XLVIII. 87 *note*, Essences and spices are to a very high degree microbicide.

Hence **microbi'cidal** *a.*, pertaining to the killing of microbes.

1897 *Allbutt's Syst. Med.* II. 715 The use of .. microbicidal agents. **1904** *Brit. Med. Jrnl.* 10 Sept. 561 The microcytase being chiefly concerned with microbicidal action.

microbiology (maɪkrəʊbaɪ'ɒlədʒɪ). *Biol.* [f. MICRO- + BIOLOGY.] The science which treats of micro-organisms; the study of microbes.

1888 *Pop. Sci. Monthly* XXXIII. 341 There was great reason for creating in the Faculty of Sciences the chair of Microbiology. **1891** *Nature* 20 Aug. 366/1 Important as are the researches into microbiology, there are other factors to reckon with. **1898** *Allbutt's Syst. Med.* V. 347 Microbiology has thrown great light upon this .. idiopathic pleurisy.

Hence **microbio'logic, microbio'logical** *a.*, of or pertaining to microbiology; **microbio'logically** *adv.*, by microbiological methods; **microbi'ologist**, a student of microbiology.

1885 *Science* V. 73 Ideas which are just now very prominent in the minds of microbiologists. **1897** *Allbutt's Syst. Med.* II. 990 This .. extremely delicate microbiological method. **1909** *Westm. Gaz.* 9 Dec. 2/1 He is .. reminded of the doctrine of the etiology of infectious diseases before the advent of the microbiologic epoch. **1942** *Industr. & Engin. Chem.* (*Analytical Ed.*) 15 Aug. 667/1 The extracted residue of dried skim milk was microbiologically inert, while the residue of alfalfa leaf meal exerted a little stimulatory action. **1956** *Nature* 4 Feb. 221/1 The relation between seven different tree-supports .. and two epiphytes was examined microbiologically. **1966** *McGraw-Hill Encycl. Sci. & Technol.* IX. 620/2 Penicillin can also be chemically or microbiologically degraded and then built up to form new penicillins. **1969** WILSON & MIZER *Microbiol. in Nursing Pract.* i. 11/2 Since Leeuwenhoek's first glimpse of bacteria and protozoa, microbiologic investigations have resulted in the accumulation of a vast body of knowledge .. that has lightened immeasurably the burden of human disease.

‖**microbion** (maɪ'krəʊbɪɒn). *Biol.* Pl. microbia. Mod. Latin form of MICROBE.

1883 *Athenæum* 27 Oct. 538/1 The treatment of diseases due to microbia. **1884** *Science* IV. 145/1 These [reports] .. by no means demonstrate that the active principle of cholera resides in a microbion.

microbiota: see MICRO- 1.

microbious (maɪ'krəʊbɪəs), *a.* [f. MICROBION + -IOUS.] = MICROBIAL (*Syd. Soc. Lex.* 1890).

microbism ('maɪkrəʊbɪz(ə)m). *Med.* [f. MICROB(E + -ISM.] Infection with microbes.

1904 *Lancet* 18 June 1724/1 The various explanations of 'return' cases were considered, including .. the possibility of a relapse of the original disease, of latent microbism, or of missed cases. **1963** *Biol. Abstr.* XLI. 553/2 (*heading*) Investigations on the role of staphylococci in cutaneous microbism.

microblast: see MICRO- 1.

microbody, -burette: see MICRO- 1, 6.

microburin (maɪkrəʊ'bjʊərɪn) *Archæol.* [f. MICRO- 1 + BURIN.] (See quot. 1970.)

1932 *Antiquity* VI. 364 A feature of the industry is the presence of the burin of upper Palæolithic type... The microburin is not mentioned either as occurring or as absent. **1955** [see IBERO-]. **1957** V. G. CHILDE *Dawn European Civilization* (ed. 6) i. 6 At Parpalló in Eastern Spain even microburins occur from the Solutrian layers upward. **1958** *Man* Apr. 57/2 The ends are then shaped either by twisting off, or by retouching, and even by the microburin technique of notching and then snapping... The microburins, the 'anti-microburins' and the obliquely snapped waste .. were all backed as well. **1970** BRAY & TRUMP *Dict. Archaeol.* 147/1 *Microburin*, a by-product of the manufacture of microliths. A blade is notched, and then snapped off... One piece becomes a microlithic tool, while the residue (the 'microburin') still shows traces of the original notch and fracture.

microburner: see MICRO- 6.

microbus ('maɪkrəʊbʌs). [f. MICRO- 1 + BUS *sb.*²] A small vehicle designed to carry passengers in seats fitted as in a bus.

1959 *Cambr. Rev.* 7 Mar. 428/2 (Advt.), Micro-buses available on continent, fitted camping facilities. Make up your own party. **1960** [see JAMBOREE]. **1962** E. KIMBROUGH *Pleasure by Busload* ii. 17 'This is a Volkswagen Microbus,' Sophy answered... No one had told me it looked as big as a trailer and that the span from ground to floorboard was a span well over three feet. **1968** *New Scientist* 19 Sept. 596/1 Caltech relied on a less streamlined red and white 1958 Volkswagen microbus. **1971** *Telegraph* (Brisbane) 14 Sept. 22/4 Mr. Ralph Nader claimed the famous Beetle was loaded with safety hazards... He claimed the VW microbus was even worse.

microcalorie, -calorimeter (etc.), **-camera, -capsule:** see MICRO- 5 a, 6, 1 b, 1.

microcard ('maɪkrəʊkɑːd). Also Microcard. [f. MICRO- 7 + CARD *sb.*²] An opaque card bearing microphotographs of a number of pages of a book, periodical, etc. (A proprietary name in the U.S.)

1944 F. RIDER *Scholar & Future of Research Library* II. i. 99 Why might we not combine the micro-texts of our books, and the catalog cards for these same books, in one single entity? .. I called this new concept .. a 'micro-card'. **1950** *Official Gaz.* (U.S. Patent Office) 24 Jan. 907/1 The Micro Library Incorporated, La Crosse, Wis.... *Microcard* for publications in card form, reproduced by printing, photographing and otherwise. Claims use since November 1947. **1950, 1953** [see MICROFICHE]. **1958** *Engineering* 31 Jan. 155/1 Micro-card can also be used on the reverse side for such purposes as abstracts in normal type and catalogue notations. **1958** *Times Rev. Industry* Mar. 61/1 For recording such material as technical periodicals or newspapers, the microcard system is often the better method. **1964** M. MCLUHAN *Understanding Media* (1967) iii. 49 Today with microfilm and micro-cards .. the printed word assumes again much of the handicraft character of a manuscript. **1973** *Computers & Humanities* VII. 168 Few agencies even assemble material on microfiches or micro-cards.

So **'microcard** *v.*, to reproduce on micro-cards; **'microcarded** *ppl. a.*

1944 F. RIDER *Scholar & Future of Research Library* II. vii. 189 What types of material, and .. what titles .. ought, therefore, to be micro-carded first. *c* **1960** *Microcards* (Microcard Foundation), Reports coming in from men in the field are collated and the completed reports are Microcarded... Literally shelves of Microcarded books and periodicals can be stored in one file cabinet.

micro-carpous, -cautery, -cellular: see MICRO- 4, 2.

‖**microcephale** (maɪkrəʊ'sɛfeɪl). *Path.* [a. F. *microcéphale.*] = MICROCEPHALUS 1.

1878 BARTLEY tr. *Topinard's Anthrop.* v. 165 All in whom the brain has not attained a certain degree of development, or the cranial cavity a given capacity at adult age, are termed microcephales. **1893** *Westm. Gaz.* 19 Apr. 2/3 Idiots, especially microcephales, have flattened retreating foreheads.

microcephali, -lia: see MICROCEPHALUS, -LY.

microcephalic (maɪkrəʊsɪ'fælɪk), *a.* and *sb. Path.* and *Anthropology.* [ad. F. *microcéphalique*, f. mod.L. *mīcrocephal-us*: see MICROCEPHALUS and -IC.] **a.** *adj.* Pertaining to, or characterized by, microcephaly. **b.** *sb.* A microcephalic person.

1856 in MAYNE *Expos. Lex.* **1864** W. TURNER in *Q. Jrnl. Sci.* I. 257 Now the Neanderthal skull cannot be regarded as microcephalic. **1873** *Eng. Cycl., Arts & Sci.* Suppl. 1552 *Microcephalics*, persons with small heads. This deformity is associated with mental defect. **1879** MAUDSLEY *Pathol. Mind* v. 176 A microcephalic idiot. **1880** *Nature* 8 Jan. 224/1 The now extinct Tasmanian race was .. microcephalic.

microcephalism (maɪkrəʊ'sɛfəlɪz(ə)m). *Path.* [f. mod.L. *mīcrocephal-us* (see MICROCEPHALUS) + -ISM.] = MICROCEPHALY.

1861 *N. Syd. Soc. Year-bk. Med.* 2 Memoir on Microcephalism. **1879** tr. *De Quatrefages' Hum. Spec.* 111 Microcephalism, idiotcy, and crétinism constitute so many teratological or pathological states.

microcephalous (maɪkrəʊ'sɛfələs), *a.* [f. mod.L. *mīcrocephal-us* (a. Gr. μῑκροκέφαλος small headed, f. μῑκρό-ς small + κεφαλ-ή head) + -OUS.] Small-headed. **a.** *Path.* and *Anthropology.* Having an abnormally small head; characterized by microcephaly. **b.** *Bot.* 'Applied to a plant that has flowers disposed in small heads' (*Syd. Soc. Lex.*).

1840 SMART, *Microcephalous*, little-headed, applied to the beryx, [a] fossil fish. **1871** DARWIN *Desc. Man* I. iv. 121 The arrested brain-development of microcephalous idiots. **1872** —— *Emotions* viii. 206 The eyes of microcephalous idiots .. brighten slightly when they are pleased. **1877** BLACK *Green Past.* iv. (1878) 34 Before I would marry one of those bedizened and microcephalous playthings.

‖**microcephalus** (maɪkrəʊ'sɛfələs). *Path.* Pl. **microcephali** (-'sɛfəlaɪ). [mod.L.: see prec.]

1. A person having an abnormally small skull.

1863 *N. Syd. Soc. Year-bk. Med.* 94 Healthy parents may produce one or several microcephali. **1879** tr. *De Quatrefages' Hum. Spec.* 111 Vogt has compared the brain of microcephali to that of the anthropomorphous apes.

2. [Cf. HYDROCEPHALUS.] A pathological condition in which the smallness of the cranium prevents the proper development of the brain.

1897 L. E. HOLT *Dis. Infancy* 702 The symptoms of microcephalus are those of idiocy and cerebral paralysis.

microcephaly (maɪkrəʊ'sɛfəlɪ). Also in mod.L. form **microcephalia.** [ad. F. *microcéphalie*, f. mod.L. *mīcrocephal-us*: see MICROCEPHALUS.] The condition of having an abnormally small head, esp. **a.** in *Anthropology*, having a skull of a capacity less than 1350 cubic centimetres (Flower *Catal. Mus. Surg.* 1879); **b.** *Path.*, having an abnormally small or atrophied skull.

1863 GORE in *Anthrop. Rev.* I. 168 The valuable essay of Wagner on the subject (*Vorstudien*, Th. 2) of micro-cephaly. **1863** *N. Syd. Soc. Year-bk. Med.* 94 On Microcephalia. **1886** *Brit. Med. Jrnl.* 30 Jan. 184/2 The theory which attributes microcephaly to premature cranial synostosis.

microceratous, -cerous, -character, -chemist, -chemistry: see MICRO- 4, 2.

microchip (ˈmaɪkrəʊtʃɪp). [f. MICRO- + CHIP *sb.*[1]] **1.** A very small chip of metal produced in machining. *rare.*

1974 *Jrnl. Engin. Materials & Technol.* July 163/2 A microchip, which forms at the tool clearance face, is the counterpart of the built-up edge which can form at the tool rake face.

2. [CHIP *sb.*[1] 2 f.] A chip or integrated circuit, esp. one in which large-scale integration is employed.

1975 *Proc. 8th Connector Symp.* 228/1 A simplified interconnection scheme provides sufficient space for attaching microchip components on the track side of an epoxy printed wiring board. **1979** *Economist* 13 Oct. 52/3 The high-growth industries of telecommunications, computers, microchips and databanks. **1979** *London Rev. Bks.* 25 Oct. 14/2 (Advt.), The global dissemination of culture and knowledge is inconceivable without the technologies of printing, cinema, television and microchip telecommunication. **1982** *Jrnl. R. Soc. Arts* Nov. 781/1 The microchip has revolutionary implications for our industry, for our economy and for our society. **1984** J. HILTON *Choosing & using your Home Computer* 36/1 The third generation [of computers] used integrated circuits... These integrated circuits were the earliest form of the microchip.

microchromosome, -cinematography (and **-graphic**): see MICRO- 1, 2 a.

microcircuit (ˈmaɪkrəʊsɜːkɪt). *Electronics.* Also **micro-circuit.** [f. MICRO- 1 + CIRCUIT *sb.*] An integrated circuit or other minute circuit.

1959 *Electronics* 4 Sept. 49/3 New circuit fabrication techniques such as are used in microcircuits. **1960** *IRE Trans. Military Electronics* IV. 461/1 (*caption*) Detailed sketch of a silicon integrated microcircuit. **1965** *Economist* 25 Sept. 1228/1 A micro-circuit is no bigger than a pin-head, replacing transistor circuits as big as a large envelope knitted out of wires. **1970** *Daily Tel.* 8 May 21 Not only do they have the advantage of smaller size: microcircuits are also more reliable and faster—a vital factor for computer use. **1971** *Physics Bull.* Jan. 45/1 The chips measure $\frac{1}{8}$ in^2 and contain 1434 microcircuit elements each, integrated into 128 memory and 46 support circuits.

So **ˈmicrocircuitry**, microcircuits collectively; the branch of electronics concerned with microcircuits.

1959 *Electronics* 4 Sept. 44/1 The microcircuitry program is concerned with the development of a circuit fabrication technique based on the combination of elementary materials rather than on the assembly of individual components. **1960** *IRE Trans. Military Electronics* IV. 459/2 Integrated microcircuitry. **1970** *Daily Tel.* 21 Sept. 19 Recent developments in microcircuitry.. have made it possible to reduce the circuitry of an amplifier to the size of an ordinary jacket button. **1974** *Country Life* 5 Dec. 1763/1 By..a brilliant piece of microcircuitry, the oscillations are translated into a constant, one second pulse.

microcirculation: see MICRO- 1.

microclase (ˈmaɪkrəʊkleɪs). *Min.* [ad. G. *mikroklas*, f. Gr. μῑκρό-ς small + κλάσις cleavage.] A potash-soda felspar occurring intercrystallized with orthoclase, from the St. Gotthard, Switzerland (*Cassell's Encycl. Dict.* 1885).

microclastic: see MICRO- 4.

microclimate (ˈmaɪkrəʊklaɪmət). Chiefly *Ecol.* and *Meteorol.* [f. MICRO- 1 + CLIMATE *sb.*] The climate of a very small or restricted area, or of the immediate surroundings of any individual or object of interest, esp. as it differs from the climate generally.

1925 *Rev. Appl. Mycol.* IV. 471 Temperature, absolute and relative humidity, aeration, insolation, &c., which prevail at various levels..are comprised by him [*sc.* L. F. Roussakov] under the term 'microclimate'. **1934** [see MICROCLIMATOLOGY]. **1951** R. GEIGER in T. F. Malone *Compendium Meteorol.* 994/1 We shall first consider microclimate as the special climate prevailing in a layer of air about two meters in height adjacent to the surface of the ground. In this layer friction between the air and the earth's surface plays a decisive role. **1958** *Engineering* 14 Mar. 352/1 A basic item influencing the design of an air-conditioning system is the 'micro-climate'— the climate existing immediately around the structure to be air conditioned. **1967** T. J. CHANDLER *Air around Us* x. 116/1 Climates can differ from one side to the other of a hedge or garden wall, or from the base of a bush to its leafy crown. Such conditions are usually described as microclimates. **1972** *Physics Bull.* June 342/1 Cool air is introduced into the microclimate between the pilot's clothing and his skin. **1973** *Times* 17 Nov. 12 Provided the compost is kept always moist a moist 'microclimate' is created around the plants.

Hence **microcliˈmatic** *a.*, **-cliˈmatically** *adv.*

1929 *Conf. Empire Meteorologists, Agric. Section* II. 131 The actual, *i.e.* the microclimatic, conditions often bear only a very remote relation to the general conditions in the habitat. **1952** *Archit. Rev.* CXII. 323 The total site area (shaded) is over 45,000 acres but more than half of this will be devoted to forestry—for microclimatic control, for experimental purposes, and as capital investment. **1972** *Nature* 10 Mar. 64/1 The immigration and establishment of local small stands of trees in microclimatically favourable habitats. **1974** *Ibid.* 15 Mar. 261/3 The alternative explanation..relates the higher soil moisture beneath vegetation to the modified microclimatic conditions in such situations.

ˌmicroclimaˈtology. *Meteorol.* [f. MICRO- 2 a + CLIMATOLOGY.] The study of micro-climates.

1934 L. A. RAMDAS in *Current Sci.* II. 445/2 The aims of 'micro-climatology' are (1) to investigate the physical laws underlying the deviations of 'micro-climate' from 'macro-climate'..and (2) to apply the theoretical results to practical ends. **1944** V. CONRAD *Methods in Climatol.* i. 14 The layering of the air is of interest..as one of the most important features from which 'Microclimatology', and especially 'Orographic Microclimatology', makes its start. **1972** *Last Whole Earth Catalog* (Portola Inst.) 83/1 This appears to be the definitive text on microclimatology: the climatic conditions within six feet or so of the earth's surface. **1974** *Daily Colonist* (Victoria, B.C.) 28 Aug. 6/4 Principles of microclimatology and its relationship to plant growth will be discussed.

Hence **ˌmicroclimatoˈlogical** *a.*, **-climaˈtologist.**

1937 *Geography* XXII. 87 (*heading*) Reality in climate: the results of recent microclimatological studies, with special references to temperatures. **1951** R. GEIGER in T. F. Malone *Compendium Meteorol.* 993/2 Location considerations in plant growth are always microclimatological in nature; whether a plant is located in an open field or at the north side of a large boulder..is a decisive factor with respect to the conditions affecting its growth. *Ibid.*, The biology of bees can be understood only if one knows the microclimate of the beehive. It is the problem of the microclimatologist to investigate these small-scale climates.

microcline (ˈmaɪkrəʊklaɪn). *Min.* [ad. G. *mikroklin* (A. Breithaupt 1830), f. Gr. μῑκρό-ς + κλίνειν to incline, as indicating that the angle between its cleavage plane differs a little from 90 degrees.] A green and blue variety of felspar.

1849 WATTS tr. *Gmelin's Handbk. Chem.* III. 442 Microcline [has] precisely the same composition as felspar. **1902** MIERS *Min.* 459 Microcline is the name given to anorthic potash felspar.

attrib. **1888** F. H. HATCH in Teall *Brit. Petrogr.* 439 Microcline structure. The mineral microcline shows..a cross hatching.

‖**micrococcus** (maɪkrəʊˈkɒkəs). *Biol.* Pl. **micrococci** (-ˈkɒksaɪ). [mod.L., f. Gr. μῑκρό-ς small + κόκκος berry.] Any one of a genus of minute spherical or slightly oval organisms, generally regarded as fission-fungi, belonging to the biological group of *Sphærobacteria* or *Schizomycetes.*

1870 T. R. LEWIS *Physiol. & Pathol. Res.* (1888) 4 A 'micrococcus colony'. *Ibid.* 29 Writers who advocate the pre-existence of a germ..to every living thing, this germ.. being called its 'micrococcus'. **1875** DARWIN *Insectiv. Pl.* vii. 173 The smallest micrococci which are distinctly discernable under a power of 800 diameters are estimated to be from ·0002 to ·0005 of a millimetre..in diameter.

attrib. **1898** P. MANSON *Trop. Diseases* xxxvii. 560 The little vesicles [of prickly heat] may pustulate, doubtless from micrococcus infection.

Hence **micrococcal** (-ˈkɒkəl) *a.*, relating to or caused by micrococci. **microcoˈccologist**, a student of micrococci.

1893 W. R. GOWERS *Man. Dis. Nerv. Syst.* (ed. 2) II. 329 The micrococcal embolism of minute vessels. **1896** *Allbutt's Syst. Med.* I. 702 We must distinguish several kinds of that disease [diphtheria] (bacillary, micrococcal, and so forth). **1902** A. LANG in *Longm. Mag.* Apr. 568 An eminent micrococcologist.

‖**Microcoleoptera** (ˌmaɪkrəʊkɒlɪˈɒptərə), *sb. pl.* *Ent.* [f. MICRO- + COLEOPTERA.] The smaller kinds of Coleoptera.

1871 WOOD *Insects at Home* 220.

microcolony: see MICRO- 1.

microcomputer (ˈmaɪkrəʊkəmˌpjuːtə(r)). Also **micro computer, micro-computer.** [f. MICRO- 1 + COMPUTER.] **a.** A small computer or computer system, usu. one built around a single microprocessor; a home or personal computer. **b.** = *microprocessor* s.v. MICRO- 1. Cf. MICRO *sb.* 3.

1971 E. F. SCHOETERS in B. de Ferranti *Living with Computer* viii. 70 The mini-computers and the smaller, cheaper, and equally powerful micro-computers. **1971** *New Scientist* 29 July 264/2 Micro computers are small 'dedicated' machines that are never reprogrammed. **1975** *Sci. Amer.* May 33/2 It was clearly just a question of time until the further integration of microscopic components would lead to a microcomputer. **1977** *Time* 5 Sept. 39/1 The age of the home computer (or microcomputer, as it is often called) is at hand. **1979** *Economist* 24 Mar. 119/1 About half of hand-held electric tools are expected to have microcomputers in them by 1987. **1982** *Sci. Amer.* Dec. 90/2 Not all microcomputers..are personal computers. A microcomputer can be dedicated to a single task such as controlling a machine tool. **1984** S. CURRAN *Word Processing for Beginners* iii. 21 Today's microcomputers often incorporate 16-bit chips, with 16-bit wide registers and/or buses.

Also **ˌmicrocomˈputing** *vbl. sb.*, computing using a microcomputer.

1976 *Digital Design* Aug. 68/2 While advances in paper-tape technology may not be as spectacular as those in, say, microcomputing, they are important. **1978** *Proc. IEEE* LXVI. 117 (*heading*) Low-cost microcomputing: the personal computer and single-board computer revolutions. **1981** B. K. PANNELL et al. (*title*) Make a success of micro-computing in your business. **1982** *Internat. Jrnl. Infrared & Millimeter Waves* III. 331 A microcomputing system for data acquisition and on-line data processing has been developed for use with Fourier transform spectrometers. **1986** *City Limits* 29 May 8 The transfer of Britain's most sophisticated technologies (especially in laser and micro-computing)..will have 'appalling' effects on the British economy.

microconidium, -constituent, -continent: see MICRO- 1.

microcook (ˈmaɪkrəʊkʊk), *v.* *U.S.* Also **micro-cook.** [f. MICRO *sb.* 4 + COOK *v.*[1]] *trans.* and *intr.* = MICROWAVE *v.*

1976 *Better Homes & Gardens* (U.S.) Feb. 85/1 Using defrost cycle, micro-cook 7 to 8 minutes. *Ibid.* May 72/4 Meatballs micro-cook in a traditional Oriental sauce. **1979** *Cuisine* Apr. 54/1 Learn to use the technique of segmented cooking: partially microcooking one item while you prepare another, [etc.]. **1979** *Chicago Tribune* 26 Apr. VII. 18/1 Some special techniques are called for when you microcook muffins.

microcopy (ˈmaɪkrəʊkɒpɪ), *sb.* [f. MICRO- 7 + COPY *sb.*] A copy of the text of a book, periodical, etc., that has been reduced in size by the use of microphotography; ***in microcopy***, in the form of a microcopy or microcopies. Also as *v. trans.*, to make such a copy of; also *absol.*; **ˈmicrocopying** *vbl. sb.*

1934 WEBSTER, Microcopy *n.* **1936** *Microphotogr. for Libraries* (Amer. Library Assoc.) 3 We microcopy because, by reducing the size of letters, we can reduce tremendously the cost of making copies. *Ibid.* 4 Whenever we contemplate reproducing something in microcopy for a number of users, we should give especial attention to materials cost. *Ibid.* 13 The production of microcopies is relatively easy and inexpensive. **1942** *Punch* 14 Jan. 4/2 By means of photographic 'micro-copying', miniature negatives of all kinds of documents can be taken on continuous lengths of.. films. **1944** F. RIDER *Scholar & Future of Research Library* II. ii. 115 All that we have to do is to take two copies of the book that we are proposing to micro-copy. *Ibid.* vi. 170 The library can usually supply a borrower at once with a duplicate micro-copy. **1950** [see *flat film* (FLAT *a.* 15)]. **1962** *B.S.I. News* Feb. 39 Specifies size ranges for transparent bases for microcopies—roll or strip microfilm, microfiches and unexposed rolls of sensitized film. **1972** *Computers & Humanities* VII. 46 The National Library will acquire most periodicals required in order to back up these services, as well as other references available in microcopy.

microcosm (ˈmaɪkrəʊkɒz(ə)m). In 5 **mycrocosme**, 5–7 **microcosme**. Also occas. in L. and quasi-Gr. forms **microcosmus, -cosmos**, 3 *Ormin* **mycrocossmós.** [ad. F. *microcosme* (14th c.), ad. med.L. *mīcrocosmus, mīcroscosmus*, ad. late Gr. μῑκρὸς κόσμος (μῑκρός small, κόσμος world). Cf. MACROCOSM.]

1. The 'little world' of human nature; man viewed as an epitome of the 'great world' or universe.

c **1200** ORMIN 17595 Mycrocossmós, þat nemmnedd iss Affterr Englisshe spæche þe little werelld. **1426** LYDG. *De Guil. Pilgr.* 12370 Merveylle nat..That thow be let in thy vyage,..Syth 'Mycrocosme', men the calle; And microcosme ys a word Wych clerkys calle 'the lasse world'. **1477** NORTON *Ord. Alch.* v. in Ashm. (1652) 62 Wherefore amonge Creatures theis two alone Be called Microcosmus, Man and our Stone. **1570** DEE *Math. Pref.* ciiij, The description of him, who is the Lesse world: and, from the beginning, called Microcosmus (that is, The Lesse World). **1597** *1st Pt. Return fr. Parnass.* I. i. 281 What an unmanerlie microcosme was this swine-faced clowne. **1603** FLORIO *Montaigne* II. xii. (1632) 301 They have thence had reason to name it [man's Nature] Microcosmos, or little world. **1604** JAMES I *Counterbl.* (Arb.) 102 The diuers parts of our Microcosme or little world within our selues. **1625** HART *Anat. Ur.* I. i. 2 God..at last made man, that microcosme, or little world, as it were an epitome or abridgment of this great vniuersall world. **1663** GERBIER *Counsel* 34 The Dimensions the Creator hath been pleased to give to the Microcosme Man. **1727** DE FOE *Syst. Magic* I. ii. 47 Among these, some studied the Microcosm of human Bodies, and searcht both Distemper and Medicin. **1768** FOOTE *Devil on 2 Sticks* I. Wks. 1799 II. 243 Woman..is a microcosm, and rightly to rule her requires as great talents as to govern a state. **1838–9** HALLAM *Hist. Lit.* III. III. iii. §19. 14 The doctrine of a constant analogy between universal nature, or the macrocosm, and that of man, or the microcosm. **1893** KROPOTKIN in *19th Cent.* Aug. 252 The molecule thus becomes a particle of the universe on a microscopic scale —a microcosmos which lives the same life.

¶ **b.** Jocularly used for 'body'.

a **1680** BUTLER *Rem.* (1759) II. 83 He puts both Ends of his Microcosm in Motion, by making Legs at one End, and combing his Peruque at the other.

¶ *nonce-use.* (See quot.)

1606 B. JONSON *Masques, Hymenæi* B 1 b, Here out of a Microcosme, or Globe (figuring Man)..issued forth the first Masque.

2. In extended sense, applied to a community or other complex unity regarded as presenting an epitome of the world, or as constituting 'a little world' in itself.

1562 EDEN *Let. to Sir W. Cecil* in *Decades* (Arb.) p. xliv, An experiment, wrought by arte to the similitude of the vniuersall frame of the worlde..and maye therfore in my iudgement more woorthely be cauled Michrocosmos, then eyther man or any other creature. **1587** GREENE *Euphues to Philautus* Wks. (Grosart) VI. 235 This citty was Microcosmos, a little Worlde, in respect of the Cytties of Greece. **1590** in Tytler *Hist. Scotl.* (1864) IV. 179 This microcosme of Britain, separate from the continent world. **1791** BENTHAM *Panopt.* I. Postscr. 79 That scene of clock-work regularity which it would be so easy to establish in so compact a microcosm. **1814** SCOTT *Wav.* ii, The more judicious politicians of this microcosm. **1826** DISRAELI *Viv. Grey* I. ii, The microcosm of a public school. **1845** FORD

Handbk. Spain I. 338 [Gibraltar] this microcosmus where all creeds and nations meet.

b. Adopted as the name of a travelling mechanical exhibition in the 18th c.

1756 B. LYNDE *Diaries* (1880) 182, P. M. went to see microcosms. *a* **1817** R. L. EDGEWORTH *Mem.* (1820) I. 110 By accident I was invited [in 1765] to see the Microcosm, a mechanical exhibition, which was then frequented by every body at Chester.

c. A 'miniature' representation *of*.

1808 ACKERMANN (*title*) The Microcosm of London, or London in Miniature. **1860** *All Year Round* No. 52. 36 He intended his wardrobe-shop to be a satirical microcosm of Petty France. **1872** MORLEY *Voltaire* vii. (ed. 2) 344 A microcosm of the whole battle. **1877** F. HEATH *Fern W.* 105 That microcosm of the Fern World, the case, or pot.

¶**d.** In the 17th c. sometimes used (? ignorantly) for: A 'world', huge mass.

1611 CORYAT *Crudities* 79 It [a mountain] is couered with a very Microcosme of clowdes. **1641** CAPT. A. MERVIN in Rushw. *Hist. Coll.* III. (1692) I. 216 Let then that Microcosm of Letters Patents..rise up in Judgment.

†**3.** *Alch.* The philosopher's stone. *Obs.*

1477 [see 1].

Hence †**micro'cosmal** *a.*, pertaining to or of the nature of a microcosm.

a **1644** QUARLES *Sol. Recant.* ch. xii. (1645) 58 Before the Sun, and Moon, and Stars appear Dark in thy Microcosmal Hemisphear. **1651** BIGGS *New Disp.* ⁋ 55 As if he were the microcosmall Councel of State's chief Physitian.

†**micro'cosmetor.** *Obs.* Also *erron.* **-meter.** [mod.L. f. Gr. μικρό-ς small + κοσμήτωρ, agent-n. f. κοσμεῖν to set in order, f. κόσμος COSMOS; after MICROCOSM.] Term used by Dolæus for the essence or principle of life. Hence †**micro-cosmetoric** *a.* (Mayne *Expos. Lex.* 1856).

1684 *Phil. Trans.* XIV. 704 The *Anima Brutorum* with him is called Microcosmeter. **1725** FREIND *Hist. Physick* I. 265 Calling in to his aid his ancient good ally, Microcosmetor, Governor of the Animal Spirits, he gives battle to the disturbers of his rest.

microcosmic (maɪkrəʊ'kɒzmɪk), *a.* [f. MICROCOSM + -IC.]

1. Of or pertaining to a microcosm or 'little world'; of the nature of a microcosm.

1816 G. S. FABER *Orig. Pagan Idol.* III. 281 The imitative Caer-Sidee represented the microcosmic Ship resting on the top of the mountain. **1871** B. TAYLOR *Faust* iii. I. 65 Man, that microcosmic fool. **1893** HUXLEY *Evol. & Ethics* 13 The microcosmic atom should have found the illimitable macrocosm guilty.

2. *microcosmic salt* [= L. *sal microcosmicus*, Bergmann *Opusc.* 1773 (ed. 1780) II. 12]: a phosphate of soda and ammonia ($HNaNH_4PO_4 + 4H_2O$), originally derived from human urine, and much used as a blow-pipe flux. †*microcosmic acid*: phosphoric acid as obtained from this salt.

1783 WITHERING tr. *Bergmann's Outl. Min.* 36 A precipitate of cobalt..which makes a blue glass with borax or microcosmic salt. **1797** *Encycl. Brit.* (ed. 3) XIV. 629–30 *Acid of Phosphorus.* This acid, called also the microcosmic acid, has already been described. **1816** *Encycl. Perth.* V. 566/1 Urine contains the fusible salt of urine, or microcosmic salt. **1902** MIERS *Mineral.* 271 The treatment in the bead of microcosmic salt.

microcosmical (maɪkrəʊ'kɒzmɪkəl), *a.* [Formed as prec. + -AL[1].] = prec. 1.

1570 DEE *Math. Pref.* c iij b, Whereby, good profe will be had, of our Harmonious, and Microcosmicall constitution. **1646** SIR T. BROWNE *Pseud. Ep.* II. iii. 69 This opinion confirmed would much advance the microcosmicall conceite, and commend the Geography of Paracelsus. **1790** SIBLY *Occult Sci.* (1792) I. 67 He [man] hath a microcosmical sun, moon, and stars within himself.

micro'cosmically, *adv.* [f. MICROCOSMIC *a.*: see -LY[2].] In relation to the microcosm.

1881 MAX MÜLLER tr. *Kant's Critique Pure Reason* I. ii. 363, I might call the two former [ideas], in a narrower sense, cosmical concepts (macrocosmically or microcosmically) and the remaining two transcendent concepts of nature. **1939** [see MACROCOSMICALLY *adv.*]. **1942** *Mind* LI. 235 A microcosmic being exists microcosmically under divine reference in constitutive *communitas* with a complement that is not absolutely other; and under self-reference in indefinitely continuing commerce of cooperation and opposition with an imaginative other.

microcosmography (ˌmaɪkrəʊkɒz'mɒgrəfɪ). ? *Obs.* [f. MICROCOSM + -(O)GRAPHY.] The description of the 'microcosm' or man. Also (*nonce-use*), microcosmic representation.

1606 BIRNIE *Kirk-Burial* Ded., Ye can see no singular thing that in some compendious Micro-cosmo-graphy does not shine in your self. **1628** EARLE (*title*) Micro-cosmographie, or, a Peece of the World Discovered; in Essayes and Characters. **1696** in PHILLIPS. **1856** in MAYNE *Expos. Lex.* In mod. Dicts.

microcosmology (maɪkrəʊkɒz'mɒlədʒɪ). *rare.* [f. MICROCOSM + -(O)LOGY.] A treatise or dissertation on the 'little world' or human body.

1856 in MAYNE *Expos. Lex.* In mod. Dicts.

microcosmopolitan: see MICRO- 1 b.

microcoulomb: see MICRO- 5.

microcoustic, erron. form of MICRACOUSTIC.

micro-crack (etc.), **-crater**: see MICRO- 1.

microcrith ('maɪkrəʊkrɪθ). *Physics.* [f. MICRO- + CRITH.] A unit of molecular weight; the half hydrogen-molecule.

1873 J. P. COOKE *New Chem.* (1874) 73, I propose to call the unit of molecular weight we have adopted a *microcrith*, even at the risk of coining a new word.

micro-crystal (maɪkrəʊ'krɪstəl). *Chem.* Also **microcrystal.** [f. MICRO- + CRYSTAL *sb.*] A crystal visible only by the microscope.

1886 *Jrnl. R. Microsc. Soc.* VI. 725 (*heading*) Preparing microcrystals. **1895** tr. *Fock's Chem. Crystall.* 42 The methods of recognizing..micro-crystals became more perfect. **1964** L. MARTIN *Clin. Endocrinol.* (ed. 4) viii. 267 Alternatively, long-acting injections of micro-crystals of œstradiol monobenzoate (Ovocyclin I.M.) may be given in doses of 10 mg.

microcrystalline (maɪkrəʊ'krɪstəlaɪn), *a.* *Geol.* and *Min.* [f. MICRO- + CRYSTALLINE.] Formed of microscopic crystals. ***microcrystalline wax***, a mixture of hydrocarbons of higher molecular weight than those in paraffin waxes and with a melting point of up to 90°C which is obtained from the residual lubricating fraction of crude oil and is used in making waxed paper, adhesives, and polishes.

1876 A. H. GREEN *Phys. Geol.* 46 The aid of a pocket lens becomes necessary..to recognise their crystals, and these [rocks] are known as Micro-crystalline. **1879** RUTLEY *Stud. Rocks* xi. 188 The central portion consists of vitreous, and at times, micro-crystalline matter. **1891** *Athenæum* 24 Jan. 126/1 A heavy, yellow, microcrystalline powder. **1943** *Jrnl. Amer. Pharmaceutical Assoc.* (*Sci. Ed.*) XXXII. 111/2 A series of 'Petro-waxes', one of which melts at about 160°F. It is a white microcrystalline wax that is available in quantity. It was thought that due to the microcrystalline structure of this wax, it might make stable ointments containing as much as 50% water. **1944** H. BENNETT *Commercial Waxes* i. 60 The designations of microcrystalline and amorphous waxes are now being used synonymously although the former is a more accurate designation. **1957** VAN DER HAVE & VERVER *Petroleum* xi. 339 As its name implies, 'micro-crystalline wax' has a very fine crystal structure; it is a flexible and often somewhat sticky product; it has a high molecular weight (550–600) and a melting point within the same range as ceresin. **1972** *Oxf. Univ. Gaz.* CII. Suppl. No. 3. 10 They [*sc.* metal objects] are boiled to remove chlorides and after drying in an infra-red cupboard are impregnated with microcrystalline wax.

Hence ˌ**microcrysta'llinity**, the property or state of being microcrystalline.

1946 *Nature* 28 Dec. 930/1 Microcrystallinity and a capacity to yield strong and pliable fibres are properties by no means confined to the linear poly-amides. **1967** *Encycl. Polymer Sci. & Technol.* VII. 207 It is possible to distinguish microcrystallinity, detectable by x-ray examination from macrocrystallinity, visible through a polarizing microscope.

microcrystallitic (ˌmaɪkrəʊkrɪstə'lɪtɪk), *a.* *Geol.* and *Min.* [f. MICRO- + CRYSTALLITE + -IC.] Belonging to microscopic crystallites.

1882 GEIKIE *Text-bk. Geol.* 104 This ground-mass..may be..still further devitrified, until it becomes an aggregation of such little granules, needles, and hairs between which little or no glass base appears (microcrystallitic).

microcrystallogeny, -crystallography, -culture, -curie: see MICRO- 2, 1, 5 a.

microcyclic (maɪkrəʊ'saɪklɪk), *a.* *Bot.* [f. MICRO- 1 b + CYCLIC *a.*] Of a plant rust: having a short life cycle.

1926 [see MACROCYCLIC *a.* 1]. **1950** E. A. BESSEY *Morphol & Taxon. Fungi* xii. 396 These last two are properly speaking microcyclic rusts. **1970** J. WEBSTER *Introd. Fungi* 376 Some rusts have only telia, with or without pycnia, and are said to be microcyclic.

microcyst ('maɪkrəʊsɪst). *Bot.* [f. MICRO- + CYST.] An enclosed swarm-cell, an encysted swarm-pore (of Myxomycetes).

1887 tr. *De Bary's Comp. Morph. & Biol. Fungi* 427 The term Microcyst was given by Cienkowski to the resting-state of the swarm-cells [of Myxomycetes]. **1902** tr. *Strasburger's Bot.* 303 They [the swarm-spores] surround themselves with a wall, and as microcysts pass into a state of rest.

microcyte ('maɪkrəsaɪt, 'mɪkrəʊ-). *Path.* [f. MICRO- + -CYTE.] A minute red blood-corpuscle. Hence **microcytic** (-'sɪtɪk) *a.*, typical or characteristic of a microcyte; characterized by microcytes; **microcytosis** (-saɪ'təʊsɪs) = MICROCYTHÆMIA.

1876 tr. *Wagner's Gen. Pathol.* 518 Microcytes..are small elements, not exceeding ·003 or ·004 mm. in diameter, brightly shining, of the same colour (or even deeper) as the red corpuscles. **1884** A. FLINT *Princ. Med.* (ed. 5) 62 These microcytes are regarded by some as red blood corpuscles in process of formation, by others as atrophied or degenerated red corpuscles. **1890** BILLINGS *Med. Dict.* II. 154/1 *Microcytosis*, production of microcytes. **1897** *Allbutt's Syst. Med.* IV. 579 Small red corpuscles or microcytes may occur in varying numbers. **1925** *Amer. Jrnl. Med. Sci.* CXXX. 684 Measurements..showed the majority of the cells to be microcytic. **1932** [see MACROCYTE]. **1938** H. DOWNEY *Handbk. Hematol.* III. xxxi. 2286 One cannot fail to notice that the average size of the red cells is less than normal; there is a distinct microcytosis. **1962** *Lancet* 12 May 1004/2 Clinical and hæmatological examinations..showed anæmia with anisocytosis, microcytosis, macrocytosis, and reticulocytosis. **1966** *Ibid.* 24 Dec. 1398/2 Prasad described a syndrome of microcytic anæmia.

‖**microcythæmia** (maɪkrəʊsɪ'θiːmɪə). *Path.* [mod.L. f. prec. + Gr. αἷμα blood.] The condition of the blood when it contains many microcytes.

1876 tr. *Wagner's Gen. Pathol.* 518 Microcythæmia is the name given..to a disease..characterized by the appearance in the blood of..microcytes.

microdactylous, -degree, -densitometer (etc.): see MICRO- 4, 5 a, 6.

microdentism (maɪkrəʊ'dɛntɪz(ə)m). [mod. f. Gr. μικρό-ς small + L. *dent-*, *dens* tooth + -ISM.] Smallness of the teeth.

1889 *Lancet* June 1152/2 Microdentism..was associated with overgrowth of the molars.

[**microdermatous**, *a.* *Path.* A spurious word originating in a misreading of MYCODERMATOUS.

1856 in MAYNE *Expos. Lex.* **1890** in *Syd. Soc. Lex.*]

micro-detector, -determination, -diffusion, -dont: see MICRO- 6, 6, 6, 4.

microdiorite (maɪkrəʊ'daɪəraɪt). *Petrol.* [f. MICRO- + DIORITE.] (See quots. 1920, 1961.)

1920 A. HOLMES *Nomencl. Petrol.* 157 *Micro-*, a prefix commonly added—..(2) to the names of phanerocrystalline rocks to indicate a microcrystalline rock or ground-mass of corresponding mineral composition and texture; e.g., *microgranite*, *microdiorite*, *microsyenite*, etc. **1961** J. CHALLINOR *Dict. Geol.* 127/1 *Microdiorite*, the medium-grained equivalent of a diorite, usually porphyritic (diorite porphyrite, or porphyrite). **1963** D. W. & E. E. HUMPHRIES tr. *Termier's Erosion & Sedimentation* iv. 94 (*caption*) The eroded surface of a microdiorite dike. **1965** G. J. WILLIAMS *Econ. Geol. N.Z.* x. 150/1 Positive nickel reactions are also produced by many of the less basic rocks from the 'mineral belt' such as the gabbros, leucogabbros and quartz microdiorites.

microdissect(ion), -distribution: see MICRO- 2 a, 1 b.

microdot ('maɪkrəʊdɒt), *sb.* [f. MICRO- (here merely emphasizing the smallness implied by *dot*) + DOT *sb.*[1]] **1.** A photograph, esp. of printed or written matter, reduced to about the size of a dot. Freq. *attrib.*

1946 J. E. HOOVER in *Reader's Digest* May 50/2 It was incredibly ingenious and effective, this micro-dot gadget. It perfectly counterfeited a typewritten or printed dot. The young Balkan agent, for example, had four telegraph blanks in his pocket, carrying Lilliputian spy orders that looked like periods; 11 micro-dots on the four papers. **1961** *Daily Mail* 8 Feb. 10/1 There was also a piece of glass with three microdots between the pieces of glass. These little dots are tiny pieces of film... By enlarging the dots again you can see what they contain. One microdot can contain a great deal of writing. **1964** M. GOWING *Britain & Atomic Energy* ix. 246 The communication of the message was in the best spy thriller traditions; it was by a micro-dot concealed in the hollow handle of a doorkey. **1965** I. FLEMING *Man with Golden Gun* viii. 108 The minor tools of espionage—codes, microdot developers, cyanide. **1968** *Listener* 1 Aug. 150/1 A house stacked with high-frequency transmitters, microdot readers.

2. A tiny capsule or tablet of lysergic acid diethylamide (LSD).

1971 *Oxford Times* 10 Dec. 1/5 Produced 2½ microdot tablets in foil which were later found to contain LSD. **1972** *Daily Colonist* (Victoria, B.C.) 5 Jan. 1/1 Called a microdot, the deceptively small, purple pill packs super-concentrated doses of the hallucinatory drug LSD. **1973** R. BUSBY *Pattern of Violence* v. 81 Gelatine micro-dots of the hallucinogenic drug LSD.

microdot ('maɪkrəʊdɒt), *v.* [f. prec. sb.] *trans.* To make a microdot or microdots of. So '**microdotting** *vbl. sb.*

1957 *Time* 28 Oct. 22 Some messages were recorded on a film which could be softened and rolled into a ball; others were microdotted, i.e., whole pages of printing were reduced on film to pinhead size. **1961** *Daily Tel.* 22 Mar. 23/5 The wireless transmitter and equipment for micro-dotting at the house. **1963** J. JOESTEN *They call it Intelligence* I. vi. 61 Colonel Abel..did a brisk business in micro-dotting. **1969** D. LAMBERT *Angels in Snow* xix. 251 He decided to micro-dot the information and despatch it to Washington.

microearthquake, -ecology: see MICRO- 1, 2 a.

ˌ**micro-eco'nomics**, *sb. pl.* (usu. const. as *sing.*). Also **microeconomics.** [f. MICRO- 2 a + ECONOMIC *sb.* 2 c.] That branch of the science of economics which deals with the individual (firm, product, consumer, etc.) rather than the aggregate.

1948 K. E. BOULDING *Economic Analysis* (rev. ed.) xiii. 259 There are two main branches of modern economic analysis, to which the names 'microeconomics' and 'macroeconomics' may conveniently be given. Microeconomics is the study of particular firms, particular households, individual prices, wages, incomes; individual industries, particular commodities. **1949** L. H. HANEY *Hist. Econ. Thought* (ed. 4) xxxvii. 734 The preceding chapters have mostly dealt with 'micro-economics'—economics concerned with the determination of *particular* prices or values. Now comes a chapter which deals with 'macro-economics', or national *aggregates* in the shape of total national income as affected by total spending or not-spending. **1960** A. CAIRNCROSS *Introd. Econ.* (ed. 3) ii. 23

When he is talking about the decisions made in an individual business the economist is in the realm of micro-economics. **1965** *McGraw-Hill Dict. Mod. Econ.* 324 Micro-economics deals with the division of total output among industries, products, and firms and the allocation of resources among competing uses. **1968** *Economist* 11 May 66/2 If the Government can provide the micro-economics that industry wants, then industry will willingly cooperate to help to provide the macro-economics that the Government needs. **1974** *Sci. Amer.* Jan. 27/2 A social decision, one not based entirely on microeconomics must be made on the value of the land to the society as a whole,

So ˌ**micro-eco'nomic** *a.*, ˌ**micro-e'conomist**.

1949 L. H. HANEY *Hist. Econ. Thought* (ed. 4) xxxiv. 692 The 'over' theories are mostly micro-economic. The 'under' theories all tend toward macro-economics, and are concerned with totals and averages, not margins. **1958** HENDERSON & QUANDT *Microecon. Theory* i. 3 Micro-economic theories are sufficiently flexible to permit many variations in their underlying assumptions. **1965** H. I. ANSOFF *Corporate Strategy* (1968) i. 16 The so-called microeconomic theory of the firm..sheds..little light on decision-making processes in a real-world firm. **1968** *Economist* 13 Jan. 46/1 Mr. Merton Peck..is mainly a 'micro-economist', interested in marketing questions and industrial problems. **1973** *Spectator* 3 Mar. 281/1 The most distinguished body of micro-economic thinkers, gathered together in one place, in the world. **1974** *Times Lit. Suppl.* 12 Apr. 398/1 Those conventional micro-economists who presume that their rather scholastic abstractions provide adequate criteria for decisions in nationalized industries.

micro-electric, -electrode: see MICRO- 4, 1.

microelectronics (ˌmaɪkrəʊiːlɛk'trɒnɪks, -ɛlɛk'trɒnɪks), *sb. pl.* (usu. const. as *sing.*). Also **micro-electronics**. [f. MICRO- 2 a + ELECTRONICS.] **a.** The branch of technology concerned with the design, manufacture, and use of microcircuits. **b.** Microelectronic devices or circuits.

1960 K. AMIS *New Maps of Hell* (1961) i. 19 Even if the problem of fitting all that machinery into a container on the human scale would require the development of a kind of micro-electronics that for the time being, one would imagine, is at a rudimentary stage [etc.]. **1967** *New Scientist* 11 May 342/2 Complete radio and TV sets have been built experimentally with 90 per cent microelectronics. *Ibid.* 342/3 There are..practical difficulties in packaging microelectronics in order to make the best use of their inherently high reliability. **1968** *Brit. Med. Bull.* XXIV. 192/2 Micro-electronics is having a profound effect on the application of computer power. **1970** *Daily Tel.* 8 May 21 Microelectronics, developed for American space and military hardware, is a way of miniaturising large circuits so that up to 100 transistors and associated components take up no more space than a pinhead. **1974** *Nature* 8 Feb. 338/2 Every week seems to bring a new idea for making use of ion implants in microelectronics.

So ˌ**microelec'tronic** *a.*

1960 *Proc. Western Joint Computer Conf.* 251/1 Microelectronic data processing systems are analyzed. **1967** *New Scientist* 11 May 342/1 Many ground and airborne radar systems, missiles and communications receivers for all three services are being developed in microelectronic form. **1973** *Sci. Amer.* Apr. 63/1 The size of microelectronic circuits has decreased to the point where their surface dimensions are measured in microns..and their thickness in angstroms.

micro-electrophoresis (etc.): see MICRO- 6.

microelement ('maɪkrəʊɛlɪmənt). [f. MICRO- + ELEMENT *sb.*] **1.** *Plant Physiol.* = MICRONUTRIENT.

1936 *Chem. Abstr.* XXX. 1496 Yields of oats..were greatest with the doubled concn. of nutrients with a special addn. of microelements. **1950** CURTIS & CLARK *Introd. Plant Physiol.* xiii. 367 We prefer the terms trace or micro elements. **1966** F. M. IRVINE tr. *Lundegårdh's Plant Physiol.* vi. 251 Manganese takes up an intermediate position between a macro- and a microelement.

2. *Electronics.* A thin, flat, miniaturized circuit made with standardized length and width for assembly into a micromodule.

1959 *Proc. IRE* XLVII. 897 (*caption*) Micro-module, exploded view, before stacking and interconnecting. As many micro-elements as desired may be assembled to form the module... A 0·01-inch space is allowed between micro-elements. **1963** S. F. DANKO et al. in E. Keonjian *Microelectronics* iii. 142 The 0·016-in.-diameter riser wires are soldered to appropriate metallized notches in the stack of microelements.

microencapsulation (ˌmaɪkrəʊɛnkæpsjʊ'leɪʃən). [f. MICRO- 2 a + ENCAPSULATION.] The process of enclosing substances in microcapsules. Hence **microen'capsulate** *v. trans.*, **-en'capsulated** *ppl. a.*, **-en'capsulating** *vbl. sb.*

1961 *New Scientist* 20 Apr. 115/2 Pre-packed flavour and aromas, contained in microscopic plastic capsules, might be added to beverages, cokes and the like—this is one of the applications envisaged for the techniques of 'microencapsulation' being developed in the United States. **1967** *Britannica Bk. of Year* (U.S.) 803/2 *Microencapsulate*, *vb.*, to enclose a small amount of a substance in a microcapsule (*microencapsulated* aspirin); *microencapsulation*. **1969** *New Scientist* 3 Apr. 18/1 These results led us to suggest the possibility of using microencapsulated enzymes for experimental enzyme replacement. **1970** BAKAN & ANDERSON in L. Lachman et al. *Theory & Pract. Industr. Pharmacy* xiii. 402/2 The process is capable of microencapsulating liquids and solids. *Ibid.*, By vertical stacking of the microencapsulating units, production rates of 50 pounds per hour have been achieved. **1970** *Daily Tel.* 2 Oct. 5/1 The different synthetic aromas are contained in small labels employing the technique of micro-encapsulation. **1971** *New Scientist* 15 July 122/3 The technique has the advantage over other attempts that are being made to microencapsulate enzymes for therapy that liposomes are constructed of 'natural' materials. **1971** *Reader's Digest* (U.S.) Oct. 206/1 (Advt.), Through a special microencapsulation process, hundreds and hundreds of tiny granules of pure aspirin are concentrated in each Bayer Timed-Release tablet.

microenvironment(al), -estimation, -event, -evolution(ary), -explosion, -explosive, -farad: see MICRO- 1, 6, 1, 1 b, 1, 1, 5.

microfauna ('maɪkrəʊfɔːnə). *Biol.* [f. MICRO- 1 + FAUNA.] A fauna made up of minute animals, or one found in a microhabitat.

1902 *Geogr. Jrnl.* X. 323 The average amount of Plankton (micro-fauna) contained in them [*sc.* mountain lakes] is only the tenth..part of that contained in the standing waters of..lowlands. **1910** H. F. OSBORN *Age of Mammals* iv. 254 Of the microfauna we first observe among the castroids that the genus *Chalicomys* replaces the *Steneofiber* of the Oligocene. **1924** *Bull. Amer. Assoc. Petroleum Geologists* VIII. 549 All of the evidence at hand is studied and weighed in the light of intensive study of the micro-faunas of the Gulf Coast region. **1947** *Antiquity* XXI. 190 Both diggers and sieve-men became very skilful at descrying even the smallest specimen... The sieve-men would pick out tiny bones of microfauna with amazing verve. **1957** G. E. HUTCHINSON *Treat. Limnol.* I. xv. 817 This rise [*sc.* in soluble copper] may contribute to the disappearance of certain members of the microfauna and microflora from the lake. **1975** *Times* 27 May 14/7 The upper part of those river-borne sediments [at Hoxne] contains a rich microfauna of small mammals, fishes and amphibia.

Hence **micro'faunal** *a.*

1935 *Bull. Geol. Soc. Amer.* XLVI. 498 The microfaunal evidence in the Wheeler Canyon section is not quite conclusive. **1964** *Oceanogr. & Marine Biol.* II. 385 The species minimum at about 5‰ salinity..has also been found in more recent investigations on..various micro-faunal groups. **1972** *Times* 11 Dec. 1/8 The microfaunal remains have shown that fishes, birds and crabs played almost as important a part in the diet of the population as that of cattle. **1973** *Nature* 7 Dec. 347/1 Experiments introducing modern lichens into the normal preparation of microfaunal samples using hydrogen peroxide failed to mineralise the plant structures.

microfelsite (maɪkrəʊ'fɛlsaɪt). *Geol.* and *Min.* [f. MICRO- + FELSITE.] A form of felsite incapable of resolution under the microscope. Hence **microfel'sitic** *a.*, of, belonging to, or consisting of, microfelsite.

1879 RUTLEY *Stud. Rocks* x. 171 It yet remains to be shown whether micro-felsitic matter is inert upon polarised light. **1888** TEALL *Brit. Petrogr.* 439 *Microfelsite*, a term first introduced by Zirkel,..is now generally defined as a microscopic substance, forming the base of some porphyries, which is characterized by the possession of a granular, scaly, and fibrous structure without the power of exerting any definite action on polarized light.

microferment, -fibril(lar): see MICRO- 1.

microfiche ('maɪkrəʊfiːʃ). Pl. microfiche, -fiches. [f. MICRO- 7 + F. *fiche* slip of paper, index-card.] A flat piece of film, usually the size of a standard catalogue card, containing microphotographs of the pages of a book, periodical, etc. Also shortened to **fiche**.

1950 *Rev. Documentation* XVII. 216/1 Perhaps the French decision of reserving the word microcard for the opaque microcopy and using microfiche for the transparency may show us the way [to avoid confusion in terminology]. **1953** *Library Sci. Abstr.* 193 The translucent microfiche is considered by some people to be better than the opaque microcard. **1959** *Times* 2 Apr. 11/7 Research work..can be economically published on *microfiche*... The cost of a *fiche* is very low, about 2s. 6d., and many research reports would not need more than two or three *fiche* to cover them. **1967** J. R. U. PAGE in De Reuck & Knight *Communication in Sci.* 151 Master microfiche are made for NASA and the Space Documentation Service. **1969** *Daily Tel.* 19 Mar. 14/8 The fiches will allow universities and other institutions to have vast reference library resources in small spaces. **1970** *Library Assoc. Rec.* Mar. 97/1 The National Aeronautics and Space Administration..makes available microfiches of the documents. *Ibid.* 97/2 The bibliographic information, together with the document and microfiche copy, is sent to NASA. **1970** *Publishers' Weekly* 8 June 152/1 A typical microfiche has 72 printed pages in an area 4 by 6 inches. **1972** J. POYER *Chinese Agenda* (1973) xiv. 210 He tossed a slim creased manila envelope..to Gillon. It felt empty... 'Microfiche,' Liu explained. **1974** *Bookseller* 8 June 2600/2 Colour printing on microfiche is now being done.

microfilaria: see MICRO- 1.

microfilm ('maɪkrəʊfɪlm), *sb.* Also with hyphen. [f. MICRO- 7 + FILM *sb.*]

1. (A length of) photographic film containing microphotographs of the pages of a book, periodical, etc.

1935 *Library Jrnl.* LX. 145/1 The only way to find out how well the film, made by M. Dagron, has preserved its original qualities during its sixty-four years, was to consider it like one of our modern micro-films and try to print enlargements from it. **1936** *Science* 1 May 403/1 Bibliofilm Service copied upon 35 mm film material in the library [*sc.* U.S. Department of Agriculture library], substituting microfilm for loan of the books and journals. **1936** *Dialect Notes* VI. 528 Documents in microfilm form..will cost approximately 1 cent a page. **1939** *Nature* 11 Mar. 392/2 The so-called micro-film..offers one means for the photographic reproduction of bulky reports. **1940** A. HUXLEY *Let.* 14 Oct. (1969) 461 All the big libraries make these micro-films now. **1948** *Times* 17 Feb. 7/4 A brochure describing the micro-film reproduction of *The Times* from its first issue in 1785 to the present day. **1957** *Listener* 24 Oct. 646/2, I should not be able to go to California or Russia. I should just have to go home and work with microfilms. **1961** L. MUMFORD *City in Hist.* xvii. 546 What is visible and real in this world is only what has been transferred to paper or has been even further etherialized on a microfilm or a tape recorder. **1972** *English Studies* LIII. 533 He reads Eckhart in Latin at the public library from microfilm.

2. Special Comb.: **microfilm reader**, a small projector used to produce a readable image from microfilm; **microfilm viewer** (see quot.).

1950 *Amer. Documentation* I. 139/2 (*caption*) Griscombe portable microfilm reader. **1962** A. GÜNTHER *Microphotogr. in Library* (Unesco) 8 A system whereby..positive microfilm strips copied from the negative master are kept near the microfilm reader offers the best advantages. **1936** *Science* 1 May 403/2 Microfilm viewer—a small monocular optical device for reading 35 mm microfilms a line at a time, suitable for inspecting film or for use while travelling.

microfilm ('maɪkrəʊfɪlm), *v.* [f. the sb.] *trans.* To record on microfilm. Hence **'microfilming** *vbl. sb.*

1940 *N. & Q.* 12 Oct. 253/2 Steps are being taken to have parish registers microfilmed... Micro-filming is a very cheap as well as speedy process. **1955** *Times* 28 July 9/4 It is intended to continue the microfilming..as and when funds permit. **1955** H. VAN THAL *Fanfare for E. Newman* v. 63 The Germans, who have always held Bizet in high respect,..micro-filmed the manuscript. **1972** M. J. BOSSE *Incident at Naha* ii. 76 Any microfilming service would do the job at ten cents a page. **1973** F. DE FELITTA *Oktoberfest* (1974) xiv. 164 There are a number of sources of wartime documentation which Yad Vashem has not yet microfilmed.

microfilter: see MICRO- 6.

microflora ('maɪkrəʊflɔːrə). *Biol.* [f. MICRO- 1 + FLORA.] A flora made up of minute plants, or one found in a microhabitat.

[**1905** *Ann. Rep. Board of Regents Smithsonian Inst. 1904* 351 Has any competent hand celebrated the mikro-flora of the highest ridges, those tiny, vivid forget-me-nots and gentians.] **1932** FULLER & CONARD tr. *Braun-Blanquet's Plant Sociol.* viii. 235 The microflora of the soil..is composed of countless bacteria, fungi, and algae. **1969** *New Yorker* 12 Apr. 85/1 The exobiologists have insisted that..the astronauts' microflora—bacteria and other organisms—have all been typed and catalogued. **1974** *Nature* 8 Feb. 361/2 This previously unknown micro-flora of blue-green and green or red algal affinities is from..the Bungle Bungle dolomite which outcrops in the Osmond Range of Western Australia.

microfoliation: see MICRO- 2 b.

microform ('maɪkrəʊfɔːm). [f. MICRO- 7 + FORM *sb.*] Microphotographic form; a microphotographic reproduction on film or paper of a manuscript, book, etc., requiring magnification to produce a readable image.

1960 *N. & Q.* Jan. 2/1 The genealogical and heraldic material listed as being already in 'microform' includes the Huddersfield Parish Registers, 1606–1812. **1962** A. GÜNTHER *Microphotogr. in Library* (Unesco) 14 The first supplementary note [to a catalogue entry] should indicate the microform. **1969** *R. & E. Coordinator* (Res. & Engin. Council Graphic Arts Industry) Apr. 4/2 Libraries make microform reproductions of everything from rare books to technical publications. **1971** *Amer. N. & Q.* X. 11/2 A selection of the major works from this catalogue is being offered in microform by the Erasmus Press. **1974** *Reprographics Q.* VII. 85/1 The cost/benefit of issuing parts lists and maintenance manuals on microforms.

microfossil, -fracture, -fracturing, -gamete: see MICRO- 1.

microgametophyte (maɪkrəʊgæ'miːtəʊfaɪt). *Bot.* [f. MICRO- + *gametophyte* (s.v. GAMETE).] A gametophyte that develops from a microspore; a male gametophyte.

1907 *Amer. Naturalist* XLI. 360 In our material of Agathis the protoplasm is unfortunately very much shrunken..but this fortunately does not interfere with the understanding of the general conditions present in the microgametophyte. **1938** G. M. SMITH *Cryptogamic Bot.* II. v. 132 Microgametophytes of other genera also have but one vegetative cell. **1959** FOSTER & GIFFORD *Compar. Morphol. Vascular Plants* viii. 161 Early stages in formation of the microgametophytes [in *Selaginella*] begin while the microspores are still within the microsporangium.

microgasometer, -metric (etc.): see MICRO- 6.

microgenic (maɪkrəʊ'dʒɛnɪk), *a.* Chiefly *Journalists' colloq.* [f. MICRO(PHONE + -GENIC b.] Of a voice: that sounds well when transmitted by microphone; well suited to broadcasting.

1931 S. GOLDWYN in *Sat. Rev.* 14 Feb. 220/1 An actor may be 'photogenic'..but that is not enough. He must also be 'microgenic', that is to say, he must have a voice that is suitable to the microphone. **1944** *Evening Standard* 5 Dec. 6/4 It seems strange that words like flak..should escape censure by the austere..while such bitter eloquence is directed against..microgenic (good for broadcasting).

micro-geology (etc.): see MICRO- 2.

micro-germ ('maɪkrəʊdʒɜːm). *Path.* [f. MICRO-
+ GERM.] A microbe. Hence **micro'germal** *a.*
1887 A. M. BROWN *Anim. Alkal.* 117 The category of
affections admittedly micro-germal, parasitic. *Ibid.* 150 It is
.. an absurdity to introduce micro-germs into the question.

microglia (maɪkrəʊ-, mɪkrəʊ'glaɪə). *Anat.* [f.
MICRO- 1 + NEURO)GLIA.] Neuroglial cells
derived from mesoderm and functioning as
macrophages (scavengers) in and about the
central nervous system (now regarded as
components of the reticulo-endothelial system);
a tissue composed of such cells. Usu. const. as
pl. So **micro'glial** *a.*
1924 *Jrnl. Nervous & Mental Dis.* LIX. 346 In 1918 del
Rio-Hortega succeeded .. in impregnating clearly and
specifically a homogeneous group of cells... These cells he
called microglia. **1929** *Amer. Jrnl. Path.* V. 452 The
microglial reaction around a sterile puncture wound of the
cerebrum. **1932** *Times Lit. Suppl.* 10 Nov. 843/3 The rod-
cells .. are in fact generally held to be a variety of microglia.
1962 *Gray's Anat.* (ed. 33) 56 The astrocytes and
oligodendroglia are ectodermal in origin .. whilst the
microglia is of mesodermal origin. **1966** W. ANDREW
Microfabric of Man x. 147 (*caption*) Microglia in gray matter
of spinal cord. Cell bodies of these cells are often angular or
elongated. *Ibid.* 148/1 The microglia .. are capable of
remarkable transformations. **1973** PALAY & CHAN-PALAY
Cerebellar Cortex vi. 178/2 Often microglia laden with such
inclusions can be found to have wandered even into the
molecular layer. *Ibid.,* The processes of a microglial cell can
even invade the confines of the myelin sheath.

**microglossary, -glossia, -gonidium,
-gramme:** see MICRO- 1 b, 3, 1, 5.

microglossia, -gonidium, -gramme: see
MICRO- 3, 1, 5.

microgranite (maɪkrəʊ'grænɪt). *Geol.* [f.
MICRO- + GRANITE.] A granite rock,
recognizable as crystalline only under the
microscope. Hence **microgra'nitic** *a.,* of, or
pertaining to, microgranite. **micro'granitoid** *a.,*
like microgranite.
1885 GEIKIE *Text-bk. Geol.* (ed. 2) 109 Where a similar
structure is so fine that it can only be recognised with the
microscope, it has been called microgranitic or euritic. **1888**
TEALL *Brit. Petrogr.* 307 The former he [Rosenbusch]
proposed to call micro-granites. **1893** [see MICRO-SYENITE].
1903 GEIKIE *Text-bk. Geol.* II. II. v. (ed. 4) 151 Where their
elements are minute the structure becomes micro-granitoid
or euritic. *Ibid.* vii. 209 Granite-porphyry (micro-granite) a
fine grained granitoid rock.

microgranulitic: see MICRO- 4.

micrograph ('maɪkrəʊgrɑːf, -æ-). [f. MICRO- +
-GRAPH.]
1. A picture or photograph of greatly reduced
size.
1874 DRAPER *Relig. & Sci.* v. (1875) 134 In her [the
Mind's] silent galleries are there hung micrographs of the
living and the dead?
2. An instrument constructed for producing
extremely minute writing or engraving (Knight
Dict. Mech. 1875). Cf. MICROPANTOGRAPH.
3. An enlarged image of an object (as seen
through a microscope) obtained either by hand
drawing or (now more usu.) photographically.
1904 *Electrochem. Ind.* Mar. 88/2 This embodies .. the
determination of oxygen content, the preparation of
micrographs, and .. the planimetric measurements of
enlarged micrographs, with calculation of the percentage of
oxygen. **1916** *Trans. Amer. Inst. Mining & Metall. Engin.*
LI. 832 A microscopic examination was made of the
threaded end of each of the 108 tensile bars. The
micrographs shown at the end of this report reproduce the
average structure of the top and bottom tensile bars. *Ibid.*
833 All micrographs are magnified 100 diameters. **1941** R.
M. ALLEN *Photomicrogr.* i. 1 The word *micrograph* used
alone has had to be broadened in meaning to include
pictures of minute objects either drawn by hand or
produced through photographic processes. **1953** *Jrnl. Appl.
Physics* XXIV. 616/1 The simplest method of obtaining x-
ray micrographs is to place the specimen in contact with a
photographic film of the maximum resolution type and
expose it to the radiation from a normal x-ray tube. All the
enlargement is obtained photographically. **1960** D. F.
LAWSON *Technique Photomicrogr.* ii. 4 Drawings made from
images projected from a microscope are referred to as
micrographs. **1968** H. HARRIS *Nucleus & Cytoplasm* iii. 59
Some electron micrographs of isolated 'polysomes' also
appeared to show the ribosomes connected by some form of
strand.

micrographer (maɪ'krɒgrəfə(r)). [f.
MICROGRAPHY: see -GRAPHER.] One who
practises micrography; one who describes or
delineates microscopic objects. So
mi'crographist in the same sense (*Syd. Soc.
Lex.* 1890).
1839-47 *Todd's Cycl. Anat.* III. 527/2 The accounts given
of it by some of the earlier micrographers. **1849** OWEN
Parthenogenesis 32 *note,* The masterly Micrographer
[Ehrenberg].

micrographic (maɪkrəʊ'græfɪk), *a.* [f.
MICROGRAPHY: see -GRAPHIC.]
1. Of or pertaining to the delineation of
microscopic objects or to micrography.
1856 GRIFFITH & HENFREY (*title*) The Micrographic
Dictionary; a guide to the examination and investigation of

the structure and nature of microscopic objects. **1895**
Nature 15 Aug. 368/2 The applications of micrographic
analysis.
2. Minutely written (as symptomatic of
nervous disorder).
1899 [see MACROGRAPHY].

micrographically (maɪkrəʊ'græfɪkəlɪ), *adv.* [f.
MICROGRAPHIC *a.* + -AL + -LY².] By means of
micrography or micrographs.
1898 *Jrnl. Iron & Steel Inst.* LIV. 191 The presence of
thin decarbonised outer layers .. may be frequently
recognized micrographically. **1908** *Analyst* XXXIII. 289
All further changes (hardening) which take place inside the
B constituents cannot be followed micrographically,
because B appears to be a uniform substance by reflected
light. **1971** (*title*) The Compact edition of the Oxford
English Dictionary: complete text reproduced
micrographically. **1974** *Nature* 30 Aug. 702/2 Grain growth
[in metals] has been studied micrographically for many
years.

micrography (maɪ'krɒgrəfɪ). [f. MICRO- + Gr.
-γραφία writing. Cf. F. *micrographie*.]
1. a. The description or delineation of objects
visible only by the aid of a microscope.
1658 PHILLIPS, *Micrography,* the description of minute
bodies by a magnifying glass. **1665** *Phil. Trans.* I. 58 He was
much surprised when he saw the Micrography of Mr. Hook.
1670 *Moral State Eng.* 41 By the study of Micrography ..
they have displaied a new Page of the Book of Nature.
1731-3 TULL *Horse-Hoeing Husb.* xvi. 233 'Tis
unreasonable to believe, that Water can have such
extraordinary Skill in Botany, or in Micrography [etc.].
1869 tr. *Pouchet's Universe* (1871) 7 Will any one accuse
micrography of giving rise to those vain illusions with which
those .. are pleased to reproach it?
b. The technique of producing micrographs
(sense 3), or of studying objects by means of
micrographs.
1908 *Analyst* XXXIII. 289 (*heading*) The micrography of
cement. **1953** *Jrnl. Appl. Physics* XXIV. 623/1 The
experiments so far made support the theoretical indications
that x-ray shadow micrography is a practicable technique at
least up to the resolution of the optical microscope. **1973**
Jrnl. Bacteriol. CXIV. 413 (*heading*) Electron micrography
of bud formation in *Metschinkowia krissii*.
2. a. The art or practice of writing in
microscopic characters. **b.** *Path.* Abnormally
small handwriting, as a symptom of nervous
disorder.
1899 [see MACROGRAPHY]. **1905** *Daily News* 3 July 12 The
achievements in micrography of Mr. Sofer, who is giving
the King a portrait composed of a biography of 44,000
letters.

micrograver, -gravimetric: see MICRO- 1, 6.

microgroove ('maɪkrəʊgruːv). [f. MICRO- 1 +
GROOVE *sb.*] A very narrow groove on a
gramophone record; a record having such
grooves. Freq. *attrib.*
1948 *Amer. Speech* XXIII. 252 CBS announces a new-
type record—microgroove. **1948** *Electronic Engin.* XX.
333/3 The groove size, from which the name 'Microgroove'
has been derived, is only 0·0027 in. to 0·003 in. **1949** *Wireless
World* Apr. 146/1 What is a 'microgroove' record? It is a
name given to the 7-, 10- or 12-in pressings in high-grade
vinylite, with a rotational speed of 33⅓ r.p.m... As it was
found necessary to reduce the groove width to about one-
third the size of normal record grooves, the name
'Microgroove' was coined originally by Columbia Records,
Inc., for their 33⅓ r.p.m. records, but it would now appear to
be used in America as a generic term for all such fine-pitch
records. **1951** SACKVILLE-WEST & SHAWE-TAYLOR *Record
Guide* 715 They increased the playing time of each side by
.. a much narrower groove-cut known as 'microgroove'.
Ibid. 717 Even a 7-inch 33⅓ microgroove would apparently
be too long—or too expensive—to meet this case. **1957**
Times 13 Dec. 18/2 The 78 r.p.m. record began to lose
favour. On the other hand, the demand for microgroove
records continued strongly and sales of both 45 r.p.m. and
33⅓ r.p.m. records increased. **1958** *Times* 13 Sept. 9/1 This
old Weingartner set has now reappeared .. skilfully
transferred to LP microgroove by Pathé-Marconi's
engineers. **1972** *Jazz & Blues* Nov. 35/2 Some microgroove
reissues contain edited versions of these titles.

microgyria, -habitat: see MICRO- 3, 1.

microhardness (maɪkrəʊ'hɑːdnɪs). [f. MICRO-
1 b + HARDNESS.] The hardness of a very small
area of a sample, as measured by an indenter.
1921 *Trans. Amer. Soc. Mech. Engin.* XLII. 1109 If we let
κ be the microhardness. **1934** *Amer. Mineralogist* XIX. 163
We have undertaken to obtain microhardness values for
each of the nine minerals from talc to corundum. **1954** A. R.
BAILEY *Text-bk. Metall.* xiii. 457 Micro-hardness testers
make it possible to obtain comparative hardness figures for
the different constituents of alloys, .. and may aid in the
identification of constituents and inclusions. **1966** D. G.
BRANDON *Mod. Techniques Metallogr.* i. 5 In soft materials it
is almost impossible to eliminate surface deformation by
repeated mechanical polishing and etching... A detectable
increase in microhardness can be observed up to 5 μm below
the polished surface.

**microhenry, microhm, -inch,
-incineration, -injection, -instability:** see
MICRO- 5 a, 5 a, 5 a, 6, 2 a, 1.

microinstruction ('maɪkrəʊɪn,strʌkʃən).
Computers. [f. MICRO- 1 + INSTRUCTION.] One
of a sequence of instructions produced by a
computer in response to some more

comprehensive instruction; *spec.* one that
corresponds to one of the smallest, most
elementary operations that can occur in the
computer and is produced in accordance with a
microprogram.
1959 E. M. GRABBE et al. *Handbk. Automation,
Computation, & Control* II. ii. 254 Many macroinstructions
can be constructed from properly sequenced
microinstructions. **1964** T. W. McRAE *Impact of Computers
on Accounting* i. 24 This problem has been solved by
programmers devising .. autocodes so that a single
macroinstruction written down by the programmer
generates the required set of microinstructions during
translation by the computer from the autocode to the
absolute machine code. **1969** P. B. JORDAIN *Condensed
Computer Encycl.* 318 Each micro-instruction is coded as
several bits, one bit for each functional unit or data path in
the computer hardware. The one-for-one correspondence
between bit positions and functional units allows for very
simple interpretation of each microinstruction.

micro-Kjeldahl, -lens: see MICRO- 6, 1.

‖**Micro-lepi'doptera,** *sb. pl. Ent.* [f. MICRO- +
LEPIDOPTERA.] A collector's term for certain
small moths.
1852 H. T. STAINTON (*title*) The Entomologist's
Companion; being a Guide to the Collection of Micro-
Lepidoptera. **1902** *Westm. Gaz.* 8 Mar. 8/1 The special
library formed by Lord Walsingham for the study of micro-
lepidoptera. **1972** L. E. CHADWICK tr. *Linsenmaier's Insects
of World* 226/1 A number of families have been included
under the collective concept of the Microlepidoptera, but
today the tendency is to consider them as separate groups.
Hence (in recent Dicts.) **microlepi'dopter,**
one of the Micro-lepidoptera. **microlepi'dop-
teran,** (*a*) *adj.*, microlepidopterous; (*b*) *sb.*, one
of the Micro-lepidoptera. **microlepi'dopterist,**
one who studies the Micro-lepidoptera.
microlepi'dopterous *a.*, of or pertaining to the
Micro-lepidoptera.
1852 STAINTON *Entom. Comp.* 3 Book-muslin .. is
therefore best adapted for Micro-lepidopterists. **1860** *Rep.
Brit. Assoc. Adv. Sci.* II. 122 (*heading*) On some peculiar
forms amongst the Micro-Lepidopterous larvæ. **1972** L. E.
CHADWICK tr. *Linsenmaier's Insects of World* 226/2 The
microlepidopterous families are not isolated in their
phylogeny.

microlepidotous: see MICRO- 4.

microlight ('maɪkrəʊlaɪt), *a.* and *sb.* [f. MICRO-
+ LIGHT *a.*¹] **A.** *adj.* Involving, pertaining to, or
designating a microlight aircraft. **B.** *sb.* =
ULTRALIGHT *sb.*
1981 *Times* 7 Mar. 2/2 Microlight flying will appeal to the
Biggles factor in most adults. *Ibid.* 2/3 The microlight
association defines the aircraft as one weighing no more than
150 kilogrammes with a minimum wing area of 10 square
metres. **1982** *Observer* 31 Jan. 2/8 The Noise Abatement
Society is being deafened by complaints about those daring
young men in their new microlight flying machines.
Warmer weather will bring out the roof-skimming
microlights—60 m.p.h. planes powered by 30 horsepower
engines—in their hundreds. **1982** *Field* 25 Dec. 1256/2 The
base weight of microlight aircraft is always more than five
kilograms. **1983** [see ULTRALIGHT *a.*] **1984** *Daily Tel.*
9 Mar. 23/4 (*caption*) Bob Calvert .. yesterday .. set a world
altitude record in a microlight by soaring 23,500 ft above
Blackburn, Lancs. **1984** *Times* 27 Dec. 2/4 She was a
passenger on a microlight plane which plunged into the sea.

microline ('maɪkrəʊlaɪn). *Microscopy.* [f.
MICRO- + LINE.] A unit of diameter for objects
viewed under the microscope.
1857 *Rep. Brit. Assoc., Trans. Sect.* 115 He (Dr. Lyons)
would propose that some definite micrometric integer
should be assumed, being a determinate part of unity. He
proposed that this measure should be denominated a
Microline.

microlinguistics (,maɪkrəʊlɪŋ'gwɪstɪks), *sb. pl.*
(const. as *sing.*). [f. MICRO- 2 a + LINGUISTIC *sb.*
b.] (See quots. 1949, 1972.) So **microlin'guistic**
a.
1949 G. L. TRAGER in *Studies in Ling.: Occasional Papers*
I. 2 The whole of the field concerned with language .. we
shall call Macrolinguistics. The three subdivisions we shall
call Prelinguistics, Microlinguistics, Metalinguistics. *Ibid.* 4
Microlinguistics .. deals with the analysis of language
systems. **1953** *Internat. Jrnl. Amer. Ling.* XIX. ii. Suppl. 28
Smith presented the conceptual scheme developed at the
Foreign Service Institute which divides linguistics into
three main compartments: .. 'microlinguistics' deals with
the analysis of linguistic systems. *Ibid.* 29 He gave an
example of the sort of methodological error which Smith's
separation of microlinguistic and metalinguistic levels
would avoid. **1955** S. & M. T. CHASE *Power of Words* x. 101
Microlinguistics .. takes a long time to reach a unit as large
as the sentence. **1963** *Amer. Speech* XXXVIII. 138 Since
distinctive articulatory features form part of a system of
contrastive correlations, any analysis based on this structure
is micro-, not extralinguistic. **1967** D. STEIBLE *Conc.
Handbk. Ling.* 78 *Microlinguistic meaning.* The term refers
to the identity or difference in meaning which results when
a part of a larger structure is replaced by a different part.
1972 HARTMANN & STORK *Dict. Lang. & Ling.* 141/2
Microlinguistics, those aspects of linguistic studies which are
concerned with the direct analysis of linguistic material, e.g.
phonology, grammar, lexicology.

microlite ('maɪkrəʊlaɪt). [f. MICRO- + -LITE.]
1. *Min.* Impure calcium pyrotantalate,
$Ca_2Ta_2O_7$.
First found in very small crystals, whence the name.

1835 C. U. SHEPHARD in *Amer. Jrnl. Sci.* XXVII. 361 Microlite, a New Mineral Species. **1868** DANA *Min.* (ed. 5) II. 513.

2. *Petrology.* = MICROLITH 1. Cf. CRYSTALLITE 2.

1878 LAWRENCE tr. *Cotta's Rocks Class.* 69 These bubbles, as well as the above-mentioned microlites. **1888** TEALL *Brit. Petrogr.* 14 Microlites differ from crystallites in possessing the internal structure of true crystals. **1926** [see CRYSTALLITE 2]. **1954** H. WILLIAMS et al. *Petrogr.* ii. 13 Extremely minute incipient crystals..are called microlites, provided they are birefringent; if they are even smaller, spherical, rod- and hair-like isotropic forms, they are called crystallites.

microlith ('maɪkrəʊlɪθ). [f. Gr. μῖκρό-ς small (see MICRO-) + λίθος stone.] **1.** *Petrology.* A term proposed in 1867 by Vogelsang for the microscopic acicular particles contained in the glassy portions of felspar, hornblende, etc. (Cf. MICROLITE 2.)

1879 RUTLEY *Stud. Rocks* x. 107 Microliths of hornblende are comparatively rare.

2. *Archæol.* A small stone tool with a sharpened edge used with a haft, characteristic of Mesolithic cultures.

1908 H. G. O. KENDALL in *Man* VIII. 103 Palæolithic Microliths.. By microliths I mean tiny flakes or other pieces of flint which have been trimmed or used by man at some part of the edge. **1927** PEAKE & FLEURE *Hunters & Artists* vii. 96 This [Capso-Tardenoisian] industry is characterized by the presence of very small flints of geometric shapes, chiefly of trapezoid, rhomboid, and triangular forms; these are commonly known as microliths. **1932** J. G. D. CLARK *Mesolithic Age in Brit.* p. xx, By a 'microlith' we understand a narrow flake blunted on one or both edges by steep secondary chipping, but devoid of secondary work on either face. **1960** *New Scientist* 11 Aug. 418/3 Finds included 52 microliths (tiny points which must have been hafted as arrow-heads and other weapons). **1971** *World Archaeol.* III. 157 Often termed 'microliths' by Old World archaeologists, these tools fall into three formal categories.

microlithic (maɪkrəʊ'lɪθɪk), a.[1] *Antiq.* [f. Gr. μῖκρός small + λίθος stone: see -IC.] Consisting or constructed of small stones. Hence, of a period, a people, etc. Characterized by the erection of microlithic monuments (opposed to MEGALITHIC).

1872 FERGUSSON *Rude Stone Mon.* ii. 40 The people.. affected..what may be called microlithic architecture. *Ibid.* 47 The cognate examples in the microlithic styles afford us very little assistance in determining either the origin or use of this class of monument.

microlithic (maɪkrəʊ'lɪθɪk), a.[2] [f. MICROLITH + -IC.] **a.** Pertaining to microliths; characterized by the presence of microliths.

1877 GEIKIE in *Nature* 4 Oct. 474/2 The abundance of the glassy microlithic base. **1882** —— *Text-bk. Geol.* 131 *Microlithic*, characterized by the abundance of microliths.

b. *Archæol.* Of or pertaining to microliths (MICROLITH 2); characterized by the use of microliths.

1923 A. L. KROEBER *Anthropol.* xiv. 407 Terminal Capsian..was a local phase..with the microlithic flint industry especially conspicuous... In Africa..the development of the extreme microlithic forms..has been most clearly traced. **1937** GARROD & BATE *Stone Age Mt. Carmel* I. i. viii. 114 We there found a layer containing an abundant microlithic industry, without pottery, superimposed on an eroded breccia with flints of Levalloiso-Mousterian type. **1947** J. & C. HAWKES *Prehist. Brit.* (rev. ed.) 19 The reduction of the size of flints to a 'microlithic' scale. **1971** *World Archaeol.* III. 157 Numbers of fragmentary flakes with backed (or 'microlithic') retouch occur in many levels of the site.

microlitic (maɪkrəʊ'lɪtɪk), a. [f. MICROLITE + -IC.] = MICROLITHIC a.[2] a.

1879 RUTLEY *Stud. Rocks* xi. 185 [The term] microlitic.. might..be given to..rocks which contain..microliths. **1903** GEIKIE *Text-bk. Geol.* II. ii. §vii. (ed. 4) 228 This microlitic felt is a distinctive character of the Andesites.

microlitre, -logic: see MICRO- 5, 1.

micrological (maɪkrəʊ'lɒdʒɪkəl), a. [f. MICROLOGY + -ICAL.]

1. Characterized by minuteness of investigation or discussion.

1879 O. W. HOLMES *Motley* §7. 53 He [*sc.* Balzac] is..a micrological, misanthropical, sceptical philosopher.

2. Of or pertaining to the study of minute objects; belonging to MICROLOGY 2.

1847 *Todd's Cycl. Anat.* IV. 71 The existing impulse towards micrological study.

Hence **micro'logically** *adv.*

1872 LOWELL *Milton Prose Wks.* (1890) IV. 88 *note*, If things are to be scanned so micrologically, what weighty inferences might not be drawn from [etc.].

micrologist (maɪ'krɒlədʒɪst). [f. MICROLOGY + -IST.] One skilled in the examination and description of minute objects. So **micrologue** ('maɪkrəʊlɒg), one who is occupied with microscopic research (*Syd. Soc. Lex.* 1890).

1841-71 T. R. JONES *Anim. Kingd.* (ed. 4) 13 The distinguished German micrologist Kölliker, whose researches..are calculated to clear up many doubtful points. **1960** [see MICRURGY].

micrology (maɪ'krɒlədʒɪ). [ad. Gr. μῖκρολογία, f. μῖκρό-ς small + -λογία: see -LOGY. Cf. F. *micrologie*.]

1. The discussion or investigation of trivial things or petty affairs; 'hair-splitting'.

1656 BLOUNT *Glossogr., Micrologie*, curiosity about things of no value; a speaking or treating of petty affairs. **1727** in BAILEY vol. II. **1820** W. TOOKE tr. *Lucian* I. 400 What a parcel of fiddle-faddle and micrology. **1829** I. TAYLOR *Enthus.* ii. (1867) 35 The philanthropist..is not found to spend his nights and days in pursuing any such subtile micrologies. **1882** FARRAR *Early Chr.* I. 525 How could one who had never learnt letters,..listen without reverence to that micrology of erudition.

2. (Properly a distinct word formed after MICROSCOPE.) That part of science which depends upon the use of the microscope; a treatise on microscopic animals and plants.

1849 in CRAIG. **1906** M. F. GUYER (*title*) Animal micrology. **1907** *Nature* 18 Apr. 582/1 The term 'micrology' has not received any general acceptance on this side of the Atlantic. **1914** (*title*) Journal of micrology.

microm, mikrom ('maɪkrɒm). [f. MICRO- + the initial letter of METRE.] A term suggested by Lord Kelvin in place of MICRON.

1898 LD. KELVIN in *Nature* 17 Nov. 57/1 Langley, fourteen years ago, used..the word 'mikron' to denote the millionth of a metre. The letter *n* has no place in the metrical system, and I venture to suggest a change of spelling to 'mikrom'.

micromachining: see MICRO- 2 a.

micromania (maɪkrəʊ'meɪnɪə). *Path.* [f. Gr. μῖκρός small (see MICRO-) + MANIA.] 'A form of mania in which the patient thinks himself, or some part of him, to be reduced in size' (*Syd. Soc. Lex.* 1890). Also, an insane habit of belittling oneself. **micro'maniac,** one affected with micromania.

1899 *Allbutt's Syst. Med.* VII. 703 Micromania is a name used in contrast to megalomania and to indicate what Dr. Mickle calls 'belittlement'. *Ibid.*, Micromania is met with.. in senile degeneration or mental degeneration of one kind or another. **1902** *Speaker* 8 Nov. 142/2 The cult of humility is a wholly spurious micromania. *Ibid.*, He is the one micromaniac of whom we have any record.

micromanipulation (,maɪkrəʊmənɪpjuː'leɪʃən). [f. MICRO- 2 a + MANIPULATION.] The performance of extremely delicate operations (such as the isolation of a single yeast cell from a culture) under the microscope, usu. with the aid of a micromanipulator; an operation so performed.

1921 *Science* 28 Oct. 411/2 (*heading*) A simple apparatus for micro-manipulation under the highest magnifications of the microscope. **1931** *Chem. Abstr.* XXV. 1409 (*heading*) Micromanipulations on latex in dark fields. **1949** *New Biol.* VII. 72 Although the chromosomes of most cells are very small objects,..in a few favourable cases it has been possible to study their physical properties by micromanipulation. **1971** *Nature* 2 July 33/1 The micro-manipulation of chromosomes of living human cells *in vitro* is a potential means of obtaining transplantable genetic material.

So **,microma'nipulator,** an instrument which is used in conjunction with an optical microscope to perform micromanipulations and which allows a microneedle, micropipette, etc., to be moved with great control through the field of view.

1921 *Science* 28 Oct. 413/1 There are two models of the micro-manipulator, a simple and a more elaborate form. **1949** A. G. SANDERS in H. W. Florey et al. *Antibiotics* II. xvi. 678 Spores from a conidium can be picked off singly with the point of a needle. Some people can do this with the needle held in the hand, others prefer to use a micro-manipulator. **1968** *Sci. Jrnl.* Nov. 18 (*caption*) Integrated circuit chip is shown above being placed in its case with aid of a micromanipulator. **1972** *Nature* 4 Feb. 263 Zeiss micromanipulators were used to position micropipettes.

micromanometer (etc.), **micromastia, -mazia:** see MICRO- 6, 3, 3.

|| **micromelus** (maɪ'krɒmɪləs). *Path.* [mod.L., f. Gr. μῖκρό-ς small + μέλος limb. (Gr. had μῖκρομελής adj., small-limbed, f. the same elements.)] A human being with all limbs dwarfed.

1890 in *Syd. Soc. Lex.* **1903** J. COATS *Man. Pathol.* 44 Partial dwarfing..may affect all four limbs, micromelus.

micromere ('maɪkrəʊmɪə(r)). *Embryology.* [f. Gr. μῖκρό-ς small + μέρος part.] The smaller of the two masses into which the vitellus of the developing ovum of *Lamellibranchiata* divides (cf. MACROMERE). Hence **'micromeral, micro'meric** *adjs.*, of or pertaining to the micromere.

1877 HUXLEY *Anat. Inv. Anim.* viii. 484 Layer of blastomeres, of which those of one hemisphere have proceeded from the micromere, and those of the other from the macromere. *Ibid.* 498 The edges of the micromeral layer. **1886** *Jrnl. R. Microsc. Soc.* Ser. II. VI. i. 224 The segmentation resembles that of other molluscs, the 'micromeres' appearing at the formative pole by separation of the 'protoplasmic' portion of the 'macromeres'.

micromeritic (,maɪkrəmə'rɪtɪk), a. [f. MICRO- + Gr. μέρ-ος part + -ITE + -IC.] Of granitoid rocks: Having a structure discernible only with the microscope.

1882 [see MACROMERITIC]. In mod. Dicts.

micromesh ('maɪkrəʊmeʃ). [f. MICRO- 1 + MESH *sb.*] Material (esp. nylon) consisting of a very fine mesh. Freq. *attrib.*

1959 *Manch. Guardian* 27 July 4/4 Plaza..have..a cheap ..micromesh. **1960** *Harper's Bazaar* Apr. 98 Seam-free in sheer micro-mesh. **1962** *Which?* Apr. 113/2 Two of the leading brands of seamless micromesh stockings. **1963** R. R. A. HIGHAM *Handbk. Papermaking* i. 6 Empty the contents on to a micro-mesh wire circle and carefully wash with distilled water. **1974** *Times* 26 Apr. 7/7 Initially only in micromesh, the tights..are in three sizes.

micro-metallography, -metallurgy, -metazoan, -metazoon: see MICRO- 2, 2 a, 1, 1.

micrometeor (maɪkrəʊ'miːtɪər). [f. MICRO- 1 + METEOR.] = MICROMETEOROID.

1957 *Seattle Times* 10 Nov. 16/5 Density of micro-meteors and meteoric dust, and the like. **1973** *Times* 16 May 1/1 The micrometeor shield was designed to protect the outer skin of the space station from minor damage but also played an important role in controlling Skylab's temperature.

Hence **micromete'oric** *a.*

1958 *Times* 30 Aug. 6/1 It also carried recording instruments to register impacts of micro-meteoric particles.

micrometeorite (maɪkrəʊ'miːtɪəraɪt). [f. MICRO- 1 + METEORITE.] A micrometeoroid; *spec.* one that has entered the earth's atmosphere (cf. the distinction between METEORITE and METEOROID *sb.*).

1949 F. L. WHIPPLE in *Science* 28 Oct. 438/1 The term *micrometeorite* is here defined as an extraterrestrial body that is sufficiently small to enter the earth's atmosphere without being damaged by encounter with the atmosphere. **1956** *Spaceflight* I. 27/1 The density of meteorites and micro-meteorites (interstellar dust) in space will also be of interest to the designers of manned research vehicles. **1967** *Technology Week* 23 Jan. 47/1 Unlike a terrestrial observatory, it will have to have airtight quarters, well-protected against radical temperature change, hard radiation and micrometeorite bombardment. **1971** I. G. GASS et al. *Understanding Earth* viii. 115/1 Many granules are so small that they do not offer sufficient air resistance to become incandescent; they sink to the ground as micrometeorites. **1973** *McGraw-Hill Yearbk. Sci. & Technol.* 277/2 Bodies less than about 0·1 mm can also be expected to survive, since their size permits them to radiate the tremendous heat energy due to friction with the atmosphere before it can cause vaporization. These smaller bodies are usually called micrometeorites, or while still in space, micrometeoroids.

Hence **micromete'oritic** *a.*

1960 H. E. NEWELL in J. A. Ratcliffe *Physics Upper Atmosphere* iii. 123 Micrometeoritic material may account for a small portion of the E-region ionization. **1974** *Nature* 20/27 Dec. 669/2 Micrometeoritic craters.

micrometeoroid (maɪkrəʊ'miːtɪərɔɪd). [f. MICRO- 1 + METEOROID *sb.*] A solid particle in space, or of extraterrestrial origin, which is small enough to survive entry into the earth's atmosphere. Cf. prec.

1954 *Mineral. Abstr.* XII. 242 There may be 'micrometeorites' (? micrometeoroids..) too small to suffer ablation and falling as cosmic dust. **1961** *Daily Tel.* 26 Aug. 1/4 Another earth satellite, Explorer 13, was put into orbit to-day. It will measure dust-like particles in space known as micrometeoroids. **1968** *Awake!* 22 Sept. 30/2 The suit will be made to protect the astronaut..from tiny particles known as micrometeoroids. **1973** [see prec.]. **1974** *Nature* 6 Sept. 17/1 It sent back more than 300 pictures of Jupiter, as well as measurements of magnetic fields, energetic particles, ..and micrometeoroids.

Hence **micromete'oroidal** *a.*

1972 *Science* 2 June 979/2 The scale of hypervelocity impact craters..on the moon extends down to submillimeter and submicron micrometeoroidal pits on rock surfaces.

micrometeorology (,maɪkrəʊmiːtɪə'rɒlədʒɪ). [f. MICRO- 2 a + METEOROLOGY.] The study of the meteorological characteristics of a small area; the study of small-scale meteorological phenomena.

1930 *Flight* 18 Apr. 442 The progress of European meteorology in the past fifteen years..is due to the introduction of micrometeorology, or detailed observations from an ever-increasing number of weather stations. **1953** O. G. SUTTON (*title*) Micrometeorology: a study of physical processes in the lowest layers of the earth's atmosphere. **1968** *New Scientist* 5 Dec. 565/1 By incorporating fluctuations of temperature and humidity, one can arrive at similar expressions for the transport of heat and water vapour. The determination of these three vertical transports is one of the central problems in micrometeorology. **1974** *Physics Bull.* Feb. 66/2 The heat balance of plants and animals and the micrometeorology of crops.

Hence **,micrometeoro'logical** *a.*, **-meteo-'rologist.**

1942 *Univ. Chicago Inst. Meteorol. Misc. Rep.* No. 3. 1 The study of the exact nature of these more or less localized thunderstorms suggests the use of a micrometeorological network of stations. Such a network exists over the Muskingum Watershed in..Ohio where the United States Soil Conservation Service..has maintained a dense observational network. The stations are no more than 8 miles apart. **1953** O. G. SUTTON *Micrometeorol.* p. vii, I have attempted to meet the needs of meteorologists..who require detailed information about physical processes in the

regions of the atmosphere where life is most abundant. It is my hope that such an account will help to increase the number of micrometeorologists. **1960** *Times* 30 Aug. 2/2 The work will involve physical and micrometeorological problems of measurement. **1968** *New Scientist* 5 Dec. 564/2 While the micrometeorologist's most productive tools are certain statistical concepts of fluid mechanics and aerodynamics, much experimental work needs to be done before these concepts can be applied to the atmosphere.

micrometer (maɪˈkrɒmɪtə(r)). [ad. F. *micromètre* (Azout 1667), f. Gr. μῑκρό-ς small + μέτρον measure: see -METER.] An instrument for measuring minute objects or differences of dimension.

1. An astronomical instrument applied to telescopes for the purpose of measuring very small angular distances.

Of this instrument, which was first invented by W. Gascoigne about 1640, there are several forms, as the ***annular*** or ***circular, dioptric*** (***catadioptric***) or ***double-image, double-refraction, duplex, filar, prism, ring, wire micrometer***.

1670 FLAMSTEED in Hone *Every-day Bk.* I. 1092, I..had Mr. Townly's Micrometer presented to me by Sir Jonas Moor. **1759** *Gentl. Mag.* 72 The method of using Mr. Dollond's new catadioptric Micrometer. **1836** *Penny Cycl.* V. 228/2 The double-refraction micrometer. **1853** HERSCHEL *Pop. Lect. Sci.* v. §17 (1873) 193 What astronomers call a 'ring micrometer'. **1866** BRANDE & COX *Dict. Sci.*, etc. II. 517/2 The prism micrometer..has this important defect [etc.]. **1883** *Encycl. Brit.* XVI. 248/1 Grubb's duplex micrometer. *Ibid.* 249/2 Double-Image Micrometers with Divided Lenses... Ramsden's dioptric micrometer.

2. An instrument applied to the microscope for the purpose of measuring small objects.

c **1790** IMISON *Sch. Art* I. 240 The new micrometer is nothing more than a stage (on which the objects are placed) moveable by a fine screw which has a hand..passing over the divisions of a graduated circle. **1855** tr. *Wedl's Rudim. Pathol. Histol.* I. i. (Syd. Soc.) 10 The glass micrometer..has supplanted the..screw micrometer. **1866** BRANDE & COX *Dict. Sci.*, etc. II. 518/1 The instruments in use among microscopists are Jackson's micrometer and the cobweb micrometer. **1877** DARWIN *Forms of Fl.* i. 16, I measured with the micrometer many specimens, both dry and wet.

3. An instrument used in machine-construction, watchmaking, etc., for obtaining an extreme degree of accuracy in measurement.

1884 F. J. BRITTEN *Watch & Clockm.* 76 The new one [a plug] may be gauged with a Micrometer or Registering Callipers.

4. *attrib.* and *Comb.*, as ***micrometer cell, eye-piece, measurement, pointer, scale, slide, square, wheel, wire***; **micrometer balance**, a balance for ascertaining minute weights with exactitude, esp. used for weighing coins; **micrometer gauge**, a gauge fitted with a micrometer, used in machine-making; **micrometer-microscope**, an apparatus for reading and subdividing the divisions of large astronomical and geodetical instruments; **micrometer screw**, a screw attached to optical and other instruments for the exact measurement of very small angles.

1875 KNIGHT *Dict. Mech.* 1431/2 Kenshaw's *micrometer-balance, invented about 1842, consists of a beam or steel-yard supported on a knife-edged fulcrum. **1898** *Allbutt's Syst. Med.* V. 443 The lines which form the divisions of the *micrometer cell may be made more distinct [etc.]. **1835** URE *Philos. Manuf.* 126 For very nice measurements Troughton's *micrometer eye-piece..may be attached to the instrument. **1902** MARSHALL *Metal Tools* 10 Another very useful type of gauge for making fine measurements is the *micrometer gauge. **1835** URE *Philos. Manuf.* 96 *Micrometer measurements taken from the spectral image..are apt to lead to great fallacies. **1849** R. V. DIXON *Heat* I. 25 The microscope E' was hence called the *micrometer microscope. **1883** *Encycl. Brit.* XVI. 249/2 A dull phosphorescence sufficient to make the *micrometer pointer..faintly visible. **1854** *Pereira's Pol. Light* 45 A very minutely grooved surface..presents an iridescent appearance in white light... *Micrometer scales frequently present the same appearances. **1788** *Trans. Soc. Arts* VI. 190 Moved by the *micrometer screw. **1883** *Encycl. Brit.* XVI. 244/1 The oblong frame, containing the *micrometer slides. **1898** *Allbutt's Syst. Med.* V. 441 The corpuscles..are reckoned by means of a series of *micrometer squares ruled over a certain area of the glass floor of the chamber or cell. **1862** *Catal. Internat. Exhib.* II. xi. 23 The tangent back sight is elevated by a rack and pinion, the latter having a *micrometer wheel for finer readings. **1806** J. A. HAMILTON in *Trans. Roy. Irish Acad.* 111 In adjusting the telescope and *micrometer wires.

micrometer, var. MICROMETRE.

micromethod: see MICRO- 6.

micrometre (ˈmaɪkrəʊmiːtə(r)). Also (*U.S.*) **-meter**. [f. MICRO- 5 a + METRE *sb.*²] A millionth of a metre: = MICRON.

The word has only recently become common (cf. quot. 1968), and now forms part of the International System of Units.

1880 *Jrnl. R. Microsc. Soc.* III. 327 The same reasoning..leads us, however, to recommend the adoption of 'micrometre' instead of 'micromillimetre', which would secure the uniformity desired, besides being a more convenient word. **1966** KAYE & LABY *Tables Physical & Chem. Constants* (ed. 13) 2, μ is widely employed as an abbreviation of μm (10^{-6} m or micrometre) and is then called micron. **1968** *Nature* 16 Nov. 651/2 By resolution No. 7 the conference [*sc.* the thirteenth General Conference of Weights and Measures] decided to proscribe further use of the name 'micron', with the symbol μ attributed to this name, for the millionth part of the metre. The symbol μ is now the recognized prefix for the decimal sub-multiple 10^{-6} and the appropriate name for the millionth part of the metre is 'micrometre', with symbol μm. **1971** I. G. GASS et al. *Understanding Earth* xiv. 336/1 (*caption*) The amplitude..used for determining the magnitude is half the displacement between the two arrows—in this case 5 micrometres. **1973** *Physics Bull.* Nov. 662/3 They contain solid particles..with dimensions of about a tenth of a micrometre, a mass of 10^{-15} g each. **1974** *Sci. Amer.* July 45 (Advt.), Neutron radiography can resolve a few micrometers.

micrometric (maɪkrəʊˈmɛtrɪk), *a.* [f. MICROMETER + -IC. Cf. F. *micrométrique.*] = next.

1835 URE *Philos. Manuf.* 126 A microscope, provided with a micrometric glass plate. **1837** *Athenæum* 28 Jan. 64/2 Diameter of Penumbra by micrometric measure = 58″. 4. **1883** *Encycl. Brit.* XVI. 243/2 Sir William Herschel's discovery..gave an impulse to micrometric research.

transf. **1880** T. W. WEBB in *Nature* XXI. 213/2 The Italian professor..inconvenienced by colour-blindness, but of micrometric vision,..has plotted a sharply-outlined chart.

micrometrical (maɪkrəʊˈmɛtrɪkəl), *a.* [f. prec. + -AL¹.] Pertaining to or of the nature of a micrometer; carried on by or resulting from the use of the micrometer.

1712 DERHAM in *Phil. Trans.* XXVII. 523, *l.u.* The enlightned part of the Moon, being 1025 Micrometrical Parts, or 20′. **1829** HERSCHELL *Ess.* (1857) 537 The micrometrical measurements of double stars. **1837** GORING & PRITCHARD *Microgr.* 48 The divisions of the scale of micrometrical eye-pieces. **1882** *Athenæum* No. 2833. 194 A third catalogue of micrometrical measures of double stars made at..Rugby,..is contained in the volume..before us.

Hence **micro'metrically** *adv.*, by means of a micrometer.

1834 MRS. SOMERVILLE *Connex. Phys. Sci.* (1849) 419 Whose motions have been micrometrically measured. **1876** G. F. CHAMBERS *Astron.* 11 This was micrometrically established in a lateral direction by Challis in 1857.

micrometry (maɪˈkrɒmɪtrɪ). [f. Gr. μῑκρό-ς small + -μετρία measuring (see -METRY) after MICROMETER.] The measurement of minute objects; the use of the micrometer.

1853 C. JOHNSON in *Bot. & Physiol. Mem.* (Ray Soc. 1854) 416 Mohl has discussed the methods of micrometry in a profound manner. **1862** *Q. Jrnl. Microsc. Sci.* II. 306 Micrometry. A good deal was written some time ago about the best form of micrometer.

micromho, -microcurie, -microfarad, -millimetre, -mineralogy, -mini: see MICRO- 5 a, 5 a, 5 a, 5 b, 2 a, 1 c.

microminiature (maɪkrəʊˈmɪnɪtjʊə(r), -ˈmɪnɪətjʊə(r)), *a.* [f. MICRO- 1 b + MINIATURE *a.*] Much reduced in size, as a result of microminiaturization; even smaller than a size regarded as miniature.

1958 *Electr. Manufacturing* Aug. 94/1 Intensive efforts at the Diamond Ordnance Fuze Laboratories..in the field of microminiature packaging have recently resulted in extremely small and compact assemblies. **1963** *Listener* 16 May 832/3 Microminiature integrator, for rocket guidance system. The integrator..is 100 times smaller than the conventionally built equipment it replaces. **1967** *Electronics* 6 Mar. 37 (Advt.), These microminiature relays are direct descendants of our military, aero/space designs. **1971** J. H. SMITH *Digital Logic* i. 5 Thin film circuits are often associated with microminiature components.

,microminiaturi'zation. Also with hyphen. [f. MICRO- 1 b + MINIATURIZATION.] Extreme miniaturization; *spec.* the development or use of techniques for making electronic components and devices of greatly reduced size (smaller than those produced by 'miniaturization').

1955 *Proc. IRE* XLIII. 1897/2 The most attractive features [of opto-electronic devices] seem to be the possible microminiaturization (which, in the present state of the art, is the ultimate in miniaturization) resulting in small weight and extremely low power consumption, [etc.]. **1959** *Listener* 28 May 930/2 The most startling recent development [in transistors] is the technology of what is called micro-miniaturization. **1963** *Daily Tel.* 22 May 21 A stage of 'micro-miniaturisation' has been reached which makes many of the marvel-working components almost invisible. **1965** *Times Rev. Industry* Winter 12/1 Micro-miniaturization is now accepted as starting at a packing density exceeding 50 parts per cubic inch. **1971** *Nature* 10 Dec. 315/3 The new on-board computer and guidance system makes great use of micro-miniaturization. **1973** *Sci. Amer.* Dec. 24/2 Its nervous system is a miracle of microminiaturization, and some of its independently evolved behavior patterns are not unlike our own.

So **micro'miniaturize** *v. trans.*, to produce in a very much smaller version; **micro-'miniaturized** *ppl. a.*

1959 J. E. SENSI in Horsey & Shergalis *Proc. Symposium Microminiaturization of Electronic Assemblies* I. v. 54 To realize fully the military and civilian potential of microminiaturized devices, optimum means of producing these devices in large quantities are necessary. **1959** *Electronics* 11 Dec. 51/2 Much of the knowledge gained in designing electronic circuits can be used directly, with only minor changes, in microminiaturizing circuits. **1963** *Listener* 16 May 832/3 Already..the sort of computer that only yesterday took up a whole room can be 'microminiaturized' so that it will go into a small suitcase. **1967** *N.Y. Times* 20 May 49 The transistorized lock..could be microminiaturized and adapted to any number of combinations. **1972** *Lebende Sprachen* XVII. 133/1 Plessey has evolved a small microminiaturized computer.

micromodule: see MICRO- 1.

micromorph (ˈmaɪkrəʊmɔːf). *Zool.* [f. Gr. μῑκρο-ς small + μορφή form.] A specimen smaller than is normal in the species.

1888 HUDLESTON *Gasterop.* (Palæont. Soc.) 112 Micromorphs..occur..in many parts of the Inferior Oolite.

micromotion (ˈmaɪkrəʊməʊʃən). Also with hyphen. [f. MICRO- 1 + MOTION *sb.*] A small bodily movement made during the performance of some task, esp. when recorded cinematographically for purposes of work study. Usu. *attrib.*, esp. designating this method of work study.

1913 F. A. TALBOT *Pract. Cinematogr.* xiv. 174 (*heading*) Micro-motion study: How increased workshop efficiency is obtainable with moving pictures. **1913** *Technical World* XIX. 189/1 'This micro-motion study furnishes a means for the transference of skill from man to machine,' the general manager further stated. **1947** J. J. GILLESPIE *Dynamic Motion & Time Study* 3 Motion study..with its motion cameras, therbligs, micromotion clocks..has become a complex, unwieldy technique. **1948** *Sci. News* VII. 107 For the so-called 'micro-motion study' of repetition movements a cine-record is not necessary. Instead, small lamps can be attached to the moving parts of the operator's body, their light being recorded over one cycle of the operation by working in a dimly lit room while the camera shutter is left open. **1961** [see MEMOMOTION].

micromutation: see MICRO- 1.

micron (ˈmaɪkrɒn). Also †**mikron**. [ad. Gr. μῑκρόν, neut. of μῑκρός small.] The one-millionth part of a metre; denoted by the symbol μ.

In the International System of Units the word has been replaced by MICROMETRE.

[**1880** *Procès-Verbaux des Séances du Comité Internat. des Poids et Mesures 1879* 41 Le Comité international des Poids et Mesures adopte, pour ses publications et son usage officiel, le système suivant des signes abréviatifs pour les poids et mesures métriques... (*table*) Mesures de longueur. ..Micron... μ.] **1885** *Jrnl. R. Microsc. Soc.* V. 140 Proposal ..(2) to use *micron* in place of *micromillimetre*. **1892** BARKER *Physics* 15 Divided into..thousandths of a millimeter; i.e. into microns. **1898** LD. KELVIN in *Rep. Brit. Assoc.* 783 Measured wave-lengths as great as 15 mikrons in radiant heat. **1905** *Brit. Med. Jrnl.* 25 Feb. 404 The lymphocytes showed all variations in size, from the smallest to some which were 15 microns in diameter. **1966** *Electronics* 14 Nov. 25 The detector..is believed to be the first photovoltaic detector of infrared radiation in the 8- to 14-micron range. **1968** [see MICROMETRE].

microneedle: see MICRO- 6.

Micronesian (maɪkrəʊˈniːʃ(ɪ)ən), *a.* and *sb.* Also (*rare*) **Mikronesian**. [f. *Micronesia* (see below: f. Gr. μῑκρό-ς small + νῆσ-ος island) + -AN.

The name, modelled after *Polynesia*, was intended to mean 'the region of small islands'.]

A. *adj.* Of or pertaining to Micronesia (a group of small islands in the western region of the North Pacific, including the Caroline, Ladrone, Marshall and Gilbert Islands, etc.), its inhabitants, language, etc.

1847 J. C. PRICHARD *Res. Physical Hist. Mankind* (ed. 3) V. 157 Micronesia, or the Micronesian Archipelago. **1877** *Jrnl. Anthrop. Inst.* VI. 392 The language of Yap..is the only Micronesian language in which the numerals are formed in the manner in question. **1884** W. TURNER *Rep. Crania* in *Rep. Sci. Results Voy. H.M.S. Challenger* X. 82 The islands of the Mikronesian group. **1945** *Language* XXI. 214 In the vocabularies of the Micronesian languages..evidence of earlier use of English has remained in the form of loan-words. **1974** *Times* 21 Jan. 12/6 Some Micronesian families connected by marriage with Japanese see themselves in a strong compradore position.

B. *sb.* **a.** A native of Micronesia. **b.** The language of the Micronesians.

1847 J. C. PRICHARD *Res. Physical Hist. Mankind* (ed. 3) V. 157 A certain difference has been noted between the Micronesians and the Polynesians in general. **1890** D. G. BRINTON *Races & Peoples* 235 Some ethnographers would make the Polynesians and Micronesians a different race from the Malays. **1896** CODRINGTON *Dict. Mota* Pref. 6 The Micronesian Group [of languages] takes in the Caroline Islands, Pellew, Marshall, and Gilbert Islands. **1899** CHRISTIAN in *Jrnl. Anthrop. Inst.* XXVIII. 288 On Micronesian Weapons, Dress, Implements, etc. **1899** ELLA *Ibid.* XXIX. 159 Melanesian and Micronesian tongues are to some extent inflexional. **1900** *Edin. Rev.* Apr. 490 The Micronesians will be the happier for this transfer. **1974** *Times* 21 Jan. 12/8 The High Commissioner..expects that a Micronesian will succeed him.

micronize (ˈmaɪkrənaɪz), *v.* [f. MICRON + -IZE, or perh. a back-formation from *Micronizer* (proprietary name in U.S.).] *trans.* To break up into very fine particles. So **'micronized** *ppl. a.*, **'micronizing** *vbl. sb.* Also **microni'zation**.

1940 *Jrnl. Econ. Ent.* XXXIII. 481/1 Good kill obtained with micronized cubé indicates that fine grinding may increase the toxicity. **1941** *Ibid.* XXXIV. 560/2 Micronization (fine grinding) of derris and cubé⁴ increased kill over that obtained by the regular product. [*Note*] ⁴Prepared by the Micronizing Processing Co., Moorstown N.J. **1952** M. E. FLOREY *Chem. Applic. Antibiotics* I. iii. 111 A ball mill for the production of a very finely divided ('micronized') mixture of potassium penicillin and glucose.

1958 *Vogue* July 5 This creamy-smooth makeup contains micronised powder, 2½ times finer than ordinary face powder. **1968** W. A. GRAY *Packing of Solid Particles* vii. 105 If, however, the particles are reduced in size to a few microns (micronized) and suitable pressure is applied, then a strong compact can be formed. **1968** *Materials & Technol.* I. viii. 263 Micronizing is used not only on sulphur but also for insecticides, fungicides, pharmaceutical preparations, grinding and polishing powders, iron oxide, etc. **1972** *Jrnl. Econ. Entomol.* LXV. 1446/1 Colorimetric analysis indicated that some decomposition took place during preparation and micronization of the dust.

micronucleus (maɪkrəʊˈnjuːklɪəs). *Zool.* Pl. -nuclei. [f. MICRO- + NUCLEUS.] The smaller of the two nuclei of a protozoon. Hence **micro'nuclear** *a.*, of or pertaining to a micronucleus.

1892 [see MACRO-NUCLEUS]. **1901** G. N. CALKINS *Protozoa* 194 The micronuclei play the most important part in conjugation. *Ibid.*, The new macronucleus is formed by the enlargement of a daughter-micronucleus. **1905** *Brit. Med. Jrnl.* 25 Feb. 441 A special ingrowth of micronuclear cells.. gave rise to the mesamœboid (mesoblastic) cells.

micronutrient (ˌmaɪkrəʊˈnjuːtrɪənt). *Biol.* [f. MICRO- + NUTRIENT *sb.*] Any of the chemical elements which are required by plants (or, less commonly, animals) in trace amounts for normal growth and development.

1943 *Ann. Rev. Biochem.* XII. 525 List of essential micronutrients.—The essentiality of boron, manganese, and zinc for higher plants is no longer open to dispute. **1953** J. RAMSBOTTOM *Mushrooms & Toadstools* viii. 80 Manganese, zinc, boron, copper, molybdenum, have been proved definitely to be micro-nutrients for certain fungi. **1970** [see MACRONUTRIENT]. **1974** *Nature* 8 Feb. 392/1 Since 1957, selenium has been recognized as an essential micronutrient for animals.

mi'cronymy. *nonce-wd.* [f. Gr. + μῑκρό-ς small + ὄνυμα name, ὄνομα, after *synonymy*, etc.] The use of short words in scientific nomenclature.

1889 *Buck's Handbk. Med. Sci.* VIII. 529/1 Astronomers have set an example in micronymy that anatomists might well follow.

micro-opaque (ˌmaɪkrəʊəʊˈpeɪk). [f. MICRO- 7 + OPAQUE *a.* (*sb.*)] A type of microform produced on card or paper instead of film. Also *attrib.* or as *adj.*

1952 *Aslib Proc.* IV. 154 Micro-opaques have made far greater psychological appeal to the user than microfilm. **1956** *Amer. Documentation* VII. 169/1 Writers in several countries have concerned themselves with the general theme of micro-opaques. **1962** A. GÜNTHER *Microphotogr. in Library* (Unesco) 7 Micro-opaque cards have another advantage in that they do not need a protective envelope and may be readily filed. **1963** *Amer. N. & Q.* June 155/1 Original public records are being published in a micro-opaque series of 3 × 5-inch cards issued by the Public Record Office of Great Britain.

micro-operation, -operative, -order: see MICRO- 1, 2a, 1.

micro-organic (ˌmaɪkrəʊɔːˈgænɪk), *a.* [f. MICRO- + ORGANIC.] Pertaining to or connected with micro-organisms.

1884 J. TAIT *Mind in Matter* (1892) 317 The micro-organic world is found to be silent as the grave on evolution.

micro-organism (ˌmaɪkrəʊˈɔːgənɪz(ə)m). *Biol.* [f. MICRO- + ORGANISM.] A microscopic animal or plant; a microbe. Hence **micro-orga'nismal** *a.*, of or induced by micro-organisms.

1880 MACCORMAC *Antisept. Surg.* 105 The presence of micro-organisms in the atmosphere..is certain. **1898** *Allbutt's Syst. Med.* V. 564 A manifestation of a micro-organismal disease.

micro-oven (ˈmaɪkrəʊˌʌv(ə)n). [f. MICRO(WAVE + OVEN *sb.*] A microwave oven. Hence **micro-'ovening** *vbl. sb.*, cooking in such an oven.

1962 *Punch* 21 Nov. 738/2 A cooked meal that is quick-frozen and then re-heated in a matter of seconds in a micro-oven. **1965** *Economist* 22 May 941/3 Two micro-ovens could do the same work in half the time, using less space. **1971** *Daily Tel.* 26 July 15/2 Thus their formula for the Big Chance: clean up some traditional greasy cafes, manufacture centrally some basic dishes for instant micro-ovening and bounce into branded home cooking.

micropædia (maɪkrəʊˈpiːdɪə). [f. MICRO- + Gr. παιδεία learning.] A section of the 15th edition of *Encyclopædia Britannica* (published in 1974) in which information is presented in a condensed form. (Cf. MACROPÆDIA, PROPÆDIA.) Hence **micro'pædic** *a.*

1974 *Daily Tel.* 12 Jan. 3/5 Consisting of 30 volumes, it will consist of what are described as a propaedia, a micropaedia and a macropaedia. **1974** *Times Lit. Suppl.* 11 Oct. 1120/4 About 180 writers are given biographies proper, the rest have to make do with a Micropaedic note.

micropalæontology (etc.), **-pantograph, -parasite, -particle, -pathology:** see MICRO- 2a, 6, 1, 1, 2.

micropegmatite (maɪkrəʊˈpɛgmətaɪt). *Min.* [f. MICRO- + PEGMATITE.] (See quot. 1888.) Hence **micropegma'titic** *a.*, having the structure of micropegmatite or of graphic granite.

1885 GEIKIE *Text-bk. Geol.* (ed. 2) 110 The structure is.. micropegmatitic where the help of a microscope is needed. **1888** TEALL *Brit. Petrogr.* 30 Graphic granite and..its microscopic equivalent, generally termed micro-pegmatite. **1896** *Nat. Sci.* Aug. 86 The garnet often streams out.. forming micropegmatitic intergrowths with other materials.

microperthite (maɪkrəʊˈpɜːθaɪt). *Min.* [f. MICRO- + PERTHITE.] (See quot. 1885.) Hence **microper'thitic** *a.*, pertaining to or resembling microperthite.

1885 GEIKIE *Text-bk. Geol.* (ed. 2) 132 *note*, F. Becke.. described this structure and names it *microperthite. Ibid.* 133 The felspar..presents the peculiar fibrous structure referred to in the foregoing description of gneiss (microperthite, microcline). **1888** TEALL *Brit. Petrogr.* 31 The microscopic equivalent of perthite termed microperthite by F. Becke. **1888** *Nature* 15 Mar. 459/2 Judging from the frequent occurrence of striated and microperthitic felspars.

micropetalous, -petrology: see MICRO- 4, 2.

microphage (ˈmaɪkrəʊfeɪdʒ). *Phys.* Also **microphag.** [ad. G. *mikrophag* (Metchnikoff), f. Gr. μῑκρό-ς small + *phag* short for PHAGOCYTE *sb.*] A certain form of the white blood-corpuscles (see quot. 1903). Also *attrib.*

1890 [see MACROPHAGE]. **1893** STARLING tr. *Metchnikoff's Comp. Pathol.* 191 In..acute inflammations it is mainly the microphages, or neutrophile polynuclear leucocytes, that are involved. **1896** *Allbutt's Syst. Med.* I. 953 The microphage cells in the spleen. **1903** COATS *Man. Path.* (ed. 5) 148 Polymorphonuclear leucocytes are called Microphags, and the cells derived from the fixed cells of the tissues, which are larger, and have large oval nuclei, are macrophags.

microphagist (maɪˈkrɒfədʒɪst). [f. Gr. μῑκρό-ς small + φαγ-, φαγεῖν to eat + -IST.] An eater of microscopic organisms.

1853 W. SMITH *Brit. Diatom.* I. p. xxxiii, Several species [of diatoms]..have been supplied in abundance by a careful dissection of the above microphagists.

microphagocyte (ˌmaɪkrəʊˈfægəsaɪt). *Phys.* [f. MICRO- + PHAGOCYTE *sb.*] = MICROPHAGE.

1896 *Allbutt's Syst. Med.* I. 79 Classifications of the varieties of leucocytes... Microphagocyte.

microphagous, -phenocryst: see MICRO- 4, 1.

†**microphily.** *Obs. rare*$^{-1}$. In 7 -philie. [Badly f. Gr. μῑκρό-ς small + φιλία friendship.] The friendship of a 'small' man with a great.

1608 D. T[UVIL] *Ess. Pol. & Mor.* 95 b, So likewise, where there is a disproportion eyther in meanes, or mindes, there can bee no other friendship, then that Microphilie, which Plato had with Dionysius the Tyrant.

microphone (ˈmaɪkrəʊfəʊn). [f. Gr. μῑκρό-ς small + φωνή sound.]

1. An instrument by which small sounds can be intensified.

1683 *Phil. Trans.* XIV. 482 Microphones or Micracousticks that is Magnifying ear instruments. **1727** in BAILEY vol. II. **1827** C. WHEATSTONE in *Q. Jrnl. Sci.* II. 69 An instrument which, from its rendering audible the weakest sounds, may with propriety be called the Microphone. **1842** BRANDE *Dict. Sci.*, etc., *Microphone*, an instrument for increasing the intensity of low sounds.

2. *spec.* An instrument (invented almost simultaneously in 1878 by Prof. Hughes and Dr. Lüdtge) by means of which the telephone is made to reproduce faint sounds with more than their original intensity. Now applied to any instrument designed to convert sound waves impinging upon it into corresponding variations in voltage or current, which may then be amplified or transmitted for reconversion into sound (as in broadcasting and the telephone) or recorded; *esp.* one made as an independent unit (colloq. abbrev. MIKE *sb.*^{5}).

This function is that of all telephone 'transmitters'. Hughes's instrument was simply a particularly sensitive one by the standards then current (hence the name: see quot. 1889), and modifications of it were for a time almost universally used as telephone transmitters, so that *microphone* became synonymous with *transmitter* and acquired its present more general meaning.

1878 HUGHES in *Proc. Roy. Soc.* XXVII. 365, I have also devised an instrument suitable for magnifying weak sounds, which I call a *microphone.* The microphone, in its present form, consists simply of a lozenge-shaped piece of gas carbon, one inch long [etc.]. **1889** PREECE & MAIER *Telephone* iv. 37 Hughes' Microphone... The microphone is nothing but a telephonic transmitter, but it owes its name ..to its power to convert vibrations of feeble intensity into undulatory currents, which, passing through a receiving telephone, produce sonorous vibrations of much greater intensity than those of the original source. **1891** F. C. ALLSOP *Telephones* ii. 20 Prof. Hughes's microphone.. forms the basis on which all the modern carbon transmitters are constructed. **1923** W. S. CHURCHILL *World Crisis 1915* 291 Already the microphone or hydrophone for detecting the beat of a submarine propeller in the distance had been discovered. **1923** E. W. MARCHANT *Radio Telegr.* vi. 76 Suppose..that the emission of waves from the transmitting aerial is controlled by means of a microphone, such as is employed in the ordinary telephone transmitter, the stream of waves given out by the antenna will be varied in accordance with the fluctuations in the current passing through the microphone. **1929** *Morning Post* 24 May 12/7 The engineer..in film-direction..has the last word as to whether the actor is speaking the line effectively for the microphone. **1935** H. C. BRYSON *Gramophone Record* iii. 59 Three main kinds of microphone are in common use: the carbon microphone, the condenser microphone, and the moving coil microphone. **1962** A. NISBETT *Technique Sound Studio* ii. 42 As an example of the sort of set-up which can be adopted in this type of studio is one where no less than six microphones were used for a quarter-hour playlet. **1970** M. L. GAYFORD in T. L. Squires *Telecommunications Pocket Bk.* iv. 36 The standard modern telephone sets now in production in most countries represent a considerable improvement over earlier sets... Improved designs of microphone and receiver give a generally better frequency response and transient response.

3. Special Comb.: **microphone boom**, a boom (BOOM *sb.*^{2} 1 d) with a microphone at the end.

1931 L. COWAN *Recording Sound for Motion Pict.* 377 *Microphone boom*, crane-like device for supporting and manipulating microphone. **1954** *Time* 12 July 47/3 Joan Diener, instead of being forced to stand near a microphone boom in order to be heard, was able to move at will in a TV studio by means of a tiny concealed microphone transmitter.

microphoned (ˈmaɪkrəfəʊnd), *a.* [f. MICROPHONE + -ED^2.] **1.** Picked up and transmitted by a microphone.

1927 *Daily Express* 21 Sept. 11/5, I heard in Archie de Bear's room at the Vaudeville..a loud speaker carrying from the stage what was only a microphoned reproduction of a gramophone record made by the Revellers.

2. Containing or furnished with a microphone.

1933 *News Chron.* 13 June 1 At one end is a high microphoned platform for the President. **1934** *Punch* 11 Apr. 416/1 Put a commentator in a microphoned observation-car on each long-distance train. **1960** *Guardian* 20 July 5/7, I lived in a room in Moscow University which everyone..said was microphoned.

microphoneme (ˌmaɪkrəʊˈfəʊniːm). *Linguistics.* [f. MICRO- 1 + PHONEME.] (See quot. 1935.) Hence **micropho'nemic** *a.*

1935 W. F. TWADDELL in *Lang. Monogr.* XVI. v. 39 A term of an ordered class of minimum phonological differences among forms is a microphoneme. **1936** *Language* XII. 56 If one restricted one's attention to the series *kill*: *till*: *pill*: *hill*, one could arrive at alternative microphonemic classes. **1953** *Trans. Philol. Soc.* 84 All that we have..are.. certain microphonemes and greater or lesser sets of microphonemes.

microphonic (maɪkrəʊˈfɒnɪk), *a.* and *sb.* [f. MICROPHON(E + -IC.]

A. *adj.* **1.** Pertaining to the microphone.

1878 *Jrnl. Franklin Inst.* CVI. 270 Microphonic Anticipations. **1879** *N. Eng. Hist. & Gen. Reg.* XXXIII. 158 Look at the amazing progress in telegraphic, microscopic, telephonic and microphonic arts! **1881** *Athenæum* 2 July 19/1 Dr. Moser read a paper 'On the Microphonic Action of Selenium Cells'. **1893** PREECE & STUBBS *Man. Telephony* 121 The adoption of the microphonic transmitter in any case necessitates the employment of a battery.

2. a. Characterized by or pertaining to the production of variations in electrical potential in response to sound waves or vibrations.

1879 *Telegraphic Jrnl.* VII. 132/1 The communication of the current with the vibrating plate..is effected by means of two small springs which are lightly pressed by the membrane..which act as a weak microphonic contact. **1919** R. STANLEY *Text-bk. Wireless Telegr.* (new ed.) II. vi. 116 With some valve designs there is a microphonic effect in L.F. amplifiers so that the slightest jar given to the apparatus, such as tapping it with the finger or even walking near it, is strongly magnified. **1931** *Jrnl. Physiol.* LXXI. p. xxix, I conclude that the effect is due to some kind of microphonic action by which vibrations produce changes in the potential between different points in the inner ear. **1940** A. WOOD *Acoustics* xvii. 478 The microphonic response of the cochlea of a cat to a pure tone of 1000 cycles/sec. is amplified and analysed with a wave analyser. **1951** *Electronic Engin.* XXIII. 429/2 An attempt has been made..to determine the absolute microphonic performance of a valve by relating its electrical output to the frequency and intensity of a sound field in which it is situated. **1970** *Nature* 11 July 184/2 The microphonic response of the cochlea.

b. Of an electrical signal: generated in response to sound waves or vibrations.

1929 *Proc. IRE* XVII. 1621 Microphonic output is caused by relative motions between the various elements of the tube. **1930** ZWORYKIN & WILSON *Photocells* ix. 114 Mechanical vibration of the elements produce what are generally called microphonic noises. **1947** *Jrnl. Appl. Physics* XVIII. 242/2 A simple experiment was set up to check Eq. (7) by mechanically driving a tube and measuring the resulting 'microphonic' output signal.

B. *sb.* **1.** *pl.* The science of magnifying sounds. *rare.*

1846 BUCHANAN *Technol. Dict.*, *Microphonics*, the science of magnifying small sounds.

2. a. A microphonic signal generated in the cochlea.

1938 STEVENS & DAVIS *Hearing* xii. 319 When the voltage of the cochlear microphonic is plotted against the logarithm of the sound-intensity..the function appears as a sigmoid curve. **1962** *Laryngoscope* LXXII. 432 Is the reduction in amplitude of the cochlear microphonics due to an impairment of sound transmission or to a more direct effect on the organ of Corti? **1974** *Nature* 10 May 162/2 The 'poor' cochlear microphonic obtained from BALB/c mice after priming is indicative of hair cell damage.

b. *Electronics.* An undesired signal or modulation produced (e.g. in a valve) by mechanical vibration. Usu. *pl.*

1929 *Proc. IRE* XVII. 1622 The simplest test for microphonics consists of an audio-frequency amplifier of fairly high gain, the tube under test being used in the first stage. **1947** *Jrnl. Appl. Physics* XVIII. 245/2 It may well be advantageous to operate the input stage of a high gain automatic volume controlled amplifier with fixed bias to reduce microphonics. **1960** *IRE Trans. Microwave Theory & Techniques* VIII. 372/1 Waveguide under a high acoustical field can definitely contribute to microphonics via the mechanism of phase modulation. **1965** GEWARTOWSKI & WATSON *Princ. Electron Tubes* v. 152 Vibration of grid wires in grid-controlled tubes is a principal source of 'microphonics'.

microphonism (maɪˈkrɒfənɪz(ə)m). *Electronics.* [f. MICROPHON(E + -ISM.] = MICROPHONY 2.

1947 *Jrnl. Appl. Physics* XVIII. 239/1 This suggests a method of design..by which the microphonism of a tube may be reduced since..most of the microphonic difficulties encountered in tubes are caused by the mechanical movement of the grid. **1950** *Proc. IRE* XXXVIII. 529/1 The effects of microphonism are most usually encountered in high-gain amplifiers.

microphonograph (ˌmaɪkrəʊˈfəʊnəgrɑːf, -æ-). [f. MICRO- + PHONOGRAPH.] An instrument combining the principles of the microphone and the phonograph, designed for rendering sound audible to deaf-mutes.

1897 *Daily News* 26 Mar. 2/2 The microphonograph he [Professor Dussaud] has just issued to the world magnifies the human voice in the same way as a lens magnifies a picture. **1898** *Nature* 13 Jan. 255/2 It is suggested that the micro-phonograph may become an important factor in the education of deaf and dumb subjects.

microphonous (maɪˈkrɒfənəs), *a.*[1] *rare*$^{-0}$. [f. MICROPHONE + -OUS.] Having the property of augmenting weak sounds.

1855 DUNGLISON *Med. Lex.*

miˈcrophonous, *a.*[2] *rare*$^{-0}$. [f. Gr. μῑκρόφων-ος (see next) + -OUS.] 'Having a slender weak voice' (Mayne *Expos. Lex.* 1856).

microphony (maɪˈkrɒfənɪ). †**1.** [ad. Gr. μικροφωνία, f. μῑκρόφων-ος weak-voiced, f. μῑκρό-ς small + φωνή voice.] Weakness of voice. *Obs. rare*$^{-0}$.

1849 in CRAIG.

2. *Electronics.* [f. MICROPHON(E + -Y[3].] The generation of microphonics in electrical apparatus.

1934 F. J. CAMM *Everyman's Wireless Bk.* v. 91 (*table*) Microphony: This may result in ringing, booming, or other sounds. **1946** *Electronic Engin.* XVIII. 336/2 The ruggedness which is required to give long service will normally ensure freedom from microphony. **1951** *Ibid.* 431/2 The design of a valve with low microphony is a long and tedious process. **1963** *Mullard Technical Communications* VII. 227/1 Microphony is occasionally experienced in a tape recorder when high gain a.f. valves are used in the first stages.

microphoto (ˌmaɪkrəʊˈfəʊtəʊ), colloq. abbrev. of MICROPHOTOGRAPH 2.

1949 *Jrnl. Geol.* LVII. 370/1 The phenomenon of corrosion between crystals (Perrin and Roubault, 1939, p. 160, pl. 5, microphotos 7 and 8). **1972** K. MASTERS *Spray Drying* xiv. 518 Each microcapsule contains numerous minute droplets of perfume oil. A microphoto of an encapsulated fragrance is shown in an article by Barreto.

microphotogram (ˌmaɪkrəʊˈfəʊtəgræm). [f. MICRO- + PHOTOGRAM.] A microphotograph.

1898 P. MANSON *Trop. Diseases* i. 20 Microphotogram shewing the necessary disposition of blood-corpuscles in slides for examination for the plasmodium.

microphotograph (ˌmaɪkrəʊˈfəʊtəgrɑːf, -æ-). [f. MICRO- + PHOTOGRAPH *sb.*]

1. A photograph reduced to microscopic size; a microscopic photograph.

1858 [see PHOTOMICROGRAPH]. **1867** *Pop. Sci. Rev.* VI. 54 'Microphotograph' is a very long name, recently introduced, to denote a very small object; it refers to the minute photographic reductions of portraits or views so often shown as curiosities under the microscope. 'Photomicrograph', on the contrary, is a name given to the photographic enlargement of a microscopic object. **1878** *Jrnl. R. Microsc. Soc.* I. 300 Microphotograph.—Mr. Langenheim..has photographed the Lord's Prayer on the ten-thousandth of a square inch. **1940** A. HUXLEY *Let.* 14 Oct. (1969) 461, I would like to have..micro-photographs suitable for reading by means of a reading machine (all the big libraries make these micro-films now) of Part III of this book. **1957** *R.A.E. News* Nov. 8/2 The National Coal Board publicity office tried to excuse..an advertisement that described a picture, about four inches by six, as a 'microphotograph'. In the O.E.D. this word certainly denotes both a small photograph of a large-or-small object and a large-or-small photograph of a small object. However, the ambiguity proved such a nuisance that after international discussion between various bodies, the words 'microphotograph' and 'photomicrograph' respectively were agreed on. **1962** A. GÜNTHER *Microphotogr. in Library* (Unesco) 5 Microphotographs are photographs which are reduced to a minute or even microscopic size. **1966** M. R. D. FOOT *SOE in France* viii. 181 A microphotograph in the false bottom of a matchbox. **1969** *Proc. R. Microsc. Soc.* IV. 142 Sixth Report of the Nomenclature Committee. The Committee recommends the following names and definitions:... *Microphotograph.* A very small photograph, intended to be viewed with a microscope.

2. A photograph of a microscopic object on a magnified scale: = PHOTOMICROGRAPH.

1860 *Photogr. News* 13 Jan. 228/1 The production of good micro-photographs appears very much to depend on the employment of a suitable collodion. **1875** tr. *Vogel's Chem. Light* xiv. 208 The beauty of the micro-photograph depends essentially on the beauty of the preparation to be photographed. **1896** *Allbutt's Syst. Med.* I. 183 Microphotographs of two pyramidal cells from a case of general paralysis of the insane. **1927** HALDANE & HUXLEY *Animal Biol.* ii. 51 Fig. 18. Micro-photograph (× 150) of a section through the ovary of a mammal (cat). **1944** R. SOUTH *Caterpillars Brit. Butterflies* 5 Of the eggs and chrysalids, the former [illustrations] are from microphotographs by A. E. Tonge and drawings by Horace Knight. **1968** *Punch* 21 Aug. 271/3 There are blackboard diagrams, and micro-photographs of sperm and ova. **1974** *Nature* 22 Feb. 511/3 Species of pine and hardwood trees, grasses and cultivated plants, for example, are represented in the atlas of 136 microphotographs.

Hence **microphotoˈgraphic** *a.*, pertaining to or connected with microphotography. **microphotoˈgraphically** *adv.*, by means of microphotography.

1858 T. SUTTON *Dict. Photogr.* 296 Micro-photographic operations. **1865** *Brit. Jrnl. Photogr.* 24 Mar. 153/1 Description of the Micro-photographic Apparatus. **1882** R. NORRIS (*title*) Physiology and Pathology of the Blood... With mikro-photographic illustrations. **1895** *Daily News* 26 July 3/1 Insect anatomy, illustrated micro-photographically.

microphotography (ˌmaɪkrəʊfəˈtɒgrəfɪ). [f. MICRO- + PHOTOGRAPHY.]

1. The art or process of making photographs of very small size.

1858 T. SUTTON *Dict. Photogr.*, *Micro-Photography.* Under this head may be included two different processes. One..consists in copying objects on an exceedingly small scale, the photograph being intended to be viewed through a magnifier... The other..consists in producing enlarged photographs of minute objects—that is, in fixing the images obtained in the microscope. **1867** SUTTON & DAWSON *Dict. Photogr.*, *Micro-Photography.* This term is now used to designate the reduction of negatives to a very minute size, and serves to distinguish it from the process denominated 'Photo-micrography'. **1900** *Westm. Gaz.* 12 Sept. 8/2 A letter printed in microphotography is gummed to his [a bee's] little back, and he is thrown into the air.

2. The art or process of producing by photography an enlarged image of a microscopically minute object: = PHOTOMICROGRAPHY.

1858 [see 1]. **1875** tr. *Vogel's Chem. Light* xiv. 209 Excellent results have been achieved in microphotography by Neyt at Ghent. **1889** *Anthony's Photogr. Bull.* II. 104 Examples may also be given of balloon, stellar, and microphotography.

microphotometer (etc.), **microphthalmia, -phthalmos:** see MICRO- 6, 3.

microphylline (maɪkrəʊˈfɪlaɪn), *a. Bot.* [Formed as next: see -INE.] Composed of minute leaflets or scales.

1872 E. TUCKERMAN *Gen. Lichenum* 245 The foliaceous *Verrucariacei*..passing..into microphylline and..into finally almost crustaceous forms.

microphyllous: see MICRO- 4.

microphysics (ˈmaɪkrəʊfɪzɪks), *sb. pl.* (const. as *sing.*). Also **micro-physics.** [f. MICRO- 2a + PHYSICS.] The part of physics that is concerned with bodies and phenomena on a microscopic or smaller scale, esp. with molecules, atoms, and sub-atomic particles.

1885 *Athenæum* 11 Apr. 477/2 He had met with a success that gave him pre-eminence in this department of micro-physics, and that was the preparation of the diamond ruling points. **1956** E. H. HUTTEN *Lang. Mod. Physics* v. 175 These rules work well enough when we describe macro-physical phenomena; but their insufficiency is revealed in micro-physics. **1962** N. R. HANSON in *Quanta & Reality* v. 86 Von Neumann advanced a 'proof' that it would be impossible to reinstate a classical determinism in microphysics; it was logically pointless to look for 'hidden variables' underlying quantum processes. **1971** *Nature* 24 Dec. 433/2 Research in Britain concentrates on the fundamental microphysics of fogs.

Hence **microˈphysical** *a.*, of or pertaining to microphysics.

1902 [see *macrophysical* s.v. MACRO- 1e]. **1936** *Discovery* Mar. 96/2 Microphysical inquiries into which chemistry is now being absorbed. **1956** E. H. HUTTEN *Lang. Mod. Physics* v. 179 Two micro-physical events are connected in a different way from two macro-physical events. **1962** S. TOULMIN in *Quanta & Reality* 16 In the macroscopic world, all statistical statements..report the overall aggregates or averages of large numbers of individual events..; but the microphysical statements of quantum mechanics were statistical in a more absolute sense. **1973** *Nature* 14 Dec. 378/3 According to Audretsch the effect of expansion is significant for particle creation when the age of the Universe is comparable to the microphysical time scale—when the Universe is only about 10^{-21} s old!

microphysiography, -physiologist, -physiology: see MICRO- 2a.

microphyte (ˈmaɪkrəʊfaɪt). [mod.f. Gr. μῑκρό-ς small + φυτόν plant. Cf. F. *microphyte.*] A microscopic plant, esp. a bacterium. Hence **microˈphytal, microˈphytic** *adjs.*, pertaining to microphytes.

1863 SLACK in *Intell. Observ.* Dec. 379 In the fermentation of wheat flour he [Lémaire] observed in the course of fifteen days, *bacterium, vibrio, spirillum, amœba, monas,* and *paramecium*, after which came what he calls *microphytes.* **1867** MURCHISON *Siluria* App. O. (ed. 4) 546 The microphytes above mentioned. **1876** PAGE *Adv. Text-bk. Geol.* xx. 440 The innumerable organisms in microphytal and microzoal deposits. **1881** J. SIMON in *Nature* No. 616. 373 The microphytic origin of an important cancroid disease of horned cattle. **1896** *Allbutt's Syst. Med.* I. 210 After the rise of modern bacteriology the first attempts made were to cultivate a specific microphyte from such tumours.

micropinocytosis, -pipette, -plankton(ic), -plastic(ity), -plate: see MICRO- 2a, 6, 1a, 1b, 1a.

micropod (ˈmaɪkrəpɒd). *Zool.* [ad. mod.L. *Micropoda*, f. Gr. μῑκρό-ς small + ποδ-, πούς foot.] Any one of the *Micropoda*, in some classifications a division of bivalve molluscs including the oyster.

1854 ADAMS, etc. *Man. Nat. Hist.* 158 Micropods (Micropoda).

micropodal (maɪˈkrɒpəʊdəl), *a.* [f. Gr. μῑκροποδ-, μῑκρόπους (f. μῑκρός small + ποδ-, πούς foot) + -AL[1].] Small-footed; esp. having the foot abnormally small though regularly developed. So **microˈpodic, miˈcropodous** *adjs.*

1857 MAYNE *Expos. Lex.* (s.v. *Micropodus*) *Micropodous.* **1859** *Chamb. Jrnl.* XI. 323 The micropodic young person. **1902** WEBSTER, *Micropodal.*

micropoise, -polariscope, -population, -pore, -porosity, -porphyritic, -powder: see MICRO- 5a, 6, 1, 4, 1.

microprint (ˈmaɪkrəʊprɪnt). [f. MICRO- 7 + PRINT *sb.*] **a.** A photographic print of text reduced by microphotography. **b.** Printed matter so reduced. Hence **ˈmicroprinting** *vbl. sb.*, the production of microprint.

1933 *Library Jrnl.* LVIII. 913/1 With these photographic prints on sensitized paper there is no more question of fire hazard and the necessity of projection is likewise eliminated. .. We have, however, to overcome one difficulty, namely to make the 'micro prints' easily legible. **1951** *Amer. Documentation* II. 151/1 Microprint is delivered in labelled, cloth slip-cases ready for shelving. **1961** T. LANDAU *Encycl. Librarianship* (ed. 2) 121/1 Microfilming and the production of microprint are camera methods. **1962** A. GÜNTHER *Microphotogr. in Library* (Unesco) 5 Micro-writing and micro-printing were known centuries ago. **1970** *Brit. Printer* Jan. 80/1 Trial runs have satisfied him that micro printing to a 10th of normal size..can be done successfully on a standard offset-litho press. **1970** *New Scientist* 31 Dec. 601/2 People of all ages have found that they can read microprint without strain.

microprism (ˈmaɪkrəʊprɪz(ə)m), *a. Photogr.* [f. MICRO- + PRISM.] Applied to an area of the focusing screen of some reflex cameras which is covered with a grid of tiny prisms and which splits up the image when the subject is not in focus; also applied to such a focusing system.

1966 H. KEPPLER *Asahi Pentax Way* 319 In using the central microprism grid for focusing, you will find that it snaps images in and out of focus with medium focal length lenses more efficiently than with either wide-angle or extremely long lenses. **1968** *Newnes Compl. Amat. Photogr.* (ed. 3) iv. 67 A new alternative [to a rangefinder] is the use of a 'microprism' zone, which gives a dotted effect when the image is out of focus. **1970** *Amat. Photographer* 11 Mar. 4 (Advt.), A very advanced camera offering a 6-1 zoom ratio and microprism focusing. **1973** *Country Life* 20 Sept. 826/1 (Advt.), Microprism focusing means speedy and accurate focusing.

microprobe, -process: see MICRO- 6, 1.

microprogram (ˈmaɪkrəʊprəʊgræm), *sb. Computers.* [f. MICRO- 1b + PROGRAM, PROGRAMME *sb.*] A program that causes any machine instruction to be transformed into a sequence of microinstructions.

1953 WILKES & STRINGER in *Proc. Cambr. Philos. Soc.* XLIX. 230 The operation called for by a single machine order can be broken down into a sequence of more elementary operations... These elementary operations will be referred to as micro-operations. Basic machine operations, such as addition, subtraction, multiplication, etc., are thought of as being made up of a micro-programme of micro-operations, each micro-operation being called for by a micro-order. **1962** HUSKEY & KORN *Computer Handbk.* XVI. 32 Once a given set of instructions has been designed into the machine by the wiring of a microprogram plugboard, the machine may be used as a stored-program computer in the normal fashion. **1969** [see MICROPROGRAMMED *ppl. a.*]. **1971** *New Scientist* 7 Jan. 27/1 This memory can hold up to 1024 words of microprogram which can be changed easily and inexpensively and tailored exactly to suit individual requirements.

microprogramming (maɪkrəʊˈprəʊgræmɪŋ), *vbl. sb. Computers.* [f. MICRO- 2a + PROGRAMMING *vbl. sb.*] The technique of making machine instructions generate sequences of microinstructions in accordance with a microprogram, rather than initiate the desired operations directly, so that by changing

the microprogram the set of possible machine instructions can be varied.

1953 WILKES & STRINGER in *Proc. Cambr. Philos. Soc.* XLIX. 230 It is also necessary that provision should be made for conditional micro-orders which play a role in micro-programming similar to that played by conditional orders in ordinary programming. **1962** HUSKEY & KORN *Computer Handbk.* XVI. 32 The concept of microprogramming suggests that the machine be designed and constructed in such a way that the individual basic command steps, such as clear the accumulator or left shift one place, are accessible for alteration. **1967** P. A. STARK *Digital Computer Programming* xix. 360 Microprogramming is a technique for letting the programmer manufacture complex instructions..from small portions of instructions. **1971** *New Scientist* 17 June 685/2 ICL is understood to be taking its own steps along the microprogramming path in its next range of computers.

So **micro'programmed** *ppl. a.*, employing microprogramming with a number of different microprograms; (as a back-formation) **micro'program** *v. trans.*; **micro'programmer**, one who writes microprograms; a specialist in microprogramming.

1956 *Jrnl. Assoc. Computing Machinery* III. 79 One of the basic requirements of a microprogrammed computer is a means of ensuring the microprogrammer ready control of the subcommands with which he is working. It is necessary that the microprogram be physically easy to set up on the machine. **1957** *Ibid.* IV. 161 The arithmetic floating point operations of addition, subtraction and multiplication can be micro-programmed with about 70 microorders. **1969** P. B. JORDAIN *Condensed Computer Encycl.* 319 It is cheaper to establish a microprogram memory which can hold many microprograms and thus allow for a large set of computer instructions which can be interpreted and implemented on simple and inexpensive computer hardware. In such computers, sometimes called microprogrammed computers, each computer instruction operation code defines the beginning of the corresponding microprogram stored in the microprogram memory. **1970** S. S. HUSSON *Microprogramming* i. 13 The user programmer tells the system or device *what to do* by placing instructions in the high-speed main storage. The microprogrammer tells the system or device *how to do it* by controlling which storage and logic elements are used and how they are used for each operation. Thus the machine instruction which the programmer considered to be the lowest level of communication with the system can now be viewed as a closed subroutine broken down into a sequence of more elementary functions called microinstructions. Each microinstruction is designed to specify the control gates that are opened at a particular point during the machine cycle. **1975** *Sci. Amer.* May 36/3 Some multichip machines have the advantage that they can be 'microprogrammed' by the user.

microprojection (ˌmaɪkrəʊprəˈdʒɛkʃən). [f. MICRO- + PROJECTION *sb.*] The process of projecting an enlarged image of a microscopic specimen.

1904 *Jrnl. R. Microsc. Soc.* 582 The firm..manufacture an optical bench and appliances for..micro-projection, and optical lantern projection. **1932** *Ibid.* LII. 134 The microprojection of a subject for reconstruction work is best accomplished by using an apparatus affixed in the vertical position, projecting the image upon a horizontal table for ease in drawing. **1972** *Jap. Jrnl. Pharmacol.* XXII. 636 The reactive points were identified with the aid of microprojection apparatus to make the composite map from the serial sections obtained from individual animals.

Hence **micropro'jector**, an apparatus for microprojection.

1932 *Jrnl. R. Microsc. Soc.* LII. 136 A method devised whereby a standard microprojector is altered to allow use in the vertical position. **1948** *Times* 15 June 7/5 He introduced into his lectures the latest methods of teaching, first by lantern slides, secondly by microprojector, and later by cine-films. **1957** B. M. ROVINSKY et al. in V. E. Cosslett et al. *X-Ray Microsc. & Microradiogr.* 277 The high resolution of the microprojector with its great sensitivity in distinguishing densities of microscopic areas makes it possible to use the device for examination of a wide range of objects.

micropsia, micropsy: see MICRO- 3.

†**micropsychy**. *Obs.* [ad. Gr. μῑκροψῡχία, f. μῑκρόψῡχ-ος pusillanimous, f. μῑκρο-ς small + ψῡχή soul.] Pusillanimity.

1651 BIGGS *New Disp.* 149 The powers..being..examinated into a dull and faint mycropsychie. **1654** GAYTON *Pleas. Notes* IV. xvii. 259 To what purpose didst thou kneel for a Licence, if thou wilt not take the liberty to fight? Though Cyd Hameti Benengeli doth not discover the reason of this Micropseuchy [*printed* Micropseachy] of the Don. **1674** BLOUNT *Glossogr.* (ed. 4), *Micropsychy*, feeble courage, faintness of heart.

micropterous (maɪˈkrɒptərəs), *a. Zool.* [f. Gr. μῑκρόπτερ-ος (f. μῑκρό-ς small + πτερ-όν wing) + -OUS.] Small winged or finned. So **mi'cropterism**, abnormally small wing-development.

1826 KIRBY & SP. *Entomol.* IV. xli. 141 Most of the micropterous tribes (*Staphylinus* L.) have a fetid smell. **1895** D. SHARP *Insects* I. 339 (Camb. Nat. Hist.) Some species are always micropterous. *Ibid.*, A curious form of variation occurs in this family [Gryllidae], and is called micropterism by de Saussure.

micropterygious: see MICRO- 4.

mi'croptic, *a. nonce-wd.* [f. Gr. μῑκρό-ς small + ὀπτικός OPTIC *a.*] Microscopic.

1800 HURDIS *Fav. Village* 104 If to the spot invisible we strain Our aching sight, and with microptic tube Bring it at last within our feeble ken.

micropublishing (ˈmaɪkrəʊˌpʌblɪʃɪŋ), *vbl. sb.* [f. MICRO- 7 + PUBLISHING *vbl. sb.*] The publication of copies of books, periodicals, etc., in microform. Hence (as a back-formation) **'micropublish** *v. trans.*; also **'micropublished** *ppl. a.*, **micro'publisher**.

1969 *R. & E. Coordinator* (Res. & Engin. Council Graphic Arts Industry) Apr. 4/1 According to a recent booklet..micropublishing sales are running at an estimated $25 million a year. **1971** *Publishers' Weekly* 23 Aug. 41/1 A new company, Congressional Information Service, which collects, indexes and micro-publishes some 450,000 pages per year of government documents. **1973** *Ibid.* 19 Mar. 52/2 Many micropublished products are compilations of public domain materials. *Ibid.* 52/3 The micropublisher is particularly affected by this unofficial copyright. **1974** *Bookseller* 8 June 2600/1 The *Oxford English Dictionary* in two volumes with a magnifying glass is a significant half way stage to micro publishing.

micropulsation: see MICRO- 1.

micropylar (ˈmaɪkrəʊpaɪlə(r)), *a.* [f. next + -AR.] Pertaining to or of the nature of a micropyle.

1869 W. S. DALLAS tr. *Müller's Facts for Darwin* 132 The formation of the 'micropylar apparatus' [in the Amphipoda].

micropyle (ˈmaɪkrəʊpaɪl). [a. F. *micropyle*, f. Gr. μῑκρό-ς small + πύλη gate.]

1. *Bot.* The foramen or orifice in the integument of an ovule, by which the pollen penetrates to the apex of the nucleus or radicle. Also, the external aperture which represents this foramen in the mature seed.

1821 tr. *Decandolle & Sprengel's Elem. Philos. Plants* 79 In the seeds of many of the Leguminous plants, a small cavity appears under the umbilicus, called *micropyle*, but its use is unknown. **1830** LINDLEY *Nat. Syst. Bot.* 181 The woody shell of the seed of Sapoteae is certainly testa,..as is proved by the presence of the micropyle upon it. **1875** BENNETT & DYER tr. *Sachs' Bot.* 429 It [the pollen] then forces itself into the micropyle and advances as far as the embryo-sac.

2. *Zool.* A special opening in a female cell for the entrance of the fertilizing cell.

1859 *Todd's Cycl. Anat.* V. [97]/2 Discoveries..as to the existence of the micropyle in fishes. **1875** RAY LANKESTER in *Q. Jrnl. Microsc. Sci.* XV. 38 The egg-shell..has a small hole at the narrower pole, which may be called a micropyle. **1893** TUCKEY *Amphioxus* 41 This..explains how it is that without the formation of a micropyle the spermatozoon can force its way into the egg.

microquantity, -rad: see MICRO- 1, 5 a.

microradiography (ˌmaɪkrəʊreɪdɪˈɒgrəfɪ). [ad. F. *microradiographie* (P. Goby 1913, in *Compt. Rend.* CLVI. 686): see MICRO- 2 a and RADIOGRAPHY.] Radiography of the fine structure of an object.

1913 P. GOBY in *Jrnl. R. Microsc. Soc.* 373 The new method of employment of X-rays, which I have the honour of introducing to you under the name of Microradiography, aims at rendering easily visible the internal structure of microscopic objects. **1944** *Jrnl. Appl. Physics* XV. 44/1 The early work on microradiography was confined chiefly to light alloys and made use of low voltage, long wave-length radiation. **1966** D. G. BRANDON *Mod. Techniques Metallogr.* 76 The two major advantages offered by microradiography as opposed to ordinary optical metallography are, firstly, the sensitivity to chemical composition and, secondly, the ability of the technique to integrate over a large volume of material. **1973** *Calcified Tissue Res.* XI. 176 This work investigated the effect of fluoride on the mineralization of rat dentine using tetracycline-labelling and microradiography.

Hence **micro'radiogram**, the original image obtained on a sensitive plate or film in microradiography; **micro'radiograph**, a photographic enlargement of a microradiogram; **ˌmicroradio'graphic** *a.*, of or obtained by microradiography.

1913 *Jrnl. R. Microsc. Soc.* 375 Plate XVI is a reproduction of a micro-radiogram, enlarged nineteen times, of the anterior and posterior limbs of the three-toed lizard. **1944** *Jrnl. Appl. Physics* XV. 43 Investigations have been made of the various factors considered to influence the sensitivity of the microradiographic method for the examination of alloys. *Ibid.* 52 (*caption*) Microradiographs of cartridge brass with Co radiation at 20 kv at 75 ×. **1957** A. ENGSTRÖM in V. E. Cosslett et al. *X-Ray Microsc. & Microradiogr.* 32 In order to take care of the inhomogeneous distribution of the absorbing material, various types of scanning photometry of the microradiogram are now being used. **1966** D. G. BRANDON *Mod. Techniques Metallogr.* 76 The detail seen in a microradiograph is projected from a slab of metal up to 0·1 mm in thickness. **1969** HOBBELL & BOYDE in Möllenstedt & Gaukler *Internat. Symposium X-Ray Optics & Microanalysis* 611 The interpretation of the microradiographic image was found to be in good correlation with the interpretation of the scanning electron microscopic image of bone surfaces.

micro-ray, -reader, -record(ing), -refractometer, -relief, -reproduction, -respirometer (etc.), **micror(h)abd**: see MICRO- 1, 7, 7, 6, 1 b, 7, 6, 1.

micro-scale (ˈmaɪkrəʊskeɪl). Also **micro scale, microscale.** [f. MICRO- 1 + SCALE *sb.*^{3}] A small or microscopic scale; *spec.* in *Chem.*, the scale of microanalysis.

Micro is freq. apprehended as an adj. qualifying *scale* (cf. MICRO- 8).

1931 [see MICRO- 8 b]. **1946** BELCHER & WILSON *Qualitative Inorg. Microanalysis* i. 3 This does not arise on the micro scale, because of the larger amounts of ethanol used to ensure complete precipitation. **1956** *Nature* 25 Feb. 378/2 Schindler's procedure, which was adapted to microscale working, was followed. 2–5 mgm. of vitamin B_{12} is dissolved in 500 µl. of 10 per cent aqueous ammonium chloride solution. **1961** *New Scientist* 16 Mar. 670/3 These materials are, however, crude on a microscale—they are porous and they contain impurities. **1964** N. G. CLARK *Mod. Org. Chem.* xxiv. 496 It became imperative to develop techniques demanding smaller samples. This was achieved in 1911 by Pregl, using 1–5 mg of material (micro-scale). **1966** D. G. BRANDON *Mod. Techniques Metallogr.* 103 It is now possible to perform a very large number of metallurgical operations in [*sic*] a microscale inside the electron microscope. **1968** [see MACRO-SCALE].

microsclere: see MICRO- 1.

microscope (ˈmaɪkrəskəʊp), *sb.* Also 7 mycroscop(e. [ad. mod.L. *microscopium*, f. Gr. μῑκρό-ς small + σκοπ-εῖν to look, see: see -SCOPE. Cf. F. *microscope*, Sp. *microscópio*, It. *microscopio*, G. *mikroskop*.]

1. a. An optical instrument, consisting of a lens or a combination of suitably adjusted lenses, (or, rarely, also of mirrors) by which objects are so magnified that details indistinct or invisible to the naked eye are clearly revealed.

1656 tr. *Hobbes' Elem. Philos.* I. IV. xxvii. 332 There are now such Microscopes..that the things we see with them appear a hundred thousand times bigger, then they would do if we looked upon them with our bare Eyes. **1662** S. P. *New Sect Latitude-men* 21 The severall discoveries we are beholden to the new invented microscope for. **1678** *Depos. Cast. York* (Surtees) 233 Polishing glasses for prospectives, and spectackles and mycroscops. **1706** *Reflex. upon Ridicule* 244 The effects of prejudice..are the same with those of microscopes. **1831** BREWSTER *Optics* v. 51 When such a lens is used to magnify the magnified image produced by another lens, the two lenses together constitute a compound microscope.

attrib. **1826** KIRBY & SP. *Entomol.* III. xxix. 193 Till..they may first enter the range of the microscope-aided eye. **1875** HUXLEY & MARTIN *Elem. Biol.* (1877) 247 Microscope-needle. **1899** CAGNEY tr. *Jaksch's Clin. Diagn.* x. (ed. 4) 431 An Abbe's or other condenser adjusted movably to the microscope-stand.

b. ***lucernal, solar, oxy-hydrogen microscopes***: instruments of the nature of the magic lantern, in which the illumination employed comes from a lamp, the sun, and an oxy-hydrogen lime-light respectively.

1740 H. BAKER in *Phil. Trans.* XLI. 516 The Solar or *Camera Obscura* Microscope, and the Microscope for opake objects. **1787** G. ADAMS *Ess. Microscope* 65 This [lucernal] microscope was originally thought of, and in part executed by my father. **1797** *Encycl. Brit.* (ed. 3) XI. 725 The improved lucernal microscope. **1839** *Penny Cycl.* XV. 188/2 A few achromatic glasses for oxy-hydrogen microscopes have been made. **1845** *Encycl. Metrop.* III. 470/2 The solar microscope differs entirely..from those above described.

c. An instrument analogous to an optical microscope in function but employing radiation other than visible light (e.g. electrons or X-rays). (Cf. *electron microscope* s.v. ELECTRON^2 2 b.)

1927 G. L. CLARK *Appl. X-Rays* i. 5 The ultraviolet microscope..discloses a fine structure which appears perfectly homogeneous under visible light rays. **1939** *Electronics & Television & Short-Wave World* XII. 637/3 The electron source..might be made completely independent from the microscope. **1957** DUNCOMB & COSSLETT in V. E. Cosslett et al. *X-ray Microsc. & Microradiogr.* 374 The purpose of the microscope is to form a picture of a surface by its X-ray emission and to analyze the elements in a selected volume of about one cubic micron in the surface by the characteristic lines emitted. **1964** G. H. HAGGIS et al. *Introd. Molecular Biol.* 346 Higher voltages on the microscope increase resolution, for a given section thickness, but reduce contrast. **1966** *McGraw-Hill Encycl. Sci. & Technol.* VIII. 371/2 In the electron, proton, x-ray, and β-ray microscopes, the image is usually recorded on a fluorescent screen or is photographed.

2. *transf.* and *fig.*

1671 MILTON *P. R.* IV. 57 Many a fair Edifice..(so well I have dispos'd My Aery Microscope) thou may'st behold Outside and inside both. **1742** POPE *Dunc.* IV. 233 The critic Eye, that microscope of Wit, Sees hairs and pores, examines bit by bit. **1839–52** BAILEY *Festus* xiv. 162 Watching the thoughts of men and angels Through moral microscopes. **1903** *Westm. Gaz.* 21 Feb. 7/1 The Board would work..under the microscope of a Committee of Censure.

3. *Astron.* (Also in mod.L. form **micro'scopium**.) A constellation south of Capricorn, introduced by Lacaille in 1752.

microscope (ˈmaɪkrəskəʊp), *v. rare.* [f. MICROSCOPE *sb.*] *trans.* **a.** To magnify. **b.** To scrutinize minutely. So **'microscoping** *vbl. sb.*, examination by microscope; **'microscoped** *ppl. a.*, *fig.* microscopically selected.

1868 G. H. LEWES *Jrnl.* 10 Jan. in Geo. Eliot *Lett.* (1956) IV. 416 With him I spent the greater part of the time at Bonn, discussing microscoping etc. **1888** T. DE W. TALMAGE in *Voice* (N.Y.) 6 Sept., He talked against you. He

microscoped your faults. **1889** J. M. ROBERTSON *Ess. Crit. Method* 87 The specialist's literature of microscoped minutiae. **1896** MRS. CAFFYN *Quaker Grandmother* 206 He looked much more likely to spring upon her unawares, and microscope her. **1919** S. PAGET *Sir V. Horsley* II. i. 143 He ..spoke his mind against that sort of pathology which hardly gets beyond the microscoping and exhibiting of diseased organs.

†**micro'scopial**, *a. Obs.* [f. mod.L. *mīcroscopium* + -AL¹.] = MICROSCOPICAL.

1738 D. BAYNE *Gout* 102 No secretion or excretion is performed without a mixture..of several sorts of particles.. as appears by microscopial observations. **1740** BAKER in *Phil. Trans.* XLI. 453 Being aware how much Imagination has frequently had to do with microscopial Observations, I distrusted my own Eyes.

microscopic (maɪkrəʊ'skɒpɪk), *a.* [ad. mod.L. *mīcroscopic-us*, f. *mīcroscopium*: see MICROSCOPE and -IC. Cf. F. *microscopique*, It. *microscopico*, Sp. *microscópico*.]

1. = MICROSCOPICAL *a.* 1. Now *rare* exc. *fig.*

1857 *G. Bird's Urin. Deposits* (ed. 5) 199 The microscopic examination of a sediment composed of cystine. **1863** RAY LANKESTER in *Q. Jrnl. Microsc. Sci.* III. 83 Nor are they generally known to microscopic observers in this country. **1877** W. THOMSON *Voy. Challenger* I. i. 15 The substances in common use in mounting microscopic preparations.

fig. **1779–81** JOHNSON *L. P., Rowe* Wks. III. 38 Few characters can bear the microscopick scrutiny of wit quickened by anger. **1850** ROBERTSON *Serm.* Ser. III. viii. 111 It is not a microscopic self-examination. **1877** STUBBS *Lect. Med. & Mod. Hist.* v. (1886) 103 The tree..bears to the microscopic investigator marks of every winter that has passed over it. **1904** *Sat. Rev.* 29 Oct. 551 The microscopic inquiry of the Dictionary of National Biography.

2. Possessing or exercising the functions of a microscope.

1732 POPE *Ess. Man* I. 193 Why has not Man a microscopic eye? For this plain reason, Man is not a Fly. **1744** THOMSON *Summer* 288 Gradual, from These what numerous Kinds descend, Evading even the microscopic Eye! *a* **1761** CAWTHORN *Antiquarians* 80 To ev'ry corner of the brass They clapp'd a microscopic glass. **1876** LOWELL *Among my Bks.* Ser. II. 278 Gulliver's microscopic eye.

fig. a **1680** BUTLER *Rem.* (1759) I. 10 His Excellence In.. magnifying all he writ With curious microscopick Wit. **1863** KINGLAKE *Crimea* (1877) II. vii. 65 His intellect being subtle and microscopic. **1903** MORLEY *Gladstone* I. 4 The microscopic subtlety of a thirteenth century schoolman.

3. Of such minute size or proportions as to be invisible or indeterminate without the use of a microscope.

176. WESLEY *Serm.* lxxiv. I. §11 Wks. (1811) IX. 314 Are Microscopic Animals, so called, *real* Animals or not? **1770** HORSLEY in *Phil. Trans.* LX. 431 The eyes of the smallest microscopic animals. **1802** BOURNON *ibid.* XCII. 300 We may..by means of a lens, perceive small microscopic crystals of thallite. **1819** CHILDREN *Chem. Anal.* 271 From the mountainous elephant to the microscopic insect. **1899** *Allbutt's Syst. Med.* VI. 891 Some of which vessels.. presented evidences of microscopic gummata.

fig. **1849** STOVEL *Canne's Necess.* Introd. 78 Every..care was taken to find..terms the most microscopic to express the littleness of those '*mere ceremonies*'. **1887** G. H. DARWIN in *Fortn. Rev.* Feb. 273 They are microscopic.. earthquakes. **1887** RUSKIN *Praeterita* II. 24 Turner's microscopic touch.

microscopical (maɪkrəʊ'skɒpɪkəl), *a.* [Formed as prec. + -AL¹.]

1. Pertaining or relating to the microscope or its use; resembling what pertains to a microscope.

1664 *Phil. Trans.* I. 28 The Microscopical view of the Edges of Rasors. **1681** GLANVILL *Sadducismus* I. (1682) 7 The certainty of which I believe the improvement of microscopical Observations will discover. **1690** LOCKE *Hum. Und.* II. xxiii. §12. 140 And if by the help of such Microscopical Eyes (if I may so call them) a Man could penetrate farther than ordinary into the..radical Texture of Bodies. **1796** BP. WATSON *Apol. Bible* ix. (ed. 2) 94 The microscopical discoveries of modern times. **1879** RUTLEY *Stud. Rocks* x. 104 Unsatisfactory in the present state of microscopical knowledge. **1883** PROCTOR in *Knowledge* 18 May 300/2 Are not microscopical papers in progress?

2. = MICROSCOPIC 3. Now *rare*.

1769 BARRINGTON in *Phil. Trans.* LIX. 31 Still smaller microscopical insects. **1771** W. JONES *Zool. Eth.* 76 The microscopical feathers upon the wing of a moth. **1871** HARTWIG *Subterr. W.* ii. 10 The aggregated remains of microscopical animals. **1880** GÜNTHER *Fishes* 114 It is the *membrana argentea*, and composed of microscopical crystals.

microscopically (maɪkrəʊ'skɒpɪkəlɪ), *adv.* [f. prec. + -LY².] By means of a microscope; so minutely as to be visible only with a microscope.

1795 HAIGHTON in *Phil. Trans.* LXXXV. 192 Metals, when microscopically examined, have convoluted fibrous appearances. **1836–9** *Todd's Cycl. Anat.* II. 122/2 One of these worms, when examined microscopically, presented a rupture in the middle of its body. **1876** BRISTOWE *Theory & Pract. Med.* (1878) 57 Microscopically, they are found to be identical in structure with the uterine muscular walls. **1879** tr. *Semper's Anim. Life* 40 The ovum cell being always microscopically small.

b. *fig.* and *hyperbolically*.

1824 SCOTT *St. Roman's* v, The company examined even microscopically the response of the stranger. **1874** tr. *Lommel's Light* 18 The rays of light which reach the microscopically small earth. **1885** C. F. WOOLSON in *Harper's Mag.* Apr. 787/2 The little advances she had made had been microscopically small.

microscopico- (maɪkrəʊ'skɒpɪkəʊ), mod. combining form of MICROSCOPICAL.

1839 LINDLEY *Introd. Bot.* I. i. (ed. 3) 7 Some beautiful microscopico-chemical experiments.

microscopist (maɪ'krɒskəpɪst, *U.S.* 'maɪkrəʊskəʊpɪst). [f. MICROSCOPE + -IST.] One skilled in the use of the microscope.

1835–6 *Todd's Cycl. Anat.* I. 405/2 We find marked discrepancies in the conclusions come to by different microscopists. **1867** J. HOGG *Microsc.* I. ii. 33 The simple hand magnifier, so often employed by microscopists in the preliminary examinations of objects. **1879** H. GRUBB in *Trans. Roy. Dublin Soc.* 188 Looked into at a convenient angle somewhat similar to that usually adopted by microscopists.

transf. **1851** WYTHES (*title*) The Microscopist, or a Complete Manual on the use of the Microscope.

microscopize (maɪ'krɒskəpaɪz), *v. nonce-wd.* [f. MICROSCOPE + -IZE.] *trans.* To work with a microscope.

1846 HUXLEY in *Life & Lett.* (1900) I. 27, I may read, draw, or microscopise at pleasure.

microscopy (maɪ'krɒskəpɪ). [f. MICROSCOPE + -Y.] The art or practice of using the microscope; the science of the microscopist.

1664–5 PEPYS *Diary* 20 Jan., To my bookseller's, and there took home Hook's book of microscopy. **1867** J. HOGG *Microsc.* I. ii. 70 The many important contributions to microscopy by Owen, Carpenter, Quekett, Ralfs, etc. **1887** *Times* 1 Sept. 6/3 The value of microscopy when brought to bear on pharmacy.

microsecond, -section: see MICRO- 5 a, 2 c.

microsegment ('maɪkrəʊsɛgmənt). *Linguistics.* [f. MICRO- 1 + SEGMENT *sb.*] A unit of sound enclosed between two open junctures.

1958 C. F. HOCKETT *Course in Mod. Ling.* vi. 60 Apart from stresses, a microsegment consists of segmental phonemes—that is, vowels and consonants. **1963** *Amer. Speech* XXXVIII. 55 Miss Sivertsen describes the phonological system within which she operates; phonemes are described in a framework of macro- and microsegments which, in turn, are divided into syllables. **1971** *Language* XLVII. 739 Each section of the description is..worked out in detail..; the main headings are phonemes, syllables, micro-segments, meso-segments, macro-segments, and mega-segments.

microseism (maɪkrəʊ'saɪz(ə)m). [f. Gr. μῑκρό-ς small + σεισμός shaking, earthquake.] A minor earthquake; in mod. use, any imperceptible disturbance of the earth's crust which is capable of being registered on a sensitive seismometer but which is not caused by an earthquake (see quots.).

1887 G. H. DARWIN in *Fortn. Rev.* Feb. 271 Earth tremors or 'microseisms' are not confined to countries habitually visited by the grosser sort of earthquakes. **1888** *Times* 24 Nov. 15/2 There may have been a succession of microseisms perceptible only to the delicate senses of quadrupeds and other dumb creatures. **1903** [see MACROSEISM]. **1924** *Bull. Seismol. Soc. Amer.* XIV. 28 They [*sc.* earth-tremors] are now generally known as microseisms. **1959** *Observer* 6 Sept. 4/8 Another advance is the linking of 'microseisms'—minute earth tremors which constantly vibrate the recording pens of seismographs—with storms at sea. **1965** A. HOLMES *Princ. Physical Geol.* (rev. ed.) xxv. 916 As a background to the P, S and L waves and their many associates there are small irregular earth tremors and quiverings going on all the time. .. These microseisms..set a limit to the degree of magnification that can usefully be employed, since they only confuse the earthquake record if they are made too big. Some of the more conspicuous microseisms are caused by distant traffic, others by the pounding of breakers on rocky coasts, while others have been traced to changes of atmospheric pressure and especially to hurricanes and typhoons. But after all such regional increases of microseismic activity have been accounted for, there still remains a world-wide background of chaotic seismic 'noise'. Don and Florence Leet have suggested that these microseisms are caused by the strained condition of the crust, which 'hums' or 'sings' like a highly strained piece of steel. **1971** *Nature* 12 Feb. 452/3 Microseisms are of practical importance in predicting the onset of a storm in areas where meteorological observations are scarce.

microseismic (maɪkrəʊ'saɪzmɪk), *a.* [f. prec. + -IC.] Pertaining to or of the nature of a faint earth tremor. (See also quot. 1972.) So also **micro'seismical** *a.*, in the same sense.

1877 *Eng. Mechanic* 10 Aug. 533/3 More than 20,000 microseismic observations, made from 1870 to 1875. **1886** J. MILNE *Earthquakes* xix. 316 The most satisfactory observations which have been made upon microseismic disturbances are those which have been made during the last ten years in Italy. *Ibid.*, A series of microseismical observations. **1972** *Gloss. Geol.* (Amer. Geol. Inst.) 452/2 *Microseismic data*, earthquake measurement or observation by instrumental means, as opposed to macroseismic observations. The term is not to be confused with the connotation of the term microseism. **1973** *Sci. Amer.* Apr. 31/1 It was a great thrill when we scanned along a seismogram made at Jamestown of an explosion on Novaya Zemlya and there—Eureka!—at the travel time predicted for a wave reflected seven times was an unmistakable tiny pulse nestling in the valley of microseismic background noise.

microseismograph (maɪkrəʊ'saɪzməʊgrɑːf, -æ-). [mod. f. Gr. μῑκρό-ς small + σεισμό-ς earthquake: see -GRAPH.] An instrument for recording slight earth tremors, as well as the feeble effects of distant earthquake shocks.

1881 *Friends' Intelligencer* XXXVIII. 556 The Microseismograph..with which Professor Palmieri..may detect the first faintest quiver which hints the coming earthquake. **1899** *Nature* 30 Mar. 523/1 The microseismograph devised a few years ago by Prof. Vicentini, of Padua.

microseismology (maɪkrəʊsaɪz'mɒlədʒɪ). [f. MICROSEISM + -OLOGY.] The study or science of minute earth-tremors.

1884 *Chamb. Jrnl.* 762 The study of these slight movements of our great Mother is called microseismology. **1884** *Athenæum* 1 Nov. 566/2 The new branch of science which is directed to the observation of these minute tremors is to be called micro-seismology.

microseismometry (maɪkrəʊsaɪz'mɒmɪtrɪ). [f. MICROSEISM + -(O)METRY.] The art or process of measuring slight earth tremors.

1889 *Nature* 7 Feb. 338/1 The account that is given of the labours of Italian observers in the field of microseismometry is meagre and unsatisfactory.

microseme ('maɪkrəʊsiːm), *a.* and *sb.* *Anthropology.* [a. F. *microsème* (Broca), f. Gr. μῑκρό-ς small + σῆμα sign, 'index'.] **a.** *adj.* Of a skull: Having a small orbital index, i.e. one below 83. **b.** *sb.* A skull having an orbital index below 83.

1878 [see MESOSEME]. **1880** *Nature* 8 Jan. 224 The now extinct Tasmanian race was..prognathous, platyrhine, microseme. **1886** A. MACALISTER in *Jrnl. Anthrop. Inst.* XVI. 150 The skulls agree with the ordinary Bushman skull in most respects, being microseme, platyrhine, tapeinocephalic, mesaticephalic. **1897** SHRUBSALL *ibid.* XXVII. 283 A special feature of the Akka skull is the microseme orbit.

microseptum, -shift: see MICRO- 1.

microsiphon (maɪkrəʊ'saɪfən). *Zool.* [f. MICRO- + SIPHON.] The small siphon, or siphuncle, characteristic of the majority of Nautiloids and Ammonoids.

1887 HYATT in *Proc. Boston Soc. Nat. Hist.* 402 None of these forms, however, attained a true microsiphon.

‖**microsiphonula** (maɪkrəsɪ'fəʊnjʊlə). *Zool.* [mod.L. dim. of prec.: see -ULE.] A larval stage in certain Cephalopods, when the microsiphon begins. Hence **microsi'phonular** *a.*, of or pertaining to the microsiphonula stage. **microsi'phonulate** *a.*, having a microsiphonula stage. **microsiphonu'lation**, the formation of the microsiphonula stage.

1887 HYATT in *Proc. Bost. Soc. Nat. Hist.* XXIII. 401 This was the beginning of the small siphon and can be appropriately termed the Microsiphonula. The microsiphonula was the typical stage of nearly all the known genera of Nautiloids. *Ibid.* 402 These organs entirely disappeared in the true microsiphonulate forms. *Ibid.*, Sannionites was a genus in which the siphon was smaller than in Endoceras, and probably..inherited the tendency to microsiphonulation at the first septum at an earlier age than in Endoceras.

microsiphuncle (maɪkrəʊsɪ'fʌŋk(ə)l). *Zool.* [f. MICRO- + SIPHUNCLE.] = MICROSIPHON.

1893 HYATT in *Proc. Amer. Phil. Soc.* XXIII. 414 The metanepionic substage must obviously begin with the advent of the characteristics of the tubular microsiphuncle.

micro-skirt(ed): see MICRO- 1 c.

microsleep ('maɪkrəʊsliːp). [f. MICRO- 1 + SLEEP *sb.*] A transitory state of sleep, esp. in a person deprived of his normal sleep; a period or occasion of such sleep.

1945 W. T. LIBERSON in *Digest Neurol. & Psychiatry* XIII. 106 Another feature which we described is 'micro-sleep', a paroxysmal sleep of 1–10 seconds. **1959** *Jrnl. Amer. Med. Assoc.* 5 Sept. 14/1 Sleep deprivation brings with it an increasing burden of drowsiness..and brief lapses of awareness or 'microsleeps'. **1969** *Sunday Times* (Colour Suppl.) 16 Feb. 44/4 Tiny seizures of sleep known as microsleeps and lasting two or three seconds have occurred in people deprived of sleep. **1970** *Sci. Jrnl.* May 14/3 The subjects developed serious anomalies in brain wave pattern accompanied by 'microsleep'—a compulsive tendency to drop off unless kept constantly active. **1974** *Times* 3 Dec. 3/1 A driver can be asleep for short periods without knowing it and without anyone else being aware of it... A neurologist ..described the state as 'micro-sleep'... They were in fact asleep for periods lasting from five to 10 seconds.

microsmatic (,maɪkrɒz'mætɪk), *a. Zool.* [f. MICR(O- + Gr. ὀσμ-ή smell + -ATIC.] Having poorly developed olfactory organs.

1890 W. TURNER in *Jrnl. Anat.* XXV. 106, I propose..to arrange the Mammalia in relation to the development of the olfactory apparatus into three groups:—(*a*) Macrosmatic... (*b*) Microsmatic, where the olfactory apparatus is relatively feeble... (*c*) Anosmatic. **1891** *Proc. Zool. Soc.* 582 The olfactory bulbs and ethmo-turbinals are present, but only moderately well-developed in this animal [*sc.* the platypus]; it therefore belongs to the group named by Sir W. Turner.. Microsmatic. **1962** *Science Survey* III. 260 In the microsmatic bats and in man only a very small area [of the nasal labyrinth] is olfactory. **1971** *Nature* 6 Aug. 396/2 Olfactory communication is now known to be important in determining the interaction between the sexes in a microsmatic higher primate, namely, the rhesus monkey.

microsocial (maɪkrəʊˈsəʊʃəl), *a.* [f. MICRO- + SOCIAL *a.* and *sb.*] Of or pertaining to a small society or community.

1909 MRS. C. WEEKES tr. *Goll's Criminal Types in Shakespeare* iii. 134 Crimes committed by her..are looked upon as typical..of micro-social family assertion, arising out of her love for the little group. **1969** A. COCKBURN in Cockburn & Blackburn *Student Power* 10 Within this framework the personnel officer can bring to bear his knowledge of micro-social dynamics.

microsociological, -sociology: see MICRO- 2 a.

microsomal (maɪkrəˈsəʊməl), *a. Biol.* [f. MICROSOM(E + -AL.] Of or pertaining to microsomes.

1897 *Jrnl. R. Microsc. Soc.* 22 The fibrils around the centrosomes have an exquisite microsomal structure. The microsomes occur in groups on the fibrils at equal distances from the centrosome. **1955** *Federation Proc.* XIV. 262/1 It appears that all the microsomal RNA is in the small particles. **1970** [see MICROSOME b]. **1971** *Nature* 9 July 84/1 Perhaps these ribosomes also make microsomal membrane proteins.

microsome (ˈmaɪkrəsəʊm). *Biol.* Also quasi-L. **micro'soma**, *pl.* **-'somata**. [mod.L. *mīcrosōma*, f. Gr. μῑκρό-ς small + σῶμα body.] **a.** A name given by Hanstein (1880) to certain small granules which abound in vegetating cells of protoplasm.

1885 GOODALE *Physiol. Bot.* 211 Imbedded in the protoplasm,..there are generally minute granules which have a high degree of refringency..; these are the microsomata of Hanstein. **1887** WARD tr. *Sachs' Physiol. Plants* 79 This..is thickly set with very numerous small granules (microsomes). **1900** EWART tr. *Pfeffer's Physiol. Plants* (ed. 2) I. ii. 43 Cytoplasm may contain minute bodies ..which..may be termed microsomes or microsomata.

b. Any of the particles which constitute the lightest fraction obtained by ultracentrifugation of cell contents under specific conditions and which are believed to be formed from fragmented endoplasmic reticulum and attached ribosomes; also (esp. formerly), a ribosome in an intact cell.

1943 A. CLAUDE in *Science* 21 May 453/2 In order to differentiate the small particles from the other, already identified elements of the cell, it may be convenient in the future to refer to this new component under a descriptive name which would be specific. For this purpose the term *microsome* appears to be the most appropriate. The term microsome..was applied originally by Hanstein (1880) to any granules, as seen in living protoplasm. The use of the word was progressively narrowed down, being retained as a general term to designate any small granules of undefined nature. Under these conditions, it seems proper to suggest that the term microsome..should be restricted to designate the small particles exclusively. **1955** *Federation Proc.* XIV. 262/1 It was found that the microsomes are morphologically identical with the vesicular and tubular elements of the endoplasmic reticula (ER) of intact cells. **1957** C. P. SWANSON *Cytol. & Cytogenetics* (1958) ii. 32 (*caption*) The structure of the cytoplasm of rat liver cells as revealed by electron microscopy, showing the endoplasmic reticulum.. and the attached particles (microsomes) which are between 100 and 200 A in diameter. **1960** *New Biol.* XXXI. 30 The microsomes themselves, which are obtained after the cell has been broken down, are vesicles made of two components: a membrane, which is rich in proteins and lipids, and very small granules... These small particles contain as much as 40–50 per cent RNA and..most of the cellular RNA is present in them. **1968** L. L. LANGLEY *Cell Function* (ed. 2) i. 9 The endoplasmic reticulum is seen..to form a series of small canals through the cytoplasm... Closely associated with the membranes which line the canals are tiny granules termed microsomes. Because they contain such a high concentration of RNA, they are often referred to as ribosomes. **1970** AMBROSE & EASTY *Cell Biol.* v. 164 Microsomes are in fact small spherical vesicles formed from disrupted endoplasmic reticulum. The microsomal fraction of homogenized cells may also contain ribosomes.

So **micro'somatous** *a.*, epithet applied to animals of minute size (Mayne *Expos. Lex.* 1856).

microsomite (maɪkrəʊˈsəʊmaɪt). *Zool.* [f. MICRO- + SOMITE.] A permanent segment formed during the embryonic stage of an insect. Hence **microso'mitic** *a.*, belonging to a microsomite.

1888 *Amer. Naturalist* XXII. 941 The secondary or microsomitic segmentation of the primitive body. *Ibid.* 942 If the macrosomites of the primitive body were to persist, as such, together with their later subdivisions (microsomites).

microsommite (maɪkrəʊˈsɒmaɪt). *Min.* [f. Gr. μικρό-ς small, as being in small crystals + *Somma*, name of one of the volcanic peaks of Vesuvius + -ITE. Named by A. Scacchi 1872 (Chester).] An impure silicate of aluminium and other bases, found in the matter discharged from volcanos.

1885 in *Cassell's Encycl. Dict.* **1900** DANA *Min.* (ed. 6) 411 Davyne is in part at least microsommite.

microspecies (ˈmaɪkrəʊˌspiːʃiːz, -ˌspiːsiːz). *Taxonomy.* [f. MICRO- + SPECIES *sb.*] A species differing only in minor characters from others of its group, often one of limited geographical range forming part of an aggregate species.

1916 J. P. LOTSY *Evolution by Means of Hybridization* i. 22 They have subsequently been called: mikrospecies, Jordanian species, subspecies, small species or elementary species indiscriminately. **1922** G. C. DRUCE *Flora Zetlandica* in *Bot. Exchange Club* VI. Suppl. 45 Twenty-two micro species of Hieracia are found in the Faroes. **1946** *Nature* 19 Oct. 535/2 The genus *Psalliota*..consists of 'species' or 'microspecies' extremely difficult to separate one from another. **1953** E. MAYR et al. *Methods & Princ. Syst. Zool.* ii. 39 Although conventionally referred to as races, reproductively isolated chromosomal populations are more logically designated (micro)species. **1963** DAVIS & HEYWOOD *Princ. Angiosperm Taxon.* xiii. 425 In large critical groups of species the difficulty of deciding to which species various subspecies should be subordinated encourages the taxonomist (often against his inclinations) to maintain numerous microspecies.

microspectrograph, -spectrophotometer (etc.): see MICRO- 6.

micro'spectroscope. [f. MICRO- + SPECTROSCOPE.] A combination of the microscope and spectroscope devised by Sorby and Browning for the examination of very minute traces of substances.

1867 J. HOGG *Microsc.* I. ii. 115 Such additions as the microspectroscope can be as easily used with it as in the old form. **1895** *Allbutt's Syst. Med.* V. 460 Human hæmoglobin invariably crystallizes in the reduced condition, as may be shown by the micro-spectroscope.

Hence **ˌmicrospectro'scopic** *a.*, of or pertaining to the microspectroscope; **microspec'troscopy**, the art or process of using the microspectroscope (*Syd. Soc. Lex.* 1890).

1871 tr. *Schellen's Spectr. Anal.* 454 Relating to the microspectroscopic and microspectroscope investigations.

microspermous, -sphere, -spherulitic, -spined, -splenic: see MICRO- 4, 1, 4.

microsporange (ˌmaɪkrəʊspɒˈrændʒ). Also in mod.L. form **-sporangium.** [f. MICRO- + SPORANGE.] A capsule containing microspores.

1881 J. S. GARDNER in *Nature* XXIV. 75 When the microsporangium or seed becomes detached. **1875** [see MACROSPORANGE]. **1882** *Gard. Chron.* XVIII. 40 The microspores..occupy the cavity of the microsporange. **1887** WARD tr. *Sachs' Phys. Plants* xlii. 746 The..micro-sporangia become expelled. **1900** in JACKSON *Gloss. Bot.*

microspore (ˈmaɪkrəʊspɔə(r)). [f. MICRO- + SPORE.]

1. *Bot.* and *Path.* A parasitic fungus which has small spores, characteristic of ringworm. = MICROSPORON.

1856 MAYNE *Expos. Lex.*, *Microsporum*..term for the cryptogamious plant in *Porrigo decalvans*,..a microspore. **1899** *Allbutt's Syst. Med.* VIII. 855 The microspores and trichophytes all belong to the same family.

2. *Bot.* The smaller of the two kinds of spores in heterosporous cryptogams; also, the homologous structure in seed plants (i.e. the immature pollen grain).

1858 CARPENTER *Veg. Phys.* §734 One containing a mass of fine powdery granules (microspores); the other including only three or four roundish fleshy bodies (megaspores). **1875** BENNETT & DYER *Sachs' Bot.* 336 The Marsiliaceæ and Selaginelleæ produce their antherozoids within the microspore itself. **1877** LE CONTE *Elem. Geol.* (1879) 355 [There are in Lepidodendrids] two kinds of spores—microspores and macrospores—corresponding to stamens and pistils. **1964** E. J. H. CORNER *Life of Plants* x. 177 The male spores [in *Selaginella*, etc.], called microspores because of their small size, are produced in large numbers in microsporangia. **1965** K. ESAU *Plant Anat.* (ed. 2) xviii. 540 A microspore develops into the male gametophyte, the pollen grain.

3. *Zool.* A spore-like form in Protozoa. Also used for MICROGAMETE.

1882 KENT *Man. Infusoria* II. 870 Microspores. The spore-like elements, of exceedingly minute size but very numerous, produced through the encystment and subsequent subdivision of many monads. **1905** McCABE tr. *Haeckel's Evol. Man* I. 140 The smaller microspores have the same shape as the larger macrospores.

Hence **micro'sporic** *a. Bot.*, of or pertaining to a microspore; **'microˌsporous** *a. Bot.*, having small seeds or grains; resembling or derived from a microspore; **ˌmicrosporo'genesis**, the development of microspores; **ˌmicrosporoge'netic** *a.*

1856 MAYNE *Expos. Lex.*, Microsporous. **1890** *Cent. Dict.*, Microsporous. **1897** WEBSTER, Microsporic. **1946** *Nature* 12 Oct. 520/1 In the microsporogenesis of buckwheat autotetraploids during the first metaphase of meiosis only very rarely were exclusively quadrivalents observed. **1961** *Developmental Biol.* III. 241 Microsporogenesis in the higher plants offers an opportunity for analyzing various stages of differentiation within the essentially closed system afforded by the microsporocyte. **1973** *Nature* 6 July 35/2 The cold treatment slowed down the microsporogenesis considerably, enabling the microsporogenetic stages to be clearly recognized.

microsporidian (maɪkrəʊspɒˈrɪdɪən), *sb.* and *a. Zool.* [f. mod.L. name of order *Microsporidia* (G. Balbiani 1883, in *Jrnl. de Micrographie* VII. 349), f. MICRO- 1 + SPORE + Gr. dim. suff. -ιδιον.] **A.** *sb.* A protozoan parasite affecting arthropods or fishes, belonging to the order Microsporidia. **B.** *adj.* Of or pertaining to a parasite of this kind.

1910 *Encycl. Brit.* IX. 386/1 The genus *Myxocystis*..has been shown..to be a true Microsporidian. **1912** E. A. MINCHIN *Introd. Study Protozoa* xvi. 411 The existence of the polar capsule in the Microsporidian spore was discovered by Thélohan. **1930** R. R. KUDO in Hegner & Andrews *Probl. & Methods of Res. in Protozool.* xxxiii. 327 The spore is perhaps the most important stage of a microsporidian from the taxonomic standpoint. **1964** T. C. CHENG *Biol. Animal Parasites* v. 141/1 The infective form of microsporidians is the spore, which is typically covered by a keratinous membrane. **1972** SWAN & PAPP *Common Insects N. Amer.* 291 Silkworms suffer from fungus, virus, and microsporidian (protozoan) infections.

microsporidiosis (ˌmaɪkrəʊspɒrɪdɪˈəʊsɪs). [f. MICROSPORIDI(AN *sb.* and *a.* + -OSIS.] = NOSEMA.

1911 FANTHAM & PORTER in *Proc. Zool. Soc.* 626 Microsporidiosis (due to *Nosema apis*) had probably been introduced from the Continent into British apiaries. **1937** W. HERROD-HEMPSALL *Bee-keeping* II. 1425 Nosema Disease (Microsporidiosis).

‖**microsporon** (maɪˈkrɒspərɒn). *Bot.* [mod.L., f. Gr. μικρό-ς small + σπορά or σπόρος seed, SPORE.] = MICROSPORE 1. Also *attrib.*

1876 tr. *Wagner's Gen. Pathol.* 217 Klebs describes as septic, or tertiary hæmorrhages those dependent on the penetration of his microsporon into the arteries or veins. **1898** P. MANSON *Trop. Diseases* xxxvii. 581, I believe that those cases of microsporon..dhobie itch are more easily cured than the trichophyton varieties. **1899** *Allbutt's Syst. Med.* VIII. 776 In microsporon ringworm also, there are round bald patches.

microsporophyl(l, -state: see MICRO- 1.

microsthene (ˈmaɪkrəsθiːn). *Zool.* [mod.L. *Microsthena* pl. (see below), f. Gr. μικρό-ς small + σθένος strength.] A member of the *Microsthena*, one of the orders in Dana's classification of the Mammalia, comprising the smallest and structurally least powerful mammals. Hence **micro'sthenic** *a.*, of or pertaining to the microsthenes. (Cf. MEGASTHENE).

1862 DANA *Man. Geol.* 345 They are of a small type..such as are styled Microsthenic in the remarks on Mammals. *Ibid.* 421 The Microsthenes..the inferior type. **1863** —— in *Amer. Jrnl. Sci.* Ser. II. XXXVI. 9 A general structural characteristic may yet be detected corresponding to these megasthenic and microsthenic qualities. **1876** DUNGLISON *Med. Lex.*, *Microsthenes*, a group of the mammalia having a small size. **1890** *Syd. Soc. Lex.*, *Microsthenes*..*Microsthenic*.

micro-stimulation, -stome, -stomatous, -stomous, -stratification: see MICRO- 1, 4.

microstrip (ˈmaɪkrəʊstrɪp). *Electr.* [f. MICRO(WAVE *sb.* + STRIP *sb.*²] A transmission line for microwaves that consists of dielectric material with a metallic film forming a conducting strip along one face and a metallic coating that serves as an earth covering the opposite face; also *collect.* (without *a*), as a material.

1952 GRIEG & ENGELMANN in *Proc. IRE* XL. 1644 (*heading*) Microstrip—a new transmission technique for the kilomegacycle range. *Ibid.* 1645/1 Because of the ease of manufacture and the apparent similarity to conventional wiring, the generic name of microstrip has been given to this transmission system. **1957** *Jrnl. Appl. Physics* XXVIII. 299/1 The 'microstrip' is a strip transmission line which consists of a thin metallic strip pasted on a dielectric layer which is in turn a coating on a ground plane. *Ibid.*, Sections of microstrip are useful as microwave filters. **1967** *Electronics* 6 Mar. 251/2 The microstrip is formed on the alumina board by depositing a silver circuit pattern and ground plane. **1971** *New Scientist* 1 July 26/1 A traditional waveguide must have dimensions comparable to the wavelength of the microwave signal it is handling—a few centimetres... No such physical restrictions apply to microstrip, which has the added advantage of a constructional technique compatible with modern microelectronics. *Ibid.* 26/2 The one [earth] plate can form the second conductor for all the microstrips used in the receiver.

'microstructure. Also micro-structure. [f. MICRO- + STRUCTURE *sb.*] Structure on a microscopic or very small scale; = FINE STRUCTURE 2.

1885 GEIKIE *Text-bk. Geol.* (ed. 2) 136 Micro-structure. **1898** *Engineering Mag.* XVI. 155/1 The Microstructure of Bearing Metals. **1956** *Nature* 25 Feb. 380/2 The inhomogeneous microstructure of the muscular tissue. **1959** B. WALL tr. *Teilhard de Chardin's Phenomenon of Man* I. i. 50 We owe our knowledge of the macro-structure and micro-structure of the universe far more to increasingly accurate measurements than to direct observations. **1960** E. H. GOMBRICH *Art & Illusion* viii. 274 The clue of texture..is basically also a clue of regularity and one which proves so reliable because the micro-structure of things is least affected by accidents. **1962** F. I. ORDWAY et al. *Basic Astronautics* iv. 153 Some hope to learn from gravitational research more about the microstructure of the building blocks of nature, the subatomic particle. **1973** *Sci. Amer.* Feb. 65/2 It is now customary to apply the term 'microstructure' to oceanic physical processes on the scale of a few centimeters or less.

Hence **micro'structural** *a.*, of or pertaining to the microstructure; **micro'structurally** *adv.*

1893 A. GEIKIE *Text-bk. Geol.* (ed. 3) 596 *Macro-structural* metamorphism, having the external structure (morphology) changed, as where an amorphous condition becomes schistose; *micro-structural*, having the internal structure (histology) wholly changed, with or without a

macro-structural alteration. **1937** O. B. DARBISHIRE tr. *A. von Buzágh's Colloid Syst.* iv. 45 With increasing crystal size the microstructural composition asymptotically approaches the stoichiometric composition. *Ibid.*, The solution of this paradox is found in a 'microstructurally correct computation'. **1966** C. R. TOTTLE *Sci. Engin. Materials* x. 224 Steels are susceptible to microstructural changes at the temperatures required for stress relief, and for this reason relief is often avoided.

microstylar: see MICRO- 4.

microstylous (maɪkrəʊ'staɪləs), *a. Bot.* [mod. f. Gr. μικρό-ς small + στῦλο-ς pillar, STYLE + -OUS.] Having a short style in association with elevated anthers.

1887 WARD tr. *Sachs' Phys. Plants* xlv. 790 When the pollen of the macrostylous flowers is transferred to the microstylous stigma.

microsurgery (maɪkrəʊ'sɜːdʒərɪ). [f. MICRO- 2a + SURGERY.] Manipulation (as by injection, dissection, etc.) of individual cells with the aid of microscopy; surgery of such delicacy as to necessitate microscopy.

1927 *Protoplasma* II. 203 Micro-surgery of plant cells shows that the impression of fluidity which one gets from mere microscopic observation is illusory. **1928** E. V. COWDRY *Special Cytol.* i. 7 With the apparatus of Chambers it is feasible to isolate a cell, to take it up with a pipette, to incise part of it and to inoculate into its cytoplasm a small amount of fluid. This microsurgery has been applied to the investigation of many problems. **1941** *Bot. Rev.* VII. 355 Harder (1926), by microsurgery, isolated the penultimate cell of a growing hypha of *Coprinus sterquilinus.* **1960** *McGraw-Hill Encycl. Sci. & Technol.* IV. 571/2 As gastrulation and embryo formation proceed, microsurgery becomes more and more the instrument of choice for analysis. The defect experiment tests the effect of removal of one part or rudiment. **1971** *Nature* 2 July 28/1 The techniques of microsurgery on single cells have been applied to a variety of cell types. **1973** *Daily Colonist* (Victoria, B.C.) 10 June 28/2 Microsurgery has been used in brain operations for the last five years, beginning in Europe.

So **micro'surgical** *a.*

1963 *Science* 5 July 46/3 (*heading*) Ruby laser as a microsurgical instrument. **1968** H. HARRIS *Nucleus & Cytoplasm* iv. 81 Nuclei which were divested of virtually all their cytoplasm by microsurgical procedures none the less retained their ability to produce specific puffing patterns. **1974** *Nature* 29 Mar. 450/1 Microsurgical removal of the root cap of *Zea* has been shown to prevent the response of the roots to gravity.

microswitch, -syringe, -system, -tasimeter, -technique, -tektite: see MICRO- 1, 6, 1, 6, 1.

microtelephone (maɪkrəʊ'tɛlɪfəʊn). *Teleph.* [f. MICRO- + TELEPHONE *sb.*] **1.** Any of various modifications of the Bell telephone transmitter which were supposed to render it more sensitive.

1879 J. OCHOVOWICZ in *Nature* 27 Mar. 482/2 The micro-telephone is regulated once for all, and transmits the feeblest word with a truly perfect precision. **1879** T. A. EDISON *U.S. Pat. 222,390* 9 Dec. 311/1 This invention I term the 'micro-telephone' in consequence of the same responding to minute vibrations.

2. [f. MICRO(PHONE.] = HANDSET.

1895 A. R. BENNETT *Telephone Syst. Europe* xvii. 296 Usually the transmitter and receiver are attached to the same handle, in 'micro-telephone' form. **1930** [see HANDSET].

microtext, -texture, -theory: see MICRO- 7, 2b, 1b.

microtherm ('maɪkrəθɜːm). *Bot.* [f. Gr. μικρό-ς small + θέρμη heat, θερμός hot.] A plant, native of an arctic or alpine region.

1875 J. G. BAKER *Bot. Geog.* 48 Microtherm, characteristic of the arctic-alpine zone. *Ibid.* 50 The seeds of many of the Microtherms..will germinate at a temperature of little over 32°. **1884** *Trans. Vict. Inst.* 38 Microtherms—plants inhabiting alpine or arctic regions. **1888** *Our Earth & its Story* (ed. Brown) II. 275 *note*, *Microtherms*, plants of the Arctic-Alpine zone. **1900** JACKSON *Gloss. Bot.*

microtine ('maɪkrəʊtiːn, -aɪn), *sb.* and *a. Zool.* [f. mod.L. subfamily name *Microtinæ* (f. generic name *Microtus* (F. von P. von Schrank *Fauna Boica* (1798) I. 66), f. MICR(O- + Gr. ὠτ-, οὖς ear): see -INA[2].] **A.** *sb.* A member of the rodent subfamily Microtinæ, which includes voles and lemmings. **B.** *adj.* Of or pertaining to this subfamily.

1926 M. A. C. HINTON *Monogr. Voles & Lemmings* I. 16 Some of the most characteristic features of the Microtine skull are shown in longitudinal vertical sections. **1936** *Proc. Prehist. Soc.* II. 53 In the case of the microtine mammals—another rapidly evolving group—detailed work along these lines has been done. **1948** A. L. RAND *Mammals E. Rockies* 165 In some areas at least in Canada the scarcity of microtines seems to cause a scarcity of certain furs. **1956** *Nature* 10 Mar. 445/2 A recognizable description of an Indian mole-vole..of the genus *Ellobius*, a microtine. **1972** T. A. VAUGHAN *Mammalogy* xv. 190 (*caption*) Population densities of several species of Microtines.

microtome ('maɪkrətəʊm), *sb.* [f. Gr. μικρό-ς small + -τόμος that cuts, f. τομ-, τεμ-, root of τέμνειν to cut.] An instrument for cutting extremely thin sections for microscopic work.

1856 CARPENTER *Microsc. & Rev.* 211 The 'microtome' of M. Strauss-Durckheim. **1864** in WEBSTER. **1875** H. G. BIRD in *Q. Jrnl. Microsc. Sci.* XV. 24 If placed dry in a rigid tube, as that of the microtome..the addition of..water will..cause the pith-cells to expand.

Hence **micro'tomic, micro'tomical** *adjs.*, relating to the use of the microtome. **mi'crotomist**, one expert in the use of the microtome. **mi'crotomy**, the scientific use of the microtome.

1885 LEE (*title*) The Microtomist's Vade-Mecum. **1887** *Amer. Naturalist* XXI. 1130 The development of microtomical technique has made it a comparatively easy matter.

'microtome, *v.* [f. the sb.] *trans.* To cut in sections with a microtome. So **'microtomed** *ppl. a.*

1893 *Brit. Med. Jrnl.* 23 Sept. 685/2 The divided roots were microtomed and examined in serial sections. **1898** *Phil. Trans. R. Soc.* B. CXC. 95 The following nerves of muscles were microtomed for detection of some fibres. **1972** *Physics Bull.* Nov. 668/1 Evidence for twisting fibrils has also been obtained from transmission electron micrographs of microtomed specimens.

microtone ('maɪkrəʊtəʊn). *Mus.* [f. MICRO- 1 + TONE *sb.*] An interval smaller than a semitone.

1920 *Outward Bound* Oct. 77/1 The ancient Greeks also recognised and used these microtones. The Greeks found twenty-four in the octave and the Indians usually recognise twenty-two. **1927** *Observer* 23 Oct. 14 But these microtones (seventy-two in the octave) give quarters of the untempered chromatic semitone. **1946** *Mod. Music* Spring 113 The Oriental sound of Hovhaness' music is realized with occidental instruments not by preparing the instruments, nor by employing microtones, but solely through the character of the melody. **1957** MANVELL & HUNTLEY *Technique Film Music* iii. 170 Volume was controlled by varying the exposure;..portamento by a rapid series of micro-tones. **1970** W. APEL *Harvard Dict. Mus.* (ed. 2) 527/1 Long a structural feature of Asian music, the use of microtones in Western music, although far from new, has been..far less extensive.

Hence **micro'tonal** *a.*, of or pertaining to a microtone or microtones; employing or producing microtones; **microto'nality**; **micro'tonally** *adv.*

1942 *Scrutiny* XI. 6 The quarter-tone or *scruti* is the microtonal interval between notes of the 'scale'. **1946** R. BLESH *Shining Trumpets* (1949) v. 106 The microtonally flatted fifth also occurs. *Ibid.* x. 234 The blues scale..gives all the opportunity needed for microtonality. **1946** *Mod. Music* Spring 113 The microtonality of Alois Haba and others presents an Oriental characteristic not found in any of the music discussed above. **1959** *Chambers's Encycl.* IX. 627/2 The microtonality of the Czech Alois Haba (1893–), who cut the scale into ¼- and ⅙- tones. **1967** *Times* 29 May 6/4 Glissandos on the microtonal harp were pure magic. **1974** *Country Life* 24 Jan. 136/1 Mozart..as an infant..could remember microtonal differences of tuning in instruments heard weeks previously.

microtopography (ˌmaɪkrəʊtə'pɒgrəfɪ). [f. MICRO- 2a + TOPOGRAPHY.] The surface features of a material, or of the earth or other body, on a small or microscopic scale.

1956 *Nature* 24 Mar. 564/1 Prof. Tolansky selected as typical subjects for examination some of his own studies on the optical testing of surface finish, of microtopography in general, the examination of micro-hardness and directional hardness [etc.]. **1962** F. I. ORDWAY et al. *Basic Astronautics* iii. 65 Photometric observations..suggest that the microtopography [of the moon] is rough, probably being pitted. **1969** *Ecology* L. 740 Lichen cover and microtopography were positively associated.

Hence ˌ**microtopo'graphic, -topo'graphical** *adjs.*

1958 *New Biol.* XXVI. 40 Even in apparently flat and uniform grassland, the distribution of the buttercup species is usually found to be associated with microtopographical features which determine slight differences in the rate of drainage and the speed with which the soil dries out during drought periods. **1960** S. TOLANSKY *Surface Microtopogr.* vi. 71 Its [*sc.* diamond's] unique hardness makes it an ideal material for microtopographic studies. **1971** *Nature* 22 Jan. 248/1, I have had occasion recently to re-read Goethe's *Theory of Colours* (1810) and have found that he described the nature of the microtopographical interference pattern given by a crystal surface.

microtrichium: see MICRO- 1.

microtron ('maɪkrəʊtrɒn). [f. MICRO(WAVE *sb.* + -TRON.] A variant of the cyclotron for accelerating electrons by passing them repeatedly through a cavity in which they are accelerated by microwaves, the amount of the acceleration on each passage being such as to allow for the increase in their time of revolution that results from their relativistic increase in mass.

1946 *Rev. Sci. Instruments* XVII. 9/1 The microtron, suggested by J. S. Schwinger and by V. Veksler, is an electron cyclotron in which the particles slip one cycle of phase on each circuit through a constant magnetic field. **1958** *Times* 21 June 4/7 It is called the 'microtron' because the electrical pulses used in acceleration are got from a pulsed microwave oscillator. **1974** *Nature* 1 Feb. 250/3 A prototype continuous microtron (a cyclic accelerator in which the electrons are accelerated by microwaves) has been constructed in Obninsk... Until now, it has proved possible to operate microtron accelerators in a pulsed mode only, with a relatively low repetition frequency.

microtubular, -tubule, -tylote: see MICRO- 1.

microunit ('maɪkrəʊ-, 'mɪkrəʊˌjuːnɪt). [f. MICRO- 5a + UNIT *sb.*] A millionth part of a unit, esp. of an international unit (as of insulin).

1900 DORLAND *Med. Dict.* 392/1 *Micro-unit*, a unit of small measurements. **1911** STEDMAN *Med. Dict.* 533/1 *Microunit*, the millionth of an ordinary unit, such as a meter, gram, ohm, etc. **1959** *Nature* 21 Nov. 1649/2 Two to three micro-units of human insulin were detectable in the experiment depicted. **1962** *Lancet* 13 Jan. 73/2 This difference is highly significant statistically..whether the figures are considered at the level of net glucose uptake or after conversion into microunits of insulin per millilitre.

microvascular, -vegetation, -viewer, -villus, -volt, -watt: see MICRO- 4, 1, 7, 1, 5a.

microwavable ('maɪkrəʊˌweɪvəb(ə)l), *a.* orig. *U.S.* Also **microwaveable**. [f. MICROWAVE *v.* + -ABLE.] Of food and food containers: suitable for cooking or heating in a microwave oven.

1982 *N.Y. Times* 17 July 1. 12/5 Pressware, a paperboard product..which is celebrated because it is not only 'ovenable' but 'microwavable' as well. **1984** *New Scientist* 3 May 46/1 Over at the supermarket the food was microwaveable. **1985** *New Yorker* 29 Apr. 30/3 Frozen food comes on plastic plates..and it's microwavable. **1985** *Listener* 5 Sept. 12/2 He had been offered..'ovenable' and 'microwavable' frozen dishes. **1986** *Chem. Week* 5 Feb. 12/3 Some of the packages will be microwaveable; one can double as a serving dish.

microwave ('maɪkrəʊweɪv), *sb.* [f. MICRO- 1 + WAVE *sb.*] **1.** An electromagnetic wave with a wavelength between about one millimetre and 30 centimetres (corresponding to a frequency between 300 gigahertz and one gigahertz); one whose wavelength is such that it is convenient to use hollow waveguides for its transmission.

The precise figures taken as extremes of wavelength or frequency are arbitrary and vary somewhat with different writers; formerly waves much longer than the present-day maximum were described as microwaves.

1931 *Telegraph & Telephone Jrnl.* XVII. 179/1 When.. trials..with wavelengths as low as 18 cm. were made known, there was undisguised surprise..that the problem of the micro-wave had been solved so soon. **1935** *Proc. IRE* XXIII. 1503 (*heading*) Diffraction of microwaves over the curve of the Earth. *Ibid.*, Radio waves below ten meters in length, at the present time termed 'microwaves', may be received at moderate distances over the horizon from the transmitter. **1940** *Amat. Radio Handbk.* (ed. 2) xvi. 232/1 Wavelengths below 1 metre are referred to as 'micro-waves' or 'centimetre waves', and demand special treatment. **1942** J. C. SLATER *Microwave Transmission* 1 The range of waves called microwaves: wave lengths perhaps in the range from a half meter to a few centimeters. **1965** *New Scientist* 10 June 724/3 Microwaves, or waves of even shorter wavelength, must be used because it is only when such short wavelengths are employed that a highly directional beam can be produced. **1968** *Maclean's Mag.* Dec. 19/1 Signals from the satellite will be received by ground stations and relayed by microwave or cable to home receivers. **1973** *Sci. Amer.* Sept. 74/2 Electromagnetic radiation at microwave frequencies is now widely used for cooking purposes. It may also be practical to use microwaves to 'cook' agricultural pests in the soil: insects, weeds, fungi and so on.

2. a. Short for *microwave oven* below; a microwave cooker. orig. *U.S.*

1974 *New Yorker* 12 Aug. 73/2 (Advt.), New, quick-cooking portable microwave. **1976** *Bon Appétit* Apr. 29/2 If you have a family that eats in relays, you'll find the microwave ideal. **1984** *Freetime* (Boots) Autumn 8/1 With a microwave, the food can be defrosted, cooked and ready to serve in a matter of minutes. **1985** *Financial Times* 19 Oct. (Suppl.) p. xiii/2 She cooked an entire dinner party menu in a microwave.

b. Cooking with a microwave oven; microwave cookery.

1977 J. M. WEBB (*title*) Microwave: the cooking revolution. **1984** *Sears Catal. 1985* Spring/Summer 10 Choose from microwave for fast action; convection to surround and brown rolls and cakes; or micro/convection.

3. a. *attrib.*

1933 *Electrician* 6 Jan. 3/1 We decided..to concentrate our efforts on the generation and efficient radiation of what may be termed a medium wavelength on the microwave scale—that is, a wavelength of the order of half-a-metre, i.e., 600 000 k.c. **1946** *Proc. IRE* XXXIV. 775/1 The extent of the microwave spectrum has been variously defined. This paper will concern itself with the range of frequencies between approximately 2000 and 30,000 megacycles per second. **1946** *Jrnl. R. Aeronaut. Soc.* L. 956/1 During the war airborne microwave radar was used to provide in the aircraft a map or picture showing the main features, e.g., towns and rivers, of the country below. **1947** *Electronic Engin.* XIX. 17 Ultra-short and microwave radio links. **1952** *Sci. News* XXV. 30 From a study of such rotational spectra of asymmetric molecules in the microwave region the distance between the atoms can be found very accurately. **1957** *B.B.C. Handbk.* 59 The vision signals from remote outside broadcast points are carried back to the main television network by BBC microwave or VHF radio links. **1959** *Daily Tel.* 18 May 12/6 The sky platform would hover in a fixed position. Helicopter type rotary wings would be turned by microwave energy beamed from stations on earth. **1964** *Ann. Reg. 1963* 163 The microwave telecommunications network linking Ankara, Karachi and Teheran. **1967** D. WILSON in Wills & Yearsley *Handbk. Managem. Technol.* iii. 44 Data transmission is concerned with the transmission of data over private or G.P.O. lines or by using microwave techniques. **1971** *Brit. Printer* Jan. 67/2 Microwave dryers are currently at an advanced stage of development. **1972** *Sci. Amer.* Feb. 13/1 Although the microwave region of the electromagnetic spectrum is not precisely defined, we use the term to describe radiation of wavelengths ranging from 30 centimeters to three millimeters.

b. *attrib.* and *Comb.* with reference to cooking in a microwave oven, esp. as ***microwave cooker, cooking***.

1962 in *Food Technol.* (1969) XXIII. 1579/1 *(heading)* General Electric microwave cooking center..heats all types of food in seconds. **1966** *Food Technol.* XX. 915/2 Microwave-puffing of foods. **1977** *Amer. Home* Nov. 61/2 Place ribs on microwave rack in shallow glass or other microwave-proof baking dish. **1978** S. BRILL *Teamsters* v. 175 A microwave reheater..prepared various cans and plastic packages of pre-cooked food. **1978** *Morecambe Guardian* 14 Mar. 26/9 (Advt.), Microwave cooker, browning dishes, now available. **1984** S. TOWNSEND *Growing Pains A. Mole* 59 My father..went to the pub and had a microwave mince and onion pie. **1984** *Which?* Dec. 542/1 Food doesn't brown well—one of the main drawbacks of microwave cookery.

c. Special Comb.: **microwave oven**, an oven in which food is cooked by passing microwaves through it, the resulting generation of heat inside the food making rapid and uniform cooking possible.

1965 *Economist* 22 May 941/2 *(heading)* Microwave ovens. A meal a minute. **1968** *New Scientist* 24 Oct. 175/1 The microwave oven..is now coming into quite wide use in homes in the United States. **1973** *Daily Tel.* 26 Apr. 11/8 Microwave ovens which are still in the experimental stage, would take eight minutes to produce a standard loaf, instead of 30.

microwave, *v.* orig. *U.S.* [f. the sb.]
a. *trans.* To cook or heat (food) in a microwave oven. **b.** *intr.* To be suitable for or undergo microwave cooking. Cf. MICROCOOK *v.*

1976 *National Observer* (U.S.) 3 Apr. 9/4, I..microwaved them two at a time for one minute. **1979** [see MICRO *sb.* 4]. **1984** *Listener* 20 Sept. 16/2 Alveston Kitchens, producer of those boil-in-the-bag and microwave-'n-serve gourmet dishes for the catering trade, have the latest technology. **1984** *Tampa* (Florida) *Tribune* 5 Apr. 8E/1 Standing time is important after a meatloaf has finished microwaving. **1986** *Family Circle* May 83/4 Microwaved veg for 4 min on High.

micro-weber: see MICRO- 5.

microweld ('maɪkrəʊwɛld), *v.* [f. MICRO- 1 b + WELD *v.*] *trans.* To join by a very small weld. So **'microwelded** *ppl. a.*, **'microwelding** *vbl. sb.*

1962 *Flight Internat.* LXXXII. 1027/1 According to Aerojet-General Corporation, a micro-welding device developed by the Corporation's Astrionics Division 'will make a reliable weld in the time it takes you to dot an 'i'... But the dot of your 'i' will be 30 times bigger than the weld.' **1963** E. KEONJIAN *Microelectronics* 380 Micro-welded connections. **1968** *Sci. Jrnl.* Nov. 17 *(caption)* The microwelding machine below is used to bond leads to the circuit. **1970** *New Scientist* 13 Aug. 338/2 An army of girls some 30 000 strong is employed..in micro-welding hair-sized connections from each silicon chip. **1975** *Country Life* 3 Apr. 838/1 The use of microwelding—an engineering skill put to very effective use as in a bracelet that seems to be a web of fine interlaced wires.

microwire, -world: see MICRO- 1.

microxea: see MICRO- 1.

‖**microzoa** (maɪkrəʊ'zəʊə), *sb. pl. Zool.* In *sing.* **-zoon** (-'zəʊɒn). [mod.L., f. Gr. μῑκρό-ς small + ζῷον animal.] A general name for infusoria, rotifers, etc. Hence **micro'zoal, micro'zoic** *adjs.*, of the nature of, containing, or consisting of microzoa.

1862 STODDART in *Q. Jrnl. Microsc. Sci.* II. 150 These small microzoa seem to be the most ubiquitous of any known beings. *Ibid.* 147 Its zoophytes and other microzoic wonders. **1876** PAGE *Adv. Text-bk. Geol.* xx. 440 The innumerable organisms in microphytal and microzoal deposits. **1884** BRADY in *Challenger Rep., Zool.* IX. 136 Microzoa from the Upper Lias of Banbury. *Ibid.* 148 In microzoic strata.

microzoan (maɪkrəʊ'zəʊən), *a.* and *sb. Zool.* [f. MICROZOA: see -AN.] **a.** *adj.* Pertaining to the Microzoa. **b.** *sb.* Any member of the Microzoa (*Cassell's Encycl. Dict.* Suppl. 1902).

micro'zoary. *Zool.* [ad. mod.L. *mīcrozōaria*, pl. of **mīcrozōarion*, f. Gr. μῑκρό-ς small + ζῳάριον dim. of ζῷον animal.] = MICROZOON.

1863 SLACK in *Intell. Observ.* Dec. 379 During the fœtid stage he [*sc.* Lemaire] observed thirty species of microzoaries.

So **microzo'arian**, *a.* and *sb.* = MICROZOAN (*Cent. Dict.* 1890).

microzone, -zoogonidium: see MICRO- 1.

microzooid (maɪkrəʊ'zəʊɔɪd), *sb.* and *a.* [f. MICRO- + ZOOID.] **a.** *sb.* (See quot.) **b.** *adj.* Pertaining to a microzooid (*Cent. Dict.* 1890).

1882 KENT *Man. Infusoria* II. 870 *Microzooids*, free-swimming zooids of abnormally minute size, which conjugate with, or become buried within the substance of the bodies of the normally sized sedentary animalcules of many Vorticellidæ.

microzoology: see MICRO- 2.

microzoon: sing. of MICROZOA.

microzoospore: see MICRO- 1.

microzyme ('maɪkrəʊzaɪm). *Phys.* Also **microzyma** (maɪkrəʊ'zaɪmə). [mod. f. Gr. μῑκρό-ς small + ζύμη yeast: cf. ZYMIC.] A zymotic microbe; one of a class of minute and lowly organized living beings, to whose presence are attributed epidemic and other zymotic diseases.

1873 HUXLEY *Critiques & Addr.* x. 242 Two of the most destructive of epizoötic diseases..are also dependent for their existence..upon extremely small living solid particles, to which the title of microzymes is applied. **1881** *Athenæum* 23 July 118/2 These microzymas and those of chalk and other rocks have the same origin as the microzymas of every living organism. **1885-8** FAGGE & PYE-SMITH *Princ. Med.* (ed. 2) 25 The word 'microzyme' was suggested by Béchamp and adopted by Sanderson. **1902** *Longm. Mag.* July 257 Water which he had obtained from the purest ice contained microzymes.

micrurgy ('maɪkrɜːdʒɪ). [f. MICR(O- + *-urgy* after METALLURGY.] The performance of delicate manipulations under the microscope, esp. on biological material such as individual cells. So **mi'crurgical** *a.*

1927 *Protoplasma* II. 189 *(heading)* The structural organization of plant protoplasm in the light of micrurgy. *Ibid.* 191 The extensive micrurgical researches that have been made on animal cells. **1935** *Industr. & Engin. Chem. (Analytical Ed.)* VII. 218/1 The word 'micrurgy' was coined by Peterfi..to describe biological microdissection and later expanded by Titus and Gray..to include dissection and examination under the microscope of non-biological material. Since the term, by its pure Greek derivation, means 'operations on a small scale or work with minute quantities', it can logically be used as a general term to include microchemistry, microanalysis, and chemical microscopy... It is here so used, and is suggested for general adoption. **1960** *New Scientist* 20 Oct. 1049/1 With the new technique of micrurgy the gap between the living cell and the micrologist had been bridged. **1973** *Nature* 2 Mar. 47/2 For micrurgical manipulation, two- or eight-celled eggs from superovulated BALB/c mice were deposited into a suspension of somatic cells and virus in an 'egg-well'.

†**'miction.** *Obs.* [ad. late L. *mictiōn-em* (also *minctiōn-em*), n. of action f. *mingĕre* to make water. Cf. F. *miction.*] The action of urinating.

1663 H. MORE *Div. Dial.* I. 372 But the Laws of Miction amongst those of the West-Indies is a pitch of Slovenliness beyond all Cynicism, the men and women not sticking to let fly their Urine even while they are conversing with you. **1689** G. HARVEY *Curing Dis. by Expect.* viii. 60 The risque of a troublesome Cure of the Wound, that seldom is performed without..difficulty of miction. **1856** MAYNE *Expos. Lex.*

micturate ('mɪktjʊəreɪt), *v.* [Incorrectly f. L. *micturīre*: see MICTURIENT. (The sense is incorrect as well as the form.)] *intr.* To urinate.

1842 *Lancet* 26 Mar. 903/2 Another, in long-winded phrase, tells us that his patient 'desires to micturate'. **1889** J. M. DUNCAN *Clin. Lect. Dis. Wom.* xxvii. (ed. 4) 220 She now complains of pain on micturating. **1899** *Allbutt's Syst. Med.* VII. 19 If the transverse spinal lesion be complete, the desire to micturate will be lost.

†**mic'turient**, *a. Obs.* [ad. L. *micturient-em*, pres. pple. of *micturīre*, desiderative vb. f. *mict-*, *minct-*, *mingĕre* to make water.] Desirous of making water.

1654 GAYTON *Pleas. Notes* IV. xxii. 274 Which..gave Sancho to perceive his condition very micturient, and cacaturient.

micturition (mɪktjʊə'rɪʃən). [agent-n. f. L. *micturīre*: see MICTURIENT. Cf. F. *micturition.*] The desire to make water; a morbid frequency in the voiding of urine. Often incorrectly used for: The action of making water.

1725 HUXHAM in *Phil. Trans.* XXXIII. 388 In the confluent kind, generally a Micturition and Dysury came on about the 12th, or 13th Day. **1799** *Med. Jrnl.* II. 200 Frequent painful micturition. **1818-20** E. THOMPSON *Cullen's Nosol. Method.* (ed. 3) 256 Without swelling of the hypogastrium or micturition. **1860** SIR H. THOMPSON *Dis. Prostate* (1868) 58 The barrier which the swollen prostate offers to micturition. **1889** J. M. DUNCAN *Clin. Lect. Dis. Wom.* xxix. (ed. 4) 236 Micturition very difficult.

mid (mɪd), *a.*, *sb.*[1], and *adv.* Forms: 1 mid(d)-, 3-6 **myd**, 4 **myde**, 4-7 **midde**, 5 **mydde**, 6 **midd**, 3- **mid.** [Com. Teut. and Indogermanic: OE. *midd* (found only in inflected forms, *midde, middes, midre, midne*, etc.) corresponds to OFris. *midde, medde*, OS. *middi*, OHG. *mitti* (MHG. *mitte*), ON. *miðr*, Goth. *midjis*:—OTeut. **medjo-*:—Indo-germanic **medhyo-*, whence Skr. *madhya*, Zend *maidya*, Gr. μέσσος (:—**methyos*), later μέσος, L. *medius*, OCeltic *medio-* (in place-names), OIrish *mide* sb., middle.] **A.** *adj.*

1. a. In partitive concord, expressing adjectivally the sense: (The) middle or midst of. (In mod. Eng. usually hyphened.)

Originally *mid* in this sense could be used without restriction, but in mod.Eng. its application has been greatly narrowed. It is still extensively used in scientific and technical language; and it is common (though rather literary than colloquial) in advb. phrases formed with *in* prep., the article being most frequently omitted, as *in mid-career, in mid-volley* (see d); but the use of phrases of this type not traditionally current is apt to seem affected. The attributive use of the combinations of *mid-* is also frequent.

c **1160** *Hatton Gosp.* Mark vi. 47 And þa æfen wæs þæt scyp wæs on midre sæ. *c* **1350** *Will. Palerne* 3605 Ac williams spere was stef wittow for soþe, & mette þat oþer man in þe midde scheld. **1375** BARBOUR *Bruce* XVIII. 132 Quhen in myd cawse war thai [etc.]. *a* **1400** *Sir Perc.* 2062 The clobe in the erthe stode To the midschafte it wode. **1489** *Paston Lett.* III. 347 It [a whale] is xj. fadam and more of length, and ij. fadam of bygnes..in the mydde fyssh. **1513** DOUGLAS *Æneis* IV. ii. 53 Begyn scho wald to tell furth hir intent And in the myd word stop, and hald hir still. **1557-75** *Diurn. of Occurr.* (Bannatyne Cl.) 104 Quhair at ane tabill sat the quenis Majestie at mydburd. **1609** T. HEYWOOD *Troia Brit.* ii. 2 Nor did that Nation first on earth begin Vnder the mid Equator. **1610** HEALEY *St. Aug. Citie of God* XVI. viii. (1620) 548 Some that haue but one eye in their mid-fore-head. **1618** M. BARET *Horsemanship* I. 48 He must obserue that the vse of the hand is not to cut and teare the Horses mouth vp to the mid-cheeke, as many heauy hands doe. **1647** J. HALL *Poems* II. 104 Thou who canst stop the Sea In her mid-rage, stop me. *a* **1667** MILTON in Birch *Life* M.'s Wks. 1738 I. 43 Next some Shepheard or companie of Merchants passing through the Mount in the time that Abram was in the midwork, relate to Sarah what they saw. **1681** DRYDEN *Span. Friar* I. i, I'll plant my Colours down In the Mid-breach. **1727-46** THOMSON *Summer* 9 Hence, let me haste into the mid-wood shade. **1742** YOUNG *Nt. Th.* IX. 954 Now Sons of Riot in Mid-Revel rage. **1753** G. WEST *Odes of Pindar*, etc. I. 228 The sacred Image, that fell down from Heav'n, In the Mid-Gally utter'd thus her Voice. **1810** SIR A. BOSWELL *Edinb.* Poet. Wks. (1871) 48 In mid-street, fit theme for laureate bard, The proper Castle of the City Guard. **1810** SCOTT *Lady of L.* III. xiv, The plough was in mid-furrow stayed. **1818** KEATS *Endym.* I. 18 The mid-forest brake, Rich with a sprinkling of fair musk-rose blooms. **1829** SCOTT *Doom of Devorgoil* III. iv, We counter'd ..even in mid-chamber. **1833** L. RITCHIE *Wand. by Loire* 59 A column of smoke rising from the mid-surface of a perpendicular rock. **1852** WIGGINS *Embanking* 86 Between the mid-tide level and the low-water level of neaps. *Ibid.*, An hour before mid-ebb, and for the same time after mid-flow. **1853** GROTE *Greece* II. lxxxviii. XI. 513 Though this seems a strange proceeding during mid-war, yet [etc.]. **1853** WHYTE MELVILLE *Digby Grand* I. viii. 206 Every oar above the surface, as though arrested in mid-stroke by a charm. **1859** TENNYSON *Elaine* 553 A Prince In the mid might and flourish of his May. *Ibid.* 874 Yet the great knight in his mid-sickness made Full many a holy vow and pure resolve. **1860** READE *Cloister & H.* xxxvii, He..suddenly rising in mid narrative, said [etc.]. **1862** G. A. LAWRENCE *Barr. Hon.* I. v. 95 Just as a fencer might do touched sharply in mid-chest by his opponent's foil. **1871** FARRAR *Witn. Hist.* ii. 82 A prophet of anarchy and naturalism, in the mid confession of his faith. **1873** RUSKIN *Fors Clav.* xxiii. 17 If the spider, or other monster in midweb, ate you. **1879** SIR G. G. SCOTT *Lect. Archit.* I. 278 By placing the glass in..the mid-thickness of the wall. **1898** *Allbutt's Syst. Med.* V. 94 Occasionally it [*sc.* a pain] is felt in the mid-axilla.

b. With article or possessive adj. interposed between the adj. and sb. *Obs.*

Prob. due to association with the construction of *on middan*: see AMID. Cf. the still surviving similar use of HALF *a.* (1 b).

c **897** K. ÆLFRED *Gregory's Past. C.* xlix. 383 Gað from ʒeate to ʒeate ðurh midde ða ceastre. *a* **900** tr. *Bæda's Hist.* v. i. §2 Ða we ða wæron on midre ðære sæ. *a* **1225** *Ancr. R.* 146 Hwui drawest tu ut þine rihte hond of midden þine boseme [tr. L. *de medio sinu*]? *c* **1420** *Liber Cocorum* (1862) 19 Be sleȝe and powre in water þenne To myd þo pot.

c. Prefixed to the name of a month or season, or the designation of a period of time. Also in †*mid eld*, middle age.

c **1000** *Sax. Leechd.* III. 162 He leng ne leofað þonn on midre ilde. **1297** R. GLOUC. (Rolls) 4005 Amidde haruest [MS. δ at myd haruest] we þe setteþ day of þis nexte ȝere. *a* **1330** *Roland & V.* 10 Opon his fest in midmay Ther on is front of gret noblay. **14..** *Stockh. Med. MS.* II. 332 in *Anglia* XVIII. 315 Betwen mydde march & mydde aprille. *c* **1485** *E.E. Misc.* (Warton Cl.) 11 At myd-undure-none wonderly I waxe. **1508** DUNBAR *Twa Mariit Wemen* 297 He was a man of myd eld. **1586** EARL OF LEICESTER *Corr.* (Camden) 251, I would haue Antwerpe towne and Burges or midd June. **1615** BRATHWAIT *Strappado* (1878) 130 Bout mid-belten twas. **1722** DE FOE *Plague* (Rtldg.) 25 It was now mid-July. **1859** TENNYSON *Geraint* 612 As a leaf in mid-November is To what it was in mid-October. **1893** F. ADAMS *New Egypt* 86 From mid-June to mid-October. **1896** HOWELLS *Impressions & Exp.* 222 The wind rises, and by mid-afternoon, blows half a gale. **1898** G. B. SHAW *Perfect Wagnerite* 34 A..melodic bogey to mid-century ears. **1902** B. GRUNDY *Thames Camp* 123, I have trouble over my mid-morning bathes on account of passing boats. **1906** *Dialect Notes* III. 146 The mid-term examinations will begin the last of January. **1923** D. H. LAWRENCE *Birds, Beasts & Flowers* 103 A disgusting bat At mid-morning. **1928** T. S. ELIOT *For Lancelot Andrewes* 76 Arnold turned from mid-century Radicalism. **1938** *Encycl. Brit. Bk. of Year* 700/1 There are 1,200 firms in Britain now operating such amenities as a ten-minute mid-morning break. **1951** I. SHAW *Troubled Air* xv. 248 The mid-afternoon coffee was put up in containers. **1952** C. P. BLACKER *Eugenics* 259 At about mid-pregnancy, identical twins differ more in size than do fraternal. **1953** *Manch. Guardian Weekly* 1 Oct. 1 The Administration party loses seats at the 'mid-term' elections. **1958** P. SHORE in N. Mackenzie *Conviction* 23 All over Britain a new mid-twentieth-century society is coming vigorously to life. **1959** P. TOWNEND *Died o' Wednesday* xii. 216 Chance customers who dropped in for mid-morning coffee, light lunches and afternoon tea. **1961** *Lancet* 5 Aug. 280/1 The gradual change in uterine activity begins as early in pregnancy as midterm. **1968** A. DIMENT *Gt. Spy Race* iv. 53 The obscure type faces which these mid-century tailors use to advertise their dens. **1972** J. MCCLURE *Caterpillar Cop* ix. 144 The last lesson before mid-morning break. **1973** *Guardian* 19 Apr. 14/2 The people who fear it [*sc.* the Watergate scandal] will hurt them are Republican candidates for next year's mid-term elections.

d. In various customary collocations or combinations with sb., as ***mid-career, -channel, -flight, -race, -river, -sentence, -stride, -thigh, -volley***. Also **mid-Atlantic**, (*a*) the middle of

the Atlantic Ocean; (*b*) something that has both British and American characteristics, or is designed to appeal to both the British and the Americans; also *attrib.* or as *adj.*; **mid-band** *a. Electronics*, of or pertaining to the middle of a band of frequencies; **mid-brain** = MESENCEPHALON; **mid-breast** *Ent.* = MEDIPECTUS; **mid-breast-bone** *Ent.* = MESOSTERNUM; **mid-calf**, (*a*) the 'pluck' of a calf; (*b*) *attrib.* or as *adj.*, describing a garment that reaches half-way down the calf of the leg; **mid-chest** *Ent.* = MESOTHORAX; **mid-cycle** *a.* and *sb. Physiol.*, (occurring at) the middle of the menstrual cycle; **mid-kidney** *Anat.* = MESONEPHRON; **mid-main** *poet.*, mid-ocean; **mid-square** *a. Math.*, describing a method of generating a pseudorandom sequence of digits by squaring an arbitrary large number, taking the middle digits of the result (usu. half the total number of digits, a zero being added at the left if necessary to make the total even), and using these as the first digits of the series and as the number to be squared to provide the next digits, and so on indefinitely; **mid-sun** (*rare*) = midday sun; **mid-totality** *Astr.*, the middle of the duration of the totality of an eclipse; **mid-town, midtown** chiefly *U.S.*, the middle of a town; a central area in a town or city; freq. *attrib.*; **mid-wicket**, in *Cricket*, † (*a*) = MID-OFF (*obs.*); when there was a corresponding fieldsman on the other side of the wicket, the two were distinguished as ***mid-wicket on*** (or MID-ON) and ***mid-wicket off*** (or MID-OFF); (*b*) a fieldsman or position between mid-off and square-leg.

1892 'MARK TWAIN' *Amer. Claimant* 65 Two shipments would meet and part in *mid-Atlantic. **1897** *Proc. Zool. Soc.* 351 *Monachus*, the Seal of the Mid-Atlantic. **1940** G. GREENE *19 Stories* (1947) 184 Central heating gave it the stuffy smell of mid-Atlantic. **1957** M. SWAN *Brit. Guiana* i. 25 He was drowned..when the ship in which he was returning to England from the United States was wrecked in mid-Atlantic. **1958** *Spectator* 7 Feb. 164/1, I crossed swords with the redoubtable Douglas Fairbanks Jr. on whether or not his television films could justly be called 'British'..; my argument was that as they aim at the American—or 'mid-Atlantic'—market, they do not deserve the name. **1962** *Radio Times* 22 Nov. 41/2 A spell in Hollywood where he was sent by the studio to which he was under contract to acquire a 'mid-Atlantic' accent. **1970** *Observer* 8 Feb. 30/6 There's another sameness too, a mid-Atlantic look. **1956** *Nature* 25 Feb. 392/2 At a *mid-band wave-length of 3·2 cm., an input-voltage standing-wave ratio of 0·9 or better can be achieved over a 10 per cent band-width. **1962** SIMPSON & RICHARDS *Physical Princ. Junction Transistors* xiii. 300 The mid-band voltage gain. **1875** HUXLEY & MARTIN *Elem. Biol.* (1877) 185 The encephalon lies in the cranial cavity, which it nearly fills, and is divisible into the hind-brain, the *mid-brain, and the fore-brain. **1826** KIRBY & Sp. *Entomol.* III. xxxv. 562 We will next say something upon those..that compose the medipectus or *mid-breast. *Ibid.* 566 The central part of the medipectus, or that which passes between the mid-legs when elevated, protended, or otherwise remarkable, is called the *mesosternum* or *mid-breast-bone. **1789** FARLEY *Lond. Art Cookery* i. xi. (ed. 6) 116 A *Midcalf. Stuff a calf's heart..and send it to the oven... When you dish it up, pour the mincemeat in the bottom... Set the heart in the middle, and lay the [fried] liver and bacon over the minced meat. **1805** ELIZ. RAFFALD *Eng. Housekeeper* (new ed.) 101 A good way to dress a Midcalf. **1816** *Yng. Woman's Comp.* 1 In a Calf,..the head and inwards are called the pluck; in some places they are called the calf's race, and in others, the mid-calf. **1967** *Harper's Bazaar* Sept. 45 The mid-calf hem for day. **1969** *Guardian* 30 July 7/1 Courrèges..does in fact show one or two midcalf dresses for late day. **1974** *Country Life* 24 Jan. 181/1 Slim, mid-calf dresses in tiny stripes. **1730–46** THOMSON *Autumn* 363 How, in his *mid-career, the spaniel, struck Stiff by the tainted gale. **1839–40** W. IRVING *Wolfert's R.* (1855) 92 He sees their concussion, man to man, and horse to horse, in mid-career. **1879** FARRAR *St. Paul* I. 207 Souls which have been arrested in mid-career by the heart-searching voice of God. **1762** MORE in *Phil. Trans.* LII. 452 It being a light Levant,..and both ships near *mid-chanel. **1879** FROUDE *Cæsar* xvi. 267 At sunrise they were in midchannel,..with the cliffs of Britain plainly visible. **1826** KIRBY & SP. *Entomol.* III. xxxiii. 379 A partition..passing down vertically into the *mid-chest. **1951** C. K. WEICHERT *Anat. Chordates* ix. 399 This is the condition at the time of ovulation, and the endometrium is said to be of the *mid-cycle type. **1952** E. S. TAYLOR *Man. Gynecol.* iii. 19 At mid-cycle a ripened ovum is extruded from the ovary. **1965** J. H. BURN *Lect. Notes Pharmacol.* (ed. 8) 93 The function of the progestogen is to prevent 'break-through' bleeding in the mid-cycle. **1974** PASSMORE & ROBSON *Compan. Med. Stud.* III. xxviii. 33/2 These pills relieve dysmenorrhoea, premenstrual tension, midcycle pain or bleeding, and regulate previously irregular periods. **1896** *Brit. Birds* I. 41 It will stop in *midflight and poise itself. **1932** W. FAULKNER *Light in August* v. 98 It did not vanish in midflight. **1948** R. GRAVES *Coll. Poems* 219 That sea-birds of all sorts that flock About the Bass, repeatedly Collide in mid-flight. **1969** *Listener* 6 Feb. 163/1 (*caption*) The Lunar Excursion Module (centre) after mid-flight reassembly of the spacecraft has taken place, to allow two astronauts to enter the module from the main unit. **1862** G. M. HOPKINS *Vision of Mermaids* (1929), Mermaids..ring the knells Of seamen whelm'd in chasms of the *mid-main. **1959** *Times* 5 Oct. 4/7 It is easy to criticize Eldon for his wasteful short bursts in *mid-race. **1571** GOLDING *Calvin on Ps.* lx. 1 (Interamnis) which may be termed in Englishe, (*Midriver). **1897** MARY KINGSLEY *W. Africa* 186 We paddled on towards it, hugging the right-hand bank again to avoid the mid-river rocks. **1901** H. G. WELLS *First Men in Moon* xiii. 104, I looked up, and stopped in *mid-sentence. **1967** *Coast to Coast 1965–66* 30 She paused in mid-sentence. **1951** *Appl. Math. Ser. Nat. Bureau of Standards* (U.S.) XII. 33 (*heading*) The *mid-square method of generating digits. **1968** P. A. P. MORAN *Introd. Probability Theory* i. 46 The midsquare method has, however, been shown to be unsatisfactory. **1932** W. FAULKNER *Light in August* xix. 436 The one stopped in the act of crouching from the leap, the other in *midstride of running. **1957** T. HUGHES *Hawk in Rain* 51 And his foot hung like Statuary in mid-stride. **1810** SOUTHEY *Kehama* XXIII. x, The Diamond City blazing on its height With more than *mid-sun splendour. *c* **1275** *XI Pains of Hell* 97 in *O.E. Misc.* 150 Summe..þat stondeþ vp to heore kneon And summe to heore *myd-þeyh. **1506–7** *Acc. Ld. Treas. Scotl.* (1901) III. 252 Item, for ij elne quhit, to be tua pair hos for the King to his myd thee, vij s. **1725** DE FOE *Voy. round World* (1840) 158 The grass..being as high as our mid-thigh. **1872** TENNYSON *Gareth & Lynette* 790 Mid-thigh-deep in bulrushes. **1879** PROCTOR *Rough Ways* (1880) 5 At the time of *mid-totality a bright light shone round the moon. **1934** WEBSTER, *Mid-town (s.v. *mid-*). **1952** S. KAUFFMANN *Philanderer* (1953) ix. 157 They went to the roof garden of a midtown hotel. **1959** J. CARY *Captive & Free* 41 The mid-town terraces which can and have so easily become slum tenements. **1963** *Listener* 31 Jan. 202/2 In the very middle of mid-town, just off (and even just on) Broadway, the whole street is sometimes used as an open-air loading bay and temporary warehouse. **1974** *Times* 19 Jan. 10/1 New York is not yet on a three-day week, but..mid-town restaurants are doing badly. **1667** MILTON *P.L.* VI. 854 Yet half his strength he put not forth, but check'd His Thunder in *mid Volie. **1744** J. LOVE *Cricket* 15 He, at *Mid wicket, disappoints the Foe. **1849** *Boy's Own Bk.* 78 Mid-wicket on, long slip, and mid-wicket-off. **1850** 'BAT' *Cricket. Man.* 44 Mid-Wicket divides the ground between the cover point and bowler.

e. Occasionally the combination of *mid* + sb. (without prep.) is used adverbially. (Probably *mid* in this use is apprehended as a prep. = *amid*: cf. *amidships*.)

1533 BELLENDEN *Livy* v. xx. (S.T.S.) II. 214 þai sufferit þe Inemyis to ascend myd montane. **1706** MAULE *Hist. Picts* in *Misc. Scot.* I. 59 Inch Keth lyeth mid-firth almost betwixt Leith and Kinghorn. **1808** FORSYTH *Beauties Scotl.* V. 298 About mid-hill there is commonly moss. **1837** SIR F. PALGRAVE *Merch. & Friar* (1844) 80 An open gallery, midheight in the guildhall wall. **1847** TENNYSON *Princess* IV. 170 To drench his dark locks in the gurgling wave Mid-channel. **1871** —— *Last Tourn.* 487 The red dream Fled with a shout, and that low lodge return'd, Mid-forest, and the wind among the boughs. **1884** CHILD *Ballads* I. 376/1 She struck him midshoulders, so that he fell to the ground. **1887** G. MEREDITH *Ballads & P.* 86 Light that Caught him mid-gallop, blazed him home.

f. In comb. with adjs. with the general sense, 'belonging to the middle portion of the designated tract or period'; as ***mid-agrarian, -arctic, -clavicular, -diastolic, -dorsal, -facial, -frontal, -Italian, -monthly, -sternal, -thoracic, -ventral, -Victorian*** (hence as *sb.*; also † ***mid-Vic*** sb. and adj. in the same senses) adjs. Also ***mid-Victorianism.***

1855 J. G. BAKER *Flower. Pl.* 9 Climatic zones... 3. *Midagrarian to Midarctic. **1902** H. J. STILES in D. J. Cunningham *Text-bk. Anat.* 1184 In a well-proportioned subject, the *mid-clavicular line, if prolonged downwards, will be found to be continuous with the vertical Poupart line. **1961** *Lancet* 9 Sept. 573/2 A hyperactive precordium with the maximum apical impulse in the left fifth intercostal space outside the midclavicular line was noted. **1898** *Allbutt's Syst. Med.* V. 944 At the apex was heard a *mid-diastolic murmur. **1879** *St. George's Hosp. Rep.* IX. 242 The fracture was in the *mid-dorsal region. **1890** *Syd. Soc. Lex.*, **Midfacial height*,..the distance from the naso-frontal suture to the alveolar border of the superior maxillary bone measured on the median line. *Ibid.*, **Midfrontal area*, the area of the skull included between two vertical lines drawn upwards from the supra-orbital arch through the frontal eminence to the coronal suture. *Midfrontal process*, the median azygous process of the fronto-nasal process in the embryo. **1895** MACKAIL *Lat. Lit.* i. 11 The keen and narrow political instinct, by which the small and straggling *mid-Italian town grew to be arbitress of the world. **1895** *Daily News* 15 Apr. 2/6 The declaration of options for the *mid-monthly settlement gave a little animation to the first part of the day's business. **1902** H. J. STILES in D. J. Cunningham *Text-bk. Anat.* 1184 The vertical lines are: the *mid-sternal, the lateral sternal, [etc.]. **1963** *Lancet* 12 Jan. 111/1 She had a severe midsternal pain which continued overnight, preventing sleep. **1898** *Allbutt's Syst. Med.* V. 980 It [i.e. the cardiac apex] may overpass the vertical *mid-thoracic line. **1904** *Amer. Naturalist* Feb. 123 The median vein lies along the *mid-ventral line of the swollen abdomen. **1925** J. T. JENKINS *Fishes Brit. Isles* 315 Its colour was almost black dorsally..with an irregular mid-ventral streak. **1933** E. HAMILTON *Halcyon Era* 6 The papers, over which the poor *Midvics yawned in ill-concealed boredom, dealt almost exclusively with Court news. *Ibid.* 32 The studied Midvic pose. *Ibid.* 39 No one was ever allowed to take anything off in Midvic days. **1901** F. H. BURNETT *Making of Marchioness* II. xiv. 280 'She was so respectable?' 'She was even a little *Mid-Victorian, dear Mary.' **1902** *Monthly Rev.* Aug. 150 The domestic style which we in England call the Mid-Victorian. **1927** Mid-Victorian [see EDWARDIAN *a.* 3]. **1965** N. ST. JOHN-STEVAS in Bagehot *Coll. Works* I. 79 Bagehot was never in the least infected by the vulgar *No Popery* of the mid-Victorians. **1969** H. PERKIN *Key Profession* iii. 81 The mid-Victorian reforms which reduced the power of the 'Heads of Houses'. **1923** *Daily Mail* 12 Feb. 13 The artist.. had an eccentric taste for *mid-Victorianism. **1927** W. E. COLLINSON *Contemp. Eng.* 62 The peg-top trousers of mid-Victorianism.

2. **a.** Occupying a central, medial, or intermediate position. Now *rare* (exc. as in b, c, d, e); superseded in ordinary use by MIDDLE *a.*

c **1440** *Jacob's Well* 187 Feendys comyn & brokyn vp..two cheynes of þat stonyn coffre. þe myd-cheyne was stylle hole. *c* **1550** *Exam. W. Thorpe* in Foxe *A. & M.* (1583) I. 534 In the secret of the midde Masse on Christmas day it is written thus: *Idem* [etc.]. **1577–8** *Reg. Privy Council Scot.* II. 665 To remove the occasioun be sum mid and indifferent way. **1612** DONNE *Elegy on Death Pr. Henry* 85 Our Soules best baiting, and midd-period, In her long journey, of considering God. **1648** BP. HALL *Sel. Th.* §63 Betwixt both these extremes, if we would have our souls prosper, a middisposition must be attained. **1656** STANLEY *Hist. Philos.* v. (1701) 196/1 Betwixt these is a mid-nature. *c* **1810** COLERIDGE in *Lit. Rem.* (1838) III. 339 The spirit of life in the mid or balancing state between fixation and reviviscence. **1819** KEATS *Isabella* xxxii, In the mid-days of autumn. **1838** MRS. BROWNING *Seraphim* II. (1892) 75 A woman kneels The mid cross under.

b. *spec.* (*a*) *Phonetics.* Of a vowel-sound: produced with the tongue or some part of it in a middle position between high and low. Freq. *Comb.*

1876 [see HIGH *a.* 4 b]. **1908** H. SWEET *Sounds of Eng.* 25 If the tongue stops exactly half-way, we obtain the normal 'mid' position, as in the first elements of *ei* and *ou*, which are mid-front and mid-back respectively. **1927** J. J. HOGAN *Eng. Lang. in Ireland* 60 He notices the representation of M.E. ē slack by a mid-vowel: 'They pronounce the words tea, sea, please, as if they were written, tay, say, plays; instead of tee, see, pleese.' **1935** *Harvard Stud. Philol. & Lit.* XVII. 44 A diphthong whose first element was at first a mid-front vowel, and later..low-front-slack, mid-back-tense, or possibly 'neutral'. **1961** R. B. LONG *Sentence & its Parts* xix. 415 For mid-central /ə/ the tip of the tongue is characteristically pulled back and elevated slightly. **1965** *Language* XLI. 346 Ngbaka shows only four sequences: high-mid, mid-high, mid-low, and low-mid. **1965** [see DOWN-GLIDE]. **1965** [see *high-tone* (HIGH *a.* 22 a)].

(*b*) Of a colour: occupying a middle position in a range of shades.

1916 *Daily Colonist* (Victoria, B.C.) 1 July 12/3 (Advt.), The colors include white, cream,..mid-brown, lemon, [etc.]. *Ibid.* 23 July 6/1 Gowns..in navy, black, mid-blue, [etc.]. **1929** *Radio Times* 8 Nov. 439/2 (Advt.), This stylish coat... In bottle green, burgundy, dk. brown, mid brown, navy and black. **1937** *Discovery* Oct. 325/2 The complementary..of mid-yellow is violet-blue. **1971** *Vogue* 15 Oct. 8 Dress..in violet, fir green and mid grey.

c. In collocations, generally hyphened, as ***mid-current, -dish, -division, -hour, -incisor, -link, -lobe, -part, -pillar, -point, -position, -region, -section, -term, -toe, -vein, -walk, -zone.***

1870 LOWELL *Among my Bks.* Ser. I. (1873) 364 The *mid-current of ever-gathering faith in duty. **1764** ELIZ. MOXON *Eng. Housew.* (ed. 9) 84 They [*sc.* oyster loaves] are proper either for a side-dish or *mid-dish. **1885** *Act 48 & 49 Vict.* c. 23 Sched. vii. 11, County of Lanark..The *Mid Division. **1415** in *York Myst.* Introd. 34 At the *mydhowre betwix iiijth and vth of the cloke. **1667** MILTON *P.L.* v. 376 These mid-hours, til Evening rise I have at will. **1703** ROWE *Ulyss.* III. i, The Mid-hour of rowling Night. **1879** FLOWER *Catal. Mus. Coll. Surg.* I. 36 The deciduous *mid-incisors, canines, and molars. **1904** *Athenæum* 25 June 821/2 Prof. W. P. Ker offers important suggestions regarding French *mid-links between the Danish and the Scottish ballads. **1870** HOOKER *Stud. Flora* 263 Lower lip spreading, *mid-lobe smallest. *c* **1440** *Promp. Parv.* 337/1 Myddys, or the *myd part of a thynge, *medium*. **1665** SIR T. HERBERT *Trav.* (1677) 121 Their mid parts circled with a Zone of vari-coloured Plad. **1535** COVERDALE *Judg.* xvi. 29 He toke holde of ye two *mydpilers, that the house stode vpon & was holden by. *c* **1369** CHAUCER *Dethe Blaunche* 660 Therwith fortune sayd checke here And mate in *mydde poynte of ye checkere. **1856** HAWTHORNE *Eng. Note-bks.* (1879) II. 80 The dreary midpoint of the..plain. **1888** J. ROSE *Mod. Machine-Shop Practice* II. xxxvii. 379/1 As the eccentric is in *mid-position (*e* being equi-distant from B and D), the valve will be in mid-position. **1896** *Rules governing Printing of Specifications* (U.S. Govt. Printing Office) 53 Mid-position. **1953** L. T. C. ROLT *Railway Adventure* iv. 106 We succeeded after some difficulty in doing this,..locking the valve in mid-position by screwing up the spindle gland nuts dead tight. **1957** R. W. ZANDVOORT *Handbk. Eng. Gram.* VI. 251 Mid-position of an adverb is apt to entail a brief pause between the adverb and the object. **1971** *Engineering* Apr. 47/1 When the sensed dimension is such that the core B is in its mid-position the primary flux is [etc.]. **1879** *St. George's Hosp. Rep.* IX. 80 In one, the left *mid-region was the part most involved. **1961** WEBSTER **Midsection*, a section midway or about midway between the extremes; midriff. **1969** *Publ. Amer. Dial. Soc.* LI. 5 *Midsection*, representation of the kayak's profile if intersected by a plane perpendicular to the keel-line at the mid-point of the craft. **1972** *Sci. Amer.* Sept. 136/3 A four-foot structure with a cathode at one end and a collector at the other and a large electromagnet surrounding the midsection. **1973** *Ibid.* July 24/2 Actually all the horns called conical incorporate a certain amount of cylindrical tubing in their midsection. **1974** *Plain Dealer* (Cleveland, Ohio) 26 Oct. 4D/1 He is not throwing any punches. Instead, he is permitting Williams to pound him in the midsection. **1869** J. MARTINEAU *Ess.* II. 231 [We] refer it to the *mid-term of ordinary life. **1894** *Geol. Mag.* Oct. 454 Projecting at a right angle to the line of the *mid-toe. **1857** T. MOORE *Handbk. Brit. Ferns* (ed. 3) 168 Venation (pinnules) consisting of a flexuous *midvein. **1860** ALLINGHAM in *Athenæum* 10 Mar. 340 By yellow-leafy *midwalk slow foots that aged Sexton. **1886** A. WINCHELL *Walks Geol. Field* 115 A constant temperature would then exist..at the *mid-zone in the crust.

d. ***mid-sixties, -nineties***, etc.: the middle years of the seventh, tenth, etc., decade of a century.

1898 *Nat. Rev.* Aug. 843 In the mid-sixties, abundant experiment had seemed to show that [etc.]. **1900** *Daily News* 1 June 6/4 The progress which has been made since the mid-nineties in the fostering of Irish not only as a literary, but as a spoken language.

e. Special collocations: **mid-angle**, an angle of 45° (*Cent. Dict.* 1890); **mid-body** *Cytology* [tr. G. *zwischenkörper* (W. Flemming 1891, in *Arch.*

f. mikrosk. Anat. XXXVII. 690)] (see quots.); **mid-brow** *sb.* and *a.* = *middle-brow* (MIDDLE A. 6); **mid-circle**, † (*a*) the great circle equidistant from the poles of a sphere; (*b*) the circle passing through the middle points of the sides of a triangle; † **mid cost**, the midrib; **mid couple**, *Sc.* † (*a*) a link for fastening garments; (*b*) *pl.* in *Law*, the documents by which an heir, assignee, etc., is connected with a precept of sasine granted to his predecessor or author; **midcrop**, a crop harvested between the main crops; **Midcult, midcult** orig. *U.S.*, middle-brow culture; also *attrib.*; † **mid-dinner**, a meal between dinner and supper; **mid-distance** = *middle distance*; **Mid-East, mid-East, Mideast** = MIDDLE EAST; also *attrib.*; **mid-European** *a.* = *Middle-European* adj. (MIDDLE A. 6); also as *sb.*; **mid-fi**, sound-reproduction equipment of a slightly lower quality than HI-FI; also *attrib.* or as *adj.*; **mid-finger** (*obs.* exc. *dial.*) = *middle-finger*; **mid-gut**, the mesenteron; **mid-impediment**, *Sc. Law* (see quot. 1838); **mid-iron** *Golf*, an 'iron' with medium degree of 'pitch' or 'loft'; also a stroke made with this; † **mid knowledge**, mediate knowledge; **mid-layer** *Biol.* = MESODERM (*Cent. Dict.*); † **mid-meat**, ? = *mid-dinner*; † **mid-motion**, mean motion; **mid-parent** *Anthropol.* (see quot. 1889); **mid-parentage**, relation to the 'mid-parent'; so **mid-parental** *a.*; † **mid-part** *adv.*, as far as the middle, half-way; † **mid-person** *Sc.*, an intermediary; † **mid-row grains** *Coal Mining* (see quot.); **mid'sagittal** *a. Anat.* = MEDIAN *a.*[1]; **mid-shot** *Cinemat.* and *T.V.* (see quot. 1953); **mid-spoon** *Golf*, a 'spoon' of medium size; † **mid-Sunday**, the Sunday next Midsummer day; **mid superior** *Sc. Law*, one who is superior to those below him, and vassal to those above him (Ogilvie 1882), a mesne lord; hence **mid-superiority**, the position of a mid-superior; **mid-watch**, the middle watch; **mid-west, mid-West** = *Middle West* (MIDDLE A. 6); **mid-western, mid-Western** *a.* = *Middle Western* (MIDDLE A. 6); **mid-westerner, mid-Westerner**, an inhabitant of the Middle West; (also in form *Midwest*, etc.); **mid-wing** *a. Aeronaut.* having the main wings placed approximately halfway between the top and bottom of the fuselage; **mid-workings**, workings with other workings above and below in the same mine or colliery (Gresley *Coal-mining Gloss.* 1883).

1896 E. B. WILSON *Cell* 338 **Mid-body* ('Zwischenkörper'), a body or group of granules, probably comparable with the cell-plate in plants, formed in the equatorial region of the spindle during the anaphases of mitosis. **1969** BROWN & BERTKE *Textbk. Cytol.* xix. 417/1 The portions of the continuous [spindle] fibers where cytokinesis is to occur, become thickened to form the mid-body, 'stem body' of Belar, or 'Flemming body' which has been seen in cytokinesis of other animals, including *Hydra*. **1928** *Sunday Express* 1 July 12/6 Delighting the low-brow, the *mid-brow, and the high-brow with equal facility. **1959** *Manch. Guardian* 10 Aug. 3/2 The dramatic policy is good average mid-brow. **1964** *Punch* 19 Feb. 268/1 When the Midbrows are first showing signs of moving in. **1966** R. A. DOWNIE tr. *O. Del Buono's Bond Affair* 158 It is superficial, banal, *midbrow* wherever psychological analysis is attempted. **1790** WILDBORE in *Phil. Trans.* LXXX. 529 If the two great circles DOE, CQA, be continued, they will meet in a point of the *midcircle 90° from O. **1883** Mid-circle [see INCIRCLE *sb.*]. *c* **1470** HENRY *Wallace* v. 824 Baith cannell bayne an schuldir blaid intwa, Throuch the *myd cost. **1583** *Invent. Roy. Wardrobe* (1815) 309 With twa buttonis or *midcuppillis of gold joynit to the saidis settis. **1832** MORE *Note* in Stair *Instit.* I. clix, Where an heir [etc.] ..takes infeftment by virtue of a procuratory of resignation or precept of seisin granted in favour of his predecessor or author, it is necessary to set forth, in the instrument, the mid-couples, or writings, whereby he is connected with the said procuratory or precept. **1957** *Times* 28 Dec. 10/1 Only the small West African *midcrops standing in the way of an absolute Brazilian control over international cocoa offerings until the gathering of the new West African main crops in the autumn. **1973** *Times* 13 July 21/8 Henry Stephens & Sons (London) reported that whatever happened, even at best, the 1973-74 crop would be a late one and the light and mid-crops would not be sufficient to meet internal demand for local industries. **1960** D. MACDONALD in *Partisan Rev.* XXVII. 592 This intermediate form—let us call it *Midcult—has the essential qualities of Masscult—the formula, the built-in reaction, the lack of any standard except popularity—but it decently covers them with a cultural fig-leaf... Midcult has it both ways: it pretends to respect the standards of High Culture while in fact it waters them down and vulgarizes them. **1962** *Listener* 22 Nov. 863/1 There may seem to be phases in broadcasting history when British broadcasting..has favoured what Dwight Macdonald has called 'midcult', something which is neither for the few nor for the many. **1966** *Ibid.* 27 Jan. 142/2 Even Wilson he feels (though he admires him), has had to sacrifice to 'Midcult' values. **14..** *Nom.* in Wr.-Wülcker 739/18 *Hoc auncinium, hoc imranda, hoc merarium*, a *myddyner undermete. **1842** FRANCIS *Dict. Arts* etc., s.v. *Distance*, The *mid-distance. **1885** *Athenæum* 23 May 669/1 In the mid-distance is a clump of sober-coloured and softly shadowed elms. *c* **1944** (*newspaper-title*) *Mid-East Mail. **1969** *Daily Tel.* 5 Feb. 24 (*heading*) Nixon decision on Mid-East 'in few days'. **1971** R. THOMAS *Backup Men* xix. 168 A juke-box blared out some Mideast music. **1972** *Newsweek* 31 July 28/1 There seemed to be some hope for a break in the Mideast diplomatic logjam. **1974** *Publishers Weekly* 7 Jan. 25 (Advt.), 3 months ago this was to be a major study of the Middle East Conflict. Today it is the first major study of the Mideast including the October War. **1960** J. STROUD *Shorn Lamb* iv. 41 Mad *Mid-Europeans camping with their chattels in the office porch. **1961** *Guardian* 1 Apr. 4/7 The hall mark of mid-European free dance. **1974** 'J. LE CARRÉ' *Tinker, Tailor* xi. 89 Toby Esterhase's faithful mid-European echo. **1970** J. EARL *Tuners & Amplifiers* 7 There is still a margin between what the audiophiles term true hi-fi and general 'domestic quality', and here an entirely new and highly popular range of equipment is emerging. Some call this '*mid-fi' equipment,..but it is noteworthy that such equipment is already rising above the basic 'domestic quality' and entering into the hi-fi fringes. **1971** *Hi-Fi Sound* Feb. 64/3 Today's hi-fi will be tomorrow's mid-fi. **1975** *Gramophone* Jan. 1389 (Advt.), Some of those 'mid-fi' stereo systems of a few years back have a good record player and good speakers. **1644** BULWER *Chiron.* 76 The *Mid-finger prest to the Palm. **1875** F. M. BALFOUR in *Q. Jrnl. Microsc. Sci.* XV. 213 The ventral wall of the *mid-gut. **1880** HUXLEY *Crayfish* ii. 66 The liver may be regarded as a much divided side-pouch of the mid-gut. **1896** KIRKALDY & POLLARD tr. *Boas' Zool.* 23 The mid-gut (mesenteron), which is usually long, and in which digestion and absorption go on. **1838** W. BELL *Dict. Law Scot.* 644 *Mid-impediment; the Roman law *medium impedimentum*; is any thing which intervenes between two events, and prevents, *quoad* the former event, the retrospective operation of the latter. **1856** MENZIES *Convey.* III. iii. 605 There shall be no mid-impediment. **1905** *Westm. Gaz.* 23 Aug. 5/1 Braid, with a magnificent *mid-iron, was dead on the pin. **1640** BP. HALL *Chr. Moder.* II. vi. 36 Betwixt which two some have placed a third, a *mid-knowledge of future conditionate Contingents. *c* **1435** *Torr. Portugal* 1189 He wold not in passe, Till they at *myd mete was. **1588** A. KING tr. *Canisius' Catech.* i. iv, To seike yerlie hir place in ye zodiake according to hir *midde motion on ye letter day of december at noone. **1885** GALTON in *Rep. Brit. Assoc.* 1212 A mean regression from 1 in the *mid-parents to $\frac{2}{3}$ in the offspring would indicate [etc.]. **1889** —— *Nat. Inher.* 87 The word 'Mid-Parent'..expresses an ideal person of composite sex, whose Stature is half way between the Stature of the father and the transmuted Stature of the Mother. **1885** —— in *Rep. Brit. Assoc.* 1209 By the use of this word ['deviate'] and that of '*mid-parentage', we can define the law of regression very briefly. *Ibid.*, The offspring of similar mid-parentages. *Ibid.* 1208 The average height of the two parents, or, as I prefer to call it, the '*mid-parental' height. **1583** *Leg. Bp. St. Androis* 1058 Or ever the preiching was *midpartdone. **1535** STEWART *Cron. Scot.* II. 505 Betuix Scotland and Ingland for till be Ane *mid persone haifand auctoritie. **1567** *Reg. Privy Council Scot.* I. 590 Mark..hes gevin and set in fewferme to his spous and bairnis be ane myd persoun, the saidis mylnis. **1609** SKENE *Reg. Maj., Stat. David II* 42 It is lesome to them to cause their campions or ane midde persone to fecht agains the defender. **1712** H. BELLERS in *Phil. Trans.* XXVII. 542 A hard grey Iron Oar, with some white spots in it, called the *Mid-row Grains. **1957** R. T. WOODBURNE *Essent. Human Anat.* i. 3/2 The median plane is a vertical plane through the body reaching the surface at the mid-line in front and behind. This plane is also known as the *midsagittal plane of the body. **1967** G. M. WYBURN et al. *Conc. Anat.* viii. 203/2 Cut the eyeball in a midsagittal plane. **1968** CHOMSKY & HALLE *Sound Pattern Eng.* 302 Consonantal sounds are produced with a radical obstruction in the midsagittal region of the vocal tract. **1953** K. REISZ *Technique Film Editing* 280 **Mid-shot*, shot taken with the camera nearer to the object than for a long shot but not so near as for a close-up; in relation to the human subject, a shot of the human figure approximately from the waist upwards. **1862** *Rambling Remarks on Golf* 13 In some links, several of these clubs, such as the *mid-spoon, baffing-spoon, driving putter, and niblick may be dispensed with; but in greens such as St. Andrews, Musselburgh, Prestwich, and some others, they all come into requisition more or less. **1906** *Price List Golf Clubs*, Bulger Mid Spoons. **14..** in *Rel. Ant.* I. 85 The Pame sonday be-fele that yere one *Mydesonday. **1850** G. ROSS *Leading Cases Law Scot.* II. 316 His taking up the *mid-superiority of the lands sold was no obstacle. **1535** COVERDALE *Judg.* vii. 19 Aboute the time whan the *myd-watch begynneth. **1901** *Munsey's Mag.* XXV. 344/2 Another kind of deep sea courage is known as 'mid-watch Pluck'. **1926** E. FERBER *Show Boat* v. 80 To the farmers and villagers of the *Midwest..the show boat meant music, romance, gaiety. **1948**, **1968** Midwest, Mid-West [see FAR WEST]. **1889** FARMER *Americanisms* 365/2 **Mid-Western States*, W. Virginia, Kentucky, Tennessee, Missouri, Kansas, and Arkansas. **1906** (*title*) The Midwestern (Des Moines, Iowa). **1923** *Collier's Mag.* 25 Aug. 24/3 One of the economic causes of Mid-Western discontent is the feeling that the Mid-West is the object of discrimination. **1936** *Mind* XLV. 218 After leaving Harvard, Boodin seemed for many years to be lost in the obscurity of a small mid-western college. **1972** M. J. BOSSE *Incident at Naha* ii. 93 You can never wholly shed a *Midwestern* background. **1927** *Scribner's Mag.* Oct. 480/2 These *midwesterners are alike unto Americans in other rural areas. **1969** I. KEMP *Brit. G.I. in Vietnam* iii. 47 A sun-tanned, crew-cut, athletic looking mid-Westerner from Green Bay, Wisconsin. **1971** *Guardian* 10 July 9/1 Stolid and conservative Mid-westerners..are..concerned about the plight of the Indians, because the Indians are part of Middle West life. **1934** *Flight* 15 Feb. 156/1 The machine is a *mid-wing cantilever monoplane with the wing in three sections. **1942** *R.A.F. Jrnl.* 16 May 16 A twin-engine mid-wing monoplane of creditable modern design.

B. *sb.*[1] *Obs.* exc. *dial.*

1. a. The *adj.* used *absol.* = MIDDLE *sb.* in various senses.

a **1300** *E.E. Psalter* cxxxv. 11 Þat led Irael fra mid of þa. *c* **1330** *Arth. & Merl.* 9765 (Kölbing) 3ete he tok þe þridde & cleued him to þe midde. *c* **1400** *Three Kings Cologne* 121 (Camb. MS.) Euerych of þe ij kyngis departed a-sonder and 3af place to her thrid felowe, and so resceyued hym to lye in þe mydde bitwix hem boþe. *a* **1542** WYATT *Ps.* li. The Author 3 Like as the pilgrim..In some fresh shade lieth down at mid of day. **1561** HOLLYBUSH *Hom. Apoth.* 21 The urine is whyte, thick, and pale above and in the midde it is clere. **1566** PAINTER *Pal. Pleas.* I. Ded. 5 Among the mid of my reioyce of those before remembred, I cannot pretermit the lamentable loss of the best approued Gonner that euer [etc.]. **1634-5** BRERETON *Trav.* (Chetham Soc.) 46 A great number of Dutchwomen, who resolved to keep their seats in the mid of the aisle. **1655** FULLER *Ch. Hist.* III. ii. §58 Next his skin he was a Hermite, and wore sack-cloth; in the midd he had the habit of a Monk. **16..** *Robin Hood newly revived* iii. in Child *Ballads* III. 145/1 It was in the mid of the day. **1700** DRYDEN *Fables, Cinyras & Myrrha* 124 'Twas now the mid of Night. **1851** *Cumbld. Gloss.*, *Mid*, the middle; the centre.

b. *Comb.*: **mid-deep** adv., as deep as the middle of the body.

1812 J. J. HENRY *Camp. agst. Quebec* 91 Jumping into the water middeep.

2. A lamb of medium class.

1831 *Sutherland Farm Rep.* 80 in *Libr. Usef. Knowl., Husb.* III, The wedder lambs are divided into three sorts, called tups, mids, and paleys.

C. *adv.* † **a.** In the middle. *Obs.*

13.. *Gaw. & Gr. Knt.* 1730 3e he lad hem bi la3, mon, þe lorde & his meyny; On þis maner bi þe mountes, quyle myd, ouer, vnder. **1426** LYDG. *De Guil. Pilgr.* 4680 To clothe the poore, wych nakyd stood Myd off the gate. **1570-6** LAMBARDE *Peramb. Kent* (1826) 197 It ran midde betweene the two Bishopricks.

b. *Comb.*

1876 G. M. HOPKINS *Wreck of Deutschland* xxxiv, in *Poems* (1967) 62 Mid-numberèd he in three of the thunder-throne! **1960** *Farmer & Stockbreeder* 23 Feb. 69/3 The Colman-Fella tedder..can be operated in conjunction with a mid-mounted mower. *Ibid.* 8 Mar. 75/2 There is much to be said for mid-mounting of tools that need accurate steerage.

mid (mɪd), *sb.*[2] Jocular shortening of MIDSHIPMAN. Cf. MIDDY 1.

1797 MRS. A. M. BENNETT *Beggar Girl* (1813) III. 120 He put on the uniform of a mid. **1836** MARRYAT *Midsh. Easy* xxv, When a mid is in love, he always goes aloft to think of the object of his affection. **1893** SLOANE-STANLEY *Remin. Midshipm. Life* xxii. 301 On reaching the gun-room they were received by the expectant Mids with a host of questions.

† **mid**, *prep.*[1] (*adv.*) *Obs.* Forms: 1-4 **mid, myd,** 1-3 **mið,** 3 **midd.** Also (before dentals and sibilants) 1-3 **mit,** 3 **my3t.** See also MIDE. [Com. Teut.; OE. *mid*, Northumb. *mið*, corresponds to OFris. *mith*, OS. *mid* (Du. *met*), OHG. (MHG., mod.G.) *mit*, ON. *með* (Sw., Da. *med*), Goth. *miþ* (in comb. *mid-*), cogn. w. Gr. *μετά* (see META-) and Zend. *maṭ* with. The word became obsolete before the end of the 14th c.; superseded by WITH.

It had approximately all the modern senses of *with*, except that of opposition (as in *to fight with*), which was the prominent sense of *wið* in OE. In OE. *mid* and *wið* were sometimes opposed, as in the first quot. below; our 'with the stream' was in OE. *mid strēame*, while *wið streame* meant 'against the stream'.]

1. Denoting association, connexion, accompaniment, proximity, addition, conjunction, communication, intercourse.

a **900** *O.E. Chron.* an. 837 Æþelhelm ealdorman ʒefeaht wið þa Deniscan on Port mid Dorsætum. *c* **950** *Lindisf. Gosp.* Luke xiii. 1 Ðara *vel* hiora blod [pilatus] ʒemengde mið asæʒdnisum hiora. *c* **1175** *Lamb. Hom.* 77 Hu scal þat bon soþþen na Mon mine likame irineð ne mid me flesliche hefde to donne. *a* **1200** *Moral Ode* 142 Betere is wori water drunch þen atter meind mid wine. *a* **1225** *Ancr. R.* 248 God Almihti..alihte adun to helle uorto sechen feolawes, & delen mid ham þet god þet he hefde. **1297** R. GLOUC. (Rolls) 5859 Ac let me speke mid my broþer vor me longeþ him to se. *a* **1300** *K. Horn* (Camb. MS.) 666 'Kyng', he sede, 'wel þu sitte, And alle þine kni3tes mitte'. *c* **1315** SHOREHAM v. 214 *Dominus tecum*..(þat hys to seggene 'god es my3tte'). *c* **1330** *Arth. & Merl.* 1468 (Kölbing), The king was wondred of þis cas & al, that euer mid him was. *c* **1350** *Will. Palerne* 3133 And þat menskful maide þat þere myd þe lies. **1377** LANGL. *P. Pl.* B. IV. 77 Wisdome and witte..toke Mede myd hem mercy to winne. **1393** *Ibid.* C. XVII. 182 And so is man þat haþ hus mynde myd *liberum arbitrium*.

b. In the same direction as (a stream, a wind).

709 *Grant* in Birch *Cartul. Sax.* I. 183 Onlong broces midstreame. *c* **1205** LAY. 13792 Þreo scipen gode comen mid þan flode. **1340** *Ayenb.* 180 Þeruore hi byeþ ase þe wedercoc þat is ope þe steple þat him went mid eche wynde.

c. In agreement with, following the action of; analogously to, like.

c **961** ÆTHELWOLD *Rule St. Benet* vii b. (1885) 29 And þus mittan witeʒan clypiʒe: 'To nahte ic wæs ʒehworfen, and ic hit nyste'. *a* **1225** *Ancr. R.* 264 Mid te gode Iosaphat, sendeð beoden uor sondesmon anon efter sukurs to þe Prince of heouene. **1377** LANGL. *P. Pl.* B. v. 75 Drynke but myd [A. v. 58 with] þe doke and dyne but ones.

2. Indicating an accompanying circumstance, condition, action, disposition of mind. With a noun expressing feeling or attitude of mind it often forms a combination equivalent to an adverb.

a **900** tr. *Bæda's Hist.* I. vii. (1890) 36 Mid his sylfes willan. *c* **1000** ÆLFRIC *Josh.* vi. 25 And hiʒ siððan leofodon mid sibbe betwux him. *c* **1175** *Lamb. Hom.* 3 Heo urnen on-3ein him al þa hebreisce men mid godere heorte and summe mid ufele þeonke. *c* **1205** LAY. 10782 Þat þu mid griðe me leten uaren forð toward Rome. *a* **1225** *Ancr. R.* 32 Þeonne ualleð adun mid þeos gretunge. **1297** R. GLOUC. (Rolls) 2932 Hii come & mette hom baldeliche mid god ernest ynou. *a* **1300** *Vox & Wolf* 148 in Hazl. *E.P.P.* I. 63 Mid thilke wordes the volf lou. *c* **1300** *Beket* 451 The kyng aros mid [*earlier version* in] wraththe ynou3. *c* **1315** SHOREHAM v. 331 Þanne ich dar segge mid gode ry3te þat [etc.].

b. = Having (an attribute or quality).

c **1220** *Bestiary* 444 Ðe deuel is tus ðe fox ilik mið iuele breides and wið swik. *Ibid.* 736 Panter..is blac so bro of qual, mið wite spottes sapen al. *a* **1225** *Leg. Kath.* 1430 Ah mit se swiðe lufsume leores ha leien [etc.].

3. Indicating (*a*) the means or instrument; (*b*) the instrumentality or cause.

a **900** tr. *Bæda's Hist.* I. xvi [xxvii] (1890) 74 To ðon þætte ..untrume mid þinre trymenisse syn ȝestrongade, & unrehte mid þinre aldorlicnesse seon ȝerehte. *a* **1000** *Cædmon's Gen.* 251 (Gr.) Forþon he heom ȝewit forȝeaf & mid his handum ȝesceop haliȝ drihten. *c* **1175** *Lamb. Hom.* 25 He seið mið þa muðe, þet nis naut in his heorte. *Ibid.* 87 þet heo sculden..merki mid þan blode hore duren. *c* **1205** LAY. 23572 And no lete noht þat wræcche uolk uor-faren al mid hungre. *c* **1220** *Bestiary* 578 And to late waken, ðe sipes sinken mitte suk, ne cumen he nummor up. *a* **1225** *St. Marher.* 4 Al þat biset is mit se ant mit sunne, buuen ba ant bineoðen. **1297** R. GLOUC. (Rolls) 835 Cloþeþ him mid þe beste cloþ þat ȝe mowe bise. *Ibid.* 11865 He was al so sik mid goute & oþer wo. **1340** *Ayenb.* 44 Ase doþ þise tavernyers þet uelleþ þe mesure myd scome.

4. With regard to; in respect of; touching.

a **1000** *Cædmon's Gen.* 2253 (Gr.) þæs sie ælmihtiȝ drihtna drihten dema mid unc twih. *c* **1200** *Trin. Coll. Hom.* 47 Wich þeau wes on þe olde laȝe mid wimmen. *c* **1205** LAY. 17808 Lauerd hu mid þe? *a* **1225** *Juliana* 10 To wurchen þi wil & al þat te wel likeð as mit tin ahne. *c* **1290** *S. Eng. Leg.* I. 190/24 'Louerd', seide Saule þo, 'ȝwat woltþov do mid me?' **1297** R. GLOUC. (Rolls) 833 Alas quaþ þe quene þo, is it nou mid him so?

5. In the sight, estimation, or opinion of.

c **950** *Lindisf. Gosp.* Matt. vi. 1 Mearde nabbas ȝe mið fader iurre seðe in heafnas is. *c* **1000** ÆLFRIC *Saints' Lives* iii. 498 þæt he him ȝeswutelode hwylc basilius wære on wurð-scype mid him. *c* **1205** LAY. 12638 þæt wes holi man..& mid godde swiðe hæh. **1340** *Ayenb.* 182 Vor him þingþ þet he is a wel guod man and wel mid gode.

6. In the possession or power of.

a **1000** *Ags. Ps.* cxxix. [cxxx.] 4 Ys seo mildheortnes mid þe [Vulg. *apud te.*] *c* **1320** *Cast. Love* 399 þer beþ rihte domes mitte [= mid þe], Alle þine werkes beþ ful of witte. **1377** LANGL. *P. Pl.* B. XVII. 167 Al þe myȝ te myd hym is in makyng of þynges.

7. In adverbial phrases. (See also MIDIDONE.)

a. ***mid alle*** (in OE. *mid ealle*, *eallum*): altogether; entirely; ..and all; at the same time, WITHAL.

a **900** *O.E. Chron.* an. 893 Swa þæt hie asettan him on anne siþ ofer mid horsum mid ealle. *c* **1000** *Ags. Leg. St. Andrew & St. Veronica* (Camb. Antiq. Soc.) 38 Hyne myd scryne myd eallum on feastum cwearterne beclysdon. *c* **1000** ÆLFRIC *Gram.* xxxviii. (Z.) 239 *Stirpitus* grundlunga oððe mid stybbe mid ealle..*radicitus* grundlunga oððe mid wyrttruman mid ealle. *c* **1200** *Trin. Coll. Hom.* 51 He gerede michel ferde mid alle and sende in to ierusalem. *a* **1225** *Juliana* 15 Ich chulle þat he wite hit ful wel & tu eke mid al. *a* **1250** *Owl & Night.* 666 Her to heo moste answere vynde Oþer mid alle beon bihinde. *c* **1305** *St. Cristopher* 172 in *E.E.P.* (1862) 64 And tuo faire wymmen mid alle seint Cristofre he broȝte.

b. ***mid the best, the most***: as good, as great as possible. So ***mid the first***, as soon as possible.

c **1205** LAY. 9801 Alle dæi þer ilæste fæht mid þan mæste. *Ibid.* 9806 þær wes hærm mid þon meste bi-uoren Ex-chæstre. *a* **1300** *K. Horn.* 1073 Aþulf, mi gode felaȝe, God kniȝt mid [*Laud MS.* wyt] þe beste, And þe treweste. *Ibid.* 1199 (Laud MS.) Schenk hus Myd þe furste.

c. ***mid childe***: with child (see CHILD *sb.* 17).

? *c* **750** *Laws of Abp. Egbert* c. 28 (*title*) in Thorpe *Laws* II. 130 Wif ðonne heo mid cylde biþ. *c* **1200** *Trin. Coll. Hom.* 21 þe holie gast wile cumen uppen þe, and godes mihte make ðe mid childe. *Ibid.*, And þus bicam ure lafdi Sainte Marie mid childe. *c* **1205** LAY. 13869 þa wif fareð mid childe. **1340** *Ayenb.* 82 þe wyfman grat myd childe.

d. ***mid iwisse***: see I-WIS *sb.*

c **1275** *Sinners Beware* 32 in *O.E. Misc.* 73 þat is in heouene blysse; Heo cumeþ þer myd iwisse, þat luuyeþ godes love. *c* **1325** *Spec. Gy Warw.* 689 He shal haue comfort and solaz Off þe holi gost..þat wole..make men haue, mid iwisse, Tristi hope to heuene blisse.

8. Placed after the word that it governs.

Beowulf 41 Him on bearme læȝ madma mæniȝo, þa him mid scoldon on flodes æht feor ȝewitan. *c* **1205** LAY. 732 Cnihtes fuseð me mid [*c* **1275** mid me]. *a* **1240** *Sawles Warde* in *Cott. Hom.* 245 For ðan þe se helende under-feng þa sin-fullan and ham mid imone hafede. *a* **1300** *Cursor M.* 21590 þe feurth to ber hir-self mid to constantinopil.

9. *absol.* or as *adv.* With the person or thing specified; together.

c **950** *Lindisf. Gosp.* Luke xiv. 15 Sume of ðæm mið vel ȝelic hlingendum [L. *quidam de simul discumbentibus*]. *c* **1000** *Sax. Leechd.* I. 158 Wið slæpleaste ȝenym þysse ylcan wyrte wos, smyre þone man mid. *c* **1200** *Trin. Coll. Hom.* 115 Swo us longe to him alse diden hise apostles and teo hus to him alse he hem dide and understonde mid on his riche. *a* **1250** *Owl & Night.* 136 Theȝ appel trendli from thon trowe, Thar he and other mid growe. *c* **1400** *Laud Troy Bk.* 15314 Ther him hid With twenti armed knyȝtes myd That were hardy & wondir strong.

mid, 'mid (mɪd), *prep.*[2] Poetical aphesis of AMID.

1808 SCOTT *Marm.* I. xxiii, Mid thunder dint and flashing levin. **1853** M. ARNOLD *Scholar-Gipsy* vii, But 'mid their drink and clatter he would fly. **1870** MORRIS *Earthly Par.*, *Man born to be King* 23 Mid the faces so well known Of men he well might call his own He saw a little wizened man.

mid, dial. pronunciation of *might*, pa. t. of MAY.

1789 CHARLOTTE SMITH *Ethelinde* (1814) III. 70 To have a little item of where I mid look for her frinds. **1796** —— *Marchmont* I. 235, I thought perhaps it middent be too late. **1891** T. HARDY *Tess* I. iii, You mid last ten years; you mid go off in ten months, or ten days.

‖**'mida.** *Ent. Obs.*$^{-0}$ [mod.L., ad. Gr. μίδας 'a destructive insect in pulse' (L. & Sc.).] The larva of the bean-fly.

1753 in CHAMBERS *Cycl. Supp.* In recent Dicts.

† **mid-age.** *Obs.* [f. MID *a.* + AGE *sb.*] = MIDDLE AGE.

c **1440** *Jacob's Well* 171 Thynk in þi 3outhe, in þi myd-age, & in þin age,.. how þou hast mysspendyd hem in synne & in euyll gouernaunce. **1509** BARCLAY *Shyp of Folys* (1874) II. 172 Whether thou be olde, yonge, or of myd age Set nat thy trust to moche on herytage. **1606** SHAKS. *Tr. & Cr.* II. ii. 104 Virgins, and Boyes, mid-age & wrinkled old. **1757** MRS. GRIFFITH *Lett. Henry & Frances* (1767) IV. 130 We.. return back, from Midage, to Childage, again.

Hence † **mid-aged** = MIDDLE-AGED.

1556 J. HEYWOOD *Spider & F.* xxxvi. 14 Frosen to death: midaged, yonge, and olde. **1821** SIR J. D. PAUL *Rouge et Noir* 69 Now mark his mid-aged neighbour.

mid air. The middle region of the air; the tract between the clouds and the part of the atmosphere near the ground. Chiefly in phrase ***in mid air***. Also *rarely* used as *adv.* (= in mid-air) and *attrib.*

1667 MILTON *P.L.* VI. 536 Zophiel, of Cherubim the swiftest wing, Came flying, and in mid Aire aloud thus cri'd. **1706** POPE *Winter* 54 No more the mounting larks, while Daphne sings, Shall list'ning in mid air suspend their wings. **1776** J. BRYANT *Mythol.* III. 229 Here towering steep The rock Aornon rises high in view E'en to the mid-air region. **1830** LYELL *Princ. Geol.* I. 300 Large quantities of fine sand, which, being in mid-air when detached, are carried by the winds to great distances. **1865** DICKENS *Mut. Fr.* I. ix, Mr. and Mrs. Boffin sat staring at mid-air. **1883** *Contemp. Rev.* June 874 A sort of spiritualistic unattached garment, floating about in mid-air. **1886** W. J. TUCKER *E. Europe* 409 All those doors mid-air lead to the lofts above. **1928** R. FRY *Let.* 25 May (1972) II. 627 Reports of aeroplanes that catch fire and grill the passengers in mid-air. **1958** 'P. BRYANT' *Two Hours to Doom* 58 Mid-air refuelling. **1970** *Guardian* 21 Aug. 5/1 If something is not done soon about these near misses, there is bound to be a mid-air collision.

midan, variant of MAIDAN.

Midas ('maɪdæs). [a. L. *Midās*, Gr. Μίδᾱς.]

1. a. The name of a fabled king of Phrygia, to whom Bacchus granted that all he touched should turn to gold (a boon that had to be withdrawn to prevent his perishing of hunger), and to whom Apollo gave ass's ears as a punishment for dullness to the charm of his lyre. Hence used *allusively*.

1568 T. HOWELL *Poems* (Grosart) 150 She..will..make the weare kyng Midas eare. **1575** G. HARVEY *Letter-bk.* (Camden) 98 Eied like an Argus, earde like a Midas. **1591** NASHE *Pref. to Sidney's Astr. & Stella* A 3 A number of Midasses. **1596** SHAKS. *Merch. V.* III. ii. 102 Thou gaudie gold, Hard food for Midas. **1728** POPE *Dunc.* III. 324 Our Midas sits Lord Chancellor of Plays! **1861** MUSGRAVE *By-roads* 211 We are looked upon as men made of money,—as so many Midases, making gold with a touch.

b. *attrib.* and *Comb.* Esp. in phr. (*the*) ***Midas touch***.

1568 GRAFTON *Chron.* II. 439 Ye must vnderstand that Princes haue sometyme Argus eyes, and Midas eares. **1670** LASSELS *Voy. Italy* II. 350 Braue Raphæl, whose only touch of a finger could, Midas like, turne gally pots into gold. **1784** COWPER *Task* IV. 507 Ten thousand casks,..Touched by the Midas finger of the State, Bleed gold for ministers to sport away. [**1879** C. M. YONGE *Magnum Bonum* III. xxxix. 899 He would talk of the touch of Midas.] **1883** *Authors & Publishers* (G. P. Putnam's Sons) 12 'From the authors he seized brains and from the public gold.' Certainly a most desirable result, and the picture of our publisher, in the guise of a prestidigitateur, exercising an infallible King-Midas touch on the material submitted to him, is a very fascinating one. **1901** E. J. DILLON in *Contemp. Rev.* Apr. 474 He is cordially hated by bankers, promoters, speculators and most men of the Midas-eared class. **1938** M. KENNEDY (*title*) The Midas touch. **1960** *Times* 18 July 3/4 Picasso, with his Midas touch, has at first try made the lino-cut a more dignified medium. **1970** *Observer* 29 Nov. 10/5 [Art] objects which start out as sincere personal statements are turned, by the fatal Midas touch of capitalism, into gold.

2. a. ***Midas's ear***: the shell of a gastropod, *Auricula Midæ*.

1713 PETIVER *Aquat. Anim. Amboinæ* 2 Auris Midæ.. Midas Ear. **1835** *Penny Cycl.* III. 109 *Auricula Midæ* (Lam.), *voluta auris Midæ* (Linn.), the Midas's ear of collectors, is a good example of the genus.

b. Midas-fly, Mydas fly, a large fly of the family Mydaidæ.

1895 J. H. COMSTOCK *Man. Study Insects* 461 The Midas-flies rival the robber-flies in size, and quite closely resemble them in appearance. **1972** SWAN & PAPP *Common Insects N. Amer.* 609 Mydas flies..are elongated, moderate to very large in size, resemble wasps and..robber flies.

miday, obs. form of MIDDAY.

mid-course. [f. MID *a.* + COURSE.]

1. a. The middle of one's course. Now chiefly in phrase ***in mid-course***.

1561 T. NORTON *Calvin's Inst.* III. 190 Hope stretcheth fayth to the vttermoste bonde, that it faint not in the midde course nor in the very beginning. **1667** MILTON *P.L.* XI. 204 Why in the East Darkness ere Dayes mid-course. **1760–72** H. BROOKE *Fool of Qual.* (1809) III. 93 Three of them, in mid-course, bore off a small ring..on the point of his lance. **1894** H. D. LLOYD *Wealth agst. Commw.* 317 The gas-company suspended its operations in mid-course.

b. In contexts of interplanetary flights. Also *attrib.*

1959 *IRE Trans. Military Electronics* III. 150/1 It will become apparent that no interplanetary mission even with the crudest requirements would have a reasonable probability of success unless some midcourse or terminal guidance is carried out. *Ibid.* 159/1 The midcourse corrections may also remove residual parallel components. **1964** *Times* 1 Aug. 6 The small rocket engine which can manoeuvre the space craft slightly in mid-course. **1969** *Times* 16 July 5/8 MCC, midcourse correction.

2. A middle course or mode of procedure.

In some recent Dicts.

middæn eard, middanerd, var. ff. MIDDENERD.

midday ('mɪddeɪ). Forms: see MID *a.* and DAY. Also 4 **miday**, 6 **myday**. [OE. *middæȝ* (also as syntactical comb.) = OHG. *mittitag* and *mitter tag* (MHG. *mittetac*, *mittac*, also syntactically in oblique cases *mitten tac* etc.; mod.G. *mittag*), MDu., MLG. *middach* (mod.Du. *middag*), ON. *miðdagr* and *miðr dagr* (Sw., Da. *middag*).]

1. The middle of the day; the time when the sun is at its highest point, noon.

971 *Blickl. Hom.* 47 þriddan siþe on midne dæȝ. *c* **1000** *Sax. Leechd.* III. 218 On þone twelftan dæȝ byð seo sceadu to underne & to none xxv fota & to middæȝe XXII. *c* **1200** *Vices & Virtues* 125 Alswa wel on buton mid-niht alswa on mid-daiȝ. *a* **1225** *Ancr. R.* 34 Abute mid dei hwose mei, & hwose ne mei þeonne, o summe oðer time, þenche o Godes rode. *a* **1300** *Floriz & Bl.* 151 Biþat hit was middai hiȝ, Floriz was þe brigge niȝ. *c* **1330** *Arth. & Merl.* 5189 (Kölbing) Miday passed & none cam. *c* **1460** *Towneley Myst.* xxvi. 522 Sich melody, myd-day ne morne, As was maide thore. **1526** *Pilgr. Perf.* (W. de W. 1531) 73 b, The lyght of the mornynge & the lyght of the myddaye..is all of one nature. **1594** T. B. *La Primaud. Fr. Acad.* II. 179 They are like to men compassed and couered with darknes at Midday. *a* **1631** DONNE *Lett.*, *To M. I. W.* 8 Like infancy or age to mans firme stay, Or earely or late twilights to mid-day. **1667** MILTON *P.L.* VIII. 112 Ere mid-day arriv'd In Eden. **1718** ATTERBURY *Serm.* (1734) I. vii. 184 Had he [Jesus] appeared at Mid-day to all the People, yet all the People would not have believed in him. **1860** TYNDALL *Glac.* I. vi. 42 The sun at mid-day shines down the glacier. **1866** G. MACDONALD *Ann. Q. Neighb.* xiii, The church was always clean and ready for me after about mid-day.

fig. **1837–9** HALLAM *Hist. Lit.* IV. IV. vii. §10. 297 Her letters..were written in the mid-day of Louis's reign.

† **b.** *Eccl.* One of the canonical hours; = SEXT.

a **1000** *Colloquy of Ælfric* in Wr.-Wülcker 101/17 Æfter þisum we sungan middæȝ. *c* **1050** *Suppl. Ælfric's Gloss.* ibid. 175/45 *Sexta*, middæȝ. *c* **1290** *St. Brendan* 225 in *S. Eng. Leg.* I. 225 þe foweles sunge ek here matyns wel riȝt,..& of þe sauter seide þe uers & siþþe also prime, & vnderne siþþe, & middai. ? *a* **1400** *Morte Arth.* 1587 He salle haue maundement to-morne or myddaye be roungene.

† **2.** The South. [Cf. L. *meridies*, F. *midi.*] *Obs.*

1481 CAXTON *Myrr.* II. i, This place Aaron is named the ryght myddaye as she that is sette in the myddle of the worlde. **1526** TINDALE *Acts* viii. 26 Aryse and goo towardes midde daye. **1604** E. G[RIMSTONE] *D'Acosta's Hist. Indies* III. ii. 121 The Southerne which blows from the Midday or South, is hote.

3. *attrib.*, as (in sense 1) ***midday-coach, -devotions, -dinner, -heat, -light, -meal, -mealtime, -post, -rest, -slumber, -splendour, -sun, -thermometer, -time, -train***; †(in sense 2) ***midday field, forest, side***. Also † **midday circle** = MERIDIAN *circle*; † **midday devil, fiend**, transl. of Vulg. *dæmonium meridianum* Ps. xc[i], for which the Eng. Bible has 'the destruction that wasteth at noonday' (cf. *meridian devil*); **midday flower**, a flower belonging to the genus *Mesembryanthemum*, which opens its flowers only for a short time at midday; † **midday line** = MERIDIAN *line*; **midday song** = sense 1 b; † **midday sphere**, ? the southern heavens; † **midday sprite**, ? = *midday devil*.

1559 W. CUNNINGHAM *Cosmogr. Glasse* 21 The meridiane or *middaie circle (saith he) is describid and drawen by the poles of the worlde [etc.]. **1861** DICKENS *Gt. Expect.* xxx, To London by the *mid-day coach. *a* **1340** HAMPOLE *Ps.* xc[i]. 6 Thou sall noght drede..of inras and *myddai deuyll. **1534** MORE *Comf. agst. Trib.* III. ii. (1553) N vij b, In this temptacion he sheweth himself such as the prophet nameth him, *demonium meridianum*, the mid day deuill. **1709** POPE *Jan. & May* 48 They style a wife..A night-invasion and a mid-day-devil. **1694** F. BRAGGE *Disc. Parables* xiii. 435 Our *midday devotions, because we are then in the midst of the dangers and temptations of the day. **1852** MISS MULOCK *Agatha's Husband* xx. (1875) 273 A *mid-day country dinner. **1382** WYCLIF *Ezek.* xx. 46 Prophecy thou to the wodi place, or wildernes, of the *myddai, or south, feeld [Vulg. *agri meridiani*]. **1388** —— *Ps.* xc[i]. 6 Of asailing, and a *myddai feend. *a* **1400** HYLTON *Scala Perf.* (W. de W. 1494) II. xxxviii, They are begyled of the myddaye fende. **1388** WYCLIF *Ezek.* xx. 47 And thou schalt seie to the *myddai forest [Vulg. *saltui meridiano*]. **1592** SHAKS. *Ven. & Ad.* 177 Titan tired in the *midday heate, With burning eye did hotly ouer-looke them. **1614** JACKSON *Creed* III. 315 As if there were no difference betwixt *mid-day-light and mid-night-darkenesse. **1554** *Lydgate's Bochas* I. i. 2 The sonne..more clere dyd shine Than it doth now in his *midday lyne. **1878** HUXLEY *Physiogr.* 7 The line indicated by the shadow at noon is known as the meridian line or mid-day line. **1861** DORA GREENWELL *Poems* 224 Come and share My *mid-day meal. **1393** LANGL. *P. Pl.* C. x. 246 At *myddày meel-tyme ich mete with hem ofte. **1857** MRS. CARLYLE *Lett.* II. 314, I may have a letter by the *midday post. **1821** BYRON *Cain* III. i, His hour of *mid-day rest is nearly over. **1612** DRAYTON *Poly-olb.* i. 172 Let vs (nobler Nymphs) vpon the *mid-daie side, Be frolick with the best. **1837** WHEWELL *Hist. Induct. Sci.* (1857) I. 14 The period of the first waking of science, and that of its *mid-day slumber.

1853 ROCK *Ch. of Fathers* III. II. 8 In like manner, *midday-song or sext, and none-song, were gone through. **1430–40** LYDG. *Bochas* IV. xi. (1494) o viij b, Towarde Septemptrion [and] vnder the *mydday spere his power raught and his regalye. **1854** J. S. C. ABBOTT *Napoleon* (1855) II. iv. 72 A brilliant moon diffused an almost *midday splendor. *a* **1529** SKELTON *Sp. Parrot* 507 So myche coniuracions for elvyshe *myday sprettes. *c* **1420** *Pallad. on Husb.* II. 159 The *mydday sonne ek stonde hit with to mete, In placis colde. **1591** SHAKS. *1 Hen. VI*, I. i. 14 His sparkling Eyes,..More dazzled and droue back his Enemies, Then mid-day Sunne, fierce bent against their faces. **1745** WESLEY *Answ. Ch.* 22 The Difference between them is as great as the Difference between the Light of the Morning and that of the Mid-day Sun. **1856** KANE *Arct. Expl.* II. vii. 78 So mild that our *mid-day thermometers gave but 7°. *a* **1300** *Cursor M.* 22512 Þe sun..quen it es þe fairest on to loke At *middai time. **1874** BURNAND *My time* xi, He could dispose of me by a *mid-day train.

midde(l(l, variant forms of MID, MIDDLE.

midden ('mɪd(ə)n). Now *dial.* (rarely *arch.*). Forms: 4 **medynge, myding,** 4–5 **myd(d)yng,** 5 **middynge, myddyn,** 5–6 **mydding,** 5–9 **midding,** 6 **myddin,** 6–7 **mydinge,** 7 **miding(e,** 7–9 **middin,** 7– **midden.** [Of Scandinavian origin: ME. *myddyng* corresponds to Da. *mødding*, altered form of *møgdynge*, f. *møg* (see MUCK) + *dynge* heap. (The ON. form would be **myki-dyngja*, but *dyngja* in the sense of 'heap' has not been found.)]

1. A dunghill, manure-heap, refuse-heap.

c **1375** *Sc. Leg. Saints* xviii. (*Egipciane*) 468 Ay valouand me in þat syne, as sow a medynge dois vithine. *Ibid.* xxx. (*Theodera*) 615 Þe mylk of sowis has he tane, þat lay by in þe myddyng. *c* **1420** *Pallad. on Husb.* I. 750 The mydding, sette it wete as it may rote. *c* **1470** HENRYSON *Mor. Fab.* I. (*Cock & Jasp.*) iii, Pietie it war, thow suld ly in this midding. **1531** *Nottingham Rec.* III. 367 A garden..next to the mydding. **1570** LEVINS *Manip.* 134/9 A Myddin, *fimarium*. **1667** *Vestry Bks.* (Surtees) 225 For takeing away the miding of ashes out of the churchyard 1*s.* 4*d.* **1718** RAMSAY *Christ's Kirk Gr.* III. xix, The wives and gytlings a' spawn'd out O'er middings and o'er dykes. **1826** E. SWINBURNE in J. Raine *Mem. J. Hodgson* (1858) II. 74 A midden is well placed on the opposite side of them. **1887** MORRIS *Odyss.* x. 412 The herded kine as full-fed of grass withal They come aback to the midden [Gr. ἐς κόπρον].

b. *Proverbs* and *allusions.*

c **1598** D. FERGUSON *Scot. Prov.* (1785) 4 A cock is crouse on his ain midding. **1588** CHURCHYARD *Challenge* (1593) 78 Much like bold Cocks that lowd on midding crowes. **1894** HALL CAINE *Manxman* VI. xiii, Any cock can crow on his own midden.

c. *fig.*

1340 HAMPOLE *Pr. Consc.* 628 A fouler myddyng saw thow never nane. **1588** A. KING tr. *Canisius' Catech.* 27 b, Forgiue me all my sinnes, and raise me poor creatur out of the midding. **1637–50** ROW *Hist. Kirk* (Wodrow Soc.) 437 Alace! I see all the middin (or dunghill) of the muck of the corruption of the Kirk of Ingland comeing on upon us. **1859** KINGSLEY *Misc.* (1860) II. 30 That everlasting midden which men call the world.

2. Short for KITCHEN MIDDEN.

[**1851** D. WILSON *Preh. Ann.* (1863) I. i. 37 True shell mounds corresponding to the Danish kitchen middens.] **1866** LAING *Preh. Rem. Caithn.* 3 In the case of the lowest Danish middens we are carried very far back in the scale both of time and civilization.

3. *attrib.*, as ***midden-fly, -head, -heap, -hill, -tike.*** **midden cock** = *dunghill cock*; **midden creel**, a basket for carrying manure; **midden crow**, the carrion crow; **midden fowl** = *dunghill fowl*; **midden hole**, a place excavated to hold a manure-heap; †**midden lair** *Sc.* = MIDDENSTEAD; **midden mavis**, a ragpicker (Jam.); †**midden mount**, a mound made of refuse; **midden pit**, a pit for holding manure; **midden stance** = MIDDENSTEAD; †**midden tulȝear**, one who fights over the 'midden', a quarrelsome person.

1818 SCOTT *Hrt. Midl.* xliii, He was as uplifted as a *midden-cock upon pattens. **1865** KINGSLEY *Herew.* xvii, The midden cock sole rival to the eagle! **1792** BURNS *Willie's Wife* iv, Her walie nieves like *midden-creels. **1831** *Montagu's Ornith. Dict.* 113 Black Neb. Corby Crow... *Midden Crow. **1728** RAMSAY *Fables* xxiii. 2 A paughty Bee Observ'd a humble *midding flie. **1900** H. G. GRAHAM *Soc. Life Scot. in 18th C.* (1901) I. 6 The *midden-fowls feasted and nursed their broods among nettles and docks. **1768** ROSS *Helenore* (1789) 85 Wese no be heard upon the *midden head. **1823** GALT *Gilhaize* II. x. 104 Its roots of rankness are in the midden-head of Arminianism. **1886** WILLOCK *Rosetty Ends* xviii. 129 Rowin' owre an' owre ane anither in the parental *midden-heap. **1564–78** BULLEIN *Dial. agst. Pest.* (1888) 9 Like vnto greate stinkyng mucle *medin hilles. **1785** BURNS *Halloween* xxii, She..ran thro' *midden-hole and a'. **1692** in *Rec. Convent. Royal Burghs Scot.* (1880) IV. 571 Item, a years [rent] of the *midding lairs at the east and west ports 1800. **1832–53** *Whistle-Binkie* (Scot. Songs) Ser. I. 88 Ilk *midden-mavis, we black jaudy, A' dread and fear thee. *a* **1670** SPALDING *Troub.* (Bannatyne Club) I. 193 The toun of Edinburghe..raised *midden montis at Heriot's Wark. **1340** HAMPOLE *Pr. Consc.* 8770 Þat alle þis world, þare we won yhit War noght bot als a *myddyng-pytt. **1844** STEPHENS *Bk. Farm* II. 654 This is easily effected by draining the '*midden' stance. **1500–20** DUNBAR *Poems* li. 14 He barkis lyk ane *midding tyk. **1535** STEWART *Cron. Scot.* (Rolls) III. 440 Seindill [is]..Ane *mydding tulȝear in ane battell bydar.

†**'middenerd.** *Obs.* Forms: 1 **middanȝeard, -eard,** 2 **middanerd, middennard, midenarde,** 3 **middæn eard, middeneard, middenerd, middenherde, myddenerd.** [OE. *middanȝeard* (later *-eard* by association with *eard* dwelling, ERD), corresp. to OHG. *mittingart*, Goth. *midjungards*. The exact formation is obscure, but the elements are OTeut. **midjo-* MID *a.* + **garđo-z* enclosure, tract, YARD. Cf. ON. *miðgarðr* MIDGARD, OS. *mittilgard*, OHG. *mittigart* and *mittilgart*; also MIDDLE-ERD.

According to Brugmann, the first element is OTeut. **midjumo-*, superlative of **midjo-* MID *a.*: cf. MIDMOST.]

The world; the earth as situated between heaven and hell; also, the inhabitants of the earth.

Beowulf 75 Maniȝre mæȝþe ȝeond þisne middanȝeard. *c* **1000** *Ags. Gosp.* John iv. 42 We witon þæt he is soþ middan-eardes hælynd. *a* **1175** *Cott. Hom.* 225 Ic wille senden flod ofer alne middennard. *c* **1205** LAY. 24778 Whar þu þat mod nime a þisse middenerde. *c* **1275** *Passion our Lord* 478 in *O.E. Misc.* 50 Hit wes welneyh mydday þo þusternesse com In alle Middenherde fort þet hit wes non. *Ibid.* 544 Iesus crist..com in-to þis myddenerd sunfulle men to ryhte.

middenstead ('mɪd(ə)nstɛd). [f. MIDDEN + STEAD. Cf. MDa. *møddingstede* (Kalkar).] The place where a dunghill is formed; a laystall.

1607 *Burgh Rec. Glasgow* (1876) I. 273 To tak in the stanis of the vttir syd of his midinge sted. **1654** *Manch. Court Leet Rec.* (1887) IV. 131 Mr. Nicholas Mosley of Collyhurst for not repaireing the middinge stidd in the Toadlane. **1860–1** FL. NIGHTINGALE *Nursing* ii. (ed. 2) 2 One of the most common causes of disease in towns is having.. middensteads close to the houses.

fig. **1889** SWINBURNE *Study B. Jonson* I. 77 A very middenstead of falsehood and of filth.

midder ('mɪdə(r)). *Med. slang.* [f. MID(WIFE *sb.* or MID(WIFERY + -ER[6].] Midwifery; a midwifery case, childbirth. Also *attrib.*

1909 A. N. LYONS *Sixpenny Pieces* iii. 23 It was no good waiting breakfast for Fatty..because Fatty's 'call' was a 'midder'. **1931** 'F. ILES' *Malice Aforethought* iv. 78 Dr. Bickleigh was wishing that a call would reach him.., a midder-case even. **1937** A. J. CRONIN *Citadel* II. vii. 153 We can't go! I've got a positive conviction I'm having a midder case next Sunday evening! **1948** M. ALLINGHAM *More Work for Undertaker* xxiv. 279 You've got a midder, you say, doctor? **1965** M. POLLAND *Thicker than Water* (1967) iii. 29 Although he..did his medicine in Edinburgh, he came here to the Rotunda for his midder.

middes, variant of MIDS.

middest ('mɪdɪst), *a. superl.* [f. MID *a.* + -EST.] Most central; in the middle.

1590 SPENSER *F.Q.* I. iv. 15 Yet the stout Faery mongst the middest crowd Thought all their glorie vaine in knightly vew. *Ibid.* II. ii. 13 The eldest did against the youngest goe, And both against the middest meant to worken woe. **1593** Q. ELIZ. *Boeth.* IV. pr. vi. 72 As..Circle is to the middest poynte: So [etc.]. *a* **1645** HABINGTON *Surv. Worcs.* in *Worcs. Hist. Soc. Proc.* III. 417 East wyndowe..consystinge of fyve panes, in the myddest pane are no Armes. **1713** C'TESS WINCHILSEA *Misc. Poems* 29 Reputation, Love, and Death, (The last all Bones, the first all Breath, The Midd'st compos'd of restless Fire). **1840** LYTTON *Pilgr. Rhine* ii, The moon was..at her middest height.

middest(e, obs. forms of MIDST.

middil(le, obs. forms of MIDDLE.

middin(g, middis(s, var. ff. MIDDEN, MIDS.

middle ('mɪd(ə)l), *a.* and *sb.* Forms: 1 **middel, midel,** 3–6 **middil,** 3–5 **midel,** 3–6 **middel, myddel,** 3, 6–7 **midle,** 4 **medel, -il,** 4–5 **medill(e, myddil(l, -ul, mydil,** 4–6 **middille, myddelle, myddyll(e, mydel(l, mydle,** 5 **medil(le, -ull(e, -ylle, middell, midil, -yl,** 5–6 **myddell, myddle,** 6 **medyl, myddle,** 7 *Sc.* **meidle,** 6– **middle.** *Comparative.* 7 **midler.** *Superlative.* 1 **midlest,** 3–4 **midlest(e,** 4 **middelest, midel(e)st, midliste, mydleste,** 4–5 **myddelest(e,** 5 **medellust, medlyste, myddlest,** 6 **mydlest.** [OE. *middel, midl-* adj., also sb. masc. (by ellipsis of *dǽl* part) = OFris. *middel* adj., OS. *middil-* in compounds (LG., Du. *middel* adj. and sb. neut. and fem.), OHG. *mittil* adj. (MHG. *mittel* adj. and sb. neut. and fem., mod.G. *mittel* adj. and sb. neut.):—WGer. **middil-*, f. **middi*:—OTeut. **midjo-* MID *a.* The Teut. langs. have also synonymous formations in which the suffix *-lo*, *-ilo* is attached directly to the root (OTeut. **med-*): OHG. *metal* adj., ON. *meðal* in advb. phrase *á meðal* between (Sw. *medel* sb.); also ON. *miðil*, whence *mill-* for *miðl-* in *á milli, á millom* between (Sw. *mellan, emellan*, Da. *mellem, imellem* between, among).]

A. *adj.*

Not in predicative use. In OE. and ME. mainly found in the superlative; the present use of the positive partly descends from compounds, in which *middel-* may be equally well taken as adj. or as sb. The superlative does not appear in our quots. later than the middle of the 16th c., but is given in the *Leeds Glossary*. The comparative, which is the prevailing form in mod.Ger., has never been current in English: for a solitary example, see quot. *a* 1682 in 2 b.

1. a. (Originally in *superlative.*) Used to designate that member of a group or sequence, or that part of a whole, which has the same number of members or parts on each side of it: said with reference to position in space, time, order of succession or enumeration, or the like. Sometimes qualifying a plural sb.

a **900** tr. *Bæda's Hist.* IV. xxiv. [xxiii.] (1890) 334 Þa wæron þus hatne & nemde, Bosa, Ætla, Oftfor, Iohannes & Wilfrið. .. Bi þæm midlestan is nu to secgenne [etc.]. *c* **900** *Laws of K. Ælfred* c. 58 Se midlesta finger. *a* **1225** *Ancr. R.* 370 Þe meidenes eoden furðre to þe midleste. *c* **1290** *S. Eng. Leg.* I. 308/313 Þe nexte finguer hatte 'leche'..'Longueman' hatte þe midleste for he lenguest is. *c* **1374** CHAUCER *Troylus* III. 615 [666] In þis myddel chaumbre þat ye se Shul youre wommen slepen wel and softe. *a* **1400** HYLTON *Scala Perf.* (W. de W. 1494) I. lxxxii, I telle the of the myddelest of hym that boughte the oxen. *c* **1450** *M.E. Med. Bk.* (Heinrich) 77 Do awey þe ouerest rynde, and take þe meddellust, & stampe hit. **1577** B. GOOGE *Heresbach's Husb.* III. (1586) 145 b, Shutte them vp the foure middle houres of the day. **1599** B. JONSON *Ev. Man out of Hum.* III. i, The middle Isle in Paules. **1706** PHILLIPS (ed. Kersey), *Base*... In Heraldry, the lowest part of an Escutcheon, consisting of the Dexter, Middle and Sinister Base-points. **1769** GOLDSM. *Hist. Rome* (1786) II. 324 He was at that middle time of life which is happily tempered with the warmth of youth. **1822–34** *Good's Study Med.* (ed. 4) I. 515 The three arterial coats are generally called external, middle and internal. **1860** TYNDALL *Glac.* I. xi. 70 The middle portion of the glacier. **1899** *Allbutt's Syst. Med.* VII. 284 Occupying the middle third, or rather middle two-fourths of the central convolutions.

b. ***middle brother, sister, son,*** etc.: the second in age of three brothers, etc. In ME. also in *superlative.*

c **1205** LAY. 2116 Cambert hehte þe oðer þat wes þe midleste broðer. *c* **1275** *Ibid.* 12909 After him was an oþer þat was þe middel broþer. *c* **1330** *Arth. & Merl.* 770 (Kölbing) Ȝete wald þe deuel ful of ond þe midel soster a gile fond. *a* **1400** *Siege of Troy* 430 in *Archiv Stud. neu. Spr.* LXXII. 21 Þenne com forþ Alisaunder Parys þe kyngis medlyste sone of prys. *c* **1447** in F. M. Nichols *Lawford Hall* (1891) App. 22 John Baddele wedded Agnes the middell daughter of Thomas Cokefeld. **1531** *Dial. on Laws Eng.* I. vii. 12 If there be thre bretherne & the mydlest brother purchase landes [etc.]. **1757** SIR J. DALRYMPLE *Hist. Feudal Property* (1758) 176 A middle brother dying without children, and leaving an elder and younger brother alive. **1818** CRUISE *Digest* (ed. 2) II. 522 She should have a writ of partition at common law, against the middle sister.

c. Of a point or line (†formerly sometimes of a concrete object): Equidistant from the extremities or boundaries; situated at the centre or middle.

c **1400** MAUNDEV. Prol. (1839) 2 He wil make it to ben cryed and pronounced in the myddel place of a Town. **1591** SHAKS. *1 Hen. VI*, II. ii. 6 The middle centure of this cursed Towne. **1667** MILTON *P.L.* IV. 195 Thence up he flew, and on the Tree of Life, The middle Tree and highest there that grew, Sat like a Cormorant. **1821** CRAIG *Lect. Drawing* 351 In the same way you will get the middle line of the mouth.

†**d.** Average, mean. *Obs.*

1699 BENTLEY *Phal.* 84 We examine the Platonic, or Stoic, or Epicurean Successions; and compute by a middle rate. **1788** PRIESTLEY *Lect. Hist.* II. x. 86 The seventeen intervals by the father's side, and the eighteen by the mother's at a middle reckoning amount to about 507 years. **1790** BURKE *Fr. Rev.* 191 The middle term for the rest of France is about 900 inhabitants to the same admeasurement.

e. Stock Exchange. ***middle price***: see quot.

1893 CORDINGLEY *Guide Stock Exch.* 42 With most outside brokers the 'cover' runs off 'at middle prices'; that is to say, the middle price between a jobber's buying and selling prices. Thus, if a quotation were $142\frac{3}{4}$–143, the middle price would be $142\frac{7}{8}$.

2. Intermediate, intervening.

a. With reference to position in space, time, or order. Also of persons: Intermediary (now *rare*: cf. *middle person* in 6, and MIDDLEMAN).

c **1200** *Trin. Coll. Hom.* 169 Warð blisfuller his [*sc.* Job's] ende, þene was his biginninge, and on þe midleste biwist þe he þolede þe ȝimere pine. *a* **1240** *Sawles Warde* in *Cott. Hom.* 257 Mi þridde suster meað spekeð of þe middel sti bituhhe riht ant luft. **1599** DAVIES *Nosce Teipsum* 59 Will, seeking good, finds manie middle ends. **1700** DRYDEN *Pal. & Arc.* III. 586 They..speed the race, And spurring see decrease the middle space. **1718** ROWE tr. *Lucan* VI. 569 The middle Space, a Valley low depress'd. **1757** FOOTE *Author* I. Wks. 1799 I. 138, I wonder what makes your poets have such an aversion to middle floors—they are always to be found in the extremities; in garrets, or cellars. **1776** ADAM SMITH *W.N.* V. ii. (1869) II. 496 All the middle buyers, who intervened between either of them and the consumer.

b. Of size, stature, rank, quality: Intermediate between the two extremes, medium. Of a course of action, an opinion: Mediating. Hence rarely of a person: †That takes a middle course, trimming. Of a colour = MID *a.* 2 a (*b*).

c **1374** CHAUCER *Anel. & Arc.* 79 Yong was this quene, of xx[ti] yere elde, Of myddell stature. *c* **1400** *Destr. Troy* 3751 A medull size, Betwene the large & the litill. **1442** *Rolls of Parlt.* V. 61/1 Beddes of the middel assise. **1525** in *Visit. Southwell* (Camden) 124 A gowne of myddle coloure. **1545** BRINKLOW *Compl.* 43 That the pore and myddel sort of the peple may be easyd therby. **1603** FLORIO *Montaigne* II. xvi. (1632) 353, I have, in my daies, seene a thousand middle, mungrell and ambiguous men..loose themselves, where I have saved my selfe. *a* **1682** SIR T. BROWNE *Tracts* 119 The first produceth a Female and large Hawk, the second of a midler sort, and the third a smaller Bird Tercellene. *a* **1716** SOUTH *Serm.* (1823) IV. 130 And therefore men of a middle condition are indeed doubly happy. **1719** DE FOE *Crusoe* I. (Globe) 3 That the middle Station of Life was calculated for all kind of Virtues and all kind of Enjoyments. **1774** BURKE *Sp. Amer. Tax.* Sel. Wks. I. 136 An Administration, that having no scheme of their own, took a middle line. **1782** PRIESTLEY *Corrupt. Chr.* I. I. 145 A middle opinion has been adopted by some Arians. **1826** SCOTT *Woodst.* i, He was a stout man of middle stature. **1858** T. D. ACLAND *Oxford*

A.A. Exam. 3 The want of better education, accessible to the middle ranks on easy terms. **1869** *Bradshaw's Railway Manual* XXI. 460 (Advt.), Brunswick Green dark middle, and pale. **1875** JOWETT *Plato* (ed. 2) V. 74 The best condition is a middle one. **1884** *Times* (weekly ed.) 5 Sept. 5/5 These societies take a middle ground between agnosticism and theism. **1902** A. E. W. MASON *Four Feathers* xiv. 135 He was a man of the middle size. **1926–7** *Army & Navy Stores Catal.* 299/1 Washable water paint... Colours..Light Stone—Middle Stone—Dark Stone. **1950** J. CANNAN *Murder Included* vii. 158 A wool frock of a dull middle-blue.

c. Middle-sized. *Obs.* in general sense. Of wool: Having the staple of medium length. †Of the voice: Moderately loud.

c **1410** *Master of Game* (MS. Digby 182) xiv, It is goode þat he haue both of þe gret and of þe smale and of the mydel. *c* **1440** *Alphabet of Tales* 87 Þe psalm was begon in a medull voyce. **1642** *Bk. Rates* 2 Balkes, great, the hundred containing 120, 12.00.00, middle..05.00.00, small.. 02.00.00. **1663** in *Kirkcudbr. War-Comm. Min. Bk.* (1855) 187 *note*, Ane great pot, meidle pot, and ane lytle pot. **1837** YOUATT *Sheep* 304 A kind of middle wool. **1859** *Stationers' Handbk.* 17 Thin post, ranging from 11 to 15 lbs.; Middle post, ranging from 16 to 18 lbs.; Thick post, comprising 19 to 23 lbs.

†**d.** Of a battle: Indecisive. *Obs.*

1625 YONGE *Diary* (Camden) 84 A middle fight.

3. In partitive concord: = '(The) middle or middle part of; mid'. Now *rare*.

785 in Birch *Cartul. Sax.* I. 339 Be midelen streame. **1382** WYCLIF *Mark* vi. 47 Whanne euenyng was, the boot was in the myddil see [1388 myddil of the see]. **1568** GRAFTON *Chron.* II. 8 Marcarus..Erle of Northumberland, and Edwyn Erle of middle England, with Edgar Athelyng [etc.]. **1590** SHAKS. *Mids. N.* II. i. 82 Neuer since the middle Summers spring Met we on hil, in dale, forrest, or mead. **1625** MILTON *Death of Fair Infant* 16 Through middle empire of the freezing aire He wanderd long. **1629** —— *Hymn Nativ.* 164 When at the worlds last session, The dreadfull judge in middle Air shall spread his throne. *a* **1631** DONNE *Sat.* i. 15 Thou wilt not leave mee in the middle street. **1632** LITHGOW *Trav.* IX. 402, I stepped downe to my middle thigh in the water. **1663** BUTLER *Hud.* I. ii. 1142 So foul [the Stocks], that whoso is in, Is to the Middle-leg in Prison. **1812** BYRON *Ch. Har.* II. xxix, Calypso's isles, The sister tenants of the middle deep. **1827** MACCULLOCH *Malaria* viii. 352 The two months of middle summer and the four of middle winter are..the freest from original attacks of..Malaria. **1860** HAWTHORNE *Marb. Faun* xxxix. 302 The holy cloud of incense,..which had risen into the middle dome.

4. *Philology.*

a. *Gram.* Intermediate between active and passive: primarily (after Gr. *μέση διάθεσις, μέσον ῥῆμα*), the designation of a 'voice' of Gr. verbs which normally expresses reflexive or reciprocal action, action viewed as affecting the subject, or intransitive conditions. Hence applied (*a*) to the system of conjugation in other Indogermanic langs. morphologically corresponding to the Gr. middle voice; (*b*) to verbal forms in various langs. serving to express a reflexive or reciprocal sense.

1751 HARRIS *Hermes* (1765) 176 That Species of Verbs, called Verbs Middle. **1844** *Proc. Philol. Soc.* I. 232 The middle verbs in the Icelandic language have been called.. reciprocal instead of reflective. **1871** EARLE *Philol. Eng. Tongue* §299 It gives to the English language a Middle Voice, or a power of verbal expression which is neither active nor passive. **1906** J. H. MOULTON *Gram. N.T. Grk.* I. 161 *note*, Formal passives with middle meaning.

b. Prefixed (after G. *mittel-* as used by J. Grimm) to the name of a language, to denote a period in the history of the language intermediate between those called *Old* and *New* or *Modern*, as in *Middle-English* (see ENGLISH *sb.* 1b), *Middle High-German, Middle-Irish*. Similarly *Middle-Latin*, by some used for Mediæval Latin.

On the other hand *Middle German* (without the limiting *High* or *Low*) is used only in a local sense, for the dialects of middle Germany (geographically and phonologically intermediate between Low and High German).

†**c.** *Phonetics.* Of consonant sounds: = MEDIAL *a.* 5. *Obs. rare*$^{-0}$. (In recent Dicts.)

5. *Geol.* Prefixed to the name or adjectival designation of a formation or period, to denote a subdivision intermediate between two others called 'Upper' and 'Lower'.

1838 *Penny Cycl.* XI. 138 Middle lias shale. **1855** OGILVIE Suppl., *Middle epoch*, in *geol.*, an epoch characterized by the presence of the new red sandstone. **1859** J. R. GREENE *Man. Protozoa* 25 They are chiefly characteristic of the Middle Eocene.

6. Special collocations: **Middle Academy**, name given to the mainly sceptic school of philosophy developed in the third century B.C. by Arcesilaus (316/15–242/1 B.C.) when he was head of the Academy founded by Plato; **Middle America**, (*a*) a geographical region comprising central America, Mexico, and the Antilles; (*b*) the 'silent' majority of Americans, regarded as a homogeneous group; hence **Middle American** *a.* and *sb.*; **middle article** = MIDDLE B. 12; **middle bachelor**, a B.A. of standing between 'senior' and 'junior', i.e. in his second year (now only *U.S.*); **middle band** *Naut.*, 'one of the bands of a sail, to give additional strength' (Adm. Smyth); †**middle bend**, some card-sharping device (see quot.); **middle-brow, middlebrow**, (*a*) *sb.*, a person of average or moderate cultural interests; (*b*) *adj.*, claiming to be or regarded as only moderately intellectual; **middle C**, *Mus.* (see quot. 1876); **middle chest** *Mil.*, the front chest on the body of an artillery caisson, so-called from its position between the rear chest on the body and the chest on the limber (*Cent. Dict.* 1890); **middle comedy** (see COMEDY[1] 2); **middle common room**, a common room for graduate students; also graduate students collectively; **middle cut file**, a file whose teeth have a grade of coarseness between the *rough* and *bastard* (Knight *Dict. Mech.* 1875); **middle deck**, the deck between the upper deck and the lower deck; † **middle dish** *Cookery*, an entrée; **middle distance**, (*a*) (see DISTANCE *sb.* 10c); (*b*) *Athletics*, a distance for a race longer than a sprint but shorter than a long-distance race, esp. one of 440 yards, 880 yards, or a mile (or corresponding metric distances); also (with hyphen) *attrib.*; **middle distillate**, a petroleum fraction that comes off at intermediate temperatures (about 180° to 340°C) in fractional distillation, from which is obtained paraffin, diesel oil, and heating oil; **middle ear**, the tympanum, sometimes also used for the tympanum together with the mastoid cells and the Eustachian tube (*Syd. Soc. Lex.* 1890); used *attrib.* in ***middle ear disease***, etc.; **middle eight** *colloq.*, the eight bars in the middle of a conventionally structured popular tune, often of a different character from the other parts of the tune; the B section in a tune of the form A, A, B, A; the 'release'; †**middle eld**, = MIDDLE AGE 1; **Middle Empire** = *Middle Kingdom*; **Middle-European** *a.*, of, pertaining to, or characteristic of central Europe or its people; cf. MITTEL-EUROPEAN *a.* and *sb.*; **middle frame**, in *Organ building* (see quot.); **middle game**, the part of a game of chess between the opening and the end-game; **middle genus**, a genus which is at the same time a species of a higher genus (*Cent. Dict.*); **middle ground**, (*a*) *Naut.* a shallow place, as a bank or bar; (*b*) *Painting* = *middle distance*; (*c*) a place half-way between extremes; an area of moderation or compromise; also *attrib.*; **middle guard** [GUARD *sb.* 3b] *Cricket*, the position occupied by a batsman so that his bat defends the middle stump; **middle height**, (*a*) the middle of the height, the distance half-way up a mountain, etc.; (*b*) medium stature; **middle horn**, one of a breed of cattle having horns that are neither long nor short (cf. *longhorn, shorthorn*); **middle income**, an average income; also (with hyphen) *attrib.*; †**Middle Inn**, ? = *Middle* TEMPLE; **Middle Kingdom**, (*a*) a name for China; (*b*) in ancient Egypt, the Eleventh and Twelfth Dynasties, which ruled from the 22nd to the 18th century B.C.; **middle lamella** *Bot.* (see quots.); **middle landlord**, in Ireland, a landlord who leases a tract of land, and sub-lets it to tenants; **middle latitude** (see quots.); **middle leg** *slang*, the penis; **middle-length** *attrib.*, (of a story, etc.) of medium length; **middle life**, (*a*) the middle of a person's life, middle age; (*b*) the life of the middle classes; **middle line**, (*a*) *Naut.* (see quot.); (*b*) *Croquet*, the line of hoops placed in the middle of the lawn; in quot. *attrib.*; **middle management** orig. *U.S.* (see quot. 1957); also (with hyphen) *attrib.*; hence **middle manager**; † **middle mast** = MAINMAST; †**middle mean**, moderation; **middle-middle**, (*a*) the middle or centre; (*b*) a member of the middle-middle-class; **middle-middle-class**, the class of society midway between the 'upper' and the 'lower' class; also *pl.* in the same sense; **middle motion** = *mean motion* (see MEAN *a.*[2] 7a); **middle name** orig. *U.S.*, (*a*) a name between one's first Christian name and one's surname; (*b*) *fig.*, the outstanding characteristic of a person; †**middle-off, -on** *Cricket* = MID-OFF, -ON (*obs.*); **middle oil**, that part of the distillate obtained from coal tar which passes over between 170° and 230° Centigrade; distinguished from the *light*, and the *heavy* or *dead* oil (Webster 1897); **middle passage**, the middle portion (i.e. the part consisting of sea travel) of the journey of a slave carried from Africa to America; (see also quot. 1949); **middle period**, the middle phase (of a culture, artist's work, etc.); also *attrib.*; **middle piece**, (*a*) in *Farriery*, the part of a horse's body between the fore and the hind legs; (*b*) *transf.* in *Pugilistic Slang*, the chest; (*c*) *U.S.* = MIDDLING 4; **middle pointed** *a.*, *Arch.*, a name for the style commonly called Decorated Gothic; **middle post**, in *Carpentry* = KING-POST 1; **middle rail**, (*a*) the rail of a door level with the hand, on which the lock is usually fixed; (*b*) the 'live' central rail of an electric railway; **middle-range** *attrib.*, designating a thing or things that occur in the middle of a range of items; **middle-rank**, a body of things or persons of intermediate status or value; also *attrib.* or as *adj.*, of neither high nor low rank or value; hence ***middle-ranking*** adj. (cf. HIGH-RANKING *a.*); **middle rib**, in beef: one of the ribs between the fore ribs and the chuck ribs; **middle-road** *attrib.*, = MIDDLE-OF-THE-ROAD; **middle school** (*a*) = MIDDLE CLASS *school*; (*b*) the middle forms in a grammar or independent school (see quot. 1960); (*c*) a separate post-primary school within the educational system of a state for children aged between about nine and thirteen years; also *attrib.*; **middle shot wheel**, a breast-wheel which receives the water at about its middle height (Knight); **middle space** *Printing*, a space intermediate in size between 'thick' and 'thin' (see quot.); **middle spear** *local* (see quot.); **Middle States**, the States which originally formed the middle part of the United States, intermediate between New England and the Southern States, namely New York, New Jersey, Pennsylvania and Delaware (*Cent. Dict.*); **middle stead** *dial.* (see quot.); **Middle Temple** (see TEMPLE); **middle term**, †(*a*) a partial degree; (*b*) *Logic*, the term which is common to the premises of a syllogism, and disappears in the conclusion; **middle timber**, that timber in the stern which is placed amidships (Adm. Smyth); **middle tint** *Painting*, 'a mixed tint in which bright colours never predominate' (Fairholt *Dict. Art* 1854); **middle-tone** = HALF-TONE *sb.* 2; **middle topsail**, a deep roached sail, set in some schooners and sloops on the heel of their topmasts between the top and the cap (Adm. Smyth); **middle tree**, †(*a*) ? a middle post in a gateway; (*b*) a pole for a cart drawn by oxen; †**middle vein**, the median vein; **middle Victorian** *a.*, belonging to the middle of the Victorian era; **middle wall**, a partition wall; **middle watch** *Naut.*, the watch from midnight to 4 a.m.; also the portion of the crew on deck duty during the middle watch; **middle watcher**, the slight meal snatched by officers of the middle watch about 2.30 a.m. (Adm. Smyth); **middle-water** *attrib.*, applied to fishing, or to ships engaged in fishing, at a medium distance from land; **middle weight**, a man of average weight; *spec.* (in various sports) used to designate an intermediate weight class; esp. in professional boxing, a boxer whose weight is not more than 11 stone 6 lbs.; also *attrib.*; **Middle West**, the north central states of the U.S.A., as distinct from the West or Far West (see quot. 1949); so **Middle Western** *a.*; **Middle White**, a Yorkshire breed of pig; †**middle wicket** = *mid-wicket* (see MID *a.* 1d) (*obs.*); †**middle woof**, applied *attrib.* to a kind of yarn; **middle years**, the years in the middle of one's life, middle age.

1659 T. STANLEY tr. *Sextus Empiricus's Pyrr. Hyp.* in *Hist. Philos.* IV. 33 Arcesilaus, Institutor and President of the *middle Academy, seems to me to participate so much of the Pyrrhonian reasons, as that his Institution and ours is almost the same. **1744** W. GUTHRIE *Morals of Cicero* p. xiii, We are now arrived at the middle Academy, the Founder of which was Arcesilas. **1845** G. H. LEWES *Biogr. Hist. Philos.* II. VIII. iv. 165 The Middle Academy and the New Academy we thus unite in one; although the ancients drew a distinction between them, it is difficult for moderns to do. **1899** M. M. PATRICK *Sextus Empiricus & Gk. Scepticism* iv. 77 Sextus himself claims a close relation between the Middle Academy and Pyrrhonism. **1970** *Oxf. Class. Dict.* (ed. 2) 95/1 The term 'Middle Academy' may also derive from Antiochus [of Ascalon]. **1898** *Pop. Sci. Monthly* Nov. 1 (*title*) Was *Middle America peopled from Asia? **1952** S. TAX (*title*) Heritage of conquest: the ethnology of Middle America. **1957** *Social & Econ. Stud.* (Kingston, Jamaica) VI. III. 380 (*title*) Haciendas and plantations in Middle America and the Antilles. **1966** WEST & AUGELLI *Middle Amer.* i. 1 Middle America is an arbitrary geographic expression which refers to a mosaic of people, places, and cultures. Mexico, Central America, and the West Indies, the area which the term usually defines, share a general focus on the Gulf of Mexico and the Caribbean Sea and an intermediate location between North and South America. **1968** *Sunday Times* 29 Sept. 8 What is seriously wrong with Mr Nixon's new Middle America is that it is virtually all white. **1971** *Guardian* 5 Apr. 4/1 Mr Agnew has continued to reflect the prejudices and confusions of Middle America. **1972** P. DICKINSON *Lizard in Cup* x. 159 We've got to show that we can build, but..Middle America will like that even less than the bombs. **1973** *Tucson* (Arizona) *Daily Citizen* 22 Aug. 28/1 The Braunlichs will also tell you that, sad as it is, middle America is leery of things it gets for free. **1926** F. F.

Blom *Tribes & Temples* I. i. 4 There are maps of most of the *Middle American countries, and the greater number of them..are remarkably inaccurate. **1969** *Collier's Encycl. Year Bk.* 3 Her [*sc.* Mrs. Richard Nixon's] looks and taste are classic Middle American, even as her husband's are. **1970** *Time* 5 Jan. 9 Who precisely are the Middle Americans?.. They make up the core of the group that Richard Nixon now invokes as the 'forgotten Americans' or 'the Great Silent Majority'. **1971** *Guardian* 5 Jan. 10/6 If the chips were to come down now, the final word would undoubtedly rest with the middle Americans. **1975** *Atlantic Monthly* Jan. 28/1 The phrase 'Middle American' was first used..by Joseph Kraft in the spring of 1968, when he was writing about the municipal workers in New York City... He specifically referred to their ethnic character: Irish policemen, Italian sanitation workers, Jewish school-teachers, and so on. *a* **1894** C. H. Pearson in W. Stebbing *Charles Henry Pearson* (1900) viii. 90 T. C. Sandars.. created the so-called *middle article—the essay on social topics. **1966** *Listener* 27 Oct. 621/3 Those 'light' middle articles which used to be a feature of the highbrow weeklies. **1758** *Ann. Reg.* 91 Two *middle batchelors of the University of Cambridge. **1840** J. Quincy *Hist. Harvard Univ.* II. 540 A Senior Sophister has authority to take a Freshman from a Sophomore, a Middle Bachelor from a Junior Sophister [etc.]. **1626** Capt. Smith *Accid. Yng. Seamen* 9 For clamps, *middle bands and sleepers, they be all of 6. inch planke for binding within. **1734** R. Seymour *Compl. Gamester* (ed. 5) II. 6 [Whist.] The other is vulgarly called Kingston-Bridge, or the *Middle-bend. It is done by bending your own or Adversary's Tricks two different Ways [etc.]. **1925** *Punch* 23 Dec. 673/3 The B.B.C. claim to have discovered a new type, the '*middlebrow'. It consists of people who are hoping that some day they will get used to the stuff they ought to like. **1928** *Observer* 17 June 26 The standard of 'middle-brow' music and plays is always rather low. **1934** C. Lambert *Music Ho!* iv. 247 Hindemith is the journalist of modern music, the supreme middlebrow of our times. **1958** Middle-brow [see glossy *a.* a]. **1972** L. Alcock *By South Cadbury* i. 22 The onerous and unrewarding task of Secretary was filled by Geoffrey Ashe, writer of distinguished middle-brow books on the problems of the historical Arthur. **1840** *Penny Cycl.* XVI. 493/1 A *middle C stop-diapason pipe. **1876** Stainer & Barrett *Dict. Mus. Terms, Middle C.* The note standing on the first leger line above the bass stave, and the first leger line below the treble stave. **1958** *Times* 28 Oct. 12/5 Lincoln College is to be the first Oxford college to establish a special common room for postgraduate students of the college. It will be known as the *Middle Common Room. **1969** *Rep. Comm. on Relations with Junior Members Univ. Oxf.* 48 One shall be a president of a Middle Common Room elected by the conference of M.C.R. Presidents. **1971** *Guardian* 21 Dec. 1/6 The ability of the junior and middle common rooms to play their essential rôle in a collegiate university. **1758** J. Blake *Plan Mar. Syst.* 2 The *middle deck tier on board in their proper places, lashed fore and aft. **1747** Mrs. Glasse *Cookery* ix. 84 Salamangundy for a *Middle Dish at Supper. **1813** *Middle-distance [see distance *sb.* 10c]. **1858** Hawthorne *Fr. & It. Note-Bks.* (1872) II. 47 Its great Duomo was seen in the middle distance. **1891** *Harper's Young People* 7 Apr. 384/2 Among *middle-distance men, as among sprinters, there are various types of runners. **1901** *Encycl. Sport* I. 56/1 It is fairer to describe a Quarter Mile as one of the middle distances. *Ibid.*, The sprinter must use different tactics to the middle-distance runner. **1929** G. M. Butler *Mod. Athletics* v. 74 Speed..should be the middle-distance runner's main objective. **1960** Middle distance [see *front-runner* s.v. front *sb.* 14]. **1956** *Nature* 10 Mar. 460/1 Prof. Morton's research work has been concerned with the constitution of petroleum, [and] with methods of separation of hydrocarbons, particularly in the *middle-distillate boiling range. **1973** *People's Jrnl.* (Inverness & Northern Counties ed.) 15 Dec. 1/1 The nature of North-Sea crude oil is more suited to what we call 'middle distillates'—diesel oil, oil fuel for heating and sulphur by-products. **1887** *Brit. Med. Jrnl.* 19 Feb. 407/1 Mr. Baker confined his remarks to abscess from *middle-ear disease. **1966** *Melody Maker* 16 Apr. 8 Doesn't sound as though there's a *middle eight. It's good, though not as good as some of their previous records. **1968** *Listener* 1 Feb. 157/3 Popular song has long been confined to an appalling eight-bar monotony. An eight-bar section, repeated; a 'middle eight' and the first eight again. *a* **1400** *Parlt. 3 Ages* 280 In his *medill elde. **1698** A. Brand *Emb. Muscovy to China* 100 China is known under several names ..the Chineses have retained two,.. Chungehoa, that is, the *Middle Empire, and Chunque, which is Middle Garden. **1939** M. Allingham *Mr. Campion & Others* 86 She's frightfully susceptible. It's her *Middle-European blood. **1949** E. Coxhead *Wind in West* iv. 115 That's enough gloom, turn on the Middle-European gaiety. **1972** C. Drummond *Death at Bar* vi. 159 Dee had liked middle-European victuals. **1881** C. A. Edwards *Organs* 42 Sixteen ribs are used in the reservoir of bellows..divided..by a wooden frame called the *middle-frame. **1894** J. Mason *Princ. Chess* 184 No true knowledge of it [*sc.* the opening] is possible independently of a fair knowledge of..the *middle game and end. **1958** *Times Lit. Suppl.* 14 Nov. 664/4 The main portion of the work..is concerned with middle-game tactics. **1959** *Listener* 5 Mar. 434/1 Coming to middle game, it is instructive to see how a great player defends himself when he is in trouble. **1801** Nelson in Duncan *Life* (1806) 146 The Channel of the Outer Deep, and the position of the *Middle Ground. **1850** *Weale's Dict. Arch.* etc. s.v., Pictures are divided into three parts: fore-ground, middle-ground, and back-ground. **1875** Bedford *Sailor's Pocket Bk.* v. (ed. 2) 136 Where a middle ground exists in a channel, each end of it will be marked by a buoy of the colour in use in that channel. **1961** A. Smith *East-Enders* vi. 102 The middleground is missing... There's no common place inside the East End for everyone as there used to be. **1972** *Language* XLVIII. 278 In the case of terms like *possible* and *impossible*, there is no middle ground; but that is simply the nature of terms which permit no qualification. **1972** *Guardian* 11 Oct. 12/2 The Laureate has to be a middle-ground man, and there are very few of them around. **1973** *Ibid.* 24 Mar. 22/6 Ultimately as the Alliance leaders know, the organisation of middleground politics is of secondary importance. **1871** 'Thomsonby' *Cricketers in Council* 25 Hold your bat up straight, on the popping crease, and ask for '*middle' guard. **1941** *Economist* 12 Apr. 475/1 Direct taxation on what have come to be known as the 'middle incomes'. **1958** B. A. Smith in N. Mackenzie *Conviction* 59 The major beneficiaries of these changes were the middle-income groups. **1971** M. McCarthy *Birds of America* 54 The subspecies they belonged to—white, middle-income intelligentsia. **1812** Sir H. Davy *Chem. Philos.* 91 The Andes, placed almost under the line, rises in the midst of burning sands; about the *middle height is a pleasant and mild climate. **1843** Borrow *Bible in Spain* xxxiv, He was a thin man of about the middle height. **1834** Youatt *Cattle* ii. 10 For these reasons we consider the *middle horns to be the native breed of Great Britain. **1450** *Paston Lett.* I. 159 Prentise is now in the *Mydle Inne. **1662** J. Davies tr. *Mandelslo's Trav.* 215 The Chineses themselves give it the name of Chunghoa, or Chungque, whereof the former signifies the *Middle Kingdom. **1848** S. W. Williams (*title*) The Middle Kingdom: a survey..of the Chinese Empire and its inhabitants. **1890** F. L. Griffith *Antiquities Tell el Yahûdîyeh* 39/1 The earliest dateable antiquities from Tell el Yahûdîyeh are of the middle kingdom. **1906** J. H. Breasted *Hist. Egypt* III. viii. 156 The stable organization, which enabled her [*sc.* Egypt] about 2000 B.C. to enter upon her second great period of productive development, the Middle Kingdom. **1928** C. Dawson *Age of Gods* viii. 173 The Middle Minoan period corresponds to the Middle Kingdom. **1969** V. G. Kiernan *Lords of Human Kind* v. 150 That China was the Middle Kingdom, the one truly civilized realm, was..an axiom to its inhabitants. **1971** J. R. Harris *Legacy of Egypt* (ed. 2) 3 Pieces of Middle Kingdom jewellery were reproduced at Byblos in the second millennium B.C. **1925** Eames & MacDaniels *Introd. Plant Anat.* ii. 25 When a pronounced secondary wall is present the primary wall is commonly called the *middle lamella. **1947** *Ibid.* (ed. 2) ii. 28 The intercellular layer is the middle layer of this group of three or five layers and the term middle lamella should be restricted to this. **1965** K. Esau *Plant Anat.* (ed. 2) iii. 34 On the basis of development and structure three parts are commonly recognized in plant cell walls: the intercellular substance or middle lamella, the primary wall, and the secondary wall. **1817** Mar. Edgeworth *Ormond* xxiii, The tenants..during the time of the late *middle landlord, had been in the habit of making their rents by nefarious practices. **1710** J. Harris *Lex. Techn.* II, **Middle Latitude*, in Navigation, is half the Summ of any two given Latitudes. **1727–41** Chambers *Cycl., Middle latitude sailing*, is used for a method of working the several cases in sailing, nearly agreeing with Mercator's way, but without the help of meridional parts. **1922** Joyce *Ulysses* 443 Are you going far, queer fellow? How's your *middle leg? **1935** Dylan Thomas *Let.* Feb. (1966) 151 Men should be two tooled and a poet's middle leg is his pencil. **1928** *Scholartis Press Catal.* July, A volume of five *middle-length (*not* short) stories by Norah Hoult. **1946** 'G. Orwell' *Shooting Elephant* (1950) 168 The usual middle-length review. *c* **1330** *Arth. & Merl.* 5391 (Kölbing) Þis were noble kniȝtes fiue & alle of *midel liue. **1719** De Foe *Crusoe* II. init., It might be allowed me to have had Experience of every State of middle Life. **1779–81** Johnson *L.P., Otway* Wks. II. 219 It is a domestick tragedy drawn from middle life. **1855** Ht. Martineau *Autobiog.* (1877) II. 115 The scene [of Deerbrook] being laid in middle life. **1895** R. L. Douglas in *Bookman* Oct. 23/1 The king..does his best in a toilsome old age to mitigate the disastrous effects of the blunders of his middle life. **1805** *Shipwright's Vade-M.* 117 **Middle line*, a line dividing the ship exactly in the middle. In the horizontal..plan, it is a right line bisecting the ship from the stem to the stern-post; and, in the..body-plan, it is a perpendicular line bisceting the ship from the keel to the height of the top of the side. **1891** *Laws Croquet* 1 The middle-line hoops. **1957** Clark & Gottfried *Dict. Business & Finance* 228/2 **Middle management*, in general, the group or class of junior executives and senior supervisory personnel in the direct line of authority and communications between the top levels of management and the first line supervisory personnel. **1966** S. Phipps *God on Monday* vi. 76 The opposite swing of the same pendulum may be seen in the groups of middle-management-type bungalows that are appearing round the fringes of English villages. **1966** *Punch* 28 Sept. 485/1 The productivity agreement says a good deal for the efficiency of the group, at least at middle-management level. **1975** *Harper's & Queen* May 101 The Saudis need to swell their middle management by 200,000. **1966** *N.Y. Times* 4 Apr. 33/1 The *middle managers have, understandably, resisted any change. **1985** *Economist* 29 June 65/1 In America,.. business-school ideas are pervasive among middle managers and are beginning to infiltrate boardrooms. **1632** Lithgow *Trav.* II. 62 We shot away their *middle mast. **1577** tr. *Bullinger's Decades* II. v. (1592) 161 In both, there must be had a *middlemeane and measure. **1914** E. M. Forster *Maurice* (1971) xlii. 202 The clientele of Messrs Hill and Hall was drawn from the *middle-middle classes. **1926** D. H. Lawrence *David* iii. 21 And only from the middle-middle of all the worlds, where God stirs amid His waters, can strength come to us. **1934** H. Read *Art & Industry* IV. 126/1 He..is a middle-middle-class man with a nice little house in the suburbs. **1936** 'G. Orwell' *Keep Aspidistra Flying* iii. 54 The derelict spinsters of the middle-middle classes. **1955** T. H. Pear *Eng. Social Differences* iii. 90 When 'middle-middles' become 'upper-middles' they..drop middle-class euphemisms. **1973** *Listener* 22 Feb. 249/3 Their milieux range from lower-middle to middle-middle class. **1669** Sturmy *Mariner's Mag.* VI. iii. 106 The Table of the *Middle-Motion of the Sun. **1835** *Harvardiana* II. 23 [He] then asks their *middle names. **1919** Wodehouse *Damsel in Distress* ii. 31 My dad ran a Bide a Wee Home for flowers, and I used to know them all by their middle names. *Ibid.* xvi. 203 Everyone told me your middle name was Nero. **1920** Ade *Hand-Made Fables* 92, I take it that Mixer is your middle name. **1926** A. Christie *Murder R. Ackroyd* xi. 144 'Modesty is certainly not his middle name.' 'I wish you wouldn't be so horribly American, James.' **1932** *N. & Q.* 3 Sept. 177/2 There is also a proverbial saying, 'Money is his middle name', 'Art is her middle name', meaning one's forte. **1972** P. Cleife *Slick & Dead* xvii. 134 If I had a dollar for every time I've said that, my middle name would be Rothschild. **1972** J. Porter *Meddler & her Murder* i. 11 Tact was far from being the Hon. Con's middle name. **1851** W. Clark in W. Bolland *Cricket Notes* 137 The *middle off, cover point, long slip, and long stop should all save one run. **1843** 'Wykhamist' *Pract. Hints Cricket* (*caption*) Short leg or *middle on. **1887** F. Gale *Game of Cricket* 139 Middle-on and middle-off were..about equal distance from either wicket, standing back some fifteen yards from the centre between the wickets, opposite each other. **1788** T. Clarkson *Essay on Slavery* (ed. 2) III. iii. 98 The captain of a ship, then on the *middle passage, had lost a considerable number of his slaves by death. **1812** *Examiner* 28 Sept. 621/1 Captains of the slave ships, on board whose ships..the.. cruelties of a middle passage had been practised. **1829** Macaulay *Pitt* Misc. Writ. 1860 II. 346 A humane bill which mitigated the horrors of the middle passage. **1949** C. Lloyd *Navy & Slave Trade* I. i. 5 The Round Trip..was commonly divided into three 'passages'. On the outward passage the cargo consisted of textiles, hardware, alcohol and antiquated firearms. These were traded on the coast for slaves, who were shipped to America and the West Indies on the notorious Middle Passage. The principal cargoes taken on there for the homeward passage were sugar, tobacco and rum. **1969** *Listener* 22 May 713/3 Even the unsqueamish stomachs of the 18th century were turned by accounts of the Middle Passage. **1873** C. M. Yonge *Pillars of House* IV. xxxvi. 50 Here's the dining room... This is the *middle period, the Stewart style part. **1894** G. B. Shaw *Music in London 1890–94* (1932) III. 157 Those features of the middle period Beethovenism of which we all have to speak so very seriously. **1930** W. S. Maugham *Cakes & Ale* i. 17 The novels of his middle period reflected..the strain. **1951** T. S. Eliot *Poetry & Drama* ii. 20 His [*sc.* Yeats's] middle-period *Plays for Dancers.* **1817** *Sporting Mag.* L. 54 Randall closed this round by a terrible blow in the *middle-piece. **1843** Ld. G. Bentinck in *Racing Life* ix. (1892) 201 Colonel Anson says he is a very clever horse, and one that must run, but thinks him rather small in the middle-piece. **1891** H. S. Constable *Horses, Sport & War* 63 A horse with big ends and a small middle-piece is more likely to become a roarer than a horse with a good middle piece and thence a good constitution. **1902** Eliz. L. Banks *Newspaper Girl* 161 Your Boston beans done in an earthen pot with the middle-piece pork just rightly browned. **1879** Sir G. G. Scott *Lect. Archit.* I. 347 It was to be the earliest phase of the later form of *Middle Pointed. **1823** P. Nicholson *Pract. Build.* 588 *Middle-post; in a roof the same as King Post. **1812** —— *Mech. Exerc.* 200 *Middle Rail [of a door]. **1842** Gwilt *Archit.* §2130 In doors, the upper rails are called top rails; the next in descending, frize rails; the next, which are usually wider than the two first, are called the lock or middle rails. **1905** Goodchild & Tweney *Technol. & Sci. Dict.* 401/2 *Middle rail*, a heavy conductor in the form of a rail carried on insulating supports, which is laid between the running rails of an electric railway to supply current to the motors. **1964** G. F. Arnold in D. Abercrombie et al. *Daniel Jones* 17 The middle-range percentages..are provided by comparisons of phonemes. **1967** M. Argyle *Psychol. Interpersonal Behaviour* ix. 161 In the matter of price, for example, some Ss [*sc.* salesmen] show the middle-range item first, others show the most expensive. **1961** *Times* 28 Dec. 11/4 That solid *middle-rank of literature. **1969** *Daily Tel.* 10 Oct. 3 Sterling, too, is a middle-rank currency these days —apparently safe from heavy selling pressure but not exactly in demand by speculators. **1972** *Guardian* 13 Nov. 2/3 Middle-rank American and Vietnamese officials in Saigon. **1959** *Encounter* Aug. 18/1 Instructions transmitted ..from on high through a number of *middle-ranking personages down to floor polishers. **1747, 1844** *Middle rib [see chuck *sb.*[4] 2]. **1963** A. L. Simon *Guide Good Food & Wines* 406/1 The *Middle Ribs* and *Chuck Ribs*, sometimes called *Wing Ribs*, are both uneconomical and ungainly as joints owing to the larger proportion of bone to meat. **1958** A. Wilson *Middle Age of Mrs Eliot* III. 343 A nice *middle-road historian's position, he thought to himself with comforting irony. **1971** *Guardian* 14 May 1/3 With no obviously dominating candidate to step into Nasser's shoes, they chose the safe middleroad candidate—Sadat. **1838** Bp. Wilberforce in Ashwell *Life* I. iv. 117 It is very desirable that ultimately we should get the *middle schools to as much uniformity as possible in the books they use. **1860** A. Jessopp *Middle-Class Exams.* 15 Middle Schools—schools which occupy that large 'terra incognita' between the National School and the Grammar School. **1914** 'I. Hay' *Lighter Side School Life* viii. 224 The occasion of his first attendance at a meeting of the Middle School Debating Society. **1933** Middle school [see Aryan *sb.* 2]. **1960** *Where?* III. 15 *Middle school*, usually the third and fourth forms of a school (a grammar school expression). **1962** E. J. King *World Perspectives in Educ.* III. vii. 142 The new Danish two-year programme established for all twelve-year-olds in 1959..was..a nationwide formalization of what used to happen in many urban middle schools. **1971** *Guardian* 20 Oct. 1/8 Surrey..County Council..passed a scheme providing for middle schools followed by 12–18 comprehensives. **1973** *New Society* 10 May 294/1 In 1970, the Department of Education and Science introduced a new category called 'middle schools' into its yearly *Statistics*... What is a middle school? The official version is..a school which straddles the traditional primary-to-secondary transfer age of eleven. **1871** *Amer. Encycl. Printing* (ed. Ringwalt) s.v. *Spaces*. Five to an em or five thin spaces; four to an em, or four *middle spaces; three to an em, or three thick spaces. **1863** W. Barnes *Dorset Gloss., Harrow of a gate*, the backer upright timber of a gate by which it is hung to its post. The one in the middle, between the harrow and the head, is the **middle spear*, which is also the name of the upright beam that takes the two leaves of a barn's door. **1784** G. Washington *Diary* 4 Oct. (1925) II. 326 The *middle States with the Country immediately back of them. **1848** J. F. Cooper *Oak Openings* I. xiii. 193 Who ever heard of the 'tribe' of New England, or..of the 'tribe' of the Middle States? **1912** M. Nicholson *Hoosier Chron.* 59 There had been an infusion of population from New England and the Middle States. *a* **1825** Forby *Voc. E. Anglia*, **Middlestead*, the compartment of a barn which contains the threshing floor; generally in the middle of the building. **1605** Bacon *Adv. Learn.* I. vii. §1 Which honour [Apotheosis], being so high, had also a degree or *middle tearme. **1725** Watts *Logic* III. ii, Syllogisms are divided into various Kinds, either according to the Question which is proved by them,.. or according to the middle Term. **1805** *Shipwright's Vade-M.* 117 **Middle timber.* **1909** Webster, *Middle tone. **1961** M. Levy *Studio Dict. Art Terms* 59 *Half-tone*, the tone value in a painting which is halfway between the dark and the light. Sometimes called Middle-Tone. **1395** in *Archæologia* XXIV. 316 De quibus..expenduntur in j *mideltree imposito in port[is] Manerii per longitudinem. **1834** *Brit. Husb.* I. 159 A tongue, or middle-tree, or shafts, are alternately fixed to the axle of the fore wheels. **1900** *Westm. Gaz.* 14 Mar. 3/2 His mental crises belong to a *middle-Victorian phase of thought. **1962** *Middle-water [see

distant-water s.v. DISTANT *a.* 8]. **1967** *Times Rev. Industry* May 28/2 The near and middle-water fleet consists of boats between 80 and 140 feet long which sail mainly from Grimsby, Fleetwood, Lowestoft, Aberdeen, Milford Haven and North Shields for fishing grounds around the Faroes, in the North Sea and to the west of the British Isles. *a* **1400** in *Rel. Ant.* I. 190 The *medyl weyn betuen ham two The coral is cleppyt also. **1448** in Willis & Clark *Cambridge* (1886) II. 8 All the tymber that..shall be ocupyed..on the *Midelwalles and on the steires. **1611** BIBLE *Ephes.* ii. 14 Who..hath broken downe the middle wall of partition betweene vs. [**1611** BIBLE *Judg.* vii. 19 Gideon..came in the beginning of the middle watch.] **1851** H. MELVILLE *Whale* xliii, It was the *middle watch—a fair moonlight. **1889** *Middle weight [see FEATHER-WEIGHT 3]. **1890** ALLANSON-WINN *Boxing* 82 'Middle' weights. **1909** *Westm. Gaz.* 9 Feb. 12/4 Some fine wrestling has been seen, more especially in the middle-weight class. **1947** E. GRUHN *Text Bk. Wrestling* (ed. 4) 84 *Middle-weight*, up to 174 lb. (79 Kilos). **1955** J. MURRAY *Weight Lifting* iii. 56 The body-weight classes used in standard international lifting competition are as follows.. 165½ pounds—Middleweight. **1972** F. BUTLER *Hist. Boxing in Brit.* xix. 132 The middleweight division was started in England in 1786... The middleweights can claim more superb champions than any section outside the heavyweight. **1898** M. H. CATHERWOOD (*title*) Heroes of the *Middle West. **1909** Middle West [see DRIPPED *ppl. a.*]. **1917** *Nation* (N.Y.) 17 May 589/2 The personal tour of the Secretary of the Treasury through the Middle West, to speak at public meetings, is a wise arrangement. **1949** *Oxf. Jun. Encycl.* III. 452/2 The Middle West region is oddly named, because the states of Ohio, Indiana, Illinois, Michigan, Wisconsin, Minnesota, Iowa, and Missouri, which make it up, are really neither middle nor west. **1909** 'O. HENRY' *Options* 310 I'm only a little Middle-Western girl. **1916** A. HUXLEY *Let.* 30 June (1969) 103 Merest text-book papers, such as would be set by a Middle Western College out your way. **1967** Middle-western [see FRATERNITY 7]. **1893** L. M. DOUGLAS *Man. Pork Trade* p. xiv (*caption*) Small and *Middle White Yorkshire Pigs. **1912** Middle White [see *fatstock* s.v. FAT *a.* 14]. **1953** A. JOBSON *Househ. & Country Crafts* vi. 65 Almost every county in England has produced its own breed of pigs, and we have amongst others Large and Middle White. **1786** *Middle wick't [see BAT *sb.*² 3c]. **1816** W. LAMBERT *Cricketers' Guide* (ed. 6) iii. 42 Middle Wicket Off. This man should stand on the off side, not far from the Bowler's wicket, and about 23 yards from the Striker's wicket. *Ibid.* 44 (*heading*) To cover the Point and Middle Wicket. **1833** NYREN *Yng. Cricketer's Tutor* (1893) 49–50 The middle wicket should stand on the off-side, not more than eleven yards from the bowler's wicket... There is no place in the whole field where so many struggles occur to save a run..as at the middle wicket. **1866** *Routledge's Ev. Boy's Ann.* 511 Thus, long-leg to one bowler may come to cover-point to the other; middle-wicket-on may be cover-slip, short-leg may be middle-wicket-off. **1547** *Act 1 Edw. VI*, c. 6 §4 Such of the said Worsted Yarn as is called..*Middle-wuffe Yarn. **1642** ROGERS *Naaman* 452 Whether in youth or *middle yeares or old age.

7. *Comb.* in parasynthetic adjs., as ***middle-coloured, -growthed, -horned, statured, †-witted, woolled.***

1849 *Florist* 195 Satisfaction, a very good-shaped *middle-coloured flower [Pelargonium]. **1690** *Lond. Gaz.* No. 2607/4 John Boone, aged 17, a straight Youth, *middle growth'd. **1811** W. H. MARSHALL *Rev. Rep. Board Agric.* III. 396 The cattle of Norfolk—evidently a variety of the *middlehorned breed, reduced in size [etc.]. **1846** MCCULLOCH *Acc. Brit. Empire* (1854) I. 495 They may..be divided..into the four classes of middle-horned, long-horned, short-horned, and polled. **1679** *Trials of Wakeman*, etc. 26 He was a *middle-statured man. **1651** WALTON *Life Wotton* d 4 in *Reliq. W.* (1672), Many *middle-witted men (which yet may mean well). **1826** K. DIGBY *Broadst. Hon.* (1848) III. *Morus* 116 There is nothing so easy as to catch the phraseology which middle-witted sophists regard as the stamp of men of judgment. **1837** YOUATT *Sheep* 304 Scarcely a *middle-woolled sheep can now be found in the whole of this county.

B. *sb.*

1. a. The middle point or part (of a line, area, volume, or anything that has spatial magnitude; also of a number, a period of time, a process, etc.). ***to knock*** (a person) ***into the middle of next week***: see WEEK *sb.* 6d.

a **900** CYNEWULF *Elene* 864 He asettan heht on þone middel þære mæran byrig beamas mid bearhtme. *c* **1050** *Voc.* in Wr.-Wülcker 396/2 *Ex centro*, of midle. *c* **1200** *Trin. Coll. Hom.* 85 Here lifes ende was bicumeliche þe middel and þe biginnenge. **1297** R. GLOUC. (Rolls) 1399 Aboute ierusalem þis noumbringe he bigan As in þe middel of þe world to noumbri eche man. *c* **1300** *Havelok* 2092 Aboute þe middel of þe nith Wok ubbe. **1377** LANGL. *P. Pl.* B. xvii. 189 Were þe myddel of myn honde ymaymed or yperssched. *c* **1380** WYCLIF *Serm.* Sel. Wks. I. 367 þis gospel telliþ þe middil of a storie of Seint Joon Baptist. **1420** *E.E. Wills* (1882) 46, I. bord mausure with a bond of seluer, & ouerguld, wyth a prent in þe myddylle. *c* **1450** *Merlin* 108 After the myddill of August, after that Arthur was crowned, he held court roiall, grete and mervelouse. **1530** PALSGR. 245/1 Myddle of the day, *midy*. **1594** SHAKS. *Rich. III*, III. v. 2 Canst thou..Murther thy breath in middle of a word, And then againe begin. **1611** BIBLE *Judg.* ix. 37 See, there come people downe by the middle of the land. **1715** LEONI tr. *Palladio's Archit.* (1742) II. 11 The middle of the upmost Wall ought to be perpendicular with the middle of the nethermost. **1749** J. MARTYN tr. *Virg. Bucol.* Life Virgil (1820) p. lxxix, The fourth Georgick, from the middle to the end, was [etc.]. **1772** PRIESTLEY *Inst. Relig.* (1782) I. 413 Pausanias..wrote about the middle of the second century. **1863** *Chambers's Encycl.* V. 715/2 In 1395 they [*sc.* the Jews] were indefinitely banished from the middle of France. **1865** TYLOR *Early Hist. Man* vi. 133 The heads, middles, and roots of plants. **1902** A. B. DAVIDSON *Bibl. & Lit. Ess.* 266 Beginnings or middles or ends of poems.

b. *U.S.* A strip of unplanted ground between rows of cotton, corn, etc. Usu. *pl.*

1829 L. COVINGTON *Diary* 28 May in *Documentary Hist. Amer. Industr. Society* (1910) I. 238 Two Ploughs breaking middles in Popular tree cut. **1907** T. F. HUNT *Forage & Fiber Crops in Amer.* 352 The field is made up into alternate beds and middles or into 'back' furrows and 'dead' furrows. **1946** *Democrat* 11 Apr. 1/5 Two and three year old kudzu stands that have not covered the middles will be greatly helped if the middles are broken out.

†2. a. The position of being among or surrounded by (a number of people) or within (a town, etc.); = MIDST. Chiefly in phr. ***in the middle of*** = in the midst of, among. *Obs.*

a **1000** *Ags. Ps.* (Spelman) cxxxv. 11 Se ðe alædde Israhel of middele heora. *c* **1000** *Ags. Gosp.* Mark ix. 36 þa nam he anne cnapan & ȝe-sette on hyra middele. *c* **1380** WYCLIF *Sel. Wks.* III. 342 But oonhede on heed of holi Chirche is Jesus Crist here wiþ us, þat is ever in þe myddil of þree þat ben gedrid in his name. **1382** —— *Gen.* xviii. 26 If Y shal fynde in Sodom fifti riȝtwis in the myddil of the cytee, I shal forȝyue to al the place for hem. *a* **1400** *Transl. N.T.* (Selwyn MS.) 2 Cor. vi. 17 (Paues 69) Wherfore God scyþ, Goo ȝe a wey from þe myddel of hem. *c* **1400** MAUNDEV. (Roxb.) Pref. 2 He will ger crie it openly in þe middell of a toune. **1548** UDALL, etc. *Erasm. Par. Acts* xxvii. 18–26 Than Paul standyng in the mydle amonge them, sayed [etc.]. **1760–72** H. BROOKE *Fool of Qual.* (1809) III. 121 [He] is come to rob me in broad day, and in the middle of my own people.

b. ***in the middle of***: while (something) is going on; 'in the thick of'. Cf. MIDST.

1609 J. MORE in *Buccleuch MSS.* (Hist. MSS. Comm.) 82 As I was yesterday in the middle of removing to my house in the Old Bayley, I [etc.]. **1760–72** H. BROOKE *Fool of Qual.* (1809) II. 111, I went and went again, in the middle of my wants, and in the middle of my sorrows, to ask..for his pay from the Admiralty. **1822** SHELLEY *Faust* II. 373 A red mouse in the middle of her singing Sprung from her mouth. **1875** JOWETT *Plato* (ed. 2) I. 373, I have often been stopped in the middle of a speech.

c. Slang phr. ***in the middle***: in a difficult, dangerous, or untenable position; in trouble. *slang* (orig. *U.S.*).

1930 *Amer. Mercury* Dec. 457/1 What's the idea? Trying to put me in the middle with the law? **1943** R. CHANDLER *Lady in Lake* (1944) xxxiv. 179 The other guy could have knocked him out to put him in the middle. **1954** 'N. BLAKE' *Whisper in Gloom* II. xvi. 217, I still don't like it. How d'ya know he's not leaving us in the middle? **1972** J. BURMEISTER *Running Scared* x. 131, I am the man in the middle. If your note giving my location should go astray..I could quietly starve to death.

3. a. The middle part of the human body; the waist.

971 *Blickl. Hom.* 141 Hie ȝegripan on hire middel. *c* **1205** LAY. 28069 þa leo me orn foren to and iueng me bi þan midle. **1297** R. GLOUC. (Rolls) 8962 Gurde aboute hire middel a uair linne ssete. ? *a* **1366** CHAUCER *Rom. Rose* 1032 Yong she was,..Gente, and in hir middel smalle. ? *a* **1400** *Morte Arth.* 4168 Schuldirs and scheldys thay schrede to the hawnches, And medilles thourghe mayles thay merkene in sondire! *c* **1470** HENRY *Wallace* VII. 307 The myddyll off ane he mankit ner in twa. **1494** in *Lett. & Papers Rich. III & Hen. VII* (Rolls) I. 400 [Ladies] with great chenys of gold about their middlys, and mervyleuse riche bees a bowt their nekkes. **1526** *Pilgr. Perf.* (W. de W. 1531) 3 Aboue yᵉ myddle he was the moost amiable stature of a man. **1653** H. COGAN tr. *Pinto's Trav.* xlvi. 268 The Water came up to our Middles. **1712** ADDISON *Spect.* No. 407 ¶5 Stroaking the sides of a long Wigg that reaches down to his Middle. **1769** E. BANCROFT *Guiana* 370 A piece of coarse blue, or brown linen, which is applied to the middle in both sexes. **1811** *Sporting Mag.* XXXVIII. 220 They hold each other tight by the middle. **1843** BORROW *Bible in Spain* xxxi, He has got it buckled round his middle beneath his pantaloons.

Comb. **1894** *Field* 1 Dec. 838/1, I sit comfortably, middle-deep under a writing table.

b. The part of a side of bacon which is left when the fore-end and the gammon are removed.

1892 P. L. SIMMONDS *Dict. Trade Products* (rev. ed.) Suppl. 473/2 *Middles*,..a name for sides of bacon and pork, there are long and short middles. **1917** G. J. NICHOLLS *Bacon & Hams* 70 These middles are cured in dry salt. **1923** R. E. DAVIES *Pigs & Bacon Curing* 29 The side may be cut into three parts, comprising the fore-end, the middle, and the gammon with corner.

4. A mean, something intermediate between two extremes of quality or degree. ***excluded middle*** (Logic): see EXCLUDED *ppl. a.*

a **1240** *Sawles Warde* in *Cott. Hom.* 247 þat ha leare ham mete þat me meosure hat þe middel of twa ueles. *Ibid.* 255 For ne mei na wunne ne na flesches licunge..bringe me ouer þe midel of mesure ant of mete. **1340** *Ayenb.* 249 Sobreté ne is oþer þing þanne to loki riȝte mesure þet alneway halt þane middel ine to moche and to lite. **1626** BACON *Sylva* §616 Bulbous Roots, Fibrous, and Hirsute Roots... The Hirsute is a Middle betweene both. **1667** *Decay Chr. Piety* v. 72 There being in this case no middle between devout reverence and horrid blasphemy. **1683** A. D. *Art Converse* 46 These two extreams we must avoid and search a middle. **1745** *De Foe's Eng. Tradesman* (1841) I. xxii. 209 To keep the safe middle between these extremes. **1790** BURKE *Fr. Rev.* 92 The pretended rights of these theorists are all extremes... The rights of men are in a sort of middle.

†5. An intermediate cause or agency. *Obs.*

a **1225** *Ancr. R.* 180 þeos cumeð also of God, auh nout ase doð þe oðre, wiðuten euerich middel. **1678** CUDWORTH *Intell. Syst.* I. iv. §30. 468 The worshipping (besides one supreme God) of other created Beings,..as middles or mediators betwixt Him and Men.

†6. a. An intervening point or part in space, time, or arrangement; something intermediate. *Obs.*

1665 MANLEY *Grotius' Low C. Warres* 397 The little River of Neths, scituate in the middle between Antwerp and Mechlin. **1667** MILTON *P.L.* IX. 605, I..with capacious mind Considered all things visible in Heav'n, Or Earth, or Middle, all things fair and good.

b. Something placed in a central position.

1796 LD. COLCHESTER *Diary* (1861) I. 35 The second course had a pig at top, a capon at bottom, and the two centre middles were turkey and a larded Guinea fowl.

†7. = MEDIUM *sb.* 4. *Obs.*

1570 DEE *Math. Pref.* cj, So that both theyr mouynges be in ayre, or both in water: or in any one Middle.

8. *ellipt.* **a.** *Logic.* = ***middle term.*** (Cf. MEDIUM *sb.* 2).

1826 WHATELY *Logic* II. iii. §2. (1827) 92 From negative premises you can infer nothing. For in them the Middle is pronounced to disagree with both extremes.

b. *Gram.* = ***middle voice*** (see A. 4a).

1818 BLOMFIELD tr. *Matthiæ's Gk. Gram.* II. 712 The proper signification of the middle is most evident in the aorists. **1906** J. H. MOULTON *Gram. N.T. Grk.* I. 155 As a matter of fact, the proportion of strictly reflexive middles is exceedingly small.

9. *Naut.* = '***middle ground***' (see A. 6).

1702 *Lond. Gaz.* No. 3844/4 The Sands..of the small Middle, in the Narrow off of Winterton near Yarmouth. **1801** NELSON in Duncan *Life* (1806) 136 The Agamemnon..could not weather the shoal of the Middle.

10. *Paper-making.* The sheet, or one of the sheets, of inferior paper placed between the two outer sheets in making pasteboard.

1859 *Stationers' Handbk.* 73 *Middles*, a paper used for forming the middle or inner portion of card and pasteboard.

11. *Football.* A return of the ball from one of the wings to mid-field in front of the goal.

1899 G. O. SMITH *Football* vi. (Badm.) 108 A middle should never be made high up in the air unless the forwards of one's side are a heavy lot. **1902** *Field* 1 Mar. 314/1 Evans actually found the mark from a middle by Corbett, but was pronounced offside.

12. (Originally ***middle article.***) A newspaper article of a particular class (treating more or less discursively some social, ethical, or literary subject), such as is in certain journals placed between the leading articles and the reviews.

1862 J. F. STEPHEN *Let.* 10 Apr. *Life* (1895) 175 Last night I finished a middle at two. **1893** G. ALLEN *Scallywag* III. 68 Working away with all his might at a clever middle for an evening newspaper. Paul was distinctly successful in what the trade technically knows as middles.

13. *Cricket.* = ***middle guard*** (see A. 6).

1866 'CAPT. CRAWLEY' *Cricket* 22 The batsman should..after asking the umpire for middle, and taking his block at a bat's length from the stumps, stand..in the position shewn. **1904** F. C. HOLLAND *Cricket* 1 What guard is to be chosen? Some cricketers take centre, some the leg stump, and many middle and leg. **1960** I. PEEBLES *Bowler's Turn* 187 He had batted on middle and off and shown a readiness to hook.

14. *colloq.* A middle-class person.

1955 T. H. PEAR *Eng. Social Differences* 101 Wealthy 'middles' are now admitted to some formerly exclusive hunts. **1967** *Listener* 21 Dec. 802/1 If a man spoke rather loudly..keeping his vowels open, then he was an Upper. If he attempted all this and just failed, then he was a Middle.

middle ('mɪd(ə)l), *v.* [f. MIDDLE *sb.* Cf. Du. *middelen*, G. *mitteln*, ON. *miðla*.]

†1. *intr.* ? To be at the middle point; ? to intervene. *Obs.*

1382 WYCLIF *John* vii. 14 Forsoþe now the feeste day medlinge [Vulg. *mediante*], or goynge bitwixe, Jhesu wente vp in to the temple.

†2. *intr.* or *absol.* To perform some kind of operation in the making of iron wire (cf. MIDDLEMAN 1). *Obs.*

1435 *Coventry Leet Bk.*, For-alsomyche as Joh. Stafford, Joh. Blakemon, sen.,..& Wal. Bonde heldon for the most part as well smethyng, brakyng middelyng and cardwire-draweng.

†3. *trans.* To take a middle view of. Also ***to middle it*** (contemptuously): to adopt a middle course. *Obs.*

1648 MANTON *Spir. Languish.* 16 We content ourselves with a lukewarmnesse and a mambling of profession midling it between Christ and the world. **1748** RICHARDSON *Clarissa* I. 173 To middle the matter between both, it is pity, that [etc.].

4. To find the middle of; to bisect.

1703 MOXON *Mech. Exerc.* 268 Draw the Line *ab*, bisect, or middle it.

5. *Naut.* To fold or double in the middle.

1841 R. H. DANA *Seaman's Man.* 76 Get up a hawser, middle it, and take a slack clove-hitch at the centre. *c* **1860** H. STUART *Seaman's Catech.* 27 How do you make a reef point? By taking five foxes and middling them. **1867** SMYTH *Sailor's Word-bk.* 479 *Middling a sail*, arranging it for bending to the yard. **1882** NARES *Seamanship* (ed. 6) 124 The sail is middled and hauled taut out.

6. a. *techn.* To place in the middle.

1883 W. H. RICHARDS *Textbk. Milit. Topogr.* (1888) 119 All the micrometers should be kept nearly 'middled', or half way through their nuts. **1898** *Chamb. Jrnl.* Mar. 188 A grandfather's clock with a bullet-hole nicely middled in its case. **1899** *Daily News* 25 July 6/6 We started to heave in on the starboard cable in order to middle the ship between her anchors.

b. *intr.* To fit into the middle.

1888 HASLUCK *Model Engin. Handybk.* (1900) 67 If these holes do not exactly middle, a small round file can be used to draw the hole over as required.

7. *trans.* in *Football.* To return (the ball) from one of the wings to mid-field in front of goal; to 'centre'. Also *absol.*

1871 *Field* 28 Jan. 61/3 The ball which had been previously middled by A. M. Jones, was driven through the goal. **1902** *Ibid.* 1 Mar. 314/1 Corbett made a run and middled.

8. *slang.* To befool, cheat.

1869 E. FARMER *Scrap Bk.* (ed. 6) 53 For I've been humbugged, middled, got the best on.

9. *Cricket.* To strike (a ball) with the middle of the bat; also with the bowler or the stroke as object.

1954 J. H. FINGLETON *Ashes crown Year* xi. 112 Hutton was in grand form. He middled Lindwall with confidence. **1955** I. PEEBLES *On Ashes* iii. 29 The batsman started by showing every sign of good form.. middling his strokes with ominous regularity. **1955** MILLER & WHITINGTON *Cricket Typhoon* x. 189 May began to middle the ball.

middle, obs. form of MEDDLE.

middle age, *sb.*

1. The period between youth and old age. Cf. *middle eld*, *middle life*: see MIDDLE *a.* 6.

1377 LANGL. *P. Pl.* B. XII. 7 And of thi wylde wantounesse tho thow ȝonge were, To amende it in thi myddel age. *c* **1440** *Ipomydon* 1588 He had an eme was stiffe and stronge; Of mydille age. **1526** *Pilgr. Perf.* (W. de W. 1531) 13 b, Some in theyr youth: some in theyr myddell age: and some in theyr last dayes. *c* **1600** SHAKS. *Sonn.* vii, Resembling strong youth in his middle age. *a* **1631** DONNE in *Select.* (1840) 24 That all thy spring, thy youth, be spent in wantonness, all thy summer, thy middle age, in ambition. **1749** FIELDING *Tom Jones* II. viii, His time of life, which was only what is called middle age. **1810** SCOTT *Lady of L.* I. xxi, On his bold visage middle age Had slightly press'd its signet sage. **1884** PAE *Eustace* 37 He was considerably past middle age.

2. ***the Middle Age***, now usually ***the Middle Ages***: the period intermediate between 'ancient' and 'modern' times; in earlier use commonly taken as extending from *c* 500 to *c* 1500; now used without precise definition, but most frequently with reference to the four centuries after A.D. 1000. Cf. mod.L. ***medium ævum***, G. ***mittelalter***, F. ***moyen âge***.

α. sing. **1621** DONNE *Sermon I Tim.* I. 15 (1661) 192 It is a perplex't question in the School, (and truly the Balance in those of the middle age, very even) whether if Adam had not sinned, the son of God had come into the world, and taken our nature and our flesh upon him. **1624** WOTTON *Elem. Archit.* sig. ¶4 After the reuiuing and repolishing of good Literature, (which the combustions and tumults of the middle Age had vnciuillized). **1753** CHAMBERS *Cycl. Supp.* s.v. *Age*, *Middle Age* denotes the space of time commencing from Constantine, and ending at the taking of Constantinople by the Turks, in the fifteenth century. *a* **1780** HARRIS *Philol. Inquiries* I. (1781) Addr. to E. Hooper, An Essay on the Taste and Literature of the middle Age. **1882** J. C. MORISON *Macaulay* 70 His acquaintance with the Middle Age generally, may without injustice be pronounced slight.

β. pl. **1616** SPELMAN *De non temerandis Ecclesiis* (ed. 2) App. 194 Thus the eldest and newest Expositors are wholly for mee, many also (& of the best of them) of the middle ages. **1699** M. LISTER *Journey to Paris* 108 It would have been some satisfaction to have seen by the Pictures, what the middle Ages, at least, had thought of them [*sc.* animals]. **1722** *Mem. Literature* VI. 296 Mr. Juncker,.. has published in the German Language an Excellent Introduction to the Geography of the middle Ages. **1819** HALLAM *Mid. Ages.* (ed. 2) III. I. ix. 304 The Middle Ages, according to the division I have adopted, comprize about one thousand years, from the invasion of France by Clovis to that of Naples by Charles VIII. **1842** BRANDE *Dict. Sci.* etc., *Middle ages*... The centuries between the ninth or tenth and the end of the fifteenth after Christ are generally comprehended under this loose denomination. **1887** J. C. MORISON *Service of Man* 177 The great hollow which is roughly called the Middle Ages, extending from the fifth to the fifteenth century.

3. *attrib.*, quasi-*adj.* (with hyphen). Belonging to the Middle Ages; mediæval. Also *attrib.* in sense 1, as ***middle-age bulge***, ***spread*** (cf. next, sense b).

1840 GEN. P. THOMPSON *Exerc.* V. 31 With the same precaution that they would have consorted with the evil spirits of middle-age romance. **1853** RUSKIN *Lect. Archit.* iv. 217 That child is working in the middle-age spirit—the other in the modern spirit. **1869** F. W. NEWMAN *Misc.* 46 Perhaps it incapacitated the Arabs and the middleage Schoolmen for all but formal reasoning. **1937** *John o' London's* 29 Jan. 742/1 (Advt.), Join the happy throng who have learnt to control the 'middle-age spread' by wearing the..supporting belt. **1963** *Times* 6 May 9/1 The butcher wants his beef before it has developed a middle-age spread. **1972** J. PORTER *Meddler & her Murder* iii. 46 She was fighting a losing battle against the middle-age bulge.

middle-aged (stress variable), *a.* [f. MIDDLE *a.* + AGE *sb.* + -ED².]

1. a. Of middle-age, neither young nor old. Also *transf.* and *fig.*

1608 TOPSELL *Serpents* 73 The elder looke to the family, placing in due order that hony which is gathered and wrought by the middle-aged Bees. **1611** CORYAT *Crudities* 252 He was a middle-aged man, as about forty yeares old. **1676** COLLINS in Rigaud *Corr. Sci. Men* (1841) II. 453 The admirable M. Leibnitz, a German, but a member of the Royal Society, scarce yet middle aged. **1709** STEELE *Tatler* No. 77 ⁋2 When I was a middle-aged Man. **1880** G. MEREDITH *Tragic Com.* (1881) 81 A middle-aged, grave and honourable man. **1918** W. OWEN *Let.* 22 July (1967) 566, I have no unused boots with me, but I left a delicate middle-aged pair in the Kitchen Cupboard. **1927** [see ÉCLAIR]. **1940** [see AUTO *sb.*² 3]. **1950** T. S. ELIOT *Cocktail Party* I. ii. 57 Only since this morning I have met myself as a middle-aged man. **1960** M. SPARK *Ballad of Peckham Rye* vii. 150 The chief barmaid had a tiny nose and a big chin; she was a middle-aged woman of twenty-five. **1974** *Broadcast* 28 Oct. 20/2 Young men go to bed with young ladies, middle-aged men (presumably) with middle-aged ladies, and old men with very young ladies.

b. Characteristic of middle-aged people. spec. ***middle-aged spread***, paunchiness in a middle-aged person; also *transf.* and *fig.* Cf. MIDDLE AGE *sb.* 3.

1886 LOWELL *Latest Lit. Ess.*, *Gray* (1891) 2 Cowper was really mad at intervals, but his poetry, admirable as it is in its own middle-aged way, is in need of anything rather than a strait-waistcoat. **1887** RUSKIN *Præterita* II. 269 His already almost middle-aged aspect of serene sagacity. **1931** H. G. WELLS *Work, Wealth & Happiness of Mankind* (1932) xv. 768 Impermanence is the lot of all encyclopædias, and though the Britannica.. shows now these marks of advanced maturity, of 'middle-aged spread', there is no reason for supposing that the spirit of Diderot is dead. **1942** D. POWELL *Time to be Born* (1943) ii. 43 Erase that middle-aged spread. **1957** J. BRAINE *Room at Top* i. 7, I hadn't then begun to acquire a middle-aged spread. **1962** *Listener* 20 Sept. 450/1 That impish sense of the ridiculous..which.. will always stop 'Tonight' from acquiring the pompous middle-aged spread that so often accompanies success.

†**2.** Belonging to the Middle Ages; mediæval. *Obs.*

1611 T. JAMES *Treat. Corruption of Scripture* Advt. to Christian Reader, sig. *2 The open or secret wrongs done vnto Fathers, auncient, middle-aged, or moderne writers, by the Papists. **1710** HEARNE *Collect.* (O.H.S.) III. 49 The reading and perusing of middle-ag'd Antiquities. **1804** MITFORD *Inquiry* 318 Of the modern and middle aged Greek. **1845** *Proc. Philol. Soc.* II. 145 The English *hunger* bears a strong resemblance to the Spanish *hambre*, formed from the middle-aged Latin *famina*. **1846** DICKENS *Pictures from Italy* 5 The first chapter of a Middle Aged novel.

Hence **middle-'agedness**.

1881 [see AGEDNESS 2].

middle-ageing, *ppl. a.* Also **middle-aging**. Becoming middle aged.

1882 HOWELLS in *Longm. Mag.* I. 53 Only a score of middle-aging veterans remained. **1916** E. POUND *Lustra* 104 With middle-ageing care I had laid out just the right books. **1956** D. M. DAVIN *Sullen Bell* II. iv. 130 The job was getting him. If not the job..his own middle-ageing self. **1969** D. LAMBERT *Angels in Snow* v. 74 A successful middle-ageing woman. **1973** *Publishers' Weekly* 8 Jan. 62/1 They get acquainted with a pair of middle-aging Jewish bachelor doctors.

middle'ageism. *nonce-wd.* [f. MIDDLE AGE + -ISM.] Mediævalism.

1840 THACKERAY *Pict. Rhapsody* Wks. 1900 XIII. 348 May we add a humble wish that this excellent painter will.. not busy himself with Gothicism, middleagism?

middle-ager. orig. *U.S.* [f. MIDDLE AGE *sb.* + -ER¹.] A middle-aged person.

1949 *Labor & Nation* Jan.–Feb. 7 Not every youngster or middle-ager..is a double dealer. **1956** *N.Y. Times Mag.* 29 July 5 (*heading*) America's unknown middle-agers. **1962** *Punch* 12 Sept. 392/3 A tough competent middleager.

middle class, *sb.* **a.** The class of society between the 'upper' and the 'lower' class. Also (now more commonly) *plural* in the same sense.

1766 QUEEN CAROLINE MATILDA OF DENMARK *Let.* 25 Dec. in *Mem. Unfortunate Queen* (1776) 21 There is no such thing here as a middle class of people living in affluence and independence. **1792** A. YOUNG *Trav. France* I. xxii. 549 Knowledge, intelligence, information, learning, and wisdom ought to govern nations; and these are all found to reside most in the middle classes of mankind; weakened by the habits and prejudices of *the great*, and stifled by the ignorance of the vulgar. **1812** *Examiner* 31 Aug. 556/1 Such of the Middle Class of Society who have fallen upon evil days. **1831** BROUGHAM *Sp.* 7 Oct. (1838) II. 617 By the people..I mean the middle classes, the wealth and intelligence of the country, the glory of the British name. **1843** BORROW *Bible in Spain* iii, Several of these were of the middle class, shopkeepers and professional men. **1891** H. D. TRAILL in *National Rev.* Mar. 15 The great body of the upper middle classes.

b. *attrib.*, as in ***middle-class education***, ***life***, ***public***, ***society***, etc.; **middle-class examination**, a name sometimes given to the 'local examinations' (see LOCAL *a.* 2 d) in their early years; **middle-class schools**, schools established for the education of the middle classes, intermediate between primary schools and the great public schools.

1848 MILL *Pol. Econ.* I. xi. §4 To get out of one rank of Society into the next above it is the great aim of English middle-class life. **1857** T. D. ACLAND *Oxford A.A. Exam.* (1858) 33 The Exeter Middle Class Examination. *Ibid.* 81 The education given in commercial and middle-class schools. **1858** *Ibid.* p. xx, The consideration of the Middle Class Examinations happened to come before the members of the Senate at a very inconvenient time. *Ibid.* 3 To prepare the way for a practical and truly English Middle-class Education. **1868** M. PATTISON *Academ. Org.* 3 For centuries our middle-class public were slowly travelling. **1890** *Spectator* 18 Oct. 518/1 The tastes of the average middle-class buyer of books.

c. Used as *adj.*, with the sense: Characteristic of the middle classes; having the characteristics of the middle classes. Esp. as ***middle-class morality***. (With depreciative implication. Cf. BOURGEOIS *a.* 2.)

1893 SALTUS *Madam Sapphira* 106 Don't talk back, it is middle-class to begin with. **1905** DICEY *Law & Publ. Opin.* vi. 186 Benthamism was fundamentally a middle class creed. **1926** F. M. FORD *Man could Stand Up* I. iii. 49 What *should* keep them apart?... Middle Class Morality? **1966** *Punch* 13 July 78/2 The tyranny of middle-class morality must be conquered, especially in the field of the homosexuality laws. **1968** A. MACLEOD *Dam* vi. 62 A concession to your middle class morality. **1975** *Times* 15 Jan. 15/5 It was refreshing to see the virtues of middle class morality applauded.

Hence **middle-classdom**, **-classism**, the middle class as a whole; their characteristics, interests, or position; **middle-classer**, one who belongs to the middle class; **middle-classness**, middle-class quality; **middle-classy** *a.*, suggestive of the middle class.

1886 MORRIS in Mackail *Life* (1899) II. 157, I met some very agreeable middle-classers there, and had much talk. **1887** *Sat. Rev.* 21 May 745 The slovenly middle-classness of Dublin. **1894** MISS BROUGHTON *Beginner* xii, I recognise the middle-classness. **1909** *Working Men's College Jrnl.* Apr. 77 Mr. Lupton..did not think the question before the House was one of aristocracy *v.* middle-classism. **1923** A. HUXLEY *Antic Hay* ix. 142 The dreadful middle-classness of her Art and Craftiness. **1926** *Glasgow Herald* 21 May 8 Highly respectable, middle-classy railway clerks. **1930** *Observer* 14 Sept. 7 The secret of Denmark's somewhat stuffy middle-classdom. **1963** *Times* 2 May 18/2 Incipient middle-classdom; outward conformity. **1970** *Guardian* 2 Mar. 9/1 There is nothing so guaranteed to preserve English middle classness..as being surrounded..by foreign parts.

middle earth. Forms: see MIDDLE and EARTH *sb.*

1. [An etymologizing perversion of MIDDLE-ERD.] The earth, as placed between heaven and hell, or as supposed to occupy the centre of the universe. Now only *arch.*, sometimes applied to the real world in contradistinction to fairyland.

c **1275** LAY. 7205 He þohte to bi-winne mid strengþe and mid ginne al þe middelerþes [*c* 1205 middel eærdes] lond. *Ibid.* 9066 Com a þisse middilherþe [*c* 1205 middel ærde] hone maidenes sune. *a* **1300** *Cursor M.* 8003 Bituix þe midel erth and þe lift. **1390** GOWER *Conf.* III. 94 Fro the seconde, as bokes sein, The moiste dropes of the reyn Descenden into Middilerthe. *c* **1440** *York Myst.* ix. 158 Fadir, what may þis meruaylle mene? Wher-to made god medilerth and man? **1522** *World & Child* (Roxb.) A v, All mery medell erthe maketh mencyon of me. **1598** SHAKS. *Merry W.* v. v. 84 But stay, I smell a man of middle earth. **1600** W. WATSON *Decacordon* (1602) 238 O monster of mankinde fitter for hell, then middle earth. **1813** SCOTT *Trierm.* I. ix, That maid is born of middle earth, And may of man be won. **1819** CRABBE *T. of Hall* x, A kind of beings who are never found On middle-earth, but grow on fairy-ground. **1860** HAWTHORNE *Transform.* xxxviii, It is difficult to imagine it [*sc.* Catholicism] a contrivance of mere man. Its mighty machinery was forged and put together, not on middle earth, but either above or below.

†**2.** The middle of the earth. *Obs.*

sea of middle earth, ***middle earth sea***, the Mediterranean. ***middle earth ocean***, an imaginary ocean in the middle of the earth.

1387 TREVISA *Higden* (Rolls) I. 53 Þe grete see of myddel erþe bygynneþ in þe west at Hercules pilers. **1494** FABYAN *Chron.* v. lxxvii. 56 In the South see of Myddell Erth. **1555** W. WATREMAN *Fardle Facions* I. iii. 34 The floude of Nilus ..passeth into the middle earth sea, with seuen armes. **1593** NORDEN *Spec. Brit.*, *M'sex.* I. 8 The forme of this land is Trianguler, much like Cicilia an Island in the middle-earth sea. **1613** PURCHAS *Pilgrimage* VII. ii. 663 So would those good men drowne a great part of the African and American World..by their imagined middle-earth Ocean.

Middle East. [f. MIDDLE *a.* + EAST *sb.*] States lying between the Near and Far East, esp. Egypt and Iran and the countries between them. Also *attrib.*

The name *Middle East* has been used with considerable freedom: see esp. quot. 1958. Cf. FAR EAST, NEAR EAST.

1902 A. T. MAHAN *Retrospect & Prospect* 237 The Middle East, if I may adopt a term which I have not seen, will some day need its Malta, as well as its Gibraltar. **1903** V. CHIROL *Middle Eastern Question* i. 5 'The Middle East', that is to say ..those regions of Asia which extend to the borders of India or command the approaches to India. **1913** *Q. Rev.* Jan. 297 The interests of Great Britain and Russia in the Middle East ..are in reality irreconcilable. **1925** A. TOYNBEE *Survey Internat. Affairs 1920–23* I. i. 3 The affairs of Turkey and the other countries of the Middle East. **1944** J. S. HUXLEY *On Living in Revolution* i. 8 Organizations like the Middle East Supply Council. **1958** LD. VANSITTART *Mist Procession* vi. 82 We had [in 1909] none of the sloppy modernism which lumps everything from the Mediterranean to Bengal as Middle East... Persia, Baluchistan, Afghanistan, India were the Middle East. **1974** *Encycl. Brit. Micropædia* VI. 871/2 *Middle East*..has come to be applied to the lands around the southern and eastern shores of the Mediterranean Sea, extending from Morocco to the Arabian Peninsula and Iran and sometimes beyond.

So **Middle 'Eastern** *a.*, of or pertaining to the Middle East.

1903 V. CHIROL (*title*) The Middle Eastern question; or, some political problems of Indian defence. **1909** A. HAMILTON *Probl. Middle East* p. xi, No study of Middle Eastern politics can avoid encroaching upon those of the Near East and of the Far East. **1925** A. TOYNBEE *Survey Internat. Affairs 1920–23* I. ii. 10 The most important permanent results of this meeting of the Supreme Council in the Near and Middle Eastern field were [etc.]. **1966** *Listener* 27 Oct. 600/1 Their children look at the world from a middle-eastern not a European standpoint. **1973** A. MANN *Tiara* iii. 28 What was the rôle of the dark girl? Her first name was Middle Eastern, not Italian.

middle-erd. *Obs.* exc. *dial.* Forms: see MIDDLE and ERD; also 4 **myddelnerde**, 2–3 **middelert**, 4 **midulert**, 5 **medlert**, 8 **midlert**, 5 **middle yorde**, **myddell yarde**. See also MIDDLE EARTH. [Formed by substitution of *middel* MIDDLE *a.* for *middan-* in *middaneard*, *-ȝeard*: see MIDDENERD. There may have been an OE. **middel(ȝ)eard* corresponding to OS. *mittilgard*, OHG.

mittilgart.] The world; the earth taken as situated between heaven and hell; also, the people dwelling on the earth.

c **1175** *Lamb. Hom.* 15 Þas laȝen weren from Moyses a þet drihten com on þis middilert for us to alesnesse of deofles onwalde. *c* **1200** ORMIN 3638 Godess þeowwess blomenn azz Inn alle gode þæwess, Her i þiss middellærdess lif. *c* **1205** LAY. 25569 Lauerd drihten crist domes waldende midelarde mund. **1297** R. GLOUC. (Rolls) 9052 Me nuste womman so vair non in þe middel erde. *c* **1315** SHOREHAM VII. 580 Wy nedde hy be ine helle y-stopped For euere mo, Ac Nauȝt her in þys myddelnerde, For to maky men offerde. **13..** *Gaw. & Gr. Knt.* 2100 More he is þen any mon vpon myddelerde. *a* **1400** *Pistill of Susan* 263 (MS. A.) Þou maker of myddelert, þat most art of miht. *c* **1460** *Towneley Myst.* iii. 100 Therfor shall I fordo All this medill-erd. ? *a* **1500** *Chester Pl.* IV. 267 Father, .. I hope for all middle-yorde you will not slaye your childe. **1513** DOUGLAS *Æneis* VI. viii. 11 Thair saw he als, with huge greit and murnyng In mydle erd most menit, thir Troianis. **1768** ROSS *Helenore* (1789) 59 This gate she could not long in midlert be.

middle finger. The finger having the position in the middle of the five; the second finger.

Cf. 'middlest finger' in MIDDLE *a.* 1 (quots. *c* 900, *c* 1290).

c **1000** ÆLFRIC *Gloss.* in Wr.-Wülcker 158/35 *Medius, uel impudicus*, middelfinger. **1398** TREVISA *Barth. De P.R.* V. xxix. (1495) 140 The thyrde fyngre is the mydle fingre, and hyght Inpudicus also. **1643** STEER tr. *Exp. Chyrurg.* vi. 21 There followed .. onely two pustels, the one in her thumbe, the other by her middle finger. **1787** HUNTER *Whales* in *Phil. Trans.* LXXVII. 385 In the fore-finger there are five bones, in the middle and ring-finger seven. **1861** [see FINGER *sb.* 1].

† **'middlegood.** *Obs.* [app. f. MIDDLE *a.* + GOOD *sb.*; cf. G. *mittelgut* ore of middle quality.] Some kind of linen fabric.

1582 *Rates Custome Ho.* D iij, Middlegood the c. elles .. xxvi.*s.* viii.*d.* **1612** *Sc. Bk. Customs* in *Halyburton's Ledger* (1867) 320 Linning cloth called Hinderlandis Middlegood and Heidlak the hundreth elnis xvi li. *a* **1618** *Rates Marchandizes* I 3, Linnen cloath vocat. Hinderlands, Middlegood, & Headlake the hundred ells .. xxvj.*s.* viij.*d.*

middlehard, variant of MIDDLE-ERD.

† **'middlehead.** *Obs.* In 3 middel-hed. [f. MIDDLE *a.* + -HEAD.] The middle.

c **1250** *Gen. & Ex.* 522 Ðis midelerdes biginning, And middel-hed, and is ending.

middleing, obs. form of MIDDLING *a.*

† **'middle-land.** *Obs.*

1. = MIDLAND *sb.* Also *attrib.* = MIDLAND *a.*, MEDITERRANEAN *a.*

1297 R. GLOUC. (Rolls) 5134 Al walis & al þe march & al middel lond ywis þat is al bituene temese & homber is. **1565** STAPLETON tr. *Bæda's Hist. Ch. Eng.* 125 Edilred kinge of the Marshes or middleland englishmen came into Kent with a terrible and fell hoste. **1650** FULLER *Pisgah* I. i. 3 Not all the water of Kishon, of Jordan, of the Red, of the Dead, of the Middle-land Sea .. should serve to quench the fire.

2. *Agric.* Land of medium elevation. In quot. *attrib.*

1790 MARSHALL *Midl. Counties* I. 269 The species of grass-land .. are chiefly, Lowland grass .. and Middleland grass, or 'Turf'; there being no Upland grass or sheepwalk within it.

Hence † **middle-lander**, an inhabitant of the Midlands.

1644 FEATLY *Roma Ruens* 42, I am sure Bede affirmeth that the Eastern Angli or English were first gained to Christ by Fœlix, .. and the middle-landers by Finanus.

† **'middlely**, *adv. Obs. rare.* In 5 middilly. [f. MIDDLE *a.* + -LY².] In a medium manner.

c **1400** *Lanfranc's Cirurg.* 320 Þou schalt streyne middilly, & not to faste.

middleman ('mɪd(ə)lmən). [f. MIDDLE *a.* + MAN *sb.*]

† **1.** ? A workman employed in some particular operation in the making of iron wire. *Obs.*

1435 *Coventry Leet Bk.*, The Cardwirdrawers and the myddelmen most nedes bye the wire that they shull wirche of the smythiers.

† **2.** *Mil.* One of the soldiers in the fifth or sixth rank in a file of 10 deep. *Obs.*

1616 *Orders establ. by Soc. of Armes, Lond.* A v, Item, That no man take the place of Leading or Middle-man .. without hee be thereunto appointed by the Captaine or Lieutenant. **1625** MARKHAM *Souldiers Accid.* 28 The fifth Ranke from the Front downeward towards the Reare, are called *Middlemen* to the reare, and the sixth Rank are called *Middlemen* to the front. **1672** T. VENN *Milit. & Mar. Discip.* v. 11 A File so drawn is distinguished according to their dignity of Place, a Leader, a Follower, two Middlemen, a Follower and a Bringer-up. **1696** PHILLIPS, *Middleman* (a term in the Art-military), he that stands middlemost in a File.

3. a. One who takes a middle course.

1741 WARBURTON *Div. Leg.* v. §6 Wks. 1788 III. 167 Neither Unbelievers nor Believers will allow to these middle men that a new-existing Soul .. can be identically the same with an annihilated Soul. **1884** A. BIRRELL *Obiter Dicta* 179 Middle men may often seem to be earning for themselves a place in Universal Biography. **1902** A. B. DAVIDSON *Called of God* vi. 168 There were three parties, the true worshippers of Jehovah, the strict idolaters, and the middle-men who were neither.

b. *nonce-use.* (See quot.)

1845 DISRAELI *Sp.* 11 Apr. in Hansard *Parl. Deb.* Ser. III. LXXIX. 565 We have a great Parliamentary middleman. It is well known what a middleman is: he is a man who bamboozles one party, and plunders the other, till, having obtained a position to which he is not entitled, he cries out. 'Let us have no party questions, but fixity of tenure'.

4. a. (Originally two words.) A person standing in an intermediate relation to two parties concerned in some matter of business: usually in somewhat unfavourable sense, as implying that direct relations between these parties would be more advantageous. Chiefly applied, in discussions on the theory of commerce, to the trader or any of the series of traders through whose hands commodities pass on their way from the maker or producer to the consumer.

1795 BURKE *Th. on Scarcity* Wks. VII. 401 If the object of this scheme should be .. to destroy the dealer, commonly called the middle man [etc.]. **1805** EAST *Reports* V. 178 The Metcalfes .. were middlemen between the vendors and the vendees. **1845** *Encycl. Metrop.* VIII. 52 In one Trade at least .. a class of middle-men, who were formerly interposed between the maker and the merchant, now no longer exists. **1861** J. G. SHEPPARD *Fall Rome* viii. 414 While to the odious middle-man, or bailiff, was left the management of those patrimonial estates. **1866** C. W. HATFIELD *Hist. Notices Doncaster* I. 100 There are middlemen and others who encourage and aid them in disposing of the stolen goods. **1880** LOMAS *Alkali Trade* 245 A considerable part of the demand for low-strength ash and alkali emanates from certain unscrupulous vendors or 'middle-men'. **1887** *Westm. Rev.* June 315 The helpless victims of grasping middlemen and a grinding competition which [etc.].

attrib. **1851** MAYHEW *Lond. Labour* (1864) II. 373 The workmen gradually became transformed from journeymen into 'middlemen', living by the labour of others... The middleman system is the one crying evil of the day.

b. In Ireland, one who leases land, and sub-lets it again at an advanced rate.

1802 MAR. EDGEWORTH *Rosanna* i. Wks. 1832 IV. 297 Mr. Hopkins was what is called in Ireland a middle-man. **1903** *Edin. Rev.* July 209 Absenteeism with its resulting evils of middlemen and rackrents was the worst bane of Ireland.

c. *Mountaineering.* The middle climber of a team. Also *attrib.*, as **middleman('s) loop, noose**, etc., a knot used by a climber to tie himself on to the middle of a rope.

1892 C. T. DENT et al. *Mountaineering* iv. 102 The 'fisherman's bend', used as a middleman noose for instance, has only 65 per cent of the strength of the rope. **1909** C. E. BENSON *Brit. Mountaineering* ii. 33 The Middleman Loop is the only one that should be used for middlemen. **1951** E. COXHEAD *One Green Bottle* vi. 160 Each child was tied on with a middleman's noose. **1968** E. FRANKLIN *Dict. Knots* 21 *Middleman's knot*, also called the *Englishman's Loop*, (in America) the *Fisherman's* or *Angler's Loop*... It is a useful loop knot tied in the bight by one of at least four different methods. Once much used for the middleman on a rope in climbing, but now superseded. **1971** J. LOVELOCK *Climbing* iii. 43 The middle man can tie on to the rope in a number of ways.

5. *U.S.* **a.** 'In *negro minstrelsy*, the man who sits in the middle of the semicircle of performers during the opening part of the entertainment, and leads the dialogue between songs.' **b.** 'In the *fisheries*, a planter.' (*Cent. Dict.*)

1870 O. LOGAN *Before Footlights* 248, I give it up, Brudder Bones, as the middle man at the minstrels always does the end man's conundrums. **1880** [see INTERLOCUTOR¹ c]. **1930** C. WITTKE *Tambo & Bones* iv. 136 Lively repartee between the endmen and the middleman.

c. *N. Amer.* One who paddles or rows in the middle of a canoe or boat.

1761 A. HENRY *Trav. & Adventures Canada* (1901) ii. 14 They engage .. the middle-men at one hundred and fifty livres and the end-men at three hundred livres, each. **1801** A. MACKENZIE *Voy. from Montreal* p. xxviii, The canoe men are of two descriptions, foremen and steersmen, and middlemen. **1839** J. K. TOWNSEND *Narr. Rocky Mts.* xv. 355 The middle-men ply their oars; the guides brace themselves against the gunwale of the boat, placing their paddles edgewise down her sides. **1968** [see BOWSMAN].

Hence **'middlemanism, 'middlemanship**, the system of employing middlemen.

1848 *Fraser's Mag.* XXXVII. 383 A sort of middlemanship, somewhat of the nature of the 'butty' system carried on in Staffordshire. **1889** G. J. HOLYOAKE in *Co-operative News* 6 Apr. 330 Middlemanism was becoming in every country a serious question. **1899** A. WHITE *Mod. Jew* 132 Their trading instincts and intuitive taste for middlemanship.

middlemost ('mɪd(ə)lməʊst), *a.* Now somewhat *rare*. [f. MIDDLE *a.* + -MOST.] That is in the very middle, or nearest the middle. Now only with reference to position; formerly also with reference to age, size, quality, etc. Cf. MIDMOST and *middlest* superl. of MIDDLE *a.*

a **1300** *Cursor M.* 10023 Þe baile midelmast o thre, Bitakens wel hir chastite. *a* **1400** *Isumbras* 184 His medilmast sone ȝit lefte he thare. **14..** in *Rel. Ant.* I. 52 Tak the rote of walwort .. and do away the overmast rynd, and tak the mydilmaste rynde. **1577–87** HOLINSHED *Chron.* I. 14/2 Cunedag the sonne of Hennius and Ragaie (middlemost daughter of Leir before mentioned). **1638** JUNIUS *Paint. Ancients* 282 Although it require great skill to paint the bodie and middlemost parts of figures, yet [etc.]. **1658** ROWLAND *Moufet's Theat. Ins.* 952 For there are these several sorts of them, the bigger, lesser, middlemost and least. **1671** H. M. tr. *Erasm. Colloq.* 14 My middlemost son hath lately entred into holy Orders. **1721** MORTIMER *Husb.* II. 222 The undermost part of the middlemost Joints are to be cut off half through. **1812** J. BIGLAND *Beauties Eng. & Wales* XVI. 517 Folding gates, the middlemost of which is of iron. **1862** BORROW *Wild Wales* xxiii. (1901) 72/1 Three men—the middlemost was praying in Welsh.

b. *absol.* The part in the middle.

1382 WYCLIF *Matt.* Prol. 1 In the whiche gospel it is profitable to men desyrynge God, so to knowe the first, the mydmeste [*MS. O* mydelmest] other the last. **1673** PENN *Chr. Quaker* vii. (1699) 60 God himself inhabits the Lowest, and Highest, and the Middlemost.

middleness ('mɪd(ə)lnɪs). *rare.* [f. MIDDLE *a.* + -NESS.] The fact or quality of being middle, average, or middle-class.

1929 D. H. LAWRENCE *Pansies* 120 Their middleness is only an unreality separating two realities. **1963** *Times* 25 May 9/5 Some few fortunates have special attributes in highest degree, the majority have varying degrees of middleness, and the tail is sadly lacking in endowments.

middle night. *Obs.* exc. *dial.* = MIDNIGHT.

Beowulf 2782 Liȝeȝesan wæȝ hatne for horde, hioroweallende middelnihtum. *c* **1205** LAY. 20607 Hit was to þere middel-niht. *a* **1300** *K. Horn* 1391 Þat schup gan ariue, Abute middelniȝte. **1893** STEVENSON *Catriona* xxi. 253 When my father and my uncles lay in the hill, and I was to be carrying them their meat in the middle night.

middle-of-the-road. 1. Phr., often used *attrib.* or quasi-*adj.*, pertaining to or designating a person who, or a course of action, etc., which, is moderate or unadventurous, tending to avoid extremes; orig. *spec.* in *U.S.* with reference to the views of the Populist party.

[**1777** P. THICKNESSE *Year's Journey* I. vi. 43 It is necessary .. to keep in the *middle* of the road, so as not to be too suddenly surprised. **1892** *Rocky Mountain News* (Denver, Colorado) 17 July 1 Side tracks are rough, and they're hard to walk, keep in the middle of the road.] **1894** *Iowa State Register* (Des Moines) 5 Sept. 8/3, I am a middle-of-the-road man, but I don't propose to lie down across it so no one can get over me. Nothing grows in the middle of the road. **1896** *Congress. Rec.* 10 Dec. 80/2 The only honest Populist is the 'middle-of-the-road' Populist. **1927** *Amer. Speech* II. 443/1 The 'middle of the road' is the sacred path followed by compromising politicians who desire to promote their own or their party's fortunes. **1950** *Ann. Reg. 1949* 331 The Japanese press said that .. efforts to establish a 'middle-of-the-road' democracy had failed. **1951** [see FUNCTIONALISM 1]. **1959** *Economist* 10 Jan. 101/1 He has been ultra-conservative, demagogically radical, or firmly middle-of-the-road. **1971** D. E. WESTLAKE *I gave at the Office* (1972) 151, There are no revolutionaries on this island, not left-wing, not right-wing, and most certainly not middle-of-the-road revolutionaries. **1973** 'S. HARVESTER' *Corner of Playground* II. i. 80 [They] wanted him, the old middle-of-the-road liberal democrat, to be their first president.

2. Of (usu. popular) music: avoiding extremes of volume, beat, etc., so as to appeal to the widest possible audience; deliberately unadventurous and inoffensive; mediocre. Abbrev. *MOR* s.v. M 6.

[**1958** L. A. G. STRONG *Treason in Egg* ii. 35 A steady middle-of-the-road musician whom they felt they could trust to lead them through the morasses of contemporary music.] **1959** *Times* 23 Sept. 13/6 The Polish composer Spisak .. has .. been represented .. by middle-of-the-road music of unpretentious amiability. **1975** *Sat. Rev. Lit.* (U.S.) 29 Nov. 45/3 Pop and so-called MOR (middle-of-the-road) [record] sales are down. **1982** BARR & YORK *Official Sloane Ranger Handbk.* 25/1 William Bartholomew of Juliana's Discotheque knows you like middle-of-the-road songs. **1983** *Washington Post* 3 Mar. D13/3 The new format .. will be middle of the road 'music, aimed at people 35 to 54 years of age'.

Hence **middle-of-the-roader**.

1896 *N.Y. Tribune* 21 July 2/2 If the Bryan faction predominates, the Middle-of-the-Roaders will bolt and nominate another candidate. **1971** D. E. WESTLAKE *I gave at the Office* (1972) 151 They are neither right-wing nor left-wing but middle-of-the-roaders.

middler ('mɪd(ə)lə(r)). Also 6 middeler, midler. [f. MIDDLE *a.* + -ER¹. Cf. MDu. *middelare* Du. *middelaar*), OHG. *mittilâri* (MHG. *mitteler*, mod.G. *mittler*).]

† **1.** An intermediary, mediator. *Obs.*

1531 FRITH *Judgem. Tracy's Test.* (1535) C iii, A middeler [1573 Wks. 79/1 mid dealer] betwene God and man. *a* **1540** BARNES *Wks.* (1573) 350/1 Heare you not playnly how we do sooner obtayne our petityon of God our owne selfe, then by any other midlers? **1551** MATTHEW (Hyl) *Isa.* xxviii. Notes, Christ .. being here mediatour or middeler betwene God & men. **1675** BROOKS *Gold. Key* Wks. 1867 V. 177 This word, μεσίτης, doth .. signify a mediator or a middler.

2. The workman who performs the middle one of three operations in the preparation of flax.

1847 *Jrnl. R. Agric. Soc.* VIII. II. 385 It is taken up by the second man or middler, who puts it through the same process.

3. *U.S.* 'A member of the middle class in a seminary which has three classes—senior, middle, and junior—as in theological seminaries' (*Cent. Dict.*).

1882 in *Minutes of Triennial Convention* (U.S.) 43 In reading Hebrew at sight Middlers and Juniors did well.

middle-rate ('mɪd(ə)lreɪt), *a.* [f. MIDDLE *a.* + RATE *sb.*] Mediocre, not first-rate.

1738 tr. *Guazzo's Art Conversation* 196 A middle-rate Beauty is most commendable in a woman. **1791** BOSWELL *Johnson* 10 Apr. an. 1775 Here (I observed) was a very middle-rate poet.

† **'middleriff.** *Obs.* [f. MIDDLE *a.* + RIFF. Cf. MLG., Du. *middelrif*.] = MIDRIFF.

1599 A. M. tr. *Gabelhouer's Bk. Physicke* 264/1 Take in Maye the Middlereefe of a kidde.

middlescent (mɪd(ə)ˈlɛsənt), *a.* and *sb.* [f. MIDDLE *a.* + *-escent* after ADOLESCENT *sb.* and *a.*]

A. *adj.* Of, pertaining to, or taking place in middle age. **B.** *sb.* A middle-aged person. Hence **midd'lescence**, the period of middle age.

Not current in the U.K.

1965 *N.Y. Times* 5 Dec. IV. 10/3 Middlescence, that awkward age between youth and premature grave in which the parent undergoes alarming physical and emotional change. *Ibid.* 10/5 The middlescent parent is a highly emotional creature of quixotic moods. **1967** *Woman's Day* (Sydney) 12 June 40/4 Although most middlescent romantic folly doesn't get beyond the planning or fantasy stage, there's a lot to be said for being in love, perhaps especially at 40. **1969** *Britannica Bk. of Year* (U.S.) 800/2 *Middlescent*, a middle-aged individual, *esp.* one who has just turned 40; *middlescence, sb.* **1973** *Daily Colonist* (Victoria, B.C.) 7 Nov. 5/1 If the corporation doesn't know how to deal with middlescence..it might find itself 'drained of crucial managerial resources', because the middlescent is a troubled man.

'middle-sized, *a.* [f. MIDDLE *a.* + SIZE *sb.* + -ED[2].] Of medium size, neither large nor small.

1632 BROME *Court Beggar* II. (1653) P 2, I thinke you able to maintaine your selfes midle-sis'd Gent. **1667** BOYLE in *Phil. Trans.* II. 582 We put it into a middle-sized Receiver. **1793** SMEATON *Edystone L.* §201 From the bigness of a pea to that of a middle-sized turnip. **1883** F. M. WALLEM *Fish Supply Norway* 30 (Fish. Exhib. Publ.) A middle-sized.. stockfish. **1898** *Allbutt's Syst. Med.* V. 4 The middle-sized bronchi.

Hence **middle-sizedness**, the condition of being middle-sized; mediocrity.

1903 G. MATHESON *Repr. Men of Bible* 86 What is their mental average? It is not greatness, it is not smallness, it is not even middle-sizedness: it is shortcoming.

middle town. 1. The centre of a town.

1855 S. RODMAN *Diary* (1927) 324/1, I went to the middle town [of Shirley Village, Massachusetts] on two first days and heard good sermons.

2. Usu. **Middletown.** A typical middle-class community. orig. *U.S.* Hence **Middletowner,** the average middle-class person.

1929 R. S. & H. M. LYND (*title*) Middletown: a study in contemporary American culture. **1954** KOESTLER *Invis. Writing* v. 65 Another factor..is the uniform dreariness of the average Russian town and its lack of architectural character... This uniformity reminds one of the middle-towns of America. **1974** *Times* 21 Feb. 4/7 'Middletown' is bored nearly to tears by the television coverage of the [election] campaign. *Ibid.*, I have watched the coverage after pounding the streets of 'Middletown', and what I have heard from political leaders has had little to do with what is bothering the many 'Middletowners' I have met. *Ibid.* 28 Feb. 18/7 Middletowners..are not political animals... Three weeks in Middletown suggests to me that no party leader has tried to find out what bothers its people.

Middleveld (ˈmɪd(ə)lfɛlt, -vɛlt). *S. Afr.* Also **-veldt.** [Partial tr. Afrikaans *Middelveld*, lit. 'intermediate region'.] A region in East and West Transvaal lower than the Highveld but higher than the Lowveld, between 3,000 and 4,000 feet above sea-level. Also *transf.*

1877 C. WARREN *Diary* 17 July in *On Veldt in Seventies* (1902) 225 We arrived at a settlement station in the Middle Veldt, forty miles from Worcester, 2800 feet above it. **1878** A. AYLWARD *Transvaal To-Day* 25 The nearer and more recently settled district called the 'Middleveld' of the Orange Free State. **1929** [see LOWVELD]. **1931** *Discovery* Aug. 259/2 There are two cotton breeding stations in the Transvaal; one at Rustenberg, where problems connected with the improvement of cottons for middle-veld areas are dealt with. **1939** tr. *E. N. Marais's My Friends the Baboons* v. 55 It was in the middle-veld between the Palala and the Magalakwen. **1955** J. H. WELLINGTON *S. Afr.* I. I. iii. 72 These two regions..have important points of dissimilarity, the chief of which are the greater altitude and humidity of the highveld and the greater areas of pre-Karoo surfaces in the middleveld. **1972** *Farmer's Weekly* (S. Afr.) 21 Apr. 11 Normal dryland conditions in the Rhodesian middleveld.

†'middleward. *Obs.* [f. MIDDLE *a.* + -WARD; in sense 2 perh. f. WARD *sb.* as in *rearward, vanward.* Cf. MIDWARD.]

1. The middle part of anything.

c **1420** *Pallad. on Husb.* VIII. 135 All the rynde is for this nothing fyne, Then oonly take the tender myddelwardes.

2. The middle body of an army.

?*a* **1400** *Morte Arth.* 1988 The kynge..Demenys the medylwarde menskfully hyme selfene. **1577–87** HOLINSHED *Chron.* III. 828/1 The earle himself led the middle-ward. **1665** MANLEY *Grotius' Low C. Warres* 673 Three Battels.. of which the Middleward being double fill'd the whole breadth of the Shore.

middle way.

1. A course between two extremes. Cf. mod.L. *via media.*

a **1225** *Ancr. R.* 336 Þe middel weie of mesure is euer guldene. **1390** GOWER *Conf.* I. 2, I wolde go the middel weie And wryte a bok betwen the tweie. **1704** NORRIS *Ideal World* II. ii. 98 Which absurd consequence..falls upon those of the middle way, who unite matter and thought in Brutes. **1725** WATTS *Logic* II. v. §2 Where two extremes are proposed.. and neither of them has certain and convincing evidence, it is generally safest to take the middle way.

2. The middle of the way; one's mid-course.

1633 P. FLETCHER *Purple Isl.* XI. xxii, Aselges..met the virgin in the middle way. **1718** POPE *Iliad* XVI. 952 Apollo dreadful stops thy middle way.

attrib. **1648** GAGE *West Ind.* 116 A plain champaign Countrey, which continued till within a league of the middle way lodge.

b. Used *advb.* Half-way, on the way.

1568 GRAFTON *Chron.* II. 981 The King remoued his campe to a village myddell way betwene Sainct Omers and Tyrwine. **1860** WHITTIER *Truce of Piscataqua* III One alone, a little maid, Middleway her steps delayed.

† middle world. *Obs.* = MIDDLE EARTH.

c **1200** ORMIN 17538 Off þise fowwre shaffte iss all þiss middell werelld timmbredd. *c* **1250** *Gen. & Ex.* 98 Of waters froren, of yses wal, ðis middel werld it luket al. **1822** SCOTT *Pirate* xxiv, He spoke mair like a man of the middle world, than she had ever heard him since she had [etc.].

middle yorde, variant of MIDDLE ERD.

middling (ˈmɪdlɪŋ), *sb.* In 6 midlyng, 7 midling. [Prob. orig. f. MID *a.* + -LING[1], suggested by the earlier Sc. MIDDLING *a.* The surviving senses, however, represent absolute or elliptical uses of the adj.

The sb. (except for the doubtful example quoted in 2 below) occurs first at the beginning of the 17th c., concurrently with the adoption of the Scottish adj. by southern writers.]

1. **†a.** Something intermediate; a mean, middle term. *Obs.*

1614–15 BOYS *Expos. Fest. Ep. & Gosp.* Wks. (1630) 573 John Baptist, the last of the Prophets, and first of Apostles, a midling as it were betweene both. **1620** T. GRANGER *Div. Logike* 89 But the midlings are disparates both to the extremes, and among themselues.

b. A person who or a thing which is mediocre or second-rate (cf. MIDDLING *a.* 3b); freq. in dial. phr. ***among the middlings***, of a mediocre class; also, in a moderate condition of health.

1877 *Sunday Mag.* 182 'How are you getting on, Dick?'.. 'Well, only among the middlings, Sir.' **1885** R. HOLLAND *Gloss. County of Chester* 226, I said to his employer, 'What sort of a man is your team-man?' The answer was, 'Well! he's just about among the middlings;' so I did not engage him. **1931** R. CAMPBELL *Georgiad* iii. 62 They're all members of the self-same school, And drilled..to enforce on all The standards of the middling and the small. **1964** R. CHURCH *Voyage Home* ii. 28 Whenever I asked after his permanently ailing wife, he beamed with benevolence and replied: 'Oh, amongst the middlings, you know, amongst the middlings.'

2. *pl.* Pins of medium size.

The sense in the first quot. is doubtful; Jamieson explains it as above. Possibly the word may be a. MDu. *middelinc*, which appears to denote some kind of nail (= *middelnagel*); cf. MLG. *middelink*, the middle finger.

1543 *Aberdeen Reg.* XVIII. (Jam.), xviiij paperis of prenis, the price xxvij sh., ane bout of midlyngis the price vj. sh., & tua hankis of wyir the price xxiiij sh. **1824** MISS MITFORD *Village* Ser. I. 227 Pincushions..capable..of containing..a whole paper of short-whites and another of middlings.

3. *pl.* Used as a trade name for the middle one of three classes into which goods are sorted according to quality. (Cf. MIDDLING *a.* 3.)

a. of fuller's teasels.

1766 *Museum Rust.* VI. 2 The next smallest which are sound, and are commonly such as grow as side heads on each branch, are thrown for a second sort, and are called *middlings.* **1797** BILLINGSLEY *View Agric. Somerset* 111 [Teasels] are sorted into..kings, middlings, and scrubs.

b. *U.S.* of cotton.

1793 WASHINGTON *Lett.* Writ. 1891 XII. 382 The middlings and ship stuff may be sold to answer the money calls which you will have upon you. **1881** *Standard* 14 Sept. 4/7 The class of cotton known as 'middlings'.

c. of flour or meal.

1743 W. ELLIS *Mod. Husbandman* IV. III. 63 Its second, or Midling, or that Meal commonly made Use of by Farmers for spending it in their Families. **1786** G. WASHINGTON *Diary* 13 Sept. (1925) III. 116 My Corn being out, or nearly so, I was obliged to have middlings and ship stuff mixed for bread. **1842** *P. Parley's Ann.* III. 126 One of the nicest, cleanest, fattest pigs that was ever killed,..fattened with nothing but peas and middlings. *a* **1845** HOOD *Lament of Toby* ii, But must I give the classics up, For barley-meal and middlings? **1893** GUNTER *Miss Dividends* 244 Some bread made of middlings. **1960** *Farmer & Stockbreeder* 12 Jan. 107/1 A balanced ration for weaner piglets is 40 parts middlings, 25 parts barley meal, [etc.]. **1969** G. E. EVANS *Farm & Village* vi. 72 The miller..used to charge us..for grinding the corn. But we got the offal as well as the flour, and the best middlings we fed to the pigs.

d. of minerals.

1869 *Amer. Jrnl. Sci.* XCVII. 9 The amount of heavy lubricating oil was largely increased, and the 'middlings' correspondingly diminished. **1909** WEBSTER, *Middling*,..*pl.* The second quality of ore obtained by washing. **1965** G. J. WILLIAMS *Econ. Geol. N.Z.* ix. 135/2 Low-grade magnetic concentrates and a high proportion of middlings.

4. *U.S.* (See quot. 1859.) Also in *sing.*

1777 *Calendar Virginia State Papers* (1875) I. 288 Bakin in hams, midlings, shoulders, &c. **1831** J. M. PECK *Guide for Emigrants* 172 To make bacon of hams, shoulders, and middlings or broadsides. **1834** D. CROCKETT *Narr. Life* xi. 79, I got also a large middling of bacon, and killed a fine deer. **1848** *Rep. Comm. Patents 1847* (U.S.) 527 The hog thus cut up into shoulders, hams and middlings undergoes further trimming. **1857** 'PORTE CRAYON' *Virginia Illustr.* i. 31 Fried middling and hot coffee were then served round. **1859** BARTLETT *Dict. Amer.*, *Middlings* 2. A term used in the West for pork, meaning the portion of the animal between the hams and shoulders. Thus the Price Current quotes hams, shoulders, and middlings. **1904** E. GLASGOW *Deliverance* 51 She has had to fry the middling in the kitchen, and mother complains so of the smell.

5. 'That portion of a gun-stock between the grasp and the tail-pipe or ramrod-thimble' (Knight *Dict. Mech.* 1875).

middling (ˈmɪd(ə)lɪŋ), *a.* and *adv.* Forms: 5 mydlyn, 6 midiling, 6–8 midling, 7 middleing, 7– middling. [App. of Sc. origin: the earliest examples in Eng. writers belong to the reign of James I.

Prob. orig. f. MID *a.* + *-ling* in adjs. like *eastling, westling* (where the suffix seems to represent a blending, in attributive use, of -LING[1] and -LING[2]). In English use of the beginning of the 17th c., the adj. appears to have been apprehended as an attributive application of the sb., which came in at the same time; Ben Jonson uses both freely.]

A. *adj.*

† 1. Intermediate between two things; forming a mean between two extremes. *Obs.*

Quot. 1645 may belong to MIDDLING *ppl. a.*

1456 SIR G. HAYE *Law Arms* (S.T.S.) 118 Bot than is vertu morale in the mydlyn way. **1614** B. JONSON *Barth. Fair* II. ii, A certaine midling thing, betweene a foole and a madman. **1645** MILTON *Tetrach.* Wks. 1851 IV. 234 As the Physician cures him who hath taken down poyson, not by the middling temper of nourishment, but by the other extreme of antidote. **1677** GALE *Crt. Gentiles* III. 103 These Demons the Romans called Semi-Gods and Medioxumi or midling Gods. **1684** tr. *Bonet's Merc. Compit.* v. 138 A middling Medicine, between a Plaster and a Cataplasm. **1733** CHEYNE *Eng. Malady* II. i. §2 (1734) 115 If Care be taken to keep up the Juices in this middling condition. **1767** tr. *Voltaire's Ignorant Philosopher* xxxii. 86 The middling state between health and disease.

2. Of medium or moderate size; moderately large. Now (exc. in ***middling size, middling degree,*** etc.) only *colloq.* or *vulgar*, as an application of sense 3b.

1596 *Aberdeen Reg.* (1848) II. 139 Thrie midling schippis, to pass to the Ilis for subdewing of the hieland men. **1598** in *Black Bk. Taymouth* (Bannatyne Cl.) 330 Off midling plaittis thair, ii do. vi; off greit plaittis thair, xiii. **1671** MARTEN *Voy. into Spitzbergen* in *Acc. Sev. Late Voy.* II. (1694) 80 He is as big as a midling Duck. **1707** MORTIMER *Husb.* (1721) II. 316 As you gather your Fruit, separate the fairest and biggest from the middling. **1792** tr. *Brissot's Trav.* 249 Quarries of Marble of a middling fineness. **1831** SIR J. SINCLAIR *Corr.* II. 269 Being able to carry a soldier of a middling size in each hand, when his arms were extended. **1853** KANE *Grinnell Exp.* xxx. (1856) 264 When colder, say —40°, with a middling breeze. **1871** BLACKMORE *Maid of Sker* (1881) 77 A middling keg of Hollands, and an anker of old rum. **1898** 'R. BOLDREWOOD' *Rom. Canvass Town* 71 You have a middling cheque, I believe.

b. *Comb.*, as ***middling-sized*** (**†-size**) adj.

a **1756** MRS. HAYWOOD *New Present* (1771) 62 Get four or five middling-sized eels. **1776** *Trial of Nundocomar* 42/1 *Q.* What sort of a man was Mahomed Comaul? *A.* A middling size man. **1840** DICKENS *Barn. Rudge* iv, A middling-sized dish of beef and ham.

† c. Average. *Obs.*

1754 HUME *Hist. Eng.* I. xii. 296 This is near half of the middling price in our time.

3. *Comm.* Used as a designation for the second of three grades of goods.

1550 *Reg. Privy Council Scot.* I. 107 The best moutoun for ixs, the midiling moutoun for viijs, and the worst moutoun for viis. **1693** LUTTRELL *Brief Rel.* (1857) III. 86 Middling wheat at 56*s.* a quarter; midling sort of rye at 36*s.* a quarter. **1859** *Stationers' Handbk.* (ed. 2) 111 Sample of the make termed Blue wove. This is a middling quality, commoner sorts would be *lower*,..better kinds *higher* in colour. **1864** DE COIN *Cotton & Tobacco* 192 Substantial upland middling cottons of good staple. **1887** *Daily News* 23 Feb. 2/6 Coffee..low middling to middling, 77*s* to 83*s*; good middling to fine middling, 83*s* 6*d* to 88*s*. **1889** *Century Dict.* s.v. *Fair a.*, *Fair to middling*, moderately good: a term designating a specific grade of quality in the market.

b. Moderately good, mediocre, second-rate.

1652 TATHAM *Scotch Fig.* IV. i. *Dram. Wks.* (1878) 161 Children, you talk not like men, you are but midling Christians. **1677** DRYDEN *Apol. Her. Poetry*, Longinus..has judiciously preferr'd the sublime Genius that sometimes erres, to the midling or indifferent one which makes few faults but seldome or never rises to any Excellence. **1756** BURKE *Subl. & B.* Introd. Wks. 1842 I. 27 The middling performance of a vulgar artist. **1833** HOOD *Epping Hunt* xxxii, All sorts of vehicles and vans, Bad, middling, and the smart. **1882** M. ARNOLD *Irish Ess.* 247 The abundant consumption of middling literature. **1895** H. BEVERIDGE in *Speaker* 14 Sept. 288/1 In the matter of trade disputes, however, he was only a middling success.

† 4. Middle-aged. *Obs.*

1610 BOYS *Exp. Dom. Epist. & Gosp.* Wks. (1622) 228 Young Lawyers, old Physitians, and midling Divines are best; an old Preacher cannot teach so painfully, and the young not so profitably, but the midling may doe both [etc.].

5. Belonging to the middle classes. ***middling class*** = MIDDLE CLASS.

1692 R. L'ESTRANGE *Fables* ccxxx. 201 There was a Middling sort of a Man that was left well enough to pass by his Father, but could never think he had enough, so long as any Man had more. **1718** *Free-thinker* No. 19. 129 The Middling People of England are generally Good-natured and Stout-hearted. **1789** ANBUREY *Trav.* II. 393 This diversion is a great favourite of the middling and lower classes. **1847** GROTE *Greece* II. xxxvii. (1862) III. 357 He was a citizen of middling station. **1897** MAITLAND *Domesday & Beyond* 65 Now if these things are being done in the middling strata of society [etc.].

absol. **1782** CREVECOEUR *Lett.* 72 The rich stay in Europe, it is only the middling and poor that emigrate.

† 6. Occupying a middle position. *Obs.*

1747 *Gentl. Mag.* XVII. 330 *note*, In many of the midling counties,..there is scarce any difference between the whole number of members at that time and this.

† 7. ***middling teeth*** (see quot.). *Obs.*

1753 CHAMBERS *Cycl. Supp.*, *Middling-Teeth*,..are the four teeth of a horse that come out at three years and a half, in the room of other four foal teeth; from which situation they derive the title of Middling.

B. *adv.* (Now chiefly *colloq.*: common *dial.* and in vulgar use.)

1. Qualifying an adj. or adv.: Moderately, fairly, tolerably.

1719 De Foe *Crusoe* II. (Globe) 411 He form'd out of one of the Iron Crows a middling good Anvil. **1779** E. Beatty in *J. L. Hardenbergh's Jrnl.* (1879) 63 The road middling hilly. **1848** Lowell *Biglow P.* Ser. I. ii. 109 Mister Sawin, sir, you're middlin' well now, be ye? **1880** H. James *Portr. Lady* v, She was thin, and light, and middling tall. **1892** Stevenson *Across the Plains* v, If a light is not rather more than middling good, it will be radically bad.

2. Fairly well; chiefly *predicatively*, fairly well in health; not very well.

1810 W. B. Rhodes *Bomb. Fur.* i. (1830) 7 We are but middling—that is, but so so. **1852** Dickens *Bleak Ho.* xxi, 'How de do?' 'Middling', replies Mr. George. **1877** P'cess Alice in *Mem.* 6 Nov. (1884) 367, I am but very middling. **1894** Hall Caine *Manxman* v. iii. 287 'We'll do middling if we get a market', said Pete.

Hence **'middlingish** *adv., dial.* or *vulgar*.

1820 J. A. Dowling *Coroners Inquest on J. Lees* 18, I believe it was a middlingish good hat before he went to the meeting. **1876** Farjeon *Love's Victory* ii, 'A gentleman, then?' 'Well, yes, sir; middlingish.'.

†**'middling,** *ppl. a. Obs. rare*$^{-1}$. [f. middle *v.* + -ing^{2}.] Acting as a go-between, intermediary.

1616 B. Jonson *Devil an Ass* I. vi. 219 What doe you say vnto a middling Gossip To bring you aye together, at her lodging?

middlingly ('mɪdlɪŋlɪ), *adv.* [f. middling *a.* + -ly^{2}.] In a middling manner; fairly, indifferently, tolerably; also, not very well in health.

1755 Johnson, *Indifferently* 3. Not well; tolerably; passably; middlingly. **1814** Moore *Mem.* (1853) II. 44, I dare say I thought but middlingly of them while they existed. **1819** J. Jebb *Corr.* (1834) II. 373 For the last two days I have felt but middlingly. **1891** H. Johnston *Kilmallie* I. viii. 133 Even then she was but middlingly pleased.

middlingness ('mɪdlɪŋnɪs). [f. middling *a.* + -ness.] The state of being middling; mediocrity.

1866 Geo. Eliot *F. Holt* v, 'Tis a poor climax, to my weaker thought, That future middlingness. **1929** D. H. Lawrence *Pansies* 120 Nothing that transcends the bourgeois middlingness. **1957** *Essays in Crit.* VII. 216 The umbrella of 'moderation'—the chief of the new slogans—means too frequently that middlingness, lack of real poetic talent and ambition has found yet another cosy corner for itself in our watered-down, democratic culture.

middow, obs. form of meadow.

middrift, -dryfe, obs. forms of midriff.

midds, middst, obs. forms of mids, midst.

middy^{1} ('mɪdɪ). *colloq.* [f. mid *sb.*^{2} + -y^{6}.]

1. A midshipman.

1818 'A. Burton' *Adventures J. Newcome* 145 A Middy rudely said, He'd sell them [*sc.* prisoners] for five pounds a head. **1833** Marryat *P. Simple* xxix, Then went two of the middies, just about your age, Mr. Simple. **1894** C. N. Robinson *Brit. Fleet* 410 The middies, with naval cadets, are now designated 'subordinate officers'.

2. In full, ***middy blouse***. A kind of loose blouse, often extending below the waistline, similar to that worn by midshipmen. Also *attrib.*

1911 *Daily Colonist* (Victoria, B.C.) 13 Apr. 24/3 (Advt.), Child's Middy Dress, in white duck. Square neck and short sleeves. **1913** *T. Eaton & Co. Catal.* Spring & Summer 31/2 Plain Galatea 'middy'. Plain Galatea waist, in Norfolk 'middy' style. **1915** E. J. Kimble *Commercial, Industr. & Technical Vocab.* 185 Middy blouse. **1917** D. Canfield *Understood Betsy* (1922) ii. 37 The neck-tie of her middy blouse fell forward. **1929** Wodehouse *Mr. Mulliner Speaking* viii. 259 A sort of middy-blouse arrangement. **1952** M. McCarthy *Groves of Academe* (1953) ix. 172 Mary Margaret, the eldest, in middy and skirt, followed. **1957** *Observer* 24 Nov. 11/1 The middy two-piece comes near the new silhouette, with a hip-length 'blouson' worn over a skirt mounted on its underbodice. **1965** Mrs. L. B. Johnson *White House Diary* 6 Aug. (1970) 307 Carol Channing in her white velvet bell-bottom trousers trimmed in red and a middy blouse top.

middy^{2} ('mɪdɪ). *Austral. slang.* [f. mid *sb.*^{1} + -y^{6}.] A measure of beer or other liquor (see quots.); the glass containing it.

1945 Baker *Austral. Lang.* ix. 169 The *middy*, a beer glass containing nine ounces, is a measure used only in N.S.W. hotels. **1956** S. Hope *Diggers' Paradise* 230 A middyglass contains ten liquid ounces. **1957** 'N. Culotta' *They're a Weird Mob* (1958) ii. 25 Those big glasses are called schooners and those small ones are called middies. **1968** *Southerly* XXVIII. 38 He ordered two more middies. **1970** *Observer* (Colour Suppl.) 15 Feb. 39/2 Getting 'full' on frosty 'middies' of beer is still a serious manly business. **1974** K. Cook *Bloodhouse* 79 'Middy of rum, Mick,' said the youth... Ten ounces of rum sold over the bar cost four dollars.

†**mide,** *prep.* and *adv. Obs.* [Related to mid *prep.* and *adv.* It has not been found in OE., but corresponds in form and use to OS. *midi*, OHG. *miti* (MHG. *mite*).] A synonym of mid *prep.* and *adv.*, employed **a.** as *adv.* (sometimes = 'wherewith'); **b.** as *prep.*, usually placed after its regimen or used *ellipt.* at the end of a sentence.

c **1160** *Hatton Gosp.* Mark xv. 41, & maneȝe oðre þe him mide ferden on ierusalem. *c* **1175** *Lamb. Hom.* 51 And hwat þa claðes bi-tacneð þe þe rapes weren mide biwunden. *c* **1205** Lay. 2831 Alle his cnihtes þe mide him weoren. *a* **1225** *Ancr. R.* 372 Nicodemus brouhte smuriles uorte smurien mide ure Louerd. *c* **1315** Shoreham I. 241 In water ich wel þe cristny her.. For mide to wessche nis noþynge þat man comeþ to so liȝte. *c* **1330** *Arth. & Merl.* 3094 (Kölbing), .vi. hundred kniȝtes he brouȝt him mide.

midear (mɪ'dɪə(r)), var. *my dear* (see my *poss. adj.* 2 b, dear *sb.*^{2}), used as a form of address.

1959 J. Braine *Vodi* xiv. 191 Anything you want, midear. **1967** J. Aiken *Ribs of Death* xxv. 176 Do-ee think it *could* be true, midear?

mid-earth. a. The middle of the earth. ***mid-earth sea***, the Mediterranean Sea. (Cf. middle earth 2.) **b.** quasi-*arch.* = middle earth 1.

1559 W. Cunningham *Cosmogr. Glasse* 143 Not farre distante from the midde Earthe Seas. **1895** A. Nutt in K. Meyer *Voy. Bran* I. 240 That tract of earth is not Accessible to many o'er mid-earth. **1895** Jane Menzies *Cynewulf's Elene* 15 Since heaven's Lord in low degree In this mid-earth a man was born.

midegaitt, variant of midgait.

midel, obs. form of middle *sb.* and *a.*

midenarde, variant of middenerd *Obs.*

miderede, obs. form of midred.

mides, midest, obs. forms of mids, midst.

mid-'ethmoid. *Anat.* = mesethmoid.

1884 Coues *Key N. Amer. Birds* (ed. 2) 160 The permanent plate,..to which the name *mesethmoid* or mid-ethmoid is more strictly applicable.

mid-'eval, *a. rare*$^{-1}$. [f. mid *a.* + eval; perhaps after *coeval*.] = mediæval.

1840 *Civil Eng. & Arch. Jrnl.* III. 365/1 The mid-eval architects.

†**mid-fasten, mid-fast.** *Obs.* [f. mid *a.* + fasten *sb.*, fast *sb.* Cf. ON. *miðfasta*, MDu., MLG. *midde-, midvasten*, MHG. *mitte(n)vaste, mitvaste* (mod.G. *mitfasten*).] = mid-lent. Also *attrib.*

c **1122** *O.E. Chron.* an. 1047 Her on þisum ȝeare wæs mycel ȝe mot on Lundene to midfestene. *c* **1205** Lay. 22256 He ferde to Æxchæstræn to þan mid-festen. **1480** *Newcastle Merch. Vent.* (Surtees) I. 2 The.. persones.. shall.. halden wppon Thursday next after Midfast Sunday [etc.].

mid feather.

1. (See quots.)

1753 [see feather *sb.* 16 d]. **1797** *Encycl. Brit.* (ed. 3) XVI. 626/1 The body of the furnace consists of two chambers, divided from each other by a brick partition called the mid-feather. **1875** Knight *Dict. Mech.*, *Mid-feather*, a water-bridge in a steam boiler furnace which occupies a middle position in the flue-space, the flame passing both above and below it. **1905** Goodchild & Tweney *Technol. & Sci. Dict.* 402/1 *Midfeather*, (*Paper Manufac.*) a partition fixed in the 'breaker' to promote circulation of the pulp. **1930** *Engineering* 22 Aug. 223/1 Numerous tests showed that, provided the midfeather was inserted at the fan end of the duct, completely uniform distribution of the dust was obtained. **1940** *Chambers's Techn. Dict.* 547/1 *Mid-feather* (*Join.*), a cross-tongue.

2. *Mining.* A support for the centre of a tunnel (Webster 1897).

mid-field. Also **midfield**. [f. mid *a.* + field *sb.*] The middle of the field (in various senses of that word). Now chiefly in *Football*. Also as quasi-*adv*.

a **1400-50** *Alexander* 955 He.. metes hym in þe myd-feld with a much nowmbre. **1533** Bellenden *Livy* II. xiii. (S.T.S.) I. 181 Þe dictator.. come on þe mydfeild of sabynis .. with his Oist of futemen. **1613** Heywood *Silver Age* II. i. Wks. 1874 III. 101 King Ptelera.. with a fresh supply Takes vp the mid-field. **1897** *Badminton Mag.* IV. 422 They [*sc.* rooks] quickly shift their position to safer quarters in mid-field. **1901** *Essex Weekly News* 29 Mar. 8/3 Woodford were the smarter team in mid-field, but they did not equal Chelmsford in front of goal. **1909** *Westm. Gaz.* 24 Nov. 12/2 C. Lyle shot well, but was very slow in midfield. **1956** *Times* 16 Apr. 13/1 Haynes, in spite of the presence of Evans in mid-field, showed himself one of the very few inside forwards in the British Isles with a spark of true genius. **1968** *Listener* 7 Nov. 625/3, I was aware.. that Gilzean would be playing mid-field: I knew my Spurs. **1973** *Liverpool Echo* (Football ed.) 17 Mar. 18/1 With Hughes pushing them forward with some strong play in mid-field, Liverpool hit back.

attrib. **1896** *Bootle Times* 18 Jan. 3/1 Midfield play ensued. **1960** *Times* 30 Nov. 3/6 Certainly they had no penetrative midfield player. **1969** [see link *sb.*^{2} 3 h]. **1974** *Times* 23 Feb. 14/8 Even eight, nine and ten-year-olds these days are taught by games masters in terms of.. 'midfield provider', 'sweeper' and the rest. **1974** *Guardian* 19 Aug. 16/2 The midfield men preferred the easy option of overlapping fullbacks to making their own breach. *Ibid.* 16/3 The painstaking midfield play of Kendall and Campbell.

†**midgait,** *adv. Sc. Obs.* Also 6 **midegaitt**. [f. mid *a.* + gait *sb.*^{1}] = midway.

1557-75 *Diurn. Occurr.* (Bannatyne Cl.) 256 He wes met be the nobilities horsmen midgait. *a* **1578** Lindesay (Pitscottie) *Chron. Scot.* (S.T.S.) II. 153 The Earle Marchall, or he come midegaitt, tyrit and grew seik that he might do no thing nor no goode at that tyme. **1596** Dalrymple tr. *Leslie's Hist. Scot.* v. 290 Bot or he was midgait, Cadhard.. slew him at the castel of Meffen.

‖**Midgard** ('mɪdgɑːd). *Myth.* [repr. ON. *Miðgarð-r*: see middenerd.] The proper name, in Scandinavian mythology, of the world inhabited by living men, in contradistinction to Asgard (*Ásgarðr*), the home of the gods. Also *attrib.*, as ***midgard sea, snake***.

1882 C. F. Keary *Outl. Prim. Belief* 73 The mid-earth serpent called Jörmungandr.. lying at the bottom of the mid-gard sea.

midge (mɪdʒ). Forms: 1 micge, mycg, mygc, mygg, 4–6 mydge, 5 migge, 5–6 myge, 6 mige, myghe, 6– midge. [OE. *mycg* masc., *mycge* wk. fem., corresponding to OS. *muggia* fem. (Essen glosses), MDu. *mugghe* (Du. *mug*), OHG. *mucca* (MHG. *mucke, mücke*, mod.G. *mücke*), Sw. *mygg, mygga*, Da. *myg*:—OTeut. types **mugjo-z, *mugjôn-*. It is uncertain whether the synonymous ON. *mý* is related, and the alleged cognates outside Teut. are very doubtful.]

1. a. A popular name loosely applied to many small gnat-like insects; by some entomologists restricted to the *Chironomidæ*.

c **725** *Corpus Gloss.* (Hessels) C 947 *Culix*, mygg. *c* **1000** *Sax. Leechd.* I. 54 Wið gnættas & micgeas. *c* **1000** Ælfric *Gloss.* in Wr.-Wülcker 122/7 *Culex*, micge. *a* **1340** Hampole *Psalter* civ. 29 He sayd & hundfle come & mydge [L. *cynomia et sciniphes*] in all paire endis. *c* **1450** *Mirour Saluacioun* 459 Some tymes diseses man a migge or els a flee. **1513** Douglas *Æneis* XII. Prol. 172 To knit hyr nettis and hir wobbys sle, Tharwith to caucht the myghe and littill fle. **1520** M. Nisbet *N. Test. in Scots* Matt. xxiii. 24 Blind leidars, clengeand a myge, bot suelliand a camele. **1551** Turner *Herbal* I. A v b, The smoke of it [wormwood], dryueth away gnates or mydges. **1625** Purchas *Pilgrims* II. 1771 *margin*, They are called Wall-lice, because they breed in Wals; but in true English they are called Midges, and in Latin *Cimices*. **1658** Rowland *Moufet's Theat. Ins.* 953 These small Summer Gnats.. are properly called in English Midges. **1668** Charleton *Onomasticon* 43 *Culices*.. Gnats, & *si parvi sunt* Midges. *a* **1732** T. Boston *Crook in Lot* (1805) 88 Midges in the summer will fly about those walking abroad in a goodly attire, as well as about those in sordid apparel. **1808** Scott *Fam. Lett.* 31 Oct., There is a foundation for the other part of the story, though no larger than a midge's wing. **1850** Rossetti *Blessed Damozel* vi, Where this earth Spins like a fretful midge. **1867** F. Francis *Angling* vi. (1880) 236 The Green Midge, a very delicate little insect. **1886** *Times* 18 Aug. 10/6 The wheat midge.. produces the red maggots which so seriously damage the ripening ears of corn. **1896** Kirkaldy & Pollard tr. *Boas' Zoöl.* 276 Midges (*Nemocera*) are usually slender with long antennæ, which in the males are often furnished with long hairs.

b. Applied to a diminutive person.

1796 Burns *Wha will buy my troggin?* ix, By a thievish midge They had amaist been lost. **1847** C. Bronte *J. Eyre* xxxvi, A more spirited, bolder, keener gentleman than he was before that midge of a governess crossed him, you never saw, ma'am. **1866** *Reader* 17 Mar. 276 As compared to the men and women about him he is a mere midge.

2. An artificial fly for fishing.

1799 G. Smith *Laboratory* II. 311 Black-midge, or gnat. Dubbing, of the down of a mole.

3. The fry of various fishes (Funk). Cf. *mackarel-midge*.

1832 Couch in *Mag. Nat. Hist.* V. 15 Midge (*Ciliata glauca*). *Ibid.* 16 It is the mackarel midge of our fishermen. .. For brevity's sake I have retained only the name Midge.

4. A kind of small one-horse 'fly' or cab.

1865 C. M. Yonge *Clever Woman* I. ii. 52 One of the midges, or diminutive flies used at Avonmouth, came to the door. **1877** *Rep. Provinc.* 133 (E.D.D.) Small flys licensed to carry two or at most three persons, to be seen on all the cab-stands about Torquay, are almost always called Midges about that town. **1896** Mrs. Oliphant *Old Mr. Tredgold* ii. (1898) 16 [Refers to Isle of Wight.] A midge is not a graceful nor perhaps a very safe vehicle.

5. *Mining.* (See quot.) Cf. midgy.

1883 Gresley *Coal-mining Gloss.*, *Midges*, lamps (not safety) carried by putters, &c.

6. *attrib.*, as ***midge-like*** adj., ***midge-tail***; **midge cap** (see quot.); **midge fly**, a midge; **midge grass**, *Holcus lanatus* (Britten & Holland, 1886).

1814 J. Hodgson in J. Raine *Mem.* (1857) I. 144 The labourers are under the necessity of wearing a sort of veil before their faces which they call *midgecaps. **1806** Wolcot (P. Pindar) *Tristia* Wks. 1812 V. 259 The Bard, to kill a *Midge-fly pours her Thunder. **1785** Burns *Death & Dr. Hornbook* xxii, Sal-alkali o' *Midge-tail clippings.

†**midgern.** *Obs.* exc. *dial.* Also 1 micgern(e, 5 medryn, mydrun, myg(g)erne, 9 *dial.* midgen, midgerum, middren, etc. (see E.D.D.). [OE. *micgern* = OS. *midgarni* OHG. *mittigarni*:—OTeut. type **midjogarnjo*^{m}, f. **midjo-* mid *a.* + **garnâ* (ON. *gorn* fem.) bowel, gut, cogn. w. **garno*^{m} yarn.] The fat about the entrails of an animal; suet; in mod. dial. use the fat about the kidneys of a pig; leaf-lard.

c **1000** Ælfric *Gloss.* in Wr.-Wülcker 162/28 *Exugium*, micgern. **14..** *Nom.* ibid. 678/22 *Hec omomestra*, a medryn. **14..** *Voc.* ibid. 599/3 *Omentum*, a paunchecloute (*vel* Myggerne). *c* **1420** *Liber Cocorum* (1862) 10 Take.. þo mydrun and þe kydnere, And hew hom smalle. *c* **1475** *Pict. Voc.* in Wr.-Wülcker 747/31 *Hoc omestrum*, a mygerne.

¶**b.** App. confused with midriff.

a **1440** *Promp. Parv.* [Several texts have *midrym*, *middryn*, instead of *midrif*, rendered *diafragma*.] **1893** *Northumb. Gloss.*, *Middern*, the midriff or diaphragm.

midget ('mɪdʒɪt). [f. MIDGE + -ET[1].]

1. An extremely small person; *spec.* such a person publicly exhibited as a curiosity.

1865 *W. Cornw. Words* in *Jrnl. R. Inst. Cornw.* Apr. 50 *Midget*, very small, a mite. **1869** MRS. STOWE *Old Town Folks* xvi. (1870) 159 Now you know Parson Kendall's a little midget of a man. **1884** *Pall Mall G.* 22 Aug. 10/2 A child..which had been exhibited by a showman..as the smallest 'Midget' in the world. **1892** E. REEVES *Homeward Bound* 7 There are 120 saloon passengers, adults, 40 children, and 2 'midgets' on board. **1903** *Review of Rev.* Apr. 347 The undersized midgets of new recruits.

2. A Canadian name for the Sand-fly.

1848 in BARTLETT *Dict. Amer.*

3. More fully ***midget-photograph***. The trade name for a very small size of photographic portrait.

1888 *Lady* 25 Oct. 374/3 A smaller frame, screen shape, .. to hold six 'midget' photographs.

4. A small vehicle, aircraft, etc.

1930 *Daily Express* 8 Sept. 3/7 The midgets will function as destroyers, and the heavier tanks will discharge the duties of land battleships. **1933** M. ARLEN *Man's Mortality* ii. 32 He climbed into the midget [*sc.* aircraft], and called out to the cadet: 'Altitude?'

5. *attrib.* **a.** In sense 'weak, puny', as ***midget effort***. **b.** 'small, small-scale, tiny', as ***midget submarine***, ***warship***, etc.; **midget golf**, a form of miniature golf, usually played indoors; so ***midget-golf course***, etc.

1908 *Daily Chron.* 7 Aug. 4/4 The spiritual intelligences.. must..laugh at our serious midget efforts to comprehend and explain the circumambient infinite. **1922** JOYCE *Ulysses* 620 Marcella, the midget queen. **1930** *Daily Express* 6 Nov. 3/7 Sydney's midget golf boom. **1930** *Daily Tel.* 1 Dec. 23/6 (Advt.), An 18-hole midget golf course complete. **1933** *Pop. Sci. Monthly* Mar. 22/1 (*caption*) Midget submarine ready for its first test. **1934** *Discovery* Nov. 324/2 The combined radio-gramophone and deaf-aid..includes..three midget valves. **1942** *Hutchinson's Pict. Hist. War* 18 Mar.–9 June 26 (*caption*) One of the Royal Navy's midget war ships, a motor gun-boat, on patrol duty round the coasts of Britain. **1945** *Jane's Fighting Ships 1943–44* 316/2 At least two classes of Japanese midget submarines are believed to exist. **1966** T. PYNCHON *Crying of Lot 49* ii. 30 He and the kid follow the old regiment to Gallipoli, where the father somehow builds a midget submarine. **1972** *Mainichi Daily News* (Japan) 7 Nov. 6/3 The National Federation of Midget Automobile Manufacturers' and Dealers' Associations revealed..that a total of 78,055 new midget automobiles were registered in October. *Ibid.*, Demand for midget commercial vehicles would increase.

'midgety, *a.* [f. MIDGET + -Y.] Very small.

1798 JANE AUSTEN *Lett.* (1884) I. 177 [My] cap..was before too midgetty to please me.

midgy ('mɪdʒɪ), *sb. Mining.* [f. MIDGE + -Y.] See quot., and cf. MIDGE 5.

1849 GREENWELL *Coal Trade Gloss.* (E.D.D.), *Midgy*, an oblong box without a front, carried upright, the use of which is to carry a lighted candle or small lamp in a current of air.

midgy ('mɪdʒɪ), *a.* [f. MIDGE + -Y.] Consisting of midges.

1806 J. GRAHAME *Birds Scot.* II. 65 When dance the midgy clouds in warping maze Confused.

mid-heaven. [MID *a.*]

1. *Astron.* and *Astrol.* The meridian, or middle line of the heavens; the point of the ecliptic on the meridian.

1594 BLUNDEVIL *Exerc.* VI. xxix. (1597) 308b, The Fiduciall line of the label crossing the Zodiaque, will shew the degree of mid heauen at that houre. **1610** HEALEY *St. Aug. Citie of God* 203 Mid-heaven, the point between the Horoscope and the west-angle. **1819** J. WILSON *Dict. Astrol.* 272 The 10th [house] is the midheaven, or medium cœli, or south angle.

2. The middle of the sky.

1612 T. TAYLOR *Comm. Titus* ii. 11 The sunne is not only risen and in our midheauen, but the light of it is seauen fold bigger then it was before. **1667** MILTON *P.L.* XII. 263 Or how the Sun shall in mid Heav'n stand still. **1871** TENNYSON *Last Tourn.* 737 The red fruit Grown on a magic oak-tree in mid-heaven.

3. The midst of heaven as the abode of angels.

1667 MILTON *P.L.* IX. 468 But the hot Hell that alwayes in him burnes, Though in mid Heav'n, soon ended his delight.

Midi[1] (midi). [Fr.] The south of France. Also *attrib.*

1883 H. JAMES *Little Tour in France* (1885) xvi. 110, I could not fail to flatter myself, on reaching La Rochelle, that I was already in the Midi. **1936** C. CONNOLLY *Rock Pool* i. 16 The jungle of the Midi bourgeoisie. **1964** E. AMBLER *Kind of Anger* ii. 41 She had a strong Midi accent and sounded like a maid. **1967** A. WILSON *No Laughing Matter* III. ii. 245 M. Garcin in his Midi accent asked.., 'Qu'est ce qu'elle dit?' **1973** *Guardian* 22 Feb. 4/4 For electoral purposes the Midi is usually divided into two—the Midi-Pyrénées and the Midi-Méditérranée or Languedoc-Rousillon.

midi[2]: see MIDI-.

MIDI[3] ('miːdɪ). Also **midi**. [Acronym f. the initial letters of *M*usical *I*nstrument *D*igital *I*nterface.] An electronic device by means of which electronic musical instruments, synthesizers, and computers can be interconnected and used simultaneously. Usu. *attrib.*

1983 *Billboard* 19 Feb. 45/3 The Roland Corp. of Los Angeles has introduced a Musical Instrument Digital Interface (MIDI), which it claims establishes a universal standard of interface for synthesizers, electronic musical instruments and computers. **1984** *New Scientist* 23 Feb. 27/1 Instruments equipped with MIDI can transmit digitally encoded information telling any other instruments linked to them when to sound and which notes to play. **1984** *Newsweek* 28 May 89/1 Some professional musicians already use MIDI connections to play several synthesizers at once from a single keyboard. **1985** *Internat. Musician* June 31/1 (Advt.), Yamaha continues the fabulous X7 range with an incredibly cheap poly, midi sequencer!

midi-, comb. f. of MID *a.*, MIDDLE *a.*, in imitation of MAXI- and MINI-, denoting garments longer than mini- but shorter than maxi-, normally extending to mid-calf. Hence **midi** *sb.*[2], such a garment. So ***midi-length***.

1967 *Word Study* Dec. 3/2 In contrast to the miniskirt a skirt whose hemline comes as low as midcalf has been called a *midiskirt*. **1968** *Chicago Tribune* 9 July 11. 1/7 A swaggering midi-coat that gives a new proportion to the trouser costume. **1969** *Sun* 13 Mar. 8/2 The newsy midi hem-length (note midi, *not* maxi). **1969** *Internat. Herald Tribune* (Paris) 6 Nov. 6/2 Almost every designer is nervously groping for the right length; it's touch and go whether the average woman will go for the maxis and midis. **1970** *Daily Tel.* 14 Jan. 15/3 Hardy Amies proved yesterday ..that the midi length only works if it is waisted or broken by a hip-belt. His spring collection was awash with midis. *Ibid.* 15/4 Midi-dresses with big ballooning sleeves, hip sashes, polo necks. **1971** *Petticoat* 17 July 23 Baggage and General midi bumper boots, £4. **1974** *Country Life* 14 Feb. 334/2 A slim-cut, midi-length trench [coat].

† **mididone**, *adv. Obs.* Also 4 **midydone**. [Orig. a syntactical phrase, *mid idone*, where MID *prep.* governs *i-done* pa. pple. of DO *v.* The literal sense is thus 'with this being done'.] Forthwith, immediately.

c **1290** *S. Eng. Leg.* I. 468/226 He helpez boþe king and knyȝht, þe pouere alle mididone. *c* **1330** *Arth. & Merl.* 4138 (Kölbing) þe cherl bent his bowe sone & smot a doke mididone.

midil, midilerth(e, midiling, obs. ff. MIDDLE *a.*, MIDDLE EARTH, MIDDLING *a.*

‖**midinette** (midinɛt). [Fr. Perh. orig. a portmanteau word f. *midi* mid-day + *dînette* light dinner: cf. 1922 *Larousse* s.v., les *midinettes* sont celles qui se contentent d'une *dînette à midi.*] A milliner's female assistant, esp. in Paris.

1909 *Westm. Gaz.* 7 Aug. 15/1 The Parisian..is tired of the absurd hat. The midinette and those of her kind have made it impossible. **1919** BEERBOHM *Seven Men* 11 A midinette who..murdered, or was about to murder, a mannequin. **1925** *Brit. Weekly* 19 Feb. 498/2 She was in the same class with the midinettes of Paris, with whom travelling Englishmen spend a passing hour and quickly forget. **1932** SELLAR & YEATMAN *And now All This* vi. 60 In the South, the beautiful *Midi*, one does *not* perceive the beautiful Race of the *Midinettes* (*hélas*). **1958** J. MACGREGOR *Glamour in Your Lens* 84 She'll..be prepared to transform herself on the spot into..a French midinette. **1961** R. SEARLE *Which Way did he Go?* 38 He firmly believes that the Boulevards abound with Midinettes who are dazzled with admiration for him. **1975** R. COBB *Paris & its Provinces* 3 Some story in which a *midinette* meets a *Duc*.

miding, obs. form of MIDDEN.

midis, obs. form of MIDS.

'midlag. *Antiq.* [Source unknown: Meyrick's explanation 'mid-leg' cannot well be correct.] An alleged name for a kind of tabard: see quots.

1824 MEYRICK *Ant. Armour* II. 84 These long tabards were peculiar to the English, being called midlags, because as they were made in imitation of the surcoat, they reached to the middle of the legs. **1830** [E. HAWKINS] *Anglo-French Coinage*, This feeble monarch [Ric. II] is represented in his state tabard or midlag.

Midland ('mɪdlənd), *sb.* and *a.* Also **midland**. [f. MID *a.* + LAND.] **A.** *sb.* **a.** The middle part of a country. Also *pl.* esp. applied to the middle counties of England; and, in hunting use, with narrower sense to the champaign country including parts of the counties of Leicester, Northampton, Warwickshire, Nottinghamshire, and Derbyshire.

1555 EDEN *Decades* 320 The three sayde prouinces occupy this mydlande of the worlde. **1612** DRAYTON *Poly-olb.* xiii. 1 Vpon the Mid-lands now th' industrious Muse doth fall. *a* **1637** B. JONSON *Discov.*, *De orationis dignitate.. Metaphora*, As if..a Gentleman of Northampton-shire, Warwickshire, or the Mid-land, should fetch all the Illustrations to his countrey neighbours from shipping. **1684** T. BURNET *Th. Earth* I. ii. 15 If the Sea lie..lower generally than the shore, and much more than the mid-land. **1727** A. HAMILTON *New Acc. E. Ind.* II. l. 216 The mid Lands seem very mountainous. **1889** C. EDWARDES *Sardinia* 340 The Sarde midlands. **1898** *Story of Midlands* 10 The Midlands are rich in mineral wealth.

b. Used *ellipt.* for the names of companies or organizations, as Midland Bank, Midland Railway.

1869 *Bradshaw's Railway Manual* XXI. 86 The question was..referred to the arbitration of Captain Galton, who decided that the Midland might work the local line. **1959** *Chambers's Encycl.* XI. 489/2 When the Midland and the Glasgow and South Western decided to throw in their lot together, approval was not given, and the only tangible result..was the adoption by the Scottish company of the Midland lake livery. **1972** C. DRUMMOND *Death at Bar* i. 14 His banking account, with the Midland, is divided into business and private.

c. The central area of the United States (see quot. 1896), esp. regarded as a dialectal area of American English.

1896 *Dialect Notes* I. ix. 438 Midland: a belt separating the North from the South and extending from the Atlantic to the Mississippi (incuding Long Island, New York City and the adjoining counties, New Jersey, Del., all but the northern strip of Penn., the upper prong of West Virginia, southern Ohio, middle Ind., middle Ill., and St. Louis county, Mo.). **1937** *Amer. Speech* XII. 316/1 For many years *Middle West*..has reigned in solitary authority..; but there seems to be a growing tendency towards the use of three other terms... Central West,..*Mid-west*,..*Midland*. This shorter and more picturesque title is still rare, but growing. As noun & adjective it occurs occasionally. **1963** R. I. MCDAVID *Mencken's Amer. Lang.* 405 The..' General American' area is really made up of two major dialects: one, Inland Northern..; the other, Midland, based on the speech of Pennsylvania and its derivatives. **1972** H. KURATH *Stud. Area Ling.* 44 The transition area between the North and the Midland reflects partly the complicated history of the settlement.

B. *adj.*

1. Situated in the middle of the land; inland; remote from the sea. ***Midland counties*** (of England): the counties south of the Humber and Mersey and north of the Thames, with the exception of Norfolk, Suffolk, Essex, Middlesex, Hertfordshire, Gloucestershire, and the counties bordering on Wales. ***Midland*** (***and Oxford***) ***circuit*** (see CIRCUIT *sb.* 5).

1601 HOLLAND *Pliny* I. 40 In the midland parts far from the sea. **1675** OGILBY *Britannia* (1698) 6 The chief Trade [of Bristol] is manag'd from Wales, and the Midland-Countries. **1785** J. PHILLIPS *Treat. Inland Navig.* p. vi, The inhabitants of the Northern..parts of England, would be little acquainted..with those of the mid-land parts. **1851** STEPHENS *Bk. Farm* I. 157 In use in Forfarshire and the midland districts. **1878** F. S. WILLIAMS *Midl. Railw.* 8 Such was the origin of the Midland Counties Railway.

b. Belonging to the Midlands. Also *pl.*

Midland dialect: (*a*) with reference to the ME. period, the dialect (divided into *East* and *West* Midland) spoken in the region between those of the 'northern' and 'southern dialects'; in addition to the central parts of England this region included South Lancashire, the Welsh borders, Lincolnshire, and East Anglia; (*b*) in A. J. Ellis's classification of modern English dialects, the dialect of an area extending from Wharfedale in Yorkshire to Stratford on Avon, and from Chester to the Lincolnshire coast.

1756 A. BUTLER *Lives Saints* I. 45 St. Cedd..first preached to the Midland English. **1837** YOUATT *Sheep* viii. 341 The Midland Long-woolled Sheep. **1849** D. ROCK *Church of our Fathers* I. I. v. 351 The chasuble, in its graceful, true old form, and appareled albs and amices, were spread throughout the Midland district. **1922** JOYCE *Ulysses* 703 The Link line railway laid..between the cattle park, Liffey junction, and terminus of Midland Great Western Railway..in proximity to the terminal stations or Dublin branches of Great Central Railway, Midland Railway of England [etc.]. **1942** *Short Guide Gt. Brit.* (U.S. War Dept.) 7 The great 'midland' manufacturing cities of Birmingham, Sheffield, and Coventry. **1954** DARBY & TERRETT (*title*) The Domesday geography of Midland England. **1971** M. LEE *Dying for Fun* xlii. 202 Ivor Canning had made his way to Oxford but..still spoke with a well-preserved Midlands accent. **1972** M. WOODHOUSE *Mama Doll* xiii. 180 The few words he did speak emerged in a Midlands accent.

c. Of or pertaining to the Midland of the United States or the regional type of American English spoken there.

1890 *Dialect Notes* I. ii. 57 But the differences in the different sections of the country are not so great that we can properly speak of a New England dialect, a southern dialect, a midland dialect. **1900** B. B. SMYTH *Plants & Flowers Kansas* 43 This is the Midland adder-tongue, as named by Prof. Knerr of Atchison. **1944** H. KURATH in *Language* XX. 151, I hope to be able to show before long, on the basis of the Atlas materials, that we must recognize a large Central or Midland speech area in addition to the Southern, the Northern, and the Northeastern (eastern New England). **1949** —— *Word Geogr. Eastern U.S.* p. v, There is an extensive Midland speech area that lies between the traditionally recognized 'Northern' and 'Southern' areas. **1959** E. TUNIS *Indians* vi. 86 Midland Indians were farmers first, but they all..hunted buffalo.

2. = MEDITERRANEAN *a.* 2. ***Midland Sea***, the Mediterranean Sea.

1579 FULKE *Heskins' Parl.* 34 From the mid lande sea to both the Oceans. **1683** T. HOY *Agathocles* 3 Fruitful Italy, The Pride, and Envy of the Mid-land Sea. **1818** BYRON *Ch. Har.* IV. clxxv, The midland ocean breaks on him and me. **1853** M. ARNOLD *Scholar-Gipsy* xxv, O'er the blue Midland waters with the gale, Betwixt the Syrtes and soft Sicily.

†**b.** Of or pertaining to the Mediterranean Sea.

1660 R. COKE *Power & Subj.* 36 In lib. 3. cap. 4 he [Diodorus] makes four kinds of Libyans to inhabit the midland coasts about Cyrene and Cirtes.

Hence **'Midlander**, one who lives in the Midlands or in the Midland of the United States; **'Midlandize** *v. trans.*, to assimilate to the Midland dialect; **'Midlandward** *adv.*, towards the Midlands.

1601 HOLLAND *Pliny* I. 91 Vpon whom ioine the mid-landers, to wit, the Gætulianders. **1865** KINGSLEY *Herew.*

xviii, The young earls went off—one midlandward, one northward. **1879** T. F. SIMMONS in *Lay Folks Mass Bk.* Introd. 58 The Northern form may have been copied mechanically by the scribe, although Midlandized in other cases. **1889** G. B. SHAW *London Music 1888–89* (1937) 243, I was at Leicester, delivering to the midlanders an impassioned appeal. **1912** BELLOC *Green Overcoat* x. 191 'I know you would!' said the big Midlander. **1932** *Times Lit. Suppl.* 14 Jan. 19/2 Himself a Midlander, he is very insistent on the special virtues which Shakespeare inherited from his Midland birth. **1972** H. KURATH *Stud. Area Ling.* 53 The proportion of 'Northerners' and 'Midlanders' in these two states as a whole differs little. **1972** *Country Life* 14 Dec. 1638/1 It is always with mild surprise that you recall that Dr. Johnson was a Midlander.., that he was born not within the sound of Bow Bells but of the bells of Lichfield Cathedral.

midle, obs. Sc. f. MEDDLE; obs. f. MIDDLE.

mid leg. [MID *a.*]
1. The middle of the leg.
1590 SIR J. SMYTH *Disc. Weapons* Ded. 10b, Their souldiors in their watches..stoode to the mid legges in dyrt and myre. **1748** *Earthquake Peru* iii. 259 A large Handkerchief, which hangs down behind to the Mid-Leg.
b. Used *advb.*: To the middle of the leg.
1829 W. H. MAXWELL *Stories of Waterloo* I. 194 His jockey boots..were in the newest style; the top..was met midleg by short tights of tea-coloured leather. **1878** H. S. WILSON *Alp. Ascents* ii. 42 We are wading mid-leg through it.
c. *Comb.*, ***mid-leg deep***, ***mid-leg high***.
1772 WESLEY *Jrnl.* 16 Mar., Snow..lay mid-leg deep in.. the streets. **1788** M. CUTLER in *Life*, etc. (1888) I. 404 We found fine feed in the road, clover mid-leg high. **1837** HAWTHORNE *Twice-told T.* (1851) II. ix. 131 A solitary passenger is seen, now striding mid-leg deep across a drift.
2. *Ent.* One of the intermediate or second pair of legs of an insect. Also *attrib.*
1826 KIRBY & SP. *Entomol.* III. xxxiii. 379 *Pedes Intermedii* (the Mid-legs). *Ibid.* III. xxxv. 534 The first or mid-leg segment is not nearly so elevated as that of the hind-legs.

mid-lent. [MID *a.*] The middle of Lent.
1470 *Paston Lett.* II. 394, I am halffe in purpose to com home with in a monythe her afftr, or abowt Med Lente. **1517** TORKINGTON *Pilgr.* (1884) 1 The ffryday a for mydlent. **1667–8** J. BRETON in Willis & Clark *Cambridge* (1886) II. 706 It is possible he may be in London by Midlent.
b. *attrib.*, in ***mid-lent Sunday***, the middle or fourth Sunday in Lent.
c **1450** *Godstow Reg.* 194 At two termes in the yere.., that is to sey, the Sonday of Sexagesyme.., and on mydlent Sonday. **1517** TORKINGTON *Pilgr.* (1884) 1 Midlente sonnday, the xxij Day of Marche. **1623–4** LAUD *Diary* 7 Mar., Mid-Lent Sunday. I preached at Whitehall. **1837** *Penny Cycl.* VIII. 31/2 Saturday after Midlent Sunday.

†**mid'lenten.** *Obs.* [f. MID *a.* + LENTEN.] = MID-LENT. Chiefly in ***midlenten Sunday***.
1377 LANGL. *P. Pl.* B. XVI. 172 Þanne mette I with a man a mydlenten sondaye. **1513** BRADSHAW *St. Werburge* II. 1600 On sonday in mydlenton the viii houre. **1538** *Aberdeen Reg.* XVI. (Jam.), Betuix this & Sonday mydlentrene nixt to cum.

midlenting (mɪd'lɛntɪŋ), *vbl. sb.* [f. MID-LENT + -ING[1].] The custom of visiting parents and giving them presents on mid-lent Sunday.
1720 WHEATLY *Bk. Com. Prayer* (ed. 3) 225 The Appointment of these Scriptures upon this Day [Midlent-Sunday], might probably give the first Rise to a Custom still retain'd in many Parts of England, and well known by the name of *Midlenting* or *Mothering*.

midler, obs. comparative of MIDDLE; obs. f. MIDDLER.

midlerd, midlert, var. forms of MIDDLE-ERD.

†**'midless**, *a. Obs.* [f. MID *sb.* + -LESS.] Having no middle.
1591 SYLVESTER *Du Bartas* I. i. 343 An un-beginning, midlesse, endlesse Ball [*sc.* the World].

midlest(e, obs. superlatives of MIDDLE.

midlife. orig. *U.S.* Also **mid-life**. [f. MID *a.* + LIFE *sb.*] **1.** (mid'life). Middle age; the part of life between youth and old age. Freq. in phr. ***in*** (also ***at***) ***midlife***.
1895 in FUNK & WAGNALLS *Stand. Dict.* **1952** DYLAN THOMAS *In Country Sleep* 16 Oh, let me midlife mourn by the shrined And druid herons' vows. **1965** *Genetic Psychol. Monographs* LXXII. 139 (*title*) Ability and social adjustment at midlife of persons judged mentally deficient. **1980** *N.Y. Times* 29 June XXI. 9/2 It is much more common for people to seek fulfillment by changing careers in midlife than it was a generation ago. **1981** *N.Y. Times Mag.* 24 May 31/3 (*heading*) Single at midlife. **1986** J. THOMPSON *Half Way* 11 Three 'Thoughts' I gave on 'The in-between times of life'..concerned adolescence, midlife and retirement.
2. *attrib.* ('midlife). **a.** *gen.*
1976 *Economist* 29 May 87/3 In a mid-life career break, he hit trouble trying to run a college. **1978** *Detroit Free Press* 5 Mar. (Parade Suppl.) 6 (*caption*) Lahr believes a mid-life breakup could affect the structure of the family for generations. **1980** *Christian Science Monitor* 9 June B8/1 A selection of..early and midlife correspondence strung together with narrative notes. **1982** *N.Y. Times* 23 Feb. C13/2 Even when the heat of a midlife affair dulls the narrator's usual cynicism, her litany of detail lets us see the lurking bitterness that she herself ignores. **1986** P. D. JAMES *Taste for Death* I. vi. 59 It had been something more profound, less explicable, than disillusionment, mid-life restlessness.

b. midlife crisis *Psychol.*, an emotional crisis occurring in midlife, characterized by the feeling that one is growing old or that life is 'passing one by'.
1965 E. JAQUES in *Internat. Jrnl. Psycho-Anal.* XLVI. 502/1 Less familiar perhaps, though nonetheless real, are the crises which occur around the age of 35—which I shall term the *mid-life crisis—and at full maturity around the age of 65. **1972** *N.Y. Times* 31 Dec. IV. 10/3 There is a marked increase in the death rate between the ages of 35 to 40 for employed men, apparently as a result of this 'mid-life crisis'. **1978** J. UPDIKE *Coup* (1979) iv. 131 Those streams and shady gardens old, harried Mohamet conjured up in the after-hours babble of his mid-life crisis. **1986** J. THOMPSON *Half Way* 11, I am now middle-aged, and can begin to look back on what was for me a midlife crisis.

†**'midlike**, *adv. Obs.* [f. MID *sb.* + -LIKE.] Moderately.
1375 BARBOUR *Bruce* III. 71 He set ensample thus mydlike.

mid-line ('mɪdlaɪn). [MID *a.*] **1.** *Zool.* A median line; also, the median plane or plane of bilateral symmetry.
1868 W. K. PARKER *Shoulder-Girdle Vertebr.* 8 There is no stoppage of the ossification at the mid-line. **1927** HALDANE & HUXLEY *Animal Biol.* xii. 285 (*caption*) The lateral nerve-trunks have united in the mid-line. **1957** R. H. SMYTHE *Conformation of Dog* 61 Behind the base of the neck in the midline of the back. **1959** SOUTHWOOD & LESTON *Land & Water Bugs Brit. Isles* 31 The males of this genus have a patch of wax-producing glands beneath the abdomen on each side of the mid-line. **1961** *Lancet* 26 Aug. 443/1 (*caption*) Coronal section of brain of patient who survived for 6 weeks. Note that the only abnormal appearances are slight dilatation of the ventricles and a tear (arrow) on the underside of the corpus callosum to the right of the midline. **1974** *Nature* 8 Mar. 165/1 The roentgenographic landmarks were joined to form triangles on both sides of the midline.
2. The middle of a line of poetry.
1882 G. M. HOPKINS *Lett. to R. Bridges* (1955) 164 The word is *more* and is a midline rhyme to *score*.

midlittoral (mɪd'lɪtərəl), *a.* and *sb. Ecol.* [f. MID *a.* + LITTORAL *a.* and *sb.*] **A.** *adj.* Designating that zone on the sea-shore which is both covered and uncovered by the neap tides. **B.** *sb.* The zone so delimited.
1948 *Austral. Jrnl. Sci. Res.* B. I. 196 (*heading*) The mid- and upper-littoral. **1949** T. A. & A. STEPHENSON in *Jrnl. Ecol.* XXXVII. 298 The most difficult zone to rename is the Balanoid. This is the middle zone on the shore... On the whole we favour the name *midlittoral zone* as being in keeping with the other terms proposed. *Ibid.*, The word *midlittoral* is less common, though it has been used by Dakin *et al.* (1948) in their recent account of the New South Wales Coast, even if not as an exact equivalent of our Balanoid zone. **1967** *Oceanogr. & Marine Biol.* V. 469 The lowest levels of the midlittoral. **1970** R. C. NEWELL *Biol. Intertidal Animals* i. 2 The second zone recognised by Stephenson and Stephenson (1949) is the midlittoral zone, characterized by barnacles and limpets. **1974** *Encycl. Brit. Macropædia* IV. 804/1 The midlittoral of sand and mud shores is usually inhabited by several types of polychaete worms, the most typical being lug-worms.

†**mid-lying**, *vbl. sb. Obs.* [f. MID *adv.*[2] + LYING *vbl. sb.*] Adultery.
c **1200** *Trin. Coll. Hom.* 13 Unrihte luue is hordom and mid-liggunge þe men drigen bi-twenen hem.

†**mid man.** *Obs.* [MID *a.*]
1. A mediator, umpire.
1646 R. BAILLIE *Anabaptism* (1647) 17 In this accomodation these mid men proceeded so far. **1652–5** —— *Lett. & Jrnls.* (Bannatyne Club) III. 179, 254, 296.
2. A man-midwife.
1706 BAYNARD in Sir J. Floyer *Hot & Cold Baths* II. (1709) 345 The Mid-men have so far consented to this fatal and pernicious Practice as never to..forbid it.

midmast, obs. form of MIDMOST.

†**midmeasure**, *v. Obs.* [f. MID *adv.* + MEASURE *v.*] *trans.* To divide in the middle.
1578 BANISTER *Hist. Man* VII. 90 This reduplication..of Pleura, is in this place, called Mediastinum, because it midmeasureth the brest.

midmest(e, obs. forms of MIDMOST.

midmore, -morewe, var. ff. MIDMORROW.

mid morn. The middle of the morning; 9 a.m.
a **1225** *Ancr. R.* 24 Also vrom Prime vort mid morwen hwon þe preostes of ðe worlde singeð hore messen. **13..** *Gaw. & Gr. Knt.* 1073 Cum to þat merk at mydmorn. **1486** *Bk. St. Albans* Ciij, Yeue the hawke therof eueri day at mydmorne and att Noone. **1876** LANIER *Clover* 5 The midmorn empties you of men.

†**midmorrow.** *Obs.* Also 4 **midmor(e)we, mydmorw**, 5 **mydmor(o)we, mydmore, myde morroo**. [f. MID *a.* + MORROW.] = MIDMORN.
13.. *S. Eng. Leg.* in *Archiv Stud. neu. Spr.* LXXXII. 308 To mydmorw, vndrin & myddAY. **13..** *Seuyn Sag.* (W.) 1626 The stiward made moche sorewe, Til hit were half wai midmorewe. *c* **1430** *Hymns Virg.* (1867) 83 At mydmore y lerned to go, And plaied as children doon in strete. **1496** *Dives & Paup.* (W. de W.) IX. xi. 363/1 For thou woldest not helpe me as I badde the, therfore as this daye mydmorowe thou shalt dye.
b. *attrib.*, as ***midmorrow day***, ***tide***.
c **1330** *Arth. & Merl.* 7982 (Kölbing) Þis was in time of May, Riȝt aboute midmorwe day. **1362** LANGL. *P. Pl.* A. II. 42 In middes on a Mountayne at Midmorwe tyde Was piht vp a Pauilon.

midmost ('mɪdməʊst), *a.* and *adv.* Forms: 1 **midmest, middemyst**, 3 **mydmest**, 3–4 **midmeste**, 4 **mydemyst, mydmest(e**, 5 **midmast**, 6 **midmest**, 7– **midmost**. [OE. *midmest*, formed with suffix -EST on WGer. **middjumo-* (OHG. *in mittamen* in the middle), OTeut. **miđjumo-* (see MIDDEN-ERD):—Indogermanic **medhyəmo-* (Skr. *madhyama*), superlative of **medhyo-* MID *a.*
OE. had also a synonymous *medemest*, formed with suffix -EST on OTeut. **medumo-* (Goth. *miduma*, OHG. *metam-* in compounds; cf. *metami*, OE. *medume*, *medeme*:—**medumjo-*, moderate):—Indogermanic **medhəmo-*, a superlative formed directly from the root **medh-*.]
A. *adj.* **1. a.** That is in the very middle, with regard to position, age, etc.
c **1000** *Sax. Leechd.* III. 112 Þanne sceal hym man læten blod on þan earme on þan middemyste ædra. **1297** R. GLOUC. (Rolls) 685 Þre doȝtren þe king adde þe eldost het gornorille þe midmeste het regan. *c* **1375** *Cursor M.* 10023 (Fairf.) The mydmest bayly of þe thre Bytokenyþ wele hir chastite. **1587** *Reg. Privy Council Scot.* IV. 205 Thai..hes dismemberit him..of the haill twa midmest fingaris. **1663** COWLEY *Verses Sev. Occas.*, *Christ's Passion* iii, My greedy eyes fly up the hill, and see Who 'tis hangs there the midmost of the three. **1697** DRYDEN *Æneid* x. 1083 Proud Mezentius ..rush'd into the Plain, Where tow'ring in the midmost Ranks he stood. **1716** POPE *Iliad* VIII. 270 High on the midmost bark the king appear'd. **1882** FARRAR *Early Chr.* I. 308 He [Philo] compares it [the Word of God] to the midmost branch of the golden candlestick.
b. *absol.* (now chiefly *poet.*) The midmost part, the middle.
1382 WYCLIF *Matt.* Prol. 1 In the whiche gospel it is profitable to men desyrynge God, so to knowe the first, the mydmeste, other the last, that [etc.]. **1865** PALGRAVE *Arabia* I. 102 A huge parallelogram, placed almost diagonally across the midmost of Arabia. **1865** SWINBURNE *Dolores* 333 From the midmost of Ida. **1905** *Edin. Rev.* Oct. 367 We are made to feel the young girl's enjoyment..even in the midmost of her grief. **1912** E. POUND tr. *Cavalcanti's Sonnets & Ballate* 19 As though I'd won unto his heart's mid-most. **1915** —— *Cathay* 7 And within, the mistress, in the midmost of her youth. **1955** —— *Classic Anthol.* II. 142, I have held him in love so long From heart's mid-most be it song Not to be lost.
2. In partitive concord: The middle or midst of.
1807 J. BARLOW *Columb.* VII. 420 Where York and Gloster's rocky towers bestride..Virginia's midmost tide. **1885–94** R. BRIDGES *Eros & Psyche* Oct. xvii, She sank Silently weeping on the temple stair, In midmost night. **1887** BOWEN *Virg. Æneid* II. 329 High in the midmost city the horse pours forth from its side Warriors armed.
3. Most intimate.
1846 HAWTHORNE *Mosses* I. i. 19 It comes flowing softly through the midmost privacy.
B. *adv.* **a.** In the middle or midst.
1700 DRYDEN *Pal. & Arc.* III. 536 The king goes midmost. **1800** COLERIDGE *Piccolom.* V. iii, Then midmost in the battle was I led In spirit. **1892** 'M. FIELD' *Sight & Song* 13 Midmost of the breeze.
b. *prep.* In the middle or midst of.
1870 MORRIS *Earthly Par.* Introd., Midmost the beating of the steely sea. **1892** *Longm. Mag.* Aug. 397 It stands midmost a marsh-country.

midnight ('mɪdnaɪt), *sb.* Forms: α. see MID *a.* and NIGHT; in 1 inflected **midder, mid(d)re, middyre niht(e**; β. 1 **middernæht**, 3 **midderniht(e**. [OE. *midniht* = MDu. *midnacht*, *middenacht*, OHG. *mittinaht* (MHG. *mitnaht*), Sw. *midnatt* (ON. had a derivative form, *miđnætti*:—**miđjonahtjo*[m]), f. MID *a.* + NIGHT. OE. had also the syntactical combination *midde niht*, frequently occurring in the dative as *middre niht*; this inflected form survived into the 13th c.; it corresponds to Du. *middernacht*, G. *mitternacht*, which from the 14th c. have been used in all cases.]
1. The middle of the night; 12 o'clock at night.
a **900** tr. *Bæda's Hist.* IV. x. (1890) 286 Þa ongon heo semninga on midde neaht cleopian þam þe hire þegnodon. *c* **950** *Lindisf. Gosp.* Luke xi. 5 Sua huelc iuer hæfeð friond & gaeð to him æd middernæht [etc.]. *a* **1000** *Phœnix* 262 Æt middre nihte. *c* **1200** *Vices & Virtues* 125 Alswa wel onbuten mid-niht alswa on mid-daiȝ. *c* **1205** LAY. 15943 Ælche middernihte heo bigunneð to fihten. *a* **1225** *Leg. Kath.* 1748 Ha wenden from hire, abuten þe midniht. **1382** WYCLIF *Judg.* vii. 19 Gedeon wente in..into a part of the tentis, bigynnynge the watchis of the mydnyȝt. **1413** *Pilgr. Sowle* (Caxton) v. xiv. (1859) 81 Sodenly the belle gan sowne the hour of mydnyght. **1535** COVERDALE *Matt.* xxv. 6 At mydnight there was a crye made. **1603** SHAKS. *Meas. for M.* IV. ii. 67 'Tis now dead midnight. **1667** MILTON *P.L.* IX. 58 By Night he fled, and at Midnight return'd From compassing the Earth. **1726–46** THOMSON *Winter* 202 As yet 'tis midnight deep. **1813** SHELLEY *Q. Mab* V. 146 Specks of tinsel, fixed in heaven To light the midnights of his native town! **1882** PEBODY *Eng. Journalism* xix. 143 There are not many subjects upon which, if he takes up his pen at ten o'clock, he cannot by midnight turn out a chatty and readable column for the next morning.
2. *transf.* and *fig.* Intense darkness or gloom; a period of intense darkness.
1593 B. BARNES *Parthenophil* Sonn. xxiii. in Arb. *Garner* V. 352 Her forehead's threatful clouds from hope removed me, Till Midnight reared on the mid-noctial line. *c* **1665** MRS. HUTCHINSON *Mem. Col. Hutchinson* (1885) I. 99 When the dawn of the gospel began to break upon this isle, after the dark midnight of papacy. **1781** COWPER *Charity* 376 Philosophy,..while his province is the reasoning part, Has still a veil of midnight on his heart. **1879** FARRAR *St. Paul* (1883) 182 It was the darkest midnight of the world's history.

†**3.** slang. ***mother midnight*** (see quots.). *Obs.*
1602 F. Hering *Anat.* 11 One while hee playeth the Apothecarie, other whiles serueth in stead of Mother Midnight. *a* **1700** B. E. *Dict. Cant. Crew, Mother Midnight*, a Midwife (often a Bawd). **1715** Mrs. Centlivre *Gotham Elect.* Wks. 1872 III. 180 [To the Midwife] And you too, Mrs. Midnight; kiss me, you old Jade you—.

4. *attrib.* passing into *adj.*

a. Of or pertaining to midnight, occurring at midnight, meeting at midnight. *spec.* as ***midnight mass.***
1390 Gower *Conf.* II. 260 That was ate mydnyht tyde. **1634** Milton *Comus* 103 Mean while welcom Joy, and Feast, Midnight shout and revelry. **1665–7** J. Lauder *Jrnls.* in *Publ. Scottish Hist. Soc.* (1900) XXXVI. 118 The rest of our Scotsmen ware so curious as to go hear Midnight Masses. **1698** [R. Ferguson] *View Eccles.* 32 The fittest and best Qualified Candidate to be A Midnight Gold Gatherer or an Emptier of Houses of Office. **1742** Young *Nt. Th.* vii. 1244 Survey this Midnight Scene. **1815** *Chron.* in *Ann. Reg.* 70 About fifty armed men came..and swore all the inhabitants to be faithful to the new system enacted by the midnight legislators of this country [*sc.* Kilkenny]. **1848** J. H. Newman *Let.* 25 Dec. (1962) XII. 382 The midnight mass was a high one. **1851** Longf. *Gold. Leg.* iv. *Refectory*, Are you such asses As to keep up the fashion of midnight masses? **1866** G. M. Hopkins *Lett. to R. Bridges* (1955) 16 It is not much more than an hour to Xmas day: I am sitting up for the midnight mass. **1905** *Westm. Gaz.* 26 Sept. 7/3 The mishap occurred to the midnight train from Liverpool-street to Norwich. **1960** A. Christie *Adventure of Christmas Pudding* 33 Who's going to brave the snow and go to midnight mass?

b. Dark as midnight.
1601 Weever *Mirr. Mart.* D 8 Whilst there I lie in midnight-dark immur'd, My friends emblazoned forth mine injurie. **1664** Butler *Hud.* ii. ii. 770 It is an Antichristian Opera Much us'd in midnight times of Popery. **1755** Young *Centaur* 99 Dungeon them in midnight Dens of Fraud and Destruction. **1855** Browning *Bp. Blougram's Apol.* 253 What's midnight doubt before the dayspring's faith? **1860** Hawthorne *Marble Faun* xi, In all that labyrinth of midnight paths.

5. *attrib.* and *Comb.*, as ***midnight-shrouded***, ***-woven*** adjs.; **midnight appointments** *U.S. politics*, appointments made during the last hours of an administration; specifically, those so made by President John Adams (*Cent. Dict.*); †**midnight banquet** = *midnight feast*; **midnight black**, an intense black colour; also *attrib.*; **midnight blue**, a very dark shade of blue; also *attrib.* or as *adj.*; †**midnight cart**, a cart for carrying away night soil; **midnight feast**, a feast at midnight; *spec.* a children's secret feast in a school dormitory or the like; **midnight matinée**, a special theatrical performance presented at midnight; **midnight oil**, used *fig.* in phrase ***to burn*** (etc.) ***the midnight oil***, to sit up or work after midnight; **midnight sun**, the sun as seen in the Arctic regions at midnight; **midnight-tide** *poet.*, midnight.
1896 C. M. Yonge in C. Coleridge *C. M. Yonge* (1903) iii. 114 She invited the other young ladies to a *midnight banquet..in their night-caps and dressing gowns. **1922** H. Crane *Let.* 2 Mar. (1965) 80 Pastel tinted flowers on a background of *midnight black. **1925** J. Gregory *Bab of Backwoods* xvi. 201 Monte made out vaguely the slim form in white, a whitish blur against a midnight-black curtain. **1916** *Daily Colonist* (Victoria, B.C.) 8 July 12/1 (Advt.), The same style [of shoe] in jungle brown, *midnight blue and bronze. **1935** R. Hichens *Afterglow* 86 A silken collar and a midnight blue tie. **1937** *Times* 10 July 15/4 Dressed in midnight-blue crêpe-de-chine. **1940** R. Chandler *Farewell, my Lovely* xxxviii. 289 His dinner clothes were midnight blue. **1972** *Guardian* 5 Dec. 11/2 Toga dress..in ..midnight blue. **1698** J. Collier *Immor. Stage* 204 To present Nature under every Appearance would be an odd undertaking. A *Midnight Cart, or a Dunghil would be no Ornamental Scene. **1938** A. Christie *Appointment with Death* i. vii. 52 This is rather fun... Rather like the *midnight feasts we used to have at school. **1964** C. Hodder-Williams *Main Experiment* i. vi. 57 'When will you be back from London?' 'Late tonight.' 'We'll have a midnight feast, then.' **1972** *Listener* 2 Nov. 614/1 Midnight feasts, practical jokes and all the fun of the dormitory. **1952** Granville *Dict. Theatr. Terms* 118 *Midnight matinée. **1963** *Daily Express* 25 Sept. 1/4, I don't honestly see why the Stationery Office have to put on a midnight matinee for the Denning Report, even if it has got a U Certificate. **1635** Quarles *Embl.* ii. ii. 33 Wee spend our mid-day sweat, our *mid-night oyle; Wee tyre the night in thought; the day, in toyle. **1744** Shenstone *Elegies* xi, I trimm'd my lamp, consum'd the midnight oil. **1882** Serjt. Ballantine *Exper.* iii. 32, I cannot say that I burnt much midnight oil. **1857** Dufferin *Lett. High Lat.* (ed. 3) 316 The nights were even brighter than the days, and afforded Fitz an opportunity of taking some photographic views by the light of a *midnight sun. **1918** W. de la Mare *Motley* 4 At cold of *midnight-tide. **1810** *Associate Minstrels* 76 Then desolation's *midnight-woven pall Shall in one sable fold envelope all.

†**'midnight**, *v.* [f. midnight *sb.*] *trans.* To plunge into midnight darkness.
1627–47 Feltham *Resolves* i. lxi. 187 Of all objects of sorrow, a distressed king is the most pitifull; because it presents most the frailty of humanity: and cannot but most midnight the soule of him that is falne.

†**'midnighting**, *vbl. sb.* [Formed as prec. + -ing[1].] ? The coming (of a star) to the meridian.
1570 Dee *Math. Pref.* d iiij b, By foreseing the Rising, Settyng, Nonestedyng, or Midnightyng of certaine tempestuous fixed Sterres.

midnightly ('mɪdnaɪtlɪ), *a.* and *adv.* [f. midnight *sb.* + -ly.] **a.** *adj.* Taking place at midnight, or every midnight. **b.** *adv.* Every midnight.
1836 *Fraser's Mag.* XIV. 107 'The Highflyer'..rushed midnightly through a village about nine miles distant. **1873** Leland *Egypt. Sketch Bk.* 194 To this day he may be seen midnightly..counting the graves and waiting his turn.

†**mid-noctial**, *a. nonce-wd.* [hybrid f. mid *a.* + *-noctial* in equinoctial.] Belonging to midnight.
1593 [see midnight 2].

midnoon (mɪdnu:n: stress variable). [f. mid *a.* + noon.] Midday; noon.
1580 Lyly *Euphues* (Arb.) 442 The Gentlewoemen in Greece and Italy, who begin their morning at midnoone. **1667** Milton *P.L.* v. 311 Seems another Morn Ris'n on mid-noon. **1725** Watts *Logic* ii. v. §7 They can tell precisely ..what Altitude the Dog-star had at Midnight or Midnoon in Rome. **1832** Tennyson *Œnone* 91 It was the deep midnoon. *a* **1864** Hawthorne *Amer. Note-Bks.* (1879) I. 157 Far towards midnoon.

b. *transf.* and *fig.*
1814 Wordsw. *Excurs.* vi. p. 305 The approved Assistant of an arduous course From his mid noon of manhood to old age! **1860** Ld. Lytton *Lucile* ii. ii. 27 A man of your years, At the midnoon of manhood, with plenty to do.

c. *attrib.* passing into *adj.* Of or pertaining to midnoon; occurring at midnoon.
1804 J. Grahame *Sabbath* (1808) 64 Here nature in her midnoon whispers speaks. **1805** Southey *Madoc in W.* vi, From early morning till the midnoon hour.

mid-ocean. [mid *a.*] **a.** The middle of an ocean.
1697 Dryden *Æneid* i. 161 Fierce Eurus..in mid Ocean left them moor'd a-land. **1881** *Athenæum* 15 Jan. 97/3 Very interesting is the account of the pelagic fishes, or those which inhabit the mid ocean. **1905** *Smart Set* Sept. 116/2 It was as surely and as irrevocably lost as though it had sunk into a thousand fathoms of midocean. **1930** S. Spender *20 Poems* 3 Like Icarus mid-ocean-drowned. **1938** *Times Lit. Suppl.* 3 Sept. 572/4 His repairs in mid-ocean to his small auxiliary engine.

b. *attrib.*, esp. in **mid-ocean ridge**, one of the mountainous ridges, several kilometres high and over a thousand wide, that rise abruptly from the abyssal plain in the middle of each ocean basin and form a connected worldwide system, marked along much of its length by a central rift that overlies earthquake foci.
1956 *Geophysical Monogr.* I. 75/1 Mid-ocean islands. **1961** Ewing & Landisman in M. Sears *Oceanogr.* i. 5 The remaining 18% [of the earth's surface]..contains parts of the mid-ocean ridge system. **1963** G. L. Pickard *Descriptive Physical Oceanogr.* ii. 10 The Mid-ocean Ridge is probably the most extensive single feature of the earth's topography. **1968** M. J. Keen *Introd. Marine Geol.* iii. 46 The abyssal plains may be cut..by mid-ocean canyons. **1968** *Times* 8 Oct. 7/7 Present-day oceans are marked by underwater mountain ranges, called mid-ocean ridges, along which molten material is injected upwards from the earth's mantle and spreads out on either side of the ridge. **1971** J. R. Heirtzler in A. E. Maxwell *Sea* IV. i. iii. 99 The Red Sea ..is bisected by the mid-ocean ridge which passes south through the Gulf of Aden and the Indian Ocean.

So **mid-oce'anic** *a.*
1961 Ewing & Landisman in M. Sears *Oceanogr.* i. 9 On every crossing the ridge has been found where it was expected, with its median rift accurately following the mid-oceanic earthquake belt. **1966** R. W. Fairbridge *Encycl. Oceanogr.* 506 The Mid-Atlantic Ridge is that portion of the mid-oceanic ridge system which lies within the limits of the Atlantic Ocean. **1970** L. R. A. Capurro *Oceanogr. for Practicing Engineers* vii. 139 The sea bottom can be divided into three major morphologic divisions: continental margin, ocean-basin floor, and midoceanic ridge.

mid-off. *Cricket.* [Short for *mid-wicket off*: see mid *a.* 1 d.] A fieldsman on the off-side, in front of the batsman and near the bowler. Also the place where this player stands.
1865 J. Lillywhite *Cricketer's Compan.* 25 Mr. Lyttelton from a fine hit, was cleverly had by Mr. Voules at deep mid off. **1867** J. Lawrence *Handbk. Cricket Ireland 1866–67* 106 Harrow drive or Mid off. **1881** *Daily News* 9 July 2 He was badly missed at mid-off from a very easy chance by Cave. **1894** *Times* 23 May 7/3 Davidson..hit the ball into the hands of mid-off. **1955** *Times* 9 May 15/2 He was dropped off him at mid-off when he had got to 29. **1959** [see deepish *a.*].

mid-on. *Cricket.* [Cf. prec.] A fieldsman on the on-side, in front of the batsman and near the bowler. Also the place where this player stands.
1870 *Times* 20 July 10/3 At 21 Smith was caught at mid-on. **1873** J. Pycroft *Cricket Field* (ed. 6) xii. 289 Some bowlers prefer to dispense with long-leg... In case of his removal it would be well to place him at mid-on. **1881** *Daily News* 9 July 2 Routledge was neatly caught by mid-on running in at 194. **1888** A. G. Steel *Cricket* (Badm. Libr.) 208 On a true hard wicket we never like to see a captain putting his mid-on or short-leg close to the batsman, to field what is called 'silly' mid-on. **1891** W. G. Grace *Cricket* 265 Mid-on is one of the easiest places in the field. **1955** *Times* 12 May 4/5 Twenty-five minutes afterwards Watson lost patience with himself and mis-hit Anderson to mid-on and then Lowson, chancing his arm in the same sort of way, was well caught also at mid-on. **1959** [see check *v.*[1] 16 d]. **1974** *Observer* 9 June 24/7 He hit one excellent four..and a single, and then holed out to mid-on.

†**midovernoon.** *Obs.* [f. mid *a.* + over *prep.* + noon.] The middle of the afternoon. (In quot. *a* 1300 app. used by mistake for midoverundern, which is the reading of other MSS.)
1297 R. Glouc. (Rolls) 7302 Fram anon amorwe uorte mid ouer non, þe bataile ilaste strong. *Ibid.* 7487 Fram þat it was amorwe þe bataile ilaste strong Vorte it was hei midouernon, & þat was somdel long. *a* **1300** *E.E. Psalter* xxxvi. 6 And he sal lede als light þi rightwisnes, And als mid over-none [Wyclif, as myddayl] þi dome þat es. *c* **1400** *Laud Troy Bk.* 10673 He was two hundred mennes ban,—Or it was passed myd-ouer-none.
fig. *c* **1430** *Hymns Virg.* (1867) 84 At vndren to scole y was sett..At mydday y was dubbid knyȝt..At hiȝ noon y was crowned king..At mydouernoon y droupid faste, Mi lust & liking wente away.

†**midoverundern.** *Obs.* [f. mid *a.* + over *prep.* + undern.] ? Midday.
a **1300** *E.E. Psalter* xxxvi. 6 He sal lede þi rihtwisnes als liht, And þi dome als midoverunder briht. *a* **1400–50** *Alexander* 3853 Þus raȝt he fra þis reuir be many ruȝe waies To it was meten to þe mere to myd-ouir-vndorne.

mid place.
†**1.** A place in the middle. *Obs.*
a **1300** *Cursor M.* 21539 Vnto þe tun bar þai þaa tre, þar war þai don als in mide place. *c* **1400** Maundev. (1839) xxviii. 280 In mydd place of that vale, vnder a roche, is an hed and the visage of a deuyl bodyliche. **1610** Healey *St. Aug. Citie of God* 350 The mid-place is neither the highest nor the lowest. **1658** W. Burton *Itin. Anton.* 131 In the mid-place between, the River Dee runnes along.

2. *dial.* (See quot.)
1871 C. Gibbon *Lack of Gold* xvi, Entering the door there was an apartment on each side, a 'mid-place'—that is, a big cupboard.

mid-'range. [range *sb.*[1]] **1.** *Statistics.* The arithmetic mean of the largest and the smallest values of a group, esp. a sample.
1949 *Ann. Math. Statistics* XX. 257 The significance tests investigated..are based on the quantity [(sample midrange)–(hypothetical mean)]/(sample range). **1951** Dixon & Massey *Introd. Statistical Analysis* xvi. 238 It is probably not advisable to use the midrange for samples of more than five observations since its efficiency drops below that of the median beyond this point. **1973** M. H. Belz *Statistical Methods for Process Industries* ii. 22 There are four commonly employed measures of sample location, the sample mean, the sample median, the sample mode and the sample mid-range.

2. a. The middle part of the range of audible frequencies. Freq. *attrib.*
1955 E. T. Canby *Home Mus. Syst.* (ed. 2) x. 160 The newest wrinkles in the speaker department are the tiny super tweeter, for crispness in extremely high tones, and the large mid-range tweeter, to take over the middle 'intelligence' highs. **1960** C. Brown *Introd. Hi-Fi* iv. 89 A third speaker to handle the mid-range can be introduced if required. **1971** *Hi-Fi Sound* Feb. 68/1 The radiogram has speaker units which are..surprisingly sensitive, particularly in the mid-range. **1975** *Gramophone* Jan. 1425/1 The tweeter maintains the smooth and wide dispersion of energy as it takes over from the bass and mid-range unit.

b. A loudspeaker designed to reproduce mid-range signals with fidelity while being relatively unresponsive to those of low or high frequency.
1955 E. T. Canby *Home Mus. Syst.* (ed. 2) x. 160 A cheap and effective alternative is an ordinary medium-sized cone speaker used as a mid-range. **1975** *Hi-Fi Answers* Feb. 68/1 It was specifically developed as a good mid-range for the new Leak 2000 series of speakers.

‖**Midrash** ('mɪdræʃ). Also 7 med-, midrasch. *Pl.* **midrashim** (mɪ'drɑ:ʃi:m). [Heb. *midrash* 'commentary' (2 Chron. xxiv. 27, Revised Version 1884), f. root *drš* to investigate, search.] An ancient Jewish homiletic commentary on some portion of the Hebrew scriptures, in which free use was made of allegorical interpretation and legendary illustration. Also, the mode of treatment characteristic of this class of commentaries.
1613 Purchas *Pilgrimage* (1614) 192 Mardochæus (saith their Medrasch) sucked the breasts of Hester. **1625** T. Godwin *Moses & Aaron* (1641) 28 The Disputer. He insisted upon allegories, and searched out mysticall interpretations of the Text. Hence himselfe was tearmed Darschan, and his exposition, or homily, Midrasch. **1878** Schiller-Szinessy in *Academy* 28 Dec. 606/1 It [the *Yalqut*] saved a goodly number of the smaller Midrashim.. from perishing altogether. **1879** Farrar *St. Paul* (1883) 501 A happy Rabbinic midrash on the non-muzzling of the ox that treadeth out the corn.

Hence **Mi'drashic** *a.*, of or pertaining to the Midrashim; of the nature of midrash.
1874 Deutsch *Rem.* 403 Midrashic literature.

midred ('mɪdrɪd). *Obs.* exc. *dial.* Forms: 1 midhridir, -hriðre, -hryð(e)re, 5 miderede, midredyn, mydred(e, -rid, -ryde, 6 midridde, *Sc.* modereid. Also 9 *dial.* midred, middrit, etc. (see E.D.D. and Jam.). [OE. *midhriðre* (:—OTeut. type **midjohriþrjo*[m]), f. *midd* mid *a.* + *hreðer* inward part; = OFris. *mithridri, midrithere, midrith, midrede.*] The diaphragm, midriff. Sometimes misused for midgern.
c **725** *Corpus Gloss.* (Hessels) I 44 *Ilia*, mid hridir, nioðan weard hype. *a* **1100** *Voc.* in Wr.-Wülcker 293/5 *Omentum*, midhriðre. *c* **1325** *Gloss W. de Bibbesw.* in *Rel. Ant.* II. 78 Miderede, *li gist rate.* **14..** *Nom.* in Wr.-Wülcker 678/5 *Hec*

diafragma, a mydrede. *c* **1450** *St. Cuthbert* (Surtees) 2388 With half þe mydrid of a swyne. **1483** *Cath. Angl.* 239 A Midredyn (*MS. A.* mydryde),..*omentum.* **1535** STEWART *Cron. Scot.* II. 432 Livar and lungis, modereid and melt. **1570** LEVINS *Manip.* 116/10 Ye midridde, *diaphragma.*

midrefe, obs. form of MIDRIFF.

midriasis, obs. form of MYDRIASIS.

midrib ('mɪdrɪb). [f. MID *a.* + RIB.]

†**1.** In phrase ***mid-rib deep***, up to the middle of the ribs (of a horse). *Obs.*

1696 *Phil. Trans.* XIX. 350 Nets trailed on the Ground by two Horses, one goeth Mid-rib deep into the Sea. **1807** P. GASS *Jrnl.* 236 A north branch..is 40 yards wide and was mid-rib deep on our horses.

2. a. *Bot.* A principal rib continuous with the petiole extending through the central part of the blade of a leaf.

1776–96 WITHERING *Brit. Plants* (ed. 3) II. 91 Scales spear-shaped, skinny, yellow, with a green midrib. **1794** in MARTYN *Lang. Bot.* **1884** BOWER & SCOTT *De Bary's Phaner.* 445 The petiole and midrib of the leaves. **1901** *Chambers's Jrnl.* May 301/2 The leaves are thoroughly dried. In testing their dryness the mid-rib or vein should not be overlooked. **1965** K. ESAU *Plant Anat.* (ed. 2) xvi. 434 In some large grasses the median part of the blade is thickened into a midrib. **1974** *Country Life* 7 Mar. 479/2 Gracillimus has narrow leaves with a silver mid-rib.

b. *Archæol.* A structure similar to the principal rib or vein of a leaf.

1929 V. G. CHILDE *Danube in Prehist.* 126 Kite-shaped daggers with rivet-holes and a rudimentary midrib. **1938** *Proc. Prehist. Soc.* IV. 283 Three flanged axes were found with a tanged spearhead with short blade and pronounced mid-rib.

3. *Bee-keeping* (see quot.).

1884 PHIN *Dict. Apiculture* Introd. 13 The word midrib has been used to denote the septum or partition between the two sheets of cells which are found in every comb.

midribbed ('mɪdrɪbd), *ppl. a Bot.* [f. MIDRIB + -ED[2].] Having a midrib.

1776–96 WITHERING *Brit. Plants* (ed. 3) III. 326.

midridde, obs. form of MIDRED.

midriff ('mɪdrɪf). Forms: 1 midhrif, midrif, 4–6 mydryf, 5 mydref(e, mydrif, myddereffe, 5–6 mydryff(e, 6 middryfe, midrefe, myddreffe, mydryfe, 6–7 midrif(f)e, 7 middrift, 6– midriff. [OE. *midhrif*, f. *midd* MID *a.* + *hrif* belly (cf. RIFF *sb.*[4]). Cf. OFris. *midref.*]

1. a. The diaphragm. ***to shake, tickle the midriff***: said of what causes laughter.

c **1000** *Sax. Leechd.* II. 278 Hwilum onginneð of þam midhrife se is betweox þære wambe & þære lifre. *c* **1400** *Lanfranc's Cirurg.* 148 He [*sc.* the œsophagus] declineþ into þe ynnere partie til þat he peerse þoruȝ þe mydrif. *c* **1440** *Promp. Parv.* 337/1 Mydryf of a beste,.. *diafragma.* **1486** *Bk. St. Albans* E viij, In the mydref that callid is the rondell also. **1533** ELYOT *Cast. Helthe* (1541) 49 The entrayles, which be underneth the myddreffe. *c* **1550** LLOYD *Treas. Health* A viij, A wounde in the braynes, hert, midrife,..or lyuer is deadly. **1596** SHAKS. *1 Hen. IV*, III. iii. 175 There's no roome for Faith, Truth, nor Honesty, in this bosome of thine: it is all fill'd vppe with Guttes and Midriffe. **1613** M. RIDLEY *Magn. Bodies* 28 An Aequator, or middle fence, that divideth the whole body in the middest between the two Poles, like a Midrift. **1641** MILTON *Reform.* II. Wks. 1851 III. 67 We would burst our midriffes rather then laugh. **1725** BRADLEY *Fam. Dict.* s.v. *Oesophagus*, It..passes through the Midriff. **1831** LAMB *Elia* Ser. II. *Newsp. 35 Yrs. Ago*, That conceit..still tickles our midriff to remember. **1847** TENNYSON *Princess* I. 198 A sight to shake The midriff of despair with laughter.

Comb. **1884** TENNYSON *Becket* III. iii, Many midriff-shaken even to tears.

b. *Fashion.* (*a*) The midportion of the torso; (*b*) that part of a woman's garment which covers the midriff, *esp.* if cut separately from the upper bodice; (*c*) *U.S.* a woman's garment which leaves the midriff uncovered.

1941 *Fashion Digest* Fall 74 Playsuit with wide-midriff and full-pleated skirt. **1948** *Harper's Bazaar* Jan. 99 Inside the elasticized bodice is a lightly boned midriff, an uplift brassiere. **1953** P. BINDER *Muffs & Morals* i. 31 The midriff mode..came in just before the Second World War... It shocked nobody. **1964** *McCall's Sewing* 12/1 Wide sashes, contrasting belts, set-in midriffs will give a lift to the waistline. **1966** L. HALLIDAY *Fashion Makers* ii. 41 A modern girl will cheerfully bare her midriff on the beach. **1970** *Daily Tel.* 23 Feb. 13 A real Slim Jane? Then only you, one prays, will dare to wear the new bare-midriff styles. **1972** E. LARSEN *Creative Dressmaker* viii. 73 Cover the midriff with a piece of lace.

†**2. a.** *transf.* A partition. (Cf. *diaphragm.*) *Obs.*

1660 BOYLE *New Exp. Phys. Mech.* Proem 12 In the midst of which frame, is..nail'd a board,..which may not improperly be call'd a Midriff. **1766** *Compl. Farmer* s.v. *Ventilator*, A square box..in the middle of which is placed a broad partition, or midriff, made to move up and down.

†**b.** Applied as a term of contempt. *Obs.*

1600 DEKKER *Shoomakers Holiday* Wks. 1873 I. 13 *Wife.* Seuen yeares husband? *Eyre.* Peace Midriffe, peace, I know what I do, peace. *Ibid.* 19 [*Eyre.*] What Nan, what Madge-mamble-crust, come out you fatte Midriffe-swag-belly whores.

midryde, obs. form of MIDRED.

mids, *sb.*, *adv.*, and *prep.* Forms: 3–6 myddes, 4 mides, mydis, -ys, 4–6 myddis, 4–7 middes, 5–6 middys, mydds, 5–7 middis, 6 mydes, myds, *Sc.* midiss, 6–7 midds, 7 *Sc.* midis, 6– mids. Also 7–9 *Sc.* (in senses 2 and 3) midse. [ME. *middes*, evolved from the advs. *in-middes*, *on-middes* (see IN-MIDS and AMIDST) which are altered forms of OE. *in middan*, *on middan* (where the prep. regularly governs the dative of *midde* sb. or of the wk. neuter adj.: see MID *a.* and *sb.*). The alteration is due to the analogy of *tó middes* in the middle (see TO-MIDS), where *to* governs the genitive as in some other phrases.]

A. *sb.*

1. The middle, middle part or point; the midst. Chiefly in phrase ***in (the) mids (of)***. *Obs.* exc. *Sc.* (see E.D.D.).

1340 HAMPOLE *Pr. Consc.* 5192 Þar-for Crist sal sytte þar þat day, Onence þe myddes of erth þus for to say. *c* **1375** *Sc. Leg. Saints* xix. (*Cristofore*) 14 Of his lyf al þe begynnynge, & þe mydis, & als þe endynge. **1375** BARBOUR *Bruce* xv. 167 Syne with his baneris hardely [The] myddis of the toune he tais. **1377** LANGL. *P. Pl.* B. II. 184 And thus fals and fauel fareth forth togideres, And Mede in þe myddes and alle þise men after. *c* **1400** *Destr. Troy* 1548 The walle..of marbill was most fro þe myddes vp, Of diuers colours. **1449** in *Cal. Proc. Chanc. Q. Eliz.* (1830) II. Pref. 55 The beames shullen be in brede atte myddes xij inches and in thiknes viij inches. *c* **1450** HOLLAND *Howlat* 1 In the myddis of May. **1530** PALSGR. 245/1 Myddes parte of a channell, *le fil dune riuiere.* *a* **1533** LD. BERNERS *Gold. Bk. M. Aurel.* (1546) I, A spyder that is in the myddes of her webbe. **1536** R. BEERLEY in *Four C. Eng. Lett.* (1880) 35 Sume cum to mattens begenynge at the mydes, and sume when yt ys allmost done. **1544** in Willis & Clark *Cambridge* (1886) I. 213 In breadythe in the mydds Fyftye and fyve Foote. **1548–9** (Mar.) *Bk. Com. Prayer*, *Communion*, The Priest standing humbly afore the middes of the Altar. **1564** HARDING *Answ. Jewel* ix. 122 King Dauid thought it very vnfitting..that..the Arke of God was putte in the myddes of skynnes, that is, of the tabernacle. **1611** BIBLE *Luke* iv. 30 He passing thorow the mids of them. *Ibid.* 35 When the deuill had throwen him in the middes. **1621** AINSWORTH *Annot. Pentat.*, *Gen.* xxiv. 22 (1639) 92 A weight called in Hebrew bekagh, which signifieth cleft or cut in the mids. **1641** HINDE *J. Bruen* xli. 129 A man who knew right well..what it was that did make a mans face to shine in the mids of his own house and in the Congregation.

†**2.** A means. *Obs.*

1520 *St. Papers Hen. VIII*, II. 32 We truste..of this your hard and goode begynning shall folowe a better myddes. **15..** *1st Bk. Discipl. Ch. Scot.* (1621) 74 He useth the ministery of men, as the most necessary middes for this purpose. **1616** J. MAITLAND *Apol. Maitland of Lethington* in *Scot. Hist. Soc. Misc.* (1904) 200, I hoip that my father his dealings sal appeir sincer..& his endis & midis lauful & honest. **1646** R. BAILLIE *Lett. & Jrnls.* (Bannatyne Club) II. 355 Your debates about the midses mak the end among your hand to be lost. *a* **1658** DURHAM *Exp. Rev.* II. iv. (1680) 129 A sinful midse for attaining an end. **1710** WODROW *Corr.* (1843) I. 144 This is the midse [method] that is fallen upon at present to prevent rents.

3. A mean between two extremes; a middle course, a compromise. *Obs.* exc. *Sc.*

1553 KENNEDY *Compend. Tract.* in *Wodr. Soc. Misc.* (1844) 143 Betuix thir twa extremiteis geve it plesit God that the myddis sulde cum furth, apperandlie it wer ane gret ease. **1582–8** *Hist. Jas. VI* (1804) 172 Quhair they conferrit lang with the Lordis upoun the xxi day of May for sum articles of peace, bot neuer concludit any midds. **1637–50** ROW *Hist. Kirk* (Wodr. Soc.) 111 The Assemblie laboured to take a mids in the mater. **1709** W. STEWART *Collect. Worship. Ch. Scot.* 244 Temperance is the Golden Mids between Abstinence and Intemperance. **1720** T. BOSTON *Fourfold State* (1797) 238 There is a mids betwixt omitting duty and the doing of it as thou dost it. **1875** W. ALEXANDER *Sk. Ain Folk* xii. 67 There's a midse i' the sea, ye ken, an' it is not wisse-like to gae sic len'ths.

†**4.** *attrib.* and *Comb.*: **midsfinger**, the middle finger; **midsman**, (*a*) a mediator; (*b*) in Ireland = MIDDLEMAN; **mids-world**, = MIDDLE EARTH.

c **1250** *Gen. & Ex.* 42 Ðo bad god wurðen stund and stede, Ðis midds werld ðor-inne he dede. **1483** *Cath. Angl.* 239/1 þe Middis fynger, *medius degitus* [sic]. *a* **1662** R. BAILLIE *Lett.* (1775) II. 401 Mr. Blair and Mr. Durham appeared as mids-men [*ed. Bannatyne Club* midmen: see MID MAN]. **1801** *Ann. Reg.* 23 What has been the main cause of the wretchedness of the Irish and the Highlanders of Scotland? The midsmen of the former, and the tacksmen of the latter.

†**B.** *adv.* In the middle or midst. *Obs.*

c **1407** LYDG. *Reson & Sens.* 5197 And myddys of the soote herbage Ther be bestys eke savage. *c* **1430** —— *Min. Poems* (Percy Soc.) 12 Middes above, in ffulle riche aray, Ther satt a child off beaute precellyng.

†**C.** *prep.* In the middle of. *Obs.*

a **1400–50** *Alexander* 1061 Þan metis him myddis þe way was meruale to sene, A hert. *c* **1475** *Partenay* 5779 Thys wonderfull and meruelous best ne but on ey hath middes the forehed. *c* **1611** CHAPMAN *Iliad* XVIII. 549 To end which two begun (Mids all) a song.

†**mids,** *v. Obs.* [f. MIDS *sb.*] *trans.* To take a middle view of.

1693 STAIR *Instit.* II. i. §41. 177 Tribonian midseth the matter thus.

mid-sea. The middle of the sea, the open sea.

1582 STANYHURST *Æneis* III. (Arb.) 73 Thee Creet Ile in mydseas dooth stand too Iuppiter hallowd. **1667** MILTON *P.L.* VII. 403 Shoales Of Fish that with thir Finns & shining Scales Glide under the green Wave, in Sculles that oft Bank the mid Sea. **1853** GROTE *Greece* II. lxxxiv. XI. 123 A gentle and steady Etesian breeze carried them across midsea without accident or suffering. **1871** R. ELLIS tr. *Catullus* lxiv. 167 He rides far already, the mid sea's boundary cleaving.

b. *attrib.* quasi-*adj.*

1579 J. STUBBES *Gaping Gulf* D vj b, When it was not yet enlarged with hir Italian dominions and midsea Iles. **1897** KIPLING *Captains Courageous* viii. 153 Three boats found their rodings fouled by these reckless mid-sea hunters.

mid-season.

†**1.** The time in the middle of the day; noon.

1610 SHAKS. *Temp.* I. ii. 239 *Pro.* What is the time o' th' day? *Ar.* Past the mid season.

2. The middle of the season.

1902 ELIZ. L. BANKS *Newspaper Girl* 166, I was wearing my new Paris hat, which, as it was mid-season, I had bought for eighteen shillings and sixpence. **1969** *Burpee Catal.* 123/2 Delicious [straw]berries in midseason.

attrib. **1882** *Garden* 14 Jan. 30/3 A mid-season house containing mixed kinds may now be started in the usual way. **1889** *Daily News* 22 Oct. 6/1 A few really tasteful and appropriate mid-season dresses. **1921** WODEHOUSE *Indiscretions of Archie* xix. 210, I was just putting old Bill through it..with a view to getting him into mid-season form. **1946** —— *Joy in Morning* v. 35 Though crushed to earth..he rises again—not absolutely in midseason form, perhaps, but perkier than you would expect. **1969** *Burpee Catal.* 81/2 Sweet Corn... A midseason corn.

midship ('mɪdʃɪp). *Naut.* [f. MID *a.* + SHIP.] The middle part of a ship or boat.

1555 *Act 2 & 3 Ph. & Mary* c. 16 §7 Any Wherry..which shall not be..iv. Foot and a Half broad in the Midship. *a* **1618** RALEIGH *Royal Navy* 33 It is a great weakening to a ship to have so much weight..at both the ends, and nothing in the Mid-ship. **1865** J. H. INGRAHAM *Pillar of Fire* (1872) 31 A singer that stood upon the bridge across the mid-ship.

b. The rower who sits in the middle of a boat.

1897 MARY KINGSLEY *W. Africa* 173 Midship backed and flapped like fury.

c. *Comb.*: **midship beam** (see quots.); **midship bend,** = *midship frame*; **midship body** (see quot.); **midship frame,** that timber or frame in a ship which has the greatest breadth; **midship port,** a porthole in the middle part of a ship.

1692 *Capt. Smith's Seaman's Gram.* II. xv. 122 The breadth upon the *Midship-beam 20 foot. *c* **1850** *Rudim. Navig.* (Weale) 95 The Midship-Beam is the longest beam of the ship, lodged in the mid ship frame, or between the widest frame of timbers. **1805** *Shipwright's Vade-M.* 117 **Midship-bend or frame*, that bend which is called Dead-Flat. **1875** KNIGHT *Dict. Mech.* s.v. *Midship-bend*, When the middle of the ship has a portion of a uniform cross-section, such is called the **midship body.* **1769** FALCONER *Dict. Marine* (1780) C 2 b, The most capacious of these represents what is called the **midship-frame.* **1836** MARRYAT *Midsh. Easy* xxx, Two of the *midship ports of the antagonist were blown into one.

midshipman ('mɪdʃɪpmən). [f. prec. + MAN. So called because stationed 'amidships' when on duty.]

1. In the navy, the designation of a rank intermediate in the line of promotion between that of naval cadet and that of the lowest commissioned officer (i.e. in the British navy that of sub-lieutenant, in the U.S. navy that of ensign).

[**1626, 1627**: see *midships-man* s.v. MIDSHIPS.] **1685** *Lond. Gaz.* No. 2054/3 Mr. Littleton, and..Mr. Brisbane, both Midshipmen Extraordinary. **1701** LUTTRELL *Brief Rel.* (1857) V. 100 Her lieutenant and 2 midship men killed. **1769** FALCONER *Dict. Marine* (1780), *Midshipman*, a sort of naval cadet, appointed by the captain of a ship of war, to second the orders of the superior officers. **1855** MRS. GASKELL *North & S.* xiv, How well he looked in his midshipman's dress. **1900** W. BAIRD *Gen. Wauchope* ii. 33 Midshipmen's amusements and practical jokes are proverbial.

2. *U.S.* 'A batrachoid fish, *Porichthys margaritatus*: so called from the rows of round luminous bodies along the belly, like the buttons of a naval cadet's coat' (*Cent. Dict.*).

1882 JORDAN & GILBERT *Synop. Fishes N. Amer.* 751 *Porichthys porosissimus*—Midshipman.

3. *Comb.*: **midshipman's butter**, the Avocado, *Persea gratissima*; **midshipman's half pay** (see quot.); **midshipman's hitch** (see quot. 1886); **midshipman's nuts**, broken pieces of biscuit as dessert (Smyth *Sailor's Word-bk.* 1867); **midshipman's roll** (see quot. 1857).

1866 *Treas. Bot.* 867/1 *Persea gratissima*... They contain a large quantity of firm pulp possessing a buttery or marrow-like taste, and are hence frequently called Vegetable Marrow or *Midshipman's Butter. **1871** KINGSLEY *At Last* ii, Avocado, or Alligator pears, alias midshipman's butter. *c* **1851** —— *Lett. & Life* (1877) I. 277 *Midshipman's half-pay (nothing a-day and find yourself). **1808** D. LEVER *Young Sea Officer's Sheet Anchor* 9 To make a *Midshipman's Hitch. **1886** *Encycl. Brit.* XXI. 591/2 *Midshipman's Hitch.*—Take two round turns inside the bight, the same as a half-hitch repeated; stop up the end; or let another half-hitch be taken or held by hand. Used for hooking a tackle for a temporary purpose. **1828** *Night Watch* II. viii. 50 'You shall have a fistful of *midshipman's nuts to crack for your supper.'.. He gave me some broken biscuits. **1846** H. MELVILLE *Typee* vi. 38, I took a double handful of those small, broken, flinty bits of biscuit which generally go by the name of 'midshipmen's nuts'. **1826** W. N. GLASCOCK *Naval Sketch-Bk.* (ed. 2) I. 8 Get your hammock slung... 'Cause, ..none o' your '*midshipman's rolls', you know! **1857** H. E. DAVENPORT *Rovings on Land & Sea* 280 If any of the hammocks are lashed in a slovenly manner, or merely bundled up in what is called a 'midshipman's roll', the owner is..made to secure it in a more ship-shape manner.

Hence **'midshipmanship**, the office or position of a midshipman.

1789 COWPER *Let.* (in *Pearson's 76th Catal.* (1894) 16), I.. rejoice with thee that thou hast succeeded in procuring a midshipmanship (there's a word for you) for the poor young

man in question. **1857** *Chamb. Jrnl.* VIII. 103 He was undergoing the preliminary ordeal of midshipmanship.

midshipmite (ˈmɪdʃɪpmaɪt). A sailor's perversion of MIDSHIPMAN. (Adopted by humorous writers as suggesting MITE *sb.*)

1833 MARRYAT *P. Simple* viii, One of them ere midshipmites. **1868** W. S. GILBERT *Bab Ball., Nancy Bell*, A bo'sun tight, and a midshipmite. **1880** *Theatre* Jan. 39 As for the Midshipmite, he creates a roar whenever he struts across the deck.

midships (ˈmɪdʃɪps), *sb.* and *adv.* [App. aphetic for AMIDSHIPS, though appearing earlier in our quots.] **A.** *sb.* The middle part of a vessel either with regard to her length or breadth.

1626 CAPT. SMITH *Accid. Yng. Seamen* 7 In a fight the Forecastle is his [the Lieutenant's] place, to make good; as the Captaine doth the halfe decke; and the quarter Maisters the midships. **1705** *Lond. Gaz.* No. 4116/3 Only her Hull from the Taffrill to the Midships remained above Water. **1762–9** FALCONER *Shipwr.* II. 901 Both stay-sail sheets to mid-ships were convey'd.

b. *Comb.*: †**midships man** = MIDSHIPMAN.

1626 CAPT. SMITH *Accid. Yng. Seamen* 2 His Mates are onely his Seconds, allowed sometimes for the two Midships men. **1627** —— *Seaman's Gram.* xiii. 61 Midships men see the tops and yards well manned.

B. *adv.* = AMIDSHIPS.

1838 *Civ. Eng. & Arch. Jrnl.* I. 384/2 Clear beam midships..32 ft. **1852** H. W. PIERSON *Missionary Memorial* 145 On retiring, we stopped midships to sing a hymn of thanksgiving. **1883** *Law Times Rep.* XLIX. 332/2 The *Clan Sinclair* with her stem took the port side of the *Margaret* abaft midships.

mid-side. [MID *a.*] The middle of the side.

c **1220** *Bestiary* 622 In water ȝe sal stonden, In water to mid side. *a* **1300** *Body & Soul* in *Map's Poems* (Camden) 338 Forth was brouȝt there, with a bridel, A corsed devel als a cote..With a sadel to the mid side. *c* **1470** HENRY *Wallace* VII. 991 Wallace selff, at mydsid off the toune, With men of armys thai was to bargane bown. **1581** BURNE *Disput.* 107 Sua that sence thay are al enterit in the scheipfauld of Christ, nocht be the dur bot be the midsyd of the house, it is [etc.]. **1651–7** T. BARKER *Art of Angling* (1820) 17 The fish may lie up to the mid-sides in the liquor.

Comb. **1794** WEDGE *Agric. Chester* 55 The cheese..is then taken and placed midside deep in brine.

mid-sky. [MID *a.*] The middle of the sky.

1634 MILTON *Comus* 957 Com let us haste, the Stars grow high, But night sits monarch yet in the mid sky. **1667** —— *P.L.* VI. 314 Two Planets rushing from aspect maligne Of fiercest opposition in mid Skie. **1860** HAWTHORNE *Marble Faun* (1879) II. iii. 37 Out of the mid-sky.

attrib. **1807** J. BARLOW *Columb.* I, Thro all the midsky zones, to yon blue pole, Their green hills lengthen.

midst (mɪdst), *sb.*, *adv.*, and *prep.* Forms: 5 **medeste**, 5–7 **myddest**, 5–8 (9 *arch. rare*) **middest**, 6 **middeste**, **mydst**, 7 **middst**, **midd'st**, **midest**, 8 **mid'st**, 6– **midst**. [First appears in the 15th c. as *middest*. Prob. two different formations have been confused: (1) an extended form of *middes*, MIDS, with the excrescent (euphonic or analogical) *t* as in *amongst*, *against*, *whilst*, and the dialectal *onst* for *once*, *nice't* (naɪst) for *nice*; (2) an absolute use of the superlative MIDDEST *a.*] **A.** *sb.*

1. The middle point or part; the centre, middle. *Obs.* or *arch.*

a **1400–50** *Alexander* 5396 He saȝe a dym cloude Full of starand sternes and stiȝtild in þe myddest A grete grysely god. *c* **1440** *Alphabet of Tales* 455 He was at þe myddest of þe brygg. *c* **1489** CAXTON *Blanchardyn* liv. 208 Subbion in the middest, and Blanchardine the hindmost. **1517** *Acc. Bk. W. Wray* in *Antiquary* XXXII. 214 King James..about the middest of march tooke his p'gresse towards Scotland. **1570–6** LAMBARDE *Peramb. Kent* (1826) 197 Hee died before he had brought the worke to the midst. **1588** KYD *Househ. Phil.* Wks. (1901) 250 Ierusalem..is in the midst of our Hemysphere. **1592** TIMME *Ten Eng. Lepers* F j, I will but touch three parts: to wit, the beginning, the middest, and the end. **1654** EARL MONM. tr. *Bentivoglio's Wars Flanders* 210 About the midst of January. *a* **1661** FULLER *Worthies, Shropsh.* (1662) III. 1 This Shire being almost in the middest of England. **1671** H. M. *Erasm. Colloq.* 319 If thou open the black stone Cyamea, thou shalt find a bean in the midst. **1695** DRYDEN *Dufresnoy's Art Painting* Pref. 44 One Play.. where there is nothing in the First Act, but what might have been said or done in the Fifth; nor any thing in the Midst, which might not have been plac'd as well in the Beginning or the End. *a* **1894** STEVENSON *Tales and Fantasies, J. Nicholson* (1905) 76 He was not past the midst of the first field.

2. The position of being in the interior of, involved or enveloped in, or surrounded by (something, or a number of things or persons, specified or implied). Now almost exclusively in the phrase ***in the midst of*** (formerly also †***among the midst of***), chiefly in the senses: Among, amid, surrounded by (a number of things or persons); while fully engaged with, 'in the thick of' (occupations, troubles, etc.); during the continuance of (an action or condition).

?*a* **1500** *Chester Pl., Salut. & Nativ.* (Shaks. Soc. 1843) 113 And one his breste written also The landes naimes and goodes bouth too, And sette also in the medeste [E.E.T.S. ed. p. 127, myddes] of thoe, God of Rome righte as a kinge. **1535** COVERDALE *Luke* iv. 35 And the deuell threw him in the myddest [1611 middes] amonge them. **1548–9** (Mar.) *Bk. Com. Prayer, Burial of Dead*, In the myddest of lyfe we be in death. **1558** KNOX *First Blast* (Arb.) 12 A woman sitteth crowned in parliament amongest the middest of men. *a* **1586** SIDNEY *Arcadia* I. (1590) 58 While you were in the middest of your sport. **1606** G. W[OODCOCKE] *Hist. Ivstine* XXXII. 109 In the midest of the battell. **1611** BIBLE *Deut.* iv. 12 And the Lord spake vnto you out of the midst of the fire. **1632** LITHGOW *Trav.* VI. 270 In the middest of all this hurley burley. **1632** SANDERSON *Serm.* 315 To plucke thee out of the middest of a froward and crooked generation. *a* **1658** CLEVELAND *Rustick Rampant* Wks. (1687) 445 Made his Way with his Sword alone..into the middest of their Troops. **1751** JOHNSON *Rambler* No. 153 ¶6 In the midst of an adventure. **1818** SHELLEY *Rosal. & Helen* 860 In the midst of a city vast and wide. **1849** MACAULAY *Hist. Eng.* iii. I. 289 Armies..were kept up in the midst of peace. **1863** GEO. ELIOT *Romola* II. i, From the midst of those smiling heavens he had seen a sword hanging. **1887** BOWEN *Virg. Æneid* III. 104 Crete, in the midst of the waters lies. *Mod.* In the midst of his enormous labours, he has found time to [etc.].

†**b.** ***to leave in the midst*** [= L. *in medio relinquere*]: to leave undecided, abstain from giving an opinion on.

1625 GILL *Sacr. Philos.* I. 107, I leave it in the middest, till further proofe of the truth be made.

c. With a possessive, usually of plural pronoun, ***(in) our, your, their midst.***

This use is scarcely found before the 19th century; the solitary example from the 16th c. does not prove that it was current. Cf. 'in her middes' (= in their midst) *Apol. Loll.* (*c* 1400) 12.

c **1586** C'TESS PEMBROKE *Ps.* cxxxv. iv, Not so his dreadfull showes he ceas'd, But did them still in Ægipts mid'st renew. **1794** C. JOHN in Southey *Life A. Bell* (1844) I. 205 If we then could have had our dear Dr. Bell in our midst, our pleasures and improvements would have been greatly heightened. **1825** J. MONTGOMERY in *Chr. Psalmist* (1828) 414 Lo, in their midst his form was seen, The form in which He died. **1864** BRYCE *Holy Rom. Emp.* xi. (1866) 200 When ..his shield [should] be hung aloft again as of old in the camp's midst, a sign of help to the poor and the oppressed. **1867** W. L. NEWMAN in *Quest. Reformed Parl.* 119 Her vast and available coalfields, her iron mines, the energy of her people, founded cities in her midst. **1869** J. MARTINEAU *Ess.* II. 133 The enduring light that broke out in their midst.

d. With omission of article, ***in midst (of)***. Now only *poet.* (*rare*).

1590 SPENSER *F.Q.* I. vii. 5 In middest of the race. *Ibid.* I. ix. 10, I ever..ioyde to stirre up strife, In middest of their mournfull Tragedy. *a* **1617** BAYNE *On Eph.* (1643) 114 To reckon him in middest of his dearest favorites. **1617** *Janua Ling.* Advt., That should haue brought thee in midst a faire orchyard. **1861** LYTTON & FANE *Tannhäuser* 112 In midst, His worn cheek channell'd with unwonted tears, The Landgrave. **1880** WATSON *Prince's Quest* 63 There towered In middest of that silent realm deflowered A palace.

¶ *poet.* with transposition of possessive adj.

1671 MILTON *Samson* 1339 And in my midst of sorrow and heart-grief To shew them feats.

†**3.** A medium, middle course or term, mean. *Sc. Obs.* Cf. MIDS.

c **1610** SIR J. MELVIL *Mem.* (1735) 19 Rather following the Extremity than the right Midst. *a* **1649** DRUMM. OF HAWTH. *Hist. Jas. II*, Wks. (1711) 30 The majesty of a prince hardly falleth from a height to a midst, but easily is precipitated from any midst to the lowest degree and station. **1678** R. BARCLAY *Apol. Quakers* vii. §2. 202 They have laboured after a Midst betwixt these two extreams. **1786** A. GIB *Sacr. Contempl.* I. VII. ii. 158 There can be no proper midst in a Soul, betwixt moral good and evil.

B. *adv.*

1. In the middle place. Only in Milton's phrase.

[Prob. to be regarded as a contracted form of MIDDEST *a.* used advb.]

1667 MILTON *P.L.* v. 165 On Earth joyn all yee Creatures to extoll Him first, him last, him midst, and without end. **1773** BURKE *Corr.* (1844) I. 426 May God grant you every blessing. Remember Him first, last, and midst. **1854** DE QUINCEY *War* Wks. 1862 IV. 271 Every nation's duty first, midst, and last, is to itself.

2. = 'In the midst'. Const. *of. poet. rare.*

1675 N. LEE *Nero* IV. i, If I gaze long, I shall my nature lose: Mid'st of my full carreer, I stop and muse. **1883** R. W. DIXON *Mano* I. vi. 16 And midst there was a goodly chantry seen. **1885–94** R. BRIDGES *Eros & Psyche* June v, The grassy plat 'Midst of her garden, where she had her seat.

C. *prep.* In the midst of; †between. Commonly written *'midst*, as if aphetic for AMIDST.

1591 SHAKS. *1 Hen. VI*, I. ii. 24, I would ne're haue fled, But that they left me 'midst my Enemies. **1593** —— *Lucr.* 566 And midst the sentence so her accent breakes, That twise she doth begin ere once she speakes. **1667** MILTON *P.L.* VI. 28 From whence a voice From midst a Golden Cloud thus milde was heard. **1682** CREECH *Lucretius* (1683) 77 The peaceful Ox contains most parts of Air, Not subject unto too much Rage, nor Fear, A temper, 'midst the Lion, and the Deer. **1704** POPE *Windsor For.* 26 And 'midst the desart fruitful fields arise. **1821** SHELLEY *Adonais* xxxi, Midst others of less note, came one frail Form, A phantom among men.

midstream (ˌmɪdˈstriːm). [f. MID *a.* + STREAM.] **1. a.** The middle of the stream. Also *fig.*

c **1315** *Greenwich Hosp. MS. Documents* (P.R.O. Box 20, bundle O, No. 12), En primis a commensere de mydstreme de Derwent. **1669** DRYDEN *Tyrannic Love* II. i, The mid-stream's his; I, creeping by the side, Am shoulder'd off by his impetuous Tide. **1735** SOMERVILLE *Chase* III. 546 Down the Mid-stream he wafts Along. **1827** E. MACKENZIE *Hist. Newcastle* II. 742 *note*, The midstream of the river, taken at low water, is considered the boundary between the coal-mines. **1849** E. B. EASTWICK *Dry Leaves* 99 He was obliged to have the boat kept in mid-stream. **1899** T. NICOL *Recent Archæol. & Bible* ii. 94 We are brought into the midstream of Biblical History.

attrib. **1894** *Outing* (U.S.) XXIV. 452/2 On the mid-stream side of the rocky islet..the bank was eight or ten feet high. **1905** *Daily Chron.* 13 Mar. 4/4 The ford would land us on a mid-stream island.

b. Used *advb.*

1872 TENNYSON *Gareth & L.* 1015 Whom Gareth met mid-stream.

2. *Med.* Used, usu. *attrib.*, to designate any portion of urine passed by an individual other than that first passed or last passed in an act of urination.

1958 *New Engl. Jrnl. Med.* CCLIX. 764 (*heading*) A comparison of bacterial counts of the urine obtained by needle aspiration of the bladder, catheterization and midstream-voided methods. **1962** *Lancet* 15 Dec. 1246/1 The urine was examined microscopically for pus cells... In men and children midstream specimens were used. **1972** *Ibid.* 2 Sept. 452/2 Specimens of midstream urine were collected in sterile universal bottles.

midsummer (ˈmɪdsʌmə(r)). Forms: see MID *a.* and SUMMER *sb.*; also, 3–5 **missomer**, 4 **mesomur**, **misomere**, **myssomer(e**, **mysomer**. [OE. *midsumor*; see MID *a.* and SUMMER; cf. ON. *miðsumar* (Sw. *midsommar*, Da. *midsommer*), MDu. *midsomer*, *middesomer*, *middensomer* (Du. *midzomer*), mod.G. *mittsommer*. In OE. also as two words, with inflexion of the adj.]

1. a. The middle of summer; the period of the summer solstice, about June 21st.

a **900** tr. *Bæda's Hist.* v. xii. (1890) 425 Swa sunnan upgong bið æt middum sumere. *c* **1055** *Byrhtferth's Handboc* in *Anglia* (1885) VIII. 311 Þæt ys on lyden solstitium & on englisc midsumor. *a* **1123** *O.E. Chron.* an. 1101 Þa to midde sumeran ferde se cyng ut to Pefenesæ. *c* **1290** *Beket* 1693 in *S. Eng. Leg.* I. 155 A-ȝein Midsomer it bi-ful. **1297** R. GLOUC. (Rolls) 10546 Suþþe he nom iwis Winchestre aboute missomer. **1389** in *Eng. Gilds* (1870) 313 Every person.. shalle pay, euery yere, ffor hys ffeste, at Myssomere, xij*d.* **1412** *Catterick Ch. Contract* (Raine 1834) 11 Be mysomer next. **1473** WARKW. *Chron.* (Camden) 6 At myssomere, the Duke of Clarence passede the see to Caleis. **1560** DAUS tr. *Sleidane's Comm.* 153 His wyfe..after aboute Midsomer, ended her life there. **1596** SHAKS. *1 Hen. IV*, IV. i. 102 Gorgeous as the Sunne at Mid-summer. **1625** N. CARPENTER *Geog. Del.* I. x. (1635) 223 Their longest day at Midsummer is 24 houres. **1714** GAY *Sheph. Week* IV. 27 At Eve last Midsummer no Sleep I sought. **1840** J. BUEL *Farmer's Comp.* 44 The crops may then mature before they are injured by the intense heats of our mid-summers.

fig. *c* **1450** *Godstow Reg.* 18 Bryng us mydsomer of heuenly blys, I pray ȝow, martyrs both, Paule and Iohn.

†**b.** *Phr.* ***to have but a mile to midsummer***: to be somewhat mad. (Cf. *midsummer madness.*)

c **1465** *Eng. Chron.* (Camden 1856) 92 Tho bestys that thys wroughte to mydsomer have but a myle.

2. = *Midsummer Day*, June 24th.

1530 PALSGR. 245/1 Mydsomer, *la sainct Jehan.* **16..** *Robin Hood & Pr. Arragon* xix. in Child *Ballads* III. 148/2 'On Midsummer next', the damsel said, 'Which is June the twenty-four'.

3. *attrib.* and *Comb.*, as ***midsummer beauty***, ***fair***, ***-night***, ***-pomp***, ***-quarter***, ***-rose***, ***-sunbeam***, ***term***, †***-tide***, ***-time***; †**midsummer ale**, a festive gathering held at midsummer; **midsummer chafer** *U.S.*, a beetle, *Rhizotrogus solstitialis* (Cent. Dict. 1890); **midsummer daisy**, *Chrysanthemum Leucanthemum* (Prior *Plant-n.* 1879); **Midsummer Day**, the 24th of June, one of the recognized 'quarterdays' in England; **midsummer eve**, †**even**, the evening before Midsummer Day; **midsummer games**, festivities held at midsummer; **midsummer growth**, a second start into growth after ceasing (Jackson *Bot. Terms* 1900); **midsummer madness**, the height of madness (cf. *midsummer moon*); **midsummer men**, *Sedum Telephium*, a plant used by girls on midsummer eve to divine whether their lovers are true; †**midsummer moon**, ? the lunar month in which Midsummer Day comes; sometimes alluded to as a time when lunacy is supposed to be prevalent; †**midsummer sights**, rural dramatic performances at midsummer; **midsummer silver**, the silver-weed, *Potentilla anserina*.

1633 MARMION *Antiquary* IV. (1641) I 3, And now next *Midsummer ale, I may serve for a fool. **1867** 'OUIDA' *C. Castlemaine* (1879) 5 The country was in its glad green *midsummer beauty. *c* **1000** *Sax. Leechd.* I. 90 Wið lifre sar genim on *midde sumeres dæȝ þa ylcan wyrte. **1297** R. GLOUC. (Rolls) 10266 Alle þe bissopes..þat ar missomer day in to this londe come. **1359** in *Eng. Gilds* (1870) 97 On mesomur day. *c* **1425** *St. Mary of Oignies* II. x. in *Anglia* VIII. 177/45 Fro þe annuncyacyone of oure lady vnto myssomer-daye. **1556** *Chron. Gr. Friars* (Camden) 29 The mydsomer day followynge was his sonne crownyd Henry the viij[th] at Westmyster. **1710** ADDISON *Tatler* No. 221 ¶2 Upon Midsummer-Day last, as he was walking with me in the Fields. **1426–7** *Rec. St. Mary at Hill* 66 On *mydsomer eve a dawber and his man..xiiij d. **1820** W. IRVING *Sketch Bk.* II. 128 On Midsummer eve, when it is well known all kinds of ghosts, goblins, and fairies, become visible and walk abroad. **1904** *Edin. Rev.* Jan. 53 The elderbush is cut on Midsummer Eve. **1352** *Wynnere & Wastoure* 166 in *Parl. Three Ages* (Roxb. Club) 95 One *Missomer euen. **1556** *Chron. Gr. Friars* (Camden) 16 On mydsomer evyn [1433] the duke with hys wyffe came to London. *c* **1566** *Scogin's Jests* (Hazl.) 145 On a time about *Midsummer faire, he.. went to Barnwell. **1577** B. GOOGE *Heresbach's Husb.* I. 6 b, The Fathers..busied them selues rather with Pageantes and *Midsommer games, then with the Vineyard. **1601** SHAKS.

Twel. N. III. iv. 61 Why this is verie *Midsommer madnesse. **1914** C. MACKENZIE *Sinister St.* II. III. v. 594 The freshmen ..celebrated the beauty of the season with a good deal of midsummer madness. **1921** GALSWORTHY *To Let* II. ix. 200 Come, be reasonable, Fleur! It's midsummer madness! **1922** JOYCE *Ulysses* 482 This is midsummer madness, some ghastly joke again. **1970** M. PETERS in *Midsummer Variations* 203 Midsummer madness they all said That summer day when we were wed. **1755** *Connoisseur* No. 56 ¶5, I likewise stuck up two *Midsummer Men, one for myself, and one for him. Now if his had died away, we should never have come together. **1877** W. JONES *Finger-ring* 169 It was an olden superstition that the bending of the leaves to the right or to the left of the orpine plants, or Midsummer men, as they were called..would never fail to tell whether a lover was true or false. **1523** FITZHERB. *Husb.* §124 Wede them clene in *myd-somer mone. **1589** *Marprel. Epit.* (1843) 14 Whether it be midsommer Moone with him or no. **1690** DRYDEN *Amphitryon* IV. i, What's this? midsummer-moon! Is all the world gone a-madding? *a* **1350** *Birth Jesus* 641 in Horstm. *Altengl. Leg.* (1875) 93 Þe schorteste niȝt þat was þo, was *missomerniȝt. **1600** SHAKS. *A.Y.L.* IV. i. 102 If it had not been for a hot Midsomer-night. **1866** M. ARNOLD *Thyrsis* vii, Soon will the high *Midsummer pomps come on. **1553–4** in Swayne *Sarum Churchw. Acc.* (1896) 99 Wyllyam lobbe for kepynge of the clocke for *mydsomer quarter xx d. *c* **1430** LYDG. *Min. Poems* (Percy Soc.) 22 All start in chaunge like a *mydsomer rose. **1577** B. GOOGE *Heresbach's Husb.* I. 16 The husbandes ..spent their time rather in Maygames and *Mid-sommer sightes, then with tylling the ground, or planting of Vines. *a* **1697** AUBREY *Nat. Hist. Surrey* (1718) III. 62 In this place [Lingfield, Surrey] the Inhabitants are very fond of Ghirlands, or Garlands, made of *Midsummer Silver, a little Herb, which continues all the Year of a bright Ash Colour, and have crowded the Church and their own Houses with them. **1809** MANNING & BRAY *Hist. Surrey* II. 340 No such custom now prevails (1808), nor do old people remember it. The Midsummer Silver is common here. **1859** GEO. ELIOT *A. Bede* xii, Warmed by the *midsummer sunbeams. **1538** *Ld. Treas. Acc. Scotl.* (1905) VI. 430 Item, Charles Geddes, in compleit payment of xl merkis for his fe of the *mydsomer terme last bipast. *c* **1330** R. BRUNNE *Chron.* (1810) 224 Fro *Midsomertide to þe Apostle S. Thomas. **1375** BARBOUR *Bruce* x. 823 Gif at *Mydsummer tyme ane ȝeir To cum, it war nocht with bata[i]ll Reskewit, than [etc.]. **1601** HOLLAND *Pliny* I. 45 The riuer Nouanus at euery midsummertime swelles and runs ouer the bankes.

midsummerish (ˈmɪdsʌmərɪʃ), *a.* [-ISH.] Having the characteristics of midsummer.

1836 MRS. GORE *Mrs. Armytage* I. 302 The days, long and Midsummerish as they were, passed away.

midsummery (ˈmɪdsʌmərɪ), *a.* [f. MIDSUMMER + -Y.] Of or pertaining to midsummer.

1866 MOTLEY *Corr.* (1889) II. 217 The weather has been mid-summery. **1883** *Century Mag.* XXVII. 108 A species of golden-rod with a midsummery smell.

† **Mid-teˈrranean**, *a. Obs.* = MEDITERRANEAN.

1598 SYLVESTER *Du Bartas* II. ii. III. *Colonies* 86 Northward with narrow Mid-terranean Sea, Which from rich Europe parts poor Africa.

† **midtholing**. *Obs.* [f. MID *prep.* + THOLE *v.* + -ING[1].] Compassion.

1340 *Ayenb.* 157 Ich ssel habbe pité and mid þolyinge.

midtime (ˈmɪdtaɪm). [f. MID *a.* + TIME.] The time in the middle (of the day, etc.).

1571 GOLDING *Calvin on Ps.* lv. 17 The midtyme was appoynted for theire Sacrifices. **1619** DRAYTON *Bar. Wars* VI. lxxiii, It being then the mid time of the Night. **1650** *Sc. Metr. Ps.* cii. 24 O take me not away In mid-time of my dayes.

midulert, variant of MIDDLE ERD *Obs.*

midwald, -wall, var. ff. (in Dicts.) of MODWALL.

midwall (ˈmɪdwɔːl). *Arch.* [f. MID *a.* + WALL.] Used *attrib.* in *midwall shaft*, a shaft or baluster, placed in the middle of the thickness of the wall, in an early type of English belfry windows.

1880 FREEMAN in *Macm. Mag.* No. 246. 453, I doubt whether a midwall shaft is to be found between the Avon and Exmoor. **1893** C. HODGES in *Reliquary* Jan. 17 The midwall shafts, which are slightly barrel-shaped, are ten inches in diameter.

ˈ**midward**, *a.*, *sb.*, *adv.* and *prep.* Forms: 1 **middeweard** (as sb. *-wearde*), **-wærd**, **-ward**, **-weard**, 2 **middewarðe**, 4 **mydwarde**, *pl.* **myddwardis**, 4–5 *Sc.* **mydwart**, 4–6 **midwarde**, 5 *pl.* **midwardis**, 5–6 **mydward**, 4– **midward**. [OE. *middeweard*: see MID *a.* + -WARD. Cf. MDu. *middewaert*. (The 12th c. form *middewarðe* may be a misreading for *middewardre* dat. fem.)]

A. *adj.*

† **1.** In partitive concord: The middle of. *Obs.*

After OE. only preceded by *in*; the definite article, when used, was placed between the adj. and sb. *In midward* as thus used has the appearance of being a prepositional phrase governing the sb.: cf. AMIDWARD, EMIDWARD.

c **893** K. ÆLFRED *Oros.* II. vi. §1 Æfter þæm Eufrate þa ea, seo is mæst eallra ferscra wætera, & is irnende þurh middewearde Babylonia burȝ. *c* **1175** *Lamb. Hom.* 43 Seoððan he him sceawede and stude inne midde-warðe helle. *a* **1300** *Cursor M.* 655 Bot yhon tre cum þou nawight to, þat standes in midward paradis. ? *c* **1325** *K. Horn* 590 (Laud MS.), Ich sal do pruesce, For þe lef wyt schelde, In mide-ward þe felde. **1340** HAMPOLE *Pr. Consc.* 6319 'Als a litel spark of fire', says he, 'In mydward þe mykel se, Right swa alle a mans wykkednes Un-to þe mercy of God es'.

2. Occupying the middle. *Obs.* exc. *arch.*

a **1300** *Cursor M.* 9921 (Cott.) Þe midward heu es þat i mene. *c* **1375** *Ibid.* 764 (Fairf.) Of al þe trees [we ete] bot of ane, þe midwarde tree ys vs out-tane. **1876** MORRIS *Sigurd* (1877) 2 The midward time and the fading, and the last of the latter days.

† **B.** *sb.* The middle, the middle part. *Obs.*

c **1000** *Ags. Ps.* xxi. 15 (Lamb.) On middeweardan innoþes mines *in medio ventris mei.* **1303** R. BRUNNE *Handl. Synne* 9664 God ys shapper of alle þyng, He wote þe mydwarde, and þe endyng. **1375** BARBOUR *Bruce* III. 682 Ane ile..may weill in mydwart be Betwuix Kyntyr and Irland. *c* **1400** *Beryn* 2759 In mydward of this gardyn stant a feire tre. *c* **1450** LOVELICH *Grail* xl. 550 But as In the Midwardis, vndirstonde þou here, that whanne he Cam to his Middyl Age, he wax A man bothe sad and Sage. *c* **1470** HENRY *Wallace* VI. 503 Als mony syne in the mydwart put he. **1505** in *Mem. Hen. VII* (Rolls) 231 The fashion of her nose is a little rising in the midward. *c* **1550** R. BIESTON *Bayte Fortune* Bjb, Yf thou were in Tems in midwarde of the sande.

† **C.** *adv.* In the middle. *Obs.*

c **1470** HENRY *Wallace* v. 920 Off kyn he was, and Wallace modyr ner, Off Craufurd syd that mydward had to ster.

D. *prep.* In the middle of. *Obs.* exc. *arch.*

a **1300** *Cursor M.* 1032 Midward þat land a wel springes. **1817** SCOTT *Harold* v. ii, Midward their path, a rock of granite grey From the adjoining cliff had made descent.

mid-water. [f. MID *a.* + WATER *sb.*] The middle portion of the water vertically, near neither to the bottom nor the surface.

1653 WALTON *Angler* xii. 183 Letting him [a minnow] swim up and down about mid-water, or a little lower. **1816** KIRBY & SP. *Entomol.* xxii. (1818) II. 295 Some move in midwater, either by the same motion of the legs as they use in walking, or by strokes, as in swimming. **1905** HOLMAN HUNT *Pre-Raph.* I. 69 Red-spotted trout poised in mid-water.

attrib. **1868** *Daily Tel.* 5 June 5/1 It is the same with herrings, cod, ling, and all the mid-water fish.

† **mid waters**, *adv. Obs.* [f. MID *a.* + WATER, with advb. *s.*] In the middle of the waters.

a **1800** *Coble o' Cargill* vi. in Child *Ballads* IV. 359 Before that he was mid-waters, The weary coble began to fill.

midway (ˈmɪdweɪ, mɪdˈweɪ), *sb.*, *a.*, *adv.* and *prep.* [f. MID *a.* + WAY. Cf. MDu. *middewech*; also Da. *midtvei.*] **A.** *sb.*

† **1.** The middle of the way or distance. *Obs.*

c **897** K. ÆLFRED *Gregory's Past C.* li. 399 Ðonne bið ðæt swa swa Segor stod on midweȝe betweox ðæm muntum & ðæm merscum ðe Sodoma on wæs. ? *a* **1400** *Morte Arth.* 2682 Sir Wychere, Sir Walchere, theis weise mene of armes, ..Mett him in the mydwaye. *c* **1400** MAUNDEV. (1839) iv. 31 Fro Calabre or fro Cecyle to Akoun, be See, is 1300 Myles of Lombardye. And the Ile of Crete is right in the myd weye. **1586** T. B. *La Primaud. Fr. Acad.* I. 68 The studie of letters is..so long and uneasie a journey, that they which thinke to finish it, oftentimes staie in the midwaie. **1677** W. HUBBARD *Narrative* (1865) I. 36 Newhaven..seated near the Midway betwixt Hudsons River and that of Connecticut. **1770** KING in *Phil. Trans.* LXI. 256 She mentioned a very steep shelf, or descent, in the midway.

† **2.** A medium; a middle course. Now *rare.*

1599 SHAKS. *Much Ado* II. i. 8 Hee were an excellent man that were made iust in the mid-way betweene him and Benedicke. **1606** —— *Ant. & Cl.* III. iv. 19 No midway 'Twixt these extreames at all. *a* **1656** BP. HALL *Rem. Wks.* (1660) 168 Our sorrow must walk in a mid-way betwixt neglect and excess. **1677** *Govt. Venice* 56 The Senat having chosen the midway, which in great dangers, and doubtful, is always the worst. **1847** EMERSON *Poems* (1857) 39 Nor mount, nor dive; all good things keep The midway of the eternal deep.

3. *U.S.* Freq. with capital initial. At an exhibition, fair, or the like: a central avenue along which the chief exhibits or amusements are placed; hence, any cheap place of amusement; *slang*, a hall. Also *attrib.*

The use originated in the inclusion of the 'Midway Plaisance' of Chicago in the grounds of the exposition held there in 1893.

1893 *Outing* Dec. 208/1 The waiters were the hardiest set on the Midway. **1901** *World's Work* Aug. 1097/2 Nowadays we frankly admit that the Midway is the strongest magnet of a big fair. **1901** *Everybody's Mag.* Oct. 424 Can I arrange with you for placing a first-class Midway on your grounds? *Ibid.* 427/1 A mile and a half of kerwhango and clash—That is the Midway show. **1927** K. NICHOLSON *Barker* 149 *Midway Confab*, news column in the *Billboard*, the weekly trade paper for outdoor show-folk. **1932** *Evening Sun* (Baltimore) 9 Dec. 31/5 *Midway*, a hall. **1949** *Sat. Even. Post* 17 Sept. 25/1, I have worked in..big-time railroad shows whose midways had the glitter of a handful of diamonds. **1956** H. GOLD *Man who was not with It* (1965) i. 3 There he is on the midway, Grack the Frenchie, talking for his Countstore.

B. *adj.*

1. Situated in the middle of the way, occupying the middle. *rare* exc. *poet.*

1605 SHAKS. *Lear* IV. vi. 6 The Crowes and Choughes, that wing the midway ayre Shew scarce so grosse as Beetles. **1742** YOUNG *Nt. Th.* IX. 1218 In Mid-way Flight Imagination tires. **1879** GEO. ELIOT *Theo. Such* 221 The midway parting of his crisp hair. **1898** G. MEREDITH *Odes Fr. Hist.* 29 No more at midway heaven.

2. † **a.** Medium, moderate. *Obs.*

1573 TYRIE *Refut. Knox* To Rdr., Als conuenient to begyle the simple reader, as to impesche and trauel men of gude ingyne and midway knawlage, to cum to the vnderstanding of the veritie. **1596** DALRYMPLE tr. *Leslie's Hist. Scot.* VII. 43 He was of midway stature. **1675** G. R. tr. *Le Grand's Man without Passion* 59, I confess that I understand not that competent or midway knowledg by him found out.

b. Of an opinion: Mediating. *rare.*

1905 JAS. ORR *Problem Old Test.* ix. 327 The midway theory advocated by Nöldeke.

C. *adv.*

1. In the middle of the way or distance; halfway. Also *U.S.* const. *of.*

a **1225** *Ancr. R.* 412 A sunedei midwei bitweonen þet and ester. **1577–87** HOLINSHED *Chron.* III. 1116/1 Lithquo, midwaie betwixt Sterling and Edenburgh. **1608** SHAKS. *Per.* v. i. 48 She..would..make a battrie through his defend parts, which now are midway stopt. **1692** R. L'ESTRANGE *Fables* cxxxiii. 123 The Hare lay'd himself down about Midway. **1794** MRS. RADCLIFFE *Myst. Udolpho* iv, The vapours floated mid-way down the mountains. **1812** J. J. HENRY *Accurate Acct. Heroes Campaign against Quebec* 192 About midway of the horn [of the moose],..there is a broad flat part. **1868** MISS YONGE *Cameos* (1879) I. xxvii. 225 Midway in the strait he met the French fleet. **1896** HOWELLS *Impressions & Exp.* 197 The band..playing in the afternoon midway of the long veranda. **1903** *Nation* (N.Y.) 17 Sept. 234 He died midway of his 70th year. **1927** *Sat. Even. Post* 24 Dec. 44/3 She stopped midway of her sentence.

2. † **a.** In a medium manner, tolerably. *Obs.*

1596 DALRYMPLE tr. *Leslie's Hist. Scot.* I. 117 Nathir sulde ony mervel heirof, quhen na man, quha leiues bot midway temperat, in the tounes of Scotland, is nocht sune rich.

D. *prep.* In the middle of. *rare.*

185. MAURY in Olmsted *Journ. Cotton Kingd.* (1861) I. 143 Norfolk [Virginia] is..midway the coast. **1868** SWINBURNE *Ess. & Stud.* (1875) 374 A boat is moored, and women..are about to enter it: one is already midway the steps of the pier.

mid-week. [f. MID *a.* + WEEK. Cf. MDu. *middeweke*, MHG. *mittwoche* (mod.G. *Mittwoch*), ON. *miðvika*, Wednesday.] The middle of the week. In Quaker language, a synonym for Fourth-day or Wednesday.

1707 S. SEWALL *Diary* 23 July, Midweek, visited Madam Leverett. **1898** *Daily News* 10 Jan. 8/7 By mid-week there was a good attendance on 'Change again.

b. *attrib.*

1706 S. SEWALL *Diary* 27 Apr., He had a Tooth pull'd out ..on Mid-week night. **1883** J. PARKER *Apost. Life* II. 35 Herein is a justification for mid-week meetings. **1898** *Cycling* 88 Two or more severe races on the Saturday, with perhaps a mid week meeting in between.

midwife (ˈmɪdwaɪf), *sb.* Forms: 4 **medewife**, **-wyve**, **meedwijf**, **midewyve**, **midwiif**, **mydwijf**, **-wyffe**, 4–5 **midwyf**, 4–6 **medwyf(e**, **mydwife**, **-wyf(e**, 5 **medwif(e**, **myddewyffe**, **medewyf**, **mydwif**, **-wyff**, 5–6 **midwyfe**, 6 **mede wif**, **meyd vyf**, 4– **midwife**. [f. either MID *a.* or MID *prep.* (*adv.*) + WIFE (in the older sense of 'woman'). On the former view the primary sense would be 'a woman by whose means the delivery is effected'; on the latter view, 'a woman who is *with* the mother at the birth'. The latter seems the more likely, though analogies are wanting for this mode of formation. The Sp. *comadre*, which is sometimes quoted, is not to the point, as the sense 'midwife' is merely developed from that of 'gossip', originally 'fellow-(god)mother'. The mod.G. *beifrau*, midwife's assistant, has also been compared.

The early (but not earliest) form *medewife* seems to be due to etymologizing association with MEED *sb.*, as *mede-* does not otherwise occur as a ME. variant of *mid-*. The colloquial pronunciation (ˈmɪdɪf) is now seldom heard.]

1. A woman who assists other women in childbirth, a female accoucheur.

1303 R. BRUNNE *Handl. Synne* 9633 Þe prest askede þe mydwyffe, 3yfe hyt were cristenede whan hyt hade lyffe. *a* **1400** *Maria Magd.* 78 in *Archiv Stud. neu. Spr.* XCI. 219 In alle my grete sorowe of my trauail of childe thou were to me a mydwife. *c* **1400** *Arth. & Merl.* 1001 (Kölbing), Ful glad was þo þe medwif And tok þeo child al so blyue. **1486** *Materials Hist. Hen. VII* (Rolls) II. 65 Alice Massy.. medwif to our derest wif the quene. **1502** *Ld. Treas. Acc. Scotl.* (1900) II. 47 Item..to the mede wif, xlij s. **1549** *Compl. Scot.* xv. 129 His mother vas ane meyd vyf. **1592** SHAKS. *Rom. & Jul.* I. iv. 54, I see Queene Mab hath beene with you: She is the Fairies Midwife. **1615** CROOKE *Body of Man* 269 Adde hereto the skilfull hand of the heads-woman or Midwife as we cal them. **1774** GOLDSM. *Nat. Hist.* (1776) II. 104 Women, in these circumstances, are said, by the midwives, to be all mouth and eyes. **1839** FR. A. KEMBLE *Resid. in Georgia* (1863) 28 A ludicrous visit this morning from the midwife of the estate.

† **2.** = MAN-MIDWIFE. *Obs.*

1577 B. GOOGE *Heresbach's Husb.* III. (1586) 139 It behoooueth the shepehearde to be skilfull in medcening of his cattell, and so cunning a midwife withal, as if neede require he may helpe his Ewe. **1711** SWIFT *Jrnl. to Stella* 29 Apr., The Admiral is your Walker's brother the midwife. **1770** *Phil. Trans.* LX. 451 Mr. John Latham, Surgeon and Midwife.

3. *fig.* One who or that which helps to produce or bring anything to birth.

1593 SHAKS. *Rich. II*, II. ii. 62 So Greene, thou art the midwife of my woe, And Bullinbrooke my sorrowes dismall heyre. **1658** OSBORN *Adv. Son* (1896) p. xxvii, There is another piece of mine ready to peep abroad, but that Mr. Wood, my Midwife, is so taken up with raising an estate in Ireland, as he cannot attend the press. **1700** DRYDEN *Pal. & Arc.* II. 562 And Midwife Time the ripen'd Plot to Murder brought. **1771** SMOLLETT *Humph. Cl.* 10 June, Let. i, This midwife of the Muses used exercise on horseback. **1883** J. T. MORSE *Jefferson* iii. (1885) 39 Jefferson..had acted as undertaker for the royal colonies and as midwife for the United States of America.

† **4.** An effeminate man. *Obs.*

1596 DRAYTON *Mortimeriados* T, No Apish fan-bearing Hermophradite, Coch-carried midwyfe, weake, effeminate.

5. midwife toad, a European toad, *Alytes obstetricans*, the male of which cares for the eggs until they hatch.

1901 H. GADOW in *Cambr. Nat. Hist.* VIII. vi. 158 *A[lytes] obstetricans*, the 'Midwife-toad', has the general appearance of a smooth toad... The pairing and the peculiar mode of taking care of the eggs by the male..has given it the specific name *obstetricans*, the midwife. **1934** *Times Lit. Suppl.* 16 June p. iv/2 A number of interesting toads have been received lately at the London Zoo, including a collection from Germany of 20 midwife toads with their eggs. **1954** G. DURRELL *Three Singles to Adventure* viii. 180 The midwife toad of Europe, instead of leaving its eggs in the nearest water to hatch unattended, hands them over to the male, who winds them round his hind legs and carries them about until they hatch. **1971** KOESTLER *Case of Midwife Toad* i. 14 Kammerer's undoing was a grotesque amphibian creature: the midwife toad, *Alytes obstetricans*.

midwife ('mɪdwaɪf), *v.* Now *rare* exc. in 2b. Also **midwive**. [f. MIDWIFE *sb.*]

1. *trans.* To act as midwife to.

1674 BREVINT *Saul at Endor* iv. 86 Whil'st she is elsewhere ..in a rich Abby Mid-wiving an Abbess, whom her Steward had unfortunately gotten with Child.

2. a. To help in bringing (a child) to the birth by acting the part of a midwife. Also with *out*.

1638 BP. H. KING in Sandys *Div. Poems* To Author 34 This Child of yours, borne without spurious blot, And Fairely Midwivd, as it was begot. **1653** in *Verney Mem.* (1894) III. 203 Madcapp saith though she sould you the mare, yett she did not sell you the colt, therefore she laies her commands on you, to midwife it out, and to tittle it upp. **1708** T. WARD *Eng. Ref.* (1710) 2 So Jove himself..Bred in his Head his Daughter Pallas, Whom Vulcan Midwiv'd [etc.]. **1736** AINSWORTH *Lat. Dict.* IV. s.v. *Pallas*, The daughter of Jupiter's own brain,..and midwived by Vulcan.

b. *fig.* To help in bringing to light or into being. (This sense not *rare*.)

1647 WARD *Simp. Cobler* (1843) 6 That he might watch a time to midwife out some ungracious Toleration for his own turne. **1725** BAILEY *Erasm. Colloq.* 124, I have something runs in my Mind, and I'm with Child to have it out... If it be a Dream, you shall be the Interpreters, or midwife it into the World. **1829** LAMB *Let. to H. C. Robinson* 27 Feb., Expectation was alert on the receipt of your strange-shaped present, while yet undisclosed from its fusc envelope... When midwifed into daylight, the gossips were at a loss to pronounce upon its species. **1959** *Times Lit. Suppl.* 4 Dec. 709/3 It also midwifed the late editor of *Commentary* himself, Elliot E. Cohen. **1971** B. MALAMUD *Tenants* 83 Lesser, dreaming of new light in his book, beheld in his dark thoughts Bill Spear, potential executioner, requesting him to midwife his bloody fable. **1972** *Sunday Tel.* 30 Apr. 7/7 As befitted the man who midwived 'That Was The Week That Was', Sir Hugh also got the best laugh at the Colonels' expense.

Hence '**midwifing** *vbl. sb.*

1382 WYCLIF *Exod.* i. 19 Thei forsothe han the kunnyng of mydwyuyng [Vulg. *ipsæ enim obstetricandi habent scientiam*]. **1750** WARBURTON in *W. & Hurd's Lett.* (1809) 47 Where was the Genius loci of the school when this disaster happened! perhaps in the office of Diana when her Temple was a burning, gone a midwifing to some Minerva of the brain.

'**midwifely**, *a.* [f. MIDWIFE *sb.* + -LY[1].] Of or pertaining to a midwife; also, characteristic of a midwife.

1607 MARKHAM *Caval.* I. (1617) 25 With other such like midwifely precepts, which I wish euery good breeder rather to hazard then proue the experiment. **1936** 'R. WEST' *Thinking Reed* i. 15 'When a woman is very tired,' he said, with a return of midwifely sententiousness, 'she does not know what is the matter with her.'

†'**midwifer.** (See quot.)

1825 D. D. DAVIS *Elem. Midwifery* 3 Julian Clement.. was soon after appointed to the new and lucrative office of Midwifer to the Princesses of France. **1828** M. RYAN *Man. Midwifery* p. vi, Professor Davis, of the London University, has proposed the term midwifer, for the word accoucheur.

midwifery ('mɪdwaɪfrɪ, 'mɪdwɪfrɪ, 'mɪdɪfrɪ). Also 5 **medewifry**, 6 **midwifrey**, **-rie**, 6–8 **midwifry**. [f. MIDWIFE *sb.* + -ERY.] The art or practice of assisting women in childbirth; the department of medical knowledge relating to this; obstetrics.

1483 *Cath. Angl.* 232/2 To be Medwyfe (MS. A. to do Medewifry), *obstetricare*. **1570** LEVINS *Manip.* 105/10 Midwifery, *obstetricium*. *a* **1673** CARYL in Spurgeon *Treas. Dav.* Ps. xxix. 9 He..shows his midwifery in helping these savage beasts when their pains come upon them. **1799** *Med. Jrnl.* II. 191 Dr. Osborn and Dr. Clarke propose to begin their lectures on the principles and practice of midwifery. **1845** MᶜCULLOCH *Acc. Brit. Empire* (1854) II. 361 The professors of Pathology,..Midwifery, and Clinical Medicine, receive no fixed salaries. **1900** H. G. GRAHAM *Soc. Life Scotl. in 18th C.* XIII. ii. (1901) 481 *note*, Midwifery was practised entirely by women.

fig. **1597** *Pilgr. Parnass.* I. 35 What wisedom manie winters hath begott Tyme's midwifrey at length shall bringe to light. *a* **1707** STEPNEY *To Earl of Carlisle* 61 So hasty fruits, and too ambitious flowers, Scorning the midwifery of ripening showers,..spring from th' unwilling earth.

b. *attrib.*

1791 J. JONES in Beddoes *Calculus* (1793) 30 Upon the principle of Smellie's midwifry forceps. **1799** *Med. Jrnl.* I. 81 The midwifery-wards in the house. **1829** GOOCH *Acc. Some Dis. Women* 75 A general practitioner, in large midwifery practice. **1884** M. MACKENZIE *Dis. Throat & Nose* II. 282 The ordinary midwifery forceps.

†'**midwifish**, *a. Obs.* [f. MIDWIFE *sb.* + -ISH.] (See quot.)

1755 JOHNSON, *Obstetrick*, midwifish, befitting a midwife; doing the midwife's office.

midwinter (mɪd'wɪntə(r)). [f. MID *a.* + WINTER. In OE. found both as compound and as two words with inflexion of the adj. Cf. OFris. *midwinter*, MDu., MLG. *mid-*, *middewinter*, MHG. *mittewinter* (mod.G. *mittwinter*), ON. *miðr vetr*, Sw. *midvinter*.] The middle of winter; spec. the winter solstice, Dec. 21st, or the period about that time. Also formerly applied to Christmas.

a **900** *O.E. Chron.* an. 827 Her mona aþistrode on middes wintres mæsse niht. *c* **1000** *Sax. Leechd.* III. 164 ȝif seo midwinter bið on wodnesdæȝ þonne bið heard winter. *c* **1200** *Trin. Coll. Hom.* 55 We auen forgult ure saules wille siðe mid winter com hiderwardes and ouercumen it. **1297** R. GLOUC. (Rolls) 7160 He sende after is barony at midewinter mid him to be. ? *a* **1400** *Morte Arth.* 77 Whas neuer syche noblay, in no manys tyme, Mad in mydwynter in tha weste marchys! **1590** GREENWOOD *Answ. Def. Read Prayers* 25 You compel men to pray against thunder and lightning at midd winter. **1697** DRYDEN *Virg. Georg.* I. 319 Nor cease your sowing till Mid-winter ends. **1882** A. W. WARD *Dickens* iii. 49 A journey across the Atlantic in midwinter is no child's-play even at the present day.

b. *attrib.* and *Comb.*, as ***midwinter month***, ***morning***, ***snow***, etc.; †**midwinter('s) day**, Christmas Day; †**midwinter('s) eve**, **even**, **night**, Christmas eve; †**midwinter('s) tide**, Christmas time.

1154 *O.E. Chron.* an. 1135, & halechede him to kinge on *mide-wintre-daei. *c* **1205** LAY. 22905 A midewinteres dæi. **1387** TREVISA *Higden* (Rolls) V. 19 Me schulde synge þe masses wiþ Gloria in excelsis a mydwynter day [orig. *in festo Natalis Domini*]. **1867** FREEMAN *Norm. Conq.* (1877) I. iii. 71 On Midwinter-day, eight hundred years back. **1300–1400** *R. Gloucester's Chron.* (Rolls) App. XX. 141 In þe þridde ȝere of his crouning A *midewinteres eue to bedeforde he com. *c* **1420** *Chron. Vilod.* 4081 Gerleyne was þat monnus name y-wys þe whiche in *midwintrus-ȝevyn to þat chirche dude gone. **1814** WORDSW. *Excurs.* v. 804 Three dark *midwinter months. **1896** *Atlantic Monthly* Feb. 203 How well the rapture of that frosty *midwinter morning is remembered. *c* **1200** *Trin. Coll. Hom.* 7 Swo abiden ure helendes tocume þat neihlacheð nuðe fram dai to daie and beð on *mide-wintres niht. *a* **1450** MYRC *Festial* 51 Þys geanology þat ys red yn mydwyntyr-nyght. **1877** BRYANT *Sella* 63 Two slippers, white As the *midwinter snow. *c* **1030** *Eccl. Laws of Cnut* Prol., On ðære halȝan *midewintres tide. *c* **1330** *Amis & Amil.* 1887 It was mid winter tide.

c. *quasi-adj.* (*fig.*), cold as midwinter.

1870 MORRIS *Earthly Par.* III. IV. 29 Because youth and maid Midwinter words of hope that day had said Before the altars. **1884** TENNYSON *Becket* I. ii, 'Tis known you are midwinter to all women.

mid-winterly, *a.* [f. MIDWINTER + -LY[1].] = MID-WINTRY.

1892 *Pall Mall G.* 16 Apr. 4/3 The thoughts of Londoners ..will naturally turn..to amusements more in accordance with the mid-winterly temperature.

mid-wintry, *a.* [f. MIDWINTER + -Y.] Of or pertaining to midwinter.

1852 MUNDY *Our Antipodes* (1857) 4 At 3 P.M. of an Australian mid-wintry but splendid day the anchor was dropped in that snug little haven. **1900** *Westm. Gaz.* 27 Aug. 8/1 The stars last night were of a mid-wintry brightness.

midwise ('mɪdwaɪz), *adv.* [f. MID *a.* + WISE *sb.*] In a medium or moderate manner.

1889 J. PAYNE *Alaeddin* 110 They ceased not to live at their sufficiency, midwise [betwixt rich and poor], without excessive spending or squandering.

†'**midwoman.** *Obs.* A midwife.

a **1300** *Cursor M.* 5543 Bremli command he and badd Midwimmen be o þe self land.

mid world. †**a.** = MIDDLE EARTH (*obs.*). **b.** An intermediate 'world' (in various applications of the word).

c **1530** tr. *Erasmus' Serm. Child Jesus* (1901) 8 Who is of wider imperye than he, whiche they in heuen magnifie, they in helle tremble at, this mydde worlde humbly worshyppeth ..? **1853** LYNCH *Self-Improv.* iii. 61 Poetry is seen in him; and the mid world of feudality and chivalry shines around in a light soft and lustrous. **1898** *Westm. Gaz.* 3 Dec. 3/2 The sombre desolation of the mid-world between the snows and the pastures.

mid-year. [f. MID *a.* + YEAR[1].]

†**1.** Midsummer. *Obs.*

c **1375** *Sc. Leg. Saints* xxv. (*Julian*) 446 þe chyld semyt þan fere mare clere þane is þe sowne in myd-ȝere.

2. *U.S.* Used *attrib.* in ***Mid-year examinations*** (also *Mid-years*), the Harvard university examinations held in the middle of the academic year (in January).

1897 HOWELLS *Landl. Lion's Head* 216 He had reckoned upon..a dance after the Mid-Years. *Ibid.* 236 A large party was given on the eve of the Harvard Mid-Year Examinations.

3. The middle of the year. Also *attrib.*

1901 *U.S. Dept. Agric. Yearbk.* 154 To teachers the series of meetings is a series of mid-year institutes. **1909** *Cent. Dict.* Suppl. s.v., Rents due at the midyear. **1932** *Irish Press* 10 Mar. 5/3 This corresponded to an annual rate of 14·6 per thousand of the estimated mid-year population for the year 1931. **1973** E. TAYLOR *Serpent under It* (1974) v. 82 This may set us back months. Instead of getting our degrees at midyears, we'll probably have to wait now until next June.

midyl, obs. form of MIDDLE *sb.*

Miehle ('miːlə). The name of Robert *Miehle*, 19th-century American printer, used *attrib.* or *absol.* to designate a flat-bed, cylinder printing press invented by him in 1884, or later developments of this machine.

1887 *Inland Printer* Oct. 35/1 (*heading*) The Miehle two-revolution press. **1894** *Amer. Dict. Printing & Bookmaking* 378/1 *Miehle Press*, a new press, lately devised by Robert Miehle, a pressman of Chicago. The bed is carried in harmony with the movement of the cylinder while printing, then it is gradually slowed up, carried smoothly over the centre, and returned for the back movement... Great speed is claimed for this press. **1915** *Southward's Mod. Printing* (ed. 3) II. viii. 101 As a standard machine of the very highest class, the Miehle is widely in use. *Ibid.* 102 (*caption*) Miehle Two-Revolution Press. *Ibid.* 104 Miehle presses are also used in tandem, coupling up two or more machines for the production of colour work. **1963** *Printing & Mind of Man: Catal. Display of Printing Mechanisms & Printed Materials Brit. Mus. & Earls Court* (Earls Court Section) 80/2 The Miehle machine, in several models, continues to be marketed and sold all over the world. The cylinder revolves continuously, is raised after the impression in order to clear the forme during its second revolution, and is then brought down on impression again by the action of a cam and eccentrics. **1966** BERRY & POOLE *Ann. Printing* 258/2 Cassell's were the first printers in this country to import Miehles... For many years the Miehle was in a class by itself for the new three-colour letterpress. **1973** J. MORAN *Printing Presses* xi. 159 The Miehle, which had great impressional strength, accurate register and durability.. kept its lead for some eighty years.

mieke, mieknesse, obs. ff. MEEK, -NESS.

mielch, mielde, obs. forms of MILCH, MILDS.

mieldew, obs. form of MILDEW.

miele, variant of MEAL *sb.*[3] *Obs.*

mielie ('miːlɪ). *S. Afr.* [Afrikaans.] = MEALIE. Also *attrib.* and *Comb.* as ***mielie cob***, ***land***; **mieliepap**, mealie meal porridge (cf. quots. s.v. MEALIE).

1804 J. T. VAN DER KEMP in *Trans.* [London] *Missionary Soc.* (ed. 2) I. 438 There is another kind of corn, which they call *bona*, and is known in the Colony by the name of *meelis*. **1818** G. BARKER *Diary* 7 Dec. (MS.), Began to clear the beans & mielies in the garden. **1835** A. SMITH *Diary* 28 Nov. (1940) II. 285 The Hottentots..had no pumpkins, melons, mielies nor calabases. **1926** O. SCHREINER *From Man to Man* i. 78 Near the mielie lands. *Ibid.* iii. 117 The maids were lighting the evening fires with mielie cobs. **1952** *Cape Times* 11 Jan. 3/4 The nearby Vergelegen Estate with its acres of corn and mielies. **1953** P. ABRAHAMS *Return to Goli* vi. 200 It was the kind of food I had not eaten for fourteen years: a thick *mielie pap*. **1959** *Cape Times* 26 Oct. 9/4 The mieliepap ..is the staple food of millions in Africa. **1971** *Cape Herald* (Bonus) 15 May 5/1 (Advt.), With mieliepap you need never fear that some of the goodness has been lost in making. **1974** *Eastern Province Herald* 23 July 13 He is wise to discard his bowler hat when crossing a field of mielies.

Mielmesse, obs. form of MICHAELMAS.

miemite ('maɪəmaɪt). *Min.* [Named by M. H. Klaproth (*Miemit*) in 1802, from *Miemo* in Tuscany, its locality: see -ITE.] A greenish variety of Dolomite.

1819 BRANDE *Chem.* 225 Magnesium. A variety found at Miemo, in Tuscany, has been called Miemite. **1843** PORTLOCK *Geol.* 214 Miemite of a rich yellowish-green, or oil yellow colour.

mien (miːn), *sb.*[1] Only *literary*. Forms: 6 **men(e**, 6–7 **meane**, 6–8 **mine**, 7 **meine**, 7–8 **meen**, **mein**, 7– **mien**. [Prob. orig. an aphetic form of DEMEAN *sb.*; afterwards partly assimilated in sense and form to F. *mine*, expression or aspect of countenance, hence *gen.* look, appearance, whence G. *miene* in the same sense.

The origin of F. *mine* is uncertain; connexion with Rom. *minare* (F. *mener*) to lead, is impossible. A Celtic origin has been suggested: cf. Breton *min* muzzle, beak, Welsh *min* lip, Cornish *mein*, *min* lip, mouth, Irish *men* mouth.]

The air, bearing, carriage or manner of a person, as expressive of character or mood.

1513 DOUGLAS *Æneis* VIII. xi. 20 Lyk as he had dyspyt and bostand men. *Ibid.* XII. Prol. 210 To hant bawdry and onlesum mene. **1593** J. ELIOT *Fruits* 167 He is an Alchymist by his mine [F. *mine*]. **1596** SPENSER *F.Q.* VI. ix. 11 Her rare demeanure, which him seemed So farre the meane of shepheards to excell, As that [etc.]. **1632** J. HAYWARD tr. *Biondi's Eromena* 158 The Princesse, who had now converted her widdowly meane into fresh teares of conjugall affection. **1713** STEELE *Englishman* No. 1. 2 It is a Jest..to talk of amending the Mein and Air of a Cripple. **1784** COWPER *Tiroc.* 829 See..Fops at all corners, lady-like in mien. **1865** TROLLOPE *Belton Est.* v, He could assume a look and mien that were almost noble. **1887** RUSKIN *Præterita* II. 174 Gordon's downcast mien did not change.

†**b.** *transf.* Appearance (of a thing). *Obs.*

a **1641** SUCKLING *Lett.* Wks. (1646) 60 Nothing, Madam, has worse Mine than counterfeit sorrow. **1684** BURNET *Th. Earth* I. I. iii. 31 Then what can have more the figure and meen of a ruine, than Crags and Rocks, and Cliffs. **1695** WOODWARD *Nat. Hist. Earth* I. 18 Some..had..Metallick or Mineral Matter..insinuated into their substance..so as to disguise them very much, and give them a face and mien extremely unlike to that of those Shells [etc.].

¶**c.** Expression (of the face). *Obs. rare.* [After F. *mine du visage.*]

1680 H. MORE *Apocal. Apoc.* 196 The mien of his face conjoyned with the posture of his body betrayed such a pitch of veneration and worship, as [etc.]. **1697** BENTLEY *Phal.* xiii. 51 The same word is inverted to a new sense and notion; which in tract of time makes as observable a change in the air and features of a language, as Age makes in the lines and mien of a Face. **1699** *Ibid.* Pref. 96 Another happy phrase, which he [Boyle] says, I have newly minted, is the Meen of a Face; which as he takes it, is much the same thing with the Behaviour of a Look or the Carriage of a Smile... Meen does not signifie behaviour, even when it's spoken of the whole Person, but the Air and Look that results from it.

d. Phrases (chiefly Gallicisms). †***with full mien***, undisguised (*obs.*). †***to make good mien upon***, to put a good face upon (*obs.*). ***to make*** (*a*) ***mien to*** do or *of* doing (something), to pretend to do or make a show of doing (something).

1649 G. DANIEL *Trinarch., Hen. IV*, xlix, That Masque put off, she comes in wth full Meine. **1683** TEMPLE *Mem.* Wks. 1731 I. 457 The Court there were surpriz'd,..but made good Mien upon it, took it gently. **1711** BLACKADER *Diary* 25 July, The French made a mien to oppose us. **1851** GALLENGA *Italy* 253 The Austrians made mien of holding out to the last.

mien (miːn), *sb.*² [Chinese, lit. = wheat flour.] Wheat flour noodles. (Cf. CHOW MEIN.)

1934 in WEBSTER. **1936** P. FLEMING *News from Tartary* v. ix. 235 At noon they woke me for a meal of mien and boiled vegetables. **1950** R. ALLEY *Leaves from Sandan Notebk.* 46 They gave him a meal of mien. **1956** B. Y. CHAO *How to cook & eat in Chinese* xix. 218 Wheat is eaten more than rice as the staple food... When it is eaten wet, it is in the form of *mien*, or unraised noodles. **1971** N. FROUD *Far Eastern Cooking for Pleasure* 82 *Mien*, Chinese noodle or wun tun paste. This dough is used for Chinese noodles, wun tun and various other patties and dumplings.

†**mien**, *v. Obs. rare*⁻¹. [f. MIEN *sb.*¹] *refl.* To comport oneself (in a specified way). Cf. DEMEAN *v.*¹ 6.

c **1680** BEVERIDGE *Serm.* (1729) I. 354 Methinks I see him looking upon them, and miening himself as angry with them.

miene, obs. form of MINE *sb.*

mier: see MIRE, MYOUR.

mierie, -ness, obs. forms of MIRY, -NESS.

mierkat, var. MEERKAT.

miersite ('maɪəzaɪt). *Min.* [f. the name of Sir Henry Alexander *Miers* (1858–1942), English mineralogist + -ITE¹.] An iodide of silver and copper, (Ag, Cu)I (with the ratio of silver to copper approximately 4:1), which is found as yellow isometric crystals at Broken Hill, New South Wales, Australia.

1898 L. J. SPENCER in *Nature* 14 Apr. 574/2 The new mineral has been named in honour of Mr. H. A. Miers, F.R.S., Professor of Mineralogy at Oxford, who first correctly determined the crystalline form of marshite, a mineral so closely resembling miersite in appearance that the two species are only distinguished by chemical tests. **1901** [see ISOMORPHOUSLY *adv.*]. **1922** *Mineral. Abstr.* I. 305 Silver iodide and copper iodide when fused together show.. specks of birefringent iodyrite in a base of isotropic miersite. **1951** C. PALACHE et al. *Dana's Syst. Min.* (ed. 7) II. 20 Both miersite and iodyrite are obtained by metathical [*read* metathetical] reaction in water solution at ordinary temperature.

Miesian ('miːzɪən), *a.* and *sb.* [Name of the German-American architect, L. *Mies* van der Rohe (1886–1969) + -IAN.] **A.** *adj.* Of, pertaining to, or characteristic of the style of architecture of Mies van der Rohe. **B.** *sb.* A devotee or follower of Mies's style.

1956 *Archit. Rev.* CXX. 238/2 The job has some obviously Miesian passages. **1958** H. R. HITCHCOCK *Archit. 19th & 20th Cent.* III. xxiii. 390 The 'Miesian' is today almost a sub-school of the new architecture. **1960** A. DREXLER *Ludwig Mies van der Rohe* 32 The measure of Mies's authority is this: it no longer seems possible to rebel against the Miesian discipline except in Miesian terms. **1963** tr. *G. Hatje's Encycl. Mod. Archit.* 194/2 Inside the enclosure there was the usual Miesian spatial continuity. **1965** M. BRADBURY *Stepping Westward* 10 The new crematorium..was designed by a devout Miesian. **1969** *Archit. Rev.* CXLVI. 313 A long, low, not quite Miesian exercise in structural and not so structural steel and glass. **1973** *Current Affairs Bull.* (Sydney) Aug. 8/2 The shell-shapes..are of Miesian derivation.

‖**mietjie** ('miːtʃiː, 'mici). Also **meitjie, michi.** [Afrikaans.] = *Klaas's cuckoo* (KLAAS).

1853 *Edin. New Philos. Jrnl.* LV. 82 The pretty notes of the *michi* and *diedrick* further enliven the growing day. **1936** E. L. GILL *First Guide S. Afr. Birds* 108 The usual call of Klaas's Cuckoo is quite well represented by its Afrikaans name 'mietjie'. **1939** [see DIEDERIK, DIEDRIK]. **1970** MCLACHLAN & LIVERSIDGE *Roberts's Birds. S. Afr.* (ed. 3) 242 The Afrikaans name [of Klaas's cuckoo] is onomatopoeic, 'Meitjie' and gives the call pretty closely.

mieu, mieve, obs. forms of MEW, MOVE.

miff (mɪf), *sb. colloq.* and *dial.* [Perh. imitative of an instinctive expression of disgust; cf. early mod.G. *muff* int. (also *miff-muff*), whence *muff* sb., a manifestation of disgust (see M. Heyne in Grimm s.v.).] A fit of peevish ill-humour; a petty quarrel; a huff, tiff: esp. in phr. ***to get, have, take a miff***, † ***to take miff***, ***to be in a miff***.

1623 C. BUTLER *Fem. Mon.* v. (ed. 2) L iv, This is not to be done..lest some of the Bees take a miffe and goe home again. **1726** ARBUTHNOT *Let. to Swift* 8 Nov., I gave your service to Lady Harvey. She is in a little sort of a miff about a ballad, that was wrote on her. **1749** FIELDING *Tom Jones* III. vi, When a little quarrel, or miff, as it is vulgarly called, arose between them. **1821** MRS. NATHAN *Langreath* I. 136, I should take miff every time I come into your house. **1825** J. NEAL *Bro. Jonathan* I. 374 If she should git another miff, we'd never be able to appease her. **1844** WILLIS *Lady Jane* II. 716 Like ladies in a miff who won't explain! **1854** DE QUINCEY *War* Wks. 1890 VIII. 378 We have a French anecdote..which ascribes one bloody war to the accident of a little 'miff' arising between the king and his minister upon some such trifle as [etc.]. **1894** T. HARDY *Life's Little Ironies* (ed. 3) 232 'Twill cause 'em to kick up a bit of a miff, for certain.

miff (mɪf), *a. rare.* [f. MIFF *sb.*] Out of humour, offended (*with*).

The first quot. may belong to MIFF *v.*

1797 COLERIDGE *Sonn., To Simplicity*, But should a friend and I Grow cool and *miff*, O! I am *very* sad! **1802** W. TAYLOR *Let. to Southey* 6 Feb. in Robberds *Mem.* I. 447 You are right about Burnett, but being miff with him myself, I would not plead against him in the least particular.

miff (mɪf), *v.* [f. MIFF *sb.*]

1. *intr.* To take offence *with* or *at*. Also *transf.* of a plant, ***to miff off***, to go off, fade.

1797 LADY A. BARNARD *Lett.* (1901) 73 We wish to have no quarrels and no miffs. They had wished to miff with us, but we are so civil,..they cannot make it out. **1879** MISS JACKSON *Shropsh. Word-bk.*, *Miff*, to take offence hastily. ''E miffed at it direc'ly.' **1883** *N. & Q.* 6 Oct. 267/2 A curious word came under my notice of late with regard to a flower losing its strength and beauty. I was speaking to a Surrey gardener about some fading plants, and he remarked that they were 'miffing off'. **1895** ELLACOMBE *Glouc. Garden* xviii, Another alpine which is very apt to 'miff off' if grown in the open border. **1907** R. FARRER *My Rock-garden* v. 71 Here it flowers once, then it miffs off without any apparent reason. **1960** F. C. STERN *Chalk Garden* vii. 73 We have sometimes been successful with it [*sc.* a peony], but it miffs off for no apparent reason.

2. *trans.* To put out of humour. Chiefly in *pa. pple.*

1811 C. MATHEWS *Let.* Dec. in A. Mathews *Mem. Charles Mathews* (1838) II. 177 You give me much gratification by your explanation of the word that miffed me. **1824** SCOTT *Redgauntlet* let. xii, 'What needs she another..?' answered my Thetis, a little miffed perhaps—to use the women's phrase—that I turned the conversation upon my former partner. **1851** MAYNE REID *Scalp Hunt.* xxx. 230 'No-o', slowly drawled Rube, apparently 'miffed' at being thus interrupted. **1889** *Kansas City* (Missouri) *Times & Star* 27 Nov., Dr. G. W. Fitzpatrick..is badly miffed because he wasn't appointed surveyor of the port. **1904** E. ROBINS *Magnetic North* I. 252 Don't get mifft, Colonel. **1907** *N.Y. Even. Post* (Semi-Weekly ed.) 2 Sept. 4 He is a little miffed to find that there are other lawyers in the Cabinet whose advice the President prefers to his own. **1957** *New Yorker* 26 Oct. 82/2 The feminine contingent..was..more than a little miffed, to learn that London..had got married. **1972** *Times Lit. Suppl.* 18 Feb. 173/3 Understandably, he is more than a little miffed by all this. **1973** *Daily Tel.* (Colour Suppl.) 23 Feb. 54/2 He told us a slightly improper story. The girls were not shocked but were rather miffed at his thinking they would not be.

miffish ('mɪfɪʃ), *a.* [f. MIFF *sb.* + -ISH¹.] = MIFFY *a.* So **'miffishly** *adv.*

1957 *New Statesman* 2 Nov. 572/2 For all his shyness and laconicism, he had a green heart—miffish and virginal perhaps, but seldom sentimental. **1968** E. HYAMS *Gardener's Bedside Bk.* 35 Failure with this lily was more common than success for so many years that gardeners still have the impression that it is very difficult and miffish. **1968** 'B. MATHER' *Springers* i. 5 He went on miffishly: 'Did I ask for the job?' **1973** —— *Snowline* xv. 180 There was a lot of banter..directed at the earnest ones, who received it in silent and miffish dignity.

miffy ('mɪfɪ), *a. colloq.* and *dial.* Also 8 **mifty.** [f. MIFF *sb.* + -Y.] Liable to 'take a miff'; easily offended. Also *transf.* of a plant.

a **1700** B. E. *Dict. Cant. Crew*, *Mifty*, apt to take Pet, or be out of Humor. **1725** in *New Cant. Dict.* **1739** CIBBER *Apol.* (1756) I. 221 She mutter'd out her words in a sort of mifty manner at my low opinion of her. **1810** BERESFORD *Bibliosophia*, etc. 119 And very lucky it was, by the way (considering how very miffy those Ladies are said to have been). **1835–40** HALIBURTON *Clockm.* (1862) 126 Well, says I, I'll tell you if you won't be miffy with me. **1850** GLENNY *Hand-bk. Fl. Gard.* 220 This [*Lotus Jacobæus*] is rather a delicate, or what is called a 'miffy' plant, being liable to damp off in winter. **1871** S. HIBBERD *Amateur's Flower Garden* 146 *M*[*yosotis*] *dissitiflora*..is a most valuable species for early flowers, but 'miffy', and therefore needing perpetual renewal. **1879** MISS JACKSON *Shropsh. Word-bk.*, *Miffy*, apt to take offence; touchy. **1894** BLACKMORE *Perlycross* 301 The slightest change of human weather is inevitably fatal to our very miffy plant [*sc.* gratitude]. **1907** R. FARRER *My Rock-garden* i. 19 A sound perennial in one place, soil and climate, but a miffy delicate untrustworthy creature half a mile away. **1934** *Gardeners' Chronicle* 19 May 330/3 A few plants invariably become 'miffy', from no apparent reason, and die out.

Hence **'miffily** *adv.*, in a miffy manner; **'miffiness**, the condition of being miffy.

1845 FORD *Handbk. Spain* I. 84 We must never compare the sensitiveness of the punctilious hidalgo with the vulgar miffyness of the newly-enriched upstart. **1958** 'A. BRIDGE' *Portuguese Escape* 104 'All right, all right,' Melplash said, rather miffily. 'There's no rush.'

mig (mɪg). *Obs.* exc. *dial.* Forms: 1 **micge, migga, migge,** 3 **migge,** 5– **mig.** [OE. *micge* wk. fem., *migga* wk. masc.:—prehistoric *migjôn-, -on, f. *mig- wk.-grade of OTeut. *mîg- (OE. *mīȝan*, ON. *míga*) to make water, cogn. w. L. *mingĕre*.] Urine; or the drainings from manure. Also *fig.*

c **1000** *Sax. Leechd.* I. 354 Drince eft buccan micgan. *Ibid.* III. 132, & his [*sc.* the man's] migga byþ hwit. *a* **1225** *Ancr. R.* 402 And tet [*sc.* Greek fire] ne mei noðing bute migge, and sond, and eisil, ase me seið, acwenchen. *c* **1400** *Apol. Loll.* 58 þe swyn of vnclennes drowniþ himself in þe mig of lecherie. **1868** ATKINSON *Cleveland Gloss.*, *Mig*, liquid manure; the fluid which runs away from the midden, or from the stall drains of a cow-house, &c.

†**migale.** *Obs. rare*⁻¹. [ad. L. *mygalē*, ad. Gr. μυγαλῆ, f. μῦς mouse + γαλέη weasel.] A shrew-mouse or field-mouse.

1382–8 WYCLIF *Lev.* xi. 30 Thes forsothe among polutid thinges shulen be holde..a mygal. **1398** TREVISA *Barth. De P.R.* XVIII. lxxv. (1495) 829 A fyrette hyghte Migale. **1609** BIBLE (Douay) *Lev.* xi. 30 The migale, and the camelean.

mige, migge, obs. forms of MIDGE.

Mighel(l)mas, Mighill: see MICHAELMAS, MICHAEL.

might (maɪt), *sb.* Forms: 1 **meaht, maht, mæht, meht, mieht, miht,** 2–3 **maht(e, meht(e,** 3 **mæht(e,** *Ormin* **mahht(e,** (3 **mayht**), 2–4 **miht(e,** 3 *Ormin* **mihht,** 3–4 **miȝt(e, myht(e,** 3–5 **myȝt(e,** (3 **miȝhte,** 4 **mit**), 3–6 *Sc.* **micht,** 4–6 **myght(e,** *Sc.* **mycht,** (4–5 **mygth(e,** 5 **myhth,** 6 **miht, mighte**), 3– **might.** See also MAUGHT, to which some of the early forms above may belong. [OE. *miht*, Anglian and Kentish *mæht*, fem. = OS. *maht* (Du. *macht*), OHG., MHG. *maht* (mod.G. *macht*), Goth. *mahts*:—OTeut. *mahti-z f. root *mag- to be able or powerful: see MAY *v.*¹ ON. had *mátt-r:—*mahtu-z from the same root, whence MAUCHT; the late OIcel. *makt* fem., MSw. *makt* (mod.Sw. *makt, magt*) fem., Da. *magt* are from German.

Outside Teut. a corresponding formation exists in OSl. *moštĭ* (:—pre-Slav. *mokti-s).]

1. a. The quality of being able (to do what is desired); operative power (whether great or small). Const. *inf. Obs.* exc. *poet.*

971 *Blickl. Hom.* 31 Forðon..he [*sc.* the Devil] næniȝe mehte wið us nafaþ. *c* **1200** ORMIN 2956 Drihhtin me ȝifeþ witt & mihht To forþenn wel min wille. **1297** R. GLOUC. (Rolls) 4853 þanne vyȝteþ hii aȝen vs, as moche as is hor miȝte. *a* **1300** *Cursor M.* 26271 þar-til has simple preist na might..wit-vten biscop ordinance. *c* **1384** CHAUCER *H. Fame* I. 41 Yf that spiritis haue the myght To make folke to dreme a-nyght. ?**1464** *Paston Lett.* II. 171 Ze have no myght, neyther power to absteyne and rewle yourself. **1500–20** DUNBAR *Poems* xxxvii. 13 The knychtis..Fell doun as deid, afferit of his licht, Quhome to behald thay had no grace nor mycht. **1606** SHAKS. *Tr. & Cr.* III. ii. 164 For to be wise and loue, Exceedes mans might, that dwels with gods aboue. **1850** TENNYSON *In Mem.* cviii, What profit lies in barren faith,..tho' with might To scale the heaven's highest height. **1869** M. ARNOLD *Urania*, But our ignoble souls lack might.

b. In various phrases; esp. ***over might***, beyond one's powers; † ***to lay might***, to do one's utmost. *Obs.* exc. in the phrase ***with all one's might***, with all one's powers; to the utmost of one's ability.

c **1175** *Lamb. Hom.* 39 þu scalt sahtnien þa þe beoð unisahte mid alle þine mahte. *c* **1200** ORMIN 945 Follȝhenn itt [hiss lare] Aȝȝ affterr ȝure mihhte. *c* **1275** *Passion our Lord* 111 in *O.E. Misc.* 40 þu [Iudas] hit seyst..and dest al þine mihte. *c* **1290** *S. Eng. Leg.* I. 30/35 [They] duden him harm bi al heore miȝhte. *a* **1300** *Cursor M.* 19625 It es to þe vte ouer might A-gain þe stranger for to fight. *Ibid.* 26294 If ..þou haf oft-sith laid might [*c* 1375 *Fairf.* done þi miȝt] his wrangwis liuelade for to right. **1390** GOWER *Conf.* III. 156 Cinichus..A Somme which was over myht Preide of his king Antigonus. *c* **1460** *Towneley Myst.* xv. 28 Tyll egypp shall thou fare with all the myght thou may. **1500–20** DUNBAR *Poems* x. 36 Be myrthfull now, at all ȝour mycht. **1611** BIBLE *Eccl.* ix. 10 Whatsoeuer thy hand findeth to doe, doe it with thy might. **1667** MILTON *P.L.* IV. 346 Th' unwieldly Elephant To make them mirth us'd all his might. **1782** COWPER *J. Gilpin* 92 He grasped the mane with both his hands, And eke with all his might.

c. As an attribute of impersonal agents: Power, efficacy, virtue. *Obs.* exc. *poet.* †Also in particularized sense, a specific virtue or active property.

c **1000** *Sax. Leechd.* I. 126 ȝenim þas ylcan wyrte heo ot sumre wundurlicre mihte helpeð. *c* **1175** *Lamb. Hom.* 47 For heo [sunne dei] hafð mid hire þreo wurdliche mihte. *c* **1200** *Trin. Coll. Hom.* 119 Fire haueð on him þre mihtes. *a* **1300** *Cursor M.* 8454 Lerd he, Bath o tres, and gress fele, Quil war þair mightes soth and lele. *c* **1386** CHAUCER *Sqr.'s T.* 125 This mirrour..Hath swich a myght þat men may in it see When ther shal fallen any Aduersitee. *c* **1402** LYDG. *Compl. Bl. Knt.* 87 The water was so holsome and vertuous, Thurgh myghte of herbes growynge there beside. **1590** SPENSER *F.Q.* I. vii. 30 One pretious stone Of wondrous worth, and eke of wondrous mights. **1599** SHAKS. *Hen. V*, II. i. 70 An oath of mickle might. **1600** —— *A.Y.L.* III. v. 82 Dead Shepheard, now I find thy saw of might. *c* **1600** —— *Sonn.* lvi, Appetite, Which but to-day by feeding is allay'd, To-morrow sharpen'd in his former might. **1820** SHELLEY *Witch of Atlas* 177 Liquors..whose healthful might Could medicine the sick soul to happy sleep. —— *Hymn Merc.* lxv,

I swear by these most gloriously-wrought portals (It is, you will allow, an oath of might). **1832** TENNYSON *Eleanore* vii, In thee all passion becomes passionless,..Losing his fire and active might.

†**d.** *pl.* Active powers (of the heart, soul, brain, etc.). ***the fivefold mights***: the five senses. *Obs.*

c **1175** *Lamb. Hom.* 75 Þe alde deouel blou on adam and on eue..swa þet heore fif-falde mihte hom wes al binumen. *c* **1200** *Trin. Coll. Hom.* 35 And þurh þes fifealde gultes forleas þe fiffeald mihten þe god him ȝef. *c* **1340** HAMPOLE *Psalter* xii. 6 When all þe myghtis of my hert ere raised in till þe soun of heuen. *c* **1380** WYCLIF *Wks.* (1880) 3 Siþþe þei myȝten..ocupie al þe myȝtis boþe of soule & body be þat clene religioun. *Ibid.* 217 Bi þis glotonye..þei..lesen..myȝttis of þe soule, as vnderstondynge, mynde & reson. *a* **1400** HYLTON *Scala Perf.* (W. de W. 1494) II. iv, Thenne shall the soule receyue the hole and the full felynge of god in all myghtes of it. **14..** *Stockh. Med. MS.* II. 64 in *Anglia* XVIII. 309 It comfortyth þe stomak & mythys degestyf. **1450–1530** *Myrr. our Ladye* 191 Adam loued god wyth all the myghtes of hys harte. **1460–70** *Bk. Quintessence* 17 If it ..a-sende vp to þe heed, it troubliþ alle þe myȝtis of þe brayn.

†**2.** Bodily strength (great or small). *Obs.*

c **1000** *Sax. Leechd.* II. 254 ȝif hæto oþþe meht ne wyrne læt him blod. *a* **1250** *Owl & Night.* 1670, & wiltu, wrecche, wiþ me vyhte? Na, nay, nauestu none Mihte. *a* **1300** *Cursor M.* 7090 He [Samson] had tuenti mens might. **1470–85** MALORY *Arthur* VI. xiii. 203 Now by my feythe..I wylle preue sir kayes myghte. **1500–20** DUNBAR *Poems* li. 17 He is ane mastyf, mekle of mycht. **1587** MASCALL *Govt. Cattle, Horses* (1627) 102 Whereas a horse is weak in couering, so much weaker shal the colt be in growing & might. **1601** SHAKS. *Jul. C.* II. iv. 8, I haue a mans minde, but a womans might. **1611** BIBLE *Jer.* li. 30 Their might hath failed, they became as women.

3. Great or transcendent power or strength; mightiness. Now somewhat *rhetorical.*

a. As an attribute of God.

971 *Blickl. Hom.* 31 Forþon his miht bið a ece, his rice ne bið ȝewemmed. *c* **1175** *Lamb. Hom.* 59 In eorðe in heuene in his mahte. **1567** *Satir. Poems Reform.* iv. 23 And puir anis did pryse thair Maker of mycht. **1650** *Scotch Psalms* XCIII. iv, The Lord that is on high is more of might by far Than noise of many waters is. **1781** COWPER *Conversat.* 473 Fruits of his love and wonders of his might.

b. Of persons or living beings, nations, etc., with reference to bodily or mental power, commanding influence, military resources, extent of dominion, etc.

a **900** tr. *Bæda's Hist.* II. viii. [ix.] (1890) 120 ȝeweox meaht eorðlices rices [of Eadwine]. **1297** R. GLOUC. (Rolls) 547 Þes were as þre kinges & men of muchel miȝte. **1390** GOWER *Conf.* III. 4 Ther mai nothing his [love's] miht withstonde. *a* **1400** *Pol. Rel. & L. Poems* (1903) 262 Loue, þou art of mikel mit. *c* **1400** MAUNDEV. (Roxb.) xxvii. 126 He es a grete lord of myȝt and of landes. *c* **1460** FORTESCUE *Abs. & Lim. Mon.* ix. (1885) 129 We haue sene a subgett off the ffrench kynges in such myght, þat he hath gyven bataill to the same kyng, and putt hym to flight. *c* **1475** *Rauf Coilȝear* 182 The gentill King, Charlis of micht. **1500–20** DUNBAR *Poems* lxxxviii. 7 Of merchauntis full of substaunce and myght. **1597** SHAKS. *2 Hen. IV*, IV. v. 130 England, shall giue him Office, Honor, Might. **1667** MILTON *P.L.* IV. 986 On th' other side Satan allarm'd Collecting all his might dilated stood. **1697** DRYDEN *Virg. Georg.* III. 363 When he [*sc.* a bull] stands collected in his might. **1818** SHELLEY *Eugan. Hills* 196 As divinest Shakespeare's might Fills Avon and the world with light. **1857** GLADSTONE *Sp.* 3 Mar., That metamorphosed consul is forsooth to be at liberty to direct the whole might of England. **1891** T. ROOSEVELT *Hist. Towns, New York* i. 2 (Funk), Spain..was a power whose might was waning.

†**c.** *pl.* in the same sense. Also, acts of power; mighty works. *Obs.*

a **1000** *Cædmon's Hymn* 2 (Gr.) Nu scylun herȝan hefaenricaes uard, metudæs maecti end his modȝidanc. *c* **1300** *St. Margarete* 169 Also yneleoue hit noȝt þt his miȝtes were so stronge Eni so holi creatoure in his wombe afonge. **1375** BARBOUR *Bruce* III. 366 God help him, that all mychtis may! *c* **1460** *Towneley Myst.* xii. 485 He that all myghtys may the makere of heuen. *a* **1550** *Christis Kirke Gr.* x, For he eschapit, throw michts of Mary.

d. Of things or impersonal agencies. (Cf. 1 c.)

c **1250** *Gen. & Ex.* 584 Fowerti dais and fowerti niȝt, So wex water mið maȝti miȝt. *a* **1300** *Cursor M.* 22679 Quen all þe stanes..Sal smitt togedir wit sli maght Als thoner dos. **1728** POPE *Dunc.* II. 318 Whirlpools and storms..With all the might of gravitation blest. **1819** SHELLEY *Peter Bell* IV. xix, He proudly thought that his gold's might Had set those spirits burning. **1831** WORDSW. *Depart. Sir W. Scott* 8 The might Of the whole world's good wishes with him goes. **1833** TENNYSON *Fatima* i, O Love, Love, Love! O withering might!

4. Superiority of strength or power as used to enforce one's will. Chiefly in contrast with *right.* Also † ***by might***: by wrongful force or violence.

a **1327** *Pol. Songs* (Camden) 254 For miht is right, the lond is laweles. **1381** in Knighton *Chron.* (Rolls) II. 139 Lat myȝt helpe ryȝt, and skyl go before wille and ryȝt before myȝt, than goth oure mylne aryght. **1559** *Mirr. Mag., Dk. York* iv, To kepe by murder that they get by might. **1573** G. HARVEY *Letter-bk.* (Camden) 3 Miht had alreddi overcumd riht. **1596** SPENSER *F.Q.* IV. ix. 6 He her unwares attacht, and captive held by might. **1657** LD. SAY & SEALE in *Eng. Hist. Rev.* (1895) X. 107 With them [your lawers] thearfore whear thear is might thear is right, it is dominion if it succeed, but rebellion if it miscarry. **1881** JOWETT *Thucyd.* I. 192 They went to war, preferring might to right.

5. In senses 1–3 formerly often strengthened by being coupled with the synonymous *main.* Now *rare* exc. in phr. ***with (all one's) might and main***, which is now only a more emphatic substitute for 'with all one's might' (see 1 b). Also as advb. phrase, ***might and main***; strenuously, vigorously.

c **950** *Lindsf. Gosp.* Luke iv. 36 Þæt is ðis word þætte in mæhte & mæȝne [*in potestate et uirtute*] ȝehateð gastum unclænum & ȝeongas. **1297** R. GLOUC. (Rolls) 218 Þes were in þisse bataile of mest miȝt & mayn. *a* **1300** *Cursor M.* 17028 For sin þat suet iesus had sua mikel might and main. *c* **1330** R. BRUNNE *Chron.* (1810) 56 Toward Wircestre he com with myght & mayn. *c* **1400** *Melayne* 282 Fyfty Lordis af gret Empryce,..Hase loste bothe Mayne & myghte. **1522** *World & Child* 195 (Manly) To serue hym truely..With mayne and all my myght. *Ibid.* 243, I haue myght and mayne ouer countrees fare. **1577** VAUTROUILLIER *Luther on Ep. Gal.* 80 The Deuill set vppon him with all might and maine. **1650** HOWELL *Giraffi's Rev. Naples* I. (1664) 48 The Card. Archb. of Naples with all his might and main..did not spare pains. **1787** MME. D'ARBLAY *Diary* 4 June, The hair-dresser..went to work first, and I second, with all our might and main. **1804** NELSON *Lett.* (1814) II. 7 They call out, might and main, for our protection. **1860** EMERSON *Cond. Life* iii. (1861) 56 The manly part is to do with might and main what you can do. **1873** BLACK *Pr. Thule* xiv, Two or three idlers ..were staring with might and main in at the door of the shop. **1888** BRYCE *Amer. Commw.* III. lxxxiv. 121 Men..who did not regard even the gods, but trusted to their own might and main.

†**6.** As rendering of L. *virtus.* **a.** A virtue. *Obs.*

c **1175** *Lamb. Hom.* 105 Nu beoð .viii. heafod mihtan þe maȝen ouercumen alle þas sunnan. *c* **1200** *Vices & Virtues* 25 An hali mihte is icleped *fides recta.* *c* **1230** *Hali Meid.* 14 [Meiðhad is] mihte ouer alle mihtes.

†**b.** *pl.* The fifth of the nine orders of angels of the celestial hierarchy according to the arrangement of Dionysius the Areopagite. Cf. VIRTUE. Also *gen.* heavenly powers, angels. *Obs.*

c **1000** ÆLFRIC *Hom.* I. 342 Uirtutes [sind ȝecwedene] mihta, ðurh ða wyrcð God fela wundra. *c* **1440** *York Myst.* i. 33 Of all þe mightes I haue made moste nexte after me, I make þe [Lucifer] als master and merour of my mighte. **1535** COVERDALE *Eph.* i. 21 And set him..aboue all rule, power, and mighte, and dominacion. **1652** BP. HALL *Invis. World* I. vii. (1847) 88 The presumption of those men, who..have taken upon them to marshal these Angelical spirits... In the second [Hierarchy] of universal regency; finding..Mights, to be the Generals of the heavenly Militia... In the third of special government, placing..Powers, forty times more than Principalities: Mights, fifty more than Powers.

7. *dial.* A considerable quantity or amount.

1834 W. A. CARUTHERS *Kentuckian in N.Y.* I. 28 I'm 'bliged to do a might of business in Baltimore afore I can go on. **1878** J. H. BEADLE *Western Wilds* ii. 29 It took a might of time. *Ibid.* 43 It was a might o' comfort, though, to see 'em 'fore they died. **1903** in *Eng. Dial. Dict.* (Yks., Suffolk). **1955** J. MASTERS *Coromandel!* i. 20 A sleeveless leather jerkin that..hid a might of queer things.

8. A possibility as distinct from a certainty.

1901 M. FRANKLIN *My Brilliant Career* xvi. 133 'We might have both been drowned,' he said sternly. 'Mights don't fly,' I returned. **1922** JOYCE *Ulysses* 344 There was just a might that he might be out. **1961** C. H. D. TODD *Pop. Whippet* 57 You don't want any *might* about it—you need to know.

†**might**, *a. Obs. rare.* Forms: 3 miȝt, 5 myght. [? f. MIGHT *sb.*: cf. ALMIGHT *a.* (OE. had *meaht* adj.:—prehistoric **mahto-*, a ppl. formation from the same root.)] = MIGHTY.

[*a* **1000** *Phœnix* 377 (Gr.) Forȝeaf him se meahta moncynnes fruma.] *c* **1250** *Gen. & Ex.* 3038 And knowen sal ben In euerilc lond min miȝte name. *c* **1460** *Play Sacram.* 85 For of a merchante most myght therof my tale ys told. *Ibid.* 182 Mace, mastyk that myght ys.

might, pa. t. of MAY *v.*[1]

†**'mightand**, *a. Obs.* [f. MIGHTY *sb.* with pr. pple. ending.] Mighty. Also *absol.*, a mighty man.

a **1300** *E.E. Psalter* xxiii. 8 Laverd strang And mightand in fight. *Ibid.* lxxxviii. 20, I sete helpe unto mightand. *Ibid.* lxxxix. 10 And if in mightandes [*v.r.* weldinges] four-skore yhere And mare, of þam swinke and sorw here.

'might-be, *sb.* and *a.* [Cf. MAY-BE, MIGHT-HAVE-BEEN.] **A.** *sb.* What might be; an unlikely possibility.

1633 AMES *Agst. Cerem.* II. 306 [He] bringeth meer conceits and might bees for proving Arguments. **1872** GEO. ELIOT *Middlem.* xii, Better than any fancied 'might-be' such as she was in the habit of opposing to the actual. **1891** LECKY *Poems* 99 He sought not far The 'might-be' in the things that are.

B. *adj.* That might be; (remotely) possible.

1934 R. CAMPBELL *Broken Record* iv. 102 This was during the Douanier rage, when every painting-railway-porter was a might-be genius. **1941** L. MACNEICE *Plant & Phantom* 26 A curfew..imposed Upon their might-be-wanderings; their might-be-applications For resurrection. **1956** AUDEN *Old Man's Road*, With might-be maps of might-have-been campaigns.

†**'mighted**, *a. Obs. rare*[−1]. [f. MIGHT *sb.* + -ED[2].] Having might. (In comb. ***cleanest-mighted.***)

1470–85 MALORY *Arthur* x. lviii. 512 He was the clenest myȝted man and the best wynded of his age, that was on lyue.

mightful ('maɪtfʊl), *a. arch.* [f. MIGHT *sb.* + -FUL; cf. G. *machtvoll.*]

1. Mighty, powerful; †efficacious.

c **1250** *Gen. & Ex.* 100 He ðe it made is miȝtful and wis. **1340** *Ayenb.* 237 Þe sacrement þet is y-mad..be þe hand of þe kueade ministre ne is naȝt..lesse miȝtuol uor to halȝy ham. **1420** *E.E. Wills* (1882) 47, I bequeth my soule into the mercy off mythfull Ihesu. **1535** STEWART *Cron. Scot.* II. 396 The michtfull maker of the sone and mone. **1586** FERNE *Blaz. Gentrie* I. 55 Musicke..is so mightfull, that it preuayleth in the taming of beastes. **1588** SHAKS. *Tit. A.* IV. iv. 5 The mightfull Gods. **1859** TENNYSON *Geraint & Enid* 95 Far liefer had I..watch his mightful hand striking great blows At caitiffs. **1876** BLACKIE *Songs Relig. & Life* 58 Not with blasts of mightful preaching. **1891** *Blackw. Mag.* CL. 837 Mightful arms and thoughtful brains.

†**b.** *absol.* Also *sb.*, a 'mightful' man. *Obs. rare.*

c **1250** *Gen. & Ex.* 3755 And two miȝtful he hauen taken, ..On dathan an oðer Abiron. *a* **1400** *Relig. Pieces fr. Thornton MS.* (1889) 53 We rede in a buke of Danyele þat a myghtfull was þat [etc.].

2. Of actions: Proceeding from arbitrary power.

1895 *Tablet* 25 May 804 These mightful assaults by the State on the Church.

Hence **'mightfully** *adv.*, **'mightfulness.**

c **1325** *Metr. Hom.* 14 He herid hel als mihti thain, And broht thaim al that war his, Mihtfullik in till his blis. **1340** HAMPOLE *Pr. Consc.* 754 If in myghtfulnes four scor yhere falle, Mare es þair swynk and sorow with-alle. *c* **1440** *Gesta Rom.* lxi. 256 (Harl. MS.) As he Iustid with a sone of the knyȝtes, he caste him downe of his horse myȝttefully. **1567** *Gude & Godlie Ball.* (S.T.S.) 108 He sall saif the mychtfullie.

might-have-been. [Cf. MAY-BE, MIGHT-BE.] That which might have been; something which might have happened; a person who might have been greater or more eminent. Also *attrib.*

1848 CLOUGH *Bothie* III. 158 He to the great might-have-been upsoaring, sublime and ideal. **1886** KIPLING *Departm. Ditties* (1888) 19 Boanerges Blitzen, servant of the Queen, Is a dismal failure—is a 'Might-have-been'. **1931** R. CAMPBELL *Georgiad* iii. 63 That moonlit people of the might-have-been. **1955** A. L. ROWSE *Expansion Eliz. Eng.* 90 The might-have-beens of history are not a very profitable subject. **1956** [see MIGHT-BE *a.*]. **1970** *Guardian* 11 Aug. 11/8 One of history's might-have-been mysteries. **1974** R. THOMAS *Porkchoppers* xxvi. 230 The name that symbolized the might-have-been world of Donald Cubbin. **1974** A. GODDARD *Vienna Pursuit* III. 174 Overwhelmed with horror for the might-have-been, she paused.

†**'mighthead.** *Obs.* [f. MIGHT *sb.* + *-hed*, -HEAD; but cf. MIGHTSOME *v.*] Mightiness.

a **1300** *E.E. Psalter* cxliv. 7 Minde of mighthed of þi softnesse [Vulg. *Memoriam abundantiæ suavitatis tuæ*].

†**'mightiful**, *a. Obs.* [f. MIGHTY + -FUL.] = MIGHTFUL.

a **1300–1400** *Cursor M.* 15161 (Gött.) Þat suete mightiful king was comen. **1421** SIR H. LUTTRELL in Ellis *Orig. Lett.* Ser. II. I. 84 Wel excellent, and myghtyfull Prince. **1548** UDALL *Erasm. Par. Luke* vii. 14 Onlesse Iesus vouchesalue with his mightifull hande to touche the biere.

†**'mightihead.** *Obs. rare*[−1]. In 4 myȝtihed. [f. MIGHTY *a.* + -HEAD.] Power.

1382 WYCLIF *Ecclus.* x. 11 Of eche myȝtihed [Vulg. *potentatus*; 1388 power] short lif.

mightily ('maɪtɪlɪ), *adv.* Forms: see MIGHTY *a.* and -LY[2]; also 4 **mythylyke**, 5 **mythyle**, 7 **mitily**. [f. MIGHTY *a.* + -LY[2].]

1. In a mighty manner, with great power or strength; with powerful effect; †also, with great effort, vigorously, vehemently.

c **888** K. ÆLFRED *Boeth.* xxxv. §4 Þæt hehste god, ðæt hit eall swa mihtiȝlice macað. *a* **1300** *Cursor M.* 23551 Sua mightili þair [*sc.* the saints'] might to fill. **13..** *Gaw. & Gr. Knt.* 2290 He myntez at hym maȝtyly. *c* **1374** CHAUCER *Troylus* v. 262 Another tyme he sholde mightily Conforte him-self, and seyn it was folye. **14..** *Stockh. Med. MS.* II. 46 in *Anglia* XVIII. 308 Þat purgyth þe neris mythylyke. *c* **1420** *Pallad. on Husb.* XI. 471 Moue it [the wyne] myghtily [L. *vehementer*] With reed al grene. **1490** CAXTON *Eneydos* xxvii. 95 Eneas made the mariners to rowe myghtyli. **1596** SHAKS. *Tam. Shr.* I. ii. 279 Do as aduersaries do in law, Striue mightily, but eate and drinke as friends. **1597** HOOKER *Eccl. Pol.* v. xxii. §4 The power of the word of God ..worketh mightily..to their conversion. **1611** BIBLE *Jonah* iii. 8 Let man and beast..cry mightily vnto God. **1680** SIR C. LYTTELTON in *Hatton Corr.* (Camden) I. 237 My L[d] Essex mitily opposes this. **1746–7** HERVEY *Medit. & Contempl.* (1818) 67 Ye..cry mightily to the Father of your spirits for faith in his dear Son.

†**2.** So as to be strong or powerful. *Obs.*

1414 BRAMPTON *Penit. Ps.* (Percy Soc.) 29 My bonys were stronge, and myghtyly made. *c* **1420** *Pallad. on Husb.* I. 399 But se that hit be tymbred myghtyly. **1464** *Paston Lett.* II. 160 Arme yowr selve as myghtyly as ye kan ageyn yowr enmyes.

3. In a great degree, to a great extent; greatly, very much. Now somewhat *rare*; very common in 17–18th c.

1593 SHAKS. *3 Hen. VI*, III. ii. 74 Therein thou wrong'st thy Children mightily. **1632** LITHGOW *Trav.* II. 74 [Athens] was after mightily inlarged by Theseus. **1667** PEPYS *Diary* 6 Feb., I sat mightily behind, and could see but little. **1711** STEELE *Spect.* No. 145 ¶2 A Gentleman..who deals mightily in Antique Scandal. **1756–82** J. WARTON *Ess. Pope* (ed. 4) II. xii. 278, I should be mightily obliged to you if you could get me a copy of his verses. **1760** GRAY *Corr.* (1843) 204 A carpet mightily finished. **1838** DICKENS *Lett.* (1880) I. 13 It amused us mightily. **1886** RUSKIN *Præterita* I. 421, I wonder mightily now what sort of a creature I should have turned out.

mightiness ('maɪtɪnɪs). [f. MIGHTY + -NESS.] The state or condition of being mighty.

13.. *S. Augustin* 1273 in Horstm. *Altengl. Leg.* (1878) 83 Þi mihtinesse we worschupeþ, lord, Boþe in dede and in word. *c* **1511** *1st Eng. Bk. Amer.* (Arb.) Introd. 30/2 Pope Iohn whose myghtynes & rychedome amounteth aboue all prynces of the world. **1526** *Pilgr. Perf.* (W. de W. 1531) 274 b, Yf he so do, the myghtynesse of the newe wyne wyll breke the vessell. **1534** MORE *Comf. agst. Trib.* III. xxvii. (1553) V viij, To shewe y[e] mightines of theyr malice. *a* **1586**

SIDNEY *Arcadia* III. (1590) 318 b, A cunning mastiffe, who knowes the..strength of the Bul, fights low..answering mightines with nimblenes. **1613** SHAKS. *Hen. VIII*, Prol. 30 Thinke you see them Great..: Then, in a moment, see How soone this Mightinesse meets Misery. **1725** POPE *Postscr. to Odyss.* (1840) 390 Language, which..rattles like some mightiness of meaning in the most indifferent subjects. **1760–72** H. BROOKE *Fool of Qual.* (1809) III. 37 The weak would have the mightiness of the law for their support. **1802** WORDSW. *Sonn.*, '*Inland, within a hollow vale, I stood*', What power is there! What mightiness for evil and for good! **1838–42** ARNOLD *Hist. Rome* III. xliv. 146 The mightiness of her energy.

†**b.** As a title of dignity ***your mightiness***.

1588 SHAKS. *Tit. A.* II. iii. 126 This Minion..braues your Mightinesse. *c* **1590** GREENE *Fr. Bacon* xvi, In royalizing Henry's Albion With presence of your princely mightiness. **1622** FLETCHER & MASS. *Prophetess* III. i, Does your Mightinesse..yet understand our faces?

c. ***High Mightiness*** (also †***High and Mightiness***): a title of dignity; esp. in pl. = Du. *hoogmogendheden*, the title of the members of the States-General of the United Provinces of the Netherlands. Now only *Hist.* Also as an ironical title.

1668 TEMPLE *Let. to De Witt* Wks. 1731 II. 88 His Majesty and their High and Mightinesses have begun..this glorious..Design of a general Peace. **1700** T. BROWN *Amusem. Ser. & Com.* iv. (1709) 43 Now for that Majestical Man and Woman there, stand off, there is no coming within a Hundred Yards of their High Mightinesses, they have revolted like the Dutch. **1707** *Lond. Gaz.* No. 4389/2 Monsieur Lintelo, Envoy Extraordinary of the States General, delivered the King a Letter from their High Mightinesses. **1733** BUDGELL *Bee* I. 71 A Letter directed to the States General, in which their High and Mightinesses are reproached. **1792** M. CUTLER in *Life*, etc. (1888) I. 486 However important their High Mightinesses of Congress may appear abroad. **1825** R. P. WARD *Tremaine* II. vii. 68 To lay my whip across his high mightyness's shoulders. **1883** BLACK *Shandon Bells* xxx, Being particular about good dinners..is beneath their high mightinesses' notice.

†'**mighting.** *Obs. rare.* Power.

a **1300** *E.E. Psalter* lxiv. 7 Gird with mightinge [Vulg. *accinctus potentia*]. *Ibid.* cv. 2 Wha sal speke of lauerd mightinges [Vulg. *potentias domini*].

†'**mightious,** *a. Obs. rare*⁻¹. In 5 **myghtyus.** [f. MIGHTY *a.* + -OUS.] Full of might or power.

c **1460** *Towneley Myst.* xvi. 220 Of bedlem a gracyus lord shall spray, That of Iury myghtyus kyng shalbe ay.

mightless ('maɪtlɪs), *a.* Now *arch.* [f. MIGHT *sb.* + -LESS.] Without might; impotent; powerless.

c **1175** *Lamb. Hom.* 111 He..bið swa mihtles on his modes streche þet [etc.]. *c* **1330** R. BRUNNE *Chron.* (1810) 280 Priue pride in pes es nettille in herbere, þe rose is myghtles, þe nettille spredis ouer fer. *c* **1450** MYRC *Festial* 55 Þys vnycorn..layth hys hed yn hur barme, myghtles without strengthe: and soo ys taken. **1553** BECON *Reliques of Rome* (1563) 172 b, Olde people yᵗ bene myghtlesse, weake, and impotente. *a* **1584** MONTGOMERIE *Cherrie & Slae* 305 Baith sichtles, and michtles, I grew almaist at ainis. **1887** MORRIS *Odyss.* x. 521 Utter thou thy praying to the mightless heads of the dead. **1888** *Ibid.* XVIII. 130 There is nought more mightless than man of all that Earth doth breed.

b. Const. *inf.*

1340–70 *Alex. & Dind.* 74 Þat may not be graunted Of me, þat miʒteles am my silf so to kepe. *a* **1450** MYRC *Festial* 82 Old men passed age and myghtles to fast. **1598** SYLVESTER *Du Bartas* II. ii. II. *Babylon* 125 Might-lesse our selves to succour, or advise.

†'**mightly,** *adv. Obs.* In 1 **meahte-, mihte-, mihtlíce**; for later forms see MIGHT *sb.* and -LY². [OE. *mihtelíce*, app. a var. of *mihtiȝlíce* MIGHTILY; for the form cf. *cræftelíce, hefelíce, grǽdelíce, ȝeþyldelíce.*] = MIGHTILY in various senses.

a **900** tr. *Bæda's Hist.* v. xix. [xxi.] (1890) 468 Mid þam he ðy mihtlicor wiðscufan mihte. *c* **1000** ÆLFRIC *Hom.* I. 108 Sæ oncneow ða Cristofer hyre yða mihtelic eode. *a* **1300** *Cursor M.* 17267 Þou spede me, lauerd! for-to spell Hu mighteli þou harud hell. **1390** GOWER *Conf.* III. 92 This soubtil water myhtely,..The strengthe of therthe perceth ofte. *c* **1410** *Master of Game* (MS. Digby 182) xv, It is þe best hounde..forto take alle manere of beestes and holde myghtliche. **1420–22** LYDG. *Thebes* I. in *Chaucer's Wks.* (1561) 363/2 A porche, bilte of square stones Ful mightely. **1480** CAXTON *Chron. Eng.* ccxxix. 241 That he myght the myʒtloker fyght and defende the reame. **1526** TINDALE *Rom.* viii. 26 The Sprete maketh intercession mightely for us. **1582** N. LICHEFIELD tr. *Castanheda's Conq. E. Ind.* I. i. 4 Whereby the Christian faith is so greatly increased..and the royall house of Portingale so mightely honoured. **1610** BIBLE (Douay) *Wisd.* viii. 1 She reacheth therfore from end vnto end mightely, and disposeth al thinges swetely. **1744** *Col. Rec. Pennsylv.* IV. 707 Finding what friendship subsisted between us and the Dutch, he approved it mightly.

[**mightsome,** *v.*, **mightsomnes,** which render L. *abundare, abundantia* in the Early English Psalter, presumably originated from misreading of early ME. **inihtsumien, -sumnis*:—OE. *ȝenyhtsumian, -sumnis*, these being the words used in the same passages in the Vespasian Psalter.

In some of the passages the Surtees editor prints *nuhtsom*, which is impossible in a northern text.

a **1300** *E.E. Psalter* xxix. 7, xlix. 20, lxiv. 14, lxxii. 12, lxxvii. 38.]

mighty ('maɪtɪ), *a.* and *adv.* Forms: 1 **mæhtiȝ, meahtiȝ, mihtiȝ,** 1–2 **mehtiȝ,** 2–4 **mihti,** 2–3 *Ormin* **mahhtiȝ,** 3 **mæhti, mahti, maʒti, miʒti, michti,** 4 **mihty, myhti, -y,** 4–5 **maʒte, miʒty, -i, myʒty, -i,** (4 **-tty,** 5 **-tie**), **miʒeti, myhety,** 3–5 **mighti,** 4–5 *Sc.* **mychty,** 4–6 **myghty,** (5 **myghti, -tty, myʒhty, myʒthty, mythty, mytheti,** *Sc.* **michtie**), 5–6 *Sc.* **mychti,** 6 **myʒghty, myghty(e,** *Sc.* **michti, -ie, -y, -tty, mychte, -ie, myghti,** 6–7 **mightie, -ye,** 4– **mighty.** [OE. *mihtiȝ* = OFris. *mechtig, machtig*, OS. *mahtig* (MLG. *mechtig*, MDu. *machtich*, Du. *machtig*), OHG. *mahtîg* (MHG. *mehtic*, mod.G. *mächtig*), ON. *mátteg-r, mǫ́ttug-r* (also contracted in inflected *máttk-*), Goth. *mahteig-s*:—OTeut. types **mahtîgo-, *mahtugo-*, f. **mahti-z, *mahtu-z*: see MIGHT *sb.* and -Y¹.]

A. *adj.* **1.** Possessing 'might' or power; powerful, potent, strong. Now only *rhetorical*, connoting a transcendent or imposing degree of power.

a. Said of God, rulers, nations, etc.

c **825** *Vesp. Psalter* xxiv. 8 Dryhten strong & maehtiȝ, dryhten mæhtiȝ in ȝefehte. *a* **900** tr. *Bæda's Hist.* I. xiv. [xxv.] (1890) 56 Ða wæs on þa tid Æðelbyrht cyning haten on Centrice, & mihtiȝ. *a* **1175** *Cott. Hom.* 231 An rice king wes, strang and mihti. *a* **1240** *Wohunge* in *Cott. Hom.* 273 Drihtin is mahti strong and kene ifihte. **1390** GOWER *Conf.* I. 16 Thei sein that god is myhti there, And schal ordeine what he wile. *c* **1470** *Gol. & Gaw.* 682 Thai mighty men vpon mold ane riale course maid. **1590** SHAKS. *Com. Err.* v. i. 282 Most mightie Duke, vouchsafe me speak a word. **1667** MILTON *P.L.* XII. 124 God..from him will raise A mightie Nation. **1697** DRYDEN *Virg. Georg.* IV. 809 Mighty Cæsar, thund'ring from afar, Seeks on Euphrates' Banks the Spoils of War. **1761** GRAY *Odin* 83, I know thee now; Mightiest of a mighty line. **1864** TENNYSON *Boädicea* 40 Fear not, isle of blowing woodland,..thou shalt be the mighty one yet!

ellipt. and *absol.* *c* **1175** *Lamb. Hom.* 129 Drihten alesde þene wrechan of þan mehtiȝan. **1340** *Ayenb.* 103 He is þe riȝt guod,..þe riȝt miȝti.

b. of persons, with reference to wealth, social position, or influence. Formerly often predicatively, const. *of, in*.

c **1375** *Sc. Leg. Saints* xli. (*Agnes*) 105 My spouse is mychtyere þane þi son, & fere richere. **1486** *Rec. St. Mary at Hill* 6 That the saide Preest..be chosen and presented..by iiij of the worthyest & myghtyest men of the said parissh. **1508** DUNBAR *Tua Mariit Wemen* 296 Syne maryit I a marchand, myghti of gudis. **1601** R. JOHNSON *Kingd. & Commw.* (1603) 40 This prince is so mightie in gold and silver. **1650** FULLER *Pisgah* II. ix. 186 They were all richly married to mighty matches of landed men.

absol. **1484** CAXTON *Fables of Æsop* I. vi. (1889) 11 The poure ought not to hold felauship with the myghty. **1651** HOBBES *Leviath.* II. xxx. 180 As well the rich, and mighty, as poor and obscure persons.

c. of persons or animals, their actions or attributes, with reference to physical strength or valour. †In early use often merely: Able-bodied. *Obs.*

c **825** *Vesp. Psalter* cxxvi. 4 Swe swe strelas in honda maehtȝes. *c* **1386** CHAUCER *Knt.'s T.* 565 Wel koude he hewen wode..ffor he was yong and myghty. *c* **1400** *Apol. Loll.* 111 Bi lawe cyuil it is not leful to a miʒty body to beg. **1432–50** tr. *Higden* (Rolls) I. 263 Thei gette myʒhty childer [1387 *Trevisa* stalworþe: *L. robustam sobolem*]. *a* **1500** in Arnolde *Chron.* (1811) 92 Yf ony..myghty beggar be within the warde. **1500–20** DUNBAR *Poems* lxxvii. 36 And syne the Bruce..cum rydand..As nobill, dreidfull, michtie campioun. *a* **1525** *Vergilius* in Thoms *E.E. Prose Rom.* II. 23 Her chyld..began to wexe bygge and stronge and myghty anough to bere armes. **1530–1** *Act 22 Hen. VIII*, c. 12 If any person..beynge hole and myghty in body..be taken in begging. **1535** COVERDALE *Gen.* x. 9 Nemrod..was a mightie hunter. **1590** SPENSER *F.Q.* II. vi. 29 Their mighty strokes their haberjeons dismayld. **1596** DALRYMPLE tr. *Leslie's Hist. Scot.* II. 163 The Scottis couragious, of a blyth hope, and a mychtie spirit, leipis to straikis. **1598** SHAKS. *Merry W.* III. i. 111 Your hearts are mighty. **1601** —— *Jul. C.* v. i. 81 On our former Ensigne Two mighty Eagles fell. **1622** R. HAWKINS *Voy. S. Sea* (1847) 126 Our ship gave a mightie blow upon a rocke. **1733** POPE *Ess. Man* III. 297 Where small and great, where weak and mighty, made To serve, not suffer, strengthen, not invade. **1839** LONGF. *Vill. Blacksm.* i, The smith, a mighty man is he, With large and sinewy hands. **1859** TENNYSON *Lancelot* 63 For so by nine years' proof we needs must learn Which is our mightiest.

d. of persons, their actions and attributes, with reference to mental ability or executive skill. Formerly often predicative, const. *in* or *inf.* ***mighty works***: in Biblical use (= Gr. δυνάμεις), miracles.

c **825** *Vesp. Psalter* li. 3 Ðu mæhtiȝ erð in unrehtwisnisse. *c* **897** K. ÆLFRED *Gregory's Past.* C. xv. 90 Se lareow sceolde beon mihtiȝ to tyhtanne on halwende lare. **1362** LANGL. *P. Pl.* A. I. 150 Þeiʒ ʒe be miʒty to mote beþ meke of ʒour werkis. **1382** WYCLIF *Acts* xviii. 24 Apollo..a man eloquent,..myʒti in scripturis. *c* **1470** HENRY *Wallace* VI. 346 Thar feild..Quhar claryowns blew full mony mychty sonis. **1535** COVERDALE *Ps.* xxviii. 4 The voyce of the Lorde is mightie in operacion [Vulg. *Vox Domini in virtute*]. —— *Matt.* xiv. 2 He is rysen agayne from the deed, therfore are his deedes so mightie. **1611** BIBLE *Matt.* xiii. 54 Whence hath this man this wisedome, and these mighty works? **1718** ECHARD *Hist. Eng.* II. II. ii. 565 b, Thomas Lydyat..of a great Soul and incomparable Learning; being a Match for the mighty Scaliger and Selden. **1737** POPE *Hor. Epist.* II. i. 137 Or what remain'd so worthy to be read By learned Critics, of the mighty dead. **1742** —— *Dunc.* IV. 211 Thy mighty Scholiast, whose unweary'd pains Made Horace dull. **1802** WORDSW. *Resol. & Independ.* xvii, And mighty Poets in their misery dead. *a* **1853** ROBERTSON *Lect.* ii. (1858) 146 Out of which a mightier master of the art than Pope could scarcely have struck the notes of true passion. **1881** BIBLE (R.V.) *Mark* ix. 39 For there is no man which shall do a mighty work [WYCLIF a virtue; 1535 COVERDALE, 1611 a miracle] in my name. [So also Acts ii. 22.]

e. of things or forces, or their operation.

c **1250** *Gen. & Ex.* 3797 A fier maʒti ðat folc fest on. *a* **1300–1400** *Cursor M.* 9384 (Gött.) For sune and mone..Had seuen sith mar þan nou of liht, And all thinges was þan..Wele mihtier þan þai er nou. **1535** COVERDALE *Exod.* xv. 10 They sancke downe as leed in the mightie waters. **1593** SHAKS. *3 Hen. VI*, II. v. 5 Now swayes it this way, like a Mighty Sea, Forc'd by the Tide, to combat with the Winde. **1611** BIBLE *1 Esdras* iv. 41 Great is trueth, and mightie aboue all things. **1781** COWPER *Charity* 283 But shipwreck, earthquake, battle, fire, and flood, Are mighty mischiefs, not to be withstood. **1806** WORDSW. *Ode Intim. Immort.* 168 And hear the mighty waters rolling evermore. **1864** TENNYSON *Enoch Arden* 767 Then he,..Because things seen are mightier than things heard, Stagger'd and shook.

f. Of drugs, liquors, spells: Potent, efficacious. †Also, of a material: Stout, strong. *Obs.*

c **1000** *Sax. Leechd.* III. 32 Ond þu weȝbrade wyrta modor eastan opone innan mihtiȝu. *a* **1240** *Ureisun* in *Cott. Hom.* 187 Min heouenliche leche þet makedest us of þi seolf se mihti medicine. *c* **1386** CHAUCER *Miller's T.* 311 This Carpenter..broghte of myghty Ale a large quart. *c* **1400** MAUNDEV. (Roxb.) xxii. 102 It es riʒt myghty wyne. *c* **1430** *Two Cookery-bks.* 12 Take myghty brothe of Beef. *c* **1448** HEN. VI *Avyse* in Willis & Clark *Cambridge* (1886) I. 367 Good and myghtty morter. **1497** *Naval Acc. Hen. VII* (1896) 242, lxvj boltes of Grete myghty canvas. **1576** BAKER *Jewell of Health* 230 Where the spyrit of the wyne shall be sufficient myghtye. **1610** ROWLANDS *Martin Mark-all* 22 Their Beere is..so mightie, that it serueth them in steade of meate, drinke, fire, and apparrell. **1781** COWPER *Anti-Thelyph.* 37 On every mind some mighty spell she cast. **1819** W. TENNANT *Papistry Storm'd* (1827) 115 Barls o' michtie beer.

†**g.** Of a legal document: Valid, efficacious. *Obs.*

c **1450** *Oseney Reg.* (E.E.T.S.) 19 This present writyng, with þe strengh of our seele we haue i-made hit myʒghty and stronge.

†**h.** Forcible, emphatic. *Obs.*

1642–7 JER. TAYLOR *Episc.* 229 The Councell of Aquileia..is full and mighty in asserting the Bishops power over the Laity.

2. Of huge proportions; massive, bulky.

1413 *Pilgr. Sowle* (Caxton 1483) IV. ii. 59 This tree is wondre stronge and myghty aretchyng in to heuen **1420–22** LYDG. *Thebes* I. in *Chaucer's Wks.* (1561) 357 b/1, The citee Thebes, of mightie square stones As I you told. **1658** SIR T. BROWNE *Hydriot.* i. (1736) 17 That large Urn found at Ashbury, containing mighty Bones. **1760** FAWKES tr. *Anacreon, Ode* lvii. 1 Bring hither, Boy, a mighty Bowl. **1810** SCOTT *Lady of L.* I. iii, And silence settled..On the lone wood and mighty hill. **1851** RUSKIN *Stones Ven.* (1874) I. xxviii. 327 A plain, deep-cut recess, with a single mighty shadow. **1895** SAFFLING *Land of Broads* 6 The older farm-houses, with their mighty kitchens.

3. a. Of things, actions, events, etc.: Very great in amount, extent or degree. In later use, chiefly colloquial or familiar.

1586 A. DAY *Eng. Secretary* I. (1625) 68 The..mutuall society betwixt man & wife being of such mighty efficacie. **1605** SHAKS. *Lear* III. v. 17 If the matter of this Paper be certain, you haue mighty businesse in hand. **1668** CULPEPPER & COLE *Barthol. Anat.* Man. II. i. 317 There is a mighty flux of blood. **1697** tr. *C'tess D'Aunoy's Trav.* (1706) 220 The difference of times makes a mighty alteration in the Events of things. **1754** FIELDING *Jonathan Wild* II. iv, That gentleman..made such mighty expedition that he was now upwards of twenty miles on his way. **1843** BORROW *Bible in Spain* xi, Huge serpents..which sometimes come out and commit mighty damage. **1865** KINGSLEY *Herew.* i, Mighty fowling and fishing was there in the fen below. **1871** R. ELLIS tr. *Catullus* lxxxiii. 2 This to the fond weak fool seemeth a mighty delight.

b. With agent-nouns, etc.: That does or is to a very great degree (what is indicated by the noun).

1692 BULSTRODE in *15th Rep. Hist. MSS. Comm.* App. II. 21 He was..a mighty Tory. **1712** STEELE *Spect.* No. 466 ¶7, I, who set up for a mighty Lover..of Virtue. **1743** BULKELEY & CUMMINS *Voy. S. Seas* 81 This Plastow was a mighty Favourite with the Captain. **1843** BORROW *Bible in Spain* xxx, He is a mighty liberal.

4. quasi-*sb.* (with *pl.*). A mighty or powerful person. Chiefly *pl.*, as in (***David's***) ***three mighties***.

1382 WYCLIF *1 Chron.* xi. 12 Eliazar, the sone of his vncle Ahoites, that was among the thre myʒty [1388 miʒti men; **1611** the three mighties. Vulg. *inter tres potentes*]. *c* **1470** *Gol. & Gaw.* 300 Quhan thai saw that mighty [the king] sa mouit in his mude. **1600** W. WATSON *Decacordon* (1602) 200 Emperors and kings and the mighties of the world. **1606** W. CRASHAW *Rom. Forgeries* E ij, Our royall Dauid and many of his Mighties. **1647** TRAPP *Comm. 1 Cor.* i. 26 Hence so many mighties miscarry. **1901** 'IAN MACLAREN' *Yng. Barbarians* iv, Speyside's officers, such mighties as Bauldie and Johnston,..clustered round their commander.

5. ellipt. in the interjections ***mighty! mighty me!*** *Sc.* and *dial.*

1867 GREGOR *Banffs. Gloss.*, *Michtie*, *interj.* expressive of surprise. *Michtie me* is another form. **1869** A. MACDONALD *Disput. Settlement* (1877) 61 (E.D.D.) Eh, mighty! that surely canna be. **1874** T. HARDY *Madding Crowd* xxxii, Mighty me! Won't mis'ess storm..when she comes back!

6. *Comb.*, parasynthetic, as ***mighty-brained, -handed, -minded, -mouthed, -spirited*** adjs.

1611 BEAUM. & FL. *Maid's Trag.* v. iii, Though he be mighty-spirited, and forward To all great things. **1855** LYNCH *Rivulet* LXXXII. iii, How came it, men of faith, to pass That ye were mighty-handed? **1864** TENNYSON *Milton* 1 O mighty-mouth'd inventor of harmonies. **1865** SWINBURNE *Atalanta* 1009, I am not mighty-minded, nor desire Crowns. **1892** W. WATSON *Lachrymæ Mus.* Poems (1898) 21 Mightiest-brained Lucretius.

B. *adv.* (Qualifying an adj. or adv., †*rarely* an adj. phrase.) In a great degree; greatly; exceedingly; very. Now *colloq.* or *familiar*, often with ironical implication; = 'vastly', 'precious'.

a **1300** *Cursor M.* 14396 Þair blisced lauerd..Þat..was..Sa mighti meke, sa mild o mode. **1535** Coverdale *Exod.* ix. 18 Tomorow..wyll I cause a mightie greate hayle to rayne. **1602** Marston *Antonio's Rev.* v. iii, He is mightie on our part. **1660** Barrow *Euclid* Pref. (1714) 2 The mighty near affinity that is between Arithmetick and Geometry. **1715** De Foe *Fam. Instruct.* i. iv. (1841) I. 91 You are a mighty good obedient thing. **1767** Gray in *Corr. G. & Nicholls* (1843) 70 To this purpose..would I write, and mighty respectfully withall. **1838** Dickens *O. Twist* xlix, This is all mighty fine. **1844** Kendall *Santa Fé Exped.* I. 32 'You'll be mighty apt to get wet', said a thorough-bred Texan. **1862** Mrs. Carlyle *Lett.* III. 105, I myself know always mighty well what I want. **1883** Stevenson *Treas. Isl.* xxix, It..looks mighty like a horn-pipe in a rope's end at Execution Dock. **1931** W. G. McAdoo *Crowded Yrs.* ii. 23 That seemed to me to be mighty good pay. **1958** *Times* 16 Oct. 17/1 They left it till mighty near no-side before they got their noses thankfully in front.

'mightyship. *nonce-wd.* [f. mighty + -ship.] Only in the mock title ***your mightyship***.

a **1726** Alsop *Tale, To Chlorinda* xv. in Dodsley *Poems* (1755) VI. 248 Is it fit, let your mightyship say..?

migma ('mɪgmə). *Geol.* [a. Gr. μίγμα mixture, f. μ(ε)ιγνύναι to mix.] A mixture of solid and molten rock.

1943 *Proc. Geol. Assoc.* LIV. 73 The migma, if the amount of its liquid portion became great enough, would flow and could intrude itself into its surroundings in typical eruptive or intrusive fashion. **1952** T. F. W. Barth *Theoret. Petrol.* iv. xiii. 364 In the root parts of the folded mountains..a migma is formed that corresponds to the magma of the higher levels. **1974** *Encycl. Brit. Micropædia* VI. 880/1 Between these extremes is a concept of a pore fluid, or migma, generated by the differential melting or partial fusion of the root portions of mountains.

migmatite ('mɪgmətaɪt). *Petrol.* [ad. Sw. *migmatit* (J. J. Sederholm 1907, in *Bull. Comm. Géol. Finlande* V. xxiii. 88), f. Gr. μίγμα (see prec.): see -ite[1].] A rock composed of a metamorphic host rock with streaks or veins of a granitic rock.

1907 J. J. Sederholm in *Bull. Comm. Géol. Finlande* V. xxiii. 110 For the gneisses here in question, characteristic of which are two elements of different genetic value,..the author proposes the name of *migmatites*. **1942** *Proc. Geol. Assoc.* LIII. 77 *Pseudodioritic migmatite* is a field-term used to name a group of fairly homogeneous foliated hornblende-rich rocks having a dioritic aspect. **1965** G. J. Williams *Econ. Geol. N.Z.* xiii. 203/2 The monazites and xenotine [*read* xenotime] in migmatites of the Charleston-Fox River area, do not seem to have produced a red colour in the adjoining felspars. **1974** *Encycl. Brit. Micropædia* VI. 880/1 Many migmatites probably represent the partial fusion of the metamorphic host during extreme metamorphism.

Hence **mig'matic**, **migma'titic** *adjs.*, composed of migmatite.

1926 *Mineral. Abstr.* III. 84 Three types of pegmatites are distinguished: I, normal pegmatites; II, contact-pegmatites ..; and III, migmatic pegmatites. **1942** *Proc. Geol. Assoc.* LIII. 67 The region around Bettyhill on the north coast of Sutherland furnishes a splendid display of migmatitic rocks produced by the injection of granitic and pegmatitic material into the different lithological types found in the Moine series. **1968** K. R. Mehnert *Migmatites* i. 5 It is inappropriate to burden petrographic investigations of metamorphic or migmatic rocks from the beginning with the question about the possible parent rock. **1969** Bennison & Wright *Geol. Hist. Brit. Isles* iii. 53 The Moinian rocks are generally metasediments showing little metamorphic segregation, although in the central migmatitic core..they are gneissose.

migmatization (mɪgmətaɪ'zeɪʃən). *Petrol.* [f. migmat(ite + -ization.] The process by which a migmatite is formed.

1932 E. G. Woods *Baltic Region* vii. 67 A great deal of migmatization having taken place has masked very effectively the relationship of these rocks to one another. **1958** *Geol. Mag.* XCV. 383 The infrastructure, although undergoing migmatization, retains the trends of the older orogenic belt from which it is largely formed. **1971** *Scottish Jrnl. Geol.* VII. 323 The frequent spatial coincidence between areas of migmatization and centres of high-grade regional metamorphism has long been recognized.

Hence **'migmatized** *ppl. a.*, converted into a migmatite.

1958 *Geol. Mag.* XCV. 383 During the Caledonian orogeny, both the old crystalline rocks and a low structural level of the Caledonian geosynclinal rocks themselves became migmatized and rose as diapirs. **1971** *Scottish Jrnl. Geol.* VII. 305 In central and eastern Sutherland the Moine rocks are extensively migmatized.

mignardise. Also mignardize, migniardise, miniardise. [a. F. *mignardise*, f. *mignard*: see prec.] **1.** Caressing treatment; affected delicacy of behaviour or appearance. Also, a fancy cake or similar delicacy, usu. served at the end of a meal.

1603 Florio *Montaigne* iii. xiii. 636 The disdainfull churlishnesse wherewith they beate them, are but mignardizes and affectations of a motherly favour. **1625** B. Jonson *Staple of N.* iii. i, Entertaine her, and her creatures, too, With all the migniardise, and quaint Caresses, You can put on 'hem. **1652** Urquhart *Jewel* Wks. (1834) 233 The gracefulness of his hand and foot, with the quaint miniardise of the rest of his body. **1689** H. Beeston in *Vota Oxoniensia*, No..Patches and spots, No Mignardize of face at all From Spanish paper or from English gall. **1931** Belloc in *One Hundred & One Ballades* 16 Elderly women full of Mignardises—The latest fruit of Adam's ancient sin. **1935** W. Stevens *Let.* 19 Dec. (1967) 303 Poulenc is a beautiful instance of *mignardise* in music. **1974** S. Coulter *Château* i. xvii. 132 Their digestive systems were dealing with Brioche de foie gras,..ananas voilé, mignardises and fruit.

2. (See quot. 1950.) Also *attrib.*

1872 *Young Englishwoman* Nov. 606/2 A band ornamented with hem-stitch and a mignardise braid. **1873** *Ibid.* June 302/1 For this larger rosette commence with the centre star by joining the ends of a length of mignardise. **1882** Caulfeild & Saward *Dict. Needlework* 111/2 Mignardise is used almost entirely to form narrow edgings for underlinen and children's dresses. *Ibid.* 112/1 Scalloped edging.—Formed of two rows of Mignardise braid. **1950** *'Mercury' Dict. Textile Terms* 345 *Mignardise*, a variety of crochet formed by inserting narrow fine ribbons into the design as the heavy part of the pattern that would otherwise be formed of crochet.

mignature, obs. form of miniature.

†**migniard**, *a.* and *sb. Obs.* Also 7 **mignard, miniard**, *Sc.* **minȝeard**. [a. F. *mignard*; related to mignon.]

A. *adj.* Dainty; mincing; caressing.

1599 Jas. I *Βασιλ. Δωρον* iii. (1603) 107 In the forme of your meat-eating, be neither vnciuill..nor affectatlie mignarde. *Ibid.* iii. 115 In your language be plaine..eschewing..all mignard and effœminate termes. **1611** Cotgr., *Mignard*, migniard, prettie, quaint, neat, feat; wanton; daintie, delicate. **1616** B. Jonson *Devil an Ass* i. iv, Loue is brought vp with those soft *migniard* handlings. **1622** A. Bysset in G. G. Smith *Middle Scots* (1902) 240 Neither have I vsed minȝeard nor effeminate, tanting, invectiue, or skornefull wordis. **1652** Urquhart *Jewel* Wks. (1834) 294 The milder sexe and miniard youth. **1653** —— *Rabelais* i. lvii. (1664) 250 Never were seene Ladies so proper and handsome, so miniard and dainty.

Hence †**migniardly** *adv.*, daintily.

1653 Urquhart *Rabelais* i. lvii. (1664) 249 Their fists miniardly begloved.

B. *sb.* [= OF. *mignarde*.] A courtesan, mistress.

1616 in *Crt. & Times Jas. I* (1849) I. 416 She says the honour..of his embassy consists in three mignards, three dancers, and three fools. **1652** Kirkman *Clerio & Lozia* 93 Idle Migniards, dinner hath waited for you till it is cold.

†**migniardize**, *v. Obs.* Also 7 **miniardize**. [f. migniard + -ize.] *trans.* To make (language) affected in character; to treat (a person) caressingly. Hence **migniardized** *ppl. a.*, **migniardizing** *vbl. sb.*

1598 Florio, *Vezzo*, a wantonnes, a quaintnes, a squeamishnes, a dandling, a dalliance, a wantonizing, a mignardizing, a pampring [etc.]. *c* **1645** Howell *Lett.* (1655) IV. xix. 49 Softnes of pronunciation proceeding from wanton spirits that did miniardize, and make the Language more dainty and feminine. *a* **1670** Hacket *Abp. Williams* i. (1693) 95 Men that are sound in their Morals, and in Minutes imperfect in their Intellectuals, are best reclaimed when they are mignarised [*sic*], and strok'd gently.

mignion, obs. variant of minion.

‖**mignon** (miɲɔ̃), *a.* Also (with fem. reference) 6 **mignone**, 7–9 **mignonne**; and see minion *a.* [F. *mignon, -onne* adj. and sb.]

A. *adj.* Delicately formed; prettily small or delicate.

1556 *Aurelio & Isab.* (1608) L vj, My mignone Isabel. [**1668** Dryden *Evening's Love* vi, That sigh too, I think, is not altogether disagreeable; but something *charmante* and *mignonne*.] **1772** Mrs. Sarah Scott *Test Filial Duty* II. 59 Salvator Rosa's wildest designs are mignonne and finical to some places in this neighbourhood. **1859** G. Meredith *R. Feverel* xxxvii, A mignonne beauty. **1873** Pater *Stud. Hist. Renaiss.* 42 Bright small creatures of the woodland, with arch baby faces and mignon forms. **1886** Marie Corelli *Rom. two Worlds* i, Her pretty mignonne face and graceful figure.

B. *sb.* A pretty child.

1827 *Souvenir* I. 71/2 (Stanf.) Little mignons, not three feet high, were there, arrayed like puppets.

Hence †**'mignon** *v. trans.*, to treat tenderly; †**'mignonness**, over-delicacy, effeminacy.

1530 Palsgr. 245/1 Mignyonnesse, *mignotise*. **1597** Daniel *Philotas* Apol., Wks. (Grosart) III. 183 For though the affection of the multitude, (whom he did not mignion)..discerned not his ends..: Yet [etc.].

mignon: see minion *sb.*

mignonette (ˌmɪnjə'nɛt). Also 8 **mign(i)onet, minionette, mennuet, minianet**, 8–9 **mignionette**. [a. F. *mignonnette*, fem. of †*mignonnet*, dim. of *mignon*: see mignon *a.*]

1. a. A plant (*Reseda odorata*) cultivated for the fragrance of its blossoms.

When trained to grow with a bushy head it is known as ***tree-mignonette. wild mignonette***, the plant *R. luteola*.

The ordinary Fr. name for mignonette is *réséda*; but Littré says that *mignonnette* is applied to this plant as well as to several others.

[**1752** Miller *Gard. Dict.* (1759) s.v. *Reseda*, 6. *Reseda foliis integris trilobisque*... Bastard-rocket..commonly called sweet *Reseda*, or *Mignonette d'Egypt*.] **1798** C. Marshall *Garden.* xix. 333 Hardy Annuals... Mignonette, (trailing) or sweet-scented reseda. **1799** Sir H. Davy in Beddoes *Contrib. Phys. & Med. Knowl.* 154 A small plant of Minianet in a state of healthy vegetation. **1817** *Bot. Register* III. 227 *Reseda odorata. β. suffrutescens.* Tree-Mignonette. **1820** *Trans. Horticult. Soc.* III. 178 With Lord Bateman [who sent the seed from France in 1742] the appellation of Mignonette originated;..he gave to it this name of endearment, by which it is not known in France. **1832** Tennyson *Miller's Dau.* xi, A long green box of mignonette. **1861** Miss E. A. Beaufort *Egypt. Sepulchres*, etc. II. xix. 116 The ground is strewed with wild mignonnette.

fig. **1847** Tennyson *Princess* Prol. 164 They..miss'd the mignonette of Vivian-place, The little hearth-flower Lilia.

b. ***Jamaica mignonette***: the name given in the West Indies to the henna plant, *Lawsonia alba* or *inermis*, which is naturalized there.

1866 *Treas. Bot.* 665/2.

c. A colour resembling that of the flowers of mignonette; greyish green or greenish white.

1885 *Daily News* 19 Feb. 2/1 The soft tints of greyish green known as 'mignonette' are to be in great favour this year. **1899** B. W. Warhurst *Colour Dict.* 47 Mignonette. Should be delicate light green.

d. A perfume derived from the flowers of the mignonette.

1897 *Sears Roebuck Catal.* 19/2 Perfumes..Crab Apple.. Mignonette..Sweet Pea. **1913** *T. Eaton & Co. Catal.* Spring & Summer 177/1 Perfumes..Jasmin Mignionette Opoponax. **1972** *Guardian* 22 Aug. 9/4 Jacksons have revived these flower perfumes..the shop plan to reintroduce other fragrancies including wallflower, mignonette, and honeysuckle.

2. A kind of lace: see quots. 1865, 1900. (More fully ***mignonette lace***.) Also, a fine kind of net.

[**1699** *Le Mercure Galant* in Mrs. Palliser *Hist. Lace* (1865) 31 *note*, On employe aussi pour les coëffures de la mignonette, et on a tellement perfectionné cette dentelle, que, etc.] **1757** Jeffrey *Coll. Dresses* ii, A pink lutestring dress covered with a white mignonet. **1762** *Lond. Chron.* 16–18 Feb. 167/3 The Ranelagh Mob... This is a piece of Gauze, Minionett,..&c., &c. which is clouted about the head. **1771** Smollett *Humph. Cl.* 13 July, Laces of Mechlin or mignionette. **1865** Mrs. Palliser *Lace* 30 The laces known at that period [1665] were—..5. Mignonette. —A light, fine, pillow lace... This lace was..at times in high favour..for head-dresses and other trimmings. **1900** Mrs. F. N. Jackson *Hand-made Lace* 182 Mignonette was a narrow lace, never exceeding two or three inches... Mignonette pattern is still largely made.

3. *attrib.* and *Comb.*, as ***mignonette-coloured*** adj., ***mignonette-green***, ***-grey*** (see 1 c), ***mignonette-pot***; **mignonette netting** (see quot.); **mignonette pepper**, coarsely ground pepper; **mignonette-vine** (see quot.).

1897 *Daily News* 2 Mar. 5/4 *Mignonette-coloured crêpe de Chine. **1888** *Lady* 25 Oct. 374/3 Alternate bows or loops of *mignonette-green and pale salmon-coloured ribbon. **1900** *Daily News* 3 Mar. 6/5 Tones of..cigar-brown, and *mignonette-grey are in great favour. **1882** Caulfeild & Saward *Dict. Needlework* 361/2, *Mignonette Netting.—This is used for curtains and window blinds, it being extremely easy, and worked with one Mesh. **1877** *Cassell's Dict. Cookery* 1177 *Mignonette Pepper. **1840** Thackeray *Pict. Rhapsody* Wks. 1900 XIII. 331 The *mignonette pots in a Cockney's window. **1896** T. W. Sanders *Encycl. Gard.* (ed. 2), *Madaria* (*Mignonette Vine).—*Ord.* Compositæ. Hardy Annual. *Nat.* California... *Flowers*, yellow.

†**mignote.** *Obs. rare*[−1]. [a. OF. *mignote* fem. of *mignot* wanton, cogn. w. *mignon*: see mignon, minion.] A wanton woman.

1489 Caxton *Faytes of A.* i. vii, Ne that he be not curyous of mygnotes, Jolyetes, ne of iewellis.

migod (mɪ'gɒd), *int.* ¶ Representation of a colloq. pronunc. of *my God!* (my *poss. adj.* 3).

1953 K. Tennant *Joyful Condemned* xx. 186 Migod, what they done to Trix! **1968** M. Richler *Cocksure* ii. 16 Migod, Mortimer thought. **1970** J. Cleary *Helga's Web* v. 78 Oh migod, isn't it terrible!

migraine ('miːgreɪn, 'maɪ-, formerly as Fr. migrɛn). [a. F. *migraine*: see megrim.] = megrim[1] 1, hemicrania. Also *attrib.* and *fig.*

1777 H. Walpole *Lett.* (1857) VI. 444 Madame de Jarnac had a *migraine*. **1837** B'ness Bunsen in Hare *Life* I. x. 446, I am obliged to take to my bed by an unusual degree of migraine. **1892** [see day *sb.* 19]. **1899** *Allbutt's Syst. Med.* VIII. 107 Ophthalmic migraine—that is paroxysmal pain in the eye or temple. **1937** *Tablet* 23 Oct. 553/2 We feel quite anxious for this young man who has fierce migraine-like black-outs. **1961** R. Graves *More Poems* 5 Love is a universal migraine, A bright stain on the vision Blotting out reason. **1971** *Brit. Med. Bull.* XXVII. 33/2 The common concept of migraine is of a syndrome in which severe unilateral periodic headache is accompanied by nausea or vomiting and preceded by a warning which is usually visual. **1971** 'D. Shannon' *Ringer* (1972) ix. 149 He's not at all well. A migraine headache. **1975** J. Symons *Three Pipe Problem* x. 72 Taking a pill for a mild migraine attack.

‖**migraineur** (migrɛnœr). [Fr. Cf. migraine.] One who suffers from migraine.

1971 *Times* 25 Jan. 6/6 The migrainous subject (or migraineur). **1971** *Daily Tel.* 11 Feb. 11/3 The general and specific measures recommended for prevention and for alleviation of the acute attack will prove a disappointment to the inveterate *migraineur* in search of relief but reflect the unpredictable and individual response to treatment. **1971** *Listener* 15 Apr. 480/3 Classical migraine is (*pace* G. B. Shaw) as uncommon among migraineurs as 'normal' vision among the rest of us.

'migrainous, *a.* [f. migraine + -ous.] Pertaining to or of the nature of migraine. Also, subject to attacks of migraine.

1889 *Lancet* 30 Mar. 640/2 All the various forms of headache—dyspeptic, migrainous,..and so on. **1897** *Trans. Amer. Pediatric Soc.* IX. 123 Migrainous epilepsy. [So called] because it commonly occurs in patients who have suffered from migraine. **1971** [see migraineur]. **1973** *Tucson* (Arizona) *Daily Citizen* 22 Aug. 32/1 Migrainous

women seldom put on weight, and they rarely develop any serious illness. **1974** *Radio Times* 6 June 66/1 Thousands of migrainous readers who read your feature 'The biggest aspirin splitter in the world'.

migram, obs. form of MEGRIM[1].
c **1450** in *Vicary's Anat.* (1888) App. ix. 230 Warke in þe swldyrs & migram in þe heue[de].

migrant ('maɪgrənt), *a.* and *sb.* [ad. L. *migrant-em*, pr. pple. of *migrāre* to MIGRATE.]
A. *adj.* Migrating; given to migration.
a. of animals; *spec.* of birds.
1672 SIR T. BROWNE *Let. Friend* §4 Passager and migrant birds.. whom no seas nor places limit. **1768** PENNANT *Zool.* II. 278 They [Grosbeaks] visit us only in hard winters, and are not regularly migrant. **1842** *P. Parley's Ann.* III. 306 The usual watering-places of the migrant animals. **1876** MRS. WHITNEY *Sights & Ins.* II. xxxvi. 651 Do you wonder we felt ourselves more like happy migrant birds than ever?
b. of persons, a tribe.
1807 J. BARLOW *Columb.* II. 178 And migrant tribes these fruitful shorelands hail. **1899** B. KING *Ital. Unity* I. 84 Migrant labourers came in gangs from the hills in harvest-time.
B. *sb.* One who or something which migrates.
a. A migratory animal; *spec.* a bird of passage.
1768 PENNANT *Zool.* II. 511 The migrants of this genus continue longest in Great-Britain in the southern counties. **1876** A. R. WALLACE *Geog. Distrib. Anim.* I. I. ii. 20 The chaffinch is a constant resident in England..; but a migrant in the south of France.
b. A person who migrates; *rarely* †a traveller.
1760 FOOTE *Minor* Ded., Wks. 1799 I. 225 The unhappy migrants may be.. at least hospitably entertained. **1864** R. A. ARNOLD *Cotton Fam.* 383 To facilitate migration from the cotton districts, and to direct the migrants to the best markets for their labour.
c. *Bot.* A plant whose distribution has changed or extended.
1905 F. E. CLEMENTS *Res. Methods Ecol.* 319 *Migrant*, a plant that is migrating or invading. **1960** N. POLUNIN *Introd. Plant Geogr.* vi. 165 These recent migrants were aided by natural means—wind, water or animals—or by Man, through intentional or accidental importation.

migrate (maɪ'greɪt, 'maɪgreɪt), *v.* [f. L. *migrāt-*, ppl. stem of *migrāre*.]
1. *intr.* To pass from one place to another; *spec.* in *Chem.* (see MIGRATION a). Also *trans.* in *pass.* to be transported.
1697 POTTER *Antiq. Greece* II. x. (1715) 292 A blow.. dissever'd the Sutures of his Skull, thro' which his Soul migrated. **1768–74** TUCKER *Lt. Nat.* (1834) I. 386 If one of us were migrated into their enormous hulks. **1784** COWPER *Task* II. 108 The sylvan scene Migrates uplifted,.. Alighting in far distant fields [Sicilian earthquake]. **1899** J. WALKER *Introd. Physical Chem.* xx. 210 Had no silver ions migrated from the anode, the rise in concentration would have been 32·2. **1931** J. C. WARE *Analytical Chem.* I. ii. 11 Ions move or migrate independently in a solution and at different rates. **1938** E. S. WALLIS in H. Gilman *Org. Chem.* I. viii. 724 The ease with which different groups migrate within the molecule is not wholly a property of the group itself, but is dependent to a varying extent on the molecule as a whole. **1967** J. H. RICHARDS et al. *Elem. Org. Chem.* xi. 194 A carbonium ion is produced as an intermediate, and a methyl group migrates from an adjacent carbon to the positive center.
2. a. *intr.* Of persons, a tribe, etc.: To move from one place of abode to another; *esp.* to leave one's country to settle in another; to remove *to* another country, town, college, etc. Also *transf.*
1770 LANGHORNE (Worc.), The Tuscans were a branch of the Pelasgi that migrated into Europe. **1784** JOHNSON *Let. to Ld. High Chancellor* Sept. in *Boswell*, If I grew much better, I should not be willing, if much worse, not able, to migrate. **1849** MACAULAY *Hist. Eng.* iii. I. 356 Almost all the noble families of England had long migrated beyond the walls. **1862** SIR B. BRODIE *Psychol. Inq.* II. iv. 117 The agricultural labourer is tempted.. to migrate to a manufacturing town. **1882** L. CAMPBELL *Clerk Maxwell* vi. 147 The advice which was pressed upon him.. that he should migrate to Trinity.
b. *Nat. Hist.* Of animals: To go from one region or habitat to another; *spec.* of some birds and fishes, to come and go regularly with the seasons (see MIGRATION).
1753 [cf. MIGRATING *ppl. a.*]. **1768** PENNANT *Zool.* I. 121 This kind of eagle sometimes migrates into Caernarvonshire. *Ibid.* 225 The birds [Fieldfares] that migrate here come from Norway. **1808–14** A. WILSON *Amer. Ornith.* II. 112 They [robins] not only migrate from north to south, but from east to west, to avoid the deep snows. **1889** A. R. WALLACE *Darwinism* 27 Of those [birds] which migrate in autumn a considerable proportion are probably lost at sea.
3. *Histol.* Of a cell: To move out of the blood-vessels into the tissues. (Cf. MIGRATORY *a.* 1 c.)
1896 [see MIGRATED *ppl. a.*].
Hence **mi'grated** *ppl. a.*; **mi'grating** *vbl. sb.*
1796 MORSE *Amer. Geog.* II. 72 Migrated Europeans from every part of Europe. **1831** TRELAWNY *Adv. Younger Son* III. 198 A migrated settler. **1884** W. J. LINTON *Poems & Transl.* (1889) 182 Knows He not, stork! the hour thy migratings begin? **1885** *Riverside Nat. Hist.* (1888) IV. 18 Diagram showing the main migrating routes of the littoral.. birds of Europe. *Ibid.* 20 The origin of the migrating habit. **1896** *Allbutt's Syst. Med.* I. 88 A large collection of migrated leucocytes.

'migrating, *ppl. a.* [f. MIGRATE *v.* + -ING[2].] That migrates, in the senses of the verb.
1753 CHAMBERS *Cycl. Supp.*, Migrating-Birds. *Ibid.*, *Migrating-Bog.*—These soft masses of earth have been sometimes known to move out of their place. **1774** GOLDSM. *Nat. Hist.* (1824) III. 70 Of all migrating fish, the Herring and the Pilchard take the most adventurous voyages. **1788** PRIESTLEY *Lect. Hist.* v. xliv. 329 The whole body of the migrating people. **1893** NEWTON *Dict. Birds* 572 These noises proceed from migrating birds.

migration (maɪ'greɪʃən). [ad. L. *migrātiōn-em*, n. of action f. *migrāre* to MIGRATE.] The action of moving from one place to another; also, an instance of this. **a.** *gen.* chiefly of things. *spec.* in *Chem.*, the (non-random) movement from one place to another of an atom or group, e.g. within a molecule as part of a rearrangement of its structure, or towards an electrode during electrolysis.
1611 COTGR., *Migration*, a migration, a remouing, or shifting of places. **1650** HOBBES *De Corp. Pol.* 133 The Tenets of Aristotle.. concerning Substance and Accidents, Species, Hypostasis, and the Subsistence and Migration of Accidents from place to place. **1695** WOODWARD *Nat. Hist. Earth* I. 45 Although such Alterations,.. Transitions, and Migrations of the Centre of Gravity:.. have actually happened, yet [etc.]. **1727–52** CHAMBERS *Cycl.* s.v., The migration of the souls of men into other animals after death. **1871** BLACKIE *Four Phases* I. 154 To pray to the gods, that our migration hence may take place with good omens. **1873** T. H. GREEN *Introd. Pathol.* (ed. 2) 100 The migration or transmission of elements from some primary growth, which.. constitute the centres of secondary formations. **1875** JOWETT *Plato* (ed. 2) I. 373 There is a change and migration of the soul from this world to another. **1879** *Encycl. Brit.* VIII. 108/2 For fused electrolytes a W-shaped tube.. is sufficient; with solutions.. the separation is more difficult, owing to the 'migration of the ions' and other causes. **1894** tr. *E. Goblet d'Alviella's Migration of Symbols* 82 Is it not the Winged Circle, whose migrations I trace in another chapter? **1898** *Jrnl. Chem. Soc.* LXXIII. I. 456 One of the following initial changes may occur. (1) Migration of the OH group. (2) Migration of the $O·SO_3H$ group as a whole. (3) Migration of a hydrogen atom of the ring, in the meta-position with regard to the side group. **1929** *Times* 13 Nov. 11/1 A serious obstacle to the work of archæologists, historians and others.. is the migration of manuscripts. **1938** A. L. RAYMOND in H. Gilman *Org. Chem.* II. xvii. 148 The migration of the benzoyl group from position three to six in monoacetoneglucose. **1962** D. H. CALAM in A. Pirie *Lens Metabolism Rel. Cataract* 439 Although the differences in migration of a group of mono-amino, mono-carboxylic acids.. are small, they are well separated by chromatography.
b. *esp.* of persons, a tribe: The action of moving from one country, locality, etc., to settle in another; also, simply, removal from one place of residence to another.
1646 SIR T. BROWNE *Pseud. Ep.* VI. vi. 302 The first man ranged farre before the Flood, and laid his bones many miles from that place, where its presumed he received them: And this migration was the greater, if.. he was cast out of the East-side of Paradise. **1766** BLACKSTONE *Comm.* II. 17 The right of migration, or sending colonies to find out new habitations. **1766** GOLDSM. *Vic. W.* i, All our adventures were by the fireside, and all our migrations from the blue bed to the brown. **1817** MOORE *Lalla R.* (1824) 290 A favourite resting place of the Emperors in their annual migrations to Cashmire. **1849** MACAULAY *Hist. Eng.* i. I. 10 In the ninth century, began the last great migration of the northern barbarians. **1891** S. C. SCRIVENER *Our Fields & Cities* 49 The poverty of the majority is the cause of the continual migration to London.
c. *Nat. Hist.* Of animals: The action of moving in flocks, shoals, etc. from one region or habitat to another; *spec.* of some birds and fishes, the periodical departure from and return to a region at a particular season of the year. Also, of plants, change or extension of distribution. ***bathic migration*** (see quot. 1877). ***equatorial migration***, ordinary meridional migration from or towards the equator.
1646 SIR T. BROWNE *Pseud. Ep.* IV. xiii. 223 By this way Aristotle through all his bookes of Animals, distinguisheth their times of generation, Latitancy, migration, sanity and venation. **1704** RAY *Creation* (ed. 4) 149 The migration of Birds.. according to the Seasons. *Ibid.*, The migration of divers sorts of Fishes. As for example; The Salmon. *Ibid.* 366 They [frogs travelling across dry land] had lived (till that time of their migration) in the Waters. **1830** LYELL *Princ. Geol.* (1875) II. III. xxxviii. 339 The former wide range of these quadrupeds implies a migration of Old World Forms into the new World. **1876** A. R. WALLACE *Geog. Distrib. Anim.* I. I. ii. 18 The term 'migration' is often applied to the periodical or irregular movements of all animals; but it may be questioned whether there are any regular migrants but birds and fishes. **1877** G. B. GOODE *Menhaden* 51 (U.S. Fish Comm. Rep.), The former may be called equatorial, the latter [*i.e.* changing to waters of less or greater depth] bathic migration. **1880** GÜNTHER *Fishes* 648 Comparatively few are subject to periodical migrations to the sea, like *Salmo*. **1905** F. E. CLEMENTS *Res. Methods Ecol.* iv. 216 Migration results when spores, seeds, fruits, offshoots, or plants are moved out of their home. **1932** FULLER & CONARD tr. *Braun-Blanquet's Plant Sociol.* xiii. 306 The first step in the development of vegetation is 'migration'. **1966** E. PALMER *Plains of Camdeboo* xvi. 270 White and Sloane wondering at the reasons for plant migrations. **1973** POLUNIN & SMYTHIES *Flowers of S.-W. Europe* ii. 86 The sierra.. has acted as a refuge for a number of montane species, which had in all probability previously undergone migrations and recessions culminating in the last ice age.
d. Of a bodily organ: Alteration of position whether from normal or pathological causes.
1890 in *Syd. Soc. Lex.*
¶ The alleged sense 'Residence in a foreign country; banishment' given in some recent Dicts. is fictitious. The word in the authority cited is a misreading of a later edition for 'extermination'.
e. *attrib.* and *Comb.* (sense c), as ***migration-route***; **migration-station**, a fixed place for the regular observation of the migration of birds.
1893 NEWTON *Dict. Birds* 561 Every species on Migration goes its own way, and what is called a *Migration-route is only the coincidence of the way taken by more or fewer of them. **1884** *Science* 17 Oct. 374/2 *Migration-stations now exist in every state and territory of the Union, excepting Delaware and Nevada.

migrational (maɪ'greɪʃənəl), *a.* [f. prec. + -AL[1].] Of or pertaining to migration or movement to another place.
1888 J. T. GULICK in *Linn. Soc. Jrnl.* XX. (*Zool.*) 223 In the case of plants and low types of animal life, the suitable situation is reached by a wide distribution of a vast number of seeds, spores, or germs, and the same situation is maintained by a loss of migrational power as soon as the germs begin to develop.

migrationist (maɪ'greɪʃənɪst). *rare.* [Formed as prec. + -IST.] **1.** An individual that participates in a migration.
1887 GOMME in *Jrnl. Anthrop. Inst.* XVII. 130 The descendants of previous ages of migrationists.
2. One who emphasizes the importance of migration in the distribution of species.
1918 L. HUXLEY *Life J. D. Hooker* II. xxxii. 98 Darwin was a migrationist; Forbes and others pushed the extension theory to excess.

migrative ('maɪgrətɪv), *a.* [Formed as prec. + -IVE.] Given to migration; migratory.
1831 J. RENNIE *Montagu's Ornith. Dict.* 322 The migrative species. *Ibid.* 534 It is a migrative bird, visiting our coasts in August. **1863** CARLYLE in *Mrs. Carlyle's Lett.* (1883) III. 181, I was as if stupefied more or less, and flying on like those migrative swallows of Professor Owen, after my strength was done.

migrator (maɪ'greɪtə(r)). [a. L. *migrātor*, f. *migrāre*: see MIGRATE.] One who migrates; also *spec.* a migratory bird.
1818 SHELLEY *Let. to Peacock* 25 July, It would be a little dangerous to the newly unfrozen senses and imaginations of us migrators from the neighbourhood of the pole. **1836** SWAINSON *Nat. Hist. Birds* I. I. iii. 97 The swallows.. are.. both the swiftest and the most distant migrators. **1852** BRISTED *Five Yrs. Eng. Univ.* 100 A migration is generally tantamount to a confession of inferiority, and acknowledgement that the migrator is not likely to become a Fellow of his own College. **1889** R. B. ANDERSON tr. *Rydberg's Teut. Mythol.* 31 Everywhere this great multitude of migrators was well received by the inhabitants.

migratorial ('maɪgrə'tɔərɪəl), *a.* *rare.* [f. MIGRATORY + -AL[1].] Of or pertaining to migration; migratory.
1865 *Daily Tel.* 28 July, Among their migratorial visitors are quails, landrels, and wrynecks. **1876** SMILES *Sc. Nat.* xi. (ed. 4) 209 Those [locusts] here alluded to are.. the best known from their migratorial flights.

migratory ('maɪgrətərɪ), *a.* and *sb.* [f. L. *migrāt-*, ppl. stem of *migrāre* to MIGRATE.]
1. Characterized by migration; given to migrating.
1755 JOHNSON, *Horde*, a clan; a migratory crew of people. **1815** ELPHINSTONE *Acc. Caubul* (1842) II. 79 The.. migratory tribes to the west of the pass of Gholairee. **1839** YEOWELL *Anc. Brit. Ch.* xi. (1847) 116 The migratory nature of the primacy seems to have weakened its stability. **1878** WOLSELEY in *19th Cent.* Mar. 449 Our population is so migratory that recruits are seldom enlisted in the parishes they were born in. **1879** FROUDE *Cæsar* v. 41 A vast migratory wave of population had been set in motion behind the Rhine and Danube.
b. Of animals; *spec.* in *Nat. Hist.*: Characterized by or given to periodical migration. Sometimes as a rendering of a mod.L. specific name, as in ***migratory locust, pigeon***.
[*a* **1672** WILLUGHBY *Ornithol.* I. ix. (1676) 17 Avium.. quæ statis anni temporibus advolant iterumque discedunt, migratoriæ dictæ. (RAY translates: Which we call Birds of passage.)] **1753** CHAMBERS *Cycl. Supp.* s.v. *Bird*, Migratory Birds, the same with birds of passage. **1793** tr. *Buffon's Birds* VI. 489 [Swallows.] Some are there permanent settlers and others migratory. **1808–14** A. WILSON *Amer. Ornith.* II. 293 *Columba migratoria*, Linnæus and Wilson.. Migratory Pigeon... The wild pigeon of the United States. **1835** W. IRVING *Tour Prairies* 206 We were on the great highway of these migratory herds. **1839** T. C. HOFLAND *Brit. Angler's Man.* iv. (1841) 107 It [the grayling] is very migratory, and frequently leaves one part of the river for another. **1875** NICHOLSON *Man. Zool.* (ed. 4) 290 The Migratory Locust (*Acrydium migratorium*) of Africa and Southern Asia. **1876** A. R. WALLACE *Geog. Distrib. Anim.* I. I. i. 20 The same species is often sedentary in one part of Europe and migratory in another.
c. Of a bodily organ, a disease, etc.: Characterized by movement from its normal position; esp. in *Histol.* of a cell: Given to migration from the blood-vessels to the tissues.
1876 QUAIN *Anat.* (ed. 6) II. 12 The pale blood-corpuscles may some of them make their way out of the blood-vessels and move freely in the surrounding tissues: hence the term 'migratory cells' (*Wanderzellen*) applied to them. **1877** tr. *H. von Ziemssen's Cycl. Med.* XV. 763 The Movable (Migratory) Kidney. **1897** *Allbutt's Syst. Med.* III. 13 One of the most characteristic features of the disease

[Acute Rheumatism] is the migratory nature of the joint affection.

2. Of or pertaining to migration.

1757 Burke *Abridgem. Eng. Hist.* Wks. X. 274 This purpose [intermixture of mankind] is sometimes carried on by a sort of migratory instinct, sometimes by the spirit of conquest. **1839** Selby in *Proc. Berw. Nat. Club* I. No. 7. 190 The wild-fowl began to..yield to that influence which directs their migratory movements. **1856** Kane *Arct. Expl.* I. viii. 80 The migratory passages of the reindeer.

B. *sb.* A migratory bird. *rare.*

1898 G. Meredith *Odes Fr. Hist.* 27 Winged migratories, having but heaven for home.

migrym, obs. form of MEGRIM[1].

Mihel, Mihel(e)mas(se, obs. ff. MICHAEL, MICHAELMAS.

‖**mihrab** (mɪx'rɑːb). Also 9 **mehhra'b, mehrab, mehreb, mirhab.** [Arab. *miḥrāb* praying-place.]

1. A niche, chamber, or slab in a mosque, indicating the direction of Mecca. Cf. KIBLAH.

1816 H. M. Williams tr. *Ali Bey's Travels* II. xvi. 217 In the wall at the end of the nave is the mehreb or niche where the Imam places himself to direct the prayer. **1836** E. W. Lane *Acct. Manners & Customs Mod. Egyptians* I. iii. 94 In the centre of its exterior wall is the *mehhra'b* (or niche). **1839** J. Pardoe *Beauties Bosphorus* 81 The *mihrab*, or niche at the eastern extremity of the edifice. **1845** R. Ford *Hand-bk. for Travellers Spain* I. 376/1 The exquisite niche, the *Mihrab* or sanctuary, in which the Koran was deposited. **1883** E. O'Donovan *Merv* xx. 242 A large deep recess, furnished with a *mirhab*, or devotional station. **1884** F. Boyle *On Borderland betwixt Fact & Fancy* 384 The Sayyid took his station at the mihrab. **1930** E. Waugh *Labels* 141 Agia Sophia..whose whole architectural rectitude has been fatally disturbed by the reorientation of the mihrab. **1931** *N. & Q.* 17 Oct. 271/1 The charm of the mosque with its *mirhab*—a false door, and its arcades—which carry nothing. **1959** *Chambers's Encycl.* VII. 763/2 The *liwan* on the side nearest to Mecca was much deeper than the others and formed a sanctuary with a central niche (*mihrab*) in its back wall. **1974** *Observer* (Colour Suppl.) 24 Nov. 43/2 The focal point of a mosque is the *mihrab*, a niche in the wall nearest to Mecca to which the congregation turns in prayer.

2. A niche motif on an Oriental prayer rug, resembling the shape of a mihrab in a mosque.

1911 G. G. Lewis *Pract. Bk. Oriental Rugs* x. 121 *Niche or Mihrab*.., the name applied to the pointed design at one end of a prayer rug. **1931** A. U. Dilley *Oriental Rugs & Carpets* viii. 201 Above this field is either one large prayer niche (called a mihrab), shaped like a tent, or a row of miniature prayer niches. **1963** tr. *I. Schlosser's European & Oriental Rugs & Carpets* 28 The mihrab, at first curved, later became steep and pointed... Scrolling stems with large flowers, or small branches..fill the border, the spandrels, and the cross panel which is usually above the mihrab. **1972** P. L. Phillips tr. *Formenton's Oriental Rugs & Carpets* 93 The mihrab, the niche in the centre of the rug, is often separated by two columns.

miht(e, obs. forms of MIGHT *sb.*

miin, mijn, obs. forms of MINE *poss. pron.*

‖**Mikado** (mɪ'kɑːdəʊ). Also 8–9 **Mikaddo.** [Japanese *mi* august + *kado* door: for the sense cf. 'Sublime Porte'.] **1.** The title of the emperor of Japan.

It was usual for European writers to describe the Mikado as a 'spiritual' emperor, and the Shogun (who was the *de facto* ruler until 1867) as a second or 'temporal' emperor.

1727 Scheuchzer tr. *Kæmpfer's Japan* III. ii. I. 211 In Spiritual Affairs, they are under the absolute jurisdiction of the Mikaddo. *Ibid.* 212 The Secular Monarch professes the religion of his forefathers, and pays his respect and duty once a year to the Mikaddo. **1845** *Encycl. Metrop.* XX. 476/1 Their Spiritual ruler is the *Mikaddo, i.e.* Sublime Porte, a term commonly used to express the Daïri himself as well as his Court. **1875** W. E. Griffis in *N. Amer. Rev.* CXX. 282 The restoration of the mikado, or true emperor [of Japan] to his ancient and rightful supreme power. **1890** B. H. Chamberlain *Things Japanese* 155 Japan.., though.. avowedly ruled by the Shōguns from A.D. 1190 to 1867, always retained the Mikado as theoretical head of the state.

2. Mikado pheasant, a pheasant native to the island of Formosa, *Syrmaticus mikado*, first described in 1906 from specimens in the Mikado's collection in Tokyo.

[**1906** W. R. Ogilvie-Grant in *Bull. Brit. Ornith. Club* XVI. 123 Among the Mikado's collection of live animals and birds, at Tokio, there are said to be a pair of Pheasants from Formosa belonging to an undescribed species.] **1922** C. W. Beebe *Monogr. Pheasants* III. 200 In appearance,..the Mikado Pheasant resembles the tragopans and impeyans, being heavy bodied and rather thick-necked. *Ibid.* 201 Several healthy hybrids with the Elliot pheasant...strongly resemble the female Mikado. **1965** P. Wayre *Wind in Reeds* xv. 211 The beautiful Mikado Pheasant, of which the male is a deep bluish purple with red wattles and a purple and white barred tail,..found only on..Taiwan. *Ibid.* 212 There the Mikado inhabits the bamboo and juniper thickets ..above five thousand feet. **1972** *Shooting Times & Country Mag.* 1 July 19/1 Next on the list for rehabilitation in Formosa (Taiwan to most, these days) is the Mikado pheasant. The Trust is breeding this bird and hopes soon to have enough for a further transplant.

Hence **Mi'kadoate**, the office of Mikado.

1899 F. V. Dickins in *Eng. Hist. Rev.* Apr. 229 The mikadoate of old Japan entered upon its final stage.

mikan ('mɪkɑːn). [Jap.] A Satsuma orange.

[**1922** T. Tanaka in *Jrnl. Heredity* XIII. 243/2 The leading orange grown in Japan is a kind of mandarin, *Unshû Mikan*, called the Satsuma orange in the United States.] **1947** J. Bertram *Shadow of War* 193 *Mikans*—the sweet, juicy mandarin oranges. **1972** *Nat. Geographic* CXLI. 672/2 Obasan offered up sliced raw fish,..and finally the Futagami specialty, *mikan*, a tangerine-like citrus. **1973** A. Broinowski *Take One Ambassador* v. 56 Drink cans, *mikan* peel..used chopsticks, everywhere.

†**mike**, *sb.*[1] *Obs. rare.* Forms: 3 mik, 4–5 myke. ? A friend.

a **1300** *Cursor M.* 2807 'Has þou her', þai said, 'ani man, Sun or doghter, mik or mau to þe langand'. **13..** *E.E. Allit. P.* A. 572 For mony ben calle[d] þaȝ fewe be mykez. *c* **1470** Harding *Chron.* LXXII. iv, He made..Hymselfe like Brethel in all semblaunce That [then was] the dukes preuy myke.

†**mike**, *sb.*[2] [? a. MDu. *micke* (mod.Du. *mik*): cf. MECK, MICHE *sb.*[2]] ? A 'crutch' or forked support on which a boom rests when lowered.

13.. *E.E. Allit. P.* B. 417 Hit waltered on þe wylde flod, ..With outen mast, oþer myke, oþer myry bawelyne.

mike (maɪk), *sb.*[3] *slang.* [Belongs to MIKE *v.*[1]] A rest; a period of idleness; a waste of time; esp. in phr. *to do* or *have a mike* = to be idle, escape from or evade work, go away. Cf. MICK[3].

1825 Egan *Life Actor* 28 The performances of the last night at the theatre are often discussed over a *mike* at the fireside the next morning respecting the abilities of the actors. *Foot-n., Mike* or *Shammock*. Technical or cant phrases amongst printers. To have a *mike* is to loiter away the time, when it might be more usefully or profitably employed. **1890** Barrère & Leland *Dict. Slang.* s.v., *Mike* (tailors), to do a *mike*, to pretend to be working or hang about. **1899** R. Whiteing *No. 5 John St.* xxiv. 238 It was pleasant to..share the tobacco and biscuit, and make sure of a good 'mike' on this side of a life to come. **1925** Fraser & Gibbons *Soldier & Sailor Words* 155 *Mike, to (to do a)*, to make off. To avoid duty. **1940** M. Marples *Public School Slang* 119 *To do a mike* (St Bees, 1915 +), to break bounds. **1955** 'N. Shute' *Requiem for Wren* iii. 83 That's a good mike for you, but you'll have plenty to do later on. **1958** *Times* 26 Sept. 19/1 The day of the cheerful veteran forward, gratefully relying upon opportunities for a mild 'mike', may be coming to an end.

Mike (maɪk), *sb.*[4] *slang.* [Shortened from *Michael.*] = MICK[1]. Phr. *for the love of Mike*, see LOVE *sb.*[1] 7 a.

1874 *Hotten's Slang Dict., Mike*, an Irish hodman, or general labourer.

mike (maɪk), *sb.*[5] Colloq. abbrev. of MICROPHONE 1; also *attrib.* Cf. MIC.

1927 *Melody Maker* June 579/3, I think it is more that he plays too loudly than that he is too near the 'mike'. **1928** Ade *Let.* 7 July (1973) 134 Open the act with a fake microphone all set and adjusted for broadcasting. You come out and talk into the 'mike' announcing the name of a fake station in the town..and say you have a very interesting program ahead and then you can read it into the mike. **1937** *Daily Herald* 16 Feb. 19/6 He is unlikely to be afflicted with 'mike' fright, because, in his line, he has found visible audiences in far more truculent mood than will be his unseen Midland Regional listeners. **1939** *Evening News* 7 Nov. 4/5 To follow the players about, the 'mike' is moved across the floor on a long arm called a 'mike boom', and its operator is a 'mike slinger'. **1943** J. B. Priestley *Daylight on Saturday* xi. 68 He delighted in entertainment, liked to make his little speech at the mike. **1956** B. Holliday *Lady sings Blues* (1973) iii. 38, I got to the mike somehow and grabbed it. **1962** *Listener* 12 Apr. 656/3 Robert Kee avoided.. entangling his mike-cable in the mob. **1971** D. E. Westlake *I gave at the Office* (1972) 188 'I am a soldier'; he said, 'not a baseball player. No interview.' Frankly, I think he had mike fright.

mike (maɪk), *sb.*[6] In slang phr. *to take the mike out of* = to take the micky out of. Cf. MICKY[1] 6.

1935 G. Ingram *Cockney Cavalcade* i. 14 He wouldn't let Pancake 'take the mike' out of him. *a* **1935** T. E. Lawrence *Mint* (1955) II. vi. 117 But, mate, you let the flight down, when he takes the mike out of you every time. **1940** *N. & Q.* 1 June 382/1 'Taking the mike out of' anyone means pulling his leg, having a game with him. **1956** J. Cannan *People to be Found* i. 14 They won't 'alf take the mike out of 'im. **1973** 'B. Mather' *Snowline* vi. 75 Watch it... The Swami don't dig taking the mike out of the gods.

mike (maɪk), *sb.*[7] *slang.* [Abbrev. of *microgram.*] A microgram, *spec.* of lysergic acid diethylamide (LSD).

1970 N. Saunders *Alternative London* xxii. 168 Lysergic Acid Diethylamide is the most common hallucinogen—and by far the most powerful, in that you only need a few millionths of a gram (micro-grams, 'mikes') to trip for eight hours. **1970** K. Platt *Pushbutton Butterfly* (1971) vi. 58 Janet Sanders could be on acid, dropping the usual LSD tab of two hundred and fifty mikes. That's the standard trip.. a penny a microgram. **1973** J. Wood *North Beat* x. 126 They wanted me to tell where I got the mikes... The acid, see?

mike (maɪk), *v.*[1] *slang.* [Of obscure origin: cf. MITCH *v.*] *intr.* To 'hang about', doing nothing or waiting for a job; to avoid work; go away, escape; also with *off.* Hence '**miking** *vbl. sb.*

1859 *Hotten's Slang Dict., Mike*, to loiter; or as a costermonger defined it, to 'lazy about'. **1887** W. E. Henley *Villon's Gd. Nt.* 3 You sponges miking round the pubs. **1894** A. Morrison *Tales of Mean Streets* 47 'I ain't settled with you yut, my gal,' he added to Lizer; 'mikin' about at 'ome an' 'idin' money.' **1930** E. Wallace *Lady of Ascot* xxii. 219, I believe in a fair day's work for a fair day's pay and no miking. **1959** B. J. Farmer *Murder Next Year* xv. 83 He knew most of the possible 'miking' holes. *Ibid.* 84 Molden was simply 'miking' on a grand scale. *Ibid.* 85 A policeman is paid to work his beat, not 'mike' with or without permission. **1959** N. Lofts *Heaven in your Hand* 145 There was nobody to send. Both my young b—s have miked off. **1974** P. Evett in J. Burnett *Useful Toil* III. 336 [He would] spy on us as we worked, and then..thunder at any one he thought was miking.

mike (maɪk), *v.*[2] *colloq.* [f. MIKE *sb.*[5]] *trans.* To place a microphone in (a place) or near (a person) for recording purposes; freq. = BUG *v.*[1] 2. So **miked** *ppl. a.*

1962 M. Procter *Body to Spare* xvi. 124 He was put in a cell with Cony, and the cell was 'miked'. **1965** D. Torr *Diplomatic Cover* v. 82 The Russian..turned a switch on the bigger recorder... Christ, they've miked us! **1968** —— *Treason Line* 19, I take it this Dean is the American Counsellor whose bungalow you're trying to mike? **1969** 'A. Hall' *Striker Portfolio* xvi. 196 My one task for the day was to find out if the room was miked because I didn't want them to hear my movements. **1969** *Rolling Stone* 17 May 12/3 What came out was a beautifully mixed and miked package of spiritual soul. **1972** *Jazz & Blues* Oct. 30/1 Mezz is too closely miked for one to be able to follow the soprano clearly at all times. **1974** *Listener* 4 Apr. 437/3 [The] film..owes a great deal to..the unobtrusive miking techniques..and the quiet manoeuvring of the crew.

mike, -lik, -ness, obs. ff. MEEK, -LY, -NESS.

mikel(l, mikil(le, mikle, obs. ff. MICKLE.

miker ('maɪkə(r)). *dial.* and *slang.* [f. MIKE *v.* + -ER[1].] = MICHER *sb.*

1890 J. D. Robertson *Gloss. Words County of Gloucester* 94 *Miker* is used for a truant. **1928** *Daily Tel.* 9 Oct. 10/5 It is reported that the casual ward of Edmonton Workhouse was known far & wide over the highway as the 'Mikers' Mecca'. **1931** C. Williams *Three Plays* 29 You always saw and sneaked your profit out Like a kerchief-miker.

Mikimoto (mɪkɪ'məʊtəʊ). The name of Kokichi *Mikimoto* (1858–1954), Japanese pearl farmer, used *attrib.* of pearls cultured by means of a technique which he perfected.

1956 R. Eunson *Pearl King* ii. 28 At Toba Bay Mikimoto pearls are harvested by the crop and sacked up like wheat. **1959** R. Kirkbride *Tamiko* iii. 20 Diamonds and great clusters of Mikimoto pearls gleamed in the candle-light. **1969** J. Bennett *Dragon* i. 6 A string of good cultured Mikimoto pearls around her neck.

mikrom, -on, variant forms of MICROM, MICRON.

mikul, obs. form of MICKLE.

mikva ('mɪkvɑː). Also **mikve(h, mikwe(h.** Pl. **mikvaoth.** [Heb. *miqwāh*, lit. collection, mass, esp. of water; pool of water.] A bath in which certain Jewish ritual purifications must be performed; the action of taking such a bath. Also *attrib.*

1843 De Sola & Raphall tr. *18 Treat. from Mishna* 356 Treatise Mikvaoth. (Contains laws that relate to diving baths for the cleansing of persons.) **1904** *Jewish Encycl.* VIII. 588 *Miḳweh*... Because of the use made of this word in connection with ritual purification.., it has become the term commonly used to designate the ritual bath... The miḳweh must contain sufficient water to cover entirely the body of a man of average size. **1962** B. Abrahams tr. *Life Glückel of Hameln* v. 108 Every Jewish community had its *mikveh*—ritual communal bath. **1966** *New Statesman* 6 May 648/2 All women about to marry must endure an interview with a woman in the rabbinate who issues a ticket to the ritual bath (*mikva*). **1968** L. Rosten *Joys of Yiddish* 242 Today, only very religious Jewish women observe the *mikva* custom—or attend a bathhouse for *mikvas*. **1970** L. M. Feinsilver *Taste of Yiddish* 249 *Mikve* immersion is also part of Orthodox conversion ritual. *Ibid.*, The average American Jewish couple would be surprised to learn..that the wife should then visit the *Mikve* before union. **1974** *Observer* (Colour Suppl.) 10 Nov. 37/3 By ancient Jewish teaching..a woman becomes virtually unclean by the act of menstruation and she must abstain from sexual relations during it and for seven days after it is finished. Before she recommences relations with her husband she should immerse herself in the *mikva* (ritual bath). Brides prior to marriage should also be purified in the *mikva* and also mothers after child-birth... Reform Jews do not use the *mikva*.

mil (mɪl). Also 8 **mill.** [ad. L. *mille* thousand. In senses 2 and 3 short for L. *millēsimum* thousandth, on the analogy of CENT 2, 3.]

1. *per mil*: per thousand. (Cf. *per cent.*)

1721 C. King *Brit. Merch.* I. 294 Ox-bones | 30400 | 0.6.8 per Mill | 10.2.8. **1753** Hanway *Trav.* (1762) I. VII. lxxxviii. 407 Koeninsburg draws in current money, 1 per mil, according to custom, being deducted. **1973** *Sci. Amer.* Feb. 66/3 Away from coastal areas..the salinity of the ocean varies from 32 to 37 grams of dissolved solid per kilogram of seawater, expressed as 32 to 37 ‰ (The symbol ‰ is read 'per mil'.)

2. A proposed coin of the value of the thousandth part of a pound sterling. See also MILL *sb.*[5] b. Also *attrib.*

1854 Humphreys *Coin. Brit. Emp.* 149 It is proposed that the smallest coin, one thousand to the pound, shall be called a *mil*. **1875** Jevons *Money* xiv. 176 The two principal schemes [of decimalization]..are the Pound and Mil scheme, and the Penny and Ten-franc scheme. **1883** *Encycl. Brit.* XVI. 734/1 Another proposal starts from the present *pound* as unit. It is to be divided into 10 *florins* (2s.), which would contain 100 *mils* (or *farthings* reduced 4 per cent.). A new coin, 10 *mils* (2s. 4d.) would probably have to be introduced. **1920** *Rep. R. Comm. Decimal Coinage* 13 in *Parl. Papers* (Cmd. 628) XIII. 467 The pound and mil provides no exact equivalent of the penny. Of the nearest equivalents 4 mils is 4 per cent. less, 5 mils is 20 per cent. more than the penny. **1920** *Glasgow Herald* 10 Apr. 4 If there were any demonstrable superiority in this 'pound mil'

system it might be worth while to face all..delays. **1960** *News Chron.* 4 May 3/2 The day when we..pay 200 mils for a packet of cigarettes has drawn a little closer. **1963** *Rep. Comm. Inquiry Decimal Currency* p. xiv, in *Parl. Papers 1962–3* (Cmnd. 2145) XI. 195 We sometimes refer to 'mil' systems..as three-place decimal systems. **1967** *Guardian* 26 Apr. 2/6 The committee..was considering an amendment to introduce the pound-florin-mil system.

3. A unit of length used in measuring the diameter of wire, = $\frac{1}{1000}$ of an inch. **circular mil**, a unit of area for measuring cross-sections of wires, tubes, and rods, being the area of a circle whose diameter is one mil.

1891 L. CLARK *Dict. Metric Meas.* **1896** F. BEDELL *Princ. Transformer* xv. 306 For conductors larger than 50,000 circular mils, flat copper ribbons are always used. **1962** A. NISBETT *Technique Sound Studio* 255 *Coarse-groove*. The groove normally used for 78 rpm recordings... Width 6 mils, depth 2·5 mils. **1973** *Sci. Amer.* July 43/1 Graphite fibers, produced by the carbonization of rayon or acrylic fibers, average about a third of a mil in diameter.

4. Used in *Pharmacy* for MILLILITRE.

Proposed (together with *decimil* for ·0001 litre, and *centimil* for ·00001 litre) by Mr. J. Humphreys in 1904. The three terms were authorized by the Board of Trade in 1905.

5. The name of a coin whose value is a thousandth part of the unit of currency, in Cyprus (and formerly in Palestine and Egypt) and Hong Kong.

1902 *Encycl. Brit.* XXXI. 292/1 *Hong Kong*,..the denominations are..the cent and the mill in bronze. **1908** G. B. RAWLINGS *Coins* xi. 317 Queen Victoria's issues for Hong Kong consisted of silver dollars, half-dollars..and mils. *Ibid.*, The mil follows the Chinese fashion and is pierced in the centre. On the one side it has a crown, V.R., and the date, and Hong Kong One Mil. **1929** *Whitaker's Almanack* 447 Palestine..*Silver*—100, 50 mils. *Bronze* 2, 1 mils. **1937** M. COMENCINI *Coins Mod. World* 42 Palestine Mandated Territory... Currency in Mils on a decimal basis, similar to that in use in Egypt. *Ibid.* 106 Egypt... *Currency unit*:..1 Piastre of 10 Milliemes or Mils. **1956** *Whitaker's Almanack* 783 Cyprus... 1,000 mils = £1 Sterling. **1968** C. NARBETH *Coin Collectors' Encycl.* 65 Cyprus... A new currency was introduced in 1955 of 100 mils (equals 2s.). **1970** C. WOOD *Terrible Hard* v. 56 'How much?' 'Forty-five mils!' **1975** G. LYALL *Judas Country* iii. 20, I served 'em a compulsory breakfast at 500 mils each.

6. A unit of angular measure equal to 1/1600 of a right angle, which is approximately the angle subtended by one metre at a distance of 1000 metres.

1907 O. M. LISSAK *Ordnance & Gunnery* xiii. 507 The horizontal deflection scale..is graduated, in sights for field artillery, to thousandths of the range. These gradations are called mils. **1920** CARTER & ARNOLD *Field Artillery Instruction* vi. 219 The angle of site scales and the deflection scales on all instruments are graduated in mils. **1920** J. K. FINCH *Topogr. Maps* 138 The vertical lines of the sketching screen, being one inch apart and twenty inches from the eye, determine an angle of fifty mils. **1941** *Amer. Math. Monthly* XLVIII. 188 Most American mobile artillery units as well as many heavy railway mounts have the scales on their sights, azimuth circles, and quadrants graduated in mils. **1955** C. R. WYLIE *Plane Trigonometry* i. 21 Show that on any circle a central angle of 1 mil intercepts an arc whose length is approximately 1/1,000 of the radius of the circle. **1970** *Daily Tel.* 1 June 15/7 The Services no longer measure bearings in 360 degrees but in 6,400 mills to a circle.

mil., var. MILL *sb.*[6] and *sb.*[7]

‖**milady** (mɪˈleɪdɪ). Also miladi. [F. *milady*: cf. MILORD.] A continental rendering of 'my lady', used as an appellation in speaking to or of an English noblewoman or great lady.

1839 JAMES *Gentl. Old School* xii, 'I did not wish to listen to your conversation, miladi', interrupted Philippina. **1873** E. FITZGERALD *Lett.* (1889) I. 361 What do you and Miladi think of these two Lines of his which returned to me the other day? **1886** *Boston* (Mass.) *Jrnl.* 13 Aug. 2/3 In the outfit of the full-dressed dog of the English milady.

milage, variant of MILEAGE.

Milan[1] (mɪˈlæn, ˈmɪlən). Forms: 5 **Melayne, -eyn, Mylleyn,** 5–6 **Mil(l)ayn(e,** 6 **Myllain, Myll-, Millan, -en, -in, -on, Myllane, Melane, Mul(l)ane, Mil(l)ion, Millian,** 6–7 **Millane, Millain(e,** 6– **Milan.** [ad. It. *Milano*.] **1. a.** The name of the chief city of Lombardy; used *attrib.* to designate certain of its manufactures, chiefly textile fabrics and steel-work, as †***Milan bonnet***, †***fustian***, †***gloves***, ***lace***, †***sleeves***; †**Milan needle**, a sail-needle; **Milan point** (see quot. 1882); **Milan steel** (*Hist.*), steel used by the armourers of Milan in the manufacture of coats-of-mail, swords, etc. (so ***Milan hauberk***, ***knife***, ***mail***)

[**1431** *Test. Ebor.* II. 13 Unam loricam de Milan.] **1495** *Naval Acc. Hen. VII* (1896) 276, vj C. mylleyn nedylles.. spent abought reparacion & amendyng of the seyd Sayles. **1503** *Acc. Ld. High Treas. Scot.* (1900) II. 234 Item for thre elne Melane fustiane. **1507** *Ibid.* (1902) IV. 15 Five Melane bonetis. **1530** in *Form of Cury* (1780) 167 A pair of Myllen Sleves of white sattin. **1532** *Proclam.* 18 Aug. in *Chron. Calais* (Camden) 116 To apparell there servauntes in..red Myllen bonnettes. **1535** STEWART *Cron. Scot.* (Rolls) I. 235 The Millane melȝeis mendit nocht ane myte, The brandis bricht sa bitterlie did byte. **1545** *Rates Custome Ho.* b viij, Millin gloues or canary the groce, xxvi.s. viii.d. **1588** in *Anc. Invent.* (Halliw. 1854) 126 A quilte..lyned with Million fustian. **1601** J. WHEELER *Treat. Comm.* 23 Milan Fustians. **16..** *K. Arth. & K. Cornw.* 168 in *Percy Fol. MS.* I. 68 He sayes, 'Collen brand Ile haue in my hand, And a Millaine knife fast by my knee.' **1622** MABBE tr. *Aleman's Guzm. d'Alf.* I. 158 A Buffe Ierkin, laid on with a costly Milane-Lace. **1828** SCOTT *F.M. Perth* xi, Canst thou take up a fallen link in my Milan hauberk? **1882** CAULFEILD & SAWARD *Dict. Needlework* s.v. *Milan Point*, The Milan Points..were fine hand made laces similar to the Spanish and Venetian Points.

†**b.** Short for *Milan steel*. *Obs.*

1464 *Mann. & Househ. Exp.* (Roxb.) 194 A stondard of mayll..and a salat wyth a vesere of meleyn. **15..** *Chevy Chase* 65 (Ashmole MS.), With swordes that wear of fyn myllan. **16..** *Eger & Grine* 169 in *Percy Fol. MS.* I. 359 My Habergion that was of Millaine fine.

2. (See quot. 1968.) Also *attrib.*

1895 *Montgomery Ward Catal.* 131/3 Misses' or children's, Union Milan and fancy braid. **1948** K. HARDY *Costume Design* x. 209 *Milan*, finer version of leghorn. **1950** '*Mercury' Dict. Textile Terms* 345/2 *Milan hat*, a hat of fine straw, originally manufactured in the province of Milan, Italy. **1968** J. IRONSIDE *Fashion Alphabet* 253 *Milan*, a fine, closely woven straw from Milan, Italy, used for expensive hats.

†**milan**[2]. *Obs. rare.* In 5 **myl(l)an,** 6 **myllaine.** [a. F. *milan*.] A kite.

c **1484** CAXTON *Fables of Æsop* I. iv. (1889) 8 The myllan. *Ibid.* II. ii. 34 The kyte or mylan. **1575** TURBERV. *Falconrie* 124 The Myllaine and the Lanerette.

milaner, -ery, obs. ff. MILLINER *sb.*, MILLINERY.

Milanese (mɪləˈniːz), *a.* and *sb.* Forms: 5 **mylannoys,** 8 **Milaneze,** 8– **Milanese.** [ad. It. *Milanese*: see -ESE.] **A.** *adj.* **1.** Of or pertaining to Milan, its inhabitants, manufactures, etc. ***Milanese lace*** (see quot. 1882).

1617 J. CHAMBERLAIN *Let.* 21 June (1939) II. 82, I met with a Milanese gentleman of some qualitie. **1753** M. W. MONTAGU *Let.* 10 Oct. (1967) III. 39 A Milanese lady being now proffessor of Mathematics in the University of Bologna. **1756–7** tr. *Keysler's Trav.* (1760) I. 384 The freedom and liberality of the Milanese ladies. **1866** G. MEREDITH *Vittoria* xxix, A printed song in the Milanese dialect. **1882** CAULFEILD & SAWARD *Dict. Needlework*, *Milanese Lace*.—This is made in the Philippine Isles, with Manilla grass. The work is a combination of Drawn Work and open Embroidery, and has not much the appearance of lace. **1896** HENTY *Knt. White Cross* xvii. 269 A superb suit of Milanese armour.

2. Of a warp knit fabric made on a Milanese loom usually from silk or rayon yarns; of a garment made of this fabric.

1897 *Sears, Roebuck Catal.* 231/1 The New Four-Button Pure Silk Glove... Guaranteed all pure Milanese silk. *Ibid.*, Black Milanese Silk Mitts, the softest, finest and most durable of all silks. **1916** *Daily Colonist* (Victoria, B.C.) 19 July 14/5 (Advt.), Nothing could be more appropriate for wear at the big Fete Saturday than one of these Suits, of Milanese Silk. **1922** *Tatler* 30 Aug. Advts. p. c, Ladies' exceedingly dainty Cami-Knickers, made of best quality Milanese Silk. **1922** *Ibid.* 5 July Advts. p. m, Pure Silk Milanese Vest.

B. *absol.* or as *sb.*

1. A native or an inhabitant of Milan.

Unchanged for pl.: cf. *Chinese*, *Maltese*. In 6 †*Milanesis*.

1484 CAXTON *Fables of Poge* iv. (1889) 297 A mylannoys named Paulus. **1582** N. LICHEFIELD tr. *Castanheda's Conq. E. Ind.* I. liv. 116 b, With them went two Milanesis, which were Lapidaries. *a* **1715** BURNET *Own Time* VI. (1734) II. 177 That the Milaneze should have a neutrality granted them. **1886** RUSKIN *Præterita* I. vi. 200 To drive to the Corso, where at that time the higher Milanese were happy and proud as ours in their park.

2. ***the Milanese***: the territory of the old duchy of Milan.

a **1715** BURNET *Own Time* VII. (1734) II. 354 If the King of France..became Master of the Milaneze. **1769** ROBERTSON *Chas. V*, II. Wks. 1851 III. 483 Seizing by surprise, or force, several places in the Milanese. **1841** W. SPALDING *Italy & It. Isl.* III. 44 The allies overran the Milanese and Piedmont.

3. The Milanese dialect.

1642 J. HOWELL *Instructions Forreine Trav.* xi. 138 There is in Italy..the Milanese, the Parmasan, the Piemontese, and others..and all these have several Dialects and Idiomes of Speech. **1818** [see GENOESE *sb.*]. **1880** *Encycl. Brit.* XIII. 493/2 It may be added that the Milanese *nün*..is really a compound or reduplication in the manner of the *ni-ni*. **1966** T. G. GRIFFITH *Migliorni's Italian Lang.* xi. 351 Porta, who gave a brilliant example of the expressive use of his own Milanese, defended dialect against Giordani.

4. Milanese fabric (see A. 2).

1927 *Glasgow Herald* 20 Apr. 10 What your supples and your Milanese may be, you alone may care. But one takes off one's hat to the 'shimmering crepe de soie'. **1945** M. D. POTTER *Fiber to Fabric* 238 Milanese has a distinctive diagonal cross effect. Originally silk, now also rayon. **1968** J. IRONSIDE *Fashion Alphabet* 241 *Milanese*, a warp-knit fabric made on a Milanese loom, used mainly for women's underwear, very fine and lustrous.

milboard, obs. form of MILLBOARD.

†**milce**, *sb. Obs.* Forms: 1 **milds,** 1–2 **milts,** 2–3 **mildce,** 2–4 **milce,** 3 **millce** (*Orm.*), **milze, milzce, mildze, milche,** 3–4 **milse, mulce,** 4 **mylse.** [OE. *milds*, *milts* fem.:—OTeut. type ***milđisjâ**, f. ***milđjo-** MILD *a.*: cf. BLISS *sb.* The *z* of early ME. forms = *ts*.]

1. Mercy, clemency, forbearance, favour. Often coupled with *ore*, *grace*, or *mercy*. Also *pl.* mercies.

Beowulf 2921 (Gr.) Us wæs a syððan Merewioinga milts ungyfeðe. *c* **825** *Vesp. Psalter* xxiv. 6 ȝemyne mildsa ðinra dryhten. *c* **1200** *Trin. Coll. Hom.* 119 Bidde we nu þe holigost þat he haue milce of us. *c* **1200** *Vices & Virtues* 81 After ðine manifealde mildces ðe ðu hafst ihafd to mankenne, do awei fram me ðese michele unrihtwisnesse. *c* **1205** LAY. 21889 We ȝeorneð þine milzce. *a* **1250** *Owl & Night.* 1083 Ic hadde of hire Milce [*MS. Cott.* milse] & ore. *c* **1250** *Gen. & Ex.* 3603 Louerd,..Merci ȝet for ðin milde mod! Or ðu ðis folc wið milche moð [*read* loc] Or do min name ut of ðin boc. **1297** R. GLOUC. (Rolls) 775 He..hopede vor to finde of hire betere mulce & grace. *a* **1310** in Wright *Lyric P.* xviii. 58 Tharefore y bidde thin mylse ant ore, Merci, lord, ynul na more! *c* **1330** *Arth. & Merl.* 667 (Kölbing), Hou Jesu of a maide þurch his milce was ybore.

2. Comb.: ***milce-hearted*** adj. [cf. OE. *milts-heort*]; **milce-witter** *a.*, knowing mercy.

c **1250** *Gen. & Ex.* 2903 Ne taȝte ic hem noȝt..Min miȝtful name adonay; Min milche witter name eley He knewen wel, and ely. *a* **1300** [see MILCER].

†**milce**, *v. Obs.* Forms: 1 **mildsian,** 1–2 **mil(t)sian,** 2 **milcian, -en,** 3 **millcenn** (*Orm.*), **milse, mylce, milce.** [OE. *mildsian*:—OTeut. type ***mildisôjan**, f. ***milđjo-** MILD- *a.*] *trans.* To have mercy on, or show mercy to (a person); to be kind, compassionate, or gracious to. Also *absol.* Hence **milciende** *ppl. a.*, merciful.

c **825** *Vesp. Psalter* I. 1 *Miserere mei*, mildsa min. *c* **888** K. ÆLFRED *Boeth.* xxxviii. §7 Nis nan riht þæt mon þone yflan hatiȝe, ac hit is rihtre þæt him mon miltsiȝe. *a* **1175** *Cott. Hom.* 235 Maȝie wiman forȝeten his oȝe cild þat hi ne milsi hire barn of hire oȝen innoð. *c* **1175** *Lamb. Hom.* 11 Muchel is us þenne neod..þet we ȝerne bidden ure milciende drihten þet [etc.]. *c* **1275** LAY. 16784 For þe loue of God al-mihti milce me and mine cnihtes. *c* **1275** *Duty of Christians* 18 in *O.E. Misc.* 141 Iblessed beo such eþeling vs mylce þat he wolde. *a* **1300** *E.E. Psalter* cxiv. 5 (Horstm.) And oure god milse sal.

†**ˈmilceful**, *a. Obs.* [f. MILCE *sb.* + -FUL.] Merciful, gracious. Hence †**ˈmilcefulness**.

a **1225** *Ancr. R.* 30 Milcefule Louerd. *Ibid.* 264 Milsfule. *a* **1225** *Juliana* 52 (Roy. MS.), Ne beoð cristene men.. merciable ant milzful. *c* **1320** *Cast. Love* 543 þou art, Fader, so milsful kyng. *c* **1330** W. HEREBERT *Antiphones* in *Rel. Ant.* I. 88 The mylde gode sped in rithfolnesse, To sunfole men sheu mylsfolnesse.

†**ˈmilcer**. *Obs. rare*[−1]. [f. MILCE *v.* + -ER[1].] One who shows mercy or pities.

a **1300** *E.E. Psalter* cxliv. 8 (MS. Egerton), Milzer & milzeherted [*L. miserator et misericors*].

†**milch**, *sb. Obs.* [? f. the vb.] The capacity or condition of giving milk; also, a yield or quantity of milk.

1634 W. WOOD *New Eng. Prosp.* I. iv, [Cattle] being generally larger and better of milch. **1642** J. EATON *Honey-c. Free Justif.* 380 Like a shrewd cow, that gives a good milch, and then kicketh it all downe, when she hath done.

milch (mɪltʃ), *a.* Forms: 3 **mielch,** 3, 6–7 **milche,** 4–6 **melche,** 5–7 **mylche,** 6 **mellche, mylch,** 6–7 **melch,** 6– **milch.** [ME. *mielch*, *milche*, repr. OE. ***milce** (in *pri-milce*, month of May, when the cows can be milked thrice in the day):—OTeut. type ***melukjo-**, f. ***meluk-** MILK *sb.*

The adj. actually found in OE. with this sense is *meolc*, *melc*, corresponding to MDu., MLG. *melk*, OHG. *melch* (MHG. *melch*, *melc*, mod.G. *melk*), ON. *miolk-r*; the stem of this adj. is identical with that of MILK *sb.*, and is probably evolved from compounds.]

1. Of domestic mammals: Giving milk, kept for milking, 'in milk'. (The opposite of *dry*.) See also MILCH COW.

c **1290** *S. Eng. Leg.* I. 351/228 ȝwane heo [*sc.* the cow] cam hom at eue, fair and round heo was, And swyþe Mielch al-so. *c* **1440** *Jacob's Well* 37 þe tythe of þe pasture to þe drye beestys owȝte to be payid as wel as to þi melche beestys. **1548** in *Rel. Ant.* II. 17 Item, ij. mellche beastes, whiche were belonginge to the norcerye. **1560** BIBLE (Geneva) *Gen.* xxxii. 15 Thirty milche camels with their coltes. **1592** SHAKS. *Ven. & Ad.* 875 Like a milch Doe, whose swelling dugs do ake, Hasting to feed her fawne. **1626** BACON *Sylva* §778 Mixtures of Water in Ponds for Cattell, to make them more Milch. **1759** CHESTERF. *Lett.* 16 Mar., I have just now bought a milch-goat, which is to graze, and nurse me at Blackheath. **1774** GOLDSM. *Nat. Hist.* III. 14 That fine milch breed, which excels the cattle of any other part of the world. **1789** G. WHITE *Antiq. Selborne* v. 324 Though barrow-hogs and young sows found no inconvenience from this food [yew-berries], yet milch-sows often died after such a repast. **1887** MORRIS *Odyss.* IX. 341 So to the milking his milch-ewes and his bleating goats he sat.

†**b.** Applied to a woman, esp. a wet-nurse. *Obs.*

c **1290** *S. Eng. Leg.* I. 472/362 þat child wolde souke and it nuste ȝwam, þare nas no milk a-boute, ne no mielch wumman. *c* **1325** *Lai le Freine* 196 He..tok it [the child] his douhter, and hir bisought, That hye schuld kepe it as sche can, For sche was melche and couthe theran. **1563** HYLL *Art Garden.* (1593) 49 And neither women in childebed, nor milch nourses,..may eate Parcely with their meats. **1662** GRAUNT *Bills Mort.* iii. 19 [Deaths] caused by carelessness, ignorance, and infirmity of the Milch-women. **1709** STEELE *Tatler* No. 15 ⁋2 One Country Milch-Wench, to whom I was committed, and put to the Breast.

c. *fig.*

1658 J. HARRINGTON *Prerog. Pop. Govt.* I. xi. Wks. (1700) 300 Thus a populous City makes a Country milch, or populous by sucking.

†**d.** applied to the breasts or teats; also *transf.* to the eyes when weeping. *Obs. rare.*

1600 J. LANE *Tom Tel-troth* 123 Pallas, the Nurse of Nature-helping Art,..From whose milch teates no pupils would depart. **1602** SHAKS. *Ham.* II. ii. 540 The instant

Burst of Clamour that she made.. Would haue made milche the Burning eyes of Heauen.

†**2.** *nonce-uses.* **a.** Of plants: Milky, full of milk. **b.** Of dew: Exuding like milk. *Obs.*

c **1420** *Pallad. on Husb.* III. 1081 Item [*sc.* plants] that beth melche in ver novelles grene [L. *uerno magis cum lactent nouella uirentia*] Beth nought to fede. **1612** DRAYTON *Poly-olb.* xiii. 171 Exhaling the milch dewe which there had tarried long, And on the ranker grasse till past the noone-sted hong.

† **milch,** *v. Obs.* [app. f. MILCH *a.*

Not repr. OE. *melcan* str. vb. or *meolcian, (ȝe)milcian* wk. vb.: see MILK *v.*]

trans. To milk (an animal). Also *fig.* Hence **milched** *ppl. a.*, **'milching** *vbl. sb.*

1570 LEVINS *Manip.* 130/7 To Milch, *mulgêre.* **1589** FLEMING *Virg. Bucol.* III. 9 And let him couple foxes too, and milch the male-kind gotes. **1648** H. FERNE *Serm.* (1649) 8 Two new-milcht Kine drawing the Arke of God. **1648** HEXHAM, *Een melckinge*, a Milking, or a Milching. **1784** TWAMLEY *Dairying* 23 The owner made a point of never keeping a Cow that was too old Milcht, or Milk'd too long from the time of Calving; or when any Cow went off her Milk.. he always replaced her with a new Milcht one. **1805** R. W. DICKSON *Pract. Agric.* II. 986 Where they [*sc.* calves] suck stale milched cows.

b. *Comb.* (the verb-stem used *attrib.*), as ***milch-barn, -bowl, -house.***

1599 *Acc. Bk. W. Wray* in *Antiquary* XXXII. 243, xv. milche boules. *Ibid.*, In the milche house. **1810** *Splendid Follies* II. 177 The equestrians.. arrived at the milch-barn.

'milch-cow. [MILCH *a.*]

1. A cow 'in milk'; a cow giving milk or kept for milking.

1424 in *E.E. Wills* (1882) 57, I wul my wyf haf half my mylche kye. *c* **1440** *Promp. Parv.* 337/2 Mylche cowe, *bassario, vel vacca mulsaria.* **1523** FITZHERB. *Husb.* §70 Melch kye and draught oxen, wyll eate a close moche barer than as many fatte kye and oxen. **1583** STUBBES *Anat. Abus.* II. (1882) 47 And so solde the former barren cowe with hir adulterate calfe, for a melch cowe. **1596** SHAKS. *Tam. Shr.* II. i. 359, I haue a hundred milch-kine to the pale. **1879** HINGSTON *Australian Abr.* ix. 102 China, as a Nation, is as weak and defenceless now as a milch cow.

transf. **1816** KIRBY & SP. *Entomol.* xvii. (1818) II. 65 Aphides and Cocci, which are the milch kine of our little pismires.

2. *fig.* A source of regularly-accruing gain or profit; *esp.* a person from whom money is easily drawn, one who 'bleeds freely'. (So F. *vache à lait.*)

1601 J. WHEELER *Treat. Comm.* 40 So profitable a Milch cowe as the English Trade was vnto the Lowe Countries. **1617** CHAMBERLAIN *Let.* in *Ct. & Times Jas. I*, II. 8 That he had been a good milch cow to Dixon.. and that he had yielded £200 a year. *a* **1700** B. E. *Dict. Cant. Crew, Milch-kine*, a Term us'd by Goalers, when their Prisoners will bleed freely to have some Favor, or be at large. **1712** ARBUTHNOT *John Bull* I. xii, John's cause was a good milch cow, and many a man subsisted his family out of it. **1885** *Ch. Times* 18 Dec. 993/4 The.. private patron.. far more frequently viewed his advowson as a milch-cow for his private profit.

milche, obs. f. MELSH, *a.* (With ***milche-hearted*** cf. early ME. *milce-herted* s.v. MILCE *sb.*)

1552 HULOET, Milche harted, *lemosus.*

milcher ('mɪltʃə(r)). [f. MILCH *a.* or *v.* + -ER[1].] An animal that yields milk; a milch-beast.

1823 E. MOOR *Suffolk Words* 229 A good milcher. **1890** 'R. BOLDREWOOD' *Col. Reformer* (1891) 417 Those miniature milchers [*sc.* goats]. **1891** T. HARDY *Tess* xvi, All prime milchers, such as were seldom seen out of this valley.

milchy ('mɪltʃɪ), *a.* [f. MILCH *a.* + -Y[1].]

†**1.** Milk-giving, yielding milk. *Obs. rare.*

1635 SIR T. HAWKINS tr. *Horace, Odes* Epode xvi. (ed. 3) 86 There, milchy Gotes come freely to the Paile.

2. ? *U.S.* 'Milky, as an oyster' (*Cent. Dict.* 1890).

milcie, var. MILCE *v. Obs.*, MILSEY *Sc.*

† **mild,** *sb.*[1] *Obs. rare.* [f. MILD *a.*[1] Cf. ON. *mildi*, OHG. *miltî.*] Gentleness, pity.

c **1430** in *Pol. Rel. & L. Poems* (1903) 197 Lete mylde & meekenes [*v.r.* mylde mekenes] melte in þin herte. **1576** GASCOIGNE *Philomene* (Arb.) 112 Then Progne phy for thee, Which kildst thine only child, Phy on the cruel crabbed heart Which was not movde with milde.

mild, *sb.*[2] Eng. and U.S. dial var. of MILE *sb.*[1]

1701 in *Essex Inst. Hist. Coll.* (1900) XXXVI. 83 To run the lien of mesuer from Ipswich meting howes.. six mields. **1725** in *Early Rec. Lancaster, Mass.* (1884) 231 We traueled to Groten 12 milds... We marcht up the riuer about 8 milds. **1777** R. LINCOLN *Diary* 7 July in *Papers* (1904) 15 They ware Engaged in Carring gun bots.. over land about one mild into Lake George. **1836** *Knickerbocker* VIII. 352, I expect we are a mild and a half from the *city.* **1886** F. T. ELWORTHY *West Somerset Word-Bk.* 476, I count 'tis up vower mild yer-vrom. **1903** *Dialect Notes* II. 321, I haven't walked a *mild* in a year. **1927** *Amer. Speech* III. 10 Most natives [*sc.* Ozarkers] use *mile* for both singular and plural, but some of the old-timers use the plural form *mild.*

mild (maɪld), *a.* Forms: 1–7 **milde**, 3–6 **myld(e**, 5 **myelde, myyld**, 5–6 **myild(e**, 6 **miled**, 3– **mild.** [Com. Teut.: OE. *milde* = OFris. *milde*, OS. *mildi* (MDu. *milde*, Du. *mild*), OHG. *milti* (MHG. *milte*, mod.G. *mild*), ON. *mild-r* (Sw., Da. *mild*), Goth. *-mild-s* (in compounds, *friaþwamildjai* masc. pl., loving, *unmildjai* masc. pl., unkind; also in derivative *mildiþa* kindness):—OTeut. **mildjo-*, **mildi-*, f. Indogermanic root **meldh-* (:*moldh-* :*mldh*), whence Gr. *μαλθακός* soft, mild, OIrish *meldach* tender, Skr. *mṛdh* to neglect, also to be moist.]

1. Of persons, their disposition and behaviour.

a. (Chiefly of a superior, e.g. a king): Kind, considerate, gracious, merciful, indulgent; not harsh or severe. Now *rare* or *Obs.*

a **725** *Laws K. Wihtræd* Prol., Ðam mildestan cyninge Cantwara Wihtræde rixiȝendum. **1387** TREVISA *Higden* (Rolls) VII. 483 þat tyme Theobald þ e mylde [L. *pius*], eorle of Campania, was in his floures. **1667** MILTON *P.L.* x. 1046 Remember with what mild And gracious temper he both heard and judg'd Without wrauth or reviling. **1725** POPE *Odyss.* XIV. 160 So mild a master never shall I find. **1832** HERAUD *Voy. & Mem. Midshipm.* ix. (1837) 157 This mild prince.. is deservedly popular with his.. subjects.

b. Applied to God, Christ, and the Virgin Mary. *Obs.* exc. in traditional collocations.

971 *Blickl. Hom.* 71 Secggaþ Siones dohtrum þæt heora cining cymeþ, milde & monþwære. *c* **1200** *Trin. Coll. Hom.* 21 þus mildeliche andswerede þe milde quen of heuene. *a* **1225** *Leg. Kath.* 2411 Milde Iesu. *a* **1300** *Cursor M.* 24748 Quen i ma mening o þat mild [the Virgin]. **1389** in *Eng. Gilds* (1870) 47 His mild modir seynt marye. **1567** *Gude & Godlie B.* (S.T.S.) 84 Thow blissit Virgin mylde. **1603** KNOLLES *Hist. Turks* (1621) 121 Libertie would availe me nothing, if Christ by his most milde incarnation had not taken away our captivitie. *a* **1729** J. ROGERS 19 *Serm.* i. (1735) 5 It teaches us.. to adore him as a mild and merciful Being, of infinite Love.. to his Creatures. **1810** SCOTT *Lady of L.* III. xxix, Ave Maria! maiden mild! **1828** JOLLY *Sunday Serv.* (1848) 206 This mild Majesty of God incarnate.. was now about to ascend to Heaven.

c. const. *to* or †dative; occas. †*with.*

971 *Blickl. Hom.* 47 God biþ milde þæm monnum þe.. on hine ȝelefaþ. *c* **1205** LAY. 14802 He [Vortimer] wes milde ælche cnafe. *a* **1250** *Owl & Night.* 1775 Wið heore cunne heo beoþ mildre. **13..** *Assump. Virg.* 888 (Add. MS.) For oure ladi here schal be mylde. *a* **1450** MYRC 29 In worde and dede þou moste be mylde Bothe to mon and to chylde. **1579** LYLY *Euphues* (Arb.) 165 Yet is he milde to those that aske forgiuenesse. **1687** A. LOVELL tr. *Thevenot's Trav.* I. 58 They erect a stone over the head of the deceased, to serve for a seat to the Angels who are to examine him, that they may be the milder to him.

d. Gentle and conciliatory in disposition or behaviour; not easily provoked, and giving no offence to others; not rough or fierce in manners.

In mod. prose used with more or less disparaging implication: cf. 6 b.

a **1000** *Guthlac* 711 (Gr.) Swa þæt milde mod.. dryhtne þeowde. *c* **1200** ORMIN 2938 Milde he [Joseph] wass.. I þatt he nollde wreȝenn þatt wimmann þatt wass gilltelæs. **1362** LANGL. *P. Pl.* A. x. 83 Drede is such a Mayster þat he makeþ Men Meoke and Mylde of heore speche. **1387** TREVISA *Higden* (Rolls) I. 173 And þere ynne beþ more mylde peple [L. *quæ gentem habet magis piam*, contrasted with *feras gentes*]. *c* **1440** *Promp. Parv.* 337/2 Myyld, and buxum, *pius, benignus, mansuetus.* **1530** PALSGR. 776/1, I have knowen hym a heedye felowe, but he is waxen mylde nowe: *je lay congneu vng testart, mays il se est bien humylié mayntenant.* **1596** SPENSER *F.Q.* v. xii. 42 Most bitter wordes they spake.. That they the mildest man alive would make Forget his patience. *c* **1645** HOWELL *Lett.* (1655) II. liv. 63 A harsh Mother may bring forth sometimes a mild daughter. **1720** POPE *Iliad* XXIV. 963 In whom the gods had join'd The mildest manners with the bravest mind. *a* **1862** BUCKLE *Civiliz.* (1873) III. ii. 53 The mildest spirit might well have been roused by this.

absol. *c* **1175** *Lamb. Hom.* 113 Drihten.. on-hefð þa mildan. *c* **1375** *Sc. Leg. Saints* xxiv. (*Alexis*) 103 Syne dyliuere was þat myld, thru goddis helpe, of a knaf chyld. **1813** H. G. KNIGHT *Alashtar* III. xiii, Let the weak bewail! Well may the mild, the woman-hearted fail.

e. of looks, language, etc.

Beowulf 1172 Sprec mildum wordum. *c* **1175** *Lamb. Hom.* 45 þa onswerede him drihten mildere steuene. *c* **1200** *Trin. Coll. Hom.* 123 þe ilke louerd.. þe þus lokeð of heuene to men mid his milde eȝen. *c* **1420** *Chron. Vilod.* 1013 Hure voys was bothe myelde & swete. **1568** GRAFTON *Chron.* II. 36 With such mylde aunsweres he put off the tyme. **1771** *Junius Lett.* xlix. (1788) 266 But this language is too mild for the occasion. **1797** *Encycl. Brit.* (ed. 3) XI. 759 Their features are extremely mild and pleasing. **1813** SHELLEY *Q. Mab* III. 158 His mild eye beams benevolence no more. **1855** MACAULAY *Hist. Eng.* xxii. IV. 754 If he sometimes stooped to be a villain—for no milder word will come up to the truth.

f. of rule, punishment, treatment of persons, influence, and the like. Now chiefly in *comparative*: Less severe.

1577 tr. *Bullinger's Decades* II. viii. (1592) 191 But this kind of quieting and setting parties at one, is verie milde in comparison of reuengement and punishment. *a* **1645** WALLER *Pens-Hurst* I. 44 Ah! cruel Nymph!.. her humble swaine.. from the winds and tempests doth expect A milder fate then from her cold neglect! *c* **1655** MILTON *Sonn.*, '*When I consider*', Who best Bear his milde yoak, they serve him best. **1776** ADAM SMITH *W.N.* IV. viii. (1869) II. 232 The penalties imposed by this milder statute. **1825** MACAULAY *Ess., Milton* (1899) 17 But.. why not adopt milder measures? **1871** FREEMAN *Norm. Conq.* (1876) IV. xvii. 73 The South.. was put under the milder rule of the Bishop.

g. in proverbial similes, ***as mild as a dove, as May, as milk***, etc.

1530 PALSGR. 626/2 Whan he is angryest of all I can make hym as mylde as a lambe. **1599** ? SHAKS. *Pass. Pilgr.* vii, Faire is my loue, but not so faire as fickle; Milde as a Doue, but neither true nor trustie. **1704** POPE *Pastorals, Spring* 81 Sylvia's like autumn ripe, yet mild as May. **1874** T. HARDY *Madding Crowd* iv, A temper as mild as milk.

†**h.** ***mild mother*** (tr. PIA MATER): see MOTHER.

2. a. Of an animal: Tame, gentle; not wild or fierce. (*Obs.* exc. as directly *transf.* from 1 d.)

c **1290** *S. Eng. Leg.* I. 39/183 þe Bollokes and þe ȝoungue steores þat weren er so wilde, Anon so huy touward heom come huy woxen tame and milde. **1377** LANGL. *P. Pl.* B. xv. 275 Egydie after an hynde cryede, And þorw þe mylke of þat mylde best þe man was susteyned. **1390** GOWER *Conf.* I. 39 Of so good mesure He song, that he the bestes wilde Made of his note tame and milde. **1671** MILTON *P.R.* I. 310 Among wild Beasts: they at his sight grew mild. **1774** GOLDSM. *Nat. Hist.* IV. 254 Mild, peaceful, and brave, it [the elephant] never abuses its power or its strength. **1801** J. JONES tr. *Bÿgge's Trav. Fr. Rep.* viii. 154 The menagerie seems to be separated into two parts, the one for mild animals, and the other for wild and ferocious. **1840** *Penny Cycl.* XVIII. 476/1 The Kinkajou is very mild in captivity.

b. Of a plant: Cultivated, not wild. *Obs. rare.*

1601 HOLLAND *Pliny* II. 168 As many vertues as the mild fig-tree hath, yet the wild is much more effectuall.

3. Of weather, etc.: Not rough or stormy, not sharp or severe; calm, fine, and moderately warm. Of a climate: Temperate.

14.. *Seven Deadly Sins* 3 in *Pol. Rel. & L. Poems* (1866) 215 Apon a mylde mornyng of may. **1530** PALSGR. 318/2 Mylde of wether, *paisible.* **1634** MILTON *Comus* 4 In Regions milde of calm and serene Ayr. **1714** GAY *Trivia* I. 144 Signs.. Of milder weather, and serener skies. **1819** SHELLEY *Prometh. Unb.* I. 793 Spring.. Whose mild winds shake the elder brake. **1892** EMILY LAWLESS *Grania* I. 1 A mild September afternoon.

fig. **1608** SHAKS. *Per.* III. i. 27 Now mylde may be thy life, For a more blusterous birth had neuer Babe.

4. Of light, or a luminous body: Shining with tempered lustre, softly radiant.

a **1645** WALLER *To Yng. Lady Lucy Sidney* 10 The rosy morne resignes her light, And milder glory to the Noon. **1768–74** TUCKER *Lt. Nat., Theol.* xviii. (1852) I. 367 The Governor of the Universe is a more discernible object,.. clothed with milder rays of glory. **1819** KEATS *Lamia* I. 382 A silver lamp, whose phosphor glow Reflected in the slabbed steps below, Mild as a star in water. **1832** STANDISH *Maid of Jaen* 21 The moon's mild orb was shining seen.

5. a. Of a medicine: Operating gently; not violent or strong in its effects. Of food, tobacco, etc.: Soft to the palate, not rough or sharp or strong in taste or odour, not over-stimulating or over-feeding. Of pathological secretions: Not acrid or irritating.

a **1400–50** *Alexander* 4824 Was neuir no mede ne no milke so mild vndire heuen. **1577** B. GOOGE *Heresbach's Husb.* II. (1586) 58 b, The smoother the leafe is, the mileder and the sweeter is the roote. **1652** CULPEPPER *Eng. Physic.* 12 The milde Arsmart is good against hot Imposthumes. **1732** ARBUTHNOT *Rules of Diet* in *Aliments*, etc. 257 Anti-acids of a milder kind. **1768** BICKERSTAFF *Lionel & Clarissa* I. (1786) 9 Why, one bottle [of hock] won't hurt you, man—this is old, and as mild as milk. **1822–34** *Good's Study Med.* (ed. 4) IV. 62 The matter discharged is whitish and mild, producing no excoriation.. or other disquiet. **1831** YOUATT *Horse* x. 171 A very mild dose of physic. **1845** ELIZA ACTON *Mod. Cookery* 122 Mild Ragout of Garlic... By changing very frequently the water in which it is boiled, the root will be deprived of its naturally pungent flavour and smell, and rendered extremely mild. **1855** *Anti-Maud* xxix, Sipping their Seltzer and Hock, and smoking a mild cigar. **1899** *Allbutt's Syst. Med.* VIII. 614 The milder form of sulphur lotion is preferable.

fig. **1781** COWPER *Charity* 502 Most satirists are indeed a public scourge; Their mildest physic is a farrier's purge.

b. Of ale or beer: In early use app. free from acidity, not sour or 'stale'; now applied to those kinds that are not strongly flavoured with hops (opposed to *bitter*). Also *absol.* = mild ale. ***mild-and-bitter***, a mixture of mild and bitter ale or beer. For the phr. ***to draw it mild*** see DRAW *v.* 40 b.

1626 BACON *Sylva* §52 A good draught of Milde Beer. **1717** PRIOR *Alma* II. 203 Suppose your eyes sent equal rays Upon two distant pots of ale, Not knowing which was mild or stale. **1818** KITCHINER *Cook's Oracle* (ed. 2) 502 Cool Tankard, or Beer Cup. A quart of mild ale, a glass of white wine, one of brandy [etc.]. **1886** 'JOHN BICKERDYKE' *Curios. Ale & Beer* 391 A pint.. of mild beer, half a pint of brandy [etc.]. **1889** A. BARNARD *Noted Breweries* I. 357 Cellars.. for racking and storing mild ales. **1894** A. MORRISON *Martin Hewitt* ii. 63 'Had his glass o'beer, has he?'.. 'Has two glasses of mild a-day... Never puts on flesh.' **1933** D. L. SAYERS *Hangman's Holiday* 157 Half of mild-and-bitter, please. **1944** DYLAN THOMAS *Let.* 21 Sept. (1966) 267 It is time for the Black Lion But there is only Buckley's unfriskly Mild. **1951** E. HYAMS *Sylvester* xxiv. 121 The chaps in the local, drinking a pint of mild and bitter. **1957** J. BRAINE *Room at Top* ii. 22 We used to.. live on onions and cheese washed down with mild-and-bitter. **1963** *Times* 25 May 9/7 'But t'brig isn't t'world', a sewing-shop overlooker says over his gill of mild. **1974** 'W. HAGGARD' *Kinsmen* vii. 70 He went to the bar. Mysteriously four evident locals were already inside and drinking mild.

c. Of a disease, or an attack of disease: Not severe or acute.

1744 BERKELEY *Siris* §3 Others had it [small-pox] in the mildest manner. **1800** *Med. Jrnl.* IV. 187 The inoculated Cow-Pox is a much milder and safer disease than the inoculated Small-Pox. **1849** MACAULAY *Hist. Eng.* iii. I. 401 The.. genius of Butler, if it did not altogether escape the prevailing infection, took the disease in a mild form.

6. a. Of bodily exercise: Moderate, gentle, easy. Of amusement or recreation: Not boisterous, not exuberant in enjoyment or mirth.

1831 YOUATT *Horse* x. 171 Mild exercise should be used. **1882** A. BAIN *Jas. Mill* 388 There should also be social amusements of a mild character, such as to promote cheerfulness rather than profuse merriment.

b. Used sarcastically to connote tameness or feebleness (in persons and their actions), where audacity, cleverness, recklessness, etc. might have been expected.

1885 *Sat. Rev.* 7 Feb. 166/1 Most of us have no wish to cheat railway Companies by travelling first class at third-class prices, but there are ingenious adventurers who practise this mild swindle. **1886** *Pall Mall G.* 2 Oct. 3 A mild attempt to anarchize English grammar. **1897** BARRÈRE & LELAND *Dict. Slang, Mild bloater*, weak young man who has pretensions to being horsey. *Mod.* We had a mild game of whist.

†**7.** *Chem.* ? Neutral. *Obs.*

1796 KIRWAN *Elem. Min.* (ed. 2) I. 6 Mild Calx (so I call lime united with fixed air). **1797** *Encycl. Brit.* (ed. 3) IX. 346/2 The brown calx of iron united with the white calx of manganese, and mild calcareous earth in various proportions. **1799** KIRWAN *Geol. Ess.* 149 The limestone of Malta contains both calcareous earth and magnesia, but most probably in a mild state. *Ibid.*, The selenite is decomposed by the mild magnesia contained in the stone.

8. a. Of soil, wood: Soft, easy to work. *dial.*

1852 S. W. HOSKYNS *Talpa* xix. 163 This'll be mild enough for anything presently; you don't call this a stiff soil? **1875** T. LASLETT *Timber* xiv. 84 The Modena, Roman, and Sardinian [Oaks] are what the workmen call milder in character—that is to say, they are easier to work, and a little less hard than the former [kinds]. **1880** JEFFERIES *Gt. Estate* ix. 164 'These old French burrs be the best stone; they be hard, but they be mild and takes the peck well.'

b. ***mild steel***: steel containing only a small precentage of carbon, of great strength and toughness, but not readily tempered or hardened.

1868 JOYNSON *Metals* 90 What is called in the trade 'homogeneous iron' is a species of 'mild-steel', and has been introduced by a Sheffield firm. **1884** W. H. GREENWOOD *Steel & Iron* 202 The mild steels produced by the Siemens and the Bessemer processes. *Ibid.* 399 The elongation of the milder qualities of steel before fracture occurs is superior to that of malleable iron.

c. *Physics.* (See quot.)

1878 J. C. MAXWELL in *Encycl. Brit.* VI. 312/1 A body which can have its form permanently changed without any flaw or break taking place is called *mild*. When the force required is small the body is said to be *soft*; when it is great the body is said to be *tough*.

¶**9.** Peculiarly used by Byron. Of a slope: Gentle. Of a wood: Not thorny.

1818 BYRON *Ch. Har.* IV. lxvii, Upon a mild declivity of hill. **1823** —— *Island* II. xx, For even the mildest woods will have their thorn.

10. Used *poet.* in the place of an adv., = MILDLY.

a **900** CYNEWULF *Crist* 249 (Gr.) þu þisne middanȝeard milde ȝeblissa þurh ðinne hercyme, hælende Crist! **1667** MILTON *P.L.* VII. 110 And thus the Godlike Angel answerd milde. **1730–46** THOMSON *Autumn* 1098 The pale deluge.. streaming mild O'er the sky'd mountain to the shadowy vale. **1739** C. WESLEY *Christmas Hymn* 21 Mild he lays his Glory by, Born—that Man no more may die. **1784** COWPER *Task* III. 443 As oft As the sun peeps and vernal airs breathe mild.

11. *Comb.* (chiefly parasynthetic and adverbial), as ***mild-aspected***, †***-aspecting***, ***-brewed***, ***-cured***, ***-eyed***, ***-faced***, ***-flavoured***, ***-mannered***, ***-mooned***, †***-persuading***, ***-scented***, ***-seeming***, ***-spirited*** (†***-sprited***), ***-spoken***, ***-tempered***, ***-worded*** adjs.

1597 DRAYTON *Heroic Ep., Isab. to Mortimer* 17 That blessed night, that *mild-aspected howre, Wherein thou mad'st escape out of the Towre. **1601** WEEVER *Mirr. Mart.* C 6 b, On Sea the *mild-aspecting heauens would guide me. **1905** W. L. COURTNEY *Father Time & Childr.* in *Queen's Christmas Carol* 95 October comes to give men cheer, With purple grapes and *mild-brewed beer! **1832** TENNYSON *Lotos-Eaters* 27 The *mild-eyed melancholy Lotos-eaters came. **1862** HOWELLS *Venet. Life* vii, A very *mild-faced old priest. **1575–85** ABP. SANDYS *Serm.* xvi. 284 Let her bee milde-worded and *milde-manered. **1821** BYRON *Juan* III. xli, He was the mildest manner'd man That ever scuttled ship or cut a throat. **1819** KEATS *Lamia* I. 156 A deep volcanian yellow took the place Of all her *milder-mooned body's grace. **1601** WEEVER *Mirr. Mart.* D 3 b, In *mild-perswading words and deedes. **1776–96** WITHERING *Brit. Plants* (ed. 3) III. 677 Prickly, or *Mild-scented Lettuce. *a* **1586** SIDNEY *Arcadia* III. (1598) 386 The sheepe [gave] *mild-seeming face. **1607** T. CAMPION *Maske* B 4 b, *Mild sprited Zephyrus haile. **1712–27** ARBUTHNOT *John Bull* I. v. Miscell. II. 12 The Neighbours reported that he was Henpeck't, which was impossible, by such a mild spirited Woman, as his Wife was. **1727** *Art Speaking in Publick* vi. 84 An Orator ought not to be too Remiss, neither in his Action, nor too *Mild-spoken. **1838** DICKENS *Nich. Nick.* xxix, You're always so mild spoken. **1747** tr. *Astruc's Fevers* 169 A cold *mild-tempered easy patient. **1575–85** *Milde-worded [see *mild-mannered*].

†**mild**, *v. Obs.* [f. MILD *a.* OE. had *mildian* intr., to become mild.] *trans.* To make mild or gentle. Also *refl.*

1340 *Ayenb.* 117 We byeþ þe more ymylded and þe dreduoller. *Ibid.* 177 Þeruore ssel þe zeneȝere him mildi ase moche are ha may beuore god. **1494** FABYAN *Chron.* VI. cxcvii. 203 This message mylded nothyng the kynges courage. **1627–47** FELTHAM *Resolves* I. xvi. 55 As for man, it [the Gospel] teaches him to tread on cottons, milds his wilder temper.

mildce, milde, var. MILCE *sb.*, MILE *sb.*[2] *Obs.*

milded: see MILE *v. Obs.*

milden ('maɪld(ə)n), *v.* [f. MILD *a.* + -EN[5].]

1. *trans.* To make mild or milder.

1603 FLORIO *Montaigne* III. xii. 620 The very names by which they call diseases doe somewhat mylden and diminish the sharpnes of them. **1820** L. HUNT *Indicator* No. 63 (1822) II. 83 What follows.. is mildened a little by the introduction of the name of Erasmus, More's intimate friend. **1900** A. B. DAVIDSON in *Expositor* Jan. 9 Polygamy and slavery were treated in two ways: their use was mildened and circumscribed.

2. *intr.* To become mild or milder.

1853 [see *mildening, ppl. a.*]. **1882** in *Imperial Dict.* Suppl.

Hence **'mildened, 'mildening** *ppl. adjs.*

1842 CARDL. WISEMAN *Prayer & Prayer-Bks.* Ess. 1853 I. 397 It is not Saul alone.. that hath felt the mildening and calming influence of David's harp. **1853** KANE *Grinnell Exp.* xxxvii. (1856) 341 The mildening temperature. **1864** LOWELL *Fireside Trav.* 315 Suffused with a tremulous, glooming glow, a mildened glory.

'milder, *v. dial.* (Lincs.) [? cogn. w. MOULDER *v.*] *intr.* To moulder, decay; to crumble *away*. *lit.* and *fig.* Hence **mildering** *ppl. a.*

1610 W. FOLKINGHAM *Art of Survey* I. ix. 20 This practise is most approuable and peculiar in mildring Clay, which otherwise by shooting and melting downe into open Trenches, would choake vp the water-passages. **1632** SANDERSON *Serm.* 353 Their estates crumble and milder away. **1647** H. MORE *Cupid's Conflict* xv, Unthankfull wretch! Gods gifts thus to reject And maken nought of Natures goodly dower. That milders still away through thy neglect. **1671** SKINNER *Etymol. Ling. Angl.*, Moulder, *agro Linc.* Milder. **1886** *S.W. Linc. Gloss.* s.v., The stone-work is so mildered. It's clean mildered away. The frost lays hold on it and it milders down.

mildernix, variant of MEDRINACKS *Obs.*

mildew ('mɪldjuː), *sb.* Forms: 1 **meledéaw, mildéaw**, 3 **mildeu**, 4–6 **myldew**, 4–8 **meldew**, 5–7 **meldewe**, 6 **myldewe, mild-, myldeawe**, 6–7 **mildewe**, 7 **mieldew**, 7–8 **milldew**, (8 **mealy-dew**), 4– **mildew**. [OE. *meledéaw, mildéaw* = OHG. *militou* (MHG. *miltou*, mod.G. with etymologizing alteration *mehlthau*), Sw. *mjöldagg*, Da. *meldug*; f. OTeut. **meliþ* (Goth. *miliþ*) honey + **ḍawwo-* DEW *sb.* The first element is in most of the Teut. langs. assimilated to **melwo-* MEAL *sb.*[1]]

†**1.** = HONEY-DEW. *Obs.*

a **1000** *Phœnix* 260 No he foddor þiȝeð mete on moldan, nemne mele-deawes dæl ȝebyrȝe, se dreoseð oft æt middre nihte. *c* **1050** *Voc.* in Wr.-Wülcker 455/19 *Nectar*, huniȝ, oððe mildeaw. *a* **1240** *Wohunge* in *Cott. Hom.* 269 Swetter is munegunge of þe þen mildeu o muðe. **1563** W. FULKE *Meteors* (1571) 53 b, Ther is another kind of swete dewes, that falleth in England called the meldewes, which is as sweet as hony. **1598** F. ROUS *Thule* T, She.. with sweete Mel-dewes doth anoint her face. **1608** TOPSELL *Serpents* 65 The Honny of Bees is longer kept pure and fine, then any Manne or Meldew. **1658** ROWLAND *Moufet's Theat. Ins.* 908 A kinde of heavenly Ambrosia falls down upon the leaves of plants (which they call honey dew, but I rather mieldew).

fig. **1600** FAIRFAX *Tasso* II. lxi. 31 While on the Christian Lords Downe fell the mildew of his sugred words.

2. A morbid destructive growth upon plants, consisting of minute fungi, and having usually the appearance of a thin whitish coating. Also, a similar growth on paper, leather, wood, etc., when exposed to damp. Usu. *collect. sing.*; also with *a* and *pl.*, denoting a particular attack of the disease.

1340 *Inquisitiones Nonarum* 334 b (Record Comm.), Maxima pars frumenti in parochia praedicta seminati distruebatur.. hoc anno.. per quendam rorem qui vocatur mildew. **1382** WYCLIF *Gen.* xli. 6 Seuene.. eerys, thinne and smytun with meldew. *c* **1440** *Promp. Parv.* 337/2 Myldew, *uredo*. **1523** FITZHERB. *Husb.* §54 They [*sc.* pasture-shepe] selden rot but with myldewes. **1570** B. GOOGE *Pop. Kingd.* III. 39 Indocus doth defende the corne, from myldeawes and from blast. **1677** PLOT *Oxfordsh.* 246 If the place be subject to the annoyances of Smutting, Meldews, Birds, &c. **1763** MILLS *Syst. Pract. Husb.* II. 411 The rust of corn, the honey-dew, the mealy-dew. **1839** *Penny Cycl.* XV. 209/2 The common orange-red mildew of the Berberry is *Æcidium Berberides*. **1850** OGILVIE, *Mildew*,.. spots on cloth or paper caused by moisture. **1859** JEPHSON *Brittany* x. 153 Damp and moss and mildew are not such deadly enemies to art as the chisel of the modern stonemason.

fig. **1640** LD. J. DIGBY *Sp. in Ho. Com.* 9 Nov. 7 [It] hath fallen againe upon the Land.. in Hailstones and Mildews, to batter and prostrate.. our liberties, to blast.. our affections. **1818** HALLAM *Mid. Ages* (1872) III. 84 Neither the blasts of arbitrary power could break them off, nor the mildew of servile opinion cause them to wither. **1874** L. STEPHEN *Hours in Library* (1892) I. iv. 138 Something of the mildew of time is stealing over the Waverley Novels.

3. *attrib.* and *Comb.*, as ***mildew-blast***, ***-drop***, ***-plant***; **mildew-gangrene, -mortification**, gangrene produced by diseased grain, such as gangrenous ergotism (*Syd. Soc. Lex.* 1890); †**mildew-grass**, grass tainted with mildew.

1634 MILTON *Comus* 640 Of sov'ran use 'Gainst all inchantments, *mildew blast, or damp. **1808** SCOTT *Marm.* II. xviii, The *mildew-drops fell one by one, With tinkling plash, upon the stone. **1523** FITZHERB. *Husb.* §54 *Myldewe-grasse is not good for shepe. **1822–29** *Good's Study Med.* (ed. 3) III. 493 *Gangræna ustilaginea*. *Mildew-mortification. **1839** *Penny Cycl.* XV. 209/2 Every precaution should be taken to prevent the spores of the *mildrew-plants from being communicated to the soil.

mildew ('mɪldjuː), *v.* Also 7 **melldew**, 8 **milldew**. [f. the sb.]

1. *trans.* To taint with mildew.

1552 [see MILDEWED *ppl. a.*]. **1605** SHAKS. *Lear* III. iv. 123 Hee.. Mildewes the white Wheate. **1747** FRANKLIN *Let.* Wks. 1887 II. 76 A great deal of hay has been lost, and some corn mildewed. **1855** MACAULAY *Hist. Eng.* xxi. IV. 541 The Licensing Act.. detains valuable packages of books at the Custom House till the pages are mildewed.

fig. **1631** BRATHWAIT *Whimzies, Almanack-maker* 14 Whole summer nights long hee lyes on his backe, as if hee were melldew'd or planet-struck, gazing on the starrie gallerie. **1807** MONTGOMERY *Molehill* 72 Tyrants, the comets of their kind, Whose withering influence.. smote and mildew'd man. **1898** BODLEY *France* II. III. i. 47 Nor are the members of the Institute, with all their learning, recluses mildewed in the dust of folios.

2. *intr.* To become tainted with mildew.

1651 R. CHILD in *Hartlib's Legacy* (1655) 14 Rank Land where Corn is apt to lodge, and consequently to Mildew. **1824** J. JOHNSON *Typogr.* II. xiii. 482 Authors sometimes detain proofs so long, that the paper allotted for those sheets will mildew. **1839** *Penny Cycl.* XV. 210/1 Mr. Knight prevented his peas from mildewing by watering them abundantly and constantly.

fig. **1864** TENNYSON *Aylmer's F.* 383 These old pheasant-lords,.. Who had mildew'd in their thousands, doing nothing.

Hence **'mildewer**.

1807 ANNA SEWARD *Lett.* (1811) VI. 389 The man.. is a noted mildewer on the profits of the noblest verse.

mildewed ('mɪldjuːd), *ppl. a.* [f. MILDEW *v.* + -ED[1].] Tainted with mildew.

1552 HULOET, Mylle dewed, *rubiginosus*. **1602** SHAKS. *Ham.* III. iv. 64 Like a Mildew'd eare. *a* **1721** POPE *Lett., to Dk. Buckhm.* Wks. 1737 VI. 26 Two or three mill-dew'd pictures of mouldy ancestors. **1813** SIR H. DAVY *Agric. Chem.* (1814) 265 Great care should be taken that no mildewed straw is carried in the manure used for corn. **1897** HARE *Story of my Life* (1900) VI. xxx. 472 The mildewed rooms have some scanty remnants of their old furniture.

fig. **1605** MARSTON *Dutch Courtesan* III. i. 128 *Tisse.* Fayth Ioyce is a foolish bitter creature. *Crisp.* A pretty mildewed wench she is. *Tisse.* And faire. **1626** E. F. *Hist. Edw. II* (1680) 24 His hypocritical Entreaties and mildewed Promises. **1923** in J. MANCHON *Le Slang*. **1930** R. CAMPBELL *Adamastor* 56 Worse than death The palsied soul, the mildewed brain. **1959** I. & P. OPIE *Lore & Lang. of Schoolch.* ix. 161 Juvenile repugnance continues to be expressed by the old standbys:.. mardy, mildewed, mingy, misery-making, [etc.].

mildewy ('mɪldjuːɪ), *a.* [f. MILDEW *sb.* + -Y[1].] Tainted with mildew; of the nature of, or resembling, mildew.

1835 DICKENS *Sk. Boz, Scenes* xiii. (1892) 113 The damp mildewy smell which pervades the place. **1838** —— *O. Twist* xxvi, Heaps of mildewy fragments of woollen-stuff. **1862** THOREAU *Excursions, Wild Apples* (1863) 296 Foggy mildewy days.

fig. **1884** R. BUCHANAN *Foxglove Manor* III. xxxiv. 147 A creed so worn out, mildewy, and old-fashioned.

†**'mildful**, *a. Obs.* [? f. MILD *sb.*[1] + -FUL. See also MILFUL.] Merciful. Hence †**'mildfulness**.

a **1225** *Juliana* 55 þe mihti mildfule godd. *a* **1300** *E.E. Psalter* cxiv. 5 Mildeful lauerd al And rightwise [Vulg. *misericors Dominus et justus*]. *c* **1440** R. GLOUC. (Rolls) 8966 (MS. δ) Mildfol. *Ibid.* 8975 (MS. ε) Myldefulle. **1489** CAXTON *Faytes of A.* III. xvii. N viij, But of ryght vryton he ought to be myldefull vnto hym. *Ibid.*, Thou hast sayde.. that to a prysoner is myldefulnes due of ryght vnto hym.

†**mild-heart**, *a. Obs.* (For forms see HEART.) [f. MILD *a.* + HEART *sb.* Cf. OHG. *milt-herzi.*] Merciful, kind-hearted.

c **950** *Lindisf. Gosp.* Matt. v. 7 Eadȝe biðon miltheorte [*c* **1000** *Ags.*, *c* **1160** *Hatton*, þa mild-heortan] forðon hiora *vel* ða miltheortnise him ȝefylges. *c* **1200** *Trin. Coll. Hom.* 121 Mild-heorte he is togenes heom. *c* **1205** LAY. 16813 þe king wes mild-heorte & heold hine stille. [**1340** *Ayenb.* 142 þe milde herten and simple.]

Hence †**mildheartful** *a.*, merciful; **mildheartlaik** (*Ormin*), †**mildheartness**, mercifulness.

c **900** *Laws of Ælfred* c. 49 Hie ða gesetton, for ðære mildheortnesse þe Crist lærde,.. þætte [etc.]. *c* **1200** ORMIN 1142 þatt he þeȝȝm þurrh hiss mildherrtleȝȝc Forrȝæfe þeȝȝre gilltess. *Ibid.* 2893 Forr aȝȝ birrþ rihhtwisnesse ben þurrh mildheorrtnesse temmpredd. *a* **1225** *Juliana* 66 Mildheortfule godd milce þi meiden. *a* **1300** *E.E. Psalter* lxxxviii. 1 Mildehertnesses of lauerd [Vulg. *misericordias Domini*].

mild-hearted, *a.* [Formed as prec. + -ED[2].] Tender-hearted, gentle, merciful.

c **1175** *Lamb. Hom.* 23 Forðon drihten is mildheorteð inoh he wule hit me forȝeuen. *c* **1200** *Trin. Coll. Hom.* 95 Mild-heorted beð þe man þe reouð his nehȝebures unselðe. *a* **1300** *E.E. Psalter* cii. 8 Rewful and mildeherted lauerd gode. **1843** MARRYAT *M. Violet* xxxiii, Mild-hearted savages.

Hence **mild-heartedness**.

1867 FREEMAN *Norm. Conq.* (1877) I. App. 553 King Ælfred's notion.. that the.. wergild was introduced by the Christian Bishops in imitation of the mild-heartedness of Christ. [Cf. quot. *c* 900 s.v. MILDHEARTNESS.].

†**'mildhede**. *Obs.* [f. MILD *a.* + *-hede*, -HEAD.] Mildness, mercifulness; meekness.

c **1290** *S. Eng. Leg.* I. 291/108 þat swete mayde [*sc.* the Virgin Mary] so hende cudde hire milde-hede, and fram heouene to him a-doun gan wende. **1340** *Ayenb.* 133 þet is ariȝt pouerte of gost and mildehede of herte. **1489** CAXTON *Faytes of A.* III. xvii. N vii, Yf myldehede is due to hym [a prisoner].

mildish ('maɪldɪʃ), *a.* [f. MILD *a.* + -ISH[1].] Somewhat mild.

1853 G. J. CAYLEY *Las Alforjas* II. 145 So they changed their cries of *m'alegro* for '*Que lastima!*' (what a pity), a mildish reparation under the circumstances.

†**mildly**, *a. Obs.* [f. MILD *a.* + -LY[1]. Cf. ON. *mildligr.*] = MILD *a.*

a **950** *Durham Ritual* (Surtees) 37 Mildelic, *propitius.* *c* **1205** LAY. 8832 Mid mildliche worden.

mildly ('maɪldlɪ), *adv.* [f. MILD *a.* + -LY[2].] In a mild manner. (See the senses of the adj.) Esp. in colloq. phr. ***to put it mildly***, to express an idea without exaggeration; freq. ironical, with an implication of understatement.

c **893** K. ÆLFRED *Oros.* I. viii. §1 His se cyning..mildelice onfeng. *a* **1225** *Ancr. R.* 136 Ine swete munegunge of þe soðe wunden þet he oð soðe rode mildeliche þolede. *c* **1250** *Gen. & Ex.* 2778 Forð he nam to sen witterlike, Hu ðat fier brende milde-like. *a* **1300** *Cursor M.* 15651 Ful mildli to þam he spak. **1387** TREVISA *Higden* (Rolls) VII. 97 Canute.. afterwarde dede more myldely [*MS. β*, myldloker, *γ*, myldelokur] wiþ seynt Edmond. *c* **1450** tr. *De Imitatione* III. li. 123, I owte in euery blamyng & repreuyng to meke myself & suffre myldely. **1593** SHAKS. *Rich. II*, v. i. 32 Wilt thou, Pupill-like, Take thy Correction mildly, kisse the Rodde..? **1626** BACON *Sylva* §375 The Aire once heated..maketh the Flame burne more mildly, and so helpeth the Continuance. **1646** MAYNE *Serm. Unity* 13 Pardon the hardnes of the language, I cannot make the Scripture speak mildlyer then it doth. **1843** R. J. GRAVES *Syst. Clin. Med.* xxviii. 360 We ought to have treated her mildly, giving small doses of calomel or blue pill. **1939** JOYCE *Finnegans Wake* 439 What I'm wondering to myselfwhose for there's a strong tendency, to put it mildly, by making me the medium. **1949** E. E. CUMMINGS *Let.* 9 July (1969) 191 Thank you much more than kindly for a most (putting it very mildly) luxurious gift. **1958** *Spectator* 22 Aug. 240/1 This, to put it mildly, seems improbable. **1972** *Listener* 6 Apr. 448/3 Suggestions that conditions [on Mars] may periodically change, causing torrential rainfall every 25,000 years or so, are—to put it mildly—highly speculative as yet.

Comb. **1567** DRANT *Horace, Ep.* I. xv. E vj, Then do I hope to drinke Lyuely and myldlie rellesde wynes. **1876** GEO. ELIOT *Dan. Der.* xxviii, The mildly-uttered suggestion. **1899** *Allbutt's Syst. Med.* VII. 681 The patient became mildly demented.

mildness ('maɪldnɪs). [-NESS.] The quality of being mild (see the adj.): **a.** as an attribute of persons, their actions, etc.

a **1310** in Wright *Lyric P.* xxv. 73 Iesu, thi mildenesse froreth me. **1377** LANGL. *P. Pl.* B. xv. 169 And alle manere meschiefs in myldenesse he suffreth. **1526** *Pilgr. Perf.* (W. de W. 1531) 31 b, To haue myldnes, gentylnes, and good maner in all our conuersacyon. **1593** SHAKS. *3 Hen. VI*, IV. iv. 20 This is it that makes me bridle passion, And beare with Mildnesse my misfortunes crosse. **1643** MILTON *Divorce* II. vii. Wks. 1851 IV. 79 The terror of the Law was as a servant to amplifie and illustrat the mildnesse of grace. **1768** STERNE *Sent. Journ., Calais* (1775) I. 5 The Bourbon is by no means a cruel race..there is a mildness in their blood. **1813** EUSTACE *Italy* (1815) III. vi. 226 The Roman Government ..though despotic and above all control,..is exercised by the Pontiff with mildness. **1839** THIRLWALL *Greece* VI. 131 Ariaspes..was generally beloved on account of the mildness of his character.

b. of things.

1605 CAMDEN *Rem.* 9 Being mellowed and mollified by the mildenes of the soyle and sweete aire. **1608** D. T[UVIL] *Ess. Pol. & Mor.* 73 b, Let him not glorie in the mildnesse of his starres. **1707** MORTIMER *Husb.* 273 The Drink..hath a delicate mildness. **1774** GOLDSM. *Nat. Hist.* (1776) V. 21 The mildness of the season. **1832** LEWIS *Lett.* (1870) 25 The perfect mildness and serenity of the weather is extraordinary.

mildrop, variant of MELDROP.

milds, miles. *dial.* Forms: 1 melde, 5 mielde, medles, 7 meedles, 8 mails, 9 melgs, meals, meols, myl(i)es, miles, milds. [OE. *melde* wk. fem., cogn. w. OHG. *melda, melde* (MHG., mod.G. *melde*), also with different ablaut-grades *malta, molto*, MLG., Du. *melde.* Some scholars suggest that the Teut. word may be cogn. w. Gr. βλίτον (? = *μλίτον) BLITE.] A name for various species of *Atriplex* and *Chenopodium.*

c **1000** *Sax. Leechd.* III. 6 Mugwyrt, organa, melde, quinque folium. *Ibid.* 54 Nim eac meldon ða wyrt. *c* **1350** *Med. MS.* in *Archæologia* XXX. 410 Medles. *c* **1450** *Alphita* (Anecd. Oxon.) 16 *Attriplex agrestis*,..ang. mielde. **1633** *Gerarde's Herbal* Suppl. to Gen. Table, Meedles, Arage. **1808** JAMIESON, *Middenmylies*... Chenopodium viride, et album, Linn.; thus denominated, as growing on dunghills. **1811** W. AITON *Agric. Surv. Ayrs.* 675 (Jam.) Chenopodium several species, Goosefoot; wild spinage, or mails. **1839** *Mag. Dom. Econ.* IV. 248 The mild succulent weeds, such as chick-weed, and miles or fat-hen. **1853** G. JOHNSTON *Bot. E. Bord.* 171 *Chenopodium album.* Myles. **1878** *Cumberld. Gloss.* Introd. 19 *Chenopodium album.* Meols, Fat hen.

†'**mildship.** *Obs.* [-SHIP.] Mildness.

c **1200** *Trin. Coll. Hom.* 49 Habbe we..mildshipe of duue. *c* **1205** LAY. 17146 Whan..mon me mid milde-scipe wulle me bisechen. *c* **1230** *Hali Meid.* 659 Miltschipe & meokeschipe of heorte. *a* **1240** *Wohunge* in *Cott. Hom.* I. 273 Meknesse and mildschipe makes mon eihwer luued.

†'**mildy**, *a. Obs.* [f. MILD *a.* + -Y.] Mild.

1598 Q. ELIZ. *Englishings* 139/24 Who..is Of mildy spirit [Gr. φύσει πρᾶος].

mile (maɪl), *sb.*[1] Forms: 1 mil, 3–7 myle, 4–6 myl, 5 *Sc.* myill, 5–6 mylle, 7 mille. [OE. *mīl* fem. = MDu. *mîle* (Du. *mijl*), OHG. *mîla, mîlla* (MHG. *mîle*, mod.G. *meile*), ON. *míla* (prob. from OE.; Sw., Da. *mil*):—WGer. **mîlja*, a. L. *mīlia, millia*, pl. of *mīle, mille* thousand. In the Rom. langs. the L. sing. is represented by F. *mille*, It. *miglio* masc., and the pl. by Pr., Sp. *milla*, Pg. *milha* fem.]

1. a. Originally, the Roman lineal measure of 1,000 paces (*mille passus* or *passuum*), computed to have been about 1,618 yards. Hence, the unit of measure derived from this, used in the British Isles and in other English-speaking countries. Its length has varied considerably at different periods and in different localities, chiefly owing to the influence of the agricultural system of measures with which the mile has been brought into relation (see FURLONG). The legal mile in Britain and the U.S. is now 1,760 yards. The Irish mile of 2,240 yards is still in rustic use. The obsolete Scottish mile was longer than the English, and probably varied according to time and place; one of the values given for it is 1,976 yards.

The use of the sing. form with a plural numeral is now only vulgar or dialectal; in the earlier part of the 19th c. it was recognized as permissible colloquially.

971 *Blickl. Hom.* 129 Ac eac swylce Gerusalem þa burh, seo is west þonon from þære stowe on anre mile. *c* **1000** ÆLFRIC *Gloss.* in Wr.-Wülcker 147/22 *Miliarium*, leouue, mile. *c* **1200** *Vices & Virtues* 127 Se ðe net þe to gonne mid him twa milen, ga mid him þrie. *c* **1290** *S. Eng. Leg.* I. 48/48 þat bote þreo Mile þanne it nas. ? *a* **1300** *Shires & Hundreds of Eng.* in *O.E. Misc.* 145 Engle lond is eyhte hundred Myle long, from penwyþ steorte þat is fyftene Mylen by-yonde Mihhales steowe. **1340** HAMPOLE *Pr. Consc.* 7683 And þat ilka myle fully contene A thowsand pases or cubites sene. *c* **1470** HENRY *Wallace* v. 782 The Inglishmen was than within a myill. **1470–85** MALORY *Arthur* IV. iv. 123 Kyng Pellinore was within thre myle with a grete hoost. **1532** MORE *Epitaph* Pref., Wks. 1419/1 Thre smal Miles from London. **1596** DALRYMPLE tr. *Leslie's Hist. Scot.* I. 27 The craig is a myl within the Sey. **1655** FULLER *Hist. Camb.* 37 An hairs breadth fixed by a divine finger, shall prove as effectuall a separation from danger, as a miles distance. **1672** PETTY *Pol. Anat.* 375 Eleven Irish miles make 14 English. **1690** MARLBOROUGH in Ld. Wolseley *Life* (1894) II. 213 A place called Macrom twelfe milles from hence. **1699** BENTLEY *Phal.* I. 97 The Mistake in the Situation, might perhaps be five Mile. **1769** GOLDSM. *Hist. Rome* (1786) II. 51 In this plain..were two little hills at about a mile distance from each other. *a* **1796** BURNS '*O, my luve's like a red, red rose*', And I will come again, my luve, Tho' it were ten thousand mile. **1838** THIRLWALL *Greece* XX. III. 154 The channel between the two points is not quite a mile broad. **1850** DICKENS *Dav. Copp.* xl, I'd go ten thousand mile.

b. (Explicitly ***square*** or ***superficial mile.***) A measure of area equal to the content of a square with a side one mile in length. So, rarely, ***cubic*** (†***cubical***) ***mile***: a measure of volume equal to that of a cube bounded by lines one mile in length.

1698 KEILL *Exam. Th. Earth* (1734) 129 Twenty six Po's will pour into the Sea one Cubical mile of water in a day. **1864** TREVELYAN *Compet. Wallah* (1866) 121 A thousand square miles.

c. A race, or a portion of a race, extending over a mile's length of the course.

1901 *Daily Tel.* 12 Oct. 10/2 Fourier..broke all automobile records... The time for the fastest mile was 66·4–5 sec.

d. *transf.* and *fig.* Chiefly *adverbially* in plural, implying a great distance or interval.

1588 SHAKS. *L.L.L.* v. ii. 54 The Letter is too long by halfe a mile. **1592** —— *Rom. & Jul.* III. v. 82 Villaine and he, be many Miles assunder. **1885** *Punch* 12 Dec. 281/1 The fellows generally bag his music, and make him play the '*Mikado*' which is miles better. **1889** RUSKIN *Præterita* 109 My eldest Irish pupil..was miles and miles my superior. **1890** 'R. BOLDREWOOD' *Col. Reformer* (1891) 282 Awful fuss always made about him. No swell within miles of him. **1919** 'C. DANE' *Legend* 64 He had heard nothing... He was miles away. **1922** JOYCE *Ulysses* 639 Bloom..picked it up.. meaning to return it to him..whose thoughts were miles away from his hat at the time. **1932** 'E. M. DELAFIELD' *Thank Heaven Fasting* I. iv. 65, I should have thought he'd be miles better than no one. **1943** J. B. PRIESTLEY *Daylight on Saturday* vii. 38 Not that the boys drew back..but..not one of them came within miles of being..Mister Right. **1951** E. PAUL *Springtime in Paris* xv. 287 Pierre Vautier, smiling, gesturing and talking a mile a minute to an attractive brunette. **1961** M. KELLY *Spoilt Kill* iii. 166 Freddy was miles out in alleging Corinna's coldness. **1961** PARTRIDGE *Dict. Slang* Suppl. 1184/1 *Miles away, be*, to be either day-dreaming or lost in thought. **1964** C. WILLOCK *Enormous Zoo* viii. 133 Ken Beaton's original estimate of the elephant, buffalo and hippo population had been miles out. **1969** A. LA BERN *Nice Class of People* ii. 11 Ann Corrie had to repeat the sentence... He was miles away. **1970** J. PORTER *Rather Common Sort of Crime* i. 17 She *was* on the scrounge. .. You could spot it a mile off. **1970** *Globe Mag.* (Toronto) 26 Sept. 9/3 The meeting..is going well. Stephen has made some miles by talking about the proposed shutdown of the Garden City Paper Mills. **1973** L. SNELLING *Heresy* I. vii. 52 The French technicians are all..very Lefty... He can keep them from getting within a mile of the set. **1974** N. FREELING *Dressing of Diamond* 176 This hasn't been done cold-bloodedly for money... Makes it all miles easier. **1974** D. GRAY *Dead Give Away* ii. 28 'Aunt Milly's miles out,' said Marion. 'As usual.'

2. Used to render its etymological equivalent in other European languages.

In Italy (where there are many different miles), Spain, and Portugal, the 'mile' has been developed from the ancient Roman measure, and its length ranges between $\frac{7}{8}$ and $1\frac{1}{4}$ English mile. In Germany, Austria, Holland, and the Scandinavian countries, on the other hand, the 'mile' seems to represent the ancient Germanic *rasta*, to which the Latin name was apparently applied arbitrarily; its values range from about $3\frac{1}{4}$ to over 6 English miles.

c **1400** MAUNDEV. (1839) v. 55 It is wel a 1880 Myle of Lombardye. **1538** ELYOT *Dict., Rasta*, a duche myle. **1559** W. CUNNINGHAM *Cosmogr. Glasse* 57, 8. of these furlonges do make an Italian or Englishe mile, which beyng multiplied by 4. makes .32. furlonges, the length of a comon Germanie mile. **1617** MORYSON *Itin.* I. 179 After I had ridden four houres space (for the Sweitzers miles are so long,..); I wondered to heare that we had ridden but one mile. **1632** LITHGOW *Trav.* IX. 415 The Hungarian miles are the longest vpon earth, for euery one of theirs, is sixe of our Scots miles, nine English. **1753** HANWAY *Trav.* (1762) I. VII. lxxxix. 408 *note*, These computed German miles are in some places four, in others five miles English.

3. ***geographical, geometrical,*** †***maritime, nautic(al mile***: a measure of length = one minute of a great circle of the earth.

Owing to the fact that the earth is not a true sphere, the 'mile' as thus defined varies considerably, the difference between the extreme values being about 62 feet; when taken as a minute of the meridian, the value increases with the latitude, in consequence of the varying curvature. It has therefore been found convenient to assign a standard value for nautical use; the British Admiralty fixed it at 6,080 feet.

1632 LITHGOW *Trav.* VIII. 362 Three hundred Maritine miles. **1697** DAMPIER *Voy.* (1729) I. 287 Italian or geometrical miles (at the rate of 60 to a degree). **1834** *Nat. Philos., Navig.* II. ii. 15 (Usef. Knowl. Soc.), A geographical or nautical mile is $\frac{1}{60}$ of a degree of a great circle of the earth. **1875** BEDFORD *Sailor's Pocket Bk.* v. (ed. 2) 201 *note*, The Nautical mile as defined by hydrographers is the length of a minute of the meridian, and is different for every different latitude. **1890** E. F. KNIGHT *Cruise of 'Alerte'* viii. 131 Trinidad is roughly 680 nautic miles from Bahia.

†**4.** As a vague measure of time; the time in which one might journey a mile; = MILEWAY. *Obs.*

c **1330** *Florice & Bl.* (1857) 504 Hire cussing laste amile And that hem thoughte litel while. **1390** GOWER *Conf.* II. 24 And thogh I stonde there a myle, Al is foryete for the while. **14..** *Sir Beues* 775 (MS. C.), A long myle he soght, Or he the bore fynde moght. *c* **1440** *Ipomydon* 1466 He had not slepyd but a while, Not the space of a myle. *c* **1450** *St. Cuthbert* (Surtees) 5059 For before a litil while Noght þe space of half a mile. **1594** SPENSER *Amoretti* lxxxvi, And maketh euery minute seem a myle.

5. *attrib.* and *Comb.* **a.** simple attrib., as in ***mile-race***; also in combinations with prefixed numeral, as ***twenty-mile walk, six-mile track.***

b. Combined with adjs., as in ***mile-deep, -high, -long, -wide***; ***mile-consuming*** ppl. adj. Also (*nonce-uses*) in attributive or adjectival uses of advb. phrases, as ***mile-away, mile(s-off.***

1897 KIPLING *Captains Courageous* 101 The tiny black buoy-flag on the shoulder of a *mile-away swell. **1932** W. FAULKNER *Light in August* i. 8 He drove on, the wagon beginning to fall into its slow and *mileconsuming clatter. **1888** J. R. LOWELL *Fitz Adam's Story* in *Heartsease & Rue* iv. 151 *Mile-deep the glaciers brooded here, they say. **1903** —— *Settler* 20 in 5 *Nations* 154 The locust's mile-deep swarm. **1963** J. LUSBY in B. James *Austral. Short Stories* 229 A black speck raced towards me along the rim of a *mile-high blood-red cliff of cumulus. **1968** *Listener* 27 June 841/2 The ozone-drenched, mile-high city of Denver. **1834** DE QUINCEY in *Tait's Mag.* I. 85/1 At times we turned off into some less tumultuous street, but of the same *mile-long character. **1870** MISS BROUGHTON *Red as Rose* I. 140 The rooks..have flapped heavily home to the *mile-off rookery. **1881** T. HARDY *Laodicean* v. v, There was a miles-off expression in hers [*sc.* her eyes]. **1866** J. G. WHITTIER *Snow-Bound* 22 Where Salisbury's level marshes spread *Mile-wide as flies the laden bee. **1903** KIPLING *Five Nations* 56, I heard the mile-wide mutterings of unimagined rivers.

c. Special comb.: **mile-a-minute** *attrib.*, travelling at a rate of a mile a minute; covering a mile a minute; **mile-eater** (cf. EAT *v.* 18 g) *colloq.*, a fast driver or traveller; **mile-heat**, a racing heat of one mile; **mile-horse**, a horse trained for a mile race; **mile-hunter**, a cyclist who is intent on accomplishing great distances; **mile-mark**, a milestone or other object placed to indicate the distance of a mile from a starting-point or from another mark; **mile-post**, a post serving as a mile-mark; also *fig.*; hence **mile-posted** *ppl. a.*; †**mile-square**, a square mile.

1957 *Railway Mag.* Nov. 752/2 In view of the Eastern, North Eastern and Scottish changes, a new table of their *mile-a-minute runs for the winter appears here. **1961** *Christian Science Monitor* 9 Jan., The daredevil courage needed to flash down a hard-packed track at better than a mile-a-minute speed. **1908** *Westm. Gaz.* 20 Aug. 12/1 These *mile-eaters go early to bed and prefer their steam-horses to our live ones. **1957** S. MOSS *In Track of Speed* i. 9 The driver himself must possess those faculties which go to make the expert mile-eater. **1802** N. MACON *Let.* 10 Sept. in J. Steele *Papers* (1924) I. 315 He says there are no regular *Mile heats at that turf. **1868** H. WOODRUFF *Trotting Horse* vi. 70 You can tell by the way he finishes..whether he will be likely to stand the mile-heat out and to repeat it. **1829** *Sporting Mag.* XXIII. 266 As to the *mile horses, I spoke of rackers, and not of trotters. **1898** *Cycling* 26 En route—Do not degenerate into a '*mile-hunter'. **1610** HOLLAND *Camden's Brit.* I. 423 London-stone, which I take to have beene a Milliarie or *Milemarke. **1892** STEVENSON *Across the Plains* 308 Christmas is not only the mile-mark of another year. **1768** in *Maryland Hist. Mag.* (1907) II. 317 As we returned (besides the *Mile Posts) we erected Marks on the Tops of all the High Ridges. **1812** *Sporting Mag.* XXXIX. 50 Beal headed Wood at every mile-post. **1909** *Westm. Gaz.* 26 Mar. 12/2 Oxford paddled up to the mile-post. **1926** ADE *Let.* 29 Aug. (1973) 107 The day in 1894 when the editor put me in

charge of a department was an important mile post. **1941** W. TEMPLE *Citizen & Churchman* i. 2 It is in reality a mile-post marking the distance away from it which thought has travelled. **1954** R. D. BURNELL *Oxf. & Cambr. Boat Race* vi. 116 Cambridge led at once... At the Mile Post they led by seven seconds. **1896** 'MARK TWAIN' in *Harper's Mag.* Jan. 294/2 The road was *mile-posted with English fortresses, so to speak. **1754** EDWARDS *Freed. Will* IV. viii. (1762) 242 'Tis improper to talk of Months and Years of the Divine Existence, and *Mile-squares of Deity.

† **mile**, *sb.*^{2} *Obs.* Forms: 1 miil, mil, 4–5 mylie, 4–6 myle, mile, 5 myld(e, milde. See also MILL *sb.*^{2} [OE. *míl* (and, prob. independently, ME. *myle*), ad. L. *milium*: see MILLET^1.] = MILLET^1.

a **800** *Ags. Voc.* in Wr.-Wülcker 32/35 *Milium*, miil. *c* **1050** *Voc.* ibid. 443/19 *Milium*, mil. **1382** WYCLIF *Isa.* xxviii. 25 Barly, and myle, and ficche. —— *Ezek.* iv. 9 Take thou to thee whete, and barli, and bene, and lent, and mylie. **1398** TREVISA *Barth. De P.R.* XVII. cv. (1495) 669 Myle [*v.r.* mile] is an herbe with a longe stalke. *c* **1420** *Pallad. on Husb.* I. 722 Eek myld is good [for geese]. **1551** TURNER *Herbal* II. 40 Lithospermon..is called gray mil..to put a difference betwene it and the other mile or millet. **1568** *Ibid.* III. Pref., Myle called in Duche Herse, in Latin *Milium*.

† **mile**, *v. Obs. rare. trans.* To ornament (a cloth) with stripes near the edge. Only in **miled** (later **milded**) *ppl. a.*; **miling** *vbl. sb.*, a stripe.

The sense seems to be certain from a comparison of quot. 1523 with an entry of 1496–7 in the same document, p. 32: 'An Awlter clothe diaper..with iiij Blewe Rayes at euery ende of the saide cloth'.

1512 in *Jacob's Hist. Faversham* (1774) 164 A lyttel olde towell pleyn miled with blewe. **1523** *Rec. St. Mary-at-Hill* (1904) 35 An aulter cloth of fine dyapre with a Cros of Sylke in the Middes..& at euery ende v. blewe Mylynges. **1548** *MS. Acc. St. John's Hosp., Canterb.*, A Towell of dyapar myleed wyth blewe. **1566** *Churchw. Acc. St. Dunstan's, Canterb.*, A towell mylded with blewe. One towelle mylded. One towelle mylded with whyt. **1590** in *Archæologia* XL. 340 Itm, two mylded napkins.

mileage (ˈmaɪlɪdʒ). Also 8 milage. [f. MILE *sb.*^{1} + -AGE.]

1. a. A travelling allowance at a fixed rate per mile; spec. *U.S.* the allowance made to members of Congress to cover the expenses of the journey between their home and the capital.

1754 FRANKLIN *Place of Union* Wks. 1887 II. 345 Members' Pay.—shillings sterling per diem, during their sitting, and milage for travelling expenses. **1776** H. GATES in Sparks *Corr. Amer. Rev.* (1853) I. 281 The militia were promised their mileage and billeting-money. **1888** BRYCE *Amer. Commw.* (1890) II. xl. 95 A small allowance, called mileage, for travelling expenses.

b. See quot.

1845 McCULLOCH *Taxation* II. vi. (1852) 280 The duty on stage-carriages consists of a licence duty of 3*l.* 3*s.* a year, and of a mileage, or duty of so much per mile travelled over, according to the number of passengers the carriage is licensed to carry.

c. A rate per mile charged for the use of railway vehicles carrying goods or passengers over another company's line.

1837 *Penny Mag.* Suppl. 31 Mar. 115/1 Mileage on the whole mail. **1863** *Great Western Mag.* Aug. 74 The Clearing House..will debit each company on the journey with its proper amount of 'mileage'. **1873** *Cassell's Mag.* VIII. 400/1 As..the Caledonian Company will receive the fares of the passengers, they will be required to pay for the use of the carriages conveying them; in other words the..Company will be charged 'mileage'. **1926** HUEBNER & JOHNSON *Railroad Freight Service* vii. 129 The prevailing rate of mileage paid by one railway to another for the use of foreign cars was three quarters of a cent per car per mile.

2. a. The aggregate number of miles of way made, used or travelled over; extent or distance in miles. Also, rate of travel in miles.

1861 SMILES *Engineers* I. 220 The total mileage of turnpike roads..was about one hundred and eighty miles. **1881** LUBBOCK in *Nature* No. 618. 412 The present mileage of railways is over 200,000 miles. **1890** *Spectator* 7 June 792 To compute the speed or mileage of quick-moving animals. **1891** T. HARDY *Tess* xliv, As the mileage lessened between her and the spot of her pilgrimage, so did Tess's confidence decrease. **1902** *Westm. Gaz.* 5 Apr. 10/1 There has been a very material decline in the traffic receipts though the mileage run has been practically the same.

b. *fig.*

1860 RUSSELL *Diary India* I. x. 155 It has been a heavy mileage of neglect for which we have already paid dearly. **1902** *Daily Chron.* 15 Oct. 3/2 A study less common than the mileage of metrical English might lead one to suppose. **1945** N. L. McCLUNG *Stream runs Fast* p. xi, There was good mileage in me yet. **1962** L. DEIGHTON *Ipcress File* xxv. 158 In the Café Budapest..'kezet csokolom' (kiss your hand) had given good mileage with the younger waitresses. **1970** W. V. QUINE *Philos. of Logic* v. 71 We can still get a little additional mileage by superimposing the virtual theory. **1971** *Rolling Stone* 24 June 36/1 Sam's got mileage that any PR firm might envy: front-page space in both San Francisco dailies,..and wire service coverage. **1971** A. PRICE *Alamut Ambush* ix. 114 The newspapers had got very fair mileage out of the bomb explosion. **1973** *Times* 5 Feb. 19/5 When.. profits began to tumble, the..senior management of the time imagined that there was no more milage in the product. **1973** *Sci. Amer.* Apr. 103/3 Mathematical notions whose foundations have been matters of continuous debate have often yielded the most mileage. **1974** T. ALLBEURY *Snowball* iii. 14 They'd enjoy stirring up the Canadians, and the French-Canadians would..get a lot of political mileage.

c. *attrib.*

1869 *Bradshaw's Railway Manual* XXI. 367 Advances are made by the Italian Government, to be made good afterwards out of the mileage subventions promised... The Italian and Pontifical Governments have given mileage guarantees. **1884** J. B. POPE *Railway Rates* 22 They [*sc.* Railway Companies] shall be allowed to vary or graduate the mileage charges according to distance. **1885** H. O. FORBES *East. Archipelago* 52 Stations..which private travellers can obtain permission to make use of on payment of small mileage dues. **1895** *Westm. Gaz.* 14 May 8/2 The mileage rate of threepence for each first-class passenger. **1908** *Westm. Gaz.* 14 Nov. 15/2 An instrument, made by one of the largest clock-makers in the world,..combines a time-piece, mileage recorder, speed indicator [etc.]. **1928** C. E. R. SHERRINGTON *Econ. Rail Transport Gt. Brit.* II. vii. 98 With the coming of the Parliamentary trains,..the equal mileage basis became..stabilized. **1969** *Observer* (Colour Suppl.) 23 Mar. 31/3 The White Car is running on Shell with the mileage ingredient. **1970** *Motoring Which?* Oct. 151/1 Check the mileage recorder—see how long the road test has been. **1971** 'J. ASHFORD' *Bent Copper* iv. 34 He left and went out to..his car, a battered Ford, which he ran on a mileage allowance. **1973** *Radio Times* 20–27 Dec. 19/1 (Advt.), Explore Canada for a week with Avis for £37·50, with no mileage surcharge. **1975** *New Yorker* 26 May 60 (Advt.), In mileage tests conducted by the Environmental Protection Agency, Seville got 13 miles per gallon in the city test.

ˈ**mile-castle.** *Antiq.* Also **milecastle.** One of a series of fortifications erected by the Romans at intervals along the lines of their military walls.

1732 HORSLEY *Rom. Antiq. Brit.* 118 These *castella* seem to have stood closest, where the stations are widest, and are by some modern authors called *mile castles* or *milliary castella.* **1935** *Antiquity* IX. 92 The recent excavations at High House Turf-Wall milecastle. **1936** *Nature* 25 July 156/2 A milecastle and three quarters of a mile of the wall itself were presented to the National Trust. **1963** E. S. WOOD *Collins Field Guide Archaeol.* II. ii. 177 The milecastles [of Hadrian's Wall] were about 75 by 60 feet, the turrets about 20 feet square.

miled, obs. form of MILD.

mileguetta, obs. variant of MALAGUETTA.

1727 BAILEY vol. II, *Mileguetta*, Cardamoms, Grains.

mileometer, var. MILOMETER.

† **miler**^{1}. *Obs. rare*$^{-1}$. [a. F. *millier* (from 11th c.):—L. *milliārium*, f. *mille* thousand.] A military corps or company of one thousand men.

c **1330** R. BRUNNE *Chron. Wace* (Rolls) 13527 By milers & by centeners Sette þey þe bataille seers.

miler^2 (ˈmaɪlə(r)). *Sporting slang.* [f. MILE *sb.*^{1} + -ER^1.] **1.** A man or a horse specially qualified or trained to run or race a mile course.

1889 E. SAMPSON *Tales of Fancy* 31, I..was in private trials one of the fastest 'milers' of my time. **1891** *Lock to Lock Times* 24 Oct. 14/1 Allen is one of the best 'milers' in the country. **1894** ASTLEY *50 Years Life* II. 100 Vexation colt..turned out a real good miler. **1955** *Times* 31 Aug. 3/5 To-night B. S. Hewson, potentially perhaps the greatest miler in the world, is to defend the trophy against a good field. **1965** *Illustr. London News* 4 Sept. 14/4 (*heading*) The first African miler to break four minutes. **1971** L. KOPPETT *N.Y. Times Guide Spectator Sports* viii. 159 The miler who excited the world's track fans in the 1920s was Paavo Nurmi, a Finn.

2. *colloq.* A walk or journey of a specified number of miles.

Properly the second element of a compound.

1856 DICKENS *Let.* 14 Nov. (1938) II. 811, I went out this morning for a 12-miler.

miles, variant of MILDS *dial.*

‖ **miles gloriosus** (ˈmiːleɪs or ˈmaɪliːz glɔːrɪˈəʊsəs). Pl. **milites gloriosi.** [f. L. *miles* soldier + *gloriosus* boastful, conceited.] The name of a comedy by Plautus (*c* 250–184 B.C.), used allusively to designate a braggart soldier. Also *attrib.*

1917 K. M. WESTAWAY *Orig. Element in Plautus* ii. 28 Other plays of Plautus contain *milites gloriosi* of smaller fame. **1936** P. FLEMING *News from Tartary* VII. iv. 343 One ..was a glib Turki from Turfan, the shoddiest type of the *miles gloriosus.* **1950** A. BONJOUR *Digressions in Beowulf* 18 In spite of Beowulf's biting allusion to Grendel's security, we should not take this as an entirely idle vaunt of some *miles gloriosus.* **1962** G. K. HUNTER *John Lyly* iv. 238 The version of *miles gloriosus* habits found here is without the menace that accompanies its adult presentation, in Pyrgopolynices (*Miles Gloriosus*) or Thraso (*Eunuchus*). **1964** *Rev. Eng. Stud.* XV. 385 A typical figure in Gleig's tales in particular was the Peninsular miles gloriosus. **1969** E. SEGAL tr. *Plautus' Three Comedies* Introd. 8 The *miles gloriosus* is by no means a Plautine invention, although the boastful officer is one of the Roman comedian's favorite characters.

Milesian (maɪˈliːʃ(ɪ)ən, mɪ-), *a.*^{1} and *sb.*^{1} [f. L. *Mīlēsius* (Gr. Μιλήσιος) of or pertaining to Miletus + -AN.] **A.** *adj.* Of or pertaining to Miletus, a city of Asia Minor, or to its inhabitants. **B.** *sb.* An inhabitant of Miletus.

Milesian tales (Gr. τὰ Μιλησιακά, L. *Milesiæ* sc. *fabulæ*), a class of voluptuous romances mentioned by ancient writers.

1550 T. NICOLLS tr. *Thucydides* IV. sig. Siiii verso, They had in their compaignie the succours of Milesyans, of Andryens and of Caristians. **1600** P. HOLLAND tr. *Livy* XLIII. 1159 The Milesians for their part said, That hitherto they had done nothing. **1602** I. B. in E. Beaumont *Salm. & Hermaphr.* Pref. Verses, Or wanton Nymphs in watry bowres haue woue, With fine Mylesian threds, the verse he sings. **1607** [see CALABRIAN *a.* and *sb.*]. *a* **1635** RANDOLPH *Hey for Honesty* (1651) IV. iii. 472 You told her, The Milesians were valiant in the daies of yore. **1649** OGILBY tr. *Virg. Georg.* III. (1684) 102 In rich Milesian Fleeces cloth'd. **1655** STANLEY *Hist. Philos.* II. (1687) 61/1 Anaximander a Milesian. **1886** *Encycl. Brit.* XXI. 319/1 The Milesian tale ..grew in the hands of Petronius and Apuleius into the satirical romance. **1961** L. MUMFORD *City in Hist.* vii. 191 Since it would be erroneous to call this Hippodamian planning, I shall follow Roland Martin and call it Milesian, after Miletus, the chief point of origin. **1968** *Encycl. Brit.* XV. 444/1 The Milesians..were already rebuilding their city on a new grid plan to the type invented..by the Milesian Hippodamus.

Milesian (maɪˈliːʃ(ɪ)ən, mɪ-), *a.*^{2} and *sb.*^{2} [f. the name of *Milesius* (Miledh), a fabulous Spanish king whose sons are reputed to have conquered and reorganized the ancient kingdom of Ireland about 1300 B.C.] **A.** *adj.* Of or pertaining to King Milesius or his people; Irish. **B.** *sb.* A member of the race descended from the companions of Milesius. Hence (sometimes *jocularly*), an Irishman.

1596 SPENSER *State Irel.* (1633) 31 All which are in truth fables, and very Milesian lyes, as the latter proverbe is: for never was there such a King of Spaine, called Milesius. **1705** M. KENNEDY (*title*) A Chronological Genealogical and Historical Dissertation of the Royal Family of the Stuarts, beginning with Milesius the stock of those they call the Milesian Irish, and of the old Scotish Race. **1771** MRS. GRIFFITH *Hist. Lady Barton* I. 54 The old Irish families stile themselves *Milesians*, from Milesius, a Spaniard, who brought over a colony of his countrymen to people the island. **1771** MACPHERSON *Introd. Hist. Gt. Brit.* 102 Some Irish annalists affirm, that the Picts..were tributary to the Milesian Scots of Ireland. **1773** —— *Ossian's Poems, Dissert.* (1806) I. p. xli, As a Scotchman, and of course, descended of the Milesian race. **1839** CARLYLE *Chartism* iv. 28 The wild Milesian features..salute you on all highways and byways. *Ibid.*, The English coachman..lashes the Milesian with his whip. **1910** D. HYDE in R. M. Dorson *Peasant Customs* (1968) II. 704 Some of the Scotch stories may have been bequeathed to the Gaelic language by those races who were displaced by the Milesian Conquest in the fifth century. **1921** *Edin. Rev.* Jan. 167 And lastly the Milesians. The Milesian being a literary and honorific cognomen of the Firbolgs' conquerors, the Gaels. **1971** *It* 2–16 June 24/1 The first groups of wholly human invaders to reach these shores ..were called the Milesians or 'Sons of Miledh'.

ˈ**milestone**, *sb.* [f. MILE *sb.*^{1} + STONE.]

1. A pillar set up on a highway or other road or course to mark the miles.

a **1746** HOLDSWORTH *Virgil* (1768) 483 The first mile-stone on the Via Appia. **1774** *Beverley & Hessle Road Act* ii. 17 Roads to be measured and mile stones erected. **1858** LYTTON *What will he do* I. iii, The cobbler seated himself on a lonely milestone.

fig. **1847** EMERSON *Repr. Men, Uses Gt. Men* Wks. (Bohn) I. 288 For a time, our teachers serve us personally, as metres or milestones of progress. **1897** *N. & Q.* 8th Ser. XII. 154/2 Ever since I have passed my eightieth milestone.

2. *slang.* (See quot.)

1812 J. H. VAUX *Flash Dict., Milestone*, a country booby.

3. *Naut. slang.* (See quots.)

1946 J. IRVING *Royal Navalese* 116 *Milestones*, the heavy, green seas which break inboard in bad weather. **1962** GRANVILLE *Dict. Sailors' Slang* 77/1 Milestones refer to the homeward trip, for, like milestones on country roads they seem to make the journey longer and harder, and one's progress slower in consequence.

milestone, *v.* [f. the sb.] *trans.* Used *fig.*, to mark (stages) as if by milestones.

1902 J. H. M. ABBOTT *Tommy Cornstalk* 157 And the road was mile-stoned by the parched hides and whitened bones of horses, mules, and oxen. *a* **1910** 'MARK TWAIN' *Autobiogr.* (1924) I. 299 You could look back over that speech and you'd find it dimly milestoned along with those commas. **1922** *Chamber's Jrnl.* Dec. 861/1 The Overland is mile-stoned with our bones. **1973** J. CLEARY *Ransom* iii. 98 Malone's life was milestoned by friends he had never made. **1973** J. WAINWRIGHT *High-Class Kill* 149 The book..will make passing reference to these things—as a means, perhaps, of milestoning his climb to the rank of chief constable.

milet, obs. form of MILLET^1.

† ˈ**mileway.** *Obs.* [f. MILE *sb.*^{1} + WAY.]

1. The space of time in which a mile may be travelled on foot; a period of twenty minutes. Hence *Astr.*, a third of an hour of angular measurement.

13.. *Evang. Nicod.* 704 in *Archiv Stud. neu. Spr.* LIII. 404 Þe sonne at his ded wex all wan wele thre myle way or mare. *c* **1350** *Will. Palerne* 1578 Alle þe surgens of salerne so sone ne coþen Haue lesed his langour and his liif saued, As þe maide meliors in a mile wei dede. *c* **1386** CHAUCER *Shipman's T.* 276, I shal nat faille surely of my day, Nat for a thousand frankes, a myle-way. *c* **1391** —— *Astrol.* I. §16 As I have said, 5 of thise degrees maken a mile-wey, and 3 mile-wey maken an houre.

2. A distance of one mile.

13.. *K. Alis.* 3487 He swam in thilke hevy armes; A mile waie with strengthe of armes. **1362** LANGL. *P. Pl.* A. VIII. 131 On Maluerne hulles, Musyng on þis Meeteles A myle wei Ich ȝeode. *c* **1470** *Gol. & Gaw.* 572 Thus thai mellit on mold, ane myle way and maire. **1530** PALSGR. 862/1 Over a myle way, *oultre vne mile.*

3. A name applied to certain roads in the neighbourhood of Oxford. Also *attrib.*

1771 *Act 11 Geo. III*, c. 19 (*title*) An Act for amending certain of the Mile-Ways leading to Oxford. *Ibid.*, Whereas such of the several Roads near the University and City of Oxford usually called the Mile-Ways, as are not Part of any Turnpike Road, are in a very bad State [etc.]. **1798** in Mrs. B. Stapleton *Three Oxford Parishes* (O.H.S.) 164 Paid Scroggs, surveyor, the Mileway money, £7 0 0.

mileyner, obs. form of MILLINER *sb.*

milfoil ('mɪlfɔɪl). Forms: 4 mille-, mylfoly, 5 myllefoyle, millefoil, melle-, myllyfoly, 5–6 mylfoile, 6 mylfoyle, myllefoly, 6–7 milfoile, 7 millefoil(e, 3, 7– milfoil. [ME. *milfoil*, a. OF. *milfoil* masc. (also *millefueille*, mod.F. *millefeuille* fem., after *feuille* leaf):—L. *milifolium*, *millefolium*, f. *mīle*, *mille* thousand + *folium* leaf. The name alludes to the many finely-divided leaves of the plant. Cf. the synonymous Gr. χιλιόφυλλος (f. χίλιοι thousand + φύλλον leaf), It. *millefoglio*, *millefoglie*, Pg. *millfolhas*.]

1. The common yarrow, *Achillea Millefolium*.

[*c* **1000** *Sax. Leechd.* I. 194 Wið ʒeswell, ʒenim þas ylcan wyrte myllefolium.] *c* **1265** *Voc. Plants* in Wr.-Wülcker 555/9 *Millefolium*, Milfoil. **14..** in *Rel. Ant.* I. 55 Tak confery, marigolde, matfelon, mylfoyle. **14..** *Stockh. Med. MS.* I. 173 in *Anglia* XVIII. 299 Take mylfoly & flour & comyn. *c* **1450** *ME. Med. Bk.* (Heinrich) 112 Take betoyne, verueyne millefoil, & quintfoile, ana, wasshe hem, & grynde hem in a morter. **1567** Maplet *Gr. Forest* 52 Mylfoile, of some Yarrow or Nosebleede, is a small and short set or shrub. **1579** Langham *Gard. Health* (1633) 397 Milfoile or yarrow: The decoction thereof doth cure the bloudy flixe and all other lasks. **1615** Brathwait *Strappado* (1878) 88 The pinke, the plantaine, milfoile, euery one. **1728** J. Gardiner tr. *Rapin On Gardens* 41 The Milfoil next her thousand Leaves displays. **1877** Besant & Rice *Harp & Cr.* i, The..yellow hawkweed, pink herbrobert, and the white milfoil.

b. The genus *Achillea*.

1789 W. Aiton *Hortus Kewensis* III. 239 *Achillea Santolina*..Lavender-cotton-leav'd Milfoil. *Ibid.*, *A. Ageratum*..Sweet Milfoil, or Maudlin. *Ibid.*, *A. tomentosa*..Woolly Milfoil... *A. pubescens*..Downy Milfoil [etc.]. **1882** *Garden* 12 Aug. 134/2 Unlike most of the Milfoils, it is ..a decidedly handsome and stately border plant.

2. In the names of plants of other genera, as **hooded (water) milfoil**, the genus *Utricularia*; **knight's milfoil**, *Stratiotes aloides*; **water milfoil**, (*a*) the genus *Myriophyllum*; (*b*) the water violet, *Hottonia palustris*.

1578 Lyte *Dodoens* I. ci. 142 Water Milfoyle or Yearrow. *Ibid.* 143 Knights Milfoyle: souldiers Yerrow. **1597** Gerarde *Herbal* II. cclxxxvi. 678 Water Milfoile or water Yarrow hath long and large leaues [etc.]. **1741** *Compl. Fam.-Piece* II. iii. 380 Likewise these in the Water-tubs,..the Water Violet, and Water Milfoil, with some others. **1760** J. Lee *Introd. Bot.* App. 319 Milfoil, Water, *Hottonia. Ibid.*, Milfoil, Water, *Myriophyllum. Ibid.*, Milfoil, Water, *Utricularia.* **1854** S. Thomson *Wild Fl.* III. (ed. 4) 205 We may find one or other of the water mill-foils. **1863** Prior *Brit. Plants* s.v., Hooded-Milfoil, *Utricularia*, L., Water Milfoil, *Myriophyllum*, L. **1866** *Treas. Bot.* s.v., Water Milfoil, *Myriophyllum*; also *Hottonia palustris.*

†**milful**, *a.* ? var. MILDFUL or MILCEFUL.

c **1400** *R. Glouc.* (Rolls) 8966 (MS. B) Mylfol. *Ibid.* 8975 (MS. B) Mylfol, (MS. δ) milfol.

†**milge**, *a. Obs.* In 5 mylge. *trans.* To dig round about. Hence '**milging** *vbl. sb.*

c **1420** *Pallad. on Husb.* II. 296 Mylge hem not [orig. *circumfodi non debent*] in tymes whan thai floure. *Ibid.* 362 In their age a mylging they desireth, Lest thai therynne al hoor yberded goo. *Ibid.* III. 522 In the semynary sholde The plauntes now be mylged euerychon.

‖**milia** ('mɪlɪə), *sb. pl. Path.* [L., pl. of *milium* MILLET[1], MILIUM.] Minute spots, resembling those of measles, which occur in miliary fever.

1876 Duhring *Dis. Skin* 119 Milia have their seat for the most part upon the face, especially on the forehead and about the eyelids. **1890** in *Syd. Soc. Lex.*

milia: see MILLY *Obs.*

miliaceous (mɪlɪ'eɪʃəs), *a.* [f. prec. + -ACEOUS.] Of the nature of milia; like millet or the millet-seed.

1684 tr. *Bonet's Merc. Compit.* XVIII. 610 Some miliaceous roughnesses..arose upon the skin. **1890** in *Syd. Soc. Lex.*

†'**miliad**. *Obs. rare.* [irreg. f. L. *mīlia*, pl. of *mille* thousand: cf. MYRIAD.] A collected thousand.

1616–61 Holyday *Persius* 298 Thou shalt not buy..This my dear scoff, my nothing, for whole miliads Of any base poets long-winded Iliads. **1732** Stackhouse *Hist. Bible* (1767) III. VI. i. 575 This miliad of wives and concubines.

†'**miliar**. *Obs. rare*$^{-1}$. In 5 milyair. [ad. L. *miliārium*.] A tall narrow vessel used in Roman baths for drawing and warming water.

c **1420** *Pallad. on Husb.* I. 1093 A milyair of leed [orig. *miliarium plumbeum*].

‖**miliaria** (mɪlɪ'ɛərɪə). [mod.L. uses of L. *miliāria*, fem. of *miliārius*: see MILIARY *a.*]

†1. The corn-bunting, *Emberiza miliaria*. *Obs.*

1706 Phillips (ed. Kersey), *Miliaria*, a Bird that feeds upon Millet, a Linnet.

2. *Path.* Miliary fever: see MILIARY *a.* 2.

1807 *Med. Jrnl.* XVII. 399 Section 2. *Exanthemata*..miliaria, urticaria,..and variola vaccina. **1822–34** *Good's Study Med.* (ed. 4) III. 408 Various species of ecpyesis, smallpox and in one instance miliaria. **1876** Duhring *Dis. Skin* 230 Miliaria is an acute, inflammatory disorder of the sweat-glands. **1890** in *Syd. Soc. Lex.*

miliary ('mɪlɪərɪ), *a.* (and *sb.*) [ad. L. *miliārius* pertaining to millet, f. *milium* MILL *sb.*[2], MILLET[1]: see -ARY.]

1. *Phys.* and *Path.* Resembling a millet-seed in size or form; resembling an aggregation of millet-seeds. ***miliary gland***: one of the sebaceous glands of the skin. ***miliary tubercle***: a greyish-white spherical body about the size of a millet-seed, common in diseased tissues of the lungs and in the membrane of the brain.

1685 Boyle *Salubr. Air* 23 The minute or miliary Glandules of the Skin. **1715** Cheyne *Philos. Princ. Relig.* I. vi. 325 Between these Scales the Excretory Ducts of the Miliary Glands of the true Skin open. **1725** Huxham in *Phil. Trans.* XXXIII. 380 There would appear in the Interstices of the Pox several miliary Pustules. **1816** Keith *Phys. Bot.* I. 68 The miliary glands of animals. **1834** J. Forbes *Laennec's Dis. Chest* (ed. 4) 325 We find a great many ulcers in the intestines, and in most of these, small miliary tubercles. **1854** Jones & Siev. *Pathol. Anat.* (1875) 241 The deposit of tubercle..occurs in the shape of small miliary granules. **1899** *Allbutt's Syst. Med.* VIII. 478 A firm, miliary or prurigo-like papular projection.

2. *Path.* Attended or characterized by spots or vesicles resembling millet-seeds or an aggregation of millet-seeds. ***miliary fever***: a specific disease characterized by the presence of a rash resembling measles, the spots of which exhibit in their centres minute vesicles of the form of millet-seed.

1737 D. Hamilton (*title*) A Treatise of a Miliary Fever. **1742** H. Walpole *Let. to Mann* 15 Apr., The Duchess of Cleveland died last night of what they call a miliary fever. **1844** T. J. Graham *Dom. Med.* 647 It [scarlet fever] may be distinguished from miliary fever by the miliary eruption being..attended by considerable perspiration. **1874** *Q. Jrnl. Microsc. Sci.* XIV. 311 A form of grey degeneration occurring in the brain and spinal cord, and designated by Drs. Batty Tuke and Rutherford, 'miliary sclerosis'.

3. *Nat. Hist.* Having numerous small granulations or projections. ***miliary gland*** (*Bot.*), a stoma or stomate.

1760 J. Lee *Introd. Bot.* III. xviii. (1765) 211 *Miliary*, like grains of Millet. **1836** Loudon *Encycl. Plants* 655 *Citron Medica*... The outer [rind] thin, with innumerable miliary glands. *Gloss.*, *Miliary*, granulate, resembling many seeds. **1852** Dana *Crust.* I. 447 A smooth even surface, excepting a neat miliary granulation. **1866** *Treas. Bot.*, *Miliary Glands*, the same as Stomates.

b. ***miliary sized***: having the size of millet-seeds.

1899 *Allbutt's Syst. Med.* VIII. 592 It [*sc.* the polygonal papule of lichen] is miliary to pepper-corn sized.

4. As *sb. Zool.* A minute tubercle on the shell or skin of some animals (Webster 1897).

miliary, obs. form of MILLIARY.

‖**milice** (milis). [F. *milice*, lit. 'warlike discipline' (Cotgr.), ad. L. *militia* warfare.] Formerly, militia; military service or training. In revived use, *spec.* a force employed by the occupied French state of 1940–44 to repress internal dissent. (In quot. 1945, by substitution for MILICIEN.)

1635 J. Hayward tr. *Biondi's Banish'd Virg.* 139 My Father not knowing how to refuse the destinated milice, bethought himselfe of sending me into Persia. **1673** Sir W. Temple *Observ. Netherl.* i. 13 The Forces of these Counts were composed of..a Milice, which was call'd *Les gens d'ordonnance*, who served on foot, and were not unlike our Train-bands. *Ibid.* vii. 227 Out of this Revenue is supplied the charge of the whole Milice. **1945** H. Nicolson *Let.* 11 Mar. (1967) 440 The *milices* had beaten him up. **1958** *Listener* 21 Aug. 277/2 The Cagoulards, who in the event became the Kernel of the Vichy Milice. **1968** A. Diment *Bang Bang Birds* vi. 98 Their disposal was left to the Gestapo and the Milice. **1974** T. Allbeury *Snowball* vi. 32 An officer..captured in Perpignan by the Milice in 1944 and handed over to the Gestapo.

milicia, obs. form of MILITIA.

‖**miliciano** (mili'θjano). [Sp.] A militiaman of the irregular Republican force formed during the Spanish Civil War. Also **miliciana**, a militiawoman of this force.

1938 J. Riesenfeld *Dancer in Madrid* viii. 159 A woman *miliciana* was being helped up by two *milicianos*. **1957** P. Kemp *Mine were of Trouble* ii. 23 Women, too, enlisted in the militias... They were also employed as jailers to guard female political prisoners, several of whom have told me that they suffered much worse treatment from the *milicianas* than from the men. *Ibid.* 27 The only opposition came from the *milicianos*, who fought with courage but without discipline or military training. **1962** D. A. Puzzo *Spain & Great Powers* iii. 69 Against German and Italian air power and matériel, the *milicianos* could not hope to advance. **1965** C. D. Eby *Siege of Alcázar* (1966) iii. 65 At the Plaza de Padilla they were stopped by some *milicianos*.

‖**milicien** (milisjẽ). [Fr.] A member of the Milice (see MILICE above).

1945 *Tomorrow* (N.Y.) Feb. 11/1 These fellow-soldiers..would..comb a building for Germans or the dreaded Miliciens. **1961** P. de Vomécourt *Who lived to see Day* ix. 107 Almost to a man the *miliciens* were thugs on the make...Many of them were convicted criminals. **1966** M. R. D. Foot *SOE in France* v. 120 Miliciens were Frenchmen who lived and worked in their home towns and villages. **1967** *Listener* 16 Nov. 640/3 He is liquidated on suspicion of being one of the *miliciens*.

milieu ('mi:ljɜ:, ‖miljø). [a. F. *milieu* middle, medium, f. *mi*:—L. *medius* (see MEDIUM) + *lieu* place.] 1. A medium, environment, 'surroundings'.

1854 Geo. Eliot *Let.* 6 Apr. (1954) II. 149, I could no more live out of my *milieu*, than the haddocks I daresay you are often having for dinner. **1877** J. A. Symonds *Renaiss. It., Reviv. Learn.* 4 The intellectual and moral milieu created by multitudes of self-centred, cultivated personalities was necessary for the evolution of that spirit of intelligence,..that formed the motive force of the Renaissance. **1893** *Fortn. Rev.* Mar. 322, I prepared a Milieu, consisting of seventy-five parts of broth and twenty-five parts of the liquid, to which I wished to habituate the Microbe. **1900** *Daily News* 15 Aug. 6/4 The story, which is set in a middle-class milieu, succeeds in being pleasantly homely. **1955** *Times* 19 May 13/5 Its [*sc.* a book's] understanding of the poet's *milieu*. **1958** H. A. Wilmer *Social Psychiatry in Action* i. 21 The crucial point, however, is that a milieu was created that permitted recovery, rather than driving patients deeper into insanity. **1975** J. Rossiter *Golden Virgin* i. 11 Whitehall, a *milieu* in which you could look revoltingly nude without a bowler hat.

2. *Comb.*, as **milieu therapy** *Psychol.*, a form of group psychotherapy which relies on the social environment evolved by the staff and patients in the treatment unit.

1940 *Amer. Jrnl. Orthopsychiatry* X. 905 In environmental (manipulative, external, reality, milieu) therapy, it is assumed that the child's difficulty is in the social situation... Since the difficulties in the child are resultants of the difficulties in the environment, a milieu therapy is the truly rational therapy. **1961** R. Kee *Refugee World* i Their [*sc.* the refugees'] removal from a filthy, over-crowded hut to shelter considered fit for human beings is disguised as 'milieu therapy'. **1963** *New Society* 5 Sept. 17/3 Community services (or milieu therapy) for young deviants. **1964** M. Argyle *Psychol. & Social Probl.* v. 71 *Milieu therapy* and *therapeutic community* treatment consists of a residential institution run on more relaxed and permissive lines than is usual. **1972** G. Sereny *Case of Mary Bell* iv. 214 There are four of these experimental units in Britain..operated loosely on Aichhorn's 'Milieu Therapy'. They are designed to provide for persistently 'asocial' children..a secure environment.

†**miligant**. *Obs.*

a **1500** *Colkelbie Sow* Proem i. 55 (Laing), A miligant and a michare.

miliner, obs. form of MILLINER *sb.*

miling, *vbl. sb.*[1]: see MILE *v. Obs.*

miling, *vbl. sb.*[2] [f. MIL(E *sb.*[1] + -ING[1].] The action of running a mile (as an athletic event).

1913 S. A. Mussabini *Compl. Athletic Trainer* 73 This is miling of the best sort, disdaining the waiting tactics which so many adopt. **1955** R. Bannister *First Four Minutes* ii. 21 It is this controlled tension about to break down that gives miling its great excitement for the spectators. **1963** *Times* 27 May 5/6 Miling..received a needed fillip..when A. J. Harris won the Surrey race in 4 min. 2·4 sec.

‖**Miliola** (mɪ'laɪəʊlə). *Zool.* Pl. -æ. [mod.L., dim. of L. *milium* millet.] An important genus of imperforate foraminifera; an animal of this genus.

1836 Buckland *Geol. & Min.* (1837) I. 385 The *Miliola*, a small multilocular shell, no larger than a millet seed, with which the strata of many quarries in the neighbourhood of Paris are largely interspersed. **1879** Carpenter in *Encycl. Brit.* IX. 376/2 The shells of the *Miliolæ*..are at present found in the shore sands of almost every sea.

miliolid ('mɪlɪəlɪd). *Zool.* [f. MILIOLA + -ID.] Any member of the foraminiferal family *Miliolida*.

1894 Lister in *Phil. Trans.* CLXXXVI. 408 The forms which had been shown to exist in the species of Nummulites and Miliolids.

mili'oliform, *a. Zool.* [f. MILIOL-A + -(I)FORM.] = MILIOLINE.

In recent Dicts.

milioline ('mɪlɪəlaɪn), *a.* and *sb. Zool.* [f. MILIOLA + -INE.] A. *adj.* Pertaining to or consisting of Miliolæ. B. *sb.* A foraminifer belonging to the genus *Miliola* or to the family *Miliolida*.

1873 Dawson *Earth & Man* 243 The milioline limestone of the Eocene, so called from its immense abundance of microscopic shells of the genus Miliolina. **1879** Carpenter in *Encycl. Brit.* IX. 376/2 Milioline shells..often show some kind of 'sculpture'. *Ibid.*, From this simple undivided spire we may pass along two divergent lines, one conducting us to the *milioline* and the other to the *orbiculine* type. *Ibid.*, In the typical Miliolines it [the structure] is more or less obscured by the extension of the later chambers over the earlier. **1884** Brady in *Challenger Rep., Zool.* IX. 137 The more strictly Milioline Foraminifera.

miliolite ('mɪlɪəlaɪt), *a.* and *sb. Geol.* and *Palæont.* In 9 *erron.* milliolite. [f. MILIOLA + -ITE[1].] A. *adj.* Formed or consisting of Miliolæ. B. *sb.* A fossil milioline foraminifer. Hence **milio'litic** *a.*, containing miliolites.

1833 Lyell *Princ. Geol.* III. 246 Coarse marine limestone through which the small multilocular shell, called milliolite, is dispersed in countless numbers. **1847** Ansted *Anc. World* xii. 289 The beds of nummulites and miliolites contemporaneous with those containing the Sheppey plants. **1872** Nicholson *Palæont.* 66 The Miliolite Limestone of the Paris basin. **1883** *Ann. & Mag. Nat. Hist.* July 68 All the species of Miliolites that we have studied are dimorphous.

milion, obs. f. MELON, MILAN, MILLION.

milioun, obs. form of MILLION.

‖**militaire** (militɛr). [Fr.] A soldier. (Cf. MILITARE *a.*)

1746 G. TOWNSHEND *Let.* 1 Oct. in J. H. Jesse *George Selwyn* (1843) I. 114 They look upon the *militaires* with abhorrence. **1827** DISRAELI *Viv. Grey* III. v. vi. 101 He was a starch *militaire*, with a blue frock coat buttoned up to his chin. **1847** THACKERAY *Van. Fair* (1848) xxxvi. 328 That young woman..forgot her charge in the society of this *militaire*. **1938** *Times Lit. Suppl.* 11 June 417/2 'Strathmore' can never be matched by an age that has learned to see *les militaires* with the cold eye of the elderly Ouida.

militancy (ˈmɪlɪtənsɪ). [f. MILITANT *a.*: see -ANCY.] **a.** The condition of being militant.

1648 W. MOUNTAGUE *Devoute Ess.* I. x. §7. 122 All humane life, especially the active part, is constituted in a state of continual militancy [*printed* malitancy]. **1826** E. IRVING *Babylon* II. VII. 180 Emblem of the Church's passage from militancy to glory upon the earth. **1856** FROUDE *Hist. Eng.* (1858) I. i. 88 The nation was in a normal condition of militancy against social injustice. **1912** in E. Pankhurst *My own Story* (1914) III. iii. 258 The leaders..have so often warned the Government that unless the vote were granted to women in response to the mild militancy of the past, a fiercer spirit of revolt would be awakened. **1913** L. A. HARKER *Ffolliots of Redmarley* xii. 156 Eloquent forgot her militancy. **1975** D. RAMSAY *Descent into Dark* ii. 56 Militancy was her bag, and..she looked like someone who spent a lot of time at the barricades.

b. In Herbert Spencer's use: The condition of being a 'militant' community; social organization framed with a view to a state of war.

1876 H. SPENCER *Princ. Sociol.* (1877) I. 708 Where..the chiefly power is small, the militancy is not great.

militant (ˈmɪlɪtənt), *a.* and *sb.* [a. F. *militant*, a. L. *mīlitant-em*, pr. pple. of *mīlitāre* to serve as a soldier, wage war (see MILITATE *v.*), f. *mīlit-*, *mīles* soldier.] **A.** *adj.*

1. a. Engaged in warfare, warring. ***Church militant***: see CHURCH 4 b.

1413 *Pilgr. Sowle* (Caxton) v. vi. (1859) 76 The chirche militant, that laboureth here in erthe. **1500-20** DUNBAR *Poems* lxx. 19 Thow, that art of mercy militant. *c* **1550** COVERDALE *Carrying Christ's Cross* viii. 94 Yet shoulde they [*sc.* the departed] in this case be discerned from the mylitaunte members, they beyng at reste. **1590** SPENSER *F.Q.* II. viii. 2 How oft do they with golden pineons cleave The flitting skyes..Against fowle feendes to ayd us militant! **1615** BRATHWAIT *Strappado* (1878) 223 For his abiding, hee's as in a Tent, Wherein hees militant, not permanent. **1672** WILKINS *Nat. Relig.* 251 Our condition, whilst we are in this world, is militant, wherein every one is without reluctancy to submit to the orders of his great captain or general. **1755** YOUNG *Centaur* v. Wks. 1757 IV. 223 This is a militant state; nor must man unbuckle his armour, till he puts on his shroud. **1873** J. H. NEWMAN *Hist. Sk.* III. I. 1 The Church is ever militant; sometimes she gains, sometimes she loses.

b. *Sociology.* Epithet employed by Spencer for a system of social organization in which efficiency in war is the primary object aimed at.

1882 H. SPENCER *Princ. Sociol.* §521 II. 662 Under the militant type [of society] the individual is owned by the State.

c. Applied to or adopted as a designation by those who seek political or industrial change by employing or advocating the use of direct action, demonstrations, etc.; freq. applied to union leaders who hold out for high wage settlements, refuse to take part in discussions, etc.

1907 M. MCMILLAN in 'B. Villiers' *Case for Women's Suffrage* 114 *Why* did the militant Suffragette ever come to the door of the House of Commons? **1914** E. PANKHURST *My own Story* I. iii. 37 That visit was one of the contributory causes that led to the foundation of our militant suffrage organisation, the Women's Social and Political Union. **1930** *Daily Express* 6 Oct. 11/6 Mr. Maxton leads a group of I.L.P. members who have brought a militant policy with them. **1960** *Economist* 8 Oct. 120/3 Mr Ted Hill's boilermakers..are incensed at the 'more militant than thou' attitude which Mr Greene is thus able to assume. **1969** *Rep. Comm. on Relations with Junior Members Univ. Oxf.* 158 Militant students believe that..they have a special position and function. **1975** *Times* 10 Apr. 17/3 The militant left are a menace to the welfare of Europe.

d. ***Militant tendency***: a Trotskyist political organization, orig. comprising the supporters of the weekly newspaper *Militant*. See B. 1 d below.

This organization has at no time been an official subdivision of the British Labour Party; however, in the mid-1980s, it was alleged to be involved in infiltration of the Labour Party, and a number of its members were expelled from Labour Party membership.

[? **1964** R. PROTZ *Let.* in *Observer* 31 Aug. (1975) 2/3 Grant and Co's insistence not only that *Militant* should be a 'tendency' paper but that it must also be a 'youth and labour' paper. **1975** B. CASTLE *Diaries* (1980) 565 Reg Underhill's document..stating..that the Marxist 'Militant' group has full-time organizers and that all but one of the eleven members of the Young Socialists' Executive have 'Militant' tendencies.] **1979** *Economist* 7 Apr. 30/3 The Militant Tendency is just another faction in the Labour Party. **1980** [see TENDENCY 1 e]. **1983** *Listener* 2 June 6/2 Minor confusions in the programme and the campaign, like Polaris and his appearance on platforms with supporters of Militant Tendency. **1984** M. CRICK *Militant* iii. 54 By 1967 the Militant tendency, as it was now becoming known..was the sole significant Trotskyist group left inside the LPYS. **1985** *Christian Science Monitor* 23 Dec. 7/2 They belong to the Militant tendency, a Trotskyite faction..dedicated to revolutionary struggle.

†**2.** Of a standard: Military. *Obs.*

1483 CAXTON *Gold. Leg.* 22b/1, The kynge of heven perdurable hath hys signes mylytant in the chirche. **1609** HOLLAND *Amm. Marcell.* Annot. b j, The militant ensignes or banners in the Romane legion.

3. Combative.

1603 FLORIO *Montaigne* I. xlix. 161 He would maintaine by militant reasons [orig. *par viues raisons*] that the waste was in his right place. **1809-10** COLERIDGE *Friend* (1865) 57 That we be sedulous, yea, and militant in the endeavour to reason aright, is His implied command. **1841** MYERS *Cath. Th.* III. §40. 147 This is a condition which must instigate to resistance in the most pacific, and to rebellion in the more militant. **1903** J. WILLCOCK *Gt. Marquess* vi. 88 The expenses of the militant Presbyterians.

B. *sb.* **a.** One engaged in war or strife.

1610 G. FLETCHER *Christ's Vict.* II. xxx, Looking down on His weake militants. **1643** SIR T. BROWNE *Relig. Med.* II. §3 Even amongst wiser militants, how many wounds have been given, and credits slain. **1814** SOUTHEY *Let. to J. White* 2 May in *Life* (1850) IV. 74 Horsley was the militant of the last generation. **1900** *Daily News* 6 Apr. 6/5 They [Anarchists in England] are divided into two bodies: 'Idealists' and 'Militants'.

b. A member of the military profession.

1842 *United Service Mag.* II. 540 Will this modicum of embryo scientific militants suffice for every regiment?

c. A person who is a militant in the senses above.

1909 *Englishwoman* Apr. 323 That bias has been greatly intensified amongst almost all classes of suffragists by the tactics of the militants. **1914** E. PANKHURST *My own Story* I, (*heading*) The making of a Militant. **1939** *Theology* XXXIX. 437 The lives of certain of the militants reveal that Jocism stands for strength through holiness and self-sacrifice. **1968** *Daily Tel.* 12 Nov. 25/1 Ultra-left militants in the Electrical Trades Union are planning another demonstration today. **1969** *New Yorker* 17 May 114/2 A mysterious black militant. **1973** *Black World* Sept. 96/2 The young militants look down upon Anna's poetry. **1975** *Daily Mirror* 29 Apr. 4 They defeated a bid by union militants for an increase which would have broken the Social Contract. **1975** *Times Lit. Suppl.* 9 May 512/5 Intransigent NUJ [*sc.* National Union of Journalists] militants who now say they will discuss no press charter with the proprietors.

d. *spec.* One who sympathizes with the views expressed in the Trotskyist newspaper *Militant*, set up in 1964; a supporter of the Militant tendency (see A. 1 d above).

[**1944** J. P. CANNON *Hist. Amer. Trotskyism* x. 193 *The Militant* was the name of the official organ of the American Trotskyists from the very beginning...*The Militant* signified the party worker, the party activist, the party fighter.] **1970** *Militant* Nov. 4/3 Now they are not ballot-rigging: they are preventing militants' names from even appearing on the ballot-papers! **1979** *Economist* 7 Apr. 30/3 The Militants hold all the seats on the Labour Party's Young Socialists' executive. **1985** *Christian Science Monitor* 23 Dec. 8/3 The booting out of Militants from party membership...will represent yet another victory for moderation.

e. *ellipt.* for *Militant tendency*.

1980 *Economist* 19 Jan. 18/2 The major advance which Militant has made inside the Labour party is to capture the official youth organisation. **1986** *Tribune* 12 Sept. 7/1 She..was one of those who walked out of the NEC's hearings into Militant.

Hence **ˈmilitantness**, the quality of being militant (1727 in Bailey, vol. II).

militantly (ˈmɪlɪtəntlɪ), *adv.* [f. prec. + -LY[2].] In a militant or combative manner.

1628 B. HALL *Serm. Lds. Parl.* 5 Apr. 48 How do they looke vp at us, as euen now Militantly-triumphant, whiles [etc.]. **1886** *Academy* 2 Oct. 215/2, I do not in the least mean that *Faust*, any more than 'Hamlet', is a militantly heathen poem. **1887** BENSON *Laud* 225 Laud's ideal was a high one, but it was..too militantly..held.

†**militar(e**, *a. Obs.* [ad. F. *militaire*: see -AR[2]. Cf. MILITARY.] Military, martial.

1533 BELLENDEN *Livy* II. xix. (S.T.S.) I. 205 It was governit be ressoun militare. **1588** J. HARVEY *Disc. Probl.* 82 What were states..without..the militar discipline of armies ..? **1624** WOTTON *Archit.* in *Reliq.* (1651) 216 They are surely fitter for Militar Architecture. **1625** BACON *Ess.*, *Vain-Glory*, In Militar Commanders and Soldiers, Vaine-Glory is an Essential Point. **1640** HABINGTON *Edw. IV* 142 The militar exercise of the French.

militaria (mɪlɪˈtɛərɪə). [f. MILITAR(Y *a.* and *sb.* + -IA[2].] Military articles of historical interest.

1964 *Exchange & Mart* 26 Mar. 12/4 Wanted: militaria, early model soldiers, uniforms, head-dress, accoutrements, paintings, by keen collector. **1970** *Times* 23 Dec. 10 During his last years he spent much of his time in trying to gather together writings, militaria and other possessions left by the Field-Marshal. **1973** *Inverness Courier* 31 July 8/4 A wider range of collectors items than ever before will be on show, and..there will be specialist stands featuring fine antique glass, weapons, militaria, old postcards, and early newspapers. **1974** *Country Life* 25 Apr. 1031/2 Sale of: Sporting Guns..Hand Guns and Nazi Militaria.

militarily (ˈmɪlɪtərɪlɪ), *adv.* [f. MILITARY + -LY[2].]

1. In a military or warlike manner.

1660 *Trial Regicides* 155 Because we were militarily affected. **1831** GEN. P. THOMPSON *Exerc.* (1842) I. 430 There is no disgrace in being militarily conquered after resisting to the last. **1870** W. R. GREG *Polit. Problems* 38 We could not interfere militarily without the assistance of a Continental Power.

2. From a military point of view.

1793 SIR M. EDEN in *Ld. Auckland's Corr.* III. 207 The Emperor's journey, civilly and militarily, has had an excellent effect. **1839** T. HOOK in *New Monthly Mag.* LVI. 2 This, militarily speaking, 'signifieth nothing'. **1898** G. W. STEEVENS *Egypt* xiv. 163 Egypt was left militarily in the most exposed situation imaginable.

militariness (ˈmɪlɪtərɪnɪs). [f. MILITARY + -NESS.] The state or condition of being military.

1834 M. SCOTT *Cruise Midge* xvi, Don't be surprised at the militariness of my lingo, for I am colonel of the regiment of foot militia here. **1897** MAITLAND *Domesday & Beyond* 152 All sense of militariness..seems to be disappearing.

militarism (ˈmɪlɪtərɪz(ə)m). [a. F. *militarisme*, f. *militaire*: see MILITARY and -ISM.]

1. The spirit and tendencies characteristic of the professional soldier; the prevalence of military sentiment or ideals among a people; the political condition characterized by the predominance of the military class in government or administration; the tendency to regard military efficiency as the paramount interest of the state.

1864 *Daily Tel.* 28 Apr. (tr. G. Garibaldi), An army, bright in glory, yet untainted with that disease of modern times, known under the sinister name of militarism. **1868** *Macm. Mag.* XIX. 156 Prussian officialism is supreme and ..Prussian militarism as well. **1891** J. W. CROSS in *Fortn. Rev.* 469 Industrialism as opposed to militarism, is now the central idea of the New World.

2. A military habit or mannerism.

1893 D. C. MURRAY *Time's Revenges* III. xlvii. 268 Their militarisms and legalities made the more openly sentimental-minded folk altogether ill at ease.

militarist (ˈmɪlɪtərɪst), *sb.* and *a.* [f. MILITARY + -IST.] **A.** *sb.* A soldier, warrior; one who studies military science; one dominated by military ideas.

1601 SHAKS. *All's Well* IV. iii. 161 This is Mounsieur Parrolles the gallant militarist, that was his owne phrase. **1860** GEN. P. THOMPSON *Audi Alt.* (1861) III cxvi. 51 Questions for the solution of the youthful militarist. **1884** J. R. SEELEY in *Encycl. Brit.* XVII. 226/1 Napoleon..a ruthless militarist, cynic, and Machiavellian.

B. *adj.* = MILITARISTIC *a.*

1934 R. CAMPBELL *Broken Record* i. 19 This form of historical instruction is no doubt at the back of the modern militarist-political unrest. **1944** J. S. HUXLEY *On Living in Revolution* iii. 33 Shall it be peaceful, cooperative, democratic, or shall it be militarist, totalitarian, brutal?

Hence **militaˈristic** *adj.*, characterized by militarism.

1905 *Athenæum* 15 July 73/1 A political organization and a moral tendency common to all nascent civilization of the militaristic order.

militarization (mɪlɪtəraɪˈzeɪʃən). [f. MILITARIZE *v.* + -ATION.] Conversion to a military status or to military methods.

1881 *Fortn. Rev.* Mar. 356 This voluntary militarization in a country where the people may calculate upon continual peace. **1891** *Sat. Rev.* 1 Aug. 133/2 There are some who.. talk about the 'militarization' of the annual rifle competitions.

militarize (ˈmɪlɪtəraɪz), *v.* [f. MILITARY + -IZE.] *trans.* To convert to military methods; to train as a soldier; to imbue with militarism.

1880 *Fortn. Rev.* Feb. 293 A war by which a military dominion is yet further militarised. **1888** *Lanc. Even. Post* 3 Feb. 2/4 Sir Charles Warren..had done his best to militarise Scotland Yard. **1889** *Times* 21 Oct. 5/4 The militarizing of the Civil Service. **1922** P. N. MILIUKOV *Russia* 205 The climax was reached when the Bolsheviks decided to militarize labor. **1972** *Daily Tel.* 11 Jan. 9/8 Will the generals militarise the Government? **1973** *Listener* 14 June 796/3 During the Cultural Revolution..Chinese politics were again militarised.

Hence **ˈmilitarized** *ppl. a.*

1922 *Edin. Rev.* July 28 Appalling slaughter and suffering, patiently endured by a militarized people.., has disillusioned the Germans.

military (ˈmɪlɪtərɪ), *a.* and *sb.* Also 6-7 -rie. [f. F. *militaire*, ad. L. *mīlitār-is*, f. *mīlit-*, *mīles* soldier. Cf. Sp., Pg. *militar*, It. *militare*.]

A. *adj.*

1. Pertaining to soldiers; used, performed, or brought about by soldiers; befitting a soldier.

1585 T. WASHINGTON tr. *Nicholay's Voy.* III. iii. 74 The Pretorian legions..began to become rulers over their maisters, vnder pretext of such a Militarie gift. **1591** GARRARD *Art Warre* 17 Which he must weare to honour the Militarie profession. **1597** SHAKS. *2 Hen. IV*, II. iii. 30 So that in Speech, in Gate,..In Militarie Rules,..He was the Marke and Glasse..That fashion'd others. **1611** HEYWOOD *Gold. Age* II. i. Wks. 1874 III. 21 Train'd my youth, In feats of Armes, and military prowesse. **1665** MANLEY *Grotius' Low C. Warres* 119 They esteem luxury, and all other licentiousness, as Military Gallantry. **1667** MILTON *P.L.* IV. 955 Was this..Your military obedience..? *Ibid.* XI. 241 Over his lucid Armes A militarie Vest of purple flowd. *a* **1718** PENN *Tracts* Wks. 1726 I. 575 Maugre all the Military Opposition of the Jews. **1776** BURNEY *Hist. Mus.* I. I. iv. 340 With respect to Military Music, the trumpet is mentioned by Homer in a simile. **1843** BORROW *Bible in Spain* xliv, The late military revolution. **1849** MACAULAY *Hist. Eng.* vi. II. 142 Tyrconnel..knew nothing of military duty. **1860** *All Year Round* No. 42. 370 They march along with their military heels, their shortened petticoats abruptly terminating.

2. a. Engaged in the life of a soldier; belonging to the army.

1597 SHAKS. *2 Hen. IV*, IV. i. 62 The Throngs of Militarie men. **1617** MORYSON *Itin.* II. 45 That dependancy which all military men already had on him. **1682** DRYDEN *Medal* 179 Thy military chiefs are brave and true.

transf. **1816** KIRBY & SP. *Entomol.* xvii. (1818) II. 65 When the military ants before alluded to go upon their expeditions.

b. Having the characteristics of a soldier; soldierly.

1588 SHAKS. *L.L.L.* v. i. 38 Most militarie sir, salutation. **1612** BACON *Ess.*, *Greatn. Kingd.* (Arb.) 472 Walled Towns, ..Ordinance, and Artillerie, they are all but a Sheep in a Lions skin, except the breed and disposition of the people be militarie. **1839** BAILEY *Festus* xii. (1852) 146 Man is a military animal, Glories in gunpowder, and loves parade. **1863** KINGLAKE *Crimea* I. 64 He was a man too military to be warlike.

3. a. Having reference to armed forces or to the army; adapted to or connected with a state of war; distinguished from *civil*, *ecclesiastical*, etc.

1590 SIR J. SMYTH *Disc. Weapons* Ded. 1 b, Our auncient proceedings in matters Militarie. **1600** J. PORY tr. *Leo's Africa* App. 373 His fourth militarie forces, are the Arabians. **1602** WARNER *Alb. Eng.* Epit. (1612) 357 Ætius.. caused this maruellous and militarie Wall then to be builded. **1612** SELDEN *Illustr. Drayton's Poly-olb.* xv. 244 Excepting those [orders] of Templars..and such like other which were more Religious then Military. **1768** BLACKSTONE *Comm.* III. 115 The public ecclesiastical, military, and maritime jurisdictions. **1804** DUKE OF GRAFTON in *Autobiog.*, etc. (1898) 3 A parent, who, had he lived, would probably have been as distinguished a character in the civil, as he had shown that he was in the military [*i.e.* naval] line. **1825** J. NEAL *Bro. Jonathan* III. 115 Washington would have lost a part, or the whole of..his military stores. **1850** W. D. COOPER *Hist. Winchelsea* 37 The Strand Gate.. leading by the new Military road to Rye.

b. In special collocations. **military academy**, a place of training in the military art (cf. ACADEMY 5); **military age**, the age at which one becomes liable for military service; **military architecture**, the science of fortification; **military art**, †**art military**, the art of war (also *fig.*); **military attaché**, an army officer serving with an embassy; also, one attached as an observer to a foreign army; hence ***military attachéship***; **military band** [BAND *sb.*[3] 4], a band attached to a military unit; **military board**, a board specially appointed to deal with the affairs of the army; **military braid** (see quots.); **military brush** = *military hairbrush*; **military chest**, the treasury of an army; **military college** (cf. COLLEGE *sb.* 4 e) = *military academy*; **Military Cross** (abbrev. *M.C.*), a decoration instituted in 1915 and awarded to officers for gallantry in the face of the enemy; **military drum**, the side or 'snare' drum; **military engineering** = *military architecture*; **military execution** (see quot. 1704); **military feud**, a feudal estate held on certain conditions of armed service to be rendered to the feudal superior; **military fever**, enteric or typhus fever; **military hairbrush**, a hairbrush without a handle; **military honours**: see HONOUR, HONOR *sb.* 5 and 5 d; **military hospital**, a hospital designed for the reception of soldiers, esp. a field hospital; **military law**, the body of enactments and rules for the government of an army; also, an enactment or rule forming part of this; **military mast**, a mast carried by a war-ship for fighting purposes only; **Military Medal** (abbrev. *M.M.*), a decoration of similar distinction to the Military Cross which was instituted in 1916 for 'other ranks'; **military-minded** *a.* [MINDED *ppl. a.* 5], having a mind of a military character; **military offence**, an offence cognizable by a military court; **military orchid, orchis**, a European orchid, *Orchis militaris*, with pinkish-grey, helmet-shaped flowers, now very rare in Britain; also called soldier orchid; **military police**, the body of soldiers responsible for police duty in the armed forces; hence ***military policeman***; **Military Secretary**, an army staff officer who acts as personal and confidential secretary to the Commander-in-Chief or certain other specified officers (see quot. 1876); hence ***Military Secretaryship***; **military service**, the service in war due from a vassal to his feudal superior (cf. SERVICE *sb.* 12); now, service in the armed forces; **military tenure**, a feudal tenure under which a vassal owed his superior certain defined services in war; **military testament**, a nuncupative will by which, in the Roman law, a soldier might dispose of his possessions without the formalities required in an ordinary testament; **military top**, an armoured platform placed on a military mast for signalling and other warlike purposes; **military two-step**, in old-time dancing, a variation of the two-step; †**military yard**, a place set apart for the training of soldiers.

1776 *Jrnls. Continental Congress U.S.* (1906) VI. 860 Resolved, That the Board of War be directed to prepare a plan for establishing a..*Military Academy. **1802** [see ROYAL *a.* 6]. **1805** J. ORROK *Let.* 7 Aug. (1927) 79 He is..a Lieut. although not in orders, which he cannot be untill he has been a few months at a..Military Academy. **1934** *Amer. Speech* IX. 313/1 The United States Military Academy. **1974** *Hartsville* (S. Carolina) *Messenger* 22 Apr. 2-A/7 He made the decision to earn an appointment to a Military Academy. **1920** WEBSTER, *Military age. **1934** G. B. SHAW *Too True to be Good* III. 88 Had I been of military age I should have been a conscientious objector. **1941** *Manch. Guardian Weekly* 26 Sept. 194/2 It would not be fair to raise the military age..without a thorough comb-out of the younger men. **1688** CAPT. J. S. *Fortification* 23 Fortification, or *Military Architecture, is a Science [etc.]. **1590** SIR J. SMYTH *Disc. Weapons* Ded. 1 And speciallie in the *Arte Militarie. **1693** CONGREVE *Old Bach.* v. xv, That you are overreached too, ha! ha! ha! only a little art-military used. **1726** SWIFT *Gulliver* IV. xii, Their prudence..would amply supply all defects in the military art. **1857** *Foreign Office List* X. 18 *Military Attaché to the Embassy, Lt. Col. E. L. Claremont, C.B. **1877** H. PONSONBY *Let.* 18 Nov. in A. Ponsonby *Henry Ponsonby* (1942) 167 We have dozens of Military Attachés with the Armies in the field. **1961** J. MASTERS *Road past Mandalay* vi. 76 It was Persia, and the Military Attaché was doubtful. **1882** *Military attachéship [see ATTACHÉSHIP]. **1775** *Westm. Mag.* May 231/1 Three *military bands, composed of fifes, drums, cymbals, etc. **1836** DICKENS *Sk. Boz*, *Scenes* xiv, A military band commenced playing. **1912** G. MILLER (*title*) The military band. **1964** A. SEXTON *Sel. Poems* 7 While a military band plays a Strauss waltz. **1800** WELLINGTON in Gurw. *Desp.* I. 233, I admire the attention to economy in the *Military board. **1950** '*Mercury*' *Dict. Textile Terms* 346 **Military braid*, a broad braid such as is worn on the tunics of soliders. **1966** *Olney Amsden & Sons Ltd. Price List* 39 Rayon Military Braid in fashion shades 66/6 gross yards. **1968** J. IRONSIDE *Fashion Alphabet* 76 *Military braid*, a flat braid with a diagonal weave. **1926** *Daily Colonist* (Victoria, B.C.) 6 Jan. 2/1 (Advt.), Gentleman's French Ivory *Military Brushes. Concave back, a fine quality bristle. **1969** *H. Knowles-Brown Ltd.* (*Hampstead*) *Christmas Catal.*, Ivory backed military brushes from; per pair £19 0 0. **1753** HANWAY *Trav.* (1762) II. v. i. 126 The *military chest..fell also into the hands of the Abdollees. **1849** MACAULAY *Hist. Eng.* vi. II. 63 The Universities were preparing to coin their plate for the purpose of supplying the military chest of his enemies. **1809** G. L. WARDLE *Charges against Duke of York* 334 Mr. Froome came to town to settle some old accounts of mine as treasurer to the Royal *Military College. **1837** W. DYOTT *Diary* 17 Jan. (1907) II. 246 Young Palmer, a candidate for the army at the Military College at Sandhurst. **1915** *London Gaz.* 1 Jan. 7/1 Royal Warrant instituting a new decoration 'The *Military Cross'. **1917** W. OWEN *Let.* 9 Apr. (1967) 451, I think Capt. Green..will get a Military Cross, which he has long deserved—for 2½ years active service. **1969** S. MAYS *Fall out Officers* viii. 52 Wearing among his campaign ribbons that of the Military Cross. **1872** *Nature* 11 Apr. 465/1 It is to the School of *Military Engineering that the young lieutenants of Engineers are sent. **1704** J. HARRIS *Lex. Techn.* I, **Military Execution*, is delivering a Country up to be ravaged and destroyed by the Soldiers, when it refuses to pay Contribution, &c. **1730** M. WRIGHT *Law Tenures* 32 *Military Feuds in most Countries began to descend to the eldest Son only. **1885–8** FAGGE & PYE-SMITH *Princ. Med.* (ed. 2) I. 131 *Morbus Castrensis* or **military fever*. **1894** *Country Gentlemen's Catal.* 148 Two Ivory *Military Hair Brushes, in Solid Leather Case, 57/-. **1972** J. PORTER *Meddler & her Murder* i. 7 A couple of quick passes with her silver-backed military hair brushes. **1778** *Crit. Rev.* Sept. 189 An account of *military honours paid to crowned heads and to other persons. **1853** Military honours [see HONOUR, HONOR *sb.* 5 d]. **1901** *Daily Chron.* 4 June, The allied troops rendered military honours to the departing commander-in-chief. **1975** *Times* 2 Aug. 2/2 The UVF, a Protestant paramilitary group, said they would receive full military honours. **1777** *Jrnls. Continental Congress U.S.* (1907) VII. 162 An Inspector General of the Army..[shall] visit the *Military hospitals..to examine the medicines and instruments. **1789** P. THICKNESSE *Year's Journey* (ed. 3) I. iii. 25 The *Silver Lion*..is..preferable to Dessein's, as the drains from the Military Hospital run under the latter. **1799** *Med. Jrnl.* I. 455 The want of proper military hospitals has been severely felt. **1860** F. NIGHTINGALE *Notes on Nursing* iii. 23 The ordinary run of military hospitals. **1969** S. MAYS *Fall out Officers* iii. 25, I was not taken to the Cambridge Military Hospital, Aldershot, as I had thought. **1737** *London Mag.* Aug. 492/2 'Tis certain the *military law may be made much stricter and more severe than the common Law can be made. **1883** *Encycl. Brit.* XVI. 295/2 The military law of England in early times existed..in a period of war only. **1887** *Daily News* 25 July 2/5 One bare pole called a *military mast. **1898** *Westm. Gaz.* 8 June 5/2 One of the Spanish shot hit the military mast of the *Massachusetts*. **1916** *London Gaz.* 5 Apr. 3647/1 Royal Warrant instituting a new medal entitled 'The *Military Medal'... We do..institute and create a silver medal to be awarded to non-commissioned officers and men for individual or associated acts of bravery on the recommendation of a Commander-in-Chief in the field. **1917** A. G. EMPEY *Over Top* 300 *Military Medal*, a piece of junk issued to Tommy who has done something that is not exactly brave but is still not cowardly. **1922** *Encycl. Brit.* XXXI. 892/1 The *Military Medal*.—Instituted in March 1916 for award to non-commissioned officers and men of the army for individual or associated acts of bravery in the field. **1957** *Ibid.* XVI. 638/1 Other awards of lesser degree in this class [awarded for gallantry] are: Distinguished Service Order, instituted in 1886 and the Military Cross (1914); only officers are eligible for the award... Also the Military Medal (1916); only 'other ranks' are eligible for the award. **1910** W. JAMES *Mem. & Stud.* (1911) xi. 288 Commonwealths fit only for contempt, and liable to invite attack whenever a centre of crystallization for *military-minded enterprise gets formed anywhere in their neighbourhood. **1939** *Ann. Reg. 1938* 266 The Portuguese are rapidly becoming a military-minded people. **1848** WHARTON *Law Lex.*, **Military offences*, those matters which are cognizable by the courts military, as insubordination, sleeping on guard, desertion, &c. **1934** M. J. GODFERY *Monogr. & Iconogr. Native Brit. Orchidaceæ* 168 *Orchis militaris* L. Soldier Orchid, *Military Orchid. **1948** J. BROOKE *Military Orchid* 1. 17 The Military Orchid had taken on a kind of legendary quality, its image seemed fringed with the mysterious and exciting appurtenances of soldiering, its name was like a distant bugle-call, thrilling and rather sad. **1969** J. E. LOUSLEY *Wild Flowers of Chalk & Limestone* (ed. 2) vii. 90 The largest..was 14 inches (35 cm.) tall with no less than 26 flowers. This must be about the finest Military Orchid seen in England. *Ibid.* 91 It is the resemblance of the hood to an ancient helmet which has led to the plant being called the Soldier or Military Orchid. **1812** W. WITHERING JR. *Withering's Brit. Plants* (ed. 5) II. 29 (*heading*) Narrow-lipped *Military Orchis. *O. militaris*. **1884** W. MILLER *Dict. Eng. Names Plants* 99/2 Orchis,.. Military. *Orchis militaris*. **1950** G. BRENAN *Face of Spain* vii. 156 Under an olive tree I picked a specimen of that rare plant, the Military Orchis, which I knew from the plate in Bentham's Flora but had never found before. **1827** J. J. SNODGRASS *Narr. Burmese War* v. 59 In every village there appeared a small party of *military police. **1933** J. BUCHAN *Prince of Captivity* I. ii. 66 The military police arrived in quest of him. **1974** J. WAINWRIGHT *Hard Hit* 52 One evening session had seen..seven full-weight smash-ups start—and end with the arrival of the Military Police. **1973** J. STRANGER *Walk Lonely Road* v. 44 My own father was a policeman. His father was a *military policeman. I suppose it's like the Services. It runs in families. **1812** J. ORROK *Let.* 26 May (1927) 130 To Colonel Torrens, *Military Secretary to His Royal Highness the Commander-in-Chief. **1853** J. H. STOCQUELER *Mil. Encycl.* 179/2 All military correspondence with the commander-in-chief should be sent through the military secretary. **1876** VOYLE & STEVENSON *Mil. Dict.* (ed. 3) 255/2 *Military Secretary*, an officer attached to the staff of the commander-in-chief, to governors of provinces, and to an officer commanding an army in the field. His duties to some extent are confidential, and he relieves the officer under whom he is serving of a great deal of personal correspondence. **1947** R. G. JESSEL *G, A, & Q* iii. 9 At the end of the course, a report on each student is sent to the Military Secretary at the War Office. **1778** E. DRAPER *Let.* 12 Feb. in *N. & Q.* (1944) 29 July 51/1 Report says, that Dick Sulivan is coming home, in that case, your Brother, I suppose, Steps into the *Military Secretaryship. **1818** HALLAM *Mid. Ages* ii. I. (1868) 79 It by no means appears, that any conditions of *military service were expressly annexed to these grants. **1863** *Act 26 & 27 Vict.* c. 65 §17 Her Majesty may direct the Lieutenants of Counties..to call out the Volunteer Corps..for actual Military Service. **1909** G. B. SHAW *Press Cuttings* 25 What women need is the right to military service. **1922** *Encycl. Brit.* XXXII. 39/2 Mr. Lloyd George persuaded the Supreme Council to accept the principle that all the enemy Powers should be obliged to abolish compulsory military service. **1797** *Encycl. Brit.* (ed. 3) XII. 14/2 Soon after the restoration of king Char. II. when the *military tenures were abolished. **1879** *Ibid.* (ed. 9) IX. 175/2 The king..had a right to the military service of such among his subjects as held lands by military tenure. **1797** TOMLINS *Jacob's Law Dict.*, **Military Testament*. **1887** *Times* (weekly ed.) 26 Aug. 8/1 Two mainmasts with *military-tops. **1911** *Ball Room* Mar. 4/1 (Advt.), Finnigan's,..Manchester... Inventor of the original *Military Two Step. **1949** V. SILVESTER *Old Time Dancing* 49 The Military Two-step is often danced with varying distances separating the partners at different times. **1950** M. GWYNNE *Old Time & Sequence Dancing* 78 Military Two Step... A championship dance. Commence as in the Veleta. **1966** *Listener* 24 Nov. 783/3 The military two-step ended with the ripping of Freddie's entire sleeve. **1630** *R. Johnson's Kingd. & Commw.* 28 That little use which he hath had of his Armes in the Artillery garden, and *Military yard. **1635** BARRIFFE *Mil. Discip.* xcix. (1643) 286 The Gentlemen of the Military yard. **1659** RUSHW. *Hist. Coll.* I. 422 The Military-yard near St. Martins in the Fields.

c. *Comb.* with other adjs., as ***military-industrial***, ***-political***, ***-scientific***, ***-technological*** adjs.

1961 D. EISENHOWER in *N.Y. Times* 18 Jan. 22/4 In the councils of Government, we must guard against the acquisition of unwarranted influence, whether sought or unsought, by the military-industrial complex. **1973** *Times* 13 Jan. 19/5 President Eisenhower, who warned the country of the dangers of a military-industrial complex, must be twitching in his grave. **1965** H. KAHN *On Escalation* 291 The military-political outcome of a war. **1960** *Encounter* Oct. 9 Military-scientific research. **1962** *Times* 26 Feb. (Canada Suppl.) p. ii/2 The 'military-technological complex' eating into American business and politics alike.

B. *sb.*

1. a. Soldiery; soldiers generally. Chiefly, ***the military***; (with sing. or plural verb).

1757 J. H. GROSE *Voy. E. Indies* 202 None..of the Parsees either meddle at all with the government, or with the military. **1772** *Ann. Reg.* 93/1 The military marched down to the ship. **1813** *Chron.* ibid. 76 The whole escorted by 400 military. **1868** M. E. G. DUFF *Pol. Surv.* 16 Their procession was interrupted by the military. **1968** *Globe & Mail* (Toronto) 3 Feb. 11/5 The military use special film to photograph hidden features of the ground below. **1968** MRS. L. B. JOHNSON *White House Diary* 8 Oct. (1970) 718 I've come to have a lot more understanding of what the military puts up with and especially the wives. **1970** *New Yorker* 3 Oct. 44/3 Other branches of the military..were not impressed.

†**b.** The military profession, the army. *Obs.*

1775 *Tender Father* I. 189 Even to the gentlemen in the military,..Mr. N—— would not allow of any material excuses.

2. A military man, esp. an officer in the army.

1736 MRS. MANLEY *Secret Mem.* I. 157 A certain Military's Wife has had more Darts for him than are necessary. **1804** ANNA SEWARD *Mem. Darwin* 149 Fox-hunting esquires, dashing militaries, and pedantic gownsmen. **1837** *Lett. fr. Madras* (1843) 94 The civilians all expect to come to us..; and the militaries go to Captain Price. **1962** *Listener* 1 Nov. 723/3 A few splendid portraits of the Austrian court nobility and of the high militaries.

Hence **'militaryism**, militarism. **'militaryment**, military experience or ability.

1776 Jefferson *Let.* Writ. 1893 II. 88 Pray regard militaryment alone. **1886** E. B. Bax *Relig. Socialism* 6 Hence the prominence of militaryism in all early civilisations. **1885** *Athenæum* 31 Oct. 569/3 In England and the United States ..militaryism is less dominant.

†**'militaster.** *Obs. rare.* [f. L. *mīlit-*, *mīles* soldier + -aster.] A soldier without military skill or knowledge.

1640 Brome *Antipodes* III. iv, *Dia...* But who comes here? a woman? *Let.* Yes; that has taken up the newest fashion Of the towne-militasters. *a* **1652** —— *Covent Gard.* v. iii, What would an upstart Militaster now, That knew no rudiments of discipline, nor Art of warre, do in a sudden service?

militate ('mɪlɪteɪt), *v.* [f. L. *mīlitāt-*, ppl. stem of *mīlitāre* to serve as a soldier, f. *mīlit-*, *mīles* soldier: see -ate[3].]

1. a. *intr.* Of persons: To serve as a soldier; to take part in warfare.

1625 W. B. *True School War* 41 This..moues many Italian Caualiers to militate in the warres of Holland. **1662** Earl Orrery *State Lett.* (1743) II. 437 The faithful Christians..militating against the hereticks. **1769** Burke *Late St. Nat.* Wks. 1842 I. 82 The supply of her armies militating in so many distant countries. **1831–40** K. Digby *Mores Catholici* (1847) III. 148 Men who militate merely for pay. **1832** De Quincey *Cæsars* Wks. 1859 X. 216 Originally it had militated for glory and power; now its militancy was for a free movement of aspiring and hopeful existence.

†**b.** *transf.* and *fig.* To contend, make war, exert power or influence; to strive. *Obs.*

1643 Prynne *Sov. Power Parl.* App. 199 Lest..whiles they seeke to deserve well of the Common-wealth, they militate to the private lust of any. **1675** Baxter *Cath. Theol.* I. III. 22 God doth not militate against himself. **1735** Berkeley *Reasons* §17 This learned professor, who at bottom militates on my side. **1781** Gibbon *Decl. & F.* xxvii. III. 64 The invisible powers of heaven..seemed to militate on the side of the pious emperor. **1799** E. Du Bois *Piece Family Biog.* III. 157 To incur the severe displeasure of his father and sir David, by disobeying the one, and militating against the peace of the other, was what he could not bear. **1851** Landor *Popery* 36 They who litigate and militate in the church about him.

c. To display industrial or political intransigence; to act in the manner of a militant (sense c).

1951 E. Paul *Springtime in Paris* xvi. 321 Busse knew all too well what happened to French Communists who showed disloyalty, or even who failed to 'militate'. **1969** *N.Y. Rev. Bks.* 30 Jan. 4/3 Simone Weil going to work in a factory and eventually starving herself to death in order to share the diet of the people of occupied France was answering the same 'call' as..Silone militating in the underground, in clandestinity.

2. Of things. †**a.** To conflict, be inconsistent *with*; also (of speech or action), to be directed *against*. *Obs.* **b.** Of evidence, facts, circumstances: To have force, 'tell' *against* (rarely †*for*, *in favour of*) some conclusion or result.

1642 Heylin *Hist. Episc.* II. 4 The discourse of Clemens ..doth militate as well against the one, as against the other. **1658** Baxter *Saving Faith* 22 Your reasons..do learnedly militate for the Assertion that I maintain. **1756** Amory *Buncle* (1770) II. 193 It militates with the revealed truths of God. **1791** Burke *App. Whigs* Wks. VI. 132 Something which militates with any rational plan. **1796** Earl Malmesbury *Diaries & Corr.* III. 355 It militated directly against the principle..laid down. **1804** tr. *La Marteliere's Three Gil Blas* II. 272 The same reasons militated in their favour. **1816** Peacock *Headlong Hall* xiii, Your observation militates on my side of the question. **1838** Sir W. Hamilton *Logic* xxxiv. (1866) II. 195 Everything may militate for, and nothing militate against, its authenticity. *a* **1852** Webster *Wks.* (1877) III. 210 Dispatches are read, which, it is said militate with one another. **1853** Mansel *Lett., Lect.*, etc. (1873) App. 102 The whole character and history of mathematical science militates against the admission of this consequence. **1864** Maine *Anc. Law* 122 Its connexion with Scripture rather militated than otherwise against its reception as a complete theory. **1874** A. J. Christie in *Ess. Relig. & Lit.* Ser. III. 65 The same reasons which militated in favour of the necessity of the Church's living authority in the first four centuries, militate for it now.

†**3.** *trans.* To fight out, debate (a question). *Obs.*

1754 A. Murphy *Gray's Inn Jrnl.* No. 78 The present question must be militated before any other question can be received. **1762** Foote *Orator* I. Wks. 1799 I. 198 When affairs of state are weighed at a common-council, religious points militated at the Robin Hood,..or politics debated near Westminster-abbey [etc.].

Hence **mili'tation**, conflict.

1659 Z. Crofton in *Morn. Exerc.* (1845) V. 387 Repentance doth not cut down sin at a blow; no, it is a constant militation, and course of mortification. **1778** B. Lincoln in Sparks *Corr. Amer. Rev.* (1853) II. 241 Dissension between the civil and military, and a militation of orders.

militaunt, obs. form of militant *a.*

militia (mɪ'lɪʃə). Also 6 **milicia**, 7 **melitia**, **mal(l)itia**. [a. L. *mīlitia*, f. *mīlit-*, *mīles* soldier. Cf. F. *milice*.]

†**1. a.** A system of military discipline, organization, and tactics; manner of conducting warfare; the arts of war. *Obs.*

1590 Sir J. Smyth *Disc. Weapons* Ded. 3 Diuers Nations that haue had notable Milicias and exercises Militarie in great perfection. **1598** Barret *Theor. Warres* III. i. 32 The true and orderly trayning of your people in this our Moderne Militia. **1605** Raleigh *Introd. Hist. Eng.* (1693) 23 The Normans had a peculiar Militia, or Fight, with Bowes and Arrowes. **1636** Massinger *Bashf. Lover* v. i, *Pisa.* Where's your Regiment? *Mart.* Not rais'd yet; All the old ones are cashier'd, and we are now To have a new Militia. **1646** J. Hall *Horæ Vac.* 162 The modern Militia differs much from the ancient, there being in it more roome for stratagems then personall valour. **1651** Hobbes *Govt. & Soc.* xiii. §14. 203 The Militia, was of old reckoned in the number of the gaining Arts. **1658** Earl Monm. tr. *Paruta's Wars Cyprus* 121 The enemy were still the same, weak, and unexperienced in the true Militia.

fig. *a* **1678** Marvell *Appleton Ho.* 330 Unhappy! shall we never more That sweet Militia restore, When Gardens only had their Towers, And all the Garrisons were Flowers.

†**b.** Military service; warfare. *Obs.*

a **1635** Naunton *Fragm. Reg.* (Arb.) 48 He first exposed himselfe to the Land service of Ireland, a Militia which then did not yeeld him food and rayment. **1656** Earl Monm. tr. *Boccalini's Advts. fr. Parnass.* II. lxi. (1674) 213 They ended their unfortunate Militia with the Romans. **1682** Sir T. Browne *Chr. Mor.* I. §18 Raise timely batteries against those strongholds built upon the rock of nature; and make this a great part of the militia of thy life. **1684** *Contempl. St. Man* I. vi. (1699) 66 He entred us into this Milita [*sic*] and Warfare. **1685** Baxter *Paraphr. N.T.* (1701) 1 Thess. ii. 15–16 Because this Preaching is the Means to save Souls, it is that Satan aimeth his Militia against it.

†**c.** Weapons; instruments of war. *Obs.*

1656 Earl Monm. tr. *Boccalini's Advts. fr. Parnass.* II. vi. (1674) 144 [Princes] should wear the powerful Militia of boundless Empire..by their side, for the security of such as are good, but..should never make use of it..[to shield] such as were guilty. **1656** Blount *Glossogr.*, *Militia*, Warfare, or all implements of War. **1694** Westmacott *Script. Herb.* (1695) 25 Box-Combs, which..bear no small part in the Militia of the Female Art.

†**2.** The control and administration of the military and naval forces of a country. *Obs.*

1622 Bacon *Holy War* Misc. Wks. (1629) 129 Now let me put a Feigned Case..of a Land of Amazons, where the whole Gouernment, Publike and Priuate, yea the Militia it Selfe, was in the hands of Women. **1641** Verney *Notes Long Parl.* (Camden) 132, [7 Dec.] Sir Arthur Hazelrigg did bring in a bill to dispose all the militia of England into two generalls for life. **1641** in Rushw. *Hist. Coll.* III. (1692) I. 525, I do heartily wish that this Great Word, this New Word, the Militia, this Harsh Word might never have come within these Walls;..I take the meaning of those Gentlemen, who introduced this Word to be, the power of the Sword,..which is a great and necessary power, and properly belonging to the Magistrate. **1641–2** *Jrnls. Ho. Comm.* 20 Jan. II. 389 They humbly beseech Your Sacred Majesty to raise up unto them a sure Ground of Safety..by putting the Tower, and other principal Forts of the Kingdom, and the whole Militia thereof, into the Hands of such Persons as Your Parliament may confide in. **1643** in Clarendon *Hist. Reb.* VII. §166 That the militia, both by sea and land, might be settled by a bill. **1647** May *Hist. Parl.* II. v. 94 He was esteemed by the Parliament (in this important businesse of setling their Militia by Land and Sea) the fittest man to take Command of the Navie.

3. a. A military force, esp. the body of soldiers in the service of a sovereign or a state; in later use employed in more restricted sense (= F. *milice*), to denote a 'citizen army' as distinguished from a body of mercenaries or professional soldiers.

1590 Sir J. Smyth *Disc. Weapons* Ded. 3 Any forraine Nation or Nations, that haue had a puissant and formed Milicia. **1625** Bacon *Ess., Greatn. Kingd.* (Arb.) 475 Let any Prince or State thinke soberly of his Forces, except his Militia of Natiues be of good and Valiant Soldiers. *Ibid.* 481 [The Spaniards are accustomed] To employ, almost indifferently, all Nations, in their Militia of ordinary Soldiers. **1665** *Surv. Aff. Netherl.* 93 The High and Mighty draw in their Money,..raise Fortifications,..Rendezvouz Militiaes, and withdraw 200 Families at least to Hamburgh. **1672** Petty *Pol. Anat.* (1691) 42 There be in Ireland, as elsewhere, two Militias; one are the Justices of Peace, their Militia of High and Petty Constables; also the Sheriffs Militia of his Servants and Bailiffs, and *Posse Comitatus...* There is also a Protestant Militia, of about 24000 Men. **1696** Phillips, *Militia*, the People and Inhabitants of a Kingdom trained up in War for the Defence of it. **1706** —— (ed. Kersey), *Militia*, a certain Number of the Inhabitants of the City and Country formed into Regular Bodies, and train'd up in the Art of War, for the Defence and Security of the Kingdom. **1776** Adam Smith *W.N.* v. i. (1869) II. 281 It [the state] may..oblige either all the citizens of the military age, or a certain number of them to join in some measure the trade of a soldier to whatever other trade or profession they may happen to carry on. Its military force is (then) said to consist in a militia. **1844** Ld. Brougham *Brit. Const.* xx. (1862) 383 A good militia, that is, a certain portion of the people called out in turn to learn the use of arms. **1865** Merivale *Rom. Emp.* VIII. lxvii. 311 A genuine militia, chosen from the citizens themselves.

†**b.** A particular species of warlike force; a branch or department of the establishment maintained for purposes of war. *Obs.*

1647 Clarendon *Hist. Reb.* v. §36 They had their eye upon another militia, the royal navy. **1654** H. L'Estrange *Chas. I* (1655) 19 Mighty preparation was made..for the reinforcing of Navall strength. Nor was the Land-Militia left unregarded.

c. *transf.* and *fig.*

1599 Sandys *Europæ Spec.* (1632) 157 Fourty hundred sure Catholikes in England alone, with foure hundred English Romane Priests to mainetaine that Militia. **1630** B. Jonson *New Inn* Argt. Act II, The Fly of the Inne is discouer'd.., with the Militia of the house, below the stayres, in the Drawer, Tapster, Chamberlaine, and Hostler, inferiour officers. *Ibid.* II. iv, He has form'd a fine militia for the Inne too. **1712–14** Pope *Rape Lock* I. 42 Know then, unnumber'd Spirits round thee fly, The light Militia of the lower sky. **1821** Scott *Kenilw.* xix, Out tumbled Will Hostler, John Tapster, and all the militia of the inn. **1838** Prescott *Ferd. & Is.* (1846) I. Introd. 38 The mendicant orders..that spiritual militia of the popes.

4. *spec.* **a.** Orig., the distinctive name of a branch of the British military service, forming, together with the volunteers, what are known as 'the auxiliary forces' as distinguished from the regular army. In later use, *spec.* as part of the British armed forces assembled in 1939. Also, a similar force raised in British North America. (Construed either as *sing.* or *plural.*)

The militia consisted of bodies raised by the several counties in numbers varying according to the population and other circumstances, the number or 'quota' to be provided by each shire being fixed by the government. From 1803, the law was that the quota might, if necessary, be raised by compulsory enlistment, a ballot being taken among the men between 18 and 35; but as sufficient numbers were latterly obtainable by voluntary enlistment, a 'Militia Ballot Suspension Act' was passed annually. The militia were bound to assemble for 28 days in every year for training, and might at any time be embodied for compulsory service within the kingdom, but could not be sent abroad except as volunteers, and then only by consent of Parliament.

1659–60 Pepys *Diary* 29 Feb., We found..the militia of the red regiment in arms. *Ibid.* 2 Mar., I hear the City militia is put into good posture. **1699** in *Archives of Maryland* (1902) XXII. 562 An Act for the Ordering and Regulating the Militia of this Province for the better Defence & Security thereof. **1724** De Foe *Mem. Cavalier* (1840) 187 They..fired..very regularly, considering them as militia only. **1755** Johnson, *Militia*, the trainbands. **1759** H. Walpole *Let. to Mann* 16 Nov., I am one of the few men in England who am neither in the army or militia. **1761** Churchill *Rosciad* Poems 1763 I. 30 Like Westminster militia train'd to fight. **1763** *Brit. Mag.* IV. 50 The following aldermen took the oaths to qualify them for colonels of the six regiments of the city militia, viz... Beckford,..col. of the white regiment... Ladbroke, col. of the blue... Rawlinson, col. of the red... Glyn, col. of the orange... Blackiston, col. of the green... Fludyer, col. of the yellow. **1903** *Westm. Gaz.* 7 July 12/2 The attempt..was opposed.. on the ground that the Militia must in future be 'more soldierly'. **1939** *War Illustr.* 16 Dec. 427/3 We have taken, besides the Militia classes which have been called up, over 85,000 voluntary recruits since the war began.

b. *U.S.* 'The whole body of men declared by law amenable to military service, without enlistment, whether armed and drilled or not' (*Cent. Dict.* 1890).

1777 W. Heath in Sparks *Corr. Amer. Rev.* (1853) I. 329 Our troops are all militia, and, although perhaps as good as any militia, yet they are not disciplined. **1789** *Constit. U.S.* I. §8 Congress shall have power..to provide for calling forth the militia. **1865** H. Phillips *Amer. Paper Curr.* II. 85 Militia were kept constantly guarding the Schuylkill. **1899** *Westm. Gaz.* 14 Mar. 2/3 The naval militia in the recent war between the United States and Spain.

5. *attrib.*, as ***militia act***, ***army***, ***bill***, ***carpenter***, ***commission***, ***force***, ***guard***, ***officer***, ***regiment***, ***service***; **militia reserve** (see quot. 1876).

1882 *Act 45 & 46 Vict.* c. 49 §1 This Act may be cited as the *Militia Act, 1882. **1813** Wellington in Gurw. *Desp.* (1838) XI. 140, I should very much doubt that a large *militia army would be very useful in the field. **1902** *Encycl. Brit.* XXVIII. 226/1 Voluntary enlistment under the new *Militia Bill [of 1852] was to be the rule. **1756** Washington *Writ.* (1889) I. 356 Forty pounds of tobacco per day, which is provided by act of Assembly for *militia carpenters. **1844** *Regul. & Ord. Army* 4 Their *Militia Commissions. **1802** *Act 42 Geo. III*, c. 72 §29 Any Act made..concerning the *Militia Forces of England. **1726** Swift *Gulliver* II. iv, A *militia guard of five hundred horse. **1775** Sheridan *St. Patr. Day* I. ii, I hate *militia officers; a set of dunghill cocks with spurs on. **1655** *Clarke Papers* (Camden) III. 23 The city have named Alderman Underwood, Alderman Tichborne, and —— to bee 3 of theire Collonells to comand theire *Militia regiments. **1876** Voyle & Stevenson *Milit. Dict.*, **Militia Reserve*, a force created by the act of 1867; its numbers not to exceed one-fourth of militia quota; the men to be enlisted for five years, during which time they remain on the strength of militia regiments, but are liable to be drafted into the army in time of war. **1818** Cobbett *Pol. Reg.* XXXIII. 83, I mean the *Militia Service and other compulsory military and naval service.

†**mi'litia**, *v. Obs.* [f. prec.] *trans.* ? To call *out* as militia.

1724 Warburton *Misc. Transl.* 106 Their Country's Cause provokes to Arms The active Pigmy Troops militia'd out, In fronted Brigades.

militiaman (mɪ'lɪʃəmən). [f. militia *sb.* + man.] A member of a militia force; *spec.* one called up in 1939 as part of the armed services at the outbreak of the war.

1780 Hamilton *Wks.* (1886) VIII. 21 The militiamen replied they were of the lower party. **1844** Ld. Brougham *Brit. Const.* xx. (1862) 383 Militiamen drafted into the regular forces. **1876** Bancroft *Hist. U.S.* VI. lii. 393 Six hundred militia-men of Virginia. **1939** *War Illustr.* 14 Oct. 129 (*caption*) Regular soldiers..and the Militiamen—all have made an excellent impression at home and in France.

Also **mi'litiawoman**, a woman in a militia force; = miliciana.

1936 *New Statesman* 21 Nov. 802/1 The C.N.T., since it contains a great many Murcians.., includes the most alarming of the faces met with in Barcelona and also most of the young militia-women. **1938** 'G. Orwell' *Homage to Catalonia* iv. 47 There were three militiawomen there who did the cooking.

†**mi'litiate**, *v. Obs.* [f. militia *sb.*: see -ate.] **a.** *trans.* To organize for warfare. **b.** *intr.* (*nonce-uses.*) To raise militia; to be occupied in soldiering. Hence **mi'litiating** *ppl. a.*

1642 *Answ. Observ. agst. King* 15 He must not have the reason that he is a King, who in extraordinary danger will not militiat his kingdome. **1759** H. WALPOLE *Let. to Mann* 16 Nov., We continue to *militiate* and to raise light troops. **1761** STERNE *Tr. Shandy* IV. xxii, I had no thoughts..in the character of my uncle Toby—of characterizing the militiating spirits of my country.

milium[1] ('mɪlɪəm). In 4 **mylium**, 6 **millium**. [a. L. *milium* millet.]

1. = MILLET[1]. *Obs.* exc. as mod.L. in *Pharmacy*. Also *Bot.* the name (Linnæus) of a graminaceous genus, 'millet-grass'.

1388 WYCLIF *Isa.* xxviii. 25 Barli, and mylium, and fetchis. **1535** COVERDALE *Ezek.* iv. 10 Take vnto the..growell sede, milium and fitches. **1598** HAKLUYT *Voy.* I. 104 They haue the seed of Millium in great abundance.

b. ***milium solis***: Graymill or Gromwell, *Lithospermum officinale*. (Cf. MILLENSOLE.)

[**1597** GERARDE *Herbal* II. clxxx. 487 Gromell is called..in shops and among the Italians *Milium solis*.] *a* **1648** LD. HERBERT in *Life* (1886) 44 Posset drinks of herbs, as milium solis, saxifragea, &c.

2. *Path.* An affection of the sebaceous glands in which hard white or yellowish tubercles resembling millet-seeds are produced, immediately below and projecting from the cuticle. Cf. MILIA.

1856 MAYNE *Expos. Lex., Milium*... Name for a white hard tubercle. **1876** tr. *Wagner's Gen. Pathol.* 331 Colloid milium of the skin. **1899** *Allbutt's Syst. Med.* VIII. 764 Milium forms firm white or yellowish masses.

b. *Surgery.* (See quot.)

1884 KNIGHT *Dict. Mech.* Suppl., *Milium Needle*, a fine needle with curved hastate point used in skin grafting.

Milium[2] ('mɪlɪəm). The proprietary name of a type of insulating fabric. Also **milium**.

1950 *Rayon & Synthetic Textiles* June 95/1 Milium has been chosen as the trademark name to designate the new 'warmth without weight' fabric development of Deering, Milliken & Company. **1951** *Official Gaz.* (U.S. Patent Office) 4 Sept. 39/1 The Vadium Corp., Wilmington, Del. Milium. For Textile Fabrics of Cotton, Rayon, Nylon, and Mixtures Thereof Having Heat Reflective and/or Heat Retentive Properties. Claims use since Apr. 20, 1950. **1954** POTTER & CORBMAN *Fiber to Fabric* (ed. 2) vi. 110 A wool outer fabric with a milium satin lining is approximately equal in warmth to an untreated satin lining plus an 8½-ounce wool interlining with the same outer fabric. **1956** *N.Y. Times* 20 Mar. 30/6 Milium is a metal-impregnated lining material valued for its lightness and insulating quality. **1968** J. IRONSIDE *Fashion Alphabet* 241 Milium insulates against cold and allows the body to retain heat, while in summer it protects from extreme heat. **1972** *Guardian* 30 June 7 This superb new Milium Ironing Board Cover..is scorch resistant.

milk (mɪlk), *sb.*[1] Forms: 1 meolc, 1–3 milc, 3 millc, 4 melke, 4–5 melk, 4–6 mylk(e, 4–7 milke, 6 mylcke, milcke, 7 milck, 3– milk. [Com. Teut.: OMercian *milc* (rare) = WS. *meolc, meoluc* fem. (whence the southern ME. *melk*), corresponding to OFris. *melok*, OS. *miluk* (Du. *melk*), OHG. *miluh* (MHG. *milich, milch*, mod.G. *milch*), ON. *miolk* (Icel. *mjólk*, Sw. *mjölk*, Da. *mælk, melk*), Goth. *miluk-s*:—OTeut. **meluk-s* fem., f. Teut. root **melk-* to milk (in the str. vb. OE. *melcan*, LG., Du. *melken*, OHG. *melchan*, MHG. *melchen*; the mod.G. *melken* is also conjugated weak):—pre-Teut. **melg-*, cogn. w. Gr. ἀμέλγειν, L. *mulgēre*, OSl. *mlěsti*, OIrish *bligim* (:—**mlg-*), to milk.

A corresponding sb. (exc. in declension) occurs in OIrish *melg* milk (:—**melgos-*). The synonymous OSl. *meleko* (Russian *moloko*, Czech *mleko*) is adopted from Teut., as it has *k* instead of the regular *g*. For the phonology of the OE. forms see Bülbring *Ags. Gramm.* §202.]

1. a. An opaque white or bluish-white fluid secreted by the mammary glands of the female individuals of the Mammalia including man, and adapted for the nourishment of their young.

a **900** tr. *Bæda's Hist.* III. xix. (1890) 244 Elles ne þeah nemne medmicel hlafes mid þinre meolc. *c* **1200** ORMIN 6446 Forr naffde ȝho nan millc till himm, ȝiff þatt ȝho nære hiss moderr. **1377** LANGL. *P. Pl.* B xv. 462 Þe cow-calf coueyteth swete mylke. **1390** GOWER *Conf.* II. 262 Warm melk sche putte..therto With hony meynd. *c* **1460** J. RUSSELL *Bk. Nurture* 93 Milke, crayme, and cruddes, and eke the Ioncate. **1471** CAXTON *Recuyell* (Sommer) 31 The melk of a goot. **1565** COOPER *Thesaurus* s.v. *Lac*, Glauciscus eaten in broth make women haue plentie of milke. **1610** SHAKS. *Temp.* II. i. 288 They'l take suggestion, as a Cat laps milke. **1616** R. C. *Times' Whistle* iii. 1048 Goats pure milck. **1661** LOVELL *Hist. Anim. & Min.* 110 Of milks the Womans is most temperate. **1725** N. ROBINSON *Th. Physick* 208 If the Ass's Milk stands twelve Hours, it will gather no Cream. **1836–41** BRANDE *Chem.* (ed. 5) 1353 Fresh milk slightly reddens litmus. **1861** *Jrnl. R. Agric. Soc.* XXII. I. 35 These milks came from the same dairy. **1896** tr. *Boas' Text-bk. Zool.* 496 The young ones [*sc.* of the Duck-billed Platypus], when hatched, are fed with milk by the mother.

b. In proverbial comparison ***as white as milk***. Also ***as like as milk to milk*** (a Latinism).

? *a* **1366** CHAUCER *Rom. Rose* 1196 Through hir smokke, wrought with silk, The flesh was seen, as whyt as milk. *c* **1420** *Anturs of Arth.* ii, One a mule as þe mylke Gaili she glides. **1596** SHAKS. *Merch. V.* III. ii. 86 How manie cowards..Who inward searcht, haue lyuers white as milke. **1638** CHILLINGW. *Relig. Prot.* I. ii. §160 They are as like your own, as an egge, or milke to milke. **1660** JER. TAYLOR *Duct. Dubit.* (1676) 417 It looks so like intemperance, as milk to milk.

c. Phrases. ***mother's-milk***: in literal and figurative contexts; also as a slang name for various liquors (see quots.). ***in milk***, † (*a*) *fig.* (a Latinism) in infancy; (*b*) in a condition to yield milk. ***brought to milk***, brought to be in milk. †***water of milk*** = milk-water (see 10).

1500–20 DUNBAR *Poems* lxxv. 37 My clype, my vnspaynit gyane, With moderis milk ȝit in ȝour mychane. **1565** JEWEL *Repl. Harding* (1611) 391 There be certaine men, that..fearing, that if they attaine to any knowledge, they shall be proud: and so they remaine still only in Milke [tr. Augustine: *et remanent in solo lacte*]. **1611** COTGR. s.v. *Laict*, *Eau de laict*..also, water of milke or drawne by stillatorie from milke. **1687** A. LOVELL tr. *Thevenot's Trav.* I. 40 The earth squeezes the poor wretch so hard, that his Mothers milk comes running out at his nose. **1727–41** CHAMBERS *Cycl., Milk*.. In the *Philosophical Transactions*, we have an account of a wether brought to *milk* by the sucking of a lamb. **1797** *Monthly Mag.* III. 486 The best three-year-old heifer, which..shall be in milk at the time of show. *c* **1821** 'W. T. MONCRIEFF' *Tom & Jerry* (1828) III. iii. 67 *Log.* What, my lily! here, take a drop of mother's milk. (Gives black child gin out of measure he has received from Landlord.) **1846** *Swell's Night Guide* 125/2 *Mother's milk*, rum boose, good liquor. **1847** JAMES *Convict* II. 50 His auditor..had sucked in such doctrines with his mother's milk. **1852** R. S. SURTEES *Sponge's Sp. Tour* l, When people talk of cream, and ask how many cows you have, they mean in milk. *c* **1863** T. TAYLOR in M. R. Booth *Eng. Plays of 19th Cent.* (1969) II. 156 Brandy do a man harm! It's mother's milk. **1922** G. M. TREVELYAN *Brit. Hist. 19th Cent.* xxiii. 363 Britons had sucked in fear of Napoleonic conquest with their mother's milk. **1966** 'L. LANE' *ABZ of Scouse* 71 *Mother's milk*, Guinness, a popular brand of stout. **1972** *Guardian* 22 Aug. 4/6 A six-month-old-baby..is being kept alive by mother's milk supplied by volunteers.

†**d.** Milk considered as in process of secretion; hence, the milk-yielding condition induced by childbirth, lactation. *Obs.*

1512 *Ld. Treas. Acc. Scotl.* (1902) IV. 356 To ane nurice to the Prince..at was prewit with sex wolkis mylk. **1616** SIR E. MOUNTAGU in *Buccleuch MSS.* (Hist. MSS. Comm.) I. 249 One nurse with one milk did suckle six of us. **1676** WISEMAN *Surg.* I. iv. 25 Milk..is certainly the occasion of many Tumours of divers kinds. **1697** DRYDEN *Virg. Past.* III. 152 When Milk is dry'd with heat, In vain the Milk-maid tugs an empty Teat.

†**e.** Put for: The period of infancy. *Obs.*

a **1637** B. JONSON *Discov., Imo serviles* (1640) 114 Wee see in men, even the strongest compositions had their beginnings from milke, and the Cradle [transl. of Quintilian I. i. 21 *a lacte cunisque*].

f. The quantity of milk drawn from a cow at a single milking.

1611 COTGR., *Mousson*, a Cowes milke,..as much as she yeelds at a milking.

g. *ellipt.* = MILKMAN I. *colloq.*

1895 W. P. RIDGE *Minor Dialogues* 79, I know *all* the comic songs..and I sing 'em whilst I'm a doing up the front steps; and the milk, *he* says he reckons it'll end in me going on the stage. **1933** A. THIRKELL *High Rising* ii. 36 The London tradesmen..called her Miss, until a fateful day when the Milk, so she told Laura, had called her Miss once too often. **1967** 'A. GILBERT' *Visitor* x. 174 She hadn't informed the postman and anyone can put out a note for the Milk. **1975** B. MEYRICK *Behind the Light* xv. 202 The disappearance of George the Milk's horse.

h. Milk-white colour. Cf. sense 11.

1899 SWINBURNE *Rosamund* I. i. 2 White I know from red, and dark from bright, And milk from white in hawthorn-flowers.

2. *fig.* **a.** As the appropriate food of infancy; often (after 1 Cor. iii. 2, Heb. v. 12) contrasted with '(strong) meat'.

c **1386** CHAUCER *Pars. T.* ¶539 Flatereres been the deueles norices, that norissen hise children with Milk of losengerie. **1426** LYDG. *De Guil. Pilgr.* 14706 With my mylk off fflaterye I was noryce, and ek guyde, In especyal vn-to Pryde. **1641** H. PETERS (*title*) Milke for Babes, and Meat for Men: or, Principles necessary to be knowne..of such as would know Christ. **1772** NUGENT *Grosley's London* I. 318 Tithes were the first milk of these rising establishments [*sc.* monasteries]. **1803** (*title*) Milk for Babes; or, a catechism in verse. **1810** *Sporting Mag.* XXXVI. 121 Neither are their consciences of that puling kind, that will submit to be fed with this milk of babes. **1860** PUSEY *Min. Proph.* 70 He was nourished, not by solid food, but by milk, i.e. by the rudiments of piety and righteousness.

b. As a type of what is pleasant and nourishing. ***pure milk***: something of the purest or finest quality.

1592 SHAKS. *Rom. & Jul.* III. iii. 55 Aduersities sweete milke, Philosophie. **1654** Z. COKE *Logick* a j, It..turneth into Milk bony Paradoxes. **1797** COLERIDGE *Kubla Khan* 53 For he on honey-dew hath fed, And drunk the milk of Paradise. **1931** *Daily Express* 15 Oct. 2/4 Men like Mr. Runciman, who hitherto represented the purest milk of the Cobdenite gospel. **1955** *Times* 6 July 11/3 Broadcasting..probably remains the most effective way, within the compass of an election campaign, of distributing the pure milk of party doctrine. **1975** 'W. HAGGARD' *Scorpion's Tail* vii. 103 For the pure milk of doctrine she cared not a damn. She saw communism as a convenient front.

c. In proverbial phrases. ***milk and honey*** (or †***mellie***): (*a*) in the Bible phrase 'flowing with milk and honey', hyperbolically descriptive of the richness of the Promised Land; hence (*b*) used to express the abundance of means of enjoyment. ***to bring*** (a person) ***to his milk*** (*U.S.*): to bring (him) to his senses; to compel (him) to acquiesce or submit; ***to come*** (or ***go***) ***home with the milk***: to arrive home at the time when the milkman calls, *i.e.* early in the morning. ***milk and roses***: said of a beautiful pink-and-white complexion. ***milk of human kindness*** (after Shaks.): compassion characteristic of humane persons. ***spilt milk***: anything which once misused cannot be recovered; see also SPILT *ppl. a.* 2 b. †***to wash the milk off*** (***one's***) ***liver***: to purge (oneself) of cowardice. †***to give down*** (***its***) ***milk***: to yield the expected assistance or profit; to consent to be 'milked'.

c **1000** ÆLFRIC *Num.* xvi. 13 Of þam lande, þe weoll meolce and hunie. **1382** WYCLIF *Ezek.* xx. 6 The loond which Y hadde purueiede to hem, flowynge with mylk and hony. *c* **1592** MARLOWE *Jew of Malta* IV. (1633) H 2 b, *Ith.* How now? hast thou the gold? *Pil.* Yes. *Ith.* But came it freely, did the Cow giue down her milk freely? **1605** SHAKS. *Macb.* I. v. 18 Yet doe I feare thy Nature, It is too full o' th' Milke of humane kindnesse. **1611** COTGR. s.v. *Souhait*, Wash thy milke off thy liuer (say we). **1614** J. DAVIES *Eclogue* 19 For fro thy Makings, milke, and mellie, flowes To feed the Songster-swaines with Arts sootmeats. *a* **1628** PRESTON *Breastpl. Love* vii. (1630) 181 They shall not give downe that milke for your comfort. **1641** S. MARMION *Antiquary* I. B j, I must flatter him, and stroke him too, he will give no milk else. **1654** H. L'ESTRANGE *Chas. I* (1655) 187 The City was sullen, would not give down their milk, and pleaded..poverty. **1775** SHERIDAN *Rivals* III. iv. 57 The thunder of your words has soured the milk of human kindness in my breast! **1783** J. KING *Th. on Difficulties*, etc. ii. 28 America is now the fancied land of milk and honey. **1826** DISRAELI *Viv. Grey* II. i, The milk and honey of the political Canaan. **1839** DICKENS *Nickleby* xxxviii. 377 What's come of my milk of human kindness? It turns into curds and whey when I look at him. **1857** J. G. HOLLAND *Bay-Path* 209 There ain't anything that'll bring you to your milk half so quick as a good double-and-twisted thrashin. **1857** S. A. HAMMETT *Sam Slick in Texas* iv. 22 When you cum to bring 'em down to thar milk, they'll turn out greener than Buffalo Bayou in September. **1860** TROLLOPE *Castle Richmond* I. vi. 113 It's no use sighing after spilt milk. **1894** HOWELLS in *Harper's Mag.* Feb. 380 The die is cast, the jig is up, the fat's in the fire, the milk's spilt. **1900** H. SUTCLIFFE *Shameless Wayne* ii, Dainty of figure she was, with a face all milk and roses. **1917** WODEHOUSE *Man with Two Left Feet* 238 You talk of a man 'going home with the milk' when you mean that he sneaks in in the small hours of the morning. **1923** W. J. LOCKE *Moordius & Co.* ii. 17 The family has nothing to do with the way the governess spends her evenings..except if she comes home with the milk after her evening out. **1947** W. S. MAUGHAM *Creatures of Circumstances* 100 Every party's got to come to an end, and next day it doesn't matter much if you went home with the milk or if you left while the fun was in full swing. **1956** G. DURRELL *My Family & other Animals* xviii. 237 Overflowing with the milk of human kindness, the family had invited everyone they could think of, including people they cordially disliked.

3. a. A milk-like juice or sap secreted by certain plants. Cf. LATEX 2.

1398 TREVISA *Barth. De P.R.* XVII. lxi. (1495) 637 The mylke of the fygge tree. **1565** COOPER *Thesaurus* s.v. *Lac*, The milke that is in greene figges. *Herba lactaria*, an hearbe that hath milke in it as spurge, &c. **1626** BACON *Sylva* §639 There be Plants, that have a Milk in them when they are Cut; as Figs, Old-Lettuce, Sow-Thistles, Spurge, &c. **1757** J. H. GROSE *Voy. E. Indies* 30 The milk of cocoa nuts. **1797** *Encycl. Brit.* (ed. 3) X. 83/1 The milks of wild-poppies, garden-poppies, dandelion, hawk-weed, and sow-thistle gave brown or brownish-red stains. **1898** *Engineering Mag.* XVI. 138/1 Analyses of the milk of a variety of rubber plants.

b. Of grain: ***in the milk***: having a milky consistency due to incomplete development. ***out of the milk***: beginning to mature.

1792 BELKNAP *Hist. New Hampsh.* III. 21 The corn then being in the milk. *a* **1817** T. DWIGHT *Trav. New Eng.*, etc. (1821) II. 341 When the kernels of wheat..are in the milk. **1878** *Ure's Dict. Arts* IV. 153 At the time when the contents of the berry [*sc.* of wheat] are in the condition technically known as 'milk'. **1899** *Evesham Jrnl.* 29 Apr. (E.D.D.), The sparrows began [*sc.* to eat the wheat] as soon as the corn was just out of the milk.

c. ***the milk in the coconut***: a puzzling fact or circumstance; a crux. *colloq.* (orig. *U.S.*).

1840 *Spirit of Times* 21 Mar. 25/2 All of 'vich'..fully accounts..for the milk in the cocoa-nut. **1853** *Knickerbocker* XLII. 50 The milk in the cocoa nut was accounted for. **1898** MRS. LYNN LINTON *Let* in G. S. Layard *Mrs. Lynn Linton* (1901) xxiv. 362 The Koran is very interesting—but oh, the milk in the cocoanut! It is so queerly disjointed and non-sequential, far more so than the Epistles, and they have their full share of that milk in the cocoanut. **1972** L. MEYNELL *Death by Arrangement* i. 17 'Nobody can really be christened Waveney: it's a river...' 'In East Anglia. Hence, as they say, the milk in the coconut. Rolffe's father..called his eleven children after East Anglian rivers.'

4. A culinary, pharmaceutical, or other preparation of herbs, drugs or the like, having some more or less real resemblance to milk.

milk of almonds = ALMOND-MILK. ***milk of lime***: hydrate of lime mixed in water. ***milk of magnesia***: a proprietary name for a white suspension of magnesium hydroxide in water, taken as an antacid. †***milk of mercury***: corrosive sublimate beaten up in fumitory water. ***milk of sulphur***: precipitated sulphur.

c **1430** *Two Cookery-bks.* 48 Take gode Milke of Almaundys, & flowre of Rys. **1626** BACON *Sylva* §50 Pistachoes..made into a Milk of themselves, like unto Almond Milk. **1686** W. HARRIS tr. *Lemery's Chym.* (ed. 2) 493 This Tincture is a dissolution of the Rosine of Benjamin made in Spirit of Wine. When it is mixed in a great deal of water, it makes a Milk. **1694** SALMON *Bate's Dispens.* (1713) 561 Milk of Mercury... Milk of Scammony. **1797** *Encycl. Brit.* (ed. 3) XII. 23/1 The name of milk is given to substances very different from milk properly so called. *Ibid.*, Milk of Sulphur. *Ibid.* 23/2 Water in which quicklime has been slaked, which..has hence been called the milk of lime. *a* **1814** *Intrigues of a Day* in *New Brit. Theatre* I. 76 A little

milk of roses. **1875** *Ure's Dict. Arts* III. 1059 Milk of Wax is a valuable varnish. **1880** LOMAS *Alkali Trade* 298 Milk of lime. **1880** *Trade Marks Jrnl.* 3 Mar. 95 Milk of Magnesia. .. Charles Henry Phillips,.. New York, United States of America; manufacturing chemist... Preparations of magnesia for medical purposes, especially hydrate of magnesia, and also proprietary medicines. **1898** *Rev. Brit. Pharm.* 41 Milk of sulphur. **1924** H. CRANE *Let.* 30 Nov. (1965) 194, I had..taken a great deal of Alkalithia and milk of magnesia. **1961** J. HELLER *Catch-22* (1962) xxvi. 282 Aarfy had a date..with a Red Cross girl.. whose father owned an important milk-of-magnesia plant.

5. ***Bristol milk***: originally a slang name for sherry; now, the name in the wine trade of a particular class of sherry.

1644 [see BRISTOL]. *a* **1661** FULLER *Worthies, Bristol* (1662) III. 35 Bristol Milk... This Metaphorical Milk, whereby Xeres or Sherry-Sack is intended. **1895** *Westm. Gaz.* 31 Dec. 1/1 Pale sherry (Bristol cream) realised £7 per dozen, and 95*s.* was the price per dozen of the sherry known as Bristol milk.

†**6.** ***milk of the moon***: 'a white, porous, friable, insipid earth, frequently found in form of a white farinaceous powder, but sometimes concreted into a mass, not unlike agaric' (Chambers *Cycl.* 1727–52).

7. A cloudy impurity found in some diamonds.

1875 *Ure's Dict. Arts* II. 24.

8. †**a.** The milt of a fish. *Obs.* [So G. *milch*, Da. *melk*, Sw. *mjölke*.]

1398 TREVISA *Barth. De P.R.* XIII. xxvi. (1495) 458 Whan the female of fysshes lay egges or pesen, the male comyth after and shedeth hys mylke vpon the egges. **14..** *Voc.* in Wr.-Wülcker 591/16 *Lactes*, roof of fyshe, or mylke of fyshe. **1718** [see MILTER].

b. The spat of an oyster before its discharge.

1858 HOMANS *Cycl. Comm.* 1480/2 The breeding-time of oysters is in April or May, from which time to July or August the oysters are said to be *sick* or *in the milk*.

9. *attrib.* and *Comb.* **a.** Simple attrib. in sense (*a*) 'made or consisting of, prepared with, or obtained from milk', as ***milk-arrowroot, -butter, -curd, -diet, -fat, -flow, -globule, -loaf, -porridge, -pottage, -pudding, -scone, -soup, -yeast***; (*b*) 'of or pertaining to milk', as ***milk-†ambry, -bloom, -board, bottle, -bowie*** (*Sc.*), ***-bowl, -bucket, -can, -car, -cart, carton, -cellar, -churn, -cog, -cooler, -dish, -ejection, -gland, -jug, -keeler, -kettle, lorry, -pail, -piggin, -pitcher, -pot, -ranch, saucepan, -secretion, -shop, -sieve, -skeel, -stall, stand, -sye*** (*dial.*), ***tanker, -tin, truck, -tub, -vein, wagon***; (*c*) 'having dealings with milk', as ***milk-boy, -folk, -girl, -lass, -nurse***; (*d*) (of animals) 'producing milk', as ***milk-ass, -camel, -sow***; also MILK-COW; (*e*) used to designate the deciduous teeth formed in the mammalian jaw during the suckling period, as ***milk-canine, -dentition, -molar, -tusk***; also MILK TOOTH.

1594 *Knaresborough Wills* (Surtees) I. 199 *Milk ambry. **1896** *Allbutt's Syst. Med.* I. 401 *Milk arrowroot and a little brandy with it is useful. **1688** in Ellis *Orig. Lett.* Ser. II. IV. 157 Though I can (to my sorrow) say why *milk-asses are provided for. **1855** TENNYSON *Maud* xxi. 70 The slender acacia would not shake One long *milk-bloom on the tree. **1602** in Grosart *Spenser's Wks.* I. p. xix, One stone or *milk-board. **1905** G. F. M'CLEARY *Infant Mortality & Infants Milk Depôts* viii. 129 (*caption*) Packing the *milk bottles in ice before sending them to the city. **1957** M. SUMMERTON *Sunset Hour* v. 67, I could hear..milk bottles being handled in and out of crates. **1959** I. & P. OPIE *Lore & Lang. Schoolch.* i. 9 Cigarette cards..are being replaced in flicking games by milk-bottle tops. **1972** C. FREMLIN *Appointment with Yesterday* xii. 93 '*Everything* goes down the waste-disposal!' But not dead matches. Or milk-bottle tops. **1972** J. MOSEDALE *Football* x. 139 He stepped on a broken milk bottle, severing all the tendons in his foot. **1724** RAMSAY *Tea-t. Misc.* (1733) II. 222 To bear the *milk-bowie nae pain was to me. **1570** *Wills & Inv. N.C.* (Surtees) I. 341, lxxxx *mylke bowlles iiij[l]. **1609** ARMIN *Maids of More-Cl.* (1880) 84 They are maids of More-clacke, homely milke-bole things. **1815** *Sporting Mag.* XLVI. 17 A new milk-bowl, of wood skilfully carved. **1847** THACKERAY *Vanity Fair* (1848) vii. 59 The groom..did not care to descend to ring the bell; and so prayed a passing *milk-boy to perform that office for him. **1865** A. & E. KEARY *Little Wanderlin* 125 After the milk-boy came the vegetable women. **1884** W. H. RIDEING in *Harper's Mag.* June 70/1 Chantrey was a milk-boy in Sheffield. **1964** F. WARNER *Early Poems* 13 A milk-boy, whistling down the wind. **1830** MISS MITFORD *Village* Ser. IV. 103 Her *milk-bucket in her hand. *c* **1830** *Glouc. Farm Rep.* 35 in *Libr. Usef. Knowl., Husb.* III, Making cheese of the first quality is more profitable than either making *milk-butter or feeding veal. **1535** COVERDALE *Gen.* xxxii. 15 Thirtie *mylck camels. **1838** DICKENS *O. Twist* xlv, Three pint-pots and a *milk-can. **1879** FLOWER *Catal. Mus. Coll. Surg.* I. 39 The *milk canine permanently retained. **1890** *Railways of Amer.* 146 The different kinds of cars which are now used..Mail car, *Milk car, Oil-car [etc.]. **1916** JOYCE *Portrait of Artist* ii. 69 Often they drove out in the milkcar. **1808** CURWEN *Econ. Feeding Stock* 64 The *milk-cart was met before it reached the town. **1964** 'E. LATHEN' *Accounting for Murder* (1965) vi. 46 He mounted the stairs..startling two typists who were precariously balancing *milk cartons. **1967** R. LOWELL *Near Ocean* 24 Milk cartons, kidney heaped to spoil, Two plates sheathed with silver foil. **1787** GARTHSHORE in *Phil. Trans.* LXXVII. 355 A woman at a *milk-cellar..was delivered [etc.]. **1931** A. UTTLEY *Country Child* iii. 48 He was backed into the loading place, waiting for the *milk-churns. *Ibid.* xxi. 278 The milk-churns were rattled and banged across the railway line. **1963** *Times* 16 Feb. 5/5 An estimated 120,000 milk churns, valued at £5 each and believed to have been taken by householders to store water, are missing from dairies. **1967** *Ibid.* 26 Sept. 1/1 He inadvertently rolled a milk churn under an oncoming express during his first day as an apprentice at Hatfield station. **1595** DUNCAN *App. Etymol.* (E.D.S.), *Mulctra, vel, -um, mulctrale*; a *milk-cog. **1844** H. STEPHENS *Bk. Farm* III. 900 Stone *milk-coolers. **1897** *Allbutt's Syst. Med.* III. 339 Small patches of adherent *milk-curd. **1863** HUXLEY *Man's Place Nat.* i. 23 The *milk dentition consists of 20 teeth. **1677** TEMPLE *Gout* in *Misc.* I. (1680) 221, I concluded..if it..continued to confine my self wholly to the *Milk-dyet. **1844** H. STEPHENS *Bk. Farm* III. 900 After it has cooled, the milk is passed through the milk-sieve into the *milk-dishes. **1950** *N.Z. Jrnl. Agric.* June 540/3 The problems related to the process of '*milk ejection' in the cow. **1901** *Daily Chron.* 7 Aug. 6/4 When a sample of milk..shall be found to contain less than 3 per cent. of *milk fat,..it shall be presumed..that the milk is not genuine. **1822–34** *Good's Study Med.* (ed. 4) IV. 74 *Galactia Præmatura*. Premature *Milk-Flow. *Ibid.* 75 *Galactia Defectiva*. Deficient Milk-Flow. **1700** T. BROWN *Amusem. Ser. & Com.* vi. (1709) 58 The Noisy *Milk-Folks, crying, A can of Milk, Ladies. **1810** *Splendid Follies* III. 66 [Madam Lynx] having caught her immaculate husband chucking the *milk-girl under the chin. **1927** HALDANE & HUXLEY *Animal Biol.* xiii. 320 The saucer-shaped depression into which the *milk-glands open. **1864** *Chambers's Encycl.* VI. 454/2 In addition to *milk globules, colostrum globules..occur in the milk. **1832** F. TROLLOPE *Dom. Manners Amer.* I. xii. 170 An intimation accompanied the *milk-jug, that the milk must be fresh. **1852** BRISTED *Five Yrs. Eng. Univ.* 60 Drowning mice in his milk jug. **1600** in W. F. Shaw *Mem. Eastry* (1870) 226 Three *milk keelers. **1596** *Wills & Inv. N.C.* (Surtees) II. 271 The milke-house stuffe..j *milke kettle 24*s.* **1805** R. W. DICKSON *Pract. Agric.* II. 993 Brass milk-kettle. *a* **1690** G. FOX *Jrnl.* (1827) I. 79 He told my troubles..to his servants, so that it was got among the *milk-lasses. **1910** *Practitioner* June 801 *Milk-loaf, scones. **1939** G. HOUSEHOLD *Rogue Male* 110, I saw..a couple of *milk lorries bobbing about..to collect the cans set out on wooden platforms by the road. **1971** W. J. BURLEY *Guilt Edged* i. 5 The milk lorry on its way back to the factory after morning collections from farms. **1849–52** *Todd's Cycl. Anat.* IV. 911/1 The fourth premolar displaces the.. tubercular *milk-molar. *c* **1826** *Earl Richard* ix. in Child *Ballads* (1886) II. 462 My mither was a gude *milk-nurse. *c* **1440** *Mylke payle [see *milk-stop*]. *c* **1475** *Pict. Voc.* in Wr.-Wülcker 793/23 *Hoc multrum*, a mylkepayle. **1831** SCOTT *Jrnl.* 1 Jan., Cadell is of opinion if I meddle in politics,..I shall break the milk-pail. **1579–80** NORTH *Plutarch, P. Æmilius* (1595) 267 Womens brests are not alwaies full of milke (as *milke pans are..). **1840** T. A. TROLLOPE *Summer in Brittany* I. 40 A brown dish of the size and shape of a milk-pan. **1885** MISS MURFREE *Prophet Gt. Smoky Mts.* iii. 57 She carried her *milk-piggin. **1855** *Harvard Mag.* I. 420 We were..a good deal incommoded by the diminutive size of the *milk-pitchers. **1567** HARMAN *Caveat* (1869) 86 Baken, chese and *mylke porrage. **1711** SWIFT *Jrnl. to Stella* 15 May, My breakfast is milk porridge. **1535** COVERDALE *Judg.* iv. 19 Then opened she a *mylke pot, & gaue him to drynke. **1838** DICKENS *O. Twist* xxvii, Mr. Bumble..made a closer inspection of the milk-pot. **1620** MIDDLETON *Chaste Maid* II. ii. 109 Herrings and *milk-pottage. **1899** ANNIE E. HOLDSWORTH *Valley Gt. Shadow* iv, Beef-tea and *milk-pudding had had their day. **1907** *Yesterday's Shopping* 213/2 *Milk saucepan with earthenware lining. **1975** J. SYMONS *Three Pipe Problem* xvii. 163 He burnt the milk saucepan dry. **1856** *Farmer's Mag.* Jan. 7 The Physiology of *Milk-Secretion. **1847** DICKENS *Dombey* (1848) xxi. 207 A neighbouring *milk-shop. **1883** *Encycl. Brit.* XV. 797/2 The privy council has issued an order, under the Contagious Diseases (Animals) Act of 1878, called the Dairies, Milkshops, and Cowsheds Order. **1844** *Milk-sieve [see *milk-dish*]. **1483** *Cath. Angl.* 240/1 A *Milke skele, *mulgarium*. **1767** MRS. GLASSE *Cookery* App. 343 *Milk soop the Dutch way. **1897** *Allbutt's Syst. Med.* IV. 191 From three and a half, to four pints [of milk] a day may be given to an adult..in the form of a milk soup. **1797** *Monthly Mag.* III. 531 A *milk sow was offered at the opening of the assembly. **1950** *N.Z. Jrnl. Agric.* Apr. 378/3 *Milk stands erected as part of the releaser room..have given satisfactory results. *c* **1440** *Promp. Parv.* 338/1 *Mylke stop, or payle, *multra, vel multrum*. *c* **1440** *Medulla Gram.* in *Promp. Parv.* 79 *note*, *Colum*, a *mylke syhe. **15..** *Wowing Jok & Jynny* 28 in *Bannatyne MS.* (Hunter. Cl.) 388 Ane milk syth. **1846** J. BAXTER *Libr. Pract. Agric.* (ed. 4) I. 209 The whole mass.. with the cream and new milk is run through the searce into the milk-sye. **1965** in P. Jennings *Living Village* (1968) 66 The milk..is collected by a *milk tanker. **1972** *Guardian* 16 Oct. 10/2 Until the rains came..villagers were collecting water in buckets from milk tankers in High Furness. **1868** ATKINSON *Cleveland Gloss.*, *Milk-tin, the metal vessel in which the milk is set to cream. **1910** *Daily Chron.* 22 Apr. 1/3 The..express..ran into a *milk truck and a guard's van. **1947** E. HODGINS *Mr. Blandings builds his Dream House* vii. 94 Her husband got run over by the milk truck. **1973** R. L. SIMON *Big Fix* (1974) xx. 170 A trio of milk trucks from a dairy. **1805** R. W. DICKSON *Pract. Agric.* II. 1017 The *milk-tub is covered up by a board. **1799** CORSE in *Phil. Trans.* LXXXIX. 211 The first or *milk tusks of an elephant never grow to any size. **1844** H. STEPHENS *Bk. Farm* II. 445 The *milk-veins along the lower part of the abdomen become larger. **1883** *Wheelman* Apr. 28/1 A superannuated 'bus-driver, with a conveyance strongly resembling a *milk-wagon. **1960** T. HUGHES *Lupercal* 46 Light and birdsong come Walloping up roads with the milk wagon. **1876** tr. *Wagner's Gen. Pathol.* 86 *Milk-yeast can grow fungus-like, if submerged.

b. objective, as ***milk-carrier, -dealer, -heater, producer, -seller, strainer, -tester, -vendor; milk-breeding, -curdling, -drinking, -making, -marketing*** (also vbl. sbs.), ***-producing*** (also vbl. sbs.), ***-yielding*** adjs. Also (of the secretions of plants) ***milk-giving, -bearing*** adjs.

1855 SIR E. SMITH in *Syst. Nat. Hist.* I. 28 The *milk-bearing tissue so readily inferred to exist from the white exuding juice of the cut dandelion [etc.]. **1656** BLOUNT *Glossogr.*, *Lactifical*, *milk-breeding, milk-making, milk-yeelding. **1805** *Mod. London* App., Cream is sold by the *Milk-carriers at 1*s.* 4*d.* per pint. **1897** *Allbutt's Syst. Med.* III. 287 'Rennin', a *milk-curdling ferment. **1805** R. W. DICKSON *Pract. Agric.* II. 969 Cows for the supply of the *milk-dealer. *c* **1175** *Lamb. Hom.* 7 Drihten þu dest þe lof of *milc drinkende childre muðe. **1898** *Daily News* 4 Apr. 2/1 The productive or *milk-giving [rubber] trees. **1905** *Westm. Gaz.* 5 Oct. 5/2 Ovens, grillers,..*milk-heaters,.. sterilisers, and other things are all there. **1656** *Milk-making [see *milk-breeding*]. **1933** *Statutory Rules & Orders* No. 789. 21 This scheme may be cited as the *Milk Marketing Scheme, 1933, and applies to England and Wales. **1936** Milk Marketing [see GRADE *sb.* 5 c]. **1968** *Listener* 4 July 15/2 In the new milk marketing case this truth is emphasised... Under the Milk Marketing Scheme the milk producers sell their milk to the Milk Marketing Board. **1870** *Rep. Comm. Agric. 1869* (U.S. Dept. Agric.) 449 The annual meeting of the *Milk Producers' Association of Massachusetts and New Hampshire. **1950** *N.Z. Jrnl. Agric.* Feb. 163/3 It is the responsibility of the milk producer to ensure..that only milk of the highest quality leaves the farm. **1946** *Nature* 12 Oct. 523/1 The recording movement may..progress to greater service to the *milk-producing industry. **1975** *Country Life* 12 June 1590/1 Different cows have different milk-producing capabilities. **1600** J. PORY tr. *Leo's Africa* III. 132 Next vnto them stand the *milke-sellers. **1686** S. SEWALL *Letter-Bk.* (1886) I. 33 Five Duz. of *milk strainers of the smaller sort. **1872** W. S. JONES *Let.* 20 Mar. in G. N. Jones *Florida Plantation Rec.* (1927) 199 The milk strainer is also in bad repair. **1902** *Daily Chron.* 5 Dec. 6/5 It is quite easy for the consumer to protect himself—in quality, by purchasing a 1*s.* 6*d.* *milk tester. **1851** MAYHEW *Lond. Labour* I. 191/2 The *milk-vendors sell..twenty quarts per day. **1611** COTGR., *Laictier*, milkie,..*milke-yeelding. **1897** *Daily News* 28 Sept. 8/3 The herd is entirely of the milk-yielding.. Ayrshires.

c. parasynthetic and instrumental, as ***milk-barred, -blended, -borne, -budded, -faced, -fed, -hued, -outstretched, -washed*** adjs.

1849 M. ARNOLD *Strayed Reveller* 197 Jasper and chalcedony, And *milk-barr'd onyx-stones. **1902** *Westm. Gaz.* 3 Mar. 11/3 The compound called '*milk-blended butter'. **1904** *Daily Chron.* 14 July 5/1 Epidemics of definite '*milk-borne' diseases. **1905** F. L. DODD *Municip. Milk* 6 Epidemics of milk-borne scarlet fever. **1865** SWINBURNE *Dolores* xl, And *milk-budded myrtles with Venus..he trod. **1815** MILMAN *Fazio* III. i. That *milk-faced mercy will come whimpering to me. **1856** KANE *Arct. Expl.* II. i. 13 The two last of the family, who will then..be tolerably *milk-fed, I shall reserve for my own eating. **1887** *Pall Mall G.* 16 Aug. 5/1 The well-known *milk-hued gem. **1886** T. HARDY *Mayor of Casterb.* i, New, milk-hued canvas. **1600** FAIRFAX *Tasso* XII. xxxi, The gentle beast with *milke out stretched teat; (As nurses custome) proffred thee to feed. **1598** F. ROUS *Thule* B 4, Viceina whose most pure *milk-washed hart Neuer supposde what fraud before did plot, Told him [etc.].

d. similative, as ***milk-blue, -dim, -green, -like, -mild, -pale*** adjs. Also MILK-WARM.

1917 D. H. LAWRENCE *Look! We have come Through!* 77 The *milk-blue, morning lake. **1945** W. DE LA MARE *Burning-Glass* 41 Pulsing beneath the silken skin The milk-blue blood rills out and in. **1955** E. POUND *Section: Rock-Drill* xc. 65 Moon's barge over milk-blue water. **1926** H. READ *Coll. Poems* 55 Oh, turn your *milk dim eyes To outer things! **1912** D. H. LAWRENCE *Let.* 2 June (1962) I. 130 The pale, *milk-green river. **1813** T. BUSBY tr. *Lucretius* v. 1028 *Milk-like nurture from her bosom flowed. *c* **1800** *Misc.* (1829) 52 Grass cut Virginia, or *milk-mild Oronoko [tobacco]. **1895** W. B. YEATS *Poems* 33 And at his cry there came no *milk-pale face Under a crown of thorns and dark with blood. **1910** W. DE LA MARE *Three Mulla-Mulgars* xviii. 248 At each thorn-tip, as the flame licks near, wells out and gathers a milk-pale globe of poison.

10. a. Special combinations, as **milk-abscess**, an abscess occurring in the breasts of women during lactation; **milk bank**, a bank (BANK *sb.*[3] 7 f) of human milk; **milk-bar**, a place where drinks made from milk (and often also other refreshments) are sold (see BAR *sb.*[1] 28); **milk-blooded** *a.*, cowardly, spiritless; **milk-blotch**, an eruption of the skin in sucking infants, *porrigo larvalis*; **milk-brother**, a foster-brother; **milk-cell** *Bot.*, the cell in which the milky juice or latex of plants is contained; **milk chicken**, a chicken that has been fed on milk and ground oats; **milk chocolate**, †(*a*) a beverage made from chocolate and milk; (*b*) eating chocolate (CHOCOLATE 2) made with milk; (*c*) a brown colour; also *attrib.*; †**milk-circle** = MILKY WAY; **milk-coffee**, coffee made with milk; white coffee; also *attrib.*, of a light brown colour; **milk-crust**, an eruption of the skin in infants, *crusta lactea* (*Syd. Soc. Lex.* 1890); †**milkdame**, a wet-nurse; **milk-diphtheria**, epidemic diphtheria spread by means of infected milk; **milk-duct**, *Anat.*, any one of the several ducts which convey milk from the secretory glands through the nipple to the exterior (*Syd. Soc. Lex.*); **milk escutcheon**, an area covered by a reversed arrangement of the direction of the hair on the udder and thighs of a milch cow; **milk factor**, a factor causing disposition towards mammary cancer which is transmitted to offspring in milk; **milk factory**, a factory in which cream is extracted from milk; **milk-farm**, a dairy farm; **milk-farmer**, a dairy farmer; **milk-fever**, a slight feverish attack which sometimes occurs in women two or three days after childbirth; also, a similar complaint in milch cows; **milk-fish**, (*a*) a clupeoid fish, *Chanos chanos*, from the Indo-Pacific (*Cent. Dict.* 1890); (*b*) *Austral.* = TREPANG; **milk-float**,

(*a*) a float (FLOAT *sb.* 14) for the conveyance of milk; (*b*) a small electrically-driven milk-cart; **milk-flour**, a preparation of desiccated milk; **milk-fungus**, any fungus of the genus *Lactarius*; **milk-giver**, one who or that which gives milk; also *fig.*; **milk-glass**, (*a*) a semi-translucent or opalescent glass, cryolite glass; (*b*) a glass vessel applied to the breast to receive a superabundant flow of milk (*Syd. Soc. Lex.*); **milk-house**, a dairy, a place for the storing or sale of milk; also *attrib.*; **milk-kinship**, the kinship arising from adoption or fostering; **milk kitchen**, a special kitchen at a maternity hospital or the like, where babies' feeds are prepared; **milk-leg**, 'white swelling', a painful swelling, usually of the lower extremities, very common after parturition; **milk line** *Embryol.* [tr. G. *milchlinie* (O. Schultze 1892, in *Anat. Anzeiger* VII. 266)], (the line occupied by) a ridge of thickened ectoderm that appears on either side of mammalian embryos, extending from the front to the rear limb buds, on which the mammary glands later form in females; †**milkmadge**, a milk-maid; **milk-mirror** = *milk escutcheon*; **milk-mite** = CHEESE-MITE (*Cent. Dict.*); **milk-name**, the name given to a Chinese child at a ceremony held one month after birth: it is later superseded by more formal names but continues to be used in particular situations (see quot. 1911); †**milk-pap**, a teat or nipple; **milk powder**, a preparation of desiccated milk; **milk-pump** = *breast-pump* (Mayne *Expos. Lex.* 1857); **milk-quartz**, an opaque white variety of quartz (cf. *milky quartz*); **milk-ranch** *U.S.* (California), a dairy farm (Schele de Vere 1872); a ranch producing milk; **milk ridge** *Embryol.* [tr. G. *milchleiste* (O. Schultze 1893, in *Verhandl. d. physik.-med. Ges. zu Würzburg* XXVI. 173)] = *milk line*; **milk-room** orig. *U.S.*, a room in a house or dairy in which milk is kept; **milk-round**, (*a*) = *milk-route*; (*b*) *transf.*, a regular trip or tour in which one calls at several places; spec. *R.A.F. slang* (see quot. 1945); hence ***milk-roundsman***; **milk-route** orig. *U.S.*, a route on which milk is regularly collected from farmers or delivered to customers; **milk-run** = *milk-round*; **milk-scab, -scall**, the same as *milk-blotch* and *milk-crust*; **milk-scarlatina**, epidemic scarlatina spread by means of infected milk; **milk-score**, a tally or other account of the purchase and sale of milk; **milk sea**, a particular kind of phosphorescent appearance on the sea (also *milky sea*); **milk-shake** orig. *U.S.*, a beverage composed of milk, flavouring, etc., mixed by shaking or agitation; **milk-shield** = *milk escutcheon*; **milk-sick** *a.*, affected with milk-sickness; also as *sb.* = *milk-sickness*; **milk-sickness** *U.S.*, an endemic disease in cattle peculiar to the Western States of America, and sometimes communicated to man through the consumption of infected meat; **milk-spot**, (*a*) a lustrous white callosity frequently observed upon the surface of the pericardium; (*b*) a white mucous patch in secondary syphilis (*Syd. Soc. Lex.*); (*c*) a form of tooth-rash (*Ibid.*); **milk stout**, formerly, a kind of sweet stout made with lactose; also *attrib.* and *fig.*; **milk-sugar**, sugar of milk, lactose; **milk-teething**, the process of cutting the milk-teeth; **milk-thrush** = APHTHA; **milk-tie** = *milk-kinship*; **milk-toast** *U.S.*, toast which is softened in milk; **milk-train**, (*a*) a railway train chiefly transporting milk, usu. very early in the morning; (*b*) *R.A.F. slang* (see quot. 1943); **milk-tube**, (*a*) *Bot.*, a laticiferous tube; (*b*) a milking tube; **milk-vessel**, (*a*) a dairy utensil for holding milk; (*b*) the udder of a cow; (*c*) *Bot.*, one of many tubes in which a milky fluid is secreted; **milk-walk**, a milkman's regular round for the sale of milk; also, a dairy business; †**milk-water**, a cordial water distilled from milk and herbs; † **milk way** = MILKY WAY; also *fig.*; **milk-whisky** = KOUMISS; †**milk-wife** = *milk-woman*; **milk-wine**, a beverage obtained from fermented milk; **milk-woman**, a woman who carries round milk for sale.

1799 UNDERWOOD *Dis. Childr.* (ed. 4) III. 111 *note*, A Treatise..in which the *milk-abscess, and sore nipples are fully considered. **1948** *Archit. Rev.* CIV. 21 (*caption*) Mothers' *milk bank. **1972** *Guardian* 22 Aug. 4/6 If there should be a shortage of mother's milk, the hospital will get supplies from the National Milk Bank. **1935** *Forres Gaz.* 20 Nov. 1/2 The *milk bar, or place where milk drinks are sold, is a popular institution all over Australia, and plans are on foot for installing..them in Britain. **1938** E. WAUGH *Scoop* II. iv. 200 Legend..told and retold over the milk-bars of Fleet Street. **1957** J. BRAINE *Room at Top* xxx. 254 A milk bar near the railway station. **1971** J. PHILIPS *Escape a Killer* (1972) I. v. 69 There's a milk bar in the village. **1847** E. BRONTË *Wuthering Heights* I. xi. 259, I wish you joy of the *milk-blooded coward. **1910** *Blackw. Mag.* Feb. 183/2 The sooner we give up all this milk-blooded, blue-spectacled, pacificist talk the better. **1797** *Ibid.* I. 97 *Milk-blotches appear first on the forehead. **1890** *Syd. Soc. Lex.*, Milk-blotch. **1897** *Strand Mag.* Christm. No. 617/1 Ivan was what is termed in Russian the '*milkbrother' of Alexia Bobrofsha. **1884** BOWER & SCOTT tr. *De Bary's Phaner.* 195 Those solitary spindle-shaped initial cells of the *milk-cells do not exist. **1890** *Syd. Soc. Lex.*, Milk-cells. **1902** *Encycl. Brit.* XXXI. 882/2 Chickens fattened quite young..and known as *petits poussins* or '*milk chickens'. **1723** J. NOTT *Cook's & Confectioner's Dict.* sig. 18 (*heading*) To make *Milk Chocolate. **1752** M. W. MONTAGU *Let.* 16 Feb. (1967) III. 5 As soon as I am risen, I constantly take 3 cups of milk coffee, and two hours after that a large cup of milk chocolate. **1752** [see *milk chocolate* above]. **1904** 'SAKI' *Reginald* 101 They all sat down to play progressive halma, with milk-chocolate for prizes. **1910** *Encycl. Brit.* X. 614/2 Milk powder..is largely employed in the preparation of so-called milk chocolates. **1926** C. BEATON *Diary* 15 Apr. in *Wandering Yrs.* (1961) iv. 80, I..bought some bars of milk chocolate. **1955** *Radio Times* 22 Apr. 21/3, 14 milk chocolate caramels. **1958** S. HYLAND *Who goes Hang?* xiv. 63 A large table splendidly covered with milk-chocolate-coloured leather. **1969** *Vogue* 15 Mar. 81/1 An edging of milk chocolate suede. **1974** 'E. LATHEN' *Sweet & Low* xii. 124 The creamy satisfaction of milk chocolate. **1601** HOLLAND *Pliny* I. 16 That white, which hath taken the name of the *Milk circle [marg. *Galaxi*]. **1695** J. LIGHTBODY *Every Man his own Gauger* 62 If you would make *Milk Coffee, you must, to every Pint of Water, put a quart of Milk. **1972** H. OSBORNE *Pay-Day* II. iv. 42 The girl at the desk..was a milk-coffee negress. **1582** STANYHURST *Æneis* IV. (Arb.) 118 Her owne *mylckdame in byrth soyl was breathles abyding. **1887** *Brit. Med. Jrnl.* 7 May 1020/1 *Milk-diphtheria at Camberley and York Town. **1881** J. P. SHELDON *Dairy Farm.* 7/2 This *milk escutcheon, or shield, then, is one of those theories of which [etc.]. **1939** J. J. BITTNER in *Public Health Rep.* (U.S. Public Health Service) LIV. 1115 The breast cancer observations..may be explained by a theory..assuming that three 'factors' are needed... These factors are: (A) A 'breast cancer-producing influence' transferred through the milk of high-cancer stock females to their progeny. This has been designated as the '*milk factor' in the tables. **1943** C. G. GESCHICKTER *Dis. Breast* xxxv. 800 This so-called milk-factor or milk-influence has been extracted from the mammary glands of lactating cancer-susceptible mice by Bittner and shown to increase the incidence of mammary cancer whether injected in, or fed to young mice. **1966** WRIGHT & SYMMERS *Systemic Path.* I. xxviii. 990/1 There is no evidence that a milk factor plays any part in the occurrence of carcinoma of the breast in women. There is no way by which such a factor can be demonstrated. **1886** BAGOT *Handbk. Dairy Factories* 8 Factories [in Ireland]..where the whole milk is purchased from the farmer—we call *milk factories. **1867** *Crim. Chronol. York Castle* 195 She had a small *milk-farm, which the prisoner managed. **1805** R. W. DICKSON *Pract. Agric.* II. 968 The sort of cow most adapted to the intentions of the *milk-farmer must of course vary. **1758** J. S. *Le Dran's Observ. Surg.* (1771) Dict. Cc b, *Lactea Febris*, the *Milk-Fever attending Women for some Days after their Delivery. **1894** 'MARK RUTHERFORD' *Catharine Furze* IV, My belief is, she'll have milk fever. **1880** *Proc. Linn. Soc. New South Wales* V. 128 Another species [of Trepang] is the '*milk fish', or 'cotton fish', so called from its power of emitting a white viscid fluid.., which clings to any object like shreds of cotton. **1905** D. S. JORDAN *Guide to Study of Fishes* II. iii. 44 The *Chanidæ*, or milkfishes, constitute another small archaic type, found in the tropical Pacific. They are large, brilliantly silvery, toothless fishes. *Ibid.* 45 The single living species is the *Awa*, or milkfish, *Chanos chanos*, largely used as food in Hawaii. **1962** K. F. LAGLER et al. *Ichthyol.* vi. 203 The irregular movements of the Asiatic milkfish (*Chanos*) into and out of fresh water make it amphidromous. **1971** *Daily Colonist* (Victoria, B.C.) 30 Mar. 5/4 Taiwan and Indonesia produce much needed sea protein in traditional milkfish 'farm ponds'. **1974** *Nat. Geographic* Dec. 788/2 Across southern Asia, from the Philippines to India, commercial aquaculturists have begun to raise milkfish, a food species that subsists on plant life. **1887** *Bury Times* 3 Sept. 6/4 He noticed the defendant driving a *milk float towards him at a great speed. **1935** N. COLLINS *Three Friends* viii. 143 A horse attached to a milk float wore a hat made of newspaper. **1951** *Engineering* 20 July 95/3 Pedestrian-controlled vehicles (such as hand-operated electric milk floats). **1974** M. BABSON *Stalking Lamb* xi. 73 An electric milk float trundling down the street. **1902** *Chambers's Jrnl.* 22 Feb. 191/1 The *milk-flour is completely soluble in water. **1888** CLODD *Story of Creation* (1894) 129 The Marsupials, or pouched *milk-givers. **1874** KNIGHT *Dict. Mech.* 931 It [Cryolite] is found in great abundance and purity in Greenland, and serves to make a fine *milk-glass. **1589** PUTTENHAM *Eng. Poesie* III. xxiv. (Arb.) 290 Who would not thinke it a ridiculous thing to see a Lady in her *milke-house with a veluet gowne? **1596** *Wills & Inv. N.C.* (Surtees) II. 271 The milke-house stuffe. **1891** T. HARDY *Tess* xvii. (1892) 146 It was a large room over the milk-house. **1885** W. R. SMITH *Kinship & Marr.* v. 149 We find among the Arabs a feeling about *milk-kinship so well established that [etc.]. **1965** *Nursing Times* 5 Feb. 181/1 In some hospitals the labour wards and the *milk kitchens were each centralized. **1899** *Allbutt's Syst. Med.* VI. 216 Tense, shiny, smooth, white or mottled skin, marked often by dilated veins, whence comes the name *milk-leg or white leg. **1893** *Jrnl. R. Microsc. Soc.* 304 Prof. O. Schultze finds in the embryos of pig, rabbit, mole, fox, and cat, that the first rudiment of the mammary glands is seen as a linear epithelial thickening on each side of the body... This '*milk-line' stretches from the anterior to the posterior limb-rudiment. **1946** B. M. PATTEN *Human Embryol.* ix. 241 Some animals (for example, the sow and the bitch) develop a series of nipples spread over nearly the entire length of the milk line. *Ibid.*, Not infrequently supernumerary nipples may occur at other levels along the course of the milk line. **1960** F. D. ALLAN *Essent. Human Embryol.* xix. 179 The primordia of the [mammary] glands form thickened strips of ectoderm located bilaterally from axilla to groin which are called the milk ridges or lines. **1582** STANYHURST *Æneis* IV. (Arb.) 114 Shal I now, lyke a castaway *milck-madge, On mye woers formoure bee fawning? **1881** J. P. SHELDON *Dairy Farming* 6/2 The '*milk-mirror' or 'escutcheon' theory of M. Guenon. **1836** J. F. DAVIS *Chinese* I. vii. 288 The birth of a son is of course an occasion of great rejoicing; the family or surname is first given, and then the '*milk name', which is generally some diminutive of endearment. **1911** J. D. BALL *Chinese at Home* vii. 75 The milk name.. clings to him or her through life, being used by parents, relatives, and most intimate friends, as well as by superiors. **1931** C. L'E. EWEN *Hist. Surnames* 8 The Chinese receive a number of names..the 'milk-name' when a month old. **1975** O. SELA *Bengali Inheritance* iii. 23 His milk name had been Chan Yan-Wo, and at school he had changed it to Richard.., the first step in accepting Western ways. **1607** SHAKS. *Timon* IV. iii. 115 Those *Milke pappes That through the window Barne bore at mens eyes. **1834** *India Jrnl. Med. Sci.* I. I. 32/2 **Milk Powder*... Specimens of an article he has advertised under the designation of Pulverised Milk. **1910** *Encycl. Brit.* X. 614/2 Milk powder is manufactured under various patents. *Ibid.*, Milk powder made from skim-milk keeps well for considerable periods. **1972** D. BLOODWORTH *Any Number can Play* xii. 96 A big American air force general with a complexion like milk-powder. **1836** T. THOMSON *Min., Geol.*, etc. I. 64 Rock crystal,..rose quartz, *milk quartz, siderite. **1856** *Calif. Pathfinder* (San Francisco) 13 Nov. 2/4 The *milk ranch that burned down beyond the Mission yesterday morning. **1909** BAILEY & MILLER *Text-bk. Embryol.* xvi. 449 In embryos of six to seven mm., or even less, a thickening of the epidermis occurs in a narrow zone along the ventrolateral surface of the body (Strahl). In embryos of 15 mm. this thickening, known as the *milk ridge, extends from the upper extremity to the inguinal region. **1960** Milk ridge [see *milk line* above]. **1836** *Knickerbocker* VIII. 706 In the rear, is quite a city of additions, in the shape of bed-rooms, bath-rooms, *milk-rooms, buttery [etc.]. **1970** *Cape Times* 28 Oct. 21/1 (Advt.), Lean-to, barn for animals, dairy and milk room, 4 calf pens. **1900** *Oxford Times* 13 Jan. (Advt.), Wanted, a single man to serve a *milk-round. **1927** R. B. FORRESTER *Fluid Milk Market Eng. & Wales* 96 Retail Delivery. Milk Rounds...no close or detailed survey of actual roundsman systems has ever been made in this country. **1945** PARTRIDGE *Dict. R.A.F. Slang* 39 *Milkround*, a run made fairly regularly by a Squadron or a Force, if it returns to its station or base in the early morning. **1952** E. F. DAVIES *Illyrian Venture* x. 191 We did a 'milk-round' of all the jails in Vienna, picking up and setting down prisoners at every stop. **1958** *Times* 9 Aug. 7/7 Strange though the urgent masochism of the milk round may seem, that is how the great majority of Americans still see us, from the windows of a coach. **1970** *Times* 17 Nov. 19/8 Like other business organisations, we make what is known as the annual milkround, going to every university at the recruiting time. **1972** *Guardian* 8 Feb. 13/7 Fund-raising must be..centralized, instead of the monthly 'milk rounds' by volunteers. **1972** *Accountant* 14 Sept. 327/1 'Farmer's Wife' branded goods—cream, yogurt, butter, eggs, potatoes, bread, margarine, bacon, sausages and poultry—constitute an increasingly important part of the milk division's turnover and profit. Sales are helping to maintain regular milk rounds when other industries find rising costs of such personal service a constant headache. **1940** F. KITCHEN *Brother to Ox* xiii. 202, I want to say what a pleasant job it is being a *milkroundsman. **1874** *Rep. Comm. Agric. 1873* (U.S. Dept. Agric.) 246 The most economical method of managing the delivery of milk at the factory is by establishing *milk routes. **1897** 'MARK TWAIN' *Following Equator* xliv. 464 The vested rights..are frequently the subject of sale or mortgage. Just like a milk-route. **1959** N. MAILER *Advts. for Myself* (1961) 372 The milk companies.. are saved most of the costs of local distribution by delivering the orange juice on their milk route. **1925** *Milk-run [see RUN *sb.*[1] 4 i]. **1943** K. TENNANT *Ride on Stranger* (1968) ix. 103 Shannon did not know anyone who wanted half a milk-run. **1944** J. H. FULLARTON *Troop Target* iii. 24 Isobel married that joker with a milk-run out Henderson way. **1944** T. H. WISDOM *Triumph over Tunisia* vi. 54 It was General Doolittle who organised the 'milk-run' Fortress raids on the ports of Tunis and Bizerta. **1964** *Observer* (Colour Suppl.) 11 Oct. 17/2 Similar risks must be taken by transport aircraft pilots, flying their daily 'milk runs' to supply jungle-bound positions along the 1,000-mile frontier [of Borneo]. **1969** *Daily Tel.* 11 Oct. 11/5 Another way of island hopping down to Grenada..is to catch the early morning 'milk-run' plane from Antigua, which calls in at Dominica, St. Lucia, Martinique and Barbados, collecting and unloading passengers, mail and newspapers as it goes. **1972** *Guardian* 30 Dec. 13 Woe betide any who suddenly discovers he has to go to Brussels the next morning. The businessmen's milkrun is always booked days ahead. **1856** MAYNE *Expos. Lex.*, **Milk-Scab*, another common term for *Porrigo larvalis*, or *Crusta lactea*, or milk-blotch... **Milk-scall*. Same as *Milk-scab*. **1887** *Brit. Med. Jrnl.* 19 Feb. 409/2 Mr. Power's report of the Hendon *milk-scarlatina outbreak. **1687** T. BROWN *Saints in Uproar* Wks. 1730 I. 77 A pack of vermin, bred up to..rubbing out of *milk-scores. **1712** ADDISON *Spect.* No. 482 ⁋4 He is better acquainted with the Milk-Score, than his Steward's Accounts. **1898** F. T. BULLEN in *Nat. Rev.* Aug. 859 That beautiful, inexplicable phenomenon of the '*milk sea' suddenly appeared! **1889** *Harper's Bazaar* 4 May 330/3 You needs some *milk shake..an' I got some nice new w'iskey to putt in. **1911** H. S. HARRISON *Queed* vii. 85 You ain't feelin good, are you, Doc? You're lookin' white as a milk-shake. **1937** *Daily Herald* 20 Feb. 11/3 (*caption*) Mrs.—..sampling a milk shake after she had opened a milk bar in Tottenham Court-road yesterday. **1952** 'J. TEY' *Singing Sands* xii. 196, I had a coupla bananas and a milk shake in Leicester Square. **1953** E. TAYLOR *Sleeping Beauty* xiii. 200 She saw herself translated to the Corner House, but to the same sundaes and parfaits and milk-shakes. **1968** *Blues Unlimited* Sept. 10 Joe worked in the kitchens at the Cafe six nights a week, pouring cokes and milk shakes. **1881** *Milk-shield [see *milk-escutcheon*]. **1885** MISS MURFREE *Prophet Gt. Smoky Mts.* ii. 46 The bars of the *milk-sick pen. *Ibid.*, She [a cow] lay down an' died o' the milk-sick. **1834** HOFFMAN *Winter in West* (1835) II. 66, I passed a deserted village, the whole population of which had been destroyed by the '*milk sickness'. **1859** BARTLETT *Dict. Amer.*, *Milk Sickness*, a fatal spasmodic disease, peculiar to the Western States. **1897** *Allbutt's Syst. Med.* IV. 530 These thickenings, which resemble the *milk-spots on the heart, are not [etc.]. **1942** *R.A.F. Jrnl.* 13 June 32 'There you are, gentlemen,'

boomed a rich, *milk-stout voice. **1959** M. GILBERT *Blood & Judgement* i. 12 A lady..[was] addressing herself to a glass of milk stout. **1965** S. M. TRITTON *Tritton's Guide to Better Wine & Beer Making for Beginners* 133 Milk Stout... Pour hot..water over the patent malt and stir in the flaked barley... Boil the hops in 2 pints of water... Dissolve sugar and lactose..and add to bulk. Follow by the yeast and ferment to completion. **1974** G. MANN *Home Wine & Beer Making* 99/1 Sweet, or milk, stout dark and sweet, but still with an underlying bitter twang. **1846** *Penny Cycl.* Suppl. II. 635/2 *Milk-sugar is an integral constituent of the milk of the mammalia. **1822–34** *Good's Study Med.* (ed. 4) I. 30 *Milk teething. **1855** DUNGLISON *Med. Lex.*, *Aphthæ*... Thrush or sore mouth... White Thrush. *Milk Thrush. **1870** LUBBOCK *Orig. Civiliz.* iii. (1875) 89 The symbol of adoption represented not the birth, but the *milk-tie. **1855** J. R. BESTE *Wabash* II. 260 Large platters of *milk toast. This delicacy is made of slices of toast, buttered and sprinkled with pepper and salt, and laid in a dish of warm milk, which serves as a sauce to the rest. **1903** K. D. WIGGIN *Rebecca* xxiii. 258 She's just asked me for some milk-toast. **1853** *Knickerbocker* XLII. 532 The '*milk-train*' still had the right of way. **1897** [see HIGHBALL 2]. **1930** WODEHOUSE *Very Good, Jeeves!* ix. 251 Her intention was..to..leave by the next train, even if that train was a milk-train, stopping at every station. **1943** HUNT & PRINGLE *Service Slang* 46 *The Milk Train*, appropriate name for the modern 'Dawn Patrol' on early morning reconnaissance flights. **1955** *Railway Mag.* May 359/1 A daily milk train which was worked by the L.N.E.R. **1877** *Rep. Vermont Dairymen's Assoc.* VIII. 106 The milk must be drawn by means of a catheter, or *milk tube. **1884** BOWER & SCOTT tr. *De Bary's Phaner.* 198 The sharp difference of structure between the sieve- and milk-tubes is always particularly clear. **1902** *Encycl. Brit.* XXV. 409/1 In one genus (*Lactarius*) 'milk-tubes', recalling the lactiferous tubes of many vascular plants, are found. **14..** *Voc.* in Wr.-Wülcker 573/39 *Coagulatorium*, a *mylkefessell. **1566** in Peacock *Eng. Ch. Furniture* (1866) 41 He haith melted yt [a 'hallywater fatt'] and made mylke vessell thereof. **1855** SIR E. SMITH in *Syst. Nat. Hist.* I. 29 Milk vessels from the stipules of the *Ficus elastica*. **1842** J. AITON *Dom. Econ.* (1857) 210 He must examine..the calf itself, —its head, and above all, its milk-vessel and its teats. **1805** *Mod. London* App., *Milk-Walks, that is, a certain proportion of neighbouring streets served by a particular person. **1851** H. MAYHEW *London Labour* I. 435/2 My father had a milk-walk. *c* **1864** BROUGH & HALLIDAY in M. R. Booth *Eng. Plays of 19th Cent.* (1973) IV. 240, I have a horse and cart, Miss Penelope, and a first-rate milk walk. **1905** G. B. SHAW in *Grand Mag.* Feb. 111 He..had..bought an agent's business as a doctor buys a practice or a dairyman a milkwalk. **1917** WODEHOUSE *Man with Two Left Feet* 247 He was..owner of a milk-walk in the most fashionable part of Battersea. **1697** KIDDER *Horneck* (1698) 53 He wd sup with an Apple or two, with a little Bread, and small Ale, or *Milk-water. **1769** MRS. RAFFALD *Eng. Housekpr.* (1778) 365 To distill Milk Water. **1555** EDEN *Decades* 245 The parte of heauen cauled *Via Lactea*, that is the *mylke waye. **1593** G. HARVEY *New Let. Notable Cont.* B, The ascending scale and Milk-way to heauenly excellency. **1511** *MS. Acc. St. John's Hosp., Canterb.*, Payd to pe *mylke wyffe for a hoole yere. **1911** M. I. NEWBIGIN *Mod. Geogr.* vii. 189 A *milk-wine or koumiss, produced by the fermentation of milk, is the characteristic drink. **1642** *Ord. & Declar. Ho. Parlt., Lord's Day* 6 Or [that they suffer] any *milke-woman to cry milke on that day. **1879** F. R. STOCKTON *Rudder Grange* v. 56 She had spent the night in a wooden rocking-chair at the milk-woman's.

b. Prefixed to names of plants, chiefly in the sense 'containing milk', as **milk-bush**, (*a*) = *milk-hedge*; (*b*) a milk-yielding shrub of the apocynaceous genus *Wrightia*, native of India; (*c*) a similar shrub, *Wrightia saligna*, native of Queensland (Morris *Austral Eng.* 1898); (*d*) in South Africa and Australia, a name used for several shrubby plants, often succulent, which have a milky latex, esp. various species of *Euphorbia* (cf. sense *a*); **milk-grass** = CORN-SALAD; **milk-hedge**, a shrub or small tree, *Euphorbia Tirucalli*, native of Africa, and cultivated or naturalized in parts of India; **milk lentil** = MILKWORT (?); **milk-parsley**, *Peucedanum palustre*; **milk pea**, a prostrate leguminous plant of the genus *Galactia*, esp. *G. glabella* and *G. mollis*, native of the warmer parts of America; **milk-plant**, (*a*) MILK PEA; (*b*) = *milk-bush* (*d*); **milk purslane**, *Euphorbia maculata*; †**milk-reed** = SPURGE; **milk thistle**, (*a*) = LADY'S THISTLE; (*b*) = SOW-THISTLE; **milk-tree**, (*a*) = *milk-hedge*; (*b*) any tree yielding a wholesome milky juice, esp. the COW-TREE; (*c*) an apocynaceous tree, *Tanghinia venenifera*, native of Madagascar, the poisonous seed of which is employed by the natives in trials by ordeal; †**milk-trefoil**, *Medicago arborea*; **milk-vetch**, a plant of the leguminous genus *Astragalus*; **milk-wood (tree)**, (*a*) a Jamaican milk-yielding tree, *Pseudolmedia spuria*; (*b*) a species of *Bignonia*; (*c*) the Australian paper-bark tree, *Melaleuca leucadendron* or other Australian trees of the genus *Alstonia*; (*d*) one of the sapotaceous ironwood trees, *Sideroxylon inerme*, native of the Cape of Good Hope; (*e*) a sapotaceous timber-tree, *Mimusops obovata*, native of South Africa.

1780 MUNRO *Narr.* (1789) 80 Thorn hedges are sometimes placed in gardens; but in the fields the *milk bush is most commonly used. **1818** C. I. LATROBE *Jrnl. Visit S. Afr. 1815–16* 133 The milk-bush (*ficus*), a tree not unlike a Portugal laurel. **1861** J. A. GRANT *Jrnl.* 27 May in *Walk across Afr.* (1864) v. 79 After we had entered the first milk-bush enclosure, there were several cleanly-swept windings. **1882** FLOYER *Unexpl. Baluchistan* 15 Pitching the tent so as to enclose three large milk bushes. **1883** 'R. IRON' *Story Afr. Farm* I. i. 3 The milk-bushes with their long, finger-like leaves..were touched by a weird and an almost oppressive beauty as they lay in the white light. **1893** 'R. IRON' *Dream Life* 13 Jannita sat alone beside a milk-bush. **1907** *Nature* 17 Jan. 288/1 The common milkbush of the karroo and karroid regions of the interior, viz. Euphorbia mauritanica. **1926** [see CAUSTIC *a.* 1 e]. **1965** *Austral. Encycl.* VI. 84/1 Milkbush, a popular name for several shrubs or small trees with a milky sap, especially *Wrightia saligna* in the family Apocynaceæ. **1966** E. PALMER *Plains of Camdeboo* xvi. 259 The milk bush grows here, the *Euphorbia mauritanica* of botanists, with its long, smooth, fleshy, yellow-green stems. **1744** in W. Ellis *Mod. Husbandm.* (1750) III. III. xxi. 161 In June, at a Distance, the Fields look as if all covered with spilt Milk; which is from a Flower, for that reason called *Milk-Grass*. **1780** MUNRO *Narr.* (1789) 80 A horse will have his head and eyes prodigiously swelled from standing for some time under the shade of a *milk hedge. **1840** E. E. Napier *Scenes & Sp. Foreign Lands* II. vi. 183 The..green rows of the milk hedges. **1787** tr. *Linnæus' Fam. Plants* I. 182 *Selinum*... *Milk Parsley. **1974** *Country Life* 3 Oct. 923/1 The double-brooding swallowtail..—from milk-parsley-eating caterpillar..to Britain's largest butterfly. **1874** GRAY *Less. Bot.* 142 *Galactia*.. *Milk-Pea. **1845–50** MRS. LINCOLN *Lect. Bot.* App. 104 *Galactia mollis*... *Milk plant. **1965** *Austral. Encycl.* VI. 84/1 Milk plant is sometimes applied to members of the genus *Euphorbia*. **1611** COTGR. s.v. *Laictier, L'herbe laictiere*. Tythimal, Spurge, *Milke-reed, Wolues-milke. **14..** *Voc.* in Wr.-Wülcker 610/5 *Scariola*, the *mylkthystel. **1562** TURNER *Herbal* II. 146 Leucacantha..named in English milkthystel. **1787** W. WITHERING *Brit. Plants* (ed. 2) II. 875 *Carduus marianus*... Leaves with a net-work of white veins... Milk Thistle. Ladies Thistle. **1866** *Treas. Bot.* 1072 *Sonchus oleraceus* and *S. asper* or Milk Thistle. **1880** BRITTEN & HOLLAND *Dict. Eng. Plant-Names* 335 Milk Thistle... *Sonchus oleraceus*, L., in allusion to its milky juice. **1883** W. ROBINSON *Eng. Flower Garden* 270/2 If a few plants are raised in the garden and planted out in rough and somewhat bare places or banks, &c., the Milk Thistle will soon establish itself permanently. **1960** *Oxf. Bk. Wild Flowers* 34/1 Corn Sowthistle or Field Milk-thistle (*Sonchus arvensis*). A perennial with a hollow stem and milky juice. *Ibid.* 150/2 Milk Thistle (*Silybum marianum*). This rather rare annual or biennial Thistle has large, solitary, often drooping, purple flower-heads. **1698** FRYER *Acc. E. India & P.* 105 The Hedges and Lanes are chiefly set with two sorts of Bushes, called by us *Milk-Trees. **1830** LINDLEY *Nat. Syst. Bot.* 214 A milk-tree called Hya-hya in Demerara. **1885** LADY BRASSEY *The Trades* 112 The milk-tree (*Tanghinia lactaria*) yields a sap in colour and taste like milk, if drunk while fresh. **1597** GERARDE *Herbal* III. xi. 1121 Of *milke Trefoile, or shrub Trefoile. *Ibid.* II. cccccii. 1058 Of *milke Vetch. **1760** J. LEE *Introd. Bot.* App. 319 Bastard Milk Vetch, *Phaca*. **1856** MAYNE *Expos. Lex.*, *Milk-Vetch, Stemless*. Common name for the *Astragalus escapus*. **1725** SLOANE *Jamaica* II. 21 *Milk-wood Tree. The bark of this tree being deeply gash'd yields a great quantity of milk. **1759** MILLER *Gard. Dict.* (ed. 7) s.v. *Bignonia*, Tree Milkwood, having Pods, with five Leaves,..commonly called in America, White or Milkwood, and Tulip Flower. **1862** L. PAPPE *Silva Capensis* (ed. 2) 24 *Sideroxylon Inerme Lin.* (Milk-wood; Melkhout)... Wood whitish, very hard, close, and durable. **1887** MRS. DALY *Digging & Squatting* 43 Ironbark trees, casuarinas, and the bright green milkwood tree grew here. **1889** J. H. MAIDEN *Useful Native Plants Austral.* 570 *Melaleuca leucadendron*... Called 'Milkwood' in the Northern Territory. **1907** T. R. SIM *Forests & Forest Flora Cape Good Hope* 252 *Sideroxylon inerme*. (White Milkwood;..). *Ibid.* 254 *Mimusops obovata*. (Red Milkwood;..). **1908** E. J. BANFIELD *Confessions of Beachcomber* I. i. 37 On Timana are gigantic milkwood trees (*Alstonia scholaris*) which need great flying buttresses to support their immense height. **1917** [see JAKKALSBESSIE]. **1928** D. COTTRELL *Singing Gold* III. i. 191 A thin ribbon of smoke showed against great milkwood trees. **1932** [see JAKKALSBESSIE]. **1946** L. G. GREEN *So Few are Free* (1948) x. 137 Vaillant noted a large milkwood tree growing out of a rocky crevice. **1973** PALMER & PITMAN *Trees S. Afr.* III. 1737 The wooden rails of the little railway on the Durban Bluff in the early days..were hewn out of milkwood trees.

¶**11.** Used as *adj.* = MILKWHITE. *rare*⁻¹.

1853 M. ARNOLD *Sohrab & Rustum* 162 That vast sky-neighbouring mountain of milk snow.

milk, *sb.*² Colloq. abbrev. of MILKSOP.

1881 *Punch* 10 Sept. 110/2 Patriotic? Well, them as talks Muggins like that to our gurls must be milks. **1923** in J. MANCHON *Le Slang*.

milk (mılk), *v.* Forms: 1 meolc(g)ian, milcian, mylcian (*Northumb.* ȝemilciȝa), 3, 5, 7 milke, 4 melke, 4–6 mylke, 6 molke, mylcke, 6– milk. [OE. *milcian, meolcian*, f. *milc, meolc* MILK *sb.*; cf. ON. *miolka* (OIcel. *mjólka, molka*, MSw. *molka*, Sw. *mjölka*, Da. *malke*). OE. had also the str. vb. *melcan* (*mealc, molcen*) inherited from OTeut. (see MILK *sb.*¹); no clear traces of this have been found later than the OE. period; a solitary instance of *molken* pa. pple. occurs in 1527, but it translates the Ger. *gemolken*.]

I. In literal sense.

1. a. *trans.* To extract milk by handling from the teats of (a cow, goat, ewe, etc., rarely, a woman). Also *absol.*

to milk the ram, the bull: *fig.* to engage in an enterprise doomed to failure. (Cf. *mulgeat hircos*, Virg. *Ecl.* iii. 91.)

c **1000** *Sax. Leechd.* III. 178 Hyt bið æac god ceap to milcian. *a* **1000** in Cockayne *Shrine* 130 Se ȝeþyrsta mon meolcode ða hinde. *c* **1290** *S. Eng. Leg.* I. 351/230 Heo ne ȝaf a-morewe noþe lasse, þei heo were i-milked an eue. **1387** TREVISA *Higden* (Rolls) I. 359 Olde wyfes..were i-woned.. forto schape hem self in likness of hares for to melke here neiȝhebores keen. **1393** LANGL. *P. Pl.* C. XVIII. 10 An hynde oþer-while To hus selle selde cam and suffrede to be melked. *c* **1400** MAUNDEV. (1839) vi. 71 For as meche as sche had to meche Mylk in hire Pappes,..sche mylked hem on the rede Stones. *a* **1450** *Paston Lett.* I. 98 He speke with wemen which were mylkand kyne. **1530** PALSGR. 636/1, I mylke a womans brest, *je tire du laict dune femme*. **1591** SHAKS. *Two Gent.* III. i. 302 *Speed.* Inprimis She can milke. *a* **1656** HALES *Tract Sacr.* Tracts (1677) 40 That fell out which is in the common proverb, *sc.* Whilst the one milks the Ram, the other holds under the Sieve. **1718** POPE *Let. to Lady M. W. Montagu* 1 Sept., When she milked, it was his morning and evening charge to bring the cows to her pail. **1725** RAMSAY *Gentle Sheph.* v. ii, To leave the green-sward dance when we gae milk. **1806** *Med. Jrnl.* XV. 382 This cow being troublesome..he had..milked her himself.

b. To extract or draw (milk). Chiefly *passive*.

1398 TREVISA *Barth. De P.R.* XIX. lxv. (1495) 901 That mylke is beste that is next to the complexyon of mankynde: ..And the nere it is mylked the better it is. **1527** ANDREW *Brunswyke's Distyll. Waters* G iv, The mylke whiche is molken in the mornynge. **1846** J. BAXTER *Libr. Pract. Agric.* (ed. 4) I. 196 If the same milk had been put into the milk-pans directly after it is milked.

†**c.** To cause (milk) to flow. Also with *out*.

c **1400** MAUNDEV. (Roxb.) ix. 36 And for scho had to mykill mylke in her pappes,..scho mylked it oute apon þe reed stanes. **1544** PHAER *Regim. Lyfe* (1560) A vij b, Also ye muste shave hys heade, and mylke theron womans mylke.

†**d.** To obtain milk from by sucking. *Obs.*

1605 SHAKS. *Macb.* I. vii. 55, I haue giuen Sucke, and know How tender 'tis to loue the Babe that milkes me.

e. To keep (cattle) for the purpose of milking.

1898 *Westm. Gaz.* 4 Apr. 10/1 The largest farmer in England..milks at least a thousand cows.

f. *colloq.* To put milk into or on to.

1877 *Trans. Devon Soc. Adv. Sci.* IX. 134 Have you *milked* your tea? **1969** J. WAINWRIGHT *Big Tickle* 52 She milked and sugared both mugs of tea.

2. a. *intr.* To give or yield milk. In early use of women (? = sense 3 *absol.*); now only of cattle.

971 *Blickl. Hom.* 93 þa breost þa þe næfre meolcgende næron. *c* **1400** *Rom. Rose* 5418 For liche a moder she can cherishe And milken as doth a norys. **1765** *Museum Rust.* IV. 225 The eating of the first shoots of rye makes ewes milk extraordinarily. **1886** C. SCOTT *Sheep Farming* 178 Some of the breeds of sheep milk very heavily.

†**b.** To eject milk. *Obs.*

c **1450** MYRC *Festial* 110 þerwyth [she] toke out hyr swete pappe, and mylked on hys þrote.

†**3.** *trans.* To suckle. *Obs.*

1382 WYCLIF *Isa.* lx. 16 With the tete of kingis thou shalt be mylkid. *c* **1475** *Partenay* 6456 Glorius virgin..which milkest with-all The sone of god with thy brestes brod. **1573** L. LLOID *Pilgr. Princes* (1607) 1 b, A Bitch..fedde him and milkt him.

II. *transf.* and *fig.*

4. a. *trans.* To drain away the contents of; to get money out of, 'bleed' pecuniarily; to exploit, turn into a source of (usually) illicit profit. In early use const. *from*.

c **1526** FRITH *Disp. Purg.* To Rdr. A vj, This theyr painful purgatorye..hath of longe time but deceaued the people and mylked them from theyr monye. **1532** MORE *Conf. Tindale* Wks. 639/2 They mylke them so euaungelically, that when their maisters call theim home, they gyue theim a very shrewed rekening. **1537** BIBLE (Matthew) *Ezek.* xviii. *Comm.* (end), Or yt the prestes benefyces were not sufficient for them to lyue on, with out soch pyllage: or yet that the pore people coulde by any other meane be mylcked from that thynge, wherwyth they, their wyues, their housholde and chyldren shulde lyue. **1591** LYLY *Endym.* III. iii. 23 Loue hath as it were milkt my thoughts, and drained from my hart the very substance of my accustomed courage. **1695** VENTRIS *Rep.* (1716) II. 28 He would milk her Purse and fill his own large Pockets. **1721** RAMSAY *Prospect of Plenty* 51 [Spain] grasps the shadows, but the substance tines, While a' the rest of Europe milk her mines. **1893** SALTUS *Madam Sapphira* 204 'They have got something', he would insist, 'or else Tooth is milking his client'. **1904** *Daily News* 8 Oct. 6/2 It will be possible for the Department to 'milk' these grants as much as they like.

Comb. **1658** J. JONES *Ovid's Ibis* 41 Milk-purse Lawyers (so Erasmus termes them) are far more tolerable then Cut-purse tyrants.

b. *U.S. slang. to milk the market, street*, to hold stock so well in hand as to make it fluctuate at will, and so yield any financial result desired.

1870 MEDBERY *Men & Myst. Wall St.* 336 To use the slang of the financial quarter, they 'milk the street'. **1883** *Harper's Mag.* 820/2 The..process of 'milking the market'.

c. *Horse-racing*. (See quot.)

1862 *Times* 2 Jan. 8/6 By such tricks as 'milking'—*i.e.* by keeping a horse a favourite at short odds for a race in which he has no chance whatever, only to lay against him [etc.]. **1865** *Hotten's Slang Dict.* s.v. *Milk*... When a horse is entered for a race which his owner does not intend him to win, and bets against him, the animal is said to be 'milked'.

d. To 'tap', steal the message from (a telegraph or telephone wire); to intercept (a telegram).

1879 PRESCOTT *Sp. Telephone* 108 The..simplicity of the means by which a wire could be milked..struck the whole of the party. **1899** *Tit-Bits* 3 June 185/1 'Milking' telegrams is a fairly common practice.

e. *Theatr. slang*. (See quots.)

1939 HIXSON & COLODNY *Word Ways* xvi. 142 To over-play an audience for applause is called *milking the audience*. **1942** BERREY & VAN DEN BARK *Amer. Thes. Slang* §593/24 *Milk a scene* or *the audience*, to try to get more laughs or applause out of a part than it deserves. **1962** *Times* 15 May 13/3 Too many of the other acts, however, have no idea how to..milk a laugh. **1971** M. BABSON *Cover-up Story* ix. 107 They milked the applause for all it was worth, then Bart held up his hand again.

†**5.** To 'handle' a person enticingly; to draw *on* by wiles. *Obs.*

1623 FLETCHER *Rule a Wife* II. iv, All this is but in seeming To milke the lover on.

6. a. To elicit, draw *out*.

a **1628** PRESTON *New Cov.* (1630) 477 To milke consolation out of the promises. **1662** GURNALL *Chr. in Arm.* III. 176 If ever you had but the sweetness of any one promise in it [*sc.* the water of life] milked out unto you. **1831** MRS. CARLYLE *Early Lett.* (1889) 189, I took nothing in hand the whole day but milking news from her (a rather rural metaphor), which she with unabating copiousness supplied.

b. To drain *away, out of*.

1652 NEEDHAM tr. *Selden's Mare Cl.* Ep. Ded. 6 Hee never made any farther use of them than to milk away the Subjects monie under pretence of building Ships. **1891** C. E. NORTON *Dante's Purgat.* xxiv. 152 Here it is not forbidden to name each other, since our semblance is so milked away by the diet. **1900** KIPLING in *Daily Mail* 24 Apr. 4/4 Dysentery that milks the heart out of a man.

7. To extract juice, virus, etc. from.

1746 *Mass. Acts & Resolves* (1878) III. 307 Any liberty obtained..from any Indian or Indians, for cutting off any timber, wood, hay, milking pine-trees,..shall not be any bar to said guardians in their said action or actions. **1871** R. ELLIS tr. *Catullus* lxviii. 112 Strainer of ooze impure milk'd from a watery fen. **1896** *Westm. Gaz.* 31 Jan. 2/1 A large black snake..not milked for, say, eight days, will give as much as four and a half grains of liquid poison.

8. To manipulate as one does the teat in milking.

1642 H. MORE *Song of Soul* I. II. lxxxiii, He..with his fingers milked evermore The hanging frienge. **1905** *Brit. Med. Jrnl.* 1 July 16 The other loops of distended bowels may then be 'milked' between the rubber-covered fingers.

†**9.** *nonce-use.* To instil with the mother's milk.

1682 DRYDEN & LEE *Dk. Guise* IV. i. (1683) 39 You..milk'd slow Arts Of Womanish Tameness in my Infant Mouth.

milk-and-water. Milk diluted with water; hence *transf.* and *fig.*

†**1.** The colour of milk and water; a bluish white colour. Also, a kind of cloth of this colour. *Obs.*

1511 *Acc. Ld. High Treas. Scot.* (1902) IV. 245 For iij elnis Franche claith of the new mylk and wattir, to be him ane coit. **1515–16** *Ibid.* (1903) V. 75, xvj elne of claith callit mylk and watter. **1555** in *Beck's Draper's Dict.* (1886) s.v., xj yards of mylke and watter, 18s. **1562** *Richmond. Wills* (Surtees) 152 To Charles my Sone..one clock [cloak] of colour callid milk and watter. **1571** in *Wills & Inv. N.C.* (Surtees) I. 363, xv yeardes of blewe carsay xv^s—j pece of mylk & watter j^l ij^s [etc.].

2. Feeble or insipid discourse; mawkish or weakly amiable sentiment.

1819 BYRON *Let. to Murray* 1 Feb., The discouragement of the milk and water they have thrown upon the First [Canto]. **1844** THACKERAY *Crit. Rev.* Wks. 1886 XXIII. 208 Inspired by that milk-and-water of human kindness. **1867** TROLLOPE *Chron. Barset* II. li. 79 The conversation had had so much of milk-and-water in its composition, that [etc.]

3. *attrib.* as *adj.* Like milk diluted with water; hence 'wishy-washy', insipid, feeble, mawkish, weakly amiable.

1783 *Jrnl. Amer. Congr.* (1823) IV. 209 Change the milk-and-water style of your last memorial; assume a bolder tone. **1823** BYRON *Juan* VIII. xc, All their pretty milk-and-water ways. **1848** THACKERAY *Van. Fair* viii, My rascals are no milk-and-water rascals. **1870** FRISWELL *Mod. Men of Lett.* i. 14 A milk-and-water damsel of the real Dickensian ideal.

Comb. **1864** KIMBALL *Was he successful?* iv. 36 A pale, milk-and-water-looking youth.

Hence **milk-and-'water** *v. intr.*, to feed upon milk and water. Also **milk-and-'waterish, -'watery**, *adjs.*, **milk-and-'wateriness**.

1807 SCOTT *Fam. Lett.* Nov. (1894) I. iii. 87 It..would be giving the signal to build some vile milk-and-waterish legendary tale upon so beautiful a subject. **1819** *Metropolis* II. 94 As milk-and-watery as a Roman senator. **1834** *Westm. Rev.* XX. 268 The ancient beauty.., however, opines in the milk-and-wateriness of her benevolence, that 'an adjustment of the question on this footing would satisfy all reasonable persons'. **1836–9** DICKENS *Sk. Boz, Tuggses at Ramsgate*, Five children milk-and-watering in the parlour. **1865** —— *Mut. Fr.* IV. iii, This gentleman..is more milk and watery with you than I'll be.

milk-cow. Now *dial.* = MILCH-COW 1, 2.

1535 COVERDALE *1 Sam.* vi. 7 Two mylke kyne vpon y^e which there neuer came yock. **1606** *Choice, Chance,* etc. (1881) 48 What a spight it was to see..a milk-cowe to be stung by a hedgehog. **1727** A. HAMILTON *New Acc. E. Ind.* I. xxv. 315 Whether our East-india Company got or lost by that War, I know not..; but this I know, that the Chief lost a good Milk Cow. **1794** W. HUTCHINSON *Hist. Cumberld.* I. 210 *note*, Several farmers keep about twenty milk cows. **1862** CARLYLE *Fredk. Gt.* XIII. i. (1872) V. 5 Hanover was the Britannic Majesty's beloved son; and the British Empire his opulent milk-cow.

milken ('mɪlk(ə)n), *a.* Now *rare* or *Obs.* [f. MILK *sb.*^{1} + -EN^5. OE. had *mylcen*, but the word was prob. formed afresh in the 16th c.]

1. Consisting of milk; *occas.* abounding in milk.

1570 LEVINS *Manip.* 62/39 Mylken, *lacteus.* **1607** R. C[AREW] tr. *Estienne's World of Wonders* 18 The hony and milken riuers. *a* **1618** RALEIGH *Pilgrimage* 16 There will I..drink mine euerlasting fill Vpon euery milken hill. **1677** SIR W. TEMPLE *Gout* in *Misc.* I. (1680) 229 A constant course of the Milken-dyet.

2. Of the colour of milk, milk-white.

a **1586** SIDNEY *Arcadia* IV. (1598) 407 A pretty palenesse (which did leaue milken lines vpon her rosie cheekes). **1633** T. ADAMS *Exp. 2 Peter* i. 16 She [i.e. truth] reacheth forth to us her milken hand.

3. *fig.* Soft, mild, gentle.

1648 GAGE *West. Ind.* v. (1655) 15 A quiet and milken sea. **1650** TRAPP *Comm. Num.* xxxi. 3 Lactantius being (according to his name) a mild and milken man.

4. *milken way, race* = MILKY WAY.

a **1586** SIDNEY *Astr. & Stella* Song v. ii. (1591) G 2 b, I said thy eyes were starres, thy breasts the milken way. **1596** C. FITZ-GEFFREY *Sir F. Drake* F 2 b, O you once matchlesse monarches of the seas, But now aduanced to an higher place..In that faire palace neere the milken race. **1612** BACON *Ess., Fortune* (Arb.) 376 The way of fortune is like the milken way in the skie.

milker ('mɪlkə(r)). [f. MILK *v.* + -ER^1.]

1. One who milks (cows, etc.); one who draws milk from the udders of cattle. ***milker's cramp***, a form of cramp to which milkers are liable.

c **1475** *Pict. Voc.* in Wr.-Wülcker 793/23 *Hic mulsor*, a mylker. **1598** FLORIO, *Caprimulgo*..a milker of goates. **1641** BEST *Farm. Bks.* (Surtees) 134 In hyringe of mayde servants yow are to make choice of such as are good milkers. **1891** T. HARDY *Tess* xvii. (1892) 140 The milkers formed quite a little battalion of men and maids. **1899** *Allbutt's Syst. Med.* VIII. 14 Milker's cramp.

†**2.** = MILT. Cf. MILK *sb.*^{1} 4 and Du. *melker*.

c **1475** *Pict. Voc.* in Wr.-Wülcker 765/26 *Hec lactis*, mylkere.

3. An animal that yields milk, esp. a milch cow. Chiefly with adj., *good, bad*, etc.

1807 A. YOUNG *Agric. Essex* (1813) II. 276 They [Yorkshire cows] are excellent milkers. **1886** *All Year Round* 14 Aug. 34 Weed out the bad milkers, and never keep a cow after her fifth calf. **1891** *Eng. Illustr. Mag.* No. 88. 299 The gentle lowing of the milkers in the stockyard.

4. An apparatus for milking cows mechanically. Also, *cow-milker* (Knight *Dict. Mech.* 1875).

5. One who 'milks' a telegraphic message.

1891 *Cassell's Sat. Jrnl.* Sept. 1036/2.

Hence **'milkeress**, a milkmaid.

1839 *John Bull* 28 July 354/1 The red-elbowed cow-milkeress of Cornwall.

milkful ('mɪlkfʊl), *a. Obs.* exc. *dial.* [f. MILK *sb.*^{1} + -FUL.] Abounding in or replete with milk.

1589 FLEMING *Virg. Georg.* II. 35 Kine downward stretch their milkfull vdders. **1608** SYLVESTER *Du Bartas* II. iv. IV. *Decay* 1053 O Milk-full Vales, with hundred Brooks indented. **1882** J. WALKER *Jaunt to Auld Reekie* 227 Milkful crummies rowtin' up the loans.

milkiness ('mɪlkɪnɪs). [f. MILKY *a.* + -NESS.]

1. The state of being milky; the condition of resembling milk in appearance or quality.

1696 FLOYER *Anim. Humours* viii. 88 The Saltness and Oyliness of the Blood, which absorbing the Acid of the Chyle, it loses its Milkiness. *a* **1722** LISLE *Husb.* (1757) 395 This milkiness of the eyes shows that such sheep are far gone. **1891** *Anthony's Photogr. Bull.* IV. 96 If no milkiness appears, a solution of common washing soda..should be made. **1899** *Allbutt's Syst. Med.* VI. 444 The milkiness [of certain ascitic fluids] is due to the presence of albumin.

b. Of sidereal and meteorological phenomena: Cloudy whiteness.

1791 HERSCHEL in *Phil. Trans.* LXXXI. 77 Among them is..Orionis, a cloudy star..but it does not seem to be connected with the milkiness any more than the rest. **1860** TYNDALL *Glac.* I. xxvii. 196 After which a milkiness slowly stole over the heavens. **1879** NEWCOMB & HOLDEN *Astron.* 458 So distant as to cause the individual stars to disappear in a general milkiness or nebulosity.

2. *fig.* Mildness, softness, gentleness; weakness. (Very common in the 18th c.)

1692 DRYDEN *Cleomenes* I. i. 4 Would I could share thy Balmy, even Temper, And Milkiness of Blood. **1753** SMOLLETT *Cnt. Fathom* (1784) 51/2 One may therefore easily conceive with what milkiness of resignation he bore the loss of the whole. **1768–74** TUCKER *Lt. Nat., Hum. Nat.* xxxiv, There is a softness and milkiness of temper that cannot say nay to any thing. **1864** HAWTHORNE *S. Felton* (1883) 378 The doctor..by no means increasing the milkiness of his mood by frequent applications to the black bottle.

milking ('mɪlkɪŋ), *vbl. sb.* [f. MILK *v.* + -ING^1.] The action of the verb MILK.

1. The drawing of milk from the udders of cows or other animals.

c **1440** *Promp. Parv.* 477/1 Stoppe, vessel for mylkynge, ..*multra.* *c* **1574–5** G. HARVEY *Lett.-bk.* (Camden) 144 P. watchd her going a milking a mile from ye towne. **1834** YOUATT *Cattle* iii. 18 Their qualities may be referred to three points; their working, fattening, and milking. **1860** TYNDALL *Glac.* I. iii. 24 Milking was over when we returned to the châlet.

2. *concr.* The quantity of milk drawn from a cow or from a dairy at one time or operation.

1538 ELYOT *Dict.*, *Mulctra*, the mylkyng, the payle, wherinto it is milked. **1611** COTGR., *Mousson*, a Cowes..milking; as much as she yeelds at a milking. **1850** J. STRUTHERS *Life* Poet. Wks. I. p. xxix, The whole milking went to the floor.

3. *techn.* The steeping of cloth in sour milk during the bleaching process.

1837 WHITTOCK, etc. *Bk. Trades* (1842) 31 The next process is called the milking, or the souring.

4. *attrib.*, as ***milking cow, cramp, gear, machine, pail, pot, -shed, side, †skeel, stool, time, trade, tube, yard, -yoke***; **milking bail** = BAIL *sb.*^{3} 5; **milking-loan** *dial.* (see quot.); **milking-parlour**, a shed specially equipped for milking cows; **milking shorthorn**, a type of shorthorn developed specially for producing milk.

1890 W. H. S. ROBERTS *Hist. Oamaru* 54 A stockyard and *milking-bail had also been erected. **1784** TWAMLEY *Dairying* 97 The people..who buy Cows, always make a large bag in a *Milking Cow their first object. **1890** *Syd. Soc. Lex.*, **Milking-cramp.* **1891** T. HARDY *Tess* xvii. (1892) 145 Without the *milking-gear nobody could have guessed what he was. **1844** H. STEPHENS *Bk. Farm* III. 824 The shepherd or cattle-man taking it as a part of his duty to bring them to a certain spot of the field to be milked, and which is usually named the *milking loan. **1850** *New England Farmer* II. 282 Gutta percha patent *milking machines are in use on Long Island. **1891** *Daily News* 14 Oct. 2/6 A good deal of curiosity was attracted..by Mr. J. Gray's 'milking machine'. **1945** 'G. ORWELL' *Animal Farm* v. 37 A windmill, which could..supply the farm with electrical power..and would also run ..an electric milking machine. **1974** 'E. LATHEN' *Sweet & Low* xiii. 131 Shots of..the dairies,..complete with milking machines. **1548** ELYOT *Dict.*, *Mulctrale*, a *mylkyng payle. **1897** CROCKETT *Lads' Love* xvi, The white streams hissed..into the milking pails. **1946** *Agric. Overseas Rep.* I. 8 The *milking parlour arrangement is only at the experimental stage. **1952** *Blackw. Mag.* Feb. 97/1 A thoroughly sound, commonsense opinion on..a milking-parlour. **1972** *Country Life* 2 Nov. Suppl. 3 The Farm buildings include 2 milking parlours, cubicles for 120, stock yards. **1511** *MS. Acc. St. John's Hosp., Canterb.*, For a new *mylkyng pot jd. ob. *a* **1930** 'H. STONE' in Murdoch & Drake-Brockman *Austral. Short Stories* (1951) 125 It was a silent *milking shed that evening. **1937** *Discovery* July 214/2 The rear parts serve as tool and store sheds, the front as byre and milking-shed. **1970** *Kenya Farmer* Feb. 36/1 'Oh Gawd!' said Fred the farmer as he came stomping up the verandah steps, his boots looking more as if he had walked from Timboroa than from the milking sheds two hundred yards away. **1910** *Encycl. Brit.* V. 539/2 The non-pedigree *milking Shorthorn of the north of England is an excellent cow. **1957** Milking Shorthorn [see *dairy shorthorn* s.v. DAIRY *sb.* 4]. **1844** STEPHENS *Bk. Farm* II. 456 There is one side of a cow which is usually called the *milking side. **1577** *Wills & Inv. N.C.* (Surtees) I. 421 In The Kitchinge And Larder House ..iiij *milken skeales, and one wassinge toobe. **1830** MISS MITFORD *Village* Ser. IV. 103 Her little brother following with the *milking-stool. **1611** SHAKS. *Wint. T.* IV. iv. 246 Is there not *milking-time? **1725** POPE *Odyss.* IX. 263 Full pails, and vessels of the *milking trade. **1881** J. P. SHELDON *Dairy Farm.* 58/1 A silver 'syphon' or '*milking-tube'. **1888** W. SENIOR *Near & Far* 281 The magpie fluted sweetly from the three gum-trees by the *milking-yard. **1910** J. MASEFIELD *Ballads & Poems* 42 Sleepy men bear *milking-yokes Slowly towards the cattle-byre.

milking ('mɪlkɪŋ), *ppl. a. rare.* [f. MILK *v.* + -ING^2.] That milks.

1821 CLARE *Vill. Minstr.* I. 203 Milking maids and boys. **1847** TENNYSON *Princess* v. 213 You did but come as goblins in the night,..Nor burnt the grange, nor buss'd the milking-maid. **1891** T. HARDY *Tess* xxii. (1892) 178 One or two of the milking-men.

†**'milkish**, *a. Obs.* [f. MILK *sb.*^{1} + -ISH.] Milky.

1398 TREVISA *Barth. De P.R.* v. xlv. (1495) 162 Amonge the colours of vryne some bytoken defawte of digestion as white mylkysshe and yelowe. **1698** FRYER *Acc. E. India & P.* 322 The Occidental [pearls] are of a Milkish Colour.

milkless ('mɪlklɪs), *a.* [f. MILK *sb.*^{1} + -LESS.]

1. Having no milk, devoid of milk.

c **1620** Z. BOYD *Zion's Flowers* (1855) 33 The sucklings..Doe from their milklesse mother's brests draw blood. **1816** 'QUIZ' *Grand Master* v. 120 With musty bread, and milkless tea. **1903** *Contemp. Rev.* Mar. 311 Helpless babes were slowly dying at their milkless breasts.

fig. **1643** T. GOODWIN *Child of Light* 179 Hast thou found a promise, which is a breast of consolation, milklesse?

2. *Bot.* Not secreting 'milk' or latex. (Said of certain fungi.)

1871 COOKE *Handbk. Brit. Fungi* I. 217 Russula..Gills nearly equal, milkless, rigid, brittle, with an acute edge.

milk-livered, *a.* Cowardly, 'white-livered'.

1605 SHAKS. *Lear* IV. ii. 50 Milk-Liuer'd man, That bear'st a cheeke for blowes. **1760–72** H. BROOKE *Fool of Qual.* (1809) III. 20 You..hare-hearted, milk-livered poltroon.

'milkmaid. [f. MILK *sb.*^{1} + MAID.]

1. A woman that milks or is employed in a dairy.

1552 HULOET, Mylker or mylke mayde. **1570** FOXE *A. & M.* (ed. 2) 2294/2 Elizabeth..hearyng..a certeine milke-mayde singing pleasauntly, wished her self to be a milke-mayde as she was. **1697** DRYDEN *Virg. Past.* III. 153 In vain the Milk-maid tugs an empty Teat. **1768** BEATTIE *Minstr.* I. xxxix, Crown'd with her pail the tripping milk-maid sings. **1849** JAMES *Woodman* ii, Barons' heirs would be marrying milkmaids.

Comb. *c* **1860** PATMORE in B. Champneys *Mem.* (1900) I. x. §5. 141 So splendid a beauty with so milkmaid-like an absence of pretension.

2. Local or book name of several plants (see quots.).

1853 *Naturalist* III. 225 *Ilex aquifolium albo-pictum*, White-spotted-leaved Common Holly; known also by the name of Milkmaid. **1886** BRITTEN & HOLLAND *Plant-n.* 335 Milk Maid, or Milk Maids (1) *Cardamine pratensis*,..(2) *Stellaria Holostea*,..(3) *Lotus corniculatus*,..(4) The flowers of *Convolvulus sepium*,..(5) *Primula vulgaris*, L. var. (the 'oxlip'). **1887** F. FRANCIS *Saddle & Mocassin* 88 Myriads of daisies and 'milkmaids' powder it [the grass] with snowy flakes.

milkman ('mɪlkmən). [f. MILK *sb.*^{1} + MAN.]

1. A man who sells milk.

1589 RIDER *Bibl. Schol.*, A milke man, *lactarius.* **1656** BLOUNT *Glossogr.*, *Lactary*, a Dairyhouse, and may be used for a Dayry-man, Milk man, or Chees-monger. **1679** *Trials of Green, Berry*, etc. 65 On Friday morning our Milkman came and told us, that one Mr. Godfrey was found murdered. **1838** DICKENS *O. Twist* x, The butcher throws down his tray,..the milk-man his pail.

2. A man who milks cows.
1902 *Contemp. Rev.* Dec. 831 The milkmen had donned their blouses of grey hemp-linen.

†**'milk,meat.** *Obs.* [f. MILK *sb.*¹ + MEAT.] Food made with or from milk.
c **1440** *Promp. Parv.* 338/1 Mylke mete, or mete made wythe mylke. *c* **1450** *Two Cookery-bks.* 106 Milkemete. Take faire mylke and floure [etc.]. **1699** *Phil. Trans.* XXI. 62 The various sorts of Cheese, and some other Milk-Meats, made in Italy. **1764** HARMER *Observ.* x. iv. 154 One would have imagined..the Septuagint would have been at no loss in translating passages which speak of cheese, or in determining what they meant, if some other kind of milk-meats were meant in them.

milkness ('mɪlknɪs). *Obs.* exc. *Sc. dial.* [f. MILK *sb.*¹ + -NESS.] The aggregate yield of milk of a cow, ewe, etc., or of a dairy of milking cattle. Also milk and its products generally, dairy produce.
1492 *Acta Dom. Concil.* (1839) 289/2 The saidis personis sall..pay..for þe proffit of þe mylkness of þe said five ky [etc.]. *Ibid.*, For þe proffit of þe mylknes of þe said iiijˣˣ of ȝowis be þe said thre ȝeris xlviij stane of cheiss, price of þe stane ijs. **1536** BELLENDEN *Cron. Scot.* (1821) I. 46 The residew of the Scottis..debaitit thair miserabill liffis,..with scars and hard fude; levand, in the somer, on milknes,..and in the winter, of wild flesche of the montanis. **1674** in *Proc. Soc. Ant. Scot.* (1896) XXX. 19 At least ane stirk to be brought up betwixt each twa [cows], reserving to the said persones the milkness. **1678** *Ibid.* 21 Reserving ther milknes to the said Duncane. *a* **1774** FERGUSSON *Drink Ecl.* Poems (1845) 52 Crummie nae mair for Jenny's hand will crune Wi milkness dreepin' frae her teats adown. **1842** J. AITON *Dom. Econ.* (1857) 89 Meat very soon communicates a taint to milkness in all its states of..preservation.

milko ('mɪlkəʊ), *sb.* and *int.* Also **milk-o, milk-oh.** [f. MILK *sb.*¹ + O *int.*] **A.** *sb.* A milkman. *slang.*
1911 *Answers* 11 Feb. 362/3 Milk-O! on the Make... Many of the milk-o! fraternity boast [of]..their..stealings. **1933** *Bulletin* (Sydney) 31 May 12/1 It is difficult to imagine a man looking like Il Duce while filling a billycan, but I have seen our milko perform the feat. *Ibid.* 5 July 20/3 One of Sydney's milk-ohs. **1958** *Daily Mail* 25 Oct. 5/2 The milko ..has become the *milk salesman.* **1968** D. IRELAND *Chantic Bird* i. 6, I remember the milk tap I turned on in old Bay Road, the milko chased me all the way home.
B. *int.* A shout made by a milkman to indicate that milk is available.
1916 'TAFFRAIL' *Pincher Martin* xii. 232 'E wus drivin' one o' these 'ere milk-carts an' shoutin' 'Milk-o!' artside th' 'ouses. **1967** L. DEIGHTON *London Dossier* 132 The milkman shouting 'milko' as he leaves milk on a doorstep.

,milk-'punch. A drink made of spirits mixed with milk, etc.
1704 T. POCOCK in *Torrington Mem.* (Camden) 181 He treated me this evening with a bowl of milk punch. **1764** ELIZ. MOXON *Eng. Housew.* 153 To make Milk Punch. Take two quarts of old milk, a quart of good brandy, the juice of six lemons or oranges,..and about six ounces of loaf sugar, mix them altogether [etc.]. **1837** DICKENS *Pickw.* l, It smells, I think, like milk-punch.

'milksile. *Obs.* exc. *dial.* Also 5 **-sele, -syle.** [f. MILK *sb.*¹ + SILE. Cf. *milk-sye*, MILSEY.]
1. A strainer for milk. (See *E.D.D.*)
1459 *Durham Acc. Rolls* (Surtees) 89, j Milksyle.
2. *lady's milksile*: the milkmaid, *Cardamine pratensis* (Britten & Holland, 1886).

'milk-snake. [See quot. 1863.] A handsome colubrine snake, *Ophibolus eximius*, common in many localities in the United States.
1842 HOLBROOK *N. Amer. Herpetol.* III. 69 *Coluber eximius*..House Snake or Milk Snake, *Vulgo.* **1863** WOOD *Nat. Hist.* III. 131 The Milk Snake, or House Snake (*Coluber eximius*) is common in many parts of North America, and has derived its popular names from its habit of entering houses and its fondness for milk, which some persons fancy it obtains from the cows.

'milksop. [f. MILK *sb.*¹ + SOP *sb.*]
†1. A piece of bread soaked in milk. *Obs. rare.*
c **1420** *Liber Cocorum* (1862) 53 Melle white brede in dysshes aboute, Powre in wellyd mylke, with outen doute, Þat called is mylke soppys in serves For Satyrday at nyȝt.
†**b.** *fig.* in *pl.* 'Soft sayings'. *Obs.*
1577 HANMER *Anc. Eccl. Hist.* 71 Lingering in their milksoppes and smoothe Exhortacions.
†**c.** *milksop dishes*, dishes made of 'milkmeats'.
1628 EARLE *Microcosm.* (Arb.) 47 Quaking Tarts and quiuering Custards, and such milke sop Dishes.
2. †**a.** An infant not advanced beyond a milk diet. *Obs. rare.*
c **1460** *Towneley Myst.* xii. 469 *Secundus pastor.* hayll, lytyll tyn mop..hayll lytyll mylk sop! hayll, dauid sede!
b. *fig.* An effeminate spiritless man or youth; one wanting in courage or manliness.
[**1246–56** in *35th Rep. Dep. Kpr. Rec.* (1874) App. 17 A villein called Robert Milcsop.] *c* **1386** CHAUCER *Monk's Prol.* 22 Allas she seith that euere þat I was shape To wedden a Milksope or a coward ape. **1568** GRAFTON *Chron.* II. 847 The Erle of Richmond Capitayne of thys rebellion, he is a Welshe milksop. *a* **1619** FLETCHER, etc. *Knt. Malta* II. i, Thou milksop,..canst thou feare to see A few light hurts, that blush they are no bigger? **1749** FIELDING *Tom Jones* XI. vii, I ought to be d—n'd for having spoiled one of the prettiest fellows in the world, by making a milk-sop of him. **1876** L. STEPHEN *Eng. Th. in 18th C.* II. 377 Fielding has a contempt for Richardson as a milksop.

c. *attrib.* and *Comb.*
1549 CHALONER *Erasm. on Folly* Pij, Farre more milke-soplyke and womannishe to cast foorth teares. **1750** *Student* I. 141 The milksop looks and mincing steps of the pretty gentlemen. *a* **1839** PRAED *Poems* (1864) II. 97 Like a fool Ripe from a milksop boarding-school.
Hence **'milksoppishness, 'milksopism,** the characteristics of a milksop. **'milksopping** *a.*, imbued with 'milksopism'. **'milksoppy** *a.* = MILKSOPPING.
1832 J. WILSON in *Blackw. Mag.* XXXII. 392 This new dandyfied era of milksoppism. **1888** STEVENSON *Black Arrow* I. ii, Y'are a milk-sopping baby, so to harp on women. **1871** T. A. TROLLOPE *Durnton Abbey* II. viii. 126, 'I think I won't take any brandy this morning', said Reginald, blushing painfully at the consciousness of his milk-soppishness in this respect. **1886** G. ALLEN *Maimie's Sake* xi, About eighty-seven per cent. of male humanity belongs absolutely to the milksoppy section.

milkstone ('mɪlkstəʊn). [f. MILK *sb.*¹ + STONE.]
1. A name for various white stones (see quots.).
1856 MAYNE *Expos. Lex., Milk-Stone.* Common name for the *Galactites.* **1860** PIESSE *Lab. Chem. Wonders* 2 Two rounded whitish flint pebbles such as boys call milk-stones. **1890** *Syd. Soc. Lex., Milk-stone.* Same as *Galactites.* Also, the same as *Morochthus.*
2. **a.** *Path. pl.* 'Hard concretions resulting from the retention or extravasation of milk in the breast, and its gradual inspissation and calcification by the absorption of its watery constituent' (*Syd. Soc. Lex.* 1890).
b. A hard deposit formed in or on dairy equipment by precipitation from milk.
1949 *N.Z. Jrnl. Agric.* Nov. 487/2 Milkstone is the casein of milk which has become attached to metal in the form of encrustations. **1963** *New Scientist* 14 Nov. 387 The alloy resisted the build-up of 'milkstone' better than polished stainless steel.

'milk-tooth. One of a temporary set of mammalian teeth which are replaced by the permanent teeth (cf. *milk-canine, molar*, etc.).
1727–52 CHAMBERS *Cycl.* s.v. *Tooth*, Twelve foal-teeth or milk-teeth [of a horse]. **1835** *Todd's Cycl. Anat.* I. 68/1 The milk teeth..by the end of the seventh year have given way to the..permanent series. **1886** C. SCOTT *Sheep Farming* 15 At a month old a lamb will have eight incisors or milk teeth, which are temporary.

milk-warm, *a.* Of the approximate temperature of milk fresh-drawn from the cow; new-milk warm.
c **1410** *Master of Game* (MS. Digby 182) xii, Caste þer in oyle of camamyle mylke warme III. dropes. *a* **1608** DEE *Relat. Spir.* I. (1659) 253 The first part let her drink (being milk warm) by little and little. **1766** SMOLLETT *Trav.* II. xxxii. 135 They had baths of cool water for the summer: but in general they used it milk-warm. **1837** *Flemish Husb.* 62 in *Libr. Usef. Knowl., Husb.* III, This mess is given milk-warm to the calf. **1894** KIPLING *Seven Seas* (1896) 36 Milk-warm wi' breath o' spice an' bloom. **1918** A. HUXLEY *Defeat of Youth* 34 At your mouth, white and milk-warm sphinx. **1922** —— *Mortal Coils* 177 Shelley had been drowned in this milk-warm sea.

milkweed ('mɪlkwiːd). [f. MILK *sb.*¹ + WEED *sb.*]
1. A name given to certain British wild plants with milky juice. **a.** The sow-thistle, *Sonchus oleraceus.* **b.** The brimstone-wort, *Peucedanum palustre*; called also *marsh milkweed.* **c.** The sun-spurge, *Euphorbia Helioscopia.*
1598 FLORIO *Worlde of Wordes* 199/2 Lattaria, herbe Tithimale, spurge or milk-weede. **1706** PHILLIPS (ed. Kersey), *Milk Weed.* **1736** AINSWORTH *Lat. Dict.*, Milk weed, *Sonchos* vel *sonchus.* **1796** WITHERING *Brit. Plants* (ed. 3) II. 293 *Selinum sylvestre*..Marsh Milkweed. *Ibid.* III. 675 *Sonchus oleraceus*... Sowthistle... Milkweed. **1955** G. GRIGSON *Englishman's Flora* 227 Sun Spurge... Milk-weed, Ess[ex], Herts, E[ast] Ang[lia]. *Ibid.* 392 Sow Thistle... Milkweed, Som[erset].
2. Any plant of the North American genus *Asclepias*, esp. *A. syriaca* or *Cornuti*, the common milkweed or silkweed of the United States, which has a copious milky juice, and seeds tufted with long silky hairs. *green milkweed*, the asclepiadaceous genus *Acerates.*
1814 J. BIGELOW *Florula Bostoniensis* 62 *Asclepias Syriaca*, Common Silk weed or Milk weed,..is used as a substitute for feathers, fur, cotton, &c. **1845–50** MRS. LINCOLN *Lect. Bot.* App. 77 *Asclepias syriaca* (common milkweed). **1860** GRAY *Man. Bot. U.S.* 354 *Acerates*, Green Milkweed. **1923** W. CATHER *Lost Lady* 17 The silvery milkweed was just coming on.
attrib. **1854** THOREAU *Walden* 252 One very calm October after noon, for such days especially they settle on to the lakes, like the milkweed down, having looked in vain over the pond for a loon, suddenly one, sailing out from the shore .., set up his wild laugh. **1860** GRAY *Man. Bot. U.S.* 350 *Asclepiadaceæ* (Milkweed Family). **1862** LOWELL *Biglow P.* Ser. II. No. vi, While Fancy's cushin'..Makes the hard bench ez soft ez milkweed-down. **1933** M. DE LA ROCHE *Master of Jalna* vii. 69 A milkweed pod having burst, its hoard was released and the silvery particles,..swam delicately on the light breeze. **1957** L. EISELEY *Immense Journey* 69 There passed before my eyes the million airy troopers of the milkweed pod. **1968** *Times* 2 Oct. 12/5 Butterflies reared on the milkweed species Asclepias curassavica.
3. In names of various North American insects feeding on milkweed: **milkweed beetle,** a brightly coloured beetle, *Tetraopes tetraophthalmus*; **milkweed bug,** either of two species of bugs of the family Lygæidæ, *Oncopeltus fasciatus*, the large milkweed bug, or *Lygæus kalmi*, the small milkweed bug; **milkweed butterfly** = MONARCH *sb.*¹ 3.
1842 T. W. HARRIS *Insects Injurious to Vegetation* 455/2 *Milk-weed beetle. **1954** BORROR & DELONG *Introd. Study Insects* xxii. 398 *T[etraopes] tetraophthalmus* Forster is a common species feeding on milkweed, and is often called the red milkweed beetle. **1905** V. L. KELLOGG *Amer. Insects* x. 211 The *milkweed-bug, *Oncopeltus fasciatus*, about ⅝ inch long, orange above with most of head and prothorax except the margins black, and a broad black band across the middle of the fore wings and large black blotch on their tips, is a common showy bug on various species of milkweed. **1970** *Nature* 3 Jan. 82/1 We have treated eggs of the milkweed bug, *Oncopeltus fasciatus*, with a juvenile hormone analogue. **1972** SWAN & PAPP *Common Insects N. Amer.* xii. 125 In the Small Milkweed Bug, *L[ygæus] kalmi*, the black on the pronotum is separated from the black on the front of the wings. **1974** *Nature* 12 Apr. 556/3 Experiments in this same general field carried out on the milkweed bug *Oncopeltus.* **1889** *Insect Life* I. 221 The following is a brief account of a migratory movement of enormous numbers of the common so-called *Milk-weed Butterfly. **1906** R. SOUTH *Butterflies Brit. Isles* 107 The actual number of specimens of the Milkweed, or, as it is sometimes called, Monarch butterfly, seen or caught in England..does not much exceed thirty. **1972** *Country Life* 6 Apr. 846/1 The milkweed or monarch butterfly is a denizen of North America.

'milk-white, *a.* **a.** White as milk.
Usually employed in the sense of 'pure white'; for a proposed use in botanical descriptions, see quot. 1839.
?*c* **1000** *Prudent. Gloss.* in *Germania* N.S. XI. 389/70 Of meolc hwyttre, *lacteo. Ibid.* 397/32 Meolchwitum, *lacteis.* *c* **1205** LAY. 15938 þe oder [drake] is milc-whit. *c* **1325** *Chron. Eng.* 621 (Ritson) Thre hondred steden mylk-whyte. **1595** *Alcilia* (1879) 19 The snow, Whose milke-white mantell ouerspreeds the ground. **1639** T. DE GRAY *Compl. Horsem.* 59 The horse which is milke-white. **1718** PRIOR *Dove* 78 Her blushing face the lovely maid Rais'd just above the milk-white sheet. **1808** SCOTT *Marm.* IV. vii, On milk-white palfrey forth he paced. **1839** LINDLEY *Introd. Bot.* 477 Milk-white..; dull white verging to blue. **1890** 'R. BOLDREWOOD' *Col. Reformer* (1891) 154 A broad, milk-white beach received the vast rollers.
absol. **1683** A. SNAPE *Anat. Horse* I. i. (1686) 2 The Horse will be of a milk-white or yellow-dun.
†**b.** *milk white way* = MILKY WAY. *Obs.*
1555 EDEN *Decades* 94 The tracte of heauen cauled *Lactea via*, that is the mylke whyte waye. **1594** *Taming of a Shrew* (1607) D 3 b, As faire as is the milke white way of Ioue. **1594** BLUNDEVIL *Exerc.* IV. xix. (1636) 475 Having described unto you..as many stars as are named in the Globe, and also the milkewhite way [etc.].

milkwort ('mɪlkwɜːt). [f. MILK *sb.*¹ + WORT.]
1. Any plant of the genus *Polygala*, formerly supposed to increase the milk of nurses; esp. *Polygala vulgaris*, a common British plant bearing racemes of very irregular bright blue or sometimes pink or white flowers. *bitter milkwort*: the *Polygala amara* (*Treas. Bot.* 1866).
1578 LYTE *Dodoens* I. xxxiii. 48 There be two kyndes of Mylkewurte, differing both in name and figure: whereof one is called *Glaux*, and the other *Polygala.* **1597** GERARDE *Herbal* II. clx. 448 Of Milkewoorte. **1671** SALMON *Syn. Med.* III. xxii. 420 Polygala Πολυγαλον Milkwort, a handful steeped all night in white wine..purgeth Choller. **1759** B. STILLINGFLEET tr. *Gedner's Use Curios.* in *Misc. Tracts* (1762) 191 No physician would have even suspected, that our milkwort would be usefull in the bite of serpents,.. unless the principles of botany had led him to it. **1873** MISS THACKERAY *Wks.* (1891) I. 70 Dandelions and milk-wort among the beds.
2. A primulaceous plant, *Glaux maritima*, common on the sea-coast and in salt marshes. Also *sea milkwort.*
1578 LYTE *Dodoens* I. xxxiii. 48 *Glaux.* Milkewurte, or sea Tryfoly. **1597** GERARDE *Herbal* II. clix. 448 The true *Glaux* or Milkwoort groweth very plentifully in salt places and marshes neere the sea. *Ibid.*, It shall suffice to call it in English Sea Milkewoort. **1640** PARKINSON *Theat. Bot.* Index 1741/2 Blacke Milkewort, or Sea Milkewort.
3. (*Our*) *Lady's milkwort*: lungwort, *Pulmonaria officinalis.*
1578 LYTE *Dodoens* I. lxxxv. 125 We call it in English.. Cowslip of Ierusalem:..in base Almaigne Onser vrouwen melck cruyt,..that is to say, Our Ladies Milkeworte, bycause the leaues be full of white spottes.
4. Any plant of the genus *Euphorbia.*
1640 PARKINSON *Theat. Bot.* 184 *Tithymalus sive Lactaria.* Spurge or Milkeworte. **1753** CHAMBERS *Cycl. Supp.* Add., *Milk-wort*, or *Wart-wort*, is also a name sometimes given to the *Euphorbia.* **1886** BRITTEN & HOLLAND *Plant-Names* App., Milkwort, *Euphorbia Helioscopia* and other species (Essex).
5. *pl.* Name for the root of *Campanula rotundifolia* (Jam. 1880).

milky ('mɪlkɪ), *a.* [f. MILK *sb.*¹ + -Y.]
1. **a.** Having the appearance of milk, or of water into which milk has been dropped. Also (chiefly *poet.*), resembling milk in colour, milk-white.
milky-white: in poetical use = MILK-WHITE; in prose use, rather, white resembling that of milk diffused through water.
1384 [see MILKY WAY]. **1398** TREVISA *Barth. De P.R.* XV. lxvi. (1495) 511 Sibel callyth frensshmen, Galles, that is whyte and sayd that in one yere mylky neckes shall be mynyd. **1567** MAPLET *Gr. Forest* 76 The Caladrius sayth

Aristotle is of milkie colour, without any black spot. **1653** *Nissena* 8 Lips of Coral.. Eyes brighter then the Sun, Milky hands; such.. were the ravishing graces. **1697** DRYDEN *Virg. Georg.* III. 600 With Fleeces milky white. **1758** REID tr. *Macquer's Chym.* I. 395 With regard to the white powder that renders the solution milky.. it is nothing but a portion of the Lead. **1791** HERSCHEL in *Phil. Trans.* LXXXI. 81 A star with a pretty strong milky nebulosity. *Ibid.* 85 Tinged with milky nebulosity. **1818–20** E. THOMPSON tr. *Cullen's Nosol. Method.* (ed. 3) 226 A milky humour like chyle. **1850** TENNYSON *In Mem.* cxiv, The flocks are whiter down the vale, And milkier every milky sail. **1859** —— *Geraint & Enid* 150 A hart Taller than all his fellows, milky-white. **1869** G. LAWSON *Dis. Eye* (1874) 157 A piece of tough milky white looking lens capsule. **1878** HUXLEY *Physiogr.* 82 The liquid becomes milky as the carbonic acid gas.. bubbles through. **1883** *Times* 27 Aug. 8/3 The whole of the bay wore a milky look.

b. said of the juices of plants and fruits.

1577 B. GOOGE *Heresbach's Husb.* II. (1586) 109 b, The sappe.. in the Figge tree.. is milkie. **1660** HICKERINGILL *Jamaica* (1661) 24 The Coco Nuts.. in whose content, is barrell'd up.. a milky liquor. **1766** *Compl. Farmer* s.v. *Sap*, In plants, particularly in such as abound with a milky sap. **1855** SIR E. SMITH in *Syst. Nat. Hist.* I. 30 The *latex*, or milky fluid, is of immense service to man. *Ibid.* 31 The following is the mode in which the India-rubber is prepared from the milky juice. **1884** BOWER & SCOTT *De Bary's Phaner.* 184 The slightly milky latex.

c. *Path. milky ascites*: that variety of ascites in which the contained fluid is milky.

1899 *Allbutt's Syst. Med.* VI. 449 Such cases [of ascites] are described as milky, non-fatty ascites.

2. Of or consisting of milk. *rare.*

1552 HULOET, Milkye meates, or meates made of milke. *Lactaria.* **1697** DRYDEN *Virg. Georg.* III. 482 The salacious Goat.. twice as largely yields her milky Store. **1791** MRS. RADCLIFFE *Rom. Forest* III. xxvi. 339 Several peasant girls.. were dispensing the milky feast.

3. a. Containing, abounding in, or yielding milk.

1641 J. JACKSON *True Evang. T.* II. 103 The milkie fruitfulnesse of the Cow. **1675** G. R. tr. *Le Grand's Man without Passion* 36 When those two Milky Mountains become one double bag full of Blood, they are no more desired by men. **1714** GAY *Sheph. Week* Mon. 78 As my Buxoma.. With gentle finger stroked her milky care. **1870** BRYANT *Iliad* IX. 272 Argos, richly stocked In milky kine.

b. *Bot.* Yielding milk-like juice.

1765 G. WASHINGTON *Diaries* (1925) I. 210 Note, the [mulberry] Stocks were very Milkey. **1768** *Ibid.* 282 Some [wheat] whose straw and head was green but the grain of full size and Milky. **1789** J. MORSE *Amer. Geogr.* 52 About the time that it begins to turn from its milky state and to ripen, they run their canoes into the midst of it. **1861** BENTLEY *Man. Bot.* 583 The Goodenia Order.—Herbs or rarely shrubs, not milky. *Ibid.*, The Stylewort Order.—Herbs or under-shrubs, not milky. **1884** BOWER & SCOTT *De Bary's Phaner.* 432 In milky plants provided with phloemportions.. these also are accompanied by laticiferous tubes.

c. Of food: Promoting the secretion of milk.

1886 C. SCOTT *Sheep Farming* 50 Cabbages.. are also preferable.. for ewes at lambing time, and are very 'milky'.

d. Of an oyster: Full of spawn. Cf. MILK *sb.* 8 b.

1865 *Chambers's Encycl.* VII. 324/1.

4. *transf.* and *fig.* **a.** Of persons, their actions, attributes, etc. Soft, gentle; in bad sense, timorous, effeminate, weakly amiable; also (*slang*), cowardly.

1602 *2nd Pt. Return fr. Parnass.* I. iv. (Arb.) 17 See what a little vermine pouerty altereth a whole milkie disposition. **1607** SHAKS. *Timon* III. i. 57 Has friendship such a faint and milkie heart, It turnes in lesse then two nights? **1658** MANTON *Exp. Jude* 20 Peter writeth in a milky, sweet, middle way. **1764** FOOTE *Patron* III. Wks. 1799 I. 352 If you find the audience too indulgent, inclined to be milky, [etc.]. **1782** MRS. H. COWLEY *Bold Stroke for Husb.* I. ii, I long to set a pattern to those milky wives, whose mean compliances degrade the sex. **1813** BYRON 5 Sept. in Moore *Lett. & Jrnls.* (1830) I. 426 They made.. me (the milkiest of men) a satirist. **1883** J. PARKER *Tyne Ch.* 3 People who.. spoke a soft and milky language. **1884** W. C. SMITH *Kildrostan* 92, I hate Your meek and milky girls, that dare not kiss A burning passion, clinging to your lips. **1936** J. CURTIS *Gilt Kid* ii. 18 They just talk that way to make you turn milky. **1938** G. GREENE *Brighton Rock* II. i. 62 I'm not milky... I just don't want another killing. **1954** 'N. BLAKE' *Whisper in Gloom* xvi. 217 Look at da kid. He's not milky. **1969** H. CARVIC *Miss Seeton draws Line* ix. 171 'Getting milky?' scoffed Doris.

b. Of a noise, song, etc.: soft. *poet.*

1924 E. SITWELL *Sleeping Beauty* x. 38 Goats gold as wheat With a kind white milky bleat. **1925** —— *Troy Park* 76 A white bird sang a milky song Of easy heaven and feathered rest.

5. *Comb.*, as ***milky-coloured, -farinaceous, -looking, -sapped, -toothed, -watery*** adjs.; **milky cap**, one of the gill-bearing fungi, *Russula lactea*; †**milky circle**, the milky way; **milky-fever, -hedge, -parsley, -scall, -sea** = *milk-fever, -hedge*, etc. (see MILK *sb.* 10, 10 b); **milky tree** = COW-TREE 1.

1887 HAY *Brit. Fungi* 112 *Russula lactea*, The *Milky-cap. **1646** SIR T. BROWNE *Pseud. Ep.* VII. iv. 346 The Galaxia or *milky Circle. **1906** W. B. YEATS *Poems 1899–1905* 268 Hold up your hands to him, that you may pluck That *milky-coloured neck out of the noose. **1896** *Allbutt's Syst. Med.* I. 411 The most satisfactory diet.. is a *milky-farinaceous one. **1747** tr. *Astruc's Fevers* 355 A fever, with a swelling of the breasts can be taken for no other than a *milky fever. **1797** *Encycl. Brit.* (ed. 3) XII. 23/2 **Milky-Hedge*, the English name of a shrub growing on the coast of Coromandel. **1862** MILLER *Elem. Chem., Org.* (ed. 2) 268 A *milky-looking fluid or emulsion. **1640** PARKINSON *Theat. Bot.* 928, I have entituled it.. Wild *milkie Parsley. **1759** MILLER *Gard. Dict.* (ed. 7) s.v. *Selinum*, Milky Parsley. **1923** D. H. LAWRENCE *Birds, Beasts & Flowers* 19 Folded upon itself.. And *milky-sapped, sap that curdles milk and makes *ricotta*. **1822–34** *Good's Study Med.* (ed. 4) IV. 487 Whence the French name of *croute de lait* and our own of *milky scall. **1871** KINGSLEY *At Last* i, That most rare and unexplained phenomenon of a '*milky sea'. **1905** E. F. BENSON *Image in Sand* i. 2 Brown-faced, *milky-toothed Arabs were there. **1666** J. DAVIES *Hist. Caribby Isles* 49 Others have venemous qualities, as the *Milkie tree. **1886** J. R. REES *Pleas. Bk.-Worm* v. 168 Languishing *milky-watery young men.

Hence **'milkily** *adv. rare.*

1881 WATSON in *Jrnl. Linn. Soc.* XV. 247 The shell is milkily transparent. **1903** N. MUNRO in *Blackw. Mag.* June 813/2 The byre was warm and odorous milkily.

milky ('mılkı), *sb. slang.* Also **milkie.** [f. MILK *sb.*[1] + -Y[6], -IE.] A familiar or nursery name for: (*a*) a milkman or milk-boy; (*b*) milk.

1886 H. BAUMANN *Londinismen* 108/1 *Milky*, milkman. **1922** JOYCE *Ulysses* 363 Go home to nicey bread and milky and say night prayers with the kiddies. **1923** 'R. CROMPTON' *William Again* xii. 203 ''Ello, kids!' said the milk-boy... ''Ello, Milky!' **1946** P. H. SIMPSON *If you'd care to Know* 134 Box in which the 'milkie' places the bottled milk. **1966** 'L. LANE' *ABZ of Scouse* 68 She keeps her milkie on ther doorstep fer ars (hours). **1975** *Evening News* 21 Apr. 4/4 He appeared his normal easy-going self and all he said to me was, 'Hullo milkie.'

Milky Way. [f. MILKY *a.* + WAY *sb.*, transl. of L. *via lactea*. Cf. *milk way* (MILK *sb.*[1] 10).]

1. = GALAXY 1.

c **1384** CHAUCER *H. Fame* II. 429 Se yonder loo the Galoxie Whiche men clepeth the melky weye. **1551** RECORDE *Cast. Knowl.* (1556) 105 The Milkye way in heauen, which many men in England do call Watlyng streete. **1615** CROOKE *Body of Man* 455 As we thinke the *via lactea* or Milky Way in heauen is occasioned by an infinite number of small starres. **1732** POPE *Ess. Man* I. 102 Far as the solar walk, or milky way. **1868** LOCKYER *Elem. Astron.* i. §1 (1879) 11 This belt is the Milky Way.

2. *fig.* and allusively. **a.** A way brilliant in appearance, or leading to heaven. Also *attrib.*

1649 W. M. *Wandering Jew* (1857) 56 The path to Heaven is a milky way; not a bloudy. **1670** EACHARD *Cont. Clergy* 60 Goodness is the milkey-way to Jupiter's palace. **1851** H. MELVILLE *Moby Dick* I. xl. 291 Leaving a milky-way wake of creamy foam. **1916** D. H. LAWRENCE *Amores* 93 Pleiads of people are Deployed around me, and I see The street's long outstretched Milky Way.

†**b.** *poet.* The region of a woman's breast. *Obs.*

1622 WITHER *Fair Virtue* E, Whatsoeuer others say, There's alone the Milkie-way, That to beauties walkes doth goe. **1630** DRUMM. OF HAWTH. *Flowres Sion* 48 From her heauie Eyne Along her Cheekes distilling christall Brine, Which downe-wards to her yuorie Brest was driuen, And had bedewed the milkie-Way of Heauen. *a* **1704** T. BROWN *On Beauties* Wks. 1730 I. 43 Two snowy mounts, so near her heart... Between those hills, a milky way there leads. **1721** RAMSAY *Tartana* 243 Behold her heav'nly face and heaving milky way.

mill (mıl), *sb.*[1] Forms: *α.* 1 **mylen**, 1–2, 6–7 **myln**, 3–7 **mulne**, 4–7 **mylne**, 5 **myllne**, **myllen**, 7, 8–9 *dial.* **miln**; *β.* 1 **myll**, 3–4 **mulle**, 4 **mille**, 4–5 **mylle**, 4–6 **melle**, 5 **myl**, 6–7 **myl(l**, 6– **mill**. [OE. *mylen* masc. and fem.:—prehistoric **mulīno-*, **mulīna*, a. late L. *molīnum*, *molīna* (whence F. *moulin*, Pr. *molin-s*, *moli-s*, Sp. *molino*, Pg. *moinho*, It. *mulino*, *molino*), f. *mola* mill, f. *mol-* root of *molĕre* to grind: see MEAL *sb.*[1] The late L. word was early adopted into the other Teut. langs.: cf. MDu. *molene* fem. (Du. *molen*, †*meulen* masc.), OHG. *muli(n* fem. (MHG. *mül*, mod.G. *mühle*), ON. *mylna* fem., perh. from Eng. (Sw. *mölla*, Da. *mølle*).

For the loss of the *n* cf. *kiln*, in most dialects pronounced (kıl).]

1. a. A building specially designed and fitted with machinery for the grinding of corn into flour. Also forming the second element in certain obvious combinations, as *water-*, *wind-mill*, *flour-*, *grist mill*, many of which are treated under the first element.

c **961** ÆTHELWOLD *Rule St. Benet* lxvi. (Schröer 1885) 127 þæt is wæterscype, mylen [*c* **1020** (Logeman) myll], wyrtun and ʒehwylce misenlice cræftas [etc.]. **982** in Kemble *Cod. Dipl.* III. 189 Se mylenham and se myln ðærto. *a* **1100** *Gerefa* in *Anglia* (1886) IX. 261 Faldian, fiscwer and mylne macian. *a* **1225** *Ancr. R.* 88 Vrom mulne & from cheping, from smiðe, & from ancre huse, me tiðinge bringeð. **13..** *Gaw. & Gr. Knt.* 2203 What! hit wharred, & whette, as water at a mulne. *c* **1374** CHAUCER *Former Age* 6 Onknowyn was þe quyerne and ek the melle. *c* **1400** *Destr. Troy* 1604 There were bild by the bankes of þe brode stremes, Mylnes full mony. **1426** LYDG. *De Guil. Pilgr.* 5422 Thys greyn was to the melle brouht. **1481** CAXTON *Godeffroy* xx. 51 They sawe vij myllenes, whiche stode at brygge nyghe the town and sette them a fyre. **1568** GRAFTON *Chron.* II. 526 A Miller that kept a Mill adioinyng to the wall. **1601** FULBECKE *1st Pt. Parall.* (1602) 39 She shal not so be indowed of a milne, but shall haue the third part of the profit of the milne, because the milne cannot be seuered. *a* **1632** G. HERBERT *Jac. Prudent.* 153 The mill cannot grind with the water that's past. *a* **1766** J. CUNNINGHAM *Miller* 2 In a plain pleasant cottage, conveniently neat, With a mill and some meadows. **1770** GOLDSM. *Des. Vill.* 11 The never-failing brook, the busy mill. **1818** CRUISE *Digest* (ed. 2) VI. 496 Edward Manning being possessed of the moiety of a mill for the term of fifty years, made his will. **1903** *Blackw. Mag.* Sept. 365/1 A leet.. whose waters work the mill below.

b. In figurative and other phrases. ***to draw water to (one's) mill***: to seize every advantage. ***to go (pass, etc.) through the mill***: to pass through a definite course of labour or experience; similarly, ***to put through the mill. to bring more sacks to the mill***: to supplement argument with argument or weight with weight. ***much water runs by the mill that the miller knows not of***: many things happen before us of which we know nothing.

1522 SKELTON *Why nat to Court?* 107 They may garlycke pyll Cary sackes to the myll. **1546** J. HEYWOOD *Prov.* (1867) 60 Muche water goeth by the myll, That the miller knowth not of. **1590** NASHE *Pasquil's Apol.* I. C ij b, To the next, to the next, more sacks to the Myll. **1622** MABBE tr. *Aleman's Guzman D'Alf.* I. (1630) 136 When there was nothing to be done at home, your Lackies.. would.. fright me with Snakes, hang on my backe, & weigh me downe, crying, More sackes to the Mill. **1649** HOWELL *Pre-em. Parl.* 10 Lewis the eleventh.. could well tell how to play his game, and draw water to his owne Mill. **1677** W. HUGHES *Man of Sin* II. viii. 118 The Invention of bringing more water to the Popes Mill. **1818** SCOTT *Heart Midl.* in *Tales my Landlord* 2nd Ser. III. iv. 96 Frank here won't hear of our putting her through the mill. **1837** *Knickerbocker* IX. 356, I had been 'through the mill' of a pre-concerted, artificial revival. **1840** R. H. DANA *Two Yrs. before Mast* 50 I've been through the mill. **1868** H. WOODRUFF *Trotting Horse* vi. 76 It was thought that they would be ruined for service if they were 'put through the mill'. **1887** *Contemp. Rev.* Jan. 10 Certain persons who have gone through the mill of what is known as our 'higher education'. **1890** 'R. BOLDREWOOD' *Col. Reformer* (1891) 147 Going to do wonders, and make important changes. That will wear off—we've all passed through that mill. **1903** G. GISSING *Private Papers H. Ryecroft* 138 His hardships were never excessive; they did not affect his health or touch his spirits; probably he is in every way a better man for having.. 'gone through the mill'. **1904** J. C. LINCOLN *Cap'n Eri* ii. 29 Jerry's the only one of us three that's been through the mill. **1940** H. READ *Annals of Innocence* II. i. 75 A boy who is destined to be a teacher, a doctor, a technician or a scientist, must go through the mill and acquire the necessary qualifications. **1959** I. & P. OPIE *Lore & Lang. Schoolch.* x. 200 *Running the Gauntlet.* Although well known by this name, the ordeal is also termed.. 'Through the Mill'. **1965** *Listener* 1 July 21/1, I am a collector—and one who has gone through the mill. I started.. in the basement with bus tickets.

c. A mechanical apparatus, whether simple or complicated, for grinding corn.

Not found until the 16th century; the quots. 1535 hardly prove its currency, as Luther, whom Coverdale very often follows, has *mühle* in both passages. The older word for a handmill was QUERN; in the case of a water-mill or wind-mill, there was little occasion to separate the notion of the machinery from that of the containing fabric which was necessarily connected with it.

1535 COVERDALE *Exod.* xi. 5 The mayde seruaunte which is behynde yᵉ myll. —— *Matt.* xxiv. 41 Two shal be gryndinge at the Myll. **1563–87, 1573–80** [see HAND-MILL]. **1614** MARKHAM *Cheap Husb.* (1668) I. v. 40 If you cause these Beans to be spelted upon a Miln, and so mixt with Oats, it will recover him. **1674** BOYLE *Grounds Mech. Hypothesis* 21–2 A Water-mill, or a Wind-mill, or a Horse-mill, or a Hand-mill. **1791** COWPER *Odyss.* xx. 135 She rested on her mill, and thus pronounced The happy omen by her lord desired. **1903** *Pilot* 22 Aug. 179/2 San niang tsû then produced a small mill and ground the wheat to flour.

2. a. A machine or apparatus for grinding or reducing to powder or pulp some solid substance. Also, a building fitted with machinery for this purpose. Often as the second element of obvious combinations, as in *coffee-*, *pepper-mill*, *paper-*, *powder-mill*, etc.

1560 GRESHAM in Burgon *Life* (1839) I. 294 The Quene's Majestie should do well to macke.. iiij or vi mylles for the macking of powdyr. **1596** LAMBARDE *Peramb. Kent* 453 Two Milles of rare deuise.. the one emploied for the making of all sortes of Paper.. the other exercised for the drawing of Iron into Wyres [etc.]. **1666–7** in *Boyle's Wks.* (1772) VI. 551 Tin always.. must be prepared.. by stamping, or knocking mills, which reduce the whole body to a very small sand. *Ibid.* 552 The tin-slag, may, by being exposed to the open air and rain for a time, be sooner prepared in the mill, and melted down. **1712–14** POPE *Rape Lock* III. 106 The board with cups and spoons is crown'd, The berries crackle, and the mill turns round. **1800** tr. *Lagrange's Chem.* II. 71 The result will be a sulphate of lead of a beautiful whiteness, and exceedingly fine, if it be washed in a large quantity of water, and then carefully mixed in a mill. **1889** C. G. W. LOCK *Pract. Gold-mining* 226 A new mill for reducing cement, known as Drake's cement-mill.. is in form of a tube [etc.]. *Ibid.* 437 The order in which the stamps drop varies in different mills.

fig. *a* **1633** G. HERBERT *Jacula Prud.* 747 Gods Mill grinds slow; but sure. **1850** TENNYSON *In Mem.* lxxxviii, Ground in yonder social mill We rub each other's angles down. **1870** LONGF. tr. *Von Logau, Retribution*, Though the mills of God grind slowly, yet they grind exceeding small.

b. An instrument designed to express the juices from any succulent matter by grinding or crushing; usually with defining prefix, as *cane*, *cider mill*.

1676 WORLIDGE (*title*) Vinetum Britannicum: or, a Treatise of Cider... And a Description of the new-invented Ingenio or Mill, For the more expeditious and better making of Cider. **1697** DRYDEN *Virg. Georg.* II. 757 Then Olives, ground in Mills, their Fatness boast. **1794** J. CLARK *Agric. Hereford.* 40 The [*sc.* cider] mill consists of a stone like a mill-stone (runner) set on its edge, with an axle through the center [etc.]. **1853** URE *Dict. Arts* (ed. 4) II. 284 They give the name *virgin oil* to that which is first obtained from the olives ground to a paste in a mill.

c. *Sc.* A snuff-box; originally, †one in which tobacco could be ground to powder by a simple mechanism. (Cf. MULL.)

1776 C. KEITH *Farmers' Ha'* vi. (1794), Wi' mill in hand, and wise adage He spent the night. *a* **1780** SHIRREFS *Poems* (1790) 215 And there, o'er pot o' beer right spruce, And mill

in hand, The carls crack'd awa' fell crouse About the land. **1805** G. M'INDOE *Million Potatoes* in Chambers *Pop. Hum. Scot. Poems* (1862) 150 In the laird's nieve John ramm'd his mill, The laird ca'd in anither gill.

3. a. In the 15–16th c., applied by extension to any machine worked by wind or water power in the manner of a corn-mill, though not used for the purpose of grinding. In later use applied to various machines for performing certain operations upon material in the process of manufacture; often with defining word, as in *flatting-*, *fulling-*, *rolling-*, *saw-mill*.

1417–18, etc. [see *fulling-mill* s.v. FULLING *vbl. sb.*]. **1463–4** *Rolls of Parlt.* V. 502/2 Wollen Cloth, fulled in milles called Gygmylles and Toune Milles. **1596** [see 2]. **1621** ELSING *Debates Ho. Lords* (Camden) App. 138 Ireland and Norton came back and .. surprised one milne used for other works of his trade. **1725** WATTS *Logic* IV. i. §1 In order to make mills and engines of various kinds. **1727–41** CHAMBERS *Cycl.*, *Mill* .. among gold-wire-drawers, is a little machine consisting of two cylinders of steel, serving to flatten the gold, or silver wire, and reduce it into laminæ, or plates... They have also *mills* to wind the gold-wire or thread on the silk. *Ibid.*, There are also *Silk*-Mills, for spinning, throwing, and twisting silks. **1863** P. BARRY *Dockyard Econ.* 242 The productive power of this mill is astonishing: it will manufacture armour-plates from 20 to 40 feet long [etc.].

fig. **1771** SMOLLETT *Humph. Cl.* 10 June Let. iii, He observed, that her ladyship's brain was a perfect mill for projects. **1848** LOWELL *Biglow P.* Ser. I. iv. Poet. Wks. (1879) 200 Babel was .. the earliest mill erected for the manufacture of gabble. **1883** G. H. BOUGHTON in *Harper's Mag.* Apr. 694/1 Model villages, .. all turned out of the same mill.

b. A machine invented by Antoine Brucher in the 16th c. for the stamping of gold and silver coins.

In the English Mint it permanently superseded the earlier practice of striking with the hammer in 1662.

1661 *Order in Counc.* in Folkes *Table Eng. Silver Coins* (1745) 104 Materials for the coining of money by the mill. **1662** *Ibid.*, Several proposals .. about coining his majesty's moneys by the mill and press. **1695** W. LOWNDES *Amendm. Silver Coin* 93 All the Moneys we have now in England .. are reducible to Two Sorts .. one stampt with the Hammer, and the other Prest with an Engine, called the Mill. **1817** RUDING *Ann. Coinage* I. 139 The advantage of this machine (which is known by the name of The Mill and Screw) over the old mode of striking with an hammer, consists [etc.]. **1854** HUMPHREYS *Coin. Brit. Emp.* 113 Pierre Blondeau .. who had carried to perfection the .. modes of stamping coins by the mill and screw, was invited to England... He produced patterns of half-crowns, shillings, and half-shillings, coined by the new mill and screw, by which means a legend was impressed for the first time upon the edge.

c. *Calico* and *Bank-note printing*: A roller of hardened steel having impressed upon it, from a hand engraved die, a pattern which by pressure is transferred in intaglio to the calico-printing cylinder or note-printing plate.

1839 URE *Dict. Arts* 218 The first roller engraved by hand is called the die; the second .. is called the mill. **1875** KNIGHT *Dict. Mech.*, *Mill*... The hardened steel roller having the design in *cameo*, and used for impressing in *intaglio* a plate .. or a copper cylinder.

d. A hollow revolving cylinder in which leather is 'tumbled' in contact with oil, tan, or any ameliorating liquid.

1884 KNIGHT *Dict. Mech.* Suppl. 606/2 The mill is used for stuffing light leather, and for other purposes. After stoning, skiving, and shaving, the sides are put in the mill with some tan liquor to soften them and make them porous.

4. A building or other place or establishment fitted with machinery in which a certain industry, manufacture or manufacturing process is carried on; esp. with prefixed word, as in *cotton-*, *silk-*, *silver-mill*, etc., q.v. under the first element.

1502 *Acc. Ld. High Treas. Scot.* (1900) II. 143 Item .. to the Franch armorar to set up his harnas myln. **1531** *Ibid.* VI. 34. **1630** *R. Johnson's Kingd. & Commw.* 347 Six mills, in which they make plate for armour. **1674** RAY *Collect. Words, Smelting Silver* 113 The Smelting and Refining of Silver at the Silver Mills in Cardiganshire. **1835** URE *Philos. Manuf.* 287 He [Mr. Graham] cannot admit a new hand into his mill unless he has joined the combination. **1854** RONALDS & RICHARDSON *Chem. Technol.* (ed. 2) I. 132 Large quantities of saw-dust accumulate at the mills. **1881** RAYMOND *Mining Gloss.*, *Mill*, 1, Eng. That part of an iron works where puddle-bars are converted into merchant-iron. **1905** *Edin. Rev.* Apr. 478 He .. built mills in the neighbouring villages .. for the manufacture of tools [etc.]. **1919** *Brit. Manufacturer* Nov. 26/2 In the linen industry a 'mill' means the works where flax is spun into yarns, while a 'factory' means the place of the further evolution of the yarns being woven into cloth.

5. A machine which performs its work by rotary motion, esp. a lapidary's mill.

1839 URE *Dict. Arts* 1096 It [the seal engraver's lathe] consists of a table on which is fixed the mill. *Ibid.*, Having fixed the tool .. in the mill, the artist applies to its cutting point, or edge, some diamond-powder [etc.]. **1860** TOMLINSON *Arts & Manuf.* Ser. II. *Pens* 44 Each of these lengths is then pointed at each end at a machine called a *mill*, consisting of a circular single-cut file and a fine grit-stone. **1879** *Encycl. Brit.* X. 663/2 The [glass] articles are held in the hand, and applied to the mill while rotating. **1882** *Ibid.* XIV. 299/1 Another form of lapidary's mill consists [etc.].

6. *slang.* **a.** Shortened form of TREADMILL.

1835 DICKENS *Sk. Boz.* (1836) 1st Ser. I. 334 The mill's a d—d sight better than the Sessions. **1842** BARHAM *Ingol. Leg.* Ser. II. *Misadv. Margate*, A landsman said, 'I twig the chap—he's been upon the Mill.' **1888** *Pall Mall G.* 6 June 7/1 When after three days of the mill I got off at night I found my feet were four or five times their ordinary weight.

b. *transf.* A prison or guard-house.

1851 H. MAYHEW *London Labour* I. 352/2 A few weeks after I was grabbed for this, and got a month at the mill... When I came out of prison, I went to Epsom races. **1853** WHYTE-MELVILLE *Digby Grand* I. ix. 229 The latter worthy .. gave a policeman such a licking the other night, that he was within an ace of getting 'a month at the mill'. **1889** H. H. MCCONNELL *Five Years a Cavalryman* 194 Very few, indeed, are they who during their term of service can say: 'They never had *me* in the mill.' **1916** E. C. GARRETT *Army Ballads & Other Verses* 21 And they put me in 'the mill'. **1928** L. H. NASON *Sergeant Eadie* 78 Why, put 'em in the mill! **1951** J. JONES *From Here to Eternity* IV. xlii. 636 'You were here when one of the old ones was in the mill, weren't you, Jack?' 'Two,' Malloy said. 'Both of them during my first stretch.' **1960** WENTWORTH & FLEXNER *Dict. Amer. Slang* 339/1 *Mill*.., a prison; a guardhouse.

7. *U.S. slang.* A typewriter.

1913 *Writer's Bulletin* Oct. 103/2 After I got a good idea I would hustle to my 'mill' and pound out some copy. **1922** N. A. CRAWFORD *Weavers With Words* 22 And sometimes .. I'll start to say, 'Jim, got a good cigarette?' and turn toward his battered old 'mill'. **1932** C. D. MACDOUGALL *College Course in Reporting* 498 *Mill*, typewriter. **1948** MENCKEN *Amer. Lang.* Suppl. II. 717 Writers' cramp was cured .. on the advent of the *mill*, i.e., the typewriter.

8. a. A pugilistic encounter between two persons.

1819 T. MOORE *Tom Crib's Memorial to Congress* 36 We who're of the fancy-lay, As dead hands at a mill as they. **1825** C. M. WESTMACOTT *Eng. Spy* I. 270 To cut a dash at races or a mill. **1864** [HEMYNG] *Eton School Days* vii. 77 We are waiting to see your mill with Butler Burke. **1869** BLACKMORE *Lorna D.* ii, They who made the ring intituled the scene a 'mill', whilst we who must be thumped inside it tried to rejoice in their pleasantry.

b. *U.S.* A circling movement of cattle. (Cf. MILL *v.*[1] 12.)

1897 E. HOUGH *Story of Cowboy* 146 By shouts and blows he did all he could to break the 'mill' and get the cattle headed properly. **1903** A. ADAMS *Log of Cowboy* iv. 27 We soon had a mill going which kept them [*sc.* cattle] busy and rested our horses. **1942** E. E. DALE *Cow Country* 55 Those behind them would follow and a 'mill' would be established in which the animals would swim around and around in a circle until they drowned unless it were quickly broken up and the leaders again headed for the opposite shore.

9. *Mining.* **a.** An excavation in rock, transverse to the workings, from which material for filling is obtained (Webster 1897). **b.** A passage underground through which ore is shot (*Ibid.*).

10. *slang.* The engine of an aircraft or a 'hot rod' racing car.

1918 *Atlantic* Sept. 414 Motor is 'moulin'—to start it, one 'turns the mill'. **1923** G. H. MCKNIGHT *Eng. Words & their Backgrounds* 56 *Tail* and *joystick* and *mill* (French *moulin*) were names for different parts of the airship. **1937** E. C. PARSONS *Great Adventure* vi. 60 To nurse one of the grunting old mills up to that height, .. and keep it running for an hour, was in itself quite a stunt. **1948** MENCKEN *Amer. Lang.* Suppl. II. 724 There are others [*sc.* new terms] that remain the private property of the men working in automobile plants and of those who sell or repair cars. A few specimens; Bald-head. A worn tire... Mill. An engine [etc.]. **1954** R. F. & B. W. YATES *Sport & Racing Cars* ii. 24 The additional motor 'moxie' provided by a reground camshaft is truly amazing, and all of this without running too much risk of a cranky 'mill' at low idling speeds. **1954** *Amer. Speech* XXIX. 100 *Mill*, .. any engine. *Ibid.* 97 *Full mill*, .. an engine with all necessary speed racing accessories. **1975** B. GARFIELD *Hopscotch* xv. 152 This was an old car but it must have had a souped-up mill.

11. *attrib.* and *Comb.*, as *mill-bag*, *-bridge*, *-brook*, *-builder*, *-burn*, *-clack*, *close*, *-gearing*, *-girl*, †*-knave*, *-labour*, *-lade*, *-lead*, *-lord* , *-lot*, *-owner*, *-process*, *-rent* , *-roller*, *-room*, *-sluice*, *-wall*, *-yard*; *mill-cut*, *-like -spun* adjs.

1832 J. P. KENNEDY *Swallow Barn* I. xv. 155 With the large canvass *mill-bags spread out for saddles. **1851** R. GLISAN *Jrnl. Army Life* (1874) vi. 58, I .. endeavored to throw [it] in a mill-bag style over my shoulder. **1833** TENNYSON *Poems* 41, I stepped upon the old *mill-bridge. **1636** *Official Rec. Springfield, Mass.* (1898–9) I. 159 The lotts .. are ordered to lye adjoining to *Mill Brooke. **1864** T. L. NICHOLS *40 Yrs. Amer. Life* I. ii. 20 Grist-mills which ground our corn, and saw-mills which supplied our timber, were upon a mill brook. **1866** G. M. HOPKINS *Poems* (1967) 171 The streams are full And millbrook-slips with pretty pace Gallop along the meadow grass. **1759** SMEATON in *Phil. Trans.* LI. 148 All our modern *mill-builders [etc.]. **1843** BETHUNE *Sc. Fireside Stor.* 111 The mill from which the *mill burn .. sweeped nearly half round the village. **1768** *Ann. Reg.* 73 His servant-man .. carried him into the *mill-close. **1925** *Glasgow Herald* 2 Apr. 9 To import into this country a sufficient number of *mill-cut houses to supply the shortage. **1825** J. NICHOLSON *Operat. Mechanic* 364 The appropriate modes described under the article '*Mill-geering'. **1856** WHITTIER *Mary Garvin* 18 O *mill-girl watching late and long the shuttles' restless play! **1609** SKENE *Reg. Maj.*, *Stat. Will.* 3 All they quha hes milns .. sall haue ane maister, and tua servants *mil-knaves. **1862** KINGSLEY in *Life* (1877) II. 138 *Mill-labour effeminates the men. **1868** PEARD *Water-farm.* iv. 39 The dangers produced by *mill-lades and sluices. **1609** SKENE *Reg. Maj.*, *Chalm. Air* c. 11 §4 Myllers .. take the fry, or smolts of salmon, in the mylne dame or *lead, contrair the ordinance of the law. **1897** *Daily News* 21 Apr. 6/2 The water flowing in the mill-lead. **1854** *Poultry Chron.* I. 148 The '*mill-like motion of the gizard'. **1918** MRS. E. LIDDELL in J. Gott *Lett.* 66 Here is a man who, alike in the mill-like grinding of life in Leeds .. and amid the urgent claims of a diocese, always found time to love and to remember. **1880** DISRAELI *Endym.* lxiii, Perhaps we shall get rid of them all some day—landlords and *mill-lords. **1746** *Boston News-Let.* 16 Nov., Seven Acres .. to be laid out to the Right of the 30 Acre *Mill-Lot, granted to Thomas Richardson. **1835** URE *Philos. Manuf.* 348 Assassins who had hired themselves .. to murder *mill-owners. **1854** HUMPHREYS *Coin. Brit. Emp.* 113 They are exceedingly well executed by the *mill process, and have the laureated bust of the protector, with OLIVAR. D.G. [etc.]. **1872** RAYMOND *Statist. Mines & Mining* 136 The ore .. produces very base bullion by mill process. **1894** R. S. FERGUSON *Hist. Westmorld.* 165 Mills .. still pay *mill-rents to this day. **1834** M. SCOTT *Cruise Midge* xx. (1836) 332 It being part of Rory's trade to prepare *mill-rollers and other large pieces of hard-wood required for the estates below. **1696** *Lond. Gaz.* No. 3186/4 Ordered that none but .. those concerned in the Coinage, be permitted to enter the Melting-houses, *Mill-rooms [etc.]. **1833** B. SILLIMAN *Man. Sugar Cane* 45 The length of the mill-room A is 64 feet. **1844** STEPHENS *Bk. Farm* I. 273 The protective effects of running water, such as water-falls from *mill-sluices. **1825** J. NICHOLSON *Operat. Mechanic* 389 *Mill-spun yarn answers better for the coarse as well as the finer fabrics. **1870** MORRIS *Earthly Par.* I. I. 157 While the smooth *millwalls white and black Shook to the great wheel's measured clack. **1824** *New Hampsh. Hist. Soc. Coll.* I. 246 A saw mill torn down and twelve thousand of boards in the *mill-yard carried away. **1936** *Discovery* Sept. 288/1, I saw the mill cat crossing the wall from our garden to the mill yard. **1955** J. R. R. TOLKIEN *Return of King* 296 The low wall of the mill-yard.

12. Special Combinations, as **mill band**, an endless belt for the wheels of mill machinery; **mill-banding**, belting for the wheels of mill machinery; **mill-bar (iron)**, rough bar iron as drawn out by the puddlers' rolls; **mill-bed**, the cast-iron bed of a machine for breaking flax, expressing oil, etc.; **mill-beetle**, the cockroach; **mill bill**, a steel adze fixed in a wooden thrift used for dressing and cracking millstones; **mill-boom**, the barrier of floating timber stretched about a saw-mill to retain floating logs; **mill-brack**, a rent in cloth made during the process of fulling (see BRACK *sb.*[1] 3); **mill-bundle** (see quot.); **mill-cake**, (*a*) the mass resulting from the incorporation of the ingredients in the process of manufacture of gunpowder; (*b*) linseed cake (Knight *Dict. Mech.* 1875); †**mill-case** (see quot. 1611); **mill-cinder**, the slag from the puddling-furnace of a rolling-mill (Raymond *Mining Gloss.* 1881); **mill-clack**, †(*a*) = CLACK 3; (*b*) *Her.* a representation of a mill-clack; **mill-cog**, one of the cogs of the wheel on the driving shaft of a wind-mill or water-mill; **mill-course** = MILL-RACE; **mill-dog**, (*a*) a dog used for turning a mill; (*b*) in Canada, a kind of clamp for securing logs in a saw-mill; **mill-dust**, the fine floury dust thrown out during the process of grinding corn; **mill-eye**, the eye or opening in the runner of a mill through which the meal escapes; **mill-fever**, a form of low fever prevalent amongst the young hands in linen mills; **mill-file** (see quot. 1884); **mill finish**, of paper, not subjected to any extra processing after being made; †**mill-fleam**, a mill-stream; **mill-gang** *Warping*, that part of the warp which is made by a descending and ascending course of the threads round the warping-mill (Knight *Dict. Mech.* 1875); **mill-gold**, ? gold obtained by stamping; **mill-hand**, one employed in a mill or factory; **mill-head**, (*a*) that part of a horse-mill from which the driving-gear is suspended; (*b*) (see quot. 1825); **mill-head**, **-headed** *adjs.*, having a milled head; †**mill-holm**, a watery place about a mill-dam (Ray *N.C. Words* 1674); †**mill-hoop** = *mill-case*; **mill-hopper** = HOPPER 3, 4; **mill-iron** = ? MILL-PICK or MILL-RIND; **mill-jade**, a mill-horse; **mill-lodge** *dial.*, a mill-pond; **mill log** *U.S.*, a log cut at a saw mill; †**mill-mail**, toll paid in feudal times for grinding corn at the superior's mill; †**mill-money**, money coined in the mill and press, not struck with the hammer (cf. *mill-sixpence*, *-tester*); **mill-moth** = *mill-beetle*; **mill-ore** *Mining*, metallic ore fit for stamping or crushing; **mill-pin**, (*a*) ? = *mill-spindle*; (*b*) *Her.* a representation of this; **mill-pot**, ? a basket contrived to capture and retain fish; **mill-power**, water-power for driving a mill; also, a unit for measuring this (see quots. 1903, 1911); **mill privilege**, **right** *U.S.*, the privilege or right of using water for driving a mill; **mill-puff** *dial.*, a kind of flock used for stuffing mattresses, etc.; **mill-ream** (see quot.); †**mill-reek** *dial.*, a disease to which workers in lead-mines are subject; **mill-ring**, (*a*) the space in a mill between the runner and the frame surrounding it; (*b*) the meal which remains about the millstones (regarded as a perquisite of the miller); (*c*) the dust of a mill (Jam.); **mill-run**, (*a*) *Gold Mining*, the work of an amalgamating mill between two 'clean-ups'; (*b*) a mill-race; (*c*) *Mining*, a test of a given quantity of ore by treatment in a mill; (*d*) applied to timber sawn to the usual specifications; (see also quot. 1957); also *transf.*, of average or mediocre

quality, 'run-of-the-mill'; hence **mill-run** *v.*, *Mining*, to yield (a given percentage) at a mill-run; **mill-sail**, the sail of a wind-mill; so **mill-sail-shaped** *a.* (see quot.); **mill-saw**, a saw for use in a saw-mill; **mill-saw file**, a file used for sharpening mill-saws; **mill-saw web**, the blade of a mill-saw; **mill-scale**, *Metallurgy*, a deposit of iron oxide formed on iron or steel during hot working; **mill-seat**, a site suitable for a water-mill; **mill-seed** (see quot.); **mill-shaft**, (*a*) a metal shaft used for driving machinery in a mill; (*b*) the tall chimney of a mill; **mill site** *U.S.* = *mill-seat*; **mill-sixpence**, a sixpence coined in a mill; **mill-spindle**, a vertical shaft supporting the 'runner' of a flour-mill; **mill-staff**, an oak staff designed to test the flat face of a millstone; **mill-stank**, a mill-pond; † **millstock** = *fulling-stock*; **mill-stream**, a mill-race; also *fig.*; **mill tail** (see quot. 1835); also *attrib.* and *fig.*; **mill-tester**, a tester coined in a mill; **mill-timber**, ? timber that has been dressed in a saw-mill; † **mill-tooth**, a grinding or molar tooth; **mill town, village**, a town or village characterized by the presence of mills; † **mill-trough**, (*a*) a corn-bin; (*b*) a mill-race or -pond; **mill-wash**, ? = MILL-TAIL; **mill-way**, a thoroughfare leading to a mill; **mill-work**, (*a*) the machinery used in mills or factories; (*b*) the designing or erection of the machinery in mills or factories; **mill-worker**, one who works at or in a mill; † **mill-yemer**, one who has the custody of a mill. Also MILL-DAM, MILL-HORSE, MILL-HOUSE, MILL-INK, etc.

1858 P. L. SIMMONDS *Dict. Trade Products* 247/2 **Mill-band maker*, a manufacturer of bands for machine shops, and for driving wheels. **1869** *Bradshaw's Railway Manual* XXI. App. 103 Manufacturers of.. Engine Hose, Fire Buckets, Mill Bands, &c. **1957** J. BRAINE *Room at Top* ix. 86 The smells of East Warley tugging at me for attention..—malt, burning millband, frying fish. **1894** *Daily News* 11 Dec. 7/4 Unpuncturable Canvas Lining, for *mill-banding, driving belts,..and cycle tyres. **1839** URE *Dict. Arts* 706 Passing through the remaining grooves till it comes to the square ones, where it becomes a *mill-bar. *Ibid.* 707 This iron called mill-bar iron, is however of too inferior a quality to be employed in any machinery. **1825** J. NICHOLSON *Operat. Mechanic* 406 Fig. 436 represents the section of a *mill-bed. **1771** J. R. FORSTER tr. *Osbeck's Voy.* I. 170 The *Mill beetles ..annually come in ships from the East Indies. **1631** WINTHROP *Let.* in *New Eng.* (1825) I. 381 Bring..mill stones..with bracings ready cast, and rings, and *mill-bills. **1897** in *Sheffield Trade List* 27 Mill Picks and Bills to order. **1877** *Michigan Rep.* XXXV. 518 Complainants had a large quantity..of timber..in their *mill-boom at East Tawas. **1552** *Act 5 & 6 Edw. VI*, c. 6 §27 If..Cloth..prove..to be full of Holes, *Mill-bracks, or to be holely. **1859** *Stationer's Handbk.* (ed. 2) 74 *Bundle of Paper* (*mill bundle), a parcel of paper tied in one bundle as it comes from the mill. **1839** URE *Dict. Arts* 629 The *mill-cake powder of Waltham Abbey is submitted to a mean theoretic pressure of 70 to 75 tons per superficial foot. **1594** PLAT *Jewell-ho.* III. 56 The worme..which is found in a *mill-case, or where Bakers vse to boult their meale. **1611** COTGR., *Archure*, a..mill-case; the open chest that holds the mill-stones. **1638** FORD *Fancies* III. iii, His tongue trouls like a *mill-clack. **1874** PAPWORTH & MORANT *Ord. Brit. Arm.* 957 Az. a millclack in fess or *Mills*. **1707** MORTIMER *Husb.* (1721) II. 42 The Timber is useful for *Mill-coggs. **1802** MAR. EDGEWORTH *Rosanne* iv, The neighbours all joined in restoring the water to the *mill-course. **1402** *Pol. Poems* (Rolls) II. 53 But thou, as blynde Bayarde, berkest at the mone, as an olde *mylne dog when he bygynnith to dote. **1877** *Lumberman's Gaz.* 24 May, Parties are attempting to introduce Mill Dogs which are infringements of mine. **1880** *Ibid.* 28 Jan., A. Rogers..is the inventor and owner of a mill dog. **1543** TRAHERON *Vigo's Chirurg.* II. iii. 18 The place..muste be playstred with floure of barleye, and wyth *myldust. **1822–34** *Good's Study Med.* (ed. 4) I. 257 There can be little doubt, that much of the mill-dust..is derived from the powder furnished by these [mill-] stones. **1641** BEST *Farm. Bks.* (Surtees) 103 Measure the meale therein..just as it commeth from the *milne-eye, and afore it be temsed. **1825** J. NICHOLSON *Operat. Mechanic* 147 To find the weight of a quantity of stone equal to the mill-eye. **1889** *Brit. Med. Jrnl.* 30 Mar. 704/1 The disturbance of health called '*mill-fever', which attacks young hands. **1884** KNIGHT *Dict. Mech.* Suppl., **Mill File*, a thin flat file used in machine shops for lathe work and draw filing. **1907** CROSS & BEVAN *Text-bk. Paper-Making* (ed. 3) x. 270 In hand-made paper the '*mill-finish' is obtained by pressing the sheets of paper one against another. **1952** E. J. LABARRE *Dict. Paper* (ed. 2) 163/2 Mill finish is synonymous with machine finish, and merely indicates that the paper has received its finish on the paper-machine. **1475–6** *Durham Acc. Rolls.* (Surtees) 646 Pro le scowrynge medietatis de le *myln-fleme. **1486–7** *Ibid.* 650 Operantibus super le mylnfleme. **1877** RAYMOND *Statist. Mines & Mining* 289 The following is the currency and gold value of *mill-gold. **1865** *Daily Tel.* 6 Dec. 4/4 The party which would now refuse the suffrage to the *mill-hands. **1805** R. W. DICKSON *Pract. Agric.* I. Plate xviii, The *mill-head is erected on a floor about seven or eight feet above the ground floor. **1825** J. NICHOLSON *Operat. Mechanic* Gloss., *Mill-head*, the head of water which is to turn a mill. **1865** KINGSLEY *Herew.* i, A duck put into Bourne pool would pass underground into the mill-head of the said village. **1790** ROY in *Phil. Trans.* LXXX. 153 The insertion of a small *mill-head key, on a square pin fitted to receive it. **1805** *Trans. Soc. Arts* XXIII. 296 By the help of the *mill-headed nut. **1611** COTGR., *Archure*, a *mill-hoope, or mill-case; the open chest that holds the mill-stones. **1570** LEVINS *Manip.* 80/8 A *Mil-hopper, *infundibulum*. **1858** CARLYLE *Fredk. Gt.* v. vi. (1872) II. 110 A stiff-backed, close-fisted old gentleman, with mill-hopper chin. ? *c* **1343** *Durham Acc. Rolls* (Surtees) 543 In.. ij *Milnyrenes. **1471–2** *Ibid.* 643 Pro factura del milniryns dictorum molendinorum. **1610** B. JONSON *Alch.* III. iii, Would you haue me stalke like a *mill-iade, All day, for one, that will not yeeld vs graines? **1891** *Jrnl. Oldham Microsc. Soc.* May 101 The shades of green in our *mill-lodges are continually changing. **1891** *Morn. Post* 23 Dec. 3/2 A number of boys were skating on a mill lodge at Stubbins, near Bury. **1795** T. B. HAZARD *Diary* (1930) 171/2, I helpt brother Robert flote *mill logs to mill. **1849** D. NASON *Jrnl.* 99, I asked the guide if there were any mill-logs among it. **1287** *Yorks. Inquis.* (Yorks. Rec. Soc.) II. 61 [In Newland] *milnemale [6*d.*]. **1613** FLETCHER, etc. *Captain* I. iii, Only to live to make their children scourge-sticks And hoord up *mill-money. **1658** ROWLAND tr. *Moufet's Theat. Ins.* 998 There are three sorts of Blattæ; the soft Moth, the *mill Moth, and the unsavoury or stinking Moth. **1877** RAYMOND *Statist. Mines & Mining* 294 The *mill-ore produced has been of high grade. **1523** LD. BERNERS *Froiss.* I. cccxxv. 507 Sir George of Besmede..bare in his armes syluer, a *myllpyn gowles, a border endented gowles. **1630** in *Descr. Thames* (1758) 66 No Fisherman..shall use..any Weel called a Lomb, or a *Mill Pot, or any other Engine, with the Head thereof against the Stream. **1833** *Chambers's Edinb. Jrnl.* II. 167/3 This stream..at some after time may be turned to account as a *mill power. **1903** *Trans. Amer. Soc. Mech. Engin.* XXIV. 983 Wherever water-power is sold it is customary to use the turbines as meters... From tables and curves made up from..tests of..turbines,..data are obtained from which to compute the actual discharge. This is referred to a given head and thence reduced to mill-powers, the values of which vary with the locality. **1911** *Encycl. Brit.* XIV. 92/2 A mill-power is defined as 38 cub. ft. of water per sec. during 16 hours per day on a fall of 20 ft. This gives about 60 h.p. effective. **1734** *New Hampsh. Probate Rec.* (1914) II. 508, I also give unto my son..the one half of my *mill Priviledge on the southerly side of ye River at Lole-End. **1892** *Rep. Vermont Board Agric.* XII. 134 Many mill privileges with excellent water power are afforded. **1851** *Catal. Gt. Exhib.* II. 496 Specimens of mattress-wools, woollen *millpuffs, and flocks. **1881** *Instr. Census Clerks* (1885) 64 Mill Puff Maker. **1884** *West. Morn. News* 3 Sept. 1/2 Milpuff Pillows... Full-size Milpuff Beds. **1859** *Stationers' Handbk.* (ed. 2) 101 A ream of writing paper ..is required to contain 18 quires of 24 good sheets and 2 quires of 20 sheets of *outsides*,..472 sheets in all, good and bad—this is called a **mill ream*. **1754** J. WILSON in *Ess. & Observ. Edinb. Soc.* I. 459 The disease which the people at Leadhills call the *mill-reek. **1794** *Mass. Hist. Soc. Coll.* III. 147 The principal object of the original settlers being lumber, more attention was paid to *mill-rights than to the soil. **1847** W. I. PAULDING *Antipathies* III. iii, in J. K. & W. I. Paulding *Amer. Comedies* 262 There's a man at Jack O'Lantern's that owns land and mill-rights. **1811** G. S. KEITH *Agric. Surv. Aberd.* 506 (Jam.) A number of the mill-masters apply the *mill-ring to the feeding of horses. **1828** *Earl Richard, Queen's brother* xlii. in Child *Ballads* II. 467 And she would meal you with millering [*sic*]. That she gathers at the mill. **1875** W. MCILWRAITH *Guide Wigtownshire* 136 A workman, in making an excavation near the mill-ring, came on a large, flat stone, aneath which were the remains of a clay urn. **1874** RAYMOND *Statist. Mines & Mining* 292 The *mill-runs have been as high as 3 oz. gold with from 30 to 60 oz. in silver. **1877** LD. HATHERLEY in *Law Repts., App. Cas.* II. 842 What is called a mill-lade or mill-run. **1881** *Chicago Times* 1 June, The supply of choice mill-run lumber was generally quite limited. **1882** *Rep. to Ho. Repr. Prec. Met. U.S.* 306 The ore gives mill-runs of $60 to the ton. **1898** *Daily News* 8 Mar. 2/7 The mill-run during February has been irregular. **1928** FOY & HARLOW *Clowning through Life* 299 He thought himself far too good for the ordinary mill run of melodramas which prevailed at that house. **1957** *N.Z. Timber Jrnl.* Nov. 59/2 *Mill run.* Usually implies all saleable output of timber from a sawmill. *c* **1449** *Pol. Poems* (Rolls) II. 222 Wylloby. Oure *Mylle-saylle wille not abowte, Hit hath so longe goone emptye. **1835** LINDLEY *Introd. Bot.* III. Gloss. (1839) 451 *Mill-sail-shaped*; having many wings projecting from a convex surface; as the fruit of some umbelliferous plants. **1856** 'MARK TWAIN' *Let.* 14 Nov. in *Adventures T. J. Snodgrass* (1928) 25 Everybody was a bobbin up and down like a *mill saw. **1897** in *Sheffield Trade List* 15 Mill Saws, Mill Saw Webs [etc.]. *Ibid.*, Mill Saw Files, one round edge. **1880** *Encycl. Brit.* XIII. 357/1 During rolling this film [of oxide] becomes somewhat thick and peels off, forming '*mill-scale'. **1902** BREARLEY & IBBOTSON *Analysis of Steel-Works Materials* VII. 229 (*heading*) Mill scale. **1940** SIMONS & GREGORY *Steel Manuf.* xvi. 109 The charge consists of steel scrap and grey phosphoric..to which are added millscale..or iron ore, and lime or limestone. **1968** T. H. ROGERS *Marine Corrosion* vi. 78 Steel with mill-scale either in or on the surface, when exposed to sea water, will pit very severely wherever any couple between scale and steel occurs. **1770** G. WASHINGTON *Diaries* (1925) I. 365 Mr. Ballendine and myself leveled Doeg Run in order to fix on a *Mill Seat. **1792** *Descr. Kentucky* 56 The cheapness of mill seats and mill work in the United States. *a* **1817** T. DWIGHT *Trav. New Eng.*, etc. (1821) II. 27 Directly under the bridge commences a romantic fall, which..furnishes a number of excellent mill-seats. **1842** J. AITON *Domest. Econ.* (1857) 194 As some of the shells still remain among the meal, they are separated from it by hand-sieves; these shells, thus separated, and having the finer particles of meal adhering to them, called **mill-seeds*, are preserved for sowins. **1833** J. HOLLAND *Manuf. Metal* II. 141 Turning very large articles, such as the outsides of cylinders, *mill-shafts, cannon, &c. **1898** *Daily News* 21 Nov. 8/6 We should stir ourselves, and clap the stopper on these belching mill-shafts. **1831** J. M. PECK *Guide for Emigrants* 196 There are but few good *mill sites in the State. **1896** C. H. SHINN *Story of the Mine* 81 Water claims and mill sites were taken up almost as soon as work had fairly begun on the Comstock. **1956** H. EVANS *Mountain Dog* 107 Earth and stones had been bulldozed to the water's edge to form a millsite. **1598** SHAKS. *Merry W.* I. i. 158 Seauen groates in *mill-sixpences. **1639** MAYNE *City Match* II. iii. 14 Had I..but forty Mark..And were that fortie Mark Mil sixpences, I would despise you. **14..** *Voc.* in Wr.-Wülcker 596/31 *Molucrum*, [the *mylle spyndelle]. **1880** JEFFERIES *Gt. Estate* 166 He laid down the millpeck, and took his *millstaff to prove the work he had done. **14..** *Iter Camer.* xi. in *Sc. Acts* (1814) I, þai [*sc.* millers] tak smoltis in þe *myll stank again þe inhibicioun of law. **1546** in W. H. Turner *Select. Rec. Oxford* (1880) 182 For carege of one *myllstock for the fullyng myll. *c* **931** in Birch *Cartul Sax.* II. 377 Of hlippenham in to þam *milestreame, Of þam mylestreame innan þa norð lange dic. **1794** COLERIDGE *Parl. Oscill.* 33 Both plunged together in the deep mill-stream. **1815** D. DRAKE *Nat. View Cincinnati* i. 58 In summer and autumn, it [*sc.* Licking River] is a moderate mill-stream. **1840** *Knickerbocker* XVI. 22 A wooden bridge which crossed a mill-stream. **1939** JOYCE *Finnegans Wake* 175 But the Mountstill frowns on the Millstream while their Madsons leap his Bier. **1975** J. B. HARLEY *O.S. Maps* iii. 44 In Ordnance Survey usage the term 'mill race' is given to the water leading to a mill, and 'mill stream' to the water leaving it. **1835** J. ABBOTT *Expos. Princ. Hydraulic Engine* 126 **Mill tail*, the water which has passed through the wheel race; or is below the mill. **1922** BLUNDEN *Shepherd* 64 No water ever ran so blithe As that same mill-tail stream, I'd say. **1925** —— *Eng. Poems* 24 Master-fish by bridges In freshened milltails leaping. **1951** E. PAUL *Springtime in Paris* ix. 171 If the priests were right, and Busse, as a card-carrying Communist, was doomed to the foulest mill tails of hell, [etc.]. **1636** DAVENANT *Wits.* I. i. B3b, His wives Bracelet of *Mill-Testers. **1804** *Naval Chron.* XI. 156 Laden with mahogany and *mill-timber. **1731** ARBUTHNOT *Aliments* (1735) 223 The best Instruments ..for cracking of hard Substances..[are] Grinders, or *Mill-Teeth. **1890** *Syd. Soc. Lex.*, *Mill tooth*, a molar tooth. **1847** D. P. THOMPSON *Locke Amsden* x. 199 [The paper] came into town all damp from the press of *Mill-Town Emporium. **1902** S. E. WHITE *Blazed Trail* xxi. 155 He arrived out of breath in a typical little mill town. **1925** T. DREISER *Amer. Trag.* (1926) I. II. vi. 195 He decided to remain— later sitting down to dinner with a small group of milltown store and factory employees. **1944** *Reader's Digest* Dec. 16/1, I used to live, years ago, in a mill town in the Deep South. *c* **1000** *Ags. Gloss.* in Wr.-Wülcker 198/25 *Canalis*, þruh, *vel* *mylentroh. *c* **1440** *Promp. Parv.* 338/1 Mylle trow, or benge (mill troughe, or beugge, *sic*, *P.*), *farricapsa*. **1530** PALSGR. 245/1 Myll troughe or broke, *auge*. **1863** A. D. WHITNEY *Faith Gartney's Girlhood* xxiii. 218 It needs just such a man [as minister] among *mill-villages like these, he says. **1861** W. LONGSTAFFE in *Siege Pontefract Castle* (Surtees) Introd. 17 An old bridge over the *millwash. *c* **1325** in Kennett *Par. Ant.* I. 566 Item una acra apud le *mulnewey. **1598** MANWOOD *Lawes Forest* xxiii. (1615) 228 If any man haue stopped or strayted any Church-way, Mill-way, or other wayes in the Forest or Purlieu..you shall do us to weet thereof. **1770** G. WASHINGTON *Diaries* (1925) I. 381 Ball and his People went about 12 oclock to Framing the *Mill Work. **1791** W. JESSOP *Rep. River Witham* 8 Have an increase of power for Mill-work. **1799** *Hull Advert.* 29 June 2/2 A colour manufactory..together with the mill-work and several utensils. **1814** R. BUCHANAN (*title*) Practical Essays on Mill Work. **1892** *Daily News* 12 Dec. 2/3 Machinery and millwork. **1835** URE *Philos. Manuf.* 348 An astonishing difference between their intelligence and that of the *mill-workers. **1895** *Daily News* 3 Sept. 2/4 The strike of thirty thousand millworkers in Dundee. **1530** in J. Allen *Hist. Liskeard* (1856) 268 *Millemers and downemers. **1604–5** *Ibid.* 234 Le millheymers and downheymers.

† **mill**, *sb.*[2] *Obs.* Also 6 myll(e, mill(e. [a. F. *mil.* Cf. MILE *sb.*[2]]

1. = MILLET[1]. ***Turkey mill*** = Turkey millet.

1525 LD. BERNERS *Froiss.* II. ccxxiii. [ccix.] 697 Bredde, made of a grayne called mylle. **1533** ELYOT *Cast. Helthe* (1541) 10b, Meates inflatynge or wyndye: Beanes..Mille. Cucumbers. **1545** RAYNOLD *Byrth Mankynde* 52 Ryse, myll, & many other thynges. **1597** GERARDE *Herbal* I. lv. 77 It is called..Turkie Mill or Turkie Hirsse. **1610** W. FOLKINGHAM *Art of Survey* I. xi. 35 Tare, Cich and Mill loue moisture. **1660** F. BROOKE tr. *Le Blanc's Trav.* 323 They..get Mill, Rice, Pulse, and other graine.

b. *mill-seed* = MILLET-SEED.

1565 COOPER *Thesaurus*, *Cenchrites*, a precious stone, hauying in it thinges lyke mill seede.

2. ***mill of the sun***, transl. of mod. Latin *milium solis*: see MILIUM[1] 1 b.

1559 MORWYNG *Evonym.* 139 Take the rotes of fenell.. mill of the sunne, *scariolæ*, of everye one like much.

† **mill**, *sb.*[3] *Obs.* [? f. MILL *v.*, or short for some comb. of MILL *sb.*[1]] Ground oak-bark for tanning.

1626 BACON *Sylva* §625 The Conservation of Fruit would be also tried in Vessels, filled with Fine Sand,..Or in Meal and Flower; Or in Oakwood; or in Mill. **1697** *Lond. Gaz.* No. 3285/4 All other Makers or Dressers of Leather in Wooze, Mill, Oyl, Salt, Allom. **1711** *Ibid.* No. 4862/4 Skins ..to be tanned, tawed or dressed in Wooze, Mill, Alom.

† **mill**, *sb.*[4] *slang. Obs.* = MILL-KEN.

1607 DEKKER & WILKINS *Iests to make you Merie* 43 A word or two of the mill, *quasi* breakehouse. *Ibid.*, A strong Iron barre made sharpe at one end, and they which trade with that are called Mils. **1676** *Warning for House-Keepers* (title-p.), Thieves and Robbers which go under these titles, viz. the Gilter, the Mill, the Glasier [etc.].

mill (mɪl), *sb.*[5] [Shortened from L. *millēsimum* thousandth part, on the analogy of CENT. Cf. MIL.] **a.** A money of account in the U.S., being one-thousandth of a dollar (one-tenth of a cent). **b.** A proposed coin in value the one-thousandth of a pound (to replace the farthing) in a projected system of decimal coinage for Great Britain.

An alleged sense 'a thousandth part of anything' appears in recent U.S. dictionaries, but without quotations.

1786 in *Amer. Museum* (1789) II. 182 Mills, the lowest money of account, of which one thousand shall be equal to the federal dollar, or money unit. **1791** JEFFERSON in *Harper's Mag.* Mar. 535/1 At 20 cents pr lb it is 8 mills per dish. **1809** KENDALL *Trav.* I. xviii. 193 The denominations of money in the United States are dollars, cents or hundredth parts of dollars, and mills or thousandth parts. **1811** P. KELLY *Univ. Cambist* I. 9 A uniform way of keeping Accounts has been established in the United States (by an act of Congress in 1789) namely, in Dollars of 10 Dimes, 100 Cents, or 1000 Mills. **1821** J. Q. ADAMS *Rep. Weights &*

Meas. 55 Ask a tradesman..in any of our cities what is a dime or a mille, and the chances are four in five that he will not understand your question. **1882** SCUDDER *Noah Webster* ii. 71 A premium for copyright of five mills a copy. **1896** H. W. BROUGHTON in *Westm. Rev.* June CXLV. 668 Let the $\frac{1}{1000}$ of a pound, the coin to be issued in lieu of the farthing, be called a 'mill', and let ten of these make a 'victoria'. **1902** *Encycl. Brit.* XXXI. 292/1 The denominations [of coins in Hong Kong] are the dollar and 50, 20, and 5 cents in silver, and the cent and mill in bronze. **1974** *News & Reporter* (Chester, S. Carolina) 24 Apr. 1-A/8 Board Chairman J. F. (Buddy) Martin told him that in 1970 the county had raised from one mill to two the amount of money that was available for the hospital from the county.

c. *attrib.*, as ***mill tax***.

1848 *Indiana Hist. Soc. Publ.* (1895-1903) III. 514 The former will pay on a mill tax $200. **1853** in *Trans. Mich. Agric. Soc.* (1856) VII. 293 A mill tax is annually levied to purchase books for these libraries. **1903** *Scribner's Monthly* Oct. 486 They support the Universities by a direct mill tax levied upon the assessed valuation of the State.

mill (mɪl), *sb.*^{6} Also **mil**. Colloq. abbrev. of MILLIMETRE (esp. in *Photogr.*, designating a size of film).

1960 E. MORGAN *You're a Long Time Dead* 386 *Sandy*, I'll be getting pictures of you in that outfit, don't worry, as good as anyone can take—*Best Man*, What, on 35 mill? **1971** *Guardian* 25 Oct. 8/3 'Is it videotape or 35 mill?' she asks. **1974** S. GULLIVER *Vulcan Bulletins* 26 'What do you want?' 'Eighty-one mil. mortar bombs.'

mill., mill (mɪl), *sb.*^{7} Also **mil**. Colloq. abbrev. of MILLION.

1955 R. J. SCHWARTZ *Compl. Dict. Abbrev.* 112/3 *Mill.*, million. **1975** *New Yorker* 20 Jan. 29/1 Thanks a mil for your letter. **1975** D. LOWDEN *Bellman & True* xi. 55 'How much will he take then?' 'Anything we can give him, up to two mill.'

mill (mɪl), *v.*^{1} Also 6 **myll, mil**. [f. MILL *sb.*^{1}]

I. *trans.* To subject to the operation of a mill.

1. To pass (cloth or other material) through a fulling-mill; to thicken (cloth, etc.) by fulling.

1552 *Act 5 & 6 Edw. VI*, c. 6 §1 And beinge well scowred, thicked, mylled, and fully dried, everie yarde of everie suche Clothe shall waye thre pound at the leste. **1633** *Proclam.* in Rymer *Foedera* XIX. 447/2 All such white Worcester Clothes..as shall be milled in Gloucestershire. **1706** BOYER *Ann. Q. Anne* IV. 27 All broad-cloaths..after the same are fully mill'd and furnish'd. **1844** G. DODD *Textile Manuf.* iii. 103 The cloth..is then 'milled', 'fulled', or 'felted', that is, beaten until the fibres of the wool become so locked into each other [etc.].

transf. **1902** *Brit. Med. Jrnl.* No. 2146. 378, It [*sc.* the folded 'form'] is then 'milled' or pounded with heavy oak hammers.

2. a. To grind (corn) in a mill; to produce (flour) by grinding.

Chiefly in *passive*, used in market reports and the like.

1570 LEVINS *Manip.* 123/31 To Mil, *molere*. **1830** *Kyle Farm Rep.* 47 in *Libr. Usef. Knowl., Husb.* III, The grain thrashed is set down on one side,..and, when milled, the meal is entered separately. **1902** *Q. Rev.* July 327 By Lord Stanley's Act of 1843 a certain advantage was given to flour milled in Canada.

b. To pound or powder (tobacco).

1782 COWPER *To Rev. W. Bull* 38 This oval box, well filled With best tobacco finely milled. **1887** BLACKMORE *Springhaven* xxvi, Shaving with his girdle-knife a cake of rich tobacco, and then milling it complacently betwixt his horny palms.

c. To hull seeds by means of a mill. Also *intr.*, to undergo hulling or milling.

1863 BUCKMAN in *Gard. Chron.* 23 May 493 The best plan ..to pursue is to mill the Sainfoin seed, in which case its outer covering is removed. *Ibid.*, The Burnet..will not mill, but simply gets its wings broken off.

d. *Porcelain manufacture.*

1875 FORTNUM *Maiolica* v. 4 The vitreous substance.. being milled with water to the consistency of cream.

e. *Soap manufacture.*

1902 *Chambers's Jrnl.* Apr. 204/1 When quite hard, this fine soap is milled, or cut into very small shreds, after which it is pressed in moulds into fancy shapes. **1967** *Everyman's Encycl.* XI. 271/2 The chips are transferred to a mixer where the dyes and perfumes are added, which are then milled to make the soap plastic and homogeneous.

f. *slang.* To send to the treadmill; to send to prison (cf. MILL *sb.*^{1} 6).

1838 DICKENS *O. Twist* II. xxv. 83, I shouldn't have been milled if it hadn't been for her advice. But..what's six weeks of it?

3. To roll (metal); to flatten (metal) under a roller or beater.

1677 [see MILLED *ppl. a.* 4]. **1691** T. H[ALE] *Acc. New Invent.* 60 When this way of Milling Lead for Sheathing of Ships was first invented.

4. a. To stamp (coins) by means of the mill and press (see MILL *sb.*^{1} 3 b).

1687 A. LOVELL tr. *Thevenot's Trav.* II. 89 They [*sc.* coins] are stamped (as all the rest of their money) with the hammer, and not milled.

b. To flute the edge of (a coin or any piece of flat metal); to produce uniform or regular markings upon the edge of (a coin).

1724 SWIFT *Drapier's Lett.* iii. Wks. 1751 VIII. 329, I find the Half-pence were milled; which..is of great Use to prevent Counterfeits. **1855** MACAULAY *Hist. Eng.* xxii. IV. 805 The new crowns and half-crowns, broad, heavy and sharply milled, were ringing on all the counters. **1875** KNIGHT *Dict. Mech.* 1441/1 Castaining's machine for milling coin was introduced into the French mint in 1685. **1889** *Science* 20 Dec. 414 These bearings are conical, and milled through.

5. To beat or whip (chocolate, etc.) to a froth. ***to mill up***, to beat together. Also *fig.*

1662 H. STUBBE *Indian Nectar* ii. 9 They dissolved it [*sc.* chocolata] (being pouder'd) and milled it, tempering it by little and little with water in an Indian cup. **1747** MRS. GLASSE *Cookery* xvi. (1767) 290 Mill the cream till it is all of a thick froth. *Ibid.*, Then..over that whip your froth which you saved off the cream very well milled up. **1764** ELIZ. MOXON *Eng. Housew.* (ed. 9) 116 Take four ounces of chocolate,..and boil it in a pint of cream, then mill it..with a chocolate stick. **1769** MRS. RAFFALD *Eng. Housekpr.* (1778) 207 Mill them with a chocolate mill, to raise the froth, and take it off with a spoon as it rises. **1829** LANDOR *Imag. Conv.* Wks. 1853 II. 83/2 A chaplain milling an egg-posset over the fire. **1859** DICKENS *T. Two Cities* II. vii, A second milled and frothed the chocolate. **1897** KIPLING *Captains Courageous* vii. 142 Graaa—ouch! went the conch, while sea and sky were all milled up in milky fog.

fig. **1817** COLERIDGE *Satyrane's Lett.* i. in *Biog. Lit.*, etc. (1882) 245 What Pericles would not do to save a friend's life, you may be assured I would not hazard merely to mill the chocolate-pot of a drunken fool's vanity.

6. To throw, as undyed silk.

1844 G. DODD *Textile Manuf.* v. 151 Directions were also drawn up for..grassing, milling, and hand-scutching the flax. **1875** KNIGHT *Dict. Mech.*, *Mill*..to throw undyed silk.

7. To tumble (leather) within a wheel or cylinder containing some softening or tanning liquid.

1885 C. T. DAVIS *Manuf. Leather* xxvii. (1897) 415 Then they [*sc.* the sides] are put into a pin-wheel and milled for ten minutes.

8. To cut (metal) with a milling-tool.

1875 KNIGHT *Dict. Mech.*, *Mill*..a machine designed for milling where only a light or medium cut is required. **1884** *Ibid.* 607/1 By means of the swinging sleeve true circles of greater or less diameter can be milled on the face of the work.

9. To saw (timber) in a saw-mill.

18.. *Art Age* IV. 46 (Cent.), Lumbermen charge the consumer for the full measurement of the boards [for floors] before they are milled.

10. *Mining.* **a.** To crush or pound into fragments; to grind to powder.

1883 *Standard* 20 Jan. 1/5 The whole of the quartz removed has been milled. **1895** *Times* 19 Feb. 3/6 For the year 1894 there was milled 2,827,365 tons.

b. To yield under the process of crushing or grinding.

1877 RAYMOND *Statist. Mines & Mining* 247 The quartz ..will mill about $20 to the ton. **1897** *Westm. Gaz.* 19 Oct. 8/3, I would not like to say that it will mill that. It will certainly mill 1 oz.

II. 11. *slang.* **a.** To beat, strike, thrash; to fight, overcome; to smash, break, break open. Also *intr.* or *absol.* to box; occas. with *away*.

c **1700** *Street Robberies Consider'd*, Mill, to beat. **1753** *Discov. J. Poulter* (ed. 2) 39 Mill the Cull to his long Libb; kill the Man dead... Mill the Quod; break the Gaol. *Ibid.* 40 Mill his Nobb; break his Head. **1810** *Sporting Mag.* XXXVI. 231 The Black..threatens to mill the whole race of fighters of the day. **1825** C. M. WESTMACOTT *Eng. Spy* I. 282 Milling the glaze. **1840** THACKERAY *Cox's Diary* Wks. 1900 III. 223 Tug..milled away—one, two, right and left,—like a little hero as he is. **1864** [HEMYNG] *Eton School Days* vii. 75 Butler Burke was going to mill Chorley. *Ibid.* 77 Are you going to mill, or are you not?

b. ***to mill doll, dolly***: to beat hemp or flax as a prison occupation. Cf. MILL-DOLL *sb.*

1714 A. SMITH *Highwaymen* (ed. 2) I. 141 Having been often punisht at hard Labour in Bridewell, which beating of Hemp the Thieves call Mill dolly. **1733** BUDGELL *Bee* IV. 477 Then mill on dear Polly,..The Hemp thou art beating may hang him to-Morrow. **1780** R. TOMLINSON *Slang Past.* vi. 7 When sitting with Nancy, what sights have I seen!..But now she mills doll. **1785** GROSE *Dict. Vulg. Tongue*.

III. To go round like a mill.

12. a. *intr.* Of cattle: To keep moving round and round in a mass; also, to move in a circle. Also *transf.* (of persons, vehicles, etc.) and *fig.*

1888 T. ROOSEVELT in *Century Mag.* Apr. 862/1 The cattle may begin to run, and then get 'milling'—that is, all crowd together into a mass like a ball, wherein they move round and round. **1895** KIPLING *2nd Jungle Bk.* 79 The deer and the pig and the nilghai were milling round and round in a circle of eight or ten miles' radius. **1910** W. M. RAINE *Bucky O'Connor* 227, I expect you were able to make out, even if I did get the letters to milling around wrong. **1911** H. QUICK *Yellowstone Nights* v. 127 The main thing the matter was that failure o' his a-millin' through his mental facilities. **1919** L. F. CODY *Memories Buffalo Bill* 302 Indians and soldiers milled, the Indians fighting with their knives, the soldiers with their guns. **1927** H. E. FOSDICK *Pilgrimage to Palestine* 262 We look down upon the throng milling around the Chapel of the Sepulcher. **1935** *Punch* 29 May 648/2 The sergeants are milling round like madmen with last-minute instructions. **1957** J. KEROUAC *On Road* (1958) v. 33 First we milled with all the cowboy-dudded tourists..at bars. **1968** R. M. PATTERSON *Finlay's River* III. 164 To follow their wanderings in detail would be pointless. They milled around like that for the next two days, obsessed with this ridge-climbing idea.

b. *trans.* To cause to 'mill' or mass in a circle.

1901 *Munsey's Mag.* XXV. 406/2 At last the cattle..ran with less energy, and it was presently easy to 'mill' them into a circle and to turn them where it seemed most desirable.

c. *fig.* To turn *over* in one's mind.

1905 *Smart Set* Oct. 17/1 No,..I ain't buyin' no dishes. I was just kind o' millin' things over to myself. **1923** R. D. PAINE *Comrades of Rolling Ocean* xvii. 298 Judson, on guard in the cabin, was milling this problem over. **1958** 'A. GILBERT' *Death against Clock* viii. 111 Barney's milled it over and over..and we can't think of any reason. **1964** M. GOWING *Britain & Atomic Energy* ix. 250 Nor did they [*sc.* the American engineers] want to spend much time in milling over alternative approaches to problems for which they had chosen..their own solution.

13. *intr.* Of a whale.

1840 F. D. BENNETT *Whaling Voy.* II. 221 A whale 'milled', or turned suddenly round, upon receiving the harpoons. **1874** SCAMMON *Marine Animals* 311 Gloss., *Mill*, to turn in an opposite direction, or nearly so; as, 'The whale was running to windward, but "milled", and ran to leeward'.

mill (mɪl), *v.*^{2} *slang.* [Possibly a use of prec.: cf. MILL *v.*^{1} 11.] *trans.* Orig. in phrase ***to mill a ken***, to rob a house. Later, to steal.

1567 HARMAN *Caveat* 84 To myll a Ken, to robbe a house. **1609** DEKKER *Lanth. & Candle Lt.* ciij b, If we niggle or mill a bowsing ken. **1621** B. JONSON *Gipsies Metamorph.* (1640) II. 65 Can they Cant, or Mill? are they masters of their Arts? *a* **1700** B. E. *Dict. Cant. Crew*, *Mill*, to Steal, Rob, or Kill. **1753** *Discov. J. Poulter* (ed. 2) 10 When we went a Milling that Swagg, that is, a Breaking open that Shop. **1811** *Sporting Mag.* XXXVII. 13 He had milled my wipe. **1818** SCOTT *Hrt. Midl.* xxx, One might have milled the Bank of England, and less noise about it.

mill, obs. form of MIL.

millable (ˈmɪləb(ə)l), *a.* [f. MILL *v.*^{1} or *sb.*^{1} + -ABLE.] **a.** Suitable for milling (sense 1).

1905 A. COCKAYNE in *13th Rep. Dept. Agric.* (N.Z.) Appendix x. 402 Most of the Phormium [in flax swamps] was short, but there were considerable quantities of good millable fibre... All the millable flax is being rapidly cut down, and no doubt these swamps will in time become good agricultural land. **1955** *Times* 2 May 23/5 As far as millable grades were concerned, the wheat market showed little feature during the past week. **1959** *Cape Argus* 15 Aug. 1/5 The fire..destroyed about 2,000 tons of millable cane before it could be brought under control. **1963** *Times* 23 Feb. 5/1 The millable oat championship went to a Blenda sample from Mr. W. Sharp, of Banff, Aberdeen.

b. Suitable for cutting in a sawmill.

1924 *Times Trade & Engin. Suppl.* 29 Nov. 250/2 It is proposed..to open up 500,000 acres of farming land and 1,000,000,000 feet of millable bush. **1969** *Northern Territory News* (Darwin) *Focus '69* 83/1 There is a considerable stand of timber again reaching 'millable' stage. **1972** *Country Life* 16 Mar. 653/3 Some sort of grading [of timber]..based on veneer, planking and millable butts in the case of hardwoods.

millage (ˈmɪlɪdʒ). *U.S.* [f. MILL *sb.*^{5} + -AGE.] The rate of taxation in mills per dollar to which a given place is liable.

1891 in *Columbus* (Ohio) *Dispatch* 20 Feb., There are cities in which the rate is higher than in Toledo, for instance, Findlay 35·7 mills, Lima 33·4 mills, Tiffin 30·4 mills,..but in the eastern or southern part of the State, excepting Ironton, as great millage as Toledo is not presented in the tables.

Millain(e, -an(e, -ayn(e, obs. ff. MILAN^1.

millainer, -aner, obs. forms of MILLINER *sb.*

millathowme, obs. form of MILLER'S THUMB.

ˈmillboard. [Altered from *milled board*: see MILLED *ppl. a.* 4.] A kind of stout pasteboard, made of a pulp of old rope, sacking, paper, and other coarse matter and 'milled' or rolled with high pressure. Also, a 'board' or piece of this material. ***millboard cutter*** (see quot. 1884).

1712 *Lond. Gaz.* No. 5014/5 Duties upon.. Pastboard, Millboard, Scaleboard. **1812** J. SMYTH *Pract. of Customs* (1821) 155 Mill Boards are the thickest sort of Pasteboard, used by Book-binders for the covering of Books. **1884** KNIGHT *Dict. Mech.* Suppl., *Mill Board Cutter*, a machine for cutting to size mill and card boards for binding, etc.

b. A specially prepared 'board' for sketching.

1854 THACKERAY *Newcomes* I. xxvii. 258 Those smooth mill-boards, those slab-tinted sketching blocks [etc.]. **1859** GULLICK & TIMBS *Paint.* 217 Milboards are..well adapted for sketching in oil colours from nature.

ˈmill-dam. [MILL *sb.*^{1}] A dam constructed across a stream to interrupt its flow and raise its level so as to render it available for turning a mill-wheel. Also, the entire area covered by the water held in check by the dam.

1182 in Kennett *Par. Ant.* (1818) I. 187 Per le mulnedam ..in veterem rivulum et ipsam mulnedam. **1394-5** *Durham Acc. Rolls* (Surtees) 599 Mosse pro le Milndam. *c* **1440** *Alphabet of Tales* 183 He went furth vnto þe myln dam of þe abbay, & þer he lowpid in & drownyd hym. *c* **1575** in *Balfour's Practicks* (1754) 581 Thay tak smoltis or salmond in the miln-dammis. **1632** *Morpeth Ct. Leet Rec.* in *Archæol. Æliana* XVI. 72 For Castinge hir yarne into the millne dame ..and dampnum iijs. **1763** *Brit. Mag.* IV. 51 As thirteen boys were sliding near a mill dam..the ice broke by the miller's suddenly drawing up the sluices. **1880** JAMIESON, *Mill-dam*,..the water collected, by means of a dam, to supply a mill.

attrib. **1833** TENNYSON *Poems* 33 Fishing in the milldam-water.

milldew, obs. form of MILDEW *sb.*

†**mill-doll**, *sb. Obs. slang.* [f. MILL *v.*^{1} + DOLL *sb.*^{1}] The bridewell. Cf. MILL *v.*^{1} 11 b.

1781 MESSINK *Choice of Harlequin* (Farmer), *'Keeper of Bridewell's Song'*, I'm Jigger Dubber here, and you are welcome to mill doll. **1823** 'JON BEE' *Dict. Turf.* **1812** J. H. VAUX *Flash Dict.*, *Mill-doll*, an obsolete name for Bridewell house of correction in Bridge-Street, Blackfriars.

'mill-doll, *v.* *Whaling.* [Prob. in some way connected with the phr. in MILL *v.*^{1} 11 b. (Cf. DOLLY *sb.* 4 b.)] (See quot.)

1820 SCORESBY *Acc. Arctic Reg.* I. 310 *note*, Mill-dolling, consists in breaking a passage through thin ice .. by a sort of ram, let fall from the bowsprit.

mille (mɪl), *sb.* In certain card games: A counter representing ten 'fishes' or 'points'.

1830 'EIDRAH TREBOR' *Hoyle Made Fam.* 37. **1876** CAPT. CRAWLEY *Card Player's Man.* 196 (Quadrille), *Mille* is a mark of ivory which is sometimes used, and stands for ten fish. **1878** H. H. GIBBS *Ombre* 8 The small round counters, which used to be called Milles, count as ten points.

mille, obs. form of MILE.

millecrate, variant of MELICRATE *Obs.*

1563 HYLL *Art Garden.* (1593) 111 Buglosse steeped in wine, and tempered with Millecrate.

† **millecuple**, *a.* *Obs.* [irreg. f. L. *mille* thousand, after *decuple*.] Thousand-fold. Hence † **millecu'plation**, the action of increasing a thousand-fold.

1659 H. MORE *Immort. Soul* III. iv. 367 Every Object that is near would not onely seem double, but centuple, or millecuple. **1678** CUDWORTH *Intell. Syst.* I. § 37. 173 Nor any Triplication or indeed Milleclupation [*sic*] of them improve the same into Reason and Understanding. **1754** HILDROP *Misc. Wks.* II. 47 If any of these [*sc.* People] should .. be created your Lordship's Peers, they would be in the same millecuple Proportion greater, and wiser, and better than they were before.

milled (mɪld), *ppl. a.* [f. MILL *v.*^{1} + -ED^1.]

† **1.** ? Polished by some mechanical process. *Obs.*

1622 F. MARKHAM *Bk. War* I. x. 39 All these seuerall parts of Armor is rather to bee of a Russet or blacke colour then mil'd.

2. Of coins: **a.** Coined or struck by the mill and press; made in a mill. **b.** Having the edge fluted or grooved by the operation of milling.

1659 *Lond. Chanticleers* xii. 26 He has got my box of mill'd sixpences and Harry groates. **1662** in Folkes *Table Eng. Silver Coins* (1745) 111 Milled unites of the same weight. **1697** DRYDEN *Æneis* Ded. (f) 2, I had certainly been reduc'd to pay the Publick in hammer'd Money for want of Mill'd; that is in the same old Words which I had us'd before. **1702** ADDISON *Dial. Medals* iii. 153, I have seen several modern Coins .. that have had part of the Legend running round the edges, like the *Decus et Tutamen* in our milled money. **1854** HUMPHREYS *Coin. Brit. Emp.* 116 In 1663 the first issue of the improved milled coinage took place. **1880** *Academy* 29 May 406 A selection of rare .. milled shillings from Elizabeth to George III.

c. *transf.* Marked with transverse grooves or ribs; *esp.* of the head of a screw, etc., serrated to afford a hold for adjustment.

1705 J. PETIVER in *Phil. Trans.* XXV. 1953 The Striæ are flat and milled, like the edges of a new Shilling. **1803** MUDGE *ibid.* XCIII. 404 At E E are seen two milled-headed screws. **1861** C. W. KING *Ant. Gems* (1866) 167 These borders are milled, or formed of small strokes set close together. **1872** NICHOLSON *Palæont.* 106 Above the Acetabulum .. there is a .. ring, more or less 'milled', for the attachment of the muscular fibres which move the spine. **1898** *Cycling* 38 A milled or hexagonal ring K is then screwed over the inner steering tube.

† **d.** Of stockings and caps: ? Ribbed. *Obs.*

1684 OTWAY *Atheist* I. i, Buzzing about your Ears concerning Poets, Plays .. mill'd Stockings .. and everything else which they do not understand. **1691** *Satyr agst. French* 7 Nay, we are grown so arrogantly vain, Our Stockings must be Mill'd, our Shooes Campaign. **1789** *Trans. Soc. Arts* I. 25 Cambrick, Lace, Milled Caps, and various Kinds of Paper. **1809** A. HENRY *Trav.* 34, I .. covered myself only with .. a molton, or blanket coat; and a large, red, milled worsted cap.

3. Pressed, rolled, 'fulled'.

1642 *Rates Merchandizes* 48 Double Sayes, or Flanders Searges... Mild Sayes the piece .. 06.00.00. **1670** *Lond. Gaz.* No 517/4 A Stuff Cloak lined with Mill'd serge. **1802** in *Spirit Publ. Jrnls.* (1803) VI. 283 Her coachman .. within the cumbrous circumference of a double-milled great coat. **1831** Double-milled [see DOUBLE C 4].

4. Flattened by rolling or beating; esp. in ***milled board*** (= MILLBOARD), ***milled lead***.

1677 *Lond. Gaz.* No. 1232/4 The late Invention for Milled Lead. **1691** T. H[ALE] *Acc. New Invent.* (title-p.), The Mill'd-Lead-sheathing, and the Excellency and cheapness of Mill'd-Lead in preference to Cast Sheet-Lead. **1707** *Lond. Gaz.* No. 4342/4 At the Pastboard Warehouse .. are sold brown Mill'd Boards ready beat, fit for Bookbinders. **1711** *Act 10 Anne* c. 18 § 37 All Pastboards, Mildboards and Scaleboards which shall be imported. **1858** *Skyring's Builders' Prices* (ed. 48) 105 Milled Lead, per cwt. £1 7*s* 0*d*. **1859** *Stationers' Handbk.* 74 *Milled Boards*, strong flexible boards, of various thicknesses and sizes, made from old tarred rope. **1868** *Ibid.* (ed. 4) 119 *Milled*, a term applied to paper, when rolled to an ordinary surface.

5. Whipped or beaten to a froth.

1760–72 H. BROOKE *Fool of Qual.* (1809) I. 171 They .. breakfasted on a pot of milled chocolate.

6. a. Ground in a mill. **b.** Hulled. **c.** Pressed in a mill to extract juice.

1813 T. DAVIS *Agric. Wilts* Gloss., *Milled Hop*, hop clover-seed cleaned from the husk. *a* **1831** BENTHAM *Lang.* Wks. 1843 VIII. 317/1 Milled corn is not cold; ice is cold. **1884** G. W. CABLE *Creoles of Louisiana* xxxii. (1885) 249 Milled breadstuffs still sought the cheapest rates of freight.

7. (See quot.; perh. not the same word.)

1886 C. SCOTT *Sheep-Farming* 18 When they [ewes] have been crossed with rams of a different breed, they are called crones, crocks, or milled ewes.

‖ **mille-feuille** (milfœj). Pl. **mille-feuilles**. [Fr., lit. 'a thousand leaves'.] A rich pastry consisting of thin layers of puff pastry filled with jam, cream, etc. Also *attrib.* and *fig.*

1895 G. A. SALA *Thorough Good Cook* xiv. 426 Mille Feuilles (Italian Pyramid). **1902** S. BEATY-POWNALL *'Queen' Cookery Bks.* XI. vi. 169 *Millefeuilles, Gâteau* (also known as *Gâteau Milfras*). **1918** A. BENNETT *Roll-Call* I. viii. 169, I should like a strawberry ice, and a lemon-squash, and a millefeuille cake. **1945** N. MITFORD *Pursuit of Love* xviii. 146 Soon Davy was falling upon *éclairs* and *mille feuilles* with all the abandon of a schoolboy. **1967** *Listener* 21 Dec. 802/2 When strangers meet, and nature calls, our society splits into a *mille-feuille* of social strata: each one of us clinging to our own euphemism. **1971** COOMBES & WAKELIN *Good Housek. Advanced Cooking is Fun* xv. 218 *Mille-feuilles*... Spread stiffly whipped cream onto the centre of the puff paste layer.

millefiore (mɪlɪfɪ'ɔərɪ). Also **-fiori**. [a. It. *millefiori*, f. *mille* thousand + *fiori* pl. of *fiore* flower.] (Also ***millefiore glass***.) A kind of ornamental glass made by fusing together a number of glass rods of different sizes and colours, and cutting the mass into sections which exhibit ornamental figures of varying pattern, and are usually embedded in colourless transparent glass to make paper-weights, etc.

1849 PELLATT *Curios. Glass Making* 25 Millefiore Glass. *Ibid.* 110 The *Mille-Fiore*, or star-work of the Venetians. **1874** *Jrnl. Archæol. Assoc.* Dec. 440 It is of early Millefiori glass, the mass looking much like chalcedony.

‖ **millefleurs** (milflœr). Also **millefleur**. [F.; in sense 1 f. *eau de millefleurs*, lit. 'water of a thousand flowers'.]

a. A perfume distilled from flowers of different kinds.

a **1850** J. ATKINSON in A. Davis *Package & Print* (1967) plate 8 (Advt.), Essence of Millefleur, Bouquet, Marechalle. **1854** THACKERAY *Newcomes* v, When you appeared in your neat pulpit with your fragrant pocket-handkerchief (and your sermon likewise all millefleurs). **1868** MISS BRADDON *Dead Sea Fr.* iii, The letters exhaled a faint odour of millefleurs.

b. (Freq. hyphenated or written as two words.) A pattern of flowers and leaves used for tapestry, porcelain, etc. Usu. *attrib.*

1908 J. F. BLACKER *Chats on Oriental China* x. 123 The colour is not nearly as brilliant as in the '*mille fleurs*' class, though the same wavy porcelain is to be noted. **1933** *Burlington Mag.* July 35/1 The style of the tapestry .. the particular type of *mille fleurs* pattern. **1933** *New Statesman* 14 Oct. 444/1 The two mille fleur boots, entirely encrusted with sharp microscopic forget-me-nots. **1938** *Burlington Mag.* June p. xxix/1 The fifteenth century French armorial tapestry with its typical *mille-fleurs* decoration of varied flowers and leafwork on the coveted red ground. **1960** H. HAYWARD *Antique Coll.* 183/2 *Mille fleurs*, decoration occurring on Chinese porcelain with panels of growing plants reserved on a flower-covered ground. **1970** *Centennial Acquisitions Mus. Fine Arts Boston* 57 (*caption*) The relatively small size of this *mille-fleurs* .. tapestry suggests that it may be part of a larger hanging.

milleflorous (mɪlɪ'flɔərəs), *a.* *Bot.* [f. L. *mille* thousand + *flōr-*, *flōs* flower + -OUS.] Having very numerous flowers.

1856 in MAYNE *Expos. Lex.* **1890** in *Syd. Soc. Lex.*

millefoil(e, obs. forms of MILFOIL.

millefoliate (mɪlɪ'fəʊlɪət). *Bot.* [f. L. *mille* thousand + *foli-um* leaf + -ATE^2.] 'Having leaves that are very much incised, so as to resemble many smaller leaves' (*Syd. Soc. Lex.* 1890).

millegrain ('mɪlɪgreɪn). Also **milligrain**. [f. L., *mille* thousand + GRAIN *sb.*^{1} 12.] (See quot. 1951.) Also *attrib.*

1948 W. A. JACKSON *Jewellery Repairing* iv. 49 If the setting be a millegraine one and the tiny beaded edge be worn down .. a new edge can sometimes be brought up by the burnisher. **1951** M. FLOWER *Victorian Jewellery* 253 *Millegrain*, a kind of setting in which the metal gripping to stone is decorated with a line of tiny grains or beads. **1960** H. HAYWARD *Antique Coll.* 183 *Millegrain setting*, a means of setting a gemstone whereby the stone is held in a mount ornamented with a band of very small beads of metal. **1970** E. BRUTON *Diamonds* xx. 349 In the nineteenth century many small diamonds were set in a form known as milligrain, in which the metal used to hold the diamonds was crenelated by drawing a hardened steel ring round the metal.

millelote, obs. form of MELILOT.

milleme, var. MILLIEME.

millemeter, obs. form of MILLIMETRE.

‖ **Mille Miglia** ('mille 'miʎʎa). [It., lit. 'a thousand miles'.] The name of a sports-car race run over approx. one thousand miles of roads in Italy from 1927 to 1957; also *fig.*

1933 B. LYNDON *Combat: Motor Racing Hist.* viii. 133 The entry list suggested that there would be a merciless fight between the Bugatti team and the Alfa-Romeos, which had just won the Mille Miglia. **1957** S. MOSS *In Track of Speed* ii. 27 The Italians had made a real Roman holiday of the Mille Miglia and .. had come to regard themselves as almost unbeatable. **1963** P. DRACKETT *Motor Rallying* v. 75 The galloping Gaul's remarkable record included first in the Alpine and German and second in the Mille Miglia. **1966** W. COURT *Power & Glory* III. xviii. 166/1 The Mille Miglia, run in traditional form on 23 occasions between 1927 and 1957, was a .. throw back to the days that had ended with Paris–Madrid. **1969** J. LEASOR *They don't make them like that any More* i. 1 The pinheaded nutters in the Minis .. roared about as though they were overtaking each other in the Mille Miglia. **1970** M. O'BRINE *Crambo* xvii. 77 He took a four-berth cabin .. that .. had cockroaches doing a Mille Miglia around the wash-basin.

millen, obs. form of MILAN.

† **millenar**, *sb.* and *a.* *Obs.* *rare*$^{-1}$. [ad. L. *millēnārius*: see MILLENARY.] = MILLENARIAN.

1654 VILVAIN *Theol. Treat.* iv. 118 Prophecies in the old Testament of the Messiah .. Millenars apply .. to Christ's second coming. *Ibid.* vii. 198 The Millenar doctrine was .. general in the next age after Apostles.

millenarian (mɪlɪ'nɛərɪən), *a.* and *sb.* Also 8–9 **millennarian**. [f. L. *millēnārius* (see MILLENARY) + -AN.] **A.** *adj.*

1. Of or pertaining to the millennium; holding the doctrine of the millennium.

1631 HEYLIN *St. George* 46 So the Papists adore Papias a Millenarian Hereticke. **1785** *Gentl. Mag.* LV. 392 Those Millennarians, believing the certainty of Christ's second coming, and his Millennarian Kingdom, lived not the holy life enjoined them. **1853** W. H. GOOLD in *Owen's Wks.* XI. 3 Goodwin may have held some millenarian views akin to the notion of a fifth monarchy.

b. Suited or appropriate to a millenarian.

1684 T. BURNET *Th. Earth* II. 175 As to the epistle of Barnabas, .. the genius of it is very much millenarian.

2. In the etymological sense: Relating or pertaining to a thousand.

In mod. Dicts.

B. *sb.* One who holds or believes that Christ will reign on earth in person for a thousand years; a believer in the millennium.

[**1552** *Articles of Religion* xli, Thei that goe aboute to renewe the fable of heretickes called Millenarii, be repugnant .. to holie Scripture.] *a* **1674** CLARENDON *Surv. Leviath.* (1676) 221 He makes his Reign longer upon Earth than ever the Millenarians imagin'd. **1787** *Minor* IV. ii. 206 Was I a millenarian, I probably should not hesitate to pronounce it the spot intended for the thousand years enjoyment after the day of judgment. **1883** *Encycl. Brit.* XVI. 318/1 The millennarians of the ancient church. **1890** *Spectator* 6 Sept. 305 It is hard to be honestly contemptuous of a convinced Millenarian.

millenarianism (mɪlɪ'nɛərɪənɪz(ə)m). [f. prec. + -ISM.] The doctrine of or belief in the coming of the millennium.

1856 [see EBIONITISM]. **1864** *Chamber's Encycl.* VI. 459/2 From this time, the church formally rejected millenarianism in its sensuous 'visible' form. **1881** STANLEY *Chr. Instit.* v. (ed. 2) 85 The whole history of early Millenarianism implies the same incapacity for distinguishing between poetry and prose. **1894** J. H. BLUNT *Dict. Sects* (ed. 2) 329 Millenarianism is to a certain degree not unorthodox, but .. Millenarians who uphold the doctrine of a sensual or Judaic Millennium are unequivocally condemned by theologians. **1937** A. REESE *Approaching Advent Christ* 304 Millennarianism has need to pray frequently to be saved from its friends. **1957** *Oxf. Dict. Chr. Ch.* 900 In the early Church, Millenarianism was upheld principally among the Gnostics and Montanists, but also upheld by more orthodox writers... Although primitive Millenarianism lingered on .. down to the end of the 4th cent., it received its death-blow from Origen. **1961** B. R. WILSON *Sects & Society* II. ix. 189 Mrs Eddy .. was unrelenting in her attacks on spiritualism, mesmerism .. and millenarianism.

millenarism. [f. MILLENAR + -ISM.] = MILLENARIANISM.

1650 BP. HALL *Rev. Unrevealed* viii, The First Paradox of Millenarism. **1894** F. C. CONYBEARE *Apology of Apollonius* 358/1 Millenarism of Gospel. **1957** P. WORSLEY *Trumpet shall Sound* 232 Where millenarism survives in countries with popular secular political organizations, it is generally escapist and quietist. **1962** N. COHN in S. L. Thrupp *Millennial Dreams in Action* II. 32 The oldest form of millenarism of which much is known is the messianic hope of the Jews. *Ibid.* 35 Marxists have sometimes tried to interpret the millenarism of the Spirituals .. as a protest by poor peasants. **1971** *Catholic Dict. Theol.* III. 280 This decision amounted to an assessment that a mitigated Millenarism .. was an error in faith, even if it could not yet be called a heresy.

millenarist ('mɪlɪnərɪst), *sb.* (and *a.*) In 9 **millennarist**. [f. MILLENAR-Y + -IST.] = MILLENARY *sb.* Also *attrib.* or as *adj.*

1862 E. B. ELLIOTT *Horæ Apoc.* (ed. 5) I. 21 The works of both Irenæus and of other early Millennarists. **1894** F. C. CONYBEARE *Apology of Apollonius* 287 They began to compromise with the world .. and they laid up their old millenarist system of faith and morality. **1957** P. WORSLEY *Trumpet shall Sound* vii. 137 These Papuans are typical of all millenarists. **1962** M. ELIADE in S. L. Thrupp *Millennial Dreams in Action* III. 143 The millenarist movements became savagely anti-Christian. **1967** R. A. MARKUS in *Cambr. Hist. Later Greek & Early Medieval Philos.* 408 He had .. abandoned all traces of millenarist thinking. **1971** *Catholic Dict. Theol.* III. 279 Justin .. has been cited .. as a Millenarist. *Ibid.*, This is frankly Millenarist. *Ibid.* 280 In the Middle Ages Joachim of Flora revived Millenarist ideas.

millenary ('mɪlɪnərɪ), *a.* and *sb.* Also 7 **millinary**. [ad. L. *millēnāri-us* consisting of or containing a thousand (in Eccl. Latin used *sb.* in

the sense B 4 below), f. *millēnī* a thousand each, f. *mille* thousand. Cf. F. *millénaire*.]

A. *adj.*

1. a. Consisting of or pertaining to a thousand, esp. a period of a thousand years.

a **1641** Bp. Mountagu *Acts & Mon.* (1642) 250 Yet the Jews..gave not over complaints and petitions.., a Millenary number of Complainants there were. *a* **1646** J. Gregory *Posthuma, Καῖναν Δεύτερος* (1649) 84 After six daies, that is six thousand Years duration of the World there shall bee a seventh daie, or Millenarie Sabbath of Rest. **1727** Arbuthnot *Tables Anc. Coins,* etc. 13 The millenary Sestertium..is marked with a line cross the top thus HS. **1783** Cowper *Let. to J. Newton* 30 Nov., I have wondered in former days at the patience of the Antediluvian world; that they could endure a life almost millenary, with so little variety as seems to have fallen to their share. **1796** Pegge *Anonym.* (1809) 270 The elliptical expressions, *in the year 20*, or *in the year 88*, wherein the millenary and the centenary numbers are omitted, are not altogether modern. **1855** W. H. Mill *Applic. Panth. Princ.* (1861) 132 The millenary periods of Greek and Roman domination. **1888** *Pall Mall G.* 12 May 6/1 In 1886 was the millenary commemoration of the Domesday Book.

b. Commanding one thousand men.

1608 Willet *Hexapla Exod.* 274 There were sixe hundred tribunes or millenarie officers. **1632** Holland *Cyrupædia* 167 Cyrus commaunded the Persian millenarie Colonels.. to come unto him.

c. *Hist.* ***millenary petition***: a petition presented by a number of Puritan ministers (represented as one thousand) on the progress of James I to London in April 1603, praying for certain changes in ecclesiastical ceremonial, etc. ***millenary plaintiffs***: the ministers who presented this petition.

1603 Bp. W. Barlow *Confer. Hampton Crt.* (1604) 2 Agentes for the Millenarie Plaintiffes. **1733** Neal *Hist. Purit.* II. 5 The Puritans presented their Millenary Petition, so called because it was said to be subscribed by a thousand hands. **1874** Green *Short Hist.* viii. §ii. 464 The Millenary Petition..which was presented to James the First..by nearly eight hundred clergymen.

2. a. Of or pertaining to the millennium, or those believing in the millennium.

1577 Hanmer *Anc. Eccl. Hist.* (1663) 50 He said there should be the term of a Millenary feast allotted for marriage. **1651** Jer. Taylor *Serm. Summer Half-yr.* xii. 154 We are apt to dream that God will make his saints raigne here as kings in a millenary kingdom. **1690** Baxter *Kingd. Christ* ii. (1691) 12 The Millenary Opinion was..early received by some followers of Papias.

b. *transf.* and *fig.*

1700 Dryden *Pal. & Arc.* Ded. to D'chess Ormond 81 When at Your second Coming You appear, (For I foretell that Millenary Year) The sharpen'd Share shall vex the Soil no more. **1722** Pope *Let. R. Digby* 10 Oct., 'Tis like the Kingdom of the Just upon Earth... Why will you ever, of your own accord, end such a Millenary Year in London?

B. *sb.*

1. a. An aggregate of one thousand; esp. a continuous period of one thousand years; ten centuries.

1550 Bale *Eng. Votaries* II. 10b, Thys mood deuylsh Syluestre, after the full accomplyshement of thys myllenary of yeares,..ded many tymes..make sacryfyce to yᵉ deuyll. **1622** Malynes *Anc. Law-Merch.* 11 Others doe account the same by thousands, or millinaries. **1646** Sir T. Browne *Pseud. Ep.* vi. i. 278 He conceaveth the Elementall frame shall end in the seventh or Sabbaticall millenary. **1684** T. Burnet *Th. Earth* II. 35 Johannes Damascenus..takes seven millenaries for the entire space of the world. **1704** Hearne *Duct. Hist.* (1714) I. 31 It [this Period of 4000 Years] fills up the Vacancies which the Silence of the Scripture has left towards the End of the Fourth Millenary. **1855** J. H. Newman *Callista* (1890) 44 We danced through three nights, dancing the old millenary out, dancing the new millenary in. **1875** E. White *Life in Christ* III. xxiii. (1878) 332 If that prophetic millenary stands, by a figure of days, for years.

b. A thousandth anniversary or its celebration; a millennium.

1897 F. Harrison (*title*) Millenary of King Alfred. **1955** *Times* 18 Aug. 9/6 The few simple features which moulded the town in the past govern its shape still, so that, for all that it is new, it is recognizably Kassel. (The town celebrated its millenary in 1913). **1974** E. Lemarchand *Buried in Past* vi. 114 The borough plans to celebrate its alleged Millenary in August. I say alleged, because its claim to have received a charter from King Edgar in the year 973 has been discredited for some time. **1975** *Church Times* 14 Feb. 18/3 St. John's, Little Missenden, celebrates its millenary.

2. *Hist.* One of the signatories of 'Millenary Petition' (see A. 1 c above).

1691 Wood *Ath. Oxon.* I. 351 Dʳ. Sparke was..called to the Conference at Hampton-Court..appearing in the behalf of the Millinaries.

3. An officer in command of a thousand men.

1555 W. Watreman *Fardle Facions* II. x. 211 The Centuriane obeied the Millenarie, that had charge of a thousande. **1598–1600** Hakluyt *Voyages* I. 62 Ouer ten Millenaries or captains of a 1000 he [Chingis Cham] placed, as it were, a Colonel.

4. A believer in the millennium; one who holds that Christ will reign in person over the earth for a period of one thousand years.

1561 T. Norton *Calvin's Inst.* III. xxv. 264b, In a little after there folowed the Millenaries, whiche limited the reigne of Christe to a thousande yeares. **1605** Chapman, etc., *Eastw. Hoe* v, I have had of all sorts of men..vnder my Keyes: & almost of all Religions i' the land, as Papist, Protestant,..Millenary, Famely o' Loue,..&c. **1645** R. Baillie *Lett. & Jrnls.* (Bannatyne Cl.) II. 313 Send me the rest of Forbes:..I marvell I can find nothing in its index against the Millenaries: I cannot think the author a Millenarie. **1708** *Brit. Apollo* No. 39. 1/2 The Millenaries found their Opinion upon several Texts. *c* **1810** Coleridge in *Lit. Rem.* (1838) III. 262 The Catholic Millenaries looked forward to carnal pleasures in the Kingdom of Christ. **1860** *All Year Round* No. 38. 270 Of Millenaries or Chiliasts there have been three classes.

millenary, -n(d)er, obs. ff. MILLINERY, -NER.

†**millenier.** *Obs. rare*⁻¹. [a. OF. *millenier*, ad. L. *millēnārius*.] = MILLENARY *sb.* 2.

1689 *Def. Liberty agst. Tyrants* 69 The ordinary Judges of Jerusalem, to wit the Milleniers, and the Centurions.

millenier, obs. form of MILLINER *sb.*

†**millenize,** *v. Obs.* [f. L. *millēn-ī* (see MILLENARY) + -IZE.] *intr.* To favour millenarian views.

1593 Bell *Motives conc. Rom. Faith* Ded. (1605) 1 If Tertullian..erred montanizing;..if Eusebius arrianizing: ..if Ambrose millenizing [etc.].

millennial (mɪˈlɛnɪəl), *a.* and *sb.* Also *erron.* **millenial.** [f. L. type **millenni-um* (see MILLENNIUM) + -AL¹.]

A. *adj.* **1.** Of a thousand years.

1807 J. Barlow *Columb.* I. 763 Millenial cedars wave their honors wide. **1819** Byron *Proph. of Dante* III. 11 The bloody scroll of our millennial wrongs. **1830** Tennyson *Kraken* 6 Huge sponges of millenial growth and height. **1899** D. G. Hogarth in *Authority & Archæol.* 231 The middle of the second millennial period B.C.

2. Of or pertaining to the millennium, or Christ's anticipated reign of a thousand years on earth.

1664 H. More *Exp. 7 Epist.* Pref. cvijb, This is that illustrious Reign of Christ in his Millenniall Empire of Love. **1690** Baxter *Kingd. Christ* ii. (1691) 12 The Millennial Opinion I have never been a censorious opposer of. **1742** Young *Nt. Th.* IX. 703 Their [*sc.* the planets'] reciprocal, unselfish aid Affords an emblem of millennial love. **1825–9** Mrs. Sherwood *Lady of Manor* III. xviii. 12 The last millennial glory. **1877** Sparrow *Serm.* xxvii. 229 But in Millenial times, how will things be changed!

b. *transf.* and *fig.*

1859 Geo. Eliot *A. Bede* vii, Every tenant was quite sure ..there was to be a millennial abundance of new gates,..and returns of ten per cent. **1897** Mrq. Salisbury *Sp. Ho. Lords* 19 Jan., You must not think that we are the victims of millennial anticipations if we hope that something may be done by an arbitration treaty.

B. *sb.* A thousandth anniversary, or its celebration.

1896 *Westm. Gaz.* 9 Mar. 1/3 In order to celebrate the millennial of Hungary with proper respect.

Hence **miˈllennialist**, one who believes in a millennial reign of Christ on earth (Webster 1847 citing *Stowe*); also as *adj.* **miˈllennially** *adv.*, during a thousand years or during the millennium.

1851 G. S. Faber *Many Mansions* 326 The Abyss, in which he will be millennially confined, is that proleptic Hell. **1903** D. D. Rutledge *Christ, Anti-Christ & Millennium* xi. 291 One Post-Millennialist misunderstood this view. *Ibid.* 301 The reply of the Post-Millennialists is to the effect that Revelation xx. is all symbolical and..cannot be relied on. **1932** A. Stewart *Christianity, Communism, Adventism* 5 'Jesus will soon be here' said one, an ardent pre-millennialist. *Ibid.* xi. 111 Post-millennialists..labor with abounding hope. **1967** R. Robertson in B. R. Wilson *Patterns Sectarianism* ii. 72 A more strictly millennialist belief that 'the end of all things is at hand'.

miˈllennialism. [-ISM.] Belief in the coming or the present existence of the millennium (MILLENNIUM 2).

1906 *Pall Mall Gaz.* 4 Jan. 1 In a spirit of fatuous millennialism the constabulary force..was being reduced. **1937** A. Reese *Approaching Advent Christ* 305 The indictment..fails to take notice of the panics that Post-millennialism provoked in the Middle Ages. **1945** D. H. Kromminga *Millennium in Church* 6 My own view I would designate as Covenantal Millennialism. **1967** J. Wilson in B. R. Wilson *Patterns Sectarianism* x. 353 The upsurge of post-adventual millennialism induced some to make comparison of their own country with the location of the forthcoming Kingdom of God.

millennian (mɪˈlɛnɪən), *sb.* and *a.* Also 7 **millenian.** [Formed as MILLENNIAL *a.* + -AN.]

A. *sb.* A believer in the millennium.

1657–83 Evelyn *Hist. Relig.* (1850) II. 230 Chiliasts, or Millenians..held that our Blessed Lord should reign on earth a thousand years. **1827** G. S. Faber *Sacr. Calend. Prophecy* (1844) I. 277 The gradual corruption of the once holy millennians.

B. *adj.* **1.** Of or pertaining to the millennium.

1806 G. S. Faber *Diss. Proph.* (1814) I. 51 The millennian reign of Christ upon earth. **1851** —— *Many Mansions* 193 A Millennian Kingdom upon Earth.

2. Belonging to a period of a thousand years.

1867 Burton *Hist. Scot.* (1873) I. xii. 411 It [*sc.* the terror caused by the expectation of the end of the world in A.D. 1000] is known as the millennian panic.

Hence †**miˈllennianism**, the doctrine of the millennians. †**miˈllennianite** = MILLENARY *sb.* 4.

1692 Wood *Ath. Oxon.* II. 49 'Tis said that he [Sir W. Ralegh] wrot a Tract of Millinanism [**1721**, II. 96 Milleninanism]. *a* **1845** Mrs. Bray *Warleigh* xliv, The constable, who was a Millennianite, was with some difficulty stopped in the midst of his harangue.

millenniarism (mɪˈlɛnɪərɪz(ə)m). [f. next + -ISM.] = MILLENARIANISM (*Cent. Dict.* 1890).

millenniary (mɪˈlɛnɪərɪ), *a.* [f. MILLENNI-UM + -ARY.] = MILLENNIAL 2.

1828 Pusey *Hist. Enq.* I. 81 The millenniary dreams of apocalyptic writers. *Ibid.* II. 289 Fanatical expectations of a visible millenniary kingdom of Christ.

†**millennist, millenist.** *Obs.* [Either f. MILLENN(IUM) or f. L. *millēn-ī* (see MILLENARY) + -IST.] One who believes in the millennium, a millenarian. So **ˈmillenism**, millenarianism.

1664 H. More *Synopsis Proph.* 512 Every faction will be content to be Millennists upon condition that Christ may reign after their way or mode. **1676** *Doctrine of Devils* 121 So was the Church in respect of Millenisme, Arrianisme [etc.]. **1755** Johnson, *Millenist.* **1795** Seward *Anecd.* (ed. 2) I. 318 So feeble-minded as to be a Seeker and Millennist.

millennium (mɪˈlɛnɪəm). Pl. **millenniums**, *occas.* **millennia.** [ad. mod.L. type **millennium*, f. L. *mille* thousand + *annus* year, on the analogy of *biennium*, *triennium*, etc.]

1. A period of one thousand years. Also, a thousandth anniversary.

a **1711** Ken *Hymnarium* Poet. Wks. 1721 II. 54 They on one Theme Milleniums spend. **1762** Macpherson *Ossian's Poems, Dissert.* (1806) I. p. xxxv, It is..needless to fix its [the kingdom of the Scots] origin a fictitious millenium before. **1840** De Quincey *Mod. Superstit.* Wks. 1862 III. 341 We may pass by a vast transition of two and a half millennia. **1832** Tennyson *Two Voices* 89 Let Thy feet, millenniums hence, be set In midst of knowledge. **1899** E. Markham *Man with Hoe*, etc. 33 The wise King out of the nearing heaven comes To break the spell of long milleniums.

2. The period of one thousand years during which (according to one interpretation of Rev. xx. 1–5) Christ will reign in person on earth.

a **1638** Mede *Wks.* v. (1672) 892 The Millennium of the Reign of Christ is that which the Scriptures call The Day of Judgment. **1772** Priestley *Inst. Relig.* (1782) II. 417 Arguments [are] advanced..against the literal interpretation of the millenium. **1890** R. Buchanan *Coming Terror* (1891) 62 Possibly, until the Millennium, there will always be drones.

3. *fig.* and in figurative context: A period of happiness and benign government.

1820 Byron *Mar. Fal.* IV. ii. 156 But this day, black within the calendar, Shall be succeeded by a bright millenium. **1857** Toulmin Smith *Parish* 421 The millennium will indeed have come for professional vagrants. **1899** *Edin. Rev.* Jan. 187 A millennium, which lasted a fortnight, succeeded his [George IV's] visit.

Hence **miˈllenniumism**, the doctrine of the millennium. **miˈllenniumite**, one who believes in the millennium.

1832 *Fraser's Mag.* V. 121 Who writes Political Economy, and Phrenology, and Millenniumism, but Scotchmen? **1837** *New Monthly Mag.* XLIX. 341 The movement party, with its train of optimists, millenniumites, and other indescribable shades and varieties of perfectibility-men.

†**millensole.** *Obs.* Also 6 **myllin soole, millium sole.** [Corruption of *milium solis*: see MILIUM¹ 1 b and MILL *sb.*² 2.] Gromwell.

1545 *Rates Custome Ho.* bviij, Myllin soole the pounde iiii d. **1582** *Ibid.* Diij, Millensole... Millium sole.

millepede (ˈmɪlɪpiːd). *Zool.* Also 7 **millipeed**, 7–8 **millepide**, 8, 9 (in Dicts.) **milleped**, 8–9 **millipede.** [ad. L. *millepeda* woodlouse, f. *mille* thousand + *ped-*, *pēs* foot. Cf. F. *mille-pieds*.]

1. Any one of the chilognathan myriapods (esp. of the British genera *Iulus* and *Glomeris*), in which the numerous legs are usually placed on each of the segments in double pairs, except the three or four pairs immediately behind the head.

1601 Holland *Pliny* xx. ii. 37 The Millipeed, which the Greeks call Seps, a long Worme with hairie feet. [**1706** Phillips (ed. Kersey), *Millepeda*, a Worm, having a great number of furry Feet; a Palmer.] **1835** Kirby *Hab. & Inst. Anim.* II. xvi. 65 These [Chilognathans] are called Millipedes. **1877** Huxley *Anat. Inv. Anim.* vii. 391 In the Millipedes, the sternal region is rudimentary.

2. Any one of several terrestrial isopod crustaceans, esp. the common woodlouse, *Oniscus asellus*; the armadillo, *Armadillo vulgaris*; and the slater, *Porcellio scaber*.

1651 French *Distill.* iv. 101 Take..of Millepides (*i*) Wood-lice one hundred. **1667** E. King in *Phil. Trans.* II. 428 Millepedes and Earwigs. **1757** Parsons *ibid.* L. 406 This body seems to be a Milleped, or Wood-louse. **1883** Wood in *Gd. Words* Dec. 764/1 The millepedes..are plentiful under the stones and flower-pots. **1890** *Syd. Soc. Lex.*, *Millepede*,..the *Oniscus armadillo*.

3. = CENTIPEDE.

1705 tr. *Bosman's Guinea* 379 It is not more prejudicial than the Sting of the Millepedes. **1756** A. Russell *Nat. Hist. Aleppo* 264 The third kind of *Mal*, which they call the pinch of a millepedes, begins like the two others, but [etc.]. **1861** Hulme tr. *Moquin-Tandon* II. v. ii. 265 The Scolopendra are..commonly termed Millipedes.

4. *attrib.* or as *adj.*: Thousand-footed.

1834 *Fraser's Mag.* X. 562 Many frightful hydra-headed and millipede insects.

millepore (ˈmɪlɪpɔə(r)). *Zool. Obs.* exc. *Hist.* [ad. mod.L. *millepora*, f. *mille* thousand + *porus* passage, PORE *sb.*, or ad. F. *millépore*. (See the note s.v. MADREPORE.)] Any one of

the *Hydromedusæ* (formerly regarded as zoantharian corals) of the genus *Millepora* or of the family *Milleporidæ*, in which the coral-like calcareous skeleton is covered with minute pores.

1751 STACK in *Phil. Trans.* XLVII. 449 The several species of vermicular tubes found in the sea, the madrepores, millepores, lithophytons, corallines, sponges. **1862** STODDART in *Q. Jrnl. Microsc. Sci.* II. 149 Millepores, Madrepores, Seriatopores [etc.].

Hence **mille'poriform** *a.*, having the form or appearance of a millepore (*Cent. Dict.* 1890). **'milleporine** *a.*, pertaining to or having the characters of the hydrozoan family *Milleporina*; resembling a millepore (*Cent. Dict.*). **mille'poreous** *a.* = *milleporous* (Mayne *Expos. Lex.* 1856). **'milleporite**, a fossil millepore. **mille'porous** *a.*, belonging to or resembling a millepore; having thousands of pores (Mayne).

1755 J. ELLIS *Corallines* Contents d, Foliaceous milleporous Eschara. **1802–3** tr. *Pallas' Trav.* (1812) II. 128 We occasionally noticed single entrochites, or almost obliterated traces of milleporites.

millepunctate (mɪlɪ'pʌŋkteɪt), *a.* [f. L. *mille* thousand + *punctātus* marked with points, f. *punctum* POINT *sb.*: see -ATE².] Covered with a multitude of points (*Syd. Soc. Lex.* 1890). So **mille'punctated** *a.*, in the same sense (Mayne *Expos. Lex.* 1856).

miller¹ ('mɪlə(r)). Forms: α. 4 **mulnere, mylnere,** 5 **milnare, mylnar, melner,** 5–7 **mylner,** 6 **myllner,** 7 **millner,** 5–8, 9 *dial.* **milner.** β. 4 **mellere, millere,** 5 **mylur, myllar**(e, 6 **myller, millar,** 7 **miler,** 4– **miller.** [Not found before the 14th c.; the α and β forms perh. represent formations of that period on the two ME. forms of MILL *sb.*¹ (*mylne, myll*) + -ER¹.

The late appearance of the word is unfavourable to the assumption of an OE. **mylnere*; if such a form existed, it might, with some of the synonyms in continental Teut., represent a WGer. adoption of late L. *molīnārius* (whence F. *meunier*) f. *molīna* MILL *sb.*¹ Cf. OS. *muliniri* (MDu. *molenare, mulner, muldener,* MLG. *molner,* mod.Du. *molenaar, mulder*), OHG. *mulināri* (MHG. *mülnære, müllner,* mod.G. *müller*), ON. *mylnari* (Sw. *mjölnare,* Da. *møller*). That the Eng. word was adopted from Du. or LG. is not altogether impossible.]

1. a. One whose trade is the grinding of corn in a mill; the proprietor or tenant of a corn-mill. Also (? *dial.*) applied to that workman in a mill who has charge of the actual grinding.

The OE. word was *mylnweard* (lit. 'mill-keeper': see MILLWARD), denoting the custodian or manager of the mill belonging to the lord. The word *miller* would have the same application so long as 'the lord's mill' continued to be one of the customary appurtenances of a manor.

α. **1362** LANGL. *P. Pl.* A. II. 80 Monde þe Mulnere [*later texts* mellere, mylnere], and moni mo oþure. *c* **1425** WYNTOUN *Cron.* VI. xvi. 1625 This milnare had a dowchtyr fayre. **1432–50** tr. *Higden* (Rolls) IV. 319 A mylner callede Athus. **1523** FITZHERB. *Bk. Surv.* 10 But dout ye nat the mylners wyll be no losers. **1619** in Ferguson & Nanson *Munic. Rec. Carlisle* (1887) 278 We amercye Archilles Armestronge for keping his wief to play the milner,..iiis. 4*d.* **1725** *Lond. Gaz.* No. 6384/7 John Hodgson,..Milner.

β. **1386** CHAUCER *Prol.* 542 Ther was also a Reue and a Millere. *Ibid.* 545 The Millere was a stout carl. *c* **1425** in Wr.-Wülcker 650/22 *Hic molendinarius,* mylur. *c* **1440** *Promp. Parv.* 337/2 Myllare. *molendinarius.* *c* **1515** *Cocke Lorell's B.* 3 A myller dusty poll than dyde come. **1646** SIR T. BROWNE *Pseud. Ep.* VII. xiii. 365 Gillius..who..made enquiry of Millers who dwelt upon its shoare received answer, that it [*sc.* the Euripus] ebbed and flowed foure times a day. **1824** R. STUART *Hist. Steam Engine* 133 A similar irregularity in the motion of corn-mills..had early exercised the ingenuity of millers.

fig. **1657** COKAINE *Obstinate Lady* Poems (1669) 301 My noble milner of words, thou that dost grind thy speeches with a merry pronunciation.

¶**b.** In proverbs imputing to millers' dishonesty in the taking of toll.

The proverb given by Ray seems to mean that there are no honest millers, and to allude to the use of the thumb in taking toll of flour. It is probable that this is the original form, and that Chaucer and Gascoigne played upon the phrase, taking the 'thumb of gold' to mean one that brings profit to the owner.

c **1386** CHAUCER *Prol.* 563 Wel koude he [*sc.* the miller] stelen corn and tollen thries And yet he hadde a thombe of gold pardee. **1576** GASCOIGNE *Steele Gl.* (Arb.) 79 When smithes shoe horses, as they would be shod, When millers toll not with a golden thumbe. **1678** RAY *Prov.* (ed. 2) 176 An honest miller hath a golden thumb. **1876** MRS. EWING *Jan of Windmill* xxxii, Was 'ee ever in a mill? 'ee seems to have a miller's thumb.

c. Proverb. ***too much water drowned the miller***: used to express that one can have too much of a good thing. Hence in figurative phrase ***to drown the miller***: to add too much water to spirits, dough, etc. (in this use also to ***put the miller's eye out***); also †*Sc.* 'to become bankrupt' (Jam.). For more recent examples see *Eng. Dial. Dict.*

1805 A. SCOTT *Poems* (1808) 136 Honest men's been ta'en for rogues, Whan bad luck gars drown the miller. **1816** SCOTT *Antiq.* xxi, The hale folk here..hae made a vow to ruin my trade, as they say ower muckle water drowns the miller. **1822** —— *Pirate* xvi, 'A fine, a fine', said the Udaller, '..he shall drink off the yawl full of punch, unless he gives us a song on the spot!' 'Too much water drowned the miller', answered Triptolemus. **1834** ESTHER COPLEY *Housekpr.'s Guide* x. 233 If after..'putting out the miller's eye' by too much water, you add flour to make it stiff enough for rolling out [etc.].

d. One who regulates or works any machine called a 'mill'. Chiefly in parasynthetic compounds, as ***cloth-, saw-, scribbling-miller***, etc.

1839 URE *Dict. Arts* 992 The use of this machine [a lamp called a *steel mill*] entailed on the miner the expense of an attendant, called the miller, who gave him light. **1888** BARRIE *When a Man's Single* i, The saw-miller's letter. **1900** *Daily News* 10 Oct. 7/3 He was a cloth miller.

2. Applied **a.** to certain white or white-powdered insects, as (*a*) the cockchafer, *Melolontha vulgaris*; (*b*) a neuropterous insect, *Sialis lutaria*; (*c*) a small moth often used by anglers; also, the ghost moth, *Hepialus humuli* (E.D.D.); **b.** to certain hairy caterpillars. See also *dusty miller*, DUSTY *a.* 5.

1668 CHARLETON *Onomasticon* 47 *Blatta*... *Molendinaria*, the Miller, because always whited with a delicate Down. **1681** GLANVILL *Sadducismus* II. 144 A Fly like a great Millar flew out from the place. **1829** *Glover's Hist. Derby* I. 177 White miller or owl fly..yellow miller or owl fly. **1858** H. W. BEECHER *Life Th.* (1859) 170 Would you put the lamp out in your house because moths and millers burn their wings in it? **1869** E. NEWMAN *Brit. Moths* 251 The Miller (*Acronycta leporina*). **1883** MISS BURNE *Folk-Lore Shropsh.* 194 Another amulet..is composed of a 'miller', or hairy caterpillar.

3. Applied to certain vertebrates, as **a.** one of the rays, *Myliobatis aquila*; **b.** *dial.* the young of the spotted flycatcher, *Muscicapa grisola*; **c.** the hen-harrier, *Circus cyaneus*, and Montagu's harrier, *C. cineraceus*; **d.** the whitethroat, *Sylvia rufa* or *cinerea*; **e.** the ringed plover (*Manx Bird-names* in *Zoologist* Feb. 1897).

1620 J. MASON *New-found-land* in *Capt. John Mason* (Prince Soc. 1887) 152 What should I speake of..Cunners, Catfish, Millers, thunnes, &c.? **1836** YARRELL *Brit. Fishes* II. 446 From..the crushing power of these teeth, the fish has acquired the additional name of the Miller. **1885** SWAINSON *Prov. Names Birds* 49 In Salop the name of Miller is given to young flycatchers. *Ibid.* 132 Hen harrier.. Miller. **1893** NEWTON *Dict. Birds* 572 Miller, a name given to the grey males of *Circus cyaneus* and *C. cineraceus*..; and also locally to the Whitethroat.

4. *Austral.* = *floury miller* (FLOURY *a.* d).

1896 *Rec. Austral. Museum* II. 107 The same kind of *Cicada* is known by different names in different localities, such as 'Miller', 'Mealy-back', etc. **1941** BAKER *Dict. Austral. Slang* 46 *Miller*, a nickname for a cicada.

†**5.** A vaulting trick in horsemanship = *miller's pass* (see 8 b). *Obs.*

1641 W. STOKES *Vaulting Master* C 3 The fifth Passe, called the Miller.

6. *slang.* **a.** A pugilist. †Also, a murderer. *Obs.*

a **1700** B. E. *Dict. Cant. Crew*, *Miller*, a Killer or Murderer. **1812** *Sporting Mag.* XXXIX. 143 Next rings the fame of gallant Crib A cool and steady miller. **1823** 'JON BEE' *Dict. Turf*, *Millers*—second rate boxers, whose arms run round in rapid succession [etc.]. **1830** S. WARREN *Diary Physic.* vii. (1832) I. 135 The Captain..being a first-rate 'miller', as the phrase is,..let fall a sudden shower of blows.

†**b.** Applied to a vicious horse. *Obs.*

1825 C. M. WESTMACOTT *Engl. Spy* I. 236 An incurable miller.

7. A milling-machine.

In mod. Dicts.

8. a. *attrib.* and *Comb.*, as ***miller-maiden***; **miller-dog**, a kind of dog-fish, *Galeus canis*; †**miller-grape**, a kind of grape; **miller-moth**, a white or 'mealy-scaled' moth (cf. sense 2); †**miller-pit** = MILL-POOL; †**miller quarrier**, one who quarries (millstones) for a miller.

1848 *Zoologist* VI. 1974 *Miller Dog, *Galeus vulgaris*. **1763** MILLS *Pract. Husb.* IV. 381 The *meunier*, or *miller grape, delights in light sands. **1828** MISS MITFORD *Village* Ser. III. 237 Our simple *miller-maiden. **1819** SAMOUELLE *Entomol. Compend.* 382 *Miller moth (*Noctua leporina*). **1878** T. HARDY *Ret. Native* IV. vii, White miller-moths flew into the air. **14..** *Nom.* in Wr.-Wülcker 725/8 *Hic assicus*, a *mylnerpyt. **1497** *Acc. Ld. High Treas. Scot.* (1877) I. 328 Giffin to the foure *millar quareouris in Dunbar for stanis wynnyng and breking, iiij lib. xviij s.

b. With possessive: **miller's coat**, a coat of fence in use in the sixteenth century, apparently a buff-coat or similar defence of leather (*Cent. Dict.* 1890); **miller's dog**, a kind of dog-fish, *Galeus canis*; **miller's-maze**, ? = *miller's round*; †**miller's pass** = sense 5 (see quot. 1653); **miller's round**, a kind of dance; **miller's soul**, a large white moth, probably the ghost-moth, *Hepialus humuli*. Also MILLER'S THUMB.

1836 YARRELL *Brit. Fishes* II. 390 It is known by the names of Penny Dog and *Miller's Dog. **1880–4** F. DAY *Brit. Fishes* II. 292 *Galeus vulgaris*..miller's dog, from its light gray colour. **1597–8** BP. HALL *Sat.* IV. iii. 59 Some of thy stallion-race Their eyes boar'd out, masking the *millers-maze. **1641** W. STOKES *Vaulting Master* Plate 5 The *Millers Passe. **1653** URQUHART *Rabelais* I. xxxv, He brought himself betwixt the horses two eares, springing with all his body into the aire, upon the thumb of his left hand, and in that posture turning like a windmill, did most actively do that trick which is called the Millers Passe. **1579** SPENSER *Sheph. Cal.* Oct. 52 Carroll lowde, and leade the *myllers rownde. **1585** J. HIGINS *Junius' Nomenclator*, *Pyrallis*..a candle flie; a stout or *millers soule. **1894** T. HARDY *Life's Ironies* 253 He saw one of those great white miller's-souls, as we call 'em—that is to say, a miller-moth.

Miller² ('mɪlə(r)). *Cryst.* The name of W. H. *Miller* (1801–80), English scientist, used *attrib.* with reference to the method for specifying the positions of planes in crystals that he used in his *Treatise on Crystallography* (1839), esp. in ***Miller index*** (INDEX *sb.* 9 c).

1890 G. H. WILLIAMS *Elem. Crystallogr.* ii. 31 To change the signs of any Miller symbol is to change the plane to its parallel and therefore equivalent plane on the opposite side of the crystal. **1900** MOSES & PARSONS *Elem. Mineral.* I. i. 10 The Miller Indices may be obtained from Weiss's parameters by first dividing each by the common multiple of their numerators and taking the reciprocal of the result. **1940** GLASSTONE *Text-bk. Physical Chem.* v. 336 The fact is represented by a bar over the Miller index, e.g., $(1\bar{1}1)$ for a face which has intercepts *a*, -*b* and *c*, on the axes *OX*, *OY* and *OZ* respectively. **1966** C. R. TOTTLE *Sci. Engin. Materials* iii. 55 When a plane is to be described, the notation used is that of Miller indices. The plane is extended to cut the *x*, *y*, and *z* axes, and the intercepts in steps of the unit cell dimensions *a*, *b*, *c* are written down. The reciprocals of these intercepts are next obtained, and fractions cleared to give the smallest integers again. *Ibid.* 59 There are six such planes in the cell, all having the last index in the Miller notation equal to 0, since they are all parallel to the hexagonal axis.

Miller effect. *Electronics.* [named after John Milton *Miller* (1882–1962), U.S. physicist.] The effect whereby capacitance (esp. inter-electrode capacitance) in the output of a valve or transistor increases its input impedance.

1931 in S. R. ROGET *Dict. Electr. Terms* (ed. 2) 209/2. **1934** J. H. REYNER *Television* x. 130 In radio practice these bypass condensers approximate to 100 or 300 μμF. and reduce the Miller effect considerably. **1967** *Electronics* 6 Mar. 130/1 In applying this principle, called the Miller effect, to a transistor, the equivalent base-to-emitter capacitance.. becomes the rated value of the capacitor multiplied by the voltage gain of the transistor. **1971** J. H. SMITH *Digital Logic* iv. 74 This feedback effect of a capacitor from the output of an amplifier to its input, is known as the Miller effect.

milleress ('mɪlərɪs). *rare.* [f. MILLER¹ + -ESS.] A miller's wife.

1680 J. AUBREY in *Lett. Eminent Persons* (1813) III. 391 My father was a miller, and my mother a milleresse, and I am now a ladie.

Millerian (mɪ'lɪərɪən), *a. Cryst.* [f. the surname *Miller* + -IAN.] Of or pertaining to W. H. Miller or his system of specifying the positions of crystal faces (cf. MILLER²).

1896 C. J. WOODWARD *Crystallogr. for Beginners* iii. 24 In the Millerian system..fractions of the parameters are taken, and the denominators of these fractions form the indices. **1944** C. PALACHE et al. *Dana's Syst. Min.* (ed. 7) I. 25 When the lattice is rhombohedral, Millerian three-index symbols are also given. **1964** HARTSHORNE & STUART *Pract. Optical Crystallogr.* i. 9 If *hkl* are the Millerian indices, the intercepts along the axes are *a*/*h*, *b*/*k*, *c*/*l*.

millering ('mɪlərɪŋ), *vbl. sb.* [f. MILLER¹ + -ING¹.] The work or trade of a miller.

1798 WASHINGTON *Lett.* Writ. (1893) XIV. 4 To carry on the millering and distillery business. **1817–18** COBBETT *Resid. U.S.* (1822) 337 Any of the men..could do the millering very well.

Millerite¹ ('mɪləraɪt). *U.S.* [f. the proper name *Miller* (see below) + -ITE¹.] A believer in the doctrines of William Miller (*died* 1849), an American preacher who interpreted the Scriptures as foretelling the early coming of Christ and the end of the world. So **'Millerism**, the doctrines of William Miller.

1843 *Niles' Reg.* 240/3 Millerism. Father Miller lately visited Rochester, New York, and devoted one whole week to dealing out exhortations. **1846** O. BROWNSON *Wks.* VI. 221 St. Paul writes to the Thessalonians not to believe the Millerites of their time. *a* **1852** F. M. WHITCHER *Widow Bedott Papers* (1883) xii. 44 When Millerism was makin' such a noise,..the Wiggletown folks raly thought ther was something in it. **1854** E. G. HOLLAND *J. Badger* xv. 418 Millerism came along showing large maps of the world's chronology..and all that. **18..** WHITTIER *World's End* Prose Wks. 1889 II. 424 One of the most ludicrous examples of the sensual phase of Millerism. **1961** B. R. WILSON *Sects & Society* III. xii. 239 There was little organisation..of the scattered converts from Millerism and Campbellism in Britain in the 1860s. **1962** G. SHEPPERSON in S. L. Thrupp *Millennial Dreams in Action* II. 51 He emphasizes how the reaction against Millerism..'speeded the adoption of a fervent postmillennialism'.

millerite² ('mɪləraɪt). *Min.* [ad. G. *millerit*: named by W. Haidinger in 1845 after W. H. Miller, professor of mineralogy at Cambridge 1832–1870: see -ITE¹.] Native sulphide of nickel, usually occurring in brassy or bronze crystals; capillary pyrites.

1854 DANA *Syst. Min.* (ed. 4) II. 49 Millerite, *Haid.* Capillary Pyrites. Sulphuret of Nickel [etc.]. **1881** RUSKIN *Let.* in *St. George* (1903) VI. 358, I would have kept the millerite, but the specimen was not pretty.

miller's thumb. Also 5 **millathowme.** [Suggested by the proverbial phrase under MILLER¹ 1 b; the head of the fish so called has some resemblance to a thumb.]

1. A small freshwater fish, *Cottus gobio* (*Aspidophorus cataphractus*); the bullhead.

*c*1440 *Promp. Parv.* 337/2 Myllarys thowmbe, fysche (*King's Coll. MS.* millathowme, fische), *capito.* 1530 Palsgr. 245/1 Myllers thombe a fysshe, *chabot.* *c*1614 Fletcher, etc. *Wit at sev. Weap.* v. i, *Clow.* 'Twill ne're be a true water. *Cun.* Why thinke you so? *Clow.* I warrant you, I told a thousand Millers thumbs in it. 1634 T. Johnson *Parey's Chirurg.* xx. iv. (1678) 457 The little Fish which the French call Chabot, we a Millers Thumb. 1741 *Compl. Fam.-Piece* II. ii. 350 Bull-Head, or Miller's Thumb, is to be met with in Holes, or among Stones, in clear Water. 1895 *Cornh. Mag.* Oct. 387 A bullhead or 'miller's thumb' has proved too much for a water rail.

2. Applied to other fishes, as a. the whiting-pout, *Gadus luscus*; b. *U.S.*, any fresh-water sculpin of the genus *Uranidea*; c. (see quot. 1838).

1838 J. Couch *Cornish Fauna* I. 37 Rock Goby, *Gobius niger*.. Miller's Thumb, Black Goby. 1880-4 F. Day *Brit. Fishes* I. 287 *Gadus luscus*... Names—Bib, pout, whiting-pout [etc.]. It is likewise said to be 'Miller's thumb'. 1882 Jordan & Gilbert *Synops. Fishes N. Amer.* 693 *Uranidea* .. Miller's Thumbs. *Ibid.* 696 *U. richardsonii*.. Miller's Thumb, Blob, Muffle-jaw, Bullhead.

3. Applied locally to certain small birds (see quots.).

1838 J. Couch *Cornish Fauna* I. 13 White Throat.. Wood Wren.. Willow Wren.. Chiff Chaff.. Lesser White Throat. The three or four latter Species are sometimes seen crossing the Channel to us, in Spring; and are confounded together by Sailors under the name of Miller's Thumbs. 1878 *Cumberld. Gloss.* 63/2 Milly thoom, Miller's thumb, the willow wren. 1885 Swainson *Prov. Names Birds* 25 Golden-crested wren.. Miller's thumb. *Ibid.* 32 British long-tailed titmouse.. Millithrum, *i.e.* Miller's thumb.

millesimal (mɪˈlɛsɪməl), *a.* and *sb.* [f. L. *millēsim-us* thousandth + (f. *mille* thousand) -AL[1].] A. *adj.* Thousandth; consisting of thousandth parts. Also, of or belonging to a thousand, dealing with thousandths. B. *sb.* A thousandth (part).

1719 I. Pound in *Phil. Trans.* XXX. 1022 The addition of the equation of Numb. B. gives the true angle of Commutation in the same Millesimals of a Circle. 1741 Watts *Improv. Mind* I. i. Wks. 1753 V. 188 He laboured long in millesimal fractions. 1873 I. Gregory *Brit. Metric Syst.* Note to Rdr., Calculating in units with fractions in decimals, centesimals or millesimals. 1874 *8th Rep. Warden of Standards* xxiii, The legal allowance of error for gold coin in millesimal fineness is 0·002 in excess or deficiency.

†**millesm.** *Obs.* Also 7 -sme. [a. F. *milliesme*, now *millième*:—L. *millēsim-um*, neut. of *millēsimus*: see prec.] A thousandth part.

1635 Gellibrand *Variation Magn. Needle* 2 The Horizon supposed.. to be divided into 360 parts, and each part subdivided into Centesmes or Millesmes. 1640 W. Crabtree in *Phil. Trans.* XXVII. 289 We intend to use the Centesmes or Millesmes of Degrees, because of the ease in Calculation.

millet[1] (ˈmɪlɪt). Forms: 5, 7 milet, 6 myllet(t, mylet, millette, 8 millett, mellet, 6- millet. [a. F. *millet*, dim. of *mil*: see MILL *sb.*[2]]

1. A graminaceous plant, *Panicum miliaceum*, native of India but extensively cultivated as a cereal in the warmer parts of Europe, growing three or four feet high, and bearing on a terminal spike or panicle a large crop of minute nutritious seeds. a. The grain.

*c*1400 Maundev. (Roxb.) xxx. 134 Þai ete milet and rysz. 1562 Turner *Herbal* II. 57 Millet in brede norisheth lesse then other cornes do. 1634 Peacham *Gentl. Exerc.* II. vii. 125 A handfull of Millet Oates, and Panicle. 1772 *Ann. Reg.* 165/2 He has subsisted chiefly for these ten years past on raw onions and millet. 1865 Miss Cary *Ball. & Lyrics* 227 Turn in the little seed, brown and dry, Turn out the golden millet.

b. The plant.

1577 B. Googe *Heresbach's Husb.* (1586) 31b, Millet called in Latine *Millium*,.. having as it were a thousand graines in an eare. 1653 H. Cogan tr. *Pinto's Trav.* xxviii. 109 Great plains full of wheat, rice, beans, pease, millet, panick [etc.]. 1762 Mills *Syst. Pract. Husb.* I. 448 Millet, either green, or after its grain is threshed out, is very good fodder for cattle. 1859 Jephson *Brittany* xi. 177 Besides the usual crops, I observed extensive fields of millet.

2. Applied to other graminaceous plants, esp. *Sorghum vulgare* (African, Black, Indian, Turkey Millet) and *Setaria italica* (Italian or German Millet). (See quots.)

1548 Turner *Names of Herbes* 54 Milium indicum is nowe muche sowen in Italy... It were better to cal it.. turkish millet. 1597 Gerarde *Herbal* I. liii. 73 *Milium nigrum.* Blacke Millet. *Ibid.* I. lv. 77 Tvrkie Millet is a stranger in England. 1640 Parkinson *Theat. Bot.* 1136 *Melica sive Sorghum.* Indian Millet. *Ibid.* 1137 Turkie or Indian Millet, and of some [called] Italian Millet. 1764 Grainger *Sugar Cane* IV. 567 Let Indian millet rear its corny reed. 1765 *Museum Rust.* v. 74 The African millet, *sorghum, milium nigrum.* 1839 *Penny Cycl.* XV. 225/1 Caffre millet (*Holcus Cafer*) is a native of the Cape of Good Hope. *Ibid.* 225/2 Drooping millet (*Sorghum cernuum*) is cultivated in Arabia, Syria, and various parts of the Levant. 1846-50 A. Wood *Class-bk. Bot.* 596 *Piptatherum nigrum.* Black-seeded millet. 1861 Swinhoe *N. China Camp.* 372 The chief produce of the country is the Kaouleang, or Barbadoes Millet (*Sorghum*). 1864 *Chambers's Encycl.* VI. 461/2 *Penicillaria spicata*, or *Pennisetum typhoideum*, is very extensively cultivated in Africa... It often receives the names Egyptian Millet and Guinea Corn. 1869 E. A. Parkes *Pract. Hygiene* (ed. 3) 178 The Hindu diet consists of some of the millets (cholum, raggee) [etc.]. 1874 *Treas. Bot.* 1318/1 Millet, Texas, *Sorghum cernuum.* 1889 J. H. Maiden *Useful Native Plants Austral.* 97 *Panicum decompositum*,.. 'Australian millet', 'Umbrella grass'... One of the most valuable of the Darling Downs (Queensland) grasses. 1896 *Australasian* 14 Mar. 488/5 One of the very best of the grasses found in the hot regions of Central Australia is the Australian millet, *Panicum decompositum.*

¶ *grey millet*: see GREY *a.* 8.

3. †a. *pl.* A skin disease attacking the fetlocks of horses. *Obs.*

1523 Fitzherb. *Husb.* § 110 Myllettes is an yll sorance, and appereth in the fetelockes behynde.

b. *sing.* A disease of the mouth, most common in infants, in which small white points or patches appear.

1842 Guy *Hooper's Physician's Vade Mecum* 352 Stomatitis, with alteration of the Secretion—Muguet—Millet.

†4. = CENCHRINE. *Obs.*

1608 Topsell *Serpents* (1658) 743 Of the Millet or Cenchrine. 1661 Lovell *Hist. Anim. & Min.* 253 Myllet, or Cenchrine... They are.. venimous in the second degree... They are spotted like millet seed, about two cubits in length, attenuated towards the taile, the colour is darke like the Millet, and is then most ireful when this herb is highest.

5. *attrib.* and *Comb.*, as ***millet-field, flour, grain, -meal, pudding, -straw***; **millet-ale, beer**, a fermented liquor made from millet-seed; **millet-rash**, miliary fever. Also MILLET-GRASS, MILLET-SEED.

1834 Pringle *Afr. Sk.* I. 19 The honey-mead, the *millet-ale, Flow round. 1890 *Syd. Soc. Lex.*, *Millet beer, a fermented liquor made from millet-seed in Roumania. 1873 'Ouida' *Pascarel* I. 107 We went through the *millet-fields at sunrise. 1747 tr. *Astruc's Fevers* 334 Many pustules.. of the bigness of *millet-grains. 1765 *Museum Rust.* V. 76 The millers.. return a good third of a bushel of *millet-meal for every bushel sent to them. 1747 Mrs. Glasse *Cookery* ix. 107 A *Millet Pudding. You must get half a Pound of Millet-seed [etc.]. 1762 W. Gelleroy *London Cook* 175 A Mellet Pudding. 1822-34 *Good's Study Med.* (ed. 4) IV. 440 Species IV. Exormia Milium. *Millet-Rash. 1844 Stephens *Bk. Farm* II. 379 They considered *millet-straw as the best for cattle.

‖**millet**[2] (ˈmɪlɛt). [Turk. *millet* nation, group of co-religionists, f. Arab. *milla* religion.] A division of the subjects of the Ottoman Empire according to allegiance to a religious leader (see quot. 1902). Often used *spec.* of non-Muslims.

[1861 G. Finlay *Hist. Greek Revolution* I. i. 9 The Greek language was the language of the Church and the law which ruled the whole assemblage of nations called by the Othoman administration, *Roum meleti*, or Roman nation.] 1900 'Odysseus' *Turkey in Europe* vii. 296 The Turk divides the population of the Ottoman Empire into Millets, or religious communities. 1902 *Encycl. Brit.* XXX. 395/1 All Moslems.. are included in the *millet*.. of Islam. The Rûm, or Roman (*i.e.*, Greek) *millet* comprises all those who acknowledge the authority of the Œcumenical Patriarch,.. the Bulgar *millet* comprises the Bulgarians who accept the rule of the exarchate; the other *millets* are the Katolik (Catholics), Ermeni (Gregorian Armenians), Musevi (Jews) and Prodesdan (Protestants). 1933 *Times Lit. Suppl.* 14 Dec. 890/2 The system of organization in *millets*.. which existed under the Sultans goes back to the early days of Islam. 1942 *Turkey* (Geogr. Handbk. Ser. B. R. 507, Admiralty, Naval Intelligence Div.) I. viii. 290 Each *millet* had complete autonomy, under the authority and leadership of an ecclesiastical functionary. 1971 A. Mango *Discovering Turkey* i. 69 The Ottoman Empire.. was a multi-national state,.. the criterion of differentiation among its subjects was religion and not nationality. *Millet*.. which in modern Turkish means 'nation', was until recently used to describe a religious community. 1973 *Times Lit. Suppl.* 29 June 754/2 They could coexist in the same territory under the same loose domination, as many different *millets* did in the Ottoman Empire.

millet, obs. variant of MULLET.

'**millet-grass.** The genus *Milium*, esp. *M. effusum*, a tall handsome grass, widely distributed throughout the northern hemisphere.

1597 Gerarde *Herbal* I. iv. 6 *Gramen Miliaceum.* Millet Grasse. 1796 Withering *Brit. Pl.* (ed. 3) II. 122 Soft Millet. Millet Grass. Wet woods, common. 1864 *Chambers's Encycl.* VI. 461/2 The Millet Grass (*Milium effusum*) of Britain.

'**millet-seed.** a. The seed or grain of millet. Also *attrib.*, as **millet-seed papula**, an isolated pimple as seen in miliary fever; **millet-seed rash**, miliary fever.

1599 T. M[oufet] *Silkwormes* 66 Their egges.. are likest of all things to Millet seede. 1671 Salmon *Syn. Med.* I. 113 The Measles are Pustules like Millet-seed. 1707 *Curios. in Husb. & Gard.* 350 Little Cray-fish, no bigger than Millet-seeds. 1822-34 *Good's Study Med* (ed. 4) I. 176 An efflorescence on the surface [of the skin] sometimes in the form of minute red millet seed papulæ. 1851 Carpenter *Man. Phys.* (ed. 2) 429 Minute lobules.. about the average size of a millet-seed. 1890 *Syd. Soc. Lex.*, *Millet seed rash.*

b. *Petrol.* Used *attrib.* to designate (grains of) sand of almost spherical shape as a result of abrasion produced by the wind.

1935 T. Eastwood *Northern Eng.* (*Brit. Regional Geol.*) 7 Thick red sandstones (Penrith Sandstone).. betray their origin as desert sand by the presence of 'millet-seed' grains. 1971 I. G. Gass et al. *Understanding Earth* xiii. 169/2 In desert sands.. the quartz grains are described as 'millet-seed' sands, a reference to the almost perfect, spherical shape.

mill-foil, variant of MILFOIL.

millful (ˈmɪlfʊl). [f. MILL *sb.*[1] + -FUL.] As much as a mill will contain; †*spec.* the quantity produced at one operation by a thread-mill.

1799 *Hull Advertiser* 23 Feb. 3/2 Nine thread-mills and upwards of 500 millfuls of twined thread.

'**mill-horse.** [f. MILL *sb.*[1] + HORSE *sb.*]

a. A horse used for turning or working a mill.

1552 Huloet, Myll horse, *molarius equus.* 1577-87 Holinshed *Chron.* II. 17/1 As if a man would reason thus: Before saint Patrike his time there was no horssemill in Ireland: *Ergo* before his time there was no milhorsse. *a*1586 Sidney *Arcadia* II. (1590) 197 His *Impresa* was, a mill-horse still bound to goe in one circle. 1650 B. *Discolliminium* 19 Hob, my blind Mil-horse. 1781 C. Johnston *Hist. J. Juniper* II. 219, I was obliged to drudge on like a blinded mill-horse.

b. *transf.* and *fig.*

1600 W. Watson *Decacordon* (1602) 47 And so by consequent all runne Hysteron Proteron, a milne horse, a King Pope, a Curch Spaniard. 1673 Dryden *Amboyna* II. i, You are the mill-horses of mankind. 1890 *Spectator* 21 June, Will the work of intellectual mill-horses suit the.. more sensitive natures of women?

c. *attrib.*

1859 Mill *On Liberty* v. 203 The official body are under the constant temptation of sinking into indolent routine, or, if they now and then desert that mill-horse round, of rushing into some half-examined crudity which has struck the fancy of some leading member of the corps. 1881 Ruskin in *Lett. Art & Lit.* (1894) 65 It cost Turner forty years of mill-horse toil. 1903 *Contemp. Rev.* Oct. 514 Her mill-horse round of vain repetitions.

'**mill-house.** A building in which milling or grinding is carried on; †in early use = MILL *sb.*[1] 1.

*c*1300 *Havelok* 1967 Summe grop tre, and sum grop ston, And driue hem ut, þei he weren crus, So dogges ut of milne-hous. *c*1440 *Promp. Parv.* 337/2 Myllehowse, *molendina.* 1508 Dunbar *Flyting w. Kennedie* 243 Chittirlilling, ruch rilling, lik schilling in the milhouse. 1657 R. Ligon *Barbadoes* (1673) 90 [Sugar-making.] From the Mill-house to the boyling house. 1766 *Compl. Farmer* s.v. *Flax*, It requires a less expensive mill-house [*sc.* for flax dressing]. 1888 Warren & Cleverly *Wanderings 'Beetle'* 129 A bridge bearing four tumble-down mill-houses.

milli- (ˈmɪlɪ), combining form of L. *mille* thousand, used esp. in the metric system of weights and measures to denote the thousandth part of the unit, as MILLIARE ($\frac{1}{1000}$ of an are), ***-barn*** [BARN *sb.* 1 d], ***-calorie*** (or ***-calory***), ***-curie***, ***-gal*** [GAL[2]], ***-henry*** [HENRY[3]], ***-joule***, ***-kayser***, ***-kelvin***, ***-lambert***, ***-micron***, ***-mol(e*** [MOLE *sb.*[7]] (hence ***-molar*** adj.), ***-poise*** [POISE *sb.*[2]], ***-rad***, ***-radian***, ***-rem***, ***-roentgen***, ***-watt***; also combined with *micro-* to denote division by a thousand million (corresponding to the single prefix NANO-), as in ***millimicroampere***, ***-mole***, ***-second***. '**millidegree**, a thousandth of a degree centigrade (kelvin); ˌ**millie'quivalent**, one thousandth of a gramme-equivalent; **milliosmol**, **-mole** (mɪlɪˈɒzmɒl, -məʊl) [f. blend of OSMOTIC *a.* and MOLE *sb.*[7]], an amount of any osmotically effective ion in solution equal to a milligramme divided by the atomic weight of the ion; hence **millios'molar** *a.*

[1816 P. Kelly *Metrology* 17 The word Milli expresses the 1000th part.]

1955 *Physical Rev.* XCVII. 88 The cross section.. has been calculated to be approximately 35 millibarns. 1958 O. R. Frisch *Nucl. Handbk.* I. 12 Nuclear cross sections are usually expressed in barns or millibarns. 1909 *Cent. Dict. Suppl.*, Millicalory. 1937 *Geogr. Jrnl.* LXXXIX. 543 The cooling power of the atmosphere at 2.0 p.m... averages 6·7 millicalories per square centimetre per second. 1953 *Brit. Jrnl. Psychol.* Nov. 280 The heat intensity required to produce pain was measured with a radiometer.. the threshold being expressed in millicalories per second per square centimetre. 1910 E. Rutherford in *Nature* 6 Oct. 430/2 This matter was left for the consideration of the standards committee; the latter suggested that the name Curie should be used as a new unit to express the quantity or mass of radium emanation in equilibrium with one gram of radium (element). For example, the amount of emanation in equilibrium with one milligram of radium would be called 1/1000 Curie or one millicurie. 1947 *Sci. News* IV. 126 One millicurie of radium expels thirty million alpha particles per second. 1963 Millicurie [see CURIE 1]. 1951 *Jrnl. Chem. Physics* XIX. 1161/1 The Curie temperatures are of the order of tens of millidegrees. 1974 *Physics Bull.* Mar. 93/2 The lighter isotope, ^{3}He, had until recently shown no anomalous behaviour even when cooled to temperatures of a few millidegrees. 1929 C. J. Engelder *Textbk. Elem. Quantitative Analysis* vii. 139 There is a gram-milliequivalent weight in 1 cc. of a normal solution. 1946 *Nature* 19 Oct. 556/2 The mean value for agouti mice is 121 milliequivalents per litre, and for black 124·5. 1965 *Math. in Biol. & Med.* (Med. Res. Council) I. 37 The computer prints out in milli-equivalents per litre all the major constituents of the plasma, cells and alveolar gases. 1914 Milligal [see GAL[2]]. 1934 *Geogr. Jrnl.* LXXXIII. 446 The Bouguer anomalies are small on the coast and decrease steadily westward to about −150 milligals in Shansi. 1969 *New Scientist* 10 July 88/2 The gal is.. a unit of one cm per second per second and a milligal thus approximately one millionth of the normal gravity of the Earth. 1909 *Cent. Dict. Suppl.*, Millihenry. 1922 Glazebrook *Dict. Appl. Physics* II. 421/1 All the coils are used in series for the higher range (9 to 105 millihenries), but only portions of each in series for the lower range (0·7 to 12 millihenries). 1950 *Engineering* 7 Apr. 398/3 In the rectifier positive lead, a 10-millihenry air-core reactor is connected. 1972 *Physics Bull.* Apr. 205/1 Methane-air can be reliably ignited by a

spark discharge of only about one millijoule. **1968** *Chem. Abstr.* LXVIII. 4308/2 The Lamb shifts of the 4*S* and 3*S* levels of the 11..are, resp., 60 ± 4 millikaysers and 138·5 ± 1·6 millikaysers. **1970** G. K. Woodgate *Elem. Atomic Struct.* i. 2 The term values T_i are written as positive numbers in units of cm^{-1}, recently re-named the Kayser (K). The new name is more commonly found when the sub-unit milli-Kayser is used; 1 mK = 10^{-3} cm^{-1}. **1972** *Physics Bull.* Feb. 85/3 Philips shows very thin metal foils between 2 and 10 μm thick being used to solve heat exchange problems at very low temperatures, a few millikelvin. **1918** Webster Add., Milli-lambert. **1920** E. N. Harvey *Nature Animal Light* iii. 64 The brightness of a surface is measured in lamberts or millilamberts... A millilambert is 1/1000 lambert. **1970** *Nature* 24 Jan. 347/2 Each pattern subtended 7° at the eye, and was projected..at an average screen illuminance of 3 millilamberts. **1956** Millimicroampere [see cosmotron]. **1960** *Cambr. Rev.* 8 Oct. 21/2 The techniques developed for handling and measuring the amounts of steroids of only a few millimicromoles likely to be present in experimental samples have made steroid chromatography a leading branch of microanalysis. **1904** C. Hering *Ready Reference Tables* I. 31, 1 milli-micron (spectroscopy) or micro-millimeter (microscopy) = 10 Angstroem units. **1966** C. R. & T. S. Leeson *Histol.* ii. 22/2 One millimicron is one thousandth of a micron, i.e., 10 Å. **1956** *Proc. CERN Symposium* II. 69 (*heading*) Recent advances in millimicrosecond counting techniques. **1964** F. L. Westwater *Electronic Computers* viii. 127 Switching speeds of a few millimicroseconds appear possible. **1934** Webster, Millimolar. **1941** *Jrnl. Physiol.* C. 61 The value of η represents the total indiffusible substance (as millimols), and of ε the difference between the total negative and positive charges on the indiffusible molecules (expressed as milliequivalents or valencies multiplied by the millimolar concentration). **1972** *Nature* 10 Mar. 57/3 Using lower than customary magnesium concentrations (in the region of millimolar), Allet finds that lithium and caesium chloride produce similar results. **1904** C. Hering *Ready Reference Tables* I. 60, 1 millimol = 0·001 mol or gram molecule. **1934** *Biochem. Jrnl.* XXVIII. 285 If we consider the titration of 1 ml. of *N*/10 acid delivered for example from a 1 ml. simple pyrex pipette..the co-efficient of variation in millimols of KOH is 25 × 10^{-5}. **1937** Pierce & Haenisch *Quantitative Analysis* vi. 83 The choice of unit, millimole or mole, milliequivalent or equivalent, depends upon the unit of volume chosen. **1954** [see isohydric *a.* b]. **1970** R. W. McGilvery *Biochem.* xxv. 614 It requires 2·3 millimoles of H^+ to react with the hemoglobin in a liter of blood before the pH can change by 0·1 unit. **1939** J. L. Gamble *Chem. Anat., Physiol. & Path. Extracellular Fluid* Notes to chart 2 The term milliosmol is used to distinguish ionic from molecular concentration. The osmolal value of a solution of Na + Cl, for instance, is double the molal value. **1942** *Ibid.* (4th printing), The milliosmolar and milliequivalence values for the univalent ions are obviously identical. The chemical equivalence of the divalent ions is twice their milliosmolar value. The term milliosmolar is used instead of millimolar to make clear the additive osmotic effect of individual ions. **1959** *Pediatric Clinics N. Amer.* VI. 272 The nephritic patient who is unable to concentrate urine..will need a water allowance..of approximately 3 ml. per milliosmol of total urinary solute. **1963** *Lancet* 12 Jan. 77/1 The last twelve patients admitted to this hospital with diabetic acidosis have had a calculated serum osmolarity greater than 300 milliosmoles per litre. **1972** *Science* 19 May 815/3 Severely disabled chicks..had plasma osmolality values (in milliosmoles per kilogram) of 335 ± 10 as compared with 309 ± 7 for controls. **1934** *Jrnl. Amer. Chem. Soc.* LVI. 998/2 We find the freezing point of our maximum density water to be 3·82°, and the viscosity at 20°, 12·6 millipoises. **1954** *Brit. Jrnl. Radiol.* XXVII. 247/1 The value is 30 millirad per week. **1973** *Times* 31 July 5/4 He said a total dose of 0·1 of a millirad—one-third of the normal background radioactive level—had been recorded during the 21 hours following the blast. **1956** *Spaceflight* I. 28/1 Despite errors caused by ionospheric refraction of the signal, the use of data from a number of stations will, it is claimed, enable the satellite's position to be established to within a fraction of a milliradian. **1971** *Sci. Amer.* June 65/1 A similar analysis of the collision kinematics indicates that the resolution in angle should be a fraction of a milliradian, which is about three minutes of arc. **1954** *Brit. Jrnl. Radiol.* XXVII. 246/1 Basic permissible weekly doses for the critical organs. Whole body exposure...0·3 millirems per week in blood-forming organs, the gonads and the eyes. **1971** *Sci. Amer.* Aug. 115/2 The U.S. Atomic Energy Commission requires that personnel working with radiation materials receive not more than 100 millirems of radiation per 40-hour week. **1955** *Sci. News Let.* 20 Aug. 116/1 A milliroentgen is one-thousandth the unit of quantity of X-rays. **1963** B. Fozard *Instrumentation Nucl. Reactors* i. 3 It is..often necessary to measure dose rate; a convenient practical unit for this quantity is the milliroentgen per hour (mr/h). **1929** *Papers Inst. Post Office Electr. Engin.* cxxix. 22 It is..sent to line at the power of 1 milli-watt. **1956** *Nature* 25 Feb. 392/1 This feature of existing methods [for the measurement of power] is particularly evident at low power-levels, of the order of 1 milliwatt, at wave-lengths of 3 cm. and less.

millia, variant of milly *Obs.*

'milliad. *rare.* [Badly f. L. *mille* thousand, after *myriad*.] A period of one thousand years.

1851 H. Torrens in *Jrnl. Asiatic Soc. Bengal* 2 Not by centuries but by milliads. **1891** L. Clark *Dict. Metric Meas.*, Milliade, a thousand years.

milliammeter (mɪlɪ'æmɪtə(r)). [f. milli- + ammeter or milliam(pere + -meter.] An instrument for measuring currents of the order of milliamperes; = *milliampere meter*.

1902 G. B. Massey in H. R. Bigelow *Internat. Syst. Electro-Therapeutics* (ed. 2) B. 150 (*caption*) Weston milliammeter, arranged specially for medical work. **1946** *Nature* 28 Dec. 943/1 The received signal was recorded continuously on a recording milliammeter. **1966** *McGraw-Hill Encycl. Sci. & Technol.* I. 323/2 A rectifier-type ac milliammeter consisting of a small copper oxide or germanium bridge rectifier feeding a conventional dc milliammeter has low losses, good overload capacity, and adequate accuracy.

milliamp ('mɪlɪæmp). Colloq. abbrev. of milliampere.

1923 *Radio Times* 28 Sept. 19/2 Another [voice], 'Five milli amps. No! Sorry! I thought you were Cardiff.' **1927** *Sunday Express* 17 Apr. 8/3 (Advt.), Every milliamp of electricity is made by the dynamo. **1957** P. Lafitte *Person in Psychol.* ii. 12 In the sciences, the fact is strictly the instrument reading..and the report of twenty milliamps..is in a sense an interpretation. **1970** D. F. Shaw *Introd. Electronics* (ed. 2) xiii. 323 Equation 13.13 (*b*) becomes V_a = 400 − 40I_a where V_a is given in volts and I_a in milliamps.

milliampere (mɪlɪ'æmpɛə(r), 'mɪlɪæm,pɛə(r)). *Electr.* Also **milliampère.** [f. L. *mille* thousand + ampere.] An electrical unit equal to the thousandth part of an ampere. Also *attrib.* **milliampere meter**, an instrument for measuring milliamperes of electricity.

1885 *Jrnl. Soc. Telegr. Engin.* XIV. 465 It [*sc.* the current] was 2·632 milliampères. **1891** in L. Clark *Dict. Metric Meas.* **1893** A. S. Eccles *Sciatica* 56 From five to eight milliampères of current. **1905** *Brit. Med. Jrnl.* 16 Sept. 620 A milliamperemeter to indicate the current going through the tube. **1922** F. W. Aston *Isotopes* 48 The bulb is arranged to take from 0·5 to 1 milliampere at potentials ranging from 20,000 to 50,000 volts. **1956** [see cosmotron].

Hence **milli'amperage**, current expressed in, or of the order of, milliamperes.

1909 *Cent. Dict.* Suppl., Milliamperage. **1937** *Discovery* Feb. 54/1 The meter then reads to the corrected milliamperage of the total body surface-area. **1961** *Med. X-Ray Protection up to 3 Million Volts* (U.S. Nat. Bureau Standards Handbk. 76) 18 A beam monitoring device fixed in the useful beam is recommended to indicate any error due to incorrect filter, milliamperage, or kilovoltage.

Millian ('mɪlɪən), *a.* and *sb.* [f. the name of John Stuart *Mill* (1806–73), English philosopher + -ian.] **A.** *adj.* Of or pertaining to Mill or his philosophical or political theories. **B.** *sb.* A follower of Mill or his theories. (See also Millite *a.* and *sb.*)

1859 J. A. Symonds *Let.* Apr. (1967) I. 183 He has a truly *Millian* contempt for public opinion. **1950** E. Nagel in Mill *Philos. Scientific Method* p. xlvii, There are doubtless no perfect Millians alive today. **1958** *Victorian Studies* I. 253 Later Millians,..such as Bain, Croom Robertson and Sully, were eclipsed by the bold but philosophically shallow eloquence of men like Huxley and Tyndall. **1972** *Times Lit. Suppl.* 14 Apr. 420/5 Practical criticism operated on the John Stuart Millian assumption that out of this bedlam the truth would ultimately emerge.

Millian, obs. form of Milan, million.

milliard ('mɪlɪəd). [a. F. *milliard*, f. *mille* thousand.] A thousand millions.

1793 A. Young *Examp. France* (ed. 3) 185, I may state their extra resources, from the regal and ecclesiastical plunder, at four *milliards*. **1823** Byron *Juan* xiv. c, I'll bet you millions, milliards. **1874** Deutsch *Rem.* 290 All those untold milliards of human beings.

milliardaire (,mɪlɪə'dɛə(r)). Now *rare.* [f. milliard after millionaire.] A person possessing a 'milliard of money'.

1924 *New Internat. Year Bk. for Year 1923* 270/2 A South-American milliardaire who can have all he wants. **1926** C. H. Herford *Mind of Post-War Germany* vii. 34 The hero, son of a milliardaire, is engaged in manufacturing a gas more powerful than all known fuels. **1927** *Spectator* 23 Apr. 720 Including..a respectable proportion of the Royal Families and aristocracy of most European countries, besides a sufficiency of 'milliardaires' from both Americas.

milliare (mɪl'ɛə(r)). [a. F. *milliare*: see milli- and are *sb.*] In the metric system, the thousandth part of an are; 154·07 square inches.

1889 E. Noel *Sci. Metrology* 12 The deciare..is not a real square measure;..the milliare..is non-existent. **1891** in L. Clark *Dict. Metric Meas.*

milliary ('mɪlɪərɪ), *a.* and *sb.* Also **miliary.** [ad. L. *milliārius* (neut. *-um*), f. *mille* thousand (paces), mile.] **A.** *adj.*

1. Pertaining to the ancient Roman mile of a thousand paces; marking a mile.

1644 Evelyn *Diary* 7 Nov., Before this was once placed a Miliary Column. **1753** *Phil. Trans.* XLVIII. 136 Milliary pillars [are] erected to mark out the distance of the ways. **1778** *Eng. Gazetteer* (ed. 2) s.v. *Spittle in the Street, Linc.*, It is pleasant riding from hence to Lincoln, in a country wholly champaign, or heath, with miliary stones all the way, of which some are thought to be Roman. **1860** J. Newlands *Carp. & Join. Assist.* Index & Gloss., *Milliary column*, a column set up to mark distances; a milestone. *Ibid.* s.v. *Column*, The miliary column, set up as a centre from which to measure distances.

†**2.** Of or pertaining to a millennium. *Obs.*

1753 Chambers *Cycl. Supp.* s.v. *Age*, Milliary or Millenary Age, *sæculum milliarium*, or *millenarium*, on medals denotes the last year of a Millennium or thousand year.

B. *sb.*

1. A stone or mark set up by the ancient Romans to form a point of departure in measuring distances of a thousand paces; a milestone.

1610 Holland *Camden's Brit.* 423 London-stone..I take to haue beene a Milliarie or Milemarke. **1741–3** Pococke *Descr. East* (1745) II. 85, I saw, about a mile from the town, an antient Roman milliary. **1865** *Reader* 18 Mar. 313/2 He found no traces whatever of the letters, and therefore he inferred that they had never been inscribed on the milliary.

†**2.** A believer in the millennium. *Obs.*

1650 Bp. Hall *Rev. Unrevealed* §4 The ancient heresy of the Milliaries, as Austin calls them.

milliary, obs. form of miliary.

millibar ('mɪlɪbɑː(r)). *Meteorol.* [f. milli- + bar *sb.*[6]] The usual unit of barometric pressure, equal to one thousandth of a bar (bar *sb.*[6] 2), i.e. 1000 dynes per sq. cm.

1910, etc. [see bar *sb.*[6] 2]. **1914** *Q. Jrnl. R. Meteorol. Soc.* XL. 187 The megadyne per square centimetre has been adopted and called the 'bar'... The bar is less convenient for printing and conversation than the millibar, its 1/1000th part, and the latter has therefore been generally adopted; it is equivalent to the pressure produced by about three-hundredths of an inch of mercury or by three-quarters of a millimetre. **1924** *Glasgow Herald* 23 Dec. 5 So far as I can judge from the synoptic chart for December 9, 7 a.m.,..the pressure at New Pitsligo at 7 a.m. seems to have been 1016 millibars, and by noon to have risen to about 1012 millibars, equivalent to 30·12 inches. **1942** V. C. Finch et al. *Elem. Meteorol.* v. 104, $\frac{1}{10}$ inch on a barometer or barograph is equivalent to about 3 millibars. Either inches or millibars may be used in numbering the isobars on a weather map. **1963** G. M. B. Dobson *Exploring Atmosphere* i. 3 A scale at the side of the frontispiece gives the average pressure at different heights in millibars (mb), where 1000 mb is approximately the average pressure at sea level.

millieme ('mɪljɛm). Also **milleme, millime.** [F. *millième* thousandth.] A unit of currency, equal to a thousandth of the main unit, orig. in Egypt, now in the United Arab Republic, the Sudan, and Tunisia.

1902 *Encycl. Brit.* XXVII. 700/1 The unit is the Egyptian pound, which is divided into 100 piastres, the piastre being again divided in 10 milliemes. *Ibid.*, Pieces of 20, 10, 5, 2, and 1 piastres in silver; 5, 2, and 1 milliemes in nickel. **1919** W. H. Downing *Digger Dial.* 34 *Milleme*, a small Egyptian coin. **1942** C. Barrett *On Wallaby* vi. 122 His son went round with a tambourine collecting stray milliemes. **1956** E. E. Evans-Pritchard *Nuer Relig.* iii. 88 A Nuer refused to accept a milleme coin..because a boy of his family, when playing with a milleme, got it into his ear and died. **1972** *Whitaker's Almanack 1973* 987 Tunisian Dinar of 1,000 Millimes. *Ibid.*, Sudanese Pound of 100 Piastres or 1,000 Milliemes. **1973** *Country Life* 20 Sept. 805/3 [Tunisia] One morning I was offered a necklace for '800 millimes and packet fags'.

†**'millifold,** *a. Obs.* [f. L. *mille* thousand + -fold.] Thousand-fold.

1609 J. Davies *Holy Roode* I 2b, Yet ere he parts, his kisses millifold, Bewray his loue, and louing diligence.

†**'milliform,** *a. Obs.* [f. L. *mille* thousand + -form.] Of a thousand shapes or aspects.

c **1581** in *Grindal's Rem.* (Parker Soc.) 471 It was like that religion, which of his own nature should be uniform, would against his nature have proved milliform, yea, in continuance nulliform.

milligrade ('mɪlɪgreɪd), *a.* [f. L. *mille* + *grad-us* step, degree.] Having a thousand degrees.

1802–12 Bentham *Ration. Judic. Evid.* (1827) I. 76 Substitute..a centigrade scale: and if that be not yet sufficient a milligrade.

milligrain, var. millegrain.

milligramme ('mɪlɪgræm). Also 9 **-gram.** [F. *milligramme*: see milli- and gram[2].] In the metric system, a weight equal to $\frac{1}{1000}$ of a gramme, or ·0154 of an English grain.

1810 *Naval Chron.* XXIV. 302 Milligram (weight of cubic millimeter of water). **1875** Bennett & Dyer *Sachs' Bot.* 776 In *Passiflora gracilis* a pressure of 1 milligram is sufficient to cause curvature in a very short time.

millilitre ('mɪlɪliːtə(r), Fr. mililitr). Also 9 **-littre;** (*U.S.*) **-liter.** [Fr.: see milli- and litre.] In the metric system, a measure of capacity equal to $\frac{1}{1000}$ of a litre, or ·061 of a cubic inch.

1810 *Naval Chron.* XXIV. 301 Millilittre, Centimeter cube. **1896** C. R. Honiball *Engin. Arithmetic & Mensuration* xli. 308 Millilitre = ·001 Litres. **1935** C. J. Smith *Intermediate Physics* (ed. 2) ix. 172 The litre and the millilitre (ml.) are now frequently chosen as the unit of volume, burettes, flasks, etc. being marked in millilitres and fractions thereof. **1960** *Science* 22 July 204/2, 1 billion of these units result from treating 15 milligrams of the proteinoid with 2·5 millilitres of hot water and allowing the clear solution to cool. **1969** *Guardian* 28 Feb. 4/4 Every patient prescribed liquid medicine by his doctor will receive a plastic spoon which will hold five millilitres of medicine; and all prescriptions will be in five millilitre units. **1974** *Daily Tel.* 10 Oct. 2/4 [He] had 120 milligrammes of alcohol in 100 millilitres of blood, 40 over the legal limit.

millimetre ('mɪlɪmiːtə(r), Fr. milimɛtr). Also **-meter.** [F. *millimetre*: see milli- and metre.] In the metric system, a measure of length equal to $\frac{1}{1000}$ of a metre, or ·0393 inch. Also *attrib.* Frequently abbreviated *millim* or *mm.*

1807 *Med. Jrnl.* XVII. 418 An incision..about the length of six millemeters (three lines). **1877** W. Thomson *Voy. Challenger* I. 41 A paper millimetre scale. **1883** McLachlan in *Ann. & Mag. Nat. Hist.* Oct. 237 Length of abdomen ♂ 37 millim. **1887** Ward tr. *Sachs' Physiol. Plants* 47 A lamella ..a few tenths of a millimeter thick.

millimetric (mɪlɪˈmɛtrɪk), *a.* [f. MILLIMETR(E + -IC.] **a.** *fig.* Minute.

1909 *Milton Memorial Lect.* 194 Those millimetric distinctions by which human character declines or ascends. **1937** E. POUND *Let.* 30 Nov. (1971) 300 As I haven't yet a projector, the small but not millimetric photos would save time. **1965** *Economist* 28 Aug. 772/2 Participation in the congress and the administrative bureaucracy is to be shared with 'millimetric' equality.

b. Of the order of a millimetre in length; employing or characterized by electromagnetic waves of this wavelength.

1962 *Newnes Conc. Encycl. Electr. Engin.* 883/2 The use of waveguides of practicable size is restricted to waves in the microwave region (i.e. centimetric and millimetric wavelengths). **1969** A. L. CULLEN in F. A. Benson *Millimetre & Submillimetre Waves* i. 5 For many puposes.. microwave radar was found to possess advantages over millimetric radar. **1973** *Physics Bull.* Feb. 99/2 The properties measured include..the absorption of millimetric microwaves. *Ibid.* Nov. 651/2 These direct measurements initially suggested that the millimetric background temperature was much *more* than 2·7 K.

†**millimillenary**, *a. Obs. rare*⁻¹. In 7 **millimillinary**. [f. MILLI- + MILLENARY *a.*] Correct within a millionth part.

1690 LEYBOURN *Curs. Math.* 311, I shall lay before you these..Proportional Conclusions in the Circle, and that to a Millimillinary solution of the Truth.

†**milli-millesm.** *Obs. rare*⁻¹. [f. MILLI- + MILLESM.] A millionth part.

1650 J. WYBARD *Tactometria* 22 The fractionall part of that solidity, $\frac{4}{21}$, being converted into milli-millesms, or Cubicall centesms.

Millin, millinary, obs. ff. MILAN, MILLENARY.

mill-in: see -IN *suffix*³.

milliner (ˈmɪlɪnə(r)), *sb.* Forms: **myllaner, -ener, -oner, -yner, mileyner, millioner, millainer,** (**millender**), 6–7 **milner**, 6–8 **millener**, 7 **millaner, millenier**, 7–8 **milaner**, 6- **milliner**. [f. MILAN¹ + -ER¹.]

1. (With capital initial.) A native or inhabitant of Milan.

1529 RASTELL *Pastyme, Hist. Fr.* (1811) 83 He was encountered by the Mylleners and the Venicyans. **1604** DEKKER *1st Pt. Honest Wh.* Plays 1873 II. 9 You know we Millaners love to strut vpon Spanish leather. *Ibid.* 42 Stranger? no sir, Ime a naturall Milaner borne. **1828** SCOTT *F.M. Perth* xi, The Milaner shall not know my work [on a Milan hauberk] from his own.

2. †**a.** A vendor of 'fancy' wares and articles of apparel, esp. of such as were originally of Milan manufacture, e.g. 'Milan bonnets', ribbons, gloves, cutlery (*obs.*). **b.** In modern use, a person (usually a woman) who makes up articles of female apparel, esp. bonnets and other headgear.

1530 in *Privy Purse Exp. Hen. VIII* (1827) 33 Paied to the Mylloner for certeyne cappes trymmed..withe botons of golde. **1531** *Ibid.* 173 Paied to xpofer mylloner for ij myllain bonettes. *Ibid.* 174 Paied to the mylloner for a knif for the king. *c* **1550** *Disc. Common Weal Eng.* (1893) 64 No not so much as a spurre, but it must be fett at the milliners hand. *Ibid.* 91 Mercers, grocers, vinteners, haberdashers, mileyners, and such as doe sell wares growinge beyond the seas. **1573** in Cunningham *Revels at Crt.* (1842) 24 To the Millioner for one yard qᵗʳ of counterfete cloth of gold. **1592** GREENE *Quip Upstart Courtier* G4b, The other a Frenchman and a Myllaner in saint Martins, and sels shirts, bandes, bracelets, Iewels, and such pretty toies for Gentle women. **1611** SHAKS. *Wint. T.* IV. iv. 192 No Milliner can so fit his customers with Gloues. **1617** MINSHEU *Ductor* 5620 An Haberdasher of small wares... In London also called a Millenier, à Lat. *mille*, i. a thousand, as one hauing a thousand small wares to sell. **1693** LUTTRELL *Brief Rel.* (1857) III. 7 Two [highwaymen] are said to be tradesmen in the Strand, one a goldsmith, th'other a milliner. **1706** PHILLIPS (ed. Kersey), *Millener*, one that sells Ribbons, Gloves, &c. **1713** GAY *Guardian* No. 149 ¶22 The milliner must be thoroughly versed in physiognomy; in the choice of ribbons she must have a particular regard to the complexion. **1742** RICHARDSON *Pamela* IV. 280 Tailors, Wigpuffers, and Milaners. **1777** SHERIDAN *Sch. Scand.* IV. iii, 'Tis a little French milliner, a silly rogue that plagues me. **1797** *Directory Sheffield* 56 Calton, Godfrey, haberdasher, and milliner. **1799** HAN. MORE *Fem. Educ.* (ed. 4) I. 191 Among milleners, mantua-makers, and other trades where numbers work together. **1827** WORDSW. in *Lit. Crit.* (ed. N. C. Smith) 258 He [T. Moore] is too lavish of brilliant ornament. His poems smell of the perfumer's and milliner's shops. **1884** *West. Daily Press* 29 May 3/7 A black butterfly is unknown to entomologists, but at present is a favourite insect with milliners.

Hence †ˈ**millineress**, a female milliner. **milliˈnerial** *a.*, pertaining to milliners or millinery. ˈ**millinering** *vbl. sb.*, milliner's work; *ppl. a.*, that works as a milliner (in quot. *fig.*).

1802 in *Spirit Publ. Jrnls.* (1803) VI. 93 The advertisements of the lady millineresses. **1831** TRELAWNY *Adv. Younger Son* cxxix, They have no Miss Edgeworth, nor any of those millinering cutters-out of human nature into certain patterns of given rules in education. **1857** GEO. ELIOT *Scenes Clerical Life* (1858) II. 99 It was hard for Mrs. Raynor to have to work at millinering—a woman well brought up. **1886** ROSA MULHOLLAND *Marcella Grace* i, To go running about after millinering and dressmaking. **1888** *Lond. Society* May 557 The dramatic interest is fairly divided with the millinerial.

milliner, *v.* [f. MILLINER 2.] To make up articles of women's clothing, esp. hats. Also *fig.*

1885 G. B. SHAW *Cashel Byron's Profession* (1886) iii. 34 We will go to Paris, and be millinered there. **1895** —— *Our Theatres in Nineties* (1932) I. 205 The displays of fashionable life..are now millinered and tailored..by the artists and tradesmen who equip the real fashionable world. **1907** in C. W. Cunnington *Eng. Women's Clothing* (1952) ii. 79 A modified *cloche* 'millinered' in a light rough-surfaced cloth.

millinery (ˈmɪlɪnərɪ). Forms: see MILLINER *sb.* [f. MILLINER *sb.*: see -ERY.]

1. The articles made or sold by milliners.

1679–88 *Secr. Serv. Money Chas. & Jas.* (Camden) 91 To Benjⁿ Drake, in full of a bill for millenary, wares [? *read* millenary wares], &c. bought of him by the Dutchess of Cleaveland. **1796** BURKE *Regic. Peace* III. (1892) 236 You will hardly expect me to go through the tape and thread, and all the other small wares of haberdashery and millinery to be gleaned up among our imports. **1855** TENNYSON *Maud* I. vi. 43 That dandy-despot, he, That jewell'd mass of millinery. **1901** MAX MÜLLER *Autobiog* 289, I could not understand how these men..could put aside the fundamental questions of Christianity and give their whole mind to what seemed to me rightly called in the newspapers 'mere millinery'.

2. The trade or business of a milliner.

1838 DICKENS *Nich. Nick.* xvii, Processes known only to those who are cunning in the arts of millinery and dressmaking.

3. *attrib.*

1741 RICHARDSON *Pamela* II. 351 What can be done in Town, as the Milanery Matters, &c., to be completed there. **1748** *Anson's Voy.* II. x. 246 European millinery ware for the women. **1880** MRS. HERVEY *Mourtray Fam.* IV. 96 My maid came to ask, if I chose to see some very pretty millinery articles. **1882** *Daily News* 4 Mar., Cotton millinery laces are still greatly run upon. **1896** *Ibid.* 26 Sept. 6/4 Chrysanthemums in all colours are the millinery flower of the moment. **1900** *Westm. Gaz.* 5 Dec. 9/1 The eminent millinery establishment. **1912** *Every Woman's Encycl.* VII. 4447/2 Get some dark green millinery wire covered. **1932** D. C. MINTER *Mod. Needlecraft* 174/1 *Lace Trimmings*..are always mounted on thin millinery wire. **1966** *Olney Amsden & Sons Ltd. Price List* 29 Millinery wires..Satin wire..7/-dozen.

millinet (mɪlɪˈnɛt). ? *Obs.* [? f. MILLIN(ERY) + -ET¹.] 'A sort of coarse, stiff, thin muslin' (Worcester 1860).

1832 MRS. CHILD *Girl's Own Bk.* (ed. 4) 118 Baskets of millinet and straw... Pieces of millinet should be cut [etc.].

milling (ˈmɪlɪŋ), *vbl. sb.* [f. MILL *v.*¹ + -ING¹.]

1. The action or process of subjecting something to the operation of a mill.

a. The action or business of grinding (esp. corn) in a mill.

high milling, milling in which the wheat grain is reduced to flour by successive crackings or slight and partial crushings, alternating with siftings and sortings of the product, resulting in a flour of extreme whiteness and nutritive quality. ***low milling***, milling in which the corn is reduced to flour by a system of mashing, repeated scraping and squeezing, usually attended with some heating of the product, and a single bolting.

1466 *Mann. & Househ. Exp.* (Roxb.) 346 Item, delyverd to Blowbolle fore mellenge and otemelle, vj.d. **1669** WORLIDGE *Syst. Agric.* (1681) 158 The description and manner of drying and Milling thereof [i.e. madder roots].. I leave to those that are better experienced therein. **1877** *Amer. Miller* Mar. 39/1 The process of milling in the United States is carried on under two different systems, namely, low milling and high, or grits, milling. **1879** *Encycl. Brit.* IX. 344/2 Thus we have these various systems:—(1) flat milling or grinding; (2) high milling or granulation; (3) roller milling or crushing; (4) disintegrator milling or crushing. **1903** *Q. Rev.* Oct. 641 There is little hope, however, of rural milling being revived.

b. The treatment of a substance or material in any of the machines known as mills; e.g. the operation of fulling cloth, rolling metals, crushing minerals, etc.

c **1617** LEDSAM & WILLIAMS in *Buccleuch MSS.* (Hist. MSS. Comm.) I. 208 The drawing of gold and silver wire, and milling of it after the manner of England and France. **1679** HOUGHTON *Collect. Husb. & Trade* No. 266 (1727) II. 211 Lead is mightily improv'd of late by a new invention of milling. **1727–41** CHAMBERS *Cycl.*, *Milling*, or *throwing of silk*, is the last preparation of silk before dyeing... To prepare the silk for *milling*, they first put it in boiling water. **1872** RAYMOND *Statist. Mines & Mining* 35 The prices of labor, lumber, and charges for milling [*sc.* quartz] during the year, have not varied much. **1875** KNIGHT *Dict. Mech.*, *Milling*,..the mastication and grinding of slip for porcelain. **1884** W. S. B. MCLAREN *Spinning* I. (ed. 2) 12 We have seen a piece of worsted cloth..shrink after two hours' milling into one-third of its former dimensions. **1892** HASLUCK *Milling Machines* 1 Milling is a term now generally understood as meaning the shaping of metals with rotary cutters.

2. *Coining.* The operation of producing by special machinery a crenation or series of transverse lines on the edge of a coin as a protection against clipping. Now only *concr.* the crenation itself.

Another sense, 'the action of upsetting the edge of a coin, so as to make raised flanges protecting the devices on the faces', given in Knight *Dict. Mech.* and the U.S. Dictionaries, is not known at the English Mint, where this operation is called 'marking'.

1817 RUDING *Ann. Coinage* I. 141 A graining has been devised for the protection of their [the smaller coins] outer edge. This, which is generally known by the technical term Milling, was first used in 1663. *Ibid.* 142 The whole operation of Milling is yet kept a profound secret in the Mint. **1876** MATHEWS *Coinage* i. 7 The saw-like edge possessed by modern coins is called the milling.

3. *slang.* **a.** The action of robbing or stealing. **b.** The action of beating or fighting with the fists, a beating. †**c.** 'Old term for kicking in horses' (*Encycl. Sport* 1897).

1567 HARMAN *Caveat* 67 They wyll send them into some house..to steale and robbe, which they call in their language, Milling of the ken. **1670** R. RHODES *Floras Vagaries* 16 We have all the Querks and Nicety of Roguery, Prigging,..Milling, all, all, Sir. **1815** *Sporting Mag.* XLVI. 148 All three got a merited milling in a few minutes.

4. The action of MILL *v.*¹ 12 a.

1874 J. MCCOY *Hist. Sk. Cattle Trade* 101 Drovers consider that the cattle do themselves great injury by running round in a circle, which is termed in cow-boy parlance, 'milling'. **1924** *Scribner's Mag.* Dec. 607 Jack.. stood outside the door and watched the milling of the excited, hysterical women. **1943** C. H. WARD-JACKSON *Piece of Cake* 41 *Milling, milling around*, flying at high speed in and out across one another's path; or flying in a defensive circle, with the nose of one aircraft a few yards from the tail of another.

5. a. Simple *attrib.*, as ***milling-cutter, -power, -right, -tool***; also with the sense 'suitable for being milled', as ***milling-gold, -ore, -wheat***. Also **milling machine**, (*a*) *Engin.*, a machine in which a work-piece fixed to a carriage is subjected to the action of rotating cutters; (*b*) a machine for fulling cloth.

1884 F. J. BRITTEN *Watch & Clockm.* 177 *Milling cutters have the advantage of retaining their sharpness for a considerable time. **1895** *Daily News* 3 Dec. 9/3 The average yield of free *milling gold is about 1¼ ounce per ton. **1876** J. ROSE *Pract. Machinist* xvi. 301 The position occupied by the *milling-machine in modern practical mechanics is almost as important as that occupied by the lathe or planing-machine. **1888** *Encycl. Brit.* XXIV. 661/2 The cloth to be fulled is well saturated with hot soap and water..and rubbed between rollers in the milling-machine while so heated and soaped. **1953** L. E. DOYLE *Metal Machining* xii. 266 A milling machine must hold and rotate a cutter and have means to hold a workpiece and move it uniformly in at least one direction. **1962** W. J. ONIONS *Wool* xi. 245 In the operation of milling..fabrics are thickened and shrunk to a desired width..The operation is usually carried out in the rotary milling machine. **1877** RAYMOND *Statist. Mines & Mining* 257 A large part of the ore is *milling-ore. **1856** OLMSTED *Slave States* 540 Running water, frequently affording excellent *milling power. **1870** *Law Rep., Comm. Pl.* V. 671 The exercise of a *milling right on a river. **1876** J. ROSE *Pract. Machinist* xvi. 303 One of the main advantages of *milling-tools is that the work will, in nearly all cases, be true. **1895** *Model Steam Engine* 90 A Milling tool is similar to a steel cog-wheel. **1865** *Public Opinion* 4 Mar. 218/2 Where are the *milling and corn trades, formerly so prosperous in Ireland? **1887** *Pall Mall G.* 23 Sept. 2/2 It ..makes so excellent a *milling wheat that [etc.].

b. In the sense 'pertaining to pugilism or pugilists', as ***milling-match, mug, phrase***.

1819 T. MORE *Tom Crib's Mem.* (ed. 3) 49 Account of the *Milling-match between Entellus and Dares. **1812** *Sporting Mag.* XL. 249 The qualifications of the renowned Jem Belcher's weight, a *milling mug and fearless resolution. **1814** BYRON *Let. to Moore* 3 Aug., London..is the only place to take the conceit out of a man—in the *milling phrase.

milling (ˈmɪlɪŋ), *ppl. a.* [f. MILL *v.*² + -ING².]

1. *slang.* Fighting, pugilistic.

1812 J. H. VAUX *Flash Dict.*, *Milling-cove*, a pugilist. **1815** SCOTT *Let. to Dk. of Buccleuch* Aug. in Lockhart *Life*, Shaw, the milling Life-Guards' man.

2. That carries on a mill or mills.

1886 *Leeds Mercury* 16 Feb. 6/6 The large milling firms in London. **1902** *Daily Chron.* 6 Oct. 7/6 Information circulated in milling circles yesterday.

3. Of cattle, fish, etc.: Going round in a circle. Cf. MILL *v.*¹ 12.

1901 *Munsey's Mag.* XXIV. 483/2 They were passing in front of the milling herd. **1919** L. F. CODY *Memories Buffalo Bill* xiii. 289 Here the buffalo thundered along in their milling herd, while Will and the assembled cowboys circled them. **1931** H. F. PRINGLE *Theodore Roosevelt* I. viii. 99 The milling crowds of the cities.

ˈ**mill-ink.** A mill-rind: in *Her.*, a conventional figure or representation of this.

1572 [see INK *sb.*²]. **1874** PAPWORTH & MORANT *Ord. Brit. Arm.* 956 Or on a mill-ink sa. five estoiles of the first. *Jaque.*

millio: see MILLY *Obs.*

million (ˈmɪljən). Forms: 4 **melione, milyon**, 4–5 **mi-, myloun**, 4–7 **milion**, 5 **myl(l)ione, melyone, mi-, myllyon**, *Sc.* **mylȝon(e, mulȝeon**, 6 **myllyant, -io(u)n, -ian, mylion, millian**, 7 *Sc.* **milleoune**, 4, 6- **million**. [a. F. *million* (1359 in Hatz.-Darm.) = Sp. *millon*, Pg. *milhão*, ad. It. *millione* (now written *milione*), f. *mille* thousand + *-one* augmentative suffix. From Fr. the word has passed into the Teut. langs.; G. *million*, Du. *miljoen*, Sw., Da. *million*.]

1. The cardinal number equal to a thousand thousands. (Often used indefinitely or hyperbolically for an enormous number.)

a. As sb. or quasi-sb., with plural.

(*a*) In singular. Usually *a*, emphatically *one million*; in phrases expressing rate, *the million*. Also in phr. ***thanks a million***: see THANK *sb.*

1370–80 *XI Pains of Hell* 316 in *O.E. Misc.* 232 Þen kneled Poul, and Mihel And a Milioun Angeles, wel. *c* **1386**

CHAUCER *Sompn. Prol.* 21 Now sire quod he han freres swich a grace That noon of hem shal come to this place? Yis quod this Angel many a Millioun. *c* **1420** *Anturs of Arth.* 706 (Douce MS.) Prestes with processione to pray were prest, With a mylione of masses to make þe mynnynge. **1480** CAXTON *Chron. Eng.* ccxxx. 243 Ye shal vnderstonde that a myllyon is /M/M/. **1576** FLEMING *Panopl. Epist.* 391 What is he among a myllian that is not surprised with sorrowe, when [etc.]. **1591** SHAKS. *Two Gent.* II. i. 105 Oh, 'giue ye-good-ev'n: heer's a million of manners. **1629** WADSWORTH *Pilgr.* i. 5 Through a Million of dangers we arriued the Spanish coasts. **1710** PALMER *Proverbs* 334 'Tis a million to one but they wish it had never been done. **1726** SWIFT *Gulliver* IV. v, A million of yahoos might have been killed. **1778** MISS BURNEY *Evelina* (1791) II. xxvii. 171 He had a million of things to say to me. **1800** MRS. HERVEY *Mourtray Fam.* II. 6 We charged him with a million of thanks. **1815** J. SMITH *Panorama Sci. & Art* I. 524 The sun is a million of times larger than the earth. **1885** *Manch. Exam.* 24 July 5/1 He could count his soldiers by the million. **1934** J. B. PRIESTLEY *Eng. Journey* ix. 316 This [ship-] yard..had been a spectacular failure in which over a million of money had been lost.

(*b*) In plural: *millions.*

1362 LANGL. *P. Pl.* A. x. 148 Mony Milions mo of Men and of Wymmen. **1494** FABYAN *Chron.* VII. 471 Thre millyons of scutes of golde. **1576** FLEMING *Panopl. Epist.* 277 His head being fraught wt myllians of imaginations. **1597** J. KING *On Jonas* (1618) 18 Ten and ten millions of men. **1611** BIBLE *Gen.* xxiv. 60 Be thou the mother of thousands of millions. **1615** MURE *Misc. Poems* xiv. 12 Till contrarie fortoun..Metamorphos'd his thowsands in milleounes of lyce. **1708** J. PHILLIPS *Cyder* I. 345 The polish'd Glass, whose small Convex Enlarges to ten Millions of Degrees The Mite. **1834** *Penny Cycl.* II. 339/1 Hundreds of thousands of millions of millions. **1893** R. T. JEFFREY *Visits to Calvary* 366 After millions of millenniums.

(*c*) After a numeral adjective, *million* sometimes occurs as a collective plural. (Cf. *dozen, hundred.*) Now *rare* or *Obs.*

c **1530** *Crt. of Love* 589 Yet eft again, a thousand milion, Rejoysing, love, leding their life in blis. *c* **1590** GREENE *Fr. Bacon* ii. 160 A thousand thousand million of fine bells.

b. As adj. or quasi-adj. (in prose use, always with *a* or prefixed multiplier), followed immediately by a plural (or collective) noun. Also in phr. (chiefly *U.S.*) (*like*) ***a million dollars***: excellent, splendid, magnificent (usu. prec. by *to feel* or *to look*).

1843 BORROW *Bible in Spain* xv. 107 The roar of a million cannon. **1846** LANDOR *Imag. Conv., Windham & Sheridan* Wks. 1853 II. 179/2 The crown-lands in Ireland,..are large enough to support half a million subjects. **1868** LYNCH *Rivulet* CLXV. iii, From Thee million spirits have their name. **1885** W. WATSON *Poems* (1892) 106 Her veins are million but her heart is one. **1925** WODEHOUSE *Carry on, Jeeves!* iii. 55 It was one of those topping mornings, and I had just climbed out from under the cold shower feeling like a million dollars. **1933** E. E. CUMMINGS *eimi* 109 Something which might be port..'Looks like a million dollars'—and which tastes like awfully watered vino rosso à l'américain. **1933** ADE *Let.* 13 Nov. (1973) 176 Those [farm buildings] that have been repaired..and painted look like a million dollars compared with most of the nearby so-called improvements. **1947** *Time* 17 Mar. 43 You'll go home feeling like a million dollars, rested and refreshed as never before! **1956** D. GASCOYNE *Night Thoughts* 35 You'd look a million dollars at your worst. **1969** C. ALLEN *Text-bk. Psychosexual Disorders* (ed. 2) xx. 400 If..abnormal habits are allowed to become fixed, the patient becomes a million times more difficult to treat. **1973** *Times* 23 Apr. 5/6 A formula not a million miles removed from that of BBC 2's now defunct *Late Night Line-up.* **1973** BOYD & PARKES *Dark Number* xiii. 150 Dorothy looked, as they say, a million dollars: brushed, scrubbed, wholesome and sane. **1974** WODEHOUSE *Aunts aren't Gentlemen* ix. 75 His refusal to do as Miss Cook asked was unequivocal. 'Not in a million years' was the expression he used.

c. The cardinal form *million* is also used as an ordinal when followed by other numbers, the last of which alone takes the ordinal form.

1866 J. H. NEWMAN *Gerontius* §3 Divide a moment, as men measure time, Into its million-million-millionth part.

2. Elliptical uses. **a.** A million coins or units of money of account of some understood value, esp. (in British use) a million pounds or (in the U.S.) dollars.

1362 LANGL. *P. Pl.* A. III. 255 Coueyte not his goodes For Milions of Moneye. *c* **1422** HOCCLEVE *Learn to Die* 397 Many a milioun Of Gold and siluer. *c* **1430** *Batayle of Eyngecourte* 82 in Hazl. *E.P.P.* II. 96 Our kynge they solde, For a myllyant of golde. *c* **1470** HENRY *Wallace* IV. 142 Of cler gold a fyne mylȝone and mor. **1570** *Ibid.* VII. 1280 Thocht he him gaif ane mulȝeon of gold. *c* **1586** C'TESS PEMBROKE *Ps.* CXIX. I. iv. [verse 72], Millions then, and mines adieu, Gold and silver, drosse you be. **1625** MASSINGER *New Way* I. iii, We must be strangers, Nor would I haue you seene here for a million. *a* **1704** T. BROWN *Sat. Fr. King* Wks. 1730 I. 59 I'd not be, for a million, in thy jerkin. **1790** BEATSON *Nav. & Mil. Mem.* I. 391, Increasing the national debt to near eighty millions Sterling. **1841** R. P. WARD *De Clifford* III. vii. 111 By loans,..and other speculations, he achieved his million, and now acts the grandee. **1902** *Westm. Gaz.* 10 June 2/2 This four millions was taken account of in the Budget statement.

b. ***the million***: the multitude; the bulk of the population.

1602 SHAKS. *Ham.* II. ii. 457 The Play I remember pleas'd not the Million. **1762** FOOTE *Lyar* I. Wks. 1799 I. 283 If you would descend a little to the grovelling comprehension of the million, I think it would be as well. **1894** K. GRAHAME *Pagan P.* 29 The two-and-sixpenny edition for the million.

c. ***a million to one***: a million chances to one; hence, an expression indicating very low probability. Freq. *attrib.*

1761 STERNE *Tr. Shandy* IV. ix. 73 Calculate it fairly..and it will turn out a million to one, that..the forceps should have the ill luck just to fall upon..that one part. **1900** C. H. CHAMBERS *Tyranny of Texas* I. 9 The article hasn't a million to one chance of being finished this afternoon. **1962** P. BRICKHILL *Deadline* v. 78 So I'm supposed to..roam Paris for weeks on the million-to-one chance of spotting someone. **1974** J. WAINWRIGHT *Hard Hit* 103 It might go wrong—there's a million-to-one chance.

d. *pl.* In full, ***millions fish***; = GUPPY[1].

1906 *Chambers's Jrnl.* Apr. 345/2 A tiny fish known locally by the name of 'millions'. **1908** *Science* 18 Dec. 885/2 'Millions' are among the most active natural enemies of mosquitos. **1924** *Glasgow Herald* 2 June 11/2 In Barbadoes..the natives are accustomed to keep in their rain barrels the minute fish known as 'millions'... Hence the absence of mosquitoes. **1966** D. W. TUCKER tr. *Sterba's Freshwater Fishes of World* (ed. 2) 568 *Lebistes reticulatus*... Guppy, Millions Fish. Venezuela, Barbados, Trinidad, parts of northern Brazil and Guiana.

e. (*one*) ***in a million***: (a person, thing, etc.) that is very rare, unusual, or valuable.

1900 CONRAD *Ld. Jim* viii. 99 The occasion was obscure, insignificant—what you will: a lost youngster, one in a million—but then he was one of us. **1906** E. NESBIT *Railway Children* xiii. 288 Take care of your Mother... She's a woman in a million. **1925** WODEHOUSE *Carry on, Jeeves!* i. 30 You know, Jeeves, you're by way of being rather a topper... One in a million, by Jove! **1931** *Times Lit. Suppl.* 5 Feb. 96/3 Emily was, of course, a chimp..in a million.

f. ***gone a million***: (having) completely lost, done for, in a hopeless state. *Austral.* and *N.Z. colloq.*

1916 C. J. DENNIS *Battle of Wazzir* in A. H. Chisholm *Making of Sentimental Bloke* (1963) 131 Fer young Bill wus gone a million, an' 'e never guessed the game. **1922** A. WRIGHT *Colt from Country* 142 What hope would you have when that came out? You'd be gone a million. **1930** K. S. PRICHARD *Haxby's Circus* xvi. 187 If it weren't for you, I'd be gone a million on the minx. **1941** *Coast to Coast* 209 No doubt about it, Sim was right. If they drop their bundles they're gone a million. **1958** *N.Z. Listener* 23 May 6/4 We scraped in in that game, only because Elvidge scored his usual try... Otherwise, we were gone a million.

3. *attrib.* and *Comb.*, (*a*) simple attrib. or objective, as ***million maker***; ***million-billowed***, ***-dollared*** (*absol.* in quot. = 'a person who has a million dollars'), ***-eyed***, ***-footed***, ***-handed***, ***-minded***, ***-pointed***, ***-voiced*** adjs.; (*b*) parasynthetic, as instrumental, as ***million-***peopled adj.; **million-act**, an act of parliament authorizing a lottery to be held in 1694 and succeeding years, by which a million pounds was to be raised by the sale of lottery tickets at ten pounds each; so ***million lottery***; **million-dollar** *a.*, worth or costing a million dollars; (also *transf.* and *fig.*) expensive-looking; magnificent, splendid; very attractive; **millionheiress**, an heiress to a 'million of money'; **million-seller**, a gramophone record, book, etc., of which a million copies have been sold.

1694 J. BRISCOE (*title*) A Discourse on the late Funds of the *Million-Act, Lottery-Act, and Bank of England. **1895** W. WATSON *Apologia*, He..beholds..In *million-billowed consentaneousness, The flowing, flowing, flowing of the world. **1892** A. E. LEE *Hist. Columbus, Ohio* II. 90 The General Assembly..passed this *milliondollar bill. **1921** *Discovery* Feb. 48/1 The water hyacinth..is a beautiful aquatic plant..but its spread in St. John's River and the enormous sums spent in attempting its suppression have earned it the name of the 'million-dollar weed'. **1932** *Amer. Speech* VII. 250 Bing Crosby plaintively croons that he has 'Found a Million Dollar Baby in the Five and Ten Cent Store'. **1959** *Listener* 5 Mar. 432/1 A man in a million-dollar suit. **1961** J. HELLER *Catch-22* (1962) xxvii. 296 I've got this million-dollar leg wound that will take me out of combat. **1972** *News & Observer* (Raleigh, N. Carolina) 30 Dec. 4/2 We don't hear much [nowadays] about..million dollar rains, and undertakers. **1857** J. G. WHITTIER *Barefoot Boy* in *Poetical Works* II. 230 Let the *million-dollared ride! Barefoot, trudging at his side, Thou hast more than he can buy. **1893** CHR. ROSSETTI *Verses* 101 Wisdom that loveth thee grows *million-eyed. **1865** W. WHITMAN *Drum-Taps* 61 When *million-footed Manhattan, unpent, descends to its pavements. **1885** W. B. YEATS *Island of Statues* II. iii, in *Dublin Univ. Rev.* July 137/1 Though I be Far fleeter than the million-footed sea. **1847** EMERSON *Poems* (1857) 47 The *million-handed painter pours Opal hues and purple dye. **1919** W. DE MORGAN *Old Madhouse* 457 His mind took kindly to the interruption of this young man's nuptials with an American *millionheiress of startling beauty. **1942** BERREY & VAN DEN BARK *Amer. Thes. Slang* §417 *Millionheiress*, a woman who is a millionaire. **1710** SWIFT *Jrnl. to Stella* 15 Sept., Colonel Fremd, and I, went to see the *million lottery drawn at Guildhall. **1849** ROBERTSON *Serm.* Ser. I. i. (1866) 10 The *million-minded Poet. **1819** SHELLEY *Prometh. Unb.* I. 551 A *million-peopled city. **1923** *Million-pointed [see *million-voiced* below]. **1969** N. COHN *AWopBopaLooBop* (1970) iii. 27 He [*sc.* Elvis Presley] has racked up twenty worldwide *million sellers. **1971** *Shout* Dec.. They performed Ship of Love & of course the near-millionseller Story Untold. **1972** *Jazz & Blues* Sept. 11/2 Fats Domino cut 16 million-sellers in this town. **1894** 'MARK TWAIN' *Those Twins* 322 The two sat unconscious of the *million-voiced music of the mosquitos. **1923** BELLOC *Sonnets & Verse* 149 To-night in million-voicèd London I Was lonely as the million-pointed sky.

million, obs. form of MELON, MILAN[1].

millionaire (mɪljəˈnɛə(r)). Formerly also in Fr. form. [a. F. *millionnaire*, f. *million*: see MILLION.] **1. a.** A person possessed of a 'million of money', as a million pounds, dollars, francs, etc.; a person of great wealth.

1826 DISRAELI *Viv. Grey* I. ix, Were I the son of a Millionaire, or a noble, I might have all. **1830** GEN. P. THOMPSON *Exerc.* (1842) I. 225 He was what the French call a millionnaire. **1853** MISS MITFORD in L'Estrange *Life* (1870) III. xiv. 254 Mrs. Stowe, from the poorest of the poor, is become quite a millionaire.

b. quasi-*adj.* Possessing a million of money.

1865 *Sat. Rev.* 11 Nov. 614 A few millionaire families.

c. ***Millionaires' Row***: a street containing the residences of very rich people.

1950 'J. GUTHRIE' *Is this what I Wanted?* iii. 56 Charles drove off past the park, the Broad Walk and Millionaire's Row. **1954** 'N. BLAKE' *Whisper in Gloom* iii. 43 [The Bentley]..swept through the doorway of 'Millionaires' Row'. **1964** B. WYNNE *Spies Within* iv. 37 What about their radio, in 'Millionaires' Row'? **1972** *Guardian* 19 Dec. 11/1 My Gozan friend had ragged, empty pockets..but he lived on millionaires' row.

2. Used *attrib.* of a town with more than a million population.

1936 C. B. FAWCETT in Salamon & Kuchar *Mélanges de Géogr. offerts à V. Švambera* 52 A 'millionaire-city' is to be understood as a conurbation which contains at least one million inhabitants. **1958** D. L. LINTON in *Geography* XLIII. 258 The emergence of millionaire cities and even five-million cities in tropical countries is now widespread and continuing. **1961** *Land Use in Urban Environment* (Univ. of Liverpool, Dept. Civic Design) 11 The great concentration of population, housing, offices and factories in the millionaire cities.

Hence **millio'nairedom**, the condition of being a millionaire. **millio'nairess**, a female millionaire. **millio'nairish** *a.*, of or pertaining to a millionaire. **millio'nairism**, the existence or rule of millionaires as a characteristic of a social system.

1881 J. PAYN *Grape from a Thorn* xiii, Even though he married an heiress or even a Millionairess. **1887** *Atlantic Monthly* LX. 222 Stuffs which none but an empress or a millionairess would dare to look at. **1888** *Pall Mall G.* 8 Feb. 4/2 The schoolboy of to-day, with his millionairish ideas of pocket-money. *c* **1890** A. MURDOCH *Yoshiwara Episode* 23 He had not as yet struck the path that leads unto millionairedom. **1891** *Harper's Mag.* Jan. 320/2 Our political turmoil, our demagogism, our millionairism. **1906** L. BELL *Carolina Lee* 38 You'll have to go on being a millionairess, whether you will or no. **1958** [see BEERAGE]. **1971** *Nature* 17 Dec. 377/1 Mrs Mary Lasker, a New York millionairess and philanthropist. **1973** *Daily Tel.* 29 Oct. 15/4 We could be millionairesses if we were concerned only with money.

millio'naireship. [-SHIP.] The position or state of a millionaire.

1901 *Chambers's Jrnl.* Apr. 217/2 The flour industry gave the late Mr. Charles A. Pillsbury the means of millionaireship. **1930** W. O. STAPLEDON *Last & First Men* 78 For the Individual, the goal imposed by his religious teaching was continuous advance in aeronautical prowess, legal sexual freedom, and millionaireship.

millionary (ˈmɪljənərɪ), *a.* and *sb.* [f. MILLION + -ARY, after F. *millionnaire*: see MILLIONAIRE.]

A. *adj.*

1. Possessing millions (of money).

1816 JEFFERSON *Writ.* (1830) IV. 284 All this to feed the avidity of a few millionary merchants. **1897** KIPLING *Captains Courageous* 230 He had a dread that these millionary people..might take undue interest in his companion.

2. Pertaining to or consisting of millions (Pinkerton, cited by Webster 1864).

B. *sb.* = MILLIONAIRE.

1834 *Fraser's Mag.* IX. 116 And sighs—the millionary sighs—for more. **1835** MRS. GORE *Mammon* II. 81 Fortunately for the new millionary, his wife, like the spouse of John Gilpin, possessed a frugal mind. **1873** M. COLLINS *Squire Silchester* II. vi. 70 Could not some English millionary give a few hundred thousands to endow such an institution?

millioned (ˈmɪljənd), *a.* [f. MILLION + -ED[2].]

1. Numbered by the million.

In the Shaks. quot. *milliond* may be a form of *million.* (So often in mod. dialects.)

c **1600** SHAKS. *Sonn.* cxv, But reckening time, whose milliond accidents Creepe in twixt vowes, and change decrees of Kings. **1749** *Deity* 41 Thy hand thou open'st, million'd myriads live. **1899** 'H. DELUSCAR' *Merris* 157 The ramping, millioned mob.

2. Possessed of millions (of money).

1747 P. WHITEHEAD *Honour* (1748) 44 The million'd Merchant seeks her [Honour] in his Gold. **1858** O. W. HOLMES *Aut. Breakf.-t.* ii, A few Northern millionaires more or less thoroughly millioned.

millioner (ˈmɪljənə(r)). [f. MILLION + -ER[1].] = MILLIONAIRE.

1882 LOWELL *Last Poems* (1895) 38 No millioner, poor I fill up With wishes my more modest cup.

millioner, obs. form of MILLINER *sb.*

millionfold (ˈmɪljənfəʊld), *a.* and *adv.* [f. MILLION + -FOLD.] **A.** *adj.* A million times as much or as many. **B.** *adv.* A million times (in amount); in a millionfold proportion: always with the indefinite article *a.*

1865 MASSON *Rec. Brit. Philos.* 256 Strengthened, enlarged, and educated by millionfold repetitions and associations. **1869** PROCTOR *Light Sci. Leis. Hours* (1871) 296 The radius..might be increased a million-fold.

millionism (ˈmɪljəniz(ə)m). [f. MILLION + -ISM.] The state of possessing a million (of money).
1858 O. W. HOLMES *Aut. Breakf.-t.* xii, The tea-spoon is of white silver,..solid, but not brutally heavy,—as people in the green stage of millionism will have them.

millionist (ˈmɪljənɪst). *rare*⁻¹. [f. MILLION + -IST.] A millionaire.
1834–43 SOUTHEY *Doctor* ccxxxiii, His revenue is less than that of many a..commercial Millionist.

millionize (ˈmɪljənaɪz), *v.* [f. MILLION + -IZE.] *trans.* **a.** To multiply by a million or millions. **b.** To enrich greatly or to the extent of millions (of money).
c **1700** *Eternity* in *Coll. Poems* 90 Ages, Worlds, Thousands, Myriads Millionize, Fatigue Conception, 'twill not all comprize Thee, O Eternity! **1841** R. OASTLER *Fleet Papers* I. xii. 96 Which enables a very large capitalist to ruin a whole neighbourhood, and millionize himself.
Hence **ˈmillionized** *a.*, accustomed to millions.
1849 SMYTH in *Archæologia* XXXIII. 201 To our now millionized conceptions the foregoing 'accompts' appear to be in a very moderate ratio.

millionnaire, French form of MILLIONAIRE.

millionocracy (ˌmɪljəˈnɒkrəsɪ). *nonce-wd.* [f. MILLION + -(O)CRACY.] The rule of millionaires.
1860 O. W. HOLMES *Elsie V.* i, The millionocracy..is not at all an affair of persons and families, but a perpetual fact of money with a variable human element.

†**ˈmillionous**, *a.* *Obs. rare*⁻¹. [f. MILLION + -OUS.] Numbered by the million.
1666 G. ALSOP *Char. Prov. Maryland* (1869) 42 They [water-fowl] arrive in millionous multitudes in Mary-Land about the middle of September.

millionth (ˈmɪljənθ), *a.* (*sb.*) Also 7–8 **millioneth.** [f. MILLION, on the analogy of HUNDREDTH.] The ordinal number belonging to the cardinal MILLION. ***millionth part***, one of a million equal parts into which a whole is or may be divided. Also *absol.*, *attrib.*, and quasi-*sb.*
1673 FLAMSTEED in Rigaud *Corr. Sci. Men* (1841) II. 164 So that I find the earth is but the millionth part of the sun. **1684** T. BURNET *Th. Earth* I. 312 'Tis not the millioneth part of the universe that is known to us. *c* **1763** BAYES in *Phil. Trans.* LIII. 410 There would be the odds of the millioneth power of 2 to one. **1838** DE MORGAN *Ess. Probab.* 28 A millionth of certainty. *a* **1853** ROBERTSON *Lect.* i. (1858) 14 It is but the millionth part of the injury which may arise from a bad law. **1876** *Catal. Sci. Apparatus S. Kens. Mus.* (1877) 49 Millionth Measuring Machine. **1893** SIR R. BALL *Story of Sun* 94 The millionth part of a second.

milliped, variant of MILLEPEDE.

Millipore (ˈmɪlɪpɔə(r)). Also **millipore.** [f. MILLI- + PORE *sb.*¹] Designating membrane filters made by the Millipore Filter Corporation of Watertown, Mass., or by a foreign subsidiary of this company.
1956 *Jrnl. Bacteriol.* LXXI. 499 Direct staining procedures for microorganisms collected on the 'millipore filter'. **1962** F. I. ORDWAY et al. *Basic Astronautics* iv. 131 Air moves through the opening into the 2-cm diameter chamber at the rear of which is located a millipore filter in a removable housing. **1967** *Oceanogr. & Marine Biol.* V. 171 Filtration through fine Millipore filters removes more of the finely dispersed material. **1969** *Methods in Microbiol.* I. vii. 207 The standard Millipore filters.

millisecond (ˈmɪlɪsɛkənd). [f. MILLI- + SECOND *sb.*¹] One thousandth of a second.
1922 GLAZEBROOK *Dict. Appl. Physics* II. 421/1 The arrangement of the coils is astatic and the time constant is about 1·6 milliseconds at the maximum. **1929** *Papers Inst. Post Office Electr. Engin.* CXXII. 11 It would be difficult to read to an accuracy of less than about 10 milliseconds. **1960** E. DELAVENAY *Introd. Machine Transl.* vi. 82 The lexical memory of the machine should provide random access to any word in not more than 10 milliseconds. **1973** C. EGLETON *Seven Days to Killing* i. 16 The car disintegrated, and a millisecond later the blast wave shattered the windscreen in the cab of the truck.

millisite (ˈmɪlɪsaɪt). *Min.* [f. the name of F. T. *Millis* (see quot. 1930) + -ITE¹.] A light grey or white hydrated basic phosphate of sodium, potassium, calcium, and aluminium, (Na,K) $CaAl_6(PO_4)_4(OH)_9.3H_2O$.
1930 LARSEN & SHANNON in *Amer. Mineralogist* XV. 329 The name millisite is proposed for the species after F. T. Millis who sent the original specimens to the U.S. National Museum. **1942** *Ibid.* XXVII. 294 Millisite is invariably associated with wardite as alternating layers in spherules or crusts. It is light gray to white in color, and normally is present as layers of fine fibers normal to the layering. **1965** *Jrnl. Geol. Soc. Austral.* XII. 261 Crandallite and millisite occur in the lateritic profiles derived from apatite and barrandite and the weathering, in the presence of phosphate, of the carbonate and volcanic rocks [on Christmas Island].

millistere (ˈmɪlɪstɪə(r)). [a. F. *millistère*: see MILLI- and STERE.] In the metric system: A thousandth part of a STERE.
1810 *Naval Chron.* XXIV. 301 Millistere, cubic Decimeter.

millitary, millium, obs. ff. MILITARY, MILIUM.

Millite (ˈmɪlaɪt), *a.* and *sb.* [f. the name *Mill* (see MILLIAN *a.* and *sb.*) + -ITE² 1 a.] = MILLIAN *a.* and *sb.*
1917 J. MORLEY *Recoll.* I. iv. 52 It was, in fact, the pure milk of the Millite word. *Ibid.* vi. 87 He [*sc.* Bagehot]..was not in the least an orthodox Millite. **1949** G. B. SHAW *Sixteen Self-Sketches* x. 56 Both societies were strongly Millite.

millium sole: see MILLENSOLE.

millivolt (ˈmɪlɪvɒlt). *Physics.* [f. MILLI- + VOLT.] The thousandth part of a volt.
In quot. 1861 *volt* is being used for what is now called an ohm.
1861 *Electrician* 9 Nov. 3/2 The application of the French system of notation in the table, is evidently faulty, the thousandth part of a volt being one milivolt [*sic*], and not one kilovolt, as stated. **1885** *Jrnl. Soc. Telegr. Engin.* XIV. 196 Differences of potential greater than such millivolts as are concerned in thermo-electricity. **1890** in *Century Dict.* **1971** *Jrnl. Gen. Psychol.* LXXXIV. 11 A sensitivity of about 60 to 200 millimetres per millivolt was used for the average preparation.
Hence **milliˈvoltmeter**, an instrument for measuring voltages of the order of millivolts.
1907 H. H. NORRIS *Introd. Study Electr. Engin.* xii. 346 The instrument..usually known as a milli-voltmeter. **1971** *Nature* 15 Jan. 167/2 Screen leads connected the coils to a millivoltmeter arranged to read from −50 to +50.

milliweber (ˌmɪlɪˈwiːbə(r)). *Physics.* [f. MILLI- + WEBER.] The thousandth part of a weber.
1897 in WEBSTER.

mill-ken. *slang. Obs.* [f. MILL *v.*² + KEN.] A housebreaker.
1669 *Nicker Nicked* in *Harl. Misc.* (1809) II. 108 Kidnappers, vouchers, mill-kens, piemen, decoys [etc.]. **1673** in R. Head *Canting Acad.* 191 The fourth is a Mill-ken, to crack up a Door. **1743** FIELDING *Jon. Wild* I. v, The same capacity which qualifies a Mill-ken..to arrive at any degrees of eminence..would likewise raise a man in what the world esteem a more honourable calling.

mill-lands, *pl.* [MILL *sb.*¹] Certain lands which by legal custom appertained to a corn-mill, esp. in Scotland.
1563 *Reg. Privy Council Scot.* I. 245 Tua mylnis of North Berwick, with the myllandis, multuris, and sukkin thairof. *c* **1680** DALLAS *Stiles* (1697) 724 The Towns, Lands, Milns, Miln-Lands, Patronages, Teinds, and other after-mentioned [etc.]. **1710** *Contract* in *Sheriff Court-bk. Inverness* (MS.) (5 Apr. 1723), The miln of Davochgarrioch, miln Lands, multures, sucken, sequells and Knaveship of the samyn [etc.]. **1892** BLOMFIELD *Hist. Over Heyford* 15 All rents and farm of the mill-lands and tenements.

ˈmill-leat. [MILL *sb.*¹] An artificial channel for the conveyance of water to a mill.
1609–10 *Act 7 Jas. I*, c. 19 §1 A newe Milleate or Trench for the Conveyance of the said Water to the said Milles. **1706** PHILLIPS (ed. Kersey), *Leat* or Mill-leat, corruptly Milleat, a Trench for conveying Water to or from a Mill. **1832** *Act 2 & 3 Will. IV*, c. 64 Sched. (O) 9 Along Hall's Mill lane to the point at which the same meets the Mill leat.

millman (ˈmɪlmən). [f. MILL *sb.*¹ + MAN *sb.*] **a.** A man who has charge of and works a mill of any kind. **b.** A man employed in a mill.
1551–2 *Act 5 & 6 Edw. VI*, c. 6 §6 Yf..any Clothe..prove ..thoroughe the defaulte or negligence of the Milman or otherwise to be full of holes [etc.]. **1837** HAWTHORNE *Twice-told T.* (1851) I. vii. 136 The whole population of Parker's Falls, consisting of shopkeepers, mistresses of boarding houses, factory girls, millmen, and schoolboys. **1874** RAYMOND *Statist. Mines & Mining* 501 You cannot ask the mill-man to vary the weight or speed of his stamps. **1885** *Manch. Exam.* 25 Mar. 5/4 The puddlers and millmen.. resolved..to give their services, for a week, gratuitously.

ˈmill-ˌmountain. ? *Obs.* [Of obscure origin; the 1633 editor of Gerarde says the plant was sold under this name at Winchester.] Fairy flax, *Linum catharticum.*
1633 *Gerarde's Herbal* II. clxvii. 560 Take a handfull of Mill mountaine [etc.]. **1640** PARKINSON *Theat. Bot.* 1336. **1828** J. E. SMITH *Eng. Flora* II. 119 Purging Flax. Mill-mountain.

†**ˈmillocke.** *Obs. rare*⁻⁰. [f. MILL *sb.*¹ + -OCK.] A little mill.
1570 LEVINS *Manip.* 159/12 Millocke, *parua mola.*

millocracy (mɪˈlɒkrəsɪ). [f. MILL *sb.*¹ + -(O)CRACY.] The rule of mill-owners; the body of mill-owners regarded as a dominant class.
1843 CARLYLE *Past. & Pr.* III. i, In hydra-wrestle, giant 'Millocracy' so-called..wrestles and wrings. **1956** G. S. HAIGHT in *Geo. Eliot Lett.* VI. 286 A small boarding school for girls..drawn largely from the millocracy, rich and profoundly ignorant. **1970** R. BLAKE *Conservative Party* i. 21 Why should not the landed aristocracy join hands with the socially dispossessed..against the northern 'millocracy'?

millocrat (ˈmɪləʊkræt). [f. MILL *sb.*¹ + -(O)CRAT.] A member of the mill-owning class viewed as a ruling caste.
1839 MRS. F. TROLLOPE *M. Armstrong* xiii, Millocrats who pile thousands upon thousands, and acres upon acres. **1851** W. E. AYTOUN in *Blackw. Mag.* LXX. 227, I prefer a feudal baron to a modern millocrat.
Hence **miˈllocratism**, the rule of the millocrats.
1849 LYTTON *Caxtons* XIII. iv. II. 334 The misery which accompanies the reign of millocratism.

millon, obs. form of MELON, MILAN¹.

ˈmill-pick, -peck. [f. MILL *sb.*¹ + PICK *sb.*, PECK *sb.*²] An iron tool for giving to mill-stones the requisite corrugated surface.
c **1357** *Durham Acc. Rolls* (Surtees) 560, 6 Milnpikkes. **1525** in W. H. Turner *Select. Rec. Oxf.* (1880) 55 The makyng of spyndyll and the myll pyckes. **1588** in Nichols *Progr. Q. Eliz.* (1823) III. 3 Furred throrough with mynnyover and calloper like myll pykes. **1880** JEFFERIES *Gt. Estate* 163 The millpeck is a little tool like a double adze.
b. *Her.* A figure or representation of a mill-pick.
1562 LEIGH *Armorie* (1597) 92b, The Frenchmen take it [the Fusil] for a spindell,..and the Dutchmen take it for a milpeck. **1634** PEACHAM *Gentl. Exerc.* III. 150 Very honourable and ancient. As the Crosse Moline (given by the ..family of Molineux) Mil-peckes, and most irons appertaining to the Mill. **1874** PAPWORTH & MORANT *Ord. Brit. Arm.* 979 Arg. three mill-picks gu. *Pickworth.*
So †**mill picker**, one who fashions the grinding surfaces of millstones.
c **1515** *Cocke Lorell's B.* 5 Here is wyll wyly the myl peker.

ˈmill-pond. [MILL *sb.*¹] The water retained above a mill-dam for driving a mill. Also *attrib.*
1697 DAMPIER *Voy.* I. 217 It was quite calm, and the Sea as smooth as a Mill-pond. **1766** SMOLLETT *Trav.* I. xix. 301 In the month of November, when the Mediterranean is always calm and smooth as a mill-pond. **1886** A. WINCHELL *Walks Geol. Field* 51 The farmer's fields contributed the material that lies in the bottom of the mill-pond.
attrib. *a* **1706** EVELYN *Sylva* III. iv. (1776) 521 Lay therefore your boards a fortnight in the water, (if running, the better, as at some mill-pond head).
b. *humorous.* [Anticipated, and perhaps orig. suggested by, the use in quots. 1813.] The Atlantic, esp. that part of the ocean traversed by ships passing between Britain and North America. Cf. HERRING-POND.
[**1813** 'H. BULL-US' *Diverting Hist. John Bull & Bro. Jonathan* (ed. 2) i. 5 He put himself in a boat, and paddled over the mill-pond to some new lands. *Ibid.* ii. 12 The tenants began to carry their grain to different parts of the great mill-pond.] **1885** G. ALLEN *Babylon* xi. (1886) 79 And now, while Minna Wroe was waiting at table in Regent's Park,..how was our other friend Hiram Winthrop employing his time beyond the millpond?

ˈmill-pool. [MILL *sb.*¹] A mill-pond.
c **800** in Birch *Cartul. Sax.* I. 418 In þone mylen pol of þam pole to þære port stræte. *c* **883** *Ibid.* II. 174 On myle pul of mylen pulle in afene stream. *c* **1530–40** J. HEYWOOD *Play of Wether* 461 (Brandl) Our floodgate, our mylpoole, our water whele. **1604** BRETON *Grimellos Fortunes* D iv, This.. man, drawing one daie a Mill-poole, among other fish, lighted on a verie great Eele. **1808** *Sporting Mag.* XXX. 248 The mill-pool of Mr. Rodwell of East Harling, Norfolk. **1905** *Macm. Mag.* Nov. 6 The chub are beginning to rise in the mill-pool.

ˈmill-post. [f. MILL *sb.*¹ + POST *sb.*]
1. The post on which a windmill was formerly often supported. Often in similative phrases, as the type of something thick and massive; hence *jocularly*, a massive leg.
a **1327** *Pol. Songs* (Camden) 70 The Kyng..Makede him a castel of a mulne post. **1378–9** *Durham Acc. Rolls* (Surtees) 588, 2 milnepostes, 4*s.* **1562** J. HEYWOOD *Prov. & Epigr.* (1867) 204 A pooddyng pricke is one, a mylpost is an other. **1592** G. HARVEY *Pierces Super.* Wks. (Grosart) II. 244 He hath thwittled the milpost of his huge conceit to a pudding-pricke. **1668** R. L'ESTRANGE *Vis. Quev.* (1708) 27 A dressing with Dr. Whackum's Plaister, that shall fetch up a Man's Leg to the size of a Mill-post. *a* **1704** T. BROWN *Walk round Lond., Quaker's Meet.* (1709) 21 His Mill-post Legs are well adapted for the Load of his Body. **1727** SWIFT *Wonder of Wonders* Wks. 1755 II. II. 57 Her legs are as thick as mill-posts. **1739** 'R. BULL' tr. *Dedekindus' Grobianus* 4 Let dangling Stockings, with becoming Air, Leave to the Sight your brace of Mill-posts bare. **1855** LADY HOLLAND *Syd. Smith* I. vii. 163 Out-of-doors reigned Molly Mills,..with her short red petticoat, legs like mill-posts [etc.]. **1858** HOGG *Life Shelley* II. 247 The daughters of Erin lost no opportunity of exhibiting their millposts to an unprejudiced and observant stranger.
2. *U.S.* 'A post upon which the cap of a smock-mill, bearing the sails, turns' (*Cent. Dict.* 1890).

ˈmill-race. [f. MILL *sb.*¹ + RACE *sb.*] The current of water that drives a mill-wheel; the channel in which the water runs to the mill.
1478–9 *Durham Acc. Rolls* (Surtees) 647 Operantibus in muracione murorum et posicione del Milnrasses et le bay ejusdem molendini. **1536–7** *Ibid.* 702 Le mylnerasse de Scaltok. **1832** BEWICK *Mem.* 49 Others were digging a mill race of about a quarter of a mile in length. **1874** GREEN *Short Hist.* ii. §7. 100 To rescue his hawk..he once plunged into a millrace, and was all but crushed by the wheel.

millree, -reye, obs. forms of MILREIS.

mill-rind (ˈmɪlraɪnd). Also 6–9 **-rynd,** 7–8 **milrine.** [f. MILL *sb.*¹ + RIND *sb.*] The iron which supports the upper millstone of a corn-mill, and carries the eye which rests upon the end of the mill spindle.
1542 *Rutland MSS.* (1905) IV. 325 A spendyll and a melle rynd for the lyttel Itallyon melle. **1870** *Eng. Mech.* 11 Mar. 624/1 'Back lash', frequently occasions a 'break down' by fracturing the 'millrynd'. **1888** J. WARD in *Jrnl. Derbysh.*

Archæol. Soc. X. 54 Mr. Jno. Evans..suggest that they were for the insertion of a 'millrine'.

b. *Her.* A conventional representation of this.

1562 LEIGH *Armorie* (1597) 34b, Yee should cal it a Ferdemolene, which is as much to say, as a Milrind. **1680** MACKENZIE *Heraldry* 46 A cross milrine. **1727** BAILEY vol. II, s.v., A *Cross Milrine*, is a Cross that has the 4 Ends clamped and turned again..only the *Milrine* hath but 2 Limbs, whereas the *Cross Moline* hath 4. **1874** PAPWORTH & MORANT *Ord. Brit. Arm.* 956 Or on a millrind sa. five estoiles arg.

'mill-round. The circular path travelled by a mill-horse. In quots. *fig.*

1851 EMERSON *Ess.* Ser. I. vi. *Motto*, O Friend..The mill-round of our fate appears A sun-path in thy worth. **1897** *Allbutt's Syst. Med.* VIII. 377 Melancholics left to their own thoughts are assuredly beating the mill-round of their disorder deeper and deeper.

Mills (mɪlz). The name of Sir William *Mills* (1856–1932) used *attrib.*, as ***Mills bomb, grenade***, etc., to designate a type of hand grenade, serrated on the outside to form shrapnel on explosion, invented by him.

1916 *War Illustr.* 30 Sept. 162/1 (*caption*) 'Lobbing' a Mills grenade. **1917** G. M. AINSLIE *Hand Grenades* 8 Grenade hand no. 5. Mark I. Mills hand grenade. **1917** A. G. EMPEY *From Fire Step* xii. 74 The standard bomb used in the British Army is the 'Mills'. It is about the shape and size of a large lemon. **1923** KIPLING *Irish Guards in Gt. War* I. 75 The Mills bomb..was not born till the autumn of 1915. **1935** C. DAY LEWIS *Time to Dance* 38 But the aeronauts, knowing iron the coinage here, had brought Mills bombs and revolvers. **1942** J. T. GORMAN *Mod. Weapons War* vii. 121 The segmented jacket of a Mills bomb or hand-grenade is not unlike that of a pomegranate's ridged outer rind. **1973** J. WAINWRIGHT *Pride of Pigs* 17 Any damn fool can work a Mills hand grenade..slip your finger through the split-ring, jerk out the pin and throw. *Ibid.*, He smuggled a Mills bomb home in..his kitbag as a memento of El Alamein. **1974** *Daily Tel.* 6 May 1/6 A fully-primed Mills bomb which had been used as a mantelpiece ornament for 56 years was handed to police at Nottingham yesterday.

Mill's Methods (mɪlz 'meθədz). *Logic.* The Methods of Agreement, of Difference, of Joint Agreement and Difference, of Residues, and of Concomitant Variations which form the five canons of inductive inquiry proposed by J. S. Mill (1806–73) for discovering, and establishing the validity of, causal relations between phenomena. Cf. METHOD *sb.* 2c.

1896 J. WELTON *Man. Logic* II. v. v. 141 (*caption*) As Mill's Methods have obtained general currency they demand some examination. **1922** W. E. JOHNSON *Logic* II. x. 217, I hold..that Mill's methods can and should be exhibited as strictly formal. **1942** D. RUNES *Dict. Philos.* (1944) 197/2 *Mill's methods*, inductive methods formulated by John Stuart Mill for the discovery of causal relations between phenomena. **1953** S. E. TOULMIN *Philos. of Sci.* i. 9 The accumulation of confirming instances, Mill's Methods and the probability-calculus: such things form the staple of most expositions. **1965** P. CAWS *Philos. of Sci.* xxxiii. 251 Mill's methods..are an elegant recipe for detecting the constant conjunctions of which Hume speaks. **1973** H. C. BYERLY *Primer of Logic* v. xiii. 423 (*heading*) Mill's methods for discovering causes: agreement and difference.

millstone ('mɪlstəʊn). Forms: see MILL *sb.*[1] and STONE *sb.* [f. MILL *sb.*[1] + STONE *sb.*; cf. Du. *molensteen*, MHG. *mülstein* (mod.G. *mühlstein*), Da. *møllesten*.]

1. One of a pair of circular stones (the upper of which rotates upon the lower or 'nether'), used for grinding corn in a mill. ***nether millstone***: see NETHER *a.*

c **1050** *Ags. Voc.* in Wr.-Wülcker 273/1 *Limu*, mylenstan. *Ibid.* 430/28 *Lima*, feol, oððe mylenstan. *c* **1290** *S. Eng. Leg.* I. 316 580 A Mulleston, he scholde al-to-driue. *c* **1380** WYCLIF *Wks.* (1880) 61 It spediþ to him þat a mylneston of assis be hangid in his necke. **1393** LANGL. *P. Pl.* C. XXI. 295 Sette mahon at þe mangonel and mulle-stones þroweþ. *c* **1450** *Mirour Saluacioun* 4041 A pece of a mylnestone threwe doune there a womman. **1560** BIBLE (Geneva) *Rev.* xviii. 21 Then a mightie Angel toke vp a stone like a great milstone, & cast it into the sea. **1609** SKENE *Reg. Maj.* I. 151 They malitiouslie occupyes ane greater space betwix the happer and the mylnstane, for their awin profite. **1622** DRAYTON *Poly-olb.* xxvi. 391 Shee Mil-stones from the Quarrs, with sharpned picks could get. **1751** J. FERGUSON in *Fam. Rose Kilravock* (Spald. Cl.) 443 The water-wheel moves a train for turning two mill-stones. **1877** BRYANT *Song of Sower* ii, Steadily the millstone turns Down in the willowy vale.

b. Stone suitable for the making of millstones.

1661 J. CHILDREY *Brit. Baconica* 153 Millstone is digged in this shire.

c. ***carpenter's millstone*** (see quot.).

1859 R. HUNT *Guide Mus. Pract. Geol.* (ed. 2) 55 The carpenter's millstone, is a hard and close variety of the Yorkshire sandstones.

d. *Her.* A representation of a millstone (usually depicted with the mill-rind attached).

1688 R. HOLME *Armoury* III. 341/1 He beareth Sable, a Mil-Ston Argent. **1874** PAPWORTH & MORANT *Ord. Brit. Arm.* 1100 Az. three millstones ppr. *Melveton.*

2. In phrases: ***to see far in*** (***into, through***), ***to look into*** (***through***), ***to dive into a millstone***, used chiefly in ironical commendation of pretended extraordinary acuteness.

1546 J. HEYWOOD *Prov.* (1867) 21 She thought Ales, she had seene far in a milstone Whan she gat a husbande. **1577** STANYHURST *Descr. Irel.* in *Holinshed* (1808) VI. 18 He would see further in a milstone than others. **1580** LYLY *Euphues* Wks. 1902 II. 67 Your eyes are so sharpe, that you cannot onely looke through a Milstone, but cleane through the minde. **1625** HART *Anat. Ur.* II. vii. 92 They..could see as farre into a milstone as any of our..Physitians. *a* **1704** T. BROWN *Lett. to Gentl. & Ladies* Wks. 1709 III. II. 93 Thou ..can'st see as far into a Mill-stone, as the oldest Match-maker in Town. **1871** C. GIBBON *Lack of Gold* ii, That's all the length your learning helps you to see through a mill-stane.

¶**b.** (***his***) ***eyes drop millstones***: said of a hard-hearted person. (Perhaps suggested by the hyperbolical phrase in quot. *c* 1400.)

[*c* **1400** *Beryn* Prol. 35 Teris..As grete as eny mylstone.] **1594** SHAKS. *Rich. III*, I. iii. 354 Your eyes drop Mill-stones, when Fooles eyes fall Teares. **1606** —— *Tr. & Cr.* I. ii. 158. **1607** *Cæsar & Pompey* II. iv. C 3, Mens eyes must mil-stones drop, when fooles shed teares.

†**c.** Of dice: ***to run a millstone.***

1680 COTTON *Compl. Gamester* (ed. 2) 11 Placing the one [die] a top the other, not caring if the uppermost run a Mill-stone (as they use to say) if the undermost run without turning. **1680** KIRKMAN *Eng. Rogue* IV. xvi. 226 Knapping, is when you strike one Die dead, either at Tables or Hazzard let the other run a Milstone, as we use to say.

3. *fig.* **a.** A heavy burden (suggested by Matt. xviii. 6); **b.** a grinding or crushing instrument.

a **1720** SEWEL *Hist. Quakers* (1795) I. IV. 272 When I was between the mill-stones, and as one crushed with the weight of his adversary. **1787** BENTHAM *Def. Usury* x. 109 The mill-stone intended for the necks of those vermin..the dealers in corn, was found to fall upon the heads of the consumers. **1875** STUBBS *Const. Hist.* II. xiv. 99 John's heart was of millstone, Henry's of wax. **1877** 'RITA' *Vivienne* IV. iv, It is the millstone they hang round our necks.

†**4.** The appellation of a form of taxation in Spain.

1630 *R. Johnson's Kingd. & Commw.* 232 There doe not want also other meanes and devices to raise money, as the imposition of the Milstone; which as it is supposed,..will amount to two millions of gold yearely. **1642** HOWELL *For. Trav.* (Arb.) 74 The Tally and taillage of France, the Milstone of Spaine,..the Gabels of Italy.

5. *Bell founding.* (See quot.)

1756 *Dict. Arts & Sci.* s.v. *Foundery of Bells*, The stake is surrounded with a solid brick-work perfectly round, 5 or 6 inches high, and of a diameter equal to that of the bell. This they call a mill-stone.

6. *attrib.*, as ***millstone-maker, -quarry***; **millstone bridge** (see quot.); **millstone dress** = DRESS *sb.* 3c; **millstone dresser,** (*a*) a machine for cutting grooves in the grinding-face of a millstone (Knight *Dict. Mech.* 1875); (*b*) one who dresses or prepares millstones (*Cent. Dict.* 1890); **millstone hammer, pick** = MILL-PICK (Knight); †**millstone rag,** a coarse stone suitable for the making of millstones; †**millstone silver,** the fee payable for the grinding of corn.

Also in many technical terms, as ***millstone-alarm, -balance, -bush, -crane, -curb, -driver, -exhaust, -feed, -hoist***: see Knight *Dict. Mech.* 1875 and *Suppl.* 1884.

1875 KNIGHT *Dict. Mech.* 1443/1 **Millstone-bridge*, the bar across the eye of a millstone by which it is supported on the head of the spindle. **1875** *Ibid.*, The draft of a *millstone dress is the degree of deflection of its furrows from a radial direction. **1876** DUNGLISON *Med. Lex.*, **Millstone-makers' Phthisis*, a form of severe bronchitis dependent on the inhalation of the fine particles which separate in the manufacture of millstones. **1806** *Gazetteer Scotl.* (ed. 2) 9 Two *millstone quarries of excellent quality are wrought to good account. **1709** HEARNE *Collect.* 16 Apr. (O.H.S.) II. 187 Coarse *millstone rag. **1661** *Min. Baron Crt. Stitchill* (1905) 21 Dew for payment of Grass maill & *mylle stain silver at thes term of Mertinmas.

millstone grit. *Geol.* [f. MILLSTONE + GRIT *sb.*[1]] A hard siliceous rock belonging to the carboniferous series and occupying in Britain and elsewhere a stratigraphical position immediately below the coal-measures.

1786 WHITEHURST *Orig. St. Earth* (ed. 2) 182 Millstone-Grit,..a coarse sandstone, composed of granulated quartz and quartz pebbles. **1813** BAKEWELL *Introd. Geol.* 136 A mass of coarse grit-stone, called by Mr. Whitehurst mill-stone grit. **1876** PAGE *Adv. Text-bk. Geol.* xiv. 250 Thick beds of quartzose sand-stone known as the millstone grit.

'mill-tail. [f. MILL *sb.*[1] + TAIL *sb.*] The water which runs away from a mill-wheel; also, the channel in which the water runs away.

1611 COTGR. s.v. *Moulin*, He that hurts himselfe to helpe others, will dye of thirst at the Mill-tayle. **1667** *Boston Rec.* (1881) VII. 33 Will Whitwell hath liberty..to wharfe one the North side of the mille taile for landing wood. **1724** *De Foe's Tour Gt. Brit.* I. III. 87 The Mill Tayl, or Floor for the Water below the Wheels is Wharft up on either Side with Stone. **1887** SIR R. H. ROBERTS *In the Shires* x. 166 [He] tells me the mill-tail is full of fish!

attrib. **1875** CROLL *Climate & T.* vi. 113 This..water.. would flow off in currents with almost mill-tail velocity.

Milltown: see MILTOWN.

†**'millward.** *Obs.* Forms: 1 mylenwyrd, myleweard, 4 milwarde, 5 millewarde, mylnard, 6 *Sc.* mylvart, 7 *Sc.* milwar(e, 8–9 *Sc.* millart, 9 *dial.* millard, -ert. [OE. *myle(n)weard*, f. *mylen* MILL *sb.*[1] + *weard* WARD *sb.*, keeper.] Originally, the keeper of a (manorial) mill; in later use = MILLER[1] 1.

c **1000** ÆLFRIC *Gloss.* in Wr.-Wülcker 141/1 *Molendinarius, uel molinarius*, mylenwyrd. *c* **1050** *Voc.* ibid. 448/18 *Molendarius*, myleweard. *c* **1305** *Pilate* 6 in *E.E.P.* (1862) 111 þe meleward þat hire fader was. **1380** *Poll Tax* in Rogers *Oxf. City Doc.* (1891) 11 De Willelmole Mulleward et Johanna vxore eius xviij.*d.* **1387** TREVISA *Higden* (Rolls) IV. 319 He gat a sone on oon Pila a milwardes douȝter þat heet Atus. *c* **1430** *Pilgr. Lyf Manhode* III. xvii. (1869) 144 Millewardes also that filleth here resoun with oute clepinge of resoun. **1598** *Aberdeen Reg.* (1848) II. 175 Alexander Marschall, mylvart at the nather mylne of this burght. **1650** *Croy Parish Session Min. Bk.* 16 Aug. (MS.), Alexander McPhail Milware. *Ibid.* 15 Sept., Ye minister having askit ye elderie..giffe yai did try any privat hanting betwixt ye said William Dolas and his Milwars wyffe yai..Declairis yat yai could not [etc.]. *c* **1760** SKINNER *Christmas Ba'ing* xxv. in *Misc. Poet.* (1809) 130 The millart's man, a suple fallow, Ran's he had been red wud. **1880** MRS. PARR *Adam & Eve* xiii, I've brushed till my arms ache, but my things is still like a millard's. **1881** *Instr. Census Clerks* (1885) 62 Corn miller. .. Millard.

mill-weir (mɪl'wɪə(r)). [f. MILL *sb.*[1] + WEIR.] = MILL-DAM.

1044 in Kemble *Cod. Dipl.* IV. 92 Andlang streames ðæt it cymð to ðam mylewere. **1890** in *Century Dict.*

millwell, variant of MULVEL.

'mill-wheel. [f. MILL *sb.*[1] + WHEEL *sb.*]

1. A wheel used to drive a mill, esp. a water-wheel used for that purpose.

c **1000** *Sax. Leechd.* III. 232 Seo heofon..tyrnð onbutan us, swiftre þonne ænig mylnn-hweol. *c* **1460** *Towneley Myst.* xii. 126 Syr, a letter of youre grace, Here comys slaw-pase ffro the myln whele. **1591** SPENSER *Daphn.* lxii, So all the world..round about doth goe Like a Mill-wheele in midst of miserie. **1610** SHAKS. *Temp.* I. ii. 281 Imprison'd, thou didst painefully remaine A dozen yeeres:..where thou didst vent thy groanes As fast as Mill-wheeles strike. **1789** J. PILKINGTON *View Derby* I. 344 Cogs for mill-wheels are made of it. **1871** B. TAYLOR *Faust* (1875) I. iv. 78, I feel as stupid from all you've said, As if a mill wheel whirled in my head.

b. *Her.* A figure or representation of this.

1688 R. HOLME *Armoury* III. 341/1 He beareth Azure..a Mill Wheel, or a Clock Wheel, Argent. **1874** PAPWORTH & MORANT *Ord. Brit. Arm.* 1122 Gu. three mill-wheels or. *Chawcers.*

c. *fig.* or in figurative context.

1861 MRS. NORTON *Lady La G.* III. 122 Till in his brain the grief he tries to cheat, A dreary mill-wheel circling seems to beat. **1891** KIPLING *Light that Failed* (1900) 210 The mill-wheel of thought swung round slowly.

†**2.** A form of grindstone employed for polishing armour. *Obs.*

1473–4 *Acc. Ld. High Treas. Scot.* (1877) I. 65 Gevin to Cuthbert Knychtsone..for mylne quhelis for the dich[t]ing of the Kingis harnes.

millwin, variant of MULVEL.

'millwright. [f. MILL *sb.*[1] + WRIGHT.] An engineer or mechanic whose occupation it is to design or set up mills or mill machinery.

1481–90 *Howard Househ. Bks.* (Roxb.) 197 The same day, I payd to Bochen the mylle wryte vj.s. viij.d. **1562–3** *Act 5 Eliz.* c. 4 §23 Tharte or Occupation of a Smithe..Myll-wright, Carpenter [etc.]. **1650** B. *Discolliminium* 14 A French Millwright who was an exquisite workman. **1702** SAVERY *Miner's Friend* 28 According to the different Genius and Abilities of the Mill-right. **1866** HATFIELD *Hist. Notices Doncaster* I. 203 Experiments..were made by a mill-wright.

attrib. **1835** URE *Philos. Manuf.* 35, I have frequently been at a loss, in walking through several of the millwright factories, to know whether the polished shafts..were at rest or in motion.

Hence **'millwrighting** *vbl. sb.*, the labour or trade of a millwright; also as *ppl. a.*

1821 A. CONSTABLE *Let.* 25 June in J. Constable *Correspondence* (1962) I. 200 Several millwrighting jobs coming in [so] that I cannot keep my money in my pocket. **18..** *Engineering* LXVII. 63 (Cent.) Engineering and millwrighting, though synonymous, are often two distinct branches in a shop. **1949** K. S. WOODS *Rural Crafts Eng.* II. iv. 76 Where local smiths have lost the art the bills are sent away to millwrighting firms.

†**'milly.** *Obs.* Also 7 millya, millio, mil(l)ia. [a. Pg. *milho* MILLET[1]: cf. MEALIE.] A kind of millet.

a **1600** MAY in *Hakluyt's Voy.* III. 571 In this pangaia we had certaine corne called *millio.* **1613** PURCHAS *Pilgrimage* (1614) 650 The Guineans..stamp their milia as we do spice, ..and grinde it..till it be dowe, which they temper with fresh water and salt, and make rolls thereof. **1629** CAPT. J. SMITH *Trav. & Adv.* Wks. (Arb.) 856 Their bread is made of..Cuskus a small white seed like Millya in Biskay. **1665** *Golden Coast* 14 Their Corn is of two sorts, 1 Milly. 2 Mais. 1 Milly, and that hath long Ears, and is a seed of colour like Hemp-seed, and long like Canary-seed, having no shells, but growing in a little husk, which is very white within. *Ibid.* 76 Their bread is of Millia, or Mais, baked on a warme Harth.

millyon, miln(e, obs. ff. MILLION, MILL *sb.*[1]

millyum ('mɪljəm), representing a colloq. pronunciation of *million. rare.*

1940 E. POUND *Cantos* liv. 40 Jobs for two millyum men. *Ibid.* lvi. 58 Thus saved several millyum lives of those chinamen. **1955** —— *Section: Rock-Drill* lxxxix. 53 And in '34 presumably will be 2 millyum.

milner, obs. variant of MILLER[1] and MILLINER *sb.*

milo (ˈmaɪləʊ). Also **millo, milo maize.** [ad. Sotho *maili.*] One of a group of drought-resistant varieties of the grass *Sorghum vulgare*, introduced from Africa to suitable regions elsewhere. Also *attrib.*

1882 *Rep. Comm. Agric. Georgia 1881–82* 23 My attention was some time since called to the claims of 'Ivory wheat' and 'Millo Maize' to a place in our long list of profitable food crops. **1887** *Florida Dispatch* 10 Jan. 34/3 The head of yellow millo maize is formed in sections of smaller heads, lying very close and compact. *Ibid.* 14 Feb. 165/3 Mr. Jones recommends the substitution of Kaffir corn, Milo Maizo, etc., for a part of the corn crop. **1920** *U.S. Dept. Agric. Farmers' Bull.* No. 1147. 3 Milo has long since passed the experimental stage as a farm crop in the southwestern United States... Milo made its first appearance in this country soon after 1880. **1965** T. CAPOTE *In Cold Blood* (1966) i. 7 One of these barns..housed a dark, pungent hill of milo grain. **1970** H. DOGGETT *Sorghum* iii. 88 The milos of the U.S.A. stem from one introduction. **1972** *Islander* (Victoria, B.C.) 12 Mar. 11/1 Milomaize is a white corn, something like wheat. We ground it in an old coffee grinder for bread, also boiled it for porridge. **1973** *Houston* (Texas) *Chron.* 21 Oct. 26 Cotton, wheat, milo, corn and soybean production can be increased tremendously.

milometer (maɪˈlɒmɪtə(r)). Also **mileometer.** [f. MILE *sb.*[1] + -OMETER.] An instrument which is fitted to a vehicle to record the distance in miles travelled by it.

1953 A. SMITH *Blind White Fish in Persia* 218 Every time another 1,000 miles was registered by the milometer, those in front would cheer a little. **1963** 'B. GRAEME' *Almost without Murder* xv. 170 We hit a toll road, whereupon the milometer ticked off the miles with boring rapidity. **1968** *Punch* 31 July 172/1 One army jeep being driven aimlessly around by Georg in order that its mileometer shall record that monthly mileage total considered by higher authority appropriate for army vehicles. **1974** *Times* 9 Oct. 14/1 Guilty..of..offering for sale cars whose milometers had been altered to show a lower reading. **1975** G. LYALL *Judas Country* xxi. 153 From the mileometer I'd guess she was only just run in.

milor(d (mɪˈlɔːd, ‖milɔr). [a. F. *milord* (in 16th c. *milour*), a. Eng. *my lord* (see LORD *sb.* 15). Cf. It. *milordo*; also the following Scottish example:

1596 DALRYMPLE tr. *Leslie's Hist. Scot.* I. 14 Thair ar Knichtes, Barrounis and mony vthiris Nobilis, quhome we cal milordis.]

(A French designation for an English lord; often applied to any wealthy Englishman); *spec.* an Englishman travelling in Europe in aristocratic style. Hence **miˈlordliness, miˈlordism.**

[**1598** J. CHAMBERLAIN *Let.* 17 Sept. (1939) I. 45 Yet me thincks still I am out of my element when I am among Lords, and I am of Rabelais minde that they looke big *comme un millord d'Angleterre*.] **1758** M. W. MONTAGU *Let.* May (1967) III. 149 He brags of having done his duty in waiting on the two Milordi. **1822** L. SIMOND *Trav. Switzerland* I. 357 Accustomed to the *Milords Anglais* of former times. **1824** BYRON *Juan* XVI. xxxviii, 'Jest!' quoth Milor. **1863** SALA *Qualk the Circumnav.* 70 An eccentric child of Albion, a milord, afflicted with the 'spleen'. **1876** GEO. ELIOT *Dan. Der.* liv, The milord, owner of the handsome yacht. **1920** A. HUXLEY *Leda* 44 They behaved like English aristocrats in a French novel... I tried to imitate their milordliness. **1931** R. CHURCH *High Summer* I. i. 8 A tall young man, very shy and nervous, very English, but trying to hide these insular virtues behind the assumption of lofty milordism. **1945** E. WAUGH *Brideshead Revisited* I. viii. 185 It's not as though he lived like a Milord. **1954** [see EDWARDIAN *sb.* 3]. **1961** A. WILSON *Old Men at Zoo* i. 9 The Zoo authorities had been very indulgent to a number of 'milord' whims that were perhaps more in keeping with an aesthetic undergraduate. **1969** *Listener* 6 Feb. 180/3 The great man scampered about, huffing and puffing, playing the magnificent milord.

Milori (mɪˈlɔərɪ). Also **Milory.** The name of the 19th-cent. French colour-maker A. *Milori* used *attrib.* in **Milori blue**, a particularly pure variety of Prussian blue (PRUSSIAN *a.* 2); **Milori green** = *chrome green* (CHROME 3).

1885 J. S. TAYLOR *Fields's Chromatogr. Modernized* 194 *Milory green*, syn. Chrome Green. **1899** B. W. WARHURST *Colour Dict.* 47 *Milori*, full to dark greens; also Chinese blue. **1924** F. W. WEBER *Artists' Pigments* 2 Prussian Blue..was put on the market under quite an array of names.. Turnbull's Blue, Paris Blue,..Milori Blue, Chinese Blue [etc.]. **1951** R. MAYER *Artist's Handbk.* ii. 77 There is a great difference in clarity and beauty of colour as well as in permanence between the common varieties of Prussian blue and the very best, well-washed grades, such as the pure Chinese or Milori blues. **1963** *New Yorker* 8 June 20 Wool carpets only come in these colors:..Milori Green. **1967** [see IRON-BLUE c].

milpa (ˈmɪlpə). [Mexican Sp.] In Central America and Mexico, a small cultivated field, usually of corn or maize; also, designating a method of cultivation practised in tropical regions (see quot. 1936).

1844 J. GREGG *Commerce Prairies* I. 150 The *labores* and *milpas* (cultivated fields) are often..without any enclosure. **1869** J. R. BROWNE *Adventures Apache Country* 164 Our houses were closely picketed in the milpas, or corn-fields, down by the river. **1934** A. HUXLEY *Beyond Mexique Bay* 216 The peasant may need only two or three acres for his *milpa.* **1936** *Nature* 26 Dec. 1090/1 The cultivation of maize ..is on the milpa system; that is, a plot, after being burned off, is cultivated for two years, when it is allowed to revert to forest conditions, taking about eight to ten years to become completely re-established and ready for burning off again. **1956** R. REDFIELD *Peasant Society & Culture* iv. 118 To the Maya Indian labor on the milpa is dignified by its connections with religion and manly virtue. **1964** *Sci. Amer.* Nov. 101/1 In Central America the Mayas,..who depended greatly on the milpa system of agriculture, were forced to abandon their cities and move north into Mexico. **1974** *Environmental Conservation* I. 17/1 This is the so-called 'slash-and-burn' or 'milpa' system, as practised in the humid tropics.

Milquetoast (ˈmɪlktəʊst). orig. *U.S.* Also with small initial. [f. the name of Caspar *Milquetoast*, a cartoon character created by H. T. Webster in 1924.] A timid or unforthcoming person. Also *attrib.* or as *adj.*

1938 M. FISHBACK *Safe Conduct* vi. 70 Don't be a Milquetoast either, and be afraid to add it [*sc.* the bill] up. **1939** C. MORLEY *Kitty Foyle* xxx. 305 What is it makes a man with brains so milquetoast when he gets away from the blackboard? **1961** M. BEADLE *These Ruins are Inhabited* iii. 34 American men are Milquetoasts. **1972** L. O'DONNELL *Phone Calls* vi. 73 You couldn't expect Norah to respect a Milquetoast. **1973** *Observer* (Colour Suppl.) 4 Nov. 12/3 Any of those milquetoast settings that Britten gave Wilfred Owen's poems in the 'War Requiem'. **1974** *Ottawa Citizen* 3 Sept. 71/1 I'm wondering if a judge would let me change my perfectly good but milquetoast name to something no one will forget, like—Jake Sexchamp.

milreis (ˈmɪlreɪs). Now *Hist.* Also 6 **millreye,** 6, 8 **milrey,** 7 **milreise, milleray,** 8 **mill-ree, milrea,** 9 **milree.** [a. Pg. *milreis*, f. *mil* thousand + *reis* (see REIS).] Formerly, a Portuguese gold coin and money of account equal to 1,000 REIS; also, a Brazilian silver coin (see quot. 1885). Replaced by new currency in Portugal in 1911 (see quot. 1913); and in Brazil in 1942 (see CRUZEIRO).

In the 17th cent. the Portuguese milreis was valued at between 13*s.* and 14*s.*, and afterwards at 10*s.*

1589 *Discourse Voy. Spaine & Port.* 9 Missing of their Portegues and Milrayes they dreamed on in Portingall. **1598** W. PHILLIP tr. *Linschoten* I. iii. 4 The Master and Pilot haue ..each man 120 Milreyes, euery Milreyes being worth.. seauen guilders. **1611** COTGR., *Milrai*, a Milleray; a coyne of gold worth betweene 13 and 14 shillings sterl. **1694** tr. *Milton's Lett. State* Wks. 1738 II. 205 Seven thousand of our Pounds, or twice as many Milreys of Portugal Money. **1721** C. KING *Brit. Merch.* I. 348 They have cost..22 Millrees per Pipe at a Medium. **1885** *Pall Mall G.* 17 Mar. 5/2 Government intend to propose certain measures tending to restore to par the real value of the milreis—namely, 2*s.* 3*d.* **1890** *Daily News* 25 Jan. 5/6 The paper milrei is now worth 26*d.* **1913** *Statesman's Yearbk.* 1155 The Decree of the Provisional Government of May 22, 1911, established a new monetary system... The unit is the gold *escudo*, of 100 *centavos*, which is equivalent to the 1-milreis gold piece.

milrine, obs. f. MILL-RIND.

milse, var. MILCE *sb.*

milsey (ˈmɪlsɪ). *Sc.* Forms: 6 **milsie,** 9 **milcie,** 9– **milsey.** [Contraction of *milk-sye* (see MILK *sb.* 9 a). Cf. *milk-sieve* (ibid.: perh. an interpretative rendering of this word) and MILK-SILE.] A milk-strainer.

1724 *Rob's Jock* iv. in *Ramsay's Tea-t. Misc.* (1775) I. 182 A milsie and a sowen-pail. **1811** W. AITON *Agric. Ayr.* 451 The milk is dropped through a sieve (provincially called a milsey).

attrib. **1801** J. THOMSON in *Mod. Scott. Poets* (1893) XV. 317 It minds me o' a milcie-clout Nae sooner filled than it rins out.

milsi, milstone, var. ff. MILCE *v.*, MILLSTONE.

milt (mɪlt), *sb.* Forms: 1 **multi, milti,** 1, 3–6 **milte,** 4–6 **mylte,** 5–6 **mylt,** 6 **melte,** 4, 6– (now *dial.*) **melt,** 6 **milt.** [OE. *milte* str. masc., also wk. fem., spleen = OFris. *milte* fem., spleen, MDu. *milte* (Du. *milt*) fem., spleen, also milt of fish, OHG. *milzi* neut. (MHG. *milze* neut., mod.G. *milz* fem.), ON. *milti* neut., spleen (OSw. *mjälte, mjälter, milter*, mod.Sw. *mjelte* masc., Da. *milt*, spleen, Norw. *mjelte* masc., spleen, milt of fish):—OTeut. types **miltjo-*, **miltjôn-*, perh. f. the root of MELT *v.*, with reference to the supposed digestive function of the spleen. The sense 'spawn of fish' may have been adopted from Du.; as the milt of a fish is of soft substance like the spleen, the transferred use was not unnatural, but it was no doubt helped to gain currency by the resemblance in sound between *milt* and *milk* (Du. *milch*: see MILK *sb.*), the older name for the soft roe of fish. The sense also exists in Norwegian, where it is to be noted that *mjelte* milt is homophonous with *mjelte* a milking, connected with ON. *mjalta* to milk.

The spelling *multi* in the Epinal Glossary cannot be explained with certainty, but it certainly cannot represent an ablaut-variant, of which there is no trace in any Teut. lang.]

I. 1. The spleen in mammals; also, an analogous organ in other vertebrate animals.

a **700** *Epinal Gloss.* 594 *Lien*, multi. *c* **725** *Corpus Gloss.* (Hessels) L. 172 *Lien*, milte. *Ibid.* S. 472 *Splenis*, milte. *c* **1000** *Sax. Leechd.* II. 242 Hu se milte bið emlang & gædertenge þære wambe hæfð þynne filmene sio hæfð fætte & þicce ædra. *c* **1250** *Death* 171 in *O.E. Misc.* 178 Nu schal for-rotien..þi mahe and þi milte þi liure and þi lunge. **1398** TREVISA *Barth. De P.R.* v. xli. (1495) 157 The substaunce of the mylte is blacke. *c* **1489** CAXTON *Sonnes of Aymon* i. 52 His nayles stacke in to my lyuer and my mylte. **1533** ELYOT *Cast. Helthe* (1541) 22 The splene or mylte is of yl juice, for it is the chamber of melancholy. **1658** ROWLAND tr. *Moufet's Theat. Ins.* 1110 In the milts of Sheep..innumerable worms are oft-times found. *c* **1720** W. GIBSON *Farrier's Guide* I. ii. (1738) 12 The Spleen, or Milt is a soft, spungy Substance. **1764** *Museum Rust.* II. li. 146 The melt or spleen was very small and thin. **1847** W. C. L. MARTIN *Ox* 130 Inflammation of the spleen or melt.

b. *attrib.* and *Comb.*, as **milt-grown** *a.*, affected by an enlarged spleen; **milt-like** *a.*, resembling the substance of the mammalian milt; **milt-pain,** a disease amongst swine; **milt-sickness,** a disease of the spleen amongst cattle; so **milt-sick** *a.*; †**milt-vein** (see quot.); **milt-wort** = MILTWASTE.

1731 *Gentl. Mag.* I. 101[The world] has an ugly hoskey cough, and is *milt-grown. **1822–34** *Good's Study Med.* (ed. 4) I. 187 One [polypus] is termed *miltlike by Professor Munro. **1704** *Dict. Rust. et Urb.*, *Milt-pain is a Disease in Hogs, proceeding from greediness of eating Mast. **1882** *Times of Natal* 8 June, He never knew of a case of illness from eating a *melt-sick ox. *Ibid.*, An ox suffering from *melt-sickness. **1597** A. M. tr. *Guillemeau's Fr. Chirurg.* 29 b/2 In the left hande, shee [the Liver vayne] is called the *miltvayne. **1611** COTGR., *Scolopendrie*, Spleenwort, *Milt-wort, Finger-fearn. **1668** WILKINS *Real Char.* Index, Miltwort [*text* p. 71 *Miltwast*].

2. *transf.* (See quot. 1599.)

1587 MASCALL *Govt. Cattle* (1596) 106 If a colt when he is fold do not cast his milt, husbandmen say he will not liue long,..some colt will cast two miltes, no horse that liues xii. yeares hath any milt within him. **1599** A. M. tr. *Gabelhouer's Bk. Physicke* 23/1 In the first foalinge of a Mare, her Foale hath..on the tung a peece of fleshe which resembleth the Milt of an Oxe, and of some is also called a Milt. **1677** JOHNSON in *Ray's Corr.* (1848) 128 Horsemen have not agreed what that is the foal is said to sneeze, which they call a milt.

II. 3. The roe or spawn of the male fish; the 'soft roe' of fishes.

1483 CAXTON *Gold. Leg.* 77 b/1 Open the fysshe and take to the herte the galle and the mylte. **1530** PALSGR. 245/1 Mylte [of] a fysshe, *la laicte; laicte de poisson.* **1596** DALRYMPLE tr. *Leslie's Hist. Scot.* I. 19 Quhen now thay ar gutted, and the meltis takne out, thay [etc.]. **1611** COTGR., *Laicte*, the milt, or soft roe, of fishes. **1653** WALTON *Angler* viii. 162 You shall scarce or never take a Male Carp without a Melt, or a Female without a Roe or Spawn. **1718** J. CHAMBERLAYNE *Relig. Philos.* (1730) II. xxii. §36 Some of the Females discharge their Spawn, and the males their Melt or Seed in the Water near each other. **1884** BRAITHWAITE *Salmonidæ Westmld.* i. 3 Milt is found in the males and ova in females.

b. *attrib.*, as **milt-like** *a.*, resembling the contents of the soft roe of a fish.

1808 *Edin. Rev.* XI. 322 The milt-like fluid of the drones might be seen in the cells.

milt (mɪlt), *v.* [f. prec.] *trans.* 'To impregnate the roe or spawn of the female fish' (J.).

1694 MOTTEUX *Rabelais* v. xxxi. (1737) 143, I..saw..Fish ..milting, spawning. **1884** *Field* 6 Dec. 787/1 A female [char] gave 146 eggs, which were milted from a male of the same hybrid race.

milter (ˈmɪltə(r)). Also 7 **meltere,** 8 **miltor.** [f. MILT *sb.* + -ER[1]; perh. adopted from the equivalent Du. *milter.*] **a.** A male fish, esp. in spawning time. **b.** = MILT *sb.* 3.

1601 HOLLAND *Pliny* I. 245 If a man do the same with a female in spawning time, hee shall haue as many milters follow after her. **1653** WALTON *Angler* viii. 164 Three Melters for one Spawner. **1718** JACOB *Compl. Sportsman* 121 The Spawner lays her Spawn, and upon it the Melter drops his Milk. **1758** *Descr. Thames* 172 Then the Male, or Miltor, advances, and covers the Spawn with his Belly. **1834** MEDWIN *Angler in Wales* I. 332 At this time also the melter is more easily distinguished from the roe. **1883** *Blackw. Mag.* Feb. 281 A greater stock of 'Spawners' and 'Milters' than its tributaries have room to contain.

†**milth,** *sb. Obs.* [f. MILD *a.* + -TH[1].] Mercy. Hence †**milth** *v. intr.*, to have mercy (*of, to*). †**ˈmilthlich** *adv.*, kindly. †**ˈmilthness** *sb.*, mildness.

a **1300** *E. E. Psalter* xxiv. 6 Laverd, of þine reuthes mine þou mare, And of þine milþes of werld þat are. *Ibid.* xxiv. 11 Laverd, milþe to my sinne. *Ibid.* lv. 1 Milþe of me, lauerd, for man fortrade me. *Ibid.* lxxvi. 8 Or he sal awai kerue is milþe in ende Fra geting and geting of strende. *Ibid.* lxxxvii. 12 Wher ani in thrughes sal telle þi milthnes. *c* **1300** *St. Brandan* 51 He welcomede ous everechon miltheliche and suete.

†**ˈmilting,** *vbl. sb.* (See quot. 1587.)

1587 MASCALL *Govt. Cattle* (1596) 45 The milting of Oxe, Cow, or other beast is called of husbandmen, when he will sodaine lie down if ye shall stay neuer so little, being at plough or cart. **1614** MARKHAM *Cheap Husb.* (1623) 99 Of milting of a beast. Milting, is when a beast will oft fall.

Milton (ˈmɪltən). **1.** Name of the English poet John *Milton* (1608–74) used in the phr. ***mute inglorious Milton*** (see quot. 1751) to symbolize the idea of native ability frustrated by lack of opportunity.

1751 GRAY *Elegy* 8 Some mute inglorious Milton here may rest. **1883** *Authors & Publishers* (G. P. Putnam's Sons) 61 We do not believe that our American prairies conceal any Charlotte Brontës to whom the opportunity for expression and fame has been denied, or that a careful search through American villages would develop any 'mute, inglorious Miltons' rusting away their undeveloped lives. **1922** H. L. MENCKEN *Prejudices* (1923) 3rd Ser. iii. 89 A genuine artist ..would have thoughts and feelings of his own, and the impulse to give them objective form would be irresistible... There are no mute inglorious Miltons, save in the

hallucinations of poets. The one sound test of a Milton is that he functions as a Milton. **1933** J. BUCHAN *Prince of Captivity* I. iv. 125 We've got to see that our Miltons don't remain mute and inglorious, but above all that our Hampdens are not left to rot on a village green. **1948** T. S. ELIOT *Notes Def. Culture* vi. 102 The Equality of Opportunity dogma..derives emotional reinforcement from the belief in the mute inglorious Milton. This myth assumes that a great deal of first-rate ability—not merely ability, but genius—is being wasted for lack of education.

2. [Perh. a different word.] *slang*. An oyster.

1841 THACKERAY *Professor* ii, in *Bentley's Misc.* Sept. 285 Mrs. Grampus herself operated with the oyster-knife, and served the Milton morsels to the customers. **1845** 'BON GAULTIER' *Bk. Ballads* 35 Fill me once more the foaming pewter up! Another board of oysters, ladye mine! To night Lucullus with himself shall sup, These mute inglorious Miltons are divine.

miltonia (mɪl'təʊnɪə). [mod.L. (J. Lindley 1837, in *Bot. Reg.* XXIII. 1976), f. the name of Charles William Wentworth Fitzwilliam, Viscount *Milton*, later 3rd Earl Fitzwilliam (1786–1857), English politician and horticulturist + -IA[1].] An epiphytic orchid of the tropical, South American genus so called, belonging to the family Orchidaceæ and bearing brilliantly coloured flowers.

1838 J. LINDLEY *Sertum Orchidaceum* plate 21 It [sc. *Miltonia candida*] differs in the structure of its column and labellum..from the original Miltonia. **1890** W. WATSON *Orchids* xli. 315 Miltonias are easily propagated. **1930** T. W. BRISCOE *Orchids for Amateurs* viii. 120, I have found the addition of a small portion of partly decayed oak or beech leaves has had very beneficial results on all the Miltonias. **1963** *Times* 6 Feb. 12/3 One exhibit of orchids contains many beautiful cypripediums and miltonias.

Miltonian (mɪl'təʊnɪən), *a.* and *sb.* [f. the name of the poet John *Milton* + -IAN.] **A.** *adj.* Of or relating to Milton, or resembling his style or imagery. **B.** *sb.* An admirer or imitator of Milton.

1708 J. PHILIPS *Cyder* I. 1 Thy gift Pomona in Miltonian verse Adventrous I presume to sing. **1816** KEATS *Epist. C. C. Clarke* 57 Miltonian storms, and more, Miltonian tenderness. **1842** DICKENS *Let.* 19 Oct. (1974) III. 352, I have been *going*, every day, to write to you about the Miltonians. **1872** LOWELL *Milton* Prose Wks. 1890 IV. 76 It is merely a Miltonian way of saying that he took regular exercise. **1907** *Illustr. London News* 4 May 672/1 Nearly all Englishmen are either Shakesperians or Miltonians... Each represents something in the make-up of England. **1947** A. J. A. WALDOCK *Paradise Lost* i. 9 Grierson..observed, supervised and corrected; but not yet had England produced a New Miltonian. **1960** *Times* 22 Sept. 15/4 The most dyed-in-the-wool Miltonian.

Miltonic (mɪl'tɒnɪk), *a.* (and *sb.*) [f. *Milton*: see prec. and -IC.]

1. *adj.* = prec.

1708 GAY *Wine* 15 Inspir'd, sublime, on Pegasean wing By thee upborne, I draw Miltonic air. **1818** BYRON *Juan* Ded. x, If Time, the Avenger, execrates his wrongs, And makes the word 'Miltonic' mean 'sublime' [etc.]. **1886** SWINBURNE *Misc.* 14 A Shakespearean adept may be a Miltonic believer.

2. quasi-*sb.* Miltonic language.

1712 HENLEY *Spect.* No. 396 ¶2 That Mungrel miscreated (to speak in Miltonic) kind of Wit, vulgarly termed the Pun.

3. *sb. pl.* Verses of Milton; verses, or style, typical of Milton.

1792 COWPER *Wks.* (1837) XV. 237 Having translated all the Latin and Italian Miltonics, I was proceeding merrily with the Commentary on the Paradise Lost. **1928** O. BARFIELD *Poetic Diction* x. 177 No one would have dreamed of employing the stale Miltonics, which lay at the bottom of so much eighteenth-century 'poetic diction', in *prose*, however imaginative. **1944** F. R. LEAVIS in *Scrutiny* XII. 202 Johnson's disapproval of Gray's Pinderick sublimities goes with his disapproval of Miltonics.

Hence **Mil'tonically** *adv.*

1853 DE QUINCEY *Autobiogr. Sk.* I. i. 2, I here record the entire list of my brothers and sisters..and Miltonically I include myself. **1905** *Q. Rev.* July 8 To speak Miltonically, the Muse utters the oracle, and her 'prophet' renders it in rhyme.

Miltonism ('mɪltənɪz(ə)m). [f. *Milton* + -ISM.] A form of expression imitating Milton. Also **Mil'tonicism**.

1802 LAMB *Lett.* (1888) I. 190 Cowper's blank verse detains you every step with some heavy Miltonism. **1936** F. R. LEAVIS *Revaluation* ii. 46 A common, limply pompous Miltonicism. **1938** E. POUND *Let.* 8 May (1971) 316, I do, however, prefer your 'supreme Hippocrates' [line 137]... Miltonism tho' it may be.

Miltonist ('mɪltənɪst). [f. *Milton* + -IST.] A follower of Milton in his views on divorce.

1806 SYMMONS *Milton* (1810) 250 A party, distinguished by the name of Miltonists, attested the power of his pen, and gave consequence to his pleading for divorce. **1836** SOUTHEY *Cowper* III. 81 Hayley..had reasons for being what in the days of the Commonwealth was called a Miltonist.

Miltonize ('mɪltənaɪz), *v.* [f. *Milton* + -IZE.]

a. *trans.* To impart a Miltonian dignity to. **b.** *intr.* To imitate the literary style of Milton. Hence **'Miltonizing** *ppl. a.* and *vbl. sb.*

1893 *Athenæum* 25 Feb. 254/3 This [*sc.* painting] is a noble example of Palmer's ability to Miltonize landscape. **1903** *Academy* 4 Apr. 336 Mr. Johnstone has..gone to Milton for his model, and Miltonizes as best he may. **1936** F. R. LEAVIS *Revaluation* iv. 116 The meditative-Miltonizing poetic modes. **1944** —— in *Scrutiny* XII. 189 The author of *The Vanity of Human Wishes* has, as critic, no weakness..for the Miltonizing habit of his age. **1953** H. HOUSE *Coleridge* iii. 65 This Miltonising is not a mere matter of poetical echoes..it is part of a conscious political act. **1958** *Essays & Stud.* v. 69 These larger Miltonizing politico-social pieces like *Religious Musings*.

miltor, milts, miltschipe, var. ff. MILTER, MILCE, MILDSHIP.

Miltown ('mɪltaʊn). *Pharm.* Also (*erron.*) **Milltown**. A proprietary name for meprobamate; a tablet of this drug.

1954 F. M. BERGER in *Jrnl. Pharmacol. & Exper. Therap.* CXII. 413 2-Methyl-2-*n*-propyl-1, 3-propanediol carbamate was unique in that it possessed a muscle relaxant and sedative action of an unusual kind. This compound has been named Miltown. **1956** A. HUXLEY *Let.* 20 Oct. (1969) 810 The conference on meprobamate was quite interesting and I made some pleasant acquaintances—Dr. (F. M.) Berger, the inventor of Miltown, [etc.]. **1957** *Trade Marks Jrnl.* 27 Feb. 191/2 Miltown... Pharmaceutical preparations in pill, tablet and powder form, or in liquid form for intravenous injection, all for use in the treatment of tension, as muscular relaxants and as anti-convulsants. Carter Products, Inc... New York. **1960** C. FITZ GIBBON *When Kissing had to Stop* vii. 91 All myths are to a greater or lesser extent tranquillisers in one way or another. But a government can't function on Milltown. **1964** M. MCLUHAN *Understanding Media* (1967) vii. 77 Would it not seem suddenly to be a conspiracy to make the artist a frill, a fribble, or a Milltown? **1969** [see MEPROBAMATE].

miltsiekte (mɪlt'siːktə). *S. Afr.* Also **meltziekte, miltsiek**. [Afrikaans, f. *milt* spleen + *siekte* sickness.] = ANTHRAX 2.

1835 A. SMITH *Diary* 1 Feb. (1939) I. 241 Bloedsiekte, or anthrax. It is also known in Afrikaans as miltsiekte. **1877** *Queenstown Free Press* 1 Dec. (Pettman), The oldest and most experienced of Kurveyors confess themselves flabbergasted by meltziekte. **1947** H. C. BOSMAN *Mafeking Road* xi. 63 After making their purchases they whiled away the time in discussing politics and the mealie-crops and the miltsiekte. **1959** *Cape Times* 12 Mar. 2/2 Miltsiek has broken out in certain areas in the Bushmanland. **1972** L. G. GREEN *When the Journey's Over* (1973) v. 51 You had to guard your oxen against redwater, *meltsiekte* and lung sickness.

miltwaste ('mɪltweɪst). Also 6–7 **-wast**, 7 **-waist**. [f. MILT *sb.*[1] + WASTE.] The finger-fern, one of the spleenworts, *Asplenium Ceterach*.

1578 LYTE *Dodoens* III. lxv. 406 Of brode or large Splenewort or Miltwast. *Ibid.* III. lxvii. 408 This herbe is called..in English..Scaleferne, Finger ferne..and Myltewaste. **1657** B. W. *Expert Phisician* 189 Agrimony, Burnet, Miltwaist, Mercury, each a handful. **1866** *Treas. Bot.* 258/2 A commonish native fern called Miltwaste or Scale Fern.

milty ('mɪltɪ), *a.* [f. MILT *sb.* + -Y.] Resembling or of the nature of the milt or spleen.

1662 J. CHANDLER *Van Helmont's Oriat.* 306 Nothing is milty or like to the milt, if it do not swell with the properties of the milt.

miltz (mɪlts). *Cookery*. [ad. G. *milz*.] The spleen. (Cf. MILT *sb.*)

1909 *Daily Chron.* 25 Feb. 3/5 No more cooking of chleb borsch schave and stuffed miltz. I shall have a cook of my own. **1951** L. W. LEONARD *Jewish Cookery* xiv. 189 The butcher will be glad to make the incision in the side of a beef miltz as large as you desire. **1966** *Bloom's Jewish Restaurant Menu, Entree*..Stuffed Miltz.

milvine ('mɪlvaɪn), *a.* and *sb.* [ad. mod.L. *milvīn-us*, f. L. *milv-us* kite + -INE.]

A. *adj.* Pertaining to a kite; belonging to the genus *Milvus* or the family *Milvinæ*. **B.** *sb.* A member of the genus *Milvus* or of the family *Milvinæ*; a kite.

1727 BAILEY vol. II, *Milvine*, belonging to a Kite or Glede. **1842** BRANDE *Dict. Sci.* etc., *Milvines*, Milvini, a family of Raptorial birds, of which the kite (*Milvus*) is the type.

Hence **milvinous** (mɪl'vaɪnəs) *a.*, in the same sense (Mayne *Expos. Lex.* 1856).

milwarde, -well, -wyn, var. forms of MILLWARD, MULVEL.

milz(c)e, variant forms of MILCE *sb. Obs.*

mim (mɪm), *a.* orig. *Sc.* and *dial.* [Imitative of the action of pursing up the mouth; cf. MUM.]

a. Affectedly modest, demure, primly silent or quiet. Also 'affecting great moderation in eating and drinking' (Jam.).

?**1679** MCWARD in *Earnest Contend. Faith* (1723) 323 The best of our Synods (for as mim as we have made it to this Day) are justly chargeable with the Blood of that renowned Martyr [Guthrie]. **1715** RAMSAY *Christis Kirke Gr.* II. 48 She was..mim that day. **1768** ROSS *Helenore* (1789) 106 Now Nory all the while was playing prim, As ony lamb as modest, and as mim; And never a look with Lindy did lat fa'. **1785** FERGUSSON'S *Prov.* 24 Maidens should be mim till they're married, and then they may burn kirks. **1816** SCOTT *Bl. Dwarf* ii, Did I not say it wasna want o' spunk that made ye [*sc.* the young Laird] sae mim? *a* **1825** FORBY *Voc. E. Anglia*, *Mim*, primly silent, with lips closed lest a stray word should escape. **1880** MRS. PARR *Adam & Eve* xiii, Worth twenty o' that stuck-up London consarn, with her pasty face and mim ways. **1891** R. T. COOKE *Huckleberries* 96 She was a mim, soft-spoken woman, but guileful and gliding as a snake. **1959** 'J. ROSS' *Boy in Grey Overcoat* viii. 93 That mim curl of grey hair across the back of her head. **1960** AUDEN *Homage to Clio* 56 Before you catch it for your mim look and gnostic chirrup.

b. Used adverbially.

1786 BURNS *Holy Fair* xvi, See, up he's got the word o' G—, An' meek an' mim has view'd it.

c. *Comb.*, as *mim-looking*, *-spoken*; also **mim-mouthed**, 'reserved in discourse, not communicative, implying the idea of affectation of modesty' (Jam.). Also *fig.* Hence **mim-mouthedness**.

1721 RAMSAY *Lucky Spence* iii, Mim-mou'd Meg. **1820** *Smugglers* I. xiii. 164 I'm no for being mim mou'd when there's no reason; but a man has gude, whiles, cast a knot on his tongue. **1849** C. BRONTE *Shirley* vii, Some o' t' bonniest and mimest looking too. **1889** *Sat. Rev.* 12 Jan. 37/1 That 'mimmouthedness' which has become a fashion of late. **1896** 'LESLIE KEITH' *Indian Uncle* xi. 189 Douce, plod-plodding, mim-spoken lads.

mimamsa (miː'mɑːmsa). Also **mimansa**. [Skr. *mīmāṁsā* profound thought, consideration, investigation, f. *man* to think, consider.] The name of one of the six systems of orthodox Hindu philosophy, called more fully the *Pūrva-*, or 'earlier', *mimamsa*, which was founded by Jaimini and concerns itself with the interpretation of Vedic ritual and text.

The term also occurs in the name of a closely-related school, the *Uttara*, or 'later', *mimamsa*, often called *Vedānta*, which deals with the nature of Brahma.

1788 *Asiatick Researches* I. 352 Of the Philosophical Schools it will be sufficient here to remark, that..the two Mimánsà's, of which the second is often distinguished by the name of Védánta, [seem analogous] to the Platonick. **1811** W. WARD *Acct. Writings, Relig. & Manners Hindoos* I. ii. 370 Like the schools of philosophy among the Greeks, these several systems have each originated with a single and a different head, or founder..Jŭyŭminee of the Mēēmangsa. **1841** M. ELPHINSTONE *Hist. India* I. II. v. 215 The prior Mímánsá, which teaches the art of reasoning with the express view of aiding the interpretation of the Védas, is, so far, only a school of criticism. **1861** H. H. WILSON *Ess. & Lect. Relig. Hindus* I. 12 Jaimini, by Śiva's orders, composed the Mímánsá, which is heretical, in as far as it inculates works in preference to faith. **1915** *Encycl. Relig. & Ethics.* VIII. 648/2 The Mīmāṁsā teaches that the relation of word and meaning is not dependent on general agreement, but that the meaning is naturally inherent in the word. **1964** *Language* XL. 113 He did not go any further with his study of the *mīmāṁsā* system. **1971** *Illustr. Weekly India* 11 Apr. 35/2 The Indian philosophical systems such as Buddhism, Nyaya, Vaisheshika, Yoga and Mimamsa.

†**mimature.** *Obs. rare*⁻¹. [f. L. *mīm-us* MIME *sb.* + -ATE[3] + -URE.] Mimicking, mimicry.

1638 MAYNE *Lucian* (1664) 253, I shall present her to you various, and in diverse shapes, and shall approve my selfe not outdone by you in Mimature. Imagine her, then.

mimbar ('mɪmbɑː(r)). Also 9 **mambar, monbar**, 9– **minbar** (the best form). [Arab. *minbar* pulpit.] The pulpit in a mosque. Also *attrib.*

1816 *Travels of Ali Bey* II. vi. 84 El Monbar, or The Tribune of the Priest of Fridays, is on one side of the Makam Ibrahim, at fourteen feet distance, and in front of the northern angle of the Kaaba. **1836** E. W. LANE *Acct. Manners & Customs Mod. Egyptians* I. iii. 94 To the right of this [*sc.* the mihrab] is the *mim'bar* (or pulpit). **1839** T. J. NEWBOLD *Pol. & Statistical Acct. Straits of Malacca* I. v. 249 The Khatib..recites the Khatbeh..in the mosque, from the three steps of the mimbar, a species of rostrum. **1855** R. F. BURTON *Pilgrimage* II. xvii. 141 The Mambar, or pulpit, was the invention of a Medinah man of the Beni Najjar. **1875** *Encycl. Brit.* II. 446/2 Near this was a pulpit (*mimbar*). **1885** T. P. HUGHES *Dict. Islam* 349 *Minbar*, generally pronounced *mimbar*... The pulpit in a mosque from which the khuṭbah (or sermon) is recited. It consists of three steps, and is sometimes a moveable wooden structure, and sometimes a fixture of brick or stone built against the wall. **1932** *Times Lit. Suppl.* 10 Nov. 840/1 The charming panels in the side walls of the *mimbar* steps at the Ravali Masjid. **1967** V. PRITCHARD *Eng. Medieval Graffiti* 35/1 There is a whole panel of swastika-peltae, in a simplified form, carved on a wooden mimbar in Kairwan, North Africa.

mime (maɪm), *sb.* [a. L. *mīm-us*, a. Gr. μῖμος. Cf. F. *mime*, Sp., Pg., It. *mimo*.]

1. *Antiq.* A performer in the dramatic pieces described in sense 4.

[*a* **900** *O.E. Martyrol.* 25 Aug. 152 Se wæs ærest sumes kaseres mima, þæt is leasere, ond sang beforan him scandlicu leoð ond plegode scandlice plegan.] **1784** T. DAVIES *Dram. Misc.* III. 51 The antient mimes were so expert at the representation of thought by action. **1888** LOWELL *Heartsease & Rue* 51 Mime and hetæra getting equal weight With him whose toils heroic saved the State.

2. a. A mimic, jester, buffoon; a pantomimist.

1616 B. JONSON *Epigr.* I. cxxix, Think'st thou, Mime, this is great? **1642** MILTON *Apol. Smect.* 9 Whereas he tels us that Scurrilous Mime was a personated grim lowring foole. **1760** FOOTE *Minor* I. (1767) 14 He is an admirable mime, or mimic, and most delectable company. **1828** SCOTT *F.M. Perth* xvii, That which may well shock the nerves of a prince of mimes and merry-makers. **1840** CARLYLE *Heroes* (1858) 251 Della Scala stood among his courtiers, with mimes and buffoons (*nebulones ac histriones*) making him heartily merry. **1902** J. CONRAD *Heart Darkn.* 142 In motley, as though he had absconded from a troupe of mimes.

b. in figurative context.

1877 MORLEY *Crit. Misc.* Ser. II. 245 That dance of mimes which passes for life among the upper classes.

3. *transf.* and *fig.* An imitator.

1677 GALE *Crt. Gentiles* II. III. 82 Mimes or imitators make only phantasmes or pictures not things... The Mime wil neither know nor think aught of those things he imitates as to good or evil. **1902** CORNISH *Naturalist Thames* 166 Those..famous mimes, the Indian mynahs.

4. a. *Antiq.* A kind of simple farcical drama among the Greeks and Romans, characterized by mimicry and the ludicrous representation of familiar types of character; a dialogue written for recital in a performance of this kind. Also occasionally applied *transf.* to similar performances or compositions in modern times.

1642 MILTON *Apol. Smect.* 9 Scaliger describes a Mime to be a Poem imitating any action to stirre up laughter. **1693** DRYDEN *Persius' Sat.* II. (1726) 255 *note*, Liberius in the Fragment of his Mimes, has a Verse like this. **1790** MALONE *Eng. Stage* in *Shaks. Wks.* I. II. 118 The *Exodiarii* and *Emboliariæ* of the Mimes are undoubtedly the remote progenitors of the Vice and Clown of our ancient dramas. *a* **1834** COLERIDGE *Shaks. Notes* (1849) 12 The mimes of Sophron were written in prose. **1850** TENNYSON *In Mem.* cv, No more shall wayward grief abuse The genial hour with mask and mime. **1904** J. A. NAIRN *Herodas* Introd. 22 A Mime is a piece depicting actual life, generally the life of the common people, and employing their language.

b. (The art of) gesture, movement, etc. (as distinct from words) used to express emotion and dramatic action or character; dumb show; = PANTOMIME *sb.* 4.

1932 I. MAWER *Art of Mime* II. i. 125 The aim of mime is not a performance of certain physical exercises which can be welded into some kind of whole, nor is it merely 'gesture'—gesture is one branch only. **1953** *Ballet Ann.* VII. 22 There is always a great misunderstanding of the word *mime*. .. In ballet it means the formal gesture language used in the narration of the classics. **1967** *Listener* 13 Apr. 503/3 Some sort of research is required..to find out the best way of using mime on television.

†**5.** An imitation. *Obs. rare.*

1650 T. VAUGHAN *Anthroposophia* To Rdr., Excellent patterns commend their Mimes.

6. *attrib.*, as *mime-ballet*, *-drama*, *-play*, *-writer*; † **mime-man**, a mimic.

1955 *Times* 11 May 7/6 Two mime-ballets by Rocca and Dallapiccola respectively. **1931** A. NICOLL *Masks, Mimes & Miracles* i. 78 The Oscan mime drama became one of the most popular divertisements there. **1968** J. WINEARLS *Mod. Dance* (ed. 2) vii. 145 There have been Masques, Dance Plays, Mime Dramas and every combination of the fundamental expressions of movement and voice. **1630** B. JONSON *New Inn* v. i, Tipto, and his Regiment of mime-men [*printed* (1631) mine-men], al drunk dumbe. **1894** *Daily News* 7 May 3/4 'Jean Mayeux', the new 'mime play',..will be performed at the Princess's. **1957** N. FRYE *Anat. Crit.* iv. 285 Classical mime-writers like Herodas.

mime (maɪm), *v.* [f. prec. sb. Cf. F. *mimer*; Gr. has μιμεῖσθαι to imitate.]

1. a. *intr.* To act or play a part, with mimic gesture and action and usually without words.

1616–1837 [see the *vbl. sb.*]. **1897** *Westm. Gaz.* 18 May 10/2 Mlle. Jane May..can sing and act as well as mime.

b. *transf.* and *fig.*

1728 NORTH *Mem. Music* (1846) 36 Our paltry imitators are mistaken when they attempt to mime it upon a silent stage. **1843** CARLYLE *Past & Pr.* III. xv, Miming and chattering like a Dead-Sea Ape. **1887** RIDER HAGGARD *Jess* xviii, We cannot bedeck our inner selves and make them mime as the occasion pleases, and sing the old song when their lips are set to a strange new chant.

c. *trans.* To represent by mimic action.

a **1894** STEVENSON *Weir of Hermiston* iv, She made it [the hearthrug] a rostrum, mimeing her stories as she told them. **1915** M. E. PERUGINI *Art of Ballet* xiii. 115 The two well-known dancers..mutely mimed the actions and emotions of the leading characters. **1959** W. GOLDING *Free Fall* xiv. 250 The maker they mimed for you in your Victorian slum was the old male maker, totem of the conquering Hebrews.

d. Of a singer, to present a pre-recorded song by mime, usu. on television.

1965 G. MELLY *Owning-Up* xi. 131 A weekly [T.V.] programme featuring the new releases and illustrating them visually by..the artists miming to their own records. **1966** *Crescendo* Jan. 8/1 He seems content to mime 'Tears' to a gaggle of unbelieving teen-agers on *Top Of The Pops.* **1966** *Listener* 11 Aug. 204/3 Since the singers and dancers are so expert in miming to their own recordings, it is possible to eliminate all microphones from the stage.

2. *trans.* To imitate, mimic.

1733 *Introd. Verses to Fielding's Intrig. Chambermaid*, Mark, in his mirth how innocent he plays! And while he mimes the mimick, hurts not Bayes. **1890** *Harper's Mag.* Feb. 422/2 Miming the cuttle-fish devouring its prey.

Hence '**miming** *vbl. sb.*; **mimed** *ppl. a.*

1616 B. JONSON *Epigr.* I. cxv, [He] Acts old Iniquitie, and in the fit Of miming, gets th'opinion of a wit. **1642** MILTON *Apol. Smect.* Wks. 1851 III. 262 But in an ill houre hath his unfortunate rashnesse stumbl'd upon the mention of miming. **1837** HOWITT *Rur. Life* VI. xi. 520 All kinds of pageants, mimings, masks, and frolics. **1910** *Daily Chron.* 9 Apr. 7/5 The marvellous power of facial expression to convey an emotion..is brought home..by the intense interest one feels in these 'mimed' plays. **1965** *Melody Maker* 3 Apr. 16 Miming is slowly disappearing from the pop scene. **1965** *Listener* 2 Dec. 908/3 Mimed opera... It soon became painfully obvious that sound was out of synchronization with vision. *Ibid.* The first programme of the series was made almost unwatchable by the process of miming.

mimeo ('mɪmiːəʊ), *sb.* [Abbrev. of MIMEOGRAPH *sb.*] A copy of a document, newspaper, etc., reproduced by means of a mimeograph (see MIMEOGRAPH *sb.*). Also *attrib.*, as *mimeo mag*, *newspaper*, *stencil*. Hence **mimeo, mimeo-stencil** *vbs. trans.*, to reproduce by means of a mimeograph; **mimeoed** *ppl. a.*

1943 J. S. HUXLEY *TVA* 139 TVA, Mimeo, 1941. **1967** KARCH & BUBER *Offset Processes* vi. 243 Within a few minutes a phototube will scan and transfer all details to a mimeo-stencil or offset plate. **1967** *Maclean's Mag.* Jan. 56 Why Sandra Peredo's patronizing attitude toward the little magazines? She states, for instance, that the mimeo mags are interested in dirty words and anti-Establishment statements as their main themes. **1969** *Harper's Mag.* May 82 We learn later that the statement was mimeoed and a few reporters were walking off with it. **1972** M. JOOS in *Language* XLVIII. 260 Having mimeo-stenciled a number of text pages without the footnoting for which I was leaving room on each stencil, I was now putting the stencils through my typewriter a second time. **1973** *Times* 17 Apr. (Liberia Suppl.) p. ii/5 These tribes have their own newspapers called mimeo-newspapers.

mimeograph ('mɪmiːəʊgrɑːf, -græf), *sb.* [irreg. f. Gr. μιμέομαι 'I imitate' + -GRAPH.] A duplicating machine for producing copies from a stencil; also *attrib.*

From 1903 to 1948 a proprietary name.

1889 *Voice* (N.Y.) 19 Sept., The 'mimeograph' and the 'autocopyist'..will give any number of copies of a letter. **1903** *T.P.'s Weekly* 6 Nov. 720/1 A typewriter who could multiply for him copies of these stories on the mimeograph. **1914** [see DUPLICATING *vbl. sb.*]. **1935** M. M. ATWATER *Murder in Midsummer* xviii. 160 Miss Marsh ran off on the mimeograph sheets of instructions all neatly tabulated. **1952** S. KAUFFMANN *Philanderer* (1953) v. 84 The mimeograph ink of the mail-room. **1963** F. C. ARCHER *Gen. Office Pract.* (ed. 2) xvii. 233 Mimeograph paper comes in a variety of colors to contrast or to harmonize with the ink. **1967** KARCH & BUBER *Offset Processes* iv. 72 Letter shops, once using mimeograph-type equipment, added the offset process..to expand..their production.

Hence '**mimeograph** *v. trans.*, to reproduce by means of a mimeograph; '**mimeographed** *ppl. a.*

1895 MARY E. BAMFORD in *Chicago Advance* 6 June 1290/2 The copies were mimeographed at last, thanks to her mother's help. **1903** MISS FAITHFULL *W. Lond. Typewr. Off. Circular*, Terms for mimeographing. Mimeographed Circulars can be sent by the ½d. post. **1912** J. C. DANA *Mod. Amer. Library Econ.* v. 6 Mimeographed copies of tests for books and printed forms for book notes are to be distributed when needed. **1937** M. L. HANLEY *Word Index to Joyce's Ulysses* p. xii, Mimeographing: Dan Marlow. **1946** *R.A.F. Jrnl.* May 152 The *Bulletin*..was an unpretentious affair of a few mimeographed sheets. **1949** SHURR & YOCOM *Mod. Dance* 3 Would you consider mimeographing this material? **1972** *Jrnl. Social Psychol.* LXXXVII. 23 Choices were to be indicated on a mimeographed answer form.

mimer ('maɪmə(r)). [f. MIME *v.* + -ER¹.] A mime or mimic, a buffoon or jester.

1755 JOHNSON [quoting Milton *Samson* 1325, where *Mimirs* in the first edition is a misprint, corrected in the Errata to *Mimics*]. **1819** H. BUSK *Vestriad* II. 128 The Muse, who taught th' enliv'ning dance, In Greece to mimers, and to gods in France. **1835** W. IRVING *Newstead Abbey* Crayon Misc. (1863) 298 We had mummers and mimers too.

‖**mimesis** (maɪ'miːsɪs). [Gr. μίμησις imitation, f. μιμεῖσθαι to imitate, f. μῖμος MIME *sb.*]

1. *Rhet.* A figure of speech, whereby the supposed words or actions of another are imitated. Also *transf.*

1550 R. SHERRY *Treat. Schemes & Tropes* sig. E3 Mimisis, that is a folowing eyther of the wordes or manoures whereby we expresse not onlye the wordes of the person, but also the gesture. **1593** H. PEACHAM *Garden of Eloquence* (1954) 138 Mimesis is an imitation of speech whereby the Orator counterfaiteth not onely what one said, but also his utterance, pronunciation, and gesture. **1650** TRAPP *Comm. Eccles.* xi. 9. 154 Solomon..by a Mimesis brings in a wild yonker thus bespeaking himself. Rejoice [etc.]. **1681** FLAVEL *Meth. Grace* xxxiv. 568 Satan called here (by a Mimesis) the god of this world, not simply and properly, but because he challenges to himself the honour of a god. **1962** S. E. FINER *Man on Horseback* xii. 240 This is to reckon without *mimesis*. Among unstable states, particularly those with a rage for innovation, military intervention has proved to be highly contagious. **1962** *Listener* 13 Dec. 1006/1 Bunyan stands with Malory and Trollope as a master of perfect naturalness in the mimesis of ordinary conversation. **1965** M. BRADBURY *Stepping Westward* vi. 292 Walker had never before heard in anyone's speech vocabulary—*mimesis*, *epistemology*, *mythopoeic*. **1965** M. COHEN in M. Black *Philos. in Amer.* 115 If Le Corbusier has encouraged the doctrine of *mimesis* in designing the chapel at Ronchamp, he has rejected it firmly at the Villa Savoie.

2. *Biol.* = MIMICRY 2.

1845 STRICKLAND in *Lond.* etc. *Philos. Mag.* XXVIII. 356 This term [Iconism], suggested by the Rev. Dr. Ingram,.. appears preferable to Mimesis, which I had originally proposed to use. **1885** in *Cassell's Encycl. Dict.* **1896** A. H. KING *Ethnology* 196 With the growing needs of society, it could not fail to develop by various processes—mimesis, reduplication, repetition [etc.].

3. *Sociol.* The deliberate imitation of the behaviour of one group of people by another as a factor in social change.

1934 A. J. TOYNBEE *Study of Hist.* III. 245 The problem of bringing the uncreative rank and file of a growing society into line with the creative pioneers..cannot be solved in practice, on the social scale, without also bringing into play the faculty of sheer mimesis—one of the less exalted faculties of Human Nature which has more in it of drill than inspiration. **1962** *Listener* 8 Feb. 257/3 There is..an important distinction between *mimesis*, which is imitation of those above you, and solidarity, which is imitation..of those with whom you find yourself in a common situation. **1965** P. LASLETT *World we have Lost* ix. 213 Only if imitation, mimesis, is taken to constitute 'solidity' can the phrase the solid middle class be made to apply to any substantial part of the population.

mimester ('maɪmstə(r)). *rare.* [f. MIME *v.* + -STER.] = MIME *sb.* 2, a mimic.

1873 T. COOPER *Paradise of Martyrs* (1877) 299 The mimesters who beclout themselves anew with rags of Rome.

† **mimetene, mimetese, mimetesite.** *Min.* [Orig. F. *mimétèse* (Beudant 1832) meant to represent Gr. μιμητής imitator. *Mimetene*, *mimetesite* (G. *mimetesit*, Breithaupt 1841), and MIMETITE are alterations intended to make the name less anomalous in form.] Older names for MIMETITE.

1835 C. U. SHEPARD *Treat. Min.* II. II. 46 Mimetene. **1843** CHAPMAN *Min.* 33 Mimetese. **1867** *Pract. Mechanic's Jrnl.* 1 Sept. 190 An arseniated plumbic apatite (mimetesite).

mimetic (maɪ'mɛtɪk), *a.* (and *sb.*) [ad. Gr. μιμητικός, f. μιμεῖσθαι to imitate: see MIMESIS.]

A. *adj.*

1. Addicted to or having an aptitude for mimicry or imitation. Also, pertaining to imitation.

1637 WHITING *Albino & Bellama* 9 But Fucus, lead by most mimetick Apes, Could not depinge Don Fuco's antick shapes. **1762** GOLDSM. *Cit. W.* lxxix, The mimetic troops.. begin their campaign [at the theatres] when all the others quit the field. **1769** R. WOOD *Ess. Genius Homer* To Rdr. 2 We shall confine our inquiry to Homer's Mimetick Powers. **1843** CARLYLE *Heroes* (1858) 316 Chatham himself lives the strangest mimetic life, half-hero, half-quack, all along. **1845** R. W. HAMILTON *Pop. Educ.* iv. (ed. 2) 70 The..mimetic tendency of infancy. **1876** GEO. ELIOT *Dan. Der.* lxii, Crying when she expected him to cry, and reflecting every phase of her feeling with mimetic susceptibility.

2. Characterized by, or of the nature of, imitation.

1669 GALE *Crt. Gentiles* I. III. i. 18 Mimetic Poesie: which the Platonists distribute into..Eicastic, and..Phantastic. **1744** HARRIS *Three Treat.* Wks. (1841) 33 The mimetic art of poetry has been hitherto considered, as fetching its imitation from mere natural resemblance. **1883** H. JENNINGS *Phallicism* ix. 99 Among the Greeks all dancing was of the mimetic kind. **1899** *Allbutt's Syst. Med.* VII. 338 Cases..in which with lesion of the optic thalamus there has been no defect in the mimetic movements.

3. = MIMIC *a.* 3.

1756 J. G. COOPER in *World* No. 159 V. 169 They may be enabled to make an exit as they have lived, in mimetic grandeur. **1841** D'ISRAELI *Amen. Lit.* (1859) I. 59 When the Duke of Normandy visited..Edward the Confessor, he beheld in England a mimetic Normandy. **1892** STEVENSON *Across the Plains* 266 A false and merely mimetic poverty.

4. a. *Zool.* and *Bot.* Of animals or plants: Characterized by 'mimicry' or resemblance in external appearance to some essentially different animal or plant, or to some inorganic object. Of appearances or processes: Of the nature of 'mimicry'.

1851 WOODWARD *Mollusca* I. 56 A second class of analogical resemblances are purely external and illusive, they have been termed mimetic. **1861** H. W. BATES in *Trans. Linn. Soc.* XXIII. 502 Mimetic analogies..are resemblances in external appearance, shape and colours between members of widely distinct families. **1870** NICHOLSON *Man. Zool.* Gen. Introd. §7 (1875) 19 It appears that the mimetic species is protected from some enemy by its outward similarity to the form which it mimics. **1882** *Garden* 28 Jan. 53/2 There are also cases of mimetic variation.

b. *Path.* (See quots.)

1856 MAYNE *Expos. Lex.*, *Mimetic*, applied to diseases that resemble, or appear like imitations of others.

c. *Cryst.* (See quot. 1888.)

1881 W. J. LEWIS in *Nature* No. 616. 355 Twin and mimetic crystals. **1888** TEALL *Brit. Petrogr.* 440 *Mimetic.* Tschermak proposed to call those crystals mimetic which possess externally a high degree of symmetry, but are built up by polysynthetic twinning of crystals having a low grade of symmetry. Thus chabasite is termed a mimetic rhombohedral crystal. **1895** STORY-MASKELYNE *Crystallogr.* Index, Mimetic crystals.

5. *Gram.* (See quot.) *rare.*

1877 MARCH *Comp. Ags. Gram.* §40. 27 Mimetic changes are those occurring through the influence of other words.

†**B.** *sb.* ? A mime, buffoon.

1631 R. H. *Arraignm. Whole Creature* Ep. Ded. 8 It is rather fit for the Mimeticks to dispute, then for mee to determine.

† **mi'metical**, *a. Obs. rare.* [Formed as prec. + -ICAL.] = MIMETIC *a.* 2.

a **1617** BAYNE *On Coloss.* (1634) 360 He doth unfold it by a mimeticall expressing the charges that these false teachers gave. **1764** HURD *Dial.* vii. *Foreign Trav.* (1765) III. 5 A Dialogue in the old mimetical, or poetic form.

mimetically (maɪ'mɛtɪk(ə)lɪ), *adv.* [f. prec. + -LY².] In a mimetic or imitative manner; by mimesis.

1647 TRAPP *Comm. Col.* ii. 21 The words of those impostours, which are here mimetically or by way of imitation related. **1795** MACKNIGHT *Comm. Epistles* (1820) II. 574 The apostle writes mimetically here, personating the false teachers. **1857** H. SPENCER in *Westm. Rev.* Apr. 464 The deeds of the god-king, chanted and mimetically represented in dances round his altar.

mimetism ('maɪmɪtɪz(ə)m). *Biol.* [f. MIMET-IC + -ISM.] = MIMICRY.

1882 in OGILVIE. **1918** B. MIALL tr. *Hamon's Lessons of World-War* ix. 271 Men hide their guns..under canopies of leaves, in order to conceal them from the view of aeroplanes. Man adopts the mimetism of Nature. **1970** *Times Lit. Suppl.*

18 Dec. 1480/5 The later history of the Inca dynasty is a depressing one of mimetism and osmosis.

mimetite ('maɪmɪtaɪt). *Min.* [ad. G. *mimetit* (Haidinger 1845), f. Gr. *μιμητ-ής* imitator + -ITE. (See MIMETENE.)] 'Arsenate of lead, found in yellow to brown crystals, resembling pyromorphite' (Chester *Dict. Min.* 1896).
1852 BROOKE & MILLER *Phillip's Min.* 481.

mimetry ('maɪmɪtrɪ). *Cryst.* [f. MIMET-IC + -RY.] = PSEUDOSYMMETRY.
1895 in *Funk's Stand. Dict.*

mi-mi, variant of MIA-MIA.

mimi, var. MAIMAI.

‖**mimiambi** (maɪ-, mɪmɪ'æmbaɪ), *sb. pl.* (In Dicts. as sing. **mimiambus.**) [L., a. Gr. *μιμίαμβοι pl.*, f. *μῖμο-ς* MIME *sb.* + *ἴαμβος* IAMBUS.] Mimes written in iambic or scazontic verse.
1706 PHILLIPS (ed. Kersey), *Mimiambus*, a kind of Verse, anciently us'd in Lampoons, Farces, &c. **1721** in BAILEY. **1905** *Academy* 4 Nov. 1145/1 The mimiambi of Herodas.

mimiambic ('maɪ-, 'mɪmɪæmbɪk), *a.* and *sb.* [ad. mod.L. *mīmiambic-us*, f. *mimiambī*: see prec.]
A. *adj.* Pertaining to or of the nature of mimiambi. Of a poet: That wrote mimiambi.
1700 COLLIER *2nd Def. Short View* 7 Another Mimiiambick poet. **1846** *Smith's Dict. Biogr. & Mythol.* II. 695/2 Matius..a mimiambic poet.
B. *sb. pl.* = MIMIAMBI.
1845 *Encycl. Metrop.* X. 412/1 Contemporary with Laberius and Publius was Cneius Matius, who wrote Mimiambics, which differed from the Mimes of the two former authors only by being written in scazontics. **1894** *Athenæum* 27 Jan. 108/3 The mimiambics of Herondas have already made a sensation in the learned world.

mimic ('mɪmɪk), *a.* and *sb.* Forms: 6–7 **mimmick, mimicke, -ique,** 6–8 **-ick,** 7 **mimik, mymik,** 7– **mimic.** [ad. L. *mīmic-us*, ad. Gr. *μιμικός*, f. *μῖμ-ος*: see MIME *sb.* and -IC. Cf. F. *mimique*, Sp. *mímico*, Pg., It. *mimico*.]
A. *adj.*
1. †a. Exercising the profession of a mime or buffoon; having the characteristics of, or resembling, a mime (*obs.*). b. Addicted to or having aptitude for mimicry; imitative.
1598 MARSTON *Sco. Villanie* III. x. H vij b, The long fooles coat, the huge slop, the lugg'd boot From mimick Piso all doe claime their roote. **1647** WARD *Simp. Cobler* 26 They would disdain to be led about the Apes, by such mymick Marmosets. **1667** MILTON *P.L.* v. 110 Oft in her absence mimic Fansie wakes To imitate her. **1708** ROWE *Roy. Convert* II. i, Some mimick Fantom wears the lovely Form. **1726** ARBUTHNOT *It cannot rain but it pours* in *Swift's Wks.* 1751 VI. 200 Aristotle saith, that Man is the most Mimick of all Animals. **1730** SWIFT *Market-hill* Wks. 1751 X. 146 Sly Hunters..To catch a Monkey by a Wile, The mimic Animal amuse, They place before him Gloves and Shoes. **17..** COWPER *Transl. fr. V. Bourne, Parrot* iii, 'Sweet Poll!' his doting mistress cries, 'Sweet Poll!' the mimic bird replies. **1821** BRYANT *Ages* iii, Let the mimic canvass shew His calm benevolent features.
2. Of actions, expression of countenance, etc. †a. Pertaining to or characteristic of a mime; histrionic; hence, hypocritical. *Obs.* b. Pertaining to, or of the nature of, mimicry or imitation.
1602 MARSTON *Antonio's Rev.* I. v, Woulds't have me.. wring my face with mimic action? **1624** GATAKER *Transubst.* 113 Where are all those..mimicke gestures and apish fooleries that their Masse-bookes enjoyne? **1638** SIR T. HERBERT *Trav.* (ed. 2) 10 They circle the grave with mimmick gestures and ejaculations. *c* **1645** HOWELL *Lett.* (1655) I. 219 No simpring smiles, no mimic face, Affected gesture, or forc'd grace. **1727** SWIFT *Misc., On Dreams* 10 The busy Head with mimick Art runs o'er The scenes and Actions of the Day before. **1797** MRS. RADCLIFFE *Italian* xxvi, Vivaldi concluded, that his dream had mocked him with a mimic voice. **1865** TYLOR *Early Hist. Man.* ii. 19 As I taught him the written signs of our language, Massieu taught me the mimic signs of his.
3. That is a copy of, or imitatively resembles, what is properly denoted by the name; imitative as opposed to real.
Unlike its approximate synonyms, 'counterfeit', 'mock', 'simulated', etc., the word does not now imply any deceptive intention or effect, being applied primarily to artistic or playful imitation, and usually suggesting that the copy is ludicrously diminutive or insignificant as compared with the reality imitated.
1625 K. LONG tr. *Barclay's Argenis* III. xix. 213 This mimicke Goddesse, who usurped divine honours. **1641** MILTON *Ch. Govt.* v. Wks. 1851 III. 119 To frame out of their own heads as it were with wax a kinde of Mimick Bishop limm'd out to the life of a dead Priesthood. **1726** POPE *Odyss.* XVI. 54 A bowl..Around whose verge a mimic Ivy twines. **1749** SMOLLETT *Regicide* IV. iii, Not all this pride Of mimic virtue..Shall shelter thee, deceiver! **1751** FRANKLIN *Lett.* Wks. 1840 V. 225, I send you some [needles], that have had their heads and points melted off by our mimic lightning. **1757** MRS. GRIFFITH *Lett. Henry & Frances* (1767) II. 193 Instances in brutes of what we partially stile mimic reason. **1812** *Gen. Hist.* in *Ann. Reg.* 212 The mimic monarch [of Hayti] has been encountered with superior force by his rival. **1822** SCOTT *Life in Forest*, Along the silver streams of Tweed 'Tis blithe the mimic fly to lead. **1839** ALISON *Hist. Europe* liv. §62 (1850) VIII. 524 The mimic warfare of the opera stage. **1875** JOWETT *Plato* (ed. 2) V. 399 If any one dies in these mimic contests, the homicide is involuntary.
4. *Path.* (See quot.)
1890 *Syd. Soc. Lex., Mimic convulsion*, same as *Facial spasm. Mimic facial palsy*, an immobility and relaxation of the facial muscles which are supplied by the paralysed nerve... *Mimic spasm*, sudden and transient contraction of the muscles supplied by the portio dura of the seventh pair of cerebral nerves.
B. *sb.*
1. †A mime, burlesque actor (*obs.*); a performer who imitates the manner, attitudes, or voice of another in order to excite laughter; hence, in wider sense, one who practises or is skilled in mimicry or ludicrous imitation.
1590 SHAKS. *Mids. N.* III. ii. 19 Anon his Thisbie must be answered, And forth my Mimmick comes. **1599** B. JONSON *Cynthia's Rev.* III. iv, Waited on By mimiques, jesters. **1609** DEKKER *Gvls Horne-bk.* vi. 31 Draw what troope you can from the stage after you: the Mimicks are beholden to you, for allowing them elbow roome. *c* **1660** WOOD *Life* 8 Oct. (O.H.S.) I. 336 He was a great mimick, and acted well in several playes. **1697** POTTER *Antiq. Greece* I. iv. (1715) 19 [They] preferr'd a Mimick, or a Stage-player before the most Valiant Captain. **1739** CIBBER *Apol.* (1756) I. 123 The mimick..is a great assistant to the actor. **1772** BOSWELL 21 Mar. in *Johnson*, A mimick can not only give you the gestures and voice of a person whom he represents; but even what a person would say on any particular subject. **1830** *Ann. Reg., Chron.* 249 Deaths..Mr. Ralph Sherwin, mimic and comedian. **1849** MACAULAY *Hist. Eng.* ii. I. 196 The mimics, revellers, and courtesans who crowded the palace.
b. 'A mean or servile imitator' (J.). Occasionally of a thing: Something that mimics or feebly resembles.
1624 WOTTON *Archit.* I. 7 What are the most iudicious Artisans but the Mimiques of Nature? **1711** ADDISON *Spect.* No. 225 ¶7 Cunning is only the Mimick of Discretion. **1791** BURKE *To Member of Nat. Assemb.* Wks. 1792 III. 346 When full grown, it [vanity] is the worst of vices, and the occasional mimic of them all. It makes the whole man false. **1818** BYRON *Ch. Har.* IV. clii, Turn to the mole which Hadrian rear'd on high, Imperial mimic of old Egypt's piles. **1840** DICKENS *Barn. Rudge* xxiv, Despisers of mankind—apart from the mere fools and mimics, of that creed—are of two sorts. **1871** PALGRAVE *Lyr. Poems* 22 The cottage gable, bare and high, Poor forlorn mimic of the mountain crest.
†2. A writer of mimes, mimographer. *Obs.*—[0]
1721 BAILEY, *A Mimick*, a Writer of Lampoons or short jests.
3. *Zool.* and *Bot.* A mimetic animal or plant. Also *appos.* in ***mimic beetle*** (see quot. 1855).
1855 W. S. DALLAS in *Syst. Nat. Hist.* I. 408 This position is always assumed by these Beetles [*Histeridæ* and *Byrrhidæ*] when alarmed; and, from this assumption of a death-like attitude, some of the commonest species have received the name of *Mimic Beetles.* **1893** NEWTON *Dict. Birds* s.v. *Mimicry*, It is pretty clear that the *Mimeta*..is rightly named the mimic, since it is a comparatively weak bird, and must benefit by being mistaken for the strong, pugnacious and noisy *Philemon.*
4. 'Play-acting', mummery (*obs.*); mimicry, imitation. *rare.*
a **1631** DONNE *Poems* (1650) 6 Compar'd to this, All honour's mimique; All wealth alchymy. **1832** *Fraser's Mag.* V. 197 The son of the soldier already will dare To mount the old charger, in mimic of war.

mimic ('mɪmɪk), *v.* [f. MIMIC *sb.*]
1. *trans.* To ridicule by imitating or copying (a person, his speech, manner, gestures, etc.).
1697 BURGHOPE *Disc. Relig. Assemb.* 121 To misrepresent his words and mimick his gestures. **1700** DRYDEN *Ovid's Met.* XI. *Ceyx & Alcyone* 330 Morpheus..express'd The Shape of Man, and imitated best; The Walk, the Words, the Gesture cou'd supply, The Habit mimick, and the Mien bely. **1770** LANGHORNE *Plutarch* (1879) I. 229/2 Androcles ..accused Alcibiades..of mimicking the sacred mysteries. **1821** SHELLEY *Chas. I*, ii. 98 He mocks and mimics all he sees and hears. **1838** DICKENS *Nich. Nick.* xiii, Mimicking the voice and manner of the usher. **1871** C. GIBBON *Lack of Gold* vi, The laird was mimicking the miller's voice and manner as well as he could. **1891** KIPLING *Light that Failed* (1900) 91 'This is disgraceful', said Maisie, mimicking Mrs. Jennett's tone.
2. a. To imitate or copy with minute accuracy in external characteristics, e.g. in voice, gesture, style, or manner of doing anything. Chiefly in contemptuous use, as implying servile, unintelligent, or otherwise ridiculous imitation.
1687 DRYDEN *Hind. & P.* I. 40 The buffoon Ape.. mimick'd all sects and had his own to chuse. **1697** —— *Virg. Past.* v. 116 Alphesibœus, tripping, shall advance; And mimick Satyrs in his antick Dance. **1761** CHURCHILL *Rosciad* Poems 1763 I. 50 Just in the way that monkies mimic man. **1843** MACAULAY *Ess., Addison* (1899) 724 Thus much..is certain, both Swift and Voltaire have been successfully mimicked, and that no man has yet been able to mimic Addison. **1844** THIRLWALL *Greece* VIII. 27 The rest only mimicked the hero [*sc.* Alexander the Great]..in their demeanour, and in the trappings and state of royalty. **1871** L. STEPHEN *Playgr. Eur.* (1894) viii. 168 The absurdity of mimicking a man who was his junior.
b. with an action or attribute as object.
1726 SWIFT *Gulliver* II. iii, He observed how contemptible a Thing was human Grandeur, which could be mimicked by such diminutive Insects as I. **1726** DE FOE *Hist. Devil* II. x. (1840) 328 The devil is known to mimic the methods, as well as the actions of his maker. **1849** MACAULAY *Hist. Eng.* ii. I. 165 When a sect becomes powerful..men crowd into it,.. conform strictly to its ritual, mimic its peculiarities. **1858** BUCKLE *Civiliz.* (1869) II. viii. 570 They mimicked the voice of liberty—they aped her very gestures. **1905** W. H. MALLOCK in *19th Cent.* Sept. 497 The devil had mimicked the art of the Creator.
c. of immaterial or inanimate things personified.
1712 GRANVILLE *Poems* 173 Who wou'd with Care some happy Fiction frame, So mimicks Truth, it looks the very same. **1712** STEELE *Spect.* No. 514 ¶2 Vice has learned so to mimick Virtue, that it often creeps in hither under its Disguise. **1750** JOHNSON *Rambler* No. 77 ¶3 The prattle of affectation mimicking distresses unfelt. **1854** PATMORE *Angel in Ho.* I. II. vii, The leaves, all stirring, mimick'd well A neighboring rush of rivers cold. **1878** STEVENSON *Edinburgh* (1889) 8 Behold the palace re-awakened and mimicking its past.
3. To represent imitatively, as by drawing, painting, etc. Of things: To have a close resemblance to, to have or assume the appearance of.
1770 T. WHATELY *Observ. Gardening* 23 Such whimsical wonders, however, lose their effect, when represented in a picture, or mimicked in ground artificially laid. **1814** WORDSW. *Excursion* VI. 315 Like..clouds that mimicked land Before the sailor's eye. **1819** KEATS *Lamia* II. 125 Fresh carved cedar, mimicking a glade Of palm and plantain, met from either side. **1860** READE *Cloister & H.* lxiii, He showed her how closely he could mimic marble on paper.
4. a. *Path.* Of a disease: To exhibit symptoms that have a deceptive resemblance to those of (another disease); to simulate.
1744 BERKELEY *Siris* § 90 The scurvy..which indeed must be allowed to create or mimic most other maladies. **1899** *Allbutt's Syst. Med.* VIII. 473 Nodular forms are closely mimicked by the..febrile outbursts of nodular leprosy.
b. *Med.* Of a drug: to produce an effect very similar to (that of some other cause).
1971 *Nature* 12 Feb. 497/1, *d*-Amphetamine closely mimicked the excitatory and inhibitory effects of *l*-NA. **1974** *Ibid.* 31 May 473/1 Colchicine..has been reported to mimic the effects of denervation on mammalian skeletal muscles.
5. *Zool.* To have a 'mimetic' resemblance to (something else) in form or colour.
1861 H. W. BATES in *Trans. Linn. Soc.* XXIII. 504 The Leptalides..fly in the same parts of the forest, and generally in company with the species they mimic. **1879** LUBBOCK *Sci. Lect.* ii. 62 The *Geometridæ*..closely mimic bits of dry stick.

'**mimicable**, *a.* [f. MIMIC *v.* + -ABLE.] Capable of being mimicked.
1955 J. L. AUSTIN *How to do Things with Words* (1962) viii. 96 The phatic act, however, like the phonetic, is essentially mimicable.

mimical ('mɪmɪkəl), *a.* (and *sb.*) Also 7 **mymicall.** [f. MIMIC *a.* + -AL[1].] A. *adj.*
†1. = MIMIC *a.* 1. *Obs.*
1603 HARSNET *Pop. Impost.* 104 The Puppets have alwaies a Mimicall prolocutor to tel what they meane. *a* **1618** RALEIGH *Rem.* (1644) 264 A Mimical French-man whom I entertained..for his Iests. *a* **1661** FULLER *Worthies, Kent* (1662) II. 80 A Mimical Ape. **1693** J. EDWARDS *Author. O. & N. Test.* 293 Devils..are a mimical sort of creatures.. diligent emulators of the most holy persons.
2. †Befitting a mime or burlesque actor (*obs.*); pertaining to, characterized by, or of the nature of mimicry.
1610 HEALEY *St. Aug. Citie of God* VI. i. (1620) 226 It were like Mimicall scurrility to demand any thing of any one of them [*sc.* gods], which resteth vnder the disposing of another. **1617** MORYSON *Itin.* III. 7, I beheld the mimicall gestures..of the Roman Priests. **1617** BP. HALL *Quo Vadis?* (1628) §14 A few waste complements and mimicall courtesies. **1676** WISEMAN *Surg.* I. xxiii. 132 Without speaking or opening his Eyes for many months, onely some odd mimicall gestures he used. **1709** STEELE *Tatler* No. 99 ¶1 By introducing mimical Dances, and fulsom Buffoonries. **1711** SHAFTESB. *Charac.* III. ii. 93 The petty Tyrannys and mimical Politys of some new Pretenders. **1774** WARTON *Hist. Eng. Poetry* (1775) I. i. 49 No priest shall be a poet, or exercise the mimical or histrionical art in any degree. **1840–1** DE QUINCEY *Style* Wks. 1859 XI. 171 The mimical situations of novels. **1873** *Q. Rev.* Oct. 340 She had musical and mimical talents.
†3. = MIMIC *a.* 3. *Obs.*
1624 GEE *New Shreds of O. Snare* 17 The Actor that puts life into this mimicall Artillery by motion and voice. **1663** *Proposal to use no Conscience* 2 Small mimical oaths, as when we swear by our Honor..or Faith. **1693** *Emilianne's Hist. Monast. Ord.* II. i. 232 The Nuns..did in progress of time attribute to their cutting off their Hair,..and mimical Habits, a holy Virtue.
B. *sb.* An imitator; an actor.
1688 R. HOLME *Armoury* II. 9/2 Euterpe..is the goddess of Mymicals.
Hence '**mimically** *adv.*, †'**mimicalness**.
1623 COCKERAM II, Scoffingly, *Irronically, Mimically.* **1642** FULLER *Holy & Prof. St.* III. xii. 181 So long mimically imitating mad men that he became one. *a* **1661** FULLER (Ogilvie 1882), The mimicalness of the ape. **1711** PUCKLE *Club* 107 Be neither mimically in, nor ridiculously out of the fashion.

†**mimi'cation.** *Obs. rare*—[1]. [f. MIMIC *v.* + -ATION.] A mimicking, counterfeit.
1716 M. DAVIES *Athen. Brit.* III. *Arianism* 83 Several imperfect notions and mimications of the Christian Religion.

mimicked ('mɪmɪkt), *ppl. a.* [f. MIMIC *v.* + -ED[1].] In senses of the verb.
1818 BYRON *Ch. Har.* IV. xli, The lightning rent from Ariosto's bust The iron crown of laurel's mimick'd leaves. **186.** DARWIN *Orig. Spec.* xiii. (1866) 507 Many of the mimicking forms of the Leptalis, as well as of the mimicked forms, can be shown by a graduated series to be merely varieties of the same species.

mimicker (ˈmɪmɪkə(r)). [f. MIMIC *v.* + -ER[1].] One who or something which mimics.

1847 in WEBSTER; and in later Dicts. **1861** H. W. BATES in *Trans. Linn. Soc.* XXIII. 509 Amongst the living objects mimicked by insects are the predacious species from which it is the interest of the mimickers to be concealed.

mimicking (ˈmɪmɪkɪŋ), *ppl. a.* [f. MIMIC *v.* + -ING[2].] In senses of the vb.; *Zool.* = MIMETIC *a.*

1733 CHEYNE *Eng. Malady* II. xii. §5 (1734) 244 Saint Vitus's Dance, (as it is call'd) the mimicking Distemper. **186.** [see MIMICKED]. **1872** NICHOLSON *Introd. Stud. Biol.* 52 The mimicing butterflies.. are liable at a distance to be mistaken for the distasteful *Heliconidæ*. **1877** E. LEIGH *Cheshire Dial.* s.v. *Mimick*, 'Mimicking work' is work made to look well for a time, but not to last, like bad contract work.

mimicry (ˈmɪmɪkrɪ). Also 7 **mimmickry**. [f. MIMIC *sb.* + -RY.]

1. a. The action, practice, or art of mimicking or closely imitating, either in sport or otherwise, the manner, gesture, speech, or mode of action of persons, or the superficial characteristics of a thing.

1709 STEELE *Tatler* No. 38 ¶6 A wretched Belief, That their Mimickry passes for Real Business, or True Wit. **1810** SCOTT *Lady of L.* II. xxvi, The chase I follow far, 'Tis mimicry of noble war. **1829** CUNNINGHAM *Brit. Paint.* i. 58 Mimickry, common to all children, was remarkable in me. **1870** HUXLEY *Lay Serm.* iii. (1874) 49 The successful mimicry of the measure of a Greek song. **1903** R. D. SHAW *Pauline Epist.* 175 A learned and distinguished Comedian.. daily went through his antics and mimicry on the Capitol.

b. ***in mimicry of***: in imitation of.

1814 SOUTHEY *Roderick* VIII. 107 As if in mimicry of insect play. **1839** THIRLWALL *Greece* xlviii. VI. 139 [He] wore a lion's skin, and armed himself with a club, in mimicry of Hercules.

c. An act, instance, or mode of mimicking. Also *concr.* a production by which something is mimicked.

1687 N. N. *Old Popery* 17 Those trivial upstart Mimmickries of them [*sc.* the Roman Church] practiced only within the narrow Limits of the Church of England. **1711** ADDISON *Spect.* No. 169 ¶4 We shall find it [Good-Breeding] to be nothing else but an Imitation and Mimickry of Good-nature. **1774** GOLDSM. *Nat. Hist.* (1776) IV. 219 They [*sc.* monkeys] soon begin to exert all their sportive mimickries. **1877** SHIELDS *Final Philos.* 236 The Latin apologists.. had denounced the myths and oracles of paganism as Satanic mimicries. **1879** C. H. WILSON in *Encycl. Brit.* X. 673/2 In France an imitative school.. has executed mimicries of ancient glass painting.

2. *Zool.* A close external resemblance which a living creature (or sometimes a nest, etc.) bears to a different animal, or to some inanimate object. Also used of similar resemblances in plants.

1861 H. W. BATES in *Trans. Linn. Soc.* XXIII. 509 *note*, The author [Rössler] enumerates many very singular cases of mimicry; he also states his belief that the mimicry is intended to protect the insects from their enemies. **1893** NEWTON *Dict. Birds* s.v. *Mimicry*, We must always remember that the Mimicry, however produced, is unconscious. **1931** R. N. CHAPMAN *Animal Ecol.* viii. 190 It seems likely that many controversies over protective coloration, mimicry, and resemblance might find the solution if they were investigated from the viewpoint of their contributions to the maintenance of the population of the species. **1951** *Dict. Gardening* (R. Hort. Soc.) III. 1304/1 There is often such resemblance between plants which themselves possess no special protective apparatus and those that do as to suggest that 'mimicry' occurs among them in the same way as it does among insects. **1966** E. PALMER *Plains of Camdeboo* xvi. 268 Some plants are barely recognizable as plants at all, and these are the mimicry plants which are some of the most famous plants in the world. **1968** R. D. MARTIN tr. *Wickler's Mimicry in Plants & Animals* x. 100 Some insects resembling ants live within the society of ants and devour their hosts. This latter case would seem to be a case of aggressive mimicry. **1975** *Nature* 17 Jan. 191/1 Mimicry is a phenomenon of evolutionary convergence or parallelism by which an edible mimic species gains some measure of protection from predators by virtue of its close resemblance to a model species which is unpalatable (that is, distasteful or dangerous).

miminy-piminy (ˌmɪmɪnɪˈpɪmɪnɪ), *a.* and *sb.* Also **mimminee-pimminee**. [Intended as phonetically symbolic: cf. MIM; also NIMINY-PIMINY.]

A. *adj.* Ridiculously delicate or over-refined; finicking.

1815 MRS. PILKINGTON *Celebrity* II. 229 Your miminy-piminy fears of hurting the feelings. **1863** READE *Hard Cash* xxxiii, In a miminy-piminy voice [she] said she was come to make her submission. **1881** W. S. GILBERT *Patience* II, A miminy piminy, *Je-ne-sais-quoi* young man.

B. *sb.* Finicking or affected composition.

1818 HAZLITT *Eng. Poets* viii. 293 All the tantalizing, teasing, tripping, lisping mimminee-pimminee of the highest brilliancy and fashion of poetical diction. **1825** —— *Spirit of Age* 397 The two lines immediately after.. are a mere piece of enigmatical ingenuity and scientific mimminee-pimminee.

mimique, obs. form of MIMIC.

†**ˈmimist.** *Obs. rare*[−1]. [f. MIME *sb.* + -IST.] One who imitates. (Erroneously used by Puttenham.)

1589 PUTTENHAM *Eng. Poesie* I. xi. (Arb.) 42 There were others [*sc.* poets] that.. vsed in places of great assembly, to say by rote nombers of short and sententious meetres, very pithie and of good edification, and thereupon were called Poets *Mimistes*: as who would say, imitable and meet to be followed for their wise and graue lessons.

mimmation (mɪˈmeɪʃən). *Assyrian Gram.* Also **mimation**. [f. Arab. *mim*, name of the letter *m* + -ATION, after NUNNATION.] The appending of *m* to the flexional vowels in Assyrian. (A characteristic of the Babylonian dialect of that language, as *nunnation* is of classical Arabic.)

1873 *Eng. Cycl. Arts & Sci.* Suppl. 173. **1896** W. ST. C. BOSCAWEN *Bible & Mon.* i. 30 The.. elaborate power of word-building, as well as the preservation of the mimmation .. attest this similarity. **1903** *Expositor* Oct. 280 Jaum is the same as Jau only with the Babylonian mimmation added.

ˈmimmering, *a.* ? Pseudo-*arch.* [Cf. next.] ? Doting, dreaming.

1827 G. DARLEY *Sylvia* 64 A half-brain'd loon! A mimmering driveller!

†**mimmerkin.** *Obs. Sc.* In 6 mymmerken, -in. [Cf. Du. *mijmeren* (MDu. *mimmeren*, *mimeren*) to dote; and see -KIN.] ? A dotard.

1508 KENNEDIE *Flyting w. Dunbar* 29 Mandrag mymmerkin, maid maister bot in mowis. *Ibid.* 514 Cankrit Caym,.. Tutiuillus, Marmaidyn, mymmerken, monstir of all men.

mimmick, -ry, obs. forms of MIMIC, MIMICRY.

mimmulus, obs. form of MIMULUS.

mimness (ˈmɪmnɪs). [f. MIM *a.* + -NESS.] Primness, demureness.

c **1817** HOGG *Tales & Sk., Edin. Baillie* (1878) V. 224 My angel Lady Jane.. had now lost all her jocularity and flippancy of speech; there was nothing but mimness and reserve in the Marquess's presence.

†**ˈmimograph.** *Obs. rare*[−1]. [ad. L. *mimographus*, Gr. μιμογράφ-ος: see next. Cf. †*geograph, bibliograph*.] = next.

1656 STANLEY *Hist. Philos.* v. 13 (*Plato*), Sophron the Mimographe.

mimographer (maɪˈmɒgrəfə(r)). [f. L. *mimograph-us* (a. Gr. μιμογράφος, f. μῖμο-ς MIME *sb.* + -γράφος writer) + -ER[1]: see -GRAPHER.] A writer or composer of mimes.

1638 SIR T. HERBERT *Trav.* (ed. 2) 235 Mimographers I needs must call them. *Ibid.* 267 Some are Poëtasters, or Mimographers. **1711** SHAFTESB. *Charac.* (1737) I. 196 'Tis in this that the great mimographer, the father and prince of poets, excels so highly; his characters being wrought to a likeness beyond what any succeeding masters were ever able to describe. **1858** DONALDSON tr. *C. O. Müller's Hist. Lit. Anc. Gr.* xxxix. §4 II. 215 Sophron the mimographer.

†**miˈmologer.** *Obs.*[−0] [f. Gr. μιμολόγ-ος reciter of mimes (f. μῖμο-ς MIME + -λόγος that speaks) + -ER[1]: see -LOGER.] A reciter of mimes. So **miˈmologist**.

1727 BAILEY vol. II, *Mimologer*, one who recites Rhymes. **1832** *Examiner* 21/1 She is the Psyche of the Mimologists.

†**miˈmology.** *Obs.* [ad. Gr. μιμολογία, f. μιμολόγος: see prec.] Recitation of mimes.

1727 BAILEY vol. II, *Mimology*, a making of Rhymes.

mimophyre (ˈmaɪməfaɪə(r)). *Petrology.* [f. *mimo-* (see next) + *-phyr* ending of G. *porphyr* porphyry.] An uncrystallized rock having the appearance of porphyry.

1841 *Penny Cycl.* XX. 56/2 Mimophyre. Cement argillaceous, uniting distinct grains of felspar, &c.

†**mimo-prophet.** *Obs. nonce-wd.* [f. Gr. μῖμο-ς MIME (taken in the sense of 'mimic', 'sham') + PROPHET.] A mock or pretended prophet. Hence †**mimoprophetic** *a.*

1668 H. MORE *Div. Dial., Schol.* (1713) 567 When the whole Empire of the World was promised.. to the Familists, by their Mimo-Prophet H. N. *Ibid.* 571 The Quakers.. are to be esteemed.. a Mimoprophetick sort of People.

‖**mimosa** (mɪˈməʊzə, mɪˈməʊsə). Pl. **-as**, also Lat. **-æ**. [mod.L. (Colin 1619: see Hatz.-Darm. s.v.), app. f. L. *mim-us* MIME *sb.* + *-ōsa* fem. of *-ōsus* suffix: see -OSE. The name seems to have been meant to allude to the 'mimicry' of conscious life shown by the Sensitive Plant.]

1. *Bot.* **a.** A genus of leguminous shrubs, natives of tropical and sub-tropical regions; the best known representative is the common Sensitive Plant, *M. pudica*. The genus was originally nearly co-extensive with the present sub-order *Mimoseæ*, but has been greatly narrowed by the separation of *Acacia* and other genera. Also, a plant of this genus. **b.** In popular language applied chiefly to the Sensitive Plant and to certain trees of the genus *Acacia*, esp. the Australian species otherwise known as Wattle-trees.

[**1704** J. HARRIS *Lex. Techn.* I, *Mimosæ Plantæ*, the same with *Sensative*.] **1751** J. HILL *Hist. Plants* 474 The legume of the Mimosa is articulated, and the leaves are sensitive. **1753** CHAMBERS *Cycl. Supp.*, The species of Mimosa, enumerated by Mr. Tournefort, are these: 1. The common sensitive shrub. 2. The prickly and more sensitive Mimosa. .. 5. The prickly Pernambuco Mimosa. **1775** *Nat. Hist.* in *Ann. Reg.* (1783) 93 The Mimosæ, or sensitive plants. **1801** SOUTHEY *Thalaba* I. xiv, Beneath a tall mimosa's shade.. They saw a man reclined. **1808** SCOTT *Marm.* IV. Introd. 196 For not Mimosa's tender tree Shrinks sooner from the touch than he. **1847** LONGF. *Ev.* II. ii. 42 At the tramp of a horse's hoof on the turf of the prairies, Far in advance are closed the leaves of the shrinking mimosa. **1857** LIVINGSTONE *Trav.* xi. 203 White-thorned mimosa (*Acacia horrida*). **1862** G. T. LLOYD 33 *Yrs. in Tasmania* iii. 33 The Mimosa or Wattle, which prevails throughout the most fertile lands of Tasmania. **1867** BAKER *Nile Tribut.* i. (1872) 9 A few miserable stunted thorny mimosas.

2. The bark of various Australian species of *Acacia*, used in tanning; also called *wattle-bark*.

1852–4 *Tomlinson's Cycl. Usef. Arts*, etc. (1866) II. 28 Mimosa or Wattle-bark, is procured from different species of mimosa, which grow in Australia and New Zealand.

3. A yellow colour resembling that of the mimosa. Also *attrib.*

1909 *Cent. Dict.* Suppl., *Mimosa*, same as thiazol yellow. **1928** A. CHRISTIE *Mystery of Blue Train* viii. 61 The little mimosa suit of crêpe de chine. **1966** *Harper's Bazaar* Sept. 41 Evening dress... In mimosa, toast or turquoise. **1971** R. BUSBY *Deadlock* xiii. 201 The immaculate coffee-coloured tussore suit.. with a fresh mimosa shirt.

4. *attrib.* and *Comb.*, as ***mimosa-bush, family, scrub, shrub, -thorn***; ***mimosa-yellow*** adj; **mimosa-bark** = sense 2; **mimosa gum** = *gum arabic* (see ARABIC *a.* 2).

1848 W. WESTGARTH *Australia Felix* xvii. 255 The other exports of Australia Felix consist chiefly of tallow, ..*mimosa bark, and gum-wood. **1856** F. FLEMING *S. Afr.* xii. 264 A broad valley, covered with rich pasturage and dotted with '*mimosa' bushes, stretched out over several acres. **1900** KIPLING in *Daily News* 16 June 4/5 McManus went for a walk through the mimosa-bushes. **1860** GRAY *Man. Bot.* 91 *Mimoseæ*, the *Mimosa Family. **1890** *Syd. Soc. Lex.*, **Mimosa gum*. **1900** DOYLE *Green Flag* 4 Thick clumps of *mimosa scrub. **1830** R. DAWSON *Pres. State Austral.* v. (1831) 202 Gum arabic, which exudes from the *mimosa shrubs. **1894** SIR G. H. PORTAL *Mission Uganda* 35 Clumps of *mimosa thorns. **1898** *Daily News* 6 Sept. 4/7 They stood behind the thin breastwork of mimosa thorn bushes. **1775** MASSON *Journeys at Cape* in *Phil. Trans.* LXVI. 290 We encamped under a large *mimosa tree. **1910** *Encycl. Brit.* VIII. 747/1 The following list includes the principal coal-tar colours.. *mimosa yellow.

mimose (mɪˈməʊs). *Petrology.* [a. F. *mimose*.] A uniformly greyish coloured lava composed of compact feldspar closely united with pyroxene.

1841 *Penny Cycl.* XX. 56/2 Mimose. Laminated felspar, and augite.

mimosine (mɪˈməʊsiːn). *Chem.* Also †**mimosin**. [ad. G. *mimosin* (J. Renz, at the suggestion of K. Suessenguth, 1936 in *Zeitschr. f. physiol. Chem.* CCXLIV. 154), f. MIMOS(A + -INE[5].] An amino-acid, $C_5H_4O_2N{\cdot}CH_2CH\ (NH_2)COOH$, found in the tree *Leucæna glauca* and in *Mimosa pudica*, the sensitive plant.

1937 *Brit. Chem. Abstr.* A. III. 50/2 The sap from the tubular cells of young shoots and leaf stalks of *Mimosa pudica*, L., and *Leucaena glauca*, Benth., yield mimosin. **1949** T. A. HENRY *Plant Alkaloids* (ed. 4) 5 Kostermanns has also investigated mimosine with results indicating that it is a derivative of 3:4-dihydroxypyridine. **1971** *Toxicon* IX. 241 When animals ingest.. mimosine they suffer from growth retardation, alopecia, skin irritation and cataract formation.

mimosite (mɪˈməʊsaɪt). *Palæont.* [ad. mod.L. *Mīmŏsitēs* (see J. H. Balfour *Man. Bot.* 1849, §1189): see MIMOSA and -ITE.] Any fossil remains of plants supposed to have belonged to the sub-order *Mimoseæ*.

1882 in OGILVIE; and in later Dicts.

mimotannic (mɪməʊˈtænɪk), *a.* *Chem.* [f. MIMO(SA + TANNIC *a.*] ***mimotannic acid***: a variety of tannic acid found in the mimosa.

1857 MILLER *Elem. Chem., Org.* v. §4 (1862) 403 The essential constituents of catechu are mimotannic acid and catechin. **1874** GARROD & BAXTER *Mat. Med.* 235 Kino contains a species of tannin, called mimotannic acid (or catechu-tannic acid).

mimotype (ˈmɪməʊtaɪp). *Zool.* [f. Gr. μῖμο-ς MIME *sb.* (taken in the sense of 'mimic') + TYPE *sb.*] 'A type or form of animal life which in one country is the analogue or representative of a type or form found in another country, to which it is not very closely related' (*Cent. Dict.*).

1881 T. GILL in *Smithsonian Rep.* 460 The quasi-representative forms are not only isotypes, but simply mimotypes. Foot-n. *Mimotypes*, forms distantly resembling each other, but fulfilling similar functions.

Hence **mimotypic** (mɪməʊˈtɪpɪk) *a.*, relating to or having the character of a mimotype.

1890 in *Century Dict.*; and in later Dicts.

mimp (mɪmp), *sb.* and *a.* [Phonetically symbolic: cf. MIM.]

A. *sb.* A pursing up of the lips.

1786 J. BURGOYNE *Heiress* III. ii. 54, I am preparing the cast of the lips for the ensuing winter—thus—It is to be call'd the Paphian mimp. **1822** M. EDGEWORTH *Let.* 16 Jan. (1971) 321 The famous learned Mrs. Somerville..no *set* smile or prim look—no *mimps* with her mouth.

B. *adj.* Prim, precise, affected, mim.

1882 in *Lanc. Gloss., Mimp*, prim, precise, affected.

So **'mimpetty mimp** *adv.*, in prim silence.

1798 CHARLOTTE SMITH *Yng. Philos.* I. 168, I am so teased and so lectured by the old folks that I sit mimpetty mimp before them merely for peace sake.

mimp (mɪmp), *v. dial.* [Cf. MIMP *sb.*]

†**1.** *trans.* To purse *up* (one's mouth).

1710 *Brit. Apollo* III. No. 35. 2/2 She mimp'd up her Mouth with scorn.

2. *intr.* 'To speak or act in an affected or mincing manner; to toy or play with one's food in an affected manner' (E.D.D.).

c **1861** STATON *Rays from Loominary* 41 Peggy coom mimpin up besoide him, lookin bonnily confused. **1880** MRS. PARR *Adam & Eve* vi. 83, I thought you'd be mimpin' and mincin', and that nothin' ud please 'ee.

†**'mimpins.** *Obs.* ? *School slang.* (See quot.)

1820 L. HUNT *Indicator* No. 35 (1822) I. 275 There used to be a mystery called mimpins, which as Dr. Johnson would say, made a pretty sweetmeat.

mimsey ('mɪmzɪ), *a. dial.* Also **mimsy, mimzy.** [f. MIM *a.*: cf. *clumsy, flimsy, tipsy.*] 'Prim, prudish; contemptible' (E.D.D.).

Lewis Carroll's *mimsy*, which may be an invented word, has influenced all subsequent uses.

1855 'L. CARROLL' *Rectory Umbrella & Mischmasch* (1932) 139 All mimsy were the borogoves. *Ibid.* 140 *Mimsy*, (whence *mimserable* and *miserable*). 'Unhappy.' **1880** *Antrim & Down Gloss., Mim, Mimsey*, prim, prudish. **1895** S. CHRISTIAN *Sarah* (ed. 4) 262 She is no mimzy miss to be scared, or a reed to break if you lean your hand on it. **1911** C. MACKENZIE *Passionate Elopement* xxi. 186 Four shillings and sixpence, ma'am, for a little mimsy book not so thick as the magick history of Jack the Giant Killer. **1920** D. H. LAWRENCE *Touch & Go* 6 Good plays? You might as well say mimsy bomtittle plays, you'd be saying as much. **1933** W. DE LA MARE *Lord Fish* 171 Treading mimsey as a cat. **1934** *Times Educ. Suppl.* 24 Mar. p. iv/2 A people unimaginative enough to accept a mimsy and scrannel 'P.R.' in place of the organ music, the soul-uplifting harmony of 'Proportional Representation'. **1936** *Punch* 10 June 650/1 'It's the glamour of it,' sighed Josephine. 'Whenever I smell a programme I go quite mimsey—honestly I do.' **1937** 'N. BLAKE' *There's Trouble Brewing* i. 24 An affected mimsy sort of voice that she reserved presumably for cultural pronouncements: Nigel preferred her normal, unmitigated boom. **1956** J. CANNAN *People to be Found* vii. 91 With horror they had seen the lawns of the Botanic Gardens torn up and replaced by a mimsy pseudo-Elizabethan rose-garden. **1963** *Times* 8 Feb. 14/3 Moreover his interpolated variation in the first act, danced to the normally unused *andante* of the *pas de trois* and consisting largely of slow *pirouettes en attitude*, looked as mimsey as the borogroves [*sic*], and could not be regarded as successful.

‖**mimulus** ('mɪmjʊləs). *Bot.* Also 8 **mimmulus.** [mod.L.; app. dim. of L. *mīmus* MIME *sb.* The application by Linnæus (sense 2) is supposed to allude to the resemblance of the flowers to a mask.]

†**1.** The Louse-wort or Red Rattle, *Pedicularis sylvatica. Obs.*

1706 PHILLIPS (ed. Kersey), *Mimmulus*, the Herb Rattle, or Louse-wort. **1727** BAILEY vol. II. **1794** *Curtis's Bot. Mag.* VIII. 283 Mimmulus is a classical word for the Pedicularis, or Lousewort.

2. [Linnæus 1741, in *Acta Soc. Reg. Scient. Upsaliensis* 82.] An annual or perennial herb of the large genus so called, belonging to the family Scrophulariaceæ and widely distributed in America, Asia, and Africa, esp. *Mimulus luteus*, the monkey-flower, a yellow-flowered perennial, native to western North America but naturalized elsewhere.

M. moschatus is commonly known as the musk plant.

1768 P. MILLER *Gardeners Dict.* (ed. 8) s.v. Mimulus. Upright Mimulus with oblong linear leaves. **1794** *Curtis's Bot. Mag.* VIII. 283 Linnæus first gave to it [sc. *Mimulus ringens*] the name of *Mimulus*. **1824** LOUDON *Encycl. Gardening* Index, Mimulus, monkey-flower. **1882** *Garden* 10 June 406/3 Single Mimuluses in variety..have been the most brilliant outdoor hardy flowers I have. **1900** L. H. BAILEY *Cycl. Amer. Hort.* II. 1018/1 There is nothing difficult in the culture of Mimulus. Some of the finest plants have been self-sown on a rubbish heap. **1905** *Longm. Mag.* Jan. 253 The showy yellow flowers of the North American mimulus may be seen. **1963** *Times* 25 Apr. 14/6, I think of a turn in a wood and a solitary exquisite butterfly-orchis; of a wide green hillside and a patch of mimulus beside a grooved trickle of water. **1974** A. SCOTT-JAMES *Sissinghurst* xiii. 143 The mimulus continues as the centrepoint.

‖**mimus** ('maɪməs). *Ornith.* [mod.L. use of L. *mimus* MIME *sb.*] A genus of American birds including the mocking-bird, *M. polyglottus*; a bird of this genus.

1706 PHILLIPS (ed. Kersey), *Mimus*, ..the Indian Mock-bird, not much unlike the Jay, but somewhat smaller.

attrib. **1896** NEWTON *Dict. Birds* 958 In the *Mimus*-group the tarsus is anteriorly scutellated.

†**'mimy,** *a. Obs. rare*⁻¹. [f. MIME *sb.* + -Y¹.] Of or pertaining to a mime or mimic.

1683 O. U. *Parish Ch. No Conventicles* 4 When his mimy Face should appear, with Gravity and Laughter at the same instant.

†**min,** *sb.*¹ *Obs.* Forms: 1, 4 **myne, mine,** 3 **mune-,** 3–4 **min,** 4 **minne,** 4–5 **myn(ne.** [OE. *myne* masc., = OS. *muni-* (in *munilîc* lovable), ON. *mun-r* mind, desire, love, Goth. *mun-s*:—OTeut. **muni-z*, f. wk.-grade of the Indogermanic root **men-* (: **mon-*: *mn-*): see MIND *sb.*]

1. a. Mind, purpose, intention (OE. only). **b.** Remembrance, memory, mention. *to make min of*: to mention.

Beowulf 2572 Læssan hwile..þonne his myne sohte. *a* **1300** *Cursor M.* 5174 Yee ha sin þat yee mak of him ani min. *Ibid.* 8835 To haf o þat tre lastand min. *a* **1450** MYRC 1852 On þy power þen haue þow mynne, þat þou myȝt a-soyle of alle synne. *c* **1460** *Towneley Myst.* xxiv. 361 Now, gramercy agayn! Mekill thank and myn and this shalbe ment.

2. *Comb.*: **min-day** = MIND-DAY; also *attrib.*

a **1225** *Ancr. R.* 22 Ine anniuersaries, þet is ine mune-dawes of ower leoue vreond. **1532** in Weaver *Wells Wills* (1890) 84 A myndey cowe that I had of my mother.

†**min,** *sb.*² *Sc. Obs.* Shortened form of MINNIE *sb.*, mother.

1... *Johnnie Faa* in Child *Ballads* IV. 284 (Cent.) I'm Johnny Faa o' Yetholm town, There dwall my min and daddie O.

min (mɪn), *sb.*³ Shortened form of MINUTE *sb.*¹

1890 in *Cent. Dict.* **1892** *Field* 14 May 735/3 He ..'clocked' 2 min 2 sec all the way. **1959** P. BULL *I know Face* i. 18 Miss Pereira..told me to meet her in the ABC up the street in ten mins.

min, *sb.*⁴: see MIN *a.*²

†**min,** *a.*¹ *Obs.* Also 3 **minne,** 4–5 **myn(n)e,** 4–6 **myn.** [a. ON. *minne* (:—**minra*) = OFris. *minnera, minra*, OS. *minnero* (MDu. *minre, minder*, Du. *minder*), OHG. *minniro* (MHG. *minre, minner*, mod.G. *minder*), Goth. *minniza*:—OTeut. **minnizon-*, **minwizon-*, cogn. w. Gr. μινύθειν to make or grow smaller, L. *minuĕre* to diminish. L. *minor* less.

The alleged OE. *min* does not exist; the word in the supposed examples is *minne* with the sense 'wicked, harmful', prob. cognate with *mán* MAN *a.* and *sb.*²]

Less. Always coupled with *more.*

a **1300** *E.E. Psalter* ix. 5 Þou snibbid genge mare and minne, Forworthed wiked for his sinne. **13..** *Gaw. & Gr. Knt.* 1881 Þere he schrof hym schyrly, & schewed his mysdedez, Of þe more & þe mynne, & merci besechez. *c* **1400** *Rule St. Benet* 175 Who so makes myrth mor or min, In god behoues his ioy begin. *c* **1440** *York Myst.* ix. 34 My Fadir knewe both more and mynne,..That al þis worlde shuld synke for synne. **1571** H. CHARTERIS *Lyndesay's Wks.* Adhort. a vj b, Idolateris..Reid heir ȝour lyfe at large, baith mair and min.

Min (mɪn), *a.*² and *sb.*⁴ **A.** *adj.* Of or pertaining to the Min district or dialect in Fukien province, S.E. China. **B.** *sb.* The dialect of this district.

1902 *Encycl. Brit.* XXVII. 27/1 The Min forts at the entrance of the Foochow river. **1910** *Ibid.* VI. 202/1 The French fleet attacked and destroyed..the forts which were built to guard the entrance to the Min river. **1959** *Chambers's Encycl.* III. 488/2 The Min dialects of Fukien, with well-marked varieties in Foochow and Amoy. **1964** M. A. K. HALLIDAY et al. in J. A. Fishman *Readings Sociol. of Lang.* (1968) 146 There are six major dialects in modern China: Mandarin, Cantonese, Wu, North Min, South Min and Hakka. **1975** *Language* LI. 258 Cháozhoū, a Mǐn dialect spoken on the southeast coast of mainland China.

†**min,** *v.*¹ *Obs.* Forms: 1 (***mynian,** ***mynnan),** *3rd sing. pres.* **myneþ,** *subj.* **meneȝe;** 4–5 **myn(n.** [OE. **mynian*, f. *myne* MIN *sb.*¹] *intr.* To intend, purpose; to direct one's course, go.

a **1000** *Guthlac* 1061 Þær min hyht myneð to gesecenne. *a* **1000** in Cockayne *Shrine* 163 Ic lære ælcne ðara þe maȝa si & maniȝne wæn hæbbe þæt he meniȝe to þam ilcan wuda. **13..** *Gaw. & Gr. Knt.* 982 Þe lorde..Mynned merthe to be made vpon mony syþez. *a* **1400–50** *Alexander* 4787 Vp at a maȝte mountane he myns with his ost.

†**min,** *v.*² *Obs.* Forms: 2–4 **mine,** 3–4 **munne, min(ne,** 4–5 **myn(e, mynne.** [a. ON. *minna* (:—OTeut. type **minjan*, **menjan*, f. root **men-*: see MIND *sb.* The first quot. may belong to OE. *mynegian*: see MING *v.*]

1. *trans.* To remind.

c **1200** *Trin. Coll. Hom.* 139 And he minede alle men to forleten here sinnes, and beten. *a* **1400–50** *Alexander* 4613 Ne neuire na mercy ȝow emell as mynes me ȝ our pistill. *a* **1450** *Le Morte Arth.* 169 Syr, of thinge I wolle you mynne.

2. impers. ***me mins*** = I recollect, I remember, I think. Const. *of, on.*

a **1300** *Cursor M.* 5274 Ne minnes yow noght, now mani dai, Of a drem, lang siþen gan? **13..** *Sir Beues* (A.) 185 'Ȝe', ȝhe seide, 'of a wilde bor I wene, me mineþ boute for, Al of þe feure!' *a* **1400–50** *Alexander* 1625 For in þe marche of Messedone me mynes [*MS. Dublin* me menys] on a tyme, þat [etc.]. *c* **1460** *Towneley Myst.* xxviii. 200 Cryst saide his self, mynnes me, That [etc.].

3. *trans.* To remember, to have or bear in mind; to call to mind or remembrance, recollect.

13.. *Gaw. & Gr. Knt.* 995 On þe morne, as vch mon mynez þat tyme. *c* **1400** *Destr. Troy* 1434 Happye is þe here In no hate lengis,..Ne mynnes no malis þat is of mynd past. *a* **1400–50** *Alexander* 1094 As ȝone ȝondire hiȝe hill sall ay hald his place, So sall þi name fra now furth be mynned in mynde. **14..** in *Polit. Relig. & Love Poems* (1903) 219 My merci, if þou it mynned, Y haue schewed it þee on many wise.

b. *intr.* and *refl.* Also, to think (of something or some one). Const. *of, on, upon.*

a **1300** *Cursor M.* 112 A lastand warc apon to myn. *Ibid.* 8252 Of cercles þat he toke a-wai Offrand he made at min on ai. *a* **1340** HAMPOLE *Psalter* viii. 5 What is man þat þou ert mynand of him? **13..** *E.E. Allit. P.* A. 583 Fyrst of my hyre my lorde con mynne. **1377** LANGL. *P. Pl.* B. xv. 454 Ȝe mynnen wel how Mathew seith how a man made a feste. *a* **1425** *Cursor M.* 21873 (Trin.) Hongres & deeþ vpon to mynne. *c* **1460** *Towneley Myst.* xxviii. 136 Myn ye noght that I you told..That my body shuld be sold.

4. *trans.* To commemorate.

a **1225** *St. Marher.* 2 Þe eadi meiden þat we munnið to dei.

5. *trans.* To say, tell, mention, record, relate.

a **1300** *Cursor M.* 23953 Of hir truli it es mi tale, Hir murning for to min. ? *c* **1325** *Old Age* iv. in *E.E.P.* (1862) 149 Iset ic am wiþ sunne þat i ne mai noȝt munne. *a* **1375** *Lay Folks Mass Bk.* App. iv. 456 Seþþe trewely trouwe þer-Inne, And fulliche out of ȝor mouþ hit mynne, þer-to liht muche mede. *c* **1400** *Destr. Troy* Prol. 37 Amonges þat menye,—to myn hym be nome,—Homer was holden haithill of dedis. *a* **1600** *Flodden Field* lxxii. in Child *Ballads* III. 358 The first word that our prince did myn, 'Welcome, dukes and erles, to mee!'

min, obs. form of MINE.

‖**mina**¹ ('maɪnə). *Pl.* **minæ** ('maɪniː), **minas** ('maɪnəz). Also 7 **myna, mine,** 8 **minah;** *pl.* 7 **minaes, mynaes.** [L. *mina*, ad. Gr. μνᾶ (see MNA), prob. from a Babylonian source: cf. MANEH.]

1. A unit of weight anciently used in Western Asia, Greece, and Egypt.

In Greek-speaking countries it contained 100 drachmas; it varied according to locality and time, but was not far from 1 lb. avoirdupois; 100 minas made a talent. In Assyria and Babylonia there seem to have been two different *minas*, one being double of the other.

1603 HOLLAND *Plutarch* Explan. Words, *Mina* or *Mna*, a weight, answering to *Libra*, that is to say, a pound. **1771** RAPER in *Phil. Trans.* LXI. 487 It weighed 72 Attic Minas. **1845** P. SMITH in *W. Smith's Dict. Gr. & Rom. Ant.* s.v. *Talentum*, Another standard of the talent, which was used in commercial transactions,..the mina of which was called the *commercial mina*... This mina is mentioned..as weighing 138 drachmae. **1903** *19th Cent.* Aug. 271 The Babylonian ordinary mina was equal to 982·4 grammes. Sixty minae made one talent.

2. A denomination of money anciently current in Greece and Greek-speaking countries, = 100 drachmas. (Rendered 'pound' in the English versions of the N.T.)

1579–80 NORTH *Plutarch, Lysander* (1595) 486 A tallent of siluer, two and fifty Minas [etc.]. **1638** SIR T. HERBERT *Trav.* (ed. 2) 242 Each supper stood him in a hundred Mynaes of gold, each mina or dina, in our money valuing six and twenty shillings and eight pence. **1659** STANLEY *Hist. Philos.* XI. (1687) 768/2 He [Protagoras] was the first, that took a hundred Minæ for a gratuity. **1685** COTTON tr. *Montaigne* xxxiv. (1711) I. 312 He was presently awarded ten Attick Mines. **1776** ADAM SMITH *W.N.* I. x. (1869) I. 141 Four minæ were equal to thirteen pounds six shillings and eight pence. **1838** THIRLWALL *Greece* xxxiii. IV. 296 Cyrus had promised them a largess of five minas a-piece. **1845** P. SMITH in *W. Smith's Dict. Gr. & Rom. Ant.* s.v. *Talentum*, The [Attic] mina was 4*l.* 1*s.* 3*d.*.. The Aeginetan mina was, according to the existing coins, 5*l.* 14*s.* 7*d.* **1877** C. GEIKIE *Christ* liv. (1879) 657 He gave them each, only a mina, one hundred drachmae.

3. = MANEH.

1737 WHISTON *Josephus* p. cl, Maneh, Mna, or Mina, as a coin = 60 Shekels. **1797** *Encycl. Brit.* (ed. 3) XII. 37/2 [Ezekiel] tells us that the minah or maneh was valued at 60 shekels.

‖**mina**² ('maɪnə). Forms: 8 **maynat,** 8–9 **mino, minor,** 9 **minah, minar, miner, myna, mynah, myneh, maina,** 9– **mina.** [Hindī *mainā.*] A name applied to several different sturnoid passerine birds of India and countries further east, belonging to the genera *Acridotheres* and *Eulabes*, esp. *Eulabes* (formerly *Gracula*) *religiosa*, the common talking starling of India. In Australia also applied to various species of the genera *Manorhina* and *Myzantha*.

1769 LADY M. COKE *Jrnl.* 11 Aug. (1892) III. 131 A number of fine Birds presented themselves before me: an Noble Mino that I wanted to Buy, but [etc.]. **1800** *Misc. Tracts in Asiat. Ann. Reg.* 4/2 The maynat. **1813** J. FORBES *Oriental Mem.* I. 47 The myneh is a very entertaining bird, ..articulating several words in the manner of the starling. **1831** TRELAWNY *Adv. Younger Son* III. 246 The mina, of deeper blue than the sky. **1848** GOULD *Birds Australia* IV. pl. 79 Yellow-throated Miner. **1859** LANG *Wand. India* 263 A minar was chased by a small hawk. **1879** M. STOKES *Ind. Fairy Tales* iv. (1880) 18 So the dog went to a maina and said: 'What shall I do to hurt this cat?' **1888** D. MACDONALD *Gum Boughs* 146 Yellow-legged minahs, tamest of all Australian birds. **1893** Myna, Maina, Minor [see GRACKLE 1].

b. *Comb.*, as ***mina-bird, -grackle.***

1782, 1842 Minor Grakle, mino grakle [see GRACKLE 1]. 1864 *Chambers's Encycl.*, *Mina bird.*

minable, var. MINEABLE *a.*

minace, obs. Sc. form of MENACE *v.*

minacious (mɪˈneɪʃəs), *a.* [f. L. *minācī-*, *minax* (f. *minārī* to threaten) + -OUS. Cf. It. *minaccioso.*] Menacing, threatening; of a threatening character; full of threats or menaces.

1660 H. MORE *Myst. Godl.* III. iii. 63 Whether the face of Heaven..look upon us with a..sad and minacious countenance. *a* 1711 KEN *Hymnotheo* Poet. Wks. 1721 III. 349 He ghostly Wants supplies, gives inward Joys, Which most minacious Crosses overpoise. 1889 ABP. BENSON in *Life* II. 286 He went away with a kind of minacious 'Very well'.

absol. 1824 *Blackw. Mag.* XVI. 68 You have often a touch of the minaceous [*sic*].

Hence **miˈnaciously** *adv.*, **miˈnaciousness.**

1674 *Rec. Presbyt. Inverness* (S.H.S.) 43 Donald dow Mack conachie..menaciouslie threatened the Minister. 1864 *Q. Rev.* Oct. 571 The attitude of the Papal communion before this new enemy is that of a startled, trembling minaciousness. 1895 *Punch* 21 Dec. 300/2 Two..terriers, which barked minaciously at my legs.

minacity (mɪˈnæsɪtɪ). [f. L. *minăc-em*, *minax* threatening (see MINACIOUS *a.*) + -ITY.] 'Disposition to use threats' (J.); denunciation.

1656 in BLOUNT *Glossogr.* 1841 L. HUNT *Seer* II. (1864) 76 Nor is the district without its historical minacities. 1854 MILMAN *Lat. Chr.* VI. iii. (1864) III. 481 The warning was couched in words of prophetic minacity.

†**minacy.** *Obs.* Also 6–7 menacy. [ad. L. *minăciæ* threats, f. *mināc-*, *minax* threatening: see MINACIOUS and -ACY.] = MENACE.

1565 STAPLETON tr. *Bede's Hist. Ch. Eng.* 17 Saynt Albane ..litle heeded the menacies [L. *minas*] of the Prince. 1645 FEATLY *Dippers Dipt* (1646) 79 According to that dreadfull menacy in the second Commandment. *a* 1670 HACKET *Abp. Williams* II. (1693) 17 Yet was I left under that minacy and the minacer..left to his course against me.

Minæan (mɪˈniːən), *sb.* and *a.* Also **Minean.** [f. L. *Minæus*, f. Arab. *Maʿīn*, + -AN.] **A.** *sb.* **a.** A native or inhabitant of an ancient kingdom of southern Arabia. **b.** The Semitic language of the Minæans. **B.** *adj.* Of or pertaining to the Minæans, their kingdom, or their language. So **Miˈnaic** *sb.* and *a.*

1601 HOLLAND tr. *Pliny's Nat. Hist.* XII. xiv. 366 There is another tract by it selfe confronting this countrye [*sc.* Arabia], wherein the Minæans doe inhabite. 1833 A. CRICHTON *Hist. Arabia* I. iv. 148 The Minæans were rich in palm-groves, flocks, and fertile fields. 1844 C. FORSTER *Hist. Geogr. Arabia* I. ii. 133 We find Carman reg., the Minæan metropolis..peopled by Pliny with the Charmæi. 1886 *Encycl. Brit.* XXI. 654/1 The other [dialect], which expresses the causative by *sa*.., is the Minaic. To this latter branch belong the numerous South Arabic inscriptions recently found in the north of the Ḥijáz, near Ḥejr where the Minæans must have had a commercial settlement. *Ibid.*, The singular manner in which districts containing Sabæan inscriptions and those containing Minaic alternate with one another. 1902 in Gottheil & Jastrow *Semitic Study Ser.* I. (Advt.), Selected Sabaean and Minaean inscriptions. 1934 L. H. GRAY *Introd. Semitic Compar. Ling.* i. 6 South Arabic is represented only by inscriptions (Minaean,..Qatabanian, ..). 1936 F. STARK *Southern Gates Arabia* 5 The Arabian empires rose and fell—Minean, Sabæan, Katabanian. 1951 W. F. ALBRIGHT in H. H. Rowley *Old Testament & Mod. Study* ii. 32 The difference between Sabaean and Minaean, the former of which has an *h*-causative whereas the latter has the *s*-causative. 1974 *Encycl. Brit. Macropædia.* I. 1044/1 Four main states are known to have established themselves in South Arabia—Maʿīn (of the Minaeans), Saba' (of the Sabaeans), Qatabān (Qitbān) and Ḥaḍramawt. *Ibid.* XIX. 1084/1 Yemen..was successively the centre of the Minaean (13th to 7th centuries BC), Sabaean.., and Himyaritic.. civilizations.

minah, variant of MINA[1] and MINA[2].

minal, variant of MONAUL.

minam, var. MENNOM *Obs.* exc. *dial.*, a minnow.

1656 SPELMAN *Villare Angl.* Pref. 3 What Dragg-net.. can be so cast to catch all Minams that come under it?

Minamata disease (mɪnəˈmɑːtə). *Path.* [Named after *Minamata*, the name of a town in Kumamoto prefecture, Japan, where it was first recognized.] A disease, caused by ingestion of alkyl mercury compounds, which is characterized by impairment of cerebral functions such as speech, sight, and muscular coordination and which is usually permanent and sometimes fatal.

1957 *Acta Path. Jap.* VII. 605 The so-called Minamata-disease may be recognized as a toxic encephalopathia. The toxic substances contained in fish and shell-fish have not been yet found. 1971 *Sci. Amer.* May 15 The Minamata disease, as it came to be called, produced progressive weakening of the muscles, loss of vision, impairment of other cerebral functions, eventual paralysis and in some cases coma and death. 1973 *Biol. Conservation* V. 143/2 Minamata disease first appeared in cats, which died from eating fish scraps from the village kitchens. 1975 *Times Lit. Suppl.* 19 Sept. 1042 (*caption*) Demonstrators for the victims of 'Minamata Disease', a defect of the central nervous system caused by eating fish poisoned by mercury in industrial waste.

Minangkabau (ˌmɪnæŋkəˈbaʊ), *a.* and *sb.* Also **Manikabowe, Menangkabau, Menangkabo,** 8 **Menangcabow(e),** 9 **Menangkabow, Minangkabauer.** Pl. **Minangkabau, -baus.**

A. *adj.* Of or pertaining to Minangkabau, a Malay territory in the highlands of Sumatra. **B.** *sb.* A native or inhabitant of Minangkabau.

1783 W. MARSDEN *Hist. Sumatra* 279 Between the Menangcabow people, those of Rou.., and the Achenese, wars used to be perpetual. 1808 *Asiatick Researches* X. iii. 165 The Menangkábow race..seem at an early period to have ruled the whole island of Sumatra. 1821 J. LEYDEN tr. *Malay Annals* ii. 37 All the Menangcabows were surprised at his appearance. 1839 T. J. NEWBOLD *Pol. & Statistical Acct. Straits of Malacca* I. v. 200 The inhabitants [of Naning]..are always styled 'Manikábowes', or settlers from Menángkábowe, in Sumatra. *Ibid.* II. xiv. 219 The information..was derived..from various Menangkabowe chiefs of Rumbowe and Naning. 1911 J. FRAZER *Golden Bough: Magic Art* (ed. 3) I. iii. 58 The Minangkabauers of Sumatra..will call in the help of a wizard. *Ibid.* 193 The Minangkabau people of Sumatra. 1947 R. O. WINSTEDT *Malays* viii. 154 Some of the sayings of the Minangkabau tribes of Negri Sembilan rise to poetry. 1968 *Encycl. Brit.* XV. 144/1 The Menangkabau have much in common with the coastal Malay, but differ radically in social organization. 1972 M. SHEPPARD *Taman Indera* 65 The *Randai*, the Minangkabau dance drama from West Sumatra.

†**ˈminant**, *a. Obs.* [f. L. *minant-em*, pr. pple. of *minārī* to threaten.] That threatens.

1646–8 G. DANIEL *Poems* Wks. 1878 I. 197 A Minant Exhalation.

‖**minar** (mɪˈnɑː(r)). Also 7 mynar. [a. Arab. *manār*, f. root of *nār* fire.] A lighthouse, a tower, or turret. Cf. MINARET.

1665 SIR T. HERBERT *Trav.* (1677) 142 High slender Turrets which the Mahometans..term..Minars, i.e. Towers. *Ibid.* 318 A Tower, Mynar [*edd.* 1634, 1638, manor]. 1864 *Chambers's Encycl.* s.v., In India, *Minars*, or pillars of victory, are frequently erected in connection with mosques... They..are divided into stories by projecting balconies, like the minarets. 1898 G. SMITH *Twelve Ind. Statesm.* iii. 100 The Taj itself..was illumined by the electric light from its four minars and the mosques on either side.

minar, variant of MINA[2].

minaret (ˈmɪnərɪt). Forms: α. 7 minoret, 8 minarat, mineret, 9 menaret, 7– minaret; β. 8–9 minaree, minareh, menareh. [a. Arab. *manārah*, *manārat* (in Turkish pronunciation *mināre*), f. root of *nār* fire: cf. MINAR. The immediate source may be F. *minaret*; cf. Sp. *minarete*, Pg. *minareto*, It. *minaretto.*] A tall slender tower or turret, connected with a mosque, surrounded by one or more projecting balconies from which the muezzin calls the people to prayer.

α. 1682 WHELER *Journ. Greece* v. 364 They have built a Minoret, or tall, slender Steeple; out of which they make a Noise, to call People together, at their set times of Prayer. 1695 MOTTEUX *Saint-Olon's Morocco* 72 Two Mosques, whose Minarets are of a considerable height. 1728 MORGAN *Algiers* I. iv. 157 This Khalifa was the first who erected Minarets in the Mosques. 1760 *Ann. Reg.* 87 All the minerets..were thrown down. 1812 BYRON *Ch. Har.* II. xxxviii, The cross descends, thy minarets arise. 1839 LANE *Arab. Nts.* I. 18 The..menaret of each mosque. 1869 TOZER *Highl. Turkey* I. 51 The minarets and the castle which crowns the highest position produce a striking effect.

β. 1775 CHANDLER *Trav. Asia M.* (1825) I. 59 Amid these the tall minarees rise, and white houses glitter, dazzling the beholder. 1798 TWEDDELL in *Rem.* (1815) I. 235 One of the minarehs of St. Sophia. 1839 LANE *Arab. Nts.* I. 379 The muëddins on the menarehs had chanted the Selam of Friday.

b. *transf.* and *fig.*

1860 TYNDALL *Glac.* I. ii. 13 This beautiful minaret of ice. 1870 B. HARTE *Dickens in Camp* i, The dim Sierras, far beyond, uplifting Their minarets of snow.

c. *attrib.*, as ***minaret-top***, ***-tower***.

1856 KANE *Arct. Expl.* I. xviii. 224 A solitary column or minaret-tower. 1867 LADY HERBERT *Cradle L.* i. 37 The only call for prayer is from the minaret top.

minareted (ˈmɪnərɪtɪd), *a.* Also **minaretted.** [f. MINARET + -ED[2].] Possessing, furnished with, or characterized by minarets.

1844 LD. HOUGHTON *Palm Leaves* 138 In the minaretted distance gleamed Purple and faint-green relics of the day. 1893 W. S. BURRELL & EDITH E. CUTHELL *Ind. Mem.* 37 The family mosque, a tiny minareted building.

minargent (mɪˈnɑːdʒənt). [f. (ALU)MIN(IUM + ARGENT.] A kind of aluminium-bronze.

1875 in KNIGHT *Dict. Mech.* s.v. 1889 BRANNT *Krupp & Wildberger's Metallic Alloys* 322 Minargent. This alloy, which has a very beautiful white color, is composed of copper 1000 parts, nickel 700, tungsten 50, aluminium 10.

minasragrite (mɪnəsˈrɑːgraɪt). *Min.* [f. *Minasragra*, name of its locality near Cerro de Pasco, Peru + -ITE[1].] An acidic hydrated vanadyl sulphate, $(VO)_2H_2(SO_4)_3 \cdot 15H_2O$, found as a blue efflorescence of monoclinic crystals on patronite.

1915 W. T. SCHALLER in *Jrnl. Washington Acad. Sci.* V. 7 The following very brief notes of four new minerals are given in order to secure priority... Minasragrite is a blue hydrous vanadium sulphate from Minasraga Peru. 1934 *Amer. Mineralogist* XIX. 198 Specimens of patronite in the Harvard mineral collection..showed in places a vivid blue incrustation which proved to be minasragrite. 1968 I. KOSTOV *Mineral.* II. ix. 517 Minasragrite, found with patronite from the well known vanadium deposit of Minasragra..in Peru, is monoclinic.

minas(s)e, obs. Sc. forms of MENACE *v.*

minati, obs. form of MANATEE.

minatorial (mɪnəˈtɒrɪəl), *a.* [f. MINATORY + -AL[1].] Minatory, threatening.

1885 in *Cassell's Encycl. Dict.*; and in later Dicts.

Hence **minaˈtorially** *adv.* = MINATORILY.

1847 in WEBSTER; and in later Dicts.

minatorily (ˈmɪnətərɪlɪ), *adv.* [f. MINATORY + -LY[2].] In a minatory or threatening manner.

a 1670 HACKET *Abp. Williams* I. (1693) 103 His other Works being prohibited so strictly and minatorily, that Bishops might not read them.

minatory (ˈmɪnətərɪ), *a.* and *sb.* Also 6 **minotary, mynatory,** 6–7 **minatorie.** [ad. OF. *minatoire*, ad. late L. *minātōrius*, f. *minārī* to threaten.]

A. *adj.* Expressing, uttering, or conveying a threat; also, of the nature of a threat or menace; threatening, menacing.

1532 MORE *Confut. Tindale* Wks. 612/1 Those wordes be mynatory and threttes. 1543 GRAFTON *Contn. Harding* 522 Kyng Rychard..reiected the dukes request with many spitefull and minotary woordes. 1577 STANYHURST *Descr. Irel.* in *Holinshed* (1808) VI. 29 With rough and minatorie speeches [he] began to menace them. 1644 BULWER *Chirol.* 59 This minatory Agitation of the Hand. 1851 CARLYLE *Sterling* I. xiii, Considerable clouds of Invasion..hung minatory over the North and North-East of Spain. 1898 BODLEY *France* II. IV. vii. 425 A doctrine minatory to the army of France.

†**B.** *sb.* A threat, a menace. *Obs. rare.*

1572 BURLEIGH in Digges *Compl. Ambass.* (1655) 334 With some sweet minatories, he intrated that he might be staied. 1686 EVELYN *Diary* 22 Sept., The Emperor sending his Minatories to the King of Denmark.

Hence **ˈminatoriness**, threateningness. *rare.*

1961 J. N. FINDLAY *Values & Intentions* viii. 344 Acknowledging a God capable of such universal minatoriness.

minature, obs. form of MINIATURE.

‖**minauderie** (minodri). [Fr., f. *minauder* to put on affected expressions, f. *mine* expression of face: see MIEN.] Coquettish airs.

1763 H. WALPOLE *Let. to Mann* 11 Aug., The Duchess.. is a heap of minauderies and affectations. 1823 SCOTT *Peveril* xl, [She] neglected nothing that effrontery and minauderie could perform to draw upon herself some portion of the King's observation. 1849 THACKERAY *Pendennis* xlvii, How much pleasanter than the minauderies of the young ladies in the ball-rooms.

‖**minaudière** (minodjɛr). [Fr. fem. adj., lit. affected, coquettish.] †**1.** An affected or coquettish woman. *Obs.*

1716 M. W. MONTAGU *Let.* 21 Nov. (1965) I. 282 The Saxon Ladys..are very genteely dress'd after the French and English modes,..but the most determin'd Minaudieres in the whole world. They would think it a mortal sin against good breeding if they either spoke or mov'd in a natural manner. 1818 LADY MORGAN *Fl. Macarthy* III. ii. 93 She struck me to be a mere *minaudiere*!

2. A small case for a woman's cosmetics, jewellery, etc.

1940 *Shopping News* (Springfield, Mass.) 15 May, Rectangular in shape, the minaudiere opens to disclose a good size mirror; there are also five lidded compartments —for powder, rouge, and eye shadow, money, keys, cigarette lighter and tortoise-shell comb. 1957 A. ADBURGHAM in *Punch* 18 Dec. 728/3 Parisian tailors have been trying..to persuade their [male] clients to forgo pockets altogether and carry a *minaudière*. 1967 *N.Y. Times* 22 June 43, I found that my regular minaudière was terribly small and I always had to stuff things in my pocket. 1969 *New Yorker* 8 Mar. 17 (Advt.), Rare shells..have been fashioned into exquisite minaudières for the hand.

minaul, variant of MONAUL.

†**minaway.** Chiefly *Sc. Obs.* Also 7 **minnaway,** 8 **minuwae,** 9 **minowaye, minua.** Phonetic adoption of F. *menuet*, MINUET *sb.*

?1695 *Ballad, Constant Coridon* ii, No Minnaway Dance, or Boree, Was ever so sweet a strain. 1787 BURNS *Let. to W. Nicol* 1 June, She..tipper-taipers when she taks the gate, first like a lady's gentlewoman in a minuwae. 1816 HOGG *Poetic Mirror* (1817) 202 The Otar dancit ane minowaye. 1821 [see MINCE *v.* 6 b]. 1826 GALT *Last of Lairds* xiv, Like a maid of honour dancing a minaway wi' the lord-chancellor.

mince (mɪns), *sb.* [f. MINCE *v.*]

1. Minced meat; mincemeat.

a 1850 ROSSETTI *Dante & Circ.* II. (1874) 274 Then let them hew me to such mince As a man's limbs may make. 1863 [see HASH *sb.*[1] 1]. 1869 MRS. STOWE *Old-town Folks* xxvii. (1870) 305 'We children' were employed in chopping mince for pies. 1899 O. SEAMAN *In Cap & Bells* (1900) 84 Those pies at which you annually wince, Hearing the tale how happy months will follow Proportioned to the total mass of mince You swallow.

2. An act of 'mincing' in speech or gesture.

Richardson 1837 has a quot. in which *mince* is a misprint for *minde*. The sense appears in many later Dicts., and though no authority is cited, it is so completely according to analogy that it might be used without producing any sense of novelty.

3. *Rhyming slang.* = MINCE-PIE 3. (Usu. in *pl.*)

1937 in PARTRIDGE *Dict. Slang* 522/1. **1958** F. NORMAN *Bang to Rights* 149 'I know what's on there' said the boggie looking Solie straight in the minces. **1960** *News Chron.* 16 Feb. 6/5 She gives me a double glinty butchers out of those sharp minces of hers. **1962** R. COOK *Crust on its Uppers* (1964) iii. 28 'One pack dealer's choice,' he says, minces all gleaming. *Ibid.* iv. 32 A general look of dislike in the minces, which tremble a bit in their sockets.

mince (mɪns), *v.* Forms: *α.* 4–6 **mynce**, 5–6 **mynse**, 5 **mence**, (7 **minze**), 6–7 **minse**, 6– **mince**; *β.* *dial.* 5 **mynsh**, 7 **minche**, 9 **minsh**, 6– **minch**. [Late ME. *mynce*, *mynsh*, ad. OF. *mincier*, *minchier* (mod.F. *mincer*), accentual variant of *menuisier*:—popular L. **minūtiāre*, f. L. *minūtia* (see MINUTIA), f. *minūtus* MINUTE *a.* Cf. It. *minuzzare* and (*am*)*mencire*.]

1. a. *trans.* To cut or chop (meat, etc.) small, or in little pieces. † Also, to cut up tobacco.

α. ?*c* **1390** *Form of Cury* (1780) 12 Mynce Oynouns and cast þer to Safronn and Salte. *c* **1420** *Liber Cocorum* (1862) 18 Above þese herbus a lytul larde Smalle myncyd. *c* **1430** *Two Cookery-bks.* 41 Þen mence Sawge. *c* **1460** J. RUSSELL *Bk. Nurture* 400 Mynse hem [*sc.* partridges, etc.] smalle in þe siruppe. **1555** W. WATREMAN *Fardle Facions* I. 48 Rawe fleshe very finely minced. **1611** MIDDLETON & DEKKER *Roaring Girle* II. i. C 3 Shee that minces Tobacco. **1693** J. DRYDEN in *Dryden's Juvenal* XIV. (1697) 353 The least Remains of which they mince, and dress It o'er again to make another Mess. **1726** SWIFT *Gulliver* II. i, [At dinner] The Wife minced a bit of Meat, then crumbled some bread on a Trencher, and placed it before me. *a* **1756** MRS. HAYWOOD *New Present* (1771) 159 Mince very fine the white of a chicken. **1863** MRS. GASKELL *Sylvia's L.* xxxiv, The sergeant asked for pepper and salt; minced the food fine and made it savoury. **1887** *Spon's Househ. Managem.* 284 Mince the flesh of a hen lobster to the size of small dice.

absol. **1875** JOWETT *Plato* (ed. 2) I. 230 And who has to kill and skin and mince and boil and roast? The cook, I said.

β. **1760–72** H. BROOKE *Fool of Qual.* (1792) I. 291 A small joint of meat,.. served us cold, hashed and minched, from one week to the other. **1821** [see 7]. **1880** JAMIESON, *To Minch, Minsh*, to cut into small pieces.

b. To chop up or grind small with a knife or mincing-machine and cook (meat, usually the remains of a joint, etc., left from a previous meal).

Mod. We will have the cold meat minced for dinner to-day.

c. *transf.* To cut (a person) in small pieces.

1602 SHAKS. *Ham.* II. ii. 537 She saw Pyrrhus make malicious sport In mincing with his Sword her Husbands limbes. **1607** —— *Timon* IV. iii. 122 Spare not the Babe.. Thinke it a Bastard.. And mince it sans remorse. **1648** GAGE *West Ind.* 200 Fearing that many would fall upon him cowardly and mince him small in pieces. **1742** POPE *Dunc.* IV. 120 Revive the Wits! But murder first, and mince them all to bits. **1819** SHELLEY *Cyclops* 359 He.. minces their flesh and gnaws their bone With his cursed teeth. **1896** FARMER & HENLEY *Slang*, *Mince* (medical students'), to dissect.

β. **1635** HEYWOOD *Hierarchie* II. 64 Thinking to minch me into parts and fleece Me of my right.

†**d.** To cut or slash. *Obs. rare.*

a **1560** BECON *Jewel of Joy* Wks. II. 19 b, Theyr dublets and hoses,.. for the most parte are so mynsed cutte and iagged, that [etc.]. **1582** STANYHURST *Æneis* II. (Arb.) 63 Lyk on a mountayn thee tree dry wythered oaken Sliest by the clowne Coridon rusticks with twibbil, or hatchet. Then the tre deepe minced, far chopt dooth terrifye swinckers.

†**e.** The alleged proper term for: To carve (a plover). *Obs.*

1486 *Bk. St. Albans* F vij b, A Plouer Mynsed. **1513** *Bk. Keruynge* in *Babees Bk.* 151 Wynge that quayle mynce that plouer thye that pegyon. **1661** RABISHA *Cookery Dissected* 253 Mince that Plover. **1840** H. AINSWORTH *Tower of London* xxxix, In the old terms of his art, he leached the brawn,.. minced the plovers, thighed the pigeons.

2. *transf.* and *fig.* To cut up, subdivide minutely. Also with *up*. †*to mince away*: to nullify by multiplied petty exceptions.

α. *a* *c* **1450** *St. Cuthbert* (Surtees) 6758 All northumberlande prouynce He thoght as croms of brede to mynce. **1581** MULCASTER *Positions* xxxix. (1887) 190 To mince his labour so, as ech one can haue but some litle. **1639** FULLER *Holy War* v. xxi. (1640) 264 We will not take notice of Germanie as it is minced into pettie Principalities. **1689** T. R. *View Govt. Europe* 62 The Jesuits there have.. minc'd away all the old remains of Morality and Conscience. *a* **1748** WATTS *Improv. Mind* II. vi. §2 (1801) 241, I have always thought it a mistake in the preacher to mince his text or his subject too small, by a great number of subdivisions. **1853** MARSDEN *Early Purit.* 244 Their [*sc.* the Puritans'] sermons were not studiously minced up in tiny fragments.

refl. **1643** SIR T. BROWNE *Relig. Med.* I. §8 Nor contented with a general breach or dichotomy with their Church do subdivide and mince themselves almost into Atoms.

β. **1637** RUTHERFORD *Lett.* 11 Mar., And let Christ have all your love, without minching or dividing it. **1712** M. HENRY *Life P. Henry* Wks. 1853 II. 647/1 In his expositions, he reduced the matter of the chapter.. read to some heads; not by a logical analysis, which often mincheth it too small.

†**3.** To diminish, take away from. *Obs.*

α. **1646** J. BENBRIGGE *Vsura Accom.* 20 He that minceth his estate, doth diminish the Magistrate's Right [= Taxes].

β. **1499** in *N. Riding Rec.* (1894) 178 Wherby the seid wode in mynshed and hurt. **1606** BIRNIE *Kirk-Buriall* (1833) 35 Lawlesse publicans, lyke Hophnees with elcrookes to minche and not Samueles, to mense the offerings of God.

4. a. To lessen or diminish in representation; to make little of, minimize; to disparage; to palliate, extenuate (faults). Now *rare*.

a **1591** H. SMITH *Serm.* (1637) 395 Wee mince our sins as though they needed no forgivenesse. **1609** W. M. *Man in Moone* (Percy Soc.) 46 To mince and extenuate any laudable part in her, but to display and augment whatsoever deformity you know by her. **1638** FORD *Lady's Trial* I. iii, Be gone Futelli, doe not mince one syllable Of what you heare. *a* **1676** HALE *Prim. Orig. Man.* II. vii. 186 The Author of the Dissertation.. seems to mince the Universality of the Flood. **1685** DRYDEN *Sylvæ* Pref. a 3 b, If to mince his meaning,.. I had.. omitted some part of what he [*sc.* Lucretius] said,.. I certainly had wrong'd him. **1727** SWIFT *Gulliver, Let. fr. Capt. G. to Sympson* 14 You have either omitted some material circumstances, or minced or changed them in such a manner that I do hardly know mine own work. **1736** AINSWORTH *Lat. Dict.*, To mince or pass a thing slightly over. **1839** BAILEY *Festus* v. (1848) 41 Ye see I do not mince the truth for ye.

†**b.** *absol. Obs.*

1615 JACKSON *Creed* IV. II. vi. §5 Abraham.. was then rejustified not by works though not without faith, as Bellarmine minceth, but by faith without works, as the Apostle strongly and peremptorily infers. **1621** *1st Bk. Discipl. Ch. Scot.* Pref. (1641) A 3, Some of the Disciples.. at first did mince, and sparingly speake, but afterward practise and loudly preach; that [etc.]. **1681** GLANVILL *Sadducismus* II. (1726) 455 Who confidently and without mincing, denied that there was any such Being.

c. *to mince the matter*: in early use, to extenuate or make light of the particular matter in question. Now only in negative contexts, to moderate one's language in condemnation, to express oneself politely or delicately. So *to mince matters*.

a **1535** [see MINCING *vbl. sb.* 2]. **1604** SHAKS. *Oth.* II. iii. 247 Iago, Thy honestie and love doth mince this matter, Making it light to Cassio. **1649** BP. HALL *Cases Consc.* (1650) 160 Some Doctors.. would either excuse, or mince the matter. **1668** OWEN *Nat. & Power Indw. Sin* Wks. 1851 VI. 315 Here it [*sc.* the law] minceth not the matter with Sinners. **1679** J. GOODMAN *Penit. Pard.* III. v. (1713) 335 A learned Jew endeavours to mince the matter, and to turn the story into an allegory. **1741** RICHARDSON *Pamela* II. 82 Well, Tom, said he, don't mince the matter. Tell me, before Mrs. Andrews, what they said. **1778** MME. D'ARBLAY *Diary* 26 Aug., His determination not to mince the matter, when he thought reproof at all deserved. **1840** CARLYLE *Heroes* ii. (1858) 239 A candid ferocity, if the case call for it, is in him; he does not mince matters! **1857** W. COLLINS *Dead Secret* II. ii. (1861) 49 A man's speculative view depends—not to mince the matter—on the state of his secretions. **1891** MRS. OLIPHANT *Jerus.* IV. iii. 483 Language of condemnation.. made when men did not mince matters.

d. †To report (expressions) euphemistically (*obs.*); to moderate (one's language), restrain (one's words) within the bounds of politeness or decorum. Also *to mince it*. *to mince an oath*: to substitute some euphemistic perversion for it (also used in sense 5).

1599 SHAKS. *Hen. V*, v. ii. 130, I know no wayes to mince it in loue, but directly to say, I loue you. **1606** —— *Ant. & Cl.* I. ii. 109 *Ant.* Speake to me home, Mince not the general tongue, name Cleopatra as she is call'd in Rome. **1720** SWIFT *Let. Advice Yng. Poet* Misc. (1722) 107 My young Master, who at first but minc'd an Oath, is taught there to mouth it gracefully, and to swear, as he reads French, *Ore rotundo*. **1754** RICHARDSON *Grandison* III. vii. 112 Shall I give it you in plain English? You don't use to mince it. **1826** DISRAELI *Viv. Grey* II. ii, I will not mince my words. **1897** S. S. SPRIGGE *Life T. Wakley* xxxii. 294 These were hard sayings, but men did not mince their words in those days.

5. a. *trans.* To utter in an affectedly refined manner; to pronounce with affected elegance, 'clip' (one's words). Also with *out*. **b.** *absol.* or *intr.* To speak with affected elegance or delicacy of pronunciation.

1549 COVERDALE, etc. *Erasm. Par. Thess.* 3 We came not unto you with bragging,.. nor curiously mincing a sorte of great wordes. **1807** CRABBE *Par. Reg.* II. Wks. 1834 II. 179 Low spake the lass, and lisp'd and minced the while. **1862** MRS. H. WOOD *Channings* II. v. 75 'You—are—very—kind—to—take—up—Arthur Channing's cause!' they mince out. **1874** L. STEPHEN *Hours in Library* (1892) I. x. 347 [The] fine gentleman who minced his mother tongue. **1888** MRS. H. WARD *R. Elsmere* III. xliii. 255 'Ah—"Reculer pour mieux *faire* sauter!"'—said Sir John, mincing out his pun as though he loved it.

6. a. *intr.* To walk with short steps or with affected preciseness or nicety; to walk in an affected manner; to show affectation or affected delicacy in manner of gait. Also *to mince it*.

1562 *Jack Juggler* (Roxb. Club) 9 She minceth, she brideleth, she swimmeth to and fro. **1567** DRANT *Horace, Ep.* I. xiv. E v, Thou hast no trippinge trull to mince it with the now That thou mighst foote it vnto her as nimble as a cow. **1593** DRAYTON *Ecl.* vii. 13 Now Shepheards.. in neate Jackets minsen on the Playnes. **1598** SHAKS. *Merry W.* v. i. 9 *Fall.* Away I say, time weares, hold vp your head & mince. **1611** BIBLE *Isa.* iii. 16 The daughters of Zion are hautie, and walke with stretched forth necks, and wanton eyes, walking and mincing [*marg.*, tripping nicely] as they goe, and making a tinkeling with their feet. **1616** R. C. *Times' Whistle* etc. (1871) 133 Then gan she trip it proudlie one the toe, And mince it finely vpon London streetes. *a* **1639** W. WHATELEY *Prototypes* I. xix. (1640) 240 Mincing with ones feete, or any other affected kind of going, is an act of haughtinesse. **1736** AINSWORTH *Lat. Dict.*, To mince it in walking. **1753** FOOTE *Eng. in Paris* I. Wks. 1799 I. 36 The men are all puppies, mincing and dancing, and chattering. **1826** *Blackw. Mag.* XX. 484 She.. minced, and primmed, and tossed her head. **1868** MISS ALCOTT *Lit. Women* xix, It was a comical sight to see her mince along. **1892** STEVENSON & L. OSBOURNE *Wrecker* ii. 28 My aunt might mince and my cousins bridle, but there was no getting over the solid physical fact of the stone-mason in the chimney-corner.

b. *trans.* To perform or enact mincingly.

1603 DEKKER *Batchelar's Banq.* xi, Fine Dames and dainetye Girles.. whoe can finely mince their measures. **1605** SHAKS. *Lear* IV. vi. 122 Behold yond simpring Dame,.. that minces Vertue & do's shake the head to heare of pleasures name. **1648** J. BEAUMONT *Psyche* III. clxxxii, To the ground Three times she bows, and with a modest grace Minces here spruce retreat. **1821** in A. Lowson *J. Guidfollow* (1890) 233 [The witch] Could mince a minua on mist, Or caper on a cloud!

7. *Comb.* The verb-stem used *attrib.* **a.** with object-noun, as in †**mince-speech**, one who 'minces' his language; **b.** in the sense of 'minced', as in †***mince-collop***, MINCEMEAT, MINCE-PIE.

α. **1621** BRATHWAITE *Nat. Embassie*, etc. (1877) 278 Mins-speech, nuff-pace sleeke-skin, and perfum'd breath.

β. **1821** GALT *Ayrsh. Leg.* xxv. (1895) 223 A steam-engine that minches minch-collops as natural as life.

†**'minceative**, *a.* and *sb. Obs.* In 7 **mynsative**, **minsitive**. [f. MINCE *v.* + -ATIVE.]

A. *adj.* ? Mincing, affected. **B.** *sb.* ? One given to mincing.

1601 B. JONSON *Poetaster* IV. i, Neuer say, your Lordship, nor your Honour; but, you, and you my Lord, and my Ladie: the other they count too simple and minsitiue. **1606** *Sir G. Goosecappe* I. ii. B ij b, Tis the mind of man,.. to affect new fashions; but to our Mynsatiues for sooth, if he come like to your *Besognio*, or your bore, so he bee rich or emphaticall, they care not.

minced (mɪnst), *ppl. a.* [f. MINCE *v.* + -ED[1].]

1. Of meat, etc.: Cut up or chopped into very small pieces. ***minced collops***: see COLLOP[1] 2 c. See also MINCED MEAT, MINCED-PIE.

c **1420** *Liber Cocorum* (1862) 17 Frye smalle mynsud onyone In oyle. *c* **1430** *Two Cookery-bks.* 15 Also mencyd Dates, Clowes, Maces [etc.]. *c* **1450** *Ibid.* 110 Take vynegre and poudre gingere, salt, and cast a-pon þe mynced shulder [of mutton]. ? *a* **1584** *Tom Thumbe* 100 in Hazl. *E.P.P.* II. 181 His mother.. Into a pudding thrust her sonne instead of minced fat. **1821** LAMB *Elia* Ser. I. *Grace before meat*, One who professes to like minced veal. **1893** *Mrs. Beeton's Cookery Bk.* 111/1 Minced Fowl—an Entrée (Cold Poultry Cookery).

b. *fig.* (See MINCE *v.* 2.)

1581 MULCASTER *Positions* viii. (1887) 53 Writers make to many, and to finely minced distinctions. **1606** SHAKS. *Tr. & Cr.* I. ii. 279 Is not birth, beauty,.. and so forth: the Spice and salt that seasons a man? *Cres.* I, a minc'd man and then to be bak'd with no Date in the pye, for then the mans' dates out.

2. Uttered or performed in a mincing or affected manner. ? *Obs.*

1545 BRINKLOW *Compl.* i. 8 The mombled and mynsed Masse (wherby neither God is glorifyed, nor the hearers edifyed). **1553** BECON *Reliques of Rome* (1563) 117 The minsed musike that now beareth chief rule in Churches.

†**3.** Diminished; deprived of some essential part, mutilated. *Obs.*

1609 J. RAWLINSON *Fishermen Fishers of Men* 34 A minced and curtall mainteinance. **1695** SAGE *Fund. Charter Presb.* (1697) 216 Giving us only a Minced account of this Petition. **1707** *Vulpone* 15 [Of the Scotch Representation at the Union.] To agree to such a minced Representative, and give away the Birth-rights of their Lords, Barons and Boroughs.

b. Of an oath: see MINCE *v.* 4 d.

1880 BREWER *Reader's Handbk.* (1885) 606 Mr. Mantalini.. is.. noted for.. his minced oaths [etc.].

minced meat.

1. a. Meat cut or chopped up very small.

1578 LYTE *Dodoens* I. ciii. 146 Chopte or minsed meate. **1585** T. WASHINGTON tr. *Nicholay's Voy* III. xi. 90 b, Pies of minced meate, and rice. **1626** BACON *Sylva* §46 With a good strong Chopping-knife, mince the two Capons.. as small as ordinary Minced Meat. **1839** LANE *Arab. Nts.* I. 123 Stuffed with rice and minced meat.

b. = MINCEMEAT 1 b. Also *attrib. rare* or *Obs.*

1762 GELLEROY *Lond. Cook* 236 Mix your minced meat and sweetmeats accordingly. **1824** MISS MITFORD *Village* Ser. I. 235 The apple-room, the pear-bin, the cheese-loft, the minced-meat closet were household words. **1885** in *Cassell's Encycl. Dict.*

2. *fig.* Any thing cut up very small; *esp.* in phrases: see MINCEMEAT 2.

1649 G. DANIEL *Trinarch., Hen. IV*, xxxiv, Neighbour Kings.. Hee Courts by his Ambassadors; and fitts with a new minc't-meat, seueral appetites. **1668** DRYDEN *Evening's Love* IV. ii, The sun and moon, and those little minced-meats of them. **1772** NUGENT *Hist. Fr. Gerund* II. 208 So as to displume him,.. so, in short, as to make minced-meat of him. **1898** A. BALFOUR *By Stroke of Sword* xxi. Father Miguel.. was straightway resolved into minced meat.

†**'mincedness.** *Obs. rare*[−1]. [f. MINCED *ppl. a.* + -NESS.] Affected delicacy.

1583 STUBBES *Anat. Abus.* I. (1879) 78 Their coynesse in gestures, their minsednes in woords and speaches.

minced-pie.

1. = MINCE-PIE 1. Now only *U.S.*

α. *a* **1607** R. JOHNSON *Pleas. Conceites Old Hobson* (Percy Soc.) 9 Cramming their bellies with minced pyes. **1655** MOUFET & BENNET *Health's Improv.* (1746) 297 Dates are usually put into.. minced pies. **1748** MRS. HARRISON *House-Kpr.'s Pocket-Bk.* ii. (ed. 4) 6 Christmas or Minced Pyes, are generally brought in with the first Course. **1753** *Scots Mag.* Oct. 491/1 The fore corner of my hat was considerably elevated and shortened, so that it resembled.. the corner of a minced pye. **1762** GELLEROY *Lond. Cook* 237 Minced Pies

with Eel, or Oysters. **1872** SCHELE DE VERE *Americanisms* 506 Minced-pies represent in America the English Christmas-pies.

β. **1609** DEKKER *Worke for Armorours* Wks. (Grosart) IV. 117 And vpon Christmas day (in stead of minched pyes) had no better cheere then prouant.

2. = MINCE-PIE 2.

1739 GRAY *Let. to West* 22 May, Sugar-loaves and minced-pies of yew.

ˈmincemeat. [Altered from MINCED MEAT: see MINCE *v.* 7 b.]

1. †**a.** = MINCED MEAT 1 a. *Obs.*

1747 MRS. GLASSE *Cookery* iv. 60 Then lay in your Dish a layer of Mince-meat.

fig. **1742** POPE *Dunc.* IV. 228 *note*, Stobæus, .. an author, who gave his Common-place book to the public, where we happen to find much Mince-meat of old books.

b. A mixture made of currants, raisins, sugar, suet, apples, almonds, candied peel, etc., and sometimes meat chopped small; used in mince-pies.

1845 ELIZA ACTON *Mod. Cookery* 358 Mince Pies. Butter some tin pattypans well, and line them evenly with fine puff paste rolled thin; fill them with mincemeat [etc.]. **1886** G. R. SIMS *Ring o' Bells*, etc. IV. ii. 129 My wife makes her own mincemeat and her own plum-puddings.

2. *to make mincemeat of* (a person), and similar phrases: To cut or chop him into very small pieces; to destroy, to annihilate. Also, to beat decisively or easily in a contest.

a. **1663** COWLEY *Cutter Colman St.* II. iv, I'll hew thee into so many Morsels, that [etc.]... Thou shalt be Mince-meat, Worm, within this Hour. **1708** MRS. CENTLIVRE *Busy Body* II. iii, If I should find a man in the house I'd make mince-meat of him. **1853** LD. STRANGFORD in *Croker Papers* (1884) III. xxviii. 296 They blame you for letting Johnny Russell off so easily [in a review], when you might have made mincemeat of him. **1876** *Coursing Calendar* 193 Maniac made mincemeat of Smoker, who was so stiff that he could scarcely raise a gallop. **1902** L. STEPHEN *Stud. Biog.* IV. ii. 76 Macaulay .. makes mincemeat of Southey's .. expositions of political economy. **1955** *Times* 20 June 13/4 Thames R.C. made mincemeat of all their opponents in the Grand Eights.

β. *a* **1774** D. GRAHAM *Writings* (1883) I. 136 Which made him minch-meat for the grave.

Hence **ˈmincemeat** *v. trans.*, to cut to pieces.

1879 ATCHERLEY *Boërland* 202 Concluding that I was about to be mincemeated by a Basuto impi. **1897** GUNTER *Susan Turnb.* ii. 15 Bring him up here, or .. I'll mincemeat you!

mincemeaty, *a.* [f. MINCEMEAT + -Y[1].] Suggestive of mincemeat.

1870 P. BROOKS in A. V. G. Allen *Phillips Brooks* (1908) 246 Huxley's new *Lay Sermons* .. is like .. most books for the people that popularize science. It is patronizing and mincemeaty.

mince-ˈpie. [Alteration of MINCED-PIE: see MINCE *v.* 7 b.]

1. A pie containing mincemeat (see MINCEMEAT 1 b).

Usually, one of the small pies (now commonly round, but cf. quots. 1807 below and 1753 s.v. MINCED-PIE) which form a prominent part of English Christmas fare.

a. **1600** [see 3]. **1661-2** PEPYS *Diary* 6 Jan., We had, besides a good chine of beef and other good cheer, eighteen mince pies in a dish, the number of the years that he hath been married. **1673** SHADWELL *Epsom Wells* IV. Wks. 1720 II. 247 For currants to make mince-pyes with. **1711-12** SWIFT *Jrnl. to Stella* 2 Jan., I see nothing here like Christmas, except brawn and mince-pies in places where I dine. **1747** MRS. GLASSE *Cookery* 116 Lent Mince Pies. **1807** SOUTHEY *Espriella's Lett.* III. 384 Old bridges dangerously narrow, and angles in them like the corners of an English mince-pie, for the foot-passengers to take shelter in. *a* **1825** PARR in Chambers *Bk. Days* (1864) II. 755/2 Please to say Christmas-pie, not mince-pie; mince-pie is puritanical. **1867** TROLLOPE *Chron. Barset* I. xix. 167 There was roast pork and mince-pies, and a bottle of wine.

β. **1846** M. A. RICHARDSON *Local Histor. Table-bk.* VIII. 377 'Tis I that's to .. send thee to Satan to make minch Pies. **1889** *N.W. Linc. Gloss.*, *Minch-pie*, a mince-pie. It is said that *mince-pies* and *minch-pies* are not quite the same. *Minch-pies*, we are told, have meat in their composition; *mince-pies* have not.

2. *transf.* A yew-tree or other shrub cut or trimmed to the shape of a mince-pie.

1756 MRS. DELANY in *Life & Corr.* (1861) III. 435 The gardens laid out in the old-fashioned way of mince-pies, arbours, and sugarloaf yews.

3. *Rhyming slang.* An eye. (Usu. in *pl.*)

1857 'DUCANGE ANGLICUS' *Vulgar Tongue* 13 *Mince pies*, eyes. **1892** *Sporting Times* 29 Oct. 1/2 And I smiled as I closed my two mince-pies. **1893** CROOK & DALY *Jerusalem's Dead (song)* 5 My mince-pies are waterin' jes like a pump. **1906** E. DYSON *Fact'ry 'Ands* xvii. 229 He thinks he'll never be able t' shut his mince pies again. **1922** JOYCE *Ulysses* 418 Got a prime pair of mincepies, no kid. **1928** M. C. SHARPE *Chicago May* xxxi. 288/1 Mince pies, eyes.

4. *attrib.* and *Comb.*

1600 ROWLANDS *Lett. Humours Blood* ii. 8 Or Mincepie-like Ile mangle out the slaue. **1906** *Month* Jan. 35 Pitt's 'mince-pie' Administrations, as they were sarcastically called.

mincer (ˈmɪnsə(r)). [f. MINCE *v.* + -ER[1].]

1. A person who minces or chops small.

1611 MIDDLETON & DEKKER *Roaring Girl* II. i. C 3 b, *Green.* Troth, this [tobacco] is finely shred. *Lax.* Oh women are the best mincers. **1850** SCORESBY *Cheever's Whalem. Adv.* v. (1859) 67 The mincer with a two-handed knife slashes it nearly through into thin slices.

b. A mincing-machine.

1885 *Pall Mall G.* 31 Mar. 3/2 How many mincers are in use at workhouses which [etc.]. **1904** *Daily News* 19 May 9 In the East-end .. there is a large trade in converting horse flesh by means of the mincer. One thing is certain—these are not sold as horse flesh sausages.

†**2.** One who diminishes or disparages. *Obs.*

Tennyson's use (quot. 1847) is fig. of 1, but prob. echoes some example of the sb. in this sense or of MINCE *v.* 4.

1619 PURCHAS *Microcosmus* lxxiv. 737 She accounted his Fame a Mincer, and .. a Halfe-reporter of his Prosperitie and Wisedome. [**1847** TENNYSON *Princess* IV. 494 Mincers of each other's fame.]

3. One who minces words; one who speaks mincingly or in an affected manner.

1587 FLEMING *Contn. Holinshed* III. 1284/2 Nicholas Stanleie, whome Leland the minser and refiner of all English names dooth most curiouslie in Latine call *Nicholaum Stenelegium*. **1867** A. J. ELLIS *E.E. Pronunc.* I. iii. §4. 194 The mincer, so far from dropping the front of the tongue from the palate, raises the middle part and produces (lj) which degenerates into (i), as in Modern French.

‖**Mincha** (ˈmɪnxɑː). Also **Minchah, Minha(h.** [Heb. *minḥāh*, lit. gift, offering.] (See quot. 1962.)

[**1706** I. ABENDANA *Discourses Polity of Jews* iv. 118 The Captives of Babylon .. sent Money to their Brethren at Jerusalem, wherewithal they might buy them Burnt-Offerings .. and prepare them Manna, (for so 'tis read corruptly for Mincha a Meat-Offering).] **1819** L. ALEXANDER *Hebrew Ritual* 25 Afternoon prayers, .. Tephillath Minchah... The Hebrew word .. *Minchah* .. signifies a gift as offering; but is generally used by Jewish ritualists for the evening. *Ibid.* 68 About two o'clock in the Afternoon they go to the Synagogue to *Mincha*, which is the Afternoon Service. **1892** I. ZANGWILL *Childr. Ghetto* I. 169 Knowest thou what, Moses? .. we shall be too late for Minchah. **1957** L. STERN *Midas Touch* III. xx. 153 Israel pronounced the *Mincha* prayers and eighteen benedictions. **1962** *New Jewish Encycl.* 322/2 *Minḥah*, Hebrew term for the Jewish daily afternoon service. In Biblical times the term *Minḥah* was applied to the 'meal-offering', but it acquired its present meaning in the days of the *Misnah*. The *Minḥah* prayer is recited before sunset. **1973** *Synagogue Light* Sept. 48/2 In the early afternoon, during *Mincha* Service, the Confession is recited.

†**ˈminchen.** *Obs.* Forms: 1 mynecenu, -cænu, munecenu, 3 mun(e)chene, 4-5 mynchoun, 4-6 -yn, 5 -on, -eon, -un, -ine, 5-6 -ion, 5, 8-9 -en, 6-7 minchun, -eon, 6, 8 mynchin, 7 minching, 7-9 -in, -en, (9 mynekin); 4-5 meynchen(e, -yn; 4-5 menchon, -en, 5 -one, 7 -ion, mention; 4-5 monchyn, -on(e, -en, 5 -ioun. [OE. *mynecenu* (:—prehistoric **munikinī*) fem. of *munuc* MONK.] A nun.

The distinction suggested in quot. 1844 between 'minchens' and 'nuns' does not seem to have any foundation in the use of the words.

c **1000** ÆLFRIC *Gloss.* in Wr.-Wülcker 155/26 *Monacha*, *uel monialis*, mynecenu. *c* **1205** LAY. 28476 And heo wes .. munechene. *c* **1315** SHOREHAM 7 *Sacraments* 1780 Sudeakne mey be ywedded nauȝt, Monek, munechene, ne frere [*MS.* muneche, ne no frere]. **1387** TREVISA *Higden* (Rolls) VI. 403 Sche was i-made mynchoun [*v.r.* monchon, meynchyn]. **1395** *E.E. Wills* (1882) 6 My suster Thomase Blount, Menchoun of Romeseye. *c* **1420** *Chron. Vilod.* 3927 þere was a mynchun wᵗ-inne þat abbay þo, þe wheche was come off heyȝe lynage. *c* **1450** *St. Cuthbert* (Surtees) 7164 þar war, in diuers mansiouns Duelland, monkys and monchiouns. **1485** CAXTON *Paris & V.* (1868) 39, I would rather make you a noune or a menchon. **1495** *Will of Terbuck* (Somerset Ho.), Euery mynchion wᵗ in the same abbey. **1538** in *Lett. Suppress. Monasteries* (Camden) 228 Many of the mynchys [*read* mynchyns] be also agyd. *a* **1539** in *Archæologia* XLVII. 54 That euery nunne and mynchin of this house .. obserue ther deuyne seruice. **1603** STOWE *Surv.* 134 Pertayning to the Minchuns, or nuns of Saint Helens. **1611** SPEED *Hist. Gt. Brit.* VII. v. 215 Ermengith a mention. *Ibid.* xi. 256 Lady Nithgith .. was a Menchion. **1658** PHILLIPS, *Minchings*, an ancient word for those consecrated, whom we call Nuns. **1844** LINGARD *Anglo-Sax. Ch.* (1858) I. v. 198 *note* 1 The mynekins were so called from the Saxon 'munuc', because they observed the rule of the monks, while the nuns observed the rule of the canons.

transf. **1531** ELYOT *Gov.* III. xviii, A Mynchen in the temple of Diana.

b. *attrib.*, as *minchen clothing*; also in the names of places, as *Minchen lane*, *-meadow*, *-wood*.

1387 TREVISA *Higden* (Rolls) VI. 473 þis Wilfritha was nouȝt verrayliche a mynchoun .. but for drede of kyng Edgar .. sche took mynchene cloþynge. **1598** STOW *Surv.* 97 A thirde lane out of Tower-streete, on the North side, is called Mincheon or Minion lane. **1640** SOMNER *Antiq. Canterb.* 69 The which Wood retaines to this day the name of Minchen-Wood. *a* **1691** AUBREY *Nat. Hist. Wilts* (1847) 49 About Priory St. Maries, and in the Minchin-meadowes there, .. there is infinite variety of plants.

minchery (ˈmɪntʃərɪ). *Hist.* Forms: 7 mincherie, minchionrea, 8 minshery, 9 mynchery, 8- minchery. [f. MINCHEN + -RY.

First recorded as the proper name of the conventual building at Littlemore near Oxford, and thence adopted in general application by archaizing writers.]

1661 WOOD *Life* (O.H.S.) I. 403 An antient house called *Mincherie*, or *Minchionrea*, that is 'the place of nunns', founded there of old time. **1710** HEARNE *Collect.* (O.H.S.) III. 84 A great many .. Bones of Men, etc., found at the Minshery by Littlemore. **1841** F. E. PAGET *Tales of Village* (1852) 225 Upon condition that a mynchery (as the Saxon nunneries were called) should be forthwith erected. **1893** W. D. MACRAY *Catal. Bodl. MSS.* V. III. 474 The view of Littlemore Minchery is given in three states.

‖**minchiate** (minˈkjate). [It., sb. pl.; in Florio (1611) *menchiatte*.] A card game chiefly played in Tuscany, a modification of tarot. Also, as *plural* (the original use), the cards used in the game.

1768 BARETTI *Acc. Manners & Cust. Italy* II. 219 The games I mean, are those which we form out of those cards called *Minchiate* and *Tarrocco's*. *Ibid.*, Both the minchiate and the tarrocco's consist of five suits instead of four, as common cards do. **1803** R. SMITH in *Archæologia* XV. 140 There is no game on the cards, .. that requires closer attention .. than this of Minchiate. *Ibid.*, A complete set of Minchiate cards, such as have been long in use at Florence. *Ibid.* 141 A Minchiate pack consists of ninety-seven cards, of which fifty-six are called *Cartiglia*, forty *Tarocchi*, and one *Matto*. **1905** *Athenæum* 18 Nov. 684/1 For those with a taste for long-drawn out pleasures, tarot and minchiate—for others, basset, trappola, [etc.]—succeeded each other as fashionable games.

minchun, variant of MINCHEN *Obs.*

mincing (ˈmɪnsɪŋ), *vbl. sb.* [f. MINCE *v.* + -ING[1].]

1. The action of chopping or cutting up into very small pieces; †*concr.* a small shred or piece (of meat, etc.).

1598 FLORIO, *Sminuzzoli*, mincings, mammocks, shreds or small peeces. **1626** BACON *Sylva* §54 Mincing of meat, as in Pies, .. saueth the Grinding of the Teeth. **1638** RAWLEY tr. *Bacon's Life & Death* (1650) 47 Gravies of Meat, and the Mincings of them small well-seasoned. **1899** *Allbutt's Syst. Med.* VIII. 797 Scarification consists in a mincing of the lupus tissue by the knife.

2. The action of extenuating, minimizing, palliating, or glossing over a matter; the suppression of part of a fact or statement.

a. **1533** MORE *Debell. Salem* Wks. 964/2 The myncynge of suche matters. *a* **1591** H. SMITH *Wks.* (1866-7) I. 449 A spiritual ear can hear God reproving this land for this mincing of his worship. **1701** NORRIS *Ideal World* I. ii. 131 What means this mincing and this disguising of a plain and unavoidable truth? **1866** FELTON *Anc. & Mod. Gr.* I. 100 If they [Homer's characters] get angry, out it comes, .. with no mincing of phrase.

β. **1604** T. WRIGHT *Passions* (1620) 290 It is admirable how the minching and particularizing of the object of delight increaseth and augmenteth delight.

3. The action or habit of speaking or acting in an affectedly nice or elegant manner.

1613 SHAKS. *Hen. VIII*, II. iii. 31 Which guifts (Sauing your mincing) the capacity Of your soft Chiuerell Conscience, would receiue. **1828** SCOTT *F.M. Perth* xii, Such shalt thou be, for all thy mincing and ambling [etc.].

4. *attrib.* and *Comb.*, as **mincing-horse**, a wooden horse or stand on which whale-blubber is minced or chopped; **mincing-knife**, a knife used in mincing meat, etc.; also in whaling, for cutting up blubber into small pieces; **mincing-machine**, a machine for mincing meat, etc.; also for cutting up blubber; **mincing-spade**, a spade used for cutting up blubber.

1586 *Wills & Inv. N.C.* (Surtees) II. 149, ij minsinge knives. **1634** in *Anc. Invent.* (Halliw. 1854) 18, 3 beefe forks, 2 mincinge knyves, 1 cleaver [etc.]. **1874** C. M. SCAMMON *Marine Mammals* 238 The blubber is transported in strap-tubs to the mincing-horse, where the ordinary two-handled knife is used. **1875** KNIGHT *Dict. Mech.*, *Mincing-machine*, .. a sausage-machine. **1884** *Ibid.* Suppl., *Mincing-knife* (Whaling). *Ibid.*, *Mincing machine*, a machine with knives on a roller, used in cutting blubber small for trying. *Ibid.*, *Mincing spade.* **1885** *Pall Mall G.* 31 Mar. 3/2 The Eastbourne board of guardians have ordered a mincing machine to be supplied for the use of aged and toothless paupers in their workhouse.

mincing (ˈmɪnsɪŋ), *ppl. a.* [f. MINCE *v.* + -ING[2].]

1. That minimizes, extenuates, or diminishes.

1581 T. HOWELL *Deuises* (1879) 233 My symple meaning plaine, not carued with mincing stile. **1593** RAINOLDS *Overthrow Stage-pl.* (1599) 108 My speech was too minsing, when I named bawderie. If I had termed it most filthy beastly bawderie, my wordes had bene broder, though not brode enough yet. *a* **1640** J. BALL *Answ. to Canne* I. (1642) 127 Your minsing figure of extenuation. **1778** MRS. SCOTT in Doran *Lady of last Cent.* x. (1873) 242, I hate those mincing names, designed only to palliate wrong actions. **1827** SCOTT *Jrnl.* 10 Mar., The mincing English edition in which he has hitherto been alone known.

2. Of speech, gait, mien, etc.: Affectedly dainty or elegant.

1530 PALSGR. 830/2 A mynsynge pace, *le pas menu.* **1596** SHAKS. *Merch. V.* III. iv. 67 Ile .. turne two minsing steps Into a manly stride. *c* **1645** HOWELL *Lett.* (1650) II. 4 The fawning and soft glances of a mincing smile. **1727** POPE, etc. *Art of Sinking* 111 The Finical Style, which consists of the most curious, affected, mincing metaphors. **1776** MME. D'ARBLAY *Early Diary* 2 Dec., Her voice low, and delicate, and mincing. **1848** DICKENS *Dombey* i, Possibly her mincing gait encouraged the belief, and suggested that her clipping of a step of ordinary compass into two or three, originated in her habit of making the most of everything. **1861** GEO. ELIOT *Silas M.* iii, 'Oho', said Dunsey .. trying to speak in a small mincing treble. **1893** A. GRIFFITHS *Secrets Prison Ho.* II. IV. ii. 63 She walked with a mincing, self-satisfied air down the passage.

b. Of a person: Speaking, walking, or behaving, in an affectedly dainty or nice manner.

1560 INGELEND *Disob. Child* D j b, This myncing Trull. **1590** SPENSER *F.Q.* II. ii. 37 Fitt mate for such a mincing mineon. **1634** MILTON *Comus* 964 As Mercury did first devise With the mincing Dryades On the Lawns. **1700** DRYDEN *Fables* Pref. C 1 b, Distinguish'd from each other as

much as the mincing Lady Prioress and the broad-speaking gap-tooth'd Wife of Bathe. **1849** JAMES *Woodman* vii, I can be as delicate and mincing as a serving maid should need be. **1887** A. J. C. HARE *Story my Life* xxiv. (1900) VI. 94 [She] frightened a mincing curate out of his life.

c. In jingling reduplication. ? *nonce-use.*

1822 MOORE in *Mem.* (1853) IV. 7 The mincing-pincing style of talking among the French women.

Hence **'mincingness.**

1866 GEO. ELIOT *F. Holt* xix, That frigid mincingness called dignity.

Mincing Lane ('mɪnsɪŋ leɪn). Used *absol.* and *attrib.* with reference to an auction-room for tea and other commodities which was originally situated in the London street of this name.

1913 *Times* 13 Oct. (Finance & Commerce) 18/1 The Mincing-lane Tea and Rubber Share Brokers' Association (Limited). **1914** in *Conc. Oxf. Dict.* **1923** *Westm. Gaz.* 31 Jan., You must go to Mincing-lane for an excuse for the rise [in the price of tea]. **1959** *Chambers's Encycl.* XI. 235/2 Business in rubber, tea, coffee, cocoa, sugar, spices and condiments was carried on at the offices of Mincing Lane until the destruction of the Commercial Sale Room by bombing in 1941. *Ibid.* XIII. 490/2 Requirements [of tea] are mainly obtained by purchases in the Mincing Lane auctions. **1970** *E. Afr. Standard* (Nairobi) 23 Jan. 5/5 Mincing Lane is pretty confident of higher prices for Africans by the end of the first quarter of this year.

mincingly ('mɪnsɪŋlɪ), *adv.* Also 6 **mins-**, 7 **minz-**, **minchingly.** [f. MINCING *ppl. a.* + -LY[2].]

†**1.** In small pieces. *Obs.*

1598 FLORIO, *Sminutamente*, mincingly,..in small peeces.

2. †Sparingly, in grudging measure (*obs.*); in a minimizing or extenuating manner.

a. **1594** HOOKER *Eccl. Pol.* I. xi. §5 The iustice of one that requiteth nothing mincingly, but all with pressed and heaped and euen ouer-inlarged measure. **1699** F. BUGG *Quakerism Exposed* To Rdr. 1 Several do Certifie (tho' mincingly) that they have Publicly Charged him with Lies. **1736** AINSWORTH *Lat. Dict.*, Mincingly, or slightly, *leviter.* **1892** *Chicago Advance* 18 Feb., [Jeremiah] must speak the truth... And better to speak it plainly, than mincingly.

β. *a* **1624** BP. M. SMITH *Serm.* (1632) 256 It is written of Galba, that he gaue pinchingly and minchingly, as though he had not beene Emperour.

3. In a mincing or affectedly elegant manner.

1596 NASHE *Saffron-Walden* M 3, A turne or two hee mincingly pac't with her about the roome. **1598** FLORIO, *Mangiare a miccino*, to eate minsingly, a crum, a iot. **1657** J. SERGEANT *Schism Dispach't* 601 Though it seeme to speak coyly and mincingly. **1741** RICHARDSON *Pamela* (1824) I. xxix. 293 She trips up and down mincingly, and knows not how to set her feet. **1838** DICKENS *Nich. Nick.* xxxiv, He led her mincingly away. **1878** HESBA STRETTON *Needle's Eye* II. 146 She tossed her head higher, and stepped more mincingly than usual.

transf. **1824** *New Monthly Mag.* X. 133 Crow-quills that move mincingly between embossed margins. **1841** *Tait's Mag.* VIII. 69 A soul of large capacity will not sip mincingly.

mincks, obs. form of MINX.

mind (maɪnd), *sb.*[1] Forms: 1 **ȝemynd**, 2-3 **imunde**, 3 **ymunde**, 2-4 **munde**, 2-7 **minde**, 3-4 **muynde**, **muinde**, 4-5 **mende**, **meende**, (5 **myynde**), 4-7 **mynd(e**, 3- **mind.** [ME. *mynd*, repr. (the prefix *ȝe-* being lost as in all other sbs.) OE. *ȝemynd* fem. (also neut.) = OHG. *gimunt*, Goth. *gamund-s* memory:—OTeut. **gamunđi-z*, f. **ga-* prefix (see Y-) + **mun-* wk.-grade of the root **men-*, *man-*, *mun-* (:—Indogermanic **men-*, *mon-*, *mn-*) to think, remember, intend. A parallel formation with different ablaut-grade is OTeut. **gaminþjo*ᵐ neut., whence Goth. *gaminþi* memory, ON. *minni* neut. (Sw. *minne*, Da. *minde*) memory, memorial. Other derivatives of the root are OE. *munan*, *ȝemunan* to think, remember (= ON. *munu*, Goth. *gamunan*), *myne* thought (see MIN *sb.*[1]), *manian* to admonish. Outside Teut. the root (Skr. *man*) is represented by innumerable derivatives, e.g. Skr. *mati* thought (= L. *mens*:—OAryan *mn̥ti-*), *manas* mind (= Gr. *μένος* rage); Gr. *μέμονα* I yearn, L. *meminī* I remember, *monēre* to advise.]

I. Memory.

†**1.** The faculty of memory. *Obs.*

c **1000** ÆLFRIC *Hom.* (Th.) I. 288 Þurh þæt ȝemynd se man ȝeðencð þa ðing ðe he ȝehyrde, oþþe ȝeseah, oþþe ȝeleornode. **1340** HAMPOLE *Pr. Consc.* 774 His mynde es short when he oght thynkes. *c* **1386** CHAUCER *Man of Law's T.* 429 She seyde she was so mazed in the see That she forgat her mynde by hir trouthe. **1387** TREVISA *Higden* (Rolls) II. 191 He was so myȝty of mynde [L. *tanta memoria viguit*] þat he rehersed two þowsand names arewe by herte. *c* **1440** *Promp. Parv.* 332/1 Meendfulle, or of good meende, *memoriosus.*

2. The state of being remembered; remembrance, recollection. Chiefly in phrases, as †**a.** (*to be*) *in mind*, to be remembered, be kept in memory. So *to come in mind*, to occur to one's thoughts.

a **1000** *Boeth. Metr.* vii. 39 Þær se wisdom a wunað on ȝemyndum. **1297** R. GLOUC. (Rolls) 636 Ȝo wolde þat ire name were eueremo in munde. **1377** LANGL. *P. Pl.* B. XI. 49 Coueytyse-of-eyes cam ofter in mynde þan dowel or dobet amonge my dedes alle. **1390** GOWER *Conf.* II. 67 The whos knyhtnode is yit in mende, And schal be to the worldes ende. **1500-20** DUNBAR *Poems* lxiii. 28 Als lang in mynd my wark sall hald..As ony of thair werkis all.

b. *to have, bear, keep,* (†*hold*) *in mind*: to remember, retain in memory. Now only with mixture of sense 7: To keep before one, keep one's attention fixed upon. Also in Arithmetic, † *to keep in mind*: to 'carry'.

a **900** tr. *Bæda's Hist.* IV. xxiv. (ed. Miller) 344 Þa aras he from þæm slæpe, & eal þa þe he slæpende song fæste in ȝemynde hæfde [L. *memoriter retinuit*]. *c* **1200** *Trin. Coll. Hom.* 209 Listeð nu..and undernimeð hit on heorte and habbeð hit on minde. *c* **1290** *S. Eng. Leg.* I. 67/460 Aȝein kuynde huy sounguen þere, ase þei huy hadden in muynde hou muche he was anoured er of foules. *c* **1386** CHAUCER *Man of Law's T.* 1029 In the olde Romane geestes may men fynde Maurices lyf I bere it noght in mynde. **1387** TREVISA *Higden* (Rolls) VII. 415 He dede oon dede þat is worþy to be kepte in mynde [*v.r.* munde]. *c* **1425** *Cursor M.* 6095 (Trin.) In mynde shal ȝe holde þis day. **1431** *Rec. St. Mary at Hill* 27 Also haue in mende of ij chales. **1550** CROWLEY *Epigr.* 1228 The Lorde wyll haue all theyr iuell doynges in mynde. *c* **1586** C'TESS PEMBROKE *Ps.* cxv. v, Iehovah..us in mind doth beare. **1612** COLSON *Gen. Treas., Art Arithm.* G gg 4, Which maketh 17. pence, I write 7. in a place further towards the right hand, and keepe 1. in minde, then 2. times 9. is 18. and 1. in minde maketh 19. **1656** WILLSFORD *Arithm.* 33, 4 times 5 is 20, for which subscribe a cypher, and keep 2 decimalls in minde;..then say 4 times 3 is 12, and 2 in minde is 14. **1827** DISRAELI *Viv. Grey* VI. v, Bearing in mind the exact position..in which I stand. **1881** MRS. CRAIK *Sydney* I. vii. 154 Will you keep in mind that we have got to be better friends? **1895** SIR A. KEKEWICH in *Law Times Rep.* LXXIII. 662/2 Keeping that fact in mind.

†**c.** *to come, fall, run* (to a person) *to mind*: to occur to his recollection. *Obs.*

c **1374** CHAUCER *Troylus* II. 553 [602] And euery word [she] gan vp and doun to wynde, That he hadde seyd as it come here to mynde. *c* **1375** *Sc. Leg. Saints* xii. (*Mathias*) 219, & alsa rane hyme þane to mynd, þ at he, as a wykyt man & vnkynd, had slane hyr sone. *c* **1412** HOCCLEVE *De Reg. Princ.* 22 Me fel to mynde how that, not long ago [etc.]. **1433** LYDG. *St. Edmund* III. 61 in Horstm. *Altengl. Leg.* (1881) 415 But now to mynde kometh the champioun Off Estyngland..Callid seynt Edmund.

d. *to bring, call to mind*: to summon to remembrance, remember, set before one.

1433 LYDG. *St. Edmund* III. 381 in Horstm. *Altengl. Leg.* (1881) 420 The olde serpent..Brouht onto mynde his stat, his regalye Off tyme passid [etc.]. **1509** HAWES *Past. Pleas.* xvi. (Percy Soc.) 65 Be not to pensyfe; call to mynde agayne How of one sorowe ye do now make twayne. **1697** DRYDEN *Virg., Past.* IX. 76 These, and more than I to mind can bring. **1788** BURNS *Auld Lang Syne* i, Should auld acquaintance be forgot And never brought to mind? **1868** DICKENS *Uncomm. Trav.* xxi, Calling these things to mind as I stroll among the Banks.

e. *to be (go, pass) out of mind* (also † *of, from mind*): to be forgotten. So † *to set out of mind*, to forget, disregard. *Obs.* exc. in the proverb, 'Out of sight, out of mind', and 'time out of mind' (see f).

c **1381** CHAUCER *Parl. Foules* 69, & al schulde out of mynde That in this worlde is don of al mankynde. **1421** HOCCLEVE *Complaint* 80 Forgeten I was, all owte of mynde a-way. *a* **1425** *Cursor M.* 3196 (Trin.) Þi dede shal neuer of mynde go. *c* **1450** tr. *De Imitatione* I. xxiii. 30 Whan man is oute of siȝt, sone he passiþ oute of mynde. **1539** TAVERNER *Erasm. Prov.* (1552) 30 Oure Englyshe prouerbe..Oute of syght, oute of minde. ? *a* **1550** *Droichis Part Play* 89 in *Dunbar's Poems* (S.T.S.) 317 One thowsand ȝeir is past fra mynd, Sen I was generid of his kynd. **1704** M. HENRY *Friendly Visits* 16 Though they are out of sight they are not out of Mind.

f. *time out of mind*, used as adv. phr. = from time immemorial; occas. † *in, from time out of mind.* (†Also *rarely*, for an inconceivably long future time: cf. sense 7 c.) Formerly also *of, from, out of time that no mind is* (*of*); *before, without time of mind*; and simply *out of mind.* Similarly *sith, in, within time of mind, time within mind of man* = within the memory of man.

? **1386** *Rolls of Parlt.* III. 225/2 As out of mynde hath he used. **1414** *Ibid.* IV. 60/1 By old tyme, and sithe tyme of mynde. **1432** *Ibid.* 417/1 [The inhabitants of Lymington petition] That hough tyme oute of mynde..there were wont many diverse Shippes..to come..yn to the saide Havenes. **1455** *Ibid.* V. 337/1 Had, enjoyed and prescribed, fro the tyme that no mynde is. **1473-5** *Cal. Proc. Chanc. Q. Eliz.* (1830) II. Pref. 61 Unto the which maner the advoweson of the church..ys and withoute tyme of mynde hath be appendaunt. **1530** PALSGR. 591/1 This countray is nothyng so well inhabyted as it hath ben within tyme of mynde. **1544** tr. *Littleton's Tenures* (1574) 36 By tytle of prescription, that is to say, from time whereof is no mind. **1566** PAINTER *Pal. Pleas.* II. 307 My..sleepinge body, under toumbe, shall dreame time out of mynde. **1592** SHAKS. *Rom. & Jul.* I. iv. 69. **1623** T. SCOT *Highw. God* 12 To follow that faith which his forefathers professed time out of minde. **1700** DRYDEN *Sigismonda & Guisc.* 140 The Cavern-mouth alone was hard to find, Because the Path disus'd was out of mind. **1898** G. W. E. RUSSELL *Coll. & Recoll.* xxii. 292 A favourite theme of satirists time out of mind.

3. [? Developed from 2 c.] *to put* (a person) *in mind*: to remind. Const. *of*; also *how* or *that* with clause, *to* with infin.

1530 PALSGR. 674/2 Within this syxe dayes I wyll put hym in mynde of his promesse. **1665** SIR T. HERBERT *Trav.* (1677) 120 This being in Asia puts me in mind, That no part of the World is so subject to earth-quakes as Asia is. **1711-12** SWIFT *Jrnl. to Stella* 30 Jan., Stella used to do such tricks formerly; he puts me in mind of her. **1839** JAMES *Gentl. Old Sch.* xii, Pray..put my young friend, Ralph, in mind, that he promised me a visit this afternoon. **1853** LYTTON *My Novel* III. xxix, You put me in mind of an old story. *Ibid.* V. ii, Jarvis, put me in mind to have these inexpressibles altered.

†**4.** That which is remembered *of* (a person or thing); the memory or record *of.* Also in phr. *of good mind* = 'of happy memory'. *Obs.*

c **1000** ÆLFRIC *De Vet. Test.* (init.), Þa ȝimeleasan men,..heora ȝemynd is forȝiten on halȝum ȝewritum. **1387** TREVISA *Higden* (Rolls) I. 5 But besines of writers to oure vnkunnynge hadde i-holde and i-streyned mynde of olde dedes [L. *memoriam transactorum*]. **1489** in *Exch. Rolls Scotl.* X. 121 *note*, The charter of umquhile owre grauntsir and faider of gud mynd quham God assoilze.

5. a. The action or an act of commemorating; something which serves to commemorate; a commemoration, a memorial.

971 *Blickl. Hom.* 189 And feower syllice stanas on þære ilcan stowe aleȝdon, to ȝemynde & to cyþnesse þæs apostolican siȝes oþ þysne andweardan dæȝ. *c* **1320** R. BRUNNE *Medit.* 196 Yn a memorand of hym with outyn ende, He seyd, 'makeþ þys yn my mende'. *c* **1386** CHAUCER *Knt.'s T.* 1048 (Harl. MS.) And westward in þe mynde and in memory Of mars he haþ I-maked such an oþer [altar]. **1388** WYCLIF *Luke* xxii. 19 Do ȝe this thing in mynde of me. **1412-20** LYDG. *Chron. Troy* II. xvii. (1513) K iij, Nynus..an ymage dyde make..And sette it vp, for consolacion And for a mynde, and a memoryall. **1423** JAS. I *Kingis Q.* lxxxv, Here bene the princis..In mynd of quhom ar maid the bukis newe. **1433** LYDG. *St. Edmund* I. 769 in Horstm. *Altengl. Leg.* (1881) 390 At his comyng he bilt a roial toun Which stant ther yit for a manier mynde For his arryuaile into this Regioun. ? *a* **1500** *Wycket* (1828) p. xiv, The breade is the fygure or mynde of Christes bodye in earth.

†**b.** *spec.* The commemoration of a departed soul, esp. by a requiem said or sung on the day of the funeral in any month or year following. Also, in OE., the annual commemoration of a saint. Chiefly in MONTH('S MIND, TWELVEMONTH('S or YEAR('S MIND.

a **900** *O.E. Martyrol.* 2 May 70 On þone æfteran dæȝ þæs monðes bið þæs halȝan biscopes ȝemynd sancte Athanasi. **1387** TREVISA *Higden* (Rolls) VII. 315 At Wynchestre he took his fader tresorie, and ȝaf moche for his fader mynde [*v.r.* munde; L. *pro patris memoria*]. **14..** in *Collectanea Topogr.* (1836) III. 260 That xx.s. be yeve to eche of the places wher as our bodyes lyith, for holding of the mendys. **1418** *E.E. Wills* (1882) 32, Y bequethe to..holde my Mynde euery ȝere duryng vij ȝere next folwyng after my desese,..vij li. **1486** *Rec. St. Mary at Hill* 11 In due fourme as to a yerely mynde perteyneth. **1526** in Strutt *Mann. Cust.* etc. (1776) III. 172 For yerely obytes, and yerelye myndes. **1649** JER. TAYLOR *Gt. Exemp.* III. Disc. xviii. 112 In the monethly minds and anniversary commemorations. **1660** —— *Duct. Dub.* II. ii. Rule vi. §55 Upon the Anniversary, or the monthly, or weekly minds.

†**6.** Mention, record. Chiefly in phr. *to make mind*: const. *of* or with *clause.*

c **1325** *Deo Gracias* 38 in *E.E.P.* (1862) 125 Holichirche Muynde of hit maas. **1377** LANGL. *P. Pl.* B. IX. 121 Of such synful shrewes þe sauter maketh mynde. *c* **1410** LOVE *Bonavent. Mirr.* vi. (Gibbs MS.), And ȝytte þowe þer was so myche nede I fynd noo mynde of furrures or pylches. *c* **1412** HOCCLEVE *De Reg. Princ.* 1723 The bible makiþ no maner of mynde Wheþer þat pharao lay by hire oght. **1433** LYDG. *St. Edmund* III. 765 in Horstm. *Altengl. Leg.* (1881) 427 Blyssid Fremund,—afforn heer put in mynde. **1450-1530** *Myrr. our Ladye* 70 Specyally on fryday, where is made mynde of oure lordes holy passyon. *Ibid.* 191 Holy scrypture..makyth no mynde that he was vnobedyente [etc.].

II. Thought; purpose, intention.

†**7. a.** The action or state of thinking about something; the thought *of* (an object). Chiefly in phrase *to have mind of* (also *on, upon*): to think of, give heed to. Also const. *how* or *that* and clause, and *to* with inf. (= be careful *to do*). Similarly *to take mind to, upon. Obs.*

971 *Blickl. Hom.* 83 Se þe nu forhoȝaþ þæt he Godes bebodu healde, oþþe æniȝ ȝemynd hæbbe Drihtnes eaþmodnesse. *a* **1250** *Owl & Night.* 252 So doþ þat beoþ of þine cunde, Of lihte nabbeþ hi none imunde. *c* **1275** *Passion of our Lord* 6 in *O.E. Misc.* 37 Lute ymvnde hi hedde of gode. **1303** R. BRUNNE *Handl. Synne* 5867 Pers, I haue mynde of þe. *c* **1325** *Poems temp. Edw. II* (Percy) lxvi, And ȝet is ther non man That to God taketh mynde With ryȝte. *c* **1380** *Lay Folks Catech.* (MS. L) 607 Fyrst haue mende how god made heuyn and erthe. *c* **1412** HOCCLEVE *De Reg. Princ.* 4997 þat þei þat haue of him lest þought & mynde By þis peynture may ageyn him fynde. *c* **1440** *Alphabet of Tales* 93 Þer was a bruther þat gretelie was turment with mynd of a womman þat he saw som tyme. *c* **1450** *Cov. Myst.* xxv. (Shaks. Soc.) 240 But now mervelous mendys rennyn in myn rememberawns. **1493** *Festivall* (W. de W. 1515) 7 He shall fynde yᵉ mynde of deth yᵉ principall salue of all manner synnes. **1550** CROWLEY *Last Trumpet* 245 Haue minde, therfore, thyselfe to holde Within the bondes of thy degre. **1560** DAUS tr. *Sleidane's Comm.* 302 b, Yᵗ..they will have some consideration, and mynde of hym [L. *ut ipsius rationem habeant*]. **1589** R. ROBINSON *Gold. Mirr.* (Chetham Soc.) 34 Haue minde vpon thy mercy Lord.

†**b.** *to put* (a person) *in mind*: to suggest an idea to (him). *Obs.*

1579 GOSSON *Sch. Abuse* (Arb.) 37 He feared that hee shoulde rather put men in minde to commit such offences.

†**c.** *out of mind*: more than one can calculate.

a **1400-50** *Alexander* 3018 He had of men out of mynde many mayn hundreth.

8. That which a person thinks about any subject or question; one's view, judgement, or opinion. Now chiefly in phrases: see 9.

a **1400** *Octouian* 888 The good wyf seyd: 'Be Seynt Denys, Swyche ys my mende'. **1512** *Act 4 Hen. VIII*, c. 19 *Preamble*, The seid Frensche Kyng..abydyng in his seid indurat & pervart opynyons & erronyous mynde. **1530** PALSGR. 680/1 I reason with one in a mater to fele his mynde in it. **1560** DAUS tr. *Sleidane's Comm.* 1 b, Such as could not be there present he desyred to send their myndes in wryting.

1593 SHAKS. *3 Hen. VI*, III. ii. 17 Widow, we will consider of your suit And come some other time to know our minde. **1689** *Col. Rec. Pennsylv.* I. 250 The Governor Desired Every Member of yᵉ board would deliver his minde, and give him advice therein. **1706** POPE *Let. to Wycherley* 10 Apr., Pray let me know your mind in this, for I am utterly at a loss. **1781** J. MOORE *View Soc. It.* (1790) II. lxv. 294 Would to heaven these doubters would keep their minds to themselves.

9. Phrases. **a.** ***to speak one's mind*** (*out*): to give one's judgement or opinion; *esp.* to express one's sentiments candidly or plainly, to speak freely. Similarly ***to tell*** (a person) ***one's mind, to let*** (a person) ***know one's mind***. For *a piece* or *bit of one's mind*, see PIECE *sb.* 2 d, BIT *sb.*² 4.

1508 FISHER *7 Penit. Ps.* cii. Wks. (1876) 140 A mannes entent or mynde spoken by his owne mouth moueth more the herer than it were shewed & spoken by ony other. **1530** PALSGR. 478/2 And I may catche hym ones, I shall tell hym more of my mynde. **1596** SHAKS. *Tam. Shr.* IV. iii. 75 Your betters haue indur'd me say my minde. **1600** —— *A. Y. L.* II. vii. 59 Giue me leaue To speake my minde. **1676** MARVELL *Mr. Smirke* 44 'Tis happy that some or other of this Few chances ever and anon to speak their minds out, to shew us plainly what they would be at. **1806–7** J. BERESFORD *Miseries Hum. Life* VII. lxxvii, I let them know my mind in a manner that pretty effectually secures me from this 'misery', for the rest of that sitting. **1845** BROWNING *Soul's Trag.* I. 207 I've spoke my mind too fully out.

b. ***to be of*** (†rarely ***in***) ***a*** (specified) ***mind***: to hold an opinion. ***to be of*** (another's) ***mind***: to be of his way of thinking, agree in opinion.

1585 T. WASHINGTON tr. *Nicholay's Voy.* Ep. Ded., Hee was alwaies of opinion and minde, that..learning, is not to be sought for in bookes. **1593** SHAKS. *Rich. II*, V. ii. 107 Sweet Yorke, sweet husband, be not of that minde. **1600** —— *A. Y. L.* V. iv. 75 He sent me word, if I said his beard was not cut well, hee was in the minde it was. **1690** LOCKE *Hum. Und.* II. xvii. §20 If these men are of the Mind, That they have clearer Ideas of infinite Duration, than of infinite Space. **1717** LADY M. W. MONTAGU *Let. to Pope* 1 Apr., I don't doubt you'll be of my mind. **1871** *Routledge's Ev. Boy's Ann.* Apr. 242 I'm of Bradshawe's mind in the matter.

c. ***in my mind***: in my judgement or opinion, as I think. ? *Obs.* Similarly ***to my mind*** (cf. 14 b).

1523 LD. BERNERS *Froiss.* I. xxiv. 34 The kyng..sayd, in his mynde, there was no realme coude be compared to yᵉ realme of Fraunce. **1596** SHAKS. *Merch. V.* IV. i, Anthonio, gratifie this gentleman, For in my minde, you are much bound to him. **1602** —— *Ham.* I. iv. 14 (Qo. 1604) But to my minde..it is a custome [etc.]. **1663** COWLEY *Ess.* iii. *Obscurity*, It is, in my Mind, a very delightful Pastime. **1813** HOBHOUSE *Journey* (ed. 2) 501 The modern cestus,..is not, in my mind, an agreeable ornament. **1866** MRS. GASKELL *Wives & Dau.* I. xvi. 182 The other is but a loutish young fellow, to my mind.

d. ***to be of one*** or ***a mind***: to agree in judgement, purpose, or opinion; to be unanimous. †***with one mind***: unanimously, with one accord.

?**1496** in *Lett. & Papers Rich. III & Hen. VII* (Rolls) II. 67 If we hadde alle here ben of oone mynde in folowyng directly the Kinges mynde. **1570** *Satir. Poems Reform.* x. 178 With ane mynde thay did consent togidder Dauid to slay. **1601** SHAKS. *All's Well* I. iii. 244 He and his Phisitions Are of a minde. **1611** —— *Cymb.* V. iv. 212, I would we were all of one minde, and one minde good. *a* **1712** GRANVILLE *Ess. Unnat. Flights Poetry* 74 And, by the Tyrant's Murder, we may find That Cato and the Gods were of a Mind. **1875** JOWETT *Plato* (ed. 2) IV. 537 When men have anything to do in common, that they should be of one mind is a pleasant thing. **1877** SPURGEON *Serm.* XXIII. 70 Here they were, all of a mind, and all ready to start.

†**e.** ***against the mind of*** (a person): in opposition to his judgement, wish, or opinion, without his approbation or consent. Also ***without the mind of***. *Obs.*

1512 *Act 4 Hen. VIII*, c. 20 *Preamble*, The said John.. fortuned to be slayn..ayenst the will and mynde of your seid Beseecher. **1553** BECON *Reliques Rome* (1563) 213 The Councell which is celebrated without the mynde and consent of the Romyshe Byshop. **1668** CULPEPPER & COLE *Barthol. Anat.* III. x. 151 Cassenius against the mind of all Anatomists draws its original from the Pinnæ of the Nose. **1698** HEARNE *Duct. Hist.* I. III. ix. 324 Themistocles.. brought the Athenians back to their City, which they fortified, and added the Pyreum to it much against the Spartans' Mind.

10. Purpose or intention; desire or wish. *Obs.* exc. in phrases: see 11.

1297 R. GLOUC. (Rolls) 9544 Þo was it muche is munde To come & winne engelond. **1523** LD. BERNERS *Froiss.* I. clxxvi. 213 With hym went a varlet, who was priuy to his mynde. *c* **1555** HARPSFIELD *Divorce Hen. VIII* (Camden) 125 God's mind was to astringe and bind the Church perpetually to it. **1588** SHAKS. *Tit. A.* V. iii. 1 Vnckle Marcus, since tis my Fathers minde That I repaire to Rome, I am content. **1597** BACON *Ess., Suitors* (Arb.) 40 Manie ill matters are vndertaken, and many good matters with ill mindes. **1656** in *Burton's Diary* (1828) I. 302 To enquire with what mind this was done. **1667** MILTON *P.L.* V. 452 Sudden mind arose In Adam, not to let th' occasion pass.

11. Phrases. †**a.** ***to fulfil one's mind, bring one's mind to pass***: to accomplish one's purpose, satisfy one's desire. ***to have*** or ***obtain one's mind***: to get what one wants. ***for one's mind's sake***: to gratify one's whim. *Obs.*

1509 HAWES *Past. Pleas.* xvi. (Percy Soc.) 75 Longynge ryght sore my mynde to fulfyll. **1530** PALSGR. 499/1 It shall coste me a fall, but I wyll have my mynde. *Ibid.* 865/1 For my myndes sake, *pour satisfaire a ma phantasie*. **1598** F. ROUS *Thule* N 2 b, And she as women wont will haue her minde. **1614** RALEIGH *Hist. World* II. v. iv. §1. 585 This war he vndertooke as it were for his mindes sake: hauing receiued no iniurie. **1671** H. M. tr. *Erasm. Colloq.* 82 Because I see that thou dost so earnestly desire it, I will fulfil thy mind as well as I can.

†**b.** ***by, according to the mind of*** (a person): by desire or after the direction of. (Cf. 14 b.) *Obs.*

1523–4 *Rec. St. Mary at Hill* (1904) 322 Paid to the Orgon maker by þe mynde of Mʳ person for mendyng the Orgons, iij s iiij d. **1618** *Vestry Bks.* (Surtees) 74 Item more they receyved which was given by Willⁱᵃᵐ Ord, and lent to fower poore folk according to his minde, xl s.

c. ***to know one's own mind***: to form and adhere to a decision without shilly-shallying; to have a line of action and keep to it.

1824 SCOTT *St. Roman's* xii, The report..that the young Earl of Etherington..intended to pass an hour, or a day, or a week, as it might happen, (for his lordship could not be supposed to know his own mind,) at St. Ronan's Well. **1864** TENNYSON *En. Ard.* 475 And others laugh'd at her and Philip too, As simple folk that knew not their own minds. **1888** [see CHOP *v.*² 4 c].

d. ***to make up one's mind***: see MAKE *v.*¹ 96 k.

e. †***to be of divers*** or ***many minds***: to waver in purpose, to chop and change (*obs.*). ***to be in two minds***: to vacillate between two intentions; similarly ***to be in twenty minds***.

1530 PALSGR. 428/1, I am of dyverse myndes, *je me varie*. .. I wolde be glad to deale with hym, but the man is of so dyverse myndes that there is no holde at hym. **1738** SWIFT *Pol. Conversat.* 55 You'll never be mad, you are of so many Minds. **1751** R. PALTOCK *P. Wilkins* (1884) I. xxi. 208, I was in twenty minds whether to take her first, and then catch the chickens, or to let her go off, and then clap upon them. **1850** DICKENS *Dav. Copp.* xxv, This missive (which I was in twenty minds at once about recalling, as soon as it was out of my hands). *Ibid.* xli, I was in several minds how to dress myself on the important day. **1853** —— *Child's Hist.* II. 171 Jack [Cade]..was in two minds about fighting or accepting a pardon. **1881** E. D. BRICKWOOD in *Encycl. Brit.* XII. 197/2 However bold the horse may be, he will soon refuse water if his rider be perpetually in two minds when approaching a brook.

†**f.** ***to be in*** or ***of mind***, to be disposed or minded, to purpose, desire (*to do* something); occas. ***to be in great mind, of good mind, in a good mind*** (cf. 13 a). ***of mind***, with purpose or intention (*to do* something). ***to run*** (*one*) ***in mind***, to become a purpose or resolution. ***to bring one in mind***, to persuade. *Obs.*

c **1375** *Sc. Leg. Saints* vi. (*Thomas*) 248 Þane rane hym in mynde in hy þat he vald firste quyke þam fla. *a* **1400–50** *Alexander* 1254 Sir meliager was in grete mynd a man owt to send To alexander. **1513** MORE *Rich. III* in Grafton *Chron.* (1568) II. 763 He secretly..caused the Queene to be perswaded and brought in minde, that it..should be ieopardous the king to come vp so strong. **1523** LD. BERNERS *Froiss.* I. ccccli. 796 Wherof complayntes came to the heryng of the duke of Berrey, who was in mynde to remedy it. **1586** *Let. Earle Leycester* 13 Neither did I it of minde to circumvent her. **1599** *Reg. Privy Council Scot.* (1884) VI. 40 His Majestie being of gude mynd that the said Sir George be satisfeit of the saidis debursmentis, as ressone requyris. *a* **1617** BAYNE *Lect.* (1634) 233 Pharaoh [was] in a good minde, as wee say, to let the people goe. **1661** C. LYTTELTON in *Hatton Corr.* (Camden) 24, I doe not find my brother of the mind he seemed at first to be of to buy it. *a* **1814** *Gonzanga* II. i. in *New Brit. Theatre* III. 113 Oh lud! if I can but get her in the mind to have me.

g. ***to pay no mind, not to pay any mind***: to pay no heed or attention (*to* someone or something); not to care or worry. *U.S. colloq.* and *dial.*

1916 *Dialect Notes* IV. 269, I pay no mind to that. **1932** W. FAULKNER *Light in August* xiii. 275, I aint never paid it no mind. **1969** *Rolling Stone* 28 June 19/2 He..doesn't pay any mind if his calf shows when he crosses his legs. **1971** *Black World* Oct. 63/2, I don't pay her no mind.

12. ***to change one's mind***, to alter one's purpose, opinion, way of thinking, disposition towards others, etc. Similarly, ***one's mind changes***.

1591 SHAKS. *Two Gent.* III. ii. 59 You are already loues firme votary, And cannot soone reuolt, and change your minde. **1601** —— *Jul. C.* II. ii. 96 If you shall send them word you will not come, Their mindes may change. **1615** W. LAWSON *Country Housew. Gard.* (1626) 44, I haue changed my mind concerning the disease called the worme. **1617** MORYSON *Itin.* I. 121 Cardinall Allan an Englishman, having used to persecute the English..had changed his mind, since the English had overthrowne the Spanish Navy. **1719** J. ALLEN in J. Duncombe *Lett.* (1773) I. 214, I have lived to change my mind, and am almost of the contrary opinion. **1842** TENNYSON *Dora* 45 It cannot be: my uncle's mind will change! **1883** F. M. CRAWFORD *Dr. Claudius* vi, Her first impulse was to change her mind and not go after all.

13. ***to have a mind***: **a.** (With expressed inf.) To wish, desire, be inclined or disposed *to do* (something). Also with qualifying word, ***to have a great, good,*** etc., ***mind, to have no mind***. Somewhat *arch.* exc. in ***to have a good*** or ***great mind, to have half a mind***, now = to be strongly disposed or inclined (to do something which one can do if one wishes), to have nearly made up one's mind (to do it). (See also MONTH'S MIND.)

The confused form *I'm a good mind* is still current in some localities as a vulgarism.

a **1400** in *Rel. Ant.* II. 44 For the greet mynde that he hath to done his maystris wille. *c* **1550** BALE *K. Johan* (Camden) 12, I have a great mynd to be a lecherous man. **1618** BOLTON *Florus* (1636) 268 Pompey driven away, and fled, he had a more minde to take order for securing the Provinces, than to pursue him. **1632** CHAPMAN & SHIRLEY *Ball* III. i. (1639) D 3 b, Harke you Mounsieur, this gentleman has a great Minde to learne to dance. **1666** S. PARKER *Free & Impart. Censure* (1667) 181 And now I have a mind to set up for a Maker of Hypotheses. *a* **1674** CLARENDON *Hist. Reb.* XIII. §179 The duke of Lorrayne had a very good mind to get a footing in Ireland. **1711** ADDISON *Spect.* No. 45 ¶6 As I had a mind to hear the Play, I got out of the Sphere of her Impertinence. **1726** SHELVOCKE *Voy. round World* (1757) 462 They had half a mind to refuse me a passage. **1833** L. RITCHIE *Wand. by Loire* 26 It was lucky for us that we did not follow the nuptial procession (which we had more than half a mind to do). **1852** R. S. SURTEES *Sponge's Sp. Tour* (1893) 65 I'm a good mind to have his throat cut. **1853** LYTTON *My Novel* x. iii, She had half a mind to reply.—'Is that so strange?' But her respect for Harley stopped her. **1858** CARLYLE *Fredk. Gt.* VI. ii. (1865) II. 47 My Brother and I had all the mind in the world to laugh. **1870** ROGERS *Hist. Gleanings* Ser. II. 102 He had little mind to be a martyr, but he had still less a mind to be a knave. **1871** FREEMAN *Norm. Conq.* (1876) IV. xvii. 54 He had no mind to be a mere conqueror.

b. with ellipsis of the *inf.* (In relative and 'if' clauses.)

a **1674** CLARENDON *Hist. Reb.* VIII. §38 Without.. restraining them from making incursions where they had a mind. **1737** [S. BERINGTON] *G. di Lucca's Mem.* (1738) 261 When they have dropp'd all [the wild Boars] that are dangerous, and as much as they haue a mind, they open their Toils. **1826** SCOTT *Let. to J. B. S. Morritt* 6 Feb. in *Lockhart*, I have no idea of these things preventing a man from doing what he has a mind. **1848** THACKERAY *Lett.* 1 Aug., Those who had a mind were free to repair to a magnificent neighbouring saloon. **1874** WHYTE MELVILLE *Uncle John* xxi. III. 22 They could..burn us out if they had a mind.

¶ In mod. colloquial use the *to* of an inf. suppressed by ellipsis is often retained. (See TO *prep.*)

The quots. below enclosed in square brackets are probably to be explained as instances of the idiom by which a prep. governing a relative expressed or understood is removed to the end of the sentence (cf. quots. 1674, 1711, 1726 in d). But the indefiniteness of the antecedent and the presence of a transitive verb in the sentence render the passages liable to be taken as anticipations of the modern colloquial practice, which may indeed have been partly developed from expressions of this kind.

[**1671** H. M. tr. *Erasm. Colloq.* 519 Enquire what thou hast a mind to. **1734** LD. CHESTERF. in *Lett. C'tess Suffolk* (1824) II. 115 Amoretto was with difficulty prevailed upon to eat and drink as much as he had a mind to. **1744** ELIZA HEYWOOD *Female Spect.* No. 4 (1748) I. 189 As our sex has the privilege of saying whatever we have a mind to. **1827** SCOTT *Highl. Widow* v, In order to gain his consent to do something he had no mind to.] **1852** MRS. STOWE *Uncle Tom's C.* ii, I don't need to hire any of my hands out, unless I've a mind to. **1871** *Lippincott's Mag.* 27 Mar. 282 You can call me when you are a-mind to. **1895** 'HEATHERBELL' in *Scott. Antiquary* X. 79 They..thought they could deal as they had a mind to with his property.

c. with dependent clause.

1673 TEMPLE *Observ. United Prov.* ii. 95 They had no mind that Her Ambassador should be present. **1705** PENN in *Pa. Hist. Soc. Mem.* X. 65, I believe he had no mind it should be done whilst I was there.

d. With *to* and *sb.*: †To be favourably disposed towards (a person) (*obs.*); to have a liking for (an occupation); to wish to possess or obtain (something). Now somewhat *arch.*

1530 PALSGR. 580/1, I have a mynde to one, I have a favoure to hym. **1605** *Lond. Prodigal* I. ii, I have a great mind to this gentleman in the way of Marriage. **1616** B. JONSON *Devil an Ass* I. ii, They doe say, H'will meet a man (of himselfe) that has a mind to him. If hee would so, I haue a minde and a halfe for him. **1674** BUTLER *Hud.* I. i. 214 That ..Compound for Sins, they are inclin'd to, By damning those they have no mind to. **1683** TEMPLE *Mem.* Wks. 1731 I. 457, I never had less mind to any Journey in my Life. **1711** STEELE *Spect.* No. 145 ¶6 There visits among us an old Batchelor whom each of us has a Mind to. **1726** SWIFT *Gulliver* II. ii, In a few Days, I was able to call for whatever I had a Mind to. **1876** GEO. ELIOT *Dan. Der.* lviii, The blacksmith said to me the other day that his 'prentice had no mind to his trade.

e. With *for*, †*of*: To wish for, desire.

1616 [see d]. **1775** JOHNSON *Let. to Taylor* 8 Apr., When shall I come down to you? I believe I can get away pretty early in May, if you have any mind of me. **1790** *Bystander* 134 When he has a mind of a little fun. **1855** PRESCOTT *Philip II*, II. iii, Philip had no mind for a second collision with the papal court. **1871** *Routledge's Ev. Boy's Ann.* Jan. 45 We have no mind for a sousing.

14. a. Bent or direction of thoughts, desires, inclinations, etc. In phrases, as ***one's mind is*** (or ***runs***) ***on***, one attends to, thinks of, is interested in. ***to set*** (***have, keep***) ***one's mind on***: to desire to attain or accomplish, put or keep before one as an object of desire. ***to give one's mind to***: to addict oneself to (a study or practice); to bend one's energies towards accomplishing or attaining (an object).

a **1400–50** *Alexander* 269 Ȝe behald me sa hogely, quareon is ȝour mynd? **1475** SIR J. PASTON in *P. Lett.* III. 129 My mynde is now nott most uppon bokes. **1509** BARCLAY *Shyp of Folys* (1874) II. 106 For a ryche man settynge theron his mynde Shal into heuen right hardly passage fynde. *Ibid.* 169 Gyue nat your myndes to gylefull vsury. **1677** HORNECK *Gt. Law Consid.* iv. (1704) 105 The wolf..sent to school to learn to spell, could make nothing of all that was said to him but *sheep*. His mind still ran upon that. **1827** DISRAELI *Viv. Grey* v. xv, I've set my mind upon your joining the party. **1850** DICKENS *Dav. Copp.* xxxv, Sordid and selfish as I knew it was..to let my mind run on my own distress so much. **1859** TENNYSON *Vivien* 476 And since he kept his mind on one sole aim. **1861** STANLEY *East. Ch.* vi. (1869) 254 But each of the sacraments must often have been deferred to a time when the candidates could give their whole minds to the subject.

b. ***to one's mind***: according to one's wish, to one's taste or liking, as one would have it to be. Also †***according to, after one's mind***.

1530 PALSGR. 580/1, I have a person or a beest accordyng to my mynde, I have them in suche awe as I desyre. **1535** COVERDALE *Ecclus.* vii. 26 Yf thou haue a wife after thine owne mynde, forsake her not. —— *1 Macc.* iv. 6 Which had nether harnesse ner sweardes to their myndes. **1719** DE FOE *Crusoe* II. (Globe) 509 It was however, some Time before we could get a Ship to our Minds. *c* **1790** IMISON *Sch. Art* II. 92 You may brighten it to your mind by the above mixture. **1847** HELPS *Friends in C.* (1873) I. viii. 130 Commands are expected to be fulfilled..exactly to the mind of the person ordering.

15. a. Inclination, tendency, or way of thinking and feeling, in regard to moral and social qualities; moral disposition; a spirit or temper of a specified character. †***to bear a*** (specified) ***mind***: to entertain (such and such) sentiments. For *frame of mind* see FRAME *sb.* 6.

1500–20 DUNBAR *Poems* ix. 129 Off mynd dissymvlat, Lord! I me confess. **1560** DAUS tr. *Sleidane's Comm.* 3 b, Luther..reproveth his cruell and bloudy mynde. **1591** SHAKS. *Two Gent.* v. iii. 13 Feare not: he beares an honourable minde, And will not vse a woman lawlesly. **1633** EARL MANCH. *Al Mondo* (1636) 29 To be willing to die, and content to liue is the minde of a strong Christian. **1777** BURKE *Let. Sheriffs of Bristol* Wks. 1842 I. 207 But the war is not ended; the hostile mind continues in full vigour. **1859** TENNYSON *Guinevere* 334 For manners are not idle, but the fruit Of loyal nature, and of noble mind. **1867** FREEMAN *Norm. Conq.* (1877) I. App. 748 He was then brought to a better mind by a rebuke from a Christian. **1884** CHILD *Ballads* I. 278/1 Hugo was evidently not in a state of mind to go [*sc.* to mass].

†**b.** The way in which one person is affected towards another; disposition or intention towards others. *to bear good mind to*: to be well disposed towards. *Obs.*

1470 TIPTOFT *Cæsar's Comm.* x. (1530) 12 Whome he had knowen and sene so specyally aboue other to bere hys good myne [? *read* mynde] and fydelyte toward hym. **1530** PALSGR. 449/2, I beare hym good mynde, *je suis affectionné enuers luy*. *c* **1550** BALE *K. Johan* (Camden) 74 Ye knowe very well she beareth the Churche good mynde. **1568** GRAFTON *Chron.* II. 707 The more number of the nobilitie, bare towarde king Henry..their good minds and fixed hartes. **1580** STOW *Chron. Eng.* Ep. Ded. ¶iij b, Not doubting but your Lordship..will..vouchesafe to accepte this Monument of my affectionate minde. **1591** SHAKS. *Two Gent.* I. ii. 33, I would I knew his minde. **1611** BIBLE *Acts* xii. 20 *marg.*, Herode bare an hostile mind intending warre.

16. State of thought and feeling in respect to dejection or cheerfulness, fortitude or fearfulness, firmness or irresoluteness, and the like.

1500–20 DUNBAR *Poems* lxvii. 7 Quho had all riches vnto Ynd, And wer not satisfiet in mynd. **1530** PALSGR. 674/2 He was never quyette in his mynde tyll I did put hym in a suertye. **1610** SHAKS. *Temp.* IV. i. 163 A turne or two Ile walke To still my beating minde. **1611** BIBLE *Acts* ii. 6 The multitude were confounded [*marg.* troubled in mind]. *a* **1631** DONNE *Paradoxes* (1652) 24 For our minds is heavy in our bodies affliction. **1667** MILTON *P.L.* IX. 1120 Not at rest or ease of Mind, They sate them down to weep. *Ibid.* 1125 High Passions..shook sore Thir inward State of Mind. **1743** SHENSTONE *Past. Ballad* III, O how, with one trivial glance, Might she ruin the peace of my mind! **1852** M. ARNOLD *Empedocles* I. ii. 29 Nature, with equal mind, Sees all her sons at play.

III. Mental or psychical being or faculty.

17. a. The seat of a person's consciousness, thoughts, volitions, and feelings; the system of cognitive and emotional phenomena and powers that constitutes the subjective being of a person; also, the incorporeal subject of the psychical faculties, the spiritual part of a human being; the soul as distinguished from the body.

a **1340** HAMPOLE *Psalter* cxviii. 93 For i lif in þi laghe, it may noght slip out of my mynde. *c* **1440** *Generydes* 480 She ..told hym all that lay sore in hir mynd. **1530** PALSGR. 430/2, I am wery for occupyeng of the mynde to moche. **1598** SHAKS. *Merry W.* IV. vi. 30 While other sports are tasking of their mindes. **1643** R. BAILLIE *Lett. & Jrnls.* (1841) II. 109 While they stand, the scribe and others number them in their mind. **1690** LOCKE *Hum. Und.* I. ii. §5 No Proposition can be said to be in the Mind..which it was never yet conscious of. **1692** —— *Educ.* §31 Due care being had to keep the Body in Strength and Vigour, so that it may be able to obey and execute the Orders of the Mind. **1768, 1834** [see CROSS *v.* 13]. **1794** W. ROBERTS *Looker-On* No. 88 III. 425 Suppose a person..to store up in his mind certain leading passages from Scripture. **1827** SOUTHEY *Penins. War* II. 352 No such thought had ever entered Reding's mind. **1851** BP. C. WORDSW. *Mem. Wordsw.* I. 81 His mind was filled with gloomy forebodings. **1871** MORLEY *Voltaire* (1886) 6 Hardly a sentence is there that did not come forth alive from Voltaire's own mind. **1887** MISS E. MONEY *Dutch Maiden* (1888) 56 Now, will you turn this over in your mind?

b. Instances of philosophical definition of this.

1704 NORRIS *Ideal World* II. iii. 133 By Mind I think we are properly to mean that power which both perceives and wills. **1785** REID *Intell. Powers* I. ii. 42 We do not give the name of mind to thought, reason, or desire; but to that being which thinks, which reasons, which desires. **1843** MILL *Logic* I. iii. §8 Mind is the mysterious something which feels and thinks. **1846** G. MOORE *Power of Soul over Body* (ed. 3) 73 Unfortunately the word mind has been almost universally employed to signify both that which thinks, and the phenomena of thinking.

c. ***on one's mind***: occupying one's thoughts; said esp. of something which causes anxiety.

1850 DICKENS *Dav. Copp.* xxxiv, I knew my aunt sufficiently well to know that she had something of importance on her mind. **1853** LYTTON *My Novel* VI. v, I asked him if he had not anything on his mind. **1864** TENNYSON *En. Ard.* 396 Annie, there is a thing upon my mind.

d. ***one's mind's eye***: mental view or vision, remembrance.

c **1412** HOCCLEVE *De Reg. Princ.* 2895 Haue often him byfore your myndes ye. **1602, 1818** [see EYE *sb.*[1] 4 d]. **1883** S. C. HALL *Retrospect* II. 320 One such scene is in my mind's eye at this moment.

e. Used with reference to God.

1612 BACON *Ess. Atheism* (Arb.) 330, I had rather beleeue all the fables in the *Legend*, and the *Alcaron*, then that this vniuersall frame is without a minde. **1690** LOCKE *Hum. Und.* IV. x. (end), That eternal infinite Mind, who made and governs all Things. **1732** POPE *Ess. Man.* I. 266 Just as absurd, to mourn the tasks or pains The great directing Mind of All ordains. **1807** WORDSW. *Ode Intimat. Immortality* viii, Haunted for ever by the eternal mind.

f. In generalized sense: Mental or psychical being: opposed to *matter*.

1759 JOHNSON *Rasselas* xlviii, The immateriality of mind, and..the unconsciousness of matter. **1879** LINDSAY *Mind in Lower Anim.* I. 51 Little is at present known of the phenomena of mind in the lowest classes of animals. **1898** ILLINGWORTH *Divine Immanence* i. §1. 4 Thus matter, as we know it, is everywhere and always fused with mind.

g. A person regarded abstractly as the embodiment of mental qualities (thought, feelings, disposition, etc.).

c **1580** SIDNEY *Ps.* xxxiv. ix, To humble broken minds, This Lord is ever, ever neare. *c* **1600** SHAKS. *Sonn.* cxvii. 5 That I haue frequent binne with vnknown mindes. **1642** LOVELACE *To Althea, from Prison* iv, Mindes innocent and quiet take That for an Hermitage. **1776** MICKLE tr. *Camoens' Lusiad* Introd. 35 Some of the Portuguese courtiers, the same ungenerous minds perhaps who advised the rejection of Columbus because he was a foreigner. **1864** BRYCE *Holy Rom. Emp.* vii. (1875) 109 The Papacy..under the guidance of her greatest minds, of Hildebrand, of Alexander [etc.].

h. In collective sense; *spec.* = SENSE *sb.* 18 b.

1812 SIR H. DAVY *Chem. Philos.* 13 In this age it was peculiarly easy to deceive, but difficult to enlighten, the public mind. **1837** HT. MARTINEAU *Soc. Amer.* III. 206 If the national mind of America be judged of by its legislation, it is of a very high order. **1883** *Daily Tel.* 10 Nov. 5/1 This cleavage of the religious mind of Europe into two extreme camps. **1951** E. BARKER *Princ. Social & Pol. Theory* II. vi. 72 We sometimes speak of the 'mind' of a meeting, or the 'sense' of a meeting... We only mean that there is a common *content* of the many minds, and the many senses, which are present and active in the meeting. **1971** *Scotsman* 20 May 1/7 Mr Herron said he was not ruling the report out of order. 'I want to take the mind of the Assembly on this.'

18. a. In more restricted application: The cognitive or intellectual powers, as distinguished from the will and emotions. Often contrasted with *heart*.

c **1200** ORMIN 17572 & sawle iss ec wurrþlike shridd þurrh Godd..Wiþþ witt & wille & minde. *c* **1350** *Will. Palerne* 4123 Wel I wot..þat he [the werwolf] has mannes munde more þan we boþe. **1382** WYCLIF *Matt.* xxii. 37 Thou shalt loue the Lord thi God, of al thin herte, and in al thi soule, and in al thi mynde. *c* **1412** HOCCLEVE *De Reg. Princ.* 997 Mynde, ee, and hand, non may fro othir flitte. *c* **1639** COWLEY *On Death of Sir H. Wotton*, He did the utmost Bounds of Knowledge find, He found them not so large as was his Mind. **1784** COWPER *Tiroc.* 722 Possessor of a soul refined, An upright heart, and cultivated mind.

b. Intellectual quality, intellect, mental power.

c **1586** C'TESS PEMBROKE *Ps.* XLIV. x, His eye of deepest minde Deeper sincks then deepest working. **1826** DISRAELI *Viv. Grey* II. ix, Blue eyes, lit up by a smile of such mind and meaning! **1827** *Ibid.* VI. iv, But his pupil appears to be a man of mind. **1855** TENNYSON *Maud* I. I. vii, But these are the days of advance, the works of the men of mind. **1876** 'OUIDA' *Winter City* iii, You mean there can be no mind in an imitation.

c. ABSENCE, PRESENCE *of mind*: see those words.

19. a. The healthy or normal condition of the mental faculties, the loss or impairment of which constitutes insanity; one's 'reason' or 'wits'. Chiefly in phrases, as ***(to be, go) out of one's mind***, †***out of mind***, *(Sc.)* ***by one's mind***; ***to lose one's mind***; ***to be in one's right mind***, etc.

c **1369** CHAUCER *Dethe Blaunche* 511 For he had welnye loste his mynde. **1412–20** LYDG. *Chron. Troy* (E.E.T.S.) 4276 Almost for wo he went out of his mynde. *c* **1440** *Gesta Rom.* lxix. 317 (Harl. MS.) þe maister of þe ship was halfe out of mynde. **1509** BARCLAY *Shyp of Folys* (1874) I. 295 Than lepe they about as folke past theyr mynde. **1596** DALRYMPLE tr. *Leslie's Hist. Scot.* x. 353 Normond with this ansuer was halfe by his mynd. **1605** SHAKS. *Lear* IV. vii. 63, I feare I am not in my perfect mind. **1847** TENNYSON *Princess* VII. 84 And still she fear'd that I should lose my mind. **1849** MACAULAY *Hist. Eng.* v. I. 663 He was drunk, they said, or out of his mind, when he was turned off.

b. in wills, etc., ***of sound*** (or ***unsound***) ***mind***, †***in good mind***, †***whole of mind***, etc.

1395 *E.E. Wills* (1882) 4, I Alice West,..in hool estat of my body, and in good mynde beynge. **1418** *Ibid.* 30 Hole of mynde & in my gode memorie beyng. **1430** *Ibid.* 85 Beyng in full mende. **1438–9** *Ibid.* 129 Beyng yn hole mynde & goode witte. **1818** CRUISE *Digest* (ed. 2) V. 541 To prove that the said Nicholas was of unsound mind at the time of the said fine taken. **1826** [see MEMORY 2 b].

†**c.** One's waking consciousness. *Obs.*

c **1384** CHAUCER *H. Fame* II. 56 And with that vois soth for to seyne My mynde came to me ageyne.

†**IV. 20.** A quantity, number, or amount (of something). [Of obscure development: cf. 7 c.]

c **1250** *Gen. & Ex.* 3676 Fro lond ortigie cam a wind, And broȝte turles michel mind. *c* **1330** R. BRUNNE *Chron. Wace* (Rolls) 1888 In fewe ȝeres al þe kynde Of folk, þey woxen mykel mynde. *Ibid.* 16436 þorow roten eyr, þorow wykkede wyndes, In alle stedes men dide gret myndes. **13..** *Propr. Sanct.* (Vernon MS.) in *Archiv Stud. neu. Spr.* LXXXI. 113/24 Heuene-kyngdom is lyk ȝut To a net..þat of alle ffissches kuynde, Gedereþ in to him muche muynde. *a* **1400–50** *Alexander* 1245 Slik a mynd vn-to me ware meruaill to reken, Thretti thousand in thede of thra men of armes.

V. 21. a. *attrib.* and *Comb.*, as ***mind-conditioning***, ***-content***, ***-dependence***, ***-doctor***, ***-event***, ***-force***, ***-hunger***, ***-malady***, †***-parts***, ***-picture***, ***-searching***, ***-wandering***, ***-world***; ***mind-altering***, ***-changing***, ***-constructed***, ***-dependent***, ***-destroying***, ***-healing***, ***-infected***, ***-like***, ***-made***, †***-mudding***, ***-numbing***, ***-perplexing***, ***-ravishing***, ***-sick***, ***-stretching***, †***-stricken***, ***-torturing***, ***-weary*** adjs.

1972 *N.Y. Times* 3 Nov. 39/3 A deluge of *mind-altering drugs. **1974** *Publishers Weekly* 7 Jan. 50/2 LSD..and other mind-altering drugs. **1597** MORLEY *Introd. Mus.* 116 What strange humor or *mind-changing opinion tooke you this morning? **1956** A. HUXLEY *Let.* 14 Mar. (1969) 791 Soma, in India, was taken only by the priests... I dare say some of the tropical takers of mind-changing stuff may have hit upon the Indian device independently. **1973** *Houston* (Texas) *Chron. Texas Mag.* 14 Oct. 4/1 PDAP defines mind-changing chemicals as alcohol, all narcotics, marijuana and such organics as peyote, i.e., anything inducted into the body to alter the mind. **1945** R. KNOX *God & Atom* ix. 131 There is a steady policy, all over eastern Europe, of anti-religious *mind-conditioning. **1930** J. LAIRD *Knowl., Belief & Opinion* xii. 284 By a mentefact, I mean that which is *mind-constructed. **1940** *Mind* XLIX. 428 The word as an element in language is a very special kind of fact,..as a thought-thing or mind-constructed thing. **1936** H. MULDER *Cognition & Volition in Lang.* 163 The intellectual components of a *mind-content. **1923** C. D. BROAD *Sci. Thought* viii. 251 We must distinguish a more and a less radical sense of '*mind-dependence'. **1951** *Mind* LX. 114 The mind-dependence is dependence on some mental process. **1881** A. C. FRASER *Berkeley* I. iii. 32 It is an argument for the phenomenal, and therefore *mind-dependent, nature of the material world. **1927** *Aristotelian Soc. Suppl. Vol.* VII. 56 Even if sense-data and images, or presentations, are taken to be existentially and qualitatively mind-dependent, to 'inspect' them will plainly be a process very different from that of noticing or scrutinizing mental operations. **1933** *Mind* XLII. 362 Berkeley's failure to demonstrate the mind-dependent character of the secondary qualities. **1886** HALDANE & KEMP tr. *Schopenhauer's World as Will & Idea* II. 211 A mere juggling with words, of which the most shocking example is afforded us by the *mind-destroying Hegelism. **1975** *Deb. Senate Canada* 20 June 6984/1 In an age when our society is becoming complex, when many of the industrial functions are becoming routine and boring, and some of them, I am told by some people on assembly lines, are becoming mind destroying, there is some advantage to that kind of thing. **1940** *Mind* XLIX. 352 It is a book worth reading..because of her power to look afresh at what is done and what should be done by the *mind-doctor. **1936** AUDEN *Look, Stranger!* 37 Every tramp's a landlord really In *mind-events. **1861** J. B. DALGAIRNS *Holy Communion* i. 13 It is hard to say whether we know not more of *mind force..than of the strange aggregate of wondrous forces which we call matter. **1937** R. A. WILSON *Birth of Lang.* 82 The life-force, or mind-force..works within the sensuous material of the world. **1826** HOR. SMITH *Tor Hill* (1838) III. 41 The placid beauties of the country, in whose *mind-healing influences he never failed to find consolation. **1941** V. WOOLF *Between Acts* 22 No one ventured so long a journey, without staving off possible *mind-hunger, without buying a book on a bookstall. *a* **1586** SIDNEY *Arcadia* I. (1590) 70 b, These fantasticall *mind-infected people, that children and Musitians cal Louers. **1940** *Mind* XLIX. 414 The answer, 'Our mind can grasp the world because the world is *mind-like' is a typical *idealistic* argument. **1953** J. S. HUXLEY *Evolution in Action* iv. 89 All living substance has mental, or we had better say mind-like, properties. **1912** J. H. MOORE *Ethics & Educ.* 36 *Mind-made ghosts of ideas. **1957** J. PASSMORE *100 Yrs. Philos.* iii. 58 The general principle that every object of experience is mind-made. **1646** FULLER *Wounded Consc.* iv. (1647) 25 There is such a gulfe of disproportion betwixt a *Mind-malady and Body-medicines. **1642** H. MORE *Song of Soul* II. i. III. xxxi, To chase away *Mind-mudding mist. **1898** F. HIRD *Cry of Children* (ed. 2) ii. 22 The existence of this *mind-numbing slavery is only proved by careful examination into individual cases. **1971** *Guardian* 28 Jan. 11/3 The cost of the gesture could be of mind-numbing proportions. *a* **1586** SIDNEY *Arcadia* IV. (1598) 394 Thinking perchance her feeling sence might call her *mind-parts vnto her. **1631** QUARLES *Samson* ii. 8 In whose eares she brake This *mind-perplexing secret. **1868** SALA in *Lamb's Wks.* I. p. xix, Wealth and piety scarcely fill up the *mind-picture one would draw of Lord Byron. **1593** NASHE *Christs T.* 10, I for-sooke all my immortall pleasures, and *mind-rauishing melody. **1940** W. S. CHURCHILL *Into Battle* (1941) 229 Untiring vigilance and *mind-searching must be devoted to the subject. **1959** *Brno Studies in English* I. 128 That Gissing had considerable mind-searchings over this incident we cannot doubt. **1577** HARRISON *England* II. i. (1877) I. 29 Although manie curious *mindsicke persons vtterlie condemne it as superstitious. **1972** *Guardian* 29 Jan. 11/4 The sheer size of Bangladesh's needs is *mind-stretching. **1974** *Columbia* (S. Carolina) *Record* 25 Apr. 16-D/5 Working with Kissinger is demanding, exhilarating, fascinating, exciting and even mind-stretching, according to four State Department intimates. *a* **1586** SIDNEY *Arcadia* II. (1590) 135 b, This noble-man..had bene so *mind-striken by the beautie of vertue in that noble King. **1595** DANIEL *Civ. Wars* III. xciv. 60 O thou *mind-tortring misery Restles ambition, borne in discontent. **1890** W. JAMES *Princ. Psychol.* I. xi. 417 This reflex and passive character of the attention..never is overcome in some people, whose work, to the end of life, gets done in the interstices of their *mind-wandering. **1899** —— *Talks to Teachers* xi. 114 If he wants to get ideas on any subject, he sits down to work at something else, his best results coming through his mind-wanderings. **1923** U. L. SILBERRAD *Lett. J. Armiter* xiii. 264 But—I am tired! Foot-

weary as well as *mind-weary. **1890** W. JAMES *Princ. Psychol.* I. vi. 154 Somewhere, then, there *is* a transformation... The question is, Where—in the nerve world or in the *mind-world? **1951** W. DE LA MARE *Winged Chariot* 44 The world without; the mind-world in our head.

b. Special comb.: **mind-bender**, a person who, or thing which, influences or alters the mind; *spec.* a psychedelic drug; so **mind-bending** *a.*; **mind-blower** *slang*, something that blows one's mind (see BLOW *v.*[1] 24j); so **mind-blowing** *a.*; (as a back-formation) **mind-blow** *v.*, **mind-blown** *a.*; **mind-body** *Philos.* and *Psychol.*, usu. *attrib.*, a term used in relation to the question of whether a distinction can be made between mental and physiological events; **mind-boggling** *a.*, that causes the mind to boggle or be overwhelmed; **mind-changer**, (*a*) a person who changes his mind; (*b*) a psychedelic drug; **mind-cure**, the curing of a disease by the influence of the healer's mind upon the patient's; **mind-curer**, (*a*) one who cures diseases of the mind; (*b*) one who practises 'mind-cure'; **mind-curist** = *mind-curer* (*b*); †**mind-day**, the day on which a person's death is commemorated, *esp.* the anniversary; **mind-dust**, in materialist evolution hypotheses, the particles of 'mind' or mental substance of which mind-stuff is composed; also *attrib.*; **mind-expanding** *a.* = PSYCHEDELIC *a.*; so **mind-expander**; **mind-healer**, **-healing** = *mind-curer*, *-cure*; †**mind-hill**, a memorial mound or cairn; †**mind-making**, commemoration; †**mind-place**, a place where the memory of a saint is observed; **mind-read** *v. trans.*, to discern what is passing in the mind of (another person); **mind-reader**, one who professes to discern what is passing in another's mind, a thought-reader; so **mind-reading** *vbl. sb.*; **mind-set**, habits of mind formed by previous events or earlier environment which affect a person's attitude (cf. *mental set* s.v. MENTAL *a.*[1] 5); **mind-sight** (*rare*), mental vision (after *eyesight*); **mind-stuff**, W. K. Clifford's name for the supposed rudimentary form of psychical existence, which he regarded as the reality of which matter is the phenomenal aspect; †**mind-taking**, consideration (*upon* a matter); †**mind-token**, a memorial; **mind-transference**, telepathy.

1963 J. KENNAWAY (*title*) The *mind benders. *Ibid.* xxv. 158 Oonagh has said that there were instincts in man laid too deep for the most skilful mind-bender to probe. **1966** *New Scientist* 15 Dec. 639/3 *The mind-bender*, a persuasive person who, for subversive political purposes or financial gain (often both), bends others to his will. Increasingly, he employs drugs, particularly of the hallucinogen group. **1967** *Sci. News Let.* 22 July 80 STP is a new, untested drug, resembling both amphetamine pep pills and the active ingredient in mescaline, the cactus-derived mind-bender. **1970** K. PLATT *Pushbutton Butterfly* (1971) vii. 70 LSD, marijuana—any of the mind-benders. **1973** B. TURNER *Hot-Foot* xvi. 122, I felt.. as if I were hearing a soapy disc-jockey play the groovy zip of some discordant group of mind-benders. **1965** *Economist* 25 Sept. 1215/3 The Socialist Labour League, furious exegetes of the gospel according to Trotsky, with their *mind-bending vocabulary full of 'Pabloism' and that mythical entity the 'rank-and-file'. **1966** *New Scientist* 21 Apr. 151/1 Already 'mind-bending' gases for military purposes are said to be at an advanced stage of development. **1970** *Sunday Times* 25 Jan. 29 The theoretical mathematics of the situation [*sc.* the mining of metals] are positively mind-bending. **1971** *New Scientist* 27 May 531/1 Heroin and other mind-bending agents. **1973** *Times* 25 May 4/3 Viscount Weymouth this afternoon unveiled the mind-bending paintings and sculpture-painting with which he has encrusted the walls of his stately home inches deep, acres wide and of fathomless significance. **1970** *Listener* 22 Oct. 540 It can *mind-blow a long-haired GI to know he'll have to live straighter to survive in Sweden than in the Army or in America. **1968** *New Scientist* 27 June 703/1 Two chemicals with almost identical structures can have very different psychedelic properties: one might be a real *mind-blower and the other as ineffective as a sugar lump. **1969** *Gandalf's Garden* VI. 11/1 Mindblower, an experience or idea which changes one's thought-pattern, enlivening the mind and emotions. **1967** *Jazz Monthly* Dec. 16/3 While the music lasted little of this was evident; the spectacular *mind-blowing ferocity of it all simply carried the group through. **1968** *Times* 4 May 21 The poet celebrates the mindblowing effects of LSD and laments at the same time his lost childhood. **1973** *Guardian* 8 May 18/1 For the hopeful voyeur of sheer obscenity in modern urban life, Glasgow is hard to beat. 'Mind blowing', was the concise description of a former civil servant. **1974** H. MCCLOY *Sleepwalker* ii. 16 A mind-blowing mustard yellow for the woodwork and on the walls a psychedelic splash of magenta and orchid and lime. **1969** B. PATTEN *Notes to Hurrying Man* 23 Bloated We lie dreamless, *mind-blown in its ruins. **1907** *Mind* XVI. 620 The essential significance of the *mind-body relationship. **1920** S. ALEXANDER *Space, Time & Deity* II. 355 The acts of its mind-body would take the place of our organic or motor sensa. **1925** I. A. RICHARDS *Princ. Lit. Crit.* 84 The Mind-Body problem is strictly speaking no problem. **1963** A. KAPLAN in P. A. Schilpp *Philos. R. Carnap* 841 The situation is like that of the attempts to soften the mind-body dualism by introducing subtle interactions. **1970** H. FEIGL in C. V. Borst *Mind-Brain Identity Theory* I. 35 The crucial.. puzzle of the mind-body problem, at least since Descartes, has consisted in the challenge to render an adequate account of the relation of.. mental facts (intentions, thoughts, volitions, desires, etc.) to the corresponding neurophysiological processes. **1964** *Punch* 19 Feb. 257/1 A lot of *mind-boggling statistics. **1973** C. BONINGTON *Next Horizon* x. 146 A monstrous bergschrund, a huge, mind-boggling chasm about fifteen feet across. **1931** *Punch* 4 Nov. 494/2 Things and opinions change so quickly in these days that no one is going to crow over a graceful *mind-changer. **1958** A. HUXLEY in *Sat. Even. Post* 18 Oct. 110/3 Within a few years there will probably be dozens of powerful but—physiologically and socially speaking—very inexpensive mind-changers on the market. **1965** Mind-changer [see HALLUCINOGENIC *a.*]. **1885** W. F. EVANS (*title*) Healing by Faith; or, Primitive *Mind-cure. **1856** MISS YONGE *Daisy Chain* II. ix. 427 Dr. May, *mind-curer, as well as body-curer. **1886** BUCKLEY in *Century Mag.* June 234/1 The Mormons, Spiritualists, Mind-curers [etc.]. **1894** 'MARK TWAIN' *Lett.* (1920) 316 A patient had actually been killed by a *mind-curist. *a* **900** tr. *Bæda's Hist.* IV. xxx. (1890) 374 Ðy dæȝe þe his *ȝemynddæȝ wære and his forðfor. *a* **1380** *Eufrosyne* 665 in Horstm. *Altengl. Leg.* (1878) 182 Vche ȝeer þei don his mynde-day holde Anon to þis day. **1438** *E. E. Wills* (1882) 109, I bequeth for my mynde day, xx li. **1890** W. JAMES *Princ. Psychol.* I. vi. 146 Evolutionary psychology demands a *mind-dust. *Ibid.* xiii. 492 It is the mind-dust theory, with all its difficulties in a particularly uncompromising form. **1970** *Times* 26 Mar. 7 Hallucinogenic.. agents such as L.S.D., mescaline and other so-called *mind-expanders. **1973** *Black World* Apr. 16/1 The play is truly a mind-expander. **1963** *News-Call Bulletin* (San Francisco) 29 May 1/6 Professors Richard Alpert and Timothy Leary.. started several years ago to experiment with 'psychedelic' or '*mind-expanding' drugs. **1972** D. BLOODWORTH *Any Number can Play* xv. 135 This dim, suffocating chamber.. was.. decorated with.. mind-expanding daubs in fluorescent paint. **1883, 1891** *Mind-healing [see CHRISTIAN SCIENCE]. **1900** *Century Mag.* LIX. 635/1 The doctrines of faith-healing, mind-healing, and Christian Science. **1382** WYCLIF *Josh.* xxii. 10 Whanne thei weren comen to the *mynde hyllis of Jordan [Vulg. *ad tumulos Jordanis*]. **1496** *Dives & Paup.* (W. de W.) I. iii. 35/1 Euery masse syngynge is a specyall *mynde makynge of Crystus passyon. *c* **1449** PECOCK *Repr.* Prol. 4 Pilgrimage in going to the memorialis or the *mynde placis of Seintis. **1968** H. WAUGH *Con Game* viii. 81 These psychiatrists are too damned smart. All the time I was talking to him I had the feeling he was *mind-reading me. **1972** J. QUARTERMAIN *Rock of Diamond* xxiv. 156 If I mind-read you, you're looking for a fall guy to do your dirty work. **1888** *Pop. Sci. Monthly* Dec. 154 The professional '*mind-reader'.. takes his clew from indications which his subject is absolutely confident he did not give. **1882** *Proc. Soc. Psych. Research* I. 17 It was shewn that *mind-reading so called, was really muscle-reading. **1934** *Agric. Hist.* June 86 The 'oats' motif can be traced throughout Johnson's life. As a schoolboy the young Sam was given oatmeal porridge for breakfast, and if he was like many children, this may have given him a *mind-set for life. **1964** *Spectator* 6 Mar. 303/2 It was thereafter always a wonderful fight, although the mindset one brought to it made it impossible to recognise what was happening. **1971** *Amer. Benedictine Rev.* Dec. 424 The mind-set and aspirations of a vibrant hellenistic culture. **1587** GOLDING *De Mornay* v. (1592) 48 Neither the Sunne, nor any thing vnder the Sunne, can well be seene without the Sunne: likewise neyther God nor any thing belonging to God can be seene without God, how good eyesight or *mindsight so euer we haue. **1849** HARE *Par. Serm.* II. 243 The more we gaze at them the more is our mindsight improved to discern them. **1930** BLUNDEN *Leigh Hunt* ii. 22 The grace which the mind-sight of those merry young scholars awoke in him. **1935** —— *Edward Gibbon* 15 He felt that there was in the world actual need of a history such as I have mentioned hovering in the mindsight of his age. **1947** S. SPENDER *Poems of Dedication* 27 She drinks his acres of light Which.. Beyond mind-sight and eye-sight Reach a womb where his rays Penetrate her night. **1878** W. K. CLIFFORD in *Mind* III. 65 Mind-stuff is the reality which we perceive as Matter. That element of which.. even the simplest feeling is a complex, I shall call **Mind-stuff*. A moving molecule of inorganic matter does not possess mind, or consciousness; but it possesses a small piece of mind-stuff. **1930** A. D. LOVEJOY *Revolt Against Dualism* viii. 272 Mind-stuff is not supposed to be the same kind of thing as either data or the awareness of them. **1937** E. UPWARD in C. Day Lewis *Mind in Chains* 42 A poet's images or a novelist's characters are not created out of pure mind-stuff, but are suggested to him by the world in which he lives. *c* **1449** PECOCK *Repr.* I. xix. 114 The remembraunce and *mynde taking upon these vij maters is so necessarie a meene into the loue and drede of God. **1382** WYCLIF *Isa.* lvii. 8 And bihynde the dore.. thou settedest thi *mynde tocne [Vulg. *memoriale tuum*]. **1886** *Science* 17 Dec. 559/1 Mr. Hodgson is now engaged.. in some experiments on the subject of *mind transference, or the occasional communication of mental impressions independently of ordinary perceptions. **1897** 'MARK TWAIN' *Following Equator* 317 Here was a clear case of mental telegraphy; of mind-transference.

mind (mɪnd), *sb.*[2] *Archæol.* Also **minn.** [Middle Irish *mind*, mod.Irish *mionn*.] A name given to crescent-shaped ornaments found in Ireland, supposed to have been used as diadems.

1862 *Catal. Spec. Exhib. S. Kens.* 41, No. 851. Gold-ornament, believed to be the ancient Celtic 'mind' or head-ornament. Formed of a thin semi-lunar plate of gold with raised ribs. **1880** W. B. DAWKINS *Early Man in Brit.* 358 The golden coronets or minns.. worn in Ireland in legendary times. **1881** W. K. SULLIVAN in *Encycl. Brit.* XIII. 257/1 The richer.. kings wore.. a golden *mind* or diadem.

†**mind**, *a. Obs.* [OE. *ȝemynde*:—prehistoric **gamundjo*[m], f. OTeut. **gamundi-*: see MIND *sb.*[1]]

1. With dat. of person: Present to one's thought.

c **1220** *Bestiary* 611 Oc he arn so kolde of kinde Ðat no golsipe is hem minde. *a* **1225** *St. Marher.* 12 Me þu makest to asteoruen wið þe strenðe of þine beoden, þe beoð þe so imunde. *a* **1275** *Prov. Ælfred* 601 in *O.E. Misc.* 135 And ower alle oþir þinke God be þe ful minde.

2. Of a person: Mindful, taking thought: const. *of*, *for*, *about*, *gain*; also with inf.

a **1000** *Elene* 1063 (Gr.) Þa ȝen Elenan wæs mod ȝemynde ymb þa mæran wyrd ȝeneahhe for þam næȝlum. *a* **1300** *Cursor M.* 21895 And he gain us, sa meke and mind, Sua mikel luues nathing als ur kind. *Ibid.* 26457 Qua-so wrethes his lauerd king, and he o merci find him mind. *Ibid.* 28952 Þat þou be noght for þi flexs mind bot for to sustain maneskind. **1303** R. BRUNNE *Handl. Synne* 727 And y am euer so mynde For to pray for al mankynde.

mind (maɪnd), *v.* Forms: 4–5 **mende**, 4–7 **mynd(e**, 5–7 **minde**, 6– **mind.** [f. MIND *sb.*[1]

The OE. (*ȝe*)*myndgian* to remember, remind (f. *ȝemyndiȝ* mindful, f. *ȝemynde* MIND *sb.*[1]), usually cited in Dicts. as the source of this vb., is not immediately connected.]

1. a. *trans.* To put (one) in mind *of* something; to remind. Also, †to admonish, exhort. Also const. †*til*, *on*, and with *clause* or *inf.* Now *rare.*

1340 HAMPOLE *Pr. Consc.* 230 Knawyng of all þis shuld hym lede And mynd with-alle, til mekenes and drede. *c* **1400** *Destr. Troy* 4210 Ne mynd not þes men of þe mykyll harme, That a sone of our folke before hom has done. **1599** SHAKS. *Hen. V*, IV. iii. 13 Farewell good Salisbury, and good luck go with thee. And yet I doe the wrong, to mind thee of it. **1645** EVELYN *Diary* Easter Monday, The season of the yeare.. minding us of returning Northwards. **1657** SPARROW *Bk. Com. Prayer* (1661) 67 Minding the people what they are about. **1658–9** *Burton's Diary* (1828) III. 575 It was minded you by my learned countryman, that no law was rightly made, but by King, Lords, and Commons. **1669** COL. T. MIDDLETON in *State Papers, Dom.* 575, I hope you will mind the treasurers about the workmen, as they would fain have money. **1670–98** LASSELS *Voy. Italy* Pref. 3 These must be minded that I am writing of the Latin country. **1693** EVELYN *De la Quint. Compl. Gard.* I. 56, I must not forget minding those who dig along a Wall, to take care not to come too near the Foundations. **1713** SWIFT *Let. to W. Draper* 13 Apr., I have been minding my lord Bolingbroke.. to solicit my lord-chancellor to give you a living. **1788** BURNS *I Love My Jean* ii, There's not a bonie bird that sings, But minds me o' my Jean. **1847** TENNYSON *Princess* IV. 109 They mind us of the time When we made bricks in Egypt. **1851** MRS. BROWNING *Casa Guidi Wind.* 76 Spain may well Be minded how from Italy she caught,.. A fuller cadence and a subtler thought. **1890** W. A. WALLACE *Only a Sister* 95 [He] began to curse and swear like a trooper at Elizabeth for not minding him on what he was doing.

†**b.** To bring (an object) *to* one's mind. *Obs.*

1590 SPENSER *F.Q.* II. ii. 10 That, as sacred Symbole, it may dwell In her sonnes flesh, to mind revengement. **1600** ABP. ABBOT *Exp. Jonah* x. 219 In the last place I haue noted, that misery mindeth God vnto vs. Then the greater our miserie is, the more is our mind on our maker.

2. a. To remember, have in one's memory; to think of (a past or absent object). Now *arch.* and *dial.*

1382 WYCLIF *Rom.* Prol. i, Therfore he afermeth hem nedi to be confermed, the vices of her paynymrie rathere myndende. **15..** *Myst. Resurr.* in *Rel. Ant.* II. 156 Now she spekes of the scornes, Now she remembers the thornes,.. Now she spekes of his pacience, Now she myndes his obedience, That unto deth was. *c* **1586** C'TESS PEMBROKE *Ps.* LXXVII. viii, Nay, still thy acts I minde; Still of thy deedes I muse. **1586** WARNER *Alb. Eng.* II. vii. (1589) 28 King Achelous minding her for whom began that broile, Alcmenas Sonne remembring too, whose cause he did defend. **1625** B. JONSON *Staple of N.* II. iv. 100 Hee minds A curtesie no more, then London-bridge, What Arch was mended last. **1666** J. FRASER *Polichron.* (S.H.S.) 42 He minded often his mother Queen Margaret's advice. **1667** MILTON *P.L.* II. 212 Our Supream Foe in time may much remit His anger, and perhaps thus farr remov'd Not mind us not offending. **1786** BURNS *Halloween* xv, Ae Hairst afore the Sherra-moor, I mind't as weel's yestreen. **1864** TENNYSON *En. Ard.* 848, I mind him coming down the street. **1896** A. E. HOUSMAN *Shropshire Lad* iii, The lads you leave will mind you Till Ludlow tower shall fall.

b. with obj. a *clause*, or †with direct obj. and *complement*. Also *absol.*

1621 AINSWORTH *Annot. Pent., Gen.* iii. 24 Minding himselfe an exile and pilgrime here one earth. **1721** WODROW *Hist. Suff. Ch. Scot.* I. 455 The Instances of invading of Pulpits are yet fewer, that is, none at all, as far as I mind, in the preceeding Years. **1723** *Wodrow Corr.* (1843) III. 2, I mind, before Mr. Webster's death, he spoke to me about one of that name. **1800–24** CAMPBELL *Power of Russia* ix, But, Poles, when we are gone, the world will mind Ye bore the brunt of fate. **1860** DICKENS *Uncomm. Trav.* ix, The lovers.. so superlatively happy, that I mind when I.. went with my Angelica to a City church. **1861** HUGHES *Tom Brown at Oxf.* xviii, Tunes.. as ha' been used in our church ever since I can mind. **1893** STEVENSON *Catriona* xxiii, I minded how easy her delicacy had been startled with a word of kissing her in Barbara's letter. **1897** RHOSCOMYL *White Rose Arno* 144, I mind you promised us a Welsh army by the time we reached this place.

c. In *imperative*, or in context implying a counsel or warning: To take care to remember, to bear in mind (a fact communicated or already known, a duty to be done, etc.). Chiefly with obj. a *clause*.

[**1340** *Ayenb.* 262 Ymende þet þis boc is uolueld ine þe eue of þe holy apostles Symon an Iudas.] **1422** tr. *Secreta Secret., Priv. Priv.* xxiv. 154 Mynde thow how thow arte dedly. *c* **1450** *Osney Reg.* (E.E.T.S.) 1 It is to be myndyd that Robert Doyly and Roger of Iuory.. come to the conquest of Inglonde with Kyng William bastarde. **1675** R. BURTHOGGE *Causa Dei* 19 But it must be minded that though the Son of Man shall Judge the World, yet that he shall come to do so.. in the Glory of his Father. **1787** BURNS *Let.* 17 Apr. (in *Pearson's Catal.* May (1888) 8), In making up the accounts of my copies, please mind that I am paid for the following number of copies, which money I retain in my own hands. **1878** BROWNING *La Saisiaz* 14 Mind to-morrow's early meeting.

d. *intr.* with *of, on, upon*: To remember. (Now *dial.*) Also quasi-*refl.* in ***I mind me, he minds him***, etc. (*arch.*)

1422 tr. *Secreta Secret., Priv. Priv.* xxi. 148, I ne may not mynde me that the Emperours of Rome..wer vnlettride while that hare lordshupp was well gouernyd in his streynth. **1699** R. L'Estrange *Erasm. Colloq.* (1725) 92 Yet it seems reasonable enough, that the poor man should mind him of that in Hosea. **1810** *Cromek's Rem. Nithsdale Song* 219 O ask your heart gif it minds o' me! *a* **1855** Thackeray *Ballad of Bouillabaisse* x, I mind me of a time that's gone, When here I'd sit, as now I'm sitting. **1871** Mrs. H. Wood *Dene Hollow* i, I mind me that something was said about that paper at the time, resumed the Squire. **1896** 'L. Keith' *Indian Uncle* ii. 21 'Did Adam ever mention him before?' 'Never, that I mind of.'

3. *trans.* In pregnant senses.

†**a.** To mention, record. Also *absol. Obs.*

c **1450, 1494** [see minded 1]. **1513** Bradshaw *St. Werburge* i. 2972 And was incarnate, scrypture dothe mynde, In the vyrgynall wombe of blessed marye. **1530** Palsgr. 636/1, I mynde a thyng, I make mencyon of a thyng or mater. *Je mencionne.*

†**b.** To remember or mention in one's prayers, to pray for. *Obs.*

c **1420** *Anturs of Arth.* 230 (Douce MS.) To mende vs with masses, grete myster hit were. **1444** *Test. Ebor.* (Surtees) II. 106 To yᵉ vicar of Mitton a pare of get bedds for to myn my saule and mynde me in his prayers. **1688** M. Shields in *Faithf. Contendings* (1780) 327 Mind us when at the throne of grace.

c. To 'remember', i.e. to give to (those who need); to remember in a will. *dial.*

1714 Ramsay *Elegy on J. Cowper* ix, And to keep a' things hush and lown He minds the poor. **1886** Willock *Rosetty Ends* xix. (1887) 143 Aboot twenty o' the leadin' inhabitants had been mindit by Ebenezer to the extent o' sums ranging frae seventeen pounds to fifty-five pounds.

4. To perceive, notice, be aware of; to have one's attention attracted by (something presented to one's eyes or outward perceptions). Also *rarely* with *clause* as obj. *Obs.* exc. *dial.*

c **1489** Caxton *Blanchardyn* viii. 33 He mynded and dyde byholde his Ioyouse esperyte. **1596** Shaks. *Tam. Shr.* i. i. 254 My Lord you nod, you do not minde the play. **1610** —— *Temp.* ii. ii. 17 I'le fall flat, Perchance he will not minde me. **1701** Norris *Ideal World* i. i. 21 A finite intelligence..may sometimes..think of somewhat else than what he is doing, so as to be said in a manner not to mind what he is about. **1703** T. N. *City & C. Purchaser* 32 A Term used commonly ..but I did never mind it in any one of the Treatises of the ..Italian Architects. **1708** Swift *Tritical Ess.*, And Archimedes, the famous Mathematician, was so intent upon his Problems, that he never minded the Soldier who came to kill him. **1709** E. W. *Life Donna Rosina* 63 He not minding the figure that stood near the wall told his Master there was no body. **1781** J. Moore *View Soc. It.* (1790) I. vi. 66 One of the company had already passed [the picture] without minding it. **1789** Mrs. Piozzi *Journ. France* I. 2, I recollect minding that his..story struck Dr. Johnson exceedingly. **1821** Clare *Vill. Minstr.* I. 159, I minded him oft when at church, How under the wenches' fine bonnets he'd glower. **1880** *Antrim & Down Gloss.* s.v., See! d'ye mind the way she's walkin'.

absol. **1667** Milton *P.L.* ix. 519 Shee busied heard the sound Of rusling Leaves, but minded not.

5. a. To attend to, give heed to. Often, to give heed to (a person, his wishes, etc.) with the intention of obeying.

1559 Bp. Scot in Strype *Ann. Ref.* (1824) I. App. vii. 422 If men wolde diligently mind St. Paul's wordes. **1673** *Vain Insolency of Rome* 28 A short History, which I minded, when I heard it, the more heedfully. **1709** Mrs. Manley *Secret Mem.* (1736) III. 107 The Emperor is no more minded than a Baby in Leading-strings. **1738** Swift *Pol. Conversat.* 124 First it should swim in the Sea (do you mind me?) then it should swim in Butter. **1739** Chesterf. *Lett.* (1792) I. xxxi. 107, I looked upon it as a sign that you liked and minded my letters. *Ibid.* lix. 167 It signifies nothing to read a thing once if one does not mind and remember it. **1782** Miss Burney *Cecilia* iv. v, I have had..much ado to make him mind me, for he is all for having his own way. **1819** Shelley *Cyclops* 494 By all means he must be blinded, If my counsel be but minded. **1824–9** Landor *Imag. Conv.* Wks. 1846 II. 90 Would our father have minded the caitiffs?..Would he.. have minded parliament? **1866** G. Macdonald *Ann. Q. Neighb.* ii, But if your reverence minds what my wife says, you won't go wrong.

b. with obj. a *clause.*

1642 H. More *Song of Soul* i. iii. vi, They neither minded who, nor what I ask. **1669** Sturmy *Mariner's Mag.* 17 Mind at Helmne what is said to you carefully. **1709–10** Steele *Tatler* No. 132 ¶9 Old Reptile..winked upon his Nephew to mind what passed.

c. *absol.* or *intr.* To pay heed or attention. Chiefly *colloq.* in *imperative*, used to call attention to, or emphasize, what the speaker is saying.

1806–7 J. Beresford *Miseries Hum. Life* (1826) i. Introd., So I bar Latin, mind. **1832** Coleridge *Table-t.* 17 Mar., Something feminine—not effeminate, mind—is discoverable in the countenances of all men of genius. **1853** Lytton *My Novel* iv. xxiii, Now mind, mother, not a word about Uncle Richard yet. **1855** Browning *Fra Lippo* 113 But, mind you, when a boy starves in the streets..Why, soul and sense of him grow sharp alike. **1959** *Listener* 22 Jan. 154/2 The Japanese—who were scattered over a very large part of Asia at that time, mind you—would have all fought it out to the death. **1969** *Ibid.* 3 Apr. 467/2 And so to the book's title. It's not, mind you, 'why we are in Vietnam', but a question.

6. †**a.** *trans.* To have in view, have a mind to (an action, plan, etc.); to contemplate, purpose, intend, aim at (doing something); also, to plan, provide for (something external to oneself). Sometimes with clause as obj. *Obs.*

1513 Bradshaw *St. Werburge* i. 575 In meane whyle the kynge mynded maryage. **1513** More in *Hall's Chron., Edw. V.* (1550) 2 Which thyng in all apparaunce he resisted, although he inwardly mynded it. **1564** *Reg. Privy Council Scot.* I. 310 The saidis Lordis na wyise willing to call in doubt the autoritie and credit of the saidis lettres.., bot rather mynding that all strangearis, freindis, and confideratis of this realme..find all favour [etc.]. **1596** Spenser *State Irel.* Wks. (Globe) 615/1 And that noble prince begann to cast an eye unto Ireland, and to mynd the reformation of thinges there runn amiss. **1622** Bacon *Hen. VII* 246 If this King did no greater Matters, it was long of himselfe; for what he minded, he compassed. **1660** Sharrock *Vegetables* 94 A convenient descent must be minded. **1663** Gerbier *Counsel* (1664) 55 Those that mind the making use of Chalk in their walls, must [etc.]. **1691** T. H[ale] *Acc. New Invent.* p. lxvii, He could find no foot-steps of their having minded the Power of such Conservacy.

b. With *infinitive* as obj.: To have a mind *to do* something; to wish, be inclined, purpose, intend. *Obs.* exc. *dial.* (see E.D.D.).

1513 More in *Hall's Chron., Edw. V.* (1550) 1 The duke not entendynge so longe to tary but mindyng..to preuent the time. **1548–9** (Mar.) *Bk. Com. Prayer, Communion*, All other (that mynde not to receive the said holy Communion). **1593** Shaks. *3 Hen. VI*, iv. i. 106 Belike she minds to play the Amazon. **1634** in *Black Bk. Taymouth* (Bannatyne Cl.) 440 In the North, quhair I mynd to stay for tuo monethes. **1671** Milton *Samson* 1603, I sorrow'd at his captive state, but minded Not to be absent at that spectacle. **1683** D. A. *Art Converse* 2 If you mind to play the logician. **1791** Boswell *Johnson* an. 1763, Roubiliac..minding to put a trick on him, pretended to be so charmed with his performance, that [etc.].

c. *ellipt.* (in relative clause).

1573 *Satir. Poems Reform.* xlii. 463 Quhilk, gif thay mynd as thay pretend, Thay wald haue begun at this end. **1890** W. A. Wallace *Only a Sister* 124 He was wandering round the shelves, taking down a book here and there as he minded.

†**d.** To direct one's thoughts *toward. Obs.*

1633 W. Struther *True Happiness* 145 So if we minde toward heaven, wee must walk through the world as Strangers.

7. a. To bend one's attention to (e.g. something that one is doing or occupied with); to direct or apply oneself to, bring one's mind or energies to bear upon, or practise diligently.

to mind his book (colloq.; now obs. or arch.), of a schoolboy, to be diligent in his studies. ***to mind one's business***, to attend to it, prosecute it diligently; hence ***to mind one's own business***, to attend to one's own affairs and leave other people's alone (see business 16 d).

c **1400** *Destr. Troy* 9305 Achilles..Myche myndit the mater, in the mene tyme, And to bryng hit aboute besit hym sore. **1530** Palsgr. 636/1, I mynde a thynge, I regarde it, or set my mynde upon it. *Je mets le cueur dessus*, or *je prens au cueur.* It can nat go forwarde with the, for thou myndest it nat. **1577** B. Googe *Heresbach's Husb.* i. (1586) 13b, A man would thinke you had neuer minded any other profession. **1611** Bible *Rom.* viii. 5 For they that are after the flesh doe minde the things of the flesh. **1625**, etc. [see business 16 d]. **1660** *Trial Regic.* 52 All those..had a mind for Peace, that minded their duty, and Trust, and Allegiance to their King. **1662** Gerbier *Princ.* 1 Whereas Building is much minded in these times. **1712** Addison *Spect.* No. 383 ¶1 Bidding him be a good Child and mind his Book. **1732** Berkeley *Alciphr.* ii. §19 If some certain persons minded piety more than politics. **1835** J. H. Newman *Par. Serm.* (1837) I. xviii. 272 Mind little things as well as great. **1877** Spurgeon *Serm.* XXIII. 360 He went back to Samaria and minded his business. **1889** Browning *Pope & Net*, So much the more his boy minds book.

†**b.** To care for, like, value, wish for. *Obs.*

1648 Gage *West Ind.* 137 The only want of wheat is not a want to them that mind bread of Wheat more then of Maiz, for in two dayes it is easily brought. **1666** Stillingfl. *Serm.* (1673) 13 They [the kine of Bashan] minded nothing but ease, softness, and pleasure. **1748** Smollett *Rod. Rand.* ii. (1760) I. 10 His heir..minded nothing but fox-hunting.

8. a. In negative, interrogative, and conditional sentences: (Not) to care for, trouble oneself or be concerned about, be affected by. Hence: (Not) to object to, be troubled or annoyed by, dislike (something proposed, something offered to one, etc.). Often in polite or tentative formulas, as ***I should not mind*** (something) = I should rather like it, I should be glad to have it or do it; ***do you*** or ***would you mind*** (doing something)? = be so kind as to do it; ***do you mind?***: also used to mean 'do you mind not doing that?', i.e. 'please do not do that'; ***don't mind me*** (*colloq.*): take no notice of me; do not worry about me; do as you please; often ironical; ***if you don't mind***, if you have no objection.

1608 Shaks. *Per.* ii. v. 20 Now absolute she's in't, Not minding whether I dislike or no. **1710** Steele *Tatler* No. 206 ¶2, I did not mind his being a little out of humour. **1747–96** Mrs. Glasse *Cookery* xxiii. 365 They will look quite yellow, and stink, but you must not mind that. **1750** Lady Bradshaigh in *Richardson's Corr.* (1804) VI. 95, I do not mind him of two straws. **1776** Foote *Capuchin* i. Wks. 1799 II. 389 Why, yes, you may venture, Sir Harry: it is not minded in London. **1777** Sheridan *Sch. Scand.* iv. i, Never mind the difference, we'll balance that another time. **1860** Dickens *Uncomm. Trav.* vi, I am rather faint, Alexander, but don't mind me. **1863** *Ibid.* xx, Would you mind my asking you what part of the country you come from? **1867** Trollope *Phineas Finn* (1869) I. viii. 69 'It's the meanest trade going... I don't know whether you are in Parliament, Mr. Finn.' 'Yes, I am; but do not mind me.' **1874** Whyte Melville *Uncle John* xviii. II. 200, I shouldn't mind a cup of tea myself. **1875** Jowett *Plato* (ed. 2) I. 85 Let us take his advice, though he be one only, and not mind the others. **1889** 'J. S. Winter' *Mrs. Bob* (1891) 48 Stay, do you mind ringing the bell for me first? **1901** G. B. Shaw *Devil's Disciple* ii. 39, I never care much for my tea. Please dont mind me. **1911** —— *Doctor's Dilemma* iii. 70 *B.B.* Well, what is our friend Dubedat? A vicious and ignorant young man with a talent for drawing. *Louis.* Thank you. Dont mind me. **1926** M. A. von Arnim *Introd. to Sally* ii. 16 You go a'ead, sir, when she come back, and don't mind me. **1961** J. I. M. Stewart *Man who won Pools* xvii. 167 He was trying to put a hand on Phil's arm. '*Do you mind?*' Phil had never got it out more arrogant. Moore fell back. **1967** S. Knight *Window on Shanghai* iii. xx. 86 Ah, how philosophic I wax (and wane?) Don't mind me. **1973** L. Koenig *Little Girl* (1974) iii. 34 'Don't mind me,' she said, dragging the chair back..and filling its place with the table... 'But the table belongs here.'

b. Hence occasionally in an affirmative sentence: To object to, dislike.

1861 Cunningham *Wheat & Tares* 136 Yet her heart smote her now, for Ella minded going dreadfully and was unusually nice and affectionate.

c. *absol.* and *intr.* = (not) to care, trouble oneself, object, etc. Const. ***about***. Often in colloq. imper. phr. ***never mind*** = don't let it trouble you, it does not matter; also offensively (see quot. 1837) = it is none of your business.

1786 Miss Burney *Diary* 25 July, She begged me not to mind, and not to hurry myself, for she would wait till it was done. *a* **1814** *Gonzanga* ii. i. in *New Brit. Theatre* III. 112 Never mind, father, don't be obstroperous about it. **1837** Dickens *Pickw.* xxiv, There must be something very comprehensive in this phrase of 'Never mind', for we do not recollect to have ever witnessed a quarrel in the street,..in which it has not been the standard reply to all belligerent inquiries. 'Do you call yourself a gentleman, sir?'— 'Never mind, sir'. **1837** S. R. Maitland 6 *Lett. Fox's A. & M.* 70 *note*, The person whom Fox calls the Bishop of Penestrum (for we will not mind about a supposed misspelling). **1849** Thackeray *Pendennis* xxxi, The public don't mind a straw about these newspapers rows. **1884** Mrs. Ewing *Mary's Meadow* ii, Mother was very angry, but Father did not mind. **1898** *Times* 5 Oct. 3/3 Sir Herbert Kitchener told them never to mind and to come as they were.

d. ***I don't mind if I do***: a colloq. phr. of acceptance or agreement, used esp. in accepting the offer of a drink.

c **1847** J. S. Coyne in M. R. Booth *Eng. Plays of 19th Cent.* (1973) IV. 193 You *are* a regular brick, and I don't mind if I do take some of your pickles. **1849** C. Brontë *Shirley* I. vii [*sc.* viii]. 184 'Take another glass,' urged Moore. Mr. Sykes didn't mind if he did. **1870** D. J. Kirwan *Palace & Hovel* v. 65 Tell ye me 'istry, is it? Vell. I don't mind if I do. *Ibid.* 69 'I'll give you a drink, me oul wiper.'.. 'Well, Billy, I don't mind if I do.' **1926** C. Beaton *Diary* in *Wandering Yrs.* (1961) 143 Everyone 'talked common'... 'I don't mind if I do; oo-er!' **1932** A. Christie *Peril at End House* viii. 101 'Come and have a drink,' I said... 'I don't mind if I do.' **1946** T. Kavanagh *Tommy Handley in Holidayland* 5 'Bitter, sir?' interrupted the Colonel [Chinstrap]..., 'I don't mind if I do.' **1967** J. Porter *Dover & Unkindest Cut* xi. 122 'Another cup of tea, Mr Dover?' 'I don't mind if I do,' said Dover, passing his cup.

9. To bear in mind and be careful *to do* (something); to remember and take care *that* something is done. ***mind you do*** (so and so) = don't fail to do it.

1641 Best *Farm. Bks.* (Surtees) 16 In setting of their barres they are allwayes to minde to sett that side of the barres inwarde. **1710** Swift *Jrnl. to Stella* 12 Oct., But I will mind and confine myself to the accidents of the day. **1782** Miss Burney *Cecilia* viii. vii, But pray mind that she is kept quiet. **1837** Disraeli *Venetia* i. xix, Never mind about your handwriting; but mind you write.

10. a. To be careful about, take care of; to employ carefully or heedfully; to take heed (what one does). ***mind your eye***, 'look out', keep your eyes about you (see eye *sb.*[1] 2 a). ***to mind one's P's and Q's***: see P 3 b. ***to mind one's step***: see step *sb.* 6.

1737 Bracken *Farriery Impr.* (1757) II. 33 It is an easy Matter to..skreen Blemishes in the Hoof, if you don't mind your Eye. **1759** Sterne *Tr. Shandy* I. i, I wish either my father or my mother..had minded what they were about when they begot me. **1809** Malkin *Gil Blas* v. i. ¶2, I began to mind a little what I was about. **1840** Dickens *Barn. Rudge* xxx, He would recommend him..to mind his eye for the future. **1892** Mrs. H. Ward *D. Grieve* ii. ii, 'Mind what you're about', cried Purcell, angrily.

b. To be wary concerning, be on one's guard against, look out for (something that is to be avoided). Now only in the imperative or in contexts conveying counsel or warning.

1690 Locke *Hum. Und.* ii. xxxiii. §8 And though those [impressions] relating to the health of the body, are, by discreet people, minded and fenced against. **1881** Ruskin *Morn. in Florence* 25 You may let your eye rest..on the glow of its glass, only mind the steps half way. **1881** A. C. Grant *Bush Life Queensl.* x. (1882) 94 'You better mind that fellow, Mr. Fitzgerald', said the Native.

c. *absol.*, esp. in colloq. phr. ***if you don't mind*** = if you are not careful (to avoid something).

1691 Wood *Life* 9 Apr. (O.H.S.) III. 359 Being in hast, not minding, [she] set the cotton..on fire. **1839** James *Gentl. Old Sch.* xiii, Take care..they'll see you, if you don't mind, as you get over the bank in the moonlight. **1894** R. Bridges *Feast Bacchus* iv. 1290 You'll certainly be his death, unless you mind.

d. ***to mind out***: to look out, be careful; freq. ***imp. colloq.*** and *dial.*

1886 R. Holland *Gloss. County of Chester* 227 *Mind out*, ..to be on one's guard. **1890** *Dialect Notes* I. 65 Mind out what you are doing. **1892** *Ibid.* 233 That is the word with the

bark on it; you better mind out. **1894** W. Raymond *Love & Quiet Life* xii. 136 If I don't min' out, woone o' these days .. he'l vall off. **1938** J. Stuart *Beyond Dark Hills* iii. 59 John's got a bad boy. He'll go to the pen if he don't mind out—that boy will. **1946** *Amer. Speech* XXI. 56 English children whizzing around on bicycles.. will warn each other to keep out of the way by shouting 'Mind out!'.

11. *trans.* To take care of, take charge of, look after; to have the care or oversight of. *spec.* to look after (a baby or child), esp. in the absence of its parents; to look after (a shop or store) (also *transf.*).

1694 Dryden *Love Triumphant* Epil. 34 The wife, that was a cat, may mind her house. **1732** Neal *Hist. Purit.* I. 26 They were.. to exhort them to stay at home and mind their families. **1802** Mar. Edgeworth *Moral T.* (1816) I. 246 The men.. were gone to dinner: I stayed to mind the furnace. **1839** G. C. Lewis *Gloss. Herefordshire* 67, I ha left Bill at home to mind the children. **1873** W. Collins *New Magd.* xviii. II. 8 The lodge-keeper's wife.. is minding the gate. **1876** C. C. Robinson *Gloss. Mid-Yorks.* 84/1 Minding the bairns and the house. **1884** Mrs. Ewing *Daddy Darwin's Dovecot* iv, Let me mind your pigeons. **1899** Kipling *Stalky & Co.* 63 Arrah, Patsy, mind the baby; just ye mind the child awhile! **1902** *Dialect Notes* II. 239 Mind the baby while I'm gone. **1953** A. Upfield *Murder must Wait* x. 93 He accused me of neglecting the baby and said he'd.. let his .. secretary mind it. **1957** J. Blish *Fallen Star* vi. 75 The cabin door opened and the Commodore came out... 'Who's minding the store?' I asked him. 'Hanchett. We're on autopilot and he's watching the instruments.' **1963** J. H. Harris *Weird World Wes Beattie* (1964) iii. 32 If you will just mind the shop, I'll be on my way. **1970** G. F. Newman *Sir, You Bastard* ii. 70 The CID room was quiet. DC Jones was minding the shop. **1971** *Where* Nov. 343/2 A certificate is issued specifying the number of children and the hours and days when they can be minded. **1973** P. O'Donnell *Silver Mistress* vi. 109 'Who's running your section at the moment?' 'I am. With limited authority... I'm just minding the shop.'

12. *intr.* To matter, be important. (Not in standard use.)

1915 F. H. Lawrence *Let.* 16 Mar. in T. E. Lawrence *Home Lett.* (1954) 680, I had a room without a door or a window.. but that did not mind. *Ibid.* 682 Bullets really don't mind much. **1961** *Listener* 5 Oct. 500/1 (*child's composition*) You migth see a earwig gust coming out of [an apple] but that dosenet mind gust pick it of.

minded ('maɪndɪd), *ppl. a.* [f. mind *sb.*[1] and *v.* + -ed.]

†**I.** [From the vb.] **1.** That has been mentioned. Also ***fore-minded*** = forementioned. *Obs.*

c **1450** *Godstow Reg.* 147 Þe fore sayde Iohn perschore.. scholde warantiȝe to þe fore-myndyd religiouse women,.. þe fore-sayde londes. *Ibid.* 424 The mynded luke yaf to the mynded William at the entryng vij. mark. **1494** Fabyan *Chron.* v. xcii. 68 He then buylded the Castell before myndyd.

II. [From the sb.] **2.** 'Having a mind' *to do* something; intending, disposed, inclined. Also (*rarely*) with clause. ***to be so minded***: to be inclined to do what has been mentioned.

1503–4 *Act 19 Hen. VII* c. 28 *Preamble*, His Highnes is not mynded.. to calle & somone a newe parliament. **1530** Palsgr. 482/1 He was so mynded yesterday, but I have chaunged his purpose nowe. *a* **1533** Ld. Berners *Gold. Bk. M. Aurel.* (1559) Ooiij b, For if that the goddes giue me longe life, I am mynded for to amende. **1653** H. Cogan tr. *Pinto's Trav.* lxx. 285, I am not minded to make mention of them. **1703** Moxon *Mech. Exerc.* 249 They are minded to make their Plastering very streight and very smooth. **1775** Sheridan *Rivals* iv. i, Ne'er a St. [*sic*] Lucius O'Trigger in the kingdom should make me fight, when I wa'n't so minded. **1816** Scott *Antiq.* xxxvii, I am no minded to answer ony o' thae questions. **1861** Mrs. Carlyle *Lett.* III. 73 Mr. C. was minded to go nowhere this summer. **1874** H. H. Gibbs *Ombre* 29 Discarding at once himself.. if he be so minded. **1887** Bowen *Virg. Æneid* iv. 638, I am minded to finish the rite.. Sacred to Stygian Jove.

†**3.** Having a certain disposition (favourable or hostile) towards a person or thing. ***well-minded***: well-disposed, friendly. *Obs.*

1513 More in *Grafton's Chron.* (1568) II. 758 Which [*sc.* Clarence's death] he [Richard] resisted openly, how be it somewhat (as men demed) more faintly than he that were hartily mynded to his welth. **1577–87** Holinshed *Chron.* I. 148/2 This worthie prince minded well toward the common wealth of his people.. did studie [etc.]. **1579** W. Wilkinson *Confut. Familye of Loue* 3 He.. standeth minded agaynst God, and his Church. **1613** Shaks. *Hen. VIII*, iii. i. 58 We come.. to know How you stand minded in the weighty difference Betweene the King and you. **1677** W. Hubbard *Narrative* 98 A well minded Squaw that was among them.

4. a. Qualified by advs. (forming combinations which when used *attrib.* are often hyphened): Having one's habitual thoughts, tastes, or sympathies, inclined in a specified direction.

1611 Bible *Rom.* viii. 6 For to be carnally minded, is death: but to be spiritually minded, is life and peace [Coverdale 1535, *has* fleshly mynded, goostly mynded]. **1890** Imperially-minded [see imperially *adv.* 1 b]. **1903** *Daily Chron.* 9 Jan. 3/3 Rather monotonous even to the most commercially and statistically-minded.

¶**b.** The combinations with adv. have sometimes been used in the senses more properly expressed by parasynthetic formations with the corresponding adj.

1712 A. Philips *Distrest Mother* iv. vii. 43 Pyrrhus is nobly minded; and I fain Would live to thank him for Astyanax. **1828** *Sporting Mag.* XXII. 229 This man was strongly minded. **1843** Ruskin *Mod. Paint.* ii. iii. iv. §10 We are in the constant hope of seeing this finely-minded artist shake off his lethargy.

c. With prefixed sb. forming adjs. with the sense 'interested in or enthusiastic about (the thing specified)'.

1928 [see *air-minded* adj. s.v. air *sb.*[1] B. III. 1]. **1932** *Daily Express* 27 June 11/3 Get travel-minded. **1933** *Times Lit. Suppl.* 30 Mar. 205/3 Today we are an inland-dwelling folk, car-minded and mechanical. **1949** Helicopter-minded [see 'copter, copter]. **1956** *Planning* 23 July 153 PEP is intensely research-minded, and would rather not reach any conclusion than plump for one which cannot survive searching criticism. **1966** C. Mackenzie *Paper Lives* viii. 109 You *must* get computer-minded and appreciate that with the development of automation more and more people will be out of employment. **1972** *Guardian* 18 Aug. 9/2 There is also a bowling green for the sports-minded customer.

III. 5. Having a mind of a specified character. Chiefly in parasynthetic formations with prefixed adj. (The more common words of this formation, as *absent-*, *bloody-*, *double-*, *feeble-*, *healthy-*, *high-*, *noble-*, *strong-minded*, are either given as Main words, or are illustrated under their first element.)

1503 [see high-minded *a.*]. **1528** [see fleshly *a.*]. **1589** Puttenham *Eng. Poesie* i. (Arb.) 33 Being a quiet mynded man and nothing ambitious of glory. **1603** Dekker *Batchelor's Banq.* vii. *heading*, The humor of a couetous minded woman. **1872** Lever *Ld. Kilgobbin* (1875) 172 Supporters, one-minded with them in everything. **1872** Ruskin *Eagle's N.* §207 You want to know what sort of a minded and shaped creature it is.

Mindel ('mɪndəl). *Geol.* The name of a tributary of the Danube in Bavaria, W. Germany, adopted by A. Penck (in Penck & Brückner *Die Alpen im Eiszeitalter* (1901) I. 1. 110) and used *attrib.* to designate the second (antepenultimate) Pleistocene glaciation in the Alps, and in conjunction with Riss to designate the following interglacial period. Also *absol.*

1910 [see Günz]. **1939** [see interglacial *a.*]. **1957** G. E. Hutchinson *Treat. Limnol.* I. i. 6 Relatively early in the Pleistocene, probably at the time of the Mindel glaciation, the Caspian was occupied by a high-level lake. **1972** *Sci. Amer.* Mar. 60/1 Deposits laid down in the subsequent interglacial period, the Mindel-Riss, contain a few fossil remains of a true cave bear. A bear skull preserved in Mindel-Riss sediments at Swanscombe in England shows the domed forehead that is characteristic of the species.

minder ('maɪndə(r)). Also 5 **mendowre**. [f. mind *sb.*[1] and *v.* + -er[1].]

†**1.** One who remembers. *Obs. rare.*

c **1440** *Promp. Parv.* 332/1 Meende haver, or mendowre, *memor.*

¶**2.** As transl. of τὸ νοοῦν (the thinking subject).

1587 Golding *De Mornay* vi. 86 [Plotinus] his conclusion is, that the Mynder, the Mynding, and the Mynded, are in the Godhead all one thing.

3. One who minds. †**a.** One who sets his mind upon (something). *Obs.*

1650 O. Sedgewick *Christ the Life* 25 The Apostle speaks of Some who are Lovers of themselves.. and who are Minders of themselves; they mind Earthly things.

b. One whose business is to 'mind' or attend to something; often with defining word as ***card-***, ***cattle-***, ***engine-minder***; *spec.* (*a*) a machine-minder; (*b*) one who minds (see mind *v.* 11) a baby or child; a baby-sitter.

1835 Ure *Philos. Manuf.* 214 His machine should reduce the minder and the screwer to one person. **1863** [see *baby-minder* s.v. baby *sb.* B. 1 b]. **1867** *Even. Stand.* 14 Feb., Henry Clearby, a minder of carts. **1874** *Sunday Mag.* 610 'Minders', I echoed. 'Yes, women who make a trade of baby minding, taking them by the day at so much a head'. **1884** W. S. B. McLaren *Spinning* (ed. 2) 215 When the lap is large enough, it is taken off by the card-minder. **1885** *Spectator* 30 May 698/2 The engine minder who goes to the parish doctor because a spark has flown in his eye. **1888** *Encycl. Brit.* XXIII. 709/2 If he is a machinist, he may superintend or be a 'minder' or he may be a layer-on or a taker-off of the sheets. **1902** *Westm. Gaz.* 4 Apr. 6/2 One of the King's cattle-minders. **1938** *Amer. Speech* XIII. 271 The man who runs the presses is a *pressman* in America, but a *machinist* or a *machine minder* or simply a *minder* in England. **1941** [see *child-minder* s.v. child *sb.* 22]. **1957** *Times* 25 Nov. 11/4 Of course we will not worry about the children, we assure the kind minder as we blow farewell kisses. **1970** *Financial Times* 13 Apr. 4/5 Among minders, the proportion on litho presses is forecast to go up from 20 per cent. in 1967 to 28 per cent. in 1972. **1971** *Daily Tel.* 4 Nov. 9/3 Mothers, forced to work to make ends meet, ship their toddlers to unregistered minders, paid to keep an eye on them in 'cramped rooms, with no toys or stimulus'.

c. *slang.* A person employed to protect a criminal; a thief's assistant.

1924 E. Wallace *Room 13* xii. 61 Glancing down into the street, he distinguished one of the 'minders' his father had put there for his protection. **1928** —— *Flying Squad* xvi. 144 Whizzers.. had 'minders', whose business it was to kick and disable the poor souls who found themselves robbed and attempted to recover their own. **1960** *Observer* 25 Dec. 7/6 A climbing team.. was most often three-handed. Driver, minder, and climber... The minder stays at the foot of the pipe or ladder. His job is to safeguard the climber's rear and collect any gear he may sling down. **1968** C. Drummond *Death & Leaping Ladies* vi. 160 At school he was a juvenile fence and money-lender, with a couple of tough, simple-minded older boys as his 'minders'. **1973** E. McGirr *Bardel's Murder* ii. 35 Comes of a whole family of wrong 'uns... A high class 'minder' around the big gambling set.

4. A child who is 'minded' or taken care of at a 'minding school'.

1865 Dickens *Mut. Fr.* i. xvi, 'Those are not his brother and sister?'.. 'Oh, dear no, ma'am. Those are Minders'. 'Minders?' the Secretary repeated. 'Left to be Minded, sir'. **1903** *Treasury* Sept. 1046 There had been a dame school, kept by an old woman... She was quite illiterate, and her pupils were simply minders.

Mindererus (mɪndəˈrɪərəs). *Pharmacy.* [Latinized name of R. M. *Minderer* of Augsburg (*died* 1621) who first recommended its use.] ***spirit of Mindererus***, †***Mindererus's spirit***: a solution of acetate of ammonia, which is used medicinally as a febrifuge. (Now often with lower-case initial.)

1776 Fothergill in *Phil. Trans.* LXVI. 589 Spirit of Mindererus, volatile spirit of sal ammoniac. **1842** Francis *Dict. Arts*, etc., *Mindererus's Spirit*. **1871** Napheys *Prev. & Cure Dis.* iii. xi. 1646 Spirits of mindererus are of service.

mindful ('maɪndfʊl), *a.* Forms: see mind *sb.*[1] [f. mind *sb.*[1] + -ful.]

1. a. Taking thought or care *of*; heedful *of*; keeping remembrance *of*. Also const. with *obj. clause* and *how* or *that*.

a **1340** Hampole *Psalter* lxii. 7 If J was myndefull of the of my bede. **1382** Wyclif *Heb.* ii. 6 What thing is man, that thou art myndeful of him? **1579** B. Googe tr. *Mendoza's Prov.* 49 That where hee [*sc.* Cæsar] was verie mindefull of all other thinges, hee neuer would remember any iniurie doone vnto him. **1661** Marvell *Corr. Let.* xxvi. Wks. (Grosart) II. 63 We beseech you be mindfull that the 29th of May be kept for a thanksgiving. **1736** Berkeley *Discourse* Wks. 1871 III. 421 In all their actions to be ever mindful of the last day. **1849** Macaulay *Hist. Eng.* iv. I. 428 He had always been mindful of his health even in his pleasures. **1873** Black *Pr. Thule* x, Mindful of the fastidious ways of his friend.

b. Having remembrance *of*. *nonce-use.*

1859 Tennyson *Geraint & Enid* 191 Guinevere, not mindful of his face.. desired his name.

c. const. with *inf.*

1581 J. Bell *Haddon's Answ. Osor.* 420 To be Baptized in Churchyardes.. was an auncient custome.. that so such as were to be Baptized might be made yᵉ more myndfull to confesse a rising agayne from yᵉ dead. **1664** Evelyn *Kal. Hort., Mar.* (1679) 13 Be mindful to uncover them [the plants] in all benign, and tolerable seasons. **1692** Sprat *Contriv. Blackhead* i. 19, I was not so mindful to preserve the Letters that came to me. **1889** Gretton *Memory's Harkb.* 324 The monks were always mindful to establish themselves where there was water close at hand.

d. without const.

1567 Turberv. *Ovid's Epist.* 141 b, So she with mindefull wrath Upon my corse for thee awroken is. **1605** Camden *Rem.* 32 Antient families have given those names to their heires, with a mindefull and thankefull regard of them. **1728** Pope *Dunc.* i. 93 Much to the mindful Queen the feast recalls. **1747** Collins *Ode to Liberty* 16 Let not my shell's misguided power E'er draw thy sad, thy mindful tears. **1854** S. Dobell *Balder* i, Point with mindful shadow day and night, Where we lie dust below.

†**2.** Minded, inclined *to do* something. Also with ellipsis of vb. of motion. *Obs.*

1632 Lithgow *Trav.* ii. 59 A great number of passengers .. that were all mindefull to Zante. *Ibid.* 61 The Turkes retired till morning, and then were mindfull to give vs.. a second alarum. **1672** in *L'pool Munic. Rec.* (1883) I. 285 Any that shall bee mindfull to build upon or improve any such wast. **1681** Chetham *Angler's Vade-m.* xxxii. §1 (1689) 173 Tired and mindful to rest.

mindfully ('maɪndfʊlɪ), *adv.* [f. prec. + -ly[2].] In a mindful manner; 'attentively; heedfully' (J.); thoughtfully, earnestly, intently.

1382 Wyclif *Job* xxxv. 5 Behold heuene, and loke, and myndefulli see the cloudis, that is heȝere than thou. *c* **1540** *Compl. Roderyck Mors* xxiv. G viij b, We must regard, that our mouthe, spirit and hart be eleuated together mindfully in faith. *a* **1568** Ascham *Scholem.* ii. (Arb.) 122 Tullie did.. purposelie and mindfullie bend him selfe to a precise and curious Imitation of Plato. **1585** T. Washington tr. *Nicholay's Voy.* i. ii, The Ambassadour being mindfully bent to his charge. **1871** *Daily News* 20 Jan., He has mindfully left for me a message.

mindfulness ('maɪndfʊlnɪs). [Formed as prec. + -ness] The state or quality of being mindful; 'attention; regard' (J.); †memory; †intention, purpose.

1530 Palsgr. 245/2 Myndfulnesse, *pencee*. **1561** T. Hoby tr. *Castiglione's Courtyer* ii. (1577) G iv, To lose.. the mindfulnesse of them. **1577–87** Holinshed *Chron.* I. 169/2 There was no mindfulnesse amongest them of running awaie. **1612** T. Taylor *Comm. Titus* iii 1 (1619) 541 To keepe in mens memories the mindfulnesse of their duties. **1817** Moore *Lalla R.* (ed. 2) 72 That deep-blue, melancholy dress Bokhara's maidens wear in mindfulness, Of friends or kindred, dead or far away. **1820** Jay *Prayers* 355 Let us not forget our souls, in our mindfulness of the body.

minding ('maɪndɪŋ), *vbl. sb.* [f. mind *v.* + -ing[1].] The action of the verb mind.

1. The action of remembering, regarding, paying attention to, or caring for; also (now only *dial.*), remembrance, recollection.

c **1449** Pecock *Repr.* ii. ix. 191 Into suche now seid remembrauncis and myndingis to be gendrid and had.. mai and wole serue at ful Holi Scripture [etc.]. **1534** More *Comf. agst. Trib.* iii. Wks. 1257/2 This matter cosin lacketh, as I belieue, but either full fayth or sufficiente mynding. **1611** Bible *Rom.* viii. 7 The carnal mind [*marg.* the minding of the flesh] is enmitie against God. *a* **1652** J. Smith *Sel. Disc.* ix. 482 To awaken and exhort every one to a serious minding of religion. **1701** Howe *Carnality Relig. Content.* Wks.

(1846) 230 Souls for their too intent minding of earthly things are called enemies to the Cross of Christ.

2. *dial.* A reminder; = MINGING *vbl. sb.* 1. Also, *pl.* 'the marks on a stone about to be sawn, for the guidance of the sawyers' (E.D.D.).

1601 HOLLAND *Pliny* XXIV. xvii. II. 202 If a man or woman happen to be sick of any disease, at what time as this Aproxis is in the flower, although he or shee bee throughly cured of it, yet shall they have a grudging or minding [L. *admonitionem*] thereof as often as it falleth to flower againe. **1893** *Wiltshire Gloss.* s.v., After a severe illness you are apt to have 'the mindings on't' now and again.

3. *Comb.*, as **minding-school**, a dame-school of which the chief purpose is to keep the children out of mischief.

1865 DICKENS *Mut. Fr.* I. xvi, I keep a minding-school: I can take only three.

†**'minding**, *ppl. a. Obs.* [f. MIND *v.* + -ING².] That reminds.

c **1449** PECOCK *Repr.* II. ii. 137 The vsing of hem [*sc.* images in churches] as rememoratijf or mynding signes is not reproued by eny ground of feith.

mindless ('maɪndlɪs), *a.* [f. MIND *sb.*¹ + -LESS.]

1. Chiefly of persons and their attributes: Destitute of mind; unintelligent, senseless. Also, †that is out of his mind, stupefied, insane.

c **1000** ÆLFRIC *Hom.* II. 326 Se wisdom.. hine sylfne ætbret fram..myndleasum ȝeðohtum. *a* **1400–50** *Alexander* 5399 Oure mode kyng was so maied myndles him semed. **1509** BARCLAY *Shyp of Folys* (1570) 118 As men mindelesse. **1513** DOUGLAS *Æneis* IV. ii. 30 And, half myndles, agane sche langis sair. **1592** DAVIES *Immort. Soul* IX. ii, God first made Angels bodiless, pure Minds; Then other Things, which mindless Bodies be. **1633** *Orkney Witch Trial* in *Abbotsford Cl. Misc.* I. 151 Scho was senceles and myndles for ane long speace. *a* **1679** W. OUTRAM *Serm.* (1682) 468 Nor is the Devil asleep or mindless. **1843** RUSKIN *Mod. Paint.* I. I. i. 5 The mindless copyist studies Raffaelle, but not what Raffaelle studied. **1866** *Sat. Rev.* 19 May 602/2 What an amount of mindless rubbish a well-educated gentleman has the audacity..to lay before the public. **1885** J. MARTINEAU *Types Eth. Th.* I. 35 It..stands fast in mindless immobility.

2. Unmindful, thoughtless, heedless, disregardful, negligent, forgetful, careless *of.*

a **1547** SURREY *Æneid* IV. (1557) F iij b, Beastes and fowles ..Laide downe to slepe by silence of the night..; mindlesse of trauels past. **1641** HINDE *J. Bruen* viii. 30 So mindlesse of their owne duties. **1697** DRYDEN *Æneid* V. 225 Mindless of others Lives..and careless of his own. **1795** *Hist.* in *Ann. Reg.* 22 The ministers of Russia,..mindless of this representation, insisted on the appointment. **1895** SIR J. CROWE *Remin.* ix. 242 The younger men..dive for sixpences, mindless of sharks.

b. const. *in, whether.*

1641 HINDE *J. Bruen* xviii. 58 Being both mindlesse in observing, and carelesse in retaining what they heare. **1786** ANNA SEWARD *Lett.* (1811) I. 232, I choose..the strongest which spontaneously occur, to express my idea..; mindless whether they do, or do not form a part of the fashionable vocabulary of Lord Fillagree and Lady Pamtickle.

Hence **'mindlessly** *adv.*, in a mindless or unintelligent manner. **'mindlessness**, the state or condition of being mindless, heedlessness; *occas.* total privation of mental power.

1646 T. COLEMAN *Brotherly Exam. Re-ex.* 5 There was either ignorance or mindlessnesse in him that sets it downe. **1681** H. MORE *Exp. Dan.* vi. 171 He observed the luxury and dissoluteness of Philopator and his mindlesness of his affairs. **1704** M. HENRY *Fam. Relig.* Wks. (1853) I. 266/2 Your backwardness and mindlessness will be their greatest discouragement. **1857** *Nat. Mag.* II. 15 A poor idiot-girl who always came,—but as I thought mindlessly,—burst into tears and exclaimed, My mother, my Mother! **1899** *Allbutt's Syst. Med.* VIII. 304 We should have mindlessness before complete organic decay and death take place. *Ibid.* 383 The general aspect is that of mindlessness. **1963** *Times* 11 June 3/7 Dumitrescu worked away mindlessly like a machine at the head of the group. *a* **1966** M. ALLINGHAM *Cargo of Eagles* (1968) xv. 170 Temper and hysteria had fought mindlessly for the upper hand. **1972** *Publishers' Weekly* 21 Aug. 71/3 The result is mindlessly entertaining.

†**'mindly**, *a.* [f. MIND *sb.*¹ + -LY¹.]

1. Mindful.

1435 MISYN *Fire of Love* I. v. 10 Whylk fyer byrnand in þam þat is chosyn, myndely euer makes þame vp forto loke, and dede in þer desyre continuly to with-hald. *c* **1445** LYDG. *Nightingale* 128 Enprinte that fall [*sc.* Lucifer's] right myndely in thy herte.

2. Pertaining to the mind; mental.

1434 MISYN *Mending Life* xii. 128 Myendly [*sic*] sight truly is takyn vp heuenly to behald be schadoly syght ȝit & meroly, not clere and opyn. **1587** GOLDING *De Mornay* vi. (1592) 62 The Father created the mindly shapes, and gaue the gouernment of them to this second Minde. *Ibid.* 81 By his mindly Inworking he is the verie eternitie it selfe. **1832** *Fraser's Mag.* VI. 732 There to put off your lingering mindly drop of mortality, and be one of the blessed.

'mindsman. *nonce-wd.* A man of mind.

1837 C. LOFFT *Self-formation* I. 96 Those whose ambition it is to separate themselves from the herd, to rise to the rank of mindsmen.

†**'mindy**, *a. Obs. rare.* [OE. *myndiȝ, ȝemindiȝ*, f. (*ȝe*)*mynd* MIND *sb.*¹] Mindful. Hence **'mindiness** (Ormin), mindfulness.

c **975** *Rushw. Gosp.* Mark xiv. 72, & myndiȝ wæs petrus wordes ðætte cweden wæs him ðe hæland. *c* **1200** ORMIN 11508 Forr sawle onnfoþ att Drihhtin Godd Innsihht & minndiȝnesse. **1435** MISYN *Fire of Love* II. xi. 98 That parfite lufe to god byndis with-oute lowsynge & makis man myndy of his god.

mine (maɪn), *sb.* Forms: 4–7 **myn(e**, 6 **moine, myene, miene, mynne**, *Sc.* **mynd(e**, 4– **mine.** [a. F. *mine* (1314 in Hatz.-Darm.), whence Pr., Sp., It. *mina*; also G., Da. *mine*, Du. *mijn*, Sw. *mina*.

The origin of the Fr. word is doubtful. The evidence seems to point to the derivation of the sb. from the vb. (see MINE *v.*), which in the earliest instances had the general sense to excavate, make underground passages, undermine. (The alleged 9th c example of med.L. *mina plumbi* 'lead-mine' given by Du Cange is from a spurious charter.) This renders it difficult to accept the otherwise plausible connexion of the sb. with the OCeltic **meini*- ore, metal (Welsh *mwyn*, Irish *méinn*).]

1. a. An excavation made in the earth for the purpose of digging out metals or metallic ores, or certain other minerals, as coal, salt, precious stones (in 16th–17th c. occas. building stones, sand). Also, the place from which such minerals may be obtained by excavation.

royal mine, mine royal: in English Law, any mine yielding more gold or silver than will cover the cost of working: all such mines being liable to be claimed as the property of the Crown.

1303 R. BRUNNE *Handl. Synne* 10737 A perylous chaunce to hym fyl; For, a grete party of þat yche myne Fyl dowun yn þe hole, and closed hym ynne. **1390** GOWER *Conf.* II. 83 Ferst forto gete it out of Myne, And after forto trie and fyne. *c* **1407** LYDG. *Reson & Sens.* 6080 Of awmber ryche and fyn, Pulshed ful clene out of the Myn. **1467–8** *Rolls of Parlt.* V. 582/2 Mynes of Coles and Leede, and all other Possessions. **1535** COVERDALE *1 Macc.* viii. 3 The Mynes of syluer and golde that are there. **1551** ROBINSON tr. *More's Utopia* I. (1895) 64 Them they condempned into ston quarris, and in to myenes to dygge mettalle. **1555** EDEN *Decades* I. III. 11 By reason of a myne of stones which was nere vnto the same, seruynge well bothe to buylde with, and also to make lyme. ? **1568** in Pettus *Fodinæ Reg.* (1670) 54 The Governours, Assistants, and Commonalty for the Mines Royal. **1638** RAWLEY tr. *Bacon's Life & Death* (1650) 3 Stones continue longer, if they be laid towards the same Coast of Heaven, in the Building, that they lay in the Mine. **1649** BLITHE *Eng. Improv. Impr.* (1653) 149 Bring in severall Loades of Sands either out of the streets or wayes, or from a sand-pit or mine once or twice a week. **1672** BOYLE *Ess. Gems* 31 In East-India,..they are wonderfully unskillful at digging Mines; as I have gathered from the Answers of some, who..went to visit the Diamond Mines, as they call them. **1696** PHILLIPS (ed. 5), *Mine* is also that part of the Earth where Metals and Minerals are found, and out of which they are digg'd. **1698** KEILL *Exam. Th. Earth* (1734) 37 If we descend into the Mines or Pits, we shall find the matter there to be three or four times heavier than the earth above. **1813** BAKEWELL *Introd. Geol.* (1815) 276 The deepest mine that has been worked in Europe..is one at Truttenberg in Bohemia. **1870** YEATS *Nat. Hist. Comm.* 113 Gold and silver mines abound in the Andes. **1882** *Rep. to Ho. Repr. Prec. Met. U.S.* 96 The hydraulic and drift-mines during the last year have produced large sums.

†**b.** *hyperbolically.* An abundant mass of gold.

1656 COWLEY *Pindar. Odes, Extasie* ix, The Horses were of temper'd Lightning made,..The noblest, sprightful'st Breed, And flaming Mines their Necks array'd.

c. *fig.* An abundant source of supply; a store from which (something specified) may be obtained in plenty.

1541 R. COPLAND *Guydon's Quest. Chirurg.* O ij, Specyally aboute the pryncipal membres that are the mynes of strength. **1561** T. HOBY tr. *Castiglione's Courtyer* I. B ij b, Some in rydinge, some in playnge at fence, euerye man accordinge to the moine of his mettall [It. (1547) 6 b, *ciascuno secondo la minera del suo metallo*]. **1601** SHAKS. *Phœnix & Turtle* 36 So betweene them Loue did shine, That the Turtle saw his right, Flaming in the Phœnix sight; Either was the others mine. *a* **1764** LLOYD *Dial.* Poet. Wks. 1774 II. 4 You must have a fund, a mine, Prose, poems, letters. **1819** BYRON *Juan* I. xi, Her memory was a mine; she knew by heart All Calderon and greater part of Lopé. **1905** *Athenæum* 30 Dec. 887/2 Her book is a mine of valuable information.

†**d.** *transf.* A subterranean cavity. *Obs.*

1604 SHAKS. *Oth.* IV. ii. 79 The baudy winde that kisses all it meetes, Is hush'd within the hollow Myne of Earth And will not hear't. *c* **1611** CHAPMAN *Iliad* XVII. 51 When a whirlewind..tosseth therewithall His fixt root from his hollow mines.

e. *dial.* (See quot.)

1750 W. ELLIS *Mod. Husbandm.* VI. I. xvi. 92 The Middlesex Farmers about Harrow..get a..great deal of Sullidge out of the Bottom of Drains in Roads, Commons, and other Places, which they here call a Mine.

2. a. Mineral or ore. Now only used for iron ore. Also with defining prefix, forming adjs. (often used *ellipt.*): ***all-mine***, designating the best quality of pig-iron, made from ore only; ***part-mine***, designating pig-iron made from ore mixed with cinder.

orange mine: see ORANGE *sb.*¹ B 2 c.

c **1400** MAUNDEV. (Roxb.) xxxiii. 149 Þe erthe es full of myne of gold and siluer. **1460–70** *Bk. Quintessence* 3 Good gold naturel, and of þe myn of þe erþe, is clepid of philosophoris sol in latyn. **1581** LAMBARDE *Eiren.* II. vii. (1588) 305 Every occupier of any maner of Ironworks, which shall cary any coles, Mine, or Iron, to or from the same. *a* **1650** BOATE *Irel. Nat. Hist.* xvi. (1652) 126 In Ireland,..in some places the Oar of the Iron is drawn out of Moores and Bogs, in others it is hewen out of Rockes, and in others it is digged out of Mountains: of which three sorts the first is called Bog-mine, the other, Rock-mine, and the third with severall names, White-mine, Pin-mine, and Shel-mine. **1651** FRENCH *Distill.* v. 166 Take of the Mine of allum, or allum stones. **1674** RAY *Collect. Words, Prep. Tin* (E.D.S.) 12 The water runs out, and carries away with it the mine that is pounded small enough to pass the holes. **1861** FAIRBAIRN *Iron* 53 To increase the quantity of mine or ore to the charge. **1900** *Daily News* 24 Oct. 2/4 Pig iron sells slowly at..65*s.* for part-mine, 62*s.* 6*d.* to 70*s.* for all-mine.

fig. **1608** MACHIN *Dumb Knt.* I. i. B 4 b, The mine Which doth attract my spirit to run this marshall course, Is the faire guard of a distressed Queene.

†**b.** Applied *spec.* to gold. *Obs.*

1627 P. FLETCHER *Locusts* II. xxi, Poore Soules, they dare not soile their hands with precious mine. **1633** —— *Purple Isl.* VIII. xxvi, Thus wallowing on his god, his heap of mine, He feeds his famished soul with that deceiving shine.

3. *Mil.* In ancient warfare, a subterranean passage excavated under the wall of a besieged fortress, for the purpose either of directly giving entrance to the besiegers, or of causing the wall to fall by removal of its foundation. In modern warfare, a subterranean gallery in which gunpowder is placed, for blowing up the enemy's fortifications; the charge of powder contained in such a gallery. Hence, in recent naval warfare, a receptacle filled with dynamite or other explosive, placed under water, and provided with means by which it can be made to explode so as to destroy an enemy's vessel passing close to it. ***contact-mine***: see CONTACT *sb.* 6. Also, a receptacle containing explosive placed in or on the ground as a weapon of war; freq. with qualifying word indicating the kind or use: for *acoustic*, *land*, *magnetic*, etc., *mine*, see under the first elements.

1483 *Cath. Angl.* 240/1 A Myne, *cunus, via subterranea, cunulus, cuniculus.* **1523** LD. BERNERS *Froiss.* (1812) I. cix. 132 Then he called to hym his myners, to thyntent that they shulde make a myne vnder all the walles. **1533** BELLENDEN *Livy* V. viii. (xix.) (S.T.S.) II. 173 Þai made ane mynde [*MS. B.* myn] vnder þe erde to mak ane gate be quhilk þai mycht cum to þe castell of Veos. **1568** GRAFTON *Chron.* II. 981 Sir Alexander Baynam..caused a myne to be enterprised to enter into the towne, but the Frenchmen perceyuing that, made a countermine. **1574** WHITGIFT *Def. Answ.* 141 To buyld vp the walles of Jerusalem, whiche you haue broken downe: and to fill vp the Mines that you haue digged. **1599** SHAKS. *Hen. V*, III. ii. 61 To the Mynes? Tell you the Duke, it is not so good to come to the Mynes: for looke you, the Mynes is not according to the disciplines of the Warre. **1695** PRIOR *Ballad* 36 Cannons above, and mines below, Did death and tombs for foes contrive. **1781** GIBBON *Decl. & F.* (1869) I. xxiv. 689 A mine was carried under the foundations of the walls. **1844** H. H. WILSON *Brit. India* II. 476 The fort was carried by storm after the destruction of part of its defences by the successful explosion of a mine. **1853** HERSCHEL *Pop. Lect. Sci.* §24 (1873) 18 As if a succession of mines had been sprung. **1880** *Encycl. Brit.* XI. 309/2 The arrangements for exploding submarine mines or fixed torpedoes, where hostile vessels are passing close to them, are somewhat of the same character. **1889** J. T. BUCKNILL *Submarine Mines* XX. 219 Just as the mines themselves form a grand obstruction to the passage of large vessels..so smaller obstructions can..impede..the passage of small craft whose aims may be to attack the mines. **1890** [see *land-mine* s.v. LAND *sb.*¹ 12]. **1915** W. OWEN *Let.* 8 Jan. (1967) 313, I am not exposed to chances of mine or torpedo. **1942** *War Illustr.* 16 Oct. 238/1 A man can walk over a mine easily enough, but a tank or lorry'll send them up a proper earthquake. **1968** VISCT. MONTGOMERY *Hist. Warfare* xviii. 416 In 1855, in the Baltic, Russia made the first serious use of floating mines.

fig. **1639** S. DU VERGER tr. *Camus' Admir. Events* 30 All the subtilties, which he invented to intrap her, were as so many vented mines, without any effect. **1647** MAY *Hist. Parl.* III. vi. 100 Many Mynes and Countermynes were every day working..on both sides. **1722** DE FOE *Col. Jack* (1840) 286 An unseen mine blew up all this tranquillity.

4. (See quot.)

1869 *Routledge's Ev. Boy's Ann.* 632 The mine..is a firework in which a number of crackers..are thrown up into the air.

5. *attrib.* and *Comb.* **a.** simple attrib., as ***mine-agent, -crater, -dust, -fire, -head, -mouth, -owner, -pump*** (in quot. *attrib.*), ***-shaft, -slime, -stamp*** (STAMP *sb.*³ 9), ***-warfare, -water, -worker***; **b.** objective, as ***mine-digger, -digging***.

1855 J. R. LEIFCHILD *Cornwall Mines* 262 What exactly suits the views of a *mine-agent, may not exactly suit yours. **1917** 'CONTACT' *Airman's Outings* 269 Two huge *mine-craters sentinel it, left and right. *a* **1691** BOYLE (J.), A *mine-digger may meet with a gem, which he knows not what to make of. **1648** OWEN *Toleration* Wks. 1851 VIII. 176 Which penalty..was inflicted unto banishment, imprisonment, *mine-digging. **1886** J. BARROWMAN *Gloss. Scottish Mining Terms* 45 **Mine dust*, the riddlings of calcined ironstone. **1813** SCOTT *Trierm.* III. xxxiii, Foul vapours rise and *mine-fires glare. **1923** *Daily Mail* 16 Mar. 9 The present intention is to send labour squads..to successive *mine-heads. **1886** J. BARROWMAN *Gloss. Scottish Mining Terms* 45 **Mine mouth*, the point where a mine leaves the surface of the ground. **1877** RAYMOND *Statist. Mines & Mining* 341 *Mine-owners are naturally elated and hopeful under this new..condition of affairs. **1824** R. STUART *Hist. Steam Engine* 117 The *mine-pump end of the lever-beam. **1831** CARLYLE *Sart. Res.* I. iv, On the whole, as in opening new *mine-shafts is not unreasonable, there is much rubbish in his Book. **1921** *Chambers's Jrnl.* Apr. 262/1 A savage land of rocks and lakes and *mine-slime and active and derelict mine-workings. **1926** J. MASEFIELD *Odtaa* xiv. 233 It is a kind of a *mine-stamp, or engine of some sort. **1953** D. LESSING *Five* III. 128 The mine-stamps thudded day and night, coming loud or soft, according to the direction of the wind. **1910** *Blackw. Mag.* June 895/2 The immense development of *mine warfare. **1957** *Encycl. Brit.* XV. 531/2 A self-contained continental power..has little to lose and everything to gain by unrestricted mine warfare. **1974** *Saturday* (Charleston, S. Carolina) 20 Apr. 3-A/2 Like wood, the fiberglass hull is non-magnetic and is considered good for mine warfare. **1882** *Rep. to Ho. Repr. Prec. Met. U.S.* 640 A very ingenious utilization of a portion of the *mine-waters is made. **1901** *Edin. Rev.* Apr. 496 An agreement..that the *mine-workers should receive an

advance of 10 per cent. in their rates of wages. **1928** *Britain's Industr. Future* (Liberal Industr. Inquiry) IV. 266 The pensioning of older mine-workers. **1975** *Times* 18 Feb. 2/1 Mineworkers' leaders in the traditionally militant areas of Scotland and Yorkshire yesterday voted to back the £140m pay deal negotiated by their national union leaders with the National Coal Board last week.

6. Special comb.: **mine adventure**, a speculation in mines; **mine-adventurer**, one who takes part in a mine adventure; **mine-boy** *S. Afr.*, a native African who works in the mines; **mine-captain**, the overseer of a mine (Worcester, 1860); **mine-car** (see quots.); **mine-clearing**, the operation of freeing a harbour from mines; **mine-detector**, an instrument which, by its reaction to metal, indicates the presence of mines; **mine-dial** (see quot.); **mine-dragging**, the operation of dragging the bottom of the sea in order to remove the mines laid by the enemy; **mine dredger**, an apparatus for taking up mines laid; **mine-dump** *S. Afr.*, a pile of refuse material on the surface of a mine, esp. a gold-mine (cf. DUMP *sb.*[4] 1); **mine earth** (see quot. and cf. sense 2); **mine-field**, a portion of the sea in which mines have been laid; also, an area of land in which mines have been laid; also *fig.*; **mine greys**, 'thin beds of shelly limestone' (E.D.D.); **mine ground** (see quot.); **mine-hunt** *v. intr.*, to hunt or sweep for mines; **mine-hunter** = *mine-sweeper*; **mine-hunting** = *mine-sweeping*; **mine-iron** = *mine pig*; **mine-lamp**, a lamp used in a mine; also *fig.*; **mine-layer**, a ship or aeroplane equipped to lay mines; **mine-laying**, the operation of laying explosive mines; also *attrib.* or as *adj.*; † **mine man**, a miner; **mine-master**, (*a*) *Mil.* one who superintends the laying of mines; (*b*) the overseer of a mine; **mine-pig**, pig-iron made from mine or ore, as distinguished from *cinder-pig*; **mine-pit**, a pit or shaft belonging to a mine; **mine ship** *Naut.*, (see quot.); **mine-sinker**, a device for keeping a mine submerged; **mine-sowing** = *mine-laying*; **mine-spirit**, a spirit supposed to inhabit a mine (cf. FAIRY *sb.* 4b); **mine-stone, -stuff**, ore, *esp.* ironstone; **mine surveyor** (see quot.); **mine-sweeper**, a ship for mine-sweeping; **mine-sweeping** = *mine-dragging*; **mine-thrower** [tr. G. *minenwerfer*], a trench-mortar; **mine tin**, tin worked out of the lode; cf. *moor-tin*, *stream-tin*; **mine-tipple** *N. Amer.* [TIPPLE *sb.*[3]], a tip (TIP *sb.*[5] 3) at a mine; **mine-town**, a town of which the population consists chiefly of miners; **mine-viewer** = *mine surveyor*; **mine-work**, (*a*) *Mil. pl.* subterraneous passages of the nature of mines; (*b*) a system of 'workings' or excavated passages belonging to a mine.

1700 *Broadside*, List of all the Adventurers in the *Mine Adventure, May the First, 1700. **1703** Steele *Tend. Husb.* II. i. 26, I consider'd all the Stocks..and Mine-Adventures, till she told me [etc.]. **1778** *Eng. Gazetteer* (ed. 2) s.v. *Pullox-Hill*, A gold mine was discovered here..by the society of royal *mine-adventurers. **1945** P. Abrahams *Song of City* 73 The tom-tom beat of the Maraba..danced away the seething bitterness that is attendant with repression... On the morrow the houseboy would be a good..houseboy!.. And the *mine-boy. **1953** P. Lanham *Blanket Boy's Moon* I. v. 51 One Monare, a mine-boy, friend of Ntoane here, was watching. **1954** P. Abrahams *Tell Freedom* III. iii. 108 Fights often flare up between mine-boys and house-boys. **1956** F. S. Atkinson in D. L. Linton *Sheffield* 270 Diesel locomotives with large *mine-cars are being used extensively underground, particularly in Yorkshire. **1967** *Gloss. Mining Terms* (*B.S.I.*) x. 11 *Mine car*, a large tub (usually spring mounted and over 60 ft..capacity) used primarily for mineral haulage underground. **1905** *Q. Rev.* Jan. 204 Several smaller craft were destroyed in the operation of *mine-clearing. **1943** *Hutchinson's Pict. Hist. War* 12 May—3 Aug. 125 (*caption*) The soldier in the foreground is sweeping the ground with a *mine detector and wearing earphones as he listens intently for the buzz indicating the presence of a mine. **1945** *Finito! Po Valley Campaign* 41 The glass-topped Topf mines that fooled the mine-detectors. **1955** E. S. Gardner *Case of Glamorous Ghost* (1960) x. 121, I used what is known as a mine detector ..an electronic device so designed that when it is moved over the surface of the ground it will give a peculiar squeal when it is moved over a metallic object. **1701** Moxon *Math. Instrum.* 12 *Mine-dial*, a Box and Needle with a brass Ring, divided into 360 degrees, with several Dials Graduated thereon, generally thus made for the use of Miners. **1905** *Blackw. Mag.* Jan. 167/1 On May 12 *mine-dragging operations in Talien Bay cost him a torpedo-boat. **1904** *Daily Chron.* 9 Aug. 5/1 Our ships, preceded by *mine dredgers, steamed towards Lungantan. **1926** S. G. Millin *S. Africans* iii. 77 They are the *mine-dumps, the refuse of stamp-mill and cyanide tank. **1956** V. Jenkins *Lions Rampant* v. 76 Dominating the landscape..are the huge yellow-white mine dumps which mark the gold mines. **1971** *Gloss. Soil Sci. Terms* (Soil Sci. Soc. Amer.) 11/1 *Mine dumps*, areas covered with overburden and other waste materials from ore and coal mines, quarries, and smelters, and usually with little or no vegetative cover. **1883** Gresley *Coal-mining Gloss.*, *Mine Earth (N.S.). Synonymous with ironstone in beds: a term used as much as 200 years ago. **1886** *Pall Mall G.* 21 Aug. 1/2 It has been already shown by similar attacks upon *mine fields unprotected in this way that the removal of such obstacles is a simple enough affair. **1889** J. T. Bucknill *Submarine Mines* xiv. 168 Secrecy is essential... Any artifice which ingenuity can suggest should be undertaken... False reports concerning the mine fields should be spread. **1917** A. Conan Doyle *His Last Bow* viii. 298 It would brighten my declining years to see a German cruiser navigating the Solent according to the minefield plans which I have furnished. **1938** *Encycl. Brit. Bk. of Year* 432/2 Other anti-tank agencies being given consideration are mine-fields and 'catch trenches' (*i.e.* tank traps). **1942** *Times* 8 June 4/6 The 'Cauldron', an area.. between..the upper and lower gaps which Rommel forced through our minefield. **1957** *Encycl. Brit.* XV. 532/2 By the end of 1914 Britain had established extensive mine-fields in the English Channel. **1963** *Times* 16 Feb. 4/6 This bold venture into the mine-fields of satire is one to be supported and preserved. **1968** Visct. Montgomery *Hist. Warfare* xxi. 512 Wavell once compared the tactics of war in the desert to war at sea; minefields were laid in the desert very much as they were in the sea. **1973** *Times* 30 Nov. 19/1 He is..operating..in a political minefield, requiring more circumspection than he has always managed. **1862** A. C. Ramsay, etc. *Descr. Catal. Rock Spec.* (ed. 3) 149 In many of the localities in the Weald these limestones are known by the name of *mine greys. **1883** Gresley *Coal-mining Gloss.*, *Mine Ground, strata containing ironstone in layers. **1964** *Navy News* Nov. 5/5 After refitting and converting.. H.M.S. *Iveston* commissioned on October 16th as a Coastal *Minehunter. **1974** *Times* 18 Apr. 1/4 It is the diver's job to locate the unexploded bomb on the canal floor after it has been picked up by the mine-hunter's sonar equipment. **1915** Kipling *Fringes of Fleet* 74 He's *mine-hunting, I expect, just now. **1964** *Navy News* Nov. 5/5 She will join the First Minehunting Squadron in December and will be based at Port Edgar in the Firth of Forth. **1974** *Observer* 17 Mar. 8/4 Minehunting ships—the Navy's new name for minesweepers. **1974** *Saturday* (Charleston, S. Carolina) 20 Apr. 3-A/2 The mine-hunting vessels include two with wood hulls and one with an experimental fiberglass hull... All three mine hunting vessels have sonar to detect mines and other objects like bombs. **1838** *Civil Eng. & Arch. Jrnl.* I. 144/1 The iron is..to be made wholly of pure or *mine-iron. **1820** Shelley *Sens. Plant* I. 63 As *mine-lamps enkindle a hidden gem. **1909** *Q. Rev.* Oct. 575 Six second-class cruisers of the Naval Defence Act have been converted into *mine-layers. **1923** W. S. Churchill *World Crisis 1915* 260 The mine-layer *Nousret* had on March 18 thirty-six mines ready for laying. **1939** *War Illustr.* 16 Dec. 435 Raid by British warplanes..on the German seaplane base at Borkum. They had been looking for the mine-layers —and they had found them. **1944** *Aeronautics* July 32/3 Suitable for duties as a torpedo bomber, a dive bomber, or a mine layer, the Fairey Barracuda was first reported in action on the 3rd April 1944. **1911** *Q. Rev.* Oct. 466 The money..is now expended upon a large and increasing fleet of *mine-laying and mine-sweeping ships. **1921** *Flight* 19 May 348/2 The American naval authorities are reported to have been carrying out in Chesapeake Bay experiments in mine-laying from the air. **1928** C. F. S. Gamble *Story N. Sea Air Station* xviii. 310 The U.C. boats were of a type designed both for mine-laying and torpedo work. **1939** *Flight* 30 Nov. 429/2 The mine-laying machines cannot behave as the enemy reconnaissance machines have been behaving of late, namely arriving at a great height and hurrying away at the first hint of defence activity. **1955** *Times* 24 May 8/4 The risk of more serious incidents, such as Egyptian minelaying and Israel retaliation, should also lessen. **1958** P. Kemp *No Colours or Crest* iii. 37 The fast mine-laying cruiser *Manxman*. **1579–80** North *Plutarch, P. Æmilius* (1595) 268 They are confuted by the common experience of these *mine men, that dig in the mines for mettall. **1755** Johnson, *Adit*,..a term among the minemen. **1598** Barret *Theor. Warres* v. iii. 133 There must be, *Mine-maisters, Smithes [etc.]. **1665** *Phil. Trans.* I. 112 The Requisits to a perfect knowledge of the Metallick Art, and of the qualities of the Mine-master. **1683** in Cochran-Patrick *Rec. Coinage Scotl.* (1876) II. 200 That he or his deputie or the myn master be judges in all debaits about myns and levells. **1881** Raymond *Mining Gloss.*, *Mine-pig, Eng. See *Pig-iron*. **1884** W. H. Greenwood *Steel & Iron* iv. 56 Cinder-pig in contradistinction to all mine pig—i.e., pig smelted entirely from ore or mine—is obtained by [etc.]. **1650** Trapp *Comm. Num.* iv. 3 A labouring even to lassitude; compared therefore to..digging in *mine-pits. **1862** A. C. Ramsay, etc. *Descr. Catal. Rock Spec.* (ed. 3) 148 These still go by the name of 'mine-pits', and must not be confounded with the 'marl-pits', or those other deeper openings. **1706** Phillips (ed. Kersey) **Mine Ships* or *Powder-Ships*, Ships fill'd with Gun-powder, enclos'd in strong Vaults of Brick or Stone; to be brought up, and fired in the midst of the Enemies Fleet. **1889** C. Sleeman *Torpedoes* (ed. 2) vi. 119 The only practicable method of testing the efficiency of *mine anchors or sinkers is to moor a buoyant mine to an anchor. **1926** *Spectator* 21 Aug. 271/1 He..produced 50,000 minesinkers at a very low cost. **1940** Bartlett & Williams *War of 1939* II. iii. 104 The Germans..had turned to indiscriminate *mine-sowing. **1940** *War Illustr.* 5 Jan. 568/3 Particular attention being paid to the favourite areas of the mine-sowing seaplanes in the Thames Estuary. **1756–7** tr. *Keysler's Trav.* (1760) IV. 144 It is said that the miners of Idra have formerly been so superstitious as to set some provisions for the *mine-spirit every day. **1612** Sturtevant *Metallica* 35 Prepared or roasted oares, *Mine-stones, or Mettle-stones beeing the fitt matter of Metallique liquours. **1703** T. N. *City & C. Purchaser* 185 'Tis the first Iron that runs from the Mine-stone when 'tis melting. **1862** A. C. Ramsay, etc. *Descr. Catal. Rock Spec.* (ed. 3) 148 The sites ..where the 'iron-mine' or 'mine-stone' was extracted. **1839** Ure *Dict. Arts* 969 During this operation, all the water and *mine-stuff are drawn off by the pit. **1860** *Eng. & For. Min. Gloss.* (S. Staffs.), **Mine Surveyor*, a person who dials the working of a colliery as often as requisite, and makes plans of the mines got and ungot. **1905** *Westm. Gaz.* 27 Sept. 4/2 *Mine-sweepers are to play a great part, it seems certain, in future naval warfare. **1914** *Illustr. London News* 22 Aug. 286/3 Mine-sweepers..precede the fleet to sea and clear its path of hostile mines. **1940** Bartlett & Williams *War of 1939* II. iii. 106 Mine damage at this time was not confined to merchant vessels, the British minesweepers *Mastiff* and *Aragonite* being sunk with casualties. *Ibid.* 107 The British Admiralty were quick..to appeal for two hundred additional drifters to act as minesweepers. **1972** *Daily Tel.* 21 Jan. 2/8 More mine-sweepers and helicopters will be used from this summer to improve coastal fishery protection. *Ibid.*, Helicopters..will make spotter sweeps to help the minesweepers to guard the six-mile limit fishing areas against unauthorised vessels. **1904** *Daily Chron.* 9 Nov. 5/2 Five *mine-sweeping steamers have been sunk by Japanese shells. **1905** *Ibid.* 12 Sept. 3/1 He took part in the risky game of mine-sweeping. **1915** *Chambers's Jrnl.* May 294/2 The operation of taking up mines is known as 'mine-sweeping'. **1958** *Times* 11 Nov. 9/1 Two coastal mine-sweeping flotillas..are already under N.A.T.O. command. **1973** *Listener* 26 Apr. 535/1 Mine-sweeping operations off Haiphong. **1915** *Illustr. London News* 13 Feb. 204/2 The Germans..had actually provided..themselves with mortars of this description, the so-called *minen-werfer*—*mine-throwers. **1923** *Daily Mail* 17 Jan. 7 They captured 7 Frenchmen, 15 local policemen, 3 minethrowers, and a machine gun. **1602** Carew *Cornw.* (1723) 15 b, A foote of.. the *Myne Tynne..[will weigh] fiftie two pound. **1839** Ure *Dict. Arts* 1244 Mine tin requires peculiar care in its mechanical preparation or dressing. **1930** J. Dos Passos *42nd Parallel* I. 111 In the middle of squirrels and *minetipples. **1974** *Beautiful Brit. Columbia* Spring 27/2 Coal is still mined there in large quantities. The highway passes underneath a portion of the mine tipple. **1802** *Brookes' Gazetteer* (ed. 12), Platen, a *mine-town of Bohemia. **1839** Ure *Dict. Arts* 1271 At the pleasure of the skilful *mine-viewer. **1583** Stocker *Civ. Warres Lowe C.* IV. 49 b, The Enemie had in suche sorte wrought his *Mine woorkes, as that he had gotten into a Monasterie within the Citie. **1665** *Phil. Trans.* I. 112 Other chief Overseers of the Mine-works. **1900** Baring-Gould *Bk. Dartmoor* 231 An old mine-work, now filled with water.

mine (maɪn), *poss. pron.* Forms: 1 mín, 2–4 min, 3–6 myn(e, 4 mein, miin, 6 mijn, *Sc.* mynn(e, 3– mine. In 1–3 inflected as str. adj. (2–3 *dat. sing. fem.* mire); in 4 *sing.* min, *pl.* mine. [Com. Teut.: OE. *mín* = OFris., OS. *mîn* (Du. *mijn*), OHG. *mîn* (MHG. *mîn*, mod.G. *mein*), ON. *mín-n* (Sw., Da. *min*), Goth. *mein-s*:—OTeut. **mîno-*, f. **me-*: see ME *pers. pron.*

A case-form (whether ablative, locative, or instrumental is uncertain) of this possessive adj. serves in all early Teut. langs. as the genitive of the pronoun of 1 pers. sing.: OE. *mín*, OFris., OS., OHG. *mîn*, ON. *mín*, Goth. *meina*. The OE. *mín* as genitive did not survive into ME. (uses like *malgre min* being not survivals, but imitations of French); and is therefore not illustrated here.]

The possessive pronoun of the first person sing.

1. Qualifying a following sb. Now only *arch.* or *poet.* before a vowel or *h*; otherwise superseded by MY, q.v. for the various uses.

Already in the 13th c. the rule in southern and midland Eng. was to use *myn* before vowels and *h*, and *my* before consonants, and this subsisted until the 18th c., though occasional examples of *mine* before consonants are found even in the 16th c. In Sc. the longer form was commonly used in all contexts down to the 15th c.

c **1000** *Ags. Gosp.* Luke xv. 24 For-þam þes min sunu wæs dead. *a* **1175** *Cott. Hom.* 225 þanne beo ic ʒemeneʒed mines weddes. *c* **1200** Ormin 2956 Drihhtin me ȝifeþ witt & mihht To forþenn wel min wille. *c* **1205** Lay. 8407 þe oðer wes mire suster sune. *Ibid.* 28220 þat ich habbe minne æm awræke mid þan bezste. *a* **1225** *Ancr. R.* 406 Bute ȝif ich parti urom ou, þe Holi Gost, þet is, min and mines Federes luue, ne mei nout kumen to ou. *c* **1374** Chaucer *Compl. Mars* 57 Then seyde he thus—myn hertes lady swete [etc.]. *c* **1375** *Sc. Leg. Saints* Prol. 169 At Petir firste I wald begyne, And sa furtht to myn purposs win. **1400** in *Ancestor* July (1904) 14, I bequeth to Hawys myn wyff all myn necessaries that arn in myn place. **1467** in *Bury Wills* (Camden) 46, I wyll that John myn sone haue myn seid place callyd Upwode Halle. **1484** Caxton *Fables of Æsop* I. vi, He shall be myn mortal enemy. **1526** Tindale *John* xvi. 26 At that daye shall ye axe in myne name. **1558** in Strype *Ann. Ref.* (1824) I. ii. 72, I do send you at this present mine faithful Chaplain. **1596** Shaks. *1 Hen. IV*, III. iii. 93 Shall I not take mine ease in mine Inne. **1628** Hakewill in *Ussher's Lett.* (1686) 399 During mine abode in the University. **1726** Swift *Gulliver* II. vii, Till I had gotten a little below the level of mine eyes. **1756** C. Lucas *Ess. Waters* I. Ded., [It] would be very far from desireable, in mine estimation. **1871** R. Ellis tr. *Catullus* lxiv. 223 Rather, first in cries mine heart shall lighten her anguish.

b. In association with another possessive, *mine* is by some used (without intention of archaism) instead of *my*.

1559 Hales in Foxe *A. & M.* (1583) II. 2117/1, I haue.. discouered myne, yours, and Englands enemies. **1610** Shaks. *Temp.* III. iii. 93 His, and mine lou'd darling. **1611** —— *Cymb.* v. v. 230 Oh Gentlemen, helpe, Mine and your Mistris. **1761** Mrs. F. Sheridan *Sidney Bidulph* III. 165 As mine and my child's future welfare must be [etc.]. **1804–6** Syd. Smith *Mor. Philos.* (1850) 209, I bought them both the same day, mine and your ticket.

† **c.** Phr. *min dieu* repr. F. *mon Dieu!* my God! *Obs.*

c **1330** *Arth. & Merl.* 961 (Kölbing) 'A, min dieu', seyd the justise, 'þine tales ben gode & wise'.

2. Placed after the sb. Now only *arch.* in vocative.

c **1200** Ormin Ded. 1 Nu, broþerr Wallter broþerr min. *c* **1205** Lay. 12064 ȝif hit wule Appolin þat is deore lauerd min. *a* **1250** *Owl & Night.* 711 (Jesus MS.) Hwy axestu of craftes myne. *a* **1300** *E.E. Psalter* vii. 6 (Horstm.) Fylegh saule mine þe faa. *c* **1330** *Arth. & Merl.* 1442 (Kölbing) Tel me now, sone mine, Whi [etc.]. *Ibid.* 4977 Y dar legge heued min, þat [etc.]. *c* **1386** Chaucer *Clerk's T.* 309 This is ynogh Grisilde myn quod he. *c* **1402** Lydg. *Compl. Bl. Knt.* 639 O gladde sterre, O lady Venus myne! *c* **1550** Cheke *Matt.* xxvi. 25 Js it J Mr mijn, quoth he. **1567** *Gude & Godlie Ball.* (S.T.S.) 38 O Father myne, how lang haif I Thy trew and faithfull seruand bene. **1592** Shaks. *Rom. & Jul.* II. iii. 82 *Rom.* Thou chid'st me oft for louing Rosaline. *Fri.* For doting, not for louing pupill mine. **1611** Florio, *Mamma*,.. also Mam, Mother-mine, or Mammie, as children first call their Mothers. **1852** Bristed *Five Yrs. Eng. Univ.* 67

There, reader mine! Is that last page grave and solid enough for you?

†3. In idiomatic phrases, *mine* ALONE, *mine* ONE, *mine* UNWITTING, MAUGRE *mine*; see those words.

4. As predicative adj.: Belonging to me.

c **1000** ÆLFRIC *Exod.* xix. 5 Eall eorðe ys min. *c* **1175** *Lamb. Hom.* 35 Me were leofere þenne al world þat hit were min. *c* **1200** ORMIN 17964 þiss blisse iss min la fuliwiss. *a* **1300** *Cursor M.* 970 (Cott.) Of alkin fruit haf þou þe nine For i wil þat þe tend be mine [*Gött.* mein, *riming with* neien]. **1362** LANGL. *P. Pl.* A. v. 90, I wusshe hit weore myn. *c* **1385** CHAUCER *L.G.W.* Prol. 145 Blessed be seynt Valentyne! For on his day I chees yow to be myne. **1484** CAXTON *Fables of Æsop* I. vi, The fyrst part is myn by cause I am your lord. **1535** COVERDALE *John* vii. 16 My doctryne is not myne, but his that hath sent me. **1603** SHAKS. *Meas. for M.* v. i. 497 Giue me your hand, and say you will be mine. **1697** DRYDEN *Virg. Eclog.* x. 54 Ah! that your Birth and Bus'ness had been mine. **1832** TENNYSON *May Queen* Conclus. x, It's not for them: it's mine. **1864–8** BROWNING *James Lee's Wife* IV. v, Such as you were, I took you for mine.

5. *Elliptically*, equivalent to MY with a sb. supplied from the context.

a **1175** *Cott. Hom.* 223 For þan þe [þu] were hihersam þines [wifes] wordum mor ðan mine. *c* **1205** LAY. 676 He deð him selua freoma þa helpeð his freondene swa ich wlle mine. *c* **1386** CHAUCER *Reeve's T.* 165 Lay doun thy swerd and I will myn alswa. **1395** *E.E. Wills* (1882) 7 To preye for my lordes soule Sir Thomas West, and for myn. *c* **1500** *Melusine* 157 Your wylle & myne be one. **1592** SHAKS. *Rom. & Jul.* II. iii. 59 My hearts deare Loue is set, On the faire daughter of rich Capulet: As mine on hers, so hers is set on mine. **1625** K. LONG tr. *Barclay's Argenis* III. xix. 211 If more holily and religiously wee esteeme of my Fathers preserver and mine. **1786** G. HORNE *Duty Contend. Faith* 8 *note*, When a man deceives me once, says the Italian proverb, it is his fault; when twice, it is mine. **1843** BORROW *Bible in Spain* xxxii, I am pleased with your company, as I make no doubt you are with mine. **1866** J. C. MAXWELL in *Phil. Trans.* CLVI. 268 In M. Meyer's experiments the time of vibration is shorter than in most of mine.

6. *absol.* **a.** Those who are mine; chiefly, my family, my kindred.

c **950** *Lindisf. Gosp.* John xvii. 10 Mino alle ðino sint & ðino mino sint. *c* **975** *Rushw. Gosp.* ibid., Mine alle ðine sindun & ðine mine sindun. *a* **1300** *Cursor M.* 5371 He has saued me and mine fra mikel nede. *c* **1300** *Harrow. Hell* 64 Y shal þe bringe of helle pyne, ant wyþ þe alle myne. *c* **1386** CHAUCER *Melib.* ¶915, I..foryeue yow outrely alle the offenses Iniuries and wronges þat ye haue doon agayn me and myne. *c* **1400** *Laud Troy Bk.* 16851 ȝit I hope that I & myne Schal venge his dethe on the & thine. **1456** SIR G. HAYE *Law Arms* (S.T.S.) 164 Unharmyt of me or ony of myn. **1594** SHAKS. *Rich. III*, II. i. 24, I will neuer more remember Our former hatred, so thriue I, and mine. **1683** *Robin Consc.* 15 Both I and mine alas would starve. **1829** WORDSW. *Mem.* II. 209, I and mine will be happy to see you and yours here or anywhere. **1884** A. PHELPS *Let.* 14 Dec. in E. S. Phelps *Mem.* (1891) 275 God is so unspeakably good to me and mine. **1891** SIR J. PAGET in *Mem. & Lett.* (1901) 387 The unhappiness of being here alone is greater than the happiness of seeing things which, if any of 'mine' had been with me, I should [etc.].

†**b.** That which is mine; my property; also, my affair, my business. *Obs.*

Beowulf 2737 Ic on earde bad mælȝesceafta, heold min tela. *a* **1225** *St. Marher.* 8 Ich..hit neauer nuste þat he of min hearm hefde. *c* **1300** *Harrow. Hell* 97 Seþþe he wes boht wyþ myn, wyþ resoun wolle ich hauen hym. *a* **1300–1400** *Cursor M.* 2429 (Gött.) Of þin wil i neuer a dele, Bot leuer me es of mine þu haue. **1382** WYCLIF *John* xvi. 14 Of myne he schal take. *c* **1450** tr. *De Imitatione* III. lv. 132 To þe I committe me & all myne to correcte. **1555** EDEN *Decades* I. III. 17 b, Myne and Thyne (the seedes of all myscheefe) haue no place with them. **1568** GRAFTON *Chron.* II. 86 Your grace hath hetherto cherished mee but for mine, but now I will go to him that is more redier to geue then to take. **1596** SHAKS. *Tam. Shr.* II. i. 385 She shall have me and mine. **1603** —— *Meas. for M.* II. ii. 12 Goe to; let that be mine.

c. *of mine*: belonging to me: see OF *prep.* 44.

†7. Comb. **mine-take-it**, app. a phrase in some childish game. *Obs.*

1694 S. JOHNSON *Notes Past. Let. Bp. Burnet* I. 28 The ridiculous Ownership we have, is the ridiculous English word, Mine-take-it; which all the Children in England Know, is equivalent to Your's-take-it.

mine (maɪn), *v.* Forms: 4 **mini, myny,** 4–6 **myne,** (7 **moine**), 4– **mine.** *Pa. pple.* 4 **ymyned.** [ad. F. *mine-r* (from 12–13th c.) = Pr., Sp., Pg. *minar*, It. *minare*; related to *mine* MINE *sb.*

The view of Diez, that the vb. is identical with popular L. *mināre* to lead, drive, is not without semasiological plausibility (cf. DRIVE *v.* 10); but the normal phonetic representative of *mināre* in Fr. is *mener*. Scheler's hypothesis, that F. *miner* was a learned adoption of med.L. *mināre* used in technical works, would remove the phonological difficulty, but seems in itself somewhat unlikely.]

1. **a.** *intr.* To dig in the earth; esp. in a military sense, to dig under the foundations of a wall, etc., for the purpose of destroying it. Also, to make subterraneous passages. ? *Obs.*

13.. *K. Alis.* 1216 Alisaundre quic hoteth his hynen, Under heore walles to myne. *c* **1330** R. BRUNNE *Chron.* (1810) 179 R. had minoures, þat myned vndere þe walle. **1375** BARBOUR *Bruce* XVII. 600 With armyt men enew tharin, And instrumentis als for to myne. *c* **1425** WYNTOUN *Cron.* VIII. xxxvii. 5538 Wndyre the erde he gert thaim myne. *c* **1440** *Gesta Rom.* xxx. 110 (Harl. MS.), He saw..an hidowse pitte, and an orible dragon þere in, myning at the tree. **1480** CAXTON *Chron. Eng.* v. (1520) 43/1 Do you myne depe tyll your men come to the ponde. **1483** *Cath. Angl.* 240/2 To Myne, *arapagere, cunire.* **1568** GRAFTON *Chron.* II. 327 They beganne to mine vnder the Castell. **1609** C. BUTLER *Fem. Mon.* (1634) 57 Then, making more room beneath, by moining and carrying out the earth, they [*sc.* wasps] hang an other comb under the first, by little pins. **1614** RALEIGH *Hist. World* II. v. iii. §9. 465 The Enemie mined; and they countermined.

b. *transf.* and *fig.*

1340 *Ayenb.* 108 þanne nymþ he his pic and his spade and beginþ to delue and to myny and geþ in-to his herte. *c* **1374** CHAUCER *Troylus* II. 628 [677] His manhod and his pyne Made loue with-Inne hire for to myne. **1387–8** T. USK *Test. Love* I. Prol. (Skeat) l. 5 Dul wit and a thoughtful soule so sore have myned and graffed in my spirites. *c* **1407** LYDG. *Reson & Sens.* 6918 Water that droppeth euer in oon Myneth ful depe in-to A stoon. **1426** —— *De Guil. Pilgr.* 4282 Thys mortal werm wyl neuere fyne Vp-on hys mayster for to myne. *Ibid.* 11872 And many kankres wych on hem myne. *c* **1430** —— *Min. Poems* (Percy Soc.) 233 In amerous hertys brennyng of Kyndenesse, This name of Jhesu moost profoundly doth myne. **1605** BACON *Adv. Learn.* II. xxv. §6 To search and mine into that which is not reuealed.

2. **a.** *trans.* To dig or burrow in (the earth); also, to make (a hole, passage, one's way) underground.

c **1400** MAUNDEV. (1839) xxvi. 267 A Fox schalle..mynen an hole. *Ibid.*, So longe he schalle mynen and perce the Erthe, til that he schalle passe thorghe. **1555** W. WATREMAN *Fardle Facions* I. vi. 93 The Troglodites myne them selues caues in the grounde, wherin to dwell. **1813** SCOTT *Rokeby* II. ii, Condemned to mine a channell'd way, O'er solid sheets of marble grey.

b. *transf.* and *fig.* To make a hollow or groove in; to burrow below the surface of; to make (a passage) by burrowing.

c **1477** CAXTON *Jason* 20 b, How well the stone is myned and holowed by contynuell droppyng of water. **1802** ER. DARWIN *Orig. Soc.* IV. 35 The cruel larva mines its silky course. **1811** PINKERTON *Petral.* II. 551 This stump and the trunk, hollowed and mined by the subterranean heat. **1816** KIRBY & SP. *Entomol.* xxii. (1818) II. 279 A subcutaneous larva..that mines the leaves of the rose. **1820** HAZLITT *Lect. Dram. Lit.* 165 He may be said to mine his way into a subject, like a mole.

c. To supply with subterranean passages; to make subterranean passages under.

1820 SHELLEY *Witch Atl.* lx. 5 Through fane, and palace-court, and labyrinth mined With many a dark and subterranean street. **1862** MERIVALE *Rom. Emp.* (1865) VII. lix. 245 The site of Jerusalem itself is mined with vaults and galleries.

†3. To bury in the ground. *Obs. rare*$^{-1}$.

c **1420** *Pallad. on Husb.* III. 334 The long endurid, old, forfreton vine Is not to helpe..To delue hit vnder al, but to reclyne Hit lyke a bowe and vnder lond hit myne.

4. **a.** To dig away or remove the foundations of (a wall, fort, etc.); to undermine in order either to cause collapse or to effect a hostile entrance. ? *Obs.*

c **1380** WYCLIF *Sel. Wks.* II. 408 If þe hosebonde man wiste what hour þe þeef were to come, certis he wolde wake, and suffre him not to myne his hous. **1388** —— *Job* xxiv. 16 Thei mynen housis in derknesses. ? *a* **1400** *Morte Arth.* 351 Merke vn-to Meloyne, and myne doune the wallez. *c* **1400** *Brut or Chron. Eng.* (E.E.T.S.) 136 William Bastard..hade taken al þe lande aboute Hastynge, & hade also mynede þe castell. *c* **1430** *Pilgr. Lyf Manhode* III. vi. (1869) 139 The kyng first bifore wente, and mynede the foundement. **1513** DOUGLAS *Æneis* v. viii. 42 To mynd the castell on the rochis hie, Lurkand in harnes wachis round about. **1570** LEVINS *Manip.* 139/22 To Mine, *suffodere.*

transf. **1807** J. BARLOW *Columb.* I. 375 Pastaza mines proud Pambamarca's base. **1824** BRYANT *Green River* ii, The plane-tree's speckled arms o'ershoot The swifter current that mines its root.

b. *fig.* To attack, overcome, ruin, or destroy by slow or secret methods; to undermine. Occas. with *down, away.*

c **1412** HOCCLEVE *De Reg. Princ.* 3133 They at þe fulle kunne his herte myne. **1426** LYDG. *De Guil. Pilgr.* 15650 Whan Ire doth myn herte myne. **1600** SHAKS. *A.Y.L.* I. i. 21 Hee..mines my gentility with my education. **1605** B. JONSON *Volpone* III. i, I haue done Base offices in.. Whispering false lies, or mining men with prayses. **1751** J. BROWN *Shaftesb. Charac.* 239 'Till..irreligion and licentiousness appear; mine the foundations of the fabric, and sink it in the general abyss of ignorance and oppression. *a* **1814** *Love, Honor & Interest* I. i. in *New Brit. Theatre* III. 260 While love is mining down The strength and virtue of my own esteem. **1847** LYTTON *Lucretia* 31 The wreck of man is fretted and mined away by small pleasures and poor excitements.

absol. **1748** JOHNSON *Van. Hum. Wishes* 332 The rival batters, and the lover mines.

5. In modern warfare: To lay mines (see MINE *sb.* 3) under, for the purpose of destruction.

1630 HAYWARD *Edw. VI* 60 They mined the walls, laid the powder and rammed the mouth. **1686** *Lond. Gaz.* No. 2158/1 A Deserter..had informed the Imperial Generals that the said Towers were Mined. **1775** JOHNSON *West. Isl.* Wks. X. 482 It is built upon a rock, as Mr. Boswell remarked, that it might not be mined. **1820** GREVILLE *Mem.* 10 Dec. (1874) 41 The Prussians arrived, mined the arches, and attempted to blow up the bridge. **1851** GLADSTONE in Morley *Life* (1903) I. III. vi. 403 The ground is mined and the train is laid. **1862** THACKERAY *Philip* vii. I. 135 Old Parr Street is mined, sir,—mined! And some morning we shall be blown into blazes. **1885** *N. Amer. Rev.* Sept. 274 Although the waters may be reported as mined in all directions, a bold test would show them to be clear of such dangers.

6. *trans.* To obtain (metals, etc.) from a mine.

1398 TREVISA *Barth. De P.R.* XVI. xciv. (1495) 585 In Capodoce is yelow salt digged and myned. *Ibid.* XIV. ii. (Tollem. MS.), Noble metal is myned out of veynes of mounteynes. **1866** ROGERS *Agric. & Prices* I. xxiii. 599 The Eastern produce [of tin] not being yet introduced into Europe, if indeed it were mined at that time. **1878** D. C. DAVIES *Slate & Slate Quarrying* 78 The stone is mined underground and brought up by shafts to the surface. **1878** *Fraser's Mag.* XVIII. 273 Lignite..is mined near Brousa. **1885** *Manch. Exam.* 10 July 5/3 Gold and other mineral wealth..are as yet not mined on any considerable scale.

7. *intr.* To dig for the purpose of obtaining minerals, etc.; to make a mine; to work in a mine.

? *c* **1400** [see MINERAL *sb.*[1]]. ? **1568** in Pettus *Fodinæ Reg.* (1670) 60 She grants unto them to search, dig, and mine for the Callamine stone in all places of England. **1677** *Phil. Trans.* XII. 912 The Earth they Mine in, is very red. **1748** *Anson's Voy.* I. v. 50 The workmen break off the rocks, and do not properly mine into them. **1819** BYRON *Juan* I. cxxxii, Coals Are safely mined for. **1828** SCOTT *F.M. Perth* xxii, He considered Ramorny as one whom nature had assigned to him as a serf, to mine for the gold which he worshipped.

8. *trans.* To dig in or penetrate for finding ore, metals, etc.

1839 URE *Dict. Arts* 748 Lead veins have been traced even further down,..but they have not been mined. **1867** W. W. SMYTH *Coal & Coal-mining* 78 The..rich coalfield..of Westphalia: which, although mined..as early as 1302, has only within the last quarter of a century risen to a high degree of importance. **1899** *Westm. Gaz.* 2 Aug. 3/1 We must leave the reader to mine this rich quarry for himself.

9. *U.S.* (See quot. 1937.)

1937 *Amer. Speech* XII. 105 They *mine* the soil; that is, they use up fertility without restoring it. **1972** *New Yorker* 25 Nov. 42/3 When they moved here, the land had been farmed out—'mined', the local phrase was—and the one undiscouraged crop was the wild strawberries.

mineable ('maɪnəb(ə)l), *a.* Also 6– **minable.** [f. MINE *v.* + -ABLE.] Capable of being mined (in any sense of the vb.).

1570 LEVINS *Manip.* 2/46 Myneable, *fossilis.* **1579–80** NORTH *Plutarch, Camillus* (1595) 144 He beganne to vndermine it (finding the earth all about very minable). **1589** *Late Voy. Sp. & Port.* (1881) 60 General Norris having ..found one place thereof myneable,..did presently set work-men in hand withal. **1611** SPEED *Hist. Gt. Brit.* IX. xxiv. (1623) 1208 One place was found mineable, where the Generall the fourth day of this siege set men on worke. **1647** SPRIGGE *Anglia Rediv.* II. iii. (1854) 91 Being well informed that the ground wheron it stood was minable. **1893** *Columbus* (Ohio) *Dispatch* 11 Sept., Coal is being found in mineable deposits in all parts of the world. **1971** *Sci. Amer.* May 17/1 There are minable cinnabar deposits in many regions around the world, and man was attracted to its use as early as prehistoric times. **1972** *Nature* 14 Apr. 332/1 And is it likely that economically minable lead ores are equally distributed between North America and the rest of the world?

mined (maɪnd), *ppl. a.* [f. MINE *v.* + -ED[1].]

1. That has been excavated.

c **1400** tr. *Secreta Secret., Gov. Lordsh.* 87 It ys lyk in manere to stoones of mynyd hilles, and of planetz, and of þinges hauynge soule.

2. Produced from mines.

1903 *Daily Chron.* 9 Aug. 3/3 The value of her mined wealth has mounted up from 314,000,000 marks in 1871 to 1,263,000,000 marks in 1900.

3. Furnished with mines.

1870 *Instr. Milit. Engin.* I. 76 The following description of a mined magazine, is suitable for a site where [etc.].

mined, obs. form of MIND *v.*

'minehood. *nonce-wd.* [f. MINE *poss. pron.* + -HOOD.] The fact of being 'mine'.

1662 J. SPARROW tr. *Behme's Rem. Wks., 2nd Apol. to Tylcken* 17 He inclineth himself to my Minehood, and my Ihood inclineth it self up into him.

minekin, obs. form of MINIKIN *sb.*

†**'mineless,** *a. Obs.* [f. MINE *sb.* + -LESS.] Without mines.

1614 SYLVESTER *Little Bartas* 866 There, without stroak to conquer in the field; And mine-less make their tumbling wals to yeeld.

minem, obs. form of MINIM.

minement, obs. form of MUNIMENT.

‖**minenwerfer** ('miːnənvɛrfər, 'miːnənwɜːfə(r)). *Mil.* [G., f. *minen* (pl.) mines + *werfer*, f. *werfen* to throw.] A German trench mortar. Cf. *mine-thrower*, MINNIE[2].

Also called *minnenwerfer* from an expansion of MINNIE[2], the British soldiers' nickname for this gun.

1915 A. D. GILLESPIE *Lett. from Flanders* (1916) 80 About Christmas time the Germans fetched up a thing called a *Minen Werfer*, a kind of trench mortar which throws 60 lbs. of gun cotton. **1915** [see *mine-thrower*]. **1916** F. M. FORD *Let.* Aug. (1965) 68 The Germans seem to have nothing but minenwerfers. **1917** A. G. EMPEY *Over Top* 300 *Minnenwerfer*, a high-power trench mortar shell of the Germans, which makes no noise coming through the air... Tommy nicknames them 'Minnies'. **1923** KIPLING *Irish Guards in Gt. War* I. 101 He retaliated..along the line of seven-inch minenwerfers.

mineon, obs. form of MINION *sb.*[1]

miner[1] ('maɪnə(r)). Forms: 3–4 **mynur,** 4–5 **minour(e, myno(u)r, mynowre,** 5 **minere, mynere, -oure,** *Sc.* **myndoure,** 5–7 **myner,** 7 **minor, mioner, myoner,** 5– **miner.** [ME. *mynur*, *minour*, a. OF.

minëor, minour (mod.F. *mineur*), f. *miner* to MINE: see -OR 2 b.]

1. a. One who excavates the ground, or makes subterranean passages; *esp.* one who undermines a fortress, etc.; now *Mil.* a soldier whose special duty is the laying of mines. ***Sappers and Miners***: see SAPPER.

c **1275** *Luue Ron* 123 in *O.E. Misc.* 97 Ne may no Mynur hire vnderwrote. *c* **1330** R. BRUNNE *Chron.* (1810) 179 R. had minoures, þat myned vndere þe walle. *c* **1400** *Destr. Troy* 4774 Mynours then mightely the moldes did serche, Ouertyrnet the toures, & the tore walles. *c* **1470** HENRY *Wallace* IX. 1139 Mynouris sone thai gert perss throw the wall. **1530** PALSGR. 245/2 Myner under the grounde, *pionnier.* **1606** *Arraign. late Traitors* in *Harl. Misc.* (Malh.) III. 48 [Guy] Fawkes the minor, justly called The Devil of the Vault. **1645** LD. FAIRFAX *Let. to Lenthall conc. Sherborn Castle* 15 Aug. 4 The Myoners having fully wrought the Mine through the Castle wall. **1692** LUTTRELL *Brief Rel.* (1857) II. 470 A miner and another person were taken fixing a train. **1709** STEELE *Tatler* No. 38 ¶13 A great Body of Miners are summoned to the Camp to countermine the Works of the Enemy. **1711** *Milit. & Sea Dict.* I, *Miners*, Men appointed to work in the Mines, being a particular Company of themselves, commanded by a Captain of the Regiment of Fuzileers. **1816** BYRON *Ch. Har.* III. lviii, Here Ehrenbreitstein, with her shatter'd wall, Black with the miner's blast.

b. *transf.* and *fig.*

c **1614** CORNWALLIS in Gutch *Coll. Cur.* I. 158 Jesuites, and Priests, the only moths, and miners of this commonwealth. **1742** YOUNG *Nt. Th.* I. 352 Death's subtle seed within, (Sly, treacherous miner!) working in the dark, Smil'd at thy well-concerted scheme. **1784** COWPER *Task* I. 273 Hillocks green and soft, Raised by the mole, the miner of the soil. **1879** JEFFERIES *Wild Life in S. Co.* 215 Sometimes when waiting quietly on a bank, you may see the miner [a rabbit] at work. **1897** W. ANDERSON *Surg. Treat. Lupus* 2 Rarely attempting to deal with the apparently healthy tissues which conceal the bacillary sappers and miners who are at work in advance of the main body.

†**c.** Phr. ***to fix*** or ***attach the miner, to fix miners.***

1676 *Lond. Gaz.* No. 1123/3 We fixed the Miner to the Ravelin, and filled up the Ditch. **1684** *Ibid.* No. 1951/3 The Imperialists had on the 20th attached their Miners to the Wall of the Upper Town in four several places. **1685** TRAVESTIN *Siege Newheusel* 23 This night we attempted to fix our Miners. **1685** *Lond. Gaz.* 17–20 Aug. 1 We made a lodgment in the Ditch in order to fix the Miner. **1704** *Collect. Voy.* (Churchill) III. 737/2 Being afterwards advanc'd to the Ditch, they fix'd their Miners. **1834** SIR W. NAPIER *Penins. War* XIII. iii. (1846) IV. 43 The besiegers.. attached the miner to the scarp.

2. One who works in a mine; one engaged in extracting minerals from the earth.

1303 R. BRUNNE *Handl. Synne* 10733 Þys mynur soȝte stones vndyr þe molde, þat men make of, syluer and golde. **13..** *Metr. Hom.* (Vernon MS.) in *Archiv Stud. neu. Spr.* LVII. 287 A Mynour wonede in a Citee, Mynours þei makeþ in hulles holes As men don þat secheþ coles. **1377** LANGL. *P. Pl.* B. Prol. 221 Masons and mynours and many other craftes. *c* **1400** *Destr. Troy* 1532 Mynors of marbull ston & mony oþer thinges. **1489** CAXTON *Faytes of A.* I. xiv. 38 Mynours that coude ful craftly digge vndre the erthe. **1555** EDEN *Decades* 22 The myners dygged the superficiall or vppermost parte of the earthe of the mynes. **1607** TOPSELL *Four-f. Beasts* (1658) 525 This (he saith) may be tryed in Laborers, Mioners, Diggers, and Husbandmen. **1625** N. CARPENTER *Geog. Del.* II. ix. (1635) 153 Minors and such as digg deepe into the earth. **1774** GOLDSM. *Nat. Hist.* (1776) I. 78 If we examine the complexion of most miners, we shall be very well able to form a judgment of the unwholsomness of the place where they are confined. **1881** RAYMOND *Mining Gloss.*, *Miner*, Penn. The workman who cuts the coal, as distinguished from the laborer who loads the wagons, etc. **1901** *Census Schedule, Instruct.*, Miners.. should always state the kind of mine in which they work —as, Lead-miner.

3. A name applied to various burrowing insects or larvæ. (See also *leaf-miner.*)

1816 KIRBY & SP. *Entomol.* xvii. (1818) II. 81 Another species of ant, which I shall call the miners (*Formica cunicularia*, L.). **1890** ELEANOR A. ORMEROD *Injur. Insects* (ed. 2) 49 [Celery and Parsnip Fly]. The 'miner' maggots go through their changes from the egg to the perfect fly so rapidly [etc.].

4. A kind of plough.

1805 R. W. DICKSON *Pract. Agric.* I. 12 The *Miner* is another plough, which is used for opening ground to a great depth; it is made very strong, but with a share only. *Ibid.* 385 The land may be opened up as deep as possible by the common plough, having others, such as that which has been termed a *miner*, following in the bottom of the furrow. **1845** *Encycl. Metrop.* XIV. 232/1 The miner is very similar to the binot.

5. A vessel used for the purpose of laying submarine mines.

1898 *Daily News* 8 June 2/7 In a sudden squall, the miner he was on collided with the steam launch Volta.

6. *attrib.* and *Comb.*, as ***miner-like*** adj.; **miner ant**, see sense 3; **miner's friend**, a name for the Davy safety-lamp; **miner's inch** = INCH 1 d; **miner's right**, in Australia and New Zealand, a licence to dig for gold.

1816 KIRBY & SP. *Entomol.* xvii. (1818) II. 84 The negro and *miner ants. **1842** FRANCIS *Dict. Arts*, etc., **Miner's Friend*, or *Miner's Lamp.* **1867** J. A. PHILLIPS *Min. & Metall. Gold & Silver* 152 *note*, The *miner's inch of water, in California, is the quantity which will flow through an opening one inch square under a mean head of six inches. **1880** S. HARPER in *Pioneer Mining Co., Debenture Prospectus* 3 If the above property be carried out in a *miner-like manner.. it will not fail to become one of the best Mines. **1855** in *Occasional Papers Univ. Sydney Austral. Lang. Res. Centre* (1966) No. 9. 15 It shall be lawful for the Governor .. to cause documents to be issued each of which shall be called 'The *Miner's Right' and shall be granted to any person applying for the same upon payment of a fee of one pound. **1858** in *Ibid.* 16 It is not generally known, .. that .. any one interested in the workings at the gold-fields should hold a Miner's Right which can be had at the Treasury. **1863** *Rules & Regulations Otago Gold Fields* 7 Every person residing on a Gold Field and engaged in mining for gold, shall take out a Miner's Right; such Miner's Right to be carried on the person, and produced for inspection when demanded. **1868** V. PYKE *Province of Otago* 41 The only qualification is the possession of a 'Miners' Right'. **1890** 'R. BOLDREWOOD' *Miner's Right* i. (1899) 7, I am a real gold-digger.. and the holder of a Miner's Right, a wonderful document, printed and written on parchment. **1950** *N.Z. Jrnl. Agric.* Feb. 189/2 Exhibits [in an Arrowtown museum, Central Otago, include].. a miner's right. **1959** BAKER *Drum* 127 *Miner's right*, a licence to dig for gold granted to a miner, orig. in the 1850s.

b. In names of diseases contracted by miners, as ***miner's anæmia, -asthma, -consumption, disease, elbow, -lung, nystagmus, phthisis, -rot, sickness, -worm.*** (See *Syd. Soc. Lex.*)

1898 P. MANSON *Trop. Diseases* xxxvi. 557 In Europe it [i.e. ankylostomiasis] is sometimes known as '*miners' anæmia'. **1855** J. R. LEIFCHILD *Cornwall Mines* 285 There is a disease called the *miner's consumption. **1879** *Miner's nystagmus [see NYSTAGMUS 2]. **1959** *Chambers's Encycl.* X. 152/2 Owing to the inadequate illumination in mines a large number of miners get a condition known as 'miner's nystagmus'. **1962** H. C. WESTON *Sight, Light & Work* (ed. 2) ix. 262 The occupational disease known as *miner's nystagmus* is so named on account of the ocular movements commonly associated with it. **1898** *Allbutt's Syst. Med.* V. 244 'Grinders' rot', '*miners' rot' and so forth. **1903** *Daily Chron.* 21 Oct. 4/2 An Ayrshire medical man, who wrote to the Home Secretary asking whether his Department is doing anything to stop the disease known as '*miners' worm'.

†**'miner²**. *Obs.* [Anglicized form of MINERA. Cf. G. *miner*, MDu. *minere, mineer.*] = MINERA. Also, a mineral impregnation.

1471 RIPLEY *Comp. Alch.* VI. xxvii. in Ashm. (1652) 167 And make them then together to be Dysponsat By Congelacyon into a myner metallyne. **1562** TURNER *Baths* I Then seynge that there can not be found any other miner or mater to be the chefe ruler in these baths. *Ibid.* (1568) 3 Two thinges whereby the miner or metall, or vayne of a bath may be knowne.

miner, variant of MINA *sb.*²

‖**mi'nera**. *Obs.* [med.L., ad. OF. *miniere, minere* mine = Pr. *meniera*, Sp. *minera*, Pg. *mineira*, It. *miniera*:—Com. Rom. type **minaria* (a med.L. *minaria* is found in the 13th c.), f. **mina, minare*: see MINE *sb.* and *v.*] The matrix in which a metal or a precious stone was supposed to grow; in later use, the ore of a metal. Also *fig.*

1652 GAULE *Magastrom.* 42 He hath discovered the *Minera* of man, or that substance out of which man.. was made. **1655** T. VAUGHAN *Euphrates* 120 This made the Philosophers seek a more crude minera, whose fume was moist. **1667** *Phil. Trans.* II. 469 Extracting the perfect Mettals out of their Minera's without Lead.. by casting a Powder upon the Minera. **1673** RAY *Journ. Low C.* 246 A large piece of the minera or matrix of Emeralds, with the stones growing in it. **1754** HUXHAM in *Phil. Trans.* XLVIII. 839 Thus the dust, or minera, or ashes of iron, are harmless, and may be swallowed safely. **1890** *Syd. Soc. Lex.*, *Minera*, .. a mine, also used frequently to designate a mineral which contains a shining metallic substance.

†**'minerable**, *a. Obs.* [a. OF. *minerable*, f. med.L. MINERA: see -ABLE.] = MINERAL *a.*

1560 WHITEHORNE *Ord. Souldiours* (1573) 24 b, The other writers beleved that it [salt-peter] was minerable.

mineragraphy (mɪnə'rægrəfɪ). *Min.* [f. MINERA(L *sb.* + -GRAPHY.] = MINERALOGRAPHY.

1924 *Amer. Mineralogist* IX. 177 Mineragraphy, the study of minerals in polished section with the metallographic microscope for the purpose of determining their identity and paragenesis, has generally been carried on under vertical illumination. **1965** G. J. WILLIAMS *Econ. Geol. N.Z.* ix. 136/2 (*heading*) Mineragraphy of titano-magnetite.

So **mine'ragrapher**, one who practises mineragraphy; **minera'graphic** *a.*

1931 *Amer. Mineralogist* XVI. 209 In the course of some recent mineragraphic work on the manganiferous iron ores of the Cuyuna Range.. it was necessary to make quick identification of the various oxides of iron and manganese. **1953** *Austral. Jrnl. Chem.* VI. 443 The most comprehensive mineragraphic report.. records the presence of more than 30 mineral species. **1964** *Weekly News* (Auckland) 10 June 8/5 The mineragrapher determines the intimacy of the admixture of minerals composing the ore. **1965** G. J. WILLIAMS *Econ. Geol. N.Z.* ix. 136/2 Titanium being an embarrassment in any metallurgical process, attention has been given to mineragraphic studies with a view to locating this element.

mineral ('mɪnərəl), *sb.* Forms: 4–7 **minerall**, 5 **minorale**, 5–7 **myneral**, 6 **minorall**, **mynoralle**, *Sc.* **manerialle**, 6–7 **mynerall**, 7 **minerale**, **minrall**, 4– **mineral.** [a. (perh. through OF. *mineral*) med.L. *minerāle*, neut. of *minerālis* MINERAL *a.* Cf. F. *minéral*, Sp., Pg. *mineral*, It. *minerale*, G. *mineral* (pl. *mineralien*).]

1. a. Any substance which is obtained by mining; a product of the bowels of the earth. In early and in mod. technical use, the ore (of a metal).

?*c* **1400** LYDG. *Æsop's Fab.* Prol. 25 Who, that myneth lowe in the grounde, Of gold and siluer fyndith the myneral. **1471** RIPLEY *Comp. Alch.* VI. xx. in Ashm. (1652) 166 Mineralls be nurryshyd by mynystracyon; Of Moysture radycall. **1576** FLEMING *Panopl. Epist.* 288 Some dig for mettalls and minneralls to erect stately buildinges. *c* **1615** BACON *Adv. Sir G. Villiers* vi. §16 The minerals of the kingdom, of lead, iron, copper, and tin, .. are of great value. **1634** HABINGTON *Castara* I. (Arb.) 28 In a darke cave.. It doth like a rich minerall lye. **1656** BLOUNT *Glossogr.*, *Mineral*, any thing that grows in Mines, and contains metal. **1667** MILTON *P.L.* VI. 517 Part hidd'n veins diggd up.. of Mineral and Stone. **1704** J. HARRIS *Lex. Techn.* I, *Minerals*, are hard Bodies dug out of the Earth or Mines, (whence the Name) being in part of a Metalline, and in part of a Stony Substance. **1727** DE FOE *Syst. Magic* I. i. (1840) 7 As one to music, another to working in and finding out metals and minerals in the earth. **1839** *Penny Cycl.* XV. 235/2 By this plan the ore or mineral is divided into more convenient masses for extraction. **1858** LD. ST. LEONARDS *Handy Bk. Prop. Law* xvi. 105 With special provisions as to minerals and the interests therein of remainder-men. **1881** RAYMOND *Mining Gloss.*, *Mineral*, in miners' parlance, ore.

fig. **1598** F. ROUS *Thule* Q 4 He sees where death with greedie spade, Meanes vp to dig the minerals of his hart.

†**b.** *pl.* The science of minerals. [Perh. with allusion to the *Liber Mineralium* (or *De Mineralibus*) of Albertus Magnus.] *Obs.*

c **1590** MARLOWE *Faust.* i, He that is grounded in astrology, Enrich'd with tongues, well seen in minerals, Hath all the principles magic doth require.

†**2.** Mining or metallurgical industry or art. *Obs.*

c **1470** HENRYSON *Mor. Fab.* v. (*Parl. Beasts*) xliv, Richt as the minor in his minorale Fair gold with fire may fra the leid weill win. **1570–6** LAMBARDE *Peramb. Kent* (1826) p. v, It is the manner.. of such as seek profit by Minerall, first to set men on woorke to digge and gather the Owre: Then [etc.].

†**3.** A mine. *Obs.*

1598 BP. HALL *Sat.* VI. i. 87 Shall it not be a wild-figg in a wall, Or fired Brimstone in a Minerall? **1602** SHAKS. *Ham.* IV. i. 26 O're whom his very madnesse like some Oare Among a Minerall of Mettels base Shewes it selfe pure. **1602** *Life T. Cromwell* I. ii, My study, like a mineral of gold, Makes my heart proud wherein my hope's enroll'd.

4. a. A material substance that is neither animal nor vegetable; a substance belonging to the 'mineral kingdom'. ? *Obs.*

1602 WARNER *Alb. Eng.* XIII. lxxvi. 316 Vigitiues, as trees, fruits, herbes, and such: Dead-Beings too, as Mynerales. **1661** LOVELL *Hist. Anim. & Min.* Introd. 78 As for Minerals, they are bodies perfectly mixt; inanimate, not having sense or motion. **1695** WOODWARD *Nat. Hist. Earth* IV. 174 Nor do Metalls only sort and herd with Metalls in the Earth; and Minerals with Minerals. **1874** J. H. COLLINS *Metal Mining* 20 Any natural substance which is not of animal or vegetable origin, and which is in all parts of the same composition, is called a mineral. Among miners, however, the term is only applied to such substances as are usually obtained from mines.

†**b.** *spec.* in *Alchemy.* One of the three varieties of the philosophers' stone (the others being *lapis animalis* and *lapis vegetabilis*). *Obs.*

It is doubtful whether quot. 1610 may not belong to 4 or 4 c.

1390 GOWER *Conf.* II. 87 The thridde Ston in special Be name is cleped Minerall... This Mineral, so as I finde, Transformeth al the ferste kynde. **1610** B. JONSON *Alch.* I. i, All your alchemy and your algebra Your minerals, vegetalls, and animalls.

†**c.** A mineral medicine or poison. See also ÆTHIOPS MINERAL. *Obs.*

1563 T. GALE *Antidot.* II. 54 Make all these mynoralles in fyne pouder and mixe with the Oyle. **1588** GREENE *Perimedes* Wks. (Grosart) VII. 20 Our late Phisitions haue found out a singular minerall, called Hope: applie this to your stomack as a soueraine simple against disquiet and feare. **1604** SHAKS. *Oth.* I. ii. 74 That thou hast practis'd on her with foule Charmes, Abus'd her delicate Youth, with Drugs or Minerals. **1611** —— *Cymb.* V. v. 50 She did confesse she had For you a mortall Minerall. **1622** FLETCHER *Sea Voy* V. i, [Famine] as the wise man says, Gripes the guts as much as any minerall. *a* **1634** CHAPMAN *Alphonsus* IV. (1654) 49 [They] Gave me a mineral not to be digested, Which burning eats, and eating burns my heart. **1730** BURDON *Pocket Farrier* 40 Sweet Oil a Spoonful, Æthiops Mineral an Ounce.

d. = MINERAL WATER. (Usu. in *pl.*)

1885 *List of Subscribers* (United Telephone Co.) p. xv, We have had a run upon minerals, and are nearly out. *Ibid.*, We are out of minerals. Kindly send us.. one gross of seltzer, one gross of soda. **1922** JOYCE *Ulysses* 597 They might hit upon some drinkables in the shape of a milk and soda or a mineral. **1927** *Glasgow Herald* 15 Apr. 11 There will be.. supper with ale and minerals at Osborne's Hotel.

5. In modern scientific use, each of the species or kinds (defined by approximate identity of chemical composition and physical properties) into which inorganic substances as presented in nature are classified.

1813 BAKEWELL *Introd. Geol.* Pref. (1815) 9 The number of simple minerals which form rocks and strata is small. **1823** H. J. BROOKE *Introd. Crystallogr.* 80 Cleavage alone cannot be relied on for determining the primary form of a mineral. **1896** A. H. CHESTER (*title*) A Dictionary of the Names of Minerals.

6. *attrib.* and *Comb.*, as ***mineral dealer, -train***; ***mineral-bearing*** adj.; **mineral dressing**, treatment of ore so as to remove gangue and concentrate the valuable constituents; so ***mineral dresser***; **mineral map**, a map for the purpose of showing the localities where

minerals are to be found; **mineral right** (see quots.); **mineral rod**, a divining-rod for finding mineral veins.

1877 RAYMOND *Statist. Mines & Mining* 174 The croppings of a heavy *mineral-bearing lode are clearly traceable. **1878** GURNEY *Crystallogr.* 57 This is generally sold by the *mineral dealers. **1895** *Funk's Stand. Dict.*, **Mineral dresser*, a machine for trimming or dressing mineralogical specimens. **1957** *Sci. News* XLVI. 35 This upgrading [of ores] is the work done by the mineral dresser. **1939** A. M. GAUDIN *Princ. *Mineral Dressing* i. 1 Mineral dressing is commonly regarded as the processing of raw minerals to yield marketable products and waste by means that do not destroy the physical and chemical identity of the minerals. **1957** *Sci. News* XLVI. 37 The methods of mineral dressing most in use before World War I were limited to gravitation in pulsing or streaming currents of water.., the use of magnets on ferro-magnetic ores, and such hydro-metallic processes as the cyanidation of gold and the leaching of copper. **1974** *Encycl. Brit. Macropædia* XI. 1063/2 Modern processes in mineral dressing have become increasingly directed toward using fundamental principles governed by laws of physics, chemistry, and electricity. **1876** *Nature* 14 Dec. 150/1 Along with this is a *mineral map of New South Wales, showing the localities of the principal minerals. **1839** *Penny Cycl.* XV. 237/2 Certain stipulations are then entered into between the company and the proprietor of the land in which the vein or deposit is situated, or should the *mineral right not belong to him, with [etc.]. **1881** RAYMOND *Mining Gloss.*, *Mineral right*, the ownership of the minerals under a given surface, with the right to enter thereon, mine, and remove them. **1809** KENDALL *Trav.* III. 101 The mysteries of the *mineral-rods are many. **1849** T. L. CLINGMAN in C. Lanman *Lett. from Alleghany Mts.* 187 Travelling about the country under the guidance of *mineral rods* or dreams in search of mines. **1902** A. D. MCFAUL *Ike Glidden* xxi. 184 They've sent for Squire Blunt to come up here in the morning, with a mineral rod, to assist them. **1894** LD. TWEEDMOUTH in *Daily News* 5 Oct. 5/6 Our express had a short distance to the north of Northallerton run into a *mineral train.

mineral ('mɪnərəl), *a.* [a. F. *minéral*, ad. med.L. *minerālis* pertaining to mines, f. *minera*: see MINERA. Cf. Sp., Pg. *mineral*, It. *minerale*. The adj. is in Eng. of later appearance than the sb., and is in some uses not to be distinguished from the attributive use of the sb.]

†**1. a.** Pertaining to mines or mining. Of persons: Skilled in mining matters. *Obs.*

1592 STOW *Annals* 11 The saide Philosopher.. in this land taught the knowledge of myneral workes. *c* **1600** NORDEN *Spec. Brit., Cornw.* (1728) 18 It were not amiss that Minerall Artistes dyd strayne their skyll to make a more generall proofe by a more exacte searche. *Ibid.* 70 The howse of Mr. Windesore, situate amonge the minerall hills. **1602** CAREW *Cornwall* 13 Sir Francis Godolphin.. entertained a Duch myneral man. **1667** COLEPRESSE in *Phil. Trans.* II. 481 John Gill, a Man well experienced in Mineral affairs. **1672** BOYLE *Ess. Gems* 31 As I have been inform'd, not only by some Mineral Writers of good credit, but also by eye witnesses. **1706** PHILLIPS (ed. Kersey), *Mineral Courts*, certain peculiar Courts for regulating the Concerns of Lead-Mines, as Stannary-Courts are for Tin.

¶**b.** *nonce-use.* Deeply buried; recondite.

a **1615** DONNE *Ess.* (1651) 28 Nothing was too Minerall, nor centrick for the search and reach of his wit.

†**2.** ***mineral virtue***: the supposed occult power by which metals are developed. *Obs.*

1477 NORTON *Ord. Alch.* i. in Ashm. (1652) 19 The vertue Minerall. **1750** tr. *Leonardus's Mirr. Stones* 22 By an example which we shall bring from the animal seed, it will appear, in what manner the mineral virtue operates in stones.

3. a. Having the nature of a mineral (MINERAL *sb.* 1); obtained from the bowels of the earth.

1581 in *Trans. Jewish Hist. Soc. Eng.* (1903) IV. 98 The vth corruption [of copper ore] is Calcator, beinge the mother or corpus of vitriall, and a myneral substance. **1600** J. PORY tr. *Leo's Africa* Introd. 11 Heere also you haue minerall salt. **1612** WOODALL *Surg. Mate* Wks. (1653) 207 Under the name of mineral salt is comprehended the salts of all metals [etc.]. **1617** MORYSON *Itin.* III. 80 Minerall salt which in Poland they dig out of pits like great stones. **1695** WOODWARD *Nat. Hist. Earth* IV. 175 By Experience.. in any Place or Mine, a Man may be enabled to give a near Conjecture at the Metallick or Mineral Ingredients of any Mass commonly found there. **1712** BLACKMORE *Creation* III. 422 Endless Store Of Min'ral Treasure and Metallic Oar. **1875** *Ure's Dict. Arts* III. 304 When the mineral ores lie in nearly vertical masses, it is [etc.].

b. Impregnated with mineral substances; esp. in ***mineral spring***. (See MINERAL WATER.) Also of colour, †indicating mineral impregnation. Also *attrib.*

1632 LITHGOW *Trav.* II. 57 Two Riuers, Acheron and Cocytus; who for their minerall colours, and bitter tasts, were surnamed the Riuers of Hell. **1783** S. TENNEY *Let.* 1 Sept. in *Mem. Amer. Acad. Arts & Sci.* (1793) II. 43, I mentioned some mineral springs in the vicinity of this place. **1797** *Encycl. Brit.* (ed. 3) IX. 346/1 About two leagues to the eastward is a brackish mineral spring. **1834** *W. India Sk. Bk.* II. 139 Invalids, many of whom come.. for the.. mineral baths. **1843** W. W. MATHER et al. *Geol. N. Y.* IV. 308 In this district the only mineral springs of interest are the salines, the sulphur springs, [etc.]. **1911** *Daily Colonist* (Victoria, B.C.) 22 Apr. 1/4 Craig.. was probably fatally shot by a burglar late tonight in his room at a mineral springs resort. **1972** *Gloss. Geol.* (Amer. Geol. Inst.) 456/1 *Mineral spring*, a spring whose water contains enough mineral matter to give it a definite taste, in comparison to ordinary drinking water, esp. if the taste is unpleasant or if the water is regarded as having therapeutic value.

4. a. Of material substances: Neither animal nor vegetable in origin; inorganic.

1599 B. JONSON *Cynthia's Rev.* V. ii, I haue an excellent mineral Fucus, for the purpose. **1601** HOLLAND *Pliny* II. 454 Men vpon a couetous mind would needs seeke for siluer, and not satisfied therwith, thought good withall to find out Minerall vermilion. **1605** BACON *Adv. Learn.* II. x. §9 Mineral medicines have been extolled. **1685** BOYLE *Salub. Air* 35 Some Metalline ores, and some mineral earths themselves have been observ'd by Mineralogists. **1794** SULLIVAN *View Nat.* II. 104 Other opinions, indeed, would fix it a solid mineral bitumen. **1796** KIRWAN *Elem. Min.* (ed. 2) II. 5 The other, extracted from some maritime plants, but most frequently of mineral origin, and thence called Mineral Alkali. *Ibid.* 51 Mineral Carbon, impregnated with Bitumen. **1797** *Encycl. Brit.* (ed. 3) IX. 347/2 Mr. Rinman ..has found that dephlogisticated calces of iron, and particularly its solutions in mineral acids, have no binding power. **1834** *Cycl. Pract. Med.* III. 109/2 Of medicines, the vegetable tonics are scarcely so serviceable as the mineral. **1843** J. A. SMITH *Product Farming* (ed. 2) 139 Of Manures of Mineral Origin, or Fossil and Artificial or Chemical Manures.

b. Pertaining to inorganic matter. ***mineral kingdom***: see KINGDOM 5.

1876 *Encycl. Brit.* V. 520/2 The study of the remaining elements and of their compounds constituting inorganic, or, as it is also termed, mineral chemistry.

5. a. Special collocations and combinations: **mineral candle** (see quot.); **mineral caoutchouc** = ELATERITE; **mineral chameleon** (see CHAMELEON 5); **mineral charcoal**, 'a charcoal-like substance, often found between layers of coal' (Chester *Dict. Names Min.*); **mineral coal**, †(*a*) a variety of coal in which there are no traces of vegetable structure (*obs.*); (*b*) native coal, in contradistinction to charcoal; **mineral cotton**, †**mineral crystal** (see quots.); **mineral jelly**, vaseline (Webster *Suppl.* 1902); **mineral oil**, a general name for petroleum and the various oils distilled from it; **mineral pitch**, asphaltum; **mineral soil**, any soil in which the organic constituents are small in proportion to the inorganic ones; **mineral solution** (see quot.); **mineral tallow** = HATCHETTITE; **mineral tar** = PISSASPHALT; **mineral teeth**, artificial teeth; **mineral wax** = OZOCERITE; **mineral wool**, a variety of mineral cotton, slag-wool (Raymond *Mining Gloss.* 1881). Also MINERAL WATER.

1890 *Century Dict.*, **Mineral candle*, a kind of candle made from a semi-fluid naphtha obtained from wells sunk in the neighbourhood of the Irrawaddy river in Burma. **1801** *Encycl. Brit.* Suppl. II. 230/2 *Mineral caoutchouc. **1805** R. JAMESON *Syst. Min.* (1816) II. 401 *Mineral Charcoal. **1802** PLAYFAIR *Illustr. Hutton. Theory* 150 *Mineral-coal.. is the same which Dr. Hutton derives from the vegetable juices.. carried into the sea and there precipitated.. to become afterwards mineralized. **1854** RONALDS & RICHARDSON *Chem. Technol.* (ed. 2) I. 37 Mineral or pit coal. **1875** KNIGHT *Dict. Mech.*, **Mineral cotton*, a fiber formed by allowing a jet of steam to escape through a stream of liquid slag, by which it is blown into fine white threads. **1706** PHILLIPS (ed. Kersey), **Mineral Crystal* (among Chymists), a Composition of Salt-peter well putrify'd, and Flower of Brimstone. **1805** R. JAMESON *Syst. Min.* (1816) II. 358 *Mineral Oil, or Petroleum. **1796** KIRWAN *Elem. Min.* (ed. 2) II. 45 *Mineral Pitch, Asphaltum. Mineral Tar exposed to a moderate heat, and the action of the air, hardens into this substance. **1924** F. E. BEAR *Soil Managem.* iv. 26 The tendency of *mineral soils to be similar in chemical composition, irrespective of their source of origin, is very nicely shown in the following table. **1960** TEUSCHER & ADLER *Soil & its Fertility* i. 10 The fundamental distinction should be made between mineral soils and organic soils, depending upon the proportion of organic matter which they contain... In general, a soil is designated as organic when it contains 20 per cent or more of organic matter. **1855** OGILVIE Suppl., **Mineral solution*, arsenical liquor, or *liquor potassæ arsenitis*. **1796** KIRWAN *Elem. Min.* (ed. 2) II. 47 *Mineral Tallow. Its colour is white, its consistence that of Tallow, it feels greasy and stains paper. *Ibid.* 44 *Mineral Tar, Barbadoes Tar. This is Petrol still further altered by exposure to the air. **1851** C. CIST *Sk. Cincinnati in 1851* 220 *Mineral Teeth. One factory. **1885** *List of Subscribers, Classified* (United Telephone Co.) (ed. 6) 230 Manufacturers of Mineral Teeth and every Dental Requisite. **1864** WEBSTER, **Mineral wax*.

b. in names of pigments: **mineral black**, a native impure variety of carbon; **mineral blue**, a variety of Prussian blue, made lighter by the addition of alumina; **mineral brown** (see quot. 1930); **mineral grey**, a pale blue-grey pigment obtained in the making of ultramarine from lapis lazuli; **mineral green**, Scheele's green, arsenite of copper; **mineral lake** (see quot. 1902); **mineral purple**, (*a*) see quot. 1850; (*b*) purple of Cassius (*Cassell's Encycl. Dict.* 1882); **mineral violet** = *manganese violet*; **mineral white**, permanent white (see PERMANENT 1 d); **mineral yellow**, a lead pigment made by digesting litharge with common salt.

1849–50 WEALE *Dict. Terms Archit.* etc., **Mineral black*. **1869** T. W. SALTER *Field's Chromatogr.* (new ed.) xvii. 342 Under the names of Euchrome and *Mineral Brown, they [*sc.* Cappah browns] have been introduced into commerce for civil and marine painting. **1930** MAERZ & PAUL *Dict. Color* 167/1 *Mineral brown*, this name, or its synonym, *Metallic Brown*, is occasionally found given to specific colors in paints. It has.. long been used to refer to any native earth colored by iron oxide, etc. **1869** T. W. SALTER *Field's Chromatogr.* (new ed.) xix. 375 *Mineral gray.. is obtainable from the lapis lazuli, after the blue and ash have been worked out. **1958** M. L. WOLF *Dict. Painting* 179 A substance known as gangue (vein-stone) is often offered as mineral gray, but it is not a successful substitute. **1815** J. SMITH *Panorama Sci. & Art* II. 382 If to this sulphate of copper be added a solution of arseniate of potass, a beautiful green precipitate is formed, called Scheele's green, or *mineral green. **1902** WEBSTER Suppl., **Mineral lake*, a pink pigment consisting of a glass colored with tin chromate. **1850** G. FIELD *Painters' Art* 79 Purple Ochre, Or *Mineral Purple, is a dark ochre, native of the Forest of Dean. **1913** B. BROWN *Painter's Palette* iv. 21 Taking these paints.. and making them.. account for themselves in the matter of value, we find that their values fall on the value-scale thus: .. O.—Burnt Sienna. Rose Madder. *Mineral Violet. **1934** H. HILER *Notes Technique Painting* ii. 132 Mineral violet (manganous metaphosphate). **1958** M. L. WOLF *Dict. Painting* 170 Manganese pigments... The violets are particularly varied, some of the shades including mineral-, permanent-, and Nuernberger violet. **1875** E. SPON *Workshop Receipts* 93/2 White Pigments..*Mineral white. —Precipitated carbonate of lead. **1844** HOBLYN *Dict. Med.*, **Mineral Yellow*, Patent Yellow, a pigment consisting of chloride and protoxide of lead.

†**minera'leity.** *Obs.* [f. MINERAL *a.*, after *corporeity*, etc.] The attribute of being mineral.

1757 tr. *Henckel's Pyritol.* 148 A material cause and property of mineraleity.

†'**mineraline**, *a. Obs.* [f. MINERAL *sb.* + -INE.] Composed of mineral substances.

1674 R. GODFREY *Inj. & Ab. Physic* 33 A Mineralline dose which another.. unlearned Chymist gave him. *Ibid.* 171 Their perverse Mineraline Remedies.

†'**mineralist.** *Obs.* [f. MINERAL *sb.* + -IST.]

1. One who is skilled in or employed with minerals; a mineralogist.

1631 CAPT. SMITH *Advt. Planters* 3 Better there may be, for I was no Mineralist. **1670** PETTUS *Fodinæ Reg.* Table, *Mineralist*, such as deal in Minerals. *a* **1728** WOODWARD *Nat. Hist. Fossils* (1729) I. I. 84 The.. Mineralists of Germany.. all agree that the Ludus Paracelsi is the tessellated Pyrites. **1796** MORSE *Amer. Geog.* I. 660 The mountain.. has several of the appearances described by mineralists.

2. One who follows Paracelsus in the use of minerals in medicines.

1628 FORD *Lover's Mel.* I. ii, Mountebanck, Empiricks, Quacksaluers, Mineralists [etc.].

minerality (mɪnə'rælɪtɪ). [f. MINERAL *a.* + -ITY.] The quality of a water containing mineral salts.

1890 in *Syd. Soc. Lex.*

mineralizable (mɪnərə'laɪzab(ə)l), *a.* [f. MINERALIZE *v.* + -ABLE.] Capable of being mineralized.

1890 in *Century Dict.*

mineralization (mɪnərəlaɪ'zeɪʃən). [f. MINERALIZE *v.* + -ATION.]

1. a. The action or process of mineralizing, or the state of being mineralized.

1757 tr. *Henckel's Pyritol.* ix. 145 The mineral damps, that lodge any where for mineralisation, may happen to be of different mixtions. **1798** HATCHETT in *Phil. Trans.* LXXXVIII. 580 This tarnish is principally a commencement of mineralization on the surface. **1837** BUCKLAND *Geol. & Min.* I. 352 *note*, As happens when vegetables are converted into coal, under the process of mineralization. **1885** GOODALE *Physiol. Bot.* 39 Mineralization of the [cell-] wall may be general or local... General mineralization of the wall depends most frequently on silicic acid. **1895** OLIVER tr. *Kerner's Nat. Hist. Plants* I. 264 The final result of the decomposition of organic bodies by bacteria has been termed mineralization. **1898** *Q. Jrnl. Geol. Soc.* LIV. 81 The silicification, or more generally the mineralization, of these conglomerates is, in my opinion, the result of secondary processes of infiltration and crystallization. **1918** *Mining Mag.* XIX. 196/2 The supposed essential similarities between the conglomerates and ordinary lode deposits and quartz veins seem rather to have been based on ignorance of the various factors identical to formation of fissure deposits than on clear conceptions as to how the conglomerates received their mineralization. **1935** *Amer. Jrnl. Sci.* XXX. 115 'Mineralization' was shown to be a process of chemical action in which the mineralizer, HCl, was regenerated after performing transport and combination of the Fe_2O_3 with the MgO. **1971** *Nature* 24 Dec. 460/2 We intend to use this method to monitor the growth and dissolution of crystals in gels, especially in connexion with mineralization and demineralization in biological systems.

b. *concr.* A product of this process, a petrifaction.

1799 W. TOOKE *View Russian Emp.* I. 109 In which mineralizations the tender white rind.. is preserved quite in its natural appearance.

2. *Mining.* The condition of being well supplied with ore.

1899 *Daily News* 3 May 6/6 A sufficient proof.. that City men believe in the mineralisation of the country. **1970** *Daily Tel.* 24 Oct. 13/3 Two of the three drills encountered insignificant mineralisation. **1971** *Nature* 6 Aug. 393/2 In regions of mercury mineralization, however, up to 100 μg/kg has been reported.

mineralize ('mɪnərəlaɪz), *v.* Also 7 **minerallise**, 8–9 **mineralise**. [f. MINERAL *sb.* and *a.* + -IZE.]

1. *trans.* To combine with (a metal) so as to convert (it) into the state of ore. ? *Obs.*

1655 T. VAUGHAN *Euphrates* 29 When it is Minerallised by it self, and without any fæculent mixture, then [etc.]. **1757** tr. *Henckel's Pyritol.* 151 Sulphur in its separate state ..mineralises, or reduces metals to an ore-state. **1796** HATCHETT in *Phil. Trans.* LXXXVI. 291 This yellow colour probably occasioned the supposition that the lead was

mineralized by the tungstic acid. **1813** BAKEWELL *Introd. Geol.* 221 They [metals] are usually combined with some substance by which they are mineralized. **1855** J. R. LEIFCHILD *Cornwall Mines* 84 Iron, lead, and mercury,.. when mineralized by sulphur, form respectively the following sulphurets, iron pyrites, galena, and cinnabar. **1880** D. C. DAVIES *Metallif. Min. & Mining* (ed. 2) 4 These metalliferous minerals occur in nature in two distinct forms:—1st. Native..2nd. Mineralised, or associated with other minerals, and in combination with the gases or earthy admixtures.

2. a. *trans.* To convert into a mineral substance.

1799 W. TOOKE *View Russian Emp.* I. 109 Here are seen ..leaves, and roots of birch-trees..entirely mineralized by iron. **1823** BUCKLAND *Reliq. Diluv.* 9 The bones found in caverns are never mineralised. **1872** W. S. SYMONDS *Rec. Rocks* v. 142 The rocky axis, even in that far remote period was as consolidated and mineralised as at present. **1911** *Encycl. Brit.* XVIII. 255/1 Shales, sandstones and igneous rocks may be silicified and mineralized under suitable conditions. **1973** *Nature* 7 Dec. 347/1 Experiments introducing modern lichens into the normal preparation of microfaunal samples using hydrogen peroxide failed to mineralise the plant structures.

b. *intr.* for *refl.* To become mineralized. In quot. *fig.*

1845 MOZLEY *Ess., Laud* (1878) I. 192 A mind, by undergoing a certain ordeal, mineralises and turns into hard transparent crystal.

3. *trans.* To impregnate with mineral matters.

1789 PILKINGTON *View Derby.* I. 235 M. de Fourcroy imagines, that some waters contain the liver of sulphur; and that others are mineralized by hepatic gaz.

4. *intr.* To seek for minerals; to study minerals.

1792 A. YOUNG *Trav. France* 26 Can he clamber the rocks to mineralize? **1857** MRS. CROSSE *Mem. A. Crosse* 171 [He] was walking with his eyes fixed on the ground (a habit acquired from mineralising).

5. *passive.* To be stocked with ore.

1890 *Melbourne Argus* 28 May 7/6 A great quantity of stone, well mineralised, in the level. **1899** *Daily News* 23 May 7/2 By cablegrams:..Lode is heavily mineralised, in so far as 3 feet, average assay value 10 dwts. per ton.

mineralized (ˈmɪnərəlaɪzd), *ppl. a.* [f. MINERALIZE *v.* + -ED[1].]

1. Changed to a mineral.

1797 *Encycl. Brit.* (ed. 3) XI. 428/1 *Mineralised ores.* **1878** A. H. GREEN *Coal* i. 16 Coal is little else but mineralised vegetable matter. **1890** *Nature* 27 Feb. 392 The bone-corpuscles differ from the dentine-corpuscles in becoming completely embedded in the mineralized matrix.

2. Impregnated with minerals; containing mineral substances.

1893 *Nation* (N.Y.) 27 July 70/3 Were there not lines of weakness in the earth, along which lavas and hot mineralized solutions could penetrate. **1896** *Allbutt's Syst. Med.* I. 319 Many other slightly mineralised warm-waters..might be mentioned. **1906** *Act 6 Edw. VII* c.20 §4 (1) The expression 'mineralized methylated spirits' means..spirits which, in addition to being methylated..have mixed with or dissolved in them..mineral naphtha. **1915** K. TORNBERG tr. *Rasch's Electric Arc Phenomena* vii. 149 The radiation from the luminous arc flame of mineralized carbons, thus, is not always sufficient to compensate for any considerable deficiency occasioned by artificial lengthening of the arc. **1967** *Martindale's Extra Pharmacopoeia* (ed. 25) 86/2 Mineralised methylated spirits is the only variety that may be sold by retail in Great Britain for general use.

3. *Mining.* Of a district: Abounding in ore.

1881 RAYMOND *Mining Gloss., Mineralized*, charged or impregnated with metalliferous mineral. **1895** *Tablet* 2 Feb. 158 It was also a highly mineralized country, and a highly 'payable' country.

mineralizer (ˈmɪnərəlaɪzə(r)). [f. MINERALIZE *v.* + -ER[1].]

1. a. A substance that combines with a metal to form an ore, as sulphur, arsenic, etc.

1795 NICHOLSON *Dict. Chem.* 503 The commonest mineralizers are sulphur, arsenic, and fixed air. **1807** AIKIN *Dict. Chem.* II. 105/1 *Mineralizer* is any substance found in natural combination with a metal. **1854** J. D. WHITNEY *Metallic Wealth U.S.* ii. 81 Silver, tin, copper, lead, zinc, and iron are obtained almost exclusively in the form of ores, that is, in combination with a mineralizer.

b. *Petrol.* A volatile substance dissolved in a magma which aids the formation of minerals by altering the properties of the magma but is not necessarily present in the final mineral; also, a substance which promotes the artificial synthesis of a mineral.

1909 A. HARKER *Nat. Hist. Igneous Rocks* xii. 290 Mineralisers are, before all, powerful fluxes. One of their most important offices is that of reducing the viscosity of a magma. **1921** *Jrnl. Geol.* XXIX. 205 The presence of mineralizers has lowered the temperature of freezing below the inversion range of these minerals. **1943** R. D. GEORGE *Minerals & Rocks* xx. 434 When a rock is poured out of a volcano the mineralizers have a chance to escape before they have done their work. **1958** J. H. DE BOER in Everett & Stone *Struct. & Properties Porous Materials* 290 We had a mixture of alumina and silica—I don't remember if it was in the right proportion—but heating at a relatively low temperature.. mullite was already formed with lithium as a mineralizer. **1974** L. N. KOGARKO in H. Spenser *Alkaline Rocks* VI. iv. 480/2 Mineralizers may not enter into the composition of minerals but exert catalytic action on the process of their growth.

2. The mineral with which a water is impregnated.

1799 *Med. Jrnl.* II. 358 The principal mineralisers of this water are the sulphats of iron and alumin.

mineralizing (ˈmɪnərəlaɪzɪŋ), *ppl. a.* [f. MINERALIZE *v.* + -ING[2].] That mineralizes.

1796 HATCHETT in *Phil. Trans.* LXXXVI. 286 Although the substance was indisputably proved to be an ore of lead, yet the mineralizing principle of it remained unknown. **1875** LYELL *Princ. Geol.* I. II. xvii. 405 In some instances, alumina ..is the mineralizing material. **1890** *Athenæum* 18 Jan. 88/1 The action of fluorine as a mineralizing agent has been widely recognized.

†**mine'rallic**, *a. Obs.* [f. MINERAL + -IC.]

1778 PRYCE *Min. Cornub.* p. ix, Tin..is..more rich in its minerallick Ore than Copper.

†**'mineralness.** *Obs.* [f. MINERAL *a.* + -NESS.] The quality of being impregnated with minerals.

1661 J. CHILDREY *Brit. Baconica* 33 The Mineralness of these waters appears.

mineralocorticoid (ˌmɪnərələʊˈkɔːtɪkɔɪd). *Biochem.* [f. MINERAL *sb.* + -O + CORTICOID.] Any of the steroid hormones produced in the adrenal cortex which are esp. concerned with maintaining the salt balance in the body; any analogous synthetic compound.

1950 H. SELYE *Physiol. & Path. of Exposure to Stress* 646 Mineralo-corticoids predispose to the formation of lung edema. **1964** L. MARTIN *Clin. Endocrinol.* (ed. 4) v. 165 The mineralocorticoids promote the retention of salt and water and the excretion of potassium by the renal tubules. **1965** LEE & KNOWLES *Animal Hormones* iv. 70 The division of adrenal cortical hormones into glucocorticoids and mineralocorticoids is a convenient one. **1970** PASSMORE & ROBSON *Compan. Med. Stud.* II. vi. 12/2 Nowadays, the mineralocorticoid of choice in the treatment of defective secretion of endogenous aldosterone is the synthetic agent 9α-fluorocortisol.

mineralogic (mɪnərəˈlɒdʒɪk), *a.* Now chiefly *U.S.* [Formed as next.] = MINERALOGICAL.

1811 PINKERTON *Petral.* I. 242 The description of the latter has been given by several mineralogic authors. *Ibid.* II. 129 Saxony, the very focus of mineralogic knowledge. **1952** G. SARTON *Hist. Sci.* I. xxi. 560 A mineralogic analysis. **1972** *Science* 3 Nov. 497/1 Approximately one-third of the book is devoted to mineralogic and petrologic attributes of sandstones.

mineralogical (mɪnərəˈlɒdʒɪkəl), *a.* [f. MINERALOGY: see -LOGICAL.] Of or pertaining to mineralogy; concerned with the study of minerals; used in the study of minerals.

1791 BEDDOES in *Phil. Trans.* LXXXI. 64 This rule has been found to hold good by so many mineralogical travellers that [etc.]. **1859** DARWIN *Orig. Spec.* x. (1873) 272 The frequent and great changes in the mineralogical composition of consecutive formations. **1867** J. HOGG *Microsc.* I. iii. 208 The sharp edge of a mineralogical hammer. **1876** PAGE *Adv. Text-bk. Geol.* v. 99 Geological, mineralogical, and chemical considerations are thus inseparably interwoven.

mineralogically (mɪnərəˈlɒdʒɪkəlɪ), *adv.* [f. MINERALOGICAL *a.* + -LY[2].] In a mineralogical manner; with regard to mineralogy.

1801 CHENEVIX in *Phil. Trans.* XCI. 239 Whether we consider it mineralogically or chymically, it certainly is an interesting substance. **1845** *Encycl. Metrop.* VI. 562/1 The most important point of view under which mica slate can be considered mineralogically is [etc.].

mineralogist (mɪnəˈrælədʒɪst). [f. MINERALOGY + -IST.]

1. One who is versed in or studies mineralogy.

1646 SIR T. BROWNE *Pseud. Ep.* II. i. 49 Yet are there also many Authors that deny it, and the exactest Mineralogists have rejected it. **1791** NEWTE *Tour Eng. & Scot.* 429 The patrons of church livings,..would naturally, like King Charles, desire that his spiritual pastor might be a good chymist, a good mineralogist, and a good botanist. **1830** HERSCHEL *Stud. Nat. Phil.* 139 The number of simple minerals actually recognised by mineralogists does not exceed a few hundreds. **1860** PIESSE *Lab. Chem. Wonders* 33 The shop of Mr. Tennant, the mineralogist. **1879** *Cassell's Techn. Educ.* IV. 310/2 John James Ferber, the eminent Swedish mineralogist.

2. *Zool.* A name given by collectors to the gasteropods of the genus *Phorus*, which attach stones to the margin of their shells: a carrier shell.

1851 S. P. WOODWARD *Mollusca* I. 136 Most of the phori attach foreign substances to the margins of their shells as they grow; particular species affecting stones,..are called 'mineralogists',..by collectors.

mineralogize (mɪnəˈrælədʒaɪz), *v.* [f. MINERALOGY + -IZE.] *intr.* To look for minerals.

1804 MAR. EDGEWORTH *Ennui* vi, Wks. 1832 XI. 143 While he was not studying, he was botanizing or mineralogizing with O'Toole's chaplain. **1807** SOUTHEY *Espriella's Lett.* II. 43 Some to mineralogize, some to botanize, some to take views of the country.

mineralography (mɪnərəˈlɒgrəfɪ). *Min.* [f. MINERAL *sb.* + -O + -GRAPHY.] The study of the physical and chemical microstructure of minerals, *spec.* of polished sections using the reflecting microscope.

1916 J. MURDOCH *Microsc. Determination Opaque Minerals* p. iii, This new method [*sc.* using the reflecting microscope]..opens an entire new field of geologic science that promises to do for the ores what petrography has done for the rocks; for this the name of 'Mineralography' is proposed. **1921** H. L. ALLING in *Jrnl. Geol.* XXIX. 194 The rock-forming minerals can be studied..as the end products of crystallization of melts—geophysical chemistry, or as here proposed—mineralography. **1937** *Amer. Mineralogist* XXII. 492 Attention is restricted to instrumental and manipulative procedure with the opaque minerals; no consideration is given..to those more interpretative and philosophical phases of mineralography, such as textures.. deformation, alteration etc. **1942** *Chem. Abstr.* XXXVI. 1267 (*heading*) The imprint method in mineralography.

Hence **mineralo'graphic** *a.*, of or using mineralography.

1916 J. MURDOCH *Microsc. Determination Opaque Minerals* p. v, Mineralographic methods show that..the sulphide minerals tend to be microscopically mingled and intergrown in most intimate fashion. **1937** *Amer. Mineralogist* XXII. 492 Many requests..have come for description or discussion of mineralographic technique as employed at Harvard. **1971** *Daily Tel.* 29 Apr. 25 (Advt.), Mineralographic and related analyses on ores and metallurgical products.

mineralogy (mɪnəˈrælədʒɪ). [f. MINERAL *sb.* + -LOGY. Cf. F. *minéralogie* (1732 in Hatz.-Darm.), G. *mineralogie*, Sp. *mineralogía*, It. *mineralogia.*] **1.** The science which treats of minerals.

1690 BOYLE *Prev. Hydrostat. Way of Estimating Ores* Advt. 149 This..will not perhaps be unwelcome to some that Love Mineralogy, much better than they vnderstand it. **1796** KIRWAN *Elem. Min.* (ed. 2) I. Pref. 5 In the preceding decennial period, from 1774 to 1784, mineralogy may be said to have for the first time assumed its rank among the sciences. **1876** PAGE *Adv. Text-bk. Geol.* v. 97 The student must on no account learn to underrate the value of Mineralogy as a branch of Geology.

2. (A description of) the mineralogical features of a region or a specimen.

1798 R. JAMESON (*title*) An outline of the mineralogy of the Shetland Islands, and of the Island of Arran. **1878** *Mineral. Mag.* II. 106 (*heading*) The geognosy and mineralogy of Scotland. **1933** P. G. H. BOSWELL *On Mineral. Sedimentary Rocks* p. v, Having devoted much time to a digest of the literature of the mineralogy of sediments, I published a review of the work. **1952** *Jrnl. Geol.* LX. 107 These processes..have produced significant changes in the mineralogy and textural relationships of the plutonic acidic rocks. **1971** I. G. GASS et al. *Understanding Earth* i. 27/2 Chemical weathering is very effective in producing a mineralogy which differs greatly from that of the igneous and metamorphic rocks.

mineraloid (ˈmɪnərəlɔɪd). *Min.* [a. G. *mineraloid* (J. Niedźwiedzki 1909, in *Centralbl. f. Min., Geol. u. Paläont.* 662), f. *mineral* MINERAL *sb.*: see -OID.] A substance that might be regarded as a mineral but is amorphous rather than crystalline.

1913 A. F. ROGERS in *Proc. Amer. Philos. Soc.* LII. 608 The question of names for colloidal or amorphous minerals arises... Niedzwiedzki has proposed the term *mineraloid* for the natural amorphous substances. **1917** —— in *Jrnl. Geol.* XXV. 526 Lechateliérite is a glass and may be considered along with other natural glasses as a mineraloid. *Ibid.* 540 The hydrocarbons may be included under Niedzwiedski's term *mineraloid*. As Niedzwiedski used this term for all naturally occurring amorphous substances, this changes somewhat the original definition of mineraloid. Such substances as opal, cliachite, limonite, collophane, halloysite, etc., are definite enough to be called minerals even though they are amorphous. The term 'mineraloid' seems appropriate for the less definite mineral-like substances. **1941** C. S. HURLBUT *Dana's Man. Min.* (ed. 15) iii. 94 There are a number of mineral substances whose analyses do not yield definite chemical formulas and further show no signs of crystallinity. They have been called gel minerals or mineraloids. **1944** A. HOLMES *Princ. Physical Geol.* iv. 37 Only a few noncrystalline substances are regarded, by common usage, as minerals, and these are generally distinguished as mineraloids. **1951** [see JORDISITE]. **1972** G. S. FAY *Rockhound's Manual* iii. 37 Mineraloids are substances which look like and are often grouped with minerals, but mineraloids have an amorphous, or noncrystalline, structure as is evident when viewed under high-power microscopes. Opal is a mineraloid.

mineral water. a. Originally, water found in nature impregnated with some mineral substance, usually, such as is used medicinally. Also (with *a* and *plural*) a kind of such water. **b.** Later, applied also to artificial imitations of natural mineral waters, e.g. soda-water, seltzer-water; and subsequently extended to include other effervescent drinks, as lemonade and ginger-beer.

1562 TURNER *Baths* 9 Thys minorall water is cleare..and springeth out of sande. **1577** B. GOOGE *Heresbach's Husb.* (1586) 903 Their drinesse they cure with baths, and their throat with drinking mineral waters. **1694** SALMON *Bate's Dispens.* (1713) 406/2 To be drank at several Draughts, as you drink Mineral-waters, for the cutting and loosening of gross Humours. **1747** tr. *Astruc's Fevers* 340 The purgative mineral waters, as those of Val, &c. prove the most universal remedy. **1831** J. DAVIES *Man. Mat. Med.* 91 We apply the name Mineral Waters to such as contain in solution one or more foreign substances in sufficient quantity to exercise a more or less marked action on the animal economy. These waters are either natural or artificial.

attrib. **1851** in *Illustr. Lond. News* 5 Aug. (1854) 119/2 Mineral-water manufacture. **1903** *Daily Chron.* 16 Mar. 3/7 There are 3,500 mineral-water manufacturers in the United Kingdom.

†**'minerist.** *Obs.* [f. MINERA + -IST.] A mining expert.

1683 PETTUS *Fleta Min.* I. Pref., This art is very profitable to Minerists and such as work in Mines.

†**ˈminerous,** *a. Obs.* [f. MINERA + -OUS. Cf. It. *mineroso.*] Containing minerals.

1611 FLORIO, *Mineroso*, minerous, miny, full of mines. **1612** DRAYTON *Poly-olb.* iii. 212 That naturall power.. Which in that minerous earth insep'rably doth breed.

Minerva (mɪˈnɜːvə). Also 4 **mynerfe, mynerff,** 4–6 **minerve,** 6 **mynerve.** [a. L. *Minerva*, earlier *Menerva*:—pre-L. **menes-wā* (cf. Skr. *manasvin* 'full of mind or sense', *Manasvinī* name of the mother of the moon) f. **menes-* = Skr. *manas* mind, Gr. *μένος* courage, fury, f. root **men-*: see MIND *sb.*]

1. The Roman goddess of wisdom, anciently identified with the Greek Pallas Athene, 'the goddess of wisdom, warlike prowess, and skill in the arts of life' (L. & Sc.). † *in spite of Minerva* (tr. L. *invītā Minervā*): contrary to one's natural bent, without natural aptitude.

1375 BARBOUR *Bruce* IV. 262 He callit hir his deir mynerfe. **1390** GOWER *Conf.* I. 79 A Sacrifice unto Minerve. **1503** HAWES *Examp. Virt.* iv. 2 A noble vyrgyn there dyde her serue That fyrst made harnes called Mynerue. **1589** PUTTENHAM *Eng. Poesie* III. xxv. (Arb.) 311 That which he doth by long meditation rather then by a suddaine inspiration,..(and as they are woont to say) in spite of Nature or Minerua. **1611** SHAKS. *Cymb.* v. v. 164 For Feature, laming The Shrine of Venus, or straight-pight Minerua. **1638** JUNIUS *Paint. Ancients* 333 In spight (as the common saying is) of Minerva, that is, our nature not giving way to it. **1835** THIRLWALL *Greece* iii. I. 67 The goddess Athené, whom, with the Romans, we name Minerva.

†**b.** *fig.* (*a*) Used for: Wisdom, ability. (*b*) With allusion to the myth that Minerva (Athene) was born from the head of Jupiter. *Obs.*

1615 CHAPMAN *Odyss.* XIII. 179 Then, the Strand They strew'd with all the goods he had, bestow'd By the renown'd Phæacians, since he show'd So much Minerua. **1665** GLANVILL *Scepsis Sci.* xvi. 99 Self-love engageth us for any thing, that is a Minerva of our own. **1685** *Gracian's Courtiers Orac.* 178 Every one then ought to labour to know his Destiny, and to try his Minerva. *a* **1734** NORTH *Exam.* III. vi. §26 (1740) 442 The Thing itself [is] no better than a Minerva of his own fertile Brain.

2. *transf.* A woman having the stately mien of Minerva as represented in sculpture.

1877 READE *Woman Hater* iii, Ashmead..chuckled internally at the idea of this Minerva giving change in a *café*.

3. Short for *Minerva machine* (see 4).

1883 *B'ham Daily Post* 11 Oct., Printers.—Youth Wanted, accustomed to Minerva.

4. *attrib.* and *Comb.*, as ***Minerva birth***; ***Minerva-like*** adj. **Minerva machine** *Printing* (see quot.). **Minerva press,** (*a*) the name of a printing-press formerly existing in Leadenhall Street, London; hence, the series of ultra-sentimental novels issued with the imprint of this press *c* 1800; (*b*) (*Printing*) = *Minerva machine*.

1632 BROME *North. Lasse* Ded., A Countrey Lass I present you, that *Minerva-like was a brayn-born Child, and Jovially begot. **1894** H. GAMLIN *Romney* 51 Reynolds was fortunate in having so Minerva-like a model. **1888** JACOBI *Printer's Vocab.*, **Minerva machine*, a small platen jobbing machine—the original Cropper machine. **1828** CARLYLE *Misc.* (1857) I. 173 So *Meister* was ranked among the legal coin of the *Minerva Press. **1850** *Athenæum* 7 Dec. 1274/1 The relief provided for the Begum [in *Pendennis*].. is Minerva Press every grain of it. **1866** *Ibid.* 10 Nov. 602/2 Such a flow of Minerva-press melo-dramatic diction. **1888** *Encycl. Brit.* XXIII. 705 (art. *Typography*) Fig. 11, Minerva Press.

minerval (mɪˈnɜːvəl), *sb.* [a. L. *minerval*, f. *Minerva*: see prec.] A gift given in gratitude by a scholar to a master; also, money paid to a schoolmaster for teaching.

1603 HOLLAND *Plutarch's Mor.* 454 You are well enough served and receive a due Minervall for your schoolage. **1674** CHARLETON in *Lett. Eminent Persons* (1813) I. 5 To accept my mean oblation,..not as an ornament to her public library, but a minerval or simple testimony of my respects and gratitude. **1700** J. BROME *Trav. Eng., Scot.*, etc. iii. (1707) 117 The School..was Built and Endowed by King Edward..with a generous Minerval for a Master and Usher. **1885** W. CORY *Lett. & Jrnls.* (1897) 513 At the end of our year's Greek reading, they [girls] gave me a minerval, to wit, the simple 'Autobiography of George Napier'.

†**Miˈnerval,** *a. Obs.* [ad. L. *Minervālis*: see MINERVA and -AL[1].] Pertaining to Minerva.

1625 C. BROOKE *On Sir A. Chichester* 201 Thus he spun Honor's Minervall web.

minery (ˈmaɪnərɪ). [ad. med.L. *minēria*, *mināria*, f. *mināre* to MINE.]

1. A place where mining operations are carried on; †also, a mine.

[**1279** *Northumb. Assize Rolls* (Surtees) 266 Quod Aldeneston' et mynaria ejusdem et homines ejusdem minariæ..fuerint alienati.] **1567** MAPLET *Gr. Forest* 13 It is found also in Mineries in maner like to Grauell and Sande. **1577** FRAMPTON *Joyfull News* III. (1596) 103 Euery day they discouer in those countries great Mineries of metals. **1633** T. ADAMS *Exp. 2 Peter* iii. 5 If we dig into her inwards, we find metals, mineries, quarries. **1670** PETTUS *Fodinæ Reg.* 88 Every other Trespass done upon the Minerie shall be fined at 2d. **1799** W. TOOKE *View Russian Emp.* II. 506 Certain wrought goods for the army and navy, as cannon-balls from the mineries. **1876** W. WHITE *Holidays Tyrol* xvii. 134 A thank-offering from the minery to the church. **1898** RAYMOND *Two Men o' Mendip* iii, I'll ride across to the mineries, myzelf, so quiet as I can.

attrib. **1681** in *Phil. Trans. Abr.* (1722) II. 369 Which came from the Washing of Lead in the Minery Ponds.

†**b.** *fig.*

a **1653** BINNING *Chr. Love* ii. Wks. (1847) 528 All these lusts..are the mineries of contentions, and strifes, and wars.

†**2.** A military mine. *Obs.*

1591 SPARRY tr. *Cattan's Geomancie* 86 Vnlesse it bee to put fire vnto Myneries or Artillerie.

†**b.** Materials for mining. *Obs.*

1687 RYCAUT *Knolles' Hist. Turks* II. 312 The besiegers had endeavoured to pass the Ditch in Boats, and so carry over their Minery.

†**3.** The science of mining. *Obs.*

1777 tr. *Born's Trav. Hungary* xiii. 107 A naturalist endowed with a proper knowledge of minery.

minestra (mɪˈnɛstrə). [It.] An Italian vegetable soup; = MINESTRONE.

1750 [see MACARONI 1]. **1871** *Monthly Packet* Sept. 362 One of the waiters here came up to me, announcing that 'la minestra' was ready. I had ordered no soup. **1907** J. WEBSTER *Jerry Junior* xii. 184 They supped on *minestra* and *fritto misto*. **1935** M. MORPHY *Recipes of all Nations* 127 This is the traditional 'minestra' served at Easter and Christmas in the province of Parma. **1941** 'M. HOME' *Place of Little Birds* vi. 89 Donati..himself saw to the making of the *minestra*. **1948** E. POUND *Pisan Cantos* (1949) lxxviii. 65 'No, there is nothing to pay for that bread.' 'Nor for the minestra.' **1972** P. EVE *European's Cook Bk.* 130 *Minestra and Minestrone.* The basic difference between these two soups is that the former is all vegetable whereas the Minestrone is made with meat stock.

minestrale, obs. form of MINSTREL.

minestrone (mɪnɪˈstrəʊnɪ). [It.] A thick soup containing vegetables and rice or pasta.

1891 E. DURET *Pract. Househ. Cookery* i. 63 The minestrone is a real Italian national soup. It is composed of a mixture of vegetables and rice. **1903** [see FRITTO MISTO]. **1922** *Blackw. Mag.* Feb. 143/2 There were slices of melon, olives and tunny and a minestrone. **1936** AUDEN & ISHERWOOD *Ascent of F6* II. iii. 95 Just as you like. What about soup? Minestrone, I think? **1959** *Sunday Times* 29 Mar. 21/6 There are..dozens of versions of Minestrone, which is a really solid soup thick with vegetables and cheese and rice or pasta and intended, with bread and wine, to constitute the entire midday meal of hungry working people. **1972** N. FROUD *World Bk. Soups* 26 A really good Italian minestrone should have a foundation of salt pork or gammon and white haricot beans.

minette[1] (mɪˈnɛt). *Min.* [a. F. *minette.*]

1. (See quot. 1888.)

1878 LAWRENCE tr. *Cotta's Rocks Class.* 166 It is sometimes difficult to distinguish minette from mica-porphyry. **1878** BONNEY & HOUGHTON in *Q. Jrnl. Geol. Soc.* XXXV. 166 We propose the analogous term minette-felsite. **1888** TEALL *Brit. Petrogr.* 350 *Minette*, this is a local name used by miners in the Vosges for a rock essentially composed of dark mica, orthoclase and a felspathic matrix. It was introduced into geological literature by Voltz in 1828.

2. A low-grade oolitic iron ore found mainly in Luxemburg and Lorraine. Freq. *attrib.*

1902 *Encycl. Brit.* XXIX. 584/2 Of these [ores] the chief is the lean but very cheap 'Minette' ore of the enormous deposits of Luxemburg and Lorraine. **1919** J. M. KEYNES *Econ. Consequences Peace* iv. 90 The German Delegation made strong efforts to secure the inclusion of a provision by which coal and coke to be furnished by them to France should be given in exchange for *minette* from Lorraine. **1940** *Economist* 13 July 40/1 A new process of steelmaking..was ..applied by Continental steelmakers to the phosphoric pig-iron produced from their minette ores. **1966** P. T. FLAWN *Mineral Resources* vi. 139 The famous minette iron ores of Lorraine were exploited first on the outcrop in Germany and then followed down dip into France.

minette[2] (mɪˈnɛt). The smallest of regular sizes of portrait photographs.

1897 in WEBSTER.

minever, variant of MINIVER.

minew, obs. form of MINNOW.

ming (mɪŋ), *sb.*[1] *dial.* [f. *ming*, MENG *v.*]

a. A mixture. **b.** (See quot. 1856.)

1823 *Caledonian Merc.* 4 Dec. (Jam.), Various sorts of mixtures, in none of which tar is an ingredient. These mings do not clot the fleece as tar does. **1856** P. THOMPSON *Hist. Boston* 715 Land of different proprietors lying mixed, is said to be lying in ming. **1866** J. E. BROGDEN *Prov. Words Lincs.*

Ming (mɪŋ), *sb.*[2] [Chinese, lit. 'bright, clear'.] The name of a dynasty which ruled in China from 1368 to 1644; a ruler belonging to this dynasty. Also *attrib.*

[**1671** J. OGILBY tr. *Montanus' Atlas Chinensis* 485 Thus ended a Prince, perhaps the greatest in the World..: Together with him, the Name of the Empire, viz. Taiming, that is, Of great Brightness, after it had continu'd two hundred sixty six Years..was utterly extinguish'd. **1676** *China & France* 19 The antient Kings of China were of the Family of Min, which signifies Light.] **1795** W. WINTERBOTHAM *Hist., Geogr. & Philos. View Chinese Empire* i. 5 The whole of their emperors, abstracting from those who are said to have reigned in the fabulous times, are comprehended in twenty-two dynasties... 21. Ming,.. 1368. 22. Tsing, 1645. **1836** J. F. DAVIS *Chinese* I. v. 185 The first Emperor of the Ming dynasty, which expelled the Mongols in 1366, had been servant to a monastery of bonzes, or priests of Budh. **1854** *Hist. China* v. 56 Houng-nan, or the first Ming, died in 1398, after a reign of thirty years. **1940** E. POUND *Cantos* lx. 91 And Japan kept peace even all through the great Ming rebellion. **1967** D. BLOODWORTH *Chinese Looking Glass* vii. 68 When in the 17th century the eunuchs betrayed their Ming ruler, and the Forbidden City of Peking fell to rebels, the Emperor wrote a valedictory message on his yellow robe and strangled himself with his silken girdle.

b. Used *attrib.* and *absol.* of the porcelain of the Ming period (of which the finest examples are extremely rare and valuable).

1892 J. D. BALL *Things Chinese* 309 A street hawker may be seen..ladling iced syrup out of Ming bowls, and there is hardly a butcher's shop without a large Ming jar. **1898** W. G. GULLAND *Chinese Porc.* I. 3 We must also remember that a large amount of Ming porcelain must have been destroyed at the end of the Ming dynasty. **1907** E. WHARTON *Fruit of Tree* II. xiii. 209, I want to show you a set of Ming I picked up the other day. **1936** R. LEHMANN *Weather in Streets* III. iv. 318 Just because she hasn't even the guts to put her own stockings on—she's to be treated like a Ming vase. **1939** T. S. ELIOT *Old Possum's Pract. Cats* 24 Down from the library came a loud *ping* From a vase which was commonly said to be Ming. **1970** *Oxf. Compan. Art* 234/2 The standard Ming porcelain body was refined and white, capable of thin potting when necessary, and covered with a fairly even, clear glaze.

c. Used *attrib.* to denote colours characteristic of Ming porcelain, as ***Ming blue, green, yellow.***

1926 *Textile Mercury* 19 June 566/3 The Textile Colour Card Association's..new greens are Locarno, elfin, ming,.. and Paradise greens. **1931** B. RACKHAM in R. L. Hobson et al. *Chinese Ceramics* ii. 141 The blue..is quite different from the many tones of Ming blue,..and whatever may be the attractive qualities of the Ming blues in isolation, there can be no doubt that this later blue and white porcelain is far more effective. **1935** J. P. MARQUAND (*title*) Ming yellow. **1966** *Country Life* 30 June 1761/2 Shift-dresses..in white, Ming-green, navy or camel. **1969** *Vogue* 1 Mar. 99 White wool tabard, edged with waves of Ming blue.

†**ming,** *v. Obs.* Forms: 1 **myng-, mynegian, menegian,** 2–3 **munegen, -eȝen,** 3 **minegen, -eȝen, -iȝen, moneȝen, muniȝen,** 5 **miniye, mynye, munye,** 4–7 **minge(n,** 4–6 **mynge(n,** 4–5 **menge(n,** 4 **meneȝe(n, menewe, monewe, munge(n, mynewe,** 6– **ming.** [OE. (*ȝe*)*mynegian*, *myngian* wk. vb.:—WGer. **munigôjan* (cf. OHG. *bi-munigôn*), f. OTeut. **muni-* (OE. *myne*: see MIN *sb.*[1]).]

1. *trans.* To put in mind, remind (a person); to admonish. Const. *of* (in OE. genit. case), *on*, *to* with *inf.*; also with dependent clause.

a **1023** WULFSTAN *Hom.* (1883) 210/9 Drihten..us þonne myngað þæs sunnandæges weorces. *c* **1175** *Lamb. Hom.* 147 þet lueð world wunne he muneȝed. *c* **1290** *S. Eng. Leg.* I. 413/368 Seint Iohan him [i.e. the Bishop] chargede of is warde; and muneguede him wel ofte þat he him wuste swiþe wel. **1415** HOCCLEVE *To Sir J. Oldcastle* 424 The sighte us myngith to the seint to preye. —— *Min. Poems* 71/144 Mynge him ther-on. *c* **1425** *Eng. Conq. Irel.* 84 He miniyed the Erle of his beheste.

b. *absol.* with clause.

c **1200** *Trin. Coll. Hom.* 215 Prest specð inne chirche of chirche neode and mineȝeð þat me niwe cloðes oðer elde bete.

2. To bring into remembrance; to commemorate; to mention. (In OE. with obj. in *genitive*.)

c **1000** *Ags. Ps.* (Th.) xliii. argt., Dauid..myngode þæra gyfa, þe he his fædrum and his foregengum sealde. *c* **1200** *Trin. Coll. Hom.* 169 He minegede alle his wrecche siðes þe he þolede on þis wrecche worelde. *c* **1315** SHOREHAM I. 1892 More godsibrede nys þer nauȝt þane hys y-meneȝed here. *c* **1320** *Cast. Love* 1193 Marie, Mayden schene,..For deol mungen I ne may þe pyne þ[t] þ[u] þoledest þulke day. *a* **1450** MYRC 1915 More, I pray þat þow me mynge, In þy masse when thow dost synge. **1522** *World & Child* 426 (Manly) Ye must loue God aboue all thynge, His name in ydelnes ye may not mynge. **1598** BP. HALL *Sat.* IV. ii. 80 Could neuer man worke thee a worser shame Than once to minge thy fathers odious name. **1623** LISLE *Ælfric on O. & N. Test.* To Rdr. 13 This that I minged last was not the least motiue I had. *a* **1656** *Sir Cawline* xxi. in Child *Ballads* II. 59/1 For because thou minged not Christ before, The lesse me dreadeth thee. **1674** RAY *N.C. Words* 48 To *Ming* at one, to mention. **1787** GROSE *Prov. Gloss.*, To *ming* at one, to remind, give warning or allude to a thing.

3. To remember. Also *refl.* to bethink oneself.

1362 LANGL. *P. Pl.* A. VII. 88 He is holden, ich hope to haue me in muynde, And munge me in his memorie. **1377** *Ibid.* B. IV. 94 And thanne gan Mede to mengen here and mercy she bisought. **1596** BP. HALL *Elegy on Dr. Whitaker* 100 The memorie of his mightie name Shall liue as long, as aged Earth shall last:.. Aye ming'd, aye mourn'd.

4. *intr.* To give an account; to relate.

13.. *E.E. Allit. P.* A. 855 For þay of mote couthe neuer mynge. *c* **1350** *Will. Palerne* 1067 Hit tidde after bi time as þe tale minges. *c* **1460** *Emare* 926 The Kyng yn herte was full woo, When he herd mynge tho Of her that was his qwene.

ming(e, variant ff. of MENG *v. Obs.* exc. *dial.*

†**minge,** *v. Obs. rare.* [ad. L. *mingĕre* to void urine.] *trans.* To discharge as urine.

1611 *Tarlton's Jests* (1844) 43 A horse mingeth whay, madam, a man mingeth amber, A horse is for your way, madam, but a man for your chamber.

minge (mɪndʒ), *sb. dial.* or *slang.* [Origin obscure.] The female pudendum; hence, by extension, women regarded collectively as a means of sexual gratification.

1903 *Eng. Dial. Dict.* IV. 118/2 *Minge*, the female pudendum. **1925** FRASER & GIBBONS *Soldier & Sailor Words* 156 *Minge*, female society (similar to Binge—*q.v.*), *e.g.*, 'His failing is Binge and yours Minge.' **1936** J. CURTIS *Gilt Kid* viii. 80 I'm going to give you a kick in the minge if

you don't shut up. **1974** *New Direction* IV. iv. 19/2 They've all..scented and talced their minges.

‖**mingei** (miŋ'gei). Also **Mingei.** [Jap., f. *min* people + *gei* arts.] Japanese folk-art; traditional local Japanese handicraft. Also *attrib.*

1960 B. Leach *Potter in Japan* viii. 183 Sen cha (green tea) taste, different from 'Matt cha' and certainly not 'Mingei'. **1967** H. H. Sanders *World of Jap. Ceramics* 177 The brown clay of Ryūmon-ji, when decorated with white slip..was considered..to be one of the distinctive *mingei* products of Japan. **1969** *Sat. Rev.* (U.S.) 13 Sept. 90/1 *Mingei*, or folk art, restaurants..with décor drawn from Japan's rich folk tradition, hand-made plates and bowls by master potters.

mingel, obs. form of MINGLE *v.*

†**'mingent**, *a. Obs. rare.* [ad. L. *mingent-em*, pr. pple. of *mingĕre*.] Discharging urine.

c **1685** *Dk. Buck'hm.'s Confer.* (1714) 22 She..continued in mingent Circumstances from the Morning till Night.

mingily ('mɪndʒɪlɪ), *adv.* [f. MINGY *a.*: see -LY².] Meanly, stingily.

1958 *Listener* 6 Nov. 722/2 The most mingily ungenerous gathers backed by elastic.

mingimingi ('mɪŋɪmɪŋɪ). Also **mingi.** [Maori.] An evergreen shrub, *Cyathodes acerosa* (or *C. fasciculata*) belonging to the family Epacridaceæ, native to New Zealand, Victoria, and Tasmania, and bearing tiny, green flowers and red or white berries. Cf. MICKY².

1889 T. Kirk *Forest Flora N.Z.* 213 The wood of the mingi is of a light-brown colour. **1906** T. F. Cheeseman *Man. N.Z. Flora* 411 *C[yathodes] acerosa*... Abundant from the North Cape southwards. Sea-level to 2500 ft. Mingimingi. **1929** W. Martin *N.Z. Nature Bk.* II. viii. 126 The mingi-mingi..is a rigid, pungent-leaved shrub with either white or red berries. **1963** *Weekly News* (Auckland) 10 July 37/3 The small shrub called mingimingi or black teatree is as good as manuka as a source of heat. **1966** G. W. Turner *Eng. Lang. Austral. & N.Z.* viii. 168 Another shrub *mingi* is said by Morris to have the form *micky* in the South Island. This is likely, as the South Island dialects of Maori have *k* for North Island *ng*.

†**'minging**, *vbl. sb. Obs.* [f. MING *v.* + -ING¹.]

1. The action of the verb MING; an admonition; a warning or reminder. In 17–18th c. a premonitory symptom. (Cf. MINDING *vbl. sb.* 2.)

a **940** *Laws of Æthelstan* v. vii, Ne forlæte he..þa mynegunge. **1674** Ray *N.C. Words* 48 *Mynegung* an admonition, warning or minding; so it is usually said, I had a *minging*, suppose of an Ague or the like Disease, that is, not a perfect Fit, but so much as to put me in mind of it. **1703** M. Warwick in Floyer *Hot & Cold Bath.* II. 298 When the Wind is Northward, I meet a little minging of Pains, but no contraction.

2. A memorial.

c **1175** *Lamb. Hom.* 45 Uwilc sunne-dei is to locan alswa ester dei for heo is muneȝing of his halie ariste. *a* **1225** *Ancr. R.* 136 Cus þe wunde studen, ine swete munegunge of þe soðe wunden. *c* **1250** *Gen. & Ex.* 1623 Sette he up ðat ston for muniging.

mingle ('mɪŋg(ə)l), *sb.* Now *rare.* [f. MINGLE *v.*] The action of mingling, the state of being mingled; mixture. Also *concr.* a mingled mass, a mixture.

1548 Elyot *Dict.*, *Aceruatim*, on heapes, without ordre, in a mengle [1545 mengley]. **1606** Shaks. *Ant. & Cl.* I. v. 59 He was not sad... He was not merrie, Which seem'd to tell them, his remembrance lay In Egypt with his ioy, but betweene both. Oh heauenly mingle! *Ibid.* IV. viii. 37 Trumpetters With brazen dinne blast you the Citties eare, Make mingle with our ratling Tabourines. **1621** Lady M. Wroth *Urania* 156 Neither Masque nor properly any one thing, but a mingle of diuers sorts. **1668** Dryden *Dram. Poesy* Ess. (ed. Ker) I. 61 Scenes admirable in their kind, but of an ill mingle with the rest. **1714** Swift *Let. to Ld. Bolingbroke* 7 Aug., To represent persons and things without any mingle of my own interest or passions. **1720** T. Boston *Fourf. State* (1797) 385 In a mingle of many different seeds the expert gardener can distinguish between seed and seed. **1811** *Ora & Juliet* IV. 76 Her thoughts were a mingle of thankfulness and dread.

b. *Comb.*, in †*mingle-coloured* adj.

1593 Nashe *Christ's T.* (1613) 62 Her high roofe was mingle-coloured with mounting drops of bloud. **1660** *Mercurius Publ.* 24–31 May 349 A mingle-coloured wrought Tabby Gown of Deer colour and white.

mingle ('mɪŋg(ə)l), *v.* Forms: 5 **myngel**, *Sc.* **mengill**, 5–6 **mengel**, **mengle**, **myngle**, 6 **mengyll**, **mingel**, **-il**, **myngell**, 6– **mingle**. [Late ME. *mengel*, frequentative f. MENG *v.*: see -LE 3. Cf. MDu., Du. *mengelen* (which may possibly have suggested the formation), MHG., mod.G. *mengeln*, of the same meaning.]

1. *trans.* To mix (things together or one thing *with* another) so that they become physically united or form a new combination; to combine in a mixture, to blend.

1495 *Naval Acc. Hen. VII* (1896) 225 Talowe..mengeled with pytche. **1526** *Pilgr. Perf.* (W. de W. 1531) 3 Electrum is a myxture of syluer & golde myngled togyder. **1535** Coverdale *Ps.* ci. 9, I..mengle my drynke with wepynge. **1687** A. Lovell tr. *Thevenot's Trav.* I. 31 There is a little Bason..and over it a cock of warm water; and..above..another cock, for cold water, so that you may mingle them as you please. **1706** London & Wise *Retir'd Gard.* I. II. xii. 167 Take some Mould mingled with soft Hay. **1839** Ure *Dict. Arts* 826 The sulphuret of antimony mingled with its gangue may be subjected to the same mode of assay. *a* **1852** Webster *Wks.* (1877) III. 317 The bones of her sons..now lie mingled with the soil of every State from New England to Georgia.

†**b.** *fig.* To put together so as to make one, to 'pool'. *Obs.*

1611 Shaks. *Cymb.* I. vi. 186 Some dozen Romanes of vs..haue mingled summes To buy a Present for the Emperor.

†**c.** Const. *to. Obs. rare.*

1563 Hyll *Art Garden.* (1593) 18 To this water also mingle a little dunge.

d. *poet. nonce-use.* To put in as an ingredient.

1842 Tennyson *Vision Sin* IV. xxxvi, Fill the cup, and fill the can! Mingle madness, mingle scorn!

2. To bring together, intersperse, or associate (material or immaterial things, persons, etc. *with* or *among* others), to unite or join in company. Also *to mingle up*.

c **1450** tr. *De Imitatione* III. lviii. 135 Grace..suffriþ not itself to be menglid with straunge þinges. **1494** Fabyan *Chron.* I. cxl. 126 They were greatly myngelyd or medelyd wᵗ other nacions. **1526** *Pilgr. Perf.* (W. de W. 1531) 217 He myngleth yᵉ trewth with errour & heresy. **1596** Shaks. *1 Hen. IV*, III. ii. 63 The skipping King..Mingled his Royaltie with Carping Fooles. **1598** Grenewey *Tacitus' Ann.* I. viii. (1622) 14 Besides this, womens quarrels were mingled among. **1630** Prynne *God no Impostor* 16 Reprobates are mingled with the Elect, as the weedes, the tares are with the corn and grasse. **1726** Swift *Gulliver* IV. vii, To devour everything that came in their way, whether herbs, roots, berries, the corrupted flesh of animals, or all mingled together. **1817** Jas. Mill *Brit. India* II. IV. iv. 151 In an instant the two regiments were mingled at the push of the bayonet. **1840** Dickens *Barn. Rudge* iii, A strong tendency to mingle up present circumstances with others which have no manner of connexion with them. **1859** Jephson *Brittany* i. 2 We must mingle our regrets when our only fare is a *gigot*. **1875** Lyell *Princ. Geol.* II. III. xlvi. 544 Mingled with the rest, the corpses of two men and one woman. **1875** Jowett *Plato* (ed. 2) V. 235 The order of the voice, in which high and low are duly mingled, is called harmony.

b. *refl.*

14.. *How Good Wife taught Dau.* 86 Thoill thaim nocht..mengill thame [*sc.* women] with neuir vith ladry. **1535** Coverdale *1 Esdras* viii. 70 Both they and their sonnes haue mengled them selues with the daughters of them. **1702** Echard *Eccl. Hist.* (1710) 65 He caus'd soldiers..to mingle themselves among the people in private apparel. **1725** De Foe *Voy. round World* (1840) 258 It is impossible to describe how the sound [of falling water], crossing and interfering, mingled itself. **1856** Kane *Arct. Expl.* I. xxix. 384 The renewed chorus..mingling itself sleepily in my dreams with school-boy memories.

†**c.** To associate (a person) *in* common action.

c **1607** Donne *Lett.* (1651) 60, I owe you so much of my health,..as I would not mingle you in any occasion of repairing [1839 ed. impairing] it.

†**d.** To join (conversation, friendship, etc.) *with* another person. Also *to mingle eyes*, look into each other's eyes. *Obs.*

1606 Shaks. *Ant. & Cl.* III. xiii. 156 To flatter Cæsar, would you mingle eyes With one that tyes his points. **1611** — *Wint. T.* I. ii. 109 To mingle friendship farre is mingling bloods. *Ibid.* IV. iv. 471 Oh cursed wretch, That knew'st this was the Prince, and wouldst aduenture To mingle faith with him. **1650** Howell *Giraffi's Rev. Naples* I. 20 The Bishop..being not able to com himself to mingle speech with him.

e. *Card-making.* (See quot. 1867.)

1837 [see MINGLING *vbl. sb.*]. **1867** Fry *Playing-Card Terms* in *Philol. Soc. Trans.* 57 *Mingle*, to place papers, or cardboards, intended to be pasted, in such a way, that the paster can readily take up the sheets in the order in which they are to be pasted.

3. To form or make up by mixing various elements or ingredients, to concoct, compound.

1611 Bible *Isa.* v. 22 Woe unto them that are..men of strength to mingle strong drinke. **1667** Milton *P.L.* VI. 277 Hence then,..to the place of evil, Hell, Thou and thy wicked crew; there mingle broiles, Ere this avenging Sword begin thy doome. **1871** Blackie *Four Phases* I. 153 The man whose duty it was to administer the drug mingled in a bowl. *absol.* **1635** Pagitt *Christianogr.* I. iii. (1636) 121 He took the Cup of the fruit of the Vine mingling, giving thankes [etc.].

†**b.** To mix up so as to cause confusion in, to confound. *Obs.*

1549 Latimer *Ploughers* (Arb.) 32 Thys is the marke at the whyche the Deuyll shooteth,..to mingle the institucion of the Loordes supper. **1551** Bible (Matthew) *Gen.* xi. 7 Let vs..myngle theyr tonge euen there, that one vnderstand not what an other sayeth.

4. *intr.* Of things material and immaterial: To unite or combine in some intimate relation; to join together (or *with* another); to mix, blend.

1530 Palsgr. 634/2 Oyle and water wyll never mengyll togyther. **1597** Shaks. *2 Hen. IV*, v. ii. 132 The Tide of Blood in me,..Now doth it turne, and ebbe backe to the Sea, Where it shall mingle with the state of Floods. **1671** Milton *P.R.* IV. 453, I heard the rack As Earth and Skie would mingle. **1756–7** tr. *Keysler's Trav.* (1760) III. 176 Which discharge themselves into the Topino, and under that name mingle with the Chiascio. **1787** G. White *Selborne* i. 4 The soil becomes an hungry lean sand, till it mingles with the forest. **1860** Tyndall *Glac.* II. App. 427 In nature, mechanical and molecular laws mingle, and create apparent confusion. **1885** W. C. Smith *Kildrostan* 52 When a wave, Broken and spent, ebbs back, what should it do But mingle with the new wave flowing in, And swell its volume?

5. Of a person: To mix or join oneself in any kind of association *with* others; to have intercourse *with*; to move about *among*, or *in* a gathering. Also, to be associated or take part with others *in* some action or combination.

1605 Shaks. *Macb.* III. iv. 3 Our selfe will mingle with Society, And play the humble Host. **1683** Temple *Mem.* Wks. 1731 I. 380 Some of the Train'd Bands..mingled among them. **1685** Otway *Windsor Castle* 24 Imagine Fate t' have..mingled in the Throng. **1769** Robertson *Chas. V*, VI. Wks. 1813 VI. 106 He is dead to the world and ought not to mingle in its transactions. **1818** Shelley *Homer's Hymn Moon* 21 The Son of Saturn with this glorious Power Mingled in love and sleep—to whom she bore Pandeia. *c* **1820** S. Rogers *Italy, Bologna* 32 Observed, nor shunned the busy scene of life, But mingled not. **1852** Thackeray *Esmond* I. x, Nor caring to mingle with the mere pleasures and boyish frolics of the students. **1870** E. Peacock *Ralf Skirl.* I. 8 They often mingled in Court society. **1872** Yeats *Growth Comm.* 138 The Batavians mingled afterwards with the Frisians. **1885** *Law Times* LXXX. 10/1 He is very anxious to avoid any appearance of mingling in party disputes.

mingleable ('mɪŋg(ə)ləb(ə)l), *a.* ? *Obs.* [f. MINGLE *v.* + -ABLE.] That may be mingled; miscible.

1666 Boyle *Orig. Formes & Qual.* 196 Distill'd Liquors, readily & totally mingleable with Water. **1682** Grew *Anat. Plants, Disc. Mixture* App. 237 So as to become easily mingleable with any unoyly Liquor.

mingled ('mɪŋg(ə)ld), *ppl. a.* [f. MINGLE *v.* + -ED¹.] In senses of the verb.

1535 Coverdale *Lev.* xix. 19 Nether sowe thy felde with myngled sede. **1611** Bible *Jer.* xxv. 20 All the mingled people. *a* **1729** J. Rogers 19 *Serm.* (1735) 330 Even the best of us appear contented with a mingled, imperfect Virtue. **1746** Hervey *Medit.* (1818) 32 See their mingled graces transfused into their offspring. **1859** Kingsley *Misc.* (1860) I. 40 Her mingled justice and mercy.

b. Of textile fabrics: Woven in mixed colours.

1655 E. Terry *Voy. E. India* 118 Silk, of which they make Velvets, Sattins, Taffataes, either plain, or mingled, or striped in party-colours. **1659** Howell *Vocab.* xxv, Mingled cloath, *panno mischio, o panno vergato*.

Hence †**'mingledly** *adv. rare.*

1573 Baret *Alv.* H 381 Here and there, mingledly, *sparsim*. **1650** W. Sclater *Comm. Malachy* 24 Duties to him performed, mingledly, of feare and love.

mingle-mangle ('mɪŋg(ə)l'mæŋg(ə)l). Also 6 **myngle mangle**, **mingle mangel.** [A varied reduplication of MINGLE *sb.*] A mixture; †a mess of mixed food for swine. Chiefly in contemptuous or disgusted use, a confused medley (of things or persons).

1549 Latimer *3rd Serm. bef. Edw. VI* (Arb.) 98 They say in my contrye, when they cal theyr hogges to the swyne troughe Come to thy myngle mangle, come pyr. **1549** Coverdale, etc. *Erasm. Par. Jas.* 25 Their doctrine is ouer muche tempred with myngle mangle. **1603** Dekker *Wonderful Year* Dj, The maine Army consisting..of a mingle-mangle, viz. dumpish Mourners, merry Sextons [etc.]. **1623** Lisle *Ælfric on O. & N. Test.* To Rdr. 37 Tell me not it [the English tongue] is a mingle-mangle. **1741** S. A. Laval *Hist. Reform* IV. VIII. 1035 A Speech..no better than a Mingle-mangle of base Adulations. **1860** *All Year Round* No. 70. 476 This mingle-mangle of dirty lanes, solemn, sorrow-stricken gaols [etc.].

b. *attrib.* or as *adj.* Like a mingle-mangle or hotch-potch, mixed confusedly.

1577 Hammer *Anc. Eccl. Hist.* (1663) 73 Tatianus..patched together, I wot not what kind of mingle-mangle consonancy of the Gospels. **1589** J. Rider *Bibl. Schol.*, In mingle mangle wise, or confusedlye. *a* **1641** Bp. Mountagu *Acts & Mon.* (1642) 468 Professing a mingle-mangle hotch-potch religion. **1799** Southey *St. Gualberto* xxv, The mingle-mangle mass of truth and lies. **1888** *Pall Mall G.* 2 Oct. 9/1 The wine drunk nowadays was a mingle-mangle mixture of all things except that which was good.

So **'mingle-mangle** *v. trans.*, to make a mingle-mangle of; whence **'mingle-mangler**. Also **mingle-'mangleness.**

1549 Coverdale, etc. *Erasm. Par. Jas.* iv. 7–17 Who so euer backbiteth his neighbour, he either condemneth the lawe,..or backbiteth it as though it were to muche myngle mangled, and walowyshe. **1550** Latimer *Last Serm. bef. Edw. VI* (1562) 119 Yet ther be Leaueners yet styll and mingle manglers, that haue sowred Christes doctrine, with the leauen of the Pharises. **1614** J. Taylor (Water-P.) *Nipping Abuses* B 3 b, How pitteous then mans best of wit is martyr'd,..So mingle mangled and so hack't and hewd. **1694** Motteux *Rabelais* IV. lx. (1737) 247 Then is sacrific'd to him, Haberdines, Poor-Jack, minglemangled, mishmash'd. **1827** Southey *Lett.* (1856) IV. 56, I wish you could see what is done, which for oddity, mingle-mangleness, and out-of-the-wayness may vie with anything that has ever preceded it.

minglement ('mɪŋg(ə)lmənt). [f. MINGLE *v.* + -MENT.] The action of mingling; an instance or result of this, a mixture.

1674 N. Fairfax *Bulk & Selv.* 28 'Tis taking in a daily minglement of bigger bodies. **1823** Moore *Loves of Angels* III. xii. 259 That happy minglement of hearts. **1868** *Contemp. Rev.* VIII. 560 The difficulty is, not to produce minglement of race, but to keep blood pure.

mingler ('mɪŋglə(r)). [f. MINGLE *v.* + -ER¹.] One who mingles, in senses of the verb.

1581 *Act 23 Eliz.* c. 8 §1 The said Melter, Myngler or Corrupter, Causer or Procurer thereof, shall forfeyte [etc.]. **1605** Verstegan *Dec. Intell.* vii. 203 Chaucer..was in deed a great mingler of English with French. **1678** Cudworth *Intell. Syst.* 306 Proclus..was indeed a confounder of the Platonick theology, and a mingler of much unintelligible stuff with it. **1888** A. S. Wilson *Lyric of Hopeless Love* 121 No sense of mine can hear or spy The mingler of the spell.

mingling ('mɪŋglɪŋ), *vbl. sb.* [f. MINGLE *v.* + -ING^1.] The action of the vb. MINGLE.

1513 MORE *Edw. V*, Wks. 63/2 The mengling of whose bloodes together, hath bene the effusion of great parte of the noble bloode of this realme. **1626** BACON *Sylva* §232 Sound is likewise Meliorated by the Mingling of open Aire with Pent Aire. **1819** T. CHALMERS in *Mem.* (1850) II. 250 From my extensive minglings with the people, I am quite confident in affirming [etc.]. **1837** WHITTOCK, etc. *Bk. Trades* (1842) 99 (*Card-maker*) The various sorts of paper of which a card-board is composed are then placed alternately in the manner called by the trade 'mingling'. **1883** *Athenæum* 1 Dec. 695/1 There was a constant mingling of merchant princes and illustrious professors.

mingling ('mɪŋglɪŋ), *ppl. a.* [f. MINGLE *v.* + -ING^2.] That mingles, in senses of the verb. Hence '**minglingly** *adv.* (Webster 1847–54).

1735 SOMERVILLE *Chase* II. 408 The Forest seems One mingling Blaze. **1812** BYRON *Ch. Har.* II. xxiii, When mingling souls forget to blend, Death hath but little left him to destroy!

† **mingly.** *Obs. rare.* Also 6 **mengl(e)y.** [? Alteration of *mengle*, MINGLE *sb.*, after MEDLEY.] A mixture or medley.

1545 ELYOT *Dict.*, *Aceruatim*, in heapes, without ordre, in a mengley [1548–52 mengle]. **1565** COOPER *Thesaurus*, *Cinnus*.. a mengly [**1578** mingly] of diuers thinges together.

Mingrelian (mɪŋ'griːlɪən, mɪn-), *sb.* and *a.* Also 7–8 **Mengrelian.** [f. *Mingrelia* (see below) + -AN.] **A.** *sb.* **a.** A member of the people inhabiting Mingrelia, an area of the Kutais region of the Caucasus. **b.** The language of this people. **B.** *adj.* Of or pertaining to this people.

1639 [see CIRCASSIAN *sb.* 1]. **1690** LOCKE *Hum. Und.* I. iii. 18 The Mengrelians, a People professing Christianity. *a* **1791** [see GEORGIAN *a.*^{2} 1]. **1876** *Encycl. Brit.* V. 257/2 The Mingrelians.. extend from the Zenesquali on the east to the Ingur and the Black Sea on the west, while the lower course of the Rion may be considered as constituting their limit on the south. **1883** *Ibid.* XVI. 437/1 The Mingrelians (still almost exclusively confined to the Mingrelian territory, and numbering 197,000) are closely akin to the Georgians. **1921** [see KIRGHIZ *sb.* and *a.*]. **1939** L. H. GRAY *Foundations of Lang.* xii. 375 South Caucasian.. consists of four languages: Georgian.., Mingrelian, Laz, and Svanian. **1959** *Chambers's Encycl.* VIII. 356/1 The chief languages are:.. Mingrelian, Lazic, Svanetian. *Ibid.* XI. 430/1 The Georgians, Mingrelians and Armenians of the Caucasus. **1973** *Observer* 15 Apr. 39/1 The Beria Papers by Alan Williams... Brash English journalist and rip-roaring Russian defector, with linguistic help from beautiful Mingrelian.

mingy ('mɪndʒɪ), *a. colloq.* Also † **mingee.** [Perh. f. M(EAN *a.*^{1} + ST)INGY *a.*, or a blend of MANGY *a.* and STINGY *a.*] Mean, stingy, niggardly; disappointingly small.

1911 J. W. HORSLEY *I Remember* xi. 254 'Mingee' for greedy. **1912** R. BROOKE *Let.* May (1968) 382, I called you a mingy and coprologous Oxford poetaster. **1918** W. OWEN *Let.* 19 Aug. (1967) 569, I rushed off a note in time for this evening's post, which may seem very mingy. **1926** C. BEATON *Diary* in *Wandering Yrs.* (1961) vii. 148 A mingy little tray he had picked up from heaven-knows-where. **1930** E. V. LUCAS *Down Sky* 223 It's dear, but we are not going to be mingy. **1940** [see CLIP *sb.*^{1} 2 e]. **1972** *Guardian* 30 Aug. 9/5 The opening for filling steam irons with distilled water is usually mingy, and the thing overflows.

Comb. **1959** *Times* 28 Dec. 3/1 Both.. were determined.. not to let the mingy-minded weather spoil the jubilee match. **1966** 'L. LANE' *ABZ of Scouse* 68 *Mingy-arsed bastard*, a miserly person.

Hence as *sb.*, a mean person. *rare.*

1939 M. EGAN *To Love & Cherish* II. 48 Don't be a mingy, father; they only cost a shilling.

Minha(h, varr. MINCHA.

minheer, obs. form of MYNHEER.

mini ('mɪnɪ), *sb.* **1.** Abbrev. of *minicar*, *minicab* (see MINI- b); *spec.* the proprietary name of a small car made by British Leyland (formerly the British Motor Corporation). Also *attrib.* and *Comb.*

1961 *Economist* 24 June 1327/2 Taxi-men and mini-men have tested their vocabularies in London this week: the mini-men are confident of profit. **1961** *Engineering* 17 Nov. 658 The Mini's astonishing success is due purely and simply to good engineering. **1962** *Listener* 18 Oct. 634/2 The designer of the Morris Minor and the 'minis'. **1963** *Times* 19 Apr. 17/1 The company also announces the appointment of Mr. A. A. Issigonis, designer of the 'mini' range and the technical director, to the corporation's board. **1964** *Times* 11 Feb. 11/7 At present a young man who passes a test in a mini is legally entitled to drive an eight-wheeler weighing 24 tons at 60 m.p.h. on a motorway. **1970** G. F. NEWMAN *Sir, You Bastard* iii. 99 Sneed squeezed his mini on to the drive where four other cars were parked. **1971** *Times* 6 Aug. 7/6 Feeding the fantasies of mini-drivers, convincing them.. that anything the film's crack stunt-drivers could do they could do.

2. Abbrev. of *mini-skirt* (see MINI- b).

1966 *Guardian* 27 July 6/4 The new thing about the Scherrer mini is that it flares. **1967** *Punch* 4 Jan. 1/1 The lengths of female laid bare by minis. **1968** *Listener* 12 Dec. 790/3 One after another, Arab states are banning the mini. **1971** B. MALAMUD *Tenants* 42 She wore.. a plain white mini with purple tights.

mini ('mɪnɪ), *a.* [Abbrev. of MINIATURE *a.* Cf. next.] Very small, tiny.

1963 *Daily Tel.* 17 Dec. 13 A 'mini' census covering one householder in ten will be taken by the Government in 1966. **1966** *Ibid.* 14 Nov. 10/3 M. Redlus insists: 'My minis will be the most mini in Europe but they'll be decent.' **1966** *Punch* 7 Dec. 857/1 Leg make-up.. gives sitting-down confidence to the wearer of the miniest skirt. **1966** *Sunday Express* 18 Dec. 23/5 Of course 25,000 cases is pretty mini. **1967** *Word Study* Dec. 3/2 There's nothing mini about their wages. **1969** *Daily Tel.* 25 Sept. 21/1 Girls prance on the longest legs, in the mini-est skirts and the kinkiest boots.

mini-, *pref.*, combining form of MINIATURE *a.* (reinforced by the first letters of MINIMUM *a.*), used to designate things that are very small of their kind.

A prefix much in vogue from the 1960s. Only a selection from the virtually unlimited number of combs. is illustrated here. The examples are arranged in alphabetical order of the combs. for convenience of reference.

1966 *Daily Tel.* 24 Oct. 11/1 The demand for a prototype female briefcase has been underlined by a strong season of mini-bag fashions—little swinging double-sided dog lead bags that made the absence of a briefcase for women all the more apparent. **1962** *Punch* 12 Dec. 878/1 A cycle firm is bringing out a mini-bike. **1970** *Time* 2 Nov. 56 Half-size (or even smaller) motor-cycles... Recession or no, minibikes seem to be all over, but nowhere are they more visible than in Los Angeles. **1960** *House & Garden* Oct. 135 (Advt.), Hygena think of details—..like built-in bread bins,.. Minibins, refrigerators. **1968** *Economist* 10 Feb. 46/3 Capital investment shows no signs (yet) of re-energising—and it shouldn't, despite the mini-boom. **1968** *Observer* 22 Dec. 21/7 A mini-bottle of Gala's nail polish (Little Gems 4s. 4d. a bottle). **1970** *Jrnl. Gen. Psychol.* LXXXIII. 155 Either *S* or *E* could activate the green light by depressing the button on a minibox situated in front of each of them. **1961** 'R. M. DASHWOOD' *Provincial Daughter* 55 Squalid piles of dust, marbles and minibricks. **1966** *Times Rev. Industry* Sept. 63/3 With the 'mini-budget' having withdrawn another £500m. from internal demand. **1971** *Daily Colonist* (Victoria, B.C.) 24 Nov. 1/7 The vessels were described as 'mini-bulkers', small ships.. for ferrying cargoes. **1936** *Miniature Camera Mag.* Dec. 4/2 It is perhaps to be expected that all sorts and conditions of industries and businesses should have sprung up around the successful Minicamera. **1964** *Punch* 21 Oct. 592/1 Mini-holidays, mini-cameras, mini-tellies. **1971** *Author* LXXXII. 108 Outside such writer-populated districts as Hampstead or Chelsea, even minor authors may be mini-celebrities, and so news. **1968** *Economist* 27 Apr. 79/2 America.. might well take chief responsibility for producing the Olivetti mini-computers as that is where chief demand lies. **1973** *Business Week* 8 Dec. 69/1 Today, a $2,000 minicomputer is more powerful, more reliable, and easier to use than the big, $100,000 machines of a decade ago. **1963** *Aeroplane* 24 Jan. 25/2 A one-man autogyro with an estimated selling price of £1000 was demonstrated recently in South Africa... This 'mini-copter' is said to be in production already. **1971** *Time* 19 Apr. 60 But, like a stabbing pain that passes quickly, the mini-crisis was a warning that the dollar faces more trouble. **1967** *Spectator* 15 Sept. 300/2 Now a new type of winter holiday is offered by several lines—the 'mini' cruise. **1969** *Daily Tel.* 13 Feb. 27/6 Results in the 'mini-elections' in India's four northern States.. show the once all-powerful Congress Party to be humbled also in the Punjab and Bihar. **1969** *Times* 27 Jan. 10/8 It will have a 30-acre 'mini-farm' for practical training on its doorstep. **1973** C. BONINGTON *Next Horizon* xix. 259 There was a long pause and then we saw the green miniflare which was the signal to follow. **1954** *Sat. Rev.* (U.S.) 24 Apr. 60 The world famous Philips Minigroove 33⅓ Long Playing Records. **1968** *New Yorker* 16 Mar. 43 Armed with three 7·62-mm. machine guns, called miniguns, which could fire a hundred rounds per second. **1969** I. KEMP *Brit. G.I. in Vietnam* vi. 117 The deep sustained roar of the dragonships' mini-guns. **1963** *Daily Tel.* 12 Nov. 17/3 A proposal that 'mini-houses' should be built to cater for people in lower income groups. **1963** *Ibid.* 6 June 15/5 (*heading*) Mini-jet as Paris 'ferry' to air show. **1967** *Word Study* Dec. 3/1 The sphere of clothing is.. well represented with.. *mini-jupe*, [etc.]. **1973** *Publishers Weekly* 18 June 35/1 Underage hopefuls in mini-jupes. **1969** *Sunday Times* 6 Apr. 53 Of course, describing these as mini-kilts makes the purist splutter in his porridge. **1974** *People's Jrnl.* (Inverness & Northern Counties ed.) 24 Aug. 3/5 Last Friday, during the great float-out, the pair donned mini-kilt outfits and became hostesses to the many guests attending the ceremony. **1963** *Daily Tel.* 13 Apr. 15/4 The mini-lifeboats.. will be normally manned by a crew of two. **1963** *Aeroplane* 21 Mar. 9/2 The third D.H. 125 'mini-liner' is shortly to go into service with Bristol Siddeley Engines. **1973** *Courier & Advertiser* (Dundee) 7 Aug. 7/2 The Fred Olsen mini-liner Basel is due over the weekend with 500 tons of paper from Norway. **1972** *N.Y. Times* 4 June 4/8 The six-mile Crazylegs minimarathon. **1963** *Times* 29 May 15/2 Most of these countries have tiny internal markets—'mini-markets' Mr. Gates calls them. **1966** J. PORTER *Sour Cream* iv. 45, I must have been out of my mini-mind to let myself be manoeuvred into this ridiculous, and dangerous, situation. **1965** *Guardian* 25 Aug. 16/8 Irresponsible action by a few mini-minded strikers. **1959** *Motor Show Catal.* 497 Mini-Minor Saloon de Luxe. **1973** *Guardian* 8 May 2 (*heading*) Mini-Nuclear arms seen as 'wishful-thinking'. **1954** *Life* 29 Nov. 83 The new 'mini-pig'.. is ideal for medical research, which is what he was bred for. **1970** *Daily Tel.* 29 May 5/1 The new mini-pigs.. at about 140 pounds are four to five times lighter than the farm variety. **1970** *New Scientist* 29 Jan. 187/1 The minipill was developed for one reason alone: because it was believed to provide safe contraception. **1967** *Sunday Times* 14 May 12/7 Expo's own minirail system passes on a slender viaduct. **1967** *Word Study* Dec. 3/2 A financial analyst reports the good news that 1967 has experienced only a mini-recession. **1970** *Times* 17 Mar. 27 Another aspect of the current apprehension is linked to the 'mini-recession' in the American motor industry. **1967** *Courier-Mail* (Brisbane) 14 Nov. 18 The collection will include mini-shifts which can double as pant tops teamed with matching slacks or shorts, or can be co-ordinated with bikinis for beach wear. **1969** *Daily Tel.* (Colour Suppl.) 24 Jan. 17/2 A girl in a mini-shift. **1971** *Time* 1 Feb. 32 In Paris, minishorts are an every-night, run-of-the-disco affair. **1973** *Times* 27 Nov. 16/2 The arrival of the mini-short in preference to the old baggy maxi-pants. **1967** *Time* 17 Mar. 36 For added balance, ski bobbers wear mini-skis fitted with braking crampons on both feet. **1974** *Maclean's Mag.* Jan. 25/3 On our GLM mini skis, we were led out to the beginners' hill, which could not have been more than 100 feet long away over almost perfectly level ground. **1966** *Economist* 31 Dec. 1385/1 The 'mini-states' must, for the sake of their own reputations and the UN's, accept a system of weighted voting. **1968** *N.Y. Times* 26 Jan. 70 South Africa's economic predominance radiates from here to the three ministates of Botswana, Lesotho and Swaziland. **1973** *Nation* (Barbados) 16 Dec. 4/2 Without the eventual federation of the unit territories or a confederation of independent mini-states, the West Indies have no future. **1959** *Chambers's 20th Cent. Dict.* Suppl., Mini-sub(marine). **1966** *New Scientist* 22 Sept. 655/2 The mini-sub *Alvin* which was used for recovering the H-bomb lost off the Spanish coast. **1963** *Flight Internat.* LXXXIII. 25/1 There has been a great deal of unofficial talk about 'mini-submarines' carrying one or two Polaris apiece, and also of a larger vessel carrying eight missiles. **1973** *Reader's Digest* Apr. 58/2 To complement the divers, mini-submarines less than 20 feet long are used by the airman for underwater surveying. **1968** *Saturday Night* (Toronto) Sept. 36 Elaine Bedard, wearing a flared pink leather minisuit, awaited him in his Mercedes-Benz. **1971** 'V. X. SCOTT' *Surrogate Wife* 254 Under the coat she wore a cream-coloured mini-suit. **1967** *Times* 18 May 23 Whisky is to be exported from Scotland by pipeline and 'minitanker', the shipping firm of Christian Salvesen and Co., of Leith, announced yesterday. **1971** *New Scientist* 2 Sept. 520 Petrol is supplied free, either by the client filling up at the company's garage or from a mini-tanker which regularly visits the special parking places. **1967** *Economist* 29 Apr. 484/3 BMC has come off even worse, working short time on truck manufacturing and likely to drop its ill-fated mini-tractor. **1966** *Punch* 14 Sept. 380/3 Hardy Amies's mini-trousers Are the latest passion-rousers. **1960** *Guardian* 30 Dec. 12/1 The first of the new vehicles to be used for road patrols will be Austin Minivans. **1968** H. C. RAE *Few Small Bones* II. viii. 142 Small personal items were taken by mini-van to the new flat. **1966** *Economist* 10 Dec. 1112/2 The day may eventually come when the big powers will stand back and permit a nuclear mini-war between smaller countries.

b. Special combinations: **minicab** [CAB *sb.*^{3}], a car like a taxi but available only if ordered in advance; **minicam**, a miniature camera; so as *v. trans.*; **minicar**, (*a*) a small motor car (cf. MINI *sb.* 1); (*b*) a child's toy model of a motor car; **minicell** *Biol.*, a miniature cell, without nuclear material, produced by the division of individuals of a particular strain of the bacterium *Escherichia coli*; **mini-coat**, a short coat, one not reaching to the knee; **mini-dress**, a dress with a mini-skirt; **Mini-Moke, mini-moke**, a small motor vehicle resembling a jeep; cf. MOKE^4; **mini-ness** = TININESS; **Minipiano**, (a proprietary name of) a small piano; also **minipiano; Miniprinter**, a proprietary name of a type of small machine for printing tickets, **mini-skirt, miniskirt**, a very short skirt; hence **miniskirted** *a.*, wearing or having a mini-skirt.

1960 *Economist* 12 Nov. 711/3 Current regulations regarding London taxis would not allow the introduction of what Mr. Dennis Vosper, speaking for the Home Office, called 'minicabs'. **1961** *Daily Tel.* 6 June 19/6 London's taxi war, between regular taximen and minicab operators, took a new turn yesterday. **1965** *Spectator* 12 Mar. 322/3, I travelled by mini-cab from Baker Street to Kensington. **1973** *Times* 29 Nov. 4/7 A mini-cab operator.. was sentenced to four years. **1937** *Amer. Speech* XII. 236/2 A professor at the University of Wisconsin minicammed his students during an examination. **1939** WEBSTER Add., *Minicam*, short for *miniature camera*. **1940** GRAVES & HODGE *Long Week-End* xxv. 432 Their photographs, largely contributed by 'minicam' amateurs. **1948** C. DAY LEWIS *Otterbury Incident* iii. 28 Penknives, Minicars, balls.. the sort of oddments you keep in your pocket. **1949** *Light Car* Dec. 599/2 Three-wheelers... The 122 c.c. Bond Minicar. **1963** *Spectator* 1 Nov. 558 To say Britain came late into the minicar race is to miss the point. **1967** H. I. ADLER et al. in *Proc. Nat. Acad. Sci.* LVII. 321 A newly isolated strain of *Escherichia coli* K12 regularly produces a large number of unusually small anucleate cells during the logarithmic phase of growth. These small cells do not divide... In this report we communicate information regarding some of the basic properties of these minicells. **1971** *Nature* 3 Sept. 11/1 Although minicells, small enucleate *Escherichia coli*, have been used occasionally by molecular biologists, it seems safe to say that they became available too late in the game. **1966** *Guardian* 8 Sept. 7/3 Topcoats were mini-coats—a little more than loose jackets. **1967** *Britannica Bk. of Year* (U.S.) 338 Rabbit had been dyed in new and heady shades—orange, mauve, navy, shocking pink, bright green—to fashion double-breasted minicoats and pea jackets. **1965** *Christian Sci. Monitor* 20 Nov. 30 The fashion pages of British papers sport mini-dresses. **1966** *Daily Tel.* 17 Oct. 10/6 The skinny model girl loped down the runway at Marlborough House in her horizontally-striped mini-dress. **1962** *Ibid.* 13 Feb. 15/4 In the BMC vehicle, named Mini-Moke, the drive is confined to the front wheels. **1972** D. FRANCIS *Smokescreen* i. 10 No one had bothered to put the canvas over the Minimoke. **1974** H. MACINNES *Climb to Lost World* iii. 46 Jonathan drove a mini-moke with Greek lettering emblazoned upon it. **1964** *Punch* 21 Oct. 592/1 Car itself victim of over-exposure, flaunting its mini-ness. **1967** *New Scientist* 13 Apr. 94/1 The current preoccupation with 'mini-ness' has now extended into the realm of.. microbiology. **1934** *Trade Marks Jrnl.* 4 Apr. 434/2 Minipiano... Pianos. Brasted Bros. Ltd.,.. London,.. piano manufacturers; and C.A.V. Lundholm Aktiebolag (a Joint Stock Company organised under the laws of Sweden), ..Sweden; merchants. **1943** H. W. VAN LOON *Lives* xviii. 558 He.. went over to the little minipiano which had been wished on Frits and now stood at the foot of the stairs. **1947**

A. H. Howe *Sci. Piano Tuning* (rev. ed.) xxi. 96 Tuning the 73 note minipiano is quite different from the conventional mode. **1949** *Electronic Engin.* XXI. 461/2 It is intermediate in size between a minipiano and a small upright piano. **1949** *Railway Gaz.* 6 May 510/2 The equipment exhibited by Westinghouse Garrard Ticket Machines Limited at.. Olympia, includes... The Westinghouse mini-printer,.. with four or six printing units. **1958** *Times* 11 Feb. 15/3 The company also supplies rapid and mini printers, as used in booking offices of the London Transport Executive. **1965** *Vogue* Aug. 53 Mini skirt,.. snakeskin belt. **1965** *Economist* 20 Nov. 862/1 The Fashion House Group of London dumbfounded the.. audience of American buyers quite as much by the sight of the British aggressively selling as by their mini-skirts and kooky outfits. **1970** G. F. Newman *Sir, You Bastard* viii. 243 There were more miniskirts around three o'clock on a warm May afternoon. **1971** B. Malamud *Tenants* 54 Had Mary Kettlesmith described his acrobatics with her miniskirt? **1966** *Listener* 30 June 955/1 The mini-skirted or levied young. **1972** F. Warner *Maquettes* 19 Pretty, miniskirted, and attractive young lady.

miniaceous (mɪnɪˈeɪʃəs), *a.* [f. L. *miniāce-us*, f. *minium* native cinnabar, also red-lead: see -ACEOUS.] Of a cinnabar-red colour. = MINIATE *a.*

1688 R. Holme *Armoury* II. 313/1 Miniaceous colour, a scarlet, or vermilion colour. **1846** Dana *Zooph.* (1848) 643 Cortex miniaceous within.

miniard, miniardize: see MIGNIARD, -IZE.

miniate (ˈmɪnɪət), *a.* *rare*—^{0}. [ad. L. *miniāt-us*, pa. pple. of *miniāre* to MINIATE.] (See quots.)

1890 *Syd. Soc. Lex.*, *Miniate*, coloured like red-lead; vermilion-coloured. **1900** Jackson *Gloss. Bot. Terms*, *Miniate*, the colour of red lead; more orange and duller than vermilion.

miniate (ˈmɪnɪeɪt), *v.* [f. L. *miniāt-*, ppl. stem of *miniā-re* (f. *minium*: see MINIUM) + -ATE^{3}.] *trans.* To colour or paint with vermilion; to rubricate or (in extended sense) to illuminate (a manuscript). Also *transf.*

1657–83 Evelyn *Hist. Relig.* (1850) I. 30 Flowery parterres of roses, lilies, tulips.. dressed, figured, fringed, folded, miniated and decked by the hand of Him who made the heavens. **1670** Blount *Glossogr.* (ed. 3), *Miniated*, painted, or inlaid; as we read of Porcellane-dishes miniated with gold. **1774** Warton *Hist. Eng. Poetry* (1781) III. *Gesta Rom.* 5 All the capitals in the body of the text are miniated with a pen. **1862** Burgon *Lett. fr. Rome* ii. 16 Vermilion is introduced abundantly. Thus, the first verse of St. John's gospel is miniated.

miniator (ˈmɪnɪeɪtə(r)). [a. L. *miniātor*, agent-noun f. *miniāre*: see MINIATE *v.* Cf. It. *miniatore*, Sp. *miniador* (Minsheu).] One who 'miniates' (a manuscript), a rubricator, an illuminator.

1865 M. Pattison in *Q. Rev.* Apr. 339 But for copies 'de luxe',.. copyist and miniator still continued in request.

miniatous (mɪnɪˈeɪtəs), *a.* [f. L. *miniāt-us*, pa. pple. of *miniāre*: see MINIATE *a.* and -OUS.] Of the colour of minium or red-lead; miniate.

1826 Kirby & Sp. *Entomol.* IV. xlvi. 279 Miniatous,.. the colour of red lead.

miniature (ˈmɪnɪətjʊə(r), ˈmɪnɪtjʊə(r)), *sb.* and *a.* Also 7–8 **mignature, miniture, miniture.** [ad. It. *miniatura*, a. med.L. *miniātūra*, f. *miniāre* to rubricate, illuminate: see MINIATE *v.* Cf. F. *miniature* (1653 in Hatz.-Darm.).

The small size characteristic of paintings in miniature has led to a pseudo-etymological association of the word with the L. *min-* expressing smallness (in *minor* less, *minimus* least, *minuĕre* to diminish), which has prob. affected the development of the transferred and figurative senses.]

A. *sb.*

†**1.** The action or process of rubricating letters or of illuminating a manuscript. *Obs.*

1645 Evelyn *Diary* 18–23 Jan., MSS. of remarkable miniature. **1686** [G. Hickes] *Spec. B. Virginis* 9 If the names of other Saints are distinguished with Miniature, Her's ought to Shine with Gold.

2. *concr.* A picture in an illuminated manuscript, an illumination; also, illuminated work in general.

1680 Evelyn *Diary* 2 Sept., [There] were 3 or 4 Romish breviaries, with a great deal of miniature and monkish painting and gilding... There is also the processe of the philosophers great elixer, represented in divers pieces of excellent miniature. **1803** Astle *Orig. Writing* viii. 195 Miniatures preserved in some of the finest and best executed manuscripts in Europe. **1895** E. M. Thompson *Eng. Illum. MSS.* 36 It is a very beautiful manuscript, written on fine vellum.., and decorated with miniatures.

3. The designation of the branch of pictorial art developed from the art of the mediæval illuminator; the painting of 'miniatures' (in sense 4 below). Chiefly in phrase *in miniature*.

1656 Blount *Glossogr.*, *Miniature*,.. the art of drawing pictures in little, being commonly done with red lead. **1669** A. Browne *Ars Pictoria* 77 The Art of Miniture or Limning. **1679** Everard *Popish Plot* 3 She further produced a picture in mignature of the said Chancellor. **1712** tr. *Pomet's Hist. Drugs* I. 14 A sort of Pink for Painting in Oil and Miniature. **1759** Johnson *Idler* No. 64 ¶4, I.. heard every day of a wonderful performer in crayons and miniature, and sent my pictures [*sc.* portraits] to be copied. **1771** H. Walpole *Vertue's Anecd. Paint.* IV. 90 Painters in Enamel and Miniature. **1821** Craig *Lect. Drawing* vi. 345 The practice of portrait painting in miniature. **1887** Propert *Miniature Art* Pref. 5 Materials.. illustrative of the history of miniature.

4. *concr.* A portrait 'in miniature'; a portrait painted on a small scale and with minute finish, usually on ivory or vellum; formerly always in water colour, but now often in oil.

1716 Lady M. W. Montagu *Lett.* 10 Oct. (1887) I. 129 There are a vast quantity of paintings, among which are many fine miniatures. **1765** H. Walpole *Vertue's Anecd. Paint.* I. 73 His [Holbein's] miniatures have all the strength of oil-colours joined to the most finished delicacy. **1815** J. Smith *Panorama Sci. & Art* II. 743 Miniatures are painted with extreme precision and brilliancy... They may be executed either with oil or water-colours. **1854** Thackeray *Newcomes* I. 53 A feeble miniature of the lady with yellow ringlets.

5. *transf.* and *fig.* A reduced image; a representation on a small scale. Also *occas.* a minutely finished production.

a **1586** Sidney *Arcadia* II. (1590) 150 As the Ladies plaid them in the water,.. the water (making lines in his face) seemed.. with twentie bubbles, not to be content to haue the picture of their face in large vpon him, but he would in ech of those bubbles set forth the miniature of them. *a* **1680** Rochester *Let. fr. Artemiza in Town*, Kiss me, thou curious Minature of Man [*sc.* a Monkey]. **1697** Dryden *Æneis* Ded., Ess. (ed. Ker) II. 157 Tragedy is the miniature of human life; an epic poem is the draught at length. *a* **1711** Ken *Preparatives* Poet. Wks. 1721 IV. 35 The great Creator's Power and Wisdom shine, Concenter'd in this Miniature Divine [*sc.* a fly]. **1827** De Quincey *Murder* Wks. 1862 IV. 9 As to Shakspere.. witness his incomparable miniature in Henry VI of the murdered Gloucester. **1842** Tennyson *Gard. Dau.* 12 A miniature of loveliness, all grace Summ'd up and closed in little. **1856** Emerson *Eng. Traits, Land* Wks. (Bohn) II. 18 In variety of surface, Britain is a miniature of Europe.

b. *in miniature*: on a small scale; in a brief or abridged form.

1700 Southerne *Fate of Capua* IV. iv, How have I hung upon the little lines Of that dear face,.. To find the mother there in miniature. **1704** Swift *T. Tub* Wks. 1768 I. 32 Their persons I shall describe particularly and at length; their genius and understandings in mignature. **1813** T. Busby *Lucretius* I. II. *Comm.* 34 That which is correct in miniature will be true in the large. **1860** Maury *Phys. Geol. Sea* (Low) xvi. 698 Land and sea breezes are monsoons in miniature. **1872** Spurgeon *Treas. Dav.* Ps. lxv. 4 This verse is a body of divinity in miniature.

c. Minuteness of workmanship. *rare*—^{1}.

c **1790** Imison *Sch. Art* I. 243 The human mind is infinitely insufficient to explore the amazing and inconceiveable gradations of miniature in every part of nature.

d. *Chess* [tr. G. *miniatur*]. A problem involving few men, *spec.* one in which not more than seven pieces are used; a game of relatively few moves.

1903 *Brit. Chess Mag.* 91 It shows the composer's various styles better to give No. 76, which is a four-move 'miniature'. **1907** S. S. Blackburne *Terms & Themes Chess Probl.* 29 Very light-weight problems are known as 'miniatures'. **1970** A. Sunnucks *Encycl. Chess* 309 There is no fixed number of moves which determine whether a game can be classified as a miniature, but the term is generally used to describe a game of under 20 moves.

e. Something that is much smaller than the size normal for things of its class; *spec.* (*a*) a very small bottle of spirits; (*b*) a miniature camera.

1939 *Sun* (Baltimore) 26 June 18/2 The sale of so-called 'miniatures' in Baltimore is fostering juvenile drinking. **1954** A. Lee *Round Many a Bend* vii. 68 Sunday was also the day on which we sold most 'miniatures'. (*footnote*) This is the name for the small bottles of spirits in the trade. **1955** [see DEFINITION 5 c]. **1958** *Spectator* 1 Aug. 167/3 The miniatures are obviously going to be the fashionable gimmick. The Pye pocket portable measures only 4 × 7 × 1½ inches. **1962** 'H. Howard' *Double Finesse* vi. 67 Didn't I see you knock back a miniature of whisky? **1971** C. Bonington *Annapurna South Face* x. 123 We had plenty of whisky—over four hundred miniatures and seventy-two full bottles.

f. A short piece of music.

1958 *Listener* 18 Dec. 1051/1 This has no connexion whatsoever with the writing of miniatures or the use of short lyric forms. **1962** *Ibid.* 15 Mar. 489/2 Schumann was a master of epigram, and the epigrammatic *Einfall* was most eminently suited to his vocal and instrumental miniatures.

¶ **6.** A lineament.

1629 Massinger *Picture* IV. i, There are lines Of a darke colour, that disperse themselues Ore euery miniature of her face. **1636** —— *Gt. Dk. Flor.* v. ii, There's no miniature In her faire face, but is a copious theme Which would.. make a volume. What cleare arch'd browes? what sparkling eyes?

7. *attrib.* and *Comb.*, as ***miniature art, colour, drawing, -kind, painter, painting, -picture, portrait***; **miniature-initial**, an ornamental initial having a miniature picture painted within it.

1711 Shaftesb. *Charac.* (1737) I. 143 *note*, When a Piece is of the Miniature-kind; when it runs into the Detail, and nice Delineation of every little particular. **1733** *School of Miniature* 15 Miniature Colours. *Ibid.* 17, I advise all Miniature Painters to practise it. **1765** T. H. Croker et al. *Compl. Dict. Arts & Sci.* II. s.v. *Marbling*, The consistence of the solution should be nearly that of strong gum-water, used in miniature painting. **1781** (*title*) Miniature Pictures. Written Originally by Mr. Gray... Newly adapted to The most Fashionable and Public Characters. **1797** *Encycl. Brit.* (ed. 3) XII. 146 Miniature-painting. **1806** Surr *Winter in Lond.* (ed. 3) III. 85 A very small miniature portrait of a gentleman. **1883** *Encycl. Brit.* XVI. 439/2 With regard to miniature art in Germany.. little can be said. **1895** E. M. Thompson *Eng. Illum. MSS.* 43 The first fifty-six leaves are occupied by a series of most exquisite miniature drawings. *Ibid.* 60 The.. ornamental-initial (to be distinguished from the miniature-initial).

B. *adj.* **a.** Represented or designed on a small scale; much smaller than the normal size; tiny; *spec.* of a camera (see quot. 1943); hence applied to photography, films, etc., involving the use of such a camera.

1714 Gay *Fan* I. 170 Here shall the Pencil bid its Colours flow, And make a Miniature Creation grow. **1740** Cheyne *Regimen* 180 He might, no doubt, have foreknown every thing.. by the self-motive Powers of his created miniature Judges. **1816** Accum *Chem. Tests* (1818) 321 Very little can be determined in these miniature assays. **1822–56** De Quincey *Confess.* (1862) 122, I.. took a very miniature suite of rooms. **1869** S. R. Hole *Bk. about Roses* x. 151 The Miniature or Pompon Provence,.. the 'baby Roses' and the 'pony Roses' of our childhood. **1872** Jenkinson *Guide Eng. Lakes* (1879) 150 This stream contains many lovely miniature cascades. **1887** (*title*) Payne's Miniature Scores. No. 1. Mozart Quartet in G major. **1893** G. B. Shaw *Widowers' Houses* III. 73 With photographic portrait of Blanche on miniature easel on the top. **1911** *Daily Colonist* (Victoria, B.C.) 9 Apr. 1/5 The Department of militia has issued notice of a competition at local miniature ranges to be fired between the 11th and 19th of April. **1913** A. G. Fulton *Notes on Rifle Shooting* 7 Miniature shooting teaches almost all that is necessary to make a man a good shot with the Service rifle. **1914** *Physical Rev.* Apr. 255 From them a miniature universe could be constructed exactly similar in every respect to the present universe. **1917** *Autocar Handbk.* (ed. 7) i. 13 (*heading*) The miniature car. **1921** *Sci. Amer.* 25 June 514/2 (*caption*) Miniature camera with magazine mounted for use.. and the miniature projector. **1941** J. du Mont (*title*) 200 miniature games of chess. **1943** C. Duncan *Man. Miniature Camera* (ed. 2) iii. 12 When the Royal Photographic Society found it necessary to define the term 'miniature camera' they ruled that it was one designed to make negatives 'not larger than six square inches'. **1943** *Gloss. Terms Electr. Engin.* (*B.S.I.*) 144 Miniature film radiography. **1953** J. du Mont (*title*) Chess: more miniature games. **1956** A. L. Sowerby *Dict. Photogr.* (ed. 18) 466 The Leica, though by no means the first camera to make small pictures, was undoubtedly the camera which popularised miniature photography. **1958** *Spectator* 1 Aug. 167/2 The new miniature transistor radios. **1959** *Chambers's Encycl.* VII. 246/1 Increased use of mass miniature radiography is resulting in many suspicious cases being discovered which cannot be definitely diagnosed. *Ibid.* XIV. 778/2 The technical quality of the present-day miniature film approximates closely to that of full-sized film. **1970** *Jrnl. Gen. Psychol.* LXXXIII. 4 The more sophisticated paradigms simulating the therapy-interview situation.. and miniature systems of conditioning in the mass.

b. Applied to a dog of a breed or variety smaller than average; also as *sb.*

1902 *Daily Tel.* 13 Feb. 6/4 [Cruft's Dog Show at Royal Agricultural Hall]. In one of the annexes of the hall are shown the Griffons, the Maltese and other miniatures. **1903** R. B. Lee *Hist. & Descr. Mod. Dogs Gt. Brit. & Ireland: Terriers* (ed. 3) xv. 401 Little dogs of these colours and toy white English terriers will not have any kind of classification, unless special arrangements are made for grouping them as a section of their own, called 'smooth-coated terriers (miniature) other than black and tan'. **1904** H. Compton *20th Cent. Dog* I. 301 The miniature black and tan terrier—to give it its new Kennel Club title—is more familiarly known.. by its original one of the 'Toy Terrier'. **1912** *Encycl. Brit.* VII. 375/2 *Non-Sporting* [Dogs].—Bulldog, bulldog (miniature).. black and tan terrier (miniature). **1924** [see BENCH *v.* 3 c]. **1945** C. L. B. Hubbard *Observer's Bk. Dogs* 53 A miniature Dachshund should be a sturdy little sportsman. **1948** —— *Dogs in Brit.* III. xx. 319 The Miniature Poodles in Britain are mostly descended from imported French dogs although many are 'bred down' from small standard Poodles. **1959** *Observer* 1 Feb. 12 The breed standard describes miniature poodles as active and intelligent... Height at shoulder should be under 15 in.

c. Applied to a version of golf played on a miniature course.

1915 F. M. Hueffer *Good Soldier* I. i. 10 Sitting together ..in front of the club house, let us say, at Homburg.. watching the miniature golf. **1930** *Glasgow Herald* 25 Sept. 17/5 Miniature Golf Course in Glasgow. What is claimed to be a real golf course in miniature is being laid out. **1930** *Daily Express* 6 Oct. 8/3 The Government's experts have been investigating the subject because of the demand the miniature golf establishments are creating for materials. **1966** J. Ball *Cool Cottontail* (1967) xi. 118 He and his date played miniature golf, had dinner, and saw a movie.

miniature (ˈmɪnɪətjʊə(r), ˈmɪnɪtjʊə(r)), *v.* [f. MINIATURE *sb.*]

1. *trans.* To embellish (a manuscript) with miniatures.

1716 M. Davies *Athen. Brit.* III. 85 A MS... in Golden Letters upon Vellum miniatur'd.

2. To represent or describe in miniature.

a **1706** Evelyn *Diary* an. 1686 (1955) IV. 531 His booke of Birds, Fish: flowers, shells &c drawn & miniatured to the life. **1833** *New Monthly Mag.* XXXVIII. 402 Take this round orb; it miniatures the world. **1865** S. Lanier *Poems* (1884) 231 Still shine the words that miniature his deeds. **1895** H. Callan *From Clyde to Jordan* xxix. 302 Is not the whole Anglo-Egyptian situation miniatured in this incident?

3. To reduce to miniature dimensions. Hence **miniaturing** *vbl. sb.* (in quot. *attrib.*).

1881 *Nature* No. 622. 514 Three sets of achromatic lenses forming a focal power of forty at ten inches, or a miniaturing power of one fortieth.

miniaturist (ˈmɪnɪətjʊrɪst, ˈmɪnɪtjʊərɪst). [f. MINIATURE *sb.* + -IST. Cf. F. *miniaturiste.*]

1. One who executed the miniature-illuminations of a manuscript; a miniator.

1851 Millington tr. *Didron's Chr. Iconogr.* I. 260 It is possible.. that the deficiency is owing to an error of the miniaturist. **1892** J. H. Middleton *Illum. MSS.* 255 When the scribe, the rubricator, the illuminator and the

miniaturist..had completed the manuscript it was ready for the binder.

2. One who paints miniature pictures or portraits.

1856 THACKERAY *Christmas Bks.* (1872) 52 A couple of young artists, young Pinkey the miniaturist and George Rumbold the historical painter.

miniaturization (ˌmɪnɪt-, ˌmɪnɪətjʊəraɪˈzeɪʃən). [f. MINIATURE *a.* + -IZATION.] The process of miniaturizing; an instance of this.

1947 *Technical News Bull., U.S. Bureau of Standards* Jan. 8/1 With the end of the war and the declassification of the principle of the VT fuse, industry is manifesting interest in the program of miniaturization of electronic devices. **1950** *Engineering* 21 Apr. 447/1 The trend towards 'miniaturisation', i.e. the production of smaller components and greater compactness of layout, is continuing. **1960** KOESTLER *Lotus & Robot* II. viii. 211 That patient biding of one's time to avenge an assumed insult by a subtle twist—a miniaturization of the mediaeval vendetta. **1967** M. CHANDLER *Ceramics in Mod. World* iv. 134 If miniaturization was to proceed, clearly much higher permittivities were needed.

miniaturize (ˈmɪnɪt-, ˈmɪnɪətjʊəraɪz), *v.* [f. as prec. + -IZE.] *trans.* To produce in a smaller version; to render small.

1946 *Jrnl. R. Aeronaut. Soc.* L. 945/1 The weight added to the aircraft by the installation is about 120 lb., but..this weight is based on a war-time design which could be miniaturised. **1950** *Ibid.* LIV. 281/2 There has been a general move to miniaturise radio components with consequent saving in bulk and weight. **1957** *Times* 28 Aug. (Radio and TV Suppl.) p. xv/2 The printed circuit gives the designer added ability to miniaturize his equipment. **1957** *Spaceflight* I. 77/2 A single satellite would be quite unable to carry all the instruments which scientists want to send aloft, even when they are miniaturized. **1963** A. SMITH *Throw out Two Hands* xiii. 135 The camp had been miniaturised. Micro-huts had been built, with midget cooking-pots smouldering over dwarf fires. **1972** *Lebende Sprachen* XVII. 133/1 Nowadays micro-film can be miniaturized to the point where the library on the desk can be of virtually any size required.

Hence **ˈminiaturized** *ppl. a.*

1951 *Electronic Engin.* XXIII. 478/2 Miniaturized components generally are becoming more and more readily available. **1967** M. CHANDLER *Ceramics in Mod. World* iv. 135 A whole new technology for the production of miniaturized capacitors. **1971** *N.Y. Times Bk. Rev.* 19 Dec. 7/4 The pages fall open easily,..four of the original appearing in each page of the miniaturized volumes.

minibus (ˈmɪnɪbʌs, formerly ˈmɪnɪbəs). [f. L. *minimus* least, smallest, after *omnibus*. The modern use is influenced by the prefix MINI-.] (See quots.)

1845 *Scotsman* 15 Feb. 3/5 (Advt.), Important sale of horses, harness, and carriages... One excellent 12-inside *omnibus*, nearly as good as new... One handsome *minibus*, in good order. **1849** CRAIG, *Minibus*, a light covered vehicle, constructed for the expeditious conveyance of passengers for short distances. **1857** OTTÉ tr. *Quatrefages' Rambles Nat.* II. 143 A tolerably good road now joins Biarritz to Bayonne. Various omnibuses and minibuses..carry on an active traffic. **1864** *Macm. Mag.* X. 205/2 When the first street cab or 'minibus' was set up in it [St. Andrews]. **1958** *Oxford Mail* 9 June 1/1 A Morris Mini-bus which could possibly save rural services threatened with extinction through high running costs went on exhibition today... It carries twelve people, including the driver, and is designed to operate without a conductor. **1960** *Guardian* 19 Nov. 5/6 The company arrived by mini-bus. **1962** [see COMMERCIAL *sb.* 2]. **1965** M. MORSE *Unattached* v. 180 Transport difficulties.. were largely solved when the worker secured the use of a mini-bus. **1972** *Daily Tel.* 19 Feb. 11/3 The company minibus (or coach if there are enough of you interested) is available for excursions.

Minié (ˈmɪnɪeɪ). The name of the inventor of the Minié bullet (see below) used *attrib.*, as ***Minié ball, bullet***, an elongated bullet invented by M. Minié of Vincennes, which, when fired, was expanded by the powder contained in an iron cup inserted in a cavity at its base; ***Minié rifle***, a rifle adapted for firing the Minié bullet (see quot. 1876).

1853 STOCQUELER *Milit. Dict.*, *Minie Rifle*, or *Culot Ball*, a new species of fire-arm. **1858** GREENER *Gunnery* 350 In 1847 and 1848 Captain Minié..proposed a hollow iron cup to fill up the cavity in Delvigne's bullet, and from this circumstance we get the name of Minié rifle. **1859** LEVER *Dav. Dunn* xiii. 113 Under all that hailstorm of Minié-balls. **1876** VOYLE & STEVENSON *Milit. Dict.* s.v., In 1851 a rifle musket of the Minié pattern was supplied to the English army... It was found to be defective in practice, and was superseded by the Enfield rifle in 1853. **1884** H. BOND *Milit. Small Arms* 202 This discovery caused..the Minié rifle (an ordinary rifle firing a Minié bullet) to become the favourite arm.

minifer, variant of MINIVER.

minification (ˌmɪnɪfɪˈkeɪʃən). [f. MINIFY *v.* + -ATION, after MAGNIFICATION.] Diminution or reduction in size, appearance, importance, etc.

1904 *Jrnl. R. Microsc. Soc.* June 281 A magnifying power which exactly balances the ten-fold minification before spoken of. **1961** L. MUMFORD *City in Hist.* viii. 242 These are symptoms of the end: magnifications of demoralized power, minifications of life. **1974** *New Scientist* 3 Oct. 61/1 The illustrations are generous in number and in size, though, talking of size, in many cases an indication of the minification would have been instructive.

minify (ˈmɪnɪfaɪ), *v.* [Incorrectly f. L. *minor* less, *minimus* least, after *magnify*.]

1. *trans.* To diminish in estimated size or importance; to regard or represent (something) as smaller than it really is.

1676 *Doctrine of Devils* Ep. Rdr., Their magnifying his body into an immensity sometimes; and then again at the same time minifying him in the smallest atomes of a wafer-cake. **1834–43** SOUTHEY *Doctor* cxcvii. (1862) 524 Is man magnified or minified by considering himself as under the influence of the heavenly bodies? **1892** LOUNSBURY *Stud. Chaucer* II. v. 304 The achievements of these celebrated men were minified rather than magnified.

2. To reduce in actual size or importance; to lessen.

1866 *Contemp. Rev.* I. 91 These are powerless,—we will not say altogether to repress and eradicate these evils, but to minify them.

Hence **ˈminified** *ppl. a.*, **ˈminifying** *vbl. sb.* and *ppl. a.*

1837 J. DIXON *M'Nicoll's Wks.* Mem. D. M'Nicoll 20 It [Divine truth] is crude or well-digested,..minified or sublime, just in proportion to the qualities of his [the instructor's] mind. **1850** T. PARKER *Wks.* (1863) IV. 205, I have not seen anything very great in General Taylor, though I have diligently put my eye to the magnifying glasses of his political partizans; neither have I seen anything uncommonly mean and little in him, though I have also looked through the minifying glasses of his foes. **1906** J. ORR *Problem O.T.* viii. 266 On these [phenomena] the minifying end of the critical telescope is persistently turned.

minik (ˈmɪnɪk). Short for MINIKIN (sense 5).

1899 *N. & Q.* 9th Ser. IV. 535 *Minik*. This name is applied by match-makers to their smaller-sized wooden splints.

minikin (ˈmɪnɪkɪn), *sb.* and *a.* Forms: 6 **mynykyn, menekyn, -in, menyking, 6–8 miniken, minnekin, 7 mynnikin, 7–8 miniking, 6–9 minnikin, minikin.** Also 7 **minckins** (*sing.*). [ad. early mod.Du. *minneken* (MDu. *minnekijn*), f. *minne* love + *-kijn* -KIN.]

A. *sb.*

1. A playful or endearing term for a female. *Obs.* exc. *dial.* (see quot. 1879).

a **1550** *Image Ipocr.* in *Skelton's Wks.* (1843) II. 419/1 Your riche ringes,..Which your mynykyns And mynyon babbes,..When masse and all is done, Shall were at afternone. **1605** *Lond. Prodigal* III. iii. E 3 Minckins looke you doe not follow me. **1608** DAY *Hum. out of Br.* II. v, You take your parts too low, you are trebble Courtiers, and will neuer agree with these Country Mynnikins. **1618** B. HOLIDAY *Technog.* v. vi. (1630) O 3 *Melan* [to *Musica*].. Come, my little Minikin, thou and I will be play-fellowes. **1640** GLAPTHORNE *Hollander* II. C 4 b, Surely the Minikin is enamoured on me. **1706** PHILLIPS (ed. Kersey), *Minnekin* or *Minks*, a nice Dame, a mincing Lass. **1879** MISS JACKSON *Shropsh. Word-bk.*, *Minikin*, a slight, delicate, affected girl —'sich a minikin as 'er is'.

†**2.** A thin string of gut used for the treble string of the lute or viol. Also *attrib.*, as ***minikin string***.

1541 *Rutland MSS.* (1905) IV. 325 For ij dossen off lewte stringes callyd 'menekyns'. **1545** ASCHAM *Toxoph.* I. 2 b, In luting..a treble minikin string must alwayes be let down, but at suche time as when a man must nedes playe. **1580** *Acc. Bk. W. Wray* in *Antiquary* XXXII. 81, ij knotes of menykinges, iiij d. **1667** PEPYS *Diary* 18 Mar., Mr. Cæsar told me a pretty experiment of his, of angling with a minnikin—a gut-string varnished over. *a* **1670** HACKET *Abp. Williams* I. (1693) 147 Sir Francis Answered him with the Old Simile, That his Lordship was no good Musician, for he would peg the Minikin so high, till it crack'd. **1676** T. MACE *Musick's Mon.* 65 Be careful to get Good Strings, which would be of three sorts, viz. Minikins, Venice-Catlins, and Lyons. **1721** C. KING *Brit. Merch.* I. 284 Lutestrings Catlings..Minikings.

b. esp. in the phrase † ***to tickle (the) minikin***, to play the lute or fiddle. (Frequently used by early 17th c. dramatists, often with allusive suggestion of sense 1.)

1601 ? MARSTON *Pasquil & Kath.* I. 14 When I was a yong man and could tickle the Minikin,..I had the best stroke, the sweetest touch, but now..I am falne from the Fidle, and betooke me to thee [the Pipe]. **1608** MIDDLETON *Fam. Love* I. iii, Of which consort you two are grounds, one touches the Base, and the other tickles the minikin. **1635** [GLAPTHORNE] *Lady Mother* II. i. in Bullen *O. Pl.* II. 131 Thou dost tickle minikin as nimbly.

fig. phrase. **1606** DEKKER *News from Hell* H j b, *Perge mentiri*. Tickle the next Minkin [*sic*].

†**c.** *transf.* of a high-pitched voice. *Obs.*

1602 MARSTON *Ant. & Mel.* III. ii, *Cast.* Good, very good, very passing passing good. *Fel.* Fut, what trebble minikin squeaks there, ha? good? very good, very very good?

3. *transf.* and *fig.* A small or insignificant thing; a diminutive creature.

1761 COLMAN *Genius* No. II. in *Prose Sev. Occas.* (1787) I. 22 A make-weight in the scale of mortality; a minim of nature; a mannikin, not to say minnikin. **1787** *Minor* IV. viii. 232 I shan't advance a minikin beyond the truth. **1804** WOLCOT (P. Pindar) *Ep. to Ld. Mayor* Wks. 1816 IV. 278, I shall suppose, That Addington's invet'rate foes Impede this honest scheme of thine. Then take this minikin of mine. **1808** E. S. BARRETT *Miss-led General* 166 A son—a very minnikin indeed. *Ibid.* 168 *Le pauvre petit garçon*, the fiddler's minnikin.

4. A small kind of pin (cf. B. 5 below).

1706 PHILLIPS (ed. Kersey), *Minnekins*, the smallest sort of Pins, us'd by Women for their Clothes. **1755** in JOHNSON. **1857** MRS. MATHEWS *Tea-Table Talk* I. 235 [An] apprentice ..with haply a provident row of minikins darned with precision on his sleeve. **1881** in *Leicestersh. Gloss.*

5. (See quot.; also MINIK.)

1852–4 *Tomlinson's Cycl. Useful Arts* (1866) II. 143/1 The large [match] splints or the second size called minnikins.

6. *Typogr.* A size of type smaller than 'brilliant'.

1890 JACOBI *Printing*.

7. *Comb.*: † **minikin tickler**, a fiddler.

1607 MARSTON *What you will* IV. i, A fiddler, a scraper, a miniken tickler, a pum, pum.

B. *adj.*

1. Dainty, elegant, sprightly. Now contemptuously: Affected, mincing.

a. of a person; formerly of a girl or woman, but now applied to a person of either sex. Also in jingling combinations, ***minikin-finikin, -finical.***

1573 TUSSER *Husb.* (1878) 20 The credite..of mistresse, to minnekin Nan. **1598** FLORIO, *Mingherlina*, a daintie lasse, a minnekin smirking wench. **1600** HOLLAND *Livy* XXXIX. vi. 1026 Then came up the maner of having at bankets singing miniken wenches, and such as could play upon the dulcimers. **1696** TRYON *Misc.* iv. 121 Fare..such as the Proud Wives and Miniking Daughters would scarce offer to their..Dogs. **1768** BICKERSTAFF *Lionel & Clarissa* I. (1781) 9 A coxcomb, a fop..A minikin, Finikin, French powder-puff. **1858** HAWTHORNE *Fr. & It. Note-bks.* II. 143, I wish I could put into..one sentence the pettiness, the minikin-finical effect of this little man. **1888** *Sheffield Gloss.*, *Minikin*, delicate, effeminate. Frequently used in the phrase, 'he's a minikin-finikin fellow'.

b. of a person's actions, attributes, etc.

1545 ASCHAM *Toxoph.* I. 10 b, The minstrelsie of lutes, pipes, harpes, and all other that standeth by suche nice, fine, minikin fingering..is farre more fitte for the womannishnesse of it to dwell in the courte among ladies. **1781** T. TWINING in *Sel. Papers Twining Fam.* (1887) 101 What have you and I to do with..the minikin duties of civility and *bienséance*? **1872** S. MOSTYN *Perplexity* I. x. 190 None of your minikin governess-schemes for me.

Comb. **1876** BROWNING *Pacchiarotto* viii, And his voice, that out-roared Boanerges, How minikin-mildly it urges.

†**2.** Of a voice: Shrill. (Cf. A. 2 c above.)

1602 MARSTON *Ant. & Mel.* v. i, I had rather haue a seruant with a short nose, and a thinne haire, then haue such a high stretcht minikin voice. **1608** SHAKS. *Lear* III. vi. 45 (Qtos. 1–2) For one blast of thy minikin mouth, thy sheepe shall take no harme.

3. Of a thing: Diminutive in size or form; miniature; tiny. Also in † ***minikin name***, a pet name, endearing diminutive.

1589 R. HARVEY *Pl. Perc.* 9 Euery cut-purse vseth them [their words] at the Old Bayly, that hath had any skill in his miniken Handsaw. **1617** COLLINS *Def. Bp. Ely* II. x. 444 The Church is the better for beeing without them [*sc.* miracles], without sicke dogges healed, and lame cattes cured by your minikin-miracles, done at Minich. **1756** MRS. F. BROOKE *Old Maid* No. 34 (1764) 279 Polly Instep, the dancing-master's daughter, insists upon being called Pally, 'because (says she)..it is the minikin name for Pallas'. **1778** [W. MARSHALL] *Minutes Agric.* 1 July an. 1775 Make it into light minikin cocks. **1784** COWPER *To the Halibut*, In thy minikin and embryo state. **1826** HOOD *Fairy Tale* i, A little house some years ago there stood, A minikin abode. **1847** *Tait's Mag.* XIV. 449 He was pervious all over, and allowed minnikin arrows..to rouse his rage. **1851** THACKERAY *Eng. Hum.* iv. (1858) 188 They [*sc.* pastorals] are to poetry what charming little Dresden figures are to sculpture; graceful, minikin, fantastic. **1887** RUSKIN *Præterita* II. 154 In the distance..the great walnut-trees have become dots, and the farmsteads, minikin as if they were the fairy-finest of models to be packed in a box.

†**4.** Used to designate some kind of baize. *Obs.*

1604 *Lismore Papers* Ser. II. (1887) I. 108, Vij yeards halfe of minikin bayste to make yᵉ same gowne. *a* **1616** BEAUM. & FL. *Scornf. Lady* I. (1616) C 2, Steward this is as plaine as your olde minikin breeches. **1721** C. KING *Brit. Merch.* II. 306 Bays (Double or Minikin) by the same Tariff.

5. ***minikin pin*** (see A. 4 above).

1742 *Phil. Trans.* XLII. 57 Minikin Pins, or small Pins. **1843** HOOD *Drop of Gin* iii, No prospect in life worth a minnikin pin.

Hence **ˈminikinly** *adv.*

1580 BARET *Alv.* G 30 Galantly, gaily, minikinly [1573 *reads* minionly]. **1623** tr. *Favine's Theat. Honour* II. vi. 110, I think it a matter hard to..represent a Floure de Luce minikinly trussed, but by an excellent Painter.

minim (ˈmɪnɪm), *a.* and *sb.* Forms: 5 **mynyn, mynnym, 6 mynym(me, minnum, 6–7 minime, minum, (6 minnem, 7 minem, min(n)om, minimme, (minume), 6– minim.** [ad. L. *minim-us* smallest, a superlative f. the root *min-*: see MINOR. The sb. represents various elliptical or absolute uses of the adj. in med.L. Cf. F. *minime* adj. and sb.]

A. *adj.* Smallest, extremely small. †Of a particle: Atomic. *Obs.*

a **1670** HACKET *Christian Consolat.* ii. in Heber *Taylor* (1822) I. 108 For nailing our great sins to the cross of Christ, and for acquitting us from the innumerable fry of minim sins. **1684** tr. *Bonet's Merc. Compit.* XVIII. 620/2 [Quick-silver] is a Body most exactly mixt, and its minime Parts do pertinaciously one stick to another. **1690** N. LEE *Massacre of Paris* III. ii, Fat Porcpise Bauds, the Mermaids too of Honour, The Minim Pages, all the twinkling Host So fill'd, the Snare of Hell must crack to hold you. **1821** *Blackw. Mag.* VIII. 663 The savage tribes..sent forth their puny fleets Athirst for blood, and wing'd with minim sails. **1876** GEO. ELIOT *Dan. Der.* v. xxxviii, A minim mammal which you might imprison in the finger of your glove. **1876** R. BRIDGES *Growth of Love* lv, For man, a minim jot in time and space.

B. *sb.*

1. *Mus.* A symbol for a note half the value of a semibreve and double the value of a crotchet; a note of this value. Also *attrib.*, as ***minim rest***.

In ancient music this note was of the shortest duration, hence its name *nota minima*; in modern music it is second in value to the semibreve. The symbol is figured with an open head, in shape round, inclining to oval (formerly lozenge-shaped), and with a tail.

c **1440** *Promp. Parv.* 338/1 Mynyn' of songys (*Harl. MS.* 2274, *P.*, mynym), *minima*. **14..** *Proverbs* in *Antiq. Rep.* (1809) IV. 408 He maakithe so his mynnyms fro the square, that it shall sownde wronge. **1550** Marbeck *Bk. Com. Prayer noted* A ij, The iii. [note is] a prycke and is a mynymme. **1587** Golding *De Mornay* xii. (1617) 184 Our life is lesse than a short Minim in comparison of a whole song. **1592** Shaks. *Rom. & Jul.* II. iv. 22 He fights as you sing pricksong,..he rests his minum, one, two, and the third in your bosom. **1609** Douland *Ornith. Microl.* 39 A Minime is a Figure like a Sembreefe hauing a tayle, ascending or descending. **1622** Peacham *Compl. Gentl.* xi. (1634) 101 A minim rest. **1782** Burney *Hist. Mus.* II. iii. 185 A Long and a Breve..differ no more in their effect on the ear, than a Minim and Crotchet.

transf. **1596** Spenser *F.Q.* VI. x. 28 Great Gloriana.. Pardon thy shepheard, mongst so many layes As he hath sung of thee..To make one minime of thy poore handmayd.

2. *Calligraphy.* A single down stroke of the pen; esp. in Court- or Secretary-hand, the short down stroke in the letters *m, n, u*, etc.; also *attrib.* † ***to be in one's minims***: to be learning to write 'straight strokes'.

1603 Holland *Plutarch's Mor.* 1029 Those who when they write a running hand in haste, doe not alwaies make out the letters full, but use pricks, minims and dashes. **1607** Dekker & Webster *Westw. Hoe* II. i, She tooke her letters very suddenly: and is now in her Minoms. **1612** Brinsley *Lud. Lit.* 39 Striuing..to make minimes, and such like letters sharp at tops & bottoms, or iust to the proportion of their copies. **1658** Cocker *Pen's Triumph* 14 For Set Secretary... Your minums must be all alike, as the down-right stroke of the *a*, the strokes of the *i, m, n, u*, and the first of the *w*. **1674** Jeake *Arith.* (1696) 293 And so increasing the Minnoms according to the Index of the Figural Number. *c* **1680** Cocker *Pens Perfection* 6 You must shape the nib of your pen to the breadth of the minum stroke. **1771** Luckombe *Hist. Printing* 254 So far [IIII] they [the Romans] could easily number the miniums [*sic*] or strokes with a glance of the eye. **1890** *Collectanea* (O.H.S.) II. 290 Mr. Jacobs reads 'pointeur'. It might be read 'poniteur', there being three minims between the *o* and the *t*.

3. The least possible portion (of something), a 'jot'; in scientific use, †an atom, minute particle.

1592 Nashe *Four Lett. Confut.* (1593) 54 Canst thou exemplifie vnto mee..one minnum of the particular deuice of his play that I purloind? **1599** —— *Lenten Stuffe* 28, I vary not a minnum from him. **1657** Trapp *Comm. Ps.* ii. 12 'When his wrath is kindled but a little'. It is sometimes let out in minnums. **1662** Stillingfl. *Orig. Sacr.* III. ii. §16 Therefore Tully asks that question, *Cur declinet uno minimo, non declinet duobus aut tribus?* why only it declines one minime, and not two or three. **1686** Goad *Celest. Bodies* III. ii. 440 The Red Earth may be more resolvable into Minims, than a White Chalk, or Marble. **1766** Amory *Buncle* (1770) IV. 94 By impregnating the most generous white wine, with the minims or leasts of antimony. **1884** *Public Opinion* 5 Sept. 290/2 He has not the smallest intention of..yielding one minim of the rights and interests of Germany.

4. A creature or thing of the least size or importance. Chiefly used contemptuously of a person. ***minim of nature***, one of the smallest forms of animal life.

1590 Bp. Andrewes *Serm.* (1629) 279 They be the base people, the minims of the world. **1609** *Ev. Woman in Hum.* II. i. D 3, What will ye? heere he is, you minime. **1667** Milton *P.L.* VII. 482 At once came forth whatever creeps the ground..not all Minims of Nature; some of Serpent kinde Wondrous in length. **1679** V. Alsop *Melius Inquirendum* II. viii. 367 The Minims of Justice ought to vail to the Magnalia of Charity. **1762** Goldsm. *Cit. W.* cxv, With what a degree of satirical contempt must they..see.. minims, the tenants of an atom, thus arrogating a partnership in the creation of universal nature! **1823** Lamb *Elia* Ser. II. *Tombs in Abbey*, These insignificant pieces of money, these minims to their sight. **1863** Cowden Clarke *Shaks. Char.* xii. 314 He must be a minim of a historian who confines himself to those facts only. **1873** Browning *Red Cott. Nt.-cap* 228 This insect on my parapet,—Look how the marvel of a minim crawls!

5. (With capital initial.) A friar belonging to the mendicant order (*Ordo Minimorum Eremitarum*) founded by St. Francis of Paula (c. 1416–1507). Also *attrib.*

1546 Langley tr. *Pol. Verg.* VII. v. 142 b, The order of Minimes or lest brethren were founded by one Franciscus Paula. **1638** Baker tr. *Balzac's Lett.* (vol. III.) 49 The Fathers of the Minimme Order. **1671** Woodhead *St. Teresa* II. xxxv. 232 The Fathers Minims were then come hither to found. *a* **1718** Penn *Maxims* Wks. 1726 I. 825 He [the covetous man] always looks like Lent: a sort of Lay-Minim. *a* **1774** Goldsm. tr. *Scarron's Com. Romance* (1775) I. 124 Two Minim friars of the Trinity of the Mount..ran to my assistance. **1885** W. W. Roberts *Pontif. Decrees* Introd. 53 The Minims Le Seur and Jacquier were permitted to bring out the treatise.

6. (See quot.) [In Fr. *minime* (†*couleur de minime, gris de minime*, Cotgr.); according to Littré from the colour of the robe of the Minim Friars: see 5.]

1659 Howell *Vocab.* xxv, Minim colour; *Minimo, ô color di nocella*. **1706** Phillips (ed. Kersey), *Minim* or *Dark Minim*, a brown, tawny, or dun Colour.

†**7.** *Printing.* A certain small size of type: ? = minion. *Obs.*

1706 Phillips (ed. Kersey), *Minim* is also a small sort of Printing-Letter. **1818** in Todd.

8. The smallest unit of fluid measure, about equivalent to one drop of liquid; the sixtieth part of a fluid drachm. Also *attrib.*, as ***minim-measure***.

1809 R. Powell tr. *Pharmacopœia* (ed. 2) 3 The fluidrachm contains Sixty minims. **1890** *Syd. Soc. Lex.*, *Minim-measure*, a measure usually holding a drachm graduated into sixty parts. **1899** *Allbutt's Syst. Med.* VI. 37 A minim or two of a..trinitrine solution may often be added.

9. A very small Roman bronze (or occas. silver) coin, usu. produced locally. Pl. **minimi**, **minims**.

1896 W. C. Hazlitt *Coin Collector* ix. 247 *Minim*, a term which, for want of a better one, has been assigned to a class of bronze money of Roman type, probably of the fourth or fifth century B.C., which may have been of local or provincial origin, and is of unusually small module. **1935** *Discovery* July 196/2 A hoard of 800 minims, small coins in some cases not more than 5 mm. in diameter, buried beneath the floor of the stage. **1962** C. R. Josset *Money in Brit.* i. 7 An attempt to overcome the shortage was made by a local production of crude bronze coins which are known as 'minimi' because of their smallness. **1971** *Daily Tel.* 13 July 9/1 Two rare British silver minims, or small coins, of the first century A.D. have been discovered during excavations taking place on a Roman occupation site in Chapel Street, Chichester.

minim, variant of mennom, minnow.

minimal ('mɪnɪməl), *a.* [f. L. *minim-us* smallest, least (see minim) + -al[1].]

a. Extremely minute in size; of the nature of or constituting a minimum; of a minimum amount, quantity, or degree; that is the least possible.

1666 G. Harvey *Morb. Angl.* x. 89 Choler being set on fire, and acting upon Melancholy, or rather calcining it into small acuated minimal bodies. **1878** *Smithsonian Rep.* 367 The strength of which [elements of an electric battery] was reduced so as to produce a minimal contraction. **1891** *Brit. Med. Jrnl.* 17 Jan. 142/1 Without charge, save a minimal one for drugs. **1894** Lister in *Phil. Trans.* CLXXXVI. 428 Multitudes of minute nuclei of minimal size. **1899** *Allbutt's Syst. Med.* VI. 846 The minimal limit [of the field of vision] in health is 55 degrees.

b. spec. *Linguistics.* (*a*) Distinguished only by a single feature; usu. applied to a pair of similar forms; (*b*) other uses (see quots.).

(*a*) **1939** *Amer. Speech* XIV. 122 Words can be distinguished by the minimal opposition of vowel nasality and [n]. **1942** C. F. Hockett in *Language* XVIII. 7 The term 'contrastive pair', meaning any pair between which there are differences in a context of similarity, any pair usable for the listing of features, is used here instead of the traditional term 'minimal pair'. **1950** D. Jones *Phoneme* vi. 15 When a distinction between two sequences occurring in a language is such that any lesser degree of distinction would be inadequate for clearly differentiating words in that language, the distinction is termed a 'minimal one'... Minimal distinctions are very commonly effected by the addition or subtraction of a phoneme. **1955** C. F. Hockett *Man. Phonol.* vi. 212 Before analysis is complete, one cannot be certain that a given pair is 'minimal' in a strict phonologic sense—that there is but a single difference, at the level of ultimate phonologic constituents. **1961** H. A. Gleason *Introd. Descr. Ling.* (ed. 2) i. 16 In calling *bill* and *pill* a minimal pair we assume that they differ by only one phoneme. **1964** R. A. Hall *Introd. Ling.* 81 Minimal pairs are not essential to show that two sounds do not belong to the same phoneme. **1971** *Archivum Linguisticum* II. 48 In the days of 'classical' phonemics much play was made of the 'minimal pair' in order to establish throughout a language such lexical differences as those between *pin, bin, tin, din*, [etc.].

(*b*) **1930** H. E. Palmer *Princ. Romanization* 52 We may designate by the term *monophone* any phone of the first or second degrees of abstraction of which the concrete members are so similar in point of production and of acoustic effect even when observed by a competent observer, that it may be regarded as a minimal unit of pronunciation (i.e. practically insusceptible of sub-division). **1941** G. L. Trager in L. Spier et al. *Lang., Culture & Personality: Ess. in Memory of E. Sapir* 133 Intensity of tone is manifested as relative height of pitch: maximal intensity is *high* tone, minimal intensity is *low* tone, medial intensity is *middle* tone. **1949** J. R. Firth in *Trans. Philol. Soc. 1948* 142 The weak, neutral, or 'minimal' vowel. **1955** Quirk & Wrenn *Old Eng. Gram.* 129 Taking the consonants of a word as its minimal root. **1962** B. M. H. Strang *Mod. Eng. Struct.* vi. 84 They [*sc.* central nouns] can follow directly in minimal constructions (i.e. be head-word to) a closed system of words we shall call *determiners*. **1964** R. A. Hall *Introd. Ling.* 15 Morphemes..are the minimal units which carry meaning. **1971** D. Crystal *Ling.* 187 The grammar..*could* be analysed in terms of identifying a set of minimal units.

c. In *Art*, used of a form of painting and sculpture which is characterized by the use of simple or primary forms, structures, etc., often geometric and massive.

[**1958** *Listener* 23 Oct. 647/1 Creating huge, minimal forms with the palette knife in a few colours.] **1965** R. Wollheim in *Arts Mag.* Jan. 26 In a historic passage Mallarmé describes the terror, the sense of sterility, that the poet experiences when he..confronts the sheet of paper.. and no words come to him... Why could not Mallarmé, after an interval of time, have simply got up from his chair and produced the blank sheet of paper *as* the poem which he sat down to write?.. Such a gesture..would provide us with an extreme instance of what I call minimal art. **1967** C. Greenberg in E. Lucie-Smith *Movements in Art since 1945* (1969) i. 13 The working out of this problem, whose solution seems to have arrived in the form of what is called Primary Structures, ABC, or Minimal Art. **1969** *Britannica Bk. of Year* (U.S.) 800/2 *Minimal sculpture*, sculpture in the idiom of minimal art. **1969** *Time* 3 Jan. 42 Minimal forms still massively demand their unrewarding space, but they are countered by weirdly eccentric shapes that are frankly frivolous, at least unpredictable. **1969** E. Lucie-Smith *Movements in Art since 1945* viii. 240 His sculptures have been described as 'minimal art', or as examples of the 'single-unit Gestalt'. **1971** *Rolling Stone* 24 June 36/5 It remained only for minimal sculpture to come along, with its emphasis on the self-contained object (sometimes just a log, rock, or mound of dirt). **1973** *Times* 30 June 12/4 There will be works of American, Continental and British artists, abstract expressionism, Pop, kinetic, minimal and conceptual art.

d. In *Music*, used of a form of composition which is characterized by the repetition of short phrases incorporating changes very gradually as the music proceeds.

1974 M. Nyman *Experimental Mus.* vii. 119 (*heading*) Minimal music, determinacy and the new tonality. *Ibid.* 144 As in the American minimal music so all the workings of the process are easy to follow audibly. **1980** *New Grove Dict. Mus.* XVIII. 481/2 Systematic, or 'minimal', music may consist of extended reiterations of a motif or group of motifs. .. Alternatively, the element of repetition may be governed by a system: the progressive lengthening of the repeated material.., changing discrepancies from simultaneity.., or large-scale rhythmic schemes based on integers. **1985** *Radio Times* 20 July 85/1 It is indeed hard to see how such a gigantic work..can be considered 'minimal' in any way.

minimalist ('mɪnɪməlɪst), *sb.* and *a.* [f. minimal *a.* + -ist, or (in sense 1) ad. F. *minimaliste*, tr. Russ. *men'shevík* Menshevik *a.* and *sb.*]

A. *sb.* **1.** (Also with capital initial.) = Menshevik *sb.*; more widely, a person who advocates small or moderate reforms or policies.

1907 I. Zangwill *Ghetto Comedies* 408 'Ah, you're a Maximalist,' said the beadle. 'No, I am only a Minimalist. I merely want the minimum—that we save our own lives.' **1917** [see Bolshevik *sb.*]. **1918** E. P. Stebbing *From Czar to Bolshevik* iii. 25 The Social Democrats consisted chiefly of Bolsheviks with a smaller Menshevik group. The Social Revolutionaries were subdivided into Maximalists and Minimalists. **1922** *Blackw. Mag.* June 820/2 The delegation represented not only Communists, but also Minimalists and the converted intelligentsia. **1954** *Ann. Reg. 1953* 153 There were the 'maximalists' (Germany and the Netherlands),.. and the 'minimalists' (France) who wanted the E.P.C. to be little more than a system of inter-governmental association and co-operation.

2. *Art.* A practitioner or proponent of minimal art (minimal *a.* c).

1967 C. Greenberg in E. Lucie-Smith *Movements in Art since 1945* (1969) i. 13 The Minimalists appear to have realized..that the far-out in itself has to be the far-out as an end in itself. **1973** *Phaidon Dict. 20th Cent. Art* 254/1 The immediate predecessors of the Minimalists were Ad Reinhardt and Josef Albers, who brought to their canvases the 'exclusive, negative, absolute, and timeless' quality so desired by the Minimal artists.

3. *Mus.* A composer of minimal music (minimal *a.* d).

1982 *N.Y. Times* 23 Nov. C11 Mr. Gibson, who..has also worked with Steve Reich, Philip Glass and other 'minimalists'.

B. *adj.* **1.** = Menshevik *a.*; *gen.*, advocating moderate policies.

1917 *Times* 23 June 7/1 At the 'All Russia' Congress of the Workmen's and Soldiers' Delegates the 'Minimalist Socialists' have defined their programme. **1972** *Times* 19 Oct. 1/6 A minimalist summit, dealing only with well tried issues of economic integration.

2. *Art.* Of or pertaining to minimal art.

1969 *Manch. Guardian Weekly* 1 May 20 Tony Smith, usually taken as the original minimalist sculptor..is well represented by large sculptures. **1973** *Times Lit. Suppl.* 9 Nov. 1363/4 The pop, minimalist, new realist, and other artists who have succeeded the abstract impressionists.

3. *Mus.* Of or pertaining to minimal music.

1977 *Rolling Stone* 5 May 73/2 The so-called 'minimalist' ambience currently so fashionable among young bands who've spent too much time listening to Iggy and taking him seriously. **1985** *Sunday Tel.* (Colour Suppl.) 7 Apr. 36/1 Glass is often described as a 'minimalist' composer, along with such Americans as Steve Reich, Terry Riley and.. John Adams.

Hence '**minimalism**.

1969 *Manch. Guardian Weekly* 1 May 20 Call it minimalism if you like, but the real point is that the thing insists on being just itself and nothing more. **1977** *New Wave Mag.* VII. 12 Numbers are fast and slow. Some are only about thirty seconds long. This ain't minimalism. It's a sense of humour. **1985** *Radio Times* 20 July 85/1 In the 1960s he [*sc.* Steve Reich] began exploring the musical effects of repeated musical patterns that incorporate gradual changes over an extended period. The style came to be called minimalism.

minimality (mɪnɪ'mælɪtɪ). [f. minimal *a.* + -ity.]

1. *Linguistics.* The quality or character of being minimal.

1953 C. E. Bazell *Ling. Form* i. 10 The criterion of minimality is fulfilled in either case. **1963** J. Lyons *Structural Semantics* ii. 29 What can be done, however, is to apply the criterion of minimality after the establishment of the several meaning-relations between sentences in context. **1969** *Word* XXV. 235 Because of the minimality requirement in the definition of the morpheme, the second class is not equivalent to a class of bound morphemes.

2. = minimalism 2.

1969 E. Lucie-Smith *Movements in Art since 1945* viii. 242 Judd's colleague, Robert Morris, defends minimality in equally emphatic terms.

minimally ('mɪnɪməlɪ), *adv.* [f. MINIMAL *a.* + -LY².] To a minimal extent or degree.

1935 H. F. TWADDELL in *Lang. Monogr.* XVI. 42 In American English, the forms *beet*: *bit*: *bait*: *bat* are minimally phonologically different. **1936** *Amer. Speech* XI. 298 They generally cite only minimally different pairs. **1951** R. FIRTH *Elem. Social Organiz.* i. 35 Even minimally, their orientations are affected by its presence. **1971** *Sci. Amer.* Sept. 40/5 In order to meet not only the food requirements but also a minimally reasonable quality of life, the contributions that can be made by the use of energy in various forms are essential. **1973** *Nature* 6 July 40/2 *In vitro* methods for the short-term culture of erythrocytic forms of *Plasmodium knowlesi* and for isolating free merozoite preparations minimally contaminated with host cells. **1973** *Publishers Weekly* 13 Aug. 52/1 Such a glaring omission will surely put off some serious movie buffs. Probably, however, sales will be damaged only minimally.

†'**minimate**, *v. Obs. nonce-wd.* [f. L. *minim-us* (see MINIM) + -ATE³.] *trans.* To reduce to the smallest size.

1623 BP. ANDREWES *Serm. Nativ.* xvi. (1629) 154 When was it, that He was so *capite minutus*? Sure, never lesse, never so little, never so minorated, so *minimated*..as now.

minimax ('mɪnɪmæks), *sb.* and *a.* [f. MINI(MUM *sb.* and *a.* + MAX(IMUM.] The smallest of a set of maxima; usu. *attrib.* (passing into *adj.*: see b), *spec.* designating (*a*) a strategy that minimizes the greatest loss or risk to which a participant in a game or other situation of conflict will be liable; (*b*) the theorem of game theory that states that, for a finite, zero-sum game with two players, the smallest maximum loss that a player can make himself liable to by a suitable choice of strategy is equal to the greatest minimum gain that he can guarantee himself. Cf. MAXIMIN *sb.* and *a.*

[**1928** J. VON NEUMANN in *Mathematische Annalen* C. 307 (*heading*) Beweis des Satzes Max Min = Min Max. **1944** —— & MORGENSTERN *Theory of Games* xvii. 154 A slightly more general form of this Min-Max problem arises in another question of mathematical economics.] **1941** COURANT & ROBBINS *What is Math.?* vii. 345 (*heading*) Minimax points and topology. **1947** A. WALD in *Econometrica* XV. 282 We shall refer to an admissible decision function η for which (1·6) takes its minimum value as a minimax solution of the problem. *Ibid.* 283 An element a_0 in *A* is said to be a minimax strategy of player 1 if $\text{Inf}_b K(a, b)$ takes its maximum value with respect to *a* for $a = a_0$. **1949** *Ibid.* XVII. 230 Often Nature's strategy is completely unknown. In that case Wald suggests that the statistician play a minimax strategy: that is, the statistician should select that decision procedure which minimizes the maximum risk. **1951** *Ann. Math. Statistics* XXII. 466 The minimax risk is $\frac{1}{2}(1 - a)$. **1957** LUCE & RAIFFA *Games & Decisions* i. 2 Although Borel gave a clear statement of an important class of game theoretic problems and introduced the concepts of pure and mixed strategies, von Neumann points out that he did not obtain one crucial result—the minimax theorem—without which no theory of games can be said to exist. **1958** *Engineering* 21 Mar. 369/2 Player B, on the other hand, will determine the largest value in each column, and the smallest of these, the 'minimax'. **1961** L. WEISS *Statistical Decision Theory* v. 89 The minimax criterion has been criticized as being too conservative. **1962** *Sci. Amer.* Dec. 114/2 Both firms were guided by the principle of the minimax, choosing the best of the worst outcomes. **1968** *Brit. Med. Bull.* XXIV. 232/2 This would be the Bayesian Strategy of decision theory.., but other strategies, such as minimax or restricted Bayes, could also be used. **1970** [see MAXIMIN *sb.* and *a.*]. **1972** *Computer Jrnl.* XV. 277 (*heading*) On minimax solutions of linear equations.

b. Used predicatively as adj.: equal to, or resulting in, a minimax value.

1952 *Ann. Math. Statistics* XXIII. 587 For such weight functions the supremum of the risk over all $\theta \in \Omega$ is infinite for every decision function, so that every decision function is minimax. **1965** WOZENCRAFT & JACOBS *Princ. Communication Engin.* ii. 118 The decision rule which has the smallest maximum probability of error is called the minimax decision rule. Which of the eight rules is minimax? **1970** R. B. ASH *Basic Probability Theory* viii. 250 Find a minimax test, that is, a test that minimizes max (α, β). It is immediate from the definition of admissibility that an admissible test with constant risk (i.e., $\alpha = \beta$) is minimax.

minimax ('mɪnɪmæks), *v.* [f. prec. sb.] **a.** *trans.* To make equal to a minimax value. **b.** *intr.* To adopt or employ a minimax strategy. So '**minimaxing** *vbl. sb.* and *ppl. a.*

1964 GOULD & KOLB *Dict. Social Sci.* 573/2 The goal may be assumed to take the form of maximizing (or, in game theory, minimaxing) the expected value, over some time interval, of a utility function. **1968** *Listener* 4 Apr. 438/1 Just like that 50-50 combination of heads and tails, the minimaxing peasant might pick a 40-60 combination of wheat and millet. **1973** *Nature* 23 Feb. 507/1 The fundamental mechanism underlying all this work [on machines designed to play games] has been a cycle of processes: lookahead, evaluation and minimaxing.

miniment, obs. form of MUNIMENT.

minimeter (mɪ'nɪmɪtə(r)). [f. MINIM + -METER.] 'Alsop's term for an apparatus for measuring minims' (*Syd. Soc. Lex.* 1890).

1855 in DUNGLISON *Med. Lex.*

minimifidian (,mɪnɪmɪ'fɪdɪən), *a.* and *sb.* [f. L. *minim-us* least + *fid-ēs* faith + -IAN.]

a. *adj.* Reducing faith to a minimum. **b.** *sb.* One who has the least possible faith in something. Hence **minimi'fidianism**.

1825 COLERIDGE *Aids Refl.* (1848) I. 164 Again, there is a scheme constructed on the principle of retaining the social sympathies, that attend on the name of believer, at the least possible expenditure of belief... And this extreme I call Minimi-fidianism. *Ibid.* 295 The Minimi-fidian party err grievously in the latter point. **1882** *Spectator* 2 Dec. 1547 Lady Bloomfield's 'supernatural' stories..are not of a kind to challenge the scrutiny of a minimifidian in pneumatology.

miniminess. *nonce-wd.* [f. L. *minim-us* (see MINIM) + -NESS.] The condition of being very small or insignificant.

1615 BP. ANDREWES *Serm. Nativ.* x. (1629) 87 But these, though they agree well, yet none of them, so well, as this, that it [Bethlehem] was *minima*: the very *miniminesse* (as I may say) of it.

minimism ('mɪnɪmɪz(ə)m). [f. L. *minim-us* (see MINIM) + -ISM.]

1. *nonce-use.* Absorption in minute details.

1820 COLERIDGE in *Blackw. Mag.* VII. 630/2 Your advice-mongers..whose critical minimism..might remind one of those tiny night-flies, that, as they hurry across one's book, contrive..to cover a word at a time.

2. *Theol.* The disposition to minimize the implications of an accepted dogma; the minimizing view of what is involved in a dogma, esp. that of papal infallibility.

1874 J. H. NEWMAN *Cert. Diffic. Anglic.* (1876) 339 Such a tone of mind [*sc.* a generous loyalty towards ecclesiastical authority] has a claim..to be met and to be handled with a wise and gentle *minimism*. **1884** W. PALMER *Narr. Events* Suppl. iv. 278 The doctrine of Minimism, adopted by Newman from Bishop Fessler..gives liberty to the theologian to examine whether the Papal decree on any given point is or is not infallible.

†**minimistic** (mɪnɪ'mɪstɪk), *a.* [f. L. *minim-us* (see MINIM) + -ISTIC.] Characterized by or of the nature of MINIMISM 2.

1897 *19th Cent.* July 100 Seeing how very far the ancient ..Church..was from accepting alien orders on the minimistic principles for which anglicans contend.

Minimite ('mɪnɪmaɪt). [f. MINIM (sense 5) + -ITE.] A friar belonging to the order of Minims. In quot. *attrib.*

1879 *Encycl. Brit.* IX. 695/1 The building of a chapel in 1436 is generally considered as marking the first beginning of the Minimite order.

minimization (,mɪnɪmaɪ'zeɪʃən). [f. MINIMIZE *v.* + -ATION.] The action of reducing to, or estimating at, the least possible amount or degree.

1802 BENTHAM *Princ. Judic. Procedure* Wks. 1843 II. 9 How to unite the maximization of redress for the injured in the character of pursuers, with the minimization of hardship ..in the character of defendants. **1830** —— *Offic. Apt. Maximized* Pref. 9 Maximization of official aptitude, and minimization of official expense. **1889** *Sat. Rev.* 9 Feb. 167/2 Dr. Struthers's minimization of sea-sickness. **1940** *Jrnl. Obstetr. & Gynaecol. Brit. Empire* XLVII. 236 As regards anaesthesia, the minimization of shock is the main indication. **1969** *Nature* 29 Nov. 845/1 The arrangement of molecules..points to a minimization of the electric quadrupole-quadrupole interaction energy of the crystal. **1973** *Ibid.* 27 Apr. 556/1 Some potential energy calculations on β-pleated sheets have been done by Chothia.., who finds that a right-handed twist in the direction of the polypeptide chain, which corresponds to dihedral angles within one zone of the conformational map, makes for minimization of energy. **1974** *Clin. Pharmacol. & Therapeutics* XV. 444/2 The new method, called *minimization* for brevity, is compared here with randomization in regard to its vulnerability to experimenter bias and chance skewing.

minimize ('mɪnɪmaɪz), *v.* [f. L. *minimus* (see MINIM) + -IZE.]

1. *trans.* **a.** To reduce to the smallest possible amount, extent, or degree. **b.** To estimate at the smallest possible amount.

1802 BENTHAM *Princ. Judic. Procedure* Wks. 1843 II. 8 The adjective branch..may be said to have two specific ends: the one positive, maximizing the execution and effect given to the substantive branch: the other negative, minimizing the evil [etc.]. **1825** —— *Offic. Apt. Maximized, Observ. Peel's Sp.* (1830) 27 You may maximize attendance, and you may minimize it. **1882** J. H. BLUNT *Ref. Ch. Eng.* II. 413 The vestments of the clergy were to be minimized. **1884** *Chr. World* 28 Aug. 649/5 Let no one think..Jesus ever minimised the exceeding sinfulness of sin. **1888** BRYCE *Amer. Commw.* II. xlii. 124 Other causes were at work to mitigate and minimise their evils.

2. *intr.* To take the most moderate view possible of what is implied by an accepted dogma.

1875, **1898** [see MAXIMIZE *v.* 2].

3. *intr.* To attain a minimum value.

1973 *Physics Bull.* Dec. 725/3 One of the unexpected discoveries made using HVEM is that for a particular incident electron energy the diffracted intensity may minimize rather than maximize. **1975** *Ibid.* Jan. 13 Other parameters used to measure the intensity of the solar cycle tend to minimize at this time.

Hence '**minimized** *ppl. a.*; '**minimizing** *vbl. sb.* and *ppl. a.*

1868 J. H. BLUNT *Ref. Ch. Eng.* I. 90 Comparing the original design for Christ Church with its minimized execution. **1874** J. H. NEWMAN *Cert. Diffic. Anglic.* (1876) 332 That principle of minimizing so necessary..for a wise and cautious theology. **1875** GLADSTONE *Vaticanism* 51 Dr. Newman and the minimising divines. **1878** —— *Glean.* (1879) I. 112 We are now..witnessing the expansion of the minimised demands of the Conference. **1906** *Athenæum* 3 Mar. 264/1 We cannot support his minimizing of Froude's inaccuracy.

minimizer ('mɪnɪmaɪzə(r)). [f. MINIMIZE *v.* + -ER¹.] One who minimizes. Chiefly in *Theol.*

1867 *Union Rev.* V. 361 Anglicans in 1866, see numbers of those who went over in the interval stigmatised as 'minimisers'. **1874** J. H. NEWMAN *Cert. Diffic. Anglic.* (1876) 321 A few years ago it was the fashion among us to call writers, who conformed to this rule of the Church, by the name of 'Minimizers'. **1880** LITTLEDALE *Plain Reas.* lxxxix. 162 The two parties..are now called *Maximizers* and *Minimizers*; the Maximizers pushing the dogma of Infallibility to its furthest possible extent..; the Minimizers endeavouring to reduce within the narrowest limits so dangerous a proposition.

minimum ('mɪnɪməm), *sb.* and *a.* *Pl.* **minima** ('mɪnɪmə); 7–8 *erron.* **minimaes, minima's.** [a. L. *minimum*, neut. of *minimus* least, smallest: see MINIM.] **A.** *sb.*

†**1.** *Nat. Philos.* The smallest portion into which matter is divisible; an atom. Also, the hypothetical smallest possible portion of time or space. *Obs.*

1663 HARVEY *Archæol. Philos. Nova* II. I. vi. 29 For minima's are indivisibles, otherwise they could not be *minima*. *Ibid.* 30 There is a *minimum* and *maximum* in all natural bodies. *Ibid.* vii. 32 Neither are we to imagine, that God did create all the *minima's* of the world, before he united them to one Mass. **1691** RAY *Creation* I. (1692) 19 Why do they [atoms] decline the least interval that may be, and not a greater? Why not two or three *minima* as well as one? **1739** HUME *Hum. Nat.* I. ii. §1 (1888) 27 The imagination reaches a *minimum*, and may raise up to itself an idea, of which it cannot conceive any sub-division. *Ibid.*, Because they are remov'd beyond that distance, at which their impressions were reduc'd to a *minimum*, and were incapable of any farther diminution.

b. A creature of the smallest size. *Obs. rare*⁻¹.

1796 *Mod. Gulliver* 25 Architecture must have been a science earlily studied by these minimæs of mankind.

2. The least amount attainable, allowable, usual, etc. Also in the phrase ***to reduce to a minimum.***

1676 W. ROW *Contn. Blair's Autobiog.* xii. (1848) 390 That was the minimum that was to be required of every intrant. **1740**, **1806** [see MAXIMUM 2]. **1823** BENTHAM *Not Paul* 128 Of the length of this interval three years is the minimum. **1857** MRS. CARLYLE *Lett.* II. 323 The maximum of bother to arrive at the minimum of comfort. **1861** SMILES *Engineers* II. 217 Means should be provided..to reduce the recoil of the waves to a *minimum*. **1863** GEO. ELIOT *Romola* xlvi, The minimum of time had been given him for decision. **1871** TYNDALL *Fragm. Sci.* (1879) I. i. 20 Her motion, and consequently her *vis viva*, is then a minimum. **1900** *Westm. Gaz.* 29 Jan. 11/3 About 60 per cent. of the parcels which we [barge-owners] carry are what is known as minimums of twenty tons. **1903** H. B. SWETE in *Expositor* June 412 There must be at least two disciples acting in Christian fellowship. .. But this *minimum* is assured of Christ's presence no less than the largest congregation.

‖**3.** *Psychol.* In mod. Latin phrases ***minimum audibile, sensibile, tangibile, visibile*** (see quots.).

1709 BERKELEY *Th. Vision* §54 There is a *Minimum Tangibile*, and a *Minimum Visibile*, beyond which Sense cannot perceive. **1836-7** SIR W. HAMILTON *Metaph.* xviii. (1859) I. 350 The *minimum visibile* is the smallest expanse.. which can consciously affect us,—which we can be conscious of seeing. *Ibid.*, In this sense [of hearing], there is, in like manner, a *Minimum Audibile*, that is, a sound the least which can come into perception and consciousness. **1874** J. SULLY *Sensation & Intuition* 45 Impressions of sound and light,.. which approached very closely the *minimum sensibile*.

4. *Math.* = *minimum value*: see B. below.

1743 EMERSON *Fluxions* 123 When a Quantity is required to be the greatest or least possible, under certain Conditions, it is called a Maximum or Minimum. **1807** HUTTON *Course Math.* II. 304 Others again decrease continually; and so have no minimum... But, on the other hand, some.. decrease to a certain finite magnitude, called their Minimum, or least state... And lastly, some quantities have several maxima and minima.

5. The lowest amount or degree of variation (of temperature, a spectrum, etc.) attained or recorded.

1823 J. MITCHELL *Dict. Math. & Phys. Sci.* 512/1 On increase of temperature, the spirit [in the thermometer] goes forward and leaves the index, which therefore shows the minimum of temperature since it was set. **1831** BREWSTER *Optics* vii. 73 The two *Minima* of each of the three primary spectra coincide at the two extremities of the solar spectrum. **1860** MAURY *Phys. Geog. Sea* (Low) vii. §348 At the same hours, the needle attains the maxima and minima of its diurnal variations. **1894** W. L. DALLAS in *Indian Meteorol. Mem.* VI. 2 The heat given out by the sun goes through a cycle which reaches..its minimum at the time of minimum sunspots.

6. *attrib.* and *Comb.*, as ***minimum period***; **minimum thermometer**, one which records automatically the lowest point to which the temperature has fallen since its last adjustment.

1860 TYNDALL *Glac.* I. xvi. 113 A minimum-thermometer. **1868** [see MAXIMUM 5 b].

B. *adj.* **a.** [The sb. used appositively.] That is a minimum; that is the lowest attainable, allowable, usual, etc.

1810 [see minimum rate in sense b]. **1845** STOCQUELER *Handbk. Brit. India* (1854) 301 Its minimum height from the sea is 900 feet. **1899** *Allbutt's Syst. Med.* VIII. 849 The rule is to begin with a minimum dose. **1904** *Daily News* 25 Feb. 12/3 Parliament..has enacted that a minimum number of trains with a minimum mileage shall be run.

b. Special collocations: ***minimum rate, wage***; **minimum free form** (see quot. 1926); **minimum lending rate** *Econ.*, the minimum percentage at which a central bank will discount bills; in Britain, an official successor to bank-rate (see BANK *sb.*³ 8 b), whose level was determined by the Government from October 1972 until August 1981; cf. *MLR* s.v. M 5; **minimum value** (of a function) *Math.*, its value when it ceases to decrease and begins to increase, as the value of the variable changes continuously; **minimum vocabulary** (see quot. 1944).

1926 L. BLOOMFIELD in C. F. Hockett *Leonard Bloomfield Anthol.* (1970) 130 A minimum free form is a *word*.. which may be uttered alone (with meaning) but cannot be analyzed into parts that may (all of them) be uttered alone (with meaning). **1958** C. F. HOCKETT *Course in Mod. Ling.* xix. 171 Minimum free forms and lexemes also do not meet this requirement. **1972** *Times* 14 Oct. 21/8 The Bank of England's minimum lending rate, which yesterday replaced Bank rate, begins life at 7¼ per cent. **1979** A. HEERTJE *Basic Econ.* vii. 106 The key rate of interest is the *minimum lending rate* (MLR) which can be set by the Bank of England, acting on government instructions. **1981** *Daily Mail* 31 July 2/1 Geoffrey Howe..revealed that Minimum Lending Rate would be abolished on August 20. **1810** BENTHAM *Packing* (1821) 44 But this is the minimum rate. **1866** *Leisure Hour* 8 Dec. 783/2 All the workmen insist on is a *minimum* rate of wages. **1909** *Act 9 Edw. VII* c. 22 §4 Trade Boards shall, subject to the provisions of this section, fix minimum rates of wages for timework for their trades. **1974** Minimum rate [see *minimum wage* below]. **1885** WATSON & BURBURY *Math. Th. Electr. & Magn.* I. 19 [It] has a minimum value when [etc.]. **1944** B. RUSSELL in P. A. Schilpp *Philos. B. Russell* 14, I mean by a 'minimum vocabulary' one in which no word can be defined in terms of the others. All definitions are theoretically superfluous, and therefore the whole of any science can be expressed by means of a minimum vocabulary for that science. **1947** *Mind* LVI. 358 Every minimum vocabulary adequate to describing the world of ordinary experience must contain at least one universal-name. **1860** *Trades' Societies & Strikes: Rep. Comm. appointed by Nat. Assoc. for Promotion of Social Sci.* 299 And so the minimum wage which the Institute stipulates for..is constantly reduced. **1908** *New Age* 18 July 223/2 A serious objection to the fixing of a minimum wage in England for employed is that it would be most difficult to make provision for the large number of incompetent, inferior, and slow workers. **1940** *Economist* 6 July 4/2 The establishment, by law or by bargaining, of a decent minimum wage in all trades is an indispensable foundation. **1974** *Encycl. Brit. Micropædia* VI. 916/1 Minimum-wage legislation or machinery for fixing minimum rates now exists in most of the nations of Latin America, Africa, and Asia, as well as in more industrialized countries.

c. In combs. used *attrib.*, as **minimum-cost**, involving the smallest possible cost; **minimum-iron**, of a garment: requiring only a small amount of ironing; **minimum-security**, of a prison: having a minimum amount of restrictions on prisoners.

1962 A. BATTERSBY *Guide to Stock Control* vi. 52 The best period may be found by a minimum-cost procedure.., that is, by minimizing the total costs of ordering and stockholding. **1959** *Harrods News* Summer 11 Little girl's sundress of minimum-iron cotton. **1963** A. J. HALL *Textile Sci.* v. 267 Very large amounts of cotton and viscose rayon materials are finished with what is now known as ..'minimum-iron' finishes. **1965** G. JACKSON *Let.* 18 Apr. in *Soledad Brother* (1971) 73, I can also obtain a parole faster there or a transfer to some minimum security camp. **1970** *Globe & Mail* (Toronto) 25 Sept. 1/6 A 26-year old escaper from the William Head minimum security prison near Victoria.

minimus ('mɪnɪməs), *sb.* and *a.* Pl. minimi ('mɪnɪmaɪ). [a. L. *minimus*: see MINIM.]

A. *sb.* **1.** A creature of the smallest size; a small or insignificant creature.

1590 SHAKS. *Mids. N.* III. ii. 329 Get you gone you dwarfe, You *minimus*. **1879** G. MACDONALD *Sir Gibbie* I. xx. 273 An evil cloud of anger at the presumption of the unknown minimus [*sc.* 'a tiny ragged urchin'] began to gather. *Ibid.* III. v. 83 Mr. Sclater beheld only the minimus which the reversed telescope of his own enlarged importance..made of him.

2. 'The fifth or smallest digit of the hand or foot' (*Syd. Soc. Lex.* 1890).

1881 MIVART *Cat* iv. 99 The fifth [toe, or digit, of the forepaw] is the *minimus*, or little digit.

3. *Numism.* (See quot.)

1852 T. WRIGHT *Celt, Roman, & Saxon* xiv. 430 On many Roman sites..are found very small coins in brass... These coins from their diminutive size, are termed by numismatists *minimi*, and are supposed to have been struck during the period between the abandonment of the island by the imperial government and the establishment of the Saxon kingdoms.

4. *Path.* Short for *lupus minimus*, the least virulent form of LUPUS. In quot. *attrib.*

1889 J. M. DUNCAN *Dis. Women* xxv. 205 But there are other cases where, without inflammation, and generally in minimus cases, the sensitiveness is extreme.

B. *adj.* In some schools, appended to a surname to designate the youngest (in age or standing) of three or four boys having the same surname. Abbreviated *min.* or *mini.* (Cf. MINOR A. 7 b.)

1791 in *Eton School Lists* (1863), Langford *mi*... Langford *min.* **1808** *List of Eton Coll.*, Cookson *mi.* Cookson *mini.* **1852** ROWCROFT *Conf. Etonian* I. 72 The boys at Eton are not known by their Christian names, and when there are more than one bearing the same surname,..the individuals are distinguished by the addition of maximus, major, minor, and minimus. **1891** BLEW *Vyner's Not. Venat.* (1892) Pref. 8 Musters minimus. **1899** E. PHILLPOTTS *Human Boy* 101 Corkey minimus.

mining ('maɪnɪŋ), *vbl. sb.* [f. MINE *v.* + -ING¹.]

1. a. The action of the verb MINE in various senses.

1523 LD. BERNERS *Froiss.* I. ccli. 372 They coude nat geat it by no assaute, nor none other wayes at their ease, without it were by mynynge. **1579–80** NORTH *Plutarch, Camillus* (1595) 145 Now when his mining fell out according to his good hope, he gaue an assaulte to the walles. **1645** MILTON *Tetrach.* Wks. 1851 IV. 257 St. Paul having thus clear'd himselfe, not to goe about the mining of our Christian liberty. **1764** GRAINGER *Sugar Cane* IV. 305 They..'melt with minings of the hectic fire'. **1776** ADAM SMITH *W.N.* I. xi. (1869) I. 181 Mining..is considered..as a lottery. **1845** DARWIN *Voy. Nat.* xii. (1879) 258 The rage for mining has left scarcely a spot in Chile unexamined.

b. with qualifying word prefixed, as ***gold-, lead-, tin-mining; placer-, vein-mining; hydraulic-mining***, etc., for which see those words.

†**2.** *concr.* A (military) mine. *Obs.*

1598 BARRET *Theor. Warres* 136 Pioners to make trenches, Rampiers, Minings.

3. *attrib.* and *Comb.*, as ***mining-camp, captain, company, -district, engineer, -lamp, -man, population, recorder, -speculation, -statute, -tool, -town, -township*** (Austral.), ***-work***; **mining geology**, geology as applied to mining; **mining-hole**, a hole bored to receive a blasting-charge in mining; **mining-ship**, one that carries and lays down submarine mines in naval warfare.

1902 'MARK TWAIN' in *Harper's Monthly Mag.* Feb. 431/2 Don't you put on any exclusiveness in a mining-camp. **1966** 'E. LATHEN' *Death shall Overcome* i. 9 Wall Street is power. The talk..closes mining camps in the Chibougamou. **1853** *Harper's Mag.* Mar. 442/2 We are accompanied by Captain John Cox, the mining captain. **1859** L. SAWYER *Diary* 23 Sept. in *Way Sk.* (1926) 116 The ..river mining companies which have not already proved failures. **1838** *Murray's Handbk. N. Germany* 421 The mining district of the Erzgebirge. **1872** *Vermont Board Agric. Rep.* I. 629 Captain Thomas Pollard..had formerly been mining engineer. **1897** 'MARK TWAIN' *Following Equator* 687 The mining engineers from America. **1941** R. PEELE (*title*) Mining engineers' handbook. **1906** J. PARK *Textbk. Mining Geol.* i. 1 Economic or Mining Geology, which bears more directly on mining, and the development of the mining industry. **1839** URE *Dict. Arts* 852 The ore.. was attacked by a single man, who bored a mining hole. **1893** *Dublin Rev.* July 652 The most perfect combination of mining-lamp and fire-damp indicator yet produced. **1874** R. W. RAYMOND *Statistics of Mines* 499 He talked over the scheme with many railroad and mining-men. **1930** J. DOS PASSOS *42nd Parallel* I. 128 The bars..were full of ranchers and miningmen. **1854** A. DELANO *Life on Plains* xxvii. 382 There is arable land enough..to supply the whole mining population with vegetables, fruit and grain. **1876** *White Pine News* (Hamilton, Nevada) 22 July 3/1 An election took place on Treasure Hill on Thursday for Mining Recorder. **1968** Mining recorder [see FILE *v.*³ 1 c]. **1905** *Westm. Gaz.* 28 Jan. 2/2 If the Russians took mines out ten miles from the shore in a mining-ship and laid them there. **1824** R. STUART *Hist. Steam Engine* 121 The failure of some of the great mining speculations. **1555** EDEN *Decades* 49 All maner of dygginge or mynynge tooles. **1829** DR. WILLARD in R. G. Thwaites *Early Western Trav.* (1905) XVIII. 359 The mining towns are mostly dependent on their supplies from abroad. **1856** *Hutchings Mag.* July 33/2 [We had] to..make a 'pilgrim's progress' to the nearest mining town. **1902** ELIZ. L. BANKS *Newspaper Girl* 87 The mining towns of Lancashire and Yorkshire. **1944** N. W. ROSS *Westward the Women* 133 She appeared in the mining town of Murray. **1890** 'R. BOLDREWOOD' *Col. Reformer* (1891) 283 The mining township of Turonia. **1633** T. JAMES *Voy.* 69 Wee continued our myning worke.

mining ('maɪnɪŋ), *ppl. a.* [f. MINE *v.* + -ING².]

1. That mines, in the senses of the verb.

1561 NORTON & SACKV. *Gorboduc* I. ii. (1590) B iiij b, That myning fraude shall finde no way to creepe, Into their fenced eares. *a* **1639** WOTTON in *Reliq.* (1651) 526 The mining Conies shroud in rockie Cels. **1816** BYRON *Ch. Har.* III. xciv, The..Rhone..whose mining depths so intervene, That they can meet no more.

2. mining bee, a solitary bee of the family Andrenidæ, including many British and American species which nest in tunnels in the ground, sometimes grouped in colonies.

1893 L. N. BADENOCH *Romance Insect World* iii. 72 (*caption*) Profile view of nest of a Mining Bee (Andrena vicina). **1912** SANDERSON & JACKSON *Elem. Entomol.* xvii. 268 None of the short-tongued bees live in colonies, and many of them make their nests in the ground, which has given them the name of 'mining bees'. **1974** *Country Life* 21 Feb. 351/1 The spoil-heaps excavated by mining-bees (*Andrena armata*) when they make their nests.

†**mini'ographer.** *Obs.*⁻⁰ [f. L. *mini-um* (see MINIUM) + *-ographer*. Cf. med.L. *miniografare* (Du Cange).] (See quot.) So †**mini'ography**.

1656 BLOUNT *Glossogr.*, *Miniographer*..he that paints or writes with Vermilion, or any red colour. **1727** BAILEY vol. II, *Miniography*, a writing with Vermilion.

minion ('mɪnjən), *sb.*¹ and *a.* Forms: 6–7 **minyon, mynyon(e, mynion, mineon,** 6 **mynny(e)on, mygnyon, mynon, mignyon,** *Sc.* **moyn3eoun, mun3(e)oun, min3eo(u)n, myn3on, -3eoun,** 7 **minnion, (minione),** 7–8 **mignion,** 7–9 **mignon,** 6– **minion.** [a. F. *mignon* (also fem. *mignonne*) sb. and adj.

The ultimate etymology is disputed; according to some the word is a derivative of OHG. *minnja, minna* love; others refer it to Celtic *min-* small.]

A. *sb.*

1. A beloved object, darling, favourite.

a. A lover or lady-love. Chiefly, and in later use exclusively with contemptuous or opprobrious sense, a mistress or paramour. Now *rare* or *Obs.*

1500–20 DUNBAR *Poems* lxxv. 52 Quod scho, 'Now tak me be the hand,..My chirrie and my maikles mun3oun'. **1548** LATIMER *Ploughers* B iiij b, They pastyme in their prelacies ..with theyr daunsyng minyons. **1590** SPENSER *F.Q.* II. ii. 37 A mincing mineon, Who in her loosenesse tooke exceeding ioy. **1597** J. PAYNE *Royal Exch.* 27 Sum gay professors (kepinge secret minions) do love there wyues..to avoyde shame. *a* **1677** BARROW *Serm.* Wks. 1716 I. 250 What will not a fond lover undertake..for his minion although she be..the worst enemy he can have? **1815** BYRON *Parisina* x, The minion of his father's bride,—He, too, is fetter'd by her side.

b. One specially favoured or beloved; a dearest friend, a favourite child, servant, or animal; the 'idol' of a people, a community, etc. Often *fig.*, as in ***minion of fortune***. Now only in contemptuous sense.

1566 PAINTER *Pal. Pleas.* I. 44 One of his dearest frends named Araspas which was..the very minion, playe felow and companion of Cyrus from his youth. **1581** PETTIE *Guazzo's Civ. Conv.* III. (1586) 150 b, I cannot abide the folly of some fathers who make some one of their children their darling and minion. **1596** SHAKS. *1 Hen. IV*, I. i. 83 A Sonne..Who is sweet Fortunes Minion, and her Pride. *Ibid.* ii. 30 Gentlemen of the Shade. Minions of the Moone. *c* **1626** *Dick of Devon* I. ii. in Bullen *O. Pl.* II. 13 That wonder of the land and the Seas minyon, Drake, of eternall memory. *a* **1627** HAYWARD *Edw. VI* (1630) 17 For enterprises by armes, he was the Minion of that time, so as few things he attempted, but he atchieued with honour. *a* **1631** DONNE *Serm.* cxv. Wks. 1839 V. 24 John the minion of Christ upon earth. **1735** SOMERVILLE *Chase* III. 125 That pamper'd Steed, his Master's Joy, His Minion, and his daily Care. **1753** HANWAY *Trav.* (1762) I. VII. xc. 411 His disinterested practice,..and his great charity to the poor, render him the minion of the people. **1859** MACAULAY *Pitt* Biog. (1860) 176 Pitt was..the minion, the child, the spoiled child of the House of Commons. **1865** DICKENS *Mut. Fr.* II. vii, All offered up sacrifices to the minion of fortune and the worm of the hour!

c. *esp.* A favourite of a sovereign, prince, or other great person; *esp.* opprobriously, one who owes everything to his patron's favour, and is ready to purchase its continuance by base compliances, a 'creature'.

1501 DOUGLAS *Pal. Hon.* III. lx, The kingis min3eoun roundand in his eir, Hecht Veritie. *a* **1548** HALL *Chron.*, *Hen. IV*, 7 b, Item the same kyng put oute divers shrives lawefully elected and put in their romes divers other of his owne minions. *a* **1593** MARLOWE *Edw. II* (1598) B 3, The king is loue-sicke for his minion. *a* **1635** NAUNTON *Fragm. Reg.* (Arb.) 16 Her Ministers and Instruments of State.. were many,..but they were onely Favourites, not Minions. **1639** G. DANIEL *Vervic.* 147 The fall Of Mignion Somerset. **1726** SWIFT *Gulliver* IV. x, I had no Occasion of bribing, flattering, or pimping, to procure the Favour of any great Man, or of his Minion. **1828** D'ISRAELI *Chas. I*, II. vii. 162 The portrait of Buckingham is usually viewed in the caricature of a royal minion. **1888** BRYCE *Amer. Commw.* II. lxiii. 455 It is no wonder if he helps himself from the city treasury and allows his minions to do so.

d. *transf.* applied to things.

a **1640** DAY *Peregr. Schol.* (1881) 65 Violets, roses, and lillies, and like mineons and darlings of the springe. **1699** SOUTH *Serm.* (1842) III. 54 That one [thing] which is the sole minion of their fancy and the idol of their affections. **1793** COLERIDGE *Songs of Pixies* iii, When noontide's fiery-tressed minion Flashes the fervid ray.

e. As a form of address: †(*a*) endearingly = darling, dear one (*obs.*); (*b*) contemptuously = hussy, jade; servile creature, slave.

1560 ROLLAND *Crt. Venus* I. 194 Myn3eoun, quhairfoir do 3e sustene Sic displesure in hert be countenance. *a* **1586** SIDNEY *Arcadia* II. (1598) 163 b, Minion said she (indeed I was a pretie one in those daies though I say it) I see a number of lads that loue you. **1591** SHAKS. *Two Gent.* I. ii. 92 You (Minion) are too saucie. **1600** HEYWOOD *2nd Pt. Edw. IV*, P 2 b, Come away minion you shall prate no more. **1825** SCOTT *Betrothed* vi, 'Go hence, thou saucy minion', said the monk. **1835** LYTTON *Rienzi* II. iii, Peace, minion! draw back!

†**2.** A gallant, an exquisite. *Obs.*

1547 BOORDE *Introd. Knowl.* i. (1870) 117, I wyll get a garment, shal reche to my tayle; Than I am a minion, for I were the new gyse.

†**3.** A small kind of ordnance (see quot. 1644).

1547 in *Archæologia* LI. 262 Gonnes of Brasse.. Culverynes vjˣ. Sacres vjˣ. Mynnyons xᵉⁿ. **1587** HARRISON *England* II. xvi. (1877) I. 281 Minion poiseth eleauen hundred pounds, and hath three inches and a quarter within the mouth. **1644** WHITELOCK *Memorials* (1853) I. 273 They lost five drakes, a minion, and two leather guns. **1644** NYE *Gunnery* (1670) 77 Minions of the largest size, are three inches and a quarter Diameter in the mouth... The ordinary Minion, the mouth 3 inches high. **1894** C. N. ROBINSON *Brit. Fleet* 217 Sakers (5-pounders) and minions (4-pounders) were mounted on skids.

4. a. A kind of peach, in full ***minion peach***. [= F. *pêche mignonne*.] **b.** A small kind of lettuce.

1699 EVELYN *Kal. Hort.*, Aug. (ed. 9) 100 Minion Peach. *Ibid.* 170 Peaches and Nectarins..Maudlin, Mignon. **1706** LONDON & WISE *Retir'd Gard.* I. viii. 37 [Peaches.] The Minion is very large, but not so round as long. **1707** MORTIMER *Husb.* (1721) II. 148 Of this sort there are two others, viz. George Lettices..and the Minion which is the

least sort. **1766** *Compl. Farmer* s.v. *Peach-tree*, The French mignon; this is a most excellent melting peach.

5. *Printing.* (In full *minion type* or *letter*.) The name of a type intermediate in size between 'nonpareil' and 'brevier'. [So F. *mignonne* (*mignone*, Fournier *Man. Typogr.* 1766).]

1659 HOWELL *Vocab.* li, Letters of all sorts, as.. Non-paril, Minion, Breviere [etc.]. **1770** [LUCKOMBE] *Hist. Printing* 152 (Specimens of Printing Types) Minion. **1824** J. JOHNSON *Typogr.* II. 83 Why this letter was denominated Minion, we have not yet been informed. **1865** M. PATTISON *Ess.* (1889) I. 72 A pocket Greek Testament in mignon letters. **1894** D. C. MURRAY *Making of Novelist* 19 Three columns of leaded minion.

6. *attrib.* and *Comb.*: **a.** (sense 1) as ***minion maintainer***; ***minion-guided*** adj.; ***minion-like*** adv. (Cf. also B. 1.)

1599 *Broughton's Let.* v. 17 An whoremaster and a minion maintainer. **1605** CAMDEN *Rem.* 18 Hitherto will our sparkefull Youth laugh at their great grandfathers English, who had more care to do well, than to speake minion-like. **1612** DRAYTON *Poly-olb.* xvii. 23 That with the fern-crown'd Flood he [the Wey] minion-like doth play. **1773** *Gentl. Mag.* XLIII. 455 Third Henry's feeble minion-guided rule.

†**b.** (sense 3), as ***minion bore***, ***gun***; **minion drake**, some kind of small cannon; **minion proof** *a.*, proof against minion shot; **minion shot**, shot used with a minion, also, the range of a minion. *Obs.*

1633 WINTHROP *New Eng.* (1853) I. 148 A vessel.. to be minion proof, and the upper deck musket proof. **1647** CLARENDON *Hist. Reb.* VI. §248 Two small iron minion-drakes (all the artillery they had). **1648** —— *St. Papers* II. 415 The Vice-Admirals.. were within minion shot one of the other. *a* **1661** FULLER *Worthies, Cornw.* (1662) I. 212 Two small Mynion-Drakes.. were planted on a little Barrough within Randome-shot of the Enemy. **1699** DAMPIER *Voy.* II. 144 He had 2 or 3 small brass Guns of a Minion bore. **1727** A. HAMILTON *New Acc. E. Ind.* I. xxx. 374[I] had eight minion Guns to scour the Sands.

B. *adj.* Now *rare.* (Cf. MIGNON *a.*)

1. Dainty, elegant, fine, pretty, neat. **a.** of a person, his actions, attributes, etc.

15.. *Songs Costume* (Percy Soc.) 58 Off servyng men I wyll begyne... For they goo mynyon trym. **1529** FRITH *Antithesis* 100 b, Some enter [the fold] thorow their curious singinge and minyon dawnsinge. **1530** *Songs* in *Anglia* XII. 591, I shal deck your mynyon face that yt shal shyne in euery place. **1542** UDALL *Erasm. Apoph.* 125 A young ruffleer trymmyng hymselfe after ye moste galaunte and mynion facion. *Ibid.* 189 b, A passyng faire damysel, beeyng a mynion dooer in syngyng. *a* **1553** —— *Royster D.* (Arb.) 86 Who so to marry a minion Wyfe, Hath hadde good chaunce and happe. **1579** PUTTENHAM *Partheniades* xi, O mightye Muse, The mignionst mayde of mounte Parnasse. **1605** CAMDEN *Rem.* 28, I may be charged by the minion refiners of English, neither to write State-English, Court-English, nor Secretarie-English. **1718** ROWE tr. *Lucan* I. 313 In silken Robes the minion Men appear, Which Maids and youthful Brides shou'd blush to wear. **1864** TENNYSON *Aylmer's F.* 533 My lady,—who made.. A downward crescent of her minion mouth.

b. of a thing, an animal.

1528 *St. Papers Hen. VIII*, I. 307 His Hynes lykythe youre mynyon howse so well, that [etc.]. **1543** *Test. Ebor.* (Surtees) VI. 175 To my lorde of Northfolke a mynyon geldinge. *a* **1552** LELAND *Itin.* V. 123 Wreshil a very fayre and mynion Castle. **1581** J. BELL *Haddon's Answ. Osor.* 264 What shall he regarde the lofty grace of Cicero?.. or his mynion deuises and toyes?

2. Dearly loved, favourite, pet. (Cf. F. *péché mignon*, one's 'darling sin'.)

a **1716** SOUTH *Serm.* (1823) III. 257 A secret love to some base minion lust. *Ibid.* VI. 167 When the tempter shall dress up any beloved minion sin. *a* **1849** H. COLERIDGE *Ess.* (1851) I. 89 They will have some pet production, some favourite passage, some minion thought.

minion (ˈmɪnjən), *sb.*² [a. F. *minion* (Cotgr.), f. L. *minium.*]

†**1.** = MINIUM. *Obs.*

1621 BURTON *Anat. Mel.* III. ii. III. iii. (1651) 477 Let them paint their faces with minion and cerusse. **1654** R. CODRINGTON tr. *Iustine* xliv. 517 The Countrie doth abound with Lead, and Brass, and with Minion also. *Ibid.* xliv. 514.

2. Calcined iron ore, 'used with lime as a water-cement' (Ogilvie 1850).

1793 SMEATON *Edystone L.* §213 What I used was the siftings of the iron stone, after calcination at the iron furnaces... This material, among the furnace men in these parts, is called *Minion. Ibid.* §214 *Minion*, or iron stone burnt. **1873** *Weale's Dict. Terms, Minion*, the siftings of iron-stone after calcination at the iron-furnaces.

†**'minion**, *v. Obs. rare.* [f. MINION *sb.*¹] *trans.* To treat as a minion; to caress. Implied in †**'minioning** *vbl. sb.*

1604 MARSTON *Malcontent* IV. i, Sooner hard steele will melt with Southerne wind.. Then women vow'd to blushlesse impudence, With sweet behauiour and soft minioning, Will turne from that where appetite is fixt.

minion, var. *munnion*, obs. f. MULLION.

†**'minionate**, *a. Obs. rare*⁻¹. In 5 **mynyonat**. [f. MINION *a.* + -ATE.] = MINION *a.* 1.

c **1495** *Epitaffe*, etc. in *Skelton's Wks.* (1843) II. 391 Ladyes, damosels, mynyonat and gorgayse.

minionette (mɪnjəˈnɛt), *sb. U.S. Printing.* [f. MINION *sb.*¹ + -ETTE.] (See quot.)

1871 *Ringwalt's Amer. Encycl. Printing, Minionette*, a very small size of type, used chiefly in small ornamental borders.

†**minio'nette**, *a. Obs. rare*⁻¹. [ad. F. *mignonnette* fem. adj., after MINION *a.*] Small and pretty.

1749 H. WALPOLE *Lett.* (1857) II. 163 His minionette face.

minionism (ˈmɪnjənɪz(ə)m). [f. MINION *sb.*¹ and *a.* + -ISM.] †**a.** The quality of being 'minion'; a manifestation of this quality (*obs.*). **b.** Partiality for a minion or favourite. *rare*⁻¹.

1611 FLORIO, *Mignardaggine*, minionisme, wantonnesse. *Mignardigie*, mignardises, minionismes. **1611** COTGR., *Mignonneté*, minionisme, quaintnesse, trimnesse, delicacie, sprucenesse, featnesse, finesse. **1818** COLERIDGE in *Lit. Rem.* (1838) III. 198 Yet how many points.. must be brought together before we can fairly solve the intensity of James's minionism, his Kingly egotism [etc.].

†**'minionize**, *v. Obs. rare.* [f. MINION *sb.*¹ + -IZE.] **a.** *trans.* To raise to the position of a minion; hence †**'minionized** *ppl. a.* **b.** *intr.* (See quot. 1604.)

1604 R. CAWDREY *Table Alph., Mignionise*, play the wanton. **1609** J. DAVIES *Holy Roode* I j b, His Minions.. Whom, of base Groomes, his Grace did Minnionize. **1616** [T. G.] *Rich Cabinet* 3 b, Anger, made Great Alexander.. kill his minionized friend Clytus.

†**'minionly**, *adv. Obs.* [f. MINION *sb.*¹ and *a.* + -LY².] In a 'minion' manner; delicately, elegantly.

1539 TAVERNER *Erasm. Prov.* (1545) 100 At Athens he wolde.. liue mynionly and elegantly. **1633** J. DONE *Hist. Septuagint* 171 A house.. very stately and minionly decked and trimmed.

†**'minionness.** *Obs. rare*⁻¹. [f. MINION *sb.*¹ + -NESS.] The condition or behaviour of a minion.

a **1533** LD. BERNERS *Gold. Bk. M. Aurel.* (1546) R j, He muste suffre hir nice mynionnesse [orig. Sp. *sus regalos*], for euery faire woman will passe hir life in plesure.

†**'minionship.** *Obs. rare*⁻¹. [f. MINION *sb.*¹ + -SHIP.] The position of a minion or favourite.

c **1645** HOWELL *Lett.* I. I. xvii, The Favourit Luines strengthneth himself more and more in his minionship.

†**'minious**, *a. Obs. rare*⁻¹. [f. L. *minium* MINIUM + -OUS.] Of the colour of minium, red.

1646 SIR T. BROWNE *Pseud. Ep.* VI. ix. 320 They which hold the [Red] Sea receiveth a red and minious tincture from springs.. that fall into it. [Whence **1656** in Blount; and in later Dicts.]

miniscule (ˈmɪnɪskjuːl). Erron. var. MINUSCULE *a.*

1898 J. SOUTHWARD *Mod. Printing* I. xxii. 139 Each of the text letters already named has its own lower case or 'miniscule' letters. **1948** *N.Y. Times* 12 Dec. VII. 5 Now once again these miniscule land areas have faded from our interests. **1955** *Ibid.* 10 Apr. x. 27 Upland meadows are carpeted with miniscule wild flowers. **1961** *Economist* 16 Dec. 1118/1 Many 'gardens' would be miniscule affairs. **1967** [see INTEGRATED *ppl. a.* b]. **1970** *Daily Tel.* 24 Apr. 1/3 If these conditions were fulfilled the risk from the pill was 'miniscule'. **1973** *Orcadian* 2 Aug. 4/4 The most interesting feature of this miniscule nation.. is the strength of its national culture.

minise, obs. form of MINISH.

mini-series (ˈmɪnɪsɪəriːz). orig. *U.S.* Also **miniseries.** [f. MINI- + SERIES.] A television series (see SERIES 9 b), usu. of short duration, that treats a single, complete theme or plot in a predetermined number of episodes.

1972 *TV Guide* (U.S.) 28 Oct. 4/2 If a miniseries fails to earn healthy ratings, the network can replace only the parts viewers don't like. **1973** *Esquire* Dec. 151/1 *The Blue Knight* has been made into a four-hour TV 'mini-series', with William Holden as the lead. **1977** *Time* 31 Oct. 56/2 The network has stayed ahead of CBS with.. miniseries like *79 Park Avenue.* **1978** G. VIDAL *Kalki* viii. 183 You have the mini-series for NBC. **1984** *Listener* 5 Jan. 10/1 At this stage, a big budget movie rather than a television miniseries was in prospect. **1985** *Woman's Own* 22 June 36/1 Another TV mini-series, this time about the life and loves of George Washington.

minish (ˈmɪnɪʃ), *v.* Now only *arch.* Forms: 4-5 **menus(e**, (4 **mynus(c)h**, **menus(c)h**, *Sc.* **menes**, **myniss**, 5 **menuze**), 4-6 **mynyssh(e**, 5 **minussh**, (**minys**, **minise**, **-issh**, **mynes(ch**, **mynuyssh**, **mynyss**), 5-6 **mynys**, 6 **mynish(e**, (**-issh**, **-essh**, **-usshe**, **myn(n)yshe**), **minishe**, **-issh(e)**, **mynysch(e**, *Sc.* **menis(che**, 6- **minish**. [ad. OF. *menusier*, *menuisier* = Pr. *menuzar*, It. *minuzzare*:—vulgar Latin **minūtiāre*, f. *minūtus* MINUTE *a.* Cf. MINCE *v.*]

1. *trans.* To make fewer in number or less in size; to make less in amount or degree; to reduce in power, influence, etc. (rarely †const. *of*).

c **1375** [see MINISHING *vbl. sb.*]. **1382** WYCLIF *Wisd.* xi. 8 Whan thei weren mynusht [Vulg. *minuerentur*].. thou ȝeue to them abundende water. *c* **1386** CHAUCER *Pars. T.* ⁋ 303 (Cambr. MS.) Ek ȝif he withdrawe or menuse the almesse of the poore. *c* **1440** *Alphabet of Tales* 31, I remevid þis stone in þe feld, to þe entent þat I wolde enlarge myne awn ground & mynys oþer mens ground. **1465** *Paston Lett.* II. 175 And yff they wold wyrke ayenst me to minussh my power. **1513** DOUGLAS *Æneis* I. Prol. 371 Latyne wordis.. That in our leid ganand translatioun hes nane, Les than we menis thar sentence and grauite. **1535** COVERDALE *Ps.* cvi[i]. 39 When they are minished & brought lowe thorow oppression. **1538** STARKEY *England* I. i. 14 Vertues.. be no les vertues, nor mynyschyd of theyr excellency, by any such frantyke fansy. *a* **1548** HALL *Chron., Hen. V* 46 b, His armie by sickenesse was sore minished and appaired. **1614** JACKSON *Creed* III. xxi. §18 The testimonies of the Law and Prophesies, serued as a light.. to minish the terrors of the night. **1826** SCOTT *Woodst.* iii, I may come to trouble, since it may be thought I have minished their numbers. **1848** LOWELL *Biglow P.* Poems 1890 II. 68, I would not.. minish by a tittle the respect due to the Magistrate.

absol. **1509** HAWES *Past. Pleas.* (Percy Soc.) 111 She [Nature] werketh upon all wonderly, Bothe for to minysshe and to multeply.

b. To break up *into* (powder, parts).

1382 WYCLIF *2 Kings* xxiii. 15 And that heeȝ auter he.. mynuschede in to poudre. **1851** LANDOR *Popery* 33 Our kingdom is minished into parts and parcels.

†**c.** To reduce (a coin) by clipping or sweating. *Obs. rare.* Cf. DIMINISH *v.* 1 b.

1622 [see MINISHED *ppl. a.*].

2. To remove, withdraw (a portion *of* or *from* something).

c **1483** CAXTON *Chaucer's Cant. T., Proheme*, I had made it accordyng to my copye and by me was nothyng added ne mynusshyd. **1525** *Test. Ebor.* (Surtees) V. 207 Shall mynysche noe part of yere. **1581** W. STAFFORD *Exam. Compl.* i. (1876) 19 We are forced, either to minishe the third part of our householde, or to raise the thirde part of our reuenewes. **1860** PUSEY *Min. Proph.* 342 What they minish from the measure, that they add to the wrath of God.

b. *absol.*

c **1400** *Apol. Loll.* 3 Not presumand to put to His lawe, ne to minys þerfro. ? **1421** *Lett. Marg. Anjou & Bp. Beckington* (Camden) 28 And ever to have libertee to adde and minise chaunge and amende. **1506** *Bury Wills* (Camden) 108 Myn executours shall mynysshe as they thynke accordyng to conciens. **1526** TINDALE *Rev.* xxii. 19 And yf eny man shall mynnyshe of the wordes off the boke of this prophesy.

3. To decry the importance or worth of; to depreciate, belittle.

1402 *Pol. Poems* (Rolls) II. 53 Thi baffyng, lye thou never so lowde, may not menuse this seint [Wyclif]. *Ibid.* 85 Thou assentist thi silf in tresoun, menusynge the kyngis majeste. **1866** J. B. ROSE tr. *Ovid's Metam.* 136 Vaunted the Titan deeds, and minished those Of the great gods.

4. *intr.* To become less in quantity, number, size, power, etc.

1398 TREVISA *Barth. De P.R.* IV. vii. (1495) 90 As fatnesse wexyth the blode mynysshyth. **1494** FABYAN *Chron.* V. cxviii. 94 Careticus.. prouyd the strengthe of his enemyes, and sawe y^t^ they increasyd, and his knyghtis lassed and mynysshed. **1511-12** *Act 3 Hen. VIII*, c. 3 Preamble, Archerie.. is right litell used but dayly mynessheth decayth and abateth. **1535** COVERDALE *2 Sam.* iii. 1 But Dauid wente and increased, and the house of Saul wente and mynished. **1535** STEWART *Cron. Scot.* III. 539 Quhilk causit science to grow.. And vice to menische ilk da les and les. **1901** HENLEY *Hawthorn & Lavender* 7 The sovran sun, As he goes southing, weakening, minishing, Almighty in obedience.

Hence **'minished** *ppl. a.* Also **'minisher.**

1564 BECON *Wks.* Pref. A v, He is not Episcopus, but Aposcopus, not a Minister, but a Minisher. **1590** SPENSER *F. Q.* I. xi. 43 The paw yett missed not his minisht might. **1622** BACON *Hen. VII* 215 In making all clipped, minished, or impaired Coines of Siluer, not to bee currant in payments.

minishing (ˈmɪnɪʃɪŋ), *vbl. sb.* [-ING¹.] The action of the verb MINISH, in various senses.

c **1375** *Sc. Leg. Saints* xxxvii. (*Vincencius*) 184, & þare-fore wil nocht ony wyse þou to my Ioy mak lessing, na to my reward menesinge. **1485** *Rolls of Parlt.* VI. 338/2 Savyng only to the abatement, discharge, mynesyng, and relesyng of the Fee Ferme of the said Towne. **1513** MORE *Rich. III* in Stow *Ann.* (1592) 743 Inticing him to many things highly redounding to the minishing of his honour. **1551** TURNER *Herbal* I. Prol. A iij b, Euery man.. will become a Phisician, to the hynderaunce and minishyng of the study of liberall artes. **1651** R. CHILD in *Hartlib's Legacy* (1655) 137 The dulling and minishing of the Spirit. **1860** DORA GREENWELL *Patience of Hope* 18 [It] has set the ideals of Christ and Humanity so far apart, that the wealth of the one can only be attained through the minishing of the other.

†**'minishment.** *Obs.* [f. MINISH *v.* + -MENT.] The action or process of lessening; diminution.

1533 MORE *Debell. Salem.* Wks. 967/2 If you fynde.. that the putting away of that lawe, be better.. for this lande without the minishment of the fayth in the same. **1577-87** HOLINSHED *Chron.* III. 1140/1 That the castell with all.. munitions of warre, should be wholie rendred without wasting, hiding, or minishment thereof. **1664** ATKYNS *Orig. Printing* 9 That they shall keep all the Lands, Honours, and Dignities.. whole, without any manner of minishment.

minisse, -issh, obs. ff. MENACE, MINISH.

†**mini'stello.** *Obs.* [f. MINISTER + It. dim. suffix *-ello.*] A petty minister.

1659 GAUDEN *Tears of Ch.* II. xiv. 194 Consider, I beseech you, what pitifull Ministellos, what pigmy Presbyters,.. this Nation in after-ages is like to have if [etc.].

minister (ˈmɪnɪstə(r)), *sb.* Forms: 3-6 **ministre**, 4 **minystre**, **mynystyr**, **mynystere**, **mynistere**, **minster**, 4-6 **mynyster**, **-ister**, **-istre**, 5 **minstre**, **mynestre**, **-ter**, **mynstre**, **minestre**, **mynnyster**, *Sc.* **mynistir**, 4- **minister**. [a. OF. *menestre*, *ministre*, a. L. *minister* servant, f. **minis-*, *minus* less, parallel in formation to the correlative *magister* MASTER *sb.*, f. *magis* more. Cf. Sp., Pg., It. *ministro*, G. *minister.*]

1. †**a.** A servant, attendant. *Obs.*

c **1375** *Sc. Leg. Saints* xxii. (*Laurentius*) 121 Fadyr, quhare gais þu bot ministeris? *a* **1500** *Chaucer's Dreme* 2132 With ladyes, knightes, and squieres, And a grete ost of ministeres,

With instrumentes and sounes diverse. **1513** BRADSHAW *St. Werburge* I. 1728 The mynysters were redy theyr offyce to fulfyll To take vp the tables at theyr lordes wyll. **1572** SIR T. SMITH in Ellis *Orig. Lett.* Ser. II. III. 15 Scarcely the ministers cowld have rowme to bring the meate or the drinck to the table. **1611** BIBLE *2 Kings* vi. 15 When the servant [*marg.* minister] of the man of God was risen early. **1612** WOODALL *Surg. Mate* Wks. (1653) 406 Let the Surgeon have at hand at the least two or three ministers or servants besides himself, to assist him in the work. **1781** GIBBON *Decl. & F.* xxxi. III. 206 A multitude of cooks, and inferior ministers, employed in the service of the kitchens.

b. One who waits upon, or ministers to the wants of another. *arch.*

1818 BYRON *Ch. Har.* IV. clxxvii, Oh! that the Desert were my dwelling-place, With one fair Spirit for my minister. **1868** FITZGERALD tr. *Omar* lv, And lose your fingers in the tresses of The Cypress-slender Minister of Wine.

2. a. One who acts under the authority of another; one who carries out executive duties as the agent or representative of a superior. Now *rare.*

c **1290** *S. Eng. Leg.* I. 301/65 Godes ministres aunglesbeoth, seint Miȝhel and oþere mo. *c* **1327** *Rolls of Parlt.* II. 430 His writings and other goods, &c., arrested by the King's ministers. **1390** GOWER *Conf.* I. 61 Pride..hath with him in special Ministres five ful diverse, Of whiche,..The ferste is seid Ypocrisie. *c* **1412** HOCCLEVE *De Reg. Princ.* 2535 If þe ministres do naght but iustice To poore peple, in contre as þei go, Thogh þe Kyng be vniust, yit is his vice Hid to þe peple. **1432–50** tr. *Higden* (Rolls) II. 339 Iosue, the minister of Moyses, rewlede the peple of Israel. **1526** *Pilgr. Perf.* (W. de W. 1531) 139 b, The goostly ennemy our olde aduersary & all his mynysters put to flyght & confusyon. **1535** COVERDALE *Rom.* xiii. 6 He is the minister of God for thy wealth. *c* **1586** C'TESS PEMBROKE *Ps.* CIII. xii, Spirits of might,..You ministers that willing work his will..His praise extoll. **1593** SHAKS. *2 Hen. VI*, v. ii. 34 O Warre, thou sonne of hell, Whom angry heauens do make their minister. **1628** COKE *On Litt.* 147 The Kings Baily should be but his Minister to distreine for his rent. **1667** MILTON *P.L.* v. 460 His wary speech Thus to th' Empyreal Minister he fram'd. **1681–6** J. SCOTT *Chr. Life* (1747) III. 314 The first and supreme Minister by which Christ rules his Kingdom is the Holy Ghost. **1750** JOHNSON *Rambler* No. 81 ¶6 The community, of which the magistrate is only the minister.

b. Const. *of*: One who is employed by another to carry into effect (a purpose or intention) or to convey (a gift, etc.). Also *transf.* of things. *Obs.* exc. as coloured by religious use.

c **1380** WYCLIF *Serm.* Sel. Wks. I. 18 Jesus Crist dide more miracle, and bad hise disciples serve þe puple at þe mete, to teche us þat we ben mynystris and not autouris of miracle. *c* **1386** CHAUCER *Can. Yeom. Prol. & T.* 747 Al to symple is my tonge to pronounce As Ministre of my wit, the doublenesse Of this Chanon. **1580** LYLY *Euphues* (Arb.) 354 Philautus determined, hab, nab, to sende his letters,..and ..he thus beganne to frame the minister of his loue. **1593** SHAKS. *2 Hen. VI*, III. i. 355 For a minister of my intent, I haue seduc'd a head-strong Kentishman. **1720** OZELL tr. *Vertot's Rom. Rep.* II. XII. 215 Catiline..had been the Minister of the Cruelties of Sylla. **1722** WOLLASTON *Relig. Nat.* ix. 186 Why doth the scene of thinking lie in our heads, and all the ministers of sensation make their reports to something there. **1784** COWPER *Task* v. 816 Those fair ministers of light to man That fill the skies. **1866** LIDDON *Bampton Lect.* vi. (1875) 321 The Angels are ministers of the Divine Will.

†**c.** An officer entrusted with the administration of the law, or attached to a court of justice. *Obs.*

c **1386** CHAUCER *Nun's Pr. T.* 223, I crye out on the Ministres quod he That sholden kepe and reulen this Citee. *c* **1450** *Godstow Reg.* 149 Vndurshreuys, or oþer ballyfs or mynysters what-so-euer they be. **1483** *Anc. Cal. Rec. Dublin* (1889) I. 303 The clerkys and mynnysters of the courte of Tolsyll. **1526** TINDALE *Matt.* v. 25 Lest..the iudge delivre the to the minister. **1538** STARKEY *England* I. iii. 83 Gud mynystrys of justyce are to few. **1723** *Royal Proclam.* in *Lond. Gaz.* No. 6135/3 Before the next Magistrate or Minister of Justice.

†**d.** An officer subordinate to another, an underling. *Obs.*

1442 *Rolls of Parlt.* V. 54/2 Custumers..have diverse persones to be here Clerkes, Deputees and Ministres in here seide Offices. **1601** LD. MOUNTJOY in *Moryson's Itin.* II. (1617) 174 It grieveth me to see her Majesty so ill served in her Musters,..for all the Ministers in that kind, are but ciphers or false numbers. **1602** *Ibid.* 256 Errours of subordinate Ministers in these matters of accompts and reckonings. **1625** GLANVILLE *Voy. Cadiz* (1883) 29 The Captaine is to give them [his superior's commands] in charge to all other officers and ministers in the shipp.

3. A high officer of state. **a.** A person appointed by the chief of a state to act for him in a particular department of government; one entrusted with the administration of a department of state; a minister or secretary of state, as ***minister*** †***at*** (now ***for, of***) ***war, minister for foreign affairs***, etc. †***first minister***, the same as ***prime minister***. †***premier, prime minister***, see the adjs.

In plural often without article = the Ministry, the members of the Government.

1625 BACON *Ess., Envy* (Arb.) 516 This publique Enuy, seemeth to beat chiefly, vpon principall Officers, or Ministers, rather then vpon Kings and Estates themselues. **1741** *Lords' Protest* in Morley *Walpole* vii. (1889) 163 We are persuaded that a sole, or even a First Minister, is an officer unknown to the law of Britain. **1745** HARDWICKE in G. Harris *Life* (1847) II. 109, *Chancellor*... Your Ministers, sir, are only your instruments of government. *King*—(*smiles*)—Ministers are the King, in this country. **1795** ANNA SEWARD *Lett.* (1811) IV. 140, I blame ministers for such an evident waste of English blood and treasure. **1803** LD. MELVILLE in Morley *Walpole* vii. (1889) 162 That power must rest in the person generally called the First Minister, and that minister ought, he [*sc.* Pitt] thinks, to be the person at the head of the finances. **1805** JEFFERSON *Writ.* (1850) IV. 45 That there is only one minister who is not opposed to me, is totally unfounded. **1836** DICKENS *Sk. Boz, Tales* ii, Well, Brogson, what do Ministers mean to do? Will they go out or what? **1838** GREVILLE *Mem.* II. (1885) I. 87 In the first place the Colonial Minister should have made some arrangement [etc.]. **1843** BORROW *Bible in Spain* xiii, Isturitz became head of the cabinet, Galiano minister of marine, and a certain Duke of Rivas minister of the interior. **1868** M. E. G. DUFF *Pol. Surv.* 16 The King..immediately dismissed his Ministers. **1877** D. M. WALLACE *Russia* (ed. 2) I. 315 The Procureur..is directly subordinated to the Minister of Justice. *Ibid.* 322 The Minister for Foreign Affairs explained that [etc.].

b. A political agent accredited by one sovereign state to another; an envoy from one country to another charged with the duty of protecting and furthering the interests of the state by which he is accredited.

1709 *Lond. Gaz.* No. 4547/1 He received the compliments of the Foreign Ministers residing here. **1711** SWIFT *Jrnl. to Stella* 5 Dec., The Elector of Hanover's Minister here has given in a violent memorial against the peace. **1789** *Const. U.S.* ii. §3 The president..shall receive ambassadors and other public ministers. **1860** MALMESBURY *Mem. Ex-Minister* (1884) II. 234 In consequence of this violent act of invading Romagna, Louis Napoleon has recalled his Minister from Turin, leaving a *chargé d'affaires*. **1880** W. CORY *Mod. Eng. Hist.* I. 158 *note*, The term Minister is applied..to an envoy residing in a foreign capital.

c. Minister of State, a government minister, now usu. regarded in the U.K. as holding a rank below that of a head of department; **Minister of the Crown**, a minister or the head of a department in the U.K. government (see also quot. 1946); **Minister without Portfolio**, a government minister who has Cabinet status but is not in charge of a specific Department of State.

1696 PHILLIPS, *Minister* of State, is one upon whom a Prince reposes the Administration of his Kingdom. **1735** BOLINGBROKE *Diss. upon Parties* (ed. 2) p. xxv, But This will not become a *Matter of State*, though you are a *Minister of State*. **1864** SALISBURY in *Q. Rev.* CXVI. 253 Ministers of State are case-hardened by practice. **1950** W. S. CHURCHILL in *Hansard Commons* 31 Oct. 16, I like to see this reverence and respect for the past and all we owe to those who have gone before, and to see Ministers of State shake themselves clear from the obsession into which they fall from time to time. **1957** *Act 5 & 6 Eliz. II.* c. 20 §13 'Minister of State' means a member of Her Majesty's Government in the United Kingdom..who neither has charge of any public department nor holds any other of the offices specified in the Second Schedule to this Act. **1958** A. CHANDA *Indian Administration* III. i. 64 The appointment of Ministers of State to take charge of independent portfolios was an innovation [in India]... In France, a Minister of State ranked higher than a Minister and was usually entrusted with some special functions. In the UK, a Minister of State was, however, a minister of the second rank, functioning as the principal aide to a Cabinet Minister. **1963** HARVEY & BATHER *Brit. Constitution* xv. 251 When the work is particularly heavy or involved, or when it entails frequent visits abroad, Ministers of State, who act as deputy ministers, may be appointed. **1970** J. HARVEY *How Brit. is Governed* xii. 147 In departments where the work is particularly heavy, the present-day practice is to appoint Ministers of State who virtually act on behalf of the minister.

1776 J. HATSELL *Coll. Cases Priuilege Parl.* v. 196 The increase of their consequence in the state, and their influence in the management of public affairs, rendered them more an object of the attention of the Ministers of the Crown. **1844** ERSKINE MAY *Law of Parl.* xvii. 262 Another form of communication from the Crown to either house of Parliament, is in the nature of a verbal message, delivered, by command, by a minister of the Crown to the house of which he is a member. **1848** DISRAELI in *Hansard Commons* 20 June 961 Surely, the people of this country are not accustomed to wait to express their opinion, till it may chance to be elicited by some captious expression of a Minister of the Crown. **1892** W. R. ANSON *Law & Custom of Constitution* II. i. 10 The present dependence of the Ministers of the Crown, for their existence as a Ministry, upon the maintenance of a majority in the House of Commons. **1937** *Act 1 Edw. VIII & 1 Geo. VI* c. 38 §3 If and so long as any Minister of the Crown to whom this section applies is a member of the Cabinet. **1946** *Act 9 & 10 Geo. VI* c. 31 §8 (2) 'Minister of the Crown' means the holder of an office in His Majesty's Government in the United Kingdom, and includes the Treasury, the Admiralty, the Board of Trade, the Army Council, and the Air Council. **1956** ABRAHAM & HAWTREY *Parl. Dict.* 113 Ministers of the Crown... In its widest sense..it means any member of the Government, of whatever rank (this does not, of course, include parliamentary private secretaries, who have no official status at all). **1975** *Listener* 7 Aug. 183/1 A speech by a Minister of the Crown.

1915 *Hansard Commons* LXXII. p. iv, Minister without Portfolio—Rt. Hon. the Marquess of Lansdowne, K.G. **1921** H. H. ASQUITH in *Ibid.* 23 June 1630, I was the first Prime Minister in modern times during the last half-century or more, to have in his cabinet a Minister Without Portfolio. **1954** LD. TEMPLEWOOD *Nine Troubled Yrs.* x. 136 The Law Officers at once intervened to say that a Minister with a special Portfolio could not be a Minister without Portfolio. **1955** *Times* 30 June 8/5 M. Nguyen Huu Chau, Minister without portfolio in the Government of southern Viet Nam. *Ibid.* 18 July 8/3 The Bishop of Derby will open a debate on mining subsidence in the House of Lords on Wednesday, when the Government's views will be put forward by Lord Munster, Minister without Portfolio.

4. Ecclesiastical and religious uses.

a. In Pre-Reformation English, applied to a person in orders officially charged with some function in the celebration of worship in a particular church, chapel, chantry, etc. In the rubrics of the Book of Common Prayer the word denotes the clergyman, or any of a number of clergymen, engaged in conducting worship on a particular occasion.

c **1315** SHOREHAM I. 1539 Ȝef her nys suiche mynystre non, þys temple stent iuere. **1482** *Rolls of Parlt.* VI. 209/2 The noumbre of ministres daily servyng Almyghty God in the seid Chapell. **1501** in *Bury Wills* (Camden) 89, I beqwethe to the vicars and to the chawntery prestys..to eche of them vj. *d.* and to mynysters and queresteres after the rate. **1549** *Bk. Com. Prayer, Communion*, Then shall this generall confession bee made, in the name of all those that are minded to receyue the holy Communion, eyther by one of them, or els by one of the ministers, or by the Prieste hymselfe. **1662** *Ibid.*, When all have communicated, the Minister shall return to the Lord's Table... Then shall the Priest say the Lord's Prayer.

b. In phrases such as ***minister of the church, of the gospel***, and the scriptural phrases ***minister of God, of Jesus Christ, of the sanctuary***, applied as general designations for a person officially charged with spiritual functions in the Christian Church. Hence from the 16th c. onwards (after the example of foreign Protestant, esp. Calvinistic, use) employed *absol.* in the same sense, at first chiefly by those who objected to the terms ***priest*** and ***clergyman*** as implying erroneous views of the nature of the sacred office. The use of ***minister*** as the designation of an Anglican clergyman (formerly extensively current, sometimes with more specific application to a beneficed clergyman) has latterly become rare, and is now chiefly associated with Low Church views; but it is still the ordinary appellation of one appointed to spiritual office in any non-episcopal communion, esp. of one having a pastoral charge. The term ***minister of religion***, as applied to a 'clergyman' or 'minister' of any religious denomination, is common in official use.

minister's man: in Scotland, a man who acts as personal servant to a parish minister, and is employed by him in various offices connected with the church and parish.

1340 *Ayenb.* 236 þe gerdel huermide þe ministres of holy cherche ssolle ham gerde ope þe lenden is chastete. **1485** CAXTON *Chas. Gt.* 196 The bysshop wyth other mynystres of the chyrche dyd halowe the fonte. **1560–1** MACHYN *Diary* (Camden) 249 Parson Veron the Frenche man dyd pryche ther, for he was parson ther, and ys menyster. **1583** STUBBES *Anat. Abuses* II. (1882) 106 Such [names] as at anie hande a Minister of the Gospell ought not to bee called by. **1590** *Articles agst. Cartwright* in Fuller *Ch. Hist.* IX. vii. 198 We do object..against him, that he, being a Minister (at least a Deacon) lawfully called,..hath forsaken,..and renounced the same orders Ecclesiastical. *Ibid.* 199 The manner of Ordination of Bishops, Ministers and Deacons. **1609** B. JONSON *Sil. Wom.* II. v, Get me a minister presently, with a soft low voice to marry vs. **1641** J. TRAPPE *Theol. Theol.* 253 A Minister, if any man, had need to bee godly. **1678** WANLEY *Wond. Lit. World* v. iii. §8. 474/1 Sixtus [I].. ordered that holy things and vessels should be touched by none but Ministers. **1698** J. COLLIER *Immor. Stage* 137 To make the Ministers of Religion less upon the score of their Function, would be a Penalty on the Gospel. **1704** NELSON *Fest. & Fasts* II. iii. (1705) 395 Bishops..only have Authority to send Ministers into the Lord's Vineyard. **1722** DE FOE *Relig. Courtsh.* i. 13 Ministers are but Men. **1726** AYLIFFE *Parergon* 71 Tho' the word Minister sometimes denotes an Office, as that of a Priest or Deacon; and sometimes it is put for a Rector of a Parish. **1727** SWIFT *What passed in London* Wks. 1755 III. I. 187 The like might be observed in all sorts of ministers though not of the church of England. **1813–15** *Proc. Ch. Miss. Soc.* IV. 338 The minister of the Gospel ought not to be left alone among a heathen people. **1833** *Tracts for Times* No. 11. 12 The minister of the Independent chapel. **1837** LOCKHART *Scott* vii. (1839) 48/1 Macdonald..then officiated as minister to a small congregation of Episcopalian nonconformists. **1867** GEO. ELIOT in Cross *Life* III. 5 Renan's appearance is something between the Catholic priest and the dissenting minister. **1901** *Scotsman* 29 Mar. 6/8 Everyone..was.. familiar with the duties which a minister's man had to perform.

Comb. **1589** R. HARVEY *Pl. Perc.* (1590) 17 How dare these fellowes aspire to further authoritie in Minister-making.

c. Applied to non-Christian religious functionaries. *Obs.* exc. *occas.* with reference to Jews.

c **1400** MAUNDEV. (Roxb.) xix. 87 þe mynisters þat kepez þat ilk mawmet. *Ibid.* xxxiv. 153 þe prestez and ministres of ydoles er obedient to him. **1582** N. LICHEFIELD tr. *Castanheda's Conq. E. Ind.* I. vii. 18 A white Moore which was a Minister of the Moores of Mousambicke. **1687** A. LOVELL tr. *Thevenot's Trav.* II. 164 One of their Ministers goes along with the Man that carries the Child; and when they are come to the River-side the Minister says these words [etc.]. **1770** LANGHORNE *Plutarch* (1879) I. 166/2 The priests and ministers of the gods.

d. The title of the superior of certain religious orders; also ***minister general***. In the Society of Jesus, each of the five assistants of the general.

1450 *Rolls of Parlt.* V. 195/2 Nicholas, nowe Maistir or Minister of the ordre of Seynt Gilbert of Sempyngham. *c* **1470** HENRY *Wallace* II. 289 Thomas Rimour in to the Faile [*sc.* monastery] was than, With the mynystir, quhilk was a worthi man. **1727–41** CHAMBERS *Cycl.* s.v., Minister is also the title which certain religious orders give to their superior. In this sense we say, the *minister* of the Mathurins, or Trinitarians. *Minister*, among the Jesuits, is the second

superior of each house. The general of the Cordeliers order is also called the *minister general*. **1884** *Catholic Dict.* (1885) 580/1 *Minister*, among the Franciscans and Capuchins the head of the order is the minister-general... Again, the general of the Society of Jesus has five assistants, called ministers, who are elected by the general congregation.

†**e.** An assistant clergyman, curate (an application of sense 2 d). *Obs.*

1624 in *Ripon Ch. Acts* (Surtees) 364 To Mr. Thompson, my minister at Dighton, 40s. To Mr. Beilbe, now vicar of Pately Bridge, which was my minister at Dightonn, one whole suite of my workeday apparell.

†**5.** *Law.* An executor of a will; an administrator of an estate. *Obs.*

1433 *Rolls of Parlt.* IV. 472/1 That he be not..greved by the Kyng, nor his heirs, nor his Ministres in tyme to come. **1463** in *Somerset Medieval Wills* (1901) 197 My trieu executors, feoffees and ministers, as they wille answere afore God. **1546** in *Trans. Cumb. & Westm. Archæol. Soc.* X. 26, I gif to Godfray muncastor j quy by the Discrecion of my mynistour.

†**6.** One who administers (medicine). *Obs.*

1559 Morwyng *Evonym.* Advert., Without any great profit to the pacient or worship to the minister, because their medicines are negligently prepared.

7. *U.S.* The catfish, *Amiurus nebulosus.* = *horned pout* (horned *a.* 2 b).

[From sense 4 b: see quot. 1872.]

1839 D. H. Storer in Storer & Peabody *Rep. Fishes, Reptiles & Birds Mass.* 102 The Horned Pout..is known in the interior of the state by the vulgar names of 'Horn pout', and 'Minister'. **1849** Thoreau *Week Concord Riv.* 34 The Horned Pout..[is] sometimes called Minister. **1872** Schele de Vere *Americanisms* 382 A species [of the Catfish] is known also as *Mudpout*,..and irreverently, from its black color perhaps, as *Minister*. **1884** G. B. Goode *Fisheries U.S.: Nat. Hist. Aquatic Animals* 628 The common 'Horned Pout', 'Bullhead', 'Bull-pout', or 'Minister' of the Northern and Eastern States is the most generally abundant and familiar representative of this family [*sc.* Siluridæ].

minister (ˈmɪnɪstə(r)), *v.* Forms: see prec. sb. [a. OF. *ministrer*, ad. L. *ministrāre*, f. *minister* minister *sb.* Cf. Sp., Pg. *ministrar*, It. *ministrare*.]

I. Transitive uses.

†**1.** To serve (food or drink). *Obs.*

13.. *E.E. Allit. P.* B. 644 Abraham..Mynystred mete byfore þo men þat myȝtes alweldez. **1426** Lydg. *De Guil. Pilgr.* 3286 Off that foode..He Gaff to etyn to hem alle Thys newe mete most vnkouth, Mynystryng yt in-to ther mouth. *c* **1440** *Gesta Rom.* lxx. 322 (Harl. MS.) Euery day he mynystrid to þe Emperour of drynke. **1662** H. Stubbe *Ind. Nectar* ii. 10 Chocolatte..which they minister in great cups of above a pint.

2. To furnish, supply, impart (something necessary or helpful). Now only (*arch.* or *literary*) with immaterial object.

c **1380** Wyclif *Wks.* (1880) 377 Bi occasion of grace of god mynystred to eny creature. **1390** Gower *Conf.* III. 119 His Monthe assigned ek also Is Averil, which of his schoures Ministreth weie unto the floures. *c* **1400** Maundev. (Roxb.) vii. 23 Þai hafe na moisture bot þat þe forsaid ryuer ministers. *c* **1450** *Mirour Saluacioun* 4206 To whame so salutere techinges he mynystres so freely. **1517** Torkington *Pilgr.* (1884) 40 The lyght ys ther mynystred by many lampes. **1533** P'cess Mary in Ellis *Orig. Lett.* Ser. I. II. 30 Ye thereyn shulde mynestre unto me veraye acceptable pleasor. **1535** *Goodly Primer* (1834) 33 He that doth minister house, license, place, time, or help, to the works of this abominable lust. **1553** Eden *Treat. Newe Ind.* (Arb.) 33 The sea also ministred vnto them great abundaunce of shelfishe. **1605** Bacon *Adv. Learn.* I. vi. §16 They minister a singuler helpe and preseruative against vnbeleefe and error. **1613** Purchas *Pilgrimage* (1614) 90 How great a quantity soeuer [*sc.* of glassie sand] is by ships carried thence, is supplied by the Winds, which minister new sands. **1653** H. Cogan tr. *Pinto's Trav.* lxxix. 320 We were thus ministring matter for the company to laugh at us. **1742** Young *Nt. Th.* viii. 598 Wisdom,..Was meant to minister, and not to mar, Imperial pleasure. **1862** Stanley *Jew. Ch.* (1877) I. xvi. 317 The story..was able to minister true consolation. *a* **1872** Maurice *Friendship Bks.* iii. (1874) 83 The wisdom and consolation which it [learning] ministered to the common wayfarer.

†**b.** To communicate, make known. *Obs.*

1535–6 *Act 27 Hen. VIII*, c. 63 (Deputy's oath) Yf any defaulte ye fynde therein ye shall mynyster and shewe it unto theym.

†**c.** To prompt, suggest. In quot. *absol. Obs.*

1603 Shaks. *Meas. for M.* iv. v. 6 Sometimes you doe blench from this to that As cause doth minister.

†**3.** To dispense, administer (a sacrament, the 'elements' or the like). *Obs.*

c **1400** *Lay Folks Mass Bk.* App. iii. 123 To ministre þis moste worschipeful sacramente. **1510–20** *Everyman* 742 Thou mynystres all the sacramentes seuen. **1549** *Bk. Com. Prayer, Commun.* 118b, As yᵉ prist ministreth the Sacrament of the body, so shal he [*sc.* the deacon]..minister yᵉ Sacrament of the bloud. **1637** *Sc. Prayer Bk., Confirmation* (Rubric), It was ordained that confirmation should be ministred to them that were of perfect age. **1816** J. Wilson *City of Plague* iii. i. 197 'Tis but two nights ago I thither went To minister the sacrament.

4. To apply or administer (something healing); also *absol.* and *fig.* ? *Obs.*

1398 Trevisa *Barth. De P.R.* vii. lix. (1495) 275 Agaynst the Canker men shall mynistre medycynes whyche brennen and frete the deed flesshe. **1426** Lydg. *De Guil. Pilgr.* 1540 For they mynystre ther oynement To boystously, & no thing soffte. **1484** Caxton *Fables of Poge* x, [He] mynistyred alwey his pylles to euery man that came to hym for ony remedy. **1542–3** *Act 34 & 35 Hen. VIII*, c. 8 An Acte that persones being no comen Surgeons maie mynistre medicines owtwarde. **1590** Barrough *Meth. Physick* i. v. (1639) 8 If the patient be any thing costive, you may minister this decoction. **1619** Fletcher *M. Thomas* iii. i, Such a Physicke May chance to find the humour: be not long Lady, For we must minister within this halfe houre. **1680** Otway *Orphan* i. i, As calmly as the wounded Patient bears The Artist's hand that Ministers his Cure.

†**5.** To execute or dispense (justice, law); to administer (punishment). *Obs.*

1454 *Rolls of Parlt.* V. 239/2 After the cours of lawe to mynystre justice. **1467–8** *Ibid.* 622/2 This Londe was full naked and bareyn of Justice, the Peas not kepte, nor Lawes duely mynystred within the same. *c* **1550** Bale *K. Johan* (Camden) 52 Her custome ys to mynyster ponyshment To kynges and princes beyng dyssobedyent. **1596** Dalrymple tr. *Leslie's Hist. Scot.* I. ii. 169 Justice and æquitie he ministerit amang his awne wᵗ gret commendatione.

†**6.** *Law.* To administer (an interrogatory, oath or the like). *Obs.*

1425 *Rolls of Parlt.* IV. 271/1, I ynne his name, shall answer to ye boke last mynystred by ye partie of my Lord Mareschall, and synglerly to each article yrof. *a* **1541** Wyatt *Defence* Wks. (1861) p. xxx, What they mean by denying of this: minister interrogatories. Let them have such thirty-eight as were ministered unto me. **1562** *Act 5 Eliz.* c. 1 §5 Every Archebushopp..shall have full power..to tender and minister the Othe. *a* **1631** Donne *Serm.* viii. 84 Is he not thy Father? is an Interrogatory ministered by Moses. **1722** De Foe *Plague* (1756) 46 To minister unto them Oaths for the Performance of their Offices.

†**7.** To guide, direct, manage (affairs, etc.). *Obs.*

c **1374** Chaucer *Boeth.* iii. met. vi. 61 (Camb. MS.) On allone is fadyr of thynges. On allone mynystreth alle thinges. *c* **1380** Wyclif *Wks.* (1880) 391 And ȝitt þai claymen so ferforþli þes tiþis, þat no man lawfully may wiþ-holde hem or minystre hem save þai. **1492** in *10th Rep. Hist. MSS. Comm.* App. v. 323 They that ony maters shall have in courte to be mynstred. **1540–1** Elyot *Image Gov.* (1549) 104 A counsaile, wherby the affaires of the citee..shoulde be ruled and ministred.

†**b.** To execute the duties of (an office). *Obs.*

1542 Udall *Erasm. Apoph.* 284 b, That he had in suche wyse executed & ministred yᵉ office of a capitaine that [etc.].

II. Intransitive uses.

8. To serve, wait at table; to attend to the comfort or wants of another; to render aid or tendance. Const. *to*, *unto*, †*for* (a person, his wants); also †*dat.* of person.

c **1380** *Antecrist* in Todd 3 *Treat. Wyclif* 124 He þat mynystriþ me folowe he me seiþ Crist. **1382** Wyclif *Luke* xxii. 27 Forwhi who is the more, he that restith, other he that mynistrith? **1388** —— *Isa.* lx. 10 The kyngis of hem schulen mynystre to thee. **1393** Langl. *P. Pl.* C. xix. 97 Maidenes and marteres ministred hym her in erthe. **1432–50** tr. *Higden* (Rolls) II. 353 The peple of Israel ministrede [orig. *servivit*] to Eglon the fatte kynge of Moab. **1509** Fisher *Funeral Serm. C'tess Richmond* Wks. (1876) 297 In theyr sykenes..mynystryng vnto them with her owne handes. **1611** Bible *Mark* x. 45 The Sonne of man came not to bee ministred vnto, but to minister. **1667** Milton *P.L.* v. 444 Mean while at Table Eve Ministerd naked. **1732** Law *Serious C.* v. (ed. 2) 69 To assist, protect, and minister for them who shall be heirs of Salvation. **1816** J. Wilson *City of Plague* ii. iv. 131 For these three months, Hath she been ministering at the dying bed. **1866** G. Macdonald *Ann. Q. Neighb.* xvii. (1878) 342 Add to your kindness this day, by letting my wife and me minister to you.

9. To serve or officiate in worship; to act as a minister of the Church.

c **1330** R. Brunne *Chron.* (1810) 80 Þei ordeynd a couent, to ministre in þat kirke. *c* **1400** *Apol. Loll.* 11 If minstris of þe kirke wele not frely minster to hem þat þei [schuld?] frely minster to, not but if mony or oþer þing be ȝeuen to hem. **1521** Bp. Longland in Ellis *Orig. Lett.* Ser. iii. I. 252, I mynystred as my weykenes wold serve, in pontificalibus. **1563–83** Foxe *A. & M.* II. 1613/2 Such Byshops as Minister not, but Lord it. **1672–5** Comber *Comp. Temple* (1702) 53 While he that Ministred repeated this Office, all present were to joyn with him. **1710** Prideaux *Orig. Tithes* ii. 86 Who then Ministred in holy things. **1855** Milman *Lat. Chr.* (1864) xiv. vi. IX. 213 The Teutons..were compelled to possess one qualification, the power of ministering in that Latin Service.

10. To be helpful or serviceable; also, to be conducive, contribute *to* something.

1696 Whiston *Theory Earth* iv. (1722) 332 The Waters..were so dispos'd as to minister to his Necessities. **1711–12** Smalridge *12 Serm.* (1717) 343 Fasting is not Absolutely..Good, but Relatively, and as it ministers to Other Virtues. **1831** Lytton *Godolphin* 3, I ministered to their amusement. **1850** McCosh *Div. Govt.* ii. i. (1874) 137 The useful..ministers to the love of the beautiful.

Hence **'ministered** *ppl. a.*

c **1425** *Found. St. Bartholomew's* (E.E.T.S.) 31 Plenty of mynystryd grace from God.

minister, obs. form of minster.

ministeriable (mɪnɪˈstɪərɪəb(ə)l), *a. rare.* [f. ministeri(al *a.* + -able.] = ministrable *a.*

1923 J. A. Spender *Life H. Campbell-Bannerman* II. 127 His test of complete co-operation was that Lord Rosebery should be definitely within the circle of ministeriable ex-Ministers.

ministerial (ˌmɪnɪˈstɪərɪəl), *a.* and *sb.* [ad. F. *ministériel*, ad. med.L. *ministeriālis*, f. L. *ministerium* ministry. But the word appears to have been generally apprehended as a direct derivative of minister *sb.*, and this view of the etymology has influenced the sense.] **A.** *adj.*

1. Pertaining to, or entrusted with, the execution of the law, or of the commands of a superior; pertaining to or possessing delegated executive authority.

ministerial act: an act which is a necessary part of a person's official duty, or which is required by law in a given state of circumstances, so that the agent is exempt from responsibility for its propriety or consequences.

1577 tr. *Bullinger's Decades* (1592) 836 And there is also one sort of power which is free and absolute, and another sort of power which is limited, which is also called ministeriall. **1647** N. Bacon *Disc. Govt. Eng.* i. xxiii. (1739) 41 He was partly ministerial, and partly judicial. *a* **1680** Butler *Rem.* (1759) II. 104 He is but subordinate and ministerial to his Wife, who commands in chief. **1765** Blackstone *Comm.* I. 427 There is yet a fourth species of servants, if they may be so called, being rather in a superior, a ministerial, capacity; such as stewards, factors, and bailiffs. **1824** J. Marshall *Const. Opin.* (1839) 325 The warrant of a ministerial officer may authorize the collection of these penalties, &c. **1846** McCulloch *Acc. Brit. Empire* (1854) II. 221 The ministerial or executive duties of the sheriff are multifarious. **1863** H. Cox *Instit.* i. vii. 92 He..puts questions to the vote,..and performs various functions of a ministerial character.

2. Concerned as a subordinate agent, or as an instrument or means; subsidiary; instrumental.

1607 Topsell *Four-f. Beasts* (1658) Pref., As Life is the Ministerial Governor and Mover in this World, so is Learning the Ministerial Governor and Mover in Life. *a* **1619** Fotherby *Atheom.* i. xi. §4 (1622) 118 The most abiect and ministeriall parts of his body. *Ibid.* ii. i. §8. 186 Inferior and ministeriall Arts. **1665** Sir T. Herbert *Trav.* (1677) 238 Cyrus..with Harpagus..were ministerial together in the subduing Astyages. *a* **1674** Clarendon *Hist. Reb.* xiii. §7 The States of Holland thought they had merited much in suffering their ships to transport him, and so being ministerial to his greatness. **1713** Derham *Phys.-Theol.* iv. xi. 195 From the Teeth, the grand Instruments of Mastication, let us proceed to the other Ministerial Parts. **1840** De Quincey *Rhetoric* Wks. 1859 XI. 29 We may admit arts of style and ornamental composition as the ministerial part of rhetoric. *a* **1859** —— *Conversat.* Wks. 1860 XIV. 167 In speaking above of conversation, we have fixed our view on those uses of conversation which are ministerial to intellectual culture. *a* **1871** Grote *Eth. Fragm.* v. (1876) 136 The supreme, or architectonic, ends, are superior in eligibility to the subordinate, or ministerial.

3. Pertaining to the office, function, or character of a minister of religion.

1561 T. Norton *Calvin's Inst.* iv. vi. 34 There may be vnder hym [Christ] an other ministerial hed (as they terme it) that may be his vicegerent in earth. **1597** Hooker *Eccl. Pol.* v. lxxvii. §2 Ministeriall power is a marke of separation, because it seuereth them that haue it from other men. **1653** Milton *Hirelings* Wks. 1851 V. 347 It will not be deni'd that in the Gospel there be but two ministerial Degrees, Presbyters and Deacons. *a* **1716** Blackall *Wks.* (1723) I. 199 Not that 'tis lawful for any Man to invade the ministerial Office, who is not call'd and ordain'd thereto. **1894** H. Gardener *Unoff. Patriot* 65 The exigencies of his ministerial life had so far made it necessary for him to leave the plantation but twice.

4. Of or pertaining to a minister of state; of or belonging to or having relations with a public minister or ministry; siding with or supporting the Ministry as against the Opposition.

1655 Digges *Compl. Ambass.* Pref., The cheif ministerial parts lay upon Burleigh and Walsingham. **1735–8** Bolingbroke *On Parties* Ded. 21 There are Persons, who take to Themselves the Title of ministerial Writers. *Ibid.* 8 They who could never brook a Regal, will have the Merit of saving their Country from the Danger of a Ministerial Tyranny. **1747** H. Walpole *Lett.* (1846) II. 200 My connexions with anything ministerial are as little as possible. **1830** Ld. Valletort in *Hansard's Parl. Deb.* XXIV. 1233 Those who sat on the Ministerial side of the House. **1850** Ht. Martineau *Hist. Peace* v. i. (1877) III. 183 Parliament was to be dissolved on the first ministerial reverse. **1863** H. Cox *Instit.* iii. viii. 723 The supreme ministerial authority is delegated by the Crown to a Secretary of State. **1879** Gladstone *Gleanings* I. viii. 229 Ministerial responsibility comes between the Monarch and every public trial and necessity, like armour between the flesh and the spear. **1889** *Daily News* 14 May 3/3 Ministerial cries of 'Oh,' and cheers from the Irish members. **1969** *Sci. Jrnl.* Sept. 6 As an example of apparent ministerial unconcern he refers to recent exchanges in Parliament on this very problem. **1973** H. Trevelyan *Diplomatic Channels* i. 16 There are the 'grey eminences' in the corridors of power, who shun the light, who learn when to feed those dangerous animals, ministers, pacing up and down their party cages, who acquire an unrivalled knowledge of how government actually works beneath the misleading surface of ministerial responsibility. **1974** *Times* 19 Sept. 1/4 In a ministerial broadcast on all channels last night Mr Wilson said [etc.].

B. *sb.*

†**1.** *pl.* Subsidiary provisions. *Obs.*

1647 Trapp *Comm. Matt.* v. 18 The ministerials of this law shall pass away together with this life.

2. *Hist.* An executive household officer under the feudal system. (Cf. Du Cange s.v. *Ministeriales.*)

1818 Hallam *Mid. Ages* (1872) I. 182 Prelates and barons, who surrounded themselves with household officers called ministerials. **1849** Kemble *Saxons in Eng.* II. viii. 391 They [the clergy] were called upon to take their place with other landowners, lords, or ministerials in the popular councils.

ministerialism (ˌmɪnɪˈstɪərɪəlɪz(ə)m). [f. prec. + -ism.]

1. Partisanship of the ministry in power.

1830 *Fraser's Mag.* II. 258 His unbending ministerialism ..cut him off from Whig sympathy. **1873** *Daily News* 28 July 4/7 An exaggerated Ministerialism is ill met by an exaggerated sectarianism.

2. The ideas and conduct characteristic of a minister of religion.

1884 Fullerton in *Sword & Trowel* July 342 There are scores of men whose sole ambition seems to be to sink their manliness in ministerialism.

mini'sterialist. [f. MINISTERIAL *a.* + -IST.] A supporter of the Ministry in office.

1793 BURKE *Policy of Allies* Wks. VII. 152 *note*, This was the language of the ministerialists. **1820** W. IRVING in *Life & Lett.* (1864) I. xxvii. 455 The visitors are men of different politics, though most frequently ministerialists. **1882** *Times* 24 Oct. 9 Those Ministerialists who are not in office themselves.

ˌministeri'ality. *nonce-wd.* [f. MINISTERIAL *a.* + -ITY.] The quality or fact of being ministerial.

1858 DE QUINCEY *Language* Wks. IX. 95 It is a capital error, under the idea of its ministeriality, to undervalue this great organ of the advancing intellect.

ministerially (ˌmɪnɪ'stɪərɪəlɪ), *adv.* [f. MINISTERIAL *a.* + -LY².] In a ministerial manner or capacity; as a minister (in any sense of the word).

1601 DEACON & WALKER *Spirits & Divels* 145 The husbandman (by applying and mixing wheat with earth,) may ministerially be saide to bring foorth the said wheat. **1652** GAULE *Magastrom.* 207 Whether the good angels can do miracles? Ministerially and instrumentally they may, but not principally and authoritatively. **1752** J. GILL *Trinity* ii. 38 The angel of the Lord..spoke in his own name, and not ministerially in his who sent him. **1848** C. A. JOHNS *Week at Lizard* 201 My informant was called on to visit ministerially one of the..persons.., then..lying on his death-bed. **1885** *Law Times* 11 Apr. 421/1 [He] must have been acting judicially and ministerially.

mini'sterialness. *rare.* [f. MINISTERIAL *a.* + -NESS.] The quality of being ministerial.

1836 PUSEY in Liddon, etc. *Life* (1893) I. xvii. 401 The Ministerialness of the act consists in that it has pleased God that the absolution should be conveyed through a minister.

ministerie, obs. form of MINISTRY.

ministering ('mɪnɪstərɪŋ), *vbl. sb.* [f. MINISTER *v.* + -ING¹.] The action of the verb MINISTER; ministration, administration.

c **1380** WYCLIF *Sel. Wks.* III. 437 Prests shulden have betere ordre in minstryng of sacraments. **1530** PALSGR. 583/1, I heale one by mynystrynge of medycines to hym, *je medicine.* **1611** BIBLE *Rom.* xii. 7 Or ministery, let vs wait, on our ministring. **1824** LAMB *Elia* Ser. II. *Capt. Jackson*, The anxious ministerings about you. **1901** *Macm. Mag.* Apr. 412/2 The Church of Ireland clergy as a rule do a deal of ministering to the Roman Catholic sick and poor.

attrib. **1535** COVERDALE *1 Chron.* x. 28 Some of them had the ouersight of the mynistrynge vessell. **1566** (*title*) A briefe discourse against the outwarde apparrell and ministring garments of the Popishe church.

ministering ('mɪnɪstərɪŋ), *ppl. a.* [f. MINISTER *v.* + -ING².] That ministers or serves; serving as a subordinate agent; performing helpful services; administering, officiating; esp. in phr. ***ministering angel***: *spec.* a kind-hearted person, usu. a woman, who helps and comforts people in distress; freq. a nurse.

1535 COVERDALE *Heb.* i. 14 Are they [*sc.* Angels] not all mynistrynge spretes? **1602** SHAKS. *Ham.* v. i. 263 A Ministring Angell shall my Sister be. **1654** JER. TAYLOR *Real Pres.* 71 The Greek Church universally taught that the Consecration was made by the prayers of the ministring man. **1764** FOOTE *Mayor of G.* I. Wks. 1799 I. 162 Is it your Worship's will that I lend a ministring hand to the maim'd? **1808** SCOTT *Marm.* VI. 30 O Woman!.. When pain and anguish wring the brow, A ministering angel thou! **1886** A. WEIR *Hist. Basis Mod. Eur.* (1889) 27 Though despotic, [both monarchs] were conscious of the ministering nature of their office. **1912** 'SAKI' *Chron. Clovis* 223 Martin Stoner rose heavily to his feet and followed his ministering angel along a passage..into a large room lit with a cheerfully blazing fire. **1922** JOYCE *Ulysses* 349 A sterling good daughter was Gerty just like a second mother in the house, a ministering angel too with a little heart worth its weight in gold. **1924** A. HUXLEY *Little Mexican* 140 Emmy was good, was kind, a ministering angel. **1931** M. D. GEORGE *England in Transition* iv. 92 Nurses paid by the parish—creatures compared with whom Mrs. Gamp would have been almost a ministering angel. **1956** F. F. DARLING *Pelican in Wilderness* i. 10 Such detached thought as I could muster was of feeling sorry for the air hostess. She remained throughout the gentle ministering angel, imperturbable as she picked her way through the shambles. **1974** W. FOLEY *Child in Forest* II. 188 She came in her nurse's uniform, and I thought 'ministering angel' a very apt description.

‖**ministerium** (mɪnɪ'stɪərɪəm). *Eccl.* [L.: see MINISTRY.]

1. (See quot.)

1858 *Direct. Angl.* 233 *Ministerium*, the Epistle corner of the altar. So called from the Sacred Ministers preparing the chalice, &c., there when the elements are removed from the credence.

2. The body of ordained ministers of the Lutheran church in any district, charged with the ruling of the congregation and the selection of candidates for clerical preferment.

1881 *Philad. Record* No. 3457. 1 In to-day's session of the Lutheran Ministerium a report on Muhlenberg College showed [etc.]. **1882–3** *Schaff's Encycl. Relig. Knowl.* III. 2126 Schmuker, S. S...was admitted into the ministry by the Lutheran Ministerium of Pennsylvania in 1820.

ministership ('mɪnɪstəʃɪp). [f. MINISTER *sb.* + -SHIP.] The office of a minister; the position or fact of being a minister.

1565 JEWEL *Def. Apol.* (1611) 412 How vainely you snap ..now at our Superintendentships: now at our Ministerships. **1742** H. WALPOLE *Lett. to Mann* 3 Mar. (1857) I. 137 Think of his talking of making it dangerous for anyone else to accept the first ministership! **1863** *Daily Tel.* 8 Oct., We are obliged to write of Sir James Hudson's Ministership as a thing of the past. **1872** *Daily News* 1 Oct. 5, I am not a footman, and the ministership you would give me under a régime such as this would be a menial office.

ministery, obs. form of MINISTRY.

ministrable ('mɪnɪstrəb(ə)l), *a.* and *sb.* [a. F. *ministrable* in the same sense: cf. -ABLE.]

A. *adj.* Fit or likely to become a minister; = CABINETABLE *a.* **B.** *sb.* One who is likely or hopes to become a minister.

In quot. 1968 a use of the Fr. word.

1921 *Contemp. Rev.* Mar. 289 The anti-British feeling [in France]..oozes out of declarations by Ministers and Ministrable politicians. **1927** *Blackw. Mag.* Feb. 277/2 Those that are ministrables have done the best for themselves. **1968** *Economist* 9 Mar. 53/2 The *ministrables* were more inclined to vote for the government than against it.

†**ministral**, *a. Obs. rare.* [a. F. *ministral*, L. *ministrāl-is*, f. L. *minister*: see MINISTER *sb.* and -AL¹.] Pertaining to a minister or agent.

1727 BAILEY vol. II, *Ministral*, belonging to a minister. **1851** G. S. FABER *Many Mansions* 105 When our Bodies shall be glorified, they will be capable..of a divestment of their glory, should such a divestment be..necessary for accomplishing the ministral purposes of the Deity.

ministralle, obs. form of MINSTREL.

ministrant ('mɪnɪstrənt), *a.* and *sb.* [a. L. *ministrant-em*, pr. pple. of *ministrāre* to MINISTER.]

A. *adj.* That ministers. Const. *to.*

1667 MILTON *P.L.* x. 87 Him Thrones and Powers, Princedoms, and Dominations ministrant Accompanied to Heaven Gate. **1718** POPE *Odyss.* x. 413 Ministrant to their Queen, with busy care Four faithful handmaids the soft rites prepare. **1805** SOUTHEY *Madoc in W.* xii, The place To that despondent mood was ministrant. **1871** B. TAYLOR *Faust* (1875) I. i. 31 The sweet, consoling chant, Which, through the night of Death, the angels ministrant Sang.

B. *sb.* One who ministers.

1818 KEATS *Endym.* I. 285 Strange ministrant of undescribed sounds. **1874** S. COX *Pilgr. Ps.* xv. 323 The heavenly ministrants do, we know, look down on us with.. compassion. **1884** BROWNING *Founder of Feast* 14 When, night by night..Music was poured by perfect ministrants. **1885** *L'pool Daily Post* 23 Oct. 4/7 Ministrants at the altar.

†**'ministrate**, *v. Obs.* Also *pa. pple.* 6–7 *Sc.* ministrat(e. [f. L. *ministrāt-*, ppl. stem of *ministrāre* to MINISTER.]

1. *trans.* To administer.

1533 BELLENDEN tr. *Livy* III. xvi. (S.T.S.) II. 8 M. Claudius had complenit a litill þat na Iustice was ministrate to him. **1559** in Tytler *Hist. Scotl.* (1864) III. 391 Their minister shall have full liberty..to ministrate the sacraments, publicly and privately. **1639** MARQ. HAMILTON *Explan. Meaning Oath & Covenant* 12 [They] refuse the participation of the holy sacraments as they are now ministrate. **1727** BAILEY vol. II, *To Ministrate*, to minister or serve.

2. *intr.* To minister *to.*

1887 BROWNING *Parleyings, Furini* 154 Learn how they ministrate to life and death.

ministration (ˌmɪnɪ'streɪʃən). [ad. L. *ministrātiōn-em*, n. of action f. *ministrāre* to MINISTER. Cf. obs. F. *ministracion* (14th c.).]

1. The action (*rarely*, an act) of ministering or serving; the rendering of aid or service.

a **1340** HAMPOLE *Psalter, Cant.* 524 Grete thing he did til hur in quantite of grace, gretter in mynystracyon of Aungell. **1382** WYCLIF *2 Cor.* iii. 7–8 If the mynistracioun of deeth defformyd by lettris in stoones was in glorie..hou not more the mynistracioun of spirit schal be in glorie? **1560** DAUS tr. *Sleidane's Comm.* 49 b, Let them not be covetous, nor for theyr ministration extorte money gredelye. *a* **1683** OWEN *True Nat. Gosp. Ch.* Wks. 1853 XVI. 110 Ministration unto the poor of the Church, for the supply of their temporal necessities is an ordinance of Christ. **1712** M. HENRY *Daily Commun.* II. (1847) 126 What a security is the ministration of those good spirits against the malice of evil spirits! **1875** JOWETT *Plato* I. 206 Nor is any one to be blamed for doing any honourable service or ministration to any man.

†**b.** Exercise of official functions. *Obs.*

1651 HOBBES *Govt. & Soc.* x. §15. 162 Content with the nomination of Magistrates, and publique Ministers, that is to say, with the authority without the ministration.

†**c.** Agency, instrumentality. *Obs.*

1398 TREVISA *Barth. De P.R.* IV. iv. (1495) 85 The vertues of the spirites werke their effectes in al the lymmes of the body by mynystracion and seruyse of humours. **1555** EDEN *Decades* 80 What so euer god by the ministration of nature hath created.

2. *spec.* The action of ministering in religious matters; service as a priest or minister; *pl.* the services of ministers of religion.

1535 COVERDALE *Acts* i. 17 For he was nombred with vs & had opteyned the felashippe of this mynistracion. **1548–9** [see MINISTRY 3]. **1660** SOUTH *Serm.* (1727) IV. i. 62 At the thirtieth Year of their Age they began their Levitical Ministration. **1841** A. R. C. DALLAS *Past. Superintend.* 5 A snare had long been spread for us..leading us to injure our means of usefulness, through a depreciation of order in our ministrations. **1884** *Law Times* 14 June 122/2 There should be a provision for religious ministrations.

†**b.** A ministerial office or employment. *Obs.*

1550 CROWLEY *Waie to Wealth* (E.E.T.S.) 145 Ye have benefices, or other spirituall promotions, as you call theym, for ye are ashamed to call them ministracions.

†**3.** The action of administering the sacraments, justice, law, an estate or revenue, etc.; administration; *occas.* executorship. *Obs.*

c **1340** HAMPOLE *Prose Tr.* (1866) 25 Thes holy menne lefte not witterly the ministracion of the lokynge and the dispendynge of worldely goodis. **1422** *E.E. Wills* (E.E.T.S.) 50, I wole þat he haue hem vpon this condicion,..þat he lete hem note off ministration of myn other goode. **1432–50** tr. *Higden* (Rolls) V. 109 The ministracion of baptym and of beryenge. **1439** *E.E. Wills* (E.E.T.S.) 128 Wich of hem as laboureth for the execucion of his will, and taketh vpon him mynystracion shall [etc.]. **1442** *Rolls of Parlt.* V. 57/1 The ministration of the revenuez. **1512** *Act 4 Hen. VIII*, c. 20 *Preamble*, Your true Subgectes beyng in Compeny with hym for mynystracion of your lawes. **1527** *Rastell's Abridg. Stat.* 99 b, Any other that take vppon them the mynystracion of the forest. **1533** MORE *Debell. Salem* Wks. 1023/1 Their authorite in ministracion of the sacramentes. *c* **1550** COVERDALE *Calvin's Treat. Sacram.* etc. F j b, The mynistracion of holye baptime. *Ibid.*, The due ministracyon of holy wedloke. **1579** FULKE *Heskins' Parl.* 309 Many corruptions, that were crept into the Church about the ministration of the cup.

4. The action of supplying, providing, or giving (something). Const. *of.*

1460–70 *Bk. Quintessence* 15 þanne comforte him wiþ ministracioun of oure quinte essencie afore seid. **1547** BOORDE *Brev. Health* 2 The ministracion of phisicke. **1862** TYNDALL *Mountaineer.* i. 3 The ministration of unwholesome food. **1873** BROWNING *Red Cott. Nt.-cap* 184 Yours the care That any world..be easy of access Through ministration of the moneys due.

ministrative ('mɪnɪstreɪtɪv), *a.* [ad. L. **ministrātīv-us*, f. *ministrāre*: see MINISTER *v.* and -IVE.] Pertaining to or of the nature of ministration; affording service or assistance.

1833 J. H. NEWMAN *Arians* I. v. (1876) 125 His ministrative office in the revealed Economy of the Godhead. **1850** GLADSTONE *Homer* II. 105 When Minerva alters the personal appearance of Telemachus, [etc.]..she uses no sign or ministrative act.

ministrator ('mɪnɪstreɪtə(r)). *rare.* [a. L. *ministrātor*, agent-n. f. *ministrāre*: see MINISTER *v.*] One who ministers or administers; †a testamentary executor.

1523 FITZHERB. *Husb.* §165 Prayer..must nedes be done in the chyrche by the mynystratours of the same before the people. **1559** *Richmond Wills* (Surtees) 132 Whome I maike juntly together executores and ministratores of yis my last wyll and testament. **1598** *Durham Wills* (Surtees No. 38) 332 Widowe Maire,..lawfull ministrator to hir laite husband. **1654** R. CODRINGTON tr. *Iustine* XIII. 208 Who would therefore wonder that the world should be conquered by such ministrators. *a* **1734** NORTH *Exam.* (1740) 74 The Law, and the Ministrators of it. **1884** *Schaff's Encycl. Relig. Knowl.* s.v. *Angels*, They were the ministrators of the law.

†**ministra'toriously**, *adv. Obs. rare*⁻¹. [f. late L. *ministrātōri-us* (see next) + -OUS + -LY².] In the capacity of an administrator.

1563–83 FOXE *A. & M.* I. 432/1 A man cannot onely ministratoriously geue any temporal or continuall gift, eyther as well to his naturall sonne, as to his sonne by imitation.

†**ministratory**, *a. Obs. rare*⁻¹. [ad. L. *ministrātōri-us*, f. *ministrātor*, agent-n. f. *ministrāre*: see MINISTER *v.* and -ORY.] Having the function of ministering.

1625 GODWIN *Moses & Aaron* (1655) 255 To shew his ministratory office.

ministre, -trele, obs. ff. MINISTER, MINSTREL.

ministrer ('mɪnɪstrə(r)). [f. MINISTER *v.* + -ER¹.] One who ministers or serves.

?**14..** in *Wars Eng. in France* (1864) II. 525 Officers royalle and mynystroures belongyng aftir the custome of Fraunce. **1509–10** *Act 1 Hen. VIII*, c. 16 §1 Wages due..to the Officers and Ministrours of the same. **1530** PALSGR. 245/2 Mynistrer of justyce, *droicturier.* **1836** *New Monthly Mag.* XLVIII. 219 My business is not with the 'sincere and conscientious' ministrer of comfort.

ministress ('mɪnɪstrɪs). [f. MINISTER *sb.* + -ESS. Cf. F. *ministresse* (Cotgr.).] A woman who ministers or serves. Also *transf.* and *fig.*

1600 *Hosp. Incur. Fooles* a j, Nature (diuine ministresse) contending..to imprint in them the seale and forme of Diuinitie. **1662** J. SPARROW tr. *Behme's Rem. Wks., Apol. conc. Perfect.* 48 It should, as a Noble Ministresse or Maid of Honour to its Bridegroom the Soul, draw the Soul thereunto. **1744** AKENSIDE *Pleas. Imag.* I. 373 Thus was Beauty sent from heaven, The lovely ministress of truth and good In this dark world. **1891** C. E. NORTON *Dante's Hell* xxix. 159 The ministress of the High Lord—infallible Justice.

ministring, obs. form of MINISTERING.

ministry ('mɪnɪstrɪ). Forms: 4 mynysterye, -ie, mynysterie, minstri, 5–6 mynistery, 5–8 ministery, 6 mynystry, ministeree, minstrie, -y, 6–7 ministerie, -trie, 8 ministrey, 6– ministry. [ME. *ministerie*, ad. L. *ministerium* office, service, f. *minister*: see MINISTER *sb.* Cf. F. *ministère* (16th

c.), Pr. *ministeri*, Sp., Pg., It. *ministerio*. Cf. MISTER *sb.*[1]]

1. The action of ministering; the rendering of service; the performance of any office or labour for another. Now only in religious use or coloured by association with this.

1382 WYCLIF *Ezek.* xliv. 14, I shal ȝeue hem porters of the hous, in al the mynysterie therof. *c* **1450** tr. *De Imitatione* III. xi. 78 þou hast ordeined also angels in to mannys mynistery. **1526** *Pilgr. Perf.* (W. de W. 1531) 257 b, More pleasaunt was to hym yᵉ poore seruyce of his mortall creatures than shold haue ben yᵉ gloryous mynystery of aungels. *c* **1555** HARPSFIELD *Divorce Hen. VIII* (Camden) 245 That woman doth not pertain to matrimony with whom..there was no matrimonial ministry. **1576** FLEMING *Panopl. Epist.* 354 The Oxe is a fellowe labourer with his maister,..so that wee finde speciall benefites redounding to vs, by and through the vse of their ministerie. **1681–6** J. SCOTT *Chr. Life* (1747) III. 379 Another of those Ministries which Princes are obliged to render his Church, is, to chasten and correct the irregular and disorderly Members of it. **1777** ROBERTSON *Hist. Amer.* v. (1778) II. 112 People who were unacquainted with the ministry of domestic animals, or the aid of machines, to facilitate any work of labour. **1892** TENNYSON in *Mem.* (1897) II. 421 My idea of heaven is the perpetual ministry of one soul to another.

†**2.** A mode or kind of service; a specific department of usefulness; a function, office. *Obs.*

1432–50 tr. *Higden* (Rolls) III. 461 Whiche suppose benefites grauntede to vs for necessites as thynges grevous, seyenge þe ministerys of artes as wickede thynges, destroyenge at the laste the lawes off lyvynge. **1546** LANGLEY *Pol. Verg. De Invent.* Pref. 5 They that have excogitated..any..handy craftes or ministeries to the maintenance, aid and comfort of the Body. **1553** BALE *Vocac.* 9 b, From the shippe, from yᵉ costomehowse, & from other homily ministerys, called he not yᵉ stought, sturdye & heady sort of men. **1635–56** COWLEY *Davideis* II. *note* 30 The daughters of Cocalus washt Minos at his arrival in Sicilie. But the more ordinary, was to have young and beautiful servants for this and the like ministeries. **1644** MILTON *Areop.* (Arb.) 75 It is not possible for man to sever the wheat from the tares..; that must be the Angels Ministery at the end of mortall things.

3. The functions, or any specific function, pertaining to a minister of religion; the action, or an act, of ministering in holy things.

1382 WYCLIF *Col.* iv. 17 Se the mynisterie, that thou hast takun of the Lord, that thou fulfille it. *c* **1400** *Apol. Loll.* 32 It semiþ þat God enioniþ to doctors and dekunis þe minstri of presthed, and of dekunhed, þat are riȝtful. **1432–50** tr. *Higden* (Rolls) IV. 405 Seynte Petyr ordeynede ij. bischoppes at Rome, other ij. helperes to hym..to fullefille the ministery off pristes to the peple. **1548–9** (Mar.) *Bk. Com. Prayer, Communion* (Rubric), The Priest that shal execute the holy ministery, shall put upon hym the vesture appoincted for that ministracion. **1581** MARBECK *Bk. of Notes* 602 In the Baptime, the outward ministerie or mysticall washing doth regenerate. **1612** T. WILSON *Chr. Dict.*, To Prophesie sig[nifieth]..to bee present at the publicke ministry, and partake in the Doctrine thereof. **1635** SWAN *Spec. M.* (1670) 311 A certain Priest..was suspended from his ministry at the Altar. **1667** MILTON *P.L.* VII. 149 This high Temple to frequent With Ministeries due and solemn Rites. **1704** NELSON *Fest. & Fasts* I. xi. (1705) 133 Whereas the other Apostles chose this or that Province as the main Sphere of their Ministry, St. Paul over-ran as it were the whole Roman Empire. **1868** W. B. MARRIOTT (*title*) Vestiarivm Christianvm. The Origin and Gradual Development of the Dress of Holy Ministry in the Church.

†**b.** A ministerial office or charge. *Obs.*

1588 J. UDALL *Demonstr. Discipl.* ii. (Arb.) 24 A minister ought not to be ordained before there be a ministery whervnto he is to be allotted.

c. The ministration of a particular minister.

1623 N. ROGERS *Str. Vineyard* 168 Many who haue heard the Word with thee, beene of the same Parish, vnder the same Ministery. **1879** GEO. ELIOT *Theo. Such* ii. 50 The roofs that have looked out..below the square stone steeple, gathering their..olive-green mosses under all ministries.

d. The office of minister of the church, or of a religious body or congregation.

1824 SCOTT *St. Ronan's* xvi, A weak constitution.. induced his parents..to educate him for the ministry. **1845** S. AUSTIN *Ranke's Hist. Ref.* II. 37 He was reproached with having intruded himself uncalled into the ministry. **1900** *Daily News* 11 Dec. 11/3 The Rev. A. B. has retired from the ministry of the M — Congregational Church.

e. The body of men set apart for spiritual functions in the Christian church or in any religious community. Now *rare.*

1566 *Reg. Privy Council Scot.* I. 494 Hes assignit for sustentatioun of the said ministerie certane victuales and money..to be tane up and disponit be the said Ministerie and thair Collectouris or Chalmerlanis. *a* **1578** LINDESAY (Pitscottie) *Chron. Scot.* (S.T.S.) II. 315 The maist pairt of the nobilitie and ministrie var in Edinburgh. **1604** E. G[RIMSTONE] *D'Acosta's Hist. Indies* v. xiii. 364 There were in them [*sc.* temples] places for the ministerie, colleges, schooles, and houses for priests. **1659** SOUTH *Serm.* (1727) I. iii. 84 We have Christ consulting the Propagation of the Gospel;..sending forth a Ministry, and giving them a Commission. **1847–54** in WEBSTER. [And in later Dicts.] **1848** A. THOMSON *Orig. Secess. Ch.* 164 Patronage..was the most effective instrument of placing a hireling ministry in the pulpits of Scotland.

4. The condition or fact of being employed as an executive agent or instrument; agency, instrumentality. Now only with religious colouring.

1581 LAMBARDE *Eiren.* I. v. (1588) 28 All others..be ordained by the meane of the great Seale, and by the ministerie of the L. Chauncellor. **1672** CAVE *Prim. Chr.* III. ii. (1673) 264 Not by the Ministery of her servants..but with her own hands. **1705** ATTERBURY *Serm.* 28 Oct. 29 The Ordinary Ministry of Second Causes. *a* **1718** PARNELL *Hermit* 231 'Twas my Ministry to deal the Blow. **1753** SMOLLETT *Ct. Fathom* (1784) 44/1 The messenger, doubly rejoiced at her atchievement, which not only recommended her ministry, but also gratified her malice, returned to her principal. **1817** COLERIDGE *Biog. Lit.* xii. (1882) 120 This becomes intelligible to no man by the ministry of mere words from without. **1891** A. PHELPS *Note-Bk.* i. 24 Heroic believers become such by the ministry of heroic pains.

†**b.** (Good or bad) conduct as an executive agent. *Obs.*

1700 TYRRELL *Hist. Eng.* II. 894 The Kingdom..felt the Effects of their ill Ministery.

5. The body of ministers charged with the administration of a country or state. †In the 18th c. often used without article.

1710–11 SWIFT *Lett.* (1767) III. 83 The ministry hear me always with appearance of regard. **1779** WILKES *Corr.* (1805) V. 213 You told him, that you had voted with ministry as long as any man of honour could. **1791** BURKE *App. Whigs* Wks. VI. 145 A Whig ministry, and a whig house of commons. **1795** —— *Regic. Peace* iii. Wks. VIII. 324 The parliament has assented to ministry; it is not ministry that has obeyed the impulse of parliament. *a* **1859** MACAULAY *Hist. Eng.* xxiv. (1861) V. 124 The date from which the era of ministries may most properly be reckoned is the day of the meeting of the Parliament after the general election of 1695. **1865** LD. IDDESLEIGH *Lect. & Ess.* (1887) 251 The Cabal Ministry were in power. **1879** MᶜCARTHY *Own Times* xxiii. II. 186 Their existence as a Ministry was only a question of days.

b. The name given to certain departments of the British government.

1916 *Whitaker's Almanack* 223/2 Munitions, Ministry of, Minister, Rt. Hon. D. Lloyd George, M.P. **1942** *R.A.F. Jrnl.* 18 Apr. 24 The Ministry of Food announces that the milk ration for children will be increased. **1963** *Listener* 28 Feb. 368/1 It [*sc.* the Treasury] has also done hitherto the work of a ministry of economic affairs. *Ibid.* 7 Mar. 422/1 The Ministries of the three Services are to be reorganized under a unified Ministry of Defence. **1968** *Times* 16 Dec. 7/1 An attempt at a Ministry takeover and a threat to a much valued independence.

6. With reference to foreign nations: A ministerial department of government; a minister and his associated subordinates. Also, the building in which the business of a (specified) government department is transacted.

1877 D. M. WALLACE *Russia* (ed. 2) I. 302 Immediately below these three institutions stand the Ministries, ten in number. *Ibid.* 305 The Governor..is the local representative of the Ministry of the Interior.

7. *Hist.* The name applied to the houses of certain religious orders. [med.L. *ministerium.*]

1889 W. LOCKHART *Ch. Scot. in 13th C.* 25 *note*, Their [the Red Friars'] houses were called hospitals or ministries.

ˈministryship. *rare*$^{-1}$. [f. MINISTRY + -SHIP.] The office of a minister of state.

1730 PULTENEY in *Swift's Lett.* (1768) IV. 249, I suppose it is not yet in your view to entail the ministryship in your family.

minitabund (ˈmɪnɪtəbʌnd), *a. rare*$^{-1}$. [ad. L. *minitābund-us* threatening, f. *minitā-rī*, frequentative f. *minārī* to threaten.] Threatening.

1890 *Sat. Rev.* 14 June 720/2 Mr. Stanley, who passes, minitabund to Lord Salisbury, throughout the land.

minitant (ˈmɪnɪtənt), *a. rare*$^{-1}$. [ad. L. *minitant-em*, pr. pple. of *minitārī*: see prec.] Threatening, forming a menace.

1854 R. G. LATHAM *Native Races Russian Emp.* 327 Azov was made into a naval arsenal, minitant to the Crimea.

minite, obs. form of MINUTE *sb.*

†**ˈminitive,** *a. Obs. rare*$^{-1}$. [aphetic form of DIMINUTIVE.] Diminutive.

1602 *Narcissus* (1893) 425 Loves little minitive god.

minitrack (ˈmɪnɪtræk). Also **Minitrack.** [f. *mini*mum-weight *track*ing.] A system for tracking satellites in which a very light-weight oscillator is fixed in the satellite and its position is calculated from the phase difference between radio signals received by each of a spaced pair of fixed aerials on the ground. Usu. *attrib.*

1956 *Spaceflight* I. 27/2 A system of radio triangulation, called Minitrack, using phase comparison techniques, will establish the satellite's position and orbital path. *Ibid.* 28/1 Minitrack will enable a limited amount of research information to be telemetered to earth. **1958** *Observer* 2 Feb. 1/3 The minitrack stations have highly sensitive directional antennae which can 'focus' on the satellite. They also collect on tape recorders all the information it transmits. **1961** *Daily Tel.* 18 Jan. 20/4 One of two remote-controlled rotating aerials at the minitrack radio tracking station at Winkfield, Berks, which is now nearly ready to go into operation. **1966** *McGraw-Hill Encycl. Sci. & Technol.* VIII. 504/1 A two-axis Minitrack system was constructed so as to measure the north-south and east-west angular positions simultaneously. **1974** G. PERRY in H. Miles *Artificial Satellite Observing* vii. 145 The NASA Minitrack system provides directional observations with an accuracy of about 100 seconds of arc.

miniture, obs. form of MINIATURE.

minium (ˈmɪnɪəm). *Obs.* exc. *Hist.* [a. L. *minium* native cinnabar; also, red lead.]

1. = VERMILION. Also *attrib.*

1398 TREVISA *Barth. De P.R.* XIX. xxvi. (1495) 878 Minium is a red colour and the Grekis founde the matere therof in Ephesym. In Spayne is more suche pigment than in other londes. **1604** E. G[RIMSTONE] *D'Acosta's Hist. Indies* IV. xi. 238 The Antients made great accompt of this Minium or vermillion, holding it for a sacred colour. **1866** H. SHAW *Art Illum.* 2 The use of minium, or vermilion, in marking..particular words of manuscripts, is of very high antiquity.

2. = RED LEAD. Sometimes ***red minium.*** Also, †the colour of red lead.

1650 J. F. *Chym. Dict.*, *Minium* is the Mercury or rather Crocus of Lead precipitated. **1665** HOOKE *Microgr.* 52 White, Yellow, Orange, Minium, Scarlet, Purple. **1686** AGLIONBY *Painting Illustr.* 133 In a little Book of Designs.. I have..two or three little Things of his in Red Minium. **1732** J. PEELE *Water-Colours* 38 The Minium, or Red Lead, is as heavy and strong a Colour as most we have. **1806** SMITHSON in *Phil. Trans.* XCVI. 267, I have found minium native in the earth. **1882** A. S. HERSCHEL in *Nature* No. 642. 362 One or two ounces of powdered minium, or red-lead.

3. *transf.* Red earthy matter resembling minium.

1613 PURCHAS *Pilgrimage* (1614) 90 The winds..doe.. carry downe alongst the streame a great quantitie of that red Earth or Minium of Libanus whereby it passeth. **1703** MAUNDRELL *Journ. Jerus.* (1732) 35 A sort of Minium, or red Earth, washed into the River.

miniver (ˈmɪnɪvə(r)). Forms: 3 **menivieyr, menuver,** 3–5 **menyvere,** 3–4, 7–8 **meniver,** 4 **meyneveir, menevayr, -veyr, -voir, menivere, menuveyr, -voyr, menyvaire,** 4–5 **menevere, menyver,** 5–6 **menever, mynever,** 6 **miniveere,** 6, 9 **minivere,** 6–9 **minever,** 7 **minerver,** 7, 9 *dial.* **minifer, -fa,** 9 **mineveer,** 6– **miniver.** [a. F. *menu vair* (14th c. in Godef.), 'the furre Mineuer; also, the beast that beares it' (Cotgr.); lit. 'little vair' (*menu*:—L. *minūtus* MINUTE *a.*, and *vair*: see VAIR).]

1. A kind of fur used as a lining and trimming in ceremonial costume.

French lexicographers say that *menu vair* is the fur of the *petit-gris*, a variety of the common squirrel. What the Eng. *miniver* meant in early use is uncertain; some have supposed that it was the white fur of the Siberian squirrel; the application may have varied at different times, but etymology would suggest that it must have been an artificially spotted or variegated fur, with a smaller pattern than that of *vair*. In 1688 R. Holme explains *miniver* as 'plain white fur', and this (notwithstanding Cotgrave's divergent explanation) may have been the meaning of the word as used with reference to the costume of judges and the lower nobility in the 16–17th c. In this sense the term was revived in the official regulations for the coronation of Edward VII, and it has since had some currency in the description of the ceremonial costume of peers.

pured miniver, miniver pure = AF. *meniver puré*, 'powdered miniver'; but in modern times the adj. has been misinterpreted as 'pure white'.

a **1300** *Floris & Bl.* 515 (Hausknecht) A mantel of scarlet Ipaned al wiþ meniver. **1377** LANGL. *P. Pl.* B. xx. 137 For a mantel of menyuere he made lele matrimonye Departen ar deth cam. *a* **1450** *Knt. de la Tour* (1868) 65 Her good and gay clothing and furres of gray[,] meniuere and letuse. **1463–4** *Rolls of Parlt.* V. 505/1 Furres of Mattrones, Funes, Letyce, pured Grey, or pured Menyver. **1470–85** MALORY *Arthur* XII. i. 593 A lykely knyghte and wel apparaylled in scarlet furred with myneuer. *a* **1548** HALL *Chron., Hen. VIII* 214 The knightes of the bath in Violet gounes with hoddes purfeled with Miniuer lyke doctors. **1593** DRAYTON *Ecl.* iv. 178 His Hood of Miniveere. **1611** COTGR. s.v. *Vair, Menu Vair*, Mineuer; the furre of Ermines mixed, or spotted, with the furre of the Weesell called *Gris*. **1647** WARD *Simp. Cobler* 76 It seems in fashion for you to..dapple your speeches with new quodled words. Ermins in Minifer is every mans Coat. **1688** R. HOLME *Armoury* III. iii. 50/2 They [*sc.* Viscounts] have no Ermine on their Mantles, but three doublings of Miniver, or plain White Furr, the Baron having but two on the cape of his Mantle. **1766** ENTICK *London* IV. 33 If they be of Cambridge, they wear white meniver. **1867** JEAN INGELOW *Story Doom* VI. 214 And served in gold, and warmed with minivere. **1901** *Lond. Gaz.* 4 Oct. 6477 That the robe or mantle of the Peers be of crimson velvet, edged with miniver, the cape furred with miniver pure, and powdered with bars or rows of ermine (*i.e.*, narrow pieces of black fur).

¶ Recent Dicts. attribute to the word the sense that belongs to *menu vair* in Fr. heraldry, viz. a fur distinguished from *vair* in that the shield *menu vair* has six rows of spots instead of four. But this use has never been recognized in English heraldry.

2. †**a.** The animal from which the fur was supposed to be obtained (*obs.*). **b.** *dial.* The stoat or ermine, *Mustela erminea*, when wearing its white winter coat.

1665 SIR T. HERBERT *Trav.* (1677) 189 Furs of Foxes, Sables,..Miniver, Beaver, Otter, Squirrel and the like. *a* **1825** FORBY *Voc. E. Anglia*, *Minifer*, the white stoat or ermin. **1895** P. H. EMERSON *Birds*, etc., *Norf.* 345 In winter, of course, he [*sc.* the stoat] is often white, with a black tip to his tail—hence his name of 'minifa'. **1895** *Daily News* 27 Nov. 6/3 To this day the white stoat is called 'minifer' in Norfolk.

3. *attrib.* and *Comb.*, as ***miniver cap, hood, mantle, skin.***

1589 RIDER *Bibl. Schol.*, A *Menever cappe, *redimiculum*. **1600** DEKKER *Gentle Craft* Wks. 1873 I. 72 Shall Sim Eyre learne to speake of you Lady Maggy? vanish mother Mineuer-Cap. **1632** MASSINGER *City Madam* IV. iv, You wore..sometimes A dainty Miniver cap. **1393** LANGL. *P. Pl.* C. XXIII. 138 For a *menyuer mantel he made leel matrimonye Departe er deþ come. **1656** EARL MONM. tr.

Boccalini's Advts. fr. Parnass. I. x. (1674) 12 *Minerver-skins, Sables, and other very pretious Furrs.

minivet ('mɪnɪvɪt). [Etym. obscure.] Any bird of the campophagine genus *Pericrocotus*.

1862 JERDON *Birds of India* I. 418 The Red Shrikes or Minivets (as Mr. Blyth has called them in the Museum Asiatic Society). *Ibid.* 425, I have found this Minivet extensively spread throughout India. **187.** *Cassell's Nat. Hist.* IV. 30 The Grey Minivet (*Pericrocotus cinereus*). **1880** A. R. WALLACE *Isl. Life* iii. 44 The brilliant little minivets are almost equally universal.

mink (mɪŋk). Also 5–6 mynk(e, 8 minck, 8–9 minx. [Found in Sw. as *mänk, menk*, 'a stinking animal in Finland'. (The word is app. not known as Finnish.)]

1. The skins or fur of the animals mentioned below (see sense 2); a garment made of this fur.

1466 *Mann. & Househ. Exp.* (Roxb.) 371 My mastyr bout of the skynner of Bury xx. mynkes prise xiij.s. viij.d. **1530** PALSGR. 245/2 Mynkes a furre, *minques*. **1545** *Lanc. Wills* (1857) II. 63 My gowne faced withe mynkys and welted withe tawnye velvet. **1707** E. CHAMBERLAYNE *Pres. St. Eng.* III. ii. 256 Of Furrs, Filches,.. Mincks, Sables, 40 Skins is a Timber. **1883** *Harper's Mag.* Dec. 90/1 The bewitching little muff trimmed with mink. **1951** F. LOESSER in Swerling & Burrows *Guys & Dolls* (1960) II. i. 44 (*song-title*) Take back your mink. *Ibid.* 45 Take back your mink Those worn out pelts And go shorten the slevees [*sic*] For somebody else. **1969** S. ELLIN in *Ellery Queen's Grand Slam* (1971) 19 Two cars, a new mink whenever you feel like it. **1972** J. GILL *Tenant* III. ii. 87 On their tenth wedding anniversary he had given her a silver mink.

2. a. A small, semi-aquatic, stoat-like mammal belonging to any of several species of the genus *Mustela*, esp. the American mink, *M. vison*, which is farmed for its dark brown fur.

1624 CAPT. SMITH *Virginia* II. 27 Weesels, and Minkes we know they haue, because we haue seene many of their skinnes. **1771** J. R. FORSTER tr. *Kalm's Trav. N. Amer.* II. 61 The English and the Swedes gave the name of Mink to an animal of this country. **1792** PENNANT *Arctic Zool.* I. 100 Minx Otter. **1812** J. SMYTH *Pract. of Customs* (1821) 220 Its skin is blacker than that of an Otter..; 'as black as a Mink' being a proverbial expression in America. **1839** *Penny Cycl.* XV. 253/2 *Minx*, a name for the Vison-weasel. **1834** MᶜMURTRIE *Cuvier's Anim. Kingd.* 62 *M*[*ustela*] *lutreola*, Pall. (The Mink or Norek.) It frequents the banks of rivers, &c., in the north and east of Europe... It is the Mink of the United States. **1883** *Fisheries Exhib. Catal.* (ed. 4) 160 Specimens of Otters, Fishers, Minks, Musk-rats, Weasels, Seals. **1914** W. T. HORNADAY *Wild Life Conservation* iv. 146 In farming communities, the Mink, Weasel, Skunk, Raccoon, and even the Opossum all become so destructive to poultry as to constitute pests. **1965** D. MORRIS *Mammals* 282 American Mink are farmed extensively for their lustrous, rich-brown pelts, and these animals have been deliberately introduced into other parts of the world because of their economic importance... In Britain, specimens which have escaped from fur farms have set up breeding colonies that are causing some concern.

b. A dark brown colour.

1955 *Punch* 16 Mar. 349/2 Colours are black, white, mink, and blue. **1961** *Guardian* 16 Jan. 4/7 There is a new colour available in the range [of blankets]—'mink'. **1971** *Vogue* 15 Sept. 30 This exciting trouser suit..[is] available in Mink/Black and Mulberry/Dark Navy.

3. = KINGFISH d.

1888 GOODE *Amer. Fishes* 122 The King-fish, *Menticirrus nebulosus*, also known as.. the 'Sea Mink' in North Carolina.

4. *attrib.*, as ***mink coat, farm, farmer, farming, head, oil, ranch, ranching, skin, stole, tail, throat***.

1928 A. CHRISTIE *Mystery of Blue Train* x. 71 Perfectly dressed in a long mink coat and a little hat of Chinese lacquer red. **1958** *Daily Mail* 21 Mar. 5/2 A mink coat for his wife? 'Good gracious, I don't think so.' **1975** 'M. DUKE' *Death of Holy Murderer* 7 An inside pocket of her mink coat. **1965** in P. Jennings *Living Village* (1968) 246 On the mink farm.. mating took place early in March. **1967** *Guardian* 26 Aug. 3/6 There is a mink farm near by, and.. householders have been protesting.. about the smell. **1961** A. WILSON *Old Men at Zoo* i. 53 A drunken failed mink farmer from Essex. **1916** *Yukon Territory* (Canada Dept. Interior) 188 The following practical hints on mink farming have been recently published. **1902** Mink head [see *mink throat* below]. **1965** *Harper's Bazaar* June 46 To take care of cuticles, some extravagant materials are used—the latest being mink oil. **1974** *Times Herald Record* (Middletown, N.Y.) 22 Apr. 12/2 What about *mink oil*? It is close to the human lipid and helps to control the moisture balance and moisture retention. **1948** A. L. RAND *Mammals E. Rockies* 92 In Alberta the number of mink ranches has increased steadily from 35 in 1929 to 773 in 1943. **1916** *Yukon Territory* (Canada Dept. Interior) 188 Mink ranching will become an important industry. **1678** *Rec. Court of New Castle on Delaware* (1904) 349, 22 mincq skins great and smal. **1812** J. SMYTH *Pract. of Customs* (1821) 220 Mink skins. **1969** E. LATHEN' *Murder to Go* (1970) 230 Mrs. Chester Brewster.. in a mink stole. **1974** D. RAMSAY *No Cause to Kill* II. 111 A mink stole or a diamond bracelet. **1892** *Daily News* 15 Oct. 7/2 Mink tail is much used by those who cannot afford sable. **1902** *Ibid.* 18 Dec. 4/2 The mink throat has pretty white markings, whilst the mink head is plain brown.

b. *fig.* in *attrib.* and *Comb.* uses: opulent, sumptuous, wealthy.

1960 *Spectator* 4 Nov. 681 A mink-stoled Republican residential suburb of Chicago. **1966** *Radio Times* 22 Sept. 22/1 Kenton gives the mink touch to half-price electric heating.

Hence **'minkery** *U.S.*, a 'kennel' or breeding place for minks.

1877 COUES *Fur Anim.* vi. 182 Mr. Resseque's minkery consists of twelve stalls.

minke ('mɪnkə). [f. the name *Meincke*; see quot. 1971.] In full, ***minke whale***. A small whalebone whale, *Balænoptera acutorostrata*; also called the piked whale or lesser rorqual.

1939 *Geogr. Jrnl.* XCIII. 190 Minke and killer whales were cruising quietly in all parts of the bay [*sc.* the Bay of Whales in the Antarctic]. **1970** *Islander* (Victoria, B.C.) 19 July 13/1 We watched seven killer whales kill and eat a minke whale. **1971** F. D. OMMANNEY *Lost Leviathan* ii. 39 It [*sc.* the piked whale or lesser rorqual] is also known to the Norwegians as the Minke whale after a whaling gunner named Meincke who accidentally shot one in mistake for a Blue and thus achieved a rather dubious immortality. **1973** *Sci. Amer.* Aug. 43/1 The danger exists that intensive hunting of sperm and minke whales could eventually reduce both species to the level of severe endangerment.

minks, obs. form of MINX.

minky. Also **minky-winky**. *colloq.* Quasi-childish nonce-words for MILK *sb. rare*$^{-1}$.

1930 D. H. LAWRENCE *Nettles* 8 Eat your pap, little man, like a man! Drink its minky-winky, then, like a man! *Ibid.* 9 Drop of whiskey in its minky?

minn: see MIND *sb.*[2]

minnaway: see MINAWAY (= minuet).

minne, minnekin: see MIN, MINIKIN.

minne-drinking ('mɪnə,drɪŋkɪŋ), *vbl. sb.* [f. G. *minne* love + DRINKING *vbl. sb.*] Originally, a heathen practice among Germanic tribes at grand sacrifices and banquets, in honour of the gods or in memory of the absent or deceased. Later, a similar practice said to survive in certain localities in Germany.

1880 J. S. STALLYBRASS tr. *Grimm's Teutonic Mythol.* I. iii. 62 Minne-drinking, even as a religious rite, apparently exists to this day in some parts of Germany.

‖**minnelied** ('mɪnəliːt). Pl. -lieder (,liːdə(r)). [G., f. *minne* love + *lied* song.] A love-song written by a minnesinger, or in the style of the minnesingers.

1876 STAINER & BARRETT *Dict. Mus. Terms* 292/2 Minnesingers.. devoted their talents to the production of love songs (Minnelieder). **1881** *Encycl. Brit.* XII. 90/1 The first lyrical writer of Holland was John I... who practised the *minnelied* with success.

minnem, minner: see MINIM, MINNOW.

minnenwerfer: see MINENWERFER.

Minnepoesy ('mɪnə,pəʊɪsɪ). *arch. rare.* [f. G. *minne* love + POESY *sb.*] = next.

1845 LONGFELLOW *Poets & Poetry of Europe* 182/2 In the fresh and youthful Minnepoesy, all art has acquired the appearance of nature.

Minnepoetry ('mɪnə,pəʊɪtrɪ). *arch. rare.* [f. G. *minne* love + POETRY.] The poetry of the Minnesingers.

1887 *Amer. Jrnl. Philol.* Dec. 454 The classical representative of Minnepoetry, Walther von der Vogelweide.

‖**Minnesinger** ('mɪnəsɪŋə(r)). [Ger. (also *minnesänger*) f. *minne* love + *-singer* (also *sänger*) SINGER.] One of the German lyrical poets and singers of the 12th, 13th, and 14th centuries, so called because love was the chief theme of their songs. Hence **'minnesinging** *vbl. sb.* (*attrib.*).

1825 E. TAYLOR (*title*) Lays of the Minnesingers, or German Troubadours. *Ibid.* 199 The great fostering place of the Minnesinging art. **1829** SCOTT *Anne of G.* iv, The foolery of minstrels and strolling minnesingers. **1871** LONGF. in *Life* (1891) III. 176 Mr. Kroeger's Specimens of the Minnesingers, which I want him to publish.

transf. **1845** LONGF. *Walter von der Vogelweid* xi, Round the Gothic spire, Screamed the feathered Minnesingers.

Minnesong ('mɪnəsɒŋ). [ad. G. *minnesang*, f. *minne* love + *sang* SONG *sb.*; cf. MINNESINGER.] One of the songs of the Minnesingers. Also *collect.*

1845 LONGFELLOW *Poets & Poetry of Europe* 182/2 This is the reason that all the Minnesongs.. seem still to resemble each other. **1907** F. C. NICHOLSON *Old German Love Songs* p. iii, English works on the subject of the German Minnesong are.. scanty in number. **1915** K. BREUL *Cambr. Songs* 36 Several.. of the 'Cambridge Songs' may be considered as direct forerunners of the early Minnesong.

Minnesota (mɪnɪ'səʊtə). [See next.] In phr. ***Minnesota Multiphasic Personality Inventory***: a personality test made up of over 500 items, the responses to which are graded for various personality traits in accordance with criteria calculated from groups of normal subjects and subjects with clinically diagnosed psychiatric disorders. (Cf. *M.M.P.I.*).

1946 *Jrnl. Appl. Psychol.* XXX. 517 The present paper presents preliminary data on the use of the Minnesota Multiphasic Personality Inventory (MMPI) with respect to differential diagnosis, with secondary findings upon the subject of overall identification of 'abnormals' from people in general. **1952** L. W. FERGUSON *Personality Measurement* viii. 235 (*caption*) Classification of items in the Minnesota Multiphasic Personality Inventory. **1973** *Jrnl. Genetic Psychol.* CXXII. 65 The tasks presented to the subjects consisted of Block Counting.. and the Depression scale from the Minnesota Multiphasic Personality Inventory (MMPI).

Minnesotan (,mɪnɪ'səʊtən). [f. the name of *Minnesota* (see below) + -AN.] A native or inhabitant of Minnesota, a State in the north-central United States.

1888 D. D. FIELD *Speeches, Arguments & Misc. Papers* (1890) III. 369 Nebraskan, Kansan, Arkansan, Minnesotan, are the true designations of the citizens of those flourishing States. **1939** F. SCOTT FITZGERALD *Let.* Mar. (1964) 53 He's a Minnesotan and seems to me an altogether admirable fellow. **1965** MRS. L. B. JOHNSON *White House Diary* 20 Jan. (1970) 229 Next we visited the Shoreham, which was full of Minnesotans.

minnie ('mɪnɪ), *sb.*[1] *Sc.* and *north. dial.* Also 6 mynnye, -nie, 8–9 minny. [Of obscure origin; perh. a child's alteration of *mammy*.] A familiar word for mother.

1500–20 DUNBAR *Poems* lxxv. 16 Sen that I borne wes of my mynnye, I nevir wowit weycht bot 3ow. **1600** W. WATSON *Decacordon* (1602) 144 A lacke what ailes my minnie at me heigh hoe. **1681** COLVIL *Whigs Supplic.* (1751) 158 My Minnie hath the lave on't. **1790** BURNS *Tam Glen* iv, My minnie does constantly deave me, And bids me beware o' young men. **1816** SCOTT *Antiq.* xl, Light loves I may get mony a ane, But minnie ne'er anither. **1858** KINGSLEY *Andromeda*, etc., *Oubit* 3 My minnie bad me bide at hame until I won my wings.

Minnie, minnie ('mɪnɪ), *sb.*[2] *Military slang.* Also **minny**. [Abbrev. of G. *minenwerfer* trench-mortar.] A German trench-mortar, or the bomb discharged by it. Also *attrib.* Hence as *v. trans.*, to attack with such a trench-mortar.

1917 A. G. EMPEY *From Fire Step* 36 A German 'Minnie' (trench mortar) had exploded in the next traverse. **1927** E. THOMPSON *These Men, thy Friends* 116 A minnie had been established in the enemy line. **1930** BLUNDEN *De Bello Germanico* iv. 46 He might have 'minnied' or gunned us out in a few light-hearted rounds. *Ibid.* vi. 73 The German minnie-man knew how to upset our domestic programme. **1933** —— & NORMAN *We'll shift our Ground* 14 M. M. for bombing a minny-crew out. **1950** G. WILSON *Brave Company* iii. 40 That bloody moaning Minnie... It's a hell of a weapon.

minnie, minny ('mɪnɪ), *v. Sc.* and *north. dial.* [f. MINNIE *sb.*[1]] *trans.* To mother; to act as a mother towards (a lamb); to find (a lamb) its mother; also *refl.*, of a lamb: to find (itself) a mother.

1772 in *Sc. Nat. Dict.* (1965) VI. 283/1 Four or six lambs broke off from the flock of eild sheep.. and run [*sic*] to the ewes, and minnied or mothered themselves by sucking. **1825** JAMIESON Suppl., s.v., It is given as a proof of the accuracy of a shepherd's acquaintance with his flock.. that, after the lambs have been separated from the ewes, he can *minnie ilka lamb*. **1861** F. O. MORRIS *Rec. Animal Sagacity & Character* 117 There was not a single ewe.. which did not minny her lambs—that is, assume the character of mother towards the offspring from which she had been separated.

minnie, -nikin, var. ff. MINNOW, MINIKIN.

†**'minning**, *vbl. sb.*[1] *Obs.* [f. MIN *v.* + -ING[1].]

1. Remembrance, memory; memorial.

c **1250** *Gen. & Ex.* 3344 Moysen dede ful ðe gemor, In a gold pot, for muning ðor. *a* **1300** *Cursor M.* 3196 Þi dede in minnyng sal last ai. *Ibid.* 25584 To haf mining o þi dede þat þou boght sua dere. **13..** *St. Erkenwolde* 269 in Horstm. *Altengl. Leg.* (1881) 272 More he menskes men for mynnynge of ri3tes þen for al þe meritorie medes. *c* **1400** *Rule St. Benet* xlv. 31 Sain benet cumandis.. þat ta þat faile in þe kirke at te minning of þe salmes.. sal [etc.].

b. A commemoration of a departed soul; also, a peal of bells rung on such an occasion: see MIND *sb.* 5 b.

c **1420** *Anturs of Arth.* 236 (Douce MS.) Here hertly my honde, þes hestes to holde, Withe a myllione of masses to make þe mynnyng. *c* **1460** *Towneley Myst.* xxxi. 158 Youre goodys ye shall forsake.. And nothing With you take Bot site a wyndyng clothe; youre Wife sorow shall slake, Youre chylder also both, Vnnes youre mynnyng make. **1524** *Test. Ebor.* (Surtees) V. 188, I will that.. the said Sir William shall every yere cause a mynnyng to be rongyn.

2. Mention.

a **1300** *Cursor M.* 5169 Quar ar yee mas minning now O ioseph. *Ibid.* 8518 Childer had he wit wijfes sere O quilk i mak no mining here.

3. *pl.* Premonitory symptoms (of a disease): = MINDING *vbl. sb.* 2, MINGING *vbl. sb.* 1.

1724 BAILEY (ed. 2), *Minnings of a Disease*, the previous or foregoing Symptoms of it.

4. *attrib.* or *Comb.*, as **minning-date, minning-day** = MIND-DAY.

a **1330** *Syr Degarre* 2 Hys wyvys mynnyng day. **1426** *Will of Hyton* (Somerset Ho.), Memoriale vocat. myneng day. **1543** *Lanc. Wills* (1857) I. 67 And yᵗ every of thafforesayd xvij yeares that vjˢ viijᵈ be dysposed upon an obyte or mynnynge day. **1556** OLDE *Antichrist* 157 b, A certain nombre of masses, certayn mynnyng dates, certain meritorious praiers. **1661** BLOUNT *Glossogr.* (ed. 2), *Minnyng days*. **1777** BRAND *Pop. Antiq.* (1849) II. 314.

†**'minning**, *vbl. sb.*[2] *rare*$^{-1}$. [f. *min vb. (f. MIN *a.*) + -ING[1].] Lessening, diminution.

c **1357** *Lay Folks Catech.* (T.) 125 Withouten ony merryng of hir modirhede, Withouten ony mynnyng of hir maidenhede.

minnion, minnite, obs. ff. MINION, MINUTE.

minnom, obs. form of MINIM.

minnow ('mɪnəʊ). Forms: [4 *Sc.* menoun,] 5 menawe, 5–8 menow, (5 *pl.* menwus), 6 menewe, menowe, 6–8 minew, 6–8, 9 *dial.* minnie, -ny, 7 menew, mynnowe, minoe, -ow, 7–9 mennow, 9 *dial.* or *slang* minner, 6– minnow. [Prob. repr. OE. **mynwe* wk. fem. = OHG. *munewa, munua* (? for **muniwa*) glossing L. *capedo* i.e. *capito*, a fish with a large head. The recorded OE. *myne* str. masc. (pl. *mynas*) glosses L. *capito* and *mena*; it is not certain what fish was meant; the L. *capito* is also rendered *ǽlepúta* EEL-POUT. The forms, and perh. the application, of the word have been influenced by association with F. *menu* (*poisson*) small (fish). Cf. MENISE.

The Sc. form *menoun* in Barbour may perhaps represent an AF. formation on the Eng. word. Cf. mod.Sc. *menon*, MENNOM.]

1. a. A small cyprinoid freshwater fish, *Leuciscus phoxinus* or *Phoxinus lævis*, common in the streams, lakes, and ponds of Europe. Often loosely applied to any small fish; in Eng. dialects chiefly to the stickleback (*Gastrosteus*). In the U.S. it is applied (sometimes with prefixed defining word) to many different fishes of small size, chiefly cyprinoids; and in Australasia to fishes of the genus *Galaxias*.

In early quots. the application of the name is uncertain. [**1375** BARBOUR *Bruce* II. 577 Trowtis, elys, and als menovnys.] **14..** *Nom.* in Wr.-Wülcker 704/44 *Hic solimicus*, a menawe. *c***1420** *Liber Cocorum* (1862) 54 Trouȝte, sperlynges and menwus. **1496** *Bk. St. Albans, Fishing* (1883) 30 The menow whan he shynith in the water, thenne is he byttyr. **1558** *Act 1 Eliz.* c. 17 §4 Places where Smeltes, Loches, Mynneis,..or Eeles, hathe been used to bee taken. **1611** COTGR., *Fregureul*, the little fish called, a Mennow. **1635–56** COWLEY *Davideis* I. 1024 The mute Fish witness no less his Praise... From Minoes to those living Islands, Whales. **1668** CHARLETON *Onomasticon* 160 *Phoxinus Lævis, seu varius*..the Minow, or Minoe. **1706** PHILLIPS (ed. Kersey), *Menow*, a little Fresh-water Fish, otherwise call'd a Cackrel. **1787** BEST *Angling* (ed. 2) 60 The minnow, though one of the smallest fishes, is as excellent a one to eat as any of the most famed. **1808** WOLCOT (P. Pindar) *One more Peep at R.A.* Wks. 1816 IV. 405 To move a mennow, who would wish—In paltry brooks a paltry fish —While Nature offers him to roll a whale! **1820** in *Smithsonian Collect.* (1877) XIII. IX. i. 32, 51st species, Red Minny, Rutilus ? Ruber. **1877** JORDAN *ibid.* 32 *note*, I add here a fine small fish,..it is said to live in the small streams which fall into the Elkhorn and Kentucky. It is a slender fish, only 2 inches long... It is commonly called Red-minny. *Ibid.* 30 *note*, Length [of Warty Chubby] from 3 to 4 inches, often called Minny or Red-Fin. **1879** JEFFERIES *Wild Life in S. Co.* 356 The minnie, as the stickleback is locally called. **1880** GÜNTHER *Fishes* 596 Other similar genera [*sc.* of carps] from the fresh waters of North America, and generally called 'Minnows', are *Pimephales* [etc.]. *Ibid.* 599 The 'Minnow' (*Leuciscus phoxinus*), abundant everywhere in Europe, and growing to a length of seven inches. **1898** MORRIS *Austral Eng.* s.v., *Manga*..a New Zealand fish... It is often called the *Whitebait* and *Minnow*.

b. *transf.* and *fig.*, as a type of smallness. ***a Triton of*** or ***among the minnows***: one who appears great by contrast with the insignificance of all those around him.

1588 SHAKS. *L.L.L.* I. i. 251 That low-spirited Swaine, that base Minow of thy Myrth. **1607** —— *Cor.* III. i. 89 Heare you this Triton of the Minnowes? **1796** LAMB *Let. to Coleridge* 27 May (end), My civic and poetic compliments to Southey if at Bristol. Why, he is a very Leviathan of Bards! —the small minnow, I! **1906** A. NOYES *Drake* II. in *Blackw. Mag.* Apr. 470 Those five small ships mere minnows clinging to the flanks Of that Leviathan.

2. *Angling.* **a.** A minnow attached to a hook in such a manner as to serve as a bait for other fish. **b.** An artificial fish made in the form and colour of a minnow, and used as a bait.

1615 MARKHAM *Country Contentm.* I. xiv. (1668) 72 His best bait is a little small Roch, Dace, or Menew. **1622** PEACHAM *Compl. Gentl.* xxi. (1634) 252 For your live baits, they are wormes of all kinds,..Gudgens, or Loches, Mynnowes, &c. **1651** T. BARKER *Art of Angling* (1653) 4 The angling with a menow..for a Trout is a pleasant Sport. **1655** WALTON *Angler* I. v. (1661) 96, I have..an artificial Minnow..the mould or body of the minnow was cloth, and wrought upon or over it thus with a needle, the back [etc.]. **1767** JOHNSON in *Ray's Corr.* (1848) 128 They will not only take a worm, or minnow, or other small fish, but swallow the bait with the hook down into the stomach. **1883** *Fisheries Exhib. Catal.* 212 Flexible Minnows..Caledonian Minnows ..Phantom Minnows.. Protean Minnows. **1894** *Daily News* 22 Aug. 5/1 The fact that he [a salmon] bites at a fly or angel minnow is..ascribed to anger.

3. *attrib.* and *Comb.*, as ***minnow-can, crate***; **minnow-fisher**, (*a*) an angler who fishes with a minnow as bait; (*b*) one who fishes for minnows; **minnow-fishing**, fishing with a minnow for bait; **minnow-rod**, a rod used for spinning with a minnow; **minnow-tackle**, fishing tackle used for spinning a minnow; **minnow-tansy**, a dish of fried minnows seasoned with tansy; **minnow-trace**, a trace intended to carry a minnow; **minnow-twisting** *vbl. sb.*, erratic movement or behaviour, resembling that of a minnow.

1893 *Outing* (U.S.) XXII. 86/2 The inside of her *minnow-can was lifted with care over the side. **1883** *Fisheries Exhib. Catal.* 214 Folding *Minnow Crate. **1863** ATKINSON *Stanton Grange* (1864) 152 The wonderful skill of a *minnow-fisher. **1895** *Bailey's Mag.* May 358/1 There is no accusation of easy times that can be justly applied to the minnow-fisher. **1655** WALTON *Angler* I. xviii. (1661) 234 The nimble turning of that [*i.e.* a sticklebag], or the Minnow, is the perfection of *Minnow-fishing. **1839** T. C. HOFLAND *Brit. Angler's Man.* iv. (1841) 70 The first [manner of baiting with a minnow]..is particularly calculated for a clear water, as your tackle is finer than in any other mode of minnow-fishing. *Ibid.*, The *minnow-rod should be of bamboo cane. *Ibid.* 72 Various kinds of *minnow-tackle may be purchased. **1655** WALTON *Angler* I. xviii. (1661) 231 In the spring they make of them excellent *Minnow-Tansies. **1839** T. C. HOFLAND *Brit. Angler's Man.* iv. (1841) 71 You must now prepare a *minnow-trace of three yards of gut. **1935** L. MACNEICE *Poems* 52 The *minnow-twistings of the latinist who alone Nibbles and darts through the shallows of the lexicon.

b. quasi-*adj.* Very small, tiny.

1824 DIBDIN *Libr. Comp.* 623 The tribe of little minnow pocket-editions.

Hence **'minnowy** *a.*, abounding in minnows.

1826 CAMPBELL *Field Flowers* 23 What pictures of pebbled and minnowy brooks.

minnowed ('mɪnəʊd), *a. poet.* [f. MINNOW + -ED².] Containing or abounding in minnows.

1889 W. B. YEATS *Wanderings of Oisin* 71 Hour by hour He ruffles with his bill the minnowed streams.

minnuet, minnum, obs. ff. MINUET *sb.*, MINIM.

minny, dial. variant of MINNIE *sb.*¹, MINNOW.

mino, minoe, obs. ff. MINA², MINNOW.

Minoan (mɪ'nəʊən, maɪn-), *a.* and *sb.* [f. L. *Mīnōs* (Gr. Μίνως), the name of a legendary king of Crete + -AN.] **A.** *adj.* Of or pertaining to ancient Crete, *spec.* to the Bronze Age civilization extending from the early part of the third to the end of the second millennium B.C., or to its people, culture, or language; also, to this civilization (or aspects of it) discovered elsewhere in the Aegean area. **B.** *sb.* **a.** An inhabitant of Minoan Crete or other parts of the Minoan world. **b.** The language or scripts associated with the Minoan civilization. Hence **Mi,noani'zation**; **Mi'noanized, Mi'noanizing** *adjs.*

The precise chronology of the successive phases and of the collapse of Minoan civilization is highly controversial.

1894 A. J. EVANS in *Jrnl. Hellenic Stud.* XIV. 367 At a time when 'Minoan' Crete and Mycenaean Greece had..evolved independent systems of writing. **1902** *Nature* 20 Nov. 58/1 The dominion of the proud Minoan thalassocrats disappeared. *Ibid.*, The hieroglyphic of their tutelary deity may have been used by the Minoans as a sort of heraldic device. **1904** *Ibid.* 15 Sept. 482/2 It was this faïence that the Minoan potters imitated. **1921** *Spectator* 5 Mar. 293/1 A hanging lamp..with a yellow and orange shade with a sort of Minoan design on it in orange, terracotta, and black. **1931** *Times Lit. Suppl.* 16 Apr. 308/1 He makes free use of his belief that the language of the Minoan script is Greek. **1939** J. D. S. PENDLEBURY *Archaeol. Crete* iv. 230 The Minoanization of the Mainland. *Ibid.*, Though superficially Minoanized, the mainland still kept a good deal of its native culture and taste. **1950** G. E. DANIEL *100 Yrs. Archaeol.* vi. 195 Perhaps a bill of lading in Egyptian and Minoan. *Ibid.*, It seems likely that the language of the Minoans was Anatolian. **1950** H. L. LORIMER *Homer & Monuments* i. 38 The strongly Minoanizing régime of LH II. **1956** *Jrnl. Hellenic Stud.* LXXVI. 1 Documents in the script known as 'Minoan Linear B' were unearthed at Knossos in Crete over fifty years ago. **1966** C. H. GORDON (*title*) Evidence for the Minoan language. **1970** BRAY & TRUMP *Dict. Archaeol.* 149/1 'Minoan' is strictly a cultural term. Surviving bones show that the Bronze Age Cretans were a racially mixed group. **1970** *Oxf. Classical Dict.* (ed. 2) 1060/2 A Minoan colony of pre-eruption days [at Thera] is being excavated.

Min of Ag (mɪn əv 'æg), colloq. abbrev. of *Ministry of Agriculture*(, Fisheries and Food).

1946 M. DICKENS *Happy Prisoner* vi. 106 D' you know what the Min. of Ag. want Fred to do... They want him to plough up the hill field. **1962** *Observer* 6 May 21/3 A man at the Board of Trade will talk about 'those Min of Ag people'. **1972** *Guardian* 22 Mar. 13/1 'The Archers' began..[as] a sort of broadcast Min of Ag handout.

Minol ('maɪnɒl). Also **minol**. [Prob. f. MIN(E *sb.* + -OL.] A mixture of ammonium nitrate, T.N.T., and aluminium used as the explosive in depth charges.

1946 *Battle of Atlantic* (H.M.S.O.) 57 About this time [*sc.* January 1943] the shattering power of our naval depth-charge was increased by the use of a new explosive called 'Minol'. This would crack the pressure hull of a U-boat at 25 feet. **1947** CROWTHER & WHIDDINGTON *Science at War* iv. 161 From January 1943, all Mark VII depth charges were filled with Minol. **1972** *Materials & Technol.* IV. xix. 725 The ammonals..and the minols—ammonium nitrate 40%, TNT 40% and aluminium 20% —were used for commercial and military applications, but are liable to evolve gases owing to the interaction of aluminium with moist ammonium nitrate.

minom, obs. form of MINIM.

minor ('maɪnə(r)), *a.* and *sb.* Forms: 3–4 **menor**, 4 **mynor**, 4–5 **menour**, 5 **menoure, -owre, -eour, minore**, 6– **minor**. [a. L. *minor*, nom. sing. masc. and fem. (neut. *minus* MINUS, declension-stem *minōr-*) smaller, lesser, junior, f. Indogermanic root **min-* small: cf. L. *minuěre*, Gr. μινύθειν, OE. *minsian* to diminish, OTeut. **minwiz* less, **minwizon-* lesser: see MIN *a.*

OFr. had *menour* (whence most of the ME. forms):—L. *minōrem* accus., beside *meindre* (mod.F. *moindre*):—L. *minor*. In early mod.Fr. the Latin word was adopted in special uses as *mineur*. Cf. Sp., Pg. *menor*, It. *minore*.]

A. *adj.*

I. 1. ***friar minor***, † ***minor friar***: a Franciscan.

Rendering of med.L. *Fratres Minores*, lit. 'lesser brethren', the name chosen by St. Francis for the order founded by him, as expressing the humility which he desired its members to cultivate. Cf. B. 1.

The plural is now *friars minor*; formerly *friar minors, friars minors*, were common.

1297 R. GLOUC. (Rolls) 10241 Þe ordre bigan of frere menors þulke sulue ȝer [*i.e.* 1210] ywis. *c***1400** MAUNDEV. (Roxb.) xxxi. 139 Twa frere meneours of Lombardy. *c***1440** *Promp. Parv.* 333/1 Menour frere, or frere menowre, (*P.* menowre friyr), *minor*. **1526** *Pilgr. Perf.* (W. de W. 1531) 140 Though the frere minor gyue great example of holynes, ..yet [etc.]. **1635** PAGITT *Christianogr.* I. iii. (1636) 93 The Friers Minors onely, are esteemed to be 60 thousand. **1670** G. H. *Hist. Cardinals* III. I. 238 They elected Pietro Filardo, a Minor Fryer. **1727–51** CHAMBERS *Cycl.* s.v. *Friar*, Franciscan, or grey, or minor, or begging, friars. **1862** *Chambers's Encycl.* IV. 518/1 The Franciscans were properly denominated 'Friars Minor' (*Fratres Minores*).

II. = LESSER in various specific applications. (Not followed by *than*.)

2. a. Used as the distinctive epithet of the lesser (in various senses) of two things, species, etc., that have a common designation; also applied to those members of a class that collectively form a subdivision as being smaller than the rest; opposed to *major*. Chiefly in certain special collocations, many of which originated in med. or mod.Latin; in most of these *lesser* may be substituted. So ***minor poem, public school, road***; also ***minor canon, excommunication, orders, prophets*** (see those sbs.). † ***Minor Fellow*** (Cambridge): a junior fellow; ***minor planet***: one of the asteroids or small planets between Mars and Jupiter; ***minor league*** (chiefly *N. Amer.*), the lower associations of teams in baseball, etc. (opp. MAJOR *a.* 1 e); also *attrib.* and *fig.*; hence ***minor leaguer***; ***minor loyalty***: adherence to an institution, church, trade union, or the like, which is subordinate to loyalty to one's country or its government; ***minor piece***: in *Chess* (see quot. 1847); ***minor suit***: in *Bridge*, diamonds or clubs; ***minor tactics***: the tactics or handling of bodies of troops in the immediate face or expected presence of the enemy.

1654 TRAPP (*title*) A commentary..upon the XII Minor Prophets. **1670** WALTON *Lives* IV. 21 He was made Minor Fellow in the year 1609..Major Fellow of the Colledge, March 15, 1615. **1679–88** *Secr. Serv. Money Chas. & Jas.* (Camden) 92 John Tinker, one of the minor canons of the collegiate church of St. Peter's, Westmʳ. **1683** J. POYNTZ *Tobago* 29 The Brazil Tree... Brazilleto, is a Minor or Junior Brazil. **1819** KEATS *Let.* 2 Jan. (1958) II. 26 It is my intention to wait a few years before I publish any minor poems. **1820** J. S. BINGHAM tr. *E. Dal Rio's Incomparable Game of Chess* I. ii. 26 Two minor Pieces, for a Rook and two Pawns, may be considered an equal contract. **1847** H. STAUNTON *Chess-Player's Handbk.* I. iii. 24 The Bishop and Knight, in contradistinction to the Queen and Rook, are called *minor Pieces.* **1861** G. F. CHAMBERS *Astron.* I. ix. 51 A numerous group of small bodies revolving round the Sun which are known as the Minor Planets. **1863** *Handbk. Chess & Draughts* 19 The Knight and Bishop, in contradistinction to the Rook and Queen, are termed minor pieces. **1875** C. CLERY (*title*) Minor tactics. **1885** A. B. LETTS *A.B.C. of Minor Tactics* 59 Minor tactics..come into use not only on the field of battle but also off it. **1889** *Sporting Life* (Philadelphia) 29 May 1/2 It will mean..the relegation of four-fifths of the men not in those leagues to the minor leagues. **1899** *Allbutt's Syst. Med.* VII. 765 The first fits occur during retarded dentition..as very slight 'minor' attacks. **1906** *Cincinnati Enquirer* 1 Apr. IV. 2/1 The Coast team is a strong aggregation, fit to cope with the best of minor leaguers. **1916** R. F. FOSTER *Auction Bridge for All* v. 23 Clubs and diamonds are called minor, or losing suits. *Ibid.*, A much larger percentage of minor suit declarations fail to make good the contract than major suits. **1927** CARR-SAUNDERS & JONES *Survey Social Struct. Eng. & Wales* 83 To discuss the 'minor loyalties' which such associations create. **1928** H. ROWAN-ROBINSON *Some Aspects Mechanization* 3 The study of the minor tactics of petrol-driven forces. **1932** *Time* 28 Mar. 29/1 After six years in the minor leagues he has become catcher for the Washington Senators. **1936** 'J. TEY' *Shilling for Candles* vii. 81 The Grammar schools..turned out a very fine type of boy. Better often..than came from the minor public schools. **1942** E. PAUL *Narrow St.* xxxiv. 304 Daladier was well along with his minor league Kampf. He had repealed the forty-hour week, reduced the wages for overtime and removed the limit of hours. **1962** *Listener* 23 Aug. 285/1 Auden in the 'thirties was no better than Osborne in the 'fifties; both operated in a very minor league. **1963** 'W. HAGGARD' *High Wire* v. 54 The junction of the minor road to Maldington with the main to London. **1967** P. ANDERTON *Play Bridge* iii. 24 One does not readily take-out from a major suit into a minor suit at the level of 'Two' unless a five-carder is shown. **1968** A. DIMENT *Bang Bang Birds* vii. 119 He knotted the tie, from a very minor public school, round his stiff collar. **1970** *New Yorker* 28 Feb. 32/1, I played minor-league baseball in Valdosta, Georgia—Class D. **1972** *N.Y. Times* 1 June 55/3 The New York Raiders of the World Hockey Association yesterday signed a smallish minor-leaguer named Alton White. **1973** E. LEMARCHAND *Let or Hindrance* xiii. 162 The accident had happened on an unfrequented

minor road. **1973** D. CHANDLER *Marlborough* xv. 318 Fourth are 'minor Tactics'—the actual fighting methods employed at unit level to gain a local success.

b. In less definite sense: Comparatively small or unimportant; not to be reckoned among the greater or principal individuals of the kind. (Not now used with reference to physical or spatial magnitude, exc. as this involves importance.) Often in ***minor poet***.

A favourite use with Sir T. Browne, and common in subsequent writers.

1623 B. JONSON *Time Vind.* (1640) 95 The unletter'd Clarke! major and minor Poet! **1643** SIR T. BROWNE *Relig. Med.* II. §1 Neither in the name of *Multitude* do I onely include the base and minor sort of people. **1646** —— *Pseud. Ep.* v. xiii. 254 Petty errors and minor lapses. *a* **1682** —— *Tracts* (1684) 36 The providence of Nature hath provided this shelter for minor fishes. **1693** *Humours Town* 36 Gaining the Author..Reputation..with the Minor Criticks. *Ibid.* 106 Minor Authors, Beaux, and the rest of the illiterate Blockheads. *a* **1734** NORTH *Exam.* III. vii. §65 (1740) 551 The Troubles that fell upon the Minor Abhorrers. **1771** *Junius Lett.* xlv. (1788) 257 The minor critic, who hunts for blemishes. **1780** BURKE *Sp. Econ. Reform* Wks. III. 262 These minor principalities. **1844** STEPHENS *Bk. Farm* II. 596 Three principal cross-rails.. besides a minor-rail. **1860** *Cornh. Mag.* Dec. 745 A minor theatre. *Ibid.* 750 The minor parts will be mistakenly rendered or slurred. *Ibid.*, Your minor gentlemen may walk about in palatial drawing-rooms with hats upon their heads [etc.]. **1879** MᶜCARTHY *Own Times* xxix. II. 387 The air was filled with the voices of minor singers. **1897** *Spectator* 27 Nov. 771 Herrick, Crashaw, Christopher Smart, and, in our own time, Rossetti, would be ranked as minor poets because of a certain aloofness from the great human concerns. **1899** *Allbutt's Syst. Med.* VI. 751 In all minor neuralgias.

†**c.** ***St. James (the) minor***: = St. James the Less (see LESS *a.* 3). *Obs.*

?**14..** *Stasyons of Jerus.* 515 in Horstm. *Altengl. Leg.* (1881) 362 This was James þe mynoure. **1687** A. LOVELL tr. *Thevenot's Trav.* I. 205 St. James the Minor, first Patriarch of Jerusalem. **1727–41** CHAMBERS *Cycl.* s.v., Thus we say, St. James minor; Asia minor.

d. *Ent.* In collectors' names of certain moths.

1775 M. HARRIS *Eng. Lepidoptera* 9 Beauty, minor. **1869** E. NEWMAN *Brit. Moths* 398 The Minor Shoulder-knot (*Epunda viminalis*).

e. Surgery. ***minor operations***, those operations which do not involve danger to life (*Syd. Soc. Lex.* 1890); hence, ***minor operation*** or ***operating instrument***, an instrument for the performance of such operations. ***minor surgery***, the smaller operations required in the treatment of slight wounds and injuries (*Ibid.*).

1862 *Catal. Exhib.* II. XVII. 125/2 Minor Operating Instruments, a complete set. **1895** *Arnold's Catal. Surg. Instr.* 45 Minor operation and hernia instruments.

f. Football. ***minor point***: A 'try' (in the Rugby game). Also, see quot. 1899.

1896 *Field* 1 Feb. 172/2 Ashford improving on the minor point by kicking a splendid goal. **1899** MACNAGHTEN in *Football* (Badm. Libr.) 39 In the Eton field game there are thus two possible points to be scored—first the major point, or 'goal',..and the minor point, or 'rouge', three of which are equivalent to a goal.

3. *Math.* †**a.** (See quot.) *Obs.*

1571 DIGGES *Pantom.* IV. Xiv b, The diameter of the comprehending sphere being a line rationall, the Icosaedrons side is a line irrationall, called of Euclide Minor. *Ibid.* Yj, The comprehending spheres diameter being rational, his conteyning circles semidiameter is an irrational of that kinde which Euclide calleth Minor.

b. ***minor axis*** (of an ellipse): the axis perpendicular to the major or transverse axis, and passing through the centre.

1862 *Catal. Internat. Exhib.* II. xi. 15 The difference between major and minor axis being ·012 of an inch. **1885** LEUDESDORF *Cremona's Proj. Geom.* 275 The polar reciprocal of an ellipse (hyperbola) with respect to a circle having its centre at a focus and its radius equal to half the minor (conjugate) axis is the circle described on the major (transverse) axis as diameter.

c. ***minor determinant***: a determinant whose matrix is formed from that of another determinant by erasing one or more rows and columns.

1850 SYLVESTER in *Philos. Mag.* Nov. XXXVII. 365 Now conceive any one line and any one column to be struck out, we get..a square, one term less in breadth and depth than the original square; and by varying in every possible manner the selection of the line and column excluded, we obtain, supposing the original square to consist of *n* lines and *n* columns, n^2 such minor squares, each of which will represent what I term a First Minor Determinant relative to the principal or complete determinant. Now suppose two lines and two columns struck out from the original square. .. These constitute what I term a system of Second Minor Determinants; and..we can form a system of *r*th minor determinants by the exclusion of *r* lines and *r* columns.

4. *Logic.* ***minor term***: the subject of the conclusion of a categorical syllogism. ***minor premiss***, ***proposition***: that premiss of a syllogism which contains the minor term.

1581 J. BELL *Haddon's Answ. Osor.* 152 For the same purpose the minor proposition must bee denyed. **1650** BAXTER *Saints' R.* II. vi. §1 (1651) 250 The Major Proposition will not sure be denied... All the work therefore will lie in confirming the Minor. **1727–41** CHAMBERS *Cycl.* s.v. *Syllogism*, They [*i.e.* the two propositions of a syllogism] are both called..*premises*..and.. both are called *antecedents*, only the first the *major*, and the latter the *minor*. **1827** WHATELY *Logic* iii. (ed. 2) 96 The proper order is to place the Major premiss first, and the Minor second; but this does not constitute the Major and Minor premises; for that premiss (wherever placed) is the Major which contains the Major term, and the Minor, the Minor. **1843** MILL *Logic* II. ii. §1 The premiss..which contains the middle term and the minor term is called the minor premiss of the syllogism.

5. That constitutes the minority. Also rarely in predicative use: In a minority.

1642 CHAS. I *Answ. to Printed Bk.* 13 That the Minor part of the Lords might joyn with the Major part of the House of Commons. **1659** BAXTER *Key Cath.* xx. 99 If a minor party ..may step into the Tribunal, and pass sentence against the Catholick Church [etc.]. **1774** T. HUTCHINSON *Diary* 3 Oct., A person had the major vote for Alderman... Another person..had the minor vote in the election. **1796** JEFFERSON *Writ.* (1859) IV. 150 There may be an equal division where I had supposed the republican vote would have been considerably minor. *Ibid.* 152 In every other, the minor will be preferred by me to the major vote.

6. *Mus.* **a.** Applied to intervals smaller by a chromatic semitone than those called *major*; as ***minor third***, ***sixth***, ***seventh*** (and sometimes ***minor fourth*** and ***fifth***, more usually called *diminished* or *imperfect*). Hence also applied to the note distant by a minor interval from a given note. Also, in acoustical theory, applied to the smaller of two intervals differing by a minute quantity, as ***minor tone*** (vibration ratio $\frac{10}{9}$, being less by a comma than the *major tone*, $\frac{9}{8}$); so, occasionally, ***minor semitone*** (usually called *chromatic semitone*). **b.** Applied to a common chord or triad containing a minor third between the root and the second note; hence to a cadence ending on such a chord. **c.** Denoting those keys, or that mode, in which the scale has a minor third (also, usually, a minor sixth, and often a minor seventh). (In naming a key, *minor* follows the letter, as *A minor*.)

1694 W. HOLDER *Harmony* (1731) 49 If A to B [lengths of strings] be as 6 to 5, they sound a Trihemitone, or Third Minor. *Ibid.* 50, $\frac{4}{5}$ sound a Third Major,..$\frac{5}{8}$ a Sixth Minor. *Ibid.* 114 There are two sorts of Tones; viz. Major and Minor... Tone Minor (10 to 9)..is the difference between Third Minor and Fourth. *Ibid.* 121 From F to ♯F, is a Minor Hemitone, 25 to 24. *Ibid.* 129, 7th Minor..9 to 5. **1742** NORTH *Life Ld. Kpr. Guilford* 298 He [*sc.* Holder] makes great ado about dividing Tones Major, Tones Minor, Dieses and Commas, with the Quantities of them. **1777** SIR W. JONES *Ess. Imit. Arts* Poems, etc. 200 The minor mode of D is tender. **1776** BURNEY *Hist. Mus.* I. Diss. i. 19 All the ancient modes were in what we should call minor keys. **1797** *Encycl. Brit.* (ed. 3) XII. 511 *note*, Thus far we have only treated of fifths, fourths, thirds major and minor, in ascending. *Ibid.* 512/2 The first are called *perfect chords major*, the second *perfect chords minor*. **1811** BUSBY *Dict. Mus.* s.v. *Key*, The natural keys of C major and A minor. **1855** BROWNING *Lovers' Quarrel* xviii, We shall have the word In a minor third There is none but the cuckoo knows. **1878** W. H. STONE *Sci. Basis Music* v. §83, $\frac{25}{24}$ = *Minor Semitone*. **1889** E. PROUT *Harmony* (ed. 10) vii. §171 This form is known as the *Harmonic* Minor Scale, the other two being called *Melodic* Minor Scales.

d. Minor chords and keys, as compared with major, have usually a mournful or pathetic effect; hence various figurative allusions.

1820 J. SEVERN in Keats *Lett.* (1958) II. 342 Here I must change to a Minor Key—Miss C fainted..I was very ill.. Keats assended his bed. **1869** T. H. HIGGINSON *Army Life* 222 This minor-keyed pathos used to seem to me almost too sad to dwell upon. **1874** BURNAND *My Time* xvi. 142 His conversation was pitched in a minor key. **1900** *Daily News* 17 Oct. 4/7 ——'s address..was pitched in a painfully minor mode.

7. Following the sb. qualified. **a.** In certain combinations correlative with similar combinations of MAJOR, e.g. ***quint***, ***tierce minor***, ***bob-minor***: see QUINT *sb.*², TIERCE, BOB *sb.*³ **b.** In boys' schools, appended (as a Latin adj.) to a surname to distinguish the younger (in age or standing) of two namesakes. (Abbreviated *mi.*)

1791 [implied in MI²]. **1852** ROWCROFT *Conf. Etonian* I. 71 A member of the fifth form, Green minor by name. **1899** E. PHILLPOTTS *Human Boy* 108, I bet she will, when Corkey minor turns up.

III. 8. Under age; below the age of majority. Now *rare*.

1579–80 *Reg. Privy Council Scot.* III. 272 We, being yit minor, within the aige of fourtene yeiris..annull all the saidis infeftmentis. **1597** SKENE *De Verb. Sign.* s.v. *Homagium*, [Homage] sulde be maid bi the vassall being *minor*, or *maior*, to his ouer-lorde. **1622** BACON *Hen. VII* 145 At which time neuerthelesse the King was Minor. **1658** SIR T. BROWNE *Hydriot.* ii. 9 Many..were persons of minor age, or women. **1754–62** HUME *Hist. Eng.* I. xiv. 351 A wife..had made her minor son an instrument in this unnatural treatment of his father. **1818** HALLAM *Mid. Ages* (1872) II. 273 The public security..was thought incompatible with a minor king. **1844** H. H. WILSON *Brit. India* II. x. II. 431 A regard for the interests of the minor Raja.

B. *sb.* [The adj. used *ellipt.*]

1. A Franciscan friar. Cf. A. 1. Also Comb. ***Minor-Observantine*** = OBSERVANTINE.

13.. *Poem Times Edw. II* 163 in *Pol. Songs* (Camden) 331 Menour and Jacobin, And freres of the Carme, and of Seint Austin. *a* **1325** *Trental St. Gregory 11* in *Anglia* XIII. 303 To mynor ne to frere Austyn To caryne [*read* carme] ne to Jacobyn. *c* **1330** R. BRUNNE *Chron.* (1810) 330 He sent for Jon Comyn, þe lord of Badenauh; To Dounfres suld he come, vnto þe Minours kirke. **1447** BOKENHAM *Seyntys* (Roxb.) 301 He..to the menours ordre went. *c* **1550** BALE *K. Johan* (Camden) 18 Jacobytes, Mynors, Whyght Carmes, and Augustynis. **1700** TYRRELL *Hist. Eng.* II. 882 The Preaching Friars and Minors exhorted him. **1761** *Ann. Reg.* 146 In the neighbourhood of Bagni..three convents of the brothers of Minor-observantins of the order of St. Francis.

2. *Logic.* The minor term or the minor premiss or proposition of a syllogism.

c **1380** WYCLIF *Wks.* (1880) 382 Gabriel schal blow his horne or þai han preuyd þe mynor. **1540** COVERDALE *Confut. Standish* g viij, Of an euell Maior and Minor foloweth a weake conclusion. **1660** BOND *Scut. Reg.* 246 The Major no man can deny, the Minor is inviolable, and the Conclusion perfect and sound. **1711** in *10th Rep. Hist. MSS. Comm.* App. v. 175 The minor, or the assumption, is uncontroulable. **1840** MACAULAY *Clive* Ess. (ed. Montague) II. 463 Here the Commons stopped. They had voted the major and minor of Burgoyne's syllogism; but they shrank from drawing the logical conclusion.

3. A person under (legal) age; = INFANT 2.

1612 DAVIES *Why Ireland*, etc. 88 King Richard the second..for the first tenne yeares of his raigne was a Minor. **1771** SMOLLETT *Humph. Cl.* 5 June, My uncle then gave him to understand that I was still a minor. **1848** KINGSLEY *Saint's Trag.* III. iii. 143 The minor's guardian guards the minor's lands. **1892** GILLESPIE *Bar's Priv. Internat. Law* (ed. 2) 312 A Dutch minor, who is by the law of Belgium major, cannot dispose of his real property in Belgium without [etc.].

transf. and *fig.* *c* **1680** BEVERIDGE *Serm.* (1729) I. 35 Our christian being thus confirmed he is now looked upon in the eye of the church as no longer a minor.

4. *Mus.* Short for *minor key*, *mode*, etc.: see A. 6.

1797 *Encycl. Brit.* (ed. 3) XII. 547 *note*, Such a piece is.. upon A, with mi, la, and its minor. **1841** JEBB *Lect. Cathedral Serv.* ii. 15 A judicious use of the swell and a change from major to minor in the course of the Psalm. **1844** MRS. BROWNING *Drama of Exile* Poems 1850 I. 83 Floated on a minor fine Into the full chant divine.

b. In figurative or allusive use: see A. 6 d.

1844 MRS. BROWNING *Perplexed Music* Poems 1850 I. 329 The strain unfolds In sad, perplexed minors. **1873** BROWNING *Red Cott. Nt.-cap* 268 Over this sample would Corelli croon, Grieving, by minors, like the cushat-dove.

5. *Math.* †**a.** *Arith.* = SUBTRAHEND. *Obs.*

1612 COLSON *Gen. Treas.*, *Arит. Arithm.* Bbb2b, Of Substraction... The first number is to be called the *Maior*, grosse sum, sum total, or superior number... The second is named the *Minor*... The third is called the Remainer.

b. ***minor of a determinant*** = ***minor determinant*** (see A. 3 c).

1850 SYLVESTER in *Philos. Mag.* XXXVII. 366 The whole of a system of *r*th minors being zero. *Ibid.*, We shall have only to deal with a system of *first* minors.

6. A name for moths of the genus *Miana*.

1843 HUMPHREYS & WESTWOOD *Brit. Moths* I. 179 *Miana literosa* (the rosy minor). *Miana strigilis* (the marbled minor). **1862** F. O. MORRIS *Brit. Moths* II. 115–117.

7. *Football.* A minor point.

1890 *Stratford on Avon Herald* 24 Oct. 2/1 No other points being scored, the 'good old second' were left victorious by 1 try and 2 minors to 1 minor. **1896** *Field* 1 Feb. 171/3 The bid for goal led to a minor being conceded by the visitors.

8. In boys' schools: One's younger brother or 'minor' namesake.

1863 [HEMYNG] *Eton School Days* vii. 82 Let my minor pass, you fellows!.. Here, Chudleigh, just make room there.

9. Short for 'minor theatre', 'minor work'.

1821 P. EGAN *Real Life in London* I. vi. 92 Mr Gloss'em, who is a *shining character* in the theatrical world, at least among the minors of the metropolis. **1837** T. HOOK *Jack Brag* xvii, She is engaged at one of the Minors, and calls herself, in the bills, Roseville. *a* **1849** H. COLERIDGE *Ess.* (1851) II. 153 Why is this play set down among Shakspeare's minors? **1931** *Times Lit. Suppl.* 1 Jan. 1/2 The vast galleries of the patented theatres and the cramped benches of the 'minors' were thronged with a new audience.

10. In American universities and colleges, a subject or course of study to which less attention is given, or for which fewer credits are given, than for a major. Also, this subject seen a qualification. (See also quot. 1969.) Cf. MAJOR *sb.*² 6.

1890 in T. W. Goodspeed *Hist. Univ. Chicago* (1916) 142 The plan of majors and minors..has been arranged in order to meet this difficulty. **1909** WEBSTER, *Minor*,..a subject of study,..pursued by a candidate for a higher degree, less time being devoted to it than to the major subject. **1919** *Univ. Texas Bull.* No. 1925. 105 The student will note that it is possible to arrange his minor... [so] as to take in effect two majors. **1926** [see ELECTIVE *sb.* 2]. **1948** *Ada* (Okla.) *Even. News* 2 July 6/2 Alliene Pryor-Smith..will graduate at East Central in July, with a major in history and a minor in sociology. **1969** *Amer. Heritage Dict.*, *Minor*... One studying a minor: *a chemistry minor*.

11. In *Bridge*, = *minor suit*; also, a card in a minor suit.

1927 [see MAJOR *a.* 1 d]. **1958** *Listener* 4 Dec. 965/1 Which two aces?.. They are both of the same rank, *i.e.* both minors. **1960** *Times* 16 Nov. 17/4 A two-suiter in the minors only, with Diamonds as long as, or longer than the clubs.

minor ('maɪnə(r)), *v.* Chiefly *N. Amer.* [f. MINOR *a.* and *sb.*] *intr.* Of a university student: to take, or qualify *in*, a minor (see prec., sense B. 10).

1934 in WEBSTER. **1967** *Oxf. Mag.* 10 Feb. 205/1 [Canada] They intend to major in life sciences and minor in Phys. Ed.

minor, obs. or erron. f. MINA², MINER, MINOT.

minorage ('maɪnərɪdʒ). [f. MINOR + -AGE.] The condition of being under age; minority.

1888 E. SALT *Hist. Standon* 84 During the minorage of the heir.

minorale, -all, obs. forms of MINERAL.

† **minorand.** *Arith. Obs.* [ad. med.L. *minōrandus* (sc. *numerus*), gerundive of *minōrāre*: see next.] = MINUEND.

1709–29 V. MANDEY *Syst. Math., Arith.* 13 The Remainer added to the Subducend, if the Sum makes the Minorand, 'tis right.

minorate ('maɪnəreɪt), *v.* [f. med.L. *minōrāt-*, ppl. stem of *minōrāre* to diminish, f. L. *minōr-em* less: see MINOR.] *trans.* To diminish, depreciate.

1534 *Act 26 Hen. VIII*, c. 6 §11 This present acte..shall not extende..to..or minorate any liberties..or auctoritie of any lorde marcher. **1623** [see MINIMATE *v.*]. **1628** A. LEIGHTON in *Camden Misc.* VII. p. vi, Magnanimious Henry whom we do not name to minorate the parts of our present Soveraigne. **1682** SIR T. BROWNE *Chr. Mor.* III. §10 Forget not how assuefaction unto anything minorates the passion from it. **1727** BAILEY vol. II, *Minorated*, diminished, or made less. **1789** J. MORSE *Amer. Geogr.* 212 Their design is by quantity to depreciate the value of their bills; and lands mortgaged for public bills will be redeemed in these minorated bills. **1922** JOYCE *Ulysses* 387 Assuefaction minorates atrocities (as Tully saith of his darling Stoics).

† **mino'ration.** *Obs.* [agent-n. f. med.L. *minōrāre*: see prec. and -ATION.]

1. A lessening, diminution.

1607 WALSALL *Life Christ* C 4, This willing minoration and exinanition of himselfe. **1646** SIR T. BROWNE *Pseud. Ep.* II. v. 86 The Loadstone, whose effluencies are both continuall, and communicable without a minoration of gravity. **1649** JER. TAYLOR *Gt. Exemp.* I. Ad Sect. v. 58 The excuse and minoration of our actuall impieties. **1696** PHILLIPS, *Minoration*, a diminishing, or making less. **1856** in MAYNE *Expos. Lex.*

2. Mild purgation by laxatives.

1684 tr. *Bonet's Merc. Compit.* VI. 229 Some minoration of the crude matter must be procured first by Clysters.

† **'minorative**, *a.* and *sb. Obs.* [f. MINORATE *v.* + -IVE. Cf. F. *minoratif* (Cotgr.).] **a.** *adj.* That diminishes or lessens. Of medicines: Gently laxative. **b.** *sb.* A gently laxative medicine.

1543 TRAHERON *Vigo's Chirurg.* IX. Add. 225 Clysters sometymes do supplye the rowme of minoratyve medicines. **1633** HART *Diet of Diseased* III. xiv. 284 When..wee feare lest nature faint before perfect concoction, we may sometimes use a gentle minorative. **1747** tr. *Astruc's Fevers* 112 Nothing but minorative apozems should be ordered. *Ibid.* 232 Others give minoratives more frequently.

Minorca (mɪ'nɔːkə). Also 9 **Menorca.** [Sp. *Menorca.*] The name of the second in size of the Balearic islands. Used *attrib.*, as ***Minorca-fowl*** (also *Minorca*), a much esteemed black variety of the domestic fowl introduced from Spain; ***Minorca holly*** (see quot.). Hence **Mi'norcan** and the equivalent † **Minorquin,** † **Menorquine** [Sp. *Menorquin*]. **a.** *adj.* of or belonging to the island of Minorca; **b.** *sb.* an inhabitant of Minorca; also, the language of the inhabitants of Minorca.

1760 SMOLLETT *Contin. Hist. Eng., Geo. II*, ann. 1756 I. 327 Five and twenty Minorquin bakers were hired. **1785** *Gentl. Mag.* LV. I. 66 The Minorquins, when they see an Englishman, follow him. **1839** *Penny Cycl.* XV. 97/2 In character and manners, the Menorquines resemble the natives of Mallorca. **1848** E. S. DIXON *Orn. & Dom. Poultry* 251 In North Devon they call the Spanish Fowls 'Minorcas'. **1853** *Naturalist* III. 225 *Ilex Balearica*, the Minorca Holly; a very distinct variety of the Common Holly, being readily distinguished by its yellow green leaves. **1882–3** *Schaff's Encycl. Relig. Knowl.* III. 2065 During the British sway, a number of Minorcans and Greeks were introduced by Mr. Turnbull [into Florida]. **1897** BAGHOT DE LA BERE *New Poultry Guide* II. 38 Blue Andalusians, black Minorcas, and white Leghorns, all universally admitted to be prolific layers.

Minoress[1] ('maɪnərɪs). *Obs.* exc. *Hist.* Forms: 4 **menouresse,** 5 **meneresse,** 7 **minoress.** [ME. *menouresse*, a. OF. *menouresse*, f. *menour* MINOR *sb.* 1: see -ESS. (In med.L. *minōrissa.*)] A nun of the second order of St. Francis, known as Poor Clares, whose house outside Aldgate gave its name to the *Minories*, a street still existing in the City of London.

Susters Meneresses (quot. 1451) is after OF. *sereurs meneuresses*.

1395 *E. E. Wills* (1882) 7 The Religiouse Wommen the Menouresses dwellyngge withoute algate of london. **1451** *Rolls of Parlt.* V. 224/1 The Abbesse and Covent of the Susters Meneresses withoute Algate. **1631** WEEVER *Anc. Funeral Mon.* 755 These Nunnes were of the order of S. Clare, and called Minoresses. **1897** *Cath. Dict.* (ed. 5) 726/2 The first monastery of Franciscan nuns or Minoresses formed in England (1293) was outside Aldgate.

minoress[2] ('maɪnərɪs). *rare*⁻⁰. [f. MINOR + -ESS.] A female minor.

1882 in OGILVIE.

Minorist ('maɪnərɪst). *rare*⁻¹. [f. MINOR + -IST.] = MINORITE *sb.* 1.

1836 *Tracts for Times* No. 75. 9 The Fratres Minores (Minorists or Franciscans) adopted the new usage.

Minorite ('maɪnəraɪt), *sb.* and *a.* [f. MINOR + -ITE.] **A.** *sb.*

1. A friar minor or Franciscan.

1577–87 HOLINSHED *Chron.* II. 41/2 Malachias, the minorit or greie frier. **1613** PURCHAS *Pilgrimage* (1614) 427 Iohn à Monte Coruino, a Minorite. **1760** JORTIN *Erasm.* II. 118 Then follows a short letter to some Minorites, who defamed Erasmus. **1883** JESSOP in *19th Cent.* July 99 The Minorites were the Low Churchmen of the 13th century.

2. † **a.** A person of minor rank (*obs.*). **b.** *allusive nonce-use.* One busied about minor matters.

1644 MILTON *Areop.* (Arb.) 41 Our inquisiturient Bishops, and the attendant minorites their Chaplains. *a* **1670** HACKET *Abp. Williams* II. (1693) 102 The Respondent takes no notice that a Bishop wrote the Letter: For why not rather some Minorite among the Clergy? **1807** SOUTHEY *Espriella's Lett.* (1814) I. 233 The ordinary pursuits of mankind are not as innocent as that of these experimental Minorites or Minims.

B. *adj.* Of the order of Friars Minor.

1563–87 FOXE *A. & M.* (1596) 236/2 The order of the minors or minorit friers descended from one Francis..of.. Assisium. **1598** HAKLUYT *Voy.* I. 53 A Frier Minorite, called Simon de Sanct. Quintin. *a* **1604** HANMER *Chron. Irel.* (1633) 73 There was another Livinus a French man, a Fryer minorite. **1766** ENTICK *London* IV. 310 On the scite.. there anciently stood the abbey of Minorite nuns. **1892** K. GOULD *Conversat. Döllinger* x. 245 S. Bonaventure, a member of the Minorite order.

minority (mɪ'nɒrɪtɪ). [ad. F. *minorité* or med.L. *minōritās*, f. L. *minōr-em* MINOR: see -ITY. Cf. Sp. *minoridad*, Pg. *minoridade*, It. *minorità.*]

† **1.** The condition or fact of being smaller, inferior, or subordinate. *Obs.*

1533 MORE *Answ. to Poysoned Bk.* Wks. 1051/2 The minoritie, and the obedyence yᵗ the scripture speketh of in Christ, is all ment of his manhod. **1592** KYD *Sol. & Pers.* IV. ii. 62 What, art thou that petty pigmie that chalenged me at Rhodes, whom I refused to combat for his minoritie? **1646** SIR T. BROWNE *Pseud. Ep.* III. vi. 117 There may, I confesse, from this narrow time of gestation ensue a minority, or smallnesse in the exclusion. **1727–51** CHAMBERS *Cycl.* s.v. *Character*, ∠ Is the sign of minority.

2. a. The state of being minor or under age; the period during which a person remains under age; nonage; *in*, † *within minority*, under age.

1547 *Reg. Privy Council Scot.* I. 78 Dispensand with thair minorite and less age,..without payment of ony teind penny. **1579–80** NORTH *Plutarch, Comp. Theseus & Rom.* (1595) 45 Theseus..stole awaye Helen in hir minoritie, being nothing neere to consent to marrye. **1617** MORYSON *Itin.* III. 217 The Pupill..is held under daies or in minority till he be twenty one yeres old. **1632** LITHGOW *Trav.* I. 7, I ..being young, and within minority. **1642** FULLER *Holy & Prof. St.* v. xviii. 432 The minority of Princes ought not to lessen their Subjects reverence unto them. **1751** H. WALPOLE *Lett.* (1846) II. 404 It is become the peculiarity of the House of Orange to have minorities. **1856** EMERSON *Eng. Traits, Wealth* Wks. (Bohn) II. 76 A youth in England, emerging from his minority. **1874** GREEN *Short Hist.* vi. §1. 265 The long minority of Henry the Sixth, who was a boy of nine months old at his father's death. **1920** *Act 10 & 11 Geo. V* c. 64 §2 A husband of full age,..whose wife is in minority, shall be her curator during her minority.

† **b.** The early part of life, youth. *Obs.*

1632 LITHGOW *Trav.* IX. 415 Such a man can neither seduce his minority with ill examples, nor marre his waxen age with a false impression. **1728** R. MORRIS *Ess. Anc. Archit.* p. xix, A Principle imbibed in Minority.

c. *transf.* and *fig.* Now *rare.*

1611 DONNE *Anat. World, 1st Annivers.* (1625) 12 When Stag, and Rauen, and the long liu'd tree..dy'de in minoritee. **1631** WEEVER *Anc. Funeral Mon.* 160 An old booke in broken English, which crept into the world in the minoritie of Printing. **1632** tr. *Bruel's Praxis Med.* 59 This disease..doth sticke close to the patient, vnlesse it bee taken away by medicines in its minority. **1646** SIR T. BROWNE *Pseud. Ep.* I. vii. 25 Yet are our authorities but temporary and not to be imbraced beyond the minority of our intellectuals. **1653** MILTON *Hirelings* Wks. 1851 V. 373 For the Magistrate..to make the Church his meer Ward, as always in Minority,..is neither just nor pious. **1742** YOUNG *Nt. Th.* VI. 616 In this her dark minority, how toils..the human soul!

3. a. The smaller number or part; a number which is less than half the whole number; *spec.* the smaller party voting together against a majority in a deliberative assembly or electoral body.

1736 AINSWORTH *Lat. Dict.*, *Minority* (lesser number). **1755** in JOHNSON. **1789** BURKE *Corr.* (1844) III. 95 We are a minority; but then we are a very large minority. **1790** —— *Fr. Rev.* (ed. 2) 186 In a democracy, the majority of the citizens is capable of exercising the most cruel oppressions upon the minority. **1809–10** COLERIDGE *Friend* (1865) 137 The tone of men, who are conscious that they are in a minority. **1828** MACAULAY *Ess., Hallam* ad fin., Conspiracies and insurrections in which small minorities are engaged. **1886–94** H. SPENCER *Autobiogr.* II. liii. 298 It is my habit to say what I think, though I may so show myself one of a very small minority, or even a minority of one. **1898** *Allbutt's Syst. Med.* V. 1004 The insufficiency of the mitral valve, which occurs in a minority of cases of exophthalmic goitre. **1903** R. D. SHAW *Pauline Ep.* II. i. 86 Men of pure Gallic blood must in Paul's time have been greatly in the minority.

b. A small group of people separated from the rest of the community by a difference in race, religion, language, etc. Also in quasi-*adj.* use.

1921 H. W. V. TEMPERLEY et al. *Hist. Peace Conf. Paris* V. ii. 112 These treaties provide for the protection of racial, linguistic, or religious minorities included within the boundaries of the specified States. **1930** *Economist* 29 Nov. 1001/1 The Nazis and the Stahlhelm have been conducting reprisals against the Polish minority in Germany. **1937** *Times* 24 Feb. 13/3 The concessions made by the Prague Government to sections of the German minority..are disconcerting to any plans..for a large-scale minorities campaign. **1945** *Ann. Reg. 1944* 26 Some broad general declaration by the United Nations deprecating the ill-treatment by a state of its minorities. **1945** L. WIRTH in R. Linton *Sci. of Man* 347 The existence of a minority in a society implies the existence of a corresponding dominant group enjoying higher social status and greater privileges. **1970** *Washington Post* 30 Sept. B. 14/4 A hard-hat worker who loses his job to a minority worker. **1973** *Black Panther* 3 Mar. 13/3 In civil rights, aid to minority business enterprises is stressed, rather than to the minority poor. **1975** *Atlantic Monthly* Jan. 29/1 By 'minority' today, we mean a disadvantaged group of citizens. *Ibid.*, Today, by a 'minority' we mean not the privileged at the top, but the underprivileged at the bottom.

4. In voting, the number of votes cast for or by the party opposed to the majority.

1774 BURKE *Sp. Amer. Tax.* Wks. II. 414 The minority did not reach to more than 39 or 40. **1788** JEFFERSON *Writ.* (1859) II. 533 The minorities in most of the accepting States have been very acceptable.

5. *attrib.* and *Comb.*, as **minority carrier** *Electronics*, a charge carrier of the kind carrying the smaller proportion of the electric current in a semiconducting material (cf. *majority carrier* s.v. MAJORITY 7); **minority debt,** a debt incurred by a person while under age; **minority group,** a group forming a minority (sense 3 b); **minority language,** a language spoken by a minority group if different from that of the majority; **minority man,** one who is in a minority or tries to secure recognition of the claims of minorities; **minority member,** a member appointed to a board, committee, or the like to represent a minority; **minority movement,** a movement to secure justice or proper representation for minorities; **minority platform** *U.S.*, the 'platform' put forward by the minority of a party; **minority report,** a separate report framed by those members of a committee or other body who are unable to agree with the majority; **minority rights,** rights granted to minorities to act as a safeguard of their interests and help prevent discrimination against them by the majority; **minority teller,** one who counts or records votes for a minority; † **minority waiter** (meaning obscure; by some explained as 'a waiter out of work', by others as 'an extraordinary tide-waiter', i.e. one not regularly employed).

1951 *Minority carrier [see *majority carrier* s.v. MAJORITY 7]. **1962** SIMPSON & RICHARDS *Physical Princ. Junction Transistors* iv. 60 Another variation in charge in the vicinity of the junction arises from the injection or extraction of minority carriers under conditions of forward or very small reverse bias respectively. **1969** J. J. SPARKES *Transistor Switching* i. 3 The current from one junction to the other is carried by minority carriers. **1897** *Daily News* 13 May 8/5 The half-crown cigars were also *minority debts? **1905** *Daily Chron.* 24 June 6/6 He has raised £45,000..out of which he paid his minority debts. **1942** LOCKE & STERN *When Peoples Meet* I. iv. 125 Such..inclusion of *minority groups is in marked and often ironic contrast to the more normal 'divide and rule' policy..of dominant groups. **1964** M. ARGYLE *Psychol. & Social Probl.* vii. 94 Several studies show that prejudice increases with the density of the minority group in an area. **1971** R. BENDIX in A. Bullock *20th Cent.* 357/1 The citizenship of racial minorities remains an unresolved problem. Members of minority groups are denied rights which are formally theirs. **1939** L. H. GRAY *Foundations of Lang.* v. 118 *Minority-languages may thus be not merely linguistic in interest, but may also constitute political problems of all degrees of importance. **1927** *Observer* 1 May 17/1 It was a curious moment..to choose for legislation calculated..to revive the power of '*minority men' and direct actionists in Britain. **1874** *Porcupine* 31 Jan. 693/2 The city of London has already conceded a *minority member. **1927** *Daily Tel.* 6 Sept. 7/3 He did not agree with the *Minority Movement. **1901** *N. Amer. Rev.* Feb. 271 The captors were able to defeat the *minority platform. **1833** *Reg. Deb. Congress U.S.* 2 Mar. 1927 A new set of majority and *minority reports are to be launched upon the public. **1940** B. DE VOTO (*title*) Minority report. **1958** *Everyman's Encycl.* XII. 532/2 With Sidney Webb..she [*sc.* Beatrice Webb] issued the minority report which initiated the Socialist agitation for the reform of the old Poor Law. **1924** R. W. SETON-WATSON *New Slovakia* vi. 104 Such international opinion as regards the '*Minority rights' provided for by the Peace Treaties, as a moral obligation assumed by all members of the League of Nations. **1955** I. L. CLAUDE *National Minorities* xii. 166 Whenever the issue must be squarely faced, the U.S. takes the lead..in opposing the concept of special minority rights. **1972** 'E. LATHEN' *The Longer the Thread* viii. 74 She was a Puerto Rican—yet she had never served on a commission about minority rights. **1902** *Daily Chron.* 27 Feb. 5/1 He had to occupy the unusual position of being the *minority-teller at the table. **1775** SHERIDAN *Rivals* II. i, I told Thomas that your Honour had already inlisted five disbanded chairmen, seven *minority waiters, and thirteen billiard markers.

b. quasi-*adj.* Of, for, composed of, or appealing to a minority (of people); freq. with the suggestion of 'serious, intellectual, highbrow' (as opposed to MASS *sb.*[2] 10).

1930 F. R. LEAVIS (*title*) Mass civilization and minority culture. **1932** Q. D. LEAVIS *Fiction & Reading Public* II. iv. §3. 199 Enough attention has perhaps been given to the effects of minority values. **1941** *Partisan Rev.* Mar.–Apr. 111 Leisured people who have been brought up in a minority culture. **1944** L. MACNEICE *Christopher Columbus* 9, I am in favour of occasional special [radio] programmes for small minority audiences. **1958** R. WILLIAMS *Culture & Society* III. iii. 235 Those extreme forms of the idea of a 'minority culture'. **1959** *20th Cent.* Nov. 324 Serious minority programmes [on television] at peak hours. *Ibid.* 333 A place remains for it [*sc.* sound radio]..in the evenings

for special minority interests and for music. **1960** *Housewife* Apr. 10/2 The Editor.. considers very few subjects indeed too 'minority' or too apparently trivial to be given a sensible airing. **1971** *Guardian* 22 Feb. 8/1 Even from the BBC.. a complete diet of minority-interest programmes.. would not be.. acceptable. **1972** P. BLACK *Biggest Aspidistra* I. iv. 42 The heat was taken off the minority drama.

† **'minorize,** *v. Obs. rare*$^{-1}$. [f. MINOR *a.* + -IZE. Cf. MINORATE *v.*] *trans.* To depreciate.

1615 SIR E. HOBY *Curry-combe* i. 34 Hee that will take vpon him to Minorize the learning of Authors.

† **minorque.** *Obs. rare*$^{-1}$. [Fr.: see MINORCA.] A kind of cloth.

1792 A. YOUNG *Trav. France* II. xix. (1794) II. 539 They make.. camblets, calimancoes, minorques, coarse cloths.

minorship ('maınəʃıp). [f. MINOR + -SHIP.] The state of being a minor (Ogilvie 1882).

‖ **minot** (mino). [F., f. *mine* a measure of 6 bushels.] An obsolete French measure of capacity, varying according to locality and the nature of the commodity to be measured: the standard value was 3 (French) bushels = about 39.36 litre.

1585 T. WASHINGTON tr. *Nicholay's Voy.* IV. xxxiii. 155 b, Those which were found aswel in grayn, as fruits of yerely reuenues the quantity of 500. minots. **1668** *Lond. Gaz.* No. 259/4 His Majesty.. intends.. to abate 4 Crowns upon each Minot [*printed* minor], or measure of four French bushels of Salt. **1727** BRADLEY *Fam. Dict.* s.v. *Bread*, They take a Minot of this Flower.. leaven and boult it, and cover it well with the same Flower or Meal. **1727–41** CHAMBERS *Cycl.* s.v. *Measure*, The minot consists of three bushels; the mine of two minots. **1820** RANKEN *Hist. France* VIII. VIII. vi. 393 The minot contained three bushels.

minotary, obs. form of MINATORY.

Minotaur ('mınətɔː(r)). *Gr. Myth.* [ad. Gr. Μινώταυρ-ος (L. *Minōtaur-us*, OF. *Minotaur*, F. *Minotaure*), f. Μίνως Minos + ταῦρος bull.]

a. A fabulous monster, the son of Pasiphaë, wife of Minos king of Crete, and a bull, represented as having the body of a man and the head of a bull. He was confined in the Cretan labyrinth and fed with human flesh. He was slain by Theseus, who thus freed Athens from her annual tribute of seven youths and seven maidens to be devoured by the monster. Hence used *allusively*.

c **1385** CHAUCER *L.G.W.* 2104 (*Ariadne*) The mynatour [*v.rr.* Mynotawr(e, -taure, Mynataur]. **1390** GOWER *Conf.* II. 304 Minotaure. *c* **1470** HENRYSON *Mor. Fab.* v. (*Parl. Beasts*) xiv, The minotaur, ane monster meruelous. **1500–20** DUNBAR *Fenȝeit Freir* 66 The Menatair [*v.r.* Mynataur] marvelus. **1591** SHAKS. *1 Hen. VI*, v. iii. 189 There Minotaurs and vgly Treasons lurke. **1592** DANIEL *Compl. Rosamond* lxix, Heere I inclos'd from all the world a sunder, The Minotaure of shame kept for disgrace. **1876** GEO. ELIOT *Dan. Der.* III. xxii, But don't give yourself for a meal to a minotaur like Bult. **1900** *United Service Mag.* Jan. 427 All those who were the hope and future strength of the race were devoured by the Imperial Minotaur [*sc.* Napoleon] in pursuit of his dream of universal domination. **1939** SPENDER & REES tr. *Büchner's Danton's Death* I. iv. 42 The people is a Minotaur that must be fed with corpses every week if it is not to eat the Committee alive. **1945** AUDEN *Sea & Mirror* ii. 51 Home to your promiscuous pastures where the minotaur of authority is just a roly-poly ruminant and nothing is at stake. **1950** T. S. ELIOT *Cocktail Party* III. 163 We talk of darkness, labyrinths, Minotaur terrors. **1964** A. W. GOULDNER in I. L. Horowitz *New Sociol.* 196 The lair of this minotaur [*sc.* Max Weber].. is still regarded by many sociologists as a holy place.

b. A representation of this, esp. *Her.*

c **1386** CHAUCER *Knt.'s T.* 122 And by his Baner born is his penoun Of gold ful riche, in which ther was ybete The Mynotaur which þat he slough in Crete. **1572** BOSSEWELL *Armorie* II. 49 R. beareth azure, a Minotaure d' Argente. **1776** BURNEY *Hist. Mus.* (1789) I. II. iii. 337 In a medal inscribed Caleno the Minotaur is seen.

minouet, obs. form of MINUET *sb.*

minour, obs. form of MINER.

† **mi'novery.** *Law. Obs.* [app. a corrupt form of MANŒUVRE. The source from which Cowell obtained the word is unknown.] (See quot.)

1607 COWELL *Interpr., Minovery*.. signifieth some trespasse or offence committed by a man's handie work in the Forest, as an engyn to catch Deere.

[Hence in Dicts.; those of recent date substitute the form *manovery*.]

minow, obs. form of MINNOW.

minowaye, variant of MINAWAY (= minuet).

Minox ('maınɒks). The proprietary name of a type of miniature camera.

1952 *Brit. Jrnl. Photogr.* 5 Sept. 433/1 Several miniature miniatures have already appeared on the market. One notable example is the Minox. This uses 16-mm. film.. and the negatives produced give moderate size enlarged prints of good quality. **1962** L. DEIGHTON *Ipcress File* ii. 20 Chico.. would have been making time with the Minox camera. **1966** J. BINGHAM *Double Agent* v. 72 Golchenko.. took out the rolls of Minox film. **1966** *Trade Marks Jrnl.* 6 Apr. 463/1 Minox... Photographic apparatus and instruments and parts and fittings there for.. Minox Gesellschaft mit Beschränkter Haftung (a Limited Liability Company organised under the laws of the German Federal Republic), .. Giessen-Heuchelheim, Germany; manufacturers. **1969** K. BENTON *24th Level* vi. 116 [He] took out his Minox.. and took photographs.

† **Minozin.** *Obs.*

1680 *Lond. Gaz.* No. 1567/4 A sad Minozin colour cloth Coat.

minrall, minre, obs. ff. MINERAL, MINE *pron.*

minse, -sed, -sen, -ser, obs. ff. MINCE, etc.

minsh, -ery, obs. forms of MINCH, -ERY.

† **minsical,** *a. Obs. rare*$^{-1}$. [? f. MINCE *v.* + -ICAL.] ? Mincing, dainty.

a **1586** SIDNEY *Wanstead Play* in *Arcadia*, etc. (1605) 571 A woman, of a minsicall countenance, but.. not three quarters so beautious as your selfe.

† **'minsing.** *Obs.* [f. **minse* vb. (cogn. w. MIN *v.*) + -ING[1].] Remembrance.

c **1330** R. BRUNNE *Chron. Wace* 326 Of hym ys mynsyng wiþ-outen ende, ffor he made a cite of ioye After his name, & calde hit Troye. —— *Chron.* (1810) 201 Þi misdede be in þi mynsyng, Euer more to drede, eft to do suilke þing.

minsitive: see MINCEATIVE.

minster[1] ('mınstə(r)). Forms: 1, 4–6 mynster, 3–6 mynstre, 2 minister, 3 munster, -tre, 4 mynyster, -tre, menestre, mynstire, 4–5 mynstere, mynistre, 5 mynester, mynstir, ministre, minstre, 1, 6– minster. [OE. *mynster*:—prehistoric **munistrjo*, a. popular L. **monisterium* = Eccl. L. *monastērium* MONASTERY. Cf. OHG. *munistri* (MHG., mod.G. *münster*), MDu. *monster* (early mod.Du. *munster*), ON. *mustari*.]

† **1.** A monastery; a Christian religious house.

a **900** tr. *Bæda's Hist.* I. xxxiii. (Schipper), Wæs se æresta abbud þæs ylcan mynstres [L. *eiusdem monasterii*] Petrus haten. *c* **1205** LAY. 29357 Gurmund falde þa munstres and an heng alle þa munkes. **1387** TREVISA *Higden* (Rolls) I. 261 Faste by þe mynystre [L. *cenobium*] of Seint Michel is marbil i-founde. *c* **1450** *St. Cuthbert* (Surtees) 6695 A mynstere, Duellyng for monkes and him in fere. *c* **1475** *Partenay* 2596 Faire maillers, that ministre roiall. **1513** BRADSHAW *St. Werburge* II. 91 Erle Leofrice repared.. The mynstre of Werburge, gyuyng therto liberte.

2. The church of a monastery; a church which had its origin in a monastic establishment; also applied gen. to any church of considerable size or importance, esp. a collegiate or cathedral church.

c **960** *Laws K. Edgar* I. i, Man agife ælce teoðunge to þam ealdan mynstre [L. *ad matrem ecclesiam*] þe seo hyrnes tohyrð. **1056–66** *Inscription* (at Kirkdale Ch. Yorksh.), Orm Gamal svna bohte scs Gregorivs minster ðonne hit wes æl tobrocan & tofalan. **1297** R. GLOUC. (Rolls) 3230 Þe heye munstre of winchestre. **13..** *E.E. Allit. P.* A. 1063 Þe almyȝty was her mynyster mete, þe lombe þe saker-fyse þer to reget. **1389** in *Eng. Gilds* (1870) 30 Seynt Willyams toumbe in ye mynstre of ye trinyte. *c* **1450** *Merlin* vi. 98 Than thei.. yeden a-gein in-to the mynistre to heir oute the masse. **1470–85** MALORY *Arthur* XIII. ix. 624, I shal assay to bere hit [the shield], and soo bare hit oute of the mynstre. *c* **1599** *Acc. Bk. W. Wray* in *Antiquary* XXXII. 278 The colligiat churche or minster.. in Ripo'. *a* **1645** HABINGTON *Surv. Worcs.* in *Worcs. Hist. Soc. Proc.* II. 191 The cloyster of the Mynster of Worcester. **1675** OGILBY *Brit.* (1698) 20 The Cathedral or Minster [at Lincoln] is a stately structure. **1771** SMOLLETT *Humph. Cl.* 4 July, As for the minster [at York], I know not how to distinguish it, except by its great size. *a* **1878** SIR G. G. SCOTT *Lect. Archit.* (1879) I. 200 Yorkshire is especially the land of minsters and abbey-churches. **1898** LEACH in *Beverley Ch. Act Bk.* (Surtees) Introd. 34 The word minster itself is peculiarly one used not of monasteries but of secular churches—York, Beverley, Ripon, Southwell, Lincoln, Lichfield, Wimborne, these are the churches to which the title of minster has clung,.. and they were one and all churches of secular canons.

† **b.** *transf.* A temple. *Obs.*

c **1200** ORMIN 7580 Þeȝȝ comenn inntill Ȝerrsalæm & inntill Godess minnstre. *a* **1400–50** *Alexander* 2174 When he was full þare & fedd he flittis with his ost, To Tergarontes he teȝe þare tiȝt was a mynstre. *c* **1400** MAUNDEV. (1839) xvi. 174 Before the Mynstre of this Ydole is a Vyvere. **1562** PHAER *Æneid* VII. Z iv b, Three hundred mynsters chief along the towne wyde open stands. **1581** NUCE *Seneca's Octavia* II. ii. 174 b, Whom as a God in minsters we adorne.

3. *attrib.* and *Comb.*, as ***minster-aisle*** (also *fig.*), ***-church, -door, -fund, -gale, -garth, pile, -quire, -yard***; † **minster book,** a book used in church.

c **1450** *St. Cuthbert* (Surtees) 4263 Þe *mynster yles were made as warde. **1863** HAWTHORNE *Our Old Home, Lichfield* I. 211 Overarched by a minster-aisle of venerable trees. *c* **1200** *Trin. Coll. Hom.* 109 Alse þe holi *minster-boc seið. **1828** SCOTT *F. M. Perth* iii, I believe she thinks the whole world is one great *Minster-church. **13..** *St. Erkenwolde* 128 in Horstm. *Altengl. Leg.* (1881) 269 *Mynster-dores were makyd opone, quene matens were songene. **13..** *E.E. Allit. P.* C. 268 As mote in at a munster dor, so mukel wern his chawlez. **14..** *Sir Beues* (M.) 4275 The kyngis doughter was.. to the mynester durre I-led, Vnto sir Myles was she wed. **1829** G. POULSON *Beverlac* 681 Trustees of the *minster fund. *c* **1400** *St. Alexius* (Cotton) 200 Withowtyn att the *mynster yate. **1393** *Test. Ebor.* (Surtees) I. 185 My graven in the *mynster Garth. **1866** NEALE *Sequences & Hymns* 131 Lincoln's *minster pile. **1634–5** BRERETON *Trav.* (Chetham Soc.) 72 Erected in the *minster-quire. **1842** W. WHITE *Directory Lincs.* 124 *Minster yard.

† **'minster**[2]. *Obs.* [From the name of *Münster* a German city, capital of Westphalia.] A kind of linen cloth originally imported from Münster.

1612 *Sc. Bk. Customs* in *Halyburton's Ledger* (1867) 321 Minsters the rowle contening xv hundreth elnis, iiicxx li. **1698–9** HOUGHTON *Collect. Husb. & Trade* No. 343 (1727) II. 382 Of minsters from Germany 74246 ells.

minster, obs. form of MINISTER *v.*

minstracy, -trall, -tralsie, -sy, obs. ff. MINSTREL, -TRELSY.

† **'minstraly.** *Sc. Obs.* Forms: 4 menstrely, 4, 6 -traly, 6 menstrallie, -tralie, -ye. [f. MINSTREL + -Y.] = MINSTRELSY.

c **1375** *Sc. Leg. Saints* xxxiii. (*George*) 191 Til haf had menstrely & in all degre haf mad myry. *Ibid.* 662 Þane wes mad gret Ioy in hy with syndry kynde of menstraly. **1500–20** DUNBAR *Poems* lxxviii. 13 For mirth, for menstrallie and play. **1549** *Compl. Scot.* vi. 65 Appollo.. vitht his sueit menstralye. **1567** *Gude & Godlie Ball.* (S.T.S.) 37 Quhen that he.. hard the menstrallie [*v.r.* menstraly] anone, The dansing, and the greit blyithnes [etc.].

minstre, obs. form of MINISTRY.

minstrel ('mınstrəl), *sb.* Forms: α. 3 menestral, (*pl.* menestraus); β. 4 mynystrel, ministrele, minestrale, 4–5 mynystral, 5 mynistralle, 6 mynystrell, mynnystrelle, (7 *arch.* ministrel); γ. 4 menstrelle, 4–5 menstrale, -alle, 4–6, 7 *Sc.* menstral, 5 *Sc.* menstraille, 5–6 menstrell, 6 menstrall; δ. 4 mynstraell, -tral(e, (munstral), 4–5 minstral(e, mynstralle, 4–6 mynstrel(le, minstralle, 5 minstrall, 5–6 minstrelle, 6 minstril, mynstrell, 6–7 minstrell, 7 minstrill, 6– minstrel. [a. OF. *menestral, -terel, ministral, -terel* (F. *ménestrel*) = Pr. *menestral* officer, person employed, attendant, musician:—late L. *ministeriāl-em* one having an official duty, f. *ministerium*: see MINISTRY.

OF. had a synon. *menestrier* (mod.F. *ménétrier* village musician), f. *menestrel* with alteration of suffix. The It. *ministrello*, Sp. *ministril*, Pg. *ministrel*, are formed after Fr.]

† **1.** *gen.* A servant having a special function. *Obs. rare*$^{-1}$.

a **1225** *Ancr. R.* 84 An oðer half, nimeð nu ȝeme of hwuche two mesteres þeos two menestraus [*sc.* the flatterer and the backbiter] serueð hore louerde, þe deofle of helle.

2. a. In early use (i.e. down to the end of the 16th c.), a general designation for any one whose profession was to entertain his patrons with singing, music, and story-telling, or with buffoonery or juggling. In modern romantic and historical use commonly with narrowed and elevated application: A mediæval singer or musician, esp. one who sang or recited, to the accompaniment of his own playing on a stringed instrument, heroic or lyric poetry composed by himself or others; *spec.* one of the Old English period.

The use of the word in romantic poetry and fiction has so coloured its meaning that the application to a mere jester, mountebank, or conjuror, originally common, would now seem inappropriate.

1297 R. GLOUC. (Rolls) 5509 Menestrel he was god ynou & harpare in eche poynte. **1362** LANGL. *P. Pl.* A. Prol. 33 And summe Murþhes to maken as Munstrals cunne. ? *a* **1366** CHAUCER *Rom. Rose* 764 Ther mightest thou see these floutours, Minstrales, and eek Iogelours. *c* **1386** —— *Sir Thopas* 134 Do come he seyde my Mynstrales And geestours for to tellen tales Anon in myn Armynge. **14..** *Nom.* in Wr.-Wülcker 693 *Hic prestigiator*, mynstralle. **1423** in T. Sharp *Diss. Pageants Coventry* (1825) 207 Thei have retained Matthew Ellerton.. & John Trumpor Mynstrells as for the Cite of Coventry. *c* **1440** *Alphabet of Tales* ccclvi. 245 He saw mynstrallis & iogullurs. *Ibid.*, He said, hym had levur clethe Criste þer-with, or pure men, þan for to giff þaim to mynstrallis, for, he said, it was no noder to giff to mynstrals bod for to offyr to fendis. **1508** in Lysons *Envir. Lond.* (1792) I. 226 To the menstorell upon May-day, 0 0 4. **1535** COVERDALE *Matt.* ix. 23 When Iesus came into the rulers house, and sawe the minstrels [so **1611**] and the people raginge. **1539** CROMWELL in Merriman *Life & Lett.* (1902) II. 236 Item youe shall allowe to Mr. Brereton and Mr. Gryffith their chaplaynes and minstralles. **1553** EDEN *Treat. Newe Ind.* (Arb.) 25 Al the musicions & minstrels.. playe on theyr instrumentes. **1559** ABP. HETHE in Strype *Ann. Ref.* (1824) I. App. vi. 403 Kinge Davyd.. placed himselfe amongest the mynystrells. **1597** *Maldon, Essex* Liber C. 146 b, The said John Cooke.. shall.. the said John Hill.. instructe.. in the.. arte misterie and facultie of a minstrell. **1706** PHILLIPS (ed. Kersey), *Minstrel*, a Player on the Violin; a Fidler, or Piper. **1767** PERCY *Ess. Anc. Eng. Minstrels* 9 The privileges and honours which were so lavishly bestowed upon the northern scalds, were not wholly with-held from the Anglo-Saxon Minstrels. **1768** BEATTIE (*title*) The Minstrel. **1805** SCOTT (*title*) The Lay of the Last Minstrel. **1839** T. WRIGHT *Ess. Lit. & Learning under Anglo-Saxons* 2 All literary genius centres on one person, the minstrel, who equally composed and sang. **1846** WRIGHT *Ess. Mid. Ages* I. ii. 68 The [Anglo-Norman] minstrel shows himself everywhere a bitter satirist upon ecclesiastics. **1850** O. WINSLOW *Inner Life* vi. 181 The banquet is ready and the minstrels are tuning their harps. **1892** J. EARLE *Deeds of Beowulf* 136 Rieger.. understands that the minstrel did not merely narrate, but improvised. **1928** W. W. LAWRENCE *Beowulf & Epic Trad.* 46 The lines at the beginning [of *Widsith*] introducing the minstrel, and those at the end glorifying his profession. **1951** D. WHITELOCK *Audience of Beowulf* 77 The poet, if he had not wished, was not forced to make the minstrel sing of the

Creation. **1966** E. G. STANLEY *Continuations & Beginnings* 129 Sometimes a minstrel working in the oral-formulaic tradition coined a phrase, for every phrase must have been new before it grew old.

¶ **b.** Used derisively with pun on *minister*.

1589 NASHE *Almond for Parrat* 8b, I forgette to tel you what a stirre he keepes against dumbe ministers, and neuer writes nor talkes of them, but hee calleth them minstrels.

3. *transf.* Used *poet.* or *rhetorically* for a musician, singer, or poet.

1718 PRIOR *Solomon* II. 71 Music's force can..make..the lynx forget His wrath to man, and lick the minstrel's feet. **1819** WORDSW. *To Dr. Wordsw.* i The Minstrels played their Christmas tune To-night beneath my cottage-eaves. **1831** —— *Yarrow Revisited* i. 8, I stood, looked, listened, and with Thee, Great Minstrel of the Border! **1839** —— *Th. on Banks Nith* 56 Sweet Mercy! to the gates of Heaven This Minstrel lead, his sins forgiven. *a* **1881** ROSSETTI *House of Life* ix, Behold this minstrel is unknown; Bid him depart, for I am minstrel here.

4. Chiefly in *plural* and with prefixed defining word, as ***Christy, Negro, nigger minstrels***: The designation assumed by certain bands of public entertainers in the U.S. and subsequently also in England, who, with blacked faces and wearing grotesque costumes, performed interludes representing Negro life in the southern states, with songs and music ostensibly of Negro origin.

1843 in G. C. D. Odell *Ann. N.Y. Stage* (1928) IV. 668 The Ethiopian Serenaders, or Boston Minstrels. **1846** *Illustr. London News* 24 Jan. 61/2 The Ethiopian serenaders. A party of American minstrels..commenced..a series of concerts. **1864, 1871** [see NEGRO 3]. **1873** [see CHRISTY]. **1904** *Daily Chron.* 29 Mar. 3/6 April 9 has been fixed for the last performance of the Mohawk Moore and Burgess Minstrels at St. James's Hall.

5. *slang.* (See quots.)

1967 M. M. GLATT et al. *Drug Scene* 115 *Minstrel (black and white)*, Durophet. **1971** E. E. LANDY *Underground Dict.* 133 *Minstrel*, 12.5 mg. capsule of an amphetamine and a sedative.

6. *attrib.*

1715–20 POPE *Iliad* xxiv. 81 This Minstrel God,..Stood proud to Hymn, and tune his youthful Lyre. **1767** PERCY *Ess. Anc. Minstrels* in *Reliq.* (1794) I. p. liv, The old Minstrel-ballads are in the northern dialect. **1810** SCOTT *Lady of L.* VI. xiv, Free from thy minstrel-spirit glanced, Fling me the picture of the fight. **1813** —— *Trierm.* I. xix, The attributes of those high days Now only live in minstrel-lays. **1865** *Chicago Tribune* 10 Apr. 1 Buckley and Budd's minstrel house is in blast. **1870** O. LOGAN *Before Footlights* 414 A clever actor..who wrote a burlesque..for a minstrel show. **1885** W. B. YEATS *Island of Statues* II. iii, in *Dublin Univ. Rev.* July 139/2 He who hath the halcyon's wing As flaming minstrel-word upon his crest. **1947** A. EINSTEIN *Mus. Romantic Era* xvii. 331 Of his [*sc.* S. C. Foster's] songs, *Oh! Susanna* was one of the oldest (1848) and was most widely circulated by the 'minstrel shows'. **1949** *Radio Times* 15 July 18/3 A black-faced minstrel show with bones, tambourines, corner men, stump speech. **1975** *Listener* 3 Apr. 454/3 At the time of the Civil War, the minstrel show became less complex in its treatment of Negro life.

Hence **ˈminstrel** *v. trans.*, to sing of, celebrate in song. **ˈminstreless**, a female minstrel. **ˈminstrelling** *vbl. sb.*, the performance of music. †**ˈminstrelship**, (*a*) minstrelsy, the performance of music; (*b*) (with possessive pronoun) the personality of a minstrel.

1471 in T. Sharp *Diss. Pageants Coventry* (1825) 35 It' paid to the waytes for mynstrelship..vjᵈ. *a* **1578** LINDESAY (Pitscottie) *Chron. Scot.* (S.T.S.) I. 381 With singing and danceing, minstrelling and playing. **1647** *Haddington Presbyt. Rec.* in *Baron Crt. of Stitchill* (1905) Introd. 35 Profane minstrellings in time of dinner or supper tends to great debauchery. **1817** *Blackw. Mag.* I. 169 No monument tells, 'mid the wilderness green, Where the minstreless lies of the Border the last. **1822** T. L. PEACOCK *Maid Marian* xvi. 218 I'll knock your musical noddles together... That will be a new tune for your minstrelships. *Ibid.* 219 Touch thou shalt not: my minstrelship defies thee. **1873** LELAND *Egypt. Sketch Bk.* 127 Such poets as Bayard Taylor, who once minstrelled an Arab's horse.

minstrelsy (ˈmɪnstrəlsɪ). Forms: *α.* 4 **menestrelsy, -tralcie, menistralsi;** *β.* 4 **menstralcye,** 5 **menstralcy, -sie, -sy;** 4 **menstracie, menstracy,** 5 **menstrasy(e;** *γ.* 4 **mynystralsye;** *δ.* 4 (**mistralsi, munstralsye**), **minstralcie, -cye, mynstralcie,** 4–5 **minstralcy, mynstralcye, -sy,** 4, 8 **minstralsy,** 5 **mynstralsi, -sie, mynstrelsee, -cye, mynstrylsy,** 5–6 **mynstralcy, -sye, mynstrelsy,** 6 **minstrelcy,** 6–7 **minstralsie,** 7 **minstrelsie;** 4 **minstracie, mynstrasy, -trecye, -trisye,** 5 (**munstrassye**), **mynstracy;** 7– **minstrelsy.** [ad. OF. *menestralsie, -trancie*, f. *menestrel* a minstrel: see MINSTREL.]

1. The art, occupation, or practice of a minstrel; the practice of playing and singing; in mod. use only *poet.* and *arch.* †***to make minstrelsy***, to produce music.

1303 R. BRUNNE *Handl. Synne* 4716 He hadde no grace to sey with-alle His graces ryghte deuoutely For þe noyse of þe mynstralsy. **13..** *Seuyn Sag.* (W.) 3363 Than was thare made grete menestrelsy. *a* **1350** *St. Thomas* 38 in Horstm. *Altengl. Leg.* (1881) 20 þare was..grete mirth of sere menistralsi [*v.r.* mistralsi]. *c* **1350** *Will. Palerne* 1155 Alle maner menstracie þere was mad. **1362** LANGL. *P. Pl.* A. III. 11 Þer was Murþe and Munstralsye Meede with to plese. **1393** *Ibid.* C. XVI. 196 What manere mynstralcie..Hast þow vsed? *c* **1440** *Bone Flor.* 168 Thorow the towne the knyghtes sange,..Makeyng swete mynstralcy. **1535** COVERDALE *Ecclus.* xl. 20 Wyne and mynstralsye reioyse the hert. **1602** *2nd Pt. Return fr. Parnas.* I. ii. (Arb.) 11 He did chaunt his rurall minstralsie. **1697** COLLIER *Ess. Mor. Subj.* II. (1709) 24 To have our Passions lie at the mercy of a little Minstrelsy. **1768** BEATTIE *Minstr.* I. xvi, Save one short pipe of rudest minstrelsy. **1862** GOULBURN *Pers. Relig.* 104 The minstrelsy of psalms and hymns, and spiritual songs. **1867** FREEMAN *Norm. Conq.* (1877) I. v. 274 Verses which breathe the true fire of the warlike minstrelsy common to Greek and Teuton.

†**b.** Harmony. *Obs.*

1605 CAMDEN *Rem., Rhymes* 18 Which delighted in nothing more then in this Minstrelsie of meeters.

2. A body of minstrels; an assemblage or gathering of minstrels.

c **1350** *Will. Palerne* 5011 So many maner minstracie at þat mariage were. *c* **1386** CHAUCER *Sqr.'s T.* 260 Toforn hym gooth the loude Mynstralcye. *c* **1440** *Gesta Rom.* lxiv. 276 (Harl. MS.), Oþer worthi lady ȝede to þe same chirch, with gret mynstracy afore hire. **1480** CAXTON *Chron. Eng.* ccxli. 267 Euery man in good aray and euery crafte with his mynstralsye. **1667** MILTON *P.L.* VI. 168 Ministring Spirits, trained up in Feast and Song; Such hast thou arm'd, the Minstrelsie of Heav'n. **1740** SOMERVILLE *Hobbinol* III. 231 Before him march in Files The rural Minstralsy. **1800–24** CAMPBELL *On Camp Hill near Hastings* iii, At the Conqueror's side There his minstrelsy sat harp in hand. **1855** PRESCOTT *Philip II*, I. iv. I. 49 The minstrelsy played before them till they reached the royal residence.

†**3.** *collect.* A number or collection of musical instruments. Also, a kind of musical instrument.

c **1386** CHAUCER *Manciple's T.* 9 Pleyen he koude on euery Mynstralcie. **1447** BOKENHAM *Seyntys* (Roxb.) 186 The voys of orgons and of dyvers menstralcy. **1523** LD. BERNERS *Froiss.* I. ccxcix. 443 The spanyerdes..departed, makyng great noyse of trumpettes and other mynstrelsies.

4. Minstrel poetry; *occas.* a body of minstrel poetry.

1802 SCOTT (*title*) Minstrelsy of the Scottish Border. **1830** H. N. COLERIDGE *Grk. Poets* (1834) 35 The Iliad and the Odyssey..are compilations..arranged by successive editors, but still compilations of minstrelsies, the works of various poets in the heroic age. **1845** CRAIK *Hist. Lit. Eng.* V. 150 That remarkable body of national song known as the Jacobite minstrelsy.

minstryng, obs. form of MINISTERING *sb.*

mint (mɪnt), *sb.*[1] Forms: 1 **mynyt, -it, -et, munet,** 1–2, 4–5 **menet,** 5 **myntte,** 5–7 **mynt,** 6 **minte,** 6– **mint.** [OE. *mynet* neut., repr. (with change of gender) WGer. **munita* fem., a. L. *monēta*: see MONEY. Cf. OFris. *menote, munte* fem., OS. *munita* fem. (MDu. *munte*, Du. *munt* fem.), OHG. *munizza* fem., *muniz* masc. and neut. (MHG. *münze*, mod.G. *münze* fem.). From LG. the word passed into the Scandinavian langs.: ON., Sw., Da. *mynt*.]

1. A piece of money, a coin; money. *Obs.*

From 16th c. only *slang*: possibly reintroduced in this use from LG.

c **725** *Corpus Gloss.* (Hessels) N 144 *Nomisma*, mynit. *c* **975** *Rushw. Gosp.* Matt. xxii. 19 Eawað me mynet [*c* **1000** *Ags. Gosp.* mynyt, *c* **1160** *Hatton* menet; Vulg. *numisma*] þæs gæfles. *c* **1000** *Sax. Leechd.* II. 192 ȝenim pipores swilce an mynet ȝeweȝe, diles sædes swilce .iiii. mynet ȝeweȝen. **1340** *Ayenb.* 241 Vor pouerte is þet menet huermide me bayþ þe riche of heuene. *c* **1420** *Pallad. on Husb.* III. 1069 These [*sc.* pigs] if me spende, or mynt for hem reseyue. **1567** HARMAN *Caveat* (1869) 83 Mynt, golde. **1621** B. JONSON *Metam. Gypsies* in *Horace*, etc. (1640) 54 Strike faire at some Jewell That mint [1641 *fol.*, mine] may accrue well. **1666** HEAD *Eng. Rogue* I. iv. 33. *a* **1700** B. E. *Dict. Cant. Crew.* **1848** MRS. GASKELL *M. Barton* xxiii, You'll want money... You must take some of the mint I've got laid by in the old tea-pot.

2. a. A place where money is coined; usually, a place where lawful money is coined under the authority and direction of the state. ***Master of the Mint*** (perh. orig. in sense 1): the chief officer and custodian of the mint.

(Since 1869 the offices of Master and Worker of the Mint have been nominally held by the Chancellor of the Exchequer, who has direct control of the establishment.)

1423 *Rolls of Parlt.* IV. 256/2 The maister of the mynte aforeseid [*previously called* maistre of the koyne]. *c* **1475** *Pol. Poems* (Rolls) II. 286 For and ther were a mynte ordeyned ny therby. *a* **1552** LELAND *Itin.* (1769) IV. 125 There was..a Mint of Coynage in Coventrye. **1553** in Strype *Eccl. Mem.* (1721) III. App. v. 8 Her Majestie hath ordered and established to be made within her mintes these seueral coynes. **1603** JAS. I in Ellis *Orig. Lett.* Ser. I. III. 67 The Warden of our Mynt and Woorkmaster of our Moneys there. **1670** LADY MARY BERTIE in *12th Rep. Hist. MSS. Comm.* App. v. 21 At the Tower..I saw the lyons and Mint. **1706** PHILLIPS (ed. Kersey), *Master of the Mint*, an Officer now call'd *The Warden of the Mint*. **1787** *Phil. Trans.* LXXVII. 204 *note*, The experiments..were made..at his Majesty's Mint in the Tower. **1836** in *Rep. Committee Roy. Mint* (1837) App. 28 The Cash Account of the Master of the Mint. **1853** HUMPHREYS *Coin-coll. Man.* I. vi. 66 The Carthaginians..had a national mint established in the Acropolis of Carthage.

b. A set of machines for coining.

1592 R. D. *Hypnerotomachia* 7 This Image was..mooved about with such a noyse..as if the mynte of the Queene of England had been going there! **1642** CHAS. I *Sp.* Wks. 1662 I. 412, I have sent hither for a Mint. **1832** BABBAGE *Econ. Manuf.* xi. (ed. 3) 94 The mint which was sent a few years since to Calcutta was capable of coining 200,000 pieces a day.

3. *transf.* and *fig.* A place in which the fabrication (of anything) is carried on; a source of invention or fabrication.

1555 EDEN *Decades* 331b, The..matrices of moste estemed ryches, and the myntes of al treasures are the mountaynes. **1588** SHAKS. *L.L.L.* I. i. 166 A man..That hath a mint of phrases in his braine. **1610** BP. CARLETON *Jurisd.* 141 If that decree were forged,..with many moe: Let the Romane forgery be acknowledged, and the Masters of that mint knowne. **1709** SACHEVERELL *Serm.* 15 Aug. 16 The Pulpit, and the Press, those Mints of Atheism. **1715** BENTLEY *Serm.* x. (1809) 348 Rome..should possess the sole mint of all spiritual licences and pardons. *a* **1792** WOLCOT (P. Pindar) *Ode to Pretty Milliner* Wks. 1794 III. 327 A kiss!—a thousand kisses let me add—Ten thousand from thy unexhausted mint. **1850** TENNYSON *In Mem.* lxxix, But thou and I are one in kind, As moulded like in Nature's mint. **1874** L. STEPHEN *Hours in Library* (1892) I. v. 192 All these [tales] bear the unmistakable stamp of Hawthorne's mint. **1905** R. F. HORTON *Child & Relig.* vii. 276 The Bible ought to be taught to every English child, as..the Mint of our noblest speech.

†**4. a.** Coinage. *Obs.*

1483 in *Lett. & Papers Rich. III & Hen. VII* (Rolls) I. 45 A lettre undre the kinges prive seall concernyng the mynte of Irlande. **1622** BACON *Hen. VII* 235 For Minte, and Warres, and Marshall Discipline, (things of Absolute Power) he would neuerthelesse bring to Parliament.

b. In phrase ***to pass the Mint*** (with allusion to the assaying department of the Mint).

1656 BLOUNT *Glossogr.* To Rdr. A4b, So when any considerable Supplement of New English Words have legally pass'd the Mint and Test of our Vertuosi, the same liberty [of reprinting with additions] may be allowed this Work.

5. †**a.** A quantity (of money) coined. *Obs.*

1579 FENTON *Guicciard.* I. (1599) 16 They were plentifully furnished..with so rich a mynt of money [*orig. tanta copia di danari*], that it sufficed against all wants.

transf. **1598** J. DICKENSON *Greene in Conc.* (1878) 100 He vanished, leauing mee extreamely discontented; for I had ready a mint of questions.

b. Hence, a vast sum (of money); rarely *transf.* a vast amount (of something costly).

1655 FULLER *Ch. Hist.* IX. vi. §19. 172 A mass, a mint, a mine of mony could easily be advanced to defray the expences thereof. **1729** BRADLEY *Riches of Hop-garden* 2 Expect Mints of Money to tumble into their Laps for a little Secret. **1833** MARRYAT *P. Simple* i, He must have lost a mint of money. **1869** BLACKMORE *Lorna D.* xxi, He was so tasselled, and so ruffled with a mint of bravery. **1874** SPURGEON *Treas. Dav.* Ps. xciv. 16 Our John Knox would be worth a mint at this hour, but where is he?

6. *attrib.* and *Comb.*, as **mint-bill**, a bill or promissory note given by the officers of the mint to the importer of bullion deposited for coining; **mint condition** = *mint-state*; **mint duties**, certain taxes formerly appropriated to the maintenance of the Royal Mint; **mint hog** *slang*, an Irish shilling; †**mint house**, a building in which money is coined; †**mintmaker**, 'a moneyer'; †**mint man**, one engaged or skilled in coining; also *transf.*; **mint par, parity (of exchange)**, the ratio between the gold equivalent of the currency units of two countries; the rate of currency exchange between two countries based on this ratio; **mint phrase**, a phrase coined for a purpose; **mint price**, the standard price of bullion as recognized at the mint; **mint-stamp** *Numism.* = MINT-MARK (also *fig.*); **mint-state** *Numism.*, the condition in which a coin comes from the mint (also *transf.*, of a postage-stamp); also applied to books and other objects in pristine condition; **mint-token**, a token of a nominal value issued by legal authority from a mint; **mint value** = *mint price*. Also MINT-MARK, MINT-MASTER.

1707 *Lond. Gaz.* No. 4330/5 The New Edict in France for making their *Mint-Bills current throughout the Kingdom. **1839** *Penny Cycl.* XV. 253/1 It [coin] is delivered to the owner weight for weight, as expressed in the mint bill which had been given. **1902** *Connoisseur* May 67/2 Nothing is more marked in present day stamp collecting than the insistence ..upon what is expressively termed a '*mint' condition in unused specimens. **1923** *Punch* 7 Feb. 130 Here we have Holbein's portrait of the first earl... His *chef-d'œuvre*, in mint condition. **1956** I. MURDOCH *Flight from Enchanter* i. 9 The books were chaotic, but in mint condition, since reading was not a popular activity. **1975** 'D. RUTHERFORD' *Mystery Tour* iii. 59, I did have half a dozen vintage Rolls-Royces..but..it was becoming more and more expensive to keep the cars in mint condition. **1782** G. & F. GARBETT in *Rep. Committee Roy. Mint* (1837) App. 221 Certain duties upon brandy and strong waters under the title of *Mint duties. **1806** CARR *Stranger in Irel.* iii. 65 The genuine Irish shillings, called by the low Irish *Mint hogs. **1605** STOW *Ann., Jas. I*, 1414 The next day he saw..the *mint-houses. **1796** MORSE *Amer. Geog.* II. 248 The Hungarian gold and silver employed mint-houses, not only in Hungary, but in Germany, and the continent of Europe. *c* **1483** CAXTON *Dialogues* 2 Of *myntemakers [F. *monnoyers*] and pybakers. **1605** TIMME *Quersit.* I. xvi. 82 The which is wel known to..euery gold-smith and *mintman. **1624** BACON *War w. Spain* (1629) 2 He that thinketh Spaine to be some great Ouermatch for this Estate..is no good Mint-man; But takes greatnesse of Kingdomes according to their Bulke and Currency. **1752** CARTE *Hist. Eng.* III. 384 They proposed to coin their plate to pay them: but the mintmen stole off with their stamps and irons. **1882** *Mint par [see PAR *sb.*[1] 2a]. **1891** G. CLARE *Money-Market Primer* 74 A Mint Par can only be established between countries that employ the same standard of value. **1928** W. F. SPALDING *Dict. World's Currencies & Foreign Exchanges* 134/2 The mint par of exchange is the rate of exchange at which the standard coin of one country is convertible into that of another country according to the terms of their respective mint laws. **1965** PERRY & RYDER *Thomson's Dict. Banking* (ed. 11) 376/2 The

Mint Par between two countries never varies unless one of them alters its coinage regulations. **1928** L. D. Edie *Money, Bank Credit & Prices* iii. 52 A so-called *mint parity existed between all gold standard countries. **1940** G. Crowther *Outl. Money* ix. 317 The 'mint parity' being $4.86⅔ = £1, whenever the exchange rate..fell..it became cheaper to buy gold from the Bank of England..and..sell it to the Federal Reserve Bank for dollars. **1965** Seldon & Pennance *Everyman's Dict. Econ.* 285 *Mint Parity of Exchange*, the exchange rate between two currencies both of which are legally convertible at fixed rates into..gold... The mint parity then expresses the ratio between the two legal rates. **1626** B. Jonson *Staple of N.* iv. iv. 74, I wyll tyde This affayre for you; giue it freight and passage, And such *mynt-phrase, as 'tis the worst of canting, By how much it affects the sense it has not. **1758** J. Harris *Money & Coins* ii. ii. 56 The market price of bullion might be frequently above the *mint price. **1892** H. R. Grenfell in *Pall Mall G.* 24 Dec. 2/3 Law has instituted the so-called mint price for gold. **1817** D'Israeli *Cur. Lit.* 1st Ser. III. 183 That all men..should take the *mint-stamp of their thoughts from the Council of Trent. **1837** in *Rep. Committee Roy. Mint* Index 22 The Mint stamp is for the security of the refiner. **1902** *Daily Chron.* 16 Jan. 7/7 The Niger Coast 5*s.* [*sc.* postage stamp] in violet on 2*d.*, and the 10*s.* in vermilion on 5*d.*, both unused and in *mint state. **1931** *Times Lit. Suppl.* 16 Apr. 305/3 Copies of 'Waverley' ..are excessively rare in mint state. **1716** *Lond. Gaz.* No. 5439/3 A small Copper Coin, under the Name of *Mint-Tokens, shall be current throughout his Dominions for half a Rixdollar.

mint (mɪnt), *sb.*² Forms: 1–6 **minte**, 1, 4–6 **mynte**, 3–7 **mente**, 5–6 **mynt**, 6 **mynthe**, 6– **mint**. [OE. *minte* wk. fem. (? Mercian *mint* str. fem.) = OHG. *minza* (MHG., mod.G. *minze*):—WG. **minta*, a. L. *menta*, *mentha*, Gr. *μίνθη* (also *μίνθος*). A synonym of unexplained form is WGer. **muntja*, represented by M.Du. *munte* (Du. *munt* fem.), OHG. *munza* (MHG., mod.G. *münze*). The obsolete Eng. form *mente* may be influenced by F. *mente* (now written *menthe*), whence also the MDu. variant *mente*.]

1. a. Any one of the aromatic labiate plants of the genus *Mentha*, esp. *M. viridis*, Garden Mint or spearmint, well known in cookery. Until the 18th c. frequently with *a* and in *pl.*

c **975** *Rushw. Gosp.* Matt. xxiii. 23 Forþon ȝe þe tæȝþiȝaþ mintæ [*c* **1000** *Ags. Gosp.* mintan] & dile & cymen. *c* **1260** *Gloss. Names Plants* in *Rel. Ant.* I. 37 *Menta*, mente, minten. ? *a* **1366** Chaucer *Rom. Rose* 731 A litel path..Of mentes ful and fenel grene. **1398** Trevisa *Barth. De P.R.* xvii. cvi. (Tollem. MS.), Mynte of gardynes is an herbe þat multiplyeþ it selfe. *c* **1400** *Lanfranc's Cirurg.* 60 Mintis stampid wiþ salt. *c* **1450** *ME. Med. Bk.* (Heinrich) 69 Take smalache, & myntes, & rewe, and betonye. **1530** Palsgr. 660/2 Plucke these roses whyle I plucke these myntes. **1565** Cooper *Thesaurus*, *Menta*, *mentæ*,..Mintes. **1593** B. Barnes *Parthenophil* Ode xi. in Arb. *Garner* V. 456 Fragrant violets, and sweet mynthe, Matched with purple hyacinth. **1618** Latham *2nd Bk. Falconry* (1633) 143 Mintes is hot and dry in the third degree. **1733** Tull *Horse-Hoeing Husb.* i. 11, I plac'd a Mint, with half its Roots in the Glass. *Ibid.*, The Mints stood just upon the ends of the Trough. **1876** Harley *Mat. Med.* (ed. 6) 471 Mint has long been used in Medicine.

b. With defining word, as **bergamot mint**, *M. citrata*; **brandy mint**, peppermint, *M. piperita*; **brook, fish, horse, water, wild mint**, *M. sylvestris* and other wild species; **brown, mackerel mint**, old names for *M. viridis*; **corn mint**, *M. arvensis*; **crisp(ed, cross, curled mint**, *M. crispa*.

1578 Lyte *Dodoens* ii. lxxiv. 243 The garden Myntes are of foure sortes, that is to say, Curlde Mynte, Crispe Mynte, Spere Mynte, and Harte Mynte. The wilde Mynte is of two sortes, that is, the Horse Mynte, and the Water Mynte. **1597** Gerarde *Herbal* ii. ccxv. 553 The first Mint is called.. browne Mint, or red Mint. The second..crosse Mint, or curled Mint. The third..Speare Mint, common Garden Mint, our Ladies Mint, Browne Mint and Macrell Mint. The fourth..Hart Woort or Hart Mint. *Ibid.* ccxvii. 555 Water Mint, Fish Mint, Brooke Mint, and Horse Mint. **1744** J. Wilson *Synops. Brit. Pl.* 87 Pepper-mint. They call this Brandy-mint in Westmoreland. **1796** Withering *Brit. Plants* (ed. 3) III. 525 *Corn Mint*. Watery places and moist corn fields. **1831** J. Davies *Manual Mat. Med.* 179 The most used of them are, the Crisped Mint, *Mentha crispa*, Lin.; the Green Mint, *M. Viridis*,..the Elegant Mint, *M. gentilis*, Lin.

c. = peppermint 2 b. Also a sweet, or chocolate, flavoured with or containing mint. Also as *adj.*

1894 E. Skuse *Compl. Confectioner* 138 (*heading*) Cheap common mints. **1958** 'R. Crompton' *William's Television Show* v. 161 Their pockets bulged with..pear drops, mint fancies, almond delight. **1964** *Listener* 1 Oct. 498/2 Mouth mint-happy, I drift to the bed. **1966** P. V. Price *France: Food & Wine Guide* 95 Really good mint chocolates are.. appreciated by French friends. **1970** D. Marlowe *Echoes of Celandine* vi. 90 A bag of mints. **1973** *Harrod's Christmas Catal.* 35/1, 1 metre box of crispy mints—a special chocolate blended in our own factory. £5.25.

2. Applied with defining word to plants of allied genera, e.g. *Calamintha* and in *U.S. Pycnanthemum* and *Monarda*. See also catmint.

1548 Turner *Names of Herbes* 22 *Calamintha*..called in english cornemint and calamynt. **1597** Gerarde *Herbal* ii. ccxviii. 556 Calamint, or mountaine Mint. **1846–50** A. Wood *Class-bk. Bot.* 417 *Monarda didyma*, Mountain Mint. *M. punctata*, Horsemint. *Ibid.* 419 *Pycnanthemum incanum*, Mountain Mint. **1886** Britten & Holland *Plant-n.* s.v., *Calamintha officinalis* is in *Yks.* Cap Mint or Cat Mint; ..*Teucrium Scorodonia* is Rock Mint in *Som.* and Wild Mint in *Suss.*; *Ajuga reptans* is Wild Mint in *Berks.*

3. *attrib.* and *Comb.*: *mint-green* adj.; **mint cake** *dial.*, (*a*) a cake made of flour and dripping or lard, flavoured with sugar and chopped fresh mint, and rolled out very thin (E.D.D.); (*b*) a sweetmeat flavoured with peppermint (*Ibid.*); **mint jelly**, mint-flavoured jelly, usu. eaten with roast lamb; **mint julep** (see julep 2); **mint rock**, a sweetmeat (see rock *sb.*) flavoured with peppermint; **mint-sling** *U.S.*, a drink containing some alcoholic beverage flavoured with mint; **mint-stick**, a stick of mint-rock or similar sweetmeat; **mint tea** = *mint-water*; **mint tree**, an Australian labiate tree, *Prostanthera lasiantha* (*Treas. Bot.* 1866); **mint vinegar**, mint-flavoured vinegar; **mint-water**, a cordial distilled from mint. Also mint-sauce.

1825 Mrs. Cameron *Seeds of Greediness* 2 (in *Houlston Tracts* I. No. 22) Apples, *mint cakes, and other things.. very tempting to children. **1958** E. Newby *Short Walk in Hindu Kush* xiv. 170 Drinking some coffee and munching Kendal mint cake. **1971** D. Haston in C. Bonington *Annapurna South Face* xvii. 211 Food level was porridge, mint cake and assorted synthetic drinks. **1971** M. Thompson in *Ibid.* App. D. 272 There was far too much sugar and too much fudge and mint cake. The Kendal Mint Cake really came into its own at very high altitude. **1967** Mrs. L. B. Johnson *White House Diary* 9 Mar. (1970) 493, I wore my *mint-green silk and sat..on his right. **1973** J. Shub *Moscow by Nightmare* ix. 97 The mint-green Winter Palace. **1922** Gordon & Rohde *Cookery* 157 **Mint Jelly*... Pick fresh young mint. Boil the sugar in the vinegar for 5 minutes. **1951** T. Sterling *House without Door* ii. 22 The lamb was tender... She ate the mint jelly separately. **1966** I. Jefferies *House-Surgeon* xiii. 245 There was red-currant jelly, white-currant jelly, mint jelly..and mint sauce. **1809** 'D. Knickerbocker' *Hist. N.Y.* II. vii. ii. 180 The inhabitants..were notoriously prone to get fuddled and make merry with *mint-julep and apple-toddy. **1817** Paulding *Lett. fr. South* (1835) I. 21 The best compounder of mint-juleps of any man in Virginia. **1845** Eliza Acton *Mod. Cookery* 540 Mint Julep. **1853** J. G. Baldwin *Flush Times Alabama* 81 Great was he too at mixing an apple toddy or mint julep. **1943** *R.A.F. Jrnl.* Aug. 16 When he spoke one tasted mint juleps and water melons. **1970** A. Launay *Cocktails & Snacks* 64 *Mint Julep*. 6 or 7 mint leaves.., shaved ice, ⅔ cocktail glass bourbon whisky. **1952** *New Statesman* 29 Mar. 370/2 The sweets are unsophisticated and long-lasting—Bottomley's *mint rock, Judy Barratt's humbugs. **1804** *Balance* 15 Mar. 86 (Th.), Three *Mint Slings. **1812** 'H. Bull-Us' *Diverting Hist. John Bull & Bro. Jonathan* xiii. 98 The Yankeys abhor horse-racing, cock fighting, and mint-slings. **1832** J. P. Kennedy *Swallow Barn* I. xi. 110 It is a vulgar error..to appropriate the mint sling to the morning. **1964** *Cookbk.* (Amer. Heritage) 345 The Mint Sling and Apple Toddy..are variations on the more traditional Slings and Toddies given here. **1862** *New York Tribune* 13 June (Cent.), The soldiers hunger for dates, figs, *mint-stick [etc.]. **1872** Schele de Vere *Americanisms* 395 Sage-tea and *Mint-tea were..familiar to all nurses. **1845** E. Acton *Mod. Cookery* (ed. 2) v. 137 *Green *mint vinegar*... The mint itself,..will keep well in vinegar, though the colour will not be very good. **1957** E. Craig *Collins Family Cookery* 893 *Mint Vinegar*... Fill up jars with the mint.., then pour in mild vinegar to overflowing. **1666** *Phil. Trans.* I & II. No. 12. 212 *Mint-water. **1843** R. J. Graves *Syst. Clin. Med.* xii. 131 A draught composed of two drachms of mint water [etc.].

†**mint**, *sb.*³ *Obs.* [Of obscure origin; possibly contraction of minute *sb.* (cf. mint-while).]

1. A small insect, mite, weevil.

14.. *Voc.* in Wr.-Wülcker 623 *Bibiones*, *uermes*, *Anglice* myntys. *c* **1475** *Pict. Voc.* ibid. 767/8 *Nomina vermium*..*Hec mica*, a mynte. **1789** W. Marshall *Glouc.* I. 330 *Mints*, mites. **1842** in Akerman *Wilts Gloss.*

2. A denomination of weight, $\frac{1}{20}$ of a grain; = mite.

a **1600** *MS. Rawlinson D.* 23 Pref. 1 b, The weyghtes called myntes which is the smallest weyhte here sette downe, saving the weyghtes called droytes, Theise weyghtes called myntes hathe no abbrevyacion sette here downe.

mint (mɪnt), *sb.*⁴ *Sc.* and *north. dial.* Also 4 **munt**, 4–6 **mynt**. [f. mint *v.*¹]

1. Purpose, intention.

a **1300** *Cursor M.* 463 Bot he was merred of hys mint, Fulson he fand vnsterne stint. **13..** *E.E. Allit. P.* A. 1160 Bot of þat munt I was bi-talt.

2. An attempt, effort; an attempt to strike; a blow aimed; a threatening gesture or movement.

c **1330** R. Brunne *Chron. Wace* (Rolls) 12367 He [Arthur] sey wel how he [Dynabrok] made his mynt, & wiþ his mace he teysed his dynt. **13..** *Gaw. & Gr. Knt.* 2345 Fyrst I mansed þe muryly, with a mynt one, & roue þe wyth no rof. *Ibid.* 2350 Þat oþer munt for þe morne, mon, I þe profered, Þou kyssedes my clere wyf. *c* **1400** *Ywaine & Gaw.* 2613 A ful fel mynt to him made. **1513** Douglas *Æneis* v. viii. 11 Now bendis he wp his burdoun with a mynt, On syde he bradis for till eschew the dint. **1573** *Satir. Poems Reform.* xxxix. 361 He..Brocht thame to miserie maid ane mynt to wrang vs. *a* **1584** Montgomerie *Cherrie & Slae* 1158 'Ȝit', quod Experience, 'at thee Mak mony mints I may'. **1589** J. Melvill *Autobiogr.* (Wodrow Soc.) 273 His brother.. making a mint, maid the lown to flie. *a* **1699** J. Fraser *Mem.* vi. §2 (1738) 139 Nor made I ever any extraordinary Mint to seek God, but [etc.]. **1728** Ramsay *To Starrat* 39 The lawly mints of my poor moorland muse.

mint (mɪnt), *v.*¹ Now *dial.* or *arch.* Forms: 1 **myntan**, 2 **mintan**, 2–3 **munten**, 3–6 **mynt**, 3–7 **minte**, 4, 6 **mente**, 5 **munt**, 6 **ment**, **mynte**, 3– **mint**. [OE. *myntan*, perh. from **myntjan*, f. *myne* thought, intention: see min *sb.*]

†**1.** *intr.* and *trans.* To think. *Obs.*

c **1000** *Judith* 153 (Gr.) Mynton ealle, þæt se beorna breȝo & seo beorhte mæȝð in ðam wliteȝan træfe wæron ætsomne. *a* **1300** *Cursor M.* 28979 For euer ai prai wit-vten stint, He þat graithli to god has mint. *a* **1310** in Wright *Lyric P.* x. 37 Of munnyng ne munt thou namore. *c* **1330** R. Brunne *Chron. Wace* (Rolls) 7225 Þey seide til oþer, 'what haue ȝe mynt?'

2. With *inf.* (rarely with *clause*). To purpose, intend; also, to make an effort, attempt, endeavour; to venture.

Beowulf 712 Mynte se manscaða manna cynnes sumne besyrwan in sele þam hean. **1154** *O.E. Chron.* (Laud MS.) an. 616 Ða mynte Laurentius þe ða wæs ercebiscop on Cænt. þæt he wolde suþ ofer se. **1154** *Ibid.* an. 1137 And ȝif he leng moste liuen, alse he mint to don of þe horder-wycan. *a* **1300** *Cursor M.* 10759 Hir to haf had he noght mint, If he moght anigat it stint. **1390** Gower *Conf.* III. 261 Sondri times as sche minte To speke, upon the point sche stinte. **1530** Palsgr. 421/2, I am aboute to do a thynge, or I ment or purpose to do a thynge, *je tache.* **1596** Dalrymple tr. *Leslie's Hist. Scot.* ix. 193 The Erle of Surrie..minted nocht to cum an inche ner vs. **1633** Rutherford *Lett.* xxix. (1862) I. 105 Jesus is looking up that water and minting to dwell amongst them. **1713** *Humble Pleadings for Good Old-way* 137 We the people that adhere to him have minted to plead with this church. **1725** Ramsay *Gentle Sheph.* i. i, To speak but till her I dare hardly mint. **1871** W. Alexander *Johnny Gibb* xii. (1873) 76 He's ready to confess Christ afore men aifter a fashion that I hae never mintit to dee yet.

†**b.** With ellipsis of verb of motion. *Obs.*

Beowulf 762 Mynte se mæra, þær he meahte..þanon fleon. *a* **1325** *Prov. Hendyng* xxx, Mon þat munteþ ouer flod, whiles þat þe wynd ys wod abyde fayre ant stille. **1660** D. Dickson *Serm.* Sel. Writ. (1845) I. 135 We are like Peter who minted to his Master on the water.

c. *absol.*

1513 Douglas *Æneis* xii. xiv. 49 Ne went it [the stone] all the space, as he dyd mynt, Nor, as he etlyt, perfornyst nocht the dynt.

3. *trans.* To intend; to attempt; to aim (a blow).

c **888** K. Ælfred *Boeth.* xxxv. §3 Ac wit sculon swaþeah secan þæt þæt wit ær mynton. *c* **1200** *Trin. Coll. Hom.* 11 And þat wreche man [leueð] þat swilche þing him mai letten of þat þe god him haueð munt. *a* **1300** *Vox & Wolf* 244 in Hazl. *E.P.P.* I. 66 Wat hauest thou i-munt, weder wolt thou? *a* **1330** *Otuel* 182 For ȝef ani of ȝou so hardi be, þat any strok munteþ to me. *c* **1400** *Ywaine & Gaw.* 3437 What so my sister ever has mynt, Al hir part now tel i tynt. **1818** Scott *Rob Roy* xxv, I will cleave to the brisket the first man that mints another stroke. *a* **1825** Forby *Voc. E. Anglia*, *Mink*, *Mint*, to attempt, to aim at.

†**b.** To direct, address (speech). *Obs.*

c **1491** *Chast. Goddes Chyld.* xviii. 49 As he minteth us his speche wythouten ony taryeng of worde.

4. *intr.* To aim a blow; to take aim in shooting; to make a threatening movement. Const. *at*, *to*.

13.. *Gaw. & Gr. Knt.* 2262 With alle þe bur in his body he ber hit [his axe] on lofte, Munt as maȝtyly, as marre hym he wolde. *Ibid.* 2274 Nawþer fyked I, ne flaȝe, freke, quen þou myntest. *c* **1400** *Ywaine & Gaw.* 2448 Unto Sir Ywayn he mynt, And on the shelde he hit ful fast. **1423** Jas. I *Kingis Q.* cv, For oft, There as I mynt full sore, I smyte bot soft. *c* **1425** Wyntoun *Cron.* viii. xvi. 2606 Thai myst bot seldyn quhare thai wald mynt. **1530** Palsgr. 635/1, I dyd ment at a fatte bucke but I dyd hyt a pricket. *a* **1600** Montgomerie *Misc. Poems* ix. 16 Vhair thou mints thou missis not the mark. —— *Sonn.* liv. 9 Bot hola, Muse! thou mints at such a mark, Vhais merit far excedes thy slender skill. **1600** *Gowrie's Conspir.* D 3, Minting to his Highnes heart with the dagger.

†**b.** To make a movement to seize something. Const. *to*. *Obs.*

1613 in R. M. Fergusson *Hume* (1899) 199 Dispersoning of him and minting to ane quhinger to have struckin him thairwith. *a* **1828** *Earl Lithgow* xxxi. in Child *Ballads* II. 469/1 It's thrice she minted to the brand.

c. To point.

a **1400–50** *Alexander* 1089 Seraphis aperis,..Toward a miȝti montayne him myntis with his fynger.

5. To make an attempt; to aim *at*, aspire *to*.

a **1300** *Cursor M.* 28314 Quen i til ony gode dede mynt Ful eth it was do me to stint. *c* **1440** *Promp. Parv.* 338/2 Myntyn, or amyn towarde, for to assayen. **1721** Ramsay *Keitha* 81 The lasses wha did at her graces mint, Hae by her death their bonniest pattern tint. **1820** Scott *Monast.* xvii, They that mint at a gown of gold, will always get a sleeve of it.

†**6.** *trans.* To mention, speak of. *Obs.*

c **1375** *Cursor M.* 14021 (Fairf.) Simonde..wondred & saide in his poȝt bot wiþ his mouþ he mynt [*earlier texts* said] hit noȝt. *c* **1400** *Destr. Troy* 431 This Medea the maiden, þat I mynt first.

Hence **'minting** *vbl. sb.*

1508 Dunbar *Flyting w. Kennedie* 4 Bot had thay maid of mannace ony mynting In speciall, sic stryfe sould ryse but stynting. *a* **1653** Binning *Serm.* (1743) 605 God in Christ accepts of endeavours and mintings. **1703** Thoresby *Let. to Ray* s.v. *Munt*, I know your Meaning by your munting.

mint (mɪnt), *v.*² Forms: see the sb. [f. mint *sb.*¹ OE. had *mynetian* = OHG. *munizôn* (mod.G. *münzen*), Du. *munten*.]

1. *trans.* To make (coin) by stamping metal.

1546 Langley *Pol. Verg. De Invent.* ii. xiii. 57 b, Phedon began syluer coyne in the yle Egina. It was mynted in Rome. **1691** Locke *Lower. Interest* 148 Had all the Money in King Charles the II. and King James the II. time been Minted according to this new proposal, this raised Money would have been gone as well as the other. **1862** Merivale *Rom. Emp.* lvii. (1865) VII. 149 Gold and silver money, minted for the occasion. **1881** *Metal World* No. 3. 37 No more half-crowns or fourpenny bits will be minted.

b. *transf.* ? *nonce-uses.* To make (paper money, a seal).

1736 BERKELEY *Querist* II. 125 Whether it was not madness in France to mint bills and actions, merely to humour the people. **1871** MISS YONGE *Cameos* (1877) II. xxi. 324 The Great Seal was cancelled in order that another for both England and France might be minted.

c. ***to mint gold, money*** (mod. colloq.): to gain or 'make' money with facility. Cf. COIN *v.*[1] 1 c.

1842 MRS. STONE *W. Langshawe* II. vii. 78 If he can but weather the corner, he'll mint gold.

d. *fig.* To produce (something regarded as comparable to coin); to 'coin' or invent (a word or phrase); in contemptuous use, to invent, fabricate (something counterfeit). Cf. NEW-MINT *v.*

1593 [see NEW-MINT *v.*]. *a* **1643** CARTWRIGHT *Siege* V. iv, Nature's sincerer kingdome, where she mints And shapes refin'd delights. **1648** GATAKER *Myst. Cloudes* 2 They might, by some colourable glosses, and nice distinctions newly minted, make them seem [etc.]. **1652** R. BOREMAN *Countr. Catech.* x. 25 Broaching new opinions..such as shall be minted in the braines of their Tutors. **1659** *Gentl. Calling* iv. (1660) 38 That it may every Year appear in some new piece of Dress, have some Oaths fresh minted to set it off. *a* **1680** CHARNOCK *Attrib. God* (1834) II. 565 Such was [his] usurpation,..as if he had power to mint gods. **1698** C. BOYLE *Bentley's Epist. Phal.* (ed. 2) 73 One Happy Phrase, newly minted by the Dr. *a* **1711** KEN *Edmund* Poet. Wks. 1721 II. 226 Curs'd Heresies and Schisms they all disclaim, Minted in Hell, and kindled by its Flame. *a* **1800** S. PEGGE *Anecd. Eng. Lang.* (1803) 35 Queen Elizabeth was very successful in minting the Latin word *Fœminilis.* **1895** SIR H. MAXWELL in *Forum* (N.Y.) Oct. 159 The name has not yet been minted which shall serve to distinguish the Unionist party of the twentieth century.

2. To convert (bullion) into coin or money. ? *Obs.*

1569 SIR T. GRESHAM in Ellis *Orig. Lett.* Ser. II. II. 318 Seing this monney..doth appertain to merchauntes, I would wishe the Quenes Majestie to put it to use..as to mynt hit into her own coyne. **1668** *Lond. Gaz.* No. 287/3 The Barres of Silver which arrived lately, are to be suddenly minted. **1670** PETTUS *Fodinæ Reg.* 42 Metall being thus Coyned or Minted, it is called Coyn.

†**b.** *transf.* To fashion or convert *into. Obs.*

a **1680** CHARNOCK *Attrib. God* (1682) 30 The Mouth takes in the meat,..the liver refines it and mints it into blood.

c. *fig.* To impress (something) with a stamp or character. Also with *out, upon.* Also, to stamp (an impress) *upon.*

1664 H. MORE *Myst. Iniq., Apol.* 544 Though it were in our power to mint Truth as we please..yet we should find that it would not serve all Emergencies. **1641** MILTON *Reform.* II. 45 But by what example can they shew that the form of Church Discipline must be minted, and modell'd out to secular pretences? **1760–72** H. BROOKE *Fool of Qual.* (1809) II. 75, I would..he had now been present..to have his soul melted and minted as mine has been. *Ibid.* 107, I was melted down and minted anew, as it were.

mint (mɪnt), *a. ellipt.* for *in mint condition* (see MINT *sb.*[1] 6).

1902 *Connoisseur* Jan. p. xiv, A hitherto unknown stamp.. unused (mint). **1928** *Humphris'* (Norwich) *Catal.* No. 149. 13/1 'Mint' signifies As New. **1952** J. CARTER *A.B.C. for Bk.-Collectors* 59 A cloth-bound, a boarded or a wrappered book may be called immaculate, mint, pristine, [etc.]. *Ibid.* 120 Dust-jacket defective, otherwise mint. **1968** P. OLIVER *Screening Blues* 3 Other conditions reflect the popularity of singer or song, and some [records], grey on one side and 'mint' on the other, betray hard service in a juke-box. **1975** *Deval & Muir* (Takeley, Hertfordshire) *Catal.* No. 35. 16/1 This book is one of the prettiest small publications of the period... Apart from discolouration of the free end-papers, virtually a mint copy.

mintage ('mɪntɪdʒ). [f. MINT *v.*[1] or *sb.*[1] + -AGE.]

1. The action or process (*occas.* the privilege) of coining or minting money; coinage.

c **1570** *MS. Rawlinson D.* 23 lf. 13 A treatyse concerninge the myntage of the monyes. **1611** SPEED *Hist. Gt. Brit.* VII. xxxviii. §14. 342 He did [enrich] certaine Cities with the Mintage of his money, whereof in London were eight houses,..at Lewis two [etc.]. **1779** *Gentl. Mag.* XLIX. 410 A curious account by the President of the Roman mintage under Honorius and Arcadius. **1820** D. TURNER *Tour Normandy* II. 261 From time immemorial, the chapter has enjoyed the right of mintage. **1824** BYRON *Juan* XV. vii, Bright as a new Napoleon from its mintage. **1853** HUMPHREYS *Coin-Coll. Man.* I. xxiv. 344 Coins of Roman mintage.

2. *transf.* and *fig.* The fabrication or production of something compared to coin; the 'coining' or deliberate formation of a new word, etc.

a **1631** DONNE *Valed. Weeping* 4 Let me powre forth My teares before thy face,..For thy face coines them, and thy stampe they beare, And by this Mintage they are something worth. **1657** W. MORICE *Coena quasi Κοινὴ* Diat. vi. 315 They had the monopoly and mintage of godliness. **1662** SIR A. MERVYN *Sp. Irish Aff.* 2 It is now in its Mintage, and our care must be, that the Miter be not stampt instead of the Crown. **1745** WARTON *Pleas. Melancholy* 88 Which Reason's mintage fair Unmoulds, and stamps the monster on the man. **1839** DE QUINCEY *Recoll. Lakes* Wks. 1862 II. 116 A new word of German mintage. **1883** MAINE *Early Law & Cust.* 15 Few literary theories of modern mintage have more to recommend them.

3. *concr.* The product of a (particular) mint; a coin, or the coins collectively, minted by a specified person or in a specified place or country. Also *transf.* and *fig.* (cf. 2).

1638 T. CAREW in *Cary's Malvezzi* To Translator 10 Or what the Crusca yet For currant Tuscan mintage will admit. **1651** CLEVELAND *Poems* 3 Thus did Natures mintage vary, Coyning thee a Philip and Mary. **1839** J. STERLING *Poems* 167 Stamped in clay, a heavenly mintage, All from dust receive their birth. **1851** SIR F. PALGRAVE *Norm. & Eng.* I. 42 The Romans..purposely sowed and buried their mintage. **1871** FARRAR *Witn. Hist.* iv. 147 Christianity.. stamped them..and made them current amid the coins of a debased mintage. **1887** *Athenæum* 5 Nov. 598/1 A timely withdrawal of the worn coins may lead to the substitution of a better class of mintages. **1888** *Ch. Times* 341/3 Parodies of his most studied turns of phrase, witty travesties of his mintages.

4. The charge for or cost of coining; the duty paid for minting or coining.

1645 *Virginia Stat.* (1823) I. 308 To allow for the mintage 12*d.* per pound soe there will remaine £9500 sterl. The mintage allowed and deducted. **1825** *Blackw. Mag.* XVIII. 240 Mintage, altarage, and small dues, are almost unknown. **1869** [see COINAGE 1]. **1875** JEVONS *Money* xiv. 168 Some small savings would accrue from the less amount of mintage required.

5. The stamp or impression placed on a coin. In quots. *fig.*

1634 MILTON *Comus* 529 And the inglorious likenes of a beast Fixes instead, unmoulding reasons mintage Character'd in the face. *a* **1664** KATH. PHILIPS *Friendship* Poems (1667) 78 Those kind Impressions which Fate can't controul, Are Heaven's mintage on a worthy Soul. **1822** BYRON *Werner* III. i, Methinks it wears upon its face my guilt For motto, not the mintage of the state. **1882** *Times* 6 Feb., Who thus became stamped with the common mintage of their colleagues' manners.

6. *attrib.*, as ***mintage place, system.***

c **1630** RISDON *Surv. Devon* §276 (1810) 287 Con... implieth the mintage place. **1898** *Westm. Gaz.* 6 Apr. 7/2 The early efforts of the Edwards to set the coin of the Realm on a proper mintage system.

'mint-drop. [f. MINT *sb.*[2] + DROP *sb.*]

1. 'A sugar-plum flavoured with peppermint' (*Cent. Dict.* 1890).

2. *U.S. slang.* With pun on MINT *sb.*[1]: A coin.

1835 HAWTHORNE *Passages from Note-Bks.* in *Atlantic Monthly* (1866) Jan. 3/2 The bar-keeper had one of Benton's mint drops for a bosom-brooch! **1837** *Congress. Globe* 29 Sept. App. 339/3 [The money flowed to Mobile] by the aid of 'the far-famed Specie circular', in 'mint drops' and 'hard currency'. **1840** J. P. KENNEDY *Quodlibet* 106 [There's] Specie Circlor and Mint Drops, and the Lord knows what. **1872** SCHELE DE VERE *Americanisms* 291 When the Hon. T. H. Benton..put his whole strength forward..to introduce a gold currency, he accidentally called the latter mint-drops, with a slight attempt at a pun... For many years gold coins were largely known as Benton's mint-drops.

Mintech (mɪn'tɛk). Also **Mintec, Min. Tech.** Colloq. abbrevs. of *Ministry of Technology.*

1967 *Guardian* 26 Aug. 6/6 A Min Tech review of the whole problem. **1967** *Spectator* 15 Dec. 750/3 The gritty 'technological' phrasemaking of you-know-who and his Mintech. **1970** *Guardian* 25 Feb. 10/3 Mintech exists... They really do give this little name..to the great big Ministry of Technology. **1970** *Punch* 17 June 920/1 Every available taxpayer's penny is needed for wasting at Min-Tech. **1971** *New Scientist* 17 June 673/1 The civilian aspects of the defence research establishments—so laboriously cultivated under Mintech auspices.

minted ('mɪntɪd), *ppl. a.*[1] [f. MINT *v.*[2] + -ED[1].] Coined, made into coin or money; in the form of coin. Also *transf.* and *fig.*

1598, etc. [see NEW-MINTED *ppl. a.*]. **1640** *Two Lanc. Lovers* 60 (Halliw.) Pretending an indisposition of health, or some other minted excuse. *a* **1678** MARVELL *Dial. Soul & Pleas.* 58 Wheresoe're thy foot shall go The minted gold shall lie. **1820** C. R. MATURIN *Melmoth* (1892) III. xxx. 202 The sterling gold of a heart-minted look. **1852** JAMES *Pequinillo* II. 55 A hundred good and well-minted sequins. **1874** HOLLAND *Mistr. Manse* xxi, The minted silver that his largess scattered wide.

minted ('mɪntɪd), *ppl. a.*[2] [f. MINT *sb.*[2] + -ED[2].] Flavoured with mint.

1881 C. E. TURNER in *Macm. Mag.* XLIV. 311 A silver jug with a kind of sparkling minted *kvass*, the pleasant odour of which filled the whole room.

minter ('mɪntə(r)). Forms: 1 **mynetere, mynytere,** (*Northumb.* **mynittre**), 2 **menetere, minitere,** 3–4 **munetere,** 4–5 **mynter,** 6– **minter.** [OE. *mynetere* = OS. **munitari* (MDu., Du. *munter*), OHG. *munizzâri*, a. L. *monētārius*, f. *monēta*: see MONEY. The modern word may partly descend from OE., and partly be an independent formation on MINT *v.*[2] + -ER[1].]

†**1.** Used to render L. *nummularius* ('money-changer'). *Obs.*

c **950** *Lindisf. Gosp.* Matt. xxi. 12, xxv. 27, etc. *c* **1000** *Ags. Gosp.* ibid. *c* **1300** *Life Jesu* 853 (Horstm.) And Muneteres also þat oncouþe Men miȝten moneie finde.

2. One who coins or stamps money; a moneyer.

c **1000** ÆLFRIC *Hom.* (Th.) II. 554 Godes feoh..bið befæst myneterum to sleanne. *a* **1131** *O.E. Chron.* an. 1125 Man scolde beniman ealle þa minitere þe wæron on Engle lande heora liman. **1423** *Rolls of Parlt.* IV. 256/2 *margin*, Mynters and Goldsmithes. **1549** LATIMER *Ploughers* (Arb.) 27 Since priests haue bene minters, money hath bene wourse then it was before. **1605–6** *Act 3 Jas. I*, c. 27 §9 Other Officers Minters and Workemen..in any the Kinges Majesties Mintes. **1780** NOBLE *Mint & Coins Durham* 3 They..employed the same Minters as Edward the Confessor. **1828–40** TYTLER *Hist. Scot.* (1864) I. 278 Foreigners appear to have been the great coiners or minters of those times.

transf. *a* **1631** DONNE *Serm.* (1640) vii. 62 God stamped his Image upon us, and so God is..our Minter, our Statuary.

3. *fig.* An inventor; a deliberate fabricator; = COINER *sb.* 3.

1654 GAYTON *Pleas. Notes* IV. xi. 242 O generation of fictitious Mynters! who knows not that Apollo is a Deity Errant. **1702** C. MATHER *Magn. Chr.* VII. 11 A most prodigious Minter of Exorbitant Novelties. **1818** in TODD.

†**4.** [A distinct word, f. MINT *sb.*[1] + -ER[1].] A resident in the precincts of the ancient Mint in Southwark, once a reputed sanctuary for debtors. *Obs.*

a **1700** B. E. *Dict. Cant. Crew, Rum-dukes*, the boldest Fellows amongst the Alsatians, Minters, Savoyards, &c. **1706** LUTTRELL *Brief Rel.* (1857) VI. 20 The riotous proceedings of the minters in Southwark. **1723** *Weekly Jrnl.* 20 July, The Southwark Mint..got to be such a pest, that special statutes..were passed ordering the abolition... The exodus of the..train of 'Minters'..included some thousands.

minting ('mɪntɪŋ), *vbl. sb.*[1] [f. MINT *v.*[2] + -ING[1].] The action of MINT *v.*[2], *lit.* and *fig.*

1549 LATIMER *Ploughers* (Arb.) 27 If the Apostles mighte not leaue the office of preaching to be deacons, shall one leaue it for myntyng? **1579** FENTON *Guicciard.* (1618) 17 For money, his Mines and mintings furnished aboue all wants that could happen. **1665** PEPYS *Diary* 11 Dec., He [*sc.* the king] was forced to borrow thereupon till the tools could be made for the new minting in the present form. **1715** *Lond. Gaz.* No. 5339/1 The Minting of the..Copper-Pieces..is.. suspended. **1841** D'ISRAELI *Amen. Lit.* (1867) 131 The minting of new words. **1894** *Athenæum* 1 Sept. 294/2 An enormous collection of old coins, the residue of a century's minting.

b. *attrib.*, as ***minting apparatus, house, -mill.***

1772 *Hist. Rochester* 10 He established three minting houses. **1875** KNIGHT *Dict. Mech.*, *Minting-mill*, a coining-machine. **1903** *Daily Chron.* 29 Sept. 4/6 A complete minting apparatus was discovered.

minting, *vbl. sb.*[2]: see MINT *v.*[1]

mintjac, variant of MUNTJAC.

'mint-mark. [MINT *sb.*[1]] A mark placed upon a coin to indicate the mint at which it was struck.

1797 *Encycl. Brit.* (ed. 3) XII. 167/2. **1826** HAWKINS *Anglo-Gallic Coins Brit. Mus.* 87 *note*, The mint mark is a cross patonce. **1853** HUMPHREYS *Coin-coll. Man.* I. vi. 49 There is on this coin a small figure of Æsculapius, a sort of mint mark.

fig. *a* **1849** H. COLERIDGE *Ess.* (1851) I. 226 What can the loyal poet do, but..impress it with the mint-mark of his own devoted fancy? **1887** LOWELL *Democr.*, etc. 108 That spontaneousness which is the mint-mark of all sterling speech.

'mint-master. [f. MINT *sb.*[1]: cf. Du. *munt meester*, G. *münzmeister.*]

1. An officer of the mint whose duty it is to superintend the coinage of money.

1528 in *Lett. & Pap. Hen. VIII*, IV. II. 1723 Th'artycles that we ben sworn to consernyng the mynt maysters. **1622** MALYNES *Anc. Law-Merch.* 279 The principall Officer is the Warden of the Mint; next is the Mint-master. **1762–71** H. WALPOLE *Vertue's Anecd. Paint.* (1786) I. 15 *note*, Of William is a curious seal, as Mint-master. **1845** SELBY in *Proc. Berw. Nat. Club* II. No. 13. 160 *note*, In Æthelred's mint were upwards of forty mintmasters. **1879** H. PHILLIPS *Notes Coins* 14 The daughter of the mint-master stood in one scale while her weight in Massachusetts shillings was poured into the other for her dowry.

2. *fig.* A 'coiner' of new ideas, words, etc. Common in 17th c.; now *rare* or *Obs.*

1599 *Broughton's Let.* ix. 30 The graund Mintmaster of learning in our age. *Ibid.* 47 You will be counted..the mintmaster of fancies. **1641** MILTON *Animadv.* Wks. 1851 III. 204 The odde coinage of your phrase, which no mint-maister of language would allow for sterling. **1690** LOCKE *Hum. Und.* III. x. §2 The great Mint-Masters of these kind of Terms, I mean the School-men and Metaphysicians.

Minto ('mɪntəʊ). Also **Mintoe, mintoe.** [f. MINT *sb.*[2]] The proprietary name of a type of boiled sweet flavoured with peppermint.

1935 *Trade Marks Jrnl.* 16 Oct. 1298/2 Nuttall's Mintoes. .. Boiled sugar sweetmeats flavoured with mint. William Nuttall Limited,..Doncaster; manufacturing confectioners. **1949** DYLAN THOMAS *Let.* 13 Oct. (1966) 328 Yesterday I broke a tooth on a minto. **1953** —— *Under Milk Wood* (1954) 2 Coughing like nannygoats, sucking mintoes, fortywinking hallelujah. **1957** *Skuse's Compl. Confectioner* (ed. 13) 63 *Mintoes.* Boil the sugar, glucose and water.. knead in the oil of peppermint and..spin out and cut. *Ibid.* 64 (caption) Kiss Cutting on 'Mintoe' Machine. **1963** *Listener* 21 Mar. 501/2, I wanted to keep on sucking mintoes for ever.

Minton ('mɪntən). The name of Thomas *Minton* (1766–1836), used *attrib.* to designate the pottery made at Stoke-on-Trent, Staffs., from 1793 onwards, by him and his successors. Also *ellipt.*, = Minton ware.

1857 J. MARRYAT *Hist. Pott. & Porc.* (ed. 2) xii. 302 Staffordshire is now the site of the great manufactures. From among these may be mentioned Minton, Copeland, Ridgway. **1863** W. CHAFFERS *Marks Pott. & Porc.* 125 Minton's, established in 1791 by Mr. Thomas Minton... The name, indented on the ware, is generally adopted both for china and earthenware. **1888** [see TILE *sb.*[1] 1 c]. **1926** S. T. WARNER *Lolly Willowes* I. 11 An amateur of china, who had dowered all his nieces..with Worcester, Minton, and Oriental. **1960** R. COLLIER *House called Memory* iii. 44 The best silver tea-service and the Minton tea-set. **1967** 'R. RAINE' *Wreath for Amer.* ii. 30 A small silver tray bearing

two Minton cups and saucers. **1972** R. PLAYER *Oh! Where are Bloody Mary's Earrings* vii. 182 A scraping of boots on the Minton tile floor.

ˌmint-ˈsauce. [f. MINT *sb.*[2] + SAUCE *sb.*]

1. A sauce made of finely chopped mint mixed with vinegar and sweetened with sugar; it is usually eaten with roast lamb.

1747 MRS. GLASSE *Cookery* 4 It will eat like Lamb with Mint Sauce. **1769** EARL CARLISLE in Jesse *G. Selwyn & Contemp.* (1843) II. 363 Sir P. Lambe.. said he would give Lady Henrietta mint sauce. **1826** MRS. DODS *Cook & Housw. Man.* 169 Mint Sauce for Hot or Cold Roast Lamb.

2. With punning allusion to MINT *sb.*[2]: Money.

1828 EGAN *Finish Tom & Jerry* (1871) 53, I.. only hope that he gets lots of mint-sauce. **1838** DICKENS *Nich. Nick.* xxxiv, It is to melt some scraps of dirty paper into bright shining, chinking, tinkling, demd mint sauce.

†mint-while. *Obs. rare.* [App. for *minute-while*: see MINUTE *sb.* 1. Cf. MINT *sb.*[3]] The duration of a minute.

1393 LANGL. *P. Pl.* C. XIII. 217 An vnredy reue þi residue shal spene, That menye mothþe was [maister] ynne in a mynte-while. *Ibid.* xx. 194 As we may seo a wynter, Isykles in euesynges, thorgh hete of þe sonne Melteþ in a mynt-while [1377 *B-text* mynut while] to myst and to water.

minty (ˈmɪntɪ), *a.* [f. MINT *sb.*[2] + -Y[1].]

a. Abounding in mint. **b.** Resembling the flavour of mint.

1878 B. TAYLOR *Deukalion* III. i. 98 Where the minty meadow breath makes cool Thine ardent brow. **1904** *Daily News* 27 Dec. 10 Among the flavours avoided like the plague by every self-respecting blender [of tea] are those described in the trade as 'herby', 'stemmy', 'mousy', 'minty' [etc.].

minua, variant of MINAWAY.

†minuate, *v. Obs. rare.* [irreg. f. L. *minu-ĕre* to lessen + -ATE[3].] *trans.* To make less, diminish.

1657 TOMLINSON *Renou's Disp.* 235 Its faculty is to minuate the spleen.

†minuca. *Obs. rare.* In 6 mynuca. [app. med.L.; cf. med.L. *nucha* in the same sense (? a. Arab. *nuχχ* marrow, or *nuχṭ* spinal marrow).] The spinal cord.

1548–77 VICARY *Anat.* ii. (1888) 19 The Sinew.. [has] his beginning from the braine, or from Mynuca, which is the marowe of the backe.

minuend (ˈmɪnjuːɛnd). *Arith.* [ad. L. *minuend-us* (sc. *numerus*), gerundive pple. of *minuĕre* to diminish.] The number from which another number is to be subtracted.

1706 W. JONES *Syn. Palmar. Matheseos* 12 The greatest of the given Numbers is called the Minuend. **1892** BARN. SMITH & HUDSON *Arith. for Schools* 11 The smaller number is called the subtrahend. The greater is called the minuend.

‖**minuˈendo,** *adv. Mus. Obs.* [It., gerund of *minuire* to diminish.] = DIMINUENDO.

attrib. **1834** *Georgian Era* IV. 452/1 A certain singer's minuendo notes.

minuet (mɪnjuːˈɛt), *sb.* Also 7 **minnuet, minuett,** 7–8 **minouet, menuet,** 8 **minuit**; and see MINAWAY, MINUETTO. [ad. F. *menuet*, subst. use of *menuet* adj., small, fine, delicate, dim. of *menu* small: see MENU, MINUTE *a.* The form of the Eng. word was perh. influenced by the It. *minuetto*, which is adapted from Fr., as are Sp., Pg. *minuete*, Sp. *minue*.

The pronunciation (ˈmɪnjuːɪt or ˈmɪnjuːɛt), given in Dictionaries, is now seldom heard.]

1. A slow, stately dance, in triple measure, for two dancers; derived from France in the latter part of the seventeenth century, and fashionable throughout the eighteenth.

1673 DRYDEN *Marr. à la Mode* II. i, And what new *Minouets* have you brought over with you! their *Minouets* are to a miracle. **1676** ETHEREDGE *Man of Mode* IV. i, I am fit for Nothing but low dancing now, a Corant, a Boreè, Or a Minnuét. **1706** PHILLIPS (ed. Kersey), *Menuet*, or *Minuet*, a sort of French Dance, or the Tune belonging to it. **1762** GOLDSM. *Nash* 34 Each ball was to open with a minuet, danced by two persons of the highest distinction present. **1778** MRS. E. MONTAGU in Doran *Lady Last Cent.* ix. (1873) 231 To excel in dancing a minouet. **1810** SIR A. BOSWELL *Edinb.* Poet. Wks. (1871) 52 To walk a minuet with becoming grace. **1864** TENNYSON *Aylmer's F.* 207 A stiff brocade in which.. she, Once with this kinsman,.. Stept thro' the stately minuet of those days.

2. The music used to accompany this dance. Hence, a piece of music in the same rhythm and style, consisting of two sections (the second of which is often called a *trio*); frequently forming one of the movements of the Suite, and, later, of compositions in Sonata-form.

1686 *Lond. Gaz.* No. 2119/4 There are designed to be published several Overtures or Sonatta's, containing Variety of Humors, as Grave Aires, Minuetts, Borees, &c. **1717** GAY *Epist. Pulteney* 144 He.. Hums a soft minuet. **1762** JEFFERSON *Writ.* (1892) I. 341 They carried away.. half a dozen new minuets I had just got. **1762–71** H. WALPOLE *Vertue's Anecd. Paint.* (1786) IV. 75 As a dancing-master would, if he expected Orpheus should return to play a minuet to them.

3. *attrib.* and *Comb.*, as ***minuet dance, -dancer, dancing, form, -step, -time, -tune.***

1831 CARLYLE *Misc.* (1857) II. 268 The graceful *minuet dance of Fancy. **1712** STEELE *Spect.* No. 308 ¶6 John Trot .. has the Assurance to set up for a *Minuit-Dancer. **1840** DICKENS *Barn. Rudge* iv, Sim.. sprang from his seat, and in two extraordinary steps, something between skating and *minuet dancing, bounded to a washing place. **1875** OUSELEY *Mus. Form* vii. 43 The original *minuet form always consisted of a piece in triple time and of moderate speed. **1711** STEELE *Spect.* No. 148 ¶1 The Gentleman who .. practised *minuet-steps to his own Humming. **1728** FIELDING *Love in Sev. Masques* II. i, The airy Sir Plume, who always walks in the minuet-step. **1851** THACKERAY *Eng. Hum.* iv. (1858) 188 A *minuet-tune played on a bird-organ.

Hence **minuet** *v.*, to dance a minuet; also *fig.*; **minueting** *vbl. sb.* Also **minuˈetic, minuetish** *adjs.*

1742 RICHARDSON *Pamela* IV. 114 A Glut of minuitish Airs. *a* **1847** ELIZA COOK *Dancing Song* v, See the sweet rose Bend to the blue-bell, in light minueting! **1856** BAGEHOT *Lit. Stud.* (1879) II. 34 You should do everything, said Lord Chesterfield, in minuet time. It was in that time that Gibbon wrote his history... You perceive the minuetic action accompanying the words. **1881** G. M. HOPKINS *Lett. to R. Bridges* (1955) 125 The magic nib has.. minuetted and gavotted into the syllables of your name. **1890** *Temple Bar* Feb. 297 Twenty years ago people minuet-ed. **1972** *Newsweek* 17 July 21/3 MacGregor might have to minuet with White House aides for a Presidential audience.

‖**minuetto** (minuˈetto, mɪnjuːˈɛtəʊ). [It.] = MINUET.

1724 *Short Explication Foreign Words in Musick Bks.* 46 *Minuetto*, a Minuet, a French Dance so called, or the Tune or Air belonging thereunto. **1888** *Academy* 21 Jan. 51/2 The wonderful largo was at times rough, and the minuetto taken at too rapid a rate. **1923** [see GRAPE *sb.*[1] 1]. **1971** BLOM & WESTRUP *Everyman's Dict. Mus.* (ed. 5) 431/2 *Minuetto* (It.). This, not 'Menuetto', is the correct It. name for the Minuet.

†miˈnuity. *Obs. rare.* [ad. OF. *minuité*, irreg. f. L. *minūtus* MINUTE *a.*] A trifle.

1612 SHELTON *Quix.* I. III. vi. (1620) 174, I would not haue my soule suffer in the other world for such a minuity as is thy wages.

†ˈminulize, *v. Obs. rare*[−1]. [Perh. an imperfect recollection of Gr. *μινυρίζειν*.] *trans.* To warble lightly or softly.

1600 TOURNEUR *Transf. Metam.* xxviii, The Thrush, the Lark, and nights-ioy nightingale, There minulize their pleasing laies anew.

minum, variant of MENNOM *dial.*, minnow.

minum(e, obs. forms of MINIM.

minument, obs. form of MUNIMENT.

minus (ˈmaɪnəs), quasi-*prep.*, *adv.*, *a.*, and *sb.* Also 5 **mynus.** [a. L. *minus* neut. of *minor* less: see MINOR *a.*

The quasi-prepositional use (sense 1), from which all the other Eng. uses have been developed, did not exist in Latin of any period. It probably originated in the commercial language of the Middle Ages. In Germany, and perhaps in other countries, the Latin words *plus* and *minus* were used by merchants to mark an excess or deficiency in weight or measure, the amount of which was appended in figures. The earliest known examples of the modern sense of *minus* are German, of about the same date as our oldest quotation. In Widmann's book on commercial arithmetic (1489) the signs (−) and (+) occur for the first time in print, and are directed to be read as *minus* and *mer*. In the *Bamberger Rechenbuch* (1483) the tare to be deducted from the weight of a package is called *das Minus*. In a somewhat different sense, *plus* and *minus* had been employed in 1202 by Leonardo of Pisa for the excess and deficiency in the results of the two suppositions in the Rule of Double Position; and an Italian writer of the 14th c. used *meno* to indicate the subtraction of a number to which it was prefixed. For the passages referred to, see Cantor, *Vorlesungen über Geschichte der Mathematik* II. (ed. 2, 1899).

The origin of the symbol (−), read as *minus*, is disputed; some have conjectured that it arose as a merchants' mark, while others believe it to descend from the *obelus* (see OBELISK 2) used by ancient critics to indicate that a passage should be removed from the text. It has certainly no historical connexion with the mark ♰ (explained as the letter ψ inverted) used by Diophantus for the same purpose. In Denmark the sign (÷) is used for *minus*.]

1. a. quasi-*prep.* Placed between two expressions of number or quantity to indicate that the second of them must be subtracted from the first. In mathematical use only as the oral rendering of the symbol (−). Hence, in non-technical use: With the deduction of, exclusive of (some specified portion or constituent element of the whole). Cf. LESS *a.* 4, and the equivalent F. *moins*, G. *weniger*.

1481–90 *Howard Househ. Bks.* (Roxb.) 417, v. yerdys, mynus the nayle, welwet blake. **1727–52** CHAMBERS *Cycl.* s.v. *Character*, Thus 14 − 2, is read, 14 *minus*, or abating, 2. **1808** J. W. CROKER *Sk. St. Irel.* (ed. 2) 42 Competitors offer the whole value of the produce minus that daily potatoe. **1811** EAST *K.B. Rep.* XIII. 214 There was not 100*l.* due.. but only that sum minus the rebate of interest for the times which the bills had then to run. **1830** M. DONOVAN *Dom. Econ.* I. 123 It might be supposed.. that acetic acid is alcohol *minus* carbon. **1849–52** *Todd's Cycl. Anat.* IV. 962/2 An imperfect cranium, composed principally of the cranial, *minus* the facial, bones. **1859** MILL *Liberty* ii, If all mankind minus one, were of one opinion. **1874** J. CAIRD *University Addr.* (1898) 16 The least and lowest fact of outward observation is not a bare fact, an independent entity, fact *minus* mind.

b. *predicatively* in colloquial use: Deprived of, 'short of', without (something). Also rarely *minus of.* Hence *occas.* as *adj.*, standing in the position of a loser, worse off than before; also, unprovided, destitute of something implied.

1813 *Chron.* in *Ann. Reg.* 44 He was considerably *minus* at the last Newmarket meeting. **1823** BYRON *Juan* VI. xxi, Which leaves you minus of the cash. **1836** *Lett. fr. Madras* (1843) 33 Twelve boatmen.. with very small matters of clothes on, but their black skins prevent them from looking so very uncomfortable as Europeans would in the same *minus* state. **1840** J. B. FRASER *Trav. Koordistan*, etc. II. xv. 310 We reached our munzil of Toorkomanchai about six in the evening, *minus* one horse. **1861** CALVERLEY *Lines 14th Feb.* (II.) 10 Yea! by St. Valentinus, Emma shall not be minus What all young ladies.. Expect to-day. **1903** *Review of Rev.* Apr. 385/2 The Englishman got back to civilization minus his left arm.

2. a. Used as the oral equivalent of the symbol (−) in its algebraical interpretation, as forming with the expression to which it is prefixed the representation of a negative quantity, e.g. in '− 3', '− *x*', which are read as *minus* 3, *minus x*; *spec.* as part of an examiner's mark, as in *α* − (read as alpha minus).

1579 DIGGES *Stratiot.* II. iv. 38 The same or like Signes multiplied produce + *Plus*. Contrarie or diuerse Signes produce alway − *Minus*. **1932** A. HUXLEY *Brave New World* iv. 75 He.. called to a lounging couple of Delta-Minus attendants to come and push his machine out. **1958** [see BETA 3]. **1962** M. DRABBLE *Summer Bird-Cage* i. 13, I.. got on the train, where I read.. *Tender is the Night* (beta minus).

b. Hence *attrib.* or as *adj.* in ***minus quantity***, a quantity which has the sign (−), a negative quantity; popularly often misused for 'something non-existent'; also *transf.*, insignificant.

1863 W. PHILLIPS *Speeches* xvii. 392 Such states are a *minus* quantity. **1916** R. FRY *Let.* 14 Aug. (1972) II. 401, I fear my recommendation would generally prove a minus quantity. **1922** WODEHOUSE *Clicking of Cuthbert* ix. 221 He might be a pretty minus quantity in a drawing-room or at a dance, but in a bunker or out in the open with a cleek, Eunice felt, you'd be surprised. **1965** F. SINCLAIR *Most Unnatural Murder* xv. 174 Cherub and Phyl wouldn't play; Phyl's a bit of a minus quantity, anyway, from that angle.

c. *adj.* Of the nature of a 'minus quantity' or deficit; also *colloq.* lacking, non-existent; absent.

1800 *Proc. Parlt.* in *Asiat. Ann. Reg.* 49/2 There were six millions *minus*. **1852** C. A. BRISTED *Five Yrs. Eng. Univ.* 53 His mathematics are decidedly *minus*, but the use of them is past long ago. **1853** DICKENS *Down with Tide* in *Househ. Words* 5 Feb. 483/2 Being, when called upon to answer for the assault, what Waterloo described as 'Minus', or, as I humbly conceived it, not to be found. **1858** A. MAYHEW *Paved with Gold* III. xiv. 342 If we ain't minus in less than no time, we're blowed upon. **1867** CARLYLE *Remin.* (1881) II. 144 The villain of a partner eloped, and left him possessor of a *minus* 12,000*l.* **1897** *Encycl. Sport* I. 62 *Penalise*. Strictly speaking, a penalty is a minus handicap, *i.e.* the man who is giving the other competitors starts, is placed behind the line from which the distance to be run is reckoned.

d. *adv.* and *adj.* Negatively (electrified).

1747 FRANKLIN *Lett.* Wks. 1887 II. 71 *B* is electrized *plus*; *A*, *minus*. And we daily in our experiments electrize bodies *plus* or *minus*, as we think proper. **1789** NICHOLSON in *Phil. Trans.* LXXIX. 270 It affords the means of producing either the plus or minus states in one and the same conductor. **1849** NOAD *Electricity* (ed. 3) 5 A body having more than its natural quantity [of electric fluid] is electrified *positively* or *plus*, and one which has less is electrified *negatively* or *minus*. **1854** J. SCOFFERN in *Orr's Circ. Sci., Chem.* 225 Its counterpart of − or minus electricity.

fig. **1817** COLERIDGE *Statesm. Man.* 54 Apparent contraries, which are yet but the two poles, or *Plus* and *Minus* states, of the same influence.

e. Followed by the name of a colour to designate the complementary colour, i.e. that of white light from which the specified colour has been removed; so ***minus colour***.

1901 CADETT & SHEPHERD *Orthochromatic & Three-Colour Photogr.* 24 [In the Sanger Shepherd process] the prints for the minus green or pink, and minus blue or yellow positives are printed together on a special film. **1901** *Chambers's Jrnl.* 4 May 366/2 The prefix 'minus' attached to a primary colour.. [implies] that this particular colour is cut out of the spectrum of white light, and that the negatively-named compound is a blend of the hues remaining. 'White minus red', 'white minus green', and 'white minus blue' would be the complete expressions; they are ordinarily termed complementary colours. **1936** *Discovery* Jan. 2/1 It [*sc.* Monastral Fast Blue BS] is a true 'minus-red' pigment for three-colour printing. **1939** J. H COOTE *Making Colour Prints* 17 The three colours which are used for 'subtraction' are described as 'minus' colours. **1970** D. L. MACADAM *Sources of Color Sci.* 130 Red, green, and blue, being the colors in positive synthesis, minus red, minus green, and minus blue, or cyan blue, bright crimson and yellow are the printing colors.

3. *sb.* in various applications: **a.** The mathematical symbol (−); also ***minus sign.*** **b.** An operation of subtraction, a quantity subtracted or taken away; a loss, deficiency. **c.** A negative quantity.

1654 WHITLOCK *Zootomia* 385 For the *Algebra* (as I may tearm it) or *Nature of Reprehension*, giveth the *Plus* to the *Reprover*, and the *Minus* to the *Reproved*. **1668** BRANCKER *Introd. Algebra* 4 The Sign for *Subtraction* is − *i.e. Minus*, or the Negative Sign. **1685** WALLIS *Algebra* xvi. 69 The Signs + and − (or *Plus* and *Minus*) the former of which is a Note of Position, Affirmation or Addition; the other of Defect, Negation, or Subduction. **1708** PRIOR *Turtle & Sparrow* 329 Now weigh the pleasure with the pain, The plus and minus, loss and gain. **1836** E. HOWARD *R. Reefer* xxvi, A slatefull of plusses, minusses, *x*, *y*, *z*'s. **1876** GEO. ELIOT *Dan. Der.* VI. xlviii, That new gambling, in which the

losing was not simply a *minus* but a terrible *plus* that had never entered into her reckoning.

Hence '**minus** *v.* (*nonce-wd.*) *trans.*, to subject to a loss or privation.

1801 COLERIDGE *Let. to Southey* 13 Apr. in *Life of S.* (1850) II. 146 Alas! you will have found the dear old place sadly minused by the removal of Davy.

minuscular (mɪˈnʌskjʊlə(r)), *a. Palæogr.* [f. L. *minuscul-us*: see MINUSCULE and -AR.] Of the nature of a minuscule; composed of minuscules.

1756 SWINTON in *Phil. Trans.* L. 177 After the introduction of the Omega of the minuscular form..upon the Parthian coins. **1882–3** *Schaff's Encycl. Relig. Knowl.* s.v. *Alpha*, The ω is of that uncial form which resembles the minuscular.

minusculated (mɪˈnʌskjʊleɪtɪd), *a. nonce-wd.* [f. MINUSCULE + -ATE[3] + -ED[1].] Written as a 'minuscule' or small letter.

1843 HUMPHREYS *Brit. Moths* II. 125 Somewhat resembling the Greek minusculated letter A.

minuscule (ˈmɪnəskjuːl, mɪˈnʌskjuːl, ˈmɪn(j)əskjuːl), *a.* and *sb.* [a. F. *minuscule*, ad. L. *minuscula* (sc. *littera*), fem. of *minusculus* rather less, dim. of *minor* (neut. *minus*): see MINOR *a.* and MINUS *a.*] **A.** *adj.*

1. †**a.** *Printing.* Of a letter: Small, not capital, 'lower-case'. *Obs.* **b.** *Palæogr.* Of a letter: Small (see B. b). Also, written in minuscules.

1727–41 [see MAJUSCULE *a.*]. **1850** A. WAY in *Archæol. Jrnl.* VII. 356 A little mark at the close of the first line, resembling a minuscule C is somewhat indistinct. **1883** I. TAYLOR *Alphabet* I. 71 The letters of the beautiful minuscule manuscripts of the 10th and 11th centuries. These minuscule letters are cursive forms of the earlier uncials. **1900** *Expositor* Mar. 175 Annotations are found in the minuscule codices.

2. *gen.* Extremely small. Also, unimportant.

See also MINISCULE.

1893 *Nation* (N.Y.) 20 July 51/1 The theories that are put forth by minuscule scholars as personal contributions to the advance of science. **1898** *Edin. Rev.* Apr. 420 Only think of the minuscule touches of advance that Ictinus added to his predecessors' designs. **1904** *Nutt's Catal.* Sept. p. ix, Sir Gawain at the Grail Castle. Three Versions, translated..by Jessie L. Weston. Minuscule 4to. **1963** *Ann. Reg. 1962* 17 Such minuscule militants as the boot and floor polish manufacturers. **1969** *Listener* 30 Jan. 155/3 One is impressed inevitably by the intensity and concentration of human effort on a project whose rewards, however satisfying, are bound to be minuscule. **1972** *Time* 17 Apr. 24/1 The Gallup organization, in all of its national soundings, has shown McGovern running between a minuscule 3% and 6% when pitted against his rivals for the nomination.

B. *sb.* †**a.** *Printing.* A small or 'lower-case' letter as opposed to a capital. *Obs.* **b.** *Palæogr.* A small letter, as opposed to a capital or uncial; the small cursive script which was developed from the uncial during the 7th–9th centuries; also, a manuscript in this writing.

1705 H. WANLEY in *Phil. Trans.* XXV. 1996 Some MSS. written with Minuscules. [**1727–41** CHAMBERS *Cycl.*, *Minusculæ*, in printing, denotes the small, or running letters.] **1782** BURNEY *Hist. Mus.* II. 32 A notation for three octaves, the gravest of which he expressed by capitals, the mean by minuscules, and the highest by double letters. **1851** SIR F. PALGRAVE *Norm. & Eng.* I. 228 The initial difference of a minuscule or a capital. *a* **1876** EADIE *Comm. Thess.* (1877) 23 A few minuscules read αὐτοὺς ἡμᾶς. **1883** I. TAYLOR *Alphabet* II. 160 The minuscule arose in the 7th century as a cursive monastic script.

minussh, obs. form of MINISH.

†'**minutable**, *a. Obs. rare.* [f. MINUTE *v.* + -ABLE.] Suitable for making a minute of.

1778 [W. MARSHALL] *Minutes Agric. Digest* 2 He threw every thing he thought minutable, into a series of Minutes.

[**minutal**. Explained as: A diminutive. Error due to misinterpreting L. *minutal* mincemeat.

[**1589** RIDER *Bibl. Schol.* 802 A Iussell, or meate made with diverse things, chopped together. I Minutal, n. **1656** BLOUNT *Glossogr.*, *Jussel* (*minutal*) meat made with divers things chopped together. *Rider.*] **1658–96** PHILLIPS, *Jussel*, a minutal from *jus*. [See JUSSEL.]]

†'**minutary**, *a. Obs.* [f. MINUTE *a.* and *sb.* + -ARY.]

1. ? Pertaining to minute quantities.

1610 HEALEY *St. Aug. Citie of God* XV. xxvii. *Vives' Comm.* 569 One cubit is generally taken for sixe of our common cubits, or for three hundred minutary cubits [orig. *Apud geometras..vel in sex cubitos vnus deputatur, si generaliter, vel trecentos, si minutatim dicatur*].

2. Consisting of minutes (of time).

1655 FULLER *Ch. Hist.* III. Ded., No mortal man can assign the minutary juncture of Time, when preparing grace ..ended, and saving grace..did first begin. *a* **1661** —— *Worthies, Berks* (1662) I. 95 This their Clock gathering up the least Crume of Time, presenting the Minutary fractions thereof.

†**minu'tation**. *Obs.* [f. MINUTE *v.* + -ATION.] The action of making minutes (of observations, etc.). (Frequent in Bentham.)

1802–12 BENTHAM *Ration. Judic. Evid.* (1827) II. 127 By this division, writing, minutation and recordation..is necessitated.

minute (ˈmɪnɪt), *sb.*[1] Forms: 4 mynut, 4–6 mynute, 4–7 minut, 5 mynwt, mynnate, 6 mynite, -ewte, -iute, *Sc.* minuth, munet, -it, 6–8 mynuit, 7 min-, mynutte, minit, minnite, 4– minute. [In senses 1–3 and 6 a. F. *minute* fem. (whence G. *minute*, Du. *minuut*), ad. L. *minūta*, subst. use of the fem. of *minūtus* MINUTE *a.* In senses 4 and 5 ad. L. *minūtum* (the neuter of the same adj.) used subst. in various applications in late Latin. Sp., Pg. and It. have *minuto* masc. (ad. L. *minutum*) in senses 1–3, but *minuta* (after Fr.) in sense 6.

Senses 1–2 (whence sense 3 is derived) represent the med.L. *minuta*, more fully *pars minuta prima*, denoting the $\frac{1}{60}$ of a unit in the system of sexagesimal fractions (med.L. *minutiæ physicæ*), which, originally derived from Babylon, was used, like the modern decimals in scientific calculations as more easy to handle than 'vulgar fractions' (*minutiæ* simply). The lower denominations of the system were (*partes minutæ*) *secundæ* (our 'seconds'), *tertiæ*, *quartæ*, etc., the understood denominators being the successive powers of 60. The system (ὁ τῆς ἑξηκοντάδος τρόπος) was recognized by Ptolemy (*c*150 A.D.), who applied it to the degree (μοῖρα) of the circle, to the sixty sections into which he divided the radius, and to the day; the application of the system to the division of the hour is much later, perhaps not earlier than the 13th c. Ptolemy has no terms corresponding to the med.L. *minutæ*, *secundæ*, etc., but merely uses μέρος 'part' or ἑξηκοστόν 'sixtieth'. The word *minuta* is referred to as a term of the 'mathematici' (app. meaning 'minute' of the circle) by St. Augustine *De diversis Quæstt. octoginta tribus* xlv, who also mentions *minutæ minutarum*, 'minutes of minutes' (see 2), *i.e.* seconds.

Sense 6 is from F. *minute*, though Littré has no example before 16th c., and the one quot. for med.L. *minuta* in this use is of date *c*1500. The primary notion seems to be that of a rough copy in *small* writing (L. *scriptura minuta*) as distinguished from the 'engrossed' document.]

I. A sixtieth (or other definite part) of a unit.

1. a. The sixtieth part of an hour (divided into sixty seconds). In earlier use frequently †***minute of an hour***, †***minute while***. Also, one of the lines upon a dial which mark the minute spaces.

The *minutum* of early mediæval writers, which was one-tenth of an hour, has no historical connexion with this. For the system of time-reckoning to which it belongs, see ATOM *sb.* 7.

1377 LANGL. *P. Pl.* B. XI. 372 He miȝte amende in a Minute while al þat mys standeth. *Ibid.* XVII. 228 Ysekeles in eueses þorw hete of þe sonne, Melteth in a mynut while to myst & to watre. **1390** GOWER *Conf.* II. 9 For the lachesse Of half a Minut of an houre [= L. *unius momenti tardacione*] ..He loste all that he hadde do. *a* **1485** *Promp. Parv.* 338/2 (MSS. K., S.) Minute of an howur, *minuta*. **1552** LYNDESAY *Monarche* 6014 The small Minuth of one hour To thame salbe so gret dolour, Thay sall thynk thay haif done remane Ane thousand yeir in to that pane. **1588** SHAKS. *L.L.L.* V. ii. 797 Now at the latest minute of the houre, Grant vs your loues. **1591** —— *1 Hen. VI*, I. iv. 54 Wherefore a guard of chosen Shot I had, That walkt about me euery Minute while. **1603** OWEN *Pembrokeshire* i. (1892) 1 Our longest sommers daies must be of XVII houres and fortie three mynuttes longe. **1684** R. WALLER *Nat. Exper.* 9 From 35, to 50 Drops [*sc.* of moist particles] have fallen in a Minute of an Hour. **1702** *Lond. Gaz.* No. 3844/1 The Great Guns were fired at a Minute's distance. **1817** T. L. PEACOCK *Nightm. Abbey* xv, The hour-hand had passed the VII.—the minute-hand moved on;—it was within three minutes of the appointed time. **1843** *Penny Cycl.* XXVII. 107/1 There are other repeaters which also strike the minutes.

b. Vaguely used for: A short space of time; also, a point of time, an instant, moment. Also in phr. ***up to the minute***, completely modern.

1390 GOWER *Conf.* III. 77 Every houre apointeth so, That no minut therof was lore. **1412–20** LYDG. *Chron. Troy* (E.E.T.S.) 2817 þe cok..of þe tyme a mynute wil not passe To warnen hem þat weren in þe place, Of þe tydes and sesoun of þe nyȝt. *c* **1485** *Digby Myst.* IV. 518, I myght not leve, nor endure On mynnate, bot I am sure The third day ryse shall hee. **1590** SHAKS. *Mids. N.* II. ii. 112 Content with Hermia? No, I do repent The tedious minutes I with her haue spent. *c* **1600** —— *Sonn.* xiv, Nor can I fortune to breefe mynuits tell; Pointing to each his thunder raine and winde. **1697** DAMPIER *Voy.* I. 80, I could not expect to find them at a minutes call. **1736** AINSWORTH *Lat. Dict.*, A minute [moment or instant], *momentum, punctum temporis*. **1795** tr. *C. P. Moritz's Trav.* 93 Composing a sermon.. should not thus have been put off to the last minute. **1800** LAMB *Let. to Manning* 5 Oct., I have barely time to finish, as I expect her and Robin every minute. **1871** R. ELLIS tr. *Catullus* lxvii. 38 You, from your owner's gate never a minute away? **1898** FLOR. MONTGOMERY *Tony* 13 The train will be starting in a minute. **1913** *Vanity Fair* (N.Y.) Dec. 9/2 Look at your Christmas shopping in this light... Don't put it off until the last minute. **1920** F. M. FORD *Let.* 27 July (1965) 117 Does 'for a minute' = 'at present'? or that you wouldn't think for a minute of knowing our establishment? **1937** A. J. CRONIN *Citadel* ix. 75 Doctor! I think you'd be interested in our new indexometer. It has a multiplicity of uses, is absolutely up to the minute..and the price is only two guineas. **1955** R. MACAULAY *Last Lett. to Friend* (1962) 208 Having the two children made it fun; they loved every minute of it. **1956** E. S. GARDNER *D. A. takes Chance* iii. 24 A very attractive young woman, vivacious, up to the minute, a thoroughly modern young woman. **1958** *Spectator* 22 Aug. 249/1 These ought to be worth a trial to give ballet that shake-up it badly needs. Not merely for Art's sake, but, any minute now, for the sake of the box office. **1972** *Daily Tel.* 26 Aug. 20/4 A good atmosphere helps me to do my best, and while at the minute it doesn't feel like an Olympic Games, I think I can psych myself up when the time comes.

c. A particular instant of time; also occas. the appointed or fitting moment. ***the minute*** (***that***)..: as soon as.

1598 SHAKS. *Merry W.* V. v. 1 The Windsor-bell hath stroke twelue: the Minute drawes-on. *a* **1640** CAREW *To A. L.* 70 O love me, then, and now begin it, Let us not lose this present minute. *a* **1721** KEILL *Maupertius' Diss.* (1734) 15 The Minute we recur to an Almighty Agent,..it should be said that such Laws imply a Contradiction. *a* **1745** SWIFT *Direct. Serv., Gen.* Wks. 1751 XIV. 11 He had but just that Minute stept out. **1799** LAMB *Let. to Southey* 20 Mar., My plan is but this minute come into my head. **1859** GEO. ELIOT *A. Bede* i, I can't abide to see men throw away their tools i' that way the minute the clock begins to strike.

d. A distance expressed in the number of minutes needed for it to be traversed (on foot, etc.).

1886 *Taunt's New Map Thames* (ed. 5) Advts. 45 Hotel.. Adjoining the River, 3 minutes from Railway Station. **1907** *Daily Chron.* 18 Sept. 3/7 (Advt.), St. Pancras Station..is within a few minutes of the City. **1922** JOYCE *Ulysses* 224 Can you send them by tram? Now?..—Certainly, sir. Is it in the city? —O, yes... Ten minutes. **1931** R. CAMPBELL *Georgiad* I. 17 Up-to-date methods: breezy situation: And only twenty minutes from the station. **1934** G. B. SHAW *On Rocks* I. 203 The Isle of Cats... Down the river, Sir Arthur. Twenty minutes from your door by underground. **1962** J. G. BENNETT *Witness* vii. 86, I went to his apartment, a few minutes from where we lived.

2. *Geom.* (*Astr.*, *Geog.*, etc.) The sixtieth part of a degree. †***minute of a minute***: the sixtieth of a minute, a second.

The sign for minutes is ′, thus 5° 8′ = five degrees eight minutes.

c **1391** CHAUCER *Astrol.* I. §8 A degree of a signe contieneth 60 minutes. **1549** *Compl. Scot.* vi. 50 The circle artic is xxiij degreis xxx munitis fra the pole artic. **1603** OWEN *Pembrokeshire* (1892) 1 Longitude 17 degrees, and 20 minuttes west. *Ibid.*, 52 degrees which is 40 mynuttes higher then that of the Cittie of London. **1652** GAULE *Magastrom.* 68 Those numbers and minutes, yea numbers of numbers and minutes of minutes (which Astrologicall Mathematicians pretend to work by). **1755** B. MARTIN *Mag. Arts & Sci.* I. x. 58 Each Degree is supposed to consist of 60 Minutes, thus marked (′). **1862** BACHE *Discuss. Magn. & Meteorol. Observ.* II. 9 The scale divisions have been converted into minutes of arc.

3. a. *Arch.* The sixtieth or occas. some other part of the MODULE. ? *Obs.*

1696 in PHILLIPS. **1727–52** CHAMBERS *Cycl.*, *Minute*, in architecture, usually denotes the sixtieth, sometimes only the thirtieth part, or division of a module. [In recent Dicts.]

b. *Art.* A unit of a scale of head measurement by which the proportions of the face may be regulated or defined; the forty-eighth part of the height of the human head. [So F. *minute*.]

1875 SIR T. SEATON *Fret Cutting* 132 Draw a line corresponding to the line within the oval, and divide this also into four equal parts. One of these parts must be subdivided into twelve parts, these are called minutes. *Ibid.* 133 The length of a head—from forehead to back—in a full-grown person, is three parts eight minutes for a man, and three parts eleven minutes for a woman.

II. Something small.

†**4.** A coin of trifling value; a 'mite'. *Obs.*

1382 WYCLIF *Mark* xii. 42 Tweye mynutis [Vulg. *duo minuta*, Gr. λεπτὰ δύο], that is, a ferthing. **1543** BECON *Nosegay* Ded. B j b, Yet let vs with the poore widowe of the Gospell at the leest gyue two minutes. **1589** J. RIDER *Bibl. Schol.*, A Minute or Q, which is halfe a farthing, *minutum*.

†**5.** Something minute or small. **a.** *pl.* Little fishes, 'small fry' (cf. MENISE). **b.** A small particular, a detail; a minutia. **c.** Something of small size or slight importance. *Obs.*

1598 FLORIO, *Pesciolini*, all manner of minutes, frye, or small fishes. **1626** B. JONSON *Staple of N.* I. v. 138 Let me heare from thee euery minute of Newes. *a* **1628** F. GREVIL *Sidney* (1652) 90 That Heroicall design..how exactly soever projected, and digested in every minute. —— *Alaham* II. Chorus ii. (1633) 39 When I propound in grosse, you minutes play. **1647** JER. TAYLOR *Lib. Proph.* XVI. 213 And such are all the sects and all the pretences of Christians, but pieces and minutes of Christianity. **1654** —— *Real Pres.* 238 They have made it to be unintelligible, inexplicable, indefensible, in all their minuits and particularities. *a* **1660** HAMMOND *Serm.* (Prov. i. 22) (1664) 46 The last minute of my last particular. *a* **1670** [see MIGNIARDIZE].

III. 6. a. A rough draft (of something to be further elaborated); a note or memorandum for the direction of an agent or servant, or for preserving the memory of current transactions or events; a brief summary of events or transactions, esp. (usually *pl.*) the record of the proceedings at a meeting of an assembly, corporate body, society, company, committee, or the like. †***in minute***: in the form of a minute or minutes. ***minute of dissent***, a minute recording a person's disagreement with something.

1502 in *Lett. & Papers Rich. III & Hen. VII* (Rolls) I. 147 He received a mynite of instructions. **1522** CLERK in Ellis *Orig. Lett.* Ser. III. I. 314 The Pope..caused it [the mynute] to be staied, and an other minute to be made which was not sped bifor his death. **1531** CROMWELL in Merriman *Life & Lett.* (1902) I. 340, I haue sent herein Inclosed the Mynewte with your Instruccions. **1640–1** *Kirkcudbr. War-Comm. Min. Bk.* (1855) 37 Ordaines James, the next Committie day, to produce the said minute of contract. **1682** EVELYN in *Pepys' Diary*, etc. (1879) VI. 140 These were only minutes relating to ampler pieces. **1697** in W. S. Perry *Hist. Coll. Amer. Col. Ch.* I. 52, I began to take their sense in minute as right as I could. *c* **1710** CELIA FIENNES *Diary* (1888) 276 To him are added in the House of Commons also scribes or secretaryes which record and take minutes also. **1713** POPE *Guard.* No. 92 ¶8 It is my business whenever we meet to take minutes of the transactions. **1728** MORGAN *Algiers* II. v. 316, I some where said my memory was

treacherous; nor do I ever keep minutes. **1741** MIDDLETON *Cicero* I. vi. 511 It was his custom to keep the minutes or rough draught of all his pleadings. **1771** P. PARSONS *Newmarket* II. 187 My paper of heads or minutes perished in a different manner. **1776** in *Archæol.* (1789) IX. 365 That such curious communications..be extracted from the Minutes of the Society, and formed into an Historical Memoir. **1827** SCOTT *Surg. Dau.* i, Lawford drew up a proper minute of this transaction, by which he himself and Grey were named trustees for the child. **1851** DICKENS *Bill-sticking* in *Househ. Words* II. 605 These are the minutes of my conversation with His Majesty, as I noted them down shortly afterwards. **1860** MOTLEY *Netherl.* vii. (1868) I. 409 The minute of a letter to Elizabeth..was submitted to the ambassador. **1876** GRANT *Burgh Sch. Scotl.* Pref. 8 The minutes of his town council. **1886** KIPLING *Departmental Ditties* (ed. 2) 23 No longer Brown reverses Smith's appeals, Or Jones records his Minute of Dissent. **1890** GROSS *Gild Merch.* I. 149 The minutes of both Companies were kept in the same book. **1930** *Times* 15 Mar. 7/1 All the members have signed the report, but Lord Ebbisham did so subject to a 'minute of dissent' which is attached to the main report.

b. An official memorandum authorizing or recommending the pursuance of a certain course. ***treasury minute***: a minute or memorandum issued by the treasury.

1564 *Reg. Privy Council Scot.* I. 301 In terms of minute 27th November. **1783** BURKE *On Fox's East Ind. Bill* Wks. IV. 75 In his minute of consultation, Mr. Hastings describes forcibly the consequences which arise [etc.]. **1798** WELLINGTON in Gurw. *Desp.* (1837) I. 9 A very able minute in the Secret department. **1817** TIERNEY in *Parl. Deb.* 768 That committee, by a Treasury minute of the 5th of April, 1816, was required to examine and report what offices had been created since the year 1793. **1845** MCCULLOCH *Taxation* II. v. (1852) 230 This fraudulent practice has been indirectly legitimated by a Treasury Minute of the 4th of August, 1840. **1863** H. COX *Instit.* I. v. 29 The Bank of England..was directed to suspend cash payments by a Minute of Council. **1880** GEN. ADYE in *19th Cent.* No. 38. 694 Lord Napier..in a masterly minute pointed out the various evils of the whole system.

†**c.** An agreement, precise understanding. *Obs.*

1720 *Wodrow Corr.* (1843) II. 519 At Edinburgh I have come to a minute with the printer.

d. *Sc. Law.* A memorandum of intention presented to the court by a party to a suit.

1848 SHAND *Pract. Crt. Sess.* I. 343 *note*, A minute of abandonment of the cause, in such form as the following, is put into process. **1904** *Dundee Advertiser* 19 Nov. 7 Yesterday a minute was lodged in the Bill Chamber of the Court of Session stating that no answers are to be lodged to the note by the Free Church [etc.].

IV. 7. *attrib.* and *Comb.*, as **minute bell**, the tolling of a bell at intervals of a minute, used as a sign of mourning or distress; **minute-book**, †(*a*) a 'book of short hints' (J.); (*b*) a book containing systematic records of the transactions of a society, court, or the like; **minute clock**, a stop clock used in making tests of gas (Knight *Dict. Mech.* 1884); **minute-flourish**, a fanfare of trumpets sounded minute by minute; **minute-glass**, a sand-glass that runs for a minute; **minute-gun**, the firing of a gun at intervals of a minute, used as a sign of mourning or distress (also *attrib.*); **minute-hand**, the long hand of a time-piece which indicates the minutes; †**minute-jack** (? cf. JACK *sb.*^{1} 6), one who changes his mind every moment, a fickle or changeable person; **minute jumper**, an electric clock in which the hands move only at the end of each minute, the minute-hand moving over a whole minute at each step (*Cent. Dict.* 1890); †**minute-line** *Naut.*, a log-line; **minute-lust**, momentary desire; **minute mile** (see quot. 1867); †**minute-motion**, the mechanism of the seconds hand of a watch; **minute-repeater**, a watch which 'repeats' the minutes; **minute space**, the duration of a minute; **minute steak** (see quot. 1934); **minute stroke**, the measured 'minutely' stroke of an oar; **minute tide**, (*a*) = *minute while* (see sense 1); (*b*) (see quot. 1865); **minute-to-minute** *attrib.*, from one minute to the next; †**minute-watch**, a watch that distinguishes minutes of time or on the dial of which minutes are marked (also †***minute pendulum watch***); **minute-wheel**, the wheel that moves the minute-hand of a clock or watch; hence **minute-wheel nut**, **pinion** (see quot. 1884); †**minute while** (see sense 1); **minute-writing**, the art or practice of recording minutes or administrative memoranda. Also MINUTE-MAN.

1827 KEBLE *Chr. Y., 1st Sunday Advent* xii, Faith's ear, with awful still delight, Counts them like *minute bells at night. **1736** AINSWORTH *Lat. Dict.*, A *minute book, *liber vel libellus memorialis.* **1772** *Ann. Reg.* 66* The minute-book of recognizances belonging to the Lord Mayor's court. **1838** *Act 1 & 2 Vict.* c. 118 §22 The Minute Book of the Court of Session and Teind Court. **1904** *Athenæum* 24 Dec. 881/2 A 'History of the Society of Apothecaries',..compiled from the Minute-Books of the Society. **1802** MRS. RADCLIFFE *Gaston de Blondev.* Posth. Wks. 1826 I. 87 The trumpets, that charged so loud and shrill their *minet-flourishes. **1626** CAPT. SMITH *Accid. Yng. Seamen* 29 Turne vp the *minute glasse, obserue the hight. **1867** SMYTH *Sailor's Word-bk.* 480 Minute and Half-minute glasses. **1728** G. CARLETON *Mem. Eng. Officer* 205 The first Guns that were fir'd from Gorge's battery were the *Minute-Guns for his Funeral. **1747** *Gentl. Mag.* XVII. 246/1 Minute guns were fired by the whole squadron. **1884** *Times* (Weekly ed.) 11 Apr. 2/3 The boom of the minute guns on the hill beyond could be heard above the funeral music of the bands. **1936** H. NICOLSON *Diary* 28 Jan. (1966) 241 The King's funeral. I stay in..all morning and do not hear more than the minute-guns firing dolefully in the distance. **1970** *Brewer's Dict. Phr. & Fable* (rev. ed.) 714/2 *A Minute gun*, a signal of distress at sea, or a gun fired at the death of some distinguished person. **1726** SWIFT *Gulliver* I. ii, He was amazed at..the Motion of the *Minute-Hand, which he could easily discern. **1892** E. REEVES *Homeward Bound* 184 Clock faces marking six, twelve, and twenty-four hours, mostly without minute hands. **1607** SHAKS. *Timon* III. vi. 107 Cap and knee-Slaues, vapours, and *Minute Iackes. **1644** *Minut-line [see *log-line* in LOG *sb.*^{1} 9]. **1696** PHILLIPS, *Log-line or Minute-line.* **1635** QUARLES *Embl.* II. xi. 106 The fleshly wanton, to obtaine His *minit-lust, will count it gaine To lose his freedome. **1867** SMYTH *Sailor's Word-bk.*, **Minute mile*, the sixtieth part of a degree of longitude or latitude. **1684** T. BURNET *Th. Earth* II. iv. 210 In a Watch, ..you may have a fancy to have an Alarum added, or a *Minute-motion. **1843** *Penny Cycl.* XXVII. 107/1 These by way of distinction are called *minute-repeaters. **1621** WITHER *Motto* A 8, I haue not of my selfe, the powre, or grace, To be, or not to be; one *minute-space. **1934** WEBSTER, **Minute steak*, a small thin steak that can be quickly cooked. **1959** *Good Food Guide* 204 The grills.. range from 6/6 (minute steak) to 9/6 (mixed grill, including vegetables). **1966** *Listener* 27 Jan. 134/3 The minute steak is the gastronomic symbol of the age. **1833** MARRYAT *P. Simple* xxx, The crew dropped their oars into the water without a splash, and pulled the *minute stroke. **14..** RYMAN *Poems* in *Archiv. Stud. neu. Spr.* LXXXIX. 255 This lyfe vnto celestiall Is but a *mynute tyde. **1865** MACGREGOR *Rob Roy in Baltic* (1867) 163 This is called the 'minute tide', in which a swelling of the water once every minute fills up and empties again a quiet pool a little withdrawn from the river's course. **1948** 'G. ORWELL' in *Adelphi* XXIV. 249/2 One ought, apparently, to live in a continuous present, a *minute-to-minute cancellation of memory. **1968** G. M. B. DOBSON *Exploring Atmosphere* (ed. 2) v. 105 In practice certain precautions have to be taken to allow for the minute-to-minute changes in the general electric field. **1660** BOYLE *New Exp. Phys. Mech.* xi. 79 A *Minute-Watch we kept by us on this occasion. **1705** *Daily Courant* 5 Sept., Dropt in St. James's Park, September the 3rd, 1705, a Gold Minuit Pendulum Watch, &c. **1797** *Encycl. Brit.* (ed. 3) V. 74/2 The minute and hour hands turn on the end of the arbor of the *minute-wheel. **1884** F. J. BRITTEN *Watch & Clockm.* 177 [The] Minute Wheel Pinion, or 'Nut'..[is] the pinion in the motion work of watches that drives the hour wheel. **1895** *Daily News* 10 Sept. 5/4 An Under-Secretary, trained in a bureaucracy where *minute-writing has been brought to the highest pitch of perfection.

†**minute**, *sb.*^{2} *Law. Obs.* [ad. Law Latin *minūta*, vbl. noun f. *minuĕre* to diminish.] = MINISHING.

1495 *Rolls of Parlt.* VI. 501/1 Of the Ferme of all Asartis, Wastes, Purpresture and minutez, of the parcelles of the Forest.

minute (mɪˈnjuːt, maɪˈnjuːt), *a.* Also 5–6 **mynute**. [ad. L. *minūt-us* (whence F. *menu* small), pa. pple. of *minuĕre* to make small, diminish.]

†**1.** Chopped small. *Obs. rare.*

c **1420** *Pallad. on Husb.* IV. 492 Hem summe in cedur scobe, & summe in stre Mynute, and summe in smal chaf, wel witholde.

†**2.** Of imposts, etc.: Lesser; esp. in ***minute tithes*** = 'small tithes'. *Obs.*

[**1464** *Rolls of Parlt.* V. 569/1 Sume ferme by the name of the Manent' firme com' post terras dat'..and sume under the name of minute firme to you.] **1542–3** *Act 34 & 35 Hen. VIII*, c. 16 §1 The fermes of diuers purprestures, assertes, sergeantes, & minute rentes. **1546** in *Eng. Gilds* (1870) 222 The preste..hathe the mynute tythes of the village of Bysshopton. **1647** CLARENDON *Hist. Reb.* IV. §38 The Dependence of the Church,..(except their minute Tythes) was entirely upon this Law. **1696** PHILLIPS, *Minute Tithes*, small Tithes, such as usually belong to the Vicar; as Wooll, Lambs, Piggs, Butter, Cheese, Eggs, Honey, &c.

3. Very small in size, extent, amount, or degree.

In the 17th and 18th centuries the comparative *minuter* frequently acquires the sense 'smaller or more insignificant than another', without the implication of extreme smallness.

a **1626** BACON *New Atl.* 40 Wee haue also Glasses and Meanes, to see Small and Minute Bodies, perfectly and distinctly. **1665** *Phil. Trans.* I. 31 An Instrument to shew all the Minute Variations in the pressure of the Air. **1698** FRYER *Acc. E. India & P.* 39 Those [chapels] of a minuter dimension were open. **1699** POMFRET *Cruelty & Lust* 79 Suppose the Accusation justly brought, And clearly prov'd to the minutest fault. **1713** DERHAM *Phys.-Theol.* IV. ii. 106 One single Minutest Thread or Fibre. **1742** YOUNG *Nt. Th.* VI. 690 With this minute distinction,..Nature revolves, but man advances. **1748** *Anson's Voy.* I. v. 43 The neighbouring coast, and the minuter isles adjacent. *Ibid.* II. x. 237 Vast quantities of..callicoes and chints,..together with other minuter articles, as goldsmiths work, etc. **1816** BENTHAM *Chrestom.* 24 The distance in question is so minute as to be incapable of measurement. **1832** BABBAGE *Econ. Manuf.* (ed. 3) 83 The minuter cavities can only be filled under an exhausted receiver. **1867** H. MACMILLAN *Bible Teach.* vi. (1870) 118 The seed vessels in this plant are exceedingly minute. **1871** TYNDALL *Fragm. Sci.* (1879) I. i. 23 What is true of the earth..is also true of her minutest atom. **1880** GEIKIE *Phys. Geog.* ii. 57 It is possible to measure very minute changes of temperature.

4. Of very little consequence or importance; trifling, petty.

Minute philosopher is an echo of Cicero's *quidam minuti philosophi* (De Senect. xxiii, also De Div. I. xxx), where the adj. appears to have this sense, though in Eng. use it is sometimes apprehended as if belonging to sense 5.

c **1650** DENHAM *Old Age* IV. 249 Some minute Philosophers pretend, That with our dayes our pains and pleasures end. **1668** WILKINS *Real Char.* To Rdr., If any shall suggest that some of the Enquiries here insisted upon ..do seem too minute and trivial, for any prudent Man to bestow his serious thoughts and time about. Such Persons may know [etc.]. **1732** BERKELEY *Alciphr.* I. §10 These minute philosophers..are a sort of pirates who plunder all that come in their way. **1748** *Anson's Voy.* III. ix. 396 The Mandarine..returned all that had been stolen..even to the minutest trifle. **1772** BURKE *Corr.* (1844) I. 377 Your grace dissipates your mind into too great a variety of minute pursuits. **1872** MINTO *Eng. Prose Lit.* II. iii. 279 As Lord Chancellor,..he proved unequal to the minuter duties of the office.

5. Of investigations, regulations, records, etc. (and hence of persons): Characterized by attention to very small matters or details; very precise or particular; very accurate.

168. AUBREY *Lives, Hobbes* To Rdr. (1813) I. 594 For that I am so minute, I declare I never intended it [etc.]. **1716** ADDISON *Freeholder* No. 42 ¶14 We cannot be too minute and circumstantial in accounts of this nature. **1751** JOHNSON *Rambler* No. 86 ¶5 He knew with how minute Attention the ancient Criticks considered the Disposition of Syllables. **1788** REID *Aristotle's Log.* IV. ii. 71 He is more full, more minute and particular than any of them. **1799** WELLINGTON in Gurw. *Desp.* (1837) I. 25 His minute private diary. **1807** T. THOMSON *Chem.* (ed. 3) II. 383 A very minute and accurate series of experiments. **1833** HT. MARTINEAU *Brooke Farm* i. 10 A reporter as faithful as he was minute. **1864** PUSEY *Lect. Daniel* (1876) 376 A minute, natural, accurate, history. **1875** JOWETT *Plato* (ed. 2) V. 96 Minute regulations are apt to be transgressed.

minute (ˈmɪnɪt), *v.* [f. MINUTE *sb.*^{1}]

1. *trans.* To ascertain or determine to the minute the time, duration, or rate of; to 'time' accurately. Also † ***to minute out***: to assign (time) precisely.

1605 CAMDEN *Rem.* 92 About the yeare of our Lord 1000 (that we may not minute out the time). *a* **1661** FULLER *Worthies, Suffolk* III. (1662) 62 All Accidents are minuted and momented by Divine Providence. **1762** *Phil. Trans.* LII. 582 The above observations were minuted from a stop-watch of Mr. Ellicott's. **1773** G. WHITE *Selborne* 8 July (1789) 153, I have minuted these birds with my watch for an hour together,..they return..about once in five minutes. **1775** *Ibid.* 1 Nov. 198 A good rush,..being minuted, burnt only three minutes short of an hour. **1784** BLAGDEN in *Phil. Trans.* LXXIV. 217 Scarcely any one had sufficient presence of mind to minute the time by his watch. **1813** MAR. EDGEWORTH *Patron.* (1832) I. iii. 42 [They] went to see High Blood rubbed down..exercised and minuted. **1822** BEDDOES *Brides' Trag.* II. iii, Do not minute The movements of the soul. **1825** *Sporting Mag.* XV. 340, I did not minute this run, but..it must have been a trimming one. **1862** SMILES *Engineers* III. 277 Captain Scoresby,.. minuted the speed of the train. **1888** *Temple Bar* Jan. 29 The Bishop..sat by with his watch on the table, for he had to minute each interview.

2. a. To draft (a document, a scheme); to record in a minute or memorandum; to enter in the minutes or records of a society, company, or the like; to make a minute of the contents of (a document). ***to minute down***, to make a note of.

a **1648** LD. HERBERT *Hen. VIII* (1683) 48 All which minuted by Louis de Longueville..was at last thus fully concluded. *Ibid.* 84 The design for the Interview with Francis continued; which being minuted by our Ambassador,..was continued by his successor. **1662** EVELYN *Chalcogr.* 94 It might not seem requisite to minute the works which he has published. **1711** *Lond. Gaz.* No. 4842/3 All such disabled Seamen and Marines as are minuted to be taken into the said Hospital. **1712** ADDISON *Spect.* No. 439 ¶3 The Cardinal is represented as minuting down every thing that is told him. **1778** [W. MARSHALL] *Minutes Agric., Observ.* 153 *note*, I minuted it as an extra observation. **1789** FRANKLIN *Ess.* Wks. 1840 II. 151 Nothing was concluded [*sc.* at the next meeting] so as to be minuted. **1836** H. ROGERS *J. Howe* v. (1863) 141 His thoughts on this occasion he minuted down. **1876** BANCROFT *Hist. U.S.* IV. xxvi. 19 The Empress of Russia with her own hand minuted an edict for universal tolerance. **1888** BRYCE *Amer. Commw.* II. II. xlviii. 228 A Town-clerk, who keeps the records, and minutes the proceedings of the meeting. **1897** P. WARUNG *Tales Old Regime* 139 Yes, your Excellency. Shall I minute that observation? **1898** G. W. E. RUSSELL *Coll. & Recoll.* xxxiv. 465 The paper..is minuted by each, and..gradually passes up..to the Under-Secretary of State.

absol. **1892** LD. LYTTON *King Poppy* I. 351 Whereon His Majesty thus minuted.

b. To inform (someone) about a matter by means of a minute or memorandum.

1918 G. S. GORDON *Let.* 13 Dec. (1943) 87 Milford has minuted me about the Oxford Trivium. **1952** *Punch* 10 Sept. 353 He had minuted General Ismay. **1964** M. GOWING *Britain & Atomic Energy* v. 174 Lord Cherwell was still minuting Mr Churchill that the British diffusion method was much superior. **1974** 'J. LE CARRÉ' *Tinker Tailor* xxvi. 221 In no case should I phone him or minute him; even the internal lines were taboo.

3. ***to minute over***: to reckon up, enumerate point by point.

a **1770** CATH. TALBOT *Lett.* (1808) 60 The most agreeable thought (as I experienced last night when we were minuting over all these things) will be, that it cannot be long [etc.].

4. *intr.* With *by*: To pass minute by minute.

a **1806** H. K. WHITE *To Thought* v, And count the tedious hours, as slow they minute by.

Hence ˈ**minuting** *vbl. sb.*, the recording of minutes; ˈ**minuting** *ppl. a.*, that minutes.

1737 J. CHAMBERLAYNE *St. Gt. Brit.* II. III. (ed. 33) 121 Minuting-clerk to Master General. **1856** DICKENS *Dorrit*

(1857) II. viii. 387 The work of form-filling, corresponding, minuting, memorandum-making. **1882** *London Police Court Rep.*, Those having the minuteing and the carrying out of the details and business of the Court.

minuted (ˈmɪnɪtɪd), *a.* [f. MINUTE *v.* + -ED¹.]

1. Recorded or set forth in a minute or note.

1716 M. DAVIES *Athen. Brit.* II. To Rdr. 38, I hope those minuted Layes of Seraphick Contemplations,..will engage the studious Youth of both Sexes, to be favourable to this undertaking. **1802–12** BENTHAM *Ration. Judic. Evid.* (1827) I. 279 Publication by authority, whether of the minuted *viva-voce* testimony, or of the ready-written depositions.

2. Timed or numbered by minutes.

1829 SOUTHEY *Sir T. More* II. 352 He is like the mail coach traveller,..and must therefore take at his minuted meals whatever food is readiest. **1859** MRS. GASKELL *Round the Sofa* II. 70 Some sore internal bruise sapping away his minuted life.

†**ˈminuteless,** *a. Obs.* [f. MINUTE *sb.*¹ + -LESS.] Not to be measured by minutes.

1652 GAULE *Magastrom.* 68 The starres, whose numbers are numberless and motions minuteless.

minutely (ˈmɪnɪtlɪ), *a.* [f. MINUTE *sb.* + -LY¹.] Happening every minute.

1605 SHAKS. *Macb.* V. ii. 18 Now do's he feele His secret Murthers sticking on his hands, Now minutely Reuolts vpbraid his Faith-breach. **1658** *Whole Duty Man* xvii. §7 All that we possess is in minutely danger of losing. **1720** *Humourist* 93, I have staid four Hours in Minutely Expectation. **1802** COLERIDGE *Lett.* (1895) 390 Our minutely conduct towards each other. **1865** *Even. Exchange* 10 Feb. 1/1 The hourly and minutely fluctuations of the.. Markets.

minutely (mɪˈnjuːtlɪ, maɪ-), *adv.*¹ [f. MINUTE *a.* + -LY².]

1. †**a.** Into small pieces (*obs.*). **b.** On a minute scale; with minute subdivision.

1599 A. M. tr. *Gabelhouer's Bk. Physicke* 89/2 Contunde all that is to be contundede, & cut the rest minutly, then mixe it to a paeste with good wine. **1613** R. CAWDREY *Table Alph.*, *Minutely*, smally. **1869** PHILLIPS *Vesuv.* x. 279 Realgar occurs minutely but well crystallized.

Comb. **1836** E. HOWARD *R. Reefer* li, The..minutely-sanded beach.

2. In a minute manner, kind, or degree; with great or absolute precision or preciseness; with exactness.

1732 BERKELEY *Alciphr.* I. §10 Considering things minutely, and not swallowing them in the gross. **1736** BUTLER *Anal.* I. v. Wks. 1874 I. 105 Observations of this kind cannot be supposed to hold minutely, and in every case. **1821** J. W. CROKER *Diary* 24 Aug., The King went minutely through the museum, and other parts [etc.]. **1863** H. COX *Instit.* III. vii. 680 He most minutely and learnedly investigated the ancient course of the Exchequer. **1895** LD. ESHER in *Law Times Rep.* LXXIII. 650/1 It is not necessary to disclose minutely and in detail every material fact. **1903** *T. P.'s Weekly* 18 Sept. 495/1 Mr. John Hollingshead has minutely described a little dinner with Dickens.

†**b.** Intimately. *Obs.*

1823 J. BADCOCK *Dom. Amusem.* 106 The ingredients are more minutely disseminated than can be performed by hand.

minutely (ˈmɪnɪtlɪ), *adv.*² [f. MINUTE *sb.*¹ + -LY².] Every minute, minute by minute.

1599 NASHE *Lenten Stuffe* 22 [The red herring]..is the onely vnexhaustible mine that hath rais'd and begot all this, and minutely to riper maturity fosters and cherisheth it. **1637** SANDERSON *Serm.* (1681) II. 89 We,..by most unworthy provocations daily and minutely tempt His patience. **1654** HAMMOND *Fundamentals* viii. 66 As if it were minutely proclaimed in thunder from heaven. **1708** J. PHILIPS *Cyder* II. 263 Their frying Blood compells to irrigate Their dry furr'd Tongues, else minutely to Death Obnoxious, dismal Death, th' Effect of Drought. **1803** COLERIDGE *Lett.* (1895) 439 The sharpshooters were behind exercising minutely. **1807** tr. *Three Germans* II. 52 A friend, whom I now minutely expect at the castle gates. **1845** WILBERFORCE in A. R. Ashwell *Life* (1880) I. 269 Two daughters..played daily, hourly, minutely..by a very clever, reaching mother, for coronets and a settlement.

ˈminuteman. Also minute-man, minute man. [f. MINUTE *sb.* + MAN.] **1.** *Hist.* One of a class of militiamen, during the American revolutionary period, who held themselves in readiness for instant military service.

1774 in *N. Eng. Hist. & Gen. Reg.* (1875) XXIX. 107 Minute or Picquet men in the Town of Brookfield. **1775–83** THACHER *Mil. Jrnl.* (1823) 17 Active men in every town have formed military companies under the name of minute men. **1903** F. NORRIS *The Pit* 43 Ample fireplaces, where once the minute-men had swung their kettles.

transf. **1863** J. WEISS *Life Th. Parker* I. 11 The same old cause, whose minute-men are again first in the field [1861].

b. In extended uses, a 'watchdog' or political activist; a member of an organization devoted to specific political issues. Also *gen.* (with small initial), a vigilant, observant, or enterprising person.

1923 *Minute Men of the Constitution Roster* (inside front cover), The Minute Men of the Constitution is a non-partisan association, organized to obtain delegates from Illinois to the Republican and Democratic State and National Conventions... The above is a movement for good government. **1930** P. R. LEACH *That Man Dawes* x. 190 Dawes called..a number of close friends and organized 'The Minute Men of the Constitution'. The purpose of the Minute Men..was to function as an open-eyed body of men throughout the state to watch elections, prevent vote frauds at the polls and counteract unfair propaganda. The society was not secret, had no passwords or meeting places and was non-political. **1952** *Manch. Guardian Weekly* 23 Oct. 3/1 An appeal went out for minute-men to tap the moneybags in their own localities. **1961** *Guardian* 25 Nov. 7/2 The Minute Men and Birchites. **1961** WEBSTER, *Minuteman*, one who resembles a Revolutionary minuteman esp. in qualities of vigilance and readiness to take prompt action. **1964** D. BELL *Radical Right* i. 4 Three elements [in the 1960s] conjoined to attract public attention to the radical right... The John Birch Society... Seminars of anti-Communist 'schools'... And, third, there was the disclosure of the existence of extreme fanatic groups, such as the Minutemen, who organized 'guerilla-warfare seminars', complete with rifles and mortars, in preparation for the day when patriots would have to take to the hills to organize resistance against a Communist-run America. **1964** *Economist* 19 Dec. 1350/2 The Minutemen, a mysterious, probably negligible, vigilante group, has drawn the gloomily righteous conclusion that America has seen its last free election. **1965** T. H. WHITE *Making of President 1964* iii. 89 Across the sky of politics there began to float new names like the John Birch Society, the Minutemen, the National Indignation Convention, [etc.]. **1970** *Peace News* 17 Apr. 8/1 It would be easy for the casual observer to link the Panthers with..the Minutemen and American Nazis.

2. (With capital initial.) A type of intercontinental ballistic missile (see quot. 1971).

1961 *Daily Tel.* 2 Feb. 1/4 The American Air Force achieved a spectacular advance today when it launched the first Minuteman missile. **1969** *Guardian* 6 Dec. 2/2 They claim that the three five-megaton warheads fitted to these missiles are unnecessarily large and accurate for use against any target but the hardened US Minuteman missile sites. **1971** E. LUTTWAK *Dict. Mod. War* 130/1 The Minuteman series are three-stage missiles with solid-propellant motors designed as simplified and low-cost weapons for launching from 'hard' silo sites. They need very brief pre-launch preparation.

minuteness (mɪˈnjuːtnɪs). [f. MINUTE *a.* + -NESS.] The quality of being minute.

1. Extreme smallness; an instance of this.

1666 BOYLE *Orig. Forms & Qual.* Exp. ix. 396 Whose Corpuscles, by reason of their Minuteness, swimme easily for a while in the Water. **1754** RICHARDSON *Grandison* (1811) II. v. 84 The discretion of a person is often most seen in minutenesses. **1751** EARL ORRERY *Remarks Swift* (1752) 86 A convex mirrour, by which every object is reduced to a despicable minuteness. **1770** C. JENNER *Placid Man* I. I. iv. 35 All the minutenesses which distinguish the domestic manners of one nation from another. **1830** HERSCHEL *Stud. Nat. Phil.* 250 Particles of inconceivable minuteness. **1872** RUSKIN *Eagle's N.* §122 The noble human sight, careless of prey, disdainful of minuteness, and reluctant to anger.

2. Attention to minute details; precision as to details; critical exactness.

1640 SIR K. DIGBY in *Lismore Papers* Ser. II. (1888) IV. 137, I am afraid..that minutenesse would rather appeare tedious then punctuall to you. **1726** SWIFT *Gulliver* IV. ix, The Justness of their Similies, and the Minuteness, as well as Exactness of their Descriptions, are indeed inimitable. **1774** GOLDSM. *Nat. Hist.* (1776) I. 193 Such..may consult Hawksbee, Morgan, Jurin, or Watson, who have examined the subject with great minuteness. **1853** LYTTON *My Novel* III. xvi, He had studied it with the minuteness with which a scholar studies a dead language. **1858** BUCKLE *Civiliz.* (1869) II. vii. 364 The chemist by his minuteness, and the geologist by his grandeur, touch the two extremes of the material universe. **1884** LADY VERNEY in *Contemp. Rev.* Oct. 545 Every gown..is chronicled with affectionate minuteness.

†**b.** Excess of detail, 'niggling'. *Obs.*

1748 *Anson's Voy.* III. x. 412 There is a stiffness and minuteness in most of the Chinese productions.

minuter (ˈmɪnɪtə(r)). [f. MINUTE *v.* + -ER¹.]

1. One who writes minutes, a note-taker.

1825 *Celebrated Trials*, etc. IV. 172 Thomas Gurney, the minuter, was called, who deposed from his minutes. **1911** *Pitman's How to take Minutes* 14 The minuter must take sufficient notes of the proceedings.

2. *Sc. Law.* One who moves the court by minute.

1904 *Dundee Advertiser* 19 Nov. 7 They do not admit that the judgments of the Court in the cases of Bannatyne and others v. Lord Overtoun and others, and Young v. Macalister,..settle or determine the rights of the minuters in the present suspension.

minuterie (mɪˈnjuːtərɪ). [Fr., = clockwork, timing mechanism, minuterie, f. *minute* MINUTE *sb.*¹] **a.** A light switch incorporating a timing mechanism that automatically turns it off a short time after it has been (manually) turned on. **b.** An electric light controlled by such a switch.

1955 W. GADDIS *Recognitions* I. ii. 72 Crémer opened the door, and the light of the minuterie threw his flat shadow across the sill. **1958** E. DUNDY *Dud Avocado* I. iii. 52 Racing from minuterie to minuterie to keep the stairs in a blaze of 40-watt bulbs. **1962** A. WILLIAMS *Long Run South* v. i. 160 He went up in the lift and pressed the minuterie. **1963** 'D. RUTHERFORD' *Creeping Flesh* iii. 153 The stairs were illuminated with a tasteful glow. No penny-wise *minuterie* here. **1971** M. MCCARTHY *Birds of America* 302 On the second landing he found it..in the weak light of the *minuterie*.

‖**minutia** (mɪˈnjuːʃɪə). Pl. minutiæ (-ɪiː). Also 8 *pl.* minutias; *erron.* 8–9 *pl.* minutia, *sing.* minutiæ. [a. L. *minūtia* smallness, pl. *minūtiæ* trifles, f. *minūtus* MINUTE *a.*] A precise detail; a small or trivial matter or object. Usually *pl.*

In Chesterfield's *Letters* the French *minutie* frequently occurs as synonymous with minutia.

1751 EARL ORRERY *Remarks Swift* (1752) 52, I should hope that all the *minutiæ* of his idle hours might be entirely excluded. **1759** JOHNSON *Idler* No. 47 ¶12 He..often declares himself weary of attending to the *minutiæ* of a shop. **1768** BLACKSTONE *Comm.* III. xxvii. 446 No exceptions to formal *minutiæ* in the pleadings will be here allowed. **1782** ELIZ. BLOWER *Geo. Bateman* I. 106 On the observance of some little minutias, no small share of the beauty.. depended. **1796** BURNEY *Mem. Metastasio* II. 270 Descending to the minutia of all the events and occasions which may be imagined. **1797** MRS. A. M. BENNETT *Beggar Girl* (1813) II. 217 Strict attention to every minutiæ of her domestic arrangement. **1804** EUGENIA DE ACTON *Tale without Title* II. 208 She..determined..to unfold every minutiae of her former circumstances. **1804** tr. *Piguenard's Zoflora* I. 4 Those minutia concerning him, which may even have the appearance of puerility. **1849** MISS PARDOE *Francis I*, xiv. 343 They were arranged with a punctilious minutia. **1882** SERJT. BALLANTINE *Exper.* II. 191 The minutiæ were very exact and carefully executed.

†**miˈnutial,** *a. Obs.* [f. MINUTIA + -AL¹.] Of the nature of minutiæ; pertaining to details.

1612 T. TAYLOR *Comm. Titus* ii. 14 In smaller, and minutiall matters to carrie an vnbounded..zeale, were to call for a sword to kill a flie. **1778** [W. MARSHALL] *Minutes Agric., Digest* 16 The minutial management of Farms. **1796** —— *W. England* II. 170 In minutial practices..the Vale [of Exeter] pursues the Devonshire method.

†**miˈnution.** *Obs.* [ad. L. *minūtiōn-em*, n. of action f. *minuĕre* to lessen.] A diminishing or making less; a lowering; *spec.* a lowering of the system by blood-letting.

1386 *Almanac* (1812) 52 Mynucyons to be made by blode lattyng or ventosyng es ful profytabul. **1607** J. CARPENTER *Plaine Mans Plough* 124 The Phisitians..prescribe.. sometimes unctions, sometimes minutions. **1656** BLOUNT *Glossogr.*, *Minution*, a diminishing or making less.

minutiose (mɪˈnjuːʃɪəʊs), *a.* [ad. L. *minūtiōs-us*, f. *minūtiæ*: see MINUTIA. Cf. F. *minutieux*.] Dealing with minutiæ.

1868 F. HALL *Benares* 15. **1892** —— in *Nation* (N.Y.) 1 Dec. 412/1 He has achieved, among minutiose philologists, an eminence which..is likely to be recognized as all his own.

minutious (mɪˈnjuːʃɪəs), *a.* [ad. F. *minutieux*, f. *minutie* MINUTIA: cf. prec.] Attentive to minutiæ; characterized by minute attention to detail.

1819 *Metropolis* III. 252 Minutious and troublesome attentions. **1891** *Fortn. Rev.* May 802 His leisure was too limited to allow him to be pedantic or minutious. **1899** *Month* Apr. 433 [He] sent them [the proofs] back covered with minutious criticism.

†**minuˈtissim,** *a. Obs. rare*⁻¹. [ad. L. *minūtissim-us*, superl. of *minūtus* small: see MINUTE *a.*] Extremely minute.

1768–74 TUCKER *Lt. Nat.* (1834) I. 475 The whole human body, together with all its..minutissim glands.

†**miˈnutulous,** *a. Obs.* [f. L. *minūtul-us* (dim. of *minūtus* MINUTE *a.*) + -OUS.] Very small.

1651 BIGGS *New Disp.* ¶248 Minutulous drops of pus.

minuwae: see MINAWAY (= minuet).

minx (mɪŋks). Also 6 mynxe, minxe, mincks, 6–7 minkes, 7–8 minks. [Of obscure origin; possibly a corruption of *minikin*, with the added *s* not uncommon *dial.* in playful terms of endearment, e.g. *ducks*, *darlings*, *pets*: cf. *Minckins* in quot. 1605 s.v. MINIKIN 1. Sense 2 agrees closely with the sense of LG. *minske* = G. *mensch* neut.]

†**1.** A pet dog. Also as proper name. *Obs.*

1542 UDALL tr. *Erasm. Apoph.* 127 b, There been litle mynxes, or puppees that ladies keepe in their chaumbers for especiall iewelles to playe withall. *Ibid.*, When I am houngry I am a litle mynxe full of playe, and when my bealy is full, a mastife. [**1605** SYLVESTER *Du Bartas* II. iii. IV. *Captains* 386 Milk-white Minks and Lun (Gray-bitches both, the best that ever run).]

2. a. A pert girl, hussy. Now often merely playful.

1592 *Nobody & Someb.* E 2 b, Thus, you minx, Ile teach you ply your worke. **1594** LYLY *Moth. Bomb.* I. iii. 17 Your minxe had no better grandfather than a Tailer. *c* **1600** DAY *Begg. Bednall Gr.* II. i. (1881) 31 Come, Minx, what Iewell did you give this Rogue. **1636** HEYWOOD *Love's Mistr.* v. i. Wks. 1874 V. 155 That Minks [Psyche] is come from hell, And heere she harbours. **1695** CONGREVE *Love for L.* II. i, How, hussy! was there ever such a provoking minx! **1706–7** FARQUHAR *Beaux' Strat.* I. i, You deserve to have none, you young Minx. **1742** FIELDING *J. Andrews* IV. xiii, 'She! a little ugly minx', cries Slipslop, 'leave her to me'. **1812** CRABBE *Tales* xiii. 136 She thinks To make her fortune, an ambitious minx! **1838** DICKENS *Nich. Nick.* ix, 'I scorn your words, Minx', said Miss Squeers. **1861** HUGHES *Tom Brown at Oxf.* xxix, She is a dressed-up little minx, who runs after all the young men of the parish. **1882** *Mrs. Raven's Tempt.* III. 181 We shall be sorry if this young minx brings more trouble on the Agates.

b. A lewd or wanton woman.

1598 FLORIO, *Magalda*,..a trull or minxe. **1602** *North's Plutarch, Seneca* (1612) 1214 Nero..tooke from him this minxe that knew the tricks of the occupation. **1604** SHAKS. *Oth.* IV. i. 159 This is some Minxes token. **1621** BURTON *Anat. Mel.* III. iii. I. ii. (1651) 600 If thou be absent long, thy wife then thinks, Thou'rt drunk, at ease, or with some pretty minks. **1678** DRYDEN *Limberham* I. i, They are a Couple of alluring wanton Minxes. **1728** GAY *Polly* I. (1777) 24 And so, sir, I leave you and your minx together. **1939** JOYCE *Finnegans Wake* 80 What are you doing your dirty minx and his big treeblock way up your path? *Ibid.* 496 There wasn't an Archimandrite of Dane's Island and the townlands nor a

minx from the Isle of Woman . . would come next or nigh him. **1941** J. SMILEY *Hash House Lingo* 38 *Minx*, prostitute.

†**c.** ***mistress minx.*** *Obs.*

c **1590** MARLOWE *Faustus* vi. 162 What are you, Mistress Minx, the seventh and last? **1592** NASHE *P. Penilesse* (ed. 2) 10 b, Mistris Minx, a Marchants wife, that wil eate no Cherries forsooth, but when they are at twenty shillings a pound. **1671** KIRKMAN & HEAD *Eng. Rogue* IV. (1874) 139 How now, Mrs. Minks. **1735** MISS COLLIER *Art Torment.* 50 Let me tell you, Mistress Minx, 'twould much better become my station, than yours.

Hence (*nonce-wds.*) †**minx** *v. intr.* (with *it*), to play the minx; **minxishness, minxship**, the condition or quality of a minx.

1609 BP. W. BARLOW *Answ. Nameless Cath.* 303 The Apologue describes Venus trans-formed waiting maide, who beeing trick't vp like a Gentle-woman, mink'st it a while til she spied a Mouse, but then made it knowne shee was a Cat. **1632** MASSINGER *City Madam* II. ii, On these terms Wil your minxship be a Lady. **1885** L. WINGFIELD *Barbara Philpot* I. x. 271 Was not the sex built up of foibles and minxishness?

minx, obs. form of MINK.

minxish ('mɪŋksɪʃ), *a.* [f. MINX + -ISH[1].] Having the character of a minx; like a minx. Hence **'minxishly** *adv.* Also (*rare*) **minxy** ('mɪŋksɪ) *a.*; (*dial.*) **'minxin** *a.*

1870 *Porcupine* 12 Feb. 443/3 Through a door, left slightly ajar, he . . sees another minxish 'Girl of the Period' waiting the return of her companion. **1883** M. R. LAHEE *Acquitted though Guilty* 55 Hoo wur a honest dacent woman: noan-like the, the minxin slut. **1919** W. DE MORGAN *Old Madhouse* xxv. 387, I do *not* believe that Lucy . . is half as minxish as she made out. **1927** *Daily Express* 27 Apr. 3/2 The mannequin wore it minxishly, for it was a frock for a minx. **1935** *Times Lit. Suppl.* 3 Oct. 613/3 A weak, attractive, minxish child. **1939** C. MORLEY *Kitty Foyle* 91 We got some right minxy columbines round here.

miny ('maɪnɪ), *a. rare.* Also **miney**. [f. MINE *sb.* + -Y[1].]

1. Pertaining to a mine; mineral.

1611 FLORIO, *Mineroso*, minerous, miny. **1662** J. CHANDLER *Van Helmont's Oriat.* 322 The minie and saltish minerals of the microcosme [Lat. *microcosmi fodinas minerales atque salinas*]. **1907** *World* 16 July 113/1 What do you say to mines? No, there's nothing miney about me.

2. Of the nature of a mine; subterraneous.

1730–46 THOMSON *Autumn* 800 Unveil The miny caverns . . Of Abyssinia's cloud-compelling cliffs.

3. 'Abounding in mines' (Webster 1828–32).

minyan ('mɪnjɑːn), *sb.*[1] Pl. **minyanim**. [Heb. *minyān*, lit. 'count, reckoning'.] The quorum of ten males over thirteen years of age required for formal Jewish worship.

1753 *Jewish Ritual* 53 This . . is executed by the Priest in the Presence of ten Jews, which Number of Jewish Men, they call in Hebrew, A Minyon. **1891** M. FRIEDLÄNDER *Jewish Relig.* 472 Women are disqualified for forming the quorum (*minyan*) required for public worship. **1893** I. ZANGWILL *Childr. Ghetto* (ed. 3) I. xii. 111 There was never lack of *Minyan*—the congregational quorum of ten. **1960** L. P. GARTNER *Jewish Immigrant* vii. 215 In the early 1860's [in Leeds], there were barely the ten Jews required for a minyan. **1962** B. ABRAHAMS tr. *Life Glückel of Hameln* iv. 78 A company of more than two *minyanim*. **1973** *Jewish Chron.* 2 Feb. 10/1 After a life of almost 33 years the congregation's list of members had of late diminished to the point where a minyan had become very difficult to secure.

Minyan ('mɪnɪən), *a.* and *sb.*[2] [f. L. *Minyae*, Gr. Μινύαι Minyans + -AN.] **A.** *adj.* Also 6 **Mynian**, 9 **Minyean** (mɪnɪ'iːən) [Gr. Μινύειος, adj. f. Μινύαι.] **a.** Of or pertaining to the Minyans. **b.** Designating a type of very smooth grey pottery first found at Orchomenus and originally attributed to the Minyans. **B.** *sb.* A member of a possibly historical ancient people said to have inhabited parts of central Greece (chiefly Orchomenus in Boeotia and Iolchus in Thessaly), with whom the legends concerning Jason and the voyage of Argo are associated. Also with *pl.* **Minyae, Minyai.**

1598 CHAPMAN tr. *Homer's Seaven Bookes of Iliades* 35 Those who in Aspledon dwelt, and Mynian Orchomen. **1709** I. LITTLEBURY tr. *Herodotus' Hist.* I. IV. 416 Their Answer was, that they were Minyans, Grandsons of those Heroes who sail'd in the *Argos*. *Ibid.*, When the Lacedemonians heard they were of Minyan Extraction, they sent another Messenger. **1867** MAX MÜLLER *Chips* II. xvi. 67 The Minyans . . reigned chiefly in Iolkos, in Southern Thessaly. **1881** H. SCHLIEMANN in *Jrnl. Hellenic Stud.* II. 152 A wall of unwrought stones . . which Professor Sayce holds to be the ancient Minyean city wall. **1894** tr. *A. Holm's Hist. Greece* I. vii. 65 The oldest accounts of the Minyae are to be found in Homer where the Boeotian Orchomenus is mentioned as a Minyan city. **1912** WACE & THOMPSON *Prehist. Thessaly* 21 Minyan Ware. This class of pottery was first found in any quantity by Schliemann at Orchomenos. **1925** V. G. CHILDE *Dawn European Civilization* v. 78 It is only in Central Greece that Minyan ware occurs in such quantities . . . True Minyan is wheel-made and has a silver-grey colour to the reduction of the iron oxides in the clay. **1928** C. DAWSON *Age of Gods* viii. 190 The Greek mainland was conquered by a new people from the north, the bearers of the so-called Minyan culture. **1929** F. W. HASLUCK *Christianity & Islam under Sultans* II. xxv. 366 The role of the magician-philosopher-engineer Plato . . proves to be similar to that of the Minyans in Boeotia. **1958** L. COTTRELL *Anvil of Civilisation* x. 138 These invaders are characterised by a certain type of plain-grey pottery called Minyan. **1964** E. VERMEULE *Greece in Bronze Age* iii. 72 The tribal name Minyan must be strenuously distinguished from the archaeological label 'Minyan' for the invaders who bring the Middle Helladic Age to Greece. We have no idea at all what these newcomers called themselves. **1969** A. TOYNBEE *Some Probl. Greek Hist.* I. ii. 16 The Minyai were a maritime commercial people who came by sea. *Ibid.*, We shall find independent legendary evidence of a Cretan origin for . . the Minyan settlements. **1970** BRAY & TRUMP *Dict. Archaeol.* 149/2 *Minyan Ware*, a grey or yellow wheel-made ware of high quality . . . It was ancestral to Mycenaean pottery, and may represent a movement of new peoples into the Aegean area.

minyon, minys, obs. f. MINION, MINISH.

Min Yuen (mɪn jʊ'ɛn). [ad. Chinese *min yuan* people's movement.] Name of an underground Communist supply organization formed during the Malayan Emergency, 1948–1960. Also *attrib.*

1951 *Communist Banditry in Malaya* (Federation of Malaya, Dept. Information) 9 During the year [*sc.* 1949] the main incidents were carried out by small gangs operating either as killer squads or as part of the Min Yuen Organization. It was the duty of this latter Organisation to arrange for the collection of food supplies and money from the local population, and for the dissemination of Communist propaganda. **1954** V. BARTLETT *Rep. from Malaya* iii. 41 There is a branch of the Communist Party known as Min Yuen (literally 'the Helpers'), which collects food for the terrorists. **1966** E. O'BALLANCE *Malaya* iv. 92 Supporting the insurgent army was the clandestine Min Yuen, an underground organisation that provided money, food, intelligence and communications. *Ibid.*, Min Yuen is a contraction of Min Chung Yuen Thong, which has been variously translated as 'popular mass movement' or 'people's revolutionary movement'. **1970** T. LILLEY *Projects Section* ii. 20 The Min Yuen—the Communist Liberation Army's supply organisation. **1971** N. BARBER *War of Running Dogs* ii. 32 The Min Yuen (which means 'Masses Movement'), . . consisted of ostensibly normal, innocent citizens who would in fact back up the army.

minyulite (mɪ'njuːlaɪt). *Min.* [f. the name of *Minyulo* Well, Dandaragan, W. Australia, near which the mineral was first found + -ITE[1].] A hydrated basic phosphate of potassium and aluminium occurring as colourless to white needles and fibres similar to wavellite.

1933 SIMPSON & LEMESURIER in *Jrnl. R. Soc. Western Austral.* XIX. 13 In examining the Minyulo outcrop there was seen to be a fibrous mineral, closely resembling wavellite, which occurred in small quantities in a hard phosphatic ironstone carrying partly altered apatite nodules. . . The mineral has been proved in the laboratory to be a well defined new species for which the authors suggest the name Minyulite. **1961** *Mineral. Abstr.* XV. 210/2 Minyulite . . occurs on Visean shales and phthanites in Belgium as fine silky fibers, ranging 60 to 300 μ, often grouped together in radiating rosettes (1 to 3 mm).

minzingly, obs. form of MINCINGLY *adv.*

Miocene ('maɪəsiːn), *a. Geol.* Also **meiocene**. [irreg. f. Gr. μείων less + καινός new, recent.]

1. The epithet applied to the middle division of the Tertiary strata (as containing remains of fewer now existing species than the PLIOCENE), and to the geological period which it represents.

1831 [see EOCENE *a.* 1]. **1833** LYELL *Princ. Geol.* III. 54 The next antecedent tertiary epoch we shall name Miocene. **1877** *Nature* 7 June 101/2 The European miocene flora. **1880** DAWKINS *Early Man* i. 10 The Meiocene group.

2. quasi-*sb.*

1882 GEIKIE *Text Bk. Geol.* VI. iv. iii. § 1. 862 The flora indicates a decidedly tropical climate in the earlier part of the Miocene. **1885** *Athenæum* 24 Oct. 541/1 The . . Eppelsheim deposits in Germany are still left in the miocene.

Hence **Mio'cenic** *a.*

1863 LYELL *Antiq. Man* xv. 314 Between the close of the miocenic and the commencement of the glacial epoch. **1889** *Lancet* 6 July 45/1 A gigantic animal of the middle of the miocenic period of the Wyoming.

miogeoclinal (ˌmaɪəʊdʒiːəʊ'klaɪnəl), *a. Geol.* [abbrev. of next.] = MIOGEOSYNCLINAL *a.* So **mio'geocline** = MIOGEOSYNCLINE.

1971 *Nature* 2 July 41/1 Several models . . can be invoked to explain the eventual orogenic deformation of miogeoclinal continental margins. *Ibid.* 42/1 Fossil arcs . . must face away from the miogeocline in the activation model but towards the miogeocline in the collision model. **1972** [see MIOGEOSYNCLINAL *a.*]. **1972** *Sci. Amer.* Mar. 33/1 The present Atlantic marine deposits closely resemble the ancient miogeoclinal foldbelts of the Paleozoic era and earlier.

miogeosynclinal (ˌmaɪəʊdʒiːəʊsɪn'klaɪnəl), *a. Geol.* [ad. G. *miogeosynklinal* (H. Stille *Einführung in den Bau Amerikas* (1940) i. 15), f. Gr. μείων less: see GEOSYNCLINAL *a.* and *sb.*] Of or pertaining to a miogeosyncline. So **miogeo'syncline**, a geosyncline in which the process of sedimentation appears to have been accompanied by little or no volcanism; *esp.* one situated between a larger, volcanic geosyncline (a eugeosyncline) and an area of the crust that has achieved stability (a craton).

1942 *Bull. Geol. Soc. Amer.* LIII. 1642 In contrast to the Magog eugeosyncline, the Champlain belt contains dominant carbonates of shallow-water origin, unaffected by subsequent volcanism; it is a miogeosyncline. *Ibid.* 1643 The eastern, miogeosynclinal belt has the well-described sequence of southeastern Idaho. **1951** *Mem. Geol. Soc. Amer.* XLVIII. 4 As volcanic rocks are practically absent in the orthogeosynclines that adjoin the North American early Paleozoic craton, they are thus miogeosynclines. **1969** BENNISON & WRIGHT *Geol. Hist. Brit. Isles* iii. 58 No vulcanicity is known and the succession is probably indicative of deposition on an unstable shelf at the margin of a miogeosyncline. **1971** *Nature* 24 Sept. 252/1 The West Andean geosyncline was divided into a 'eugeosynclinal' volcanic (coastal range) zone and a 'miogeosynclinal' sedimentary (longitudinal valley) zone during the Jurassic. **1972** *Sci. Amer.* Mar. 30/2 When one examines the structure of ancient folded mountains, one finds that the classic geosyncline is divided into a couplet: two adjacent and parallel structures consisting of a eugeosyncline (true geosyncline) and a miogeosyncline (lesser geosyncline), often shortened to eugeocline and miogeocline.

Miohippus (maɪəʊ'hɪpəs). [mod.L. (O. C. Marsh 1874, in *Amer. Jrnl. Sci.* 3rd Ser. VII. 249), f. MIO(CENE *a.* + Gr. ἵππος horse.] A small fossil horse of the genus once so called, known from North American remains of the Oligocene period, and now included in the genus *Anchitherium*.

1877 T. H. HUXLEY in *Pop. Sci. Monthly* Jan. 294 Next [in the equine series] comes the *Miohippus*, which corresponds pretty nearly with what I spoke of as the *Anchitherium* of Europe. **1933** A. S. ROMER *Vertebr. Paleont.* xvii. 325 In *Mesohippus* . . and the somewhat larger *Miohippus* we find the beginning of a series of functionally three-toed horses. **1958** C. L. & M. A. FENTON *Fossil Bk.* xxxii. 419 *Mesohippus* was followed by *Miohippus*, a larger and somewhat more horselike beast.

miol, variant of MEAL *sb.*[4]

mioling, obs. form of MIAULING.

Miolithic (maɪə'lɪθɪk), *a. Archæol.* Also **meiolithic**. [irreg. f. Gr. μείων less + λίθος stone + -IC.] = MESOLITHIC *a.* 2.

1877 *Academy* 3 Nov. 434/3 Prof. Mantovani introduces the term Miolithic to denote a period intermediate between the palaeolithic and neolithic ages. **1896** A. J. EVANS in *Rep. Brit. Assoc.* 908 A late quaternary deposit, for which Professor Issel has proposed the name of 'Meiolithic'.

miombo (mɪ'ɒmbəʊ). Also **miomba**. [Swahili.] A tree of the tropical African genus *Brachystegia*, belonging to the family Leguminosæ; woodland composed mainly of these trees. Also *attrib.*

1864 J. A. GRANT *Walk across Afr.* vi. 88 The wands from the Miombo, a kind of banyan, afford the natives the fibre which they attach to their wool. **1910** *Encycl. Brit.* XI. 772/2 The silk-cotton tree (*Bombax ceiba*), miomba, tamarisk, copal tree . . are frequent [in German East Africa]. **1934** *Jrnl. Ecol.* XXII. 220 A strip of 'Miombo' through which a narrow, fairly shallow ravine . . was running. **1947** *E. Afr. Ann.* 1946–7 95/2 The considerable forests of Unyamwezi, largely miombo, provide much honey. **1948** *Cape Argus* 3 Dec. 5/4 Surrounded by uninhabited miombo bush. **1959** R. W. J. KEAY in *Vegetation Map Afr.* Explanatory Notes 9/1 In these woodlands, commonly known by the vernacular name 'myombo', several species of *Brachystegia* . . are dominant. **1966** C. A. W. GUGGISBERG *S.O.S. Rhino* iii. 53 Black rhinoceroses frequent savannah country, mopane and miombo forests, bushveld and dry thornbush. **1970** A. T. SEMPLE *Grassland Improvement* i. 14 African farmers have found that their ground-water supplies improve when they extend their settlements in the 'miombo' (*Brachystegia* woodland).

mioner, obs. form of MINER.

mionite, -phylly: see MEIONITE, -PHYLLY.

miops, obs. form of MYOPE.

miosis (maɪ'əʊsɪs). *Path.* Also **myosis**. [f. Gr. μύ-ειν to shut the eyes + -OSIS.] Contraction of the pupil of the eye.

1819 *Pantologia*. **1875** H. WALTON *Dis. Eye* xxxiii. (ed. 3) 935 Myosis occurs in progressive locomotor ataxy. **1890** BILLINGS *Med. Dict.* II. 160/2 *Miosis* (G[erman]), myosis. **1892** A. DUANE tr. *E. Fuchs's Text-bk. Ophthalm.* iv. 257 There is a series of alkaloids which produce either dilatation of the pupil (mydriasis) or its contraction (miosis). [*Note*] From μείωσις, contraction; hence miosis, and not myosis, as it is generally written (Hirschberg). **1910** *Trans. Ophthalm. Soc.* XXX. 163 Miosis on the right side was associated with dilatation of the left pupil. **1947** F. B. WALSH *Clinical Neuro-Ophthalmology* 201 Miosis has already been defined as indicating a pupil 2 mm. or less in diameter. **1964** W. B. SMITH *Allergy & Tissue Metabolism* vii. 78 The pharmacological effects of reserpine administration are: . . miosis (contraction of pupil of the eye), ptosis [etc.].

Hence **mio'sitic** *a.*[1] and *sb.* = MIOTIC.

1855 DUNGLISON *Med. Lex.*, *Myositic*, causing contraction of the pupil, as opium. **1874** GARROD & BAXTER *Mat. Med.* 459 Pupil Contractors (Myositics). **1899** *Allbutt's Syst. Med.* VI. 403 Calabar bean was not . . in use as a myositic.

miosis, miostemonous, miotaxy: see MEI-.

miotic (maɪ'ɒtɪk), *a.* and *sb.* Also **myotic**. [f. MIOSIS: see -OTIC.] **a.** *adj.* Pertaining to or causing miosis. **b.** *sb.* An agent which produces miosis.

1864 tr. *Donder's Anom. Accomm. Eye* 621 It is true that all myotic action could not be denied to the agents which were formerly placed in this category. *Ibid.*, The want of an efficient myotic was long felt in ophthalmic surgery. **1887** *Buck's Handbk. Med. Sci.* V. 97/1 Eserine or physostigmine . . is the most powerful of myotics. **1892** A. DUANE tr. *E.*

Fuchs's Text-bk. Ophthalm. iv. 259 The action of miotics is of shorter duration than that of the mydriatics. **1918** *Jrnl. Amer. Med. Assoc.* 29 June 1992/2 There are contradictory opinions expressed on the effect of miotic drugs in cases of incomplete sphincter. **1946** *Nature* 28 Sept. 432/1 The work ..developed to include other problems, such as the mechanism..of lachrymation, of the action of myotics, etc. **1971** *Lancet* 6 Nov. 1040/2 The use of a miotic..should be regarded as mandatory whatever the mydriatic previously instilled.

mioul, miour(e, miowe, var. MIAUL *v.*, MYOUR, MIAOW.

mipafox (ˈmɪpəfɒks). [f. bis(*mono-isopropylamino)fluorophosphine oxide*, its chemical name.] An organic phosphorus compound, $[(CH_3)_2CHNH]_2POF$, which is used as an insecticide.

1953 *Recommended Common Names for Pesticides (B.S.I.)* II. 5 Mipafox: fluorobis*iso*propylamino-phosphine oxide. **1956** *Nature* 28 Jan. 186/1 It has recently been found that 8 × 10⁻⁷ *M* mipafox..completely inhibits the non-specific serum cholinesterase. **1971** *Brit. Jrnl. Pharmacol.* XLI. 21 The ileum was then incubated with mipafox (10 μg/ml) for 75 min.

‖**mi-parti** (miːpɑːtiː), *a. Her.* Also 8 **-party**. [Fr., pa. pple. of *mipartir* to divide in half, f. *mi-* (:—L. *medium* middle) + *partir* to divide.] (See quots.)

1725 COATS *Dict. Her., Mi-party*, is a Word used by French Heralds, denoting that the Escutcheon is half Way down parted per Pale, and there cross'd by some other Partition. **1896** WOODWARD *Heraldry* I. 478 *Mi-parti*—said of dimidiated arms, and of an ordinary parti per pale.

Mipolam (ˈmɪpəlæm). Also **mipolam**. A proprietary name for plastics composed of polyvinyl chloride which are used for chemically resistant piping and containers.

1936 *India-Rubber Jrnl.* 4 Nov. 19/2 Mipolam is a purely thermoplastic mass, and behaves accordingly in electrical tests. **1939** H. R. SIMONDS *Industr. Plastics* (1940) xiii. 324 A new polyvinyl chloride plastic in Germany known as Mipolam is resistant to acids and to many other chemicals and is being used for beer, alcohol and other prime containers, and also in the form of piping and pumping fixtures in chemical plants. **1943** *Jrnl. R. Aeronaut. Soc.* XLVII. 140 The group of polymerization resins includes, among others, the plastic of German production—mipolam —remarkable for its high fire resistance, toughness and elasticity. **1951** *Trade Marks Jrnl.* 24 Oct. 980/1 Mipolam. .. Mouldable plastics for use in manufactures. Dynamit-Actien-Gesellschaft Vormals Alfred Nobel & Co... Troisdorf, Cologne, Germany; manufacturers. **1969** R. F. LANG tr. *Henglein's Chem. Technol.* 215 Mipolam pipes can be enlarged thermally, beaded, bent and cemented with solvents.

Miquelet (ˈmɪkəlɪt). Also 9 **miquelete, miquelite, miguelet(e.** [a. F. *miquelet*, ad. Sp. *miquelete, miguelete*, f. Cat. *Miquel*, Sp. *Miguel*, Michael. (For the supposed origin of the name see quot. 1845.)] **a.** In the 17th c., a member of a body of Catalonian banditti who infested the Pyrenees. **b.** Before and during the Peninsular war, a Spanish guerrilla soldier; also, a member of a corps of French irregulars raised by Napoleon in 1808 for service against the Spaniards. **c.** In modern Spain, the designation of the soldiers of certain local regiments of infantry, chiefly employed on escort duties.

1670 *Lond. Gaz.* No. 476/4 The Miquelets or Mountaineers were again got together in a little Village,.. neer the Pyrenean hills. *a* **1700** B. E. *Dict. Cant. Crew, Miquelets*, Mountaneers (in Spain) or Spanish Rapparies. **1721** *Lett. Mist's Jrnl.* (1722) II. 176 No more, you Holiday Fools, throw away your Six-pences,..to see a Spanish Miquelet swallow a Toad. **1779** *Gentl. Mag.* XLIX. 501 The miquelets or mountaineers who so cruelly harrassed the French armies. **1827** SOUTHEY *Penins. War* II. 358, 10,000 Miquelets and Somatenes..had been sent..to take advantage of any insurrection that might be attempted in Barcelona. **1829** SIR W. NAPIER *Penins. War* v. iv. 57 Francisco Milans and Milans de Bosch, with their Migueletes, keep the mountains to the northward of Barcelona. **1843** BORROW *Bible in Spain* xxiv, One of those singular half soldiers half guerillas, called Miguelets. **1845** FORD *Handbk. Spain* I. I. 41 A regular body of men was organized for that purpose [as a government escort] all over Spain, and were called 'Miquelites', from, it is said, one Miquel de Prats, an armed satellite of..Cæsar Borgia. **1879** STEVENSON *Trav. Cevennes* (1886) 186 Militiaman and Miquelet and dragoon..they had all been sabreing and shooting.

Mir (mɪə(r)), *sb.*¹ Also **meer**. [a. Hindi and Pers. *mīr*, ad. Arab. *amīr* leader, commander: see AMEER, EMIR.] = AMEER, EMIR.

1625 PURCHAS *Pilgrimes* I. III. xii. 282 The Mir of Aden sent a Boat and a Messenger aboord. **1787** C. HAMILTON *Hist. Relation Rohilla Afgans N. Provinces Hindostan* 41 Omdat al Moolk..was at this period Meer Buchshy or Paymaster-General of the Empire. **1792** R. HERON tr. *Niebuhr's Trav. Arabia* II. XXIII. vii. 155 Mr Kniphausen had agreed with Mir Naser, Prince of Bender Rigk,..that the Dutch should..be allowed to seat their factory there. **1800** F. GLADWIN tr. *Ayeen Akbery* I. II. 231 (*heading*) The office of Meer Behry, or Admiralty. **1840** J. B. FRASER *Trav. Koordistan* I. iii. 80 The jealousy of the Meer extends only to strangers travelling in the country without apparent business. **1873** E. BALFOUR *Cycl. India* (ed. 2) III. 284/1 Mir Jaffir, in 1702, was appointed dewan of Bengal... He was of a poor brahmin family..but was..converted to mahomedanism. **1885** T. P. HUGHES *Dict. Islam* 350/1 *Mīr*. A title of respect used for the descendants of celebrated Muḥammadan saints. More generally used for Saiyids, or descendants of Fāṭimah, the Prophet's daughter. **1928** *Blackw. Mag.* May 709/1 To get the savour of the Mir's table talk, you must hear a little more about its setting. **1973** C. BONINGTON *Next Horizon* xviii. 252 On my first morning I attended the Court of the Mir of Hunza... At ten o'clock, the Mir, an absolute monarch with complete control over the internal affairs of his 20,000 people, walks from his palace to the Durbah. *Ibid.* 253 The Mir sits on a small rostrum, and his Court, in strict order of precedence, squat on carpets in two lines on either side of him. **1973** *Observer* (Colour Suppl.) 30 Sept. 51/1 In some circumstances,..the Mir (ruler) of Hunza could, from personal knowledge of his State's history, verify ages.

‖**mir** (mɪə(r)), *sb.*² [Russ.] A village community in pre-revolutionary Russia. Also *attrib.*

1877 D. M. WALLACE *Russia* I. viii. 179 The Mir is the most peculiar of Russian institutions. **1878** E. C. GRENVILLE-MURRAY *Russians To-Day* 21 The Mir system may be summed up in a few words; it has simply caused the peasant to exchange the domination of his old master for the more grinding tyranny of many masters. **1905** J. H. ROSE *Devel. European Nations* xi. 294 The ownership of the soil of Russia by the Mirs, the communes of her myriad villages. **1916** C. E. BECHHOFER *Russ. at Cross-Roads* 71 No period is known in Russian history when the Mir did not exist. **1925** *Contemp. Rev.* Jan. 60 They pointed out that the land-holding peasant..did not cease to be a member of the *mir*. **1967** *Listener* 2 Nov. 558/3 The break-up of the *mir* and the ..transition from communal to hereditary tenure. **1975** *Times* 8 Jan. 15/7 The democratic and civic traditions of Russia, from Kievian Rus to the *mirs* and the Zaporozhean Republic.

Mir (mɪə(r)), *sb.*³ [ad. *Mirabad*, the name of a town in the Sarawan district, S.W. of Arak, Iran.] A rare and fine quality Saraband rug woven in Mirabad. Also *attrib.*

1900 J. K. MUMFORD *Oriental Rugs* xi. 197 In the Sarawan district the *tereh* Mir, so called from the village where it is said to have originated, is the almost universal design. *Ibid.*, Artisans in other localities have copied the Mir Saraband, changing the borders or coloration to suit their fancy. **1931** A. U. DILLEY *Oriental Rugs & Carpets* iv. 125 All the fine Sarabands, known as Mir from the town of that name which an earthquake destroyed, were 'Farma-yashti', or special-order weavings. **1953** A. C. EDWARDS *Persian Carpet* ix. 144/2 *Miri* no doubt refers to the Mir carpets of the early nineteenth century which were the prototypes of the present-day Serabands. **1972** P. L. PHILLIPS tr. *Formenton's Oriental Rugs & Carpets* 69 The botch design came from the Seraband region and..was used at the beginning in the Mir carpets. **1973** *Times* 2 Apr. 6/5 (Advt.), A superb Mir carpet in soft pastel dyes.

mir, obs. form of MYRRH.

mirabelle (mɪrəˈbɛl). Also 8 **mirabel**. [a. F. *mirabelle*.] **1.** A variety of plum.

1706 LONDON & WISE *Retir'd Gard'ner* I. 41 The Mirabel is a small Plum. **1840** *Penny Cycl.* XVIII. 287 Varieties of plums..Mirabelle. **1860** *All Year Round* No. 56. 130 There are varieties of the Mirabelle plum..which annually bloom profusely in England. **1890** *Syd. Soc. Lex., Mirabelle*, the fruit of *Prunus armenoides*. *Mirabelle of Corsica*, the fruit of *Physalis alkekengi*.

2. An alcoholic spirit distilled from mirabelles, *spec.* those grown in Alsace, France.

1940 H. J. GROSSMAN *Guide to Wines, Spirits & Beers* xviii. 185 The brandy obtained from plums is known by several names, depending on the country of origin:.. Quetsch or Mirabelle when it comes from Alsace in France. **1963** *Times* 24 Apr. 11/7 'Try that,' he said, proffering a spoon dipped into the last vat of limpid 85° Mirabelle. **1967** N. FREELING *Strike Out* 67 Bernhard's last bottle of mirabelle.

‖**mirabile dictu** (mɪˈrɑːbɪliː ˈdɪktuː), *Lat. phr.* [L. *mirabile*, neut. of *mirabilis* wonderful + *dictu*, supine of *dicĕre* to say. cf. Virgil *Georgics* ii. 30 quin et caudicibus sectis (mirabile dictu) truditur e sicco radix oleagina ligno.] Wonderful to relate.

1831 *Athenæum* 12 Mar. 173/2 An unassuming young female relative, whom she gives in marriage to the son of her (*mirabile dictu!*) honest attorney. **1837** J. F. COOPER *Recoll. Europe* I. 318 The late king was the Miller, and, *mirabile dictu*, the Archbishop of Paris did not disdain to play the part of the Curé. **1841** DICKENS *Let.* 21 July (1969) II. 334 A man is coming here at 8, to settle (mirabile dictu) the matter of Mrs. Macrone's book. **1861** S. B. BIRCH *Constipated Bowels* ii. 15 The tradesman..is permitted to go so far as to usurp the functions of the physician, and is even encouraged (*mirabile dictu!*) to prescribe himself on the strength of the pharmacopœia. **1943** L. MARCHAL *Vichy* xiii. 195 The Marshal was anxious to save Otto Abetz, who, *mirabile dictu*, was considered in certain Vichy circles as a 'friend of France'.

†**mirabili'arian**, *a. Obs.* [f. L. *mīrābiliārius* (see next) + -AN.] = MIRABILIARY *a.*

1624 BP. MOUNTAGU *Immed. Addr.* 218 In opinion of Tertullian, it is no safe proceeding by this [*sic*] Mirabiliarian courses, to iustifie Inuocation of Saints or Angels.

†**mira'biliary**, *sb.* and *a. Obs.* [ad. late L. *mīrābiliārius* miracle-monger, applied by Augustine to the Donatists.] **A.** *sb.* One who deals in the marvellous; a collector of marvels.

1600 O. E. *Repl. Libel* II. iii. 50 The Mirabiliaries were likewise condemned, for that by myracles, and prophecies, they sought to confirme their religion. **1605** BACON *Adv. Learn.* II. i. §4 The vse of this worke..is nothing lesse then to giue contentment to the appetite of Curious and vaine wittes, as the manner of Mirabilaries [*sic*] is to doe.

B. *adj.* Characteristic of 'miracle-mongers'.

1624 GEE *Hold Fast* 44, I haue formerly related some iugling mirabiliarie tricks acted of late in this City.

†**mi'rabilis**. *Obs.* Short for AQUA MIRABILIS.

1673 DRYDEN *Marr. à la Mode* III. i. 35 She..opens her dear bottle of Mirabilis. **1687** SEDLEY *Bellamira* III. i, Have you any mirabilis?

†**mi'rabilist**. *Obs.* [f. L. *mīrābilis* wonderful + -IST.] One who works wonders.

1599 HARSNET *Agst. Darell* 220 Vnto which kinde of people, and seducing Mirabilistes, Master Darrell in his practises with Somers, may well bee resembled. **1601** DEACON & WALKER *Answ. to Darell* 47 The most admirable mirabilist, among all the mirabilistes vnder the heauens.

mirabilite (mɪˈræbɪlaɪt). *Min.* [a. G. *mirabilit* (Haidinger 1845) f. mod.L. (*sal*) *mīrābil-is* 'wonderful salt', the name given by Glauber to sulphate of soda ('Glauber's salt'): see -ITE.] Native sulphate of soda.

1854 DANA *Syst. Min.* (ed. 4).

†**mira'bility**. *Obs.* [ad. L. *mīrābilitās*, n. of quality f. *mīrābilis*: see next and -ITY.] ? Admirable quality.

a **1691** FLAVEL *Navig. Spirit.* (1770) 232 An art of exquisite excellency, ingenuity, rarity, and mirability.

†'**mirable**, *a.* and *sb. Obs.* [ad. L. *mīrābilis*, f. *mīrārī* to wonder: see -ABLE.]

A. *adj.* Wonderful, marvellous.

c **1450** *Mirour Saluacioun* 899 Now fylowes it for til here hire mirable Conceyving. *c* **1450** *Cov. Myst.* (Shaks. Soc.) 389 A! myrable God, meche is thy myth. **1606** SHAKS. *Tr. & Cr.* IV. v. 142. **1606** HOLLAND *Sueton.* 271 With mirable sentences and Apophthegmes.

B. *sb.* Something wonderful; a wonder.

1646 GAULE *Cases Consc.* 33 The Arted Witch, or one onely speculative upon the abstruse Mirables of Nature. **1653** H. WHISTLER *Upshot Inf. Baptism* 45 Ye grave Fathers & Bretheren, who find among the Mirables of Oxford Library that Coat [etc.].

mirabola(m, -lan(e, obs. ff. MYROBALAN.

†**mira'bundous**, *a. Obs.* [f. L. *mīrābundus* (f. *mīrārī* to wonder) + -OUS.] Wonderful.

1694 MOTTEUX *Rabelais* (1737) V. 229 Our Auricles, percuss'd by Fame sonorous, Your mirabundous Acts have brought before us.

†'**mirach**. *Obs.* Forms: 5–6 **mirac**, 6 **myrac, myracke**, 6–7 **mirach(e**, 7 **myrach(e**. [med.L., a. Arab. *marāqq* pl., 'the thin or tender parts of the belly' (Lane), f. root *raqqa* to be thin or weak.] A name for the abdomen.

c **1400** *Lanfranc's Cirurg.* 169 Alle þese þingis þanne ben comprehendid in a skyn þat is fleischi & of lacertis maad, & is clepid mirac, & is clepid þe vttere wombe. **1528** PAYNEL *Salerne's Regim.* Ciij b, These ventositees gether to gyther betwene the places of the bealye called mirac. **1541** R. COPLAND *Guydon's Quest. Chirurg.* H ij, Of howe many and what & howe many partes is the myrac composed. **1621** BURTON *Anat. Mel.* I. iii. II. ii. (1651) 200 If from the myrache, a swelling and wind in the Hypocondries. **1693** tr. *Blancard's Phys. Dict.* (ed. 2).

†**mi'rachial**, *a. Obs.* In 7 **myrachiall**. [f. med.L. *mirachia* hypochondria (f. *mirach*: see prec.) + -AL¹.] Hypochondriacal.

1621 BURTON *Anat. Mel.* I. ii. IV. iv, Of Hypocondriacall or flatuous melancholy, which the Arabians call Myrachiall.

miracidium (ˌmaɪərəˈsɪdɪəm). *Zool.* Pl. **miracidia**. [mod.L., f. Gr. μειρακίδιον, dim. of μειράκιον boy, stripling.] The ciliated, first larval form of a digenetic trematode. Also *attrib.* So **mira'cidial** *a.*

1898 A. SEDGWICK *Student's Text-bk. Zool.* I. v. 229 The miracidium generally becomes a sporocyst, rarely a redia. **1904** C. W. STILES *Illustr. Key to Trematode Parasites of Man* 18 Miracidium ciliated, develops after eggs leave the host. **1952** J. CLEGG *Freshwater Life* viii. 127 The miracidium stage [of *Bucephalus*] is passed in the freshwater Mussels *Anodonta* and *Unio*. **1962** J. D. SMYTH *Introd. Animal Parasitol.* xxxii. 388 The miracidial immobilisation test is based on the immobilisation of miracidia in immune serum. **1963** *New Scientist* 29 Aug. 441/3 Those [schistosome] eggs which reach the outside world hatch in fresh water and the microscopic miracidia which emerge swim around. **1971** *Oxf. Bk. Invertebr.* 24/1 When the pasture is damp, the first larva [of the liver fluke], the miracidium, hatches and this swims by its cilia in the film of water on the pasture until it encounters a snail. **1974** *Nature* 22 Mar. 361/2 A better understanding of the intricacies of how miracidia and cercariae find and penetrate hosts.

miracle (ˈmɪrək(ə)l), *sb.* Forms: 4 **maracle, -kle, meracull, -kill, mercle, miracil, -cyl, -kel, myrakil(l, -kyl**, 4–5 **meracle, myrrakull**, 4–6 **myracle**, 5 **mirakelle, -ylle**, 5–6 **mirackle, miracule**, 6 **mirakill, mirakle, myrackle**, 2– **miracle**. [a. OF. *miracle*, ad. L. *mīrāculum* object of wonder (in Eccl. L. miracle), f. *mīrārī* to wonder, f. *mīr-us* wonderful. Cf. Pr. *miracle*, Sp. *milagro*, Pg. *milagre*, It. *miracolo*.]

1. a. A marvellous event occurring within human experience, which cannot have been brought about by human power or by the operation of any natural agency, and must

therefore be ascribed to the special intervention of the Deity or of some supernatural being; chiefly, an act (e.g. of healing) exhibiting control over the laws of nature, and serving as evidence that the agent is either divine or is specially favoured by God. Phrases, *to do*, † *make*, *work*, † *show a miracle*.

The L. *miraculum* in this sense, though common in patristic and later theology, is foreign to the Vulgate, in which the Gr. words rendered 'miracle' in the English Bible—σημεῖον 'sign', τέρας 'wonder', δύναμις 'power' or 'mighty work', are translated respectively by *signum*, *prodigium*, and *virtus*.

1154 *O.E. Chron.* an. 1137 (Laud MS.), He maket þur ure Drihtin wunderlice & manifealdlice miracles. *a* **1225** *Leg. Kath.* 1426 þæt wes miracle muchel. *c* **1250** *Kent. Serm.* in *O.E. Misc.* 30 þis was þe commencement of þo miracles of ure louerde þet he made flesliche in erþe. *a* **1300** *Cursor M.* 177 Iesu..did þe meracles sua rijf þat þe Iuus him hild in strijf. *Ibid.* 9512 Quat man es moght se sa bright, þat suilk a man cuth think in thoght þat mustre þat mercle moght? *c* **1330** R. Brunne *Chron.* (1810) 23 God did faire miracle for Elfride þat houre. *a* **1340** Hampole *Psalter* xvii. 16 He shewyd many myrakils. **1377** Langl. *P. Pl.* B. xv. 438 þorw myracles..al þat marche he torned To cryst and to crystendome. *c* **1380** Wyclif *Wks.* (1880) 288 þou seist þat myraclis & lyues of holy men approuen þis dowynge of þe chirche. *c* **1400** Maundev. (1839) xii. 139 This was the firste Myracle..that Machomete dide in his ȝouthe. *c* **1440** *Sir Gowther* 743 (Breul) He..gyffus to þo mad hor wytte, And mony odur meracullus yytte. *c* **1511** *1st Eng. Bk. Amer.* (Arb.) Introd. 35/1 Saint Thomas doeth more myracles, than ony seynt in heuen. **1591** Shaks. *1 Hen. VI*, v. iv. 41 Chosen from aboue..To worke exceeding myracles on earth. **1608** Bp. Hall *Epist.* i. vi. 73 Miracles must be iudged by the doctrine which they confirme; not the doctrine by the miracles. **1611** Bible *John* iv. 54 This is againe the second miracle that Iesus did. **1699** Burnet 39 *Art.* iv. 62 A Miracle is a Work that exceeds all the known Powers of Nature. **1756–7** tr. *Keysler's Trav.* (1760) I. 466 A St. Ignatius performing a miracle, by Rubens, on another altar. **1865** Mozley *Mirac.* i. 5 Miracles or visible suspensions of the order of nature for a providential purpose, are not in contradiction to reason. **1872** Tennyson *Gareth & Lynette* 1292 Wonders ye have done; Miracles ye cannot.

b. In generalized sense.

a **1225** *Ancr. R.* 158 Al were he, þuruh miracle, of barain iboren [etc.]. **1390** Gower *Conf.* III. 106 That therof mai be non obstacle, Bot if it stonde upon miracle. *c* **1430** Lydg. *Min. Poems* (Percy Soc.) 13 Lyke to the watyr of Archideclyne, Wiche be meracle were turned into wyne. **1590** Shaks. *Com. Err.* v. i. 264 Then you fled into this Abbey heere, From whence I thinke you are come by Miracle. **1671** Milton *P.R.* i. 337 Who brought me hither Will bring me hence... By Miracle he may, reply'd the Swain. **1742** Young *Nt. Th.* iv. 131 Am I fond of life, Who scarce can think it possible, I live? Alive by miracle! **1855** Milman *Lat. Chr.* ix. ix. IV. 256 By what was believed to be miracle, which might be holy art. **1869** Liddon *Serm. Spec. Occas.* viii. (1897) 164 When we take up the Book of Jonah, that which strikes us first of all..is the degree in which miracle pervades the whole narrative.

2. *transf.* in various uses, *esp.* as applied hyperbolically to an achievement seemingly beyond human power, or an occurrence so marvellous as to appear supernatural. Also with defining word prefixed designating a remarkable development in some specified area.

c **1386** Chaucer *Knt.'s T.* 1817 A myracle ther bifel anon. **1586** *Let. to Earle Leycester*, etc. 12 The bottomlesse graces and immeasurable benefits bestowed upon me by the Almightie..I must..admire..accounting them as well miracles as benefites. **1633** T. Stafford *Pac. Hib.* i. xiv. 84 Captain Flower at Lysmore, wrought miracles against the Rebels in those parts. **1638** Junius *Paint. Ancients* 95 Now these miracles of Nature may seeme to fall out by meere chance. **1692** Dryden *Cleomenes* ii. ii. 17 O Miracle! He blushes! **1738** Wesley *Ps.* cxxxix. v, Lord to thy Works of Nature join Thy Miracles of Grace! **1824** R. Stuart *Hist. Steam Engine* 35 It would, indeed, have been a miracle had a copy, of any equally unimportant book, been found at such a distance of time in that unenviable situation. **1850** Scoresby *Cheever's Whalem. Adv.* xi. (1859) 145 She was within a miracle of being upset. **1860** Pusey *Min. Proph.* 257 The moral miracles were, in these hundreds of thousands, God's over-powering grace. **1903** *Daily Mail* 11 Sept. 3/1 There are two theories to account for the radium 'miracle'. **1959** M. Crosland tr. *Rovan's Germany* 78 The fact that millions of new arrivals were housed and employed..is the most miraculous aspect of the 'German miracle'. **1963** *Listener* 21 Feb. 321/2 This contract production is an important factor in the Polish miracle. **1973** A. Price *October Men* ix. 128, I don't mind him being part of the Italian economic miracle.

b. Phrase, *to a miracle*: so well or successfully as to seem miraculous; marvellously well.

1643 Trapp *Comm. Gen.* xxxi. 27 Hypocrites are likened to bull-rushes, which are green and smoothe; and he is curious to a miracle, that can find a knot in them. **1672** Dryden *Assignation* i. i, Gad, sir, everything becomes you to a miracle. **1758** J. S. *Le Dran's Observ. Surg.* (1771) 335 Things went on to a Miracle. **1840** Dickens *Old C. Shop* xvi, Nelly..was soon busily engaged in her task, and accomplishing it to a miracle. **1882** Stevenson *New Arab. Nts.* (1884) 94, I understand my part to a miracle.

c. *concr.* A wonderful object, a marvel; a person or thing of more than natural excellence; a surpassing example *of* some quality.

c **1400** Maundev. (Roxb.) vii. 24 ȝit es þe heued of þat beste with þe hornes halden and keped at Alisaunder for a miracle. **1577** B. Googe *Heresbach's Husb.* iv. (1586) 167 The bird appeereth as it were a myracle of nature. **1595** Daniel *Civ. Wars* v. xiv. (1609) 117 That magnanimous King, Mirror of vertue, miracle of worth. **1597** Shaks. *2 Hen. IV*, ii. iii. 33 O Miracle of Men! **1602** Carew *Eng. Tongue* in *Camden's Rem.* (1614) 44 Take the miracle of our age Sir Philip Sidney. **1617** Moryson *Itin.* iii. 64 The Bridge at London is worthily to be numbred among the miracles of the world. **1709** J. Lawson *New Voy. Carolina* 145 The Humming-Bird is the Miracle of all our wing'd Animals. **1712** Addison *Spect.* No. 543 ¶3 Sir Isaac Newton, who stands up as the miracle of the present age. **1797** Coleridge *Kubla Khan* 38 It was a miracle of rare device. **1845** Craik *Sk. Hist. Lit. Eng.* V. 174 To Garrick, a miracle of an actor,..we owe [etc.].

†**3.** A miraculous story; a legend. *Obs.*

c **1386** Chaucer *Sir Thopas* Prol. 1 Whan seyd was al this miracle, euery man As sobre was that wonder was to se.

4. One of a class of dramatic representations of the Middle Ages based on the life of Our Lord and the legends of the Saints. Now usually called *miracle play* (see 5).

1303 R. Brunne *Handl. Synne* 4659 þat make swyche pleyys to any man As myracles and bourdys. *c* **1386** Chaucer *Wife's Prol.* 558 To pleyes of myracles and to mariages. *c* **1394** *P. Pl. Crede* 107 At marketts & myracles we medleþ vs nevere. **1798** in *Archæologia* (1800) XIII. 237 But those theatrical pieces called 'Miracles' were their delight beyond all others. **1852** Hallam *Lit. Ess. & Char.*, *E. Europ. Drama* 4 Geoffrey, afterwards abbot of St. Alban's, while teaching a school at Dunstable, caused one of the shows, vulgarly called miracles, on the story of St. Catherine to be represented in that town.

5. *attrib.* and *Comb.* (chiefly objective), as *miracle-abode*, *-author*, † *miracles-doing*, *drug*, *miracle-making*, *-monger* (hence *-mongering*), *-worker*, *-working*. Also *miracle-bred*, *-breeding*, *-proof* adjs.; **miracle man**, one who performs miracles; † **miracle minter**, one who 'coins' fictitious miracles; **miracle play** = MIRACLE 4; † **miracle player**, one who takes part in a miracle play; **miracle rice**, a modern hybrid rice seed that yields more than the traditional varieties; † **miracle shop**, contemptuously for a shrine at which miracles are reputed to be wrought.

1807 Wolcot (P. Pindar) in *Monthly Mag.* Feb. 1 Methinks I see them [*sc.* Chaucer's pilgrims] on the road To Becket's *miracle-abode. **1749** Lavington *Enthus. Meth. & Papists* (1820) 237 One of their famous *miracle-authors declares, that one brother was so elevated..that he boasted of having visions of angels attending him. **1928** W. B. Yeats *Tower* 62 Even the grey-leaved olive tree *Miracle-bred out of the living stone. **1814** Mrs. J. West *Alicia de Lacy* III. 174 By pacing at midnight the flinty aisle of some *miracle-breeding chapel. *c* **1440** *Alphabet of Tales* 305 þe tone of þaim fell vnto þe syn of lichorie, & her-for God deprivid hym of *meracles-doyng. *c* **1449** Pecock *Repr.* ii. viii. 188 Bi the seid euydencis of myraculis doing. **1953** J. Ramsbottom *Mushrooms & Toadstools* xxiii. 279 Penicillin was really on the stage at last; it dwarfed other performers into insignificance. It was hailed as a '*miracle drug'. **1962** *Lancet* 2 June 1137/1 A miracle drug that will charm away any and every form of infection. **1970** P. Moyes *Who saw her Die?* xvi. 209, I got hold of the streptomycin..and the miracle drug worked. She was cured. **1677** Gilpin *Demonol.* (1867) 181 When his [Satan's] agents can go no further in the trade of *miracle-making, he [etc.]. **1572** Forrest *Theophilus* 1235 in *Anglia* VII, Bruited abroade this great *myracle Man. **1914** F. L. Packard (*title*) The miracle man. **1926** A. Conan Doyle *Hist. Spiritualism* I. iii. 54 He [*sc.* Andrew Jackson Davis] was a miracle man, the inspired, learned, uneducated apostle of the new dispensation. **1951** L. MacNeice tr. *Goethe's Faust* 185 In priestly robes and wreath a miracle-man Will now fulfil what he in hopes began. **1959** I. & P. Opie *Lore & Lang. Schoolch.* x. 179 They are willing to acclaim anyone who habitually comes top of the class without apparent effort, naming him Genius, The Brains, Miracle Man. **1603** Harsnet *Pop. Impost.* 103, I should haue acquainted you how the *Miracle-minter in his miracle booke doth solemnly tell vs, that [etc.]. **1584** R. Scot *Discov. Witchcr.* viii. i. (1886) 125 Why doo not these (meaning *miraclemongers) appoint some Siloah to swim in? **1613** Purchas *Pilgrimage* (1614) 93 We leaue to you the stile of Mirabiliary Miracle-mongers. **1856** R. A. Vaughan *Mystics* (1860) I. 36 All the pretences, both of heathen and of Christian miracle-mongers. **1881** A. B. Bruce *Chief End Rev.* iv. 182 Legendary tales due to the..*miracle-mongering spirit of the..reporters. **1852** Hook *Ch. Dict.* (1871) 517 *Miracle-plays were a kind of church performance in the middle ages representing the miracles wrought by the holy confessors, and the sufferings by which the perseverance of the martyrs was manifested. **1875** Ward *Eng. Dram. Lit.* (1899) I. 41 Miracle-plays, on the other hand, are more especially concerned with incidents derived from legends of the Saints of the Church. *a* **1400** *Serm. agst. Miracle-plays* in *Rel. Ant.* II. 46 Therfore to pristis it is uttirly forbedyn not onely to been *myracle pleyere but also to heren or to seen myraclis pleyinge. **1711** Shaftesb. *Charac.* (1737) II. 328 The safest station in Christianity is his who can be mov'd by nothing of this kind, and is thus *miracle-proof. **1969** *Americana Ann.* 408 The introduction of U.S.-supplied '*miracle rice' notwithstanding, the country [*sc.* Laos] was still unable to produce enough rice for its own people. **1972** *Times* 8 May 14/1 Dr Norman Borlaug, the discoverer of the 'miracle' rice and wheat strains..was awarded the Nobel Peace Prize in 1970. **1629** Donne *Serm.* xxiv. (1640) 239 In the Romane church (where miracles for every naturall disease may be had at some Shrine or *miracle-shop, better cheap, then a Medicine..). **1561** T. Norton *Calvin's Inst.* C.'s Pref. A iv b, The Lorde hath made vs ware agaynste suche *miracle workers. **1857** Stanley *Mem. Canterb.* ii. (ed. 3) 103 His [Becket's] fame as the great miracle-worker of the time, was increasing every month. **1923** Kipling *Independence* 29 He was something of a magician, if not a miracle-worker. **1970** G. Greer *Female Eunuch* 277 She twice..took a little pill... She thinks they are little miracle workers. **1605** Bacon *Adv. Learn.* ii. xi. §3 They haue exalted the power of the imagination to be much one with the power of *Miracle-working faith. **1867** Macfarren *Harmony* iv. (1876) 152 This miracle-working harmony.

miracle ('mɪrək(ə)l), *v.* *nonce-wd.* [f. MIRACLE *sb.*] **a.** *refl.* ? To be revealed by miracle. **b.** *intr.* To work miracles.

1611 Shaks. *Cymb.* iv. ii. 29 Ime not their Father, yet who this should bee Doth myracle it selfe, lou'd before mee. *a* **1656** Hales *Tracts* (1677) 169 Their undaunted fortitude, their power of miracling.

miracle, corrupt form of MEREL, a game.

† **'miraclely**, *adv.* *Obs.* In 4 **meraclelyche**. [f. MIRACLE *sb.* + -LY[2].] By a miracle.

c **1420** *Chron. Vilod.* 1432 þey cryede god mercy alle þat ny3t—And meraclelyche god toke hede þerto.

† **'miracler.** *Obs.* [f. MIRACLE *v.* + -ER[1].] One who works miracles.

1676 *Doctrine of Devils* Ep. to Rdr. A ij, Who the greater Miracler, Christ or Belial?

† **'miraclist.** *Obs.* [f. MIRACLE *sb.* + -IST.] One who records miracles.

1603 Harsnet *Pop. Impost.* 113 Heare the Miraclist report it, who himselfe was an Actor. *Ibid.* 125 The first honour the Miraclist doth bestow vppon it [the cross] is this: that it serued to discouer Sara to haue a deuil [etc.].

† **mi'racular**, *a.* *Obs.* [f. L. *mīrāculum* MIRACLE *sb.* + -AR.] Of or pertaining to miracle.

1728 North *Mem. Music* (1846) 15, I waive the cure of Saul's frenzy by Musick as miracular. **1812** Coleridge in *Lit. Rem.* (1836) I. 371 A scripture miracle, therefore, must be so defined, as to express, not only its miracular essence, but likewise the condition of its appearing miraculous.

† **mi'raculate**, *v.* *Obs.* [f. L. *mīrāculum* MIRACLE *sb.* + -ATE[3].] *trans.* To produce by means of a miracle.

1633 T. Adams *Exp. 2 Peter* i. 2 The vessels whereinto Christ miraculated wine, were filled up to the brim.

† **miracu'lific**, *a.* *Obs.* [f. L. *mīrāculum* MIRACLE *sb.* + -IFIC.] Performing miracles.

1772 Nugent tr. *Hist. Fr. Gerund* I. 478 Saint Francis Xavier, the divine Heliotrope, or sacred Sun-flower, as he followed, in the course of his miraculific life..that planet [etc.].

† **mi'raculist.** *Obs.* [f. L. *mīrāculum* MIRACLE *sb.* + -IST.] **a.** One who works miracles; in quot. quasi-*adj.* **b.** A believer in miracles.

1666 H. Stubbe (*title*) The miraculist Conformist; or, an Account of several miraculous Cures performed by the Stroking of the Hands of Valentine Greatarik. **1804** Southey in *Ann. Rev.* II. 200 It will be equally intelligible to the reasoner and the miraculist. **1825** Hone *Every-day Bk.* I. 1394 Their biographers were miraculists.

miraculize (mɪ'rækju:laɪz), *v.* [f. L. *mīrāculum* + -IZE.]

1. *trans.* To make miraculous; to consider as miraculous.

1711 Shaftesb. *Charac.* (1737) II. ii. v. 335 You are searching Heaven and Earth for Prodigys, and studying how to miraculize every thing. **1891** Max Müller *Anthrop. Relig.* Pref. (1892) 16 A real historical fact..which from very early days was miraculised and misinterpreted.

2. ? To work upon by miracle. *nonce-use.*

1751 Lavington *Enthus. Meth. & Papists* iii. (1754) 164 Whatever Miracles Mr. Wesley may bring to account; I judge, that I ought to be impartial,..though, in Consequence, I should be miraculized into Dread and Shame.

† **miracu'losity.** *Obs.* [as if f. L. *mīrāculōs-us* (see next) + -ITY.] The quality of being miraculous.

1608 T. James *Apol. Wyclif* 33 He preached against the pretiosity, speciosity, and miraculositie, and sundry other sophistications about images. **1653** Gataker *Vind. Annot. Jer.* 185 They do rather directly infringe and remoove the miraculosity of them.

miraculous (mɪ'rækjʊləs), *a.* Also 6 **maryculousse, miraculus**, 6–7 **myraculous(e.** [ad. F. *miraculeux*, ad. med.L. *mīrāculōs-us*, f. *mīrācul-um* MIRACLE *sb.*: see -OUS.]

1. a. Of the nature of a miracle; produced or effected by miracle; beyond the agency of natural laws; supernatural.

1502 *Ord. Crysten Men* (W. de W. 1506) v. ii. 366 These operacyons dyuynes and marycolousses. **1605** Shaks. *Macb.* iv. iii. 147 A most myraculous worke in this good King. **1651** Hobbes *Leviath.* iii. xxxvi. 231 The miraculous power of foretelling what God would bring to passe. **1671** Milton *Samson* 587 Why else this strength Miraculous yet remaining in those locks? **1704** Nelson *Fest. & Fasts* xxiii. (1739) 287 The miraculous Gifts which the Apostles received. **1856** Max Müller *Chips* (1880) II. xvi. 3 Men who had no sense for the miraculous and supernatural. **1884** F. Temple *Relat. Relig. & Sci.* v. (1885) 156 They profess to have miraculous power.

† **b.** Concerned with miracles. *Obs.*

c **1540** tr. *Pol. Verg. Eng. Hist.* (Camden) I. 176 Ihon, archebusshop of Yorcke... went into Beverlaye,..where at this daye he is remembered with miraculus memorie. **1585** T. Washington tr. *Nicholay's Voy.* iii. xix. 106 Of whom they do say..miraculous fable. **1845** *Encycl. Metrop.* II. 868/1 The testimony by which the miracles of our Lord are accredited is..distinguished, by its strength, from that which supports any other miraculous accounts.

2. *transf.* and *hyperbolically.* (Cf. MIRACLE *sb.* 2.) Resembling a miracle; so extraordinary as to appear supernatural; marvellous; astonishing.

In some of the earlier instances the sense may be directly based on the primary sense of L. *miraculum*, 'object of astonishment'.

1573 (*title*) A letter sent by a Gentleman of England to his frende contayning a confutation of a French mans errors in the report of the myraculous starre now shyninge. **1601** HOLLAND *Pliny* II. 585 The miraculous workes that Q. Marcius Rex performed. **1601** R. JOHNSON *Kingd. & Commw.* (1603) 127 Neither is it miraculous amongst them to see a manne live above an hundred and thirty or forty yeares. **1602** SHAKS. *Ham.* II. ii. 623 For Murther, though it haue no tongue, will speake With most myraculous Organ. **1698** FRYER *Acc. E. India & P.* 75 [A mountain] on whose Summit was a miraculous Piece hewed out of solid Stone. **1710** T. FULLER *Pharm. Extemp.* 150 'Twas communicated to me..as a miraculous Experiment, against bleeding at the Nose. **1742** YOUNG *Nt. Th.* I. 395 Of man's miraculous mistakes, this bears The palm, 'That all men are about to live': For ever on the brink of being born.

b. (See quot. 1965.) *dial.*

1879 F. M. FETHERSTON *Oops & Doons T. Goorkrodger* 27, I say when a man's drunk, *he's miraculus and mad.* **1925** L. P. SMITH *Words & Idioms* 142 *Miraculous* has changed its meaning to 'very drunk'. **1965** *Sc. Nat. Dict.* VI. 286/1 *Miraculous*, in a stupefied or incapable condition, esp. from drink, very intoxicated.

3. a. Of things (formerly also of persons): Having the power to work miracles; wonder-working.

1596 DALRYMPLE tr. *Leslie's Hist. Scot.* VI. 334 In takne of his rare and excellent halynes,..he was miraculous, canonizet and reknet with the haly number. **1610** SHAKS. *Temp.* II. i. 86 His word is more then the miraculous Harpe. **1618** ROWLANDS *Sacred Mem.* 29 He miraculous did heale them all. **1703** MAUNDRELL *Journ. Jerus.* (1732) 132 A certain Sacrilegious Rogue took an opportunity to steal away this Miraculous Picture. **1781** GIBBON *Decl. & F.* xxxi. III. 247 The miraculous tomb of St. Fælix. **1850** MRS. JAMESON *Leg. Monast. Ord.* (1863) 79 The flask is always supposed to contain the miraculous oil which flowed under her shrine. **1872** MORLEY *Voltaire* (1886) 6 Some miraculous soil, from which prodigies and portents spring.

b. In names of plants: **miraculous berry**, in Western tropical Africa, applied by the English residents to the fruit of *Sideroxylon dulcificum*, from its extraordinary power of rendering sour substances intensely sweet (*Treas. Bot.* 1866); **miraculous fruit**, the fruit of *Thaumatococcus* or *Phrynium Danielli*, native of the Soudan (Moloney *Forestry W. Afr.* 1887, p. 428).

†**4.** As *adv.*

1766 *Gentl. Mag.* July 331/1 The scenes,..Shifting backwards and forwards,..And painted miraculous fine.

miraculously (mɪˈrækjʊləslɪ), *adv.* [f. prec. + -LY².] In a miraculous manner; by or as by miracle; in a miraculous degree.

1494 FABYAN *Chron.* VI. cxcvi. 201 Any whyle they were there in great argument for this matyer..a rode there beynge..spake myraculously and said, that Dunstans waye was good and trewe. **1554** *Act 1 & 2 Phil. & Mary* c. 10 §4 He hathe hitherto miraculouslye preserved the Quenes Maᵗⁱᵉ from many greate and imminent perills and dangers. **1596** DALRYMPLE tr. *Leslie's Hist. Scot.* I. 40 Lochbroune in commendatione has the first place, copious in herring miracoulouslie. **1656** WOOD *Life* (O.H.S.) I. 203 *note*, An elegie on the miraculously learned bishop of Armagh [Usher]. **1774** PENNANT *Tour Scotl. in* 1772, 236 Preserved miraculously for two hundred years. **1885** *Manch. Exam.* 6 Apr. 5/2 Savages ..prove almost miraculously quick in hearing and seeing.

miraculousness (mɪˈrækjʊləsnɪs). [f. MIRACULOUS *a.* + -NESS.] The condition, quality, or state of being miraculous.

1587 GOLDING *De Mornay* xxvi. (1592) 410, I will not alledge any miraculousnes. **1676** TOWERSON *Decal.* 297 They could..outshine the laity..by the miraculousness of their works. **1754** SHERLOCK *Disc.* (1759) I. I. 67 The Miraculousness of an Escape adds to the Pleasure and Joy of it. **1873** M. ARNOLD *Lit. & Dogma* (1876) 151 The more the miraculousness of the story deepens,..the more does the very air and aspect of things seem to tell us we are in wonderland.

‖**mirador** (miraˈdor). Also **miradore**. [Sp., f. *mirar* to look.] **a.** A watch-tower. Also *fig.* **b.** A turret or belvedere on the top of a Spanish house.

1670 DRYDEN *Conq. Granada* I. i, Your valiant Son, who had before Gain'd Fame, rode round to ev'ry Mirador. **1797** *Encycl. Brit.* (ed. 3) IV. 9/2 Few are without a mirador or turret for the purpose of commanding a view of the sea. **1832** W. IRVING *Alhambra* I. 112 The delightful belvidere, originally a mirador of the Moorish Sultanas. **1888** *Pall Mall G.* 4 Sept. 14/1 The curious miradores, or turrets on the tops of the houses. **1950** G. BRENAN *Face of Spain* iv. 80 We went into the house. One wing, that of the *mirador* or tower, had been set aside for our books and furniture. **1955** J. THOMAS *No Banners* xxxi. 310 The *miradors* (watch-towers) around Buchenwald were manned by *Wehrmacht* troops. **1971** *Homes & Gardens* Aug. 36/1 Spanish women were generally kept in the background, and watched the world from behind their wooden *miradors.* **1971** *Nat. Geographic* Oct. 547/1, I spent several weeks last spring in this brilliant mirador of capitalist colonialism on the edge of China.

mirage (ˈmɪrɑːʒ, miːˈrɑːʒ). [a. F. *mirage*, f. (*se*) *mirer* to look at oneself in a mirror, to be reflected.] **1. a.** Originally, and still most commonly, that species of optical illusion, common in hot countries, and especially in sandy deserts, which consists in the appearance of a sheet of water at some distance from the spectator, where no water actually exists; now frequently extended to include other forms of optical illusions similarly produced by atmospheric conditions, e.g. the appearance in the sky of a reflected image of a distant object.

[**1803** W. H. WOLLASTON in *Phil. Trans.* XCIII. 1 The phenomenon known to the French by the name of *mirage*, which their army had daily opportunities of seeing, in their march through the deserts of Egypt.] **1837** CARLYLE *Fr. Rev.* (1872) II. I. iv. 29 Mirage, or shadow of still waters painted on the parched ground. **1861** *Court Life at Naples* II. 106 The thirsty traveller in the desert pants to attain the cooling stream in the far distance. Alas! 'tis but a mirage! **1865** LIVINGSTONE *Zambesi* xiii. 270 The mirage lifted them at times half-way to the clouds. **1885** JENNINGS & LOWE in *Expositor* Aug. 130 Isaiah (xxxv. 7) certainly mentions the 'mirage'.

b. *fig.*

1812 SOUTHEY *Ess.* iv. 81 Against this Goliath of the philosophistical Canaanites [Godwin], Mr. Malthus stept forth, at a time when the *mirage* in which Goliath had made his appearance was pretty well dispersed, and had left him in his natural dimensions. **1825** COLERIDGE *Aids Refl.* (1848) I. 130 If the self-examinant will..exchange the safe circle of religion and practical reason for the shifting sand-wastes and *mirages* of speculative theology. **1876** LOWELL *Among my Bks.* Ser. II. 141 They lie beyond the horizon of the every-day world and become visible only when the mirage of fantasy lifts them up.

c. A wave-like appearance of warmed air visible just above ground level. Also *attrib.*

1913 A. G. FULTON *Notes on Rifle Shooting* 18 When mirage can be seen, it provides the best means of estimating allowances for gentle but tricky winds. **1958** J. A. BARLOW *Elem. Rifle Shooting* (ed. 5) iv. 50 The effect of wind on such air disturbance is readily remarked, since the result of a cross wind is to give the impression of the mirage flowing either slowly or swiftly in the same direction as the wind, just like a clear stream of water over a pebbly bed. **1962** *Amer. Speech* XXXVII. 270 *Mirage puddle*, a heat-caused illusion which makes the road appear wet in the distance.

2. *attrib.* and *Comb.*, as **mirage dream**, **-water**; ***mirage-bright***, ***-lifted***, ***-making***, ***-reflected*** adjs.

1924 E. SITWELL *Sleeping Beauty* xvii. 65 Mirage-bright It lies, that dusty gold. **1908** *Daily Chron.* 3 Aug. 3/2 It was like one of those mirage dreams which lure the gambler to his doom. **1874** J. G. WHITTIER *Sea Dream* in *Atlantic Monthly* Aug. 160 And watched the mirage-lifted wall Of coast, across the dreamy bay. **1902** J. H. M. ABBOTT *Tommy Cornstalk* i. 13 And the wide rolling downs quivered and danced with the same beautiful mirage-making islands of kopjes. **1923** R. GRAVES *Whipperginny* 9 Mirage-reflected drink At the clear pool's brink. **1918** E. SITWELL *Clown's Houses* 11 Then, mirage-waters as they flow, Or dream-perfumes, they fade and go.

Hence **miˈrage** *v.*, to affect with mirage; **miˈrageous** *a.*, of or pertaining to a mirage; **miˈrageously** *adv.*, as a mirage; **miˈragy** *a.*, of, pertaining to, or of the nature of a mirage.

1890 GUNTER *Miss Nobody* iii, Atmosphere so clear that thirty miles would look as ten, did not a blazing sun make a heat mist that seems to mirage everything. **1895** W. WRIGHT *Palmyra & Zenobia* xxiii. 259 Magnified by the miragy atmosphere. **1905** *Blackw. Mag.* July 81/2 By the side of a deep mirageous lagoon there sprang up a deep mirageous homestead. *Ibid.*, I pictured her mirageously there on the deep verandah, looking out, waiting for me.

miraged (mɪˈrɑːʒd), *a.* [f. MIRAGE + -ED².] Seen in a mirage; of the nature of a mirage.

1920 *Blackw. Mag.* June 817/2 A dim outline of miraged date palms. **1925** *Chambers's Jrnl.* Aug. 486/2 Framed anew, in mystic space—Miraged dream past all believing—Looms the cradle of a race.

‖**miramolin** (mɪˈræməʊliːn). *Hist.* Also **maramoline**. [Sp., corruption of Arab. *amīru'l mūminīn* 'Commander of the Faithful'.] The European designation in the Middle Ages of the Emperor of Morocco.

1779 *Hist. Mod. Europe* I. 392 He invited the miramolin of Africa into Spain. **1840** BROWNING *Sordello* Wks. 1896 I. 126/2 Saracenic wine The Kaiser quaffs with the Maramoline.

Miranda (mɪˈrændə). *U.S. Law.* [f. the name Ernesto A. *Miranda* (see quot. 1966).] The name given to a set of rules specified by the Supreme Court in the U.S. whereby law enforcement officers are required to apprise a person suspected of a crime of his rights to counsel and his privileges against self-incrimination prior to his being interrogated. Also *attrib.*

[**1966** *Washington Post* 14 June A7/1 Here are excerpts from yesterday's Supreme Court opinion on the admissibility of statements obtained in questioning of a person in police custody, and on the Fifth Amendment protections such a person is to be afforded against self-incrimination. This opinion..encompasses four cases—Ernesto A. Miranda v. the State of Arizona, [etc.].] **1967** *Time* 3 Mar. 49/1 The Supreme Court's famous *Miranda* decision..wrought vast changes in police procedure. *Ibid.* 49/2 *Miranda* does not seem to have helped Miranda and his mates. **1970** W. WAGER *Sledgehammer* xxii. 173 I've got quite a few motions—the complete kit. I'll start with *Miranda* when the trial begins. **1972** J. MILLS *Report to Commissioner* 270 Do you know what a Miranda warning is? **1973** *N.Y. Law Jrnl.* 2 Aug. 13/5 At this point Miller read to Dixon his four required warnings under Miranda.

†**miˈrandous**, *a.* [f. L. *mīrand-us* (gerundive pple. of *mīrārī* to wonder at) + -OUS.] Wonderful.

1652 GAULE *Magastrom.* 47 Because of some mirandous or stupendious things, either effected or foretold, &c.

miration (maɪəˈreɪʃən). *U.S. regional colloq.* [Abbrev. of ADMIRATION.] An expression of admiration, wonder, or surprise; a fuss, to-do. So **miˈrate** *v. intr.*, to feel or express surprise or astonishment.

1893 in H. Wentworth *Amer. Dial. Dict.* (1944) 390/2. **1903** *Dialect Notes* II. 321 *Mirate*, to wonder at; to admire. **1909** *Ibid.* III. 349 *Miration*, an expression of admiration. 'He made a great miration over the baby.' **1926** in J. F. Dobie *Rainbow in Morning* (1965) 82 He may have made *a great miration* over the place, but it's my private opinion that he has something up his sleeve. **1935** Z. N. HURSTON *Mules & Men* (1970) I. vi. 125 Aw, man, you done seen Tookie and her walk too much to be makin' all dat miration over it. **1946** *Publ. Amer. Dial. Soc.* VI. 20 *Miration*, exaggerated and pretentious wonderment, a carrying-on. 'They made a great miration about my killing that squirrel.' **1950** *Ibid.* XIV. 46 *Mirate*, to make a miration over; to express surprise, admiration over a person or thing. **1950** A. LOMAX *Mr. Jelly Roll* (1952) I. 4 This lady displayed me in saloons, setting me on the bar and..making mirations.

mirbane (ˈmɜːbeɪn). [Of obscure origin: F. *mirbane* is in Littré 1885.] ***essence of mirbane***, ***oil of mirbane***, nitrobenzol used in perfumery.

1857 MILLER *Elem. Chem.*, *Org.* ix. (1862) 656 It [Nitrobenzol] has a very sweet taste, and an odour resembling that of bitter almonds, which has led to its use in perfumery under the name of Essence of Mirbane.

mirc, mircken, mirckenes, obs. ff. MURK *a.*, MURKEN, MURKNESS.

mird, *v. Sc.*

1. *intr.* To meddle. Also, to sport amorously.

1614 BP. P. FORBES *To a Recusant* 27 (Jam.) Except that there perhaps he thought some occasion might be catched to calumniat, or that there was ministred to him some matter of mirding. **1768** ROSS *Helenore* (1789) 91 'Tis nae to mird with unco fouk ye see, Nor is the blear drawn easy o'er her ee. *c* **1768** —— in Whitelaw *Bk. Sc. Song* (1875) 360/1 He there wi' Meg was mirdin' seen. **1806** R. JAMIESON *Pop. Ball.* II. 335 Wi' lasses I ne'er mean to mird or to mell.

2. *trans.* To attempt, to venture.

?*c* **1740** J. SKINNER *Christmas Ba'ing* vii. *Misc. Coll. Poetry* (1809) 125 He squeel' to her like a young gyte, But wad na mird to gang Back a' that day. **1863** JANET HAMILTON *Poems & Ess.* 300 But the nameless, though giftit, are caul' i' the yird, Ere a sang or a word i' their praise she wull mird!

mird, variant of MERD *Obs.*, excrement.

Mirdita (ˈmɜːdɪtɑː). Also **Mirditë** (ˈmɜːdɪtə). The name of a region on the river Drin in Albania used *attrib.* and *absol.* to designate the tribal people living there. Also anglicized as **Mirdite** (ˈmɜːdaɪt).

1861 G. FINLAY *Hist. Greek Revolution* I. I. ii. 43 The Mirdites are considered the most warlike of the Christians. **1920** *Q. Rev.* Jan. 65 The late Mirdite Prince, Prenk Bib Doda. **1939** A. TOYNBEE *Study of Hist.* IV. 367 The present Mirdite territory would have been a natural site for the plantation of a Mardaite settlement by a seventh-century Roman statesman. **1954** M. HASLUCK *Unwritten Law in Albania* xv. 154 There had been attacks on the Montenegrins by the Mirditë, which had followed on plenary assemblies of the Mirditë tribes. **1959** *Chambers's Encycl.* I. 220/1 The Mirdita region south of the Black Drin gorge.

mire (maɪə(r)), *sb.*¹ Forms: 4–8 myre, 4–6 myr, 4–5 myere, 4 meore, mir, mure, muyre, 5–7 myer, 5–6 moyre, 6 mier, 4– mire. [ME. *mire*, a. ON. *mýr-r* fem. (mod.Icel. *mýri*, Sw. *myr*, Da. *myre*, *myr*):—OTeut. **miuzjâ*:—**meuzjâ* f. **meus*- (cf. OE. *méos* moss, OHG. *mios*, MHG. *mies*), ablaut-var. of **mus*-: see MOSS.]

1. a. A piece of wet, swampy ground; a boggy place in which one may be engulfed or stick fast. Also in generalized sense, swampy ground, bog.

13.. *Exec. Simon Fraser* in *Pol. Songs* (Camden) 216 Now Kyng Hobbe in the mures ȝongeth. **13..** *Sir Beues* (A.) 2023 And in a mure don him cast. **1387** TREVISA *Higden* (Rolls) VI. 379 It stondeth in water mareys and meores. **1393** LANGL. *P. Pl.* C. IV. 384 Bote stande as a stake þat stykeþ in a muyre. **14..** *Sir Beues* (MS. S.) 638 So he smote on her sweres þat her hedes fel on þe myres. *a* **1400–50** *Alexander* 2986 Sum ware dreuyn doun in dikis sum in depe myrys [*MS. Dubl.* mires]. *c* **1440** *Sir Gowther* 417 (Breul) He toke his speyre..And spard nodur myre ne more; Forthe at þo yatus on hors he went. **1542** UDALL *Erasm. Apoph.* 222 When he had dispeched theim out of the moyre. **1616** SURFL. & MARKH. *Country Farme* 539 Where the ground.. yeeldeth forth such a continuall moisture, that the smallest trampling or treading therupon bringeth it to a verie myre. **1789** BLAKE *Songs Innoc.*, *Little Boy Lost* 7 The mire was deep. **1887** RIDER HAGGARD *She* xxviii, For three whole days through stench and mire..did our bearers struggle along.

transf. **1819** SHELLEY *Mask of Anarchy* x, Over English land he passed, Trampling to a mire of blood The adoring multitude.

b. *fig.* esp. in phrases, e.g.: ***to bring, drag, lay, leave, stick in the mire***; ***to find oneself in the mire***.

c **1380** WYCLIF *Wks.* (1880) 286 Synne..bryngiþ his doere into þe same myre þat he eschewiþ. *c* **1386** CHAUCER *Prol.* 508 He sette nat his benefice to hyre, And leet his sheepe

encombred in the Myre. —— *Manciple's T.* 186 A thousand folk hath rakel Ire ffully fordoon and broght hem in the Mire. **1390** GOWER *Conf.* II. 93 And of his Slouthe he dremeth ofte How that he sticketh in the Myr. *c* **1440** *York Myst.* xxxvii. 256, I schall þe prove be right resoune, þou motes his men in to þe myre. **1535** COVERDALE *Ps.* lxviii. 1 The waters are come in euen vnto my soule. I sticke fast in the depe myre. **1559** *Mirr. Mag., Mortimer* xv, The subtyll quean [i.e. Fortune] behynde me set a trap, wherby to dashe and laye all in the myre. **1607** SHAKS. *Timon* I. ii. 60 Honest water, which nere left man i' th' mire. **1622** BACON in Spedding *Life* (1874) VII. 385 That thrice noble prince.. will help to pull me.. out of the mire of an abject and sordid condition. **1742** YOUNG *Nt. Th.* VI. 216 For sordid lucre plunge we in the mire? **1859** KINGSLEY *Misc.* (1860) I. 338 Drowning in the horrible mire of doubt. **1884** *Pall Mall G.* 9 Sept. 1/2 Sir Edmund Hornby.. when he leaves the general for the particular finds himself in the mire.

2. a. Wet or soft mud, slush, dirt. Often in allusions to 2 Pet. ii. 22.

c **1330** R. BRUNNE *Chron.* (1810) 70 William was oglyft, his helm was fulle of myre. **1471** RIPLEY *Comp. Alch.* IV. v. in Ashm. (1652) 145 Clay and Myer. **1526** *Pilgr. Perf.* (W. de W. 1531) 206 Whiche threwe stones and clottes of myre at hym. **1535** COVERDALE *2 Pet.* ii. 22 The sowe that was waszhed [is turned agayne] vnto hir walowynge in the myre. [So **1611.**] **1667** MILTON *P.L.* IV. 1010 What follie then To boast what Arms can doe, since thine no more Then Heav'n permits, nor mine, though doubld now To trample thee as mire. **1755** YOUNG *Centaur* ii. Wks. 1757 IV. 157 He is an immortal being, that would lose none of its most darling delights, if he were a brute in the mire. **1755** JOHNSON, *Mire*, mud; dirt at the bottom of water. **1837** LYTTON *E. Maltrav.* II The roads were heavy with mire. **1871** R. ELLIS tr. *Catullus* xvii. 9 Headlong into the mire below topsy-turvy to drown him.

b. *fig.* or in figurative context.

13.. *E.E. Allit. P.* B. 1113 Þaȝ þou be man fenny, & al tomarred in myre whyl þou on molde lyuyes. **1765–78** TUCKER *Lt. Nat.* (1834) II. 279 Thus the mire of sordid appetite must be the soil wherein to plant them all. **1882** MRS. LYNN LINTON in *Life* xvii. (1901) 238 Turn where you will you see pain and sacrifice—the root of the lily in the mire.

c. *nonce-uses.* A mass of dirt.

1871 BROWNING *Pr. Hohenst.* 1338 Until a stumble, and the man's one mire! **1877** TENNYSON *Harold* IV. iii, What late guest,.. caked and plaster'd with a hundred mires, Hath stumbled on our cups?

d. Dung. *rare.*

1922 JOYCE *Ulysses* 649 Bloom.. with Stephen passed through the gap of the chains.. and, stepping over a strand of mire, went across towards Gardiner street lower.

3. *attrib.* and *Comb.*, as *mire-fir, -hole*; *mire-bestrowed, -deep, -smirched* adjs.

1834 H. MILLER *Scenes & Leg.* xii. (1857) 187 Helen hastily lighted a bundle of mire-fir. **1835** HALIBURTON *Clockm.* Ser. I. (1837) 73 Over ditches, creeks, mire holes, and flag ponds. **1859** DICKENS *T. Two Cities* III. i, The mire-deep roads. **1908** HARDY *Dynasts* III. VI. viii. 281 Cavalry in the cornfields mire-bestrowed. **1960** S. PLATH *Colossus* 12 Common barnyard sows, Mire-smirched, blowzy.

4. Special comb.: **mire-bumper** *Sc.*, the bittern (Jamieson 1808–25); **mire-crow**, the laughing gull, *Larus ridibundus*; **mire-duck** *Sc.*, the wild duck, *Anas boscas* (Swainson *Prov. Names Birds* 1885); also *U.S.* the common duck (*Cent. Dict.*); **mire-pipes** *dial.*, stockings without feet. Also MIRE-SNIPE.

1678 RAY *Willughby's Ornith.* 347 The Pewet or Black-cap, called in some places the Sea-Crow and Mire-Crow. **1807** J. HALL *Trav. Scotl.* II. 608 Mire-pipes or stockings without feet.

† **mire**, *sb.*[2] *Obs.* Cf. PISMIRE. [ME. *mire* (?:—OE. **míre* wk. fem., found only in Benson's *Anglo-Saxon Dict.*, but possibly genuine) corresponding to MDu. *miere* (Du. *mier*), MLG., mod.LG. *mire* (whence rare mod.HG. *miere*).

If the word is the formal equivalent of Sw. *myra* (OSw. also *myr*), Da. *myre*, the OTeut. type may have been either **meuzjôn-* (= Welsh *mywion*, ants) or *miurjôn*, related by ablaut to ON. *maur-r* (Norw. *maur*, OSw. *mör*) whence the synonymous northern ME. MAUR. Another hypothesis is that the Eng. and LG. forms represent an OTeut. **mîrôn-*, unconnected with the Scandinavian words and not otherwise found exc. perh. in the doubtful Crim-Goth. *miera*; some scholars would refer this to the root **mîg-* (see MIG), so that the etymological notion would be the same as that in the synonymous LG. *mig-ente* (Woeste), *mig-æmeken* (Schambach); if so the compound PISMIRE expresses the idea twice over. Outside Teut. several langs. have names for the ant of similar sound to the Teut. words here mentioned, though the difficulties in the way of admitting etymological connexion have not yet been removed: cf. Zend *maoiri*, Gr. μύρμηξ (and L. *formica* from **mormica*), OSl. *mravija* (Russ. *muraveĭ*), OIrish *moirb*, Welsh *mór*.]

An ant. (Cf. MAUR, PISMIRE.)

c **1220** *Bestiary* 234 De mire is maȝti. *Ibid.* 273 De mire muneð us mete to tilen.

‖ **mire** (mir), *sb.*[3] [F. *mire*, vbl. sb. f. *mirer* to look at, to sight a gun.]

1. Gunnery. ***quoin of mire*** [= F. *coin de mire*]: see quot.

1797 *Encycl. Brit.* (ed. 3) VIII. 233/2 The quoin of mire, which are pieces of wood with a notch on the side to put the fingers on, to draw them back or push them forward when the gunner points his piece.

2. *Astr.* (See quot.)

1885 E. S. HOLDEN in *Sidereal Messenger* (Minn.) III. 301 A mire or meridian mark, eighty feet distant.

† **mire**, *a. Obs.* [f. MIRE *sb.*[1]] Miry.

c **1420** *Pallad. on Husb.* I. 791 Yit if thy garth be mire, a diche may stonde. **1441** in *Plumpton Corr.* (Camden) p. lx, The said misdoers followed, and drove them into a mire more. **1557** TUSSER *100 Points Husb.* xxxviii, When pasture is gone, and the fildes mier and weate. *c* **1656** MILTON *Sonn. to Lawrence*, Now that the Fields are dank, and ways are mire.

mire (maɪə(r)), *v.*[1] Forms: 5–7 myre, 6–7 myer, 6 myar, myir, 4– mire. [f. MIRE *sb.*[1]]

I. *trans.* **1. a.** To plunge or set fast in the mire. (Chiefly in *passive.*) Also *refl.*

1559 *Mirr. Mag., Hen. VI*, xxxiv, Who moyled to remove the rocke out of the mud, Shall myer him selfe. **1574** HELLOWES *Gueuara's Fam. Ep.* (1577) 354 There be so many quagmires, wherein to be myred. **1576** NEWTON *Lemnie's Complex.* (1633) 179 As among Fishes, Eeles, and other slippery Fishes that lye still myering themselves in mudde. *a* **1656** USSHER *Ann.* VI. (1658) 706 The Souldiers of Cæsar and Antonius were mired in the fens of Philippi. **1752** CARTE *Hist. Eng.* III. 207 Some of them were mired in it [*sc.* a slough]. **1832** LYELL *Princ. Geol.* II. 276 Where terrestrial quadrupeds were mired.

b. *fig.* To involve in difficulties. Formerly often, †to discomfit or confound, *esp.* in a dispute.

c **1400** *Beryn* 3388 And nowe we be I-myryd, he letith vs sit aloon. **1560** ROLLAND *Crt. Venus* II. 936 With the missiue that sa oft did him myir. *c* **1570** *Durham Depos.* (Surtees) 264 He.. was so myerd and blinded, by reason of the said stroks. **1577–87** STANYHURST *Chron. Irel.* 86/1 in *Holinshed*, This is a doubtie kind of accusation.. wherein they are stabled and mired at my first deniall. **1688** PRIDEAUX *Valid. Orders Ch. Eng.* 74 You having been mir'd amongst abundance of Absurdities.. already. **1728** EARBERY tr. *Burnet's St. Dead* I. 39 But further we shall be mired in the Difficulties of their Hypothesis. **1778** *Conciliation* 7 Mir'd and flound'ring in th' unbottom'd Pit. **1847** EMERSON *Poems* (1857) 185 Or mired by climate's gross extremes. **1852** J. BRUCE *Biog. Samson* iii. (1854) 70 It [marriage] threatened to mire him for ever in domestic wrangling and broils. **1896** FR. H. BURNETT *Lady of Qual.* xvi, A devil grins at me and plucks me back, and taunts and mires me.

c. Of bogs, mud, etc.: To hold fast, entangle.

1889 T. N. PAGE *In Ole Virginia* (1893) 175 The marsh on either side would have mired a cat. **1892** A. E. LEE *Hist. Columbus* (Ohio) I. 273 The bog.. began to dry up, but not sufficiently to prevent it from hopelessly miring the village cows.

2. To bespatter or soil with mire or filth; to defile. *lit.* and *fig.*

1508 KENNEDIE *Flyting w. Dunbar* 472 And myrit thaym wyth thy mvk to the myd mast. **1530** PALSGR. 636/1, I myar, I beraye with myar. *Je crotte.* **1566** DRANT *Horace, Sat.* I. i. A ii b, Janyvere That myrethe all the costs wyth slete. **1599** SHAKS. *Much Ado* IV. i. 135 Smeer'd thus and mir'd with infamie. **1622** MABBE tr. *Aleman's Guzman d' Alf.* I. 228 Being myred in the Winter with durt. **1751** JOHNSON *Rambler* No. 116 ⁋2, I.. did not come home.. mired and tanned. **1851** BORROW *Lavengro* lxix, I wonder how my horse's knees are; not much hurt, I think—only mired. **1852** M. ARNOLD *Tristram & Iseult* III. 171 Her palfrey's flanks were mired and bathed in sweat. **1868** TENNYSON *Lucretius* 159 Strangers at my hearth Not welcome, harpies miring every dish.

II. *intr.* **3. a.** To sink in the mire, be bogged. Also with *down.*

1607 SHAKS. *Timon* IV. iii. 147 Paint till a horse may myre upon your face. **1762** MILLS *Syst. Pract. Husb.* I. 152 It ploughed very tough, and the cattle mired in some places. **1778** [W. MARSHALL] *Minutes Agric.* 25 Oct. an. 1775 No horse could have dragged his legs after him—he must have mired-down. **1835** H. EVANS *Jrnl.* in *Mississippi Valley Hist. Rev.* (1927) XIV. 195 In crossing some of these creeks some of our horses and pack mules mired down. **1840** W. SEWALL *Diary* (1930) 221 The roads being soft.. I mired down. **1865** VISCT. MILTON & CHEADLE *N. West Passage by Land* 283 We had been delayed and harassed every day by the horses miring. **1941** *Amer. Speech* XVI. 184 *Mire down*, to stick in mud.

b. To defecate. *rare.*

1922 JOYCE *Ulysses* 48 An archway where dogs have mired. *Ibid.* 649 Slowly.. he [*sc.* the horse] mired.

† **mire**, *v.*[2] *Obs.* Also 7 **myre.** [a. F. *mirer* = It. *mirare*, Sp., Pg. *mirar*:—popular L. *mīrāre* to look at, from class. L. *mīrārī* (pre-class. *mīrāre*) to wonder: see MIRACLE *sb.*] *trans.* To look at in a mirror.

c **1430** *Pilgr. Lyf Manhode* I. cv. (1869) 56 A mirrour.. in whiche al the world may mire him wel and considere him. **1640** tr. *Verdere's Rom. Rom.* III. 106 She by the light of two Tapers.. myred her self in his eyes.

† **mire**, *v.*[3] *Obs.* [a. L. *mīrārī*: see MIRACLE.

The dial. *mire* 'to wonder' is perh. aphetic for *admire.*]

intr. To wonder.

1582 STANYHURST *Æneis* IV. (Arb.) 104 Heere but alas he myred what course may be warelye taken.

mire, obs. dat. sing. fem. of MINE *pron.*

mire, obs. form of MAR *v.*; variant of MERI.

mired (maɪəd), *ppl. a.* [f. MIRE *v.*[1] + -ED[1].]

1. a. Stuck fast in the mire, bogged.

1621 BURTON *Anat. Mel.* II. iii. vi. (1624) 285 As a myred horse that struggles at first with all his might and maine to get out. **1857** KINGSLEY *Two Y. Ago* II. 91 Cowards, old Odin held.. sank.. like mired cattle, to all eternity in the unfathomable peat-slime.

b. *transf.* and *fig.* Involved in difficulty, perplexed.

1513 DOUGLAS *Æneis* IX. iii. 106 Rutylianys wolx affrayit wyth myndis myrit.

2. Bespattered with mire; soiled or discoloured with mud or mire.

1586 WARNER *Alb. Eng.* I. iv. (1612) 13 The.. Sunne.. did shine vpon the oosie plashes myerd. **1891** 'Q' *Noughts & Crosses* 207 My mired boots played havoc with the neatly sanded floor. **1897** T. C. DE LEON *Jealous God* v, in *Novelette Trilogy* 127 Lifting tenderly the mired, limp and senseless form of a shriveled old woman, struck down by them [*sc.* 'bus horses].

mire-drum (ˈmaɪədrʌm). *dial.* Forms: 4–8 myre-dromble, 4 mir-drommel, 5 myre-dromylle, 6 myr-drumnyl, 7 mire-drumbel, 7– mire-drum. [ME. *myre dromble*, formed by substitution of MIRE *sb.*[1] for the first portion of some variant of the name for the bittern, which appears in OE. as *ráradumbla, ráredumla.*

The original form and etymology of the word are obscure, but the OE. form (with which cf. *rárian* to ROAR) seems to be more primitive than those in continental Teut., which have evidently been influenced by popular etymology. OHG. had *horotumil* (as if 'mire-tumbler', f. *horo* mire + stem of *tumôn, tûmalôn* to tumble) and *horo tûbil* (as if 'mire-diver'). The MHG. *rôrtumel*, mod.G. *rohrdommel*, MDu. *roesdommer, rosdomp*, mod.Du. *roerdomp*, have the first element assimilated to the word for reed. MHG. and early mod.G. have several forms with inserted *r* in the second element, as *roredrumbel, -drummel, -trummel, rardrümmel*, etc. (see Diefenbach *Gloss.* s.v. *Onocrotalus*); the alteration may be of onomatopœic origin, and perh. arose independently in Ger. and Eng.]

The bittern.

1398 TREVISA *Barth. De P.R.* XII. xxviii. (Tollem. MS.), The mirdrommel is calde onacrotalus. *Ibid.* xxxvi, A myre dromble, þat is a brid of þe marreyes. **1483** *Cath. Angl.* 50 A Buttir, *vbi* myre dromylle. **1500** *Ortus Voc.* in *Cath. Angl.* 50 *note*, Myrdrumnyl or a buture. **1668** CHARLETON *Onomasticon* 103 The white, and spoon-bill'd Heron, or Shoveler, or Mire-drumbel. **1678** RAY *Willughby's Ornith.* 282 The Bittour or Bittern or Mire-drum. **1794** W. HUTCHINSON *Hist. Cumbld.* I. 18/2 The bittern... In the spring it makes a loud bellowing kind of noise. From which it is called in Cumberland Mire-Drum. **1866** *Inverness Courier* 4 Jan., We refer to the bittern of British Zoology, provincially, the bog-bumper and miredrum.

mirepoix (mirpwa). *Cookery.* [f. the name of the Duc de *Mirepoix* (1699–1757), French diplomat and general.] A mixture of diced vegetables used for flavouring or served as a vegetable dish.

1877 E. S. DALLAS *Kettner's Bk. of Table* 65 Set the steak to boil,.. add to it a Mirepoix of red wine, and let it simmer. .. As for taste it is perilous to attempt to improve upon a good Mirepoix. *Ibid.* 304 Mirepoix.. is.. the convenient name for the faggot of vegetables that flavours a stew or sauce. **1877** *Cassell's Dict. Cookery* 425/2 *Mirepoix*, a flavouring for made dishes. **1906** *Mrs. Beeton's Bk. Househ. Managem.* lxi. 1648 A mirepoix is the foundation for flavouring sauces, braised meats, and a number of thick soups. **1936** LUCAS & HUME *Au Petit Cordon Bleu* 173 *Mirepoix*, carrot, onion, celery, turnip, and French beans cut into very small, even dice. **1960** *Guardian* 15 June 16/4 A mirepoix.. is.. another interesting way of serving early vegetables.. cut into dice.

mire sauce, variant of MERESAUCE *Obs.*

ˈmire-snipe. *Sc.* [f. MIRE *sb.*[1] + SNIPE: cf. ON. *mýri-snípa* (Edda Gl.).] The common snipe, *Scolopax gallinago.*

Also in phr. *to catch a mire-snipe*, to fall in the mire; hence *fig.* an accident, mishap (Jam.).

c **1450** HOLLAND *Howlat* 213 The Martoune, the Murcoke, the Myresnype. **1847** *Zoologist* V. 1908 The snipe.. known by the name of the mire-snipe.

miret. *dial.* (Cornwall). The common tern.

1838 J. COUCH *Cornish Fauna* I. 27 Common Tern.. Miret; a name which from this Species is extended indiscriminately to the whole genus.

mirex (ˈmaɪərɛks). orig. *U.S.* [etym. unknown.] An organochlorine insecticide active esp. against ants.

1962 *Bull. Entomol. Soc. Amer.* VIII. 89/1 The Committee on Insecticide Terminology announces the following proposed common names... Mirex. Dodecachloro-octahydro-1,3,4,-methano-2H-cyclobuta(cd)pentalene. **1963** *Jrnl. Econ. Entomol.* LVI. 296/1 The newly developed mirex.. (formerly known as GC 1283) is an analog of Kepone and has exhibited excellent ant poison characteristics with low toxicity to higher animals. **1972** *Nature* 18 Feb. 353/1 'Mirex', the chief weapon used against the fire ant, has been criticized because of its persistence in the environment and its possible toxicity to animals and fish.

mirhe, obs. form of MYRRH.

† **miri.** *Obs. rare.* [a. OF. *mirie, mire*:—L. *medicum.*] A physician.

c **1400** *Rule St. Benet* (Prose) 22 For pi sal sho do als te wyse miri [*L. medicus*] dos, þat wyl hele þe seke. *Ibid.* 23 Þan sal þabbes do als te sleȝe miri [*L. medicus*].

miri, obs. form of MERRY *a.* and *adv.*

miriad, obs. form of MYRIAD.

mirid (ˈmaɪərɪd, ˈmɪrɪd), *sb.* and *a.* [f. mod.L. family name *Miridæ*, f. the generic name *Miris* (J. C. Fabricius *Entomologia Systematica* (1794) IV. 183), f. L. *mīrus* wonderful, extraordinary: see -ID[3].] **A.** *sb.* A leaf bug of the family Miridæ, formerly called Capsidæ (see CAPSID *a.* and *sb.*[1]),

which includes a large number of insects that live on the sap of plants, often causing damage to the plants affected. **B.** *adj.* Of or pertaining to an insect of this kind.

1941 *Bull. Illinois Nat. Hist. Survey* XXII. 2/1 The eggs of most mirids hatch early in the season. *Ibid.* 3/2 A majority of mirid species produce only one generation per year. **1957** RICHARDS & DAVIES *Imms's Textbk. Entomol.* (ed. 9) III. 461 Other Mirids do considerable damage to cultivated plants. **1962** METCALF & FLINT *Destructive & Useful Insects* (ed. 4) vi. 225 Anyone who sits down in a grassy, weedy spot in early summer..can scarcely fail to make the acquaintance of some of the hundreds of kinds of mirids that crawl about over the vegetation and feed on its sap. **1972** SWAN & PAPP *Common Insects N. Amer.* xii. 117 The mirids comprise a fairly large family commonly called plant bugs or leaf bugs.

†**mi'ridical,** *a. Obs.*—⁰ In 7 *erron.* **miradical.** [f. late L. *mīridic-us* (Quicherat), f. *mīr-us* wonderful + *dic-* wk. stem of *dīcĕre* to say: see -AL¹.] Speaking wonderful things. Hence †**mi'ridically** *adv.*

1652 GAULE *Magastrom.* 215 Those things that are miridically done by the Devill and magicians. **1656** BLOUNT *Glossogr.*, *Miradical* [sic], that speaks strange things.

mirie, obs. form of MERRY.

mirific (maɪ'rɪfɪk), *a. rare.* Forms: 5 **myrifyke, myryfyke,** 8 **mirifick,** 7- **mirific.** [a. F. *mirifique*, ad. L. *mīrificus*, f. *mīrus* wonderful + *-ficus* (see -FIC). Cf. It., Pg. *mirifico*, Sp. *mirífico*.] Doing wonders; exciting wonder or astonishment; marvellous. Now chiefly *jocular*.

1490 CAXTON *Eneydos* vi. 24 Hiely decored by merueyllous artes and myryfyke. *a* **1693** *Urquhart's Rabelais* III. iv. 45 In..very few years you should be sure to see the sancts..more numerous, wonder-working, and mirifick. **1727** BAILEY vol. II, *Mirifick.* **1832** *Examiner* 291/2 They have accomplished something mirific. **1848** THACKERAY *Bk. Snobs* xxxi, That man educates a mirific family. **1853** *Blackw. Mag.* LXXIII. 635 The mirific diminishment of the contents of the brandy-bottle.

†**mi'rifical,** *a. Obs.* Also 7 **mirificall.** [Formed as prec. + -AL¹.] = prec.

1603 HOLLAND *Plutarch's Mor.* 1196 That yeeld sweet odors most mirificall. **1656** BLOUNT *Glossogr.*, *Mirifical* ..marvellous. **1829** T. L. PEACOCK *Misfort. Elphin* 173 Merry England..was..a phrase which must be a mirifical puzzle to any one.

mirifically (maɪ'rɪfɪkəlɪ), *adv.* [f. MIRIFICAL *a.* + -LY².] So as to excite wonder or admiration; wonderfully, superbly.

1922 W. J. LOCKE *Tale of Triona* v. 49 Into the lounge filled with mirifically vestured fellow-creatures.

†**mi'rificence.** *Obs.*—⁰ [ad. late L. *mīrificentia*, f. *mīrificus* (cf. MAGNIFICENCE).] The attribute of doing wonders.

1727 BAILEY vol. II, *Mirificence*, doing wonders.

†**mi'rificent,** *a. Obs. rare.* [f. L. *mīrificent-*, altered stem (cf. MAGNIFICENT) of *mirific-us* MIRIFIC.] Doing wonders; wonder-working.

1664 H. MORE *Myst. Iniq.* xviii. 66 The more general Notion of Enchantment, Agrippa defines..to be nothing but The conveiance of a certain mirificent power into the thing enchanted by virtue of the words and breath of the Enchanter.

†**mi'rificously,** *adv. Obs.* [f. L. *mīrific-us* MIRIFIC *a.* + -OUS + -LY².] Wonderfully.

1657 TOMLINSON *Renou's Disp.* 602 It mirificously conduces to the freeing the liver.

mirily, mirines, obs. ff. MERRILY, MERRINESS.

miriness ('maɪərɪnɪs). Also 6 **myrinesse,** 7 **mieriness.** [f. MIRY *a.* + -NESS.] Miry condition or quality.

a **1608** SIR F. VERE *Comm.* (1657) 21 A dike or causey,.. most used in winter by reason of the lownesse and myrinesse of the country. **1649** BLITHE *Eng. Improv. Impr.* (1653) 12 Another cause of Barrenness is Bogginess or Mieriness. **1755** JOHNSON, *Miriness*, dirtiness, fullness of mire.

mirinesse, obs. form of MERRINESS.

miring ('maɪərɪŋ), *vbl. sb.* Also 6 **mireing.** [f. MIRE *v.* + -ING¹.]

1. The state of becoming entangled in a mire.

1556 *Act 8 Eliz.* c. 8 §1 Wᵗʰout daunger and peryll of the mireyng drowning and perishing of the same [horses]. **1657** R. LIGON *Barbadoes* (1673) 29 Because their Cattle shall not be in danger of miring or drowning. **1888** *Century Mag.* Mar. 657/2 As long as everything is frozen solid there is..no danger from miring.

2. The action of covering with mire; a bespattering.

1641 'SMECTYMNUUS' *Answ.* (1653) Post. 89 The tearing of Hoods and Cowles, the miring of Copes,..in the scuffle.

mirinkaleon: see MYRMELEON.

†'**mirish,** *a. Obs.* Also 8 **myrish.** [f. MIRE *sb.*¹ + -ISH.] Of the nature of mire; miry; foul.

1630 J. TAYLOR (Water P.) *To Honour of O'Toole* Wks. II. 17/2 Thou Hast made them skip o'r bogs and quagmires mirish. **1719** D'URFEY *Pills* (1872) IV. 326 In that same myrish, bloody Fen.

mirites, obs. variant of MIRRITE.

mirk, mirky, etc., var. forms of MURK, etc.

mirled (mɜːld), *ppl. a. Sc.* [var. of MARLED *ppl. a.*²] Speckled, spotted.

1885 *Times* 4 June 10/6 Exhibition of Collies... A curiously marked blue mirled and white specimen.

mirligoes ('mɛrlɪgoz), *sb. pl. Sc.* Also **merligoes, merrily-goes, mirlegoes, mirlygoes.** [Cf. Sc. dial. *mirl* to turn round, to be giddy.] Dizziness, vertigo; *esp.* in the phrase ***in the mirligoes***: in a state of dizziness.

1773 FERGUSSON *Ghaists* 46 Or else some kittle cantrip thrown, I ween, Has bound in mirlygoes my ain twa ein. **1816** SCOTT *Old Mort.* xxviii, My head's sae dizzy with the mirligoes. **1893** J. A. BARRY *S. Brown's Bunyip*, etc. 99 They havena muckle likin' for sic a med'cin'. It gives them the mirligoes.

‖**mirliton** ('mɜːlɪtɒn). *Mus.* Also *erron.* **mirloton.** [F. *mirliton* reed pipe; of onomatopœic origin (Littré).] A toy instrument resembling a kazoo.

1819 MOORE *Mem.* (1853) III. 9 The crowd of dancers, mountebanks, mirloton players [etc.]. **1865** M. EYRE *Lady's Walks S. of France* xx. 217 In returning home the pilgrims unite in bands, singing;..while others, provided with *mirlitons*, play the wildest accompaniments. **1894** G. DU MAURIER *Trilby* I. II. 155 Taffy and Jeannot and Little Billie made the necessary music on their *mirlitons*. **1895** in *Funk's Stand. Dict.* **1938** [see KAZOO]. **1970** P. OLIVER *Savannah Syncopators* 109 *Kazoo*, submarine-shaped tube mirliton, played in blues bands.

mirly, variant of MARLY *a.*² *Sc.*

†**mirmillon.** *Obs. rare*—⁰. [ad. L. *mirmillōnem.*] A kind of gladiator.

1656 BLOUNT *Glossogr.*, *Mirmillon.*

mirmydan, -den, -don, obs. ff. MYRMIDON.

mirnyong, var. MIRRNYONG.

miro ('mɪərəʊ), *sb.*¹ *New Zealand.* [Maori.] A large, evergreen tree, *Podocarpus ferrugineus*, of the family Taxaceæ, native to New Zealand, or the timber produced by it. Also ***miro-tree***.

1832 G. BENNETT in *London Med. Gaz.* X. 793/1 The Miro tree..is named Miro by the natives of New Zealand. **1835** W. YATE *Acc. N. Zealand* (ed. 2) 45 Miro..grows to the height of from forty to sixty feet, with a diameter of not more than thirty inches. **1875** LASLETT *Timber* 308 The miro-tree is found in slightly elevated situations in many of the forests in New Zealand. **1905** W. B. *Where White Man Treads* 19 When the red miro berries were ripe..the Maori smiled. *Ibid.*, On the ranges of the interior there are certain waterless districts, where the miro is abundant. **1926** H. GUTHRIE-SMITH *Tutira* (ed. 2) 99 Black pine, miro. **1966** *Encycl. N.Z.* II. 568/2 Miro was known and cherished by the Maoris because of its fleshy covered fruit, about an inch long, on which the native pigeon feeds... Miro is found in lowland forests throughout North, South, and Stewart Islands. **1971** *Daily Tel.* 23 Dec. 3/7 [On Pitcairn Island] Henry may give Warren..a block of scarce miro wood for carving.

miro ('mɪərəʊ), *sb.*² Also **miro-miro,** 9 **mirro mirro.** [Maori, adopted as a generic name by R. P. Lesson in *Traité d'Ornithologie* (1831) 389.] Either of two New Zealand flycatchers of the genus *Petroica*, the black-and-white tomtit, *P. macrocephala*, or the greyish-brown New Zealand robin, *P.* (formerly *Miro*) *australis*.

1843 J. E. GRAY in E. Dieffenbach *Trav. N.Z.* II. 191 *Miro Forsterorum*..Turdus minutus..Mirro mirro of the natives of Queen Charlotte's Sound. **1848** R. TAYLOR *Leaf from Nat. Hist. N.Z.* 9/1 *Miromiro*, small land bird, very tame; can be caught by the hand. **1879** *Trans. N.Z. Inst.* XII. 119 The miro-miro is the little Petroica toitoi, which runs up and down trees peering for minute insects in the cavities in the bark. **1930** W. R. B. OLIVER *N.Z. Birds* 458 *Genus Petroica*..Distinguished from Miro by its smaller size. *Ibid.* 460 White-breasted Tit. Miromiro. **1966** R. A. FALLA et al. *Field Guide to Birds N.Z.* 200 Tomtit... Other names: Miromiro (North Island).

mirobalan(e, -bolan, obs. ff. MYROBALAN.

miroir, obs. form of MIRROR *sb.*

mirondones, obs. pl. of MYRMIDON.

‖**miroton** (mirotɔ̃). *Cookery.* [Fr.] (See quots.)

1725 BRADLEY *Fam. Dict.*, *Miroton*, a culinary Term, being a Kind of Farce, and usually serv'd up for a Side dish, and may be made several Ways. **1877** *Cassell's Dict. Cookery* 1177 *Miroton*, small thin slices of meat about as large as a crown piece made into ragoûts of various kinds, and dished up in a circular form.

mirour, obs. form of MIRROR *sb.*

†**mirourer.** *Obs.* Also **mirorer.** [f. *mirour* MIRROR *sb.* + -ER².] A maker of or dealer in mirrors.

1309 in *Cal. Let. Bk. D. Lond.* (1902) 38 [25 Nov. 1309 Roger de Elvedene] mirourer [admitted]. **1320** *Rolls of Parlt.* I. 382/2 Ad Petitionem Johannis le Mirorer.

mirr, mirra, obs. ff. MYRRH.

mirre, obs. f. MERRY.

mirrer, obs. f. MIRROR.

mirrette, obs. f. MERIT.

mirrh(e, obs. ff. MYRRH.

mirrines(se, obs. forms of MERRINESS.

mirriounis, obs. Sc. pl. form of MORION.

‖**mirrnyong** ('mɜːnjɒŋ). *Austral.* Also **mirnyong.** [Native word.] A mound of shells, ashes, and other debris accumulated in a place used for cooking by Australian Aborigines; an Aboriginal kitchen-midden.

1878 R. B. SMYTH *Aborigines Victoria* I. 238 (*heading*) Mirrnyongs, shell-mounds, and stone-shelters. *Ibid.* 239 The sites for *Mirrn-yong* heaps appear to have been chosen generally in localities near water. **1888** R. M. JOHNSTON *Syst. Acct. Geol. Tasmania* 337 (Morris), With the exception of their rude inconspicuous flints, and the accumulated remains of their feasts in the 'mirnyongs', or native shell-mounds, along our coasts,..we have no other visible evidence of their former existence. **1896** A. H. KEANE *Ethnol.* v. 94 Australia, numerous *mirrnyongs* (ash-heaps, shell-mounds, &c.) mainly confined to the eastern and southern regions. **1964** *Mod. Encycl. Austral. & N.Z.* 666/1 *Mirrnyong Heaps or Kitchen Middens*, aboriginal cooking areas which have grown through thousands of years of use. Consist of ashes, shells and other debris; some have an area of 5,000 sq ft and are 10 ft high. Mainly found in coastal and Murray Valley areas. **1965** *Austral. Encycl.* I. 35/1 Continued use of the same cooking-place builds up enormous deposits of ashes, such as those in Riverina and Murray River districts of New South Wales, Victoria and South Australia, where the ovens or Mirrnyong heaps are up to 125 feet long, 50 feet wide, and 12 feet thick.

mirr-n'yong, var. MURRNONG.

mirrold, obs. form of MIRROR *sb.*

mirror ('mɪrə(r)), *sb.* Forms: 4-8 **mirrour(e,** 4-7 **mirour,** 4-6 **myrour(e, myrrour(e,** 4-5 **meror, merour(e,** 4 **merrour(e, merrur, mirrur, mirur,** 5 **mero, merowe, merowr, merrowre, merur(e, murrour, myrowre, myrrore, myrrow,** 6-8 **miroir,** 6 **miror, mirrhour, mirrold,** *Sc.* **murrur,** 7-8 **mirroir, myrhorr,** 6- **mirror.** [ME. *mirour*, a. OF. *mirour, mireor, mireoir*, earlier (11th c., Rashi) *miradoir* (mod.F. *miroir*):—popular L. **mīrātōrium*, f. **mīrāre* to look at (class. L. *mīrārī* to wonder, admire, whence MIRACLE): see -ORY. Pr. had *mirador-s*, and It. *miratore, miradore*, in the same sense (both rare); Sp., Pg. *mirador* has the meaning of watch-tower.

The Eng. spelling *mir(r)oir*, almost confined to the 17th c., is due to the influence of mod.Fr.]

I. Literally (or with obvious metaphor).

1. a. A polished surface which reflects images of objects, formerly made of metal, now ordinarily of glass coated with amalgam; a looking-glass. Also *rarely*, the coated glass of which mirrors are made.

c **1225** *Dict. J. de Garlande* in Wright *Voc.* 123 Willelmus, vicinus noster, habet..specula (myrrys [? *read* myrurys]). *c* **1315** SHOREHAM 7 *Sacraments* 727 To-slyfte A[l þy] myrour þou myȝt fol wel, Bote nauȝt þe ymage schifte. **1413** *Pilgr. Sowle* (Caxton 1483) IV. xxvi. 71 In a ful lytel myrroure thou myght see as grete an ymage as in another that is double more. **1483** *Cath. Angl.* 236 To loke in Merowe, *speculari.* **1590** SPENSER *F.Q.* I. iv. 10 And in her hand she held a mirrhour bright. **1601** HOLLAND *Pliny* II. 478 No plates might be driuen by the hammer, nor mirroirs made, but of the best and purest siluer. **1634** SIR T. HERBERT *Trav.* 59 Stones..so well polisht, that they equall for brightnesse a steele mirrour. **1766** FORDYCE *Serm. Yng. Wom.* (1767) II. viii. 43 Next morning the mirror is consulted again. **1848** DICKENS *Dombey* xxiii, Mirrors were dim as with the breath of years. **1898** G. B. SHAW *Plays* II. *Candida* 81 A varnished wooden mantelpiece, with neatly moulded shelves, tiny bits of mirror let into the panels.

b. *fig.*

c **1374** CHAUCER *Troylus* I. 365 Thus gan he make a myrrour of his mynde. **1593** B. BARNES *Parthenophil* Madr. xi. 4 in Arb. *Garner* V. 370 Thine Eyes, mine heaven!.. made mine eyes dim mirrolds of unrest. **1602** SHAKS. *Ham.* III. ii. 24 Playing..whose end..is, to hold as 'twer the Mirrour up to Nature. *a* **1633** G. HERBERT *Jacula Prud.* 296 The best mirrour is an old friend. **1677** GALE *Crt. Gentiles* II. IV. 94 The Divine Law is called perfect, as it is an absolute perfect Miroir or Glasse. **1784** COWPER *Task* II. 291 The fleeting images that fill The mirror of the mind. **1881** GARDINER & MULLINGER *Stud. Eng. Hist.* I. ix. 174 Such books serve to hold up the mirror to the time.

c. *transf.* Applied to water (chiefly *poet.*).

1595 SPENSER *Epithal.* 63 And in his waters, which your mirror make, Behold your faces. **1637** HEYWOOD *Dialogues* Wks. 1874 VI. 258 Their chrystall waves are Myrrhors. **1667** MILTON *P.L.* IV. 263 A Lake, That to the fringed Bank ..Her chrystall mirror holds. **1713** ADDISON *Cato* I. vi, So the pure limpid stream..Works itself clear, and as it runs, refines; Till, by degrees, the floating mirror shines. **1866** G. MACDONALD *Ann. Q. Neighb.* xiii, The stars above shining as clear below in the mirror of the all but motionless water.

2. *spec.* **a.** A glass or crystal used in magic art.

13.. *Seuyn Sag.* (W.) 2009 Virgil made another ymage, That held a mirour in his hond, And oversegth all that lond. *c* **1386** CHAUCER *Sqr.'s T.* 226 Alocen and Vitulon And Aristotle that writen in hir lyues Of queynte Mirours and of prospectiues. **1481** CAXTON *Reynard* xxxii. (Arb.) 84 Now ye shal here of the mirrour. The glas that stode theron was of suche vertu, that [etc.]. **1533** GAU *Richt Vay* 12 Alsua thay that wsis corsis, christal, murrur, bukis, vordis and.. coniuracione to find hwid hurdis in the ȝeird [etc.]. **1859** GEO. ELIOT *A. Bede* i, With a single drop of ink for a mirror,

the Egyptian sorcerer undertakes to reveal . . far-reaching visions of the past.

†**b.** A small glass formerly worn in the hat by men and at the girdle by women. *Obs.*

1599 B. JONSON *Cynthia's Rev.* II. i, Call for your casting-bottle, and place your mirrour in your hat.

3. *Optics.* A polished surface, either *plane, convex*, or *concave*, that reflects rays of light; a speculum. ***burning mirror***: a concave mirror which, by concentrating the reflected rays of the sun at a focus, causes them to set fire to objects.

1762 H. WALPOLE *Vertue's Anecd. Paint.* (1765) I. vi. 125 Among the stores of old pictures at Somerset-house, was one . . representing the head of Edward VI. to be discerned only by the reflection of a cylindric mirrour. **1768–74** TUCKER *Lt. Nat.* (1834) II. 675 A convex mirror strengthens the colours and takes off the coarseness of objects by contracting them. **1822** IMISON *Sci. & Art* I. 262 Plane mirrors are those whose surfaces are perfect planes, and whose section is a straight line. Such are vulgarly called looking-glasses. **1839** G. BIRD *Nat. Philos.* 301 The point . . being consequently equal to half the radius of the concavity of the mirror.

II. Figurative uses.

4. a. That which gives a faithful reflection or true description of anything. Cf. LOOKING-GLASS 1 b.

Formerly common in titles of books, after med.L. *speculum*.

c **1385** CHAUCER *L.G.W.* Prol. 307 What [seith] vincent in his estoryal myrour. *c* **1440** *Eng. Conq. Irel.* 117 That same boke . . was . . as merrowre of al his dedys. **1563** SACKVILLE *Induct. Mirr. Mag.* vii, A Mirour well it might bee calde. **1647** CLARENDON *Hist. Reb.* I. §94 It seemed the more reasonable to enlarge upon the nature and character and fortune of the duke; as being the best mirroir to discern . . the spirit of that age. **1751** JOHNSON *Rambler* No. 156 ¶ 10 The stage, which pretends only to be the mirrour of life. **1874** SAYCE *Compar. Philol.* v. 176 Language is the mirror of society, and accordingly will reflect every social change.

b. Used of a person. *poet.*

1563 SACKVILLE *Induct. Mirr. Mag.* xvii, Those Whom Fortune in this maze of miserie Of wretched chaunce most wofull myrrours chose. **1594** SHAKS. *Rich. III*, II. ii. 51 But now two Mirrors of his Princely semblance, Are crack'd in pieces by malignant death. *c* **1637** WALLER *On Ben Jonson* 1 Mirrour of Poets, Mirrour of our Age.

5. a. That which exhibits something to be imitated; a pattern; an exemplar. Now *rare*.

a **1300** *Cursor M.* 23867 Cristen folk . ., In eldrin men ur mirur se Quat for to folu, quat for to fle. *c* **1386** CHAUCER *Frankl. T.* 726 O Teuta queene thy wyfly chastitee To alle wyues may a Mirour bee. *c* **1440** *York Myst.* xxi. 93 For men schall me þer myrroure make. **1568** GRAFTON *Chron.* II. 81 Wherefore this Princes actes may be a myrour unto all Princes. **1683** *Brit. Spec.* 18 Thou art a Mirror to all Christian Kingdoms. **1765** COWPER *Lett.* 24 June, A servant . . who is the very mirror of fidelity and affection for his master. **1801** STRUTT *Sports & Past.* Introd. 7 Sir Tristram, a fictitious character held forth as the mirror of chivalry.

†**b.** Hence of persons: A model of excellence; a paragon. *Obs.*

c **1369** CHAUCER *Dethe Blaunche* 974 She wolde haue be at the beste A chefe myrrour of al the feste. **1599** SHAKS. *Hen. V*, II. Prol. 6 They sell the Pasture now, to buy the Horse; Following the Mirror of all Christian Kings. **1615** BRATHWAIT *Strappado* (1878) 71 Whilest thy renowme great mirrour of the North, Showne in our time, wants one to set it foorth. **1785** BURKE *Sp. Nabob of Arcot's Debts* Wks. 1842 I. 343 Our mirror of ministers of finance did not think this enough for the services of such a friend as Benfield.

†**c.** That which reflects something to be avoided; a warning. *Obs. rare.*

1377 LANGL. *P. Pl.* B. XVI. 156 þow shalt be myroure to manye men to deceyue. **1475** *Bk. Noblesse* (Roxb.) 39 But alway [they] brake the saide trewes . . as it shewethe openly, and may be a mirroure for ever to alle cristen princes to mystrust any trewes taking by youre saide adversarie or his allies and subjectis. **1633** T. STAFFORD *Pac. Hib.* II. iii. 145 He might for ever bee poynted at as an exemplary mirror for all insolent Traytors.

III. 6. Applied to various objects resembling a mirror in shape or in lustre.

a. *Arch.* A small oval ornament.

1847–54 WEBSTER, *Mirror*, in architecture, a small oval ornament cut into deep moldings, and separated by wreaths of flowers. **1901** STURGIS *Dict. Archit. & Build.*, *Mirror*, a panel surrounded by a moulded or otherwise ornamented frame and suggesting the idea of a mirror. Practically the same as a Cartouche, Rondel or Medallion, but the mirror in this sense is usually a detached panel.

b. *Ornith.* A bright patch of colour on the wings of ducks and other birds; = SPECULUM.

1903 *Blackw. Mag.* Mar. 359/2 The black tips of the long wings waving in the wind, showing the large white 'mirrors' on the first three feathers distinctly.

c. Short for *mirror cloth* (see 7 b).

1899 *Daily News* 14 Jan. 2/4 So glossy is the cloth . . that it is now called 'mirror', in allusion to the sheen of its highly-polished surface.

IV. 7. *attrib.* and *Comb.*

a. simple attrib., objective, etc., as ***mirror-bearer, -gazer, -hall, -light, -scroll, -silverer, -silvering, -stand, -trick***; ***-mirror-topped*** adj.

Also in names of scientific instruments in which the index is a beam of light reflected from a mirror, as in ***mirror barometer, galvanometer, thermometer***.

1885 PATER *Marius* I. vi, Placed in their rear were the *mirror-bearers of the goddess. **1898** LODGE in *Daily News* 7 Jan. 2/4 Such an instrument was the beautiful '*mirror-galvanometer' of Lord Kelvin. **1937** G. BARKER *Calamiterror* 9 The *mirror-gazer self-betrayed. **1923** BLUNDEN *To Nature* 10 From the *mirror-lights on the dressing table. **1970** R. LOWELL *Notebk.* 207 Your wall-mirror in a mat of plateglass sapphire, *mirror-scroll and claspleaves, holds our faces. **1829** SIR R. CHRISTISON *Treat. Poisons* xiii. (1832) 375 A somewhat later account of the disease by Dr. Bateman, as he observed it in *mirror-silverers. **1897** *Allbutt's Syst. Med.* II. 931 In *mirror-silvering it [mercury] was also employed. **1817** J. CONSTABLE *Let.* 10 July in *Corr.* (1964) II. 228, I am glad I have not made a purchase of the *mirror stand (called a Canterbury). **1960** H. HAYWARD *Antique Coll.* 187/1 *Mirror-stand*, an adjustable mirror mounted on a shaft and tripod base, resembling a pole-screen; popular at the end of the 18th cent. **1949** D. SMITH *I capture Castle* III. xiv. 260 A *mirror-topped table. **1950** M. ALLINGHAM *Mr. Campion & Others* xiii. 270 He remembered Geoffrey's face at the other end of the mirror-topped table. **1940** W. FAULKNER *Hamlet* IV. i. 247 Something to be repudiated with contempt, like a *mirror trick.

b. similative, as ***mirror-eye, -faculty, finish, -floor, -sheen, surface***; ***mirror-bright, -dark, -flat, -like, -polished, -resembling, -scaled*** adjs. Also in the designations of textile fabrics with lustrous surface, as ***mirror moiré, velvet***; and of colours, as ***mirror-black, -grey, -pink*** adjs.

1890 *Century Dict.*, **Mirror-black*, an epithet applied to any ceramic ware having a lustrous black glaze. **1900** *Daily News* 7 Aug. 3/5 There is an amount of steel and brass work to be kept *mirror-bright. *a* **1955** W. STEVENS *Opus Posthumous* (1957) 51 Your gowns . . came shining as things come That enter day from night, came *mirror-dark. **1923** D. H. LAWRENCE *Birds, Beasts & Flowers* 98 The red-gold *mirror-eye [of a fish] stares and dies. **1951** KOESTLER *Age of Longing* II. viii. 306 She felt herself reflected in their watchful mirror-eyes, and was forced to see herself as they saw her. **1711** SHAFTESB. *Charac.* (1737) I. 199 Besides the difficulty of the manner it-self, and that *mirrour-faculty, . . it proves also . . a kind of mirrour . . to the age. **1897** *Sears, Roebuck Catal.* 112/3 Heavy nickel plated and polished to a *mirror finish. **1926–7** *Army & Navy Stores Catal.* 199/3 Polishing wool . . gives to silver, electro-plate, gold, etc., that beautiful 'mirror' finish of newly manufactured articles. **1971** *Engineering* Apr. 118/2 A second tool produces the final truly 'mirror' finish. **1923** D. H. LAWRENCE *Birds, Beasts & Flowers* 98 This red-gold, water-precious *mirror-flat bright eye. *a* **1849** J. C. MANGAN *Poems* (1859) 73 On the *mirror-floor of Ocean's wave. **1887** *Daily News* 19 May 5/6 A *mirror-grey satin dress. **1772** MASON *Eng. Garden* I. 23 Whose mighty mind . . *mirror-like Receiv'd, and to mankind with ray reflex The sov'reign Planter's primal work display'd. **1832** MISS MITFORD *Village* Ser. v. 151 Two narrow shady lanes cross each other, leaving just room enough . . for a clear mirror-like pond. **1894** *Westm. Gaz.* 20 Sept. 3/3 Another splendid gown . . was of '*mirror moiré'. **1936** J. STEINBECK *In Dubious Battle* iv. 29 One line of worn and *mirror-polished rails extended ahead. **1937** *Discovery* Feb. 57/1 Pickle mirror-polished silver sheet in sulphuric acid. **1927** W. B. YEATS *October Blast* 9 All those things whereof Man makes a superhuman *Mirror-resembling dream. **1934** —— *King of Gt. Clock Tower* 40 The *mirror scalèd serpent is multiplicity. **1960** S. PLATH *Colossus* 22 River lapsing Black beneath bland *mirror-sheen. **1874** FARRAR *Christ* (1894) 161 The *mirror surface of their lake. **1893** *Daily News* 27 Nov. 6/1 Vivid tones of pink and red are seen in *mirror velvets.

c. Special comb.: **mirror carp**, the looking-glass carp, *Cyprinus carpio*; **mirror drum**, a scanning device, used in early television transmitters and receivers, which consists of a rotating drum with its curved surface covered with a number of equally spaced plane mirrors, there being as many mirrors as there are scanning lines in the picture; **mirror embroidery** = *mirror-work*; **mirror-fashion** *adv.*, in the manner of mirror-writing; **mirror fugue** *Mus.*, a fugue that can be played in a reversed or inverted manner, as if read in a mirror placed at the end of or underneath the music; **mirror-glass**, glass used in a mirror; also, a mirror (in quot. *fig.*); also *attrib.*; **mirror image**, something that resembles an image in a mirror in having left and right interchanged or its constituent parts arranged in reverse order (but being otherwise identical); also *transf.* and *fig.*; **mirror machine** *Nuclear Physics*, a linear device in which plasma is confined by means of magnetic mirrors; **mirror nucleus** *Nuclear Physics*, a nuclide having as many neutrons as another nuclide (of the same atomic number) has protons, and as many protons as the other has neutrons; also (more correctly) **mirror nuclide**; **mirror-painting** (see quot. 1960); also, the process of such painting; **mirror-picture** = *mirror-painting*; also, a picture as seen in a mirror; **mirror-plate**, a plate of glass suitable for a mirror; also, a type of metal plate used for fixing two things together; **mirror ray**, the spotted ray, *Raia maculata*; **mirror room**, a room with mirrors set into the walls; **mirror scale**, a scale provided with an adjacent mirror so that parallax errors may be avoided when taking readings; **mirror-script** = *mirror-writing*; †**mirror-stone** = MUSCOVITE; **mirror-wall**, a wall entirely covered with a mirror; **mirror-work**, small rounds of mirror appliquéd on fabric; **mirror-writer**, one who practises *mirror-writing*; hence (as a back-formation) **mirror-write** *v.*; **mirror-writing**, writing which appears as though viewed in a mirror, reversed writing (a characteristic of aphasia).

1880–4 F. DAY *Brit. Fishes* II. 159 The *mirror-carp, or carp king, *Cyprinus rex cyprinorum*, *C. specularis*, *C. macrolepidotus*. **1927** *Wireless World* 20 Apr. 480/2 As the *mirror drum revolves, these seven beams trace seven lines at once on the screen, and then pass over another adjacent track of seven lines until the entire screen has been covered. **1935** M. G. SCROGGIE *Television* iii. 22 The scanner which has been used for the last few years to transmit the B.B.C. programmes by the Baird low-definition system, and also in a large proportion of the receivers, is the mirror drum. **1968** *Brit. Med. Bull.* XXIV. 261/2 The National Biomedical Research Corporation is developing a mirror-drum scanner, of a type pioneered at Harwell. **1967** E. SHORT *Embroidery & Fabric Collage* i. 17 (*caption*) Indian 'Shisha' or *mirror embroidery. **1899** *Allbutt's Syst. Med.* VIII. 25 A young lady . . who wrote more fluently '*mirror' fashion with the left hand. **1931** D. F. TOVEY *Compan. to 'Art of Fugue'* 61 The original edition [of Bach's 'Art of Fugue'] . . should not have printed the *mirror-fugues in succession instead of in mirror-reflection. **1962** *Listener* 27 Dec. 1109/2 The fifth fugue is again for strings only, as are the rectus versions of the 'mirror' fugues XII and XIII [of Bach]. **1973** *Times* 23 Apr. 16/2 A concert-goer who can recognize a mirror-fugue merely by listening to it has no need of assistance. *c* **1440** *Promp. Parv.* 339/1 *Myrowre glasse, *speculum*. *a* **1560** BECON *Jewel of Joy* Wks. II. 42 b, O what a myrrour glasse and spectacle is here offered vnto vs. **1876** J. S. INGRAM *Centenn. Exposition* ix. 287 Inside was an oblong square, formed of mirror-glass, which reached to the top of the case. **1934** *Heal & Son Catal.: Better Furnit.* 8 Dressing-table, . . pink mirror-glass top. **1953** *Glass for Glazing* (*B.S.I.*) 18 (*heading*) Mirror glass. **1885, 1929** *Mirror image [see ENANTIOMORPH]. **1937** 'G. ORWELL' *Road to Wigan Pier* xii. 244 Fascism . . is a sort of mirror-image . . of a plausible travesty of Socialism. **1949** Mirror image [see ASYMMETRIC a. b]. **1961** *Lancet* 26 Aug. 447/2 The hemispheres are not exact replicas but mirror images of each other. **1962** W. NOWOTTNY *Lang. Poets Use* vi. 141 The formal correspondence between the lines . . makes 'time is setting with me' the mirror-image of 'The wan moon is setting ayont the white wave'. **1964** *Language* XL. 247 The phonological disintegration characteristic of the aphasic's linguistic regressions is a mirror-image of the child's acquisition of its sound pattern. **1966** *New Statesman* 27 May 775/3 The Black Muslim creed is the mirror image of the white racialist one. **1972** J. MCCLURE *Caterpillar Cop* v. 68 An element of variety had been introduced by building the bungalows in pairs and making one the mirror image of the other. **1954** R. F. POST *16 Lect. Controlled Thermonucl. Reactions* (Univ. Calif. Radiation Laboratory, UCRL-4231, 2 Feb.) p. vi, A general principle involved in the *mirror machine's conception was the establishing as an initial condition that the plasma should be created by injection and trapping of a space-charge neutralized energetic ion beam into an otherwise evacuated chamber. **1958** *New Statesman* 6 Sept. 266/3 In the mirror machines the molecules of heavy hydrogen are violently injected into a chamber and go spiralling along until magnetic forces at the ends of the chamber reflect them and send them spiralling back again —from one magnetic mirror to another. **1969** *New Scientist* 25 Sept. 639/1 If mirror machines are feasible, then a fusion reactor based on the system would be relatively easy to build. **1947** H. A. BETHE *Elem. Nucl. Theory* ii. 7 If the binding energies of a pair of nuclei which differ only in the interchange of neutrons and protons are compared, a difference in binding energy which increases with the charge of the nuclei is found. Examples of such '*mirror' nuclei are: $^{1}H^{3}$ $^{2}He^{3}$; $^{3}Li^{7}$ $^{4}Be^{7}$; . . $^{14}Si^{29}$ $^{15}P^{29}$. **1962** H. D. BUSH *Atomic & Nucl. Physics* vi. 127 Evidence for the equality of *n—n* and *p—p* forces is provided by certain positron emitters where the parent and product of the decay are mirror nuclei. **1955** RICHTMYER & KENNARD *Introd. Mod. Physics* (ed. 5) x. 510 Among the many unstable nuclides . . a set of particular importance are the so-called '*mirror nuclides'. **1960** H. HAYWARD *Antique Coll.* 187/1 **Mirror-painting*, a type of glass picture in which the glass was first coated at the back with an amalgam of tin and mercury to make it into a mirror. The parts to be painted were then scraped away and painted in as required. **1970** G. SAVAGE *Dict. Antiques* 275/1 Most surviving mirror-paintings are Chinese and belong to the 18th century... Mirror-painting, being on the back of a sheet of glass, meant working in reverse. **1939** *Burlington Mag.* May p. xv/1 A pair of decorative Chinese *mirror-pictures in Chippendale frames. **1959** E. PULGRAM *Introd. Spectogr. of Speech* v. 46 Oscillograms of repetitive waves whose half-cyles are not mirror pictures of one another. **1964** *Amer. N. & Q.* Jan. 72/1 *Mirror pictures* . . this kind of repeated or reflected picture of a picture of a picture, ad infinitum. **1839** URE *Dict. Arts* 572 The casting of *mirror-plates was commenced in France about the year 1688. **1940** *Chambers's Techn. Dict.* 550/1 *Mirror plate*, . . (1) Plate glass for silvering.—(2) A fixing device in the form of a small metal plate, one end being screwed . . to the object . . and the other fixed to the base. **1966** A. W. LEWIS *Gloss. Woodworking Terms* 56 *Mirror plate*, small metal plate screwed to the backs of frames, etc., so that they can be fixed to a wall. **1863** COUCH *Brit. Fishes* I. 104 Those staring marks, from which this fish has sometimes been called the *Mirror Ray. **1926** A. HUXLEY *Jesting Pilate* I. 70 These *mirror rooms at Amber. **1901** M. W. TRAVERS *Exper. Study Gases* vi. 56 *The *mirror scale* (Jolly). In reading barometers, manometers, etc., it is usual to employ a glass scale ruled in millimetres. The scale is etched on the surface of a strip of glass about 5 mm. in thickness, which is then silvered on the second surface. **1961** M. D. ARMITAGE *Basic Princ. Electronics & Telecommunications* xi. 290 (*caption*) Use of mirror scale. **1890** W. JAMES *Princ. Psychol.* I. x. 399 The subjects, e.g., often write backwards, or they transpose letters, or they write *mirror-script. **1668** CHARLETON *Onomasticon* 255 *Selenitis*, . . *Lapis Specularis* . . *Mirrour-stone, or Muscovy Glass. **1964** *Listener* 20 Aug. 264/2 A prism, or perhaps tent-shaped room, some eighty feet high, whose two inclined faces are all mirror; hidden in the ridge are two film cameras... So that film image as well as the constantly moving crowd are repeated *ad infinitum* in the *mirror-wall, as if it were the inside of a kaleidoscope. **1969** *Guardian* 1 July 9/2 *Mirror-work is a traditional Indian craft which looks enchanting . . densely applied to a gipsy-type waistcoat or belt. **1973–4** *Oxfam Catal.* 12 Typical Gujarat embroidery and mirrorwork covers this bag. **1960** I.

BENNETT *Delinquent & Neurotic Children* ix. 367 Left-handed, tends to *mirror-write, poor wrist coordination. **1881** IRELAND in *Brain* Oct. 367 The .. change in the brain-tissue from which the image is formed in the mind of the *mirror-writer. **1960** I. BENNETT *Delinquent & Neurotic Children* ix. 370 *Mirror-writer, below average in every subject. **1776** G. CAMPBELL *Philos. Rhetoric* I. II. iii. 420 If the analogy of the language must be preserved in composition, to what kind of reception are the following entitled .. homedialect, bellysense, and *mirrour-writing? **1881** IRELAND in *Brain* Oct. 361 Buchwald and Erlenmeyer have directed attention to what they call Spiegelschrift or mirror-writing. **1924** R. M. OGDEN tr. *Koffka's Growth of Mind.* v. §6. 293 Certain children can read mirror-writing at first just as well as they can ordinary writing. **1969** 'E. MCBAIN' *Shotgun* iii. 35 A blotter was the only other thing on the desk. Carella automatically checked it for any mirror writing that might have been left on it. **1970** D. BOWDEN tr. *Luria's Traumatic Aphasia* xiii. 332 (*caption*) Writing disturbance in visual agraphia; 'mirror writing'.

mirror ('mɪrə(r)), *v.* [f. MIRROR *sb.*] *trans.* To reflect in the manner of a mirror.

1820 KEATS *Lamia* II. 47 He .. bending to her open eyes, Where he was mirror'd small in paradise. **1823** F. CLISSOLD *Ascent Mt. Blanc* 23 The glassy pinnacles of the surrounding Alps mirrored the varying lights of the hemisphere. **1896** A. E. HOUSMAN *Shropshire Lad* xv, Look not in my eyes, for fear They mirror true the sight I see.

b. *fig.* To reflect, or represent something (to the mind). Also to ***mirror back***.

1827 DISRAELI *Viv. Grey* v. i, Those glorious hours, when the unruffled river of his Life mirrored the cloudless heaven of his Hope. **1883** S. C. HALL *Retrospect* II. 41 The brightness of the outer world is mirrored in imperishable verse. **1890** TOUT *Hist. Eng. fr.* 1689, 110 Literature and language faithfully mirrored back the age.

c. *refl.* To see oneself reflected in a mirror.

1891 C. E. NORTON *Dante's Purgat.* ix. 57 White marble so polished and smooth that I mirrored myself in it.

Hence '**mirroring** *vbl. sb.* and *ppl. a.*

1852 M. ARNOLD *Empedocles* 18 Hither and thither spins The wind-borne mirroring Soul. **1873** —— *Lit. & Dogma* (1876) 173 A perfectly faithful mirroring of the thought of Jesus.

mirrored[1] ('mɪrəd), *a.* [f. MIRROR *sb.* + -ED[2].] Fitted with a mirror or mirrors.

1820 KEATS *Lamia* 579 Still mimick'd as they rose Along the mirror'd walls by twin-clouds odorous. **1890** *Daily News* 8 Jan. 2/4 The action of the magnet .. was visibly represented by means of the mirrored galvanometer.

mirrored[2] ('mɪrəd), *ppl. a.* [f. MIRROR *v.* + -ED[1].] Reflected, as by a mirror; also *fig.*

a **1861** WOOLNER *Beautiful Lady* (1863) 122 Those mirrored marvels of the lake. **1905** *Q. Rev.* July 100 The mirrored image of life.

mirrorize ('mɪrəraɪz), *v.* [f. MIRROR *sb.* + -IZE.] *trans.* To show up as in a mirror.

1598 TOFTE *Alba* (1880) 54 A Monster then I may her mirorise, Since she delights in such strange Tragedies. **1873** S. WILBERFORCE in Ashwell *Life* (1879) I. viii. 337 All that sea of glass which lay spread before the Throne, mirrorizing, measured, compassed, completed.

†'**mirrorly**, *a. Obs.* Also 5 **meroly**. [f. MIRROR *sb.* + -LY[1].] Resembling a mirror.

1434 MISYN *Mending Life* 128 Myendly sight truly is takyn up heuenly to behald be schadoly syght ȝit & meroly.

mirrory ('mɪrərɪ), *a.* [f. MIRROR *sb.* + -Y.] Having the nature of a mirror; mirror-like.

1885 R. F. BURTON *Arab. Nts.* (abr. ed.) I. 140 The seas sank to mirrory stillness.

mirt, mirtel: see MYRT, MYRTLE.

mirth (mɜːθ), *sb.* Forms: 1 **myriȝþ, miriȝþ, myr(ȝ)þ, mir(ȝ)þ, myrhþ, mirhþ, merȝþ,** 2 **murþh, merhþ(e,** 3 **mirþh, muri(h)þe, mur(e)hþe, mur(e)ȝþe, muru(h)þe, mureþe, murcþ,** 3–5 **murþ(e,** 3–6 **mirthe,** 4 **muirth,** 4–6 **merth(e, myrthe,** 4–7 **myrth,** 3– **mirth.** [OE. *myr(i)ȝþ* str. fem. (cf. MDu. *merchte*):—OTeut. **murgiþâ*, n. of quality f. **murgjo-* MERRY *a.*]

†**1. a.** Pleasurable feeling, enjoyment, gratification; joy, happiness. Often used of religious joy. *Obs.*

c **888** K. ÆLFRED *Boeth.* vii. § 1 Be þæm þu meaht onȝietan ðæt þu þær nane myrhðe on næfdest. *c* **1000** ÆLFRIC *Gen.* iii. 24 He adræfed wæs of neorxena wonges myrðe. *c* **1175** *Lamb. Hom.* 13 Murðhe sculen wunian on londe. *a* **1225** *Ancr. R.* 132 Treowe ancren .. resteð ham inne swuche þouhte, & habbeð murðe of heorte, ase þeo þet singeð. *a* **1225** *Leg. Kath.* 1422 Þer ha heuen up hare honden to heouene; & .. ferden, wið murðe, icrunet, to Criste. *a* **1340** HAMPOLE *Psalter* Prol., & oft sith in til soun & myrth of heuen. **1377** LANGL. *P. Pl.* B. XVIII. 127 'Haue no merueille' quod Mercy, 'myrthe it bytokneth'. **1390** GOWER *Conf.* II. 107 Of whom I scholde merthe take. *c* **1440** *York Myst.* xlvii. 114 Nowe maiden meke and modir myne, Itt was full mekill myrþe to þe, þat I schulde ligge in wombe of þine. **1508** DUNBAR *Twa Mariit Wemen* 42 Bewrie, .. ȝe weddit wemen ȝing, Quhat mirth ȝe fand in maryage, sen ȝe war menis wyffis. **1659** H. PLUMPTRE in *12th Rep. Hist. MSS. Comm.* App. v. 6 Wishing that all your yeares yet to come may passe over with mirth and jollityes. **1696** TATE & BRADY *Ps.* ii. 11 Rejoyce with awful Mirth.

b. *pl.* Delights, joys.

a **1225** *Leg. Kath.* 1712 Monie ma murhðen þen alle men mahten wið hare muð munnen. *Ibid.* 2217 Þæt wes on an Wodnesdei þæt ha þus wende, martir, to þe murhðes þæt neauer ne wonieð. *a* **1300** *Cursor M.* 1004 Paradis is a priue stedd þar mani mirthes er e-medd. *c* **1420** *Anturs of Arth.* xiv, Whene þou sittis in thi sette, Withe all mirthes at thi mete, Some dayntes þou dele. *c* **1440** *York Myst.* xxiv. 144 To make þere myrthis more.

†**c.** Put for: A cause of joy. *Obs.*

a **1000** *Runic Poem* 75 (Gr.) Dæȝ byþ .. myrȝþ and tohiht eadȝum and earmum. *a* **1225** *Leg. Kath.* 2382 Þe is mi lauerd & mi luue, mi lif & mi leofmon, mi wunne .. mi murhðe & mi mede. *c* **1425** *Cursor M.* 10887 (Trin.) For þi of þe beþ born a burþ Synful men to ioye & murþ.

2. Rejoicing, esp. manifested rejoicing; merry-making; jollity, gaiety. Phrase, †***to make mirth(s***, to rejoice.

c **1205** LAY. 1794 Muchel wes þa murðe þe þat folc makode. **13..** *K. Alis.* 1575 Murthe is gret in halle. **1375** BARBOUR *Bruce* XVI. 237 Thou hass mair causs myrthis till ma, For thou the ded eschapit swa. **1390** GOWER *Conf.* I. 45 Maii, Whan every brid hath chose his make And thenkth his merthes forto make. *c* **1470** HENRY *Wallace* VI. 619 To meit thai went, with myrthis and plesance. **1470–85** MALORY *Arthur* I. ii. 37 And so in alle haste they were maryed in a mornynge with grete myrthe and Ioye. **1590** SPENSER *F.Q.* I. xii. 40 Their exceeding merth may not be told. **1605** SHAKS. *Macb.* III. iv. 11 Be large in mirth, anon wee'l drinke a Measure The Table round. **1822** SCOTT *Pirate* xxii, Life without mirth is a lamp without oil. **1837** W. IRVING *Capt. Bonneville* I. 238 The genial festival of Christmas, which .. lights up the fireside of home with mirth and jollity.

†**3. a.** Something which affords pleasure or amusement; a diversion, sport, entertainment. *Obs.*

c **1386** CHAUCER *Prol.* 767 Of a myrthe I am right now bythoght To doon yow ese and it shal coste noght. **1390** GOWER *Conf.* II. 241 And thus the dai, schortly to telle, With manye merthes thei despente. **1470–85** MALORY *Arthur* XII. vi. 601 And euery day ones for ony myrthes that alle the ladyes myȝt make hym he wold ones euery day loke toward the realme of Logrys. **1472–5** *Rolls of Parlt.* VI. 156/1 Lordes, .. Yomen, and other Comyners, have used the occupation of shotyng for their myrthes and sportes with Bowes of Ewe. **1534** MORE *Comf. agst. Trib.* II. Wks. 1171/1 You require my minde in the matter, whether menne in tribulacion may not lawfully .. coumfort themselfe, with some honest mirth. **1577** NORTHBROOKE *Dicing* (1843) 100 Such vaine, ydle, and filthy pastimes and myrthes should surcease. **1606** SHAKS. *Ant. & Cl.* I. iv. 18 To giue a Kingdome for a Mirth, to sit And keepe the turne of Tipling with a Slaue.

†**b.** Musical entertainment, melody. *Obs.*

c **1320** *Sir Tristr.* 1254 Ich man was lef to liþe, His mirþes were so swete. **1377** LANGL. *P. Pl.* B. VIII. 67 Vnder a lynde vppon a launde lened I a stounde, To lythe þe layes þe louely foules made. Murthe of her mouthes made me þere to slepe. **1485** CAXTON *Paris & V.* 4 [They] wyth one accorde dysposed them self for to gyue somme melodyous myrthe to the noble mayde. *c* **1532** DU WES in Palsgr. 942 To make myrth as byrdes, *degoiger.* **1579** SPENSER *Sheph. Cal.* Dec. 40 Somedele yblent to song and musickes mirth.

4. a. Gaiety of mind, as manifested in jest and laughter; merriment, hilarity; in early use, †jocularity, fun, ridicule (*obs.*). †Also, a jest.

1390 GOWER *Conf.* III. 253 Thei hire sihe of glad semblant, Al full of merthes and of bordes. **1560** DAUS tr. *Sleidane's Comm.* 28 b, Which Luther got afterwardes, and translated it into Duche, not without much myrthe and pastime [L. *non sine scommatis multoque sale*]. **1591** HARINGTON *Orl. Fur.* Pref. ¶vj, Then, for Comedies. How full of harmeles myrth is our Cambridge Pedantius? **1599** SHAKS. *Much Ado* II. i. 343, I was borne to speake all mirth, and no matter. **1655** STANLEY *Hist. Philos.* III. (1701) 88/1 Aristophanes taking this Theme interweaves it with much abusive Mirth. *a* **1674** CLARENDON *Hist. Reb.* XIII. §30 He was of an excellent humour, .. and under a grave countenance, covered the most of mirth. **1712** ADDISON *Spect.* No. 381 ¶1, I have always preferred Chearfulness to Mirth. The latter I consider as an Act, the former as an Habit of the Mind. Mirth is short and transient, Chearfulness fixed and permanent. *a* **1716** SOUTH *Serm.* (1744) VII. vii. 151 For if these [great crimes and great miseries] be made the matter of our mirth, what can be the argument of our sorrow? **1760–74** TUCKER *Lt. Nat.* (1834) II. 129 Joy, when occasioned by the contrast of very dissimilar objects, along which it proceeds by continual leaps and bounds from one to the other, becomes mirth. **1774** GOLDSM. *Retal.* 24 Who mix'd reason with pleasure and wisdom with mirth. **1841** W. SPALDING *Italy & It. Isl.* II. 216 A reckless mixture of seriousness with mirth. **1832** HT. MARTINEAU *Demerara* iii. 33 Cassius grinned with some feeling deeper than mirth.

b. personified.

? *a* **1366** CHAUCER *Rom. Rose* 817 Ful fair was Mirthe, ful long and high; A fairer man I never sigh. **1632** MILTON *L'Allegro* 152 These delights, if thou canst give, Mirth with thee, I mean to live. **1770** GOLDSM. *Des. Vill.* 222 Where grey-beard mirth, and smiling toil retir'd. **1816** BYRON *Monody on Sheridan's Death* 110 Mirth, That humbler Harmonist of care on Earth.

†**c.** Put for: The object of one's mirth.

1601 SHAKS. *Jul. C.* IV. iii. 114 Hath Cassius liu'd To be but Mirth and Laughter to his Brutus, When greefe and blood ill temper'd, vexeth him? **1611** —— *Wint. T.* I. ii. 166 He's all my Exercise, my Mirth, my Matter. **1708** OZELL tr. *Boileau's Lutrin* III. 52 The Flout of Boys, and Mirth of every Feast.

5. *Comb.* objective and obj. genitive, as ***mirth-maker, -marrer,*** †***-monger, -provoker; mirth-inspiring, -lit, -loving, -making, -marring, -moving, -provoking*** adjs.; †**mirth-day**, a holiday, festival; †**mirth-song**, a song of (religious) joy.

1778 [W. MARSHALL] *Minutes Agric., Digest* 118 Let the Amusements of those *Mirth-Days be athletic and exhilarating. **1725** POPE *Odyss.* IV. 302 Bright Helen mix'd a *mirth-inspiring bowl. **1849** C. BRONTË *Shirley* II. iv. 100 Lifting up her *mirth-lit face to the gallery. **1853** HICKIE tr. *Aristoph.* (1872) II. 543 The unrestrained, *mirth-loving act of worship. **1636** MASSINGER *Gt. Dk. Florence* v. ii, Such chopping *mirth-makers as shall preserve Perpetuall cause of sport. **1969** *Daily Tel.* 15 Feb. 14/6 Kenneth Horne .. was acknowledged as one of radio's top *mirth-makers. **1638** BRATHWAIT *Barnabees Jrnl.* I. (1818) 37 They eat, drink, laugh, are still *mirth-making. **1652** J. WRIGHT tr. *Camus' Nat. Paradox* IV. 129 Who playing the *Mirth-marrer at this Triumph, put Water into this fuming Wine. **1771** FOOTE *Maid of B.* I. Wks. 1799 II. 209 That .. water-drinking, *mirth-marring, amorous old hunks. **1641** J. TRAPPE *Theol. Theol.* iv. 191 Then woe to our *mirth-mongers that laugh now. **1588** SHAKS. *L.L.L.* II. i. 71 A *mirth-mouing iest. **1895** W. ARCHER *Theatr. 'World' 1894* lii. 341 The pun, as a '*mirth-provoker', is dead. **1859** LANG *Wand. India* 287 Each in his own peculiar way, could relate a story, .. in such a manner as to make it wonderfully *mirth-provoking. **1561** DAUS tr. *Bullinger on Apoc.* (1573) 81 The *myrth-songes, or Carols of Gods excellent creatures.

† **mirth**, *v. Obs.* Forms: 3 **mirþhen**, 4–5 **myrth(e,** 4 **merþe, murthe,** 4–7 **mirth(e.** [f. MIRTH *sb.*]

1. *intr.* To be glad, rejoice.

a **1300** *E.E. Psalter* xxxi. 14 Faines in Laverd and glades in quert And mirþhes [L. *gloriamini*] alle rightwise of hert.

2. *trans.* To gladden, delight; to provide sport or entertainment for.

a **1300–1400** *Cursor M.* 7254 (Gött.) Bi a piler þan was he [Samson] sett, To mirth þe gomys at þair mett. **13..** *E.E. Allit. P.* A. 861 He myrþez vus alle at vch a mes. **1377** LANGL. *P. Pl.* B. XVII. 240 Þe weyke and fyre wil make a warme flaumbe For to myrthe the men with þat in merke sitten. **1387–8** T. USK *Test. Love* I. i. (Skeat) l. 11 Blisse of my joye, that ofte me murthed, is turned in-to galle. *c* **1400** *Destr. Troy* 7910 To se the maner of þo men, & mirth hym a stound. **1435** MISYN *Fire of Love* 10 With byrnynge lufe playnly our myndes myrthand. *a* **1600** *Flodden F.* ii. (1664) 20 Then Minstrels mirthed all the land.

mirþer, obs. form of MURDER *v.*

mirthful ('mɜːθfʊl), *a.* [f. MIRTH *sb.* + -FUL.]

1. a. Of persons, their dispositions, moods, etc.: Full of mirth; joyous, gladsome, hilarious.

a **1300** *Cursor M.* 10611 Þar bileft þat mirthful mai, Drightin hir ledd in al hir wai. *c* **1475** *Rauf Coilȝear* 357 Befoir that mirthfull man menstrallis playis. **1500–20** DUNBAR *Poems* x. 36 Be myrthfull now, at all ȝour mycht, For passit is ȝour dully nycht. **1634** SIR T. HERBERT *Trav.* 14 Brasse buttons, pieces of Pewter, spur-rowels, or what else the mirthfull Saylers exchange. **1726** POPE *Odyss.* XX. 415 A mirthful frenzy seized the fated croud. *a* **1745** BROOME tr. *Anacreon's Odes* liv. 8 Hence, hoary Age!—I now am young, And dance the mirthful Youths among. **1821** CLARE *Vill. Minstr.* I. 45 Each mirthful lout The ale-house seeks. **1940** W. FAULKNER *Hamlet* IV. i. 279 His constant expression of incorrigible and mirthful disbelief had left him now.

b. Of places, seasons, etc.: Characterized by mirth or rejoicing. Of sounds or utterances: Expressive of mirth, joyous, merry.

c **1450** HOLLAND *Howlat* 998 In mirthfull moneth of May. **1500–20** DUNBAR *Poems* xlviii. 163 Thane all the birdis song with voce on hicht, Quhois mirthfull soun wes mervelus to heir. **1634** SIR T. HERBERT *Trav.* 198 This Ceremony .. to Libidinists may seeme mirthfull and charitable. **1807** CRABBE *Par. Reg.* III. 847 But most his Reverence loved a mirthful jest. **1834** LYTTON *Pompeii* III. ii, There is nothing very mirthful in your strain. **1846** KEBLE *Lyra Innoc.* (1873) 131 Mirthful bower or hall.

2. Of things: Affording mirth, amusing.

1593 SHAKS. *3 Hen. VI*, v. vii. 43 And now what rests, but that we spend the time With stately Triumphes, mirthfull Comicke shewes. **1877** *Athenæum* 13 Oct. 475/2 The piece .. is one of the most mirthful and original that has, during late years, been seen on the stage.

mirthfully ('mɜːθfʊlɪ), *adv.* [f. MIRTHFUL + -LY[2].] In a mirthful manner, joyously; in an amusing manner; humorously.

c **1470** *Gol. & Gaw.* 216 The meriest war menskit on mete, at the maill, With menstralis myrthfully makand thame glee. **1665** SIR T. HERBERT *Trav.* (1677) 182 As was mirthfully experimented upon one of Alexander's Pages. **1856** HAWTHORNE *Eng. Note-Bks.* (1879) II. 229 Always saying something mirthfully. **1862** LYTTON *Str. Story* I. 104 She would enter mirthfully into the mirth of young companions round her. **1885** *Spectator* 25 July 976/1 He mirthfully describes the shooting in cold blood of 2,000 rebels .. as an *envoi à l'ambulence.*

mirthfulness ('mɜːθfʊlnɪs). [f. MIRTHFUL + -NESS.] The quality or state of being mirthful; joyfulness; jocosity, facetiousness.

1867 A. DUNCAN *Mem. D. Duncan* 2 Cheerfully doing what he could to contribute to their gratification and innocent mirthfulness. **1906** *Hibbert Jrnl.* Apr. 572 She impresses all who approach her by her constant mirthfulness.

†'**mirthing**, *vbl. sb. Obs.* [f. MIRTH *v.* + -ING[1].] The action of the vb. MIRTH; rejoicing.

a **1300** *E.E. Psalter* lxxxviii. 16 [15] Milthe and sothnes sal forgan þi face: seli folke þate mirthinge [L. *jubilationem*] kan.

mirthless ('mɜːθlɪs), *a.* [f. MIRTH *sb.* + -LESS.] Wanting in mirth, joyless; sad, dismal.

c **1381** CHAUCER *Parl. Foules* 592 Daunsith he murye that is mytheles. **1509** BARCLAY *Shyp of Folys* (1570) 172 O mirthless muse of eloquence barayne. **1567** GOLDING *Ovid's Met.* IX. (1593) 226 My colour pale, my bodie leane, my heavie mirthlesse cheere. **1627** DRAYTON *Sheph. Sirena* 26 Whilst his gamesome cut-tayld Curre With his mirthlesse Master playes. *a* **1800** J. WARTON *Fashion* 63 As mirthless infants, idling out the day, With wooden swords, or toothless puppies play. **1847** C. BRONTË *J. Eyre* xi, It was a curious laugh; distinct, formal, mirthless. **1899** *Blackw. Mag.* July 48/1 A circle of mirthless young men.

Hence '**mirthlessly** *adv.* Also '**mirthlessness**.

1890 CLARK RUSSELL *Ocean Trag.* II. xxiv. 252 He laughed harshly and mirthlessly. **1727** BAILEY vol. II, *Mirthlessness*, sadness, melancholiness.

mirthquake ('mɜːθkweɪk). *colloq.* Also **mirthquaker.** [f. MIRTH *sb.* + QUAKE *sb.*, after EARTHQUAKE.] An entertainment that excites convulsive mirth.

1928 *Daily Express* 24 Apr. 4/2, I found Prince George.. among the first to see Harold Lloyd's new 'mirthquake'. **1938** *N.Y. Times* 13 Jan. 19/1 Robert Benchley's new mirthquake *After 1903—What?* Always in hot water—that's Benchley, America's Mogul of Mirth. **1939** *Amer. Speech* XIV. 4 A 'screamario' is the scenario for a comedy, which proves to be a 'mirthquake'. **1942** BERREY & VAN DEN BARK *Amer. Thes. Slang* §281/4 Something humorous; joke. .. Mirthquake, mirthquaker. **1965** LEITNER & LANEN *Dict. French & Eng. Slang* 90/1 *Mirthquake*,..film, pièce, etc., très amusant.

mirthsome ('mɜːθsəm), *a.* [f. MIRTH *sb.* + -SOME.] Characterized by mirth; mirthful, joyous.

1823 *Mirror* I. 326/1 Mirthsome birds With wild song fill the air. **1841** *Fraser's Mag.* XXIII. 459 This was a blythesome bridal, yet less mirthsome than mony I mind of.

Hence '**mirthsomeness**. Now *rare.*

1648 W. BROWNE *Polexander* III. IV. 122 Coming up to him with the mirthsomeness of a man that brings good newes. You have no more enemies, said he. *Ibid.* v. 135 Two [statues] represented the Pleasures as well by their youth, their mirthsomeness,..as [etc.].

mirtill, mirtle, obs. forms of MYRTLE.

† '**mirtus.** *Obs.* Also 6 **myrthus.** [a. L. *myrtus*: see MYRTLE.] Myrtle.

1398 TREVISA *Barth. De P.R.* XVII. ci. (1495) 667 Some Mirtus is whyte and some is blacke. **1513** DOUGLAS *Æneis* V. ii. 63 And sayand this, he gan his templis tway Covir with myrthus, that is his moderis tre.

miry ('maɪərɪ), *a.* Forms: 4-6 **myry(e,** 6-7 **mierie, miery, myery, myrie,** 6 **myerry,** 7 **merie, mirie,** 8-9 **mirey,** 5- **miry.** [f. MIRE *sb.*[1] + -Y[1].]

1. Of the nature of mire or marshy ground, swampy.

1398 TREVISA *Barth. De P.R.* XVIII. lxxxvii. (1495) 836 The Sowe is frende to fenne and to myry places. **1494** FABYAN *Chron.* VII. 433 The feelde where the hooste laye, was so wete and myry, that men and horses were greuoslye noyed. **1596** SPENSER *F.Q.* v. x. 23 Onely these marishes and myrie bogs, In which the fearfull ewftes do build their bowres. **1622** S. WARD *Woe to Drunkards* (1627) 38 Though the pit bee deepe, merie and narrow. **1763** MILLS *Pract. Husb.* IV. 332 The ground..had better be dry, than mirey wet. **1833** HOOD *Epping Hunt* lxxvii, Some fell in miry bogs.

fig. **1602** F. HERING *Anat.* 5 Ouer head and eares in the myrie puddle of grosse Ignorance.

2. Abounding in mire, muddy.

c **1440** *Alphabet of Tales* 335 þe strete þat he rade in was passand myrye. **1574** tr. *Marlorat's Apocalips* 40 As the cleere and vnmuddie water that glydeth with a quiet streame, differeth from troubled and myrie froth. **1630** *R. Johnson's Kingd. & Commw.* 135 Women footing it in the mierie streets. **1714** GAY *Trivia* I. 239 Deep thro' a miry Lane she pick'd her Way, Above her Ankle rose the chalky Clay. **1833** HT. MARTINEAU *Berkeley the Banker* I. i, When the days get damp and dark, and the roads miry.

fig. *a* **1652** J. SMITH *Sel. Disc.* i. 14 Several steps and ascents out of this miry cave of mortality. **1768-74** TUCKER *Lt. Nat.* (1834) II. 356 Nor that the miry road of labour, trouble, suffering, and imperfection, should be made the necessary passage thereto.

3. Covered or bespattered with mud or mire.

1496 *Bk. St. Albans, Fishing* 3 [The hunter] his clothes torne wete shode all myry. **1530** PALSGR. 318/2 Myerry or dirty, berayed with dyrte, *boueux*. **1714** GAY *Trivia* I. 25 When late their miry sides stage-coaches show. **1864** R. A. ARNOLD *Cotton Fam.* 54 Hodge comes in all miry from his work.

4. *fig.* Dirty, defiled; despicable.

1532 MORE *Confut. Tindale* Wks. 614/1 Tindall..layeth hys myrye handes vpon the knowen catholike churche of Christ. **1613** PURCHAS *Pilgrimage* I. ii. 10 Beyond that myrie heap of earthie waters. **1877** E. JOHNSON *Antiq. Mat.* 69 A name under which men drove a miry business.

†*Comb.* **1589** NASHE *Almond for Parrat* 5 Thinke you this myrie mouthed mate, a partaker of heauenly inspiration, that thus aboundes in his vncharitable railings.

5. 'Dirty' in colour. *rare.*

1850 *Zoologist* VIII. 2644 Those [*sc.* eggs] of the plover were somewhat discoloured, and were beginning to get what may be called miry.

miry, obs. form of MERRY *a.*

‖**miryachit** (miːr'jɑːtʃiːt). Also *erron.* **myri-.** *Path.* [Russian *miryachit'* (inf.) to be epileptic (Pavlovsky).] A peculiar nervous disease observed in Siberia and in some non-European countries, the chief characteristic of which consists in mimicry by the patient of everything said or done by another.

1890 in *Century Dict.* **1897** *Trans. Amer. Pediatric Soc.* IX. 168b, The group of nervous disorders which include the 'jumpers' described by Beard, the latah of the Malays, the myriachit of Siberia. **1902** QUAIN *Dict. Med.* 440 The subjects of Myriachit react only to impulses entering through the efferent optic and auditory channels.

‖**mirza** ('mirzaː). *sb.* Also 7 **mirzey, mursi,** 7-8 **murza,** 8-9 **meerza,** 8 **myrza.** [Pers. *mirzā*, *mīrzā*, short for *mīrzād*, f. *mīr* (a. Arab. *amīr*: see AMEER, EMIR) a prince + *zād* born.] In Persia: **a.** A royal prince; as a title, it is placed after the name. **b.** The common title of honour prefixed to the name of an official or a man of learning.

1613 PURCHAS *Pilgrimage* (1614) 422 These Nagayans have their divers hords subject to their severall Dukes whom they call Murzes. **1634** SIR T. HERBERT *Trav.* 70 The Persian Prince, hunted him backe againe, not daring to abide a Combat with that happy Mirza. **1698** FRYER *Acc. E. India & P.* 381 When the other Party..creeps with a dejected countenance to the feet of the Cadi, calling him Mirza. **1770** *Ann. Reg.* 25 Several of their mirzas or chiefs.. entered into a negociation..with the Russians. **1788** GIBBON *Decl. & F.* lxv. VI. 351 The same success attended the other mirzas and emirs in their excursions. **1885** GOLDSMID in *Encycl. Brit.* XVIII. 628/1 [Persia.] The somewhat common prefix 'mirza' is usually taken by the high functionaries of state.

Mirzapur ('mɜːzəpʊə(r)). Also **Mirzapore.** The name of a town in the state of Uttar Pradesh in Northern India used *attrib.* and *absol.* to designate a type of carpet manufactured there.

c **1882** *Cardinal & Harford's Price List Oriental Carpets & Rugs* 10 Indian carpets from Masulipatam, Mirzapore, etc. .. The Mirzapore can be manufactured in less time than any other. **1900** J. K. MUMFORD *Oriental Rugs* (1901) xiv. 264 The designs of the old Mirzapur carpets..showed a pronounced Hindu character. **1967** *Times* 23 Feb. 24/6 (Advt.), Really superb plain off-white 'Mirzapur' carpets with 1 in. virgin wool pile.

† **mis,** *a.*[1] *Obs.* Also **mys(se.** [Partly the prefix MIS-[1] (4) used as a distinct part of speech (cf. next); partly a reduced form of AMISS.

Some of the attributive collocations illustrated below are not essentially different from compounds of the prefix with a sb. They are placed here because they are app. intended as two words and do not appear at any period as established compounds.]

Bad; wrong; wicked. In predicative use: Amiss.

c **1350** *Will. Palerne* 716 þurth a mys metyng þat swiche a maide wold Leye hire loue so lowe. *c* **1374** CHAUCER *Troylus* IV. 1348 That men the quene Eleyne shal restore, And Grekes us restore that is mis. **1390** GOWER *Conf.* III. 274 So that whil I live I myhte amende that is mys. *a* **1425** *Cursor M.* 16496 (Trin.) My tresoun is so mys. *c* **1430** *Hymns Virgin* (1867) 110 Ne plese hire not with no mis plawe. *c* **1447** in F. M. Nichols *Lawford Hall* (1891) App. 23 The said enformacion of the said bille ys mysse. *c* **1450** BURGH *Secrees* 1922 In Oold mys humours. **1470-85** MALORY *Arthur* XVII. ii. 692 For yf I be a mys creature or an vntrue knyghte. **1556** *Chron. Gr. Friars* (Camden) 51 To for-geve hym hys mysse insample.

mis (mɪz), *a.*[2] and *sb.* Also **miz, mizz.** Colloq. abbrev. of MISERABLE *a.*, MISERY.

1886 in H. BAUMANN *Londinismen.* **1918** *Chambers's Jrnl.* Mar. 156/2 He won't get any peace now we've seen him. We'll make his life a mizz. **1939** N. MONSARRAT *This is Schoolroom* II. ix. 205 'I'm mis,' she volunteered immediately, in a muted babyish voice. **1952** 'C. BRAND' *London Particular* x. 121 Rosie was ackcherly utterly *mis.* about..poor, darling Thomas. **1954** J. B. PRIESTLEY *Magicians* ii. 27 Don't look so miz. Are you hating it? **1968** *Times* 24 Feb. 21/3 We feel a teeny bit miz—reality does depress. **1974** *Observer* 27 Oct. 5/5, I wouldn't care to guess what proportion of the population has some sexual problem that makes them mis.

† **mis,** *adv. Obs.* Also **miss(e, mys(se.** [Partly MIS-[1] treated as a separate word (as in *to gon mis* for *to misgon*); partly a reduced form of AMISS. Cf. MLG. *mis, miss(e*, Du. *mis.*] Wrongly; badly; mistakenly; amiss.

to do mis(s: see MISS *sb.*[1]

[*c* **950** *Lindisf. Gosp.* John iii. 20 Hælc monn forðon seðe yfle *vel* mis doeð..*omnis enim qui male agit.*] *a* **1225** *Ancr. R.* 210 Summe iuglurs beoð þet..makien cheres, & wrenchen mis hore muð. *a* **1240** *Lofsong* in *O.E. Hom.* I. 205 Ich habbe ..iȝeuen mis and inumen mis and mis etholden. *a* **1300** *Cursor M.* 14207 Iesus said, 'miss yee vnderstand'. **1303** R. BRUNNE *Handl. Synne* 634 Whan þou wost þat þou seyst mys. *c* **1350** *All Saints* 186 in Horstm. *Altengl. Leg.* (1881) 144 þe tyme..þat has bene spended mys. *c* **1350** *Will. Palerne* 141 Al þe making of man so mysse had ȝhe schaped. *c* **1374** CHAUCER *Boeth.* IV. pr. v. (1868) 131 þan I merueile me..whi þat þe þinges ben so mys entrechaunged. **1415** HOCCLEVE *To Oldcastle* 83 Thow lookist mis, thy sighte is nothyng cleer. *c* **1430** *Pol. Rel. & L. Poems* (1903) 193 þou hast goon mys! come hoom ageyne! *c* **1450** LOVELICH *Merlin* 270 (Kölbing) Forsothe ȝe seyn mys bothe two.

mis, obs. form of MISS *sb.*[1] and *v.*[1]

Mis, Mis, obs. abbreviations of *mistris*, MISTRESS.

mis- (mɪs), *prefix*[1] (also 1 (*rare*), 2-7 **miss-**, 3-6 **misse-, mysse-**, 3-7 **mys-**, 4-5 **mes-**), represents OE. *mis-* = OFris., OS. *mis-* (MDu. *mis(se)-*, *mes(se)-*, Du. *mis-*), OHG. *missa-*, *missi-*, *misse-*, *mes-* (MHG. *mis(se)-*, G. *miss-*), ON. *mis-*, Goth. *missa-* (in *missadêþs* MISDEED, *missaleiks* different, various, see MISLICH, and *missaqiss* 'speaking diversely', disagreement, tr. Gr. σχισμα):—OTeut. **misso-* (whence **missjan* MISS *v.*), repr. a pre-Teut. formation with ppl. suffix *-to* on a root ending with a dental. The adj. **misso-* seems to have had two senses: (1) divergent, astray, (2) mutual, alternate (cf. Goth. *missō* mutually). The first of these supports the identification of the root with the Teut. **mīþ-* to avoid, conceal (see MITHE *v.*); the two senses may be accounted for by the supposition that the primitive notion expressed by the root was that of difference or change. Phonologically, the Teut. root might represent a pre-Teut. form either with *t* or *th.* On the former view, some scholars regard it as cogn. w. L. *mittĕre* to send, let go; but the sense seems too remote. On the other assumption, it would be cognate with Skr. *mith* 'to meet as friend or antagonist, alternate, engage in altercation' (M. Williams), *mithu* 'alternately, falsely, wrongly', *mithas* 'mutually, reciprocally, alternately', *mithya* 'invertedly, contrarily, incorrectly, wrongly'; cf. OSl. *mitě, mitusĭ* alternately. The root **meith-* in these words is by some regarded as an extension of **mei-* to change: see MEAN *a.*[1]

In OE. and ME. MSS. the compounds of *mis-* (as of other prefixes) are written sometimes as two words, sometimes continuously, the hyphen being never used. From the 16th c. onwards the compounds are regularly printed as one word, with or without the hyphen, which becomes, however, less and less frequent, and is now employed chiefly in new or rarely-used formations, and in words like *mis-say* or *mis-cite*, where its omission would tend to disguise the identity of the compound or suggest a wrong pronunciation. (In Sir T. More's Works 1557, the spelling of the compounds as two distinct words was retained, e.g. *misse remember, mysse rule.*) The spellings *mispel, mispend*, etc. for *mis-spell, mis-spend*, etc. were once common and are found as late as the end of the 18th century.

The predominant meaning of the prefix in English, as in the other Teutonic languages, is that of 'amiss', 'wrong(ly)', 'bad(ly)', 'improper(ly)', 'perverse(ly)', 'mistaken(ly)', and this is the only one now recognized in the formation of new compounds. But even in OE. there are instances of its use as a mere negative prefix and also as a pejorative intensive with words of sinister meaning (see 7 and 8 below).

In early ME. a great extension of the use of the prefix took place, *mis-* being freely combined with words of indigenous and of foreign origin alike. Many of the new compounds appear to have been suggested by French formations with *mes-* (see MIS-[2]); thus we have *misbelieve* after OF. *mescreire* (mod. *mécroire*), *misfortune* and *mishap* after OF. *mescheance* (see MISCHANCE); a word like *misjudge* has prob. a double origin, being partly of native formation, and partly an adaptation of OF. *mesjuger.* The most prolific period for the formation of *mis-* compounds was the 17th c., to which a considerable number of those illustrated in this article belong; Bacon, Donne, and Bp. Hall are noteworthy as employing them largely. They still continue to be formed with considerable freedom, but in certain cases *ill-* and *mal-* are now preferred where writers of earlier periods would have preferred *mis-*.

In the ME. period *mis-* became to some extent a separable prefix; thus we have *inumen mis* and *misnumen, don mis* and *misdon, seyn mis* and *misseyn*, side by side. (See further under MIS *a.* and *adv.*) Even as late as the 16th c., the prefix was sometimes co-ordinated with an adj. or adv., as in the example *very erroniouse and misopinions* (see MISOPINION). A related phenomenon, of which an instance is found as late as the 17th c., consists in the dropping of the prefix before the second of two compounds coupled together, e.g. *ich abbe misseien mid eȝen, mid mine eren iherd* (Lamb. Hom. p. 189), *myslyuyng and techynge* (Wyclif), *mis gyed and led, yee mis happe and cheeue* (Hoccleve), *for thou hast mis-said or done* (J. Davies *Ecl.* 1614).

In OE. *mis-* was prefixed to verbs, active and passive participles, nouns of action and condition, and adjectives. In ME. its composition with agent-nouns and adverbs followed as a matter of course, and the principle of prefixing it to any word of the above classes, existing either actually or potentially, became soon established. Hence, in a group of formally related words such as *misrepresent* vb., *misrepresentation, misrepresentative* adj. and sb., *misrepresentatively* adv., *misrepresenter, misrepresenting* vbl. sb. and ppl. a., it is possible (unless there is historical evidence to the contrary) that each member may have been formed independently of any of the others.

All those compounds of *mis-* with respect to which there is evidence of a continuous history during any period, or which belong to a group, are treated in their alphabetical places. Those illustrated in the present article are for the most part nonce-words of obvious meaning.

1. Prefixed to verbs, with the meaning 'amiss', 'badly', 'wrongly', 'perversely', 'mistakenly'.

In OE. about 40 of such compounds are recorded, of which less than half are represented in ME. or mod.E. (see MISBEDE, MISDO, MISFARE, MISFERE, MISLEAD, MISLIKE, etc.).

As now apprehended, the prefix normally implies not censure of the act itself, but only of its manner. With this restriction, nonce-words may be formed very freely. In the 17th c. the use was much wider, and many of the formations of that period would now be inadmissible.

1603 FLORIO *Montaigne* II. xii. 284 *Missacknowledging [F. *mescognoissant*] both himselfe and his labours. 1657 J. WATTS *Vind. Ch. Eng.* 53, I am mistaken, and have *misadded. 1709 STRYPE *Ann. Ref.* v. 89 The Bp. of Carlile on the Papists side, and Sandys on that of the Protestants are misadded to the aforesaid Disputants. 1641 BP. HALL *Answ. Vind. Smectymnuus* §2. 19 These are all..which have so *mis-altered the Leiturgie, that it can no more be known to be itself then [etc.]. 1873 F. HALL *Mod. Eng.* App. 344 *note*, He *misanalysed *is being built* into *is being + built*. 1611 COTGR., *Mesarriver*, to *misarrive, to happen, or come vnfortunately vnto. 1636 SANDERSON *Serm.* (1681) II. 64 To mis-judge and *mis-asperse those that are set over them. 1614 J. DAVIES *Ecl.* in Browne *Sheph. Pipe* G 3, Hast thou any sheep-cure *mis-assaid? *a* 1849 J. C. MANGAN *Poems* (1859) 375 Thus all too mournfully *mis-atoning For that black ruin his word had made. 1900 *Blackw. Mag.* Apr. 492/2[Disraeli] to whom completely opposite proclivities have been *misattributed. 1646 PRYNNE *Susp. Susp.* Ep. Ded., Having neither any private interest nor design to *misbyas my judgment. 1638 MAYNE *Lucian* (1664) 354 As if we *misbusied our selves in a vain, womanish exercise. *a* 1631 *Miscanonize [see MISCHRISTEN]. 1624 DONNE *Devot.* (ed. 2) 127 They had mis-placed, *mis-centred their hopes. 1798 W. ETON *Survey Turkish Empire* Pref. xii, They are generally..related..with circumstances which so totally *mischaracterise the action, that [etc.]. 1611 FLORIO, *Misuenire*..to mischance or *miscom. 1624 BP. HALL *True Peace Maker* in *Var. Treat.* (1627) 540 If either the superiors *miscommand, or the inferiors disobey. 1615 SYLVESTER *Job Triumph.* I. 518 Remit, O Lord, what I have ill omitted: Remove (alas!) what I have *mis-committed. 1605 TIMME *Quersit.* II. vii. 138 Thou shalt not *miscompare that..to dead coales. 1615 SYLVESTER *Job Triumph.* IV. 256 Therefore doth Job open his mouth in vain: And voyd of knowledge, yet, yet, *mis-complain. 1898 T. HARDY *Wessex Poems* 12 Grieved that lives so matched should *miscompose. 1579 LODGE *Def. Plays* 8 Your day owl hath *misconned his parte. 1847 BUSHNELL *Chr. Nurture* viii. (1861) 214 We are to see that we do not *miscondition the state of childhood. 1583 GOLDING *Calvin on Deut.* xxxi. 184 Wee doe *misconsider our owne frailetie when we desire that God shoulde worke miracles dayly. *a* 1656 BP. HALL *Let. Parænetical* Rem. Wks. (1660) 400 An old Church, ..*mis-daubed with some untempered..morter. 1877 M. ARNOLD *Sonnet, Divinity* Poems I. 261 God's wisdom and God's goodness!—Ay, but fools *Mis-define these till God knows them no more. 1613 BP. HALL *Holy Panegyrick* Wks. (1625) 474 One God, one King, was the acclamation of those ancient Christians: and yet it was *mis-desired of the Israelites. 1610 DONNE *Pseudo-martyr* 14 That the Romane Religion doth..*mis-encourage and excite men to this vicious affectation of danger. 1649 J. H. *Motion to Parl.* 42 It is easie for men of acute wits to mis-judge and *mis-expect Nature. *a* 1618 J. DAVIES (Heref.) *Rights of Living & Dead* Wks. (Grosart) II. 64 To say thou wast the Forme (that is the soule) Of all this All; I should thee *misenroule In Booke of Life. 1645 RUTHERFORD *Tryal & Tri. Faith* (1845) 43 The saints can *mis-father their love, and love where God loveth not. 1881 F. T. PALGRAVE *Vis. Eng.* 206 The vapour and echo within he *mis-held for divine. 1687 BOYLE *Martyrd. Theodora* vi. (1703) 86 Whatever wilfulness may be *mis-imputed to us. 1610 DONNE *Pseudo-martyr* 97 To *mis-incite men to an imagined martyr-dome. *Ibid.* 118 The Romane Church, which *mis-inflames the minde to false Martyrdome. *a* 1625 FLETCHER *Four Plays, Honour* i. (1647) 29/1 If either of ye *miskil one another, what will become of poor Florence? 1835 WILLIS *Pencillings* II. liv. 122 If he was not a rogue, nature had *mislabelled him. 1746 in E. D. Dunbar *Social Life* (1865) 358 A part of the lands..suffered damage by being *mis-laboured, and other parts by not being at all laboured. 1674 N. FAIRFAX *Bulk & Selv.* Contents, Two or three things of another sort, ..*mismingled. 1876 MRS. WHITNEY *Sights & Ins.* x. 109 You have mingled, and perhaps not mismingled the stories. 1864 *Spectator* 17 Dec. 1444/2 The facts (at least so far as they are *misnarrated by either or both Evangelists). 1650 B. *Discolliminium* 11 It is a dangerous thing to *mis-obey Magistrates. 1852 HAWTHORNE *Grandfather's Chair* (1879) II. iii. 85 Virgil whose verses..have been..*misparsed..by so many..idle school-boys. 1658–9 in *Burton's Diary* (1828) III. 331, I understand that you and your clerk are reflected upon, as for *mispenning your order. 1879 MEREDITH *Egoist* xxxi, Might he not have caused himself to be *misperused in later life? 1749 H. WALPOLE *Let.* 23 Mar., Pigwiggin's Princess has *mis-piged. 1709 SACHEVERELL *Serm.* 5 Nov. 12 Whosoever Presumes to..*Mispresent any Point in the Articles. 1885 [W. H. WHITE] *Mark Rutherford's Deliverance* i, The same arguments, diluted, muddled, and mis-presented. 1885 *American* IX. 229 In some directions we are *misproducing. 1624 DONNE *Devot.* (ed. 2) 81 Keepe me back, O Lord, fro them who *misprofesse artes of healing the Soule. 1610 —— *Pseudo-martyr* 96 The Romane Doctrine..doth *mis-prouoke her disciples to a vicious affection of imaginarie Martyrdome. 1496 *Dives & Pauper* (W. de W.) IX. ii. 349I Yf thou occupye ony thynge *mys purchaced. 1659 in *Burton's Diary* (1828) IV. 425 The question was *misput. It ought not to have been put with a negative in it. 1870 LOWELL *Study Wind.* 295 [Religious poetry] a painful something misnamed by the noun and *misqualified by the adjective. 1817 J. GILCHRIST *Intell. Patrimony* 78, I could not, indeed so strangely *mis-reason as to suppose that [etc.]. 1653 WATERHOUSE *Apol. Learning* 249 There is nothing that more dishonoureth Governours than to *misreceive moderate addresses. 1602 J. DAVIES *Mirum in Modum* D 2 b, Th' outward Sences Which oft misse apprehend, and *misse referre. 1662 TUKE *Adv. 5 Hours* IV, The censorious world, who, like false glasses..*Misreflect the object. 1644 MILTON *Bucer on Div.* Wks. 1851 IV. 294 If Ezra and Nehemiah did not *mis-reform. 1658 A. FOX *Würtz' Surg.* Ep. Ded. 9 If he find any thing..*mis-reprinted. 1879 SWINBURNE in *Gentl. Mag.* Aug. 176 A comedy miserably misreprinted in Dodsley's Old Plays. 1642 SIR E. DERING *Sp. on Relig.* 35 This..being *mis-resented abroad. 1442 T. BECKINGTON *Corr.* (Rolls) II. 191 Howe true men..might be in subtil wise *misrewarded. 1633 BP. HALL *Hard Texts, N.T.* 392 The doctrines of that wicked Impostor..put an ill savour..upon all that were *mis-seasoned with them. 1598 FLORIO, *Misuéndere*,..to *mis-sell. 1674 N. FAIRFAX *Bulk & Selv.* Contents, Sense mistakes and *misshews, and thereby reason often misled. 1896 *Dublin Rev.* Apr. 274 St. Thomas's mare was *mis-shod at the village forge. 1598 SYLVESTER *Du Bartas* II. Ded., Wks. (Grosart) I. 94 It will not seem then that we have *mis-sung. 1614 J. DAVIES *Ecl.* in Browne *Sheph. Pipe* G 3 b, Albe that I ne wot I han mis-song. 1654 J. P. *Tyrants & Prot. Set forth* 33 The Mariners eye is upon the star, when his hand is on the stern;..if he *misteers, the whole is in danger. 1626 in *Archæol. Cant.* (1902) XXV. 18 We present Robert Broome for shutting or *mis-stopping our usual way on going perambulation of our parish. *a* 1640 JACKSON *Creed* XI. ii, So far hath the misapprehended doctrine of predestination..*missuaded some as they [etc.]. 1647 WARD *Simp. Cobler* 28 If they [*sc.* tailors] might bee..discharged of the tyring slavery of *mis-tyring women. 1596 SPENSER *F. Q.* V. xi. 54 She..with corruptfull brybes is to untruth *mis-trayned. *a* 1626 BACON *Charge Sess. Verge* (1662) 19 That which is miswrought will *miswear.

b. In the 14–16th c. a few verbs like MISDEEM, MISTHINK, in which the prefix had originally its normal function, developed new senses in which it had the force of 'unfavourably'. Then also arose a few new formations, such as MISBODE, MISDOUBT, MISDREAD, in which *mis-* was prefixed to a verb expressing suspicion or fear, in order to render more fully the notion of uneasy feeling contained in the vb. These new senses and combinations, however, now survive only as *arch.* or *dial.*

2. Prefixed to pples. and ppl. adjs. with the same meaning as in 1. Such compounds may be formed without reference to the corresp. infinitives, which in many cases are not extant.

So OE. *misboren*, *misbroȝden*, *mishwierfed*, *misscrýdd*, and *mishæbbende*, *misweaxende*, the corresp. infinitives *misberan*, etc. being unrecorded.

A few of the formations illustrated below are quasi-parasynthetic, as *misminded*, *misnatured*, *misprincipled*.

1654 BP. HALL *Let. Apol.* 6 To compose our *mis-alienated hearts to perfect love and concord. 1641 SMECTYMNUUS *Vind. Answ.* §2 This *misaltered Liturgie. 1643 MILTON *Divorce* 47 They shall recover the *misattended words of Christ to the sincerity of their true sense from manifold contradictions. 1563–87 FOXE *A. & M.* (1596) 61/1 It may be easilie espied, this epistle to be feigned and *misauthorised. 1864 CARLYLE in *Lett. Jane W. Carlyle* (1883) III. 198 The house was new,..small, *misbuilt every inch of it. 1611 FLORIO, *Misuenúto*, *miscome, decaied. 1893 A. FORBES in *Daily News* 1 May 3/1 The poor *mis-commanded,..over-marched, outnumbered fighting men. 1643 HERLE *Answ. Ferne* 38 A *misconcealed statute. 1713 *Hist. Grand Reb.* II. 302 Honours..*mis-confered become the Nations curse. 1831 CARLYLE *Schiller* in *Misc. Ess.* (1840) III. 12 Among the crowd of uncultivated and *miscultivated writers. 1854–66 PATMORE *Angel in Ho.* II. II. 251 *Misdespairing word and act May now perturb the happiest pact. 1633 BP. HALL *Hard Texts, N.T.* 293 Uncertaine and *Mis-devised traditions of men. 1649 G. DANIEL *Trinarch., Hen. IV*, c, Cannot find Contempt enough for *misenforced Lawes. 1780 M. NOBLE *Mint & Coins of Durham* 65 The supposed letter B will be found to be *mis-engraved C. 1891 SWINBURNE *Stud. Pr. & Poetry* (1894) 22 The most execrably *misedited book that ever (I should hope) disgraced the press. *c* 1600 *B. Mus. Add. MS.* 10303 *title*, The death of Blaunche the Dutchesse..no doubte *mysse entituled for this shoulde be Chaucers dreame. 1633 BP. HALL *Hard Texts, O. T.* Amos. iii. 14 Those *mis-erected altars. 1844 KINGLAKE *Eothen* xvi. 232 If you look at pictures, you see Virgins with *mis-foreshortened arms. 1614 BP. HALL *Contempl., O. T.* v. iv, It is both unmannerly and irreligious to be *misgestured in our prayers. 1622 *Ibid.* XVII. iv, Those *mis-hallowed hills. 1882 SWINBURNE *Tristram of Lyonesse* 19/12 His mishallowed and anointed steel. *c* 1600 SIR J. HORSEY *Trav.* (Hakl. Soc.) 243 His highnes maibe *misincenced. 1615 CHAPMAN *Odyss.* XIV. 258 Some God *mis-inspired. 1728 SAVAGE *Bastard* 47 Thus Unprophetic, lately misinspir'd, I sung. 1641 BP. HALL *Mischief of Faction* Rem. Wks. (1660) 70 The *mis-kindled heat of some vehement spirits. 1581 MULCASTER *Positions* xxxvi. (1887) 138 To haue wittes misplaced, and their degrees *mislotted by the iniquitie of Fortune. 1850 E. WARBURTON *Reginald Hastings* II. 65 The misshapen and *misminded dwarf. 1881 SWINBURNE *Mary Stuart* I. ii. 42 To join my name with my *misnatured son's. 1627 W. SCLATER *Exp. 2 Thess.* (1629) 159 The tidings of the *misnoised inhibition of preaching. 1839 DE QUINCEY *Recoll. Lakes* Wks. 1862 II. 183 All over his *misorganized country. 1903 A. LANG in *Longman's Mag.* Feb. 382 [The book] is so much *mispaged as to be totally useless. 1748 RICHARDSON *Clarissa* (1811) VIII. 158 Winking and pinking, *mis-patched, yawning, stretching. 1624 QUARLES *Job Militant* xi. I 2 b, My dayes are gone, my thoughts are *mis-possest. [Cf. *Job* xvii. 11 and marg.] *a* 1684 LEIGHTON *Serm.* Wks. 1830 III. 209 The..persecutors of our holy religion..are very wrongfully *misprejudiced against it. 1659 H. L'ESTRANGE *Alliance Div. Off.* 31 The violent passions of other men *mis-principled. 1646 BP. HALL *Free Prisoner* v. 120 Here we were out of danger of this *mis-raised fury. 1653 H. MORE *Conject. Cabbal.* (1713) 148 The *misreflected Echo of the sound. 1900 *Westm. Gaz.* 13 Feb. 9/1 It is the old story of *mis-reposed trust by easy-going directors in the executive of the business. 1610 BP. HALL *Apol. Brownists* §12 If the sway of your *misresolued conscience be..vnresistable. 1802–12 BENTHAM *Ration. Judic. Evid.* (1827) V. 87 Punishment that has been called **mis-seated* punishment: punishment *in alienam personam*. 1592 SHAKS. *Rom. & Jul.* v. iii. 205 This Dagger..is *misheathed in my Daughters bosome. 1681 BAXTER *Answ. Dodwell* i. 1 Some tender place that is so impatient of a *mis-supposed touch. 1850 CARLYLE *Latter-d. Pamph.* i. 56, I will lead you to the Irish Bogs,..to *mistilled Connaught. 1640 BP. HALL *Humble Remonstr.* 11 That any ingenuous Christian should bee so farre *mis-transported as to condemne a good prayer. 1626 —— *Contempl., O.T.* xx. 97 To set on foot the iust title of Joash, and to put him into the *misvsurped throne of his father Ahaziah.

3. Prefixed to vbl. sbs. with the same meaning as in 4. (Such compounds may be formed without reference to a verb.)

1661 J. STEPHENS *Procurations* 147 Except the mistakes in printing..others of mispointing and *misaccenting with some other literal escapes. 1670 BLOUNT *Law Dict.* Pref., Cowel also, especially in the Folio Edition, (besides the *misalphabeting) is extreamly misprinted. 1625 BP. MOUNTAGU *App. Cæsar* 3 They seldome or never talke of any *misbeing, misordering, misdemeaning. *a* 1641 —— *Acts & Mon.* (1642) 394 For mis leading and *mis-bringing up of youth and children. 1629 SIR R. BOYLE in *Lismore Papers* (1886) II. 324 The pretended *miscocqueting..of the yron sent by me. 1586 HOOKER *Answ. Travers* §24 Whatsoeuer was..by *miscollecting gathered out of darke places. 1611 FLORIO, *Misueniménto*..a mischancing or *miscomming. 1645 MILTON *Tetrach.* Wks. 1851 IV. 171 Granting no divorce, but to the want, or *miscommunicating of that. 1865 *Mis-craving [see MIS-WISH *sb.*]. 1866 G. STEPHENS *Runic Mon.* I. p. xvii, All the talk about '*miscuttings'. 1598 SYLVESTER *Du Bartas* II. i. II. (1641) 93/2 The *mis-eating of a certain fruit. 1621–31 LAUD *Serm.* (1847) 175 The sin..is committed by man's *mis-endeavouring, or want of endeavouring. 1645 BP. HALL *Rem. Discontent* 146 The sting of the guilty *mis-enjoying of them will be sure to stick by us. 1496 *Dives & Pauper* (W. de W.) v. ix. 206/2 They drawe folke to synne by *mys entysyng. 1665 *Phil. Trans.* I. 229 The *Misgraving the Bended end of the Springing Wire. *a* 1586 SIDNEY *Arcadia* II. (1629) 185 When they knew their *mismeeting and saw each other..striuing who should run fastest to the goale of death. 1804 EUGENIA DE ACTON *Tale without Title* III. 59 Will not our readers lament this mis-meeting. 1851 CARLYLE *Sterling* II. v. 200 There are several things misseen, untrue, which is the worst species of *mispainting. 1611 COTGR., *Mespartement*, a *misparting; an vnhonest, vnfit, or vnseemelie diuision. *a* 1626 BACON *Controv. Ch. Eng.* in *Resuscitatio* (1657) 178 All which Errours, and *Misproceedings, they do fortifie..by an addicted Respect, to their own Opinions. 1865 J. GROTE *Explor. Philos.* I. 249 It depends solely upon the realizing, in my view quite *mis-realizing, of logical terms. 1651 HOBBES *Leviath.* I. v. 21 By *mis-reasoning, or by trusting them that reason wrong. 1862 F. HALL *Hindu Philos. Syst.* 190 In this misreasoning. 1552–3 *Act 7 Edw. VI*, c. 1 §7 Fines..upon any Shirief..for not returning or *misreturning of any Write. 1652 H. L'ESTRANGE *Amer. no Jewes* 73 Some infirmities, which by Venery, and *misriding and *miswalking they have contracted. 1901 W. E. LINGELBACH in *Trans. Roy. Hist. Soc.* (1902) XVI. 59 In case a report or presentment of *mis-shipping was brought to the notice of the authorities. 1882 *Atlantic Monthly* L. 695 A slight *misspacing, very common in newspaper print. 1680 WALLER *Div. Medit.* XV. 110 The slipping, or breaking of a string or the *mistopping [= mis-stopping] of a fret. 1496 *Dives & Pauper* (W. de W.) VI. xiv. 256/1 That a man kepe well his handes & his bodye from *mystouchynge. 1872 BUSHNELL *Serm. Living Subj.* 34 Our pitiful *mistraining is assuredly to be corrected.

4. Prefixed to nouns of action, condition, and quality, with the meaning 'bad', 'wrong', 'erroneous', 'perverse', 'misdirected'.

Of such compounds 13 are recorded in OE., of which MISDEED, MISLORE, MISREDE, and MISWORK are the only representatives in subsequent periods.

1894 GOLDWIN SMITH in *19th Cent.* Feb. 226 The misprints and *misaccentuations..contributed to its failure. *a* 1661 FULLER *Worthies* (1840) I. 306 Let them sink into obscurity, that hope to swim in credit by such *mis-achievements. *a* 1849 E. A. POE *Sphinx* Wks. 1865 II. 436 To under-rate or to over-value the importance of an object, through mere *misadmeasurement of its propinquity. 1650 R. HOLLINGWORTH *Exerc. Usurped Powers* 58 The magistrates *mis-administration. 1825 COLERIDGE *Aids Refl.* (1848) I. 286 The *misallotment of worldly goods and fortunes. 1642 C. VERNON *Consid. Exch.* 28 The said undue discharges and *misallowances. 1509 BARCLAY *Shyp of Folys* 21 If all the Foly of our Hole Royalme were named Of *mys apparayle. 1862 CARLYLE *Fredk. Gt.* XIII. ii. (1873) V. 26 *Misappointment of your Captains is a fatal business. 1834 DE QUINCEY *Autob. Sk.* Wks. 1854 II. 20 His extravagant *mis-appraisement of Knolles. 1623 BP. HALL *Great Impostor* Wks. (1625) 503 Being ouercome with the false delectablenesse of sinne, it yeelds to a *misse-assent. 1646 R. BAILLIE *Anabaptism* (1647) Pref. b, The ground of this *mis-assertion I take to be a twofold misapprehension. 1888 *Charity Organis. Rev.* Oct. 436 To prevent a mis-association of the sexes. 1706 BAYNARD *Cold Baths* (1709) II. 341 Infants ..may be writh'd..by the least *mis-bandage into any inform Figure. 1596 SPENSER *F.Q.* IV. iii. 11 The meede of thy *mischalenge and abet. 1845 STODDART *Gram.* in *Encycl. Metrop.* I. 131/1 A *miscoinage of Ben Jonson's coarse and pedantic wit. 1826 BENTHAM in *Westm. Rev.* VI. 499 Not only mis-selection..but *miscollocation likewise. *a* 1628 F. GREVIL *Mustapha* III. i. Wks. (Grosart) III. 357 In Tyrants state neuer was man undone By *miscomplaints. 1618 BP. HALL *Righteous Mammon* Wks. (1625) 699 The euill dispositions that doe commonly attend wealth, are Pride and *Misconfidence. 1822–34 *Good's Study Med.* (ed. 4) IV. 160 Labour impeded by *mis-configuration of the fetus. 1819 W. S. ROSE *Lett.* ii. 21 Misconstructions and *misconjugations. 1648 BP. HALL *Select Th.* §6 The *miscredulity of those who will rather trust to the Church than to the Scripture. 1854 [S. R. BOSANQUET] *The First Seal* 71 This wilderness of *misculture and unprofitableness. 1822–34 *Good's Study Med.* (ed. 4) III. 243 Those cases in which the [spinal] *miscurvature is very considerable. 1905 *Daily Chron.* 9 Jan. 4/5 The offence is known in railway parlance as '*misdeclaration of freight'. 1822–34 *Good's Study Med.* (ed. 4) I. 29 Genus I:—Odontia. *Misdentition. 1617 BP. HALL *Quo Vadis?* Ep. Ded., Returning as emptie of grace..as full of words, vanitie, *mis-dispositions. 1624 —— *True Peace-Maker* Wks. (1625) 542 To falsifie the writings of..Authors, by secret expurgations, by wilfull *mis-editions. 1659 HEYLIN *Examen Hist.* II. 66 The *mis-effects of that war. 1829 BENTHAM *Justice & Cod. Petit.* 58 Neither the inefficiency, nor the whole of the *misefficiency, can be brought into view. 1822 GOOD *Study Med.* IV. 131 Seminal *Misemission. 1603 FLORIO *Montaigne* II. xxxiv. (1632) 415

Victories, which one onely disaster, or *mis-encounter, might make him lose. **1822** GOOD *Study Med.* I. 94 Psellismus Blæsitas. *Misenunciation. **1592** *Arden of Feversham* G 4 And aske of God,..Vengeance on Arden, or some *misevent, To shewe the world, what wrong the carle hath done. **1583** GOLDING *Calvin on Deut.* xci. 564 To bee caryed away by their *misexample. **1685** BAXTER *Paraphr. N.T.* Matt. xxiv. 3 Though Christ do not presently blame their *mis-expectations. **1657** J. SERGEANT *Schism Dispach't* 200 These two *mis-explications of Dr. H.'s duly consider'd. **1614** SYLVESTER *Parl. Vertues Royall* 195 Wks. (1621) 853 When by *mis-heed, or by mishap, hee coms.. into the Sacred Rooms. **1652** BP. HALL *Invis. World* I. §9 Here then was this *mis-humility, that they thought it too much boldness to come immediately to God. **1665** WITHER *Lord's Prayer* 121 This *misimputation to God, is continued, though he hath said, (yea sworn) the contrary. **1894** *Eclectic Mag.* Jan. LIX. 20 The hugest and ugliest shed constructible by human *mis-ingenuity. **1680** BAXTER *Answ. Stillingfl.* xxiv. 37 All will not prevent the *mis-intimations even of such worthy Men as you. **1822** GOOD *Study Med.* IV. 37 Galactia. *Mislactation. **1571** GOLDING *Calvin on Ps.* lii. 4 He bursteth not out into *mislanguage too wreake himself. **1822** GOOD *Study Med.* IV. 37 Paramenia. *Mismenstruation. *Ibid.* 438 Paruria. *Mismicturition. *a* **1631** DONNE *Obseq. Ld. Harrington* 132 As small pocket-clocks, whose every wheele Doth each *mismotion and distemper feele. **1904** *Daily Chron.* 8 Jan. 4/6 Drowned through *Misnavigation on the Congo. **1835–6** *Todd's Cycl. Anat.* I. 60/1 Certain morbid conditions of the system, in which there is any process of *mis-nutrition. **1643** MILTON *Divorce* II. ix. Wks. 1851 IV. 83 That our obedience be not *mis-obedience. **1822–34** *Good's Study Med.* (ed. 4) IV. 97 A misformation or *misorganisation of the parts. *Ibid.* 242 Parostia. *Mis-ossification. **1901** *Sotheby's Catal.* May 53 We think that the..*mispagination was an error on the part of the printers. **1633** BP. HALL *Hard Texts, N.T.* 8 The inward *mis-passion of the heart. **1865** J. GROTE *Explor. Philos.* I. Introd. 13 This error I have called ultra-phenomenalism or *mis-phenomenalism. **1896** L. ABBOTT *Christ. & Soc. Probl.* xi. 305 The very phrase 'administration of justice' is a *mis-phrase. **1812** SOUTHEY *Ess.* (1832) I. 154 If some strange *mispolicy does not avert this..natural course of things. [Several other instances in Southey.] **1822–34** *Good's Study Med.* (ed. 4) IV. 156 Those apprehensions which are often entertained by a pregnant woman respecting the *misposition of the child. **1653** BAXTER *Christian Concord* 110 No mans *mis-practice is any reasonable cause of excepting against our Agreement. **1621** BP. MOUNTAGU *Diatribæ* 5 Having once by a *mis-preconceit fashioned their thoughts thereunto. **1905** *Daily News* 26 Jan. 12 The *misproposals of the present Government. **1659** H. L'ESTRANGE *Alliance Div. Off.* 31 Through whose *mis-providence these errours have come to pass. **1865** J. GROTE *Explor. Philos.* I. Introd. 9 A very mistaken view, which I have called generally the wrong psychology or *mis-psychology. **1496** *Dives & Pauper* (W. de W.) IX. vi. 355/2 Them that have mysgoten them by *myspurchace, or by withholdynge of dette. **1851** CARLYLE *Sterling* I. viii, Sordid misbeliefs, *mispursuits and *misresults. *a* **1483** *Liber Niger* in *Househ. Ord.* (1790) 59 To counsayle upon whome to cast the losses of suche *mysse pourveyaunce. **1867** CARLYLE *Remin.* (1881) II. 128 'Sense of the ridiculous'..is withal very indispensable to a man; Hebrews have it not..hence various *misqualities of theirs. **1864** *Daily Tel.* 13 June, The *mis-reception of evidence. *c* **1843** CARLYLE *Hist. Sk.* (1898) 104 Struggling all thy years against poverty and *misrecognition. **1886** GURNEY, etc. *Phantasms of Living* II. 390 The mis-recognition would then be very similar. **1894** J. L. ROBERTSON *Scott's Poet. Wks.* Pref., The discovery of several *mis-references. **1831** *Fraser's Mag.* III. 203 This is a favourite *mis-rhyme. *a* **1670** HACKET *Abp. Williams* I. (1693) 72 That *mis-sentence, which pronounced by a plain and understanding Man, would appear most Gross and Palpable. *c* **1810** COLERIDGE in *Lit. Rem.* (1838) III. 296 They rejected the fact for the sake of the *mis-solution. *a* **1656** BP. HALL *Let. Parænetical* Rem. Wks. (1660) 399 Meer tricks of *mis-suggestion. **1818** SCOTT *Rob Roy* ii, An erasure in the ledger, or a *mis-summation in a fitted account. **1780** BENTHAM *Princ. Legisl.* Wks. 1843 I. 75 Where..there is no *missupposal in the case. **1876** TENNYSON *Q. Mary* IV. ii, The huge corruptions of the Church, Monsters of *mistradition. *a* **1862** O'CURRY *Manners Anc. Irish* (1873) III. 384 This, unless figurative, is clearly a mistake or a *mistranscript. **1868** H. H. GIBBS *Chev. Assigne* Pref. p. i, There are several *mistranscriptions. **1849** *Fraser's Mag.* XXXIX. 598 Trouble and joy in strange *misunion blent. **1882** ABP. BENSON *Let.* in *Life* (1901) 219 Wherever my *miswisdom..draws my eyes down from the Pattern showed us in the Mount.

5. Prefixed to agent-nouns.

1625 BP. MOUNTAGU *App. Cæsar* 232 Wicked *mis-agents in respect of living. *a* **1618** SYLVESTER *St. Lewis* 670 Wks. (Grosart) II. 236 Who..could better brook A *miss-Fault-finder, than a Fawner's looke. **1547** *Reg. Privy Council Scot.* I. 75 Thai salbe reput and halding as *misfavouraris of this realme. **1574** tr. *Marlorat's Apocalips* 39 *marg.*, Hypocrites and *misprofessors of religion. **1638** MEDE *Disc. Texts* xlvi. Wks. II. (1672) 258 All prophaners and *misreceivers of those Sacred pledges. **1891** *Sat. Rev.* 30 May 667/1 The incorrigible *misrhymer who jingles 'burden' and 'pardon'.

6. Prefixed to adjs. with the sense of 'wrongly', 'erroneously', 'perversely'.

1620 BP. HALL *Hon. Marr. Clergy* III. iii, Whether the catholike Bishop that wrote this, or the *mis-catholike masse-priest that reproues it, be more worthy of Bedleem. **1641** —— *Answ. Vind. Smectymnuus* §2. 22 My eyes are so Lyncean, as to see you proudly *mis-confident. **1893** STEVENSON *Catriona* x. (1903) 110 It is most *misconvenient at least. **1837** SYD. SMITH *Let. Archd. Singleton* iii. Wks. (1850) 641/2 In defeating this *mis-ecclesiastic law. **1614** SYLVESTER *Little Bartas* 822 Without *mis-fond affection.

7. Expressing negation (of something good or desirable); equivalent to DIS-, IN-, or UN-.

In OE., *misȝieman, mishieran, misspówan, mistríewan, misweorþian* are instances in which this meaning is more or less clearly developed.

1649 EARL MONM. tr. *Senault's Use Passions* (1671) 82 Men..seem to have a design to hasten their *misadvantages. **1859** TENNYSON *Holy Grail* 175 And once by *misadvertence Merlin sat In his own chair. **1816** COLERIDGE *Lett.* (1895) 658 If pain and sorrow and self-*miscomplacence had not forced my mind in on itself. **1855** A. H. STEPHENS in Johnston & Browne *Life* (1878) 288 That..the Supreme Court would hold it to be *misconstitutional. **1893** STEVENSON *Catriona* 108 It is most *misconvenient at least. **1704** F. FULLER *Med. Gymn.* (1718) 76 The Pus, the Slough, and all the *Mispurities of the Sore. **1382** WYCLIF *Ecclus.* xxv. 29 The wrathe of a womman and the *mysreuerence [1388 vnreuerence, Vulg. *irreverentia*]. **1850** *Tait's Mag.* XVII. 2/1 A rental of ten pounds yearly would be, for many families, a deed of *misthrift.

8. Prefixed to words denoting something wrong or bad, serving as an intensive.

In OE. we have *misscręnce* by the side of *ȝe-scręnce* = withered.

1570 in J. P. Collier *Old Ballads* (Percy Soc. 1840) 79 What *mis-deformed wights Of women borne there bee. **1656** EARL MONM. tr. *Boccalini's Advts. fr. Parnass.* I. lxxxvii. 171 The..reproaches..which Poets..make.. against such *misdemeriting men [orig. *huomini di tanto demerito*]. *Ibid.* II. xcv. 388 His Majesty thought he had no waies *mis-demerited [orig. *demeritato*] by that his forgetfulness. *Ibid.* I. ii. 4 The *misdemerits [orig. *il demerito*] of this fellow. **1533** BELLENDEN *Livy* III. xxiii. (S.T.S.) II. 40 We..covatis nocht bot ȝow to be penitent of ȝoure *mysfalt. *c* **1470** HARDING *Chron.* CLXXVI. iii, That ruled had in mykell *mysryote. ? *a* **1500** *Felon Sewe of Rokeby* in R. Bell *Anc. Poems*, etc. (1857) 134 Ye wolde hav ren awaye, When moste *misstirre had bin. **1592** WYRLEY *Armorie* 152 *Capitall de Buz*, Bicause from England he was late *mistraid [= mis-strayed].

9. The existence of pairs of words like *misbelieve* and *disbelieve*, *mislike* and *dislike* gave rise to confusion between the prefixes and to the (often unmeaning) substitution of *mis-* for *dis-* (and even *des-*), as in †*misguise*, †*mismay*. To the same confusion are due the dial. *misdain*, *misdainful* (after *disdain*), *miscry* for *descry*, and *mislest*, corruption of *molest*; also the obs. *mislaundre* for *dislaundre* DISCLANDER.

mis- (mɪs), *prefix*[2] (Forms: 3–5 **mes-**, 4 **mess(e)-**, 4–5 **myss(e)-**, 3– **mis-**) in compounds adopted from French represents OF. *mes-* (mod.F. *més-*, *mes-*, *mé*) = Pr. *mes-*, *mens-*, Sp., Pg. *menos-*, OIt. *menes-*, *minis-*, It. *mis-* (also med.L. *mis-*):—Com. Rom. *minus-*, a use of L. *minus* adv. 'less, not', as a prefix with the signification 'bad(ly)', 'wrong(ly)', 'amiss', and with negative force, in comb. with verbs, adjectives, and nouns.

The list of words derived immediately from OFr. compounds of *mes-* is not large, the most important being MISADVENTURE, MISCHANCE, MISCHIEF, MISCONTENT, MISCREANT, MISEASE, MISNOMER, MISPRIZE; but the number due directly or indirectly to the influence of such compounds is prob. much larger (cf. MIS-[1]). In English the prefix became ultimately identical in form (as it was in meaning) with MIS-[1].

Mischief, mischievous, and *miscreant* are the only compounds of MIS-[2] having the stress on the prefix. This is due to the fact that they early ceased to be felt as compounds, and while they followed the rule of stress-change in French-derived words, *mischance* and the rest fell under the influence of the native compounds of MIS-[1], and so have their stress on the root.

mis-, *prefix*[3]: see MISO-.

mis', var. MISS *sb.*[2] 5.

†**misac'cept**, *v. Obs. rare.* [MIS-[1] 1.] *trans.* To take (a word) in a wrong sense. Hence †**misac'cepter**.

1697 J. SERGEANT *Solid Philos.* 88 My Intention..is..to settle the True and Genuine Sense of such Words, to be applied afterwards to the Mis-accepters of them, as occasion requires. *Ibid.* 288 Those Words, which have been Abus'd or Mis-accepted by Trivial Philosophers.

misaccep'tation. *rare*⁻⁰. [MIS-[1] 4.] The taking of a word in a wrong sense.

1721 BAILEY, *Misacceptation*, a wrong Understanding or Apprehension of any thing. **1755** in JOHNSON.

†**misac'ception.** *Obs.* [MIS-[1] 4: see ACCEPTION 4.] = prec.

1628–9 BP. HALL *Serm. to Lords* 18 Feb. Wks. 1808 V. 385 The Apostle..contemning all impotent mis-acceptions, calls them what he finds them, A froward generation. **1697** J. SERGEANT *Solid Philos.* 109 What Prodigious Inconveniences do arise from the Mis-acceptions of one of those many Different Senses such Words may bear. **1727** in BAILEY vol. II.

†**mi'saccident.** *Obs.* [f. MIS-[1] 4 + ACCIDENT *sb.*, after *mischance*.] = MISCHANCE, MISHAP.

1623 in H. Foley *Rec. Eng. Prov. S.J.* I. 95 His majestie was verie sorrie for the mis-accident that happened at the French Ambassador's. **1633** BP. HALL *Occas. Medit.* vi. 16 Here is a great world in a little roome, by the skill of the workeman, but in lesse roome, by mis-accident. **1648** —— *Breathings Devout Soul* (1851) 187 Secular mis-accidents.

†**misa'ccount**, *v. Obs.* [MIS-[1] 1.] *trans.* To misreckon, misjudge.

c **1374** CHAUCER *Troylus* V. 1185 He thoughte he mis-acounted hadde his day. **1603** FLORIO *Montaigne* III. xiii. 639 How often..hee hath beene deceived, and mis-accompted his owne judgement. **1655** J. SEDGWICK in *E. Calamy's Serm.* 17 Oct. 1654. 28 Misaccounting his years summe.

misact (mɪs'ækt), *v.* [MIS-[1] 1.] *trans.* and *intr.* To act badly. Also † **mis'acting** *vbl. sb.*

1609 J. RAWLINSON *Fishermen* 35 So if the Minister did misact but an earthly Prince only, his fault were more tolerable. **1614** T. ADAMS *Physicke fr. Heaven* Wks. (1633) 300 The Player, that misacts an inferiour and vnnoted part, carryes it away without censure. **1651** W. LYFORD *Serm.* (1654) 4 In case of misactings. **1665** WITHER *Lord's Prayer* 159 Truely repenting his other misactings. **1925** *Contemp. Rev.* Nov. 624 The wonderful scene in Pimen's cell..was completely 'mis-acted', if I may use a non-existing word.

†**mis'action.** *Obs.* [MIS-[1] 4.] A wrong action; misdoing.

1693 W. FREKE *Sel. Ess.* xxxi. 182 The only occasion of his [*viz.* God's] Contempt of us, is our Misaction, and our Aberration from his Law.

†**mis'actor.** *Obs.* [MIS-[1] 5.] A misdoer.

1659 C. NOBLE *Mod. Ans. to Immod. Queries* 14 Here's a down right quarrel to the..management of State Affairs; the mis-actors herein he names to be some Lawyers.

misa'dapt, *v.* [MIS-[1] 1.] To adapt wrongly.

1862 MRS. N. CROSLAND *Mrs. Blake* II. 307 By a gradual misapplication of ideas, some persons have grown to 'mis-adapt' the thought.

misadap'tation. [MIS-[1] 4.] Defective adaptation, want of adaptation.

1878 MORLEY *Diderot* I. iv. 94 The marvels of misadaptation in the Universe. **1888** H. S. HOLLAND *Christ or Eccl.* 5 Every day has some fresh discovery to make to us of..misadaptation, disorder, confusion.

misa'ddress, *v.* [MIS-[1] 1.] *trans.* To address wrongly or impertinently. Also **misa'ddressed** *ppl. a.* and **misa'ddressing** *vbl. sb.*

1648 BOYLE *Seraphic Love* (1660) 49 A fervent Love seems little less than Devotion misaddrest. **1858** CARLYLE *Fredk. Gt.* II. VII. v. 225 This one [letter]..by mere misaddressing, ..fell into the hands of vigilant Rittmeister Katte. **1885** MCCONKEY *Hero of Cowpens* xxiv. 228 These..cautions seem singularly misaddressed, to the man who had never been known to be surprised from Quebec to Cowpens. **1892** STEVENSON *Vailima Lett.* (1895) 163 Receiving misaddressed letters.

misa'djusted, *ppl. a.* Badly adjusted.

1860 I. TAYLOR *Ess.* 276 They are in a misadjusted condition.

misa'djustment. [MIS-[1] 4.]

1. Want of adjustment.

1827 I. TAYLOR *Transm. Anc. Bks.* (1859) 410 The wrong chronological conceptions which have arisen from the mis-adjustment of them as to their order of time. **1888** MARTINEAU *Study Relig.* II. IV. iii. 384 Apparent misadjustments of this world's goods.

2. *U.S.* Lack of agreement or harmony.

1878 GARFIELD in *N. Amer. Rev.* CXXVI. 450 The mis-adjustment between the Secretary of War and the army.

misadventure (mɪsæd'vɛntjʊər, -tʃə(r)), *sb.* Forms: 3–6 (9 *arch.*) **misaventure**, (3–6 **-eur**, 4 **-ur**, 4–6 **-our**, 6 **-aventre**), 5– **-adventure**. See also MISAUNTER. [a. OF. *mesaventure* (12th c.), f. *mesavenir* to turn out badly, after *aventure* ADVENTURE *sb.*: see MIS-[2].

The spelling with *-ad-* appears first in the 15th c., but does not become regular till the end of the 16th c., when the stress also finally settled in its present position.]

1. Ill-luck, bad fortune. Nearly always in particularized use: A piece of bad fortune; a mishap or misfortune.

c **1290** *S. Eng. Leg.* I. 364/11 Muche reuþe was into al þat lond of þis misauenture. *c* **1330** R. BRUNNE *Chron. Wace* (Rolls) 9218, & preye Iesu our Saueour To schulde vs fro mysauentour. *c* **1407** LYDG. *Reson & Sens.* 4238 The sorrowes and mysaventures..That loves folkys ha suffred there. *c* **1425** *Eng. Conq. Irel.* 68 Good aduentures comen oft slowly & aloon, bot mesaduentures ne cometh neuermore aloon. **1500–20** DUNBAR *Poems* xx. 44 Hald God thy friend, ..He will the confort in all misaventeur. *c* **1510** BARCLAY *Mirror Gd. Manners* (1570) D v, Joy sauced is with payne,.. Mixt with misadueture be chaunces prosperous. **1592** SHAKS. *Rom. & Jul.* v. i. 29 Your lookes are pale and wild, and do import Some misaduenture. **1614** RALEIGH *Hist. World* II. (1634) 407 All under the Sunne are subject to worldly miseries and misadventures. **1792** BURKE *Pres. St. Aff.* Wks. VII. 103 The grand, solid body..proceeded leisurely..to support the expedite body in case of misadventure. **1822** SHELLEY tr. *Calderon's Magico Prodigioso* ii. 102 Among my misadventures This shipwreck is the least. *a* **1850** ROSSETTI *Dante & Circle* I. (1874) 151 Through this my strong and new misaventure, All now is lost to me. **1878** BOSW. SMITH *Carthage* 323 Not a misadventure or a hitch occurred. **1885** *Manch. Exam.* 3 June 5/1 There was a mistake, or a misunderstanding, or a misadventure of some sort.

2. Phrases. **a.** † *at*, *by misadventure* (see also 3): by an unlucky accident. † **b.** *to bid* (a thing) *misadventure*: to curse. *to do* (a person) *misadventure*: to bring disaster or ruin upon. † **c.** In imprecatory expressions.

a. *c* **1330** R. BRUNNE *Chron.* (1810) 166 His nese & his ine he carfe at misauentoure. **1470–85** MALORY *Arthur* III. vii. 107 And soo he smote of her hede by mysauenture. *Ibid.* VII. vi. 221 Alle that euer thou dost is but by mysauenture and not by prowesse of thy handes. **1820** SHELLEY tr. *Dante's Convito* 55 If by misadventure chance should bring Thee to base company. **1873** BROWNING *Red Cott. Nt.-cap* II. 669 Made aware By misadventure that his bounty..comforted a visitant.

b. *c*1330 *Arth. & Merl.* 4384 (Kölbing) Boþe o lif & eke tresour þai dede þe paiens misauentour. *Ibid.* 8361 He.. bad þe time mesauenture, þat he cunteked wiþ king Arthour.

c. *a*1300 *K. Horn* 344 (Camb. MS.) Went [= go] vt of my bur, Wiþ muchel mesauenteur. *c*1386 CHAUCER *Friar's T.* 36 'Pees, with mischance and with misaventure', Thus seyde our host, 'and lat him telle his tale'. *c*1450 *Merlin* 68 And she seide 'Mysauenture haue that it kepeth eny counseile'.

3. *Law.* Homicide committed accidentally by a person in doing a lawful act, without any intention of hurt; now chiefly in phr. ***homicide*** or ***death by misadventure***.

[*c*1290 BRITTON (1865) I. ii. §2 Cum nule felounie ou mesaueunture soit avenue.] 1509–10 *Act 1 Hen. VIII*, c. 7 Yf eny persone hathe happened to be slayne by myssaventre and not by no mannys Hande. 1581 W. STAFFORD *Exam. Compl.* iii. (1876) 85 A man that had trespassed the lawe of misadueuture. 1596 BACON *Max. & Use Com. Law* I. (1630) 30 If diuers bee in danger of drowning by the casting away of some boate.. and one of them get to some plancke.. and another to save his life thrust him from it, whereby hee is drowned, this is neither *se defendendo* nor by misadueuture, but iustifiable. 1614 —— *Charge touching Duels* 20 For the case of misadueuture it selfe, there were Citties of refuge. 1769 BLACKSTONE *Comm.* IV. IV. xiv. 182 Homicide *per infortunium*, or misadventure. *Ibid.*, Where a parent is moderately correcting his child, a master his servant or scholar, or an officer punishing a criminal, and happens to occasion his death, it is only misadventure. 1800 *Addison's Rep.* 8 Homicide by misadventure is an unlawful killing by accident. 1903 *Blackw. Mag.* Dec. 772/1 Death by misadventure in the ordinary execution of her duty.

†misad'venture, *v. Obs.*$^{-0}$ [nonce-formation on It. (see quot.).]

1611 FLORIO, *Misauenturáre*, to misadueuture.

†misad'ventured, *a. Obs.*$^{-1}$ [f. MISADVENTURE *sb.* Cf. OF. *mésaventuré*.] Unfortunate.

1592 SHAKS. *Rom. & Jul.* Prol. 7 (Qo.) Whose misaduentur'd pittious ouerthrowes, Doth with their death burie their Parents strife.

misadventurer (mɪsæd'vɛntjʊrə(r)). *rare.* [f. MISADVENTURE *sb.* + -ER[1].] One who meets with or suffers misadventures; an unfortunate person.

1886 HARDY *Mayor Casterbr.* II. xviii. 250 His mood was no longer that of the rebellious, ironical, reckless misadventurer.

misadventurous (mɪsæd'vɛntjʊərəs), *a.* Also 5 **mysauentrous**. [In the early quot. a. OF. *mesaventureux*; in the mod. instances f. MISADVENTURE + -OUS.] Unfortunate, unlucky.

*c*1400 tr. *Secreta Secret.*, *Gov. Lordsh.* 114 Kepe þe fro vche mysauentrous man, þat ys lesnyd of any membre. *a*1693 *Urquhart's Rabelais* III. xxii. 180 He was.. so unfortunately misadventrous in the Lot of his own Destiny, that [etc.]. 1742 C. JARVIS *Don Quixote* (1749) II. II. i. 104 The obstinacy, with which he was bent upon the search of his misadventurous adventures. 1817 COLERIDGE *Biog. Lit.* xx. (Bohn) 201 A few misadventurous attempts to translate the arts and sciences into verse. 1842 H. TAYLOR *Edwin the Fair* IV. i. 180 Our misadventurous Synod.

Hence **misad'venturously** *adv.*, by misadventure.

1632 STRAFFORD in Browning *Life* (1891) 300, I am hartely sorrye for him and for myself too, that.. should thus misaduenturousely light vpon a man, that [etc.].

misad'vertence. *rare.* [MIS-[1] 4.] Carelessness, thoughtlessness, absent-mindedness.

1870 TENNYSON *Holy Grail* 43 Once by misadvertence Merlin sat In his own chair, and so was lost.

misad'vice. [MIS-[1] 4.] Wrong advice.

1632 SHERWOOD, Misaduise, *mesadvis.* *a*1684 LEIGHTON 18 *Serm.* vii. (1745) 113 When they are abused by Misadvice and corrupt Counsel. 1775 LORD CHATHAM *Sp.* in *Modern Orator* (1847) 71 To rescue him from the misadvice of his present Ministers.

misad'vise, *v.* [MIS-[1] 1.]

†**1.** *refl.* To take a wrong counsel; to act unadvisedly. *Obs.*

[1370–80: see MISADVISED.] *c*1386 CHAUCER *Wife's Prol.* 230, I sey nat this by wyves that ben wyse, But-if it be whan they hem misavyse. 1602 WARNER *Alb. Eng.* XI. lxvii. (1606) 285 In making Loue vnmeant thou didst thy selfe but misaduise.

2. *trans.* To advise wrongly.

*a*1548 HALL *Chron.*, *Hen. IV*, 8 b, Ruled and misavised by the evell.. councell of perverse.. persons. 1659 in Rushw. *Hist. Coll.* I. 607 They accused John de Gaunt.. and Lord Latimer, and Lord Nevil, for misadvising the King. 1679 BEDLOE *Narr. Popish Plot* Ep., To have Some of their Chief Friends thereabouts, that may misadvise Great Persons. 1727 in BAILEY vol. II. 1827 POLLOK *Course Time* IX. (1860) 266 Nor failed to misadvise his future hope And faith, by false unkerneled promises. 1849 GROTE *Hist. Greece* II. lvi. (1862) V. 91 He.. had fatally misadvised his countrymen into making important cessions.

Hence †**misadvising** (? *ppl. a. absol.*, ill-advised persons; or = MIS *a.* + ADVISING *vbl. sb.*).

*a*1461 *Pol. Poems* (Rolls) II. 253 Many a wondurfulle dysgyzyng, By unprudent and myssavyzyng.

†mis-ad'vised, *ppl. a. Obs.* [f. prec. + -ED[1] or f. MIS[1] 2 + ADVISED.] Wrongly advised; ill-advised; injudicious.

1370–80 *XI Pains of Hell* 237 in *O.E. Misc.* 229 He haþ ben muche mys-Auyset, Godus Comaundemens he haþ dispyset. 1400 in *Roy. & Hist. Lett. Hen. IV* (Rolls) I. 37 We was nevere so mys avised to worch agayn the Kyng no his lawes. *c*1460 *Play Sacram.* 639 Voydeth from my syght & yt wyghtly ffor ye be mysse a vysed. 1469 in *10th Rep. Hist. MSS. Comm.* App. v. 306 Affray made of purpose or by mysse-advised men. *a*1529 SKELTON *Ware the Hauke* 22 To make complaynte Of such mysaduysed Parsons and dysgysed. 1590 SPENSER *F.Q.* III. ii. 9 Ye misavised beene t'upbrayd A gentle knight with so unknightly blame. 1643 PRYNNE *Sov. Power Parl.* II. (ed. 2) 76 It would rest in the meere power.. of a wilfull or misadvised King.. to deprive the Kingdome of the.. use.. of Parliaments. 1780 BENTHAM *Princ. Morals* (1789) ix. §6 In such case the act may be said to be mis-advised.

Hence †**misad'visedly** *adv.*, ill-advisedly, imprudently; †**misad'visedness**, the quality or condition of being misadvised.

*a*1548 HALL *Chron.*, *Edw. IV* (1550) 30 Lest it shoulde be laied to her charge, that she had doen any thyng misaduisedly. 1548 UDALL *Erasm. Par. Luke* ix. 85 If the teacher dooe not presumpteouslye vsurp to hymself the gifte of learnyng.. ne vndiscretely or mysaduisedly shewe foorth the same as though it wer of his owne. 1780 BENTHAM *Princ. Morals* (1789) ix. §16 In the case of *mis*-advisedness with respect to any circumstance. *Ibid.* §17 Un-advisedness coupled with heedlessness, and mis-advisedness coupled with rashness correspond to the *culpa sine dolo*.

†misad'visement. *Obs.* = MISADVICE.

1594 LODGE *Wounds Civ. W.* v. I 4 b, These are verie indiscreet counsailes neighbor Poppey, and I will follow your misaduisement.

†misa'ffect, *v. Obs.* [MIS-[1] 1, 7.]

1. *trans.* To affect injuriously.

1621 BURTON *Anat. Mel.* I. i. III. i, Fracastorius.. calls those melancholy, whom abundance of.. black choler hath so misaffected, that they become mad thence. 1650 CHARLETON *Paradoxes* 60 When the Palate is misaffected with paine.

2. To dislike.

1586 BACON *Let. to Ld. Treas.* Wks. 1830 XII. 473 They [*sc.* objections] were delivered by men that did misaffect me. 1641 MILTON *Animadv.* Postscr. 74 That peace which you have hitherto so perversely misaffected.

†misa'ffected, *ppl. a. Obs.* [Partly f. prec. + -ED[1], partly f. MIS-[1] 2 + AFFECTED. Cf. OF. *mesafaitié* evil-disposed.]

1. Affected by illness or disease; diseased.

1621 BURTON *Anat. Mel.* I. iii. II. iv. (1651) 204 Such are for the most part misaffected and prone to this disease. 1694 *Phil. Trans.* XVIII. 17 The Liver.. which by some is adjudged to be particularly.. misaffected in this Distemper.

2. Ill-disposed, disaffected.

1633 BP. HALL *Occas. Medit.* (1634) xxi. 126 By how much more excellent any object is, by so much more is our weake sense mis-affected in the first apprehending of it. 1645 *Some Observations* 3 An ill Rhetorician to a misaffected and ignorant People may make this seem very odious.

misa'ffection. Now *rare* or *Obs.* [MIS-[1] 4.]

1. Perverted affection; disaffection.

1621 BP. MOUNTAGU *Diatribæ* 425 Your ill disposition, and mis-affection vnto him. 1635 J. HAYWARD tr. *Biondi's Banish'd Virg.* 28 The misaffections and disaffections of his sonnes. 1635 BP. HALL *Char. Man* 41 How earthly and grosse with misaffections.

2. Physical disorder; disease.

1673 O. WALKER *Educ.* 71 Divers misaffections in the eyes, by Spectacles. 1822–34 *Good's Study Med.* (ed. 4) III. 398 Flatulency or some other misaffection of the stomach. *Ibid.* 401, IV. 44, 295, 524. 1847 BUSHNELL *Chr. Nurture* II. i. (1861) 238 The seminal damages and misaffections derived from sinning ancestors.

†misa'ffectionate, *a. Obs.*$^{-1}$ [MIS-[1] 6.] Evil-disposed.

1533 MORE *Let. to T. Cromwell* Wks. 1428/2 Which condicion hath neuer growne.. of any obstinate minde or misse affectionate appetite.

misa'ffirm, *v. rare.* [MIS-[1] 1.] *trans.* To affirm wrongly or falsely.

*a*1614 DONNE *Βιαθανατος* (1644) 27 They mis-affirme that this act alwaies proceeds from desperation. 1649 MILTON *Eikon.* Pref., By onely remembring them the truth of what they themselves know to be heer missaffirmd.

misagree, *v.* [MIS-[1] 7.]

1. *intr.* To disagree. Now *dial.*

1530 PALSGR. 636/2, I never wyst them misagre afore in my lyfe. *a*1542 WYATT *Defence* 264 If they misagree in words, and not in substance, let us hear the words they vary in. 1847 HALLIWELL, *Misagree*, to disagree. 1875 PARISH *Sussex Gloss.* s.v., I doant see how anyone can be off from misagreeing with these here people next door.

2. To be inconsistent or out of harmony.

1571 GOLDING *Calvin on Ps.* x. 10 It wil not misagree that the sayd talantes and teethe should by a similitude be called strong souldyers.

misai, obs. form of MISSAY.

mis'aim, *v. rare.* [MIS-[1] 1.] To aim amiss.

1590 SPENSER *F.Q.* I. viii. 8 Missing the marke of his misaymed sight. 1692 DRYDEN *Cleomenes* II. ii. 21 My languishing Regards Are like mis-aiming Arrows, lost in Air. 1813 SCOTT *Rokeby* IV. xxii, Some tale.. of shaft misaimed.

misa'lignment. Also misalinement. [MIS-[1] 4.] Bad or imperfect alignment.

1924 J. F. HOBART *Tulley's Handbk.* (ed. 7) II. xv. 582 Misalignment refers either to that of the turbine and generator, or that of the rotating and stationary elements. 1937 *Marconi Rev.* May–Aug. 27 The tracking does not allow phase misalignment greater than ±5 degrees. 1947 *Brit. Jrnl. Psychol.* Dec. 57 It is easy to present a misalinement to an operator, and then screen his eyes just before he makes his corrective movement. 1963 C. R. COWELL et al. *Inlays, Crowns & Bridges* xii. 130 Difficulty is rarely encountered with cases of gross misalignment [of the teeth]. 1974 *Sci. Amer.* May 54/3 There is often a misalignment of the eyes too.

So **misa'ligned** *a.*

1948 *Aircraft Power Plants* (Northrop Aeronaut. Inst.) 216 The crank extension shaft may be misaligned. 1954 S. DUKE-ELDER *Parsons' Dis. Eye* (ed. 12) xxix. 483 In concomitant squint, as opposed to paralytic squint, although the eyes are misaligned, they retain their abnormal relation to each other in all movements. 1962 A. NISBETT *Technique Sound Studio* iv. 81 (*caption*) Misaligned recording or reproducing head. 1973 *New Scientist* 22 Nov. 544 Directional roof aerials pointed accurately at Wrotham for optimum BBC reception are, likely as not, hopelessly misaligned for signals from Croydon.

†misalle'gation. *Obs.* [MIS-[1] 4.] A false allegation; a misleading citation (of an authority).

1633 (*title*) A Discharge of Five Imputations or Misallegations. 1647 JER. TAYLOR *Lib. Proph.* viii. 155, I must consider.. the mis-allegations of Scripture, their inconsequent deductions [etc.].

†misa'llege, *v. Obs.* [MIS-[1] 1.] *trans.* To cite falsely as supporting one's contention.

1566 STAPLETON *Ret. Untruths to Jewell* Ep.**, What kinde is there of Authors, that you haue not Corrupted, Misalleaged, False Translated, and Abused? 1625 BP. MOUNTAGU *App. Cæsar* 299 If I have misalledged, falsified, or else misapplyed my Authors and Authority. 1642 J. BALL *Answ. to Can* i. 10, I wonder if men doe not tremble thus to .. misalledge the holy scripture. *a*1670 HACKET *Cent. Serm.* (1675) 323 The Devil did Misalledge the Psalm of David, because he gave it a sense repugnant to the text of Moses.

So **misa'lleged** *ppl. a.*, **misa'lleging** *vbl. sb.*

15.. in Strype *Ann. Ref.* (1709) I. App. xi. 36 Excusinge the mysalledginge of Words. 1620 BP. HALL *Hon. Marr. Clergy* I. ix. 53 Those two mis-alledged Authors, to whom hee ascribes vs. 1629 H. BURTON *Truth's Triumph* 343 A mis-alledged place, or a mis-conceiued allegation. *a*1684 LEIGHTON *Expos. Creed* Wks. (1859) 442/2 There shall be no misalleging or misproving, or misjudging there.

misa'lliance. [f. MIS-[1] 4 + ALLIANCE, after F. *mésalliance*.] An improper alliance, association, or union; *esp.* in reference to marriage = MÉSALLIANCE.

1738 WARBURTON *Div. Legat.* III. iii. I. 350 The only Greek Masters he [*sc.* Plato] followed, were Pythagoras and Socrates... This was a monstrous Misalliance. 1755 CHESTERF. in *World* No. 114 IV. 84 Brutes.. never degenerate, except in cases of mis-alliances with their inferiors. 1762 BP. HURD *Lett. Chivalry* viii. 71 Their purpose was to ally.. the Gothic, and the classic unity; the effect of which misalliance was to.. expose the nakedness of the Gothic. 1768 *Woman of Honor* II. 159 No remains of her former notions of mis-alliance, interfere to lessen her present vexation. 1839–40 W. IRVING *Chron. Wolfert's Roost* (1855) 189 They would have considered their mares disgraced, and their whole stud dishonoured by such a misalliance. 1840 THACKERAY *Paris Sk.-bk.* (1872) 34 A grocer's daughter would think she made a misalliance by marrying a painter. 1876 MEREDITH *Beauch. Career* III. viii. 138 He had no wish to meet his uncle, whose behaviour in contracting a misalliance.. appeared to him to call for the reverse of compliments.

misallo'cation. [MIS-[1] 4.] Failure to allocate in an efficient or correct way what is to be assigned or distributed.

1950 *Jrnl. Pol. Econ.* Apr. 118 The crop-share lease has not resulted in the gross misallocation of land that would have occurred. 1961 *Ann. Reg. 1960* 474 There can be no doubt that misallocation and waste continued in 1960. 1965 H. KAHN *On Escalation* viii. 152 There has been a startling misallocation of official emphasis. 1971 *Nature* 9 July 82/2 Mondale's argument that the shuttle is a far grosser misallocation of priorities than the SST.. may carry great weight.

misally (mɪsə'laɪ), *v. rare.* [MIS-[1] 1. Cf. F. *mésallier*.] *trans.* To ally or join inappropriately.

1697 VANBRUGH *Æsop* I. 11 *Hort.* Sir, I keep my Chamber, and converse with my self; 'tis better being alone, than to mis-ally ones Conversation. 1796 BURKE *Let. to Noble Lord* Wks. VIII. 52 They are a misallied and disparaged branch of the house of Nimrod. 1860 READE *Cloister & H.* xxxvii, These beauties being misallied to homely features, had turned her head.

misandry: see MISO-.

†mis'answer, *sb. Obs.* [MIS-[1] 4.]

1. A wrong answer.

1496 *Dives & Pauper* (W. de W.) v. xix. 222/2 Yf a clerke erre in answerynge and by his mys answere folowed manslaughter.

2. Failure to correspond to requirements.

1614 BP. HALL *Contempl.*, *O.T.* VI. 156 Hee that after the misse-answere of the one talent, would not trust the euill seruant with a second.

†mis'answer, *v. Obs.* [MIS-[1] 1.] *trans.* To give a wrong or perverse answer to (a person).

*c*1400 *Rule St. Benet* 24 Yef ani man askis hir ohte þat es a-gain resun, sho sal noht.. mis-ancewer þam. *a*1450 *Knt. de La Tour* xviii. 26 Alle women that ben gretherted and misansueringe her husbondes. 1535 *Horæ in usum Sarum* 155 I haue synned.. whan I haue mysanswered myn euen chrysten reioysynge.

misanthrope ('mɪsænθrəʊp). Forms: α. 6–7 **misantropos**, 7 **misanthropos**, *pl.* **-thropi**. β. 7 **misanthrop**, 8 **-thrope**. [ad. Gr. μισάνθρωπος

(adj.), f. μῑσ(ο)- (μισεῖν to hate) + ἄνθρωπος man. Cf. F. *misanthrope* (Rabelais).

The stressing of the Greek form in the 17th c. was *mis'anthropos*.]

A hater of mankind; a man-hater; one who distrusts men and avoids their society.

α. **1563** A. NEVILLE in *Googe's Eglogs* (Arb.) 23 Defye them all. μισάνθρωποι and squynteyd Monsters ryght They are. **1579–80** NORTH *Plutarch* (1595) 171 Timon, surnamed *Misanthropus* [ed. **1676** *Misantropos*]. **1607** SHAKS. *Timon* IV. iii. 53. **1612** BACON *Ess., Goodness* (Arb.) 205 *Misanthropi*, that make it their Practise, to bring Men, to the bough. **1612** T. JAMES *Jesuits Downefall* 5 Nether Zoilus, Aristarchus, Timon, or other Misanthropos. **1678** SHADWELL *Timon* v. 74 Hee'll ne'r return; he truly is *Misanthropos*.

β. **1683** D. A. *Art Converse* 55 A misanthrop in such a measure that can praise nothing that is praise worthy. *a* **1745** SWIFT *On Death Dr. S.* Wks. 1751 VII. 254 Alas, poor Dean! his only Scope Was to be held a Misanthrope. **1794** SULLIVAN *View Nat.* I. 10 It is said, that the most religious men are in general the most inflexible misanthropes. **1849** MACAULAY *Hist. Eng.* ii. I. 169 Ill as he [*viz.* Charles II] thought of his species, he never became a misanthrope.

b. Used as *adj.* = next.

1757 MRS. GRIFFITH *Lett. Henry & Frances* (1767) II. 129 My philosophy is neither of the cynic or misanthrope kind. **1875** JOWETT *Plato* (ed. 2) III. 79 The finer..natures..may become misanthrope and philanthrope by turns.

misanthropic (mɪsæn'θrɒpɪk), *a.* [f. prec. + -IC. Cf. F. *misanthropique*.] Pertaining to, resembling, or characteristic of, a misanthrope; characterized by misanthropy; man-hating.

1762 *Biogr. Dict.* XI. 65 [Swift's epitaph] shews a most unhappy misanthropic state of mind. **1812** BYRON *Ch. Har.* I. lxxxiv, He..view'd them not with misanthropic hate. **1824** SCOTT *St. Ronan's* v, A misanthropic recluse. **1881** *Med. Temp. Jrnl.* XLVII. 163 Insomnia does not so much produce special local affections as a miserable misanthropic state.

misan'thropical, *a.* [Formed as prec.: see -ICAL.] = prec.

1621 T. GRANGER *Expos. Eccl.* iv. 9 An illustration of the vanities of Misanthropicall couetousnesse. **1751** SMOLLETT *Per. Pic.* (1779) II. lxxi. 259 His disposition was altogether misanthropical. **1841** MACAULAY *Ess., Hastings* (1850) 604 He had thrown down his pen in misanthropical despair. **1864** C. KNIGHT *Pass. Working Life* II. 51 No desertion of old friends rendered me misanthropical.

b. *absol.* (See DO *v.* 11j.)

1836–7 DICKENS *Sk. Boz., Characters* i, Old fellows..who ..do the misanthropical in chambers, taking great delight in thinking themselves unhappy.

Hence **misan'thropically** *adv.*

1834 H. MILLER *Scenes & Leg.* xvi. (1857) 243 Misanthropically accumulating into one gloomy heap all that is terrible in the judgments of God. **1864** [F. W. ROBINSON] *Mattie* II. 283 He thought, a little misanthropically, it did not matter.

misanthropist (mɪ'sænθrəpɪst). [f. Gr. μισάνθρωπ-ος MISANTHROPE + -IST.] = MISANTHROPE.

Todd, s.v. *Misanthrope*, says 'It is now usual to say *misanthropist*'. But this form is now very rare.

1656 BLOUNT *Glossogr., Misanthropist*, he that hates the company of men. **1791** CUMBERLAND *Observer* No. 138 V. 130 Passages..where he [*sc.* Menander] speaks in the character of a misanthropist. **1876** L. STEPHEN *Eng. Th. 18th C.* II. XII. iv. 372 The sturdy moralist had a hearty dislike for the misanthropist.

Hence **mi'santhropism** = MISANTHROPY.

1832 *Fraser's Mag.* V. 535 Parading an ultra-misanthropism, and complaining of a morbid and melancholy mind.

misanthropize (mɪ'sænθrəpaɪz), *v.* [f. Gr. μῑσάνθρωπ-ος MISANTHROPE + -IZE.]

1. *intr.* To be a misanthrope; to hate mankind.

1846 *Blackw. Mag.* LIX. 169/1 Misanthropizing under the pangs of grief or unrequited love. **1849** KINGSLEY *Misc.* (1859) II. 264 What a place for some 'gloom-pampered man' to sit and misanthropize. **1891** F. M. WILSON *Primer on Browning* 190 Abandoning the world to misanthropise in a distant solitude.

2. *trans.* (in quot. *absol.*) To cause to be misanthropic.

1838 F. W. ROBERTSON *Let.* in Brooke *Life & Lett.* 20 All that has grieved and disappointed and misanthropised will be fully explained.

misanthropy (mɪ'sænθrəpɪ). [ad. Gr. μῑσανθρωπία, f. μῑσάνθρωπος MISANTHROPE. Cf. F. *misanthropie* (16th c.).] Hatred of mankind; the character, nature, or condition of a misanthrope.

1656 BLOUNT *Glossogr., Misanthropie*, an hating of men. **1725** SWIFT *Let. to Pope* 29 Sept., Upon this great foundation of Misanthropy, (tho' not in Timon's manner) the whole building of my Travels is erected. **1780** HARRIS *Philol. Enq.* Wks. (1841) 538 Bad opinions of mankind naturally lead us to misanthropy. **1828** MACAULAY *Ess., Hallam* (1850) 75 Misanthropy is not the temper, which qualifies a man to act in great affairs, or to judge of them. **1866** W. R. ALGER *Solit. Nat. & Man* III. 123 Misanthropy ..will be found almost always to be the revenge we take on mankind for fancied wrongs it has inflicted on us.

misantour, obs. form of MISAUNTER.

misantropos: see MISANTHROPE.

†**misa'paid**, *ppl. a.* (pseudo-*arch.*) *Obs.* [MIS-[1] 2.] ? Discontented. (Cf. MISPAY.)

1614 J. DAVIES *Ecl.* in Browne *Sheph. Pipe* G 3 b, Thou.. Who whilom no encheson could fore-haile; And caitiue-courage nere made misapaid.

misa'ppear, *v.* *rare*$^{-1}$. [MIS-[1] 1.] *intr.* To appear erroneously.

a **1614** DONNE *Βιαθανατος* (1648) 155 If any small place of Scripture, mis-appeare to them to bee of use for justifying any opinion of theirs.

misa'ppearance. *rare.* [MIS-[1] 4, 7.]

1. Failure to appear, non-appearance.

a **1683** SCROGGS *Courts-leet* (1714) 116 If Judgment be given against the Tenant or Defendant as upon a Misappearance, because the principal Party does not appear.

2. Appearance in a perverted form.

1844 EMERSON *Ess.* Ser. II. i. 23 Certain priests..appeared to the children..like dead horses; and many the like misappearances.

,misappe'llation. [MIS-[1] 4.] The action of calling by a wrong name.

1816 BENTHAM *Chrestomathia* Wks. 1843 VIII. 77 Of the act of misappellation thus committed, now then observe the consequence. **1885** *Law Times* LXXIX. 438/1 Partly in consequence of its misappellation..the Bill escaped much observation.

†**misa'ppliably**, *adv.* *Obs.* [f. MISAPPLY + -ABLY.] So that one's remarks can be misapplied.

a **1631** DONNE *Lett.* (1651) 28 In which I know I speak not dangerously nor misappliably to you.

misappliance (mɪsə'plaɪəns). *rare*$^{-1}$. [f. MIS-[1] 4 + APPLIANCE.] Placing (of oneself) amiss.

1903 H. JAMES *Ambassadors* III. 58 He scarce knew where to sit for fear of a misappliance.

,misappli'cation. [MIS-[1] 4.] The action of misapplying; often used of misappropriation of funds (†occas. *absol.* in that sense).

1607 BEAUM. & FL. *Woman-Hater* I. iii, Hee brings me informations,..which with his malitious misapplication, hee hopes will seeme dangerous. **1681** FLAVEL *Meth. Grace* i. 11 He may seem to..tast some sweetness in the delicious promises..of the Gospel by a misapplication of them to himself. **1704** LD. TWEEDDALE in *Lond. Gaz.* No. 4037/3 The Misapplications of..Funds. **1722** DE FOE *Col. Jack* (1840) 111 Having been charged with some misapplications, [he] was obliged to take shelter in England. **1864** PUSEY *Daniel* (1876) 113 The misapplication of the ancient Symbol. **1885** *Law Times* LXXIX. 7/1 The plaintiff specified one misapplication of a sum of £25. **1902** GREENOUGH & KITTREDGE *Words & Their Ways* 217 Language develops by the felicitous misapplication of words.

misapply (mɪsə'plaɪ), *v.* [MIS-[1] 1.] *trans.* To apply to a wrong person or object; to make a wrong application of.

1571 GOLDING *Calvin on Ps.* lxix. 29 Such a one [*sc.* manner of speech] as is not misapplyed too our small capacitie. **1592** SHAKS. *Rom. & Jul.* II. iii. 21 Vertue it selfe turnes vice being misapplied. **1655** FULLER *Ch. Hist.* I. i. 1 Idolaters, who, from misapplying that undeniable Truth of God's being in every thing, made every thing to be their God. **1698** COLLIER *Immor. Stage* iv. 145 Thus the Marks of Honour, and Infamy are misapplyed. **1711** G. HICKES *Two Treat.* (1847) II. 377 The presbyterians have abused and misapplied this doctrine. **1742** YOUNG *Nt. Th.* II. 274 She.. notes each moment misapply'd. **1782** MISS BURNEY *Cecilia* vi. vi, His phrases are almost always ridiculous or misapplied. **1784** COWPER *Task* III. 402 Misapplying his unskilful strength. **1825** COBBETT *Rur. Rides* 123 These enclosures and buildings are a waste; they are means misapplied. **1863** H. FAWCETT *Pol. Econ.* III. xiv. (1876) 476 Capital may be misapplied and wasted.

absol. **1732** POPE *Prol. Sat.* 301 Who reads, but with a lust to misapply.

Hence **misa'pplied** *ppl. a.*, **misa'pplying** *vbl. sb.* Also **misa'pplier**, one who misapplies.

[**1450** Misapplying: see MISDISPENSE.] **1587** GOLDING *De Mornay* cxxxiiii. (1592) 547 His misapplying..of hys skil. **1629** H. BURTON *Truths Triumph* 59 Their mis-applyed philosophicall diuinity. **1699** COLLIER *Def. Short View* 84 Unfair Citing and Misapplying. **1736** CARTE *Ormonde* II. 369 The Misappliers of his revenue. **1903** *Blackw. Mag.* Oct. 535/1 He thumps it with the same misapplied vigour.

misa'ppreciate, *v.* [MIS-[1] 1.] *trans.* To fail to appreciate rightly; to make a wrong estimate of.

1828 DE QUINCEY *Wks.* (1859) XI. 54 The real value of his speech was never at any time misappreciated by the judicious. **1865** D. MASSON *Rec. Brit. Philos.* 271 Unappreciated or misappreciated because of their higher nature.

'misappreci'ation. [MIS-[1] 4.] Erroneous estimation or valuation.

1854 FABER *Growth in Holiness* (1872) xi. 178 Want of sympathy with contemplation leads to a misappreciation of austerity. **1868** NETTLESHIP *Ess. Browning* i. 19 The lovers fail by reason of their mistresses' misappreciation.

misa'ppreciative, *a.* [MIS-[1] 6.] Not properly appreciative.

1866 LOWELL *Carlyle* Prose Wks. (1890) II. 111 A man may look..on an heroic master, with the eyes of a valet, as misappreciative certainly, though not so ignoble.

,misappre'hend, *v.* [MIS-[1] 1.] *trans.* To apprehend wrongly; not to understand rightly; to attach a wrong meaning to. †Also, with acc. and inf., to suppose erroneously (that..).

a **1653** BINNING *Serm.* (1845) 567 All our Mischief proceeds from this, that we Misapprehend and Mistake that which we would gladly have. *a* **1661** FULLER *Worthies, Wiltsh.* (1662) III. 155 Country-People who live far off in our Land misapprehend them (distanced more then 12 miles) to be near together. **1726** ATTERBURY *Serm.* I. ix. 322 Here is a Law, attended with none of these Inconveniences; the grossest Minds can scarce misapprehend it. **1856** SIR B. BRODIE *Psychol. Inq.* I. ii. 61 Let me not be misapprehended as giving our knowledge for more than it is actually worth. **1875** JOWETT *Plato* (ed. 2) III. 218, I do not think that I misapprehend your meaning.

absol. **1658** T. WALL *Character Enemies Ch.* 42 To mis-apprehend, denotes a man. Tis head-strong persistance that degrades him into a Beast.

Hence **misappre'hended** *ppl. a.*, **misappre'hending** *vbl. sb.* Also **misappre'hendingly** *adv.*, through misapprehension.

1646 SIR T. BROWNE *Pseud. Ep.* I. iv. (1686) 10 Fallacious foundations, and misapprehended mediums. **1665** GLANVILL *Scepsis Sci.* xiii. 72 Mis-apprehended, or ill-compounded phantasmes. **1702** SIR G. KNELLER in *Pepys' Diary* VI. 237, I ask your pardon for Misapprehending. **1862** F. HALL *Hindu Philos. Syst.* 16 Unless a man identifies himself, misapprehendingly, with his body. **1886** *New York Sch. Jrnl.* XXXI. 259 The most misapprehended word in all modern educational literature is the word, 'method'.

misappre'hensible, *a.* *rare*$^{-1}$. [MIS-[1] 6.] Capable of being misapprehended.

1829 BENTHAM *Justice & Cod. Petit.* p. xiii, A determinate and never misapprehensible..standard of reference.

,misappre'hension. [MIS-[1] 4.] The action of misapprehending or condition of being misapprehended; the misunderstanding of the meaning of anything.

1629 H. BURTON *Truth's Triumph* 312 His eyes are not dazeled..by a mis-apprehension and mis-application of the true light. **1665** BOYLE *Occas. Refl.* v. vi. (1848) 317 [He] commanded the Fidlers to be thrust out of his Seraglio, upon a mis-aprehension that they were playing, when they were but tuning. **1737** BERKELEY *App. to Querist* §165 Wks. 1871 III. 537 Whether such difference in opinion be not an effect of misapprehension. **1860** TYNDALL *Glaciers* II. xiv. 304 An opinion, founded on a grave misapprehension. **1885** *Law Rep.* 29 Chanc. Div. 545 The Vice-Chancellor there was under a misapprehension.

,misappre'hensive, *a.* [MIS-[1] 6.] Apt to misapprehend. Hence **misappre'hensively** *adv.*, through misapprehension; **misappre'hensiveness**, the quality of being misapprehensive.

1646 H. LAWRENCE *Comm. & War w. Angels* 120 Because men are either insincere and unfaithfull, or misapprehensive and darke. **1862** F. HALL *Hindu Philos. Syst.* 142 The good and evil works of the misapprehensive man serve to fetter him. *Ibid.* 246 The soul..when it is misapprehensively viewed as a reflexion. **1869** BROWNING *Ring & Bk.* IX. 1526 Gently, O mother, judge men—whose mistake Is in the mere misapprehensiveness! **1880** J. W. SHERER *Conjuror's Dau.* 130 Henry had been always dull and misapprehensive.

misa'ppropriate, *a.* *rare.* [MIS-[1] 7.] Inappropriate. Hence **misa'ppropriately** *adv.*

c **1831** SIR H. HALFORD in W. Munk *Life* (1895) 83 The disease, misappropriately called cholera morbus. **1897** SMEATON *Smollett* x. 135 Her misappropriate use of the language of that circle is most felicitously rendered.

misa'ppropriate, *v.* [MIS-[1] 1.] *trans.* To appropriate to wrong uses; chiefly, to apply dishonestly to one's own use (money belonging to another).

1857 TOULMIN SMITH *Parish* 145 A part of what had been wrongfully misappropriated being restored. **1887** *Times* 10 Oct. 3/3 The prisoner..had been in the habit of misappropriating fees which he received.

,misappropri'ation. [MIS-[1] 4.] Appropriation to wrong uses.

1794 BURKE *Sp. agst. W. Hastings* Wks. 1827 VIII. 367 Another class of women, who suffered by the violent misappropriation of the revenues of the Nabob. **1838** W. H. PRESCOTT *Hist. Reign Ferdinand & Isabella* III. II. xxv. 490 He made a strict inquisition into the funds of the military orders, in which there had been much waste and misappropriation. **1847–54** in WEBSTER. **1860** WORCESTER cites *Ch. Ob.* **1922** JOYCE *Ulysses* 718 Forgery, embezzlement, misappropriation of public money. **1952** M. A. ELLIOTT *Crime in Mod. Society* iii. 59 Misappropriation of funds of private character is seldom punished unless there is a glaring embezzlement.

misarchist: see MISO-.

misard, obs. form of MISER *sb.*

misaritie, variant of MISERITY.

misa'rranged, *pa. pple.* and *ppl. a.* [MIS-[1] 2.] Wrongly arranged.

1848 DE QUINCEY *Goldsmith* Wks. 1857 VI. 232 To unsettle false verdicts, to recombine misarranged circumstances, and to explain anew misinterpreted facts. **1873** SKEAT *P. Pl.* III. 143 *note*, 77, 78. Misarranged in all the copies.

misa'rrangement. [MIS-[1] 4.] Bad or wrong arrangement.

1784 COWPER *Task* v. 111 Here glitt'ring turrets rise, upbearing high (Fantastic misarrangement) on the roof Large growth [etc.]. **1832** SOUTHEY *Hist. Penins. War* III. 37 By a misarrangement arising from mere inattention, they had been served..with meat on a meagre day. **1897** SKEAT

Chaucerian & other Pieces p. li. That the Trinity MS. agrees with the Harleian as to misarrangement of the subject-matter.

misarray (mɪsəˈreɪ). [MIS-[1] 4.] = DISARRAY.
1810 SCOTT *Lady of L.* v. xxvii, Then uproar wild and misarray Marr'd the fair form of festal day.

misarticuˈlation. [MIS-[1] 4.] Inability to articulate correctly.
1959 *Jrnl. Speech & Hearing Res.* II. 244 (*heading*) A phonetic study of misarticulation of /r/. **1972** *Language* XLVIII. 492 It is important that the study of misarticulation be integrated into this dependency relationship, for the mutual benefit of speech therapy and linguistic theory.

misaˈscription. Also with hyphen. [MIS-[1] 4.] False ascription.
1923 E. K. CHAMBERS *Elizabethan Stage* II. xii. 30 He light-heartedly accuses my friend Mr. Pollard, me, and others of perpetuating an old mis-ascription. **1946** *Mod. Lang. Notes* LXI. 61 The initial and continued misascription of the fourteen line poem, 'The Muses, fairest light in no darke time', to John Cleveland. **1971** A. KIRK-GREENE in J. Spencer *Eng. Lang. W. Afr.* 137 These lexical items [in West African English] consist of creation in two ways: deliberate coining and misascription.

misaˈssign, *v. rare.* [MIS-[1] 1.] *trans.* To assign erroneously.
1660 BOYLE *New Exp. Phys. Mech.* ii. 38 We have not mis-assign'd the cause of this Phænomenon. **1879** A. B. GROSART in *T. Howell's Poems.* p. x. *note*, Wood misassigns Abp. Parker's verse-Psalter to him.

misassimiˈlation. *rare.* [MIS-[1] 4.] Incomplete or unsuccessful assimilation.
1934 E. SITWELL *Aspects Mod. Poetry* 69 Here, too, is another misassimilation of Hopkins by the same writer.

misattriˈbution. [MIS-[1] 4.] Attribution, usu. of a work of art, literature, etc., to the wrong person. Hence **misaˈttributor**, one who makes a misattribution.
1873 M. ARNOLD *Lit. & Dogma* (1876) 399 The misattribution to the Bible..of a science..which is not there. **1927** *Sunday at Home* Jan. 216/1 The hurried journalist is a great misquoter and a great misattributor too. **1963** *Times* 4 June 14/4 Highmore, even until recent years, has suffered from misattributions, either of his best work to others, Hogarth in particular, or of the inferior work of others to him. **1973** *Times* 3 Nov. 15/6 Misattributions of this kind should be avoided. **1975** *Sotheby & Co. Catal.* 28–29 July 4/2 Books may not be returned nor will their sale be set aside ..for possible misattribution of authorship where the authorities are in disagreement.

misaunter (mɪˈsɔːntə(r)). *Obs.* exc. *north. dial.* Also 3–4 **-aunture, -auntre, -antour,** 4 **-awentoure,** 5 **-anter, -awnter.** [Contracted form of *miˈsauenture* (see MISADVENTURE). Cf. MISHANTER.] = MISADVENTURE.
1297 R. GLOUC. (Rolls) 4187 Alas alas þou wrecche mon, woch mesaunture Aþ þe ybroȝt in to þis stede. *c* **1330** *Arth. & Merl.* 6180 (Kölbing) þe painem starf wiþ misantour. *c* **1374** CHAUCER *Troylus* I. 766 If I wiste what she were For whom that thee al this misaunter ayleth. *c* **1375** *Sc. Leg. Saints* xix. (*Christofore*) 4 þat þaim ne may ony mysawentoure fal þat day. **1405** *Lay Folks Mass-Bk.* 65 That god saue thaim fra al missaunters. *c* **1440** *Promp. Parv.* 339/1 Mysawnter, or myscheve. *infortunium.* **1876** *Whitby Gloss.*, *Misaunter*, a misadventure. 'Ful o' mishaps an misaunters'.

misaventeur, -our, -ur(e: obs. ff. MISADVENTURE.

†**misaˈver,** *v. Obs.* [MIS-[1] 1.] *intr.* To speak erroneously.
1615 SYLVESTER *Job Triumph.* IV. 215 And let the prudent mark..That void of knowledge, Job hath misaverr'd.

misaˈward, *v. rare.* [MIS-[1] 1.] *trans.* To award wrongly. So **misaˈwarding** *vbl. sb.*
a **1625** SIR H. FINCH *Law* (1636) 226 Misawarding of Processe. **1887** A. M. BROWN *Anim. Alkaloids* 6 Here an honour seems to have been somewhat misawarded.

misbapˈtize, *v.* [MIS-[1] 1.]
1. *trans.* To misname, miscall.
1610 MARKHAM *Masterp.* I. xv. 43 The vnskilfull Farrier ..doth euer mis-baptise the name of the horses infirmity. **1625** F. MARKHAM *Bk. Honour* II. ix. §9 To haue kept all the Rules of proportion..would..have..misbaptized my Title by turning an Epistle into a tedious discourse.
2. To baptize wrongly.
1819 KEATS *K. Stephen* I. ii. 33 A fierce demon, 'nointed safe from wounds, And misbaptized with a Christian name.

†**misˈbear,** *v. Obs.* [f. MIS-[1] 1 + BEAR *v.*[1]]
1. *refl.* To misbehave or misconduct oneself.
c **1300** *Beket* 1248 Ic ne miȝte do hit for nothing theȝ he him hadde misbore. *c* **1386** CHAUCER *Melib.* ¶911 Ye have mysbore yow, and trespassed unto me. *c* **1400** MAUNDEV. (1839) xii. 135 3if ony of here Wyfes mysberen hem aȝenst hire Husbonde. **1496** *Dives & Pauper* (W. de W.) IV. xxiv. 191/1 Yf they mysbere them, ther patrons may depryue them of ther benefyce. **1502** *Ord. Crysten Men* (W. de W. 1506) IV. xxi, Yf he..mysbere hym unto the sacramentes.
2. See MISBORN.
Hence, †**misˈbearing** *ppl. a.*, ill-behaved.
a **1400** in *Hampole's Wks.* (1896) I. 159 þat noon schulde be proude ne mysberynge aȝens oþere.

†**misˈbearing,** *vbl. sb.* [MIS-[1] 3.] **a.** ? Wrongful bearing. **b.** Misconduct.
c **1330** R. BRUNNE *Chron.* (1810) 336 Dan Waryn he les tounes þat he held With wrong he mad a res & misberyng of scheld [Langtoft *Ke citez et viles perdist par l'escu*]. *c* **1449** PECOCK *Repr.* v. xv. 564 Al this..foule and mys bering and vniust chalenging and blamyng.

misbecome (mɪsbɪˈkʌm), *v.* [MIS-[1] 1.] *trans.* To fail to become; to suit ill; to be unsuitable or unbecoming to.
1530 PALSGR. 637/1 It mysbecometh, as a garment mysbecometh one, or any other comunycacion, or other behavour. **1597** SHAKS. *2 Hen. IV*, v. ii. 100 Speake..What I haue done, that misbecame my place. **1624** WOTTON *Archit.* in *Reliq.* (1672) 35 A Frank light can mis-become no Ædifice whateuer. **1638** BP. WILKINS *New World* v. (1707) 39 An Opinion altogether misbecoming a Philosopher. **1749** FIELDING *Tom Jones* XV. vi, Nothing could misbecome me more, than to presume to give any hint to one of your great understanding. **1855** MACAULAY *Hist. Eng.* xiv. III. 464 He declined no drudgery..provided only that it were such drudgery as did not misbecome an honest man. **1889** SWINBURNE *B. Jonson* 108 Such sweeping denunciation of all contemporary poetry as would not have misbecome the utterance of incarnate envy.

misbeˈcoming, *ppl. a.* [f. prec. + -ING[2], or f. MIS-[1] 2 + BECOMING *ppl. a.*] Not becoming, unbecoming, unsuitable, unfitting.
1611 COTGR., *Messeant*, ill-fitting, ill-suiting, misbecoming. **1634** MILTON *Comus* 372 As that the single want of light and noise..Could stir the constant mood of her calm thoughts, And put them into mis-becoming plight. **1651** T. STANLEY *Poems* 62 Cast off for shame ungentle maid That misbecoming joy thou wearst. **1707** NORRIS *Treat. Humility* v. 213 Pride is never so odious and misbecoming as now. **1743** FIELDING *J. Wild* III. xiv, It is..very far from being an improper or misbecoming habitation. **1820** SCOTT *Abbot* xi, When a paroxysm of laughter has seized him at a misbecoming time and place.

misbeˈcomingly, *adv.* [-LY[2].] Unbecomingly, unfittingly.
1612 *Two Noble K.* v. iii. (1634) 81 Those darker humours that Sticke misbecomingly on others, on them Live in faire dwelling. **1635** J. HAYWARD tr. *Biondi's Banish'd Virg.* 180 He did it so misbecomingly..as made him loathsome to such as saw him act it. **1707** NORRIS *Treat. Humility* vii. 298 It makes it [*sc.* pride] sit..still the more misbecomingly upon us.

misbeˈcomingness. [-NESS.] The quality or condition of being misbecoming; also, in particularized use, an unbecoming characteristic.
1644 DIGBY *Nat. Bodies* xxviii. §8 One great misbecomingnesse he was apt to fall into, whiles he spoke: which was an vncertainty in the tone of his voyce. **1674** N. FAIRFAX *Bulk & Selv.* Ep. Ded., 'Tis a misbecomingness to have a doing Philosophy set forth by a talking Philosopher. *a* **1704** LOCKE *Notes Ephes.* v. 3 Wks. 1714 III. 376 What indecency or misbecomingness is it among Christians to name covetousness?

†**misˈbede,** *v. Obs.* Forms: 1 **misbéodan,** 3–4 **mis-, mysbeode,** 4 **-bide,** 4–5 **-bede;** *pa. t.* 1 **misbéad,** 4 **-bed(e;** *pa. pple.* 1 **misboden,** 4 **mysbode(n.** [OE. *misbéodan* (= MDu. *missebieden*, MLG. *misse-, misbeden*, MHG. *missebieten*, ON. *misbjóða*), f. *mis-* MIS-[1] 1 + *béodan* (see BID *v.*[1] A).] *trans.* To ill-use, ill-treat; to injure, abuse. (In OE. with obj. in *dative.*) Also *intr.* const. *till.*
a **975** *Canons Edgar* v. in Thorpe *Laws* II. 244 Gif him ænig man healice misboden hæbbe. *a* **1023** WULFSTAN *Hom.* xxii. (1883) 112 Ðy ne misbeode cristenra manna ænig oðrum ealles to swyðe. *a* **1122** *O.E. Chron.* (Laud MS.) an. 1083 He misbead his munecan on fela þingan. *a* **1250** *Owl & Night.* 1541 Me hire may so ofte mysbeode þat heo do wile hire owe neode. *c* **1330** R. BRUNNE *Chron.* (1810) 104 Whan Lowys herd þat sawe, þat Roberd was so dede, Ageyn right & lawe, tille Henry he misbede. **1362** LANGL. *P. Pl.* A. VII. 45 And mis-beode [B. VI. 46 mysbede] þou not þi bondemen. *c* **1386** CHAUCER *Knt.'s T.* 51 Or who hath yow misboden, or offended? **1387** TREVISA *Higden* (Rolls) III. 225 The peple of Rome made stryf as þough þey were mysbode of the senatoures. ? *a* **1400** *Morte Arth.* 3083 That no lele ligemane ..Sulde..biernez myse-bide, that to þe burghe longede. **1496** *Dives & Pauper* (W. de W.) VII. xxvii. 318/2 Yf thou lene to my poore people, thou shalt not therfore mysbede hym. **1846** BROCKETT *Gloss. N.C. Words, Mis-boden*, injured. [Quotes Chaucer.]

†**misbeˈfall,** *v. Obs.* [MIS-[1] 1.]
1. *impers.* With dat. of the person affected: To happen unfortunately, turn out badly.
a **1225** *Ancr. R.* 200 þe ueorðe [unðeauwe] is Gledschipe of his vuel: lauhwen oðer gabben, ȝif him mis-biueolle [*MS. T.* mis-times, *C.* mistimeð]. **1390** GOWER *Conf.* I. 57 For elles, bot a man do so, Him may fulofte mysbefalle. *c* **1425** *Eng. Conq. Irel.* 124/15 Thegh hym yn thyke [= thylke] vyage mys byfelle. *c* **1430** *Pilgr. Lyf Manhode* I. lxix. (1869) 40, I wole telle yow how it bifel of hem, and how it misbefel hem.
2. Of events: To happen unfortunately. Also in ppl. adj. **misbefallen.**
1591 *Troub. Raigne K. John* (1611) 48 Deep sorrow throbbeth mis-befaln euents. **1645** WITHER *Vox Pacif.* 117 Scarce a man Among a thousand, searcheth out those things Which mis-befall. **1648** W. BROWNE *Polexander* III. iv. 128 Something..is misbefalne Zelmatida.
3. Of persons: To come to harm.
c **1430** *Pilgr. Lyf Manhode* I. lvi. (1869) 203 Wherefore so lightliche fallen þei nouht, ne so soone misbefallen.

misbeˈget, *v. rare.* [MIS-[1] 1.] *trans.* To beget unlawfully.
c **1330** *Arth. & Merl.* 1113 (Kölbing) þou art a cursed þing, Misbiȝeten oȝaines þe lawe. **1390** GOWER *Conf.* III. 80 His fader, which him misbegat, He slouh. **1607** SHAKS. *Timon* III. v. 29 Which [quarrelling] indeede Is Valour misbegot, and came into the world, When Sects, and Factions were newly borne. **1860** READE *Cloister & H.* II. 363 Buss the old folk and thank them for misbegetting of thee.

†**misbeˈget,** *ppl. a.* and *sb.* Also 3 **-biȝite,** 4 **-bigete, -biȝete, -beyete,** 5 **begeten.** [f. MIS-[1] 2 + *beȝet(en*, ME. pa. pple. of BEGET *v.*] = MISBEGOTTEN.
1297 R. GLOUC. (Rolls) 987 Leste it heode out of kunde þorȝ child mis bi ȝite [*later MSS.* mys bi gete, mis biȝete]. **13..** *Seuyn Sag.* 1052 (W.) And of the child..He segh hit was a mis-beyete. *c* **1330** *Arth. & Merl.* 1021 (Kölbing) þou misbiȝeten þing, þou hast ylowe a gret lesing. *a* **1400** *Octouian* 259 Thy mysbegeten chylderen two.

misbeˈgin, *v. rare.* [MIS-[1] 1.] *trans.* To begin amiss or badly. So **misbeˈgun** *ppl. a.*
1583 GOLDING *Calvin on Deut.* lxxv. 461 By applying their minds to al wicked shifts for ye maintenance of ye thing y[t] they had misbegun. **1587** —— *De Mornay* xxiii. (1592) 353 a Song mistuned, or a Gambauld misbegun. **1864** *Louie's last term* (N.Y.) 9 Another mis-begun day.

misbeˈgotten, *ppl. a.* and *sb.* Also **misbegot.** [MIS-[1] 2.] **A.** *adj.*
1. Unlawfully begotten; illegitimate; bastard.
1554 T. MARTIN *Marr. Priests* B iv, Those haue we seen to be the most gredy getters for their misbegotten heires. **1595** SHAKS. *John* v. iv. 4 That misbegotten diuell Falcon-bridge. **1603** HOLLAND *Plutarch's Mor.* 1133 Where no other youthes do exercise but misbegotten bastards. **1700** DRYDEN *Fables, Cinyras & Myrrha* 354 (1721) 136 Mean time the mis-begotten infant grows. **1749** FIELDING *Tom Jones* I. iii, It goes against me to touch these misbegotten wretches, whom I don't look upon as my fellow creatures. **1789** BURNS *Fragm. inscr. to C. J. Fox* 15 A sorry, poor, misbegot son of the Muses. **1875–86** [see B].
b. *transf.* and *fig.*
1593 SHAKS. *Rich. II*, I. i. 33 In the deuotion of a subiects loue,..And free from other misbegotten hate. **1760** LLOYD *Poems* (1762) 97 When Falshood stole them to disguise Her misbegotten brood of lies. **1820** HAZLITT *Lect. Dram. Lit.* 15 Germany first broke the spell of misbegotten fear. **1858** BUSHNELL *Nat. & Supernat.* xiii. (1864) 421 Our misbegotten opinions.
2. Used as a term of opprobrium.
1571 GOLDING *Calvin on Ps.* xxiv. 5 That misbegotten generation, whiche was proude of the only visour of their ceremonies. **1641** MILTON *Ch. Govt.* iii. Wks. 1851 III. 110 Some misbegotten thing, that..vaunts and glories in her stolne plumes. **1815** BYRON *To Moore* 12 June, Murray.. has been cruelly cudgelled of misbegotten knaves. **1838** SOUTHEY *Doctor* cxxxvii. (1848) 346, I should never like to trust my precious limbs upon the back of such a misbegotten beast. **1839** BAILEY *Festus* (1848) 18/1 This dim, dwarfed, misbegotten sphere. **1886** STEVENSON *Dr. Jekyll* 100 There was something abnormal and misbegotten in the very essence of the creature.
B. *sb.* A bastard; also, as a term of abuse (cf. A. 2). Now only *dial.*, in form *misbegot.*
1546 BALE *Eng. Votaries* I. (1560) 21 b, Saint Cuthbert y[e] great God of the North..was a misbegotten also. *c* **1550** T. INGELEND *Disob. Child* E iv, What wordes haue we here, thou misbegotten? **1875–86** *W. Somerset Gloss., Misbegot*, adj. and sb. Base born; a bastard. **1877** *Holderness Gloss., Misbegot*, a bastard.

misbehadden, Sc. form of MISBEHOLDEN.

misbeˈhave, *v.* [MIS-[1] 1.]
1. *refl.* and (later) *intr.* To behave wrongly; to conduct oneself improperly.
1475 *Rolls of Parlt.* VI. 134/1 They never offended nor mysbehaved theym in the mater of the compleynts.. specified. **1530** PALSGR. 636/2 You were to blame to mysbehave you to hym so sore as you dyd. **1648** *Art. Peace* xxix. in Milton *Wks.* 1851 IV. 538 Such other Person or Persons..to be named and appointed in the place or places, of him or them, who shall so die or misbehave themselves. **1759** FRANKLIN *Ess.* Wks. 1840 III. 462 The said mayor, by becoming a promoter and ringleader of such an insult, had exceedingly misbehaved himself. **1764** BURN *Poor Laws* 289 The punishment of a servant misbehaving, is to be either by commitment to the house of correction, or [etc.]. **1860** EMERSON *Cond. Life* vi. (1861) 131 If we misbehave we suspect others. **1871** BROWNING *Hervé Riel* vii, Not a ship that misbehaves. **1884** *Law Times Rep.* XLIX. 775/2 The court can order costs to be paid by a trustee who has misbehaved.
†**2.** *trans.* To conduct or manage improperly.
1540 HYRDE tr. *Vives' Instr. Chr. Wom.* (1592) O 4 The naughtinesse of misbehaving her body.
So **misbeˈhaving** *vbl. sb.* and *ppl. a.*
1451 *Rolls of Parlt.* V. 216/1 Noyse and claymour of the seid mysbehavyng renneth openly. **1496–7** *Act 12 Hen. VII*, c. 2 Perjurie and other divers offenses and mysbehavynges. **1529** *Act 21 Hen. VIII*, c. 20 Bill or informacyon..agaynst any person for any mysbehavynge afore rehersed. *c* **1610** in Gutch *Coll. Cur.* II. 12 That all common women, and misbehaving people..withdraw themselves out of this Fair. **1891** *Spectator* 7 Mar. 331/2 For the purpose of inflicting a sort of penance on a misbehaving clergyman's soul.

†**misbeˈhaved,** *ppl. a.* [MIS-[1] 2.] Ill-behaved.
1592 SHAKS. *Rom. & Jul.* III. iii. 143 Like a misbehaved and sullen wench.

misbeˈhaviour. [MIS-[1] 4.] Bad behaviour, improper conduct; †an instance of this.
1486 *Act 3 Hen. VII*, c. 1 Bill or Information..against any Person for any Misbehaviour afore rehersed. **1512** *Act 4 Hen. VIII*, c. 19 §11 What so euer persone or persones do..

commytt eny mysbehavoure in eny maner wyse touchyng the premisses. **1516** in *Eng. Gilds* 329 To..ponysch all such mysbyhauyors and fauttes as haue be, or be nowe, or schalbe. **1674** Brevint *Saul at Endor* 207 An Officer..who was cashiered for some Mis-behavior. **1712** Steele *Spect.* No. 503 ⁋1 The misbehaviour of people at church. **1765** Blackstone *Comm.* I. xvi. 442 The law does not hold the tie of nature to be dissolved by any misbehaviour of the parent. **1855** Thackeray *Newcomes* lxxvii. II. 347 The just feelings of displeasure with which I could not but view his early disobedience and misbehaviour.

misbe'holden, *ppl. a.* Also *dial.* **-behodden**, *Sc.* **-behad(d)en**. [f. MIS-[1] 2 + *beholden*, pa. pple. of BEHOLD *v.* The orig. meaning seems to have been 'improperly guarded, unguarded'; cf. OE. *behealden* cautious.] Unbecoming, indiscreet; disobliging: usually qualifying *word.*

1600 T. Heywood *2nd Pt. Edw. IV*, I. ii. (1613) M i b, We shew thee not one discontented looke, Nor render him one misbeholden word. **1828** *Craven Gloss.* (ed. 2) II. 294 Bud thou minds I nivver gav him another misbehodden word. **1837** Hogg *Siege Roxb.* iv. *Tales & Sk.* VI. 105 The first side that lifts a sword, or says a misbehadden word. **1869** *Lonsdale Gloss.*, *Misbehodden*, disobliging, offensive. 'I nivver gav her a misbehodden word'.

misbe'lead, *v. rare.* In 4 *pa. pple.* misbilad. [MIS-[1] 1.] *trans.* To lead astray.

c **1320** *Cast. Love* 428 Ac as a Mon mis-I-rad On vche half he is mis-bilad. **1909** Galsworthy *Strife* II. ii. 251 *Thomas.* I haf ears to my head... *Jago.* Your ears have misbeled you then.

misbelief (mɪsbɪ'liːf). [MIS-[1] 4, 7.]

1. Erroneous or unorthodox religious belief; wrong faith; heresy.

a **1225** *Leg. Kath.* 2393 Leste ȝe eft wepen echeliche in helle..as ȝe schullen alle, buten ȝef ȝe forleten..ower misbileaue. **1340** Hampole *Pr. Consc.* 5521 Þe haithen men of mysbylyefe. **1377** Langl. *P. Pl.* B. xv. 402 Mekometh in mysbileue men and wommen brouȝte. **1481** Caxton *Godfrey* c. 152 Grete hate..hath ben bytwene the Turkes of thoryent and the Turkes of Egypt..By cause they discorde in theyr creaunce and mysbyleue. **1529** More *Dyaloge* I. Wks. 144/2 If the woorship of ymages wer ydolatrie than y[e] churche beleuing it to be lawful..were in a misbelieue & in a deadly error. **1639** Laud *Wks.* (1849) II. 6 Perfidious misbelief could not be welcome, or, rather, indeed, perfidious misbelievers or schismatics could not be welcome. **1670** Milton *Hist. Eng.* Wks. 1738 II. 61 Paulinus omitting no opportunity to win the King from misbelief. **1829** Southey *Sir T. More* II. 93 In producing superstition and misbelief on one hand, and unbelief on the other. **1865** Pusey *Truth Eng. Ch.* 13 The authors..did not speak out..the unbelief or misbelief which they suggested. **1879** A. W. Haddan *Apost. Succ. Ch. Eng.* p. vii,[A doctrine] which the tendency of modern belief or misbelief leads men to scorn as childish.

2. *gen.* Erroneous belief; false opinion or notion.

c **1386** Chaucer *Can. Yeom. T.* 660 Ye shul han no mysbileeue Ne wrong conceite of me in youre Absence. **1387** Trevisa *Higden* (Rolls) VI. 397 Þis and oþere suche lewed tales Englisshe men holdeþ by a mysbyleve [L. *incredulitate*] þat haþ ful longe i-dured. **1426** Lydg. *De Guil. Pilgr.* 18623 And thynges that thow doste obserue, Alle is but ffoly and mysbyleve. **1496** *Dives & Pauper* (W. de W.) I. xlv 87/1 They haue no suche fantasye ne mysbyleue in dremes. **1513** Douglas *Æneis* x. xi. 56 Gif thou wenis that all the victory..May be reducit and alterat clar agane, A mysbeleve thou fosteris all in vane. **1651** Baxter *Inf. Bapt.* 18 If they prevail to perswade the people of the necessity of practice, in so doing they put on them both the misbelief and the mispractice. **1905** *Athenæum* 8 July 39/2 The misbeliefs of bygone times.

†**3.** Want of belief; disbelief; incredulity.

138. Wyclif *Sel. Wks.* III. 108 God hardede Pharaois herte for þe mysbyleve þat he hadde to God. **1483** Caxton *Gold. Leg.* 215/1 O how thy moste beaute hast thou lost for thyn incredulyte and mysbyleue. **1587** Golding *De Mornay* vi. (1592) 84 Simple distrusts or misbeleefes of the things which they vnderstand not. **1591** *Troub. Raigne K. John* (1611) 38 The traitors breath, Whose periurie..Beleaguers all the skie with mis-beleefe. *a* **1649** Drumm. of Hawth. *Poems* Wks. (1711) 51/1 Misbelief Of these sad news. **1653** H. More *Antid. Ath.* III. xvi. (1712) 142 A contemptuous misbelief of such like Narrations concerning Spirits, and an endeavour of making them all ridiculous and incredible.

¶**4.** An alleged term for a 'company' of painters.

1486 *Bk. St. Albans* f vij, A misbeleue of paynteris.

Hence †**misbe'liefful** *a.*, unbelieving; †**misbe'liefness**, unbelief.

c **1320** *Cast. Love* 1428 [Saint] Thomas misbileuenesse. *c* **1420** *Wyclif's Bible* Ecclus. i. 36 Mysbileueful [1382 mys leeful, 1388 vnbileueful] to the dred of the Lord [Vulg. *incredibilis timori Domini*].

misbe'lieve, *v.* [MIS-[1] 1, 7. Cf. OF. *mescrere*, mod. *mécroire.*]

1. *intr.* To believe amiss; to hold an erroneous belief. Also with *clause.*

1382 Wyclif *Deut.* i. 26 Mysbileuynge [1388 vnbileueful, Vulg. *increduli*] to the word of the Lord God. *a* **1425** *Cursor M.* 18698 (Trin.) Thomas..Stonde studfaste now herfore And mis bileue [*other MSS.* mistr(o)u] þou no more. **1526** *Pilgr. Perf.* (W. de W. 1531) 190 Who so euer confesse ..all ye articles of our fayth, saue onely one, & in that one do mysbyleue, he is an heretyke. **1596** Spenser *F.Q.* IV. xii. 26 She..comming to her sonne, gan first to scold And chyde at him that made her misbelieve. **1644** Milton *Bucer on Div.* Wks. 1851 IV. 335 The holy Spirit does not make the mis-beleeving of him who departs, but the departing of him who mis-beleevs, to be the just cause of freedom to the brother or sister. **1647** Trapp *Comm. John* xx. 8 As Mary Magdalene had told them, so they mis-believed, that it [the Lord's body] was taken away to some other place.

2. *trans.* Not to believe; to distrust (a person); to disbelieve (a thing). *Obs.*

c **1450** Lovelich *Merlin* 1505 And Neuere j schal the Misbeleve For non Man that owht can on þe preve. **1653** H. More *Antid. Ath.* I. ix. (1712) 26 If bare possibility may at all intangle our assent..we cannot fully misbelieve the absurdest Fable. **1699** Burnet 39 *Art.* xv. 139 We find the same Zachary guilty of misbelieving the Message of the Angel to him. **1728** Bailey, *To Misbelieve*, to distrust.

†**misbe'lieved**, *a. Obs.* [f. MISBELIEF + -ED[2]; or perh. f. MIS-[1] 2 + BELIEVED *ppl. a.* (cf. *smooth-spoken*).]

1. Holding a wrong belief or false religion; heretical; infidel, heathen.

a **1225** *St. Marher.* 1 Þe ȝet weren monie ma þen nu beon misbileuede men. **13..** *Guy Warw.* (A.) 3397 Sarrazins þat misbileued be. **1387** Trevisa *Higden* (Rolls) II. 309 Hit was þe manere of mysbeleued men [L. *ethnicorum*] forto kepe a dede body nyne dayes wiþ oute oignement. **1398** —— *Barth. De P.R.* XIII. ix. (Bodley MS.), Þis ryuer [Jordan].. departeþ þe contrey of riȝt beleued men fro þe contrey of mysbileued men. **1494** Fabyan *Chron.* I. ii. 9 Diana a Goddesse of mysbyleued people.

absol. *c* **1330** *Arth. & Merl.* 1900 (Kölbing) Þus ended sir Fortiger, þat misbileued. **1340** *Ayenb.* 252 Þe bougres and þe misbylefde.

2. Unbelieving, incredulous.

c **1374** Chaucer *Troylus* III. 838 O thou wikkid serpent Jelosye! Thow mysbylevid, envyous folye.

misbe'liever. [MIS-[1] 5.] One who holds a false or unorthodox belief; a heretic or infidel.

1470–85 Malory *Arthur* XIII. xiv. 631 The other wey betokeneth the way of synners and of mysbyleuers. **1509** Barclay *Shyp of Folys* (1570) 198 Of these misbeleuers more to write or tell..It were but foly. **1596** Shaks. *Merch. V.* I. iii. 112 You call me misbeleeuer..And spet vpon my Iewish gaberdine. **1651** C. Cartwright *Cert. Relig.* I. 114 Though Protestants have done little..to convert meer Infidels, yet in the other kinde, viz. in converting mis-believers they have done much. **1728** Morgan *Algiers* I. vi. 180 In the very first Encounter..with the Misbelievers, Sheikh Abdallah..was hurried into the other World. **1830** Wordsw. *Armenian Lady's Love* xx, Innocent, and meek, and good, Though with misbelievers bred. **1867** Freeman *Norm. Conq.* (1877) I. vi. 465 Roger..sought..to wage warfare against the misbeliever. **1868** J. H. Blunt *Ref. Ch. Eng.* I. 525 The correction of misbelievers was originally part of the ordinary jurisdiction of every bishop.

misbe'lieving, *vbl. sb.* [MIS-[1] 3.] Misbelief.

1340 *Ayenb.* 134 And þerof byeþ y-come alle þe maneres of eresye and of misbeleuinge. **1644** [see MISBELIEVE 1]. **1737** J. Willison *Affl. Man's Companion* VII. iv. (1744) 140 What is it but a Misbelieving of God?

misbe'lieving, *ppl. a.* [MIS-[1] 2.] Holding a false belief; heretical, unorthodox.

c **1330** *Arth. & Merl.* 5982 (Kölbing) Þe misbileueand paiem starf. **1340** *Ayenb.* 69 Þe bougres and þe mysbyleuinde. **1470–85** Malory *Arthur* v. x. 178, I aduyse ..to make vs redy to mete with these sarasyns and mysbyleuyng men. **1585** T. Washington tr. *Nicholay's Voy.* IV. xxxvi. 160 b, The righteous iudgements of God towards the mis-beleeuing. **1642** Rogers *Naaman* 577 A misbelieving Turke or Iew. **1691** Dryden *K. Arthur* I. Wks. 1701 II. 491 Lift high thy thund'ring arm, let every blow Dash out a mis-believing Briton's Brains. **1816** Southey *Poet's Pilgr.* I. 3 When Martel..from the yoke Of misbelieving Mecca saved the West. **1873** B. Gregory *Holy Cath. Ch.* xv. 161 Each denominational church has the right ..of excommunicating..misbelieving members.

transf. **1847** De Quincey *Sp. Mil. Nun* Postscr., Wks. 1854 III. 96 Confessions that..were absolutely mobbed and hustled by a gang of misbelieving (*i.e.* miscreant) critics.

Hence **misbe'lievingly** *adv*, incredulously.

1882 Miss Braddon *Mt. Royal* I. iii. 92 He would have shrugged his shoulders misbelievingly.

†**misbe'love**, *v. Obs. rare.* [MIS-[1] 1, 7.]

1. *trans.* To love amiss.

1614 Sylvester *Parl. Vertues Royall* 371 Wks. (Grosart) II. 127 Th' one loves not, th' other mis-beloves What best to fear, and least presume behooves.

2. Not to love; to hate.

1545 Raynold *Byrth Mankynde* Prol. C vi, By this reason phisitians and chyrurgians wyves shold greatly be abhorryd and mysbeloued of theyr husbandes.

misbe'seem, *v.* [MIS-[1] 1.] = MISBECOME. (In 17th c. freq. in the pres. pple. with an obj.)

1598 Bp. Hall *Sat.* Postscr., One thinkes it misbeseeming the Author because a Poem, another vnlawfull in it selfe because a Satyre. **1627** Hakewill *Apol.* (1630) 104 Neither can this action misbeseeme the worthinesse of so glorious a peece. **1773** Steevens *Shaks. Wks.*, *Ham.* III. ii. *note*, Nor.. would it much misbeseem us to remember..that we likewise are men. **1884** J. Payne *1001 Nights* IX. 336 Examples of Mohammedan fervour..that would not have misbeseemed the strictest epochs of religious enthusiasm.

misbe'seeming, *ppl. a.* = MISBECOMING.

c **1610** Beaum. & Fl. *Philaster* IV. (1622) 48 Goe sell those misbeseeming cloathes thou wearest. *a* **1677** Barrow *Serm.* (1810) II. 144 To condescend to such a misbeseeming employment..as the washing of his disciple's feet.

misbe'stow, *v.* [MIS-[1] 1.] *trans.* To bestow wrongly or improperly.

1532 More *Confut. Tindale* Wks. 355/2 To bestowe his witte..about some better busines then Tindall missbestoweth it now. **1583** Golding *Calvin on Deut.* xxxv. 206 If yee complayne of that time as though it were misbestowed. **1641** Milton *Animadv.* iv. 65 The misbestowed wealth which they were cheated of. **1748** Richardson *Clarissa* (1811) IV. vii. 40 All his compliments are misbestowed. **1815** Southey *Roderick* XXIV. 247 Oh, for a month Of that waste life which millions misbestow. **1841** Fr. A. Kemble *Rec. Later Life* (1882) II. 148 This is the way that fool Fortune misbestows her favours.

So **misbe'stowal**, wrong bestowal.

a **1866** J. Grote *Moral Ideas* (1876) 133 The misbestowal of love..does of course do much harm.

†**misbe'think**, *v. Obs.* [MIS-[1] 1.] *refl.* and *pass.* To think amiss: **a.** to be mistaken; **b.** to have wrong thoughts.

c **1275** in *O.E. Misc.* 45 Peter þo onswerede..Neuer er ich hyne ne yseyh þu ert mys-by-þouht. **13..** *Sir Beues* (A.) 55 Þe leuedi hire mis-be-þouȝte And meche aȝen þe riȝt ȝhe wrouȝte. *c* **1380** *Sir Ferumb.* 5825 He þe gat.., Thar-for ert þow mys-byþoȝte, To procury hym to slee.

†**misbe'tide**, *v. Obs.* [MIS-[1] 1.] *impers.* and *intr.* = MISBEFALL 1, 2.

c **1330** R. Brunne *Chron. Wace* (Rolls) 11833 Y trowe þei schul ȝit mis-bytide ffor þer couetise & þer pryde. *c* **1400** *Laud Troy Bk.* 6734 Alas, that euere him mys-be-tid! *c* **1430** *Syr Gener.* (Roxb.) 5480 If his help be my guyde, Neuer shal I misbetid.

misbeyete: see MISBEGET *ppl. a.*

†**misbi'hede**, *v. Obs.* [MIS-[1] 1.] *pass.* To be misguided.

13.. *Childh. Jesus* 438 Þo speken þis maistres gret: Josep, þou art mis bi hed.

mis'birth. *rare.* [MIS-[1] 4. Cf. OE. *misbyrd.*] = ABORTION.

1648–60 Hexham, *Een Misbaert*,..A Misbirth,..or an Abortive. **1833** Carlyle *Misc. Ess.*, *Cagliostro* (1888) V. 83 The everlasting Pit had opened itself and from its still blacker bosom had issued..all manner of shapeless misbirths. **1887** W. Stokes tr. *Tripartite Life Patrick* (Rolls) 207 No children save mis-births used to be born to Carthenn.

†**mis'bode**, *sb. Obs.* [Representing OE. *misbod, corresp. to *misbéodan* MISBEDE: cf. BODE *sb.*[2]] Wrong, offence.

c **1200** *Trin. Coll. Hom.* 79 He..þe ne þoleð and forebereð noht a misbode. *c* **1205** Lay. 11095 Al Rome he fordude þurh his muchele misbode. **1613** R. Cawdrey *Table Alph.*, *Misbode*, wrong. [Hence in later Dicts.]

mis'bode, *v. rare*[−1]. [MIS-[1] 1.] *trans.* To forebode (something evil).

1626 in *Cosins' Corr.* (Surtees) I. 89 My only desire to be with you..is to knowe what you must not or dare not write, for I misbode some great matter.

So **mis'boding** *vbl. sb.* and *ppl. a.*

a **1659** Bp. Brownrig *Serm.* (1674) I. ii. 33 [He] forbids four sorts of Characters to be set upon a Signet, as misboding Characters. **1739** Lillo *Arden of Feversham* v, Her misboding sorrow for his absence Has almost made her frantic. **1819** Lingard *Hist. Eng.* II. xii. 69 With a misboding heart he obeyed the summons. **1825** *Ibid.* VI. iv. 239 The misbodings of fanaticism.

misboden, pa. pple. of MISBEDE.

misborn (mɪs'bɔːn), *ppl. a.* ? *Obs.* [MIS-[1] 2.]

1. Prematurely born; abortive. Hence, deformed or mis-shapen from birth.

c **1000** *Sax. Leechd.* I. 228 Gif cild misboren sy. *c* **1230** *Hali Meid.* 34 Ʒif hit is misborn..& wont eni of his limen. **1382** Wyclif *1 Cor.* xv. 8 At the laste of alle, he was seyn and to me, as to a mysborn child [Vulg. *tamquam abortivo*]. **1390** Gower *Conf.* I. 192 A povere child..in the name Of thilke which is so misbore We toke. **1496** *Dives & Pauper* (W. de W.) VI. iii. 234/1 They that be mysborn moost comonly they haue an harde ende. **1570** Levins *Manip.* 172/35 Mysborne, *obortiuus* [sic]. **1600** Surflet *Countrie Farme* VII. xi. 817 It must either be transplanted, or else it woulde prooue out of course like a misborne thing. **1605** Camden *Rem.*, *Languages* 19 That which the Latines call *Abortus*,..they [the Anglo-Saxons] called Miss-borne.

2. Born of unlawful union; hence, base-born.

1590 Spenser *F.Q.* I. vi. 42 Ah! misborn Elfe, In evill houre thy foes thee hither sent. **1624** Bp. Mountagu *Gagg* 204 Thou Lyer, and misborne Elfe of the Father of lies. *a* **1641** —— *Acts & Mon.* (1642) 535 The mis-begotten, and mis-born changeling of an hereticall father. **1718** Motteux *Quix.* (1733) I. 108 He wou'd not be allow'd to be a lawful Knight; but a Mis-born Intruder.

mis'bound. [f. MIS-[1] 2 + BOUND *ppl. a.*[2] 6.] Of a book: badly or wrongly bound.

1802 D. Wordsworth *Jrnl.* 5 Feb. (1941) I. 107 The Chaucer not only misbound but a leaf or two wanting. **1889** Skeat *Barbour's Bruce* Pref. p. lxvii, The Bodleian copy is quite perfect; it is only misbound. **1952** J. Carter *ABC for Bk.-Collectors* 120 When a leaf or leaves, or an entire gathering, has been wrongly folded or misplaced by the binder, it is called misbound. Provided that nothing is missing, and that the amount of matter misbound is not too great or its misplacing too glaring, collectors commonly take a more charitable view of the result than readers.

†**mis'breyde.** *Obs.* Also **-brayde.** [f. MIS-[1] 4 + *breyde*, BRAID *sb.* Cf. OE. *misbróden* 'distortum', pa. pple of *misbreȝdan (see BRAID *v.*[1]), also ON. *misbrigði* trespass.] Offence, misdeed.

1303 R. Brunne *Handl. Synne* 3492 Ʒyf a man haue mysdo or seyde, And men hym blame for þat mysbreyde. *c* **1380** *Sir Ferumb.* 1037 Maugree haue þou..for þy foul mysbreyde.

mis'calculate, *v.* [MIS-[1] 1.] *trans.* To calculate, compute, or reckon wrongly.

1705 Arbuthnot *Coins*, etc. (1727) 112 There may be in such a multitude of passages, several misquoted,

misinterpreted, and miscalculated. **1788** BURNS *Let.* 17 Dec., You miscalculate matters widely, when you forbid my waiting on you, lest it should hurt my worldly concerns. **1836** THIRLWALL *Greece* II. xii. 155 They probably miscalculated the effects of the public success. **1878** BOSW. SMITH *Carthage* 194 Or was it that Hannibal miscalculated the distance..of the route which he chose?

b. *absol.* or *intr.*

1697 COLLIER *Ess. Mor. Subj.* II. (1709) 39 To look for so obliging a World as this comes to, is to miscalculate extremely. **1840** MACAULAY *Ess., Clive* (1854) 531/2 The conspirators found that they had miscalculated. **1895** *Atlantic Monthly* LXXVI. 68 They had evidently miscalculated about my departure.

Hence **mis'calculating** *ppl. a.*

1851 I. TAYLOR *Wesley & Methodism* 205 An ill-judging weakness, a miscalculating caution.

,miscalcu'lation. [MIS-[1] 4.] Wrong or faulty calculation or reckoning.

1720 *Biblioth. Bibl.* I. 73 Their want of Intercalations, and their miscalculations of Eclipses. **1858** J. MARTINEAU *Stud. Christ.* 320 The miscalculation of one age is checked by that of a succeeding; opposite errors cancel each other. **1903** MORLEY *Life Gladstone* III. VIII. ix. 146 Events show this to have been the capital miscalculation.

mis'calculator. [MIS-[1] 5.] One who makes miscalculations.

1873 HAMERTON *Intell. Life* IV. ii. 153 Let us not think too contemptuously of the miscalculators of time.

miscall (mɪsˈkɔːl), *v.* Also 8 **miscal.** [MIS-[1] 1.]

1. *trans.* To call by a wrong name; to give a wrong name to; to misname. Often with *compl.*

1398 TREVISA *Barth. De P.R.* XIX. cxxviii. (1495) 936 A vessell wyth fowre fete is myscallyd Trisilis. **1593** SHAKS. *Rich II*, I. iii. 263 *Gau.* Call it a trauell that thou tak'st for pleasure. *Bul.* My heart will sigh, when I miscall it so, Which findes it an inforced Pilgrimage. **1650** J. HALL *Paradoxes* 49 Suppose you miscall happinesse content. **1697** T. BROWN *Dispensary* II. Wks. 1709 III. II. 80 Lest I should mis-call you, and not give you your right Title. **1742** RICHARDSON *Pamela* III. 185 That violent Passion which we mad young Fellows are apt to miscal Love. **1796** MORSE *Amer. Geog.* I. 216 The Partridge of New England is the Pheasant of Pennsylvania, but is mis-called in both places. **1812** H. & J. SMITH *Rej. Addr., Theatre* 14 No room for standing, miscall'd standing room. **1822** T. L. PEACOCK *Maid Marian* xii. 165 No one shall miscall a forester. He who call Robin Robert of Huntingdon..or..Marian Matilda Fitzwater [etc.]. *a* **1853** ROBERTSON *Lect. & Addr.* ii. (1858) 59 One of those miserable publications miscalled religious. **1886** GURNEY, etc. *Phantasms of Living* II. 2 His ..explanation..depended on his miscalling his experience, and referring it to the class of dreams.

b. To misread, mispronounce. *dial.*

1853 CADENHEAD *Bon Accord* 205 (E.D.D.) Woe to the loun that a word wad misca'. **1866** GREGOR *Banffsh. Gloss.*, *Misca'*..(2) To read imperfectly. **1881** MISS YONGE *Lads & Lasses Langley* iv. 146 He no sooner opened his mouth to read than half-a-dozen hands were held out, in token that he had miscalled a word.

2. To call by a bad name; to call (a person) names; to revile, abuse, malign. Now *dial.*

c **1449** PECOCK *Repr.* v. xv. 563 Thei not oonli scornen it [*sc.* the sacrament of the altar], but thei haaten it, mys callen it bi foule names. **1596** SPENSER *F.Q.* IV. viii. 24 Whom she [*sc.* Slander] with leasings lewdly did miscall And wickedly backbite. **1603** HOLLAND *Plutarch's Mor.* 124 They deserved to be..punished, for so miscalling and reviling him. **1643** SIR T. BROWNE *Relig. Med.* (1656) II. §4 By opprobrious Epithets we miscall each other. **1725** RAMSAY *Gentle Sheph.* I. i, She..Misca'd me first, then bade me hound my dog. **1789** BURNS *Capt. Grose's Peregr.* x, Whae'er o' thee shall ill suppose, They sair misca' thee. **1866** READE *G. Gaunt* (ed. 2) II. xvi. 313, I can't bear any man on earth to miscall her but myself. **1872** *Routledge's Ev. Boy's Ann.* 6/2 Here's Kathleen and Susy been miscallin' me dreadful.

Hence **mis'calling** *vbl. sb.* Also **mis'caller.**

1690 LOCKE *Hum. Und.* IV. iv. §9 Miscalling of any of those Ideas..hinders not, but that we may have certain.. Knowledge of their several Agreements and Disagreements. **1816** SCOTT *Antiq.* xii, A' the slights and taunts that hurt ane's spirit mair nor downright misca'ing. **1866** GREGOR *Banffsh. Gloss.*, *Misca'er*, one who reads imperfectly; as, 'He's an unco' misca'er fin he reads'. **1884** A. A. PUTNAM *10 Yrs. Police Judge* xvii. 171 The miscalled threw a clothes-pin and hit the miscaller somewhere.

mis'called, *ppl. a.* [MIS-[1] 2.] Wrongly named.

1822-34 *Good's Study Med.* (ed. 4) III. 169 In those cases of miscalled cataracts. **1838** DICKENS *Nich. Nick.* vi, Let miscalled philosophers tell us what they will. **1904** *Q. Rev.* Oct. 467 The hyraces—the miscalled coneys of Scripture.

miscanter (mɪsˈkæntə(r), -æ-). *north. dial.* [var. of MISAUNTER, of obscure origin; cf. MISHANTER.] Misadventure, mishap.

1781 HUTTON *Tour to Caves* Gloss. (E.D.S.), *Miscanter*, a misadventure. **1808** J. STAGG *Apparition* vii. (1808) 75 Oft by miscanter this way led, The nighted traveller's seen, A frightful ghaist. **1869** *Lonsdale Gloss.*, *Miscanter*, misadventure. **1878** *Cumbld. Gloss.*, *Miscanter*,..a defeat, mishap.

†**mi'scape,** *v. Obs.* [app. f. MIS-[1] 1 + SCAPE *v.*]

1. *intr.* To have a mishap, come to grief.

1377 LANGL. *P. Pl.* B. x. 283 (MS. Rawl.) Archa dei meskapud and ely brak his nekke. **1477** NORTON *Ord. Alch.* iv. in Ashm. (1652) 49 Use one manner of Vessell in Matter and in Shape, Beware of Commixtion that nothing miscape [*several Ashm. MSS. have* mishappe].

2. *trans.* To escape (a person) sinfully.

a **1535** FISHER *Spirit. Consol.* Wks. (1876) 359 Many deeds, words, and thoughtes, miscaped me in my lyfe.

miscarriage (mɪsˈkærɪdʒ). [MIS-[1] 4.]

†**1. a.** Misconduct, misbehaviour. *Obs.*

1618 SIR H. MOUNTAGU in *Buccleuch MSS.* (Hist. MSS. Comm.) I. 253, I have received..the note that imports the miscarriage of the new Justice of Peace. It was very insolent, if the information be true. **1645** in *Essex* (Mass.) *Antiquarian* (1904) VIII. 6 Wife of Mr. Samuel Hall fined for miscarriage in words against the constable of Salsbery. **1682** WOOD *Life* 17 June (O.H.S.) III. 22 The chancellor's letters for regulating the rudeness and miscarriag of the Masters in Convocation.

†**b.** An instance of this; an error of conduct; a misdemeanour, misdeed. *Obs.*

1635 BP. HALL *Char. Man* 34 Miscariages of children, miscasualties, unquietnesse [etc.]. **1647** TRAPP *Comm. Jas.* ii. 7 A sad thing that a Heathen should see such hellish miscarriages among Christs followers. **1649** ROBERTS *Clavis Bibl.* 337 His [*sc.* Job's]..irreverent miscarriages against God under his afflictions. **1710** NORRIS *Chr. Prud.* vi. 288 As to the personal Miscarriages of the Minister, our prudent Christian will not for these disesteem his Office. **1749** FIELDING *Tom Jones* VIII. xi, The miscarriages of my former life. **1760-72** H. BROOKE *Fool of Qual.* (1792) III. 232 Many miscarriages and woful defaults are recorded of Saul, as a man, yet, as a king, he was held perfect in the eyes of the people. **1829** SCOTT *Rob Roy* Introd. (1865) 495/1 [They] conducted themselves with such loyalty..to his Majesty, as might justly wipe off all memory of former miscarriages.

2. a. (A person's) mismanagement or maladministration (of a business); ill-success, failure (of an enterprise, etc.). Now *rare.*

1651-2 SIR E. NICHOLAS in *N. Papers* (Camden) I. 286 The miscarriage of the business in the Downs was not inferior to any treason that I have heard of. **1674** *Baker's Chron.* (an. 1625) 453/2 He excused himself, laying a great part of the miscarriage on the stubbornness of the Earl of Essex. **1706** DE FOE *Jure Divino* p. v, Some People, who are too apt to make Misconstruction, watch for my Miscarriage. *a* **1715** BURNET *Own Time* (1724) I. 251 He did not wonder at the miscarriage of the late King's counsels. **1784-5** BURNS *Poem on Pastoral Poetry* in *Poems & Songs* (1968) I. 191 Scarce ane has tried the Shepherd-sang But wi' miscarriage? **1800** *Chron.* in *Asiat. Ann. Reg.* III. 113/2 The sagacious and intrepid commander, to whom success and miscarriage ..are now alike indifferent. **1807** VANCOUVER *Agric. Devon* (1813) 431 The miscarriage of one crop only..would.. involve him in ruin. **1880** 'MARK TWAIN' *Lett. to Publishers* (1967) 123 Chatto waits..without asking a solitary question about the book, and then pitches into *me* about the miscarriage.

b. An instance of this; a failure; a blunder, mistake. Now *rare* exc. as in e.

1614 R. BAILLIE *Satan* 3 When a hard piece of worke is put in the hand of an Apprentice for the first assay of his skill, the beholders are justly afraid for a miscarriage in his young and inexperienced hand. **1650** [see CARRIAGE 10]. **1667-8** MARVELL *Corr.* Wks. (Grosart) II. 234 That the division of the Fleet was a miscarriage. **1714** GARTH *Dispens.* v. (ed. 7) 61 Your Cures..aloud you tell, But wisely your Miscarriages conceal. **1824** TRAVERS *Dis. Eye* (ed. 3) 338, I have now adverted to the principal miscarriages of the operation. **1834** MACAULAY *Ess., Pitt* (1850) 300/2 An inquiry into the circumstance which had produced the miscarriage of the preceding year.

†**c.** Mishap, disaster. *Obs.*

1725 DE FOE *Voy. round World* (1840) 46 If I should meet with any..miscarriage in the voyage. **1776** JOHNSON *Let. Mrs. Thrale* 1 Apr., His wife died at last, and before she was buried he was seized by a fever, and is now going to the grave. Such miscarriages..fill histories and tragedies.

†**d.** An unfortunate lapse (*into*). *Obs.*

1754 H. WALPOLE *Lett.* (1846) III. 76 The chimney-pieces, except one little miscarriage into total Ionic..are all of a good King James the First Gothic.

e. *miscarriage of justice*: a failure of a court to attain the ends of justice.

1875 *Act 38-9 Vict.* c. 77 Order xxxix, Unless in the opinion of the Court..some substantial wrong or miscarriage has been..occasioned in the trial of action. **1878** PEEK in *Contemp. Rev.* XXXII. 105 In cases where the defendant is poor or ill-defended, there is often positive miscarriage of justice. **1882** SERJT. BALLANTINE *Exper.* vi. 160 In both.., through no fault of the judge, there was a miscarriage of justice. **1891** *Daily News* 5 Feb. 7/1 It was submitted..to their lordships that there had been a miscarriage, and that the order of reference should be revoked.

3. Untimely delivery (of a woman): usually taken as synonymous with *abortion* = expulsion of the fœtus before the twenty-eighth week of pregnancy.

'Some pathologists have sought to establish a distinction between *abortion* and *miscarriage* (see quot. 1822), but this is not generally recognized.' *N.E.D.* In popular speech, however, *abortion* is used chiefly of the induced termination of pregnancy, but *miscarriage* is never so used.

1662 GRAUNT *Bills Mort.* v. 38 Miscarriages and Abortions. **1710-11** SWIFT *Jrnl. to Stella* 15 Feb., I dined at Sir John Germain's, and found lady Betty but just recovered of a miscarriage. **1754-64** SMELLIE *Midwif.* II. 67 She had eight children, besides two miscarriages. **1822** GOOD *Study Med.* IV. 176 If the exclusion [of the fœtus] take place within six weeks after conception, it is usually called Miscarriage; if between six weeks and six months, Abortion; if during any part of the last three months before the completion of the natural term, Premature Labour. **1967** M. M. BOOKMILLER et al. *Textbk. Obstetr.* (ed. 5) xxii. 333/2 The term early abortion refers to expulsion of the fetus up to 12 weeks' gestation. When expelled from 12 to 28 weeks it is called a late abortion and from 28 to 36 weeks it is said to be premature termination of pregnancy. Many laymen still associate the word abortion with illegal interference and prefer to call a spontaneous termination of pregnancy a miscarriage. The nurse should be guided accordingly. **1970** *Sci. Jrnl.* June 75/2 Most hospitals regard the loss of a pregnancy before 20 weeks as a miscarriage. **1971** RUGH & SHETTLES *From Conception to Birth* (1972) x. 157 There are generally signs of an impending miscarriage (another term for a spontaneous abortion). **1974** PASSMORE & ROBSON *Compan. Med. Stud.* III. xlii. 1/2 Abortion may be defined as the termination of pregnancy before the fetus is viable. In Britain this is considered to be before the 28th week of pregnancy. However, fetuses expelled before the 28th week occasionally survive, and to allow for this possibility the 20th week is sometimes used as the watershed between viability and non-viability... In many North American centres abortion is defined as the expulsion of a fetus weighing less than 500 g. A precise definition is required for medico-legal purposes and in Britain abortion means the termination of pregnancy before the 28th week. Miscarriage is synonymous with abortion and is often more acceptable to the lay public.

fig. **1688** CROWNE *Darius* II. Dram. Wks. (1874) III. 398 They who poorly fell Were embrios, and miscarriages of war.

4. The failure (of a letter, etc.) to reach its destination.

1650 LD. BEAUCHAMP in *Nicholas Papers* (Camden) I. 179, I have been very unfortunate in the miscarryage of your former addresses. **1670** BLOUNT *Law Dict.* s.v. *Duplicat*, A second Letter written and sent to the same party and purpose, as a former, for fear of a miscarriage of the first,.. is called a *Duplicat.* **1877** RAYMOND *Statist. Mines & Mining* 172 The miscarriage of a paper by Mr. Alexander Trippel prevents me from presenting..some further notes. **1893** W. M. THOMAS *Lett. Lady M. W. Montagu* II. Contents p. vi, Miscarriage of letters.

5. Failure to carry or convey properly.

1862 'SHIRLEY' (J. Skelton) *Nugæ Crit.* iv. 195 Public carriers must carry the public safely, or take the consequences; and neither a voluntary, nor an extorted consent, will relieve them from the legal results of miscarriage.

†**mis'carriageable,** *a. Obs. rare*[−1]. [f. prec. + -ABLE.] Liable to be led astray.

a **1656** BP. HALL *Rem. Wks.* (1660) 418 Why should we be more mis-carriageable by such possibilities..than others?

†**mis'carried,** *ppl. a. Obs.* [f. MISCARRY *v.* + -ED[1].] Gone astray.

1656 SIR R. BROWNE in *Nicholas Papers* (Camden) III. 285 The subject of that my miscarried letter..was that [etc.].

†**mis'carrier.** *Obs. rare*[−1]. [f. next + -ER[1].] A seducer, beguiler. (See MISCARRY *v.* 7.)

1596 NORDEN *Progr. Pietie* (1847) 172 Turning our hearts from our Maker, we become one in consent with our miscarrier.

miscarry (mɪsˈkærɪ), *v.* [MIS-[1] 1. Cf. OF. *meskarier* to go from the right path.]

†**1.** *intr.* To come to harm, misfortune, or destruction; to perish; (of a person) to meet with one's death; (of an inanimate object, e.g. a ship) to be lost or destroyed. *Obs.*

a **1340** HAMPOLE *Psalter* xxxvi. 23 Bot weriand til him sal myskary [Vulg. *maledicentes autem ei disperibunt*]. *c* **1386** CHAUCER *Prol.* 515 He..dwelte at hoom, and kepte wel his folde, So that the wolf ne made it nat miscarie. **1444** *Rolls of Parlt.* V. 114/1 So that there myght neither Clusters of Grapes, ne hole Grapes..entre..into the Vessels..yat myght cause yat Wyne after that to reboille or myscare. **1447** BOKENHAM *Seyntys* (Roxb.) 142 And that noon hous where were hyr passyonarye Wyth feer ner lyhtnyng shuld never myskarye. **1526** *Pilgr. Perf.* (W. de W. 1531) 12 b, Not one of them all miscaryed, but were all safe and sounde. *c* **1550** R. BIESTON *Bayte Fortune* B iv, But yet he must regarde, for drede his welth miscary. **1586** J. HOOKER *Hist. Irel.* in *Holinshed* II. 92/1 In this conflict, Patrike Fitzsimons, with diuerse other good housholders, miscaried. **1601** R. JOHNSON *Kingd. & Commw.* (1603) 63 The great ships bringing corne from Siria and Egipt..doe seldome miscarrie. *a* **1604** HANMER *Chron. Irel.* (1809) 371 [He] shortly after miscarried at Athlone, by the fall of a Turret. **1668** SIR W. TEMPLE *Let. to King* Wks. 1731 II. 58 If we had miscarried, your Majesty had lost an honest diligent Captain and sixteen poor Seamen. **1737** [S. BERINGTON] *G. di Lucca's Mem.* (1738) 126 He left the Government..of all to his eldest Son in case he should miscarry. **1749** R. JAMES *Diss. Fevers* (ed. 2) 3 Many Patients miscarry even under this Treatment, perhaps more than recover.

†**b.** *pass.* in the same sense. *Obs.*

1387-8 T. USK *Test. Love* II. iv. (Skeat) I. 106, I had routhe to sene thee miscaried. **1470-85** MALORY *Arthur* XII. iv. 599, I am sore ashamed that I haue ben thus myscaryed, for I am bannysshed oute of the Countrey of Logrys for euer. **1565** *Act 8 Eliz.* c. 13 §1 Divers Shyppes..have by the lacke of suche Markes of late yeres ben myscaried peryshed and lost in the Sea. **1605** SHAKS. *Lear* V. i. 5 Our Sisters man is certainely miscarried. **1654-66** EARL ORRERY *Parthen.* (1676) 581 Learning that his first Ambassadors..were miscarried, he employed others.

†**2.** *intr.* and *refl.* To go wrong or astray; to behave amiss, do wrong; to misbehave. *Obs.*

c **1325** *Metr. Hom.* 112 Lat thou noht this child miscarye. **138.** WYCLIF *Sel. Wks.* III. 38 þouȝ þat it myskarie whanne it comeþ to age, þe childheed þei moun save. **155.** LYNDESAY *Interl. Auld Man & Wife* 57 Maister, quhairto sowld I my self miskary, Quhair I, as preistis, may swyve and nevir mary? **1632** LITHGOW *Trav.* VIII. 348 [They] may not marry, and yet may mis-carry themselues in all abhominations. **1649** ROBERTS *Clavis Bibl.* 368 Solomon more miscarrying in that [*sc.* prosperity] then Job in this [*sc.* adversity]. **1732** BERKELEY *Alciphr.* II. §20 Wks. 1871 II. 92 Crates..having had a son miscarry at London, by the conversation of a minute philosopher.

3. *intr.* Of a person: To fail in one's purpose or object; to be unsuccessful.

1612 T. TAYLOR *Comm. Titus* ii. 12 Many men are crossed and miscarrie in their outward estate, because they are vngodly persons. **1642** FULLER *Holy & Prof. St.* IV. iii. 252 Here Wolsey miscarried in the Masterpiece of his policy. **1711** ADDISON *Spect.* No. 35 ¶1 Among all kinds of Writing, there is none in which Authors are more apt to miscarry than

in Works of Humour. **1815** W. H. IRELAND *Scribbleomania* 261 Good luck; without which..it is odds but he miscarries in his suit. **1841–4** EMERSON *Ess., Self-Reliance* Wks. (Bohn) I. 32 If our young men miscarry in their first enterprises, they lose all heart. **1875** MAINE *Hist. Inst.* ix. 256 If you sue for a bull, you will miscarry if you describe him as a bull.

b. const. *of.*

1781 COWPER *Conv.* 372 We dare not risk them [*sc.* our talents] into public view, Lest they miscarry of what seems their due. **1832** A. W. FONBLANQUE *Eng. under 7 Administr.* (1837) II. 259 He has..pitiably miscarried of his object.

4. Of a business, design, etc.: To go wrong; to come to nought; to be a failure; to prove unsuccessful or abortive. †Also *pass.*

1607 SHAKS. *Cor.* I. i. 270 What miscarries Shall be the Generals fault. **1639** FULLER *Holy War* II. xlv. (1840) 112 When a great action miscarrieth, the blame must be laid on some. **1654** MARQ. ORMONDE in *Nicholas Papers* (Camden) II. 142 It is ordinary when a busines is miscaryed to blame the ways taken to effect it. **1726** SWIFT *Gulliver* IV. vii, If they find their Project hath miscarried, they return Home. **1827** HALLAM *Const. Hist.* iv. (1876) I. 212 A similar proposition in the session of 1601 seems to have miscarried in the Commons. **1893** J. STRONG *New Era* 252 Motive miscarries if method is wrong.

†**b.** Of plants, seeds, etc.: To be abortive or unproductive; to fail. Also *transf. Obs.*

1588 SHAKS. *L.L.L.* IV. i. 114 My Lady goes to kill hornes, but if thou marrie, Hang me by the necke, if hornes that yeare miscarrie. *a* **1682** SIR T. BROWNE *Tracts* (1683) 77 [A plant] not subject to miscarry in Flowers and Blossomes. **1707** MORTIMER *Husb.* (1721) II. 124 The worst Enemies to this Plant are a sort of Flea that fastens upon its Shoots, and makes it miscarry. **1740** TULL *Horse-Hoeing Husb.* 254 In other Parts of the same Fields, where a much less Number of Seeds had miscarried, the Crop was less.

5. To be delivered prematurely *of* a child; to have a miscarriage. (†In first quot. *passive.*)

1527 ANDREW *Brunswyke's Distyll. Waters* C iij b, Women whiche be myscaryd of the mydwyfe in the byrthe of her chylde. **1560** DAUS tr. *Sleidane's Comm.* 113 b, She had dyverse tymes mis-caried of chylde. **1662** GRAUNT *Bills Mort.* v. 37 The Question is, Whether Teeming-women died, or fled, or miscarried? *a* **1715** BURNET *Own Time* (1766) I. 244 She had once miscarried of a child. **1786** J. HUNTER *Treat. Ven. Dis.* (1810) VI. II. i. 433 The mother..miscarried of her third child at the end of five months. **1822–34** *Good's Study Med.* (ed. 4) IV. 171 The case of a lady..who had miscarried of a fetus under three months old.

fig. **1712** POPE *Let. to J. C.* 5 Dec., Wks. (1737) 89 You have prov'd your self more tender of another's embryo's, than the fondest mothers are of their own, for you have preserv'd every thing that I miscarry'd of. **1805** MOORE *To Lady H—* viii, And some lay-in of full-grown wit, While others of a pun miscarried.

†**b.** Said of the child. *Obs.*

1597 SHAKS. *2 Hen. IV.* V. iv. 10 If the Child I now go with, do miscarrie. *Ibid.* 15 But I would the Fruite of her Wombe might miscarry.

6. *intr.* Of a letter, etc.: To fail to reach its proper destination; to get into wrong hands.

1613 SHAKS. *Hen. VIII*, III. ii. 30 The Cardinals Letters to the Pope miscarried, And came to th'eye o' th' King. **1710** SWIFT *Jrnl. to Stella* 26 Sept., My penny-post letter, I suppose, miscarried: I will write another. *a* **1839** PRAED *Poems* (1864) II. 10 Has the last pipe of hock miscarried? **1842** BORROW *Bible in Spain* xxxv, I supposed..that my letter had miscarried. **1866** CRUMP *Banking* v. 101 If a bill miscarry—unless payable to 'bearer'—the unlawful possessor can neither acquire nor convey any title thereto.

b. *pass.* in the same sense. ?*Obs.*

1665 J. STRYPE in *Lett. Lit. Men* (Camden) 183, I..think my Tuesday letter was miscarried, because no Answer to it. **1786** JEFFERSON *Writ.* (1859) II. 16 If my letter of advice is miscarried.

†**7.** *trans.* To cause (a person) to go wrong; to lead astray; to mislead, delude, seduce. *Obs.*

c **1450** *Cast. Persev.* 2348 in *Macro Plays* (1904) 147 Whoso wyl schryuyn hym of his synnys all, he puttyth þis brethel to mykyl myschefe, Mankynde he þat myskaryed. **1513** DOUGLAS *Æneis* II. xi. 107 Than wod for wo, so was I quyte miscareit, That noder god nor man I left wnwareit [*Quem non incusavi amens hominumque deorumque?*] **1562** A. SCOTT *Poems* (S.T.S.) i. 75 It maid na mis quhat madinnis þai miscareit. **1580** A. FLEMING in Baret *Alv.* A aaj, Manie words of like spelling, and..different in signification, may miscarrie young beginners. **1596** SPENSER *State Irel.* Wks. (Globe) 623/1 The judges, whoe are men and may be mis-carryed by affections, and many other meanes. **1611** SPEED *Hist. Gt. Brit.* IX. vii. 476/1 Impotent passions carrying him, and miscarrying him. **1633** BP. HALL *Hard Texts O.T.* 121 He was not miscarried into any..enormous crime. **1650** TRAPP *Comm. Num.* xx. 11 The best may be mis-carried by their passions. ? *a* **1700** *Bonny Lizie Baillie* xi. in Child *Ballads* IV. 267 O bonny Duncan Grahame, Why should ye me miscarry?

†**8.** In physical sense: To carry to destruction.

1632 LITHGOW *Trav.* VI. 262 If any of them had missed [his footing], his sliding downe had miscarried them both ouer the Rocke.

Hence **mis'carrying** *ppl. a.*

1611 BIBLE *Hosea* ix. 14 Giue them a miscarying wombe, and drie breasts. **1637** RUTHERFORD *Lett.* (1664) xc. 184 Such are the rovings of our miscarrying hearts. *Ibid.* cxxxv. 263 What is the dry and miscarrrying hope of all them who are not in Christ, but confusion and wind?

mis'carrying, *vbl. sb.* [-ING¹.] The action of the vb. MISCARRY; miscarriage.

1568 *Jacob & Esau* v. ix, O Lorde saue thou my sonne from miscarying. **1658–9** in *Thurloe St. Papers* VII. 627 *note*, The miscarryinge of a packitt. **1736** BUTLER *Anal.* I. iv, These things..imply temptation, and danger of miscarrying,..with respect to our worldly..happiness. **1822–34** *Good's Study Med.* (ed. 4) IV. 132 Women who are in the habit of miscarrying.

†**mis'case.** *Obs.* [f. MIS-¹ 4 + CASE *sb.*¹ (sense 1).] Misfortune, mishap.

1297 R. GLOUC. (Rolls) 10047 Þe meste miscas com to him sulf attelaste Vor he vel of is palefrey & brec is fot bi cas. *a* **1400** *Isumbras* 784 And coverde he hase alle his myscas, He lyffes nowe fulle richely. *c* **1450** *Godstow Reg.* 416 Yf hit so happened..that the forsaid houses..were I-brent thurgh ony mysse-case.

mis'cast, *sb.* [MIS-¹ 4.] †**1.** Miscalculation. *Obs.*

1599 SANDYS *Europæ Spec.* (1632) 210 That their private ambitions, feares and miscasts did drive them to make so abiect..a choyce.

2. *Theatr.* An actor or actress who is miscast (see MISCAST *v.* 4); an instance of miscasting.

1907 G. B. SHAW *Lett. to G. Barker* (1956) 81 Barker was capable of anything in the way of casting..Miss Sterling McKinlay was..a very obvious miscast. **1908** *Ibid.* 142 It was not her fault; it was simply a miscast.

mis'cast, *v.* [MIS-¹ 1.]

†**1.** *trans.* To cast with evil intent. *Obs.*

1390 GOWER *Conf.* I. 283 If it so befelle That I..sihe On me that sche miscaste hire yhe, Or that sche liste noght to loke.

2. To miscalculate, misreckon. Also *absol. Obs.* exc. *dial.*

1598 SYLVESTER *Du Bartas* I. i. 416 You have mis-cast in your Arithmetick. **1614** RALEIGH *Hist. World* v. ii. §8. 604 The number is somewhat misse-cast by Polybius..he reckons nine hundred horse too many. **1633** EARL MANCH. *Al Mondo* (1636) 107 In reckoning of time most men miscast it. **1677** *Conn. Col. Rec.* (1852) II. 308 This Court findeing that the List of Stoneington was in the last year miscast three hundred and twenty one pownd. **1876** ROBINSON *Whitby Gloss.*, *Miskest*, to err in casting up accounts. 'All miskessen together'.

†**3.** To mislay. *Obs.*

1600 HOLLAND *Livy* 1234 How all these complete bookes of T. Livius should miscarrie, it is not certenly knowne. Some hope there is, that they are but mis-cast and laid out of the way.

4. *Theatr.* In passive, of an actor: to be cast in an unsuitable rôle; of a play: to have unsuitable actors performing in it; also *fig.*

1927 *Observer* 10 July 15/1 We say that so-and-so was good or adequate or miscast or unhappy in his part. We do not appraise the acting as we appraise the play. *Ibid.* 21 Aug. 9/4 'The Climax'..was brought to England seventeen years ago... It was then admittedly miscast. **1944** M. J. MACMANUS *Eamon de Valera* xiii. 288 Poor Mr. Thomas..was sadly miscast on the diplomatic stage. **1957** *Observer* 8 Sept. 10/4 As Tigre, M. Barrault is mournfully miscast. **1972** *Daily Tel.* 9 Feb. 13/6 This was partly because John Neville was miscast in the main role.

mis'casting, *vbl. sb.* [MIS-¹ 3.]

1. Miscalculation; in mod. use, technically, wrong addition (of accounts).

1542–3 *Act 34 & 35 Hen. VIII*, c. 21 For misrecytall or nonrecytall of Leases..or for lacke of the certentie myscasting rating or setting foorthe of the yerelie values..of the Premisses. **1621** MOLLE *Camerar. Liv. Libr.* III. i. 149 When there is a miscasting in the beginning of an account. **1692** WASHINGTON tr. *Milton's Def. People Eng.* M.'s Wks. 1738 I. 516 Ballance your Accounts, and you will find that by miscasting, you have lost your Principal. **1797** TOMLINS *Jacob's Law Dict.*, Miscasting or Miscomputing. **1887** *Daily News* 4 Mar. 7/3 A miscasting of the books in one instance was over 3,000*l.*

2. Bad casting (of metal)

1901 *N. & Q.* Ser. IX. VIII. 430/2 The difficulty arises from the bell-founder's miscasting.

3. *Theatr.* The allotting to an actor of a part which does not suit him.

1926 *Spectator* 25 Sept. 470/2 In a long list of characters there is not one case of miscasting. **1927** *Observer* 26 Sept. 13/4 Those instances of what I thought was miscasting have made me long to try my hand at casting a play. **1946** *Weekly Rev.* 20 June 156/1 The extraordinary mis-casting of the Elder who was made up to look like an emaciated crook suffering from T.B. **1971** *Daily Tel.* 24 Nov. 10/4 Act Four [of 'Swan Lake'] suffered..from the miscasting of Miss Mason.

mis'casualty. *Obs.* or *dial.* [MIS-¹ 4.] Mischance, mishap.

1588 J. HARVEY *Disc. Probl.* 18 They..imputed the mishap, or miscasualtie unto the multitude of their owne transgressions. **1604** EDMONDS *Observ. Cæsar's Comm.* 95 Men haue two wayes to come by wisdome, either by their owne harmes, or by other mens miscasualties. *a* **1639** WOTTON in *Reliq.* (1685) 683 A Souldier, filling his Flask out of a Barrel of Powder, set by Miscasualty both on fire. *a* **1825** FORBY *Voc. E. Anglia* (1830), *Miscasualty*, an unlucky accident.

mis'catalogued, *ppl. a.* [MIS ¹ 2.] Erroneously or inaccurately entered in a catalogue.

1963 [see *information retrieval* s.v. INFORMATION 8]. **1974** *Times* 10 Jan. 4/6 Low-season sales are always well scrutinized by dealers looking for miscatalogued bargains.

miscegenation (ˌmɪsɪdʒɪ'neɪʃən). [irreg. f. L. *miscē-re* to mix + *gen-us* race + -ATION.] Mixture of races; *esp.* the sexual union of whites with Negroes.

1864 (*title*) Miscegenation: The Theory of the Blending of the Races, applied to the American White Man and Negro. Reprinted from the New York Edition. **1878** STANLEY *Dark Cont.* I. 44 By this process of miscegenation, the Arabs are already rapidly losing their rich colour. **1889** *Boston* (Mass.) *Jrnl.* 27 Feb. 4/4 Miscegenation in Kentucky... The penalty for miscegenation is three years' imprisonment. **1902** *Pilot* 27 Dec. 540/2 The danger of 'miscegenation'..ought to warn us against introducing Oriental settlers into South Africa. **1927** M. M. BENNETT *Christison* ii. 29 'Miscegenation' being official jargon for what Governor Bourke called 'detaining black women by force'. **1971** *Sunday Times* 20 June 29/6 [He] must inaugurate 'creative miscegenation' by marrying a Chinese girl.

fig. **1865** E. BURRITT *Walk to Land's End* 64 It is an..effort to engraft Christian ideas upon the heathen stock of Grecian mythology... In beautiful..contrast with this ostentatious group of Christian and pagan miscegenation is [etc.]. **1884** J. HAWTHORNE *N. Hawthorne & Wife* II. 178 The lower regions of palaces come to strange uses in Rome; a cobbler or a tinker perhaps exercises his craft under the archway; a work-shop may be established in one of the apartments; and similar miscegenations.

So (mostly nonce-wds.) **'miscegen** [back-formation] = *miscegenate*; **'miscegenate** *sb.* [see -ATE² 3], the issue of a union between people of different races; **'miscegenate** *v.*, to produce miscegenation; **'miscegenated** *ppl. a.*, produced by miscegenation; **misce'genesis** (in quot. **misci-**) = MISCEGENATION; **miscege'netic, misce'genic** *adjs.*, pertaining to or involving miscegenation; **ˌmiscege'nationist, 'miscegenator, mi'scegenist,** one who favours miscegenation; also, one who contracts a union with one of another race; **mi'scegeny,** miscegenation.

1864 [CROLY, etc.] *Miscegenation* 7 To *miscegenate*; i.e. to mingle persons of different races. *Ibid.* ii. 19 The Griquas, or Griqua Hottentots, are a miscegenated race. *Ibid.* v. 28 A miscegenetic community. *Ibid.* vii. 34 The purest miscegen will be brown, with reddish cheeks. **1865** *Reader* 20 May 561/2 (art. Emancipation), There are philogynists as fanatical as any 'miscegenists'. **1865** S. S. COX *Eight Yrs. Congress* 354 A very sprightly suffragan of the miscegen stamp. *Ibid.*, The result would be an average miscegen and a superior patriot. **1872** SCHELE DE VERE *Americanisms* 289 A Miscegenationist, named Williams, was tarred and feathered, and dumped into the river at Grenada, Mississippi. **1880** WINCHELL *Preadamites* vi. 81 The policy of North American miscigenesis, which has been recommended..as an..expedient for obviating race collisions. **1881** SALA *Amer. Revis.* 316 Two such 'Miscegenators' have been hanged by the mob in Virginia. **1898** C. F. ADAMS *Imperialism* 10 It has saved the Anglo-Saxon stock from being a nation of half-breeds—miscegenates. **1941** 'R. WEST' *Black Lamb* I. 527 It was a fusion, lovely but miscegenic, of the Byzantine and the baroque styles. **1935** *Punch* 14 Aug. 176/1 Since miscegeny is not a bad British trouble, *Shanghai* is a film that is more likely to interest America than ourselves.

miscelane, -lin, -ling, obs. forms of MASLIN².

miscelden, -din, obs. forms of MISTLETOE.

†**miscella'narian.** *Obs.* [f. MISCELLANY + -ARIAN.] A writer of miscellanies.

1711 SHAFTESB. *Charac.* (1737) III. Misc. I. i. 8, I..like my Fellow-Miscellanarians, shall take occasion to vary often from my proposed Subject. *Ibid.* 113.

†**miscellane,** *a.* and *sb. Obs.* Also 7 -el(l)an, -elane, -illane. [ad. L. *miscellāneus* (see MISCELLANEOUS): cf. *momentane.*]

A. *adj.* Mixed; miscellaneous; combining various elements. (Cf. MASLIN² *attrib.*)

1603 HOLLAND *Plutarch's Mor.* 131 Choler is a miscellane seed (as it were) and a dregge, made of all the passions of the mind. **1608** J. KING *Serm.* 5 Nov. 32 A linsey wolsey, miscellan, medlyreligion. **1612** BREREWOOD *Lang. & Relig.* v. 39 Paulus Diaconus his miscellane history [sc. *Historia miscella*]. **1642** J. EATON *Honey-c. Free Justif.* 139 These miscillane Christians never knew what an horrible thing the least motion of sin is in the sight of God. [Cf. B. quot. 1642.] **1658** W. BURTON *Itin. Antonin.* 62 One [colony]..drawn out from among the gowned Citizens, as well as the miscellane sort of people.

B. *sb.* A mixture, medley, miscellany. (Cf. MASLIN².)

1600 BP. W. BARLOW *Serm.* (1601) D 5 b, The miscellan of all nations. **1626** BACON *Sylva* §670 It is thought to be of vse, to make some Miscellane in Corne. **1642** J. EATON *Honey-c. Free Justif.* 137 [They] preach neither true law nor true Gospel, but a miscillane and marring of both. **1664** J. WILSON *A. Commenius* v. iv, Some have call'd life a Stage-play..; Others agen, a miscelane of years, Or Chequer-work of hopes, and fears.

‖**miscellanea** (mɪsə'leɪnɪə). [neut. pl. of L. *miscellāneus* (see MISCELLANEOUS): in Latin used for 'hash of broken meat' and 'a writing on miscellaneous subjects'. Used also in Fr.]

A collection of miscellaneous literary compositions; a literary medley or miscellany. Also, a miscellaneous collection of notes, or the like.

1571 ALLEY (*title*) The poore mans Librarie... Here are adioyned..certaine..annotations which may properly be called Miscellanea. **1653** FLECKNOE (*title*) Miscellania, Or, Poems of all sorts, with divers other Pieces. **1690** TEMPLE *Ess., Learning* Wks. 1731 I. 291 Upon the Miscellanea's first Printing in Paris, Monsieur Boileau made this short Satyr. **1710** SWIFT *Jrnl. to Stella* vi, [He] has written some mighty pretty things; that in your 6th *Miscellanea*, about the Sprig of an Orange, is his. **1784** *New Spect.* No. 6. 3, I..begin my miscellanea with a Private Anecdote. **1836** H. N. COLERIDGE *Lit. Rem. S. T. Coleridge* I. L'Envoy p. xiii, I should misinform you grossly if I left you to infer that his collections were a heap of incoherent *miscellanea.* **1897** J. W. CLARK *Barnwell* Introd. 11 Miscellanea likely to be useful for reference.

† **misce'llaneal**, *a.* (*sb.*) *Obs.* [f. L. *miscellāne-us* (see next) + -AL¹.] Miscellaneous. Also *sb. pl.* = MISCELLANEA. So † **misce'llanean** *a.*

1632 GUILLIM *Heraldry* I. vi. 38, I tooke occasion to peruse certaine Miscellanean notes of Seales. *a* **1633** W. AMES *Fresh Suit agst. Cerem.* II. 209 Concerning certayn miscelaneall notions and testimonies against..Ceremonies. **1654** VILVAIN *Epit. Ess.* v, Miscellaneal Essais. The fifth.. Century of Miscellaneals. **1703** T. S. *Art's Impr.* p. xxvii, Miscelaneal Experiments and Observations.

miscellaneous (mɪsəˈleɪnɪəs), *a.* [f. L. *miscellāne-us*, f. *miscellus* mixed (f. *miscēre* to mix): see -EOUS.]

1. With a sing. sb.: Consisting of members or elements of different kinds; of mixed composition or character. With a pl. sb.: Of various kinds.

1637 SALTONSTALL *Euseb. Const.* 53 The people being thus a long time divided betweene divers opinions, it produced a miscellanious confusion in Religion. **1671** MILTON *P.R.* III. 50 A miscellaneous rabble, who extol Things vulgar. **1711** SHAFTESB. *Charac.* (1737) III. Misc. I. i. 1 That Charitable and Courteous Author, who.. introduc'd the ingenious way of Miscellaneous Writing. **1766** GOLDSM. *Vic. W.* i, My second boy..received a sort of miscellaneous education at home. **1790** BURKE *Fr. Rev.* Wks. 1808 V. 47 Dr. Richard Price..preached..a very extraordinary miscellaneous sermon. **1821** W. IRVING *Life & Lett.* (1864) II. 49, I have been leading a 'miscellaneous' kind of life at Paris, if I may use a literary phrase. **1862** STANLEY *Jew. Ch.* (1877) I. xvii. 322 In this miscellaneous assemblage were to be seen worshippers of the most various characters. **1899** Æ. J. G. MACKAY *Lindesay's Chron. Scot.* (S.T.S.) I. p. lxxxvii, One of the miscellaneous volumes of the Wodrow Manuscripts.

† **b.** Mingled. *Obs.*

1698 W. CHILCOT *Evil Th.* iv. (1851) 44 The miscellaneous horror and exultation of that dreadful day.

2. Of persons: Having various qualities or aspects; treating of various subjects: many-sided. †Also, general (as opposed to *technical*).

1646 SIR T. BROWNE *Pseud. Ep.* I. viii. §9. 32 [Athenæus] being miscellaneous in many things, he is to be received with suspicion; for such as amasse all relations, must erre in some. **1711** SHAFTESB. *Charac.* (1737) III. Misc. I. i. 8 Nor ought the Title of a Miscellaneous Writer to be deny'd me, on the account that I have grounded my Miscellanys upon a certain Set of Treatises already publish'd. **1773** BURNEY *Mus. Germany*, etc. (1775) II. 305 As technical terms will be unavoidable in this description, I advise my miscellaneous readers to pass it over. **1831** WORDSW. *Prose Wks.* (1876) III. 313 A great theatrical writer,..and miscellaneous to that degree, that there was something for all classes of readers. **1839** LONGF. *Hyperion* I. vi. Prose Wks. 1886 II. 45 The Baron of Hohenfels was rather a miscellaneous youth, rather a universal genius.

Hence **miscellaneity** (ˌmɪsələˈniːɪtɪ), miscellaneousness.

1905 *Daily Chron.* 13 Nov. 4/5 The miscellaneity of the Hellenic 'masses' thus enjoying the hospitality of the King.

misce'llaneously, *adv.* [-LY-.] With variety or diversity; in various ways, on miscellaneous subjects, etc.

1751 EARL ORRERY *Remarks Swift* (1752) 41 He has written miscellaneously. **1850** *Tait's Mag.* XVII. 740/1 They are more miscellaneously clever, and can make themselves more 'generally useful'. **1905** *Q. Rev.* Jan. 42 He collected miscellaneously, and in all probability.. indiscriminately.

misce'llaneousness. [-NESS.] Miscellaneous quality, character, or condition.

1727 BAILEY vol. II, *Miscellaneousness*, mixture or mixedness together without Order. **1755** JOHNSON, *Miscellaneousness*, composition of various kinds. **1871** GEO. ELIOT *Middlemarch* xxii, The..miscellaneousness of Rome, which made the mind flexible with constant comparison. **1887** LOWELL *Old Eng. Dram.* (1892) 59 The gratuitous miscellaneousness of plot..in some of the plays of John Webster.

miscellanist (mɪˈsɛlənɪst). [f. MISCELLANY + -IST.] A writer of miscellanies.

1810 BYRON in *Mem. F. Hodgson* (1878) I. 168 My third [letter] will be conveyed by Cam, the miscellanist. **1862** F. HALL *Hindu Philos. Syst.* 35 A late miscellanist, more celebrated for versatility and self-confidence than for exactness. **1889** SAINTSBURY *Ess. Eng. Lit.* (1891) 219 We may..consider him [Leigh Hunt] first as a poet, secondly as a critic, and thirdly as..a miscellanist.

miscellany (ˈmɪsələnɪ, mɪˈsɛlənɪ), *sb.* Also 7 **missel(l)-**, **miscel-**, 8 **misell-**. [app. ad. F. *miscellanées* fem. pl. (ad. L. *miscellānea* neut. pl.: see MISCELLANEA), only in sense 2.]

1. A mixture, medley.

1617 BACON in *Resuscitatio* (1657) 81 A Miscellany and Confusion of Causes of all Natures. **1620** *Hic Mulier* C 3 b, This Misselanie or mixture of deformities. **1668** DRYDEN *Dram. Poesy* Ess. (ed. Ker) I. 84 As for Falstaff, he is not properly one humour, but a miscellany of humours or images, drawn from so many several men. **1703** MAUNDRELL *Journ. Jerus.* (1721) 40 A confus'd miscellany of Trees. *Ibid.* 18 A Miscellany of Christians and Turks together. **1833** LYTTON *Eng. & Engl.* (ed. 2) II. 287 Turn your eyes now to the ultra Radicals, what a motley, confused, jarring, miscellany of irreconcilable theorists! **1847** TENNYSON *Princess* v. 190 Not like the piebald miscellany, man, Bursts of great heart and slips in sensual mire. **1886** STEVENSON *Treas. Isl.* iv, Under that, the miscellany began—a quadrant, a tin canikin, an old Spanish watch and some other trinkets of little value.

† **b.** *miscellany madam*: 'a female trader in miscellaneous articles; a dealer in trinkets and ornaments of various kinds' (Nares). *Obs.*

1599 B. JONSON *Cynthia's Rev.* IV. i, I would bee..one of your miscelany madams. *Ibid.*, As a miscellany madame [I would] inuent new tyres, and goe visite courtiers.

2. *pl.* Separate treatises or studies on a subject collected into one volume; literary compositions of various kinds brought together to form a book. (Common in titles of books.)

1615 P. WENTWORTH (*title*) The Miscellanie, or, a Registrie, and Methodicall Directorie of Orizons. *a* **1626** BACON *Let. to Bp. Ely* Wks. 1830 XII. 91 This hath put me into these miscellanies, which I purpose to suppress, if God give me leave to write a just and perfect volume of philosophy. **1629** J. LIGHTFOOT (*title*) Ervbhin or Miscellanies Christian and Judaicall. **1678** NORRIS *Misc.* (1699) Pref. 1 To you I humbly present this Collection of Miscellanies, for the entertainment of your liesure hours. **1711** [see MISCELLANEOUS 2]. **1733** SWIFT *On Poetry* 318 And when they join their pericranies, Out skips a book of Miscellanies.

3. A book, volume, or literary production containing miscellaneous pieces on various subjects.

1638 HERBERT *Trav.* II. 262 The Alcoran is a miscellany of other prodigious things. **1671** SALMON *Syn. Med.* To Rdr. *3 Wonder not, Courteous Reader, at the Appearance of this early, or rather untimely fruit; a Miscelany only intended for our own private use. **1704** *Faction Display'd* xiii, Those only purchase everliving Fame, That in my Misellany plant their Name. **1707** (*title*) The Monthly Miscellany: or, Memoirs for the Curious. **1791** BOSWELL *Johnson* (1831) I. 205 He.. wrote 'The Life of Cheynel', in the miscellany called 'The Student'. **1801** *Med. Jrnl.* V. 107 What appears to me an error in your truly valuable Miscellany. **1872** R. MORRIS (*title*) An Old English Miscellany. **1873** H. ROGERS *Orig. Bible* iv. (1874) 163 The Bible, in fact, is a 'Miscellany'—a very various one.

4. *pl.* Persons of various classes. *rare.*

1840 CARLYLE *Let.* Aug. in R. Blunt *Carlyles' Chelsea Home* (1895) 16 Blackguards, improper females, and miscellanies sauntered.

† **miscellany**, *a. Obs.* [ad. L. *miscellāne-us*: the form perh. suggested by prec. sb. (But cf. *momentary*).] = MISCELLANE, MISCELLANEOUS.

1629 *Bacon's War w. Spain* 70 A Veterane Army, compounded of Miscellany Forces of all Nations. **1629** (*title*) Certaine Miscellany Works of The Right Honovrable, Francis Lo. Verulam. **1651** CLEVELAND *Poems* 26 The Misselany Satyr, and the Fawn. **1659** PEARSON *Creed* (1839) 29 By their miscellany deities at Rome,..they showed no nation was without its God. **1684** (*title*) Miscellany Poems Containing a New Translation of Virgills Eclogues, Ovid's Love Elegies [etc.]. **1738** SWIFT *Pol. Conversat.* Introd. 66, I have read..all the miscellany Poems that have been published for twenty Years past. **1756** AMORY *Buncle* (1825) I. 1 Miscellany thoughts upon several subjects.

† **miscelleny.** *Obs. rare*⁻¹. [Alteration of *miscellen*, MASLIN², after *miscellany*.] = MASLIN².

1745 tr. *Columella* II. xi, It is proper to sow miscelleny, or barley todder [orig. *farraginem*] in a place that is plowed and sown every year.

misceline, reading in mod. edd. of Jonson's *Volpone* for *misc'line* (see MASLIN² c).

miscelling, obs. form of MASLIN².

miscelto, -tow, obs. forms of MISTLETOE.

† **mis'censure**, *sb.* [MIS-¹ 4.] Wrongful or undeserved censure.

1613 *Voy. Guiana* in *Harl. Misc.* (Malh.) III. 171 All men's actions are subject to miscensure. **1645** WITHER *Vox Pacif.* 117 A self-respect May cause mis-censures to be cast upon The Publike Justice. *a* **1684** LEIGHTON *Comm. 1 Pet.* ii. 6 (1693) 292 They cast him [*sc.* Christ] away by their miscensures and reproaches put upon him.

† **mis'censure**, *v. Obs.* [MIS-¹ 1.] *trans.* To censure wrongfully or undeservedly.

1611 CORYAT *Crudities* 364, I hope the candid reader will not miscensure me for inserting this into my obseruations. **1645** WITHER *Vox Pacif.* 33 Ten hundred thousand tongues Shall censure them, who now mis-censure thee. **1665** —— *Lord's Prayer* 35 Nor will [I] miscensure their charitable hope, who [etc.].

Hence † **mis'censuring** *vbl. sb.*

1657 SANDERSON *Serm.* Pref. (1674) E 2 b, To prevent (if I could) the mis-censuring of these Sermons.

† **mis'certify**, *v. Obs.* [MIS-¹ 1.] *trans.* To certify inaccurately. So † **miscer'tificate**, inaccurate certification.

1540 *Act. 32 Hen. VIII*, c. 22 Many prebendes..bene double certified..and some by wrong names or otherwise miscertifyed. *Ibid.* c. 45 By reason..of miscertificat of the said possessions.

mischance (mɪsˈtʃɑːns, -æ-), *sb.* Forms: see CHANCE *sb.*; also 5 **miscaunce**, **-chanche**, **meshaunce**. [a. OF. *mesch(e)ance*, *-aunce*, also *meschance*, *mescance*:—L. type **minuscadentiam*: see MIS-² and CHANCE *sb.*]

1. Ill-luck, ill-success. In early use often with stronger sense, disaster, calamity.

1297 R. GLOUC. (Rolls) 2902 Ouer homber he fley anon to wite him fram meschance. **1362** LANGL. *P. Pl.* A. IX. 51 God saue þe from mischaunce, And ȝiue þe grace uppon grounde. *c* **1475** *Partenay* 5642 Anon it happned to hym gret miscaunce. **1591** SHAKS. *1 Hen. VI*, I. i. 89 Lords view these Letters, full of bad mischance. **1622** BACON *Hen. VII* 181 They..let downe with Cords..seuerall Messengers (that if one came to mischance, another might passe on). **1822** HAZLITT *Table-t.* Ser. II. iv. (1869) 83 We are the sport of imbecility and mischance. **1833** TENNYSON *Lady of Shalott* IV. ii, Beholding all his own mischance, Mute, with glassy countenance. **1855** MOTLEY *Dutch Rep.* II. iii. (1866) 191 If mischance should follow the neglect of this warning.

personified. *c* **1386** CHAUCER *Knt.'s T.* 1151 Amiddes of the temple sat meschaunce, With disconfort and sory contenaunce. **1742** GRAY *Spring* 38 Brush'd by the hand of rough Mischance.

2. In particularized use: A piece of bad luck. a mishap, an unlucky accident; †*spec.* an accidental injury or mutilation. In early use also, †a state of unhappiness, an evil fate.

a **1300** *Cursor M.* 1182 In takinning als o þi penance þe sal be send a lang meschance. **1393** LANGL. *P. Pl.* C. xx. 229 Mynne ȝe nat, riche men to which a meschaunce þat dives deyed? *a* **1450** MYRIC 1899 Fowrty dayes for þat myschawnce þow schalt be in penaunce. **1577** in Ellis *Orig. Lett.* ser. II. III. 56 Upon Monday here fell a mischaunce betwene two of my Lo. Chamberleyns men, and the on of them was killed in Powles churche yarde. **1587** GOLDING *De Mornay* i. (1617) 7 When a man loseth an eye, an arme, or a legge, we do commonly say, it is a mischance. **1685** WOOD *Life* 23 July (O.H.S.) III. 155 He had got a mischance by gunpowder. **1758** JOHNSON *Idler* No. 55 ¶7, I had secured it [*sc.* a book] against mischances by lodging two transcripts in different places. **1838** DICKENS *Nich. Nick.* xxiv, First the right sandal came down, and then the left, and these mischances being repaired [etc.]. **1863** HAWTHORNE *Our Old Home* (1879) 145 The vicissitudes and mischances of sublunary affairs.

3. Phrases. † **a.** *to fare, go to mischance*; *to cast, chase, drive, put to mischance. to give* (a person) *mischance*: to bring bad luck to, to overwhelm with disaster. *to bid* (a person) *mischance*: to wish him bad luck.

c **1330** R. BRUNNE *Chron. Wace* (Rolls) 7282 þey cald hym traitour wyþ manace, & to meschaunce þey scholde hym chace. *c* **1374** CHAUCER *Troylus* II. 222 Lat us daunce, And cast your widwes habit to mischaunce. *Ibid.* v. 359 Thy swevenes..Dryf out, and lat hem faren to mischaunce. **1377** LANGL. *P. Pl.* B. XIII. 325 And blame men bihynde her bakke and bydden hem meschaunce. *c* **1385** CHAUCER *L.G.W.* 333 Enuye I preie to god ȝeue hire myschaunce. *c* **1430** *Syr Gener.* (Roxb.) 142 What with swerd and with launce Many oon he gafe myschaunce. *c* **1460** G. ASHBY *Dicta Philos.* 47 Otherwise your werkys gone to mischanche. *c* **1470** HENRY *Wallace* VI. 282 How he had put his pepill to myschance.

† **b.** In exclamations and imprecations, esp. in *with mischance!* = deuce take it! Also *How mischance..?* How the devil..? *Obs.*

13.. *Guy Warw.* 2533, & ȝif ich Gij mete may, Wiþ meschaunce y schal him gret. *c* **1374** CHAUCER *Troylus* IV. 1362, Or how mischaunce sholde I dwelle there? *c* **1386** —— *Manciple's Prol.* 11 Is that a cook of Londoun, with meschaunce? *c* **1386** —— *Man of Law's T.* 816 The lordes styward—god yeve him meschaunce! *c* **1400** *Rom. Rose* 7581 What? welcome with mischaunce now! **1402** *Jack Upland* in *Chaucerian Pieces* (Skeat) 203 Than so shulde they be better than Christ himselfe, with miscaunce! *c* **1430** LYDG. *Min. Poems* (Percy Soc.) 34 She..hir husband disceyvethe, allas! meschaunce! **1526** SKELTON *Magnyf.* 502 God gyue you a very myschaunce!

c. *by mischance*: by an unlucky accident.

AF. *par mescheaunce* (Britton) = 'by misadventure'.

1535 *Act 27 Hen. VIII*, c. 6 If it shall happen any of the said mares by mischaunce or casualte for to die. **1625** MILTON *Death Infant* 44 Wert thou some Starr which from the ruin'd roofe Of shak't Olympus by mischance didst fall? **1662** GRAUNT *Bills Mort.* viii. 48 Slain in Wars, killed by mischance, drowned at Sea. **1848** THACKERAY *Van. Fair* xliv, When they met by mischance, he made sarcastic bows or remarks to the child. **1859** TENNYSON *Marr. Geraint* 112 And these awoke him, and by great mischance He heard but fragments of her later words.

d. Proverbs.

14.. *Hermes Bird* lxii. in Ashm. *Theat. Chem.* (1652) 225 A Chyldys Byrde, and a Chorlys Wyfe, Hath ofte sythys sorow and mischaunce. **1611** COTGR. s.v. *Malheur*, Mischances neuer come single.

mis'chance, *v. Obs.* or *arch.* [MIS-¹ 1.]

1. *intr.* To happen unfortunately. Also with dat. of person.

1552 HULOET, Mischauncen, *male euenire.* *a* **1578** LINDESAY (Pitscottie) *Chron. Scot.* (S.T.S.) I. 40 Belieueing no falshoode to mischance him efterwart in respect of his hartlie messaige that come to him fre the maistratis. **1591** SPENSER *M. Hubberd* 64 And still I hoped to be up advaunced,..but still it hath mischaunced. **1809** E. S. BARRETT *Setting Sun* I. 68 It so mischanc'd, A horde barbarian,..Landing, spread death wherever they advanc'd.

2. *pass.* To be unfortunate; to have bad luck.

a **1542** WYATT in *Tottel's Misc.* (Arb.) 36 Stephan said true, that my natiuitie Mischanced was with the ruler of May. *a* **1578** LINDESAY (Pitscottie) *Chron. Scot.* (1728) 11 He burnt the more for anger within himself, that he was so mischanced in this behalf. *c* **1586** C'TESS PEMBROKE *Ps.* LXXXIX. viii, All that him hate, be me shall be mischaunced.

3. *intr.* To have the ill-luck *to do* so-and-so.

1600 FAIRFAX *Tasso* XIX. xcviii, On an ambush I mischanst to light Of cruell men.

Hence **mis'chancing** *vbl. sb. rare.*

1611 FLORIO, *Misueniménto*,..a mischancing. **1929** W. FAULKNER *Sartoris* v. 357 A period of history which had seen brothers and husband slain in the same useless mischancing of human affairs.

mis'chanced, *a.* [f. MISCHANCE *sb.* + -ED.]

† **1.** Unlucky, unfortunate, ill-fated. *Obs.*

c **1470** HENRY *Wallace* VIII. 320 Curssand fortoun off his myschansit [*ed.* 1570 mischancefull] cace. **1552** HULOET, Mischaunced, *infortunatus.*

2. Gone wrong.
1875 O. SCHMIDT *Doctr. Descent* xi. 255 From these [the Annulosa] diverged on one side the Testacea, who might perhaps be called mischanced vertebrata, and on the other the true vertebrate animals.

misˈchanceful, *a.* Now *arch.* or *poet.* [f. MISCHANCE *sb.* + -FUL.] Unlucky, unfortunate.
1303 R. BRUNNE *Handl. Synne* 3924 ȝyf þou were euer payde of myschaunceful þyng þat befyl to any man. **1570** [see MISCHANCED, quot. *c* 1470]. **1594** H. HELMES *Gesta Grayorum* (1688) 22 This mischanceful Accident..was a great Discouragement. **1872** BLACKIE *Lays Highl.* 202 Where wert thou when Sire Adam first Drew his mischanceful breath? **1875** BROWNING *Aristoph. Apol.* Wks. 1896 I. 734 Woe—woe! What man was born mischanceful thus!

mischancie: see MESCHANCIE.

mischancy (mɪsˈtʃɑːnsɪ, -æ-), *a.* Chiefly *Sc.* [f. MISCHANCE *sb.* + -Y.] Unlucky.
1513 DOUGLAS *Æneis* IX. vii. 137 His freind and fallow deyr That sa myschancy was. **1819** *Blackw. Mag.* V. 637 Country Laird, attracted from afar, With some mischancy Writer to engage. **1858** TROLLOPE *Three Clerks* xlvi. (1867) 538 Circumstances were mischancy with Mr. Nogo. **1860** READE *Cloister & H.* xix, If ever I was so mischancy as to last so long as Ghysbrecht did.

†**misˈchange**. *Obs.* [MIS-¹ 4.] Change for the worse.
1561 HOLLYBUSH *Hom. Apoth.* 20b, The harte also shrink[eth] together by reason of excessiue feare, heuinesse & mis-change. [*marg.* Soudain alteracion.] **1595** T. MAYNARDE *Drake's Voy.* (Hakl. Soc.) 6 They gave us instructions for directinge our course, if, by foule weather or mischange, any should be severed.

†**misˈchanging**, *vbl. sb.* [MIS-¹ 3.] Wrongful interchange or substitution.
1382 WYCLIF *Wisd.* xiv. 26 The mischaunging [1388 chaungyng] of birthe [Vulg. *nativitatis immutatio*].

mischanter: see MISHANTER.

misˈcharge, *sb.* [MIS-¹ 4.] 'A mistake in charging, as an account; an erroneous entry in an account' (1828–32 Webster).

misˈcharge, *v.* ? Now *rare.* [MIS-¹ 1.] *trans.* To charge wrongly or falsely.
1571 GOLDING *Calvin on Ps.* xvii. 3 He was mischarged with wrongfull hatred. **1583** —— *Calvin on Deut.* xl. 240 If wee doe but misconster some one worde that is well spoken beholde wee mischarge the partie. **1639** in *T. Lechford's Note-Bk.* (1885) 164 The said W...H...did..overreckon misreckon..& mischarge upon this Complt divers particulare things hereinafter expressed. *a* **1676** HALE *Sheriff's Acc.* x. (1683) 106 The most of the rest of the complaints were touching particulars mischarged, or not charged. **1833** J. C. HARE in *Philol. Mus.* II. 222 [This] has led us to mischarge the Greek verb with a double anomaly.

†**misˈcharging**, *vbl. sb. Obs.* [MIS-¹ 3.] Misaiming (of a weapon).
a **1548** HALL *Chron., Edw. IV*, 247b, He was with mischarging of a speare..pytyfullye slayne.

mischeantly, variant of MESCHANTLY *Obs.*
1600 *Reg. Privy Council Scot.* VI. 97 Maist crewellie, barbarouslie and mischeantlie.

†**misˈcheer**, *v. Obs.* [MIS-¹ 7.] *trans.* To dishearten.
c **1412** HOCCLEVE *De Reg. Princ.* 2380 The kyng haþ schame, and eke it hem mys-cherith.

mischief (ˈmɪstʃɪf), *sb.* Also 4–5 **mes-**, 4–6 **mys-**, **mis-**; 4 **-chif**, **-cheyf**, **-chive**, **chyve**, 4–5 **-cheef**, **-cheff(e**, **-chyef**, 4–6 **-chef(e**, **-cheve**, *Sc.* **-cheif(f)**, 5 **-cheeffe**, *Sc.* **-cheyff**, 6 **-cheefe**, **-chyfe**, *Sc.* **-cheif(f)e**, **-sheif**, 6–7 **-chiefe**, 7 **-chieve**; also 4 **mechef**, **myshef**, 6 **mishief**, **mychief**; *pl.* 4 **-cheves**, **-cevis**, 4–5 **-chevys**, 6 **-chives**, 6–7 **-chieves**, 5– **-chiefs**. [a. OF. *meschief*, *meschef*, *mechef* (mod. *méchef*), vbl. sb. f. *meschever* (see MISCHIEVE): cf. Pr. *mescap*, OCat. *menyscab*, OSp. *mescabo*, OPg. *mazcabo* (Sp., Pg. *menoscabo* loss, deterioration).]

†**1. a.** Evil plight or condition; misfortune; trouble, distress; in ME. often, need, want, poverty. *Obs.*
a **1300** *Cursor M.* 20050 Womman sal peris o na barn, Ne nan wit mischiue be forfarn. *c* **1325** *Song Deo Gratias* 49 in *E.E.P.* (1862) 125, I schal seie Deo gracias In myschef and in bonchef boþe. *c* **1350** *Will. Palerne* 5131 Be merciabul to alle men þat in mechef arn. *c* **1386** CHAUCER *Prol.* 493 He ne lafte nat, for reyn ne thonder, In siknesse ne in meschief, to visyte The ferrest in his parisshe. *c* **1400** MAUNDEV. (1839) xxviii. 287 That no man ȝeve him..nouther of Mete ne Drynk: and so schalle he dye in myschef. **1433** *Rolls of Parlt.* IV. 424/2 They bee nowe in grete myschief and necessite. **1523** LD. BERNERS *Froiss.* I. xii. 12 The kyng and the yong Spencer, seyng theym selfe thus beseged in thir myschiefe, and knewe no Comfort that myght come to them. **1590** C'TESS PEMBROKE *Antonie* 1997 O breast where death (Oh mischief) [orig. (*hà méchef*)] comes to choake vp vitall breath. *a* **1605** MONTGOMERIE *Misc. Poems* iii. 54 Hir mirrines with missheif ay is mixt. **1628** EARLE *Microcosm., Childe* (Arb.) 21 Hee arriues not at the mischiefe of being wise. **1679** PENN *Addr. Prot.* I. (1692) 55 Alas! we are not the same; that's our Mis-chief.

b. With *a* and *pl.* A misfortune, calamity.
a **1350** *St. Andrew* 56 in Horstm. *Altengl. Leg.* (1881) 4 For pete þat he had in mynde Of þe grete mescheuys of mankynde. *c* **1380** WYCLIF *Sel. Wks.* III. 204 Þenk..how God haþ savyd þe fro deeþ and oþer miscevis. *a* **1400–50** *Alexander* 399 Lo, maister, slike a myschefe! **1481** CAXTON *Godfrey* vi. 25 Alle the meseases & the myschiefs that the peple of our lord endured that tyme. **1633** FORD *'Tis Pity* II. v, But Heaven is angry, and be thou resolv'd Thou art a man remark'd to taste a mischief.

†**c.** Phr. ***at mischief, at great*** (etc.) ***mischief*** [= OF. *a meschief, a grant meschief*]: in (great) misfortune, in evil plight; in distress; *esp.* in fight, at a disadvantage. *Obs.*
c **1330** R. BRUNNE *Chron. Wace* (Rolls) 9855 Netheles þey were at meschef, ffor to ascape þem were ful lef. **1375** BARBOUR *Bruce* XI. 604 The erll and his thus fechtand war At gret myscheiff. **1430–40** LYDG. *Bochas* VIII. i. (1558) 3b, Thou died in preson at mischefe like a wretch. **1441–2** *Chron. London* (1827) 130 [He] hadde hym at myschief redy to a popped hym in the face with his dagger. **1470–85** MALORY *Arthur* IX. xxxii. 389 Allas said syr Tristram vpon my heede there is somme good Knyghte at meschyef. **1558** G. CAVENDISH *Poems* (1825) II. 75 By cruel fortune at myschefe she ended. **1567** *Gude & Godlie Ball.* (S.T.S.) 206 Of lait I saw thir lymmaris stand Lyke mad men at mischeif. **1579** SPENSER *Sheph. Cal.* Sep. 10 Or bene they chaffred? or at mischiefe dead? [*gloss*, an vnusuall speache, but much vsurped of Lidgate, and sometime of Chaucer].

2. a. Harm or evil considered as the work of an agent or due to a particular cause.
1480 *Robt. Devyll* (1797) 31 Greate myscheyf haue I do, and muche yll As to robbe and slea. **1535** COVERDALE *Ps.* lv. 3 They are mynded to do me some myschefe, so maliciously are they set agaynst me. **1545** BRINKLOW *Lament.* 26b, Ye haue..done most myschefe in shuttynge vp of Godes worde from the people. **1590** SHAKS. *Mids. N.* II. i. 237 If thou follow me, doe not beleeue But I shall doe thee mischiefe in the wood. **1613** —— *Hen. VIII*, II. i. 22. **1647** CLARENDON *Hist. Reb.* VI. §102 They..who had contrived the mischieve. **1727** DE FOE *Syst. Magic* I. iii. (1840) 72 The devil is seldom out of call when he is wanted for any mischief. **1818** SCOTT *Rob Roy* xxxvii, It was hardly possible two such damned rascals should colleague together without mischief to honest people. **1857** RUSKIN *Pol. Econ. Art* ii. (1868) 136 It is quite wonderful how much mischief may be done even by small capacity.

b. An injury wrought by a person or other agent; an evil arising out of or existing in certain conditions. Now only in *collect. pl.* with the sense 'evil consequences', and in phr. ***to do oneself a mischief.***
c **1385** CHAUCER *L.G.W.* 2331 *Philomela*, This false thef Hath don this lady yit a more myschef. **1530** TINDALE *Pract. Prel.* C vij, If any resisted them what so euer mischeuen they went about. **1580** LYLY *Euphues* (Arb.) 338 Of two mischiefes the least is to be chosen. **1598** YONG *Diana* 47 A mischeefe neuer comes alone. **1611** BIBLE *Ps.* lii. 2 Thy tongue deuiseth mischiefes. **1693** *Mem. Cnt. Teckely* I. 50 The Turks..would not fail to work them 1000 mischiefs by means of the new Garrison of Newhaussel. **1726** SWIFT *Gulliver* II. i, I..made three huzzas, to shew that I had got no mischief by my fall. **1774** BURKE *Sp. Amer. Tax.* Wks. 1842 I. 165 Infinite mischiefs would be the consequence of such a power. *a* **1862** BUCKLE *Civiliz.* (1869) III. ii. 47 General mischiefs depend upon general causes. **1871** SMILES *Charac.* ii. (1876) 58 The social mischiefs resulting from a neglect of the purifying influence of women.

c. ***to make mischief***: to create discord or dissension, esp. by talebearing. Cf. MISCHIEF-MAKER.
1884 *Cassell's Fam. Mag.* May 374 She was always making mischief between them [*sc.* two lovers].

3. a. *Law.* A condition in which a person suffers a wrong or is under some disability, esp. one which it is the object of a statute to remove or for which equity affords a remedy. Phr. †***to be at a mischief.***
1596 BACON *Max. Com. Law* III. (1630) 26 Pleadings must be certain, because the aduerse party may know wherto to answer, or else he were at a mischief, which mischiefe is remedied by a demurrer. *Ibid.* IX. 48 Hee tooke his graunt subiect to that mischiefe at first. **1642** COKE *On Litt.* II. 124 The mischiefe before this Act was, That in a Writ of Dower, *Unde nihil habet*, there were dayes of common retourn.. which was mischievous to the woman, in respect of the long delay. **1768** BLACKSTONE *Comm.* III. ii. 19 Every scheme.. hath been hitherto found to be..productive of more mischiefs than it would remedy. **1792** N. CHIPMAN *Rep.* (1871) 80, C. having notice, was not within the mischief and therefore not within the equity of the remedy. **1818** CRUISE *Digest* (ed. 2) IV. 524 If the adhering to such determinations is likely to be attended with inconvenience, it is a matter fit to be remedied by the legislature; which is able to prevent the mischief in future. **1828–32** WEBSTER s.v., A new law is made to remedy the mischief.

†**b.** Distinguished from *inconvenience*; see quots. and INCONVENIENCE 3c.
[**1509**: see INCONVENIENCE *sb.* 3.] **1532** *Dial. on Laws Eng.* II. xlvi. 94b, The law wyll rather suffre that myscheyf then the said inconuenience. **1596** SPENSER *State Irel.* Wks. (Globe) 618/1 True Justice punnisheth nothing but the evill act or wicked woord; yet by the lawes of all kingdomes it is a capitall crime to devise or purpose the death of the King. .. And therfore the lawe in that case punnisheth the thought; for better is a mischeif, then an inconvenience. **1622** [see INCONVENIENCE *sb.* 3c]. **1670** RAY *Prov.* 121 Better a mischief, then an inconvenience. That is, better a present mischief that is soon over, then a constant grief and disturbance. *a* **1709** [see INCONVENIENCE 3c].

4. †**a.** A disease or ailment. *Obs.* **b.** In medical parlance used simply to indicate a morbid condition without further definition.
1552 HULOET, Myschiefe beynge close or secrete, *vlcus.* **1599** SHAKS. *Much Ado* I. iii. 13 To apply a morall medicine, to a mortifying mischiefe. **1601** HOLLAND *Pliny* I. XVII. xxiv. 539 The running mange or tettar, is a mischeefe peculiar unto the Fig tree. **1755** POTT *Chirurg. Observ.* 135 A hernia where the abdominal tendon has no share in the mischief. **1843** R. J. GRAVES *Syst. Clin. Med.* ix. 98 Traces of inflammatory mischief. **1860** WINSLOW *Obsc. Dis. Brain* 12 The mischief established within the cranium, disorganizing the delicate tissue of the brain. **1899** *Allbutt's Syst. Med.* VI. 130 When the mischief is confined to the lung.

5. a. Hurtful character or influence; mischievousness. Now *rare* or *Obs.*
1646 SIR T. BROWNE *Pseud. Ep.* II. v. §2. 84 The conceit [that glass is poison] is surely grounded upon the visible mischiefe of glasse grossely or coursely powdered; for that indeed is mortally noxious. **1803** R. HALL *Sentiments Pres. Crisis* 45 The innocence of the intention abates nothing of the mischief of the precedent. **1822** GOOD *Study Med.* IV. 78 This is a disorder of far greater mischief and violence than the preceding.

b. The phrase ***the mischief*** (***of..***) ***is*** (***that***) is used idiomatically to single out the most unfortunate aspect or vexatious circumstance of an affair.
1660 F. BROOKE tr. *Le Blanc's Trav.* 374 The mischief is, if we carry them out of their own air they die immediately. **1677** W. HUGHES *Man of Sin* III. i. 5 Their dear Francis.. admired for a glorious Saint, was in his life time commonly taken for a silly Fool, by their own Confession. And the mischief is, for no small reason neither. **1708** SWIFT *Let. conc. Sacr. Test* Wks. 1751 IV. 170 But the mischief was, these Allies would never be brought to allow that the common Enemy was quite subdued. **1751** JOHNSON *Rambler* No. 155 ¶7 The mischief of flattery is..that it suppresses the influence of honest ambition. **1882** OGILVIE s.v., I have money enough, but the mischief is I have left my purse at home. **1896** A. E. HOUSMAN *Shropsh. Lad* lxii, And faith, 'tis pleasant till 'tis past: The mischief is that 'twill not last.

†**6.** Evil-doing, wickedness. *Obs.*
1470–85 MALORY *Arthur* IX. xix. 367 By thy meschyef and thy vengeaunce thou hast destroyed the mooste noble Knyght. **1535** COVERDALE *Gen.* vi. 5 Yᵉ earth was corrupte in ye sight of God and full of myschefe. **1593** Q. ELIZ. *Boeth.* I. pr. v. (1899) 15 Of mischefz or fraudes of thy slaunderers [orig. *sceleribus fraudibusque delatorum*]. **1596** DALRYMPLE tr. *Leslie's Hist. Scot.* I. 161 With a plumpe he fercelie fallis in al kynde of mischeife [orig. *in omnia flagitiorum & turpitudinum genera*]. **1611** BIBLE *Acts* xiii. 10 O full of all subtilty and all mischiefe.

7. A cause or source of harm or evil: often applied to a person whose conduct or influence is harmful; a worker of mischief; also, in milder sense, one who causes petty annoyance or acts in a vexatious or annoying manner.
1586 A. DAY *Eng. Secretary* I. (1625) 42 He was called.. the Plague of the Common-Weal, the mischiefe of men. **1599** B. JONSON *Ev. Man out of Hum.* v. v, O, my good Mischiefe! art thou come? **1643** TRAPP *Comm. Gen.* xvi. 12 Mahomet, the mischiefe of mankinde. **1660** F. BROOKE tr. *Le Blanc's Trav.* 174 One of the jarrs of water broke, which was a great mischiefe to them, and a very important losse. **1671** MILTON *Samson* 1039 The contrary she proves, a thorn Intestin, far within defensive arms A cleaving mischief. *a* **1704** T. BROWN *Sat. agst. Woman* Wks. 1730 I. 55 The sex are all Pandoras, mischiefs all. **1708** MRS. CENTLIVRE *Busy Body* IV. iv, B'ye, b'ye, dearee! Ah mischief! how you look now! B'ye, b'ye. **1780** COWPER *Progr. Err.* 302 The sacred implement I now employ Might prove a mischief, or at best a toy. **1816** BYRON *Ch. Har.* III. xlix, Many a tower for some fair mischief won. **1825–80** JAMIESON, *Mischief*, a vexatious or ill-deedie person; as, 'Ye're a perfect mischief'. **1890** *Spectator* 5 July Unionists such as Mr. Caine..are positive mischiefs to the party. **1891** J. EVELYN *Baffled Vengeance* 191 A curly-headed mischief known by the name of Jimmy.

8. Vexatious or annoying action or conduct; chiefly, conduct causing petty injury or trouble to others by way of sport, without any ill-will. Also, a tendency to or disposition for such conduct.
1784 COWPER *Tiroc.* 207 Childish in mischief only and in noise. **1820** W. IRVING *Sketch Bk., Leg. Sleepy Hollow* (1821) II. 303 He was always ready for either a fight or a frolic; had more mischief than ill-will in his composition. **1834** MARRYAT *P. Simple* II. viii. 118 The midshipmen are ..full of fun and frolic. I'll bet a wager there'll be a bobbery in the pig-sty before long, for they are ripe for mischief.

9. Phrases, chiefly expletive and imprecatory.
†**a.** ***with a mischief***: (*a*) used as an expletive, esp. parenthetically in questions, as ***What with a mischief..?*** (also ***What a mischief..?***); (*b*) = with a vengeance. *Obs.*
1538 ELYOT *Dict.* Add., *Abi in malam rem*, go hens with a mischefe. **1565** COOPER *Thesaurus* s.v., *Malus*, *Quid tua (malum) id refert?* what, with a mischiefe, haste thou to doe with it? **1572** T. SMITH in Ellis *Orig. Lett.* Ser. III. IV. 8 What a mischeefe meanethe hee to write unto mee of new Starres and Astronomers, and telleth me nothinge of my comeing home? **1611** COTGR. s.v. *Chemise*, Hee raised them with a mischiefe, roused them with a vengeance. *a* **1625** FLETCHER *Nice Valour* II. i. (1647) 152 Hold still the chaire, with a grand mischiefe to you. **1630** J. TAYLOR (Water-P.) *Wks.* II. 96/2 The matronly medicines..of this..woman, will in a little time make her encrease with a vengeance, and multiply with a mischiefe. **1640** NABBES *Bride* III. ii, Y'are welcome with a mischiefe to the occasion that brought you hither. **1722** SWIFT in J. Duncombe *Lett.* (1773) II. 5, I wonder how a mischief you came to miss us. **1822** SCOTT *Nigel* xxvii, Bide doun, with a mischief to ye.

b. In imprecatory sentences, e.g. ***A mischief on..! A mischief take..!***
1519 *Interl. Four Elem.* 535 A myschyfe on it! *c* **1550** BALE *K. Johan* (Camden) 95 It is Sedicyon, God gyve hym a very myschefe. *a* **1553** UDALL *Royster D.* IV. iii. (Arb.) 62 A mischiefe take his tokens. **1609** B. JONSON *Sil. Wom.* II. iv. (1616) 545 Did I not tell you? mischiefe! **1668** DRYDEN *Even. Love* IV. Wks. 1701 I. 317 And a mischief of all foolish disguisements, for my part.

c. Hence (like *the plague*, etc.) *the mischief* is used *colloq.* and *dial.* as a euphemistic substitute for 'the devil', chiefly in the phr. ***to play the mischief (with)***, and in questions ***What (how***, etc.) ***the mischief..?*** (cf. a). Also ***to go to the mischief, like the mischief.***

1583 HOLLYBAND *Campo di Fior* 283 What the mischiefe is this that thou hast for thy sadelle? **1614** B. JONSON *Barth. Fair* I. i, What the mischief do you come with her; or she with you? *a* **1616** BEAUM. & FL. *Wit without M.* v. I 2 Ith name of mischiefe what did you meane? **1807–8** W. IRVING *Salmag.* (1824) 125 This unlucky characteristic played the mischief with him in one of his love affairs. **1818** MISS FERRIER *Marriage* xv, Boys may go to the mischief, and be good for something. **1865** TROLLOPE *Belton Est.* xxxi. 375 Why the mischief should he not set about the work at once? **1867** —— *Chron. Barset* II. xii, That butcher in Silverbridge was playing the mischief with him. **1876** T. E. BROWN *Doctor* 36 And them givin' sheet Like the mischief. **1892** KIPLING *Barrack-r. Ballads* 24 You 'eathen, where the mischief 'ave you been? **1895** *Century Mag.* June 279/2 And there's kindnesses and kindnesses, Mr. Ludovic. There's some that cost like the mischief. **1907** J. M. SYNGE *Lett. to Molly* (1971) 123, I am coughing away like the mischief today. **1922** JOYCE *Ulysses* 354 She wished.. they'd take the ..twins and their baby home to the mischief out of that. **1942** BERREY & VAN DEN BARK *Amer. Thes. Slang* §20/5 Indefinite eminence in degree. (Preceded by..'like')... The (very) mischief.

†**d.** ***words of mischief***: abusive language, abuse. *rare*⁻¹. (Cf. MISCHIEVE *v.* 4.)

1555 W. WATREMAN *Fardle Facions* I. vi. 86 They curse him, and reuyle him with all woordes of mischiefe.

10. *Comb.* (chiefly objective), as ***mischief-doer, -founder, -master, -monger, -sufferer, -taker***; ***mischief-boding, -doing, -hatching, -loving, -tainted, -working*** adjs.; **mischief night**, an evening, orig. 30 April, now 4 November, on which children indulge in mischievous pranks; also *attrib.*

1814 SCOTT *Ld. of Isles* III. xxv. A *mischief-boding ray. **1822** COBBETT *Weekly Reg.* 4 May 304 Representing me as a *mischief-doer to the country. **1800** COLERIDGE *Piccolom.* IV. i, Thus compel Into my service that old *mischief-founder. **1835** J. P. KENNEDY *Horse-Shoe Robinson* xxxiv. 295 Some *mischief-hatching fiend. **1810** *Splendid Follies* II. 51 The *mischief-loving imp. **1587** GOLDING *Ovid's Met.* XIII. 158 Would God this *mischeef mayster had in verrye deede beene mad. **1620** SHELTON *Quix.* II. iv. 23 That Cheater, that arrant *Mischiefe-monger. **1888** *England* 18 Aug. 11/1 The Grand Old Mischief Monger at the head. **1865** W. S. BANKS *List Provincial Words Wakefield* 47 **Mischief neet.* Boys, thirty years ago, used to go about damaging property, believing the law allowed them, on this night. Happily the practice is over at Wakefield, and the time forgotten. **1871** *N. & Q.* 17 June 525/1 The eve of May Day was formerly known as 'Mischief Night' throughout South Lancashire, and prior to the epoch of the 'new policeman', many were the strange pranks, rude practical jokes, and mortifying degradations committed. **1959** I. & P. OPIE *Lore & Lang. Schoolch.* xii. 255 In the nineteenth century April the thirtieth..was..the traditional Mischief Night... How Mischief Night has..come to be transferred to the other end of the year is one of the mysteries of the folklore calendar. *Ibid.* 279 '20 Boys in Mischief Night Raid at Ayton.' **1969** —— *Children's Games* ii. 68 They even celebrated Mischief Night on 4 November as do their northern contemporaries. **1972** 'J. RIPLEY' *My Word you should have seen Us* 119 It was 'Mischief Night'—the evening before 'Bonfire Night'—and an annual happening peculiar to the northern provinces. **1552** HULOET, *Myschiefe sufferer, or taker, *sceleratus.* **1598** F. ROUS *Thule* B, That rout of *mischief-tainted theeues. **1902** *Fortn. Rev.* Jan. 41 A child in the *mischief-working hands of his own childishness.

mischief ('mɪstʃɪf), *v. arch.* Forms: see prec. sb. [f. MISCHIEF *sb.* Cf. the earlier MISCHIEVE.]

1. *trans.* To inflict injury upon; = MISCHIEVE *v.* 3.

1483 *Cath. Angl.* 241/1 To Mischefe, *erumpnare.* **1533** MORE *Debell. Salem* Wks. 971/1 He wil of lykelihode hate & mischief any man by whome he taketh any harme. **1605** ARMIN *Foole upon F.* (1880) 25 He, that mischiefes many, sometimes wrongs himselfe. **1611** SPEED *Hist. Gt. Brit.* IX. xx. (1623) 967 Britaine hauing so many Sea-townes and Outlets to mischiefe the English trafficke. **1682** BUNYAN *Holy War* 195 Whomever I mischief, whomever I wrong, to me it is musick, when to others mourning. **1855** SINGLETON *Virgil's Ecl.* iii. I. 15 If you had not somehow mischiefed him, You would have died.

2. To do physical harm to; = MISCHIEVE 3 b.

c **1470** HENRY *Wallace* VIII. 248 The flearis than with erll Patrik relefd To fecht agayn, quhar mony war myscheifd. **1483** in *Surtees Misc.* (1890) 29 The crosse in the merkyth place is lyke..to myschef sume man. **1573** TUSSER *Husb.* (1878) 62 The rack is commended for sauing of doong, so set as the old cannot mischiefe the yoong. **1607** MARKHAM *Caval.* v. (1617) 57, I haue seene them run away, ouerthrowe..the Coach, and mischiefe the Coach-man. **1667** *Decay Chr. Piety* (1668) 74 'Tis a certain Indication of madness to tear and mischief those things that would be useful to us. **1702** C. MATHER *Magn. Chr.* VI. v. (1852) 393 Having set his dog to mischief his neighbor's cattel. **1858** TRENCH *Parables* xx. (1877) 356 The barren tree mischiefed the land, 'troubled' it, as Bishop Andrewes renders the word.

refl. *a* **1470** GREGORY in *Hist. Coll. Cit. Lond.* (Camden) 213 There myght noo man come unto them ovyr the pavysse for the naylys that stode up-ryghte, but yf he wolde myschyffe hym sylfe. **1547** BOORDE *Brev. Health* clxxi. 61 At length they do fal mad, or do mischefe them selfe. **1624–5** in *Notes & Gleanings* (Exeter 1889) II. 177 To..cut theire owne throats or otherwise murder or mischeife themselves. **1719** DE FOE *Crusoe* I. 191 When the two Ladders were taken down, no Man living could come down to me without mischiefing himself.

absol. **1658** SIR T. BROWNE *Pseud. Ep.* II. v. 100 A Bullet of Wax will mischief without melting. **1672** R. WILD *Poet. Licent.* 33 Their Breath will mischief far beyond a Gun.

3. *intr.* To suffer injury; = MISCHIEVE 1.

a **1510** DOUGLAS *K. Hart* II. 71 Len me thy cloke, to gys me for ane quhyle; Want I that weid in fayth I will mischeif. **1598** F. ROUS *Thule* B, Which done she weepes vpon her pitchie dore, That she should in ere she had mischief'd more.

mischiefful ('mɪstʃɪfful), *a.* Now *dial.* [f. MISCHIEF *sb.* + -FUL.] Full of mischief.

†**1.** Unfortunate, disastrous. *Obs.*

1303 R. BRUNNE *Handl. Synne* 4622 Also y telle by iustyng, þer-of cumþ myschefful þyng. *c* **1470** HENRY *Wallace* III. 410 Thar selff was caus of this myschefull chance. *Ibid.* IV. 748.

2. Of persons: Full of or prone to do mischief; mischievous. Now *dial.*

1541 PAYNELL *Catiline* xlii. 69 The common weale, through the cursed counsell of mischiefull cytesyns is brought into so great daunger. **1834** LANDOR *Exam. Shaks.* Wks. 1853 II. 284/2 This is the mischief-fullest of all the devil's imps. **1896** *Warw. Word-bk.*, *Mischiefful*, mischievous.

3. Involving mischief. *rare*⁻¹.

1772 FOOTE *Nabob* III. Wks. 1799 II. 318 For mischiefful matters there wasn't a more ingenious..lad in the school.

'mischief-,maker. One who makes mischief (see MISCHIEF 2 c); one who foments discord, esp. by talebearing.

1710 M. HENRY *Disp. Reviewed* Wks. 1853 II. 466/2 None but a tale-bearer, that great mischief-maker, will reveal such secrets. **1785** HUTTON *Bran New Wark* (E.D.S.) 188/121 At present there er in ivvery neak ta manny mischief-makers. **1848** LD. BROUGHAM *Of Revolutions* Wks. 1857 VIII. 332 The trade of the agitator, the professional mischief-maker. **1862** MRS. CARLYLE *Lett.* III. 138 Elizabeth, who is weak enough to believe what mischief-makers tell her.

So **'mischief-,making** *vbl. sb.* and *ppl. a.*

1715 ROWE *Lady Jane Gray* v. Wks. 1728 III. 74 I'll.. know What 'tis the Mischief-making Priest intends. **1818** BYRON *Juan* I. xxv, A little curly-headed,..And mischief-making monkey. **1825** SCOTT in Lockhart *Life* (1839) VIII. 118 Byron loved mischief making. **1896** W. BLACK *Briseis* xx, A piece of mischief-making between two school-girls —about a music-master.

†**mis'chievable**, *a. Obs.* [f. MISCHIEVE *v.* + -ABLE (in an active sense).] Mischievous, harmful.

1680 FILMER *Patriarcha* iii. §7 If a King did strictly swear to observe all the Laws, he could not without Perjury give his Consent to the Repealing..of any Statute..which would be very mischievable to the State.

†**mis'chievance.** *Obs.* [? f. MISCHIEVE *v.* + -ANCE.] Harm, injury, damage.

1600 HOLLAND *Livy* II. xv. 549 Unlesse they would be executors of their owne wrongs, and seeke their owne mischievance. **1628** [SIR F. HUBERT] *Life & Death Edw. II* cclvii, Nor [let] common curses, caus'd by public greeuance, Draw iudgment down on you for their mischieuance.

mischieve (mɪs'tʃiːv), *v.* Now *dial.* or *arch.* Also (4–5 mes-, 4–6 mys-), 4–5 -chieve, -chyeve, 4–6 -cheve, 5 -cheeve, -chewe, 5–6 *Sc.* mischeif, -cheive, 7 mischive. [a. OF. *meschever* to be unfortunate, come to grief, f. *mes-* MIS-² + *chever* CHEVE: cf. Sp. *menoscabar* to impair.

That the Scottish forms in *f* belong to this word rather than to MISCHIEF *v.* is attested by the rimes and the modern pronunciation.]

†**1.** *intr.* To suffer harm or injury; to meet with misfortune; to come to grief, 'miscarry'. *Obs.*

c **1330** R. BRUNNE *Chron.* (1810) 171 He said, 'þei salle mischeue', whan he þat tiþing herd. **1377** LANGL. *P. Pl.* B. XII. 119 And his sones al-so for þat synne myscheued. *c* **1420** *Pallad. on Husb.* I. 614 And up thai wol atte eve Into a tree lest thai by nyght myscheve. **14..** in *Q. Eliz. Acad.* 85 Whene pryde is moste in prys..þenne schall englonde myschewe. *a* **1450** HOCCLEVE *Learn to die* 544 in *Min. Poems* 198 He mischeeueth where as he wende han recouered be. **1450–1530** *Myrr. our Ladye* 34 Yt hathe not bene sene, that euer eny place myscheued where goddes seruyce was deuoutly kepte. **1604** EDMONDS *Observ. Cæsar's Comm.* 78 To make supplications for all soules, and specially for such as had mischieued in France in the time of that warre.

2. *trans.* To afflict or overwhelm with misfortune; to bring to destruction or ruin.

1388 *Pol. Poems* (Rolls) I. 272 The chyrche is grevyd,.. And so sume be myschevyd. *c* **1440** *Alphabet of Tales* 3 Why hase þou loste and myschevid so many sawlis as þou hase done? **1451** *Rolls of Parlt.* V. 224/2 Thaugh he [*sc.* John Cade] be dede and myscheved. **1513** DOUGLAS *Æneis* II. x. 112 And tho beheld I all the citie mischevit. **1526** SKELTON *Magnyf.* 2360 So I am lapped in aduersyte, That dyspayre well nyghe had myscheued me! **1621** BP. MOUNTAGU *Diatribæ* 212 You may haply fall foule, where you may be mischieued for euer. **1883** R. W. DIXON *Mano* I. xi. 34 They who thy fair head mischieved Of such a deed the cost shall well aby.

3. To inflict injury or loss upon; to do harm to; to injure, damage.

1475 *Bk. Noblesse* (1860) 41 Many folde tymes we have ben deceived and myschevid thoroughe suche dissimuled trewes. **1500–20** DUNBAR *Poems* xxii. 5 Excess of thocht dois me mischeif. *a* **1600** MONTGOMERIE *Misc. Poems* v. 7 Melancholie mischeivis my mind, That I can not rejose. **1645** BP. HALL *Treat. Content.* 71 The Male-content, whether hee bee angry or sad, mischieves himself both wayes. **1687** R. L'ESTRANGE *Brief Hist. Times* I. 7 Whatsoever Mischiev'd the One, must needs do the Other a Service. **1707** *Reflex. upon Ridicule* 177 Desire of mischieving those who are happier than they.

b. To do physical or bodily harm to; to wound, hurt.

c **1400** *Destr. Troy* 7429 A sad man full sone, þe sun of Theseus, Segh Achilles myscheuyt. **1465** *Paston Lett.* II. 205 Ther fylle uppon me befor Sevayne dore xij. of hes men ..and ther they wold have myscheved me. **1513** DOUGLAS *Æneis* X. xiii. 20 A gret speyr, quharwith he feyll myschevit. **1530** PALSGR. 637/1 Beware of yonder horse, for he wyll myscheve as many as come within his reache. **1649** MILTON *Eikon.* x. 412 The onely Armes that mischiev'd us in all those Battels and Incounters. **1682** FLAVEL *Fear* 74 Francis Spira..would have mischieved himself had not his friends prevented him. **1725** SLOANE *Jamaica* II. 6 Some they.. mischiev'd to Death with certain Pricks of small Sticks sharply pointed. **1825–80** JAMIESON, To *mischieve*, to hurt. **1836** J. STRUTHERS *Dychmont* in *Poet. Wks.* (1850) II. 67 With dye vats chok'd, with engines deav'd And countless nuisances mischieved.

†**4.** To abuse, slander. (Cf. MISCHIEF *sb.* 9 d.)

1656 MANASSEH BEN ISRAEL *Vind. Jud.* 15 Men mischieving the Iewes to excuse their own wickednesse. **1674** SCRIVENER *Course Div.* II. v. 388 Sometimes you shall hear from them somewhat religiously (as it were) spoken, when they intend thereby to mischive and abuse it [sc. Religion]. **1785** W. FORBES *Dominie* 14 Some strain'd their lungs, And very loud me mischiev'd With their ill tongues.

†**mis'chieved**, *ppl. a. Obs.* [f. MISCHIEVE *v.* + -ED¹. Cf. OF. *meschevé* unfortunate.] Ruined.

1580 TUSSER *Husb.* x. (1878) 23 Happie is he..that can take heede by the fall of a mischieued man.

mis'chieving, *vbl. sb.* Now *dial.* or *arch.* [f. MISCHIEVE *v.* + -ING¹.] †**a.** Mishap, misfortune, disaster. *Obs.* **b.** Injury, hurt, damage.

1297 R. GLOUC. (Rolls) 7706 þeruore þerinne wel [*read* uel] mony mis cheuing. **1432** *Rolls of Parlt.* IV. 405/2 For reboylyng or wexyng long or unresonable excesse of suche lyes, or sum other untrowed meschevyng..thei wex all noght or litell of value. *c* **1447** in *Jarrow & Wearmouth* (Surtees) 241 Yᵉ said kepper and his felowe durste nott abide wᵗ in yᵉ said place for drede of mychevyng. **1737** WHISTON *Josephus, Hist.* II. xviii. §4 He abused both to the mischieving of his countrymen.

†**mis'chieving**, *ppl. a. Obs.* [f. MISCHIEVE *v.* + -ING².] Hurtful, injurious.

1621 LADY M. WROTH *Urania* 313 He might chuse the most mischeuing, and most speeding hurt for him.

mischievous ('mɪstʃɪvəs), *a.* Forms: α. 4 **mischuos, myschefous**, 4–5 **meschevous**, 4–6 **mis-, myschevous**, 5 **meschievous, -chyevous, myschevos, -us, -es, myschyvys, myshevouse**, 6 **mischevos, mischefous, mischevus, mischiefous, mischivous, mischeevous**, *Sc.* **mischeivous, mischeifais**, 7 **mischeifous**, 6– **mischievous.** β (now only *dial.*, *vulg.*, and *joc.*). 6–8 **mischevi(e)ous**, 7– **mischievious, mischeivious.** [a. AF. *meschevous* (*c* 1400), f. OF. *meschev-er* MISCHIEVE *v.* or *meschef* MISCHIEF *sb.*: see -OUS.

The stressing on the second syllable was common in literature till about 1700; it is now dialectal, vulgar, and jocular.]

†**1.** Unfortunate, calamitous, disastrous. Chiefly of events; also occas. of persons, miserable, needy, poverty-stricken. *Obs.*

c **1330** R. BRUNNE *Chron.* (1810) 158 Whan kyng R. herd of þat mischuos tide [orig. *la meschaunce*], & how his schippis misferd. *c* **1380** WYCLIF *Wks.* (1880) 389 þis almes-ȝevynge haþ made alle owre rewme..full pore and nedy and myscheuous. *c* **1412** HOCCLEVE *De Reg. Princ.* 4713 þogh þat a man disceuere & pleyne To many a lord his mescheuous myserie. *c* **1450** *Merlin* 5 Synne draweth bothe man and woman to myshevouse ende. **1556** LAUDER *Tractate* 453 Quho list to pryde pretend, May be assurde of ane mischeuous end. **1563–83** FOXE *A. & M.* II. 810/2 Who sayde..that before this day seuenth night Hunne should haue a mischieuous death.

absol. *a* **1380** *St. Augustine* 870 in Horstm. *Altengl. Leg.* (1878) 76 þe vessel..of holichirche..He wolde breke and melte hit smal, þe mescheuous to parte wiþ al.

2. Of persons and animals, or their dispositions: Producing or designing mischief or harm; inflicting damage or injury; having a harmful influence or intent.

Now *rare*, owing to the predominance of sense 4.

1473 WARKW. *Chron.* (Camden) 11 The Lorde Say..and other myscheves peple that were aboute the Kynge. **1535** COVERDALE *Susanna* 28 Yᵉ two elders came also, full of myscheuous ymaginacions agaynst Susanna, to bringe her vnto death. **1563** WINȜET *Cert. Tractates* Wks. (S.T.S.) II. 33 Quhen that mischeuous Nestorius..began to ryve the flok of Christe. **1595** SPENSER *Epithal.* 342 Ne let mischivous witches with theyr charmes..Fray us. **1601** SHAKS. *Jul. C.* II. i. 33 Thinke him as a Serpents egge, Which hatch'd, would as his kinde grow mischieuous, And kill him in the shell. **1677** in *12th Rep. Hist. MSS. Comm.* App. v. 37 Some mischievous persons to dishonour my Lord Chancellour.. stole the Mace and the two purses. **1724** RICHARDSON *De Foe's Tour Gt. Brit.* (1769) IV. 35 A People uncivilized, warlike, and very mischievous, commonly called Highland-men; who, being the true Race of antient Scots, speak Irish. **1860** WHARTON *Law Lex.* (ed. 2) s.v. *Animals*, Domestic animals, or animals not naturally mischievous, such as dogs or oxen.

3. Of things, events, actions: Fraught with or entailing mischief or harm; having harmful effects or results.

α. *c* **1380** WYCLIF *Wks.* (1880) 390 þis mischeuous peruertynge of cristis ordenance. *c* **1471** *Pol. Poems* (Rolls) II. 277 Thayre myschevus dedis avaylid ham noughte. **1553** EDEN *Treat. Newe Ind.* (Arb.) 31 They committed

innumerable wronges and mischieuous actes. **1582** STANYHURST *Æneis* II. (Arb.) 51 Through wals downe razed wee draw thee mischeuus engyn. **1669** STURMY *Mariner's Mag.* c 3 b, The mischievous Storm continuing. **1736** BUTLER *Anal.* I. iii. Wks. 1874 I. 53 Vicious actions are, to a great degree, actually punished as mischievous to society. **1792** BURKE *Corr.* (1844) III. 398 The opinions, principles, and practices, which I thought so very mischievous. **1870** LOWELL *Among my Bks.* Ser. I. (1873) 195 A mischievous fallacy. **1888** BRYCE *Amer. Commw.* I. xxvi. 403 To resist a momentary impulse of their constituents which they think mischievous.

β. **1571-2** *Reg. Privy Council Scot.* Ser. I. II. 121 Thair mischevious querrell. **1648** J. BEAUMONT *Psyche* x. cclxvii, Th' alarmed Gadarens..loading him with chains and fetters, hop'd They now had his mischievious torrent stop'd. **1675** TRAHERNE *Chr. Ethics* 323 Love without discretion is a mischievious thing. **1747** in *Col. Rec. Pennsylv.* V. 111 The many mischevious consequences that arose [etc.]. **1913** MRS. P. CAMPBELL *Let.* 5 Feb. in *B. Shaw & Mrs. Campbell* (1952) 81 Some mischeivious personal experience.

4. Of persons, their conduct, etc.: Disposed to or characterized by acts of playful malice or petty annoyance.

α. **1676** WYCHERLEY *Pl. Dealer* v. i, Don't we esteem the Monky a Wit amongst Beasts, only because he's mischievous? **1726** SWIFT *Gulliver* II. i, And well remembering how mischievous all Children among us naturally are to Sparrows, Rabbits [etc.]. **1856** MISS YONGE *Daisy Chain* II. ix. 432 She..was only waked by Meta, standing over her with a sponge, looking very mischievous. **1865** CARLYLE *Fredk. Gt.* XIX. viii. (1872) VIII. 260 M. de Voltaire had..a big Ape, of excessively mischievous turn; who used to throw stones at the passers-by.

β. **1847** C. M. YONGE *Scenes & Characters* xv. 194 You thought mischievous was meant in Hannah's sense, when she complains of master Reginald being very mische-vious. **1861** —— *Young Step-Mother* xxxi. 476 For shame, to be so *mischievieous*; such a great boy as you. **1952** F. SWINNERTON in *Bks. of Month* Nov.-Dec. 31/1 Wells,..friendly with everybody, mischevious, quick-thinking, nonsensically inventive.

5. *Comb.*, as ***mischievous-eyed, -minded*** adjs.; †**mischievous-stomached** *a.*, ill-tempered.

1577 B. GOOGE *Heresbach's Husb.* (1586) 125 b, Moyles that..are..rugged of their body, and mischeuous stomaked [orig. *animo indomito*]. **1641** *True Rel. Dev. Des. Pap. Oxf.* A 3 Mischievous minded wretches. **1887** P. MCNEILL *Blawearie* xv. 116 'Hey, chappie', cried out a mischievous-eyed wench, quite unable to restrain her mirth.

mischievously (ˈmɪstʃɪvəslɪ), *adv.* [f. prec. + -LY^{2}.] In a mischievous manner.

†**1.** Unfortunately, disastrously, miserably. *Obs.*

c **1330** R. BRUNNE *Chron. Wace* (Rolls) 14107 Mescheuously þen fel such cas þat sire Wawayn slayn þer was. *c* **1380** WYCLIF *Wks.* (1880) 387 þer schuld no man haue be mischeuously nedy. **1430-40** LYDG. *Bochas* IV. xxiii. *heading*, Duke Brennus delighting to rob and steale, mischievouslye ended. **1567** *Gude & Godlie B.* (S.T.S.) 182 Except ȝe mend,..ȝe sall end all mischeuouslie. **1660** R. COKE *Power & Subj.* 166 The same judgment is to be given upon him, who mischievously ended his life with pain.

†**2.** Wickedly. (Cf. MISCHIEF *sb.* 6.) *Obs.*

1470-85 MALORY *Arthur* x. vii. 424 His squyers they said hit was foul done, and meschyeuously.

3. In such a manner as to produce injury or damage; with injurious effect, result, or intention.

1500-20 DUNBAR *Poems* lxxiv. 17 Sic deidlie dwawmes so mischeifaislie..hes my hairt ouirpast. **1512** *Act 4 Hen. VIII*, c. 20 *Preamble*, The said..myschevously disposed persons. **1583** STUBBES *Anat. Abus.* II. (1882) 6 To dispense with them that shall thus mischieuouslye behaue themselues. *a* **1614** DONNE *Βιαθανατος* (1644) 74 Not likely to write any thing in jest mischievously interpretable. **1647** CLARENDON *Hist. Reb.* IV. §154 The King was very mischievously advised. **1775** ADAIR *Amer. Ind.* 339 By mischievously endeavouring to foment a civil war. **1839** THIRLWALL *Greece* xi. II. 76 Though it was often mischievously abused, it may be questioned whether it was not a salutary precaution. **1885** *Truth* 28 May 839/2 Lord Beaconsfield never exercised his patronage so mischievously as when he raised Dr. Ryle to the Bench.

4. With playful maliciousness.

1730 W. HARTE *Ess. Sat.* 8 The Verse..nicely pointed in th' Horatian way Wounds keen, like Syrens mischievously gay. **1786** tr. *Beckford's Vathek* (1883) 89, I had rather his teeth should mischievously press my finger than the richest ring of the imperial treasure. **1803** LAMB *Let. to Coleridge* 13 Apr., I mischievously wished that by some inauspicious jolt the whole contents might be shaken.

mischievousness (ˈmɪstʃɪvəsnɪs). [-NESS.] The quality or condition of being mischievous; injuriousness, harmfulness, perniciousness.

1567 *Lucres & Eurialus* G ij b (Roxb.) 150 Myscheuousnes be not too be encreased but too be lessed. **1647** TRAPP *Comm. Rev.* xii. 3 A Dragon the devil is called ..for his mischievousnesse. *a* **1715** BURNET *Own Time* III. (1724) I. 525 Many were sensible of the mischievousness of such a precedent. **1790** MARSHALL *Rur. Econ. Midl.* 56 A striking instance of the..mischievousness of mice. **1829** BENTHAM *Justice & Cod. Petit., Abr. Petit. Justice* 3 The system..would remain as it does in all its mischievousness. **1884** *Manch. Exam.* 1 Dec. 5/4 The tendency to scandal-mongering..only equalled..in mischievousness by the spirit of rationalism.

misch-masch, var. MISH-MASH *sb.*

mischmetal(l (ˈmɪʃmɛt(ə)l). Also **misch metal.** [ad. G. *mischmetall*, f. *misch-en* to mix + *metall* METAL *sb.*] A mixture of lanthanons containing about 50 per cent cerium which is obtained usu. by electrolysis of the fused chlorides from monazite and is used in lighter flints.

1923 B. S. HOPKINS *Chem. Rarer Elements* x. 168 The most important of these [cerium alloys] is the alloy called misch metal, mixed metal, commercial cerium, or simply 'cerium'. **1924** J. W. MELLOR *Comprehensive Treat. Inorg. & Theoret. Chem.* V. xxxviii. 608 A. Sieverts and G. M. Goldegg studied the action of hydrogen and nitrogen on the mischmetals. **1954** H. E. KREMERS in C. A. Hampel *Rare Metals Handbk.* xvi. 343 The most common ferrous alloy of the rare earths is the common lighter flint, which contains about 30 per cent iron, the balance being misch metal. **1966** PHILLIPS & WILLIAMS *Inorg. Chem.* II. xix. 18 A particularly interesting lanthanide alloy is 'misch-metall', with 50 per cent Ce, 25 per cent La, and the rest mostly Nd and Pr. This alloy is added to partly purified iron when it preferentially removes elements such as C, O, S, N, and P into the slag as lanthanide compounds.

mis'choice. [MIS-^{1} 4.] Wrong or improper choice.

a **1684** LEIGHTON *Comm. 1 Pet.* i. 13 (1693) 132 The great error of Mans mind..is the diverting of the soul from God, ..and this mischoyce is the very root of all our miseries. **1882** *Advance* (Chicago) 1 June, A mis-choice at such a time would be a misfortune. **1891** *Daily News* 2 Nov. 4/8 The mis-choice or misuse of a pronoun. **1896** J. WATSON *Mind of Master* v. 99 Sin is not merely a mistake or a misfit; it is a deliberate mischoice.

mis'choose, *v.* [MIS-^{1} 1.] *trans.* and *intr.* To choose wrongly; to make a wrong choice (of).

c **1250** *Gen. & Ex.* 190 In ðe moste and in ðe leste he [*sc.* Adam] forles His louerd-hed quuanne he mis-ches. *a* **1407** SCOGAN *Moral Ballad* 187, I wolde be sory, if that ye mis-chese. **1597** HOOKER *Eccl. Pol.* v. lxv. §5 Unlesse they [*sc.* ceremonies] be either greatly mischosen..or els [etc.]. **1601** STOW *Ann.* 1286 (an. 1596) But that we mischose the daie attempting so great a worke vpon his daie of rest. **1665** BOYLE *Occas. Refl.* I. vii. (1848) 89 If th' end be not mischosen, the means are to be estimated by their tendency thereunto. **1847** EMERSON *Repr. Men, Shakspere* (1850) 149 The madness with which the passing age mischooses the object on which all candles shine.

So **mis'choosing** *vbl. sb.*, **mis'chosen** *ppl. a.*

c **1400** *Rule St. Benet* (Verse) 2247 þai sal cum To reknyng on þe day of dome For þer myschesing þam omang. **1597** HOOKER *Eccl. Pol.* v. lxii. §20 This and the like mischosen resemblances. **1643** MILTON *Divorce* Wks. 1851 IV. 52 To ..shut up..the one with a mischosen mate, the other in a mistaken calling. *Ibid.* 87 Whom..onely marriage ruins, which doubtlesse is not the fault of that ordinance, for God gave it as a blessing, nor alwayes, of mans mis-choosing. **1895** *Century Mag.* Aug. 577/1 [A cat] whose mis-chosen tail was already a source of questioning self-contemplation.

†**mis'christen,** *v.* *Obs.* [MIS-^{1} 1.] = MISBAPTIZE 1.

a **1631** DONNE *Serm.* (1649) II. xxiv. 201 They did not onely mis-canonize men, made Devills Saints, but they mis-christened men, put names to persons..that never were.

mischsprache (ˈmɪʃʃpraːxə). [G., 'mixed language'.] = *mixed language* (MIXED *ppl. a.* 11).

[**1885** M. GRÜNBAUM in *Sammlung gemeinverständlicher wissenschaftlicher Vorträge* XX. 613 (*title*) Mischsprachen und Sprachmischungen.] **1930** J. T. HATFIELD et al. *Curme Vol. Ling. Stud.* 12 The question as to the justification of calling this tongue German and whether it is a *Mischsprache*. **1963** *English Studies* XLIV. 9 There are cases where..a scribe *half*-transforms his original, producing a sort of *Mischsprache*.

misch(t)y, dial. var. MISCHIEF *sb.*

1890 S. S. BUCKMAN *John Darke's Sojourn in Cotteswolds* xvi. 150 Er's harmless enow when he comes yereby, er 'oodn't do none mischy. **1895** HARDY *Jude* I. i. 9 Just now he's a-scaring of birds for Farmer Troutham. It keeps un out of mischty. **1896** —— *Under Greenw. Tree* II. v. 117 Bless ye, my sonnies! 'tisn't the pa'son's move at all. That gentleman over there..is at the root of the mischty [mischief, 1872, 1876, 1891 eds.].

mischuos, obs. form of MISCHIEVOUS.

miscibility (mɪsɪˈbɪlɪtɪ). [f. MISCIBLE: see -ITY.] The quality or condition of being miscible; capability of being mixed (*with* something else).

1754 *Phil. Trans.* XLVIII. 683 The miscibility of platina with metallic bodies. **1786** *Ibid.* LXXVI. 118 Miscibility with water. **1896** *Blackw. Mag.* May 685 The miscibility of racial traits. **1898** *Allbutt's Syst. Med.* V. 248 The solubility, miscibility with fluids, and cohesiveness of the dust.

miscible (ˈmɪsɪb(ə)l), *a.* (*sb.*) [ad. L. type **miscibilis*, f. *miscēre* to mix: see -IBLE. Cf. F. *miscible.*] **a.** Capable of being mixed (*with* something). Usu. *spec.* of a liquid: capable of forming a true solution *with* another liquid.

1570 DEE *Math. Pref.* *iij, When you haue two thinges Miscible, whose degrees are truely knowen. **1660** STANLEY *Hist. Philos.* IX. (1687) 567/1 The Soul of the World God inkindled in the midst..; which (Soul) being not easily miscible, was not without difficulty contemperated. **1750** G. HUGHES *Barbados* 106 Tho' oils in general..are not miscible with water. **1790** BURKE *Fr. Rev.* 163 All these had kept the landed and monied interests more separated in France, less miscible. **1807** T. THOMSON *Chem.* (ed. 3) II. 380 Alcohol has a strong affinity for water, and is miscible with it in every proportion. **1885** GOODALE *Physiol. Bot.* (1892) 221 Two liquids which are not miscible—for instance, oil and water. **1960** HAMILL & WILLIAMS *Princ. Physical Chem.* ix. 244 While phenol and water at this temperature and pressure are only partly miscible the addition of acetone increases their mutual solubility. **1964** G. I. BROWN *Introd. Physical Chem.* xxiii. 252 Ether will dissolve a little water (about 1·2 per cent at room temperature) to form a homogeneous solution, and water will also dissolve a little ether (about 6·5 per cent at room temperature) to form a similar solution. Within these limits ether and water are completely miscible. As their mutual solubilities are limited, however, ether and water are only partially miscible.

†**b.** *sb.* A substance that will mix with another.

1660 INGELO *Bentiv. & Ur.* II. (1682) 126 Produc'd by the Commixture of such antecedent Miscibles. **1678** R. RUSSELL tr. *Geber* II. I. II. iii. 43 In Animals..there is not a perficient Proportion, nor miscibles of Proportion, nor Qualities of Miscibles.

Hence **'miscibleness** *rare*$^{-0}$, miscibility.

1736 BAILEY (fol.), *Miscibleness.*

mis-cipher (mɪsˈsaɪfə(r)), *v.* *rare.* [MIS-^{1} 1.] *trans.* To express wrongly in cipher; †to affix a wrong numeral figure to.

1644 MARQ. ORMONDE *Let.* in Carte *Coll.* (1735) 290 The person's name, from whom it was sent..[was] certainly mis-cyphered. **1657** J. SERGEANT *Schism Dispach't* 172 He proceeds, upon this mistake of his own and the Printer's mis-ciphering it, to call my sixth the seventh. **1893** S. R. GARDINER in *Hamilton Papers* (Camden) 22 Aversion [*note: Sic.?* mis-ciphered for 'diversion'].

mis-citation (mɪssaɪˈteɪʃən). [MIS-^{1} 4.] Incorrect citation.

1634 BP. HALL *Residue Contempl.* 190 What a mis-citation is this? 'Moses commanded'. The law was Gods, not Moseses. **1896** SAINTSBURY *Hist. 19th Cent. Lit.* v. 250 He made his own case worse by mis-citation.

mis-cite (mɪsˈsaɪt), *v.* [MIS-^{1} 1.] *trans.* To cite or quote incorrectly. Also **mis'citing** *vbl. sb.*

1591 SYLVESTER *Du Bartas* I. iii. 939 So Antichrists.. Miss-cite the Scriptures. *a* **1609** DONNE *Lett., To Sir H. Goodyere* (1651) 161 For this particular Author, I looked for more prudence..in him, in avoiding all miscitings, or misinterpretings. **1620** BP. HALL *Hon. Marr. Clergy* I. i, If Satan haue mis-cited the psalme 'Hee shall giue His angels charge ouer thee', for temptation. **1700** COLLIER *2nd Def. Short View* 20 Is the Testimony miscited? **1899** *Westm. Gaz.* 20 May 3/2 Nor do I blame [him]..for mis-citing the Act of Parliament which he venerates.

†**mis'clad,** *pa. pple.* *Obs.* [MIS-^{1} 2.] Wearing wrong clothes.

1494 FABYAN *Chron.* III. liv. 35 [He] chaunged his.. Armure and dydde vpon hym the Armoure of a Brytayne, and by that meane as a Bryton mysclad [etc.].

mis'claim, *sb.* [MIS-^{1} 4.] A wrong or mistaken claim.

a **1626** BACON (J.), Error, misclaim, and forgetfulness, become suitors for some remission of extreme rigour.

mis'claiming, *vbl. sb.* [MIS-^{1} 3.] Wrongful claiming.

1583 GOLDING *Calvin on Deut.* cxiii. 694 Notwithstanding his misclaiming of the priuiledge.

mis'class, *v.* [MIS-^{1} 1.] *trans.* To put in the wrong class.

1782 AYSCOUGH *Catal. MSS. Brit. Mus.* II. 907 Manuscripts which had been misclassed, or overlooked.

,misclassifi'cation. [MIS-^{1} 4.] Erroneous classification.

1827 HARE *Guesses* Ser. I. (1873) 80 The misclassifications ..produced by a general term. **1901** W. CALLAWAY in *Publ. Mod. Lang. Assoc. Amer.* XVI. 155 In such a mass of details occasional..misclassifications are inevitable.

miscle, variant of MISSEL, mistletoe.

†**mis'cleping,** *vbl. sb.* *Obs.* [MIS-^{1} 3.] Misnaming.

1387-8 T. USK *Test. Love* I. x. (Skeat) I. 46 Thus is night turned in-to day, and day in-to night,..not in dede, but in miscleping of foliche people.

misc'line, obs. form of MASLIN^{2}.

mis'code, *v.* [MIS-^{1} 1, 3.] *trans.* To code incorrectly. So **mis'coding** *vbl. sb.*

1965 *Math. in Biol. & Med.* (Med. Res. Council) II. 54 Gross mistakes in the date are probably rare, and are due only to mispunching and/or miscoding. **1970** *Sci. News Let.* 23 May 510 The mutant DNA miscoded a single amino acid in the sequence of structural protein in the membrane. As a result..the entire membrane was defective.

mis'cognizant, -isant, *a.* *Law.* Also 7 -conusant. [a. AF. **mesconisant*, *-usant* = OF. *mescognoissant*, *-conissant*, f. *mes-* MIS-^{2} + *cognoissant*, pres. pple. of *cognoistre* (mod. F. *connaître*) to know.] Ignorant *of*.

1540 *Act 32 Hen. VIII*, c. 9 §5 That no maner of personne ..shall be ignorante or miscognisaunt of the..penalties therin specified. **1586** *Act. 28 Eliz.* c. 1 in Bolton *Stat. Irel.* (1621) 386 To the intent no person or persons shall be ignorant or misconisant of the penalties herein contayned. **1628** COKE *On. Litt.* 99 The King shall not be intended to be misconusant of the Law.

†**miscognize,** *v.* *Obs.* *rare*$^{-1}$. [ad. OF. *mescognoiss-*, stem of *mescognoistre* (mod. F. *méconnaître*): for the form cf. COGNIZE and RECOGNIZE.] *trans.* To fail to appreciate or acknowledge.

1603 HOLLAND *Plutarch's Mor.* 1092 The good never intervert, nor miscognize the favour and benefit which they have received.

miscolle, obs. variant of MISKAL.

†miscollection. *Obs.* [MIS-[1] 4.] A wrong inference.
1610 Bp. Hall *Apol. Brownists* §6 Wks. (1625) 555 In his words and yours I finde both a miscollection, and a wrong charge. **1615** Sylvester *Job Triumph.* xx. 413 Wks. (Grosart) II. 159, I conceive your mis-conceits, from hence; Your mis-collections, and your wrested Sense.

miscoloration. [MIS-[1] 4.] Discoloration.
1822–34 *Good's Study Med.* (ed. 4) IV. 540 Miscolourations of the same character as moles, freckles, and sunburn.

mis'colour, *v.* [MIS-[1] 1.] *trans.* To give a wrong 'colour' to (facts, etc.); to misrepresent.
1809 Syd. Smith *Serm.* I. 31 The imagination always miscolours the facts in these cases. **1844** *Q. Rev.* LXXIV. 91 Many of the leading politicians..perverted by the bitterness of party miscoloured and distorted to the public..the motives [etc.]. **1879** Howells *L. Aroostook* 139 You have no right to miscolor my words.

mis'coloured, *a.* [MIS-[1] 6.] Improperly coloured.
1658 Hexham, *Misverwet*, Ill-dyed, or Mis-coloured. *a* **1684** Leighton *Comm. 1 Pet.* iii. 21 Wks. (1859) 223/2 Looking through the miscoloured glass of their own malice. **1822–34** *Good's Study Med.* (ed. 4) IV. 531 Miscoloured hair.

mis'colouring, *vbl. sb.* [MIS-[1] 3.] Attributing a false colour.
1669 Pepys *Let.* 21 Nov., The miscolouring, misfiguring, diminishing, or undue magnifying, of an object.

†mis'comfort, *sb. Obs.* [MIS-[1] 7.] Distress, desolation, trouble; = DISCOMFORT *sb.* 2.
c **1330** R. Brunne *Chron. Wace* (Rolls) 2992 He ne wyste what lond ne port He was aryued, for mys-confort. *a* **1340** Hampole *Psalter* lxxii. 19 How ar þai made in miscomforth [*in desolacionem*]. **1387–8** T. Usk *Test. Love* I. iv. (Skeat) l. 4 Than thought me that Love gan a litel to hevye for miscomfort of my chere. **1483** *Cath. Angl.* 241/1 A Miscomforthe, *mesticia*. **1526** *Pilgr. Perf.* (W. de W. 1531) 42 b, To theyr great confusyon & miscomfort.

†mis'comfort, *v. Obs.* [MIS-[1] 7.] *trans.* To trouble, distress, disturb.
1303 R. Brunne *Handl. Synne* 8508 To chastyse hym ..þat he myscumfort eft noun oþer. *a* **1340** Hampole *Psalter* lxxii. 19 How ar þai miscomforthed. *Ibid.* cxix. 4 Aruys sharpe of þe myghty with kolis myscomfortand [*cum carbonibus desolatoribus*]. **1470–85** Malory *Arthur* x. xxix. 460 Fyghte frely..& myscomforte yow noughte for ony knyȝt. **1483** *Cath. Angl.* 241/1 To Miscomforthe, *desolari*.

ˌmiscompreˈhend, *v.* [MIS-[1] 1.] *trans.* To comprehend wrongly, misunderstand.
1813 T. Busby *Lucretius* I. II. *Comm.* vi, The preceptor of Nero seems to have miscomprehended the poet. **1899** Baring-Gould *Bk. of West* I. 16, I am quite certain to be miscomprehended by them.

ˌmiscompreˈhension. [MIS-[1] 4.] Misunderstanding.
1856 J. W. Kaye *Life Sir J. Malcolm* I. xv. 499 In either case, of disobedience or miscomprehension, he had proved himself..unworthy of the confidence. **1891** Kipling *Life's Handicap* p. ix, [They] stare at each other hopelessly across great gulfs of miscomprehension.

ˌmiscompuˈtation. [MIS-[1] 4.] Miscalculation, misreckoning.
1647 Clarendon *Hist. Reb.* II. §71 A very gross miscomputation. *a* **1674** *Ibid.* VIII. §2. **1728** Morgan *Algiers* I. iv. 116 Many Writers..make great Miscomputations in their References of the Hejira to our Aera.

†miscompute, *sb. Obs.*[−1] [MIS-[1] 4.] = prec.
1646 Sir T. Browne *Pseud. Ep.* VII. xviii. 380 As he maketh the account, and Budeus *de Asse* correcting the miscompute of Valla, delivereth it.

miscom'pute, *v.* [MIS-[1] 1.] *intr.* To miscalculate, misreckon.
1672 Wallis in Rigaud *Corr. Sci. Men* (1841) II. 532 Excuse me if I have in haste miscomputed. **1726** T. Madox *Firma Burgi* Pref. bj, I intended it should make onely a Pamflet..But I miscomputed.

miscon'ceit, *sb.* Now *arch.* [MIS-[1] 4.] = MISCONCEPTION. (Common in the 17th c.)
1576 in *Grindal's Wks.* (Parker Soc.) 408 To remove the scrupulousness and misconceits of some few. **1596** Spenser *F.Q.* IV. vi. 2 Full of melancholie and sad misfare Through misconceipt. *a* **1600** Hooker *Eccl. Pol.* VI. (1648) 119 A misconceit whereby they imagine every act which they doe knowing that they doe amisse..to bee mere sinne against the Holy Ghost. **1635** Sibbes *Confer. Christ & Mary* (1656) 4 She had a misconceipt of Christ, as if he had been the gardiner. *a* **1716** South *Serm.* (1744) VII. ii. 40 That general misconceit of the Jews, about the kingdom of the Messiah. **1855** Singleton *Virgil* II. 172 Whether is it by misconceit of course, Or driv'n by storms..Ye've come within the margents of our flood. **1870** Swinburne *Ess. & Stud.* (1875) 105 Taintless of jealousy or misconceit.

miscon'ceit, *v. arch.* [MIS-[1] 1.] *trans.* To have a wrong conception or false idea of; to think erroneously (that..).
1595 Munday *John a Kent* (Shaks. Soc.) 20 You wrong them, madame, if you misconceite That you or they shall be unnobly usde. **1599** Nashe *Lenten Stuffe* 73 If you would not misconceit that I studiously intended your defamation. **1606** J. Ford *Honor Triumphant* (Shaks. Soc.) 5 Else had I misconceited mine owne hopes, and beene gravelled in mine owne conceipts. **1677** Gilpin *Demonol.* (1867) 176 If this humour..misconceit inspiration or prophecy. **1871** R. Ellis tr. *Catullus* xvi. 4 You that..Misconceit me, sophisticate me wanton.

†miscon'ceited, *a. Obs.* [MIS-[1] 6.] **a.** Wrongly supposed. **b.** Having a wrong idea *of*.
1600 Breton *Melan. Humours* (Grosart) 10/2 Feede not thy self with misconceipted goode. **1633** Bp. Hall *Hard Texts, N.T.* 118 Those wch are fondly and proudly misconceited of their..wisdom.

miscon'ceive, *v.* [MIS-[1] 1.]
1. *intr.* To have a false conception or entertain wrong notions (*of*). Also with clause, †to suspect (= MISDEEM *v.* 6 b).
c **1386** Chaucer *Merch. T.* 1166 He that misconceyveth, he misdemeth. *c* **1585** *Faire Em* III. 1236 You know it's for your cause It pleaseth thus the King to misconceive of me. **1611** Bible *2 Macc.* iii. 32 The high Priest suspecting lest the king should misconceiue [Coverdale suspecte] that some treachery had beene done to Heliodorus by the Iewes. **1862** F. Hall *Refut. Hindu Philos. Syst.* 90 Even if I granted, that some men thus misconceive, still such a mistake would not be one of perception, but one of inference.
2. *trans.* To form an erroneous conception of; to misapprehend (a word, an action, etc.); to mistake the meaning of (a person).
1597 Hooker *Eccl. Pol.* V. i. §1 To yeeld them..reasonable causes of those things, which, for want of due consideration heretofore, they misconceiued. **1605** Timme *Quersit.* Pref. iii, A bad heart misconceiueth good actions. **1642** Milton *Apol. Smect.* Wks. 1851 III. 254 As for others who..have yet decreed to mis-interpret the intents of my reply, I suppose they would have found as many causes to have misconceav'd the reasons of my silence. **1794** Burke *Sp. agst. W. Hastings* Wks. 1827 VIII. 250 If I have understood the matter wrong, or misconceived your design. **1828** Scott *F.M. Perth* vi, I cannot suffer my feelings..to remain unexplained, without the possibility of my being greatly misconceived. **1841** J. F. Cooper *Deerslayer* I. i. 10 The Mengwe fill the woods with their lies, and misconceive words and treaties. **1867** Freeman *Norm. Conq.* (1877) I. iv. 229 The translator seems to misconceive his meaning.

miscon'ceived, *ppl. a.* [MIS-[1] 2.]
1. Wrongly or erroneously conceived.
1595 Spenser *Epithal.* 337 Ne let false whispers..Breake gentle sleepe with misconceiued dout. **1629** H. Burton *Truth's Triumph* 343 A mis-alledged place, or a mis-conceiued allegation. **1640** Bp. Hall *Episc.* I. i. 3 Being wedded to the love of this misconceived pomp. **1800** *Proc. E. Ind. Ho.* in *Asiat. Ann. Reg.* II. 133/1 He believed..when he first read that paper, that it was a hasty and misconceived production. **1884** Sir E. E. Kay in *Law Times Rep.* (N.S.) I. 323/1 All I can say is, that this motion seems to be misconceived, and that it must be refused with costs.
†2. Having a misconception or wrong idea.
1591 Shaks. *1 Hen. VI*, v. iv. 49 No misconceyued, Ione of Aire hath beene A Virgin from her tender infancie. *a* **1612** Harington *Epigr.* (1633) I. 56 Take heed henceforth you be not misconceived.

miscon'ceiver. [MIS-[1] 5.] One who forms misconceptions.
a **1625** Fletcher *Nice Valour* II. i, What a mis-conceiver 'tis. **1684** Baxter *Answ. Theol. Dial.* 21 An erring Conscience is no Lawmaker, but a misconceiver. **1827** Hare *Guesses* (1859) 199 Armed at all points against carpers and misconceivers. **1891** E. Abbott *Philomythus* Introd. 45 A misconceiver of it [*sc.* truth].

miscon'ceiving, *vbl. sb.* [MIS-[1] 3.] Misconception.
a **1586** Sidney *Arcadia* III. (1629) 232 And to be fallen from all happinesse, not by any misconceiuing, but by his owne fault. **1616** Bacon *Exceptions to Coke's Rep.* Wks. 1827 VII. 372 Any mistaking either in the declaring thereof unto him, or in his misconceiving of the same. **1685** Baxter *Paraphr. N.T.* John iv. 25 Even the Samaritans expected the Messiah: But with misconceivings of him.

miscon'ceiving, *ppl. a.* [MIS-[1] 2.] That misconceives; having false notions. In first quot., *causally*, productive of misconception.
1590 Spenser *F.Q.* III. x. 47 And misty dampe of misconceyving night. **1598** Yong *Diana* IV. 114, I was then so trustles and misconceiuing of my selfe, that [etc.]. **1628** Strafford in Browning *Life* (1891) 295 They were the wise intelligent men, and we..the ignorant, the misconceiving.

†misconcept. *Obs.* [MIS-[1] 4.] Misconception.
1616 W. Haig in Russell *Haigs* (1881) vii. 157 To have been..freed..of all misconcept they may have bred in your Majesty of me.

miscon'ception. [MIS-[1] 4.] The action or an act of misconceiving; a notion resulting from misconceiving.
1665 Glanvill *Scepsis Sci.* x. 53 It cannot be that our knowledge should be other, then an heap of Misconception and Error. **1672** Harvey *Anat. Consumptions* (ed. 2) ii. 4 The great errors and dangers, that may result out of a misconception of the names of things. **1809–10** Coleridge *Friend* (1865) 97 There is another use of the word reason,.. and more exposed to misconception. **1873** Symonds *Grk. Poets* xii. 417 To suppose that the Greeks were not a highly moralized race is perhaps the strangest misconception to which religious prejudice has ever given rise.

†miscon'clude, *v. Obs.*[−1] [MIS-[1] 1.] *intr.* To draw wrong conclusions.
1636 T. Goodwin *Child of Light* 34 Concerning which, men are more apt..to make..false Syllogismes, and to misconclude, then about any other spirituall truth.

†miscon'cluder. *Obs.*[−1] [MIS-[1] 5.] One who draws wrong conclusions.
1684 Baxter *Par. Congreg.* 8, I am specially obliged to answer such misconcluders, lest they make my writings a means of deceit against my sence.

miscon'clusion. [MIS-[1] 4.] A wrong or false conclusion.
a **1631** Donne *Lett. to Pers. Hon.* (1651) 164 We must take heed of making misconclusions upon the want of it [*sc.* unity in religion]. **1634** Bp. Hall *Fash. of World* 379 Away, then, with all the false-positions, and misconclusions, all the fantasticall, or wicked thoughts of the world.

mis'conduct, *sb.* [MIS-[1] 4.]
1. Bad management; mismanagement. Often quasi-*spec.*, malfeasance or culpable neglect of an official in regard to his office.
1710 Palmer *Proverbs* 2 Princes have lost their crowns by the mis-conduct of the first year of their reigns. **1736** Lediard *Life Marlborough* II. 357 This new Commander, by some unaccountable Misconduct,..suffer'd himself to be surprized. **1788** Burke *Sp. agst. W. Hastings* Wks. 1827 VIII. 314 Whenever in any matter of money there is concealment, you must presume misconduct. **1863** H. Cox *Instit.* III. ii. 599 Censure..of ministers of the Crown for misconduct of diplomatic affairs.
2. Improper conduct; wrong behaviour. Now often, in judicial trials, *spec.* in the sense of 'adultery'.
a **1729** Rogers 19 *Serm.* (1735) xii. 236 It..highly concerned them to reflect, how great Obligations..the Memory of their past Misconduct..laid on them..to walk with Care and Circumspection. **1748** Thomson *Cast. Indol.* II. lxxii, Let wisdom be by past misconduct learned. **1869** Freeman *Norm. Conq.* (1875) III. xii. 111 Stirred up by the misconduct of their eldest son. **1879** Blakiston *Teacher* 6 When a teacher feels his temper ruffled by a child's misconduct.
†b. *pl.* Instances of misconduct. *Obs.*
1711 Addison *Spect.* No. 256 ⁋4 Such as are guilty..of the same Slips or Misconducts in their own Behaviour. **1771** Goldsm. *Hist. Eng.* I. 106 His misconducts were incurable. **1857** Gen. P. Thompson *Audi Alt.* I. iii. 8 All malpractices and misconducts shall be smothered by the exercise of brute force at our expense.

miscon'duct, *v.* [MIS-[1] 1.]
1. *trans.* To mismanage.
1755 Johnson, *To misconduct*, to manage amiss; to carry on wrong. **1794** Burke *Sp. agst. W. Hastings* Wks. 1827 VIII. 125 The administration misconducted the people oppressed. **1885** *Law Times* LXXVIII. 167/1 The second [sale], though not misconducted, had not realised the value of the property.
2. *refl.* To misbehave oneself.
1883 Sir Edward Fry in *Law Rep.* (11 Q.B. Div.) 596 A barrister may be..reprimanded by the judge if he misconducts himself in court. **1901** *Daily Colonist* (Victoria, B.C.) 11 Oct. 2/1 The Jacksons..induced girls to misconduct themselves with the belief that it was a necessary part of their religious devotions. **1922** Joyce *Ulysses* 318 Belle in her bloomers misconducting herself. *Ibid.* 457 He made improper overtures to me to misconduct myself at half past four p.m. on the following Thursday.

miscon'jecture, *sb. rare.* [MIS-[1] 4.] Erroneous conjecture.
1646 Sir T. Browne *Pseud. Ep.* v. xxi. 272 We hope they wil plausibly receave our attempts, or candidely correct our misconjectures. **1822** Galt *Sir A. Wylie* I. xxxii. 317 There may be some misunderstanding or misconjecture.

miscon'jecture, *v. rare*[−1]. [MIS-[1] 1.] *intr.* To make wrong conjectures.
a **1626** Bacon *Ch. Eng. Controv.* in *Resuscitatio* (1657) 166 Many Pressing, and Fawning Persons do misconjecture, of the Humours, of Men in Authority.

miscon'junction. [MIS-[1] 4.] A wrong conjunction.
1867 Bushnell *Mor. Uses Dark Th.* 128 There is no misconjunction so absurd as that of safety and wrong. **1898** *Atlantic Monthly* Apr. 461/1 The road..was..a diabolical misconjunction of slipperiness and supreme adhesiveness.

mi'sconsecrate, *v. rare*[−0]. [MIS-[1] 1.] *trans.* To consecrate improperly.
1872 in Latham.

mi'sconsecrated, *ppl. a.* [MIS-[1] 2.]
a. Consecrated to a wrong purpose. **b.** Improperly consecrated.
1634 Bp. Hall *Def. Crueltie* 428 Our prayers were the gale ..that tore these mis-consecrated flags, and sayles. **1880** Burton *Reign Q. Anne* I. i. 42 He evaded the Communion, and so escaped desecration through the misconsecrated elements.

misconse'cration. [MIS-[1] 4.] Improper or invalid consecration.
1664 H. More *Myst. Iniq.* 132 This succession may be interrupted by the misordination or misconsecration of a priest or bishop.

mis'construable, *a.* [f. MISCONSTRUE *v.* + -ABLE.] Capable of misconstruction.
a **1734** North *Exam.* I. ii. §160 If he had been taken up as a presupposed Prostitute out of the Goal..it had been misconstruable.

miscon'struct, *v.* [MIS-[1] 1.]
†1. Chiefly *Sc.* = MISCONSTRUE. *Obs.*
1637 Gillespie *Eng. Pop. Cerem.* II. i. 7 Except as it is misreported..and misconstructed..by the false Calumnies of our Adversaries. **1666** Abp. Sharp *Let. to Dk. Rothes* in

Kirkton *Ch. Hist.* (1817) 213 *note*, To have their carriage, inclinations, and actions..misconstructed. **1678** SIR G. MACKENZIE *Crim. Laws Scot.* I. i. §4. 12 The doing what may tend to misconstruct, or raise jealousies. **1685** EARL OF ARGYLE *Last Sp.* in Wodrow *Hist. Ch. Scot.* (1722) II. 545, I pray you do not misconstruct my Behaviour this Day. **1795** MᶜKNIGHT *Apost. Epist.* (1820) I. 183 Dost thou form a wrong opinion of the goodness of God? Dost thou misconstruct it?

2. To construct badly. *rare*⁻¹.
1823 DE QUINCEY *Lett. to Yng. Man* Wks. 1860 XIV. 39 He fails to construct some leading idea, or he even misconstructs it.

miscon'struction. [MIS-¹ 4.]
1. The action of misconstruing; the putting of a wrong construction on words or actions.
1513 MORE in Grafton *Chron.* (1568) II. 760 Sometime a thing right well entended, oure misconstruction turneth it to worsse. **1605** SHAKS. *Lear* II. ii. 124. **1662** *Bk. Com. Prayer* Pref., Words and phrases..liable to misconstruction. **1677** HORNECK *Gt. Law Consid.* ii. (1704) 58 Misconstructions of the ways of God. **1790** PALEY *Horæ Paul.* 210 To rectify the misconstruction that had been put upon his words. **1846** *Mirror of Literature* Sept. 119 Being well aware that misconstructions are apt to be placed on the projector of any new scheme. **1885** *Law Times Rep.* LII. (N.S.) 675/1 The language..is open to misconstruction.
2. Faulty or bad construction. *rare.*
1819 W. S. ROSE *Lett.* II. 21 Misconstructions and misconjugations allowed in the Tuscan and rejected in the Italian. **1822–34** *Good's Study Med.* (ed. 4) III. 56 Some misconstruction or misaffection of the cerebral organs. *Ibid.* 408.

miscon'structive, *a.* [f. MISCONSTRUCT + -IVE, after prec.] Characterized by misconstruction.
1649 BP. HALL *Cases Consc.* III. vii. 299 A conceit sensibly weak, and mis-constructive.

mi'sconstrue, *v.* Also (β) 6–7 misconster, (-tre, -ture). [MIS-¹ 1. For stress cf. CONSTRUE.]
1. a. *trans.* To put a wrong construction upon (words or actions); to mistake the meaning of (a person); to take in a wrong sense.
a. c **1374** CHAUCER *Troylus* I. 346 Ful ofte thy lady wole it misconstrue, And deme it harm in her opinioun. **1513** MORE in Grafton *Chron.* (1568) II. 791 But these words king Edward made to be misconstrued, and enterpreted, that Burdet ment the Crowne of the realme. **1587** GOLDING *De Mornay* xi. (1592) 158 Thou misconstrewest al the good which the bountifull prouidence of God doth vnto thee. **1601** SHAKS. *Jul. C.* v. iii. 84 Alas, thou hast misconstrued euery thing. **1611** BIBLE *Transl. Pref.* ¶ 1 It is sure to bee misconstrued, and in danger to be condemned. *a* **1656** BP. HALL *Rem. Wks.* (1660) 241, I beseech you..misconstrue me not. **1675** OTWAY *Alcibiades* IV. iii, Alas, dear Friend, misconstrue not my Zeal. **1791** MRS. RADCLIFFE *Rom. Forest* viii, I know that young ladies are apt to misconstrue the unmeaning gallantry of fashionable manners. **1849** MACAULAY *Hist. Eng.* v. I. 583 Words, it was said, may easily be misunderstood by an honest man. They may easily be misconstrued by a knave. **1861** DICKENS *Lett.* 8 July (1880) II. 144, I fear you may sometimes have misconstrued my silence.
β. **1533** MORE *Apol.* 85 They..of theyr owne fauour to them selfe, mysse constre [Wks. (1557) 869/2 mysse construe] the good mannys mynde. **1579** GOSSON *Sch. Abuse* To Rdr., His schollers were woont, how plaine soeuer he spake, to misconster him. **1596** SHAKS. *Merch. V.* II. ii. 197 Least through thy wilde behauiour I be misconsterd in the place I goe to. **1640** GLAPTHORNE *Ladies' Priviledge* I. Wks. 1874 II. 100 You misconster The intention of my lookes, I am not angry Though much distemper'd. **1678** COLEMAN in *Trial of C.* 59 So as to make them mis-conster all our endeavours. **1869** *Lonsdale Gloss.*, *Misconster*, corr[uption] of misconstrue.
absol. **1609** F. GREVIL *Mustapha* IV. ii. F 2, Enuy tooke hold of worth, doubt did misconster. **1612** BP. HALL *Contempl.*, *O.T.* IV. *Birth of Moses* Wks. (1625) 868 Then, he aggrauates, and misconstrues. **1842** C. LEVER *Jack Hinton* (1843) xlviii. 308 It is so easy, when people have no peculiar reasons to vindicate another—to misconstrue—perhaps condemn.
†b. *intr. to misconstrue of* (in the same sense).
1581 RICH *Farew.* (1846) 145, I confesse I have trespassed in misconsteryng of your lines. **1588** GREENE *Pandosto* (1607) 4 He then began to..misconsture of their too priuate familiarity.
2. *trans.* To infer wrongly. *rare*⁻¹.
1813 SCOTT *Rokeby* IV. xxi, A kindly smile..So kind, that, from its harmless glee, The wretch misconstrued villany.
So **mi'sconstruing** *vbl. sb.* and *ppl. a.*
1513 MORE in Grafton *Chron.* (1568) II. 791 By the misconstruing of the lawes of the realme for the princes pleasure. **1603** KNOLLES *Hist. Turks* (1621) 1290 A perverse interpretation or misconstruing of words. **1636** COWLEY *Sylva* Wks. (Grosart) I. 25/2 Lest the misconst'ring world should chance to say [etc.].

mis'construed, *ppl. a.* [MIS-¹ 2.] Construed amiss.
1682 DRYDEN & LEE *Dk. Guise* IV. i, To know The true intent of my mis-constru'd Faith. **1718** PRIOR *Solomon* III. 203 The long depending cause, And doubtful issue of misconstrued laws. **1762** WESLEY *Jrnl.* 5 Feb. (1827) III. 77 A misconstrued text in the Revelation. **1866** J. MARTINEAU *Ess.* I. 127 A labyrinth of misconstrued relations.

mis'construer. Also 6 misconsterer. [MIS-¹ 5.] One who misconstrues.
1592 CHETTLE *Kind-harts Dr.* (1841) 8 If enuious misconsterers arme themselues against my simple meaning. **1649** BP. HALL *Cases Consc.* III. x. 352 The scripture hath..set down the severall six dayes, wherein each part of it was distinctly formed: which those misconstruers are fain to understand of the distinct notifications given to the Angels concerning this almighty work.

†mis'construous, *a. Obs.* [f. MISCONSTRUE *v.* + -OUS.] Apt to misconstrue.
1632 LITHGOW *Trav.* I. 4 Misconstruous lack-iudgment.

miscon'tent, *sb. rare.* [MIS-¹ 4.] Discontent.
1683 *Sir J. Melville's Mem.* 155 There was at this Time a universal Miscontent [*Bannatyne Club ed.* miscontentement] in the Country. **1827** H. E. LLOYD *Timkowski's Trav.* II. 310 Divorce is frequent among them; the least miscontent on either side is sufficient to procure it.

miscon'tent, *a. arch.* and *dial.* Also 5–6 myss-, 6 miss-, mes-. [f. MIS-¹ 6, 7 + CONTENT *a.* Cf. *discontent* (from 1494) and F. *mécontent* (from 1642).] Not content; discontented, dissatisfied; ill-pleased. Const. *with, of.*
c **1489** *Corr. Plumpton* (Camden) 170 In any thing which ye are myscontent with. **1519** HORMAN *Vulg.* §13. 73, I am sore miscontent with thy outragious laughynge afore the peple. **1571** *Satir. Poems Reform.* xxviii. 101 Of this lyfe the Lord was miscontent. **1591** SPARRY tr. *Cattan's Geomancie* Ep. to Rdr. A 4 None..after the vnderstanding and reading therof will be miscontent to confesse that [etc.]. **1637–50** Row *Hist. Kirk* (Wodrow Soc.) 314 The King was miscontent that no more mischief was done. *a* **1670** SPALDING *Troub. Chas. I* (1829) 7 [He] got not good payment of his fee..whereat he was miscontent. **1870** MORRIS *Earthly Par.* I. (1896) 212 Nor be ye with him miscontent For that with little ornament Of gold and folk to you he came.

miscon'tent, *v.* [f. MIS-¹ 1, 7 + CONTENT *v.*, after OF. *mescontenter* (14th c.).] *trans.* To dissatisfy, displease; *refl.* to become discontented.
1498–9 *Plumpton Corr.* (Camden) 133, I am right sory..that he shold myscontent your mastership & give you cause of accion. **1530** PALSGR. 637/1, I have served hym this seven yere, and I never myscontented hym. **1567** J. SANFORD *Epictetus* A 8 b, Thou shalte be troubled..& shalte miscontente thy selfe with God and men. **1611** FLORIO, *Miscontentáre*, to miscontent. **1920** M. HEWLETT *Light Heart* v. 33 'I have had words come by me,' she said, 'that you are beguiling my Thordis. That miscontents me.'

†misconten'tation. *Obs.* [MIS-¹ 4, 7. Cf. *discontentation.*] Dissatisfaction.
1523 WOLSEY in Fiddes *Wolsey* Collections (1724) 140 His graces..miscontentation. **1591** SPARRY tr. *Cattan's Geomancie* 127 The man shall not be put from the Court, but hee shall continue there to his great miscontentation.

†miscon'tented, *a. Obs.* [MIS-¹ 6, 7. Cf. *discontented.*] Discontented, dissatisfied, displeased.
1534 LD. BERNERS *Gold. Bk. M. Aurel.* (1546) D vij, It was no reson, that suche as came to his seruyce shoulde retourne myscontented. **1575–85** ABP. SANDYS *Serm.* xviii. §7. 312 So it fareth with miscontented mindes. Their own desires plague them. *a* **1670** SPALDING *Troub. Chas. I* (Spalding Club) I. 78 Ane Meingzie of miscontentit puritanes. **1826** GALT *Last of Lairds* vii, Had she gotten a gentleman of family, I would not have been overly miscontented.
So **†miscon'tentedly** *adv.*, discontentedly.
1561 T. NORTON *Calvin's Inst.* III. 296 Neither ought we to take it miscontentedly that the outward man be destroyed so that the inwarde man be renued.

†miscon'tenting, *vbl. sb. Obs.* [MIS-¹ 3, 7.] Discontent, displeasure.
1495 *Act 11 Hen. VII*, c. 10 *Preamble*, The murmore grudge and myscontenting of such youre seid subgettes. **1658** HEXHAM, A misliking, or a miscontenting.

miscon'tentment. *Obs.* exc. *arch.* [f. MIS-¹ 4, 7 + CONTENTMENT. Cf. OF. *mescontentement* (from 16th c.) and Eng. *discontentment.*] Discontent, dissatisfaction; grievance.
1579 FENTON *Guicciard.* v. (1599) 210 The French king with melancholy moodes and miscontentments tooke occasion to dismisse from his Court the Spanish Embassadors. *a* **1586** SIDNEY *Arcadia* I. xv. (1590) 67 Hauing through some adventure, or inwarde miscontentment withdrawne him selfe from any bodies knowledge, where he is. *a* **1670** SPALDING *Troub. Chas. I* (Spalding Club) I. 220 It pleisit his Majestie to send thir miscontentmentis in paper..to Edinbrugh. **1860** MOTLEY *Netherl.* xviii. (1868) II. 379 Alexander..his eyes declaring miscontentment—asked [etc.].

†miscon'tinuance. *Law. Obs.* [AF.; see MIS-².] Continuance by unlawful process.
In some Law Dicts. confused with DISCONTINUANCE.
1540 *Act 32 Hen. VIII*, c. 30 Any myscontynuance or discontinuance or mysconveing of process. **1607** COWELL *Interpr.*, *Miscontinuance*, Kitchin, fol. 231 [*error for* 331]. See *Discontinuance* [*ed.* **1672** *adds* Is the same with Discontinuance]. **1628** COKE *On Litt.* 325 There is..a Discontinuance of Processe consisting in not doing, where the Processe is not continued... There is another erronious proceeding and that consisteth in misdoing, as when one Processe is awarded in stead of another, or when a day is giuen which is not legall, this is called a miscontinuance and if the Tenant or Defendant make default it is error, but if he appeare, then the miscontinuance is salued, otherwise it is of a Discontinuance. **1771** JENKINS *Rep.* II. v. 57 A miscontinuance is where the continuance is made by undue process; a discontinuance is where no continuance is made at all.

misconusant, variant of MISCOGNIZANT.

†miscon'vert, *v. Obs.* [MIS-¹ 1.] *trans.* To convert to wrong uses.
1601 *Act 43 Eliz.* c. 4 §1 Misconvertinge or misgovernemente, of any Landes Tenementes Rentes. **1603** *B.N.C. Munim.* W. 20 (Rodborough), [Tenements] have for a long time been so misused and misconverted.

miscon'vey, *v.* Now *rare.* [MIS-¹ 1.] *refl.* To convey a wrong impression of one's meaning.
1839 S. WILBERFORCE *Let.* in E. S. Purcell *Life Card. Manning* (1895) I. xiii. 275, I hope he has misconveyed himself to H. E. Manning. **1864** *Saunders' News Letter* 17 Dec., Lest I should have misconveyed myself to the jury.

†miscon'veying, *vbl. sb. Obs.* [MIS-¹ 3.] Mismanagement.
1540 *Act 32 Hen. VIII*, c. 30 The pursueing myscontynuying [*v.r.* mysconveying] or discontynuyng.

mis'cook, *v.* Chiefly *Sc.* [MIS-¹ 1.] *trans.* To cook badly; to spoil in cooking. Also *fig.* to mismanage.
1508 DUNBAR *Tua Mariit Wemen* 455 Bot folk a cury may miscuke, that knawledge wantis. **1570** *Satir. Poems Reform.* xvi. 8 This commoun weill he hes miscuikit. **1638** BAILLIE *Lett.* (Bannatyne Cl.) I. 70 These who, by their..imprudencies, had miscooked all the matter. **1825** JAMIESON, To *Miscook* to mismanage any business; as 'Ye've miscookit a' your kail'. **1864** MRS. CARLYLE *Lett.* III. 206 Food miscooked. **1868** F. E. PAGET *Lucretia* 234 In just retribution for his miscooking his master's chops.

mis'cookery. [MIS-¹ 4.] Bad cooking.
1655 MOUFET & BENNET *Health's Improv.* xiii. 112 The Tongues of Beasts are..never faulty of themselves, but marred oftentimes by miscookery.

mis'copy, *sb.* [MIS-¹ 4.] An error in copying.
1881 R. G. WHITE *Two Hamlets* in *Atlantic Monthly* Oct. 477/2 It [sc. *sallied*] might be..a misprint or a miscopy of *sullied.* **1899** Æ. J. G. MACKAY *Lindesay's Chron. Scot.* (S.T.S.) I. p. clv, 'Fiftie' is a miscopy for 'fifteen'.

mis'copy, *v.* [MIS-¹ 1.] *trans.* To copy incorrectly.
1825 COLERIDGE *Lit. Rem.* (1836) II. 324 These may have been..ignorantly miscopied. **1877** RUSKIN *Fors Clav.* lxxxi. 250 However..miscopied, the message..remains clear. **1903** *Strand Mag.* Nov. 504/1 Did this little imp miscopy your letters?

†mis'cord, *v. Obs.* [a. OF. *mescorder*: see MIS-² and CORD *v.*²] *intr.* Not to correspond.
1387–8 T. USK *Test. Love* II. xiv. (Skeat) l. 27 In his first beginninge he was a man right expert in resons and swete in his wordes; and the werkes miscorden.

misco'rrect, *v.* [MIS-¹ 1.] *trans.* To correct wrongly.
1697 DRYDEN *Virg.* Life, He passed the first Seven Years of his Life at Mantua, not Seventeen, as Scaliger miscorrects his Author. **1789** T. TWINING *Aristotle's Treat. Poetry* Note 232 ΑΔΥΝΑΜΙΝ: which it was obvious enough for the transcriber to miscorrect into ἀδυναμιΑν.

misco'rrection. [MIS-¹ 4.] An erroneous correction.
1685 H. MORE *Paralip. Prophet.* vii. 42 Ptolemy not concerned in those Miscorrections, they not happening in the years the Eclipses are set down in.

mis'counsel, *sb.* [MIS-¹ 4.] Wrong advice.
1496 *Dives & Pauper* (W. de W.) v. x. 208/2 Through his mysse counseyll..he slough all mankynde both goostly and bodely. **1678** MARVELL *Growth Popery* Wks. 1875 IV. 384 Before we give [our money] we would be secure it should be applied to this purpose, and not by miscounsels be diverted to others.

mis'counsel, *v.* [MIS-¹ 1. Cf. OF. *mesconseillier.*] *trans.* To counsel or advise wrongly.
1389 in *Eng. Gilds* (1870) 87 If any broyer or syster..mysconsel or lye his broyer. **1413** *Pilgr. Sowle* (Caxton 1483) II. iii. 55 Yf the fende haue mysconceyled them, they hadden also counceyll in that other side. **1530** PALSGR. 637/1 You wene you take the ryght waye, but you are myscounsayled. **1591** SPENSER *M. Hubberd* 128 Things miscounselled must needs miswend. **1616** DONNE *Serm.* (1660–1) III. 333 Can I think him fit to give me counsel, that mis-counsels himself in the highest business, Religion? **1643** PRYNNE *Sov. Power Parlt.* I. (ed. 2) 11 These two great Favorites the Spensers who miscounselled and seduced him. **1841–3** ANTHON *Class. Dict.* 576 Having been bribed to miscounsel the people. **1877** RUSKIN *Fors Clav.* lxxvi. 116 The share that other people have had in counselling or miscounselling me.
So **mis'counselled** *ppl. a.*, **mis'counselling** *vbl. sb.*
c **1460** FORTESCUE *Abs. & Lim. Mon.* xiv. (1885) 144 The myscounsellynge off hym in many oþer cases. **1643** PRYNNE *Sov. Power Parlt.* IV. 19 Not daring to trust his prodigall mis-counselled King with moneys. **1823** GALT *R. Gilhaize* II. x. 106 The provocation given to the people of Scotland by the King's miscounselled majesty.

mis'count, *sb.* [MIS-¹ 4. Cf. OF. *mescont*, *mesconte.*] A wrong count, reckoning, or calculation.
1586 J. HOOKER *Descr. Irel.* in *Holinshed* II. 49/1 Aswell in the miscount of yeares as other vnlikelihoods found therein. **1637** RUTHERFORD *Lett.* (1664) lix. 132 O that he would take his own blood for counts & miscounts, that I might be a free man, & none had any claim to me, but onely, onely Jesus. **1897** *Daily News* 13 May 5/3 The Speaker has, owing to a miscount, been compelled to give a casting vote. **1903** *Fluff-Hunters* 137 She knew how many beans make five, and never made a miscount.

mis'count, *v.* [MIS-¹ 1. But cf. OF. *mesconter*, mod.F. (*se*) *mécompter.*]
1. *trans.* To miscalculate, misreckon.

a **1548** HALL *Chron., Hen. VIII*, 124 In their computacion they had mistaken and miscounted in their nomber an hundreth yeres. **1611** COTGR., *Mesconté*, misreckoned, miscompted. **1646** RUTHERFORD *Lett.* 9 Jan. (1664) 537 Christ cannot miscount one of the poorest of his lambs. **1793** *Tour thro' Theat. War* 47 A man less wretched might easily miscount time, and so did he. **1816** SCOTT *Antiq.* xli, After twice miscounting the sum, he threw the whole to his daughter.

2. *intr.* (†also *refl.*, after Fr.) To make a wrong calculation.

1390 GOWER *Conf.* I. 147 And if so be that he misconteth, To make in his answere a faile. **1530** PALSGR. 637/1 Tell it agayne, you have myscounted your selfe, I warrant you. **1603** HOLLAND *Plutarch's Mor.* 1045 These philosophers doe miscount greatly, and stray farre from reason and proportion.., if so be that Geometricall demonstrations do availe ought. **1659** BP. PATRICK *Div. Arith.* (1660) 6 Thus do all men generally miscount in the dayes of their health. **1687** A. LOVELL tr. *Thevenot's Trav.* I. v. 131 The trouble in going up [the steps], makes one often miscount. **1840** WHEWELL *Philos. Induct. Sci.* I. 133 In such a case we may forget in the intervals of the strokes, and miscount.

3. † **a.** To estimate wrongly. *Obs.* **b.** To regard erroneously (*as*).

a **1684** LEIGHTON *Comm. 1 Pet.* ii. 17 (1693) 393 Men miscount themselves at home, they reckoning that they ought to be regarded. **1847** TENNYSON *Princess* IV. 315 While my honest heat Were all miscounted as malignant haste.

mis'counting, *vbl. sb.* [MIS-^{1} 3.] Misreckoning.

?*a* **1366** CHAUCER *Rom. Rose* 196 To taken other folkes thing, Through robberie or myscounting [*MS.* myscoueiting; Fr. *cest cele qui fait..bescochier et mesconter*]. **1655** FULLER *Ch. Hist.* VI. 274 The miscounting of Dialects for Tongues causlessly multiplieth the number of those Languages. **1861** RILEY *Liber Albus* II. 115 *note*, The word 'miskenning' meaning miscounting or mispleading.

† **mis'covetise.** *Obs.* [MIS-^{1} 4.] Evil desire.

1496 *Dives & Pauper* (W. de W.) VII. iv. 280/2 Men sholde take no thynge for ony mys couetyse ayenst the lordes wyll.

† **mis'craft.** *Obs.* [MIS-^{1} 4.] Malpractice.

1496 *Dives & Pauper* (W. de W.) V. xviii. 221/1 Yf the woman..do ony mys crafte to let hyrself or ony other from berynge of childern.

miscreance^1 ('mɪskriːəns). Now *arch.* Also 4–5 mes-, 5 mys-: see CREANCE. [a. OF. *mescreance* (mod.F. *mécréance*) = Pr. *mescrezenza*, It. *miscredenza*: see MIS-^{2} and CREANCE.] False belief or faith; misbelief.

1390 GOWER *Conf.* II. 175 Se nou the foule mescreance Of Greks in thilke time tho, Whan Venus tok hire name so. **1415** HOCCLEVE *Min. Poems* 16/252 For thow sholdist reconsyle Thee to him, & leue thy mescreaunce. **1484** CAXTON *Ryall Book* C viii, They falle ofte..in heresyes and in myscreaunce. **1540** *Act 32 Hen. VIII*, c. 26 Allured to.. misbeleue miscreaunce and contempt of God. **1590** SPENSER *F.Q.* II. viii. 51 Paynim..if thou wilt renounce thy miscreaunce,..Life will I graunt thee. **1863** YULE tr. *Jordanus' Mirab. Descr.* (Hakl. Soc.) xiv. 56 Their preachers [*sc.* Mohammedans] run about..in order to turn all to their own miscreance. **1864** KINGSLEY *Rom. & Teut.* xi. 311 The Crescent was master of the Cross; and beyond the Pyrenees all was slavery and 'miscreance'. **1876** RUSKIN *Fors Clav.* lxxii. 384 By the faith that is in it, what..good it can..do, by the miscreance in it, what mischief it can do.

† **miscreance**^{2}. *Obs. rare.* [irreg. f. MIS-^{2} + L. *crē-(crēscĕre)* to grow + -ANCE. Cf. OF. *mescreu* misgrown.] = MISGROWTH.

1658 A. FOX tr. *Würtz' Surg.* III. Introd. 218 Earth is the mother of all fruits, yet hath it many miscreance [orig. *viel Missgewaechse*]. **1658** —— tr. *Würtz' Childr. Bk.* 359 Unless there be some miscreance, or other unshapednesse about them.

miscreancy ('mɪskriːənsɪ). [f. MISCREANT + -ANCY, after *miscreance*.]

1. Misbelief; = MISCREANCE^1 1. Now *arch.*

1611 COTGR., *Mescreance*, miscreancie, misbeleefe. **1630** in Rushw. *Hist. Coll.* (1659) I. App. 33 Treasons..against the Celestial Majesty, as Schism, Heresie, Miscreancy. **1726** AYLIFFE *Parergon* 208 The more usual Causes of this Deprivation are such as these..Schism, Heresy, Miscreancy, Atheism. **1840** DE QUINCEY *Essenes* in *Blackw. Mag.* XLVII. 469/2 Does the audacity of man present us with such another instance of perfidious *miscreancy*? God the Jehovah anxious for the honour of Jupiter and Mercury!

2. Villainy, depravity. Also semi-*concr.*

1804 J. LARWOOD *No Gun Boats* 30 In the envious miscreancy of the men..*la Sexe* does not participate. **1851** W. ANDERSON *Expos. Popery* (1878) 75 The attempt of a perjured miscreancy to deliver England up to the domination of the obscene Italian Impostor. **1875** CALDER *Nat. Tribes Tasmania* 68 The savages..had long been the objects of the miscreancy of the sealers, and hated the white race accordingly.

miscreant ('mɪskriːənt), *a.* and *sb.* Also 4–6 -creaunt, 6 -croyaunte. [a. OF. *mescreant* :—popular L. **minuscrēdentem*: see MIS-^{2} and CREANT *a.*^{1}] A. *adj.*

1. Misbelieving, heretical; 'unbelieving', 'infidel'. Now *arch.*, with some notion of sense 2.

c **1330** *Arth. & Merl.* 5227 (Kölbing) Grete hepes him lay about Of mani paiem miscreaunt. **1419** in Ellis *Orig. Lett.* Ser. II. I. 87 Sir John Oldcastell, that was myscreant and unboxome to the lawe of God. **1532** MORE *Confut. Barnes* VIII. Wks. 774/1 Al miscreant Painyms, all false Jewes, al false heretikes. **1562** LEGH *Armory* 26 b, If he [a Christian] ..kill an heathen gentleman..he shall beare the armes.. without any difference, sauing only ye word of ye same miscreant gentleman. **1633** T. ADAMS *Exp. 2 Peter* iii. 4 All their [*sc.* Atheists'] virulent and miscreant positions shall perish with them in unquenchable flames. **1715** ROWE *Lady Jane Gray* v. Wks. 1728 III. 69 To break thro' all Engagements made with Hereticks, And keep no Faith with such a Miscreant Crew. **1823** SCOTT *Quentin D.* xvii, Such a miscreant dog as this Boar of Ardennes, who is worse than a whole desert of Saracen heathens. **1844** MACAULAY *Misc. Writ.* (1889) 310 No outrage committed by the Catholic warrior on the miscreant enemy could deserve punishment. **1865** KINGSLEY *Herew.* vi, The gates of the pit were too narrow for their miscreant souls.

2. Depraved, villainous, base.

1593 G. HARVEY *Pierce's Super.* 176 The Ring leader of the corruptest bawdes, and miscreantest rakehells in Italy. **1725** POPE *Odyss.* XVII. 667 All the miscreant race of human kind. **1818** COBBETT *Pol. Reg.* XXXIII. 381 The miscreant ministers and judges and spies who had been the abettors of that tyrant House. *c* **1820** S. ROGERS *Italy* (1839) 245 A miscreant crew, That now no longer serve me. **1850** S. DOBELL *Roman* i. Poet. Wks. (1875) 18 That..sneaks downcast With craven tail and miscreant trepidation To kennel and to collar.

B. *sb.*

1. A misbeliever, heretic; an 'unbeliever', 'infidel'. Now *arch.*

138. WYCLIF *Sel. Wks.* III. 303 A litel covent of Sathanas synagoge, þat ben moche worse þan heþene myscreauntis. *c* **1400** *Three Kings Cologne* 2 þese þree kynges, þat of myscreauntes were þe first byleuyng men. **1470–85** MALORY *Arthur* XXI. xiii. 860 These foure knyghtes dyd many batayles vpon the myscreantes or turkes. **1550** J. COKE *Eng. & Fr. Heralds* §55 (1877) 73 Alvred kynge of Englande.. fought agaynst the Danes and other myscreantes .LVI. battayles. **1554** T. MARTIN *Marr. of Priests* Bb iij b, If the vnbeleuer or miscroyaunte dooe departe, let him departe. **1597** HOOKER *Eccl. Pol.* v. lxiii. §1 We are not therefore ashamed of the Gospell of our Lord Iesus Christ because miscreants in skorne haue vpbraided vs. **1632** LITHGOW *Trav.* x. 477 A blasphemous miscreant, against their Pope, their Lady, and their Church. **1668** M. CASAUBON *Credulity* (1670) 81 Enough to make any miscreant, (professing outwardly Christianity) to blush. **1719** DE FOE *Crusoe* (Globe) 584 With a Caravan of Miscreants, as he call'd them, that is to say, Christians. **1788** GIBBON *Decl. & F.* lviii. VI. 42 [Soliman's] generosity to the miscreants was interpreted as treason to the Christian cause. **1840** DE QUINCEY *Essenes* in *Blackw. Mag.* XLVII. 469/1 Now he [*sc.* Josephus] will reveal himself (in the literal sense of the word) as a *miscreant*. **1873** DIXON *Two Queens* IV. XIX. v. 27 A miscreant who had raised his impious hands against the Vicar of Christ.

transf. **1660** F. BROOKE tr. *Le Blanc's Trav.* 17, I know many miscreants, that doubt whether the world hath such a beast [*sc.* a unicorn]. *a* **1681** WHARTON *Wks.* (1683) 45 There ..ever have been some Hereticks and Miscreants, who rail ..against Astrology.

2. A vile wretch; a villain, rascal.

1590 SPENSER *F.Q.* II. vi. 39 'Vile Miscreaunt', (said he) 'whither dost thou flye The shame and death, which will thee soone invade?' **1593** SHAKS. *Rich. II*, I. i. 39 Thou art a Traitor, and a Miscreant. **1657** EVELYN *Diary* 25 Dec., As we went up to receive the Sacrament the miscreants held their muskets against us. **1710** STEELE *Tatler* No. 101 ¶1 These Miscreants are a Set of Wretches we Authors call Pirates. **1780** BENTHAM *Princ. Legisl.* xiii. §1 The miscreant who would commit murder that he might succeed to an inheritance. **1835** LYTTON *Rienzi* I. iii, He belongs to a horrible gang of miscreants, sworn against all order and peace. **1870** E. PEACOCK *Ralf Skirl.* III. 251 The miscreant, fully armed, set out on his errand of blood.

Hence †**miscre'antic** *a.*, villainous.

1793 J. WILLIAMS *Life Ld. Barrymore* 87 The miscreantic, pallid, hell-born, pestilential group. **179.** [J. WILLIAMS] *Crying Epistle* 59 *note*, Mr. Pitt has apparently as little respect for individual worth..as the most vile and miscreantic of his predecessors.

'**miscreantly,** *adv.* *rare*$^{-1}$. [f. MISCREANT + -LY^2.] Wretchedly.

a **1734** NORTH *Life Sir Dudley North* (1744) 123 The common Sort, who are miscreantly poor, and the most faithless Wretches upon Earth.

miscre'ate, *v.* *rare.* [MIS-^{1} 1.] *trans.* To create amiss. Also **miscreating** *vbl. sb.* and *ppl. a.*

1603 HARSNET *Pop. Impost.* 83 What a wonderfull Saint-maker is Tyburne by this, that in a quarter of an houre shall miscreate a Saint [etc.]. **1670** LD. BROOKE *Monarchy* lxxi. Wks. (Grosart) I. 30 Yet both the head and members finite are And must still by their miscreating marre. **1841–4** EMERSON *Ess.* Ser. I. iv. (1876) 110 We miscreate our own evils. **1880** MEREDITH *Tragic Com.* (1881) 47 The thick-featured sodden satyr of her miscreating fancy.

'**miscreate,** *pa. pple.* and *ppl. a.* [MIS-^{1} 2.] = next. Also *absol.*

1590 SPENSER *F.Q.* II. x. 38 He..Ymner slew of Logris miscreate. **1599** SHAKS. *Hen. V*, I. ii. 16 That you should.. nicely charge your vnderstanding Soule, With opening Titles miscreate. **1607** R. WILKINSON *Merchant Royall* 15 To see a woman created in Gods image so miscreate..and deformed, with her..foolish fashions. **1868** BROWNING *Ring & Bk.* VI. 1478 Creation purged o' the miscreate, man redeemed. **1871** SWINBURNE *Songs bef. Sunrise* Prel. 53 Fancies and passions miscreate By man in things dispassionate.

miscre'ated, *ppl. a.* [MIS-^{1} 2.] Created or formed improperly or unnaturally; mis-shapen, misformed. Also used as an abusive epithet.

In the first quot. a mistranslation.

1585 T. WASHINGTON tr. *Nicholay's Voy.* IV. xxxvi. 160 b, These wretched Græcians are left vnder the miserable seruitude of these miscreated Mahometists [orig. *des mescreans Mahometistes*]. **1590** SPENSER *F.Q.* II. vii. 42 For nothing might abash the villein bold, Ne mortall steele emperce his miscreated mould. **1596** NASHE *Saffron Walden* G 2 b, An Oration, including the miscreated words and sentences in the Doctors Booke. **1667** MILTON *P.L.* II. 683 What art thou,..That dar'st..advance Thy miscreated Front athwart my way? **1712** HENLEY *Spect.* No. 396 ¶2 That Mongrel miscreated (to speak in Miltonic) kind of Wit, vulgarly termed the Pun. **1778** WESLEY *Wks.* (1872) XIV. 278 A miscreated phantom, called 'The Spiritual Magazine'. **1826** J. WILSON *Noct. Ambr.* Wks. 1855 I. 167 Every scraper on catgut as intent on the miscreated noise, as if [etc.]. **1831** TRELAWNY *Adv. Younger Son* ii. 26 Ill-finished, dwarfish, or miscreated abortions. **1868** SWINBURNE *Blake* 42 This monstrous nomenclature, this jargon of miscreated things in chaos.

miscre'ation. [MIS-^{1} 4.] **a.** The action of creating badly or improperly. **b.** *concr.* A miscreated thing; something ill-formed or mis-shapen.

1852 GILFILLAN *Martyrs Sc. Covenant* vii. 132 One of the vast creatures of the bygone chaos—the magnificent miscreations of Geology, interesting..as a fossil remain. **1871** C. KINGSLEY in *Devon. Assoc. Trans.* IV. 378 Great dirty warrens of houses,..peopled with savages and imps of our own miscreation. **1880** SWINBURNE *Stud. in Song* 202 Formless form, incarnate miscreation.

miscre'ative, *a.* [MIS-^{1} 6.] Creating or forming amiss.

1819 SHELLEY *Prometh. Unb.* I. 448 The all-miscreative brain of Jove. **1890** SWINBURNE *Autumn Vision* vi, Darkening with its miscreative spell Light.

miscre'ator. [MIS-^{1} 5.] One who miscreates.

1818 BYRON *Ch. Har.* IV. cxxv, Circumstance, that unspiritual god And miscreator.

† **mis'credence.** *Obs. rare*$^{-1}$. [Alteration of MISCREANCE after *credence*.] Misbelief.

1603 HOLLAND *Plutarch's Mor.* 1346 The Governour of Cilicia is..doubtfull..whether there be gods or no ? upon infirmity, as I take it, of miscredance and unbeliefe.

† **mis'credent.** *Obs.* [Alteration of MISCREANT after L. *crēdent-em* (see CREDENT). Cf. It. *miscredente*.] = MISCREANT *sb.*

1480 *Robt. Deuyll* (1827) 49 The myscredaunte Sarasyns. **1577** STANYHURST *Descr. Irel.* in *Holinshed* (1808) VI. 36 A dungeon appointed for offendors and miscredents. **1847** HALLIWELL, *Miscredent*, a miscreant. *Devon.*

mis'credit, *sb.* [MIS-^{1} 7.] Disbelief.

1565 W. ALLEN in Fulke *Def. Purg.* xi. 101 b, There dare no man..affirme that the doctrine of Purgatory is hourtfull to vertuous life, the only miscreditt whereof, hath vtterly banished al good Christian condicions.

mis'credit, *v.* [MIS-^{1} 7.] *trans.* To disbelieve.

1554 J. PHILPOT *Exam. & Writings* (Parker Soc.) 351, I can not otherwise do in believing them, but miscredit thee. **1565** STAPLETON tr. *Bæda's Hist. Ch. Eng.* Pref. 4 To miscredit the perfect behauiour of our primitiue church, and the miracles wrought therein. **1652** BENLOWES *Theoph.* Pref., If thou wilt not prejudice thine own Charity by miscrediting me.

mis'credited, *ppl. a.* [MIS-^{1} 2.] Disbelieved.

1837 CARLYLE *Fr. Rev.* I. VII. vii. 372 The miscredited Twelve hasten back to the Château for an 'answer in writing'.

mis'creed. *poet.* [MIS-^{1} 4.] A mistaken creed.

a **1821** KEATS *Sonnet on Fame* ii. Wks. (1884) 413 Why then should man..Spoil his salvation for a fierce miscreed? **1822** SHELLEY *Hellas* Prol. 106 Tyranny which arms Adverse miscreeds..To stamp..Upon the name of Freedom.

mis'criticize, *v.* *rare.* [MIS-^{1} 1.] To criticize adversely or wrongly.

1877 SWINBURNE *Lett.* (1960) III. 275 Attacked and miscriticized in the Saturday Review and the Academy.

† **mis'crooked,** *a.* *Obs. rare*$^{-1}$. [MIS-^{1} 6.] Bent awry, deformed.

1398 TREVISA *Barth. De P.R.* VI. x. (Tollemache MS.), She strecceþ oute his lymis..to kepe..þe childe þat he be not defacit with miscrokid lymes.

mis'crop, *v.* *rare.* [MIS-^{1} 1.] *trans.* To sow (a field) with a crop out of rotation. Also *absol.*

1844 H. STEPHENS *Bk. Farm* III. 1222 A field may be miscropped in order to bring it the more quickly into the legitimate rotation of the farm. *Ibid.* 1317 A better notion of farming than to miscrop prevails.

mis'cry, *v.* *dial.* ? *Obs.* Also miscree. [app. alteration of DESCRY *v.*^{1}, by substitution of the prefix MIS-^{1} 9.] *trans.* To descry, discover, detect.

1645 N. DRAKE *Diary Siege Pontefract* (Surtees) 76 One of them was taken, being miscryed by the boy which went out the night before. **1674** RAY *N. C. Words* 33 *Miscreed*: descryed, This I suppose is also only a rustick word, and nothing else but the word *descried* corrupted. **1703** THORESBY *Let. to Ray* Gloss., *Miscryed*, discovered. **1847** HALLIWELL, *Miscreed*, discovered, detected, decried, depreciated. *North.*

mis'cue, *sb.* Also mis-cue, miss cue. [f. MIS-^{1} 4 (or perh. orig. stem of MISS *v.*^{1}) + CUE *sb.*^{3}]

a. A failure to strike the ball properly with the cue.

1873 BENNETT & 'CAVENDISH' *Billiards* 9 So long as the point of the cue was flat and unyielding, if the ball was not struck precisely in the centre, the consequence was a miss cue. *Ibid.* 33 A miss-cue. **1906** *Westm. Gaz.* 22 May 9/3 When Roberts wanted only two to complete his 'points' for the afternoon he made a mis-cue.

b. Hence in other sports, and *transf.* or *fig.*, an error resulting in a failure of some sort.

1883 in *Amer. Speech* (1965) XL. 130 When I escort a lady I..have a..Havana And puff it all the time And should she make a small miscue And knock it from my mouth, [etc.]. **1920** ADE *Hand-Made Fables* 26 It suggested that there had been a Miscue at the Christening. **1942** BERREY & VAN DEN BARK *Amer. Thes. Slang* §170/2 Error; mistake; blunder... Miscue. **1958** J. A. BARLOW *Elem. Rifle Shooting* (ed. 5) v. 56 The idea..is to be able to put sufficient force behind the bolt to eliminate any chance of a miscue—in other words, a failure to close the bolt. **1970** *Washington Post* 30 Sept. D1/7 One Oriole scored, another took third on the miscue and John Oates' sacrifice fly made it 2-2.

So **mis'cue** *v.*, to make a miscue; also *transf.* and *fig.*; **mis'cued** *ppl. a.*; **mis'cueing** *vbl. sb.*

1894 *Sheffield Daily Tel.* 29 Mar. 8/5 Dawson had a promising opening of potting the red, but mis-cued. **1929** *Times* 1 Nov. 7/4 At the end of the last of these breaks he missed a difficult *massé* cannon, through partly miscueing. **1941** G. HEYER *Envious Casca* xii. 219 Mathilda shied away from the thought, miscued, and straightened herself. **1941** J. SMILEY *Hash House Lingo* 38 *Miscue*, make an error. **1955** I. PEEBLES *On Ashes* x. 100 Bailey tried to hook Johnston and miscued so that the ball bounced off his pads. **1962** *Times* 3 Jan. 3/7 His miscued strokes always went up to score disconcertingly. **1962** *Sunday Times* 25 Feb. 22/7 Miss Truman was now mis-cueing. **1970** *Sunday Tel.* 1 Nov. 32/7 Southgate went nearest to a goal when Neale cut in from the left but Walker miscued badly.

†**'misculate,** *ppl. a. Obs. rare*$^{-1}$. [ad. late L. *misculāt-us*, pa. ppl. of *misculāre* (whence OF. *mesler*, etc.: see MEDDLE *v.*).] Mingled.

1632 LITHGOW *Trav.* VIII. 364 In this misculat iourneying of paine & pleasure.

†**mis'dain,** *v. Obs.* [See MIS-^{1} 9. But cf. MISDEEM.] *trans.* To be mistrustful of. So **mis'dainful** *a. dial.*, suspicious.

1558 GOODMAN *How to Obey* 201 Papistes..Of whom to be misdained or slandered, is in the eyes of the godly, no small commendation. **1879** [see MISDEEMFUL].

mis'date, *sb.* [MIS-^{1} 4.] A wrong date. Hence **mis'dateful** *a.*, abounding in wrong dates.

1858 CARLYLE *Fredk. Gt.* x. v. II. 642 They abound in small errors, in misdates, mistakes. **1862** *Ibid.* XIII. ix. III. 536 Poor Bielfeld being in this Chapter very fantastic, misdateful to a mad extent.

mis'date, *v.* [MIS-^{1} 1.] *trans.* To assign or affix a wrong date to; to date wrong. Also *absol.* Also **mis'dated** *ppl. a.*

1586 STANYHURST *Cont. Chron. Irel.* Ep. in Holinshed II, If he misdate, he is named a falsifier. *a* **1626** BACON *Charge agst. Earl of Somerset* in *Baconiana* (1679) 31 That you did deface,..and misdate all Writings that might give light to the Impoisonment. **1671** *Rhode Island Col. Rec.* (1857) II. 422 Why and how the letter was soe long a cominge..wee cannot but wonder; save as wee may suppose it was misdated. **1728** MORGAN *Algiers* II. iv. 289 This Author seems to have misdated those occurrences. **1742** YOUNG *Nt. Th.* v. 777 In hoary youth Methusalems may die; O how mis-dated on their flatt'ring tombs! **1815** *Paris Chit-chat* (1816) III. 144 His card of invitation was accidentally mis-dated, and he did not arrive till the day after the feast. **1858** CARLYLE *Fredk. Gt.* v. vi. I. 606 Trusting to memory alone, she misdates, mistakes, misplaces. **1892** *Times* 23 Jan. 13/6 Mis-dated newspapers. *Ibid.*, The practice of mis-dating newspapers and other periodical publications.

mis'deal, *sb. Cards.* [f. next.] An error in dealing.

1850 *Bohn's Handbk. Games* 255 The turn up being anterior to the mis-deal. **1862** 'CAVENDISH' *Whist* (1879) 8 A misdeal loses the deal. **1886** *Euchre: how to play it* 108.

mis'deal, *v.* [f. MIS-^{1} 1 + DEAL *v.*; in first sense after Du. *misdeelen*.]

†**1.** *intr.* To distribute unfairly. *Obs.*

1481 CAXTON *Reynard* (Arb.) 7 Knowe not ye how ye mysdeled on the plays whiche he threwe down fro the carre?

2. To deal or act improperly.

1561, etc. [see MISDEALING.]

3. *Cards.* To make a mistake in dealing: usually *intr.*, but occas. *trans.*

[**1746** HOYLE *Whist* (ed. 6) 10 If the Dealer should happen to miss Deal.] **1850** *Bohn's Handbk. Games* 254 On mis-dealing the entire hand. **1861** DICKENS *Gt. Expect.* viii, She won the game, and I dealt. I misdealt. **1891** *Spectator* 10 Jan., She can never be persuaded that she has misdealt until the cards have been carefully counted..three times.

fig. (cf. 2). **1868** BROWNING *Ring & Bk.* IV. 435 Fie on you, all the Honours in your fist, Countship, Househeadship,—how have you misdealt!

mis'dealing, *vbl. sb.* [MIS-^{1} 3.] Wrong or improper dealing; †wrong-doing, evil conduct.

1561 DAUS tr. *Bullinger on Apoc.* (1573) 14 b, Let us take heede that we put not Gods so great benefites from vs through our owne misdealynges. **1571** GOLDING *Calvin on Ps.* xxxiv. 15 To abstein from al misdealing and to enure themselves to weldoing. **1587** —— *De Mornay* xx. (1592) 319 They..which refreyne from misdealing for feare of mans Lawe. **1863** H. COX *Instit.* I. x. 229 Misdealings with the public revenue. **1902** *Westm. Gaz.* 4 Feb. 3/2 Captain N.., as an old cavalry officer, could not stomach the scandalous misdealing with horses that had taken place.

misde'cide, *v.* [MIS-^{1} 1.] *intr.* To make a wrong decision.

1802-12 BENTHAM *Ration. Judic. Evid.* (1827) I. 270 It is ..possible for the judge..to misdecide, without any regard to the evidence. **1830** *Examiner* 659/2 Nor can they misdecide from incompetency or any other cause of misdecision, without incurring shame.

misde'cision. [MIS-^{1} 4.] Wrong decision or judgement.

1802-12 BENTHAM *Ration. Judic. Evid.* (1827) I. 28 The danger of..misdecision on the part of the judge. *Ibid.* II. 137, IV. 48. **1849** GROTE *Greece* II. xlvi. V. 528 The dikast trial at Athens..had in it only the same ingredients of error and misdecision as the English jury.

misdeed (mɪsˈdiːd). [OE. *misdǽd* = OS. *misdâd*, OFris. *misdede*, MLG. *misdât* (MDu. *misdaet*, Du. *misdaad*), OHG. *missi-*, *missetât*, *misso-*, *missidât* (MHG. *missetât*, G. *missetat*), Goth. *missadêþs*: see MIS-^{1} 4 and DEED *sb.*] An evil deed; a wrong action; an offence; a crime. †In ME. also in collective sense = misdoings.

c **879** ÆLFRED *Gregory's Past. C.* liii. 413 Mine misdæda bioð simle beforan me. *a* **1200** *Moral Ode* 130 A hwilke time se eure Mon of þinchþ his mis-dede [*MS. Trin.* misdade]. *c* **1200** ORMIN 10618 Þat missdede þat wass don þurrh Adam & þurrh Eve. *c* **1290** *S. Eng. Leg.* I. 32/86 Lo here godes lomb, þat bi-nimeth þe worldes mis-dede. **1340** *Ayenb.* 114 Voryef ous oure misdedis ase we uoryeueþ to ham. *c* **1386** CHAUCER *Pars. T.* ℙ206 He was woundid for oure mysdede, and defouled by oure felonyes. **1470-85** MALORY *Arthur* XVI. xiv. 683 Ye lefte me..and suffred me in perylle of deth ..And for that mysdede now I ensure you but deth, for wel haue ye deserued it. **1535** COVERDALE *Ps.* l. 9 Turne thy face fro my synnes, and put out all my myszdedes. **1663** BUTLER *Hud.* I. iii. 349 Like caitiff vile, that for misdeed Rides with his face to rump of steed. **1726** POPE *Odyss.* XXII. 290 That impious race to all their past misdeeds Would add our blood. **1841** ELPHINSTONE *Hist. India* II. 53 These misdeeds were not entirely unmixed with good actions.

†**mis'deedy,** *a. Obs.* [f. prec. + -Y. Cf. MDu. *misdadich*, Du. *misdadig*, MDa. *misdædig*.] Doing wrong.

13.. *Cursor M.* 18279 (Gött.) For mani wick and misdedi [*a* **1425** *Trin.* mis dedy] Has þu nu here tint forþi.

†**mis'deem,** *sb. Obs.* [prob. f. next, but cf. DEEM *sb.*] Misjudgement.

1593 LYLY in *Phœnix Nest* Wks. (1902) III. 477 Such life leads Loue entangled with misdeemes. **1602** WARNER *Alb. Eng.* XII. lxxv. 313 What should we say his Ioy, that his Mis-deemes did sort to this?

mis'deem, *v.* Now chiefly *arch.* and *poet.* (See also MISDAIN.) [MIS-^{1} 1. Cf. ON. *misdœma*.]

1. *trans.* To form an unfavourable judgement of, think evil of. *Obs.*

c **1375** *Sc. Leg. Saints* xi. (*Symon & Iudas*) 370 Ws afferis til helpe saklas men, bot to mysdeme na man kene. [Leg. Aur. *Nocentes perdere non decet.*] **1509** BARCLAY *Shyp of Folys* (1570) 63 When he by gelousy His wife suspecteth.. Or her misdeemeth, and kepeth in straitly. *a* **1529** SKELTON *Bouge of Court* 137 The seconde was Suspecte, which that dayly Mysdempte eche man. **1590** SPENSER *F.Q.* I. vii. 49 Till all unweeting an Enchaunter..made him to misdeeme My loyalty. *Ibid.* III. x. 29 As much disdeigning to be so misdempt, Or a war-monger to be basely nempt. **1628** GAULE *Pract. Theories* (1629) 96 His Iealousie hasts not to reuenge, while he cannot but misdeeme her. **1767** LEWIS *Statius* II. 370 He..saw his Friends misdeem'd in Crouds resort, To bask beneath the Sunshine of the Court.

†**2.** *intr.* To form an unfavourable judgement, think ill (*of*). *Obs.*

1388 WYCLIF *Num.* xiv. 11 How long schal this puple bacbite me [*gloss*, ether mysdeme of me]? **1496** *Dives & Pauper* (W. de W.) I. xlv. 86/2 To mysdeme of his euen crysten. **1548** UDALL, etc. *Erasm. Par. Matt.* i. 19 True honesty is neyther redy to misdeme, nor hasty to reuenge. **1671** MILTON *P.R.* I. 424 What but thy malice mov'd thee to misdeem Of righteous Job.

3. To have a wrong opinion of, be mistaken in one's view of.

c **1384** CHAUCER *H. Fame* 92 That take hit [*sc.* my tale] wel, and scorne hit noght, Ne hit misdemen in her thoght. **1570** *Henry's Wallace* II. 352 Be war that ȝe do nocht misdeme my taille. **1593** G. FLETCHER *Licia* To Rdr., Men unfitte to knowe what love meanes; deluded fondlie with their owne conceit, misdeeming so divine a fancie. **1616** BRETON *Invect. agst. Treason* (Grosart) 5/2 Where Wisdomes care can neuer truthe misdeeme. **1677** GILPIN *Demonol.* (1867) 257 Though such men are under God's favour, yet they misdeem it, and think God is angry with them. **1784** COWPER *Task* IV. 685 Hence too the field of glory, as the world misdeems it. **1848** LYTTON *Harold* II. ii, Nor misdeem me, that I, humble, unmitred priest, should be thus bold. **1875** LOWELL *Under Old Elm* VIII, If ever with distempered voice or pen We have misdeemed thee, here we take it back.

b. *trans.* To suppose (a person or thing) erroneously to be (something else); to mistake (a thing) *for* another.

1667 DRYDEN *Secr. Love* v. Wks. 1701 I. 185 My grace to Philocles mis-deem'd my Love! ? **1802** WORDSW. *Sonn.*, '*Desponding Father*', Misdeem it not a cankerous change. **1829** SOUTHEY *All for Love* VI. xxiv, Thy thoughts possest With one too painful theme, Their own imaginations For reality misdeem. **1872** A. DE VERE *Leg. St. Patrick, St. P. at Cashel* 65 Demons misdeemed for gods.

c. with adj. or phr. as compl.

1835 TRENCH *Sonnet 'Look, dearest, what a glory'*, If, having shared the light, we should misdeem That light our own. **1852** ROBERTSON *Serm.* Ser. IV. xxxviii. (1863) 291 As if some poor miserable minister or teacher, rejoicing over his success, were to misdeem the work his own. **1885-94** R. BRIDGES *Eros & Psyche* Mar. I. ii, The wealth which men misdeem of much avail.

4. To form a wrong judgement (*of*); to hold a mistaken opinion.

a **1300** *Cursor M.* 27742 Wreth..Flites, scendes and misdenisse [*c* **1375** *Fairf.* fliting shindis & misdemis; *a* **1400** *Cott. Galba* It makes fliteing and misdemes] Man aun wiit it fra him cleuisse [*other texts* flemis]. *c* **1386** CHAUCER *Merch. T.* 1166 He that misconceyveth, he misdemeth. *a* **1618** SYLVESTER *Wks.* (Grosart) II. 335/1 Then doome not rashly, lest you may misdeem. **1629** H. BURTON *Truth's Triumph* 225 Misdeeming and doubting of the remission of sinnes. **1667** MILTON *P.L.* IX. 301 Misdeem not then, If such affront I labour to avert From thee alone, which [etc.]. **1779** MASON *Eng. Garden* III. 536 Whom elder Thales, and the Bard of Thebes Held first of things terrestrial; nor misdeem'd. **1791** COWPER *Iliad* I. 528, I..much misdeem Of my endeavour, or my prayer shall speed. **1814** CARY *Dante, Hell* xxxii. 118 Farther on, If I misdeem not, Soldanieri bides. *Ibid.*, *Paradise* XXVI. 73 At his sudden waking, he misdeems Of all around him. **1839** WORDSW. *Mem. Tour Scotl.* 1803 iii, Leaving each unquiet theme Where gentlest judgments may misdeem. **1884** BIBLE (R.V.) *Deut.* xxxii. 27 Lest their adversaries should misdeem.

b. To suppose mistakenly.

1596 SPENSER *State Irel.* Wks. (Globe) 609/1, I will rather thinke the cause of this evill..to proceede rather of the unsoundness of the Counsells..which [etc.]..then of any such..appoyntment of God, as you misdeeme. **1600** HAKLUYT *Voy.* (1810) III. 186 Least any man should misdeeme that God doth resist all attempts intended that way. **1817** SHELLEY *Rev. Islam* XII. x, He misdeems That he is wise, whose wounds do only bleed Inly for self. **1839-52** BAILEY *Festus* 223 He by..instigating all the soul's vain aims, Misdeems to cause thee lose God.

†**5.** *trans.* To have a suspicion or inkling of; to suspect the existence or occurrence of (some evil).

1494 FABYAN *Chron.* v. cxvii. 92 The Kynge not mysdemynge eny thyng of this Conspyred treason. *a* **1553** UDALL *Royster D.* IV. iii. (Arb.) 62 Surely, this fellowe misdeemeth some yll in me. *a* **1607** T. BRIGHTMAN *Brightm. Rediv.* III. (1647) 78 While wee were in Ignorance, we lay secure in our sin,..never mis-deeming our estate. **1607** TOPSELL *Four-f. Beasts* (1658) 177 The Fox..misdeemeth no harm, and entreth into the hive which is wrought close into the mouth of his den.

†**b.** *to misdeem* (a person) *for* —: to suspect him to be —. *Obs.*

c **1500** *Melusine* 265/15 [He] was so Lyke a Sarasyn that no man mysdymed hym for other than a Sarasyn.

†**6.** *intr.* To suspect something evil. *Obs.*

c **1430** *Syr Gener.* (Roxb.) 222 Jewel thoght of treason and tray..Thoo he mysdemed in this case, Whan she cam not of so long while He supposed ther yede som gyle. **1556** J. HEYWOOD *Spider & F.* iii. 25 Hath fortune wrought my foes at this time hither, And not so much as warnde me to mis-deeme. **1561** SACKVILLE *Gorboduc* I. i. 39 (Manly), If thinges do so succede As now my ielous mind misdemeth sore. **1596** LODGE *Marg. Amer.* 55 The emperour conceiuing new suspitions upon this second assault, began to misdeeme.

†**b.** const. *clause.* To suspect (that..). *Obs.*

a **1530** HEYWOOD *Play of Love* (Brandl) 516 Anone she mysdemed That I was not merely disposed, And so myght she thynke, for I disclosed No worde nor loke, but such as shewed as sadly as [etc.]. **1581** SAVILE *Tacitus, Hist.* I. xxviii. (1591) 17 [He] gaue most men to misdeeme by his dealing, that he was somewhat of counsel with the case [orig. *præbuit plerisque suspicionem conscientiæ*]. **1600** FAIRFAX *Tasso* x. xxxviii, Nor say I this for that I ought misdeeme That Egypts promis'd succours faile vs might.

mis'deemer. [MIS-^{1} 5.] One who misjudges.

1616 *Manifest. Abp. Spalato's Motives* App. iii. 6 This some misdeemers impute to their penury.

mis'deemful, *a. dial.* (See also MISDAINFUL.) [f. MISDEEM *v.* + -FUL.] Having a false judgement *of*; suspicious *of*.

c **1750** SHENSTONE *Wks.* (1777) I. 304 He too, misdeemful of his wholesome law, Ev'n he, expiring, gave his treasur'd gold To fatten monks on Salem's distant soil! **1879** MISS JACKSON *Shropsh. Word-bk.*, *Misdeemful*, suspicious. *Misdeenful, misdainful*, same as above—corrupted forms.

mis'deeming, *vbl. sb.* [MIS-^{1} 3.] Misjudging; false judgement; †suspicion.

? **1468** *Paston Lett.* II. 313 But for gelosye and mysdemyng of peple that hafe me yn greete awayt. **1491** CAXTON *Vitas Patr.* (W. de W. 1495) I. xxxvii. 50 b, To the ende that they..sholde haue noo suspecyon ne misdemyng. **1571** GOLDING *Calvin on Ps.* iv. 2 His innocencie was overwhelmed..with the misdeemings of the common people. **1590** SPENSER *F.Q.* I. iv. 2 After that he had faire Una lorne, Through light misdeeming of her loialtie. **1612** J. MASON *Anat. Sorc.* 33 To take away all occasion of misdeeming.

mis'deeming, *ppl. a.* [MIS-^{1} 2.] Misjudging; mistaken (of persons, their opinions, etc.); *dial.* suspicious. *Obs.*

? **1468** *Paston Lett.* II. 313 The world ys to mysdemyng and redy to make dyvysyon and debate. **1584** BABINGTON *Confer. Frailty & Faith* (1596) 45 A suspicious misdeeming mind of euery bodie. **1590** SPENSER *F.Q.* I. ii. 3 Covered with darkenes and misdeeming night. **1648** J. BEAUMONT *Psyche* v. lxiii. (Grosart) I. 83 O no, misdeeming Sovereign; I am sent The soft Ambassador of Peace to you. **1760-72** H. BROOKE *Fool of Qual.* (1809) IV. 98 Pardon the misdeeming transports of your lover. **1819** SHELLEY *Cenci* v. i. 87 The misdeeming crowd Which judges by what seems. **1848** A. B. EVANS *Leicestersh. Words, Misdeeming*, suspicious. 'She's sadly misdeeming'.

†**misde'light,** *sb. Obs.* [MIS-^{1} 4.] Delight in something wrong.

? **13..** *All Saints* 510 in *Archiv Stud. neu. Spr.* LXXIX. 440 If any wyked sprete had brouȝt hym in myssedelyte.

†**misde'light,** *v. Obs.* [MIS-^{1} 1.] *pass.* To be wrongly delighted.

1640 BP. HALL *Chr. Moder.* I. x. 92 This hony-bagge hath ever a sting attending it; so as we are commonly plagued.. in that wherein we were mis-delighted.

misde'liver, *v.* [MIS-^{1} I.] *trans.* **a.** To deliver to the wrong person or at the wrong place. **b.** To hand down improperly.

1858 CARLYLE *Fredk. Gt.* VI. ii. II. 17 Message misdelivered by my Official Gentleman. **1885** *Law Times Rep.* LII. 324/2 The goods were misdelivered by the defendants to another firm. **1893** WESTCOTT *Chr. Aspects of Life* (1897) 408 The testimony of the Church is misdelivered if [etc.].

misde'livery. [MIS-^{1} 4.] Wrong delivery.

1859 SALA *Tw. round Clock* 34 The misdelivery of a letter. **1867** BRANDE & COX *Dict. Sci.*, etc. III. 89/2 (*Printing*) In case of any misdelivery a sheet is spoiled. **1885** *Law Times* LXXVIII. 386/1 The misdelivery by the company amounted to conversion.

†**misde'mean,** *sb. Obs.* [MIS-^{1} 4.] Misbehaviour, misdemeanour.

1602 W. BAS *Sword & Buckler* xxiii, To thinke it any misdemeasne in vs, If we..doe fall againe Into our ancient Sword and Buckler vaine. **1742** in B. Peirce *Hist. Harvard Univ.* (1833) App. 86 Sundry crimes and misdemeans whereof he was convicted. **1773** J. ROSS *Fratricide* I. 308 (MS.), A Criminal arraign'd For..some heinous misdemean.

misde'mean, *v.*^{1} [f. MIS-^{1} I + DEMEAN *v.*^{1}]

1. *refl.* To misbehave, misconduct oneself.

[**1558** in Strype *Ann. Ref.* (1709) I. i. 42 One of the Canons of Litchfield has also preached lewdly, and misdemeaned himself (those are the words in the Minutes of the Council-Book).] **1577–87** HOLINSHED *Chron.* (an. 1381) III. 434/2 Neither did the townesmen of S. Albons..thus outragiouslie misdemeane themselues. **1613** SHAKS. *Hen. VIII*, v. iii. 14 You that best should teach vs, Haue misdemean'd your selfe. *a* **1618** RALEIGH *Prerog. Parl.* (1628) 18 Iustices..that had vsed extortion, or bribery, or had otherwise misdemeaned themselues. **1689** *Col. Rec. Pennsylv.* I. 256 They did not judge the Keeper to have highly misdemeaned himself in his office of Keeper of the board Seale. **1736** CARTE *Ormonde* I. 260 Sir Luke Fitzgerald misdemeaned himself before the board by uncivil words. **1857** *Hurlstone & Norman's Rep.* (1858) II. 221 The said William Baker did..unlawfully misdemean and misconduct himself in his said service by neglecting..his said master's service.

b. *intr.* in the same sense.

1765 C. SMART tr. *Phædrus* IV. ix, When our neighbours mis-demean, Our censures are exceeding keen.

†**2.** *trans.* To misuse, abuse. *Obs.*

a **1625** SIR H. FINCH *Law* (1636) 47 Hee that misdemeaneth authority that law giueth him..shall be a wrong doer *ab initio*.

misde'mean, *v.*^{2} *rare*$^{-1}$. [f. MIS-^{1} 8 + DEMEAN *v.*^{2}] = DEMEAN *v.*^{2}

1843 LYTTON *Last Bar.* IV. ix, My Lord Scales, lift the curtain; nay, sir, it misdemeans you not.

misdemeanant (mɪsdɪˈmiːnənt). [f. MISDEMEAN *v.*^{1} + -ANT, or f. MISDEMEANOUR by substitution of suffix.] A person convicted of a misdemeanour.

1819 J. J. GURNEY *Notes on Visit to Prisons* 78 The only division of these females being that of misdemeanants from felons. Amongst the men, the classification is much more complete; for, the misdemeanants are divided into three classes, and the felons into four. **1843** *Penny Cycl.* XXV. 150/1 Misdemeanants of the first division. **1865** *Act 28–9 Vict.* c. 126 §67 In every Prison to which this Act applies Prisoners convicted of Misdemeanor, and not sentenced to Hard Labour, shall be divided into at least Two Divisions, One of which shall be called the First Division;..and a Misdemeanant of the First Division shall not be deemed to be a Criminal Prisoner within the Meaning of this Act. **1896** *Times* 30 July 5/6 Dr. Jameson and his fellow-prisoners.. were placed in the apartments reserved for first-class misdemeanants.

b. *transf.* A person guilty of misconduct.

1886 A. M. ELLIOTT in *Amer. Jrnl. of Philol.* VII. 146 They were no set of political convicts or social misdemeanants. **1892** W. BEATTY-KINGSTON *Intemperance* 34 To be compelled to slake their thirst with water would be no great hardship to these confirmed misdemeanants.

†**misde'meaned,** *ppl. a. Obs.* [MIS-^{1} 2.] Ill-conducted.

1586 HOOKER *Descr. Irel.* in Holinshed II, Bewailing with great remorse of conscience his former misdemened life.

†**misde'meaning,** *vbl. sb. Obs.* [MIS-^{1} 3.] Misconduct, misdemeanour.

1487 *Rolls of Parlt.* VI. 389/1 For othre misdemenyng of the said John Morys ayenst your Highnesse. **1492** *Plumpton Corr.* (Camden) 265 Consideringe the said Dame Joyce was innocent, & nothinge knowinge of his misdemeaninge. **1562–3** *Act 5 Eliz.* c. 9 §7 Heinous Perjuries and other Offences and Misdemeaninges. **1625** [see *misbeing*, MIS-^{1} 3]. **1706** PHILLIPS (ed. Kersey), *Misdemeanour*, a misdemeaning, or behaving one's self ill.

misde'meanist. [f. next: see -IST.] Misdemeanant.

1862 LEVER *Barrington* xviii, Never did a misdemeanist take his 'six weeks' with a more complete consciousness of penalty than did Polly sit down to that piano.

misde'meanour, -or, *sb.*^{1} Forms: see DEMEANOUR. [MIS-^{1} 4.]

1. a. Evil behaviour, misconduct. Now *rare*.

1494 FABYAN *Chron.* II. clvii. 146 For the whiche mysse demeanure of this woman, that she had innaturally slayne hir lorde and husbonde [etc.]. **1561** *Child-Marriages* (1897) 78 Whan he perceyvid this Respondent to be with child, he perceyvid her noughtie lief and misdeamenour. **1568** GRAFTON *Chron.* II. 629 This great riote and vnlawfull misdemeanour. **1579** *Termes of Law* 63 His..misdemeaner shall cause the officer..to loose his office. *a* **1639** W. WHATELEY *Prototypes* II. xxvi. (1640) 68 You..that are so wickedly gevin over to idlenesse, and drunkennesse..be ashamed of such more than beast-like misdemeanor. **1723** SHEFFIELD (Dk. Buckhm.) *Wks.* (1753) II. 104 A thousand slanders..will never here be able to give a suspicion of misdemeanor. **1775** JOHNSON *Tax. no Tyr.* 60 The whole town of Boston is distressed for the misdemeanour of a few.

b. An instance of this; a misdeed, offence.

1494 FABYAN *Chron.* VI. ccvi. 218 Some mysdemeanures and rules that were occupyed and exercysed in his absence. **1592** NASHE *Four Lett. Confut.* 52 God forbid that our forheades should for euer be blotted with our forefathers misdemeanors. **1601** R. JOHNSON *Kingd. & Commw.* (1603) 78 These misdemenors against all sence and reason. **1659** PEARSON *Creed* (1839) 490 By great and scandalous offences, by incorrigible misdemeanours, we may incur the censure of the Church of God. **1709** SWIFT *Adv. Relig.* Wks. 1751 IV. 129 If any apparent Transgression..would be imputed to him for a misdemeanor, by which he must certainly forfeit his..Station. *a* **1716** SOUTH *Serm.* (1744) IX. xii. 359 God takes a particular notice of our personal misdemeanors.

2. *Law.* One of a class of indictable offences which were formerly regarded as less heinous than those called felonies; ***high misdemeanour***: see quot. 1706. (All distinctions between a felony and a misdemeanour were abolished by the Criminal Law Act of 1967.)

1487 *Rolls of Parlt.* VI. 402/1 An Acte giving the Court of Star Chamber authority to punish divers misdemeanors. **1503–4** *Act 19 Hen. VII*, c. 14 §8 Such reteynours and offences and other Mysdemeanours as shalbe doon.. contrary to the forme of this acte. **1614** BACON *Charge touching Duels* 22 Practice to impoison, though it tooke no effect, way-laying to murder,..haue been adiudged haynous misdemeanors punishable in this Court. **1660** *Trial Regic.* 113 He charged the Prisoner at the Bar with Treason and high misdemeanors. **1706** PHILLIPS (ed. Kersey), *High Misdemeanour*, a Crime of a hainous Nature, next to High Treason. **1769** BLACKSTONE *Comm.* IV. i. 5 This general definition comprehends both crimes and misdemesnors; which, properly speaking, are mere synonymous terms. *Ibid.* vi. 80 Words spoken amount only to a high misdemesnor, and no treason. **1807** JEFFERSON *Writ.* (1830) IV. 103 The trial of Dayton for misdemeanor may as well go on at Richmond. **1807** SIR S. ROMILLY in Hansard *Parl. Deb.* Ser. I. IX. 327 He conceived that if ministers should give such a pledge.., it would be a high crime and misdemeanour. **1821** HOLFORD *Th. on Crim. Prisons* 36 Any person convicted of any misdemeanor, except libel.

3. Short for: A person imprisoned for misdemeanour; = MISDEMEANANT. (Cf. next word.)

App. in regular prison use till *c* 1820, when *misdemeanant* took its place.

1812 'A Prisoner' in *Examiner* 7 Sept. 574/2 The acts of Parliament required him to keep the felons and misdemeanours separate. **1815** *Rep. Comm. K.B.* (*etc.*) *Prisons* (Parl. Papers) 229 Four felons, nine misdemeanors, and one fine. *Ibid.* 230 The female misdemeanors I generally class with the female debtors. **1818** *Min. Evid. Comm. Prisons Metrop.* VIII. 109 For debtors, male and female, and vagrants and misdemeanors.

attrib. **1814** *Min. Evid. St. Gaols London* (Parl. Papers) App. i. 33 There are three [prisoners] for misdemeanors in the other misdemeanor ward.

†**4.** Mismanagement. *Obs. rare*$^{-1}$.

Cf. DEMEANOUR 4. But the use in the quot. was probably suggested by MANURE.

1644 BP. HALL *Serm.* Wks. 1808 V. 236 Never was there any sterility, whereof there may not be a cause given; either ..some naturall fault in the soil, or misdemeanure of the owners.

†**misde'meanour,** *sb.*^{2} *Obs.* [f. MISDEMEAN *v.* + *-our*, -OR^2.] A person guilty of a misdemeanour.

1533 *Chron. Calais* (Camden) 154 If they fynde any mysdemeanours, suspect persons or straungers stirring in the strets. **1533–4** *Act 25 Hen. VIII*, c. 3 §1 The same mysdemeanours, Felons, Robbers and burglaries [*sic*] have ..the pryvylege..of theire clergie.

†**misde'meanour,** *v. Obs. rare*$^{-1}$. [f. MISDEMEANOUR *sb.*^{1}] = MISDEMEAN *v.*^{1}

1620 J. WILKINSON *Coroners & Sherifes* 52 If any one shal refuse to enter bond or misdemeanor himselfe.

†**misde'part,** *v. Obs. rare*$^{-1}$. [MIS-^{1} I.] *trans.* To distribute unfairly.

c **1386** CHAUCER *Man of Law's Prol.* 9 Thou blamest Crist, and seyst ful bitterly, He misdeparteth richesse temporal.

misderi'vation. [MIS-^{1} 4.] A wrong derivation.

1905 *Athenæum* 464/3 This misderivation is no doubt responsible for the change of spelling of 'flet' to 'fleet'.

misde'rive, *v.* [MIS-^{1} I.]

†**1.** *trans.* To divert into a wrong channel. *Obs.*

1649 BP. HALL *Cases Consc.* III. vii. 298 Mis-deriving the well meant devotions of..pious soules into a wrong channell.

2. To assign a wrong derivation to.

1817 COLERIDGE *'Blessed are ye'* 16 To exaggerate and misderive the distress of the labouring classes in order to make them turbulent. **1822–34** *Good's Study Med.* (ed. 4) I. 103 Alimon, alimonia, alimentum.. have been commonly mis-derived by the lexicographers from *alo*, 'to nourish'.

misde'scribe, *v.* [MIS-^{1} I.] *trans.* To describe inaccurately.

1827 BENTHAM *Ration. Judic. Evid.* Wks. V. 599 When any other circumstance is misdescribed in the pleadings. **1884** *Fortn. Rev.* Dec. 847 The events..have been systematically misdescribed by..the Liberal press.

Hence **misde'scribed** *ppl. a.*, **misde'scriber**.

1889 GASQUET *Hen. VIII & Eng. Monast.* II. 495 Those kindly misdescribers, Sir Walter Scott and the author of the 'Ingoldsby Legends'. **1891** ATKINSON *Moorland Par.* 153 These misnamed, or rather misdescribed pits.

misde'scription. [MIS-^{1} 4.] Incorrect description.

1848 ARNOULD *Marine Insur.* 172 If the party insuring purposely misdescribed the vessel..the policy might be held void for such misdescription. **1885** *Law Times* LXXIX. 47/1 'Accountant' was held to be a misdescription of an accountant's clerk. **1886** DICEY *Eng. Case agst. Home Rule* (ed. 2) 225 The very heading of the Bill is a misdescription.

misde'scriptive, *a.* [MIS-^{1} 6.] Giving an inaccurate description (*of*).

1903 *Law Q. Rev.* Jan. 9 His title is therefore misdescriptive of his book. **1938** R. G. COLLINGWOOD *Princ. Art* v. 80 Calling it by that misdescriptive name, we patronizingly license the child to go on with it.

misde'sert. *Obs.* or *arch.* [MIS-^{1} 4.] The condition of being undeserving; ill-desert.

1596 SPENSER *F.Q.* VI. i. 12 My haplesse case Is not occasiond through my misdesert But through misfortune. **1656** EARL MONM. tr. *Boccalini's Advts. fr. Parnass.* 306 Those miserable creatures, who for their secret misdeserts, are..condemned to tug at an Oar. **1865** PUSEY *Truth Eng. Ch.* 192 Many of us, for our misdeserts, may be unfit for the immediate presence of God.

†**misde'serve,** *v. Obs.* [MIS-^{1} I.] **a.** *intr.* To deserve ill. **b.** *trans.* To fail to deserve.

1657 J. SERGEANT *Schism Dispach't* 77 If any be found misdeserving in the same manner. **1672** *Essex Papers* (1890) I. 47 In assuring my selfe anew of yr friendship which I have never misdeserved.

†**misde'serving,** *vbl. sb. Obs.* [MIS-^{1} 3.] Misdesert.

1540 PALSGR. *Acolastus* I ij b, Throughe thy mysdeseruing. **1611** SPEED *Hist. Gt. Brit.* VII. xxx. 317 Not stained with any aspersion of mis-deseruing. *a* **1649** DRUMM. OF HAWTH. *Hist. Jas. II*, Wks. (1711) 30 His past demerits and misdeservings.

misde'voted, *pa. pple.* [MIS-^{1} 2.] Improperly devoted; devoted to a wrong object.

1612–15 BP. HALL *Contempl.*, *O.T.* XVIII. *Asa* Wks. (1625) 1328 There were some misdeuoted to the worship of the true God. **1856** KINGSLEY *Misc.* (1859) I. 333 Twenty pages of comment on it would not have been misdevoted.

misde'votion. [MIS-^{1} 4.] Wrong or misdirected devotion.

1612 DONNE *Progr. Soul, 2nd Anniv.* 511 Here..where mis-devotion frames A thousand Prayers to Saints. **1614** BP. HALL *No Peace with Rome* §20 The priuate mis-deuotion of some superstitious old wife! **1649** MILTON *Eikon.* Wks. 1738 I. 429 The vanity, superstition, and mis-devotion of which place [*sc.* a private chapel], was a scandal.

†**misde'vout,** *a. Obs.* [MIS-^{1} 6.] Wrongly devout.

1610 DONNE *Pseudo-martyr* 359 Some kings in a mis-deuout zeale..neglected the office of gouernement to which God had called them. **1651** BP. HALL *Soliloquies* xxiii. 287, I have grieved to see poor misdevout souls under the Papacy, measuring their orisons, not by weight but by number.

mis'diagnose, *v.* [MIS-^{1} I.] *trans.* To diagnose wrongly, make a wrong diagnosis of (a condition); also, to diagnose wrongly the condition of (an individual).

1928 *Daily Express* 6 Oct. 8/6 Internal troubles which have been misdiagnosed are the most common. **1949** G. RYLE *Concept of Mind* iv. 107 The..distresses of which such feelings are diagnosed, or mis-diagnosed, as signs are not themselves feelings. **1963** *Lancet* 12 Jan. 95/1 In spite of general recognition for nearly half a century that the two conditions simulate each other, nobody can say how often torsion is misdiagnosed as 'orchitis'. **1968** *Globe & Mail* (Toronto) 5 Feb. 13/6 Many children with minimal brain dysfunction are still being misdiagnosed. **1972** *Village Voice* (N.Y.) 1 June 36/3 His primary theme, however, is that far too many of the kids being drugged have been misdiagnosed.

misdiag'nosis. [MIS-^{1} 4.] A wrong diagnosis.

1949 G. RYLE *Concept of Mind* iv. 105 Such misdiagnoses are more common in children than in grown-ups. **1965** J. POLLITT *Depression & its Treatment* iii. 43 Migraine, angina pectoris, and prolapsed intervertebral disc are the commonest misdiagnoses in this field. **1971** *Daily Colonist* (Victoria, B.C.) 28 Feb. 28/5 This is a depressingly high rate of misdiagnosis.

mis'dial, *v.* [MIS-^{1} I.] *intr.* To dial (usu. by mistake) a number other than that required on a telephone.

1964 W. MARKFIELD *To Early Grave* (1965) xii. 244 You *could* have been all along misdialing. **1967** J. GARDNER *Madrigal* i. 6 He misdialled, then got it right... The signal brut-brutted at the far end of the line. **1970** *Guardian* 27 Apr. 10/2 The Post Office say the numbers are similar to his, and people misdial.

†**mis'diet,** *sb. Obs.* [MIS-^{1} 4.] Wrong diet, improper feeding.

1528 PAYNELL *Salerne's Regim.* Pref. A j b, By our mysse dyete, and to moche surfettynge. **1590** SPENSER *F.Q.* I. iv. 23 A dry dropsie..Which by misdiet daily greater grew. **1620** SANDERSON *Serm.* I. 145 A man may have..little distempers in his body, through mis-dyet or otherwise. **1665** J. FRASER *Polichron.* (S.H.S.) 287 A place unfit for him, considering the aire and misdyet he was ingaged to grapple with.

mis'diet, *v.* ? *Obs.* [MIS-[1] 1.] *trans.* To diet improperly. Hence **mis'dieter**.

1496 *Dives & Pauper* (W. de W.) I. xxx. 68/2 Yf a man mysdyete hym & ete & drynke out of mesure. **1607** WALKINGTON *Opt. Glass* 4 Those who distemper and misdiet themselves with untimely..surfeting. *Ibid.* 16 If consorting with misdieters, he bath himself in the muddy streames of their luxury. **1617** HIERON *Wks.* II. 253 To giue his patient a charge..to take heed how hee mis-diet himselfe.

mis'dieting, *vbl. sb.* ? *Obs.* [MIS-[1] 3.] Improper feeding.

1486 *Bk. St. Albans* c viij b, The leest mysdyeting and mysentendyng sleth h[ir]. **1496** *Dives & Pauper* (W. de W.) I. xxi. 56/2 By mysdyetynge of the moder whyle she is with childe. *a* **1656** BP. HALL *Balm of Gilead* vi. §6 Wks. 1808 VIII. 158 This great body, by mis-dieting and wilful disorder, contracted these spirituall diseases.

†**mis'dight**, *pa. pple.* *Obs.* [MIS-[1] 2.] Ill-clothed; badly furnished or prepared; ill-treated, brought to misfortune.

a **1400** *Songs of London Prentices* (Percy Soc.) 3 But if might Goe before right, And will Before skill, Then is one Mill misdight. **1596** SPENSER *F.Q.* v. vii. 37 Her heart gan grudge for very deepe despight Of so unmanly maske in misery misdight. **1597** BP. HALL *Sat.* III. vii. 66 Despised Nature suit them once aright, Their bodie to their coate: both now mis-dight. **1607** R. C[AREW] tr. *Estienne's World of Wonders* 245 Their wine..Wherewith they bene each one so oft misdight [orig. *le vin, dont chacun d'eux s'enyure*].

misdi'rect, *v.* [MIS-[1] 1.] *trans.* To direct wrongly; to give a wrong direction to.

1603 FLORIO *Montaigne* II. xvii. (1632) 367 Fearing lest the contention of his will should make him to misse-direct his hand. **1768** BLACKSTONE *Comm.* III. xxiv. 390 In the hurry of a trial the ablest judge may mistake the law, and mis-direct the jury. **1868** MISS YONGE *Cameos* I. iii. 21 He himself remained to misdirect the pursuers. **1885** *Law Rep.* (14 Q.B. Div.) 694 The Court in banc will..grant a new trial on the ground that the jury were misdirected. **1897** P. WARUNG *Tales Old Regime* 129 Through the going out of the light, the blow was misdirected.

misdi'rected, *ppl. a.* [MIS-[1] 2.] Wrongly directed or applied; misguided; sent to a wrong address. Hence **misdi'rectedness**.

1790 T. BURGESS *Div. Chr.* 17 The vanity of mis-directed reason. **1828-43** TYTLER *Hist. Scot.* (1864) III. 96 In a spirit of erroneous and misdirected zeal. **1850** MARSDEN *Early Purit.* (1853) 381 The divinity of the times..was at once artificial, and to a great degree misdirected. **1886** KIPLING *Departm. Ditties*, etc. (1888) 48 It was a misdirected wire, Her husband was at Shaitanpore. **1965** A. FARRER in J. Gibb *Light on C. S. Lewis* 38 The primary function of mental pain, says Lewis, is to force our misdirectedness on our attention.

misdi'rection. [MIS-[1] 4.]

1. a. Wrong or improper direction or guidance; the action of misdirecting or the condition of being misdirected; direction to a wrong address.

1768 BLACKSTONE *Comm.* III. xxiii. 373 A new trial..is now very commonly had for the misdirection of the judge at *nisi prius*. **1830** GEN. P. THOMPSON *Exerc.* (1842) I. 228 The great object of fear to the middle classes, is the apprehended violence and misdirection of those with whom they think they would have to join. **1857** WHEWELL *Hist. Induct. Sci.* (ed. 3) I. 216 The mis-direction of their efforts. **1860** MRS. CARLYLE *Lett.* III. 48 The two notes..were received together (on account of misdirection). **1875** *Act 38 & 39 Vict.* c. 77 Order xxxix, A new trial shall not be granted on the ground of misdirection..unless..some substantial wrong or miscarriage has been thereby occasioned in the trial of the action.

b. Of the action of a conjurer, thief, etc.: distraction, guidance (of a person's attention) away from (something).

1943 A. CHRISTIE *Moving Finger* x. 124 A conjuring trick. .. You've got to make people look at the wrong thing and in the wrong place—Misdirection, they call it. **1949** *Amer. Speech* XXIV. 40 When the performer directs your attention, by word, glance, or gesture, away from a secret function, he calls the process *misdirection*. **1955** *Publ. Amer. Dial. Soc.* XXIV. 16 The thieves can apply misdirection (verbal, kinesic, tactile) to take his mind off his wallet—if only for a few seconds—and he will be astonished to find that he has been robbed. **1971** P. O'DONNELL *Impossible Virgin* iv. 71 There had been callers at the house... None of them had been genuine... It was all part of a misdirection play.

2. A wrong direction, line, or course.

1861 CRAIK *Hist. Eng. Lit.* II. 517 Whatever of misdirection any of them may have given for a time to the form of our poetry. **1887** H. S. HOLLAND *Christ or Eccles.* (1888) 8 We..wonder whether the entire movement of human life has not..taken some terrible misdirection.

†**misdi'spend**, *v.* [MIS-[1] 1.] *trans.* To spend improperly.

c **1380** *Lay Folks Catech.* (L.) 793 Who euer mysdispendys myȝtys of sowle or body or ony oþer goodis agaynst godys law. **1390** GOWER *Conf.* I. 52 That I scholde schrive As touchende of my wittes fyve, And schape that thei were amended Of that I hadde hem misdispended. *c* **1412** HOCCLEVE *De Reg. Princ.* 1303 Some riche is large, and his goode mysdespendethe In mayntenaunce of synne.

†**misdi'spense**. *Obs. rare*[-1]. [MIS-[1] 4.] Wrong expenditure.

1450 *Rolls of Parlt.* V. 180/2 The mysdispence and applying of the same.

†**misdi'stinguish**, *v.* *Obs.* [MIS-[1] 1.] *intr.* To distinguish wrongly, make wrong distinctions.

1594 HOOKER *Eccl. Pol.* III. iii. §1 So that if wee imagine a difference where there is none, because wee distinguish where we should not, it may not bee denyed that we misdistinguish. *Ibid.* III. ii. §2 Herein for two things wee are reproved; the first is misdistinguishing **1654-66** EARL ORRERY *Parthen.* (1676) 353 You may acknowledge the Error of such a misdistinguishing.

misdistribution. [MIS-[1] 4.] Wrong or faulty distribution. So **misdi'stribute** *v.*

1914 G. B. SHAW *Misalliance* Pref. p. xxxvi, Obstructing the way of the proper organization of childhood, as of everything else, lies our ridiculous misdistribution of the national income. **1920** S. ALEXANDER *Space, Time & Deity* II. III. ix. 280 Evil is misdistribution, and vice is a feature of character which wills such misdistribution. **1958** *Archit. Rev.* CXXIV. 338/1 The misdistribution of people has inevitably brought problems, chiefly that of lack of housing. **1968** *Economist* 27 July 39/1 The schools are to have another $33 million, similarly misdistributed.

misdi'vide, *v.* [MIS-[1] 1.] *trans.* To divide wrongly.

1882 in OGILVIE.

misdi'vision. [MIS-[1] 4.] **a.** An incorrect division.

1890 *Cent. Dict.* s.v., *Newt*, *newte*, an erroneous form due to misdivision of *an ewte*. **1905** JESPERSEN *Growth Eng. Lang.* 73 The result being the same misdivision of the word.

b. *spec.* in *Cytology*. The abnormal transverse (instead of longitudinal) division of a centromere at meiosis or mitosis.

1939 C. D. DARLINGTON in *Jrnl. Genetics* XXXVII. 341 (*heading*) Misdivision and the genetics of the centromere. *Ibid.* 346 Misdivision in..107 univalents consisted of the centromere dividing into two halves, as it does normally; but to these halves the wrong chromatids were attached or no chromatids at all. *Ibid.*, The simplest misdivision is that where two short arms are carried to one pole, two long arms to the other. **1972** tr. *J. Sybenga's Gen. Cytogenetics* v. 223 It happens occasionally that the centromeric region breaks up (mis-division), which results in two half chromosomes (the arms) each with a part of the centromere. *Ibid.*, After centromere mis-division, functional telocentric chromosomes may arise.

misdo (mɪs'duː), *v.* Forms: see DO *v.*[1] [OE. *misdón* = OFris. *misdua*, MDu., Du. *misdoen*, OHG. *missa-*, *missituon*, *-duan* (MHG. *missetuon*, G. *misstun*): see MIS-[1] 1 and DO *v.*[1]]

1. *intr.* To do evil or wrong; to do harm or injury *to*, *unto*, *against*. Now *rare* or *Obs.*

c **950** *Lindisf. Gosp.* John iii. 20 Hælc monn..seðe yfle *vel* mis doeð. *a* **1023** WULFSTAN *Hom.* I. (1883) 270 Ac to fela is þæra, þe ær þisan misdydan. **1154** *O. E. Chron.* (Laud MS.) an. 1135 Durste nan man misdon wið oðer on his time. *c* **1200** ORMIN 3974, & ȝiff þatt iss þatt he missdoþ Onn aniȝ kinne wise, Itt reoweþþ himm. *c* **1250** *Gen. & Ex.* 3555 He hauen sineged and misdon. *a* **1300** *Cursor M.* 7914 Ga to dauid king, and sai He has misdon again mi lai. *c* **1375** *Sc. Leg. Saints* xxxvi. (*Baptista*) 436 [He] with-stud in na degre agane þame þat in ony thing til hyme mysded. **1470-85** MALORY *Arthur* XVI. xvi. 686 Fair swete Ihesu that I haue mysdoo haue mercy vpon my sowle. *c* **1500** *Melusine* 261 There nys none that may say that euer we mysdyde..ayenst our souerayne lord. **1561** NORTON & SACKV. *Gorboduc* I. i, I knowe nothynge at all, Wher in I haue misdone vnto his Grace. **1618** WITHER *Motto, Nec Careo* Juvenilia (1633) 531 To see my Friend misdoe, I want not eyes, Nor Love to cover his infirmities. **1671** MILTON *P. R.* I. 225 The erring Soul Not wilfully mis-doing, but unware Misled. **1676** DRYDEN *State Innoc.* v. i, I have misdone; and I endure the Smart. **1875-86** *W. Somerset Gloss.*, *Misdo*, to transgress; to do amiss.

2. *trans.* With pronominal or vague object: To do amiss. ? *Obs.*

a **1060** *Laws of Æthelred* (Liebermann) 258 ȝif hit ȝeweorpeð þæt man unwilles..æniȝ þing misdeð. *a* **1200** *Moral Ode* 100 Al þet we misduden her ho hit wulleð kuðe þere. **1297** R. GLOUC. (Rolls) 491 Ere Ion..bisouȝte is grace of þat he adde misdo. *c* **1320** R. BRUNNE *Medit.* 462 What haþ he mysdo to dey þus? **1390** GOWER *Conf.* I. 122 Godd it thee foryive If thou have eny thing misdo Touchende of this. *c* **1440** HYLTON *Scala Perf.* (W. de W. 1494) II. xl, They haue kyssed and made frendes: and all is forgyuen that was mysse done. **1528** MORE *Dyaloge* III. Wks. 225/1 The thinges that they mysdo. **1592** KYD *Sp. Trag.* II. v. 28 O poore Horatio, what hadst thou misdonne. **1671** MILTON *Samson* 911 To shew what recompense Toward thee I intend for what I haue misdone. **1837** CARLYLE in *Lett. Jane W. Carlyle* (1883) I. 70, I know not whether this book is worth anything, nor what the world will do with it, or misdo.

b. To do (work), perform (a duty) improperly.

1840 CARLYLE *Heroes* iv. 274 The work committed to him will be misdone. **1858** —— *Fredk. Gt.* x. v. II. 642 He could have done us this little service..and he..has been tempted into misdoing it! **1893** *Advance* (Chicago) 23 Mar., To misapprehend and mis-do the duty now fronting us.

†**3.** To do evil or wrong to (a person); to harm, injure, wrong. *Obs.*

a **1225** *Ancr. R.* 124 ȝif ei mon oðer ei wummon mis-seið oðer mis-deð ou. *c* **1275** LAY. 22456 And ich þe wolle loke to þat no king ne sal þe mis-do [*c* 1205 woh don]. *c* **1357** *Lay Folks Catech.* (T.) 370 To be tholemode when men misdos us. **1377** LANGL. *P. Pl.* B. xv. 252 Misdoth he no man ne with his mouth greueth. **1470-85** MALORY *Arthur* v. xii. 181 Madame ther shal none of my subgettys mysdoo you ne your maydens. **1530** PALSGR. 637/1, I nouther mysded hym nor myssayd hym. **1597** LYLY *Wom. in Moon* III. i. 24, Pardon me, That I misdid thee in my witles rage.

†**b.** To injure (an inanimate object). *Obs.*

1387 TREVISA *Higden* (Rolls) I. 111 Mysbyleued men mysdede neuere þat chirche. *c* **1400** *Chron. Eng.* lxxii. in *Archiv Stud. neu. Spr.* LII. 12 The walles were so stronge that noo man myght hem mysdoo.

†**4.** To destroy, put out of existence. *refl.* To do away with oneself. *Obs.*

c **1250** *Gen. & Ex.* 2642 Hamonel [? Hamones] likenes was ðor-on; ðis crune is broken, ðis is misdon. **1592** KYD *Sp. Trag.* IV. v. 6 Faire Isabella by her selfe misdone. **1599** *Warn. Faire Wom.* II. 669 Is not The better part of me by me misdone? My husband, is he not slaine? **1600** HEYWOOD *2nd Pt. Edw. IV*, Wks. 1874 I. 142 Drownd in a butte of Malmsey! that is strange, Doubtless he neuer would misdoe himself? **1613** J. DAVIES (Heref.) *Muses Teares* D 2 b, Seuere Torquatus, did his Sonne mis-do For charging, 'gainst his Chardge, his brauing Fo. **1619** in Heath *Grocers' Comp.* (1829) App. 348 A burial-place for children dying without baptism, and for such as had misdone themselves.

misdoer (mɪs'duːə(r)). Now *rare*. [MIS-[1] 5.] A wrong-doer, evil-doer, offender, malefactor.

c **1320** R. BRUNNE *Medit.* 503 Nat onely a mysdoer now he ys holde, But as a lewed fole he ys eke tolde. **1387** TREVISA *Higden* (Rolls) I. 115 Whan þeues and mysdoeres were þere byheded, þe hedes were i-left þere. **1433** *Rolls of Parlt.* IV. 422/1 Pilours Robbours or eny other open mysdoers. **1495** *Act 11 Hen. VII*, c. 2 If eny persone or persones geve eny other mete or drinke to the seid mysdoers being in stokkes ..or the same prisoners favour in their mysdoyng. **1535** COVERDALE *Luke* xxiii. 39 And one of the myszdoers that hanged there blasphemed him. **1596** SPENSER *State Irel.* (Globe) 610/1 Feare of law, which restrayneth offences, and inflicteth sharpe punishment to misdoeres. *a* **1670** SPALDING *Troub. Chas. I* (Spalding Club) I. 50 To summond thir misdoeris at the marcat crossis of Aberdein.. to compeir befoir the secreit counsall. **1802-12** BENTHAM *Ration. Judic. Evid.* (1827) IV. 590 Without having succeeded so far as to have produced in the breast of the misdoer any permanent..repentance. **1818** SCOTT *Hrt. Midl.* xvi, He may be called the father of a' the misdoers in Scotland. **1903** *Expositor* Nov. 339 The laws of physical nature..are not gentle in their treatment of misdoers, nor.. of those involved in the misdoing of others.

mis'doing, *vbl. sb.* [MIS-[1] 3.] Wrong-doing, evil-doing; also *Law*, the improper performance of an act.

1340 *Ayenb.* 157 Ich me ssel ase moche ase ich may wyþoute misdoinge a-yens ham paye and condecendre. *c* **1386** CHAUCER *Melib.* ¶741 He that supporteth him and preyseth him in his misdoinge. **1495** [see prec.]. *c* **1540** COVERDALE *Goostly Psalmes* Wks. 1846 II. 579 And after thy great benignite Forgyve thou all my mysdoynge. **1628** [see MISCONTINUANCE]. **1632** J. HAYWARD tr. *Biondi's Eromena* 8 My conscience doth not accuse me of misdoing. **1675** W. SHEPPARD *Actions*, etc. xii. 357 Of an Action upon the Case for Doing, not Doing, or Mis-doing. **1880** 'OUIDA' *Moths* I. 102 The glance and the blush were not for the shame of her own misdoing. **1903** [see prec.].

b. An instance of wrong-doing, a misdeed. Chiefly in *pl.*

1543 *Necessary Doctrine* I ij, He shall..haue pardon..of all his missedoinges. **1547-8** *Ordre of Commvnion* 13 Wee do earnestly repent..for these our misdoynges. **1692** R. L'ESTRANGE *Fables* ccclxxxviii. 361 That All-seeing Eye.. that Observes all our Mis-doings. **1848** THACKERAY *Van. Fair* xlvii, Harbouring of priests, obstinate recusancy, and Popish misdoings. **1898** L. STEPHEN *Stud. Biogr.* I. v. 168 We may forgive a misdoing which caused no permanent misery.

mis'doing, *ppl. a.* [MIS-[1] 2.] Doing wrong.

1554 *Interlude of Youth* (1557) C iv b, Whan ye se mysdoing men Good counsell geue them.

†**mis'doom**, *sb.* *Obs.* [MIS-[1] 4.] Misjudgement.

1606 *Sir G. Goosecappe* I. iv. in Bullen *O. Pl.* III. 23 Such misconstructions, and resolud misdoomes Of my poore work.

†**mis'doom**, *v.* *Obs.* [MIS-[1] 1.] To misjudge.

1615 SYLVESTER *Job Triumph.* II. xix. 287 Know, there shall Judgment com, To doom them right, who Others (rash) misdoom.

mis'doubt, *sb.* Now *arch.* and *dial.* [MIS-[1] 4.] Apprehension of evil; hence *gen.* mistrust, suspicion.

1592 KYD *Sp. Trag.* II. iv. 20 Ile conquer my misdoubt, And in thy loue and councell drowne my feare. **1593** SHAKS. *2 Hen. VI*, III. i. 332 Steele thy fearfull thoughts And change misdoubt to resolution. **1621** G. SANDYS *Ovid's Met.* x. (1626) 209 And thee Adonis, her misdoubts disswade From such encounters. **1680** CROWNE *Misery Civ. War* v. 70 The bird that sees the bush where once it self Was lim'd,.. Cannot but hover round it with misdoubt. **1823** GALT *Entail* II. xxx, I hae a misdoot that a's no right and sound wi' her mair than wi' him. **1893** SIR E. ARNOLD in *Westm. Gaz.* 11 Oct. 7/2 It seems time for enlightened minds to lay aside misdoubt regarding the continuity of individual life. **1899** C. H. HERFORD in *Shaks. Wks.* (Eversley ed.) IV. 404 The tragic compunctions and misdoubts of Faustus.

mis'doubt, *v.* Now chiefly *dial.* or *arch.* [f. MIS-[1] 1 + DOUBT *v.* Cf. obs. F. *mesdoubter* refl. to suspect (1518 in Godefroy).]

1. *trans.* To have doubts as to the existence, truth, or reality of (a thing).

c **1540** tr. *Pol. Verg. Eng. Hist.* (Camden No. 36) 156 The citizens..in nothing misdoubtinge their power [orig. *satis suis freti uiribus*]. **1570** J. DEE *Math. Pref.* 6 That..I did misdoute your zelous mynde to vertues schole. **1621-31** LAUD *Serm.* (1847) 191, I will never misdoubt the piety of this nation in the performing this duty. **1684** R. WALLER *Nat. Exper.* 61 Misdoubting the sufficiency of the Ligature to sustain the air. **1862** TROLLOPE *Orley F.* xxvii, She did not say that she misdoubted the wisdom of her son's counsels. **1875-86** *W. Somerset Gloss.*, *Misdoubt*, to misbelieve; to doubt. **1887** P. MCNEILL *Blawearie* 129 This was the voice of Teenie Bell: there was no misdoubting it.

absol. **1601** SHAKS. *All's Well* I. iii. 130 Manie likelihoods inform'd mee of this before, which hung so tottring in the ballance, that I could neither beleeue nor misdoubt.

b. With clause: To doubt (*but*) *that*..; to have doubts as to *how*...

1640 G. SANDYS *Christ's Passion* IV. 42/26 Who beares not his own burden, that none may Misdoubt, the Innocent became their prey. **1709** STRYPE *Ann. Ref.* iii. 74 We need not..misdoubt but that it is his, under whose name it goes. **1865** DE MORGAN in Graves *Life Sir W. R. Hamilton* (1889) III. 622 Misdoubting that the subscription plan had the sanction of the relatives. **1891** ATKINSON *Moorland Par.* 14 [He] gravely shook his head, and misdoubted how it would work.

2. To have doubts about the character, honesty, etc. of (a person); to be mistrustful or suspicious of.

c **1585** *Faire Em* II. 573 Iealousy..Hath so bewitched my lovely Manviles senses That he misdoubts his Em, that loves his soul. **1598** SHAKS. *Merry W.* II. i. 192, I doe not misdoubt my wife: but I would bee loath to turne them together. **1619** GATAKER *Spirituall Watch* (1637) 109 Peter then..misdoubted not himselfe, nor his own inability, but he would and should doe as then he said. **1818** SCOTT *Rob Roy* xxii, I dinna misdoubt ye. **1882** MISS C. F. WOOLSON *Anne* 371 We put him in charge of a woman, who said she'd take care of him, but I misdoubt her. **1902** A. LANG in *Blackw. Mag.* Apr. 481/1 His witnesses were misdoubted.

3. To have misgivings, suspicion, or forebodings in regard to.

1563-87 FOXE *A. & M.* (1596) 248/1 They began to misdout their speeding. **1588** SHAKS. *L. L. L.* IV. iii. 194, I beseech your Grace let this Letter be read, Our person misdoubts it: it was treason he said. **1593** —— *3 Hen. VI*, V. vi. 14 The Bird that hath bin limed in a bush, With trembling wings misdoubteth euery bush. **1663** H. COGAN tr. *Pinto's Trav.* lxxv. 307 Presently misdoubting the businesse, she went..to impart the sad news unto her Mother. **1857** DICKENS *Lett.* (1880) II. 9, I much misdoubt an amateur artist's success in this vast place. **1870** MORRIS *Earthly Par.* II. III. 496 Much they misdoubted what these came to do.

†**b.** To hesitate or scruple (*to do* something). *Obs.*

1581 J. BELL *Haddon's Answ. Osor.* II. 176 The holy Ghost misdoubteth not to speake in the Scriptures, after this usuall phrase of speech [orig. *sacræ literæ non dubitant voces huiusmodi vsurpare*].

4. To fear or suspect the existence or occurrence of (something regarded as evil).

c **1540** tr. *Pol. Verg. Eng. Hist.* (Camden No. 36) 159 The kinge, misdoubtinge some treason [orig. *fraudem suspicatus*]. *a* **1586** SIDNEY *Arcadia* III. (1629) 250 Hee misdoubted each mans treason, and coniectured euery possibility of misfortunc. **1597** BEARD *Theatre God's Judgem.* (1612) 170 The Turks secure and misdoubting nothing. **1603** DRAYTON *Bar. Wars* I. xlix, Warn'd by Danger to misdoubt the worst. **1633** G. HERBERT *Temple, Ch. Porch* xxviii, Yet in thy thriving still misdoubt some evil. **1653** GATAKER *Vind. Annot. Jer.* 6 Because he misdoubted discovery as wel by the one as by the other. *a* **1721** SHEFFIELD (Dk. Buckhm.) *Wks.* (1753) I. 64 My fearful conscious eyes Look often back, misdoubting a surprize.

absol. **1700** DRYDEN *Wife of Bath's T.* 116 Misdoubting much, and fearful of the event. **1850** MRS. BROWNING *Poems Island* xxx. Poems II. 189 And who would murmur and misdoubt, When God's great sunrise finds him out?

†**b.** *transf.* To fear for, have fears about. *Obs.*

1630 R. N. tr. *Camden's Hist. Eliz.* I. 14 This also troubled the French King, who could not but misdoubt France [orig. *Galliæ non poterat non timere*], if by this new marriage England should fall againe to the Spaniard, his Enemy.

5. With clause (occas. with simple obj.): To fear or suspect (that something is or will be the case).

1596 SPENSER *F. Q.* VI. iii. 47 Misdoubting least he should misguyde His former malice to some new assay. **1605** in *Buccleuch MSS.* (Hist. MSS. Comm.) 81 They misdoubt they shall not be able to raise many voluntaries. *a* **1648** LD. HERBERT *Hen. VIII* (1683) 406 Neither did the King misdoubt that the putting of Arms into so many of his Subjects hands would redound to his prejudice. **1813** BYRON *Br. Abydos* I. v, Much I misdoubt this wayward boy Will one day work me more annoy. **1818** SCOTT *Hrt. Midl.* xxxviii, And that leddy was the Queen hersell?.. I misdoubted it when I saw that your honour didna put on your hat. **1865** DICKENS *Mut. Fr.* III. xv, Mr. Boffin stared here, and stared there, as misdoubting that he must be in some sort of fit. **1885** *Harper's Mag.* May 830/2, I misdoubt the ladies won't like it.

b. With acc. and inf.: To suspect (a person or thing) of being (so-and-so). ? *Obs.*

1599 SANDYS *Europæ Spec.* (1632) 172 [He] is strongly misdoubted to practise with the Emperour for the joyning the Catholike and Lutheran forces in one. **1625** BP. MOUNTAGU *App. Cæsar* 275 You misdoubt the Testimony to be forged, because it was forgotten to name the place.

c. *refl.* and *intr.* To suspect; to have suspicions *of*; to be suspicious *of*. *Obs.* or *arch.*

1637 HEYWOOD *Dial.* viii. 109 Dost thou misdoubt thee Of nothing lost? hast all thy tooles about thee? **1814** CARY *Dante, Paradise* XXIV. 86, I not a whit misdoubt of its assay. **1843** JAMES *Forest Days* I. ii. 12 Get thee gone, slut!..what dost thou know of friars' cells? Too much, I mis-doubt me. **1846** TRENCH *Mirac.* xviii. (1862) 300 The neighbours may have misdoubted of the work, as having been done on the Sabbath.

Hence **mis'doubted** *ppl.a.*

1687 H. MORE *App. Antid.* (1712) 181 Suspected Innocency and misdoubted Truth.

†**mis'doubtful**, *a.* *Obs.*$^{-1}$ [MIS-^{1} 6.] Suspicious. So **mis'doubtfully** *adv.*, suspiciously.

1575 R. B. *Appius & Virg.* civ, When men wyll seeme misdoubtfully, Without an why, to call and crie. **1596** SPENSER *F. Q.* V. vi. 3 She gan to cast in her misdoubtfull mynde A thousand feares.

mis'doubting, *vbl. sb.* [MIS-^{1} 3.] = MISDOUBT *sb.*

1571 GOLDING *Calvin on Ps.* lxviii. 18 Our nature is forward to misdoubting. **1606** G. W[OODCOCKE] *Hist. Ivstine* I. 5 This man..casting about..to found out the depth of this their misdoubting. **1823** J. F. COOPER *Pioneers* xi, The misdoubtings of our arrogant nature. **1877** LADY WOOD *Sheen's Foreman* I. 264 She..had a little misdoubting of the success of an evening's entertainment.

mis'doubting, *ppl. a.* [MIS^1 2.] Distrustful, suspicious.

1652 *Eliza's Babes* 75, I must now ask thee pardon for those misdoubting thoughts. **1814** BYRON *Corsair* III. viii, Mis-doubting Corsair! **1868** HOLME LEE *B. Godfrey* xvi, Mis-doubting vagabond that you are.

mis'draught. *rare.* [MIS-^{1} 4.]

†**1.** Misbehaviour. (Cf. DRAUGHT *sb.* 20 b.) *Obs.*

c **1440** CAPGRAVE *Life St. Kath.* I. 821 Whanne she covde aspye ony mysdraught [*MS. Rawl.* mysdrawte] Of man or of woman, that thei were nyce.

2. A draught (of air) in a wrong direction.

1838 *Civil Engin. & Arch. Jrnl.* I. 212/2 The mortar..falls out in powder, and leaves gaping chinks for misdraught between the bricks.

mis'draw, *v.* [MIS-^{1} 1.]

†**1.** *trans.* To draw amiss. *Obs.*

Cf. OF. *mestraire le merel* (*la merele*), jouer mauvais jeu, éprouver un revers; *un trait de merele*, un coup de la fortune (Godefroy).

1390 GOWER *Conf.* I. 18 So that under the clerkes lawe Men sen the Merel al mysdrawe. **1885** *Proc. Soc. Psychical Res.* III. 427 There were also 40 diagrams..all misdrawn.

†**2.** To entice, allure, mislead. *Obs.*

1382 WYCLIF *Deut.* xvii. 17 He shal not haue many wyues, that mysdrawen [Vulg. *alliciant*] the soule of hym. **1599** SANDYS *Europæ Spec.* (1632) 122 So they be in the latine, and not purposely written..to misdraw the multitude.

†**3.** *intr.* To go astray. (Cf. DRAW *v.* 68.)

c **1290** *S. Eng. Leg.* I. 304/168 þe luþere lucifer, þo he was is [*sc.* St. Michael's] felawe.., for-to he gan misdrawe.

Hence †**mis'drawing** *ppl.a.* (in quot. *absol.*); **mis'drawn** *ppl. a.*, badly or wrongly drawn (up).

c **1374** CHAUCER *Boeth.* III. pr. xii. (1868) 104 ȝif þere were a ȝok of mysdrawynges in diuerse parties [orig. *detrectantium jugum*]. **1867** BAGEHOT *Eng. Constitution* 268 The practical arguments and the legal disquisitions in America are often like those of trustees carrying out a misdrawn will.

mis'drawing, *vbl. sb.* [MIS-^{1} 3.] A faulty drawing or delineation.

1872 PROCTOR *Ess. Astron.* iv. 59 A small misdrawing in an orthographic presentation of a planet. **1905** C. F. KEARY in *Author* 1 Feb. 144 Leslie's misdrawings of mob-capped maidens.

†**mis'dread**, *sb.* [MIS-^{1} 4.] Dread of evil.

1608 SHAKS. *Per.* I. ii. 12 (Qo. 1) The passions of the mind, That haue their first conception by misdread.

†**mis'dread**, *v.* *Obs.* [MIS-^{1} 1.]

1. *refl.* and *intr.* To have fear, be in dread.

c **1350** *Will. Palerne* 1567 Misdrede ȝow neuer; I wil fulfille alle forwardes feiþli in dede! **1597-8** BP. HALL *Sat.*, *Defiance to Envie* 25 Needs me then hope, or doth me need misdread?

2. *trans.* To dread (some evil).

1606 G. W[OODCOCKE] *Hist. Ivstine* XXXI. 104 To auoyd a mischiefe which he misdreaded. *Ibid.* XXXV. 113 Alexander ..misdreding no hostility prepared against him at all.

mis'drive, *v.* [MIS-^{1} 1.]

†**1.** *trans.* ? To commit (a wrong). *Obs.*

c **1330** R. BRUNNE *Chron.* (1810) 116 If trespas be misdryuen, & do þin owen socoure, & I wille make amendes.

2. To drive in a wrong direction.

a **1631** DONNE *Serm.* lxxxiv. Wks. 1839 IV. 58 They are miscarried, misdriven,..with the spirit of giddiness. **1674** N. FAIRFAX *Bulk & Selv.* 74 A curious frame..so featly set together..that should but any one pin of it be mis-driven.. you hazard the cracking..of the whole. **1885** SIR H. TAYLOR *Autobiogr.* I. 298 The Government..was so much misled, or rather misdriven, as to supersede him in office.

mise (miːz, maɪz), *sb.*^{1} Also 5-6 **myse**, 5, 8 **myze**, 6 **misse**, 7 **mize**. [a. AF., OF. *mise* action of placing or setting, expenses, account, wager, arbitration (whence med.L. *misa*, *misia*), fem. abstract noun f. *mettre* (pa. pple. *mis*) to place.]

†**1.** *pl.* Expenses or costs. *Obs.*

c **1450** *Godstow Reg.* 88 The mysis and expensis I-had by the defaute of the said John and Robert. **1469** *Anc. Cal. Rec. Dublin* (1889) I. 333 And also rollys to be made of the misis and costes. **1492** in Rymer *Fœdera* (1711) XII. 490 The Mises and Expenses the which he hath doon for th'entertaining of the Men of Werr.

2. A grant, payment, or tribute made to secure a liberty or immunity, as (*a*) by the inhabitants of Wales to a new Lord Marcher, king, or prince on his first entrance into their country, (*b*) by the inhabitants of the County Palatine of Chester on a change of earl.

? *a* **1500** *Chester Pl.* (E.E.T.S.) 439 Ofte I sett vppon falce Assyze rayvinge poore with layinge myze. **1535** *Act 27 Hen. VIII*, c. 26 §23 That all..lay and temporall..personnes nowe beyng Lordes Marches [*v.r.* Marchers]..shall..have all suche myses and profittes of thir tenauntes as they have had or used to have at the first entre into their Landes. **1548** *Act 2 & 3 Edw. VI*, c. 36 §52. *c* **1567** in *Cardiff Rec.* (1901) III. 279 As concernyng myses the which the said Erle [of Pembroke] and lorde [Herbert of Cardiff] do clayme to have of their tennauntes at their fyrst entry. **1648** *British Bell-man* 7 Impositions, by way of Excise, Loane, Myzes, Weekly and Monethly Assesments. **1656** *King's Vale-Royal Eng.* 15 We perceive, that the Inhabitants of the said County of Chester, have paid, and must pay rightfully, at the change of every Owner of the said Earldom, 3000. Marks, called a Mize. And the inhabitants of the County of Flint, being parcel of the said County Palatine, must likewise pay 2000. Marks, which is also called a Mize. **1665** P. HENRY *Diaries & Lett.* (1882) 172 At Malpas at a parish-meeting..three mizes sess'd for yᵉ ensuing year. **1709** STRYPE *Ann. Ref.* Introd. §2. 13 Nor did she [Q. Eliz.] forget her Myzes; that is, what was due to her from the People of Wales, by antient Custom due to the Princes of Wales,..at their first Entrance upon the supreme Government.

3. A settlement by agreement.

In *Eng. Hist.* applied to the two settlements made in January and May, 1264, between Henry III and his rebellious barons, called the *Mise of Amiens* and *Mise of Lewes* respectively.

[*a* **1293** T. DE WYKES *Chron.* an. 1264 in *Hist. Angl. Script.* (1687) II. 63 Statutum quoddam quod Misam Lewensem inusitato nomine nuncupabat.] **1700** TYRRELL *Hist. Eng.* II. 1027 Until such time as the Peace between the said Lord the King, and the Barons at Lewes, according to a certain *Mise* or Agreement, should be fully concluded. *Ibid. marg.*, The *Mise* at Lewes. **1875** STUBBS *Const. Hist.* xiv. §177 (1896) II. 92 The Mise of Amiens..received the papal confirmation on the 16th of March.

4. *Law.* The issue in a writ of right.

1544 tr. *Nat. Brevium* 2 Ioynynge the myses vpon the mere. **1544** tr. *Littleton's Tenures* 101 He..may well have a writ of right agaynst him yᵗ recovered, for thys that the mise shallbe joyned onely upon the clere right. **1726** W. NELSON *Lex. Maneriorum* (1733) 47 [The Court of the Manor] 'tis a Court which may try the Mise joined upon a Writ of Right. **1773** BLACKSTONE *Comm.* III. xx. 305 In a writ of right, the mise or issue is, that the tenant has more right to hold than the demandant has to demand. **1853** JUDGE LEE in *Grattan's Rep. Virginia* (1855) X. 355 Upon the mise joined on the mere right, every affirmative matter going to the right and title of the demandant..is necessarily put in issue.

†**b.** ***at one's own mise***: by one's own pleading. [Cf. AF. *par sa mise et par soen assent* (Britton II. xviii).]

1453 *Rolls of Parlt.* V. 270/2 In cas that they..appere nat, that than they that appered nat, by auctorite aforseid be atteynt and convict..as veryly and in the same forme and effect, as they were atteynt and convict at theire own myse.

5. *Comb.*, as ***mise-gatherer***; **mise-book**, a book containing the ratings for the gathering of the mise in the various towns and villages of the County Palatine; **mise-layer**, an assessor of taxes; **mise-money** = 2 (above).

1673 *Mize-book [see MISE *v.*]. **1725** J. JOLLEY (*title*) The Head Constable's Assistant; or, a Mize-Book for the County Palatine of Cheshire. **1886** *Cheshire Gloss.* (citing *Cheshire Sheaf* II. 361), There was, and perhaps still is, at Chester a mise-book, in which every town and village in the county is rated for this tax. **1597** *Crt. Leet Rec. Manch.* (1885) II. 130 Reynolde Parkynson and Anthonie Shepparde to the office of *mysegatherers for this year to come. **1604** *Salford Portmote Rec.* (1902) 41 Henrye Kelley and ffrancis Hutchenson were appointed misegatherers. *Ibid.* 114 There shalbee a Laye layd by the *Myselayers for provysion of Bucketts and Hookes. **1615** in *Crt. Leet Rec. Manch.* (1885) II. 308 That A reasonable ley shalbe assessed and taxed by the myselayers..whereby sixe ladders [etc.]..maye be presentlye provided for the Comon good of all the inhabitants. **1617** in *N. & Q.* Ser. VII. (1891) XI. 66 *Mize Money. **1679** BLOUNT *Anc. Tenures* 162 The tenants shall pay him a certain sum of money called Mise-money, in consideration whereof, they claim to be acquit of all fines and amerciaments, which are recorded at that time and in Court Rolls and not levyed. **1706** PHILLIPS (ed. Kersey), *Mise-Money*, Money given by way of Composition or Agreement, to purchase any Liberty.

†**mise**, *sb.*^{2} *Obs.* [Of obscure origin. Cf. MISER *sb.*^{2}] app. = PANADA.

c **1440** *Promp. Parv.* 339/2 Myse, or mysys, *mice, in plur.* **1611** COTGR., *Eau panée*, a Panado, a Mise.

†**mise**, *v.*^{1} [app. back-formation f. MISER *sb.*^{1}] *intr.* To be miserly. Hence **mising** *ppl. a.*

1579 E. HAKE *Newes owt of Powles Churchyarde* D j b, They scratch, they scrape, they mise, they muse. **1595** LODGE *Fig for Momus* Sat. iv. 21 A miserable mysing wretch, That liues by others losse, and subtle fetch.

mise (miːz, maɪz), *v.*^{2} [f. MISE *sb.*^{1}] *trans.* To rate for the mise.

1673 SIR P. LEYCESTER *Hist. Antiq. Cheshire* IV. 309 The Township of Limme..is in our Common Mize-book Mized at 01*l.* 16*s.* 00*d.* *Ibid.* 351 Runcorn Superior and Inferior.. are Mized together in our Common Mize-book, and are very hard Mized. **1886** *Cheshire Gloss.*, *Mise*, to value for rating purposes.

mise, obs. pl. of MOUSE; var. MESE *sb.*^{2} and *v.*

misease (mɪs'iːz), *sb. arch.* Forms: see MIS-^{2} and EASE *sb.*; also 3 **meoseise**, 4 **myseis**, **myssis**, **mishese**, **meseysey** (?), 5 **myssaes**. [a. OF. *mesaise* (from 13th c.), f. *mes*- MIS-^{2} + *aise* EASE.]

1. Distress, affliction; trouble, misery; extreme suffering or discomfort. Also *pl.* *Obs.* exc. *arch.*

a **1225** *Ancr. R.* 114 Al þet flesch þuncheð sur oðer bitter, þet is, pine & weane, & teone, & alle meoseise. *c* **1330** R. BRUNNE *Chron. Wace* (Rolls) 2460 þe vnkynde þou wilt vp reyse, þe kynde þou puttest to meseysey. *c* **1375** *Cursor M.* 3596 (Fairf.), Squa has now elde þis ysaac led þat he in mysese [*Cott.* langur] lijs in bed. **1382** WYCLIF *Gen.* iii. 16, I shal multiply thi myseses and thi conceyuyngis. *c* **1386** CHAUCER *Pars. T.* ¶ 102, I go with-oute returning..to the lond of

misese and of derknesse, where-as is the shadwe of deeth. *c* **1440** *York Myst.* xx. 213 Mysese [*Towneley* sorow] had neuere man more. *c* **1450** *Merlin* 64 And so endured the kynge in grete mysese for love of Ygerne. **1470–85** Malory *Arthur* ix. xix. 367 Alle the mysease that sir tristram hath was for a letter that he fond. **1483** Caxton *Gold. Leg.* 148/3 Wherfore are ye in so grete mesease for brede? Yf ye haue none thys day ye shal haue to morn. **1490** —— *Godfrey* vi. 25 Alle the meseases & the myschiefs that the peple of our lord endured that tyme. *c* **1611** Chapman *Iliad* xiii. 521 His dart, Meriones Pursude, and Adamas so striu'd, with it, and his misease, As doth a Bullocke puffe and storme. **1848** Lytton *Harold* II. v. ii. 25 'Gurth, has my father ailed? There is that in his face which I like not'. 'He hath not complained of misease', said Gurth, startled. **1900** F. S. Ellis *Rom. Rose* I. 7/178 Covetise eggs men on, for their misease, To gather, but to scatter not.

†**2.** Lack of the necessaries of life or of the means of living; poverty, need, want. *Obs.*

c **1200** *Trin. Coll. Hom.* 43 *Diuicias et paupertates ne dederis michi sed tantum uictui necessaria*, louerd ne gif þu me noþer ne woreld winne ne meseise ac mi bare bileue. *a* **1300** *Cursor M.* 4770 Þat he..ar grant þam son menskli to dei, Ar þat misese [*Gött.* hunger] lang for to drei. *a* **1325** *Prose Psalter* xliii. 26 Þou for-ȝetest our mesais [*inopiæ nostræ*] and our tribulacioun. **1362** Langl. *P. Pl.* A. i. 24 Þat on Clothing is from Chele ow to saue: And þat oþer Mete at Meel for meseise of þiseluen. **1389** in *Eng. Gilds* (1870) 31 Quat broyer or syster..falle in mischefe er mys-ese..he schal han Almesse. **1490** Caxton *Godfrey* ci. 153 Seyng that our men suffred so moche famyne and mesease.

3. Uneasiness, disquiet.

1905 R. H. Sherard *O. Wilde* vi. 75, I noticed with some misease that..he seemed to have the middle class contempt for the title of knighthood.

†**mis'ease**, *a.* *Obs.* [app. an adj. use of misease *sb.* modelled on F. *aise* adj. (? for **aaise* = *à aise* at ease); cf. the forms *eese*, *eise*, s.v. easy *a.*] Distressed, miserable; in want.

a **1225** *Ancr. R.* 46 Hwo se is ful meseise, of alle beo heo cwite. *Ibid.* 162 Uorto urouren ancre þet is meseise [*v.r.* in meseise]. *c* **1290** *St. Julian* 106 in *S. Eng. Leg.* I. 259 Þis holie Man..mani Miseise Man in is hous wel loueliche vnder-fonge. **1377** Langl. *P. Pl.* B. vii. 26 And amende mesondieux þere-myde and myseyse folke helpe. *c* **1440** [see miseased]. *c* **1450** *Merlin* 94 He..yaf his godes..to mysese peple of his reame.

absol. ? *a* **1400** *Morte Arth.* 667 To mendynantez and mysese in myschefe fallene.

†**mis'ease**, *v.* *Obs.*[−0] [a. obs. F. *mesaiser*, OF. *mesaisier*, f. *mesaise* misease *sb.*] *trans.* To trouble, inconvenience.

1530 Palsgr. 637/1 If you take this waye, it wyll mysease you.

†**mis'eased**, *a.* Also 5 missaysid. [f. misease *sb.* + -ed[2].] **a.** In want. **b.** Troubled, distressed.

c **1440** *Eng. Conq. Irel.* (Rawl. MS.) 115 The mayny, that was myssaysid [*Dubl. MS.* myssayse] and hungry, founde ther mette and drynke y-now. **1553** Grimalde *Cicero's Offices* (1558) To Rdr., To make sound the sicke mind (in case it be miseased and hath a wil to be relieved).

†**mis'easely**, *adv.* *Obs.* In 3 miseislich. [app. f. misease + -ly[2].] ? Miserably.

a **1300** *Earth* ix. in *E.E.P.* (1862) 151 Whan erþ haþ erþ wiþ streinþ þus geten, alast he haþ is leinþ miseislich i-meten.

†**mis'easeness.** *Obs. rare*[−1]. [f. misease *sb.* + -ness.] Trouble, affliction.

14.. *Wyclif's Bible* Job v. 21 (MS. Bodl. 277), þu schalt not drede myseesnesse [Vulg. *calamitatem*] whanne it comiþ.

†**mis'easety.** *Obs.* In 4 myseiste, -este, -eisetee. [f. misease + *-te(e*, -ty.] = misease.

1382 Wyclif *Mark* iv. 19 Myseiste [*v.r.* myseeses, Vulg. *ærumnæ*] of the world. *Ibid.* xii. 44 But this of hir myseste [Vulg. *penuria*] sente alle thingis that she hadde.

†**mis'easy**, *a.* *Obs.* [a. OF. *mesaisé*, *-aisié* (also *-aisi*), f. *mes-* mis-[2] + *aisé* easy *a.*] Miserable, wretched.

c **1290** *St. Julian* 120 in *S. Eng. Leg.* I. 259 A Miseisiore man þane he þouȝte, no man ne miȝte iseo. **1387–8** T. Usk *Test. Love* i. iii. (Skeat) I. 150 Unneth may I ligge for pure misesy sorowe.

‖**mise au point** (miz o pwɛ̃). [Fr.] A focusing or clarification of an obscure subject or problem.

1946 *Word* II. 113 A general *mise au point* of the linguistic side of semantic problems is thus overdue. **1949** *Archivum Linguisticum* I. 126 The Geneva School retorted with an important *mise au point.* **1971** *Ibid.* II. 64 For a recent *mise au point*, see P. H. Matthews,..in *New Horizons in Linguistics.*

mis'educate, *v.* [mis-[1] 1.] *trans.* To educate wrongly. Also **mis'educated** *ppl. a.* [mis-[1] 2], wrongly educated.

1827 Pollok *Course T.* ix. 167 The miseducated fancies ..Of superstitious men. **1856** G. Wilson *Gateways Knowl.* 86 The tongue is deliberately mis-educated. **1858** Carlyle *Fredk. Gt.* vii. viii. II. 277 His fault was the general one, of having miseducated the Prince. **1897** *Lady's Realm* June 216/1 Servants are not only more educated; they are miseducated.

misedu'cation. [mis-[1] 4.] Wrong or faulty education.

1624 Bp. Hall *Epist.* vi. vi. 394 Our Land hath no blemish comparable to the mis-education of our Gentry. **1831** Carlyle *Sart. Res.* ii. iii, As for our Miseducation, make not bad worse. **1840** Kingsley *Misc.* (1859) I. 237 Spiritual faculties, which it is as wicked to stunt..by miseducation as it is to maim our own limbs.

‖**mise-en-page** (mizɑ̃paʒ). [ad. Fr. *mise-en-pages* imposition.] The design of printed pages, including the layout of text and illustrations; also, the composition of pictures.

1926 R. Fry in J. M. Cameron *Victorian Photographs* 13 Here the artist has been able to control everything, the *mise-en-page*, the disposition of the drapery, and the illumination. **1930** *Times Lit. Suppl.* 3 July 556/1 More intent on realizing the volumes than on the mise-en-page. **1938** *Burlington Mag.* Sept. p. xiii/1 There is hardly a single plate..which can be considered a really satisfactory *mise-en-page.* **1939** *Ibid.* Apr. 177/1 No difference as far as the mise-en-page is concerned between the portrait said to be by Bellini and a Turkish work. **1957** *Listener* 5 Dec. 947/2 The wrapper is deplorable..and the *mise-en-page* rather poor.. nevertheless a book to be thankful for. **1959** *Times* 26 Mar. 3/4 Neither the tonal harmony..nor the *mise-en-page* is always quite strong enough in these latter pictures. **1963** *Ibid.* 18 Apr. 7/6 Of special interest are the publications in which students are given the opportunity of gaining practical experience in the design of the book and the *mise-en-page.* **1968** *Listener* 25 Jan. 106/3 Television cannot emphasise in the manner of a newspaper's *mise-en-page.* **1972** *Guardian* 19 June 11/2 Aubrey Beardsley.. contributed..the art of *mise en page*..the art of making dramatic use of big blank spaces.

‖**mise-en-scène** (mizɑ̃sɛn). [Fr.] **a.** The staging of a play; the scenery and properties of a stage production; the stage setting.

1833 W. C. Macready *Diary* 14 Dec. (1912) I. 85 Saw the play, *Coriolanus*, in so disgraceful a state that it was useless to bestow a word upon the *mise en scène.* **1840** A. Bunn *Stage* II. xi. 298 More attention was paid to the *mise en scène* than to the acting. **1891** 'L. Malet' *Wages of Sin* I. iii. ii. 131 Only look at the walls of our exhibitions, look at the *mise en scène* of our theatres! **1911** G. B. Shaw *Blanco Posnet* Pref. 340 The *mise-en-scène* of a play is as much a part of it as the words spoken on the stage. **1951** *Oxf. Compan. Theatre* 715/1 Perhaps Antoine..never realized the force of some of his *mises-en-scène.* **1961** K. Tynan *Curtains* iii. 391 In the newer *mises en scène* one got a feeling of dehydrated Luhtishness. **1974** *Listener* 17 Jan. 92/3 The newspaper office *mise-en-scène*..gave it [*sc.* a radio play] early vitality.

b. *transf.* and *fig.* The setting, surroundings, or background of an event or action.

1872 E. Braddon *Life in India* i. 8 Novelists..sometimes select India as the *mise en scène* of their tales. **1894** [see impressionize *v.*]. **1901** *Q. Rev.* CXCIII. 314 She [*sc.* Queen Victoria] was unrivalled in her sense of the proper *mise en scène* of a formal ceremonial. *a* **1916** H. James *Ivory Tower* (1917) 270, I manage to treat myself to some happy.. mise-en-scène or exploitation of my memory of (say) California. **1924** Earl of Birkenhead *Amer. Revisited* vi. 165 She would have dictated peace, I should imagine, at Buckingham Palace; for the *réclame* of the *mise-en-scène* would, on the whole, have been greater than that of Versailles. **1940** Wodehouse *Eggs, Beans & Crumpets* 12 You have simply got to get your atmosphere right... Chance your arm with the *mise en scène*, and before you can say 'what ho', you've made some bloomer. **1972** J. Hodgson *Uses of Drama* xvi. 183 In certain dramatized situations 'people' are actors, and the rush of social events, mise-en-scene.

†**mis'egging**, *vbl. sb.* *Obs.* [f. mis-[1] 3 + egging *vbl. sb.*[1]] Unlawful instigation.

1496 *Dives & Pauper* (W. de W.) vii. viii. 286/2 Yf a man ..by mys eggynge take awaye an other mannes seruaunt he doth theft.

Misegun, vulgar corruption of mazagan.

1818 Scott *Rob Roy* xiv, 'Am trenching up the sparry-grass, and am gaun to saw sum Misegun beans'.

misel, var. mizzle.

miselden, obs. f. mistletoe.

miself, obs. f. myself.

miselle, obs. f. mizzle.

miselled, obs. f. measled *ppl. a.*

miselto(e, obs. ff. mistletoe.

miselve(n, obs. ff. myself.

mis'emphasis. [mis-[1] 4.] Incorrect emphasis.

1927 *Sat. Rev. Lit.* 12 Mar. 651/1 The historic church has too frequently specialized in morbid and bogey-ish suggestions until the natural trend of a faith that *is* faith has been diverted to misemphasis on guilt and introspective self-analysis under the obsession of fear. **1962** R. B. Fuller *Epic Poem on Industrialization* 3 Full of fanciful misemphasis. **1965** H. Kahn *On Escalation* viii. 152 This example of past misemphasis is now widely known and is often cited by analysts.

misem'ploy, *v.* [mis-[1] 1.] *trans.* To employ amiss; to use for a wrong or improper purpose; to put to wrong uses.

1609 W. M. *Man in the Moone* (1849) 16 Much riches were you bequeathed, the more is the pittie you have so little grace to misemploy them. **1654** H. L'Estrange *Chas. I* (1655) 5 Considering how those moneys were mis-imployed, indeed rather thrown away. **1681** Dryden *Abs. & Achit.* 613 'Tis sin to misemploy an hour. **1712** Addison *Spect.* No. 535 ¶1 That vain and foolish Hope, which is misemployed on Temporal Objects. **1852** Grote *Greece* ii. lxxviii. IX. 335 The force of Athens, misemployed and broken into fragments, is found..unable to repel a new aggressor. **1860** Mill *Repr. Govt.* (1865) 66/1 Not that the depositaries of power will not, but that they cannot, misemploy it.

misem'ployed, *ppl. a.* [mis-[1] 2.] Wrongly or improperly employed. Also *absol.*

1646 Fuller *Wounded Consc.* (1841) 324 In case his leg be set, he..flies out, unjointing it again by his misemployed mettle. **1647** Ward *Simp. Cobler* 28 What a multitude of mis-employ'd hands, might be better improv'd in some more manly Manufactures. **1905** *Daily News* 30 Aug. 5 Workers and loafers, unemployed, misemployed, and unemployable.

misem'ploying, *vbl. sb.* [mis-[1] 3.] Misemployment.

1686 Horneck *Crucif. Jesus* xx. 574 These general gifts, upon his abuse and misemploying of them, are gradually removed. *a* **1711** Ken *Preparatives* Poet. Wks. 1721 IV. 6 The pass'd can be no more, Whose misemploying I deplore.

misem'ployment. [mis-[1] 4.] Wrong employment or use; improper application.

1597–8 *Act 39 Eliz.* c. 6 §1 The..misimploymentes Falsityes defrauding of the Trustes. *a* **1661** Fuller *Worthies, Rutlandshire* (1662) ii. 348 The pious and liberal gift is much abused by the avarice and mis-imployment of the Governors thereof. *a* **1676** Hale *Prim. Orig. Man.* i. i. (1677) 4 An improvident expence, and misemployment of their time and faculties. **1705** Stanhope *Paraphr.* II. 267 By our Negligence and Mis-employment they prove at last to have been bestowed in vain. **1846** Grote *Greece* i. xvi. I. 497 A misemployment of abstract words. **1877** M. Arnold *Last Ess. on Church* 155 The risks which beset practice from the misemployment of such criticism.

misen, obs. form of mizen.

†**mis'english**, *v.* *Obs.* [mis-[1] 1.] *trans.* To mistranslate into English. Also, to make an English word of illegitimately. Also *absol.* So **mis'englishing** *vbl. sb.*

1567–9 Jewel *Def. Apol.* (1611) 257 Not nipping the Scriptures, nor misse-englishing them. **1641** Smectymnuus *Vind. Answ.* Pref., Hee tells us..of misenglishing Tertullian. *Ibid.* §6 With what face can the Remonstrant charge us with infidelity in quotation and mis-englishing? **1737** Byrom *Rem.* (Chetham Soc.) II. i. 137, I thought.. that the word *inanimating* was mis-englished.

misenite ('mɪsənaɪt). *Min.* [f. *Miseno*, the name of a promontory near Naples, where the mineral is found.] Hydrous sulphate of potassium found in white silky fibres.

1854 Dana *Syst. Min.* (ed. 4) II. 377.

†**mis'enter**, *v.* *Obs.* [mis-[1] 1.] *trans.* To enter erroneously.

1675 *Conn. Col. Rec.* (1852) II. 360 This was ordered Septr. 3, 75,—and was miss-entered here.

†**mis'entering**, *vbl. sb.* *Obs.* [mis-[1] 3.] Erroneous entering, misentry.

1580–1 *Act 23 Eliz.* c. 3 §2 No Fyne..shalbee reversed.. by any Writte of Errour, for false..Lattin..misentring of any Warraunte of Attorney [etc.]. **1607** Norden *Surv. Dial.* i. 34 The misconceiuing misentring by the Surveyor, may be erroneous.

†**misen'treat, -in'treat**, *v.* *Obs.* [mis-[1] 1.] *trans.* To treat badly; to ill-treat, ill-use.

1450 *Rolls of Parlt.* V. 189/2 Arestyng and misentretyng, ayenst the lawes of God and libertees of the Church, the Dean. **1483** Caxton *Gold. Leg.* 399/3 A clerke..sayd it was not honest..to mysentrete the holy body by vyolente hondes. **1519** Horman *Vulg.* 4 Pristhod is holy, and ought nat to be misintreatted. **1583** Golding *Calvin on Deut.* lxxiii. 448 S. Paule warneth maisters y[t] they should not mis-intreat their seruaunts.

†**misen'treating**, *vbl. sb.* *Obs.* [mis-[1] 3.] Ill-treatment.

1531 *Elyot's Instr.* in *Governor* (1883) 72 Complaining to the Pope of the misintreating of us. **1581** Lambarde *Eiren.* ii. iii. (1588) 135 Violent handlings and misentreatings of the person.

mis'entry. [mis-[1] 4.] An erroneous entry.

1602 Fulbecke *1st Pt. Parall.* 70 Because he did make a misentrie once into a rolle in a Court where hee was Steward. **1697** *View Penal Laws* 18 No Common Brewer shall be prosecuted for any Misentry—if [etc.]. **1768** Blackstone *Comm.* III. 407 And if any mis-entry was made, it was rectified by the minutes.

†**mise'piscopist.** *Obs. rare*[−1]. [f. Gr. μισ(ο)- miso- + ἐπίσκοπος bishop + -ist.] A hater of episcopacy.

1659 Gauden *Tears Ch.* iv. xxiv. 640 Those Misepiscopists..who most envied..that honour to..other Bishops.

miser ('maɪzə(r)), *a.* and *sb.*[1] Also 6 myser, myzer, 7 mizer. *β.* 6–7 misard, 9 *dial.* miserd, misert, etc. [a. L. *miser* wretched, unfortunate.

The *β* forms are due to association with the suffix -ard. Sp. and It. *misero* have, like the Eng. word, the two meanings of (1) wretched, (2) avaricious.]

†**A.** *adj.*

1. Miserable, wretched. *Obs.*

1542 Udall *Erasm. Apoph.* 108b *marg.*, Manne of all creatures moste miser. **1558** Phaer *Æneid* ii. E iv b, Again to wepons fourth I flewe, and death moste myser call [*L. mortemque miserrimus opto*]. **1567** Turberv. *Epit.* etc. 8 Thus must I Miser liue till shee..Doe pittie mee. *a* **1586** Sidney *Arcadia* ii. (1622) 174 Shee assured her selfe I was such a one as would make euen his miser-minde contented with that he had done. **1612** *Pasquil's Night-cap* (1877) 58 And looking forth did see that miser wight, which (like a drowned mouse) stood dropping there.

2. [attrib. use of B. 2.] Miserly. *arch.* or *dial.*

1598 SYLVESTER *Du Bartas* II. i. III. 781 Treasures, scrap't by th' Vsury and Care Of miser-Parents [orig. *des ayeuls vsuriers*]. **1612** W. PARKES *Curtaine-Dr.* (1876) 30 A miser father finds a thriftlesse sonne. **1729** SAVAGE *Wanderer* III. 155 The miser-spirit eyes the spendthrift heir. **1789** BURNS *To Mary in Heaven* iv, Still o'er these scenes my mem'ry wakes, And fondly broods with miser care! **1810** J. MONTGOMERY *W. Indies*, etc. (ed. 3) 18 Dark through his thoughts the miser purpose roll'd To turn its hidden treasures into gold. **1855** SINGLETON *Virgil* III. 63 Ah! fly fell regions, fly a miser shore [orig. *fuge litus avarum*].

β. **1825–80** JAMIESON, *Misert*, extremely parsimonious.

Comb. **1602** BRETON *Mother's Blessing* (Grosart) 10/2 Where thou shalt see the mizer-minded-dogge, Frie in the furnace of his molten gold.

B. *sb.*

†1. A miserable or wretched person; a wretch. *Obs.* (*arch.* in Scott.)

1542 UDALL *Erasm. Apoph.* 108 b, So did the philosophier call hym a miser, that had no qualitee aboue the commen rate of manne. *a* **1548** HALL *Chron., Hen. VIII*, 242 b, He paciently suffered the stroke of the axe, by a ragged and Boocherly miser, whiche very ungodly performed the Office. **1584** R. SCOT *Discov. Witchcr.* VIII. ii. (1886) 128 If these cold prophets..tell thee prosperitie and deceive thee, thou art made a miser through vaine expectation. **1591** SHAKS. *1 Hen. VI*, v. iv. 7 Decrepit Miser, base ignoble Wretch. **1608** TOPSELL *Serpents* 99 Being destitute of.. comfort, like a silly Miser..hee trudged home to his owne lodging. **1820** SCOTT *Monast.* xxiv, And who..is the old miser who stands beside him? **1831** —— *F. M. Perth* xv, See thou keep thy scoffs, to pass upon misers in the hospital.

2. One who hoards wealth and lives miserably in order to increase his hoard. Also, in wider use, an avaricious, grasping person, a niggard.

α. c **1560** *Misogonus* II. ii. 91 (Brandl), The misers wealth doth hurt his health. **1599** SHAKS. *Hen. V*, II. iv. 47 Defence ..Which of a weake and niggardly proiection, Doth like a Miser spoyle his Coat, with scanting A little Cloth. **1634** MILTON *Comus* 399 The unsun'd heaps Of Misers treasure. **1691** NORRIS *Pract. Disc.* 265 To see an old shaking Miser among his Bags, like a Scare-Crow in a Field of Corn. **1764** GOLDSM. *Trav.* 51 As some lone miser, visiting his store, Bends at his treasure, counts, recounts it o'er. **1818** BYRON *Juan* I. cxxiv, Sweet to the miser are his glittering hopes. **1842** NEWMAN *Par. Serm.* V. iii. 50 A miser praising almsgiving..is unreal.

β. **1588** GREENE *Perimedes* F, This Melissa flourishing thus in happy fame, the old misard her Father..sought out ..a yoong Gentleman. **1623** COCKERAM I, *Cimbicke*. A misard, or niggard. **1879** MISS JACKSON *Shropsh. Word-bk.*, *Miserd*, a miser, an avaricious man. **1886** *Cheshire Gloss.*

b. †*miser's gallon*: 'a very small measure' (Nares). ***miser's sauce***: see quot. 1877.

1630 J. TAYLOR (Water-P.) *Armado* Wks. I. 82 The *Drunken Sisse*..Her Ordnance are Gallons, Pottles, Quarts, Pints, and the mizers Gallon. **1877** *Cassell's Dict. Cookery*, *Miser's Sauce.*—Mince some young onions, a little parsley, ..and grate a dessert-spoonful of horse-radish. Mix these ingredients with an equal quantity of oil and vinegar.

†c. A niggard in the use *of*. *Obs.*

1630 J. TAYLOR (Water-P.) *Wks.* I. 130 Wine and Ale was so scarce, and the people there such Mizers of it, that [etc.].

†'miser, *sb.*² *Obs.* Also 6 mizer. [Origin uncertain; perh. a use of F. *misère*, which according to Cotgrave had the sense of a drink made from the washings of bee-hives.] A kind of sop made with the crumb of bread, etc.

1594 NASHE *Unfort. Trav.* K, They may crumble it [*sc.* bread] into water well inough, and make mizers with it. **1670–74** HAN. WOOLLEY *Queen-like Closet* (1684) 169 To make Misers for Children to eat in afternoons in Summer. Take half a pint of good small Beer, two spoonfuls of Sack, the Crum of half a penny Manchet [etc.].

miser ('maɪzə(r)), *sb.*³ Also mizer. [Origin uncertain.] A boring instrument used in sinking wells, consisting of an iron cylinder having an opening in the side with a cutting lip, which is attached to the lower end of a boring-rod.

1842 *Civil Eng. & Arch. Jrnl.* V. 168/2 The 'miser' can bring up a cubic yard of earth each time it is raised. **1843** *Min. Proc. Inst. Civil Eng.* (1844) II. 59 The advantages of a large diameter were manifest to all practical men, particularly when the auger or 'miser' was used. **1875** E. SPON *Sinking & Boring Wells* 56 The valve in the old form of mizer is subject to various accidents which interfere with the action of the tool. *Ibid.* 57 The conical bottom of the miser has a triangular-shaped opening.

miser ('maɪzə(r)), *v.*¹ *rare.* [f. MISER *sb.*¹] *trans.* To hoard *up* in a miserly fashion.

1888 G. MACDONALD *Elect Lady* xvi. 144 Before people had money, they must have misered other things! Some girls miser their clothes, and never go decent. **1902** *Cassell's Suppl.*, *Miser*, to keep or hoard like a miser; to save (with *up*).

miser ('maɪzə(r)), *v.*² [Related to MISER *sb.*³] *trans.* To bring *up* (earth) by means of a miser. Also *absol.* Hence **'misering** *vbl. sb.*, boring with a miser.

1842 *Civil Eng. & Arch. Jrnl.* V. 420/1 The misering was continued until the depth of 189 ft. 10 in. was attained. **1843** HOLTZAPFFEL *Turning* II. 552 *note*, In boring large holes, the earth is generally excavated by the process of 'misering up'. **1855** OGILVIE Suppl., *Miser*, an iron cylinder..in which the earthy matters are collected, or misered-up, in the process of sinking.

miserabilism ('mɪzərəbɪlɪz(ə)m). [ad. mod.L. *miserabilism-us*, f. L. *miserābil-is* MISERABLE: see -ISM.] A form of pessimism (see quot.). So **'miserabilist**, an advocate of miserabilism; **miserabi'listic** *a.*, practising or advocating miserabilism.

1882 J. W. BARLOW *Ultim. Pessimism* 8 The third..of these unscientific species combines the characteristic evils of both wrathful and quietistic pessimism. It has been aptly termed Miserabilism (*Miserabilismus*). The miserabilistic pessimist spends his life in sulky grumbling at his lot, without making the slightest effort to improve it. He is not active, nor has the grace to be resigned. **1902** *Q. Rev.* Oct. 632 Leopardi's pessimism is of the 'miserabilist' kind.

miserability (ˌmɪzərə'bɪlɪtɪ). *rare*⁻¹. [f. MISERABLE: see -ITY.] Miserableness.

1838 HAWTHORNE *Amer. Note-bks.* (1883) 180 The utter and ludicrous miserability thereof made us laugh.

miserable ('mɪzərəb(ə)l), *a.* and *sb.* [a. F. *misérable* (from 14th c.), ad. L. *miserābil-is* pitiable, f. *miserārī* to be pitiful, f. *miser* wretched.]

A. *adj.*

1. Of persons: **a.** Existing in a state of misery; wretchedly unhappy in condition. Now *rare*.

1526 TINDALE *1 Cor.* xv. 19 Then are we off all men the miserablest. **1536** *Prymer of Salysbery* fol. clviij b, I am a wretched: and a miserable synner. **1548–9** (Mar.) *Bk. Com. Prayer, Litany*, Haue mercy vpon vs miserable synners. **1560** DAUS tr. *Sleidane's Comm.* 273 a, He..besecheth him for Christes sake..not to worke any extremitie against hym, beyng a myserable Prince [*miserum sane principem*]. **1588** SHAKS. *Tit. A.* III. ii. 28 To bid Æneas tell the tale twice ore How Troy was burnt, and he made miserable. **1604** E. G[RIMSTONE] *D'Acosta's Hist. Indies* V. xii. 360 It was a thing very common..that the Divell..answered in these false Sanctuaries deceiving this miserable people. **1667** MILTON *P.L.* XI. 500 O miserable Mankind, to what fall Degraded, to what wretched state reserv'd! **1710** BEVERIDGE *Thes. Theol.* II. 383 How miserable wilt thou be without Christ, Satan always domineering over..thee.

absol. **1484** CAXTON *Fables of Æsop* IV. v. (1889) 107 Every one ought to do wel to the straunger and forgyue to the myserable. **1711** STEELE *Spect.* No. 84 ¶2 In the Regard for the Miserable, Eucrate took particular Care, that the common Forms of Distress..should never obtain Favour by his Means.

b. Mentally full of misery; wretchedly unhappy in feeling. Now often in somewhat trivial sense: Wretchedly uneasy or uncomfortable.

1591 SHAKS. *Two Gent.* IV. i. 35 My youthfull trauaile, therein made me happy, Or else I often had beene often miserable. **1696** SWIFT *Let.* (1768) IV. i, He is the miserablest creature in the world; eternally in his melancholy note, whatever I can do. **1766** GOLDSM. *Vic. W.* xvii, Go and be miserable, for we shall never enjoy one hour more. **1802** MRS. E. PARSONS *Myst. Visit* IV. 152 Mr. Clifford..seemed very miserable by the loss of his box. **1847** C. BRONTË *J. Eyre* ii, I cry because I am miserable. **1859** TENNYSON *Enid* 7 The pang That makes a man, in the sweet face of her Whom he loves most, lonely and miserable. **1866** [see 3].

absol. **1890** *Spectator* 15 Mar., Not by subordinating religious principle to the desires of the miserable.

2. Needy, poverty-stricken; wretchedly poor. *Obs.* exc. as merged in 1 a.

1585 *Reg. Privy Council Scot.* Ser. I. III. 747 Ydill beggaris and miserable personis. **1590** SWINBURNE *Testaments* 30 They be poore and needie, such as the law tearmeth miserable persons. **1697** DAMPIER *Voy.* (1699) 464 The Inhabitants of this Country [New Holland] are the miserablest People in the World. The Hodmadods of Monomatapa, though a nasty People, yet for Wealth are Gentlemen to these. **1706** PHILLIPS (ed. Kersey), *Miserable*, wretched, unfortunate, distressed, poor. **1842** BORROW *Bible in Spain* xxxiv, San Vincente, a large dilapidated town, chiefly inhabited by miserable fishermen.

3. Of conditions, events, etc.: Full of or fraught with misery; causing wretchedness.

1500–20 DUNBAR *Poems* lxi. 50 My lyf hes bene so miserable. **1535** COVERDALE *2 Kings* xiv. 26 The Lorde considered the myserable affliccion of Israel. **1594** SHAKS. *Rich. III*, I. iv. 2 O, I haue past a miserable night, So full of fearefull Dreames, of vgly sights. **1666** DRYDEN *Ann. Mirab.* Pref., Ess. (ed. Ker) I. 11 The destruction being..so vast and miserable, as nothing can parallel in story. **1726** SWIFT *Gulliver* II. viii, What could I expect but a miserable death of cold and hunger? **1813** SHELLEY *Q. Mab* v. 248 Disease, disgust, and lassitude, pervade Their valueless and miserable lives. **1866** MRS. CHARLES *Winifred Bertram* i. 13 Auntie says it is not of the least use to make one's self miserable about miserable things that never happened at all.

b. In weakened sense: Causing extreme discomfort.

1850 *Beck's Florist* 233 It was a miserable morning..when we started for Slough in our open conveyance. **1856** FROUDE *Hist. Eng.* (1858) I. v. 403 The journey in the wild weather was extremely miserable.

4. Of things: Exciting, or such as to excite, pity; pitiable, deplorable. Now *rare* exc. with mixture of sense 5.

1552 ABP. HAMILTON *Catech.* Pref. (1884) 5 Bot and the samyn office be done negligently, thair is na thing afore God mair miserabil, mair hevy and mair damnabil. **1665** SIR T. HERBERT *Trav.* (1677) 307 Superstition I detest; but that it should become a derision, is miserable and to be pitied. **1726** SWIFT *Gulliver* II. vii, To show the miserable effects of a confined education. **1870** MAX MÜLLER *Sci. Relig.* (1873) 272 His success was after all a miserable failure.

5. Pitiably unworthy, inadequate, or meagre; contemptible, despicable; paltry, 'sorry', 'poor'.

1500–20 DUNBAR *Poems* lxiii. 37 Ane vthir sort, more miserabill, Thocht thai be nocht sa profitable. **1534** WHITINTON *Tullyes Offices* I. (1540) 58 Ambycion and contencion for honour is a vyce vtterly very miserable. **1535** COVERDALE *Job* xvi. 2 Miserable geuers of comforte are ye. **1597** *Pilgrim. Parnass.* II. (1886) 8 [He] often scratcheth his witts' head for the bringinge of one miserable period into the worlde. **1620** T. GRANGER *Div. Logike* 350 The Proposition is miserable. For a false adiunct is put a true adiunct, happie. **1723** CHAMBERS tr. *Le Clerc's Treat. Archit.* I. 137 Their Bases and Corniches will be confounded together, which must needs have a miserable Effect. **1743** WESLEY in *Wks.* 1872 I. 412 One of the most miserable sermons I ever heard. **1794** BURKE *Sp. agst. W. Hastings* Wks. 1827 VIII. 301 This miserable balance of 60,000*l.* **1818** in *Harper's Mag.* (1884) June 126/1 The corn is miserable..; we have to pound it. **1841** L. HUNT *Seer* (1864) II. 34 It would be the miserablest and most despicable of all mistakes. **1873** HALE *In His Name* vi. 60 He had lost certainly half an hour in that miserable altercation.

b. *colloq.* Applied to very weak tea. Also *absol.*

1842 LOVER *Handy Andy* xv. 130 The large bowl of *miserable* Mrs. O'Grady had prepared. **1900** E. GLYN *Visits Eliz.* 205 There was only a *miserable* tea left.

6. Miserly, mean, stingy. Now *dial.*

1484 CAXTON *Fables of Æsop* IV. iv. (1889) 106 The myserable auarycious, the more goodes that they haue the more they desire to haue. **1522** [implied in MISERABLENESS 2]. **1597** HOOKER *Eccl. Pol.* V. lxv. §20 The liberall harted man is by the opinion of the prodigall miserable, and by the iudgement of the miserable lauish. **1611** COTGR. s.v. *Fourmage*, Cheese is good when a miserable hand giues it. **1621** BURTON *Anat. Mel.* II. i. IV. ii. (1651) 228 That he be not too niggardly miserable of his purse. **1646** QUARLES *Judgem. & Mercy* Wks. (Grosart) I. 78/1 If I am covetous it is interpreted providence; if miserable, it is counted temperance. **1816–60** WHATELY *Comm.-pl. Bk.* (1864) 235 In Norfolk and Suffolk, among the common people, the word *miserable* is the only one in use to signify what we call penurious. **1853** *N. & Q.* Ser. I. VII. 544. **1859** MRS. GASKELL *Round the Sofa* II. 101 A certain kind of sober pleasure in amassing money, which occasionally made them miserable (as they call miserly people up in the north).

†7. Having pity, compassionate. *Obs.*

1584 *Three Ladies Lond.* F j b, Therefore pray ye Sir, be miserable to me, and let me go. **1600** HEYWOOD *1st Pt. Edw. IV*, IV. iv. I j b, My sonnes..itha Gaile,..and outstep [= outcept] the King be miserable, hees like to totter. **1630** J. TAYLOR (Water-P.) *Wks.* II. 80/1 Although my crime is vnmeasurable, yet I hope your Lordship will not forget to become miserable.

8. *Comb.*, as ***miserable-looking*** adj.

1839 DARWIN *Jrnl. Voy. Beagle* 3 A hospital, containing about a dozen miserable-looking inmates.

B. *sb.* A miserable person; one who is in misery, extreme unhappiness, or great want.

[In mod. use chiefly after F. *misérable*.]

1534 LD. BERNERS *Gold. Bk. M. Aurel.* (1559) H h vj b, These miserables after that they be appoincted and set in their offices, where of they be nothynge woorthy [etc.]. **1640** tr. *Verdere's Rom. of Rom.* III. 131 Parmolina (so is this miserable called that speaks to you) loves you with passion. **1679** EVERARD *Disc.* 23 We need not admire at the Tribulation which these poor miserables do suffer. **1768** STERNE *Sent. Journ., Dwarf*, So many miserables, by force of accidents driven out of their own proper class. **1815** SOUTHEY *Roderick* xxv, Saying thus, he seized the miserable. **1833** GEN. P. THOMPSON *Exerc.* (1842) II. 480 The same kind of effect, that a clean shirt and a razor have upon the miserable who was in want of them. **1896** 'IAN MACLAREN' *Kate Carnegie* 287 It ill became such miserables [*sc.* students in grimy towns] to be insolent.

'miserableness. [-NESS.]

1. The quality or condition of being miserable; wretchedness, miserable unhappiness.

1613 PURCHAS *Pilgrimage* I. xiii. (1614) 74 He found a miserable death, where others with miserablenesse seeke a blessed life. **1701** COLLIER *M. Anton.* (1726) 178 Does any natural defect force you upon grumbling, miserableness, or laying your faults upon your constitution. **1830** COLERIDGE *Lett.* (1895) 751 During my long chain of bodily miserablenesses. **1890** *Spectator* 5 July, 'My God! what a genius I had when I wrote that book', said Swift, half-mad and wholly miserable... Wordsworth, without any miserableness or despair, was..of the same opinion.

†2. Miserliness, niggardliness, stinginess. *Obs.*

1522 SKELTON *Why nat to Court* 1029 Suche gredynesse, Suche nedynesse, Myserablenesse, With wretchydnesse. **1641** QUARLES *Enchyr.* II. xvii, It is lesse reproach, by miserablenesse, to preserve the popular love, than by liberality to deserve the private thanks. **1681–6** J. SCOTT *Chr. Life* II. iv. §3 Wks. 1718 I. 289 His Prosperity either shrivels him into Miserableness, or melts him into Luxury. **1706** PHILLIPS (ed. Kersey), *Miserableness*, Covetousness, Niggardliness, Stinginess.

3. Wretched or mean character or condition.

1633 BP. MORTON *Disch. 5 Imputations* 199 To the end that you may see the miserablenesse of your Cause, which must be supported by such Frauds..as his have beene.

miserably ('mɪzərəblɪ), *adv.* [f. MISERABLE + -LY².]

1. In a miserable manner; in such a manner or to such an extent as to excite pity; in misery; in extreme unhappiness or discomfort.

1432–50 tr. *Higden* (Rolls) IV. 5 He herde that his moder scholde die miserably. *c* **1440** *Alphabet of Tales* 244 And þan come tythandis at þe pope was myserablie dead. *a* **1500** *Bernard. de cura rei fam.* (E.E.T.S.) 1 As he his howsalde sulde contene, And his famele miserabilly sustene. **1535** COVERDALE *Micah* ii. 10 Because off their Idolatry they are corrupte, and shall myserably perish. **1657** WOOD *Life* (O.H.S.) I. 216 The effigies..miserably defaced when Oxon was besieged. **1726** SWIFT *Gulliver* III. iv, In the mean Time, the whole Country lies miserably waste. **1753** *Scots Mag.* Feb. 100/1 Five were miserably scorched. **1782** COWPER *Lett.* 18 Nov., We promise, however, that none shall touch it but such as are miserably poor. **1822** SHELLEY tr. *Calderon's Mag. Prodig.* II. 44 The melancholy form Of a great ship..Drives miserably! **1881** RUSSELL *Haigs* vii. 154 This unnatural strife..which had ended in her husband being thus miserably incarcerated.

b. Pitiably, deplorably, despicably.

1597 *Pilgrim. Parnass.* II. (1886) 6, I want a worde miserablely! I must looke for another worde in my dictionarie. **1741** MIDDLETON *Cicero* II. x. 414 Bassus was miserably unwilling to deliver up his Legion.

2. So as to cause misery or distress; calamitously, disastrously. ? *Obs.*

1538 STARKEY *England* 22 Some put in pryson and myserably handlyd. **1584** POWEL *Lloyd's Cambria* 100 [They] set the cathedrall on fire, and..spoiled and burnt the towne miserablie. **1596** DALRYMPLE tr. *Leslie's Hist. Scot.* II. 300 The Jnglis men of weir..afflicted vs sair, and misaribilie. **1603** KNOLLES *Hist. Turks* (1621) 59 [They] miserably and without resistance wasted the countrey about Emissa. **1728** MORGAN *Algiers* II. ii. 227 He continued his Excursions, miserably ravaging all the Italian Coasts.

b. So as to make one feel wretched.

1806 J. BERESFORD *Miseries Hum. Life* VI. xxxviii, On the road—one of the wheels of your carriage beginning to creak miserably.

†**3.** In a miserly fashion, covetously. *Obs.*—0

1611 COTGR., *Sordidement*,..basely, miserably, for (deere) lucres sake. **1736** AINSWORTH, Miserably (covetously), *Avarè, illiberaliter.*

4. Meanly, wretchedly, badly.

a **1586** SIDNEY *Arcadia* II. xix. §4 (1590) 187 b, The same loue makes me ashamed to bring you to a place, where you shalbe so..miserably entertained. **1840** MACAULAY *Ess., Ld. Clive* (1843) III. 113 The younger clerks were so miserably paid.

5. Used as a pejorative intensive (cf. *wretchedly*).

1715 POPE *Iliad* I. 180 Sanson's map..is miserably defective both in Omissions and false Placings. **1810** J. FOSTER in *Life & Corr.* (1846) I. lxxviii. 415 The miserably deficient improvement of a life of which the best part is now gone. **1871** CARLYLE in Mrs. Carlyle *Lett.* I. 392 She had a miserably bad sore throat.

miseraic(k, -aike, etc., obs. ff. MESARAIC.

†**mise'ration.** *Obs.* [ad. L. *miserātiōn-em*, n. of action f. *miserārī* to have compassion, f. *miser* wretched.] Pity, compassion, mercy.

1382 WYCLIF *2 Esdras* ix. 31 God of myseracîouns [Vulg. *Deus miserationum*]. **1432–50** tr. *Higden* (Rolls) I. 5 Diuine miseracion [orig. *divina miseratio*] hath prouided vse of letters in to the remedy of the imperfeccion of man. **1522** SKELTON *Why nat to Court* 1041 God of his miseracyon Send better reformacyon! **1533** BELLENDEN *Livy* I. ii. (S.T.S.) I. 17 Hir sonnys war commandit but ony miseracioun to be cassin in tyber. **1609** BIBLE (Douay) *Zech.* vii. 9 *comm.*, Doe ye mercie, and miserations [Vulg. *miserationes facite*]. **1638** JUNIUS *Paint. Ancients* 72 The sight of so many afflicted ones provoking teares by a mutuall miseration.

†**miseratour.** *Obs. rare*—1. [a. L. *miserātor*, agent-n. f. *miserārī* to pity.] One who pities.

1609 BIBLE (Douay) *Isa.* liv. 10 *comm.*, Our Lord thy miseratour [Vulg. *miserator tuus*].

miserdom ('maɪzədəm). [f. MISER *sb.*[1] + -DOM.] The habits and practices of a miser.

1887 *Pall Mall G.* 11 Feb. 2/1 A Tory Government yielding to senseless and uncalled-for pressure for miserdom is a sight for men and gods. **1887** *Advance* (Chicago) 13 Oct. 641 In all the annals of miserdom or rapacity.

misere, obs. form of MISERY.

‖**misère** (mɪ'zɛə(r), Fr. mizɛr). *Cards.* [Fr. = poverty, MISERY.] **1.** In boston and solo whist, a declaration by which the caller undertakes not to take a trick.

1830 'EIDRAH TREBOR' *Hoyle* 32 [Boaston.] If he is to play Misere, the elder hand leads, and in this case there are no trumps. *Ibid.* 34 In playing any of the four modifications of 'Misere'. **1888** A. S. WILKS & C. F. PARDON *How to Play Solo Whist* 2 The monotony of the very bad hands which in Whist were dealt out to him..he is now enabled to vary by calling 'misère'. *Ibid.* 6 The misère caller should..claim the full penalty for every such offence. *Ibid.* 9.

2. = MISERY.

1897 E. DOWSON *Let.* c 10 June (1967) 385 Writing to you has somewhat cheered me, but all my misères will return in a moment. **1903** [see GOD-FORSAKEN *ppl. a.*]. **1964** *Punch* 2 Sept. 359/3 Recommended to those who still enjoy being stunned by the grandeurs of empire with the *misères* guaranteed absent.

‖**misereatur** (mɪzɛrɪ'eɪtə(r)). *Eccl.* [3 pers. sing. pres. subj. of L. *miserērī* to have pity or mercy.] = May (God) have mercy; being the first word of the Absolution used in the Western Church.

c **1450** *Bk. Curtasye* 154 in *Babees Bk.*, To schryue þe in general þou schalle lere þy Confiteor and misereatur in fere. *a* **1470** GREGORY in *Hist. Coll. Cit. Lond.* (Camd.) 167 He..layde hym downe prostrate, sayng there hys *Confyteor*, and alle the prelatys sayde *Misereator*. **1845** J. JONES *Man. Plain-chant* 25 The *Confiteor, Misereatur*, and *Indulgentiam*, are recited, not sung.

‖**miserere** (mɪzə'rɪərɪ, -'rɛə-). Also 6 messerery, 7 misereri. [imper. sing. of L. *miserērī* (see prec.).]

1. a. The fifty-first Psalm (fiftieth in the Vulgate), beginning *Miserere mei Deus* ('Have mercy upon me, O God'), being one of the Penitential Psalms.

a **1225** *Ancr. R.* 44, & mid te miserere, goð biuoren ower weoude & endeð ðer þe graces. **1539** PERY in Ellis *Orig. Lett.* Ser. II. II. 153 Sayeinge the sawme of 'Messerery' ower us. **1583** FOXE *A. & M.* 1493/2 And so was brought..by the Sheriffes toward Smithfield, saying the Psalme *Miserere* by the way. *a* **1693** *Urquhart's Rabelais* III. xxiii, If ever..I may lay hold upon thee..thou shalt have the *Miserere* even to the *Vitulos* [cf. Vulgate Ps. l. fin.]. **1656** BLOUNT *Glossogr.* *Miserere*,..is commonly that Psalm, which the Judge gives to such guilty persons as have the benefit of Clergy allowed by the Law. **1829** W. IRVING *Diary* 16 Apr. in *Life & Lett.* (1862) II. 310 Miserere in the cathedral in the evening. **1845** E. HOLMES *Mozart* 65 Arriving at Rome in the Holy Week, they hurried to the Sistine Chapel, to hear the *Miserere* at matins.

b. With reference to the time it takes to recite the *Miserere.* (Cf. F. *demeurer un bon miséréré.*)

[*c* **1450** *ME. Med. Bk.* (Heinrich) 111 Seþe hem by þe space of þis psalme seyenge: miserere mei deus.] **1558** WARDE tr. *Alexis' Secr.* (1568) 26 Let all boyle together for the space of one Miserere. **1665** *Phil. Trans.* I. 97, I have heard one say, that had seen it, that it did not set Wood on Fire but after the time of saying a *Miserere.*

c. A musical setting of this psalm.

1776 BURNEY *Hist. Mus.* (1789) IV. 569 Metastasio, to whom I transmitted a copy of this *Miserere.* **1779** H. WALPOLE *Let. to C'tess Ossory* 15 Nov., I was last night at Lady Lucan's to hear the Misses Bingham sing Jomelli's 'Miserere'. **1845** E. HOLMES *Mozart* 67 The 'Miserere' of Allegri.

¶**d.** = KYRIE 1 b.

?*c* **1620** R. PATRICK in S. Arnold *Cathedral Mus.* (1790) (*title*) The Te Deum, Benedictus, Miserere, Nicene Creed [etc.].

2. *transf.* A cry of 'Have mercy!'; a prayer or ejaculation in which mercy is asked for.

a **1616** BEAUM. & FL. *Woman's Prize* III. i, No more aymees, and miseries [*read* misereres] Tranio Come near my brain. **1657** J. D[AVIES] tr. *Lett. Voiture* xi. I. 19, I repeated to her in your behalf, a whole *Miserere.* *a* **1700** KEN *Hymnotheo* Poet. Wks. 1721 III. 75 The Mourners, who the Penitent espy'd, A universal *miserere* cry'd. **1804** *Edin. Rev.* V. 152 A main fault that pervades the whole is the monotonous cry of *miserere* for the poor Irish. **1845** LONGF. *Arsenal at Springfield* ii, What loud lament and dismal Miserere Will mingle with their awful symphonies [*sc.* of firearms]. **1882** J. H. BLUNT *Ref. Ch. Eng.* II. 350 The sweet Alleluias and the plaintive Misereres of the English Prayer Book.

†**3.** In full ***miserere mei*** ('miːraɪ), lit. 'have mercy on me': a name for the 'iliac passion', a form of colic attended with stercoraceous vomiting. *Obs.*

1611 COTGR., *Reply*..the voiding of the excrements at the mouth; a disease called, *Miserere mei.* **1648** JENKYN *Blind Guide* iv. 116 You were under a quotidean fury, or sick of the miserere mei. **1722** QUINCY *Lex. Physico-Med.* (ed. 2), *Miserere mei*, this is apply'd to some Cholicks, where the Pains are so exquisite, as to draw Compassion from a Bystander. **1766** AMORY *Mem.* II. 50 In the excruciating torments of that most dreadful distemper a *miserere.* **1783** POTT *Chirurg. Wks.* II. 148 If it proves fatal by mortification, it is taken for a *passio-illiaca*, or *miserere.*

4. = MISERICORD 2 c. (An incorrect use.)

1798–1801 J. MILNER *Hist. Winchester* II. 36 The stalls with their misereres, canopies, pinnacles, &c. *Ibid. note*, That small shelving stool, which the seats of the stalls formed when turned up in their proper position, is called a *Miserere.* **1863** I. WILLIAMS *Baptistery* II. xxiii. (1874) 80 The Misereres here have place, As hiding from the day of Grace The quaint device, and snakes that twine,..Which speak the serpent's brood below. **1869** TOZER *Highl. Turkey* I. 80 The stalls..are provided with misereres, which..are seldom used, as the monks generally stand during the whole service. **1959** *Punch* 30 Dec. 675/2, I..selected a train with the longest carriages I could find... To get the full vista, I sat on the miserere at the front.

attrib. **1848** B. WEBB *Sk. Continental Ecclesiol.* ii. 39 Four beautiful stalls, with miserere-seats and canopies. **1872** *N. & Q.* Ser. IV. IX. 405/1 Miserere carvings. *Ibid.* 472/2 Miserere stalls.

'**miserhood.** *rare.* [-HOOD.] Miserliness.

1867 BUSHNELL *Mor. Uses Dark Th.* 221 Hate, jealousy, petulance, miserhood, envy,—every sort of obliquity has its own disfigurement. *Ibid.* 253.

misericord (mɪ'zɛrɪkɔːd), *sb.* Also 4–5 mysere-, 4–6 mi-, myseri-, mysery-. [a. OF. *misericorde*, ad. L. *misericordia*, f. *misericors* (see next).]

1. Compassion, pity, mercy. Also as *int. Obs.* except *arch.*

a **1315** SHOREHAM I. 1183 To oure lorde Mercy he cryþ, and biddeþ hym Mercy and misericorde. *c* **1386** CHAUCER *Pars. T.* ⁋731 Thanne is misericorde..a vertu, by which the corage of man is stired by the misese of him that is misesed. *c* **1489** CAXTON *Sonnes of Aymon* xi. 284 Gode lord..by thy pite & mysericorde graunt to Rowlande his prayer. **1549** *Compl. Scot.* viii. 72 Quhy vil ȝe nocht haue misericord & pytie of ȝour natiue cuntre? **1651** tr. *De-las-Coveras' Don Fenise* 144 [He] abandoned himselfe to divine mercie, and to the misericord of the waves. **1657–83** EVELYN *Hist. Relig.* (1850) II. 217 The Divine misericord did not utterly abandon our lapsed parents in this condition. **1705** VANBRUGH *Confederacy* I. iii, Misericorde! what do I see! **1922** JOYCE *Ulysses* 380 They had had ado each with other in the house of misericord where this learning knight lay.

2. *Hist.* and *Antiq.* Senses derived from monastic uses of L. *misericordia.* **a.** An indulgence or relaxation of the rule.

1820 SCOTT *Monast.* xix, Indulgence shall be given to those of our attendants who shall, from very weariness, be unable to attend the duty at prime, and this by way of misericord or *indulgentia.*

b. An apartment in a monastery in which certain relaxations of the rule were permitted, *esp.* one in which those monks ate to whom special allowances were made in food and drink.

c **1529** in *Archæologia* (1882) XLVII. 51 That noo suche householdes be then kepte..butt oonly oon place which shalbe called the mysericorde where shalbe oon sadde lady of the eldest sorte ouersear and maistres to all the residue that thidre shall resorte. *c* **1535** *Surv. Yorksh. Monast.* in *Yorksh. Archæol. Jrnl.* (1886) IX. 212 A nother chambre by the same called Mysericorde. **1545** in *London & M'sex Archæol. Trans.* IV. 357 *note*, That Mr. Dean and his successors shal have the Misericorde, the greate Kitchen [etc.]. **1883** *Athenæum* 24 Feb. 255/2 [Mr. Turle's house] was one of the largest of the houses..next after that of the abbot... It stood between the dorter and the misericorde. **1898** J. T. FOWLER *Durham Cath.* 59 The misericorde or 'loft'.

c. A shelving projection on the under side of a hinged seat in a choir stall, so arranged that, when turned up, it gave support to one standing in the stall. Also *attrib.*

c **1515** in Willis & Clark *Cambridge* (1886) I. 484 Iron worke and other small necessaries..as copper to hang the misericordes with [etc.]. **1874** MICKLETHWAITE *Mod. Par. Churches* 2 The chancel seats hung on hinges and provided with misericords. **1893** *Reliquary* VII. 129 Of the ancient misericords [in Limerick Cathedral] nineteen are perfect. **1904** *Athenæum* 20 Aug. 250/3 There are four misericord stalls at Wysall.

3. A dagger with which the *coup de grâce* was given. [So med.L. *misericordia*, F. *miséricorde.*]

14.. *Voc.* in Wr.-Wülcker 653/20 *Hic pugis* [read *pugio*], myserecord. *Ibid.* 654/16 *Hec cica*, misericord. **1484** CAXTON *Chivalry* 63 Mysericorde or knyf with a crosse is gyuen to a knyght to thende that yf his other armures faylle hym that he haue recours to the myserycorde or daggar. **1859** *Archæol. Jrnl.* XVI. 356 A *misericorde*, or dagger of mercy, dug up in a field near Deddington. **1869** BOUTELL *Arms & Armour* iii. 49 It was adjusted at the waist, as was the mediæval *misericorde*, on the right side.

†**misericord**, *a. Sc. Obs.* [a. OF. *misericord*, L. *misericord-em* (*-cors*), f. *miseri-*, stem of *miserērī* to pity + *cord-*, *cor* heart.] Compassionate, pitiful, merciful.

1456 SIR G. HAYE *Law Arms* (S.T.S.) 269 Jugis suld be ay misericordes, and full of clemence and pitee. **1567** *Gude & Godlie B.* (S.T.S.) 168 How suld we thank that Lord, That was sa misericord. **1583** *Leg. Bp. St. Androis* 448 Ye man be gude, my Lord, And to yor man misericord.

†**miseri'cordially**, *adv. Obs. rare*—1. [f. L. *misericordia* mercy + -AL[1] + -LY.[2] Cf. OF. *misericordialment.*] Mercifully.

1659 BROME *Queen & Conc.* IV. iii. 81 If misericordially This gracious Fæminine preserve your lives Ex ore lupi.

†**miseri'cordious**, *a. Obs.* [a. OF. *misericordieux* (from 12th c.), or ad. med.L. *misericordiōs-us*, f. *misericordia* (see MISERICORD *sb.*).] Compassionate, merciful.

1483 CAXTON *Cato* e iiij b, Yf he neuer pardonned..he shold not seme to be myserycordyous ne mercyful. *a* **1500** *Melusine* 313 There nys so grete a synnar in the world but that is more piteable & mysericordyous whan the synnar repenteth hym..of his..synne. **1528** *Sheph. Kal.* xiv. L j b, By youre myserycordyous pyteye. **1634** W. TIRWHYT tr. *Balzac's Lett.* 91 The misericordious Justice of God. **1648** W. BROWNE *Polexander* III. III. 79 That misericordious Goodnesse from whom I have so often petition'd you.

†**miseri'cordy.** *Obs.* [ad. L. *misericordi-a*: see MISERICORD *sb.*] Mercy.

14.. *Chaucer's Boeth.* III. met. xii. (Caxton), The Lord and lugge of sowles was meoued to myserycordyes. **1491** CAXTON *Vitas Patr.* (W. de W. 1495) II. 243 b/2 To haue mercy of me poore synnar & Indygne of thy grete myserycordye.

†**mi'sericors**, *a. Sc. Obs. rare*—1. [a. OF. or L. *misericors*; cf. MISERICORD *a.*] Compassionate.

1535 STEWART *Cron. Scot.* II. 566 Gratius God quhilk is misericors [*rime* perforce].

miserism ('maɪzərɪz(ə)m). *rare*—1. [f. MISER + -ISM.] Miserliness.

1798 ANNA SEWARD *Lett.* (1811) V. 155 Mr Newton has put an immense sponge upon Dr Falconer's reproach to his miserism.

†**mi'serity.** *Sc. Obs.* Also **misaritie.** [app. f. L. *miser* + -ITY after *prosperity.*] Misery.

1530 LYNDESAY *Test. Papyngo* 404 Quhat mortall cheangis, quhat miseritie! [*rime* calamitie]. **1533** GAU *Richt Vay* (1888) 51 Ye miserite of this vane vardil. **1552** LYNDESAY *Monarche* 165 Sum tyme in vaine prosperitie, Sum tyme in gret Misaritie.

†**miserlike**, *adv. Obs.* Of obscure origin and meaning.

c **1250** *Gen. & Ex.* 2658 Ðor-fore seide ðe ebru witterlike, Ðat he spac siðen miserlike. [Petrus Comestor: *Unde et Hebræi impeditioris linguæ eum fuisse autumant.*]

miserliness ('maɪzəlɪnɪs). [f. next + -NESS.] The quality or condition of being miserly; niggardliness, closefistedness.

1645 USSHER *Body Div.* 304 Frugality without liberality [degenerateth] into sordid miserlinesse. **1860** GEO. ELIOT *Mill on Fl.* I. 227 In old-fashioned times, an 'independence' was hardly ever made without a little miserliness. **1865** LEWES in *Fortn. Rev.* II. 692 Economy is rejection of whatever is superfluous; it is not Miserliness.

miserly ('maɪzəlɪ), *a.* [f. MISER *sb.* + -LY[1].] Pertaining to or characteristic of a miser; niggardly, stingy.

1593 NASHE *Christ's T.* 29 b, If there were any that had dudgen-olde coughing miserly Fathers they could not endure. **1860** WINSLOW *Obsc. Dis. Brain* vi. 169 If benevolent, he [*sc.* the insane person] becomes

parsimonious and miserly. **1870** DICKENS *E. Drood* vii, He was a miserly wretch who grudged us food to eat, and clothes to wear. **1875** JOWETT *Plato* (ed. 2) III. 104 The youth who has had a mean and miserly bringing up.

transf. **1869** LOWELL *Under the Willows* vii, To spend in all things else, But of old friends to be most miserly.

† **'miserous,** *a. Obs.* [a. OF. *misereux*, f. *misère*: see MISERY.] Miserable.

c **1475** in Miss Wood *Lett. Roy. Ladies* (1846) I. 108 She hath been long in the miserous prison of Ludgate. **1530** PALSGR. 319/1 Myserable wretched or myserouse. **1560** PHAER *Æneid* VIII. (1562) Bb iij b, O plague most miserous.

misery ('mɪzərɪ). Also 4-6 **misere, mysere,** 4-7 **miserie,** (5 **mesury**), 5-6 **mysery(e,** 6 **misserie.** [a. OF. *miserie* (12th c.), ad. L. *miseria*, f. *miser* (see MISER).

The 15th c. form *mi'sere* seems to be a later re-adoption from OF. *misere* (mod.F. *misère*).]

1. A condition of external unhappiness, discomfort, or distress; wretchedness of outward circumstances; distress caused by privation or poverty.

c **1374** CHAUCER *Troylus* IV. 272 Wrecche of wrecches, out of honour falle In-to miserie. *c* **1425** *Eng. Conq. Irel.* 43 Shew hym the mesury that thay Sufferid for his Sake. *c* **1450** LOVELICH *Grail* xliii. 450 And so longe abod he here In povert and In gret Misere. **1470-85** MALORY *Arthur* II. viii. 84 In grete pouerte myserye & wretchidnes. **1535** COVERDALE *2 Esdras* ii. 17 Ye se the myserye yt we are in, how Ierusalem lyeth wayst. **1610** SHAKS. *Temp.* II. ii. 41 Misery acquaints a man with strange bedfellowes. **1667** MILTON *P. L.* x. 810 But say That Death be not one stroak,..but endless miserie. **1705** ADDISON *Italy* 5 The extream Misery and Poverty that are in most of the Italian Governments. **1829** LYTTON *Devereux* I. i, Early marriages were misery; imprudent marriages idiotism. **1836** MACGILLIVRAY tr. *Humboldt's Trav.* xix. 273 The converts live in great poverty, and their misery is augmented by prodigious swarms of mosquitoes. **1849** MACAULAY *Hist. Eng.* iv. I. 433 The sight of his misery affected his wife so much that she fainted. **1886** RUSKIN *Præterita* I. 432 The misery of unaided poverty.

personified. **1750** GRAY *Elegy* Epit., He gave to Mis'ry all he had, a tear. **1799** COWPER *Castaway* 59 But misery still delights to trace Its semblance in another's case.

2. a. With †*a* and *pl.* A miserable condition or circumstance; a cause or source of wretchedness.

1509 FISHER *Funeral Serm. C'tess Richmond* Wks. (1876) 306 After that he [*sc.* Lazarus] was restored to the myseryes of this lyfe agayne, he neuer laugh. **1548-9** (Mar.) *Bk. Com. Prayer, Offices* 24 b, The miseries of this wretched world. **1572** HULOET s.v., It is a great mysery to be very beautifull. **1615** STOW *Ann.* Pref. ¶ 5 What a hellish misery it is to have vnreconciliable warres in one small kingdome. **1660** F. BROOKE tr. *Le Blanc's Trav.* III. xvi. 398 The misery is, divers of them have fallen to frequent their Superstitions and Idolatries. **1697** DRYDEN *Æneid* x. 1076 The Gods from Heav'n survey the fatal Strife, And mourn the Miseries of Human Life. **1788** COWPER *Negro's Compl.* 43 By the miseries that we tasted, Crossing in your barks the main. **1842** BORROW *Bible in Spain* vii, He was going to expose himself to inconceivable miseries and hardships. **1849** MACAULAY *Hist. Eng.* v. I. 628 All the miseries of fallen greatness and of blighted fame.

b. *concr.* A miserable person or place.

1790 MME. D'ARBLAY *Diary* (1842) V. 181, I am sure she would gladly have confined us both in the Bastile, had England such a misery. **1888** *Lady* 25 Oct. VIII. 374/2 'Small street Arabs', she answered. 'The little miseries out of the gutters'.

c. ***misery me!***, an interjection expressing self-pity, distress, or general wretchedness.

1888 W. S. GILBERT *Yeomen of Guard* II. 48 Misery me, lackadaydee! He sipped no sup and he craved no crumb, As he sighed for the love of a ladye! **1968** N. MARSH *Clutch of Constables* i. 15 'O misery, misery, misery me,' she wrote with enormous relish.

3. The condition of one in great sorrow or distress of mind; miserable or wretched state of mind; a condition characterized by a feeling of extreme unhappiness.

1535 COVERDALE *Job* iii. 20 Wherfore is the light geuen, to him that is in mysery? and life vnto them that haue heuy hertes? **1599** *Return fr. Parnass.* I. i. 472 Thanks, gentle nimphes, for this sweete harmonie! Soe musick yealdes some ease to miserie. **1667** MILTON *P. L.* II. 563 Of good and evil much they argu'd then, Of happiness and final misery. **1729** BUTLER *Serm.* Wks. 1874 II. 35 It is acknowledged that rage, envy, resentment, are in themselves mere misery. **1833** TENNYSON *Two Voices* 2 Thou art so full of misery, Were it not better not to be? **1852** MRS. STOWE *Uncle Tom's C.* xxxiv. 311 It seemed as if I had misery enough in my one heart to sink the city.

†**4.** Miserliness, niggardliness. *Obs.*

1531 ELYOT *Gov.* III. xxii. (1880) II. 345 This was but miserye and wretched nygardeshippe in a man of suche honour. **1579-80** NORTH *Plutarch, Galba* (1595) 1107 His meane and simple ordinary of dyet..was imputed misery and niggardlines in him. **1600** HOLLAND *Livy* III. 131 The Senate right sparingly (such was their miserie), decreed.. one daies thanksgiving..and no more. **1624** WOTTON *Elem. Archit.* 66 A little misery in the Premises, may easily breed some absurdity of greater charge in the Conclusion.

†**5.** A mean or despicable condition. *Obs.*

1607 DEKKER *Knt.'s Conjur.* (1842) 76 Into so lowe a miserie (if not contempt,) is the sacred art of poesie falne [etc.].

6. *dial.* Bodily pain; *U.S. dial.* (with *a*) a pain. *to **put*** (a person or animal) ***out of*** (his) ***misery***: see PUT *v.*^{1} 48 d.

1825 FORBY *Voc. E. Anglia, Misery*, acute pain in any part of the body. '*Misery* in the head', means a violent head-ache. **1867** LATHAM *Black & White* 38 Massa, I have such a misery in my back. **1895** *Century Mag.* Aug. 543/1 [His] most memorable remark was that he had 'a misery in his stomach'.

7. *Cards.* = MISÈRE 1. Common *colloq.*

8. *Comb.*, as *misery-line, -threshold*; *misery-making, -stricken, -thirsting* adjs.

1813 SHELLEY *Q. Mab* VI. 126 Thou framedst A tale..to glut Thy misery-thirsting soul. **1865** DICKENS *Mut. Fr.* II. xiv, Perverted uses of the misery-making money. **1896** *Daily Tel.* 10 Mar. 6/7 The misery-stricken people of Italy. **1902** W. JAMES *Varieties Relig. Experience* vi. 135 The sanguine and healthy-minded live habitually on the sunny side of their misery-line. *Ibid.* v. 135 We might speak of a 'pain-threshold', a 'fear-threshold', a 'misery-threshold'.

misese, obs. form of MISEASE.

mise'steem, *sb.* [MIS-^{1} 4. Cf. F. *mésestime.*] Want of esteem or respect; disrespect.

1850 OGILVIE, *Misesteem*, disregard; slight. **1881** F. T. PALGRAVE *Vis. Eng.* 111 They of the great race Look equably ..on foe And fame and misesteem of man below. **1898** BODLEY *France* II. III. v. 258 The office of minister must remain in misesteem.

mise'steem, *v.* [MIS-^{1} 1. Cf. F. *mésestimer.*] *trans.* To have a wrong estimation of. Also **mise'steeming** *vbl. sb.*

1611 SPEED *Hist. Gt. Brit.* VIII. iii. §8. 402 Albeit some Heralds make Harold by birth but a Gentleman of one, and the first descent,..yet..it may seeme he is mis-esteemed, seeing his Father was Goodwin a Duke by degree. **1647** H. MORE *Song of Soul* II. i. I. i, I must him tell, that he doth misesteem Their strange estate. **1685** BUNYAN *Pharisee & Publican* 51 What kind of righteousness of thine is this, that standeth..in a mis-esteeming of Gods Commands? **1848** LYTTON *Harold* VI. vi, I pray you not so to misesteem us. **1850** GROTE *Greece* II. lxvii. VIII. 477 The practical teachers of Athens and of Greece, misconceived as well as misesteemed. **1900** HENLEY *Verses War, Envoy*, That race is damned which misesteems its fate.

mis'estimate, *sb.* [MIS-^{1} 4.] Wrong estimate or valuation.

1843 MILL *Logic* II. v. iv. 398 A positive mis-estimate of evidence actually had. **1852** H. ROGERS *Ess.* (1874) I. vii. 363 The presumption of this..intellect, its total misestimate of the exigencies of the great problems with which it had to deal.

mis'estimate, *v.* [MIS-^{1} 1.] *trans.* To estimate erroneously, have a false estimate of.

1841 CARLYLE *Heroes* ii. 75, I believe we mis-estimate Mahomet's faults even as faults. **1849** J. CUMMING *Christ Receiving Sinners* vi. 124 If you see a person mis-estimating every thing around him, thinking..that rags are royal purple.

misesti'mation. [MIS-^{1} 4.] False or incorrect estimation.

1809 SYD. SMITH in Lady Holland *Mem.* (1855) II. 64 The delay occasioned by the mis-estimation of my own powers.

mis'execute, *v.* [MIS-^{1} 1.] *trans.* To execute, carry out, or perform improperly.

1647 CLARENDON *Hist. Reb.* III. §234 A person so obnoxious to them, in the mis-executing his..office of Chief Justice in Eyre. **1894** *Voice* (N.Y.) 1 Feb., All the laws, good and bad, are so misexecuted by Tammany as [etc.].

misexe'cution. [MIS-^{1} 4.] Improper execution.

1535 *Act 27 Hen. VIII*, c. 24 §9 Fynes..for none execucion or mysexecucion..of suche writtes. **1809** W. BLAKE *Descr. Catal.* 34 All is misconceived, and its mis-execution is equal to its misconception.

misex'pending, *vbl. sb.* [MIS-^{1} 3.] = next.

1646 QUARLES *Judgem. & Mercy* Wks. (Grosart) I. 82/1 The misexpending of my pretious time.

misex'penditure. *rare*$^{-1}$. [MIS-^{1} 4.] Wrong expenditure.

1795 HAMILTON *Wks.* (1886) VII. 89 A misexpenditure of so much money.

†**misex'pense.** *Obs.* [MIS-^{1} 4.] = prec.

1598 SYLVESTER *Du Bartas* I. ii. (1641) 9/1 Lesse should I wail their misse-expence of leasure, If [etc.]. **1627** *Beggers Ape* C 2 b, O wretched end of idle vanity, Of misexpence and Prodigality. **1646** QUARLES *Sheph. Oracles* viii. ad fin., This fruitlesse hower's misexpence. **1665** BOYLE *Occas. Refl.* v. i. (1848) 297, I will not be forward to condemn him of a mis-expence.

misex'plain, *v.* [MIS-^{1} 1.] *trans.* To explain incorrectly.

1674 BOYLE *Excell. Theol.* II. iv. 172 Divers phænomena of nature, that had been left unexplained, or were left misexplained by the Schools. **1864** GROSART *Lambs all Safe* 53 Misexplaining the incident as meaning only childlike-dispositioned adults, robs it of all its meaning. **1869** FARRAR *Fam. Speech* iii. (1870) 129 *note*, A second-hand reflection of Greek thoughts, often both mistranslated and misexplained.

misexpo'sition. [MIS-^{1} 4.] Incorrect exposition.

1524-5 *Archæol. Jrnl.* (1874) XXXI. 64 By inadvertence and misexposition of the saide Acte. **1645** MILTON *Tetrach.* Wks. 1851 IV. 247 Let them..give God his thanks, who hath..scowr'd off an inveterat misexposition from the Gospel. **1673** BAXTER *Let.* in *Acc. Sherlocke* ii. 168 You misexpound Rom. 7. and upbraid others with the consequents of your misexposition.

misex'pound, *v.* [MIS-^{1} 1.] *trans.* To expound wrongly.

1673 [see prec.].

misex'press, *v.* [MIS-^{1} 1.] *refl.* To express oneself faultily.

c **1718** *Life R. Frampton* (1876) 122 If in such a royal auditory he had misexprest himself. **1847** FR. A. KEMBLE *Rec. Later Life* III. 305 You have misunderstood me, or I misexpressed myself.

misex'pression. [MIS-^{1} 4.] Incorrect expression.

1651 BAXTER *Inf. Bapt.* 324 The two former I hope are but mis-expressions of a tolerable sence. *a* **1832** BENTHAM *Deontol.* (1834) II. 221 Impute his neglect..to misconception, or misexpression, or forgetfulness.

misex'pressive, *a.* [MIS-^{1} 6.] Expressing a wrong meaning. Hence **misex'pressiveness.**

1816 BENTHAM *Chrestom.* 109 Instead of being negatively and simply unexpressive, it is positively misexpressive. *Ibid.* Wks. 1843 VIII. 40 The inexpressiveness, or rather the misexpressiveness, of the language. **1832** AUSTIN *Jurispr.* (1879) II. 542 The terms promulged and unpromulged.. are not less misexpressive than written and unwritten.

†**mis'fait.** *Obs.* In 4 **mysfait,** 5 **mesfeat.** [a. OF. *mesfait*, mod.F. *méfait* (= Pr. *mesfait*, It. *misfatto*), f. *mesfaire*, *méfaire* to misdo.] Misdeed.

1377 LANGL. *P. Pl.* B. XI. 366, I haue wonder of þe..Why þow ne suwest man and his make þat no mysfait hem folwe? **1481** CAXTON *Godfrey* viii. 29 All their mesfeates and trespeaces were redressyd.

mis'faith. [MIS-^{1} 4.] Disbelief; mistrust.

1382 WYCLIF *Ecclus.* ii. 18 Who dreden the Lord, shul not ben of mysfeith [1388 unbileueful] to the wrd of hym. **1859** TENNYSON *Vivien* 382 A woman and not trusted, doubtless I Might feel some sudden turn of anger born Of your misfaith.

†**mis'fall,** *sb.* [MIS-^{1} 4.] Mishap, misfortune.

1340 *Ayenb.* 84 Kueade mysfalles and zorȝes. *Ibid.* 86, 182. *c* **1489** CAXTON *Blanchardyn* xii. 44 Ye wyll scandalyze & vttre your mysfal that is now happed to you of one man.

†**mis'fall,** *v. Obs.* [MIS-^{1} 1. Cf. MLG., MDu., Du. *misvallen*, MHG. *missevallen*, Ger. *missfallen.*]

1. *intr.* To suffer misfortune, come to grief.

a **1300** *Cursor M.* 7820 His hend he wrang..þat godds folk suld sua mis-fall. *c* **1330** R. BRUNNE *Chron. Wace* (Rolls) 2005 Humbert gan þer mys-falle..ffor he dreynte þerin. **1375** BARBOUR *Bruce* XII. 365 And thai may happin to mysfall.

2. *impers.* or said of the event: To happen unfortunately, fall out amiss. ***it misfell me***: misfortune befell me.

1340 *Ayenb.* 193 Hit is wel riȝt þet hit misualle to him ..þet deþ harm uader oþer moder. *c* **1386** CHAUCER *Knt.'s T.* 1530 Al-though thee ones on a tyme misfille Whan Vulcanus had caught thee in his las. **1481** CAXTON *Reynard* (Arb.) 55 Whiche mysfylle her euyl, ffor the false felle foxe awayted wel his tyme [etc.]. **1509** BARCLAY *Shyp of Folys* (1570) 70 Thou art blinde and mad to set thy brayne All thing to venge by wrath that doth misfall. **1530** PALSGR. 637/2 Sythe you wyll nat be ruled, if it mysfall with you, you can blame no body but yourselfe. **1596** SPENSER *F.Q.* v. v. 10 Thereat she gan..to upbrayd that chaunce which him misfell. **1615** SYLVESTER *Job Triumph.* 157 Yet did not Job, for all that him mis-fell, Murmur at God.

†**mis'fame,** *sb. Obs. rare*$^{-1}$. [MIS-^{1} 4.] Evil fame or report.

1480 CAXTON *Trevisa's Higden* III. xxiii. 112 b, He had grete Joye of euyll loos and mysfame.

mis'fame, *v. rare*$^{-1}$. [MIS-^{1} 1.] *trans.* To spread a false report concerning.

a **1850** ROSSETTI *Dante & Circ.* I. (1874) 42 This false and evil rumour which seemed to misfame me of vice.

†**mis'fare,** *sb. Obs.* [f. MIS-^{1} 4 + FARE *sb.*^{1}] Going wrong or astray; mishap, misfortune.

a **1300** *Cursor M.* 315 His sun..þat wat All þinges þat haldes stat, And halds þam up fro misfare þat þai ne worth to noght. **1387** TREVISA *Higden* (Rolls) II. 213 Sterynge and meuynge in lymes wiþ oute eny mysfare [orig. *motus membrorum sine errore*]. *c* **1470** HENRY *Wallace* x. 1060 Mekill dolour it did him in his mynd, Off thair mysfayr. **1496** *Dives & Pauper* (W. de W.) x. ii. 372/2 They were more enclyned to lecherye for welfare than to robberye for mysfare. **1596** SPENSER *F.Q.* VI. iii. 24 Crying aloud to shew her sad misfare Unto the knights.

†**mis'fare,** *v. Obs.* Forms: see FARE *v.*^{1} [OE. *misfaran* = OFris. *misfara*, MHG. *missevarn*, ON. *misfara*: see MIS-^{1} 1 and FARE *v.*^{1}]

1. *intr.* To fare ill, come to grief, be unfortunate.

c **1000** ÆLFRIC *Hom.* (Th.) I. 100 Sume..cweðað ðæt hi þurh bletsunge misfarað, and ðurh wyriȝunge ðeonon. *a* **1023** WULFSTAN *Hom.* xviii. (1883) 104 Eala, ȝefyrn is, þæt ðurh deofol fela þinga misfor. *c* **1230** *Hali Meid.* 34 For nis ha neauer wiðute care leste hit ne mis-feare. *c* **1350** *Will. Palerne* 1359 þi fader and al his folk so misfaren hadde, þat alle here liues in a stounde hadde be lore. *c* **1420** *Sir Amadace* (Camden) xxi, A dede cors opon a bere lay A woman alle mysfare. **1496** *Dives & Pauper* (W. de W.) VII. xxviii. 319/1 In what londe usurye is used openly that londe shall mysfare. **1621** *Gude & Godlie B.* (S.T.S.) 232 Do ȝe the contrair, ȝour housis will misfair. **1633** HEYWOOD *Eng. Trav.* v, If shee misfare I am a man more wretched in her losse, Then had I forfeited life and estate.

b. Of an enterprise: To miscarry, fail.

c **1375** BARBOUR *Bruce* (Edinb. MS.) x. 529 For it wes hys ententioun To put hym till all aventur Or that a sege on hym

mysfur. **1513** DOUGLAS *Æneis* IX. Prol. 66 Now war me laith my lang laubour mysfur.

2. To go wrong; to transgress.

c **897** K. ÆLFRED *Gregory's Past. C.* i. 29 Forðon oft for ðæs lareowes unwisdome misfarað [orig. *offendant*] ða hieremenn. *c* **1250** *Gen. & Ex.* 1911 If he saȝ hise breðere mis-faren, His fader he it gan vn-hillen. *a* **1300** *Cursor M.* 866, I sagh wel þat i misfard. **1390** GOWER *Conf.* II. 115 Er thou so with thiself misfare. **1487** *How Good Wife Taught Dau.* 282 And kep thame fra neyd and mystair, That pouerte gar thame nocht mysfair.

3. *trans.* (*Sc.*) **a.** To do amiss. **b.** To cause to go wrong.

1461 *Liber Pluscardensis* XII. viii, He that all as made As langand gouernance of his Godhade Nathing mysfaris, bot all dois for the best. *a* **1578** LINDESAY (Pitscottie) *Chron. Scot.* (1728) 172 He shall..misfair the Government and Guidment of his Country.

†**mis'faring**, *vbl. sb. Obs.* [MIS-[1] 3.] Wrong-doing; transgression.

1595 SPENSER *Col. Clout* 758 For all the rest do most-what fare amis, And yet their owne misfaring will not see. For either they be puffed up with pride [etc.].

†**mis'faring**, *ppl. a. Obs.* [MIS-[1] 2.]

a. Transgressing, misbehaving.

c **1290** *S. Eng. Leg.* I. 305/180 He [*sc.* Lucifer] may corsi euere-more his mis-farinde pruyte. *a* **1300** *Leg. Rood* (Ashm. MS.) 50 Eraclius þe emperour.. Of þis mysuaryngе prute [*Vernon MS.* mis farinde pruyde] hurde telle ilome. **13..** *K. Alis.* 6470 Alle they [*sc.* the devil's sons] beon mysfaryng. **1413** *Pilgr. Sowle* (Caxton) IV. xxxviii. (1859) 65 So that the kynge put awey that foule, mysfarynge old one.

b. In evil plight.

c **1450** *Guy Warw.* (Camb.) 1118 He sawe a knyghte rydynge; Hys ryght arme was mysfarynge.

†**mis'fashion**, *v. Obs.* [MIS-[1] 1.] *trans.* To put out of shape; to make of a wrong shape.

1570 LEVINS *Manip.* 164/43 To Misfashion, *deformare.* **1594** BLUNDEVIL *Exerc.* VIII. (1636) 757 He saith that they must needs mis-fashion the Regions, and make the.. longitudes, and latitudes, to be untrue. **1608** J. DAYE *Humour out of Breath* III. v, What toyle I had to fashion them to loue, And how 'tis doubled to misfashion them. **1647** WARD *Simp. Cobler* 35 What is amisse in the mould, will mis-fashion the prosult.

mis'fashioned, *ppl. a.* [MIS-[1] 2.] Badly formed; deformed, mis-shapen.

1500–20 DUNBAR *Poems* xxviii. 25 Thocht God mak ane misfassonit man, ȝe can him all schaip new agane. **1548** GESTE *Pr. Masse* F iv, What a misfashioned argumentation is this. **1594** HOOKER *Eccl. Pol.* Pref. iii. §9 Through their misfashioned preconceit. **1633** BP. HALL *Hard Texts O.T.* 610 Such a scrip—as no wise shepheard would beare, as being mis-fashioned.

mis'fashioning, *vbl. sb.* [MIS-[1] 3.] Disfigurement; deformity.

1469 *Paston Lett.* II. 343 Let hym bryng the hat upon hys hid for mysfacyonyng of it. **1581** MULCASTER *Positions* XXX. (1887) 110 Sicknesse assaileth vs three ways:..by misfashioning, when either the whole bodie, or some parte therof, wanteth his due forme [etc.].

†**mis'fate.** *Obs.* [MIS-[1] 4.] Evil fate.

1614 SYLVESTER *Parl. Vertues Royall* I. *Panaretus* 1495 Were't throw their own mis-fate, in having none, Or having Vertues, not to have them known. **1652** BENLOWES *Theoph.* II. xxxiii, Misdeeds their own misfate engage.

†**mis'favour.** *Obs.* [MIS-[1] 7.] Disfavour.

a **1660** *Contemp. Hist. Irel.* 1641–52 (1880) III. I. 142 The clergie..deliuered their opinions in his misfauour.

misfeasance (mɪsˈfiːzəns). *Law.* Also 7 -feisance, 7–8 -fesance, 8 -fesans, 9 -feazance. [a. OF. *mesfaisance*, f. *mesfaisant*, pres. pple. of *mesfaire*, *méfaire* to misdo: see MIS-[2] and FEASANCE.] A transgression, trespass; *spec.* the wrongful exercise of lawful authority or improper performance of a lawful act.

1596 BACON *Max. & Uses Com. Law* I. (1636) 32 He is subject to an action upon the case for his misfeisance. **1675** W. SHEPPARD (*title*) Actions upon the Case for Deeds, viz. Contracts, Assumpsits [etc.]..and for other Male-Feasance and Mis-feasance. **1689** *Trial Pritchard v. Papillon* 9 That were a Misfesance, or a Male-execution of their Office. **1768** BLACKSTONE *Comm.* III. 208 Any misfeasance, or act of one man whereby another is injuriously treated or damnified, is a transgression, or trespass in it's largest sense. **1781** W. JONES *Law Bailments* 54 A distinction seems very early to have been made in our law between the *non*feasance, and the *mis*feasance of a *conductor operis.* **1863** KINGLAKE *Crimea* II. 13 The custom of awarding wild, violent praise to the common performance of duty, and even now and then to actual misfeasance. **1875** DIGBY *Real Prop.* (1876) vi. 303 *note*, All cases of damage caused by misfeazance (commission of wrongful acts).

transf. **1840** *New Monthly Mag.* LIX. 242 The long-acre copse..which had so often sheltered the misfeasance both of my gun and lips. **1882** HUGHES *Mem. D. Macmillan* 6 He had..discovered some small misfeasance in the shop and had accused his apprentice of it.

†**mis'fease,** *v. Obs. rare*⁻¹. [Back-formation f. prec.] *trans.* To do evil to.

1571 in *Archæologia* XLV. 62 Whose son or servant shall be found to misfease Iohn a wood, sexton, in word or deed.

misfeasor (mɪsˈfiːzə(r)). *Law.* Also 7 -fesor, 9 -feazor. [a. OF. *mesfesour*, *-feisour*, agent-n. f. *mesfaire*, f. *mes-* MIS-[2] + *faire* to do.] One who commits a misfeasance.

1631 *Star Chamb. Cases* (Camden) 62 They take upon them to punish these misfesors. **1884** *Law Rep.* 26 Chanc. Div. 146 The punishment which is reserved for wilful misfeasors.

mis'feature, *sb.* [MIS-[1] 4.] A distorted feature; a bad feature or trait.

a **1821** KEATS *Sonn., Human Seasons*, He [*sc.* man] has his Winter too of pale misfeature. **1871** CARLYLE in *Mrs. Carlyle's Lett.* I. 42 Some misfeature of pronunciation, which I have now forgotten. **1890** R. BRIDGES *Shorter Poems* I. 5 All summer's dry misfeatures.

mis'featured, *ppl. a.* [MIS-[1] 2.] Having bad features.

1868 BROWNING *Ring & Bk.* I. 593 A dark misfeatured messenger.

mis'featuring, *ppl. a.* [MIS-[1] 2.] Distorting the features.

1885 TENNYSON *Wreck* ix, The strange misfeaturing mask that I saw.

†**mis'feel,** *v. Obs. rare*⁻¹. [MIS-[1] 1.] *intr.* To have sinful feelings.

c **1200** in *O.E. Hom.* I. 305 Ich habbe..Misifelet.

†**mis'feeling,** *ppl. a. Obs. rare.* [MIS-[1] 2.] Used in the earlier version of Wyclif's Bible to render L. *insensatus* 'senseless'.

1382 WYCLIF *Ecclus.* xvi. 20 In all these thingus mys felende, or vnwittie, is the herte. *Ibid.* xxii. 14 With a mys felende go thou not awey [1388 an vnwijs man].

†**mis'feign,** *v. Obs. rare*⁻¹. [MIS-[1] 1.] *intr.* To feign with a wrong intention.

1590 SPENSER *F.Q.* I. iii. 40 By him, who has the guerdon of his guile, For so misfeigning her true knight to bee.

mis'felt, *ppl. a.* [MIS-[1] 2.] Felt incorrectly or imperfectly.

1935 L. MACNEICE *Poems* 42 We whose senses give us things misfelt and misheard.

†**mis'fere,** *v. Obs.* Forms: see FERE *v.*[1] [OE. *misféran*: see MIS-[1] 1 and FERE *v.*[1]]

1. *intr.* To do wrong, transgress; to misbehave (const. *mid*, *with* = towards).

c **1000** ÆLFRIC *De Vet. Test.* (Gr.) 7 Saul..þæt folc bewerode wið þa hæðenan leoda heardlice mid wæmnum, þeah þe he misferde on maneȝum oðrum þingum. *a* **1300** *Vox & Wolf* 212 in Hazl. *E.P.P.* 65 Men seide, that thou on thine liue Misferdest mid mine wiue. **1387** TREVISA *Higden* (Rolls) VIII. 147 Þe outrage of riche men, þat misferde with pore men [orig. *divitum insolentiam qua pauperes indigne tractabantur*]. **1390** GOWER *Conf.* I. 241 Bot only that thou hast misferd Thenkende.

2. *intr.* and *pass.* To fare ill; to come to grief; to be unfortunate or unsuccessful.

c **1205** LAY. 26229 Ȝif Arður mis-ferde þene he come to fihte. *c* **1330** R. BRUNNE *Chron. Wace* (Rolls) 7965 Alle þat þey made a day vpright, ffallen was doun vpon þat nyght; ..þat saw þe kyng hit misferde so. *c* **1375** *Sc. Leg. Saints* xxi. (*Clement*) 197, & his fadir fore doule & wa he trewyt in þe se mysferde. *a* **1425** *Cursor M.* 18311 (Trin.) Þere I was wiþ my foos mysferde [*Cott.* was vm-sett].

3. ? *trans.* ? To overthrow.

c **1330** R BRUNNE *Chron.* (1810) 224 Whan Sir Edward herd, þat þei had Lyncoln taken, & þe Juerie misferd, þer tresorie ouerschaken [*cf. supra* þei robbed þam & slouh].

mis'field, *v.* [MIS-[1] 1.] *trans.* To field (a ball) badly. Hence **mis'fielded** *ppl. a.*

1870 *Times* 10 Aug. 5/5 Both of these [*sc.* hits for four].. were unaccountably misfielded by Smith, who rarely makes mistakes. **1890** *Daily News* 18 Sept. 3/6 Key misfielded the ball. **1894** *Punch* 22 Dec. 298/3 The course of a 'misfielded' ball between leaving bowler's hand and returning thereto. **1954** J. B. G. THOMAS *On Tour* vi. 66 Dixon..looked at the South African wing for a moment and misfielded. **1974** *Times* 8 Jan. 7/8 The new beak picks up the pill and chucks at McCallum who misfields it.

Also as *sb.*, failure to gather the ball properly.

1909 *Daily Chron.* 25 Feb. 8/4 Guy's scored after a misfield of a high kick by Batchelor.

mis'figure, *sb. rare.* [MIS-[1] 4.] Disfigurement, deformity.

c **1375** *Sc. Leg. Saints* xl. (*Ninian*) 682 Othir be þe to hafe remede of þis mysfigur, or be dede. **1857** HEAVYSEGE *Saul* II. II. iv. 149 As a thing which long pressed out of form, Does, after being restored to its true shape..start back All foul and crumpled to its old mis-figure.

mis'figure, *v.* Now *dial.* [MIS-[1] 1; after *disfigure* (cf. MIS-[1] 9).] *trans.* To disfigure; to distort the form of; to disguise.

1648 J. GOODWIN *Right & Might* Pref. 1 That men.. should be able to misfigure the liberall and ingenuous face of your actions into an absolute deformity. *a* **1677** MANTON *Serm. John* xvii. 3 Wks. 1872 X. 149 Some great..governor of the order of the world, whom they mightily transformed and misfigured in their thoughts. **1870** E. PEACOCK *Ralf Skirl.* III. 99 He may misfigure hissen next time as he likes, I shall knaw him.

mis'figured, *ppl. a.* Now *dial.* [MIS-[1] 2.] Disfigured.

1624 GATAKER *Transubst.* 134 You may not marvaile why his answer is so diffused, deformed and mis-figured. **1886** *S.W. Linc. Gloss.* s.v. *Misfigure*, She's misfigured worse than ever I seed her. **1895** *E. Angl. Gloss.*, *Misvigured.*

mis'figuring, *vbl. sb.* [MIS-[1] 3.] Disfiguring; misrepresenting of figure.

1685 H. MORE *Illustration*, etc. 34 Even to the misfiguring his own visage by the distemper of his passion. **1699** PEPYS *Let. to Ld. Reay* 21 Nov., The miscolouring, misfiguring, diminishing, or undue magnifying, of an object.

misfire (mɪsˈfaɪə(r)), *sb.* [f. next. Cf. MISS-FIRE.] **a.** A failure to discharge or explode.

1839 URE *Dict. Arts* 478 A mis-fire is hardly ever experienced with the fire-arms made at the Royal manufactory. **1859** *Musketry Instr.* 18 The instructor will naturally attribute 'mis-fires' to a dirty rifle. **1881** GREENER *Gun* 28 A misfire of the charge in the mortar. **1888** *Times* (weekly ed.) 21 Dec. 12/3 Did you leave him after three or four misfires?

attrib. **1902** *Westm. Gaz.* 26 Feb. 9/3 A misfire ball cartridge, or one that had been used but had not exploded.

b. The state or action of misfiring.

1966 B. C. MACDONALD *Car Doctor* iv. 45 If there is a regular or rhythmical type of misfire, together with a blackish exhaust, then the mixture is too rich. **1973** J. B. EDWARDS in Springer & Patterson *Engine Emissions* ii. 47 A significant level of misfire may exist in a poorly maintained and/or adjusted engine.

misfire (mɪsˈfaɪə(r)), *v.* [MIS-[1] 1. Cf. phr. *to miss fire*, s.v. MISS *v.*[1]] **a.** *intr.* Of a gun or its charge: To fail to be discharged or exploded.

1752 in *Scots Mag.* (1753) Aug. 401/2 The little gun was in use to snap or misfire. [**1881** GREENER *Gun* 43 The weapons were..tiresome to charge and discharge, and continually miss-firing.] **1902** *Westm. Gaz.* 16 Apr. 8/1 Both guns in the fore-barbette had misfired.

b. Of an internal-combustion engine: to fail to explode the charge, or to explode it at the wrong instant. So **mis'firing** *vbl. sb.*

1905 *Motor Cycle* 6 Mar. 218/3 If an engine is back firing, that is, giving explosions in the silencer, it is also misfiring. Misfiring may result from a defect in the ignition system. **1928** MONTAGU & BOURDON *Cars & Motor-Cycles* III. 1244 An engine is said to misfire when the gas in one or more of the cylinders does not ignite. **1966** B. C. MACDONALD *Car Doctor* ix. 80 Other causes of misfiring are: incorrect valve timing, weak or broken valve springs, sticking valves, too much carbon in engine, [etc.]. **1974** HAYNES & WARD *Audi 100 Owners Workshop Manual* iv. 89/2 If the engine misfires regularly, run it at a fast idling speed.

c. *fig.* To fail, to be misdirected, to make a mistake. So **mis'fired** *ppl. a.*

1942 BERRY & VAN DEN BARK *Amer. Thes. Slang* §170/6. **1949** KOESTLER *Promise & Fulfilment* xii. 132 The other after-effects of the misfired operation were in the same strain. **1974** 'J. GRAHAM' *Bloody Passage* viii. 120 'What a wonderful idea,' he said, and then the thing misfired slightly.

misfit (mɪsˈfɪt), *sb.* [f. MIS-[1] 4 + FIT *sb.*[3]] **1.** A garment or other article which does not fit the person for whom it is intended. Also *transf.* and *fig.*; *spec.* a person unsuited to his environment, work, etc.

1823 J. BEE *Dict. Turf*, etc., *Misfits*—clothes which do not suit the wearer's shape. Hence, ''tis a misfit', when a story, or some endeavour fails of its effect, then 'it von't fit'. **1851–61** MAYHEW *Lond. Labour* III. 232/2 There are a number of [artificial] eyes come over from France, but these are generally what we call misfits. **1862** MISS BRADDON *Lady Audley* II. ii. 19 Her mouth..was an obvious misfit for the set of teeth it contained. **1865** *Cornh. Mag.* June 645 There are some unfortunate people in this world, whose names are —how can I express it?—whose names are, Misfits. **1865** KNIGHT *Passages Work. Life* III. x. 213 [The] shoemaker.. would occasionally have a misfit or two on his hands. **1903** C. E. OSBORNE *Father Dolling* vi, Amid the streets of Landport Father Dolling was no deplorable misfit. **1936** *Discovery* Sept. 280/1 The selection and training of personnel to eliminate as far as possible the misfit and (what is far more prevalent) the partial misfit who just stands the test of results but has really missed his vocation. **1939** T. S. ELIOT *Family Reunion* I. ii. 55 The very moment when you are wholly conscious Of being a misfit, of being superfluous. **1959** *Times Lit. Suppl.* 30 Jan. 57/1 He is a determined individualist, wears Afrika Korps uniform while serving in the British Army and is something of a misfit. **1975** *Times* 20 Aug. 4/8 The police..said young misfits were taking as their victims other car drivers.

attrib. **1910** *Encycl. Brit.* XIV. 223/2 The advantage of this combination is that..it..lessens the danger of making 'misfit' pig iron, *i.e.* that which, because it is not accurately suited to the process for which it is intended, offers us the dilemma [etc.]. **1961** A. MILLER *Misfits* xi. 117 Nothin' but misfit horses, that's all they are, honey.

2. *Physical Geogr.* A stream which, if its average flow in the past was at present-day levels, would be expected to have eroded a larger or a smaller valley than it has done. Usu. *attrib.* or as *adj.*

1910 LAKE & RASTALL *Text-bk. Geol.* iii. 47 In this case the lower part of valley A is left dry, or with an insignificant stream only, which appears to be too small to have eroded the valley in which it flows. Such a stream is called a misfit. **1932** *Jrnl. Geol.* XL. 486 (*heading*) Misfit streams. **1964** *Prof. Papers U.S. Geol. Survey* No. 452-A. 6/1 Streams recognized as misfit are so usually underfit that the two names are frequently interchanged. **1968** R. W. FAIRBRIDGE *Encycl. Geomorphol.* 706/2 The most commonly recognized case of a misfit stream is the underfit river.

mis'fit, *v.* [Partly f. MIS-[1] 1 + FIT *v.*, partly f. prec. sb.] *trans.* and *intr.* To fail to fit, fit badly.

1885 W. ALLINGHAM in *Athenæum* 3 Oct. 435/1 No luck misfits thee, Ivy, great or mean, Mirthful or solemn. **1887** *Twin Soul* II. iii. 32 Every truth..is a link in one eternal and infinite chain, and cannot possibly misfit with or contradict

any other. **1894** *Outing* (U.S.) XXIV. 244/2 His garments all misfitted him so astonishingly.

So **mis'fitting** *vbl. sb.* and *ppl. a.*

1851 I. TAYLOR *Wesley & Methodism* 233 The *misfitting* of the twelve volumes [of Wesley's Writings] to the times current. **1896** *Allbutt's Syst. Med.* I. 464 Mis-fitting boots.

†**mis'fong,** *v. Obs.* [f. MIS-[1] 1 + *fong*, FANG *v.*[1] Cf. OE. *misfón* to make a mistake.] *trans.* To take wrongly.

c **1250** *Owl & Night.* 1374 (Cott. MS.), þah heo [*sc.* mine song] beo god me hine mai misfonge An drahe hine to sothede.

†**mis'footing,** *vbl. sb. Obs. rare*[−1]. [MIS-[1] 3.] Going astray.

1446 LYDG. *Nightingale Poems* 23/209 Myn handes were nayled fast vn-to the tre, And for mysfotyng, where men wente wrong, My feete thurgh-perced.

†**misfor'give,** *v. Obs. rare*[−1]. [MIS-[1] 1.] *trans.* = MISGIVE 1. (Cf. FORGIVE *v.* 7.)

c **1374** CHAUCER *Troylus* IV. 1426 But yet to lete hir go His herte misforyaf him ever-mo.

mis'form, *v.* [MIS-[1] 1.] *trans.* To form or shape amiss; to mis-shape.

1413 *Pilgr. Sowle* (Caxton 1483) IV. xxx. 78 Ther wylle be fourged a fowle deformed hede and nedes must be mysformed all the body after. **1580** BLUNDEVIL *Horses Diseases* iii. 2 Those [diseases] that doe come.. by errour of nature, in misforming the yoong. **1609** BIBLE (Douay) *Jer.* xviii. *comm.*, A potter can make a new vessel of the same clay being misformed in casting. LD. BROOKE *Monarchy* ccccxxi. Wks. (Grosart) I. 151 He shall find all wisdoms that suppress, Still by misforming, make their own forms less.

misfor'mation. [MIS-[1] 4.] Malformation. (Frequent in Good.)

1822–34 *Good's Study Med.* (ed. 4) I. 439 Where these defects depend on organic misformation, they will mostly be found without a remedy. **1842** J. H. NEWMAN *Par. Serm.* VI. xxiv. 390 Cases of.. what may be called misformation of the reason.

mis'formed, *ppl. a.* [MIS-[1] 2.] Badly formed or shaped; mis-shapen.

1590 SPENSER *F.Q.* I. ii. 43 How long time.. Are you in this misformed hous to dwell? **1610** G. FLETCHER *Christ's Tri.* 60 Such horrid gorgons, and misformed formes Of damned fiends. **1864** [CROLY, etc.] *Miscegenation* xvi. 65 The dirty, ignorant, and misformed Irish girl from the emigrant ships. **1883** J. W. SHERER *At Home & in India* 176 He.. of the misformed arm.

mis'fortunate, *a.* Now chiefly *Sc.* and *U.S.* [MIS-[1] 6.] Unfortunate.

1530 PALSGR. 319/1 Mysfortunate. **1553** T. WILSON *Rhet.* 45 But what seeke I for misfortunate men,.. seyng it is an harder matter.. to finde out happie men? **1573** L. LLOYD *Pilgr. Princes* (1607) 3 Thus was the misfortunate end of so fortunate a beginning. **1664** H. MORE *Myst. Iniq.* xix. 73 Harbours of retirement.. to the Nobler sort of Persons who are.. misfortunate in their affairs. **1733** P. LINDSAY *Interest Scot.* 11 The misfortunate Trader that fails. **1782** ELIZ. BLOWER *Geo. Bateman* III. 21 But her's misfortunate in all her undertakings. **1818** SCOTT *Hrt. Midl.* xlvi, 'Married, Effie!' exclaimed Jeanie—'Misfortunate creature! and to that awfu' ——'. **1834** SIR H. TAYLOR *Artevelde* II. IV. iv. 165 In that misfortunate wasting of his strength. **1855** HALIBURTON *Nat. & Hum. Nat.* I. 186 These arguments.. do harm if the misfortunate critter is rubbed agin the grain. **1860** READE *Cloister & H.* lv, Maligning the misfortunate.

Hence **mis'fortunately** *adv. Sc.*, unfortunately.

1727 J. KEITH *Mem.* (Spalding Cl.) 71 We expected immediately to have open'd the trenches, but very misfortunately we had no cannon. **1881** BLACKIE *Lay Serm.* viii. 246 One of those men of small notions,.. who, when perched misfortunately on high places [etc.].

misfortune (mɪsˈfɔːtʃən, -uːn), *sb.* [f. MIS-[1] 4 + FORTUNE *sb.*]

1. Bad or adverse fortune; ill-luck.

1502 ARNOLDE *Chron.* 60 b/2, For his mysse fortune they wepe and waile. **1535** COVERDALE *Ps.* lxxii. 5 They come in no misfortune like other folke. **1579** *Termes of Law* 62 When any man by mysfortune is slaine by an horse or by a cart. **1590** SPENSER *F.Q.* III. iii. 5 When so her father deare Should of his dearest daughters hard misfortune heare. **1647** CLARENDON *Hist. Reb.* I. §20 The common misfortune of Princes, that in so substantial a part of their Happyness.. as depended upon their Marriage, Themselves had never any part. **1742** *Act 15 Geo. II*, c. 30 Persons who have the Misfortune to become Lunaticks. **1874** MOZLEY *Univ. Serm.* ix. 195 Misfortune, adversity, soften the human heart.

personified. **1596** SHAKS. *Merch. V.* II. iv. 36 And neuer dare misfortune crosse her foote, Vnlesse she doe it vnder this excuse. **1650** WALLER *Poems* (1664) 180 Here weeps Misfortune, and there triumphs Crime. **1742** GRAY *Eton* 57 Black Misfortune's baleful train! **1838** LYTTON *Leila* I. ii, Misfortune set upon my brow her dark and fated stamp.

b. An instance of this.

1494 FABYAN *Chron.* VII. ccxxviii. 257 After which season ..fell to the Frenshe Kynge many and dyuerse mysfortunys. **1553** EDEN *Treat. Newe Ind.* (Arb.) 39 A misfortune which chaunced in the goulfe of the sea Atlantic. *a* **1680** BUTLER *Rem.* (1759) II. 12 Nor shall our past Misfortunes more Be charg'd upon the ancient Score. **1767** GRAY in *Corr. w. Nicholls* (1843) 69, I have many *désagrémens* that surround me; they have not dignity enough to be called misfortunes, but they feel heavy on my mind. **1781** GIBBON *Decl. & F.* xxx. III. 177 He might perhaps be affected by the personal misfortunes of his generous kinsmen. **1860** WARTER *Sea-board* II. 181 To be deprived of Burial.. has ever been looked upon as amongst the greatest of misfortunes.

c. Proverbial phrases.

1622 MABBE tr. *Aleman's Guzman d'Alf.* I. iii. 29 *marg.*, Misfortunes seldome come alone. **1647** CLARENDON *Hist. Reb.* I. §71 Let the fault or misfortune be what and whence it will. **1717** G. REDPATH in Burns *Mem. Wodrow* (1838) I. p. vii, Which is not our crime but our misfortune. **1717** ADDISON tr. *Ovid's Met.* III. *Cadmus* ad fin., You'll find it his misfortune, not his fault. **1840** DICKENS *Barn. Rudge* xxxii, Misfortunes, saith the adage, never come singly. **1862** SIR B. BRODIE *Psychol. Inq.* II. iii. 83 The overabundance of leisure ..is often a misfortune rather than a fault.

2. *dial.* and *colloq.* ***to have*** or ***meet with a misfortune***: to have an illegitimate child. Hence used simply for: An illegitimate child, bastard.

1801 *Har'st Rig* liii, She wi' a Misfortune met, And had a bairn. **1835** MRS. CARLYLE *Lett.* I. 42 It would be difficult for me to say that an Annandale woman's virtue is the worse for a misfortune. **1836** MARRYAT *Midsh. Easy* iii, 'If you please, ma'am, I had a misfortune, ma'am', replied the girl, casting down her eyes. **1866** CARLYLE *Remin.* (1881) II. 156 A special 'misfortune' (so they delicately name it), being of Esther's own producing. 'Misfortune' in the shape ultimately of a solid tall ditcher. *a* **1881** —— in *New Lett. Jane W. Carlyle* (1903) I. 59 ['Wee Jen'] Ann Cook's 'misfortune'.

†**mis'fortune,** *v. Obs.* Also 5 mes-. [MIS-[1] 1.] **a.** *impers.* or said of an event: To happen unfortunately. **b.** *intr.* Of a person: To happen by mischance *to do* something. **c.** To be unfortunate, come to grief.

1466 *Mann. & Househ. Exp.* (Roxb.) 173 It mesfortened me.. to hurte my lege. **1470–85** MALORY *Arthur* IX. ii. 340 And soo it mysfortuned hym, another stronge knyght met with hym. **1533** MORE *Apol.* 94 b, Whych thynge to se so mysfortune betwene any two crysten folke, is a thynge myche to be lamented. **1533** —— *Answ. Poysoned Bk.* Wks. 1102/1 As for this argument of mine.. I missefortuned to make so feble, y[e] he taketh euen a pleasure to play with it. **1599** *Vestry Bks.* (Surtees) 276 Whatsoever shall happen to faille or misforten about the clock. **1615** E. HOWES in Stow *Ann.* Pref. ¶7 The Queene after mariage was conceiued with childe, but it misfortuned.

mis'fortuned, *a.* Now *rare.* [f. MISFORTUNE *sb.* + -ED[2].] Affected by misfortune, unfortunate.

1582 STANYHURST *Æneis*, etc. (Arb.) 109 Also se that thither you bring thee martial armoure That the peasaunt left heere, with al his misfortuned ensigns. *a* **1578** LINDESAY (Pitscottie) *Chron. Scot.* (S.T.S.) I. 8 This potent prince.. vas murdreist be ane misforttunit gown. **1645** MILTON *Tetrach.* 44 While charity hath the judging of so many private greevances in a misfortun'd Wedlock. **1876** BLACKIE *Lang. & Lit. Highl. Scot.* i. 5 The Highlanders.. were not exactly in the position of that misfortuned people [*sc.* the Poles]. **1881** —— *Lay Serm.* i. 70 Coming into misfortuned collision with the great forces of the universe.

mis'fortuner. *rare*[−1]. [f. MISFORTUNE *sb.* + -ER[1].] One who meets with a misfortune.

a **1774** GOLDSM. *Intended Epil. 'Stoops to Conq.'*, Doctors, who cough and answer every misfortuner 'I wish I'd been called in a little sooner'.

†**mis'founding,** *vbl. sb. Obs.* [f. MIS-[1] 3 + *founding*, f. FOUND *v.*] ? Mistaken endeavour.

c **1460** *Towneley Myst.* xxviii. 242 In all youre skylles more and les for mysfowndyng fayll ye. *Ibid.* 275 He shewid hym not to you, for mysfoundyng ye rafe.

mis'framed, *ppl. a.* [MIS-[1] 2.] Badly framed, formed, or fashioned; ill-formed, ill-constructed.

c **1510** BARCLAY *Mirr. Gd. Manners* (1570) A ij, A man with hoare heres uncomely doth incline To misframed fables. **1539** ABP. PARKER *Corr.* (1853) 11 Not with ambiguous sophistication to fortify their misframed judgments. *a* **1578** LINDESAY (Pitscottie) *Chron. Scot.* (S.T.S.) I. 143 Ane peace of ane misframit gune that brak in the schutting.

mis'framing, *vbl. sb. rare*[−1]. [MIS-[1] 3.] Mis-shaping.

1533 MORE *Apol.* xiii. Wks. 874/1 In the misse framing of hys matter more towarde deuision then vnitye.

†**mis'gang.** *Obs.* Also **-gong.** [Partly a. ON. *misganga* straying, misconduct, partly f. MIS-[1] 4 + GANG *sb.*[1]] Going astray, misbehaviour.

13.. *Cursor M.* 17235 (Gött.) Of þi misgang þu wend again. *a* **1325** *Maudelein* 21 in Horstm. *Altengl. Leg.* (1878) 163 For hir sinne & hir misgong.

†**mis'get,** *pa. pple. Obs.* [f. MIS-[1] 2 + *get*, pa. pple. of GET *v.*] Misbegotten.

1390 GOWER *Conf.* III. 283 For of the false Moabites Forth with the strengthe of Amonites, Of that thei weren ferst misgete, The poeple of god was ofte upsete.

misgilt: see MISGUILT.

misgive (mɪsˈgɪv), *v.* [MIS-[1] 1, 7.]

1. *trans.* Of one's 'heart', mind, etc.: To suggest (to one) doubt or apprehension; to cause to be apprehensive (*that*); to incline to suspicion or foreboding. (See GIVE *v.* 22; the personal obj. was orig. a dative.)

1513 MORE in Grafton *Chron.* (1568) II. 777 Were it, that before such great thinges mennes harts.. misgeueth them. *c* **1592** MARLOWE *Jew of Malta* II. ii, My heart misgives me that.. He's with your mother. **1593** SHAKS. *3 Hen. VI*, IV. vi. 94 So doth my heart mis-giue me, in these Conflicts, What may befall him. **1667** MILTON *P.L.* IX. 846 Yet oft his heart, divine of something ill, Misgave him. **1712–13** SWIFT *Jrnl. to Stella* 14 Feb., I was afraid to knock at the door; my mind misgave me. **1727** GAY *Begg. Op.* I. vi, I am as fond of this child as though my mind misgave me he were my own. **1849** MACAULAY *Hist. Eng.* v. I. 559 The minds of the questioners misgave them that the guide was not the rude clown that he seemed. **1865** KINGSLEY *Herew.* xii, Torfrida's heart misgave her.

b. *absol.* or *intr.* Said orig. of the mind, etc., and hence (now *rarely*) of the person (also *refl.*) = To have misgivings.

1604 SHAKS. *Oth.* III. iv. 89 Fetch me the Handkerchiefe, My minde mis-giues. **1612** BP. HALL *Contempl.*, *O.T.* IV. Wks. (1625) 872 Those seruices, which we are forward to, aloofe off, wee shrinke at, neere hand, and fearfully missegiue. *a* **1641** BP. MOUNTAGU *Acts & Mon.* (1642) 300 He began somewhat to misgive himselfe, and to feare detection. **1726** POPE *Odyss.* XXII. 175 Learn, if by female fraud this deed were done, Or (as my thought misgives) by Dolius' son. **1838** LYTTON *Leila* I. vi, The Zeguis might misgive, did they see me leave the palace with you. **1872** C. J. VAUGHAN *Earnest Words* (1878) 154 When we.. misgive ourselves as to the possibility of spiritual endurance. **1887** HALL CAINE *Deemster* xxxix, When this man came my mind misgave.

†**c.** *trans.* To suggest fear of. *Obs.*

1587 GOLDING *De Mornay* xvii. 308 Repentance presupposeth a fault, and conscience misgiueth the insewing of punishment for the same [orig. *s'en propose la pène*].

2. *intr.* To fail; to go wrong, miscarry. Of a gun: To fail to go off; to miss fire. Chiefly *Sc.*

1579 *Reg. Privy Council Scot.* Ser. I. III. 227 The said George Hume presentand ane pistolet to him, quhilk had slane him gif scho had not misgevin. **1629** *Ibid.* Ser. II. III. 13 Thair purpose misgave thame. **1654** EARL MONM. tr. *Bentivoglio's Wars Flanders* 250 If the design of assaulting England misgive. **1703** BRAND *New Descr. Orkney, Zetland*, etc. 112 Upon which the 1st. and 2d. Brewings misgave likewise, but the 3d. was good. **1752** in *Scots Mag.* (1753) Aug. 401/1 It [*sc.* a gun] misgave with him thrice at a black cock. **1799** J. ROBERTSON *Agric. Perth* 248 Oats for the first year frequently misgive. **1833** CHALMERS *Const. of Man* vi. (1834) I. 228 The abortive enterprises of.. Utopianism.. have all of them misgiven. **1880** MRS. C. H. MACGILL *Mem. H. Macgill* 61 Fall back in thought on the question who He is, and your hope will not misgive.

3. *trans.* To bestow amiss; to cite wrongly.

1611 COTGR., *Mesdonner*, to misgiue, or bestow amisse. **1639–40** LAUD *Hist. Chanc. Oxf.* in *Rem.* (1700) II. 192, I knew nothing of any of their Liberty misgiven or misused, till about a Fortnight since. *a* **1713** ELLWOOD *Autobiog.* (1714) 318 Quotations.. misgiven, misapplied, or perverted.

mis'given, *ppl. a.* [MIS-[1] 2.] Wrongly given.

1887 RUSKIN *Præterita* II. 254, I remember.. his swift correction of my misgiven Wordsworth's line.

mis'giver. *rare.* [f. MISGIVE *v.* + -ER[1].] One who misgives.

1625 K. LONG tr. *Barclay's Argenis* II. iv. 76 Great are the gods portents, but greater farre Our inward feares; all men misgivers are. **1894** *Westm. Gaz.* 8 Feb. 3/2 The misgivers really hold the situation in their own hands.

mis'giving, *vbl. sb.* [f. MISGIVE *v.* + -ING[1].] The action of the vb. MISGIVE; a feeling of mistrust, apprehension, or loss of confidence.

1601 SHAKS. *Jul. C.* III. i. 145 And my misgiuing still Falles shrewdly to the purpose. **1612** BP. HALL *Contempl.*, *O.T.* IV. *Plagues of Egypt*, His very misgiuing hardens him the more. **1705** STANHOPE *Paraphr.* I. 75 [To] look stedfastly up to this Tribunal, without any manner of Misgiving or Concern. **1781** COWPER *Conversat.* 770 Conscious of her crimes, she feels instead A cold misgiving, and a killing dread. **1803–6** WORDSW. *Ode Intim. Immort.* 148 Blank misgivings of a Creature Moving about in worlds not realised. **1840** DICKENS *Old C. Shop* i, I had a strong misgiving that his nightly absence was for no good purpose. **1849** MACAULAY *Hist. Eng.* ii. I. 185 The bulk of the Scottish nation,.. with many misgivings of conscience, attended the ministrations of the Episcopal clergy. **1883** H. DRUMMOND *Nat. Law in Spir. W.* vii. (1884) 230 The misgiving which will creep.. over the brightest faith.

mis'giving, *ppl. a.* [-ING[2].] That misgives; having misgivings.

1598 R. TOFTE in *Shaks. Cent. Praise* 25 My misgiving minde presaging to me ill. **1646** P. BULKELEY *Gosp. Covt.* II. 172 With a.. misgiving heart, fearing lest our own mouth should judge us. **1711** M. HENRY *Forgiv. Sin* Wks. 1857 II. 522 Sinners carry about with them a misgiving conscience. **1814** WORDSW. *White Doe* VI. 82 He heard, and with misgiving mind. **1845–6** TRENCH *Huls. Lect.* Ser. I. vii. 198 This is the true answer to every misgiving question of a like kind.

Hence **mis'givingly** *adv.*, with misgiving.

1834 DE QUINCEY *Autob. Sk.* Wks. 1854 II. 63 Misgivingly I went forwards, feeling.. that.. I was continually nearing a danger. **1850** L. HUNT *Autobiog.* II. xi. 77 A reform in Parliament,.. which the younger ones.. advocated but fitfully and misgivingly.

†**mis'gloze,** *v. Obs. rare*[−1]. [f. MIS-[1] 1 + GLOZE *v.*[1]] *trans.* To misinterpret.

1387–8 T. USK *Test. Love* II. i. (Skeat) l. 59, I have ordeyned hem, which that auctorite, misglosed by mannes reson, to graunt shal ben enduced.

misgo (mɪsˈgəʊ), *v.* Now *dial.* Pa. t. and pa. pple. as in GO *v.* Cf. MISWEND. [MIS-[1] 1.]

1. *intr.* To go from the right path; to go astray; to go the wrong way. Often in *fig.* context.

1340 *Ayenb.* 94 Fol he is þet can þane riȝte way and be his wytinde mysgeþ. *c* **1386** CHAUCER *Reeve's T.* 298 'Allas!' quod she, 'I hadde almost misgoon; I hadde almost gon to the clerkes bedde'. **1387–8** T. USK *Test. Love* II. x. (Skeat) l. 143 And there thou hast miswent, eschewe the path from hensforward, I rede. *c* **1430** LYDG. *Min. Poems* (Percy Soc.) 241 Duryng my lyf with many gret trespace, By many wrong path wher I have mys-went. **1509** BARCLAY *Shyp of Folys* 271 b, But in my iournay if that I haue mysgo By bytynge wordes or scarsnes of scyence. **1600** FAIRFAX *Tasso* XIV. xviii,

All thy souldiours wandred and misgone. **1875–86** *W. Somerset Gloss.* s.v. *Miswent.*

b. Of a thing: To go astray.

1864 MRS. CARLYLE *Lett.* III. 242 Send me a single line.. by return of post, that I may be sure the thing has not misgone.

2. *intr.* and *pass.* To go astray, go wrong in conduct or action; to err, make a mistake.

a **1300** *Cursor M.* 16148 O galilee þan es he born, þe folk he dos mis-ga [*Fairf.* & bringis our folk in wa]. *a* **1350** *St. Nicholas* 307 in Horstm. *Altengl. Leg.* (1881) 15 þe iew sayd þan: 'þou has mis-gone, For to me payd þou neuer none'. *c* **1400** *Rule St. Benet* (Prose) 5 þe abot sal be blamid if þe cuuent mis-ga. *c* **1450** *Bk. Curtasye* 363 in *Babees Bk.*, ȝif any mann hase in court mys-gayne. ? *a* **1500** *Plowman's Tale* 756 Such mister men ben all misgo. [Echoed by Spenser *Sheph. Cal.*, July 201.] **1500–20** DUNBAR *Poems* ix. 70 Plane I rewoik in thir quhair I miswent. **1605** MARSTON *Du. Courtezan* II. D, Lord, how was I misgone, how easie ti's to erre. **1875–86** *W. Somerset Gloss., Miswent, p.t.* and *p.p.*, went astray; gone astray. In these tenses common, but obs. in the *pr.t.*

3. Of a business, etc.: To go wrong, miscarry.

1766 NICOL *Poems* 21 (E.D.D.) But if a' mercy things misgae. **1843** CARLYLE *Past & Pr.* (1858) 125 The business had all misgone in the interim! **1866** —— *Remin.* I. 169 Some whole fleet of cargoes had by sudden change of price during the voyage ruinously misgone. **1866** GREGOR *Banffsh. Gloss.*, *Mis-gae*, to miscarry; as, 'A doot the thing 'ill mis-gae'.

†**4.** Of a firearm: To miss fire. *Sc. Obs.* [The usual word is *misgie*, MISGIVE.]

1586–7 *Reg. Privy Council Scot.* Ser. I. IV. 139 The said Archibald.. schote ane pistolett at him..; and seeing the same misgaa, he.. presentit ane uthir pistollet at him.

mis'going, *vbl. sb.* Now *rare.* [MIS-¹ 3.] Going astray; trespass, transgression.

a **1300** *Cursor M.* 17235 (Cott.) O þi misgaing þou weind again [cf. MISGANG, quot. 13..]. **1387** TREVISA *Higden* (Rolls) I. 31 þe staat of mysgoynge [orig. *status deviationis*]. **1398** —— *Barth. De P.R.* XIV. li. (Tollemache MS.) Londe of misgoynge and of erryng [orig. *terra deuii et erroris*]. **1855** THACKERAY *Newcomes* xlv, Let those pity her who can feel their own weakness and misgoing.

mis'gotten, *pa. pple.* and *ppl. a.* Also 5 **mysgettyne.** [MIS-¹ 2.]

1. Wrongly acquired or obtained; ill-gotten.

c **1412** HOCCLEVE *De Reg. Princ.* 664 As yt mysgoten was, mys was despendid. *a* **1425** *Cast. Persev.* 2628 in *Macro Plays* 155 Mys-gotyn good þee schal schende. **1550** CROWLEY *Epigr.* 703 The goodis mysgoten, that men do ther at wynne. **1596** SPENSER *F.Q.* VI. i. 18 Leave.. that misgotten weft To him that hath it better justifyde. **1649** BP. HALL *Cases Consc.* IV. ix. (1654) 369 Secretly mis-gotten dispensations. **1903** W. S. JACKSON *Nine Points of Law* vi. 171 Here was he with a trunk-load of misgotten gold wandering haphazard.. over two countries.

2. = MISBEGOTTEN.

c **1425** *Seven Sag.* (P.) 1075 He saw wyl with hys eye.. That the childe was mys-gettyne. **1652** BENLOWES *Theoph.* II. xxxi. 27 Misgotten Brat! **1904** *Blackw. Mag.* July 89/1 Cornwallis sahib.. had beaten Tippu, and those misgotten Mysore *log* [= men].

mis'govern, *v.* [MIS-¹ 1. (F. *mesgouverner* is cited only from Palsgrave 637/2.)]

†**1.** *trans.* In obs. uses corresponding to those of GOVERN *v.*; to mismanage, misdirect, misconduct.

c **1440** *Jacob's Well* 148 He techyth his dyscyples, to mysgouerne here tungys. **1493** *Festivall* (W. de W. 1515) 75 Then Iohan blamed hym and sayd yᵗ he had mysgouerned the chylde. **1513** MORE in Grafton *Chron.* (1568) II. 807 Brydeling and punishing of such as there had misgouerned themselues. *a* **1577** GASCOIGNE *Wks.* (1587) To Rdr. ¶¶¶ j b, If any (misgouerning their owne wittes) doe fortune to vse that for a Spurre, which I haue heere appoynted for a Brydle. **1621** T. WILLIAMSON tr. *Goulart's Wise Vieillard* 76 They.. feele.. grieuous woundes in their bodies, either for that their children misgouerne themselues, or their wiues behaue themselues vsurpingly.

†**b.** *intr.* for *refl. Obs.*

? *a* **1500** in Grose, etc. *Antiq. Rep.* (1809) IV. 407 A Shawme.. yf it be blowne withe to a veheme[n]t wynde, It makithe it to mysgoverne oute of his kynde.

2. *trans.* To direct and control the affairs of (a state, etc.) wrongly or badly; to mismanage the government of.

1587 *Mirr. Mag., Iago* vi. (1610) 73 Misgouern'd both my Kingdome and my life, I gaue my selfe to ease. **1665** BOYLE *Occas. Refl.* IV. xi. (1848) 231 Our wonder, that the Rulers of States.. should oftentimes mis-govern them. **1710** M. HENRY *Life Lieut. Illidge* Wks. 1853 II. 578/1 Our own wills have undone us; they have misgoverned us. **1889** *Sat. Rev.* 30 Mar. 371/2 All Oriental nations under Oriental rule are misgoverned.

†**misgovernail.** *Obs.* [MIS-¹ 4.] **a.** Bad steering. **b.** Mismanagement, misrule, misgovernment; disorder.

1439 *Rolls of Parlt.* V. 29/2 By.. misgovernaile of suche Maistres and Mariners with suche Shippes. *c* **1440** *Gesta Rom.* xxv. 93 (Harl. MS.) That wacchemen shulde.. visite eche house, þat þere was no misgouernayle þere in. *c* **1470** HARDING *Chron.* CXLIX. ii, Whom his father exiled for misgouernaile.

mis'governance. *Obs.* exc. *arch.* Also 5–6 *Sc.* **-goverance.** [MIS-¹ 4.]

†**1.** Misconduct, misbehaviour; evil living or conduct. *Obs.*

c **1386** CHAUCER *Monk's T.* 22 Had never worldly man so heigh degree As Adam, til he for misgovernaunce Was drive out of his hye prosperitee. **1456** SIR G. HAYE *Law Arms* (S.T.S.) 150 Be caus of the misgoverance of sik ane ungracious creature, all a hale company may tak.. scathe and schame. *c* **1470** HARDING *Chron.* CV. xiv, He had.. repentaunce For his trespas and misgouernaunce. **1495** *Act 11 Hen. VII*, c. 11 *Preamble*, Yong people.. be growen to ydelnes vices and other divers mysgovernaunces. **1512** *Act. 4 Hen. VIII*, c. 20 *Preamble*, The same mysgoverned persons shall lyf in robbyng and mysgovernaunce duryng ther lyves. **1627** P. FLETCHER *Locusts* IV. xxi, Those who disgrac't by some misgovernance (Their owne, or others) swell with griefe or spight.

†**2.** Mismanagement, misdirection, misuse. *Obs.*

1390 GOWER *Conf.* II. 150 For if ther fell him eny schame, It was thurgh his misgovernance. **1413** *Pilgr. Sowle* (Caxton 1483) I. i. 2 By theyr owne mysgouernaunce they forlettyth the ryght way of vertu. ? *a* **1500** in Grose, etc. *Antiq. Rep.* (1809) IV. 407 The sounde borde crasede forsith the instrumente, Throw mysgovernaunce to make notis whiche was not his intente. **1579** SPENSER *Sheph. Cal.* May 90 All will be soone wasted with misgouernaunce. **1621** BP. HALL *Heauen upon Earth* §7 These vnruly affections are not more necessary in their best vse, then pernicious in their misgouernance. **1678** SIR G. MACKENZIE *Crim. Laws Scot.* I. ix. (1699) 40 He who burns a House.. by misgovernance and not of set purpose.

3. Bad government of a country or state.

1447 BOKENHAM *Seyntys* (Roxb.) 28 To what myschaunce The cyte he brouth, thorgh mysgouernaunce. *c* **1460** FORTESCUE *Abs. & Lim. Mon.* xiv. (1885) 144 Murmor ageynes the kynges person, ffor þe mysgouernaunce off his reaume. *a* **1578** LINDESAY (Pitscottie) *Chron. Scot.* (S.T.S.) I. 171 They tuik god to witnes that they sould be guiltles of the misgoverance of the realme. **1641** BAKER *Chron.* (1660) 160 That the Realm of England should be destroyed through the misgovernance of King Richard. **1878** STUBBS *Const. Hist.* III. xviii. 243 He is liable to be defamed for misgovernance.

†**4.** Lack of restraint. *Obs.*

1463 in Heath *Grocers' Comp.* (1869) 61 Yf anye debatis arose betwixt anye two members, for misgovernaunce of wordes. *c* **1470** *Hors, Shepe & G.* (Roxb.) 27 Beware of surfete and misgouernaunce.

mis'governed, *ppl. a.* [MIS-¹ 2.]

†**1.** Characterized by misconduct; ill-conducted; immoral. *Obs.*

c **1440** *Jacob's Well* 270 Noȝt only to gode & sobre souereynes but also to mysgouernyd. *c* **1460** G. ASHBY *Dicta Philos.* 438 Misgoverned men and vicious. **1509** BARCLAY *Shyp of Folys* 12 b, His mysgouerned maners. ? *a* **1550** in *Dunbar's Poems* (1893) 309 Misgovernit ȝowth makis gowsty age. **1611** SPEED *Hist. Gt. Brit.* IX. xvii. (1623) 884 Many misgouerned and loose persons.

†**2.** Unruly, unrestrained; misdirected. *Obs.*

1593 SHAKS. *Rich. II*, v. ii. 4 Where rude mis-gouern'd hands.. Threw dust and rubbish on King Richards head. **1627** DRAYTON *Agincourt* 65 The beauteous Margarite, whose misgouern'd spleene So many sorrowes brought vpon her life. *a* **1639** DONNE *Ess.* (1651) 69 How strong and misgovern'd faith against common sense hath he.

3. Badly ruled or managed; mismanaged.

1834 *Tait's Mag.* I. 732 The poor misgoverned child. **1875** STEDMAN *Vict. Poets* ii. (1887) 54 The punishment of a misgoverned career is that it hinders even the man of genius from being justified during his lifetime.

mis'governing, *vbl. sb.* [f. MISGOVERN *v.* + -ING¹ or MIS-¹ 3 + GOVERNING *vbl. sb.*] The action of the vb. MISGOVERN. †**a.** Misconduct. *Obs.* **b.** Misgovernment.

1487 *How Good Wife Taught Dau.* 256 For falt of aw and of teching Bryngis thame oft to mysgouernyng. **1593** SHAKS. *Lucr.* 654 Blacke lust, dishonor, shame, mis-gouerning. **1609** DANIEL *Civ. Wars* I. xxxiii, Besides, the times, with all iniustice fraught, Concurr'd, with such confus'd misgouerning. **1711** in *10th Rep. Hist. MSS. Comm.* App. v. 112 The people.. dethroned their King under pretence of misgoverning. **1845** CARLYLE *Past & Pr.* I. v, A Governing Class.. which.. could not.. be kept from misgoverning, corn-lawing, and playing the very deuce with us.

mis'government. [MIS-¹ 4.]

†**1.** Evil conduct; unruly or disorderly behaviour; misconduct. *Obs.*

In the first quot. strictly two words.

c **1384** CHAUCER *H. Fame* 1975 Of good, or mysgouernement. **1573** L. LLOYD *Marrow of Hist.* (1653) 140 Tarquinius Superbus.. for his misgovernment and lust in the City against the chast matrons.. was.. banished Rome. **1581** PETTIE tr. *Guazzo's Civ. Conv.* III. (1586) 127 b, Through idlenesse, or gluttonie, or some such misgouernment. **1599** SHAKS. *Much Ado* IV. i. 100 Thus pretty Lady I am sorry for thy much misgouernment. **1602** WARNER *Alb. Eng.* (1612) Epit. 384 Through his owne obstinate headinesse and misgouernment. **1665** GLANVILL *Def. Van. Dogm.* To Tho. Albius, The unreasonable heats, frequent partialities [etc.]... The resentment I have of which misgovernments [etc.].

†**2.** Error or irregularity in the management, conduct, or use of anything; mismanagement. *Obs.*

1601 *Act 43 Eliz.* c. 4 §1 Misconvertinge or misgovernemente of any Landes Tenementes Rentes. **1650** JER. TAYLOR *Holy Living* i. §1 (1686) 9 If such misgovernment and unskilfulness make them fall into vitious and baser company. **1777** HOWARD *St. Prisons* (1780) 181 No.. servant of any judge to take a fee on occasion of a petition or complaint, founded upon the foregoing orders, or any misgovernment.

3. Bad government of a country or state; maladministration of public affairs. Hence, disorder, anarchy (cf. *misrule*).

1592 *Nobody & Someb.* (1878) 293 King Archigallo that now raignes In tiranny and strange misgovernment. *c* **1620** COKE in *Bacon's Wks.* (1827) VII. 376 Tending to.. the raising of faction or other misgovernment. **1783** BURKE *Sp. Fox's E. India Bill* Wks. 1792 II. 386 Whether, with this map of misgovernment before me, I can suppose myself bound.. to continue.. the management of these countries in those hands? **1849** MACAULAY *Hist. Eng.* iv. I. 522 The misgovernment of James.. completely turned the tide of public feeling. **1889** *Sat. Rev.* 30 Mar. 371/2 The chronic misgovernment.. which usually accompanies Turkish rule.

mis'governor. [MIS-¹ 5.] One who misgoverns.

1509 BARCLAY *Shyp of Folys* 257 b, O Lothsome lust: o mad mysgouernour Of all mankynde. *a* **1649** DRUMM. OF HAWTH. *Hist. Jas. III*, Wks. (1711) 49 The nobility of Scotland should be ready.. to seise upon the king's favourites, and misgovernours of the state. **1829** GEN. P. THOMPSON *Exerc.* (1842) I. 179 A nation bound by the act of past misgovernors. **1862** CARLYLE *Fredk. Gt.* XII. viii. (1873) IV. 187 Traitors, misgovernors worthy of death. **1884** *Sat. Rev.* 12 July 40/1 The misgovernors of Egypt.

†**mis'graffed,** *pa. pple. Obs.* [MIS-¹ 2.] Grafted amiss; *fig.* badly matched.

1590 SHAKS. *Mids. N.* I. i. 137 The course of true loue neuer did run smooth, But either it was different in blood.. Or else misgraffed, in respect of yeares.

mis'graft, *v. rare*⁻⁰. [Inferred from *misgrafted.*] To graft wrongly.

1846 in WORCESTER.

mis'grafted, *ppl. a.* [MIS-¹ 2.] Grafted wrongly or unsuitably.

1738 WARBURTON *Div. Legat.* I. Ded. p. vi, The Barren Leaves of misgrafted Free-thinking.

†**mis'gree,** *v. Obs.*⁻⁰ [MIS-¹ 7.] To disagree.

1530 PALSGR. 518/1, I discorde, I mysgre, *je descorde.* **1570** LEVINS *Manip.* 46/41 To Misgrée, *dissentire.*

†**mis'grieved,** *pa. pple. Obs.* [MIS-¹ 8.] Grieved or offended.

1543 GRAFTON *Contn. Harding* 578 He desired hym not to bee misgreued that he did thus leaue hym. **1579** TOMSON *Calvin's Serm. Tim.* 236/1 That they may not thinke much or be misgreeued. **1641** J. TRAPPE *Theol. Theol.* 179 They are such, as are misgrieved at the matter of the word.

mis'ground, *v.* [MIS-¹ 1.] *trans.* To ground falsely.

1827 HALLAM *Const. Hist.* I. vii. 418 *note*, That he had misgrounded his opinion on a certain precedent, which [etc.].

mis'grounded, *ppl. a.* [MIS-¹ 2.] Falsely grounded; ill-founded.

1598 SYLVESTER *Du Bartas* II. Ded. to Earl of Salisbury 12 Cause-less Envie, and mis-grounded Hate. **1630** PRYNNE *Anti-Armin.* 253 O vnhappy flocke that must be led by such a young misgrounded Shepheard. **1633** BP. HALL *Hard Texts, N.T.* 33 Your frequent and misgrounded putting away of your wives. *a* **1684** LEIGHTON *Comm. 1 Pet.* i. 14 It is a foolish misgrounded fear. **1700** ASTRY tr. *Saavedra-Faxardo* II. 295 Sometimes, upon a mis-grounded Apprehension, Money is expended to no purpose.

mis'grow, *v. rare*⁻⁰. [MIS-¹ 1.] *intr.* To grow amiss.

1647 HEXHAM, *Miswassen*, to Misgrowe.

mis'grown, *pa. pple.* and *ppl. a.* [MIS-¹ 2.] Grown out of shape; mis-shapen.

c **1611** CHAPMAN *Iliad* xx. 36 Lame Mulciber, his walkers quite misgrowne. **1848** tr. *Richter's Levana* iii. §16. 25 An interlaced, misgrown, banyan forest. **1866** GREGOR *Banffsh. Gloss., Misgrown*, stunted.

mis'growth. [MIS-¹ 4.] A distorted or abortive growth.

1647 HEXHAM, *Een Miswas in kruyden, boomen, &c.*, a Misgrowth in hearbes, trees, &c. **1819** COLERIDGE in *Lit. Rem.* (1836) II. 204 A misgrowth or *lusus* of the capricious ..genius of Shakspeare. **1848** CLOUGH *Amours de Voy.* III. 170 Our strivings, mistakings, misgrowths, and perversions. **1883** A. W. WARD *Eng. Poets* II. 443 A disgraceful illustration of too common a misgrowth of patriotism.

†**mis'guess,** *v. Obs.* [MIS-¹ 1.] *intr.* To guess wrongly.

1533 MORE *Debell. Salem* Wks. 976/2 He mysse gesseth amonge and weneth it were one, where in dede it was another. **1665** HOOKE *Microgr.* 74 Not withstanding this mis-ghessing.

mis'guggle, *v. Sc.* Also **-goggle, -grugle.** [f. MIS-¹ 8 + *guggle, gruggle* to handle roughly or clumsily (see *Eng. Dial. Dict.*).] *trans.* To handle roughly, maul; to mar, spoil, bungle.

1742 R. FORBES *Jrnl.* in *Ajax's Sp.*, etc. (1755) 33 She bad me had aff my hands, for I misgrugled a' her apron. **1814** SCOTT *Wav.* xviii, Donald had been misguggled by ane of these doctors about Paris. **1818** —— *Hrt. Midl.* viii, Overturning and mishguggling the government and discipline of the kirk. **1825–80** JAMIESON, *To misgoggle*, to spoil,.. as, 'He's fairly misgogglit that job'.

mis'guidance. [MIS-¹ 4.] Guidance in a wrong direction; misdirection.

1640 BP. HALL *Episc.* Ep. Ded. 4 The misguidance of many well meaning soules.. which are impetuously carried away in the throng. **1711** SHAFTESB. *Charac.* (1727) I. 113 By a small mis-guidance of the Affection, a Lover of Mankind becomes a Ravager. **1840** CARLYLE *Heroes* v. (1841) 258 He wanders.. in a world of which he is as the spiritual light, either the guidance or the misguidance. **1844** KINGLAKE *Eothen* xiii. (1878) 171 The Nazarene, whose mis-guidance had been the cause of our difficulties. **1859** I. TAYLOR *Transmission Anc. Bks.* xxii. 410 Under the mis-guidance of these chronological errors.

† **mis'guide**, *sb. Obs.* [f. MIS-^{1} 4 + GUIDE *sb.* III.] Misguidance; irregular behaviour.

1596 SPENSER *Hymn Heav. Love* 144 Nor spirit, nor Angell.. Could make amends to God for mans misguyde. **1602** WARNER *Alb. Eng.* IX. xliv. 210 Proserpin her offence (Growen through Mis-Guides, Venial perhaps) we censure in suspence. ? **16..** *Beggar-Laddie* xv. in Child *Ballads* V. 119 And for a' the lassie's ill misguide, She's now the young knight's lady.

mis'guide, *v.* [MIS-^{1} I.]

† **1.** *refl.* To go astray, go wrong; to conduct oneself badly or manage one's affairs improperly.

1390 GOWER *Conf.* III. 373 He may sone himself misguide, That seth noght the peril tofore. **1483** CAXTON *G. de la Tour* k vij b, How the badde.. wymmen.. were punysshed, as they mysgyded them. **1535** STEWART *Cron. Scot.* I. 423 Quhen that thai se.. thair king Misgyde him self in ony kynd of thing. **1651** CULPEPPER *Astrol Judgem. Dis.* (1658) 43 The disease came by the mans own misguiding himself.

2. *trans.* To mismanage, misgovern, misrule. Hence (mod. *Sc.*), to treat badly or improperly; to abuse, injure, spoil.

1494 FABYAN *Chron.* VII. 502 The realme before tyme had been mysseguydyd by offycers. **1572** *Satir. Poems Reform.* xxxiii. 163 The Parische Kirkis.. thay sa misgyde That nane for wynd and rane thairin may byde. **1671** MILTON *Samson* 912 To shew what recompence Towards thee I intend for what I have misdone, Misguided. **1681** COLVIL *Whigs Supplic.* (1751) 94 When they misguided church and state. **1787** [J. BEATTIE] *Scoticisms* 55 The boy misguides his cloaths.—Abuses, or sullies. **1893** STEVENSON *Catriona* xv, There were whiles when his dander rase to see the Lord's sants misguided.

3. To guide in a wrong direction, misdirect, mislead.

1509 BARCLAY *Shyp of Folys* (1570) ¶¶ iij, Blinde foolishenes Misgideth the mindes of people hye and lowe. **1594** NASHE *Unfort. Trav.* 49 When Phaeton his chariot did misguide. **1596** SPENSER *F.Q.* VI. iii. 47 Misdoubting least he should misguyde His former malice to some new assay. **1667** *Decay Chr. Piety* xvi. §3 Those leaders.. who misguide their tractable admiring followers. **1680** COTTON *Compl. Gamester* 8 But his drunkenness misguided his hand, so that he ran him only through the arm. **1709** POPE *Ess. Crit.* 202 To blind Man's erring judgment, and misguide the mind. **1759** GOLDSM. *Polite Learning* vi, The truth is, vanity is more apt to misguide men than false reasoning. **1880** MCCARTHY *Own Times* IV. 338 The curious ignorance of the condition of American.. feeling which misguided England's policy.

absol. **1696** LOCKE *Let.* 21 Nov. in F. Bourne *Life* II. xv. 453 Outward hearing may misguide but internal knowledge cannot err. **1837** CARLYLE *Fr. Rev.* I. I. ii, The nobles.. have nearly ceased either to guide or misguide.

mis'guided, *ppl. a.* Also 5 -kidyd. [MIS-^{1} 2.]

† **1.** Ill-conducted, ill-behaved, immoral. *Obs.*

c **1490** *Plumpton Corr.* (Camden) 77 If I knew that she wold be a myskidyd woman, I shold never speake word.. for hir. **1500–20** DUNBAR *Poems* lx. 20 Druncartis, dysouris, dy[v]owris, drewellis, Misgydit memberis of the dewellis. **1523** in *Acc. Fam. of Innes* (1864) 97 Alexander has bene ane misgidit man prodigus and has waistit.. his.. gudis.

2. † **a.** Mismanaged, misruled. *Obs.* **b.** Badly trained or reared.

1562 WINȜET *Cert. Tractates* Wks. (S.T.S.) I. 4 Manassing.. destruction of ȝour.. misreulit, and misgydit gouernment. **1842** J. AITON *Domest. Econ.* (1857) 300 Misguided apple and pear-trees may be recovered in a very few years.

3. Guided in a wrong direction; misdirected or misled in action or thought; hence, having a wrong purpose or intention; erring in thought or action.

1659 PHILIPOTT *Vill. Cant.* A j, That fiction of Brute.. obtruded upon us by seduced and misguided Histories. **1660** MILTON *Free Commonw.* 18 To give a stay.. to this general defection of the misguided and abus'd multitude. **1660** *Trial Regic.* 101 Others might do it by a misguided Conscience. *a* **1776** HUME *Ess.* (1777) I. ix. 68 An ambitious, or rather a misguided [*earlier edd.* ignorant], prince arose, who [etc.]. **1825** LAMB *Elia* Ser. II. *Barbara S*—, Some comic actor,.. in the misguided humour of his part, threw over the dish such a quantity of salt [etc.]. **1828** SCOTT *F.M. Perth* xxxii, Far different had been the fate of the misguided Heir of Scotland, from that which was publicly given out. **1903** R. D. SHAW *Pauline Ep.* 137 Unworthy and misguided party cries had arisen among them.

Hence **mis'guidedly** *adv.*, **mis'guidedness**.

1809 KNOX in Jebb & K. *Corr.* (1834) I. 555 Ignorance, misguidedness, and.. infelicity of circumstances. **1868** BROWNING *Ring & Bk.* IX. 932 A poor hard-pressed.. thing Has rushed so far, misguidedly perhaps. **1874** MORLEY *Compromise* 96 Perversely and misguidedly self-asserting.

mis'guider. [MIS-^{1} 5.] One who misguides.

a **1572** KNOX *Hist. Ref.* Wks. 1846 I. 206 Maister James, principall mysgydar now of Scotland. **1648** SALTMARSH *Some Drops* 50 That a new-star is to prepare for a misguider, and your story of Barchochebas upon it, it hath more lightsomnesse than light in it. **1741** RICHARDSON *Pamela* IV. 234 Pride, Vanity, Thoughtlessness, were my Misguiders. **1796** ELIZA HAMILTON *Lett. Hindoo Rajah* (1811) I. 138 The misguider of the mind of Zaarmilla has.. mixed some truth with the abundance of his falsehoods. **1824** SCOTT *Redgauntlet* let. xi, My gudesire was nae manager—not that he was a very great misguider.

mis'guiding, *vbl. sb.* [MIS-^{1} 3.]

† **a.** Evil conduct; misbehaviour; disorder. **b.** Misrule; mismanagement; ill-treatment. *Sc.* **c.** Misdirection.

? *c* **1470** G. ASHBY *Active Policy* 431 Mysreule & extorcion Mysguiding, Robbery & neclygence. **1480** CAXTON *Chron. Eng.* ccxlviii. u 7 b, Thurgh mysguydyng of the barge it ouerthrewe on the pyles. **1520** *Caxton's Chron.* III. 25/2 He slewe .l. thousande of yᵉ olde sage faders of greate vertue bycause they tolde hym his mysgydynge. **1530** PALSGR. 470/2 Reformacions of mysgydyng [F. *reformacions des abus*] be very necessary in a comen welth. **1535** STEWART *Cron. Scot.* II. 214 King Occa.. Throw misgyding wes slane into the feild. **1588** *Reg. Privy Council Scot.* Ser. I. IV. 266 For allegeit misgyding of sum of the saidis collegeis. **1786** BURNS *On Sc. Bard* viii, He ne'er was gien to great misguidin, Yet coin his pouches wad na bide in. **1898** *Westm. Gaz.* 7 Oct. 3/2 The.. perversion of our taste and misguiding of our æsthetic instincts.

mis'guiding, *ppl. a.* [MIS-^{1} 2.] That misguides, misdirecting.

1753 H. JONES *Earl of Essex* (1756) 43 The narrow censures of misguiding crowds. **1811** SHELLEY in Hogg *Life* (1858) I. 406 A man under a misguiding preconception. **1891** *Daily News* 15 Oct. 4/6 The.. misguiding criticisms of Tory newspapers.

Hence **mis'guidingly** *adv.*, 'in a way to mislead' (1847–54 Webster).

† **mis'guilt**, *sb. Obs.* In 4–5 -gilt, -gylt(e, -gelt. [f. MIS-^{1} 8 + GUILT *sb.*] Offence, misdeed, crime.

a **1300** *Cursor M.* 14732 Þe moneurs for þair misgilt, þair bordes [Jesus] ouerkest, þair penis spilt. *c* **1350** *Will. Palerne* 3996 Let me make a-mendis for al my mis-gelt. *Ibid.* 4397, etc. ? **1370** *Robt. Cicyle* (Hall.) 61 Thynke how thou was owte pylte Of thy lande, for thy mys-gylte. **14..** *Leges Burgorum* li, Gif þat a burges be attachyt.. for det or for ony misgilt. *c* **1430** *Hymns Virgin* (1867) 123 Thys mys-gylt þou for-yeue me!

† **mis'guilt**, *v. Obs.* In 4 *pa. pple.* misgilt, -gelt. [f. MIS-^{1} 8 + GUILT *v.*] To do wrong: used *intr.* or with pronominal obj.

13.. *Sir Beues* (A.) 1581 What haue ich so meche misgilt? *a* **1325** *Maudelein* 24 in Horstm. *Altengl. Leg.* (1878) 163 Euer he schoneþ þat haþ misgilt.

† **mis'guise**, *sb. Obs.* [MIS-^{1} 9.] Disguise. So † **mis'guised** *ppl. a.*, † **misguising** *vbl. sb.*

1581 *Satir. Poems Reform.* xliv. 332 Ȝour filthie, fals misgysing, Of haly Kirk ȝour temerar dispysing. **1603** HARSNET *Pop. Impost.* xxii. 149 These misguised bewitched creatures. **1646** W. DELL *Rights Reform.* Ep. Ded. A 2 b, The power of God.. shall as soon be made void, as the true Doctrine of the Gospel, though called Errour, Heresie, and Schisme, and have all the misguises of Hell put upon it.

† **mis'gye**, *v. Obs.* [f. MIS-^{1} I + *gye*, GUY *v.*^{1}] *trans.* To misguide; *refl.* to misbehave.

c **1386** CHAUCER *Monk's T.* 543 Tho wiste he [*sc.* Nero] wel he hadde him-self misgyed. **1406** HOCCLEVE *Lu Male Regle* 228 Sotil deceyuours, By whom the peple is mis gyed & led. *c* **1500** *Lancelot* 1663 If thei tak not full contrisioune, And pwnys them that hath ther low mysgyit.

† **mish**^{1}. *Cant. Obs.* [Shortening of COMMISSION *sb.*^{2}] A shirt.

1671–80 HEAD *Eng. Rogue* I. iv. 44. *a* **1673** in *Head's Canting Acad.* 19 What though I no Togeman wear, Nor Commission, Mish, or slate.

mish^2 (mɪʃ). Colloq. abbrev. of MISSIONARY *sb.*

1939 J. CARY *Mr. Johnson* 164 That's wot's wrong with some of these teetotal mishes. **1946** C. S. ARCHER *China Servant* vii. 105 You've no idea what a bunch of mishs will do, when sex rears its head.

mish, obs. form of MISS *v.*^{1}

mishaif, Sc. form of MISHAVE.

† **mis'hale**, *a. Obs.* [MIS-^{1} 7. (Etymological perversion of *mi'sale* MESEL.)] Unhealthy, sick.

c **1325** *Metr. Hom.* 132 Forthi thou, and the sones ilk ane, Sal be mishale als was Naamane [*cf. infra* unhale].

mishandle (mɪs'hænd(ə)l). *v.* [MIS-^{1} I. Cf. G. *misshandeln*, Du. *mishandelen.*] *trans.* To handle or treat badly or improperly; to handle roughly or rudely; to maltreat, ill-treat.

[**1390**: cf. MISHANDLING *vbl. sb.*] **1530** PALSGR. 637/2 It is nat well done to myshandell hym thus as you do. *Ibid.* 689/1, I restore a mater, or processe that was mysse handled. **1533** MORE *Apol.* xxxv. Wks. 899/2 To be so wrongefullye myssehandeled and punyshed, for onelye speakynge agaynste mysseorder and abusions. **1581** J. BELL *Haddon's Answ. Osor.* 257 b, There be some that are so beastly brutish that will mishandle the wordes and deedes of others, be they never so well spoken. **1616** BACON *Tract Commendams* Wks. 1827 VII. 319 The proceedings wherein had either been mis-reported or mis-handled. **1823** SCOTT *Quentin D.* xxi, It is a shame to see how they have mishandled the old man. **1828** SOUTHEY *Lett.* (1856) IV. 93 He mishandled good subjects with great success. **1904** WEYMAN *Abb. Vlaye* vii, Solomon is old, and they may mishandle him.

mis'handled, *ppl. a.* [MIS-^{1} 2.] Ill-managed; maltreated, ill-treated.

c **1610** SIR J. MELVIL *Mem.* (Bannatyne Cl.) 370 Charging us to tak cair of his mishandled estait. **1896** A. WHYTE *Bible Char.* 178 Poor mishandled Esau could not say that.

mis'handling, *vbl. sb.* [MIS-^{1} 3.] Rough handling; improper treatment; maltreatment.

1390 GOWER *Conf.* II. 189 The wardes of the cherche keie Thurgh mishandlinge ben myswreynt. **1533** MORE *Apol.* xxxv. Wks. 900/2 The proues of al such myssehandlyng may.. be brought foorth. **1658** A. FOX *Würtz' Surg.* II. vii. 68 Not regarding the mis-handling, it happeneth in some fals.. that the skin goeth off from the bone. **1886** STEVENSON *Kidnapped* xiii. 119 He had looked on, day by day, at the mishandling of poor Ransome. **1904** *Longman's Mag.* Jan. 254 Even my mishandling cannot rob the earth of its quickening power.

mishant, variant of MESCHANT.

mishanter (mɪ'ʃæntə(r)), **mischanter** (mɪs'tʃæntə(r)). *Sc.* and *north. dial.* Also MISCANTER. [Var. of MISAUNTER, prob. influenced by *mishant*, *mischant* (see MESCHANT). The form *mischanter* is app. due to assimilation to the synonymous *mischance.*] Misadventure, mishap.

1755 R. FORBES *Ajax's Sp.* 31 They had some allagust that some mishanter had befa'n us. **1784** BURNS *Welcome Illeg. Child*, Mischanter fa' me, If ought of thee, or of thy mammy, Shall ever daunton me, or awe me. **1824** SCOTT *Redgauntlet* let. xii, Mischanter on the auld beard o' ye! **1866** GREGOR *Banffsh. Gloss*, *Mischanter*, a hurt; a bruise. **1871** W. ALEXANDER *Johnny Gibb* (1873) 256 For there's sae mony mishanters 't we hear o' happenin' wi' the like o' 'im.

mishap (mɪs'hæp, 'mɪs-), *sb.* Forms: see HAP *sb.*^{1}; also 5 myschap, 6 mishhapp. [f. MIS-^{1} 4 + HAP *sb.*^{1}, prob. after OF. *mescheance* MISCHANCE.]

1. Evil hap; bad luck; misfortune. Now *rare.*

c **1386** CHAUCER *Monk's T.* 255 What man that hath freendes thurgh fortune, Mishap wol make hem enemys. **1470–85** MALORY *Arthur* VII. vii. 221 Thorou myshappe I sawe hym slee two knyghtes at the passage of the water. *c* **1530** *Pol. Rel. & L. Poems* (1866) 32 Wyse laboure & myshappe seldom mete to-gyder. **1591** SHAKS. *1 Hen. VI*, I. i. 23 Shall we curse the Planets of Mishap? **1633** G. HERBERT *Temple* 132 *Artillerie* i, From small fires comes oft not small mishap. **1667** MILTON *P.L.* x. 239 It cannot be But that success attends him; if mishap, Ere this he had return'd. **1684** *Contempl St. Man* I. ii. (1699) 21 The greatest felicity of the World, was tyed to the greatest Mishap. **1807–8** W. IRVING *Salmag.* xvii. (1860) 381 It is either my good fortune or mishap, to be keenly susceptible to the influence of the atmosphere. **1826–34** WORDSW. *To May* 66 And what if thou, sweet May, hast known Mishap by worm and blight.

2. In particularized use: An unlucky accident.

c **1330** R. BRUNNE *Chron.* (1810) 175 Many grete mishappes, many hard trauaile. *c* **1450** *Merlin* 5 A worthy man to whom were fallen many myshappes with-in shorte time. *c* **1586** C'TESS PEMBROKE *Ps.* CXXI. v, From ev'ry mishapp.. Safe thou shalt by Jehovas hand be guarded. **1588** SHAKS. *Tit. A.* I. i. 152 Secure from worldly chaunces and mishaps. **1667** DRYDEN *Ind. Emp.* v. ii, I might have liv'd my own Mishaps to mourn. **1781** COWPER *Conversat.* 321 Alas for unforeseen mishaps! **1836** W. IRVING *Astoria* I. 17 The pleasures, dangers, adventures, and mishaps, which they had shared together in their wild wood life. **1896** *Law Times* C. 438/2 The musical portion of the service had to be curtailed.. in consequence of a mishap to the organ.

Proverb. **1509** BARCLAY *Shyp of Folys* (1874) II. 251 One myshap fortuneth neuer alone.

b. A fall from chastity. *rare.* (Cf. MISFORTUNE *sb.* 2.) Cf. dial. *mishap-child*, a bastard.

1857 P. CUNNINGHAM *Walpole's Lett.* I. 95 *note*, Lady Betty was the friend and correspondent of Swift. In early life she made a mishap.

† **mis'hap**, *v. Obs.* [MIS-^{1} I.]

1. *intr.* Of a person: To meet with mishap or misfortune; to come to grief. Also, to have the misfortune *to do* something.

c **1330** R. BRUNNE *Chron. Wace* (Rolls) 4967 For þou myshappedest y þe first ende, Now schaltow spede er þat þou wende. **1377** LANGL. *P. Pl.* B. x. 283 *Archa dei* myshapped and ely brake his nekke. **1402** HOCCLEVE *Let. of Cupid* 217 For many a man by woman hath mishapped. *c* **1450** *Merlin* 24 Yef Vortiger hadde be ther, they hadde not so myshapped. **1533** MORE *Apol.* 192 b, Mo men then so many, haue misse happed to be.. mysse punyshed.

2. Of an event or *impers.*: To happen unfortunately. Often with dative pron.

c **1330** R. BRUNNE *Chron. Wace* (Rolls) 13280 Grace til hym wold non bytide, But euere mys happed [*a* **1400** *Petyt MS.* mishapned] on his syde. **14..** *Arth. & Merl.* 795 (Douce MS.) For hit was myshapped so, In his herte hym was ful wo. *c* **1450** *Merlin* 471 Gawein was euer pensif for his vncle,.. that hym sholde eny thinge myshappe. **1533** MORE *Apol.* 95 A thynge.. myche more to be lamented, when yt myshappeth to fall betwene a man & his wyfe. **1592** LD. VAUX in Ellis *Orig. Lett.* Ser. III. IV. 109 This mishappethe me by Andrewe Mallories lewdest misleading my sonne. **1633** B. JONSON *Tale Tub* III. i, Some things mishap'd, that he is come without her. **1647** HEXHAM, *Misschieden*, to Mishap, or to Fall out Ill.

b. Of a weapon: To fall unluckily.

1480 CAXTON *Chron. Eng.* i. a 4, As this Brute shold shete vn to an hert his arwe myshapped.. and so there Brute quelled his fadre.

So † **mis'happing** *vbl. sb.*, mishap.

c **1330** R. BRUNNE *Chron.* (1810) 68 Alle his mishappyng felle, he com in to Pountif [*Descendist en P. à sa confusioun*].

mis'haply, *adv.* [MIS-^{1} 6.] By mischance.

1470–85 MALORY *Arthur* VII. vi. 220 By myshap thou camyst behynde hym and myshapely thou slewe hym.

† **mis'happen**, *v. Obs.* [MIS-^{1} I.]

1. = MISHAP *v.* I.

c **1330** R. BRUNNE *Chron.* (1810) 289 Boste & deignouse pride & ille avisement Mishapnes oftentide. ? *a* **1400** *Morte Arth.* 3454 Mane, amende thy mode, or thow myshappene. **1530** PALSGR. 637/2 It is no wonder thoughe he myshappen, for he is ever quarellynge.

2. = MISHAP *v.* 2.

a **1400** [see MISHAP *v.* 2, quot. *c* 1330]. *c* **1430** *Pilgr. Lyf Manhode* IV. xxiii. (1869) 188 Whan any wole flee in to þe skyes, and afterward happeneth him to falle, oþer mishapneth. **1530** PALSGR. 637/2 He that trusteth ever to happe it

myshappeneth hym somtyme. **1550** COVERDALE *Spir. Perle* v. (1588) 41 No evil mishappened vnto him therof. **1590** SPENSER *F.Q.* I. iii. 20 Affraid, least to themselves the like mishapen might. **1610** HOLLAND *Camden's Brit.* I. 59 If ought should mishappen. **1611** COTGR., *Mesadvenir à*, to mishappen, to succeed ill vnto.

So †**mis'happening** *vbl. sb.*, mishap.

c **1330** R. BRUNNE *Chron.* (1810) 290 On þo þat God lufes lest mishappenyng salle falle.

†**mis'happy**, *a. Obs.* [MIS-[1] 7.] Unhappy.

c **1386** CHAUCER *Melib.* ¶602 Sorweful and mishappy is the condicioun of a povre begger. *c* **1440** *Promp. Parv.* 339/2 Myshappy, or vnhappy, *infortunatus.*

So †**mis'happiness**, unhappiness, unluckiness.

a **1541** WYATT in *Tottel's Misc.* (Arb.) 47 What wit haue wordes so prest, and forceable, That may conteyn my great mishappinesse? **1639** BAILLIE *Lett.* (Bannatyne Cl.) I. 143 The mishappines of the affair, which could not be..so compassed as to give content to all.

†**mis'harrit**, *pa. pple. Sc. Obs.* [? f. MIS-[1] + HARRE + *-it* = -ED.] ? Unhinged.

1501 DOUGLAS *Pal. Hon.* I. xix, I agane..Crap in the muskane aikin stok misharrit.

†**mis'have**, *v. Obs.* Also 6 *Sc.* **mishaif, mischawe.** [f. MIS-[1] 1 + HAVE *v.* 12. Cf. HAVING *vbl. sb.* 3. (In OE. *mishæbbende* = ill, unwell.)] *refl.* To misbehave oneself.

1528 *Sc. Acts Jas. V* (1814) II. 323/2 Gefe ony tyme had bene þ^t^ we had mishad ws. *c* **1560** A. SCOTT *Poems* (S.T.S.) iii. 49 Bot ȝit ȝe may mishaif ȝow in sum caice, And ȝe defend no^t^ damissellis defame. **1562** *Aberdeen Reg.* (1844) I. 346 For the iniuring of diuerse nychtbouris..and for mischawing of himself in sic sindry wayis. **1744** MRS. DELANY *Life & Corr.* (1861) II. 287 Barrow has mishaved himself so much that he must go.

misheant, variant of MESCHANT.

mishear (mɪs'hɪə(r)), *v.* Also 3 **misiheren** (see Y-HERE). [In OE. *mishíeran*: see MIS-[1] 1 and HEAR *v.*[1]] *trans.* †**a.** In OE., to disobey. **b.** To hear amiss, incorrectly, or imperfectly. Also *absol.* or *intr.*

c **961** *Æthelwold Rule St. Benet* v. (Schröer 1885) 62 Se þe eow ȝehyrð, he ȝehyrð me, and se þe eow mishyrð, he mishyrð me. *a* **1023** WULFSTAN *Hom.* xviii. (1883) 104 And þæt mancynn to swyðe gode mishyrde. *a* **1225** *Ancr. R.* 296 On elpi word þet tu mis-iherest. **1483** *Cath. Angl.* 241/2 To Mishere, *obaudire.* **1552** HULOET, Misheare, *obaudio.* [Cf. COOPER *Thesaurus* (1565), *Obaudio*, to heare hardely or vnwillingly.] **1595** SHAKS. *John* III. i. 4 Thou hast mispoke, misheard, Be well aduis'd, tell ore thy tale againe. **1815** J. C. HOBHOUSE *Substance Lett.* (1816) II. 70/1 My informant misheard or mistook a metaphor for a fact. **1877** TENNYSON *Harold* v. i, Your second-sighted man..Misheard their snores for groans. **1884** *Harper's Mag.* Dec. 142 Perhaps he had misheard the unknown voice.

So **mis'hearer**.

1483 *Cath. Angl.* 241/2 A Misherer, *obauditor.*

mis'hearing, *vbl. sb.* [MIS-[1] 3.] †**a.** Sinful hearing or listening. *Obs.* **b.** Hearing incorrectly or imperfectly.

1483 *Cath. Angl.* 241/2 A Misherynge, *obauditus, obaudicio.* **1493** *Dives & Pauper* II. xix. i vj, Goddes name is taken in veyne by mysheryng For if thou haue liking to here grete othes [etc.]. **1832–4** DE QUINCEY *Cæsars* Wks. 1859 X. 32 The universal mishearing in the outermost ring of the audience. **1860** PUSEY *Min. Proph.* p. vii, The question how the translators came so to render it, by what misreading or mishearing, or [etc.]. **1881** *Blackw. Mag.* Apr., [Errors] such as arise from mishearing.

†**mis'hearken**, *v. Obs.* [MIS-[1] 1.] *intr.* **a.** To listen sinfully. **b.** To mishear.

c **1200** in *O.E. Hom.* I. 305 Ich habbe..Mishercnet. *c* **1580** JEFFERIE *Bugbears* IV. v. 3 in *Archiv Stud. neu. Spr.* (1897) XCIX. 40 Art sure he did tel thee, or didest thou missehарken?

mishellene (mɪs'hɛliːn). [ad. Gr. μῑσ-έλλην, f. μῑσ(ο)-, f. μῑσ-εῖν to hate + Ἕλλην HELLENE, after PHILHELLENE *a.* and *sb.*] One who dislikes or is opposed to Greece or the Greeks. Hence **mishe'llenic** *a.*

1958 R. LIDDELL *Morea* I. 16 Those two learned, grumpy, and extremely mishellenic travellers, Edward Dodwell and Sir William Gell. *Ibid.* 23 To the grumpy Mishellene, it is all merely boring and tiresome. **1972** W. ST. CLAIR *That Greece might still be Free* xxxi. 350 Henry Lytton Bulwer.. became violently pro-Turkish in the Greek-Turkish questions later in the century. David Urquhart..also became a noted mishellene.

mishent, obs. variant of MESCHANT.

[**misher(s)ing.** see ABISHERING.]

mishit ('mɪshɪt), *sb.* [MIS-[1] 4.] In cricket, tennis, etc., a faulty or bad hit.

1882 *Australians in Eng.* 25 He made two mishits which fell harmless. **1898** *Westm. Gaz.* 1 Jan. 5/1 Caught at mid-off by Hirst, off a mis-hit. **1928** *Daily Tel.* 11 May 18/1 Lyon has never played a better innings... I did not notice that he made even a mis-hit. **1963** *Times* 11 June 4/6 Bear's bold effort ended in a mishit to leg slip.

So **mis'hit** (also erron. **miss-hit**) *v. trans.*, to hit (a ball) faultily. Also **mis'hitting** *vbl. sb.*

1904 P. F. WARNER *How we recovered Ashes* ix. 189 Gregory..mis-hit Braund and Rhodes caught him easily at backward point. **1930** *Times* 17 Mar. 4/4 Three minutes from the end Craig made his only mistake of the game, miss-hitting a bumping ball. **1963** *Times* 6 May 3/5 Some flashes of brilliance,..together with a good deal of mishitting,.. suggests that the final next Sunday may provide an attractive game. *Ibid.* 13 June 3/2 Booth batted sensibly for an hour to claim 33 out of 47 before mishitting a towering catch to backward point. **1974** *Country Life* 21 Feb. 360/1, I wondered whether he had mishit his tee shot.

mishlaw, variant of MUSHLA.

mish-mash ('mɪʃmæʃ), *sb.* Also 5 **mysse-masche, 7 mish-mass, 9 misch-masch; mish-mosh, mish-mush.** [A reduplication of MASH *sb.*[1] Cf. G. *mischmasch*, Da. (? from LG.) *miskmask.*] A confused mixture; a medley, hodgepodge, jumble.

c **1450** *Mankind* 49 in *Macro Plays* 3 But, ser, I prey yow þis questyon to claryfye: Dryff-draff, mysse-masche. **1585** HIGINS *Junius' Nomenclator* 362 A confused or disordered heape of all things together: a mishcmash. **1600** HOLLAND *Livy* XXVI. xl. 615 A very mish mash [orig. *conluvio*] and sinke of vile and wretched persons. **1634** SIR T. HERBERT *Trav.* (1638) 27 A mish-mash of Arabick and Portuguise. **1676** *Doctrine of Devils* 146 That Gallimawphey Mish-mass, of most Monstruous..Conceits and Practises. **1806** W. TAYLOR in Robberds *Mem.* (1843) II. 257 The Mishmash of Manuscript, printed extract [etc.]. *c* **1855** 'L. CARROLL' (*title*) Mischmasch. **1860** PUSEY *Min. Proph., Haggai* i. 2 The Samaritans..(amid their mishmash of worship, worshipping, as our Lord tells them, they know not what). **1876** GEO. ELIOT *Dan. Der.* xxii, A ridiculous mish-mash of superannuated customs and false ambition. **1957** *Time* 2 Sept. 34/2 Paul Gregory's *Crescendo*, a mish-mash of American music, with Ethel Merman, Rex Harrison, Louis Armstrong, &c. **1959** N. MAILER *Advts. for Myself* (1961) 335 You call this a report?.. It is nothing but a mish-mosh. **1962** *John o' London's* 18 Jan. 68/2 How did the cast make out amid the mish-mush? **1964** G. MARX *Let.* 24 Feb. (1967) 305, I suggest you learn how to pronounce 'mishmash'. It is not pronounced 'mash',..but rather as though it were spelled *mosh.* **1965** P. ZIEGFELD *Ziegfelds' Girl* i. 7 How the elegant and impeccably British Mr. Maugham had come to write this mishmash nobody could figure out. **1975** *Listener* 30 Oct. 589/2 The original *Panorama* had consisted of a mish-mash of disconnected and frequently frivolous items.

attrib. **1652** *News fr. Low-Countr.* 1 When, first, the first confused Masse Did, from its mish mash medly, passe. *a* **1922** T. S. ELIOT *Waste Land Drafts* (1971) 27 From such chaotic misch-masch potpourri What are we to expect but poetry?

Hence **'mishmash** *v.*, to make a 'mish-mash' or confused mass of; to throw into confusion.

1694 MOTTEUX *Rabelais* IV. lx. (1737) 247 Then is sacrific'd to him Haberdines, Poor-Jack, minglemangled, mishmash'd. **1791** LEARMONT *Poems* 199 Steghin gluttons.. Mish-mashin' creatures for their greed or gust. **1866** GREGOR *Banffsh. Gloss.*, *Meesh-mash*, to mingle; to throw into a confused mass.

‖**Mishnah, Mishna** ('mɪʃnə). Also 7–8 **misna, mischna,** (*pl.* **mischnaios**). [post-Biblical Heb. *mishnāʰ*, pl. *mishnōth* and *mishnāyōth* (1) repetition, (2) instruction, f. *shānāʰ* to repeat, in post-Biblical Heb. to teach or learn (oral tradition).] The collection of binding precepts or *halakhoth* (see HALACHAH) which forms the basis of the Talmud and embodies the contents of the oral law. Also, a paragraph of the mishnah.

1610 T. FITZHERBERT *Policy & Relig.* II. xiv. 191 The first collection was made by Iudas, the sonne of Simon,..and this was called *Misna.* **1613** PURCHAS *Pilgrimage* (1614) 169 The *Mischnaios*, and *Gemara* made vp the whole Talmud. *Ibid.* 170 Their *Mischna* or Talmud text. **1723** MATHER *Vindic. Bible* 300 The Jews affirm that the most remarkable copies of the Mischna, written in the second age after Christ, were marked with points. **1768–74** TUCKER *Lt. Nat.* (1834) II. 673 Drawn from the Fathers, the Councils, or the Mishna. **1867** *Chamb. Encycl.* IX. 281/1, 524 chapters (Perakim), which contain the single Mishnas. **1883** *Encycl. Brit.* XVI. 503/2 A mishnah, if genuine, never begins with a passage of the Pentateuch.

Hence **Mishnic, -ical** ('mɪʃnɪk, -ɪkəl), also **Mishnaic** (mɪʃ'neɪɪk), †'**Misniac, -acal** *adjs.*, pertaining or relating to, characteristic of, the mishnah.

1718 PRIDEAUX *Old & New Test.* II. II. 67 The Tanaim or the Mishnical doctors. **1723** MATHER *Vindic. Bible* 301 Ephodeus assures us that all the ancient Misniack books were pointed. *Ibid.* 362 After these let the Misniacal Doctors be considered. **1867** *Chamb. Encycl.* IX. 281/1 The individual enactments of the Mishnic doctors. **1898** *Expositor* July 77 Very late Biblical or even Mishnic Hebrew. **1878** *Encycl. Brit.* VIII. 561/1 The Mishnaic usage. **1953** *Jrnl. Theol. Stud.* IV. 7 St. Mark is an apocalyptic, St. Matthew is a mishnaic writer. **1973** *Jewish Chron.* 2 Feb. 22/4 The Amoraim ('interpreters'), the post-Mishnaic teachers in the great schools of Palestine..and Babylon.

†**mis'honour**, *sb. Obs.* [MIS-[1] 7.] Dishonour.

a **1300** *Cursor M.* 23644 þe wicked..of alle þai sal hat mishonur.

So †**mishonour** *v.*, to dishonour.

1570–6 LAMBARDE *Peramb. Kent* (1826) 174 God was blasphemed, the holy Virgine his mother mishonoured.

mis-hook (mɪs'hʊk), *v. Cricket.* [f. MIS-[1] 1 + HOOK *v.* 8c.] *trans.* To hook (a ball) faultily.

1955 *Times* 19 July 12/1 The new ball was losing its shine, when he mishooked a bouncer gently to mid-wicket. **1963** *Times* 12 June 4/4 Bear completely mishooked a ball and was caught at 19.

So **'mishook** *sb.*, a faulty hook.

1961 *Times* 16 May 4/1 Minney..was caught off a mis-hook.

†**mis'hope**, *sb. Obs.* [MIS-[1] 7. Cf. MDu. *mishope*, MSw. *mishop.*] Despair.

a **1300** *Cursor M.* 27050 For sli mis-hope þat þai lij in, ne dar þai nakin god bigin. *c* **1400** *Rule St. Benet* (Prose) 9 þat ye ne falle in na mis-hope, bot in godis trouȝ to liue. *c* **1450** *St. Cuthbert* (Surtees) 5889 Mys hope of þair synn. **1506** *Kalender of Sheph.* I j b (1892) III. 93 Myshope.

†**mis'hope**, *v. Obs.* [MIS-[1] 7. Cf. MDu. *mishopen*, MHG. *missehoffen*, MSw. *mishoppa.*]
1. *trans.* To fail to hope in.

a **1240** *Lofsong* in *Cott. Hom.* 213 Ich ne mishopie þe nout.

2. *intr.* To despair.

1303 R. BRUNNE *Handl. Synne* 8439 þat a man myshope noght þogh he haue grete temptyng of þoght. *a* **1340** HAMPOLE *Psalter* xliii. 20 Myshopand of thi goednes. *c* **1380** WYCLIF *Serm.* Sel. Wks. I. 346 How myȝte þis Ladi myshope þat ne she shulde come to hevene?

misick, obs. form of MIZZICK *dial.*

misidentifi'cation. [MIS-[1] 4.] Erroneous identification.

1902 *Encycl. Brit.* XXV. 468/1 The chief defects in practice were (1) frequent failure to identify, (2) liability to mis-identification. **1946** F. E. ZEUNER *Dating Past* III. v. 132 The implications of such misidentifications..are obvious. **1968** *Listener* 27 June 828/3 Much more serious..is..the kind of terrible events which were foreshadowed in the novel *Fail Safe*, whereby one has accidental misidentification leading to some international disaster. **1973** *Nature* 13 July 74/3 They criticize Theyer's micro-palaeontological work by giving chapter and verse on a series of supposed misidentifications and miscorrelations.

So **misi'dentify** *v.*, to identify erroneously.

1895 L. STEJNEGER in *Ann. Report U.S. Nat. Museum 1893* 449 The specimens so recorded which I have had an opportunity to examine have either been misidentified, or else the locality was very doubtful. **1924** *Geogr. Jrnl.* LXIV. 457 A marks the position of Camp IV. (26,700 feet) and G the point reached by Mallory, Norton, and Somervell in 1922, which was probably misidentified and placed too high in the theodolite measure of 1922, made in very difficult circumstances. **1951** *Essays in Crit.* I. 332 He [*sc.* Iago] pretends ignorance, he pretends helpfulness, he intentionally misidentifies. **1952** *Mind* LXI. 422 He misidentifies the test he is using. **1971** *Nature* 19 Mar. 149/3 This name has been widely used for specimens of the genus in the Mediterranean and northern Europe. Templeman regards them all as having been misidentified.

mis-iheren: see MISHEAR *v.*

Misima, var. MASSIM.

misimagi'nation. [MIS-[1] 4.]
Wrong imagination.

1618 BP. HALL *Righteous Mammon* Wks. (1625) 700 Who can without indignation look vpon the prodigies which this mis-imagination produces in that other sex?

misi'magine, *v.* [MIS-[1] 1.] *trans.* To imagine erroneously. So **misi'magined** *ppl. a.*

1625 DONNE *Serm.* 24 Feb. (1626) 44 God hath no where told thee, that hee hath done any such thing as an ouertender Conscience may mis-imagine. *a* **1684** LEIGHTON *Comm. 1 Pet.* Wks. (1868) 231 Had he come down, as some have misimagined it, only to set us this perfect way of obedience.

misim'pression. [MIS-[1] 4.]
A wrong impression.

1670 BAXTER *Cure Ch. Div.* 351 Even he that overcometh in the main yet seldome so far conquereth as to receive no misimpression upon his mind. **1869** SIR J. T. COLERIDGE *Mem. J. Keble* xiii. 301, I can scarcely avoid saying a few words to prevent a misimpression as to himself. **1884** SIR J. A. PICTON in *N. & Q.* 5 Apr. 271/2 [She] is under a misimpression as to any connexion between these two words.

misimprision. Error for MISPRISION.

1611 SPEED *Hist. Gt. Brit.* IX. xxi. 781/1 Whose fault as shee thought..was rather through misimprision then will.

misim'prove, *v.* Now *rare.* [MIS-[1] 7.]
1. *trans.* To employ wrongly (cf. IMPROVE *v.* 2); to fail to use to good purpose; to abuse, use ill. *Obs.* or *U.S.*

1658 H. MOSELEY *Healing Leaf* 15 What should become of him that had ten Talents, if he had misimproved them? **1680** MATHER *Irenicum* 19 That good principle of..moderation towards Brethren of differing Judgments, hath been.. perversely misimproved. **1737** J. WILLISON *Affl. Man's Companion* VII. i. (1744) 128 The most Part of Men..misimprove their Health. **1798** *Missionary Mag.* No. 22. 133 We warned the people against misimpoving so high a privilege. **1826** LONGF. in *Life* (1891) I. vii. 87 You either overrated my abilities and advantages..or I have sadly misimproved them both.

2. To improve injudiciously; to 'make worse for mending'. Also *absol.*

1847 MILLER *First Impr. Eng.* xvi. (1857) 266 Nowhere.. had the hand of improvement misimproved so sadly. **1853** G. JOHNSTON *Nat. Hist. E. Bord.* I. 115 This, our only station for the plant,..has been..tampered with and mis-improved of late.

misim'proved, *ppl. a. Obs.* or *U.S.* Also 8 **-improven.** [MIS-[1] 2.] Wrongly employed; not used to good purpose; abused.

1661 HICKERINGILL *Jamaica* 95 Nor did this licentiousnesse long want the misimproved subtlety of a Gentleman. **1717** WODROW *Corr.* (1843) II. 286 Our sins and misimproven privileges. **1820** W. JAY *Prayers* 208 Our misimproved time and talents.

† **misim'provement.** *Obs.* [MIS-^{1} 4.] Failure to employ properly, abuse, misuse.

1644 [H. PARKER] *Jus Populi* 41 If the commonwealth hath an interest in slaves, how can such mis-improvement thereof be answered to God? *a* **1748** WATTS *Improv. Mind* II. iv, We are justly chargeable with criminal sloth, and misimprovement of the talents. **1774** ABIGAIL ADAMS in *Fam. Lett.* (1876) 48 The misimprovement of our great advantages. **1806** A. STEWART in *Mem.* (1822) 232 Our sin in the misimprovement of former privileges.

misim'prover. *Obs.* or *U.S.* [MIS-^{1} 5.] One who misimproves.

1712 BLACKWELL in H. G. Graham *Social Life Scot.* x. (1899) II. 133 [Every enjoyment that came from Providence] could but feed to the slaughter of the misimprover. **1746** D. BRAINERD *Diary* 11 Oct. (1902) I. 314 My mind was perplexed with fears that I was a misimprover of time.

misincli'nation. [MIS-^{1} 4.]
A wrong inclination.

1652 SCLATER *Civ. Magistracy* (1653) 16 If any are found of the same misse-inclinations now. **1673** O. WALKER *Educ.* 21 It is much easier to bend a natural mis-inclination to its neighbour virtue—than to its opposite.

misin'cline, *v.* [MIS-^{1} 1.] To incline in a wrong direction.

1652 BP. HALL *Invis. World* III. §11 See him, by misinclining his own will, apostatizing from his Infinite Creator.

misin'clined, *ppl. a.* [MIS-^{1} 2, 7.] **a.** Wrongly inclined. **b.** Disinclined.

a **1716** SOUTH *Serm.* (1744) X. i. 8 Our affections [are] mis-inclined. **1837** S. R. MAITLAND *Voluntary Syst.* (ed. 2) 12 If you've any thing..that you could let me have reasonable, I should not be misinclined to deal with you.

misin'fer, *v.* [MIS-^{1} 1.] *trans.* To infer wrongly; also, †to draw a wrong inference from.

1597 HOOKER *Eccl. Pol.* v. lii. §4 Nestorius..did..mis-inferre that in Christ those natures can by no coniunction make one person. **1640** SIR E. DERING *Carmelite* (1641) B ij, You corrupt one Text and mis-inferre two other. *a* **1663** SANDERSON *Serm., Ad Clerum* (1681) 67 Such conclusions as are mis-inferred hence. **1700** COLLIER *2nd Def. Short View* 101 Because Modesty is the Character of Women, [I] misinfer, that no Woman must be shewn without it.

mis'inference. [MIS-^{1} 4.] Wrong inference.

1627 W. SCLATER *Exp. 2 Thess.* (1629) A iv b, Plausibly perhaps by mis-inference. **1647** TRAPP *Comm. 2 Pet.* iii. 16 When we put words into the mouths of these oracles by mis-inferences or mis-applications.

misin'ferring, *vbl. sb.* [MIS-^{1} 3.] = prec.

1627 BP. HALL *Epist.* IV. iv. 343 Is it the voice of treason, or religion? And, if traiterous, whether flatly, or by mis-inferring?

misin'form, *v.* [MIS-^{1} 1.] *trans.* To inform amiss; to give wrong or misleading information to.

In the first quot. prob. two words (see MIS *adv.*).

1390 GOWER *Conf.* I. 178 It nedeth of no bakbitinge That thou thi ladi mis enforme. **1530** PALSGR. 605/1, I..bring one from the trewe opinion by misenformyng. *a* **1608** DEE *Relat. Spir.* I. (1659) 67 You may also mark how the Devil at this time did misinform E. K. **1651** HOBBES *Leviath.* II. xxx. 175 To let the people be..mis-informed of the grounds..of those his essentiall Rights. **1667** MILTON *P.L.* IX. 355 Least ..She dictate false, and missinforme the Will To do what God expressly hath forbid. **1701** NORRIS *Ideal World* I. iv. 188 Our senses..do not..deceive or misinform us as to the meer existence of things. **1807** G. CHALMERS *Caledonia* I. III. ix. 457 Pontoppidan misinformed, and deluded, his prince, upon a thousand points of history. **1974** *Physics Bull.* Jan. 3/2 All the above is well known... Those attempting to misinform the World Scientific Community are fully aware of my real circumstances.

absol. **1611** BIBLE *2 Mac.* iii. 11 That some of it belonged to Hircanus,..and not as that wicked Simon had misinformed. **1625** BP. MOUNTAGU *App. Cæsar* 256 You misinforme against him for concluding with the Papists. **1678** MARVELL *Growth Popery* 43 However the King's Counsel may misinform.

misin'formant. [MIS-^{1} 5.] One who gives wrong information.

1860 in WORCESTER, citing Wilberforce. **1882** *Standard* 11 Nov. 5/7, I am at a loss to know what your mis-informant can mean by the expression.

misinfor'mation. [MIS-^{1} 4.]

1. The action of misinforming or condition of being misinformed.

1587 FLEMING *Contn. Holinshed* III. 1009/1 A..riuer, which the Britons called Isk; Ptolomeus by misinformation nameth it *Isaca.* **1654** in *Nicholas Papers* (Camden) II. 60, I must now contradict..what by Lt Gen. Middleton's very unkind and unfriendly misinformation I mistold you in my last. **1668** CLARENDON *Vindic.* Tracts (1727) 37 Either by misinformation or negligence of the clerk..the county of Warwick was inserted. **1756** JOHNSON *K. of Prussia* Wks. 1796 XII. 239 He declares himself..against the use of torture, and by some misinformation charges the English that they still retain it. **1800** *Asiat. Ann. Reg.* 312/2 By the misinformation of our guides, we were led to Amergurh. **1861** J. S. MILL *Utilitarianism* v. 85 Courts of law allow voluntary engagements to be set aside..sometimes on the ground of mere mistake, or misinformation.

2. Erroneous or incorrect information.

a **1661** HOLYDAY *Juvenal* (1673) 262 According to the common misinformation, which the Romans had concerning the Jews. **1743** T. BIRCH *Life Boyle* B.'s Wks. 1772 I. p. cvi, Not only our weather-glasses, but likewise our senses, may give us misinformation about cold. **1846** J. W. CROKER in *C. Papers* 22 Aug. (1884), Lord George is again under some misinformation. **1901** KIPLING *Kim* vii. 163 He was, by virtue of his office, a bureau of misinformation.

† **b.** With *a* and *pl.* *Obs.*

1627 LORNE in Willcock *Gt. Marquess* (1902) App. iii. 355 Whom they have incensed agains me by their misinformations. *c* **1640** J. SMYTH *Lives Berkeleys* (1883–5) II. 407 A misinformation of those that waited in his sicknes. **1788** JEFFERSON *Writ.* (1859) II. 63 It says that Congress removed to Hartford, but this is a misinformation.

misin'formative, *a.* [MIS-^{1} 6.] That gives wrong information. So **misin'formatory** *a.*

1912 *Times Lit. Suppl.* 15 Feb. 64/3 To modify these few misinformative parts of a work which otherwise is.. valuable. **1927** *Observer* 3 Apr. 25/3 A so-called Informatory Double that does not contain top card strength is better termed 'misinformatory'.

misin'formed, *ppl. a.* [MIS-^{1} 2.] Incorrectly informed; having an incorrect or imperfect knowledge of or acquaintance with the facts.

c **1447** in F. M. Nichols *Lawford Hall* (1891) App. 23 The said pe de gre aboue is mysse enfourmed bothe of weddyng of Agnes Forde and [etc.]. **1635** QUARLES *Embl.* II. vi. (1718) 85 She abuses Her mis-inform'd beholder's eye. **1735** BERKELEY *Free-think. in Math.* §6 Wks. 1871 III. 304, I own myself misinformed, and shall gladly be found in a mistake. **1815** A. BURN in *Mem.* III. (1816) 121 A weak and misinformed conscience. **1895** *Times* 9 Jan. 4/4 A few of the less important ones [*viz.* statements] were found to be misinformed or misleading.

misin'former. [MIS-^{1} 5.] = MISINFORMANT.

1635 in *Lismore Papers* Ser. II. (1889) III. 222 Those malicious misinformers whose..lyes turned my sinces into ..a confused load of greife. **1637–50** Row *Hist. Kirk* (Wodrow Soc.) 525 That all incendiaries, and misinformers of the subjects anent his Majestie..be punished. **1894** *Columbus* (Ohio) *Disp.* 17 Jan., Your informer, or rather misinformer.

misin'struct, *v.* [MIS-^{1} 1.] *trans.* To instruct amiss.

1547–64 BAULDWIN *Mor. Philos.* (Palfr.) 147 When they haue beene..misinstructed..by a fawning and fleering flatterer. **1597** HOOKER *Eccl. Pol.* v. xlix. §3 Let vs not thinke that our Sauiour did misinstruct his disciples. **1843** *Blackw. Mag.* LIV. 31 He..subsides into the mere singing-master, to misinstruct the rising generation.

misin'struction. [MIS-^{1} 4.] Erroneous instruction.

1642 MILTON *Apol. Smect.* Wks. 1851 III. 299 Correcting by the clearnesse of their owne judgement the errors of their mis-instruction. **1664** H. MORE *Antid. Idolatry* x. 116 By reason of the blinde Mis-instructions of their Church. **1839** *Spirit Metrop. Conserv. Press* (1840) II. 157 The official project..for the mis-instruction of our poorer countrymen. **1854** H. ROGERS *Ess.* (1874) II. i. 59 Bent and perverted by ..early misinstruction. **1898** *Daily News* 26 May 4/7 The Eton Greek Grammar..was one of the worst ever compiled for the delusion and misinstruction of youth.

misin'telligence. [f. MIS-^{1} 4 + INTELLIGENCE, prob. after F. *mésintelligence.*]

1. Misunderstanding between two parties; disagreement, discord. Now *rare* or *Obs.*

1639 DRUMM. OF HAWTH. *Sp. for Edin.* Wks. (1711) 216 Whatever those mis-intelligences have been, which might have estranged..us from your majesty. **1654–66** EARL ORRERY *Parthen.* (1676) 645 Her heart and face were in perfect mis-intelligence. **1765** MACLEANE tr. *Mosheim's Eccl. Hist.* XVII. ii. I. i. §21 (1768) IV. 323 There had subsisted.. an, almost, uninterrupted misintelligence between the French monarchs and the Roman pontiffs.

2. Misunderstanding of the meaning of something; wrong impression as to facts.

1779 H. WALPOLE *Let. to Rev. W. Cole* 28 Jan., I showed one or two of them [*sc.* some tales] to a person..who may have mentioned them, and occasioned Mr. Lort's misintelligence. [**1818** TODD, *Misintelligence*,..2. Misinformation; false accounts.] **1822** SHELLEY *Sel. Lett.* (1882) 192 Their stupid misintelligence of the deep wisdom and harmony of the author.

3. Lack of intelligence or sagacity. *rare.*

1848 *Tait's Mag.* XV. 703 [tr. Fr.] There reigns in our stables a rudeness, a misintelligence, which does not allow our undertaking the necessary operations for taming these animals. **1876** LOWELL *Lett.* (1894) II. 196 No doubt the government is bound to protect the misintelligence of the blacks, but surely not at the expense of the intelligence of the men of our own blood.

misin'telligible, *a.* *rare*$^{-1}$. [MIS-^{1} 6.] Capable of being wrongly understood.

1847–8 DE QUINCEY *Protestantism* Wks. 1858 VIII. 89 It is not even intelligible, and, what is worse still, sure to be mis-intelligible.

† **misin'tend,** *v.* *Obs.* [MIS-^{1} 1.] *trans.* To intend, purpose, or direct wrongfully.

1592 KYD *Sol. & Pers.* I. iv. 127 Cut short what malice Fortune misintends. **1598** DICKENSON *Greene in Conc.* (1878) 111 Such recreations not misintended, hinder melancholy.

† **misin'tended,** *ppl. a.* *Obs.* [MIS-^{1} 2.]
Maliciously aimed.

1594 SPENSER *Amoretti* xvi, The Damzell broke his misintended dart.

† **misin'tending,** *vbl. sb.* *Obs.* In 5 **mysentendyng.** [app. f. MIS-^{1} 3 + INTEND *v.* + -ING^1, but the meaning 'tend, care for' is not recorded for INTEND or F. *entendre.*] ? Want of care, inattention.

1486 *Bk. St. Albans* c viij b, The leest mysdyetyng and mysentendyng sleth [hir].

misin'tention. *rare*$^{-1}$. [MIS-^{1} 4.]
Wrong intention.

1626 BP. HALL *Contempl., O.T.* xx. 74 The act is no other then what the infinite iustice of God would iustly worke by their mis-intentions.

misin'terpret, *v.* [MIS-^{1} 1. Cf. F. *mésinterpréter.*] *trans.* To interpret erroneously or in an incorrect sense; to give a wrong interpretation to. occas. *absol.* Also **misin'terpreting** *vbl. sb.*

1589 *Reg. Privy Council Scot.* Ser. I. IV. 427 The motioun of my voyage..wilbe diverslie skansit upoun, the misinterpreting quhairof may tend..to my grite dishonnour. **1593** SHAKS. *Rich. II*, III. i 18 Neere to the King in blood, and neere in loue, Till you did make him mis-interprete me. **1645** MILTON *Tetrach.* 83 That all misinterpreting, and occasion of fraud, or death may be remov'd. **1651** HOBBES *Leviath.* II. xxvii 153 False Teachers, that..mis-interpret the Law of Nature. **1711** STEELE *Spect.* No. 80 ⁋1 All their Words and Actions were misinterpreted by each other. **1821–2** SHELLEY *Chas. I*, III. 54 Mark too, my lord, that this expression strikes His Majesty, if I misinterpret not. **1880** MCCARTHY *Own Times* xxxii. III. 63 They entirely misinterpreted the significance of the stories.

misin'terpretable, *a.* [MIS-^{1} 6.] Capable of misinterpretation; liable to be misinterpreted.

1604 *Supplic. Masse Priests* §14 The letter of Scripture (mis-interpretable by every contentious spirite). **1684** E. S. *Answ. H. More's Expos. Apoc.* 169 How mis-interpretable the Bible is..is too notoriously known. **1828** CARLYLE *Misc. Ess., Werner* (1840) I. 110 The two most showy, heterogeneous, and misinterpretable writers of his day.

,misinterpre'tation. [MIS-^{1} 4. Cf. F. *mésinterprétation.*] Erroneous interpretation.

1576 *Lichfield Gild Ord.* (E.E.T.S.) 32 By the abvsynge, mysinterpretacion or mystakinge of these ordynaunces. **1624** DONNE *Serm.* (1640) ii. 17 S. Matthew..sayes in a word, which can admit of no mis-interpretation That that was fulfilled which Esay had said. **1684** T. BURNET *Th. Earth* III. 13 We are oblig'd to free it from those false glosses or mis-interpretations, that..make it wholly ineffectual. **1711** STEELE *Spect.* No. 4 ⁋2 One would think a silent Man ..should be very little liable to misinterpretations. **1874** CARPENTER *Ment. Phys.* I. iv. (1879) 168 A far more frequent cause of false perceptions, however, lies in the misinterpretation of real Sense-impressions. **1896** *Allbutt's Syst. Med.* I. 211 The histological misinterpretations it contains are so numerous [etc.].

misin'terpreter. [MIS-^{1} 5.] One who misinterprets.

1599 NASHE *Lenten Stuffe* Wks. (Grosart) V. 293 The lawyers and selfe-conceited misinterpreters. **1643** MILTON *Divorce* Introd., Wks. 1851 IV. 12 He is no better then a Pharise..whom as a misinterpreter of Christ I openly protest against. **1661** BOYLE *Style of Script.* 227 His solid defence of divers of its truths against its misinterpreters. **1825** COLERIDGE *Aids Refl.* (1848) I. 246 To present each article in its true Scriptural purity, by exposure of the caricatures of misinterpreters.

mis'join, *v.* [MIS-^{1} 1.] *trans.* To join or connect wrongly, inappropriately, or unsuitably; *spec.* in *Law* (cf. MISJOINDER).

1540 *Act 32 Hen. VIII*, c. 30 Ye issues haue ben misioyned. *Ibid.*, Mysjoyning of thissue. **1667** MILTON *P.L.* v. 111 Oft in her absence mimic Fansie wakes To imitate her [*sc.* Nature]; but misjoyning shapes, Wilde work produces oft. **1687** DRYDEN *Hind & P.* II. 140 Luther, more mistaking what he read, Misjoins the sacred Body with the Bread. **1790** *Sempronia* III. 61 It misjoins nor thoughts, nor words, nor deeds. **1857** [see next].

mis'joinder. *Law.* [MIS-^{1} 4.] Improper joinder of parties in an action or of causes of action in a suit.

1852 *Act 15 & 16 Vict.* c. 76 §35 In case it shall appear at the Trial of any Action that there has been a Misjoinder of Plaintiffs. **1857** KERR *Blackstone's Comm.* III. xx. 324 In actions of tort the plaintiff may always remedy a misjoinder of defendants, by entering a *nolle prosequi*, as to the defendant misjoined. **1883** [see JOINDER b].

mis'judge, *v.* [MIS-^{1} 1.] *trans.* To judge wrongly; to judge ill of; to have false opinions of.

1533 MORE *Debell. Salem* x. Wks. 952/2 And therefore no more mysse iudge any manne. **1633** EARL MANCH. *Al Mondo* (1636) 171 If you know the goodnesse of a mans life, mis-judge him not by any strangenesse of his death. *c* **1779** JOHNSON *L.P., Waller* (1868) 109 That Clarendon might misjudge the motive of his retirement is the more probable. **1891** E. PEACOCK *N. Brendon* II. 3 How you misjudge us women!

b. *absol.* or *intr.* To err in judging; to form wrong opinions *of*.

1562 *Act 5 Eliz.* c. 5 §23 And because no maner of person shall misjudge of thintent of this Estatute. **1678** DRYDEN *All for Love* II. Wks. 1701 II. 70 You misjudge: You see through Love, and that deludes your sight. **1725** POPE *Odyss.* IV. 38 Too long, mis-judging, have I thought thee wise. **1868** BROWNING *Ring & Bk.* x. 1467 Have we misjudged here, over-armed our knight?

So **mis'judged** *ppl. a.*, **misjudging** *vbl. sb.* and *ppl. a.* (hence **mis'judgingly** *adv.*).

1526 *Pilgr. Perf.* (W. de W. 1531) 64 Suspicyon or mis-iudgynge of that thynge that is vncertayne. **1598** MARSTON *Sco. Villanie* II. vi. 199 Hence thou misiudging Censor. **1643** MILTON *Divorce* (1645) A 2 b, Let me arreed him, not to be the foreman of any mis-judg'd opinion, unlesse his

resolutions be firmly seated. **1677** GILPIN *Demonol.* III. ii. 10 All kind of distresses are obnoxious to the worst of misjudgings from malevolent minds. **1788** CHARLOTTE SMITH *Emmeline* (1816) IV. 314 Did he not wish to see his misjudging father? **1836–7** DICKENS *Sk. Boz, Scenes* xi, His graceful demeanour, stiff, as some misjudging persons have..considered it. **1838** LYTTON *Leila* III. i, 'I did not read that face misjudgingly,' thought the queen. **1849** MACAULAY *Hist. Eng.* ii. I. 153 The misjudging friends of liberty.

mis'judgement, -'judgment. [MIS-¹ 4.] Wrong, mistaken, or perverted judgement.

1526 *Pilgr. Perf.* (W. de W. 1531) 93 Misiudgement is whan of a lyght suspycyon..we iudge our neyghbour to speke, thynke, or do yᵗ thynge that is mortall synne. **1633** BP. HALL *Hard Texts, N.T.* 157 To runne so far into the mis-judgement of their mindes. **1796** PEGGE *Anonym.* (1809) 368 They cannot carry off a misjudgment, or a rash saying, with the..indifference of a younger person. **1873** SPENCER *Stud. Sociol.* ix. (1877) 207 The bias thus causing misjudgments in cases where it is checked by direct perception, causes greater misjudgments where direct perception cannot check it.

mis'judger. [MIS-¹ 5.] One who misjudges.

1877 F. J. FURNIVALL *Leopold Shaks.* Introd. p. lxxxv, For all misjudgment and crime comes death to the misjudger.

‖**miskal** ('mɪskəl). Forms: 6 met-, mitical, -gal, 7 medical, mesticall, meticalle, mettegal, miticale, miscolle, 8 muscal, 9 mes-, met-, mitch-, mith-, miskal, -kel, -call, mitkul. [Arab. *miþqāl* (locally *misqāl*, *mitqāl*), f. *þaqala* to weigh. The 17th cent. forms in Eng. come mostly through Sp. *mitical*, Pg. *matical*, *metical*.]

1. An Arabian measure of weight, equivalent to 24 carats or about 1½ dirhems; the corresponding English weight is given variously for different countries at from 71 to 74 grains Troy.

1555 EDEN *Decades* (1885) 263, xi. Fanans and a quarter, is one Mitigal: And .vi. Mitigales and a halfe, make one vnce. **1613** PURCHAS *Pilgrimage* VI. vii. (1614) 687 Euery Mittigall being a Duckat of Gold, and a third part. **1687** A. LOVELL tr. *Thevenot's Trav.* I. 67 The Medical is a Drachm and a half. **1698** FRYER *Acc. E. India & P.* 406 Their lowest Weight is a Miscolle;..whereof 6 make an Ounce. **1753** HANWAY *Trav.* (1762) I. v. lxiv. 293 The muscal through all Persia is the same..6 dunk 1 muscal 6 muscals 1 dram. **1836** LANE *Mod. Egypt* II. 372 The cheera't (or carat),..as above mentioned, is the 24th part of a mitcka'l. **1884** J. PAYNE *1001 Nights* IX. 83 Make it not large, a mithcal in weight and no more. **1886** YULE & BURNELL *Hobson-Jobson* Suppl., *Miscall*,..an Arabian weight, originally that of the Roman aureus and the gold dīnār; about 73 grs. **1902** *Encycl. Brit.* XXXI. 627/1 The unit of weight [in Persia] is the miskâl (71 grains), subdivided into 24 nakhods (2·96 grains).

2. In Morocco, a money of account.

1695 MOTTEUX tr. *St.-Olon's Morocco* 145 The Meticalle or Ducat for the generality is nothing real, but such a manner of counting as by Francs or Livres in France. **1845** G. C. RENOUARD in *Encycl. Metrop.* XXII. 285/1 (art. *Morocco*), 1 Mithkál, or ducat, (an imaginary coin) = 10 waklyahs = 3*s.* 4*d.* *Ibid. marg.*, Miskel.

†**mis'keep,** *v. Obs.* [MIS-¹ 1.] *trans.* To keep, guard, or observe badly or wrongly.

13.. *Evang. Nicod.* 915 in *Archiv Stud. neu. Spr.* LIII. 408 We sall noght trow..þe knyghtes þat him myskeped has Sen he in graue was layd. *c* **1412** HOCCLEVE *De Reg. Princ.* 1301 If it be wrong dispendid or mys-kept. **1530** PALSGR. 638/1 The beste thyng in the worlde, if it be myskept, wyll marre in processe of tyme. *a* **1618** SYLVESTER *Du Bartas, Mem. Mort.* II. lxxv. (1621) 1053 Misers mis-keep, and Prodigals mis-spend them. [*a* **1649** DRUMM. OF HAWTH. *Cypress Grove* Wks. (1711) 120 Prodigals mispend them, wretches miskeep them.]

†**mis'keeping,** *vbl. sb. Obs.* [MIS-¹ 3.] Improper or faulty keeping, observance, etc.

c **1375** *Sc. Leg. Saints* xxxvi. (*Baptista*) 817 Gif þe dekine eschapit thru miskepyng ore subtilite. **1387–8** T. USK *Test. Love* III. v. (Skeat) l. 42 To lese his love by miskeping, thorowe his owne doing. **1457–8** *Anc. Cal. Rec. Dublin* (1889) I. 298 Becawys of har myskepyng of har sayd swyne. **1496** *Dives & Pauper* (W. de W.) I. xxi. 56/2 Cause of bodely sekenesse is..by myskepynge of the childe in the youthe. **1540** *Act 32 Hen. VIII*, c. 48 Al..wastes imbesselinges miskeapinges..of the sayd artilleries.

†**misken,** *sb. Obs.* Also -kin. [? Dim. of MDu. *meese*, Du. *mees* titmouse.] A titmouse.

1585 HIGINS *Junius' Nomenclator* 60/1 *Parus*..a titmouse, misken. **1616** SURFL. & MARKH. *Country Farm* 729 The Miskin is more subiect vnto the gowt than any bird that is.

misken (mɪs'kɛn), *v. Sc.* and *north. dial.* [f. MIS-¹ 1, 7 + KEN *v.*¹, prob. after ON. *miskenna* not to recognize (a person).]

1. *trans.* Not to know; to be ignorant of.

c **1375** *Sc. Leg. Saints* vii. (*Jacobus Minor*) 210 Lord, remyt þis gilt þam to, for þai myskene quhat þai do. **1513** DOUGLAS *Æneis* I. viii. 126 Quha knawis nocht the lynaige of Enee? Or quha miskennis Troye, that ryall cietie? **1552** ABP. HAMILTON *Catech.* (1884) 48 Miskennying the rychteousnes of God. *a* **1553** WEDDIRBURNE *Ball. Prayis Wemen* 3 (Bann. MS. 694), The veritie and trewth thay do misken, Thruch thair obdurat obstinatioun. **1829** BROCKETT *N.C. Gloss.*, *Misken*, to be ignorant of.

2. To have wrong ideas about; to misunderstand.

c **1375** *Sc. Leg. Saints* iii. (*Andrew*) 355 þu miskennis, and saweris nocht þe thinge he god will haf in thocht. **1535** STEWART *Cron. Scot.* II. 250 The warld, thame self, and God for to misken. **1660** DICKSON *Writings* (1845) I. 25 The impenitent..miskens both God and himself. **1737** J. WILLISON *Affl. Man's Companion* VII. vii. (1744) 203 How ready am I to misken and mistake him, when he changeth his Dispensations toward me! **1899** *Cumbld. Gloss.*, *Misken*, to form a mistaken idea with regard to a person.

absol. *c* **1375** *Sc. Leg. Saints* vii. (*Jacobus Minor*) 174 For nerhand all þe puple now myskennand trowis in Ihesu. *c* **1470** HENRY *Wallace* x. 459 Throuch thi falsheid thin awn wyt has myskend.

b. *refl.* To have false ideas about oneself, one's position, etc.

1456 SIR G. HAYE *Law Arms* (S.T.S.) 6 He miskend himself and forȝett quha had gevin him that grete beautee. **1573** *Satir. Poems Reform.* xlii. 424 That na wayis thay thair selfis misken. **1791** LEARMONT *Poems* 266 Ye sair misken yoursel' Or thans ye wadnae tell me sic a tale. **1825–80** JAMIESON s.v., *To misken one's self*, to assume airs which do not belong to one, to forget one's proper station.

3. Not to know; to fail to recognize, mistake the identity of.

1549 *Compl. Scot.* vii. 70 Thai vald haue clair myskend it, be rasone that it vas sa mekil altrit. **1646** RUTHERFORD *Lett.* (1664) II. xlviii. 536 Ye shall misken him, & he shall appear a new Christ. **1652** LOVEDAY tr. *Calprenède's Cleopatra* I. 45 He misken'd her not in the lustre of those glorious ornaments in which she then shin'd. **1722** RAMSAY *Three Bonnets* II. 14 Wks. 1877 II. 384 Gin that I had nae mair miskend ye. **1824** SCOTT *St. Ronan's* xvi, No man fell so regularly into the painful dilemma of mistaking, or, in Scottish phrase, *miskenning*, the person he spoke to.

4. To refuse to recognize or notice; to affect ignorance of; to overlook, disregard, disown.

1508 DUNBAR *Tua Mariit Wemen* 380 Quhen he..payntit me as pako, proudest of fedderis, I him miskennyt, be Crist; & cukkald him maid. **1533** [see MISKENNING *ppl. a.*]. **1552** LYNDESAY *Monarche* 190 Thare Predecessouris, Peter and Paull, That day wyll thame mysken, at all. **1588** A. KING tr. *Canisius' Catech.* 231 b, Nother misken we the iustice of God or denyes it. **1637** RUTHERFORD *Lett.* (1862) I. lxxxix. 231 My Lord miskent all and did bear with my foolish jealousies. **1724** in Calderwood *Dying Test.* (1806) 226 Misken these new ones, hold you by the old. **1737–50** RAMSAY *Sc. Prov.* xxviii. 8 Poor fowk's friends soon misken them. **1819** SCOTT *Leg. Montrose* xiii, Were I you, Ranald, I would be for miskenning Sir Duncan.

with clause. **1686** G. STUART *Joco-ser. Disc.* 14 I ken this County weel eneugh, Miskenn I tell'd ye.

misken, variant of MISKIN, dunghill.

†**mis'kenning,** *vbl. sb. Old Law.* [f. MIS-¹ 3 + OE. **cęnning*, vbl. sb. f. *cęnnan* to make known, declare: see KEN *sb.*¹] A mistake or variation in pleading before a court. Also, a fine exacted for this.

Found in several alleged charters of Eadweard, but these are either forged or modernized in the 12th c.

11.. *Charter of Eadweard* in Earle *Charters* 340 And icc an heom eft alswa ðat hi habben ðarto sace and socne, toll and team, infangeneðef and flemenesfermð, griðbriche and hamsocne, forestal and miskenninge. **1114–18** *Leges Henrici* xxii. in Liebermann *Gesetze* I. 561 Sepe etiam ex inscicia placitancium cause transeunt in ius aliorum: exaggeracione rerum..transeunt etiam in mislocutione—miskenninge. ?**1131** *Charter Hen. I*, ibid. I. 525 Et amplius non sit miskenninga in hustenge neque in folkesmote neque in aliis placitis infra ciuitatem. **1136** *Charter of Stephen* in Stubbs *Sel. Charters* (1895) 121 Omnes exactiones et injustitias et mescheningas, sive per vicecomites vel per alios quoslibet male inductas, funditus exstirpo. *c* **1250** *Gloss. Law Terms* in *Rel. Ant.* I. 33 Miskenninge, *Mespris par oi, u de fet.* **1267** in *Lib. de Antiq. Leg.* (1846) 104 Quod non occasionentur propter miskenninga in suis loquelis, videlicet, si bene non omnino narraverint. **1387** TREVISA *Higden* (Rolls) II. 95 Miskenynge, chaunginge of speche in court. **1607** COWELL *Interpr.* **1658** PHILLIPS, *Miskenning* [**1706** or *Miskonning*].

mis'kenning, *ppl. a. Sc.* [MIS-¹ 2.] Misunderstanding, ignorant; neglectful, forgetful.

1533 BELLENDEN *Livy* v. xx. (S.T.S.) II. 216 To þame þat ar nocht myskennand na gude dedis suld be remembrit in reproche. **1552** ABP. HAMILTON *Catech.* (1884) 25 Wilful ignorant and miskennand men.

mis'kick, *v.* [MIS-¹ 1.] *intr.* In various sports, to fail to kick the ball properly.

1901 *Daily Express* 18 Mar. 8/4 Having to deal with a dropping ball which he could not properly judge, [he] miskicked. **1963** *Times* 21 Feb. 3/6 Lancaster presented Harris with an open goal, but the Watford winger completely miskicked. **1973** *Times* 24 Apr. 8/8 He miskicked and mishandled and could take pleasure only from his two successive penalty shots.

So **mis'kick** *sb.*

1973 *Times* 1 Jan. 17/6 His miskick only emphasized his mistake.

miskin¹ ('mɪskɪn). Also **misken.** Variant (mainly s.w. midland dial.) of MIXEN.

1601 [BP. W. BARLOW] *Defence* 8 A very heape and misken of shamelesse vntruethes. *a* **1603** *Order-bk. Worcester* in Nichols *Progr. Q. Eliz.* I. 533 Every person having any donghills or myskyns. **1625** FLETCHER & SHIRLEY *Nt. Walker* III. 216 Would you mellow my young pretty Mistress In such a misken? **1656** W. D. tr. *Comenius' Gate Lat. Unl.* 139 Our home-bred ones turn over miskens, and refuse things flung out. **1789** W. MARSHALL *Glouc.* I. 330 *Miskin*, the common term for a dunghill; or a heap of compost. **1896** *Warw. Gloss.*, *Miskin*, a compost pit.

attrib. **1665** S. HARWARD *Treat. Propag. Plants* in Markham *Way to Get Wealth* III. iv. 103 Good rank mould, tempered with short muck and misken water.

†'**miskin².** *Obs. rare*⁻¹. [? Dim. of MDu. *muse*, a. OF. *muse* (mod.F. *musette*, *cornemuse*) bagpipe.] (See quots.)

1593 DRAYTON *Ecl.* ii. 5 Now would I tune my Miskins on this Greene [*marg.* A little Bagpipe]. **1678** PHILLIPS, *Miskin*, (old word) a little Bagpipe.

miskin, variant of MISKEN *sb.*

†**miskin-fro.** *Obs.*⁻⁰ [f. MDu. *mesken*, *meiskijn* (= mod.Du. *meisje*) dim. of *meid* young woman + FROW *sb.*] A maidservant.

1632 COTGR., *Meschine*, a wench, maid seruant, miskin fro.

†**mis'kissing,** *vbl. sb. Obs. rare*⁻¹. [MIS-¹ 3.] Improper kissing.

1387 TREVISA *Higden* (Rolls) IV. 219 Let no myskissynge have prise of ȝoure boþe lyvynge [*orig. Convictus vestros non vincant oscula conchæ*].

Miskito (mɪ'skɪtəʊ), *a.* and *sb.* Also **Misskito, Mosquito, Musquito.** [f. *Misquito*, a section of the eastern coast of Nicaragua.] **A.** *adj.* Of or pertaining to an American Indian people living on the Atlantic coast of Nicaragua and Honduras. **B.** *sb.* **a.** A member of this people. **b.** The language of this people.

1789 O. EQUIANO *Interesting Narr. Life O. Equiano* II. xi. 172 He had a mind for..cultivating a plantation at Jamaica and the Musquito Shore... I found with the Doctor four Musquito Indians... One of them was the Musquito king's son. **1830** *Honduras Almanack* 11 The canoe, a paddle and a harpoon, are the Mosquito man's whole wealth. **1907** F. W. HODGE *Handbk. Amer. Indians* I. 948/2 *Mosquito Indians*, a tribe named from its habitat on Mosquito lagoon. **1911** *Encycl. Brit.* XVIII. 902/2 The Mosquito Coast is so called from its principal inhabitants, the Misskito Indians, whose name was corrupted into Mosquito by European settlers and has been entirely superseded by that form except in the native dialects. **1932** *U.S. Bureau Amer. Ethnol. Bull.* No. 106. 10 Ethnographical Survey of the Miskito and Suma Indians of Honduras and Nicaragua. **1959** *Chambers's Encycl.* I. 343/2 The Lenca, Xicaque,..and coastal Misquito of the Atlantic pocket of Nicaragua-Honduras missed the stream of Maya-Nahua influence. **1964** *Amer. Speech* XXXIX. 47 The Mosquitos are Caribs. **1964** E. A. NIDA *Toward Sci. Transl.* ix. 194 In Miskito, a language of Nicaragua and Honduras, one encounters the following transliterations. **1966** C. F. & F. M. VOEGELIN *Map N. Amer. Indian Lang.* (*caption*) Misumalpan Family 1. Miskito.

mis'know, *v.* [MIS-¹ 1 and 7. In early use largely Sc.; cf. MISKEN.]

†**1.** *intr.* ? To have an evil conscience. *Obs.*

a **1300** *Cursor M.* 17314 Me think ȝe haf to me misknawen of þat prophetz þat ȝe gart hang.

†**2.** *trans.* Not to know or be aware of; to be ignorant of. Also with clause as obj. *Obs.*

c **1375** *Sc. Leg. Saints* iii. (*Andrew*) 902 þe bischope þan, as Innocent, þat misknew al hyr entent. **1513** DOUGLAS *Æneis* VI. xi. 57 Misknawing quhat this ment. **1552** ABP. HAMILTON (*title*), The Catechisme;..ane..Instructioun..in materis of our Catholik Faith..whilk na gud Christin man..suld misknaw. **1560** ROLLAND *Crt. Venus* I. 62 That I was thair..thay did misknaw. **1581** in *Cath. Tractates* (S.T.S.) 121 Gif ye haue red the antiquitie, ye can not misknau this.

†**b.** in pa. pple. *misknown* = unknown (*to*).

1558 KENNEDY *Compend. Tract.* in *Wodrow Soc. Misc.* (1844) 159 Because it wes evir misknawin to the Kirk of God. **1562–3** *Reg. Privy Council Scot.* I. 230 Quhilk article..suld not haif bene misknawin to the said Thomas. **1632** LITHGOW *Trav.* VII. 328 Our way we Know, and yet vnknowne to other, And whiles misknowne to vs.

3. To know badly; to have a wrong idea of; to misapprehend, misunderstand. Also *absol.*

1535 STEWART *Cron. Scot.* II. 5 Than tha misknaw God and Fortoun so far, Na wounder is suppois tha get the war. **1645** BP. HALL *Rem. Discontents* 108 If therefore we misknow, the fault is in the mean, through which we doe imperfectly discover them. *a* **1663** C. HARVEY *Sch. of Heart* XXII. iii, Some things thou knowest not, mis-knowest others. **1831** CARLYLE *Sart. Res.* I. iii, Great men are too often unknown, or what is worse, misknown. **1865** RUSKIN *Sesame* 162 What she half-knows, or mis-knows. **1879** J. C. MORISON *Gibbon* 26 It would be greatly to misknow Gibbon to suppose that his studies were restricted to the learned languages.

b. *refl.* = MISKEN 2 b. Chiefly *Sc.* ? *Obs.*

1530 PALSGR. 638/1 Whan a man mysknoweth hym selfe it is a daungerouse thyng for hym. **1565** *Reg. Privy Council Scot.* I. 370 The greit honour we did unto thame..maid thame to misknaw thame selffis. **1617** JAS. I *Let.* in *Bacon's Wks.* (1830) XII. 329 You were afraid that the height of his fortune might make him misknow himself.

4. Not to recognize (a person); = MISKEN *v.* 3.

c **1375** *Sc. Leg. Saints* xxv. (*Julian*) 317 & twa lyand [he] has persawyt, þat he mysknew, fore þai ware hyd. *c* **1480** HENRYSON *Mor. Fab.* 48 Knew thou not weill I was both Lord and King Of beastes all? Yes (quod the Mouse) I knaw, But I misknew because yee lay so law. *c* **1500** *Melusine* 102 Seeyng that he mysknewe the place for cause of the new toune & toure. **1570** *Satir. Poems Reform.* x. 19 Na word he said, quhairthrow I did misknaw him, Because in sic ane stait I neuer saw him. **1840** CARLYLE *Heroes* iv. (1858) 275 Why should we misknow one another, fight not against the enemy, but against ourselves, from mere difference of uniform?

5. To refuse to recognize or notice; = MISKEN *v.* 4.

1483 CAXTON *Cato* i vj, To thende that thou be not reputed for unkynde proude or misknowyng the..seruyse which they haue done to the. **1533** BELLENDEN *Livy* v. xx. (S.T.S.) II. 215 As Ignorant or mysknawing sic thingis as

semys to my estate [orig. *meæ condicionis oblitum*]. **1572** *Satir. Poems Reform.* xxxiii. 255 Thay ar sa riche, that thay do vs misknaw. **1575** FENTON *Gold. Epist.* (1582) 75 In their prosperitie they misknow vs. **1632** LITHGOW *Trav.* v. 212 He priuately wronged me, which I misknew, as vnwilling.. to be too forward to seeke a redresse. **1633** BP. HALL *Occas. Medit.* (1851) 111 We misknow our parents: not acknowledging any friend, but the tailor that brings us a fine coat.

absol. **1558** KENNEDY *Compend. Tract.* in *Wodrow Soc. Misc.* (1844) 126 He that misknawis shalbe misknawin.

So **misknowing** *ppl. a.*, ignorant.

c **1374** CHAUCER *Boeth.* II. pr. viii. (1868) 61 Fortune.. euere mysknowynge of hir self [L. *sui semper ignaram*].

† mis'knowing, *vbl. sb. Obs.* [MIS-[1] 3, 7.]

1. Ignorance.

c **1374** CHAUCER *Boeth.* III. met. xi. (1868) 101 Alle the dyrknesse of his mysknowynge. *c* **1375** *Sc. Leg. Saints* xxiii. (*vii Sleperis*) 43 As he trewyt be mysknawine, þat let hyme wyt na suthtfast thing. **1530** PALSGR. 245/2 Mysknowyng, *descognoissance*.

2. Wrong or spurious knowledge.

1623 BP. HALL *Great Impostor* Wks. (1625) 503 The vnderstanding of man is euery way deceitfull in ouerknowing, mis-knowing, dissembling. **1892** F. S. ELLIS *Lexical Concordance Shelley* p. viii, Well would it be for the world if no more was known of any poet's life, except through his works, than is known of Shakespeare's; how greatly should we then be delivered from misknowing!

3. Used for: MISKENNING.

1384 in Arnolde *Chron.* (1502) C j b/2 That in the cite in noo plee be mis knowing.

mis'knowledge, *sb.* [MIS-[1] 4, 7.]

† 1. Failure to recognize or acknowledge. *Obs.*

a **1533** LD. BERNERS *Gold. Bk. M. Aurel.* (1546) Mm vij b, The mysknowlage that thou makest to me. **1549** *Compl. Scot.* iii. 27 To puneis vs for the mysknaulage of his magestie.

2. Spurious knowledge; misunderstanding.

1579 FENTON *Guicciard.* (1618) 219 Their men at armes, by negligence and misknowledge had charged their owne foot-men. **1653** A. WILSON *Jas. I*, 18 Lest men might presume further upon the misknowledg of my meaning to trouble this Parliament. **1679** G. R. tr. *Boaistuau's Theat. World* II. 338 If there be so much misery.. it was joined to man since his mis-knowledge of God. **1866** CARLYLE *Remin.* (1881) I. 77 The dismal perception that this sham of knowledge had been flat misknowledge. **1891** *Athenæum* 26 Dec. 862/3 Mr. Wagner's misknowledge extends to other than philological matters.

† mis'knowledge, *v. Sc. Obs.* [MIS-[1] 7.] *trans.* To refuse to acknowledge.

1600 *Reg. Privy Council Scot.* (1884) VI. 85 [Ogilvy had] stcirit [up the complainer's tenants.. to] misknawlege him [and to withhold from him his maills and duties].

misky ('mɪskɪ), *a.* Now *dial.* (see *Eng. Dial. Dict.*) Misty.

1680 KIRKMAN *Eng. Rogue* IV. viii. 108 Having a brave opportunity to drink.. I swallowed so much.. that my eyes were miskie.

mis'labelling, *vbl. sb.* [MIS-[1] 3.] Incorrect labelling.

1952 M. GARDNER *In Name of Science* i. 5 The government charged that displays of the book [sc. *Look Younger, Live Longer* by G. Hauser] next to jars of blackstrap constituted, because of the book's sensational claims, a 'mislabeling' of the product. **1960** *Times* 20 Sept. (Pure Food Suppl.) p. i/5 There still remains.. the possibility of.. mislabelling in retail shops. **1964** *Economist* 6 June 1098/2 Some American firms.. have been charged with mislabelling.

mis'laid, *ppl. a.* See MISLAY *v.* 2.

1781 COWPER *Let. to J. Newton* Wks. 1837 XV. 109 In the mislaid letters I took notice of certain disagreeable doubts you had expressed.

mislaird, variant of MISLEARED.

mislane, obs. form of MASLIN[2].

† mislaundre. *Obs.* [Alteration of *dislaundre*, DISCLANDER: see MIS-[1] 9.] Scandal, disgrace.

1531 in *Archæologia* (1882) XLVII. 60 Redresse of the said myslaundre.

mislay (mɪs'leɪ), *v.* [MIS-[1] 1. Cf. Du. *misleggen*, ON. *misleggja*.]

1. *trans.* To lay, place, or set wrongly; to misplace; to err in placing (a thing). Now *rare.*

1402 *Pol. Poems* (Rolls) II. 97 For Alrede his clerke wrote his reson, that thou mysse layst, and dokkist it as the likist. **1591** SYLVESTER *Du Bartas* I. i. 417 You have mis-cast in your Arithmetick, Mis-laid your Counters. **1601** BP. W. BARLOW *Serm. Paules Crosse* 35 Fire.. if mislayed or abused, burneth the house. *a* **1631** DONNE 6 *Serm.* (1634) ii. 34, I have not mislayed my foundation; my foundation is Christ. *a* **1656** VINES *Lord's Supp.* (1677) 286 Upon this ground wrongly mislaid and mistaken. *a* **1704** LOCKE *Cond. Und.* Introd. §4 Wks. 1714 III. 394, I am apt to think the Fault is generally mislaid upon Nature.

† b. *fig.*

1671 CROWNE *Juliana* III. 35 Oh heavens! her grief mislayes her noble reason.

2. To lay (a thing) by accident in a place where it cannot readily be found.

1614 WOTTON in *Reliq.* (1672) 436, I have (I know not how) mislayed the Character which I left you, therefore I pray send me.. a Copy. **1726–31** WALDRON *Descr. Isle of Man* (1865) 28 If anything happens to be mislaid, and found again, in some place where it was not expected. **1765** FOOTE *Commissary* I. (1782) 11 Be sure you don't mislay the pearl necklace. **1825** SCOTT *Jrnl.* 5 Dec., I cannot conceive what possesses me.. to mislay papers. **1852** MRS. CARLYLE *Lett.* II. 202, I am certain it is not mislaid.. I have searched too thoroughly.

† 3. To allege incorrectly. (Cf. LAY *v.*[1] 26 c.) *Obs.*

1596 BACON *Max. Com. Law* (1630) 21 The yeare must be alledged in fact, for it may be mislaid by the plaintiffe, and therefore the defendants.. must alledge it precisely.

Hence **mis'laying** *vbl. sb.* Also **mis'layer.**

1612 BACON *Ess., Judicat.* (Arb.) 450 The mislaier of a Meerestone is too blame. **1649** BP. HALL *Cases Consc.* I. ix. 82 The casualty of their mis-laying doth not alter their propriety; they are still his that lost them. **1898** BP. MOULE *Colossian Stud.* viii. 166 This little document has lately after a long mislaying, been in my use again.

misle: see MISTLE, MIZZLE.

mislead (mɪs'li:d), *v.* Pa. t. and pa. pple. **misled.** [OE. *mislǽdan* = MLG., MDu., Du. *misleiden*, OHG. *misseleiten* (G. *missleiten*), Sw. *missleda*, Da. *mislede*: see MIS-[1] 1 + LEAD *v.*[1].]

1. *trans.* To lead astray in action or conduct; to lead into error; to cause to err.

c **1015** ÆLFRIC *Past. Ep.* xlvi. in Thorpe *Laws* (1840) II. 384 Gif he.. leornian nele, ac mislæt his hyrmen. *a* **1300** *Cursor M.* 28264 Mi spussed wyfe i haue misledd bath in burdyng and in bedde. **1422** tr. *Secreta Secret., Priv. Priv.* 142 He dothe many thyngis.. wherof Some byth damagid, Some byth myslade. **1594** T. B. *La Primaud. Fr. Acad.* II. 255 When the affection of the heart.. is misled and deceiued by humane reason. **1603** FLORIO *Montaigne* I. xix, Let not pleasure so much mislead or transport us, that we.. forget, how many waies, our joyes,.. be subject unto death. **1671** MILTON *P.R.* I. 226 The erring Soul Not wilfully mis-doing, but unware Misled. **1736** BUTLER *Anal.* I. iv. Wks. 1874 I. 78 Men are misled by external circumstances of temptation. **1781** COWPER *Retirem.* 126 The roving eye misleads the careless heart. **1814** SCOTT *Ld. of Isles* III. v, Though by ambition far misled, Thou art a noble knight. **1856** SIR B. BRODIE *Psychol. Inq.* I. iii. 98 Juries have.. been misled by the refinements of medical witnesses.

absol. **1625** BACON *Ess., Friendship* (Arb.) 179 Scattered Counsels.. will rather distract, and Mislead, then Settle, and Direct. **1671** MILTON *P.R.* IV. 309 What can they teach, and not mislead? **1861** H. LAW *Beacons of Bible, Lamech* 10 Patience, the gentle guide to penitence, misleads to hard indifference.

b. *refl.* To misbehave, misconduct oneself.

c **1374** CHAUCER *Troylus* IV. 48 The folk of Troye hemselven so misledden, That with the worse at night homward they fledden. **1390** GOWER *Conf.* III. 236 How thei for love hemself mislede.

† c. ? To adduce wrongly. *Obs.*

1654 GATAKER *Disc. Apol.* 80 Manie Papists have misled Scripture in their.. labouring to prov the single life of the Priests to be of Divine Command.

† 2. To mismanage. *Obs.*

1390 GOWER *Conf.* III. 141 And his astat.. In such manere forto lede, That he his houshold ne mislede. **1494** FABYAN *Chron.* VII. 502 To.. make serche of certayne thynges than myslad and euyll gyded within the realme.

3. In physical sense (or *fig.*): To lead or guide in the wrong direction.

1575 FENTON *Gold. Epist.* (1582) 16 Others supposing themselues to be misse-led and gone astray, are notwithstanding in the high way to their felicitie. **1590** SHAKS. *Mids. N.* II. i. 39 Are you not hee, That.. misleade night-wanderers? **1635–56** COWLEY *Davideis* I. Wks. 1710 I. 309 An Angel whose.. Might Put by the Weapon, and misled it right. **1667** MILTON *P.L.* IX. 640 A Flame Which.. Misleads th' amaz'd Night-wanderer from his way. **1837** LYTTON *E. Maltrav.* 5 The lights have rather misled me.

Hence **mis'leadable** *a.*, capable of being misled.

1836 *For. Q. Rev.* XVII. 122 This last most misleadable, if not most leadable, age.

mis'leader. [MIS-[1] 5.] One who or something which misleads or causes people to err; also, †one who misrules or misgoverns (quot. 1390).

1390 GOWER *Conf.* I. 261 Thou Bonefas, thou proude clerk, Misledere of the Papacie. **1579** TOMSON *Calvin's Serm. Tim.* 774/2 A great number.. which.. were misleaders, & loued to disguise matters. **1596** SHAKS. *1 Hen. IV*, II. iv. 508 That villanous abhominable mis-leader of Youth, Falstaffe. **1611** SPEED *Hist. Gt. Brit.* IX. xi. (1623) 679 To deliuer the Realme from the misleaders of the King. **1703** ROWE *Ulysses* v. Wks. 1747 I. 410 Thou rash Misleader of this giddy Crowd. **1753** RICHARDSON *Grandison* III. i. 3 Delicacy, too, is often a misleader. **1853** MILL *Diss. & Disc.* (1859) II. 546 That Cleon, and men of his stamp.. were by no means the worst misleaders of the Athenian people. **1868** J. DORAN *Saints & Sinners* II. 83 He denounced both song and music as misleaders.

mis'leading, *vbl. sb.* [MIS-[1] 3.] The action of the verb MISLEAD; †misconduct.

a **1300** *Cursor M.* 27926 Fole behalding, misleding o late. **1480** CAXTON *Descr. Brit.* 22 Scottes and pictes by misleding of Maximus the tyraunt pursiewed Britayne. **1597** *Pilgr. Parnass.* v. (1886) 23 Nere let the pilgrims to this laurell mounte Fainte, or retire.. Through the misleading of some amorous boye. **1645** MILTON *Colast.* Wks. 1851 IV. 348 Which may in time bring in round fees to the Licencer, and wretched mis-leading to the People. **1768–74** TUCKER *Lt. Nat.* II. 408 To other persons perhaps they might prove misleadings, stumbling-blocks. **1884** *Law Rep.* 27 Chanc. Div. 630 There has not been any misleading.

mis'leading, *ppl. a.* [MIS-[1] 2.] That leads astray or causes to err.

1638 JUNIUS *Paint. Ancients* 10 Such a mis-leading labyrinth of confused.. precepts. **1649** MILTON *Eikon.* B 2, [A blindness] more gross or more misleading. **1834** DE QUINCEY *Autob. Sk.* Wks. 1854 II. 137 Natives as well as strangers.. have fallen victims.. to the misleading and confounding effects of deep mists. **1864** PUSEY *Lect. Daniel* (1876) 487 It would then have been simply misleading, to have used these words at all. **1878** JEVONS *Primer Pol. Econ.* 47, I have heard it said that land is capital, intelligence is capital, and so forth. These are all misleading expressions.

Hence **mis'leadingly** *adv.*, **mis'leadingness.**

1862 T. A. TROLLOPE *Lent. Journey* i. 2 The period of the, somewhat misleadingly so called, *renaissance*. *a* **1866** J. GROTE *Treat. Moral Ideals* (1876) 379 An element of deceptiveness and misleadingness. **1881** *Contemp. Rev.* May 828 The misleadingness of the utterances of disease and grief. **1957** *Essays in Crit.* VII. 342 The misleadingness of any implication that I was scraping the barrel for evidence. **1975** *Nature* 10 Jan. 79/2 One example of the misleadingness of demonstration must suffice.

mis'lear, *v. Obs.* exc. *dial.* [OE. *mislǽran*: see MIS-[1] 1 and LERE *v.*] *trans.* To misteach; to mislead, misguide; to lead astray.

c **1000** ÆLFRIC *Saints' Lives* v. 119 þa ongunnon heora maȝas mycclum be-hreowsian þæt hi æfre þa martyras mislæran woldon. *c* **1275** LAY. 4311 Ac Brenne hafde luþer men þat hine mislerede. *c* **1305** in *E.E.P.* (1862) 57 Er he ischryue were þe deuel was wel ȝurne about him to mislere. **1878** *Cumbld. Gloss.*, *Mis-leer't*, led astray.

So **†mis'learing** *vbl. sb.*, bad training.

13.. *Seuyn Sag.* (W.) 1391 For mi sones mislering, Ye schulle habbe evil ending!

misleared (mɪ'sle:rd), *a. Sc.* and *north. dial.* Also **-leert, -laird.** [f. MIS-[1] 2 + *leared*, LERED *ppl. a.*] Unmannerly, ill-bred; not knowing what is due to oneself or one's position in society.

1692 *Sc. Presbyt. Eloq.* (1738) 140 I'll not be greedy, nor misleard. **1786** *Har'st Rig* lviii. (1794) 21 The Embrugh wives them a' exceed For sad mislear'd ill words indeed! **1808** STAGG *Bridewain* vi. Poems 4 Some gat sae mislear'd wi' drink. **1820** SCOTT *Monast.* iv, What made you, ye misleard loons.. come yon gate into the ha', roaring like bullsegs, to frighten the leddy? **1832** HENDERSON *Prov.* 30 The deil's greedy, but you're mislear'd. **1897** CROCKETT *Lad's Love* x. 102, 'I could get on a heap faster!' cried the mis-leared lassie, her impudence rising instantly.

mis'learn, *v.* [MIS-[1] 1.] *trans.* To learn badly or incorrectly.

1678 *Yng. Man's Call.* 149 Things once mislearned are exceeding hardly unlearnt. **1872** RUSKIN *Fors Clav.* xix. 16, I learned nothing from it, and the public mislearned much. **1900** *Pilot* 23 June, Those who had mislearned the lesson which they had sought to teach them.

† mis'learned, *ppl. a. Obs.* [MIS-[1] 2.] **a.** Ill-taught, badly trained; *Sc.* = MISLEARED. **b.** Perversely learned.

1632 RUTHERFORD *Lett.* (1664) II. xii. 449 Like a tarrowing & mislearned childe. **1637** *Ibid.* I. ci. 201, I would be rich, but dare not be mislearned and seek more in that kinde. **1642** T. LECHFORD *Plain Dealing* (1867) 85 Master Robert Parker.. who.. wrote that mislearned Book *De Politea Ecclesiastica*. **1649** BP. HALL *Cases Consc.* Addit. i. (1654) 384 A mis-learned Advocate.

† mis'learning, *vbl. sb. Obs.* [MIS-[1] 7.] Want of learning.

1382 WYCLIF *Ecclus.* iv. 30 And of lesing of thi myslernyng [Vulg. *de mendacio ineruditionis*] be thou confoundid.

mis'led, *ppl. a.* [pa. pple. of MISLEAD *v.*] Led astray; misguided; †ill-conducted.

a **1300** *Cursor M.* 27735 Lates misledd, lightness o rage. **1594** KYD *Cornelia* III. 39 Esops mysled Country swaine, That fownd a Serpent pyning in the snow. **1614** RICH *Honestie of this Age* (1844) 27 Her former misled life. **1634** MILTON *Comus* 200 To give due light To the misled and lonely Travailer. **1711** in *10th Rep. Hist. MSS. Comm.* App. v. 114 To take pitty.. on his mislead people. **1826** E. IRVING *Babylon* II. 384 Poor misled men, who are themselves ignorant of the spirit that driveth them.

misleden, obs. form of MASLIN[2], MISTLETOE.

† mis'leeful, *a. Obs. rare*[—1]. [f. MISLEVE *sb.* + -FUL.] Unbelieving.

1382 WYCLIF *Ecclus.* i. 36 Be thou not rebel, and mys leeful [Vulg. *incredulus*] to the dred of the Lord.

misleen, -len, obs. forms of MISTLETOE.

mislen: see MASLIN[2].

mislest (mɪ'slɛst), *v.* [Alteration of MOLEST by substitution of MIS-[1] 9 for the first syllable.] *trans.* To molest, injure.

c **1573** *Durham Depos.* (Surtees) 259 Whether the said Rosse, Mathew Ogle, or Toppinge dyd then draw any wepon or mislest them sells. **1847** HALLIWELL, *Mislest*, to molest. *Var. dial.* [See *Eng. Dial. Dict.*] **1863** in Robson *Bards of Tyne* 81 Ther' sha'nit yen biv tongue or pen, Mislist wor toon or trade.

misletoa, -to(e: see MISTLETOE.

† mis'leve, *sb. Obs.* [f. MIS-[1] 4 + LEVE *sb.*] Misbelief.

c **1200** *Trin. Coll. Hom.* 73 þe mannes shrifte þe þurh his misleue herberȝeð þe fule gost on his heorte. **13..** *E.E. Allit. P.* B. 1230 Hade þe fader.. neuer trespast to him in teche of mysseleue.

† mis'leve, *v. Obs.* [f. MIS-[1] 1, 7 + LEVE *v.*] To believe wrongly; to misbelieve; to disbelieve.

c **1200** *Trin. Coll. Hom.* 137 His fader.. hadde dumb ben siðe he þe engel mislefde. *a* **1225** *Ancr. R.* 68 þe treowe is misleued. *c* **1250** *Gen. & Ex.* 3906 Ðat folc misleuede ðoron. *c* **1330** R. BRUNNE *Chron. Wace* (Rolls) 1336 A temple.. þat whilom þe folk mys-lyuande Worschiped þer-inne

Maumetry. *c* **1375** *Sc. Leg. Saints* xxxix. (*Cosme & Damyane*) 367 Myslewand ȝet þat it wes he. **14..** in *Tundale's Vis.* (1843) 82 Nay, sayde the sole, thou mys levest, I am not ho that thou wenest.

So †**mis'leving** *vbl. sb.* and *ppl. a.*

a **1300** *Cursor M.* 20904 Þis ilk simon he yede to rome at turn misleuand lede. *Ibid.* 27431 He will..his misleuyng noght for-sak. *c* **1330** R. Brunne *Chron. Wace* (Rolls) 1348 To holden hem yn mys-leuynge. *a* **1450** *Cov. Myst.* (Shaks. Soc.) 43 Ow, what menyht this myslevyng man?

misley, misleyne, obs. ff. MIZZLY, MASLIN².

†**'mislich,** *a. Obs.* [OE. *mislic, misse-, mist-, mystlic* = OS. *mislîc*, OFris., MLG., LG. *mislîk*, MDu. *mis(se)-, mes(se)lijc* (Du. *misselijk*), OHG. *missa-, missi-, mis(se)lîh* (MHG. *mis(se)lîch*, G. *misslich*), ? Icel. *mislíkr* (MSw. *mislika*, Da. *mislig*), Goth. *missaleiks*: see MIS-¹ and -LY¹.]

1. Diverse, unlike, various.

c **888** K. Ælfred *Boeth.* xxxiii. §5 (Sedgefield) 82 þu fyldest ðas eorðan mid mistlicum cynrenum netena, & hi siððan aseowe mistlicum sæde treowa & wyrta. **971** *Blickl. Hom.* 43 þæt hie heora synna cunnon on rihtlice ȝeandettan; forþon þe hie beoþ toþon mislice. *a* **1122** *O.E. Chron.* an. 979 (MS. C) þy ilcan ȝeare was ȝesewen blodiȝ wolcen..& þæt ..on mistlice beamas wæs ȝehiwod. *a* **1225** *Ancr. R.* 4 þe inre [rule] is euere iliche: þe uttre is misliche. *a* **1240** *Wohunge* in *Cott. Hom.* I. 281 Selcuðes þat misliche and monifald hauen bifallen.

2. Wandering. (Cf. next 2.)

a **1100** in Napier *O.E. Glosses* 98/3695 Errabundis .i. *uagabundis*, mistlicum.

†**'misliche,** *adv. Obs.* Forms: 1 mis(t)líce, 2-4 misliche, 4 misseliche, -ly. [OE. *mis(t)líce*, adv. corresp. to prec.: see -LY². Cf. MDu. *misse-, messelike*, OHG. *misselîcho*, MHG. *mis(se)lîche*.]

1. In various ways; diversely, variously.

c **888** K. Ælfred *Boeth.* xxxvi. §4 (Sedgefield) 106 Ealle men ȝe goode ȝe yfele wilniað to cumanne to goode, þeah hi his mislice wilnien. *a* **1100** *O.E. Chron.* an. 1036 (MS. D), & his ȝeferan he to-draf; & sume mislice ofsloh. *a* **1175** *Cott. Hom.* 231 Ac þis ȝesceod he hadde isett bi-tweone frend and fend þat þan hi come mistlice to berie [etc.]. *a* **1225** *Ancr. R.* 6 Vor þi mot þeos riwle chaungen hire misliche efter euch ones manere. **1340-70** *Alisaunder* 1160 Of menne þat myslych wer murdred therin.

2. In various directions; astray.

a **1100** *O.E. Chron.* an. 1072 (MS. D) Her Eadwine eorl & Morkere eorl hlupon ut & mislice ferdon on wuda. *c* **1175** *Lamb. Hom.* 119 He scal misliche faran on monie gedwilþan. *c* **1205** Lay. 6270 Fulle seouen ȝere heo misliche foren [*c* 1275 hii misferde þere]. *c* **1320** *Cast. Love* 947 (Halliwell), I se the myslyche i-gon and unȝemed [*Vernon MS.* mis-lyken & al for-ȝemed, Fr. *esgarez*].

3. Wrongly.

a **1250** *Owl & Night.* 1773 þeos riche men..þat leteþ þane gode man þat of so fele þinge can & yeueþ rente wel Mislyche. *c* **1350** *Will. Palerne* 207 But missely marked he is way. *Ibid.* 711 Crist it for-bede þat ich more of þat matere so misseliche þenke!

mislicken: see MISLIPPEN.

†**mis'lie,** *v. Obs.* [MIS-¹ 1.] *intr.* To lie in a wrong position.

c **1386** Chaucer *Miller's T.* 461 And eft he routeth, for his heed mislay.

†**mis'life.** *Obs.* [MIS-¹ 4.] Wrong living.

1606 Warner *Alb. Eng.* xv. c. 395 Can Iustice sleepe where such Mis-life is found?

†**mis-'light,** *v. Obs.* [MIS-¹ 1.] *trans.* To lead astray by its light.

1648 Herrick *Hesper., The Night-piece, to Julia*, No Will-o'-th'-Wispe mis-light thee; Nor Snake..bite thee.

mis'like, *sb.* [f. MISLIKE *v.*]

†**1.** = MISLIKING *vbl. sb.* 1. *Obs.*

a **1300** *Cursor M.* 9907 Þis castel es o luue and grace [9881] ..Wit mislik sal he neuer be ledd, þe man þat þiderwerd es fledd.

2. Want of affection; dislike (*of*), distaste (*for*), objection (*to*). †*to grow in mislike of*: to become unpopular with. Now *rare*.

a **1569** Kingesmyll *Confl. w. Satan* (1578) 54 As a man that swaloweth a most pleasant drinke without any mislike of taste. **1587** Fleming *Contn. Holinshed* III. 1275/2 He grew in mislike of the nobilitie in continuall prouoking them to anger. **1593** Shaks. *3 Hen. VI*, iv. i. 24 **1605** Marston *Dutch Courtezan* ii. i. B 3 b, O let not my secure simplicity, breed your mislike. **1645** Ussher *Body Div.* (1647) 284 When the party withdraweth itselfe, in mislike, or loathsomness. **1845-6** Trench *Huls. Lect.* Ser. i. vii. 112 Julian's mislike of the rising faith. **1885-94** R. Bridges *Eros & Psyche* Feb. xxi, The goddess, whose mislike had birth From too great honour paid the bride on earth.

b. With *a* and *pl.*

1557 North *Gueuara's Diall Pr.* (1619) Prol. 1. ¶2 What envie doth hee expose himselfe to, and multitude of mislikes, that hath the charge of governing others? **1610** Holland *Camden's Brit.* i. 84 Upon a mislike that they tooke to him..they deprive him of his Empire. **1620** E. Blount *Horæ Subs.* 222 Dispraising will nourish a mislike of such things, as deserue commendations.

†**3.** Disaffection, disagreement, dissension. *Obs.*

a **1586** Sidney *Arcadia* ii. xxvi. (1590) 218 The mislike growne among themselues did wel allay the heat against her. **1590** *Act Privy Council* (1899) XIX. 300 [This] may breed a general murmure and mislyke amongst the rest. **1654** Earl Monm. tr. *Bentivoglio's Warrs Flanders* 75 Greater mislikes arising among the citizens, they came to blows.

†**4.** Wasting or consumption in animals or plants; sickliness, disease. *Obs.*

1552 Huloet, s.v. *Mislykinge, Tabidus*, he that is in a mislyke. **1613** Markham *Eng. Husbandman* i. ii. iii. (1635) 132 [If] you finde a certain mislike or consumption in the plant. **1614** —— *Cheap Husb.* 92 Of Leannesse, Mislike, Scurfe, and Manginesse in Swine. **1622** R. Hawkins *Voy. S. Sea* (1847) 49, I never have seene any man to whom they have bred mis-like, or done hurt with eating much of them.

†**mis'like,** *a. Obs. rare.* [MIS-¹ 7.] Unlike.

1570 Levins *Manip.* 122/40 Mislike, *dissimilis.* **1597** A. M. tr *Guillemeau's Fr. Chirurg.* 22/2 Small sproutes, not mislike vnto the feet of the fishe Purpura.

mis'like, *v.* Now chiefly *literary* or *dial.* [OE. *mislícian* = OHG., MHG. *misselîchên*, ON. *mislíka*: see MIS-¹ 1 and LIKE *v.*¹]

1. *trans.* To be displeasing to; to displease, offend. Orig. const. dative (†occas. in ME. with *to*).

c **897** K. Ælfred *Gregory's Past. C.* xxi. 158 Ðonne eow misliciað ða medtrymnessa þe ȝe on oðrum monnum ȝesioð. *c* **1000** Ælfric *Exod.* xxi. 8 Gif heo mislicað þam hlaforde, forlæte hiȝ. *c* **1200** Ormin 18287, & tiss maȝȝ þe full innwarrdliȝ Misslikenn. *c* **1250** *Gen. & Ex.* 1728 Ðo saȝ laban ðat iacob bi-gat Michil, and him mislikede ðat. *c* **1330** R. Brunne *Chron.* (1810) 173, I trowe þe Sarazins our comyng mislikes. **138.** Wyclif *Serm.* Sel. Wks. II. 395 If it myslike to þis pope. **1413** *Pilgr. Sowle* (Caxton 1483) iii. viii. 55 To be wroken vppon tho that aught haue mysliked them. **1573** Tusser *Husb.* (1878) 63 The daie of S. Stephen old fathers did vse: if that doe mislike thee some other daie chuse. **1585-7** T. Rogers 39 *Art.* vi. (1625) 32 Against them which..deface and put out such texts as mislike them. **1870** Morris *Earthly Par.* III. iv. 275 Because the Gods are wise, and thriftless deed Mislikes them. **1874** Pusey *Lent. Serm.* 56 If thou thinkest that thou..mayest take what thou likest, and leave what mislikes thee.

absol. *a* **1250** *Owl & Night.* 344 For harpe & pipe & foweles song Mislikeþ if hit is to long. **1603** Drayton *Heroic. Ep.* iv. (1619) 34 That pleaseth well, and This as much mislikes.

†**b.** To be out of harmony with. *Obs.*

Perhaps a distinct word f. LIKE *a.* or LIKE *v.*²

c **1470** Henry *Wallace* xi. 1261 Bot a fyr brand in his for-heid he bayr, And than him thocht it myslikyt all the lawe [*ed.* **1570** And yat him thocht myslykit all the laif].

†**2.** *intr.* To be displeased; in ME. also, to be troubled or uneasy (cf. MISLIKING *vbl. sb.* 1). *Obs.*

a **1300** *Cursor M.* 2513 Abram was þen ful mislikand Quen he herd þan o þis tyþand. *c* **1330** R. Brunne *Chron. Wace* (Rolls) 2417 Now gynnes Leyr to myslyke. *c* **1400** *Ywaine & Gaw.* 534 And knyghts and swiers war ful fayne, Mysliked none bot syr Ywayne. *c* **1585** *Faire Em* iii. 832 The repair of those gentlemen to your house hath given me great occasion to mislike. **1592** Warner *Alb. Eng.* viii. xlii. 183 First they mislike, yeat at the length for lucar were mislead. **1621** Burton *Anat. Mel.* i. ii. iv. iii. (1651) 147 When the intrals were opened, and a noysome savour offended her nose, she much misliked. **1642** Milton *Apol. Smect.* 14 They made sport, and I laught, they mispronounc't and I mislik't.

†**b.** To be displeased *with* or *at*; to disapprove *of*. *Obs.*

c **1555** Harpsfield *Divorce Hen. VIII* (Camden) 58 Who ..would most highly mislike of this divorce. **1577** Hanmer *Anc. Eccl. Hist.* (1663) 234 It was not because we misliked with that form of faith. **1578** Roydon in T. P[roctor] *Gorgious Gallery* A ij b, [He] scofte at this, and did mislike at that. *a* **1591** H. Smith *Serm.* (1637) 410 Lest Agrippa should goe back and mislike with his boldness and say no.

†**c.** with clause or inf. *Obs.*

1539 Cromwell in Merriman *Life & Lett.* (1902) II. 178, I mislike that thambassadour sayeth he shal not retourne. *a* **1586** Sidney *Arcadia* ii. (1629) 175 Misliking much such violence should bee offred..to men of our ranke. **1618** Dalton *Countr. Just.* lxix. (1630) 168 If the party shall mislike to be..bound to the peace. *a* **1656** Hales *Gold. Rem.* (1688) 397 They misliked that any such Form should be forced upon them.

3. *trans.* To be displeased or offended at; to disapprove of; to dislike.

1513 More in Grafton *Chron.* (1568) II. 778 That he much mislyked these two seuerall counsayles. **1547-8** *Ordre of Commvnion* 2 Wee would not haue our subiectes, so muche to mislike our iudgment. **1593** Shaks. *2 Hen. VI*, i. i. 140 'Tis not my speeches that you do mislike: But 'tis my presence that doth trouble ye. **1611** Bible *Trans. Pref.* ¶11 If we..doe endeuour to make that better which they left so good; no man, we are sure, hath cause to mislike vs. *a* **1634** Chapman *Alphonsus* Plays 1873 III. 219 If she mislike the kiss I'l take it off agen with such an other. **1722** De Foe *Relig. Courtsh.* i. i. (1840) 9 She cannot mislike him. **1815** Mar. Edgeworth *Love & Law* ii. ii, That daughter will.. choose the very man her father mislikes. **1878** Gladstone *Glean.* (1879) I. 208 They mistrust and mislike the centralisation of power.

transf. **1577** B. Googe *Heresbach's Husb.* ii. (1586) 95 It misliketh not a moist grauell ground.

†**4.** To take sinful pleasure in (something). *rare*⁻¹.

c **1200** in *O. E. Hom.* I. 305 Ich habbe..Misiliket swote smelles.

†**5.** *intr.* To grow sickly or unhealthy; to waste away. (Cf. LIKE *v.*¹ 4.) *Obs.*

c **1420** *Pallad. on Husb.* iv. 515 Yf that the fruyte myslike and from hem falle. **1552** Huloet, Mislyken in the bodye ..*tabe laborare.* **1601** Holland *Pliny* II. xx. xi, If a man perceive that the fish..do mislike and grow sickly. **1606** —— *Sueton.* 211 The tree..did mislike and die.

Hence **misliked** *ppl. a.*, offended.

1641 Smectymnuus *Answ.* i. (1653) 3 Misliked Persons? and why not offending persons? **1680** Baxter *Cath. Commun.* (1684) 23 When I excluded his misliked sense.

mis'likeness. *rare.* [MIS-¹ 4.]

†**1.** A distorted shape. *Obs.*

c **1440** *Eng. Conq. Irel.* 131/25 (Rawl. MS.) That thynge that was in myse-lyckenys [*Dubl. MS.* that was forshape].

2. Bad portraiture.

1822 Southey *Ep. A. Cunningham* Poet. Wks. 1838 III. 308 This countenance, such as it is, So oft by rascally mislikeness wrong'd.

mis'liker. [f. MISLIKE *v.* + -ER¹.] One who mislikes, dislikes, or hates.

1565 Cooper *Thesaurus* s.v. *Auertere, Auersus a vero*..a misliker of the truth. **1618** in Farr *S.P. Jas. I* (1848) 292 Those That were mislikers of this woman's deed. **1866** W. R. Alger *Solit. Nat. & Man* iv. 269 His mislikers considered him as 'a growling old bear'.

mis'liking, *vbl. sb.* [MIS-¹ 3.]

†**1.** The opposite of pleasure; discomfort, uneasiness; unhappiness, trouble. *Obs.*

a **1225** *Ancr. R.* 180 Vttre uondunge is hwarof cumeð likunge oðer mislikunge, wiðuten oðer wiðinnen. **1340** Hampole *Pr. Consc.* 8319 Þat na mare grevance salle þou fele, Ne na mare payne have, ne myslykyng. **1375** Barbour *Bruce* iii. 516 Gretyng Cummys to men for mysliking. **1470** *Gol. & Gaw.* 877 Na mysliking haue in hart, nor haue ye na dout. **1496** *Dives & Pauper* (W. de W.) i. xliii. 84/2 Somtyme dremes come..of myslykynge that man hath whan he is wakyng. *a* **1568** Ascham *Scholem.* i. (Arb.) 47 What soeuer I [*sc.* Lady Jane Grey] do els, but learning, is ful of grief, trouble, feare, and whole misliking vnto me. *a* **1600** T. Tymme *Silver Watch-bell* i. (1630) 10 The Peacock..with great misliking, vaileth his top-gallant, & seemeth to sorrow.

†**2.** Displeasure; indignation. *Obs.*

a **1300** *E. E. Psalter* lxxvii. 49 He sent in þam wreth of his mis-likyng [L. *indignationem*]. **1587** *Reg. Privy Council Scot.* Ser. i. IV. 209 To his Hienes mislykeing and miscontentment. **1592** Stow *Ann.* 287 Going forth with the Bishop, til they came to Windsore, he entred the Castle, to the great misliking of the Bishoppe.

3. Dislike (*of*); aversion.

a **1568** Ascham *Scholem.* ii. (Arb.) 147 This mislikyng of Ryming, beginneth not now of any newfangle singularitie. **1637** Gillespie *Eng. Pop. Cerem.* i. ix. 33 Their wish importeth a..misliking of all Festivall dayes besides the Lords day. **1638** *Sidney's Arcadia* ii. 197 Particular mens likings and mislikings [*edd.* 1590, 1629 dislikings]. **1709** Strype *Ann. Ref.* I. xl. 409 Yet her Majesty inwardly to the Secretary, and other her Counsillors, shewed much Misliking. **1866** Howells *Venetian Life* xi. 146 His own little learning has made him mistrust his natural likings and mislikings. **1891** *Tablet* 7 Feb. 210 The prevalent misliking of dogmatic and traditional conclusions.

†**4.** Mutual disaffection, dissension. *Obs.*

1564 in Ellis *Orig. Lett.* Ser. i. II. 197 Whether you understande there by anye suche mislikinge betwene them or not. **1589** Cooper *Admon.* 155 By defaming and slandering, he bringeth the parties in hatred and misliking.

†**5.** = MISLIKE *sb.* 4. *Obs.*

1552 Huloet, Mislikynge in the body, *tabes.* **1601** Holland *Pliny* I. 539 That manner of Blasting or misliking called Sideratio. *Ibid.* II. 317 In case of misliking when the habit of the body receiueth no benefit by food. **1616** Surfl. & Markh. *Country Farm* ii. liv. 302 They [*sc.* citron trees] fall..into mislikings and diseases.

mis'liking, *ppl. a.* [MIS-¹ 2.] In senses of the verb. †**a.** Unpleasant. †**b.** Disaffected. †**c.** Sickly.

1477 Norton *Ord. Alch.* v. in Ashm (1652) 70 Odours misliking, as Aloes and Sulphure. **1586** Earl Leycester *Corr.* (Camden) 385 That such a man should carye a misliking mind. **1601** Holland *Pliny* I. 504 The blackish, misliking, and vnkind herbs growing thereupon.

Hence **mis'likingly** *adv.*, with dislike.

1882 J. Hawthorne *Fort. Fool* i. xviii, Having previously determined to shake his head mislikingly.

mislin: see MASLIN², MISTLETOE.

misline (mɪsˈlaɪn), *v.* [MIS-¹ 1.] *trans.* To print with lines omitted or arranged in the wrong order. So **misline'ation**, the result of a mistake of this kind.

1922 Joyce *Let.* 20 Mar. (1966) III. 62 Besides misprints I see..that it is in part mislined. **1964** F. Bowers *Bibliogr. & Textual Crit.* vi. iv. 182 It may be that some mislineation at the beginning of *Othello* was caused by the trouble he [*sc.* the compositor] experienced in adjusting text about the ornamental initial letter.

misling, obs. form of MIZZLING.

mis'lippen, *v. Sc.* and *north. dial.* Also **mislicken** (see LICKEN). [MIS-¹ 1.]

1. *trans.* To deceive; to disappoint.

1552 *Burgh Rec. Edin.* (1871) 173 Gyf it salhappin the saidis seriandis..to mislippin or defraude ony pairty in wairnyng [etc.]. **1581-2** *Reg. Privy Council Scot.* Ser. i. III. 453 His majestie is liklie to be myslippinnit of wynis in thair default. **1683** G. Meriton *Yorksh. Dial.* 7 If wee'd nut come just when we did, Wee'd been mislicken'd out of our dinners Pegg. **1775** Watson *Hist. Halifax* 543 *Mislippen'd*, disappointed. **1807-10** Tannahill *Poems* (1846) 20, I haflins think his e'en hae him mislipened. **1888** *Sheffield Gloss.*

2. To neglect, overlook.

1581-2 *Reg. Privy Council Scot.* Ser. i. III. 451 It can not be differrit nor myslippinnit. **17..** *The Ghaist* 6 The yearding o' my bains Dinna mislippen—O remember me! **1866** Gregor *Banffsh. Gloss.*, *Mis-lippent*, neglected. **1894** Crockett *Raiders* iii, In a great job like the making of the earth, small points are apt to be mislippened (overlooked).

3. To suspect.

1816 Scott *Bl. Dwarf* iv, I thought it best to slip out quietly..in case she should mislippen something of what

we're gaun to do. **1871** W. ALEXANDER *Johnny Gibb* 243 Aw sanna begin to mislippen ye noo at the tail o' the day.

† **mis'literate**, *a. Obs.* [MIS-[1] 7.] Unlearned.
1532 *Guystarde & Sygysmonde* Lenvoy D ij, Yf ought be amys.. In addycyon or sence myslytterate.

† **mis'live**, *v. Obs.* [MIS-[1] 1. Cf. OHG. *misseleben.*] *intr.* To live a bad life.
c **1000** ÆLFRIC *Hom.* (Th.) II. 324 Nu bið mannum sceamu þæt hi mislybban sceolon. *a* **1350** *St. Matthew* 468 in Horstm. *Altengl. Leg.* (1881) 137 He teches.. þo men þat mislifand ware To mend þam self. **1579** SPENSER *Sheph. Cal.* May 87 If he misliue in leudnes and lust.

mislive, variant of MISLEVE.

† **mis'lived**, *a. Obs.* [f. MIS-[1] 6 + LIFE *sb.* + -ED[2]. Cf. LIVED *a.*] Of evil life.
c **1374** CHAUCER *Troylus* IV. 330 O olde unholsom and mislyved man. **1566** DRANT *Horace, Sat.* I. iv. B vij b, If any person were mislyude in thefte, or leachers lore.

mis'liver. *rare* or *Obs.* [MIS-[1] 5.] A person of evil life; an evil liver.
1436 *Rolls of Parlt.* IV. 511/1 Alle maner of myslyvers and avowterers. **1528** TINDALE *Obed. Chr. Man* 153 Yf he sofre hyr to be an whore and a misse lyver. **1593** NASHE *Christ's T.* 90b, The dissolutest misliuer that liues. **1604** G. BABINGTON *Comf. Notes Levit.* xiii. §5 All.. presumptuous misliuers, being most vncleane before God. **1873** B. GREGORY *Holy Catholic Ch.* 279 So many.. misbelievers and mislivers are members of the Church.

mis'living, *vbl. sb.* [MIS-[1] 3.] Evil living.
c **1325** in *E. E. P.* (1862) 119 Ful fresliche riht wol vs affray. And blame vs for vr mislyuyng. **1340** HAMPOLE *Pr. Consc.* 3773 Parchaunce byfor þair endyng, þai er amended of þair myslyvyng. *c* **1450** *Merlin* 2 Yef they will repent and forsake their myslyvinge. *c* **1480** HENRYSON *Mor. Fab.* Prol. i, To repreue the haill misleuing Of man. **1528** PAYNELL *Salerne's Regim.* Pref. A ij b, By our myslyuynge and fylthy synne. **1558** BP. WATSON *Sev. Sacram.* xvii. 108 The repentaunce that a myslyuynge manne or woman taketh for theyr myslyuynge. **1906** *Edin. Rev.* July 108 He suffered for his sins with his eyes fixed on fresh misliving.

† **mis'living**, *ppl. a. Obs.* [MIS-[1] 2.] Of evil life.
1519 HORMAN *Vulg.* 78b, A myslyvynge woman. **1550** CROWLEY *Last Trumpet* 731 For where mislyuyng curates be, The people are not good certayne. **1558** [see prec.]. **1624** BP. HALL *Serm.* in *Rem. Wks.* (1660) 16 The mis-living Christian.. crucifies Christ again.

mislo'cate, *v.* [MIS-[1] 1.] *trans.* To misplace.
1816–30 BENTHAM *Offic. Apt. Maximized, Extract Const. Code* (1830) 13 By *artificially mislocated*, understand conferred on an individual, other than him by whom the service was rendered. **1954** *Word* X. 239 In diagnosing the conflict between mentalism and mechanism he [*sc.* Bloomfield] mislocates the issue. **1959** P. F. STRAWSON *Individuals* II. viii. 244 Such an account runs the risk of mislocating the problem altogether. **1971** *New Scientist* 18 Mar. 611/1 The flash is both harder to see and it is mislocated. **1973** *Nature* 7 Sept. 12/2 Nuclear explosions fired on Amchitka are regularly mislocated by tens of kilometres.

mislo'cation. [MIS-[1] 4.] Misplacing.
a **1661** FULLER *Worthies* (1840) I. 203, I am confident herein is no mislocation. **1677** CARY *Chronol.* II. I. §1. xx. 153 The Number.. was originally the Transcriber's slip of the Pen; so likewise the mislocation of Aphobis. *a* **1832** BENTHAM *Deontol.* (1834) I. 254 Dirt.. is a sort of mislocation of matter in small particles. **1836–9** *Todd's Cycl. Anat.* II. 318/1 Mislocation of the germ during its growth. **1874** L. BACON *Genesis New England Churches* p. x, Every careless mislocation of words in the structure of a sentence. **1974** *Nature* 29 Nov. 369/2 All the main features are fairly well reproduced although there are some small mislocations.

mis'lodge, *v.* [MIS-[1] 1.] *trans.* To lodge or place in a wrong place; †to mislay.
1676 *Lond. Gaz.* No. 1071/4 Lost or mislodged by a Messengers mistake.. 6 or 7 bundles of Parchment Court Rolls. **1824** BYRON *Def. Transf.* I. i. 146 'Tis an aspiring one [*sc.* a soul], whate'er the tenement In which it is mislodged. **1827** HOOD *Hero & Leander* xxxvi, Mislodging music in her pitiless breast.

† **mis'look**, *sb.* [MIS-[1] 4.] Sinful looking.
1390 GOWER *Conf.* I. 53 Ovide telleth in his bok Ensample touchende of mislok.

† **mis'look**, *v. Obs.* [MIS-[1] 1.]
1. *intr.* To sin in looking.
c **1200** *O.E. Hom.* I. 305 Ich habbe.. Misloket. **1390** GOWER *Conf.* I. 56 That thei wolde Misloke, wher that thei ne scholde. *Ibid.* 57 Of mislokynge how it hath ferd,.. now hast thou herd.
2. To look unfavourably *on.*
c **1412** HOCCLEVE *De Reg. Princ.* 703 And now I am myslokyd on & loured.
3. *dial.* (See quots.)
1875–86 *W. Somerset Word-bk.*, *Mislook*, to mislay; to miss; to lose temporarily. **1876** *Mid-Yorksh. Gloss.*, *Mislook*, to overlook, neglectively.

† **mis'lore.** *Obs.* [MIS-[1] 4.] Evil teaching or counsel.
a **1050** *Liber Scintill.* vii. (1889) 33 Flæsclicra mislara [L. *carnalium sugge(s)tiones*]. *a* **1100** in Napier *O.E. Glosses* 228/323 *Inlecebras*, misl[ara]. *c* **1200** *Trin. Coll. Hom.* 29 Elch pine [of helle] is fremed on þre fold wise. On is þe defles tuihting and mislore.

† **mis'lose**, *v. Obs.* [f. MIS-[1] 1 + *lose*, LOOSE *v.*] Used to render L. *dissolvere.*
1382 WYCLIF *Josh.* xiv. 8 My bretheren,.. discoumfortiden [*v.r.* myslosedyn, Vulg. *dissolverunt*] the herte of the puple.

† **mis'losed**, *ppl. a. Obs.* In 5 mysloset. [f. MIS-[1] 1 + LOSE *v.*[2] Cf. OF. *meslos* blame.] Dispraised, blamed.
c **1440** *Gesta Rom.* xxxvii. 360 (Addit. MS.), Grete men are but glosede, and smale men borne downe and myslovede [*read* mislosede (*for rime*)]. *c* **1450** *Bk. Curtasye* 208 in *Babees Bk.*, In swete wordis þe nedder was closet, Disseyuaunt euer and mysloset.

† **mis'love**, *v. Obs.* [f. MIS-[1] 1 + LOVE *v.*[1]] *intr.* To love in a wrong way.
c **1450** in *Pol. Rel. & L. Poems* (1903) 134 þat I myslufede, I aske mercy.

† **mis'loving**, *vbl. sb. Obs.* [f. MIS-[1] 3 + LOVING *vbl. sb.*[2]] Dispraise, depreciation.
a **1300** *Cursor M.* 27683 Missau, and groching alsua Bakbite, mislouing [*Cott. Galba* sklander and bacbiteing].

mis'luck, *sb.* Chiefly *Sc.* [MIS-[1] 4.] Misfortune.
1623 WODROEPHE *Marrow Fr. Tongue* 301 It was his Mislucke to marry that wicked Wife. **1647** HEXHAM, *Een misluck*, a Mishap, or a Misluck. **1711** *Countrey-Man's Let. to Curat* 84 But the Misluck is, he did not believe himself. **1725** RAMSAY *Gentle Sheph.* I. i. (1877) II. 47 Wha can help misluck?
So **mis'luck** *v. intr.*, to meet with misfortune.
1647 HEXHAM, *Mislucken*, to Misluck, to Mishap. **1808** JAMIESON, To *Misluck*, to miscarry, not to prosper. **1855** CARLYLE *Misc. Ess., Prinzenraub* (1857) IV. 343 They are to ride by two different roads towards Bohemia, that if one misluck, there may still be another to make terms.

misly, obs. form of MIZZLY.

mis'made, *pa. pple.* and *ppl. a.* [MIS-[1] 2.] Badly or wrongly made; †deformed, mis-shapen.
c **1375** *Sc. Leg. Saints* ix. (*Bertholomeus*) 217 þe face.. wes awful & mysmade. **1393** in *Collect. Topogr.* (1836) III. 257 A feynyd chartre in oure alle forsaid confeffes name mysmaad. **1483** CAXTON *Gold. Leg.* 154/3 A man whiche was greuously mysmade. **1508** DUNBAR *Flyting w. Kennedie* 53 Mismaid monstour. **1640** BP. HALL *Episc.* II. xv. 172 His mis-made Presbyters. **1856** MRS. BROWNING *Aur. Leigh* III. 524 Subjoined to limping possibilities Of mismade human nature. **1881** FAIRBAIRN *Stud. Life Christ* vii. 115 The simple Galileans were not mismade, only unmade, men.

mis'make, *v.* Now *Sc.* [MIS-[1] 1.] **a.** *trans.* To make badly. †**b.** To unmake, depose. *Obs.* **c.** *refl.* To disturb oneself, put oneself out.
c **1400** *Chron. Eng.* lxxxv. in *Archiv Stud. neu. Spr.* LII. 24 Be stille, good wyff, quoth they, there of mysmake you noght. **1500–20** DUNBAR *Poems* xxviii. 10 That God mismakkis ȝe do amend. **1575** *Burgh Rec. Edin.* 9 July (1882) 41 That we haid spokine off his Graice that we haid maid his Graice and we waild mismak him. **1613** W. COWPER *Holy Alphabet* 186 Wee haue mismade our selues,.. and are not now like vnto that which God created vs. **1825** JAMIESON, To *Mismack*, *Mismake*. 1. To shape or form improperly; applied to clothes. 2. To trouble, to disturb; as 'Dinna mismake yoursell for me'. **1887** *Jamieson's Dict.* Suppl. s.v., He could threep a lee in your face, an' no mismak him.

† **mis'making**, *vbl. sb. Obs.* [MIS-[1] 3.] Bad composition.
1532 *Guystarde & Sygysmonde* Lenvoy D ij, And where nede is to adde or elles detray Pardon of mysmakinge gladly thou hym pray.

† **mis'manage**, *sb. Obs. rare*[−1]. [MIS-[1] 4.] Bad management; improper administration.
a **1716** BEVERLEY *Virginia* (1722) I. §20 That this Disappointment.. proceeded from a Mismanage of Government.

mis'manage, *v.* [MIS-[1] 1.] *trans.* and *intr.* To manage badly or wrongly. Also **mis'managed** *ppl. a.*, **mis'managing** *vbl. sb.* and *ppl. a.*
1690 LOCKE *Hum. Und.* IV. xvii. §4 The Business of Assemblies would be in danger to be mismanag'd. **1698** COLLIER *Immor. Stage* (1699) 138 The Clergy mismanage sometimes, and they must be told of their faults. **1699** —— *Def. Short View* 68 As for his Mismanaging, he must account to his Master. **1817** JAS. MILL *Brit. India* II. IV. ix. 294 The good of the community.. so formidably threatened in their mismanaging hands. **1838** LYTTON *Alice* 89 A mismanaged estate. **1885** *Manch. Exam.* 21 Feb. 5/3 In some respects our foreign policy has been mismanaged.
Hence **mis'manageable** *a.*
1883 RUSKIN *Fors Clav.* xc. 162 A kind of girl.. who is more or less spoilable and mis-manageable.

mis'management. [MIS-[1] 4.] Bad or improper management or administration.
1668 PEPYS *Diary* 13 Nov., The reason he had to suspect his mismanagement of his money in Ireland. **1690** LOCKE *Govt.* II. xix. §225 Such Revolutions happen not upon every little Mismanagement in publick Affairs. **1711** POPE *Temp. Fame* 456 Old mismanagements, taxations new. **1845** E. HOLMES *Mozart* 82 The mismanagement 'of the blessed theatrical people, who,.. delay every thing to the last'. **1878** LECKY *Eng. in 18th C.* I. iii. 423 In the English service mismanagement and languor were general.

mis'manager. [MIS-[1] 5.] A bad manager.
1683 in W. Maitland *Hist. Edin.* (1753) I. vi. 104 Mismanadgers and Imbezlers of the Common Good. **1711** STEELE *Spect.* No. 258 ¶3, I would fain ask any of the present Mismanagers, Why should not Rope-dancers [etc.] ..appear again on our Stage? **1780** BURKE *Œcon. Reform* Wks. III. 247 A long and unbroken pedigree of mismanagers. **1862** *Public Opin.* 26 July 'Contents', The Mismanagement and Mismanagers in the War Department. **1877** RUSKIN *Fors Clav.* VII. 229 He would find.. that the mismanagement could be 'arrested', instead of the mismanager.

mis'mannered, *a. north.* [MIS-[1] 6.] Ill-mannered, unmannerly.
1637 RUTHERFORD *Lett.* (1862) I. cvi. 268 Some pining and mismannered hunger. **1790** MRS. WHEELER *Westmld. Dial.* (1821) 57 Sic like mismannerd deins [= doings]. **1847** HALLIWELL, *Mismannered*, unbecoming. *Cumb.*
So † **mis'manners**, bad manners.
1697 VANBRUGH *Relapse* IV. i. (1708) 41, I hope your Honour will excuse my Mismanners to whisper before you. **1820** HOGG *Winter Even. T.* II. ix. 42, I do.. beseetsh yer pardoune for myne grit follye and mismainners.

mis'mark, *v.* [MIS-[1] 1. Cf. ON. *mismarka* to mark (a sheep) wrongly.]
† **1.** *refl.* To make a wrong guess. (Cf. MARK *v.* II.)
c **1440** *York Myst.* xxix. 123 *Petrus*... Of his company never are I was kende. þou haste þe mismarkid.
2. *trans.* To mark, note, or designate wrongly. Also in pa. pple., having wrong markings.
a **1535** MORE *Answ. Poysoned Bk.* v. ii. Wks. 1135/1 In a side [= page] after misse marked with the noumber of 249, which should haue been marked.. 259. **1699** COLLIER *Def. Short View* 90 His Objections at Big-Allyances, is somewhat unfairly transcrib'd, and the Page mismark'd. **1700** —— *2nd Def. Short View* 101 Why is Nature thus disguis'd, and Quality mismark'd? **1904** *Daily Chron.* 30 Aug. 8/1 It does not matter if the birds are a trifle mismarked.

mis'marriage. [MIS-[1] 4.] An unsuitable marriage. So **mis'marry** *v.* (*lit.* and *fig.*).
1817 MAR. EDGEWORTH *Ormond* iv. (1833) 42 He was never the same man, especially since his last mis-marriage. **1892** *Sat. Rev.* 2 July 29/2 The absurd words he mismarried. **1893** SWINBURNE *Stud. Prose & Poetry* (1894) 121 The woes ..of any couple accidentally or otherwise mismarried.

mismase, obs. form of MIZMAZE.

mis'match, *sb.* [MIS-[1] 4.] A bad match; a discrepancy; lack of correspondence; also, an unequal or unfair sporting contest.
1606 SYLVESTER *Du Bartas* II. iv. II. Argt. 6 Mis-Matches taxt. **1748** RICHARDSON *Clarissa* IV. 65 See you not.. the mismatch that there is in our minds? **1881** MRS. A. R. ELLIS *Sylvestra* II. 168 That mismatch began the mending of Philip. **1883** *Harper's Mag.* Mar. 538/1 The saucer a mismatch. **1954** F. C. AVIS *Boxing Reference Dict.* 71 *Mismatch*, a contest between two boxers of very different standards of ability. **1958** *Optima* Mar. 40/2 The mismatch between arisings and normal disposal methods. **1959** *New Scientist* 9 Apr. 802/3 There is a bad mismatch which will run right through the crystal. **1961** *Times* 21 Nov. 3/3 There had been suggestions that this [*sc.* a boxing match] had been a mismatch. **1971** *Daily Tel.* 28 Apr. 5/3 There is a definite mis-match between what universities are producing and what industry is wanting. **1973** *Computers & Humanities* VII. 139 The computer.. compares the corresponding words.. until a mismatch occurs.

mi'smatch, *v.* [MIS-[1] 1.] *trans.* To match ill, badly, or unsuitably, esp. in marriage; *pass.* to be ill-matched or ill-mated. Also **mi'smatched** *ppl. a.*, **mi'smatching** *vbl. sb.*
1599 B. JONSON *Cynthia's Rev.* v. x, *Cup.* I am studying how to match them. *Mer.* How to mis-match them were harder. **1633** T. ADAMS *Exp. 2 Peter* ii. 4 (1865) 288 How preposterous and mismatched is an erected countenance and a grovelling spirit! **1638** in *Buccleuch MSS.* (Hist. MSS. Comm.) I. 282 Here and there a mismatched suit, but none complete. **1643** MILTON *Divorce* 18 One example of mismatching with an Infidell. **1678** DRYDEN *All for Love* IV, Sure that Face Was meant for Honesty, but Heav'n mismatch'd it. **1726** LEONI *Alberti's Archit.* II. 8/1 If the Members be.. not mismatcht nor unsightly. **1848** J. H. NEWMAN *Loss & Gain* 73, I have heard persons mentioned, but, if I tried, I think I should, in some cases mismatch names and opinions. **1853** FELTON *Fam. Lett.* xliii. (1865) 317 A mismatched pair of Eleusinian steeds. **1875** KNIGHT *Dict. Mech.* 1426 The belts are of different lengths, so as to mismatch the sections as they are revolved. **1971** *Jrnl. Gen. Psychol.* LXXXV. 188 The interference occurs when the pictorial and linguistic symbolic representations of the color concepts are combined together with mismatching. **1974** *Nature* 7 June 566/2 This difference in thermal stability would indicate about 5% mismatching between the Mu MTV DNA and the tumour RNA.
Hence **mis'matchment** = MISMATCH *sb.*
1858 MRS. GORE *Heckington* III. xiii. 283 The mismatchments created by those hypocrisies of modern life which [etc.].

mismate (mɪs'meɪt), *v. rare.* [MIS-[1] 1: back-formation from MISMATED *pa. pple.* and *ppl. a.*] *intr.* and *refl.* To mate or match (oneself) unsuitably.
1891 HARDY *Group of Noble Dames* I. iii. 113 No syllable would have been breathed of how I mismated myself for love of you! **1946** *Mod. Lang. Notes* Feb. 73 This is Milton's longest account of this Biblical episode, and it is clear that here the sons of God are pious men who mismate with the daughters of him 'who slew his brother'.

mis'mated, *pa. pple.* and *ppl. a.* [MIS-[1] 2.] Ill-mated, ill-matched, unsuitably allied.
1825 J. NEAL *Bro. Jonathan* III. 382 The windows carefully mismated, no two of a size. **1858** J. G. HOLLAND *Titcomb's Lett.* v. 132 A mismated match is much worse than unmated life. **1859** TENNYSON *Enid* 1275 Not all mismated with a yawning clown. **1883** *Century Mag.* XXVI. 245/1 Several pairs of mismated oars. **1914** F. L. PACKARD *Miracle*

Man i. 10 Trousers.. torn at the ankles where they flapped around miss-mated socks and shoes. **1931** *Weekend Rev.* 16 May 743/2 It presents him [*sc.* Bulwer-Lytton].. as the child of his mismated parents. **1952** W. STYRON *Lie down in Darkness* v. 194 At that age he was clear-headed enough to understand that he was not alone in a world of mismated passions: others betrayed and were betrayed, and got tired of loving.

mismating (mɪsˈmeɪtɪŋ), *vbl. sb.* [MIS-¹ 3.] Unsuitable mating or matching; *spec.* wrong assorting (of printing types).
1900 T. L. DE VINNE *Pract. Typogr.: Treat. Type-Making* vi. 236 This difficulty tempts founders to make one set of small capitals serve for two or more distinct faces. An inexpert can seldom detect the mismating. **1934** *Punch* 10 Jan. 55/2 There is enough cruelty, halfwittedness, epilepsy, moral depravity and the mismating and obstetrical bungling that sometimes prelude these horrors. **1968** *Punch* 7 Feb. 205/3 Mis-matings are most common in such surroundings.

misˈmay, *v. Sc.* and *north. dial.* [Alteration of DISMAY or ESMAY by substitution of the prefix MIS-¹ 9. For the sense cf. MISMAKE *v.* c.] *trans.* To trouble, disturb, 'upset'; chiefly *refl.*
a **1300** *Cursor M.* 15265 Mismai yow noght, mi breþer dere, Quat-sum yee her or se. **1438** *Bk. Alex. Grt.* (Bannatyne Cl.) 21 We na wayis sould vs mismay. **1501** DOUGLAS *Pal. Hon.* I. lxii, Than as I mocht with curage all mismaid,.. Sair abaisit, beliue I thus out braid. **1825–80** JAMIESON, To *Mismae*, to disturb; as 'She never mismaed her mind'.

mismaze, variant of MIZMAZE.

†**misˈmean,** *v. Obs.* [MIS-¹ 1.] *trans.* **a.** To mean or intend wrongly. **b.** To misinterpret.
1605 VERSTEGAN *Dec. Intell.* 230 Our northerne name of Peg, misment for Margaret. **1647** WARD *Simp. Cobler* 61 Mismeane me not.

†**misˈmeaning,** *vbl. sb. Obs.* [MIS-¹ 3.] Wrong intention.
a **1586** SIDNEY *Arcadia* IV. (1622) 417 He saw the misfortune not the mismeaning of his worke, was like to bring that creature to end.

†**misˈmeaning,** *ppl. a. Obs.* [MIS-¹ 2.] Wrong-thinking.
1387–8 T. USK *Test. Love* II. ix. (Skeat) I. 88 Heretykes and misse-mening people.

misˈmeasure, *v.* [MIS-¹ 1.] *trans.* To measure or estimate incorrectly.
1742 YOUNG *Nt. Th.* v. 974 With aim mis-measur'd, and impetuous speed. *Ibid.* IX. 1330 Time, eternity! ('Tis these, mis-measur'd, ruin all mankind). **1851** E. FITZGERALD *Euphranor* 72 The moralist who worked alone and.. in his closet was most apt to mismeasure Humanity. *a* **1859** DE QUINCEY *Brevia* iv. in *Posth. Wks.* (1891) I. 261 What motive should that furnish him for mismeasuring Nineveh?
So **misˈmeasurement,** wrong measurement.
1859 MILL *Diss. & Disc.* I. 392 *note*, The habitual mismeasurement of the.. value of things. **1900** MORLEY *Cromwell* III. i. 204 Mismeasurement of forces.

misˈmetre, *v.* [MIS-¹ 1.] *trans.* To spoil the metre of. Hence **misˈmetring** *vbl. sb.*
c **1374** CHAUCER *Troylus* v. 1796 So preye I god that noon miswryte thee, Ne thee mismetre for defaute of tongue. **1509** HAWES *Past. Pleas.* (Percy Soc.) 220 Go, little boke! I praye God the save From misse metrying by wrong impression. **1513** DOUGLAS *Æneis* XIII. concl. 217 Take gud tent.. ȝhe nowder maggill nor mismetir my ryme. **1829** SOUTHEY *Sir T. More* II. 228 *note*, Whether these verses are her own composition, or whether she only remembered, and elongated, and mis-metered them. **1891** LOUNSBURY *Stud. Chaucer* III. vii. 207 No one capable of reading can manage to mismetre them.

†**misˈminded,** *ppl. a. Obs. rare*⁻¹. [MIS-¹ 2.] Perverted in mind.
1509 BARCLAY *Shyp of Folys* (1570) 25 Mad and misminded, priuate of wisedome.

misˈmove. *U.S.* [MIS-¹ 4.] A faulty move or step in action.
1877 T. B. ALDRICH *Queen of Sheba* viii. (1885) 158 He had been guilty of a mismove in attempting to take her at a disadvantage. **1901** *N. Amer. Rev.* Feb. 166 It is a distress to look on and note the mismoves, they are so strange and so awkward.

†**misˈmoved,** *a. Obs.* [MIS-¹ 6.] Moved unrhythmically.
? *a* **1500** in Grose, etc. *Antiq. Rep.* (1809) IV. 407 How may a mysmovede tymere judge a trew instrument?

Misnagid, var. MITNAGGED.

†**misˈname,** *sb.* [MIS-¹ 4.] An abusive name.
1481 in *Eng. Gilds* (1870) 315 Callenge hym knaffe, or horson, or deffe, or any voder mysname.

misˈname, *v.* [MIS-¹ 1.]
1. *trans.* To call by a wrong name; to name wrongly; = MISCALL 1. Often with compl.
1537 tr. *Latimer's Serm. bef. Convocation* C vij, They be mis-named children of lyghte for as moche as they so hate lyghte. **1603** KNOLLES *Hist. Turks* (1638) 244 Oftentimes mis-naming vnto them the places they passed by. *a* **1641** BP. MOUNTAGU *Acts & Mon.* (1642) 145 Though he misname the man, and nicknames him Darius Medus. **1711** STEELE *Spect.* No. 84 ¶4 By the Force of a Tyrant Custom, which is mis-named a Point of Honour, the Duellist kills his Friend. **1774** BEATTIE *Minstr.* II. xxxvii, In that Elysian age (misnamed of gold). **1882** FARRAR *Early Chr.* I. 497 If James and Joses and Simon were habitually called brothers when they were only cousins, it can only be said that they were needlessly and systematically misnamed.
†**2.** To call by an abusive name; = MISCALL 2.
c **1500** *Coventry Corpus Chr. Plays* 6/160 *Josoff*... Thogh thatt I dyd the mys-name, Marce, Mare! *a* **1529** SKELTON *Replyc.* Wks. I. 211 Bycause ye her mysnamed, And wolde haue her defamed. *c* **1550** BALE *K. Johan* (Camden) 85 If thu with an hatefull harte Misnamest a kyng. **1632** SHERWOOD, To misname, *improperer*.
So **misˈnamed** *ppl. a.*, wrongly named.
1839 HALLAM *Hist. Lit.* II. v. §58 A tone of sadness reigns through this misnamed Paradise of Daintiness. **1904** *Contemp. Rev.* Aug. 164 The now misnamed Pacific Ocean.

misˈnaming, *vbl. sb.* [MIS-¹ 3.]
1. The giving of a wrong name to a person or a thing; in *Law* = MISNOMER.
1539 *Act 31 Hen. VIII*, c. 13 §16 Misrecitall, misnaming or non-recitall. **1599** THYNNE *Animadv.* (1875) 61 Althoughe there be no mysnamynge of the signe [Taurus]. **1653** KITCHIN *Jurisd. Courts Leet* (ed. 2) 398 Defendant pleads misnaming of himself. **1689** *Grant* in Brand *Newcastle* (1789) II. 671 The.. misnameing or not nameing of any demise or grant.
†**2.** Calling by abusive names. *Obs.*
1641 MILTON *Ch. Govt.* I. vi. 32 And whom ye could not move by sophisticall arguing, them you thinke to confute by scandalous misnaming.

misne, obs. form of MIZEN.

†**misˈnim,** *v. Obs.* [f. MIS-¹ 1 + NIM *v.* Cf. OHG. *missenemen* to err.] **a.** *trans.* To mistake. **b.** *intr.* To make a mistake; to err, do wrong.
a **1225** *Ancr. R.* 46 ȝif ȝe.. gluffeð of wordes, oðer misnimeð uers, nimeð ower uenie dun et ter eorðe.. oðer ualleð adun al uor muchel misnimunge. *a* **1225** *Leg. Kath.* 455 ȝef þu ne misnome onont ure maumez. *c* **1250** *Gen. & Ex.* 3091 Quad pharaon, 'ic haue mis-numen'. *c* **1330** R. BRUNNE *Chron.* (1810) 211 He proued.. þat þe kyng misnam, & did grete trespas. **1340** *Ayenb.* 83 Ine oþre quereles huanne me mysnymþ.
Hence †**misˈniming** *vbl. sb.*: (*a*) error; (*b*) misappropriation.
a **1225** [see above]. **1297** R. GLOUC. (Rolls) 10465 ȝuf eni clerc vorȝeue out þe king of suich mis niminge. **1340** *Ayenb.* 160 þo þet.. ine alle þinges habbeþ discrecion and mesure wyþ-oute misnimynge.

misnome (mɪsˈnəʊm), *v.* Only in pa. pple. [Back-formation f. MISNOMER.] *trans.* To misname.
1804 EUGENIA DE ACTON *Tale without Title* II. 101 The effect of a principle superior to either pride or misnomed delicacy. **1822** T. G. WAINEWRIGHT *Ess. & Crit.* (1880) 294 *note*, The misnomed Grecian Shepherdess. **1852** LYTTON in *Blackw. Mag.* LXXI. 86/1 This *My Novel*.. was misnomed and insulted as 'a Continuation of *The Caxtons*'.

misnomer (mɪsˈnəʊmə(r)), *sb.* Also 5 **-noumer,** 7–8 **-nosmer.** [a. AF., OF. *mesnom(m)er* inf. used subst., f. *mes-* MIS-² + *nommer* to name:—L. *nōmināre* (see NOMINATE *v.*).]
1. *Law.* A mistake in naming a person or place.
1455 *Rolls of Parlt.* V. 334/1 To allege or plede.. misnoumer. **1532** *Dial. on Laws Eng.* II. xlviii. 122 He.. pledeth misnomer [*ed.* 1638 misnosmer]. *a* **1625** SIR H. FINCH *Law* (1636) 385 The defendant may plead misnosmer of himself, or no such towne. **1769** BLACKSTONE *Comm.* IV. 328 A plea in abatement is principally for a misnosmer, a wrong name, or a false addition to the prisoner. **1846** *Act 9 & 10 Vict.* c. 95 §59 No misnomer or inaccurate description of any person or place in any such plaint or summons shall vitiate the same. **1882** *Act 45 & 46 Vict.* c. 50 §241 No misnomer or inaccurate description of any person, body corporate, or place.. shall hinder the full operation of this Act.
2. *gen.* The use of a wrong name; misapplication of a term.
1635 JACKSON *Creed* VIII. xxvii. 304 The second [difficulty] pitcheth upon a misnomer of the Prophet, as whether that Prophecie.. was uttered or written by Zachariah, or.. Jeremiah. **1681** HICKERINGILL *Sin Mancatching* Wks. 1716 I. 174 The Spirit of God.. miscalls none, and never is guilty of any misnosmer. **1796** MME. D'ARBLAY *Lett.* 16 Dec., You would not accuse yourself of a misnomer in calling him cherub. **1874** L. STEPHEN *Hours in Library* (1892) II. vi. 206 A kind of misnomer which classifies all Scott's books as novels. **1882** PEBODY *Eng. Journalism* xxi. 159 The City which, by a misnomer, is called the Metropolis.
3. A wrong name or designation.
1657 W. MORICE *Coena quasi Κοινη* Def. vi. 309 The Notion of Presbytery (which sure is a misnomer). **1728** MORGAN *Algiers* II. v. 307 To pass by abundance of Misnomers he will needs call the Person I name Drub-Devil, Devil-Driver. **1818** BYRON *Juan* I. cc, My name of Epic's no misnomer. **1891** DRIVER *Introd. Lit. O.T.* (1892) 471 *note*, The term 'Chaldee' for the Aramaic of either the Bible or the Targums is a misnomer.

misˈnomer, *v.* [f. prec.] *trans.* To misname. Chiefly in pa. pple. and ppl. a. = Called by a name which is a misnomer, misnamed.
1740 RICHARDSON *Pamela* (1824) I. lxi. 404 The misnomered free-gifts which we read of in some kingdoms on extraordinary occasions. **1795** WOLCOT (P. Pindar) *Wks.* (1812) III. 435 Whose life (misnomer'd life) is death, rank death. **1848** *Fraser's Mag.* XXXVIII. 134 Louis, misnomered *le Grand.* **1854** LADY LYTTON *Behind the Scenes* I. II. ii. 186 He was beginning sorely to repent the precipitate step which he misnomered hospitality. **1884** EDERSHEIM *Life of Jesus* (ed. 2) II. 562 The wretched witticisms of what is misnomered common sense.

†**misˈnote,** *v. Obs.* [f. MIS-¹ 1 + NOTE *v.*¹] *trans.* To abuse.
a **1225** *Ancr. R.* 130 Saul, *abutens, siue abusio.* Vor Saul, on Ebreuwisch, is mis-notinge an Englisch ant te valse ancre mis-noteð ancre nome.

misˈnumber, *v.* [MIS-¹ 1.] *trans.* To number incorrectly.
1614 RALEIGH *Hist. World* v. i. §8 Which might well make it suspected, that the Armies by Sea, before spoken of, were misse-numbred. **1774** GOSTLING *Walk Canterb.* (1777) 140 The misnumbering the prebendal houses. **1906** *Bookman* Mar. (Educ. Suppl.) 25 The last twelve pieces are misnumbered, 103–114 instead of 147–158.

misˈnurture, *v.* [MIS-¹ 1.] To train up badly.
1625 BP. HALL *Contempl., O.T.* XIX. *Elisha cursing children*, He would punish the parents mis-nurturing their children.. with the death of those children.

†**misˈnurtured,** *ppl. a. Sc. Obs.* [MIS-¹ 2.] Badly brought up; ill-bred; unmannerly. Hence **misˈnurturedness.**
a **1578** LINDESAY (Pitscottie) *Chron. Scot.* (S.T.S.) II. 84 It was ane misnurtartnes [*v.r.* misnortourit] deid and he was bot ane knaif that did it. *Ibid.* 120 The scoittismen growis nevir misnortourit nor dissobedient to thair governouris. **1616** ROLLOCK *Lect.* xxxv. 343 This homelines will not be with misnourturnesse [*sic: ? misprint*], and with an opinion of paritie. **1637** RUTHERFORD *Lett.* (1664) I. xxvii. 62 That which idle on-waiting cannot doe, misnurtured crying and knocking will doe.

‖**miso** (ˈmiso). [Jap.] A paste, made from soya beans and barley or rice malt, used by the Japanese in preparing various foods.
1727 J. G. SCHEUCHZER tr. *Kæmpfer's Hist. Japan* I. I. ix. 121 Of the Meal of these Beans is made what they call *Midsu*, a mealy Pap, which they dress their Victuals withal. **1905** *Chambers's Jrnl.* 25 Mar. 270/2 Soya beans.. from which miso, soya and tofu are made. **1930** *Economist* 4 Jan. 24/1 The higher Japanese price-level is accounted for largely by such 'sheltered' goods as red beans, miso, dried bonito, [etc.]. **1966** P. S. BUCK *People of Japan* (1968) xiv. 167 Chicken with *miso* paste and raw vegetables. **1970** J. KIRKUP *Japan behind Fan* 104 A red lacquer bowl of rich *miso* soy (bean paste) soup.

miso- (maɪsəʊ, mɪsəʊ), before a vowel usually **mis-**, repr. Gr. μισο- (μισ-), combining form of the root of μισεῖν to hate, μῖσος hatred. The compounds formed in Greek with this prefix are of the same kind as those with the similar φιλο-, PHILO-, but, both in Greek and in English, they are much less numerous than in the case of the latter prefix. The most important adoptions and coinages will be found as main words, viz. MISANTHROPY, MISOGAMY, MISOGYNY, MISOLOGY, MISONEISM, and the related words; others, chiefly nonce-words, follow here. **misandry,** the hatred of males. **misarchist,** one who hates or opposes government in any form. **misoˈbasilist** [Gr. μισοβασιλεύς], a hater of kings. **misoˈcapnic** *a.* [In Bp. Montagu's Lat. edition (1619) of James I's works *A Counterblaste to Tobacco* appears as *Misocapnus*: Gr. καπνός smoke], hating tobacco smoke; so **misoˈcapnist,** a hater of tobacco smoke. **misoˈcatholic** *a.*, hating what is (Roman) Catholic. **ˈmisoclere** *a.* [eccl. Gr. κλῆρος clergy], clergy-hating. **miˈsocyny** [Gr. κυν-, κύων dog], hatred of dogs. **misoˈgallic** *a.*, characterized by hatred of the French. **misogeˈlastic** *a. nonce-wd.* [Gr. γελαστ-ός laughable (see AGELAST; cf. AGELASTIC *a.* and *sb.*)], hating laughter. **misoˈgrammatist** [Gr. γράμματα 'letters', pl. of γράμμα letter], a hater of letters or learning. **miso-Heˈllene** [cf. Gr. μισέλλην], a hater of the Greeks. **ˈmisomath,** a hater of mathematics. **misomoˈnarchical** *a.*, detesting monarchy. **misoˈmusist** [Gr. μοῦσα learning], a hater of learning. **misoˈpædist** [cf. Gr. μισοπαιδ-, μισόπαις], a child-hater. **miso-ˈparson,** a hater of parsons. **miso-ˈpaterist,** a hater of the Fathers of the Christian Church. **misopogoˈnistically** *adv.* [Gr. μισοπώγων name of a satire by the emperor Julian: πώγων beard], with a hatred of beards. **misopoˈlemical** *a.* [cf. Gr. μισοπόλεμος], war-hating. **miˈsoscopist** [Gr. σκοπεῖν to look at], a hater of sights. **miˈsosophist** [cf. Gr. μισόσοφος], a hater of wisdom; so **miˈsosophy,** hatred of wisdom; so **misoˈsophical** *a.* **misoˈtheism** [cf. Gr. μισόθεος], hatred of God or gods; so **misoˈtheist, misotheˈistic** *a.* **misotramonˈtanism,** hatred of what is 'tramontane'. **misoˈtyranny** [cf. Gr. μισοτύραννος], hatred of tyranny. **ˈmisoxene** [Gr. μισόξενος], a hater of strangers; so **miˈsoxeny** [Gr. μισοξενία], hatred of strangers. †**misoˈxygenous** *a.*, having no chemical affinity for oxygen.
1946 *Scrutiny* XIII. 249 In the absence of feminine precedents, she [*sc.* Beatrice] could do no better than what she very sensibly does do: follow masculine example, and answer to their affected misogyny with the affectation of *misandry. **1960** B. KAYE *Upper Nankin St.* xii. 232 Such women are common in.. Kwangtung Province, where there

is a tradition of misandry. **1898** L. F. Ward *Outl. Sociol.* x. 228 These *misarchists see the beneficent influences of natural law in the industrial world interfered with. **1638** in *Bk. Sc. Pasquils* (1868) 43 Frome..All monster *Misobasilists..Almighty God deliver us. **1855** Kingsley *Westw. Ho!* vii, That *Misocapnic Solomon James I. **1839** 'Joseph Fume' *Paper on Tobacco* 70 Offending the nostrils of all *misocapnists with the fumes of his mundungus. **1857** Ellis & Blackburn *Rep. Cases Q.B.* VII. 190 He would not have approved of the *misocatholic opinions. **1655** Fuller *Ch. Hist.* iv. 182 King Henry the sixth, acted herein by some *misoclere-Courtiers sent this Arch-Bishop for a New years-gift, a shred-pie. **1889** *Sat. Rev.* 26 Oct. 450/1 They ..seldom express their '*misocyny'..articulately. **1897** *Edin. Rev.* July 31 The *misogallic language and policy of Signor Crispi. **1877** G. Meredith *Ess. Comedy* in *New Q. Mag.* VIII. 2 It is but one step from being agelastic to *misogelastic. *a* **1661** Fuller *Worthies, Suffolk* (1662) iii. 68 Wat Tyler..being a *Misogrammatist (if a good Greek word may be given to so Barbarous a Rebel). **1868** Visct. Strangford *Selection* (1869) I. 345 A dastardly anti-Christian *miso-Hellene. **1872** De Morgan *Budget* 418 The great *misomath of our own day. **1644** Maxwell *Prerog Chr. Kings* 158 Our *Miso-monarchicall Statists and Sectaries. **1642** Sir E. Dering *Sp. on Relig.* 116 Our better cause hath gained by this light: which doth convince our *Miso-musists. **1895** *Pop. Sci. Monthly* Sept. 655 Children, says the *misopaedist, are not only unfeeling. **1795** G. Wakefield *Reply 2nd Pt. Paine* 54 For me, who am engaged in this controversy with our *miso-parson. **1840** G. S. Faber *Prim. Doctr. Regen.* p. xvii, Lest it should be eagerly caught up, by some strenuous *Misopaterist, as stultifying the legitimate Principle of an Appeal to Antiquity. **1842** Mrs. Browning *Grk. Chr. Poets* Poems 1890 V. 135 He and Basil..talked low and *misopogonistically of their fellow-student Julian's bearded boding smiles. **1849** Eastwick *Dry Leaves* 167 The *misopolemical Cobden. **1873** Lowell *Lett.* (1894) II. 111 He has become a thorough *misoscopist or hater of sights. **1937** *Philos.* XII. 332 The disposition to be convinced of ill-founded or unfounded doctrines, or unconvinced of well-founded ones, is a '*misosophical' disposition. **1890** *Eng. Illustr. Mag.* Nov. 130, I am a *mysosophist! All wisdom is vanity, and I hate it! **1820–30** Coleridge in *Lit. Rem.* (1838) III. 33 Schools of psilology ..and *misosophy are here out of the question. **1937** *Philos.* XII. 319 A fraternity of persons of kindred credulities could only constitute a school of 'misosophy'. **1846** De Quincey *Christianity* Wks. 1859 XII. 251 Hypocrisy, the cringing of sycophants, and the credulities of fear, united to conceal this *misotheism. **1881** H. Hartshorne *Glance 20th Cent.* 56 They unite ourselves..as *misotheists, against all that is called God. *Ibid.*, The new *Misotheistic Association. **1846** De Quincey *Mackintosh* Wks. 1862 XII. 78 Machiavelli's fierce *misotramontanism. **1874** Mahaffy *Soc. Life Greece* v. 148 The..known *miso-tyranny of the family. **1883** *Q. Rev.* Jan. 197 His fellow *misoxene of a nearer East. **1611** Speed *Hist. Gt. Brit.* ix. ix. (1623) 614 Our *Misoxenie (or hatred to strangers) was no new qualitie. **1674** Josselyn *Two Voy.* 125 Both Men and Women are guilty of Misoxenie. **1799** Sir H. Davy in Beddoes *Contrib. Phys. & Med. Knowl.* 223 The terms philoxygenous and *misoxygenous must be changed.

misob'servance. *rare.* [MIS-[1] 4.] Failure to observe rules or conditions properly. Also †**misob'servancy**.

1496 *Divos & Pauper* (W. de W.) i. xl. 80/1 Yf they use in theyr dooynge ony mysobseruaunce. **1637** Earl Monm. tr. *Malvezzi's Romulus & Tarquin* 49 Misobservancie differs from contempt. **1817** Jas. Mill *Brit. India* I. iii. v. 643 That as soon as any misobservance was laid hold of by the judge, the whole of the preceding operations..should be set aside.

So **misob'serve** *v.*, **misob'server**.

1649 Milton *Eikon.* ix. 87 The..Covnanteers (For so I call them as misobservers of the Cov'nant). **1693** Locke *Educ.* §81 If I misobserve not, they [*sc.* children] love to be treated as rational Creatures, sooner than is imagin'd.

mis'occupy. [MIS-[1] 1.] *trans.* To occupy amiss. Also **mis'occupied** *ppl. a.*

1534 More *Treat. Passion* Wks. 1330/2 He may..misse occupy his eares and heape vp in his hart a donghyl of theyr dyuelyshe vanities. *a* **1832** Bentham *Deontol.* (1834) II. ii. 113 Unoccupied or misoccupied time.

misogamy (maɪs-, mɪ'sɒgəmɪ). [ad. mod.L. *misogami-a*, a. Gr. *μῑσογαμί-α, f. μῑσόγαμος hating marriage (Stephanus), f. μῑσο- MISO- + γάμος marriage. Cf. F. *misogamie*.] Hatred of marriage.

1656 Blount *Glossogr.*, *Misogamie* (*misogamia*), hating of marriage. **18..** Lamb *Let. to Coleridge* (L.), It is misogyny rather than misogamy that he affects. **1857** *Chamb. Jrnl.* VIII. 397 Not through any foolish independence of mankind, or adventurous misogamy.

So **mi'sogamist**, a hater of marriage; **misogamic** (maɪsəʊ-, mɪsəʊ'gæmɪk) *a.*, marriage-hating.

1706 Phillips (ed. Kersey), *Misogamist*, a Marriage-hater. **1780** M. Madan *Thelyphthora* II. 89 *note*, Notwithstanding all the bitterness of that gloomy misogamist Jerome. **1877** Mrs. Forrester *Mignon* I. 34 A cynical old misogamist. **1889** *Pall Mall G.* 7 Jan. 3/2 Any doubt he may have ever cherished in his misogamic breast concerning woman's creative capacity.

misogyne ('maɪsəʊ-, 'mɪsəʊdʒɪn). Also **misogyn**. [ad. Gr. μῑσογύνης (see MISOGYNIST). Cf. F. *misogyne*.] A woman-hater.

1817 Coleridge *Biog. Lit.* (Bohn) 112 The Misogyne, Boccaccio. **1877** C. Reade *Woman-Hater* I. v. 113 Misogyn consented, but sighed. **1919** Beerbohm *Seven Men* 186 'Tis a goodly jest! The *con*firm'd misogyn a ladies' man!

So **miso'gynic**, **misogynous** (maɪs-, mɪ'sɒdʒɪnəs) *adjs.*, woman-hating.

1825 *New Monthly Mag.* XV. 247 A cynic misogynic heretic old bachelor. **1859** Meredith *R. Feverel* xxv, His misogynic soul. **1884** *Trans. Cumbld. & Westmld. Lit. Assoc.* X. 41 A woman has been, by misogynous old bachelors, said to be at the bottom of all mischief.

misogynist (maɪs-, mɪ'sɒdʒɪnɪst). Also 7 **-genyst**. [f. Gr. μῑσογύνης (f. μῑσο- MISO + γύνη woman) + -IST.] A woman-hater.

1620 *Swetnam Arraigned* i. ii. A4 [Mysogenos loq.] Swetnams name, Will be more terrible in womens eares, Then euer yet Misogenysts hath beene. **1642** Fuller *Holy & Prof. St.* i. xii. §3 Junius, at the first little better then a Misogynist, was afterwards so altered from himself, that he successively married foure wives. **1748** Richardson *Clarissa* (1811) I. 308 That surly old misogynist, as he was deemed, Sir Oliver. **1858** Thackeray *Virgin.* xxxiv. (1878) 274 'Confound all women, I say', muttered the young misogynist. **1900** W. L. Courtney *Idea of Tragedy* 104 Many critics have called him [*sc.* Euripides] misogynist, and certainly he says very hard things of the female sex.

Hence **mi'sogynism** = MISOGYNY; **misogy'nistic, -gy'nistical** *adjs.* = MISOGYNIC.

1821 *New Monthly Mag.* I. 88 The sentiment has been re-echoed by every misogynistic satirist. **1830** H. N. Coleridge *Grk. Poets* (1834) 274 Euripides did not indulge his supposed misogynism beyond the taste of his audience. **1850** J. Brown *Horæ Subs.*, *Locke & Sydenham* (1858) 10 This misogynistical rosicrucian was brought over to Oxford by Boyle. **1876** H. Kingsley *Grange Garden* I. 30 Ben Jonson in his hideous misogynism. **1891** *Harper's Mag.* Jan. 196/2 The misogynistic lament that 'Adam ever lost a rib'.

misogyny (maɪs-, mɪ'sɒdʒɪnɪ). [ad. mod.L. *misogyni-a*, a. Gr. μῑσογυνία, f. μῑσογύνης (see MISOGYNIST). Cf. F. *misogynie*.] Hatred of women.

1656 Blount *Glossogr.*, *Misogynie* (*misoginia*), the hate or contempt of women. **1658** Phillips, *Misoginy*. **18..** [see MISOGAMY]. **1882** H. C. Merivale *Faucit of B.* I. i. i. 7 He ..walked the banks apart, a thing of misogyny, in a suit of flannel.

misology (maɪs-, mɪ'sɒlədʒɪ). [ad. Gr. μῑσολογία (corresp. to μισόλογος hating reason): see MISO- and -LOGY.] Hatred of reason or discussion; also, hatred of learning or knowledge.

1833 Coleridge *Table-t.* 16 Feb, Misology, or hatred and depreciation of knowledge. **1847** Lewes *Hist. Philos.* (1853) 327 Bruno's scorn sprang from no misology. **1865** Grote *Plato* II. xxiii. 155 Tinged with misology, or the hatred of free argumentative discussion.

So **mi'sologist**, **misologue** ('maɪsəʊ-, 'mɪsəʊlɒg), a hater of reason or discussion.

1866 M. P. W. Bolton *Inquis. Philos.* 89 'Let us not', replies Socrates, 'become misologues, as some persons become misanthropes'. **1871** Jowett *Plato* I. 438 As there are misanthropists or haters of men, there are also misologists or haters of ideas. **1873** Morley *Struggle Nat. Educ.* 66 What statesmanship is that which..invests its priests with a new function, and entrusts afresh a holy army of misologists with the control of national instruction?

misomere, obs. form of MIDSUMMER.

†**mison.** *Obs.* = MISY 1.

1601 Holland *Pliny* xix. iii. II. 7 Of the excrescence name Misy [*marg.* or, Mison]. *Ibid.*, Misy [*marg.* or, Mison rather, according to Turneb.]. **1611** Florio, *Misi*, a kinde of excressence of the earth called Misons passing sweet in smell and taste.

mison, obs. form of MIZEN.

misoneism (maɪsəʊ-, mɪsəʊ'niːɪz(ə)m). [ad. It. *misoneismo* (Lombroso *L'uomo delinquente* (1889) I. 21), f. Gr. μῑσο- MISO- + νέ-ος NEW: see -ISM.] Hatred of novelty. Hence **miso'neist**, a hater of novelty; **misone'istic** *a.*, characterized by misoneism.

1886 *Pop. Sci. Monthly* Oct. 782 The fear of the unknown has been named misoneism... It is best exemplified in children and savages. **1891** H. Zimmern in *Blackw. Mag.* Feb. 206/2 'What else is it but this that we call misoneistic', continues Lombroso, 'that prevents the speedy acceptance of scientific improvements'? **1891** *Review of Rev.* Jan. 83/2 The most thoroughgoing misoneist.

†**miso'pinion.** *Obs.* [MIS-[1] 4.] An erroneous opinion.

1545 Raynold *Byrth Mankynde* 2 Certayne thynges..of the whiche bothe men..and women..haue conceauyd very erroniouse and misopinions. **1624** Bp. Hall *True Peacemaker* (1645) 102 Every fault is a crime; every mis-opinion an heresie. **1640** —— *Episc.* i. xii. 54 Were there not foule mis-opinions in the Churches of Corinth, Galatia, Thessalonica, Colosse? **1680** Waller *Div. Medit.* 35 Nothing but ignorance is the mother of this misopinion.

misor'dained, *pa. pple.* [MIS-[1] 2.] †**a.** Not guided or directed. *Obs.* **b.** Irregularly ordained. So †**misor'daining** *vbl. sb.*, misdirection.

c **1400** Mysordeyninge [see MISORDINANCE]. **1456** Sir G. Haye *Law Arms* (S.T.S.) 291 But hete, but wilfulnes of a disordinate lust,..but favour mysordanyt. **1640** Bp. Hall *Episc.* ii. xv. 172 A Nullity pronounced of those his misordained.

mis'order, *sb.* Now *rare.* [MIS-[1] 4.]

1. = DISORDER (in various senses); absence or breach of order; confusion; disorderly conduct, misbehaviour.

c **1400** *Ser J. Mandevelle & Gt. Souden* (MS. Bodl. e. Museo 160, fol. 111 b), They by & selle by craft & gyn, Theyr mysorder cawses alle myscheve. **1494** Fabyan *Chron.* ii. xlvi. 29 After hym reygned .xx. Kynges successyuely..of the whiche..is no mencyon made eyther for their rudenesse ..or discordaunt meanes, or maners..the whiche mysordre Clerkes disdayned to wryte or put in memory. *c* **1515** Bp. West in Ellis *Orig. Lett.* Ser. iii. I. 182, I have begonne my Visitacyon in my Cathedrall Churche of Ely, wher I have ffounde suche Mysorder..that [etc.]. **1586** Cogan *Haven Health* ccxiv. (1636) 228 It is better to preserve health by sobriety and temperance, than by surfet and misorder, to make the body weake and sickly. **1646** R. Baillie *Anabaptism* (1647) Pref. A, When an Army is once..put in such misorder as it begins to run. **1654** Z. Coke *Logick* 50 The misorder (ἀταξία) in this motion is not from the soul. **1849** H. Miller *Footpr. Creat.* ix. (1874) 160 The limbs seem to exhibit merely the amount of natural misarrangement and misorder.

b. An instance of disorder; an ill-ordered procedure or state of things.

1538 Starkey *England* i. iii. 20 Except we..serch out al commyn fautys and general mysordurys. **1623** Camden *Rem.* (1636) 263 His Uncles..with other of that faction, who sought to reforme the misorders of..his Counsellours. *a* **1656** Hales *Gold. Rem.* (1688) 96, I will speak of the redress of some misorders very frequent in our Age. **1709** Strype *Ann. Ref.* xlv. 462 Because he found still the Continuance of that his misorder. **1885** Edgar *Old Ch. Life Scot.* v. 234 To report to the Session what scandals and misorders existed within the bounds of his charge.

†**2.** Bad or wrong order. In first two quots. with reference to the 'ordering' of clergy. *Obs.*

1561 *Burnynge of Paules Church*, etc. (1563) O ij b, The order by whiche oure Byshops and Priestes are made nowe, is more agreeing to the..tradition of Thapostles than that misorder wherby the Popish prelates order their clergy. **1563–83** Foxe *A. & M.* 1693/2 *Boner.* Well Syr, what say you to the Sacrament of Orders? *Smith.* Ye may call it the Sacrament of misorders. **1641** R. B. K. *Parallel of Liturgy with Mass-bk.* 87 We follow punctually the misorders..we cast the Epistles ever before and the Gospels behind.

†**mis'order**, *v.* *Obs.* [MIS-[1] 1.]

1. *trans.* To put into disorder or confusion; to confuse, disturb.

1494 Fabyan *Chron.* vi. ccix. 223 The doughter of Canutus..by whome many thynges were mysse orderyd, and specyally by y[e] subtylytie of this Erle Goodwyn. **1530** Palsgr. 638/1 Who hath mysordred these thynges sythe I wente. I dyd put every thyng in his ryght place. **1555** in Hakluyt *Voy.* (1599) 262 That which shall be misordered by negligence. **1597** Shaks. *2 Hen. IV*, iv. ii. 33 The Time (mis-order'd) doth..Crowd vs, and crush vs, to this monstrous Forme. **1909** *Daily Chron.* 24 Aug. 4/3 [He] charged the Admiralty with having so misordered the Navy as to expose the nation to the gravest jeopardy every hour.

2. To ill-treat, ill-use.

1550 Coverdale *Spir. Perle* xxviii. 265 When he was mocked..scourged..and most cruelly misordered and dealt with all. **1575** *Gamm. Gurton* v. ii. (Manly), Master Doctor vpon you here complaineth That you and your maides shuld him much misorder.

3. *refl.* To misbehave, misconduct oneself; to be disorderly or ill-behaved.

1505 *Rep. Var. Coll.* (Hist. MSS. Comm. 1901) I. 5 If there be any of the bretherne..that messay or do in myssorderynge hyme selffe one anenst another. **1572** *Act 14 Eliz.* c. 5 §2 Every person or persons..taken vagrant wandring and misordering themselves. **1588** *Nottingham Rec.* IV. 220 For misorderinge hym selfe in the sarmon time. **1740** *Act. 13 Geo. II*, c. 24 The County..where such Person shall be so found begging, or otherwise misordering him or herself.

†**mis'ordered**, *ppl. a.* *Obs.* [MIS-[1] 2.]

1. Of disorderly behaviour; ill-conducted.

1529 More *Dyaloge* iv. Wks. 274/1 Where were become al good ordre among men, if euery misordred wretche myght alledge that his mischieuous dede was his desteny? *a* **1568** Ascham *Scholem.* i. (Arb.) 33 Fewe of them cum to any great aige, by reason of their misordered life when they were yong. **1605** *Play of Stucley* in Simpson *Sch. Shaks.* (1878) 168 Thou lewd misordered villain.

2. Disordered, confused, deranged; irregular.

1538 in *Lett. Suppr. Monast.* (Camden) 184 A better deade for the comen wealth and dew reformacion of the whole mysordered dyocesse can not be purposed. **1559** *Primer* in *Priv. Prayers* (1851) 101 No agreement of opinions, but, as it were, in a misordered quire, every man singeth a contrary note. **1631** Gouge *God's Arrows* i. §43 Anger is mis-ordered, when it is unadvisedly, or immeasurably moved. **1645** Rutherford *Tryal & Tri. Faith* (1845) 31 Christ must oil the wheels of mis-ordered will. **1794** Mathias *Purs. Lit.* (1798) 397 This mis-order'd world, these lawless times.

†**mis'ordering**, *vbl. sb.* *Obs.* [MIS-[1] 3.]

a. Mismanagement; misrule. **b.** Disturbance. **c.** Misconduct.

1526 *Pilgr. Perf.* (W. de W. 1531) 61 In ony other euyl kepyng of thy syght, or misorderyng of ony other of all thy senses. **1535** *Act 27 Hen. VIII*, c. 18 Misorderynge of the saide riuer by casting in of dunge. **1625** Bp. Mountagu *App. Cæsar* 3 Any misbeing, misordering, misdemeaning in any point. **1643** Prynne *Sov. Power Parl.* i. (ed. 2) 8 Who for misordering of his people was deposed by them.

†**mis'orderly**, *a.* *Obs.* [MIS-[1] 6, 7.] Unruly, disorderly; irregular, confused.

a **1568** Ascham *Scholem.* i. (Arb.) 28 Lest his ouermoch hearinge of you driue him to seeke some misorderlie shifte. *Ibid.* 91 This kinde of misorderlie meter. *a* **1656** Hales *Gold. Rem.* i. (1673) 164 Unruly and misorderly affections. **1661** *Plymouth Col. Rec.* (1855) III. 213 Misorderly carriages tending to disturbance in the towne of Eastham.

†**mis'orderly**, *adv.* *Obs.* [MIS-[1] 6, 7.] In a disorderly manner.

a **1557** *Diurn. Occurr.* (Bannatyne Cl.) 36 The Scottis without any skaith fled mis-ordourlie. **1558** Kennedy *Compend. Tract.* in *Wodrow Soc. Misc.* (1844) 142 Takand the place of authoritie mysordourlie on thame selfis. **1592**

STOW *Ann.* 1146 Being taken begging, vagrant, and wandring misorderly [cf. MISORDER *v.* 3, quot. 1572].

† **mis'ordinance.** *Obs.* [MIS-^{1} 4.] **a.** Lack of order or regularity. **b.** Misconduct.

c **1400** *Lanfranc's Cirurg.* 84 Mys-ordynaunce [*v.r.* mysordeyninge] of dietynge. **1509** BARCLAY *Shyp of Folys* 252 b, Who can rehers eche sort of folysshenes That vs mysgydeth through our mysordynaunce?

misordi'nation. [MIS-^{1} 4.] Improper ordination.

1664 [see MISCONSECRATION.]

misorien'tation. [MIS-^{1} 4.] Variation in orientation.

1952 *Acta Crystallogr.* V. 162 When aluminium is cold-rolled, the original grains break up into smaller particles. X-ray micro-beam back reflexion photographs permit the determination of the mean particle size and misorientation. **1966** D. G. BRANDON *Mod. Techniques Metallogr.* ii. 82 If two neighbouring regions differ slightly in orientation,.. and if the misorientation is extensive, characteristic radiation will only image one region at a time. **1973** *Nature* 3 Aug. 276/2 The large more misorientated subgrains (misorientation normally > 5°) could be directly related to the optical subgrains.

So **mis'orient, -'orientate** *vbs.* [MIS-^{1} 1], to orient differently or variably; also, to orient badly. (Chiefly as pa. pples.)

1951 *New Yorker* 22 Sept. 94 The result of misorienting the Secretariat and using glass so exuberantly is to create a building that functionally is often windowless on all sides. **1953** *Acta Crystallogr.* VI. 167/1 A large number of grains in which there is widely misoriented material will be irradiated. *Ibid.* 177/1 This mosaic structure consists of particles slightly misorientated with respect to one another. **1967** *Sunday Times* 9 Apr. 52 We have the uneasy suspicion that our communal sense of values has become misorientated; and so it has. **1970** *New Scientist* 8 Oct. 65/1 Adjacent grains are misoriented with respect to one another. **1973** Misorientated [see above].

† **mis'orned,** *ppl. a. Obs.* [f. MIS-^{1} 2 + **orned* after F. *orné* adorned. (Cf. ORNE *a.*^{2})] Unadorned.

15.. R. COPLAND *Helyas* Prol. in Thoms *E. Eng. Prose Rom.* (1828) III. 2 To take no regard to the languag misorned and rude.

† **mis'owning,** *vbl. sb. Obs.* [MIS-^{1} 7.] Disowning.

1661 J. DAVIES *Civil Warres* 311 Manifesting an utter dislike and misowning of theirs and the kings proceedings.

† **mis'pair.** *Obs.* In 5 myspayre. [? Alteration of DESPAIR: see MIS-^{1} 9.] ? Despair.

14.. *Sir Beues* 4264 (MS. Cant. in Hall.) The kyng Edgare Dryveth the to grete myspayre [*MS. A.* to meche te bismare].

† **mis'parlance.** *Obs. rare*$^{-1}$. [ad. OF. *mesparlance*: see MIS-^{2} and PARLANCE.] Evil speaking.

c **1570** *Pride & Lowl.* (1841) 49 And praied witnesse of his fowle misparlaunce.

mispay, *v.* [a. OF. *mespai-er*: see MIS-^{2} and PAY *v.*^{1}]

† **1.** *trans.* To displease, dissatisfy; to anger, irritate. *Obs.*

a **1225** *Ancr. R.* 198 Hwose..is wel ipaied ȝif heo is ipreised, & mis-ipaied ȝif heo nis itold swuch ase heo wolde. *c* **1330** R. BRUNNE *Chron. Wace* (Rolls) 7811 So þe barons þem nought mispaye, Ne þe comun folk affraye. *a* **1340** HAMPOLE *Psalter* cxxxviii. 23 If thou see any thynge in my way that is mispayand til the. *c* **1440** *York Myst.* v. 64 To do is us full lothe, þat shuld oure god myspaye. **1493** *Dives & Pauper* II. xix. ivj, If thou..art nat myspayed whan thou heryst them [*sc.* oaths], thou takest goddes name in veyne.

2. To pay by mistake.

1698 *Lond. Gaz.* No. 3369/4 Whoever has Mispaid such a Bill, let him enquire of John Brassey.

mispeak, mispeche, obs. ff. MIS-SPEAK, MIS-SPEECH.

misper'ceive, *v.* [MIS-^{1} 1.] *trans.* To perceive wrongly or incorrectly; to mistake.

1924 J. E. MCTAGGART in J. H. Muirhead *Contemp. Brit. Philos.* (1st Ser.) 265 Consequently H will be misperceived by G as existing in time. **1953** *Mind* LXII. 207 The bedpost was not being misperceived when I dreamed that I saw the Eiffel Tower. **1973** E. BULLINS *Theme is Blackness* 174 No, of course I don't think you're the bad guy but you're misperceiving me wrongly. **1974** *Sci. Amer.* Jan. 84 One might succeed in correcting the eyes shown here so that they are perceived as gazing downward and leftward, but at that very moment the mouth is uncorrected and expresses sorrow rather than pleasure. Conversely, one might correct the mouth and misperceive the eyes.

misper'ception. [MIS-^{1} 4.] The action of misperceiving or condition of being misperceived.

1722 WOLLASTON *Relig. Nat.* iii. 42 Wrong notions, and misperceptions of things. **1893** *Daily News* 24 Feb. 3/1 Lord R. Churchill said he must blame his aural misperception. **1949** H. C. WESTON *Sight, Light & Efficiency* iii. 108 One very familiar example of this mis-perception occurs in reading when we see a group of letters as the word they ought to represent, even though the printed word is mis-spelt.

misper'form, *v.* [MIS-^{1} 1.] *trans.* To perform improperly.

a **1656** VINES *Lord's Supp.* (1677) 172 The positive worship of God in sacraments is not easily either misperformed or neglected. **1663** H. COGAN tr. *Pinto's Trav.* xxiv. 87, I do not think any of your company can accuse me for misperforming my duty. **1817** JAS. MILL *Brit. India* III. ii. 74 The duties of the office..were..such as could not be neglected, or misperformed. **1873** BRYCE *Holy Rom. Emp.* x, To degrade him if he rejected or misperformed it [*sc.* his task].

misper'formance. [MIS-^{1} 4.] Improper performance.

1684 BAXTER *Twelve Argts.* §4. 10 Must we renounce the Communion with them all, or reserve exception against their faults and misperformances? **1885** H. W. BEECHER in *Amer. Rev.* Jan. 192 It is an argument against the misperformance of duty, and not against the imperative duty.

† **mis'person,** *v. Sc. Obs.* [Alteration of DISPERSON. by substitution of prefix: see MIS-^{1} 9.] *trans.* To treat (a person) with indignity.

1523-4 *Extracts Aberd. Reg.* (1844) I. 445 For the mispersoning of..the merchandis..in calling of thame 'Coffeis'. **1530** *Ibid.* 134 Alex. Rutherfurd, bailzie, complenzeit in iugment that he was disobeyit, strublit, and mispersonit in the executioun of his office. **1613** *Extracts Rec. Lanark* (1893) 120 Quhille hie..acknahaulege his offens in mispersoning the said Robert Lokhart [*cf. supra* impersonit].

misper'suade, *v.* Now *rare* or *Obs.* [MIS-^{1} 1.] *trans.* To persuade wrongly or into error.

1597 HOOKER *Eccl. Pol.* v. lxii. §9 The teachers error is the peoples tryall, harder and heauier by so much to beare, as he is in worth and regard greater that misperswadeth them. **1635** JACKSON *Creed* VIII. ix. 86 Job's wife did seeke to mispersuade him. **1710** NORRIS *Chr. Prud.* vii. 328 Tho' he is misperswaded in so thinking.

misper'suasibleness. *nonce-wd.* Incapability of being persuaded.

a **1684** LEIGHTON *Comm.* I. *Pet.* i. 14 Sons of mispersuasibleness [*rendering of* υἱοὺς τῆς ἀπειθείας, *Eph.* v. 6].

misper'suasion. Now *rare* or *Obs.* [MIS-^{1} 4.] Persuasion of what is erroneous; wrong conviction or conception.

1594 HOOKER *Eccl. Pol.* Pref. viii. §13 Touching the sequele of your present misperswasions. **1597** *Ibid.* v. lxviii. §11 Suppose that some haue by misperswasion liued in Schisme. **1667** *Decay Chr. Piety* viii. ¶7 Some misperswasions concerning the divine attributes, which do ..tend..to the corrupting mens manners. **1707** in Hearne *Collect.* (O.H.S.) II. 50 To confirme people in their several mispersuasions. **1829** SOUTHEY *Sir T. More* II. 207 Persons ..under a fatal but invincible mispersuasion. **1834** *Oxf. Univ. Mag.* I. 47 Till the mispersuasion is eradicated from the mind of the public.

mispickel ('mɪspɪkəl). *Min.* Also 7 -pickle, 8 -pikel. [a. G. *mispickel*, formerly also *mispütl*, *mispilt*, of obscure origin.] Native arsenosulphide of iron; arsenical pyrites; arsenopyrite. Also *attrib.*

1683 PETTUS *Fleta Minor* II. 7 All Silver Oars..free from Flint, Blent, Cobolt, Mispickle, Glimmer, Wolferan. *Ibid.*, The Blent, Cobolt, or mispickle Oars. **1789** in *Med. Comm.* II. 350 Specimens of aerated barytes that contain ramifications of mispikel. **1801** CHENEVIX in *Phil. Trans.* XCI. 215 To ascertain the quantity of metallic arsenic in mispickel. **1839** URE *Dict. Arts* 681 Mispickel is a tin-white mineral, which emits a garlic smell at the blowpipe.

Hence † **mispickly** *a.*, resembling mispickel.

1683 PETTUS *Fleta Minor* I. 230 What is splendy, mispickly, glimery or spady.

mis'place, *v.* [MIS-^{1} 1.]

1. *trans.* To put in a wrong place or in wrong hands.

1594 SHAKS. *Rich. III*, III. ii. 44 Ile haue this Crown of mine cut fro my shoulders, Before ile see the Crowne so foule mis-plac'd. *c* **1600** —— *Sonn.* lxvi, And gilded honor shamefully misplast. **1603** FLORIO *Montaigne* II. xxxi, If he have not washt a glasse well or misplaced a stoole. **1662** STILLINGFL. *Orig. Sacræ* III. i. §9 Many times arguments may be good in their order, but they are mis-placed. **1727** BRADLEY *Fam. Dict.* s.v. *Florist*, Handling a Flower..is..apt to misplace the Leaves. **1781** COWPER *Table-T.* 39 The globe and sceptre in such hands misplaced. **1822-34** *Good's Study Med.* (ed. 4) I. 60 [The teeth] may be misplaced by incurvation, or projection, or obliquity. **1867** FREEMAN *Norm. Conq.* (1877) I. vi. 489 Secondary authorities have altogether misplaced the date.

b. To assign a wrong position to.

1551 RECORDE *Cast. Knowl.* (1556) 157 To prooue that it [the earth] standeth in the myddle of the worlde,..I wyll declare certayne inuincible reasons for confutation of them that mysseplace it. **1779** FORREST *Voy. N. Guinea* 6 That..the Spaniards, in their posterior charts, misplaced Solomon's islands.

† **c.** *absol.* To misplace one's words. *Obs.*

1603 SHAKS. *Meas. for M.* II. i. 90 *Elb.* Proue it before these varlets here thou honorable man, proue it. *Esc.* Doe you heare how he misplaces?

2. To set (one's affections) on a wrong object; to place (one's confidence) amiss; †to spend (time) unprofitably. Usually in pa. pple. (cf. next).

1638 WILKINS *New World* II. (1684) 176 In the study of which, so many do misplace their younger Years. **1665** DRYDEN *Ind. Emp.* v. i, Your guilty kindness why do you mis-place? **1666** M. M. *Solomon's Prescr.* 82 Hast thou misplac't thy heart on a treacherous Friend? **1710** PALMER *Proverbs* 174 A man of honour isn't therefore to be fool'd, because he has mis-plac'd his address. **1784** COWPER *Tiroc.* 50 Power misemployed, munificence misplaced. **1838** JAMES *Robber* I. vii. 159 With that bright confidence which you shall never find misplaced, you have yielded your heart [etc.].

mis'placed, *ppl. a.* [MIS-^{1} 2.] Put in a wrong place; devoted to a wrong object; hence, out-of-place, unseasonable, ill-timed.

1595 SHAKS. *John* III. iv. 133 The mis-plac'd Iohn. **1685** BUNYAN *Pharisee & Publican* 51 This misplacing of Gods Laws, cannot..but produce mis-shaped, and misplaced Obedience. **1759** GOLDSM. *Bee* No. 3 ¶3 Misplaced liberality. **1793** A. YOUNG *Example of France* 58 Two words on this purity will not be entirely misplaced. **1797** BURKE *Regic. Peace* III. ad init., The loose, misplaced stones..of this rough, ill kept..French causeway. **1814** LAMB *Let. to Coleridge* 13 Aug., One's romantic credulity is for ever misleading one into misplaced acts of foolery. **1891** HARDY *Tess* xxxiii, The incident of the misplaced letter.

mis'placement. [MIS-^{1} 4.] The action of misplacing or the condition of being misplaced; wrong position.

1655 H. MORE *Antid. Ath.* App. *Wks.* (1662) 159 The story of the misplacement of certain Mountains on the Earth. **1676** —— *Remarks* 93 The measure of misplacement of the parts of the matter of the Universe. **1876** BRISTOWE *Th. & Pract. Med.* (1878) 867 Misplacements of the kidneys. **1881** WESTCOTT & HORT *Grk. N.T.* II. 301 The confusion arising out of the misplacement of the incident. **1906** J. H. MOULTON *Gram. N.T. Grk.* I. 84 A very curious misplacement of the article occurs in the ὁ ὄχλος πολύς of Jn. 12^9.

mis'placing, *vbl. sb.* [MIS-^{1} 3.] = prec.

1622 BACON *Holy War* Wks. 1827 VII. 131 An omission which is more than a misplacing. **1706** A. BEDFORD *Temple Mus.* ix. 192 The Misplacing of the Accent. **1891** *Athenæum* 31 Oct. 584/1 The erroneous dates have led to much misplacing of the letters.

mis'plant, *v.* [MIS-^{1} 1.] *trans.* To plant amiss; *spec.* in *Fencing* (see quot. 1767).

1692 DRYDEN *Cleomenes* II. i, Thou art..Misplanted in a base degenerate Soil. **1767** FERGUSSON *Dict. Terms Small Sword* 13 To *Misplant*, not to direct any thrust properly.

mis'play. [MIS-^{1} 4.] Wrong play.

1889 *Columbus* (Ohio) *Disp.* 1 Aug., A misplay of any kind would allow the score to be tied. **1894** *Outing* (U.S.) XXIV. 300/2 He was playing a steady, careful game,..apparently waiting for Hovey's misplays.

mis'plead, *v. rare.* [MIS-^{1} 1. AF. had *mespleder.*] *trans.* To plead wrongly or falsely.

1676 BUNYAN *Strait Gate* §44 Wks. (1692) 636/1 You that can tell how to misplead Scripture to maintain your Pride. **1681** HICKERINGILL *Sin Man-catching* Postcr., Wks. 1716 I. 206 They suffer no Man's Cause to perish..by a word misplaced, mis-recited or mis-pleaded.

mis'pleading, *vbl. sb.* [MIS-^{1} 3: cf. prec.] Wrong pleading; a mistake in pleading.

1532 *Dial. on Laws Eng.* II. xlviii. 121 The Iudges shall so instructe hym..that he shall renne into no ieopardy by his mispleadyng. **1540** *Act 32 Hen. VIII*, c. 30 Any myspleading lacke of colour..or jeofaile. **16..** T. ADAMS *Forrest of Thornes* Wks. (1629) 1059 And when the vpshot comes, perhaps the mispleading of a word shall forfeit all. **1775** DE LOLME *Eng. Const.* I. x. (1784) 96 A mispleading, or the like transgression.

† **mis'pleasance.** *Obs.* [MIS-^{1} 7.] Grief, sorrow.

1387-8 T. USK *Test. Love* I. iii. (Skeat) l. 22 There shal no misplesaunce be caused through trespace on my syde.

† **mis'please,** *v. Obs.* [MIS-^{1} 7. Cf. OF. *mesplaire.*]

1. *trans.* To displease.

c **1430** *Hymns Virgin* (1867) 90 Schulde neuere þan þis erþe for þis erþe mysplese heuene king. *c* **1450** LOVELICH *Merlin* 272 God..Js misplesid..whanne ony Synnere doth him hate. **1614** J. DAVIES *Ecl.* in Browne *Sheph. Pipe* G 6 Sith the rude world doon vs misplease That well deseruen.

2. *intr.* To be displeased *with*.

c **1450** LOVELICH *Grail* xxvi. 87 Flegentyne..hire preide þat sche sholde not with hire mysplese. *Ibid.* xxxvi. 556 Wherfore his wyf gan there to mysplese.

† **mis'point,** *v.*^{1} *Obs.* [See DISPOINT *v.*^{1} and MIS-^{1} 9.] *trans.* To balk.

1480 CAXTON *Chron. Eng.* ccxlix, Whan they apperceyued this, that they were myspoynted they saylled strayt to Depe.

mis'point, *v.*^{2} Now *rare* or *Obs.* [MIS-^{1} 1.] *trans.* † **a.** To point with the wrong finger. *Obs.* **b.** To punctuate wrongly; to mispunctuate. Also **mis'pointed** *ppl. a.*, **mis'pointing** *vbl. sb.*

1542 UDALL *Erasm. Apoph.* 87 b, The errour of myspoyntyng with the fynger. **1567-9** JEWEL *Def. Apol.* (1611) 103 You haue purposely corrupted, and mispointed the whole place. **1582** STANYHURST *Æneis*, etc. (Arb.) 157 The mis-poyncting of periods. **1635** JACKSON *Creed* VIII. xxxiii. 376 Those sophistical Novelists who thus mispoint the words of his promise... Verily I say unto thee this day, thou shalt be with me in Paradise. **1649** BP. HALL *Cases Consc.* III. vii. 299 Ambroses mis-pointed reading. **1744** C. WILLATS *Assize Serm. at York* 26 This greatly mistaken passage..could not possibly have been mistaken..if it had not been first mispointed. **1870** LOWELL *Study Wind.* 307 Misprints and mispointings.

† **mis'port**, *v. Obs.* [MIS-¹ 1.] *trans.* To import unlawfully.

c **1630** DONNE *Serm.* (1649) II. xxxiv. 305 When forain merchandize is mis-ported, the Prince may permit, or inhibit his Subjects to buy it, or not to buy it.

mis'praise, *v.* Now *rare.* [MIS-¹ 1, 7.]

1. *trans.* To dispraise, blame.

a **1300** *Cursor M.* 25842 Mai naman mis-prais þe thing þe quilk es broght to god ending. **1340** *Ayenb.* 136 He prayzeþ more þe oþre þe more he him-zelue mispraysеþ. **1481** CAXTON *Reynard* (Arb.) 7 Your Chyldren many yeris herafter shal be myspreysed and blamed therfore. **1850** BLACKIE *Æschylus* I. 196 Thus speaking, ye mispraise the holy rites Of matrimonial Hera and of Jove.

2. To praise amiss. Also *absol.*

a **1631** DONNE *Serm.* (1640) ix. 89 They, whom I have so mispraised, are the worse in the sight of God, for my overpraising. **1888** F. T. PALGRAVE in *19th Cent.* Sept. 341 The natural frailty to mispraise and overpraise.

3. ? Error for: MISPRIZE *v.*¹

1550 *Sheph. Kal.* vii. D vij, When any maketh a vow and misprayseth to doo it.

† **mis'pride.** *Obs. rare*⁻⁰. [f. MIS-¹ 4 + PRIDE *sb.*, after MISPROUD.] Improper pride.

1530 PALSGR. 245/2 Mystakyng of a man selfe or myspride, *oultrecvidance*. *Ibid.* 613/2, I loke ashosshe, or aswasshe, as one dothe upon a thing by disdayne, or mispride.

misprint ('mɪs-, formerly mɪs'prɪnt), *sb.* [f. next.] A mistake in printing; an error of the press.

1818 in TODD. *a* **1834** [see MIS-SCRIPT]. **1884** *Q. Rev.* Jan. 215 The bibliographical information..abounds in errors.. many of them no doubt mere misprints.

mis'print, *v.* [MIS-¹ 1.] **a.** *trans.* To print incorrectly; to make a mistake in printing.

1494 FABYAN *Chron.* VI. cxciv. 198 If Dame Nature had any thynge forgoten or mysprynted in her. **1532** MORE *Confut. Tindale* Wks. 772/1 Leste there myght haue bene some ouersight..by misse writing or mysse pryntynge those fygures of algorisme. **1598** T. SPEGHT *Chaucer's Wks.* B bbb vj, This place is misprinted, as well in misnaming of the signe, as the misreckoning the degrees of the sun. **1629** H. BURTON *Truth's Triumph* 97 Vega's copie hath sanctification haply mis-printed. **1729** FENTON *Wks. E. Waller, Observ.* (1729) p. xix, *Shillingsworth, Walter, Cid,* have been constantly mis-printed for *Chillingworth, Waller,* and *Sid.* **1817** COLERIDGE *Lett.* (1895) 673, I would that the misprinting had been the worst of the..ill-usage.

b. *intr.* Of deer: to leave foot-prints in a pattern different from the usual one.

1909 W. A. & F. BAILLIE-GROHMAN in Edward, Duke of York *Master of Game* 262 A hind..misprints, that is sometimes the hind foot will be placed beside the fore foot, sometimes inside or in front of it. **1957** F. J. T. PAGE *Field Guide Brit. Deer* 71 Misprint. To step irregularly; failure to register [*i.e.* to place the hind feet in the slots made by the fore feet].

misprisal (mɪ'spraɪzəl). *rare.* Also 7 -prizal. [f. MISPRIZE *v.*¹ + -AL¹ 5.] Contempt, disdain, scorn.

1620 [J. PYPER] tr. *Hist. Astrea* VII. 230 The heauens.. will accuse me of misprisall [orig. Fr. *mécognoissance*], if I liue not for you. **1652** KIRKMAN *Clerio & Lozia* 129 If the sots raile against the misprizal that I make of it. **1897** MARIE CORELLI in *Lady's Realm* Mar. 527/2 A marriage-vow sworn in falsification and misprisal of Love.

† **mis'prisement.** *Obs.* [a. OF. *mesprisement*, f. *mespriser* MISPRIZE *v.*¹] Disdain.

1484 CAXTON *Curiall* 3 Therrour of mesprysement whyche thou hast goten.

misprision¹ (mɪ'sprɪʒən). Also 5-6 mes-, mys(se-. [a. AF. *mesprisioun* (whence Law-Latin *misprisio*) = OF. *mesprison, -prision* mistake, error, wrong action or speech :—popular L. **minuspræhensiōnem*, n. of action f. **minuspræhendĕre* (OF. *mesprendre* to mistake, act wrongly, mod.F. *méprendre*): see MIS-² and PREHEND *v.*]

1. *Law.* A wrong action or omission; *spec.* a misdemeanour or failure of duty on the part of a public official.

1425 *Rolls of Parlt.* IV. 306/2 Suche misprisions and defautes of ye said Sherefs. **1491** *Act 7 Hen. VII*, c. 22 §1 Mesprision by hym commytted and doon ayenst the Kynges moost royal persone. **1622** CALLIS *Stat. Sewers* (1647) 120 To pronounce a Traytors judgement upon a Fellon, or a Fellons judgement upon a Traytor, is grand misprision. **1648** COKE *On Litt.* III. lxv. 139 If any man in Westminster Hall [etc.]..shall draw a weapon upon a Judge, or Justice, though he strike not; this is a great misprision. **1875** STUBBS *Const. Hist.* xvi. II. 476 All defaults and misprisions whereby the king was injured or the law broken.

b. ***misprision of treason, of felony***: originally, an offence or misdemeanour akin to treason or felony, but involving a lesser degree of guilt, and not liable to the capital penalty. As various statutes enacted that concealment of a person's knowledge of treasonable actions or designs should be regarded as *misprision of treason*, this term came to be used as the ordinary designation for such concealment.

Hence it was often supposed that the word *misprision* itself expressed the sense of 'failure to denounce' a crime. This imagined sense Sir E. Coke (followed by Blackstone) attempted to account for etymologically, assuming that the word was derived from the OF. *mespris* (mod.F. *mépris*: cf. MISPRIZE *sb.*¹ and *v.*¹) neglect, contempt.

1533-4 *Act 25 Hen. VIII*, c. 22 §9 Yf any person..being commaunded..to take the seid othe..obstynatly refuse that to doo..that every suche refusall shalbe..adjudged mesprysion of high treason. **1551-2** *Act 5 & 6 Edw. VI*, c. 11 Provided also..that concealment or kepinge secrete of any Highe Treason be deemed and taken only mysprision of Treason. **1572** *Act 14 Eliz.* c. 3 That yf any person or persons hereafter..counterfayte any suche kind of Coygne ..as is not the proper Coigne of this Realme... That then everye suche Offence shalbee deemed and adjudged mysprision of Highe Treason. **1579** *Expos. Termes of Law* s.v., Misprision of felonie or trespasse. **1769** BLACKSTONE *Comm.* IV. 119 Misprisions..are..generally understood to be all such high offences as are under the degree of capital, but nearly bordering thereon: and it is said, that a misprision is contained in every treason and felony whatsoever; and that, if the king so please, the offender may be proceeded against for the misprision only. **1855** KINGSLEY *Westw. Ho!* II. vi. 176 Amyas was guilty of something very like misprision of treason in not handing him over to the nearest justice.

¶ **c.** *transf.* in popular use.

a **1662** HEYLIN *Laud* (1668) 54 It was almost made an Heresie..for any one to be seen in his company, and a misprision of Heresie to give him a civil Salutation as he walked the Streets. **1769** *Junius Lett.* ii. 12 A sort of misprision of treason against society. **1855** MOTLEY *Dutch Rep.* II. i. (1866) 134 The edict..provided against all misprision of heresy by making those who failed to betray the suspected liable to the same punishment as if suspected or convicted themselves. **1862** T. A. TROLLOPE *Marietta* I. ix. 153 Guilty of mis-prision of flirting.

† **2.** Wrongful capture. *Obs.*

1442 *Rolls of Parlt.* V. 60/1 How..awners of divers Shippes, that have, be commaundement of the Kynges Counseill, sent their Shippes to the See, and they nought sette in their Shippes Maisters ne Maryners, for their mesprision on the See were putte in grete trouble.

3. The mistaking one thing, word, etc., for another; a misunderstanding; a mistake. *arch.*

1588 SHAKS. *L.L.L.* IV. iii. 98 A Feuer in your bloud! why then incision Would let her out in Sawcers, sweet misprision. **1590** —— *Mids. N.* III. ii. 90. **1594** PLAT *Jewell-ho.* III. 17 By the misprision of the Brewer of English hoppes for Flemish hoppes. **1624** SANDERSON *Serm.* I. 170 An earthly judge is subject to misprision, mis-information, partiality, corruption. **1630** CAPT. SMITH *Trav. & Adv.* Ep. Ded., To prevent therefore all future misprisions, I have compiled this true discourse. **1644** BULWER *Chiron.* 121 To use the Middle-Finger instead of the Index..is much to be condemned... Paschalius alluding to the same misprision of the Hand [etc.]. **1655** tr. *Sorel's Com. Hist. Francion* XII. 30 He intended to have foysted into his Chamber the Coffer.. but by misprision he hid it in the Chamber of Raymond. **1774** J. BRYANT *Mythol.* II. 410 The fable of the Horse certainly arose from a misprision of terms. **1817** LADY GRANVILLE *Lett.* (1894) I. 114 Lady Jersey goes on calling Lord Morley Boringdon, and..he endures this misprision. **1846** J. C. HARE *Mission of Comforter* (1850) 193 The misprision of this passage has aided in fostering the delusive notion.

b. ***misprision of the clerk***: a clerical error.

[In Britton (I. 317, 318) AF. *mesprisioun* is used with reference to misnomer: *mesprisioun de nouns, de vile*.]

1543 tr. *Act 14 Edw. III*, c. 6 That by the misprision of the clerkes of euery place, no proces shalbe adnulled or discontinued, by mistakinge in writynge one syllable or one letter to moche or to lytle. **1543** tr. *Act 8 Hen. VI*, c. 15. **1706** PHILLIPS (ed. Kersey), *Misprision of Clerks*, a Neglect or Default of Clerks in Writing, Engrossing or keeping Records.

† **c.** A malformation: app. regarded as a mistake on the part of Nature. *Obs.*

1650 BULWER *Anthropomet.* 16 To preserve what is according to Nature, and in case of misprision to reduce unto the Naturall state. *Ibid.* 212 These misprisions of Nature in this Organical part.

¶ **d.** Unjust suspicion.

1657 TRAPP *Comm. Esther* v. 2 Neither did he command her to the block, as Henry the eighth did his Anne Bullen, upon a meer misprision of disloyalty. **1705** in W. S. Perry *Hist. Coll. Amer. Col. Ch.* I. 156 Any temporary Misprisons we may for a short time (till the reason of the thing be duly considered) lye under at home.

misprision² (mɪ'sprɪʒən). *arch.* [f. MISPRIZE *v.*¹ after prec.] **a.** Contempt, scorn. **b.** Failure to appreciate or recognize as valuable.

1586 A. DAY *Eng. Secretary* II. (1595) 119 [Such men] do of seruants become sawcie:..of aduisers, arrogant: & consequently, running into euery misprision of others. **1601** SHAKS. *All's Well* II. iii. 159 That dost in vile misprision shackle vp My loue, and her desert. **1692** DRYDEN *St. Euremont's Ess.* 19 The Legions particularly had in great misprision the Adversaries Horse. **1815** SCOTT *Guy M.* iii, Those..persons who..have their hearts barred against conviction by prejudice and misprision. **1871** R. ELLIS tr. *Catullus* lxiv. 301 Peleus sister alike and brother in high misprision Held. **1895** ZANGWILL *Master* I. viii. 96 It seemed an insult to Ruth Hailey, and a misprision of her kindly wishes.

mis'prize, *sb.*¹ *rare.* Also 6 mes-, 6, 9 -prise. [f. MISPRIZE *v.*¹: cf. OF. *mespris*, mod.F. *mépris.*] = prec.

1590 SPENSER *F.Q.* II. vii. 39 Mammon was much displeased, yet no'te he chuse But beare the rigour of his bold mesprise. *a* **1843** G. FIELD in C. R. Leslie *Mem. Constable* (1843) xi, 116 Our most eminent landscape painters..have been subjected..to frequent misprise and neglect. **1898** T. HARDY *Wessex Poems* 154 When I found you, helpless lying, And you waived my deep misprise.

† **mis'prize**, *sb.*² *Obs. rare*⁻¹. [Belongs to MISPRIZE *v.*² Cf. OF. *mesprise*, mod.F. *méprise.*] Mistake.

1590 SPENSER *F.Q.* II. xii. 19 A goodly Ship..Which through great disaventure, or mesprize, Her selfe had ronne into that hazardize.

misprize (mɪ'spraɪz), *v.*¹ Also 5-6 mespryse, 5-9 -prise. [a. OF. *mesprisier, -priser* (mod.F. *mépriser*) = Sp. *menospreciar*, Pg. *menosprezar*:—L. **minuspretiāre*: see MIS-² and PRIZE *v.* Cf. MEPRIZE *v.*] *trans.* **a.** To despise, contemn, scorn. **b.** To fail to appreciate the good qualities of.

1481 CAXTON *Godfrey* liii. (1893) 94 A mescreaunt named arrius which mesprised certeyn poyntes of the fayth. **1530** PALSGR. 635/1 He that mespriseth his betters it shalbe longe or he thrive. **1549** *Compl. Scot.* iii. 28 He that misprisis the correctione of his preceptor. **1599** SHAKS. *Much Ado* III. i. 52 Disdaine and Scorne ride sparkling in her eyes, Mis-prizing what they looke on. **1637** HEYWOOD *Royal King* II. iv, It sorrows me that you misprise my love. **1660** tr. *Amyraldus' Treat. conc. Relig.* II. iii. 205 By misprising and debasing his own worth. **1805** SCOTT *Last Minstr.* v. xxx, Less lik'd he still that scornful jeer Mispris'd the land he lov'd so dear. **1894** BLACKMORE *Perlycross* 23 Her fine qualities..were misprised and under-valued.

† **mis'prize**, *v.*² *Obs.* Also 5 mes-, myspryse, 6-7 misprise. [f. OF. *mespris*, pa. pple. of *mesprendre* to commit a crime (mod.F. *méprendre*). Cf. *comprise, reprise.*]

1. *intr.* To commit an offence, do wrong.

1485 CAXTON *Paris & V.* (1868) 48, I..knowe in my self that I haue mesprysed [orig. *i'ay grandement mespris*] and faylled toward you. *c* **1489** —— *Sonnes of Aymon* ii. 59 Ye mysprysed sore whan my brother..ye made thus shamfully deye. *a* **1500** *Melusine* 79 Yf in eny poynt forsayd [I] haue myssaid or mesprysed.

2. *trans.* To mistake, misunderstand. Also with clause and *absol.*

1598 B. JONSON *Case Altered* IV. i, Monsieur Gaspar.. misprise me not. **1624** MIDDLETON *Game at Chess* V. iii, How you misprize! this is not meant to you-ward. **1657** W. MORICE *Coena quasi Κοινὴ* Def. xv. 206 There are some that misprise their faults to be their perfections.

mi'sprized, *ppl. a.*¹ [f. MISPRIZE *v.*¹ + -ED¹.] **a.** Despised, scorned. **b.** Not appreciated.

1648 J. BEAUMONT *Psyche* XVII. cxli, The best amends I can, I vow to make To my misprised slander'd Piety. **1822** HAZLITT *Table-t.* Ser. II. xi. (1869) 228 Such misprized obligations. **1880** MᶜCARTHY *Own Times* lxvii. IV. 529 The misprized Tiberius. **1899** *Allbutt's Syst. Med.* VIII. 396 The pangs of misprised love.

† **mis'prized**, *ppl. a.*² *Obs.* [f. MISPRIZE *v.*² + -ED¹.] Mistaken.

1590 SHAKS. *Mids. N.* III. ii. 74 You spend your passion on a mispris'd mood.

mis'prizer. *rare.* [f. MISPRIZE *v.*¹ + -ER¹. Cf. OF. *mespriseur.*] A despiser.

1586 A. DAY *Eng. Secretary* II. (1625) 31 Some other misprizers of my courtesies. **1884** *19th Cent.* July 132 The misprizer of the spirit and the worshipper of the body.

mis'prizing, *vbl. sb.* [f. MISPRIZE *v.*¹ + -ING¹.] = MISPRISION².

1485 CAXTON *Chas. Gt.* 132 The mysprysyng that guy had doon in hys presence. **1539** CROMWELL in Merriman *Life & Lett.* (1902) II. 205 For mesprising and avoyding of his abuses. **1601** SHAKS. *All's Well* III. ii. 33 By the misprising of a Maide too vertuous For the contempt of Empire. **1648** W. BROWNE *Polexander* III. v. 145 Our misprising of men might make you doe the same to us. **1875** D. GREENWELL *Liber Human.* 106 What can be a more ignoble misprizing of man's true dignity, than to intimate..that man has no natural thirst after righteousness?

mispro'nounce, *v.* [MIS-¹ 1.] *trans.* To pronounce incorrectly.

1593 NORDEN *Spec. Brit., M'sex* I. 21 Sometime we finde names in England giuen of the French, and mispronounced as..Beaulye for Beaulieu. **1642** MILTON *Apol. Smect.* Wks. 1851 III. 268 They mispronounc't and I mislik't. **1775** SHERIDAN *Rivals* I. ii, Mrs. Malaprop..shall treat me..with her select words so ingeniously misapplied, without being mispronounced. **1865** DICKENS *Mut. Fr.* III. xiv. 119 To correct Mr. Wegg when he grossly mispronounced a word. **1905** *Athenæum* 8 Apr. 430/3 Daily do we suffer from the conversation of persons..who misapply terms, mispronounce words.

mispro'nouncer. [MIS-¹ 5.] One who pronounces words incorrectly.

1885 *Educ. Times* 1 June 207/1 Warnings more adapted to American mispronouncers than to English.

mispronunci'ation. [MIS-¹ 4.] Bad pronunciation.

1530 PALSGR. 12 Lest the lerner shulde accustome any mispronunciation. **1832** tr. *Sismondi's Ital. Rep.* iv. 103 They were made to repeat—*ceci* and *ciceri*, and were, on their mispronunciation, immediately put to death. **1859** R. F. BURTON *Centr. Afr.* in *Jrnl. Geog. Soc.* XXIX. 234 The words Tanganyenka and Tanganyenko used by Dr. Livingstone..are palpable mispronunciations.

mispro'portion, *sb.* [MIS-¹ 4, 7.] Lack of proportion.

1825 COLERIDGE *Aids Refl.* (1848) I. 213 The temporary deformity and misproportions of immaturity. **1847** H. BUSHNELL *Chr. Nurture* (1861) viii. 219 A certain misproportion is induced which distempers all our efforts.

mispro'portion, *v.* [MIS-1 1.] *trans.* 'To join without due proportion' (Johnson).

†**mispro'portionateness.** *Obs.* [MIS-1 4, 7.] = DISPROPORTIONATENESS.

1587 GOLDING *De Mornay* xiv. (1592) 223 Mans Soule.. is troubled by the distemperature or misproportionateness of the body.

mispro'portioned, *ppl. a.* [MIS-1 2.] Badly or wrongly proportioned.

1552 HULOET, Misproporcioned, *ineffigiatus*. **1587** GOLDING *De Mornay* xiv. (1592) 222 A mishapen and misproportioned head. **1657** EARL MONM. tr. *Paruta's Pol. Disc.* 73 This monstrous body of the Roman Empire being composed of almost incompatible, ill-govern'd, and misproportioned parts. **1710** M. HENRY *Christ. No Sect* Wks. 1857 II. 458/1 When.. the exercises of devotion are either.. misplaced or misproportioned. **1879** DOWDEN *Southey* iii. 76 The rage of Popery working in his misproportioned features.

misproud (mɪs'praʊd), *a. Obs.* exc. *arch.* [MIS-1 6.] Wrongly or wickedly proud; arrogant.

1303 R. BRUNNE *Handl. Synne* 3047 3yf þou for strenkþe be mysproute, And hast bostful wrdys and loude. *a* **1400** HYLTON *Scala Perf.* (W. de W. 1494) II. xiv, And yf ony man wolde lette his mysproude wyll he wexith felle & wrothe. **1545** RAYNOLD *Byrth Mankynde* Prol. B vij, Vtterly abhorryng.. all fardyng, paynting, and counterfeit cast colours: which of some dampnable and mysproude people be dayly vsed. **1593** SHAKS. *3 Hen. VI*, II. vi. 7 Impairing Henry, strength'ning misproud Yorke. **1605** CHAPMAN, etc. *Eastw. Hoe* III. ii, Ah thou misproude Prentise, dar'st thou presume to marry a Ladies sister? **1810** SCOTT *Lady of L.* v. xxvi, Thy mis-proud ambitious clan. **1864** MISS YONGE *Bk. Golden Deeds* 169 A bold but misproud and violent prince.

†**mis'proving**, *vbl. sb. Obs.* [f. MIS-1 7 + PROVE *v.* = thrive.] Falling off, failure. So **mis'proving** *ppl. a.*, failing, unsuccessful.

1542 UDALL *Erasm. Apoph.* 101 b, To laye vnto ye Goddes ye faulte of quaillyng and mysprouyng. **1798** *Trans. Soc. Arts* XVI. 204 By too thin planting I am subject to more misproving crops. *Ibid.* 209 If I try any fresh experiment, I never condemn it for misproving one year.

mis'punctuate, *v.* [MIS-1 1.] *trans.* and *intr.* To punctuate incorrectly.

a **1849** POE *Marginalia* v, The writer who neglects punctuation, or mis-punctuates, is liable to be misunderstood. **1897** *Daily News* 3 Sept. 6/2 A mispunctuated sentence.

So **mispunctu'ation**, wrong punctuation.

1807 SOUTHEY *Espriella's Lett.* (1814) III. 65 Omissions which alter the meaning, or mispunctuations which destroy it. **1879** W. S. SIMPSON in *Mem.* (1899) 87, I have corrected one or two mispunctuations.

†**mis'queme**, *v. Obs.* [MIS-1 7.] *trans.* To displease, offend.

?*c* **1395** *Plowman's Tale* 647 But if any man these misqueme, He shal be baited as a bere. **1658** PHILLIPS *Misqueam*, (old word) to displease.

misquo'tation. [MIS-1 4.] **a.** Inaccuracy in quoting. **b.** An incorrect quotation.

1773 JOHNSON *Note on Shaks. Ant. & Cl.* I. v, The misquotation of *stall-worn* for *stall-worth*. **1833** DICKENS *Sk. Boz, Tales* ix, He could never sit by and hear a misquotation from the 'Swan of Avon' without setting the unfortunate delinquent right. **1867** LEWES *Hist. Philos.* (ed. 3) I. 90 He is guilty of a very gross misquotation of Aristotle.

mis'quote, *v.* [MIS-1 1.] *trans.* To quote incorrectly.

1596 SHAKS. *1 Hen. IV*, v. ii. 13 Looke how we can, or sad or merrily, Interpretation will misquote our lookes. **1699** COLLIER *Def. Short View* 36 Because I Misquoted *Wasting Air*, for *Wafting Air*. **1771** *Junius Lett.* lxi. 316 You answer .. by misquoting his words, and mistating his propositions. **1835** LYTTON *Rienzi* I. i, They.. misquote Latin over their cups. **1891** *Law Times* XCII. 18/1 Mr. Besant.. accused Mr. Willis of intentionally misquoting him.

absol. **1809** BYRON *Bards & Rev.* 66 With just enough of learning to misquote.

So **mis'quoter**; **mis'quoting** *vbl. sb.*

1673 [R. LEIGH] *Transp. Reh.* 147 His disingenuity is visible in his.. misquoting of Thorndikes passage of Schism. **1830** *Blackw. Mag.* XXVIII. 894 We are sad misquoters.

mis'quote, *sb.* [MIS-1 4.] An incorrect quotation, a misquotation.

1855 J. A. SYMONDS *Let.* Sept. (1967) I. 61 How very kind of M. de Condolle it was to lend Mdlle the three missquotes. *a* **1953** E. O'NEILL *Touch of Poet* (1957) I. 30 Disdainfully, emphasizing his misquote of the line from Byron. **1968** C. M. VINES *Little Nut-Brown Man* ix. 149 'Preferred not to' had a different nuance from 'was not well enough to'.. it seemed a curious misquote. **1974** *Daily Tel.* 21 Oct. 16 Mr Heath made little attempt to correct the misquotes and inaccurate statements made by various Labour politicians.

mis'rate, *v.* Now *rare.* [MIS-1 1.] *trans.* To estimate wrongly. Also **mis'rating** *vbl. sb.*

1624 HEYWOOD *Captives* I. i. in Bullen *O. Pl.* IV. 112, I have bethought mee better nowe to keepe This business secrett.. And not to make it publicke and this honest Purpose of myne by that meanes misreated. *a* **1626** BACON *Ordin. Admin. Chanc.* (1642) 2 Any pretended misrating or misvaluing. *a* **1677** BARROW *Serm.* Wks. 1686 III. xxix. 317 Either assuming false, or misrating true advantages. **1691** NORRIS *Pract. Disc.* 65 By this means we shall mis-rate both Persons and Things. **1804** EUGENIA DE ACTON *Tale without Title* III. 139 A boy, who.. greatly misrates her endowments.

mis'read, *v.* [MIS-1 1.] *trans.* To read or interpret wrongly.

1809 J. BARLOW *Columb.* x. 368 War sure hath ceased; or have my erring eyes Misread the glorious visions of the skies? **1851** ROBERTSON *Serm.* Ser. I. xvii. (1866) 297 Let not the rich misread the signs of the times. **1879** FROUDE *Cæsar* xiii. 189 He misread the disposition of the great body of citizens.

So **mis'reader**; **mis'reading** *vbl. sb.*

1847–8 DE QUINCEY *Protestantism* Wks. 1858 VIII. 150 The New Testament had said nothing directly upon the question of slavery; nay, by the misreader it was rather supposed indirectly to countenance that institution. **1849** H. MILLER *Footpr. Creat.* xv. (1874) 300 The hypothesis involves a misreading of the geologic records. **1866** KINGSLEY *Herew.* I. iii. 105 *note*, 'Ulcus Ferreus', says Richard of Ely; surely a misreading for uncus. **1885** *Law Rep. 29 Chanc. Div.* 210 A misreading of the clause.

misre'cital. [MIS-1 4.] An incorrect recital or account.

1539 *Act 31 Hen. VIII* c. 13 §16 For mysrecitall or non recitall of leases. **1634** *Jrnls. Irish Ho. Lords* (1779) I. 20 The Lords of the Committee perused the Journal-Book.. and amended what Mistakes and Misrecitals they found. **1818** CRUISE *Digest* (ed. 2) V. 23 Though founded upon a misrecital. **1850** *New Eng. Hist. & Gen. Reg.* IV. 309 It is drawn up with technical accuracy... A misrecital would have then been fatal to the suit. **1863** KINGLAKE *Crimea* I. xvii. 350 The Turkish Government soon detected in it not only a misrecital of history, but [etc.].

misre'cite, *v.* [MIS-1 1.] *trans.* To recite incorrectly; to give a wrong account or rendering of. Also *absol.*

1591 SYLVESTER *Du Bartas* I. vi. (1641) 49/2 If the Grecians doe not mis-recite. **1596** BACON *Max. Com. Law* xxv. (1630) 97 The reference of the Pattent, the date whereof was mis-recited. **1628** COKE *On Litt.* 46 b, If a man.. mis-recite a lease in point materiall which is in esse. *a* **1715** BURNET *Own Time* IV. (1724) I. 639 They [*sc.* words] were often ill heard and ill understood, and were apt to be mis-recited by a very small variation. **1827** HALLAM *Const. Hist.* xii. (1876) II. 419 The committee reported on the 29th of March, after misreciting the order of reference to them in a very remarkable manner.

So **misre'citing** *vbl. sb.* = MISRECITAL.

1572 *Act 14 Eliz.* c. 14 Any suche Mysnamynge, Mysrecyting or not true namynge or recytinge. **1688** PRIDEAUX *Valid. Orders Ch. Eng.* 70 That misreciting which you charge me with.

mis'reckon, *v.* [MIS-1 1.]

1. *trans.* To reckon, compute, or calculate (an amount) incorrectly; also, to make a wrong calculation in respect of (a certain number).

1524–5 *Rec. St. Mary at Hill* (1904) 330 For xxix *ll* of wax whiche was MisRekonyd in the byll of her Acount. *a* **1553** UDALL *Royster D.* I. iv. (Arb.) 28, I am not so olde, thou misreckonest my yeares. **1614** RALEIGH *Hist. World* II. (1634) 421 It is a familiar error in Josephus to misreckon times. **1669** STURMY *Mariner's Mag.* v. viii. 27 The mistake of a quarter of an Inch.. may make you misreckon a Gallon in the Content. **1717** BERKELEY *Jrnl. Tour Italy* Wks. 1871 IV. 567 Avellino reckons (I doubt misreckons) 30,000.

fig. **1628** BP. HALL *Serm. Lds. Parlt.* 5 Apr. 22 Bee sure, if we be forgetfull, God will not mis-reckon his owne mercies. *a* **1716** SOUTH *Serm.* (1727) VI. 397 His Heart misreckons him; and therefore when he comes to rectify his Account by the Measure God takes of Things [etc.].

2. *pass.*, *refl.*, and *intr.* To make a wrong calculation; to be out in one's reckoning. (Cf. F. *se mécompter.*)

a. *pass.* **1530** PALSGR. 638/1, I had rather paye to moche than to be mysrekened. **1586** in Ellis *Orig. Lett.* Ser. I. III. 8 Wherein no doubt he was misreckened.

b. *refl.* **1603** FLORIO *Montaigne* I. xxx. (1632) 103 He that hath once misreckoned himselfe is never seene againe. **1667** FLAVEL *Saint Indeed* (1754) 68 Thou misreckonest thyself, when thou think'st My provision is almost spent.

c. *intr.* *a* **1608** DEE *Relat. Spir.* I. (1659) 90 Where have I misreckoned, I pray you? **1614** B. JONSON *Barth. Fair* II. ii, Drinke with all companies, though you be sure to be drunke: you'll mis-reckon the better, and be lesse asham'd on't **1708** SWIFT *Sent. Ch. Eng. Man* Wks. 1755 II. I. 69 [He] must allow himself out, though.. he may not see in which article he has misreckoned. **1831** CARLYLE *Sart. Res.* I. xi, Wherefrom, if I misreckon not, your perspicacity will draw fullest insight.

†**3.** *trans.* To present an incorrect (esp. an exorbitant) account to (a person). *Obs.*

1640 BROME *Sparagus Gard.* III. ii. E 4 b, *Ex. Gen.* Who would be troubled with such pinching guests? *Gar.* I, tis good to misreckon such to be rid of 'hem. **1654** WHITLOCK *Zootomia* 335 For Arithmetick; who can misreckon a woman (they can men) in payments?

mis'reckoning, *vbl. sb.* [MIS-1 3.] Incorrect reckoning or casting of accounts; miscalculation.

1540 PALSGR. *Acolastus* b iv, To helpe to vndo hym with mysse reckenynge and false dyce. **1562** J. HEYWOOD *Prov. & Epigr.* (1867) 161 Misrecknyng is no payment. **1647** TRAPP *Comm. 2 Tim.* ii. 18 As inconsiderate Mariners, by misreckoning of a point, they have missed the haven. **1792** *Phil. Trans.* LXXXII. 103 By these precautions, almost all possibility of a misreckoning was prevented. **1845** LD. CAMPBELL *Chancellors* lxxxix. (1857) IV. 203 Seeing Lord Norris had not observed it, he went on with his misreckoning often.

misreco'llect, *v.* [MIS-1 1.] *trans.* and *intr.* To recollect wrongly or imperfectly. (A favourite word of Bentham's.)

1787 BENTHAM *Def. Usury* vi. 49 If I do not misrecollect, I remember instances. *a* **1832** —— *Mem. & Corr.* Wks. 1843 X. 60 He received, if I misrecollect not, the sum of £1000.

So **misreco'llection.**

1802–12 BENTHAM *Ration. Judic. Evid.* (1827) IV. 261 To enable him.. to reflect upon it, without danger of misrecollection. **1818** *Champion* 20 Dec. in *Athenæum* (1891) 26 Dec. 865/3 Oblivion, or misrecollection of the past. **1922** O. JESPERSEN *Lang.* iii. 70 He speaks.. of other linguistic changes as well. These he refers to the following causes... (1) Mishearing and misunderstanding; (2) misrecollection; [etc.].

†**mis'rede**, *v. Obs.* Also 4 *pa. pple.* misirad, mysrad. [OE. *misrǽdan* = MDu., Du. *misraden*, OHG. *misserâten* (G. *missraten*); cf. ON. *misráðit* (neut. pa. pple): see MIS-1 1, and REDE *v.*, READ *v.*] *trans.* To misadvise. Also *absol.*

c **960** ÆTHELWOLD *Rule St. Benet* lxiv. (Schröer 1885) 117 ȝif ȝeferræden þæne ræd on ȝemænum ȝeþeahte misredað [*v.r.* missrædað]. *c* **1200** *Trin. Coll. Hom.* 215 þenne cumeð þe werse to sume mannes heorte.. and þus him misredeð. *a* **1300** *K. Horn* 308 Sore ihc me ofdrede, He wolde horn misrede. **1320** *Cast. Love* 427 Ac as a Mon mis-I-rad [*ed. Hall.* mysrad] On vche half he is mis-bi-lad. **1340** *Ayenb.* 184 þe ilke þet ylefþ liȝtliche uint ofte þet me him.. misret.

†**misre'gard**, *sb. Obs.* [MIS-1 4.] Lack of regard, respect, or care; neglect; contempt.

1542 RECORDE *Gr. Artes* (1640) To Rdr., Contempt or misregard of learning. **1596** SPENSER *F.Q.* IV. viii. 29 When as these rimes be red With misregard. **1637** GILLESPIE *Eng. Pop. Cerem.* III. iv. 50 There was also a great contempt and misregard shewed to the King. **1655** tr. *Sorel's Com. Hist. Francion* XII. 31 He found a small Seal.. by mis-regard huddled in amongst the rest.

†**misre'gard**, *v.* Chiefly *Sc. Obs.* [MIS-1 1.] *trans.* To have no regard for; to despise, disregard.

1582 *Reg. Privy Council Scot.* (1880) III. 470 Thay wald gif his Majestie occasioun.. to think his letter.. misregardit. **1632** LITHGOW *Trav.* x. 453 The Kings safe Conduct he mis-regarded, giuing it neyther Respect not trust. **1697** in A. Fergusson *Laird of Lag* (1886) 247 They having misregarded all former admonitions of the Synod.

Hence †**misre'garder**, one who disregards.

1632 LITHGOW *Trav.* v. 228 Beeing vntamed Sauages, and mis-regarders of ciuility.

mis'register, *sb. Printing.* [MIS-1 4.] The incorrect positioning of printed matter in relation to other printed matter on the same sheet, esp. of two or more colours in relation to each other.

1931 *National Lithographer* Feb. 27/2 It was determined to study first the factors causing misregister. **1949** R. F. REED *What Lithographer should know about Paper* (Lithographic Technical Foundation, N.Y., Technical Bull. No. 8) 50 While misregister in the ordinary sense never occurs until two or more colors have been printed, it is obvious that improper printing of the first color may be.. the real cause of register trouble. **1963** C. W. LATHAM *Advanced Pressmanship* xvii. 130 When the first color plate does not register with another color plate it may be termed internal misregister or mis-hit. **1966** R. R. COUPE *Sci. of Printing Technol.* ii. 47 The need to avoid misregister in multicolour work is usually regarded as the major reason for air-conditioning, but there are many others. **1968** *Gloss. Terms Offset Lithogr. Printing* (*B.S.I.*) 30 *Mis-register*, the appearance of the printed image out of its correct position. **1970** R. F. REED *What Printer should know about Paper* (Graphic Arts Technical Foundation, Pittsburgh) iii. 33 Distortion due to wavy-edged paper is probably the most common and serious cause of misregister on sheet-fed offset presses.

Hence **mis'registered** *ppl. a.*

1963 C. W. LATHAM *Advanced Pressmanship* xvii. 130 If the plate is at fault, the same misregistered image will show the same error sheet after sheet.

mis'register, *v.* [MIS-1 1.] *trans.* To form from elements that are not properly aligned or positioned.

1969 G. L. HANSEN *Introd. Solid-State Television Syst.* xi. 265 It is imperative that the optical alignment of the light paths be precise. If they are not, the reproduced color image will be misregistered. That is, each image will not be located at exactly the same point on the camera tube.. and a blurred presentation will result. **1969** P. B. JORDAIN *Condensed Computer Encycl.* 278 If a line is misregistered irregularly, that is, if some characters are high, others low, etc., then line registration is bypassed in favor of character registration.

ˌmisregi'stration. [MIS-1 4.] Faulty or imperfect registration (i.e. alignment or positioning) of images, *spec.* of the three fields that compose a colour television picture.

1942 H. C. MCKAY *Photographic Negative* IV. x. 649 The neutralized areas will print out gray, and the lines of misregistration will print dark. **1952** *Electronics* Nov. 216/2 Color edging includes color fringing, misregistration, etc. **1960** *Electronic Engin.* XXXII. 71 Misregistration is the least favourable feature of colour television as at present conceived. **1969** P. B. JORDAIN *Condensed Computer Encycl.* 87 Character misregistration takes the form of character high, character low, or character skew. **1971** [see FACTURE 4]. **1971** H. E. ENNES *Television Broadcasting* x. 469 This beam pulling or dynamic misregistration results in colored edges.

†**misre'hearsal.** *Obs.* [MIS-1 4.] Misrecital, misquotation.

1472–3 *Rolls of Parlt.* VI. 49/1 Any mysrehersell of the premisses in any wise notwithstondyng. **1523** MORE in Wordsw. *Eccl. Biogr.* (1853) II. 60 If it mishappen me.. for lacke for good utterance, and misrehearsal to pervert.. their prudent instructions. **1631** C. MORE *Life Sir T. More* (1828) 332 They laid to his charge.. the.. misrehearsal of Tindall's arguments.

†**misre'hearse**, *v. Obs.* [MIS-[1] 1.] *trans.* To misrecite, misquote. Also *absol.*
1533 MORE *Debell. Salem* Pref., Wks. 931/1 The man hath ..misse rehearsed them to make the reader wene..I had written wronge. *Ibid.* xvii. Wks. 1009/1 He woulde make you wene here, that I bothe misserehearse and misseconstrue.

†**misre'join**, *v. Law. Obs.* [f. MIS-[1] 1 + REJOIN *v.*[1]] *intr.* To reply wrongly to a pleading.
a **1625** SIR H. FINCH *Law* (1636) 398 No repleader shall be notwithstanding that the Tenant haue..misreioyned.

†**mis'reke**, *v. Obs.* [f. MIS-[1] 1 + REKE *v.*[1]] *intr.* To go astray.
a **1250** *Owl & Night.* 490 Vor sumerestyde is al wlonk & doþ mysreken monnes þonk. *Ibid.* 675 & sone may a word mysreke þar muþ schal ayeyn horte speke.

misre'late, *v.* [MIS-[1] 1.] *trans.* To relate or recount incorrectly. Also *absol.* So **misre'lating** *vbl. sb.*, **misre'lation**, incorrect relation or account; also **misre'lated** *ppl. a.*, wrongly related or connected.
1621 BP. MOUNTAGU *Diatribæ* 489 It could not be, you should so often mistake, or mis-relate, if you had trusted your owne eyes. **1625** —— *App. Cæsar* 118 Historicall mistakings, misrelatings. *a* **1656** HALES *Gold. Rem.* II. (1673) 4 That if any thing were either omitted or misrelated, it might be rectified. *a* **1663** BRAMHALL *Def. True Liberty* Ep. Ded., To press home those things in writing..(a course much to be preferred before verbal conferences, as being..less subject to mistakes and misrelations). **1674** HICKMAN *Quinquart. Hist.* (ed. 2) 226 Some things done in England, and misrelated by the Doctor, must be rectified. **1892** *Pall Mall G.* 16 July 3/1 Here are two flagrantly misrelated participles.

†**misre'ligion**. *Obs.* [MIS-[1] 4.] False religion. So †**misre'ligious** *a.*
1623 BP. HALL *Best Bargaine* Wks. (1625) 518 The eternall state of their soules hath not seemed too deare to cast away vpon an ill bargaine of mis-religion. **1625** —— *Contempl., O.T.* XVIII. *Seduced Prophet* Ibid. 1320 No pestilence should bee more shunned then the conuersation of the mis-religious. **1648** *British Bell-man* 1 Perjury and Lyes in their Mouths, Falshoods, Treasons, Misreligions in their hearts.

misre'member, *v.* [MIS-[1] 1.]
1. *trans.* To remember wrongly, imperfectly, or incorrectly; to have an imperfect recollection of. Now chiefly *dial.*, to forget, 'disremember'.
1533 MORE *Answ. Poysoned Bk.* Wks. 1139/1 Not the pacifier but my selfe was ouersene in that place wyth a litle hast, in misse remembring one worde of his. **1641** LD. FINCH in Rushw. *Hist. Coll.* (1692) I. 226 He who twice upon Oath with time of recollection, could not remember any thing of such a Business, might well a third time misremember somewhat. **1769** BLACKSTONE *Comm.* IV. vi. 80 [Words] may be.. mistaken, perverted, or mis-remembered by the hearers. **1802–12** BENTHAM *Ration. Judic. Evid.* (1827) I. 170 The oftener a man has had to give an account of a fact the less likely he is to have forgotten it or in any point misremembered it. **1851** CARLYLE *Sterling* I. i. 8 A tumult having risen around his name..so that he could not be forgotten, and could only be misremembered. **1856** LEVER *Martins* xv, He forgets many a thing, but no man living can say that he ever misremembered a duel. **1890** W. A. WALLACE *Only a Sister?* xxix. 325 A doctor—..I misremember his name.
2. *absol.* or *intr.*
a **1631** DONNE *Lett. to Pers. Honour* (1651) 191 He is practising for the Mask, of which, if I mis-remember not, I writ as much as you desire to know in a letter. **1713** DERHAM *Phys. Theol.* 64 *note*, A Cave, which (if I misremember not) was lined with those Stalactical-Stones. **1815** W. TAYLOR in Robberds *Mem.* (1843) II. 454, I did not like to write to you without the book at my elbow, least I should misremember. **1841** LEVER *C. O'Malley* xcix, 'What do they call the convent?' 'It is a hard word, I misremember'.
So **misre'membrance** *rare.*
1542 RECORDE *Gr. Artes* (1575) 338 You would not haue me trust to memorie till I were better experte, leaste oftentimes I happen by misse remembraunce to bee abused. **1831** MACKINTOSH *Hist. Eng.* II. 200 Every misremembrance into which hurry or faintness plunged her.

†**mis'rempe**, *v. Obs.* [? f. MIS-[1] 1 + REMP *v.*] *intr.* ? To go astray.
a **1250** *Owl & Night.* 1787 Telle ic con word after worde & if þe þinkþ þat ic misrempe þu stond ayeyn and do me crempe.

mis'render, *v.* [MIS-[1] 1.] *trans.* To render or interpret incorrectly. So **mis'rendering** *vbl. sb.*
1661 BOYLE *Style of Script.* 64 The misrendring of the Original Particles. **1674** SCHEFFER *Lapland* ii. 59, I suppose they are both mistaken, and misrender'd them leaden darts. **1693** *Answ. Treat. Just Measures* 39 Those who so mistook and misrendred the design of the Brethren. **1871** LIGHTFOOT *Revision New Test.* iv. 178 'Your devotions' is not a misrendering but an archaism, signifying 'the objects of your worship'. **1883** *Harper's Mag.* Feb. 468/1 He would not admit that Shakespeare would allow Burbage to misrender Hamlet.

misre'peat, *v.* [MIS-[1] 1.] *trans.* To repeat incorrectly.
1615 BACON *Charge agst. Mr. I. S.* in *Resuscitatio* (1657) 61 Because I will not mistake, or mis-repeat, you shall hear the Seditious Libell, in the proper termes..thereof. **1645** PRYNNE *Fresh Discov.* 36 He misrepeats, and misapplies some Passages of mine. *a* **1715** BURNET *Own Time* II. (1724) I. 296 Words, they said, might be misunderstood, misrepeated and denied.

misre'port, *sb.* [MIS-[1] 4.]
†**1.** 'Evil report'; unfavourable repute. *Obs.*
1412–20 LYDG. *Chron. Troy* II. xix, Without spot of trespasse or of blame Of mysreporte in hyndrynge of our name. **1553** T. WILSON *Rhet.* 59 b, Any misreport or evil behavior of our party here tofore. **1589** COOPER *Admon.* 12 They..shall often light into..misliking of many, and thereby get misreport. **1697** STILLINGFL. *Disc. Trinity* 42 The mis-report of him came from his zeal against Sabellianism.
2. A false or erroneous report, as of the actions or character of a person.
1530 PALSGR. 585/1, I hynder ones promocion by my mysse reporte. **1535** COVERDALE *Num.* xiv. 37 Because they brought vp a myszreporte of the lande that it was euell. *a* **1649** DRUMM. OF HAWTH. *Hist. Jas. II* Wks. (1711) 26 The king at first was loth to lend an ear to misreports and calumnies of a man lately so well deserving. **1736** CARTE *Ormonde* I. 312 The apprehension he lay under of those misreports. **1865** CARLYLE *Fredk. Gt.* XVIII. vi. VII. 193 An Aide-de-Camp made a small misnomer, misreport of one word, which was terribly important. **1901** A. LANG *Magic & Relig.* 44 If they are all misreports..what is the value of anthropological evidence?
b. without article, in generalized use.
1535 STARKEY *Lett.* p. xvii, Yf I had found truth in dede thes thyngys wych by mysreport ther wyth you were commynly sayd. **1581** LAMBARDE *Eiren.* II. vii. (1602) 253 The one chargeth the other with words of misreport. **1660** INGELO *Bentiv. & Ur.* I. (1682) 65 You may have receiv'd misreport concerning him. **1748** RICHARDSON *Clarissa* (1811) VIII. 55 That I should..be the occasion..of widening differences by light misreport.

misre'port, *v.* [MIS-[1] 1.]
1. *trans.* To report (a matter) erroneously; to give a false or imperfect account of (an event, statement, opinion, or the like).
c **1430** LYDG. *Compl. Bl. Knt.* 605, I am worthy for to bere the blame If any thing here misreported be. **1592** GREENE *Conny Catch.* III. 25 This tale, because it was somewhat misreported before...is set downe now in true forme. *a* **1641** BP. MOUNTAGU *Acts & Mon.* (1642) 230 He misreporteth Herods off-spring and descent. **1722** DE FOE *Plague* Wks. (Bohn) V. 30 There has been heretofore much abuse in misreporting the disease. **1830** DE QUINCEY *Bentley* Wks. 1857 VII. 60 His behaviour..scandalously misreported by Bennet. **1874** MOTLEY *John of Barneveld* I. iv. 203 Villeroy had..been making mischief..by reporting and misreporting private conversations.
†**b.** const. acc. with inf. or pres. pple. *Obs.*
1574 tr. *Marlorat's Apocalips* 39 [They] boast themselues to be professors of the true faythe, and misreport thee to folow a false doctrine. **1579** FULKE *Heskins' Parl.* 4 You misreport S. Peter being a Lord of the higher house.
2. To give a false report or account of the statements or opinions of (a person).
1531 LATIMER *Let. to Baynton* in Foxe *A. & M.* (1583) 1747/1 Christ himselfe was misreported, & falsely accused. **1675** BAXTER *Cath. Theol.* II. I. 11 You wholly mistake and misreport us. **1699** COLLIER *Def. Short View* 127 He calls me an unfair Adversary, as if I had misreported him. **1862** RAWLINSON *Anc. Mon. Chald.* I. viii. 215 The probability would seem to be, that Berosus has been misreported.
†**3.** To speak ill of; to slander. *Obs.*
1534 MORE *Comf. agst. Trib.* II. Wks. 1209/2 Leste he should geue other folke occasion to..misreporte hym for an hypocryte. **1603** SHAKS. *Meas. for M.* V. i. 148 A man that neuer yet Did (as he vouches) mis-report your Grace. **1625** in Ferguson & Nanson *Munic. Rec. Carlisle* (1887) 280 James Blaklocke..did misreport and slaunder the wife of Alexander Addle..in calling her shepe stealer.
†**4.** *intr.* To give a false report (*of*). *Obs.*
1572 HULOET, To misreporte of an other. **1579** W. WILKINSON *Confut. Fam. Love* 10 If to slaunder and misreport be a worke of righteousnesse. **1601** J. WHEELER *Treat. Comm.* 62 The doings, which..they..doe..misreport of.
So **misre'ported** *ppl. a.*, **misre'porting** *vbl. sb.*
1513 BRADSHAW *St. Werburge* II. 2014 Go forth litell boke, Iesu be thy spede And saue the alway from mysreportyng. **1607** MARKHAM *Caval.* I. (1617) 20 It shall appeare great honor to our nation, and much shame to them who haue wrongd it with former misreportings. **1690** LOCKE *Hum. Und.* I. xxi. §62 The wrong Judgment that misleads us,..lies in misreporting upon the various Comparisons of these. **1846** GROTE *Greece* I. xvi. I. 543 A misreported exaggerated and ornamented recital.

misre'porter. [MIS-[1] 5.] One who misreports.
1553 GRIMALDE *Cicero's Offices* II. (1558) 87 Dishonest mis-reporters [orig. *maledicos*]. **1584** *Reg. Privy Council Scot.* Ser. I. III. 648 To stope the mouthis of misreportaris. **1624** GATAKER *Transubst.* 114 As this mis-reporter and mis-expounder of him affirmeth. **1748** RICHARDSON *Clarissa* (1811) VII. 264 Let misreporters say what they will.

ˌ**misrepre'sent**, *v.* [MIS-[1] 1.]
1. *trans.* To represent improperly or imperfectly; to give a false representation or account of.
1647 CLARENDON *Hist. Reb.* II. §49 Those..who had done them ill offices, and misrepresented their carriage to the King. **1677** GILPIN *Demonol.* II. ix. 390 Satan doth endeavour to misrepresent God to troubled Souls. **1726** SWIFT *Gulliver* III. viii, They had so horribly misrepresented the Meaning of those Authors to Posterity. **1846** WRIGHT *Ess. Mid. Ages* II. xiii. 87 Popular tradition generally misrepresents the actions, but not the character of its hero. **1879** FROUDE *Cæsar* xxi. 352 He had been himself misrepresented to his countrymen.
absol. **1671** MILTON *Samson* 124 This, this is he..Or do my eyes misrepresent? **1822** COBBETT *Weekly Reg.* 9 Feb. 362 If I had misrepresented, why not prove it?
2. To fail to represent correctly or adequately as agent or official representative.
1860 MILL *Repr. Govt.* (1865) 55 The constituencies to which most of the highly educated..persons..belong..are ..either unrepresented or misrepresented.
So **misrepre'sented** *ppl. a.*, **mis'representing** *vbl. sb.* and *ppl. a.*
1688 *Pulpit-Sayings* 14 Such, who pretend to be clear from the Imputation of Misrepresenting. **1699** COLLIER *Def. Short View* 90 He understands the Art of Misrepresenting. **1817** DR. T. CHALMERS in *Mem.* (1850) II. 140, I had previously read the misrepresented passage to Mr. Chalmers. **1887** *Pall Mall G.* 28 Nov. 12/1 It [a company] can recover the purchase money from the misrepresenting vendors.

ˌ**misrepresen'tation**. [MIS-[1] 4.]
1. Wrong or incorrect representation of facts, statements, the character of a person, etc.; the action of misrepresenting.
1647 in Rushw. *Hist. Coll.* IV. (1701) I. 554 Those who have..improved all opportunities..by false Suggestions, Misrepresentations, and otherwise, for the destruction of this Army. **1661** BOYLE *Style of Script.* (1675) 5 The misrepresentation made by these men of the Bible. **1711** ADDISON *Spect.* No. 50 ¶5 Our Guides deceived us with Misrepresentations and Fictions. **1814** WELLINGTON in Gurw. *Desp.* (1838) XII. 9 Misrepresentation of facts is the common practise of the writers for newspapers. **1858** LD. ST. LEONARDS *Handy-Bk. Prop. Law* v. 26 A purchaser.. who makes an actual misrepresentation, which tends to mislead the seller. **1875** HELPS *Soc. Press.* xxv. 403, I never met with a man who bore misrepresentation with thorough calmness.
2. 'Incorrect or unfaithful representation in the capacity of agent or official representative' (*Cent. Dict.* 1890).

ˌ**misrepre'sentative**, *sb.* [MIS-[1] 5.] One who fails to represent others; a bad representative.
1862 *New York Tribune* 26 Jan. (Cassell), A better reply from that misrepresentative of Indiana. **1887** *Pall Mall G.* 18 Apr. 9/1 Until the chairman appealed for order his.. opponents would not hear one of their misrepresentatives.

ˌ**misrepre'sentative**, *a.* [MIS-[1] 6.] Not properly representative (*of*).
1736 SWIFT *Let. to Sheridan* Wks. 1751 XIII. 147 The.. slavish Practices of those mis-representative Brutes. **1892** *Daily Tel.* 18 Aug., The question before the country would be whether the representative or the misrepresentative branch of the Legislature should prevail. **1902** B. KIDD *West. Civilization* 99 Interpretations..utterly misrepresentative of the real meaning of the phenomenon.

ˌ**misrepre'senter**. [MIS-[1] 5.] One who misrepresents.
1688 *Pulpit-Sayings* 15 They must not take it amiss, if as they were misrepresenters then, they are esteem'd Misrepresenters still. **1748** RICHARDSON *Clarissa* (1811) IV. 332 Ill will and passion were dreadful misrepresenters. **1760–72** H. BROOKE *Fool of Qual.* (1809) II. 9 Lawyers..are ..the pleaders and impleaders, representers and misrepresenters..of our laws. **1813** SCOTT 3 Sept. in *Fam. Lett.* (1894) I. ix. 306 All I have to fear..is that some busy misrepresenter may whisper in the Regent's ear.

misre'pute, *v.* ? *Obs.* [MIS-[1] 1.] *trans.* To estimate erroneously. Also **misre'puted** *ppl. a.*, wrongly reputed or estimated.
1628 GAULE *Pract. Theories* (1629) 232 Wis-dome chose there to bee misreputed, rather then Curiositie should be satisfied. **1643** MILTON *Divorce* 47 They shall vindicate the misreputed honour of God and his great Lawgiver. **1659** H. L'ESTRANGE *Alliance Div. Off.* 101 Those Liturgies extant under the names of misreputed Authors.

misre'semblance. *rare.* [MIS-[1] 4.] †**a.** Want of resemblance or agreement. *Obs.* **b.** Bad likeness or portrait.
a **1618** RALEIGH in Gutch *Coll. Cur.* I. 75, I shall pick out some short mis-resemblances, or disagreements, between the common law, and the civil law. **1822** SOUTHEY *Ep. A. Cunningham* Poet. Wks. 1838 III. 313 Return we now..To a lighter strain; and from the gallery Of the Dutch Poet's mis-resemblances Pass into mine.

mis'rule, *sb.* [MIS-[1] 4.]
†**1.** Disorderly conduct or living; misconduct; ill-conducted or irregular life; excess. *Obs.*
In quot. 1406 app. intended to be taken as two words (see MIS *a.*) rendering OF. *male regle.*
c **1400** *Destr. Troy* 7952 Thow might meruell the mykell of my misrewle, But þat wottes..þat þere longes no loue..To hym þat dressis for my dethe. **1406** HOCCLEVE *La Male Regle* 90 My freendes seiden vn-to me ful ofte, My mis reule me cause wolde a fit. **1484** CAXTON *Fables of Æsop* III. xi, The cryme and mysrewle of his sone. **1494** [see MISDEMEANOUR[1] 1 b]. **1570** LEVINS *Manip.* 95/43 Misrewle, *excessus, luxus.* **1613** PURCHAS *Pilgrimage* (1614) 749, I haue seen houses as full of such prostitutes, as the schooles in France are full of children. They there vse much misrule, riot and wantonnes.
2. Bad rule or government (of a state, etc.); misgovernment; the action of misruling or condition of being misruled; hence (often), a state of disorder, anarchy, or rebellion.
1399 LANGL. *Rich. Redeles* IV. 3 Where was euere ony cristen kynge..þat helde swiche an household..As Richard is þis rewme þoru myserule of oþer? **1450** *Rolls of Parlt.* V. 206/1 The Abbot and Convent..is in gret disolacion..by the mysreule and dilapidacion of divers Abbottes. **1541** A. KERR in *Hamilton Papers* I. 142 This mysrewill and breik upoun the Bordouris. **1657–8** in *Burton's Diary* (1828) II. 365 Misrule is better than no rule; and an ill government.. is better than none. **1667** MILTON *P.L.* VII. 271 And the loud misrule Of Chaos farr remov'd. **1725** POPE *Odyss.* I. 139 The heav'n born maid Enormous riot and misrule survey'd. **1777** ROBERTSON *Hist. Amer.* VI. (1851) I. 650 The authority

of government had been almost forgotten during the long prevalence of anarchy and mis-rule. **1828** SCOTT *F.M. Perth* xix, As the town is in misrule, we two, Harry, will carry her home. **1841** GEN. ABBOTT in C. R. Low *Jrnl.* ii. (1879) 195 There is such misrule here, that the country never can be quiet; people are sent out for the express purpose of getting up rows.

3. ***Lord*** (also ***Abbot, Master***) ***of Misrule***: one chosen to preside over the Christmas games and revels in a great man's house. *Obs.* exc. *Hist.*

See Brand *Popular Antiquities* (1813) I. 387 seqq; R.T. Hampson *Medii Aevi Kalendarium* (1841) I. 116, 117.

1491 in *Excerpta Historica* (1831) 88 To Ringley, lorde of mysrewle, upon a prest, £5. **1492** *Ibid.* 92 To Ringley, abbot of mysreule, £5. **1571** [see LORD *sb.* 14a]. **1577–87** HOLINSHED *Chron.* III. 1067/2 On mondaie the fourth of Januarie, the said lord of merie disports came by water to London,.. where he was receiued by Wause lord of misrule to John Mainard one of the shiriffes of London. **1633** R. EVELYN in *Archæol.* (1817) XVIII. 333, I giue free leave to Owen Flood my Trumpeter, gent. to be Lo^{d} of Misrule of all good Orders during the twelve dayes. **1654** H. L'ESTRANGE *Chas. I*, 72 That Christmas the Temple Sparks had enstalled a Lieutenant, a thing we country folk call a Lord of Misrule. **1664** H. MORE *Myst. Iniq.* 323 Their Master of Misrule at Christmas. [**1820** SCOTT *Abbot* xiv, A hall, a hall! for the venerable Father Howleglas, the learned Monk of Misrule, and the Right Reverend Abbot of Unreason!]

b. *transf.* and *fig.*

1591 LYLY *Endym.* v. ii, Loue is a Lorde of misrule, and keepeth Christmas in my corps. **1623** WEBSTER *Duchess Malfi* III. ii, *Ant.* I must lie here. *Duch.* Must! you are a lord of mis-rule. *Ant.* Indeed, my rule is only in the night. **1660** SOUTH *Serm.* (1727) IV. i. 63 Their great Master of Misrule Oliver [Cromwell]. **1822** W. IRVING *Braceb. Hall* xxvi. 227 Slingsby.. who is not merely lord of misrule in his school, but master of the revels to the village. **1850** HAWTHORNE *Scarlet Let.* viii. (1852) 99 There used to be a swarm of these small apparitions, in holiday time; and we called them children of the Lord of Misrule. **1898** K. GRAHAME *Golden Age* 15, I [*sc.* the wind] am the strong capricious one, the lord of misrule.

†**c.** ***show of misrule*** (? nonce-use): festivities such as those presided over by a Lord of Misrule.

1555 W. WATREMAN *Fardle Facions* II. viii. 182 Thei [*sc.* Brachmanes] couette no sightes, nor shewes of misrule: no disguisinges nor entreludes.

mis'rule, *v.* [MIS-^{1} 1.]

†**1.** *trans.* To manage or control badly. Also *refl.*

13.. in *Hampole's Wks.* (1896) I. 172 Þe foule fende þat mone gostle men begils þorou preway pontz of pryde þat misrewle þere witte. **1377** LANGL. *P. Pl.* B. IX. 59 Moche wo worth þat man þat mys-reuleth his Inwitte. **1390** GOWER *Conf.* III. 170 Wher such thing falleth overal That eny king himself misreule. *c* **1460** G. ASHBY *Dicta Philos.* 19 Suche folk as misreule theire spendyng. **1530** PALSGR. 638/1 If you mysrule your selfe, you maye.. catche some disease.

2. To rule or govern (a country, etc.) badly.

1390 GOWER *Conf.* III. 346 If he misreule that kingdom. **1462–3** *Pol. Poems* (Rolls) II. 268 Engeland.. Whiche hathe be mysrewled ȝerys sertayne. **1567** *Gude & Godlie B.* (S.T.S.) 197 Preistis.. Misreule the realm and court no moir. **1810** G. CHALMERS *Caledonia* II. II. v. 200 The Duke of Albany misruled his kingdom. **1883** *Pall Mall G.* 12 Sept. 10/1 He pleaded guilty to being a disturber so long as Ireland was misruled by England.

Hence **mis'ruling** *vbl. sb.* and *ppl. a.*

c **1380** WYCLIF *Wks.* (1880) 214 For here synne & mysreulynge of hem self. **1839** LD. BROUGHAM *For. Relat. Gt. Brit.* Wks. 1857 VIII. 126 Like the knell of death to the hopes of the misruling few. **1927** *Daily Tel.* 25 Oct. 8/5 If in refereeing I give a flagrant legal mis-ruling.. the Rugby Union can send for me and say what they think about me and my mis-ruling.

mis'ruled, *ppl. a.* [MIS-^{1} 2.]

1. Disorderly; lawless; unruly. *Obs.* or *arch.*

a **1400** HYLTON *Scala Perf.* (W. de W. 1494) I. xlii, A fals mysruled loue of man to hymselfe. *c* **1400** *Apol. Loll.* 101 Þat it [*sc.* a vow] be made wiþ deliberacoun, þat þe purpos or entent be not misrewlid. **1495** *Act II Hen. VII*, c. 2 §3 Vagaboundes and other mysruled persones. **1532** MORE *Confut. Barnes* VIII. Wks. 777/2 Agaynst murderers & theues and against al other viciouse & mysseruled persons. **1563** in Robertson *Hist. Scot.* (1759) II. App. 15 Except we put better order unto our misruled papists. **1829** SCOTT *Antiq.* xxvii, I may weel tak the tale hame to mysell, that hae led a misruled and roving life.

2. Badly ruled or governed.

1829 F. GLASSE *Belgic Past.* iii. 52 Misruled nations in vain wars engage. **1873** *Brit. Q. Rev.* LVII. 500 The state of Ireland.. was that of a misruled dependency.

mis'ruler. *rare.* [MIS-^{1} 5.] †**a.** A disorderly person. *Obs.* **b.** A bad ruler.

1479 in *Eng. Gilds* (1870) 416, I shall reproue & chastice the mysrewlers & mysdoers in the forsaid toune. **1897** *Edin. Rev.* July 1 Their tyrants and misrulers.

†**mis'ruly**, *a.* *Obs.* [MIS-^{1} 6.] Disorderly; unruly.

c **1412** HOCCLEVE *De Reg. Princ.* 4376, I me repent of my misrewly [*v.r.* mysreulede] lyfe. **1442** *Rolls of Parlt.* V. 55/2 Misgoverned Maisters.., and other misruly poeple. **1570** LEVINS *Manip.* 100/21 Misruly, *enormis.* **1581** in *Cath. Tractates* (S.T.S.) 90 And knok the crouins of thame quha ar misreulie. **1598** BP. HALL *Sat.* VI. i. 89 And crub the rauge of his mis ruly tongue.

miss (mɪs), *sb.*^{1} Forms: 3–6 **mis, mysse,** 3–7 **misse,** 4–5 **mys,** (5 **myss,** 6 **myshe**), 6– **miss.** [Partly f. MISS *v.*^{1}; but other formations (likewise from the OTeut. *misso-) seem to have coalesced with this. In the sense of 'loss' (branch I) the word may partly represent OE. **miss* neut., 'absence, loss' (Sweet *Anglo-Saxon Dict.*), or be ad. ON. *missi-r* masc. or *missa* fem., 'loss'. In some of the earlier examples of branch II (fault, mistake) the word appears to have been evolved (like MIS *adv.*) from the resolution of compounds of MIS- *prefix*^{1}; of similar origin are MHG., MLG., MDu. *misse* mistake, ill-success, Du. *mis* error. In the sense of 'missing a mark', etc. (branch III) it has not been found earlier than the 16th c., and may be purely a late formation on the verb; cf., however, early mod.Du. *misse* 'vanus ictus, jactus' (Kilian), which was developed from the adverbial use in *misse slaan*, to miss one's stroke. Cf. also ON. *á mis* adv., so as to miss or fail to meet, whence the ME. *on mis* (see 4 below), later AMISS *adv.*, is prob. adopted.]

I. Loss, lack. (Cf. MISS *v.*^{1} IV.)

1. a. The fact or condition of missing, having lost, or being without (a thing or person); loss, lack, privation. Const. *of* or *genitive*. (Cf. MISS *v.*^{1} 14.)

c **1470** HARDING *Chron.* CCXXX. iv, The kyng murthered.. The duke was wod, and frantike for his misse. **1494** FABYAN *Chron.* VII. ccxxix. 260 And whan he lefte his crowne, than fell honour downe, for mysse of such a kynge. **1513** MORE in Grafton *Chron.* (1568) II. 783 When the wondring of the people cast a comely red in her chekes, of the which she before had most misse. **1586** MARLOWE *2nd Pt. Tamburl.* IV. ii, As when an herd of lusty Cymbrian bulls Run mourning round about the females miss. **1592** NASHE *P. Penilesse* 9 b, If more regard were not had of him shortly, the whole Realme should haue a misse of him. **1614** RALEIGH *Hist. World* II. v. v. §4. 570 At Carthage, the misse of so great a person was diuersly construed. **1628–77** FELTHAM *Resolves* II. xxii. 40 An estate squander'd in a wanton waste, shews better in the miss, then while we had the use on't. **1886** SPURGEON *Treas. Dav.* Ps. cxliv. 15 Temporal blessings are not trifles, for the miss of them would be a dire calamity.

†**b.** Observable lack. (Cf. MISS *v.*^{1} 15.) *Obs.*

1689 S. SEWALL *Diary* 27 May, The main streets thwacked with people, and yet little miss of people in Fen-Church and Lumbard Streets. **1722** DE FOE *Plague* (1754) 248 There was no miss of the usual Throng of People in the Streets.

2. a. Disadvantage or regret occasioned by loss, absence, or privation *of* a person or thing. (Cf. MISS *v.*^{1} 16.) Chiefly in phrases, ***to have*** or ***find*** (***a***) (***great, heavy, little***) ***miss of***; ***to feel the miss of***; ***there is no*** (***great***) ***miss of***. Now *dial.* or *vulgar*.

a **1200** *Moral Ode* 234 Þenne hi cumeð eft to þe chele, of hete hi habbeð misse. **13..** *E.E. Allit. P.* A. 262 Þer mys nee mornyng com neuer here. *c* **1400** *Destr. Troy* 6707 Of soche a mon were a mysse þurgh the mekyll world. **1523** LD. BERNERS *Froiss.* I. ccxix. 279 These two kynges.. bewayled the lorde James of Bourbon, sayeng, that it was great damage of hym, and a great mysse of hym out of theyr company. **1540** *St. Papers Hen. VIII*, III. 205 Their shalbe greate myshe of ther absentie, considering ther towardnes and goode esperience. **1589** PUTTENHAM *Eng. Poesie* III. xxv. (Arb.) 282 Heywood being loth to call for drink so oft as he was dry.. sayd I finde great misse of your graces standing cups. ? **1608** BACON *Let. to Sir T. Bodley* Wks. 1830 XII. 91 In respect of my going down to my house in the country I shall have miss of my papers. **1657** W. RAND tr. *Gassendi's Life Peiresc.* 66 Leaving behind him a great misse of himself, at Padua especially. **1748** RICHARDSON *Clarissa* (1811) VIII. 114 We know the miss of you, and even hunger and thirst, as I may say, to see you. **1751** ELIZA HEYWOOD *Betsy Thoughtless* II. 267 Agreeable as her conversation was, Mr. Trueworth found no miss of her, as the lovely Harriot was left behind. **1797** MRS. A. M. BENNETT *Beggar Girl* I. 95 The poor servants will all have a miss of such a master as your honour. **1807** ANNA SEWARD *Lett.* (1811) VI. 364 With such excellent qualities of head and heart [etc.].. I think his professional talents will have no great miss of what are called the classics. **1860** GEO. ELIOT *Mill on Fl.* III. viii, I was determined my son should have a good eddication: I'd none myself and I've felt the miss of it. **1901** 'RITA' *Jilt's Jrnl.* I. xx, I'm thinking 'tis now you'll feel the miss o' your mother, my dear.

†**b.** *transf.* A person missed. *nonce-use.*

a **1631** DONNE *Eleg.* xvi. Poems (1654) 95, I found my misse, struck hands, and praid him tell.. where he did dwell.

II. Wrong, mistake. (Cf. MISS *v.*^{1} V.)

†**3. a.** Wrong, wrong-doing; offence, injury; a wrong, misdeed. ***with miss***: wrongly, amiss. *Obs.*

Not always distinguishable with certainty from MIS *adv.*

a **1225** *Ancr. R.* 86 ȝif a mon.. seið & deð so much mis þet hit beo so open sunne [etc.]. *a* **1300** *Cursor M.* 24339 To me his moder did þai þe mis. *c* **1330** R. BRUNNE *Chron. Wace* (Rolls) 4784 Þou bedes me mys & outrage! **1340** HAMPOLE *Pr. Consc.* 3289 Als Innocentes þat never dyd mys. **13..** *Gaw. & Gr. Knt.* 2391 Þou art confessed so clene, be-knowen of þy mysses. *c* **1430** *Hymns Virgin* (1867) 98 Repentynge þee of al þi mys. *c* **1470** HENRY *Wallace* II. 352 Be war that yhe with myss deyme nocht my taille. *a* **1500** *Bernard. de cura rei fam.* (1870) 7/162 Ane aulde woman þat is Licherus and wyl not lef hir mys. **1546** *Supplic. Poore Commons* (1871) 79 Defer not (moost deare Soueraine) the reformation of this mysse. **1590** SPENSER *F.Q.* III. ix. 2 What wonder then if one, of women all, did mis? **1592** SHAKS. *Ven. & Ad.* 53 He saith, she is immodest, blames her misse. *c* **1611** CHAPMAN *Iliad* v. 197 Some other way I might repair this shameful miss. **1616** J. LANE *Contn. Sqr.'s T.* XI. 60 But if hee will for neithers [sake] quitt the misse.

b. in alliterative association with *mend*, etc.

c **1320** *Sir Tristr.* 2760 Mendi þou most þat mis [*viz.* the slaying of Moraunt]. *a* **1400** *Relig. Pieces fr. Thornton MS.* 91 Þou broghte thaym to blysse Thorowe mendynge of mysse. *c* **1470** HENRY *Wallace* IV. 64 Off this gret myss I sall amendis hawe. **1470–85** MALORY *Arthur* II. ii. 78, I shalle amende all mysse that I haue done ageynst yow. **1581** *Satir. Poems Reform.* xliv. 114 And tyme requyris amendement of missis. *c* **1620** A. HUME *Brit. Tongue* (1865) 2 To mend the misses that ignorant custom hath bred. **1637–50** ROW *Hist. Kirk* (Wodrow Soc.) 164 To amend his awin misses, and to reforme abuses in his Court.

†**4.** Phr. ***on mis*** (cf. ON. *á mis*) = AMISS, q.v.

c **1230** *Hali Meid.* 17 Þet is.. þe stude & te time þe mahten bringe þe on mis forte donne. *a* **1350** *St. Anastasia* 202 in Horstm. *Altengl. Leg.* (1881) 27 Onmis þo wurdes þou vnderstode. *c* **1420** [see AMISS *adv.* 5].

†**5.** ***withoute***(***n***) ***miss***: without mistake or uncertainty; undoubtedly, certainly; = ***without fail*** in its older application. [Cf. MDu. *sonder misse.*]

a **1250** *Five Joys of the Virgin* in *Rel. Ant.* I. 49 There is joie ant eke blisse, That ever last, wid-oute misse. *a* **1300** *Cursor M.* 24758 Quat time and term þat þis bitidd.. I sal yow mon wid-vten mis. *c* **1450** LOVELICH *Merlin* 208 And whanne the devel vndirstod al this, thanne was he joyful, with-owten mis. *Ibid.* 308, 1366, 1388, 1454.

†**6.** Error, mistake. *Obs.*

a **1568** ASCHAM *Scholem.* II. (Arb.) 90 Without any great misse in the hardest pointes of Grammer.

III. Failure to hit or attain. (Cf. MISS *v.*^{1} I.)

7. a. Failure to hit something aimed at; *transf.*, an unsuccessful gramophone record (opp. HIT *sb.* 4.)

Proverb: ***a miss is as good as a mile*** (formerly † ***an inch in a miss is as good as an ell***, etc.): a failure is a failure however near one may have been to success.

1555 W. WATREMAN *Fardle Facions* I. vi. 89 He throweth his stone, fetching his ronne, and maketh lightly a narowe mysse, thoughe it be a good waye of. **1614** CAMDEN *Rem.*, *Prov.* 303 An ynche in a misse is as good as an ell. **1721** KELLY *Sc. Prov.* 35 An Inch of a miss is as good as a span [*misprinted* spaw]. **1825** SCOTT *Jrnl.* 3 Dec. (1890) I. 32 He was very near being a poet—but a miss is as good as a mile, and he always fell short of the mark. **1860** ADLER *Prov. Poet.* xi. 237 Walter.. evades the blow but the miss stretches his antagonist flat upon the ground. **1878** BROWNING *La Saisiaz* 163 What seemed hits and what seemed misses in a certain fence-play. **1887** RIDER HAGGARD *Jess* v, He has just killed half a dozen.. partridges without a miss. **1965** *Listener* 9 Sept. 391/1 Persons invited to give their verdict.. are not being asked to say whether the songs are good or bad but merely whether they will be 'hits' or 'misses'. **1966** *Melody Maker* 16 July 20 Dusty's new single may be one of her misses.

b. *Billiards.* A failure to hit the object ball, on account of which the opponent scores: in certain circumstances considered the correct play. Phr. ***to give a miss*** = to avoid hitting the object ball, esp. with the intention of putting one's ball in a safe position; also, to ***give the miss in baulk***. The opponent is said ***to score a miss***.

1844 MARDON *Billiards* 29 In playing off, it is customary to give a miss in the baulk. *Ibid.* 115 Should the striker, when in hand, play at a ball in baulk, his adversary has the option of scoring a miss. **1867** W. DUFTON *Pract. Billiards* iii. 42 The miss may be made with the butt or the point of the cue. **1873** BENNETT & 'CAVENDISH' *Billiards* 345 In most cases a miss would be the game here. **1907** WESTBROOK & WODEHOUSE *Not George Washington* II. xxi. 228 And James.. is actually giving this the miss in baulk! **1923** WODEHOUSE *Inimitable Jeeves* iii. 31 Anyway, it never even occurred to me for a moment to give her the miss-in-baulk.

c. *transf.* ***to give a miss***, to abstain from, avoid.

1919 B. RUCK *Disturbing Charm* I. ii. 10 The Professor chose (as he often did) to give lunch a miss. **1927** A. HUXLEY *Let.* 17 May (1969) 286 The result of this will be that we must, alas, give Paris a miss. **1930** *Morning Post* 16 July 8/3 The leek is.. among the.. vegetables that are too often given a miss. **1950** J. CANNAN *Murder Included* vii. 183 I'm afraid I've given church a miss this morning. **1973** BOYD & PARKES *Dark Number* ix. 91, I think the CID would be happier if you gave the whole place a miss.

8. Failure to obtain or achieve something. Now *rare.*

1609 SIR E. HOBY *Let. to Mr. T. H.* 15 Your debts were.. very clamorous: the misse of your preferment was grieuous. **1615** W. LAWSON *Country Housew. Gard.* (1626) 18 After first or second graffing in the same Stocke, being mist (for who hits all) the third misse puts your Stocke in deadly danger. **1661** R. L'ESTRANGE *Interest Mistaken* Pref. p. iv, Aërius turn'd Heretique upon the misse of a Bishoprick. **1680** BAXTER *Answ. Stillingfl.* xxviii. 41 It is not.. the miss of a Complement or Ceremony, that makes a Man a Rebel. **1753–4** RICHARDSON *Grandison* (1811) II. ii. 12 If they have had no lovers, or.. have not found a husband, they have had rather a miss than a loss, as men go. **1834** GLADSTONE in Morley *Life* (1903) I. 112, I ought to be thankful for my miss [*sc.* failure to catch the Speaker's eye].

9. *Printing.* The omitting to lay on a sheet in feeding a printing-machine.

1888 JACOBI *Printers' Vocab.*

miss (mɪs), *sb.*^{2} [Shortening of MISTRESS.

Probably this oral shortening may have been suggested by the written abbreviations 'Mis.' and 'Mis' (the latter representing the spelling *mistris*) which were common in the 16–17th c. In the following quots. it is not quite certain that 'Mis' is not a mere graphic abbreviation.

1606 *Choice, Chance, & Change* G 4 My Mistrisse.. did thus salute me. Seruante good morrow, what abroade so earlie?.. mistris quoth I, shall the seruant bee in bed after his Mis? *Ibid.* H 2, If your mistris haue a fine wit, and your wife, but a plaine vnderstanding.. if your mis. be kind and your wife dogged: wil you loue your mis. better then your wife?]

1. A kept mistress; a concubine. Less commonly, a common prostitute, whore. *Obs.* exc. *dial.*

1645 EVELYN *Diary* June, The com'on misses [at Venice] ..go abroad bare-fac'd. 1662 *Ibid.* 9 Jan., She being taken to be the Earle of Oxford's Misse (as at this time they began to call lewd women). 1675 (*title*) The Character of a Town-Misse. 1678 BUTLER *Hud.* III. i. 864 All women would be of one piece, The virtuous matron, and the miss. 1765 BICKERSTAFFE *Maid of Mill* II. x. 42 If one is a Miss, be a Miss to a gentleman I say. 1803 MARY CHARLTON *Wife & Mistress* IV. 214, I would rather chuse to see this child..the wife of an honest man, than the Miss of a Nobleman. 1809 J. ADAMS *Wks.* (1854) IX. 303 A Miss of the street. 1826 J. WILSON *Noct. Ambr.* Wks. 1855 I. 10 Can you believe what the newspapers said that the parents connived at her being Colonel Barclay's miss? 1889 in *N.W. Linc. Gloss.*

transf. 1700 DRYDEN *Fables, Cock & Fox* 56 This gentle cock..Six misses had, beside his lawful wife.

fig. 1678 BUTLER *Hud.* III. i. 969 (1694) 51 Our Money's now become the Miss Of all your Lives and Services.

2. Prefixed as a title to the name of an unmarried woman or girl (not entitled to the prefix 'lady' or some higher designation of rank).

In modern use, when *Miss* is prefixed to the surname alone, e.g. *Miss Smith*, it normally indicates the eldest (unmarried) daughter of the family; in referring to the others the Christian name is employed, e.g. *Miss Ethel (Smith)*. (But for reasons of convenience the Christian names are often inserted or omitted without regard to this rule.) When the title is applied to several persons of the same name at once, usage sanctions two forms, viz. *the Misses Smith* and *the Miss Smiths*, the former being regarded as grammatically the more proper.

1666–7 PEPYS *Diary* 7 Mar., Little Miss Davis did dance a jigg after the end of the play. 1670 FLECKNOE *Epigr.* 43 To Mis Davies, On her excellent dancing. Dear Mis, Who would not think [etc.]. 1697 VANBRUGH *Relapse* IV. i, Enter Miss Hoyden, and Nurse. c1700 FARQUHAR *Love & a Bottle* Epil., Oh Collier! Collier! thou'st frighted away Miss Cross. 1729 SWIFT *Direct. Serv.* xvi, Miss Betty won't take to her Book. 1772 in J. L. Chester *Westm. Abbey Reg.* (1876) 416 Miss Catharine Ayrton; aged three months. 1826 DISRAELI *Viv. Grey* II. IV. i. 171 Does my Lord Manfred keep his mansion there, next to the Misses Otranto? 1870 GEO. ELIOT in Cross *Life* III. 112 The Miss Gaskells were staying with them. 1880 *Theatre* Feb. 118 As Adriano Miss Josephine Yorke looked and sang admirably.

b. ***Miss Nancy*** (dial. and colloq.): an effeminate man; so ***to talk Miss Nancy***, to speak politely; also *attrib.* Hence ***Miss-Nancyfied***, ***-Nancyish*** adjs., effeminate; ***Miss-Nancyism***, effeminacy.

1824 CARR *Craven Gloss.* s.v. *Nancy*, A Miss-nancy, is an effeminate man. 1848 A. BRONTË *Tenant of Wildfell Hall* I. iii. 53 You will treat him like a girl—you'll spoil his spirit, and make a mere Miss Nancy of him. 1855 'Q. K. P. DOESTICKS' *Doesticks, what he Says* 298, I could overlook the boarding-school-ism of the Miss Nancyish 'Journal'. 1863 'G. HAMILTON' *Gala-Days* 117 A man's hair is shag... Ceasing to be shag, it does not become beauty, but foppishness, effeminacy, Miss Nancyism. 1870 A. W. DRAYSON *Young Dragoon* viii. 61 Officers and men must be thorough soldiers—not 'Miss Nancy' sort of fellows. 1874 *Southern Mag.* XIV. 353 Poh! 'Miss-Nancyfied' men! 1886 *Harper's Weekly* 20 Mar. (Cent.), Ineffable silliness, sneering at the demand for honesty in politics as Miss Nancyism. c1898 MRS. LYNN LINTON in *Speaker* (1901) 20 July 453/1, I think a dash of femininity in a man is good; but I hate a 'Miss Nancy'. 1916 W. RILEY *Netherleigh* xv. 152 Talkin' Miss Nancy as if 'e was a dancin' master. 1928 'BRENT OF BIN BIN' *Up Country* ii. 8 He actually carried sleeping attire about with him, and a tooth-brush, Miss Nancy habits derided by the men.

c. A lady entitled to be addressed as 'Miss ——'.

1840 HOOD *Kilmansegg, Marriage* xxiii, The Bride, who came from her Coach a Miss, As a Countess walk'd to her carriage.

d. ***Miss Milligan***, a kind of patience played with two packs of cards.

1899 M. W. JONES *Games of Patience* 5th Ser. x. 27 Miss Milligan Patience. 1914 C. MACKENZIE *Sinister St.* II. III. xiv. 782 She used to sit playing 'Miss Milligan'..and said.. that she had really enjoyed Patience for the first time. 1934 H. G. WELLS *Exper. Autobiogr.* I. i. 29, I have played a spread-out patience called Miss Milligan for the past fifteen years. 1938 C. MORGAN *Flashing Stream* II. ii. 205 Karen, make it four and bridge. Oh, you don't play. Five and poker. (*No answer.*) Hell, I'll play Miss Milligan. 1975 J. SYMONS *Three Pipe Problem* xviii. 200 She played all sorts of patience games from simple single-pack patiences like Miss Milligan and the elegant Windmill to complicated double-pack games like French Blockade and Triple Line.

e. A young woman, *Miss America*, *Miss England*, *Miss Europe*, *Miss World*, etc., chosen for beauty, personality, etc., to represent a country, region, etc.; also *transf.*

[1905 R. H. DAVIS (*title*) Miss Civilisation.] 1922 *N.Y. Times* 5 Sept. 19/6 Miss Margaret Gorman of Washington, winner of the 1921 contest, will be known as 'Miss America'. 1927 *Maclean's Mag.* 1 June 40 'Miss Toronto' wearing a stylish Aberley of the attractive 'Bird of Gladness' design in which she won the cup at the 1926 Beauty Contest at Sunnyside. 1929 *Daily Tel.* 8 Feb. 11/4 'Miss Europe' was chosen to-night..from among the seventeen girls who had been selected as the most beautiful women of their respective countries. 1935 M. CAMPBELL *My 30 Yrs. Speed* ix. 202 Sir Henry Segrave was killed on Lake Windermere during attempts on the water-speed record with *Miss England II.* 1953 S. SPEWACK *Under Sycamore Tree* II. i. 35 Attention, everybody. We now bring you the results of the beauty contest..to pick Miss Human Ant of nineteen fifty-three. 1958 *Listener* 23 Oct. 662/1 Sport, travelogues, space-rockets, Miss World..succeed each other rapidly and effortlessly. 1962 E. CLEAVER in A. Dundes *Mother Wit* (1973) 14/2 A..blue eyed 'white' girl is..proclaimed as.. Miss Universe. 1968 *Radio Times* 28 Nov. 70/3 The first Miss World in 1951 measured 37-23-36. 1972 G. BROMLEY *In Absence of Body* iii. 27 Poised at a desk on a low dais—as though she might have been Miss Great Britain..was a ravishing receptionist. 1974 *Times* 8 Mar. 3/4 (*heading*) Miss World stripped of title.

f. ***Miss Ann(e, Annie*** (see quots.).

1926 C. VAN VECHTEN *Nigger Heaven* 286 *Miss Annie*, a white girl. 1942 Z. N. HURSTON in A. Dundes *Mother Wit* (1973) 224/2 Miss Anne used to worry me so bad to go with me. 1965 [see CHARLEY, CHARLIE 7]. 1966 *Publ. Amer. Dial. Soc.* 1964 XLII. 45 *The Man* and *Miss Ann* refer more specifically to the boss and the fair, young white lady of the plantation... Both..are used ironically. 1970 C. MAJOR *Dict. Afro-Amer. Slang* 81 *Miss Ann*, a white woman—carry-over from Southern terminology, but now used with a good-natured sneer or with outright maliciousness.

g. ***Miss Willmott's ghost***, a large sea holly, *Eryngium giganteum*, so called in allusion to Ellen Ann Willmott (1860–1934), English horticulturist, who was responsible for the introduction of many plants.

1956 A. M. COATS *Flowers & their Histories* 89 The biennial sea-holly..has a spectral look in the twilight which might well justify its name of Miss Willmott's Ghost. It is said that when visiting gardens, Ellen Willmott used surreptitiously to drop a few seeds of this plant here and there, to surprise the owners in due course. 1963 *Oxf. Bk. Garden Flowers* 154/1 The biennial species, *E[ryngium] giganteum*, becomes quite white and desiccated after it has flowered, and is often called 'Miss Willmott's Ghost', after that great gardener Miss Ellen Willmott. 1974 R. L. FOX *Variations on Garden* 127 It [sc. *Eryngium giganteum*] is also called Miss Willmott's Ghost, Miss Willmott being a former plantswoman of the home counties with a tongue, and tastes, as sharp as a thistle's spine.

h. Occas. uses, as ***Miss Lonelyhearts*** (see LONELY *a.* 6); ***Miss Right***, a woman who would be a perfect wife; ***Miss White***, a lavatory.

1922 JOYCE *Ulysses* 347 When she wanted to go where you know she said she wanted to run and pay a visit to the Miss White. *Ibid.* 640 He would one day take unto himself a wife when Miss Right came on the scene.

3. With ellipsis of the proper name. Not now in educated use. **a.** Without article, substituted for the name of a young unmarried lady, often equivalent to 'the daughter of the house', 'the young lady of the family.'

1695 CONGREVE *Love for L.* II. x, Oh, madam, you are too severe upon miss. 1712 SWIFT *Jrnl. to Stella* 30 Dec., I saw the Bishop of Clogher's family to-day; Miss is mighty ill of a cold. 1747 GARRICK (*title*) Miss in her Teens. 1758 JOHNSON *Idler* No. 33 ¶24 Both the old lady and miss are fond of..collared eel. 1820 BYRON *Blues* I. 78 Is it miss or the cash of mamma you pursue? 1888 J. PAYN *Prince of Blood* xxviii. (1892) 229 'I hope miss is not much worse', he said.

b. *vocatively.*

1667 DRYDEN *Maiden Qu.* III, Adieu, Dear Miss! If ever I am false to thee again. 1670 [see 2]. 1740 tr. *De Mouhy's Fort. Country Maid* (1741) I. 60 And, Miss, since that is your Name, you shall go Home to your Parents. 1766 GOLDSM. *Vic. W.* xxxi, 'My sweetest Miss', cried my wife, 'he has told you nothing but falsehoods.' 1816 KIRBY & SP. *Entomol.* (1818) I. 101 'Dear Miss', said a lively old Lady to a friend of mine. a1825 FORBY *Voc. E. Anglia* s.v., Nor must one say, 'Pray, Miss, do you go to the ball this evening?' 1850 MISS YONGE *Henrietta's Wish* iv. 49, 'I beg your pardon, Miss,' said she [sc. a maidservant]. 1901 'RITA' *Jilt's Jrnl.* I. ii, He..said, 'A pleasure, miss, I assure you'... 'Miss', I repeated... 'Fancy calling me—"miss". But then he isn't a gentleman.'

c. In angry or contemptuous use.

1906 WEYMAN *Chippinge* xxii, [A mother says] 'You hate me!' 'Oh no, no!' the girl cried in distress. 'You do, miss!'

d. A pert girl.

1818 KEATS *Lett.* (1958) II. 13 She is a downright Miss without one set off—we hated her. 1864 C. M. YONGE *Trial* I. vi. 100, I came down upon little Miss at last for her treatment of the doctor. 1937 M. ALLINGHAM *Dancers in Mourning* xi. 158 A sulky little miss if ever I saw one.

e. ***miss sahib***, in India, the daughter of a mem-sahib, a European girl.

1888 KIPLING *Soldiers Three* (1889) 8 *Bund karo* all the Miss Sahib's *asbab* an' look slippy! 1892 —— & BALESTIER *Naulakha* xx. 236 'Has the miss sahib any orders,' asked Dhunpat Rai. 1971 R. DENTRY *Encounter at Kharmel* iii. 46 Oh, memsahib... Is the miss-sahib unwell? 1973 'B. MATHER' *Snowline* ix. 105, I saw the sahib... He..passed close to a group of goras and dirty miss-sahibs, who called out to him.

f. A female schoolteacher; an English governess in France.

1924 A. D. SEDGWICK *Little French Girl* I. vi. 51 The 'Misses' of her childhood. 1951 R. SENHOUSE tr. *Colette's Chéri* 21 No 'Fräulein', no 'Miss' was ever to be seen at Chéri's side. 1968 L. BERG *Risinghill* 16 Girls are caned as well as boys in Islington. 'Miss said no one should come in the class during the dinnertimes.' *Ibid.* 227 That's not a bad thing for a child to copy—to think 'Sir's mod!' or 'Miss is mod!' 1973 *Guardian* 20 Mar. 17/3, I would like to subject some of the 'misses' and some of the 'sirs' to the indignities and fears that they have heaped upon my kids.

4. A young unmarried woman; a girl, esp. a schoolgirl, or one who has lately left school; in modern use, often connoting the squeamishness or sentimentality characteristic of girls of such an age.

In literary English use now only playful or contemptuous; in trade use (distinguished from *ladies* and *children*, with reference to sizes or styles of articles of clothing), *misses* denotes girls of from about 10 to 17 years of age. The American dicts. describe the word as being in colloquial and trade use.

1667 DRYDEN *Maiden Qu.* II. i, Oh, my Miss in a Masque! have you found your Tongue? a1700 B. E. *Dict. Cant. Crew*, *Miss*, ..a little Girl. 1706 PHILLIPS (ed. Kersey), *Miss*, a Title given to a young Gentlewoman. 1715 GAY *Ep. Burlington* 75 Three boarding-schools well stock'd with misses. 1750 JOHNSON *Rambler* No. 85 ¶12 A knot of misses busy at their needles. 1796 LAMB *Let. to Coleridge* 28 Oct., To fall out like boarding-school misses. 1802 MRS. E. PARSONS *Myst. Visit* II. 172 Very unlike a novel-reading Miss. 1842 TENNYSON *Amphion* 81 The wither'd Misses! how they prose O'er books of travell'd seamen. 1858 MRS. GORE *Heckington* III. x. 213 Leave them [sc. whimsies] to such Misses as the Horsfords. 1880 in *Amer. Mail Order Fashions* (1961) 20 A Misses' bathing costume. The pattern ..is in 6 sizes for misses from 10 to 15 years of age. 1880 *Nation* (N.Y.) 12 Aug. *advt.*, The Maples.—A Family School for Young Ladies and Misses. 1885 *Spectator* 30 May 706/1 Happiest when under the tyranny of some small miss of two or three. 1892–3 *T. Eaton & Co. Catal.* Fall & Winter 11/1 In misses' and small women's coats, we are still unexcelled. 1930 E. WALLACE *Lady of Ascot* viii. 67 She catered for what they call in America the 'Miss', and had as her principal clients thousands of working girls, who, through the Carawood stores, were able to dress fashionably. 1951 *Vogue* Feb. 94/1 We pass through the Baby Linen on our way to the Misses. 1954 M. COREY *McCall's Compl. Bk. Dressmaking* 50 In junior sizes, as in misses' and women's sizes, the size that you take in a dress pattern is also the right size for your coat or your suit. 1970 *Vogue Sewing Bk.* II. 108 The Misses' figure is considered the statistically 'average' figure. 1973 *Philadelphia Inquirer* 7 Oct. 9 (Advt.), Misses' nationally famous Separates. Coordinated sets. *Ibid.*, Every winter coat for misses, juniors, women reduced Monday only.

5. = MRS. (*dial.* and *U.S.*) Also used conventionally of a married woman in public life.

1790 N. WEBSTER in *Gazette U.S.* 17 Nov. (Th.), The use of Miss for Mistress in this country is a gross impropriety. 1819 *Mass. Spy* 12 May (Th.), I concluded he had resolved to marry Miss Spruce, but found upon inquiry that his name was Spruce, and Miss Spruce was his wife. 1836 HALIBURTON *Clockm.* (1862) 451 If Miss Corncob, your wife, ain't here. 1838 DICKENS *Nickleby* (1839) xxv. 246 The company..fell to, immediately: Miss Petowker blushing very much when anybody was looking, and eating very much when anybody was *not* looking. 1854 —— *Hard T.* in *Househ. Words* 12 Aug. 598/2 Miss Josephine Sleary..was then announced... 'Here 'th Jothphine hath been and got married to E. W. B. Childerth, and shee hath got a boy.. three yearth old.' 1873 M. HOLLEY *My Opinions* 166 Miss Aster would give up her bedroom to me, or mebby she would make Mr. Aster sleep with one of the boys, and have me sleep with her. 1875 in PARISH *Sussex Gloss.* 1878 R. T. COOKE *Happy Dodd* x. 99 Mis' Potter sent that. 1888 L. D. POWLES *Land of Pink Pearl* 154 No married woman, not even excepting the Governor's wife, is ever accorded the title of 'Mrs.' but all ladies, married or single, are called 'Miss' or 'Missey' indiscriminately. 1936 MENCKEN *Amer. Lang.* (ed. 4) 124 The vulgar American misuse of..*Mis'* (pro. *miz*) for *Mrs*...was so widespread by 1790 that.. Webster denounced it as 'a gross impropriety'... It survives unscathed in the speech of the common people. 1937 N. MARSH *Vintage Murder* i. 6 What about Miss Dacres? Or should I say Mrs. Meyer? I never know with married stars. 1974 *Daily Tel.* 3 Oct. 10/6 Miss Blyton seems to have indulged in a few affairs before marrying her devoted surgeon second husband. 1975 *Times* 3 Apr. 14/4 Miss [Eileen] Fowler attributes her success in her unusual field partly to the fact that she started her working life as an actress... 'My husband was a bit overweight when we married,' she said. *Ibid.* 4 Apr. 1/1 Miss Ure..was found collapsed by her husband, Mr. Robert Shaw, the actor.

miss (mɪs), *sb.*[3] *Cards.* [Possibly a use of MISS *sb.*[1] or of MISS *sb.*[2]] At loo, an extra hand for which any of the players may discard his own.

1767 LADY M. COKE *Jrnl.* 10 June (1889) II. 22 There was to be two tables at Lu... The partys were scanty; both tables play'd with 'Miss'. 1861 H. KINGSLEY *Ravenshoe* (1862) III. 240 General Mainwaring had been looed in miss four times running. 1883 H. JONES in *Encycl. Brit.* XV. 1/1 Each player in rotation..looks at his cards, and declares whether he will play, resign, or take miss.

miss (mɪs), *sb.*[4] Colloq. abbrev. of MISCARRIAGE 3.

1897 W. S. MAUGHAM *Liza of Lambeth* x. 167, I've 'ad twelve, ter sy nothin' of two stills an' one miss. 1951 J. CANNAN *And All I Learned* v. 70, I heard of a girl who'd had eleven misses. 1959 'J. ROSS' *Boy in Grey Overcoat* x. 125, I didn't care what happened either to me or the child. I hoped I would have a miss. 1971 'D. SHANNON' *Murder with Love* (1972) viii. 138 She had a miss, that time, lost the baby.

miss (mɪs), *v.*[1] Forms: 1 missan, 3–7 misse, 4–6 mys(se, mis, myse, 5–6 myss, 6 mish, 6– miss; *pa. t.* 1–4 miste, (3 misste), 4–9 mist, 5–6 myst, 4– missed (also 5 -id, -yd -ud, etc.); *pa. pple.* 3 ymyst, 3–4 imist, 4– (as in pa. t.). [OE. *missan* = OFris. *missa*, MLG., MDu., Du. *missen*, OHG. *missan* (MHG., G. *missen*), ON. *missa* (Sw. *mista*, Da. *miste*, from the pa. t. and pa. pple.):—OTeut. **missjan*, f. participial stem **misso-*: see MIS-[1].]

I. *trans.* To fail to hit, meet, or light upon.

1. To fail to hit (something aimed at). Said either of the person aiming or of the missile. In OE. with obj. in genitive (cf. *miss of*, 23).

to miss the cushion: see CUSHION *sb.* 10 a.

Beowulf 2439 He miste mercelses and his mæᵹ ofscet. c1470 HENRY *Wallace* x. 366 The Bruce him myssyt as Wallace passyt by. a1547 SURREY in *Tottel's Misc.* (Arb.) 13 The palme play, where..With dazed eies oft we..Haue mist the ball. 1603 FLORIO *Montaigne* I. xxxiii, That ancient fellow, who, hurling a stone at a dog, missit him, and there withall hit..his step-dame. 1646 EVELYN *Diary* (Chandos ed.) 193 They were most accurate at the long-bow and

musket, rarely missing the smallest mark. **1664** INGELO *Bentiv. & Ur.* VI. 182 The next Course was perform'd much after the same manner, only Proselenes miss'd the Ring. **1748** *Anson's Voy.* II. iii. 148 The Purser..fired a pistol at Cozens, which however mist him. **1813** SCOTT *Rokeby* IV. xxvi, The gun he levell'd—mark like this Was Bertram never known to miss. **1864** TENNYSON *En. Ard.* 753 The babe.. rear'd his creasy arms, Caught at and ever miss'd it. **1867** FREEMAN *Norm. Conq.* (1877) I. v. 387 He..missed the traitor, and slew another soldier who was near him.

b. in fig. application, esp. ***to miss one's aim, one's*** (or ***the***) ***mark*** (see MARK *sb.*[1] 7 e).

1530 PALSGR. 638/1 If I mysse nat my marke, he is a busy felowe. **1591** SHAKS. *1 Hen. VI*, I. iv. 4, I..oft haue shot at them, Howe're vnfortunate, I miss'd my ayme. **1604** — *Ham.* IV. i. 43 (Qo. 2). **1602** *2nd Pt. Return fr. Parnass.* IV. iii. 1926 For that I misse this gaudy painted state, Whereat my fortunes fairely aim'd of late. **1655** FULLER *Ch. Hist.* IX. 176 The Ministers or Brethren now missing their mark, abated much of their former activity. **1735** POPE *Ep. Lady* 128 The Pleasure miss'd her, and the Scandal hit. *a* **1800** COWPER *Ep. to Prot. Lady* 38 But ills of every shape and every name, Transformed to blessings, miss their cruel aim. **1855** BROWNING *Grammarian's Funeral*, This high man, aiming at a million Misses an unit. **1874** GREEN *Short Hist.* ix. §1 Cromwell..in his later years felt bitterly that Puritanism had missed its aim.

c. Occasionally, of a missile, a blow, etc.: To chance not to hit (some object or part, not necessarily aimed at); to pass by without touching.

1749 BRACKEN *Farriery Impr.* (ed. 6) I. 300 Gun shot Wounds are seldom or never deadly (provided they miss the very Vitals). **1859** TENNYSON *Vivien* 781 One flash, that, missing all things else, may make My scheming brain a cinder.

d. *absol.* (Phr. ***hit or miss***: see HIT *v.* 22.)

c **1250** *Gen. & Ex.* 3872 Ones he smot ðor on ðe ston, And miste, and saȝ ðe water gon. **1535** COVERDALE *Judg.* xx. 16 With the slynge coulde they touch an heer, and not mysse. **1592** SHAKS. *Rom. & Jul.* I. i. 214 Well in that hit you misse, sheel not be hit With Cupids arrow. **1687** A. LOVELL tr. *Thevenot's Trav.* I. xlix. 68 In cutting off Heads, they are very dextrous, and never miss. **1742** FIELDING *J. Andrews* I. xvi, I never saw a surer shoot at a partridge. Every man misses now and then. **1859** TENNYSON *Vivien* 349 The sick weak beast seeking to help herself By striking at her better, miss'd. **1866** READE *G. Gaunt* I. vi. 154 The longer and more steadily the duellist fixes his eye on his adversary, the less likely he is to miss.

2. Not to hit upon (the right path). Usually ***to miss one's way***. (Also fig.)

a **1547** [see MISSING *vbl. sb.* 2]. **1582** N. LICHEFIELD tr. *Castanheda's Conq. E. Ind.* 13 b. The said Nicholas missed yᵉ channell, and ranne on ground. **1613** SHAKS. *Hen. VIII*, III. ii. 439 Say Wolsey..Found thee a way..to rise in: A sure, and safe one, though thy Master mist it. **1667** MILTON *P.L.* III. 735 Thy way thou canst not miss. **1742** FIELDING *J. Andrews* II. ii, He could not apprehend any mischief had happened, neither could he suspect that he missed his way. **1800** A. CARLYLE *Autobiog.* 28 Their eldest son.., having missed the road.., fell into a peat pot. **1822** SHELLEY tr. *Calderon's Mag. Prodig.* I. 76 Take which [path] you will, you cannot miss your road.

3. To fail to obtain footing on (a step, plank, etc.). Also ***to miss one's footing***. (Sc.) ***to miss a foot***.

? *a* **1550** *Freiris Berwik* 558 in *Dunbar's Poems* (1893) 303 Freir Johine attour the stair is gane In sic wyiss, that mist he hes the trap, And in ane myr he fell. **1641** J. JACKSON *True Evang. T.* II. 146 Till wee misse the bridge and fall into the ditch. **1670** [see FOOTING *vbl. sb.* 4]. **1785** BURNS *Halloween* xxvi, She..mist a fit, an' in the pool..she plumpit. **1816** SCOTT *Old Mort.* x, If he..dinna..miss ony o' the kittle steps at the Pass o' Walkwary. **1847** TENNYSON *Princess* IV. 159 Blind with rage she miss'd the plank, and roll'd In the river.

4. To fail to meet (a person with whom a meeting or interview was possible or intended). Also occas. *intr.* for *reciprocal*.

1589 NASHE *Returne of Pasquill* Wks. (Grosart) I. 91, I ranne presently to the water side to discouer your comming in; I wonder how I missed you? **1598** SHAKS. *Merry W.* III. v. 56, I will visit her, tell her so:..I will not misse her. **1663** PEPYS *Diary* 27 July, Walked over the Parke to St. James's, but missed Mr. Coventry. **1721–2** POPE *Let. to Atterbury* 14 Mar., I was disappointed..in missing you at the Deanery, where I lay solitary two nights. **1880** MEREDITH *Tragic Com.* 40 Then we missed: now we meet.

b. Of a letter: To fail to reach (a person).

1855 R. M. MILNES in *Life* (1891) I. xi. 527 Lady Ellesmere's letter missed me altogether, although directed as I desired.

5. Phrases. **a. to miss fire.** Of firearms: To fail to go off. Hence *fig.* to be unsuccessful, to fail in his or its object.

1727 GAY *Begg. Op.* I. xiii. (1729) 16 May my pistols miss fire. *a* **1734** NORTH *Exam.* I. ii. §160, I conclude only that Wilkinson was a Trapan, and after missing Fire [etc.]. **1837** DICKENS *Pickw.* vii, Never knew one of them miss fire before. **1838** D. JERROLD *Men of Char.* II. 166 That's how a man's brightest ideas sometimes miss fire. **1859** READE *Love me little* i, She missed fire—Uncle Fountain, like most Englishmen, could take in a pun by the ear, but wit only by the eye.

b. to miss stays (*Naut.*). To fail in the attempt to go about from one tack to another.

1691 *Lond. Gaz.* No. 2687/3 It was by reason he mist stays. **1758** *Chron.* in *Ann. Reg.* I. 83/1 The Invincible, one of his fleet,..missed her stays, and run upon a flat. **1821** SCOTT *Pirate* xxxiv, His mates..have been here waiting for him till they have missed stays. **1893** F. M. CRAWFORD *Children of King* i. 11 She was near missing stays.

fig. **1883** STEVENSON *Treas. Isl.* xxvi, I reckon I've missed stays!.. I'm for my long home, and no mistake.

c. [ellipt. use of 5 a.] *intr.* Of a motor vehicle or an engine: to fail to explode the mixture in a cylinder. (In quot. 1904 *transf.*) Phr. ***to miss on all*** (or ***four***, etc.) ***cylinders***: see CYLINDER *sb.* 6.

1904 *Peel City Guardian* 14 May 3/2 Hargreaves was 'missing' very badly. **1917**, **1932** [see CYLINDER *sb.* 6]. **1953** A. SMITH *Blind White Fish in Persia* x. 199 The departure from the Consulate was unceremonious, for the truck was missing badly, stalled several times and finally pulled us out through the gate. **1973** D. MACKENZIE *Postscript to Dead Let.* 8 The motor started missing a few miles back..then it died completely.

d. ***to miss a trick***: see TRICK *sb.* 13 c.

II. *trans.* To fail to attain.

6. To fail to get, obtain, receive, or acquire; to come short of, go without (what it is possible or desirable to have).

c **1250** *Gen. & Ex.* 3336 A met ðor was, it het Gomor, Ilc man is he bead, and nunmor, Him gaderen or ðe sunne-sine, Elles he sulden missen hine. **1340** HAMPOLE *Pr. Consc.* 5266 And for þe godhede es ful of blisse, þarfor þe sight of it þai sal misse. **13..** *E.E. Allit. P.* B. 189 Man may mysse þe myrþe, þat much is to prayse. *a* **1450** LOVELICH *Merlin* 782 Whanne the devel aspide..that his pray he scholde thus mis. **1582** STANYHURST *Æneis* I. (Arb.) 18 Through this wyde roaming thee Troians Italy mishing Ful many yeers wandred. **1596** SHAKS. *Merch. V.* II. i. 37 And so may I.. Misse that which one vnworthier may attaine. **1606** BACON in *Four C. Eng. Lett.* (1880) 41 Since the time I missed the solicitor's place. **1634** MILTON *Comus* 925 May thy brimmed waves for this Their full tribute never miss. **1779** JOHNSON *L.P.*, *Denham* (1868) 33 At the Restoration he obtained that which many missed, the reward of his loyalty. **1850** MISS YONGE *Henrietta's Wish* iii. 29 She could not bear that her husband should miss his yearly holiday. **1872** TENNYSON *Gareth & Lynette* 1265 So will my knight-knave Miss the full flower of this accomplishment. **1879** FROUDE *Cæsar* xi. 130 Catiline had missed the consulship, and was a ruined man.

b. To fail to capture (a person, †a fortress).

1596 DALRYMPLE tr. *Leslie's Hist. Scot.* (S.T.S.) II. 468 Becaus tha knew him not tha mist him, and sa he chaiped. **1634** SIR T. HERBERT *Trav.* (1638) 94 Curroon..attempting vainely Hasser, but missing it redelivers Rantos also into his enemies hands. **1889** 'R. BOLDREWOOD' *Robbery under Arms* xliii, What a muff Sir Ferdinand must be, he's missed me twice already.

c. Not to have the satisfaction of hearing, seeing, or witnessing (something).

1841 H. AINSWORTH *Guy Fawkes* III. i, It has been a painful spectacle.., and yet we would not have missed it. **1852** ROGERS *Ecl. Faith* (1853) 181 Painful as were the revelations which ensued, I would not have missed them on any account. **1875** JOWETT *Plato* (ed. 2) I. 142, I would not have missed the speech of Protagoras for a great deal.

7. a. With inf. or gerund: To fail (to do something). Now *arch.* or *dial.*

c **1381** CHAUCER *Parl. Foules* 75 Thou shalt nat misse To comen swiftly to that place dere. **1477** NORTON *Ord. Alch.* v. in Ashm. (1652) 77 Which would not misse..to make *lac virginis*. *c* **1540** J. HEYWOOD *Four P.P.* 368 (Manly), I thought ye wolde nat haue myst To make men lyue as longe as ye lyste. **1568** *Jacob & Esau* Prol., To send him a son by Sara he did not misse. **1664** CHAS. II. in Cartwright *Madame* (1894) 159 Pardon me for haveing mist writing to you so many posts. **1667** MILTON *P.L.* VI. 499 Th' invention all admir'd, and each, how hee To be th' inventer miss'd. **1733** TULL *Horse-Hoeing Husb.* xiv. 196 In a dry Summer both sorts of Clover are apt to miss growing. **1816** SCOTT *Old Mort.* xxxiv, The whigs never miss to find it [*sc.* good ale] out. **1820** KEATS *Isabella* xxvi, I was in pain Lest I should miss to bid thee a good morrow. **1869** BROWNING *Ring & Bk.*, *Pope* 1658 So, never I miss footing in the maze.

b. To fail to achieve (an object). Cf. 1 b.

1644 MILTON *Areop.* (Arb.) 54 To make it plain that this order will misse the end it seeks. **1738** WESLEY *Hymns*, '*But that Thou art my Wisdom, Lord*', My Soul would be extremely stirr'd At missing my Design. **1779** JOHNSON *L.P.*, *Cowley* (1868) 6 He that misses his end will never be as much pleased as he that attains it.

†**c. *to miss*** (one's) ***measure***: to fail to measure correctly. *Obs.*

1631 WEEVER *Anc. Funeral Mon.* 271 The Carpenters (missing their measure) had made it so much too short.

d. To fail to accomplish (a stroke).

1858 'CRAWLEY' *Billiards* (ed. 2) 29, I attempted a difficult canon off the white—and missed it. **1888** J. PAYN *Myst. Mirbridge* xxii, A man..must be an angel indeed who misses his stroke at billiards without a murmur.

8. To escape, avoid. Now only *dial.*, exc. with adv. *just*, *narrowly*, etc. Also, †to get clear of, elude (pursuit).

1526 *Pilgr. Perf.* (W. de W. 1531) 166 [The ball].. mysseth the hande & falleth to the grounde. **1567** *Gude & Godlie B.* (S.T.S.) 126 Throw his bitter deide I mis Of hell the dyntis dour. **1638** SIR T. HERBERT *Trav.* (ed. 2) 23 A shark (a man eating fish, and who seldome misse the hook, out of too much greedinesse). **1640** GLAPTHORNE *Wit in a Constable* IV. Wks. 1874 I. 223 The house anon I will enforme you, and what way to take To misse pursuit. **1788** P. HENRY in *Amer. Oratory* (1868) 19 (Stand. Dict.), Happy will you be, if you miss the fate of those nations, who..have groaned under intolerable despotism. **1791** W. JESSOP *Rep. Navig. Thames* 14 A cut of 400 Yards will miss a very crooked and Obstructed Part. **1890** 'R. BOLDREWOOD' *Col. Reformer* (1891) 278, I turned..across country for Delhi, and after missing a few shots, rode one hundred and thirty miles before I stopped.

with gerund. **1600** HAKLUYT *Voy.* III. 257 [This] made mee and my company as narrowly to escape staruing..as euer men did that missed the same. **1687** [see NARROWLY 4 b]. **1756** TOLDERVY *Hist. 2 Orphans* IV. 94 A hollier, who narrowly missed taking off the toes of Humphry with his carriage. **1814** SCOTT *Wav.* lxi, She..once very narrowly missed introducing Waverley to a recruiting-sergeant of his own regiment.

9. To fail to take advantage of; to let slip (an opportunity, etc.).

a **1628** PRESTON *New Covt.* (1629) 587 *marg.*, Because men misse the time they fall into misery. **1672** MARVELL *Reh. Transp.* I. 198 How frequent opportunities have I mist. **1772** PRIESTLEY *Inst. Relig.* (1782) I. 338 Would the orator Tertullus have missed so fine a topic of declamation, had there been the least colour of truth in this story? **1827** SCOTT *Highl. Widow* v, He thus missed an opportunity..of doing much good. **1841** JAMES *Corse de Leon* II. xi. 245 If we miss the precise moment..we have lost the great talisman for ever. **1902** T. M. LINDSAY *Church & Min. in Early Cent.* v. 173 It was better to be imposed upon sometimes than to miss the chance of entertaining a brother Christian.

b. To fail to catch (a train, etc.); not to be in time for. (Cf. *miss of*, 23 n.)

1823 DK. SUSSEX in S. Parr *Wks.* (1828) VII. 5, I fear to miss the Post. **1842** TENNYSON *Walking to Mail* 102 But put your best foot forward, or I fear That we shall miss the mail. **1856** [see LIE *v.*[1] 27 a]. **1886** *Manch. Exam.* 12 Jan. 4/7 Mr. Parnell himself was absent in consequence of missing his train at Crewe on the previous night.

c. In various colloq. phrases, as ***to miss the boat; to miss the bus***: see BUS *sb.*[2] 1 b.

1929 F. C. BOWEN *Sea Slang* 91 *Miss the boat*, to be late for anything. **1930** *Times Educ. Suppl.* 8 Mar. 106/3 Boys of average ability..often had to neglect other pursuits..for fear that they might 'miss the boat'. **1930** *Aberdeen Press & Jrnl.* 3 Sept. 4/5 As a medium for a dull debut, 'A Devil's Disciple' by Bernard Shaw.., to use an Americanism, missed the boat by twenty years. **1931** *Time & Tide* 29 Aug. 1001 There are ten men in the Cabinet... There are three more who, by strange irony of circumstance, have missed the train. **1934** T. E. LAWRENCE *Let.* 18 Aug. (1938) 875, I fear I have missed the boat, for lately a viking ship came from you: so I place you in Norway. **1939** H. NICOLSON *Let.* 18 July (1966) 406 But Anthony..is in fact missing every boat with exquisite elegance. **1973** *Times* 24 Mar. 2/4 Some firms were missing the boat because their managements were not prepared to be adventurous.

10. To fail to see or perceive (something that is within view); to fail to 'catch' or hear (some part of what one is listening to); to fail to apprehend or perceive intellectually.

a **1588** *Tarlton's Jests* (1844) p. xx, You may see his goodly counterfeit Hung up on everie wall. You never can misse the likennesse, For everie bodie knowes..His fathers lovelie visnomie. **1596** SHAKS. *Tam. Shr.* v. ii. 18 You are verie sencible, and yet you misse my sence. **1605** —— *Macb.* II. ii. 13, I lay'd their Daggers ready, He could not misse 'em. **1610** —— *Temp.* II. i. 54. **1666** PEPYS *Diary* 28 Dec., I sat so high and far off that I missed most of the words. **1690** LOCKE *Govt.* II. vi. §61 Wks. 1727 II. 175 The most blinded Contenders for Monarchy, by Right of Fatherhood, cannot miss this Difference. **1779** JOHNSON *L.P.*, *Savage* (1868) 320 Mr. Savage..thought his drift could only be missed by negligence or stupidity. **1781** COWPER *Retirem.* 458 What obvious truths the wisest heads may miss. **1816** SCOTT *Old Mort.* xli, Ye canna miss Widow Maclure's public, for deil another house or hauld is on the road for ten lang Scots miles. **1855** GEO. ELIOT *Ess.*, *Evang. Teaching* (1884) 164 He is meeting a hypothesis which no one holds, and totally missing the real question. **1893** LIDDON *Life Pusey* I. viii. 165 Allusive writing is open to two objections: Its point is missed by the majority of readers [etc.].

III. *trans.* To omit.

11. To omit, leave out (usually, a part of what one is reading, reciting, or writing.) Also with *out*.

1530 PALSGR. 681/1 He hath a syngular memorie, he recyted al our hole comunycacion and myssed nat a worde. **1563–83** FOXE *A. & M.* II. 2047/2 Then the said Lane being somewhat abashed, said his beliefe to these words, which he missed vnawares: Borne of the virgin Mary. **1641** SMECTYMNUUS *Vind. Answ.* §2 The Heathens had a Monitor that led them along in their prayers..that they might misse nor mistake no words. **1816** SCOTT *Old Mort.* xii, He has gone to church service with me fifty times, and I never heard him miss one of the responses in my life. **1818** BYRON *Juan* I. xi, If any actor miss'd his part She could have served him for the prompter's copy. **1870** TOULMIN SMITH *Eng. Gilds* 432 *note*, The transcriber by a slip of the pen has missed out words or parts of words.

†**b.** To leave undone through inadvertence. *Obs.*

1568 GRAFTON *Chron.* II. 747 All thinges were prepared, and no thing was missed.

12. To omit the performance of (a customary or expected action); to fail or neglect to keep (an appointment); to be exceptionally absent from (church, school, etc.); to omit to attend or be present at (some particular spectacle, ceremony, festivity, etc., out of a series or succession).

1598 SHAKS. *Merry W.* II. ii. 102 One..that will not misse you morning nor euening prayer. **1602** *Ibid.* III. i. 92 (Qo. 1), For missing your meetings and appointments. **1658** *Whole Duty Man* v. §34 He can never find in his heart so much as to miss a meal. *c* **1694** PRIOR *Lady's Looking Glass* 11 She would never miss one day A walk so fine. **1711** STEELE *Spect.* No. 51 ¶6 Others never miss the first Day of a Play. **1742** FIELDING *J. Andrews* II. iv, She..rarely missed a ball, or any other public assembly. **1819** B'NESS BUNSEN in Hare *Life* I. v. 139 Mr. Thirlwall has never missed any Tuesday evening since, except the moccoli night. **1834** HOOD *Tylney Hall* I. xii. 122, I remember the time when Dr. Cobb never missed a meet of the hunt. **1886** RUSKIN *Præterita* I. 368, I never missed chapel.

†**13.** To pass by, overlook. *Obs.*

1666 BUNYAN *Grace Abound.* §208 How many Scriptures are there against me? There are but three or four: and cannot God miss them, and save me for all them?

IV. *trans.* To be without; lack; want.

†**14.** To be without, not to have, lack; to cease to have, lose. Also with *away*. (Cf. sense 6.) *Obs.*

a 1300 *Cursor M.* 20792 He wil noght tak þe cark on him Quar þat it be sua soght or nai, þou hir bodi be mist o wai. 1340 Hampole *Pr. Consc.* 8000 Þe dampned bodyse salle fredom mys. 1377 Langl. *P. Pl.* B. xii. 101 As a man may nouȝt se þat mysseth his eyghen. c 1400 *Rom. Rose* 5646 To paradys the soner go He shal, .. Where that he shal no good misse. a 1450 *Cov. Myst.* (Shaks. Soc.) 50 Ȝoure fadyrly love lete me nevyr mysse. 1583 *Leg. Bp. St. Androis* 80 Gif he had not fled for feir, Gude Matchewell had mist his meir. 1628–77 Feltham *Resolves* i. xxxiv. 59 He hath good Materials for a foundation: but misseth where-with to rear the walls.

absol. 1573 Tusser *Husb.* (1878) 35 To borow to daie and to-morrow to mis, for lender and borower, noiance it is. a 1631 Donne *Lett. to Pers. Honour* (1651) 113 You have a fortune that can endure, and a nature that can almost be content to misse.

†b. *to be missed*: to be missing or absent; not to be found. *Obs.*

c 1374 Chaucer *Troylus* iii. 537 If that he were missed, night or day, Ther-whyle he was aboute this servyse. 1535 Coverdale *2 Kings* x. 19, I haue a greate sacrifyce to do vnto Baal Who so euer is myssed, shal not lyue. 1596 Dalrymple tr. *Leslie's Hist. Scot.* II. 6 Of the Scotis onlie war misset twa knichtis, and of the commoun peple four thousand.

†c. Contextually, to do without. *Obs.*

1533 Heywood *Pard. & Friar* Bj, This is the pardon, which ye cannot mysse. 1580 Lyly *Euphues* (Arb.) 264 Bringing vnto man both honnye and wax, .. both so necessary that we cannot misse them. 1610 Shaks. *Temp.* i. ii. 311 We cannot misse him: he do's make our fire [etc.]. 1637 Rutherford *Lett.* (1664) cl. 301 Learn daily both to possess and miss Christ in his secret bridegroom-smiles.

15. To discover the absence of; to perceive that (a person or thing) is not in the expected or accustomed place. Also (*north.*) †with *away*.

c 1200 Ormin 8919 Till þatt itt comm till efenn, & ta þeȝȝ misstenn þeȝȝre child. a 1225 *Ancr. R.* 78 Þe ueorðe time was þoa heo hefde imist hire sune, & eft hine ivond. a 1300 *Cursor M.* 17288 + 120 And when þai missed his body fast away þai fledd. 1375 Barbour *Bruce* xix. 504 On the morn, .. The Ingliss host myssit avay The Scottis men. c 1450 *St. Cuthbert* (Surtees) 5641 Þe childe waked and his belt myst. 1568 Grafton *Chron.* II. 827 They myssed hym and knewe not in what part of the worlde to make inquirie or serche for hym. 1592 Greene *Conny Catch.* ii. 21 The farmer .. thrust his hand into his pocket and mist his purse. 1693 Dryden & Earl Mulgrave *Ess. Satire* 47 Like her, who miss'd her Name in a Lampoon, And grieved to find her self decay'd so soon. 1712 Steele *Spect.* No. 280 ¶4 This Man, whom I have missed for some Years in my Walks. 1750 Gray *Elegy* 109 One morn I missed him on the custom'd hill. 1770 Sir J. Banks *Jrnl.* xvi. (1896) 376, I took decoction of bark plentifully, and in three or four days missed it [*sc.* an ague]. 1782 Cowper *Gilpin* 231 The post-boy's horse right glad to miss The lumbering of the wheels. 1814 Scott *Wav.* lxiii, It was sae dark that his folk never missed him till it was ower late. 1846 Browning *Soul's Trag.* i. 198 Well, he paid my fines Nor missed a cloak from wardrobe.

16. To perceive with regret the absence or loss of; to feel the want of.

1470–85 Malory *Arthur* xviii. v. 731 Madame said sir Bors now mys ye sir launcelot. c 1586 C'tess Pembroke *Ps.* l. iii, Not want of sacrifice doth mee offend, Nor doe I misse thy alters daily flame. 1667 Milton *P.L.* x. 104, I miss thee here, Not pleas'd, thus entertaind with solitude. 1779 Johnson *L.P., Milton* (1868) 44 Milton was too busy to much miss his wife. 1849 Macaulay *Hist. Eng.* v. I. 524 Every month his native land remembers and misses him less. 1870 Dickens *E. Drood* iii, I feel as if it would miss me, when I am gone so far away.

V. Intransitive uses.

†17. To go wrong, make a mistake, err. In OE. *impersonal*, const. dative of person. *Obs.*

In some of the latest examples the word should perhaps be referred to sense 1 d.

a 975 *Canons K. Edgar* xxxii. in Thorpe *Laws* (1840) II. 250 Ac beo se canon him æt-foran eagum; beseo to, ȝif he wille, þy læs þe him misse. c 1275 *Passion our Lord* 102 in *O.E. Misc.* 40 Þo seyde vre louerd crist .. Nymeþ gode yeme þat ye nouht ne mysse. Hwam ich biteche þat bred .. He me schal bitraye. c 1325 *Spec. Gy Warw.* 120 And, what it is, i wole þe wisse, Vnderstond, þat þu ne misse. 1489 Caxton *Faytes of A.* iv. i. 230, I telle the that thou myssest in thy sayeng in this byhalfe. 1562 Legh *Armory* 51 There you misse. For if you marke it, this is not like yt, yt were the misse. a 1568 Ascham *Scholem.* i. (Arb.) 26 If a childe misse, either in forgetting a worde, or in chaunging a good with a worse. 1633 G. Herbert *Temple, H. Script.*, Starres are poore books, and oftentimes do misse. a 1700 Dryden *Fables, Cock & Fox* 452 For art may err, but nature cannot miss. a 1754 Fielding *On Conversat.* Wks. 1784 IX. 366 If .. men .. often err in their conceptions of what would produce their own happiness, no wonder they should miss in the application of what will contribute to that of others.

†18. To be lacking or wanting. Const. dat. (of person) or *to*. *Obs.* (Cf. missing *ppl. a.*)

c 1374 Chaucer *Troylus* iii. 445 Nil I nought swere .. that he .. wolde of that him missed han ben sesed. 1535 Coverdale *Josh.* xxi. 45 And their myssed [1611 failed] nothinge of all the good that the Lorde had promysed .. it came euery whyt. a 1536 *Interl. Beauty & Good Prop. Women* ad fin., For grace doth neuer mys To them that vse good prayers dayly. 1589 Lyly *Pappe w. Hatchet* Dd, There shall not misse a name of any, that had a Godfather. 1611 Bible *1 Sam.* xxv. 7 Neither was there ought missing vnto them, all the while they were in Carmel. 1828 Scott *F.M. Perth* xiii, 'The heir of Thomas Randolph might have a better claim to be answered.' 'And, by my honour, it shall not miss for want of my asking the grace.'

†19. To fail to happen, come, etc. *Obs.*

1390 Gower *Conf.* I. 325 Who loveth wel, it mai noght misse .. Bot if that thei som weie finde. 1603 Florio *Montaigne* i. xl, Death hath come, or it will not misse.

†20. To come to an end, give out, fail. *Obs.*

a 1300 *Cursor M.* 9964 Þis castel es o beld and blis, þar mirth es neuer mar to mis. c 1374 Chaucer *Troylus* iii. 1624 That, there-as thou now brought art in-to blisse, That thou thy-self ne cause it nought to misse. c 1381 —— *Parl. Foules* 40 Til the day gan misse. c 1460 *Towneley Myst.* i. 66 Thou has .. giffen vs Ioy that neuer shall mys. a 1529 Skelton *'Now synge we'* 71 And thou shalt have blys That neuer shall mys.

21. To be unsuccessful: said of a person's designs or the person himself. Now *arch.* or *Obs.*

1592 Shaks. *Rom. & Jul.* Prol. 14 What here shall miss, our toil shall strive to mend. 1662 Pepys *Diary* 3 Nov., Though we have missed twice, yet they bring such an account of the probability of the truth of the thing, .. that we shall set upon it once more. 1687 Dryden *Hind & P.* i. 149 The bank above must fail before the venture miss. 1747 in *Col. Rec. Pennsylv.* V. 137 If they miss in their Schemes. 1813 Scott *Rokeby* iii. xxvi, If thy scheme miss.

22. a. Of crops, etc.: To be abortive or unproductive. *dial.*

1615 W. Lawson *Country Housew. Gard.* (1626) 18 Put in euery such roomth three or foure Kirnels of Apples or Peares .. and that day Moneth following, as many moe (lest some of the former misse). 1826 in *N.W. Linc. Gloss.* (1889) s.v., The turnips have all missed. 1852 *Jrnl. R. Agric. Soc.* XIII. ii. 274 The seed has been known to miss occasionally.

b. To fail to menstruate at the normal time, to miss a period.

1947 C. Willingham *End as Man* 9 A beautiful but wicked girl of a good Port George family missed one month. Then she missed another month. She went to a doctor and found out the truth. 1961 G. Greene *Burnt-Out Case* vi. i. 184, I think I have a baby on the way .. I've missed twice. 1971 'P. Hobson' *Three Graces* i. 8, I think I'm pregnant. This is the second time I've missed.

23. miss of ——. Chiefly *Obs.* or *arch.*

a. To fail to obtain, receive, acquire, attain to, or secure; = 6. (†occas. *miss on.*)

a 1250 *Owl & Night.* 581 Þu hauest ymyst of fayrhede & lutel is þi godhede. c 1357 *Lay Folks Catech.* (T.) 379 And man withouten merci of merci sal misse. c 1386 Chaucer *Shipman's T.* 352 And if that I were riche .. Of twenty thousand sheeld shold ye nat misse. 1526 Skelton *Magnyf.* 397 And of my seruyce you shall not mysse. 1599 *Return fr. Parnass.* ii. i. 638, I had like have missed of this preferment for wante of one to be bounde for my truthe! a 1625 Beaum. & Fl. *Wit at Sev. Weap.* i. i, For feare some poor Earle steale her, 't has bin threatned To redeem morgag'd land, but he shall misse on't. 1633 T. Stafford *Pac. Hib.* i. xix. 111 Ill pleased for that they missed of the booty expected. 1712 Steele *Spect.* No. 485 ¶3 He is that Sort of Person which the Mob call a handsome jolly Man; which Appearance can't miss of Captives in this part of the Town. 1742 Mrs. Montagu *Lett.* (1809) II. 144 An animal that has missed of instinct, and not lit upon reason. 1835 Macaulay *Ess., Mackintosh* (1852) 325/2 A project which .. had very narrowly missed of success. 1841 F. E. Paget *Tales of Village* (1852) 505 Placed in a state in which .. he cannot miss of everlasting happiness. 1868 Swinburne *Blake* 89 Compelled .. to an eternity of fruitless repentance for having wilfully missed of pleasure .. in this world.

†b. To make a mistake with regard to. *Obs.*

c 1386 Chaucer *Friar's T.* 118 Er we departe, I shal thee so wel wisse, That of myn hous ne shaltow never misse. c 1400 *Solomon* 30* in *Adam Davy* 97 And to knowe god & yuel þat I þerof ne mysse.

c. To fail to seize or capture; = 6 b.

a 1631 Donne *Elegy on Mris. Bulstrod* Poems (1633) 70 But thou hast both of Captaine mist and fort. 1678 *Donna Olimpia* 32 Which indeed, as to his possessions, she effected, though she missed of his life. 1737 Whiston *Josephus, Hist.* iv. ii. §5 Titus .. had captives enough .. to satisfy his anger, when it missed of John. 1833 Whittier *Pr. Wks.* (1889) I. 262 They had missed of the old chief, but had captured his son.

†d. To be without, lack; to cease to have, lose; = 14. *Obs.*

a 1300 *K. Horn* (Ritson) 126 Hue wenden mid y wisse, Of huere lyve to misse. c 1325 *Spec. Gy Warw.* 418 'Þeih sholen se god' aperteliche, In his godhede and in his blisse, Off which þei sholen neuere misse. c 1489 Caxton *Sonnes of Aymon* xxii. 486 Wyte it that ye have myssed of peas, For Charlemagne wylle noo thynge of it.

e. To fail to accomplish (a design) or realize (a hope); to fail in (an attempt or enterprise).

a 1225 *Leg. Kath.* 651 Þet þeo þe beoð icumene .. me to underneomene, moten missen þrof. 1390 Gower *Conf.* III. 349 And I [have] bot on desire, of which I misse. c 1420 Lydg. *Assembly of Gods* 108 Oft of myn entent hath he made me mys. c 1489 Caxton *Sonnes of Aymon* xiv. 321 He never myssed of no thyng that he toke in hand. 1585 T. Washington tr. *Nicholay's Voy.* ii. iv. 34 He hadde missed of his enterprise. 1649 Milton *Eikon.* 2 Rather .. then that the People should not still miss of their hopes, to be releiv'd by Parlaments. 1662 Pepys *Diary* 1 Nov., I myself did truly expect to speed; but we missed of all. 1667 *Decay Chr. Piety* ii. ¶1 Who can suspect that a cause so rightly dispos'd, should miss of its effect? 1703 Burkitt *On N.T.* Matt. xxvii. 27–31 The Jews missing of their Expectation of a Temporal King in Christ. 1719 De Foe *Crusoe* ii. (Globe) 503 If he miss'd of his Business outward bound, he was to go up to China.

f. Not to find (a person or thing) where one expects or desires to; to discover the absence of (a thing). Also, to fail to meet with (a person).

1560 Daus tr. *Sleidane's Comm.* 57 b, When they missed of their company, they wer in such a rage [etc.]. 1603 Knolles *Hist. Turks* (1621) 634 Grittus .. missing of the Moldauian, fell vpon Francis Schenden. 1610 Heywood *Gold. Age* iv. i. 54 We have mist of Saturne lately fled. 1628 Gaule *Pract. Theories* (1629) 367 They worthily misse of Christ, that seeke him where he is not. 1721 Cibber *Lady's Last Stake* v. Dram. Wks. 1757 II. 226 They are certainly gone out that way, and Sir Friendly must miss of 'em. 1769 Burke *Corr.* (1844) I. 172, I was unluckily in London and so missed of him. 1889 *N.W. Linc. Gloss.*, I miss'd on him yisterdaay, though I look'd high an' low fer him.

g. *to miss of one's aim*: = 1 b.

1621 Burton *Anat. Mel.* iii. ii. vi. v, Penelope had a company of suiters, yet all missed of their aym. 1655 Loveday tr. *Calprenède's Cleopatra* iii. 222 Oroondates enrag'd to have miss'd of his aime, drew his sword and threw himself after Artabon. 1771 Foote *Maid of Bath* iii. Wks. 1799 II. 234 Projects, the most prudentially pointed, may miss of their aim. 1876 Lowell *Ode for 4th July* ii. iii, Time has a quiver full of purposes Which miss not of their aim.

h. To fail to perceive or understand; = 10.

1678 R. Barclay *Apol. Quakers* x. §19. 310 He cannot be certain, but may still miss of the sense of it. 1704 Norris *Ideal World* ii. i. 38 The reason is so very obvious that we cannot well miss of it. 1708 Atterbury *Serm.* (1726) II. vi. 190 These .. Perfections of the Deity, are .. most easy to be understood by us; upon the least Reflection and Enquiry we cannot miss of them.

i. With gerund: To fail (to do something); = 7 a.

1658 *Whole Duty Man* i. §30 No man can miss of enjoying them [*sc.* God's mercies], but by his own default. 1663 Pepys *Diary* 20 Sept., He hath not missed one night .. of supping with my Lady Castlemaine. 1756 Washington *Lett.* Writ. 1889 I. 268 Since the first murders were committed by the Indians, I have never missed of receiving intelligence of their motions. 1840 T. Robbins *Diary* 12 Aug. (1887) II. 579 Missed of seeing my brother at Enfield. 1868 Swinburne *Blake* 6 With what excellent care and taste this has been done, no one can miss of seeing.

†j. To fail to accomplish (a stroke). *Obs.*

c 1320 *Sir Tristr.* 2389 Eft vrgan smot wiþ main And of þat stroke he miste.

k. To fail to be present at or to witness; = 6 c.

1612 Beaum. & Fl. *Cupid's Rev.* i. ad init., I had mist of this, if you had not call'd me.

l. To escape, avoid; = 8.

1628–9 Digby *Voy. Medit.* (Camd.) 85 [He] told me the Dunkerkers ranged much .. about our channell, and that in all probabilities I could not misse of a hott encounter with them.

m. To fail to take advantage of; = 9.

a 1628 Preston *New Covt.* (1629) 587 Because they do not effect the thing they go about, when they misse of their time. 1785 M. Cutler in *Life*, etc. (1888) II. 223 Missing of the opportunity by which I expected to have sent this letter last week.

n. To fail to catch (a boat, etc.); = 9 b.

1777 Franklin *Lett.* Wks. 1889 VI. 56 Should you miss of one at Boulogne, proceed to Calais.

24. miss on ——. To fail to hit upon.

1823 Lamb *Elia* Ser. ii. *Amicus redivivus*, Trite as the counsel was, and impossible, as one should think, to be missed on.

25. miss out (on) ——. To fail (esp. to achieve something); to make a mistake (over something); to omit; to be omitted.

1929 D. Scarborough *Can't Get Red Bird* xxvii. 405, I feel sorry for a poor sucker that misses out on any one of 'em. 1934 *Hound & Horn* VII. 393 They have a way of missing out on emotional experience, either through timidity and caution or through heroic renunciation. 1938 R. Franken *Gold Pennies* xix. 224 Morton lumbered behind her, fearful that he might be missing out on something. 1942 Berrey & Van den Bark *Amer. Thes. Slang* §262/2 *Fail*, .. miss out (on). 1944 D. Runyon *Runyon à la Carte* 100 He will lay them according to how he figures their word .. if Brandy Bottle misses out. 1952 G. W. Brace *Spire* (1953) xii. 105 It was Flanders who was planning the reception... But he missed out on Wilfred Stearns. 1959 *Listener* 15 Jan. 115/2 We had to by-pass Tippaburra and miss out on that Christmas Eve spree. 1960 S. H. Courtier *Gently dust Corpse* iii. 32 They .. had missed out when prosperity hit the Mallee. 1960 I. Cross *Backward Sex* 116 You and I are going to miss out, y' know. 1961 J. Wade *Back to Life* ix. 120 Sorry I missed out on that report. 1963 A. Lubbock *Austral. Roundabout* 48 We didn't want the kids to miss out... They don't often get the chance to have a bit of fun. 1965 M. Morse *Unattached* i. 38 It's a terrible feeling missing out. 1969 *New Yorker* 12 Apr. 56/2 The motivation derives from the desire not to miss out on any information that could be essential later. 1972 *National Observer* (U.S.) 27 May 21/5 (Advt.), Don't 'miss out' on any of the fresh, new kind of reporting that makes The Observer the national newspaper for the *business of living*.

miss (mɪs), *v.*^{2} [f. miss *sb.*^{2}] *trans.* To address as 'miss'.

1824 Miss Ferrier *Inher.* xlv, Did you hear how he Miss'd me to-day?—me a married woman! 1863 Mrs. Carey Brock *Margaret's Secret* viii. 115, 'I am not accustomed to hear myself called Miss Ellis,' .. 'Well, you'll be *missed* here by every one'.

miss, obs. form of mass *sb.*^{1}

missable ('mɪsəb(ə)l), *a.* [f. miss *v.*^{1} + -able.] That can be or is likely to be missed.

1924 *Glasgow Herald* 15 June 11/6 Of course it was not a record, but he holed out everything missable. 1955 [see holeable *a.*]. 1959 *Times* 11 Sept. 5/1 [He] holed all the missable putts.

missafic, erroneous form of missific.

missage, missai obs. ff. message, missay.

†mis'sake, *v. Obs. rare*$^{-1}$. [a. MDu. *missaecken* (mod.Du. *miszaken*): cf. forsake *v.*] *trans.* To deny, renounce.

1481 Caxton *Reynard* (Arb.) 116 Yf he were otherwyse .. I wold euer myssake hym.

missal ('mɪsəl), *sb.*^{1} Forms: 4 messel, 5 **myssal(l)e**, 5–6 **messall, missale**, 5–7 **missall**, (7 *erron.* **massal**), 6– **missal**. [ad. eccl. L. *missāle*, neut. sing. of *missālis* (see next). Some of the

early forms represent OF. *messel* (mod.F. *missel*).]

1. The book containing the service of the Mass for the whole year; a mass-book.

c **1330** *Arth. & Merl.* 3574 (Kölbing) Her after sone Merlin swore.. Tofore þe king on o messel. **1432** *Test. Ebor.* (Surtees) II. 21, I wyte unto my chauntry in yᵉ chapell of Sancte Anne.. my best Missall. **1480** CAXTON *Chron. Eng.* ccxxx. 245 Charlys leyde his right hond on the paten with goddes body and his lift hond on the missale. **1506** *Test. Ebor.* (Surtees) IV. 247 To yᵉ Chapell in Holbek my Messall, my Portus in prynte. *c* **1553** *Durham Acc. Rolls* (Surtees) 728 For Carryage of yᵉ new grailes and missales. **1611** BIBLE *Transl. Pref.* ¶13 Pope Nicolas the third.. brought into vse the Missals of the Friers Minorites. **1657-61** HEYLIN *Hist. Ref.* I. ii. §5. 40 Many of the inferior Clergy had not much more learning than what was taught them in the Massals and other Rituals. **1726** AYLIFFE *Parergon* 356 In the Roman Church there were always Forms of Prayer, as may be seen in their Missals, Breviaries, Rituals.. &c. **1845** T. H. HORNE in *Encycl. Metrop.* XXI. 494/1 The Council held at Toledo, in 633.. adopted the Missal and Breviary of Isidore, Bishop of Seville. **1895** G. H. PALMER in *Elem. Plainsong* 59 To S. Gregory alone belongs the credit of having compiled.. the Sacramentary and Antiphoner, i.e. what we should now call the Missal and Gradual.

¶ **b.** Used vaguely for: A Roman Catholic book of prayers, esp. when illuminated; an illuminated book of hours, or the like.

1651 BAXTER *Inf. Bapt.* 304 The reading of one of their Missals, or books of Devotion. **1838** C. B. ELLIOTT *Trav.* II. 368 The greater part of the night, as well as of the day, is passed with rosaries, crucifixes, and missals. **1845** LONGF. *Norman Baron* iii, A monk.. Who.. repeated Many a prayer and pater-noster From the missal on his knee. **1858** O. W. HOLMES *Aut. Breakf.-t.* iii, He is as tender and reverential to all that bears the mark of genius.. as a nun over her Missal. **1886** J. R. REES *Divers. Bookworm* (1887) 163 The pages of the missal are.. illuminated with elegant borders of fruit, flowers, and birds.

2. *attrib.* and *Comb.* (usually with reference to the illumination of service-books or manuscripts), as ***missal-album***, ***hand***, ***letter***, ***-like*** adj., ***-marge***, ***-page***, ***-painter***, ***-painting*** vbl. sb. and ppl. a.; **missal caps** (*Printing*): see quot.

1890 W. WHITE *Catal. Ruskin Mus. Library* 6 *Missal Album of Lady Diana de Croy. **1875** J. SOUTHWARD *Dict. Typogr.*, **Missal caps*, a style of fancy letter, used sometimes as initials to Old English or Black letter. **1831** LAMB *Let. to Dyer* 22 Feb., You never wrote what I call a schoolmaster's hand, like Mrs. Clarke;.. nor a *missal hand, like Porson. **1888** *Athenæum* 20 Oct. 514/1 The colours used for the *missal letters, and in the final touches of the rubricator. **1872** BLACK *Adv. Phaeton* vii. 94 Decorating our bedrooms with *missal-like texts. **1855** BROWNING *Men & Women* II. 237 He.. Fills his lady's *Missal-marge with flowerets. **1858** RUSKIN *Arrows of Chace* (1880) I. 129 The officers.. of the British Museum refuse to expose their best drawings or *missal-pages to light. *a* **1843** SOUTHEY *Comm.-pl. Bk.* (1849) IV. 258 In these countries the poets resemble *missal-painters;—their colours often rich, their pencilling delicate. **1883** RUSKIN *Art of Eng.* 9 The speciality of colour-method.. founded on *missal-painting. **1895** *Army & Navy Co-op. Soc.* Price List 668 Colours for illuminating and missal painting. **1903** *Edin. Rev.* Apr. 450 The patient labour of *Missal-painting monks.

missal (ˈmɪsəl), *a.* (*sb.*²) [ad. eccl. L. *missāl-is*, f. *missa* MASS *sb.*¹] Of or pertaining to the Mass; mass-. †Also *sb.*, a mass-priest.

a **1548** HALL *Chron., Hen. VIII*, 74 The Closet hanged with clothe of gold all other iewelles Missall. *Ibid.* 82 b, The alter apparelled with all Juelles myssall of great riches. **1549** LATIMER *3rd Serm. bef. Edw. VI* (Arb.) 86 It had bene good for our missal priestes to haue dwelled in that contrye. **1553** BECON *Reliques of Rome* (1563) 130* Pope Honorius the third commaunded yᵗ the Missall bread shoulde be.. lifted vp aboue the Priestes heade at the sacryng tyme. **1614** BP. HALL *No Peace with Rome* §19 Wks. (1625) 658 The Priestly Office of Christ is not a little impeached by the dayly Oblation of the Missall Sacrifice. **1637** GILLESPIE *Eng. Pop. Cerem.* Ep. A 3 b, Her sweet Voice is.. muttering some missall and magicall Liturgies. **1660** R. COKE *Power & Subj.* 162 All his Missal vestiments. **1793** HELY tr. *O'Flaherty's Ogygia* I. 41 They distinguished Thanes into missals, and seculars; the Missal-Thanes were Presbyters.

missal, obs. variant of MISSILE.

ˈmissal-book. [f. MISSAL *a.*] = MASS-BOOK.

c **1645** HOWELL *Lett.* (1650) 178 They present unto him the Cross, and the Missall book to swear upon. **1873** HALE *In His Name* viii. 71 The beautiful missal book, from which the Senior Canon was about to read. **1894** *Dublin Rev.* Oct. 246 Three early missal-books of the Roman Church, or, as they are called sacramentaries.

missale, variant of MESEL.

c **1375** *Sc. Leg. Saints* xxxvi. (*Baptista*) 366 Missale are clene mad alsa.

† **miˈssalian**, *a.* and *sb. Obs. rare.* [f. eccl. L. *missāl-is* MISSAL *a.* + -IAN.] **a.** *adj.* = MISSAL *a.* So ˈ**missaline** *a.* **b.** *sb.* A mass-priest. So ˈ**missalist**.

1624 DARCIE *Birth of Heresies* xii. 50 The vestments of these Missalian Sacrificers. *Ibid.* 51 A Pectorall.. which the Missalists terme a Chasuble. *Ibid.* 52 The Stole put ouer the Amict, at the Missalians necke. *Ibid.* 53 The Missalian Priest. *Ibid.* xxi. 84 Was there euer.. a more detestable Heresie then this Missaline transubstantiation? **1909** *Daily Chron.* 9 Oct. 4/4 The three brothers Maris might be re-incarnations of the Van Eyck brothers, or the de Limburg missalists.

missall (*Sc.*), **missar**: see MUZZLE, MISSER.

† ˈ**missary.** *Obs.* [ad. eccl. L. *missāri-us*, f. *missa* MASS *sb.*¹: see -ARY.] A Romanist or Romish priest.

1550 VERON *Godly Sayings* (1846) 34 The very missaries.. do call it.. the sacrifice of.. praise. **1657** J. SERGEANT *Schism Dispach't* 56 Such as are neither easily deceivable by our Missaries, nor possibly undeceivable by Dr. H.

† **miˈssatical**, *a. Obs.* [f. eccl. L. *missātic-us*, f. *missa* MASS *sb.*¹: see -ATIC.] Pertaining to the Mass.

a **1670** HACKET *Abp. Williams* I. (1692) 101 Since he profess'd open adherence to the Romish Church and did not renounce the Missatical corruption of their priesthood. *a* **1683** J. OWEN *Nat. & Causes Apostasy* Wks. 1852 VII. 99 Missatical sacrifices for the living and the dead.

† **mis-ˈsavour**, *v. Obs.* [MIS-¹ 1.] *intr.* **a.** To have defective sense of taste. **b.** *fig.* To have wrong notions *of*.

1402 *Pol. Poems* (Rolls) II. 53 With wrong wrytyng he wrouȝte mykil care, and.. foul fel fro the chirche, mis-saveryng of the sacrament. **1540** PALSGR. *Acolastus* H iv b, To vs also the palate myssesauoreth or mysse tasteth neuer a whytte.

† **misˈsaw.** *Obs.* Forms: 3-4, 7 **missawe**, 4 **mys(s)awe, mis(s)au(e, mys-, missagh.** [f. MIS-¹ 4 + SAW *sb.*, saying.]

1. Evil speaking, calumny, slander, abuse.

a **1225** *Ancr. R.* 124 Aȝein mis-sawe oðer misdede, lo, heranont, remedie & salue. *a* **1300** [see MISLOVING *vbl. sb.*]. *a* **1340** HAMPOLE *Psalter* xix. 3 All.. wrangis and myssaghis.. that thou suffird for vs. *c* **1375** *Cursor M.* 5877 (Fairf.) Quat wene þai wiþ missawe fra my werk ham to drawe.

¶ **2.** ? Wrong expression, perverted language.

1614 J. DAVIES *Ecl.* in Browne *Sheph. Pipe* G 4 So my sp'rits been steept In dulnesse, through these duller times missawes Of sik-like musicke (riming rudely cleept).

† **misˈsay**, *sb. Obs.* Also 4 **misai**, 5 **myssae.** [f. next.] = prec.

a **1300** *Cursor M.* 21474 Al has þis curt herd þi misai. *c* **1460** *Towneley Myst.* xxiii. 568 If thou be crist.. Com downe emangys vs all, And thole not thies myssaes [*rime* says].

mis-say (mɪsˈseɪ), *v. arch.* Pa. t. and pa. pple. **mis-said** (mɪsˈsɛd). Forms: see MIS-¹ 1 and SAY *v.*: also 4 **misain, misaie**; *pa. t.* **misede.** [ME. *misseggen, missei(n)*, etc. Cf. MDu. *misseggen*, LG. *miszeggen*, MHG. *mis(se)sagen*.]

1. *trans.* To speak evil of or against (a person); to abuse, slander, revile, vilify. Now *arch.* and *poet.*

a **1225** *Ancr. R.* 186 Biddeð ȝeorne uor þeo ou eni vuel doð oðer missiggeð. *c* **1290** *Beket* 2036 in *S. Eng. Leg.*, Hold þinne mouthþ,.. þov mis-seist mi louerd þe king. **13..** *Sir Beues* (A.) 1168 þow haddest vnriȝt, So te misain a noble kniȝt! *c* **1380** WYCLIF *Wks.* (1880) 353 Crist was so patient,.. þat whan he was mys-said he cursid not aȝen. **1470-85** MALORY *Arthur* v. i. 161 The kynge commaunded that none of them vpon payne of dethe to myssaye them ne doo them ony harme. **1541** COPLAND *Guydon's Quest. Chirurg.* E ij b, Myssaye nat the auncyentes, nor dyspryse nat Hyppocrates. **1568** *Jacob & Esau* IV. xi, Cursed be the man that shall thee curse or missay. **1631** HEYWOOD *1st Pt. Fair Maid of West* III. 33 Is she such a Saint, None can missay her? **1872** TENNYSON *Gareth & Lynette* 923 Far liefer had I fight a score of times Than hear thee so missay me and revile. **1888** MORRIS *Dream John Ball* xii. 125 These men shall the blind and the fearful mock and missay.

† **b.** To say (something) with evil, abusive, or slanderous intent. *Obs.*

a **1300** *Cursor M.* 14779 Mikel of him can þai missai. **1340** *Ayenb.* 189 By þe kueade huiche he ssel miszigge. **1470-85** MALORY *Arthur* VII. xi. 229 The myssayenge that ye myssayed me. **1530** PALSGR. 638/1, I never myssayd hym worde. **1593** DRAYTON *Ecl.* ii. 95 And sore repents what he before misse-said. **1614** SYLVESTER *Parl. Vertues Royall* Wks. (Grosart) II. 134/2 And can suffer nought 'Gainst them to be mis-done, mis-said, mis-thought.

† **2.** *intr.* To speak evil; to speak abusively, slanderously, arrogantly, or the like. *Obs.*

a **1300** *Cursor M.* 13905 þou missais, deuel es in þe. *c* **1386** CHAUCER *Manciple's T.* 249 He that hath misseyd.. He may by no wey clepe his word agayn. **1481** CAXTON *Myrr.* I. v. 28 To whom it pleseth that they messaye. **1596** SPENSER *F.Q.* IV. vi. 27 Her tongue.. brought forth speeches myld when she would have missayd.

† **b.** To speak evil of. *Obs.*

a **1300** *Cursor M.* 19420 Tua wittnes fals þai þam puruaid, To tell he had o godd missaid. *c* **1385** CHAUCER *L.G.W.* 233 And of mynne olde seruauntis thow misseyst. **1477** *Paston Lett.* III. 185 Sum evyll tong.. myss sayeth of me. **1579** SPENSER *Sheph. Cal.* Sept. 106 Their ill haviour garres men missay, Both of their doctrine, and of theyr faye.

3. *trans.* With pronominal or cognate obj.: To say amiss, wrongly, or incorrectly. Now *rare.*

a **1400** *Cursor M.* 25192 (Cott. Galba) And of oure praier crist es payd Sum tyme all if it be missayd. **1629** H. BURTON *Truth's Triumph* 254 Let men beleeue that.. which the diuine Scriptures doe say, and not which mens tongues doe mis-say. **1641** MILTON *Animadv.* §2 Wks. 1851 III. 203 Lest any thing in generall might be missaid in their publick Prayers through ignorance. **1665** WITHER *Lord's Prayer* Preamble, Beseeching him to pardon what is misdone or missaid, by others, or misunderstood by me.

b. *intr.* To say what is not right or correct; to say something wrong or amiss.

1390 GOWER *Conf.* I. 19 And natheles I can noght seie, In aunter if that I misseye. *c* **1489** CAXTON *Sonnes of Aymon* vii. 174 Ye have myssayed, For I never sawe Reynawde nor I wote not what he is. **1579** SPENSER *Sheph. Cal.* Sept. 2 Or Diggon her is, or I missaye. **1611** A. GILL in Speed *Theat. Gt. Brit.* Pref., Great love and little skill may cause mee to missay. **1816** BYRON *Siege of Cor.* Introd., Some of mosque, and some of church, And some, or I missay, of neither. **1879** BROWNING *Ivan Ivanovitch* 417 The Sacred Pictures—where skulks Innocence enshrined, Or I missay!

† **mis-ˈsayer.** *Obs.* [MIS-¹ 5.] An evil speaker, slanderer.

1340 *Ayenb.* 61 Blondere and misziggere byeþ of one scole. *Ibid.* 136, 177, 256. *c* **1400** *Rom. Rose* 2231 If that any missayere Dispyse wimmen. **1481** CAXTON *Myrr.* I. v. 28 Myssayers felons & enuyous men that wil lerne no good.

† **mis-ˈsaying**, *vbl. sb. Obs.* [MIS-¹ 3.] **1.** The action of the verb MISSAY; evil speaking; slander, abuse.

13.. in *Archiv Stud. neu. Spr.* LXXXI. 316/42 Blesset beo ȝe.. To whom þe world makeþ missiggynge. **1340** *Ayenb.* 66 þe myssiggynges þet is huanne þe on þcyneþ þannoþren and ziggeþ þe greate felonyes. *c* **1440** *Jacob's Well* 83 Myssaying; þat is, whan þou spekyst euyll of an oþer mannys goodnesse. **1526** *Pilgr. Perf.* (W. de W. 1531) 80 b, And asked of hym mercy and forgyuenes of his mis-sayenge. **1581** *Reg. Privy Council Scot.* Ser. I. III. 433 For missaying, detracting and sclandering of the baillies.

2. Mis-statement.

1650 MILTON *Eikon.* Pref. (ed. 2) A 4 To.. refute the mis-sayings of his book.

Misschelmasse, obs. form of MICHAELMAS.

mis-ˈscript. [MIS-¹ 4.] A miswriting.

a **1834** COLERIDGE *Notes & Lect.* (1849) I. 143 In treating this 'path' as a mere misprint or mis-script for 'put'. **1873** F. HALL *Mod. Eng.* 175 *note*, These mis-scripts [*analyze*, *paralyze*] look as if descendants of ἀναλύζω and παραλύζω, which are nothing.

misse, nonce-var. of MILCE, used for rime.

a **1300** in *Rel. Ant.* I. 275 That he.. bring us of this woning For his muchele misse [*rime* blisce].

missed (mɪst), *ppl. a.* [f. MISS *v.*¹ + -ED¹.] **a.** In senses of the vb. Also *dial.* of a heifer: Barren.

1615 WITHER *Sheph. Hunting* Ecl. iii, Thy mist pleasure. **1657** in *Burton's Diary* (1828) 195 It was a little missed sense, that might be mended. **1763** 'THEOPH. INSULANUS' *Second Sight* 189 His account of a missed hatchet found by a dream. **1780** A. YOUNG *Tour Irel.* I. 259 Those who buy the mist heifers are farmers in Monaghan. **1898** *Westm. Gaz.* 6 Sept. 2/3 This missed train. **1905** *Daily Chron.* 24 Aug. 4/6 The undergraduate never heard more of the missed chapels.

† **b.** ***missed way***: having missed the way; erring, straying. *Obs.*

1599 PORTER *Angry Wom. Abington* (1841) 116 To light my mist way feete to my right way.

c. Med. ***missed abortion***: the retention of a fœtus in the womb for a period after it has died; also, the fœtus itself; ***missed labour***: the retention of a fœtus in the womb beyond the normal period of pregnancy.

[**1847** H. OLDHAM in *Guy's Hosp. Rep.* V. 109 A female carries a child in the womb to the full period of gestation; but the process of labour is literally missed, and lactation follows on completion of gestation. *Ibid.*, Cases resembling this, in its principal feature of labour being missed, have been recorded.] **1864** *Med. Times & Gaz.* 22 Oct. 449/2 Dr. Greenhalgh did not consider that Dr. Williams' cases could be placed under the head of missed labour... Dr. Oldham said that he had used the term as the most appropriate he could find. It was a case in which the time of natural labour passed by without any pains, and the child was not expelled. **1878** J. M. DUNCAN in *Ibid.* 28 Dec. 730/1 In a case of missed abortion.. the important element of suspicion as to the real conditions may not have come into the mind either of the patient or her physician. *Ibid.*, This is a case in which you have.. slight protraction of pregnancy, and then the condition of missed labour. **1936** W. SHAW *Text-bk. Gynæcol.* xii. 262 In missed abortion the signs of pregnancy disappear. **1971** E. S. TAYLOR *Beck's Obstetr. Pract.* (ed. 9) xxix. 436/1 Missed labor, unlike missed abortion, is extremely rare. Pregnancy continues to term in the normal manner, but near the expected date of confinement labor starts and then ceases after a time. **1972** W. BARR *Clin. Gynaecol.* xi. 148 There is a risk that, if a missed abortion is left in situ for over four weeks, difibrination of the blood can occur.

d. ***missed approach*** [APPROACH *sb.* 13], in *Aeronaut.*, an approach that is discontinued for any reason; esp. (with hyphen) *attrib.*

1951 *Gloss. Aeronaut. Terms* (*B.S.I.*) III. 20 *Missed-approach altitude*, the minimum height at which a final approach should be discontinued if it cannot be completed. *Ibid.* 21 *Missed-approach procedure*, procedure to be followed when an aircraft cannot complete final approach. **1971** *Flying* Apr. 42/3 Sometimes, the missed-approach procedure directs you to an NDB. **1973** *Black Panther* 13 Oct. 14/2 The Aero Commander pilot requested of Midway Tower a 'missed approach' (that he be allowed to go round again and make a second landing attempt).

mis-ˈsee, *v.* [MIS-¹ 1.] *trans.* To see imperfectly; to take a wrong view of. Also *absol.*

1591 FLORIO *2nd Fruites* 81 *N.* Well maie I want in habilitie, but neuer in affection. *S.* To much affection makes you mis-see both. **1840** CARLYLE *Heroes* v. (1841) 311 The man who cannot think and see; but only.. missee the nature of the thing he works with? **1841** —— *Misc. Ess., Baillie* (1857) IV. 236 Herein he fundamentally mistook; mis-saw;—and so miswent. **1902** *Words of Eye-witness* 324 Its modest hues and stature being ridiculously mis-seen as 'purple-patched' and 'tall'.

missee, obs. form of MISSY.

mis-'seek, *v.* [MIS-^{1} I.] *trans.* and *intr.* To seek wrongly. So **mis-'seeking** *vbl. sb.*, **mis'sought** *ppl. a.*

1387-8 T. USK *Test. Love* II. xi. (Skeat) l. 48 Errour in mankynde departeth thilke goodes by mis-seching, whiche he shulde have hole. *a* **1542** WYATT in *Tottel's Misc.* (Arb.) 87 The thing, that most is your desire, You do misseeke, with more trauell and care. **1563** *Mirr. Mag.*, *Rivers* xxii, What myschiefes folow missought maryages. *a* **1628** F. GREVIL *Cœlica* lxvi, The heart of man mis-seeking for the best.

mis-'seem, *v.* Now *rare.* [MIS-^{1} I.] *trans.* To misbecome.

c **1400** tr. *Secreta Secret.*, *Gov. Lordsh.* 62 Ne wost þou noght þat yt myssemys þi dignite..whanne þou swerys? **1513** DOUGLAS *Æneis* IV. vi. 108 Nor it sall neuir me irk, na ȝit misseme, The worthy Dido to hald in fresche memory. **1590** SPENSER *F.Q.* III. iii. 53 Ne certes, daughter, that same warlike wize, I weene, would you misseeme. **1603** FLORIO *Montaigne* II. iv, He hath at lest lent him nothing that doth belye him, or misseeme him. *a* **1641** BP. MOUNTAGU *Acts & Mon.* (1642) 57 Divines ought not hold any opinion (it misseemeth their profession so to hold) which hath no footing in Scripture. **1819** *Chron.* in *Ann. Reg.* 523 A spirit that would not have misseemed the most illustrious of her ancestry. **1836** CARLYLE in *Academy* 17 Sept. (1898) 272/1 His head is getting a shade of grey..which does not mis-seem him, but looks very well.

† **mis-'seeming**, *vbl. sb. Obs.* [MIS-^{1} 3.] ? False show.

1590 SPENSER *F.Q.* I. vii. 50 With her witchcraft and misseeming sweete.

mis-'seeming, *ppl. a.* [MIS-^{1} 2.] Misbecoming, unseemly.

a **1340** HAMPOLE *Psalter* lxxii. 15 Lo this misemand thing folous. **1513** DOUGLAS *Æneis* I. Prol. 409 He..haldis missemyng, Ay word by word to reduce ony thing. *Ibid.* XII. i. 63 Of blude and frendschip na thyng myssemand [orig. *nec genus indecores*]. **1590** SPENSER *F.Q.* I. ix. 23 For never knight I saw in such misseeming plight. **1603** FLORIO *Montaigne* I. xxxvi, A thing which would no whit be misseeming or undecent.

misseif, obs. form of MISSIVE.

missel ('mɪsəl). Forms: 1, 5 mistel, (1, 3 -il), 6 mistle, miscel, 6-7 missel(l, 7 mis(c)le, missle. [OE. *mistel*, (1) basil, (2) mistletoe, distinguished in the *Leechdoms* as *eorþmistel* and *ácmistel* respectively: corresp. to OHG. *mistil* (MHG., G. *mistel*) mistletoe, early mod.Du. *mistel* 'viscum' (Kilian), 'glew' (Hexham), ON. only in comb. *mistilteinn* MISTLETOE (the Sw. and Da. *mistel* are prob. from LG.): of unascertained origin.]

† **1.** Mistletoe. *Obs.*

c **725** *Corpus Gloss.* (Hessels) V 185 *Viscus*, mistel. *c* **825** *Epinal Gloss.* 1083 *Viscus*, mistil. *c* **1450** *Alphita* (Anecd. Oxon.) 192/1 [*Viscus*] g^e. wy de chene, a. mistel. **1562** TURNER *Herbal* II. 164 b, Of the Missel or Misselto tre. **1566** WITHALS *Dict.* 22 b, Mistle, whiche groweth vpon aple trees and crabbe trees in a great numbre of white or yelow beries. **1573** TUSSER *Husb.* (1878) 33 Giue sheepe to their fees the mistle of trees. **1610** BARROUGH *Meth. Physick* I. xxiv. (1639) 41 Miscle of the Oke. **1670** SWAN *Spec. M.* 246 Missel or Misselto, groweth.. upon trees.

† **b.** *attrib.*, as ***missel-berry***, ***-birdlime***, ***-child***.

1562 TURNER *Herbal* II. 165 The thurse..shiteth out the *miscel berries. **1658** SIR T. BROWNE *Gard. Cyrus* iii. 123 The Quincunciall Specks on the top of the Miscle-berry. **1562** TURNER *Herbal* II. 164 b, The best *missel byrde lyme is freshe resemblinge a leke in Color within. **1579** LANGHAM *Gard. Health* (1633) 40 Missel birdlime, hath power to soften and ripen apostumes with rosin and wax. **1608** SIR H. PLATT *Gard. Eden* (1653) 86 There you shall finde an Oake with Mistletoe therein, at the root whereof there is a *missell-child, whereof many strange things are conceived.

† **2.** Basil, *Calamintha Clinopodium. Obs.*

c **1000** *Sax. Lechd.* I. 232 Ðenim þas wyrte þe man ocimum & oðrum naman mistel nemneþ. *Ibid.* II. 86 Eorð mistel. **12..** *MS. Bodl.* 130 lf. 54 b, Mistil. *Ocimum.*

3. Short for MISSEL-BIRD, MISSEL-THRUSH.

1845 *New Statist. Acc. Scotl.* XIV. (Ross & Cromarty) 189 The missel, blackbird,..and threstle are common. **1882** *Proc. Berw. Nat. Club* IX. No. 3. 554 The Missels were fewer than usual.

missel, variant of MESEL *a.*

? **14..** *Iter Camerar.* xx. in *Balfour's Practicks* (1754) 582 Quhen thay opin fish, thay luke not gif thay be missel fish, or not [cf. MESEL *a.* b, quot. *a* **1400**].

missel, obs. Sc. form of MIZZLE.

misselane: see MESSELLAWNY.

misselany, obs. form of MISCELLANY.

'missel-bird. Now *dial.* Also 7 missle-, 8 mizzel-. [f. MISSEL. Cf. G. *mistelfink*, Du. *mistelvink*.] = MISSEL-THRUSH.

1626 BACON *Sylva* §556 An Idle Tradition, that there is a Bird, called a Missel-Bird, that feedeth upon a seed which many times shee cannot digest [etc.]. **1646** SIR T. BROWNE *Pseud. Ep.* II. vi. 98 One kind of thrush called ἰξοβόρος, the missell thrush or feeder upon misseltoe. **1676** WILLUGHBY *Ornith.* II. xvii. 137 *Turdus viscivorus major.* The Missel-Bird or Shrite. **1731** ALBIN *Nat. Hist. Birds* 31 The Mizzel-Bird, *Turdus Viscivorus.* **1768** PENNANT *Brit. Zool.* I. 226. **1773** G. WHITE *Selborne*, *To Pennant* 9 Nov., The people of Hampshire and Sussex call the Missel-bird the storm-cock. **1879** MISS JACKSON *Shropsh. Word-bk.*

misselden, -din(e, obs. forms of MISTLETOE.

misselin, -ling, -llane, obs. forms of MASLIN^2.

misselling, misselmas, obs. ff. MIZZLING, MICHAELMAS.

'missel-thrush. [f. MISSEL. Cf. G. *misteldrossel.*] A species of thrush, *Turdus viscivorus*, which feeds on the berries of the mistletoe.

1774 GOLDSM. *Nat. Hist.* (1776) V. 320 The missel-thrush is distinguished from all of the kind by its superior size. **1774** G. WHITE *Selborne*, *To Barrington* Sept., Several magpies came determined to storm the nest of a missel-thrush. **1859** DARWIN *Orig. Spec.* iii. 59 The recent increase of the missel thrush in parts of Scotland has caused the decrease of the song thrush. **1870** MORRIS *Earthly Par.* III. IV. 124 The sharp crying of the missel-thrush.

misselto(e, obs. forms of MISTLETOE.

† **mis-'semblance.** *Obs.* [MIS-^{1} 4.] False semblance.

a **1641** SIR H. SPELMAN *Feuds* xx. Posth. Wks. (1698) 34 From such missemblances rise many errors.

missen, obs. form of MIZEN.

mis-'send, *v.* [MIS-^{1} I.] *trans.* To send wrong; to send to a wrong place or person. Chiefly in pa. pple. and ppl. a. **mis-'sent.**

14.. *Sir Beues* 1447^2 (MS.S.) He toke no leue, he is myssende. **1737** J. CHAMBERLAYNE *St. Gt. Brit.* (ed. 33) II. *Gen. List* 78 [Generall Letter-Office in Lombard-street]..Mr. Robert Parsons and Mr. John Barber, to overlook the Franks and mis-sent Letters. **1834** MAR. EDGEWORTH *Helen* II. 199 She pointed to the word 'mis-sent', written on the corner of the cover. **1839** MURCHISON *Silur. Syst.* I. xxix. 382 *note*, This sketch was missent. **1847-54** WEBSTER, *Missend*, to send amiss or incorrectly. **1841** EMERSON *Misc.* (1855) 249 It appears that there was some mistake in my creation; and that I have been missent to this earth.

† **mis-'sense**, *sb. Obs.* [MIS-^{1} 4.] Wrong sense or meaning.

a **1618** SYLVESTER *Honor's Farwel* Wks. (1621) 1159 Without Offence, without Mis-sense, or Blame.

† **mis-'sense**, *v. Obs.* [MIS-^{1} I.] *trans.* To attach a wrong sense or meaning to.

1560 JEWELL *Serm. at Paul's Cross* A iij, The false Prophets..caused the people..to missence the sacraments. **1627-47** FELTHAM *Resolves* I. lxxi. 215 Philoxenus..hearing some masons, mis-sensing his lines..falls to breaking their bricks amaine; they aske the cause, hee replyes, they spoyle his work, and he theirs.

'missense, *a. Biol.* [MIS-^{1} 4.] Causing or involving the insertion of a different amino-acid at a particular point in a polypeptide or protein molecule from that which is usual.

1961 LEVINTHAL & DAVISON in *Ann. Rev. Biochem.* XXX. 651 An alteration in any base pair by a mutagen raises the possibility of a class of so-called nonsense mutations, as well as a class of missense mutations... A missense mutation in this context is one which causes a substitution of one amino acid for another at a particular position in the protein. **1974** *Nature* 2 Aug. 412/1 The missense mutation *trpA36* results in a Gly (GGA)→Arg (AGA) amino acid substitution at position 211 of the tryptophan synthetase A protein. *Ibid.* 413/1 The anticodons of the suppressor tRNAs are complementary to the missense codons suppressed by these tRNAs.

† **'misser, -ar.** *Obs.* [ad. eccl. L. *missārius* MISSARY.] A mass-priest.

a **1560** BECON *Jewel of Joy* Wks. II. 26 b, Verely these myssars are altogyther amyse. **1604** [see MISSIFICAL].

misserie, obs. form of MISERY.

mis-'serve, *v.* Now *rare.* [In early use a. OF. *messervir* (see MIS-^{2}); later f. MIS-^{1} I + SERVE *v.*]

1. *trans.* To serve badly or unfaithfully; to do a disservice to.

1340 *Ayenb.* 20 þench hou uele ziþe þou hest misserued oure lhord Jesu crist. **1390** GOWER *Conf.* III. 224 Of that the king his god misserveth, The poeple takth that he descerveth Hier in this world. **1475** *Paston Lett.* III. 130 If it be so that ye be mysse servyd ther. *c* **1500** *Geste Robyn Hode* cxc, I was mysserued of my dynere. **1584** *Extracts Aberdeen Reg.* (1848) II. 54 Quhilk [regrating of victual] is..the caus that the pure communis of this burght ar misservit. *a* **1626** BACON *Charge Sess. Verge* (1662) 19 Whereby a man may have that he thinketh he hath, and not be abused or misserved in that he buyes. **1727** ARBUTHNOT *Coins*, etc. xix. 200 Great Men who mis-served their Country, were often fined very highly.

† **2.** To deprive of the services *of. Obs.*

1456 SIR G. HAYE *Law Arms* (S.T.S.) 147 Sen he..mycht..have had otheris at will and wale, of quhilkis he has gert the King be misservit.

† **3.** *intr.* To miss fire. *Obs.*

1661 *Justiciary Rec.* (S.H.S.) 10 George presented a Pistoll to them which misserved. **1685** *Lond. Gaz.* No. 2045/1 He presented his Pistol to the Country-man, but it mis-served.

† **mis-'service.** *Obs.* [MIS-^{1} 4, 7.] A bad service; disservice.

1587 GOLDING *De Mornay* xxiv. 409 That seruice should rather bee a misseruice than a Seruice, if it were not according to his will. *a* **1660** *Contemp. Hist. Irel.* 1641-52 (1880) II. I. 119 By those reciprocall misunderstandings a gape was open for the misservice of both kinge and kingdome.

misserye, missese, obs. ff. MISERY, MISEASE.

mis-set (mɪs'sɛt), *v.* [MIS-^{1} I. Cf. MDu. *missetten*, *missitten*, OHG. *missisezzen.*]

1. *trans.* To set in a wrong place, misplace.

c **1369** CHAUCER *Dethe Blaunche* 1210 Many a worde I ouer skipte In my tale for pure Fere Lest my wordys myssette were. *a* **1626** BACON *Charge Sess. Verge* (1662) 7 If..that Boundary of Suits be taken away or mis-set, where shall be the end?

2. To put out of humour, 'upset'. *Sc.*

1501 DOUGLAS *Pal. Hon.* II. xxii, In recompence for his missettand saw, He sall ȝour hest in euerie part proclame. **1567** *Satir. Poems Reform.* iv. 12 In tyme be war fra ainis the work misset hir. **1790** J. FISHER *Poems* 143 (E.D.D.), I..did's she bade, wha durst mis-set her? **1816** SCOTT *Bl. Dwarf* iii, I did not say frighted, now—I only said mis-set wi' the thing. **1818** —— *Hrt. Midl.* xviii, Our minnie's sair mis-set.

misset, misseuse, missey: see MESSET, MISUSE, MISSAY *v.*, MISSY.

miss-'fire. [f. phr. *to miss fire*: see MISS *v.*^{1} 5 a. Cf. MISFIRE *sb.*] A failure to discharge or explode. Also *attrib.*

1811 *Sporting Mag.* XXXVIII. 290 It was done without a miss or a miss fire. **1881** *Times* 15 Jan. 5/6 The five-barrelled Gardner fired 339, with one miss-fire in the minute, worked single handed. **1914** W. OWEN *Let.* 28 Aug. (1967) 281 After your deplorable miss-fire fashion. **1933** *Times Lit. Suppl.* 2 Mar. 148/4 Narrating the missfire of a tired New York business man who hoped his wife and daughter would fly with him.

† **mis'shameful**, *a. Obs.* [MIS-^{1} 8.] Shameful.

Perhaps the word originally written by Capgrave was intended as a form of *mischiefful.*

c **1440** CAPGRAVE *Life St. Kath.* v. 649 þou myssha[m]ful [*v. rr.* myschamful, shameful, vnshamfulle] doggeful of boost.

mis-shape (mɪs'ʃeɪp), *sb.* Now *rare.* [MIS-^{1} 4.] A bad or deformed shape or figure; deformity. Also *concr.* a mis-shapen body or person.

c **1465** *Eng. Chron.* (Camden 1856) 7 The whiche Edmund hadde a crokid bak and was a mysshape. **1542** UDALL *Erasm. Apoph.* 223 Silenus..whom for his monstreous myshape,..Jupiter, Apollo [etc.],..used for their foole. **1610** HOLLAND *Camden's Brit.* I. 530 The diuels of Crowland with their long tailed buttocks, and ugly mishapes. **1654** WHITELOCKE *Mem.* (1732) 596/1 Hardly to be called Men or Women, by reason of their mishapes. **1875** G. MACDONALD *Malcolm* I. xxii. 281 Disorder and misshape must appear to it the law of the universe.

mis-shape (mɪs'ʃeɪp), *v.* [MIS-^{1} I.] *trans.* To shape ill; to give a bad form to; to deform. *lit.* and *fig.*

1450-1530 *Myrr. our Ladye* 98 Oure..soulle..ys made to hys lykenesse but yt was defoyled and darkyd and myshape by synne. **1530** PALSGR. 637/2, I myshappe, or bring out of facyon. **1583** GOLDING *Calvin on Deut.* cix. 669 Such as mishape thinges by their inchauntments. **1590** SPENSER *F.Q.* II. v. 27 Whom..she does transforme..And horribly misshapes with ugly sightes. **1673** HOWE *Self Dedication* 292 They do strangely mis-shape religion who frame to themselves a religion made up of..doubts and fears. **1703** J. SAVAGE *Lett. Antients* viii. 49 Mishape me, if you please, into any Monstrous Form. **1798** COLERIDGE *Picture* Poems (1864) 157 A thousand circlets spread And each mis-shape the other. **1858** GREENER *Gunnery* 436 If the distance the drops fall be not sufficiently great, and they reach the water in a semi-fluid state, the resistance of the water mis-shapes them.

misshape, variant of MISHAP *v.*

mis-shaped (mɪs'ʃeɪpt), *ppl. a.* [MIS-^{1} 2.] = next.

1509 HAWES *Past. Pleas.* XXXVII. (Percy Soc.) 192 His great body, Which was mishaped ful right wonderly. **1593** SHAKS. *3 Hen. VI*, III. ii. 170 My mis-shap'd Trunke, that beares this Head. **1601** WEEVER *Mirr. Mart.* 203 Bleare-eyde, mishapt, vntoward, impious. **1709** POPE *Ess. Crit.* 171 Some figures monstrous and mis-shap'd appear, Consider'd singly, or beheld too near. **1876** T. HARDY *Ethelberta* (1890) 380 Did you ever see anything so ugly as that hand—a mis-shaped monster, isn't he?

Hence † **mis'shapedness**, deformity.

1610 HEALEY *St. Aug. Citie of God* 900 A statuary..can mold or cast it [*i.e.* a statue] new..without all the former miss-shapednesse.

† **mis-'shapement.** [MIS-^{1} 4.] Deformity.

1653 H. MORE *Antid. Ath.* III. xi. Wks. (1712) 122 What is that outward mis-shapement of Body, to the inward deformity of their Souls?

† **mis-'shapen**, *v. Obs. rare.* [? f. MIS-SHAPEN *pa. pple.*] = MIS-SHAPE *v.*

c **1440** *Alphabet of Tales* 361, I am aferd þat I sall oght be mysshapend [*cf. ante* sho was shapen to be a biche whelpe]. **1555** EDEN *Decades* To Rdr. (Arb.) 53 People myshapened with phantastical opinions. **1788** *Trifler* No. xvi. 217, I conceived that the purest favour of Providence might be so perverted and mishapened, that [etc.].

mis-shapen (mɪs'ʃeɪp(ə)n), *ppl. a.* Forms: 4-6 mys-, mischapen, (5 -on, -yn, 6 -shapin), 6-7 mishapen, 4- misshapen, (7- mis-shapen). Also 4-5 myschape, mysshap(e. [f. MIS-^{1} 2 + *shapen*, pa. pple. of SHAPE *v.*]

1. Having a bad or ugly shape; ill-shaped; deformed; monstrous.

c **1375** *Cursor M.* 8076 (Fairf.) Sagh men neuer of na cures sa misshapen creatures. *c* **1400** *Destr. Troy* 5482 Mysshapon

bestes. *Ibid.* 7758 There met hym þis Mawhown, þat was so mysshap. *c* **1440** *Promp. Parv.* 339/2 Myschape thynge yn kynde, *monstruosus.* **1530** PALSGR. 637/1 He is the moste mysshapen slovyn that ever you sawe. **1581** PETTIE tr. *Guazzo's Civ. Conv.* III. (1586) 123 b, It sildome falleth out, that a good minde is lodged in a mishapen bodie. **1594** SHAKS. *Rich. III*, I. ii. 251 On me, that halts, and am mishapen thus? **1687** DRYDEN *Hind & P.* III. 1054 A mis-shapen ugly race; The curse of God was seen on every face. **1711** ADDISON *Spect.* No. 50 ¶3 An huge mis-shapen Rock that grew upon the Top of the Hill. **1833** HT. MARTINEAU *Charmed Sea* iv. 48 Jagged, misshapen pieces of silver. **1856** EMERSON *Eng. Traits, Character*, The mis-shapen hairy Scandinavian troll.

2. *transf.* and *fig.* Badly formed, shaped, or framed; distorted; †morally monstrous or ugly.

13.. *E.E. Allit. P.* B. 1355 In notyng of nwe metes & of nice gettes, Al was þe mynde of þat man, on misschapen þinges. **1509** BARCLAY *Shyp of Folys* (1570) 8 If I should write all the euils manifolde, That proceedeth of this counterfaite abusion, And misshapen fashions I neuer should haue done. **1579** G. HARVEY *Letter-bk.* (Camden) 59 A mis-shapin illfavorid freshe copy of my precious poems. **1603** FLORIO *Montaigne* I. xxiv, Crooked and mis-shapen minds. *a* **1631** DONNE *Poems* (1650) 93 Mishapen Cavils, palpable untroths. **1633** G. HERBERT *Temple, Ch. Militant* 46 Such power hath mightie Baptisme to produce For things mis-shapen, things of highest use. **1670** in *12th Rep. Hist. MSS. Comm.* App. v. 15 Their ordnary designes [in tapestry] for the most part being deformed and mishapen. **1809** W. IRVING *Hist. New York* IV. iii. (1820) 238 Some dozen..mis-shapen, nine-cornered Dutch oaths and epithets that crowded all at once into his gullet.

†**3.** 'Without form' (*Gen.* i. 2). *Obs.*

1639 HORN & ROB. *Gate Lang. Unl.* ii. §20 A kind of darke and mis-shapen thicke fogge.

4. 'In Shakespeare, perhaps, it once signifies ill directed; as, *to shape a course*' (J.).

1592 SHAKS. *Rom. & Jul.* III. iii. 131 Thy wit, that Ornament, to shape and Loue, Mishapen in the conduct of them both.

Hence **mis-'shapenly** *adv*, **mis-'shapenness** († **mishapnesse**), deformity.

1587 GOLDING *De Mornay* ix. (1592) 123 Euen mishapnesse it self is a kind of shape. **1611** COTGR., *Monstrüeusement*, monstrously; mishapenly. **1621** BP. MOUNTAGU *Diatribæ* 94 To let you see the misshapennesse of your Argument. **1883** B. HARTE *Carquinez Woods* i. 3 At times this life seemed to take visible form, but as vaguely, as mis-shapenly as the phantom of a nightmare. **1903** G. MATHESON *Repr. Men of Bible* Ser. II. 271 It was as if a deformed creature..for the first time beheld his misshapenness.

misshood ('mɪshʊd). [f. MISS *sb.*[3] + -HOOD.] The condition of a young unmarried woman.

1861 THACKERAY *Philip* xvii, When she used to read the Wild Irish Girl or the Scottish Chiefs in the days of her misshood. **1886** *Blackw. Mag.* CXXXIX. 493 Pretty daughters..emerging from bread-and-butter-misshood.

missible ('mɪsɪb(ə)l), *a. rare.* [f. L. *miss-*, ppl. stem of *mittĕre* to send + -IBLE. (*Missibilia* occurs for *missilia* in Sidonius.) Cf. OF. (*lettres*) *missibles*.] Capable of being sent.

1789 G. KEATE *Pelew Isl.* 315 Their spears..not being in general missible beyond fifty or sixty feet. **1809** LAMB *Let. to Coleridge* 30 Oct., This Custom-and-Duty Age would have made the Preacher on the Mount take out a licence and St. Paul's Epistles would not have been missible without a stamp.

missie, var. MISSY.

†**mi'ssific, -fical**, *adjs. Obs.* Also 7 *erron.* -afique. [f. eccl. L. *missific-us*: see -IC, -ICAL.] Celebrating Mass.

1604 *Answ. Supplic. Masse-priests* viii, These Missificall Misseres. **1607** R. C[AREW] tr. *Estienne's World of Wonders* 343 Without interrupting his missificall deuotion. **1624** DARCIE *Birth of Heresies* xxii. 105 Abolishing your Pompilian and Missafique Idolatries.

†**mi'ssificate**, *v. Obs.* [f. ppl. stem of eccl. L. *missificāre*, f. *missa* MASS *sb.*[1]: see -FICATE.] *intr.* To perform Mass. So †**missifi'cation**.

1641 MILTON *Ch. Govt.* v. Wks. 1851 III. 115 What can be gather'd hence but that the Prelat would still sacrifice?.. he would missificate. **1641** R. BAILLIE *Parallel Liturgy w. Mass Bk.* 2 None but Schismaticks will denie their harmonie with the ancients in this Missification. **1694** MOTTEUX *Rabelais* IV. lxvii. (1737) 277 Fourteen missificating Arch-lubbers.

missikin ('mɪsɪkɪn). *jocular.* Also **missakin** (?), **missykin**. [f. MISSY + -KIN.] A little 'miss' or young lady.

1815 *Zeluca* III. v. 149 Zeluca flew to the bell, with an exclamation, that but for her she should have forgot the Missakin in toto. **1839** *Tait's Mag.* VI. 35 Little mannikin lords and missykin ladies. **1863** HOLME LEE *A. Warleigh* III. 271 'It will be your turn some day, missikin'... 'No, it will never be my turn, for I purpose to lead a single life'.

missil, perverted form of MESLE *Obs.*

1610 GUILLIM *Heraldry* §5. ii. 241 Those Armes..doe admit..intermixture, of one colour with another, for which cause they are of Leigh termed Missils. **1656** BLOUNT *Glossogr.*

missile ('mɪsaɪl, 'mɪsɪl), *a.* and *sb.* Also 7 -il(l, -al. [ad. L. *missilis* (neut. sing. *missile* as sb., missile weapon), f. *miss-*, ppl. stem of *mittĕre* to send: see -ILE. In OFr., Godefroy cites *missiles dardz*, and Cotgr. has *feu missile*, 'a squib, or other fire-worke throwne'.]

A. *adj.* **a.** Capable of being thrown; adapted to be discharged from the hand or from a machine or engine: chiefly in ***missile weapon***.

1611 SPEED *Hist. Gt. Brit.* IX. xvi. (1623) 840 Women and children assaill the English from their windowes with all sorts of missill things. **1627** MAY *Lucan* III. 505 The Greeks missill weapons. *a* **1711** KEN *Edmund* Poet. Wks. 1721 II. 313 The Pagans all the Traitors drave before, To shield them from the Anglians missile store. **1725** POPE *Odyss.* IX. 183 We bend the bow, or wing the missile dart. **1817** KEATINGE *Trav.* II. 2 Every missile article being immediately laid hands on by them and showered on us. **1872** E. W. ROBERTSON *Hist. Ess.* Introd. 13, The horseman ..used his spears,..as missile weapons.

b. Applied to weapons that discharge arrows, bullets, or the like. *rare.*

1819 SCOTT *Ivanhoe* xxx, Their long-bows, slings, and other missile weapons. **1855** MACAULAY *Hist. Eng.* xiii. III. 371 To alter his missile weapon [*sc.* a gun] into a weapon with which he could encounter an enemy hand to hand.

c. *transf.* and *fig.*

1756 BURKE *Subl. & B.* Wks. 1808 I. 224 The porcupine with his missile quills. **1791** COWPER *Iliad* XI. 325 With missile force of massy stones. **1813** JEFFERSON *Writ.* (1830) IV. 227 Since the invention of gunpowder has armed the weak as well as the strong with missile death. **1864** SWINBURNE *Atalanta* 60 But Meleager smote, and with no missile wound, the monstrous boar.

d. *Zool.* Applied to the filaments which *Actinia bellis* sends out on provocation.

1855 GOSSE *Mar. Zool.* I. 29 *Actinia*..destitute..of missile filaments. **1856** TUGWELL *Man. Sea-Anemones* 90.

B. *sb.*

1. a. A missile object or weapon, as a stone discharged from a sling, an arrow, a bullet.

1656 BLOUNT *Glossogr.*, *Missil* (*missile*), a dart, stone, arrow, or other thing thrown or shot. **1828-41** TYTLER *Hist. Scot.* (1864) I. 79 The missiles which they [*sc.* engines of war] threw consisted of leaden balls. **1829** SCOTT *Demonol.* x. 377 Surprisingly quick at throwing stones, turf and other missiles. **1847** TENNYSON *Princess* Prol. 45 Some were whelm'd with missiles of the wall. **1897** FRAZER *Pausanias* I. 534 Despite the cross-fire of missiles and the bitter cold. *fig.* **1833** I. TAYLOR *Fanat.* ii. 28 The word [fanaticism] is the favourite missile of that opprobrious contempt [etc.]. **1866** G. MACDONALD *Ann. Q. Neighb.* ix. (1878) 167 All my missiles of argument were lost.

b. *Mil.* A destructive projectile that during part or all of its course is self-propelling and directed by remote control or automatically.

1945 (27 Aug.), etc. [see GUIDED *a.* b]. **1945** *Sci. Amer.* Nov. 283/3 Communications systems between air and ground making possible the most intricate maneuvers..by ..pilotless missiles. **1946** *Aeroplane Spotter* 1 June 128/1 A rocket-propelled missile carries its oxygen internally, whereas a jet-propelled missile takes in its oxygen from the atmosphere. **1954**, etc. [see BALLISTIC *a.* d]. **1956** *Newsweek* 7 May 19/1 The 'Nike B' is designed as an antimissile missile as well as an improved version of the anti-aircraft 'Nike' weapons. **1959** *Times Lit. Suppl.* 13 Feb. 79/2 Some of the smaller European members of N.A.T.O. have given notice that they will not allow American intermediate-range missiles to be stationed in their territory in time of peace. **1964** *Ann. Reg. 1963* 221 Another factor may have been a realization that the arms race was becoming ruinously expensive, and..a partial test ban would prevent the United States from outpacing the U.S.S.R. in research on an anti-missile missile. **1973** *Sci. Amer.* Nov. 27/2 Under the SALT I agreement the U.S.S.R. is allowed about 25 percent more offensive missiles than the U.S.

c. *attrib.* and *Comb.*, as ***missile base, carrier, gap*** [GAP *sb.*[1] 6 a] ***silo, site, submarine***; ***missile-armed, -firing, launching*** adjs.

1959 *Daily Tel.* 20 May 10/2 The nuclear-powered, missile-armed submarine offers itself as the costly major strategic weapon of the future. **1969** *New Scientist* 28 Aug. 421/2 The Royal Navy has only three fast patrol boats in service and none of these is missile-armed. **1956** W. A. HEFLIN *U.S. Air Force Dict.* 329/1 Missile base. **1958** *Listener* 3 July 7/2 The Soviet Union's aim is to attract Iceland out of the Nato alliance because she is fearful of the American missile bases there. **1957** *Economist* 21 Dec. 1025/2 The wheels of the missile-carriers rumble towards Europe from east and west. **1958** *Listener* 20 Feb. 303 The missile-firing nuclear-powered submarine will..prove the most potent form of nuclear attack in the future. **1959** *Economist* 13 June 1020/2 The Air Force gets an additional $170 million to help close the 'missile gap'. **1962** *Listener* 19 Apr. 697/1 The passages on the 'missile gap' are a little dated, since Mr Kennedy has now told us that it scarcely ever existed. **1958** *New Statesman* 2 May 600/1 A missile-launching site. **1965** H. KAHN *On Escalation* vii. 141 The Soviets could increase pressure on us by simultaneously stationing missile-launching submarines or ships off our coasts, by sabotaging communications, [etc.]. **1967** *Economist* 28 Oct. 371/1 Their programme includes planes and medium-range missile silos as well as three Polaris-type submarines. **1974** *Times* 24 Oct. 6/8 Under the 1972 agreements the Soviet Union was allowed to have 1,618 operational land-based missile silos. **1949** *Aviation Week* 21 Feb. 11/3 (*heading*) Defense chiefs ask guided missile site. **1962** *Listener* 29 Mar. 553/1 On-site inspections of airfields and missile-sites. **1959** *New Statesman* 3 Jan. 6/3 A similar sum, according to one estimate, will be needed for the 40 Polaris missile-submarines which the Navy says it requires. **1974** L. DEIGHTON *Spy Story* xii. 119 They'll have one missile submarine close enough to fire.

2. *pl.* = L. *missilia, res missiles*, largesse (consisting of sweets, perfumes, etc.) thrown by the Roman emperors to the people.

1606 HOLLAND *Sueton.* 183 Scattered also abroad there were for the people Missils, during the whole time of those Plaies. **1647** A. ROSS *Mystag. Poet.* vi. (1675) 126 The Romans were very lavish in their missals or larges at this solemnity.

'missileman. Also **missile man, missile-man.** [f. MISSILE *a.* and *sb.* + MAN *sb.*[1]] One who is engaged in the construction, design, flying, or operation of a missile (sense B. 1 b).

1951 [see BIRD *sb.* 4 d]. **1961** *Amer. Speech* XXXVI. 234 The verb *destruct* is used by missile men to describe the push-button blowing up of a missile. **1962** *Daily Tel.* 7 Feb. 1/6 (*heading*) 300 missile men to lose jobs. **1963** *Ann. Reg. 1962* 35 The rapid development of the missile-men's craft. **1964** *Economist* 29 Feb. 803/3 The plight of the redundant missile-men.

missilery ('mɪsaɪlərɪ). *N. Amer.* Also **missilry**. [f. MISSILE *sb.* + -ERY.] Missiles collectively; a collection of missiles.

1880 *Harper's Mag.* Sept. 506/1 There were in her main-mast eighteen large grape, and sixteen musket-balls, besides smaller missilery in profusion. **1957** *Britannica Bk. of Year* 512/1 In military affairs, the prominence of the guided missile as a weapon was indicated by such terms as *missilry*, a collective term for such missiles. **1959** *Life* (Internat. ed.) 13 Apr. 20/1 We do have a mass of evidence to indicate that the Soviets have gone all-out in missilery. **1973** *Daily Colonist* (Victoria, B.C.) 27 Apr. 4/7 The [transistor] devices became important foundation stones of military aviation, missilery, and space exploration, where it is vital to save space and weight.

missilry, variant of MESELRY.

missiness ('mɪsɪnɪs). [f. MISSY *a.* + -NESS.] = MISSISHNESS.

1857 J. MILLER *Alcohol* (1858) 97 The designation of water-drinker can carry no imputation of missiness or mediocrity.

missing ('mɪsɪŋ), *vbl. sb.* [f. MISS *v.*[1] + -ING[1].]

†**1.** Absence, privation, lack. *Obs.*

a **1300** *Cursor M.* 14228 We sal find missing witerli Of vr god freind o bethani. **1393** LANGL. *P. Pl.* C. xi. 201 God wol nat lete hym sterue In myschef for lacke of mete ne for myssynge of cloþes. *c* **1440** *York Myst.* i. 48 Of myrthe neuermore to haue myssyng. *c* **1530** LD. BERNERS *Arth. Lyt. Bryt.* (1814) 499 Theyr hoost is..in great trouble for the myssynge of theyr emperoure. **1611** SPEED *Hist Gt. Brit.* IX. iv. 48 Vpon which his suddaine flight and missing, the Empresse Maud..was suspected to be guiltie of his death. **1611** SHAKS. *Cymb.* V. v. 275 My Lord,..Vpon my Ladies missing, came to me With his Sword drawne. **1634** BP. HALL *Contempl. N.T.*, *Resurrection* 282 Shee freely confesseth the cause of her griefe to be the missing of her Saviour.

2. Failure to hit, obtain, attain to, or take advantage of.

a **1547** SURREY *Æneid* II. (1557) D 2 Whether by fate, or missing of the way. **1603** FLORIO *Montaigne* I. liv, Without ever missing he would every time make it goe through a needles-eye. *a* **1628** PRESTON *New Covt.* (1629) 586 The missing of time bringeth misery. **1660** PEPYS *Diary* 28 Mar., This day we had news of the election at Huntingdon for Bernard and Pedley at which my Lord was much troubled for his friends' missing of it. **1711** ADDISON *Spect.* No. 15 ¶7 The missing of an Opera the first Night. **1748** *Anson's Voy.* III. i. 301 The currents were driving us to the northward..and we thereby risqued the missing of the Ladrones. **1749** FIELDING *Tom Jones* XIII. ii, These kind of hair-breadth missings of happiness. **1858** O. W. HOLMES *Aut. Breakf.-t.* ix, That trick of throwing a stone at a tree and attaching some mighty issue to hitting or missing.

†**b.** ***missing-wood*** (*Bowls*): see quot. *Obs.*

1753 CHAMBERS *Cycl. Supp.* s.v. *Bowling*, Bowl-room, or missing-wood, is when a bowl has free passage, without striking on any other.

†**3.** Fault, error. *Obs.*

a **1568** ASCHAM *Scholem.* II. (Arb.) 88 Shew his faultes iently,..of such missings, ientlie admonished of, proceedeth glad and good heed taking. **1664** PEPYS *Diary* 10 Aug., To see him..read it all over, without any missing, when..I could not..read one..letter of it.

'missing, *ppl. a.* [f. MISS *v.*[1] + -ING[2].]

1. Not present; not found; absent; gone. spec. ***the missing***, soldiers (sailors, etc.) neither present after an action nor known to have been killed or wounded; so ***missing, presumed dead*** (in quot., *fig.*). In wider use: (*to be*) ***among the missing***: to be absent, to absent oneself (*U.S. colloq.*).

a **1530** HEYWOOD *Play of Love* (Brandl) 24 Whiche one ones founde I fynde of all the rest Not one myssyng. *c* **1566** *Merie Tales of Skelton* in Wks (1843) I. p. lxviii, Skelton was verye angrie that his cup was mysynge. **1607** SHAKS. *Temp.* V. i. 255 There are yet missing of your Companie Some few odde Lads. **1611** BIBLE *1 Kings* xx. 39 Keep this man: if by any meanes he be missing, then shall thy life be for his life. **1671** MILTON *P.R.* II. 15 Moses was in the Mount, and missing long. **1716** SWIFT *Phyllis* 26 Wks. 1751 VII. 168 Next Morn betimes the Bride was missing. **1833** HT. MARTINEAU *Manch. Strike* i. 8 Missing from home. *a* **1845** HOOD *Waterloo Ballad* 10 Before I'm set in the Gazette As wounded, dead, and missing. **1848** ARNOULD *Marine Insur.* (1866) I. II. ii. 524 The ship is what is called a missing ship, i.e. has been so long on the voyage that the owner has reason to suspect that she has met with some casualty. **1855** T. C. HALIBURTON *Nat. & Hum. Nat.* I. i. 10 If a person inquires if you are at home, the servant is directed to say, No, if you don't want to be seen, and choose to be among the missing. **1859** in Bartlett *Dict. Amer.* (ed. 2) 273 There comes old David for my militia fine. I don't want to see him, and think I will be among the missing. **1860** TYNDALL *Glac.* I. xxvii. 212 In a moment the missing man was drawn from between its jaws [*sc.* of the fissure]. **1900** *Daily News* 26 May 4/2 War Office Statement... The term 'missing' means that a soldier's fate has not been definitely ascertained. **1917**

'CONTACT' *Airman's Outings* p. xii, Once eleven of our machines were posted as 'missing' in the space of two days. **1918** W. OWEN *Let.* 8 Oct. (1967) 581 Must now write to hosts of parents of Missing, etc. **1962** *Listener* 11 Oct. 585/1 His [*sc.* Schönberg's] music seemed dead-alive on more than one occasion... Ernest Newman..reported him missing, presumed dead, just because he did not seem to have made it in time.

2. That fails to hit.

a **1586** SIDNEY *Astr. & Stella* xxiii, The curious wits,.. With idle paines, and missing ayme, do guesse. **1603** FLORIO *Montaigne* I. xxxix, A never-missing runner at the Ring.

3. Of a crop: That has failed. ? *Obs.*

1777 *A. Hunter's Georgical Ess.* 408 Finding some beds I had sown very early with onions to be a missing crop.

4. Special collocations: **missing link**, (*a*) something lacking to complete a series; (*b*) *Zool.* a hypothetical type assumed to have existed between two related types; *esp.* a hypothetical animal assumed to be a connecting link between man and the anthropoid apes; also applied trivially to an animal (or person) supposed to resemble the latter; **missing mass** *Sci.*, the amount by which an observed or measured mass falls short of an expected or inferred mass; *spec.* in *Astr.*, the difference between the mass of a galaxy or cluster of galaxies calculated dynamically and the sum of the masses of the visible objects in the system; also, the difference between the mass there must be in the universe if it is closed and the total mass accounted for by direct observation; **missing person**, a person whose whereabouts are unknown (and who is being sought); also *attrib.* of an organization, etc., recording information about such persons; **missing word**, a term which arose in 1892 in connexion with 'competitions' instituted by certain periodicals, the object being for the competitors to guess the appropriate word to fill a gap left in a given sentence.

1851 LYELL *Elem. Geol.* xvii. 220 A break in the chain implying no doubt many *missing links in the series of geological monuments which we may some day be able to supply. **1862** G. DU MAURIER *Let.* Oct. in *Young G. du Maurier* (1951) 178, I..said that if he would take the trouble to make a post mortem on the Irish roughs I intend to kill next Sunday in the Park, he might convince himself that the 'missing link' had been found. **1875** JOWETT *Plato* (ed. 2) IV. 154 The metaphysical imagination was incapable of supplying the missing link between words and things. [**1876** tr. *E.H.P.A. Haeckel's Hist. Creation* II. xxii. 293 Although the preceding ancestral stage is already so nearly akin to genuine Men that we scarcely require to assume an intermediate connecting stage, still we can look upon the speechless Primæval Men (Alali) as this intermediate link.] **1879** *Gentl. Mag.* CCXLV. 298 The early critics of the hypotheses of evolution were not slow to fix upon 'missing links' and their nature. **1883** T. TYLER in *Time* VIII. 476 The exhibition at the Westminster Aquarium of..'The Missing Link', or, according to another description, 'The Human Monkey'. *a* **1930** D. H. LAWRENCE *Phoenix II* (1968) 569 One woman..wrote to me out of the blue: 'You, who are a mixture of the missing-link and the chimpanzee, etc.'—and told me my name stank. **1936** A. O. LOVEJOY *Great Chain of Being* viii. 235 By 1760 the triumphs of the missing-link hunters were being celebrated in verse. **1966** R. & D. MORRIS *Men & Apes* v. 126 Albertus [Magnus] made the first attempt to bridge the gap between man and the rest of the animal world by means of a kind of 'missing link' in the shape of the pygmy and the ape. **1967** *Astrophysical Jrnl.* CXLVIII. 713 It has been known for some time that the mass in ordinary galaxies is inadequate by a factor of about 40 to close the Universe... Apparently the *missing mass necessary for a closed Universe could not be *uniformly distributed* hydrogen. **1968** M. S. LIVINGSTON *Particle Physics* v. 93 The magnitude of the excitation of such a heavier particle is given by the 'missing mass' calculated from the *Q*-equation when the mass of the normal particle is assumed. **1970** *New Scientist* 9 Apr. 57/1 Information about the incoming pi meson, the target proton and the recoil proton is sufficient to calculate the 'missing mass'. **1976** G. B. FIELD in E. H. Avrett *Frontiers Astrophysics* xii. 529 The missing mass in the Coma cluster or other clusters. **1982** *Nature* 24 June 623/1 Such holes might today provide the 'missing mass' known to reside in clusters of galaxies and galactic haloes. **1876** GEO. ELIOT *Dan. Der.* III. III. xx. 39 There were safer means than advertising: men might be set to work whose business it was to find *missing persons. **1943** R. CHANDLER *Lady in Lake* (1944) ii. 15 It will mean going to the Missing Persons Bureau. **1967** R. RENDELL *Wolf to Slaughter* ii. 20 They didn't want to add to their Missing Persons list if they could help it. **1970** *Guardian* 7 Jan. 18/2 A 'missing person' poster for station notice boards will be issued soon. **1975** 'E. LATHEN' *By Hook or by Crook* xv. 147 The..kids had been missing persons all through the war. **1892** *Times* 14 Dec. 9/4 The decision of Sir John Bridge, to the effect that the '*missing word' competitions..are contrary to the law by which lotteries are forbidden. *Ibid.* 17 Dec. 7/6 'Missing Word' Lotteries. **1892** *Spectator* 17 Dec. 882/1 The fortunate guessers of the 'missing word'. **1898** GISSING *Town Traveller* xxv, The missing word this week, discovered by an East-end licensed victualler, was *pick-me-up*.

Hence †**'missingly** *adv.*, with a sense of loss.

1611 SHAKS. *Wint. T.* IV. ii. 35, I haue (missingly) noted, he is of late much retyred from Court.

missiology (mɪsɪ'ɒlədʒɪ). [f. MISSI(ON *sb.* + -OLOGY.] The study of the methods, purpose, etc., of religious missions.

1937 *Tablet* 23 Oct. 545/1 (*heading*) The science of missiology. First principles of mission work. *Ibid.*, Missiology is a new word for a new science. **1961** A. V. SEUMOIS in G. H. Anderson *Theol. Christian Mission* II. 133 Practical missiology, scientifically theological, covers the study of mission spirituality and mission methodology. **1971** *Sunday Times* (Johannesburg) 28 May 30/5 (Advt.), Senior Lecturer in Ecclesiastical History and Missiology. **1975** *Church Times* 11 July 2/5 Miss Myrtle Langley is to be head of the new department of missiology..at Trinity College, Bristol.

So **missio'logical** *a.*, of or pertaining to missiology; **missi'ologist**, one who concerns himself with missiology.

1951 *Theology* LIV. 349 The aim of missions..is.., as a distinguished Roman Missiologist has said, to 'found' the Church'. **1957** *Scottish Jrnl. Theol.* X. 300 One meets here the biblical theologian, the scientist in religions, the missionary and 'missiologist'. **1961** A. V. SEUMOIS in G. H. Anderson *Theol. Christian Mission* II. 123 The writing which marked the launching of the modern missiological movement. **1970** J. POWER *Mission Theol. Today* p. ix, There is a lacuna that so far has not been filled either by missionaries themselves or by missiologists. **1971** N. Q. KING *Christian & Muslim in Afr.* 90 Leaving aside such theological and missiological considerations, a large number of African Christians ask us to compare some of the Christians of the older generation.

mission ('mɪʃən), *sb.* [ad. L. *missiōn-em*, n. of action f. *mittĕre* (*miss-*) to send. Cf. F. *mission*, in OF. = expenses (Cotgr.), from 16th c. in sense 3, from 17th c. in sense 4; Sp. *mision*, formerly *mission* (= 'dismissal' in Orozco 1611 s.v. *Missa*); It. *missione*.]

†**1. a.** The action or an act of sending. *Obs.*

1606 SHAKS. *Tr. & Cr.* III. iii. 189 Whose glorious deedes ..Made emulous missions 'mongst the gods themselues, And draue great Mars to faction. **1611** FLORIO, *Missióne*, a mission, a sending. **1647** *Missive of Consolation* Pref. A 2, This Mission of my thoughts into my country. **1658** OSBORN *Adv. Son* Wks. (1673) 225 Nor can this Mission to the Tower be looked upon for less than the best Fortune so high a Malefactor could be capable of. **1662** PETTY *Taxes* 13 The numerous missions of Cattle and Sheep out of Ireland. **1698** FRYER *Acc. E. India & P.* 87 The Extent of the Presidency is larger in its Missions than Residency.

b. Among the Jesuits, the sending of members of the order to seminaries abroad or on missionary work; also, a body of men thus sent, or the errand on which they are sent. *Obs.*

1598 in Foley *Rec. Eng. Prov. Soc. Jesus* (1878) III. 723 Ye continuallie confluence of the rares and bestes [*sic*] wittes of our nation to the Seminaires, and ther constance in following their missions. *Ibid.* 724 Thes evident testimones of missions and remissions..sent continuallie to Fr. P. by expresse messingers. **1606** *Ibid.* 268 Beinge sent in mission to the Colledge of Siville. **1644** *Ibid.* 66.

2. A sending or being sent to perform some function or service; *Theol.* the sending of the Second or Third Person of the Trinity by the First, or of the Third Person by the Second, for the production of a temporal effect.

1609 BIBLE (Douay) *Joel* ii. comm., The mission of the Holie Ghost performed on Whitsunday. **1676** HALE *Contempl.* I. 310 The miraculous Mission of his Holy Spirit visibly and audibly. **1745** tr. *Coetlogon's Univ. Hist. Arts & Sci.* II. 1180 The Mission whereby Christ came into the World in the human Flesh. **1752** J. GILL *Trinity* vii. 138 The greatness of God's love in the gift and mission of his Son. **1846** J. C. HARE (*title*) The Mission of the Comforter. **1897** *Catholic Dict.* (ed. 5) 904/1 It cannot..be said that all three Persons are sent, because mission consists in the procession of one Person from another.

3. *Eccl.* The action of sending men forth with authority to preach the faith and administer the sacraments; also, the authority given by God or the Church to preach.

1641 J. JACKSON *True Evang. T.* III. 186 Christ..in the Mission first of his Twelve, and after of his Seventy. **1656** BLOUNT *Glossogr.*, *Mission* (says a Roman Catholick Author) is a giving of Orders, Jurisdiction and power to preach that Doctrine, which is taught by the Catholick Church, and to administer the Sacraments. **1672–5** COMBER *Comp. Temple* (1702) 291 These words, Receive the Holy Ghost..are properly used by us on the ordinary Mission of Pastors. *a* **1699** STILLINGFL., 50 *Serm.* (1707) xlviii. 729 That Christ and his Apostles did work..Miracles..and this for a Confirmation of their Divine Mission. **1727–52** CHAMBERS *Cycl.* s.v., Jesus Christ gave his disciples their mission in these words, *Go, and teach all nations*, &c. The Romanists reproach the Protestants, that their ministers have no mission. **1884** *Catholic Dict.* 584/2 Mission is inseparably connected with jurisdiction. **1894** J. T. FOWLER *Adamnan* Introd. 28 To obtain consecration and mission from Pope Caelestine I.

4. a. A body of persons sent to a foreign country, esp. for the purpose of conducting negotiations, establishing political or commercial relations, watching over certain interests, etc.

1626 BACON *New Atl.* (1627) 19 That in either of these Shipps, ther should be a Mission of three of the Fellowes, or Brethren of Salomon's House; whose Errand was onely to giue vs Knowledge of the Affaires..of those Countries, to which they were designed. **1662** PETTY *Taxes* 27 The envy which precedent missions of English [in Ireland] have against the subsequent. **1791** WASHINGTON in *Amer. State Papers* (1833) I. 127 An additional motive for this confidential mission arose in the same quarter. **1813** *Edin. Rev.* XXI. 155 The French mission was still suffered to remain in Stockholm, until the *Moniteur* mentioned the behaviour of Gustavus disrespectfully. **1816** J. PICKERING *Vocab.*, *Mission*... It was first employed as a diplomatic term, I believe, by American writers. **1845** T. H. HORNE in *Encycl. Metrop.* XVIII. 26/1 (1) Diplomatic Missions..the object of which is, affairs of State or Politics..; (2) Missions of Ceremony or Etiquette, the object of which is, notifications or compliments of congratulation or condolence..; (3) Fixed Missions, in which the Diplomatic Agent..is charged with watching over the various objects above mentioned.

b. *U.S.* A permanent diplomatic establishment, embassy, or legation.

1805 *Amer. State Papers* (1832) II. 669 As nothing was said in my communication respecting the ordinary mission, it remains of course in force. **1890** *Century Dict.* s.v., The members of the British mission at Washington.

5. a. A body of persons sent out by a religious community into foreign lands for the conversion of the heathen. Also (esp. *pl.*) the organized effort involved in the preparation and equipment of such bodies; called distinctively *foreign missions* (cf. b).

1622 BACON *Holy War* Misc. Wks. (1629) 96 The Church ..maketh her Missions, into the Extreme Parts, of the Nations, and Isles. **1648** GAGE *West Ind.* 3 Missions..of Voluntiers, Fryers mendicants, Priests or Monkes, or else of forced Jesuites. **1660** F. BROOKE tr. *Le Blanc's Trav.* 42 S. Francis Xaverius..was called the Apostle of the Indies, his order continues their mission thither stil. **1660** DRYDEN *Astræa Redux* 193 Like zealous Missions, they did care pretend Of souls in show, but made the gold their end. **1768** MACLAINE tr. *Mosheim's Eccl. Hist.* Cent. XVII. i. §18 The African missions were allotted to this austere Order by the court of Rome. **1830** *Encycl. Brit.* (ed. 7) II. 632/2 A mission consists in general of one or two friars or priests, who settle among the savages [etc.]. **1864** *Chamb. Encycl.* VI. 488/2 The mission in the south of India soon received the support of the English Society for Promoting Christian Knowledge. **1888** *Encycl. Brit.* XVI. 515/2 In 1882 the amount raised by British contributions alone to foreign missions amounted to upwards of £1,900,000.

b. With qualifying word: An organization for the evangelization, spiritual instruction, or moral betterment of various classes of people; e.g. ***home***, ***city***, ***police-court mission***. (Cf. MISSIONARY B. 1.)

1839 *Penny Cycl.* XV. 271/2 Within the last four years, 'City Missions' have been formed in London and several of the large towns. **1851** MAYHEW *Lond. Labour* I. 318 That the object of the London City Mission is most noble.. admits of no dispute. **1861** E. L. CUTTS (*title*) Home Missions and Church Extension.

c. ***Congregation of the Priests of the Mission***: a congregation founded by St. Vincent de Paul in 1624, mainly for the evangelization of the poor; also known as Lazarites.

1656 BLOUNT *Glossogr.* s.v. *Missionaries*,..Also, a particular institute in France, called the Fathers of the Mission; who go by pairs,..preach and catechize, and perform other pastoral Offices. **1727–52** CHAMBERS *Cycl.*, *Mission* is also the name of a congregation of priests and laymen, instituted by Vincent De Paul, and confirmed in 1626 by pope Urban VIII. under the title of Priests of the congregation of the mission. **1845** *Encycl. Metrop.* XIII. 488/1 The Priests of the Mission.. acted as home-missionaries.

6. a. A permanent establishment of missionaries in a country; a particular field of missionary activity; a missionary post or station.

1769 *Chron.* in *Ann. Reg.* 189 An officer that has lived seven years in the missions of Paraguay. **1825** SOUTHEY *Tale Paraguay* III. xiv, They..To the nearest mission sped and ask'd the Jesuit's aid. **1836** MACGILLIVRAY tr. *Humboldt's Trav.* viii. 100 Nocturnal birds the fat of which is employed in the Missions for dressing food. **1843** MARRYAT *M. Violet* xix, The mission of Conception..is a very large stone building. **1880** C. R. MARKHAM *Peruv. Bark* 65 Dr. Weddell descended the river Tipuani to Guanay, a mission of Lecos Indians.

b. *transf.* An organization, usually including a church with quasi-parochial institutions, established in a particular district for the spiritual betterment or conversion of the people; *spec. R.C. Ch.* (see quot. 1884).

c **1800** C. BUTLER *Acc. A. Butler* in *Lives of Saints* (1847) I. 8 The vicar-apostolic of the middle district..appointed him to a mission in Staffordshire. **1845** *Catholic Direct.* 27 Hackney... This interesting Mission was established in July, 1843. **1884** *Catholic Dict.* 585/2 In countries where the majority of the population is non-Catholic..the priests having charge of souls are not inducted into parishes, but stationed on missions. **1903** C. E. OSBORNE *Father Dolling* v, It was resolved that Magdalen College should adopt S. Martin's Maidman Street, as its mission.

7. A special series or course of religious services, sermons, instructions, etc. organized in connexion with a particular church or parish for the purpose of stimulating the piety of believers and converting the unbelieving.

1772 NUGENT *Hist. Fr. Gerund* I. 287 *note*, In the time of Lent many preachers go about from town to town, inveighing vehemently against sin, and strenuously exhorting to repentance, which is called going upon a Mission. **1826** H. D. BEST *Four Yrs. France* xiv. 301 In the second year of my sojourn, a mission was preached at Avignon. **1862** [see MISSIONER]. **1906** *Ch. Times* 26 Oct. 513 The first service of the Ruridecanal Hampstead Mission.

8. a. The commission, business, or function with which a messenger, envoy, or agent is charged; now *esp.* the errand on which a political mission is sent.

1671 MILTON *P.R.* II. 114 How to accomplish best His end of being on Earth, and mission high. **1704** NELSON *Fest. & Fasts* xi. (1705) 135 None of the rest of the Apostles stand in competition with St. Paul for this Mission [*sc.* of converting Britain]. **1820** SCOTT *Abbot* ii, 'No', answered the old woman, sternly; 'to part is enough. I go forth on my own mission'. **1836** THIRLWALL *Greece* III. 365 Phæax possessed talents well suited for negotiation,..but..he met

with such opposition as to deter him from proceeding further on the business of his mission. **1859** TENNYSON *Enid* 1376 Another hurrying past, a man-at-arms, Rode on a mission to the bandit Earl. **1863** LD. RUSSELL in R. F. Burton *Mission to Gelele* (1864) p. x, You were informed.. that you had been selected by her Majesty's Government to proceed on a Mission to the King of Dahomey, to confirm the friendly sentiments expressed by Commodore Wilmot to the King. **1873** HALE *In His Name* vi. 108 It seemed to him..that there was not one..who seemed to take the least interest in his mission.

b. orig. *U.S.* A military operation or project; esp. the dispatch of an aircraft or spacecraft on an operational flight; also *transf.*

1929 E. W. DICHMAN *This Aviation Business* v. 107 Night, heavy long-distance, slow, and large all describe a certain type of airplane designed to accomplish a particular mission. **1939** *Aircraft Yearbk.* iii. 64 Many missions were flown, day and night, by participating bombardment and attack units. **1944** *Amer. N. & Q.* Apr. 15/2 *Mission*, ordered operation against the enemy, such as dropping bombs, strafing ground troops and ships, dropping parachute troops, flying diversions (missions intended to draw the enemy away from the main objective), taking photographs, etc. **1962** J. GLENN in *Into Orbit* 43 The clock is pre-set on the ground according to a timing for retro-fire which we have computed before the mission. **1968** MRS. L. B. JOHNSON *White House Diary* 1 July (1970) 694 Lynda heard from Chuck... He had returned from a mission and..had only time to read two or three letters, write her.., stuff a few more into his pocket, and leave on another mission! **1969** *Times* 23 May 1/2 Twice during the critical hours before the separation of the lunar module..from the command service module..the mission's future looked doubtful. **1971** *Daily Tel.* 19 July 7 Apollo 15, America's eighth manned flight for the Moon, is due to be launched on a 12-day mission..from Cape Kennedy a week today.

9. That which a person is designed or destined to do; a duty or function imposed on or assumed by a person; (a person's) vocation or work in life. Also *transf.* attributed to things. Sometimes *trivial* or *contemptuous*.

a **1805** WORDSW. *Prelude* I. Introd. 5 Whate'er its mission, the soft breeze can come To none more grateful than to me. **1819** BYRON *Juan* II. clxxxii, Who..Thought daily service was her only mission. **1839** CARLYLE *Chartism* iii. (1858) 14 Work is the mission of man in this Earth. **1843** PRESCOTT *Mexico* IV. iii. (1864) 225 They..held it to be their 'mission' (to borrow the cant phrase of our own day) to conquer and to convert. **1848** LD. BROUGHAM *Of Revolutions* Wks. 1857 VIII. 322 She [*sc.* France]..has a *mission*, what we would term a vocation, to hasten and help the Discontented. **1865** LOWELL *Thoreau* Prose Wks. (1890) I. 362 Everybody had a mission (with a capital M) to attend to everybody-else's business. **1881** W. S. GILBERT *Patience* II. I am a man with a mission.

10. a. *attrib.* and *Comb.*, as ***mission-agent***, ***-boat***, ***-chapel***, ***-church***, ***-college***, ***farm***, ***-field***, ***-hall***, ***-house***, ***-journey***, ***land***, ***lecture-room***, ***-preacher***, ***-preaching***, ***-premises***, ***-room***, ***-school***, ***-seminary***, ***-service***, ***-ship***, ***-society***, ***station***, ***style***, ***-teacher***, ***-tower***, ***-vessel***, ***-work***; also ***mission-bred***, ***-trained***, ***-ward*** adjs.

1888 E. J. MATHER *Nor'ard of Dogger* 98 The work accomplished by the *mission-agents. **1903** *Month* Aug. 150 Two small *mission boats were built. **1909** *Times Lit. Suppl.* 7 Jan. 3/2 He makes capital fun of the *mission-bred Kaffir's misuse of book-learning. **1871** *Scribner's Monthly* I. 497 His church was only a *mission chapel, supported by a richer society of the same denomination. **1883** BESANT *Childr. Gibeon* II. x, He had ..a mission chapel to serve in some slum or other. **1792** in *Missionary Mag.* (1797) II. 217 He preaches twice every Lord's Day, in the *Mission church, in Calcutta. **1839** *Penny Cycl.* XV. 274/2 The Society for the Propagation of the Gospel founded a *mission college at Calcutta in 1820. *a* **1861** T. WINTHROP *John Brent* (1883) ii. 13 He had found his early way to California, bought a *mission farm, and established himself as a ranchero. **1856** *Mission Field* Jan. 5 The '*Mission Field' of the Society may be said to extend over an area of 7,000,000 square miles. **1859** L. N. R. *Missing Link* i. 10 Many churches..maintain ..their own missionaries, and have their own Home *Mission halls. **1794** C. I. LATROBE tr. *Loskiel's Hist. Mission among Indians N. Amer.* II. xii. 166 The *mission-house on the Mahony..was..burnt. **1824** W. H. KEATING *Narr. Exped. St. Peter's River* (1825) 150 At the time we passed at the Carey mission-house, this gentleman was absent on business. **1839** *Penny Cycl.* XV. 274/2 Funds for the erection of churches and mission-houses. **1902** T. M. LINDSAY *Church & Min. in Early Cent.* iv. 163 The *Mission-journey of Paul and Barnabas. **1851** *Whig Almanac 1852* 18/2 The Commissioners are required to report to the Secretary of the Interior the tenure by which the *Mission lands are held. **1851** R. NESBIT in *Mem.* xii. (1858) 305 After receiving 'licence', he preached in the *Mission Lecture Room. **1898** *Dublin Rev.* Apr. 315 A very holy Franciscan *mission-preacher. **1884** *Catholic Dict.* (1897) 634/2 In substance, *mission-preaching has been employed in every age of the Church. **1848** THOMSON *Hist. Sk. Secession Ch.* 153 More recently *mission-premises were erected. **1888** *Q. Rev.* CLXVI. 57 The multiplication of *mission-rooms in squalid districts. **1879–80** WEBSTER Suppl., **Mission-school*, a school for children who do not regularly attend a church, or who are poor and neglected. (*U.S.*) **1839** *Penny Cycl.* XV. 273/2 So successfully has the work of education been conducted in the *mission seminary. **1839** *Ibid.* 272/1 A South-Sea *mission-ship. **1856** MISS YONGE *Daisy Chain* II. xvii. 529 They..hoped shortly to be called for by the mission-ship to return. **1809** C. SIMEON in W. Carus *Life* (1847) 272 The religious dissipation of *Mission Societies. **1828** I. MCCOY in *Kansas Hist. Q.* (1936) V. 243 Here we intersected a waggon road leading from the settlements on Missouri River to Harmony *Mission Station. **1844** J. MCDONOGH *Papers* (1898) 78 One of these young men..is now at the mission station at Settra Kroo, Liberia, keeping a school for the native youth. **1876** W. BOOTH in H. Begbie *Life W. Booth* (1920) I. xxv. 417 What is a Mission Station?.. It is not a building..; it is not even a society, but a band of people united together to mission,..to christianize an entire town or neighbourhood. **1884** LADY MARTIN *Our Maoris* i. 15 The Bishop came a day or two later, as he had to visit a mission station on the way. **1971** *Scope* (S. Afr.) 19 Mar. 31/1 The maternal grandfather ..came to take up the same mission station. **1909** WELLS & HOOPER *Mod. Cabinet Work* 257 In America there has been a similar movement, known as 'The *Mission Style', which is more or less a revival of Gothic and Jacobean forms applied to modern work. **1930** J. DOS PASSOS *42nd Parallel* I. 122 I've got several magnificent mission style bungalows. **1948** A. L. KROEBER *Anthropol.* (rev. ed.) xii. 484 Since the American occupation, the buildings and ruins of the Spanish period have stood out as landmarks and have set the model for a type of architecture: the Mission style, which in essentials is nothing but Spanish Moorish architecture. **1972** M. MEAD *Blackberry Winter* x. 117 The apartment Luther had found [in 1923] was small enough for the furniture we had: a strong round folding table,..Luther's mission-style desk, [etc.]. **1897** MARY KINGSLEY *W. Africa* 557 Two *mission-teachers. **1868** B. HARTE *Angelus* Poems (1886) 7 The dome-shaped *Mission towers. **1965** *Listener* 27 May 766/1 The men at the top in Uganda and Tanganyika were both *mission-trained teachers. **1888** E. J. MATHER *Nor'ard of Dogger* 95 The fleets where *mission-vessels are stationed. **1925** T. DREISER *Amer. Trag.* (1926) I. I. i. 8 The *missionward march was taken up. **1861** (*title*) A Few Words to Bible *Mission-women. **1888** H. C. LEA *Hist. Inquis.* II. 34 Their arduous and dangerous *mission-work.

b. mission control *collect.*, a group or organization responsible for directing a spacecraft and its crew; **mission furniture** *U.S.*, a plain, solid style of furniture said to have been modelled originally on the furniture of the Spanish missions in North America; **mission oak** *U.S.*, mission furniture made of oak; **mission stiff** *U.S. slang*, (*a*) a missionary; (*b*) one who frequents missions, esp. a tramp who is religious or who pretends to be religious so as to get free food and lodging.

1964 J. L. NAYLER *Dict. Astronautics* 165 **Mission Control Center*. The Center..is due to be operational in 1964 for *Gemini* rendezvous flights. **1969** *Times* 16 July 5/8 Key abbreviations used by mission control and the astronauts will be [etc.]. **1973** *Guardian* 21 May 2/7 After the first switch-over, mission control commanded the computer to move back to the primary coolant circuit. **1900** *Harper's Bazaar* 28 Apr. 388/1 She stumbled upon an artistic small shop filled to overflowing with what the salesman called *Mission furniture. **1910** *Daily Chron.* 24 Jan. 3/5, I have often wondered why the modest designs of the mission furniture are so attractive. **1967** *Boston Sunday Herald* 9 Apr. (Show Guide) 15/1 The turn-of-the-century Mission furniture,..coming into popularity with the recent art nouveau revival. **1927** U. SINCLAIR *Oil!* 223 Inside was furniture of a style called '*mission oak'. **1973** *Washington Post* 13 Jan. F.1/8 (Advt.), Big mission oak library table. **1904** 'No. 1500' *Life in Sing Sing* 256/2 **Mission stiff*, missionary; a convert. **1931** 'D. STIFF' *Milk & Honey Route* v. 58 You may hang on to the good life for a time, while your erstwhile companions in sin dub you a 'mission stiff'. **1948** MENCKEN *Amer. Lang.* Suppl. II. 676 At the bottom of the pile are the poor wretches..who..gravitate dismally toward the big cities, to become beggars and mission-stiffs.

mission (ˈmɪʃən), *v.* [f. prec. sb.]

1. *trans.* To send on a mission; to give (a person) a mission to perform. Chiefly in *passive*.

1692 BEVERLEY *Disc. Dr. Crisp* 19 Whom the Spirit of God ..hath so Missiond, Commission'd, and Enabled. **1737** *Dream* ii, To native Heav'n they're fled, and there have Place, Till mission'd to attend her Rising Race. **1785** *Gentl. Mag.* IV. I. 66 The English..thinking that being missioned to the States of Barbary I might command some attention from the Algerines. **1818** KEATS *Endym.* I. 701 A disguis'd demon, missioned to knit My soul with under darkness. **1864** CARLYLE *Fredk. Gt.* XI. ix. IV. 106 We shall see him expressly missioned hither. **1887** *Temple Bar* Sept. 32 Parties, each led by its own captain, and missioned to its separate duty, began to go forth.

b. *nonce-use.* To send.

1824 HOOD *Two Swans* xxi, And through the shadows dun He missions like replies.

2. To conduct a religious mission among (a people) or in (a district).

1772 NUGENT *Hist. Fr. Gerund* I. 287, I have heard the Theatines say [so]..when they come to mission our souls for us. **1894** *Westm. Gaz.* 25 Apr. 7/1 The young lady missionaries who have been sent out to Algeria to mission the natives. **1894** *Mexborough & Swinton Times* 30 Nov. 5/2 The brass band missioned the streets morning and afternoon.

3. *intr.* To conduct a mission.

1898 *Athenæum* 5 Nov. 648/2 It was used by St. Augustine when he was missioning in those parts.

†**missionaire.** *Obs. rare*⁻¹. [a. F. *missionnaire.*] = MISSIONARY.

1687 [see MISSIONER b].

missional (ˈmɪʃənəl), *a. rare.* [f. MISSION *sb.* + -AL.] Relating to or connected with a religious mission; missionary.

1907 W. G. HOLMES *Age of Justinian & Theodora* II. 687 Several prelates, whose missional activities brought over whole districts and even nationalities to their creed.

missionarism (ˈmɪʃənərɪz(ə)m). *rare.* [f. MISSIONARY *a.* and *sb.* + -ISM.] = MISSIONIZING *vbl. sb.*

1890 H. S. HOLLAND in S. Paget *Henry Scott Holland* (1921) II. iv. 197 If I believe anything at all, I believe, with it, all that missionarism involves.

ˈ**missionarize**, *v.* Also **-aryize.** [f. MISSIONARY + -IZE.] = MISSIONIZE.

1829 T. ARNOLD in Stanley *Life* let. xi, No missionaryizing is half so beneficial, as to try to pour sound and healthy blood into a young civilized society. **1830** *Fraser's Mag.* I. 717 The regulation of the Church—the conversion of the Jews—the missionarizing Kamschatka and Galway.

missionary (ˈmɪʃənərɪ), *a.* and *sb.* [ad. mod.L. *missiōnāri-us* (17th c.), f. *missiōn-* MISSION + *-āri-us* -ARY. Cf. F. *missionnaire* sb. (G. Sagard *Hist. du Canada* 1636, p. 1008).] **A.** *adj.*

1. a. Relating to or connected with religious missions; sent on or engaged in a mission; proper to or characteristic of one sent on a mission; occupied in or characterized by mission-work.

In some collocations it is felt to be the sb. used attrib. ***missionary rector*** (R.C.Ch.): see quot. 1884. ***missionary box***: a box for the reception of contributions in money towards the funds of a missionary society.

1644 in Foley *Rec. Eng. Prov. Soc. Jesus* (1878) III. 89 They seemed..firmly united in the several graces of priestly and apostolical missionary vocation. **1690** TEMPLE *Misc.* II. 20 These [records] are agreed, by the Missionary Jesuits, to extend so far above Four Thousand Years. **1719** DE FOE *Crusoe* II. (Globe) 523 The Missionary Priests usually went thither [*sc.* to Macao], in Order to their going forward to China. **1813–15** (*title*) Proceedings of the Church Missionary Society for Africa and the East. **1832** DOWNES *Lett.* I. 47 Near the gate is a large missionary cross. **1841** GEO. ELIOT *Let.* 21 June (1954) I. 98 We yesterday heard him preach his last Missionary sermon. **1842** BORROW *Bible in Spain* xlvi, One of those little accidents which chequer missionary life in Spain. **1849** [see AU FAIT *advb. phr.*]. **1854** C. M. YONGE *Castle Builders* v. 69 The chimney-piece ornamented with missionary boxes and cards for shilling and penny subscriptions. **1854** in C. C. Richards *Village Life Amer.* (1912) 47 If we wanted to take shares in the missionary ship, *Morning Star*, we could buy them at 10 cents apiece. **1866** J. C. PATTESON *Let.* 1 Jan. in C. M. Yonge *Life J. C. Patteson* (1874) II. x. 160, I value much these memorials of the first Missionary Bishop of the Church of England. **1872** FROUDE in *Brit. Q. Rev.* (1873) LVII. 509 That section of the Protestants who alone possessed missionary power. **1873** C. M. YONGE *Pillars of House* II. xviii. 150 Mrs. Shapcote sent out invitations to a missionary tea in honour of him [*sc.* a missionary]. **1875** MAX MÜLLER *Chips* IV. 265 The three missionary religions, Buddhism, Mohammedanism, and Christianity. **1884** *Catholic Dict.* s.v. *Rector*, In England there is a certain number of missions in each diocese, important either on account of their having been long established or because of the size of the congregation, the priests in charge of which are styled 'Missionary-Rectors'. **1886** *Free Ch. Monthly* Dec. 365/1 Every class..to have its missionary box. **1894** ILLINGWORTH *Personality* 10 The missionary desire to commend their creed..will..increase the need of theological definition. **1932** T. S. ELIOT *Sweeney Agonistes* 23 I'll convert *you*! Into a stew. A nice little, white little, missionary stew. **1933** P. A. EADDY *Hull Down* v. 108 On some missionary hooker where they'll want to dish up two prayer meetings in the one week to all hands. **1942** A. P. JEPHCOTT *Girls growing Up* iii. 58 We redeemed ourselves..by working hard for a missionary box. **1971** J. MANTON *Sister Dora* xvi. 272 Selwyn of Lichfield.. had been the first missionary bishop in Melanesia.

transf. **1865** GROTE *Plato* I. vii. 290 The..operations announced..by Socrates..as his missionary life-purpose.

b. ***missionary position***: the position for sexual intercourse in which the woman lies underneath the man and facing him.

1969 *Daily Tel.* (Colour Suppl.) 10 Jan. 7 In six States [in the U.S.] a woman may still be awarded a divorce if her husband makes love to her in any other than the missionary position. **1971** *Vogue* Nov. 60/2 The face-to-face 'missionary position' (so called because it is virtually unknown in primitive races) is actually said to have been invented by Roman courtesans to hinder conception. **1971** 'V. X. SCOTT' *Surrogate Wife* 54 His wife would allow only one position—male-on-top—called the Missionary position by some and the Mamma-Papa position by others.

2. That is sent out or forth. Now *Obs.* or *poet.*

1691 NORRIS *Pract. Disc.* 330 The Missionary Angels, that have the..Office of Guardians here upon Earth. **1699** POMFRET *Love Triumphant* Poems (1724) 28 Cupid..Who Troops of missionary Loves commands. **1850** S. DOBELL *Roman* vi. Poet. Wks. (1875) 95 The night..calling By missionary winds and twilight birds.

B. *sb.*

1. a. A person who goes on a religious mission; *esp.* one sent to propagate the faith among the heathen.

home missionary: a person (usually a layman) employed by some religious organization to labour in the evangelization or spiritual instruction of the poor. ***city missionary***: one so employed amongst the poor of a city; chiefly, an agent of the London City Mission or of one of the similarly named organizations in other towns; so ***town missionary***. ***police-court missionary***: a person employed to attend a police-court and to work for the spiritual or moral benefit of those brought before it, and to inquire into cases of distress that are disclosed by the proceedings.

1656 BLOUNT *Glossogr.*, *Missionaries*, persons sent; commonly spoken of Priests sent to unbelieving Countries to convert the people to Christian Faith. **1691** tr. *Emilianne's Frauds Rom. Monks* (ed. 3) 296 Should the Jesuits of Italy.. send thither their Missionaries. **1726** CAVALLIER *Mem.* I. 4 The King sent through all his Kingdom Missionaries to instruct the Protestants..in the Roman Religion. **1791** WESLEY *Wks.* (1872) VIII. 316 Why are we not all devoted to God; breathing the whole spirit of Missionaries? **1851** MAYHEW *Lond. Labour* I. 70 A poor..urchin, who was spoken of by one of the City Missionaries as being a well-disposed youth. **1874** GREEN *Short Hist.* i. §3. 23 The missionaries of the new faith appeared fearlessly among the Mercians. **1891** M. WILLIAMS *Later Leaves* 390 The great

assistance magistrates receive from the thirteen missionaries attached to the different Courts. *Ibid.* 397 My Court missionary saw the two off by train.

b. *transf.*

1672 MARVELL *Reh. Transp.* I. 92 That Politick Engine who..was employed by some of Oxford as a Missionary amongst the Nonconformists of the adjacent Counties. **1747** CHESTERF. *Lett.* (1792) I. cxix. 323, I would not, at twenty years, be a preaching missionary of abstemiousness and sobriety. *c* **1789** GIBBON *Mem.* Misc. Wks. 1814 I. 270 The fanatic missionaries of sedition have scattered the seeds of discontent in our cities. **1890** R. BUCHANAN *Coming Terror* (1891) 83 My father was one of Robert Owen's missionaries.

†**c.** A 'Priest of the Mission', a Lazarite. *Obs.*

1656 [see MISSION *sb.* 5 c].

2. An agent or emissary; esp. one sent on a political mission. Now *rare* or *Obs.*

1693 *Apol. Clergy Scot.* 101 The Agents of the party would employ their little Missionaries to gather Stories from all corners of the Country. **1777** BURKE *Let. to Sheriffs of Bristol* Wks. III. 200 That this ill-natured doctrine should be preached by the missionaries of a Court I do not wonder. **1821** JEFFERSON *Autob.* Wks. 1892 I. 148 The diplomatic missionaries of Europe at Paris. **1821** SCOTT *Pirate* iv, Mr. Triptolemus Yellowley, who was the chosen missionary of the Chamberlain of Orkney and Zetland.

†**3.** A missionary body or establishment. *Obs.*

1719 DE FOE *Crusoe* II. (Globe) 529 Christianity..was once planted here by a Dutch Missionary of Protestants. **1761** *Chron.* in *Ann. Reg.* 172 There were then..612 jesuits colleges, 340 residuaries, 59 noviciates, 200 missionaries, and 24 professors houses of that society.

†**4.** *N.Z.* A Christian. *Obs.*

1834 E. MARKHAM *N.Z. or Recollections of It* (MS.) 32 They are all Missionaries as they call the Christians. **1840** *N.Z. Jrnl.* 5 Dec. 292/2 The natives..call themselves missionaries, having embraced Christianity. **1841** *Ibid.* 10 Apr. 87/2, I asked whether it was true, that he had given up all fighting intrigues, and become a missionary. **1854** R. E. MALONE *Three Years' Cruise Australasian Colonies* iii. 22 Mihaneri (missionaries—the universal name, in New Zealand, for Protestant Christians).

5. The sweet-brier, *Rosa eglanteria. N.Z.*

1881 F. LARKWORTHY *N.Z. Revisited* 30 The sweetbriar, which here [*sc.* at Tarawera] goes by the name of the 'Missionary', blocking the roads and vacant spaces. [**1898** W. P. REEVES *Long White Cloud* i. 17 The sweetbriar.. covers whole hillsides, to the ruin of pasture. Introduced, innocently enough, by the missionaries, it goes by their name in some districts.] **1912** B. E. BAUGHAN *Brown Bread from Colonial Oven* iii. 48 'Missionary', in the North Island is frequently an alternative spelling for 'sweet-brier', which is a pest. **1921** H. GUTHRIE-SMITH *Tutira* xxvii. 274 Sweet-briar..'Missionary' as it is still called, has been spread abroad by the horse.

'missionary, *v.* [f. the sb.] **a.** *intr.* To act as a missionary. **b.** *trans.* To act as a missionary towards (someone).

1862 *Independent* (N.Y.) 24 Apr. 3/1 He [*sc.* the Rev. S. H. Tyng] was always fond of missionarying. *c* **1876** J. ALBERY *Man in Possession* 1, in *Dramatic Works* (1939) II. 105, I know I *was* [dreadfully wicked], but I'm not now, Teddy. I've been missionaried, and preached to. **1884** 'MARK TWAIN' *Huck. Finn* xix. 183 Preachin's my line, too, and workin' camp-meetin's, and missionaryin' around. **1893** K. D. WIGGIN *Polly Oliver's Problem* (1894) vii. 87 Boys hate to be missionaried, and I'm sure I don't blame them.

'missionaryship. [-SHIP.] The position or status of a missionary.

1840 *Fraser's Mag.* XXII. 363 To back Wightwick in his propagandist missionaryship for the conversion of the public to architectural study. **1898** G. A. SMITH *H. Drummond* vi. (1899) 135 Drummond resigned the missionaryship.

missionate ('mɪʃəneɪt), *v. U.S.* [f. MISSION + -ATE.] *intr.* = MISSIONIZE *v.* a.

1816 J. PICKERING *Vocab.*, To *Missionate*, to perform the services of a missionary. 'A low ecclesiastical word (says a learned clerical correspondent) used in conversation' in America. **1828** *Richmond* (Virginia) *Enquirer* 19 Aug. 4/1 (Th.), [Mr. Weed] was next heard of in the southern tier of counties, missionating for the administration. **1896** *Home Missionary* Oct. 303 To make professional visits, or to 'missionate' to the farmer, will not serve the purpose. **1966** *Publ. Mod. Lang. Assoc.* LXXXI. II. 7/2 Their fellow linguists who are interested in..missionating to convert the National Council of Teachers of English. *Ibid.* 8/1 Our missionaries should at least know what they are talking about before they set out to missionate.

missioned ('mɪʃənd), *ppl. a.* Chiefly *poet.* [f. MISSION *sb.* or *v.* + -ED.]

1. Having a mission; sent on a mission or errand.

1795 SOUTHEY *Joan of Arc* III. 101 The mission'd maid reply'd, 'Go thou Dunois, Announce my mission to the royal ear'. **1804** GRAHAME *Sabbath* 431 The mission'd men, who have renounced Their homes, their country..Bearing glad tidings to the farthest isles. **1819** KEATS *Eve of St. Agnes* xxii, When Madeline, St. Agnes' charmed maid, Rose, like a missioned spirit, unaware. **1822** *Blackw. Mag.* XII. 38 The missioned Angel of Destruction.

2. That belongs to a person's mission to perform.

1798 in *Spirit Publ. Jrnls.* (1799) II. 77 Ere his mission'd toil is done.

missionee (mɪʃə'niː). *rare.* [f. MISSION *v.* + -EE[1].] One who is susceptible to the arguments of an emissary or a missionary.

1951 'J. TEY' *Daughter of Time* v. 70 George could obviously be talked into anything. He was the born missionee.

†**missio'neer,** *sb. Obs.* [f. MISSION *sb.* + -EER[1].] One who gives a commission.

a **1660** *Contemp. Hist. Irel.* 1641–52 (1880) III. II. 140 That..such commissioners..had free libertie to..treate.. accordinge instructions of theire missioneeres.

†**missio'neer,** *v. Obs.* [f. MISSION *sb.* + -EER[1]. Cf. *electioneer* vb.] *intr.* To conduct a mission. Also **missio'neering** vbl. sb. (also *attrib.*).

1715 M. DAVIES *Athen. Brit.* I. 276 A Secular Priest..now Missioneering in Yorkshire. **1716** *Ibid.* III. *Diss. Drama* 12 That insolent Popish Missioneering Calumny. *Ibid.* 26 Their common Fool's Errand of Missioneering.

missioner ('mɪʃənə(r)). [f. MISSION + -ER[1].] One sent on a mission, a missionary; *esp.* (in early use) a Jesuit missionary. In mod. use chiefly, one who conducts or is in charge of a parochial mission (in some dioceses, a permanent clerical officer).

1654 W. MOUNTAGUE *Devout Ess.* II. v. §3. 94 The missioners of France..seek to establish this practice in all places where they teach, that persons of all conditions, make some short address to God, at the striking of every clock. ? **1687** DRYDEN *Let. to Sir G. Etherege* 13 Like mighty missioner you come *Ad Partes Infidelium.* **1716** M. DAVIES *Athen. Brit.* II. 120 Other four were sent as itinerant Preachers and Missioners into all the Counties of England. **1771** GOLDSM. *Hist. Eng.* I. 51 The pope enjoined his missioner to remove the pagan idols. **1849** ROCK *Ch. of Fathers* I. iii. 274 The British style of..illumination..was carried by British missioners far to the north. **1862** FURNISS *Confession* §xv. 16 One night during the Mission he went into the church. He stood near the platform where the missioner was preaching. **1894** BARING-GOULD *Deserts S. France* II. 76 St. Fronto,..probably a missioner of the third century. **1896** *19th Cent.* Aug. 213 Our [the Jesuits'] position as theologians, missioners, preachers.

†**b.** *fig.* (cf. MISSIONARY B. 1 b, 2.) *Obs.*

1687 DRYDEN *Hind & P.* II. 565 Poems (1743) I. 285 Those are the Manufactures we export; And these the Missioners [*1st ed.* Missionaries] our zeal has made. **1751** ELIZA HEYWOOD *Betsy Thoughtless* II. 215 As every little circumstance..seems a missioner from fate. **1793** BURKE *On policy of Allies* Wks. VII. 146 You will have a missioner of peace and order in every parish.

'missioning, *vbl. sb.* [f. MISSION *v.* + -ING[1].] The conducting of a religious mission.

1886 in H. BAUMANN *Londinismen.* **1961** B. R. WILSON *Sects & Society* III. xiv. 293 Costly missioning in pagan lands.

missionist ('mɪʃənɪst). [-IST.] One who does mission work.

1909 M. B. SAUNDERS *Litany Lane* I. iii. 34 These were wood-carvers, church artists, metal-workers, window designers, architects, carpenters and missionists.

missionize ('mɪʃənaɪz), *v.* [f. MISSION *sb.* + -IZE.] **a.** *intr.* To conduct or promote a mission; to do missionary work. **b.** *trans.* To do missionary work amongst (people).

1826 *Blackw. Mag.* XIX. 464 Why do they not buy all the land in a single island, and missionize and philanthropize at their own expense. **1879** MRS. HUTCHINSON *In Tents in Transvaal* xiv. 125 One must hope..that the Kafirs..will cheerfully suffer themselves to be missionized, shot, and bayonetted into tail-coats. **1888** MRS. J. K. SPENDER *Kept Secret* III. ii. 29 You have been spending the long years in missionizing cannibals.

Hence **'missionizing** *vbl. sb.* and *ppl. a.*; **'missionizer,** one who does missionary work.

1864 [see DISSENTERISH]. **1888** *Voice* (N.Y.) 9 Feb. 4 Missionizing agencies. **1893** *19th Cent.* July 167 The missionising..function of the Church. **1901** *Publ. Circular* 25 May 583/2 Social missionizers.

missis, missus ('mɪsɪs, -ɪz, 'mɪsəs). *dial.* and *vulgar.* [Corruption of MISTRESS. The oral equivalent of the abbreviation MRS. (q.v.), which is always written exc. in the vulgar uses explained below.]

1. Wife. (*the missis* is used by a man in speaking of his own or of another man's wife.)

1833 DICKENS *Let. c* 10 Dec. (1965) I. 34 Hint this delicately to your *Missus.* **1836** —— *Let. c* 20 July (1965) I. 155 My Missis furthermore desires me to say [etc.]. **1839** CLARK *J. Noakes* lxviii (E.D.S.), Missus! I thinks as how, taa-day, Yow've put the meller's eye out! **1848** THACKERAY *Van. Fair* xxv, So he altered these words, bowing to the superior knowledge of his little Missis. **1860** GEO. ELIOT *Mill on Fl.* I. viii, And what with the Missis being laid up so, things have gone awk'arder nor usual. **1892** KIPLING *Barrack-r. Ballads* 11 Then 'ere's to you Fuzzy-Wuzzy, an' the missis and the kid. **1934** T. S. ELIOT *Rock* ii. 65 Lor-love-a-duck, it's the missus! **1946** K. TENNANT *Lost Haven* (1947) I. 23, I wouldn't let any missus of mine..go gallivanting with another chap. **1975** *Daily Mirror* 29 Apr. 25 If you fancy taking the missus for a day out, you take her virtually free.

2. Used by servants (usually without article) in speaking of their mistresses; *spec.* used by N. American Negroes and in *India* and *S. Africa* of a white employer, and loosely of any (esp. a white) woman.

1790 J. B. MORETON *Manners & Customs West India Islands* 154 Then missess fum me wid long switch. **1835** DICKENS *Sk. Boz* (1837) 2nd Ser. 87 The servant..has utterly disregarded 'Missis's' ringing. **1837** DICKENS *Pickw.* xxxvi, 'Gentlemen', said the man in blue.., 'I'll give you the ladies; come'. 'Hear, hear!' said Sam. 'The young missises'. ..'Missises, Sir'..'We don't recognize such distinctions here'. **1850** MISS YONGE *Henrietta's Wish* iv. 49 Yes, Miss Henrietta, I was coming down from Missus's room, when Mr. Godfrey stopped me. **1852** MRS. STOWE *Uncle Tom's Cabin* II. xxxiv. 203 'Missis,' said Tom, after a while, 'I can see that, some how you're quite 'bove me in everything; but there's one thing Missis might learn, even from poor Tom.' **1857** TROLLOPE *Barchester T.* II. ix. 165 'Mr. Slope called with it himself, your reverence', said the girl; 'and was very anxious that missus should have it to-day'. **1901** M. FRANKLIN *My Brilliant Career* xiii. 107 I'll tell the missus on you as sure as eggs. **1924** E. LEWIS *Harp* II. vii. 98 Does the missis hear the young masters in the stable? **1940** in H. Wentworth *Amer. Dial. Dict.* (1944) 392/2 Mighty fine for young missus. **1942** P. ABRAHAMS *Dark Testament* II. iii. 113 As soon as she saw it was a white person she ran back into the house. 'Ma! Ma! There's a missus at the door!' **1943** 'B. KNIGHT' *Covenant* (1944) II. x. 132 He smiled at the Ayah and said, 'I will speak to the *Missis* and perhaps she will be willing to go.' **1950** L. BENNETT et al. *Anancy Stories & Dial. Verse* 48 Eee-Hee Missis, is me same one Sidung yah all de time. **1952** P. ABRAHAMS *Path of Thunder* III. i. 190, I work for old missus when I was a child. **1971** *Weekend World* (Johannesburg) 9 May 2/2 Langton told her to cook. 'When I refused, he slapped my face hard, accusing me of making myself a "missus".'

Hence **'missis** *v. trans.*, to address as 'Mrs.'

1838 DICKENS *Nich. Nick.* xlii, 'Don't Missis me, ma'am' ..returned Miss Squeers.

Missisauga (mɪsɪ'sɔːgə). Also **Messasague, Messisauger, Missasago, Missasauga, Missis(s)a(u)ga(h), Mississagua,** etc. [Ojibwa, lit. 'people of the Mississagi River' (in Ontario).] **1.** A tribe of Algonquian Indians; a member of this tribe. Also *attrib.* or as *adj.*

1703 tr. *Lahontan's New Voy. N.-Amer.* I. xxv. 230 A list of the savage nations of Canada... The Missisagues. **1749** G. CLINTON *Let.* 3 June in E. B. O'Callaghan *Docs. rel. Colonial Hist. New-York* (1855) VI. 486 To meet the Missisaque Indians at Oswego. **1772** in *14th Rep. R. Comm. Hist. Manuscripts* App. X. 85 in *Parl. Papers 1895* (C. 7883) LIX. 1 The Chippawaes and Mississagaes are by far the most numerous and powerful nation with whom we have any connection in North America. **1798** B. S. BARTON *New Views Origin of Tribes & Nations N. Amer.* (ed. 2) App. 4 The Messaugers, or Messasagues. The language of these Indians is, undoubtedly, very nearly allied to that of the Chippewas. **1831** A. S. WITHERS *Chron. Border Warfare* 299 Their force consisted of four thousand warriors, and was led on by a Missasago chief. **1838** A. JAMESON *Winter Stud. & Summer Rambles Canada* I. 16 One solitary wigwam.., the dwelling of a few Missassagua Indians. *Ibid.* 296 The scene of bloody conflicts between the Hurons and the Missassaguas. **1888** *Jrnl. Amer. Folklore* I. 151 (*heading*) Notes on the history, customs, and beliefs of the Mississagua Indians. *Ibid.* 152 These are the most advanced in civilization of the Mississaguas. **1948** *Southwestern Jrnl. Anthropol.* Spring 100 These people, particularly the Missasaugas, seem to have occupied the southern end of the Park a century ago. **1960** D. JENNESS *Indians of Canada* (ed. 5) iv. 40 The cultivation of maize had spread..to some adjacent Algonkian tribes,..the Missisauga on the north shore of lake Huron. *Ibid.* xvii. 282 Many Missisauga moved into the old territory of the Hurons between lakes Huron and Erie.

2. = MASSASAUGA.

1843 W. OLIVER *Eight Months Illinois* 150 The inhabitants recognize two kinds of rattlesnakes, to wit, the wood- and the prairie-rattlesnake, or missisauga, of which the latter is much the smaller and less dangerous. **1961** *Listener* 16 Nov. 826/1 A missisauga rattler I once knifed.

missish ('mɪsɪʃ), *a.* [f. MISS *sb.*[2] + -ISH.] Like or characteristic of a miss, young lady, or schoolgirl; hence, affected, prim, squeamish, or sentimental.

1795 MME. D'ARBLAY *Diary* (1846) VI. 47, I remember how many people did not like that [*sc.* the name] of Evelina, and called it 'affected' and 'missish', till they read the book. **1853** MRS. GORE *Dean's Dau.* II. 86 Some foolish, missish scruple or other. **1865** MISS BRADDON *Eleanor's Victory* i, Another girl would have given herself all manner of missish airs. **1897** *Truth* 6 May 1123 The missish street dress, fashionable when the Queen came to the Throne, would never do for girls who play lawn tennis.

Hence **'missishness.**

1839 T. HOOK *Births, Deaths & Marriages* I. ii. 41 My own missishness..in liking to have lovers in order to teaze them. **1890** *Spectator* 13 Dec., There is far more 'grit' and far less missishness in this story than are generally to be found in books written for girls.

mississippi (mɪsɪ'sɪpɪ). Also 8 **missisipee, -ippi,** 9 **-ipie.** [A fanciful application of the name of the North American river.] A game similar to bagatelle, in which balls are driven against cushions at the side of the table so as to go through arches (of which there are 15) at the end of the table, the number of the arch counting to the player whose ball goes through it.

1728 in *Dig. Proc. Crt.-leet Savoy* (1789) 15 Playing a game commonly called Missisipee. **1777** HOWARD *State of Prisons* 159 They also play in the yard at skittles, missisippi, fives, tennis, &c. **1835** J. WILSON *Biog. of Blind* 185, I remember his occasionally playing at billiards, missisipie, shuffle-board and skittles. **1850** *Bohn's Handbk. Games* 612.

attrib. **1757** *Act 30 Geo. II*, c. 24 §14 Any Gaming with Cards, Dice,..Mississippi or Billard Tables. **1801** STRUTT *Sports & Past.* IV. i. §18 Arches similar to those upon the mississipi-table.

Mississippian (mɪsɪ'sɪpɪən), *sb.* and *a.* [f. *Mississippi* (see below) + -AN.] **A.** *sb.* **1.** A native or inhabitant of Mississippi, a state on the Gulf of Mexico.

1775 J. ADAIR *Hist. Amer. Indians* 93 'The ugly yellow French,' (as they [*sc.* Indians] term the Missisippians). **1867**

Harper's Mag. June 1/1 Two of us New Englanders, and a Mississippian. **1948** *Daily Ardmoreite* (Ardmore, Okla.) 4 May 1/6, I recognize our Negroes, as do all good white Mississippians, as a part of our citizenry. **1973** A. DUNDES *Mother Wit* 37 Mississippian David L. Cohn.

2. *Geol.* The Mississippian period or system.

1910 *Encycl. Brit.* V. 310/2 It became the practice to distinguish a 'productive' [Upper]..and an 'unproductive', barren..Lower Carboniferous; these two groups correspond in North America to the 'Carboniferous' and 'Sub-Carboniferous' respectively, or, as they are now sometimes styled, the 'Pennsylvanian' and 'Mississippian'. **1969** BENNISON & WRIGHT *Geol. Hist. Brit. Isles* ix. 184 The Carboniferous System is traditionally divided into the Lower and Upper Carboniferous in Britain and western Europe. The two systems in North America, the Mississippian and the Pennsylvanian, correspond broadly to these divisions.

B. *adj.* **1.** Of, pertaining to, or peculiar to Mississippi.

1835 J. H. INGRAHAM *South-West* II. 79 Of every variety of gaited animals..the Mississippian pacer is the most desirable. **1963** *Economist* 10 Aug. 509/2 A man who, in Mississippian terms, is a relative moderate on the race issue.

2. *Geol.* [Named after the Mississippi River, on the bluffs of which in Iowa and Missouri the system is exposed.] Of, pertaining to, or designating a period and system of the Palæozoic Era in North America that succeeded the Devonian and preceded the Pennsylvanian, and corresponds more or less to the Lower Carboniferous in Europe.

[**1870** A. WINCHELL *Sk. Creation* xii. 136 The Mountain limestone, or Lower Carboniferous mass, which I have proposed to designate the Mississippi Group, because so extensively developed in the valley of the Mississippi River.] **1891** H. S. WILLIAMS in *Bull. U.S. Geol. Survey* No. 80. 135 As these formations are bound together by a common general fauna and constitute a conspicuous feature in the geology of this region, it is proposed to call them the Mississippian series. **1933** R. C. MOORE *Historical Geol.* xvii. 257 The consensus of judgment among American geologists increasingly supports the view that the Mississippian and Pennsylvanian deposits should be reckoned as independent geologic systems rather than as subordinate divisions (series) of a so-called system that combines them. *Ibid.* 260 Red shale and sandstone..with a maximum thickness of about 3,000 feet form the upper part of the Mississippian system in much of the Appalachian region. **1967** *Oceanogr. & Marine Biol.* V. 131 Evaporite sediments of Mississippian age have caused similar uplift in nearby Nova Scotia.

† **mis'sit**, *v.* *Obs.* [MIS-^{1} 1. Cf. F. *messeoir.*] *intr.* To be unbecoming *to*; to misbecome (with dative). Also, to be inconvenient or disturbing *to*.

? *a* **1366** CHAUCER *Rom. Rose* 1194 And certes, it [a brooch] missat hir nought. *c* **1375** *Sc. Leg. Saints* xii. (*Mathias*) 44 & to þe faddir þat hyme gat his byrth ful gretumly missate. **1390** GOWER *Conf.* II. 302 For it mai be that thi desir,..Per cas to hire honour missit. **1412-20** LYDG. *Chron. Troy* v. (1513) 2 D iij b/1 And though so be that any worde mysse syt, Amende it with chere debonayre. *c* **1430** *Pilgr. Lyf Manhode* I. lxxxviii. (1869) 50 And suppose þat, to þi seemynge, j hadde maad thing missittynge.

missive ('mɪsɪv), *a.* and *sb.* Also 5 myssif, -yfe, 5-6 -yve, 6 missiwe, -yve, -eif. [ad. F. *missive* fem. (also sb. in Cotgr.), or med.L. *missīv-us* (Diefenbach), f. *miss-*, ppl. stem of *mittĕre* to send: see -IVE.

The corresponding words in med.Latin and the Romanic languages are used chiefly in phrases analogous to 'letter missive': med.L. *litteræ missivæ*, F. *lettre(s) missive(s)*, It. *littera missiva*, Sp. *letra*, *carta misiva*, Pg. *cartas missivas*, also *arma missiva* (cf. A. 2). Cf. MDu. *missijf-brief*. OF. has also *lettres missibles*.]

A. *adj.*

1. letter missive, missive letter. Usually pl. ***letters missive*** or † ***missives***.

† **a.** *gen.* A letter or epistle sent from one person to another. *Obs.*

1519 HORMAN *Vulg.* viii. 80 b, Fyne and thynne papyr, seruynge for myssyue letters. **1530** PALSGR. 35 The letters missyves of suche as be secreatores in the sayd countreis. *c* **1532** DU WES *Introd. Fr.* Ibid. 898 The second boke shall be of lettres missyves in prose and in ryme. **1637** RUTHERFORD *Lett.* (1664) I. cxiii. 219, I know missive letters goe between the Devil & young blood. **1658** PHILLIPS, A *letter Missive*, a letter which is sent from one friend to another. **1710** J. CHAMBERLAYNE *St. Gt. Brit.* I. III. x. (ed. 23) 281 Though the Number of Letters missive in England were not at all considerable in our Ancestors Days, yet it is now so prodigiously great (since the meanest People have generally learnt to write) that [etc.].

b. A letter or letters sent by a superior authority, esp. the sovereign, to a particular person or body of persons, conveying a command, recommendation, or permission. Now chiefly, in the Church of England, a letter from the sovereign to a dean and chapter nominating the person whom they are to elect bishop. (See CONGÉ D'ÉLIRE.)

1466 *Anc. Cal. Rec. Dublin* (1889) I. 323 The saide Maister John..for the Maire, Baylyffes and cominaltie..to make all myssyvve lettres in lattyne to Irishe enemyes..and others..that undrestandith not Englys. **1477** *MS. Rawl. B.* 332 lf. 42 *marg.*, A commission maad in a lettre myssif forto visite the priory of Hertford by my lord Abbot in proper persone. **1477** EDW. IV in Ellis *Orig. Lett.* Ser. I. I. 17 Whereas we have other tymes addressed our Lettres missiues vnto Robert Conestable for restitucion of the goods of Thomas Yare. **1487** *Naval Acc. Hen. VII* (1896) 66 A letter missiue Vnder the Kynges signett. **1533-4** *Act 25 Hen. VIII*, c. 20 §3 A lycence vnder the greate seale..with a lettre myssyve, conteynyng the name of the persone which they shall electe and chose; By vertue of which licence the seid Deane and Chapitour..shall..electe..the seid person named in the seid letters myssyves. **1555** EDEN *Decades* Contents (Arb.) 45 The letters missiue which kynge Edwarde the .vi. sent. **1603** HOLLAND *Plutarch's Mor.* 13 Alexander the Great had by his letters missive given commandement that the Greekes should provide Robes of purple against his returne. **1637-50** ROW *Hist. Kirk* (Bannatyne Cl.) 63 His Maiestie sent aught missive letters, dated..To..(such a man) Minister of (such a place). **1679** BURNET *Hist. Ref.* I. III. 236 The King granted a *Congé d'élire* to the Prior and Convent, with a Missive Letter, declaring the name of the person whom they should choose. **1768** BLACKSTONE *Comm.* III. 445 If a peer is a defendant, the lord chancellor sends a letter missive to him to request his appearance. **1841** HALLAM *Mid. Ages* (ed. 8) I. iv. 397 John I had long before admitted, that what was done by cortes and general assemblies could not be undone by letters missive. **1863** COX *Instit.* I. vi. 32 The Convention Parliament of 1688, elected by virtue of letters-missive written by the Prince of Orange. **1868** FREEMAN *Norm. Conq.* (1877) II. viii. 189 A good precedent for the *congé d'élire* and letter missive.

c. *Sc.* = B. 2.

1568 *Reg. Privy Council Scot.* Ser. I. I. 641 All missive lettres, contractis or obligationis for mariage [etc.]. **1693** STAIR *Inst. Law Scot.* I. x. §9 Though the buyer by a Missive Letter, wrote, that he thought he would not be able to furnish the Money. *Ibid.* IV. xlii. §25 Missive-Letters are Probative, except where they relate to more solemn Writs, such as Bonds, Bills, or Accompts. **1773** ERSKINE *Inst. Law Scot.* III. ii. §24 Missive letters *in re mercatoria* are valid, though they be not holograph.

d. *U.S.* Among Congregationalists, an official letter inviting churches to send delegates to a council.

1798 M. CUTLER in *Life, Jrnls. & Corr.* (1888) II. 4 We jointly addressed letters missive to eleven churches, all of whom complied, and the council was formed at my house. **1880** H. M. DEXTER *Congregationalism* x. 527 In what manner Councils are regularly called. This has been uniformly done by a form of written request, which has received the technical name of a Letter-Missive.

† **2.** *Sc.* ***missive bill, writing*** = letter missive.

1564 *Reg. Privy Council Scot.* I. 283 Heirupoun wer lettres direct and als missyve writtingis to this same effect sent to [etc.]. *a* **1578** LINDESAY (Pitscottie) *Chron. Scot.* (S.T.S.) II. 112 This was done all for sending of ane missiwe bill in Ingland. **1579-80** *Reg. Privy Council Scot.* Ser. I. III. 256 Missive bill of Houstoun and New Work.

† **3.** Of a weapon or engine of war: = MISSILE *a.*

1548 PATTEN *Exped. Scot.* I ij b, Most of our artillerie & missiue engins. **1603** KNOLLES *Hist. Turks* (1621) 879 Not with their missive weapons onely..but with their drawne swords. **1697** DRYDEN *Æneid* XII. 848 The feather'd Arrows fly, And clouds of missive Arms invade the sky. **1704** SWIFT *Batt. Bks.* Misc. (1711) 226 Ink is the great missive Weapon in all Battels of the Learned. **1780** in Grose, etc. *Antiq. Rep.* III. 68 Nor among the defensive machines is the missive wheel to be despised... The missive chariot may also be effectually used. *a* **1809** J. PALMER *Like Master* (1811) I. x. 141 He hurl'd the missive weapon which transpierced the heart of his adverse chief.

transf. **1667** MILTON *P.L.* VI. 519 Thir Engins and thir Balls Of missive ruin. **1695** BLACKMORE *Pr. Arth.* v. 254 Each on his Foe missive Destruction pours. *a* **1761** CAWTHORN *Poems* (1771) 19 Where dreadful flew the missive deaths around.

† **4.** That is sent; sent on an errand; also, sent as a message. *Obs.*

1610 WILLET *Hexapla, Daniel* 376 Christ is none of the missiue or ministring Angels. **1627-77** FELTHAM *Resolves* I. xlvii. 75 Scaliger defines Death to be the Cessation of the Souls functions: as if it were rather a restraint, than a missive ill. **1830** W. PHILLIPS *Mt. Sinai* I. 444 The missive words then told he.

B. *sb.*

1. A written message; a letter. Sometimes *spec.* = 'missive letter' (A. 1). Now usually, either denoting an official letter, or used as a somewhat high-flown equivalent of 'letter'.

In early use largely *Sc.*

1501 DOUGLAS *Pal. Hon.* II. v, How Acontius till Cydippe anone Wrait his complaint,..With vther lustie missiues mony one. **1560** ROLLAND *Crt. Venus* II. 635 His small missiue belyue he gaif him fro, Vnto thir thre. **1577-87** HOLINSHED *Chron.* III. 1237/1 A missiue persuasorie sent to the Scots for the marriage of their yoong queene Marie to our yoong king Edward the sixt. **1603** FLORIO *Montaigne* I. xxxix, To spend their time in wittily devising and closely hudling up of a quaint missive or witty epistle. **1605** BACON *Adv. Learn.* I. 33 The last act of his short raigne left to memorie was a missiue to his adopted sonne. *c* **1610** SIR J. MELVILLE *Mem.* (1827) 283 To the quhilk convention his Maieste directed missyues to some of the nobilite. **1647** (*title*) A Missive of Consolation: sent from Flanders, to the Catholikes of England. **1791** GIBBON *Misc. Wks.* (1814) I. 342 Had I delayed..another post, your missive of the 13th.. would have arrived in time. **1838** PRESCOTT *Ferd. & Is.* (1846) I. ix. 395 The marquis..had despatched missives, requesting the support of the principal lords..of Andalusia. **1879** FARRAR *St. Paul* (1883) 247 The circular missive from James and the Church at Jerusalem. **1885** DOBSON *At Sign of Lyre* 188 Mysterious missives, sealed with red.

2. *Scots Law.* A document in the form of a letter interchanged by the parties to a contract. Also ***missive of lease*** (or ***tack***), ***m. of sale***.

1561 *Reg. Privy Council Scot.* I. 181 The charter party, and the missive, billis, and cocquet of the said schip. **1572** *Ibid.* II. 139 The writting of missives and other writtis. **1773** ERSKINE *Inst. Law Scot.* III. ii. §2 Where an agreement concerning heritage is executed in the form of mutual missives. **1816** SCOTT *Bl. Dwarf.* x, There really should be some black and white on this transaction. Sae just make me a minute, or missive,..and I'se write it fair ower, and subscribe it before famous witnesses. **1822** R. AINSLIE *Land of Burns* 94 As gif the Almighty was bun by missives o' tack, to gi'e them seed time an' harvest. **1832** *Act 2 & 3 Will. IV*, c. 65 §9 Provided each Tenant..shall..have held such.. Tenements under a Lease or Leases, Missive of Lease, or other written title. **1838** W. BELL *Dict. Law Scot.* s.v., It would appear that missives of lease, like missives of sale, require to be stamped to found an action.

† **3.** A messenger. *Obs. rare.*

1605 SHAKS. *Macb.* I. v. 7 Whiles I stood rapt in the wonder of it, came Missiues from the King, who all-hail'd me Thane of Cawdor. **1606** —— *Ant. & Cl.* II. ii. 74. **1649** G. DANIEL *Trinarch., Hen. IV*, ccclxxvi, Where trusted Ianizaries stand about The Tyrant, Missives to his Crueltye.

† **4.** Something hurled or thrown; *esp.* a missile weapon. *Obs.*

1644 DIGBY *Nat. Bodies* xii. 100 The stringes [of a racket]..do cause the missiues [*sc.* tennis balls] to speede so fast towardes their appoynted homes. **1770** SIR J. BANKS *Jrnl.* (1896) 244 Defensive weapons they have none, and no missives except stones and darts. **1809** W. IRVING *Knickerb.* VI. viii. (1849) 366 The heavens were darkened with a tempest of missives.

¶ **5.** = MISSILE *sb.* 2.

1649 JER. TAYLOR *Gt. Exemp.* I. Ad. §7. 110 How great things God hath done for us, whether in publick Donatives, or private Missives.

† **'missively**, *adv.* *Obs.* [f. MISSIVE *a.* + -LY^{2}.] By letter.

1641 KEYLWAY in Rigaud *Corr. Sci. Men* (1841) I. 63 At least missively if not personally.

Misskito, var. MISKITO *a.* and *sb.*

missle, missletoe, obs. ff. MISSEL, MISTLETOE.

'miss-mark. *rare.* [f. MISS *v.*^{1} Cf. MARK *sb.*^{1} 7 e.] A person who misses the mark, or who fails in a purpose.

1908 HARDY *Dynasts* III. VII. ix. 520 So, as it is, a miss-mark they will dub me.

miss-maze, variant of MIZMAZE.

missment ('mɪsmənt). *dial.* [f. MISS *v.*^{1} + -MENT.] **a.** Mistake, error. **b.** Loss.

1868 TREGELLAS *Tales* 33 But howsomever, we maade a missment. **1866** W. THORNBURY *Greatheart* III. xviii. 248 There's something wrong in the level, surely, some missment (mistake), I tell 'ee. **1890** 'Q.' *Three Ships* viii, We've found 'ee a great missment.

missomer, misson(ne: see MIDSUMMER, MIZEN.

mis-'sort, *v.* [MIS-^{1} 1.] *trans.* To sort badly; to allot to a wrong place or in a wrong way. So **mis-'sorted** *ppl. a.*

1581 MULCASTER *Positions* v. (1887) 25 If they be..missorted in place. *a* **1626** BP. ANDREWES 96 *Serm.* xv. (1661) 503 Not to be mis-sorted into a place no way meet. **1821** COLERIDGE *Lett., Conversat.* etc. (1836) II. 71 The present unsorted or *mis*-sorted ministry. **1873** M. COLLINS *Squire Silchester* II. xv. 179 These missorted twins.

Hence **mis-'sort** *sb.*, an instance of mis-sorting; a thing mis-sorted.

1898 *Daily News* 20 Dec. 3/3 To be able to sort the whole 500..with not more than 30 'blinds'—mis-sorts, that is.

mis-'sound, *v.* [MIS-^{1} 1.]

1. *intr.* To sound amiss.

? *a* **1500** in Grose, etc. *Antiq. Rep.* (1809) IV. 405 A songe myssowndithe yf the prickynge be not right. *Ibid.* 409 For perversite of thy prickinge and myssoundynge of thy songe.

2. *trans.* and *intr.* To mispronounce.

a **1548** HALL *Chron., Hen. VIII*, 127 They called them Crakers, whych by missounding, was commonly called Krekers. **1599** NASHE *Lenten Stuffe* 41 By corruption of speech, they false dialect and misse-sound it. **1880** FREEMAN *Let.* 18 May in Stephens *Life & Lett.* (1895) II. 204 *W* is sure to be missounded.

missour, obs. Sc. form of MEASURE.

Missouri (mɪs-, mɪ'zʊərɪ). *U.S.* [The name of a river and a state in the U.S.] **1.** A member of an American Indian people of the Sioux family, first encountered by Europeans near the Missouri River; also, the language of this people.

1703 tr. *Lahontan's New Voy. N.-Amer.* I. 130 We.. arriv'd on the 18th at the first Village of the Missouris. **1807** P. GASS *Jrnl.* 26 Six of them were made chiefs, three Otos and three Missouris. **1933** L. BLOOMFIELD *Lang.* iv. 72 The *Siouan* family includes many languages, such as..*Missouri*, *Winnebago*, [etc.]. **1947** *St. Louis* (Missouri) *Globe-Democrat* 16 Mar., The Missouris were a comparatively insignificant tribe.

2. Colloq. phr. ***to be*** (or ***come***) ***from Missouri***: to be very sceptical; to believe nothing until it is demonstrated. (Originally *I come from Missouri. You have got to show me.*)

1900 *Missouri State Tribune* (Jefferson City) 13 Dec. 4/1 Ex-Lieut.-Gov. Chas. P. Johnson thinks he knows the origin of the extensively-used expression: 'I'm from Missouri; you'll have to show me'; at least he can recall its use twenty years ago in Colorado. **1901** *Columbia Missouri Statesman* 13 Dec. 1/3 You gentlemen are from Kentucky, Texas, Tennessee and Arkansas and seem to trust each other, but 'I'm from Missouri and you must show me'. **1912** C. MCCARTHY *Wisconsin Idea* 291 In the words of the current slang phrase, every Wisconsin legislator 'comes

from Missouri' and you have to 'show him'. **1931** *Amer. Speech* VI. 205 *I'm from Missouri*, I don't believe that; you'll have to show me, or prove it to me. **1963** J. Mitford *Amer. Way of Death* III. iv. 132 If you suggest..that Destiny led him there, he will give you an I'm-from-Missouri look.

3. *attrib.* and *Comb.*, as **Missouri antelope** = pronghorn *sb.*; **Missouri Compromise** *Hist.*, an arrangement made in 1820 which provided that Missouri should be admitted to the Union as a slave state, but that slavery should not be allowed in any new state lying north of 36° 30′; also *attrib.*; **Missouri Indian** = sense 1 above; **Missouri mule**, a mule bred in Missouri; **Missouri question** *Hist.*, the question of the conditions under which Missouri should be admitted into the Union, and the connected problems regarding slavery; **Missouri skylark**, a variety of pipit, *Anthus spraguei*.

1806 Lewis & Clark in *Deb. Congress U.S.* (1852) 9th Congress 2 Sess. App. 1046 The Missouri antelope, (called Cabri' by the inhabitants of the Illinois). **1820** in T. H. Benton *Exam. Dred Scott Case* (1857) 102 The line is.. nominated..by its popular descriptive appellation of 'the Missouri Compromise Line'. **1847** J. K. Polk *Diary* 16 Jan. (1910) II. 335 The line of the Missouri Compromise, *viz.*, 36° 30′. **1943** E. B. White *One Man's Meat* 16 The Missouri Compromise had temporarily settled the slavery question. **1949** D. S. Freeman in B. A. Botkin *Treas. S. Folklore* p. x, Wirt..did not issue his life of Henry until almost the time of the Missouri Compromise. **1765** R. Rogers *Conc. Acct. N. Amer.* 194 The inhabitants on this river are called the Missouri Indians. **1817** J. Bradbury *Trav. Interior Amer.* 41 It is customary amongst the Missouri Indians to register every exploit in war, by making a notch for each on the handle of their tomahawks. **1923** *Nation* (N.Y.) 17 Oct. 432 Then there is the Missouri mule. He it was who won the war. **1972** *Listener* 21 Dec. 858/2 Not for nothing did the idiom 'as stubborn as a Missouri mule' come into the language. **1819** J. Adams *Let.* 21 Dec. in T. Jefferson *Writings* (1903) XV. 236 The Missouri question, I hope, will follow the other waves under the ship, and do no harm. **1884** J. G. Blaine *20 Yrs. Congress* I. 15 The 'Missouri question'..formally appeared in Congress in the month of December, 1818. **1858** S. F. Baird in *Rep. Explor. Route to Pacific* (U.S. War Dept.) IX. 234 *Neocorys Spraguei*, Sclater. Missouri Skylark. **1940** E. T. Seton *Trail of Artist-Naturalist* 299 The strictly prairie birds were gone—of the Missouri skylark, for instance, I saw not one.

Missourian (mɪs-, mɪˈzʊərɪən), *sb.* and *a.* [f. prec. + -an.] **A.** *sb.* A native or inhabitant of the State of Missouri. **B.** *adj.* Of or belonging to, native or peculiar to, Missouri.

1820 *Deb. Congress U.S.* (1855) 26 Jan. 945, I cannot believe that I, or any other man or men, are better capable of governing Missourians than they are of governing themselves. **1862** *Harper's Mag.* Sept. 450/2 Teamsters, many of whom were young Missourians embarked for the first time upon a prairie trip. **1885** 'Mark Twain' in *Century Mag.* Dec. 201 The Masons gave us a Missouri country breakfast, in Missourian abundance. **1944** B. A. Botkin *Treas. Amer. Folklore* II. 318 One of the harshest of these [*sc.* slang names] is Puke, for a Missourian. **1948** Mencken *Amer. Lang.* Suppl. II. vii. 173 D. S. Crumb.. unearthed a great deal more that was specially Missourian, *e.g...buckshot land*, poor clay soil. **1957** *Encycl. Brit.* XIII. 258/2 About 1,700 armed Missourians invaded Kansas and stuffed the ballot boxes. **1973** R. Rosenblum *Mushroom Cave* (1974) 83 The junior diplomat, a glad-handing Missourian.

missourite (mɪs-, mɪˈzʊəraɪt). *Petrogr.* [f. Missour(i + -ite^1 (see quot. 1896).] A grey, granular, igneous rock composed mainly of pyroxene, leucite, and sometimes olivine.

1896 Weed & Pirsson in *Amer. Jrnl. Sci.* II. 323 This rock is a new type, and it fills a place which has hitherto been vacant in all systems of rock classification... We have therefore called it missourite from the Missouri River, the most prominent and best known geographical object in the region where it occurs. **1927** *Ibid.* XIV. 179 These granitoid augite-leucite rocks will be called missourite, although Pirsson's original Montana missourite contained less leucite and about 15 per cent of olivine. *Ibid.* 180 The presence of olivine in missourite need not be regarded as essential. **1963** *Mineral. Abstr.* XVI. 388/1 The first missourites recorded from Russia are in an outcrop of alkaline gabbroic rocks near the Lomachan River.

'miss-out. [f. vbl. phr. *to miss out*: see miss *v.*^{1} 25.] **a.** *pl.* In *Gambling*, loaded dice. **b.** In *Craps*, a losing throw: see craps b; also, the action of losing the right to throw.

1928 J. O'Connor *Broadway Racketeers* xiv. 157 The game keeper has all sorts of crooked ones, those known as 'Shapes', others called 'Miss-Outs'. **1936** *Detective Fiction Weekly* 21 Mar. 139/1 If the dice are cut as 'passers', the percentage in favor of the shooter is 'mild'; but cut for a banking or fading advantage (called 'miss-outs' or 'missing dice') the advantage is stronger. **1942** W. Faulkner *Go down, Moses* 114 The spots on them miss-out dice. **1961** in Partridge *Dict. Underworld* (1968) 846/1 *Misses*... (2) Crooked dice that are gaffed to make more miss-outs than passes. **1964** A. Wykes *Gambling* v. 109 He loses if he throws a Two, Three, or Twelve (a 'crap' or 'miss-out').

†**mis'sowne,** *v. Obs.* [f. mis-^{1} 7 + *sowne*, sound *v.*] *intr.* To be discordant; not to agree.

1382 Wyclif *Josh.* Prol., And forsothe it may not be sooth that discordith [*v.r.* myssouneth, Vulg. *dissonat*]. *c* **1465** *Eng. Chron.* (Camden 1856) 57 Articlez longyng..to the said craft of nigromancie, or mis sownyng to the Cristen feith.

missoy, variant of massoy.

mis-'speak, *v.* Also 4-7 misp-. [mis-^{1} 1.]

†**1. a.** *intr.* To speak wrongly or improperly; to speak evil. *Obs.*

c **1200** in *O.E. Hom.* I. 305 Ich habbe..Misispeken. *c* **1374** Chaucer *Troylus* I. 934, I me repente If I mis spak. *c* **1386** —— *Miller's Prol.* 31 If that I misspeke or seye, Wyte it the ale of Southwerk. **1595** Shaks. *John* III. i. 4 It is not so, thou hast mispoke, misheard. **1613** tr. *Mexia's Treas. Anc. & Mod. Times* 764/1, I doe not inferre that it is lawfull for weomen to depraue or mispeake by any means.

b. To speak disrespectfully or disparagingly *of*.

c **1380** Wyclif *Wks.* (1880) 228 Enemys of oure feiþ þat bakbiten or myspeken of vs. **1390** Gower *Conf.* I. 227 If that I myhte ofherkne..That eny man of hire mispeke. **1598** Sylvester *Du Bartas* II. iv. IV. (1641) 232 Who mis-speaks of thee, hee spets at Heav'n, And his owne spettle in his face is driven.

†**2.** *trans.* To speak evil of; to calumniate. Obs.

1582 N. T. (Rhem.) *Acts* xxiii. 5 The prince of thy people thou shalt not misspeake. **1584** Peele *Arraignm. Paris* III. i, Mis-speak not all for his amiss.

3. a. *trans.* To speak, utter, or pronounce incorrectly or improperly. *rare.*

[**1390**: see mis-speech.] **1593** Nashe *Christ's T.* (1613) 132 We care not how we mispeake it so wee haue it to speake. *a* **1631** Donne *Let. to M.M.H.* Poems (1654) 177 As a mother which delights to heare Her early childe mis-speake halfe uttered words. **1879** Butcher & Lang *Odyss.* xiv. 238 Thou hast not misspoken aught, nor uttered a word unprofitably.

b. *refl.* To fail to convey the meaning one intends by one's words.

1890 in *Cent. Dict.* **1894** *Congress. Rec.* 19 Jan. 1051/1, I simply wanted to bring that matter out plainly... I believe he misspoke himself. **1973** *Harper's Mag.* June 38/2 'The President,' Ziegler said, 'misspoke himself.' He explained that the President had noted his error in reviewing the transcript of the press conference. **1975** G. V. Higgins *City on Hill* ii. 53 If I gave that impression, I misspoke myself.

So **mis-'speaking** *vbl. sb.*

1530 Palsgr. 172 *Blaspheme*, mispekyng of God. **1650** Earl Monm. tr. *Senault's Man bec. Guilty* 199 As they have the art of speaking, they have also the cunning of mis-speaking.

mis-'speech. [mis-^{1} 4.] †**a.** Evil speaking. Obs. **b.** Incorrect speaking.

c **1350** *Will. Palerne* 1523 þan meliors mekly hire maydenes dede calle, & many of hire meyne for drede of misse-speche. **1390** Gower *Conf.* I. 178 And otherwise of no mispeche, Mi conscience forto seche, I can noght of Envie finde That I mispoke have oght behinde Wherof love owghte be mispaid. *a* **1461** *Songs & Carols 15th C.* (Warton Club) 1 Rewle thi tunge in swych a gys, That non mysspeche come the froo. **1496** *Dives & Pauper* (W. de W.) II. i. 109/2 Goddes name is taken in vayne..by myslyuynge, by myspeche, & by mysheryngе. **1895** *Atlantic Monthly* Mar. 432 Another form of misspeech, to which most of us are.. subject,—the exchange of syllables.

†**mis-'speed,** *v. Obs.* [mis-^{1} 7.] *intr.* To be unsuccessful or unlucky.

c **1330** R. Brunne *Chron. Wace* (Rolls) 6912 Now haue þey for-sake vs alle & sum,..þat often mys-spedde in þer passage. **1387** Trevisa *Higden* (Rolls) I. 243 Dayes þat þe Romaynes misspedde were i-hote nefasti, as it were nouȝt leeful. **1496** *Dives & Pauper* (W. de W.) vii. xiii. 297/2 He that wyll not paye his tythes shall myspede. **1501** *Plumpton Corr.* (Camden) 161, I send about it unto the Shereffe as sone as Hare Harlad com from you, for sume remedy ther, if he myspede.

mis-'spell, *v.* [mis-^{1} 1.] *trans.* To spell incorrectly. So **mis-spelt** *ppl. a.*

1655 Fuller *Hist. Cambr.* (1840) 160 No wonder, if they did mis-spell him whom they did mis-call, loading him with opprobrious language. **1775** Sheridan *Rivals* I. ii, That she might not mis-spell, and mis-pronounce words. **1838** Hawthorne *Twice told T., Chippings with a Chisel*, Some [of the monuments] were inscribed with misspelt prose or rhyme. **1846** Landor *Exam. Shaks.* Wks. II. 296, I wrote not down the words, fearing to mis-spell them.

Hence **mis-'spell** *sb.*, mis-spelling. *rare.*

1891 *N. & Q.* Ser. vii. XII. 351/2 He has discovered a misspell in Evelyn. **1895** *Dublin Rev.* July 37 Mis-spells occurring in proper names.

mis-'spelling, *vbl. sb.* [mis-^{1} 3.] A bad spelling; false orthography.

1695-6 *Act 7 & 8 Will. III*, c. 3 §9 That noe Indictment ..shall bee quashed..for miswriting misspelling false.. Latine. **1731** *Gentl. Mag.* I. 213 Mis-spelling or Mistake of Clerkship. **1865** Kingsley *Herew.* Prelude 21 The misspellings of English names in his work are more gross than even those in Domesday. **1898** Gissing *Town Traveller* xxv, Mis-spelling, he knew, would invalidate his chance.

mis-'spend, *v.* Also 4-8 misp-, (4-6 mysp-). [mis-^{1} 1.] *trans.* To spend amiss or wastefully; to make a bad, useless, or wasteful expenditure of.

c **1375** *Sc. Leg. Saints* xxxiv. (*Pelagia*) 44 Scho þat welth & þat beute myspendit in sic degre, þat [etc.]. **1377** Langl. *P. Pl.* B. xv. 74 How þat folke in folyes myspenden her fyue wittes. **1460** *Pol. Rel. & L. Poems* (1903) 206, I haue mysspendyd my yonge age In synne, and wantonnehed also. **1494** Fabyan *Chron.* vi. clxx. 164 Gouernours therof mysspent the patrymony therof in excesse. **1530** Palsgr. 638/1 Myspende nat your monay, you may happe to have nede of it. **1597** *Pilgrim. Parnass.* v. (1886) 19, I have beene guiltie of mispending some time in philosophie. **1697** Dryden *Æneid* Ded., Some similitude, which diverts..your attention from the main Subject, and mispends it on some trivial Image. *a* **1721** Prior *On a Pretty Madwoman* i, Our grief's misplac'd, our tears mis-spent. **1812** Byron *Ch. Har.* I. xxvii, His early youth, misspent in maddest whim. **1858** Froude *Hist. Eng.* (1858) II. vi. 15 [They] vowed to accept no benefice, lest they should misspend the property of the poor.

mis-'spender. [mis-^{1} 5.] One who misspends.

1607 Hieron *Wks.* I. 463 Mispenders of the sabbath. **1648** Milton *Observ. Art. Peace* Wks. 1851 IV. 577 The most prodigal mis-spenders of time. **1766** Johnson *Prayers & Medit.* (1817) 67, I again appear in thy presence the wretched mispender of another year.

mis-'spending, *vbl. sb.* [mis-^{1} 3.] Bad or useless expenditure.

138. Wyclif *Sel. Wks.* III. 370 þis mon schal nedis be dampned for mysspendynge of Gods tresoure. **1541** Barnes *Wks.* (1573) 364 Mispending of goodes. **1659** *Gentl. Calling* 422 Not only with the mis-spending their own estates, but other mens.

mis-'spenditure. *rare*$^{-1}$. [f. mis-spend, after *expenditure.*] Wasteful expenditure.

a **1843** Southey *Sydney* in *Fraser's Mag.* (1868) LXXVIII. 104 Compelled to lose time the value of which he understood, and the mispenditure of which he lamented.

†**mis-'spene,** *v. Obs.* Also 4 -speyne. [f. mis-^{1} 1 + spene *v.*] *trans.* To misspend, misemploy.

c **1275** Lay. 13483 Ʒef ich his god mis-spene [*earlier text* for-leose]. *c* **1320** *Cast. Love* (Halliw.) 1150 And for oure syȝht myspende allso, His eynen were blynwherved boo. **1393** Langl. *P. Pl.* C. xi. 174 And muche wo worth hym þat Inwitt mys-speyneþ [*v.rr.* myspeneþ, mys-spendeþ].

†**mis-'spense, -'ence.** *Obs.* Also misp-. [f. mis-^{1} 4.] Improper or wasteful expenditure.

1591 *Garrard's Art Warre* 61 Mispence of munition. **1597** Beard *Theatre God's Judgem.* (1612) 427 The losse of time and mispence of goods. **1627** Bp. Hall *Epist.* ii. x. 309 If your negligence, your riotous mis-spence, had empaired your estate. *a* **1677** Barrow *Serm.* Wks. 1687 I. 395 A wilful mispense of our time. *a* **1788** in Croft *Let. to Pitt on Johnson's Dict.* (1788) 40 The misspence of every minute is a new record against us in heaven.

mis-spent (stress variable), *ppl. a.* [mis-^{1} 2.] Badly or wastefully spent; ill-spent, wasted.

1500-20 Dunbar *Poems* lxvi. 3 The mispent tyme, the service vaine. **1781** Cowper *Hope* 715 The shameful close of all his misspent years. **1871** R. Ellis tr. *Catullus* lxxv. 2 So in her own misspent worship uneasily lost.

'miss-stays. [f. as misstay *v.*] Of a ship: the act or fact of failing to go about.

1878 D. Kemp *Man. Yacht & Boat Sailing* 245 A 'miss-stays' may be the consequence.

†**mis-'start,** *v. Obs.* In 3 -sturte, -storte. [mis-^{1} 1.] *intr.* To start forth amiss.

a **1250** *Owl & Night.* 677 & sone may a word mys sturte [*Cott. MS.* misstorte] þar muþ shal speke ayeyn horte.

mis-'state, *v.* [mis-^{1} 1.] *trans.* To state erroneously; to make wrong statements about.

1650 R. Hollingworth *Exerc. Usurped Powers* 39 You dare to mis-represent and mistate the minde of God. **1657** Sanderson *Serm.* Pref. §12 (1674) C 3 They mis-state the Question, when they talk of pressing Ceremonies. **1791** Cowper *Yardley Oak* 48 Unrecorded facts Recovering, and misstated setting right. **1818** Cobbett *Pol. Reg.* XXXIII. 271 When a writer mis-states facts, be sure that he drives at no very laudable conclusion. **1865** Bright *Sp., Canada* 13 Mar. (1876) 66, I am not mis-stating the case.

absol. **1864-8** Browning *J. Lee's Wife* IV. iii, Now do I mis-state, mistake?

So **mis-'stated** *ppl. a.*, **mis-'stating** *vbl. sb.*; **mis-'stater**, one who mis-states.

1643 Prynne *Sov. Power Parlt.* III. 61 Through the mis-stating of the points in question. **1665** Glanvill *Scepsis Sci.* xix. 120 The mis-stated words are the original mistake. **1859** *Chamb. Jrnl.* XI. 404 That gross misstater of fact.

mis-'statement. [mis-^{1} 4.] A wrong or erroneous statement.

1790 Burgess *Div. Christ* Notes 39 There is in this passage a mistatement of important circumstances. **1818** Cobbett *Pol. Reg.* XXXIII. 271 A very flagrant mis-statement in point of fact. **1875** Jowett *Plato* (ed. 2) III. 265 Story-tellers make the gravest misstatements about men when they say that many wicked men are happy.

mis'stay, *v.* Also **miss-stay.** [app. f. phr. *to miss stays.*] *intr.* Of a ship: To miss stays.

1829 G. Griffin *Collegians* (ed. 2) I. xii. 241 Ahoy! ahoy! Have an oar out in the bow, or she'll miss-stay in the swell. **1849** N. Kingsley *Diary* (1914) 88 We mis-stayed in but 11 feet of water, but the bottom is very muddy and not dangerous. **1885** *Standard* 5 May 6/8 C. H. Cumbell.. misstayed in Cornlough Bay; took the ground. **1906** *Westm. Gaz.* 5 Dec. 9/2 The ship, when tacking, mis-stayed.

mis-'step, *sb.* [mis-^{1} 4.] **a.** A wrong step.

1837 *Yale Lit. Mag.* III. 8 (Th.), Forgetting the round door block, he made a mis-step. **1855** Prescott *Philip II*, iv. vi. I. 460 As he was descending a flight of stairs he made a misstep and fell. **1888** B. A. Watson *Sportsman's Paradise* 193 So that..the game may not be frightened by a mis-step. **1894** *Outing* (U.S.) XXIV. 363/2 One mis-step might have resulted in a clear fall of three thousand feet. **1963** J. Walsh *Shroud* (1964) vi. 47 His headlong disregard for bodily care and his courting of the injuries or death that lay only a mis-step away. **1974** *Sci. Amer.* Oct. 87/2 A misstep would not necessarily lead to a stumble or a fall.

b. = faux pas.

a **1800** *Spirit of Farmer's Museum* (1801) 205 The Squire ..can sit on the sessions, and fine poor girls for natural missteps. **1854** Marion Harland *Alone* xxi, Watchfully, prayerfully, Ida strove to keep her feet in the path, and by no

misstep or fall, to cast obloquy upon the name she loved. **1892** *Harper's Mag.* June 152/2 Whatever we think of the first misstep of Tess in the immaturity of her girlhood. **1931** F. L. ALLEN *Only Yesterday* 101 The publishers of the confession magazines..concentrated on the description of what they euphemistically called 'missteps'. **1934** D. SARGENT *Thomas More* iii. 62 As in all diplomatic conferences each side spends a great deal of time waiting for the other side to make a misstep. **1949** *Sat. Even. Post* 1 Oct. 20/3 Russians..turn sick with fear if they make the slightest little misstep. **1974** *Publishers Weekly* 4 Feb. 64/2 Henry Keller..picks up a hitchhiker... For awhile, he shares her sexual favours... Becky is killed accidentally. The police don't care much; neither does Henry's wife, who forgives his misstep.

mis-'step, *v.* [MIS-[1] I.] *intr.* To take a wrong step; to go astray.

1390 GOWER *Conf.* II. 143 Sche schal noght with hir litel too Misteppe, bot he se it al. **1598** SYLVESTER *Du Bartas* II. i. I. (1641) 83 If man from duty never has mis-stept. **1869** S. BOWLES *Our New West* v. 102 Mules don't mis-step, and even the top-heavy pack jacks..carried their burden and themselves unharmed to the top.

mis-'style, *v. rare.* [MIS-[1] I.] *trans.* To style or term incorrectly.

a **1604** HANMER *Chron. Irel.* (1633) 103 He..came to the Church called..the Church of great Paternus, mis-stiled with the governement therof. **1613** J. DAVIES *Muses Teares* B4 Greatnes (as we mis-stile it). **1832** AUSTIN *Jurispr.* (1879) II. lv. 911 The privilege mis-styled personal.

†**mis-suc'ceeding**, *vbl. sb. Obs.* [MIS-[1] 3.] Ill-success. So †**mis-suc'cess.**

a **1656** BP. HALL *Serm.* Wks. (1662) 197 As some shifting alchymist that casts all the fault of his mis-success upon his glasse or his furnace. *a* **1661** FULLER *Worthies, Lincolnshire* (1662) II. 154 Miscarriages in his Government (many by mismanaging, more by the missucceeding of matters).

†**mis-'sue**, *v. Law. Obs.* [MIS-[1] I.] *trans.* To sue (livery) wrongly.

[**1227** in *Cal. Charter Rolls* I. (1903) 63 With soc and sac ..mundbriche, miskenning, missueing and forfeg.] **1548** STAUNFORD *Kinges Prerog.* (1567) 79 b, Yf the heire sue his generall lyuerie beefore an offyce thereof founde omittinge them in the liuerye, the liuery is missued. *Ibid.* 84 Whether in this case yᵉ missuing of yᵉ same shal be a cause of reseiser or not.

mis-'suit, *v.* [MIS-[1] I.] *trans.* To suit ill.

a **1618** SYLVESTER *St. Lewis* 588 Wks. (Grosart) II. 235 That Robe of Power, which those doth much mis-suit, Who have not on rare Vertue's richest Suit. **1860** MRS. BROWNING *Napoleon III in Italy* xviii, He will not swagger nor boast Of his country's meeds, in a tone Missuiting a great man most If such should speak of his own. **1864** BROWNING *Sludge the Medium*, Each..Is blind to what missuits him.

†**'missure.** *Obs. rare*[−1]. [ad. L. type **missūra*, f. *miss-* ppl. stem of *mittĕre* to send: see -URE.] A commission.

1615 T. ADAMS *Lycanthropy* 5 The missure, 'I send you': the mixture, 'as lambes among wolves'.

missus: see MISSIS.

†**mis-'sware.** *Obs. rare*[−1]. [f. MIS-[1] 4 + *-sware*, repr. OE. *-swaru*, *-swara* action of swearing, as in *áþswara*.] False swearing.

a **1240** *Lofsong* in *O.E. Hom.* I. 205 Wreððe and onde, lesunge, missware vuele i-holden treouðe.

†**mis-'sway**, *v. Obs.* [MIS-[1] I.] *trans.* To sway in a wrong direction.

a **1640** JACKSON *Creed* XI. xxv. §11 Other secular vanities, which usually missway us Christians to folly.

†**mis-'swaying**, *vbl. sb. Obs.* [MIS-[1] 3.] Misgovernment.

1603 J. DAVIES (Heref.) *Microcosm.* 149 The first Edward, that did first refine This Common-weale, and made the same ascend When through mis-swaying it seem'd to decline.

†**mis-'swearing**, *vbl. sb. Obs.* [MIS-[1] 3.] False swearing.

1493 *Dives & Pauper* (Pynson) II. xix. ivj, If thou haue liking to here grete othes..or any myssweryngе.

miss-woman, -word: see MISWOMAN, MISWORD.

mis-'sworn, *ppl. a.* [MIS-[1] 2.]

a. Forsworn. **b.** Whose name has been taken in vain.

1506 *Kalender Sheph.* E6 (1892) III. 62 Mysswоrone By wordes [etc.]. ? *a* **1800** *Broomfield Hill* v. in Child *Ballads* I. 395 But if I stay from Broomfield Hills, I'll be a maid mis-sworn. **1871** R. ELLIS tr. *Catullus* lxxvi. 4 A God's mis-sworn sanctity, deadly to men.

missy ('mɪsɪ), *sb.* Also 7 **missee**, 8–9 **missey**, 9 **missie**. [f. MISS *sb.*[2] + -Y dim. suffix.] An affectionate or playful appellation for a young girl: used chiefly by servants and the like. occas. *contemptuous.*

1676 in *12th Rep. Hist. MSS. Comm.* App. v. 29 A coach fitt for pretty Missee is not to be found ready made. **1780** MME. D'ARBLAY *Let.* 24 Aug. in *Diary* (1891) I. 311, I beg my best compliments to him,—and to my master and missey. **1818** *Blackw. Mag.* III. 403 An English missy, slim and pale. **1852** MRS. STOWE *Uncle Tom's C.* xiv. 124 'What's little missy's name?' said Tom at last. **1876** BLACKMORE *Cripps* liii, The pious papa and the milk-and-water missy rush into each other's arms. **1919** WODEHOUSE *Damsel in Distress* vii. 107 Those—them—over there are Ayrshires, missy. **1922** JOYCE *Ulysses* 733 Little chits of missies they have now singing. **1924** R. MACAULAY *Orphan Island* xv. 202 'You're very smart and proud, missie,' her uncle told her. **1967** P. ROTH *When she was Good* III. 274 Either you calm down with that bossy little voice, missy, or you get out.

Comb. **1831** *Society* I. 138 The missy-like astonishment you are pleased to assume.

Hence **'missyish** *a.* = MISSISH.

1887 MISS BETHAM-EDWARDS *Next of Kin Wanted* II. xviii. 245 Why do you put on this missyish air of innocence?

missy ('mɪsɪ), *a.* [f. MISS *sb.*[2] + -Y.] Pertaining to, resembling, or characteristic of a miss or young lady; = MISSISH.

1809–12 MAR. EDGEWORTH *Vivian* viii, Her ladyship.. values herself too highly, to make such a missy match. **1831** *Society* I. 88 The mean and missy feeling of seizing the first opportunity to speak to you of a man. **1859** BOYD *Recreat. Country Parson* ii. 43, I have heard..the same person called a gentlemanlike man and a missy piece of affectation. **1881** *Literary World* 14 Jan. 26/1 With nothing to recommend him physically but a missy prettiness.

missy, obs. variant of MISY.

mist (mɪst), *sb.*[1] Forms: 1– **mist**; also 3 **mijst**, 3–6 **myste**, 4–7 **myst**, **miste**, (5 **meyst**). [OE. *mist* str. masc. = MLG. (LG.), MDu. (Du.) *mist*, Icel. *mistur* (genit. *misturs*) neut. (Norw., Sw. *mist*):—OTeut. **mihstoz-*, f. *mĭg-*:—pre-Teut. **migh-*, *meigh-*, as in Gr. ὀμίχλη, OSl. *mĭgla*, Skr. *mih* and *mēgha* cloud, mist. Perhaps further related to the root of OE. *mīʒan*, MIG, and *meox* MIX *sb.*[1]]

1. a. A cloud formed by an aggregation of minute drops of water and resting on or near the ground. In generalized sense, vapour of water precipitated in very fine droplets, smaller and more densely aggregated than those of rain. Sometimes distinguished from *fog*, either as being less opaque or as consisting of drops large enough to have a perceptible downward motion (cf. quot. 1972).

c **1000** ÆLFRIC *Gen.* xv. 17 Þa þa sunne eode to setle, þa sloh þær micel mist. *c* **1050** *Suppl. Ælfric's Gloss.* in Wr.-Wülcker 175/23 *Nebula*, mist, *uel* genip. *a* **1200** *Moral Ode* 16 Ne michte ich seon bi-fore me for smike ne for miste. *c* **1290** *S. Eng. Leg.* I. 239/688 A wel deork mijst þare com al-so þat swiþe longue i-laste. *Ibid.* 317/603 Ȝwane þe sonne hath þudere i-drawe þene mist for hete. **1340** HAMPOLE *Pr. Consc.* 1445 Now gadirs mystes and cloudes in þe ayre. *c* **1375** *Sc. Leg. Saints* xl. (*Ninian*) 895 Bot myste ves in sic degre þat nan mocht a stane caste se. **1398** TREVISA *Barth. De P.R.* XI. xii. (1495) 397 Myste is frende to theues and to euyl doers for he hydyth theyr spyers and waytynges. *c* **1450** *St. Cuthbert* (Surtees) 7105 Þan fell sodaynly slike a myst, Þat whidir to wende þai ne wist. **1530** PALSGR. 740/2 Whan the moysture of the dewe stryketh upwarde agayne, it maketh a myste. **1602** MARSTON *Ant. & Mel.* II. Wks. 1856 I. 26 The flagging'st bulrush that ere droopt With each slight mist of raine. **1667** MILTON *P.L.* XII. 629 As Ev'ning Mist Ris'n from a River o're the marish glides. **1798** COLERIDGE *Anc. Mar.* I. xix, In mist or cloud on mast or shroud It perch'd for vespers nine. **1831** SCOTT *Cast. Dang.* iii, The mist had settled upon the hills, and unrolled itself upon brook, glade, and tarn. **1878** HUXLEY *Physiogr.* 40 The atmospheric moisture passes through the condition of visible cloud or mist. *Ibid.* 44 The position of a river is often marked by mist. **1972** *Meteorol. Gloss.* (Meteorol. Office) (ed. 5) 182 *Mist*, a state of atmospheric obscurity produced by suspended microscopic water droplets or wet hygroscopic particles. The term is used for synoptic purposes when..the associated visibility is equal to or exceeds 1 km; the corresponding relative humidity is greater than about 95 per cent.

fig. **1615** HIERON *Wks.* I. 438 Neither is euery myst of sorrow dissolued into teares. **1842** TENNYSON *Love & Duty* 43 Rain out the heavy mist of tears.

b. Used in proverbial phr.

c **1330** *Arth. & Merl.* 7364 (Kölbing) Ich hope..We schul hem driue, so sonne doþ mist! *c* **1420** LYDG. *Assembly of Gods* 1988 Derke as a myste, or a feynyd fable. **1535** COVERDALE *Isa.* xliv. 21 As for thyne offences, I dryue them awaye like the cloudes, and thy synnes as the myst.

c. *Scotch* (†*Scottish*, †*Scots*) *mist*: a thick, very wetting mist characteristic of the Scottish hills; hence *jocularly*, a steady soaking rain.

1589 [? LYLY] *Pappe w. Hatchet* Ded., Wks 1902 III. 394 We care not for a Scottish mist, though it wet vs to the skin. **1599** *Broughton's Lett.* viii. 27 It is no marueile you so affect the Scottish mist; for where the head doth σκοτοδινιᾶν, the tongue must needes σκοτολογεῖν. **1623** MINSHEU, *Mollinas*, soft showers, Scottish mists. *a* **1700** B. E. *Dict. Cant. Crew*, *Scotch-mist*, a sober, soaking Rain. **1770** WESLEY *Jrnl.* 16 Apr. (1827) III. 384 We..got into a Scotch mist. **1872** *Routledge's Ev. Boy's Ann.* 38/1 With a light drizzle or Scotch mist falling thickly.

d. *transf.* A cloud (of small particles) resembling a mist; a haze or haziness, as that produced by distance; hence *fig.* of time, etc.

1785 COWPER *Task* I. 360 The rustling straw sends up a frequent mist Of atoms. **1794** MRS. RADCLIFFE *Myst. Udolpho* i, The plains of Guienne and Languedoc were lost in the mist of distance. **1810** SHELLEY *St. Irvyne's Tower* v. 4 Why may not human minds unveil The dim mists of futurity? **1812** BYRON *Ch. Har.* II. ii, And o'er each mouldering tower, Dim with the mist of years, Grey flits the shade of power. **1869** FREEMAN *Norm. Conq.* (1875) III. xi. 5 Times..half shrouded in the mist of legend.

e. A colour suggestive of a mist.

1926 *Daily Colonist* (Victoria, B.C.) 21 July 16/4 (Advt.), A 4-ply worsted wool in shades of pink, mist, [etc.]. **1927** *Daily Express* 12 Mar. 3/5 Mist, a subdued mauve, suggesting the atmospheric effects of sunset. **1937** *Discovery* July 217/2 Our silk stockings are..described as..sun-tan, sandalwood, mist. **1963** *New Yorker* 29 June 57 Black, mist, rust, or olive.

2. a. Dimness of eyesight; a hazy or filmy appearance before the eyes caused by disorders of the body or by the shedding of tears.

c **1000** *Sax. Leechd.* II. 26 Læcedomas wiþ eaȝna miste. *c* **1220** *Bestiary* 102 in *O.E. Misc.* 4 Of hise eȝen wereð ðe mist. **1655** CULPEPPER, etc. *Riverius* XIV. iv. 385 They have the Head-ach, mists before their Eyes, and giddiness. **1693** SOUTH *Serm.* (1698) III. ii. 99 Where there is a Giddiness in the Head, there will always be a mist before the Eyes. **1859** TENNYSON *Enid* 1617 She did not weep But o'er her meek eyes came a happy mist. **1880** 'OUIDA' *Moths* I. 33 She felt a mist before her eyes, a tightness at her throat. **1899** *Allbutt's Syst. Med.* VII. 66 Such patients usually complain of a mist before their eyes.

b. Hence used in phrases with reference to the obscuring of the vision (physical or mental), esp. *to cast* or *throw a mist before* (a person's) *eyes*; also simply, † *to cast a mist* or *mists*: to produce mystification.

1565 COOPER *Thesaurus*, *Offundere caliginem oculis*, to cast a miste before ones eyes. **1579** GOSSON *Sch. Abuse* (Arb.) 20 The Iuggler casteth a myst to worke the closer. **1607** DEKKER *Wh. of Babylon* H4 They say you can throw mists before our eyes, To make vs thinke you faire. **1641** [see PETTIFOG *sb.*[2]]. *a* **1674** CLARENDON *Surv. Leviath.* (1676) 26 And by a mist of words..he dazles Mens eies. **1750** JOHNSON *Rambler* No. 81 ¶5 Over this law, indeed, some sons of sophistry have been subtle enough to throw mists, which have darkened their own eyes. **1824** LAMB *Elia* Ser. II. *Capt. Jackson*, He was a juggler, who threw mists before your eyes.

3. a. Applied to immaterial things conceived as enveloping a man's mind and obscuring his mental vision or outlook, or as veiling the real character or blurring the outlines of a thing.

c **888** K. ÆLFRED *Boeth.* v. §3 fin., þa mistas ðe þæt mod ȝedrefað. *a* **1000** *Boeth. Metr.* xxiii, ȝif he..of him selfum ðone sweartan mist, modes þiostro, mæȝ aweorpan. *c* **1384** CHAUCER *H. Fame* I. 352 Euery thinge ys wyste, Though hit be keuered with the myste. **1509** HAWES *Past. Pleas.* x. (Percy Soc.) 36 The fatall problemes of olde antiquyte, Cloked wyth myst and wyth cloudes derke. **1526** *Pilgr. Perf.* (W. de W. 1531) 67 b, All cloudes & mystes vtterly purged and expulsed out of our soules. **1576** FLEMING *Panopl. Epist.* 416 All mystes and fogges of ignoraunce. **1728** VENEER *Sincere Penitent* Pref. 7 Those mists and false notions which our infirmities, education or conversation may have thrown in our way. **1779–81** JOHNSON *L.P., Cowley* (first par.), All is shown confused and enlarged through the mist of panegyric. **1810** *Sporting Mag.* XXXVI. 153 There is a kind of mist or dubiosity playing about it. **1842** TENNYSON *Will Waterproof's Monol.* 39 And softly, thro' a vinous mist, My college friendships glimmer. **1849** ROBERTSON *Serm.* Ser. I. x. (1866) 170 It was faith straining through the mist. **1852** M. ARNOLD *Empedocles* II. 67 The mists Of despondency and gloom.

b. *mists of death, deathly mists.*

1729 SAVAGE *Wanderer* III. 280 Sad o'er the sight swim shadowy mists of death. **1866** B. TAYLOR *Poems, Autumnal Vespers*, Death's mist shall strike along her veins. **1878** BROWNING *La Saisiaz* 484 As soul is quenchless by the deathly mists.

†**4.** A state of obscurity or uncertainty; an 'atmosphere' of doubt. *Obs.*

1532 MORE *Confut. Tindale* Wks. 401/2 They wil clerely dissipate & discusse the myst that he fain would walke in. **1590** SHAKS. *Com. Err.* II. ii. 218 Ile say as they say, and perseuer so: And in this mist at all aduentures go. **1650** B. *Discolliminium* 54 The Grand Cause of this Realme..is yet in the myst to many..judicious men. **1678** *Hatton Corr.* (Camden) 161 My Lord wee are in a mighty mist wʰᵗ our buisnesse is heere. *a* **1715** BURNET *Own Time* III. (1724) I. 510 In this mist matters must be left till the great revelation of all secrets.

5. *attrib.* and *Comb.*, as *mist-belt*, *-cloud*, *-drop*, *-light*, *-magic*, *-mote*, *-pavilion*, *-plash*, *-sheet*, *-thread*, *-veil*, *-wreath*; *mist-blotted*, *-blurred*, *-circled*, *-clad*, *-cold*, *-coloured*, *-covered*, *-dimmed*, *-enshrouded*, *-exhaling*, *-green*, *-hung*, *-impelling*, *-laden*, *-pale*, *-shrouded*, *-tracked*, *-veiled*, *-wet*, *-wild*, *-wreathed*, *-wreathen*, *-wrought* adjs.; **mist-blower**, a device for spraying insecticide into the tops of trees; so *mist-blowing* vbl. sb.; **mist-bow**, a white arch, resembling a rainbow, sometimes seen in misty weather; **mist-flower**, a plant of the tropical American genus *Conoclinium*; †**mist-hackle**, a 'cloak' or covering of mist; **mist-net**, a net made of very fine threads, used to trap birds etc. for ringing or examination and subsequent release; also as *v. intr.*, to trap in a mist-net; hence **mist-netter**, one who uses a mist-net; **mist-pond** = DEW-POND; **mist propagation**, a method of rooting plant cuttings in which high humidity is maintained in a greenhouse by an automatic system of watering with fine spray at regular intervals; **mist propagator**, an installation for this type of cultivation; **mist-tree**, a name for *Rhus Cotinus*, the smoke-tree (*Cent. Dict.*).

1906 *Rep. Brit. Assoc. Adv. Sci.* 1905 594 Passing either east or west of this '*mist-belt' the rainfall rapidly diminishes. **1864** TENNYSON *En. Ard.* 681 A great *mist-blotted light Flared on him. **1946** POTTS & FRIEND in *Bull. Connecticut Agric. Exper. Station* No. 501. 48 The development of a *mist blower which will apply thoroughly

a small quantity of a concentrated insecticide. 1969 *Nature* 9 Aug. 558/2 Only the mistblower, which is mounted on a tractor, seems feasible for large-scale applications. 1960 *Farmer & Stockbreeder* 12 Jan. 97/2 *Mistblowing of fruit trees is a practical proposition. 1880 *Academy* 11 Dec. 415 The whole view is *mist-blurred and indistinct. 1897 *Daily News* 11 Dec. 8/3 Clouds on which brilliant *mist-bows were thrown by the morning sunlight. 1935 W. Empson *Poems* 27 Starlit, *mistcircled, one whole pearl embrowned. 1796 H. Hunter tr. *St. Pierre's Stud. Nat.* (1799) II. 363 These *mist-clad hills are islands emerging above the Horizon. 1884 Jefferies *Life of Fields* 133 The inclined plane of *mist-clouds again reflects a grey light. 1889 W. B. Yeats *Wanderings of Oisin* III. 34 Came now the sliding of tears and sweeping of *mist-cold hair. 1890 *Cent. Dict.*, *Mist-colored. 1929 W. Faulkner *Sartoris* 224 That 'ere mist-colored stallion. 1809 Shelley *Dial.* 20 Tell me.. What awaits on Futurity's *mist-covered shore. *a*1847 Eliza Cook *Winter is here* iii, The mist-covered pane. 1880 'Mark Twain' *Tramp Abroad* 398 Along their *mist-dimmed heights [i.e., of the Alps]. 1860 Pusey *Min. Proph.* 375 Countless multitudes of *mist-drops. 1848 Dickens *Dombey* xxxiii, Towards the *mist-enshrouded city. 1782 J. Scott *Amœbean Ecl.* ii. Poet. Wks. 114 Dull are slow Ousa's *mist-exhaling plains. 1860 A. Gray *Man. Bot.* 188 *Conoclinium*, *Mist-flower. 1961 A. Sillitoe *Key to Door* iv. xxvi. 389 Green fields rolling up to.. Catstone Wood, a *mist-green spearblade of sky above. 13.. *Gaw. & Gr. Knt.* 2081 Vch hille hade a hatte, a *myst-hakel huge. 1601 Weever *Mirr. Mart.* (Roxb.) 210 A *mist-hung Star-exhaled Meteor. 1777 Mason *Eng. Garden* II. 396 The sable ensign of the night Unfurl'd by *mist-impelling Eurus. 1899 F. T. Bullen *Way Navy* 85 The secret of Ireland's greenness is the *mist-laden Gulf Stream. 1930 Blunden *Poems* 40 The wolfish shadows in the eerie places Sprawl in the *mist-light. 1921 R. Graves *Pier-Glass* 12 Cold fog-drawn Lily, pale *mist-magic Rose. 1923 H. Crane *Let.* 15 Apr. (1965) 132 The eerie speed of the shutter.. catching even the transition of the *mist-mote into the cloud. 1956 *Brit. Birds* L. 450 *Mist nets, a traditional Japanese method of catching birds, were introduced to British ringers at a meeting of the Bird Observatories Committee in January, and by the early autumn of 1956 it is probable that over a hundred nets were in use. 1961 *New Scientist* 23 Mar. 728/1 The watchers gather with note-books, binoculars, mist nets, Heligoland traps and boxes of rings. 1971 *Daily Tel.* (Colour Suppl.) 18 June 7/1 Birds are.. snared in a 'mist net' (a long net erected on poles, which is of so fine a mesh that the birds cannot see it, and so fly into it, where they are entangled). 1972 *Science* 1 Sept. 806/3 Bats are mist-netted near cattle. 1973 *Country Life* 1 Feb. 263/3 Helpers.. ring large numbers of passerines, which they trap in mist-nets. 1960 *Brit. Birds* LIII. 526 The capture of rare and difficult forms.. is now within the province of every *mist-netter. 1849 C. Brontë *Shirley* III. vi. 142 He would rather have appointed tryste with a phantom abbess, or *mist-pale nun. 1925 C. Day Lewis *Beechen Vigil* 26 Now from blue mist-pavilion You may see King Silence go Royally through the forest. 1916 Blunden *Harbingers* 33 So heavily drives the rain, and lashes The open pool into white *mist-plashes. 1893 Dartnell & Goddard *Gloss. Words Wiltshire* 104 **Mist-pond*, a pond on the downs, not fed by any spring, but kept up by mist, dew, and rain... More commonly called *dew-ponds*. 1931 *N. & Q.* 22 Aug. 141/2 High up on the hills, in various parts of the country, are to be found ponds. Some call them dew ponds, but a more correct title is mist pond. [1941 *Amer. Nurseryman* 1 May 5 (*title*) Propagation under mist.] 1953 *Ibid.* 1 Aug. 63/2 Results of some of the work we have done at Koster Nursery appear to indicate the equal value of constant *mist propagation in the open. 1961 *Amat. Gardening* Suppl. 28 Oct. 34/2 A technique known as mist propagation... The main feature of this technique is the automatic provision of a fine mist spray. 1969 *New Scientist* 10 Apr. 70 (*caption*) After five weeks' mist propagation, two-leaf cuttings of Iceberg [*sc.* a rose] are well-rooted young plants. 1972 *Country Life* 1 June 1419/3 Mist Propagation equipment. Maximises health and growth of plants. 1971 'J. Fraser' *Death in Pheasant's Eye* xxxi. 187 He'd have sufficient cash to buy a proper heating and ventilating system... Aye, and perhaps a *mist propagator! 1917 D. H. Lawrence *Look! We have come Through!* 47 A thick *mist-sheet lies over the broken wheat. 1890 'R. Boldrewood' *Col. Reformer* (1891) 246 The *mist-shrouded pinnacle of.. success. 1919 V. Woolf *Night & Day* v. 62 Lonely mist-shrouded voyagings. 1957 Manvell & Huntley *Technique Film Music* iii. 164 Calm scenes of mist-shrouded lakes and shots of dew-spangled vegetation. 1888 W. B. Yeats *Phantom Ship* in *Wanderings of Oisin* (1889) 87 Hang the *mist-threads for a little while Like cobwebs in the air. 1867 M. Arnold *Heine's Grave* in *New Poems* 204 And *mist-track'd stream of the wide. 1928 Blunden *Retreat* 14 Or mist-veil brushed thee, fine as yet was wove For moonmaid's clothing. 1908 *Daily Chron.* 14 Nov. 4/4 Down the damp roadway move long lines of *mist-veiled traffic. 1776 Mickle tr. *Camoens' Lusiad* vii. 298 Distant navies rear the *mist-wet sail. 1936 L. B. Lyon *Bright Feather Fading* 48 *Mist-wild you melt now, gossamer fawn. 1811 Scott *Don Roderick* ii. lxiii, All the phantasms of my brain, Melted away like *mist-wreaths in the sun. 1849 M. Arnold *Resignation* in *Strayed Reveller* 123 Make, whistling, towards his *mist-wreath'd flock. 1864 Tennyson *En. Ard.* 633 The *mist-wreathen isle. 1909 E. Pound *Personae* 43 Slender as *mist-wrought maids and hamadryads.

†**mist**, *sb.*[2] *Obs.* [? A use of prec. sb. influenced by *mystic*, *mystery*: cf. misty *a.*[2]] Things spiritual or mystical. *in mist*: mystically.

13.. *E.E. Allit. P.* A. 462 Ryȝt so is vch a krysten sawle, A longande lym to þe mayster of myste. *c*1430 *Hymns Virgin* (1867) 41 Þese prophetis speken so in myst, What þei mente we neuere knewe. 1667 Milton *P.L.* v. 435 So down they sat, And to thir viands fell, nor seemingly The Angel, nor in mist, the common gloss Of Theologians, but with keen dispatch Of real hunger.

†**mist**, *sb.*[3] *Obs.* App. shortened form of mister *sb.*[1] = need.

*c*1400 Maundev. (Roxb.) xi. 41 Þat þai schuld lede me fra citee to citee, if miste ware. ?1469 *Paston Lett.* II. 334, I have grete myst of it.

mist (mɪst), *v.*[1] [OE. *mistian*, f. *mist* mist *sb.*[1]]

1. *intr.* To be or become misty; to gather or appear in the form of a mist; (of the eyes, outlines, etc.) to become dim, obscure, or blurred.

*c*1000 Ælfric *Gram.* xxxvi. (Z.) 216 *Caligo* me mistiað mine eaȝan. *c*1440 *Promp. Parv.* 340/2 Mystyn, or grow roky as wedur, and mysty. 1655 Vaughan *Silex Scint.* I. 70, I have deserved a thick, Egyptian damp, Dark as my deeds Should mist within me. 1818 Keats *Endym.* III. 44 When thy gold breath is misting in the west. 1821 Clare *Vill. Minstr.* I. 132 Full sweet it was to look, How clouds misted o'er the hill. 1829 Froude in *Rem.* (1838) I. 241 It began to rain and blow, and, what was worse, to mist. 1891 *Columbus* (Ohio) *Disp.* 23 Dec., Your eyes cannot but mist as you look and listen.

2. *trans.* To cover or obscure with or as with mist; to envelop in mist; to bedim (the eyes) with tears.

1430–40 Lydg. *Bochas* II. ii. (1554) 44 Flattery.. Whiche ..Misteth the iyen of euery gouernour That they cannot know their owne erroure. 1598 E. Guilpin *Skial.* (1878) 21 He sits Misted with darknes like a smoaky roome. 1600 Holland *Livy* xxix. xxvii. 730 They were misted againe, and lost the sight of land. 1605 Shaks. *Lear* v. iii. 262 If that her breath will mist or staine the stone, Why then she liues. 1628 Gaule *Pract. Theories* (1629) 373 Perhaps, her lauish weeping.. misted her eyes. 1631 Heywood *2nd Pt. Fair Maid of West* III. F 4 Let's mist our selves In a thick cloud of smoak. 1685 Sir G. Mackenzie *Religious Stoic* v. 43 That Glass is now so misted and soiled. 1820 Keats *Lamia* II. 274 No soft bloom Misted the cheek. 1858 Mrs. Oliphant *Laird of Norlaw* III. 220 Stars do not mist themselves with tender dew about the perversities of human kind as these eyes do.

b. with immaterial obj.

1598 Marston *Sco. Villanie* II. v. 198 With Caduceus nimble Hermes fights, And mists my wit. 1613 Purchas *Pilgrimage* I. ii. 14 We haue this testimonie of Moses of the Creation of the World, whose sense, if I haue missed or misted in these many words, I craue pardon. 1637 Rutherford *Lett.* (1862) I. cxviii. 294 If I were not misted, and confounded, and astonished how to be thankful. 1654 Whitlock *Zootomia* 495 This double Errour mists mens Judgments concerning them.

†**mist**, *v.*[2] *Obs.* In 3 miste, myste. [? f. *mist* pa. pple. of miss *v.*[1] Cf. Sw. *mista*, Da. *miste*.] *intr.* and *trans.* = miss *v.*[1]

*a*1250 *Owl & Night.* 764 Oft spet wel a lute lyste þar muche strengþe solde myste. *Ibid.* 825 If þe uox miste of al þis dwele At þan ende ho creophþ to hole. *Ibid.* 1640 Nule ic wiþ þe playdi na more Vor her þu myst þi ryhte lore.

mist, obs. pa. t. and pa. pple. of miss *v.*[1]; scribal variant of ME. *miȝt* (see may *v.*[1]).

†**mi'stad**, *pa. pple. Obs.* [app. f. mis-[1] 2 + *stad*, pa. pple. of stead *v.*] In sorry plight.

*a*1300 *Cursor M.* 28158 Quen i sagh oþer men mistad, Of his fare wald i be gladd.

mistakable (mɪ'steɪkəb(ə)l), *a.* [f. mistake *v.* + -able.] Capable of being mistaken, misapprehended, or misunderstood.

1646 Sir T. Browne *Pseud. Ep.* vi. i. 279 If wee consider how differently they are set forth in minor and lesse mistakeable numbers. *c*1653 Hammond *Paraphr. N.T.* Postscr. §32 Places of Scripture.. mistakable by the Enthusiast. 1822 *Examiner* 341/1 The darkest and most mistakable parts of this drama. 1864 Bowen *Logic* xii. (1870) 388 The internal peculiarities of the malady, of which the outward symptoms are only the faint and easily mistakable indications.

Hence **mi'stakableness; mi'stakably** *adv.*

1665 J. Sergeant *Sure Footing* 221 Supposing the notoriety of it secur'd the thing from mistakableness. 1844 Browning *Let. to Dowson* 10 Mar. in *Athenæum* 18 July 108/1 The good fortune which appears slowly but not mistakably setting in upon me.

mistake (mɪ'steɪk), *sb.* [f. next. Cf. Sw. *misstag*.]

1. a. *properly*, A misconception or misapprehension of the meaning of something; *hence*, an error or fault in thought or action.

1638 Junius *Paint. Ancients* 337 We doe excuse small mistakes in them. *a*1656 Ussher *Lett.* (1686) 505 'Upon the old Sabbath-day, or upon the Sunday'; by a strange kind of mistake, turning the Copulative into a Disjunctive. 1717 Lady M. W. Montagu *Let. to Lady Rich* 17 June, Your whole letter is full of mistakes from one end to the other. 1752 Hume *Ess. & Treat.* (1777) II. 5 It is easy for a profound philosopher to commit a mistake in his subtile reasonings. 1818 Cruise *Digest* (ed. 2) V. 166 Mistakes in the description of the premises. 1856 Sir B. Brodie *Psychol. Inq.* II. iv. 134 There are not a few who make the great mistake of expecting too much of life. 1856 Froude *Hist. Eng.* (1858) I. iii. 285 It will be thought.. on wider grounds, that the measure was a mistake. 1874 Micklethwaite *Mod. Par. Churches* 29 It is a great mistake to think that a building looks better for being empty.

†**b.** *a mistake of*: a misconception as to.

1649 in *Def. Rights & Priv. Univ. Oxford* (1690) 19 Mistakes of the manner and rules of proceeding. 1690 Locke *Hum. Und.* III. x. §16 Whatever Inconvenience follows from this Mistake of Words. 1712 Steele *Spect.* No. 502 ⁋1 It cannot be called a Mistake of what is pleasant. 1771 Jenkins *Cent. Rep.* (ed. 3) II. v. 57 For when the defendant appears, a mistake of the process to bring him to appear shall do no harm.

c. In generalized use.

1671 Tillotson *Serm.* Pref. b 5 b, Infallibility is an absolute security of the understanding from all possibility of mistake in what it believes. 1742 Young *Nt. Th.* ix. 32 But if, beneath the favour of mistake, Thy smile's sincere. 1813 Shelley *Q. Mab* vi. 30 Crime and misery are in yonder earth, Falsehood, mistake, and lust.

d. An instance of a woman's becoming pregnant unintentionally; an unplanned baby.

1957 *New Yorker* 12 Jan. 30/3 Owing to a 'mistake', Bernadette was probably 'caught'. She was beginning to 'show'. 1959 *Times* 2 Mar. 5/3 We all know the baby is a 'mistake',.. but surely it is a mistake which is understandable. 1963 in *Sc. Nat. Dict.* (1965) VI. 303/1 The peer lassie was pitten awa frae hame for makin a mistak.

2. Phrases. †**a.** *in, upon,* or *under a mistake*: under a misapprehension. *Obs.*

1683 *New Hampsh. Prov. Papers* (1867) I. 460 It may be I may be upon a mistake, but, according to what I know and belive, I am falsely indited. 1683 H. Prideaux in *Lett. Lit. Men* (Camden) 185 That you may be under noe mistake as to him. 1742 Young *Nt. Th.* viii. 884 For what is vice? self-love in a mistake. 1777 *Bentley's Phal.* 328 *note*, Gronovius was under a mistake, in supposing the Romans had no such sum as a Talent in their accounts. 1822 Shelley tr. *Calderon's Mag. Prodig.* I. 32 You lie—under a mistake. 1839 *Standard* 12 Apr., Some timid conservatives.. labour in the same mistake.

b. *by* (rarely *from*, †*in a*) *mistake*: erroneously, mistakenly. Also *in mistake for*.

1726 Swift *Gulliver* II. viii, It [*sc.* a tooth] was drawn by an unskilful Surgeon, in a Mistake. 1769 *Junius Lett.* xiii. (1771) I. 65 It is not that you do wrong by design, but that you should never do right by mistake. 1822 Cobbett *Weekly Reg.* 9 Mar. 579 In the year 1814; and not 1815, as I, from mistake, stated at Chichester. 1864 J. H. Newman *Apol.* 23 A story of a sane person being by mistake shut up in the wards of a Lunatic Asylum. 1906 Galsworthy *Man of Property* I. ii. 39 Old Jolyon.. gave the driver a sovereign in mistake for a shilling. 1923 *World's Work* May 563/1, I remember looking at him and.. expecting that I had been arrested in mistake for him.

c. *and no mistake*: without any doubt, undoubtedly, for certain; used *colloq.* to emphasize a preceding statement. Also used attrib., *(and-)no-mistake* = undoubted, unquestionable. Also *make no mistake* (*about*) (something): have no doubt about it.

Often stressed (anomalously) on the syllable *no*.

1818 Lady Morgan *Autobiog.* (1859) 15 He is the real thing and no mistake. 1837 Thackeray *Ravenswing* i, A tip-top swell, I can assure you, a regular bang-up chap, and no mistake. 1857 Hughes *Tom Brown* I. i, Yes, it's a magnificent Roman camp, and no mistake, with gates, and ditch, and mounds. 1884 *Harper's Mag.* Feb. 412/1 Mary Ann was mad, an' no mistake. 1885 W. S. Gilbert *Mikado* II. 27 Ah, pray make no mistake, We are not shy; We're very wide awake. 1911 G. B. Shaw *Shewing-up of Blanco Posnet* 390 It wont make any difference to us: make no mistake about that. 1962 *Listener* 27 Sept. 463/2 But the present terms do confront us with this choice: make no mistake about it. 1963 *Ibid.* 21 Feb. 341/1 Make no mistake about Mr Bennet: we are meant to disapprove thoroughly of his detachment. 1974 *Times* 22 Mar. 11/7 Make no mistake. We had a major work of television last night.

attrib. 1838 Thackeray *Fashnable Fax* Wks. 1900 XIII. 251 A reglar slap-up, no mistake, out-an'-out account of the manners and usitches of genteel society. 1848 —— *Bk. Snobs* xxiii, The real old original and-no-mistake nobility. 1858 O. W. Holmes *Aut. Breakf.-t.* xii, He is the real, genuine, no-mistake Osiris.

3. mistake-free *a.*

1969 F. I. Dretske *Seeing & Knowing* ii. 63 What we might call a mistake-free way of seeing D.

mistake (mɪ'steɪk), *v.* Forms: see take *v.* [a. ON. *mistaka* to take by mistake, refl. to miscarry (Sw. *misstaga* refl. to be mistaken), f. *mis-* = mis-[1] + *taka* to take. For the uses cf. also OF. *mesprendre* (mod.F. *méprendre*).]

†**1.** *trans.* To take wrongfully, wrongly, or in error. *Obs.*

*c*1380 Wyclif *Wks.* (1880) 345 Þis office is dispised & cristes owne office is misse-taken. 1382 —— *Deut.* v. 11 Thow shalt not mystaak the name of the Lord thi God idillich. 1387 Trevisa *Higden* (Rolls) VII. 321 He haþ nouȝt mystake as his owne þat he haþ i-fonge for a tyme. 14.. *Lat. Eng. Voc.* in Wr.-Wülcker 604/39 *Presumptuo*, to mystake. 1550 Crowley *Way to Wealth* 579 To make restitucion of that ye haue misse taken. 1614 B. Jonson *Barth. Fair* II. ii, To be euer busie, and mis-take away the bottles and cannes ..before they be halfe drunke off. *a*1631 Donne *Sat.* v. Poems (1633) 348 To see a Pursivant come in, and call All his cloathes, Copes;.. and all His Plate, Challices; and mistake them away.

†**2. a.** *intr.* To transgress, offend, do wrong. *Obs.*

*c*1330 R. Brunne *Chron.* (1810) 138 If þe Scottis kyng mistake in any braide Of treson in any þyng, ageyn Henry forsaid. ?*a*1366 Chaucer *Rom. Rose* 1540 Ladyes, I preye ensample taketh, Ye that ayeins your love mistaketh. *c*1400 *St. Alexius* (Laud 622) 94 Aȝeins no Man she mystook,.. Noiþer in word ne dede. *c*1500 *Melusine* 29, I haue mystaken ouermoche anenst your noble personne. 1822 Scott *Nigel* iv, I think the knave mistook more out of conceit than of purpose.

b. *refl.* (and *pass.*) in the same sense. *Obs.*

*c*1330 R. Brunne *Chron. Wace* (Rolls) 5145 Þaw y mystok me greuously, I prey þe of me haue þou mercy. *c*1386 Chaucer *Melib.* ⁋852 We han so greetly mistaken us, and han offended.. agayn your heigh lordshipe, that [etc.]. *a*1400 *Pety Job* 116 in 26 *Pol. Poems* 124, I pray to the, Warne me when I am mystan. *a*1425 *Cursor M.* 18788 (Trin.) His kyn wol he not forsake But we vs fouly mystake.

3. To err in the choice of, as *to mistake the* or *one's way* (*road*): to take the wrong path. Similarly *to mistake one's mark*. *Obs.* or *arch.*

1390 Gower *Conf.* II. 35 That he mistake noght his gate. 1548 Hall *Chron., Hen. VIII*, 26 By negligence of the carters yt mystooke ye way. 1603 Florio *Montaigne* II. xii.

(Frowde) 314 It is very hard to find one in perfect plight, and that doth not alwaies mistake his marke and shute wide. **1666** DRYDEN *Ann. Mirab.* cciii, [They] swallow in the fry, Which through their gaping jaws mistake the way. **1742** YOUNG *Nt. Th.* VI. 393 When blind ambition quite mistakes her road. **1791** MRS. RADCLIFFE *Rom. Forest* i, La Motte began to have apprehensions that his servant had mistaken the way.

4. a. *trans.* To misunderstand the meaning of (a person); to attach a wrong meaning to the sayings or doings of (a person).

1402 *Pol. Poems* (1859) II. 97 And so thou mysse takist Jerom, and lyest on Bernarde. *a* **1568** ASCHAM *Scholem.* II. (Arb.) 124 Erasmus..is mistaken of many, to the great hurt of studie, for his authoritie sake. **1591** SHAKS. *Two Gent.* II. v. 49 Why, thou whorson Asse, thou mistak'st me. **1637–50** Row *Hist. Kirk* (Wodrow Soc.) 312 [He] was mistaken, and his answer thrown to another sense. **1699** BENTLEY *Phal.* 460 There's no room for any suspicion, that he mistook his Author. **1709** POPE *Ess. Crit.* 557 Yet shun their fault, who, scandalously nice, Will needs mistake an author into vice. **1714** R. FIDDES *Pract. Disc.* II. 207 The old serpent..was..out of his calculation, and mistook his man. **1821** SHELLEY *Hellas* 792 Mistake me not! All is contained in each. **1837** BROWNING *Strafford* I. ii, I was away, Mistook, maligned: how was the king to know? **1891** *Pall Mall G.* 30 Oct. 5/3 On the point of resignation he has mistaken me.

†**b.** To have a wrong view of the character of (a person). Also with compl. *Obs.*

1589 WARNER *Alb. Eng.* VI. xxix. 129 Let them take me wilfull, or mistake me wanton. **1622** FLETCHER *Beggar's Bush* IV. i, *Ger.* Good fortune Master. *Flo.* Thou mistak'st me Clause, I am not worth thy blessing. *c* **1680** BEVERIDGE *Serm.* (1729) I. 535 No, mistake not your selves; so long as you are so unjust to others [etc.],..ye have no ground to hope that God will be so merciful to you.

c. ***to mistake one's man***: to judge incorrectly, or underestimate, the capabilities, character, etc., of the person with whom one has to deal.

1794 *Mass. Spy* 16 Apr. (Th.), If he supposes I am to be frightened by his pompous accusations, he has much mistaken his man. **1841** *Congress. Globe* 18 June 75/3 Mr. G. said that he was not to be coughed or cried down; gentlemen mistook their man if they supposed he was to be affected by the machinery of the political party.

5. To have a misconception with regard to (an opinion, statement, action, purpose, etc.); to misapprehend the meaning or intention of; to take in a wrong sense, attach an erroneous meaning to.

1496 *Rolls of Parlt.* VI. 511/1 As though every of the said Shires and other wordes theryn mistaken, had be well taken. **1560** DAUS tr. *Sleidane's Comm.* 172 a, This Oration..was set forth in prynte, and John Calvine made a comentary to it, leste any man should mistake it. **1597** SHAKS. *2 Hen. IV*, IV. ii. 56 My Fathers purposes haue beene mistooke. **1610** —— *Temp.* II. i. 56 He doth but mistake the truth totally. **1677** DRYDEN *Apol. Heroic Poetry* Ess. (ed. Ker) I. 179 They wholly mistake the nature of criticism who think its business is principally to find fault. **1729** BUTLER *Serm.* Wks. 1874 II. Pref. 7 An argument may not readily be apprehended, which is different from its being mistaken. **1769** *Junius Lett.* xxii. 103 It sometimes may happen, that the judge may mistake the law. **1856** FROUDE *Hist. Eng.* (1858) I. ii. 144 He over-rated the strength of his English connexion, and mistook the English character. **1880** DIXON *Windsor* IV. i. 2 He mistook the times in which he lived.

6. To make a mistake; to be in error; to err in opinion or judgement; to be under a misapprehension; to take a wrong view.

a. *intr.* Now somewhat *arch.*

1581 PETTIE tr. *Guazzo's Civ. Conv.* II. (1586) 77, I think you mistake. **1591** SHAKS. *Two Gent.* v. iv. 94 Oh, cry you mercy sir, I haue mistooke. **1631** GOUGE *God's Arrows* I. §42. 67 God can not mistake: the evill at which he is at any time angry is indeed evill. **1699** BENTLEY *Phal.* 326 That He was not the first, that made this (false) Discovery, but mistook after great Names, Goltzius, and Fazellus. **1732** POPE *Ep. Cobham* 210 Yet, in this search, the wisest may mistake, If second qualities for first they take. **1802** MAR. EDGEWORTH *Moral T.* (1816) I. x. 85 If I don't mistake. **1819** SHELLEY *Cenci* IV. iv. 56 How; dead! he only sleeps; you mistake, brother. **1861** *Jrnl. Asiatic Soc.* XXX. 198 Professor Lassen mistakes as to the locality of this place. **1891** *Speaker* 2 May 532/2 If we mistake not, he has put the believers in the guilt of Richard III in a dilemma.

b. *pass.* (***to be mistaken***, †***mistook***), and †*refl.* Const. *in* (rarely †*of*).

1599 SHAKS. *Hen. V*, II. iv. 30 You are too much mistaken in this King. **1607** DEKKER *Knt.'s Conjur.* (1842) 69 The destinies (who fought on their side) mistooke themselues, and in steede of striking the colours out of his hand, smote him. **1644** GABRIEL PLATTERS in *Hartlib's Legacy* (1655) 253 If I be not hugely mistaken, it is the self-same with..Saint-Foin. **1658** COKAINE *Obstinate Lady* V. iv. Poems (1874) 96 But I am much mistook; you are not she Whom here I was to meet. **1671** MILTON *Samson* 907, I was a fool, too rash, and quite mistaken In what I thought would have succeeded best. **1784** COWPER *Task* III. 154 That He who made it [*sc.* the earth], and revealed its date To Moses, was mistaken in its age. **1824** HOGG *Conf. Sinner* 188, I can never be mistaken of a character in whom I am interested. **1848** DICKENS *Dombey* iv, You're mistaken I dare say. **1875** JOWETT *Plato* (ed. 2) I. 431 Plato, if I am not mistaken, was ill.

†**7.** *trans.* With direct obj. (or acc. and inf.) and compl.: To suppose erroneously to be or to do... Also *passive.* *Obs.*

1596 SPENSER *F.Q.* IV. viii. 55 For me he did mistake that Squire to bee. *a* **1637** B. JONSON *Eng. Gram.* Pref. (1640), The opinion of rudenesse and barbarisme, wherewith it [*sc.* our language] is mistaken to be diseas'd. *a* **1661** FULLER *Worthies, Warwickshire* (1662) 124 Vincent of Coventrie was ..bred a Franciscan (though Learned Leland mistakes him a Carmelite). **1721** BRADLEY *Philos. Acc. Wks. Nat.* 144 Some mistake the Aureliae of certain kinds of Butterflies to be the Aureliae of Ichneumon Flies. **1736** BUTLER *Anal.* II. iii. 170 Lest I should be mistaken to vilify Reason.

8. ***to mistake*** (a person or thing) ***for*** (some other person or thing): to suppose erroneously the former to be the latter; to substitute in thought or perception the latter for the former.

1611 SHAKS. *Wint. T.* II. i. 82 You haue mistooke (my Lady) Polixenes for Leontes. **1617** MORYSON *Itin.* I. 181, I touched the poore mans box with my fingers..mistaking it for the Font of holy water. **1651** HOBBES *Leviath.* II. xxv. 131 They mistake the Precepts of Counsellours, for the Precepts of them that Command. **1711** ADDISON *Spect.* No. 120 ¶15 She [*sc.* a hen] mistakes a Piece of Chalk for an Egg, and sits upon it in the same manner. **1791** MRS. RADCLIFFE *Rom. Forest* ix, The effusions of gratitude she mistook for those of tenderness. **1828** SCOTT *F. M. Perth* xxii, Poor gossip Oliver often mistook friends for enemies. **1871** MORLEY *Voltaire* (1886) 5 Those..who have the temperament which mistakes strong expression for strong judgment.

9. a. To err as to the identity or nature of; to take to be somebody or something else; now usually in phr. ***there's no mistaking*** = it is impossible not to recognize.

1590 SPENSER *F.Q.* III. viii. 5 In hand she boldly tooke To make..Another Florimell, in shape and looke So lively and so like, that many it mistooke. **1633** MILTON *Arcades* 4 What sudden blaze of majesty Is that which we from hence descry Too divine to be mistook. **1732** POPE *Ess. Man* II. 216 If white and black blend..is there no black or white?..Tis to mistake them, costs the time and pain. **1837** DICKENS *Pickw.* ii, There was no mistaking the fact. **1874** SYMONDS *Sk. Italy & Greece* (1898) I. xv. 320 Another [astrologer] described him so accurately that there was no mistaking the man.

b. To estimate wrongly.

1785 BURNS *Jolly Beggars* 3rd Recit., I fear I my talent misteuk.

†**10.** To commit an error in regard to (a date, a number, etc.); to perform (an action) at a wrong time. *Obs.*

1704 *Lond. Gaz.* No. 4035/3 In the Circuit Gazette, the Day of the Month for the Assizes..is mistaken. **1726** SWIFT *Gulliver* III. ii, He..brought my Clothes very ill made, and quite out of Shape, by happening to mistake a Figure in the Calculation. **1734** SEYMOUR *Compl. Gamester* 79 He that mistakes his Stroke, loses 1, to that Side he is of.

†**11.** To bring by mistake *into*. *Obs.*

1663–9 DRYDEN *Wild Gallant* I. ii, Sure this fellow..was sent by Fortune to mistake me into so much money. **1667** —— *Ind. Emp.* Prol., Wks. 1725 I. 326 Grant us such Judges ..As still mistake themselves into a Jest.

†**12.** To take amiss, object to. *Obs.*

1725 DE FOE *Voy. round World* (1840) 245 Since I would be a maker of presents, she should do herself the honour to take it with her own hands and he would be very far from mistaking them, or taking it ill from his wife.

mi'stakeful, *a.* [f. MISTAKE *sb.* + -FUL.] Full of mistakes.

1880 FURNIVALL in *Trans. New Shaks. Soc.* (1880–2) 199 The scrappy and mistakeful state of the text.

mistaken (mɪ'steɪk(ə)n), *ppl. a.* Also 8 *Sc.* **-tane**. [pa. pple. of MISTAKE *v.*]

†**1. a.** Wrongly supposed to be so. **b.** Wrongly taken for something else. **c.** Taken in a wrong sense; misunderstood, misconceived. *Obs.*

1597 BRETON *Marie's Exercise* (Grosart) 5/2 Martha.. complained to Thee of her sister's mistaken and mistermed idlenes. **1660** DRYDEN *Astræa Redux* 149 The watchful travellour That by the moon's mistaken light did rise. **1744** [see MISPOINT *v.*[2]].

d. ***mistaken identity***: a phrase used to describe an error made with regard to a person's identity.

1865 *Remarkable Convictions* 26 (heading), Mistaken Identity.

2. Of persons: Labouring under a misapprehension; taking a wrong view.

1601 SHAKS. *Twel. N.* II. ii. 36 And she (mistaken) seemes to dote on me. **1660** T. BLOUNT *Boscobel* 55 An imputation (laid on them by some mistaken Zelots) of disloyalty. **1712–14** POPE *Rape Lock* IV. 151 Yet am not I the first mistaken maid, By love of Courts to num'rous ills betray'd. **1715** DE FOE *Fam. Instruct.* I. iv. (1841) I. 73 You'll find yourself mistaken in my mother. **1770** *Junius Lett.* xxxvi. 177, I think him honest, though mistaken. **1878** JEVONS *Primer Pol. Econ.* 11 A hundred years after the publication of his great book, there ought not to be so many mistaken people vainly acting in opposition to his lessons.

3. *transf.* of their opinions, actions, etc.: Wrongly conceived, entertained, or carried out; erroneous.

1676 HALE *Contempl.* I. 21 The mistaken estimate of the generality of men. **1692** R. L'ESTRANGE *Fables* xxxviii. 38 The Licentiating of any thing that is Course and Vulgar, out of a foolish Facility or a Mistaken Pity. **1700** COLLIER *2nd Def. Short View* 123 Of these Lines he gives a foul and mistaken Translation. **1742** YOUNG *Nt. Th.* V. 301 Friends counsel quick dismission of our grief: Mistaken kindness! our hearts heal too soon. **1868** FREEMAN *Norm. Conq.* (1877) II. vii. 158 We can only suppose that a mistaken feeling of loyalty hindered him. **1897** GLADSTONE *E. Crisis* 2 The unwise and mistaken views of some Powers have brought dishonour upon the whole.

mistakenly (mɪ'steɪk(ə)nlɪ), *adv.* [f. prec. + -LY[2].] In a mistaken manner; by mistake; under a misapprehension; erroneously.

1654–66 EARL ORRERY *Parthen.* (1676) 805 A Vow.. manifested to be mistakenly grounded. **1660** *Trial Regic.* 71 He was unhappily ingaged in that bloody business, I hope mistakenly. **1715** LEONI *Palladio's Archit.* (1742) II. 71 A Portico (mistakenly called Piazza in England). **1759** GOLDSM. *Bee* No. 3 ¶40 Animated with a strong passion for the great virtues, as they are mistakenly called, and utterly forgetful of the ordinary ones. **1850** ROBERTSON *Lect.* (1858) 69 It matters little whether it was rightly or mistakenly denied. **1881** SAINTSBURY *Dryden* 115 This was Amphitryon, which some critics have treated most mistakenly as a mere translation of Molière.

mistakenness (mɪ'steɪk(ə)nnɪs). [-NESS.] The condition or quality of being mistaken.

1865 J. GROTE *Explor. Philos.* I. 66 There is no reason why people should not find out the mistakenness of them..by making the attempts, and seeing the absurdity which results. **1894** *Athenæum* 20 Jan. 80/2 A little prose tale.. which in simplicity and mistakenness is like the production of a clever child.

mistaker (mɪ'steɪkə(r)). [f. MISTAKE *v.* + -ER[1].] One who mistakes or misunderstands. In early use, sometimes, one who wilfully takes things in a wrong sense.

1551–2 *Act 5 & 6 Edw. VI*, c. 1 §4 Their hathe arrisen.. diverse doubtes..rather by the curiositie of the Mynistre and mystakers, then of anye other worthie cause. **1628** BP. HALL *Old Relig.* 191 The well meaning ignorance of mistakers. **1684** tr. *Bonet's Merc. Compit.* XIX. 794 The unhappiness of the Mistakers ought to have derogated nothing from the excellency of the Medicin. **1827** in Hone *Every-day Bk.* II. 1032 Would it be impossible to make a.. mistake with regard to the mistaker? **1869** BROWNING *Ring & Bk.* XI. 2045 So, let death alone! So ends mistake. So end mistakers!

mistaking (mɪ'steɪkɪŋ), *vbl. sb.* [f. MISTAKE *v.* + -ING[1].] The action of MISTAKE *v.*; †wrong-doing; misunderstanding, misconception; the act of making a mistake. From *c* 1580 to *c* 1650 frequent in the sense of: Mistake, error.

a **1300** *Cursor M.* 27258 Enentes knightes [sal he frain] o mistakyng, And namli wrangwis warraing. *c* **1430** *Pilgr. Lyf Manhode* I. lxxvi. (1869) 44 To you dame Sapience sendeth me..to shewe you youre mistakinges. **1529** MORE *Dyaloge* I. Wks. 167/1 That we shall auoide..all such myssetakyng, as might brynge vs into any damnable errour. **1530** PALSGR. 245/2 Mystakyng of a man selfe or myspride. **1573** BARET *Alv.* M 367 The likenesse causeth mistaking. *Errorem creat similitudo.* **1579** FULKE *Heskins' Parl.* 203 As his manifold mistakins do declare. **1613** SIR H. NEVILL in *Buccleuch MSS.* (Hist. MSS. Comm.) I. 131, I would wish you not to neglect him, out of any mistaking of his worth. **1626** BACON *Sylva* §946 This Pretended Learned Man told me; It was a Mistaking in Me. **1651** HOBBES *Leviath.* IV. xliv. 336 The same mistaking of the present Church for the Kingdom of God. *a* **1654** SELDEN *Table-T.* (Arb.) 112 The way to find out the Truth is by others mistakings. **1677** R. CARY *Palæol. Chron.* II. I. xxi. 161 To prevent Confusion, as well as Mistakings, it was not permitted [etc.]. **1824** BYRON *Juan* XVI. cxviii, He first inclined to think he had been mistaken; And then to be ashamed of such mistaking. **1890** *Spectator* 7 June, Those whose eyes are opened in a new world to their fearful mistaking. **1891** KIPLING *Light that Failed* iv. 66 There was no mistaking.

mistaking (mɪ'steɪkɪŋ), *ppl. a.* [-ING[2].]

1. Misunderstanding, misconceiving; erring.

1596 SHAKS. *Tam. Shr.* IV. v. 45 Pardon old father my mistaking eies. **1688** PRIOR *Ode Exodus* vii, Still enquiring, still mistaking Man. **1692** DRYDEN *Cleomenes* v. ii. 59 And with a good mistaking Piety, First blessing him, then Heaven! **1711** SWIFT *Examiner* No. 24 ¶2 And first I declare (because we live in a mistaking world) that [etc.]. **1725** POPE *Odyss.* VII. 394 Man's of a jealous and mistaking kind. *a* **1806** HORSLEY *Serm.* (1812) II. 252 They expected not like the mistaking Jews a Saviour of the Jewish nation only.

†**2.** Of opinions, statements: Mistaken, erroneous. *Obs.*

1651 BAXTER *Saints' R.* III. ii. (ed. 2) 193 Do not say then, I cannot beleeve that my sin is pardoned..and therefore I am no true Beleever: This is a most mistaking conclusion. **1660** BOYLE *Seraph. Love* To Rdr. 3 Its mistaking Passages and unwary Expressions. **1680** BAXTER *Answ. Stillingfl.* lxiv. 87 How faulty and hurtful this mistaking passionate Separation is.

mistakingly (mɪ'steɪkɪŋlɪ), *adv.* [f. prec. + -LY[2].] Erroneously; incorrectly; mistakenly.

1652–69 HEYLIN *Cosmogr.* III. 25 Sola..mistakingly called Heliopolis, by Qu. Curtius. **1654** WHITLOCK *Zootomia* 424 The mistakingly frighted, and running Army. **1678** *Lond. Gaz.* No. 1273/4 With the Crest an Eagles head and a fire-brand in the beak, but mistakingly engraved like a flaming torch. **1794** *Rigging & Seamanship* II. 338 If the chaser should mistakingly stand on. **1807** SOUTHEY *Espriella's Lett.* (1814) III. 284 The Heaven therefore which men mistakingly desire. **1883** *Nature* XXVII. 254/2 Parents mistakingly think the measles and whooping cough necessary accompaniments of childhood.

mistal ('mɪst(ə)l). *dial.* Also 7–9 **mistall**, 8 **mystall**, 9 **mistle**, **missel**, etc. [Of doubtful origin; perh. f. MIX *sb.*[1], dung + STALL *sb.*

Connexion with Norw. *mjøstøl* resting-place near a farm, or *mjølkestødl* station in the out fields for milking purposes, is improbable.]

A stable or shed for cattle.

1673 *Depos. Cast. York* (Surtees) 29 He..saith that..he sawe the said Mary Sikes riding upon the backe of one of his cowes. And he endeavouring to strike att her stumbled and soe the said Mary flewe out of his mistall window. **1703** THORESBY *Let. to Ray* Gloss. (E.D.S.), *Mystall*, mewstall for cattle, oxen, and cows. **1808** *Complete Grazier* (ed. 3) 68 Ox-stalls, or Feeding Houses..are usually denominated [in Lincolnshire] mistles. **1847** HALLIWELL, *Missel*, a cow house. *Yorksh.* **1865** W. S. BANKS *Wakefield Words*, *Mistle*, a cowhouse. **1884** *Leeds Merc.* 3 June 2 Good Mistal, for 8 beasts, with Hay Chamber. **1885** *Law Times* LXXVIII. 187/2 Whilst the cattle were in the mistal they were supplied with water from the well in the plaintiff's land.

† **mis'taste**, *v. Obs.* [Formed after DISTASTE; cf. MIS-¹ 9.] **a.** *intr.* To be out of taste. **b.** *trans.* To spoil the taste of. **c.** To have no taste for.

1540 [see MIS-SAVOUR]. **1562** J. HEYWOOD *Prov. & Epigr.* (1867) 90 Tast not to muche, lest taste mistast thy chaps. **1613** WITHER *Abuses Stript* To Rdr., Some, no doubt, will mistaste my plainnes, in that I have so bluntly spoken [etc.].

mistate, obs. variant of MIS-STATE.

mistaught (mɪs'tɔːt), *ppl. a.* [MIS-¹ 2.] Wrongly taught; badly brought up.

1552 HULOET, Mistaught or rude, *triuialis*. **1554** *Interlude of Youth* B iv, Who learned the thou mistaught man To speake so to a gentylman? **1692** R. L'ESTRANGE *Fables* xxxviii. 38 The Disorders, of either a Mis-taught, or a Neglected Youth. **1851** D. JERROLD *St. Giles* xxii. 223 Again, did strange thoughts tingle in that mistaught little brain.

† **miste**, *v. Obs.* [f. med.L. *mistum, mixtum* (OF. *miste, mixte*): see MIXTUM. Cf. med.L. *mixtāre* = 'mixtum sumere'.] *intr.* To take the light meal known as *mixtum*.

c **1400** *Rule St. Benet* (Prose) xxxv. 26 Þa þat serue o þe kichin sal miste [orig. *accipiant..singulos biberes et panem*] bi-fore þe mikil mete bred, butter, þat tay may serue widvten gruching. *Ibid.* xxxviii. 27 Sho þat sal rede sal miste [orig. *accipiat mixtum*] ay litil, be-fore sho rede.

miste, scribal var. *mihte*: see MAY *v.*¹ 4 a.

c **1205** LAY. 18690 Ne miste [*c* 1275 mihte] he of þan eorle naþing iwinnen.

mis'teach, *sb.* [app. alteration of MISTETCH after next.] Bad habit.

1842 G. S. FABER *Prov. Lett.* (1844) II. 100 What gave these members of our Church such an unlucky misteach, that [etc.].

misteach (mɪs'tiːtʃ), *v.* [OE. *mistǽcan*: see MIS-¹ 1 and TEACH *v.*] *trans.* To teach or instruct badly or wrongly. Also, †to misdirect.

c **1000** ÆLFRIC *Hom.* (Th.) II. 50 ȝif ða lareowas.. mistæcað, oððe misbysniað, hi forþærað hi sylfe. *c* **1250** *Gen. & Ex.* 475 Al-so he mistaȝte, also he schet. **1529** MORE *Dyaloge* IV. xi. Wks. 263/2 If thei should..blame the church for misteching the people. **1549** COVERDALE, etc. *Erasm. Par. Rom.* Argt., The Romaines..beyng fyrst misse taught & by false preachers deceiued. **1656** HOBBES *Six Lessons* Wks. 1845 VII. 316 When I think how dejected you will be ..for misteaching the young men of the University. **1702** C. MATHER *Magn. Chr.* VII. 15 Their Teachers..had mistaught and mis-led the People. **1868** GLADSTONE *Juv. Mundi* x. (1870) 402 He is indeed mistaught with reference to the use of the strong hand.

absol. *a* **1661** FULLER *Worthies* (1840) III. 463 They did not only not teach in the Church, but misteach by their lascivious..behaviour. **1837** HT. MARTINEAU *Soc. Amer.* III. 295 Has not God his own ways..of teaching when man misteaches?

b. To teach (a subject) badly.

1831 CARLYLE *Misc. Ess.* (1840) III. 240 The New School, with all that it taught, untaught, and mistaught.

Hence **mis'teaching** *vbl. sb.*

1549 COVERDALE etc. *Erasm. Par. Gal.* 1 Simplenes it was, that they were through misteachyng begiled. **1587** GOLDING *De Mornay* xvi. 306 The misteaching or misexample of the Parents. **1828** [see MISTETCH *sb.*].

misted ('mɪstɪd), *a.* [f. MIST *sb.* or *v.* + -ED.] Obscured by or hidden in mist; *fig.* dulled, blurred.

1627–77 FELTHAM *Resolves* I. viii, When the brain is misted, with arising Fumes. **1637** RUTHERFORD *Lett.* (1664) xxxii. I. 74 Misted faith, & my fever conceive amiss of him. **1820** CLARE *Poems Rur. Life* (ed. 3) 58 Through the rimy misted pane. **1887** *Harper's Mag.* June 108 He walked the streets under the thinly misted moon.

misteir, obs. form of MISTER *sb.*¹

mistell (mɪs'tɛl), *v.* Also 7–8 **-tel.** [MIS-¹ 1.]

† **1.** *trans.* To number or reckon incorrectly; to miscount. Also *absol. Obs.*

1426 LYDG. *De Guil. Pilgr.* 17618 Thys hand ek falsly beyth and sylleth; And in reknynge, thys hand mystelleth. **1530** PALSGR. 638/2 You have mystolde, for there was no lesse in the purce. **1608** SYLVESTER *Tri. Faith* I. xxxv. (1621) 540 That Bizantian Prince, that did mis-tell A four-fould Essence in the onely One. **1622** BRETON *Strange News* (Grosart) 5 Their prayers are all by the dozen, when if they miss-tell one, they thinke all the rest lost. **1647** HEXHAM, *Mistellen*, to Mistell, or to Miscount.

2. a. To relate incorrectly. † **b.** To misinform.

1565 JEWEL *Repl. Harding* (1611) 181 M. Harding mis-telleth his authours tale, and auoucheth that he neuer meant. **1674** N. FAIRFAX *Bulk & Selv.* 141 One who could never mistake himself, nor mistel us. **1755** JOHNSON, *To Mistel*, to tell unfaithfully or inaccurately.

misteltewe, -tow, obs. forms of MISTLETOE.

mistely, obs. form of MISTILY.

† **mis'temper**, *sb. Obs.* [f. MIS-¹ 4 + TEMPER *sb.*] Disorder.

1549 CHEKE *Hurt Sedit.* (1641) 31 To..find by your mistemper to be themselves better ordered. *c* **1550** LLOYD *Treas. Health* T viij b, If he haue the lepre mystempre and paynes throughe al the bodye.

So † **mis'temperance**, disordered or improperly 'tempered' condition.

1541 R. COPLAND *Galyen's Terap.* 2 A iv, The mystemperaunce of yᵉ flesshe vlcerate. **1561** HOLLYBUSH *Hom. Apoth.* 26 The iaundis caused by mistemperaunce of heate.

† **mis'temper**, *v. Obs.* [f. MIS-¹ 1 + TEMPER *v.*] *trans.* To disturb or disorder.

a **1547** in *Laneham's Let.* (1871) Pref. 130 Haue youe bene mystemperyd With ale att any tyme? **1561** HOLLYBUSH *Hom. Apoth.* 21 b, Lyke to lyke mistempereth the body. **1592** WARNER *Alb. Eng.* VII. xxxiv. (1612) 166 When..Nor Husbands weale nor Childrens woe mistempered my head. **1642** SIR E. DERING *Sp. on Relig.* 120 It will not now suit this Bil, as it is now mistemper'd to that purpose.

Hence † **mis'tempering** *vbl. sb.*, disorder.

1561 HOLLYBUSH *Hom. Apoth.* 17 b, Manye wayes getteth a man the cough: somtyme of the brestes mistemperinge.

† **mis'temperateness.** *Obs. rare*⁻¹. [MIS-¹ 4.] = MISTEMPERANCE.

1561 HOLLYBUSH *Hom. Apoth.* 26 The jaundis..is caused ..ether by mistemperatness of heate, or by stoppynge in the lyuer.

mis'tempered, *ppl. a. Obs.* or *arch.* [f. MIS-¹ 2 + TEMPERED.]

1. Badly or unsuitably mixed.

1506 *Kalendar Sheph.* L 3 (1892) III. 107 Whan they [*sc.* the humours] be vnegall & mysse tempred that one domyne ouer an other. **1594** NASHE *Terrors of Night* Wks. (Grosart) III. 269 Our brains are like the firmament..and exhale.. the like grose mistempred vapors and meteors. **1633** BP. HALL *Hard Texts, O.T.* 498 Those substitutions..shall be of a mis-tempered mixture, some of them strong..others weake.

2. Disordered, deranged.

1541 R. COPLAND *Galyen's Terap.* 2 A iv, The mystempered flesshe ought to be deuysed in two dyfferences. The fyrste is whan the subiect flesshe is out of nature in an onely qualyte. **1587** HOLINSHED *Hist. Scot.* 114/1 He..vsed to sit at supper..till he were so mistempered, that being laid to sleepe, he would streight vomit out such heauie gorges, as [etc.]. **1595** SHAKS. *John* V. i. 12 This inundation of mistempred humor. **1872** BLACKIE *Lays Highl.* 33 Gentleness, and tenderness, and truth And Gospel charms to tame mistempered souls.

3. Of weapons: Tempered for an evil purpose.

1592 SHAKS. *Rom. & Jul.* I. i. 94 From those bloody hands Throw your mistemper'd Weapons to the ground.

† **'misten**, *v. Obs. rare*⁻¹. [f. MIST *sb.*¹ + -EN⁵ 2.] *trans.* To dim the senses or perception of.

1599 SANDYS *Europæ Spec.* (1632) 82 Whom neither the fumes of fierie passions doe misten, nor [etc.].

† **mis'tend**, *v. Obs.* In 4 *pa. pple.* **mysetente.** [f. MIS-¹ 1 + TEND *v.*²] *trans.* Not to give proper attention to.

13.. *E.E. Allit. P.* A 257 ȝe haf your tale myse-tente, To say your perle is al awaye, þat is in cofer.

† **'misteous**, *a. Obs. rare*⁻¹. [f. MIST *sb.* + -EOUS.] 'Misty', obscure.

1549 *Compl. Scot.* x. 85 On this misteous propheseis, thai haue intendit veyris contrar scotland, in hope to conques it.

mister ('mɪstə(r)), *sb.*¹ *Obs.* exc. *arch.* and *dial.* Forms: 3–4 **meister**, 3–5 **mester**, (4 **me(i)stere, mæster, meyster, mystare, -eir**), 4–5 **misteir, -ere, mestyer(e**, 4–6 **mistir, mystir**, 4–7 **mestier**, 4–8 **myster**, (5 **mestyer, -ire, -ur, -our, maister, mystur, -yr, -ire, -air, mystre, mistre, -tyr**, 6 **mistar**, 7 **mistier**), 4– **mister.** [a. OF. *mestier, mester*, mod.F. *métier*, (1) service, office, occupation, (2) instrument or made-up article of certain kinds, (3) need, necessity (etc.) = Pr. *mester, meistier*, Sp., Pg. *mester*, It. *mestiere*:—popular L. **misterium* for *ministerium*: see MINISTRY and cf. MÉTIER. (In 13–14th c. stressed *mi'ster*.)]

I. Occupation, service, etc.

† **1.** Handicraft, trade; profession, craft. ***man of mister***: a craftsman (cf. 5). *Obs.*

a **1300** *Cursor M.* 11840 He..dos him leches for to seke, And þai com bath fra ferr and ner, þat sliest war o þat mister. *c* **1330** R. BRUNNE *Chron.* (1810) 94 He asked for his archere, Walter Tirelle was haten, maister of þat mister. *Ibid.* 169 Respons þei gaf him þere, þei were men of mistere. *c* **1386** CHAUCER *Prol.* 613 In youthe he lerned hadde a good mister; He was a wel good wrighte, a carpenter. **1390** GOWER *Conf.* III. 142 Of hem that ben Artificiers, Whiche usen craftes and mestiers. *c* **1477** CAXTON *Jason* 21 For to mayntene the noble mestier of armes. **1538** STARKEY *England* II. i. 159 Euery man scholer apply hym selfe to hys mystere and craft. **1613** DANIEL *Coll. Hist. Eng.* I. 11 As one who well knew his mistier.

† **2.** Office, duty, business, function. Chiefly qualified by possessive pron. *Obs.*

a **1225** *Ancr. R.* 72 Holde euerich his owene mester, & nout ne reame oðres. *Ibid.* 414 Marthe mester is uorto ueden & schruden poure men, ase huselefdi. *a* **1300** *Cursor M.* 2154 Sem had fiue suns sere, Of an to spek es our mestere. *c* **1320** *Cast. Love* 478 Rihtes mester hit is and wes In vche dom Pees to maken. *c* **1386** CHAUCER *Knt.'s T.* 482, I noot which hath the wofullere mester. *c* **1400** *Rom. Rose* 6976, I am somtyme messager; That falleth not to my mister. *c* **1450** *Bk. Curtasye* 352 in *Babees Bk.*, Now speke we wylle of officiers Of court, and als of hor mestiers.

† **3.** Employment, occupation; practice. ***to do, use*** (such) ***misters***: to be so employed. *Obs.*

a **1225** *Ancr. R.* 84 Þus ha beoð bisie i þisse fule mester. *c* **1250** *Gen. & Ex.* 536 And ðe fifte hundred ȝer, wapmen bigunnen quad mester, bi-twen hem-seluen hun-wreste plaȝe. *a* **1300** *Cursor M.* 29319 Þe tent [case of cursing] es of þis okerers þat openli dose sli misters. *c* **1330** R. BRUNNE *Chron. Wace* (Rolls) 11576 We haue now al þis fyue ȝer Lyued in lechours mester. **1375** BARBOUR *Bruce* XII. 414 Thai maid knychtis, as it efferis To men that oysis thai mysteris.

† **4.** Skill or cunning in a profession; art. *Obs.*

a **1400** *Minor Poems fr. Vernon MS.* 600/547 Mester wol not fayle þi lyf, Hit nul þe neuere forsake. *c* **1450** *Merlin* 156 And he lepte vp lightly as he that hadde grete mystere. *c* **1475** *Rauf Coilȝear* 442, I haue na myster to matche with maisterfull men.

5. *Comb.* † **mister man, misters** (genitive) **man**: a craftsman, artificer; a man having a certain occupation. Also † **mister folk.** Phrases like ***all mister men, what mister man, such a mister man*** came to be analysed as 'men of all misters', 'a man of what mister', 'of such a mister'; and these were subsequently interpreted as = 'men of all classes', 'a man of what (such a) class, or kind', 'what kind of a man', etc. The idiom occurs as an archaism in Spenser and later writers, from whom it was adopted (but with misapprehension of its meaning) by Pope and Scott; it survives dialectally in Yorkshire (see E.D.D.).

a **1300** *Cursor M.* 27261 All mister men wirkand wit handes. *c* **1325** *Prov. Hendyng* 270 in *Rel. Ant.* I. 115 Of alle mester men mest me hongeth theves. **1340** *Ayenb.* 39 Ine zuyche reuen, prouost, bedeles, oþre mesteres men huiche þet hy byeþ. **13..** *St. Erkenwolde* 60 in Horstm. *Altengl. Leg.* (1881) 267 Mony a mesters mon of maners dyuerse. *c* **1386** CHAUCER *Knt.'s T.* 852 But telleth me what mister men ye been. *c* **1400** *Rom. Rose* 6332 Now am I maister, now scolere; Now monk, now chanoun, now baily; What-ever mister man am I. *c* **1430** *Pilgr. Lyf Manhode* I. cxx. (1869) 63 So þat ayens suich a mister man it is good to haue suich a gorgeer. *c* **1440** LOVE *Bonavent. Mirr.* xlvi. (Gibbs MS.), Othere mester men þat broghten with hem dyuerse instrumentys. *c* **1450** LOVELICH *Merlin* 13 What mester man Js he, this, that doth vs here al this distres? *c* **1530** *Crt. of Love* 227 Seeing full sundry peple in the place, And mister folk. **1590** SPENSER *F.Q.* I. ix. 23 To weet what mister wight was so dismayd. **1593** DRAYTON *Sheph. Garl.* vii. 47 These mister artes been better fitting thee. *c* **1620** FLETCHER & MASS. *Lit. Fr. Lawyer* II. iii, What mister thing is this? Let me survey it. **1626** QUARLES *Feast for Worms* Medit. ii, What mister word is that? **1728** POPE *Dunc.* III. 187 Right well mine eyes arede the myster wight. **1814** SCOTT *Wav.* ix, Sometimes this mister wight held his hands clasped over his head.

II. † **6.** Instrument, tool. *Obs.*

c **1450** HOLLAND *Howlat* xvi, He couth wryte wounder fair, With his neb for mistar.

III. Need, necessity.

† **7.** Need arising from the circumstances or facts of the case. ***mister is, (it) is mister***: it is necessary.

In the predicative use, the word becomes quasi-adj.

a **1300** *Cursor M.* 24810 O siluer and gold giftes to bede, Mar þan mister es to rede. *Ibid.* 28377, I ha ben mare Grenand and greueand þan mister ware. *c* **1320** *Sir Tristr.* 1388 In his schip was boun Al þat mister ware. **1340** HAMPOLE *Pr. Consc.* 7373 Helle..es..swa wyde and large, þat it moght kepe Alle þe creatures..Of alle þe world if myster ware. *c* **1350** *Will. Palerne* 1919 Mete & al maner þing þat him mister neded. *c* **1400** *Song Roland* 321 And we may son help yf me þink myster. *c* **1400** *Destr. Troy* 11815 Þat mys to amend, is maistur ye go To the corse of þat kyng in his cleane towmbe. *c* **1440** *York Myst.* viii. 52 Me liste do no daies dede, Bot yf gret mystir me garte. *c* **1450** *Erle Tolous* 434 Hyt was no mystur them to bydd. **1470–85** MALORY *Arthur* I. xv. 57, I wylle encountre with kynge bors and ye wil rescowe me whan myster is. **1543** *Aberdeen Reg.* (1844) I. 191 That the portis be mendytt and lokit and reformit as mister is. **1556** LAUDER *Tractate* 490 Be wer..And mend, geue ony myster be. **1600** in Pitcairn *Crim. Trials* (Bannatyne Cl.) II. 286 Hald me excused for my vnsemly Letter, qhilk is nocht sa veil vrettin as mister ver.

† **8.** A condition in which help is needed, or there is a lack of some necessary thing; a state of difficulty or distress; *esp.* a state of destitution, lack of means. Phr. ***in*** or ***at*** (***one's***) ***mister***. Rarely *pl.* = necessitous circumstances. In later use *Sc.*

a **1300** *Cursor M.* 803 Þai cled þam þan in þat mister Wit leues brad bath o figer. *Ibid.* 10134 For-þi rede i þaim þat yee here þat mai yow help at [*other texts* in] your mistere. *c* **1375** *Sc. Leg. Saints* I. (*Katerine*) 248 Gret mystere gert me assemble ȝou & call. *a* **1400–50** *Alexander* 1774 For mestire & miserie vnneth may þou forthe þine awen caitefe cors to clethe & to fede. **1487** *How Good Wife Taught Dau.* 288 Sic mysteris haldis madynnis in, That thai ar pynit with pouerte. **1549–50** *Extracts Burgh Recs. Stirling* (1887) 58 Neid and mister compellit hir to sell the saidis warklumes to sustene hir. **1570** BUCHANAN *Admon.* (S.T.S.) 25 Saying yat yai had enterit yame in dangeare and not supportit in mister. **1641** FERGUSON *Prov.* (1785) 24 Mister makes man of craft. **1768** ROSS *Helenore* I. 27 To come alang sweer was she to intreat, An' yet I kend her mister to be great.

† **b.** ***to have mister***: to be in straits or in necessity; to be in want of something. *Obs.*

a **1300** *Cursor M.* 19044 At þair gain come mete þai gaue, Ilkan þat þai sagh mister haue. **1375** BARBOUR *Bruce* XVII. 743 Till releif thame that had mister. **1432** *Test. Ebor.* (Surtees) II. 22 A rough felt..to be in kepyng of Agnes Weston..to lay on yᵉ pore folke yᵗ hafe mystre in yᵉ winter. *c* **1489** CAXTON *Sonnes of Aymon* ix. 249 Socoure vs for the love of Ihesus, for we have well mystre. **1567** *Gude & Godlie B.* (S.T.S.) 97 Bot he will gif and len his gude at large, Till thame that myster hes.

† **9.** Need or want of something specified. Const. *of, to.* Chiefly in ***to have mister***. *Obs.*

a **1300** *Cursor M.* 3247 Wit tresur grette and riche ring, Suilk als maiden had of mister. *Ibid.* 4718 Was neuer mare mister o bred. *Ibid.* 28275, I..lette o þam þe lighter þat þai suld haue to me mister. *c* **1330** *Arth. & Merl.* 3428 (Kölbing), ȝou worþ to hem wel gret mister. *c* **1400**

MAUNDEV. (Roxb.) xxiv. 113 God hase na mister of mete ne drink. *c* **1475** *Partenay* 6253 Tho which had grett necessite, Both mister and ned vnto som goodnesse. *c* **1489** CAXTON *Sonnes of Aymon* vii. 180 Yf they have mystre of vs, Lete vs goo helpe & socoure theym. **1533** BELLENDEN *Livy* v. v. (S.T.S.) II. 160 þe ciete had grete myster of money, havand sa mony armyis to gif wagis to. **1603** *Philotus* xv, He is richt gude, Ane man of wealth and nobill blude, Bot hes mair mister of ane Hude. **1692** *Sc. Presbyt. Eloq.* (1738) 140 England, that stands muckle in mister of a Reformation.

†**b.** with ellipsis of prep. *Obs.*

a **1300** *Cursor M.* 20793 Disput, he sais, es na mister Bituix te wis in swilk a wer. *a* **1400** *Relig. Pieces fr. Thornton MS.* 24 Thurghe þese gyftes oure Lord Ihesu lerres man all þat he hase myster till þe lyfe þat es callid actyfe.

†**c.** with inf. *to have mister*: to need, require (to do something). *Obs.*

c **1325** *Metr. Hom.* 3 Laued men hauis mar mister, Godes word for to her, Than klerkes. **13..** *E.E. Allit. P.* B. 67, I haf ȝerned & ȝat ȝokkez of oxen, & for my hyȝez hem boȝt, to bowe haf I mester. *c* **1435** *Torr. Portugal* 583 To the mownteyne he toke the wey, To rest hyme alle that day, He had mystyrr to be kyllyd [= cooled]. **1549** *Compl. Scot.* v. 36 Ve haue mistir to be vigilant ande reddy, sen the terme of cristis cumming is schort.

†**10. a.** *pl.* Necessary articles, fittings, etc.; necessaries. *Obs.*

1413 *Pilgr. Sowle* IV. xxxvii. 134b, Alle tho mystres, whiche that apperteynen to the body without, as clothyng howsynge and defense ageyne dyuerse perylles. **1513** in *Acc. Ld. Treas. Scot.* (1902) IV. 481 Item for ½ᶜ Swetyn burdis to the said Lorence for misteris in the schippis. **1609** SKENE *Reg. Maj.* 29 (Stat. Rob. I) Reseruand to the tutours their reasonable misterres and necessare expenses.

b. Something needed or necessary. *rare.*

1829 SCOTT *Hrt. Midl.* xliv, Warld's gear was henceforward the least of her care, nor was it likely to be muckle her mister.

11. A matter or respect in which some necessity or want is felt; a case of need. *Sc.* in phr. with the vb. *to beet*: see BEET *v.* 3.

1508 DUNBAR *Tua mariit wemen* 128 He.. may nought beit worth a bene in bed of my mystirs. **1513** DOUGLAS *Æneis* I. viii. 105 To hew, and tak Tymmer to beit ayris and wther mysteris. *Ibid.* VI. i. 15. **1721** RAMSAY *Scribblers Lashed* 78 To please the sighing sisters, Who often beet them in their misters. **1823** HOGG in *Blackw. Mag.* Mar. 314 If twa or three hunder pounds can beet a mister for you in a strait, ye sanna want it.

mister (ˈmɪstə(r)), *sb.*² Also 6 **myster.** [See MASTER *sb.*¹ 22, note.]

1. a. Used as a title of courtesy prefixed to the surname or Christian name of a man (not entitled to be addressed as 'Sir' or 'Lord'), and to designations of office or occupation.

The word in mod. use may be best described as the oral equivalent of the written prefix MR. (q.v. in its alphabetical place). In writing, the unabbreviated form is now used only with more or less of jocular intention; in a passage like quot. 1854 in d, most persons would now write 'Mr.' (with inverted commas).

1551 *Acts Privy Council Eng.* (N.S.) III. 397 To suffer the ij Mysters Bassetes to have accesse and speake.. with theyre brother. **1706** in *Mem. Ripon* (Surtees) II. 302 My best hat which is at Mister Rigedale's in Ripon. **1786** MRS. A. M. BENNETT *Juvenile Indiscr.* II. 42 'Squire Franklin meant to do great things for Mister Dellmore. **1840** HOOD *Up Rhine* xvii, Mister Broker, is that 'ere your carpet-bag? **1853** R. S. SURTEES *Sponge's Sp. Tour* xliv, Spraggon took advantage of a dead silence to call up the table to *Mister* Sponge to take wine,.. and by-and-by Mister Sponge 'Mistered' Mr. Spraggon to return the compliment.

b. *transf.* and *jocular.*

1760–72 H. BROOKE *Fool of Qual.* (1809) I. p. vii, O Jupiter, some water, a little water! dear mister Jupiter, water, water, water! *a* **1806** H. K. WHITE *Descr. Summer's Eve*, The snare for Mister Fox is set.

c. The word 'mister' (Mr.) as a prefix or title.

1758 GOLDSM. *Mem. Protestant* (1895) II. 244, They never spoke to us without putting Mister to our Names. **1837** LYTTON *E. Maltrav.* 43 Stop, mon cher, don't call me Mister; we are to be friends. **1860** EMERSON *Cond. Life, Culture* Wks. (Bohn) II. 373 Mr. Pitt.. thought the title of *Mister* good against any king in Europe. **1888** BURGON *Lives 12 Gd. Men* I. 440 'Well, Mr. Burgon?'.. 'Mister at the end of 20 years!.. I wish you wouldn't call me Mister'.

d. One who is entitled to be addressed or spoken of only as *Mr.* ——.

1764 FOOTE *Mayor of G.* I. i, Has his majesty dubb'd me a Knight for you to make me a Mister? **1859** MACAULAY *Biog., Pitt* (1860) 182 Plain Mister himself he [Pitt] had made more lords than any three ministers that had preceded him. **1864** BURTON *Scot Abr.* I. ii. 98 Whether the Persian Mirza expresses a Prince or a mere Mister.

e. ***Mister Big, Mister Fixit***: see MR. 2 e; ***Mister Charlie***: see CHARLEY, CHARLIE 7.

2. a. As a form of address not followed by the name; = SIR (or less respectful than that title). Now only *vulgar.*

1760–72 H. BROOKE *Fool of Qual.* (1809) I. 31, I must.. tell you, Mister, that matters are much changed. **1782** MISS BURNEY *Cecilia* IX. iii. (1882) II. 322 Mrs. Belfield,.. running into the passage,.. angrily called out [to the chairmen], 'What do you do here, Misters?' **1834** HAWTHORNE *Twice-told T., Mr. Higginbotham's Catastrophe*, 'Good morning, mister', said Dominicus. **1862** LOWELL *Biglow P.* Ser. II. *The Courtin'*, Says he, 'I'd better call agin'; Says she, 'Think likely, Mister'. **1901** *Punch* 22 Jan. 65 Please Mister, when are we going to get through?

b. Colloq. shortening of ***Mister Mate*** (MATE *sb.*² 4 a). Freq. as vocative.

1909 F. H. SHAW *Daughter of Storm* xx. 177 'All right, sir,' said the second mate to Steadman... 'West by north,' said Steadman... 'I'll go and turn in, mister.' *a* **1966** C. S. FORESTER *Hornblower & Crisis* (1967) v. 40 The mate was marking up the traverse board. 'What's the course, Mister?' asked Hornblower. **1972** *Listener* 6 Jan. 18/3 The Captain.. addressed the Mate as William, except when he thought he was getting uppish, when he called him 'Mister'.

†**3.** A (horse's) rider. (= MASTER *sb.* 4.) *Obs.*

c **1620** in J. P. HORE *Hist. Newmarket* (1885) I. 360 The horse and mister yairof that first comes over the scoir at the said Walnuik of Paislaye.

†**mister** (ˈmɪstə(r)), *v.*¹ Chiefly *Sc. Obs.* Forms: as in MISTER *sb.*¹ Also *pa. t.* **mustrid, 6 mestoret, mistorit, mystart, mistert.** [f. MISTER *sb.*¹]

1. *impers.* To be necessary or needful. Const. inf. or clause, or absol.

1424 *Sc. Acts Jas. I* (1814) II. 7 Ande gif it misteris þat secular power be callyt þerto in suppowale and helping of halykirk. ?*c* **1500** *King & Barker* 99 in Hazl. *E.P.P.* (1864) I. 9 The hors prekyd, as he was wode, Het mestoret to spor hem not. *c* **1500** *Melusine* 222 Yf it mystier, we shal guyde & lede you.. thrughe all the passages. **1583** *Leg. Bp. St. Androis* 884 Ten pund Stirveling I have heir, And mair, when misteris, you command. **1590** SPENSER *F.Q.* III. vii. 51 As for my name, it mistreth not to tell.

b. ***what misters*** (a person to do something): what need is there for him to, why need he? Also ***what misters*** (a thing)? What need is there for it?

c **1440** *York Myst.* vii. 54 What mystris þe, in gode or ille, of me to melle þe? **1490** CAXTON *Eneydos* xvi. 62 What mystreth hym to edyfie cartage? **1581** in *Cath. Tractates* (S.T.S.) 77 Quhat misterit men in this eage seik out ane neu interpretation? **1590** R. BRUCE *Serm.* (1843) 17 Quhat misterd us to have a sign? **1603** *Philotus* cxxvi, Gude-man, quhat misteris all this mowis? **1715** A. PENNECUICK *Poems* 17 What misters me for to express, My present Poverty.

2. Of things: To be necessary, needful, or requisite. Const. dat. of person.

1375 BARBOUR *Bruce* XVII. 215 And alkynd othir apparaill That mycht availl, or ȝeit mysteir Till hald castell. *a* **1400–50** *Alexander* 4281 Vs mistris neuire na medcyne for malidy on erthe. **1412** *Catterick Ch. Contract* (Raine 1834) 8 All the stuffe of the stane that misters more for the makyng of the Kirke of Katrik. *c* **1450** *Merlin* 22 Blase sought all that hym mystered to write with. *a* **1530** HEYWOOD *Weather* (Brandl) 314 At all tymys when suche thynges shall myster.

3. *trans.* To have need of, require.

1456 SIR G. HAYE *Law Arms* (S.T.S.) 268 Gif me think I mister ma, I sall have leve to produce ma. *c* **1460** *Towneley Myst.* xii. 231 We myster no sponys here, at oure mangyng. *c* **1470** HENRY *Wallace* III. 212 Harnes and hors, quhilk thai mysteryt in wer. **1513** DOUGLAS *Æneis* XII. ii. 117 Now is the tyme that I maste mister the. **1533** GAU *Richt Vay* (1888) 62 Thay quhilk ar hail thay mister notht ane lech. **1596** DALRYMPLE tr. *Leslie's Hist. Scot.* I. 125 For surelie, we mister na Magistrat. **1722** RAMSAY *Three Bonnets* IV. 146 Counting what things he now did mister.

absol. **1438** *Bk. Alexander Gt.* (Bannatyne Cl.) 2 And gif thay mister, to mak rescours. **1572** *Act 31* Mar. in *Peebles Burgh Rec.* (1872) 337 Quhair superabundance of stanis is to help vtheris thairwith that mistaris.

4. *intr.* To find it necessary *to do* something. Also with ellipsis of inf.

c **1440** *Alphabet of Tales* 6, I sall so ordand at þou sall nott myster to be a thief no mor. **1540** J. HEYWOOD *Four P.P.* 175 (Manly) That way, perchaunce, ye shall nat myster To go to heuen without a glyster! *a* **1578** LINDESAY (Pitscottie) *Chron. Scot.* (S.T.S.) I. 20 Na man misterit to tak feir of the Erle of Douglas. **1585** MONTGOMERIE *Cherrie & Slae* 805 First quhen he mistert not, he micht, He neids, and may not now.

5. To have need (*of*). Also pass. ***to be mistered of***: to have lost, feel the loss of.

c **1470** HENRY *Wallace* I. 361 Bot blynd he was.. Throuch hurt of waynys, and mystyrit of blud. **1484** CAXTON *Fables of Æsop* III. xvii, Gyue thou not that thynge of whiche thow hast nede of to the ende that afterward thow myster not of hit. *c* **1500** *Melusine* 219 He.. proffred to them his seruyse, yf they myster of it. **1552** ABP. HAMILTON *Catech.* 59 To be distrubit to thaim self sa far as thai myster to thair honest sustentatioun. *a* **1572** KNOX *Hist. Ref.* III. Wks. (Wodrow Soc.) II. 81 It mycht chance that the Kyng mycht mister of his greit gunis and artailyerie in France.

6. To be of advantage or service.

c **1489** CAXTON *Sonnes of Aymon* iv. 129 Lady moder, gramercy of so fayre a yefte as here is, For it mystreth me well. *Ibid.* vi. 141.

ˈ**mister,** *v.*² [f. MISTER *sb.*²] *trans.* To address or speak of by the title of 'Mr.'

1742 FIELDING *J. Andrews* IV. ii, 'Pray, don't mister such fellows to me', cries the Lady. **1817** HAZLITT *Pol. Ess.* (1819) 213 He would not have been content.. with Mistering his opponent, and Esquiring himself. **1830** MISS MITFORD *Village* Ser. v. (1863) 338 Mr. Warde—pshaw! he is too eminent a man to be mistered! John Warde, the celebrated fox-hunter. **1838** DICKENS *O. Twist* xiii, 'None of your mistering', replied the ruffian; 'you always mean mischief when you come that'. **1892** T. HARDY *Tess* xxvii, Darling Tessy!.. Don't, for Heaven's sake, Mister me any more.

†ˈ**misterful,** *a. Sc. Obs.* [f. MISTER *sb.*¹ + -FUL.]

1. Needy, necessitous.

c **1375** *Sc. Leg. Saints* xliv. (*Lucy*) 128 To helpe pure men & fede, & visit mysterful in ned. **1513** DOUGLAS *Æneis* I. xvi. 136 Vnkend and misterful in desertis of Libie I wandir. **1517** *Burgh Recs. Edinb.* (1869) I. 170 The reparatioun, beylding and vphalding of the licht of any misterfull alter. **1584** *Reg. Privy Council Scot.* Ser. I. III. 695 For.. sustentatioun of the puir people infectit and misterfull. **1670** RAY *Prov.* 287 Misterfull folk mon not be mensfull.

2. Needful, necessary.

a **1450** *Ratis Raving* I. 977 Thane Is it misterfull to the Till have thai placis veil in thocht.

misteri, obs. form of MYSTERY.

mis'term, *v.* [MIS-¹ 1.] *trans.* To term incorrectly; to apply a wrong term or name to.

1579 E. K. *Gloss. Spenser's Sheph. Cal.* Apr. 144 Flowre delice, that which they vse to misterme, Flowre de luce. **1592** SHAKS. *Rom. & Jul.* III. iii. 21. **1599** THYNNE *Animadv.* (1875) 28 The woorke, before this last editione of Chaucer termed 'the Dreame of Chaucer', is mystermed. **1623** MIDDLETON & ROWLEY *Sp. Gipsy* v. i, I am none of ought Your rage misterms me. **1822** *Liberal* I. 342 The factitious modes of society, which form what is mis-termed 'its well being'. **1891** L. MERRICK *Violet Moses* III. xxiii. 189 There are unions mistermed 'guilty'.

Hence **mis'termed** *ppl. a.*, **mis'terming** *vbl. sb.* and *ppl. a.*

1589 NASHE *Anat. Absurd.* C j b, [His] bald affected eloquence,.. better beseeming.. a misterming Clowne in a Comedy, then a chosen man in the Ministerie. **1593** NORDEN *Spec. Brit., M'sex* I. 8 Holding the smallest errour (yea the misterming of the place) verie criminous. **1597** [see MISTAKEN *ppl. a.* 1]. **1706** PHILLIPS (ed. Kersey), *Misnomer*, .. a misterming or miscalling.

†ˈ**misterous,** *a. Obs.* In 5 **mysterus.** [f. MISTER *sb.*¹ + -OUS.] Needy.

14.. *Langland's P. Pl.* C. III. 78 (*MS. F., northern*) þese mysterus men þat after mede wayten.

mistership, corruption of MISTRESS-SHIP.

1588 SHAKS. *Tit. A.* IV. iv. 40 How now good fellow, would'st thou speake with vs? *Clow.* Yea forsoouth, and your Mistership be Emperiall.

mistetch (mɪsˈtɛtʃ), *sb. north. dial.* Also **-tech.** [f. MIS-¹ 4 + TETCH *sb.*] A bad habit.

c **1450** *St. Cuthbert* (Surtees) 1226 We.. þat for our slepyng and mysteches, With goddis seruande we lete to wake. **1828** *Craven Gloss.*, *Mistetch*, a bad instruction, a misteaching. 'Toud mear hes gitten a sad mistetch'. **1847** HALLIWELL, *Mistech*, a bad habit. *North.*

mistetch (mɪsˈtɛtʃ), *v. north. dial.* [app. an alteration of MISTEACH after prec. sb.] *trans.* To teach bad habits to; to train badly.

1529 MORE *Dyaloge* III. xiii. Wks. 229/2 Because he that had mistetched his wife and his children, were vnmete for a great cure. **1683** G. MERITON *Yorksh. Dial.* 2 Thou macks sike Anters, Thou'l mistetch my Cow. **1828** *Craven Gloss.*, *Mistetch*, to teach bad tricks or habits, to give bad instructions. **1876** *Mid-Yorksh. Gloss.*, *Mistetch*, mistrain, or misteach.

mistetched (mɪsˈtɛtʃt), *ppl. a. north. dial.* [f. prec. sb. or vb.] Badly trained; of bad habits: commonly applied to a vicious horse.

1691 RAY *N.C. Words* (ed. 2) 49 *Mistetcht*; that hath got an ill habit, Property or Custom. A Mistecht Horse. **1787** MARSHALL *Rur. Econ. E. Yorksh.* (E.D.S.) 33 *Misteached* (pron. *mistech't*), *pp.* spoiled by improper treatment; vicious, as a horse. **1829** BROCKETT *N.C. Gloss.* (ed. 2), *Mistetched*, spoiled—said of a horse that has learnt vicious tricks. **1893** *Northumbld. Gloss.*, *Mistached, mistetched*... 'A dangerous horse is termed mistached'. **1900** *Darlington Horse Shoers' Assoc. Price List*, Cramped or Mis-stetched Horses.

mistful (ˈmɪstfʊl), *a.* [f. MIST *sb.*¹ + -FUL.] Full of mist; obscured with or as if with mist.

1599 SHAKS. *Hen. V*, IV. vi. 34, I must perforce compound With mistfull [*printed* mixtfull] eyes. **187.** W. A. SCOTT in W. H. Rankine *Hero of Dark Cont.* (1896) 25 We've seen the mistful mountains on the lone Glenshee. **1893** *Westm. Gaz.* 31 Jan. 9/2 Morns rise mistful.

†**mis'thank,** *v. Obs.* [MIS-¹ 7.] *trans.* To show resentment at.

1591 SYLVESTER *Du Bartas* I. v. (1621) 100 The Dolphin, beating 'gainst the bank 'Gan mine oblivion moodily misthank [orig. *pour taxer mon oubly*].

†**mis'thew.** *Obs.* [MIS-¹ 4.] A bad habit.

c **1325** *Prov. Hendyng* 18 (Camb. MS.), Ne be þi childe neuir so dere And he wil misþewis [*other version* vnþewes] lere, Bete him oþir wile.

mis'think, *v.* [f. MIS-¹ 1 + THINK *v.*¹]

†**1.** *intr.* To have sinful thoughts. *Obs.*

a **1225** *Ancr. R.* 62 Ich habbe ivestned, seið Job, foreward mid min eien, þet ich ne misðenche. **1615** SYLVESTER *Job Triumph.* xxxi. 458, I made a Covenant with my constant eyes, From gazing out on blazing vanities:.. Why should I once mis-think upon a Maid?

2. To have mistaken thoughts; to think mistakenly (that..). Also **mis'thinking** *vbl. sb.*

a **1530** *Crt. of Love* 483 Women.. lightly set their plesire in a place; Whan they misthink, they lightly let it passe. **1599** B. JONSON *Cynthia's Rev.* IV. iii, There is the note; and all the parts if I mis-thinke not. **1609** F. GREVIL *Mustapha* II. ii, For ignorance begetteth cruelty, Misthinking each man, euery thing can be. *a* **1631** DONNE *Elegy on Mrs. Boulstred* Poems (1654) 256 There would have been Some that would sinne, mis-thinking she did sinne. **1674** N. FAIRFAX *Bulk & Selv.* 5 If I do not much mis-think. *a* **1871** DE MORGAN *Budget* (1872) 336 One.. who takes misthinking from points of view which none but a student of history can occupy.

3. *trans.* To think ill of; to have a bad or unfavourable opinion of. Also *intr.* const. *of*, in the same sense.

1593 SHAKS. *3 Hen. VI*, II. v. 108 How will the Country.. Mis-thinke the King, and not be satisfied? **1606** —— *Ant. & Cl.* v. ii. 176. *a* **1634** CHAPMAN *Alphonsus* II. (1654) 14, I hope your grace will not mis-think of me, Who for your good.. Bethought this means to set the world at Peace. **1843** LYTTON *Last Bar.* II. ii, When I am gone, my liege.. will not misthink me, will not listen to my foes.

4. With cognate obj.: To think bad thoughts.

a **1618** SYLVESTER *Panaretus* 1196 Wks. (Grosart) II. 134 Their People.. can suffer nought 'Gainst them to be mis-

done, mis-said, mis-thought. **1667** MILTON *P.L.* IX. 289 Thoughts, which how found they harbour in thy brest, Adam, missthought of her to thee so dear?

mis'thought. [MIS-¹ 4.] Erroneous thought or notion; mistaken opinion.
1596 SPENSER *F.Q.* IV. viii. 58 Error and misthought Of our like persons, eath to be disguiz'd. *c* **1843** CARLYLE *Hist. Sk.* (1898) 342 He had no soul..or his thought would not have been such a misthought.

misthrive (mɪsˈθraɪv), *v.* [MIS-¹ 7.] *intr.* To be unsuccessful; not to thrive. Hence **mis'thriven** *ppl. a.*, unsuccessful, unprosperous; **mis'thriving** *vbl. sb.*, failure.
1567 *Gude & Godlie B.* (S.T.S.) 187 And thocht thay fuffe at it, and blaw..The mair thay blaw..The mair it dois misthryue. **1599** JAS. I *Βασιλ. δωρον* (1682) 51 This oversight hath beene the greatest cause of my mis-thriving in money matters. **1609** A. CRAIG *Poet. Recr.* (1873) 5 Amongst so many children some must mis-thrive and proue naght. **1776** C. KEITH *Farmer's Ha'* vi, And ay till this mis thriven age, The gudeman here sat like a sage. **1844** *N. Brit. Rev.* II. 34 A starving, misthriven, and wretched population.

mis'throw, *v. rare.* [MIS-¹ 1.]
†**1.** *trans.* To cast (glances) with a wrong intent.
1390 GOWER *Conf.* I. 60 Hast thou thin yhen oght misthrowe?
2. To throw (a ball) badly.
1896 *Westm. Gaz.* 14 July 4/2 To fumble the ball or misthrow it.

†**mis'þunche,** *v. Obs.* [f. MIS-¹ 1 + *þünche*, OE. *þyncan* THINK *v.*²] *intr.* To seem wrong.
a **1225** *Leg. Kath.* 982 þet tu of þet þing þet te misþuncheð, underfest þe an half & dustest adun þe oðere.

mistic, -ical, obs. forms of MYSTIC, -ICAL.

mistice, obs. variant of MESTIZO.
1704 *Collect. Voy.* (Churchill) III. 709/2, 150 *Mistices* and Negroes. *Ibid.* 732/2.

‖**mistico** (ˈmɪstɪkəʊ). [Sp. = Cat. *mestech*, taken to be a. Arab. *misṭeḥ* (lit. flat surface) broad basket, large frying-pan, etc., f. *saṭaḥa* to flatten. In F. *mistic*, *mistique*: see also MYSTIC(K.)] A coasting vessel having two sails, used in the Mediterranean.
1801 *Naval Chron.* VI. 416 The Spanish mistico Jean Baptiste. **1841** J. ALLEN *Engl. Wooden Walls* xvi. in *United Service Jrnl.* Mar. 332 A well-directed fire was opened upon the misticoes from the frigate. **1886** *List of Ships Reported* Dec., Abbrev., *Mis.* Mistico.

†**mis'tide,** *sb. Obs.* [f. next.] A mishap.
c **1400** *Cursor M.* 23599 (Edin.) Na mistid [*other texts* mischiue, mistime] mai þaim bitid, For þai er traist on ilka side.

†**mis'tide,** *v. Obs.* [OE. *mistídan*: see MIS-¹ 1 and TIDE *v.*]
1. *intr.* To happen amiss or unfortunately. In OE. *impers.* to be a failure.
1027-34 *Laws of Cnut* (Liebermann) 348, & ȝif hit tihtle siȝ, & æt lade mistide, deme se bisceop. *a* **1250** *Owl & Night.* 1501 Þu myht wene þat þe myste hwanne þu lyst bi hire side. **1421-2** HOCCLEVE *Dial.* 644 Certes, for the deffaute of good forsighte, Mis-tyden thynges þat wel tyde mighte.
2. To have misfortune.
c **1386** CHAUCER *Melib.* ⁋730 He that hath over-hard an herte, atte laste he shal mishappe and mistyde.

mistier, obs. variant of MISTER.

mistify: see MYSTIFY *v.*¹, *v.*²

mistigris (ˈmɪstɪgrɪs). [ad. F. *mistigri* knave of spades, esp. when accompanied by two cards of the same colour at 'bouillotte' and 'brelan'.] The name of the blank card in a variety of draw poker; hence, the game in which it is used.
1882 *Poker* 76 Mistigris. This is a variety of the game of Draw Poker, sometimes called Fifty-Three Deck Poker. Mistigris is a name given to the blank card accompanying every pack. **1895** *Poker Manual* 17 The Joker is sometimes called Mistigris.

†'**mistihede.** *Obs.* [f. MISTY *a.*¹ and *a.*² + *-hede*, -HEAD.] **a.** Mistiness, obscurity. **b.** Mystical significance.
c **1374** CHAUCER *Compl. Mars* 224 What meneth this? what is this mistihede? *a* **1400** HYLTON *Scala Perf.* (W. de W. 1494) II. xliii, By mystyhed it is illumyned for to see þe werkes of Jhesu in holy chirche. *c* **1413** LYDG. *Goodly Ballad* 33 Misty cloudes, that wolde overlede Trewe humble hertes with hir mistihede.

mistik, mistilto, obs. ff. MYSTIC, MISTLETOE.

mistily (ˈmɪstɪlɪ), *adv.* Also 4 **mystiliche, mistili,** 4-5 **mistely,** etc. [f. MISTY *a.*¹ + -LY².] In a misty manner; in early quots. *fig.*
With the first quot. cf. MISTY *a.*²
1340 HAMPOLE *Pr. Consc.* 4364 In þe appocalipse apparty Es sayd þus ful mistyly [etc.]. **138.** WYCLIF *Serm.* Sel. Wks. I. 149 þat þes þingis he seide bifore to hem in proverbis and mystily. *c* **1386** CHAUCER *Can. Yeom. T.* 841 Philosophres speken so mistily In this craft, that men can nat come therby. *c* **1450** *Merlin* 54 Than began Merlin to speke so mystily wher-of the boke of prophesyes is made. **1494** FABYAN *Chron.* VII. ccxlv. (1533) 173/1 Yt ys..so darkely or mystly wryten, that the reader therof shall hardely come to yᵉ knowlege of the trouthe. *a* **1633** AUSTIN *Medit.* (1635) 90 These Men having gazed long at the Starre above doe as Mistyly behold the Wise-men below. **1813** *Examiner* 31 May 348/1 The mistily seen objects behind. **1864** LOWELL *Fireside Trav.* 278 It began to rain, first mistily, and then in thick, hard drops. **1874** LISLE CARR *Jud. Gwynne* I. iv. 122 A semi-unconscious and mistily vague hope. **1897** *Cent. Mag.* Feb. 556/1 The distant palms rose mistily into the genial air.

†**mis'time,** *sb. Obs.* [f. next.] Mishap.
a **1300** *Cursor M.* 27768 In mining of his mistime He wites wend [*read* werd] and waris his time. **13..** *Ibid.* 20050 (Gött.) Womman sal noght peris of barn, Ne nane wid mistime [*Cott.* mischiue] be forfarn.

mistime (mɪsˈtaɪm), *v.* [OE. *mistímian*: see MIS-¹ 1 and TIME *v.*]
†**1.** *intr.* **a.** Of the event: To happen amiss. Const. dat. **b.** Of the person: To come to grief, suffer misfortune. *Obs.*
c **1000** tr. *Basil's Admon.* v. (1849) 44 ȝif him hwæt mistimaþ besarga his unrotnysse. *a* **1225** *Ancr. R.* 200 Lauhwen oðer gabben, ȝif him mis-bieuolle [*MS. T.* mis-times]. **1401** *Pol. Poems* (Rolls) II. 58 Litil wondir thowȝ lordis myssetyme, that han suche confusours. *c* **1420** in *Lay Folks Mass Bk.* 84/38 Lat neuer my saul on domesday mystime.
2. Not to time properly: **a.** to do or perform at a wrong time; to say or do (something) out of season; **b.** to miscalculate or mis-state the time of. Also *absol.*
1390 GOWER *Conf.* I. 49, I prai the let me noght mistime Mi schrifte. *Ibid.* III. 281 So hath such love his lust mistimed. ? *a* **1500** in Grose, etc. *Antiq. Rep.* (1809) IV. 405 The sownde of a trew songe makithe the trew concorde, But subtill prickynge mystymthe and causith grete discorde. *a* **1661** FULLER *Worthies, Monmouthshire* (1662) 53 If he is guilty in Mis-timing of his Actions, he is not the onely Historian without company in that particular. **1664** H. MORE *Myst. Iniq.* II. II. iii, As Grotius has mis-timed these Visions, so his Interpretations are accordingly absurd. **1673** SHAFTESB. *Parl. Sp.* in *Coll. Poems* 239 He desires you not to mistime it: but that it may have only the second place. **1706** *Reflex. upon Ridicule* 307 Actions mistim'd lose their value. **1752** CHESTERF. *Lett.* III. cclxxv. 259 [He] mis-times, mis-places, runs precipitately..at the mark. **1858** DORAN *Court Fools* 143 Rowley's chronicle drama abounds in anachronisms. The probable facts..are only mistimed. **1896** *Daily News* 14 July 4/6 [He] mis-timed a ball..and was out leg before wicket.

mistimed (mɪsˈtaɪmd), *ppl. a.* [MIS-¹ 2.]
†**1.** Unfortunate. *Obs.*
c **1470** HENRY *Wallace* VIII. 1212 The ost..prayit God..Him to conwoy fra all mystymyt cace.
2. Ill-timed, unseasonable, out of place.
1687 R. L'ESTRANGE *Answ. to Dissenter* 40 That's a little Uncharitable, and Miss-timed. *c* **1710** KILLINGBECK *Serm.* (1717) 63 A hasty and unguarded Expression, an incautious and mistimed Reproof. **1742** YOUNG *Nt. Th.* VIII. 792 There is a time, when toil must be preferr'd, Or joy, by mis-tim'd fondness, is undone. **1820** SCOTT *Abbot* iii, We do not recover composure by the more feeling that agitation is mistimed. **1887** *Spectator* 2 July 882/1 Proposals for reunion amongst Liberals would be absolutely mistimed.
3. Disturbed in one's habits, esp. with respect to eating and sleeping. *dial.*
1841 R. W. HAMILTON *Nugae Lit.* 356 'He has not slept for the last three nights. No wonder he is ill; he is quite mistimed'. His regular hours are interrupted. **1868** ATKINSON *Cleveland Gloss.*, *Mistimed*, subjected to irregularity as regards seasons of refreshment, especially sleep.

†**mis'timely,** *a.* (or *adv.*) *Obs.* [MIS-¹ 6.] Unseasonable (or unseasonably).
c **1680** BEVERIDGE *Serm.* (1729) II. 536 So careful should we be..of speaking any thing mis-timely.

mis'timing, *vbl. sb.* [MIS-¹ 3.] The action of the verb MISTIME.
1. a. Doing a thing at a wrong time. **b.** Miscalculation of the time of an event, etc.
1581 MULCASTER *Positions* xvi. (1887) 73 The rule of health condemnes not daunsing, but the mistyming of it. **1649** JER. TAYLOR *Gt. Exemp.* III. Disc. xiv. 11 He endures affronts, mistimings, tedious waytings. **1664** H. MORE *Myst. Iniq.* 448 The same falling out here that has in his other mistimings of Prophecy. **1693** J. EDWARDS *Author. O. & N. Test.* 152 There was no great mis-timing of the story. **1765** ELLWOOD *Autobiog.* (ed. 3) 301 If..there was any mistiming in the Case it must lie on the Part of those Plotters for timing the breaking forth of their Plot. **1873** MAXWELL *Electr. & Magn.* II. §751 The error arising from a mistiming of the current.
2. *dial.* Disturbance of regular habits.
1844 W. CROSS *Disruption* xxxii. (E.D.D.), This illness maun have maid him less fit to thole ony mistiming either of meat or sleep.

mistiness (ˈmɪstɪnɪs). [f. MISTY *a.*¹ + -NESS.] A condition of being misty; dimness, obscurity; also *concr.* or semi-*concr.* = vapour, haze, mist. Said of the atmosphere and of the eyes or sight.
1382 WYCLIF *Deut.* iv. 11 There weren in it [Sinai] derknessis, and clowde, and mystynes [Vulg. *caligo*]. **1561** T. NORTON *Calvin's Inst.* I. 89 A heavisome mistinesse is cast before our eyes. **1583** GOLDING *Calvin on Deut.* xxii. 130 God..did set a Cloude darkenesse and mistinesse before him. **1626** BACON *Sylva* §91 The Mistinesse scattereth and breaketh up suddenly. **1656** JEANES *Mixt. Schol. Div.* 38 The cloudinesse, and mistinesse of the aire. **1748** RICHARDSON *Clarissa* (1811) I. 355 Mistinesses, which give to my deluged eye the appearance of all the colours in the rainbow. **1838** JAMES *Robber* iii, The mistiness of the mid-day sunshine. **1863** MISS BRADDON *Eleanor's Victory* i, The red August sunset was melting into grey mistiness. **1878** T. BRYANT *Pract. Surg.* I. 306 The..extent of the mistiness or obscurity is governed by the..extent of the impaired portion of retina.
b. of language and thought.
[**1577** tr. *Bullinger's Decades* (1592) 24 The holy Prophets of God..did not call the worde of God darkeness, obscurenesse, or mistinesse.] **1816** J. GILCHRIST *Philos. Etym.* 40 If he makes use of a little metaphysical mistiness. **1836** E. HOWARD *R. Reefer* xx, I cannot even shelter myself under the mistiness of the peremptory *we.* **1898** *Pall Mall Mag.* Feb. 250 In the mistiness of waking thought.

misting (ˈmɪstɪŋ), *vbl. sb.* [f. MIST *sb.*¹ or *v.*¹ + -ING¹.] **1.** Mist.
1686 GOAD *Celest. Bodies* I. xiii. 70 Great fog m. misting and misling 7 p. **1713** DERHAM *Phys.-Theol.* I. iii. 20 If the Vapours..soon meet the Cold, they are then Condensed into Misting. **1905** *Westm. Gaz.* 8 July 2/2 Arriving in an Irish 'misting', drenched to the skin.
2. ***misting-up***, the act of obscuring as with mist, the process of becoming thus obscured; also *concr.*
1964 B. GASTON *Drifting Death* ii. 22, I rinsed out the face mask against misting-up. **1966** T. WISDOM *High-Performance Driving* x. 108 A film of dirt or misting up on the inside [of the windscreen] can make the fog seem twice as thick as it is in reality. **1969** *Listener* 6 Feb. 161/1 There were no major hitches during the flight, and only a few minor ones, such as the misting-up of windows.

misting (ˈmɪstɪŋ), *ppl. a.* [-ING².] Misty.
1772 *Gentl. Mag.* 394 Oct. 22, misting morning, cloudy afternoon.

†'**mistion.** *Obs.* [ad. L. *mistiōn-em*, f. *mist-*, ppl. stem of *miscēre* to mix. (Cf. MIXTION.)] Mixtion, mixture.
1612 WOODALL *Surg. Mate* Wks. (1653) 272 Mistion is such a composition of bodies, as inceration, incorporation, colliquation, and contusion do declare. **1646** SIR T. BROWNE *Pseud. Ep.* III. x. 128 In animals..many actions are mixt, and depend upon their living forme, as well as that of mistion. **1680** BOYLE *Scept. Chem.* II. 146 To evince that Nature makes other Mistions than such as I have allowed.

mistir, obs. variant of MISTER *sb.*¹

†**mis'tithe,** *v. Obs.* Also *pa. pple.* 3 **misiteoðeget,** 4 **mys-i-teyþed.** [MIS-¹ 1.] **a.** *intr.* To be dishonest in paying tithes. **b.** *trans.* To pay tithes wrongly upon.
a **1225** *Ancr. R.* 208 Mis-iteoðeget [*v.r.* tiheðe mis, teouðen mis], etholden cwide, oðer fundles, oðer lone. *c* **1380** WYCLIF *Sel. Wks.* III. 309 Alle þo þat mystiþen ony goodis ben cruely cursed. *a* **1450** MYRC 950 Hast þou wyth-holden any teyþynge, Or mys-I-teyþed?

mistitle (mɪsˈtaɪt(ə)l). *v.* [MIS-¹ 1.] *trans.* To give a wrong title or name to. Also **mis'titled** *ppl. a.*
1618 WITHER *Motto, Nec careo* Juvenilia (1633) 533 A bashfulnesse, which some mis-title, feare. **1670** MILTON *Hist. Eng.* IV. Wks. 1851 III. 141 Keaulin whom he mistitles King of East-Saxons. **1740** NORTH (*title*) Examen of an Historical Libel, mistitled A Compleat History of England. **1812** COMBE *Syntax, Picturesque* xxi, Who then will venture to declare That man's mistitled sorrow's heir? **1816** 'QUIZ' *Grand Master* VII. 187 That all he got, mis-titled pay, Kept him in constant poverty.

mistle, obs. form of MISSEL, MIZZLE.

mistless (ˈmɪstlɪs), *a.* [f. MIST *sb.*¹ + -LESS.] Free from mist.
1853 C. BRONTE *Villette* I. xiv. 270 How soft are the nights of the continent!..No sea-fog..; mistless as noon, and fresh as morning. **1884** *Edin. Rev.* 479 An unclouded and mistless sky.

mistletoe (ˈmɪz(ə)ltəʊ, ˈmɪs(ə)ltəʊ). Forms: *α.* 1 **mistiltán,** 5 **mistilto,** 6 **myscelto, -towe, miscelto, mysteltew, misteltow, -tewe, -dew, misletoa, muscelto,** 6-7 **miselto,** 6-8 **misselto,** 7 **misceltow, messelto,** 7-9 **misseltoe, mis(s)letoe,** 8-9 **miseltoe, mistleto,** 9 **-tow,** 7- **mistletoe.** *β.* 6 **mysceltyne, misceldin, misselden,** 6-7 **mis(c)elden,** 7 **misseldin(e, mistleden, meseldine,** 8 **misleden.** *γ.* 6 **mislen,** 7 **misleen.** 9 *dial.* **mislin.** [OE. *mistiltán* (= ON. *mistilteinn*, Sw., Da. *mistleten*), f. *mistil*, *-el* (see MISSEL) + *tán* twig.
The normal development (with obscuration of the final syllable) of OE. *mistiltán* is represented by the *β*-forms, of which the disyllabic *γ*-forms appear to be merely contractions. The *α*-forms, to which the current form belongs, descend from another type having secondary stress on the final syllable, which app. underwent the same development as the uncompounded word *tán* (str. masc.), from which *tá* (wk. fem.) was evolved in late WS.]
1. a. A parasitic plant of Europe, *Viscum album* (N.O. *Loranthaceæ*), growing on various trees (in Britain, frequently on the apple-tree, rarely on the oak) and bearing a glutinous fruit, from which a birdlime is prepared.
This plant was held in veneration by the Druids, esp. when found growing on the oak. It is still used in England in Christmas decorations, a bunch of it being commonly hung from the ceiling of a room or hall: see also quot. 1820.
a. *c* **1000** ÆLFRIC *Gloss.* in Wr.-Wülcker 136/11 *Uiscerago*, mistiltan. **1548** TURNER *Names Herbes* (E.D.S.) 89 Muscelto. *c* **1550** LLOYD *Treas. Health* C vij b, Mysceltowe layd to the head draweth out the corrupt humores. **1558** PHAER *Æneid* VI. P4b *marg.*, Mysteltew callyd of some misteldew growyng on trees in winter with a yelowe shiny bery. **1588** SHAKS. *Tit. A.* II. iii. 95 The Trees..Ore-come

with Mosse, and baleful Misselto. **1599** A. M. tr. *Gabelhouer's Bk. Physicke* 24/1 Take Misletoa of Hasellnuttree..Misletoa of Oackes, of Pearetree. **1663** BOYLE *Usef. Exp. Nat. Philos.* II. v. vii. 185 A young Lady ..was cured onely by the powder of true misseltoe of the oake. **1716** GAY *Trivia* II. 41 Now with bright Holly all your Temples strow, With Laurel green, and sacred Misletoe. **1768** TUCKER *Lt. Nat.* II. 371 It is thought the misletoe would be lost out of nature, if it were not continually propagated from tree to tree by the thrush. **1820** W. IRVING *Sketch Bk., Christmas Eve* (1821) III. 32 *note*, The mistletoe is still hung up in farm-houses and kitchens at Christmas; and the young men have the privilege of kissing the girls under it, plucking each time a berry from the bush. When the berries are all plucked the privilege ceases. **1866** *Treas. Bot.* 1221/1 The mistleto of the oak had such repute for 'helping' in the diseases incidental to infirmity and old age, that it was called *Lignum Sanctæ Crucis*, Wood of the Holy Cross. **1885** *Encycl. Brit.* XVIII. 265/2 The mistletoe grows on a large number of different trees, such as the apple, lime, elm, maple, willow, thorn, poplar, and even on conifers.

β. **1538** TURNER *Libellus*, *Viscum*, angli uocant Mysceltyne, aut Myscelto. **1548** —— *Names Herbes* (E.D.S.) 80 Viscum is called..in english Miscelto or Misceldin. **1590** GREENE *Never too late* (1600) 89 None comes neere the fume of the Misselden but he waxeth blinde. **1611** COTGR., *Visc*, Missell, Misseltoe, Misseldine. **1656** BLOUNT *Glossogr.*, Messelto, Meseldine, or *Mistelden* [ed. 1661 *Misselden*]. [And in later Dicts.]

γ. **1562** BULLEIN *Bulw. Def., Bk. Simples* (1579) 50b *marg.*, Misseltow or Mislen. *Ibid.* 50b, This mislen groweth ..vpon the tree through the dounge of byrdes. **1680** T. LAWSON *Mite into Treas.* 50 The Druides had Oak-Trees in great estimation; they worshipped the Misleen that grows thereon. *a* **1825** FORBY *Voc. E. Anglia* (1830), *Mislin-bush.*

b. Applied to other species of *Viscum* and other genera of N.O. *Loranthaceæ*.

American or ***false mistletoe***, *Phoradendron* (*Viscum*) *flavescens*. ***West Indian mistletoe***, *Loranthus*, *Phoradendron*, and *Arceuthobium* (Treas. Bot.).

1597 GERARDE *Herbal* III. xxxv. 1168, 2 *Viscum Indicum L'Obelij*, Indian Misseltoe. 3 *Viscum Peruuianum L'Obelij*, Misseltoe of Peru. **1806** LEWIS & CLARK in *Deb. Congress U.S.* (1852) 9th Congress 2 Sess. App. 1142 Mistletoe, thistle, wild hemp, bulrush. **1819** E. EVANS *Pedestrious Tour* 318 In this..country [*sc.* Louisiana] grows the celebrated plant called mistletoe. **1838** J. HALL *Notes on Western States* ii. 28 The mistletoe is seen hanging from the branches of the trees throughout the whole course of the Ohio. **1845–50** MRS. LINCOLN *Lect. Bot.* 186 *Viscum verticillatum* (mistletoe). **1847–60** DARLINGTON *Amer. Weeds & Pl.* 287 *Phoradendron,..P. flavescens*..Mistletoe. False Mistletoe. **1860** GRAY *Man. Bot.* 383 *P. flavescens*..(American Mistletoe).

†**2.** Basil; = MISSEL 2. *Obs.*

a **1400** *Stockholm Med. MS.* 211 Mistilto, *osinun*.

3. *attrib.* and *Comb.*, as ***mistletoe berry***, ***birdlime***, ***bough***, ***plant***, ***seed***, ***tree***; **mistletoe bird** *Austral.*, a small black, white, and crimson bird, *Dicæum hirundinaceum*, which feeds on nectar, pollen, and berries; **mistletoe cactus**, a tropical American epiphytic cactus of the genus *Rhipsalis*, esp. *R. cassytha* and other species bearing white fruits resembling those of mistletoe; **mistletoe thrush**, the missel-thrush, *Turdus viscivorus*.

1626 BACON *Sylva* §556 It may be, that Bird feedeth upon the *Misseltoe-Berries and so is often found there. **1908** E. J. BANFIELD *Confessions of Beachcomber* I. iii. 96 Flower-pecker or *Mistletoe Bird. **1944** A. RUSSELL *Bush Ways* iii. 19 Already there is a mistletoe-bird, with crimson breast, swaying itself on a mistletoe twig. **1965** *Austral. Encycl.* VI. 104/2 Mistletoe-bird, a small arboreal bird (*Dicaeum hirundinaceum*), the only representative in Australia of a group found throughout southern Asia..and belonging to a family known as flower-peckers. **1597** GERARDE *Herbal* III. xxxv. 1170 It can no where be read that *Chamæleon niger* doth beare *Misseltoe birdlime. *a* **1839** T. H. BAYLY (*title of poem*), The *Mistletoe Bough. [**1850** J. MACFADYEN *Flora Jamaica* II. 182 Rhipsalis... Pseudo-parasitic plants, growing on trees, leafless, with small flowers, and with berries white, resembling those of the mistletoe.] **1889** W. WATSON *Cactus Culture for Amateurs* 227 They [*sc.* the flowers]..are succeeded by white berries, exactly like those of the Mistletoe, whence the name *Mistletoe Cactus, by which this species [sc. *Rhipsalis cassytha*] is known. **1967** ELBERT & HYAMS *House Plants* xi. 102 *R*[*hipsalis*] *cassytha*, the Mistletoe Cactus, is a hanging mass of succulent branches dripping with white berries. **1753** CHAMBERS *Cycl. Supp.* s.v., The branches of trees full of *Misletoe plants. *Ibid.*, The radicle of a *Misletoe seed. **1719** SIR J. COLBATCH *Diss. conc. Mistletoe* 7 A Bird generally known by the Name of the *Misletoe Thrush; which Name, I suppose, it derives from its feeding upon Misletoe-Berries. **1828** J. FLEMING *Hist. Brit. Anim.* 64 Throstle Cock, Shrite,..Misselto Thrush. **1562** TURNER *Herbal* II. 164b, Of the Missel or *Misselto tre.

'mist-like, *a.* and *adv.* [f. MIST *sb.*[1] + -LIKE.] Like a mist.

1592 SHAKS. *Rom. & Jul.* III. iii. 73 Vnlesse the breath of Hartsicke groanes Mist-like infold me from the search of eyes. **1813** T. BUSBY *Lucretius* I. III. 642 The Soul's seeds.. like spreading mist, Mist like exude, and there no more exist. **1839** LONGF. *Beleaguered City* iv, The mist-like banners clasped the air, As clouds with clouds embrace. **1847** TENNYSON *Princess* VII. 334 All the past Melts mist-like into this bright hour. **1873** 'SUSAN COOLIDGE' *What Katy Did at Sch.* iii. 49 A tender mist-like colour.

mistling, obs. form of MIZZLING.

mistoinit, obs. Sc. form of MISTUNED *ppl. a.*

mistone (mɪsˈtəʊn). *rare*$^{-1}$. [MIS-[1] 4.] Discord.

1813 HOGG *Queen's Wake* 250 The harp-strings jarred in wild mistone.

†**mis'toned**, *ppl. a. Obs.* [MIS-[1] 2.] Discordant, out of tune.

? *a* **1500** in Grose, etc. *Antiq. Rep.* (1809) IV. 406 In the dyvers proporciones of the mystonyde sownde. **1562** WINȜET *Cert. Tractates* Wks. (S.T.S.) I. 20 That ane mistoneit string confoundis all zour harmonie. **1570** *Satir. Poems Reform.* xvii. 66 Mistonit stringis.

mistral (ˈmɪstrəl, mɪˈstrɑːl). Also 7 mestrall, 8–9 **maestral, maestrale.** [a. F. *mistral*, a. Pr. *mistral*:—L. *magistrāl-is* MAGISTRAL. The literal meaning is 'master-wind'; cf. Sp. *maestral* or *viento maestro* (Minsheu).] A violent cold northwest wind experienced in the Mediterranean provinces of France and neighbouring districts.

1604 E. G[RIMSTONE] *D'Acosta's Hist. Indies* III. v. 134 Southeast is by them called *Xirocque*..and his opposite, which is Norwest, *Mestrall*. **1766** SMOLLETT *Trav. France & Italy* xii, The wind that blew, is called Maestral, in the Provincial dialect, and indeed is the severest that ever I felt. **1804** C. B. BROWN tr. *Volney's View Soil U.S.* 179 The mistral of Provence. **1813** J. FORSYTH *Rem. Excurs. Italy* 29 The nights are damp, close, suffocating, when not ventilated by the maëstrale. **1891** A. LANG *Angling Sketches* 176 He reached Mentone, and there the mistral ended him.

†**mis'tram**, *v. Sc. Obs.* [Origin obscure.] *trans.* ? To derange, disorder.

1606 BIRNIE *Kirk-Buriall* xvii. (1833) E3b, By kirk-buriall kirk bounds are so mistrammed, and in many places either so eatten up with intaking Iles..that [etc.]. **1614** FORBES *On Revelation* xii. §8. 103 [Satan] being..shut out of God his house, he furiously mistrammeth his owne.

mistrans'late, *v.* [MIS-[1] 1.] *trans.* To translate incorrectly.

1532 MORE *Confut. Tindale* Wks. 428/1 The tother word, which he hath also mistranslated of like malice *ecclesia*. **1645** GATAKER *God's Eye on Israel* 3 Which place..is..commonly mistranslated and mistaken by the most. **1718** WATERLAND *Vind. Christ's Div.* xxvii. (1720) 437 The learned Doctor by wrong Pointing and Mistranslating perverts a Passage of Justin Martyr. **1822** SOUTHEY *Sel. Lett.* III. 333, I do not mistranslate *beau ideal* when I write of the fair ideal of a work of art. **1855** PUSEY *Doctr. Real Presence* 67 note E, 'Behold the blood of the covenant', has been mistranslated, 'This blood is the covenant'.

mistrans'lation. [MIS-[1] 4.] Erroneous or incorrect translation.

1694 C. LESLIE *Short Method w. Deists* iii. §1 Wks. 1721 I. 16 Mis-translations and errors either in Copy or in Press. **1731** *Act 4 Geo. II*, c. 26 §2 That Mistranslation, Variation in Form by reason of Translation, Mispelling or Mistake in Clerkship..shall be no Error. **1864** PUSEY *Lect. Daniel* 509 The statement, that the Zend books contained the doctrine of the Resurrection, was first rested on mistranslation.

mistrau, -traw, variant forms of MISTROW.

†**mis'tread**, *sb. Obs.* [MIS-[1] 4.] A wrong step; a *faux pas*.

1597 MIDDLETON *Wisd. Solomon* xix. 17 Eyes thought for to misleade, and were mislead: Feete went to make mistreads, and did mis-treade.

†**mis'tread**, *v. Obs.* [MIS-[1] 1.]

1. *trans.* To tread (one's shoes) awry.

c **1305** *Sat. Monks Kildare* in *E.E.P.* (1862) 154 Ofte mistrediþ ȝe ȝur schone, ȝur fete beþ ful tendre.

2. *intr.* To make a *faux pas*.

1597 [see MISTREAD *sb.*].

†**mis'treading**, *vbl. sb. Obs.* [MIS-[1] 3.] A mis-step; a misdeed.

1596 SHAKS. *1 Hen. IV*, III. ii. 11 For..the Rod of heauen To punish my Mistreadings. **1647** HEXHAM, *Een Mis-terde*, ..a Mistreading. **1760–72** H. BROOKE *Fool of Qual.* (1809) I. 92 Their secret lapses and mistreadings.

mistreat (mɪsˈtriːt), *v.* [MIS-[1] 1.] *trans.* To treat badly or wrongly; to ill-treat. Also **mis'treated** *ppl. a.*, ill-treated; **mis-'treating** *vbl. sb.*, ill-treatment, abuse.

1453 *Rolls of Parlt.* V. 270/2 To th' endaungeryng, trouble and mistreatyng of all Ladies. *c* **1465** *Eng. Chron.* (Camden 1856) 22 That thay sholde not mystrete the said Oweyne, lest he made the Walshmen arise. **1496** *Dives & Pauper* (W. de W.) VIII. xiii. 339/2 Robberye is called al maner mystreatynge of an other mannes good ayenst his wyll. **1799** SOUTHEY *Nondescripts* iv, *The Pig*, A poor, mistreated, democratic beast. **1862** LYTTON *Str. Story* I. xii. 77, I had seen many more patients die from being mistreated for consumption than from consumption itself. **1868** J. H. NEWMAN *Verses Var. Occas.* 11 Where iron rule, stern precedent, Mistreat the graceful day. **1886** A. WEIR *Hist. Basis Mod. Europe* (1889) 42 She..ran counter to what Russians regarded as their traditional, though long mistreated *régime*.

mistreatment (mɪsˈtriːtmənt). [MIS-[1] 4.] Bad treatment; ill-treatment.

1716 B. CHURCH *Hist. Philip's War* (1865) I. 140 The Government promising him satisfaction and redress for some mistreatment that he had met with. **1828** CARLYLE *Misc. Ess., Heyne* (1888) I. 59 Threats and mistreatment of all sorts. **18..** DE QUINCEY *Language* Wks. 1858 IX. 94 Darkness gathers upon many a theme, sometimes from previous mistreatment. **1891** CARD. MANNING in *Dublin Rev.* July 161 A century of narrow and commercial mistreatment.

mistress (ˈmɪstrɪs), *sb.* Forms: 4 **maist-, mastiresse, 4–6 maystres(se, 4–7 maistres(se, mastres, 5 mastras, maistress, -tricce, mayst-, maisteres, -erace, mestresse, 5–7 mastress(e, mistresse, 5–8 mistres, -is, 6 masteres, maisters, -triss, -teras, misterz, maistrice, -isse, mestres, maestriss, mystres, 6–7 mistriss(e, (7 misterss), 7– mistress.** [a. OF. *maistresse*, mod.F. *maîtresse* (cf. It. *maestressa* and med.L. *magistrissa*), f. *maistre*, *maître* MASTER *sb.*[1] + *-esse* -ESS. For shortened and corrupted forms see MISS *sb.*[2] and MISSIS.]

I. A woman who rules, or has control.

1. a. A woman who employs others in her service; a woman who has the care of or authority over servants or attendants.

1426 LYDG. *De Guil. Pilgr.* 3786 For she that ys a maysteresse Muste haue a seruant hyr to-beye. **1451** *Paston Lett.* I. 222, I send yow the *cerciorari* for my maistresse yowr modir. *c* **1532** DU WES *Introd. Fr.* in Palsgr. 1036 My lady Mary of Englande, my lady and mastresse. **1535** COVERDALE *Ps.* cxxii. 2 As the eyes of a mayden [loke] vnto the handes of hir mastresse. **1591** SHAKS. *Two Gent.* II. iv. 106 Too low a Mistres for so high a seruant. *c* **1614** SIR W. MURE *Dido & Æneas* III. 391 Her Dams attending see their mistris fall On piercing sword. **1715** POPE *Iliad* III. 526 The maids officious round their mistress wait. **1866** READE *G. Gaunt* II. iv. 76 That sort of..cold pity women are apt to show to women, and especially when one of them is Mistress and the other is Servant. **1866** W. COLLINS *Armadale* II. 322 Whan the maid-servant had opened the door... 'Is your mistress at home?' he asked. 'Yes, sir.' **1903** J. M. SLOAN *Carlyle Country* xxi. 192 Jane Welsh was among the best of mistresses to her servants.

Proverbial phrases. **1573** TUSSER *Husb.* (1878) 107 Such maister such man, and such mistris such maid. **1611** BIBLE *Isa.* xxiv. 2. **1612** PEACHAM *Gentl. Exerc.* To Rdr., He should neuer leaue the Mistresse to court the maid.

b. *transf.* and *fig.*

1545 ASCHAM *Toxoph.* I. (Arb.) 44, I euer thought shooting shoulde be a wayter vpon lerning not a mastres ouer learning. **1599** SHAKS. *Hen. V*, I. i. 52 The Art and Practique part of Life, Must be the Mistresse to this Theorique. **1658** DRYDEN *Death Cromwell* viii, Fortune, that easy mistress of the young, But to her ancient servants coy and hard. **1846** *Pref. Ess.* in *Charnock's Wks.* p. xii, Charnock's imagination was..the handmaid not the mistress of his reason.

2. a. The female head of a household or family, and, by extension, of an establishment of any kind.

? *c* **1400** *Rule St. Benet* (Prose) 10 Ilkain sal take discipline at oþir, als hir mastiresse þoȝ scho ware. **1413** *Pilgr. Sowle* (Caxton) IV. xxxviii. (1859) 64 She bare hyr seluen boldely, right as she were maystresse, and hadde alle the gouernement of the kyng, and his houshold. **1513** BRADSHAW *St. Werburge* I. 2317 Of whiche sayd places [*sc.* monasteries] she had the gouernaunce, As worthy maystres. **1611** BIBLE *1 Kings* xvii. 17 The sonne of the woman, the mistresse of the house, fell sicke. **1641** J. JACKSON *True Evang. T.* III. 225 The Mistris is a good Huswife, but of shrewish condition. **1711** STEELE *Spect.* No. 202 ¶ 12 That the Masters and Mistresses of such Houses live in continual Suspicion of their ingenuous and true Servants. **1773** MRS. CHAPONE *Improv. Mind* (1774) II. 72 The mistress of a family must be ever watchful. **1814** SCOTT *Wav.* liii, The future mistress of my family, and the mother of my children. **1861** FLOR. NIGHTINGALE *Nursing* 24 The mistress of any building, large or small, does not think it necessary to visit every hole and corner of it every day. **1864** TENNYSON *En. Ard.* 26 Enoch was host one day, Philip the next, While Annie still was mistress.

b. *Sc.* and *dial.* (with *the*): The wife of a principal tenant, a minister, etc. (the application varying in different localities).

1683 *Reg. Par. Forres* 10 Feb. (MS.), John the son of Thomas Urquhart of Burgorge and Flowrence Dunbar the Mistress [born]. **1786** BOSWELL *Jrnl.* 6 Sept. *note*, The tacksmen, or principal tenants, are named by their farms, as Kingsburgh, Corrichatachin; and their wives are called the mistress of Kingsburgh, the mistress of Corrichatachin. **1815** SCOTT *Guy M.* xxvi, Several of the neighbouring mistresses (a phrase of a signification how different from what it bears in more fashionable life!) had assembled at Charlieshope to witness the event of this memorable evening. **1822** GALT *Steam-Boat* xii. 296 Although Mr. Keckle had been buried but the week before, the mistress, as a' minister's wives of the right gospel and evangelical kind should be, was in a wholesome state of composity.

†**3.** A woman who has charge of a child or young person; a governess. *Obs.*

c **1320** *Sir Tristr.* 102 To hir maistresse sche gan say þat hye was boun to go To þe kniȝt þer he lay. *c* **1386** CHAUCER *Doctor's T.* 106 This mayde,..So kepte hir-self, hir neded no maistresse. *c* **1386** —— *Sqr.'s T.* 369 Thise olde wommen that been gladly wyse, As is hir maistresse,..seyde, 'madame' [etc.]. *c* **1400** *Ywaine & Gaw.* 936 Sho was al hir maystres, Her keper, and hir cownsayler.

4. a. A woman who has the power to control or dispose *of* something. † ***to be mistress***: to have the upper hand. Now *rare*.

c **1380** WYCLIF *Serm.* Sel. Wks. I. 380 Oure Ladi..is special maistiresse to distroie þes heretikes. **1577** *F. de L'isle's Legendarie* Kiij, The Cardinal knew that so long as the Queene mother was Mistresse, the accomptes should neuer be taken. *a* **1586** SIDNEY *Arcadia* III. (1590) 254 While you say I am mistresse of your life, I am not mistresse of mine owne. **1592** Q. ELIZ. in *Archæologia* XIX. 11 That any lewd..subject of myne, should make his Soveraen be supposed of less gouvernement than mistres of her word. **1687** A. LOVELL tr. *Thevenot's Trav.* I. lxx. 111 The World is turned topsie-turvie in this Island; for the Women are the Mistresses there. **1746** HERVEY *Medit.* (1818) 251 The little creature..shewed herself mistress of every grace which constitutes or embellishes harmony. **1794** MRS. RADCLIFFE *Myst. Udolpho* xxxix, You are your own mistress. **1807** CRABBE *Par. Reg.* II. 31 And now at sixty, that pert dame to see, Of all thy savings mistress, and of thee.

b. *transf.* of things more or less personified.
c **1430** LYDG. *Min. Poems* (Percy Soc.) 60 Entendement double is a maystresse, Triew people to sette at distaunce. **1509** BARCLAY *Shyp of Folys* (1570) 185 This pride is lady and maistres Ouer womankinde. **1587** GOLDING *De Mornay* (1592) Pref. 4 Christ wrought by a powre, that is mistresse of Nature. **1603** FLORIO *Montaigne* I. xi, I know his reason ..so absolute mistress over him, that she can never give him away in any vicious desire. **1614** JACKSON *Creed* III. 239 An infallible authoritie which may sit as Iudge and mistresse of all controuersies of faith. **1711–12** ATTERBURY *Serm.* (1734) II. vii. 200 The Mind of Man is..so little Mistress of strict Attention, so unable to fix itself steddily even on God. **1727** ARBUTHNOT *Coins*, etc. 243 What a miserable Spectacle was this for a Nation that had been Mistress at Sea so long? **1742** YOUNG *Nt. Th.* VIII. 533 Pleasure's the mistress of ethereal pow'rs. **1785** COWPER *Task* IV. 703 Ere yet her ear was mistress of their powers. **1842** TENNYSON *Gardener's Dau.* 57 Such a lord is Love, And Beauty such a mistress of the world. **1884** *Sat. Rev.* 7 June 731/1 England is still mistress of the situation on the Nile.

†**5. a.** The female governor of a territory, state, or people. *Obs.*
c **1366** CHAUCER *A.B.C.* 109 From his ancille he made þe maistresse Of heuene & eerþe. **1598** SYLVESTER *Du Bartas* II. ii. II. 673 That prudent Pallas, Albion's Misteris, That Great Eliza. **1686** WALLER *Poems* 244 Ages to come..Will think you Mistriss of the Indies were. **1785** COWPER *Task* V. 129 Imperial mistress of the fur-clad Russ!

b. Said of a country or state, etc. that has supremacy or suzerainty over others.
(Ancient Rome is freq. called the 'mistress of the world'.)
1375 BARBOUR *Bruce* I. 550 Arthur..Maid Bretane maistres & lady Off twelf kinrykis that he wan. **1456** SIR G. HAYE *Law Arms* (S.T.S.) 21 The kirk of Rome suld be callit lady and maistress of all cristyn kirkis. **1570–6** LAMBARDE *Peramb. Kent* (1826) 17 The Westsaxon kingdome, which in the ende became ladie and maistres of all the rest of the kingdomes. **1611** B. JONSON *Catiline* I. i. Chorus, Rome now is mistress of the whole World, sea and land, to either pole. **1785** COWPER *Task* IV. 169 A Roman meal, Such as the mistress of the world once found Delicious. **1835** THIRLWALL *Greece* I. 435 Eretria..was mistress of several islands. **1859** JEPHSON *Brittany* xvi. 255 England, mistress of Normandy and Anjou. **1893** EARL DUNMORE *Pamirs* II. 315 Russia, being then determined to make herself mistress of Central Asia.

†**c.** The chief, the first. *Obs.*
1491 CAXTON *Vitas Patr.* (W. de W. 1495) I. xxxvi. 32 b/2, The fayr vertue of charytee, whyche is the maystresse of all vertues. **1613** SHAKS. *Hen. VIII*, III. i. 152 The Lilly That once was Mistris of the Field.

†**6.** A woman, a goddess, or something personified as a woman (e.g. a virtue, a passion), having dominion over a person or regarded as protecting or guiding influence. *Obs.*
c **1369** CHAUCER *Bk. Duchesse* 797 For that tyme yowthe my maistresse Gouerned me in ydelnesse. *c* **1375** *Sc. Leg. Saints* xviii. (*Egipciane*) 745 Sa þat þu myn mastres be, & ledar in wa of sawete. **1390** GOWER *Conf.* III. 353 For Nature is under the Mone Maistresse of every lives kinde. *c* **1420** LYDG. *Assembly of Gods* 243 Wyll ye agre that Phebe your mastresse May haue the guydyng of your varyaunce? **1470–85** MALORY *Arth.* x. lxxi. 538 Wel I wote that loue is a grete maystresse. **1594** T. B. *La Primaud. Fr. Acad.* II. 61 They..do as if they meant to despite God and Nature, whome they will not followe as mistresse. **1605** SHAKS. *Lear* II. i. 42 Mumbling of wicked charmes, coniuring the Moone To stand auspicious Mistris. **1633** MILTON *Arcades* 36 The great Mistres of yon princely shrine. **1677** YARRANTON *Eng. Improv.* 6 To beat the Dutch with fighting, so as to force them from their beloved Mistriss and delight, (which is Trade and Riches thereby).

†**7. a.** A woman, or something personified as a woman, regarded as the authoress, creatress, or patroness of an art, religion, a state of life, etc.
a **1400–50** *Alexander* 4530 Minerua was a maistres of many kingis werkis. **1490** CAXTON *Eneydos* xiii. 46 Juno, the goddesse of wedlocke whiche is lady mastresse, and wardeyne, of the connexes or bondes aminicules. *a* **1500–20** DUNBAR *Poems* lxxxvii. 13 Dochtir to Pallas.., Maistres of nurtur and of nobilnes. **1577** NORTHBROOKE *Dicing* (1843) 59 Idlenesse (sayeth Chrysostome) is the mystres and beginning of all vice and wickednesse. **1604** E. G[RIMSTONE] *D'Acosta's Hist. Indies* III. iii. 127 Vntill that Experience (the mistris of these secrets) had taught them. **1708** MRS. CENTLIVRE *Busy Body* I. i, Want, the mistress of invention.

†**b.** = PATRONESS 1. *Obs.*
[**1460**: see MISTRESS-SHIP 2.] **1710** SWIFT *Jrnl. to Stella* 10 Sept., I..saw my mistress, Ophy Butler's wife, who is grown a little charmless. *Ibid.* 1 Oct., To desire him to engage Lady Hyde as my mistress to engage Lord Hyde in favour of Mr. Pratt.

8. A female possessor or owner. Chiefly ***to be mistress of***: to be possessed of; to have in her possession or at her disposal; also, to be perfectly acquainted with (a subject). ? *Obs.* (Cf. 4.)
1551 T. WILSON *Logike* Ep. A iij, I haue first laboured to bring so noble a maistresse both of reason and judgement acquainted with so noble a countrey. **1600** SHAKS. *A. Y. L.* I. ii. 4, I show more mirth then I am mistresse of. **1603** FLORIO *Montaigne* I. xl, [The soule] who is the only and soveraigne mistris of our condition. **1665** BOYLE *Occas. Refl.* v. ix. (1848) 329 The Collection..is..such, as if the Mistress of it were less handsome than she is, might give her as well Cause to be jealous of these fine things. **1703** ROWE *Fair Penit.* II. i, If I was ever Mistress of such Happiness. **1756** WASHINGTON *Lett.* Writ. 1889 I. 256 You may expect..that, without a considerable reinforcement, Frederick county will not be mistress of fifteen families. **1766** *Gentl. Mag.* Dec. 587 A strong bodied mare, mistress of 16 stone. **1782** COWPER *Parrot* IV. 13 'Sweet Poll!' his doting mistress cries. **1811** MISS AUSTEN *Sense & Sens.* xl, Elinor, not hearing much of what was said and more anxious to be alone than to be mistress of the subject.

9. A woman who has mastered any art, craft, or branch of study.
1484 CAXTON *Fables of Auian* v. (1889) 221, I am a maystresse in medecyn. **1535** COVERDALE *Nah.* iii. 4 The fayre and beutifull harlot: which is a mastresse of wychcraft. **1590** SPENSER *F.Q.* I. vii. 1 Great maistresse of her art was that false Dame. **1611** SHAKS. *Wint. T.* IV. iv. 593, I cannot say 'tis pitty She lacks Instructions, for she seemes a Mistresse To most that teach. **1712** ADDISON *Spect.* No. 92 ⁋5, I would advise all young Wives to make themselves Mistresses of Wingate's Arithmetick. **1718** ROWE tr. *Lucan* VI. 912 Hail! mighty Mistress of Hæmonian arts. **1802** ANNA SEWARD *Lett.* (1811) VI. 48 Who is such a mistress, where I am so shallow a student. **1807** CRABBE *Par. Reg.* I. 184 The Sybil of the Row..Mistress of worthless arts. [**1888** BRYCE *Amer. Commw.* VI. cii. III. 445 *note*, Degree titles.., Mistress of Polite Literature, Mistress of Music.]

10. a. A woman who has command over a man's heart; a woman who is loved and courted by a man; a sweetheart, lady-love. (Now avoided in ordinary use exc. in unequivocal contexts.)
1509 HAWES *Past. Pleas.* xviii. (Percy Soc.) 83 You are my lady, you are my masteres, Whome I shall serve with all my gentylnes. **1591** SHAKS. *Two Gent.* IV. iv. 182, I giue thee this For thy sweet Mistris sake, because thou lou'st her. **1647** CLARENDON *Hist. Reb.* I. §20 How Gallant..a thing it would be for his Highness..to fetch home his Mistres. **1697** DRYDEN *Virg. Past.* III. 103 To the dear Mistress of my Love-sick Mind, Her Swain a pretty Present has design'd. **1750** JOHNSON *Rambler* No. 28 ⁋3 How few faults a man, in the first raptures of love, can discover in the person or conduct of his mistress. **1822** LAMB *Elia*, Ser. I. *Modern Gallantry*, It was during their short courtship,..that he had been one day treating his mistress with a profusion of civil speeches. **1868** [see MISAPPRECIATION]. **1891** HARDY *Tess* xxxiii, A last jaunt in her company while they were yet mere lover and mistress.

b. Applied to animals.
1692 R. L'ESTRANGE *Fables* cxxiii, The Other Cock had a Good Riddance of his Rival..and had All his Mistresses to Himself again. **1720** GAY *Rur. Sports* 82 The dewlap'd bull ..His well-arm'd front against his rival aims, And by the dint of war his mistress claims. **1840** *Penny Cycl.* XVIII. 477/1 In France they allow twenty mistresses to each cock.

11. A woman who illicitly occupies the place of wife.
1430–40 LYDG. *Bochas* I. viii. (1494) cj, [Scylla loq.] Called in my cuntre a fals traitouresse..Of newe defamed and namyd a maistresse. **1601** R. JOHNSON *Kingd. & Commw.* (1603) 320 Every man hath his Mistresse with instruments of musicke, and such like pleasures [etc.]. *a* **1631** DONNE *Serm.* lxiv. 642 Those women, whom the Kings were to take for their Wives, and not for Mistresses, (which is but a later name for Concubines). **1694** EVELYN *Diary* 22 Apr., The quarrel arose from his taking away his owne sister from lodging in a house where this Laws had a mistress. **1727** POPE & GAY *What passed in London* Swift's Wks. 1751 VI. 271 They took to Wife their several kept Mistresses. **1819** BYRON *Mazeppa* iv, But soon his wrath being o'er, he took Another mistress, or new book. **1859** MACAULAY *Biog.*, *Pitt* (1860) 193 His Protestant mistresses gave less scandal than his Popish wife. **1865** TROLLOPE *Belton Est.* xviii. 212 For three years I was a man's mistress, and not his wife.

II. 12. A female teacher, instructress; now only, one who is engaged in a school, or one who teaches some special subject, as music, drawing, etc. Cf. 3, and MASTER *sb.* 2.
c **1374** CHAUCER *Compl. Mars* 33 She hath take him in subiecciou̇n, And as a maistresse taught him his lessoun. *c* **1374** —— *Troylus* II. 98 'Is it of love? O, som good ye me lere!' 'Uncle', quod she, 'your maistresse is not here!' **1534** LD. BERNERS *Gold. Bk. M. Aurel.* (1546) F v, He prouyded women and maystresses for to teache theim. **1663** J. HEATH *Flagellum* (ed. 2) 4 From this A. B. C. Discipline and the Slighted Governance of a Mistris, his Father removed him to the Tuition of Dr. Beard. **1697** in *Col. Rec. Pennsylv.* I. 532 Such and so many masters, ushers, mistrisses. *a* **1745** POPE *Mem. P.P.* Swift's Wks. 1751 V. 229 Even when I was at School, my Mistress did ever extol me above the rest of the Youth. **1826** MRS. DODS *Cook & Housewife's Man.* 88 The Masters and Mistresses of Boarding Schools. *Mod.* She is a mistress at the High School.

III. Used as a title or prefix.
13. a. Used vocatively as a term of respect or politeness; = MADAM, MA'AM. *Obs.* exc. *arch.* in general use. Also *W. Indies.*
c **1430** *Syr Gener.* (Roxb.) 269 'Maistres', he seid, 'god you spede!' ? **1468** *Paston Lett.* II. 313 And ye know welle, maistras, better ys afrende unknow then knowen. **1513** BRADSHAW *St. Werburge* I. 133 Blessed vyrgyn Werburge my holy patronesse, Helpe me to endyte I praye the, swete maystresse. **1534** MORE *Comf. agst. Trib.* II. Wks. 1170/2 Forsoth maisters quod he, youre husband loueth well to talke. **1588** SHAKS. *L.L.L.* v. ii. 847 Studies my Ladie? Mistresse, looke on me. **1667** MILTON *P.L.* IX. 532 Wonder not, sovran Mistress, if perhaps Thou canst, who art sole Wonder, much less arm Thy looks..with disdain. **1824** HOGG *Conf. Sinner* 91 'Pray, mistress, what is your name?' 'My name is Arabella Calvert', said the other: 'Miss, mistress, or widow, as you chuse, for I have been all the three'. **1905** R. GARNETT *Will. Shaks.* 76 Mistress, if pardon for thy spouse entreating, Thine errand know for vain. **1957** F. A. COLLYMORE *Notes for Gloss. Barbadian Dial.* (ed. 2) 57 The archaic nominative of address has survived in Barbados, and may be heard any day on the lips of any servant or huckster addressing the mistress of the household, as, *I want some more butter, mistress. Mistress, you want any useful limes?* **1966** *Evening Standard* 1 Feb. 8/4, I would be very glad to get out of this hard country [sc. Jamaica], mistress.

†**b.** In angry use (cf. MISS *sb.*^{2} 4 b). *Obs.*
1883 M. R. LAHEE *Acquitted though Guilty* vi, [Father to daughter] But let me tell thee one thing, mistress: if ever I catch thee wi' him I'll mischieve th' pair on yo'.

14. As a title of courtesy. Prefixed, **a.** to the surname (in early use also to the Christian name) of a married woman. Now abbreviated MRS. (q.v.), formerly Mis, Mis, M^{ris}. Now *dial.* and *W. Indies.*
1471 *Paston Lett.* III. 18 If it come to Mestresse Elysabeth Hyggens, at the Blak Swan. *Ibid.*, Mestresse Elysabeth hathe a son, and was delyveryd within ii. dayes afftr Seynt Bertelmew. **1552** LATIMER *Serm.* (1584) 288 Hee styred vp mistris Pilate, which tooke a nap in the morning [etc.]. **1563–83** FOXE *A. & M.* II. 2073/2 One maistresse Anne Lacie widowe in Notinghamshiere. **1628** *Obituary R. Smith* (Camden Soc.) 4 Mis Lucas, wife to Anthony Lucas..died. *a* **1631** DONNE *Lett. to Persons Hon.* (1651) 75, I hear from England of many censures of my book, of M^{ris} Drury. **1631** T. POWELL *Tom of All Trades* 141 To abate the fury of Mistrisse Overcount mine hostesse. **1782** COWPER *Gilpin* 65 Now Mistress Gilpin (careful soul!) Had two stone bottles found. **1825** HOOD *Addr. to Mrs. Fry* xiii, I like your chocolate, good Mistress Fry! **1872** SCHELE DE VERE *Americanisms* 507 *Mistress* is in the South very frequently yet heard pronounced fully, without the usual contraction into 'Missess'. **1966** *Guardian* 14 Dec. 8/4 We go..to see Mistress Gladys Walker... Here [*sc.* in Barbados], Mrs is often spoken out, in full.

b. to the Christian name or surname of an unmarried woman or girl; = MISS *sb.*^{2} *Obs.* or *dial.*
? **1461** *Paston Lett.* II. 78 To my right worchepfull Mastres Paston. *c* **1535** ELIZ. SHELLEY in Miss Wood *Lett. Roy. & Illustr. Ladies* (1846) II. 213 Your letter,..by the which I do perceive your pleasure is to know how mistress Bridget your daughter doth. **1598** SHAKS. *Merry W.* I. i. 197 O heauen! this is Mistresse Anne Page. **1707** STEELE *Corr.*, Dear Mistress Scurlock. **1710** SWIFT *Jrnl. to Stella* 25 Nov., So, here is mistress Stella again with her two eggs, &c. **1818** TODD, s.v. *Miss*, *Mistress* was then the style of grown up unmarried ladies, though the mother was living; and, for a considerable part of the [18th] century, maintained its ground against the infantine term of *miss*.

†**c.** to a title, as ***mistress mayoress.*** *Obs.*
1541 *Cal. Anc. Rec. Dublin* (1889) I. 410 Such obprobrious words as one Walter Coke shold haw spokyn by Maisteras Mayras.

d. *transf.* and *jocular.*
1577–87 HOLINSHED *Chron.* III. 862/2 Some profit the husbandmen in some parts of the realme got by the mooving of this matter, where inclosures were alreadie laid open, yer mistresse monie could preuent them. **1592** SHAKS. *Rom. & Jul.* III. v. 152 (Qo. 2), Mistresse minion you? Thanke me no thankings, nor proud me no prouds. **1596** —— *Tam. Shr.* v. ii. 42, I, Mistris Bride, hath that awakened you? **1610** —— *Temp.* IV. i. 235 Mistris line, is not this my Ierkin?

15. In the title of certain Court offices. (Cf. MASTER *sb.* III.) ***Mistress of the Robes***: in the English Royal Household, a lady of high rank, charged with the care of the Queen's wardrobe. †***great mistress***: used to represent the title of the lady entrusted with the government of the household of a foreign princess.
1710 J. CHAMBERLAYNE *St. Gt. Brit.* 542 Mistress of the Robes, Sarah Dutchess of Marlborough. **1768** *Hist. Eur.* in *Ann. Reg.* 116 The great duchess [of Tuscany], attended by her great mistress, and the ladies of honour. **1905** *Whitaker's Alm.* 85 Household of H.M. Queen Alexandra. Mistress of the Robes, The Duchess of Buccleuch.

IV. Technical senses.
16. In the game of Bowls, the jack; = MASTER *sb.*^{1} 9. Often *fig.*
a **1586** SIDNEY *Arcadia* III. xiv. (1590) 303 Zelmane (vsing her own bias to bowle neer the mistresse of her owne thoughtes). **1598** FLORIO, *Lecco*, is properly the maister or mistres at bowels or quoits. **1600** *Weakest goeth to the Wall* G 3, Though I come late, I hope to lie as neare the Mistresse as any of ye all. **1606** SHAKS. *Tr. & Cr.* III. ii. 52 So, so, rub on, and kisse the mistresse. **1630** [see JACK *sb.*^{1} 18]. **1680** COTTON *Compl. Gamester* iii. 36 The World..where most are..wrong byassed, and some few justle in to the Mistress, Fortune!

†**17.** *Bot.* = PLUMULE 1. *Obs.*
a **1722** LISLE *Husb.* (1752) 281 The little mistress or plume (from whence the flower arises).

18. A lantern used in coal-mines.
1851 GREENWELL *Coal-trade Terms, Northumb. & Durh.* 36 *Mistress*, an oblong box, wanting the front side, carried upright; the use of which is to carry a lighted candle in a current of air. **1860** *Eng. & For. Min. Gloss.* (Newcastle Terms).

V. 19. a. *attrib.* and *Comb.*, as ***mistress-market, -server***; ***mistress-like*** adv.; †**mistress-bowl** = sense 16 (cf. *master bowl*).
1598 FLORIO, *Matto*,..the *mistress bowle to caste at. **1654** WHITLOCK *Zootomia* 486 Let who will commend their *Mistresse-like-chosen Arts. **1802** MRS. GUTHRIE *Tour* xlviii. 152, I am sure that a *mistress-market must be a curious subject to the polished nations of Europe. **1609** DEKKER *Gull's Horn-bk.* iii. 16 But [be] thou a Reueller and a *Mistris-seruer all the yeare.

b. quasi-*adj.* = 'Chief', 'leading': with fem. personification, or (formerly) with a sb. grammatically fem. in L. or Fr. (Cf. MASTER *sb.*^{1} 25 a.)
1581 SIDNEY *Apol.* (Arb.) 30 So yet are they all directed to the highest end of the mistres Knowledge..*Architectonike.* **1599** SHAKS. *Hen. V*, II. iv. 133 Hee'le make your Paris Louer shake for it, Were it the Mistresse Court of mightie Europe. **1601** HOLLAND *Pliny* XVI. xliii. I. 493 Ioyners doe chuse the mistresse threadie graine [Fr. transl. *maistresse veine*] that is most streight. **1603** FLORIO *Montaigne* I. xxvii, After this general communitie, the mistris and worthiest part of it [etc.]. **1611** COTGR. s.v. *Maistresse*, *La maistresse Eglise*, a Cathedrall Church, the mistresse Church, or chiefe Church in a Towne. **1613** JACKSON *Creed* I. 110 Rome..the Mistresse-citie of the world. **1641** MILTON *Prel. Episc.* Wks.

1738 I. 30 Being born free, and in the Mistress Island of all the British. **1641** W. Stokes *Vaulting Master* D, The ninth Passe, called The Mistresse Command. **1667** Boyle *Orig. Formes & Qual.* (ed. 2) 291 Subjected to the predominant Mistresse Forme. **1899** Mackail *W. Morris* II. 198 Through the mistress-art to all the other subordinate arts.

mistress (ˈmɪstrɪs), *v.* [f. prec.] **a.** *trans.* To provide with a mistress. †**b.** To make a mistress or paramour of. **c.** To call or address as 'mistress'. **d.** *to mistress it*: to play the mistress, to have the upper hand. **e.** To become mistress of (an art). **f.** To dominate as a mistress.

1579 J. Stubbes *Gaping Gulf* D 3 b, Both she and we poore soules, are to be mastered, and, which is worse, mistrised to. **1603** Sir C. Heydon *Jud. Astrol.* xii. 318 Neither could Venus in coniunction with Mars cause any to mistresse another mans wife. **1802** H. Martin *Helen of Glenross* III. 74 Not but I am surprised too to be 'mistressed', and to hear them talking of my child. **1819** 'Robert Rabelais' *Abeillard & Heloisa* 11 Care not a farthing, but resolv'd To mistress it with men they lov'd. **1856** Reade *Never too Late* II. xxii. 218 This one is a first-rate gilder, she mistressed it entirely in three days. **1904** M. Hewlett *Queen's Quair* I. viii. 117 You are too masterful, my girl... I do not choose to be mistressed by a maid of honour.

ˈmistressdom. *rare*$^{-1}$. [See -dom.] Female despotism.

1844 *Fraser's Mag.* XXX. 449/2 We object..to the sole sway and mistressdom of the one histrionic queen.

ˈmistresshood. [See -hood.] The condition or status of a mistress (of a household).

1879 *Gentl. Mag.* Jan. 3 Her first act of mistresshood was to give her husband a power of attorney to deal with all as he would. **1883** Mrs. Lynn Linton *Ione* III. xxx. 137 The house was a standing disgrace to her mistresshood.

mistressing (ˈmɪstrɪsɪŋ), *vbl. sb.* [f. mistress *sb.* + -ing[1].] Paying court to, or dallying with, a mistress.

a **1631** Donne *To Mr. Tilman* Poems (1654) 350 As if their day were only to be spent In dressing, Mistressing, and complement. **1633** G. Herbert *Temple, Ch. Porch* xiv, Flie idlenesse, which yet thou canst not flie By dressing, mistressing, and complement. **1683** Tryon *Way to Health* 461 No Mistrissing, nor Revelling. **1783** Wesley *Wks.* (1872) XI. 525 Drinking, and dressing, and mistressing.

mistressless (ˈmɪstrɪslɪs), *a.* [-less.] Having no mistress or female head.

1873 Miss Broughton *Nancy* III. viii. 126, I have again taken advantage of the mistressless condition of the establishment. **1886** Mrs. Moberly *Lady Valeria* II. iv. 92 Altcar Court lost much of its forlorn mistressless air.

mistressly (ˈmɪstrɪslɪ), *a.* [-ly[1].]

1. Belonging to the mistress of a household. *rare.*

1748 Richardson *Clarissa* (1811) I. 298 Will he take from me the mistressly management, which I had not faultily discharged?

2. [after masterly 2.] Like one who is a 'mistress' in her art.

1786 Mackenzie *Lounger* No. 76 ¶9, I have seen some of them go through their evolutions in a very masterly and mistressly manner. **1794** Walpole *Let. to the Miss Berrys* 27 Sept., I did see the new bust of Mrs. Siddons, and a very mistressly performance it is indeed. **1804** Southey *Sel. Lett.* (1856) I. 272 You who manage a pencil in so masterly, or mistressly a way. **1898** C. G. Robertson *Voces Academicæ* 253, I thought Gerty would have burst out crying, but she controlled herself in a mistressly way.

3. Characteristic of a man's mistress. *nonce-wd.*

1939 A. Huxley *After many a Summer* I. xiii. 180 Flirting with him all through dinner, so that you got the old man hopping jealous of him. That was masterly. Or should one say mistressly?

ˈmistress-piece. Now *rare.* [f. mistress after *masterpiece*. Cf. F. *maîtresse pièce* the principal piece of a work.] A feminine masterpiece.

a **1648** Ld. Herbert *Hen. VIII* (1649) 175 Mistresse Elizabeth Blunt..was thought, for her rare Ornaments of nature, and education, to be the beauty and Mistresse-peece of her time. *a* **1661** Fuller *Worthies, Herefordshire* (1662) II. 41 Rosamund..being the Mistress-piece of beauty in that Age. **1902** *Daily Chron.* 24 Mar. 5/1 Those who hold his [Sir Walter Besant's] 'Dorothy Forster' to be his mistresspiece.

ˈmistress-ship. [f. mistress *sb.* + -ship.]

1. The condition or status of mistress or head of a household, etc.; authority of one in the position of a mistress.

1581 Mulcaster *Positions* xxxviii. (1887) 176 From the lowest in menaltie, to the highest in mistriship. *a* **1656** Bp. Hall *Rem. Wks.* (1660) 407 If any of them still usurpe a Mistress-ship over them. **1705** Bp. Bull *Corrupt. Ch. Rome* Wks. 1827 II. 290 They never acknowledged her mistressship over them. **1858** Miss Mulock *Woman's Th. about Women* 55 Having all the cares, and only half the joys of maternity or mistress-ship. **1892** *Catholic News* 23 July, There is some talk of her Majesty putting the Mistress-ship of the robes into commission. **1898** Fitchett *Fights for the Flag* 3 The struggle between the two maritime republics for the mistress-ship of the seas.

†**2.** The status of a woman to whom the title of mistress was used: always in *your mistress-ship. Obs.*

1460 *Paston Lett.* I. 533 Beseching yow of your good maisteresship to be myn good maisteres to help wit your gracious woord. *Ibid.* III. 253 Plesith it your mastresship to witte. *a* **1553** Udall *Royster D.* II. iv. (Arb.) 38 By your mistreshyps licence. **1611** Middleton & Dekker *Roaring Girl* II. i, I humbly thank your good mistresship. **1632** Massinger *City Madam* IV. iv, He made a knight, And your sweet mistress-ship ladyfied.

3. The post of mistress in a school.

1891 *Brit. & For. School Soc. Rep.* 17 There has been a change of teachers, Miss Brown having resigned the mistress-ship on her marriage. **1900** *Standard* 27 Oct., Girls' School.—Head Mistress-ship.

4. Pre-eminent skill in an art, etc. ? *Obs.*

1819 *Blackw. Mag.* V. 125 His wife has a complete mistress-ship in the art. **1837** *Tait's Mag.* IV. 589 She..imparts to her..sketches a certain style and mistress-ship which no traveller of the other sex..could have attained.

mistrest, variant of mistrist.

mistrial (mɪsˈtraɪəl). [mis-[1] 4.] A trial vitiated by some error (e.g. a disqualification in a judge or juror). Also, *U.S.*, an inconclusive trial, as where the jury cannot agree.

1628 Coke *On Litt.* 125 If there be a mistryall, (that is) if the Jury commeth out of a wrong place, or returned by a wrong Officer and giue a verdict. **1651** Brownlow *Rep.* 7 The words were spoken at C. in the County aforesaid..and so a Mistryall. **1810** East *K.B. Rep.* XII. 229 Littledale..moved to..have a new trial on the ground of a mistrial. **1884** *Law Rep.* 9 Prob. Div. 185 They insisted that there had been a mistrial on the ground of improper rejection of evidence. **1889** *Boston* (Mass.) *Jrnl.* 3 May 1/5 Another Mistrial. A Seven Days' Trial of a Case Results in a Disagreement of the Jury.

†**misˈtrist**, *sb. Obs.* Also 5 mystrest. [mis- 4.] = mistrust *sb.*

1382 Wyclif *Prol. Bible* iii. 4 God..punisshide hem..for grucchyng and mystriste to Goddis word. *c* **1440** *Generydes* 1673 In hym he hadde no maner of mystrest. **1483** *Cath. Angl.* 241/2 A Mistriste, *desperacio, diffidencia.* **15..** *Guistard & Sismond* II. (1597) C 3 b, And when they wer in comin, they put no mistrist.

†**misˈtrist**, *v. Obs.* or *dial.* Also 4–5 -triste, 4–6 -traist, 5 mystrast, 5–6 -trest, 9 -thrist. [mis-[1] 7.] = mistrust *v.*

a. *trans.* *c* **1386** Chaucer *Pard. Prol.* 41 And never shal he more his wyf mistriste. *c* **1440** *Generydes* 1399 It grevith me full soore, That ye shuld me mystrest by eny waye. *c* **1460** Sir R. Ros *La Belle Dame* 746 Sum man say how he mystristed is on sum partyse. **1552** Abp. Hamilton *Catech.* (1884) 41 And quhy suld we nocht put all our traist..in the mercy of God?.. Suerly we suld nocht mistrest him.

b. *intr.* **1390** Gower *Conf.* I. 149 Sche wissheth forto ben unbore, Er that hire fader so mistriste To tellen hire of that he wiste. *c* **1400** *Song Roland* 186 'Sistir son', said the king, 'sore I mystrist'. *c* **1470** Henry *Wallace* IX. 1623 Ner the castell he drew thaim prewaly In till a schaw; Sotheroun mystraistyt nocht. **1567** *Gude & Godlie B.* 160 At thy deith thow did mistraist, And sa fell in dispair. **1596** Dalrymple tr. *Leslie's Hist. Scot.* II. 356 Quhom the deith of Makintosche causet gretlie to defecte,..mistraisting of his actioune. **1877** *Holderness Gloss.*, Misthrist, to mistrust or doubt.

mistrouth(e: see mistruth.

†**misˈtrow**, *sb. Obs.* Also 4 -tru(n, -trou(n, -trouȝ. [f. next. For the form *mistrun* cf. the verb.] Mistrust, suspicion.

a **1300** *Cursor M.* 8433 And þat þou be noght in mistru, þar-til mak i þe here a wou. *Ibid.* 9261 He sal find, withvten mistruns, Sexti hale generacions. *Ibid.* 15354 Ilkan Of oþer had mistrun [*rime* resun]. *c* **1350** *Will. Palerne* 3314 Swiche mistrowe had meliors for þei so moche him preised. *c* **1400** *Rule St. Benet* (Prose) 19 Yef it sua bi-tide, þat any falle in mis-trouȝ; þan sal scho pray gerne to god.

†**misˈtrow**, *v. north. Obs.* Also 4 -tru(n, -tro(u)n, -trou(e, -trau, -traw(e, -treu. [ad. ON. *mistrúa*, f. *mis-* mis-[1] + *trúa* (see trow *v.*).

The form *mistrun* in *Cursor Mundi* was app. orig. used for the purposes of rime (perhaps under the influence of ON. *mistrúnaðr* disbelief), but the *n* seems to have been afterwards taken as part of the stem: cf. prec. sb.]

1. *trans.* To disbelieve (a person); to have no faith or confidence in.

a **1225** *Ancr. R.* 68 For þi þe treowe is misleued [*MS. T.* mistrowet], & þe sakelease ofte bilowen, uor wone of witnesse. *a* **1300** *Cursor M.* 3651 þat he þe mai þe less mistru [*Gött.* mistrau, *Fairf.* mistraw] þou sal sai þou ert esau. **13..** *Ibid.* 17958 (Gött.) His auen sun sal he send dune In erde, þat mani sal mistron. *c* **1450** *Merlin* 21 'Yef this be so', quod the Iuge, 'neuer shall I mystrowe the'. **1480** Caxton *Ovid's Met.* XV. vi, The fader..belived the lesyng, which was full of iniquyte, & mistrowed hys son.

2. To suspect (a person) *of* (a misdeed).

1375 Barbour *Bruce* X. 327 Thai mystrowit hym of tratory.

3. To disbelieve (a thing). Also with clause.

a **1300** *Cursor M.* 22795 Bot mistrou [*Edinb.* mistrun] þat, es na nede. *c* **1375** *Sc. Leg. Saints* xl. (*Ninian*) 1303 Mystrowand þat I mocht help þe ocht.

4. *intr.* To be unbelieving, not to believe (*in*); to be doubtful (*of*).

a **1300** *Cursor M.* 13595 þe maisters Iuus þan bigan To mistru o þis sinful seli man [*Fairf.* mistrowne queþer þis sely man, queþer he be fore blinde had he bene]. *Ibid.* 17402 Yee ar þe folk þat ai mistruus. *Ibid.* 22868 Vte of all skil it es,.. For to mistru in godds might. *c* **1380** Wyclif *Serm.* Sel. Wks. I. 368 þe vigile of Baptist telliþ how Gabriel bihiȝte him, and þis storie telliþ how Zacarie mistrowede.

Hence †**misˈtrowing** *vbl. sb.* and *ppl. a.* Also †**misˈtrowable**, †**misˈtrowful** *adjs.*, unbelieving; †**misˈtrower**, an unbeliever.

a **1300** *Cursor M.* 16643 Yee foles mistruand folk. *Ibid.* 18673 To frest if þai in trouth war tru, þair mistruing [*Gött.* mistrouning, *Fairf.* mistrowning] for to misprais. *Ibid.* 21203 Lucas..þe mistruand he tok to teche. **1375** Barbour *Bruce* x. 329 For that ilk mystrowing, Thai..put in presoun. **1382** Wyclif *Isa.* lxv. 2, I spredde out myn hondis al dai to a puple mystrouful [1388 vnbileueful, Vulg. *incredulum*]. —— *Bar.* i. 19 We weren mystrowable [1388 vnbileueful, Vulg. *incredibiles*] to the Lord oure God. **1390** Gower *Conf.* III. 56 For espiaile and mistrowinges They dede thanne suche thinges. **1456** Sir G. Haye *Law Arms* (S.T.S.) 89 May men move were agaynis the Sarrazenis or othir mistrowaris. *Ibid.* 103 The Sarazenis or othir mistrowand folk.

†**miˈstrum**, *a. Obs.* [f. mis-[1] 7 + OE. *trum* strong, after untrum *a.*] Weak.

a **1225** *Ancr. R.* 262 ȝif heo þencheð wel heron, of mistrum, oðer leane mel [*MS.T.* of mistune meal, *MS.C.* of mistrume mel] of unsauure metes, of poure pitaunce?

mistrust (mɪsˈtrʌst), *sb.* [mis-[1] 7. Cf. the later *distrust* sb.] Lack of trust or confidence; suspicion, distrust. Const. *of*, *in*, †*to*. †Also, doubt as to the truth or probability (*of* something).

c **1374** Chaucer *Troylus* II. 780 For ever som mistrust, or nyce stryf, Ther is in love, som cloud is over the sonne. **1440** *Generydes* 5760 'To you', quod she, 'now haue I noo mystrost'. **1488** Caxton *Chast. Goddes Chyldern* 35 No man shall haue mystrust of foryeuenesse of whatsomeuer synne man hathe done. *a* **1533** Ld. Berners *Huon* lxxxi. 247, I had no mystruste in him. **1601** Shaks. *Jul. C.* v. iii. 66 Mistrust of good successe hath done this deed. **1677** Marvell *Corr.* Wks. 1872–5 II. 552, I have sent for you hither to prevent mistakes and mistrusts. *a* **1699** Stillingfl. *Serm.* xlii. Wks. 1710 V. 640 The mistrust Men have of themselves would make their Fears over-balance their Hopes. **1805** Wordsw. *Prelude* x. 161 Man is only weak through his mistrust And want of hope. **1854** Milman *Lat. Chr.* VIII. ii. III. 29 These decrees were sent to the Pope, with a significant menace, which implied great mistrust in his firmness.

mistrust (mɪsˈtrʌst), *v.* Also 4–6 -trost(e. [f. mis-[1] 7 + trust *v.*, prob. after OF. *mesfier* (mod. F. *méfier*): see mis-[2].]

1. a. *trans.* Not to trust, to have no confidence in (a person); to suspect the actions, intentions, motives (etc.) of.

c **1374** Chaucer *Troylus* IV. 1606, I see wel now that ye mistrusten me; For by your wordes it is wel y-sene. *c* **1440** *Generydes* 5695 Me to mystroste trewly she is vnkynd,.. Vntrew to hir she shall me neuer fynde. *a* **1548** Hall *Chron., Edw. V*, 21 b, For whom mistrusted he that mistrusted his awne brother? **1598** Shaks. *Merry W.* v. v. 141, I will neuer mistrust my wife againe, till thou art able to woo her in good English. **1725** De Foe *Voy. round World* (1840) 207 Had it been a Spanish ship, they would not have mistrusted him. **1861** Thackeray *Four Georges* iii. (1862) 151 She kept her household lonely and in gloom, mistrusting almost all people who came about her children. **1886** G. Allen *Darwin* vii. 113 The practical English nation mistrusts philosophers.

b. *refl.* To be doubtful as to one's own powers or capabilities.

1552 Latimer *Serm.* (1584) 299 Mistrusting himselfe and hys owne doynges, and trusting in the merites of Christ. **1577–87** Holinshed *Chron.* III. 1212/1 They mistrusted themselues,..their minds being suddenlie altered, they returned. **1875** Manning *Mission H. Ghost* viii. 217 Our need to watch over ourselves and to mistrust ourselves, and to trust in God alone.

2. To entertain suspicions with regard to, have doubts about (a thing); to doubt the truth, validity, or genuineness of.

c **1375** *xi. Pains of Hell* 232 in *O.E. Misc.* 218 To god hit is most hye trespace To mys-trost his mercy and grace. **1526** *Pilgr. Perf.* (W. de W. 1531) 167 b, Mystrust not the goodnes of god. **1529** More *Dyaloge* i. Wks. 123/2 The messenger thynketh that he may well mistrust & deny the myracles. **1602** Marston *Ant. & Mel.* v. sign. I, When I see one..wallowe in a greate sloppe, I mistrust the proportion of his thigh. **1615** Bacon *Sp. Undertakers* Wks. 1826 VI. 20 As gamesters use to call for new cards, when they mistrust a pack. **1742** *Lond. & Country Brew.* I. (ed. 4) 15 Such Waters ought to be mistrusted more than any, where they are not pure, clear, and soft. **1759** Goldsm. *Bee* No. 4 ¶10 For my part I am ever ready to mistrust a promising title. **1848** Lytton *Harold* v. v. 178 Mistrust the wisdom that sees only the things of the day-light. **1871** Miss Yonge *Cameos* Ser. II. xiv. 152 Juan mistrusted this advice.

3. a. To suspect the existence of or anticipate the occurrence of (something evil). ? *Obs.*

1535 Coverdale *Judges* viii. 11 The hoost was carelesse, and mystrusted nothinge. **1590** Nashe *Pasquil's Apol.* I. B j b, No such largesse could be looked for at the hands of her Ma[iestie]..no fingring of Spanish coyne mought be mistrusted. **1598** Barret *Theor. Warres* I. i. 2 To shake off securitie, to mistrust the worst. **1603** Florio *Montaigne* I. vi, They were all asleepe mistrusting no harme. **1674** Prideaux *Lett.* (Camden) 18 It is feared..that he will speedyly be mad, if he is not soe already, which his actions doe make every on mistrust. **1728** Morgan *Algiers* II. iii. 238 The poor Prince,..mistrusting no Treachery was easily surprised.

b. with obj. a clause: To suspect *that* something has happened or will happen. ? Now *dial.* and *U.S.* †Also *pass.* (corresponding to acc. and inf. in the active): To be suspected (of doing something).

a **1450** *Knt. de La Tour* 35 The brother tolde her husbonde, the whiche alle his lyff after mistrusted that his wiff had done amys. **1554–5** Eden *Decades* (Arb.) 386 Not mystrustynge that that shulde haue hyndered theyr bargenynge. **1565** Cooper *Thesaurus*, *Suspectus in aliqua virgine*, Mistrusted to be ouer familiar with a mayden. **1621** Lady M. Wroth *Urania* 475 Shee mistrusted I loued a brother of hers. **1646** Sir T. Browne *Pseud. Ep.* I. xi. 46 Wisely mistrusting that reasonable spirits would never

firmely be lost in the adorement of things inanimate,..he [Satan] begat an opinion that they..were living creatures. **1777** *Boston Gaz.* 10 Nov. 3/3 He said he was taking his Way to Boston, but is mistrusted to be going to Long or Rhode Island. **1840** C. F. HOFFMAN *Greyslaer* I. x. 109, I mistrust that your Injun friend there..didn't help you much..in finding out old Josie. **1861** O. W. HOLMES *Elsie Venner* vii. 73, I mistrusted he didn't mean to come. **1867** *Harper's Mag.* July 147/1 They have left the Atlantic coast, given up by physicians as in the last stage of consumption—a fact that would never be mistrusted from their present robust condition. **1898** A. NICHOLAS *Idyl of Wabash* 188 Before early apples were ripe I mistrusted what was keeping him. **1904** T. ROOSEVELT in J. A. Riis *Life* viii. 187, I mistrust that it scared the Spaniard almost as much as our charge did. **1909** *Dialect Notes* III. 349, I mistrusted he was at the bottom of it. Not common.

absol. **1615** E. S. *Britain's Buss* E 4 Except the Dutch should proove more froward and fond then I can yet mistrust.

†**c.** To have an inkling of (*what* is the matter). **1707** *Curios. in Husb. & Gard.* 204 Mistrusting what it ail'd, I took the Pot out of the Water.

4. *intr.* To be distrustful, suspicious, or without confidence. Also, †not to trust *in*, to be doubtful *of*.

138. WYCLIF *Ps.* Prol. 737 To mystrosten of forȝiuenesse, and of the merci of God. **1382** —— *Bar.* i. 17 Wee han not leeued, mystrostende in to hym. **1570** LEVINS *Manip.* 194/32 To Mistruste, *diffidere.* **1711** PRIOR *Henry & Emma* 352 Near thee, mistrust not, constant I'll abide. **1725** POPE *Odyss.* II. 116 At once the gen'rous train complies, Nor fraud mistrusts in virtue's fair disguise. **1896** *Godey's Mag.* Apr. 391/2 Until I noticed..your confusion over your name, I never mistrusted.

Hence **mis'trusted** *ppl. a.*, in quot. †suspected.

1588 GREENE *Pandosto* (1843) 10 Hoping now he should be fully revenged of such mistrusted injuries.

mis'truster. [MIS-^{1} 5.] One who mistrusts.

c **1425** *Found. St. Bartholomew's* (E.E.T.S.) 38 Ther was oone amonge the wepers and waylers & mystrustres, ripyr & sadder of age. *a* **1560** BARNES *Wks.* (1573) 354/2 You Infidelles and mistrusters of God. **1643** MILTON *Divorce* Wks. 1738 I. 112 These cautious mistrusters might consider, that what they thus object lights not upon this Book. **1840** DICKENS *Old C. Shop* xvi, But now you're a universal mistruster. **1861** CRAIK *Hist. Eng. Lit.* I. 391 The enemies and mistrusters of all innovation.

mis'trustful, *a.* [f. MISTRUST *sb.* + -FUL.] Full of or marked by mistrust; wanting in confidence; distrustful, suspicious. Const. *of*.

1529 MORE *Dyaloge* IV. i. Wks. 247/2 To shewe our selfe so mistrustful & wauering, that for to serche whether our faith were false or true, we should geue hearing..to a fond frere. **1593** SHAKS. *3 Hen. VI*, IV. ii. 8, I hold it cowardize, To rest mistrustfull, where a Noble Heart Hath pawn'd an open Hand, in signe of Loue. **1667** MILTON *P.L.* II. 126. **1680** *Lond. Gaz.* No. 1548/3 We begin here to be somewhat mistrustful of the Merchandises that are brought from Germany. **1712** ARBUTHNOT *John Bull* III. ii, Why so mistrustful! Hast thou ever found us false to thee? **1847** C. BRONTË *J. Eyre* (1857) 86 She presented it across the counter, accompanying the act by another inquisitive and mistrustful glance. **1886** NIXON *Euclid Revised* Pref., So far, teachers are either unaware, or mistrustful, of such strength.

†**b.** *transf.* Causing mistrust or suspicion. *Obs.*

1592 SHAKS. *Ven. & Ad.* 826 Or stonish'd as night-wanderers often are, Their light blown out in some mistrustful wood.

Hence **mis'trustfully** *adv.*, with mistrust or suspicion, distrustfully; **mis'trustfulness**, the condition or quality of being mistrustful; want of confidence, suspiciousness.

1542 UDALL *Erasm. Apoph.* 294 The mystrustfulnesse of the Byzancians he laied on the necke of..yᵉ capitain. *a* **1586** SIDNEY *Arcadia* II. (1590) 181 b, A mistrustfulnes of my selfe, as one strayed from his best strength. **1602** WARNER *Alb. Eng.* VI. xxxiii, Mistrustfully he trusteth, and he dreadingly did dare. **1672** EACHARD *Hobbs's State Nat.* (1705) 5, I am confident there must be some occasion or other of this so very great jealousie and mistrustfulness of yours. **1873** BROWNING *Red Cott. Nt.-cap* 330 Those five Cold fingers, tendered so mistrustfully. **1879** MEREDITH *Egoist* xxvii. (1889) 258 She controlled her alert mistrustfulness.

mis'trusting, *vbl. sb.* [-ING^{1}.] The action of the vb. MISTRUST.

1526 *Pilgr. Perf.* (W. de W. 1531) 64 That couent can neuer be in peace..where the heed is suspicyous and full of mystrustynge. **1544** *Exhort.* in *Priv. Prayers* (1851) 568 Without wavering or doubtful mistrusting..in his almighty power. **1647** HEXHAM, A mistrusting, *een mistrouwinge.* **1921** *Spectator* 30 Apr. 556/2 Class bitterness and the mistrusting of the employer by the employed.

mis'trusting, *ppl. a.* [-ING^{2}.] That mistrusts, mistrustful. Hence **mis'trustingly** *adv.*

1552 HULOET, Mistrustynge, *diffidens.* *Ibid.*, Mistrustinglye, *diffidenter, dubitanter.* **1576** FLEMING *Panopl. Epist.* 93 My wauering and mistrusting mynde. *a* **1586** SIDNEY *Arcadia* VI. (1638) 488 The humble teares of a still-mistrusting lover. **1822–56** DE QUINCEY *Confess.* i, Gradually, tentatively, mistrustingly, as one goes down a shelving beach into a deepening sea. **1845** *Whitehall* lxix. 479 They parted coldly and mistrustingly.

mis'trustless, *a.* [-LESS.] Free from mistrust or suspicion; unsuspecting. Const. *of*.

1586 WARNER *Alb. Eng.* I. iv. (1612) 14 He hunts abroad, mistrustles of such wrong. **1596** R. L[INCHE] *Diella* (1877) 60 So Syrens sing vntill they haue their will, Some poore mistrustlesse Passenger to kill. **1632** QUARLES *Div. Fancies* II. xlix, Mistrustles Isaac seeing the wood, the fire, The sacrificing Knife, begins t'enquire. **1770** GOLDSM. *Des. Vill.* 27 The swain, mistrustless of his smutted face. **1839** *Blackw. Mag.* XLV. 355 A bland expression of mistrustless affection.

†**mis'trusty,** *a. Obs.* [MIS-^{1} 6.] Mistrustful, suspicious.

c **1440** *Partonope* (1862) 156 Ye shull me neuer fynde That euer mystrusty shall I to you be.

†**mis'truth.** *Obs. north.* Also 4 -trouth(e, -trowþ, -trauþe, -treutht. [MIS-^{1} 7.] **a.** Disbelief, unbelief. **b.** Unfaithfulness.

a **1300** *Cursor M.* 18676 Bot þair mistrouth, þe soth to sai, Es strenghing of vr trouth to dai. **13..** *E.E. Allit. P.* B. 996 For two fautes þat þe fol was founde in mistrauþe. *c* **1375** *Sc. Leg. Saints* v. (*Johannes*) 364 To þat entent, þat þu of þi mystreutht haf scham now. *c* **1400** *Apol. Loll.* 97 þei are brout in to mis trowþ, & hopiþ to haue helpe wiþ out God.

mistry (mɪsˈtraɪ), *v.* [MIS-^{1} 1.] *trans.* To try wrongly.

1651 BROWNLOW *Rep.* 7 *marg.*, Judgement arrested being mis-tried. *Ibid.* 17 It was moved in Arrest of Judgement, that it was mis-tried, because [etc.]. **1906** *Daily News* 5 Mar. 7/6 Murray..was..mistried by Sir Forrest Fulton, and condemned to nine months' hard labour for perjury.

mistry, obs. form of MYSTERY.

mistryall, obs. form of MISTRIAL.

mistryst (mɪsˈtraɪst), *v. Sc.* and *north. dial.* [MIS-^{1} 1, 7.]

1. *trans.* To fail to keep an engagement with. Also *absol.* or *intr.* const. *with*.

1816 SCOTT *Bl. Dwarf* iv, Ye'll be gaun yonder, Mr. Patrick; feind o' me will mistryst you for a' my mother says. **1893** STEVENSON *Catriona* xiii, 'Braw trysts that you'll can keep', said Alan. 'Ye'll just mistryst aince and for a' with the gentry in the bents'. **1894** CROCKETT *Raiders* 393 An ill speldron o' a loon that had mistrysted wi' twa lasses already.

2. *pass.* To be perplexed, confused, frightened (app. orig. = to have an unpleasant meeting with something).

1816 SCOTT *Bl. Dwarf* iii, It's a braw thing for a man to be out a' day, and frighted—na, I winna say that neither—but mistrysted wi' bogles in the hame-coming. **1818** —— *Rob Roy* xiv, They are sair mistrysted yonder in their Parliament-House, about this rubbery o' Mr. Morris. **1855** ROBINSON *Whitby Gloss.*, *Mistrysted*, frightened, put out of track. 'I hae been sair mistrysted', sorely perplexed.

mis'tune, *v.* [MIS-^{1} 1.] *trans.* To tune wrongly; to put out of tune, make discordant; to perform (music) out of tune. Hence **mis'tuned** *ppl. a.*, out of tune; †of persons, having no ear for music; **mis'tuning** *vbl. sb.*

1504 CORNISHE in *Skelton's Wks.* (1568) z v b, If he [*sc.* the harper] play wrong, good tunes he doth lette Or by mystunyng the very trew armonye. *Ibid.* z vj, Any Instrument mystunyd shall hurt a trew song. **1535** LYNDESAY *Satyre* 75 Till all our rymis be rung, And our mistoinit sangis be sung. **1587** [see MIS-BEGIN]. **1636** B. JONSON *Eng. Gram.* vii, Where for want of one [*sc.* an accent], the word is in danger to be mis-tuned. *a* **1684** LEIGHTON *Comm. 1 Pet.* iv. 8 Wks. 1830 II. 333 When thou prayest alone, while thy heart is imbittered..it is as a mistuned instrument. *c* **1750** ARMSTRONG *Misc.* (1770) II. 197 Some of the best mimicks are mistuned, and have not the least ear to harmony. **1753** CHAMBERS *Cycl. Supp.* s.v. *Diatonic*, Ptolemy's tetrachords are so mis-tuned, that Salinas has charged him with having no ear. **1755** SMOLLETT *Quix.* (1803) I. 220 A hoarse, mistuned voice. **1815** SCOTT *Ld. of Isles* v. xxviii, Hymn mistuned and mutter'd prayer. **1883** *Knowledge* 25 May 315/1 With the pianoforte tuned (or, one might say, mistuned) to equal temperament. **1914** R. STANLEY *Text-bk. Wireless Telegr.* 134 In the Telefunken transmitter the circuits are slightly mistuned, the aerial circuit having a free wave length about 2 per cent. higher than that of the primary circuit, and this mistuning is increased with the closeness of the coupling. **1970** J. EARL *Tuners & Amplifiers* iii. 73 It is possible to mistune a stereo transmission and collect a terrific amount of sideband noise. *Ibid.*, The quality of f.m. is significantly impaired by even slight mistuning.

transf. and *fig.* **1744** ARMSTRONG *Art Preserv. Health* IV. 134 The Body, by long ails mistun'd. **1836** LANDOR *Imag. Conv.*, *Pericles & Aspasia* Wks. 1846 II. 429 Idly do our sages cry out against the poets for mistuning the heart. **1858** BUSHNELL *Nat. & Supernat.* ii. (1864) 46 A scheme unstrung and mistuned.

mistur, obs. form of MISTER *sb.*^{1}

†**'misture**^{1}. *Obs. rare.* [?f. MISS *v.*^{1} on the analogy of *mixture*; but prob. suggested by MISTER *sb.*^{1} 8.] A loss, privation; = MISS *sb.*^{1} 1, 2.

1563–83 FOXE *A. & M.* 1964/2 How sore they tooke hys death to hart, and also, how hardly they could away with the misture [orig. *desiderium*] of such a man. **1592** NASHE *P. Penilesse* 20 b, It is a great misture, that we haue not men swine as well as beasts.

†**'misture**^{2}. *Obs. rare.* [ad. L. *mistūra*: see MIXTURE.] Mixture.

a **1626** BACON *Disc. Union Eng. & Scot.* in *Resuscitatio* (1657) 201 Such Imperfect Mistures, continue no longer, then they are forced.

misturn (mɪsˈtɜːn), *v.* Forms: see TURN *v.* [MIS-^{1} 1. Partly after OF. *mestourner.*]

1. *trans.* To turn in a wrong direction; to pervert, invert; to reverse the order of; to turn to a wrong use.

c **1325** in *Rel. Ant.* I. 265 Armes other legges mis-turnd wose syth [*sc.* in dreams], Langour ant mournyng that bith. **1340** HAMPOLE *Pr. Consc.* 1617 þat es to say þam sall be wa þat here mysturnes þair lyfe swa. **1382** WYCLIF *Gal.* i. 7 Ther ben summe that disturblen ȝou, and wolen mysturne the euangelie of Crist. **1390** GOWER *Conf.* I. 56 Diverse men ..Thurgh sihte of hem mistorned were, Stondende as Stones hiere and there. *c* **1440** *Jacob's Well* 142 þou mysturnyst þe tyme þat god ordeynyd, for þou makyst day of nyȝt, & nyȝt of day. *a* **1450** *Knt. de la Tour* 71 The unlefulle synne of lecherye..mistornithe the ordre of nature. **1532** MORE *Confut. Tindale* Wks. 359/1 Tindal..manifestlye misturneth the mynde and sentence of our sauiour. **1561** T. NORTON *Calvin's Inst.* III. 239 Wherupon followeth, that yᵉ doctrine of iustification is mistourned, yea ouerturned from the very foundation. **1581** J. BELL *Haddon's Answ. Osor.* 398 The state of the Question is mis-tourned by the Romanistes. *a* **1625** SIR H. FINCH *Law* (1636) 187 To reduce a water-course that is misturned.

2. *intr.* To turn in a wrong direction; to go wrong.

1390 GOWER *Conf.* I. 36 And whan this litel world mistorneth, The grete world al overtorneth. *Ibid.* III. 236 If the Monthe of Juil schal frese And that Decembre schal ben hot, The yeer mistorneth. **1413** *Pilgr. Sowle* (Caxton) I. xxiv. (1859) 29 Bokes of moralyte techen what wey a trewe pylgrym owed for to take and not for to mystorne to one syde, ne to other.

So **mis'turning** *vbl. sb.*

c **1400** *Rom. Rose* 5545 And Fortune, mishapping, Whan upon men she is falling, Thurgh misturning of hir chaunce.

mis'tutored, *ppl. a.* [MIS-^{1} 2.] Badly instructed or brought up.

a **1757** T. EDWARDS *Canons Crit.*, *Sonn.* xxviii. *To G. Onslow*, Gay, mistutored youths, who ne'er the charm Of Virtue hear. **1876** BLACKIE *Songs of Relig.*, etc. 141 Before the power of misvouched creeds and a mistutored church.

misty (ˈmɪstɪ), *a.*^{1} Also 1 **mistiȝ**, 4 **myisti, misti,** 4–5 **mysti,** 4–6 **mysty,** (6 -tie), 6–7 **mistie,** 4– **misty.** [OE. *mistiȝ*. f. *mist* (see MIST *sb.*^{1}) + *-iȝ*, -Y. Cf. MLG., MDu. *mistich.*]

1. a. Covered with, clouded or obscured by, mist; accompanied or characterized by mist; consisting of mist.

Beowulf 162 Atol æȝlæca ehtende wæs,..seomade and syrede, sinnihte heold mistiȝe moras. *a* **1327** in *Rel. Ant.* I. 265 Eyr mysty whose syth [in a dream], Desturbaunce that bith. *c* **1374** CHAUCER *Troylus* III. 1060 For I have seyn, of a ful misty morwe Folwen ful ofte a mery someres day. *c* **1430** LYDG. *Compl. Bl. Knt.* 24 Whan that the misty vapour was agoon And clere and faire was the morowning. *c* **1460** RUSSELL *Bk. Nurture* 911 in *Babees Bk.*, Wheþur hit be feyre or foule, or mysty alle withe reyn. **1592** SHAKS. *Rom. & Jul.* III. v. 10 And Iocond day Stands tipto on the mistie Mountaines tops. **1603** KNOLLES *Hist. Turks* (1638) 157 The night being dark and misty, and the moon giving little light. **1682** WOOD *Life* (O.H.S.) III. 29 Misty and rimy morning. **1718** LADY M. W. MONTAGU *Lett.* II. lii. 73 The misty rains..penetrated even the thick fur I was wrapped in. **1817** WOLFE *Burial Sir J. Moore* ii, By the struggling moon-beam's misty light. **1858** MASSON *Milton* I. 720 The mistier north is forgotten, and he longs to make Florence his home. **1877** TENNYSON *Harold* III. ii, Two young lovers in winter weather, None to guide them, Walk'd at night on the misty heather.

b. Clouded with fine particles resembling mist.

1833 TENNYSON *Miller's Dau.* 104 The very air about the door Made misty with the floating meal. **1885** *Manch. Exam.* 4 May 5/3 The air is in fact quite misty with the fine impalpable dust.

c. Blurred or blinded as with a 'mist' of tears.

1859 TENNYSON *Enid* 1620 Not so misty were her meek blue eyes As not to see before them on the path. **1897** *Romance of Lady Barton* II. 745, I never took my misty eyes off Trieste and our home.

d. Having the appearance of being shrouded in mist; indistinct in form or outline.

1797 MRS. RADCLIFFE *Italian* xii, The long-drawn prospect faded into misty light. **1818** SHELLEY *Rosal. & Helen* 1198 A troop Of misty shapes did seem to sit Beside me. **1833** N. ARNOTT *Physics* (ed. 5) II. 207 The light from adjoining points will mix at the edges, and will render the images misty and indistinct. **1898** *St. James's Gaz.* 12 Jan. 12/1 Striped across..in a misty admixture of colouring.

2. *fig.* (often with literal phraseology retained).

a. 'Dark'; obscure; unintelligible.

1377 LANGL. *P. Pl.* B. x. 181 Ac theologie hath tened me ten score tymes, The more I muse þere-Inne þe mistier it semeth. *c* **1380** WYCLIF *Serm.* Sel. Wks. I. 156 þes wordis ben mysty and derke to þe puple. **1471** RIPLEY *Comp. Alch.* XII. v. in Ashm. (1652) 185 Thys mysty talkyng. **1494** FABYAN *Chron.* 2 Ryght mysty storyes, doughtfull and vnclere. *c* **1530** *Interl. Beauty & Gd. Prop. Women* B iij b, The wordes whych thou spekyst in my presence Be so mysty, I perseyue not thy sentence. **1581** SIDNEY *Apol. Poetrie* (Arb.) 32 The Philosopher..is so hard of vtterance, and so mistie to bee conceiued, that [etc.]. **1603** FLORIO *Montaigne* II. xii. (Frowde) 236 Wherefore hath Heraclitus beene surnamed σκοτεινός, 'a darke mysty clowded fellow'? **1624** GATAKER *Transubst.* 201 What not mysticall, but mistie riddles are these? **1755** JOHNSON, *Misty*...2. Obscure; dark; not plain.

b. Resembling mist; obscuring, causing ignorance. *Obs.*

1509 HAWES *Past. Pleas.* (Percy Soc.) 2 To drawe a curtayne I dare not to presume, Nor hyde my matter with a misty smoke. **1577–87** HOLINSHED *Chron.* I. 150/1 Liuing in a time of palpable blindnesse and mistie superstition. *a* **1631** DONNE *Elegy on Mrs. Boulstred* Poems (1654) 260 Blinde were those eys, saw not how bright did shine Through fleshes misty vaile those beams divine.

c. Not illuminated with the 'light' of reason, faith, truth, etc.

1616 HAYWARD *Sanct. Troub. Soul* I. §3. 59 Mollifie my stony heart, illuminate my misty minde. **1633** P. FLETCHER *Purple Isl.* III. iv, Shed in my mistie breast thy sparkling light. **1669** PENN *No Cross* xx. §14 (1682) 511 Though times began to look somewhat mistier, and the purity and spirituality of Religion to be much declined. **1748** JOHNSON *Van. Hum. Wishes* 144 Should Reason guide thee with her brightest ray, And pour on misty Doubt resistless day. **1811** W. R. SPENCER *Poems* 185 No beam of real fire My misty nature ever knows.

d. Of thought, speech: Having no definite 'outline' or character; vague, indistinct. Said also of writers with reference to style or exposition.

1816 J. W. CROKER in *C. Papers* 28 Nov. (1884), That misty pomp of language which you..think laudable. **1855** GEO. ELIOT *Ess., Evang. Teaching* (1884) 157 Their sense of truthfulness is misty and confused. **1865** TYLOR *Early Hist. Man.* iv. 58 A misty recollection hovering about it in our minds. **1890** GROSS *Gild Merch.* I. 94 The jurists had not yet shrouded the notion in misty complexity.

e. Of persons: Clouded in intellect.

1822 *Blackw. Mag.* XII. 101 And over a skin of Italy's wine To get a little misty. **1848** H. ROGERS *Ess.* (1874) I. vi. 316 A little too misty readily to follow the argument, they got drowsy.

3. *Comb.*: parasynthetic, as ***misty-brained***; adverbial, as ***misty-bright***, ***-dark***, ***-magnific***, ***-soft*** adjs. ***misty-eyed*** adj., that brings tears to the eyes; having tears in one's eyes.

1611 SPEED *Hist. Gt. Brit.* IX. i. 1 Through the misty-darke times of which Stories..I am lastly approached to these times of more light. **1649** HEYLIN *Hist. Indep.* II. 80 *marg.*, For this you must take the faith of the mysty-brayned Pen-man, who had this..by Revelation. *c* **1810** COLERIDGE in *Lit. Rem.* (1838) III. 210 Paragraphs so vague and misty-magnific as this is. **1860** RUSKIN *Mod. Paint.* V. VII. iv. §6. 140 The rain-clouds in the dawn..not shining, but misty-soft. **1871** M. COLLINS *Mrq. & Merch.* I. vii. 215 The air was misty-bright. **1886** *Pall Mall G.* 5 Oct. 11/2 A misty-visioned political sect. **1956** W. H. WHYTE *Organization Man* (1957) III. xiii. 156 He can grow as misty-eyed as the next man at the banquet honoring the Grand Old Man. **1974** M. CECIL *Heroines in Love* vi. 151 Misty-eyed emotion and passionate declarations of love.

Hence **'mistyish** *a.*, somewhat misty.

1686 GOAD *Celest. Bodies* II. iv. 202 Mistyish Heaven.

† **'misty**, *a.*2 *Obs.* [app. the prec. adj. used by form-association for L. *mysticus*.] Pertaining to, involving, or characteristic of spiritual mysteries; mystical, spiritual.

c **1380** WYCLIF *Serm.* Sel. Wks. II. 286 And so þre mysty wittis ben tokened in þe same story. *c* **1420** LYDG. *Commend. Our Lady* 134 Thou misty arke, probatik piscyne. *c* **1449** PECOCK *Repr.* II. x. 203 O Sion, mysti douȝter. **1450–1530** *Myrr. our Ladye* 330 The mysty or spyrytuall body of cryste. **1570** LEVINS *Manip.* 111/42 Mystie, mist, *nebulosus*. Mysty, mistery, *mysticus*.

mis-'typing, *vbl. sb.* [MIS-1 3.] A bad or false typing; a typing error.

1936 F. M. FORD *Let.* 2 July (1965) 252 The 4 being a mistyping for ', I having just changed my machine.

,misunder'stand, *sb.* *rare*−1. [f. next.] Misunderstanding.

1864 MEREDITH *Sandra Belloni* xxvi, No misunderstands, mind! Wilfrid's done with.

,misunder'stand, *v.* [MIS-1 1.]

1. *trans.* Not to understand rightly; to misconceive, miscomprehend. **a.** To take (words, statements, etc.) in a wrong sense.

c **1200** *Vices & Virtues* 37 Sume mis-understondet hier ðis hali writt. *c* **1380** WYCLIF *Serm.* Sel. Wks. II. 123 þei mysundirstonden þer lawe. **1529** MORE *Dyaloge* I. xxi. Wks. 147/2 That some of them which do rede it diligently..may yet for al that, mistake & misvnderstand it. **1614** RALEIGH *Hist. World* I. iii. §9 He failed in distinguishing these two Regions, both called Eden: and..mis-vnderstood two of the foure Riuers (to wit) Pison and Gehon. **1629** H. BURTON *Truth's Triumph* 310 It is plaine hee mis-vnderstandeth..the place. **1778** MISS BURNEY *Evelina* xxi, His booby of a servant had misunderstood his orders. **1791** MRS. RADCLIFFE *Rom. Forest* i, His sense of compassion was too sincere to be misunderstood. **1864** BRYCE *Holy Rom. Emp.* xxi. (1875) 381 To praise or to decry the Empire as a despotic power is to misunderstand it altogether. **1873** RUSKIN *Pol. Econ. Art* Addenda 223 He must say all he has to say..in the plainest possible words, or his reader will certainly misunderstand them.

b. To misinterpret the words or actions of (a person).

a **1300** *Cursor M.* 19152 Iesu þat yee did on rode, þat alwais yee mis-vnderstode. **1530** PALSGR. 639/1 He that mys-vnderstandeth a man must nedes make a folysshe answere. **1680** W. ALLEN *Addr. Nonconf.* 69 When Nicodemus grosly mis-understood our Saviour, and demanded how can these things be? **1791** CUMBERLAND *Observer* No. 140 V. 151, I conceive I have been misunderstood as having carried my attack against the moral doctrines of Socrates. **1837** LYTTON *E. Maltrav.* 13 My poor girl, we misunderstand each other. **1841** EMERSON *Ess., Self-reliance* Ser. I. 58 To be great is to be misunderstood. **1847–9** HELPS *Friends in C.* (1851) I. 30 The question is, will people misunderstand you—not, is the language logically impregnable?

2. *intr.* Also with clause.

13.. *Cursor M.* 14207 (Gott.) Iesus said, 'ȝe mis-vnderstand' [*Cott.* miss yee vnderstand]. *Ibid.* 15922 'Yoene ..es ane of his þat wid vs es in band'. 'Ebberthwert nai', said he, 'ȝe misunderstand' [*Cott.* yee mis nu vnderstand]. **1822** COBBETT *Weekly Reg.* 2 Feb. 295 The effects of the system were so manifest, that nobody could misunderstand whence they sprung. **1906** KIPLING *Puzzler* in *Tribune* 15 Jan. 4/3 Giuseppe placed the monkey atop of the organ, where the beast, misunderstanding, stood on his head.

Hence **misunder'standable** *a.*, capable of being misunderstood.

1843 *P. Parley's Ann.* IV. 266 The old mamma grunted and looked very misunderstandable through her grey eyes.

,misunder'stander. [MIS-1 5.] One who misunderstands.

1529 MORE *Suppl. Soulys* Wks. 324/2 Many textes whiche as farre semed vnto the missvnderstanders to speake against purgatory, as [etc.]. **1697** J. SERGEANT *Solid Philos.* A 3 The true Sense of Aristotle's Doctrine,..being taken..from some Modern Misunderstanders, was lost. **1891** *Pall Mall G.* 26 Oct. 3/2 'Tim' is a really striking book. It is somewhat on the lines of 'Misunderstood', the chief misunderstander being the hero's own father.

,misunder'standing, *vbl. sb.* [MIS-1 3.]

1. Failure to understand; mistake of the meaning; misconception, misinterpretation.

c **1449** PECOCK *Repr.* I. xii. 60 The mis vndirstonding of the firste text. **1579** W. WILKINSON *Confut. Fam. Love* B i, All controuersies growne among men about their misunderstanding of the Scriptures. **1644** MILTON *Bucer on Div.* xxviii. 11 Through misunderstanding of the law. **1685** SOUTH *Serm.* (1697) I. viii. 347 The misunderstanding of a word. *a* **1839** PRAED *Poems* (1864) II. 184 Misrepresentations of reasons, And misunderstandings of notes.

2. The condition in which parties fail to come to an 'understanding'; an interruption of harmonious relations; dissension, disagreement.

1642 CHAS. I in Rushw. *Hist. Coll.* (1721) III. II. 5 The malignant Party, which have..begot this Misunderstanding between us and our good Subjects. **1691–2** LUTTRELL *Brief Rel.* (1857) II. 339 The accommodation which seem'd to be in view between the pope and the French, upon some misunderstanding, quite disappears. **1712** STEELE *Spect.* No. 263 ¶3 The many Misunderstandings which are created by the Malice and Insinuation of the meanest Servants between People thus related. **1849** COBDEN *Sp.* 17 America has three times, within the last few years, had a misunderstanding with two of the greatest Powers of the world. **1859** GEO. ELIOT *A. Bede* xxxiii, Some little pique or misunderstanding between them. **1867** FREEMAN *Norm. Conq.* (1877) I. ii. 38 Occasional misunderstandings seem not to have seriously interrupted their friendship.

,misunder'standing, *ppl. a.* [MIS-1 2.] That misunderstands. Also *absol.*

1610 HEALEY *St. Aug. Citie of God* 333 The misunderstanding reader..might imagine that the Pagans worshipped gods in the Temples. **1675** BAXTER *Cath. Theol.* II. v. 107 These are but the bold effusions of a misunderstanding contentious temerarious passion. **1881** *Athenæum* 23 July 103/3 Whatever is most vicious in a style which grows out of a misunderstanding worship of Keats. **1900** W. M. SINCLAIR *Unto You Young Men* iii. 72 Doubts and difficulties may make sad..the fainthearted, the misunderstanding.

Hence **misunder'standingly** *adv.*, by a miscomprehension.

1725 BRADLEY *Fam. Dict.* s.v. *Wold*, Wold,..as Stow in the Wolds, and Cotswold..is sometimes misunderstandingly confounded with *Weald*.

,misunder'stood, *ppl. a.* [MIS-1 2.] Improperly understood; taken in a wrong sense. Also *absol.*

1594 CAREW *Huarte's Exam. Wits* (1616) 172 Three mis-vnderstood lawes, which they haue learned at all aduentures. **1711** ATTERBURY *Serm.* (1734) I. xi. 291 A mis-understood Place of Scripture may overthrow One of the Prime Articles of Faith. **1790** BURKE *Fr. Rev.* 219 The most dangerous shock that the state ever received through a misunderstood arrangement of religion. **1887** STEDMAN *Vict. Poets* xi. 389 America, with her strange..misunderstood yearning for a rightful share of the culture..of the older world. **1892** ZANGWILL *Bow Mystery* 51 The incurable interest of humanity in the Unknown and the Misunderstood.

Hence **,misunder'stoodness.**

1826 BENTHAM in *Westm. Rev.* VI. 484 From non-understoodness or misunderstoodness comes oppositeness to expectation.

misure, obs. form of MEASURE.

1416 in Madox *Formulare Angl.* (1702) 16 The boundes i founde and misured of the..grounde of John Bernardes.

misusage (mɪsˈjuːzɪdʒ). Now *rare.* [MIS-1 4. Cf. OF. *mesusage*.]

† **1.** Misconduct; corrupt practice, abuse. *Obs.*

1532 [see MISUSE *v.* 3]. **1579** *Roy. Proclam.* 15 Dec., The great misusage in the execution of sundrie her Highnes graunts made to diuers persons. **1579** SPENSER *Sheph. Cal.* July 184 Palinode..Yode late on Pilgrimage To Rome,..and then He saw thilke misusage.

2. Ill-usage; maltreatment; †*pl.* instances of this.

1554–5 EDEN *Decades* (Arb.) 386 The fame of theyr mysusage so preuented them that the people of that place also offended therby, wold bring in no wares. **1583** GOLDING *Calvin on Deut.* cli. 934 Vnder this saying our Lorde hath comprehended all the misusages that wee can offer to our neighbour. **1601** HOLLAND *Pliny* (1634) I. 30 These misusages which she [*sc.* the earth] abideth aboue, and in her outward skin, may seeme in some sort tolerable. **1670** G. H. *Hist. Cardinals* II. II. 158 The rest of the Cardinals looking upon the misusage of his person, as a reflection upon the Order. **1709** STRYPE *Ann. Ref.* Introd. §1. 3 By occasion of the Hardships and Misusages she underwent before. **1837** LOCKHART *Scott* (1839) VI. 394 He had no longer any thoughts for the petty misusage of mankind. **1858** CARLYLE *Fredk. Gt.* VI. iii. II. 269 Foul misusage, not to be borne by human nature. **1886** A. WEIR *Hist. Basis Mod. Europe* (1889) 308 The Serbs..were determined only to defend themselves from misusage.

3. Bad or wrong use, misuse.

1567 in Strype *Ann. Ref.* I. (1709) 508 This Misusage of the Privilege that belonged to him, as her Ambassador. *a* **1638** MEDE *Wks.* I. (1672) 14 If the Name of God be prophaned by the disesteem and misusage of the things it is called upon. *a* **1849** POE *Whipple*, etc. Wks. 1864 III. 387 The misusage of 'like' in place of 'as'.

† **mis'usance.** *Obs.* [MIS-1 4. Cf. OF. *mesusance*.] Misrule, mismanagement.

c **1470** HARDING *Chron.* CCXXXIII. iv, Made good rule and noble ordynaunce, Auoyding all misrule and misusaunce. *a* **1670** HACKET *Abp. Williams* I. (1692) 202 [They] presaged that after he had chafed at their mis-usance, they might promise to themselves a good cast of his office.

misuse (mɪsˈjuːs), *sb.* [MIS-1 4. Cf. OF. *mesus* abuse, excess, misdeed.]

1. Wrong or improper use; misapplication.

1398 TREVISA *Barth. De P.R.* III. i. (1495) 48 Isidorr sayth by a mysuse Homo a man hath the name of humo the erthe. **1450–1530** *Myrr. our Ladye* 88 To be ware leaste by mysvse of oure free wylle we falle in blyndnesse and hardnes of harte. **1483** *Cath. Angl.* 241/2 A Misvse; *Abusus, Abusio.* **1690** LOCKE *Hum. Und.* III. x. §15 How much Names taken for Things are apt to mislead the Vnderstanding,..and that, perhaps, in words little suspected for any such Misuse. **1707** ATTERBURY *Serm.* (1726) II. iv. 112 Lest he should punish our Misuse of his Mercies, by stopping the Course of them. **1748** HARTLEY *Observ. Man* II. iv. §3. 391 A great Misuse of Time to dwell upon such Speculations. **1866** J. MARTINEAU *Ess.* I. 14 Artful misuse of the confidence of others. **1885** *Manch. Exam.* 28 Mar. 5/4 The gross misuse of his public position for private profit.

2. Ill-usage. *rare.*

1596 SHAKS. *1 Hen. IV*, I. i. 43 Vpon whose dead corpses there was such misuse, Such beastly, shamelesse transformation, By those Welshwomen done, as [etc.]. **1881** SWINBURNE *Mary Stuart* I. i. 10 The Catholics naked here to all misuse Fall off in numbered force, in means and power.

† **3.** Evil custom or conduct. *Obs.*

1509 BARCLAY *Shyp of Folys* (1570) 233 Let these fooles auoyde this mad misuse, and folowe the right way of vertuous grauitie. **1554** in Strype *Eccl. Mem.* (1721) III. xviii. 47 Thus plainly ye se one mischievous misuse in this mass. **1604** SHAKS. *Oth.* IV. ii. 109 How haue I bin behau'd, that he might sticke The small'st opinion on my least misvse?

misuse (mɪsˈjuːz), *v.* [MIS1 1. Cf. OF. *mesuser* to make a bad use (of), commit an error or misdeed.]

1. *trans.* To use or employ wrongly or improperly; to apply to a wrong purpose.

c **1374** CHAUCER *Boeth.* IV. pr. vii. (1868) 145 þe comune worde of men mysusiþ..þis manere speche of fortune. *c* **1380** WYCLIF *Sel. Wks.* III. 252 And so many men mysosiþ [? *read* mysvsiþ] her power. *c* **1460** G. ASHBY *Dicta Philos.* 378 That mysguideth his liuelode..And al his reuenues mysvseth! **1486** *Bk. St. Albans* d ij, Som folke mysuse this terme draw. **1596** SHAKS. *1 Hen. IV*, IV. ii. 13, I haue misvs'd the Kings Presse damnably. **1620** *Hist. Fr. Rush* in Thoms *E. Eng. Prose Rom.* (1858) I. 289 He had so vildly misused the order of his religion. **1754** T. GARDNER *Hist. Dunwich* III At the house is a stone coffin misused as a trough. **1765** BLACKSTONE *Comm.* I. 244 A king cannot misuse his power, without the advice of evil counsellors. **1842** TENNYSON *Godiva* 72 The Powers, who wait On noble deeds, cancell'd a sense misused. **1859** GEO. ELIOT *A. Bede* v, It turns a man's stomach t' hear the Scripture misused i' that way. **1880** 'OUIDA' *Moths* II. 117 It will not be men's fault if she misuse her liberty.

2. To subject to ill-treatment; to maltreat, ill-use.

1540 in R. G. Marsden *Sel. Pleas Crt. Adm.* I. (1894) 99 With moche other wrongs and injuries that I and other hath been mysused in tymes past. **1553** *Act 1 Mary* Sess. II. c. 3 §1 Yf any person..shall..molest..disquiet or misuse, any Preachour. **1625** PURCHAS *Pilgrims* II. 1173, I was taken by the Turks and misused and almost slain. **1632** *Star Chamb. Cases* (Camden) 128 Whereupon Walton beat the prisoner, haleing and dragginge him towardes the common goale, and otherwise misused him. **1781** COWPER *Hope* 128 Men deal with life as children with their play, Who first misuse, then cast their toys away. **1840** DICKENS *Barn. Rudge* lvi, They haven't been misusing you with sticks, or pokers,..have they, Johnny? **1884** TENNYSON *Becket* I. iv, Who misuses a dog would misuse a child—they cannot speak for themselves.

† **b.** To violate, ravish, or debauch. *Obs.*

1382 WYCLIF *Judg.* xix. 25 The which whanne al nyȝt thei hadden mysusid, thei laften hir eerly. **1538** BALE *God's Promises* v, Of late dayes thu hast mysused Bersabe, The wyfe of Urye. *c* **1540** W. SAMPSON in *Old Ways* (1892) 106 Bicause I have myseused here, I intende to make [her] a goode woman.

† **3.** *refl.* To misconduct oneself. *Obs.*

1532 in W. H. Turner *Select. Rec. Oxford* (1880) 109 For the Mysvsage of Seriaunts... Yf any of the serjaunts..doth mysuse themselfe, or geve not attendans to the Mayre, Aldermen, and Bayllyffs. **1583** *Leg. Bp. St. Androis* 953 in *Satir. Poems Reform.* xlv, I schame to tell Sa oft as I misvsit my sell, In guyding of the giftis of grace. **1581** LAMBARDE *Eiren.* II. vii. (1588) 202 If any such person..shall be taken begging, or wandring, or misusing himselfe [cf. MISORDER *v.*, quot. 1572].

† **4.** *trans.* To speak evil of; to abuse with words; to revile, deride. *Obs.*

1586 J. HOOKER *Hist. Irel.* 128/1 in *Holinshed* II, None taunting, checking, or misusing an other in anie vnseemelie wordes or deeds. **1596** SHAKS. *Tam. Shr.* I. i. 160. **1621** BURTON *Anat. Mel.* II. iii. VII. (1651) 356 Socrates was brought upon the stage by Aristophanes, and misused to his face. **1633** T. STAFFORD *Pac. Hib.* xiii. (1821) 143 Doe you not heare him misuse mee in words?

†5. 'To speak falsely of, to misrepresent'. *rare*$^{-1}$.

c **1600** SHAKS. *Sonn.* clii, All my vows are oaths but to misuse thee.

†6. To deceive, delude. (Cf. ABUSE *v.* 4.) *Obs.*

1382 WYCLIF *Ecclus.* xxv. 36 Fro thi flesh kut hir awei lest euermore sche mysvse thee. **1599** SHAKS. *Much Ado* II. ii. 28 Proofe enough, to misuse the Prince, to vexe Claudio,..and kill Leonato. **1601** SIR W. CORNWALLIS *Ess.* xxxii, Wee are misvsed by these spirites both night and day.

misused (mɪsˈjuːzd), *ppl. a.* [f. prec. + -ED^1.] Improperly used or employed; ill-treated.

c **1375** *Sc. Leg. Saints* xxxv. (*Thadee*) 17 Mysoysit beute dois Il ofte. *c* **1620** A. HUME *Brit. Tongue* (1865) 15 T, the last of these misused souldioures, keepes alwayes it's aun nature, excep it be befoer tio. **1634** MILTON *Comus* 47 The sweet poyson of mis-used Wine. **1823** SCOTT *Peveril* xxxix, Submitting to all his injustice with the endurance of a faithful and misused spaniel. **1837** J. H. NEWMAN *Par. Serm.* I. ix. 139 The poor mis-used soul is left exhausted. **1853** J. NICHOL in Knight *Mem.* (1896) 106 That misused sense of the word gallantry.

misuseful (mɪsˈjuːsfʊl), *a. rare.* [f. MISUSE + -FUL, after *useful*.] Characterized by misuse.

1890 A. LANG *Old Friends* xvi. 135 The wanton misuse, or rather the misuseful wantonness, of the Indian herb [*sc.* tobacco].

†**misˈusement.** *Obs.* [f. MISUSE *v.* + -MENT.] Ill-usage; seduction.

1561 BRENDE *Q. Curtius* IV. 56 b, And Darius coulde not be otherwyse perswaded but that she was slayne, because she woulde not consente to her mysusement.

misuser^1 (mɪsˈjuːzə(r)). [MIS-^{1} 5.] One who misuses.

1548 UDALL, etc. *Erasm. Par. Matt.* xv. 84 Not the faulte of the meates, but of the misuser. **1598** R. BERNARD tr. *Terence* (1607) 204 To him that knowes how to use them, they are good, but to the misuser of them they are ill. *c* **1643** *Maximes Unfolded* 24 The misuser of his trust may forfeit that to others. **1927** *Manch. Guardian Weekly* Oct. 315/2 An exercise in most delicate raillery at the expense of all the misusers of the English language.

misuser^2 (mɪsˈjuːzə(r)). *Law.* [a. OF. *mesuser*, inf. used as sb.: see -ER^4.] Unlawful use of a liberty or benefit such as may lead to its forfeiture.

a **1625** SIR H. FINCH *Law* (1636) 165 A franchise is.. forfeited by misusing of it. As..keeping Faire vpon two dayes when hee hath but one granted: for that is a misuser. **1664** R. ATKYNS *Orig. & Growth Printing* 19 All lesser Governments under a Monarchy may by misuser be wholly taken away, or else abated. **1766** BLACKSTONE *Comm.* II. 153 An office..may be forfeited by mis-user or non-user. **1883** *Law Times* 27 Oct. 428/1 Something which had arisen in consequence of some neglect or some misuser.

misusing (mɪsˈjuːzɪŋ), *vbl. sb.* [MIS-^{1} 3.] The action of the verb MISUSE.

1. Wrong use or employment; misuse.

c **1380** WYCLIF *Wks.* (1880) 56 Euere þe betre þat a þing is, þe worse & þe more abhominable is þe mysusynge þer-of. *c* **1393** CHAUCER *Scogan* 95 Through misusing of right. **1488–9** *Act 4 Hen. VII*, c. 6 Through the negligence of.. kepers..and by mysusyng of their Offices, the dere..is destroied. **1526** *Pilgr. Perf.* (W. de W. 1531) 238 All vnlawfull vsurpynge or misvsynge of the temporall goodes of ony persone. **1689** POPPLE tr. *Locke's 1st Let. Toleration* L.'s Wks. 1727 II. 313 Whether the Magistrate's Opinion can change..the Power he has, or excuse him to his Judge for misusing of it. **1814** MRS. J. WEST *Alicia de Lacy* II. 197 To render a strict account of our intrusted ten talents, for the mis-usings of reputation, of knowledge, of time. **1874** W. BRIGHT *Hymns* 22 Look not on our misusings of Thy grace.

†2. Misconduct. *Obs.*

1395 *Remonstrance* (1851) 153 How abhominable is the mysusinge of prelatis that holden benefisid men in seculer officis. **1532** MORE *Confut. Tindale* Wks. 346/2 He semed verye penitent of hys mysseusing of hymself, in falling to Tyndalles heresies agayne. **1540** SIR W. EURE in Ellis *Orig. Lett.* Ser. III. III. 280 For the reformacion of the mysusing of the Spiritualtie in Scotlande.

†3. Maltreatment. *Obs.*

1590 SIR J. SMYTH *Disc. Weapons* Ded. 5 b, [They] haue liued..more vpon the spoile, and misusing of the common people. **1647** HEXHAM, *Een mishandelinge*, a Mis-using.

misˈvalue, *v.* [MIS-^{1} 1.] *trans.* To value falsely or wrongly; to misesteem.

a **1626** [see MISRATE]. **1614** J. DAVIES *Ecl.* in Browne *Sheph. Pipe* G 3 b, I dread my warke Woll be misualued both of old and yong. **1875** TENNYSON *Q. Mary* III. ii, I fear the Emperor much misvalued me. **1900** *Athenæum* 21 Apr. 490/2 After having been ignored or misvalued during his life.

So **misvaluˈation.**

1903 *Daily Chron.* 26 May 3/2 This same misvaluation is perhaps responsible for the statement that [etc.].

misˈventure, *sb.* Now *arch.* [MIS-^{1} 4.] An unfortunate venture; a mischance, misadventure.

1563 HYLL *Art Garden.* (1574) A iv b, Whosoeuer thou be, That by misuenture or by will, shall chaunce this booke to see. **1755** SMOLLETT *Quix.* III. v. I. 108 All the misventures, which have this day happened to us, are designed as a punishment for the sins committed by your worship. **1831** *Fraser's Mag.* III. 131 From among so many shipwrecks and misventures one goodly vessel comes to land. **1858** CARLYLE *Fredk. Gt.* VI. i. II. 136 Pranks enough, and misventures,—half-drowning 'in the mill-race at Annamoe in Ireland', for one.

¶ In allusion to Cervantes' use of *desventura* (see DISVENTURE): Foolish 'adventure'.

1839 J. M. WILSON *Tales Borders* V. 96/2 Like all good knights of misventure, I fainted and fell down upon the floor. **1881** DUFFIELD tr. *Don Quixote* I. v. 61 My honoured uncle would read those impious books of misventures.

†**misˈventure**, *v. Obs. rare*$^{-1}$. [MIS-^{1} 1.] *trans.* To risk in bad investments.

1677 YARRANTON *Eng. Improv.* 20 Moneys misventur'd by trusting and bad Securities.

misˈventurous, *a. rare*$^{-1}$. [MIS-^{1} 7.] Not venturous; timid.

1882 CARLYLE in *Century Mag.* XXIV. 20 Misventurous Irishwomen, giving up their plan of emigration to Australia.

misvocaliˈzation. [MIS-^{1} 4.] The insertion of incorrect vowel-signs in forms of writing consisting mainly or entirely of consonants.

1932 *Times Lit. Suppl.* 14 Jan. 20/2 Surely *kābhôdh* 'glory' ..is a misvocalization of *kābhēdh* 'liver'. **1942** *Jrnl. Theol. Stud.* XLIII. 155 An act. verb is required by the context on Gunkel's restoration of the text; the misvocalization is due to the unusual form.

misˈvouched, *pa. pple.* and *ppl. a.* [MIS-^{1} 2.]

1. Alleged wrongly.

a **1626** BACON *True Greatness Brit.* Wks. 1859 VII. 56 That very..saying of Mutianus, which was the original of this opinion [that money is the sinews of war] is misvouched, for his speech was, *Pecuniæ sunt nervi belli civilis*.

2. Not well vouched for.

1876 [see MISTUTORED].

†**misˈwandered**, *ppl. a. Obs.* [MIS-^{1} 2.] In which one has gone astray.

1590 SPENSER *F.Q.* III. vii. 18 His late miswandred wayes now to remeasure right. **1620** QUARLES *Feast of Wormes* ix, They..relented, And (changing their mis-wandred wayes) repented.

†**misˈwandering**, *ppl. a. Obs.* [MIS-^{1} 2.] Going astray.

c **1374** CHAUCER *Boeth.* II. pr. viii. (1868) 61 Amyable fortune..draweth mys wandrynge men [orig. *devios*] fro the souereyne good. *Ibid.* III. pr. ii. 65 þe myswandryng errour mysledip hem in to false goodes. **1631** QUARLES *Hist. Samson* vii, Can thy miswandring eyes choose none, but her, That is the child of an Idolater? **1645** —— *Solomons Recant.* Solil. v, Wavering footsteps, and miswandring eyes.

†**misˈwaste**, *v. Obs.* [MIS-^{1} 8.] *trans.* To lavish foolishly.

c **1380** WYCLIF *Sel. Wks.* III. 400 þo seed of Gods word is better þen þo seed of mon: þerfore hit is worse to mysspende þat þen to myswaste monnys seed. *a* **1618** SYLVESTER *Spectacles* viii. Wks. (Grosart) II. 298 Their Health, Wealth, Wit, mis-wasted Are but as blossoms blasted.

†**misˈway.** *Obs.* [MIS-^{1} 4.] A wrong path.

c **1374** CHAUCER *Boeth.* III. met. xi. (1868) 100 Who so that ..coueyteth nat to ben deseyuyd by no mys-weyes [orig. *nullis deviis*] *Ibid.* v. pr. i. 149 It is to douten þat þou ne be maked weery by mysweys.

b. quasi-*adv.* in ***to go misway***, to go astray.

c **1400** *Rom. Rose* 4766 Love makith alle to goon miswey.

misˈwed, *v.* [MIS-^{1} 1.] *trans.* To marry unsuitably. Also **misˈwedded** *ppl. a.*, of a marriage: Wrongly or unsuitably contracted.

1645 MILTON *Tetrach.* Wks. 1851 IV. 167 Every ungodly and miswedded mariage. **1828–32** WEBSTER, *Miswed*, to wed improperly.

†**misˈween**, *v. Obs.* [MIS-^{1} 1.]

1. *intr.* To have a wrong opinion. Also with *clause*.

1590 SPENSER *F.Q.* II. i. Prol. iii, Why then should witlesse man so much misweene, That nothing is but that which he hath seene? **1594** —— *Astr.* xvii, Full happie man (misweening much) was hee. *a* **1640** JACKSON *Creed* XII. iv. Wks. XII. 27 The Jews..misweening that the whole family ..of God..should be comprised within the..family of Abraham.

2. *trans.* To think wrongly of, misjudge.

1614 J. DAVIES *Ecl.* in Browne *Sheph. Pipe* G 4 For thy tho Songsters are misween'd of all. **1749** MELMOTH *Fitzosborne's Lett.* II. lxxii. 105 Ne thou, O man! who deal'st the tort, misween The equal gods.

†**misˈweening**, *vbl. sb. Obs.* [MIS-^{1} 3.] Misthinking; misjudgement; mistrust.

1488 CAXTON *Chast. Goddes Chyldern* 92 A man shall put suche mysweenyng away from hym. **1571** GOLDING *Calvin on Ps.* lix. 20 They bee made drunken as wel with their owne misweening as with the flattery of the common sorte. **1590** SPENSER *F.Q.* I. iv. 1 Least..rash misweening doe thy hart remove.

†**misˈweigh**, *v. Obs. rare*$^{-1}$. In 5 **mysweye**. [MIS-^{1} 1.] *trans.* To weigh amiss.

c **1450** *Godstow Reg.* 9/157 The balance of vertues I haue mysweyed, With sleyng of tonge, or with wilfulnesse [etc.].

†**misˈwend**, *v. Obs.* [MIS-^{1} 1. (For certain uses of *miswent* see MISGO *v.*)]

1. *trans.* To turn in a wrong direction; to misapply; to lead astray; to pervert.

1340 *Ayenb.* 22 Ac uor hire euele tongen hi miswendeþ moche uolk to done wel. *Ibid.* 62 Huanne he miswent and went to þe worse half al þet he yherþ oþer yziþ. **1390** GOWER *Conf.* III. 80 Nectanabus his craft miswente. *a* **1450** *Pol. Poems* (Rolls) II. 243 Ther the Bibelle is al myswent To jangle of Job or Jeremye. *c* **1460** G. ASHBY *Dicta Philos.* 469 That the myddyl of your liffe be not spent In ydelnesse, ne in vnthrifte myswent.

2. *pass.* and *intr.* To go astray (*lit.* and *fig.*); to come to grief. Pa. pple. *miswent* = **a.** gone astray; **b.** out of gear; dilapidated; ruined.

1297 R. GLOUC. (Rolls) 7217 Vr louerd..prest aþ imad uor to smite men þat beþ mis wend. **1340** *Ayenb.* 27 þe herte of þe enuious is enuenymed and suo miswent. **1390** GOWER *Conf.* I. 21 And eche in his compleignte telleth How that the world is al miswent. *Ibid.* 331 And that makth al mi world miswende. **1413** *Pilgr. Sowle* (Caxton 1483) III. iii. 51 Good hede he took..that cord or chaine were nought myswent other wise than it shold. **1581** RICH *Farew.* (1846) 38, I now forsake the former tyme I spent, And sorry am, for that I was miswent. *a* **1586** SIDNEY *Sonn.* in *Arcadia* (1622) 494 What? is thy Bagpipe broke, or are thy lambes miswent? **1591** [see MISCOUNSEL *v.*]. **1596** SPENSER *F.Q.* IV. v. 30 Who likewise sought her lover long miswent. **1600** FAIRFAX *Tasso* II. x. 21 In this maze still wandred and miswent. **1723** *Portland Papers* (Hist. MSS. Comm.) VI. 77 He that would see a church miswent, Let him go to Cuckeston in Kent.

†**misˈwill.** *Obs.* [MIS-^{1} 4.] Wrong desire.

1496 *Dives & Pauper* (W. de W.) vii. Introd. 27/1 Her wycked couetyse and myswyll of richesse.

†**misˈwin**, *v. Obs.* [MIS-^{1} 1.] *trans.* To obtain wrongfully.

1377 LANGL. *P. Pl.* B. XIII. 42 Of þat men mys-wonne þei made hem wel at ese. *c* **1613** in *Overbury's Wks.* (1856) 10 As if the day Were come, wherein another Phaeton Stolne into Phœbus waine, had all misse-won A cleane contrary way.

mis-ˈwish, *sb.* [MIS-^{1} 4.] Wrong desire.

1865 J. GROTE *Moral Ideas* ii. (1876) 31 Mis-craving is physical disease, mis-wish is mental.

mis-ˈwish, *v.* [MIS-^{1} 1.] *trans.* To have wrong wishes with regard to.

1831 CARLYLE *Misc. Ess., Early German Lit.* (1840) III. 173 He men miswishes and misjudges, Inferiors scorns, superiors grudges.

So †**misˈwishing** *vbl. sb.*, wrong desire.

1571 GOLDING *Calvin on Ps.* xxxv. 25 This miswishing hath bin expounded.

†**misˈwite**, *v. Obs.* [MIS-^{1} 1 or 7.] To neglect.

a **1225** *Ancr. R.* 202 To..miswiten ei þing þet heo haueð to witene.

†**misˈwive**, *v. Obs.* [MIS-^{1} 1.] *trans.* To marry unlawfully.

c **1250** *Gen. & Ex.* 540 Two hundred ȝer after ðo wunes, Mis-wiuen hem gunnen seðes sunes.

†**miswoman.** *Obs.* [app. f. MIS *a.* + WOMAN.] A 'bad woman'; a strumpet.

1528 TINDALE *Parab. Wicked Mammon* 17 Mysse women tyre them selues with golde and sylke to please theyr louers. **1530** PALSGR. 831 As a mysse woman is at ones commaundement. *c* **1530** *Remedy of Love* Chaucer's Wks. (1561) 322 b, Flie the miswoman, lest she thee disceiue, Thus saith Salomon. **15..** *Guistard & Sismond* II. (1597) C 6, Sooner..Then ye wold euer haue thought to be a mis-woman.

†**misˈwonting**, *vbl. sb. Obs.* [MIS-^{1} 3.] Disuse.

1627 BP. HALL *Div. Medit.* vii, These feeble beginnings.. are soone extinguished by intermission, and by mis-wonting, perish.

misword (mɪsˈwɜːd), *sb.* Now *dial.* Also 9 **miss word.** [MIS-^{1} 4. (Cf. MIS *a.*)] A harsh, angry, or cross word.

a **1225** *Ancr. R.* 190 A mis-word þet ȝe þolieð. **1598** SYLVESTER *Du Bartas* II. iii. IV. 1015 Where..the Tyrant's sword Is not made drunk with blood for a Mis-word. **1603** HOLLAND *Plutarch's Mor.* 111 What mis-word can they have to say unto you? **1603** BRETON *Packet Mad Lett.* (1633) 38, I haue receiued your snappish Letter whereby I see you are more angry, then I thought you would haue beene for a misword or two. **1801** W. HUNTINGTON *Bank of Faith* 88 Not one creditor ever gave me a miss word in this world. **1824** MRS. CAMERON *Pink Tippet* II. 33 If a miss word was said by chance, she would never let it drop. **1872** MRS. H. WOOD *Within the Maze* i, Not a mis-word would ever have arisen between them.

mis-ˈword, *v.* [MIS-^{1} 1.] *trans.* To word (a message) incorrectly. Also **mis-ˈworded** *ppl. a.*

1883 *Advance* (Chicago) 16 Aug., A number of mis-worded telegrams. **1895** *Funk's Stand. Dict.*, *Mis-word*, to word wrongly or inaccurately; as the telegram was misworded.

mis-ˈwording, *vbl. sb.* [MIS-^{1} 3.] Wrong wording or expression.

a **1680** BUTLER *Rem.* (1759) I. 425 [They] spoil all they do by wilful Miswording of their Acts. **1804** EARL MALMESBURY *Diaries & Corr.* III. 327 A Miswording in the original Message.

†**misˈwork**, *v. Obs.* Chiefly in *pa. pple.* **miswrought.** [MIS-^{1} 1.]

1. *trans.* (with indefinite obj.) To do amiss.

a **1300** *Assump. Virg.* (Camb. MS.) 187 ȝef ihc habbe eny þing mis wroȝt, Tellez hit me. **1340** HAMPOLE *Pr. Consc.* 1993 Turne agayne þan may he noght For to amend þat he has myswroght. *c* **1407** LYDG. *Reas. & Sens.* 2930 Yif any thing I ha myswrought. *a* **1529** SKELTON *Replyc.* Wks. I. 214 Howe ye haue small contrycion Of that ye haue mys-wrought. **1554** *Interlude of Youth* C iij, And amende that thou hast myswrought.

2. *intr.* To act amiss; to commit an offence.

c **1350** *Will. Palerne* 5148 þat sche wold miswerche wrongli any time. **1413** *Pilgr. Sowle* (Caxton 1483) I. xv. 12, I am that same that hyely haue myswrought. *c* **1450** *Cov. Myst.* 121 Aȝens God thou hast myswrought.

3. *trans.* To manufacture badly.

a **1626** BACON *Charge Sess. Verge* (1662) 19 That which is miswrought will miswear.

mis'worship, *sb.* [MIS-¹ 4.] Wrong or false worship.

1626 BP. HALL *Contempl., O.T.* xx. 118 He was not more the father of a later Iereboam, then (in respect of misworship) he was the son of the first Iereboam, who made Israel to sin. **1840** CARLYLE *Heroes* i. (1841) 5 Such hideous inextricable jungle of misworships, misbeliefs.

mis'worship, *v.* [MIS-¹ 1.] *trans.* To worship amiss. Also **mis'worshipping** *vbl. sb.*; **mis'worshipper.**

1640 BP. HALL *Serm.* Wks. 1837 V. 420 In them God is made our idol, and we the misworshippers of him. **1647** WARD *Simp. Cobler* 35, I fear many holy men have not so deeply humbled themselves for their former misworshippings of God as [etc.]. *a* **1656** BP. HALL *Soul's Farew.* §3 There have not wanted nations..which have misworshipped it [heaven] for their God.

†**mis'wrench,** *v. Obs.* Only in pa. pple. 4 **myswreynt.** [MIS-¹ 1.] *trans.* To twist out of shape.

1390 GOWER *Conf.* II. 189 The wardes of the cherche keie Thurgh mishandlinge ben myswreynt.

†**mis'wrest,** *v. Obs.* [MIS-¹ 1.] *trans.* To pervert; *esp.* to pervert the meaning of (a passage).

a **1400** *Pety Job* 369 in *26 Pol. Poems* 133 All thys world now ys myswrest, To carpe thys, lorde, ayenst the. **1532** MORE *Confut. Tindale* Wks. 501/2 The heretikes wrested & misse construed the scripture (as we see that these heretikes much more mysse wrest it nowe). **1583** GOLDING *Calvin on Deut.* lxx. 31 b, Ye see how this Text hath bin miswrested.

miswrite (mɪsˈraɪt), *v.* [MIS-¹ 1.] *trans.* To write incorrectly; to make a mistake in writing (a word, etc.). Also **mis'written** *ppl. a.*

c **1000** ÆLFRIC *Gram.* l. (Z.) 294 ʒif hit byð miswriten oððe miscweden of þam rihtan cræfte. *c* **1374** CHAUCER *Troylus* v. 1795 So preye I god that noon miswryte thee, Ne thee mismetre. **1533** MORE *Apol.* vii. Wks. 858/2 These wordes seme to be miswritten, either in the principall booke, or in the copy. **1614** RALEIGH *Hist. World* II. xxii. §6 Whether it were so that Iosephus did omit, or else that he did mis-write, some number of the yeares. **1677** WALLIS in Rigaud *Corr. Sci. Men* (1841) II. 608 At your note K, I desire you to consider if there be not somewhat miswritten. **18..** KINGSLEY *Sir W. Raleigh* in *Misc.* (1859) I. 33 That the passage..is either misquoted, or miswritten by Raleigh himself, I cannot doubt. **1876** EMERSON *Ess.* Ser. II. i. 15 And substitute something of our own, and thus miswrite the poem. **1884** A. R. PENNINGTON *Wiclif* ii. 22 *note*, The miswritten word *apocrisus*, instead of *apocryphus*. **1899** PLUMMER *Sax. Chron.* II. p. xxxii, 1130 (miswritten 1080, MLXXX having been substituted for MCXXX).

miswriting (mɪsˈraɪtɪŋ), *vbl. sb.* [MIS-¹ 3.] An error in writing.

1430–1 *Rolls of Parlt.* IV. 378/1 Ony errour in myswrityng. **1632–3** LAUD *Hist. Chanc. Oxf.* Rem. 1700 II. 58 That Slip was but in the mis-writing of one word. **1677** W. MOUNTAGU in *Buccleuch MSS.* (Hist. MSS. Comm.) I. 325 There are some little miswriting[s] in the patent. **1752** J. LOUTHIAN *Form of Process* 167 Nor shall any such miswriting, &c. after Conviction, be Cause to stay or arrest Judgment. **1828** THIRLWALL & HARE tr. *Niebuhr's Hist. Rome* (1855) I. 264 The greatest difficulties in them [*sc.* the Fasti of Diodorus] arise from mis-writing. **1869** E. A. FREEMAN *O.E. Hist.* vii. 92 *note*, The text of the Chronicle has *three* years, but it seems clear that this must be a miswriting for *thirteen*.

miswrought: see MISWORK *v.*

†**mis'wune.** *Obs.* [MIS-¹ 4.] Evil habit.

c **1200** *Trin. Coll. Hom.* 13 For te quenchen..his lust þe miswune haueð on broht.

†**'misy.** *Obs.* Also 7 **mysy, missy.** [a. L. *misy* (Pliny), a. Gr. μίσυ. Cf. F. *misy*, It. *misi.*]

1. A kind of mushroom or truffle.

1601 HOLLAND *Pliny* XIX. iii. II. 7 Within the province of Cyrenaica in Affricke, there is found the like excrescence, called Misy, passing sweet and pleasant.

2. A kind of copper ore, usually identified as yellow copperas or copiapite.

There is no evidence that the word was ever used in Eng. except with reference to the mineral described by Pliny.

1601 HOLLAND *Pliny* XXXIV. xii. II. 510 Some..have written, that Mysy is engendred by the means of a fire made with pine wood, in the hollow veines..of brasse ore... But the truth is, of the foresaid stone or ore [*sc.* chalcitis] it is engendred naturally. **1616** BULLOKAR *Eng. Expos., Misy*, a kind of yellow copperas, shining like gold, brought out of Egypt and the Ile of Cyprus. **1661** LOVELL *Hist. Anim. & Min., Isagoge*, Some [minerals] have only little sparks, as misy. **1683** PETTUS *Fleta Min.* II. 90 *Missy*..which G. Agricola from Pliny, calls *Atramentum sutorium*, or shoemakers Black; but Pliny makes it a kind of Vitriol. **1722** QUINCY *Lex. Physico-Med.* (ed. 2). *a* **1775** SIR J. HILL *Materia Med.* 141.

misy, obs. form of MIZZY.

†**mis'yearning,** *vbl. sb.* In 4 **-ȝarninge.** [MIS-¹ 3.] Wrong desire.

c **1375** *Sc. Leg. Saints* iii. (*Andrew*) 451 þat..he, throw þe croice of þe blissit tre, suld exclude of misȝarninge þe tre.

†**mis'yeme,** *v. Obs.* [MIS-¹ 1.] *trans.* To neglect.

1028–*c* **1060** *Law Northumb. Priests* xxxiv. (Liebermann) 382 ʒif preost sceare misʒime beardes oððe feaxes, ʒebete þæt. *a* **1225** *Ancr. R.* 344 þe þinges in þisse riwle þet beoð misȝemed. **13..** *E.E. Allit. P.* A. 322 For hit was for-garte, at paradys greue Oure ȝore fader hit con mysseȝeme.

†**mis'yenge,** *v. Obs.* [f. MIS-¹ 1. + *ȝengen, GENG *v.*] *intr.* To go astray, miss.

a **1250** *Owl & Night.* 1229 (Cott.) ȝef me ikepþ mid iwarnesse An fleo schal toward misȝenge [*Jesus MS.* misyenge].

misyoke (mɪsˈjəʊk), *v.* [MIS-¹ 1.] *trans.* To yoke or join (in marriage) unsuitably. Also *intr.*, to be so yoked.

1645 MILTON *Divorce* I. viii. 18 Therefore saith the Apostle *2 Cor.* 6, 'Mis-yoke not together with infidels', which is interpreted of marriage. *Ibid.* II. xix. 70 Hinder'd in wedlock by mis-yoking with a diversity of nature as well as of religion. **1645** —— *Tetrach.* Wks. 1851 IV. 150 Where the yoke is mis-yok't, heretick with faithfull. **1872** TENNYSON *Last Tourn.* 566 Misyoked with such a want of man.

mis'zealous, *a.* [MIS-¹ 6.] Wrongly zealous.

1617 BP. HALL *Quo Vadis?* §16 Their mis-zealous passions hide themselues in a pleasing sweetnesse. **1641** —— *Answ. Vind. Smectymn.* 66 Let those mis-zealous men..see how they will answer it. **1641** MILTON *Animadv.* Wks. 1851 III. 196 The practizes, and combinations of Libelling Separatists, and the miszealous advocates thereof.

miszen, obs. form of MIZEN.

mit (mɪt), *sb. Obs.* exc. *dial.* Forms: 1 **mitte,** 5 **mytte,** 9 **mit.** [OE. *mitte* wk. fem.:—OTeut. type **mitjôn-*, f. root **met* to measure: see METE *v.* Cf. OHG. *mezzo* masc., '[h]eminus', MHG. *metze*, G. *metze* masc., fem., a measure for corn, salt, etc.]

†**1.** A measure of capacity, in OE. app. = two ambers; mentioned as used for corn, meal, honey, ale, wine; in 15th c. used for salt. *Obs.*

804–29 *Charters*, etc. (Thorpe) 460, xxx. ombra godes Uuelesces aloð þet limpnað to xv. mittum. *c* **1050** *Voc.* in Wr.-Wülcker 359/8 *Bata*, mittan. *c* **1450** *Godstow Reg.* 664 In the wyche xiiij. myttes of Salte [L. *xiiii. mittas salis*].

2. *dial.* 'A shallow tub, or other like vessel, used for household purposes' (Miss Jackson *Shropsh. Word-bk.*, Suppl. 1879), as ***butter-mit, kneading-mit.*** Cf. MOAT *sb.*²

1847 HALLIWELL, *Butter-mit*, a small tub in which newly-made butter is washed. *West.*

‖**mit** (mɪt), *prep. colloq.* or *jocular.* [G., with.] With (esp. with apparent ellipsis of 'me' or 'us').

1885 W. JAMES *Let.* 19 Feb. (1920) I. 241, I..suppose Mrs. Godkin will come *mit.* **1922** JOYCE *Ulysses* 505 Will some pleashe pershon not now impediment so catastrophics mit agitation of firstclass table-numpkin? **1959** D. BARTON *Loving Cup* 237 Why not come along mit.

mit, obs. form of MIGHT *sb.*; var. MITT, a mitten.

‖**mita** (ˈmiːtə). [Sp.] In the Spanish-American colonies: A certain portion of the Indian population chosen by lot for a specified period of forced labour in the public service.

1726 J. STEVENS tr. *Herrera's Hist. America* V. 56 The Mitayos Tindarunas are Tributary Indians, the Curacas, or native Lords have set apart to hire them out to work in the Mines, build Houses, and the like... These they furnish to serve in their Mitas, or Turns, for the Space of two Months, or longer. **1777** ROBERTSON *Hist. Amer.* VIII. (1851) II. 102 In Peru, each *mita*, or division, destined for the mines, remains there six months. **1812** *Ann. Reg., Gen. Hist.* 161 The inhumanity..of that regulation in the American colonies [of Spain] called the Mitas. **1880** C. R. MARKHAM *Peruv. Bark* 147 *Mitas* of Indians, for the purpose of collecting coca-leaves, were forbidden in 1569.

Mitanni (mɪˈtænɪ). Name of the people and language of Mitanni, a Hurrian kingdom centred on the Habur and Upper Euphrates which flourished in the fifteenth and early fourteenth centuries B.C. Also *attrib.* or as *adj.* So **Mi'tannian** *sb.*, an inhabitant of Mitanni; the language of Mitanni; **Mi'tannian, Mi'tannite** (*rare*) *adjs.*, of or pertaining to Mitanni, its people, or its language.

1897 A. H. SAYCE in *Proc. Soc. Biblical Archæol.* XIX. 285 Tesup was the Mitannian Air-god. **1900** —— *Ibid.* XXII. 176 The Mitannian language was highly agglutinative. *Ibid.* 182 The verb in Mitannian has hardly been differentiated from the noun. **1907** —— *Archæol. Cuneiform Inscr.* vi. 169 On the west..the Mitannians found themselves confronted by another northern population, the Hittites. **1910** *Encycl. Brit.* XIII. 539/1 Whether the Mitanni..were racially kin to the Hatti, cannot be determined at present. **1911** *Ibid.* XVIII. 182/2 From cuneiform sources we know the names of six other Mitanni rulers. *Ibid.*, The language of the Mitanni state..was neither Aryan nor Semitic. *Ibid.* 183/1 The Hittite King's interference restored the Mitannite state as a protectorate. **1933** L. BLOOMFIELD *Lang.* iv. 65 Extinct languages of an older time..Mitanni, east of Mesopotamia, from around 1400 B.C. **1939** L. H. GRAY *Foundations of Lang.* 380 Northern Mesopotamia was the home of the *Subaraean* group,..divided into Mitannian and Khurrian (or Kharrian), which were very similar, if not identical. **1948** D. DIRINGER *Alphabet* 90 Hurrian..differs but very little from the language of the Mitanni. **1948** G. R. DRIVER *Semitic Writing* iii. 131 The proto-Elamites in the East and the Hittites and the Mitanni in the north devised their own systems of pictographic and cuneiform writing. **1952** *Trans. Philol. Soc.* 117 Chance..has also apparently left us without a *ŭ*-stem among the Indoeuropean borrowings into certain languages of the ancient Near East—Mitanni, Kassite, Lycian and the like. **1955** T. BURROW *Sanskrit Lang.* i. 28 The author..was a Mitannian called Kikkuli. **1970** [see ELAMITE *sb.* and *a.*]. **1973** A. MALAMAT in D. J. Wiseman *Peoples Old Testament Times* vi. 149 The Aramaeans were always strongly influenced by the specific local environment, in Mesopotamia by the remnants of the Mitanni culture and by the Assyrians. **1973** H. A. HOFFNER in *Ibid.* ix. 223 It was these Mitannians who were responsible for the introduction into the Near East of scientific techniques for the breeding and training of chariot horses. *Ibid.* 224 The Hittite conqueror caught his Mitannian foes off guard and routed all opposition.

mitch (mɪtʃ), *v.* Now *dial.* Also 5–7 **miche,** 6 **myche,** 6–7 **mitche,** 9 **mich, meech.** [app. a. OF. *muchier, mucier* to hide, also intr. to skulk, lurk.]

†**1.** *trans.* To pilfer. *Obs.*

[*a* **1225**: cf. MICHER *sb.*] **1390** [Implied in MITCHING *vbl. sb.*]. *c* **1440** *Promp. Parv.* 337/1 Mychyn, or pryuely stelyn smale things. **1496** *Dives & Paup.* (W. de W.) I. liii. 94/1 That he myght haue myched or deled the moneye awaye, for he bare the purce. **1570** LEVINS *Manip.* 115/32 To Mych, *suffurari. Ibid.* 130/10 To Pilch, miche, *suffurari.*

2. *intr.* **a.** To shrink or retire from view; to lurk out of sight; to skulk. Also *pass.* and Const. *off.*

1558 PHAER *Æneid* v. (1573) O ij b, To woods, and mountayn caues, and holes of rocks they miching ronne. **1581** STUDLEY *Seneca's Herc. Œtæus* II. 193 b, Myche where thou mayst vnspyde. **1582** STANYHURST *Æneis* IV. (Arb.) 104 What doe ye forge? wherefore thus vaynely in land Lybye mitche you? **1602** HEYWOOD *Wom. Killed w. Kindn.* Wks. 1874 II. 113, I neuer look'd for better of that rascall Since he came miching first into our house. **1605** *Hist. Stukeley* D 3, Then will we not come miching thus by night But charge the towne and winne it by day light. **1612** CHAPMAN *Widowes T.* v. i. K 4 b, Where found you him? My truant was mich't, Sir, into a blind corner of the Tomb. **1728** BAILEY, To *Miche*, to stand off, to hang back. **1907** J. M. SYNGE *Playboy of Western World* II. 42 You're pot-boy in this place, and I'll not have you mitch off from us now. **1960** A. CLARKE *Later Poems* (1961) 84, I mitched from miracles.

b. To play truant.

1580 LYLY *Euphues* (Arb.) 279 What made the Gods so often to trewant from Heauen, and mych heere on earth, but beautie? *a* **1586** SIDNEY *Astr. & Stella* xlvi, Yet, deare, let me his pardon get of you, So long, though he from book myche to desire, Till without fewell you can make hot fire. **1624–5** *Exeter City Mun.* in *Notes & Gleanings* (Exeter) II. 187/1 Some of oʳ children pretendinge that they went to schoole went a meechinge half a yeare or more together. **1672** [H. STUBBE] *Rosemary & Bayes* 18 Like truant children forsook their school, to go miching after blackberries. *c* **1806** T. SWIFT *Town Scene* in *Poet. Reg.* (1806–7) 157 On mischief bent, the imps had mitch'd from school. **1867** W. F. ROCK *Jim an' Nell* 6 Wan vomoon Hur mitched vro' schule. **1879** in Fitzpatrick *Life Lever* I. 10 One day Charley and I mitched from school. **1888** 'Q' *Troy Town* xi. 117 Turn your back, an' they'd be mitchin' in a brace o' shakes. **1900** UPWARD *Eben. Lobb* 96 The limp and trembling boy..now looked as if he could never mich from Sabbath-school or throw a stone..again. **1933** DAVIES & THOMSON tr. *O'Sullivan's 20 Yrs. A-Growing* i. 6 What would you say for us to go mitching? *a* **1953** DYLAN THOMAS *Quite Early One Morning* (1954) 84 He cribbed, mitched, spilt ink, rattled his desk and garbled his lessons with the worst of them. **1968** *TV Times* 28 Sept.–4 Oct. 69/1, I used to mitch a lot from school because I simply dreaded it.

†**3. a.** To grumble secretly. **b.** To pretend poverty. *Obs.*

1598 FLORIO, *Nicchiare*, to lament..to miche, to grumble closely or show some signe of discontent. **1611** COTGR., *Faire le senaud*..to miche it, or a rich man to make shew of pouertie.

mitch, var. MICH *sb.* and obs. f. MUCH.

mitch-board (ˈmɪtʃbɔəd). *Naut.* [? f. *mitch* = MICHE *sb.*² + BOARD *sb.*] A support for a boom, yard, etc., when not in use.

1883 E. W. H. HOLDSWORTH *Sea Fisheries* 58 The mast of these Yarmouth luggers..is supported about the middle by a broad upright piece of wood called a 'mitch-board'. **1887** HALL CAINE *Deemster* (1888) 65 Davy jumped on deck, took a lantern, and fixed it to the top of the mitch-board. **1894** R. LEIGHTON *Wreck Golden Fleece* 18 The crutch of the mitch-board.

mitche, obs. form of MITCH *v.*

mitchel (ˈmɪtʃəl). ? *Obs.* [Possibly from the surname *Mitchel*; it can hardly represent the obsolete southern *mitchel* = MICKLE *a.*] (See quots.)

1669 in *Dict. Archit.* (Arch. Publ. Soc.) s.v., For paving the upper pawne with Mitchells per foote 8*d.* **1703** T. N. *City & C. Purchaser* 202 *Mitchels*, Purbeck-stones for Paving, pick'd all of a Size, from 15 inches square to 2 Foot. **1737** SALMON *Country Build. Estim.* (ed. 2) 3 Purbeck Paving at promiscuous Sizes..is about 7*d.* or 8*d.* per Foot; also Mitchels are valued at about 1*s.* 10*d.* per Foot. **1842** GWILT *Archit.*, *Mitchel*, a name given by workmen to Purbeck stones of twenty-four by fifteen inches when squared for building. [Perh. an error: cf. quot. 1703.]

Mitchell (ˈmɪtʃəl). The name of Sir Thomas Livingstone *Mitchell* (1792–1855), Scottish-born explorer of Australia, used *attrib.* in **Mitchell grass** to designate an Australian fodder grass of the genus *Astrebla.*

1883 F. M. BAILEY *Synopsis Queensland Flora* 660 Used for food by the natives. The most valuable fodder-grass of the colony. True Mitchell-grass. **1902** *Encycl. Brit.* XXXII. 108/2 The 'Mitchell grasses' (*Astrebla pectinata*) and its varieties, viz., the Wheat (*triticoides*), the weeping (*elymoides*), and the curly (*curvifolia*),..have the most extraordinary vitality. **1909** *Chambers's Jrnl.* Dec. 809/2 Mitchell grass is said to be able to survive a rainless period extending over three years. **1927** M. M. BENNETT *Christison*

v. 55 Curly Mitchell grass shimmered gold and silver. **1934** *Bulletin* (Sydney) 27 June 22/1 Bull Mitchell grass and its seed is easily the best feed we have. **1936** I. L. IDRIESS *Cattle King* xix. 178 Thudding through the Mitchell grass to the crackling of sticks and flying gravel, the mob galloped on. **1948** V. PALMER *Golconda* xix. 153 League upon league of crinkly Mitchell grass. **1965** *Austral. Encycl.* IV. 365/1 Four species of *Astrebla* (Mitchell grasses) are known. Because the dry leaves remain attached to the plant and support stock in times of drought, they have become famous as fodder plants.

‖**mitchella** (mɪˈtʃɛlə). *Bot.* [Mod.Lat.; named by Linnæus in 1753 after the botanist John *Mitchell* (died 1768).] A genus of trailing evergreen herbs of the N.O. *Rubiaceæ*; a plant of this genus, e.g. *M. repens*, the partridge-berry.

1824 LOUDON *Encycl. Gard.* Gen. Index (ed. 2) 1206/2 Mitchelia [*read* Mitchella]..a diminutive creeper which grows in peat soil. **1862** DARWIN in *Life & Lett.* III. 301 The Mitchella very good, but pollen apparently equal-sized. **1870** MRS. WHITNEY *We Girls* ii, Leslie was quick to spy the bit of creeping mitchella.

mitcher, variant of MICHER *sb.*

mitching (ˈmɪtʃɪŋ), *ppl. a. Obs.* exc. *dial.* Also 6–9 **miching**, 7 **micking**, **meiching**, 8–9 **meeching**. [f. MITCH *v.* + -ING[2].] Pilfering, skulking, truant-playing, pretending poverty.

1581 LAMBARDE *Eiren.* II. vi. (1588) 196 Either miching or mightie theeues. **1592** SYLVESTER *Tri. Faith* IV. v, Here, myching Jonas (sunk in sudden Storm) Of his Deliverance findes a Fish the mean. **1609** BP. W. BARLOW *Answ. Nameless Cath.* 68 A miching Curre, biting her behinde, when she cannot turne backe. **1614** DYKE *Myst. Selfe-deceit* (1615) 40 They are no miching and scraping niggards, but rather wasteful and riotous prodigals. **1621** T. WILLIAMSON tr. *Goulart's Wise Vieillard* 72 What myching couetousnesse is it, not to bee willing to part with somewhat of that which we haue. *a* **1625** FLETCHER *Noble Gent.* I. i, O my meiching varlet—I'll fit ye as I live. **1766** J. ADAMS *Diary* 2 Jan., Wks. 1850 II. 173 Meeching, sordid, stupid creatures,..they deserve to be made slaves to their own negroes! **1857** KINGSLEY *Two Y. Ago* I. 116 You loafing, miching, wrecking crow-keepers. **1866** BLACKMORE *C. Nowell* li, Not even a shark's fin, or a mitching dolphin. **1877** —— *Erema* xliii, Two miching boys, who meant to fish for minnows with a pin. **1939** DYLAN THOMAS *Map of Love* 14 When I whistled with mitching boys through a reservoir park.

mitching (ˈmɪtʃɪŋ), *vbl. sb. Obs.* exc. *dial.* Also 4–9 **miching**, 7 **micking**. [f. MITCH *v.* + -ING[1].] Pilfering, skulking, playing truant. Also Comb., as ***mitching-time***. †***in mitching wise***: in a skulking or surreptitious manner.

1390 GOWER *Conf.* II. 347 For noman of his conseil knoweth; What he mai gete of his Michinge. *c* **1480** HENRYSON *Fable Fox & Wolf* 5 This Fox..durst no more with miching intermell. **1577** STANYHURST *Descr. Irel.* in *Holinshed* (1808) VI. Ep. Ded., His historie in mitching wise wandred through sundrie hands. **1875** BLACKMORE *Alice Lorraine* I. xvii. 183 She laid upon Hilary all the burden of this lengthened mitching-time. **1889** P. H. GOSSE in *Longm. Mag.* Mar. 517 We called it [*sc.* playing truant] 'miching', pronouncing the *i* in 'mich' long, as in 'mile', whereas in Devonshire the same word, in the same sense, is pronounced with the *i* short, as in 'mill'. **1891** S. MOSTYN *Curatica* 67 The schoolboy's miching is the clergyman's Mondayishness. **1894** *Q. Rev.* July 136 These servants.. were skilful in devising means of interrupting the performance, or miching from it to the nearest tavern.

mite[1] (maɪt). Also 4–6 **myte**, (5 **moighte**, **myght**). [OE. *míte* wk. fem. = MDu., MLG. *mîte* (Du. *mijt* fem.), OHG. *mîza* fem., gnat:—OTeut. **mîtôn-*. Cf. F. *mite*, of Teut. origin.

Franck suggests derivation from the Indogermanic root **mei-* expressing smallness. Some refer the word to an ablaut-variant of the Teut. root **mait-* (Goth. *maitan*, OHG. *meizen*) to cut.]

1. a. In early use, applied vaguely to any minute insect or arachnid; sometimes *spec.* a small parasitic insect infesting hawks. Now usually restricted to certain genera of the order *Acarida* of arachnids, and chiefly applied to the cheese-mite, *Tyroglyphus* (formerly *Acarus*) *domesticus*.

c **1000** ÆLFRIC *Gloss.* in Wr.-Wülcker 122/6 *Ta*[*r*]*mus*, maþa, mite. *c* **1386** CHAUCER *Wife's Prol.* 560, I..wered vpon my gaye scarlet gytes. Thise wormes ne thise Motthes ne thise mytes Vpon my peril frete hem neuer a deel. **1472–3** *Rolls of Parlt.* VI. 59/1 Such [wools] as shall happen to rote or perych by long standyng, bityng of moightes. *c* **1475** *Pict. Voc.* in Wr.-Wülcker 767/26 *Hoc gamalion*, a myght. **1486** *Bk. St. Albans* C v, An hawke that hath mites. **1530** PALSGR. 245/2 Myte in chese, *myte*. **1601** SHAKS. *All's Well* I. i. 154 Virginitie breedes mites, much like a Cheese. **1611** COTGR., *Calendre*, the corne-deuouring Mite, or Weeuill. **1633** LATHAM *Falconry* Words Art Expl., Mites, are a kinde of vermine smaller then Lice, and most about the heads and nares of Hawks. **1658** ROWLAND *Moufet's Theat. Ins.* 1094 In English, Mites, in cheese, leaves, dry wood, and wax. **1732** POPE *Ess. Man* I. 196 Say what the use, were finer optics giv'n, T' inspect a mite, not comprehend the heav'n? **1753** CHAMBERS *Cycl. Supp.* s.v., The Mites among figs resemble beetles. **1870** NICHOLSON *Man. Zool.* xxxvii. (1875) 269 Several Mites (*Thalassarachna, Pontarachna*, &c.) have been found to inhabit salt water. **1881** E. A. ORMEROD *Injur. Insects* 62 Other kinds of mites which may very likely be found on currant bushes. **1896** tr. *Boas' Zool.* 285 Peculiar microscopic Mites..(*Demodex folliculorum*) occur in the follicles of the human nose.

b. With defining word prefixed (see quots.).

1797 *Encycl. Brit.* (ed. 3) I. 48/2 The siro, or cheese-mite, is a very minute species. *Ibid.* 49/1 The baccarum, or scarlet tree-mite, is a small species [of *Acarus*]. **1833** *Penny Cycl.* I. 69/2 Water-Mites (*Hydrachnellæ*). **1833** Itch-mite [see ITCH *sb.* 3]. **1835** KIRBY *Hab. & Inst. Anim.* xix. II. 305 A species of bat-mite [*Pteroptes*]. **1870** NICHOLSON *Man. Zool.* xxxvii. (1875) 269 The Wood-mites (*Oribatidæ*)..are to be found amongst moss and herbage, or creeping upon trees or stones. **1874** *Hardwicke's Sci.-Gossip* 234 *Tetranychus Lapidum* (Stone Mite). **1874**, **1877** Harvest-mite [see HARVEST *sb.* 7]. **1896** tr. *Boas' Zool.* 284 The Beetle-mites (genus *Gamasus*) frequently occur on Beetles, Bumble-bees, etc... An allied, but thin-skinned form, the common Bird-mite (*Dermanyssus avium*) occurs on Birds (Fowls, Canaries), and sucks their blood. **1898** E. A. ORMEROD *Handbk. Insects* 61 *Phytoptus ribis*, or the Currant Bud Mite.

2. *slang.* A cheesemonger.

[**1765** FOOTE *Commissary* III. i, Miss Cicely Mite, the only daughter of old Mite the cheesemonger.] **1785** GROSE *Dict. Vulg. Tongue*, *Mite*, a nick name for a cheesemonger, from the small insect of that name found in cheese.

3. *attrib.* and *Comb.*, as ***mite-breeding***, ***fly***, etc.; **mite-borne** *a.*, carried or transmitted by mites; so **mite-borne typhus**, scrub typhus; also called **mite typhus**.

1939 *Brit. Encycl. Med. Pract.* XII. 347 The classical form of the disease is the Japanese river fever which bears the same relation to mite-borne typhus fevers as does Rocky Mountain fever to the tick-borne. **1974** PASSMORE & ROBSON *Compan. Med. Stud.* III. xii. 73/2 The rash spares the face in louse-borne typhus but not in the mite-borne disease. **1624** GATAKER *Transubst.* 191 Corruption, putrefaction, mite-breeding [etc.]. **1774** GOLDSM. *Nat. Hist.* (1824) I. 405 These [cheeses] are never found to breed mites.., probably because the mite-fly is not to be found in Lapland. **1881** E. A. ORMEROD *Injur. Insects* 180 The Mite-infested bud. **1921** *Indian Med. Gaz.* LVI. 370/1 (*table*) Mite typhus. **1939** *Brit. Encycl. Med. Pract.* XII. 348 Scrub or rural form of tropical typhus..has been found to be mite-typhus conveyed by *T*[*rombicula*] *deliensis*. **1959** C. OGBURN *Marauders* (1960) viii. 265 He had all of the three worst scourges of the organization, in combination: mite typhus, amoebic dysentery and malaria. **1878** EMERSON *Sovereignty of Ethics*, The same original power which..works in a lobster or a mite-worm.

mite[2] (maɪt). Also 4 **myt**, 4–5 **myght**, 4–6 **myte**, 5 **myth**, 6 **myit**. [a. (? through OF. *mite*, 14th c.) MDu. *mîte* fem. (early mod.Du. *mijte*, now *mijt*) = MLG. *mîte*, *meite*, *meute* (whence early mod.G. *meite*, something very small):—OTeut. **mîtôn-*; prob. identical with MITE *sb.*[1]]

1. a. Originally, a Flemish copper coin of very small value; according to some early Flemish writers, worth $\frac{1}{3}$ of a Flemish penny, though other, chiefly smaller, values are also mentioned. In Eng. use mainly as a proverbial expression for an extremely small unit of money value. In books of commercial arithmetic in 16–17th c. it commonly appears as the lowest denomination of English money of account, usually $\frac{1}{24}d$, but sometimes $\frac{1}{64}d$, and sometimes $\frac{1}{16}d$; it is, however, unlikely that the word was ever in Eng. mercantile use. From the 14th c. *mite* has been the usual rendering (though the Wyclif versions have 'mynutis') of L. *minūtum* (Vulg.), Gr. λεπτόν in Mark xii. 43, where two 'mites' are stated to make a 'farthing' (Gr. κοδράντης, L. *quadrans*); hence the word was popularly taken as equivalent to 'half-farthing'.

1377 LANGL. *P. Pl.* B. XIII. 196 Haued nouȝt..þe pore widwe [more] for a peire of mytes, þan alle þo that offreden in-to *gazafilacium*? *c* **1483** CAXTON *Dialogues* 51 A peny, a halfpeny, A ferdyng, a myte. **1535** COVERDALE *Mark* xii. 43 And there came a poore wyddowe, and put in two mytes, which make a farthinge. **1577** D. GRAY *Storeh. Brev. Arithm.* 5 Firste giue heede howe many Mites make one Farthyng, and that beeyng 6, you shall for euery 6 Mytes cary one Farthyng to the place of farthynges. **1600** HYLL *Arithm.* III. i. Pp vij, Four Mites is the aliquot part of a peny, viz. $\frac{1}{6}$, for 6. times 4 is 24. and so many mites marchants assigne to 1. peny. **1674** JEAKE *Arith.* (1696) 77 That is 16 Mites in one Farthing. **1706** PHILLIPS (ed. Kersey), *Mite*, an ancient small Coin, about a third part of our Farthing. **1778** *Eng. Gazetteer* (ed. 2) s.v. *Littleborough, Notts.*, Many little coins like flatted peas, called mites, are also found here. **1807** SOUTHEY *Espriella's Lett.* I. 243 It will soon entirely disappear, just as the mite or half farthing has disappeared before it. **1863** TREVELYAN *Compet. Wallah* (1866) 95 We were ferried across [the Ganges] for the moderate remuneration of three mites a head.

†**b.** In proverbial phrases, as ***not worth a mite***, ***not to care a mite***, etc. (***to pay***) ***to the mite***: = 'to the uttermost farthing', without deduction.

c **1350** *Will. Palerne* 4543 William..Greiþed him..so þat non miȝt a-mend a mite worþ, i wene. *Ibid.* 5348 Al þe men vpon mold it amende ne miȝt..half a mite. *c* **1374** CHAUCER *Compl. Mars* 126 He ne roghte not a myte for to dye. *c* **1374** —— *Troylus* III. 783 [832] Yf to lese his Ioye he set a myte, Than seemeth it þat Ioye is worth but lyte. **1375** BARBOUR *Bruce* III. 198 And fra the hart be discumfyt The body is nocht worth a myt. *c* **1425** *Cast. Persev.* 247 in *Macro Plays* 84 þou synne my sowle sese, I ȝeue not a myth. *c* **1485** *Digby Myst.* (1882) I. 142 And though thei sharme and crye, I care not a myght. **1513** DOUGLAS *Æneis* III. Prol. 19 In cais thai bark, I compt it neuir a myte. **1567** *Gude & Godlie Ball.* (S.T.S.) 176 Bot quhen he had payit all to ane myit, He mon be absoluit than. **1592** GREENE *Groatsw. Wit* Wks. (Grosart) XII. 137 Greene will send you now his groat worth of wit, that neuer showed a mites-worth in his life.

c. With allusion to Mark xii. 43, (***one's***) ***mite*** is often used for: The small sum which is all that one can afford to give to some charitable or public object; hence *fig.* applied to an immaterial contribution (insignificant in amount, but the best one can do) to some object or cause.

1650 BAXTER *Saints' R.* IV. xiv. 801 Will my mite requite thee for thy golden Mines? **1687** DRYDEN *Hind & P.* III. 113 Are you defrauded, when he feeds the poor? Our mite decreases nothing of your store. **1709** SWIFT *Tritical Ess.* Wks. 1755 II. I. 140, I hope I may be allowed among so many far more learned men to offer my mite. **1747** BERKELEY *Tar-water in Plague* Wks. 1871 III. 479 It may not be amiss to contribute my mite of advice. **1784** FRANKLIN *Autobiog.* Wks. 1840 I. 103 My mite for such purpose was never refused. **1818** SCOTT *Hrt. Midl.* ix, Reuben Butler went to offer his mite of consolation to his old friend and benefactor. **1827** ROBERTS *Voy. Centr. Amer.* 255, I have been desirous ..to add my mite to the great mass of information. **1873** MORLEY *Rousseau* I. ix. 328 He subscribed his mite for the erection of a statue to him.

†**2.** A small weight; *spec.* the twentieth part of a grain troy. (See note s.v. DROIT[2].) *Obs.*

1390 GOWER *Conf.* II. 275 Lovers..thogh thei love a lyte, That scarsly woulde it weie a myte. **15..** *MS. Harl.* 660 lf. 81 b, Euery subtylle grayne [doth] contayne 20 mytes. **1601**, *a* **1606**, **1649** [see DROIT[2]]. **1725** [see BLANK *sb.* 10]. **1727** ARBUTHNOT *Tables Anc. Coins* 109 The Sevil piece of Eight ..contains 13 Pennyweight 21 Grains and 15 Mites (of which there are 20 in the Grain) of Sterling Silver. **1727–38** CHAMBERS *Cycl.* (ed. 3) s.v.

3. a. A minute particle or portion; a tiny fragment. Now only *colloq.* or *vulgar*.

1608 SHAKS. *Per.* II. Prol. 8 Loosing a Mite, a Mountaine gaine. **1614** SIR A. GORGES tr. *Lucan* IV. 148 Although we few are but a mite Mongst thousands that for him do fight. **1633** FORD *Love's Sacr.* IV. ii, I haue a sword..To..cut your throats, and mince Your flesh to mites. **1670** EACHARD *Cont. Clergy* 56 We be but mites of entity, and crumbs of something. **1691** RAY *Creation* II. 130 The Ants..drop upon them a small Mite of their stinging Liquor. **1820** BYRON *Mar. Fal.* III. i, All the pregnant hearts of our bold blood, Moulder'd into a mite of ashes. **1828** HAWTHORNE *Fanshawe* vii, A man must keep his mite of honesty.

†**b.** *Arith.* A fraction (see quot.) *Obs. rare*[−1].

1709–29 V. MANDEY *Syst. Math.*, *Arith.* 21 A Fraction or Broken Number, is that which we assign for a part or parts of any whole thing. It is also wont to be called a Mite or Fraction, because these things are broke into small parts.

4. *fig.* A 'jot', 'whit'. Now only *colloq.* (used adverbially).

1377 LANGL. *P. Pl.* B. xx. 178 Surgerye ne Fisyke May nouȝte a myte auaille to medle aȝein elde. *c* **1420** LYDG. *Assembly of Gods* 1814 Be hyt ryght or wrong, he changeth nat a myte. **1571** GOLDING *Calvin on Ps.* ii. 6 He is further of from earthly men, than that the whole multitude of them can one myte deface the glory of him alone. **1573** *New Custome* III. i. D iij b, God waieth not, who is a sprite, Of any vesture, or outward appearance a mite. **1632** TATHAM *Love Crowns the End* i. (1640) K 1 b, Since then my love is not one mite rewarded. **1886** C. D. WARNER *Their Pilgrimage* xi. (1888) 256 The White Sulphur waters..had not done her a mite of good. **1897** *Graphic* (Christm. No.) 9, I wonder whether you will help me a mite to-day. **1906** WINSTON CHURCHILL *Coniston* 191 He's a hard one to fool, too. Never suspected a mite did he? **1939** L. M. MONTGOMERY *Anne of Ingleside* i. 9 You needn't be a mite afraid to sleep in that bed. I aired the sheets to-day. **1955** H. CROOME *Mountain & Molehill* ii. 29 We were a mite surprised to see so many German names on your prospectus. **1958** *Spectator* 22 Aug. 241/2 This, to me, is a mite depressing. **1972** J. PORTER *Meddler & her Murder* viii. 107 'There was no need to go to all that expense, dear,' said Miss Jones, a mite huffily. **1972** J. WAINWRIGHT *Night is Time to Die* 66 If..the farmer buys pigs..and wishes to move them..he must obtain such a licence... This..may seem a mite bureaucratic. **1974** WODEHOUSE *Aunts aren't Gentlemen* iii. 20 Last night..it may be that I became a mite polluted, but that rarely happens.

5. A very small object; often, a very small living creature, as a tiny child. (Cf. MITING.)

In some instances this use might perh. be more properly referred to MITE[1].

1594 LYLY *Mother Bombie* II. ii, Well, without Halfepenie all my witte is not woorth a dodkin: that mite is miching in this groue, for as long as his name is Halfepenie, he will bee banquetting for the other Halfepenie. **1821** CLARE *Vill. Minstr.* I. 7 And tales of fairy-land he loved to hear, Those mites of human forms,..That through a lock-hole even creep with ease. **1852** DICKENS *Bleak Ho.* xv, A mite of a boy, some five or six years old. **1883** *Gd. Words* 639 When I was quite a little mite. **1893** *Atlantic Monthly* Feb. 283/1 What an intense spark of vitality must it be that warms such a mite [viz. a bird] in such an immensity of cold.

6. mite society, a 19th-century society whose object was to collect funds for some charitable purpose by small contributions (see sense 1 c).

1822 *Missionary Herald* (Boston, Mass.) XVIII. 21 Female Mite So[ciety] for Cher[okee] and Choc[taw] missions [gave $]25. **1823** *Baptist Mag.* IV. 133, I have also assisted in the organization of two Female Mite Societies. **1872** *Newton Kansan* 26 Sept. 3/2 The Mite Society will hold a ten cent sociable in the school room this Thursday evening. **1878** *Harper's Mag.* Jan. 203/1 By means of 'mite' societies..sufficient money was raised to inclose it [*sc.* the grave-yard]. **1883** C. F. WILDER *Sister Ridnour's Sacrifice* 262 We call upon certain poor, we attend the 'Dorcas', the socials, the festivals, and mite societies.

‖**mitella** (mɪˈtɛlə). [L. *mitella*, orig. 'headband', dim. of *mitra*: see MITRE.]

1. *Surg.* A sling for the arm.

1688 R. HOLME *Armoury* III. 434/2 The Mitella is a.. Scarf to..carry the Arme in, that is hurt or wounded. **1753** CHAMBERS *Cycl. Supp.* **1855** DUNGLISON *Med. Lex.*

2. [Adopted as a generic name by J. P. de Tournefort in *Institutiones Rei Herbariæ* (ed. 3, 1719) I. 241.] A perennial herb of the genus so called, belonging to the family Saxifragaceæ,

native to North America and north-east Asia, and bearing racemes of small flowers; usually called MITRE-WORT.

For the meaning of the name, cf. quot. 1731 and the English synonyms *bishop's cap* and *mitre-wort*.

1731 MILLER *Gard. Dict.*, *Mitella* (so call'd, of *Mitella*, Lat. a little Mitre, because the Seed-vessel of this Plant resembles a Bishop's Mitre). Bastard American Sanicle... American Mitella. **1882** *Harper's Mag.* Nov. 853/2 Why should the starry blossom of the fringed mitella seek the snow-flake as its model?

miter, obs. form of METRE; var. MITRE.

† **mi'tescent**, *a. Obs. rare*⁻⁰. [ad. L. *mītescent-em*, pr. pple. of *mītesc-ĕre*, f. *mītis* mild: see MITIGATE.] Growing mild.

1727 in BAILEY vol. II.

miteyn, obs. f. MITTEN *sb.*

mith: see MAY *v.*

mith, variant of MID *prep.* and *adv. Obs.*

‖ **mithan** ('mɪθən). Also **mytton, mythun, methin, mithong, mithun.** [Assamese *methōn.*] The GAYAL.

1845 E. J. T. DALTON in *Jrnl. Asiat. Soc. Bengal* XIV. 265 The Mytton is the only species of horned cattle possessed by the Meris. **1885** BALFOUR *Cycl. India* (ed. 3) II. 936 *Methin*, the wild cow of the hills near Cachar. **1885** HUNTER *Imper. Gaz. Ind.* I. 349 The mithan or gayal (*Gavæus frontalis*). **1890** *Pall Mall G.* 18 Aug. 7/3 To propitiate these ghosts an animal must be slaughtered—whether it be the prolific pariah dog or the valuable mythun. **1921** *Blackw. Mag.* Feb. 258/2 There was no rice, no water, no fences, no herds of mithun. **1923** *Ibid.* Feb. 186/2 The mithong were once more stalled beneath the houses. **1937** *Jrnl. R. Anthrop. Inst.* 15 Over the neck of the bound and trembling Mithan.

† **mithe**, *v. Obs.* Forms: 1 **miðan**, 3–4 **myth(e**, 3–4 **mith(e.** [A Com. W. Ger. str. vb.: OE. *míðan* (pa. t. *máð*, pl. *miðon*, *miðon*, pa. pple. *miðen*) corresponds to OFris. (*far*)*mītha* to avoid, OS. *mîthan* (MDu. *mîden*, Du. *mijden*), OHG. *mîden* to hide oneself, conceal, avoid (MHG. *mîden*, mod.G. *meiden* to shun, forbear).

For the affinities of the Teut. root **miþ-*, see MIS-¹.]

1. *trans.* To conceal, dissemble (feelings, etc.). In OE. (as in OS.) occas. with obj. in genitive.

c **888** K. ÆLFRED *Boeth.* xxvi. §1 Ne me næfre næs ealles swa ic wolde, þeah ic his miðe. *a* **1300** *Cursor M.* 29069 Quen yee fast, þen sal yee scau gladnes wit yur sembland blith, and sua yur fasting sal yee myth. *c* **1300** *Havelok* 948 His sorwe he couþe ful wel miþe. *a* **1310** in Wright *Lyric P.* iv. 24 My murthe is al with mournyng meind, ne may ich mythen hit namore.

2. *absol.* and *intr.* To remain concealed, to escape notice (in OE. also *trans.* to escape the notice of); to hide one's thoughts or feelings.

a **900** *Gloss.* in Wr.-Wülcker 222/18 *Dilitiscendo*, miþende. *a* **900** tr. *Bæda's Hist.* v. xii. (1890) 424 Moniȝ ðing ȝe eȝ[e]slice ȝe willsumlice ȝeseh, þe oðre meoðon [L. *multa quæ alios laterent*]. *c* **1000** *Sax. Leechd.* II. 298/8 þonne biþ sona sweotol æteowod on him þ ær deaȝol mað. *c* **1250** *Gen. & Ex.* 3807 Ðoȝ ðis folc miðe a stund for-dred. **1320–30** *Horn Ch.* 825 Sche might no lenger mithe; To him spac that maiden fre, And seyd, Horn, y love the.

mither: see MITRE, MOIDER *v.*, MOTHER.

mithology, etc., obs. forms of MYTHOLOGY, etc.

Mithra: see MITHRAS.

'**Mithracize**, *v.* Incorrect form of MITHRAICIZE *v.* Hence '**Mithracizing** *ppl. a.*

1876 A. WILDER in *R. P. Knight's Symbolic Lang.* p. xix, The Albigenses, it is supposed, were Manicheans or Mithracising Christians.

Mithradatic, etc.: var. ff. MITHRIDATIC, etc.

‖ **Mithræum** (mɪ'θriːəm). *Antiq.* Pl. **Mithræa.** [Mod.L. f. L. *Mithrā-s*: see MITHRAS.] A sanctuary of Mithras; a chapel (often underground) for the celebration of the Mithraic mysteries.

1878 COOTE in *Archæologia* (1882) XLVII. 206 A similarly acuminated stone was found in the Mithraeum at S. Clemente in Rome. **1900** *Pilot* 24 Mar. 94/2 The lion-headed human figure..that so often occurs in the Mithræa.

Mithraic (mɪ'θreɪɪk), *a.* [f. MITHRA + -IC. Cf. late L. *Mithriacus* MITHRIAC.] Of, pertaining to, or connected with Mithras or his worship.

1678 CUDWORTH *Intell. Syst.* I. iv. §16. 286 Zoroaster and the ancient Magi, who were best initiated in the Mithraick Mysteries. **1818** MILLINGEN in *Archæologia* (1821) XIX. 71 The crow, the scorpion, and the serpent, are animals commonly seen on Mithraic monuments. **1877** PARKER *Catacombs of Rome* Plate xv, Catacomb of Mithraic Worshippers.

Hence **Mi'thraicism** = MITHRAISM; **Mi'thraicist** = MITHRAIST; **Mi'thraicize** *v.* = MITHRAIZE.

1864 C. W. KING *Gnostics* 49 Such a connexion was actually declared by the partisans of Mithraicism. *Ibid.* 62 The author of the Apocalypse probably had the Mithraicists in view in penning this allegory. *Ibid.* 248 (Index) Mithraicising Christians. **1878** COOTE in *Archæologia* (1882) XLVII. 206 A stone commemorating this birth of Mithras was an object of adoration amongst the Mithraicists. **1888** *Pop. Sci. Monthly* Feb. 560 Mithraicism, with explanations of its alliance with Occidental Christianity. **1898** *Contemp. Rev.* Jan. 96 The Lord's Supper was modified to meet the Christians who had been converted from Mithraicism.

Mithraism ('mɪθreɪɪz(ə)m). [f. MITHRA + -ISM.] The religion of the worshippers of Mithras.

1822 HODGSON in *Archæol. Æliana* I. 307 The success of Mithraism in Gaul and Britain, must not, therefore, be attributed to novelty. **1887** J. A. FARRER in *Gentl. Mag.* Nov. 442 In its general tenets..Mithraism was the same as Zoroastrianism, out of which it sprang.

Mithraist ('mɪθreɪɪst). [f. MITHRA + -IST.] A worshipper of or believer in Mithras.

1888 *Pop. Sci. Monthly* June 283 Whether the Christians borrowed from the Mithraists or the Mithraists from the Christians. **1900** *Pilot* 24 Mar. 94/2 The Mithraists identified him [Ormuzd] with the Roman Jupiter.

Mithraistic (mɪθreɪ'ɪstɪk), *a.* [f. MITHRAIST + -IC.] = MITHRAIC *a.*

1900 *Open Court* May 290 Mithraistic Cameos. Showing Mithras born from the rocks between the Dioscuri, surrounded by Mithraistic symbols, among them the cup and bread of the Eucharist. **1920** *Glasgow Herald* 1 May 4 Hymn-writing..ran too much to gloomy terrorism and Mithraistic images of wounds and blood.

† **Mithra'itic**, *a. Obs.* [f. MITHRA + -ITIC.] = MITHRAIC *a.*

1827 G. HIGGINS *Celtic Druids* 152 A Mithraitic cave, which was found near Newcastle.

Mithraize ('mɪθreɪaɪz), *v.* [f. MITHRA + -IZE.] *intr.* To hold or affect the doctrines of Mithraism.

1890 in *Century Dict.*; and in later Dicts.

Mithras ('mɪθræs), **Mithra** ('mɪθrə). *Mythol.* Forms: 6 **Mitra**, 6–7 **Mythra**, 7 **Mithres**, 6– **Mithra**, 7– **Mithras.** [L. *Mithrās*, *Mithrēs* = Gr. Μίθρᾱς, a. OPers. *Mithra*, corresponding etymologically to Skr. *Mitra*, one of the gods of the Vedic pantheon.] One of the chief gods of the ancient Persians, in later times often identified with the sun. His worship was introduced amongst the Romans under the empire, and spread over most of northern and western Europe. Also applied by More to the Supreme Being of 'Utopia'.

1551 ROBINSON tr. *More's Utopia* II. (1895) 267 There is one chiefe and pryncipall God..whome they all commonly in their countrey language call Mythra. **1585** T. WASHINGTON tr. *Nicholay's Voy.* IV. ii. 115 [They] worshipped the Sunne, which they called Mitra. **1603** HOLLAND *Plutarch's Mor.* 1306 This Zoroastres..named the good god Oromazes, and the other Arimanius..he gave out..also that there is one in the middes betweene them, named Mithres: (and heereupon it is, that the Persians call an intercessor or mediator Mithres). *a* **1650** CRASHAW *Wks.* (1904) 365 Before the Infant Shrine Of my weake feet the Persian Magi lay And left their Mithra for my star. **1822** HODGSON in *Archæol. Æliana* I. 284 Montfaucon thinks these two attendants are also Mithrases.

attrib. **1864** C. W. KING *Gnostics* 47 The Mithras-worship at first indeed makes its appearance as a distinct creed. **1903** J. MOFFAT in *Expositor* Dec. 469 The Mithra-cult.

Mithratic (mɪ'θrætɪk), *a.* [f. MITHRA + -ATIC.] Of, pertaining to, or concerned with the worship of Mithras.

1816 FABER *Orig. Pagan Idol.* III. 178 Porphyry..tells us, that the Mithratic grotto was a symbol of the World, and that it was dedicated to Mithras in the capacity of the great demiurgic father. **1822** PORTER *Trav. Georgia*, etc. I. 673 The true faith, from a dateless epoch in Persian annals until the conquest of the Arabs, was the Mithratic mystery.

Mithriac ('mɪθrɪæk), *a.* and *sb. rare.* [a. L. *Mithriacus*, f. MITHRAS.] **a.** *adj.* = MITHRAIC. **b.** *sb. pl.* A festival of Mithras.

1818 R. P. KNIGHT *Symbol. Lang.* §168. 135 Another mode of mystic purification by baptism was the Taurobolium..of the Mithriac rites. [*Index has* Mithraic rites.] **1864** PUSEY *Lect. Daniel* viii. 537 The Satrap sent the King yearly 20,000 colts for the Mithriacs.

mithridate ('mɪθrɪdeɪt). Also 6 **mith-, methridat, mithrydate, mitridat**, 6–7 **metridat(e, methridate**, 7 **mythridate, methredate, mithrydat, mitridate, medridate.** [a. med.L. *mithridātum*, altered from late L. *mithridātīum*, orig. neut. of *Mithridātīus*, *-ēus* adj., pertaining to Mithridates (see below, sense 1 *note*), f. L. *Mithri-*, *Mithradātēs*, Gr. Μιθρι-, Μιθραδάτης. Cf. OF. *metridat* (mod.F. *mithridate*), Sp., It. *mitridato*, Pg. *mithridato*.]

1. *Old Pharmacy.* A composition of many ingredients in the form of an electuary, regarded as a universal antidote or preservative against poison and infectious disease. Hence, any medicine to which similar powers were ascribed.

So called from Mithridates VI, king of Pontus (died *c* 63 B.C.), who was said to have rendered himself proof against poisons by the constant use of antidotes.

1528 PAYNEL *Salerne's Regim.* (1541) 33 b, Auicen saythe; There be certeyne medicins..which wyl not suffre poyson to approche nere the harte, as triacle and Metridate. **1533** ELYOT *Cast. Helthe* (1541) A ij, Mithridates invented the famous medicine ageynst poyson, callid Mithridate. **1593** S. KELLWAYE *Defens. agst. Plague* 32 Take a great Onyon, make a hole in the myddle of him, then fill the place with Mitridat or Triacle, and some leaues of Rue, then [etc.]. **1605** TIMME *Quersit.* III. 177 Take of.. the treacles of mythridate, and the confection of hiacinth, of each 2 ounces. **1616** SURFL. & MARKH. *Country Farm* 387 Some make a soueraigne mithridate against the plague..with two old walnuts, three figges [etc.]. **1686** D'URFEY *Commonw. Wom.* v. ii. 47 Fools may talk of Mythridate, Cordials, Elixers. **1758** R. BROWN *Compl. Farmer* (1759) 96 Anoint it with some honey or mithridate. **1802** GIFFORD tr. *Juvenal* vi. 959 Yet, if the husband, prescient of his fate, Have fortified his breast with mithridate. **1825** SCOTT *Betrothed* xvii, Their rash recipes, their mithridate,..their amulets, and their charms.

attrib. **1694** SALMON *Bate's Dispens.* (1713) 591/2 The Mithridate Julep against Fits of the Mother.

b. *transf.* and *fig.*

1592 LYLY *Midas* IV. iv. 47 That which maketh me most both to sorrow and wonder, is that musick (a methridat for melancholy) should make him mad. **1597** TOFTE *Laura* III. xii, Cordiall of hart, right Methridate of loue. **1622** in *Naworth Househ. Bks.* (Surtees) 458 Yᵉ l're..was medridate to his hart. **1632** MASSINGER *Maid of Hon.* IV. iv, In this breach of faith My loyalty findes reward! what poysons him Proves Mithridate to me! **1812** SOUTHEY *Ess.* (1832) I. 120 Those..whom a sound understanding, and a mind well stored, have fortified, as with mithridate, against such poison. **1834** —— *Doctor* lxxvi. (1848) 162 A drop of the true elixir, no mithridate so effectual against the infection of vice.

2. In full ***mithridate mustard***, a name for the plants *Lepidium campestre* and *Thlaspi arvense*. Also ***bastard mithridate mustard***: candytuft.

1597 GERARDE *Herbal* II. xix. (1633) 261 Mithridate Mustard..the roote is long and slender. **1731** MILLER *Gard. Dict.*, *Thlaspi*,..Mithridate Mustard. *Ibid.*, *Thlaspidium*, ..Bastard Mithridate Mustard. **1760** J. LEE *Introd. Bot.* App. 319 Mithridate Mustard, Bastard, *Iberis*. **1780** J. T. DILLON *Trav. Spain* (1781) 392 A high mountain covered with mithridate. **1855** MISS PRATT *Flower. Pl.* I. 87 *Thlaspi arvense* (Mithridate Mustard, or Penny-cress).

Mithridatic (mɪθrɪ'dætɪk), *a.* Also 9 **mithradatic.** [ad. L. *mithridātic-us*, a. Gr. Μιθριδᾱτικός, f. Μιθριδάτης: see MITHRIDATE and -IC. Cf. F. *mithridatique*, Sp. *mitridático*, Pg. *mithridatico*.]

1. Of or pertaining to Mithridates VI, king of Pontus. ***Mithridatic wars***, the wars waged by Rome against this king.

1649 OGILBY tr. *Virg. Georg.* II. (1684) 79 *note*, This Tree was first shewn by Pompey to Rome in his Mithridatick Triumph. **1678** J. D. (*title*) The History of Appian... In Two Parts. The First consisting of the Punick, Syrian, Parthian, Mithridatick,..and Hannibalick, Wars. **1898** W. M. RAMSAY in *Expositor* Aug. 132 The Romans aided them to gain their freedom in the Mithradatic wars.

2. Of, pertaining to, or of the nature of mithridate. *rare*⁻⁰.

1847 in WEBSTER.

3. a. Resembling Mithridates or his alleged immunity from poisons (see MITHRIDATE 1 *note*). **b.** Pertaining to or of the nature of mithridatism.

1868 HELPS *Realmah* vi. (1869) 122 Poison has no more effect on my Mithridatic constitution than ginger-beer. **1889** E. R. LANKESTER in *Nature* 13 June 149/2 The mithradatic theory of inoculations.

‖ **mithri'daticon.** *Obs.* In 6 **metridaticon.** [med.L., a. Gr. μιθριδᾱτικόν, neut. of Μιθριδᾱτικός, MITHRIDATIC.] = MITHRIDATE 1.

1540 J. HEYWOOD *Four P.P.* 619 Mercury sublyme. and metridaticon.

mithridatism ('mɪθrɪdeɪtɪz(ə)m). [f. L. *Mithridāt-ēs* (see MITHRIDATE) + -ISM.] The condition of immunity to a poison induced by administering to an organism gradually increased doses of it.

1851 MORELL tr. *Fourier's Pass. Human Soul* I. 191 The state of Mithridatism, or unitary accord of our bodies with the neuter poisons, will depend on [etc.]. **1889** E. R. LANKESTER *Adv. Sci.* (1890) 113 We may speak of this training in tolerance of poison as 'mithridatism'.

‖ **mithridatium.** *Obs.* Also **mithridation.** [L. *mithridātium*: see MITHRIDATE.] = MITHRIDATE.

1693 tr. *Blancard's Phys. Dict.* (ed. 2), *Mithridatium*, compounded by King Mithridates. **1764** GRAINGER *Sugar Cane* II. 130 *note*, This medicine is called *Mithridatium*, in honour of Mithridates.

mithridatize (mɪ'θrɪdətaɪz), *v.* Also **mithradatize.** [f. L. *Mithridāt-ēs* (see MITHRIDATE) + -IZE.] *trans.* To render immune or proof against a poison by the administration of gradually increasing doses of it. Also *transf.*

1866 LOWELL *Lett.* I. 406 Our constitutions adapt themselves to the slow poison of the world till we become mithridatized at last. **1889** E. R. LANKESTER *Adv. Sci.* (1890) 114 Poisonous snakes are..mithridatised in regard to their own poison. *Ibid.*, Thus the animal is mithridatised. **1889** —— in *Nature* 13 June 149 The utility of the related terms 'mithradatize' and 'mithradatic' is obvious.

‖ **mithri'datum.** *Obs.* Also 7 **meth-, myth-.** [med.L.: see MITHRIDATE.] = MITHRIDATE.

1603 DEKKER *Wonderfull Yeare* D 2, For poor Methridatum and Dragon-water..were boxt in euery corner, and yet were both drunke euery houre at other mens cost. **1605** BACON *Adv. Learn.* II. x. §8 For except it be Treacle and Mythridatum,..they tye themselues to no receiptes seuerely and religiously. **1634** R. H. *Salernes Regim.* 51 Under the name of Tryacle the noble medicine

Mithridatum may be comprehended, which two be like in operation.

mithril ('mɪθrɪl). [Invented word.] Name given by J. R. R. Tolkien to a mythical precious metal.
1954 J. R. R. TOLKIEN *Fellowship of Ring* II. iv. 331 Here alone in the world was found Moria-silver, or true-silver as some have called it: *mithril* the Elvish name... The beauty of *mithril* did not tarnish or grow dim. *Ibid.*, Bilbo had a corslet of mithril-rings. **1955** —— *Return of King* V. x. 165 The coat of mithril-mail that Frodo had worn wrapped in his tattered garments. *Ibid.* VI. ix. 308 On her finger was Nenya, the ring wrought of *mithril*, that bore a single white stone flickering like a frosty star.

miticide ('maɪtɪsaɪd). [f. MIT(E¹ + -I- + -CIDE.] Any substance used to kill mites.
1946 TRAVIS & MORTON *Use of Insect Repellants & Miticides*. (U.S. Dept. Agric., Bureau Entomol. & Plant Quarantine, E-698) 4 Benzyl benzoate is very effective as a miticide. **1955** *Sci. News Let.* 18 June 392/2 Each of the six dusts is a mixture of insecticides, miticides and fungicides, and prevents damage by aphids, leaf-hoppers, spider mites, and by the plant diseases, mildew and black-spot. **1972** *Daily Colonist* (Victoria, B.C.) 30 July 47/5 Spray thoroughly now with a good miticide such as kelthane or malathion.

†**mitifi'cation.** *Obs. rare.* [n. of action f. L. *mītificāre*: see MITIFY *v.*] Mitigation.
1607 TOPSELL *Four-f. Beasts* (1658) 161 The juyce of Barly to be given to them for their mitification. **1657** TOMLINSON *Renou's Disp.* 63 Such distempers as require mitification.

†**'mitify**, *v.* *Obs. rare.* [ad. L. *mītificāre*, f. L. *mītis* mild: see -FY.] *trans.* To soften, mitigate.
1656 BLOUNT *Glossogr.*, *Mitifie*, to pacifie, or make quiet. **1744** MITCHELL in *Phil. Trans.* XLIII. 145 The virulent Acrimony of the cutaneous Contagion being inviscated, and consequently mitified, by the Semen which received it.

mitigable ('mɪtɪɡəb(ə)l), *a.* [ad. L. *mītigābilis* (implied in *mītigābiliter* adv.) f. *mītigāre* to MITIGATE.] Capable of being mitigated.
a **1677** BARROW *Wks.* (1686) II. xv. 213 The rigour of that ceremonious law was mitigable. **1822-34** *Good's Study Med.* (ed. 4) I. 50 The pain will be..far less mitigable. **1887** GURNEY *Tertium Quid* I. 182 Supposing the pain of the rack to be mitigable.

mitigal: see MISKAL.

mitigant ('mɪtɪɡənt), *a.* and *sb.* *rare.* [ad. L. *mītigant-em*, pr. pple. of *mītigāre* to MITIGATE: see -ANT¹.] **A.** *adj.* Mitigating, lenitive.
1541 R. COPLAND *Galyen's Terap.* 2 C ij, A playster made of mytygant thynges. **1727** in BAILEY vol. II. **1755** in JOHNSON. **1800** *Med. Jrnl.* IV. 558 The oxygen is the tempering, mitigant..principle of life.
B. *sb.* Something that mitigates; a lenitive.
1865 *Pall Mall G.* No. 182. 1/1 A simple disease which yields to mitigants.

†**'mitigate**, *pa. pple.* and *ppl. a. Obs.* Forms: see MITIGATE *v.*; also 6 *Sc.* mitigait. [ad. L. *mītigātus*, pa. pple. of *mītigāre*: see next.] Mitigated, alleviated.
1432-50 tr. *Higden* (Rolls) II. 387 Hit was answerede to theyme by Apollo Delphicus that pestilence to be mitigate [L. *sedari*] if [etc.]. *Ibid.* VII. 35 But their myndes not mitigate þerwith [L. *Sed adhuc non sedatis animis*]. **1531** ELYOT *Gov.* II. vi, The wise prince with that playne confession was mitigate. *a* **1533** LD. BERNERS *Gold. Bk. M. Aurel.* (1546) L vj, His chastysement was mitigate, and more easye. **1560** A. L. tr. *Calvin's Foure Serm. Song Ezech.* iv, That the pain should be mitigate. **1560** ROLLAND *Crt. Venus* Prol. 113 Sumpart ar dry and sum are mitigait. **1592** in Neal *Hist. Purit.* (1732) I. 551 That some more mitigate and peaceable course might be taken therein.

mitigate ('mɪtɪɡeɪt), *v.* Also 5 myttygate, 6 mytygate, metigat(e, mit(t)igat, mettegate, 6-7 mytigate, mittigate, 7 medigate; also *pa. t.* 6 *Sc.* metigat. [f. L. *mītigāt-*, ppl. stem of *mītigāre*, f. *mīti-s* mild, gentle. Cf. F. *mitiger* (OF. also *mitiguer*), Sp. *mitigar*, It. *mitigare*.]
1. *trans.* To render (a person, his mind, disposition, or mood) milder, more gentle, or less hostile; to appease, mollify. Now *rare*.
1432-50, **1531** [see MITIGATE *pa. pple.*]. **1513** MORE *Rich. III*, Wks. 57/1 Where the king toke displeasure, she would mitigate & appease his mind. **1584** COGAN *Haven Health* ii. (1636) 21 The Chesse..was invented..to mitigate the minds or hearts of Tyrants. **1642** *Declar. Lords & Com. London* 8 Such Commissioners were mittigated, in respect of some clauses perilous to the Commissioners, and approved of for the time to come. **1761** HUME *Hist. Eng.* I. viii. 178 The Cardinal of Pavia..tooke care..to mitigate the pope by the accounts which he sent of that princes conduct. **1855** PUSEY *Doctr. Real Presence* Note S. §75. 694 S. Leo the Great..mitigated Genseric, when Rome was taken. **1859** J. BROWN *Rab & F.* (1862) 18 The severe little man was mitigated, and condescended to say 'Rab, ma man, puir Rabbie'.
2. a. To render (anger, hatred, etc.) less fierce or violent; to appease.
1494 FABYAN *Chron.* VII. ccxxxv. 271 The preestys..to the entent to myttygate..the crueltye of the sayd tyrauntes, dyd open them the ornamentys of the sayde churche. **1513** BRADSHAW *St. Werburge* II. 1554 O glorious virgin.. Metigate the malice..of Richard our lorde. **1558** BP. WATSON *Sev. Sacram.* xviii 116 To mitigate Goddes dyspleasure. *a* **1578** LINDESAY (Pitscottie) *Chron. Scot.* (S.T.S.) I. 302 Thir goode wordis..metigat and assuadgit

the Duike of Albanieis anger. **1579-80** NORTH *Plutarch, Sylla* (1595) 503 To mitigate somewhat the peoples ill will towards him. **1656** in *Verney Mem.* (1894) III. 317 [Luce begs Sir Ralph to do his best] to medigate my lady's anger against her dauʳ. **1777** ROBERTSON *Hist. Amer.* v. (1778) II. 90 Montezuma addressed them with every argument that could mitigate their rage. **1855** PRESCOTT *Philip II*, I. III. vi. 379 The..envoys interposed to mitigate the king's anger. **1875** JOWETT *Plato* (ed. 2) IV. 17 His [Socrates'] hostility towards the sophists..was not mitigated in later life.
†**b.** To relax the violence of (one's actions, etc.).
c **1470** HENRYSON *Mor. Fab.* VII. (*Lion & Mouse*) xl, To remit sum tyme ane grit offence, And mitigate with mercy crueltie. **1509** BARCLAY *Shyp of Folys* (1570) 39 Mitigate by measure your proude hastie language. **1549** *Compl. Scot.* Prol. 13 Dame fortoune vil mittigat hyr auen crualte.
3. a. To alleviate (physical or mental pain); to lessen the violence of (a disease); to lighten the burden of (an evil of any kind).
1432-50 tr. *Higden* (Rolls) V. 389 A man nesynge, peple beynge by use to say 'Criste helpe the', and make a crosse on their mowthe to mitigate that passion. **1502** ATKYNSON tr. *De Imitatione* III. liii. 241 Comforte me, good lorde, in my exyle mytygate my sorowe. **1541** R. COPLAND *Guydon's Quest. Chirurg.* O j b, Anoynte it [*sc.* the place] with oyle of Roses..to mytygate the smert. **1553** T. WILSON *Rhet.* 5 It is wisedome..warely to mitigate, by protestacion, the evill that is in theim. **1590** SPENSER *F.Q.* I. x. 26 And dieted with fasting every day, The swelling of his woundes to mitigate. **1591** SPARRY tr. *Cattan's Geomancie* B ij, The Iasper stone.. hath vertue to mittigate Kernels of the flesh. **1655** CULPEPPER, etc. *Riverius* VI. i. 132 At first the pain wil seem to encrease; but afterward, it wil be mitigated, and cease. **1715** ADDISON *Freeholder* No. 12 ¶2 Government.. mitigates the inequality of power among particular persons. **1759** ROBERTSON *Hist. Scotl.* I. Wks. 1813 I. 29 Princes of greater abilities were content to mitigate evils which they could not cure. **1804** ABERNETHY *Surg. Obs.* 92 Nothing mitigated her sufferings so much as lint dipt in a solution of opium. **1824** J. H. NEWMAN *Hist. Sk.* (1873) II. II. iii. 256 He..gave himself up to the composition of those works which..mitigated his political sorrows. **1895** R. L. DOUGLAS in *Bookman* Oct. 23/1 The king..does his best.. to mitigate the disastrous effects of the blunders of his middle life.
†**b.** *pass.* To be relieved *of* a burden. *Obs. rare.*
1644 HASTINGS INGRAM *Let. to Ld. Denbigh* 19 Aug., Yᵉ countrie exspecteth by yoʳ justice to be mittigated of yoʳ to heavie pressures.
4. a. To abate the rigour or severity of (a law); to render less stringent or oppressive.
1532 MORE *Confut. Tindale* Wks. 641/1 Yet are the lawes of the church mitigated. **1563** *Homilies* II. *Fasting* II. 98 b, It may lawfully..alter, change, or mittigate those Ecclesiasticall decrees & orders. **1683** *Brit. Spec.* 61 Where he sees the Laws rigorous or doubtful he may mitigate and interpret them. **1965** W. MITCHELL tr. *Huyghe's Relig. Orders Mod. World* I. 6 The mendicant Orders..while in part adopting the monastic and canonical forms of organization..plainly mitigated them to enable their members to go out and preach..in the highways and by-ways.
†**b.** To lessen the stringency of (an obligation).
1651 C. CARTWRIGHT *Cert. Relig.* I. 2 Your Majesty knows ..my obligation to him, which difference in opinion shall never mitigate in point of affection.
5. a. To reduce the severity of (a punishment). Also, †to lower, moderate (a price).
a **1533** [see MITIGATE *pa. pple.*]. **1539** *Act 31 Hen. VIII*, c. 8 To diminish or mitigate the penalties. **1542-3** *Act 34 & 35 Hen. VIII*, c. 7 Suche Lordes..shall..haue the same auctoritie to mittigate, and enhaunce the price of wynes..as ..occasion shall require. **1596** SHAKS. *Merch. V.* IV. i. 203, I haue spoke thus much To mittigate the iustice of thy plea. **1621** BURTON *Anat. Mel.* I. iv. I. (1651) 454 Those hard censures..are to be mitigated. **1667** MILTON *P.L.* x. 76 That I may mitigate thir doom. **1850** DICKENS *Bill-Sticking* in *Househ. Words* II. 604 They were..fined five pounds.. but..the magistrate..mitigated the fine to fifteen shillings. **1869** TOZER *Highl. Turkey* II. 284 As she could not reverse the curse..she did what she could to mitigate it by substituting for death a sleep of a hundred years' duration.
b. To render (a condition, custom) more humane.
1835 J. B. ROBERTSON in *Von Schlegel's Philos. Hist.* (1846) 39 Christianity first mitigated, and then abolished slavery. **1869** LECKY *Europ. Mor.* (1877) I. ii. 252 Marcus Aurelius..mitigated the gladiatorial shows.
6. To moderate, reduce to a more bearable degree (heat, cold, light); to temper the severity of (a climate).
1611 TOURNEUR *Ath. Trag.* II. iii, That but mitigates The heat. **1611** BIBLE *Wisd.* xvi. 18 Sometime the flame was mitigated, that it might not burne vp the beasts that were sent against the vngodly. **1742** COLLINS *Oriental Ecl.* II. 24 Or moss-crown'd fountains mitigate the day. **1837** LYELL *Princ. Geol.* I. I. viii. 226 The winter and summer temperatures being sometimes mitigated, and at others exaggerated, in the same latitude. **1840** MACAULAY *Ess., Clive* (1899) 504 Many devices which now mitigate the heat of the climate, preserve health, and prolong life, were unknown. **1846** DE QUINCEY *Antigone* Wks. 1860 XIV. 221 There were no stage lights; but..the general light of day was specially mitigated for that particular part of the theatre. **1860** MAURY *Phys. Geog. Sea* (Low) viii. §398 This current is felt as far as the Equator, mitigating the rainless climate of Peru as it goes, and making it delightful.
7. To lessen the gravity of (an offence); to palliate.
1719 YOUNG *Revenge* III. i, Then you must pardon me, If I presume to mitigate the crime. **1862** BURTON *Bk. Hunter* (1863) 301 It may perhaps do something to mitigate Surtees's offence in the eye of the world.

8. With a quality as obj.: To moderate (the severity, rigour, heinousness, etc., *of* something).
In recent times there has been a tendency to prefer this periphrastic use to the uses in which the vb. takes a thing or condition as its object.
1571 GOLDING *Calvin on Ps.* lxviii. 34 The harshnesse of the metaphor was to bee mitigated. **1597** HOOKER *Eccl. Pol.* V. xxii. §20 We could greatly wish that the rigor of this their opinion were alayed and mitigated. **1660** WOOD *Life* (O.H.S.) I. 359 The strictness of the Lord's day was mitigated. **1702** J. PURCELL *Cholick* (1714) 165 To Mitigate the Violence of the Pain. **1718** *Free-thinker* No. 10. 69 No Consideration upon Earth can mitigate the Heinousness of the Crime. **1849** JAMES *Woodman* ix, One who..strove to mitigate the bloody rigour of a civil war. **1879** FROUDE *Cæsar* ix. 96 Cæsar interceded to mitigate the severity of the punishment.
†**9.** In physical senses: To render mild; to free from acridity; to make (land) fruitful. *Obs.*
1601 HOLLAND *Pliny* I. 379 This tree..hath in it a certaine fat liquor..and entreth into compositions of sweet ointments, for to..mitigate the other oile. **1654** R. CODRINGTON tr. *Iustine* XLIII. 507 To exercise and mitigate the fields with ploughs.
10. *intr.* To become mitigated; to grow milder or less severe. *rare.*
1633 T. JAMES *Voy.* 68 The cold did very little mitigate. **1738** H. BROOKE *Jerus. Deliv.* I. 43 But as his Years encrease, his Fires asswage Allay with Time, and mitigate with Age. **1880** McCARTHY *Own Times* IV. lvii. 235 The bitterness of popular feeling had very much mitigated.

mitigated ('mɪtɪɡeɪtɪd), *ppl. a.* [f. MITIGATE *v.* + -ED¹.] In senses of the verb. *spec.* designating or pertaining to a religious order less austere than other orders.
1671 WOODHEAD *St. Teresa* II. xxxii. 199 The Fathers of the Mitigated Rule. *Ibid.* xxxv. 232 The Mitigated Fathers Carmelites had bin attempting the same. **1694** EARL OF PERTH *Let.* 17 Sept. (1845) 44 They are called rich Clarisses, because the poor Clarisses are of a far more rigid order..; these are far more mitigated, and they gave us an entertainment of musick. **1771** SMOLLETT *Humph. Cl.* 10 May, Saying, in a mitigated tone—'Surely I am much obliged—'. **1791** BURKE *App. Whigs* Wks. 1842 I. 517 Who, though they perfectly abhor a despotick government, certainly approached more nearly to the love of mitigated monarchy, than [etc.]. **1810** *Sporting Mag.* XXXV. 36 Fined in the mitigated penalty of ten pounds. **1869** G. LAWSON *Dis. Eye* (1874) 12 The solid mitigated nitrate of silver. **1884** HUNTER & WHYTE *My Ducats & My Dau.* iii, She was dressed in mitigated mourning. **1888** [see CARMELITE *sb.* and *a.* 1 b]. **1948** W. S. MAUGHAM *Catalina* ix. 43 Since it was a convent of the mitigated order they enjoyed a good deal of freedom.
Hence **'mitigatedly** *adv.*, in a mitigated degree.
1884 H. JAMES *Little Tour in France* xviii, This young man ..was mitigatedly monastic. He had a big brown frock and cowl, but he had also a shirt and a pair of shoes.

mitigating ('mɪtɪɡeɪtɪŋ), *vbl. sb.* [f. MITIGATE *v.* + -ING¹.] The action of the verb MITIGATE.
a **1683** SIDNEY *Disc. Govt.* III. xv. (1704) 287 The power of mitigating is inseperable from that of instituting.

mitigating ('mɪtɪɡeɪtɪŋ), *ppl. a.* [f. MITIGATE *v.* + -ING².] Alleviating, extenuating, palliating.
1612 WEBSTER *White Devil* F 2, Beare me hence, Vnto this house of what's your mittigating Title? *Mon.* Of conuertites. **1749** FIELDING *Tom Jones* Wks. 1775 III. 205 I ..have more than once applied to the judge on the behalf of such [highwaymen] as have had any mitigating circumstances in their case. **1841** MACAULAY *Ess., Hastings* (1850) 636 He could see no mitigating circumstances, no redeeming merit. **1903** R. D. SHAW *Pauline Epist.* 323 The Mosaic legislation [dealing with slavery] was essentially mitigating and restricting.

mitigation (mɪtɪ'ɡeɪʃən). [ad. L. *mītigātiōnem*, n. of action f. *mītigāre* to MITIGATE. Cf. F. *mitigation* from 14th c.)] The action of mitigating; the fact or condition of being mitigated.
1. Abatement or relaxation of the severity or rigour of a law, penalty, or the like; alleviation of anything painful, oppressive, or calamitous; extenuation or palliation of an offence. *in mitigation*: by way of palliation (*of* an offence); in order to obtain a favourable modification (*of* judgement, a penalty, damages).
[**1347-8** *Rolls of Parlt.* II. 215/1 Si mitigation ne lui soit faite de sa dite ferme.] **1362** LANGL. *P. Pl. A.* v. 252 Bote for þi muchel Merci mitigacion I be-seche; Dampne me not on domes day for I dude so ille. *c* **1430** LYDG. *Min. Poems* (Percy Soc.) 206 Sobre and appeese suche folk as falle in furye, To trist and hevy do mytigacioun. **1494** FABYAN *Chron.* VII. 651 For the mytigacion of his peynfull sykenesse. **1533** MORE *Apol.* xlviii. Wks. 924/1 Therfore nede we no such chaunge of the lawes for that purpose. But on yᵉ tother side, what harme would come of hys mytygacions,..the whole summe and sequele of hys deuises doe more than manifestly shew. **1533** ELYOT *Cast. Helthe* (1539) 36 b, It somewhat profyteth in mitigation of excessiue heate. **1599** SHAKS. *Hen. V*, I. i. 70 How now for mittigation of this Bill, Vrg'd by the Commons? **1601** —— *Twel. N.* II. iii. 98 Ye squeak out your Coziers Catches without any mitigation or remorce of voice. **1622** BACON *Hen. VII* 209 Their manner was..to suffer them to languish long in Prison, and..to extort from them great Fines and Ransomes, which they termed Compositions and Mitigations. **1664** H. MORE *Myst. Iniq.* xiii. 44 As for the mitigation of the fault of either side from any exteriour circumstances, I briefly adde, That [etc.]. **1749** E. MOORE *Trial Selem* 318 These crimes

successive on your trial Have met with proofs beyond denial, To which yourself with shame conceded, And but in mitigation pleaded. **1766** BLACKSTONE *Comm.* II. 508 Though, as against the rightful executor or administrator, he cannot plead such payment, yet it shall be allowed him in mitigation of damages. **1801** *Med. Jrnl.* V. 221 She perspired.. very freely, but without affording any mitigation of her pain. **1817** COBBETT *Taking Leave Countrymen* 13 The Wolves.. flew upon the fleecy fools and devoured them and their lambs without mercy and without mitigation. **1832** HT. MARTINEAU *Homes Abroad* i. 6 A mitigation of punishment. **1875** JOWETT *Plato* (ed. 2) I. 339 The shorter address in mitigation of the penalty. **1885** J. PAYN *Talk of Town* I. 45 William Henry murmured something in mitigation about its being an acrostic. **1885** *Manch. Exam.* 24 July 5/1 All that could be done for him was to attempt some mitigation of his pain.

b. quasi-*concr.* A circumstance that mitigates.

1729 BUTLER *Serm.* Wks. 1874 II. 70 Mitigations and reliefs are provided.. for most of the afflictions in human life. **1742** YOUNG *Nt. Th.* VI. 4 This seeming mitigation but inflames; This fancy'd med'cine heightens the disease. **1864** PUSEY *Lect. Daniel* (1876) 240 Which God gave them as a mitigation of their ills.

†**2.** Softening (of words or statements); a qualification, limitation. *Obs.*

1588 FRAUNCE *Lawiers Log.* Ded. ¶¶j b, The addition, detraction, or mitigation of woordes. **1651** HOBBES *Leviath.* III. xlii. 306 Hee bringeth one Text,.. Iohn 16. 13.. where (saith he) by *all truth*, is meant, at least, all truth necessary to salvation. But with this mitigation, he attributeth no more Infallibility to the Pope, than to any man that professeth Christianity, and is not to be damned. **1709** STRYPE *Ann. Ref.* I. xliv. 445 A third letter was written to the Chancellor, with more mitigation.

†**3.** Propitiation (of a person); taming (of an animal). *Obs.*

1382 WYCLIF *Eccl.* xvii. 28 How gret the merci of God, and the mytigacioun.. of hym to men conuertende to hym [L. *et propitiatio illius convertentibus ad se*]. **1737** WHISTON *Josephus, Antiq.* XVII. v. §5 The most envenomed serpents.. admit of some mitigation, and will not bite their benefactors.

†**4.** ? A soothing remedy. *Obs.*

c **1430** LYDG. *Min. Poems* (Percy Soc.) 15 And ageyns hertis ffor mutigacions, Damysyns wiche withe her taste delyte, Fulle grete plente both of blak and white.

mitigative ('mɪtɪgeɪtɪv), *a.* and *sb.* Now *rare* or *Obs.* [ad. L. *mītigātīvus*, f. *mītigāre*: see MITIGATE *v.* and -IVE. Cf. F. *mitigatif.*]

A. *adj.* Tending to mitigate or alleviate; lenitive; also const. *of*.

c **1400** *Lanfranc's Cirurg.* 235 þou schalt ȝeue him medicyns.. þat ben mitigatif for to take awey þe akynge. **1541** R. COPLAND *Guydon's Formul.* X j b, The fyfth fourme is vnguentum dulce mollyfycatyfe, resolutyfe, and mytygatyfe of the paynes of yᵉ synewes. **1566** WARDE tr. *Alexis' Secr.* III. I. 49 b. A playster mitigatiue, and very gentle for Cankers. **1611** COTGR., *Mitigatif*, mitigatiue, lenitiue, appeasiue.

B. *sb.* Something that serves to mitigate or alleviate; a soothing remedy.

c **1400** *Lanfranc's Cirurg.* 217 Leie þerto mitigatiuis for to do awei þe akynge. *c* **1430** LYDG. *Min. Poems* (Percy Soc.) 196 Ayer of nature.. [is] a gret mytigatiff. *c* **1530** *Remedy of Love* Prol. 20 Whiche may the feruence of loue aslake To the louer, as a mitigatiue.

mitigator ('mɪtɪgeɪtə(r)). Also 7–8 -er. [agent-n. f. L. *mītigāre*: see MITIGATE *v.*] One who or something which mitigates or alleviates; †a soothing remedy.

1605 TIMME *Quersit.* I. xiii. 53 A certain red ocre.. which is.. a great mitigator of all griefes and paines. **1656** RIDGLEY *Pract. Physick* 257 Mitigaters are useful, either temperate or cold. **1711** SHAFTESB. *Charac.* (1737) III. 23 The highest glory which cou'd be attain'd by mortal man, was to be mitigator or moderator of that universal tyranny already establish'd. **1869** BUSHNELL *Wom. Suffrage* vii. 139 They are no more mitigators now, but instigators rather.

mitigatory ('mɪtɪgeɪtərɪ), *a.* and *sb.* Also 7 mitt-. [ad. L. *mītigātōri-us*, f. *mītigāre*: see MITIGATE *v.* and -ORY[2].] **A.** *adj.* Tending or serving to mitigate; lenitive, alleviating; palliative.

c **1611** CHAPMAN *Iliad* XI. 758 Then twixt his hands he brusde A sharpe and mitigatorie roote: which when he had infusde Into the greene well-cleansed wound, the paines he felt before Were well and instantly allaide. **1813** CROKER *Parl. Deb.* 18 Feb. in *Examiner* 22 Feb. 118/2 That.. Admiral had since received no mitigatory or restrained orders. **1868** J. H. BLUNT *Ref. Ch. Eng.* I. 32 Whatever mitigatory explanations might be offered by the learned.

B. *sb.* Something which serves to mitigate; a lenitive or soothing remedy; a plea in extenuation.

1656 W. D. tr. *Comenius' Gate Lat. Unl.* §806 Hee mitigateth pains, with certain mittigatories, or anodynes. *a* **1734** NORTH *Exam.* II. v. §2 (1740) 316 He talks of hard Usages, and straining Points of Law.. and such Mitigatories.

Mitin ('maɪtɪn). A proprietary name for certain mothproofing agents, spec. ***Mitin F.F.***, a substituted urea, $Cl_2C_6H_3$·NH·CO·NH·$C_6H_3(Cl)O$·$C_6H_3(Cl)SO_3Na$, which is used for treating woollen goods such as carpets.

1938 *Trade Marks Jrnl.* 17 Aug. 994/1 Mitin Moth-proof... Moth repelling and destroying preparations. J. R. Geigy.., Basle,.. Switzerland; manufacturers. **1945** *Chem. Abstr.* XXXIX. 764 A new attack based on the insecticidal activity of *p,p′*-dihalodiphenyl sulfones, sulfoxides and sulfides, and resulting in the introduction of the H_2O-sol. dye Mitin F.F. showed the fundamental toxicity of this type of compd. **1958** *House & Garden* Apr. 7/3 (Advt.), Stockwell [carpet]... All-woollen pile. Mitin-processed; guaranteed mothproof for life. **1969** *Chem. Abstr.* 18 Aug. 206/2 For the protection of wool, mohair, camel's hair, or alpaca, mixts. of 1 part dieldrin,.. Mitin FF, naphthalene.. or alkylyl-2-thiazolyl sulfide and 0·33–12 parts epoxide, polyamide, and (or) acrylic resins are used.

†**'miting.** *Obs.* Forms: 5 mytyng, myghtyng, 5–7 mytting, 6 myten, myting, myteyng. [f. MITE[2] + -ING[3].] A diminutive creature. Often used as a term of endearment or of contempt.

c **1440** *York Myst.* xviii. 113 With þat mytyng yf þat we be mette þer is no salue þat hym may saue. *Ibid.* xxxi. 305 þou mummeland myghtyng. *c* **1460** *Towneley Myst.* xii. 477 Hayll, praty mytyng! **1508** KENNEDIE *Flyting w. Dunbar* 494 A myten [*v.r.* myting], full of flyting. *a* **1529** SKELTON *E. Rummyng* 224 He calleth me his whytyng, His mullyng and his myting. —— *Agst. Garnesche* iii. 115 For alle ys nat worthe a myteyng, A mekerell nor a wyteyng. *a* **1585** MONTGOMERIE *Flyting w. Polwart* 9 Foule mismade mytting.

mitis[1] ('mɪtɪs). Also **mittis**. [a. G. *mitis* (*grün*); from the name of the manufacturer, Ignaz *Mitis* of Kirchberg (1771–1842).] ***mitis green***: Scheele's or Emerald green (see EMERALD 5 d).

1839 URE *Dict. Arts* 619 Mittis green is an arseniate of copper. **1853** WATTS tr. *Gmelin's Handbk. Chem.* VIII. 329 Cupric Aceto-arsenite. Schweinfurt Green, Vienna Green. Imperial Green, Mitis Green. **1892** CHURCH *Chemistry Paints & Painting* s.v. *Scheele's Green*, Mittis Green.

mitis[2] ('miːtɪs). *Metallurgy.* [Named by the inventor of the process, P. Östberg of Stockholm; app. from L. *mītis* mild, taken in the sense of MILD *a.* 8 b.] ***mitis casting***: a method of increasing the fluidity of molten iron (so as to render it possible to prevent the occlusion of air in the casting) by adding a minute quantity of aluminium to the charge in the crucible; also, a casting produced by this process. So ***mitis-metal, process***, etc.

1885 T. NORDENFELDT in *Ironmonger* 9 May Suppl., On 'Mitis' Castings. **1886** *Chamb. Jrnl.* 14 Aug. 527/2 The 'Mitis process'. *Ibid.* 528/1 In the United States and Sweden, Mitis Metal has already established itself as an article of commerce. **1888** *Pall Mall G.* 6 Sept. 12/1 The 1-20th part of 1 per cent. of aluminium, when added to molten wrought iron will reduce the fusing-point of the whole mass some 500 degrees, and will render it extremely fluid, and thus enable wrought iron (or what are commercially known as 'Mitis'-castings of the most intricate character) to be produced. **1894** *Jrnl. Iron & Steel Inst.* XLIV. 476 Mitis Castings.—Stambke.. describes the method in use at the Mitis foundry at Chemnitz.

mitkul, variant of MISKAL.

mitla ('mɪtlə). [Native name.] An unidentified animal said to inhabit the forests on the borders of Bolivia and Brazil.

a **1925** P. H. FAWCETT *Exploration Fawcett* (1953) xiv. 173 In the forests [of Bolivia] were various beasts still unfamiliar to zoologists, such as the *mitla*, which I have seen twice, a black dog-like cat about the size of a fox-hound. **1965** *Sun* 28 Sept. 3/1 He will spend two months looking for a mitla.. in the forests of Rio Abuna.

Mitnagged (mɪt'nɑːgɪd). Also **Misnagid**. Pl. Mitnaggedim. [ad. Heb. *mitnāggēd* opponent.] The name given by the Chasidim to their religious opponents; hence any Jew who is not a Chasid.

1904 *Jewish Encycl.* VIII. 623/1 *Mitnaggedim*, (lit. 'opponents'), title applied by the Hasidim to their opponents, *i.e.*, to the Orthodox Jews of the Slavonic countries who have not become adherents of Hasidim... 'Mitnagged' now means.. simply a non-Hasid. **1907** I. ZANGWILL *Ghetto Comedies* 409 'Me join the *Misnagdim*!' cried the cobbler in horror. 'Never will I join with those who deny the Master-of-the-Name.' **1936** M. GOLDSTEIN *Thus Religion Grows* iii. 269 The Hasidim as well as the Mitnaggedim, both were confronted by the challenge of a new heaven and a new earth. **1964** S. BELLOW *Herzog* 139 She.. seemed to be seeing the Old World—her father the famous *misnagid*.

mitochondrion (maɪtəʊ'kɒndrɪən). *Biol.* Pl. **-chondria**. [a. G. *mitochondrion* (C. Benda 1898, in *Arch. f. Anat. u. Physiol.* (*Physiol. Abth.*) 397), f. Gr. *μίτος* thread + *χονδρίον*, dim. of *χόνδρος* granule or lump (of salt).] An organelle that is present (usu. in great numbers) in the cytoplasm of all cells with a true nucleus and primarily functions to store and release energy by the reactions of the Krebs cycle (see KREBS).

1901 *Jrnl. R. Microsc. Soc.* 14 Meves believes that this term [sc. *Nebenkern*] should lapse, and himself employs for the separate granules Benda's term *mitochondria*, and for the *Nebenkern* which may be formed by their union, the term *mitochondrial corpuscle*. **1911, 1920** [see CHONDRIOSOME]. **1949** *Amer. Jrnl. Physiol.* CLVII. 136 The residue.. which contained only mitochondria and microsomes was transferred to a vial. **1962** *Science Survey* III. 169 Each mitochondrion is bounded by an outer limiting membrane, then there is a narrow space and then another membrane bounding an inner chamber. **1964** A. L. LEHNINGER *Mitochondrion* p. vii, It is now some fifteen years since the mitochondria were first recognized to be the 'power plants' of aerobic cells. **1970** *New Scientist* 24 Sept. 626/1 The amount of DNA in a chick liver cell mitochondrion.. is only about 0·5 per cent of that in a bacterium. **1971** [see KREBS].

So **mito'chondrial** *a.*, of or pertaining to a mitochondrion or to mitochondria.

1901 [see MITOCHONDRION]. **1920** L. DONCASTER *Introd. Study Cytol.* ii. 23 Some investigators maintain.. that every mitochondrial body arises only from a pre-existing one. **1962** *Lancet* 19 May 1056/1 Increased permeability of the mitochondrial membrane leads to the escape of enzymes and cofactors. **1970** *Sci. Amer.* Feb. 100/1 Heavy mitochondrial damage was followed by an almost total absence of dehydrogenase activity.

mitogenetic (maɪtəʊdʒɪ'nɛtɪk), *a. Biol.* [f. as next + -GENETIC.] Mitogenic; applied *spec.* to a type of radiation supposed by some to be emitted by dividing cells and to stimulate mitosis in other tissues.

1927 *Biol. Abstr.* I. 1042/2 The blood through the admission of air sends out mitogenetic currents... The mitogenetic oxidation reaction is cared for through oxyhemoglobin. **1928** *Ibid.* II. 406/2 Experiments.. lead the author [*sc.* A. Gurwitsch] to believe in the physical nature of what he terms mitogenetic rays. **1930** *Jrnl. Marine Biol. Assoc.* XVII. 65 Various authors have framed the hypothesis of a mitogenetic radiation emanating from cells in the act of division. Gurwitsch first of all pointed out the mitogenetic influence of cells of embryonic tissues. **1952** G. H. BOURNE *Cytol. & Cell Physiol.* (ed. 2) ii. 94 The school of Gurwitsch has.. claimed that mitogenetic radiation is closely associated with many other forms of cellular activity.

mitogenic (maɪtəʊ'dʒɛnɪk), *a. Biol.* [f. MITO(SIS + -GENIC.] Inducing or stimulating mitosis. So **'mitogen**, a substance or agent which has a mitogenic effect.

1962 *Hereditas* XLVIII. 619 (*heading*) On the effect of mitogenic plant extracts (phyto-hemagglutinin) on human white blood cells cultivated in vitro. **1963** *Proc. 9th Congr. European Soc. Haematol.* II. I. 78 (*heading*) Factors stimulating cell division in cultured leucocytes. Chemical, serological and immunological studies on mitogens. **1970** *Nature* 26 Sept. 1351/1 When certain mitogenic agents are added to lymphocytes cultured in serum, the cells are activated to transform and divide. **1971** *Ibid.* 31 Dec. 508/2 Pokeweed mitogen is one of the plant lectins which.. can be used to stimulate lymphocytes *in vitro*.

mitom, mitome ('maɪtɒm, -əʊm). *Biol.* Also in mod. Latin form. [ad. mod.L. *mitōma* (mɪ'təʊmə), f. Gr. *μίτος* thread: see MITOSIS and cf. *carcinoma*, *sarcoma*, etc.] Flemming's name for the mass of fibrils of protoplasm in the body of a cell.

1888 ROLLESTON & JACKSON *Anim. Life* p. xxi, Protoplasm.. as a rule.. is more or less vesicular, consisting of a denser substance (mitome) enclosing droplets of a more fluid character (enchylema, paramitome). **1898** KLEIN & EDKINS *Elem. Histol.* 11 The divided nuclear mitoma. **1900** JACKSON *Gloss. Bot. Terms, Mitom.*

mitomycin (maɪtəʊ'maɪsɪn). *Biochem.* [f. *mito-* (perh. representing Gr. *μίτος* thread or MITOSIS, MITOCHONDRION, etc.: the allusion is not explained by the (Japanese) authors of the name) + -MYCIN.] An antibiotic active against some bacteria and tumour cells that is produced by the soil bacterium *Streptomyces cæspitosus*; also any of the three (or more) slightly different molecular species (as those designated *mitomycin A*, *B*, and *C*) into which preparations of this antibiotic can be resolved.

1956 T. HATA et al. in *Jrnl. Antibiotics* (Tokyo) A. IX. 141 (*heading*) Mitomycin, a new antibiotic from Streptomyces. *Ibid.* 145 Mitomycins have a high antibacterial activity against gram positive and gram negative bacteria. **1958** *Antibiotics & Chemotherapy* VIII. *S*[*treptomyces*] *caespitosus*, which produces mainly mitomycin A and B in some cultural conditions, produces mitomycin C exclusively under other conditions. **1968** [see INDUCTION 9 d].

‖**mitosis** (mɪ'təʊsɪs). *Biol.* Pl. **-oses** (-'əʊsiːz). [mod.L., f. Gr. *μίτος* a thread of a warp: see -OSIS; first formed in Ger. by W. Flemming in *Zellsubstanz, Kern und Zelltheilung* (1882) xxiv. 376.] The process of nuclear division by which a cell nucleus gives rise to two daughter nuclei identical with the parent nucleus; an instance of this; commonly also used to refer to the whole process of mitotic cell division, i.e. division of the cytoplasm as well as the nucleus; also, a cell or nucleus undergoing this. Cf. KARYOMITOSIS.

1887 *Jrnl. R. Microsc. Soc.* 163 (*heading*) Showing mitosis in brain of tadpole. **1888** ROLLESTON & JACKSON *Anim. Life* p. xxii, The nuclear membrane is dissolved in mitosis and reconstituted round the new nuclei. **1891** *Lancet* 6 June 1269/1 The 'mitoses' are not of uniform size,.. but present the greatest variety in this respect in one and the same tumour. **1896** *Allbutt's Syst. Med.* I. 65 Many of the corneal corpuscles.. can.. be seen undergoing mitosis. **1918** *Surg., Gynecol. & Obstetr.* XVIII. 205/2 These cells are large and mostly polyhedric... Mitoses are found, though rarely. **1937** C. D. DARLINGTON *Recent Adv. Cytol.* (ed. 2) i. 22 Nuclei divide by the characteristic process of mitosis in the course of which the whole nucleus, apart from the nucleoli, resolves itself into longitudinally split threads, the chromosomes. **1962** D. G. COGAN in A. Pirie *Lens Metabolism Rel. Cataract* 292 Although showing few mitoses normally, the lens epithelium may be activated into lively mitotic activity when stimulated by heat. **1970** AMBROSE & EASTY *Cell Biol.* i. 20 The actual process of cell division, however, known as mitosis, is remarkably similar for all cell types.

Hence **mitosic** (mɪ'təʊsɪk) *a.* = MITOTIC.

1890 in *Century Dict.*; and in later Dicts.

†mitosome (ˈmaɪtəʊsəʊm). *Cytology. Obs.* Also 9 **mitosoma.** [a. G. *mitosoma* (G. Platner 1889, in *Arch. f. mikrosk. Anat.* XXXIII. 199), f. Gr. μίτο-ς thread + σῶμα body.] (See quots.)

1891 *Jrnl. R. Microsc. Soc.* 461 The portion of the mitosoma which becomes attached to the nucleus becomes chromatic and wanders to the anterior end of the spermatozoon. **1895** G. W. FIELD in *Jrnl. Morphol.* XI. 237 In view of the fact that the term 'Nebenkern' has come to be applied to many sorts of intracellular structures.. it seems best, since the history of the middle piece or 'Nebenkern' is now better understood, that this noncommittal term.. should be replaced by some term which gives a hint as to the nature of this body. Since the middle piece or 'Nebenkern' of the echinoderm spermatozoön is formed from the mitotic spindle, the term 'mitosome', introduced by Platner, has been adopted and will be used to designate the middle piece, = Nebenkern = *corpuscle accessoire* of other writers. **1920** L. DONCASTER *Introd. Study Cytol.* vii. 95 In the spermatocyte, as the cell enlarges, the mitochondrial bodies increase in size... In the young spermatid they unite to form a fairly compact mass near the nucleus at the side of the cell at which the tail will grow out. [*Note*] This mitochondrial mass ('mitosome') constitutes the 'Nebenkern' of some authors, but as the word has been used to designate the remains of the division-spindle.., the 'idiozome'.. and other cell-structures, it is now dropping out of use. **1925** E. B. WILSON *Cell* (ed. 3) iv. 366 One of these [elements of doubtful nature] is the spindle-remnant, sometimes called the 'mitosome'... This body was believed by some earlier observers to play an important part in the sperm-formation, and was confused with the nebenkern or with the acroblast; but later studies seem to show that it disappears without taking any definite part in the sperm-formation. **1934** L. W. SHARP *Introd. Cytol.* (ed. 3) xiv. 218 In insects generally the chondriosomes form a single more or less compact body, the nebenkern (the mitosome of Gatenby).

mitotic (mɪˈtɒtɪk), *a.* [f. MITOSIS: see -OTIC.] Pertaining to, connected with, characterized by, or exhibiting mitosis.

1888 ROLLESTON & JACKSON *Anim. Life* p. xxii, The division of the protoplasm [of a cell].. may be indirect or mitotic. **1904** *Brit. Med. Jrnl.* 10 Sept. 584 The work of Flemming and his pupils in 1884 placed beyond doubt the mitotic reproduction of lymphocytes in these situations.

Hence **miˈtotically** *adv.*, by mitosis.

1890 in *Century Dict.* **1896** *Jrnl. R. Microsc. Soc.* 494 The cells of the inner theca layer begin to divide mitotically. **1946** [see AMITOTIC *a.*]. **1973** *Nature* 30 Mar. 299/3 The thymus is usually thought of as a staging house through which pass stem cells and their mitotically amplified products.

‖**mitra** (ˈmaɪtrə). Also 7 **mi-, mythra.** [L., a. Gr. μίτρα: see MITRE *sb.*]

1. *Antiq.* A head-dress = MITRE *sb.*[1] 1 a.

1638 SIR T. HERBERT *Trav.* (ed. 2) 146 Above each doore is ingraven the Idea of a Majestique Monarch; his roabe is long, a Tiara or Mithra on his head. **1850** LEITCH tr. *C.O. Müller's Anc. Art* §383 (ed. 2) 488 A magnificent luxuriance of curling hair restrained by the mitra.

2. *Bot.* †**a.** (see quot. 1775). **b.** (see quot. 1852).

1775 ASH, *Mitra*, the name of a plant, the mitreola. **1852** HENSLOW *Dict. Bot. Terms*, *Mitra*, used synonymously with galea, for 'Helmet'. Also, the thick, rounded, and folded pileus of some fungi.

3. *Surg.* 'A fillet or bandage applied on the head' (Mayne *Expos. Lex.* 1856).

‖**mitraillade** (mitrɑjad). [Fr., f. *mitraille-r*: see MITRAILLE *v.* and -ADE.] A wholesale execution or massacre by volleys of mitraille.

1833 ALISON *Hist. Europe* (1849–50) III. xiii. §115. 123 The inhuman mitraillades of Lyons.

‖**mitraille** (mitrɑj, mɪˈtreɪl), *sb.* Also anglicized **mitrail.** [F. *mitraille*, OF. *mi(s)traille* small money, pieces of metal; an altered form of OF. *mitaille*, f. *mite*: see MITE[2].] Small missiles, as fragments of iron, heads of nails, etc. shot in masses from a cannon; now *spec.* small shot or projectiles fired from a mitrailleuse.

[**1802** C. JAMES *Milit. Dict.*, *Mitraille*, *Fr.* small pieces of old iron, such as heads of nails, &c., with which pieces of ordnance are frequently loaded.] **1868** KINGLAKE *Crimea* (1877) IV. vi. 140 His.. purpose of meeting the assaulting column.. with a pelting blast of mitrail. **1876** VOYLE & STEVENSON *Milit. Dict.* (ed. 3) s.v. *Mitrailleur*, A machine gun intended to throw *mitraille*, that is, groups of small projectiles, independently, to distances of 1000 yards.

Hence **miˈtraille**, *v. rare* [cf. F. *mitrailler*], *trans.* to assail with mitraille.

1844 TH. PARKER in J. Weiss *Life & Corr.* I. 225 The wretched Terrorists of the Revolution guillotined.. and mitrailled, I know not how many.

‖**mitrailleur** (mitrɑjœr). [Fr., agent-n. f. *mitrailler* to fire mitraille (see MITRAILLE *v.*). In Littré only in sense 2.]

1. = MITRAILLEUSE 1. Also, see quot. 1876[2].

1869 FOSBERY in *Jrnl. R. United Serv. Instit.* XIII. 540 Mitrailleur, the term I have adopted in the title of this paper, perhaps best of all expresses what is intended, namely, a weapon producing a hail storm of comparatively small projectiles. **1876** VOYLE & STEVENSON *Milit. Dict.* (ed. 3) s.v. *Mitrailleur*, The *Nobel* mitrailleur is the one used in the Russian army. It is a ten-barrelled gun on the Gatling system. *Ibid.*, Mr. Hale.. has invented a mitrailleur which fires five rockets at a time. **1883** *Pall Mall G.* 15 Sept. 1/2 The French mitrailleuse was only an adaptation of the Montigny mitrailleur.

2. One who works a mitrailleuse. *rare*[−0].

1890 in *Century Dict.*

‖**mitrailleuse** (mitrɑjøz). [Fr., fem. agent-n. formed as prec.] A breech-loading machine-gun with a number of barrels fitted together, so arranged that it can discharge small missiles simultaneously in large quantities with great rapidity, or singly in rapid succession.

It was introduced into the French army about 1868 and first brought into service in the Franco-German war of 1870–1. There are many varieties of this gun, with qualifying names prefixed.

1870 *Times* 23 July 10/3 The Emperor.. is reported to have constantly had the mitrailleuses brought to St. Cloud to be tested under his own eyes... The mitrailleuse is, perhaps, relied upon to do for France in the present war what in the last the needle-gun did for Prussia. **1872** RUSKIN *Eagle's N.* §34 Our mechanical contrivance will only make the age of the mitrailleuse more abhorred than that of the guillotine. **1902** R. W. CHAMBERS *Maids of Paradise* i. 14 A battery of Montigny mitrailleuses passed.

mitral (ˈmaɪtrəl), *a.* and *sb.* Also 8 **mytrale.** [a. F. *mitral*, ad. mod.L. *mitrālis*, f. L. *mitra*: see MITRE *sb.* and -AL[1].] **A.** *adj.*

1. Of, pertaining to, or resembling a mitre.

1610 GUILLIM *Heraldry* III. i. 190 The Field is Iupiter, a Crowne Mitrall Imperiall Sol, garnished and enriched with sundry precious Gems, Proper. *Ibid.*, *margin*, A Crowne Imperiall Mitrall. **1624** DARCIE *Birth of Heresies* xii. 54 Which Mytrall Ornament is only preserued for eminent and higher Priests. **1658** SIR T. BROWNE *Gard. Cyrus* ii. in *Hydriot.* etc. 41 The mitrall Crown, which common picture seems to set too upright and forward upon the head of Aaron.

2. a. *Anat.* **mitral valve**: The left auriculo-ventricular valve of the heart, so called from its shape (see quot. 1872); formerly it was considered as two valves. Also called *bicuspid valve.*

[**1693** tr. *Blancard's Phys. Dict.* (ed. 2), *Mitrales Valvulæ*, see *Episcopales*.] **1705** W. COWPER in *Phil. Trans.* XXV. 1974 The Mitral and Semilunary Valves of the Left Ventricle of the Heart. **1860** O. W. HOLMES *Prof. Breakf.-t.* xi. 227 Heart hits as hard as a fist,—bellows-sound over mitral valves. **1872** MIVART *Elem. Anat.* 408 The left auriculo-ventricular opening is guarded by two flaps, forming what is called the mitral valve, from a fancied resemblance to a bishop's mitre.

b. *Anat.* and *Path.* Of or pertaining to the mitral valve.

1853 MARKHAM *Skoda's Auscult.* 207 Constriction of the mitral orifice. **1857** DUNGLISON *Med. Lex.* s.v. *Regurgitation*, *Mitral regurgitation*.. means the reflux of blood through the left auriculo-ventricular opening, during the contraction of the left ventricle. **1872** *Half-Yearly Abstr. Med. Sci.* LV. 103 (*heading*) The physical signs of mitral stenosis. **1879** *St. George's Hosp. Rep.* IX. 406 With mitral and tricuspid insufficiency. **1891** *Syd. Soc. Lex.*, *Mitral area*, the area in which the sounds produced at the mitral valve are best heard. **1926** *Daily Colonist* (Victoria, B.C.) 14 Jan. 4/6 In 1921 the patient, a young girl, came up to the London Hospital suffering from mitral stenosis, or a gradual closing of one of the four valves of the heart. **1966** WRIGHT & SYMMERS *Systemic Path.* I. xxiv. 50/1 In mitral stenosis, two further complications may arise which still further burden the already overstressed heart:.. arterial fibrillation, and.. increasing incompetence of the valve with progressively greater regurgitation of blood into the left atrium during ventricular systole.

B. *sb.* = *mitral valve.*

[**1704** J. HARRIS *Lex. Techn.* I, *Mitrales*, are two Valves at the Orifice of *Vena pulmonaris*, in the Left Ventricle of the Heart.] **1835** J. HOPE in *Cycl. Pract. Med.* IV. 424/1 Extreme contraction of the mitral.. can be detected by the characters of the pulse, and the assemblage of other signs. **1897** *Allbutt's Syst. Med.* III. 450 A.. contracted mitral. **1899** *Ibid.* VI. 25 The degree of stenosis of the mitral is generally more severe than that of the tricuspid.

mitrate (ˈmaɪtreɪt), *a.* *Bot.* and *Zool.* [ad. L. *mitrāt-us* wearing a turban, f. *mitra*: see MITRE *sb.* and -ATE.] Having the shape of a mitre or bonnet.

1848 E. FORBES *Naked-eyed Medusæ* 22 The umbrella is sub-cylindrical and mitrate. **1887** W. PHILLIPS *Brit. Discomycetes* 1 Receptacle.. mitrate.

mitre (ˈmaɪtə(r)), *sb.*[1] Forms: 4–5 **mytir**, 4–7 **mytre, -er**, 5 **mytyre, mytor**, 6 **mytyr, myttor, mytter, mither, meeter**, 6– **miter**, 4– **mitre**. [ad. F. *mitre* (= Pr., Sp. *mitra*, It. *mitra*, *mitria*, ON. *mítr*, *mítra*), ad. L. *mitra*, a. Gr. μίτρα (Ionic μίτρη) belt, girdle, head-band, turban.]

1. a. *Antiq.* As rendering of Gr. μίτρα, L. *mitra*: A headband or fillet worn by ancient Greek women; also, a kind of head-dress common among Asiatics, the wearing of which by men was regarded by the Romans as a mark of effeminacy.

1382 WYCLIF *Isa.* iii. 19 In that dai the Lord shal don awei the.. armcercles, and mytris, and combys, and ribanes. —— *Judith* xvi. 10 She bond togidere hir crisp heris with a mitre. *c* **1450** *Mirour Saluacioun* 3204 Judith hire clothis didde on most ffestyvale faire and swete With mytre hire heved arraied. **1590** SPENSER *F.Q.* I. ii. 13 And like a Persian mitre on her hed Shee wore. *c* **1614** MURE *Dido & Æneas* II. 417 His curled head with Phrygian mytre. [*Æn.* IV. 216 *Mæonia mitra*] guised. **1647** A. ROSS *Mystag. Poet.* ii. (1675) 40 Bacchus used to wear a Mitre, which is the proper attire of women. **1699** GARTH *Dispens.* VI. 72 These, Miters emulate, Those, Turbans are. **1866** BRANDE & COX *Dict. Sci.*, etc., s.v., Servius makes it a matter of reproach to the Phrygians that they were dressed like women, inasmuch as they wore mitres.

¶ Used by Chapman and Pope for the Homeric μίτρη, which means a belt or girdle.

c **1611** CHAPMAN *Iliad* v. 719 Oresbius, that did wear The gaudy mitre. **1716** POPE *ibid.* 870 Oresbius, in his painted mitre gay. [Gr. ὅθι ζωννύσκετο μίτρην.]

†**b.** Applied by travellers in the 16–17th c. to the turban or the long conical cap worn by certain Asiatic peoples; also, rarely, applied to other kinds of head attire worn in remote countries. *Obs.*

1585 T. WASHINGTON tr. *Nicholay's Voy.* IV. xiv. 128 They weare.. on their head a long myter. **1604** E. G[RIMSTONE] *D'Acosta's Hist. Indies* V. xxix. 420 The maides were clothed in new garments, wearing.. vpon their heads myters made of rods covered with this mays. **1638** SIR T. HERBERT *Trav.* (ed. 2) 227 About their heads they wreath great rowles of Callico, of silke and gold,.. they call them shashes, in past times (especially those worne by Kings) Cydarims or Tyaraes, with us call'd Mithers.

2. A sacerdotal head-dress.

a. *Hebrew Antiq.* Used (after L. *mitra*, Vulg., and μίτρα, LXX.) for the ceremonial turban of the high priest (Heb. *miçnepheth*, *çānīph*); also (in Wyclif and the Douay Bible, though not in the other versions) for the head-dress of the ordinary priests (Heb. *migbāꜥāh*; Coverdale and the Bible of 1611 'bonnet', 1884 Revised 'headtire').

For the 'mitre' of the English Bible of 1611 the Vulgate has *cidaris* or *tiara* (*mitra* only in Exod. xxxix); its *mitra* is the 'bonnet' of the English Bible. Wyclif's rendering of *cidaris* by 'mytre' is noteworthy, as probably indicating that the word was already current in English (in sense 1 b).

1382 WYCLIF *Lev.* xvi. 4 He [*sc.* Aaron] shal be gyrd with a lynnen gyrdil, and a lynnen mytre he shal putte to the heed. —— *Zech.* iii. 5 Putte ȝe a cleane cappe or mytre [**1535** COVERDALE a fayre myter, **1611** a faire miter, **1884** (*Revised*) a fair mitre (*margin*, or turban)] vpon his heued. **1398** TREVISA *Barth. De P.R.* XVII. cxxix. (1495) 687 The myter of the cheyf preest was shape to the liknesse of the herbe weybrede. *a* **1400–50** *Alexander* 1589. **1614** RALEIGH *Hist. World* IV. ii. §6. 470 Iaddus the high Priest.. with his miter. **1878** B. TAYLOR *Deukalion* IV. ii. 145, I took away The High Priest's mitre, long since threadbare grown.

b. *Eccl.* A head-dress forming part of the insignia of a bishop in the Western Church, and worn also by certain abbots and other ecclesiastics as a mark of exceptional dignity. In its modern form, it is a tall cap, deeply cleft at the top, the outline of the front and back having the shape of a pointed arch; the material has usually been white linen or satin, embroidered and often jewelled; but mitres of gold or silver have also been used.

The application of *mitra* in med.L. to the episcopal head-dress was doubtless suggested by its occurrence in the description of the attire of the Jewish high-priest. (See a.)

In the Anglican church after the Reformation, the mitre, though theoretically part of the episcopal insignia, was seldom actually worn except at coronations down to that of George III. In recent times some bishops have revived its use on special ceremonial occasions.

c **1380** WYCLIF *Sel. Wks.* II. 398 Bishopis.. shulden knowe boþe Goddis lawes; and þis token þei beren on hem, whanne þei hilen hem wiþ her mytir. *c* **1393** CHAUCER *Gentilesse* 7 Al were he mytre [*Caxton* mytor] croune or dyademe. **1431** *Rec. St. Mary at Hill* 27 Also a myter of cloth of gold set with stones. *a* **1533** LD. BERNERS *Huon* lxiii. 219 He [*sc.* the abbot] called all his couent, and chargyd them.. to reuest them selues with crosse and myter & copes, to receyue Huon. **1556** *Chron. Gr. Friars* (Camden) 33 Dyvers byshoppes and abbottes in their mytteres. *Ibid.* 50 The byshoppe in his myttor. **1661** EVELYN *Diary* 20 Dec., There was a silver mitre with episcopal robes, born by the Herauld before the herse [of the Bishop of Hereford]. **1687** DRYDEN *Hind & P.* I. 395 Our Panther,.. The crosier wielded and the mitre wore. **1852** HOOK *Ch. Dict.* (1871) 508 The episcopal coronet-Mitres, though worn in some of the Lutheran churches (as in Sweden), have fallen into utter desuetude in England, even at Coronations.

transf. *c* **1645** HOWELL *Lett.* v. 48 Upon their heads they carry a Miter of paper. **1649** JER. TAYLOR *Gt. Exemp.* III. Ad Sect. xv. 161 The Crown of Thorns was his Miter. **1868** MARRIOTT *Vest. Chr.* p. xl, In Egyptian monuments we find the symbols of priesthood.. such as.. a high cap or mitre, indicative of authority.

c. Used as the symbol of the episcopal office or dignity.

1387–8 T. USK *Test. Love* II. ii. (Skeat) l. 36, I [*sc.* Love] bar both crosse and mytre, to yeve it where I wolde. **1390** GOWER *Conf.* I. 258 The Mitre with the Diademe He hath thurgh Supplantacion. **1589** WARNER *Alb. Eng.* v. xxiii. 103 What cite I forraine matters, when our natiue Stories yeeld Of Myters medling with our Sword an ouerplenteous feeld? **1641** HEYWOOD *Reader here you'l plainly see*, etc. 2 As Wolstan, Becket, Wolsey,.. And their successors,.. Would make the Miter levell with the Crowne! *a* **1660** *Contemp. Hist. Irel.* (Irish Archæol. & Celtic Soc. 1879) I. i. 101 To indeere himself unto the Councell, that they may speake a good worde for him to enjoy a meeter. **1708** HEARNE *Collect.* 10 Jan. (O.H.S.) II. 88 Learning being.. reckon'd of a very ordinary Qualification for yᵉ Mitre. **1738** POPE *Epil. Sat.* ii. 240 Stars.. (Such as on Hough's unsully'd Mitre shine, Or beam, good Digby, from a heart like thine). **1849** MACAULAY *Hist. Eng.* iv. I. 491 Baxter.. refused the mitre of Hereford. **1903** *Edin. Rev.* Apr. 526 James II.. could not get a mitre for Petre.

d. *Her.* The representation of a (bishop's) mitre. (In British heraldry borne, instead of helmet and crest, over the arms of episcopal

sees; in the arms of a few sees it occurs also as a charge.)

1610 GUILLIM *Heraldry* IV. ii. 193 He beareth Sable, a Miter with two Labels Argent. **1727–41** CHAMBERS *Cycl.* s.v., In Germany, several great families bear the mitre for their crest; to shew that they are advocates, or feudataries of antient abbies, or officers of bishops, &c. **1784** COWPER *Tiroc.* 369 In fancy sees him..ride In coach with purple lined, and mitres on its side. **1823** CRABB *Technol. Dict.* s.v., Those [*sc.* the arms of the sees] of Norwich and Chester have three mitres. **1885** *Fairholt's Costume* II. Gloss. 286 The row of strawberry leaves around the modern archbishop's mitre is an invention of modern engravers. **1894** WOODWARD *Eccles. Her.* 101 The mitre of the Bishops of Durham is represented as rising out of a ducal coronet.

e. *slang.* A hat.

1896 FARMER & HENLEY *Slang, Mitre* (University), a hat.

f. A medieval type of woman's headwear resembling a bishop's mitre. Also *attrib.*

1877 *Encycl. Brit.* VI. 469/2 Some of the more popular of these strange varieties of head-gear have been distinguished as the 'horned', the 'mitre', [etc.]. **1906** H. DRUITT *Man. Costume* vi. 258 The next development shows the cauls curving outwards and upwards, and terminating above the head in a pair of horns. This form is called the *horned, lunar, mitre* or *heart* shaped head-dress according to the shape which it assumes. **1960** CUNNINGTON & BEARD *Dict. Eng. Costume* 136/2 Mitre head-dress.

3. Used as the name of various taverns and hotels, etc., as the *Mitre Tavern*, a famous place of resort in Shakespere's time. Also *attrib.*

1608 MIDDLETON *Mad World* v. H, This will be a True feast, a right Miter supper. **1611** BARRY *Ram-Alley* II. D 3, Meete me straite At the Myter doore in Fleet-street. **1633** ROWLEY *Match at Midn.* II. E 3, Come, weele..to the Miter in Bredstreete, weele make a mad night on't. **1661–6** WOOD *City of Oxford* (O.H.S.) III. 152 This High-German..fell sick at his arrival, in the Miter inne.

4. †**a.** The 'head' or 'cap' of an alembic. *Obs.*

1591 SYLVESTER *Du Bartas* I. iii. 139 Like as in a Limbeck, th' heat of Fire Raiseth a Vapour, which still mounting higher To the Still's top; when th' odoriferous sweat Above that Miter can no further get, It softly thickning, falleth drop by drop.

b. A cowl for a chimney (*Cent. Dict.* 1890).

5. *Hist.* A base coin current in Ireland during the last half of the 13th c. (see quot).

1749 J. SIMON *Irish Coins* 15 note, Other foreign coins called Mitres, Lionines,..Eagles, &c. from the stamp or figures impressed on them, were..uttered here for pennies, though not worth half a penny.

6. *Conch.* A mitre-shell.

1840 SWAINSON *Malacology* 98 The *Mitrinæ*, or mitres, where the spire is always acute [etc.]. **1861** CARPENTER in *Rep. Smithsonian Inst. for* 1860, 180 Family Fasciolariadæ (Tulip-shells and Mitres).

7. *attrib.* and *Comb.*: *mitre-bearer, -gold, -superstition*; *mitre-crowned, -missing, -shaped* adjs.; *mitre-wise* adv.; **mitre-flower**, 'a plant of the genus *Cyclamen*' (*Cent. Dict.* 1890); **mitre-mushroom**, an edible mushroom (*Helvella crispa*), so called from the shape of the pileus; **mitre-shell**, any one of numerous species of marine univalve shells of the genus *Mitra* (the shape in some species resembles that of a mitre); **mitre-snake**, 'a slender colubrine serpent (genus *Contia*), especially *C. episcopa*, of the Mexican borderland' (Funk's *Stand. Dict.* 1895).

1835 WILLIS *Pencillings* I. xviii. 127 The long train of proctors,..*mitre-bearers, and incense-bearers. **1885** W. J. FITZPATRICK *Life T. N. Burke* I. 17 Dr. Butler..*mitre-crowned, singing the High Mass at St. Finbar's. **1820** MILMAN *Fall Jerus.* (1821) 114 The breastplate gems, and the pure *mitre-gold, Shine lamplike. **1840** L. HUNT *Dram. Wks. Wycherley, Congreve*, etc. *Biog. Congreve* p. xxxiii, Bravo, Doctor Young! With leave of thy very gloomy, *mitre-missing, and most erroneous 'Night Thoughts' [etc.]. **1854** LINDLEY *Sch. Bot.* ix. 156 c, *Helvella crispa* (the *Mitre Mushroom). **1766** *Gentl. Mag.* Apr. 169/1 The *mitre shap'd aloe. **1753** CHAMBERS *Cycl. Supp.* App., **Mitre-shell*, the English name of the smooth and slender buccinum, with a split rostrum. *a* **1628** F. GREVIL *Sidney* ii. (1652) 30 To binde this *Miter-superstition with the reall cords of truth. **1662** GREENHALGH in Ellis *Orig. Lett.* Ser. III. IV. 280 A very light cap with its corners standing straight and upwards, *mitre wise. **1844** THACKERAY *May Gambols* Wks. 1900 XIII. 442 The dinner-table set out, the napkins folded mitrewise.

mitre ('maɪtə(r)), *sb.*[2] Also **miter.** [Of somewhat uncertain origin: perh., as is usually assumed, a transferred use of prec., but the development of sense is not easy to explain.

Possibly there may be a reference to the early form of the episcopal mitre, which had a vertical band bisecting a rectilinear angle at the top.]

1. In Joinery and other mechanical arts: A joint (also *mitre-joint*) in which the line or plane of junction makes an angle of 45° with the side of each of the two pieces joined, so that the adjacent sides meet in a right angle; the shaped end or edge of a piece of material intended to form such a joint with another; an angle or slope of 45°. Now sometimes applied to any joint in which the angle made by the sides of the joined pieces is bisected by the line of junction.

keyed mitre: a mitre-joint strengthened by the insertion of keys (KEY *sb.* 9). *lapped mitre*: a combination of the lap and mitre joints.

1678 MOXON *Mech. Exerc.* IV. 60 By Miters are meant the joining of two pieces of wood, so as the Joynt makes half a Square. **1710** J. HARRIS *Lex. Techn.* II, *Mitre*, in Architecture, is the Workmen's Term for an Angle that is just 45 degrees, or half a right one; and if it be a quarter of a Right Angle, they call it a *Half Mitre.* **1825** J. NICHOLSON *Operat. Mechanic* 589 A lapped mitre. **1850** *Parker's Gloss. Archit., Mitre*, the line formed by the meeting of mouldings or other surfaces, which intersect or intercept each other at an angle. **1876** *Encycl. Brit.* IV. 489/1 A keyed mitre. **1880** *Coach Builders' Art Jrnl.* I. 71, I drive all home, and cut the mitres and joints on the body single-handed, thus making a better job by single saw cut than can be obtained by solid mitre made at bench. **1882** J. LUKIN *Picture Frame Making* 2 These [mouldings] need only be sawn to a mitre or angle of 45 deg. **1901** *S. Black's Illustr. Carp. & Build., Home Handicrafts* 28 The amateur measures off four pieces for the sides of his quadrangle [*sc.* the frame], allowing for the mitre. **1902** A. MORRISON *Hole in Wall* 337 Now a lock of that sort joins in an angle or mitre at the middle, where the two sides meet like a valve, pointing to resist the tide.

2. Short for *mitre-square*.

1678 MOXON *Mech. Exerc.* v. 85 As the Square is made to strike an Angle of 90 Degrees, and the Miter an Angle of 45 degrees, so the Bevil [etc.]. **1842** GWILT *Archit.* Gloss. s.v. *Bevel*, The make and use of it [*sc.* the bevel] are much the same as those of the common square and mitre, except that those are fixed, the first at an angle of ninety degrees and the second at forty-five. **1877** *Amateur Handicraft* 77 The carpenter's Try-square, T-Square and Mitre. **1884** KNIGHT *Dict. Mech.* Suppl. **1890** in *Century Dict.*

3. Short for *mitre-wheel*.

1844 STEPHENS *Bk. Farm* II. 291 When it happens that.. the wheels *y*', fig. 322, are..mitres. **1875** KNIGHT *Dict. Mech.* fig. 3182 d, Miters.

4. = GUSSET 2. (Cf. MITRE *v.*[2] 3.)

1882 CAULFEILD & SAWARD *Dict. Needlework* 305 In dividing the stitches to form the Gusset or Mitre, place double the number [etc.]. **1892** *Daily News* 10 Mar. 2/4 There are no buttons at the back [of the overcoat], but a finish is lent by mitres being worked in.

5. *Comb.*, **mitre-arch**, the curve formed by the mitre or junction of two curved surfaces, as in groining, etc.; **mitre-bevel** = *mitre-square*; **mitre-block, board**, (*a*) a joiner's mitre box; (*b*) = *mitre shooting-board*; **mitre box**, a joiner's templet with kerfs or guides for the saw in cutting material for mitre-joints; also, a similar tool for mitring printers' rules; **mitre-bracket**, each of the angle-brackets in the bracketing of a moulded cornice; **mitre-cap**, a cap of a newel terminating a handrail to which it is mitred; **mitre-clamp**, a clamp with mitred ends; hence *mitre-clamped*; **mitre-cramp**, a cramp to secure a glued mitre-joint while it is drying; **mitre-cut**, 'a groove cut in the surface of plate-glass for ornamentation' (*Cent. Dict.* 1890) having a bottom angle of nearly 90°; **mitre-dovetail, dovetailing**, a combination of the mitre and dovetail joints; also *attrib.*; (**cross**) **mitre drain** (see quot. 1838); **mitre-gauge** (see quot. 1875); **mitre-iron, -jack** (see quots.); **mitre-joint** (see sense 1); so **mitre-jointed** *a.*, furnished with a mitre-joint; **mitre-line**, any line which bisects a mitre-joint; **mitre-machine** = *mitring-machine*; **mitre-plane**[1] [PLANE *sb.*[2]], a plane having the iron set obliquely across the face of the stock; **mitre-plane**[2] [PLANE *sb.*[3]], the plane in which the mitre-joint lies; **mitre post**, each of the chamfered outer posts of a pair of lock-gates which, when closed, present an angular face to the stream; **mitre rule**, a plasterers' tool (see quot.); **mitre-seating** *a.*, (of a valve) that has an annular seating turned to an angle of 45°; **mitre shooting-board**, a shooting-board used in chamfering the edges of wood; **mitre sill**, the sill of a lock-gate which presents an angular face to the stream when closed; **mitre square**, a 'square' with the blade set immovably at an angle of 45° for striking lines on something to be mitred, also sometimes applied to the bevel; **mitre-valve**, a puppet valve having its face and seat inclined 45° to its axis; **mitre-wheel**, each of a pair of bevelled cog-wheels, the axes of which are at right angles, and which have their teeth set at an angle of 45°.

1725 W. HALFPENNY *Sound Building* 16 To find the Angle, or *Mitre Arch of a..Groin. **185.** *Dict. Archit.* (Arch. Publ. Soc.) s.v. *Bevel*, [An instrument] which answers for a square, a common bevel, and a *mitre-bevel of forty-five degrees. **1846** HOLTZAPFFEL *Turning* II. 503 *Mitre block. **1871** AVELING *Carpentry & Join.* 61 A saddle or block, known as a Mitre-block or box. **1884** KNIGHT *Dict. Mech.* Suppl., **Mitre Board.* **1888** *Lockwood's Dict. Mech. Engin., Mitre Board.* **1678** MOXON *Mech. Exerc.* v. 88 Another way..of Drawing, or striking out of Squares, Miters, and several Bevils..is with a Tool called a *Miter Box. **1875–84** KNIGHT *Dict. Mech.*, Miter-box. **1725** W. HALFPENNY *Sound Building* 14 To find the..*Mitre-Bracket of a Cove. **1820** P. NICHOLSON *Staircases & Handrails* 7 *Mitre-cap..is a block of wood, turned to some agreeable figure..used in dog-legged stairs to terminate the handrail. **185.** *Dict. Archit.* (Arch. Publ. Soc.) s.v. *Clamp*, *Mitre clamp. **1825** J. NICHOLSON *Operat. Mechanic* 602 Boards keyed and clamped, mortise-clamped, and *mitre-clamped. **1847** SMEATON *Builder's Man.* 90 The last method to be mentioned..may be termed *mitre-dovetail grooving. **1873** TARN *Tredgold's Carpentry* 240 *Mitre-dovetailing. **1838** *Civil Eng. & Arch. Jrnl.* I. 97/2 Other drains are made under the roadway which, from their form, are termed *cross *mitre drains.* Their plan is in shape like the letter V... The construction of mitre-drains is [etc.]. **1875** KNIGHT *Dict. Mech.*, **Miter-gage*, a gage to determine the angle of a miter-joint in picture-frames, moldings, etc. **1894** HASLUCK *Woodworker's Handy-bk.* xiii. 121 The use of an adjustable mitre gauge. **1843** HOLTZAPFFEL *Turning* I. 197 [A faggot of iron] made of a round bar in the center, and a group of bars of angular section, called *mitre iron, around the same. **1884** KNIGHT *Dict. Mech.* Suppl., **Miter Jack*, a templet used in making and fitting all kinds of small miters on moldings. **1688** R. HOLME *Armoury* III. 367/2 [A plane] for the fitting and framing of *Miter and Bevil Joynts. **1791** SMEATON *Edystone L.* p. 196 The mitre joint of two contiguous bars. *Ibid.* §276, I chose them to be *mitre-jointed at the angles. **1678** MOXON *Mech. Exerc.* v. 85 A *Miter line. **1890** W. J. GORDON *Foundry* 155 The cutting of the louvres, which a boy does on a *mitre machine. **1688** R. HOLME *Armoury* III. 367/2 The *Miter Plain. **1894** C. P. B. SHELLEY *Workshop Appl.* 44 Mitre-planes..are intended for planing across the grain. **1823** P. NICHOLSON *Pract. Build.* 173 The upper mouldings are mitred together, so that the *mitre-plane may be perpendicular to the horizon. **1838** *F. W. Simms' Publ. Wks. Gt. Brit.* ii. 6 The gates are made water tight at the *mitre posts, by being rubbed dry the one upon the other. **1845** *Encycl. Metrop.* XXV. 177/1 The *mitre or joint rule is eighteen inches long by three inches wide, and about an inch thick, bevelled off to a thin edge about an inch wide. **1888** HASLUCK *Model Engin. Handybk.* 111 The *mitre-seating cone-valves..are often considered easier to make than the ball valves. **1903** *Cassell's Cycl. Mechanics* VI. 167/2 A *mitre shooting board. **1841** BREES *Gloss. Civ. Engin.* s.v. *Lock*, The bottom framings, against which the gates are shut, are called *mitre sills. **1678** MOXON *Mech. Exerc.* v. 84 The *Miter square..is used for striking a Miter line, as the Square is to strike a square line. **1850** *Archæol. Jrnl.* VII. 403 What is technically called a mitre square. **1875** KNIGHT *Dict. Mech.*, **Miter-valve.* **1833** LOUDON *Encycl. Archit.* Gloss., **Mitre wheel.* **1844** STEPHENS *Bk. Farm.* II. 295 Each of the screws is mounted with a small mitre-wheel.

mitre ('maɪtə(r)), *v.*[1] [f. MITRE *sb.*[1]; cf. early mod.F. *mitrer, mittrer*, Sp., Pg. *mitrar*, It. *mitrare, mitriare* (Baretti), OIt. *metrare*, med.L. *mitrāre.*] *trans.* To confer or bestow a mitre upon, to raise to a rank to which the dignity of wearing a mitre belongs. Chiefly in pa. pple. *mitred*, invested *with* something by way of mitre.

c **1380** WYCLIF *Sel. Wks.* III. 25 Bischopis mytrid wiþ two hornys figuren þat þei schulden þoru good ensaumple putte þe folk fro vicis to virtues. *c* **1440** *Promp. Parv.* 341/1 Mytryn, *mitro.* **1801** COLERIDGE in C. K. Paul *W. Godwin* (1874) II. 74 It was once clothed and mitred with flame. **1804** J. GRAHAME *Sabbath* 332 Mitred with a wreath Of nightshade. **1891** C. E. NORTON *Dante's Purgat.* xxvii. 176 Wherefore thee over thyself I crown and mitre.

mitre ('maɪtə(r)), *v.*[2] Also **miter.** [f. MITRE *sb.*[2]]

1. *trans.* To join with a mitre-joint; to make a mitre-joint in; to cut or shape (the end of a piece of material) to a mitre. Also with *away, up.* ***to mitre the square***: to bisect the angle of a joint.

1731 [implied in MITRING *vbl. sb.*]. **1753** HOGARTH *Anal. Beauty* xii. 172 The profile out-line of some corner of it [*sc.* the moulding] where it is 'mitered', as the joiners term it. **1833** LOUDON *Encycl. Archit.* §1122 The slates to be all close-mitred, when two planes meet against a diagonal line, they are said to be mitred. **1842** GWILT *Archit.* §2285 (1859) 607 Steps and risers mitred to cut string, and dove-tailed to balusters. *c* **1850** *Rudim. Navig.* (Weale) 116 They are.. mitred into the gunwale. **1875** *Carpentry & Join.* 65 Such work as mitring up a box. **1881** YOUNG *Ev. Man his own Mech.* §452 The edges are bevelled or mitred away.

b. *intr.* To form a mitre, meet in a mitre-joint.

1820 P. NICHOLSON *Staircases & Handrails* 28 The part that mitres upon the riser below. **1875** *Encycl. Brit.* II. 467/2 A moulding returned upon itself at right angles is said to mitre. In joinery the ends of any two pieces of wood of corresponding form cut off at 45° necessarily abut upon one another so as to form a right angle, and are said to mitre.

2. a. *Bookbinding.* **b.** *Printing.* See quots.

1875 [cf. MITRED *ppl. a.*[2]]. **1880** ZAEHNSDORF *Bookbinding* xxii. 119 As a general rule morocco is always mitred. *Ibid.* 121 Carefully mitreing the corners where any lines are used. **1888** JACOBI *Printers' Vocab. Mitre*, to chamfer..the ends of rules in order that they may join closely in forming a border.

3. *Needlework.* To make an angle in (a straight strip or band, etc.) by cutting out a three-cornered piece and uniting the resulting edges.

1880 *Plain Hints Needlework* 27 To make corners of a hem ..they should be 'mitred'.

mitre, obs. form of METRE *v.*

mitred ('maɪtəd), *ppl. a.*[1] [f. MITRE *sb.*[1] and *v.*[1] + -ED. Cf. med.L. *mitrātus.*]

1. Entitled or privileged to wear a mitre. ***mitred abbot*** (= med.L. *abbas mitratus*): an abbot invested by the pope with the privilege of wearing a mitre; hence ***mitred abbey*** (med.L. *beneficium mitratum*), an abbey ruled by a mitred abbot.

In England before the Reformation the mitred abbots were members of the House of Lords.

c **1380** [see MITRE *v.*[1]]. **1393** LANGL. *P. Pl.* C. v. 193 More þan al þy marchauns oþer þy mytrede bisshopes, Oþer lumbardes of lukes þat lyuen by lone as Iewes. **1550** BALE *Eng. Votaries* II. Eiij, Whiche of them shuld be highest in that mitred kingdome of idlenesse. **1560** DAUS. tr. *Sleidane's Comm.* 368 The bishops..and..a few other mitred men. **1658** BRAMHALL *Consecr. Bps.* vi. 139 One Bishop and two Mitred Abbats. *a* **1661** FULLER *Worthies, Yorks.* (1662) II. 190 Selby, where after he [Henry] founded a Mitred-Abby. **1759** DILWORTH *Pope* 67 The bishop.. related that conference to a friend of his, a dignified but not a mitred clergyman. **1830** *Westm. Rev.* XII. 473 The methodist

parson and the mitred bishop. **1878** STUBBS *Const. Hist.* III. xx. 445 The mitred and parliamentary abbeys were not identical.

2. Wearing or adorned with a mitre.

c **1420** LYDG. *Story of Thebes* 4186 As a bisshop, mytred, in his stalle. **1480** CAXTON *Chron. Eng.* ccxliv. 300 Bisshops reuessed and mytered with senscers to welcome the kyng. **1562** in *Rep. on Foedera* E. II. 48 The impure assemblie of those shaven fathers, those myteryd and redd-hattyd fellowes [at Trent]. **1637** MILTON *Lycidas* 112 He shook his Miter'd locks, and stern bespake. **1687** DRYDEN *Hind & P.* I. 202 Your fangs you fastened on the mitred crown. **1790** BURKE *Fr. Rev.* 153 We will have her [*sc.* religion] to exalt her mitred front in courts and parliaments. **1805** SOUTHEY *Madoc in W.* xv, The mitred Baldwin, in his hand Holding a taper, at the altar stood. **1850** TYMMS *Bury Wills* (Camden) 229 A leaden token..bears on the obverse a mitred head. **1863** J. R. WALBRAN *Mem. Fountains Abbey* (Surtees) 147 The abbot robed and mitred..standing under a trifoliated canopy.

b. Bearing a representation of a mitre. *rare.*

1768–74 TUCKER *Lt. Nat.* (1834) II. 464, I see the mitred coach come rolling along. **1772–9** W. MASON *Eng. Garden* IV. 106 The fane conventual there is dimly seen, The mitred window, and the cloister pale.

3. Formed like a mitre; having a mitre-shaped apex; *Nat. Hist.* in specific names (= mod.L. *mitrātus*).

a **1547** SURREY *Æneid* IV. 277 With mitred hats, with oynted bush and beard. **1860** *Chamb. Encycl.* s.v. *Basilisk*, The Mitred or Hooded Basilisk (*Basiliscus mitratus*), a native of the tropical parts of America. **1887** HAY *Brit. Fungi* 140 *Helvelia lacunosa*, the Mitred Helvel. **1897** H. O. FORBES *Hand-bk. Primates* II. 137 The mitred langur, *Semnopithecus mitratus*.

mitred ('maɪtəd), *ppl. a.*[2] [f. MITRE *v.*[2] + -ED.] In the senses of the verb.

1775 ASH, *Mitred*, cut off at an angle of forty-five degrees. **1832** *Skyring's Builders' Prices* 18 Mitred and glued borders. **1842** GWILT *Archit.* §2285 (1859) 607 If grooved for balusters, circular..mitred and turned caps, such to be mentioned. **1847** SMEATON *Builder's Man.* 90 Fig. 26 represents a still neater dovetail; and, as the edges are mitred together, is termed a mitred dovetail. **1860** BURN *Gloss. Techn. Terms Building* 7 *Mitred Borders*, narrow widths of boarding placed round the front hearths to fireplaces. **1871** *Ringwalt's Amer. Encycl. Printing*, Mitred Rules. **1875** KNIGHT *Dict. Mech.*, *Mitered.* (*Bookbinding*). Said of a fillet ornamentation when the lines unite exactly at their junction without overrunning. **1880** ZAEHNSDORF *Bookbinding* xxii. 119 This [finishing with a full gilt back] is done in two ways, a 'run up' back and a 'mitred' back. **1902** *Westm. Gaz.* 16 May 3/2 Perpendicular mitred lines of insertion on the skirt.

mitre-wort ('maɪtəwɜːt). [f. MITRE *sb.*[1] + WORT.] A book-name for the genus MITELLA. *false mitre-wort*: a plant of the genus *Tiarella*.

1845–50 MRS. LINCOLN *Lect. Bot.* App. 176/2 *Tiarella cordifolia*, (mitre-wort). **1856** GRAY *Man. Bot.* (1860) 145 *Mitella*, Mitre-wort. *Tiarella*, False Mitre-wort.

mitridat(e, obs. forms of MITHRIDATE.

mitriform ('maɪtrɪfɔːm), *a.* [ad. mod.L. *mitriformis*, f. *mitra* MITRE *sb.*[1]: see -FORM]

a. *Bot.* Resembling or shaped like a mitre; conical, hollow, and open at the base, the base being sometimes irregularly indented; applied to the calyptra of mosses and to certain fruits. **b.** *Conch.* Shaped like a mitre-shell.

1830 LINDLEY *Nat. Syst. Bot.* 322 The mitriform calyptra. **1843** *Penny Cycl.* XXVI. 446/2 [Of shells] Mitriform; spire produced, conic. **1881** R. B. WATSON in *Jrnl. Linn. Soc.* XV. 404 Shell,—high, mitriform, biconical.

mitring ('maɪt(ə)rɪŋ). *vbl. sb.* [f. MITRE *v.*[2] + -ING[1].] The action of MITRE *v.*[2] in its various senses; also *concr.* the shaped end of a piece prepared to be mitred with another.

1731 W. HALFPENNY *Perspective* 31 The Mitering of the under side of every Square..must be drawn from the Point of Sight. **1778** *Encycl. Brit.* (ed. 2) I. 618 The thickness of the bracket, with its mitring to the riser. **1852** SEIDEL *Organ* 158 Sometimes pipes require even a repeated mitering. This mitering greatly influences the..tone of a pipe.

b. *attrib.*, as ***mitring tool***; also ***mitring block, board, box, saw***, etc. = mitre block, board, etc.; **mitring-machine** (see quots.).

1845 *Encycl. Metrop.* XXV. 177/1 Tools used by the plasterer... There are also various mitring tools of iron or steel. **1871** *Ringwalt's Amer. Encycl. Printing*, *Mitring Box*, a box used to facilitate the operation of cutting material that is to be mitred. *Ibid.*, *Mitring Machines*, various machines made for the purpose of mitring rules neatly and accurately. **1875** KNIGHT *Dict. Mech.*, *Mitering-machine* (*Joinery*), a machine for mitering or slanting the ends of pieces which are to be united by a miter-joint. **1875** *Carpentry & Join.* 39 *The Mitreing Box*..is used to cut pieces of moulding at the right angle for picture and other frames.

†**'mitrous**, *a. nonce-wd.* [f. MITRE *sb.* + -OUS.] Relating to a mitre or bishopric.

1791 HUDDESFORD *Salmag.*, *Monody Death of Dick* 137 When soft reclines in velvet pomp supreme Divinity, entranc'd in mitrous dream.

mitry ('maɪtrɪ), *a. Her.* [f. MITRE *sb.* + -Y[1].] Charged with a number of mitres.

1847 *Gloss. Her.*, *Mitry.* The word occurs in blazoning a bordure charged with eight mitres. **1889** ELVIN *Dict. Her.*

‖**Mitsein** ('mɪtzaɪn). *Philos.* [ad. G. *mit* with + *sein* being.] A term used by Heidegger to express the concept of man's being in its relationship with others.

1955 J. MACQUARRIE *Existentialist Theol.* iv. 89 Thus 'being-in-the-world' implies 'being-with-others' (*Mitsein*). **1957** H. BARNES tr. *Sartre's Being & Nothingness* III. iii. 413 The very existence of this grammatical form [*sc.* the word *we*] necessarily refers us to a real experience of the *Mitsein*. **1963** *Philos.* XXXVIII. 275 The whole world of human *Mitsein* is regarded by M. Bastide as his province. **1966** A. MANSER *Sartre* vi. 97 The essence of relations between consciousnesses is not Mitsein (being together), it is conflict.

mitsumata (ˌmɪtsʊ'mɑːtə). [Japanese.] A deciduous shrub, *Edgeworthia papyrifera*, bearing clusters of fragrant yellow flowers, belonging to the family Thymelæaceæ, and native to China, although widely cultivated in Japan, where its bast fibre is used in the manufacture of paper. Also *attrib.*

1889 J. REIN *Industries of Japan* III. 402 Mitzu-mata (*Edgeworthia*) paper has also a distinctly marked yellow colour. **1891** B. H. CHAMBERLAIN *Things Japanese* (ed. 2) 334 Several plants and trees contribute their bark to the manufacture of Japanese paper... The one most easily recognised by the unlearned is the *Edgeworthia papyrifera*, which has the peculiarity that its branches always divide into three at every articulation, whence the Japanese name of *mitsu-mata*, or 'the three forks'. **1936** D. HUNTER *Papermaking Pilgrimage Japan, Korea & China* iii. 45 The so-called 'vellum'—that smooth, long-fibred, natural-toned paper sometimes used in the printing of fine books and etchings..is made largely from the bark of the mitsumata shrub. **1947** —— *Papermaking* (ed. 2) ii. 57 The origin of mitsumata (*Edgeworthia papyrifera*) as a papermaking material is uncertain, but there is a record stating that in the year 1597 a papermaking family was granted the privilege of gathering mitsumata bark in a certain locality of Japan. **1974** G. USHER *Dict. Plants used by Man* 223/2 *E*[*dgeworthia*] *papyrifera*... Cultivated for the bark fibres which are used, particularly in Japan to make a hand-made paper (Nepal Paper, Mitsumata Paper).

mitt (mɪt). Chiefly in *pl.* Also **mit.** [Shortened from MITTEN *sb.*]

1. = MITTEN *sb.* 2.

1765 *Univ. Mag.* XXXVII. 324/2 Silk mitts, and silk gloves. **1795** WOLCOT (P. Pindar) *Lousiad* v. Wks. 1812 I. 304 Transform an old silk stocking into mits. **1811** *Ora & Juliet* I. 42 Dudley laughed, and took hold of her cherry fingers, that peeped out of her mits. **1828** SCOTT *Aunt Marg. Mirr.* Introd., The black silk gloves, or mitts. **1851** *Catal. Gt. Exhib.* II. 575 Lace mitts. *a* **1876** HT. MARTINEAU *Autobiog.* I. 57 The long mits she wore.

transf. **1886** *Pop. Sci. Monthly* Nov. 208 The hands and forearms of the women are tattooed with mitts, as in the Marshall Islands. **1903** *Daily Record & Mail* 30 Dec. 7 A novel device..for persons who do not know how to swim. It consists of a mitt or gauntlet... When fitted to the hand it forms webs between the fingers and the thumb. *Ibid.*, An elastic band which fastens the mitt to the wrist.

2. a. = MITTEN *sb.* 1. †Also *slang*, a glove.

1812 J. H. VAUX *Flash Dict.*, *Mitts*, gloves. **1812** J. SMYTH *Pract. of Customs* (1821) 214 Waste Silk..may..be spun to make stockings, mits, &c. but they will be coarse and ordinary. **1856** KANE *Arct. Explor.* II. i. 24 Mitts of seal-skin well wadded with sledge-straw. **1867** SMYTH *Sailor's Word-bk.*, *Mitts*, a protection for the hands, covering the thumb in one space and the fingers in another, so that men wearing them can still handle ropes.

b. *U.S.* A protective glove worn in baseball by the catcher or first baseman.

1902 *Sears Catal.* 326 Boys' Canvas Mitt, made of canvas throughout; a good, cheap mitt for boys; well stuffed. **1949** *Nat. Geogr. Mag.* June 738/1 On the ball field the Indians waved their mitts.

3. *slang.* (orig *U.S.*). **a.** A hand. **b.** ***a big mitt***: a mode of swindling at cards (see quot. 1905); hence a municipal scheme undertaken with a view to the private advantage of its promoters.

1896 ADE *Artie* xiii. 116, I thought them was gloves you had on. Gee, is them your mits? **1901** H. MCHUGH *John Henry* 10 I'm sitting on the sofa with one mitt lying carelessly on the family album and the other bunched around a $1.70 cane. **1903** *Daily Chron.* 27 May 7/2 A 'big mit,'..is a big boodle game, a graft. **1905** *Blackw. Mag.* Jan. 137/1 At the 'big mitt' game alone, an ingenious method of swindling by means of a stacked hand at stud poker, a vast profit was made. **1914** JOYCE *Dubliners* 74 He was also handy with the mits. **1940** R. CHANDLER *Farewell, my Lovely* ii. 12 'Freeze the mitts on the bar.' The barman and I put our hands on the bar. **1959** I. & P. OPIE *Lore & Lang. Schoolch.* x. 197 The commonest challenge is 'Put up your mitts'.

c. ***the glad mitt***: a warm or friendly reception; = *glad hand* (GLAD *a.* 4 e); ***the frozen*** (or ***icy***) ***mitt***: an unfriendly reception; rejection; the 'cold shoulder'. *slang.*

1904 'No. 1500' *Life in Sing Sing* 255/2 *Glad mitt*, warm welcome. **1907** J. LONDON *Road* 187 The erstwhile hospitable farmers met us with the icy mit. **1925** FRASER & GIBBONS *Soldier & Sailor Words* 156 He tried to make up to me but I gave him the frozen mit. **1937** M. SHARP *Nutmeg Tree* ix. III, I expected any number of black eyes, Julia darling, but not the frozen mitt. **1960** A. PRIOR in *Pick of Today's Short Stories* XI. 179 She'd have taken it and then handed me the frozen mitt.

d. *attrib.* and *Comb.*, as **mitt camp** *U.S. slang*, a palmist's or fortune-teller's establishment, tent, etc.; **mitt joint** *U.S. slang*, (*a*) (see quot. 1914); (*b*) = *mitt camp*; **mitt-reader** *U.S. slang*, a palmist; a fortune-teller.

1942 BERREY & VAN DEN BARK *Amer. Thes. Slang* §466/5 *Mitt camp* or *joint*, a fortune-telling establishment. *Ibid.* §626/7 *Mitt camp* or *joint*, a fortune teller's tent or booth. **1956** H. GOLD *Man who was not with It* (1965) i. 4 She would ..take the tickets to Palmistry Pauline's mitt-camp. **1914** JACKSON & HELLYER *Vocab. Criminal Slang* 59 A 'mitt joint' is a gambling house where victims are 'steered' for fleecing by means of deceptively 'sure thing' hands. **1923** C. R. COOPER *Under Big Top* 60, I have seen a couple halt before a 'mitt joint' where a greasy Mexican or Syrian or anything else but a gypsy stands. **1942** Mitt joint [see *mitt camp* above]. **1928** *Amer. Speech* III. 414 *Mitt reader*, a palmist, or fortune teller. **1956** H. GOLD *Man who was not with It* (1965) xiv. 120 How do you know? You a mitt reader like your mother.

‖**Mittagessen** ('mɪtɑːgˌɛsən). Also **Mittagsessen**, and with lower-case initial. [Ger.] In Germany: a midday meal; lunch.

1880 GEO. ELIOT *Let.* 11 July (1956) VII. 303 There is a magnificent drive to Baden which can be reached in seven hours (including time for the Mittagsessen and the rest). **1899** R. FRY *Let.* Oct. (1972) I. 174 The Galleries shut at the absurd hour of 3..in order that the officials may have some absurd meal, a *mittagessen* or something. **1941** M. TREADGOLD *We couldn't leave Dinah* xv. 238 The heavy *mittagessen* upon which Germany nourishes young and old. **1972** *Sat. Rev.* (U.S.) 25 Mar. 72/1 The *Mittagessen* (lunch) always begins with soup.

mittain(e, mittan, obs. forms of MITTEN *sb.*

†**mittane.** *Sc. Obs. rare.* Also **myttane, myttaine.** [Of obscure origin: cf. MITTELL.] A bird of prey, a kind of hawk.

1500–20 DUNBAR *Poems* xxii. 12 Forsett is ay the falconis kynd, Bot euir the mittane [*v.r.* myttell] is hard in mynd. *Ibid.* xxxiii. 73 The myttane and Sanct Martynis fowle.

mitted ('mɪtɪd), *ppl. a.* [f. MITT + -ED[2].] Wearing mitts or mittens.

1893 *Atlantic Monthly* Feb. 155/1 Reaching in deftly with mitted arms.

Mittel-Europa ('mɪt(ə)ljʊə'rəʊpə). Also **Mittel Europa, Mitteleuropa.** [Ger.] Central Europe. Also *attrib.*

1918 M. J. DAVOREN tr. *Gettlich's German Grip on Russia* 24 It is in this combination of a community of the interests of Budapest with those of the financial circles of Berlin that the idea of the new politico-commercial *consortium*, known to-day by the name 'Mitteleuropa', arose. **1918** Z. N. PREEV *Russian Riddle* iii. 36 It would be worth her while to abandon ..her grandiose plans of Mittel-Europa. **1931** *Times Lit. Suppl.* 9 Apr. 281/3 The glorification of the *Mittel-Europa* ideal which Frederick the Great failed to realize. **1950** A. CHRISTIE *Murder is Announced* v. 48 Very temperamental you'll find her. Mittel Europa refugee of some kind. **1956** AUDEN & KALLMAN *Magic Flute* (1957) 116 We'll never lack friends back in Mittel-Europa. **1971** C. FICK *Danziger Transcript* (1973) 29 He had a slight Mittel-Europa accent, but at Claridge's, who doesn't? **1975** J. SYMONS *Three Pipe Problem* xviii. 176 Would the totally unknown actress be able to resist the charm of Mitteleuropa?

Mittel-European ('mɪt(ə)ljʊərə'piːən), *a.* and *sb.* [ad. G. *mittel-europäisch*, f. *mittel* middle.]

A. *adj.* = *Middle European* adj.

[**1937** WYNDHAM LEWIS *Blasting & Bombardiering* xii. 189 With his dramatic miteuropean accent he gave this suggestion such a rich Austrian welcome as no suggestion ever had before or since.] **1939** C. BEATON *My Royal Past* xiii. 143 The destined lot of *mittel*-European royalty. **1957** P. KEMP *Mine were of Trouble* x. 187 The sinister but intriguing personality of a Mittel-European barman known as Otto. **1959** J. DRUMMOND *Black Unicorn* xv. 110 The fringe of the fashionable area, where the big shops give way to little mittel-European establishments. **1974** *Times* 31 Dec. 7/3 The pretence of Mittel-European dilettantism.

B. *sb.* A native or inhabitant of central Europe.

1950 A. CHRISTIE *Murder is Announced* xi. 118, I expect Mitzi, our Mittel European, would love that. **1958** *Times* 24 July 5/3 A mittel-European exploding with conversation like a fire-cracker.

†**mittell.** *Sc. Obs. rare.* Forms: 5 **myttal, mytall,** 6 **myttell.** [Of obscure origin: cf. MITTANE.] 'A bird of prey of the hawk kind' (Jam.).

1457 *Sc. Acts Jas. II*, c. 32 (1814) II. 51 Vper foulys of reif as ernys bussardes gleddes and myttalles [*v.r.* (1566) mittalis]. **1500–20** [see MITTANE].

‖**Mittelschmerz** ('mɪt(ə)lʃmɛrts). *Gynæcology.* Also **mittelschmerz.** [G., lit. 'middle pain'.] Pain in the lower abdomen regularly experienced by some women between menstrual periods, perhaps related to the occurrence of ovulation.

1895 *Lancet* 28 Dec. 1625/1 Dr. J. Halliday Croom read a paper on So-called Mittelschmerz, sometimes called a form of dysmenorrhœa. **1942** MAZER & ISRAEL *Diagn. & Treatm. Menstrual Disorders* ix. 135 The pain undoubtedly emanates from the ovaries, since neither hysterectomy nor resection of the presacral nerve..eliminates *mittelschmerz*, but bilateral oophorectomy does. **1971** *Vogue* Nov. 60/2 Have intercourse as near ovulation as possible. This can be detected..by the pain that some women experience (Mittelschmerz). **1971** I. A. MCDONALD *Method Obstetr. & Gynaecol.* xiii. 300 Some females regularly have a spotting of blood on day 14 of the menstrual cycle... It may be associated with lower abdominal pain (*Mittelschmerz*).

mitten ('mɪtən), *sb.* Forms: 4–5 **meteyn(e, metayn, myteyn(e, mytan, -en,** 5 **meting,** 5–6 **myttan, -en,** 5, 7–8 **mittain,** 6 **mytayne, myttayn, mytton,** 6–8 **mitton,** 6, 8–9 **mittan,** 7 **mittaine,** 7– **mittin, -ing,** 6– **mitten.** [a. F. *mitaine* (from 12th c.), of obscure origin; cf. F. *miton* gauntlet (16th c.), mitten (1738 in Littré), also Fr. dial. *mite*

mitten, and med.L. (13th c.) *mitana, mitanna* mitten, *mita* ? mitten.]

1. a. A covering for the hand, differing from a glove in having no divisions for the fingers, but provided with a separate receptacle for the thumb; worn either for warmth, or (e.g. by hedgers and other workmen) to protect the hand from injury or pain in handling something. Also (now *dial.*: see *Eng. Dial. Dict.*) applied to a thick winter glove.

c **1386** CHAUCER *Pard. Prol.* 45 He þat his hand wol putte in this Mitayn He shal haue multipliyng of his grayn. *c* **1394** *P. Pl. Crede* 428 Twey myteynes, as mete, maad all of cloutes; þe fyngers weren for-werd, and ful of fen honged. *c* **1420** *Pallad. on Husb.* I. 1167 And botis, cokirs, myttens [L. *manicas de pellibus*] mot we were. **1488** in Tytler *Hist. Scot.* (1864) II. 393 A pare of metingis for hunting. **1515** BARCLAY *Egloges* iv. (1570) C iij/1 His furred mittens were of a curres skin. **1563** *Homilies* II. *Excess of Apparel* 114b, He that ruffleth in his..corked slippers, trimme buskins, and warme mittons, is more redy to chyll for colde, then the poore labouryng man. *a* **1623** FLETCHER *Love's Cure* ii. i, Let not thy mittens abate the talons of thy authority, but gripe theft and whoredom wheresoever thou meet'st 'em. **1634** PEACHAM *Gentl. Exerc.* II. vii. 126 December must be expressed with a horrid and fearefull aspect,..at his backe a bundle of Holly,..holding in furd Mittens the signe of Capricornus. **1662** *Plymouth Col. Rec.* (1855) IV. 12 There was found his capp, with his staffe and one mitting. **1667** PEPYS *Diary* 21 Jan., The Swede's Resident..came to us out of bed in his furred mittens and furred cap. **1729** T. CONSETT *Pres. St. Ch. Russ.* 157 *note*, The vulgar people.. with their..gloves on, which are almost as large and strong as a hedger's mittins. **1742** MIDDLETON in *Phil. Trans.* XLII. 161 A large Pair of Beaver Mittings..which reach up as high as our Elbows. **1818** SCOTT *Hrt. Midl.* xxi, Hastily and confusedly searching for his worsted mittans and staff. **1840** R. H. DANA *Bef. Mast* iii, [The crew] can get their wet mittens and stockings dried. **1884** Baby's mitten [see COMBINATION 10].

fig. phrase. **1662** J. OWEN *Animadv. Fiat Lux* 311 Such stupid blockheads, as to be imposed on with Sophistry, that they may feel through a pair of Mittens.

b. Phrases. ***to cast one's mitten***: to offer a challenge (cf. GAUNTLET[1] 1 c). ***to claw up*** or ***lay up*** (a person's) ***mittens*** (Sc.): to give the finishing stroke to, to kill (cf. CLAW *v.* 8). ***to handle without mittens***: to treat unmercifully.

1589 NASHE *Martins Months Minde* G 4, I cast him here my Mitten vpon the quarrell. **1678** RAY *Prov.* (ed. 2) 76 To handle without mittins. **1699** R. L'ESTRANGE *Erasm. Colloq.* (1711) 178 He handled the Reverend Fathers without Mittens. **1742** FORBES *Jrnl. fr. Lond.* in *Ajax*, etc. (1755) 30 They may come to lay up my mittens, an' ding me yavil, an' as styth as gin I had been elf-shot.

c. *Her.*

1688 R. HOLME *Armoury* III. xviii. (Roxb.) 110/1 He beareth Gules, a left hand Male Mitton..proper.

d. *slang. pl.* (*a*) The hands. (*b*) Boxing-gloves. (*c*) Handcuffs.

1812 J. H. VAUX *Flash Dict.*, *Mittens*, the hands. **1859** *Hotten's Slang Dict.*, *Mittens*, fists. **1880** G. WEBSTER in *Sc. Nat. Dict.* (1965) VI. 306/1 My lad was made fast an' a pair o' mittens clappit on wi' little mair adee. **1883** J. GREENWOOD *Odd People* 56 That's their mittens they've got tied up in that hankercher. They're fighting coves. **1937** 'D. HUME' *Halfway to Horror* 3 'Mittens' are handcuffs; a padlock is a 'monkey'.

2. a. A sort of glove of lace or knitted work covering the forearm, wrist, and part of the hand, but not extending over the fingers; much worn by women at the beginning of the nineteenth century, and revived towards the end of it. Now more commonly MITT.

1755 JOHNSON, *Mittens*, gloves that cover the arm without covering the fingers. **1762** *Ann. Reg.* 162 Their chief business was making silk nets, purses, and mittins. **1795** WOLCOT (P. Pindar) *Pindariana* Wks. 1812 IV. 187 On week-days were black worsted mittens worn; Black silk on Sundays did her arms adorn. **1824** MISS MITFORD *Village* Ser. I. 223 The sleeves came down just below the elbow, and were finished by a narrow white ruffle meeting her neat mittens. **1838** DICKENS *Nich. Nick.* iii, 'Hem!' said Miss La Creevy, coughing delicately behind her black silk mitten.

b. *transf.* See quot.

[**1899** Cf. *mitten-wise*, 3 below.] **1900** *Daily Mail* 5 Feb. 7/1 The sleeve in its full dress adaptation is called the mitten because it falls from the shoulder, though it is attached to the bodice underneath the arm, and covers the hand right down to the knuckles.

3. Phrase (*slang* or *colloq.*). ***to get the mitten***: of a lover, to be dismissed or rejected; hence, in wider application, to be dismissed from any office or position. Similarly, ***to give*** (a person) ***the mitten***.

1838 J. C. NEAL *Charcoal Sk.* (Bartlett), Young gentlemen that have got the mitten..always sigh. **1848** LOWELL *Fable for Critics* 936 Here comes Dana,..Who'll be going to write what'll never be written Till the Muse, ere he thinks of it, gives him the mitten. **1851** [B. H. HALL] *College Words* 209 *Mitten.* At the Collegiate Institute of Indiana, a student who is expelled is said *to get the mitten.* **1867** O. W. HOLMES *Guard. Angel* xxxiii, Some said that Susan had given her young man the mitten, meaning thereby that she had signified that his services as a suitor were dispensed with. **1884** *Punch* 1 Mar. 108/2 Lifeboat hands who are found shrinking, Or with fear of danger smitten, Get, not medals, but the mitten.

4. *attrib.* and *Comb.*, ***mitten-gauntlet, -sleeve, -wise*** (adv.); **mitten-beaver**, the skin of a beaver used for making mittens [cf. F. *mitaine* inferior beaver-skins]; **mitten crab** (see quots.); **mitten-mill**, a fight with boxing-gloves.

1744 A. DOBBS *Countries Adjacent to Hudson's Bay* 26 The eight is the *Mittain Beaver, cut out for that Purpose to make Mittains, to preserve them from the Cold. **1934** *Times* 1 Feb. 17/5 If we want an English equivalent for the German *Wollhandkrabbe* it might be called the *mitten crab. **1934** *Nature* 9 June 856/1 The pincer claws are clothed with long soft hair, and a writer in the *Times* has suggested 'mitten crab' as an appropriate name for it... The mitten crab must have been introduced into German rivers before 1912... In 1923 the species was found to be established in the..Elbe and was determined as *Eriocheir sinensis.* **1959** *Chambers's Encycl.* IX. 455/1 Mitten crab, a popular name applied to a greenish grapsoid crab, *Eriocheir sinensis*, with conspicuous brown tufts of long silky hairs on the pincers of the male. **1898** *Archæol. Æliana* XIX. III. 246 The hands are covered with plate *mitten-gauntlets having gads and cuffs. **1859** MATSELL *Vocab.* s.v. (Farmer), *Mitten-mill. **1813** J. N. BREWER *Beauties Eng. & Wales* XII. II. ii. 146 A woman.. with..*mitten sleeves, a belt and cordon. **1899** *Westm. Gaz.* 22 Dec. 3/1 When a lace sleeve, instead of having actual mittens, is brought *mitten-wise over the hand.

Hence **'mitten** *v.*, *U.S.*, *trans.*, to 'give the mitten' to.

1873 CARLETON *Farm Ball.* 10 Once, when I was young as you, and not so smart, perhaps, For me she mittened a lawyer, and several other chaps.

mittened ('mɪtənd), *a.* [f. MITTEN *sb.* + -ED[2].] Furnished with, or wearing, mittens.

1834 HT. MARTINEAU *Farrers* ii. 20 Jane settled herself, aproned, shawled, and mittened, at her desk. **1876** *Whitby Gloss.* s.v., 'A mitten'd cat catches no mice'. **1895** KIPLING *2nd Jungle-Bk.* 162 The girl..laid her mittened hand..to the ice floor of the hut.

†**'mittent**, *a. Path. Obs.* [a. L. *mittent-em*, pr. pple. of *mittĕre* to send.] Said of the organ or part supposed to send peccant 'humours' to another.

1661 LOVELL *Hist. Anim. & Min.* 367 It's cured, by.. evacuating corrupted humours and helping mittent parts. **1676** WISEMAN *Chirurg. Treat.* II. v. 179 Vicious Humours peccant in quantity or quality are either thrust forth by the Part mittent,..or attracted by the Part recipient. **1684** tr. *Bonet's Merc. Compit.* XVIII. 631 We must consider whether the part mittent [L. *pars mittens*] of the Humour to the Stomach be less noble than the part suscipient.

mittilate, Sc. form of MUTILATE.

‖**mittimus** ('mɪtɪməs), *sb.* [L. *mittimus* 'we send', the first word of the writ in Latin.]

1. *Law.* A warrant under the hand and seal of a justice of the peace or other proper officer, directed to the keeper of a prison, ordering him to receive into custody and hold in safe-keeping, until delivered in due course of law, the person sent and specified in the warrant.

a **1591** GREENE *2nd Pt. Conny-Catching* Wks. (Grosart) X. 132 The knight..bad him [*sc.* his clerk] make a mittimus to send the Tinker to prison. **1625** MASSINGER *New Way* v. i, Take a Mittimus, And carry him to Bedlam. **1681** W. ROBERTSON *Phraseol. Gen.* (1693) 486 Send him away with a Mittimus to the house of Correction. **1728** VANBR. & CIB. *Prov. Husb.* v. 98 No words, Sir; a Wife, or a Mittimus. **1764** FOOTE *Mayor of G.* I. (1783) 15 Some warrants and mittimuses ready fill'd up. **1768–74** TUCKER *Lt. Nat.* (1834) I. 642, I never sign a mittimus to the house of correction, but had much rather it were done by somebody else. **1837** CARLYLE *Fr. Rev.* II. VI. i, Clapped in prison by mittimus and indictment of Feuillant Justices. **1849** MACAULAY *Hist. Eng.* iii. I. 320 The heir of an estate often..scarce attained learning enough to sign his name to a Mittimus.

†**b.** (See quot. 1641.) *Obs.*

1464 *Rolls of Parlt.* V. 516/1 Doo to be made, oure Writt' of a Mittimus unto the Tresourer and Barons of oure Exchequier. **1641** *Termes de la Ley* 204 Mittimus is a Writ by which Records are transferred from one Court to another. **1704** J. HARRIS *Lex. Techn.* I. **1727–41** CHAMBERS *Cycl.*, *Mittimus*, in law, a writ, by which records are ordered to be transferred from one court to another; sometimes immediately, as out of the King's Bench into the Exchequer; and sometimes by a certiorari into the Chancery, and from thence by a mittimus into another court.

c. *transf.* and *fig.*

1638 NABBES *Cov. Gard.* v. vi. 71 *Warr...* I sweare I understand it no more then Ignoramus himselfe. *Ralph.* Make his Mittimus and send him to schoole. **1642** BP. HALL *Free Prisoner* vii. in *Three Tractates* (1646) 123 Never was there a more close prisoner then my soul is for the time to my body;..which since it's first Mittimus, never stir'd out from this strait room. **1681** FLAVEL *Meth. Grace* xxxii. 540 His mittimus is already made for hell. *a* **1708** BEVERIDGE *Priv. Th.* I. (1816) 164 How runs the mittimus, whereby he is pleased to send me to the dungeon of afflictions.

2. *colloq.* A dismissal from office or situation; a notice to quit (*dial.*). ***to get one's mittimus***: to be dismissed; also, to get one's 'quietus'.

1596 NASHE *Saffron Walden* X j b, Out of two Noblemens houses he had his Mittimus ere he was gone. **1668** R. L'ESTRANGE *Vis. Quev.* (1708) 88 He had his Mittimus, and took the Left-hand way at parting. **1850** CARLYLE *Latter-d. Pamph.*, *Jesuitism* 15 Ignatius's black militia..have got their mittimus to Chaos again. **1857** KINGSLEY *Two Y. Ago* I. i. 24 He got his mittimus by one of Schamyl's bullets.

3. A jocular designation for a magistrate.

1630 RANDOLPH *Conceited Peddler* Wks. (1875) 38, I am no Justice of Peace, for I swear, by the honesty of a Mittimus, the venerable Bench ne'er kissed my worshipful buttocks. **1775** SHERIDAN *St. Patr. Day* II. ii, Nay, 'tis but what old Mittimus commanded.

Hence **'mittimus** *v. trans.*, to commit to jail by a warrant.

1764 FOOTE *Mayor of G.* I. (1783) 9 Had I been here, I would have mittimus'd the rascal at once. **1836** T. HOOK *G. Gurney* III. 83, I had mittimused half a dozen paupers for begging about the streets.

mittin(g, obs. forms of MITTEN *sb.*

mittle ('mɪt(ə)l), *v. Sc.* [? a. F. *mutiler* to MUTILATE; cf. *mittilate.*] *trans.* To hurt or mutilate. Hence **'mittled** *ppl. a.*

1820 A. SUTHERLAND *St. Kathleen* III. 213 The stirk that ye lat get itsel' mittled the ither day. *a* **1869** C. SPENCE *From Braes of Carse* (1898) 71 Collie left me in the bog, A mittled, mertered, drooket laddie. **1900** BARRIE *Tommy & Grizel* xxvi, Say a word against him and I'll mittle you.

mitton, obs. form of MITTEN *sb.*

mitty[1] ('mɪtɪ). *dial.* The stormy petrel.

1831 *Montagu's Ornith. Dict.* (ed. 2). **1840** *Penny Cycl.* XVIII. 44/1.

Mitty[2] ('mɪtɪ). Also **Walter Mitty**. [f. the name of Walter *Mitty*, hero of James Thurber's short story *The Secret Life of Walter Mitty* (in *New Yorker* (1939) 18 Mar.).] A person who indulges in day-dreams; one who imagines a more adventurous or enjoyable life for himself than he actually leads; the characteristics of such a person. Freq. *attrib.* or quasi-*adj.* Hence **Mi'ttyesque, 'Mittyish, Mitty-like** *adjs.*

1950 B. SCHULBERG *Disenchanted* (1951) xvii. 313 I've had daydreams of how I'd come back. Walter Mitty stuff about arriving in style. **1953** *Sunday Times* 14 June 8/4 The Mitty me, I notice, will risk his life for a trifle, but never gets his hands dirty. **1958** *Times Lit. Suppl.* 16 May 274/1 Greave takes refuge from the horrid realities of life in Mittyesque fantasies, pretending he is a high-powered American salesman. **1960** *Harper's Bazaar* Apr. 125/1 The average motoring man is..a visionary, a Walter Mitty locked in a private world of fantasy... Vintage cars seldom fail to spark off the Mitty in a man. **1960** *Sunday Express* 12 June 14/5 Women..live in a dream world of their own imagining—a Walter Mitty-ish 'Other Life'. **1961** *John o' London's* 28 Sept. 363/3 I'm in the delirious position of being able to indulge my Mitty-like obsession. **1968** S. BRITTAN *Left or Right* v. 106 The whole Walter Mitty idea of a private line from Downing Street to the White House. **1972** *Guardian* 11 July 10/5 Both men are Mittyesque failures. **1974** N. FREELING *Dressing of Diamond* 33 Bernard was doing his hospitality act... This was no Mitty performance.

‖**mitu** ('mɪtjuː). [Tupi.] = CURASSOW. Also ‖**mitupo'ranga**. [Tupi *poranga* beautiful].

The two names are applied by Marggraf to two different genera or species, but the identification is doubtful.

[*a* **1644** MARGGRAF *Hist. Rer. Nat. Brasil.* v. (1648) 194 *Mitv* vel *Mvtv* Brasiliensibus dicta avis ex Phasianorum est genere, major gallo gallinaceo. *Ibid.* 195 Reperitur & alia ejusdem species, quam *Mituporanga* vocant Brasilienses, solo rostro & pennis capitis differens [etc.].] **1753** CHAMBERS *Cycl. Supp.*, *Mitu*, or *Mitu-Porangu*;..a Brasilian bird of the pheasant-kind, according to Marggrave,..but supposed by Mr. Ray, rather to approach to the nature of the peacock or turkey-cock. **1828–32** WEBSTER, *Mitu*, a fowl of the turkey kind, found in Brazil. **1890** in *Century Dict.*; and in later Dicts.

mity ('maɪtɪ), *a.* [f. MITE *sb.*[1] + -Y[1].] Full of mites, abounding in mites: said esp. of cheese.

1681 COLVIL *Whigs Supplic.* (1751) 85 Some sold the soldiers mity meal. **1827** *Blackw. Mag.* XXII. 383 The part [of the cheese] is particularly mouldy and mity. **1904** *Longm. Mag.* May 27 Too much salt-junk and mity biscuit ain't good for you.

fig. **1778** in *Loyal Verses* (1860) 35 Do'st think it is an honest job This Mity bunch of Kings to rob?

‖**mitys** ('maɪtɪs). [Gr. μίτυς, the wax used by bees to cover the crevices of their hives.] (See quots.)

1706 PHILLIPS (ed. Kersey), *Mitys*, the gummy Wax with which a Bee-hive is first lin'd. **1816** KIRBY & SP. *Entomol.* xxvii. (1818) II. 485 [The bees] replacing the demolished cells..with mitys, which firmly fixes the comb to its support.

‖**mitzvah** ('mɪtsvaː). *Judaism.* Also **misva, mitsva(h), mitzwa.** Pl. **misvot, mitswoth, mitzvot, mitzwoth.** [Heb. *miṣwāh* commandment.] A precept; something which should be done; hence a good deed done as a religious duty, without expectation of earthly reward. Cf. BARMITZVAH.

1650 E. CHILMEAD tr. *Leon Modena's Hist. Rites of Jews* I. i. 2 Precepts of the Written Law..they call..*Mizuoth de Draita*, that is to say, *Præcepta Legis*, Precepts of the Law. The second sort are..*Mizuoth de Rabbanan*,..Precepts of the Wise men. **1753** *Jewish Ritual* 33 All the eight Cakes together, for the Service of both Nights, are call'd *Mitzwoth*, i.e. the Statutes. **1831** *Ascamot, or Laws & Regulations Jewish Congregation* vii. 52 If these three *Misvot* as well as the *Misva* of saying the *Zemirot*, shall have been given..it shall not be given to any other. **1893** I. ZANGWILL *Childr. Ghetto* (ed. 3) I. iii. 41 *Mitzvah* is a 'portmanteau-word'. It means a commandment and a good deed, the two conceptions being regarded as interchangeable. **1932** L. GOLDING *Magnolia St.* I. ii. 33 To break some of the less severe laws is almost accounted a *mitzvah*, a pious duty. **1959** W. L. GRESHAM *Houdini* xxi. 154 To Harry a good deed was something to be done quietly: 'So when you do a *mitzvah* you don't take along a brass band.' **1973** *Jewish Chron.* 2 Feb. 40/2 'Neither,' he adds scornfully, 'do we give out mitzvot according to money or position or influence.' **1973** *Synagogue Light* Sept. 11/1 There is great apprehension as to the meaning and message of this act of

removing the shoe, which forms an essential part in the right and mitzvah of *Chalitzah*.

mivvy ('mɪvɪ). *slang*. [Origin uncertain; perh. a corruption of MARVEL *sb*. The three senses may not be connected.] **1.** A marble.

1856 *N. & Q.* 5 Apr. 283/2 *Mivvies*, marbles. **1917** H. H. RICHARDSON *Fortunes Richard Mahony* I. iv. 33 You were always a good one at striking a bargain, my boy! What about: 'Four mivvies for an alley!'

2. A contemptuous term for a woman; the landlady of a lodging-house.

1881 *Punch* 10 Sept. 110/1 Lor' bless yer, they don't knaw the ropes, these old mivvies don't, more than a mug. **1887** *Punch* 10 Sept. 111/1 And talk about stodge! Jest you arsk the old mivvey as caters for me at the crib where I lodge. **1892** E. J. MILLIKEN *'Arry Ballads* 13/2 Bare-armed old mivvies you meet spread out pink in a theatre stall. **1923** J. MANCHON *Le Slang* 195 *Mivvy*, femme.

3. A person who is adept at something; a 'marvel'.

1906 E. PUGH *Spoilers* xv. 162 He's a mivvy at makin' things easy. **1959** 'O. MILLS' *Stairway to Murder* xi. 121 He's a mivvy with anything like that.

Miwok ('mi:wɒk, 'maɪwɒk). [Native name.] A Penutian Indian people of California; a member of this tribe; also, the language spoken by the tribe. Also *attrib.* or as *adj.*

1877 S. POWERS in *Contrib. N. Amer. Ethnol.* III. 346 By much the largest nation in California, both in population and in extent of territory, is the Miwok, whose ancient dominion extended from the snow-line of the Sierra Nevada to the San Joaquin River, and from the Cosumnes to the Fiesno. **1916** *Univ. California Publ. Amer. Archaeol. & Ethnol.* XII. IV. 141 With the Miwok the moiety has no subdivisions. *Ibid.* 142 That totemic symptoms of one sort or another are present in the Miwok organization cannot be denied. **1949** *Los Angeles Times* 10 Apr. II. 5/2 The name Yosemite was given to this valley by the Miwoks. **1964** GOULD & KOLB *Dict. Social Sci.* 436/1 A Miwok couple about to marry endogamously. **1966** C. F. & F. M. VOEGELIN *Map N. Amer. Indian Lang.* (*caption*) Miwok-Costanoan Family 1. Sierra Miwok. 2. Coast-Lake Miwok. **1972** *Language* XLVIII. 847, 6b is given.. by Sedlak for.. Miwok, Mongol (Dagor),.. and Siona. **1973** *Black Panther* 28 Apr. 10/1 He had come to participate in the Tuolumne Acorn Festival, an annual traditional ceremony of his people, the Miwok Indians.

† **mix**, *sb.*[1] *Obs.* Forms: 1 **miox, meox, (meohs, meohx)**, 1–4 **mix, myx**, 2 **mex**. [OE. *meox* neut. (? or masc.) = Fris. *miux, miuhs*:—OTeut. type **mihso-*, a parallel formation with **mihstu-z* (Goth. *maihstu-s*, OHG., G. *mist* masc., dung), f. wk. grade of Teut. root **mĭgh-*: see MIG.]

1. Dung; filth. Also *fig.*

c **888** K. ÆLFRED *Boeth.* xxxvi. §1 Se wisdom & eac oðre cræftas.. licgað forsewene swa swa miox under feltune. *c* **1000** *Ags. Gosp.* Luke xiii. 8 Oð ic hine bedelfe & ic hine bewurpe mid meoxe. *c* **1000** ÆLFRIC in Morris *OE. Hom.* I. 301 Seðe ahefð of meohse þone mann þe he wile. [*Qui suscitat de puluere egenum & de stercore erigit pauperem.*] *c* **1175** *Lamb. Hom.* 113 God ahef of mexe þene mon þe he wule. *a* **1250** *Prov. Ælfred* 385 in *O.E. Misc.* 126 And vyches cunnes madmes to mixe schulen i-Multen. *c* **1315** SHOREHAM iv. 239 For nys non of þe syxe [sins] þat hy ne comeþ of þane [*sc.* pride], For myx of alle myxe In heuene hy by-gan.

2. *transf.* A vile wretch.

c **1275** *Orison* 53 in *O.E. Misc.* 140 Ne myhte þe mixes þo wurse þe don Bute a-mong þeoues on rode an-hon. *c* **1350** *Will. Palerne* 125 þe quene his moder on a time as a mix þouȝt, how faire & how fetis it was & freliche schapen. ? *a* **1400** *Morte Arth.* 989, I am comyne fra the conquerour, .. Messenger to þis myx, for mendemente of þe pople.

3. As *adj.*: Filthy, foul.

a **1225** *Leg. Kath.* 204 þet euch waried weoued of þe mix maumez ron of þet balefule blod al bibledeget. *Ibid.* 2100, & tine mix maumez alle beon amanset.

mix (mɪks), *sb.*[2] [f. MIX *v.*] **1. a.** The act or result of mixing; a mixture. esp. *colloq.*: A muddle, 'mess'; (*a*) a state of being 'mixed' or confused; (*b*) a number of ingredients mixed together, or intended for mixing; *spec.* the prepared ingredients of a cake, etc., sold ready for cooking; (*c*) more generally, the proportion of different constituents that make up a product, plan, policy, etc.; a combination of various components into an integrated whole.

c **1586** C'TESS PEMBROKE *Ps.* CXLVII. iii, O make harmonious mix of voice and string. **1882** HOWELLS *Likely Story* iii. (1897) 56 She'll show the note to Miss Greenway, and you'll be ruined. Oh, poor Mr. Welling! Oh, what a fatal, fatal—mix! **1893** A. FULLER *Lit. Courtship* xv. 156, I thought of her clear eye and her healthy way of looking and talking, and I was more in a mix than ever. **1901** *Harper's Mag.* Apr. 761/1 'It has all been a mix and a muddle', she answered. **1905** *Speaker* 3 June 231/1 They made an indescribable mix and blend of colour. **1912** L. & M. GREENBAUM *Pract. Dentistry* xxvii. 457 It is best to subject the mass to the least amount of stirring conducive to a homogeneous mix. **1922** MOJONNIER & TROY *Technical Control of Dairy Products* xiii. 276 Ice cream made from mix No. 9 will feel about 12·00 per cent warmer to the tongue than ice cream made from mix No. 1. **1938**, etc. [see *cake-mix* s.v. CAKE *sb.* 9]. **1945** B. MACDONALD *Egg & I* (1946) 66, I could use automatic biscuit mix for the crust. **1959** *Life* (Internat. ed.) 13 Apr. 20/2 The new term is 'mix'. There is, says the Administration, an adequate 'mix' of forces to maintain our deterrent. **1962** *Listener* 29 Mar. 579/2 When the egg mix is light and foamy add it to the sauce. **1962** *Times* 26 Apr. 9/5 (*headline*) Canada may ban food mix sales. **1962** L. DEIGHTON *Ipcress File* xviii. 110 A bottle of Scotch, gin, some assorted mixes. **1964** M. MCLUHAN *Understanding Media* (1967) v. 60 Oral societies are made up of people differentiated.. by their unique emotional mixes. *Ibid.* 64 Chaplin.. hit upon the wondrous media mix of ballet and film. **1966** [see JERSEY[1] 1]. **1967** *Daily Tel.* 17 May 17/7 Without sufficient statistics on the question of socially mixed entry to public schools, the committee believes it impossible to induce artificially a 'social mix'. **1967** *Times Rev. Industry* Aug. 16/2 Retailing strategy will probably go on trying to maximize interest in stores by an optimum mix of heavily advertised manufacturer-branded lines and an increasing proportion of housebrand lines. **1970** *Daily Tel.* 9 Apr. 36/5 The mix of dancing, cabaret, drinking and gaming created an undesirable temptation to young people. **1971** *Guardian* 9 June 13/1 Alcoholic mixes like bitter lemon. **1971** M. MCCARTHY *Birds of America* 31 First a cake made with a mix and then a real one. **1972** *Publishers Weekly* 6 Mar. 25/1 In publishing, I think you have to have a good mix, and not try to reach just one segment of the population, but to cover all segments. **1972** *Guardian* 5 Aug. 11/8 By expelling the Russians he [*sc.* Sadat] has drastically altered the strategic mix.

b. *Printing.* (See quot.)

1897 *Daily News* 29 Nov. 6/3 A somewhat different class of Printers' errors are those that arise from what are technically known as 'mixes'—that is the accidental running together of sentences.. which have no connexion.

c. mix-up, the state of being 'mixed up' (see MIX *v.* 6). *spec.* (*a*) a state of confusion; a mess or muddle; (*b*) a fight.

1841 S. BAMFORD *Passages in Life of Radical* I. xv. 94, I had expected being conducted to London alone, and certainly was not prepared for a mix-up with these men. **1898** *Daily News* 12 Aug. 6/3 One or two boats had run into the raft, and there was a considerable mix up there. *Ibid.* 24 Nov. 7/3 Glove Contest in America. Midway the round was a rattling mix up. **1902** *Daily Chron.* 14 Oct. 3/2 The general mix-up of things in these.. latter days. **1913** *Chums* 25 Jan. 361/2 Then for a full minute the two engaged in a 'mix-up'. **1913** *Collier's* 1 Feb. 27 (*caption*) A bad mix-up. **1919** [see GOY]. **1923** WODEHOUSE *Inimitable Jeeves* viii. 85 When the driver started making a fuss, there was a bit of a mix-up. **1932** J. C. POWYS *Glastonbury Romance* (1933) II. xxiii. 737 God! What a mix-up it all is. **1971** D. E. WESTLAKE *I gave at the Office* (1972) 139 As soon as the mix-up was brought to light I was freed.

2. *Cinemat.* and *Broadcasting.* The action or result of mixing two pictures or two sounds (see MIX *v.* 7 a).

1922 [see FADE *sb.*[1] 2]. **1932** *Wireless World* 16 Mar. 276/1 A sound-mix, which corresponds to a picture-mix (when the picture dissolves into another picture) is done by starting with one microphone set at its gain figure and the second microphone set at zero gain. *Ibid.*, For a smooth mix, the two knobs must be turned as nearly as possible at the same speed. **1960** [see FADE *sb.*[1] 2]. **1961** *Listener* 2 Nov. 716/1 If phrases overlap musically the visual counterpart is a mix; and.. a mix between two different angles on the same performer is usually upsetting to the viewer. **1962** A. NISBETT *Technique Sound Studio* ix. 152 It is the way that fades and mixes are carried out.. that distinguishes the polished, finished recording from the one that sounds amateur.

mix (mɪks), *v.* Pa. t. and pa. pple. **mixed** (mɪkst). [Back-formation from the ppl. adj. *mixt* (see MIXED *ppl. a.*), a. F. *mixte*, ad. L. *mixtus*, pa. pple. of *miscēre* to mix. Cf. MIXT *v.*

Our earliest example of the vb., in any form other than the pa. pple., is of the date 1538, and it was extremely rare until Shakspere's time. Of the pa. pple. itself, the earliest examples are *c* 1480 and 1526, the latter year being the date of our first quot. for MIXT *v.* The OE. *miscian* (the alleged by-form **mixian* is spurious) which has generally been assumed to be the source of the present verb, app. did not survive into ME. Only two examples are cited by Toller, and in these the sense seems to be 'to apportion suitably'.

The L. *miscēre*:—*mik-sk-* is f. the Indogermanic root **mik-*(:*meik, moik-*), represented by Skr. *miçra* (:—**mikro-*) mixed, and by many vbs. with the sense 'to mix' in the various langs.: Skr. *miksh*, ? Gr. μίσγειν (Gr. μιγνύναι is from the cognate root *mig-*), Welsh *mysgu*, OIrish *mesc*, Lith. *maiszýti*, OSl. *mĕsiti* (Russ. *meshat'*). Whether the OE. *miscian*, OHG. *misgen*, *miskan* (MHG., MLG., mod.G. *mischen*) is cognate with the Latin or an early WGer. adoption from it, seems doubtful; the absence of the word from Goth., Scandinavian, OS., and Frisian, is an argument in favour of the latter view.]

1. a. *trans.* To put together (two or more substances, or groups or classes of things) so that the particles or members of each are more or less evenly diffused among those of the rest; to unite (one or more substances, groups, etc.) in this manner *with* another or others; to mingle, blend.

Not now employed with reference to the more intimate union of substances to form a chemical compound; in this application *combine* is the usual vb.

c **1480** *Songs & Carols* (Percy Soc.) 6 Butt now prosyrs [? *read* profyrs] glorius be myxyd with gall, Wyche bytter ys and tedius over all. **1526** *Pilgr. Perf.* (W. de W. 1531) 3 More pleasaunt to beholde than is the colour of syluer myxte with golde. **1535** COVERDALE *2 Esdras* xiii. 11 And they were all myxte together: the blast of fyre, the wynde of the flammes, and yᵉ greate storme. **1538** ELYOT *Dict.*, *Misceo*,.. to myxe [*so* 1545; 1548 *reads* myxt, 1552 myxte] or meddyll together. **1555–8** PHAER *Æneid* II. Eiij b, & mixt wᵗ dust & smoke [Virg. II. 609 *mixtoque undantem puluere fumum*] thick streames of reekings rise. **1560** BIBLE (Genev.) *Heb.* iv. 2 The worde that they heard, profitted not them, because it was not mixed [Gr. συγκεκραμένος] with faith in those that heard it. **1566** DRANT *Horace, Sat.* II. iv. G viij, Aufidius, myxt heddy wyne, and honey all in one. **1572** MASCALL *Plant. & Graff.* 86 Clense the ground of weedes, and mixe it well with good molde and fat earth. **1638** JUNIUS *Paint. Ancients* 272 He who vainly mixing many faire colours representeth nothing else in his worke but a painted tempest. **1667** MILTON *P.L.* XII. 181–2 Thunder mixt with Haile, Haile mixt with fire must rend th' Egyptian Skie. **1670** LADY MARY BERTIE in *12th Rep. Hist. MSS. Comm.* App. v. 21 Some ware all small ribban, others brode ribbans, others broad and small mixed. **1716** LADY M. W. MONTAGU *Let. to C'tess Mar* 14 Sept., Their own hair.. they mix with a great deal of false. **1800** tr. *Lagrange's Chem.* I. 129 If you mix nitrous vapour with oxygen gas, there will be no absorption. **1811** A. T. THOMSON *Lond. Disp.* I. (1818) p. lxxi, Oxygen gas and sulphurous acid gas probably combine when simply mixed together. **1819** BYRON *Juan* II. lxxv, The lots were made, and mark'd, and mix'd, and handed In silent horror.

b. With immaterial obj.: To combine, associate, or blend (different principles, methods, qualities, or one principle, etc., *with* something else).

1597 SHAKS. *2 Hen. IV*, v. ii. 46 Brothers, you mixe your Sadnesse with some Feare. **1662** STILLINGFL. *Orig. Sacr.* II. vi. §11 Now there had been no reason at all for this, if he had mixed promises together with his threatnings. **1707** FLOYER *Physic. Pulse-Watch* 277 In this case we must mix both the hot and the cold Method. **1729** BUTLER *Serm.* Wks. 1874 II. 7 The two principles are frequently mixed together, and run up into each other. **1815** ELPHINSTONE *Acc. Caubul* (1842) I. 333 They also mix trade and agency with their regular banking business. **1875** JOWETT *Plato* (ed. 2) V. 124 In the election of the Council, the legislator attempts to mix aristocracy and democracy.

† **c.** To put in or introduce as an ingredient, to intersperse. Const. *to*. *Obs.*

1607 TOPSELL *Four-f. Beasts* (1658) 187 The milk also of a Goat mixed to a Womans milk is best for the nourishment of man, because it is not too fat. *a* **1715** BURNET *Own Time* (1724) I. 18 They were very factious and insolent; and both in their sermons and prayers were always mixing severe reflections on their enemies. **1742** YOUNG *Nt. Th.* VIII. 495 Knows he, that mankind praise against their will, And mix as much detraction as they can?

d. To prepare (a compound) by putting various ingredients together.

1592 SHAKS. *Rom. & Jul.* III. iii. 44 Had'st thou no poyson mixt? **1697** DRYDEN *Virg. Georg.* III. 685 From the Founts where living Sulphurs boil, They mix a Med'cine to foment their limbs. **1818** KITCHINER *Cook's Oracle* (ed. 2) 577 Puddings are best when mixed over night. **1842** C. WHITEHEAD *R. Savage* (1845) II. iii. 203 I'll write the letter while the punch is mixing. **1887** P. MᶜNEILL *Blawearie* 100 He had mixed and otherwise prepared as much of his layering compound as he thought he might use.

e. *hyperbolically*. To confound, confuse together.

1667 MILTON *P.L.* VII. 215 They view'd the vast immeasurable Abyss.., Up from the bottom turn'd by furious windes And surging waves, as Mountains to assault Heav'ns highth, and with the Center mix the Pole.

f. In various occasional uses: To unite (persons' eyes) in interchange of glances; to join (hands). Also † *to mix one's thigh* (= 4 b).

1592 SHAKS. *Ven. & Ad.* 489 Were neuer foure such lamps together mixt, Had not his clouded with his browes repine. **1606** MARSTON *Fawn* IV. i, The Romans.. thought that a woman might mix her thigh with a stranger wantonly, and yet still love her husband matrimonially. **1713** ADDISON *Cato* III. ii. 36 Never to mix my plighted Hands with thine. **1868** TENNYSON *Lucretius* 56 And hands they mixt, and yell'd and round me drove In narrowing circles.

g. Colloq phr. *to mix one's drinks*: to drink various kinds of alcoholic liquor in succession; *spec.* to become intoxicated by drinking both wine and liquor made from grain. Also *ellipt.* and *absol.*

1898 J. D. BRAYSHAW *Slum Silhouettes* 238 'E was gettin' a bit beargered—not that 'e'd 'ad so much, but 'e would keep mixin'; first one thing an' then annuver. **1933** J. B. PRIESTLEY *Wonder Hero* vii. 269 Had a thick night last night. .. Mixed 'em a bit. Always a mistake—mixing 'em. **1950** G. GREENE *Third Man* ii. 13 If you stayed around in a hotel lounge, sooner or later.. one mixed one's drinks. **1961** J. B. PRIESTLEY *Saturn over Water* iii. 35, I mixed my drinks too much last night—I feel better now.

h. Slang phr. *to mix it*: to fight or quarrel; to start fighting; freq. const. *with*; also, to cause trouble. So *to mix it up*: to fight vigorously.

1900 A. CONAN DOYLE *Green Flag* 165 This round must decide it. 'Mix it oop, lad; mix it oop!' the iron-men whooped. **1905** C. H. DAY *Actress & Clerk* xv. 149 As Hard Knox would have himself described in the technique of the ring, the men 'mixed it'. **1906** H. GREEN *At Actors' Boarding House* 359 They're goin' to mix it up. The little un'll win out, see if she don't. My eye! dames is allus fightin'. **1918** E. M. ROBERTS *Flying Fighter* 91 He grew angry and we mixed it. I gave him a black eye. **1919** WODEHOUSE *Coming of Bill* (1920) II. xiv. 239, I thought I could stay around and part 'em if they got to mixing it. **1941** E. C. SHEPHERD *Mil. Aeroplane* 14 Many a German bomber in daylight raids over England has accepted failure rather than 'mix it' with the British fighters which came to dispute with it. **1941** *Time* 8 Dec. 22/1 The tanks.. face the approaching column... Then they begin to mix it up. **1945** *Aeronautics* Feb. 50/3 Pilots took full advantage of every opportunity of 'mixing it' with the Hun. **1950** P. TEMPEST *Lag's Lexicon* 136 *Mix it, to*, to put one man against another. To make trouble. **1958** F. NORMAN *Bang to Rights* 28 The screw who's giving evidence against you starts telling a load of bleeding lies and mixing it for you. **1973** D. LEES *Rape of Quiet Town* vi. 92 These lads don't want to fight for nothing. If they can get away without mixing it they will.

2. a. *intr.* = to be mixed. Also, to admit of being mixed; to unite with, to go (well or badly) along with.

1632 MARMION *Holland's Leaguer* III. iii, O divine counsel! that so rare a beauty Should mix with wisdom. **1647** COWLEY *Mistr.*, *Platonick Love* i, When Souls mix 'tis an Happiness; But not compleat 'till Bodies too combine. **1667** MILTON *P.L.* XI. 529 But is there yet no other way,.. how we may come To Death, and mix with our connatural

dust? *a* **1745** SWIFT *Abstr. Hist. Eng.* Wks. 1824 X. 303 The Danes..in process of time..mixed with the English. **1760–2** GOLDSM. *Cit. W.* xciv, Her dear idea mixes with every scene of pleasure. **1774** —— *Nat. Hist.* I. xix. *init.*, All the bodies of the earth are continually sending up a part of their substance by evaporation, to mix in this great alembic [the atmosphere], and to float awhile in common. *Ibid.* (1776) II. 136 At last, when the approaches of sleep are near, every object of the imagination begins to mix with that next it. **1796** C. MARSHALL *Garden.* xix. (1813) 379 The pyramidal sort [of the Star of Bethlehem] is a proper flower to pot, mixing with others very ornamentally. **1797** LAMB *Let. to Coleridge* 10 Jan., I do long to see our names together; not for vanity's sake..altogether..; and yet there is a little vanity mixes in it. **1815** ELPHINSTONE *Acc. Caubul* (1842) II. 111 The Afghaun Humsauyehs mix well with the Dooraunees. **1845** *Encycl. Metrop.* XXV. 169/1 Some builders prefer receiving the grey-stone lime ground dry, as it mixes more readily when made up into mortar. **1889** SKRINE *Mem. E. Thring* 164 He floated in their element, not soluble. It is often the way with heroes: they will not mix.

b. Of the eyes: To interchange glances. *poet.*

1879 E. ARNOLD *Lt. Asia* 29 Their eyes mixed, and from the look sprang love.

3. *trans.* To unite (persons) in dealings or acquaintance; to associate; †to join in sexual intercourse. Chiefly *refl.* and *pass.* Now *rare.*

1535 COVERDALE *Ezra* ix. (*Contents*), Eszdras is sory that the people haue myxte them selues with the Heythenish wemen. **1599** B. JONSON *Cynthia's Rev.* IV. v, Wee must mixe this gentleman with you in acquaintance. **1667** MILTON *P.L.* I. 579 Th' Heroic Race..That fought at Theb's and Ilium, on each side Mixt with auxiliar Gods. *Ibid.* XI. 686 Those ill-mated Marriages..Where good with bad were matcht,..and by imprudence mixt, Produce prodigious Births of bodie or mind. **1791–1823** D'ISRAELI *Cur. Lit.* (1866) 285/1 Ever since we have mixed ourselves with the Low Countries.

4. a. *intr.* To associate, have intercourse *with* (occas. *among*); to occupy oneself *with*, take part *in*. Also ***to mix in with***. ***to mix in***: to start or join in a fight (*slang*). Cf. 1 h and 4 c.

1667 MILTON *P.L.* VI. 21 Gladly then he mixt Among those friendly Powers who him receav'd With joy. **1697** DRYDEN *Æneid* VII. 538 She flies the town, and, mixing with a throng Of madding matrons, bears the bride along. **1711** ADDISON *Spect.* No. 69 ¶1, I am infinitely delighted in mixing with these several Ministers of Commerce. **1725** *Wodrow Corr.* (1843) III. 232, I hope still to be guarded by better principles. Indeed, it's hard mixing in with self-willed and peremptory people. **1771** *Junius Lett.* liv. (1788) 293 He never mixed with the world. **1816** SCOTT *Old Mort.* x, Have you, who used to mix so little in these unhappy feuds, become so suddenly and deeply implicated. **1846** *Mirror of Lit.* Sept. 109 Here he mixed among the primitive and rude inhabitants of the district. **1868** E. EDWARDS *Ralegh* I. xxiii. 521 He had mixed largely with his countrymen, in every rank of life. **1870** J. P. SMITH *Widow Goldsmith's Daughter* vi. 69 Of course they couldn't expect to mix in with the rich children. **1872** *Routledge's Ev. Boy's Ann.* 153/2 Mr. Polybank has only mixed in the best society. **1895** M. HALSTEAD *100 Bear Stories* 117 Elk killing didn't seem half so great an achievement as it did before the bear had mixed in with the proceedings. **1912** R. A. WASON *Friar Tuck* xxi. 158 'Well, what if he did shoot,' sez Slim, 'we wouldn't have to mix in, would we?' **1971** WODEHOUSE *Much Obliged, Jeeves* ix. 89 If you see any more gnats headed in her direction, hold their coats and wish them luck, but restrain the impulse to mix in.

b. To have sexual intercourse *with.*

1615 CHAPMAN *Odyss.* I. 123 She mixt [Gr. μιγεῖσα] with Neptune in his hollow caues. **1630** MAY *Contn. Lucan* I. 265 There goates..Doe mix with woman kinde **1774** GOLDSM. *Nat. Hist.* (1776) III. 363 Warreners assert, that the pole-cat will mix with the ferret. **1889** R. B. ANDERSON tr. *Rydberg's Teut. Mythol.* 151 They mixed with the wood sprites, and thus became the progenitors of the Huns.

c. To join battle, engage in conflict. *poet.*

1697 DRYDEN *Virg. Georg.* IV. 359 Wasps infest the Camp with loud Alarms, And mix in Battel with unequal Arms. *a* **1700** —— *Ovid's Metam.* XII. Fables 448 Where Greeks and Trojans mix'd in mortal Fight.

d. To be sociable.

1816 JANE AUSTEN *Emma* III. vii. 113 Mr. and Mrs. Elton ..showed no unwillingness to mix, and be..agreeable. **1905** *Dialect Notes* III. 88 He doesn't mix much. **1940** A. CHRISTIE *Sad Cypress* I. vi. 83 Rather a funny crowd of people, but I don't mix much. You told me once that I wasn't a good mixer. **1965** M. SPARK *Mandelbaum Gate* I. 7 He was in no great hurry for the flat, preferring hotel life where one need not mix.

5. To cross in breeding. *trans.* and *intr.*

1737 BRACKEN *Farriery Impr.* (1757) II. 55 When a good English Mare is mixed with a Barb, she produces a better Foal. **1892** A. A. CROZIER *Pop. Errors about Plants* App. 157 (Funk) Plants mix or cross in the blossom only.

6. mix up. a. *trans.* To mix intimately, to work into a mixture *with* something else.

1753 J. BARTLET *Gentl. Farriery* vi. (1754) 68 Then give him two drams of calomel, mixed up with an ounce of diapente, for two nights. **1845** *Encycl. Metrop.* XXV. 168/2 Mortar... Its composition varies..according to the various ingredients which may be mixed up with it.

b. In immaterial applications. Now only with unfavourable implication: To mix or associate irrelevantly, unsuitably, or confusingly; to confuse. Also *slang* (see quot. 1823).

a **1806** HORSLEY *Serm.* iv. (1816) I. 75 Who is he that shall determine in what proportions the attributes of justice and mercy, forbearance and severity, ought to be mixed up in the character of the Supreme Governor of the universe? **1818** BYRON *Juan* I. xx, But then she had a devil of a spirit, And sometimes mix'd up fancies with realities. **1823** 'J. BEE' *Dict. Turf, To Mix it up*, to agree secretly how the parties shall make up a tale, or colour a transaction in order to cheat or deceive another party, as in case of a justice-hearing, of a law-suit, or a *cross* in a boxing-match for money. **1846** HARE *Mission Comf.* (1850) 403 One virtue was mixt up with a thousand crimes. **1875** JOWETT *Plato* (ed. 2) III. 188 His manner of mixing up real and imaginary persons.

c. With implication of something discreditable or unpleasant: To associate *with* (inferior or discreditable company); to connect *with* or involve *in* (a compromising affair, shady dealings, etc.). Chiefly *refl.* and *pass.*

1847 MARRYAT *Childr. N. Forest* xxv, It is not fit that the heiress of Arnwood should mix herself up with foresters' daughters. **1882** E. DICEY *Victor Emanuel* v. 53 An Italian exile, who in his hot youth had been mixed up, very much against the grain, in an abortive plot for the assassination of the late King.

d. *intr.* (*Pugilism.*) Of two combatants: To interchange blows wildly and rapidly.

1898 *Daily News* 24 Nov. 7/3 The men were in the centre of the ring mixing up in the liveliest manner.

7. *Cinemat.* and *Broadcasting.* **a.** *trans.* To combine (two pictures or sounds) temporarily by fading one out as the other is faded in; freq. *intr.*, to pass from one picture *to* another in this way.

1922 L. C. MACBEAN *Kinematogr. Studio Technique* ix. 82 On occasions..it is necessary..to fade or mix titles into a scene to which they relate. **1929** *Radio Times* 8 Nov. 389/1 The D.C. Panel..which allows a producer..to mix and fade speech, music, and sound-effects. **1953** K. REISZ *Technique Film Editing* I. i. 25 From the scene in the present, Griffith simply mixed to the earlier scene and then mixed back again. **1961** G. MILLERSON *Technique Television Production* xvi. 305 Mixing opposite directions of movement can sometimes arouse feelings of expansion or impact. **1962** *Listener* 6 Dec. 983/1 Mr Cooper uses..the language and grammar of film-making in his radio plays. He will cut sharply from scene to scene; or he will mix from one scene into the next.

b. *trans.* To combine (two or more sound signals) into one, either linearly, by adding together a fraction of each in a mixer (sense 2 b), or non-linearly, by causing one signal to modulate a second in a mixer (sense 2 c).

1928 [see BALANCE *v.* 4]. **1931** C. DREHER in L. Cowan *Recording Sound for Motion Pict.* xxiv. 345 He also mixes the output of the microphones when several are used. **1958** W. F. LOVERING *Radio Communication* viii. 172 Suppressor-grid control may be used to 'mix' two signals to produce a modulated output. **1962** J. H. & P. J. REYNER *Radio Communication* ix. 364 A pentode valve was used as an anode bend detector.., while a small triode, assembled round the same cathode, generated the local oscillation, and the two were mixed by using a common bias resistor in the cathode circuit. **1974** *Encycl. Brit. Macropædia* XII. 549/1 When several microphones are used on the set, their outputs are often mixed and reproduced on a single film or tape.

mixable (ˈmɪksəb(ə)l), *a. rare*⁻⁰. [f. MIX *v.* + -ABLE. Cf. MISCIBLE, MIXIBLE, MIXTIBLE.] That can be mixed. Hence **ˈmixableness**.

[**1827** *Blackw. Mag.* XXI. 761 It consists of jarring, unmixable atoms.] **1854** WEBSTER, *Mixable.* [And in later Dicts.] **1881** WHITNEY *Mixt. Lang.* 7 Any view.. concerning the mixableness or unmixableness of language.

†ˈmixar. *Alch. Obs.*

a **1500** *Liber Patris Sap.* in Ashm. (1652) 199 Sche ys a very frendly mixar, The progeneration of a greate Elixar. *Ibid.* 201 The which ys called the greate Elixer, And ys verily made with a stronge mixar.

†mixed, *a. Obs.* [f. MIX *sb.*¹ + -ED².] Foul, polluted.

c **1300** *Havelok* 2533 Þat fule traytour, that mixed cherl.

mixed, † mixt (mɪkst), *ppl. a.* [Originally *mixt*, a. F. *mixte* (in the AF. law phrase *accioun mixte* in Britton *c* 1290: see sense 1 below), ad. L. *mixtus*: see MIX *v.* The word having the appearance of an Eng. pple in *-t*, which would regularly have an alternative form in *-ed* (cf. *blest, blessed, vext, vexed*), the form *mixed* (*myxyd*) came very early into use, and ultimately gave rise to the formation of the vbs. MIX and MIXT.

The spelling *mixt* in the 17th c. is prob. in most instances merely phonetic, but may sometimes indicate that the writer apprehended the word as an adoption of L. *mixtus* rather than as the pple. of an Eng. vb. In recent use this spelling sometimes occurs (*Hist.*) in the legal sense 1, but otherwise it is confined to writers who advocate spelling reform.]

1. *Law.* Formerly applied to an action which partook at once of the nature of a real and of a personal action: see PERSONAL 6 a.

With the abolition of real actions (see PERSONAL *a.* 6), mixed actions necessarily came to an end.

1448 [see PERSONAL *a.* 6]. **1535** *Act 27 Hen. VIII*, c. 26 §4 Al actions personals..and al actions mixte..shall be sued by originall writte. *c* **1610** BACON *Case Post-nati Scotl.* (1641) 12 But for free-hold, or lease, or actions reall, or mixt: he is not inabled, except [etc.]. **1768** BLACKSTONE *Comm.* III. 228 This action of waste is a mixed action; partly real, so far as it recovers land, and partly personal, so far as it recovers damages. **1818** CRUISE *Digest* (ed. 2) V. 532 In pleas real or mixt. **1888** T. C. WILLIAMS in *Law Q. Rev.* IV. 398 Mixed actions partook of the nature both of real and personal actions.

2. a. Mingled or blended together; formed by the mingling of different substances, individuals, etc.

1557–8 PHAER *Æneid* VI. Q iv b, Thou hedlong threwst thyself on myxyd heapes of enmyes slain. **1611** BIBLE *Prov.* xxiii. 30 They that tarry long at the wine, they that goe to seeke mixt wine. **1663** GERBIER *Counsel* g iv, A Building, either made of stone, brick, or mixt. **1696** *Lond. Gaz.* No. 3160/4 Stolen..6 Pieces Northern brown mixt Clothes. **1742** YOUNG *Nt. Th.* v. 260 With mixt manure she surfeits the rank soil. **1747** WESLEY *Prim. Physic* (1755) p. xv, Abstain from all Mixt, all High-season'd Food. **1861** [F. W. ROBINSON] *No Church* II. 238 A plate of mixed biscuits. **1869** BOUTELL *Arms & Arm.* viii. (1874) 124 Armies.. composed of mixed bands of mercenary soldiers.

b. Compounded *of* (different ingredients).

1622 BACON *Holy War* Ep. Ded., Therefore I haue chosen an Argument, mixt of Religious and Ciuill Considerations; And likewise mixt between Contemplatiue and Actiue. **1639** GENTILIS *Servita's Inquis.* (1676) 840 This is the beginning in Venice of the Office of the Inquisition mixed of Secular and Ecclesiastical Persons. *a* **1716** SOUTH *Serm.* (1823) II. 14 With an odd kind of passion, mixed of pleasure and envy too. **1742** YOUNG *Nt. Th.* VIII. 819 Nature..drinks to man, in her nectareous cup, Mixt up of delicates for ev'ry sense. **1883** R. W. DIXON *Mano* I. xi. 33 This story mixed of spiteful falsity My wicked daughter gave.

3. Consisting of different or unlike elements or parts; combining diverse natures or qualities; not of one kind, not pure or simple, as ***mixed motives***.

1530 PALSGR. 920 Myxed lyght is devyded in four partes. **1586** W. WEBBE *Eng. Poetrie* (Arb.) 69 A foote of two sillables, is eyther simple or mixt, that is, of like time or of diuers. **1590** SWINBURNE *Testaments* 123 Mixt conditions are those which are partlie arbitrarie and partlie casuall. **1645** RUTHERFORD *Tryal & Tri. Faith* (1845) 51 David was punished according to the rule of that mixed and fatherly justice, which keeps a due proportion between the sin and the punishment. **1711** ADDISON *Spect.* No. 62 ¶6 Mixt Wit therefore is a Composition of Punn and true Wit. **1742** CIBBER *Let. to Pope* 34 What a merry mixt Mortal has Nature made you? **1790** *Monthly Rev.* III. 485 The mixed atomists, who ascribe the power of thinking to some inherent power in matter. **1818** M. EDGEWORTH *Let.* 13 Oct. (1971) 114 There were mixed motives I grant... Lord Byron was distressed for money. To be sure he could have had other fortunes but then there was vanity. **1844** H. H. WILSON *Brit. India* II. 164 A person of mixed European and Indian descent. **1849** HARE *Par. Serm.* II. 469 Man is a mixt being, made up of a spiritual soul and of a fleshly body. **1903** A. CARR in *Expositor* 6 June 418 With these mixed motives Pilate wrote the title. **1939** L. MACNEICE *Autumn Jrnl.* iii. 18 None of our hearts are pure, we always have mixed motives.

4. Made up of good and bad elements; having both good and bad qualities.

1745 WESLEY *Answ. Ch.* 11, I have described them, as of a Mixt Character, with much Evil among them, but more Good. **1760–2** GOLDSM. *Cit. W.* lxviii, This gentleman, who is of a mixed reputation. **1762** *Ann. Reg.* II. 50 The life, character, transactions, and writings of that mixed man [Voltaire]. **1776** GIBBON *Decl. & F.* xii. I. 343 Every circumstance that relates to this prince appears of a mixed and doubtful nature. **1882** MOZLEY *Remin.* I. xx, As regards the older boys it is a monastery, and the results are about as mixed as in the monastery of old times.

5. Of a company of persons: Comprising individuals of different birth, rank, or character; not restricted to one class or set. Hence, in bad sense: Not 'select', containing persons who are of doubtful character or status.

1611 BIBLE *Exod.* xii. 38 And a mixed multitude went vp also with them. **1657** J. WATTS *Vind. Ch. Eng.* 199 You cannot away with mixt communions. **1705** STANHOPE *Paraphr.* II. 249 This Parable was spoken before a mixt and numerous Auditory. **1720** SWIFT *Fates Clergym.* Wks. 1751 V. 35 A free Manner of speaking in mixt Company. **1748** CHESTERF. *Let. to Son* 19 Oct., Avoid, in mixed companies, argumentative polemical conversations. **1817** BYRON *Beppo* lviii, The company is 'mix'd' (the phrase I quote is As much as saying, they're below your notice). **1902** T. M. LINDSAY *Ch. & Ministry in Early Cent.* ii. 49 The population of Corinth was as mixed as that of Alexandria.

6. a. Of a government or polity: Combining features of two or more of the recognized types (monarchy, democracy, etc.); not pure or absolute in type.

1538 STARKEY *England* II. ii. 181 For thys cause the most wyse men..affyrme a myxte state to be of al other the best and most conuenyent to conserue the hole out of tyranny. **1650** HOBBES *De Corp. Pol.* 72 This Policy they call Mixt Monarchy, or Mixt Aristocracy, or mixt Democracy, according as any of these three sorts do most visibly predominate. **1752** HUME *Ess. & Treat.* (1777) I. 12 Unbounded liberty of the press..is one of the evils attending..mixt forms of Government. **1844** LD. BROUGHAM *Brit. Const.* i. (1862) 12 The ancient republic of Sparta was a Mixed Aristocracy. *Ibid.* iii. 29 The British Constitution, the most perfect example of Mixed Government.

b. *Phonetics.* Of a vowel sound = CENTRAL *a.* 1 d.

1867 [see BACK *a.* 1 c]. **1890** H. SWEET *Primer Spoken Eng.* 4 In the vowels we distinguish three horizontal positions, or degrees of retraction of the tongue: back, mixed, front. **1918** D. JONES *Outl. Eng. Phonetics* 17 An example of a mixed vowel is the vowel in *bird*. **1966** M. PEI *Gloss. Ling. Terminol.* 164 *Mixed vowel*, Migliorini's term for middle vowel.

7. Of sciences: Involving or dealing with matter; not 'pure' or simply theoretical. Now *rare* or *Obs.* exc. in ***mixed mathematics***: see MATHEMATICS.

1641 [see MATHEMATICS]. **1706** PHILLIPS (ed. Kersey), *Mixt Mathematicks*, are those Arts and Sciences which treat of the Properties of Quantity, apply'd to material Beings, or sensible Objects; as Astronomy, Geography, Navigation, Dialling, Surveying, Gauging, &c. *a* **1834** COLERIDGE *Method* iii, We call those [sciences] *mixed* in which certain ideas of the mind are applied to the general properties of bodies. **1835** URE *Philos. Manuf.* 2 The finest model of an automatic manufacture of mixed chemistry is the five-coloured calico machine.

8. *Path.* Said of cases which present symptoms of two kinds of disease at once.

mixed fever: see quot. 1856. *mixed nævus*, 'one in which the true skin and the subcutaneous connective tissue are both involved' (*Syd. Soc. Lex.*).

1767 GOOCH *Treat. Wounds* I. 275 The assemblage of symptoms will generally be of a mixt nature. **1856** MAYNE *Expos. Lex., Mixed Fever*,..a fever having a mixture of the symptoms of an inflammatory and a typhus fever, being a combination of *Synocha* and *Typhus*. **1897** *Allbutt's Syst. Med.* II. 445 Where the case is marked by a moderate amount of œdema, and a moderate amount of paralysis, it is sometimes called mixed beriberi.

9. Comprising both sexes; involving the presence or co-operation of both sexes. ***mixed school***, one in which girls and boys are taught together.

1644 MILTON *Areop.* (Arb.) 51 Who shall regulat all the mixt conversation of our youth, male and female together, as is the fashion of this Country? **1667** —— *P.L.* IV. 768 Nor in Court Amours, Mixt Dance, or wanton Mask, or Midnight Bal. **1826** D. RAMSAY (*title*) Delineation of a mixed school in regard to its influence in promoting a Christian education. **1863** JOYCE *Sch. Management* 47 A mixed school, in which the girls do not learn needlework, is, so far as the time-table is concerned, the same as a boys' school. **1880** GROVE *Dict. Mus.* II. 339 *Mixed Voices*, the English term for a combination of female and male voices. **1889** BROWNLEE *Lawn-Tennis* 167 Ladies never play carelessly in Mixed Doubles. **1899** *Daily News* 2 Aug. 6/6 He was, he said, a convert to the mixed system in education.

10. *colloq.* Mentally confused, 'muddled'; *esp.* 'muzzy' with drink.

1872 *Leeds Mercury* 29 Aug. (Farmer), 'No, Sir, he was not drunk, and he wornt sober'. 'You say he wasn't drunk?' 'No, Sir, he was mixed'. **1880** *Punch* 4 Sept. 106 Tomkins's First Session... Rather 'mixed' after twenty-one hours' continuous sitting, he says [etc.]. **1882** H. C. MERIVALE *Faucit of B.* II. I. xxiv. 106, I am myself a man of peace, who only carried a gun four times, and grew rather 'mixed' over it.

11. a. Special collocations: † **mixed angle**, one formed by the intersection of a straight line and a curve; **mixed arch**, an arch of three or four centres; **mixed bag**, a heterogeneous collection of people, objects, items, etc.; **mixed bathing**, simultaneous bathing in the same place by people of both sexes; **mixed bed**, a flower bed containing an assortment of plants, arranged in irregular groups; **mixed blessing**, a blessing (BLESSING *vbl. sb.* 4) that has unpleasant elements in it; **mixed blood**, (*a*) descent from two or more races; (*b*) a person of mixed descent; † **mixed body**, a compound body (cf. MIXT *sb.*); **mixed border**, in a garden, a long bed containing a mixture of hardy herbaceous plants and shrubs, hardy and half-hardy plants, bulbs, etc.; **mixed breed**, a cross-breed; **mixed cadence** *Mus.* (see quot.); **mixed-celled** *a. Path.*, involving or containing cells of more than one kind; **mixed chalice**, the sacramental wine with water added to it; **mixed company**, (*a*) company comprising both men and women; (*b*) company comprising people of different classes or characters; **mixed contract** *Civil Law* (see quot.); **mixed crystal** *Physical Chem.*, a homogeneous crystal formed of more than one crystalline substance; **mixed decrement** *Cryst.* (see quot.); **mixed earth** (see quot.); **mixed economy**, an economic system containing both private and state enterprise; **mixed farming**, farming which combines the raising of livestock and the cultivation of arable crops; so ***mixed farm***; † **mixed figure** *Geom.*, one composed of straight lines and curves; **mixed flow**, flow (in a turbine or the like) that consists of two or more types (usu. radial and axial) in succession; usu. *attrib.* (with hyphen); † **mixed fraction** = *mixed number* (*b*); **mixed grill**, a dish consisting of several different grilled or fried items of food; also *fig.*; **mixed language**, a language made up of a mixture of elements from two or more languages; a creolized language; cf. MISCHSPRACHE; **mixed-manned** *a.*, pertaining to or designating a military force comprising people of more than one nationality; so ***mixed manning***; **mixed marriage**, (*a*) a marriage between persons of different religions; (*b*) a marriage between persons of different races; also *transf.* and *fig.*; **mixed media**, (*a*) = *mixed technique*; (*b*) an entertainment, work of art, etc., which combines various media; = MULTI-MEDIA *a.*; also *attrib.* or as *adj.*; **mixed metal**, an alloy; also *fig.* (in quot. *attrib.*); **mixed metaphor**, the combination of two or more inconsistent metaphors in one figure; **mixed mode** *Philos.* (see MODE *sb.* 6); † **mixed money**, money coined of mixed metal; † **mixed motion**, the descending curve of the trajectory of a projectile; **mixed nerve**, a nerve which contains afferent and efferent fibres; **mixed number**, † (*a*) a whole number expressed by two or more Arabic figures (*obs.*); (*b*) a number which consists of an integer and a fraction; **mixed person** *Law* (see quot.: after mod.L. *persona mixta*); **mixed pickles**, vegetables of several kinds pickled together; † **mixed plat** *Geom.*, a surface partly plane and partly curved; **mixed-pressure** *a. Engin.*, applied to a steam turbine powered by both high- and low-pressure steam; **mixed proportion** *Math.* = *mixed ratio*; † **mixed range** = *mixed motion*; **mixed ratio**, †**reason** *Math.* (see quot.); **mixed school** (see 9); **mixed technique** (see quots.); **mixed tithes** (L. *decimæ mixtæ*), tithes partly of the nature of 'personal' and partly of that of 'prædial' tithes, e.g. those of cheese, milk, young animals; **mixed tone**, name of one of the Gregorian tones (= *peregrine tone*); **mixed train**, a railway train made up of both passenger-carriages and goods-waggons; formerly also, a train carrying different classes of passengers.

1594 BLUNDEVIL *Exerc.* IV. i. (1636) 272 Of plaine Angles, .. some are said to be *mixt, because the one line is crooked and the other right. **1702** RALPHSON *Math. Dict.*, Angle mixed or mixtilinear. **1815** J. SMITH *Panorama Sci. & Art* I. 131 *Mixed arches are of 3 centres. **1817** RICKMAN *Archit.* 41 Mixed arches are of three centres, which look nearly like elliptical arches; or of four centres, commonly called the Tudor arch. **1936** C. C. R. MURPHY (*title*) A *mixed bag. **1943** K. TENNANT *Ride on Stranger* (1968) v. 47 This mixed bag began, not ill-naturedly, to re-arrange itself in the seating. **1973** A. BEHREND *Samarai Affair* i. 13 Representatives of the press, a mixed bag in age, but not in sex. **1901** *Graphic* 31 Aug. 268/3 The case against *mixed bathing has passed into the academic or empty stage. **1930** *New Statesman* 27 Dec. 356/1 He..could obtain any sum he pleased for writing on any subject he pleased, from the League of Nations to the ethics of mixed bathing. **1964** M. LASKI in S. Nowell-Smith *Edwardian England* iv. 167 Bexhill where mixed bathing has just [*sc.* circa 1901] been introduced, though the custom will quickly spread. **1871** W. ROBINSON *Hardy Flowers* iii. 13 A *mixed bed, carefully arranged as to the height, and tastefully as to the quality and disposition of the contents. In this kind of bed I should have no band or circle whatever, but simply a careful following out of the mixed principle. **1873** *Young Englishwoman* May 238/1 We hope this year to see a great improvement in the bedding system—mixed beds introduced in the place of those of one sort of plant, and of one colour. **1933** *Discovery* Oct. 309/2 The introduction of European influences may prove a *mixed blessing. **1960** *News Chron.* 21 Sept. 6/3 In theory it was a Good Thing... In practice it turned out a mixed blessing. **1973** *Guardian* 16 June 11/3 Mr Duggan regards Mr Bloom's twin tub machine..as a very mixed blessing; a machine..which..uses the same lot of suds time and time again. **1817** S. BROWN *Western Gazetteer* 244 About one half of the Cherokee nation are of *mixed blood by intermarriages with the white people. **1858** THOREAU in *Atlantic Monthly* Aug. 306/2 The two mixed bloods..went off up the river. **1935** HUXLEY & HADDON *We Europeans* i. 23 If a Scottish or Irish clan is of 'mixed blood', what likelihood is there of purity of descent among the millions that make up the population of any great modern nation? **1960** *Press* (Vancouver) Dec. 13 A new and dominant element, the mixed bloods, descended from French and Scottish fathers and Indian mothers. **1963** A. LUBBOCK *Austral. Roundabout* 125 The largest..group of Aborigines are those, both full and mixed bloods, who have been completely detribalized... There is a fourth group of mixed-blood Aborigines. **1973** *Guardian* 20 June 11/3 The left-overs of the Korean war—the mixed-blood children fathered and then deserted by GIs... Today only 5 per cent of children placed by Harry Holt's [adoption] agency are mixed-bloods. **1656** STANLEY *Hist. Philos.* VI. (*Aristotle*) (1687) 378/2 *Mixt bodies are twofold, imperfect and perfect. **1868** D. THOMSON *Handy Bk. Flower Garden* xii. 326 A *mixed border of hardy and half-hardy plants..would be effective anywhere. **1871** W. ROBINSON *Hardy Flowers* i. 5 The mixed border is capable of infinite variation as to plan as well as to variety of subjects. The most interesting variety is that composed of hardy herbaceous plants, bulbs, and alpine plants. **1899** G. JEKYLL *Wood & Garden* xvi. 200, I have a rather large..mixed border of hardy flowers. **1903** W. ROBINSON *Alpine Flowers* (ed. 3) I. 34 The mixed-border system rightly done enables us to cultivate..many of the more vigorous alpine plants as edgings. **1957** C. LLOYD *Mixed Border* i. 11 The mixed border stands mid-way between two extremes: the shrubbery on the one hand and the herbaceous border on the other. **1970** P. COATS *Flowers in Hist.* 39 'Mixed border' is the fashionable phrase, today, for a border of herbaceous plants with a backing of shrubs. **1974** A. SCOTT-JAMES *Sissinghurst* xiii. 137 At its [*sc.* a wall's] foot is a mixed border.. planted with roses, shrubs, herbaceous flowers and irises. **1775** in *South Carolina Hist. & Geneal. Mag.* (1916) XVII. 99 Breakfasting with his *mixed breed daughters. **1789** P. THICKNESSE *Year's Journey* (ed. 3) II. xlv. 107 If a male or female of this species [*sc.* Orang Outang] were to cohabit with an European of the contrary sex, they would..produce a mixed breed. **1838** H. COLMAN *1st Rep. Agric. Mass.* (Mass. Agric. Survey) 53, I have had some of the full-blood and some of the mixed breed. **1876** STAINER & BARRETT *Dict. Mus. Terms*, **Mixed Cadence*, an old name for a cadence, consisting of a subdominant followed by a dominant and tonic chord; so called because the characteristic chords of the plagal and authentic cadences succeed each other. **1908** *Practitioner* Feb. 235 Leucocythaemia..may be qualified by such descriptive titles as *mixed-celled leucocythaemia..or lymphocytic leucocythaemia. **1964** S. DUKE-ELDER *Parsons' Dis. Eye* (ed. 14) xxv. 369 The cells [of a melanoma of the choroid] are usually spindle-shaped; they may be cylindrical or palisade-like, arranged in columns or around blood vessels, or even endothelial in appearance; most tumours are mixed-celled. **1877** J. D. CHAMBERS *Div. Worship* 244 The course of the Church of England in respect of the *Mixed Chalice. **1816** JANE AUSTEN *Emma* II. xvii. 329 Walk half-a-mile to another man's house, for the sake of being in *mixed company till bed-time. **1820** HAZLITT in *London Mag.* Sept. 253 The conversation of authors..is better than any other. That of mixed company becomes utterly intolerable. **1901** G. B. SHAW *Three Plays for Puritans* 305 As far as my social experience goes (and I have kept very mixed company) there is no class in English society in which a good deal of Drinkwater pronunciation does not pass unchallenged save by the expert phonetician. **1973** A. BROINOWSKI *Take One Ambassador* ix. 131 Nance Donnelly ..objected..to jokes about sex in mixed company. It was alright, a bit of dirt between men... But not with ladies present. **1860** WHARTON *Law Lex.* (ed. 2), **Mixed contract*, one in which one of the parties confers a benefit on the other, and requires of the latter something of less value than what he has given; as a legacy charged with something of less value than the legacy itself. **1892** *Jrnl. Chem. Soc.* LXII. I. 265 (*heading*) Solubility of *mixed crystals, especially of two isomorphous substances. **1916** R. H. RASTALL *Agric. Geol.* i. 4 Many of the most important rock-forming minerals are not pure chemical compounds; they are to be regarded rather as mixtures of various compounds possessing the property of isomorphism; in other words they are mixed crystals. **1952** T. L. TIPPELL tr. *Guinier's X-Ray Crystallogr. Technol.* viii. 207 There are substances which can never be classified; these are mixed crystals (solid solutions) whose unit cell size varies continuously with their composition. **1963** C. R. BERRY et al. in J. J. Gilman *Art & Sci. Growing Crystals* xii. 229 Mixed crystals of AgCl and AgBr..have been grown. **1823** H. J. BROOKE *Introd. Crystallogr.* 21 A *mixed decrement is one in which unequal numbers of molecules are omitted in height and in breadth, neither of the numbers being a multiple of the other, such as three in height and two in breadth, or four in height and three in breadth. **1796** KIRWAN *Elem. Min.* (ed. 2) I. 370 Earths, resulting from the union of earths, or sands, are called *mixed, because the ingredients..may in great measure be mechanically separated. *Ibid.* 371 The only mixed earths, to which peculiar names have been assigned, are loam and mould. **1938** *Encycl. Brit. Bk. of Year* 171/2 Under this *mixed economy there is a large and developed system of trade unionism among producers, and another.. system of co-operative societies among consumers. **1949** E. ESTORICK *Stafford Cripps* xix. 362 Cripps' role as the 'master planner of Britain's mixed economy' now had its international complement. **1973** *Guardian* 1 June 12/2 Neither Lonrho's shareholders nor Labour's fundamentalists provide an argument for abandoning the mixed economy. **1892** W. E. SWANTON *Notes on N.Z.* ii. 89 The farm upon which, as in England, both sheep and cattle are carried and also crops are grown..is what is generally called a '*mixed farm'. **1917** C. S. ORWIN *Determination of Farming Costs* ii. 13 The analytical method is probably more useful in connexion with the highly-developed mixed farms of this country. **1942** *E. African Ann. 1941–2* 128/2 Friends who own a mixed farm ask us over. The first signs of their successful management are the calves... This is also a most successful pyrethrum farm. **1973** *Country Life* 15 Mar. 713/2 In the southern region of England..the average price of mixed farms of 10–49 acres with vacant possession..rose to £915 an acre. **1872** *Trans. Illinois Dept. Agric.* IX. 66 The majority of farmers, fruit-growers or others, generally succeed best by what is called *mixed farming. **1908** KIPLING *Lett. to Family* vi. 52 Providence..did not intend everlasting wheat in this section [in Canada]... Are you interested in mixed farming? **1913** W. K. HARRIS *Outback in Austral.* xxiv. 169 The district is an ideal one for 'mixed farming' (wheat and sheep). **1959** A. MCLINTOCK *Descr. Atlas N.Z.* p. xiv, Typical of the [Canterbury] plains is the patch-work of fields, indicative of a system of mixed farming, with supplementary fodder crops being necessary for stock. **1704** J. HARRIS *Lex. Techn.* I, **Figures Mixt*, are such as are bounded partly by right Lines, and partly by crooked ones, as a Semicircle. **1889** *Mixed-flow [see AXIAL *a.* 4]. **1958** *Engineering* 21 Mar. 376/1 The runner vane shape is of particular importance, especially in mixed-flow machines, where the vanes are three-dimensional surfaces. At present it is possible only in the case of axial-flow machines to define runner vane shapes in a systematic way. **1969** *Trans. Inst. Engin. & Shipbuilders Scotl.* CXII. 221 (*heading*) Mixed flow pumps and fans. **1706** W. JONES *Syn. Palmar. Matheseos* 91 To Reduce an Improper Fraction into an Integer, or *Mixt Fraction. **1913** W. PETT-RIDGE (*title*) *Mixed grill. **1922** A. HUXLEY *Mortal Coils* 201 'Two mixed grills,' I said..to the waiter. **1959** *Good Food Guide* 205 The best dishes are such things as sauté river trout, mixed grill and cold turkey. **1973** 'D. HALLIDAY' *Dolly & Starry Bird* xvii. 258 The whip..was pointing to me. I was wondering, if I got marked like a mixed grill, whether Charles would still love me. **1973** *Times Lit. Suppl.* 21 Dec. 1555/3 The audience will be a mixed-grill of faculty, students, alumni, businessmen, and perhaps a few who have simply wandered in from the rain. **1888** H. SWEET *Hist. Eng. Sounds* 55 A very intimate mixture of two languages is always a prelude to the complete extinction of the weaker one, and this is why few ..of these thoroughly *mixed languages become permanently fixed. **1922** O. JESPERSEN *Lang.* xi. 224 These [pidgin] languages are not 'mixed languages' in the proper sense of that term. **1932** W. L. GRAFF *Lang.* II. x. 390 In several instances English used by people of an entirely different linguistic type results in a mixed or creolized language, the best known example being the so-called *pidgin English* of the Far East. **1972** R. ANTTILA *Introd. Historical & Compar. Ling.* xiii. 171 The various kinds of borrowing, that is, vocabulary, adstratum phonetics, and syntax, have led to the notion of a *mixed language*. **1963** *Economist* 16 Mar. 980/3 The *mixed-manned, mixed-money nuclear force that Mr Merchant is..trying to create. **1964** *Ann. Reg. 1963* 28 On June 4 Admiral C. V. Ricketts..arrived in London to sell the mixed-manned fleet to a reluctant Mr Thorneycroft. **1963** *Times* 11 June 13/6, I fail to understand the fuss about *mixed manning for the proposed Nato nuclear surface fleet. **1698–9** *Mixed marriage [see WORLD *sb.* 4b]. **1829** K. H. DIGBY *Broad Stone of Honour: Godefridus* xviii. 212 They are the last to admit those monstrous and impious plans..which divide the children of mixed marriages, by training some to receive as truth, what others are to protest against as error. **1851** HT. MARTINEAU *Hist. Peace* v. xi. (1877) III. 434 The Catholic clergy were beginning to object to the mixed marriages which they had hitherto sanctioned. **1961** C. MCCULLERS *Clock without Hands* ix. 178 The conditions of the Negro in the North are appalling—mixed marriages, nowhere to live and lay his head. **1962** *Sunday Times* 8 July 32/5 David Franklin's libretto reinterprets the Orpheus legend in terms of a mixed

marriage between a white composer and a coloured cabaret-star turned opera-singer. **1966** *New Statesman* 15 Apr. 548/3 In this mixed marriage, she brings her talent from the world of working-girl and art student, weds it to the dandy showmanship that goes with a certain kind of aristocracy. **1970** J. BROWN *Un-melting Pot* vii. 105 Even mixed marriages between Jamaicans and Barbadians. **1972** *Listener* 21 Dec. 854/3 They understand very well the power of the Catholic Church, and the processes by which it is maintained: clerical control of the educational system, the mixed-marriage laws and the preservation of high fertility rates. **1962** R. G. HAGGAR *Dict. Art Terms* 214/2 **Mixed media*, painting with water colors and paste, Indian ink, oil color, crayon, or some similar combination. **1970** BURTON & LANE *New Directions* iii. 66 The most extensive development of mixed media work are the Theatre Folk Ballads which Charles Parker has developed. **1972** G. F. BROMMER *Drawing* iv. 49 Paul Klee experimented freely with mixed media, as did his contemporaries in the German Bauhaus. **1972** *Guardian* 24 June 9/2 The newer, mixed-media work using a lot of sound, space, smell, and participation. **1973** *Sunday Times* 28 Oct. 37/1 (Advt.), Don't miss Contemporary Dance Theatre in Robert Cohan's *Stages*! A mixed media dance production with Bob Downes open music. **1617** MORYSON *Itin.* I. 154 A statua of a woman, made of *mixt metal (richer then brasse, vulgarly called *di Bronzo*). **1756–7** tr. *Keysler's Trav.* (1760) I. 283 A blue kind of mixed metal, not unlike varnished steel. **1800** LAMB *Let. to Coleridge* (end of year), It seems the Doctor is invariably against the use of broken or *mixed metaphor. **1602** in J. Simon *Irish Coins* (1749) 104 Three score pounds in *mixt monies of the new standerd of this realme. **1603** *Ibid.* 109 To reduce the base mixt monyes of three ounces fyne to their value in silver. **1615** SIR J. DAVIES *Cases* 18 La Roigne Elizabeth, pur payer les gages del Army..que fuit mainteine..a suppresser le rebellion de Tyrone, causast vn graund quantity de Mixt Moneyes..destre coine in le Tower de London. **1669** STURMY *Mariner's Mag.* v. xii. 68 (*plate*), The *mixt or Crooked Motion. **1878** FOSTER *Phys.* III. i. 390 All the spinal nerves are *mixed nerves, composed of afferent and efferent, of motor and sensory fibres. **1542** RECORDE *Gr. Artes* (1575) 53 That number is called *myxt, that containeth articles, or at the least one article, and a digitte. *Ibid.* 324 Mixt numbers (that is whole numbers with fractions). **1690** LEYBOURN *Curs. Math.* 3 If many Digits alone, or many Digits and Cyphers stand together.. promiscuously placed one among another, such Numbers are called Mixt or Compound Numbers. *c* **1865** in *Circ. Sci.* I. 443/2, $2\frac{1}{3}$; $3\frac{5}{7}$, &c., are *mixed numbers.* **1660** R. COKE *Power & Subj.* 209 The King is a *mixt person, because he hath Ecclesiastical and Temporal jurisdiction. **1857** J. H. WALSH *Dom. Econ.* 407 For *Mixed Pickles, prepare [etc.]. **1551** RECORDE *Pathw. Knowl.* I. Defin., And if it be partlie plaine, and partlie crooked, then is it called a *Myxte platte. **1909** *Engineering* 5 Feb. 198/1 A turbine of what is called a *mixed-pressure type, having high-pressure stages, in which the live steam may..keep the turbine running during the periods of insufficient supply of exhaust steam. **1929** T. M. NAYLOR *Steam Turbines* i. 9 Mixed pressure turbines use both high-pressure and exhaust or low-pressure steam. Often the exhaust steam supplied is intermittent, and so to obtain constant power from the turbine, high-pressure steam is admitted and it is controlled by a governor to enable the turbine to work at constant power. **1971** B. SCHARF *Engin. & its Lang.* xv. 209 We may..distinguish between straight condensing turbines, pass-out turbines, back-pressure turbines, exhaust turbines and mixed-pressure turbines. **1704** J. HARRIS *Lex. Techn.* I, *Mixt Reason*, or **Proportion*. **1669** STURMY *Mariner's Mag.* v. xii. 75 Every Shot made upon the Level hath the *mixt or Crooked-Range thereof. **1727–52** CHAMBERS *Cycl.*, **Mixed ratio*, or *proportion*. **1695** ALINGHAM *Geom. Epit.* 19 **Mixt Reason*, is the comparing the sum of the Antecedent and Consequent, to the difference of the Antecedent and Consequent. **1935** E. NEUHAUS tr. *Doerner's Materials of Artist* v. 240 Painting with tempera into wet resin-oil color (*mixed technique). This technique is better suited to a deliberate, stylistic type of painting. **1969** R. MAYER *Dict. Art Terms & Techniques* 246/1 *Mixed technique*, in painting, the technique of combining tempera colors with paints of an oleoresinous medium... Mixed technique first became known in the U.S. and Britain in 1934. **1531** *Dial. Laws Eng.* II. I. 113 A *mixte tythe is properly of calues, lambes, pygges, and suche other that come parte of the grounde that thei be fedde of, & parte of the kepynge industrye, and ouersyght of the owners. *a* **1634** COKE *Inst.* II. (1642) 490 Now of tithes there be three kindes, prediall, personall, and mixt. **1672** *Cowell's Interpr.*, *Mixt Tythes*, Decimæ mixtæ. Are those of Cheese, Milk, &c. and of the young of Beasts. **1844** [W. B. HEATHCOTE] *Canticles* ii, A ninth [tone] is generally added..called '*Mixed'. **1838** *Civil Engin. & Arch. Jrnl.* I. 115/1 The *mixed train which leaves Birmingham at half-past four. **1839** *Bradshaw's Railway Time Tables* 25 Oct., The Mixed Trains consist of First Class Carriages carrying six inside, and of 2d class carriages open at the side. **1850** LARDNER *Railway Econ.* 481 Mixed trains, by which goods and passengers are indifferently carried. **1866** W. COLLINS *Armadale* I. 268 In the crowd and confusion caused by the starting of a large mixed train.

b. In Combs. used *attrib.*

1908 J. M. SULLIVAN *Criminal Slang* 16 *Mixed-ale oration*, a cheap political harangue containing bad English grammar. *Mixed-ale philosopher*, a drunken know it all. **1948** *Penguin Music Mag.* June 49 The best members of these choirs.. incorporated in..a secular mixed-voice choir. **1956** *Railway Mag.* Nov. 729/2 Many Drummond mixed-traffic 4-4-0 tender engines were tried on this route. **1963** *Guardian* 28 Jan. 7/4 Everyone asks Mr Morris..how mixed-ability classes affect the number of grammar school entrances. **1963** *Daily Tel.* 25 June 1/1 President Kennedy and Dr. Adenauer agreed in Bonn to-night that the proposed mixed-crew NATO nuclear force was 'a good instrument for serving all members of the alliance in combining their defence efforts'. **1964** *Economist* 17 Oct. 228/2 A.. contribution to the mixed-fleet command. **1969** *Jane's Freight Containers 1968–69* 444 A racing Mini being loaded into a mixed-traffic, British United Airways, VC 10. **1971** *Guardian* 17 Sept. 1/5 A delegation of six mixed-race Rhodesians. **1974** *Times* 21 May 3/1 Some teachers found that their brighter pupils started slacking when they were put in mixed-ability classes.

c. mixed up, mixed-up, involved, embroiled, intermingled; (mentally) confused, unbalanced, neurotic; hence **mixed-up-ness**, confusion. Cf. MIX *v.* 6.

1862 QUEEN VICTORIA *Let.* 15 Jan. in R. Fulford *Dearest Mama* (1968) 41, I only want your advice—not to get you further mixed up. **1884** 'MARK TWAIN' *Huck. Finn* xlii. 432 Aunt Sally she was one of the mixed-upest looking persons I ever see. **1888** 'R. BOLDREWOOD' *Robbery under Arms* II. viii. 144 How were any police..to keep the run of a few men ..among such a mixed-up mob? **1903** H. JAMES *Ambassadors* VI. xv. 206 How comes Chad so mixed up, anyway? **1927** H. T. LOWE-PORTER tr. *T. Mann's Magic Mountain* I. iv. 123 'A fine mixed-up state of affairs,' said Hans Castorp. **1937** *New Yorker* 23 Jan. 12/1 M. Dali, standing alone and thinking dark, mixed-up thoughts. **1939** D. PARKER *Here Lies* 61 I've been all sort of mixed up to-day. .. Everything so strange. **1945** G. ENDORE *Methinks the Lady* (1947) xi. 264 Such confusion, such mental mixed-up-ness, occurs at times in all of us. **1955**, etc. [see CRAZY *a.* 4 f]. **1966** J. BINGHAM *Double Agent* x. 157 Poor damned old mixed-up queer. **1967** A. LASKI *Seven Other Years* xi. 154 It wasn't even as if she had made some kind of distinction between God and Christ and seen One as protecting her and the Other being Them: just a general mixed-upness. **1973** C. BONINGTON *Next Horizon* xi. 157 Layton was like a big, slightly mixed-up puppy, in need of love and care.

mixedly ('mɪkstlɪ), *adv.* Now *rare.* [-LY².]

1. In a mixed manner; after the manner of a mixture or combination; †conjointly.

1570 BILLINGSLEY *Euclid* XII. ii. 361 Note the manner of the drift in this demonstration and construction, mixtly. **1656** S. H. *Golden Law* 56 The Israelites liv'd together in Goshen,..and not mixtly or scatteringly amongst the Egyptians. **1839** *Fraser's Mag.* XIX. 127 He lived..with the revolution, revolutionally;..with the directory, directorially; with the consulate, mixedly. **1860** I. TAYLOR *Ultimate Civiliz.* 111 In such instances the Governing Power pleases itself in thinking of men—mixedly, and alternately—as brutes and as babies.

†**b.** Promiscuously; without discrimination.

1597 BEARD *Theatre God's Judgem.* (1612) 333 He spared neither noble or ignoble, but mixtly sent them to their graues, without respect of cause or justice.

2. With intermixture of other qualities, elements, etc.; not purely, simply, or absolutely.

1579 G. HARVEY *Letter-bk.* (Camden) 66 Anye notable thinge..that..is not ether merely or mixtely outlandish. **1594** HOOKER *Eccl. Pol.* I. x. §10 The one sort [of laws] wee may for distinctions sake call mixedly, and the other meerely Humane. **1653** *Apol. J. Goodwin* 4 Things of a Religious nature are absolutely such, or mixtly.

3. *Math.* In mixed proportion (see MIXED 11).

1695 ALINGHAM *Geom. Epit.* 19 If $A : B :: C : D$ then mixtly as $A + B : A - B :: C + D : C - D$. **1709** J. WARD *Introd. Math.* II. vii. (1734) 191 If Four Quantities are Proportionals they will also be Proportional in Alternation, Inversion, Composition, Division, Conversion, and Mixtly.

mixedness ('mɪkstnɪs). [f. MIXED + -NESS.] The quality of being mixed.

1668 WILKINS *Real Char.* II. i. §3. 28. **1727** BAILEY vol. II, *Miscellaneousness*, mixture or mixedness together without Order. **1881** J. HAWTHORNE *Fort. Fool* I. xxxv, The reservations produce..that mixedness in human characters which must more or less vitiate any..generalisation. **1893** *Spectator* 15 Apr. 490/1 The mixedness of American dinner-parties.

mixel(l, obs. forms of MIXHILL *dial.*

mixen ('mɪksən). Now *dial.* or *arch.* Also 1 **micxsen, meoxin, -en**, 1, 4–5 **myxen**, 3–5 **mixne**, 4 **myxne**, 5 **myxon**, 6 **myxson, mickeson, mickson**, 4–5, 7, 9 **mexen**, 7–9 *dial.* **mixon**, 9 *dial.* **maxon, -en.** [OE. *mixen* str. fem.:—prehistoric **mihsinnja*, f. **mihso-*: see MIX *sb.*¹ and -EN³. A similar formation on the parallel stem **mihstu-* (Goth. *maihstus*, OHG. *mist* dung) is OHG. *mistunnea* dunghill.]

1. A place where dung and refuse is laid; a dung-hill or laystall; also, a heap of dung, earth, compost, etc. used for manure; †dung and refuse from sheds and cow-stalls, etc. (*obs.*).

c **950** *Lindisf. Gosp.* Luke xiii. 8 Ic delfo ymb hia & ic sendo micxseno. *a* **1000** ÆLFRIC *Sigewulfi Interrog.* xlix. (1888) 16 On þære nyðemestan fleringe wæs heora gangpyt & heora myxen. *c* **1386** CHAUCER *Pars. T.* ¶837 Though that hooly writ speke of horrible synne, certes hooly writ may nat been defouled, namoore than the sonne that shyneth on the Mixne [*v.rr.* myxen, myxene, mexen]. **1480** *Robt. Devyll* 38 Into a foule donge myxen he her caryed. **1581** in *5th Rep. Hist. MSS. Comm.* I. App. 579/2 Let all the myxsons and annoyances be caryed away byffore the spryng do cum. **1596** HARINGTON *Metam. Ajax* 42 By turning a streame of water on the mickesons, he [Hercules] scowred away that in a weeke, that an hundred could scant haue done in a yeare. **1611** COTGR., *Fumier*, a mexen, dung-hill, heape of dung. **1622** MABBE tr. *Aleman's Guzman d'Alf.* II. 53 The.. rottennest mixen that was in all the street. **1688** R. HOLME *Armoury* II. 173/1 A muck-hill is the place where the Dung is laid till it be carried into the field to manure the ground: some call it a Mixon. **1794** J. CLARK *Agric. Heref.* 23 The makings of mixens, however, is not properly attended to in general. **1865** GOSSE *Land & Sea* 12 Great mixens outside the doors, strewn with the shells of enormous limpets. **1881** BLACKMORE *Christowell* xvi, He was turning up a mixen in a meadow near the lane. *a* **1887** JEFFERIES *Field & Hedgerow* (1889) 169 He had dug up a gallon of snakes' eggs in the 'maxen'.

b. *transf.* and *fig.*

1609 BP. W. BARLOW *Answ. Nameless Cath.* 337 The Epistle would needes..haue this mixen stirred. **1684** BP. W. LLOYD *Hist. Acc. Ch. Govt.* Pref. (b), The *Gesta Pontificum*, that Mixen of ill-contrived Forgeries, which perhaps was made before Bede's time. **1880** T. HARDY *Trumpet-Major* xxxvi. III. 151 We will let it be buried in eternal mixens of forgetfulness.

c. Proverbs. †***a cock on his own mixen***: cf. DUNGHILL *sb.* 1 b. ***better wed over the mixen than over the moor***: 'better marry a neighbour than a stranger from distant parts' (E.D.D.).

a **1225** *Ancr. R.* 140 Ase me seið, 'þet coc is kene on his owune mixenne'. *a* **1661** FULLER *Worthies, Cheshire* (1662) I. 174 Better wed over the Mixon then over the Moor. **1710** *Brit. Apollo* No. 12. 3/2. **1818** SCOTT *Hrt. Midl.* xxxi, 'Better wed over the mixen as over the moor', as they say in Yorkshire. **1874** T. HARDY *Madding Crowd* xxii. I. 250.

2. A term of abuse or reproach to a woman or child: see quot. 1887. *dial.*

1764 FOOTE *Mayor of G.* I. Wks. 1799 I. 173 Who told you as much, Mrs. Mixen? **1887** T. DARLINGTON *Folk-Sp. S. Cheshire*, *Mexen*, *Mixen*,..a term of reproach to a female. 'Yo little mixen'. It seems to have originated as a comic substitute for *vixen*.

3. *attrib.*, as ***mixen-cart, -heap, -hole***; **mixen-varlet** (quasi-*arch.*), a term of abuse for a man.

1610 *Mirr. Mag.*, *King Madan* xi, I thinke the clowne that driues the mixen-cart Hath better hap than Princes such as I. **1886** *Cheshire Gloss.*, *Mixen-hole*, a midden hole. **1895** CROCKETT *Men of Moss-Hags* i. 13 Faugh, keep wide from me, mixen-varlet! **1903** F. HALL in *Eng. Dial. Dict.*, *Mixen-heap*, a dunghill.

mixer ('mɪksə(r)). [f. MIX *v.* + -ER ¹.]

1. a. One who mixes (in various senses of the vb.); *spec.* in various manufactures, the workman who performs the operation of 'mixing'.

1611 COTGR., *Meslangeur*, a mingler, mixer, blender. **1828** SCOTT *Tales of Grandf.* Ser. II. xlvii. (1841) 207/2 The wretched mixer of the poison was tried and executed. **1854** LONGF. *Catawba Wine* ix, To the sewers and sinks With all such drinks, And after them tumble the mixer. **1884** *Manch. Exam.* 16 Sept. 7/1 Professional mixers [of cotton] had been less successful in their operations. **1897** *Allbutt's Syst. Med.* II. 928 The 'mixers' and 'dippers' are particularly liable to suffer from phossy jaw [in match factories].

b. One who mixes drinks; a bartender. orig. *U.S.*

1858 LONGFELLOW *Catawba Wine* in *Atlantic Monthly* Jan. 271 To the sewers and sinks With all such drinks, And after them tumble the mixer. **1919** T. K. HOLMES *Man from Tall Timber* viii. 93 He..drank several insidious concoctions of the hotel's most famous 'mixer'. **1934** M. ALLINGHAM *Death of Ghost* xxiii. 262 There was too much gin in the cocktails, he decided, and reflected that the fault was a common one among unprofessional mixers. **1939** C. ISHERWOOD *Goodbye to Berlin* 21 Bobby is a mixer at a west-end bar.

c. *Cinemat.* and *Broadcasting.* One who operates the mixer (sense 2 b) during sound recording and is responsible for balancing different signal sources and producing transitions from one source to another.

1929 F. GREEN *Film finds its Tongue* xiii. 186 A 'mixing booth' or monitor room had been built about 15 feet up... It had glass sides through which the 'mixer' could view everything that was going on. **1948** L. LEVY *Music for Movies* iv. 35 Just before writing this I had been sitting at the control desk in a mixer's cabinet during the rehearsals for a new picture. **1957** MANVELL & HUNTLEY *Technique Film Music* iv. 183 Regular consultation with the Music Mixer is necessary to ensure that the complete intention of the composer is..being registered on the sound-track.

2. a. A machine or mechanical contrivance for mixing. Also with defining word. *spec.* a domestic electrical appliance for mixing foods, ingredients for cookery, etc. See also *cake-mixer*, *electric mixer*.

1876 *Catal. Sci. App. S. Kens. Mus.* (1877) 248 Mixoscope (colour-mixer). **1883** *Fisheries Exhib. Catal.* p. lxxxiii, Patent mixer for mixing hard water supply and lime water. **1898** *Allbutt's Syst. Med.* V. 443 The smaller end of the stirrer may be used to remove the drop of diluted blood from the mixer to the cell. **1901** *Westm. Gaz.* 1 July 7/3 The fall of a workman into a sugar mixer. **1957** M. GAIR *Sapphires on Wednesday* xi. 134 It was a kitchen,..American style, complete with refrigerator, dishwasher, mixer, and garbage disposal unit. **1960** *Harper's Bazaar* Oct. 98/2 You must become accustomed to your oven, to your mixer, to your omelette pan. **1974** *Trafford Catal.* Spring–Summer 781/1 Three machines in one—a mixer, a liquidiser and a mincer.

b. *Cinemat.*, *Broadcasting*, etc. A device designed to receive two or more separate signals, from microphones or other sources, and combine them (usu. in variable proportions) in a single output.

1929 F. GREEN *Film finds its Tongue* xi. 171 When more than one microphone was used, each of them had an amplifying dial for monitoring. A panel containing more than one such dial was called a 'Mixer'. **1935** NILSON & HORNUNG *Pract. Radio Communication* viii. 356 The program fed into the mixer does not always come directly from a microphone but may be fed in from a phonograph pick-up. **1962** A. NISBETT *Technique Sound Studio* ix. 152 Where no mixer is available, it may be that linking music, etc., can be cut in by editing the tape; but I would regard a simple mixer—with two faders—as the very minimum for creative programme work. **1968** C. N. G. MATTHEWS *Tape Recording* xi. 109 To do full justice to any group of instrumentalists you need more than one microphone and also a mixer.

c. *Electronics.* A valve or circuit that produces an output signal containing frequencies equal to the sum and the difference of the frequencies of

two input signals. Freq. *attrib.*, as ***mixer tube, valve***, etc.

1936 *Proc. IRE* XXIV. 208 (*caption*) Typical mixer circuit using 6L7 tube. *Ibid.* 210 The conversion conductance of a mixer tube. **1938** F. E. TERMAN *Fund. Radio* ix. 249 The heterodyne detector.., commonly referred to as first detector, converter, or mixer, is required to develop a difference frequency..by combining the incoming radio wave with a local oscillation differing in frequency by the desired amount. **1952** E. ARMITAGE *Wireless Fund.* xviii. 324 The frequency-changing stage of a superhet consists of two parts—(1) a beat oscillator generating a signal of constant amplitude, and (2) a mixer valve into which are fed, on to different grids, both the aerial signal and the beat oscillator signal. **1968** *Radio Communication Handbk.* (ed. 4) 48/2 Any non-linear circuit element will act as a mixer, that is to say if frequencies f_1, f_2 are combined in the element, frequencies $f_1, f_2, f_1 + f_2$ and $f_1 - f_2$ will be present in the output.

3. A person in respect of his capacity for mixing with others; a sociable person; esp. ***good mixer***, one who mixes readily with others. orig. *U.S.*

1896 ADE *Artie* xii. 105 I'm a good mixer and I've kind o' got next to the live ones. **1904** W. H. SMITH *Promoters* xx. 287 He was a most excellent 'mixer', told a story well [etc.]. **1917** WODEHOUSE *Man with Two Left Feet* 91 Some men are shy and some men are mixers. **1925** W. S. MAUGHAM in *Good Housekeeping* Sept. 15/2 He was a good mixer, and in three days he knew everyone on the ship. **1930** R. MACAULAY *Staying with Relations* xix. 281 Good plumbers, but poor mixers; that's what we are. **1937** [see CEREBROTONIC *a.* and *sb.*]. **1955** *Times* 18 Aug. 4/6 A man who is a ready mixer and with a natural flair for salesmanship may make £1,000 a year. **1967** N. FREELING *Strike Out* 148 You needed to..get on well with all the murderers? A 'good mixer'—a 'good team man'. **1975** *Listener* 24 July 126/3 He is neither so astute a tactician nor so gifted a mixer with his own men.

4. A social gathering for making people acquainted with each other. *U.S. colloq.*

1916 *Dialect Notes* IV. 277 A very successful mixer was given on Charter day. **1948** *Downers Grove* (Illinois) *Reporter* 21 Oct. 1/8 The Trojan Fathers Fall Mixer will take place Tuesday, Oct. 26 at the high school auditorium.

5. A drink with which an alcoholic liquor is diluted, as soda water, etc.; an alcoholic drink used in cocktails. Also *attrib.* orig. *U.S.*

1938 D. BAKER *Young Man with Horn* III. i. 147 They worked all possible combinations of bootleg gin and mixers, orange juice, lemon juice, grapefruit juice..and..root beer. **1948** *Sun* (Baltimore) 1 Jan. 15/1 In the case of the Tom Collins, it's largely a matter of which mixer should be used, plain soda or ginger ale. **1961** *Encounter* XVI. v. 81 Using Coca-cola as what the Americans call 'a mixer'. **1961** *Guardian* 21 Nov. 13/1 Vodka has become, like gin, an international 'mixer',..used to make martinis or to drink with tonic water. **1965** *Economist* 11 Dec. 1251/1 It [*sc.* Beechams] has just introduced a number of 'mixer' drinks to compete with Schweppes. **1968** *Daily Tel.* (Colour Suppl.) 13 Dec. 41/4 Port was traditionally enjoyed here as a mixer —mulled, say, in the way Dr Johnson liked it, with spices, orange, and cloves. **1975** T. TEAL tr. *Sjöwall & Wahlöö's Cop Killer* vii. 69 'Do you drink?' 'Yes... But..not lukewarm vodka with no mixer.'

6. A trouble-maker. *slang.*

1938 PARTRIDGE *Dict. Slang* (ed. 2) 1014/1 He's a reg'lar mixer! **1964** J. BURKE *Hard Day's Night* i. 21 He's a king mixer. *Ibid.* iv. 84 'The old mixer,' growled Paul. 'Come on —we'll have to put him right.' *Ibid.* v. 116 'Look,' said Paul slowly and deliberately, 'he's a mixer and a trouble-maker!' **1966** A. E. LINDOP *I start Counting* xviii. 226, I knew what a mixer she was, and I knew she was not capable of keeping a secret.

7. *attrib.*, as **mixer tap**, a tap through which both hot and cold water can be drawn in various proportions; **mixer valve**, a valve by which the proportions of the fluids or gases in a mixture are regulated.

1936 *Archit. Rev.* LXXX. 325/2 Mixer taps or hand showers are worth the extra cost of £2 or £3 they entail. **1972** *House & Garden* Dec.-Jan. 85/3 Mixer taps by Trufords..gold-plated. **1904** *Electr. World & Engin.* 2 Jan. 22/1 This magnet controls a compressed air valve, and this compressed air valve in turn controls a large mixer valve.

So **'mixeress**, a female mixer.

1830 W. TAYLOR *Hist. Surv. Germ. Poetry* II. 480 A poison-mixeress Ought not to sully England's royal throne.

mixey-maxy, variant of MIXTY-MAXTY.

†**'mix-grass.** *Obs. rare.* [? f. MIX *v.*] (See first quot.) Also *attrib.*

1778 [W. MARSHALL] *Minutes Agric., Digest* 73 By Mix-grass is here meant a compound of White-Clover, Rye-Grass, and Trefoil. *Ibid., Observ.* 32 It was..stacked with the mix-grass hay of Norwood. *Ibid.* 80 No Manure has this year been laid on Mixgrass-Leys.

Mix-Hellene (mɪksheˈliːn). [ad. Gr. *μιξέλλην*, f. *μιξ(ο)-* MIXO- + *Ἕλλην* HELLENE.] A person of mixed Greek and barbarian blood.

1856 GROTE *Greece* II. xcviii. XII. 645 Taking into pay a semi-Hellenic population in their neighbourhood (Mix-Hellenes, like the Liby-Phenicians in Africa). **1875** LOWELL *Spenser* Pr. Wks. 1890 IV. 286 The descendants of the earlier English settlers had degenerated as much as the Mix-Hellenes who disgusted the Latin poet.

mixhill (ˈmɪkshɪl). *dial.* Forms: 6 mixel(l, 9 maxul, 8- maxhill, mixhill. [f. MIX *sb.*[1] + HILL *sb.*] A dunghill, mixen.

1552 HULOET, Mixell and dunghyll. **1570** LEVINS *Manip.* 56/29 A Mixel, *stercorarium.* **1763** *Museum Rust.* I. lxii. 261 They generally make a maxhill on some corner of the land. **1846** HANNAM in *Jrnl. R. Agric. Soc.* VII. II. 589 Part of the ground..was manured from a mix-hill. **1887** *Kentish Gloss.*, *Maxul*, a dungheap.

mixible (ˈmɪksɪb(ə)l), *a.* ? Obs. *rare.* [f. MIX *v.* + -IBLE. Cf. MIXABLE, MISCIBLE, MIXTIBLE.] Capable of being mixed.

1607 J. DAVIES *Summa Totalis* C j b, Mixion vnites Things mixible by change; Or intermingling of their Substances: Things mixible, are they, which, though they range, Are yet contain'd in eithers Essences. **1800** *Med. Jrnl.* IV. 25 It being known that the sulphuric and septic acids are mixible with each other.

mixie-maxie, variant of MIXTY-MAXTY.

mixing (ˈmɪksɪŋ), *vbl. sb.* [-ING[1].] **a.** The action of the verb MIX. Also with *up* (see MIX *v.* 6).

1599 B. JONSON *Cynthia's Rev.* II. i, I cannot abide any thing that sauours the poore ouer-worne cut..I must haue variety, I: this mixing in fashion I hate it worse, then to burne juniper in my chamber. **1611** COTGR., *Mistionnement*, a mixing, mingling [etc.]. **1683** TRYON *Way to Health* xix. 615 These ought to be the Chief Ends and Considerations of every man in Marriage, and not the mixing of Mannours, and joyning together of Farmes. **1813** VANCOUVER *Agric. Devon* 213 The quantity of lime expended in these mixings being voluntary. **1875** KNIGHT *Dict. Mech.*, *Mixing*, (*Cloth.*) uniting wool of different colors for *mixed cloth*, called *medleys.* **1890** *Spectator* 6 Dec., The mixing-up of a local control with the working of the Purchase Act. **1893** *Athenæum* 25 Nov. 731/2 This mixing..takes place in the arrangement of the stories. **1897** *Encycl. Sport* I. 62 *Mixing*, a deliberate attempt to put in a few running strides when in a walking race.

b. *concr.* in *pl.* (*U.S. slang.*) Mixed drinks.

1861 LOWELL *Biglow P.* Ser. II. i, Le' 's liquor; Gin'ral, you can chalk our friend for all the mixins.

c. *attrib.*, as ***mixing bowl, machine, sieve***, etc. **mixing valve**, a valve in which separate supplies of hot and cold water are mixed together; = *mixer tap.*

1875 KNIGHT *Dict. Mech.*, *Mixing-machine*, Poole's machine for mixing chemicals, fertilizers, etc. *Ibid.*, *Mixing-sieve*, one by which ingredients are intimately combined by sifting together. **1881** *Encycl. Brit.* XII. 841/2 The rubber ..is mechanically incorporated with about one-tenth of its weight of that substance [*sc.* sulphur] by means of the mixing rollers. **1887** MORRIS *Odyss.* IX. 9 The wine-swain from the mixing-bowl filleth up And beareth forth, and poureth the wine in every cup. **1897** F. M. CRAWFORD *Corlione* xxv, Don Atanasio [the apothecary] laid down the broad mixing-knife he was using. **1898** *Allbutt's Syst. Med.* V. 433 The mixing pipette is provided with a rubber nozzle. **1902** R. STURGIS *Dict. Archit.* III. 977 General Morin called attention to the necessity of the 'mixing valve'. **1951** *Good Housek. Home Encycl.* 281/2 *Mixing valves*: These are used mainly for showers and baths. **1973** J. WAINWRIGHT *Pride of Pigs* 59 A corner shower with a mixing valve that really worked.

'mixing, *ppl. a.* [-ING[2].] That mixes.

1730-46 THOMSON *Autumn* 1362 The mind,..where the mixing passions endless shift.

mixion, obs. form of MIXTION.

mixite (ˈmɪksaɪt). *Min.* [Named in 1879 by A. Schrauf, after A. *Mixa*: see -ITE.] 'Hydrous arsenate of copper and bismuth, found in fibrous, green incrustations' (Chester *Dict. Min.* 1896).

1882 *3rd App. to Dana's Min.* 82 Mixite... Occurs with bismuth, ochre, bismutite, and torbernite in the Geistergang at Joachimsthal. Named in honor of Bergrath A. Mixa.

†**'mixitive**, *a. Obs. rare*[−1]. [f. MIX *v.* ? after *fugitive*, etc.] Tending to mix.

1614 W. B. *Philosopher's Banquet* (ed. 2) 26 This mixitiue application of viands.

Mixmaster (ˈmɪksmɑːstə(r)). The proprietary name of a type of electrical food-mixer. Freq. *transf.* and *fig.* (see quots.).

1931 *Good Housekeeping* (N.Y.) Oct. 223/3 (Advt.), See what you get *now* in Mixmaster. A food mixer that beats everything—a juice extractor—an automatic salad oil dripper. **1935** *Official Gaz.* (U.S. Patent Office) 11 June 278/2 Chicago Flexible Shaft Co. *Mixmaster* for Food Mixers, Fruit Juice Extractor, [etc.] filed Nov. 21, 1934. **1946** *Britannica Bk. of Year* (U.S.) 832/2 *Mixmaster*, army bomber propelled by two rear counter-revolving propellers. Made by Douglas Aircraft Co., Inc. **1951** R. MALKIN *Boxcars in Sky* xiii. 156 In the business, they refer jocularly to the helicopter by a number of descriptive names: 'eggbeater', 'windmill', and 'mixmaster', to mention a few. **1963** *Economist* 11 May 537/2 A 'mixmaster' force of ships with American missiles and international crews. **1967** *Punch* 22 Mar. 410/1 On all those important matters our opinions are divided, and so therefore are our teachers; the whole situation is confused in the extreme. The mix-master whirrs, the beaters rotate, but unfortunately the recipe is missing. **1971** M. TAK *Truck Talk* 107 *Mixmaster-special*, any transmission with two shift levers; so named because, in running through the gears, the trucker's hands are constantly in motion.

mixne, obs. form of MIXEN.

‖**mixo-** (ˈmɪksəʊ), repr. Gr. *μιξο-*, f. root of *μιγνύναι* to mix, occurring in many Gr. compounds with the sense 'mixed'; used in a few mod. scientific words founded on Greek analogies, as **mixogamous** (mɪkˈsɒgəməs) *a. Ichth.* [Gr. *γάμ-ος* marriage + -OUS.], (see quot. 1880); **mi'xogamy** *Ichth.*, the condition of being mixogamous; **mixo'haline** *a.* [Gr. *ἁλῖν-ος* of salt], brackish; **mixonephridium, mixonephrium**, in certain annelids, an organ in which the nephridium is combined with the cœlomoduct; **mixopyous** (mɪkˈsɒpɪəs) *a. Med.* [Gr. *μιξό-πυος*, f. *πῦον* pus], 'mingled, or mixed with pus; formerly applied to the urine' (Mayne *Expos. Lex.* 1856); **'mixoscope** [see -SCOPE], the name given to an apparatus for mixing colours; **mixo'scopia, mi'xoscopy** *Psychol.* [ad. G. *mixoskopie* (A. Moll *Die Conträre Sexualempfindung* (1891) v. 136), f. Gr. *σκοπεῖν* to look at], (see quot. 1939); hence **mixo'scopic** *a.* **mixo'trophic** *a.* [see TROPHIC *a.*], 'half-saprophytic' (B. D. Jackson *Gloss. Bot. Terms* 1900). See also MIXOBARBARIC, MIXOLYDIAN, and cf. MIX-HELLENE.

1880 GÜNTHER *Fishes* xiii. 177 The majority of Teleostei are mixogamous—that is, the males and females congregate on the spawning-beds, and..several males attend to the same female, frequently changing from one female to another. **1881** *Athenæum* 15 Jan. 97 Chapter xiii [of Günther's Study of Fishes deals] with..mixogamy, polygamy..as occurring amongst fishes. **1959** *Archivio di Oceanogr. e Limnol.* XI. Suppl. 243 At the final session of the Venice Symposium a revised classification of marine waters according to salinity was adopted and recommended for universal application... The term 'brackish', as a classificatory term, was avoided because of its ambiguous meaning and the term 'mixo-haline' was proposed to indicate diluted sea water. **1969** G. VEVERS tr. *Friedrich's Marine Biol.* vii. 419 Waters with intermediate salinities are known as brackish or mixohaline. **1946** E. S. GOODRICH in *Q. Jrnl. Microsc. Sci.* LXXXVI. 119 When, as in the majority of Polychaeta, the coelomostome is so completely fused to the inner end of the nephridium as to form an apparently simple large-funnelled organ..it may be called a mixonephridium... This new name is proposed to draw attention to the difference between these two kinds of organ (the metanephridium, and the compound nephromixial organ). **1963** Mixonephridium [see CŒLOMO-]. **1972** M. S. GARDINER *Biol. Invertebr.* xiii. 505/2 In a mixonephridium, the nephrostome has presumably become occluded and lost. **1958** G. A. KERKUT *Borradaile & Potts's Invertebrata* (ed. 3) viii. 287 Mixonephrium. The coelomoduct is so closely associated with the nephridium that they form an apparently simple funnelled organ. **1876** Mixoscope [see MIXER 2]. **1939** G. R. SCOTT *Encycl. Sex* 200/2 *Mixoscopia* or *mixoscopy*, the securing of sexual orgasm or excitation as a result of seeing human beings or animals engaged in copulation. **1940** HINSIE & SHATZKY *Psychiatric Dict.* 350/2 *Mixoscopia*, a form of sexual perversion, deriving pleasure from watching the act of coition between the desired one and another person. **1903** *Alienist & Neurologist* May 167 Mixoscopic. **1905** H. ELLIS *Stud. Psychol. Sex* IV. 188 Founded on the sense of vision also we find a phenomenon, bordering on the abnormal, which is by Moll named mixoscopy. This means the sexual pleasure derived from the spectacle of other persons engaged in natural or perverse sexual actions.

‖**mixo-barbaric** (ˌmɪksəʊbɑːˈbærɪk), *a.* [f. Gr. *μιξο-βάρβαρος* half-barbarian half Greek: see MIXO- and BARBARIC *a.*] Characteristic of a people partly barbarous and partly Hellenic.

1876 C. T. NEWTON *Ess. Art & Archæol.* xi. (1880) 413 All the barbaric and mixo-barbaric coinages imitated from Greek prototypes.

mixolimnion (mɪksəʊˈlɪmnɪən). Pl. **-limnia.** [f. MIXO- + *-limnion*, after EPILIMNION, HYPOLIMNION.] The upper, freely circulating layer of a meromictic lake. Cf. MONIMOLIMNION.

1937 G. E. HUTCHINSON in *Trans. Connecticut Acad. Arts & Sci.* XXXIII. 74 A meromictic lake may be regarded as consisting of an upper region capable of complete mixture at the time of the overturn, and here called the mixolimnion, and a lower region not undergoing mixture at the overturn and termed by Findenegg the monimolimnion. **1968** *Limnol. & Oceanogr.* XIII. 273 Both lakes are permanently stratified. The chemocline, separating the mixolimnion.. from the monimolimnion.., lies at 18 m in Green Lake and at 24 m in Round Lake.

mixologist (mɪkˈsɒlədʒɪst). *U.S. slang.* [f. MIX *sb.*[2] or *v.* + -OLOGIST.] One who is skilled in the mixing of drinks; = MIXER 1 b. Hence **mi'xology.**

1856 *Knickerbocker* XLVII. 615 Who ever heard of a man's..calling the barkeeper a mixologist of tipicular fixins? **1870** W. F. RAE *Westward by Rail* xv. 201 The most delicate fancy drinks are compounded by skilful mixologists in a style that captivates the public. **1908** W. G. DAVENPORT *Butte & Montana* 45 Brandy and cigarettes were furnished by an expert mixologist from the Thornton Hotel. **1952** *John o' London's* 25 Jan. 82/4 There [*sc.* at Miami], it seems, a mixer of drinks at a bar is referred to as a mixologist. The art of mixing a cocktail is consequently known as mixology.

mixolydian (mɪksəʊˈlɪdɪən), *a. Mus.* [f. Gr. *μιξο-λύδιος* half-Lydian: see MIXO- and LYDIAN.] The designation of (*a*) the highest in pitch of the modes in ancient Greek music; (*b*) the fourth of the 'authentic' ecclesiastical modes, having G for its 'final' and D for its dominant.

1589 PUTTENHAM *Eng. Poesie* II. x. (Arb.) 98 The Eolien, Mi[x]olidien and Ionien. **1603** HOLLAND *Plutarch* Explan. Words, *Mixolidian tune*, that is to say, lamentable and pitifull: meet for Tragoedies. **1760** STILES in *Phil. Trans.* LI. 709 In the Mixolydian species, the diazeuctic tone was the first interval, reckoning from acute to grave. **1776** BURNEY *Hist. Mus.* I. 390 Mixolydian mode. **1842** W. F.

DONKIN in *Smith's Dict. Gr. & Rom. Ant.* s.v. *Music (Greek)*, The seven species of the Octachord..were anciently..denoted by the names Mixolydian, Lydian [etc.],..the Mixolydian being the highest, and the Hypodorian the lowest. **1867** MACFARREN *Harmony* i. 14 The fourth mode Ambrose selected is the Hyper-Lydian, sometimes called Myxo-Lydian. **1893** H. E. WOOLDRIDGE *Chappell's O. Eng. Pop. Mus.* I. p. xi, Ecclesiastical Scale of G. 7th or Mixolydian Mode.

mixon, dial. form of MIXEN.

mixoploid ('mɪksəʊplɔɪd), *a.* (and *sb.*). *Biol.* [f. MIXO- + -PLOID.] Containing cells which are of differing ploidy or, more widely, have differing numbers of chromosomes. Also as *sb.*, a mixoploid individual.

1931 B. NĚMEC in *Rep. Proc. 5th Internat. Bot. Congr. 1930* 233 Many plants contain under normal conditions both diploid and polyploid cells. It is easy to get experimentally plants containing a varying number of polyploid cells. The author designates such plants mixoploid. *Ibid.*, Mixoploid organs tend to eliminate the polyploid cells when they form a minority, especially when they are highly polyploid. **1939** *Hereditas* XXV. 111 As a result of the agar treatment entire plants occasionally become mixoploids. **1944** *Jrnl. Heredity* XXXV. 359/2 Mixoploid tissue resulted from colchicine treatment. *Ibid.* 361/1 Individual anthers were mixoploid. **1951** *Nature* 2 June 891/1 In many species the diploid tissue grows at the expense of the tetraploid, and such a mixoploid reverts rapidly to the diploid condition. **1967** *Current Sci.* XXXVI. 307 (*heading*) Preferential elimination of diploid cells in a colchicine-induced mixoploid tissue. **1971** J. HAMERTON *Human Cytogenetics* I. vii. 224 Autosomal mosaics are less common, and about 1% of Down's syndrome patients are estimated to be mixoploids.

So '**mixoploidy**, the property or state of being mixoploid.

1931 B. NĚMEC in *Rep. Proc. 5th Internat. Bot. Congr. 1930* 233 (*heading*) Mixoploidy and the cellular theory. **1958** C. P. SWANSON *Cytol. & Cytogenetics* ix. 300 This gradual change, if caught before the completion of the entire process of doubling, will give both tissues of mixed ploidy and cells with an uneven degree of polyteny in the individual chromosomes. Mickey (1946, 1947) has also shown this type of mixoploidy to be true for the spermatogonia in the testes of the grasshopper, Romalea. **1963** LEVAN & MÜNTZING in *Portugaliae Acta Biol.* A. VII. 10 The present writers would suggest that the term mixoploidy should include all cases in which cell populations contain more than one chromosome number irrespective of whether the numbers are euploid or aneuploid. Mixoploidy, thus, covers all cases of mosaicism and chimeric constitution in which the heterogeneity between different elements involves differences in chromosome number. Mixoploidy may originate by all kinds of mitotic irregularities, by cellular and nuclear fusions, or even by amitotic processes, provided they give rise to viable products. **1971** J. HAMERTON *Human Cytogenetics* I. vii. 225 *In vitro* studies on mixoploidy should include the use of single cell clones from a mixoploid culture so that the only genetic difference is confined to a single chromosome.

mixotrophic (mɪksəʊ'trəʊfɪk), *a.* *Biol.* [a. G. *mixotroph* (W. Pfeffer *Pflanzenphysiologie* (ed. 2, 1897). I. vii. 349), f. MIXO- + Gr. τροφικός nursing.] Living by a mixture of autotrophic and heterotrophic nutrition; pertaining to nutrition of this kind.

1900 A. J. EWART tr. *Pfeffer's Physiol. Plants* I. vii. 364 By others [*sc.* plants] a portion only of the organic food is drawn from the external world, the rest being supplied by the imperfectly developed chlorophyll-apparatus; such may be termed 'mixotrophic' plants. *Ibid.*, All stages of transition between pure autotrophism and heterotrophism are exhibited among obligate or facultative mixotrophic plants. **1940** L. H. HYMAN *Invertebrates* I. iii. 58 Nutrition [of Protozoa] is holophytic, saprozoic, holozoic, or mixotrophic. **1965** BELL & COOMBE tr. *Strasburger's Textbk. Bot.* 5 Such mixotrophic organisms [*sc.* unicellular Protista] (which obtain their energy partly directly as autotrophs, and partly indirectly as heterotrophs) are regarded as the starting-point of two great developmental series which have led on the one side to the 'typical' plants and on the other to the 'typical' animals.

† '**mixschipe**. *Obs. rare*⁻¹. [f. MIX *sb.*[1] + *-schipe* -SHIP.] Wickedness.

a **1225** *Juliana* 46 (Royal MS.), Ant mi lauerdes wil ich wurche, þat is meister ouer mixschipe [*Bodl. MS.* meister of alle mixschipes] ouer al þer imei.

† **mixt**, *sb.* *Obs.* Also 7 **mixte**. [ad. L. *mixtum* neut. of *mixtus*: see MIXED *ppl. a.* Cf. F. *mixte* sb.]

1. A substance consisting of different elements mixed together; esp. in *Old Chem.*, a compound.

1644 DIGBY *Nat. Bodies* xxv. §3. 229 The causes of the figures of diuers mixtes, and particularly of some pretious stones. **1665–6** *Phil. Trans.* I. 326 He discourses of Bread, Wine, Oyle, and the other Mixtes that are made of Plantes. **1680** BOYLE *Scept. Chem.* III. 172 There may be two sorts of Mixts, whereof the one may not have any of all the same Elements as the other consists of. **1704** J. HARRIS *Lex. Techn.* I, *Mixt*, i.e. a *Mixt Body*: By which, in Chymistry and Natural Philosophy, is understood a Body not mixt or compounded by Art, but by Nature; such as Minerals, Vegetables, and Animals. **1727–41** CHAMBERS *Cycl.* s.v., *Perfect Mixts* are the class of vital or animated bodies.. *Imperfect Mixts* are inanimate bodies. **1757** *Phil. Trans.* L. 163 Where the quantity of the mixt to be assayed was very small. **1805** W. SAUNDERS *Min. Waters* 462 The blood is not merely a peculiar chemical mixt, but a living part of the animal economy.

2. In immaterial applications: A product of mixture, a compound.

1589 PUTTENHAM *Eng. Poesie* II. ix. (Arb.) 97 Now also haue ye in euery song or ditty concorde by compasse and concorde entertangled and a mixt of both. **1647** GENTILIS tr. *Malvezzi's Chief Events*, etc. 162 From that conflict it comes forth a mixt, which is not feare, but consideration.

† **mixt**, *v.* *Obs.* Also 6 **myxte, mixte**. [Inferred from the pa. pple. *mixt* (see MIXED *ppl. a.*).

In the early 16th c., although *mixt* was freely used as a pple., there seems to have been much doubt whether the inferred Eng. vb. should have the form *mixt* or *mix*. Elyot's *Lat. Dict.* (1538), s.v. *Misceo*, has *myxe*, but the edition of 1548 alters this to *myxt*.]

= MIX *v.*

1526 *Pilgr. Perf.* (W. de W. 1531) 39 b, By mixtynge water with floure, & werkynge it into paste. **1531** ELYOT *Gov.* I. xiii, Mixting serious mater with thynges that were pleasaunt. **1545** RAYNOLD *Byrth Mankynde* 123 In the whiche also myxte barly meale. *a* **1548** HALL *Chron.*, *Hen. VI* 129 Aduertisyng hym..not to..mixte his safetie and surenesse with the unstablenesse and unsuretie of his newe alye. **1563** WINȜET *Cert. Tractates* Wks. 1890 II. 60 Bot..gif we sal begin to mixt noueltie with antiquitie. **1609** BIBLE (Douay) *Jer.* Argt., In the next eleuen chapters he mixteth consolations and threats.

Hence † '**mixting** *vbl. sb.*

1535 COVERDALE *2 Macc.* xiv. 3 Alcimus (which had.. wilfully defyled himselfe, in the tyme of the myxtinge) [1611 their mingling (with the Gentiles)]. **1570** DEE *Math. Pref.* *ij, And so is this Arithmetike greately enlarged, by diuerse exhibityng and vse of Compositions and mixtynges.

† **mixt**, *a.* *Obs.* exc. *Hist.*: see MIXED *a.*

mixt, var. *mixed*, pa. t. and pa. pple of MIX *v.*

Mixtec ('mi:ʃtɛk). Also **Mixteca, Mixteco**. [Sp., f. native name.] A people of central America; a member of this people; also, their language. Also *attrib.* So **Mix'tecan**.

1850 R. G. LATHAM *Nat. Hist. Varieties Man* 409 South of Mexico we have several languages of a small..area... *Mixteca*, spoken in Oaxaca [etc.]. **1928** D. H. LAWRENCE *Woman who rode Away* 267 His mother was a Mixtec Indian woman. **1934** A. HUXLEY *Beyond Mexique Bay* 288 In the waste land..stood a church..and, beside it, the Mixtec ruins which it had been built to exorcise and sanctify. **1948** D. DIRINGER *Alphabet* I. vii. 123 The Zapotecs and Mixtecs ..in ancient times probably played the part of cultural intermediaries between the Maya Old Empire of the East, and the Toltec 'Empire' of the West. **1952** E. FISCHER-JØRGENSEN in E. P. Hamp et al. *Readings in Linguistics II* (1966) 307 An exception of a different kind is formed by languages of the Mixteco-type. In Mixteco the minimal utterance is cvcv or cvv, containing two syllabic bases. **1965** *Canad. Jrnl. Ling.* Spring 152 We made the first attempt with the sixteenth century Mixtec dictionary. *Ibid.* 153 We began on the Mixtec, first listing all the affix elements we knew. **1968** CHOMSKY & HALLE *Sound Pattern Eng.* 377 In languages such as Mixtecan or Chinese, each vowel in the word may have its own distinctive prosodic features. **1972** *Language* XLVIII. 847 Otomi nasal vowels, Mixteco,..and Zoque. **1975** *Times* 24 May 10/1, I went to Mexico with only the most cursory knowledge of..the Toltecs, the Olmecs, the Mixtecs, the Zapotecs. *Ibid.* 10/5 Friezes made up of exquisitely curved geometric patterns..were Mixtec work.

mixter-maxter, etc., var. ff. MIXTY-MAXTY.

† '**mixtible**. *Obs. rare.* [ad. mod.L. type **mixtibile*, f. L. *mixt-*, ppl. stem of *miscēre* to MIX: see -IBLE.] = MIXTIL.

1750 tr. *Leonardus' Mirr. Stones* 57 The Magnet has Hardness, an iron Colour, and the like, proceeds from the Virtue of Mixtibles or the Elements.

mixtiform ('mɪkstɪfɔ:m), *a.* *rare.* [f. L. *mixt-us*, pa. pple. of *miscēre* to MIX + -FORM.] Of a mixed shape, form, or character.

1837 CARLYLE *Fr. Rev.* I. VII. ix, The General..glances, only with the eye, at that so mixtiform National Assembly. **1837** —— in Froude *Life in Lond.* (1884) I. 108 My hearers were mixtiform dandiacal of both sexes.

† **mixtil**. *Obs. rare.* [ad. L. type **mixtile*, neut. of **mixtilis* f. *mixt-*, ppl. stem of *miscēre* to MIX: see -ILE.] A mixed body, a compound.

1654 VILVAIN *Epit. Ess.* I. xxvi, From which..all mixtils doe surmount. **1654** —— *Theol. Treat.* i. 27 Mixtils are compact of Elements into which they resolv.

mixtilinear (mɪkstɪ'lɪnɪə(r)), *a.* [f. as prec. + -AR.] Formed or bounded partly by straight, and partly by curved lines.

1702 [see *mixed angle*, MIXED *ppl. a.* II]. **1734** BERKELEY *Analyst* §34 The right Line C *c* being produced to K, there are formed three small Triangles, the Rectilinear C E *c*, the Mixtilinear C E *c*, and the Rectilinear Triangle C E T. **1803** WOODHOUSE in *Phil. Trans.* XCII. 121 The lines and mixtilinear triangle therein exhibited cannot be called natural signs. **1868** BLEDSOE *Philos. Math.* 61 The little mixtilinear figures at the ends of the triangles.

So **mixti'lineal** *a. rare*⁻¹.

1833 *Fraser's Mag.* VIII. 491 Whether in rectilineal, curvilineal, mixteleneal [*sic*], or other figures.

mix'tilion, anglicized form (in translations of documents) of med.L. *mixtiliōn-em* MASLIN[2].

c **1640** J. SMYTH *Lives Berkeleys* (1883) I. 155 Had also Drage, pilcorne, mixtilion [etc.]. **1892** KIRK in *Abingdon Acc.* (Camden) p. xxi, Small quantities of corn, mixtillion, and malt were received from the mill under the Court.

† '**mixtion**, *sb.* *Obs.* Forms: α. 5 **myxtion, -yon, -ioun**, 6– **mixtion**; β. 5 **myxyon, myxcion**, 6 **myxion**, 6–7 **mixion**. See also MISTION. [a. F. *mixtion* (from 14th c.; also *mistion*), ad. L. *mixtiōn-em* (also *mistiōn-em*), n. of action f. *miscēre* (pa. pple. stem *mixt-, mist-*); see MIX *v.*]

1. *gen.* The action, or process of mixing, or the condition or fact of being mixed. = MIXTURE I.

α. **1483** CAXTON *Gold. Leg.* 133/1 The waxe whyche is made of the bee purely wythout companye and myxtioun of one bee with another signefyeth the body of our lord Jhesu cryst. **1530** PALSGR. 246/1 Mixtion of thynges, *mixtion, confusion*. **1563** W. FULKE *Meteors* (1640) 63 Upon the mixtion of these colours..all things have their colour. **1594** R. ASHLEY tr. *Loys le Roy* 66 Being all vnited by the mixtion of bloud. **1604** CAWDREY *Table Alph.*, *Mixtion* [**1613** *mixion*] mingling, or tempering together. **1615** CROOKE *Body of Man* 279 An Embleme of the holy mixtion of seedes in Matrimony. **1644** DIGBY *Nat. Bodies* xvi. §7. 143 The qualities which we find in bodies do result out of the composition, and mixtion of the Elements. **1705** C. PURSHALL *Mech. Macrocosm* 132 Those that consider that the Mixtion of different Particles, is the Cause of the Generation.

β. **1398** TREVISA *Barth. De P.R.* I. (1495) 6 From this holy trynyte all confusion and all myxcion of persones is voyded for the fader is a nother, the sone is a nother, the holy ghost is a nother. **1483** CAXTON *Gold. Leg.* 437 b/1, He prayeth.. that by the vertue of the same myxyon the people may be unyed to god by veray loue & dyleccion. **1662** R. MATHEW *Unl. Alch.* §10. 5 By reason of the mixion of forcible Vegetatives.

2. *concr.* A product of mixing, *esp.* a medicine or drug composed of various ingredients.

α. *c* **1477** CAXTON *Jason* 81 This myxtion shall haue suche vertue that yf thy body be anoynted therwyth the fyre ne the venym of the dragon..may not noye the. **1480** —— *Ovid's Met.* XIV. vii, And other [flowers] she toke..& made dyverse myxtyons. **1549** *Compl. Scot.* ix. 80 Thai mixtions he [Mithridates] eit euyrie daye vitht ane fastan stomak. **1558** WARDE tr. *Alexis' Secr.* (1568) 34 Annoint a piece of parchement with this mixtion. **1607** R. C[AREW] tr. *Estienne's World of Wonders* 246 These their mixtions they call counterpoison. *a* **1648** DIGBY *Closet Open.* (1677) 171 Put this mixtion into a deep wooden dish. **1697** *Phil. Trans.* XIX. 657 There may be copious Supplies of Matter for such Mixtions. **1757** tr. *Henckel's Pyritol.* 122 These are..in their mixtion found of a like proportion of metal and sulphur.

β. **1502** *Ord. Crysten Men* IV. xxi. (W. de W. 1506) 232 To make these mixions where with women paynte theyr visages. **1576** BAKER *Jewell of Health* 104 b, Take the myxion, which put into a goates skynne.

b. = MIXT *sb.* I. *Obs.*

1481 CAXTON *Myrr.* II. xxi. 111 Of thyse two myxtyons [sande and the glayre of the see] is made good glasse and clere. **1555** EDEN *Decades* 333 b, Yet are there not many that do care to knowe of what substaunce or natural mixtion it [*sc.* gold] consisteth. **1646** SIR T. BROWNE *Pseud. Ep.* II. i. 55 Yet are they not to be closed up in the generall name of concretions, or lightly passed over as onely Elementary and Subterraneous mixtions. *a* **1677** HALE *Prim. Orig. Man.* IV. ii. 299 The *materia proxima* or *secunda* of all other Corporeal Beings being the simple Elements, and the next Matter of all Mixtions or Composition.

3. = MIXTURE 5.

1557 N. T. (Genev.) *Heb.* iv. 2 It..proffited not them that they hearde the worde, because they yᵗ heard it, had not the mixtion of faith. *a* **1577** SIR T. SMITH *Commw. Eng.* I. vi. (1609) 5 Ye shall finde one vtterly perfect without mixtion of the other. *a* **1619** FOTHERBY *Atheom.* II. x. §3 (1622) 304 God is a pure substance, without any mixtion. **1656** STANLEY *Hist. Philos.* v. (1687) 185/2 But the Gods being void of corporeal mixtion understand purely and sincerely.

† '**mixtion**, *v.* *Obs. rare.* [ad. F. *mixtionner*, f. *mixtion*: see prec.] *trans.* To mix, make into a mixture.

c **1500** *Melusine* 142 Vesselles full of flaxe grecyd with oyle and mixtyouned with brymstone and sulfer.

'**mixtish**, *a.* *nonce-wd.* [f. *mixt*, MIXED *ppl. a.* + -ISH[1].] Of the nature of a mixture.

a **1844** L. HUNT *Blue-stocking Revels* II. 164 So Irish, so modish, so mixtish, so wild.

mixtly, variant of MIXEDLY *adv.*

‖ '**mixtum**. *Obs. rare.* [med.L. *mixtum*, neut. of *mixtus* MIXED *ppl. a.* Cf. MISTE *v.*]

1. In monastic rule: A slight refection.

c **1490** CAXTON *Rule St. Benet* xxxviii. 131 The reder may afore his lecture take a lytyll refeccyon that is called mixtum yf nede be for by-cause of his redyng atte mete. [**1823** CRABBE *Technol. Dict.*, *Mixtum* (*Archæol.*), a breakfast, or a certain quantity of bread and wine.]

2. = MIXT *sb.* I.

1656 [? J. SERGEANT] tr. *T. White's Peripat. Inst.* 207 A Mixtum, therefore is a body of certain parts, of divers degrees of rarity and density [etc.]. *Ibid.* 215 The nature of Mixtum's, which consist in the Number and Proportion of rare and dense bodies, follows [etc.].

mixture ('mɪkstjʊə(r), -tʃə(r)). Also 6 **myxture, mixtur**. [ad. L. *mixtūra* (also *mistūra*), f. *mixt-* (*mist-*), ppl. stem of *miscēre*: see MIX *v.* Cf. OF. *mesture, misture*, F. *mixture*, It., Pg. *mistura*, Sp. *mistura, mixtura*, G. *mixtur*.]

1. a. The action, process, or fact of mixing (in the intransitive senses of the vb.) or becoming mixed; also, an instance of this.

1530 PALSGR. 420/1, I allaye, as mettals be alayde or as sylver or golde is with their myxture, *je attrempe*. **1587** GOLDING *De Mornay* (1592) 144 Or yᵉ mixtur of the elements. **1594** HOOKER *Eccl. Pol.* I. iii. §2 If the Moone should wander from her beaten way, the times and seasons of the yeare blend themselues by disordered and confused mixture. **1613** PURCHAS *Pilgrimage* (1614) 62 That mixtures in garments, seedes, and the like, were forbidden by the Law of Moses. *Ibid.* 76 This river..passeth through the Lake

Thonitis without mixture of waters by reason of this swiftnesse. **1727–41** CHAMBERS *Cycl.*, *Mixture*, in matters of drapery, denotes the union, or blending of several wools of different colours, not yet spun. **1731** ARBUTHNOT *Aliments* (1735) 22 When those Liquors are expell'd out of the Body, which by their mixture convert the Aliment into an Animal Liquid. **1842** A. COMBE *Physiol. Digestion* (ed. 4) 228 Mixtures of different kinds of food are strongly condemned by almost all writers on dietetics, as injurious to digestion. **1860** TYNDALL *Glac.* II. v. 250 From the intimate mixture of air and water we obtain foam. **1872** BAGEHOT *Physics & Pol.* ii. 69 Early in history the continual mixtures by conquest were just so many experiments in mixing races as are going on in South America now. **1876** VOYLE & STEVENSON *Milit. Dict.* s.v. *Mixing the Ingredients*, Five minutes is sufficient for a thorough mixture.

b. In the transitive sense: The action of mixing (different things). ? *Obs.*

1663 GERBIER *Counsel* 11 A good Surveyour sheweth his Art..in the fit mixture of Materials, Morter [etc.].

c. Mixed state or condition; coexistence of different ingredients or of different groups or classes of things mutually diffused through each other.

1597 HOOKER *Eccl. Pol.* v. xlvii. §4 O happie mixture, wherein things contrary do so qualifie and correct the one the daunger of the others excesse. **1615** CROOKE *Body of Man* Pref. 1 A Discourse of the constitution of mans body, as he enioyeth a perfect or apportionated health by a due Mixture of the principles whereof he consisteth; of the Temperament of each part arising from that mixture. **1712–13** SWIFT *Jrnl. to Stella* 23 Jan., There was a mixture of company.

†**d.** Mixed nature, complexity. *Obs.*

1614 RALEIGH *Hist. World* Pref. 1 How unfit, and unworthy a choice I made of my self, to undertake a work of this mixture, mine own reason..hath sufficiently resolved me.

†**e.** Sexual intercourse. Cf. MIX *v.* 4 b. *Obs.*

[Cf. **1483** MIXTION 1 b.] **1604** DEKKER *1st Pt. Hon. Wh.* vi. Wks. 1873 II. 38 *Bellafronte* [a Courtesan]..For whose true love I would..Hate the worlds mixtures, and the smiles of gold. **1615** CHAPMAN *Odyss.* VIII. 382 The Sunne their mixture saw; and came, and told. **1632** MILTON *Penseroso* 26 Thee [*sc.* Melancholy] bright-hair'd Vesta long of yore, To solitary Saturn bore; His daughter she (in Saturns raign, Such mixture was not held a stain). **1659** HAMMOND *On Ps.* xix. 9 The dread of offending God keeps the man from all impure mixtures. **1697** POTTER *Antiq. Greece* I. ii. (1715) 8 Promiscuous Mixtures had been allowed of amongst them. **1703–12** POPE *Thebais* I. 96, I..With monstrous mixture stain'd my mother's bed.

f. The mixing or blending of different races in common offspring.

1842 PRICHARD *Nat. Hist. Man* 20 The tribe of people, termed..Cafusos..are known to have sprung originally from a mixture of native Americans with the Negroes imported from Africa. **1845** YOUATT *Dog* iv. (1858) 155 The shock-dog is traced by Buffon..to a mixture of the small Danish dog and the pug.

†**g.** The fact of 'mixing' socially with others, association. *Obs.*

1764 J. SMITH in F. Chase *Hist. Dartmouth Coll.* (1891) I. 26 He intended..to send his son to obtain his education in mixture with these Indians.

2. *concr.* A product of mixing; a complex unity or aggregate (material or immaterial) composed of various ingredients or constituent parts mixed together. **a.** With the components specified (const. *of*) or implied by the context.

1460–70 *Bk. Quintessence* I. 9 Putte all þat mixture into a strong watir maad of vitriol and of sal petre, and þe siluyr wole be dissolued. **1582** N. T. (Rhem.) *John* xix. 39 Bringing a mixture of myrrhe and aloes. **1612** DRAYTON *Poly-olb.* II. 304 That braue youth, the splendor of whose eye A wondrous mixture shew'd of grace and maiestie. **1676** GLANVILL *Ess.* Pref. a iij b, The [seventh] Essay is a mixture of an Idæa, and a disguised History. **1702** ADDISON *Dial. Medals* i. Wks. 1766 III. 9 The agreeable Mixture of shades and fountains, in which the whole country naturally abounds. **1732** LEDIARD *Sethos* II. VIII. 227 His conduct..was..a fatal mixture of weakness and temerity. **1815** J. SMITH *Panorama Sci. & Art* II. 314 A simple mixture of sand and clay. **1828** SCOTT *F. M. Perth* xix, His mixture of surprise, joy, and anxiety, did not deprive him of the presence of mind which the occasion demanded. **1884** W. H. GREENWOOD *Steel & Iron* ix. 186 It is always considered better to use a mixture of several brands of iron in a charge for any casting..since such mixtures are most frequently found to be stronger than the average of the several brands taken separately. **1899** *Allbutt's Syst. Med.* VIII. 826 The vessels may be all veins,..capillaries,..or very commonly a mixture of both. **1902** T. M. LINDSAY *Ch. & Ministry in Early Cent.* vi. 258 The sorry mixture of Paganism and Christianity which [etc.].

†**b.** = MIXT *sb.* 1. *Obs.*

1604 E. G[RIMSTONE] *D'Acosta's Hist. Indies* To Rdr., In the two following books, is treated of that which concernes the Elements and naturall mixtures, as Mettalls, Plants, Beasts, and what else is remarkable at the Indies. *Ibid.* IV. xiii. 248 We..will passe to the two other mixtures, the which are plants and beasts. **1634** MILTON *Comus* 244 Can any mortal mixture of Earths mould Breath such Divine inchanting ravishment?

3. *spec.* in various concrete applications.

a. A preparation for medicinal or other purposes, consisting of two or more ingredients mixed together. In *Pharmacy*, now applied to potions or liquid medicines, in contradistinction to pills and other solid forms in which drugs may be administered. ***the mixture as before***: medicine to be taken in a similar dose as on a previous occasion (as a set phrase often found on medicine bottles); freq. *transf.* and *fig.*, something that has already been encountered, used, etc.

1592 SHAKS. *Rom. & Jul.* IV. iii. 21 What if this mixture do not worke at all? **1604** —— *Oth.* I. iii. 104 With some Mixtures, powrefull o're the blood,..He wrought vp on her. **1695** Freezing mixture [see FREEZING *vbl. sb.* 2]. **1706** PHILLIPS (ed. Kersey), *Mixture*... In a Physical Sense, several Ingredients or Drugs mixt in a Medicine. **1806** *Med. Jrnl.* XV. 513 A pint of this mixture [*sc.* of wine and water] was presented to him. **1831** J. DAVIES *Manual Mat. Med.* 295 Antispasmodic mixtures. **1834** DICKENS *Let.* 3 Sept. (1965) I. 40, I have taken a wine-glass full of 'the mixture as before' twice a day, varying the amusement with an occasional pill. **1904** *Longm. Mag.* Feb. 304, I took a sip of the horrid mixture. **1920** WODEHOUSE *Jill the Reckless* (1921) viii. 120 There he sat, surrounded by happy, laughing young men, each grasping a glass of the good old mixture-as-before. **1959** *Listener* 26 Feb. 363/1 What special or new responsibilities do these developments place upon industry? Some will say that it is the mixture as before, but in larger and more frequent doses. **1973** R. HILL *Ruling Passion* II. iv. 113 After ten minutes, all Pascoe had was the mixture as before.

b. A cloth of variegated or mottled fabric, usually of 'quiet' colouring. ***heather***, ***Oxford mixture***: see these words.

1722 DE FOE *Col. Jack* (1840) 310 Five yards of crimsom [cloth]..., and the rest of fine mixtures. **1727–41** CHAMBERS *Cycl.* s.v., The mixture, or mixed stuff, is that whose woof and warp are of wools of different colours dyed and mixed before they were spun. **1799** *Hull Advertiser* 12 Jan. 2/3 Woollen drapery, jeans, quiltings,..plains, mixtures. **1882** CAULFEILD & SAWARD *Dict. Needlework*, *Mixtures*, a term applied to any cloths of variegated colouring, such as Knickerbockers and Tweeds. **1885** Heather-mixture [see HEATHER 3].

attrib. **1784** *Europ. Mag.* Nov. 339/2 But amongst the other class of gentlemen are worn dark green, drab, or mixture cloths. **1837** DICKENS *Pickw.* xx, An elderly..man, in a black coat, dark mixture trousers, and small black gaiters. **1897** *Daily News* 8 Apr. 8/5 The shot mixture canvases. **1902** *Daily Chron.* 7 Jan. 6/3 The jacket..of a drab-mixture serge.

c. A tea, tobacco, snuff, etc. of various sorts or qualities mixed together; usually with qualifying word to indicate the variety.

1840 HILL *Pinch—of Snuff* 32 Prince's Mixture..is nothing more than plain brown Rappee scented with otto of roses. **1872** 'M. LEGRAND' *Cambr. Freshm.* 286 I'm going in to get a canister of smoking mixture to take down with me. **1895** *Price List*, The Foochow Mixture, specially prepared and packed from the Finest Foochow Teas.

d. In an internal-combustion engine, the mixture of vaporized or gaseous fuel with air that enters the combustion chamber to form the explosive charge.

[**1848** *Chambers's Edin. Jrnl.* 6 May 303/1 What is the moving power? The answer will be heard with surprise: the successive explosions of a mixture of gas and air in the boxes at the root of the wings, by which means they will be made to flap about twelve times a minute! The balloon..is a mere reservoir for gas. The explosion is to be effected in the four boxes by the electric spark.] **1894** B. DONKIN *Text-Bk. Gas, Oil & Air Engines* I. 6 Sometimes an auxiliary pump is used for compressing the mixture. **1914** W. D. NEWTON *War* iii. 19 Brun shut off mixture, and, slowing down, he swung from the motor-cycle. **1943** A. P. FRAAS *Aircraft Power Plants* vi. 107 The power loss resulting from mixtures 10 or 20 per cent leaner than that for best power is not large as compared with the reduction in fuel consumption. **1968** R. H. BACON *Car* iii. 23 Modern carburettors have..cold starting devices to give very rich mixtures when starting the engine from cold. **1973** J. LEASOR *Host of Extras* i. 21 The engine..was under no stress at all, with tiny valves that let it take such delicate breaths of mixture, it never grew fussed like engines of lesser breeds.

e. Petrol to which has been added a small proportion of oil, used as a combined fuel and lubricant in some two-stroke engines; = PETROIL.

[**1927**: see PETROIL.] **1952** *Cyclemotor Manual* ('Motor Cycling') iii. 20 Use of oil of too thick a grade may result in the mixture being too heavy to pass through the carburetter jet in sufficient quantity. **1960** J. QUEENBOROUGH *Garage & Service Station Handbk.* xv. 263 Avery-Hardoll Ltd., market the *Petroiler* which can deliver a choice of two mixtures; there are tanks for petrol (13¾ gallons) and two grades of oil (1⅜ gallons each). **1967** P. E. IRVING *Two-Stroke Power Units* vii. 131 As the proportion of oil is for convenience fixed at one figure, usually..six per cent, it may on occasion be necessary to add a little more oil or dilute the mixture with more petrol to obtain the proportion recommended for any particular engine. **1972** J. STEVENS *Scooter* iv. 99 The first scooters had engines calling for a 6% oil content in the mixture.

4. a. In mod. physical science used with restricted meaning: The mechanical mixing of two substances as distinguished from (*chemical*) *combination*; also *concr.* the product of such a mixing, in contradistinction to a *compound*. More explicitly ***mechanical*** or ***simple mixture***, originally used in antithesis with †***chemical mixture***.

1797 *Encycl. Brit.* (ed. 3) XII. 184/1 Chemical mixture is attended with many phenomena which are never observed in simple mixtures. **1865** BRANDE & COX *Dict. Sci.*, etc., s.v. *Chemistry*, Artificial mixtures of oxygen and nitrogen. **1887** REMSEN *Elem. Chem.* i. (1897) 9 Mechanical Mixtures and Chemical Compounds.—In a mixture the substances are unchanged... In a chemical compound the substances which are in combination are completely changed. They are so intimately combined that they cannot be recognised by any ordinary means.

b. A fluid containing some foreign substance in suspension: opposed to *solution*.

1765 HAMILTON in *Phil. Trans.* LV. 150, I think..we may consider the transparency of a heterogeneous fluid..as the criterion of a true solution, and where that is wanting, it is only a mixture. **1875** H. C. WOOD *Therap.* (1879) 18 Mixtures are preparations in which one or more medicinal substances are held in suspension in water. Of such nature are emulsions, in which some oily material is suspended by a gummy or an albuminous body.

5. The action or an act of adding as an ingredient; the presence of a heterogeneous element in the composition of something; quasi-*concr.* an amount or proportion of something heterogeneous that has been added to or mixed with a thing; admixture. ***without mixture***: unmixed, pure.

1526 *Pilgr. Perf.* (W. de W. 1531) 40 b, Whether..these bothe sayd thynges be togyder in your soule without ony myxture of yᵉ contrary. **1529** MORE *Dyaloge* I. Wks. 161/1 For when the gospell spekeθ of wyne onely tourned into his precious blode, what man woulde adueuture to make any mixture of water. **1560** DAUS tr. *Sleidane's Comm.* 59 b, Suche ministers as should preache Gods worde sincerely, without any mixture of mens traditions. **1611** BIBLE *Rev.* xiv. 10 The same shall drink of the wine of the wrath of God, which is powred out without mixture into the cup of his indignation. **1613** PURCHAS *Pilgrimage* (1614) 96 The Earth ..hath a kinde of bloodie mixture, somewhat like red waxe, the depth of three or foure cubites. **1625** BACON *Ess.*, *Truth* (Arb.) 499 A mixture of a Lie doth euer adde Pleasure. **1641** BAKER *Chron.* (1653) 16 His [*sc.* K. Edgar's] Pious Acts were, that he built and prepared seven and forty Monasteries... But now his mixture of Vice marred all. **1658** SIR T. BROWNE *Hydriot.* i. 2 Except the salt Ocean were handsomly contempered by a Mixture of the fresh Element. **1670** TEMPLE *Let. to Dk. Tuscany* Wks. 1731 II. 221 Such is the Composition of human Things, that nothing is pure or without Mixture. *a* **1704** B. KEACH *Key to open Script. Metaph.* (1779) 137 Adulterating the Word of God by the Mixture of their own Fancies. **1720** HEARNE *Collect.* (O.H.S.) VII. 186 His Conversation, which was generally facetious, not without a Mixture of Satyr. **1725** WATTS *Logic* I. vi. §1 In order therefore to a clear and distinct Knowledge of things, we must uncloath them of all these Relations and Mixtures, that we may contemplate them naked, and in their own Natures. **1765** A. DICKSON *Treat. Agric.* I. xix. (ed. 2) 143 The soil in which there is a great mixture of moss. **1826** LAMB *Elia* Ser. II. *Pop. Fallacies* xiii, The good things of life are not to be had singly, but come to us with a mixture; like a schoolboy's holiday, with a task affixed to the tail of it. **1845** YOUATT *Dog* vii. (1858) 211 His bark..had a slight mixture of the howl, and there was a husky choking noise in the throat.

6. *Mus.* In full ***mixture-stop***: A compound stop or furniture stop: see COMPOUND *a.* 2 f. and FURNITURE 8.

1776 HAWKINS *Hist. Mus.* IV. I. x. 147 The compound stops are the..Mixture,..and sundry others. **1811** BUSBY *Dict. Mus.* s.v. *Stop*, Mixture, or Furniture Stop. **1876** STAINER & BARRETT *Dict. Mus. Terms*, *Mixture*, an organ stop, consisting of several ranks of pipes to each note. **1876** Mixture-stop [see FURNITURE 8].

7. ***Printing.*** 'Type setting that calls for the use of three or more distinct faces or faces and bodies of type' (*Cent. Dict.* 1890).

1888 JACOBI *Printers' Vocab.*, *Mixture*, an extra charge involved on composition if three or more types are used in a work.

Hence †**'mixture** *v. Obs. rare*⁻¹, *refl.* to mix or mingle oneself *with*, to associate *with*.

1582 N. LICHEFIELD tr. *Castanheda's Conq. E. Ind.* I. xvi. 40 They will mixture themselues with you and yours [Pg. orig. *estar coeles de mestura*].

†**'mixturous**, *a. Obs. rare*⁻¹. [f. MIXTURE *sb.* + -OUS.] Of the nature of a mixture.

1657–83 EVELYN *Hist. Relig.* (1850) I. 173 Nor is this co-existence with any mixturous confusion.

mixty-maxty, mixy-maxy ('mɪkstɪ'mækstɪ, 'mɪksɪ'mæksɪ), *a.* and *sb. Sc.* and *dial.* Forms: α. 8–9 **mixtie-maxtie**, 9 **mixter-maxter**, 9– **mixty-maxty**; β. **mixie-maxie, mixey-maxey, mixy-maxy.** [A varied reduplication of *mixt* MIXED *ppl. a.* Cf. MISH-MASH.]

A. *adj.* Incongruously or promiscuously mingled; jumbled together; mixed; confused.

1786 BURNS *Earnest Cry* xxi, Yon mixtie-maxtie, queer hotch-potch, The Coalition. **1861** QUINN *Heather Lintie* (1863) 238 Degenerate things, however coud Yer mixtie-maxtie puddle Vie wi' the pure Milesian bluid O' winsome Sally Noddle. **1885** G. FRASER *Poems* 133 His points got mixy-maxy, and defied ye tae recall The guid advice he gied ye, for 'twas a' reel-rawl. **1894** *Superfluous Woman* (ed. 4) I. 75 It makes a body feel mixtie-maxtie to come upon her sudden-like amidst the pots and pans.

B. *sb.* Anything promiscuously mixed; a mixed or confused mass, a heterogeneous mixture.

1824 MACTAGGART *Gallovid. Encycl.* (1876) 189 Wi' supper in his kyte weel fed, Composed o' unco mixie maxies. **1829** BROCKETT *N.C. Gloss.* (ed. 2), *Mixty-maxty, Mixy-maxy*, any thing confusedly mixed, an irregular medley—*a mish-mash*, or hotch-potch. **1871** ALEXANDER *Johnny Gibb* ix. 68 A mixter maxter o' figures wi' the letters o' the A B C. **1895** ROY *Horseman's Word* xxxix. 429 The warld was a gey queer mixty-maxty.

mix-up: see MIX *sb.*² c.

mixy ('mɪksɪ), *a.* [f. MIX *v.* + -Y¹.] **a.** Adapted for mixing. **b.** *colloq.* Sociable.

1929 R. BRIDGES *Testament of Beauty* ii. 41 Nor that the unwholesomeness of mixy pollen was by the flowers contrived for their own benefit. **1942** BERREY & VAN DEN BARK *Amer. Thes. Slang* §363/14 Sociable,..*mixy*. **1968** P.

G. HOLLOWELL *Lorry Driver* vii. 181 Lorry drivers aren't so mixy nowadays since there are so many of them.

miz (mɪz). [Shortening of MISTRESS *sb.*]

1. Prefixed as a title to the name of a married or unmarried woman, = 'Mrs.' or 'Miss'. *southern U.S.*

1907 'O. HENRY' *Heart of West* i. 5, I ain't reflectin' none on Miz Yeager—she's the finest little lady between the Rio Grande and next Christmas. **1913** H. KEPHART *Our Southern Highlanders* xiii. 290 A married woman is not addressed as Missis by the mountaineers, but as Mistress when they speak formally, and as Mis' or Miz' for a contraction. **1937** M. MITCHELL *Gone with Wind* xlv. 800 'Don't you question Miz Wilkes' word,' said Archie. **1952** V. WILKINS *King Reluctant* I. iii. 46, I kin' 'spicion wat Miz Fell gwine ter say about dis-yere chile, Miz Virgie! **1975** E. BERCKMAN *Indecent Exposure* v. 53 Miz Tor is such a wonderful lady.

2. Repr. pronunc. of Ms[2].

1972 *Village Voice* (N.Y.) 1 June 28/3 Cavett addressed her as Mrs. Morgan and asked her if she would rather be called a miz and she said she didn't care. **1974** J. PHILIPS *Power Killers* (1975) III. iv. 183 Nice to have you back, ma'am... Or should I say 'Miz'? **1975** P. G. WINSLOW *Death of Angel* i. 48 'Smoky Angel, I believe he is called, Mrs Jones.' 'Miz,' she corrected him.

miz, mizz: see MIS *a.*[2] and *sb.*

mizen, mizzen (ˈmɪz(ə)n). *Naut.* Forms: 5 meseyn, 5–7 meson, 6 mizine, myszen, mesen, myssyne, myssen, missonne, mysson, *Sc.* mozan, 6–7 misen, 6–8 missen, misne, 7 myson, meisseine, mison, miszen, mizon, mizan(e, 7– mizen, mizzen. [a. F. *misaine* (in mod.Fr. foresail, foremast; c 1381 *migenne* in Hatz.-Darm.), believed to be ad. It. *mezzana* mizen-sail; the It. word is fem. of *mezzano* middle. Cf. Sp. *mesana*, Pg. *mezena* foresail, Du. *bezaan* (earlier *bezane*), G. *besan* (*-mast, -segel*) mizen.

The agreement of the use in Eng. and It. suggests that the divergent use in mod.Fr. is not original; the statement that It. *mezzana* originally meant 'mainsail' seems to be merely a conjecture based on the etymological meaning of the word, the precise implication of which is uncertain: some have suggested that it may be 'middle-sized'.

The 16th c. MUSALL (*Sc.*) and *myssyll* (see quot. *c* 1515 s.v. MAIN-MIZEN) appear to be synonymous, but their relation to this word is obscure.]

1. a. (Also **mizen-sail.**) A fore-and-aft sail set on the after side of the mizen-mast. Often used as synonymous with SPANKER, but more correctly applied to the 'mizen trysail', set instead of the spanker in stormy weather. †Formerly also applied to a sail of similar shape serving as the principal sail in certain small craft.

1465 *Mann. & Househ. Exp.* (Roxb.) 200 Item, for a yerde for a meseyn, xvj.*d.* **1485** *Naval Acc. Hen. VII* (1896) 37 Blokkes for the meson with iij sheves of brasse. *Ibid.* 41 Meson sailes.. ij. **1549** *Compl. Scot.* vi. 41 Heise the mysȝen, and change it ouer to leuart. **1591** PERCYVAL *Bibl. Hisp., Dict., Messana vela*, the mizine saile. **1601** HOLLAND *Pliny* II. 1 Yet are not wee content with a single maine saile.. vnlesse.. we haue fore-sailes and sprit-sailes in the Prow, misnes also hoised vp.. in the Poupe;.. and all to set vs more forward vpon our death, and to hasten our end. **1609** *John Dory* vii. in Child *Ballads* V. 132/2 They hoist their sailes, both top and top, The meisseine and all was tride-a. **1622** R. HAWKINS *Voy. S. Sea* lix. 138 To fight with sprit-saile and myson, and top-sayles loose. **1665** SIR T. HERBERT *Trav.* (1677) 389 This tempest.. forced us.. to lie by the Lee without more sail than the mizzen. **1669** STURMY *Mariner's Mag.* I. ii. 16 Loose the Misne in the Brailes. **1670** COVEL *Diary* (Hakl. Soc.) 130 A small vessel with a meson and stay sail. **1694** NARBOROUGH, etc. in *Acc. Sev. Late Voy* II. 2 We.. drove with our Missen-sail towards South-east. **1715** J. EDENS in *Phil. Trans.* XXIX. 318 Their Sails [*sc.* of a Caravel] are all Mizen Sails, that is, Triangular. **1748** *Anson's Voy.* I. vii. 73 We were obliged.. to continue under a reefed mizen till eleven at night. **1886** R. C. LESLIE *Seapainter's Log* vi. 130 The Dean is correct in his description of what was known in those days as bagpiping the mizen, by hauling the mizen-sheet to windward.

b. In figurative context.

1579 PUTTENHAM *Partheniades* in Nichols *Progr. Q. Eliz.* III. 477 Thou strike mizzen, and anker in his porte. *a* **1619** FLETCHER *Wit without M.* I. ii, My sister is a goodly portly Lady,.. she spreads satten, as the Kings ships doe canvas, every where she may spare me her misen, and her bonnets strike her maine petticoate, and yet outsaile me. **1702** VANBRUGH *False Friend* III. ii, There may be foul weather there too. I reckon at present he may be lying by under a mizen at the street door.

2. = MIZEN-MAST. Now *rare*.

1583 HAYES *Narr. Gilbert's Voy.* in *Hakluyt* (1811) III. 190 The Golden Hind succeeded in the place of Vizadmirall, and removed her flagge from the mizon unto the foretop. **1622** MABBE tr. *Aleman's Guzman d'Alf.* II. 357 Streamers that belonged to the Main-Mast, the Misne, and other fitting places for them. **1626** CAPT. SMITH *Accid. Yng. Seamen* 13 In great ships they haue two misens, the latter is called the *boneauentuer* misen. **1634–5** BRERETON *Trav.* (Chetham Soc.) 169 This carries four masts.. 4. the mizen, which is placed in the stern almost over the helm. **1867** SMYTH *Sailor's Word-bk.* s.v. *Admiral*, The white St. George's cross at the main, fore, or mizen.

3. *attrib.* and *Comb.* in the sense 'pertaining to, connected with, or near the mizenmast or mizensail', as ***mizen-boom, -brail, -cap, -halyard, -lift, -light, -parrel, -peak, -pole, -rigging, -royal, -sheet, -shroud, -skysail, -stay, -staysail, -tack, -truck, †-tye.*** Also **mizen-sail** (see 1), MIZEN-MAST, MIZEN TOP, etc.

1485 *Naval Acc. Hen. VII* (1896) 36 Meson showdes. *Ibid.* 49 Meson lyftes... Meson halyers... Meson perell... Meson shetes... Meson tyes. **1626** CAPT. SMITH *Acc. Yng. Seamen* 14 The mison stay. **1667** DRYDEN & DAVENANT *Tempest* I. i, Get the Misen-tack aboard. Haul aft Misen-sheet! **1692** LUTTRELL *Brief Rel.* (1857) II. 456 Hanging white flags.. on the mizen peak. **1757** in J. S. McLennan *Louisbourg* (1918) 209 Fore stay sail, Main and Mizen stay sail all blown away. **1768** J. BYRON *Narr. Patagonia* (ed. 2) 206 Which he desired might be hung up in the mizen-shrouds. **1835** SIR J. ROSS *Narr. 2nd Voy.* xlvi. 594 Carrying away the mizen-boom. **1841** R. H. DANA *Seaman's Man.* I. i. 4 Mizen royal yard 16 ft. Mizen skysail yard 10 ft... Mizen pole 9 ft. **1905** *Daily Graphic* 17 Jan. 4/4 Watching the mizzen truck swing among the stars. **1964** R. E. LLOYD in *Roving Commissions 1963* 228 On again next day with, to our joy, a mizzen staysail breeze.

ˈmizen-mast. *Naut.* The aftermost mast of a three-masted ship.

1486 *Naval Acc. Hen. VII* (1896) 14 A Mayne Meson mast for the said Ship. **1505** in *Ld. Treas. Acc. Scotl.* (1901) III. 86 Item,.. for ane mozan mast and ane pege mast. **1556** BURROUGH in Hakluyt *Voy.* (1599) I. 275 The Pinnesse bare her Myssen mast ouer boord with flagge and all. **1748** *Anson's Voy.* II. iv. 161 To make a mizen-mast for the *Wager*. **1895** R. LEIGHTON *Under Foeman's Flag* xxi, Her mizen-mast had been shot away in the battle.

ˈmizen-ˈtop. *Naut.* The 'top' of a mizen-mast; a platform just above the head of the lower mizen-mast.

1667 *Lond. Gaz.* No. 178/4 She wears upon her Main-top an English Ancient.. and a French upon his Mizen-top. **1806** *Med. Jrnl.* XV. 73 Lord Nelson was mortally wounded ..by a musquet-ball,.. fired from the mizen-top of La Redoubtable. **1833** MARRYAT *P. Simple* xiv, I was put into the mizen-top.

b. *attrib.*, as ***mizen-top-boy, -man, -shrouds.***

1626 CAPT. SMITH *Accid. Yng. Seamen* 14 The mison top shroudes and their ratlings. **1833** MARRYAT *P. Simple* xiii, Having recourse to one of his remedies to cure a mizen-top-boy of smoking. *a* **1860** H. STUART *Seaman's Catech.* 79 The duties of mizentop-men aloft are much the same as the other topmen... The youngest and slightest hands in the ship are usually selected for mizen-top-men.

ˈmizen-topˈgallant. *Naut.* Used *attrib.* in **mizen-topgallant-mast**, the mast above the mizen-topmast; similarly in ***mizen-topgallant brace, -mast-head, -sail, -yard***, etc.

1864 *Chamb. Encycl.* s.v., Above it [*sc.* the mizen-mast], are the mizen-topmast, the mizen-top-gallant-mast, and the mizen-royal. **1875** BEDFORD *Sailor's Pocket Bk.* vii. (ed. 2) 260 When she is immediately to hoist her ensign at the mizen top-gallant mast-head.

ˈmizen-ˈtopmast. *Naut.* The mast next above the lower mizen-mast. Also *attrib.*

1626 CAPT. SMITH *Accid. Yng. Seamen* 13 The misen top mast. **1692** *Capt. Smith's Seaman's Gram.* I. xiv. 63 Mizan Topmast Shrowds... Mizan Topmast Stay... Mizan Topmast Crowfoot. **1755** *Gentl. Mag.* XXV. 184 With the blue flag at the mizentopmast head of the *Monarch*. **1841** R. H. DANA *Seaman's Man.* I. iii. 16 The main topsail braces.. are seized to the mizen topmast-head. **1867** SMYTH *Sailor's Word-bk.* s.v. *Stay*, *The mizen-topmast stay* is that which comes to the hounds of the main-mast.

ˈmizen-ˈtopsail. *Naut.* The sail above the mizen-sail, the sail set on the mizen-topmast. Also *attrib.*

1626 CAPT. SMITH *Accid. Yng. Seamen* 13 The misen top sayle yeard. **1692** *Capt. Smith's Seaman's Gram.* I. xiv. 63 Mizan Topsail Lifts. Mizan Topsail Sheets. **1772–84** COOK *Voy.* (1790) I. 151 It was so tempestuous as to split the main topsail and the fore mizen-top sails. **1841** R. H. DANA *Seaman's Man.* I. iii. 16 The mizen topsail braces reeve up through the leading blocks.. on the main rigging. *Ibid.*, The lower block of the mizen topsail halyard is usually in the mizen tops.

mizen-yard. *Naut.* The yard on which the mizen-sail is extended.

1485 *Naval Acc. Hen. VII* (1896) 49 Meson yerdes.. ij. **1564** in R. G. Marsden *Sel. Pl. Crt. Admir.* (Selden) II. 129 Item a bade smalle bote of two toune and a myssyne yerde vj[s] viij[d]. **1627** CAPT. SMITH *Seaman's Gram.* iii. 17 You must allow the Misen Yard and Spretsaile Yard ½ inch of thicknesse to a yard in length. **1786** CUMBERLAND *Observer* No. 23 I. 224, I would hang him at the mizen yard.

mizer: see MISER *sb.*[1] and [2].

mizerion, obs. form of MEZEREON.

mizmaze (ˈmɪzmeɪz). Also 6 myse mase, 6–7 mis-mase, 7 misse-, 7, 9 mis-, 9 *dial.* mizz-, mizzy-maze. [Varied reduplication of MAZE *sb.*]

†1. A labyrinth or maze. Chiefly *fig. Obs.*

1547 SALESBURY *Welsh Dict.*, *Frustial*, a myse mase. **1587** HARMAR tr. *Beza's Serm.* 69 Salomon.. hath walked vs through the whole labyrinth & mizmaze of this life. **1612** J. DAVIES *Muse's Sacrif.* (Grosart) 10/1 Errors misse-maze, where lost is Veritie, Or blinded so, that still wrong course it takes. *a* **1624** BP. M. SMITH *Serm.* (1632) 234 In this distraction, and mismaze, I think the middle-way to be the best way. *a* **1734** NORTH *Life Dudley North* (1744) 41 The Gentlemen of the House were in a Miz-maze, and knew not how to take one Step towards extricating themselves. **1794** *Percy's Reliq.* (ed. 4) II. Gloss. s.v. *Maze*, On the top of Catharine-hill, Winchester (the usual play-place of the school), was a very perplexed and winding path, running in a very small space over a great deal of ground, called a *Miz-Maze*.

2. Mystification, bewildering delusion; a state of confusion or perplexity. Chiefly *dial.*

1604 BABINGTON *Comf. Notes Exod.* viii. 18 The Lord will cut off that difference and mismaze,.. and giue his truth victory ouer all Enchanters. **1871** PULMAN *Rustic Sk.* (ed. 3) 116, I da veel all ev a mizz-maze. **1875** *Q. Rev.* Oct. 392 The physico-theological mizmaze which.. clouded the perception of those who were following immediately in the wake of Newton. **1880** MRS. PARR *Adam & Eve* xxvii. 371, I want to be a bit quiet—my head seems all of a mizmaze like. **1880** *W. Cornwall Gloss.* s.v. *Mizmaze*, 'I'm all o' a mizzy-maze'. **1880** *E. Cornwall Gloss.*, *Mismaze*, bewilderment.

†3. Dazzling radiance. *Obs.*

a **1814** *Gonzanga* II. i. in *New Brit. Theatre* III. 110, I have now a scheme in my head, which.. will envelope you all in a mizmaze of glory.

†mizmore. *Obs.* = MASSYMORE.

1656 BLOUNT *Glossogr.*, *Mizmor* (Span. *mazmorra*), a Dungeon. **1658** in PHILLIPS.

Mizo (ˈmiːzəʊ), *sb.* and *a.* Pl. **Mizo, Mizos.** [Native name, lit. 'highlander', f. *mi* person + *zo* hill.] **A.** *sb.* A native or inhabitant of the territory of Mizoram in north-eastern India, formerly the Lushai Hills District or the Mizo Hills District. **B.** *adj.* Of or pertaining to these people. Cf. LUSHAI *a.* and *sb.*

1832 *Asiatic Res.* XVII. 375 *Krisong*.. is esteemed as being the more martial and decided character, and his influence.. with the *Mizhus*.. is consequently greater. *Ibid.*, *Ruding*, a Chief of the *Mizhú* tribe. *Ibid.* 400 The *Reiga* tribe are on the western side of the great river, beyond the *Pasi* and *Mizong* tribes. **1912** J. SHAKESPEAR *Lushei Kuki Clans* v. 110 Some Mizo (natives of these Hills) who were passing through the village also heard the song of those who knew magic. **1954** *Current Indian Statutes* II. 107 The district is largely inhabited by tribes who are collectively known as 'Mizos'—'Lusei' being one of the tribes. **1968** CHAPMAN & CLARK *Mizo Miracle* 85 The pioneer missionaries Lorrain and Savidge toured the district, learning the Mizo language and reducing it to writing. **1969** S. BARKATAKI *Tribes of Assam* 82 Mizo is a generic term which includes several sub-tribes.. Lusei, Ralte, Hmar, Pawi (Poi). *Ibid.* 83 The *lingua franca* of the Mizos which has become popularly known as the Mizo language or *Dulhian*, is the dialect of the Lusei clan. *Ibid.* 128 One can hardly imagine the difficulty with which a Mizo or Zemi Naga has to eke a livelihood out of his little patch of land. **1975** *Times* 17 May 6/1 'Hostile' Mizos have been up in arms for more than a decade. *Ibid.*, The Mizo National Front has joined hands with the underground movement of the Nagas.

Mizpah (ˈmɪzpə). [ad. Heb. *Miṣpah* place-name in ancient Palestine (Gen. xxxi. 49).] An expression or token of association ('The Lord watch between me and thee'), esp. used *attrib.* to designate an ornament with 'Mizpah' inscribed upon it, as given by a lover.

[**1887** *Mizpah* 21 Feb. 7 A deeper, more mysteriously beautiful meaning than appears at first sight, is comprehended in the word 'Mizpah'—light within light, circle within circle, revelation within revelation. *Ibid.* 19 It is our duty to examine from the Tower of Mizpah this wonderful Advent of Divinity.] **1898** *T. Eaton & Co. Catal.* Spring & Summer 133/5, 10k Mizpah ring. **1907** B. M. CROKER *Company's Servant* xv. 152 Was she wearing his presents? the sapphire brooch.. the 'Mizpah' bangle. **1909** P. WEBLING *Story of Virginia Perfect* i. 11 The thick wedding-ring, with the heavy 'Mizpah' ring squeezed on her finger over it. **1940** H. G. WELLS *Babes in Darkling Wood* I. iv. 118 Mizpah, as they say inside the engagement rings. *Ibid.*, 'Anyhow, Gemini, Mizpah!'.. 'Mizpah,' he responded. Like most English people they thought that was a pledge between two young lovers. **1961** M. K. ASHBY *Joseph Ashby* xv. 202 The pedlars.. used to bring the silver 'Mizpah' brooches. **1970** I. ORIGO *Images & Shadows* ii. 69 He gave me the gold Victorian locket—engraved with the word Mizpah, 'God watch between us two'—which he had given to his fiancée.

‖**miz'quitl**, native Mexican form of MESQUITE. (In F. Hernandez *Nova Plant. Hist.* 1651.)

1753 in CHAMBERS *Cycl. Supp.* **1797** *Encycl. Brit.* (ed. 3) XI. 672/2 The *mizquitl*, or mezquite, is a species of true acacia.

Mizrach (ˈmɪzrɑːx). [ad. mod.Heb. *mizrāḥ*, f. Heb. *mizrāḥ* east, f. *zāraḥ* to rise.] The east, the direction of Jerusalem; a sacred picture facing east; the Judaic practice of turning towards Jerusalem in prayer. Hence **Miz'rachi**, a religiously traditionalist Zionist organization, amalgamated with Hapoel Hamizrachi in 1957.

1892 I. ZANGWILL *Childr. Ghetto* I. 46 A crudely-coloured *Mizrach* on the east wall, to indicate the direction towards which the Jew should pray. **1911** *Zionist* Oct. 107/2 The Misrachi profess to see in such work a danger to orthodox Judaism of which they claim to be the bulwark in Zionism. *Ibid.* Nov. 123/2 The Misrachi Federation has issued a manifesto.. appealing for loyalty and labour for the Zionist movement. **1922** JOYCE *Ulysses* 689 His gaze turned in the direction of Mizrach, the east. **1934** M. M. KAPLAN *Judaism as Civilization* III. xiv. 174 The *Mizraḥi* organization which is orthodox in its constituency, is devoid of any systematic philosophy of Judaism. **1956** *Ann. Reg. 1955* 285 The Mizrachi (Religious) Zionists of the world. **1973** *Jewish Chron.* 19 Jan. 2/1 (*heading*) Mizrachi in stormy debates. *Ibid.*, A stormy debate as a resolution about diaspora leaders .. marked the closing session here.. of the 22nd Mizrachi-Hapoel Hamizrachi conference.

mizurko, obs. form of MAZURKA.

mizzle (ˈmɪz(ə)l), *sb.*[1] Forms: 5 **mysell**, 7 **misle**, 9 **mizzle**. [f. MIZZLE *v.*[1] Cf. MDu. *mysel* dew.] Slight or drizzling rain, drizzle.

1490 CAXTON *Eneydos* xv. 55 And tormented [them] Rygth asperly with Rayne mysell, and grete heyle stones amonge. **1686** GOAD *Celest. Bodies* I. xii. 49 Snow and Misle. *Ibid.* II. xii. 322 A misle of Vapour or Fume may be extenuated into some hundreds [of miles] at least. **1806–7** J. BERESFORD *Miseries Hum. Life* (1826) VI. iii, A mist which successively becomes a mizzle a drizzle a shower a rain a torrent. **1860** *All Year Round* No. 72. 512 The sorts of rain are natural (as cat-and-dog-rains, showers and mizzle) and unnatural. **1886** *S. W. Linc. Gloss.* s.v., There was a bit of a mizzle. *a* **1963** S. PLATH *Crossing Water* (1971) 34 This mizzle fits me like a sad jacket. **1975** P. G. WINSLOW *Death of Angel* x. 204 The neighbours would not be likely to air themselves in their gardens in a steady mizzle.

mizzle, *sb.*[2] *rare.* [f. MIZZLE *v.*[2]] Phr. ***to do a mizzle***: to depart suddenly.

1923 J. MANCHON *Le Slang* 195 *To do a mizzle*, se trotter, se barrer.

mizzle (ˈmɪz(ə)l), *v.*[1] *dial.* Forms: 5- **misel(le, my(s)sylle**, 6 **mizsel(l, mysle, myssel, mesel, misell**, 6–8 **misle**, 7 **mizell**, 7–9 **mizle, mistle**, 8 **meazle**, 9 **measle, mezel**, 6- **mizzle**. [Recorded only from the end of the 15th c.; cogn. w. the synonymous Du. dial. *miezelen*, WFlem. *mizzelen*, *mijzelen*, LG. *miseln*, *museln*; a frequentative formation with the suffix -LE 3; the base is found also in Du. dial. *miesregen* drizzle, *miezig*, *miezerig*, LG. *misig*, drizzly.]

1. *intr.* (*impers.*) To rain in very fine drops, drizzle. Also ***to mizzle of rain***.

1483 *Cath. Angl.* 241/2 To Miselle (*A.* Mysylle), *pluuitare, pluuitinare.* **1530** PALSGR. 130 *Il brvýne*, it misleth. **1579** SPENSER *Sheph. Cal.* Nov. 208 Up, Colin, up! Now gynnes to mizzle, hye we homeward fast. **1606** HOLLAND *Sueton.* 79 If it chanced to mizzle of raine, hee tooke that for a luckie signe. **1662** MABBE tr. *Aleman's Guzman d'Alf.* II. 48 The raine..came not drizling or mizling downe vpon me; but [etc.]. **1711–12** SWIFT *Jrnl. to Stella* 24 Mar., It has rained or mizzled all day. **1721** BAILEY, To *Misle*, (*q.d.* to mistle, *i.e.* to rain in a Mist, of *Mieselen*, Du.) to rain small. **1852** MISS MITFORD *Recoll.* I. 81 On the morning in question, it did not absolutely rain, it only mizzled.

†**2.** *trans.* Of a cloud (also *impers.*): To send down in a drizzling shower. *Obs.*

1584 LYLY *Sappho* IV. iii. 59 It seemed to mysell gold, with faire drops. **1592** WARNER *Alb. Eng.* VIII. xxxix. (1612) 192 Some Cloudes but misell Rayne.

mizzle (ˈmɪz(ə)l), *v.*[2] *slang.* Also in 'Shelta' form **misli**. [Of obscure origin: the Shelta *misli* 'to go' has been assigned as the source, but this may be from Eng.] *intr.* To disappear suddenly; to run or slink away, decamp, vanish, take oneself off; also *imperative* – be off! Also *dial.* 'to succumb, to yield, to give up' (*Eng. Dial. Dict.*) and *trans.* in Naut. phr. ***to mizzle one's dick***: to miss one's passage.

1781 G. PARKER *View Society* II. 231 He preferred mizzling off to France. **1823** W. T. MONCRIEFF *Tom & Jerry* I. iv. (1828) 20 Now then Dicky, mizzle!—be scarce!—broom! **1842** BARHAM *Lay St. Cuthbert* in *Ingol. Leg.* 2nd Ser. 229 Come, mizzle!—be off with you!—go! **1849** DICKENS *Dav. Copp.* (1850) xxii. 236 Now you may mizzle, Jemmy (as we say at Court). **1853** R. S. SURTEES *Sponge's Sp. Tour* i, It was a murky October day that..Mr. Sponge ..was seen mizzling along Oxford Street. **1863** C. ST. JOHN *Nat. Hist. Moray* 78 When it saw us the trout immediately turned itself round, and mizzled back into the pool it had come from. **1891** CAREW *No. 747*, xxxvii. 434 Misli in an 'our and a 'arf. **1904** A. LANG in *Morn. Post* 6 Feb., He mizzled into the general company, and I hope he enjoyed his luncheon. **1925** J. MASEFIELD *Sard Harker* III. 134 He had broken his word..and missed his passage; 'mizzled his dick', as Pompey Hopkins called it. **1970** 'R. LLEWELLYN' *But we didn't get Fox* iii. 47 There was a girl with him... He fell behind the table, and she mizzled.

mizzle (ˈmɪz(ə)l), *v.*[3] *Obs.* exc. *dial. rare.* Forms: 6 **mizzel, misle**, 7 **mizel**, 9- **mizzle**. [A frequentative formation, perh. suggested by MIZMAZE.] *trans.* To confuse, muddle; †to make tipsy; also, to mystify (a person); to give (one) wrong information.

1583 STUBBES *Anat. Abus.* I. (1879) 87 Their heades preteley mizzeled with wine. **1599** PORTER *Angry Wom. Abingt.* (Percy Soc.) 48 What though he be mump, misled, blind..? tis no consequent to me. **1601** BP. W. BARLOW *Defence* 81 They were by their owne ignorance mizeled, or by their blind guides miss-led. **1876** BOUND *Provinc. Heref.* (E.D.D.).

mizzle (ˈmɪz(ə)l), *v.*[4] *Sc.* Also 9 **mizle, misle**. [Var. of MEASLE *v.*; early mod.Flemish (Kilian) has *maschelen* 'reddish spots contracted in winter when the legs are put too near the fire'.] *trans.* To make spotty. Hence **ˈmizzled** *ppl. a.*, said *esp.* of the legs when discoloured by sitting too near the fire; also **ˈmizzly** *a.*[2] in the same sense.

1801 W. BEATTIE *Fruits Time Parings, Yule Feast*, May the French for their ambition Get mizzled shins. **1805** A. SCOTT *Poems* 146 (Jam.) Oft have I blawn the danders quick Their mizlie shins amang. **1808** in JAMIESON. **1832** A. HENDERSON *Prov.* 47 Bare shouthers mak mizzled shins.

mizzle (ˈmɪz(ə)l), *v.*[5] [Perh. f. MOAN *v.* + GRIZZLE *v.*[2]; cf. MISERY.] *intr.* To complain, whimper; used also of fretful children.

a **1935** T. E. LAWRENCE *Mint* (1950) I. xiv. 49 The question took a self-pitiful turn, and I mizzled gently in the white-walled silence. **1945** BAKER *Austral. Lang.* vi. 134 To complain: *to mizzle* and *to whinge* (whence come the nouns *mizzler* and *whinger*, and the verbal nouns *mizzling* and *whingeing*).

mizzle, Sc. form of MUZZLE *v.*

mizzler[1] (ˈmɪzlə(r)). *slang.* [f. MIZZLE *v.*[2] + -ER[1].] (See quot. 1890.)

1834 H. AINSWORTH *Rookwood* III. v, Though a needy mizzler mysel, I likes to see a cove vot's vel dressed. **1890** BARRÈRE & LELAND *Slang Dict.* (1897) s.v., *Mizzler* or *rum mizzler* (popular), one clever at effecting an escape, or getting out a difficulty.

ˈmizzler[2]. *slang.* [f. MIZZLE *v.*[5] + -ER[1].] One who complains.

1945 [see MIZZLE *v.*[5]].

mizzling (ˈmɪzlɪŋ), *vbl. sb.* [f. MIZZLE *v.*[1] + -ING[1].] The action of MIZZLE *v.*[1]; the falling of very fine rain; †fine rain or drizzle. Also *fig.*

1483 *Cath. Angl.* 241/2 A Miselynge (*A.* Myssyllynge), *nimbus.* **1523** SKELTON *Garl. Laurel* 698 Of Pliades he prechid with ther drowsy chere, Immoysturid with mislyng and ay droppyng dry. **1530** TINDALE *Deut.* xxxii. 2 My speach flowe as doeth the dewe, as the mesellynge vpon the herbes. **1572** MASCALL *Plant. & Graff.* (1592) 7 They..doe put their fruite gathered, into the middest of their Garden, in the raine & mislings, vppon the bare earth. **1656** STANLEY *Hist. Philos.* VI. (1687) 378/2 They [*sc.* clouds] are condensed..into drops of water, which if they come down very small, are called misling; if greater, rain. **1687** A. LOVELL tr. *Thevenot's Trav.* II. 73 In the Evening we had a shower of rain..which was the first, save onely a little mizling, that we had seen fall since our departure from Aleppo. **1725** BRADLEY *Fam. Dict.*, *Mizzling*; the falling of very small Rain, after a Fog in Winter or at some other Times. **1843** THOREAU *Let.* 8 June in *Atlantic Monthly* (1892) May 588, I must wait for a shower of shillings, or at least a slight dew or mizzling of sixpences, before I explore New York very far.

mizzling (ˈmɪzlɪŋ), *ppl. a.* [f. MIZZLE *v.*[1] + -ING[2].] That mizzles: **a.** of rain or the like.

1535 COVERDALE *Isa.* xviii. 4 There fel a myslinge shower, like a dew. **1655** R. DAVENPORT *K. John & Matilda* v. i. I4b, These [eyes] sheed..misling showers. **1733** ARBUTHNOT *Ess. Effects Air* iv. 87 The Air..feels more moist when the Water is..in meazling and soaking Rains, than in great Showers. **1827** *Sporting Mag.* XX. 397 Tuesday morning came in with a nasty mizzling rain. **1866** MRS. H. WOOD *St. Martin's Eve* xxviii, A slow, mizzling rain was falling.

b. of a day, weather, etc.

1641 BEST *Farm. Bks.* (Surtees) 44 If the morninge bee wette and mislinge. **1697** *Phil. Trans.* XIX. 745 Wet and Mistling Weather. **1714** GAY *Sheph. Week* Tues. 55 In misling days..With nappy beer I to the barn repair'd. *a* **1845** BARHAM *Ingol. Leg.* Ser. III. *My Letters*, Another mizzling, drizzling, day!

†**c.** *fig.*

1608 CHAPMAN *Byron* Plays (Pearson) II. 269 The misling breath of policie.

mizzlings, obs. form of MEASLINGS.

mizzly (ˈmɪzlɪ), *a.*[1] [f. MIZZLE *v.*[1] + -Y[1].] Of the nature of, or characterized by 'mizzling'.

1566 J. PARTRIDGE *Plasidas* C iiij b, The deadly shaft through misley cloudes aloft in Skies doe flie. **1666–7** PEPYS *Diary* 24 Jan., It proved dark, and a misly night. **1821** COLERIDGE in *Blackw. Mag.* X. 253 This..muzzy, mizly morning. **1853** G. J. CAYLEY *Las Alforjas* I. 187 It came on mizzly, and we put on our cloaks. **1866** BLACKMORE *Cradock Nowell* xxii, A mizzly drizzly rain set in.

mizz-maze, dial. variant of MIZMAZE.

mizzy (ˈmɪzɪ). *dial.* Forms: 4 **misy**, 7- **mizzy**. [ME. *misy*, perh. related to OE. *méos* moss, bog.] A quagmire.

13.. *Gaw. & Gr. Knt.* 749 Þe gome vpon Gryngolet glydez hem vnder, þurȝ mony misy and myre. **1674** RAY *N.C. Words* 33 Mizzy, a Quagmire. **1755** in JOHNSON. **1819** J. BUTTERWORTH (Paul Bobbin) *Sequel Lanc. Dial.* 39 (E.D.D.) They draggunt meh..thro' mizzies. **1882** *Lanc. Gloss.*, Mizzy, a soft, boggy place.

Mlimo (mˈliːməʊ). Also **Umlimo** (ʊmˈliːməʊ). [Bantu; see quots.] The name given by the Matabele and other East African tribes to their god. Also, one of the prophets or priests of this cult.

[**1833** S. KAY *Trav. Caffraria* I. ix. 236 A few indeed there were who seemed to have some confused notion of invisible powers, whom they designated *Mooreemo* and *Booreemo*, and of whom they were taught by their sorcerers to stand in constant dread.] **1861** E. CASALIS *Basutos* II. xiii. 248 Every being, to whom the natives render adoration, is called *Molimo*, the signification of which shows that it is by no means of heathen origin. It is evidently composed of the prefix *mo*, which belongs to almost all those words representing intelligent beings, and of the root *holimo*—*above, in the sky. Moholimo*, or the abbreviation Molimo, therefore, signifies, *He who is in the sky.* **1896** F. C. SELOUS *Sunshine & Storm Rhodesia* xxvi. 236 The Umlimos or prophets..exist among all the tribes in Mashunoland. **1928** P. NEILSON *Matabele at Home* ii. 38 Before the occupation by the white people of this country, it had become customary for many of the Matabele to go to the Umlimo's cave..at regular intervals, and there to make obeisance by presenting the Umlimo with cattle and beer. **1955** E. C. TABLER *Far Interior* iv. 112 These magicians were diviners and hereditary priests of the cult of *Mwari* (Sintabele, *Mlimo*), a deity that was believed to have made the world and therefore controlled the rain... Lobengula, who seems to have had no faith in the *Mlimo*, nevertheless refrained from wiping out this nest of tricky parasites. **1965** L. H. GANN *Hist. S. Rhodesia* iv. 128 The Matabele, have settled north of the Limpopo, transferred their allegiance from *Nkulunkulu*, the Zulu high god, to *Mlimo*, the Karanga deity. *Ibid.* 129 *Mlimo* originally appears to have been regarded as some remote *deus abscondidus*, the Ancient of Days, who took no notice of tribal affairs... But when the Matabele fell on evil days the god gained increasing political importance, and his cult..provided an effective machinery of revolt.

Mlle. Abbrev. of Mademoiselle (see MADEMOISELLE 1).

1792 F. BURNEY *Jrnl.* May (1972) I. 155 *Mlle Planta* had told her I was going to be married!..why what I had said.. a week a go, should not have reached this Mlle nor her informant, is marvellous. **1820** M. WILMOT *Let.* 3 Mar. (1935) 53 Poor nurse had her share—Mlle hers—and Nanny hers. **1896** C. K. SHORTER *Charlotte Brontë & her Circle* iv. 109 Madame Héger..has been gibbeted for all time in the characters of Mlle. Zoraïde Reuter and Madame Beck. **1975** B. GARFIELD *Hopscotch* i. 13 The German folded and then it was *Mlle* Stein's turn.

mm, m'm ((ə)m). Also **mm-m**, (*rare*) **mn.** [Imit.] Used to express a hesitating or inarticulate utterance of interrogation, assent, reflection, or satisfaction on the part of a speaker. Cf. UM *int.*

1922 JOYCE *Ulysses* 56 A sleepy soft grunt answered:—Mn. **1924** *Dialect Notes* V. 273 *M-*: —, — -m. **1966** G. N. LEECH *Eng. in Advertising* xxii. 197 By tomorrow they'll [*sc.* sandwiches] lose not a single 'M'm' of flavoursome moisture! **1967** *Boston Herald* 8 May 24/4 (*caption*) Mm... Another dud, but not bad for a dull movie. **1967** *Listener* 21 Sept. 367/2 Restraint is unnatural, mm? **1968** [see CHASE *v.*[1] 7 c]. **1974** D. FRANCIS *Knock Down* ii. 21 'You'd thought of that, had you?'.. 'Mm,' I said.

Mme. Abbrev. of Madame (see MADAME 1).

1806 *Young Ladies' Assistant in Writing French Lett.* i. 6 In hand-written letters, *Monsieur, Madame, Mademoiselle*, before family names, are abbreviated thus: *Mr. Mde. Mlle.*; in printed ones, we find *M.* for *Monsieur*, *Mme.* for *Madame*, *Melle.* for Mademoiselle. **1860** D. G. ROSSETTI *Let.* 9 June (1965) I. 368 My best address would be: Chez Mme Houston (as above): the said Mme is English and very obliging. **1896** C. K. SHORTER *Charlotte Brontë & her Circle* iv. 102 Mme. Héger was an accomplished spy. **1975** *Listener* 7 Aug. 190/1 Mme Laure Bernardini and her companion, Mme Thérèse, are very old.

‖**mna.** [Gr. μνᾶ: see MINA[1].] = MINA[1].

1603 HOLLAND *Plutarch's Mor.* 373 A halfe a Mna [*mispr.* Mua; corrected in Errata] of silver. **1737** WHISTON *Josephus, Of Jewish Weights & Meas.* p. cl, Maneh, or Mna—100 Shekels in weight—21,900 grains Troy. Maneh, Mna, or Mina, as a coin = 60 shekels = 7. 10. 0. **1845** *Encycl. Metrop.* I. 444/2 The Greeks had a second pound of 16 physical ounces, called the *mna*, or *mina*.

†**mnam.** *Obs. rare.* Also NAM. [a. L. *mnam* (Luke xix. 24), accusative of *mnā* MNA.] = MNA.

1377 LANGL. *P. Pl.* B. VI. 244 [He] ȝaf þat Mnam to hym þat ten Mnames hadde.

mneme (ˈniːmiː). *Psychol.* and *Physiol.* [a. G. *mneme* (R. Semon *Die Mneme als erhaltende Prinzip im Wechsel des organischen Geschehens* (1904)), f. Gr. μνήμη memory.] The capacity which a living substance or organism possesses for retaining after-effects of experience or stimulation undergone by itself or its progenitors.

1913 M. HARTOG *Probl. Life & Reproduction* 275 The mnemic possibilities of an organism may be termed, collectively, its 'mneme'. **1921** L. SIMON tr. *Semon's Mneme* 12 The capacity for such after-effect of stimulation constitutes what I have called the Mneme. **1928** J. T. MACCURDY *Common Princ. Psychol. & Physiol.* ii. 15 The mneme and memory are thus reduced, fundamentally, to physico-chemical phenomena. **1966** E. ENG tr. *Strauss's Phenomenological Psychol.* I. iii. 61 *Mneme* must not be limited to organic substances.

mnemic (ˈniːmɪk), *a.* [f. as prec. + -IC.] Pertaining to, of the nature of, or involving mneme. Hence **ˈmnemically** *adv.*, **ˈmnemicness**, the state or quality of being mnemic.

1908 *Daily Chron.* 3 Sept. 5/7 Alleging the existence of a mnemic factor in the life of plants. **1913** [see prec.]. **1921** B. RUSSELL *Analysis of Mind* iv. 78 Following a suggestion derived from Semon..we will give the name of 'mnemic phenomena' to those responses. **1921** L. SIMON tr. *Semon's Mneme* 11 Instead of speaking of a factor of memory, a factor of habit, or a factor of heredity, and attempting to identify one with another, I have preferred to consider these as manifestations of a common principle, which I shall call the mnemic principle. This mnemic property may be regarded from a purely physiological point of view, inasmuch as it is traced back to the effect of stimuli applied to the irritable organic substance. **1925** C. D. BROAD *Mind & its Place* viii. 377 Experiences which are owned in senses (2) or (3) may be said to be 'mnemically owned'. **1941** *Mind* L. 417 The only perceptible difference between conscious and non-conscious behaviour is *mnemicness*. **1943** A. M. FARRER *Finite & Infinite* xvii. 201 That already depends on the mnemic content, which disposes us to attention in one direction rather than another, because certain elements of memory are pressing closest to the gate. **1963** O. L. ZANGWILL tr. *Luria's Restoration of Function after Brain Injury* vi. 213 The patient retained the content of this

particular thought, and..his difficulties were dynamic in nature rather than mnemic. **1968** S. Bogoch *Biochem. Memory* vi. 194 That is, the glycoproteins of the nervous system represent the mnemic substances in which experiential information is encoded.

mnemon (ˈniːmɒn). *Psychol.* [f. Gr. μνήμ-η memory + -on¹.] A unit of memory (see quots. 1965, 1966).

The coiner of the term appears to be Cherkin (quot. 1966), whose forthcoming paper is mentioned by Young in 1965. Cherkin's paper was communicated to the editor of the *Proceedings* on 19 November 1965.

1965 *New Scientist* 23 Dec. 861 In the author's [*sc.* J. Z. Young's] view, memory is localized in small combinations of brain cells, which he calls 'mnemons'. **1966** A. Cherkin in *Proc. Nat. Acad. Sci.* LV. 88 The proposed unit is defined as the minimum physical change in the nervous system that encodes one memory... The name proposed for the unit is the 'mnemon' (mneme = memory; -on = suffix denoting a fundamental particle). **1971** J. Z. Young *Introd. Study Man* xix. 252 The time to begin accumulating such units of memory (mnemons) would be as soon as they are ready.

†**mnemoˈneutic**, *a. Obs. rare*⁻¹. [ad. Gr. μνημονευτικ-ός of or for reminding, f. μνημονεύ-ειν to remind, f. μνήμων (see next).] = mnemonic.

1652 Urquhart *Jewel* Wks. (1834) 212 This Mnemoneutick hexameter, *quis, quid, ubi, quibus auxiliis, cur, quomodo, quando.*

mnemonic (niːˈmɒnɪk), *a.* and *sb.* [ad. Gr. μνημονικ-ός, f. μνημον-, μνήμων mindful, f. μνᾶ-, μνᾶσθαι to remember. Cf. F. *mnémonique*, Sp. *mnemónico*, Pg., It. *mnemonico*, G. *mnemonisch.*]

A. *adj.*

1. Intended to aid the memory; pertaining to mnemonics.

1753 Chambers *Cycl. Supp.*, *Mnemonic Tables*, among the artifices to assist the memory, this is one of great use. **1866** Felton *Anc. & Mod. Gr.* I. i. iii. 40 Many of the North American tribes had invented..a set of mnemonic signs, by which the words of popular songs, once learned, could be recalled to the memory. **1870** Jevons *Elem. Logic* xvi. 141 In the next lesson certain ancient mnemonic lines will be furnished.

2. Of or pertaining to memory.

1825 *Gentl. Mag.* XCV. i. 234 The mnemonic power of the late Professor Porson. **1905** Sherard *Oscar Wilde* 246 We took immense pleasure in this mnemonic tourney.

B. *sb.*

a. A mnemonic device. b. = mnemonics.

1858 J. Martineau *Stud. Chr.* 156 Serving the purpose of a theological Mnemonic to those who want a religion ready more than deep. **1836–7** Sir W. Hamilton *Metaph.* vii. (1859) I. 122 Mnemonic, or the science of the laws of Memory. **1899** *Allbutt's Syst. Med.* VII. 449 The different sounds are best remembered by the mnemonic given by Pitman.

mnemonical (niːˈmɒnɪkəl), *a.* [f. Gr. μνημονικ-ός (see mnemonic) + -al¹.] = mnemonic *a.* 1.

1661 Hartlib in *Worthington's Diary* (1855) II. i. 45 It is the best mnemonical expedient to the acquest of languages. **1701** R. Fleming *Rise & Fall Rome Papal* (1849) 137 To remember the three heads themselves, with relation to the morning, the day, and the evening, as they are comprehended in these three mnemonical words, propose, reflect, and examine. **1839** Hallam *Hist. Lit.* II. ii. iii. §14 In these mnemonical treatises he [Bruno] introduced much of his own theoretical philosophy. **1847** Emerson *Repr. Men, Uses Gt. Men* Wks. (Bohn) I. 287 The history of the universe is symptomatic, and life is mnemonical.

Hence **mneˈmonicalist** = mnemonist; **mneˈmonically** *adv.*, in a mnemonical manner.

1867 *Q. Rev.* Oct. 427 Each one of these mysterious letters was taken, mnemonically, as the initial of some technical word that indicated one of these four methods. **1887** J. Gillow *Bibl. Dict. Eng. Cath.* III. 310 Hill, William, mnemonicalist.

mnemonician (niːməʊˈnɪʃən). [f. mnemonic + -ian.] = mnemonist.

1830 Maunder *Treas. Knowl.* i, *Mnemonician*, one skilled in mnemonics.

‖**mnemonicon** (niːˈmɒnɪkɒn). [Gr. μνημονικόν, neut. sing. of μνημονικός: see mnemonic.] A device to aid the memory.

1858 *Appleton's Cycl.* III. 410 Bode's law is not a law, properly speaking, but simply a mnemonicon for remembering the distances of the planets from the sun.

mnemonics (nɪˈmɒnɪks), *sb. pl.* [f. Gr. μνημονικά, neut. pl. of μνημονικός: see mnemonic and -ic 2 (*-ics*). Cf. F. *mnémonique*, Sp. *mnemónica*, Pg., It. *mnemonica.*] The art of refreshing, improving, or developing the memory, *esp.* by artificial aids; a system of precepts and rules intended to aid or improve the memory.

[**1706** Phillips (ed. Kersey), *Mnemonica.*] **1721** Bailey, *Mnemonicks*, Precepts or Rules and common Places to help the Memory. **1755** in Johnson. **1824** *Register of Arts & Sci.* I. 46 (*heading of paragraph*) Mnemonicks. **1837** *Pop. Encycl.* V. 6/1 The ancients were well acquainted with mnemonics. **1843** Carlyle *Past & Pr.* ii. xvii, With all conceivable appliances and mnemonics. **1866** Brande & Cox *Dict. Sci.*, etc., s.v., The common process of tying a knot in a handkerchief, &c., will exemplify the simplest species of mnemonics.

mnemonist (ˈniːmənɪst). [f. mnemon-ic + -ist.] One versed in the science of mnemonics; one who teaches how to train and improve the memory, or practises the art of memory. Also, a professional entertainer who practises recollection.

1863 Cooper in *N. & Q.* 3rd Ser. III. 383 His [*sc.* Fuller's] contemporaries gave him credit for being an accomplished mnemonist. **1883** *Encycl. Brit.* XVI. 533/1 Modifications of the systems of Feinaigle and Aimé Paris were advocated by subsequent mnemonists. **1969** *Observer* 26 Jan. 28/7 Eventually he became a mnemonist or professional 'memory man'. His powers of recall were not so far from total.

mnemonize (ˈniːmənaɪz), *v.* [f. mnemon(ic) + -ize.] *trans.* To express by a mnemonic formula. Hence **mnemoniˈzation**.

1845 *N. Amer. Rev.* July 260 This work..contains a series of numbers arranged with the various corresponding words to facilitate the rapid mnemonization of facts. *Ibid.* 263 Twelve fortunate individuals being thus mnemonized into immortality. **1850** P. Miles *Mnemotechny* i. 17 On finding an Event with its Date, that we wish to Mnemonize, or retain in the mind by Mnemotechny, we [etc.].

mnemotechnic (niːməʊˈtɛknɪk), *a.* and *sb. pl.* [f. mnemotechny + -ic. Cf. F. *mnémotechnique.*]

A. *adj.* = mnemonic *a.*

1839 *Civil Eng. & Arch. Jrnl.* II. 437/2 The mnenotechnic [*sic*] rules appended to it. **1844** Fauvel Gouraud (*title*) Phreno-mnemotechnic dictionary. **1873** Hamerton *Intell. Life* iii. x. (1875) 128 The mnemotechnic art..may be of some practical use in ordinary life.

B. *sb. pl.* [See -ic 2 (*-ics*).] = mnemonics. Also as *sing. rare.*

1845 Fauvel Gouraud in *N. Amer. Rev.* July 262 A gigantic impulse given to mnemotechnics. **1868** D. G. Brinton *Myths New World* i. (1876) 15 On what principle of mnemotechnics the ideas were connected with the knots and colors we are very much in the dark. **1922** Joyce *Ulysses* 503 See, you have forgotten. Exercise your mnemotechnic.

mnemotechnist (niːməʊˈtɛknɪst). [f. mnemotechny + -ist.] = mnemonist.

1891 *Chambers's Encycl.* VII. 240/2 The mnemotechnist who has a succession of things to be remembered..compels himself to detect some association..between each of them and one of the 'hieroglyphs' which are to serve as memorial links.

mnemotechny (ˈniːməʊtɛknɪ). [f. Gr. μνήμη memory + -τεχνία, τέχνη art. Cf. F. *mnémotechnie.*] = mnemonics.

1845 Fauvel Gouraud (*title*) Phreno-mnemotechny, or the art of memory. **1846** Worcester, *Mnemotechny*.., the art of memory, or an artificial method of improving the memory. **1850** P. Miles (*title*) Mnemotechny, or Art of Memory, theoretical and practical.

mo (məʊ), *adv.*, quasi-*sb.*¹, and *a. Obs.* exc. *Sc.* and *north.* Forms: 1 **má**, *Anglian* **mǽ** (*adv.*); **má** (*adj.*); 2–6 **ma**, 3–6 **maa, moo**, (3 **moa**), 4–6 **may**, (6 **maye, me, mooe**, *Sc.* **mea**, 7 *north.* **meay**), 3–9 **mo**, 5–9 **moe**, 6–9 *Sc.* and *north.* **mae**. [Com. Teut.: OE. *má* corresponds to OFris. *mâ, mê* (beside *mâr, mêr* adv., influenced by the adj. *mâra, mêra* more), MDu. *mee* (the MDu., mod.Du. *meer*, OS. *mêr* adv., is influenced by the adj.), OHG., MHG. *mêr* (mod.G. *mehr*; the MHG. *mê*, early mod.G. *meh*, is a shortened form), ON. *meir(r* (Sw., Da. *mer*), Goth. *mais*:—OTeut. ****maiz***. The OE. variant *mǽ* has not been accounted for; but cf. OE. *mǽst* most *adv.*

According to Brugmann, OTeut. **maiz* is unconnected with L. *mājor, magis*, but is the formal equivalent of Oscan *mais*, and represents an Indogermanic type **məis*, formed with comparative suffix *-is* (: *-*yes*: -*yŏs*) on the root **mə*- (:**mē*-: *mō*-); an ablaut-variant is found in OIrish *māo* more :—**mōyŏs*.]

†A. *adv. Obs.*

1. In or to a greater degree, extent, or quantity. ***mo and mo***: increasingly.

c **825** *Vesp. Psalter* li. 5 Ðu lufedes hete ofer freamsumnisse, unrehtwisnisse mae ðon spreocan rehtwisnisse. *c* **888** K. Ælfred *Boeth.* xxxii. §3 Hit þær ne weaxð þe ma ðe ȝimmas weaxað on winȝeardum. *a* **900** tr. *Bæda's Hist.* iv. xxix. (1890) 370 Ðæt he..to ðæm upplican lustum ma & ma onbærned wære. *c* **1175** *Lamb. Hom.* 9 Na ma ne mei me her god don for þere saule þe on þis liue god bi-ȝinnen nalde. *a* **1300** *Cursor M.* 5532 (Cott.) Þis folk multiplid ai maa [*a* **1425** *Trin.* moo & moo].

2. Longer, further, again, besides. Chiefly qualified by *any, no, none*; *ever, never* = at (any or no) future time. See also evermo, nathemo, nevermo.

c **897** K. Ælfred *Gregory's Past. C.* lii. 405 Wenestu recce he hire æfre ma? **971** *Blickl. Hom.* 247 Þæt wæter oflan and ma of heora muþe hit ne eode. *c* **1200** Ormin 4206 Þatt næfre ma ne shall he ben O nane wise filedd. *c* **1386** Chaucer *Wife's Prol.* 691 It is an impossible That any clerk wol speke good of wyues,..Ne noon oother womman neuer the mo. —— *Wife's T.* 8 But now kan no man se none Elues mo. *c* **1440** *Generydes* 2722 Nor let no mo suche thoughtez yow assayle. **1584** Peele *Arraignm. Paris* v. i, Without mislike or quarrell any moe, Pallas shall rest content. **1591** Greene *Maiden's Dr.* xv, No foreign wit could Hatton's overgo: Yet to a friend wise, simple, and no mo. *a* **1619** Fletcher, etc. *Q. Corinth* iii. ii. Song, Grief is but a wound to woe; Gent'lest fair, mourne, mourne no moe. **1812** Byron *Ch. Har.* i. xciii, Ye..Shall find some tidings in a future page, If he that rhymeth now may scribble moe.

B. quasi-*sb.* [These uses originated from the adv., but from the point of view of the later language those that survived may be regarded as elliptical uses of the adj.]

†1. With partitive genitive sing.: Something in addition; an additional quantity or amount. *Obs.*

a **1000** *Andreas* 1443 (Gr.) No þe laðes ma þurh daroða ȝedrep ȝedon motan, þa þe heardra mæst hearma ȝefremedan. *a* **1250** *Owl & Night.* 564 (Jesus MS.) Hwat dostu godes among monne? Na mo þene doþ a wrecche wrenne.

†2. A greater number; more individuals of the kind specified or implied. Const. *than. Obs.*

In OE., a verb to which *má* is the subject is put in the singular. Subsequently, *mo* in this sense was treated as an adj. with ellipsis of a plural sb, and therefore takes a plural vb.

a. In early use, with partitive genitive plural; later, const. *of.*

a **900** tr. *Bæda's Hist.* ii. ii. (1890) 102 Mid þy eower ma is. **971** *Blickl. Hom.* 61, & weana ma þonne æniȝes mannes ȝemet sy þæt hie ariman mæȝe. *c* **1175** *Lamb. Hom.* 27 Ma monna ic scolde biȝeten swa. *c* **1386** Chaucer *Prol.* 576 Of maistres hadde he mo than thries ten. *c* **1470** Henry *Wallace* ii. 192 Off ws thai haiff wndoyne may than ynew. **1546** Langley *Pol. Verg. De Invent.* vii. vi. 144 b, Of these valiant beggers there be in euery place mo then a great meny. **1549** *Compl. Scot.* iv. 29 Ther is maye of the sect of sardanapalus amang vs, nor ther is of scipions. **1630** tr. *Camden's Hist. Eliz.* i. 19 The Papists murmured, 'That moe of the Protestants were chosen of set purpose'.

†b. Without partitive genitive or its equivalent. Often = more persons. †***mo twice***: twice as many. *Obs.*

a **900** tr. *Bæda's Hist.* i. xi. [xiv.] (1890) 48 Þæt heora moniȝe heora feondum on hand eodan; & ȝyt ma wæs þe þæt don ne wolde. *c* **1200** *Trin. Coll. Hom.* 141 And muchele mo fareð on þisse sæ, þat is on þisse worelde, fuliende þe leome of penitence..þane don þe leome of maiðhod. *c* **1205** Lay. 12036 Heo..iseȝen scipen an & an while ma [*c* **1275** mo] while nan. *a* **1225** *Ancr. R.* 42 Her siggeð fifti auez, oþer an hundred, oðer mo oðer les. *Ibid.* 74 Mo sleað word þene sweord. *a* **1300** *K. Horn* 864 Her buþ paens ariued, Wel mo þane fiue. *c* **1470** Henry *Wallace* x. 113 And I haiff seyn may twys in to Scotland, With ȝon ilk king. **1563** Winȝet *Four Scoir Thre Quest.* Wks. (S.T.S.) I. 129 In mony places thryse in ye oulk, and in fer may nocht anis in the moneth. **1594** Hooker *Eccl. Pol.* i. x. §2 Unto life many implements are necessary; moe, if we seek..such a life as [etc.].

†c. ***the mo***: the majority, the greater part. *Obs.*

c **1330** R. Brunne *Chron.* (1810) 58, & for he had þe treuth, on his side were þe mo. **1399** Langl. *Rich. Redeles* iv. 86 Some helde with the mo how it euere wente. *c* **1449** Pecock *Repr.* v. vii. 522 The mo of the peple. **1526** *Pilgr. Perf.* (W. de W. 1531) 173 b, Crisostom answereth. Before the mo he hath spoken euyll of the. **1589** Puttenham *Eng. Poesie* i. xv. (Arb.) 48 Some men among the moe became mighty and famous in the world.

†d. Phrases. ***and mo, or mo***: and, or a larger number than that specified. (Frequently used to express an indefinite excess over a number stated approximately.) Similarly, ***one or mo***. *Obs.*

a **1000** *Elene* 634 (Gr.) Is nu worn sceacen .cc. [*sc.* wintra] oððe ma ȝeteled rime. *c* **1200** *Trin. Coll. Hom.* 135 His michelnesse was unhiled on ten fold wise and mo. *c* **1290** *S. Eng. Leg.* I. 313/490 For þe man þat miȝte go euereche daye fourty mile, and ȝeot sumdel mo. *c* **1320** *Sir Tristr.* 613 He .. redily ȝaf hym..Ten schilinges and ma. *c* **1470** *Gol. & Gaw.* 970 His scheild he chopit hym fra In tuenty pecis and ma. **1473** *Exch. Rolls Scotl.* VIII. 153 *note*, To mak and depute subtennandis undir him in the said landis ane or maa as he thinkis maste expedient. **1599** *Act Sed.* 3 Nov. (1790) 30 That the secretarie..mak and constitut particular deputts, ane or mae. **1617–18** W. Lawson *Orch. & Gard.* Pref. (1623) A iij b, A..way of planting, which I haue found good by 48. yeeres (and moe) experience.

†e. In phrases of which the proverb ***the mo the merrier*** is the type. *Obs.*

1375 Barbour *Bruce* xiv. 273 The ma thai be, The mair honour allout haue we. **1529** S. Fish *Supplic. Beggers* (1871) 13 To make many hospitals for..poore people? Nay truely. The moo the worse. **1571** Digges *Pantom.* i. vii. C iv b, So haue ye the sides of your scale eche to be deuided in 12. 60. 100. 1000. poynts..the mo the more commodious. *a* **1575** Gascoigne *Posies, Flowers* 30 And mo the merrier is a Prouerbe eke. **1684** G. Meriton *Yorksh. Dial.* 64 Meay the merryer, but fewer better Fair.

†f. ***mo and mo***: used to express a progressive increase in numbers. *Obs.*

c **1205** Lay. 18276 Auer þer comen ma & ma and ferden touward Octa. **1530** Palsgr. 707/1 Sythe we used to scourge beggars out of towne, we have ever sythe had mo and mo.

3. Other individuals of the kind specified; other persons or things in addition to those mentioned. Const. *than, save, but.* See also no mo.

In the combinations *many mo, a hundred mo*, etc., *mo* admits of being taken as adv.: see A 1. So also in the modern *no mo*, which must not be confounded with the OE. *ná má*, where *ná* = 'not', and *má* might be referred to sense B 2. (The first quot. may belong to A. 2.)

c **1000** Ælfric *Gram.* xiv. (Z.) 262 Donatus telð ȝyt ma to ðisum: *ni, nisi*, sed. *Ibid.* 89 [see no mo]. *c* **1200** Ormin 15496 Þuss wrohhte þær þe Laferrd Crist..hiss firrste takenn, & affterr þatt he wrohhte ma. *a* **1225** *Ancr. R.* 328 Þis beoð nu nie reisuns, & monie moa þer beoð. *c* **1275** *Passion our Lord* 686 in *O.E. Misc.* 56 Nerun and Dacyen and mo þet beoþ vor-lorene. **13..** *E.E. Allit. P.* A. 870, & wyth hym maydennez an hundreþe þowsande & fowre & forty þowsande mo. *c* **1400** *Rom. Rose* 3023 He was not sole, for ther was mo. **1413** *Pilgr. Sowle* (Caxton 1483) iv. vii. 61 This fayre grene appel tree..said..I ne bere neuer no mo but this

one appel. c1460 *Towneley Myst.* iii. 152 Take..of ich kynd beestis two, Mayll & femayll, but no mo. **1540** J. Heywood *Four P.P.* A j b, Yet haue I been at Rome also And gone the stacions all arowe, Saynt Peters shryne and many mo. **1594** Hooker *Eccl. Pol.* ii. vii. §2 The Chronicles of England mention no moe than only six kings bearing the name of Edward. **1597** *Ibid.* v. lxxviii. §12 The ancientest of the Fathers mention those three degrees of Ecclesiastical order specified and no moe. **1605** Bacon *Adv. Learn.* ii. xv. §3 And besides which axioms, there are divers moe. **1641** C. Burges *Serm.* 5 Nov. 3 In all which places, and many moe, the Originall word is [etc.]. **1725** Ramsay *Gentle Sheph.* iv. i, But first I'll Roger raise, and twa three mae, To catch her fast. **1785** Burns *Death & Dr. Hornbook* xxii, Forbye some new, uncommon weapons..Sal-alkali o' Midge-tail clippings, And mony mae. **1844** W. Jamie *Muse of Mearns* 71 (E.D.D.) Several mae that I did ken.

b. const. *of*.

1562 Turner *Baths* 13 Other writers give a geat deale mo of properties unto this bath. **1583** *Leg. Bp. St. Androis* 614 Of honest men he had na mea. **1724** in Calderwood *Dying Testimonies* (1806) 232 Would you open moe of their eyes. **1856** G. Henderson *Pop. Rhymes etc. Berw.* 14 Need I mention ony mae..O' the honest men o' the day.

†**c.** Phrases: ***withouten mo, but ma*** (Sc.) = only, alone. *Obs.*

c1290 *S. Eng. Leg.* I. 311/418 þat euerech of heom [*sc.* firmamenz], i-wis, One steorre hath with-oute mo þat planete i-cleoped is. a1300 *Cursor M.* 13489 Fiue laues and fisches tua, Bot quat don þai, wit-vten maa? **1375** Barbour *Bruce* ii. 9 For he wald in his chambre be..in priuate, With him a clerk, for-owtyn ma. c1440 *Generydes* 2682 It is your loue, quod she, withoute moo. **1560** Rolland *Crt. Venus* Prol. 88 On ane of thame alluterlie, but ma. a1600 Montgomerie *Misc. Poems* vii. 46 O worthie wicht both wyse and womanlie! O myn but mo!

C. *adj.* = more *a.*

[In OE. the construction of *má* with a partitive genitive (see B 1, 2) was sometimes inconvenient, because the sb. which was felt to be virtually the subject or object of the verb, or the regimen of the prep., did not show the nature of this relation by its inflexion. Hence the genitive was occas. replaced by the case in which the sb. would have stood if *má* had been absent, or (to express the same thing in another way) the sb. was placed in apposition with *má*. In this way *má* became practically an indeclinable adj.]

1. (With a sb. in *sing.*)

a. As the comparative of much: More or greater in amount or quantity. **b.** Additional, further.

This use has always been rare, and perhaps the later examples may be due to mere inadvertence.

971 *Blickl. Hom.* 231 Ac ma wen is þæt þu onsende þinne engel, se hit mæg hrædlicor geferan. *Ibid.* 247 Ara nu..and ma wæter of þinum muþe þu ne send. c1275 *Passion our Lord* 317 in *O.E. Misc.* 46 Hwat abyde ye nuþe to habben mo wytnesse. **14..** *Lett. Marg. Anjou & Bp. Beckington* (Camden) 69 For their moe surete, ye do the said B. and his servants to be bounden to us. **1535** Stewart *Cron. Scot.* III. 347 With small power rydand furth the way, This Striuiling, ..With far ma power hes him vmbeset. **1610** Shaks. *Temp.* v. i. 234 With..noyses Of roring,..gingling chaines, And mo diuersitie of sounds. **1650** Slingsby *Diary* (1836) 342 Never thirstinge ambiciousiy after more honor nor covetously of moe estate. **1893** *Northumbld. Gloss.* s.v. *Mae*, The mae pairt on them wis gan back agyen.

2. As the comparative of many: More in number (as distinguished from *more*, greater in amount or quantity). Const. *than*, *nor*; also negatively with *but*. Frequently qualified by *many*, also by *far*, *well*. Rarely put after the *sb.*

c1200 *Trin. Coll. Hom.* 27 And forgiue us ure gultes þe we hauen don..and ofte..and muchele mo siðe þanne we seʒen muʒen. a1300 *Cursor M.* 21883 Bot ai þe ma takens we se, Ai þe warr warnist ar we. **1398** Trevisa *Barth. De P.R.* vii. lxvi. (1495) 282 The female serpentes haue moo teeth than males. **1481** Caxton *Reynard* (Arb.) 7 Ye haue byten and nypte myn vncle..many mo tymes than I can telle. **1530** Rastell *Bk. Purgat.* i. xiii, There be no mo Goddys but one. a1641 Bp. Mountagu *Acts & Mon.* (1642) 28 Bookes of moe sorts then one. **1655** Fuller *Ch. Hist.* viii. ii. §16 According to the rules of proportion, who could expect otherwise, but, the moe men, the moe Martyrs? **1737** Ramsay *Sc. Prov.* (1750) 5 A fair maiden tocherless will get mae wooers than husbands. **1868** J. Salmon *Gowodean* iii. ii, Ane maun keep mony mae cracks to their sel',..than abroad they tell.

†**b.** Phrases. ***mo..than one or two, two or three, mo..than enough.*** *Obs.*

13.. *Gaw. & Gr. Knt.* 730 He sleped in his yrnes Mo nyʒtez þen in-noghe in naked rokkez. c1500 *Lancelot* 1197 The lady said, 'Per dee, He vsyt haith mo horses than one or two'. **1500–20** Dunbar *Poems* lxxi. 4 ʒeiris and dayis mo than two or thre.

†**c.** predicatively. *Obs.*

a1300 *E.E. Psalter* xv. 2 Tille haleghs þat in land are ma, He selkouthed alle mi willes in þa. **1375** Barbour *Bruce* xi. 636 His fayis ar ma Than he. a1400 *Sir Perc.* 926 He was ferde lesse my sonnes sold hym slo, Whenne thay ware eldare and moo. c1460 *Towneley Myst.* i. 163 Erthly bestys ..bryng ye furth and wax ye mo. c1460 Fortescue *Abs. & Lim. Mon.* v. (1885) 119 How be it thai [*sc.* harms] bith mony mo than we haue shewid yet. **1567** *Cal. Laing Charters* (1899) 208 Becawse thai war fer may nor he was, he mycht nocht stope thaim. **1611** Bible *Ps.* lxiv. 4 They that hate mee without a cause are moe then the haires of mine head. **1624** Bp. Mountagu *Gagg* 32 Ecclesiasticall constitutions are moe, more certaine; of the same authority with the Churches written Lawes. **1655** Fuller *Ch. Hist.* ii. ii. §6 Seeing you are moe in Number.

3. Additional to the number specified; further, other.

Forming an adjunct to a sb. pl., often qualified by an indefinite adj. as *many*, *any*, etc., or by a definite numeral adj. as *one*, *two*, etc.

c1000 Ælfric *Gram.* viii. (Z.) 32 Þus byð eac on ma stowum. c1320 *Sir Tristr.* 335 Þe fairest hauke he gan ta þat tristrem wan þat day; Wiþ him he left ma Pans for to play. **1382** Wyclif *Ruth* i. 11 Y haue no mo sonys in my wombe. c1449 Pecock *Repr.* ii. xi. 215 Thouȝ ther wer x. thousind mo bokis writun in Londoun..of the same Seintis lijf. c1483 Caxton *Dialogues* 30/24 Make the ynche to seethe, And put therin mo galles And more substance. **1564** Bulleyn *Dial. agst. Pest.* 4 b, [A beggar from Redesdale (Northumberland) says:] Besides vs pakers, many me men haue gud lucke. c1600 Montgomerie *Cherrie & Slae* 847 Thair be mae sences than the sicht. **1613** Shaks. *Hen. VIII*, iii. ii. 5 You shall sustaine moe new disgraces, With these you beare alreadie. a1649 Drumm. of Hawth. *Poems* Wks. (1711) 2 Day shall but serve moe sorrows to display. **1721** Ramsay *Prospect of Plenty* 206 For rowth shall cherish love, and love shall bring Mae men t'improve the soil. **1813** E. Picken *Misc. Poems* i. 151 Gie's nae mae sic wither-shins.

†**b.** put after a sb. pl.; also with a sb. sing. preceded by *many a*, and negatively. †***times mo***, at other times. *Obs.*

c1200 Ormin 8157, & ȝet he haffde suness ma Acc himm he ȝaff þatt crune. a1300 *Cursor M.* 3210 Sex scor and seuen yeir liued sarra And deid wit-outen childer ma. a1300 *Fall & Passion* 11 in *E.E.P.* (1862) 13 And in to helle sone he liȝte an wiþ him mani an mo. c1330 R. Brunne *Chron.* (1810) 26 After nyen & twenty ȝere þe dede him hiþen nam, & sex monethes mo. c1386 Chaucer *Clerk's T.* 393 Ther fil, as it bifalleth tymes mo [etc.]. **1423** Jas. I *Kingis Q.* xlii, I..sawe hir walk..With no wight mo, bot onely wommen tueyne. c1440 *Generydes* 1964 After hym ther came ij kynggez moo. **15..** *Adam Bel* 538 in Ritson *Anc. Pop. P.* 25 Syr, they be slayne,.. And many an officer mo. **1579** Spenser *Sheph. Cal.* June 57, I sawe Calliope wyth Muses moe..Theyr yvory Luyts..forgoe. a1584 Montgomerie *Cherrie & Slae* 20, I saw the cunning and the cat,..With mony beistis mo.

†**c.** with a sb. pl. qualified by *other* or with *other* used absolutely. *Obs.*

c1290 *Beket* 571 in *S. Eng. Leg.*, Seint Thomas grauntede bluþeliche þeos [*sc.* laws] and oþure mo. *Ibid.* 2079 Ofte ich habbe þe guod i-do and manie othure mo. a1300 *Cursor M.* 14449 Lazar þat ded was..he raisid, and oþer maa. **1390** Gower *Conf.* I. 181 Tuo Cardinals he hath assissed With othre lordes many mo. c1400 *Apol. Loll.* 79 And þis inconuenient mai w^t mani moo oþer. **1470–85** Malory *Arthur* i. viii. 45 Kyng Lot and mo other called hym a wytche. **1513** Douglas *Æneis* iii. iv. 6 The cruell Celeno, With all the vtheris Harpyis mony mo. **1545** Ascham *Toxoph.* i. (Arb.) 27 And infinite other mo lettes. **1622** Wither *Chr. Carol* 87 Some others play at Rowlandhoe And twenty other Gameboys moe. **1652** C. B. Stapylton *Herodian* xvii. 144 These Countries got he left unto his heires, With other moe.

¶**4.** ***mo and less***: misused for *more and less* in reference to condition or rank. *Obs. rare*$^{-1}$.

1426 Audelay *Poems* 80 Fore thi-self furst thou pray.. And fore men and women mo and lees.

mo (məʊ), *sb.*^{2} Also mo'. Colloq. or slang abbrev. moment *sb.* Chiefly in ellipt. phr. ***half a mo***: wait for half a moment, *i.e.*, for a short time.

1896 in J. R. Ware *Passing Eng.* (1909) 9/2 In half a mo'—half a mo' Your pluck and perseverance you can show. **1903** [see 'arf]. **1905** H. G. Wells *Kipps* ii. v. 234 Chitterlow hesitated. 'Half a mo', my boy,' he said. **1929** N. C. James *Sleeveless Errand* 176 Well, wait a mo, while I get my tata on. **1934** [see 'arf]. **1938** Auden & Isherwood *On Frontier* iii. i. 98 Wait a mo. Gimme a torch. **1972** J. Wilson *Hide & Seek* vi. 110 Hang on... Hang on a mo. Look, you can't pin nothing on me.

mo, *sb.*^{3} Austral. and N.Z. slang abbrev. moustache, mustache *sb.*

1936 M. Franklin *All that Swagger* xli. 383 Darcy was a man. He had a 'mo'. **1946** D. Stivens *Courtship Uncle Henry* 18 'I'll warm your pants for you..' he'd warn me, the ends of his long black mo shaking. **1947** 'A. P. Gaskell' *Big Game* 17 Never mind Henry,..we'll soon shave Hitler's mo off.

mo' (mɔː), *a.* (*sb.*) and *adv. U.S.* Also mo. An abbrev. (chiefly found in written Black English) of more *a.* (*sb.*) and *adv.*, esp. in phr. ***no mo'***.

1902 J. D. Corrothers *Black Cat Club* i. 23 Read dat piece o' yo's once mo' an' let me die a-listenin' to it! *Ibid.* ii. 40 Black cats is dead bad luck. Dey's hoodooed me mo' den once. **1944** C. Himes *Black on Black* (1973) 196 Pour me some mo' of that licker. **1953** S. A. Brown in A. Dundes *Mother Wit* (1973) 41/2 Dere ain't no mo scufflin'. **1962** N. E. Whitten in *Ibid.* 402/1 White folks don' put much stock in roots and the like no mo'. **1969** S. Sanchez in S. Henderson *Understanding New Black Poetry* (1973) iii. 272 White people Ain't rt bout nothing No mo. **1973** *Black World* Sept. 35 Me an' my baby's Got two mo' ways, Two mo' ways to do de Charleston!

-mo (məʊ), *suffix.* The final syllable of terms derived from the abl. sing. masc. of L. ordinal numerals which are used to denote book sizes by the number of leaves into which a sheet of the paper on which the book is printed has been folded, e.g. *duodecimo*, *sextodecimo*, etc., and, by analogy, *vicesimo-quarto*, *tricesimo-secundo*, etc., which may be pronounced or written as *12mo*, *16mo*, *24mo*, *32mo*, etc., or *twelvemo*, *sixteenmo*, *twenty-fourmo*, *thirty-twomo*, etc.

c1716 T. Rawlinson *Let.* in T. Hearne *Remarks & Coll.* (1901) V. 178, I..would willingly know something of y^r Sylloge Epistolar., whither MSs. & unpublish'd, or a 12mo of A^o 1640. **1742** in *N. & Q.* (1855) 2 June 419 History of the Adventures of Joseph Andrews, &c., 12mo., in 2 vols., No. 1500, with alterations. **1776** in T. Harmer *Observations Divers Passages Scripture* (ed. 2) I. 484 (Advt.), The New Testament in Greek,..2 vol. 12mo. **1801** *Schedule of Presswork Prices* in E. Howe *London Compositor* (1947) iii. 98 Twelves: Pot, such as ladies and christian ladies table part, 6mo. 35 Pica ems wide, 26 long. **1810** *Scale of Prices for Compositors' Work* Art. 6, in *Ibid.* vi. 176 English and larger type, not less than 7s... English 12mo. to be paid not less than 10s. 6d. **1841** W. Savage *Dict. Art. of Printing* 798 A sheet of paper folded into twenty-four leaves, forty-eight pages, is termed twenty-fourmo. **1894** *Amer. Dict. Printing & Bookmaking* 548/1 *Trigesimo-secundo*, the bibliographical term for thirty-twomo; written shortly 32mo. **1927** R. B. McKerrow *Introd. Bibliogr.* i. iv. 34 Duodecimo, sextodecimo, vicesimo-quarto, and tricesimo-secundo, but often called 'twelvemo', 'sixteenmo', 'twenty-fourmo', and 'thirty-twomo'. *Ibid.* ii. ii. 167 Both in a 16mo and a 32mo the watermark is, however, often absent. *Ibid.* 170 (*heading*) Twelve-mo by cutting. **1949** F. Bowers *Princ. Bibliogr. Descr.* v. 193 Sexagesimoquarto—64° *or* 64mo. **1952** J. Carter *ABC for Bk.-Collectors* 89 The principal sizes, with their common abbreviations, are: Folio...Quarto... Octavo...Duodecimo (12mo, pronounced twelvemo). Sextodecimo (16mo, pronounced sixteenmo). Vicesimo-quarto (24mo, pronounced twentyfourmo). Tricesimo-secundo (32mo, pronounced thirtytwomo). **1973** *Collins's Authors & Printers Dict.* (ed. 11) 406/2 *Sixty-fourmo*,..a book based on 64 leaves, 128 pages, to the basic sheet..abbr. 64mo (no point).

‖**moa** ('məʊə). [Maori.] **a.** A bird of the genus Dinornis, formerly inhabiting New Zealand.

[**1820** *Gram. & Voc. New Zealand Lang.* 181 *Móe O'*, a bird so called.] **1842** Bp. Williams in *Trans. Zool. Soc.* (1844) III. 237 The Natives told me of some extraordinary monster which they said was in existence,..to which they gave the name of 'Moa'. **1862** Dana *Man. Geol.* 578 The Moa (*Dinornis giganteus*) of New Zealand exceeded the ostrich in size. **1880** *Daily Tel.* 20 Sept., The other Barons are doomed, and will ere long be an extinct species, like the moa.

b. *attrib.*, as ***moa bone***.

1875 J. von Haast in *Trans. N.Z. Inst.* VII. 89 The older occupants, probably the Moa-hunters, who were inhabitants, or at least frequent visitors at the Moa Bone Point Cave. **1957** J. Frame *Owls do Cry* xiv. 61 A moa bone.

Moab ('məʊæb). *University slang.* ? *Obs.* [See quot.; at Winchester College *Moab* is the name for the lavatories.] A kind of hat: see quot. 1865.

1865 *Slang. Dict.*, *Moab*, a name applied to the turban-shaped hat fashionable among ladies, and ladylike swells of the other sex, in 1858–9. From the Scripture phrase 'Moab is my washpot' (Ps. lx. 8), which article the hat in question is supposed to resemble.—*University*. **1884** *Graphic* 20 Sept. 307/2 His stiff brown 'Moab' of the newest fashion.

Moabite ('məʊəbaɪt), *sb.* and *a.* [ad. L. *Mōabīta* (Gr. *Μωαβίτης*, repr. Heb. *mōābī*), f. *Moab*: see -ite.] **A.** *sb.*

1. One of the people of Moab, which bordered on the territory of the trans-Jordanic Israelites. In 16–17th c. occas. applied opprobriously to Roman Catholics.

1382 Wyclif *Deut.* xxiii. 3 Amonytis and Moabites [so all later versions]..shulen not goon into the chirche of the Lord. **1567** *Gude & Godlie Ball.* (S.T.S.) 104 Ze Moabitis, with hornis twa ful hie, Outwart, lyke scheip, ze beir the beistis mark. a1623 W. Pemble *Justif.* iii. iii. (1629) 111 That doctrine is part of the dregs of corrupted nature, maintained by Popish Moabites. **1903** G. Matheson *Repr. Men Bible* II. 66 The Moabite worshipped the physically beautiful.

2. *slang.* (See quots.)

a1700 B. E. *Dict. Cant. Crew*, *Moabites*, Serjeants, Bailiffs and their Crew. **1725** in *New Cant. Dict.* **1823** 'Jon Bee' *Dict. Turf* 210 *Moabites*, baliffs and their followers.

B. *adj.* Pertaining to Moab or the Moabites. ***the Moabite stone***, a monument erected by Mesha king of Moab c850 b.c., which furnishes the earliest known inscription in the Phoenician alphabet.

1870 C. D. Ginsburg (*title*) The Moabite Stone; a facsimile of the original inscription. **1883** *Athenæum* 1 Sept. 275/3 It is not to be supposed that because Berlin was taken in by the Moabite pottery, Dr. Lepsius would wish Bloomsbury to be deceived into buying a forged Deuteronomy.

Hence '**Moabitess**, a woman of the Moabites; **Moabitic** (məʊə'bɪtɪk), '**Moabitish** (-aɪtɪʃ) *adjs.*, of or pertaining to or resembling the Moabites.

1530 Coverdale *Ruth* ii. 6 The damsell the Moabitisse. **1611** Bible *ibid.*, The Moabitish damosell. **1882–3** Schaff *Encycl. Relig. Knowl.* II. 1540 The Moabitic worship.

moag, variant of mogue *v. dial.*

moa-hunter, Moa-hunter ('məʊə 'hʌntə(r)). *N.Z.* [f. moa + hunter.] The name given to early Maori inhabitants of New Zealand. Also *attrib.* Hence **moa-hunting** *ppl. a.*

1870 J. von Haast in *Proc. Zool. Soc.* 53, I have been so fortunate as to find a large Moa-hunters' encampment, with their cooking-places and kitchen-middens. **1872** —— in *Trans. N.Z. Inst.* IV. 78 Proceeding now to an examination of the traces left by the moa-hunting population. *Ibid.* 80, I discovered a moa-hunter encampment of considerable extent. **1873** A. Trollope *Austral. & N.Z.* II. xxiii. 379 From these fractures Dr. Haast draws the conclusion that there were, before the Maoris, a race of moa-hunters. **1874** A. Bathgate *Colonial Experiences* xvii. 241 The moa was hunted and used as food by man... Were these moa-hunters the ancestors of the Maories, or some more ancient race? **1892** W. L. Buller in *Trans. N.Z. Inst.* XXV. 92 Long after the moa-hunters had disappeared. **1950** R. Duff *Moa-Hunter Period Maori Culture* 7 The Moa-hunter phase of Maori culture, as defined and isolated here, is in my opinion clearly distinct from pre-European Maori culture, although it is probably ancestral to it. **1962** *Antiquity* XXXVI. 169 The existence of a widespread Moa-hunter culture in both [North and South] islands inferred by Duff has indeed been demonstrated by a number of excavations. **1974** *Nat. Geographic* Aug. 196 The men who hunted *Dinornis*..were called by later Polynesians *tangata whenua*... But the name

by which they are commonly known in English is the more appropriate one: moa-hunters.

†**moaks.** *Obs.* Pl. **moakses.** [repr. OE. *máx, másc-*, recorded only in Comb.: see MASH *sb.*[1]] A mash in brewing.

1703 SIR J. MORE *Eng. Interest* iv. 62 Two Moakses will.. take out the strength of your Malt. *Ibid.* 68 Lade or Pump out your Second Liquor..on your Moaks. **1728** BAILEY, *Moaks*, a mashing in brewing Drink.

†**moal.** *Obs.* Also 3 mal. [a. ON. *mál* = OE. *mǽl*: see MAIL *sb.*[2]] Language, speech.

c **1200** ORMIN 4270 Forr Jesuss o Grickisshe mal Onn Ennglissh iss Hælennde. *c* **1250** *Gen. & Ex.* 81 Ðes frenkis men o france moal, it nemnen 'un iur natural'.

moal(e, obs. forms of MOLE.

Moal, Moallakat: see MUʿALLAQAT *sb. pl.*

ˈ**moaler.** Some kind of railway lamp.

1843 MEESON & WELSBY *Exchequer Cases* (1845) XII. 33 Scott *v.* The Eastern Counties Railway Company... On the 18th May, 1841, the defendants..agreed to purchase..one triangular lamp,..twelve moaler lamps, four square lamps, two new side lamps [etc.]. *Ibid.* 35 The moaler, the square, and the new side lamps were delivered..and paid for.

moam(e, obs. forms of MOME.

moan (məʊn), *sb.* Forms: 3 man, 3–4 mon, mane, 3–7 mone, 4–6 moon(e, 5–7 moane, (5 moyn), 5– moan; *Sc.* 4–6 mayn(e, 5–9 mane, 8 main, 9 maen. [app. repr. an unrecorded OE. **mán*:—prehistoric OE. **main-*, whence **mainjan*, OE. *mǽnan* MEAN *v.*[2]

The sb. cannot well be identified with OE. *mán* wickedness (though the cognate ON. *mein* has the sense of 'hurt'); perhaps its phonetic coincidence with this may be the cause of its being unrecorded in OE. The word has app. no cognates in Teut. or elsewhere, as there seems to be no sufficient ground for etymologically identifying its derivative OE. *mǽnan* to complain (MEAN *v.*[2]) with *mǽnan* to intend, mean, speak of (MEAN *v.*[1]).]

1. a. Complaint, lamentation; an instance of this, a complaint, lament. Chiefly in phr. ***to make (one's) moan***: const. *of* and with *obj. clause.* Now always apprehended as a transferred use of sense 2.

For †*to mean one's moan*, see MEAN *v.*[2] 1 b.

a **1225** *Ancr. R.* 418 Þis is lodlich þing hwon me makeð mone in tune of ancre eihte. *c* **1290** *S. Eng. Leg.* I. 96/140 And huy afenge þe deth for godes loue: with-oute anie mone. *c* **1290** *Beket* 1264 *ibid.*, To þe we comieth to make ore mone: of strong lif þat we ledez. *a* **1300** *Cursor M.* 16865 Noiþer þai gaf man, ne tok emsample gode þar-bi. *c* **1375** *Sc. Leg. Saints* xxvi. (*Nycholas*) 1137 Þane in his hart he mad mayne & sichit sare. **1398** TREVISA *Barth. De P.R.* XII. xxvii. (1495) 430 The kite sekeþ his meete wepynge wyth voys of pleynynge and of moon. **1413** *Pilgr. Sowle* (Caxton 1483) I. xv. 9, I not to whome to make my mone to. *c* **1450** HOLLAND *Howlat* 41, I herd ane petuoss appele, with ane pur mane, Solpit in sorowe. *a* **1553** UDALL *Royster D.* I. ii. (Arb.) 15 Of loue I make my mone. **1572** in Digges *Compl. Ambass.* (1655) 343 There is very great moan made for the loss of Monsieur D'Candales. **1591** SHAKS. *Two Gent.* II. iii. 33 Marke the moane she makes. **1720** DE FOE *Capt. Singleton* i. (1840) 18 A carpenter..made such pitiful moan to be taken in. **1832** TENNYSON *Miller's Dau.* vi, And oft I heard the tender dove In firry woodlands making moan. **1832** —— *Mariana in South* i, But 'Ave Mary', made she moan. *Ibid.* vii, 'The day to night', she made her moan. **1853** LYNCH *Self-Improv.* vi. 135 The moan of the idle about circumstance. **1876** FREEMAN *Norm. Conq.* V. xxiii. 159 In Henry's days the people made their moan that they were ground down.

Comb. **1598** FLORIO, *Querela*, a complaint, a moane-making.

†**b.** A state of grief or lamentation. *Obs.*

1500–20 DUNBAR *Poems* lxxiv. 31 Behald my mayne, and mwrning merwalous. **1560** INGELEND *Disob. Child* G iij, Thou maiest learne what griefe, sorowe and mone, Socrates had with Xantippa his wyfe. **1591** SHAKS. *1 Hen. VI*, II. iii. 44 Thy mirth shall turne to moane. **1600** DEKKER *Gentle Craft* Wks. 1873 I. 49 T'would kill my soule to leave thee drownd in mone. **1631** MILTON *Epitaph M'ness Winchester* 55 Here be tears of perfect moan Weept for thee in Helicon.

c. A grievance, a grumble; an 'airing' of complaints. orig. *Services' slang.*

1911 'GUNS' & 'THEELUKER' *Middle Watch Musings* 12 'Guard and Steerage 'ammicks, Sir!' I wake up with a groan; Why can't I sleep till 7 a.m.? Once more I had a moan. **1927** *Daily Express* 5 Oct. 3/4 The midshipmen fling their moanful forms into chairs, and one says:—'Come on, you chaps, let's have a moan!' **1942** 'DUGGIE' in Forbes & Allen *Ten Fighter Boys* 20 We all had a moan to the C.O. about it, and he in turn was in full agreement. **1974** *Times* 6 Apr. 14/8 It's the one moan I have about international rugby. There ought..to be referees from neutral countries.

2. a. In mod. use, with onomatopœic suggestion: A prolonged low inarticulate murmur indicative of physical or mental suffering.

Differing from *groan* in that it suggests a sound less harsh and deep, and produced rather by continuous pain than by a particular access or paroxysm.

1673 MILTON *Sonn., Massacre in Piedmont*, Avenge O Lord thy slaughter'd Saints... Their moans The Vales redoubl'd to the Hills. **1708** POPE *Ode St. Cecilia* 60 Sullen moans, Hollow groans, And cries of tortured ghosts! **1789** BLAKE *Songs Innoc., Cradle Song*, Sweet moans, dove-like sighs. **1808** J. MAYNE *Siller Gun* IV. viii, John answer'd only wi' his tears, Or made a maen! [1836, III. vii, mane.] **1864** TENNYSON *Boädicea* 25 Phantom sound of blows descending, moan of an enemy massacred.

b. *transf.* of the low, plaintive sound produced by the wind, water, etc.

1813 SCOTT *Trierm.* III. Introd. iii, See how the little runnels leap, In threads of silver, down the steep, To swell the brooklet's moan! **1832** TENNYSON *Pal. Art* 280 [He] hears the low Moan of an unknown sea. **1860** TYNDALL *Glac.* I. xxvii. 211 The moan of the adjacent pines chimed in noble harmony.

moan (məʊn), *v.* Forms: (? 5), 6–7 mone, (? 5 moone), 6–7 moane, 6– moan, 9 *Sc.* mane, maen. [f. the sb., a new formation taking the place of the older MEAN *v.*[2]

It is doubtful whether the vb. *moan* occurs before the 16th c. *Mone* is often a misprint or editorial misreading for *moue* = move; in other instances the rimes show that the word is MONE *v.* (= *mun*). The two 15th c. instances here given may be genuine, but possibly the true readings are *mene, mournyd.*]

1. a. *trans.* To complain of, lament (something); to lament for (a dead person); to bemoan, bewail. Const. with simple object and object clause.

[**1471**: see MOANED *ppl. a.*] *a* **1548** HALL *Chron., Hen. VIII* 68 b, Their fall was litle moned emong wise men. **1605** STOW *Ann.* 780 This man was greatly moaned of the people. *a* **1677** BARROW *Serm.* Wks. 1716 II. 38 Doth not every man moan the scantness of his lot? **1749** SMOLLETT *Regicide* III. ii, The sick Wretch who moan'd the tedious Night. **1816** SCOTT *Antiq.* xl, Na, na, I maun never maen doing and suffering for the Countess Joscelin. **1848** THACKERAY *Van. Fair* xiv, She..bitterly moaned the fickleness of her Matilda.

†**b.** *refl.* To lament or bewail one's lot, to 'make one's moan'; = MEAN *v.*[2] 2 d. Const. *to. Obs.*

c **1425** *Castle Persev.* 1632 in *Macro Plays* 125 Mankynde! take kepe of chastyte, & mone [*printed* moue; *but cf. quots. under* MEAN *v.*[2]] þee to maydyn Marye. **1548** CRANMER *Catech.* 148 b, God hath commaunded us to..mone ourselues to him in all our troubles and aduersities. **1642** ROGERS *Naaman* 48 You should rouze up yourselves and moan yourselves to the Lord.

†**2.** To condole with (a person); to pity. *Obs.*

1593 *Tell-Troth's N.Y. Gift* (1876) 24 He looked to have his wife rebuked and himselfe moned. **1596** DANETT tr. *Comines* (1614) 332 If this misery had fallen but vpon them only that made this composition, they had not been greatly to be moned. **1669** DRYDEN *Wild Gallant* III. i, *Non.* What! Does he take no pity on me? *Const.* Prithee moane him Isabelle.

3. a. *intr.* To make complaint or lamentation. Const. *of, for.* Now only *arch.* or *poet.*, coloured by association with sense 4.

1593 Q. ELIZ. *Boethius* I. pr. v. 15 Of our complaynt [thou] haste moned [L. *doluisti*], & bewaylde the wrack of estymations Loste. **1593** SHAKS. *Lucr.* 977 Let there bechance him pitifull mischances, To make him mone. **1650** *Sc. Metr. Psalms* cii. 6, I like an owl in desert am, that nightly there doth moan. **1725** POPE *Odyss.* XI. 100 Still as I spoke the phantom seem'd to moan, Tear followed tear, and groan succeeded groan. **1833** TENNYSON *May Queen* Conclus. xiv, And what is life, that we should moan? **1855** BRIMLEY *Ess., Angel in Ho.* 206 We listen to the fierce Achilles moaning for his lost mistress.

†**b.** *trans.* (*causatively*) To cause to lament, to grieve (a person). *Obs. rare*$^{-1}$. (Perh. *moans* is a misreading for *moves.*)

a **1625** FLETCHER, etc. *Fair Maid Inn.* V. i, And yet my wife (which infinitly moanes me) Intends [etc.].

c. (See quot. 1925.) orig. *Services' slang.*

a **1922** T. S. ELIOT *Waste Land Drafts* (1971) 57 line 42 So this injurious race was sullen, and kicked; Complained too of the ship... So the crew moaned. **1925** FRASER & GIBBONS *Soldier & Sailor Words* 156 *To moan*, to complain, to grumble, to be a pessimist. (Navy—equivalent to the Army 'grouse'.) **1948** *Landfall* II. 112 He felt through his pockets for a cigarette, found a butt and lit it. Why moan?

4. a. *intr.* To make a low mournful sound indicative of physical or mental suffering. Cf. MOAN *sb.* 2.

1724 [see MOANING *vbl. sb.*]. **1798** WORDSW. *We are seven* xiii, In bed she moaning lay. **1819** SHELLEY *Cenci* III. ii. 79 The house-dog moans, and the beams crack. **1828** D'ISRAELI *Chas. I*, II. x. 245 The King..throwing himself on the bed..passionately moaned, shedding abundant tears. **1871** R. ELLIS tr. *Catullus* lxiv. 119 Mother, who o'er that child moan'd desperate, all heartbroken.

b. *transf.* of inanimate things.

1805 SCOTT *Last Minstr.* I. xii, She sits..And listens to a heavy sound That moans the mossy turrets round. **1851** KINGSLEY *Song, Three Fishers*, For men must work.. Though the harbour bar be moaning. **1902** A. B. DAVIDSON *Called of God* x. 267 You hear..the forests moan.

5. *trans.* To utter moaningly. Also with *forth.*

1819 KEATS *St. Agnes* xxxiv, Fair Madeline began to weep And moan forth witless words. **1822** SHELLEY *Dirge*, Rough wind, that moanest loud Grief too sad for song. **1859** TENNYSON *Guinevere* 130 And in herself she moan'd 'Too late, too late!' **1878** BROWNING *La Saisaiz* 75 Melodious moaned the other 'Dying day with dolphin-hues.'

Hence †**moaned** *ppl. a.*, lamented.

1471 SIR J. PASTON in *P. Lett.* III. 4 Ther was kyllyd uppon the ffelde..Sir Omffrey Bowghsher off owr contre, whyche is a sore moonyd man her.

moaner (ˈməʊnə(r)). *colloq.* [f. MOAN *v.* + -ER[1].] One who moans; a complainer, a murmurer; a pessimist.

In quots, 1927, 1932 'a singer of blues songs'.

1927 [see HONKY-TONK 1]. **1929** *Papers Mich. Acad. Sci., Arts & Lett.* X. 308/2 *Moaner*, a pessimist. **1932** *Amer. Speech* VII. 247 Clara Smith evidently deems it a mark of distinction to be known as 'The World's Greatest Moaner'. **1942** BERREY & VAN DEN BARK *Amer. Thes. Slang* §406/1 Gloomy or irritable person; pessimist..complainer; fault-finder..*moaner*. **1952** *Landfall* VI. 202 Anyone who questions too often is a 'moaner', yet in New Zealand the moaner is common. **1959** I. & P. OPIE *Lore & Lang. Schoolch.* x. 187 Croydon boys have twenty names for a cry-baby:..*moaner* [etc.]. **1969** I. KEMP *Brit. G.I. in Vietnam* v. 95 Burmeister..once said to me, 'Limey, you and Goad are the two biggest moaners in my squad.' **1969** F. SARGESON *Joy of Worm* iii. 87 But my boy, I did not intend to write you a letter to make myself out what our fellow countrymen call a 'moaner'.

moanful (ˈməʊnfʊl), *a.* [f. MOAN *sb.* + -FUL.]

1. Full of moaning or lamentation; expressing lamentation or grief. Said of a person, his actions, etc., hence of a melody, song, etc., plaintive, mournful, sad. Now somewhat *rare.*

a **1586** SIDNEY *Arcadia* I. (1598) 83 Now ceasse we to wearie the hearers With monefull melodies, for enough our griefes be reuealed. *Ibid.* IV. (1629) 414 But in such monefull march, they went towards the other Shepheards. **1586** WARNER *Alb. Eng.* I. iv, He saw a monefull sort of people. *a* **1677** BARROW *Wks.* (1686) II. 483 Do not (saith S. James) grudge (or make moanfull complaint) against one another. [Cf. quot. *a* 1677 under MOANFULLY *adv.*] **1714** GAY *Sheph. Week, Past.* iii. 26 Sparabella..Did this sad Plaint in moanful Notes devise. **1837** CARLYLE *Misc. Ess., Diam. Neckl.* (1840) V. 104 He..sobbing out the moanfulest broken howl, sank down in swoon. **1855** *Fraser's Mag.* LI. 95, I sang upon the linden like a moanful nightingale.

†**2.** Fraught with or causing lamentation. *Obs.*

1573 TWYNE *Æneid* XII. Nn iij, And houses to deface, and monefull mariages to make. *a* **1660** HAMMOND *Wks.* (1684) IV. 580 Look upon all the sad moneful objects in the world. **1662** HICKERINGILL *Apol. Distressed Innoc.* Wks. 1716 I. 314 'Tis a sad Conscience that can joy at the thoughts of this days moanful Remembrance.

Hence ˈ**moanfully** *adv.*

1621 LADY M. WROTH *Urania* 189 Monefully she would sit, dayes without words. *a* **1677** BARROW *Wks.* (1687) I. 286 Do not (saith S. James) moanfully complain one against another. [Cf. *James* v. 9 Μὴ στενάζετε κατ' ἀλλήλων.]

moanifiˈcation. *nonce-wd.* [see -FICATION.] The action of 'making moan'.

1827 B. HALL *Diary* in Lockhart *Scott* xxv. (1881) 591 When he saw that we had no intention of making any attempt at sympathy or moanification.

moaning (ˈməʊnɪŋ), *vbl. sb.* [-ING[1].] The action of the verb MOAN, in various senses.

a **1586** SIDNEY *Arcadia* I. xi. (1590) 44 Palladius.. besought her for her promise sake, to put silence so longe vnto her moning. **1648** OWEN *Righteous Zeal Encouraged* Wks. 1851 VIII. 143 Hence his complaints, hence his moanings. **1724** RAMSAY *Vision* vi, Thy graneing, and maneing, Have laitlie reich'd myne eir. **1744** ARMSTRONG *Preserv. Health* IV. 151 Nor to the rivulet's lonely moanings tune Your sad complaint. **1855** BAIN *Senses & Int.* II. ii. §9 (1864) 216 The moaning of the wind is due to the waxing and waning of the intensity of the sound. **1889** TENNYSON *Crossing the Bar*, And may there be no moaning of the bar, When I put out to sea. **1904** *Expositor* Mar. 198 The self-commiserating moanings of the modern lyrics of pessimism.

moaning (ˈməʊnɪŋ), *ppl. a.* [f. MOAN *v.* + -ING[2].] **a.** That moans.

a **1800** J. WARTON *Ode on Shooting*, Linnet, or warbling thrush, or moaning dove. **1829** F. GLASSE *Belgic Past., True Lover* 141 A sighing, moaning, am'rous youth. **1830** TENNYSON *Poems* 97 On the black and moaning sea. **1859** KINGSLEY *Misc.* (1860) II. 281 The soft melancholy alto of the moaning woods.

b. *spec.* **moaning minnie** (also with capital initials). (*a*) Either of two German types of mortar (*minenwerfer* or *nebelwerfer*); also, a shell from one of these mortars; (*b*) an air-raid siren; (*c*) = MOANER.

1941 R. GREENWOOD *Mr. Bunting at War* xiv. 192 'One up now,' said Chris, listening to the drone of an engine. 'Hope Moaning Minnie doesn't sound, and bring mother downstairs.' **1944** *Hutchinson's Pict. Hist. War* 12 Apr.–26 Sept. 376 (*caption*) When the Germans beat a hasty retreat from Cagny among the material they abandoned was this multiple mortar, or 'Moaning Minnie'. **1950** [see MINNIE[2], MINNIE]. **1962** *Sunday Times* 21 Jan. 32/4 Another said that she '..just didn't believe these moaning minnies'. **1972** *N.Z. News* 26 Apr. 6/5, I don't want to give the impression of being a moaning Minnie but may I..make a special plea to the railmen to..get back to work.

Hence ˈ**moaningly** *adv.*

1837 VERLANDER *Vestal*, etc. 80 Hark! the sad voic'd bell ..now rolling Moaningly and low. **1844** DICKENS *Mart. Chuz.* xv, High over her they [*sc.* waves] break,..and giving place to others, moaningly depart. **1857** *Fraser's Mag.* LVI. 489 The rain welters moaningly.

moanism (ˈməʊnɪz(ə)m). *rare.* [f. MOAN *v.* + -ISM.] The practice of lamenting; emotionalism.

1916 R. FROST *Let.* 24 May (1964) 34 Moanism and swounding.

moanless (ˈməʊnlɪs), *a.* [f. MOAN *sb.* + -LESS.] Without a moan.

1810 SCOTT *Lady of L.* VI. xxi, Thus, motionless, and moanless, drew His parting breath, stout Roderick Dhu!

moansome (ˈməʊnsəm), *a. nonce-wd.* [f. MOAN *v.* + -SOME.] = MOANFUL.

1883 JEAN INGELOW in *Longm. Mag.* Sept. 533 While lovesome and moansome thereon spake and falter'd the dove to the dove.

†'**moanworthy**, *a. Obs. rare*−1. [MOAN *sb.*] Worthy of lament.

1540 PALSGR. *Acolastus* D iij, This was his moneworthy communication .i. this was his pituous tale worthye to be bewayled or lamented.

moap, obs. form of MOPE *v.*

‖**moar** (mɔəɹ). Also **moor.** [Manx = Irish and Gaelic *maor*: see MAYOR 3.] (See quots.)

1656 J. CHALONER *Descr. Isle of Man* 17 Of which [courts], the Moors which are the Lords Bayliffs of the Land, give Summons. **1702** W. SACHEVERELL *Acc. Isle of Man* 2 The Towns [are govern'd] by the 4 Constables; and the Civil Constitution, by two Deemsters, 6 Coroners, 17 Moars, or Bayliffs, with several other inferiour Officers. **1811** J. JOHNSON *Jurispr. Isle of Man* 82 There is also in each parish in the island, an ancient officer called a Moar, who collects the rents and fines due to the lord [etc.].

moar(e, obs. forms of MOOR, MORE.

moarish(e, obs. forms of MOORISH.

moary, obs. form of MOORY *a.*

† **moashy.** *Obs. rare*−1. Some kind of fur.

1619 MIDDLETON *Tri. Love & Antiq.* D, Lamb, Wolf, Fox, Leopard, Minck, Stote, Miniuer, Racoone, Moashye, Woluerin, Caliber.

moat (məʊt), *sb.*¹ Forms: 4-8 **mote**, 4-6 (9- *dial.*) **mot(t**, 5-6 **moote**, 6 **moate**, 7 **moat.** [ME. *mote, mot*, app. identical with MOTE *sb.*² mound, embankment, a. OF. *mote, motte*.

The development of the sense 'ditch' from that of 'embankment' (for which cf. DIKE *sb.*¹, DAM *sb.*¹) may have taken place in Norman-French: Moisy (*Dict. Patois Normand*) says that *motte* is still used in Normandy for 'moat', and quotes from an early document (? of 16th c.) a passage containing *mote* in this sense.]

1. *Fortif.* A deep and wide ditch surrounding a town, castle, or other building, usually filled with water as a protection against assault. Also *transf.* and *fig.*

1362 LANGL. *P. Pl.* A. VI. 76 Þe Mot is of Merci þe maner al abouten. **1377** *Ibid.* B. XIX. 362 Conscience comaunded þo al crystene to delue, And make a muche mote. **1469** *Bury Wills* (Camden) 46 Alle the curtelage..wyth inne the moote. **1542** BOORDE *Dyetary* iv. (1870) 239 Yf there be a moote made aboute it [*sc.* a mansion], there should be some fresshe sprynge come to it. **1593** SHAKS. *Rich. II*, II. i. 48 The siluer sea, Which serues it in the office of a wall, Or as a Moate defensiue to a house. **1647** CLARENDON *Hist. Reb.* VI. §276 The Close in Leitchfield..; a place naturally strong, and defended with a moat. **1694** G. SAVILE *New Model at Sea* 4 It may be said now to England,..What shall we do to be saved in this World? There is no other answer, but this, Look to your Mote. **17..** S. JENYNS *Mod. Fine Lady* in Dodsley *Poems* (1763) III. 174 Until at length appears the ruin'd hall Within the grass-green moat, and ivy'd wall. **1808** LD. ERSKINE in Hansard *Parl. Debates* X. 929 Surrounded by that impregnable moat with which the Divine Providence has fortified this island, we can say [etc.]. **1820** W. IRVING *Sketch Bk., Royal Poet* I. 194 The garden ..occupies what was once the moat of the keep. **1871** FREEMAN *Norm. Conq.* (1876) IV. xviii. 153 A sort of ravine ..forms a natural moat round the greater part of the city. **1937** *Times* 16 Nov. 19/6 One pair [of ducks] yearly chose the old moat or 'mott', all among the reeds and the moorhens, [to nest in].

2. A pond, lake; esp. a fish-pond. *Obs.* exc. *dial.*

1463 *Mann. & Househ. Exp.* (Roxb.) 563 My master put into his longe mote be the hye wey att Overbury halle, in roches, ixxx. [**1472** in Blount *Law Dict.* (1691) s.v. *Mote*, Rogerus tradidit prefato Thomæ tria stagna & unam Motam Piscariam existentem infra manerium Domini de Yeffyn.] **1539** *Act 31 Hen. VIII*, c. 2 *title*, Fishing in any seuerall ponde stewe or mot with an intent to steale fishe out of the same is felony. **1598** YONG *Diana* 71 They came to a large greene meadow, wherein was a very faire great moate of cleere water. **1774** GOLDSM. *Nat. Hist.* (1776) VI. 38 The water-hen..keeps near ponds, motes, and pools of water near gentlemen's houses. **1903** *Dial. Dict., Mot*, a 'moat'; a small pond. *Chs. Nhp. War. Ess.*

3. *attrib.* and *Comb.*, as **moat-side**; **moat-garden**, one situated in a disused moat; †**moat-hen**, the moor-hen, *Gallinula chloropus* (cf. 1774 in 2); **moat-house**, a moated house.

1899 CROCKETT *Black Douglas* (ed 2) 94 Sholto stood..on the topmost step of the ascent from the *moat-bridge. **1826** HOR. SMITH *Tor Hill* (1838) II. 82 The *moat-garden. **1544** TURNER *Avium Præcip.* I 6, Trynga, Anglicè a uuater hen, or a *mot hen. **1899** TREVELYAN *Eng. Age Wycliffe* 318 He was welcomed at nightfall to the kitchen fire of the *moat-house. **1697** VANBRUGH *Relapse* IV. v, Will they open the Gate, or do they desire I should grow at their *Moat-side like a Willow?

† **moat**, *sb.*² *Obs.* Also 7 **mot, moate,** 8 **mote.** [Cf. MIT 2.] A cheese-vat.

1602 PLAT *Delightes for Ladies* III. xxii, You may deuise moates or cases [for cheese] either rounde or square of fine wicker. **1617**, **1629** Cheese mot, moate [see CHEESE *sb.*¹ 7]. **1736** BAILEY *Househ. Dict.* 171 Fill a narrow high cheese mote or vat, continually filling as the curd sinks, till the mote or vat is full.

moat (məʊt), *v.* [f. MOAT *sb.*¹] *trans.* To surround with or as with a moat, ditch, or trench. (Said of a personal agent, also of a river, fosse, etc. which serves as a moat.) Also with *about, in, round.*

c **1420** *Anturs of Arth.* 671 (Thornton MS.), I gyffe to the ..Twa baronryse in Burgoyne, with burghes so balde, That are moted abowte [*Douce MS.* batailed abouȝte]. **1509** HAWES *Past. Pleas.* xxxiv. (Percy Soc.) 175 A manour place, Moted about. **1606** HOLLAND *Sueton.* 17 The Cirque was enlarged on both sides and moted round about [L. & *in gyrum Evripo addito*]. **1680** MORDEN *Geog. Rect., Hungary* (1685) 96 Komora is..moated by the Danow. **1700** DRYDEN *Ceyx & Alcyone* 372 An Arm of Lethe with a gentle flow.. The Palace moats. **1768** MORANT *Essex* II. 599/1 It is now but a farm-house moated in. **1779** FORREST *Voy. N. Guinea* 183 A broad and straight street... It is so well raised, as never to be overflowed; and is moated on both sides. **1848** J. A. CARLYLE tr. *Dante's Inferno* (1849) 88 The deep fosses, which moat that joyless city. **1855** MOTLEY *Dutch Rep.* VI. xi. (1866) 804 Through the breach was seen a massive terreplein, well moated.

b. *transf.* and *fig.*

1617 BP. HALL *Quo vadis* (1624) §1 In moting our Iland with the Ocean he [God] meant to shut vs vp from other Regions. **1625** B. JONSON *Staple of N.* IV. i, He [a mastercook]..Makes Citadels.., Some he dri-dishes, some motes round with broths. **1641** J. TRAPPE *Theol. Theol.* iv. 181 Warding off (as well as they can) Gods blow, motting themselves up against his fire. **1652** BENLOWES *Theoph.* III. lxvi, When purple robes hide scarlet sin Ingrain'd from that life-blood, which moated their Souls in. **1740** H. WALPOLE *Lett.* (1857) I. 63 The torrent broke down the quays... We were moated into our house all day. **1742** YOUNG *Nt. Th.* v. 481 Moated round, with fathomless destruction. **1830** *Examiner* 785/1 A prodigious effusion of cant..streamed forth, to moat in as it were, the new Government. **1852** M. ARNOLD *Empedocles on Etna* II, The sea of cloud That heaves its white and billowy vapours up To moat this isle of ashes from the world.

Hence '**moated** *ppl. a.*

1592 SYLVESTER *Tri. Faith* IV. xiv, Elias' Faith..Fir'd without fire his moated Sacrifice. **1603** SHAKS. *Meas. for M.* III. i. 277 There at the moated-Grange recides this deiected Mariana. **1676** DRYDEN *Aurengz.* Ep. Ded. 1 When he sees he can hardly approach Greatness, but as a Moated Castle. **1845** CARLYLE *Cromwell* I. Introd. iii. 38 A moated mansion, with ditch and painted paling round it. **1903** AUSTIN *Flodden Field* II. 72, I would not be an hour with him alone, For all my vaunted moated maidenhood.

moat(e, obs. forms of MOTE.

moater, variant of MOTER.

moath, obs. form of MOTH *sb.*¹

moating ('məʊtɪŋ). The puddling beaten in behind the stonework of a mining shaft built up through a bed of quicksand.

1830 *Brewster's Edin. Encycl.* XIV. 338/2 The ashler and moating are progressively carried up... The water..is kept back by the clay moating. **1839** in URE *Dict. Arts* 970.

moatley, obs. form of MOTLEY.

mob (mɒb), *sb.*¹ Also 7-8 **mobb.** [Abbreviation of MOBILE *sb.*² Cf. the following:

1711 ADDISON *Spect.* No. 135 ¶10 It is perhaps this Humour of speaking no more than we needs must which has so miserably curtailed some of our Words,..as in *mob. rep. pos. incog.* and the like. *a* **1734** NORTH *Exam.* III vii. (1740) 574, I may note the Rabble first changed their Title, and were called *the Mob* in the Assemblies of this [the King's Head] Club. It was their Beast of Burthen, and called first, *mobile vulgus*, but fell naturally into the Contraction of one Syllable. **1738** SWIFT *Pol. Conversat.*, Wks. VI. 234 Abbreviations exquisitely refined; As Pozz for Positively, Mobb for Mobile.]

1. a. The disorderly and riotous part of the population, the roughs, the rabble; an assemblage of the rabble; a tumultuous crowd bent on, or liable to be incited to, acts of lawlessness and outrage. More recently also *spec.* in *Social Psychol.*

1688 *Verney Mem.* (1899) IV. 447 [13 Dec.] The Mobb carried away the very boards and rafters. [Cf. 1688 LUTTRELL *Brief Rel.* (1857) I. 486 (12 Dec.) This night the mobile were up again (etc.).] **1692** *Jacobite Conventicle* 19 But Common-wealths why should we rob, Of th' Glory of a Ruling Mob. **1695** C. HATTON in *H. Corr.* (Camden) II. 216 For thes 2 nights a great mob have been up in Holborn and Drury Lane. **1774** GOUV. MORRIS in Sparks *Life & Writ.* (1832) I. 25 We shall be under the domination of a riotous mob. **1790** BURKE *Fr. Rev.* (ed. 2) 125 Lord George Gordon ..having..raised a mob (excuse the term, it is still in use here) which pulled down all our prisons. **1849** MACAULAY *Hist. Eng.* v. I. 559 The army had become a mob. **1874** GREEN *Short Hist.* x. (1878) 729 When mobs were roaring themselves hoarse for 'Wilkes and liberty'. **1897** E. A. ROSS in *Pop. Sci. Monthly* July 390 (*heading*) The mob mind. *Ibid.*, Great mental instability marks the true mob. **1931** E. S. BOGARDUS *Fund. Social Psychol.* (ed. 2) xxv. 315 A mob is a crowd in a very high state of suggestibility. **1940** E. A. STRECKER *Beyond Clin. Frontiers* iv. 60 Lynching mobs, certain strike mobs, etc. furnish examples of positive reality-evasion action en masse. **1959** GILL & BRENMAN *Hypnosis* ix. 293 Such people are sometimes said to be hypnotized. They show regressive phenomena similar to those revealed by a mob. **1973** G. R. LESLIE et al. *Order & Change: Introd. Sociol.* xi. 289 Although scientific interest in mobs and riots as mechanisms of social change is relatively new, the phenomena themselves have existed throughout history.

†**b.** One of the mob. *Obs.*

1706 FARQUHAR *Recruiting Officer* II. (1707) 18 Enter Kite, with a Mob in each Hand drunk.

2. The common mass of people; the lower orders; the uncultured or illiterate as a class; the populace, the masses.

This is noted by Swift among the vulgarisms for which he censures Burnet's History.

1691 T. H[ALE] *Acc. New Invent.* p. xxiv, An idle Notion ..that intoxicated the beliefs of the Mob. **1695** DRYDEN tr. *Dufresnoy's Art Paint.* Pref. 26 A very Monster in a Bartholomew-Fair for the Mob to gape at for their two-pence. *a* **1715** BURNET *Own Time* (1900) II. III. v. 70 At least he [the Prince of Orange] thought religion was only for the mob. **1738** SWIFT *Pol. Conversat.* I. 91 She sat among the Mob in the Gallery. **1749** FIELDING *Tom Jones* I. ix, Refusing to gratify the good-natured disposition of the mob. [*Note*] Whenever this word occurs in our writings, it intends persons without virtue, or sense, in all stations. **1752** —— *Covent Gard. Jrnl.* 13 June, Three estates, namely kings, lords, and commons, all entirely passing by in silence that very large and powerful body which form the fourth estate in this community, and have been long dignified and distinguished by the name of 'the mob'. **1779-81** JOHNSON *L. P., Pope* Wks. IV. 42, I, says Pope, have the town, that is, the mob, on my side. **1795** SOUTHEY *Lett. fr. Spain* (1799) 50 The opinion of this forgiving power vested in the church, will, among the mob of mankind, destroy the motives to virtue. **1831** LD. BROUGHAM *Sp.* 7 Oct. (1838) II. 599, I do not mean the populace—the mob: I never have bowed to them. *Ibid.* 600 But if there is the mob, there is the people also. I speak now of the middle classes. **1868** DUFF *Pol. Surv.* 143 The mob of the great cities..is hostile to us.

†**3.** Without *the*: Disorderly or lower-class people forming a crowd. *Obs.*

1693 *Humours Town* 128 A number of undistinguishable mob. **1716** ADDISON *Freeholder* No. 44 ¶3 A cluster of mob, who were making themselves merry with their betters. **1721** DE FOE *Mem. Cavalier* (1840) 15, I saw the street..full of mob. **1751** CHESTERF. *Lett.* 18 Mar. (1774) II. 118 Every numerous assembly is *mob*, let the individuals who compose it be what they will. **1789** A. YOUNG *Trav. France* (1890) 210 Great riots at Belfort:—last night a body of mob and peasants demanded of the magistrates the arms in the magazine.

4. a. A promiscuous assemblage of people; a multitude or aggregation of persons regarded as not individually important. In Austral. and N.Z. use, without disparaging implication, a crowd; (N.Z.) a crowd, a group, a gang of workmen.

1688 CAPT. SOUTHOUSE *Taking K. James*, etc. (B. M. Add. MS. 32091-96, lf. 3), These Gent. mob [*app. meaning* the king and his friends] were much perplex'd to get a coach. **1700** DRYDEN *Cock & Fox* 328 Fancy..Compounds a Medley of disjointed Things, A Mob of Coblers and a Court of Kings. *a* **1704** T. BROWN *Praise Wealth* Wks. 1730 I. 87 The applauses the mob of quality gave to the Don's oration. **1737** POPE *Hor. Epist.* II. i. 108 But for the Wits of either Charles's days, The Mob of Gentlemen who wrote with Ease; Sprat, Carew, Sedley, and a hundred more. **1742** YOUNG *Nt. Th.* VIII. 1088 Earth's genuine sons, the scepter'd, and the slave, A mingl'd mob! a wand'ring herd! **1784** COWPER *Tiroc.* 206 Train him in public with a mob of boys. **1813** SHELLEY *Q. Mab* v. 58 Gold: Before whose image bow..The mob of peasants, nobles, priests, and kings. **1830** in J. West *Hist. Tasmania* (1852) II. 42 A mob of natives appeared at Captain Smith's hut. **1834** in R. MCNAB *Old Whaling Days* (1913) App. C. 424 A mob of natives came running into the hut where we stopped. **1845** *N.Z. Company Rep.* XIX. 70 The Pah is small, and occupied by a few Natives, the crops, as I understood, being the property of several 'mobs' in different parts of the Sound. **1852** *Austral. & N.Z. Gaz.* 10 Jan. 11/2 In Major Hornbrook's words 'the *Stedfast's* mob is a much jollier mob than that of the *Duke of Bronte*'. **1860** G. DUPPA in S. S. Crawford *Sheep & Sheepmen Canterbury* (1949) v. 48 Commence shearing with a strong mob of shearers. **1863** F. E. MANING *Old N.Z.* IV. 66 It was 'our mob' coming to the rescue. **1875** HELPS *Ess., Party-Spirit* 100 Those who think whatever the little mob in which they live pleases to think. **1877** *Ht. Martineau's Autobiog.* III. 177 Young men who deprecated the tyranny of a moneyed mob. **1884** 'R. BOLDREWOOD' *Melb. Mem.* ix, He..was one of the 'Dunmore mob', and aided generally in the symposia which were there enjoyed. **1888** —— *Robbery under Arms* xix, At the side of the crowd was a small mob of blacks. **1890** *Melbourne Argus* 16 Aug. 13/2 It doesn't seem possible to get a mob of steady men for work of that sort now. **1907** W. H. KOEBEL *Return of Joe* 257 [He] had but a few hours ago formed one of their 'mob', and [was] the most skilful bushwhacker in the district. **1941** *Coast to Coast* 214 The mob around the bar was thinning down, with chaps grabbing their bundles and going off home. **1944** *Living off Land* viii. 155 You may meet the Abo. He may be only a poor specimen on the outskirts of a township, or he may be a 'mob' of half-wild blokes in the furthest nor'west. **1960** S. ASHTON-WARNER *Incense to Idols* 23, I know one girl from another, course you do in my mob anyway. **1968** K. WEATHERLY *Roo Shooter* 27 Hunter pushed his way through the mob, every one of whom he knew,..and sat down at the table.

b. *transf.* and *fig.* A heterogeneous collection or crowd (of things). *Obs.* exc. *Austral.* Also quasi-*adv.*

1728 POPE *Dunc.* I. 65 She sees a Mob of Metaphors advance. **1742** YOUNG *Nt. Th.* IX. 1437 'Twill not make one amid a mob of thoughts. **1844** *Port Philip Patriot* 22 July 2/6 They buttoned up in front; the only suit in the mob which did so. **1892** G. PARKER *Round Compass in Austral.* v. 72 My wife..insisted on my carrying this book to you..and if it was in your mob of books, to give this copy to somebody that would appreciate it. **1934** A. RUSSELL *Tramp-Royal in Wild Austral.* xiii. 91 There'll be mobs of water on the track, we'll get mobs of beef at the runs, the stages'll be mobs shorter, an' there'll be mobs better camping grounds... And of course we'll be able to take it mobs easier. **1942** C. BARRETT *On the Wallaby* iii. 41 Even an offer of..mobs of tucker.. failed to gain me a guide.

c. orig. *Austral.* A flock or drove of animals. (The form *mop* in quot. 1836 is perh. a mistake.)

1836 in *Three Yrs. Exper. of Settler in N.S.W.* 44 (Morris) While I watched the mop [of cattle] I had collected. **1838** T. WALKER *Month in Bush* 8, I beheld a level plain,..with ..'mobs' of cattle scattered over the surface. **1843** J. COTTON *Let.* July in Billis & Kenyon *Pastures New* (1930) xiii. 227, I inspected a mob (as it is termed here) of the cattle. **1846** G. H. HAYDON 5 *Yrs. in Austral. Felix* iii. 59 The 'old men' kangaroos are always the largest and strongest in the flock, or in colonial language, 'mob'. **1850** *Househ. Words* 6 Apr. 42/2, I was going down to Sydney with a mob of horses. **1853** R. CLOUGH *Let.* 24 Sept. in J. Deans *Pioneers of Canterbury* (1937) 295, I should like to put all the calvers in

one mob. **1875** *Melbourne Spectator* 22 May 34/2 A mob of sheep has been sold at Belfast at 1*s.* 10*d.* per head. **1875** *Trans. & Proc. N.Z. Inst.* VII. 130 For about 400 birds of this large size to have been roasted in so small a compass in one mob would be a physical impossibility. **1906** J. OXENHAM *John of Gerisau* ix, At last..we sighted him [a white colt], galloping quietly along in the centre of the very last mob of all. **1933** *Bulletin* (Sydney) 5 July 21/3 The dog was turning the mob to work over the fallen animal. **1936** I. L. IDRIESS *Cattle King* vii. 63 A squatter was overlanding with a big mob of stock. **1940** *Geogr. Jrnl.* XCV. 242 There is now only one firm remaining which has a mob of mules. **1964** *Sunday Mail Mag.* (Brisbane) 27 Sept. 3/5 Behind him ..were the ragged outriders of the mob... I knew he didn't stand a chance of clearing those terrible hooves. **1968** K. WEATHERLY *Roo Shooter* 35 A small mob of wild pigs, mostly white with black spots. **1972** P. NEWTON *Sheep Thief* ii. 20 The two men had taken out a mob of ewes.

d. *Shetland dial.* A 'school' of whales.

1898 *Shetland News* 30 July (E.D.D.), It is believed this shoal [of whales] consisted of two mobs.

e. *Mil. slang.* A battalion, a regiment; a military unit.

1916 J. N. HALL (*title*) Kitchener's mob. **1916** *Anzac Book* 32 Yes; some d-d gobblers thought they would catch our mob nappin' but missed the bus. **1925** FRASER & GIBBONS *Soldier & Sailor Words* 156 *Mob*, any collection or body of troops. A very old Army term. **1948** PARTRIDGE *Dict. Forces' Slang* 120 *Mob*, unit, not necessarily in a derogatory sense. 'What mob are you from, chum?' **1972** M. PUGH *Murmur of Mutiny* iv. 34 You must have heard of Sharjah and the Trucial Oman Scouts. This mob is modelled on them.

5. *slang.* **a.** A company or gang of thieves or pickpockets working in collusion. Also, a member of such a company. ***swell mob***, a class of pickpockets who dress stylishly to carry on their occupation; see also SWELL *a.* c.

1839 H. BRANDON *Poverty, Mendicity & Crime* 164/1 *Mobs*—companions. Working with mobs. Robbing with companions. **1843** *Punch* IV. 129/1 The swell mob—they are there. **1846** LANDOR *Imag. Conv., Southey & L.* Wks. 1853 II. 156/1 Making room for the swell-mob of authors to pass by. **1851** MAYHEW *Lond. Labour* (1864) I. 234/1 Some classes of patterers..work in 'schools' or 'mobs' of two, three, or four. **1859** *Slang Dict., School*, or *mob*, two or more 'patterers' working together in the streets. **1884** *Standard* 6 June 6/3 There were about twenty mobs (pickpockets) that never got a rap.

b. *U.S.* A more or less permanent association or gang of violent criminals. ***The Mob***, a supposed permanent gang controlling much of organized crime in the U.S. and elsewhere; cf. MAFIA. Also *attrib.* and *Comb.*, amongst gangs, on behalf of a mob or 'The Mob'.

1927 *Amer. Speech* II. 385/1 Any kind of a gang was known as a push, a word credited to Australia, but I think it is a sister of the mob of the city underworld. **1930** WODEHOUSE *Very Good, Jeeves!* xi. 302 By the time he had come to the surface, a sort of mob-warfare was going on at the other side of the field. **1952** TURKUS & FEDER *Murder, Inc.* xv. 345 One mob baron..'moved in' to the extent that he had his picture taken in a friendly pose with a candidate for the vice-presidency of the United States. **1968** P. OLIVER *Screening Blues* iv. 134 Within a year control of the New York numbers racket passed into the dominion of a mob enforcer. **1969** *Guardian* 24 Jan. 7/6 The Mob from its Chicago headquarters runs the subcontinent. **1975** 'A. THACKERAY' *One Way Ticket* 23 Better watch out... It could be the Mafia, the Mob, or whatever they call it these days.

6. *attrib.* and *Comb.*: **a.** simple attrib. (senses 1 and 2), as ***mob action, -assembly, -associator, behaviour, -cause, -condemnation, control, -culture, -emotion, -fancy, favour, -fever, gentry, -government, -hysteria, -idol, -indignation, -leader, -madness, mania, -meeting, mind, -movement, -orator, -oratory, petition, -psychology, -reaction, rule, scene, -sensation, -storm, -sycophancy, -tide, -tyranny, -violence, -way, -will, -worship; mob-like*** adj. **b.** objective, as ***mob-adoring, -fearing, -inspiring*** adjs. **c.** instrumental, as ***mob-election***; ***mob-created, -guided, led*** adjs.

1972 TURNER & KILLIAN *Collective Behavior* (ed. 2) iii. 49/2 *Mob action is frequently nothing more than culturally sanctioned punishment carried out by unauthorized persons without 'due process'. **1828** E. IRVING *Last Days* 304 The *mob-adoring press. *a* **1734** NORTH *Exam.* I. ii. (1740) 66 This *Mob-assembly was drawn together for the Purpose of Terror. **1750** CARTE *Hist. Eng.* II. 135 These *mob-associators broke open houses by night. **1973** G. R. LESLIE et al. *Order & Change: Introd. Sociol.* xi. 289 The distinction between *mob behavior and riot behavior has to do with the degree to which the hostility is focussed upon a single object or class of objects. When the hostility is so directed and is concentrated on destruction of particular scape-goats, the term 'mob' is used. **1721** AMHERST *Terræ Fil.* No. 43 (1754) 226, I do not intend to enumerate all the strong holds of this prevailing *mob-cause [*sc.* High-Church]. **1929** D. H. LAWRENCE *Pornogr. & Obscenity* 9 When it comes to the so-called obscene words,..the first reaction is almost sure to be mob-reaction, mob-indignation, *mob-condemnation. **1971** D. E. WESTLAKE *I gave at the Office* (1972) 89 The gun is the primary tool in situations of *mob control. **1807–8** W. IRVING *Salmag.* (1824) 280 Your true *mob-created great man. **1968** L. DURRELL *Tunc* v. 269 A surrogate *mob-culture. **1823** MOORE *Fables* 9 Where Kings have been by *mob-elections Rais'd to the throne. **1928** D. H. LAWRENCE *Woman who rode Away* 231 A steam of wet *mob-emotion! **1929** GALSWORTHY in *Story-Teller Mag.* Aug. 597/2 Impervious by nature and training to mob-emotion Soames yet was emotionalized. Here was something that was not mere mob-sensation. **1841** C. MACKAY *Mem. Pop. Delus.* I. 329 It tickled the *mob-fancy mightily. **1835** LYTTON *Rienzi* x. iii, Too vulgar a desire of *mob favour. **1935** A. L. JAMES *Broadcast Word* i. 5 It will have cleansed our political life of its *mob-fever. **1859** HELPS *Friends in C.* Ser. II. (ed. 2) II. 97 If they are *mob-guided, *mob-fearing people. **1722** DE FOE *Moll Flanders* (1840) 200 The assurance gave the *mob gentry a check. **1770** BURKE *Pres. Discont.* Sel. Wks. I. 23 Whilst they are terrifying the great and opulent with the horrors of *mob government. **1895** W. JAMES *Let.* 24 Dec. (1920) II. 28 Three days of fighting *mob-hysteria at Washington can at any time undo peace habits of a hundred years. **1934** R. CAMPBELL *Broken Record* 59 Race-feeling, mob-hysteria. *a* **1849** H. COLERIDGE *Ess.* (1851) II. 169 Nelson was a *mob-idol indeed. **1929** *Mob-indignation [see *mob-condemnation* above]. **1782** J. TRUMBULL *M'Fingal* IV. 95 And while plebeian signs ascend, Their *mob-inspiring aspects bend. **1834** *New Monthly Mag.* XLI. 59 In their ambition to be *mob-leaders, they were, in fact, *mob-led. **1796** W. COOKE *Conversation* III. 34 That *mob-like education of the streets. **1901** E. A. ROSS *Social Control* xiii. 147 *Mob-madness leads men captive to the impressions of the moment. **1935** L. MACNEICE *Poems* 60 *Mob mania in the air. **1714** MANDEVILLE *Fab. Bees* (1733) II. 41 In all *mob-meetings, ..the entertainment in general is abominable. **1897** *Mob mind [see sense 1 above]. **1933** *Essays & Stud.* XVIII. 61 After half a century's work on the mob-mind psychologists are agreed that a crowd is an entirely different problem from an individual. **1964** GOULD & KOLB *Dict. Social Sci.* 433/2 The irrationality and excesses of which people are capable when acting under the influence of the 'mob mind'. **1923** D. H. LAWRENCE *Kangaroo* xvi. 338 But revolution is not a *mob-movement. **1817** H. C. ROBINSON *Diary* 13 Feb. (1967) 54 One Walker spoke also—a coarse *mob-orator with a stentorian voice. **1839** WHITTIER *Pr. Wks.* (1889) II. 333 The mob-orator of Clare and Kerry. **1965** *Punch* 13 Jan. 55/1 Hitler the rabble-rouser, Hitler the mob-orator. **1961** *John o' London's* 9 Nov. 517/2 His [*sc.* Hitler's] megalomaniac *mob-oratory. **1724** DE FOE *Mem. Cavalier* (1840) 312 The *mob petition from Bucks was presented to the king. **1896** W. JAMES *Let.* 11 June (1920) II. 36 The really bad thing here is the silly wave that has gone over the public mind—protection humbug, silver, jingoism, etc. It is a case of '*mob-psychology'. **1938** R. G. COLLINGWOOD *Princ. Art* v. 91 They cannot as a whole exhibit a compact mob-psychology. **1929** *Mob-reaction [see *mob-condemnation* above]. **1869** MCLAREN *Serm.* Ser. II. vii. 123 The willing spirit sets us free,..free from the *mob rule of Passions and Appetites. **1922** U. SINCLAIR *They call me Carpenter* vii. 20 They're a lot of studio bums, doing a real *mob scene on a real location. **1937** *Printers' Ink Monthly* May 39/3 *Mob scene*, a group of performers used as a background. **1929** *Mob-sensation [see *mob-emotion* above]. **1865** J. D. BURN *Three Yrs. among Working-Classes U.S.* p. xiii, A series of *mob-storms would be sure to set in. **1849** MILL in *Westm. Rev.* LI. 16 One hardly expected to hear them taunted with..*mob-sycophancy. **1881** 'MARK TWAIN' *Prince & Pauper* 127 The *mob-tide..dashed itself against the champion. **1893** *Ladies' Home Jrnl.* Feb. 6/1, I don't approve of *mob violence. **1949** LAPIERE & FARNSWORTH *Social Psychol.* (ed. 3) xxv. 471 There is a close relationship between critical social circumstances and mob violence. **1969** M. B. ARNOLD in T. Mischel *Human Action* 192 Emotions, whether mob-violence or passive love-ins, seem to have been chosen by many young people as sole guide of their actions. *c* **1800** R. CUMBERLAND *John De Lancaster* (1809) II. 280 A propensity in the town's-folk to ..administer tumultuous justice in their own *mob-way. **1924** J. MASEFIELD *Sard Harker* 51 Never had I thought that my fellow-citizens of Las Palomas would try to impose the *mob-will upon the individual. **1893** E. DOWSON *Let.* *c* 27 Aug. (1967) 288 'One View of the Question', a beautiful piece of satire on English *mob-worship.

7. Special comb.: **mob courtship**, courtship among the lower classes; **mob defence**, defence by the populace as opposed to military defence; † **mob-driver**, one who incites a mob; **mob feast** *nonce wd.*, a banquet open to every one; **mob law**, 'law' imposed and enforced by a mob; **mob-man** = MOBSMAN; **mob-master**, one who controls a mob; **mob opinion**, the opinion of the illiterate or uncultured; **mob reader**, a reader belonging to the mob; † **mob story**, a story circulating among the mob.

1883 RUSKIN *Fors Clav.* xc. 167 There are no words strong enough to express the general danger and degradation of the manners of *mob-courtship, as distinct from these. **1845** W. H. MAXWELL *Hints Soldier on Service* I. 239 No city.. afforded the same advantages, for what might be termed a *mob-defence. *a* **1734** NORTH *Exam.* I. iii. (1740) 126 Colonel Mildmay, an old Rumper, and late *Mob-driver in Essex. *Ibid.* II. v. 343 A Sideling-Writer..shall cry, O! the Papists are set up; just as his Mob-Drivers did to their Rabble. **1830** MOORE *Mem.* (1854) VI. 150 This is the third dinner..one of the others being a *mob feast, at six shillings a-head. **1823** BENTHAM *Not Paul* 347 As has been seen in the case of Saint Stephen,..a sort of *mob-law might..be stated as forming part and parcel of the law of Moses. **1747** in *New Jersey Archives* (1883) 1st Ser. VII. 428 He discoursing with several of the *mobmen,..has heard them [say]..that the King himself was unable to quell mobs in England. **1835** *Maryland Hist. Mag.* IX. 160 You may see large companies of worthies marching to and fro, and a mob man, as such, cannot be seen. *a* **1734** NORTH *Exam.* III. vii. (1740) 571 *Mob-Masters..that upon the Watch-word, are to bring forward some hare-brained Rout, which they call the People. **1769** WARBURTON in *Pope's Ep. Cobham* 135 *note*, This, though a mere *mob-opinion, is the opinion in fashion, and cherished by the Mob of all denominations. **1697** DRYDEN *Æneid* Ded. (e) 3 b, Such things as are our Upper-Gallery Audience in a Play-House... These are *Mobb-Readers. **1716** ADDISON *Freeholder* No. 9 ¶12 Do you..believe the *mob-story, that King George designs to make a bridge of boats from Hannover to Wapping?

mob (mɒb), *sb.*[2] *Obs.* exc. *Hist.* [Cf. MAB *sb.*, MOB *v.*[1], and MOB-CAP.]

†**1.** *Cant.* A strumpet. *Obs.*

1665 R. HEAD *English Rogue* I. lvii (end), We kist and parted; I sigh'd, she did sob; she for her lusty Lad, I for my Mob. **1673** —— *Canting Acad.* 13 *Mob*, a Wench or Whore. *Ibid.* 192 When a Mob he has bit, his Cole he will tell. **1697** N. LEE *Princess of Cleve* Prol., The little Mob, the City Wastcoateer.

†**2.** A négligé attire, a dishabille; also *attrib.* ***mob-dress***. *Obs.*

1665 R. HEAD *English Rogue* I. x, Their Mobs Scarfs, and Hoods all rent. **1709** *Brit. Apollo* II. No. 71. 3/2 It shines.. As Beauty does, tho' in a Mob-Dress. **1710** SWIFT *Jrnl. to Stella* 13 Dec., The ladies were all in mobs (how do you call it?) undress. **1712** STEELE *Spect.* No. 302 ¶11 Wrapping Gowns and dirty Linnen, with all that huddled Oeconomy of Dress which passes under the general Name of a Mob.

3. = MOB-CAP.

1748 RICHARDSON *Clarissa* (1811) III. iii. 29 Her head-dress was a Brussels-lace mob, peculiarly adapted to the charming air and turn of her features. **1790** MALONE *Shaks. Wks., Ham.* II. ii. 525 *note*, The ordinary morning head-dress of ladies continued to be distinguished by the name of a *mob*, to almost the end of the reign of George the second. **1793** STEEVENS *Ibid.*, In the counties of Essex and Middlesex, this morning cap has always been called a *mob*, and not a *mab*. My spelling of the word therefore agrees with its most familiar pronunciation. **1805** *Sporting Mag.* XXVI. 221 Some ladies talking of the revived fashionable headdress—mobs. **1830** MRS. BRAY *Fitz of F.* xxi, A neat little old woman, wearing a close mob and pinners.

mob (mɒb), *sb.*[3] (See quot.)

1852 SEIDEL *Organ* 150 The mob is a sort of brush, consisting of threads of wool or silk, which are glued on to a thin handle of wood or wire.

† **mob**, *v.*[1] *Obs.* [Cf. MAB *v.*, MOB *sb.*[2], MOBLE *v.*]

1. *trans.* To muffle the head of (a person); to dress untidily. Also ***to mob up***.

1664 H. MORE *Exp. 7 Epist.* Pref. b 2, Men..having.. Chins as smooth as Womens, and their Faces mob'd in Hoods. **1681** —— *Expos. Dan.* I. Notes 22 Monks and Friers mob'd in their Cools and long Coats. **1720** GAY *Eclogues, Tea-table*, Yet in the gall'ry mob'd, she sits secure. *a* **1745** SWIFT *Story Injured Lady* (1746) 3, I go always mobbed, and in an Undress. **1762** GOLDSM. *Cit. W.* xc. Wks. (Globe) 232 [He] shall sit..mobbed up in double night-caps.

2. ***to mob (it), to go a-mobbing***: to go in disguise, or attired so as to escape recognition, to the unfashionable part of a theatre, etc. Hence (? associated with MOB *sb.*[1]), to frequent low company.

[**1720**: see 1.] **1727** DE FOE *Hist. Appar.* iv. 43, I don't wonder such as these go a mobbing among those meanest of mad Things call'd Free-Masons; rough Cheats, and confess'd Delusions are the fittest things to amuse them. **1772** *Town & Country Mag.* 85/2 At the play one night with the Freemans, mobbing it in the gallery. **1782** MISS BURNEY *Cecilia* IV. vii, Warrant I'll mob with the best of them! **1825–9** MRS. SHERWOOD *Lady of Manor* I. ix. 389, I don't want you to make your appearance, I want to go incognito, to mob it, you know, to go in masquerade, and sit in the gallery. **1837** *New Monthly Mag.* LI. 36 He cannot mob it to see a play in the pit.

mob (mɒb), *v.*[2] [f. MOB *sb.*[1]]

1. a. *trans.* To attack in a mob or disorderly crowd; to crowd round and molest or annoy; to press unduly upon; to throng; also in *pass.* to be attacked or surrounded by such a mob.

1709 LUTTRELL *Brief Rel.* (1857) VI. 494 Last week a corn factor..had like to have been mobb'd. **1717** DE FOE *Mem. Ch. Scotl.* II. 27 They mobbed the Presbytery, beat and very ill treated..the Moderator. **1719** *Rhode Island Col. Rec.* (1859) IV. 259 'Tis very wonderful to me..that none of His Majesty's officers of the custom, have been mobbed, and torn in pieces by the rabble. **1810** *Sporting Mag.* XXXVI. 262 The crowd were very abusive, following us, and mobbing us. **1828** MACAULAY in *Edin. Rev.* May, Whenever any tolerable book of the same description makes its appearance, the circulating libraries are mobbed. **1884** *Manch. Exam.* 4 Oct. 4/7 The Alcade of the town having made himself obnoxious to the people, they mobbed the Courthouse. **1894** BARING-GOULD *Deserts S. France* II. 63 The populace..mobbed and derided him in the streets.

b. To force (a person) *into* (an action, etc.), drive him *from* (a place) by mobbing him. *spec.* in bird behaviour, to engage in MOBBING (*vbl. sb.*[2] 1 c).

1724 DE FOE *Mem. Cavalier* (1840) 159 The king was obliged to leave them.., for fear of being mobbed into something..unworthy of himself. **1840** HOOD *Up Rhine* 7 Between one and another, I was fairly mobbed into it. **1861** W. PHILLIPS *Disunion* 6 Throughout half the great cities of the North, every one who touches on it [the slavery question] is mobbed into silence! **1927** E. M. NICHOLSON *How Birds Live* vii. 87 An owl appears and is surrounded by a clamorous crowd of small birds which proceed to mob it. **1936** *Brit. Birds* XXX. 28 Usually when seen it was sitting in a tree, and it was much 'mobbed' by Rooks. **1938** T. H. WHITE *Sword in Stone* xvii. 250 They [*sc.* rooks] have got the courage to mob their enemies. I should think it takes some courage to mob a hawk, even if there is a pack of you. **1965** P. WAYRE *Wind in Reeds* v. 62 The falcon, sometimes.. accompanied by the tiercel, would fly out and mob us.

2. *intr.* To form a mob, to congregate in a mob or disorderly crowd; also ***to mob it***.

1711 E. WARD *Vulgus Brit.* VIII. 96 For those that Mob, like noisy Knaves, Against the Law, with Clubs and Staves. **1728** WOOLSTON *Disc. Miracles* iv. 61 If they did mob it to their own disappointment, about the Door of the House. **1753** FOOTE *Eng. in Paris* I. Wks. 1799 I. 37 They ha'nt spirit enough to mob here. **1826** HOOD *Fairy Tale* v, With dusty hides, all mobbing on together. **1840** —— *Miss Kilmansegg, Fancy Ball* ix, As many more Mob round the door To see them going to see it. **1845** W. H. MAXWELL *Hints Soldier on Service* I. 74 Perceiving their unsteadiness when mobbed together in the repulse.

3. *nonce-use.* To mix *up* with a mob.

1847 TENNYSON *Princess* VI. 289 That Which..drags me down From my fixt height to mob me up with all The soft and milky rabble of womankind.

4. *trans.* To abuse, scold, rail at. *dial.* Also *absol.*

1803 [see MOBBING *vbl. sb.*² 3]. *a* **1825** in FORBY *Voc. E. Anglia.* **1903** *Longm. Mag.* July 253 'Let her mob, she'll sune get tired.'

† **mobard.** *Obs. rare.* A 'clown', 'boor'. (A term of contempt.)

c **1440** *York Myst.* xxviii. 137 Nay such mobardis schall neuere man vs make. *Ibid.* xliv. 74 Harke, maistir..Howe þat þes mobbardis maddis nowe, þer maistir þat oure men haue slayne.

† **mobarship,** variant of AMOBRESHIP *Obs.*

1467–8 *Rolls of Parlt.* V. 589/2 A Graunte to hym..undre the Seall of oure Erledome of Marche, of th' office of Mobarship of oure Lordship of Dynby.

mobbed (mɒbd), *ppl. a.* [f. MOB *sb.*² and *v.*¹ + -ED.] Furnished with or wearing a mob; hooded. Also *Comb.* **mobbed-head**, a harlot (cf. MOB *sb.*² 1).

1681 H. MORE *Exp. Dan.* i. 22 They [*sc.* Monks and Friars] pretending to nothing but holiness..whether in these mob'd habits, or got into a more brisk dress. **1707** MRS. CENTLIVRE *Platonick Lady* Epil., Young Templars.. March hither [*sc.* to the theatre], where Mobb'd-heads too often ply. **1708** —— *Busie Body* Epil. 33 Like that dark mob'd-up Fry..Who to remove Love's Pains bestow a worse.

mobber ('mɒbə(r)). [f. MOB *v.*² + -ER¹.]

1. One who mobs, in the senses of the verb.

1744 WHITEFIELD *Brief Acc. Late Trial* Wks. 1771 IV. 105 His Majesty had no where put the reins of Government into the hands of mobbers. **1745** BYROM *Jrnl. & Lit. Rem.* (Chetham Soc.) II. II. 398 He orders no two persons be seen walking together..on pain of being deemed mobbers and rioters. **1885** *Harper's Mag.* Mar. 599 That sparrow.. disappeared in a panic, and the whole party of mobbers with him.

2. *U.S.* (See quot.)

1892 E. L. WAKEMAN in *Columbus* (Ohio) *Dispatch* 6 Oct., Those who remove the fish to the stallmens' wagons, or the costers' carts, who are called 'mobbers'.

mobbie, mobee ('mɒbɪ, 'məʊbɪ). Also 7–8 mobby, 7 mobbi, (mabby). [a. Carib *mabi* batata, drink made from batatas.]

1. In the West Indies: **a.** A spirituous liquor made from the batata or sweet potato.

1638 T. VERNEY in *V. Papers* (1853) 194 This as we call mobby is only potatoes boyled, and then pressed as hard as they can till all the juce is gon out of the root into fayre water, and after three houres this is good drink. **1750** G. HUGHES *Barbados* 34 *note*, Mobby is a Drink made with pounded Potatoes, and Water fermented with Sugar or Molasses. **1826** H. N. COLERIDGE *West Indies* (1832) 40 Their suppers being a few potatoes for meat, and water or mobbie to drink.

b. (See quot. 1859.)

1833 MRS. CARMICHAEL *Dom. Mann. W. Ind.* II. xiv. 68 Ginger beer, mobee, and orgeat are always plentiful [in the market]. **1859** BARTLETT *Dict. Amer.*, *Mobee*, a fermented liquor made by the negroes in the West Indies, prepared with sugar, ginger, and snake-root.

2. In America: The expressed juice of apples and peaches, used in the distillation of apple and peach brandy; also the brandy itself. ***mobby punch*** (see quot. 1705).

1705 R. BEVERLEY *Virginia* IV. II. xv. §74 (1722) 254 Mobby Punch, made either of Rum from the Caribbee Islands, or Brandy distill'd from their Apples and Peaches. **1860** WORCESTER, *Mobby*, the liquid or juice first expressed from apples and peaches, and afterwards distilled to make apple or peach brandy.

† **'mobbify,** *v. Obs.* [f. MOB *sb.*¹ + -(I)FY.] *trans.* To drive *out* by mob-violence.

a **1734** NORTH *Exam.* II. v. (1740) 345 This same High and Low shall..serue for Noise, and mobbify out, at Elections, conformable Loyal Gentlemen.

† **mobbing,** *vbl. sb.*¹ *Obs.* [f. MOB *v.*¹ + -ING¹.] The action of MOB *v.*¹; in quot. *attrib.*

1825–9 MRS. SHERWOOD *Lady of Manor* I. ix. 390 The mobbing-party for the theatre was determined upon and carried into effect.

mobbing ('mɒbɪŋ), *vbl. sb.*² [f. MOB *v.*² + -ING¹.] The action of MOB *v.*²

1. a. Gathering in crowds; the action of a mob in assailing a person.

a **1734** NORTH *Exam.* III. vii. (1740) 579 The Spirit of the Faction was not broken till..the Rye Conspiracy was discovered; and then Mobbings were laid aside all at once. **1741** H. WALPOLE *Lett.* 12 Nov., It is Admiral Vernon's birthday..and the night will be full of mobbing, bonfires, and lights. **1816** *Remarks Eng. Mann.* 32, I never heard any one..say that the mobbing of a London rout was any thing but insipid.

attrib. **1781** S. PETERS *Hist. Connecticut* 411 David Wooster, the rebel General, Benedict Arnold's old acquaintance and mobbing confederate.

b. *Sc. Law.* (See quot. 1959.)

1800 D. HUME *Commentaries Law of Scotl.* IV. xvi. 228 A multitude may be convened for a criminal purpose without being guilty of mobbing. **1885** *Manch. Exam.* 18 Mar. 4/7 Two of the prisoners..pleaded guilty to charges of mobbing and rioting. **1898** J. CHISHOLM *Green's Encycl. Law of Scotl.* 370 In the law of Scotland mobbing, or 'the Tumultuous Convocation of the Lieges', includes the several degrees and stages of disorder which are known in the law of England under the names of Riot, Rout, and Unlawful Assembly. **1959** *Chambers's Encycl.* XII. 327/2 Mobbing is violent or threatening action taken in an effort to obtain a definite end and this distinguishes it from rioting and breach of the peace which are disorderly conduct at large. **1973** *Observer* 4 Feb. 29/4 We almost goat ye fur mobbin' an' riotin'.

c. Esp. in bird behaviour, a type of display in which a group of small birds engages to drive off a predator, or a similar kind of display exhibited by one or two birds, in which they fly close to the object of their apparent aggression. Also *attrib.*

1919 F. FINN *Bird Behaviour* ix. 275 The mobbing of Hawks and Owls is no doubt often dictated by revenge. **1927** E. M. NICHOLSON *How Birds Live* vii. 93 Akin to fighting and play, but not identifiable with either, is the mobbing habit. **1936** *Brit. Birds* XXIX. 307 The 'mobbings' of nesting Rooks by other members of the colony..are sexual in origin. **1949** *Ibid.* XLII. 64 This behaviour is certainly in no way analogous to the so-called 'mobbing' of predatory birds. **1961** *Behaviour* IV. 288 (*title*) The motivational organisation controlling the mobbing calls of the Blackbird.

2. *Hunting.*

1781 P. BECKFORD *Hunting* (1802) 213 When hounds are at cold hunting with a bad scent, it may then be a proper time to send a whipper-in forward: if he can see the fox, a little mobbing, at such a time as this may reasonably be allowed.

3. ? Abusive treatment, scolding (see MOB *v.*² 4).

1803 *Censor* 1 Mar. 35 If he has not enough to give something to the waiter and the ostler, he must..undergo a good (or rather a bad) mobbing from these gentry.

mobbing ('mɒbɪŋ), *ppl. a.* [f. MOB *v.*² + -ING².] That gathers in a mob.

1842 F. BARHAM *Socrates* 48 Till the mobbing populace shall catch a sparkle of their radiance.

mobbish ('mɒbɪʃ), *a.* Also 8 mobish. [f. MOB *sb.*¹ + -ISH.] Resembling or characteristic of a mob; †given to mobbing (*obs.*), disorderly, tumultuous. Also, †characteristic of, or appealing to 'the mob' or lower classes; vulgar, clap-trap.

1695 *Whether Parlt. be dissolved by Death of Princess of Orange* 4 They turn more Mobbish than a Dover Court. **1699** COLLIER *2nd Def. Immor. Stage* 398 The Surveyor gives the Text a mobbish Turn, and foists in some of his own ill Language. **1711** HICKES *Two Treat. Chr. Priesth.* (1847) I. 168 His mobbish fallacious way of arguing. **1732** EARL OF OXFORD in *Portland Papers* VI. (Hist. MSS. Comm.) 156, I never was in so mobbish a place, we could scarce walk the streets for the numbers of people that flocked about us. **1793** A. YOUNG *Example of France* (ed. 3) 58 As if it was possible, after rousing, by inflammatory publications, the mobbish spirit, that you could draw the line of moderation. **1814** SCOTT *Wav.* xxxv, The group..were in ordinary Lowland dresses..which, contrasted with the arms they bore, gave them an irregular and mobbish appearance. **1831** *Blackw. Mag.* XXIX. 512 The mobbish love of destruction. **1864** CARLYLE *Fredk. Gt.* XVI. vii. IV. 355 Be judicial, arithmetical, in passing sentence on it [*sc.* Voltaire's fraud]; not shrieky, mobbish, and flying off into the Infinite! **1920** *Q. Rev.* July 166 This mobbish or, as it may be termed, 'synnomic' character of primitive mentality is well known.

Hence **'mobbishly** *adv.*

1716 M. DAVIES *Athen. Brit.* II. 250 The tumultuous Citizens of Thessalonica..having mobbishly murder'd one of the Emperor's Lieutenants. **1767** CHAUNCY *Disc.* 24 July 26 Some mobishly disposed persons.

'mobbishness. [-NESS.] Tendency to mobbism; the practice of acting in groups.

1920 *Q. Rev.* July 166 The savage enjoys no privacy, but is always in some sort of a crowd,..experiencing therefore all those peculiar mental effects which mobbishness brings in its train. **1927** W. DEEPING *Kitty* xxiv. 310 You would still hope for your super-scientist..who, by pressing a button in his laboratory, could efface all mobs and mobbishness.

mobbism ('mɒbɪz(ə)m). [f. MOB *sb.*¹ + -ISM.] Mobbish behaviour.

1794 *Mass. Spy* 16 Apr. 3/2 A few days since, we experienced a scene of the most unlicensed mobism. **1830** *Blackw. Mag.* XXVIII. 620 Nothing better than what we must call..mere mobbism.

mobble, mobby: see MOBLE *v.*, MOBBIE.

mob-cap. [? f. MOB *sb.*² The relation to Du. *mopmuts* (*muts* = cap) is not clear.] An indoor cap worn by women in the 18th and early 19th c. (see quots.). Cf. MOB *sb.*² 3. Also *transf.*

1795 T. WILKINSON *Wandering Patentee* II. 137 On she came in a frock and a little mob-cap, and sang the song. **1812** H. & J. SMITH *Rej. Addr.* v, Lady Macbeth is to have..a cotton gown, and a mob cap. **1819** COLERIDGE in *Lit. Rem.* (1836) II. 225 A mob-cap is still a word in common use for a morning cap which conceals the whole head of hair, and passes under the chin. **1846** FAIRHOLT *Costume* 396 Mob-caps, that covered the hair, were worn [*c* 1780] with a full caul and deep border, secured by a broad riband. **1849** DICKENS *Dav. Copp.* xiii, A mob-cap; I mean a cap, much more common then than now, with side-pieces fastening under the chin. **1884** EDNA LYALL *We Two* ix, [Her] smooth grey hair was almost hidden by a huge mob-cap. **1971** *Daily Tel.* 19 Jan. 11/2 There's a whole range of Victoriana too, including washable mob-cap lamp-shades in lace and embroidered cotton.

Hence **mob-capped** *a.*, that wears a mob-cap; **mob-cappish** *a.*, *nonce-wd.*

1828 MOORE *Mem.* (1854) V. 251 Her beauty was gone; her dress was even prematurely old and mob-cappish. **1905** *Author* 1 Feb. 144 Misdrawings of mob-capped maidens.

mobese (mɒ'biːz). [f. MOB *sb.*¹ + -ESE.] The cant of American professional criminals.

1955 *People* (Austral.) 19 Oct. 13/2 A few even felt..that Dewey should be 'hit'—which is mobese for gang murder. **1965** I. FLEMING *Man with Golden Gun* xiii. 173 In mobese, he was 'going to be hit'.

'mob-handed, *a. colloq.* [f. MOB *sb.*¹ + HANDED *a.* 1 b.] In considerable numbers, constituting a large body.

1934 P. ALLINGHAM *Cheapjack* xix. 254 His companions had been 'mob-handed', that is to say, working in a big group. **1966** A. PRIOR *Operators* vi. 64 Mo and his brother had returned home penniless to find the police mob-handed. **1970** *Sunday Tel.* 9 Aug. 27/7 The evergreen X class [of yachts] turned out mob-handed at 60 strong.

mo-bike ('məʊbaɪk), colloq. abbrev. of *motor bicycle.*

1925 *Punch* 22 Apr. 433/1 Just think of going out on a mo-bike in top-hats and tail-coats! **1971** *Ceylon Observer* (Mag. ed.) 19 Sept. 7/3 A Japanese mo-bike (over 180 c.c. of course!).

'mobilar, *a. nonce-wd.* [f. MOBILE *sb.*² + -AR.] Pertaining to the mob. So † **mobi'larity**.

1757 MRS. GRIFFITH *Lett. Henry & Frances* (1766) IV. 47 The mobilar Spirit infused into the People of Ireland, in 1753, has been the Root of all the Tumults and Risings in this Kingdom, ever since. *Ibid.*, It would be an useful Work for some ingenious Writer to lay open to the Public, the Difference between Popularity and Mobilarity. *Ibid.* 226.

mobile ('məʊbɪl), *sb.*¹ Also 6–7 mobil. [a. F. *mobile* (in *premier mobile*, etc.), a. L. *mōbile* neut. of *mōbilis*: see MOBILE *a.*

The later examples with the spelling *mobile* were perh. intended by the writers for the Latin *mōbile* (in Eng. pronunciation 'məʊbɪliː). A pronunciation (məʊ'biːl) is indicated by the rime in quot. 1645 under 1.]

† **1.** ***first, grand, great, principal mobile***, anglicized forms of PRIMUM MOBILE (*lit.* and *fig.*). *Obs.*

1549 *Compl. Scot.* vi. 48 Al thir nyne speris or hauynis ar inclosit vitht in the tent spere, quhilk is callit the fyrst mobil. *c* **1645** HOWELL *Lett.* v. (1650) 150 Thou First Mobile, Which makst all wheel In circle round. **1652** URQUHART *Jewel* Wks. (1834) 249 There be some that have been pretty well principled,..yet seeing the great mobil of the rest, by circumvolving them into a contrary motion, hath retarded their action [etc.]. **1704** *Collect Voy.* (Churchill) III. 32/2 This Wind proceeds from the Course of the first *Mobile.* *a* **1797** MARY W. GODWIN *Posth. Wks.* IV. lxvii. 3 A world in which self-interest..is the principal mobile. *Ibid.*, *Let. Pres. Char. Fr. Nation* 45, I begin to fear that vice, or, if you will, evil, is the grand mobile of action.

2. *Metaphysics.* A body in motion or capable of movement. Now *rare.*

a **1676** HALE *Prim. Orig. Man.* IV. ii. 292 Motion, whose Measure Time was, had a beginning, before which it was not; because no *Mobile* was more ancient than the beginning of Time. **1685** BOYLE *Enq. Notion Nat.* 355 The [Immaterial] Agent having no impenetrable Part, wherewith to impell the Corporeal *Mobile.* **1875** LEWES *Probl. Life & Mind* Ser. I. II. IV. iii. §45. 279 There can be no direction, distance, dimension, unless a mobile moves in that direction, and a sensation appreciates it.

mobile ('məʊbɪliː), *sb.*² *arch.* Also 7 mobele, 7–8 mobilee. [Shortened form of L. *mōbile vulgus* the movable or excitable crowd.] The common people; the populace, rabble, MOB.

[**1600** W. WATSON *Decacordon* (1602) 67 There followeth ..another deuice plotted of purpose to make it seeme meet to the ignorant multitude..(for note this, that popularitie is the rouer they ayme at in all their proceedings, the *mobile vulgus* being euer wauering and readiest to run vpon euery change).] **1676** SHADWELL *Libertine* v. 81 *D. Lop.* D' hear that noise? the remaining Rogues have rais'd the Mobile, and are coming upon us... Enter two Shepherds, with a great Rabble. **1679** in *Verney Fam. Memoirs* Nov. (1899) IV. vii. 259 Yᵉ mobele was very rud to yᵉ Dutch Imbasidor & his wife. **1683** HICKERINGILL *Hist. Whiggism* Wks. 1716 I. II. 166 Dr. Lamb..(an Intimate and Friend to the Duke of Buckingham) was pull'd in pieces by the Mobile and Rabble. **1686** SIR J. LAUDER (Fountainhall) *Hist. Notices Sc. Affairs* (Bannatyne Cl.) 705 The Privy Councell..repreived them..for they thought not fit to irritat the mobilee too much. **1688** W. LONGUEVILLE in *Hatton Corr.* (Camden) II. 99 The mobile has been very turbulent hereabouts. **1701** DE FOE *True-born Eng.* Misc. (1703) 34 He grants a Jubilee, And hires Huzza's from his own Mobilee. **1830** N. S. WHEATON *Jrnl.* 271 The *mobile* were fast gathering.

mobile ('məʊbaɪl), *sb.*³ [Subst. use of MOBILE *a.*] **1. a.** Also with pronunc. ('məʊbiːl). A form of decoration consisting usu. of abstract designs in metal, plastic, etc., contrived (as by suspension) so as to be mobile. Cf. STABILE *sb.*

[**1936** P. NASH in *Archit. Rev.* LXXX. 208/3 Shadows bring us to Calder, who is..so far as I know, the original inventor of mobile sculpture and so, also, of the '*objet mobile*'. The mobile object is not now confined to Calder's invention; both Max Ernst and Duchamp have made various pieces of this nature.] **1949** *Ibid.* CVI. 117 Alexander Calder's work on the 'stabile' is not as well known in England as is his work on the now well established 'mobile'. In fact Calder has always done 'still' sculpture, and the term stabile, given to it by Hans Arp, appears to be some months older than the name mobile, which was invented by Marcel Duchamp. **1952** *Granta* 29 Nov. 8/1 We find it agreeable..to hang pastel-tinted antlers on the wall near a mobile. **1957** *Times* 18 Nov. 11/1 Mobiles at Heal's include a life-size black cat, and a cut-out set of small figures costs from 4s. and can be set up by children of about 10 years without help. **1958** E. DUNDY *Dud Avocado* I. ix. 156 He picked up a wire coat-hanger and some string and a couple

of paint-brushes and a shoe, and started making them into a Mobile. **1971** D. D. BOYDEN *Introd. Mus.* (ed. 2) 524 Someone has aptly noted that chance music is rather like the mobiles of Calder. **1972** *Sci. Amer.* Mar. 76/1 They were shown an arrangement of three colored geometrical objects in a 'mobile'.

b. *transf.* and *fig.*, esp. in *Mus.* (see quot. 1967).

1961 *Punch* 11 Jan. 116/3 Admirers of the hard, glittering mobiles constructed.. by Stan Kenton may be pleased by *Standards in Silhouette*... A big, big band, making big, big sounds, in what was once a daringly experimental manner. **1967** *Listener* 2 Feb. 176/3 The crystallization of these new formal principles was the 'mobile'. It connotes a dynamic arrangement of musical thoughts in which several patterns are possible, depending on the decision of the interpreter... A 'mobile' is made up of finite (musical) thoughts of fairly conventional dimensions... As units they remain constant; but the arrangement of their sequence varies, subject to certain pre-compositional order. **1970** 'J. MORRIS' *Candywine Devel.* xvi. 184 Five electric guitars and a mobile of drums were backstopping a sleek, oxblood brown singer. **1971** E. BORROFF *Mus. in Europe & U.S.* xxvii. 656 Other works include.. *Symphonies* (1955), for fifteen soloists; *Mobile* for two pianos 1958.

2. Short for: (*a*) mobile canteen; (*b*) (*Austral.* and *N.Z.*) mobile barrier; (*c*) mobile police.

1940 *New Statesman* 9 Nov. 466/1 Go up and have a cup of tea at the mobile. **1969** *Australian* 24 May 34/4 Fifth.. over this trip and from behind the mobile here last week. **1971** W. J. BURLEY *Guilt Edged* iv. 62 Control to all mobiles: keep look out for red Mini-Cooper saloon. **1974** J. GARDNER *Corner Men* ii. 14 Put out a call. There must be some mobiles around. We need them here.

Mobile, *sb.*[4]: see MOBILIAN *sb.*

mobile ('məʊbaɪl, 'məʊbɪl), *a.* Forms: 5 **mobyle**, 6–7 **mobil**, 7– **mobile**. [a. F. *mobile*, ad. L. *mōbilis*, f. *mō-*, *movēre* to MOVE. Cf. MOBLE *a.* and *sb.*]

1. Capable of movement; movable; not fixed or stationary. **a.** In various applications. Of the sight: Wandering, not steady. Of a star: Not fixed. ***mobile spirits***, the 'spirits' by which the motor impulses were supposed to be transmitted to the muscles.

Now esp. used to distinguish transportable forms of facilities which are normally accommodated on a fixed site, as ***mobile hospital, library, shop***, etc.

1490 CAXTON *Eneydos* xix. 71 Dydo.. or euer that she coude saye ony thyng, as rauysshed helde her sighte all mobyle, wythout to areste it vpon one thynge of a long while. **1522** SKELTON *Why not to Court?* 522 Any star Fyxt or els mobil. **1649** BULWER *Pathomyot.* I. v. 23 The Motive Faculty by a wonderfull providence of Nature moves the mobile Spirits, and these moved, flie forth.. to their destinated Organs. **1727–41** CHAMBERS *Cycl.*, *Mobile*, moveable; any thing susceptible of motion, or that is disposed to be moved either by itself, or by some other prior mobile, or mover. [Not in JOHNSON 1755.] **1927** *U.S. Daily* 22 Nov. 2/3 Mobile stations must be established in such a way as to comply as concerns frequencies and types of waves, with the general provision of Article 5. **1935** *Discovery* May 151/2 The treatment of patients far removed from the well-equipped hospitals, by means of mobile units complete with laboratories. **1937** *Archit. Rev.* LXXXI. 19 (*caption*) A mobile sculpture by Alexander Calder. **1938** *Encycl. Brit. Bk. of Year* 122/1 Mobile recording vans with a new method of editing records made it possible to broadcast composite sound records of events only a few minutes after their occurrence. **1940** *Economist* 5 Oct. 422/2 Cooking facilities have been provided by the L.C.C. Some mobile kitchens are at work. **1940** *New Statesman* 5 Oct. 321/2 Feeding centres and mobile canteens. **1955** *Radio Times* 22 Apr. 11/3 Franklin Engelmann with a BBC mobile recording unit visits Dudley to meet local people. **1959** *Economist* 14 Mar. 991/1 Mobile shops have more than doubled in number since the war, and are still taking extra trade on to the roads at the rate of perhaps fifteen a week. **1960** *Library Assoc. Rec.* Aug. 262/2 *Mobile library*, a vehicle devised, equipped and operated to provide, as far as reasonably practicable, a service comparable to a part-time branch library. **1961** L. D. STAMP *Gloss. Geogr. Terms* 258/1 *Mobile or footloose industries*, broadly those generally called 'light'. **1962** *Economist* 17 Nov. 665/3 The mobile lounges will not only provide transport.. between the terminal and the parked aircraft but will also serve as waiting rooms. **1971** *Guardian* 10 June 1/1 A 22-bed mobile hospital.. was among the supplies which left for Calcutta. **1974** *Camping & Caravanning* Sept. 15/1 Fees 30p per unit per night, C.C.Y. 5p. Mobile shop. Walking distance of beach.

b. Of a limb, an organ of the body: Movable, not fixed, 'free'.

1828 STARK *Elem. Nat. Hist.* I. 133 The Nine-banded Armadillo.. body with seven, eight, or nine mobile bands. **1831** R. KNOX *Cloquet's Anat.* 579 The lower [region of the nose], which is less firm, but mobile, allows the apertures of the nostrils to be contracted, widened, or even closed. **1874** WOOD *Nat. Hist.* 285 The hind toe of each foot is very mobile. **1881** J. HAWTHORNE *Fort. Fool* I. iii, A hawk circling high in air, with steady wings and mobile, down-looking head.

c. Of a liquid, etc.: That has its particles capable of free movement.

1851 NICHOL *Archit. Heav.* 101 Streams of matter internally mobile. **1860** MAURY *Phys. Geog. Sea* (Low) i. §27 Like all fluids they are mobile. **1878** HUXLEY *Physiogr.* 56 The mobile liquid passes into a compact rigid solid. **1880** BASTIAN *Brain* 9 The coming into contact of a fragment of organic matter with projected portions of the substance of an Amœba is followed by the closure of this mobile substance round it.

d. Of a cell, molecule, etc.: Capable of separate movement, 'free'; not adnate or fixed.

1871 T. H. GREEN *Introd. Pathol.* (1873) 102 It is the mobile cells which are principally concerned. These cells are the most active. **1877** E. R. CONDER *Bas. Faith* ii. 89 Yet no less a task is laid upon the mobile molecules, momentarily renewed, momentarily perishing, of the brain.

e. ***mobile spasm***, 'Gower's term for the slow and irregular movements that occur in the extremities after hemiplegia' (*Syd. Soc. Lex.* 1891).

1899 *Allbutt's Syst. Med.* VII. 338. *Ibid.* 735 The peculiar mobile spasm known as athetosis.

f. *Sociol.* Of a person: able to move into different social levels, or a different environment or field of employment. Of a society: not rigidly stratified, in which upward or downward movement between social levels can take place, and also movement between fields of employment, etc., within the same social level.

1927 P. A. SOROKIN *Social Mobility* II. vii. 138 Such a type of social stratification may be styled open, plastic, penetrable, or mobile. *Ibid.* v. xvii. 427 Unskilled labor is more mobile than skilled labor. **1940** K. MANNHEIM *Man & Society* II. vi. 93 The significance of the mobile elements in social and cultural life. **1945** C. W. MILLS in *Jrnl. Econ. Hist.* V. Suppl. v. 39 For laissez faire, the pattern of success might involve a larger proportion of upwardly mobile persons. **1959** V. PACKARD *Status Seekers* (1960) xviii. 256 Many socially declining or downward-mobile people turn to alcohol or drugs for support.

g. *Philol.* = MOVABLE *a.* 7 b.

1955 T. BURROW *Sanskrit Lang.* iii. 80 The so-called mobile *s*. Indo-European *s* when it formed the first member of an initial consonant group, was an unstable sound, and liable to disappear under conditions which it has not been possible accurately to define. **1965** G. Y. SHEVELOV *Prehist. of Slavic* 230 The mobile consonants, i.e. consonants sometimes used, sometimes dropped on word boundaries... *n*-mobile.. *s*-mobile... Problem of *k*-mobile.

h. Special collocations: as, **mobile barrier** *Austral.* and *N.Z.*, in *Trotting*, a foldable barrier designed to facilitate a flying start; **mobile home**, a large caravan permanently parked and used as a residence.

1965 *Weekly News* (Auckland) 8 Dec. 59/1 The controversy that is developing over the use of the mobile barrier in trotting. **1954** *N.Y. Herald Tribune Bk. Rev.* 13 June 12 Books pertaining to trailer houses—or mobile homes—published within the last five years. **1961** *Daily Tel.* 22 Nov. 17/4 Mobile homes for 1,200 families could be provided on 300 vacant sites in London. **1969** *Eugene* (Oregon) *Register-Guard* 3 Dec. 5D/1 Mobile homes—the things people used to call trailer houses. **1973** *People's Jrnl.* (Inverness & Northern Counties ed.) 1 Dec. 22/5 *Mobile Home*, Coats Caravans. 32 ft. × 9 ft. 6 in. Astral Mobile Home. Double End Bedroom, Bathroom, Kitchen and Lounge. Solid Fuel Fire. £895.

2. Characterized by facility of movement. **a.** Of features: That easily change in expression.

1851 MRS. BROWNING *Casa Guidi Wind.* I. 798 And brows that with a mobile life contrive A deeper shadow. **1874** GREEN *Short Hist.* vi. §4. 309 The thin mobile lips.. picture the inner soul of the man. **1878** BESANT & RICE *Celia's Arb.* xxxii, As much astonishment as discipline would allow, expressed upon a not remarkably mobile set of features. *a* **1880** C. T. NEWTON *Art & Archæol.* iii. 79 In the Ephesian heads, the eye appears rather as if seen through a slit in the skin than as if set within the guard of highly sensitive and mobile lids.

b. Of a person, his mind, etc.: That turns or is turned easily from one thing to another; wanting in stability of purpose; also, in favourable sense, versatile.

1853 MILL in *Edin. Rev.* XCVIII. 432 They [*sc.* the Athenians] were not fickle, but (a very different quality, vulgarly confounded with it) mobile; keenly susceptible.. to the feeling and impression of the moment. **1855** LEWES *Goethe* (1864) 127 Nor will this surprise those who have considered the mobile nature of our poet. **1860** HAWTHORNE *Marble Faun* (1879) I. ix. 89 This idea filled her mobile imagination with agreeable fantasies. **1866** *Cornh. Mag.* Oct. 465 [*Art.* Naval Men] The very nature of his work.. makes an off-hand, free-spoken, decisive, and yet mobile man of him. **1867** MILL *Subj. Women* (1869) 117 Women's minds are by nature more mobile than those of men, less capable of persisting long in the same continuous effort. **1874** L. STEPHEN *Hours in Library* (1892) I. v. 187 His imagination is more intense and less mobile.

c. *rarely* of a visible object: Constantly in motion.

1882 STEVENSON *New Arab. Nts.* (1884) 145 In the mobile light of the lantern.

3. *Mil.* Of troops, etc.: That may be easily and rapidly moved from place to place. Also of police.

1879 A. G. F. GRIFFITHS *Eng. Army* iv. 107–8 Wheeled vehicles are not sufficiently mobile to conform to the rapid movement of active troops. **1897** *Westm. Gaz.* 16 Aug. 5/1 A mobile army of upwards of 25,000 men. **1938** F. D. SHARPE *Sharpe of Flying Squad* i. 11 The Flying Squad has about twenty cars, and they are very different cars to those of the Mobile Police. **1955** *Radio Times* 22 Apr. 13/3 The Police. A series of eight talks. 7. Beats and Mobile Patrols. **1967** N. LUCAS *C.I.D.* vi. 78 The new mobile patrol toured the streets with the hidden detectives scanning.. the crowds.

-mobile. Used freely in the 20th century as the second element in combinations: **a.** Portable, or travelling under its own power. **b.** In occas. uses of immobile objects or structures, usu. having a function pertaining to, or being an imitation of, an automobile or other form of transport.

Mobilian (məʊ'bɪlɪən), *sb.* Also **Mobile** (məʊ'biːl). [? f. the town of *Mobile* in Alabama + -IAN.] A lingua franca or trade language used formerly in south-eastern North America (see quot. 1907). Also as *adj.*

1840 G. BANCROFT *Hist U.S.* III. xxii. 249 The whole country south-east, south, and west of the Cherokees.. was in the possession of one great family of nations, of which the language was named by the French the Mobilian, and is described by Gallatin as the Muskhogee-Chocta. **1907** F. W. HODGE *Handbk. Amer. Indians* I. 916/1 The so-called Mobilian trade language was a corrupted Choctaw jargon used for the purposes of inter-tribal communication among all the tribes from Florida to Louisiana, extending northward on the Mississippi to about the junction of the Ohio. It was also known as the Chickasaw trade language. **1928** W. A. READ *Indian Place-Names Louisiana* 6 The identity of *Manchac* with the Mobilian *imashaka*, 'rear entrance', is rendered more plausible by my discovery of the form *Mashake*. **1937** *Amer. Speech* XII. 212 Besides the Shawnee words one Algonquian term has slipped in through the medium of the Mobilian trade language. **1947** P. S. MARTIN et al. *Indians before Columbus* 68 In the Southeast a Choctaw jargon called 'Mobilian' was spoken from Florida to Louisiana and up the Mississippi River as far north as the Ohio. **1964** *Amer. Speech* XXXIX. 16 He [*sc.* Charles P. G. Scott] attempted to push *O.K.* back to the Mobile trade language, current along the Gulf of Mexico in the eighteenth century.

mobiliary (məʊ'bɪlɪərɪ), *a.* [ad. F. *mobiliaire*, f. L. *mōbili-s* movable: see -ARY.]

1. In the Channel Islands: Relating to movable property. Also as the distinctive epithet of a court that deals with 'mobiliary' questions.

1682 WARBURTON *Guernsey* (1822) 83 On the second Monday of the term, the mobillary [*sic; also in other passages*] courts are held for the upper parishes. **1694** FALLE *Jersey* iv. 112 This Court.. is intended for the decision of Matters of less moment, as Arrears of Rents.., Arrests, Distrainings, and such like Mobiliary things. **1841** DUNCAN *Guernsey* 485 In the mobiliary court, all common debts may be sued for by way of summons.

2. Of or pertaining to household furniture. ***mobiliary art*** = *art mobilier* (ART *sb.* VI. d).

1855 tr. *Labarte's Arts Mid. Ages* i. 10 Specimens of mobiliary sculpture. **1927** [see HOME *sb.*[1] 15]. **1960** *Times Lit. Suppl.* 2 Sept. 565/4 'Mobiliary' art in the form of sculpture, carving and engraving on bone, antler, ivory and stone.

3. *Mil.* Pertaining to mobilization.

1888 *Daily News* 16 Apr. 6/3 We [the Russians] do not command the mobiliary facilities of the smaller Powers. **1896** *Westm. Gaz.* 5 Dec. 7/1 The frontier forces.. have also been placed upon a mobiliary footing.

†**mobilifi'cation.** *Obs. rare*[−1]. [f. MOBILE *a.*: see -FICATION.] = MOBILIZATION.

1794 EARL MALMESBURY *Diaries & Corr.* III. 113, I trusted no time would be lost for putting his army into a state of mobilification.

mobility[1] (məʊ'bɪlɪtɪ). [a. F. *mobilité*, ad. L. *mōbilitās*, f. *mōbilis*: see MOBILE and -ITY.]

1. a. Ability to move or to be moved; capacity of change of place; movableness. (Sometimes enumerated among the properties of matter.) Also, facility of movement.

1490 CAXTON *Eneydos* xv. 57 Wherby arose one euylle goddesse callyd fame or renommee, whiche.. by mobylite vygorouse encreaseth her forse in rennynge. *c* **1500** MORE *Wks.* ℭ iiij, I am Eternitee... Thou mortall Tyme.. Art nothyng els but the mobilite, Of sonne and mone chaungyng in euery degre. *a* **1639** WOTTON *Surv. Educ.* in *Reliq.* (1651) 318 A rod or barre of iron.. by the help of a corke.. being ballanced in water, or in any other liquid substance where it may have a free mobility, will bewray a kind of unquietude. **1669** BOYLE *Absolute Rest in Bodies* §2 The Epicureans.. ascribing to every particular Atom an innate, and unlooseable mobility, or rather, an actual motion. **1688** NORRIS *Theory Love* I. ii. 18 The two eminent Propertys of matter, viz. that of receiving various Figures, and that of Motion or Mobility. **1727** ARBUTHNOT *Tables Anc. Coins*, etc. 244 The Romans had the advantage.. by the Bulk of their Ships, and the Fleet of Antiochus in the Swiftness and Mobility of theirs. **1792** *Phil. Trans.* LXXXII. 221 The thermometers I employed had not a sufficient mobility for very nice experiments. **1794** G. ADAMS *Nat. & Exp. Philos.* IV. xlix. 347 Of all that are known in the universe, the mobility of the matter of light is the greatest. **1837** BREWSTER *Magnet.* 322 The mobility of the needle is diminished. **1841** —— *Martyrs Sci.* 97 Paul Anthony Foscarinus.. wrote a pamphlet in which he illustrates and defends the mobility of the earth.

b. Of the limbs or organs of the body: Freedom of movement; absence of fixity or rigidity; *occas.* liability to be abnormally displaced.

1528 PAYNELL *Salerne's Regim.* (1541) 115 The .ii. cause [of over-much bleeding] is mobilitie of the arterie,.. for woundes with out rest can nat heale. **1688** BOYLE *Final Causes Nat. Things* ii. 55 Nature not having given that mobility to the eyes of flies. **1831** R. KNOX *Cloquet's Anat.* 165 All that the former [*sc.* the tarsus] has gained with respect to size and solidity, it appears to have lost with reference to mobility. **1872** T. G. THOMAS *Dis. Women* (ed. 3) 59 In estimating the effects of direct pressure upon the position of the uterus, its extreme mobility must be constantly borne in mind. **1876** BERNSTEIN *Five Senses* 24 All organs adapted for touching are endowed with the greatest mobility. **1881** MIVART *Cat* 54 The mobility of the spinal column in different regions.

c. Of persons: Ability to move about. *spec.* in *Sociol.* the possibility of movement between different social levels that exists in a society (***vertical mobility***); also the possibility of

movement to different fields of employment or interest, or to new areas, within the same social level (***horizontal mobility***).

1777 JOHNSON *Let. to Mrs. Thrale* 29 Sept., Mrs... grows old, and has lost much of her undulation and mobility. **1779** *Ibid.* 16 Oct., But I am told how well I look; and I really think I get more mobility. **1900** *Amer. Jrnl. Sociol.* VI. 377 (*caption*) Mobility of type. **1927** P. A. SOROKIN *Social Mobility* II. vii. 136 The intensiveness of the vertical mobility may be measured in the same way in the field of the political and occupational stratifications. *Ibid.* 160 Horizontal mobility, in spite of the great importance of the problem, is not an object of this study. **1938** T. H. MARSHALL *Class Conflict* 111 The use of mobility as an excuse for inequality is usually associated with a measure of self-deception. **1956** C. W. MILLS *Power Elite* xv. 349 Only if the criteria of the top positions were meritorious..could we smuggle merit into such statistics of mobility. **1965** B. B. WOLMAN *Handbk. Clin. Psychol.* xxxiv. 979 While mobility has been frequently related to schizophrenia, R. Freedman ..failed to find positive correlation between high mobility and high hospital admission rates of schizophrenics. **1972** S. COTGROVE *Sci. of Society* (rev. ed.) vii. 230 Restricted mobility facilitates the protection of privileges by a stratum and the development and persistence of a unitary culture.

d. *Physics.* Of a fluid: Freedom of movement of its particles.

1817 FARADAY *Exp. Res.* ii. 6 The actual relative mobilities of the gases are inversely as their specific gravity. **1830** HERSCHEL *Stud. Nat. Phil.* 232 The perfect mobility of their [*sc.* liquids] parts among one another. **1871** TYNDALL *Fragm. Sci.* (1879) I. x. 311 The mobility of hydrogen.. being far greater than that of air.

e. *transf.* and *fig.* of immaterial things.

1866 ROGERS *Agric. & Prices* I. iv. 108 Labour, on which so many circumstances are now conferring mobility and expansion. **1889** *Spectator* 12 Oct., It is within the province of the State to promote the mobility of labour and capital.

f. *Chem.* and *Physics.* [tr. G. *beweglichkeit* (given this specific sense by F. Kohlrausch 1876, in *Nachrichten von d. K. Ges. d. Wissensch. und d. G.-A.-Universität zu Göttingen* 17 May 220).] The degree to which a charge carrier undergoes movement in a definite direction in response to an electric field, now usu. expressed as the average speed (in cm. per second) in a field of one volt per cm. divided by the net number of charges on the carrier.

1895 C. S. PALMER tr. *Nernst's Theoret. Chem.* II. vii. 315 The term mobility (Beweglichkeit) or velocity of transport will mean..the velocity with which 1 g.-ion will be transported under the influence of a pull of 1, *e.g.* 1 kilogram weight. *Ibid.* 316 If we denote the mobility of the positive and negative ions by U and V, then their respective velocities will be in the same ratio as their mobilities. *Ibid.* 317 The conductivity of a solution of a binary electrolyte is greater in accordance as it contains more free ions, and according as these have a greater mobility. **1912** *Jrnl. Chem. Soc.* CI. II. 1276 The following figures..are the results of the chief researches on the mobility of the hydrogen ion... All values are expressed in terms of the reciprocal ohm. **1924** J. R. PARTINGTON in H. S. Taylor *Treat. Physical Chem.* I. xi. 539 The equivalent conductance at infinite dilution is the sum of the mobilities of anion and kation at a given temperature. **1946** [see CARRIER 1 k (ii)]. **1950** W. J. MOORE *Physical Chem.* xv. 434 With two exceptions, the ionic mobilities in aqueous solutions do not differ as to order of magnitude, being all around 6×10^{-4} cm^2 sec.$^{-1}$ volt^{-1}. The exceptions are the hydrogen and hydroxyl ions with the abnormally high mobilities of $36{\cdot}2 \times 10^{-4}$ and $20{\cdot}5 \times 10^{-4}$. **1963** B. FOZARD *Instrumentation Nucl. Reactors* ii. 15 In a uniform electric field the electrons and ions may be regarded as acquiring a uniform drift velocity which is superimposed upon their kinetic motion and directed towards the electrodes [of the ionisation chamber]... The term mobility may be used to indicate the ease with which ions may be caused to drift.

2. a. Ability to change easily or quickly; liability to fluctuation; changeableness, instability; fickleness.

1567 FENTON *Trag. Disc.* i. 19b, [There is not] any so greate a paterne or example of her [*sc.* fortune's] mobitie [1579 mobility], as they that fynde often chaunge of estate. **1656** BLOUNT *Glossogr.*, *Mobility*, moveableness, changeableness, inconstancy. *a* **1676** HALE *Prim. Orig. Man.* IV. vii. 356 We cannot choose but daily observe in our selves a strange mobility and instability in our Imaginative and Intellective Faculty. **1829** I. TAYLOR *Enthus.* iv. (1867) 75 In the conformation of the heretic by temperament, there is more of intellectual mobility than of strength. **1873** HAMERTON *Intell. Life* IX. iv. (1875) 315 The mobility of fashionable taste. **1884** tr. *Lotze's Metaph.* 8, I do not ignore the many valuable results that are due to this mobility of imagination.

b. Of a person: The condition of being easily moved; excitability.

1824 BYRON *Juan* XVI. xcvii, So well she acted all and every part By turns—with that vivacious versatility, Which many people take for want of heart. They err—'tis merely what is call'd mobility. [*Note*, In French 'mobilité'. I am not sure that mobility is English.] **1837** C. LOFFT *Self-formation* II. 225, I had not the excitable spirit, the mobility, to use their own term, of our French neighbours. **1870** HUXLEY *Lay Serm.* ii. 27 Women are, by nature, more excitable than men —prone to be swept by tides of emotion,..and female education does its best to weaken every physical counterpoise to this nervous mobility.

c. Of the features: Facility of change of expression.

1845 E. HOLMES *Mozart* 298 Mozart's physiognomy was remarkable for its extreme mobility. The expression changed every moment. **1872** J. H. GLADSTONE *Faraday* ii. 89 That wonderful mobility of countenance. **1884** *Graphic* 4 Oct. 357 A mouth with a sympathetic mobility about it.

3. *Mil.* Of a field force and its equipment: The quality of being able to move rapidly from one position to another.

1866 E. B. HAMLEY *Operat. War* VI. i. 316 Mobility and the mutual support of all arms,..were now on the side of the French. **1871** C. H. OWEN *Mod. Artillery* III. iii. 329 Other means have been taken to give field batteries the greater mobility now required on some occasions. **1894** LD. WOLSELEY *Life Marlborough* I. 89 A new and well-ordered mobility and a facility of manœuvre was taught.

mobility² (məʊˈbɪlɪtɪ). [f. MOBILE *sb.*², MOB *sb.*¹, after *nobility*.] The mob; the lower classes.

1690 DRYDEN *Don Sebast.* IV. iii, She singled you out with her Eye, as commander in Chief of the Mobility. **1695** HICKERINGILL *Lay-Clergy* Wks. 1716 I. 321 No wonder then that the mobility did run a madding, when Oppressions will make the Nobility and Wise Men mad. **1774** FOOTE *Cozeners* I. (1778) 24, I don't mean for the mobility only;.. the best people of fashion ar'n't ashamed to follow my Doctor. **1823** BYRON *Juan* XI. xix. *note*, The select mobility and their patrons. **1843** *Blackw. Mag.* LIII. 79 They are as easily to be distinguished..from the children of the mobility, as is a well-blooded Arabian from a Suffolk punch.

mobilizable (ˈməʊbɪˌlaɪzəb(ə)l), *a.* [f. MOBILIZE *v.* + -ABLE. Cf. F. *mobilisable.*] Capable of being mobilized.

1884 *Contemp. Rev.* XLV. 885 A mobilizable army. **1892** *Harper's Mag.* June 54/2 The mobilizable commands, posts, companies, and establishments of the armed force.

mobilization (ˌməʊbɪlaɪˈzeɪʃən). [a. F. *mobilisation*, f. *mobiliser* to MOBILIZE: see -ATION.]

1. a. The action or process of mobilizing or rendering 'movable'; bringing into circulation; also in *Law*, the conversion of real into personal property. Cf. MOBILIZE *v.* 1 b.

1799 *Hist. Europe* in *Ann. Reg.* 89/1 [France] A mobilization of the national debt; by which the real stock was reduced to one-third, payable in money, and the other two in bonds to be taken in payment for national lands. **1879** BARING-GOULD *Germany* II. 249 Roman law..brought in the novel ideas of capital and the mobilisation of real property. **1890** LAW & JEWELL tr. *Gruber's Text-bk. Dis. Ear* xvii. 479 (*heading*) Mobilisation of the stapes. **1901** ROSE & CARLESS *Man. Surg.* (ed. 4) xvi. 400 A most valuable adjuvant in the treatment of fractures is massage..whilst in some cases early mobilization is also desirable. **1930** *Morning Post* 7 Aug. 11/6 The credit mobilisation in London by the Australian banks to meet Governmental commitments..was approved. **1967** *Economist* 14 Oct. 120/1 A growing number of Labour MPs are sponsoring the case for government 'mobilisation' of the £3,200 million odd of foreign shares held by private British investors. **1967** S. R. MAWSON *Dis. Ear* (ed. 2) xxi. 515 Relief of conductive deafness due to stapedial ankylosis by mobilization of stapes.

b. *Sociol.* The organizing of some hitherto unused form of social energy to bring about changes within a society.

1953 K. W. DEUTSCH *Nationalism & Social Communication* vi. 104 The processes of mobilization and assimilation may be illustrated rather strikingly in the case of Finland. **1964** G. GERMANI in I. L. Horowitz *New Sociol.* 395 We understand by mobilization the 'excess'..of group participation in relation to the level defined by the old society as 'normal'. **1968** A. ETZIONI *Active Society* xv. 393 Whatever the form of mobilization, whether it be direct or indirect, the process entails a shift of control and/or a shift of the usage of assets. **1972** TURNER & KILLIAN *Collective Behavior* (ed. 2) iv. 62/2 The crowding together of Negro Americans in the black ghettoes is a type of mobilization that has contributed to urban insurrections.

2. *Mil.* and *Naval.* The action or process of mobilizing (an army, a fleet, etc.).

1866 *Ch. Times* 14 Apr., Austria..demanding that the mobilization of the Prussian army be at once discontinued. **1883** *Manch. Exam.* 26 Nov. 4/3 The news respecting the Russian mobilization of troops is exaggerated.

attrib. **1885** *Pall Mall G.* 14 Feb. 7/1 A Mobilization Committee has been sitting at the War Office arranging for the despatch of troops to Suakin.

mobilize (ˈməʊbɪlaɪz), *v.* [ad. F. *mobiliser*, f. *mobile*: see MOBILE *a.*]

1. a. *trans.* To render movable or capable of movement; to bring into circulation.

1838 *Globe* 15 Jan. 2/2 They have 'the masses', they say. We believe they have, so far as those inorganic masses as yet have been—to borrow a French term—*mobilised*. **1864** *Realm* 27 Apr. 3 Mobilise the riches of Austria (and Free Trade is in fact only movement—circulation—life) and [etc.]. **1868** *Pall Mall G.* 24 Sept. 4 Either the Governor-General must give up his tours, or must take his Council with him. The real question at issue seems therefore to be not as to the healthiness of Calcutta, but whether the Supreme Council should be mobilized. **1899** *Allbutt's Syst. Med.* VI. 259 Oil once deposited may be again mobilised and transferred to other capillaries.

b. *Surg.* To restore mobility to (an ankylosed bone); to free or detach so as to render more accessible.

1894 O. DODD tr. *Politzer's Text-bk. Dis. Ear* 318 The stapes is mobilized by means of a single or double hook inserted between the crura. **1914** ROSE & CARLESS *Man. Surg.* (ed. 9) xxxv. 1076 If a stone is lodged behind the second piece of the duodenum, it may be possible to manipulate it up, and make it accessible above the intestine; but otherwise the duodenum must be mobilized by dividing the peritoneum on its outer edge. **1953** *N.Y. State Jrnl. Med.* LIII. 2653/1 The stapes was mobilized, and the hearing improved on the operating table. **1967** G. M. WYBURN et al. *Conc. Anat.* iv. 121/2 Next the temporal lobes [of the brain] should be mobilised from the floor of the middle cranial fossa.

c. *Sociol.* To bring into circulation (hitherto unused social assets or energies).

1953 K. W. DEUTSCH *Nationalism & Social Communication* vi. 100 Within any geographical setting and any population, economic, social, and technological developments mobilize individuals for relatively more intensive communication. *Ibid.*, Population mobilized for mass communication. **1968** A. ETZIONI *Active Society* xv. 409 Two disparate organizations seem to mobilize a collectivity more effectively than one. **1968** G. MYRDAL in W. Ewald *Environment & Change* IV. xvi. 261 Their [*sc.* the lower strata of American society's] low rate of participation in elections, when they are not mobilized and exploited by the political machines.

2. *Mil.* **a.** To prepare (an army) for active service. Also *fig.*

1853 C. L. BRACE *Home Life Germany* 256 When ever the army is to be prepared for war or mobilised, the Reserve step into their respective regiments again. **1871** L. W. M. LOCKHART *Fair to See* III. xxxiii. 100 A hundred times he had paraded the line of arguments he meant to employ, and the reserve which, in case of their failure, he held in readiness, and, so to speak, mobilised. **1951** D. B. TRUMAN *Governmental Process* ix. 271 The political party in the United States most commonly is a device for mobilizing votes.

absol. **1873** BORBSTÆDT & DWYER *Franco-Ger. War* viii. 170 It only requires a simple telegraphic order to mobilise.. to set in perfectly harmonious movement the colossal machinery spread over the whole country.

b. *intr.* (for *passive*). To undergo mobilization.

1878 LD. WOLSELEY in *19th Cent.* Mar. 437 To fill its.. stores, so that..its little army may be in a condition to mobilise. **1899** *Daily News* 18 Dec. 5/2 The Seventh Division is to mobilise at Aldershot.

Hence **ˈmobilized** *ppl. a.*, **ˈmobilizing** *vbl. sb.*

1851 GALLENGA *Italy* 463 The mobilized national guard was to leave Milan for the camp. **1882** H. SPENCER *Stud. Sociol.* §515 In rude societies..the army is the mobilized community, and the community is the army at rest. **1899** F. T. BULLEN *Way Navy* 83 The signal was made, 'Mobilised cruisers proceed independently to Portland'. **1913** in W. S. Churchill *World Crisis 1911–14* (1923) viii. 190 A very large staff would be employed at all the mobilizing centres to report upon the whole workings of the mobilization. **1953** K. W. DEUTSCH *Nationalism & Social Communication* vi. 101 The rate of growth of the mobilized population..and the changes in its sociological level could all be calculated. **1968** A. ETZIONI *Active Society* xv. 408 Strains and conflicts among the organizational arms of any mobilizing collectivity should be 'routine' and expected.

mobish, obs. form of MOBBISH.

Möbius (ˈmøːbɪəs). Also **Moebius**. The name of August Ferdinand *Möbius* (1790–1868), German mathematician, used, chiefly in ***Möbius band, strip***, to designate a surface having only one side and one edge, formed by twisting one end of a rectangular strip through 180 degrees and joining it to the other end.

1904 E. R. HEDRICK tr. *Goursat's Course in Math. Analysis* I. 546 Möbius' strip. **1941** COURANT & ROBBINS *What is Math.?* v. 260 If the Moebius strip is cut along this [center] line..we find that it remains in one piece. **1950** Möbius band [see KLEIN BOTTLE]. **1960** F. LAND *Lang. Math.* xi. 171 We have in the Moebius strip the strange object which consists of one continuous surface bounded by one continuous curve. **1965** Möbius strip [see KLEIN BOTTLE]. **1970** *New Yorker* 28 Nov. 58/3 Barbara, taking a pair of scissors..turned the clipping on fragrant Christmas gifts into a Möbius strip. **1974** *Times* 10 Sept. 14/8 If the curtain at Covent Garden three weeks hence goes up on yet another ring, circle, hoop, saucer, dish or Möbius band I shall be heard to blow my nose in an ominous falling figure..which ..betokens Doom.

†**ˈmoble**, *a.* and *sb. Obs.* Forms: 4–6 moble, (4 mobill, *Sc.* **mwbill**), 4–5 **meoble, moeble, meble**, (4 **meeble**, *Sc.* **mebile**, 5 *Sc.* **mobylle, mubulle, meuble**), 5–6 **mobil**. [a. OF. *moeble, moble* (mod.F. *meuble*) = Pr. *moble*, Sp. *mueble*, Pg. *movel*, It. *mobile*:—popular L. **mŏbil-em* for class. L. *mōbil-em*: see MOBILE.]

A. *adj.* Movable. Chiefly of possessions, e.g. in ***goods mobles, moble goods***, personal property.

c **1330** R. BRUNNE *Chron.* (1810) 300 Whan þe kyng asked half of alle þer moble þing. *c* **1340** HAMPOLE *Prose Tr.* 11 Thou sall noghte couayte þe hous or oþer thynge mobill or in-mobill of þi neghtbour. *c* **1391** CHAUCER *Astrol.* I. §21 Alle the signes, be they moist or drie, or moeble or fix. **1429** *Wills & Inv. N.C.* (Surtees) I. 80 And alle remenant and residewe of my goods moblez and vnmoblez. **1480** CAXTON *Chron. Eng.* ccxxv. 230 For whiche nedes to be sped the kyng axed the fifthe part of all the meoble goodes of englond.

B. *sb. pl.* Movable goods; 'personal' property. *rare* in *sing.*

13.. *Coer de L.* 6460 Home he wente..With that tresore and the moble. *c* **1330** R. BRUNNE *Chron.* (1810) 145 Richard ..His mobles on siluer reised þorgh Inglond alle his gode. **1375** BARBOUR *Bruce* v. 275 A man..That wes..rich of mwbill [MS. E moble] and catell. *c* **1420** *Anturs of Arth.* 199 (Douce MS.) If auþer matens or mas miȝte mende þi mys, Or eny meble [*v.r.* mobylles] one molde. *a* **1450** *Knt. de la Tour* (1868) 119 They wolde haue lefte her no thinge nor londes, heritage, nor meuble. **1456** SIR G. HAYE *Law Arms* (S.T.S.) 154 Gudis wonnyn apon inymyes..that is to say meubleis. **1513** DOUGLAS *Æneis* VIII. vi. 15 Nor ȝit had [thai] craft to conques nor wyn geyr, Nor kep thair moblis quhen it gadderit was.

moble, mobble (ˈmɒb(ə)l), *v. Obs.* exc. *dial.* Also moble. [frequent. f. MOB *v.*¹ Cf. MABBLE *v.*]

trans. To muffle (one's) head or face. Chiefly with *up*. Hence †**mobled** *ppl. a.*

1603 SHAKS. *Ham.* (Qos.) II. ii. 524 *Play.* But who, O who had seene the mobled [*1st Fol.* inobled] Queene? *Cor.* Mobled Queene is good, faith very good. **1655** SHIRLEY *Gentl. Venice* V. iii, The moon does mobble up her self sometime in't. Where she will shew a quarter face, and was The first that wore a black bag. **1668** OGILBY *Æsop* II. xi. 26 Mobbled nine dayes in my Considering-cap. **1673** MARVELL *Reh. Transp.* II. 278 The old Jades..are mobled up like so many Judges. **1879** in Miss Jackson *Shropsh. Word-bk.* s.v. *Moble*, 'Er mobles 'erself up in that owd 'ood an' shawl, an' sits by the fire, tell 'er's as nesh as nesh. *Ibid.*, Yo' mun moble yourself well up, its a despert, raw, coud night.

¶ In mod. writers echoing Shakspere's use.

1860 S. DOBELL in *Macm. Mag.* Aug. 325 But heard, far off, the mobled woe Of some new plaintiff for the light. **1877** EARL OF SOUTHESK *Meda Maiden*, etc. 120 There rested a woman,—close mantled in brown, Mobled and muffled from sandal to crown.

mobocracy (mɒ'bɒkrəsɪ). [f. MOB *sb.*^{1}, after *democracy*, *ochlocracy*: see -CRACY.]

1. The rule of the mob, government by a mob.

1754 A. MURPHY *Gray's-Inn Jrnl.* No. 95 Another Mode of civil Policy, which cannot be called by a better name than a Mobocracy. **1789** MME. D'ARBLAY *Diary* 19 Nov., Mr. Wilkes..quarrelled with a gentleman for saying the French government was become a democracy, and asserted it was rather a mobocracy. **1839** *Times* 18 July, Henceforth,.. mobocracy will be 'at a heavier discount' than ever. **1878** BAYNE *Purit. Rev.* x. 431 [They] seem to have been infected ..with the cretinous hallucinations of mobocracy.

2. The 'mob' or lowest class as a ruling body; a ruling or politically supreme mob.

1754 A. MURPHY *Gray's-Inn Jrnl.* No. 95 The Mobocracy have further the legislative and executive Part of their Laws in their own Hands. **1819** *Metropolis* II. 73 Without the nobles, the mobocracy would have it all their own way. **1856** *Chamb. Jrnl.* VI. 225 The shopocracy in the pit, and the mobocracy in the gallery. **1885** *Century Mag.* XXXI. 54 The American demagogue is the courtier of American mobocracy. **1921** G. B. SHAW *Back to Methuselah* Pref. p. lxii, Bastiat had proved convincingly that Nature had arranged Economic Harmonies which would settle social questions far better than theocracies or aristocracies or mobocracies. **1949** F. L. WRIGHT (*title*) Genius and the mobocracy.

mobocrat ('mɒbəʊkræt). [formed as prec. after *democrat*, etc.: see -CRAT.] One who advocates mobocracy; a leader of the mob, a demagogue.

1798 in *Spirit Public Jrnls.* (1799) II. 123 Republican Gazette for 1892. Written and prophesied by an eminent Mobocrat. **1845** T. W. COIT *Puritanism* 233 The demagogue, the mobocrat, the sans-culottes. **1879** BAYNE *Less. fr. my Masters* I. 75 The idiotic notion, possibly entertained by a brainless mobocrat here and there, that [etc.].

mobocratic (mɒbəʊ'krætɪk), *a.* Also 8 mobcratic. [f. prec. + -IC.] Pertaining to or of the nature of a mobocracy; that advocates mobocracy.

1775 J. TUCKER *Let. to Burke* (ed. 2) 14 Tarring and Feathering would be the mildest Punishment, which such a Rebel against this (Mob-cratic) Constitution could expect. **1836** MRS. STOWE in *Life* iv. (1889) 85 All the newspapers.. were either silent or openly 'mobocratic'. **1889** J. M. ROBERTSON *Ess. Crit. Method* 23 His dislike of mobocratic and democratic principles.

mobocratical (mɒbəʊ'krætɪkəl), *a.* [formed as prec. + -IC-AL.] Of or pertaining to mobocracy.

1754 A. MURPHY *Gray's-Inn Jrnl.* No. 95 Mr. Wilks..was not in his Heart of Mobocratical Principles. *Ibid.*, One disaffected Person cannot withstand the Mobocratical Power. **1804** FESSENDEN *Democr.* (1806) I. 98 Many plausible excuses For mobocratical abuses.

mobolatry (mɒ'bɒlətrɪ). [f. MOB *sb.*^{1} + *-olatry*, after *idolatry*.] Worship of the mob.

1864 *Daily Tel.* 8 Apr., It is no sacrifice of revenue at the shrine of mob-olatry, as the abandonment of half the malt tax was so clearly proved to be. **1882** *Dublin Morn. Mail* 15 Dec. 3 Mr. Gladstone has himself always discriminated between popularity and mob-olatry.

'**mobship.** *nonce-wd.* [f. MOB *sb.*^{1} + *-ship*, after *lordship*, *kingship*.] **a.** *jocularly*. The personality of a member of a mob. **b.** Mob-government.

1830 *Fraser's Mag.* I. 457 The two gentlemen..smile condescendingly on the mobility, cut a curvet in the air to shew their mobships that they are clever lively divinities, and finally [etc.]. **1893** HUXLEY *Evolution & Ethics* 51 The Ionian politics had passed through the whole gamut of social and political changes—from patriarchal..kingship to rowdy ..mobship.

mobsman ('mɒbzmən). [f. *mob's*, genitive of MOB *sb.*^{1}]

1. One of a mob or crowd.

1868 *Express* 20 May, To..find himself in a well-dressed, querulous, selfish mob,..to see small detachments of his fellow mobsmen conveyed by policemen through phaetons and barouches [etc.]. **1881** W. H. MALLOCK in *Contemp. Rev.* 938 Of all these thousands of men [composing a mob] each man has his own separate temperament... The passions that direct him as a mobsman may be quite dormant in private life. **1901** R. M. STILLARD *B. Sullivan* II. 10 Forrest had none of his mobsmen in the theatre that evening to repeat the disturbance.

2. (In full ***swell mobsman***.) A member of the swell mob (see MOB *sb.*^{1} 4). Also, = next.

1846 *Swell's Night Guide* p. iii, The tophic blacklegs and swell mobsman, who can pluck a pigeon with the sang froid of a ripened friendship. **1851–61** MAYHEW *Lond. Labour* II. 369 Swell-mobsmen, and thieves, and housebreakers. **1862** *Ibid.* IV. 25 'Mobsmen', or those who plunder by manual dexterity. **1856** *Q. Rev.* June 183 The swell mobsmen proper generally work together at races in gangs of from three to seven. *Ibid.*, A school of mobsmen. **1904** *Daily News* 9 Nov. 2 He belonged to a gang of swell mobsmen who frequented the West-end. **1935** A. J. POLLOCK *Underworld Speaks* 77/1 *Mobsman*, a gangster, a thug; ruffian; gunman. **1974** *Daily Tel.* (Colour Suppl.) 29 Nov. 86/4 It is doubtful if the Victorian Londoner needed warning, for the artful mobsmen, toolers and dippers, together with their stickman accomplices, were everywhere among the crowds.

mobster ('mɒbstə(r)). *slang* (orig. *U.S.*). [f. MOB *sb.*^{1} + -STER.] A member of a group of criminals; cf. GANGSTER. Also *attrib.* and *transf.*

1917 *Lincoln* (Nebraska) *Evening News* 11 July 4 Many mobsters have left the city, it is asserted, and leaders of the mob are going to be hard to find. **1940** *New Yorker* 13 July 17/1 A mob nickname he got from the mobsters. **1947** E. HYAMS *William Medium* x. 199 South African diamond mobsters. **1947** J. MULGAN *Report on Experience* x. 125, I never lived in Chicago, but have a wide vicarious acquaintance from films and paperbacks of mobster-rule and gang-law. **1957** *Observer* 3 Nov. 19/3 Mr. [Marc] Lawrence, renowned for his portraits of flinty Hollywood mobsters. **1962** D. WARNER *Death of Bogey* I. ii. 10 A scurrying horde of spivs and pimps, fiddlers and tweedlers, tearaways, mobsters. **1964** D. VARADAY *Gara-Yaka* xviii. 159 The dead mobsters were mangy, disease-ridden outcasts of the dog world. **1972** D. E. WESTLAKE *Cops & Robbers* (1973) xvi. 251, I was afraid to think about Vigano and his mobsters.

mobylle, *Sc.* variant of MOBLE *Obs.*

mocadan, variant of MOKADDAM.

mocado, variant of MOCKADO.

mocador: see MUCKENDER.

mocamp ('məʊkæmp). [f. MO(TOR *sb.* + CAMP *sb.*^{2}] (See quot. 1970.)

1967 *Times* 1 Nov. (Suppl.) p. ii/1 If you're touring Turkey, stay at BP Mocamps. Here's a welcome for campers and caravanners. **1970** *Britannica Bk. of Year* (U.S.) 798/3 *Mocamp*, a camp providing tourists with a protected area for tents and trailers and offering various conveniences and services. **1972** *Maclean's Mag.* June 54/3 In Turkey camping facilities called Mocamps are found all over the country.

†**mocawk**, variant of MACAQUE.

mocayare, obs. form of MOHAIR.

moccasin ('mɒkəsɪn). Forms: 7, 9 mockasin, 8 molkasin, morgisson, mogasheen, -i(n)son, -erson, -oson, -ason, moggi(n)son, mokasin, -awson, mackassin, maccase(e)ne, mockassin, -aseen, -ason, -eson, magassin, 8–9 mocas(s)in, 9 mowkisin, mocki(n)son, moccaso(o)n, -usin, -assin, mognesan, mogissin, mocsen, mocasson, moccassin, 8– moccasin. [a. Powhatan '*mockasin*, Odjibwa '*makisin*; other Indian dialects have the stress on the middle syllable, as in Narragansett *mo'kussin*, Micmac *m'kusun*.]

1. a. A kind of foot-gear made of deerskin or other soft leather, worn by the Indians of North America, and by the trappers and backwoodsmen who have adopted Indian customs. Also *attrib.*, as ***moccasin track***, ***awl***.

1612 CAPT. SMITH *Map Virginia* (Arb.) 44 *Mockasins.* Shooes. **1704** *New Hampsh. Prov. Papers* (1869) III. 290 *note*, Every Householder..shall provide..one good pair of snow shoes and mogasheens. **1725** S. WILLARD in *Early Rec. Lancaster, Mass.* (1884) 238 We found a mogerson tracke, and spent some time scouting after said Tracke. **1760** *Char.* in *Ann. Reg.* III. 23/2 His dress was a deer-skin jacket,.. with morgissons, or deer-skin pumps, or sandals, which were laced. **1788** M. CUTLER in *Life*, etc. (1888) I. 423 We saw frequently moccasin tracks, which appeared to have been just made. **1799** J. SMITH *Acc. Remark. Occurr.* (1870) 115 All the surgical instruments I had, was a knife, a mockason awle, and a pair of bullit moulds. **1826** J. F. COOPER *Mohicans* (1829) II. iv. 59 The impression of a moccasin in the rich and moist alluvion. **1840** R. H. DANA *Bef. Mast* xxvi. 85 Indian curiosities..such as..feathers of birds, fur mocassins [etc.]. **1877** BLACK *Green Past.* xlv, His mocassins of buffalo-hide were very elaborately embroidered.

b. A type of shoe for informal wear, resembling those worn by American Indians.

1895 *Montgomery Ward Catal.* 513/3 Infants' Moccasins, made from soft dingola stock, with silk lace and tassel. **1944** H. MCCLOY *Panic* ii. 13 The loose sweater, kilted skirt, and flat-heeled moccasins she had put on so hastily. **1970** B. KNOX *Children of Mist* iii. 53 He wore a blue sports shirt with brown shoes, his feet were in light tan moccasins.

c. *Austral.* and *N.Z.* (See quots.)

1929 H. B. SMITH *Sheep & Wool Industry Austral. & N.Z.* (ed. 3) x. 75 The shearers..arrayed in their working clothes, with bowyangs..and moccasins on (a kind of shoe made out of wool-pack, after the style of the foot-covering of the Red Indian). **1965** *N.Z. Listener* 26 Feb. 15/2 *Moccasin*, the shearer's home-made footwear, usually made of sacking or felt.

2. moccasin flower, plant, U.S. name for the orchidaceous genus *Cypripedium* (Lady's Slipper); **yellow moccasin**, *C. pubescens*.

1680 in J. Ray *Hist. Plant.* (1688) II. 1926/1 Helleborine flore rotundo luteo, purpureis venis striato. The Mockasine flower. **1700** PLUKENET *Opera Bot.* (1769) III. 101 *Helleborine Virginiana*... The Molkasin Flower. **1748** *Phil. Trans.* XLV. 159 They call it the Mocasin Flower, which also signifies in their Language a Shoe or Slipper. **1882** *Garden* 3 June 384/1 The Mocasson Flower (*Cypripedium spectabile*)..here apparently finds a congenial home. **1890** *Syd. Soc. Lex.*, *Moccasin plant*, same as *M. flower*. *Moccasin root*, the *Cypripedium pubescens*. **1902** CORNISH *Naturalist Thames* 181 Big white mocassin flowers,..and bog arum. **1954** C. J. HYLANDER *Macmillan Wild Flower Bk.* 65 The Lady's-slippers or Moccasin-flowers are easily recognizable by the inflated sac which forms the lip of the flower. **1970** R. T. NORTHEN *Home Orchid Growing* (ed. 3) 197/2 Cypripedium. These are the moccasin-flowers or ladyslippers of our woods and moist meadows.

3. [Possibly a distinct word; in any case the reason for the name is obscure.] In full **moccasin snake**: a venomous crotaline snake, *Ancistrodon* (or *Cenchris* or *Toxicophis* or *Trigonocephalus*) *piscivorus*, about two feet in length, usually of a somewhat aquatic habit, native of the Southern United States; also ***water moccasin*** (*-snake*). ***highland*** or ***upland moccasin***, the Cottonmouth, *Agkistrodon atrofuscus*, a similar or identical snake inhabiting the dry land and mountainous regions. Sometimes erroneously applied to the Copperhead snake, *Agkistrodon contortrix*, and to snakes of the colubrine genus *Nerodia*.

1784 J. FILSON *Discovery Kentucke* 27 The horned and the mockason snakes. **1784** J. SMYTH *Tour U.S.A.* I. vii. 54 The most noxious, virulent, and deleterious of the species, the rattle, moccasson, and horn-snakes. **1788** [see COPPER-BELLY]. **1791** W. BARTRAM *Carolina* 272 The moccasin snake is a large and horrid serpent. *Ibid.* 273 There is another snake in Carolina and Florida called the moccasin. **1842** HOLBROOK *N. Amer. Herpetol.* III. 33 *Trigonocephalus piscivorus*... Water Mocassin *Vulgo*. *Ibid.*, 45 The *Trigonocephalus atro-fuscus* ..is..called in Tennessee Highland Mocassin. **1849** J. E. GRAY *Catal. Specim. Snakes Brit. Mus.* 16 The Black-brown Mocassin, *Cenchris atrofuscus*. **1853** BAIRD & GIRARD *Catal. N. Amer. Reptiles* I. 19 *Toxicophis piscivorus*... Water Mocassin. *Ibid.* 165 Highland Mocassin (*Toxicophis atrofuscus*). *Ibid.* 166 Upland Mocassin (*Toxicophis atrofuscus*). *Ibid.*, Mocassin (*Nerodia sipedon* and *N. fasciata*). **187.** *Cassell's Nat. Hist.* IV. 319 The Copper-head Snake *Trigonocephalus* (*Ancistrodon*) *contortrix*, often wrongly called the Mocassin Snake..preys upon frogs and birds. **1885** *Riverside Nat. Hist.* (1888) III. 394 The so-called highland-mocassin, *Ancistrodon atrofuscus*, has not been collected since the time of its original description. It and *A. piscivorus* are undoubtedly the same species. **1965** R. & D. MORRIS *Men & Snakes* iv. 80 As recently as 1943, it was claimed that moccasin venom had been used with success in the treatment of rheumatoid arthritis.

4. *attrib.*, as **moccasin telegram** or **telegraph** *N. Amer.*, a means for the rapid or surreptitious transmission of information, orig. by an Indian runner; = *bush telegraph*.

1908 A. C. LAUT *Conquest Gt. Northwest* II. 35 Word of the white woman ran before the advancing traders by 'moccasin telegram'. **1909** A. D. CAMERON *New North* 349 And now, apprised by moccasin telegraph, we are all on the *qui vive* to catch sight of a floating bride. **1927** *Sat. Even. Post* 23 July 3/3 That agency known to white men as the Moccasin Telegraph, by which odd bits of news are flashed from one isolated native camp to another. **1969** *Islander* (Victoria, B.C.) 15 June 5/1 Word of the new constable was relayed to Simon by moccasin telegraph.

moccasined ('mɒkəsɪnd), *a.* [f. prec. + -ED^{1}.]

1. Furnished or provided with moccasins.

1829 J. F. COOPER *Borderers* III. iii. 89 The two chiefs left the piazza in the noiseless manner of the moccasined foot. **1851** MAYNE REID *Scalp Hunt.* i, This region is only trodden by the mocassined foot of the hunter. **18..** WHITTIER *Yankee Gypsies* Pr. Wks. 1889 I. 326 Quick tripping of fair moccasined feet on glittering ice pavements. **1903** *Blackw. Mag.* Apr. 497/2 Her moccasined feet, tucked into wide wooden stirrups. **1951** I. SHAW *Troubled Air* viii. 138 Moving a moccasined foot gently back and forth. **1968** M. WOODHOUSE *Rock Baby* xvii. 176 She started back towards the camp, her moccasined feet leaving damp footprints.

2. *U.S. slang.* (See quot.)

1859 BARTLETT *Dict. Amer.*, *Moccasoned*, intoxicated. South Carolina. **1872** SCHELE DE VERE *Americanisms* 35 In the South a man made drunk by bad liquor is said to have been 'bitten by the [moccasin] snake', or simply to be mocassined.

†**moccenigo.** *Obs.* In 7 **muccinigo, mutsenigo.** [a. It. *moccenigo*, *mocenigo* (Florio 1611); from the name of Tommaso Mocenigo, doge of Venice 1413–23.] A small coin formerly current in Venice, worth about ninepence.

?**1553** J. LOCKE in *Hakluyt's Voy.* (1599) II. I. 108 They haue euery pay, which is 45 dayes, 15 Mozenigos, which is 15 shillings sterling. **1605** B. JONSON *Volpone* II. i, You shall not giue mee sixe Crownes,..nor two nor one; nor halfe a Duckat; no, nor a Muccinigo. **1617** MORYSON *Itin.* I. 291 The Spanish piastro of siver is given for sixe lires,..the mutsenigo for a lire. **1655** SHIRLEY *Gentl. Venice* I. i. 3 *Mal.* .. In the mean time lend me the trifling Duccats... *Cor.* Not a Muccinigo To save thee from the Gallies.

mocco, obs. form of MOCHA^{2}.

moch (mɒx), *sb. Sc.* [app. repr. OE. *mohðe* MOTH; cf. the 15th c. Eng. forms *mowhe*, *mowghe* (Promp. Parv.).] A moth.

c **1650** P. GORDON *Short Abridgem. Brit. Distemper* (1844) 113 This earle George his first wife..forbids her husband to leave such a consuming moch in his house, as was the sacraledgeous medling with the abisie of Deir. **1871** W. ALEXANDER *Johnny Gibb* xxi. 156 Half ate'n wi' the mochs.

†moch, *a. Sc. Obs.* Also 6 moich. [Of obscure origin: cf. MOCH *v.* and MOCHY *a.*, also MUGGY *a.* and dial. *moke* sb. (Lincs.) a mist, fog, *moke* adj., hazy, dark (E.D.D.).] Moist, damp.

1501 DOUGLAS *Pal. Hon.* I. 26 Auld rottin runtis quhairin na sap was leifit, Moch, all waist, widderit with granis montit. **1513** —— *Æneis* XII. Prol. 46 Mysty vapour vpspringand,.. In smoky soppis of donk dewis wak, Moich hailsum stovis ourheildand the slak.

†moch, *v. Sc. Obs.* Also 7 moach. [? f. MOCH *a.* But cf. G. *muchen* to turn rancid or mouldy.] *intr.* To decay, rot.

1624 *Extracts Aberd. Reg.* (1848) II. 394 Not onlie sall the most pairt of thame [*sc.* the books] moch and conswme, bot [etc.]. *a* **1670** SPALDING *Troub. Chas. I* (Bannatyne Club) I. 49 The cornes..begane to moche and rott.

moch, obs. form of MUCH *a.*

Mocha[1] (ˈməʊkə). Forms: 7 mocus, 8 moco(e, mocoa, mocho(e, mochoa, 8– Mocha. [In early examples *mocus, moco, mocho*; of obscure origin, but regarded (perh. correctly) by Johnson (and apparently by Woodward in 1728) as identical with the place-name MOCHA[2] (in 18th c. often spelt *Mocho*); hence now commonly written with capital M. Cf. G. *mokkastein*, F. *pierre de Mocka* (1765 in *Encyclopédie* X. 590), Sp. *piedra de moca*, Pg. *pedra de moca*, perh. after the Eng. name.]

1. (Also ***Mocha stone, pebble.***) A variety of chalcedony resembling or identical with moss-agate, having dendritic markings due to the presence of oxides of manganese, iron, etc.

1679 *Will Dan. Bennett* (Somerset Ho.), My Mocus stone Ring. **1704** in Ashton *Soc. Life Q. Anne* (1882) I. 180 A gold Moco Stone chain set in Gold. *Ibid.* 181 One Moco Stone Bracelet. **1728** WOODWARD *Fossils* 22 The Mocho-Stone. *Note, Achates Mochoensis*..These are nearly related to the Agat-Kind,..with Delineations representing Mosses, Shrubs and Branches. **1728** —— *Catal. Foreign Fossils* 16 A Mochoa-Stone, with Delineations of Shrubs. **1753** MRS. DELANY in *Life & Corr.* (1861) III. 249 Some new acquisitions of shells, agates, mocoes, and a thousand fine things. **1769** *Public Advertiser* 29 May 3/4 Beautiful oriental Mocoas, Antiques, Seed Pearl. *Ibid.* 12 June 3/2 A Mourning Ring, Hair, Mocoa, set round with Amethyst. **1771** *Phil. Trans.* LXIII. 17 The Earl of Wandesford had one of them sawn into a slab, and it is as beautiful as a Moco. **1789** E. DARWIN *Bot. Gard.* II. 157 Pictured mochoes tesselate the ground. **1827** H. E. LLOYD tr. *Timkowski's Trav.* I. 185 An eminence which was covered with cornelians, calcedony, mocha stones, and jasper of different colours. **1843** BERKELEY in *Ann. Nat. Hist.* XI. 415 On Substances inclosed in Mochastones. [*Footnote*, This word is evidently used with considerable latitude, and by no means confined to the bodies so named in this country.] By Karl Mueller. **1864** BLACKMORE *Clara Vaughan* xl, Any Mocha stone, fortification agate, or Scotch pebble.

2. One of several brown geometrid moths lined and variegated with grey, esp. of the genus *Ephyra*; in full often ***mocha moth***, † ***stone***.

1775 M. HARRIS *Eng. Lepidoptera* 45 Mocha stone. Pale mocha stone. **1869** E. NEWMAN *Brit. Moths* 73 The False Mocha (*Ephyra porata*)... I do not know the caterpillars of the Mocha moths from each other. *Ibid.* 74 The Mocha (*Ephyra omicronaria*). *Ibid.*, The Dingy Mocha (*Ephyra orbicularia*). *Ibid.*, The Birch Mocha (*Ephyra pendularia*).

3. *dial.* 'A term applied to a cat of a black colour intermixed with brown.' (Halliwell 1847).

4. A type of English pottery, made from the late eighteenth to the early twentieth century, with white or cream body decorated with coloured bands on to which moss- or fern-like patterns have been applied. Freq. *attrib.*

1837 S. SHAW *Chem. of Compounds used in Manuf. Porc.* I. v. 346 The readiness with which they combine with earths ..renders them very useful in the Mocha and dipped ware. *Ibid.* II. i. 410 The peculiar kind of clay, in this neighbourhood,..veins of which are still kept open for supplying the same, fine in grain, and dark in colour, for the mocha dip. **1953** *N. Teulon-Porter Coll. Mocha Pott.* (Stoke-on-Trent Museum & Art Gallery Comm.) 1 There are a few collectors in the field and soon Mocha will vie for attention with lustre or transfer printed pottery. **1961** L. G. G. RAMSEY *Connoisseur New Guide Antique Eng. Pott., Porc. & Glass* 67 Mocha ware, so named because of its resemblance to the quartz mocha stone, was in demand for kitchen jugs and mugs and large cups and saucers after its invention about 1780. **1968** *Canad. Antiques Collector* June 17/2 What is Mocha Ware? Sometimes referred to as 'Leeds Ware' or 'banded creamware' it is a creamware decorated with seaweed or tree silhouettes. This was made from 1787 up to 1903.

mocha[2] (ˈməʊkə). Also 8 Mocco, 9 Moka, 9- Mocha. [The name of an Arabian port at the entrance of the Red Sea.]

1. a. In full, ***mocha coffee***: a fine quality of coffee; *originally*, that produced in the Yemen province of Arabia in which the town of Mocha is situated. [So F. *Moka*, Sp. *café de Moca*, Pg. *cafe de Moka*.]

1773 SIR J. PRINGLE *Let.* in *Encycl. Brit.* (1797) V. 124/1 The coffee ought to be of the best Mocco. **1819** S. ROGERS *Hum. Life* Poems (1839) 14 Then fragrant clouds of Mocha and Souchong Blend as they rise. **1871** M. COLLINS *Mrq. & Merch.* II. x. 292 The..lady would..sip a cup of strong Mocha. **1883** *Encycl. Brit.* XVI. 540/2 The..name of Mochá coffee is derived from the shipment of coffee there.

b. Used *attrib.* of cakes, puddings, etc., flavoured with coffee, or coffee and chocolate.

1892 A. B. MARSHALL *Larger Cookery Bk.* xii. 475 *Moka Cake*... Prepare a Genoise paste mixture.., bake for an hour and a quarter, then turn out, and, when cold, mask over with Coffee glace. **1908** J. KIRKLAND *Mod. Baker* III. lxxxi. 390 A butter cream flavoured with coffee and vanilla..will be useful for flavouring and decorating the popular cakes known as *Mocha fancies*. **1963** V. NABOKOV *Gift* v. 305 Old Stupishin, whose spoon was working its way through a wedge of mocha cake. **1972** M. J. BOSSE *Incident at Naha* ii. 102 His skin was like rich mocha chocolate. **1975** *New Yorker* 3 Feb. 26/2, I sold schnecken, cookies, apple turnovers, and mocha tarts.

c. A shade or tint of the colour of mocha coffee; a dark brown colour. Also ***mocha brown***.

1895 *Montgomery Ward Catal.* 274/3 Men's Fedora Hats. .. Colors: Blue black, mocha brown and slate. *Ibid.* 275/1 Fedora Hats... Colors: Black, dark brown, gray, tan and mocha. **1919** T. S. ELIOT *Sweeney among Nightingales* in *Poems*, The silent man in mocha brown Sprawls at the window sill and gapes. **1971** *Vogue* 15 Sept. 15 Eye shadow in earthy wine, rose, turquoise and mocha. **1974** *Harrods Christmas Catal.* 15 Leather clutch bag... Black, mocha brown, navy, rust, or terracotta.

2. a. ***mocha aloes***: an inferior kind of hepatic aloes, of dark colour and nauseous smell, brought to Aden from the interior. **b.** ***mocha senna***: 'Indian' senna, the product of *Cassia lanceolata, angustifolia*, or *elongata*.

1881 *Syd. Soc Lex., Aloes, Moka.* **1882** BENTLEY *Man. Bot.* (ed. 4) 524 The Common East Indian, Arabian, Mocha, or Bombay Senna is derived from *Cassia angustifolia*.

3. (See quot. 1968.) Also *attrib.*

1895 *Montgomery Ward Catal.* 290/2 Men's dressed mocha kid gloves. **1922** [see BOULTON *a.*]. **1938** E. BOWEN *Death of Heart* II. iv. 235 The stitching on her brown mocha gloves. **1968** J. IRONSIDE *Fashion Alphabet* 238 *Mocha*, a fine, soft, hard-wearing leather made from sheepskin from Arabia, Africa and Persia. The chief outlet was Mocha in Arabia, hence the name.

mochado, variant of MOCKADO.

mochato, obs. corrupt form of MUSTACHIO.

†moche. *Surg. Obs.* [a. F. *moche* skein, OF. *moiche* (mod.F. *mèche*) seton.] A seton.

1541 R. COPLAND *Guydon's Quest. Chirurg.* L iv b, And all other woundes without tentes and moches ought to be vnderstande to be consolydate.

moche, obs. form of MUCH *sb.*, *a.* and *adv.*

mochel(l, -il(l, obs. forms of MICKLE.

mochenese, obs. form of MUCHNESS.

‖**mochi** (ˈmɒtʃɪ). Also 7 musho. [Jap.] A cake made from pounded, glutinous rice.

In some quots. *mochi* has the honorific prefix *o-*.

1616 R. COCKS *Diary* 10 Feb. (1883) I. 109 Shezque Dono ..came to the English howse and brought a present of *mushos*, wyne, and redish. **1880** I. L. BIRD *Unbeaten Tracks Japan* I. 235 *Mochi*, a small round cake of unbaked rice dough, though insipid, is not unpalatable, and is much in favour. **1891** A. M. BACON *Jap. Girls & Women* i. 5 Cakes of mochi, or rice paste. **1936** K. TEZUKA *Jap. Food* 49 *Mochi* (glutinous rice boiled and pounded) is a special New Year food. **1960** B. LEACH *Potter in Japan* ii. 62 We were taken indoors and fed on what was described to me as good country food, which included O Mochi. These are dumplings made of pounded steamed rice of a particularly glutinous variety. *Ibid.* 239 *Mochi*, steamed and dried cakes of glutinous rice. **1970** J. KIRKUP *Japan behind Fan* 106 We would sip green tea and beer and nibble peanuts and seaweed biscuits and *o-mochi*, or sweet bean cakes.

Mochica (məʊˈtʃiːkə), *a.* and *sb.* Also **Mochican**, **Moche**, 9 **Moxa**. [Sp., f. an Indian word; cf. *Moche*, the name of an archæological site in the valley of the same name in the coastal region of northern Peru.] **A.** *adj.* Of or pertaining to the Mochica, a pre-Inca people living on the Peruvian coast, or their modern descendants, or the language spoken by them. **B.** *sb.* **a.** The name of this people or a member of it. **b.** The language of the Mochica.

1853 F. L. HAWKS tr. *Rivero & Von Tschudi's Peruvian Antiquities* v. 97 The Moxa language has strictly no declension. **1871** *Jrnl. R. Geogr. Soc.* XLI. 283 Bishop Luis Geronimo de Orè..is the only source from which we get specimens of the Puquina and Mochica languages. *Ibid.* 323 We have..the Lord's Prayer in the *Mochica*, a dialect spoken in the valleys of Runahuanac and Huarco. *Ibid.* 326 Tribes along the Peruvian coast..the *Chimus* (the *Yuncas* of Carrera); the *Mochicas* (the *Chinchas* of Garcilasso). **1877** E. G. SQUIER *Peru* viii. 128 You should have seen my Moche children forty years ago. **1927** *Geogr. Rev.* XVII. 42 The inhabitants of Chan-Chan spoke a language known as Yunga (or Yunca) or Mochica of which today vestiges survive in the vicinity of Eten. **1948** [see BICHROME *a.* and *sb.*[2]]. **1953** A. C. KINSEY et al. *Sexual Behavior Human Female* vii. 231 The Mochican pottery of ancient Peru.. depicts practically every petting and coital technique. **1959** [see HUACO]. **1961** J. B. PRIESTLEY *Saturn over Water* v. 57 A monochrome ceramic, of the Mochica Culture, representing a warrior in ambush. **1965** A. EMMERICH *Sweat of Sun & Tears of Moon* ii. 15 The Mochica also continued the use of elaborate gold headdresses by important personages. **1967** R. PENISTON-BIRD tr. *Gallo's Gold of Peru* 15 The Mochicans of the Peruvian coast..having as their centre the pyramids of the sun and moon at Moche developed the science of metallurgy before most of the Peruvian peoples. **1971** L. A. BOGER *Dict. World Pott. & Porc.* 229/2 The decoration on Mochica pottery which is painted or modeled or a combination of both, gives a vivid picture of the life and customs of the people.

†ˈmochlic, *a.* and *sb. Obs.* [a. F. *mochlique*, ad. Gr. μοχλικός pertaining to the use of levers (in reducing dislocation), f. μοχλός lever.] **a.** *adj. Surg.* Of or relating to the reduction of a dislocated bone (Mayne *Expos. Lex.* 1856). **b.** *sb. Med.* A drastic purge. So **ˈmochlical** *a.*, (of a medicine) drastic.

1657 TOMLINSON *Renou's Disp.* 390* Elaterium is numerated among mochlical Medicaments. [**1753** CHAMBERS *Cycl. Supp.*, *Mochlica*, a term by which some authors call the violent or drastic purges.]

mocho, -oa, -oe, obs. forms of MOCHA[1].

‖**mochras** (moːtʃˈrʌs). Also 9 moocherus, mucherus, muchi-ras, mochurrus. [Hindī *mōčras*:—Skr. *močarasa*.] (See quots.)

1856 A. FAULKNER *Dict. Commerc. Terms*, *Moocherus*, a gum resin yielded by the *Bombax Heptaphyllum*. **1882** J. SMITH *Dict. Plants Econ.*, *Mucherus*, a gummy substance obtained from the bark of *Bombax malabaricum*. **1885** E. BALFOUR *Cycl. India* (ed. 3), Muchi-ras. Hind. Gum from several plants,—Salmalia Malabarica and Moringa pterygosperma, also a gall from the Areca catechu. **1885** *Cassell's Encycl. Dict.*, *Mochras*.

mochree, var. MACHREE.

mochy (ˈmɒxɪ), *a. Sc.* [f. MOCH *a.* + -Y. Cf. MOKY, MUGGY.] Damp, misty.

1786 *Har'st Rig* lxxxi, Mair scouthry like it still does look, At length comes on in mochy rook. [For later quots. see E.D.D.]

mochyll, variant of MICKLE.

mocio(u)n, -cioner, obs. ff. MOTION, -ER.

mock (mɒk), *sb.*[1] Now chiefly *rare* or *arch.* Forms: 5–6 mokk(e, 5–7 mocke, 6 mok, 7 moke, 6– mock. [f. MOCK *v.*]

1. a. A derisive or contemptuous action or speech; an act of mocking or derision.

c **1440** *Alphabet of Tales* 360 Þe gude man bade styll & had a mokk [L. *maritus delusus remansit*]. **1491** CAXTON *Vitas Patr.* (W. de W. 1495) II. 195 b/2 This olde philosopher.. casted at hym many proude mockes & shamefull wordes. **1500–20** DUNBAR *Poems* xlix. 45 Wyvis thuss makis mokkis Spynnand on rokkis. **1509** HAWES *Past. Pleas.* xxxv. (Percy Soc.) 182 He..called me boye, and gave me many a mocke. **1535** JOYE *Apol. Tindale* (Arb.) 14 This saith Tindale yroniously in a mok as though it were false. *a* **1541** WYATT in *Tottel's Misc.* (Arb.) 36 Such mockes of dreames do turne to deadly payne. **1587** GOLDING *De Mornay* xv. (1617) 251 Ye may well thinke they gaue a dry mocke to all the arguments of Aristotle. **1615** SWETNAM *Arraignm. Wom.* (1880) p. xxi, Thou canst not goe in the street with her without mocks, nor amongst thy neighbours without frumps. **1679** EARL MULGRAVE *Ess. on Satire* 194 For after all his vulgar marriage mocks, With beauty dazzled, Numps was in the stocks. **1888** CHILD *Ballads* III. 178/1 Robin Hood..changes clothes with the palmer (who at first thinks the proposal a mock).

b. †***to make mock(s*** or ***a mock at***: to deride (*obs.*). ***to make a mock of***: to bring into contempt. ***to put the*** (or ***a***) ***mock(s) on*** (someone): see quot. 1943 (*Austral. slang*).

a **1460** *Gregory's Chron.* in *Hist. Coll. Citizen Lond.* (Camden) 178 For men provesyde be-fore þat the vyntage of Gascon and Gyan shulde come ovyr Scheters Hylle, and men made but a mocke ther of. **1508** DUNBAR *Tua Mariit Wemen* 279 Makand mokis at that mad fader. **1535** COVERDALE *Ps.* xliii. 9 Ye haue made a mocke at the councell of the poore. —— *Heb.* vi. 6 Yf they fall awaye (and concernynge them selues crucifye the sonne of God afreszhe, and make a mocke off him) that they shulde [etc.]. **1611** BIBLE *Prov.* xiv. 9 Fools make a mock at sin. **1693** *Mem. Cnt. Teckely* II. 125 Tekeley made a mock at this forced offer. **1714** GAY *Sheph. Week, Tues.* 19 Colin makes mock at all her piteous Smart. **1837** HAWTHORNE *Twice-told T.* (1851) II. xviii. 265 My own shadow makes a mock of my fooleries! **1891** HALL CAINE *Scapegoat* v, An evil spirit would make a mock at him. **1894** CROCKETT *Raiders* 21, I could never forgive her for making a mock of me. **1911** E. DYSON *Benno* 33 It's up t'me t'put a mock on that tripester. **1938** X. HERBERT *Capricornia* xxxii. 482 'He put the mocks on me,' roared Norman... 'What's he saying, dear?' 'He.. reckons I told the police on him.' **1943** BAKER *Dict. Austral. Slang* (ed. 3) 51 *Mocks on, put the*, to upset someone's plans, to spoil a person's calculations. Also, 'put the mock on'. **1965** W. GROUT *My Country's 'Keeper* xx. 206, I hope I am not 'putting the mock' on Norm because my feelings are the same as the rest of the Australian Test players: When O'Neill is a doubtful Test starter the job always looks grimmer.

c. Derision, mockery.

1568 GRAFTON *Chron.* II. 726 All their trauaile, paine, and expences, were to their shame loste and employed, and nothyng gayned, but a continuall mocke, and dayly derision of the French King. **1692** WASHINGTON tr. *Milton's Def. Pop.* vii. M.'s Wks. 1851 VIII. 171 Are they called so in vain, and in mock only? **1881** PALGRAVE *Visions Eng.* 247 [They] watched the Ganges-brimming jars In fiendish mock borne past their dungeon bars.

†d. An imposture. *Obs.*

1523 LD. BERNERS *Froiss.* I. clxxvi. 213 He sent me with yᵉ letter, the goodlyest chessemen than euer I sawe: He found out that mocke, bycause he knewe well that the capitayne loued well the game of the chesse.

†e. In phr. ***mocks and mows***: see MOW *sb.*

2. A thing to be derided or jeered at; something deserving of scorn.

1489 CAXTON *Faytes of A.* IV. i. 230 Other suche thinges of the whiche shulde not be reputed nor taken in Iugement but for a trifle or a mocke. **1583** *Leg. Bp. St. Androis* 127 They hald it still vp for a mocke, How Maister Patrik fedd his flock. **1627** MAY *Lucan* x. 31 If ere the world her freedome had attaind, He for a mocke had been reserv'd. **1655** FULLER *Ch. Hist.* III. iv. §20 They were a fright to few, a mock to many, and an hurt to none. **1814** BYRON *Ode to Napoleon* xvi, Foredoom'd by God—by man accurst, And that last act, though not thy worst, The very Fiend's arch mock. **1890** MRS. A. E. BARR *Friend Olivia* i. 5 A Puritan gentleman is her mock, and nothing else.

3. The action of 'mocking' or imitating; *concr.* something that mocks or deceptively resembles; an imitation, a counterfeit.

1646 CRASHAW *Musicks Duell* 108 Now reach a straine my Lute Above her mocke, or bee for ever mute. **1659** *Burton's Diary* (1828) IV. 277 It is but a mock, an image of a House of Lords. **1807** J. BARLOW *Columb.* IV. 23 While pious Valverde mock of priesthood stands, Guilt in his heart, the gospel in his hands. **1844** MRS. BROWNING *Lost Bower* xxxii, Or, in mock of art's deceiving, was the sudden mildness worn?

4. *attrib. use*: † **mock-sign**, a derisive gesture; **mock-word**, a term of derision. (Perh. rather f. the stem of MOCK *v.*)

1659 HOWELL *Vocab.* i, To make mock-signs with the fingers. *Far la castagna ò la fica cioè* [etc.]. **1845** R. W. HAMILTON *Pop. Educ.* iv. (ed. 2) 61 Religion is a mock-word on their lips.

mock (mɒk), *sb.*[2] *dial.* [Possibly repr. an OE. **moc*, related to ON. *miúk-r* soft (see MEEK *a.*), *myki* MUCK.] (See quots. 1796, 1882.)

1777 *Horæ Subsecivae* 275 (E.D.D.). **1796** W. MARSHALL *W. Eng.* I. 232 The washings of the 'mock', or pomage. *Ibid.* 328 *Mock*, pomage, or ground fruit. **1882** FRIEND *Devon. Plant names* (E.D.S.) 38 *Mock*, apples made into cheese or pommage, ready for the cider-press.

mock (mɒk), *sb.*[3] *dial.*

1. A root or stump; a log.

1844 BARNES *Poems Rural Life* 328 *Mock*, a root or stump of a cut-off bush, or large stick. **1855** *Morton's Cycl. Agric.* II. 724/2 *Mock* (Dorset), the root of a tree. **1874** MRS. WHITCOMBE *Bygone Days Devon & Cornw.* 194 The Christmas Log..is usually called 'the mock'.

2. A tuft of coarse grass or rush left by cattle in pasture land.

1844 BARNES *Poems Rural Life* 328 *Mock*,..a tuft of sedge. **1886** ELWORTHY *W. Somerset Word-bk.* 482 The cattle usually leave tufts or patches of the ranker herbage: these are always called *mocks*.

mock (mɒk), *sb.*[4] *Anglo-Irish.* [Of obscure origin.] A piece of land held in 'conacre'. Also *Comb.* **mockground** = CONACRE.

1824 *Evid. bef. Commons Comm.* 20 May 131 What do you mean by mockground?.. Do you not refer to muckground? It may be; they call it cornacre. **1862** H. COULTER *West of Irel.* 71 Conacre or Mockground as they term it in Clare... I have heard of an instance of a Mock being charged for at the rate of £10 an acre.

mock (mɒk), *a.* (Not in predicative use.) [Partly from the attributive use of MOCK *sb.*[1]; partly from the use of the stem of MOCK *v.* in combination with an object. The hyphen is still often used in the collocations of the adj. with sbs.; when these are used attributively the hyphen is almost always inserted.]

1. Prefixed to a sb. to form a designation for a person or thing that 'mocks', parodies, imitates, or deceptively resembles that which the sb. properly denotes; = sham, counterfeit, imitation, pretended.

a. of persons.

1548 LATIMER *Ploughers* (Arb.) 26, I feare me some be rather mocke gospellers then faythful ploughmen. **1591** SPENSER *M. Hubberd* 1091 They this mock-King did espy. **1652** EVELYN *Diary* 6 Mar., Then marched the mourners, General Cromwell.., his mock-parliament-men, officers, and 40 poore men in gounes. **1660** FULLER *Mixt Contempl.* (1841) 256 Many mock-ministers having banished out of divine service the use of the Lord's prayer, creed, and ten commandments. **1668** DRYDEN (*title*) An Evening's Love, or the Mock-Astrologer. **1687** A. LOVELL tr. *Thevenot's Trav.* III. 10 The Tomb of the Mock-Saint which is in the middle of the Chappel. *a* **1711** KEN *Hymnotheo* Wks. 1721 III. 217 The Envoy Thanks to the Mock-Angel paid. **1724** SWIFT *Drapier's Lett.* Wks. 1755 V. II. 30 This little arbitrary mock-monarch. **1849** MACAULAY *Hist. Eng.* vi. II. 84 A barrister..appeared for the mock plaintiff, and made some feeble objections to the defendant's plea. **1901** A. LANG *Magic & Relig.* 134 The mock-king who was annually killed at the Babylonian festival of the Sacæa.

b. of things, actions, events, etc.

c **1561** [see MOCK HOLIDAY]. **1581** SAVILE *Tacitus, Hist.* IV. xv. (1591) 179 Those mocke-expeditions of Caius the Emperour. **1623** COCKERAM, To Rdr., The mocke-words which are ridiculously vsed in our language. **1643** *Conycatching Bride, title-p.*, This..Mock-Marriage was kept privately in London. **1646** J. BENBRIGGE *God's Fury* 54 Alas, your mock-prayers, mock-fasts, your mock-duties, make his fury come into face. **1647** R. STAPYLTON *Juvenal* 213 His wooden mock knife. **1655** FULLER *Ch. Hist.* II. ii. §43 Those Idols..were so far from defending themselves, that their mock-Mouths could not afford one word, to bemoan their finall Destruction. *a* **1656** BP. HALL *Rem. Wks.* (1660) 167 The Popish mock-fasts which allow the greatest dainties in the strictest abstinence. **1682** DRYDEN & LEE *Dk. of Guise* I. i, I'll swear him Guilty. I swallow Oaths as easie as Snap-dragon, Mock-Fire that never burns. **1689** *Acc. Reasons Chas. II War States-Gen.* 6 After a Mock-Imprisonment of nine or ten days he was let out again. *a* **1700** B. E. *Dict. Cant. Crew*, *Mock-song*, that Ridicules another Song, in the same Terms and to the same Tune. *A Mock-Romance*, that ridicules other Romances, as *Don Quixot*. A Mock-Play, that exposes other playes, as the *Rehearsal*. *a* **1711** KEN *Hymns Evang.* Wks. 1721 I. 88 Mock-Thunder-bolt in his Right Hand he graspt. **1770** *Junius Lett.* xxxviii. (1820) 188 The lofty terms..resembled the pomp of a mock tragedy. **1838** THIRLWALL *Greece* IV. xxviii. 49 The mock assembly was dismissed. **1839** FR. A. KEMBLE *Resid. in Georgia* (1863) 21 The turkey-buzzards.. soar over the river like so many mock eagles. **1844** THIRLWALL *Greece* VIII. 361 A mock trial in which their enemies were judges. **1855** TENNYSON *Maud* III. vi. 33 It is time, O passionate heart and morbid eye, That old hysterical mock-disease should die. **1894** HALL CAINE *Manxman* v. ii, He..lifted his eyebrows and his hands in mock protest.

c. of qualities, sentiments, etc.

1648 SANDERSON *Serm.* II. 248 There are..many mock-graces..that..are not the things they seem to be. **1684** WINSTANLEY *Eng. Worthies* 346 One that was a Thrasonical Puff, and Emblem of mock-valour. **1712** ADDISON *Spect.* No. 309 ¶1 That superior Greatness and Mock-Majesty, which is ascribed to the Prince of the fallen Angels. **1749** J. CLELAND *Mem. Woman Pleasure* II. 12 The mask of mock-modesty was compleatly taken off. **1784** W. COXE *Trav. Poland*, etc. I. 150 This spirit of mock-reverence. **1806** T. CAMPBELL in Smiles *Mem. J. Murray* (1891) I. xiv. 326, I am not assuming any mock modesty. **1835** LYTTON *Rienzi* x. ii, The young man..had much of the..mock patriotism of the Romans. **1877** BLACK *Green Past.*, xxiv, He gave that advice with mock humility. **1880** SWINBURNE *Heptalogia* 90 Thank my stars I'm as free from mock-modesty, friend, As from vulgar fatuity. **1962** I. S. BLACK *High Bright Sun* i. 8 She had ..none of the island girls' self-consciousness, none of their mock modesty.

d. Designating an examination set by a school to give pupils practice for a specified public examination. Also *ellipt.* as *sb.*

1960 *Guardian* 22 June 6/4 A prefect enters... 'It was a long time ago that we did Mock.' **1960** *Where?* III. 15 '*Mock*' *GCE*, an internal examination..run by some schools as a rehearsal for the normal GCE examinations. **1964** C. DALE *Other People* iii. 71 June..had done Tennyson for mock GCE. **1967** *Guardian* 2 May 6/5 Some interviewers..asked if students had done 'mock' 'A' levels at school. **1969** C. FREMLIN *Possession* xvii. 138 How could she ever get through her Mocks next term?

2. a. Special collocations (usually hyphened): **mock auction**, a 'Dutch auction' (see AUCTION *sb.* 2); also, a fraudulent auction of worthless articles, in which a brisk pretence of bidding is kept up by confederates in order to elicit genuine bids; **mock auctioneer**, the auctioneer at a mock auction; **mock-colour**, a fugitive as opposed to a permanent colour or dye (cf. *false colour*: FALSE *a.* 16 b); **mock croc**: see CROC[2] 1 b; **mock-gold**, a yellow alloy composed of copper, zinc, platinum and other materials in various proportions (*Cent. Dict.* 1890); **mock-knee**, a callosity on the inner side of a horse's leg below the knee (*Syd. Soc. Lex.* 1891); **mock-lead** = BLENDE, hence **mock-leady** *a.*, containing blende; † **mock-man**, (*a*) one unworthy to be called a man; also *attrib.*; (*b*) a chimpanzee; **mock-moon** = PARASELENE; **mock-ore** = *mock-lead* (see also quot. 1681); **mock-plum** = *bladder plum* (BLADDER *sb.* 10); **mock-rainbow**, a secondary rainbow (see RAINBOW 1); **mock-sun** = PARHELION; also *fig.*; † **mock-velvet**, perh. = MOCKADO. Also in names of culinary preparations, as **mock-brawn**, the flesh of a pig's head and ox feet cut in pieces, and dressed to resemble brawn; **mock-duck, -goose**, a piece of pork from which the 'crackling' has been removed, baked with a stuffing of sage and onions (*colloq.*); **mock venison**, leg of mutton long hung, cooked after the manner of venison. Also MOCK TURTLE.

c **1766** *Cheats of London Exposed* 32, I term them *Mock-Auctions, because they are deceits throughout. **1884** DICKENS *Dict. Lond.* 28/1 The '*Mock Auction*' is a swindle. **1891** M. WILLIAMS *Later Leaves* 82 A mock auction case. **1959** *Daily Tel.* 13 Mar. 23/4 The requirement that a *mock auctioneer should display his name and address was still valid though it was not enforced by the police. **1959** *Listener* 9 July 72/1 The mock-auctioneer in back street or fairground. **1769** MRS. RAFFALD *Eng. Housekpr.* (1805) 302 To make *Mock Brawn. **1845** ELIZA ACTON *Mod. Cookery*, Index, Mock brawn. **1791** HAMILTON *Berthollet's Dyeing* I. I. ii. iv. 207 If it loses its body or ground of colour it is a *mock colour. **1877** *Cassell's Dict. Cookery* 262 *Mock Goose is a name given in some parts to a leg of pork roasted without the skin, and stuffed just under the knuckle with sage-and-onion stuffing. *a* **1728** WOODWARD *Nat. Hist. Fossils* (1729) I. I. 182 A black glossy Matter like Talc.. common in Cornwall; and call'd there *Mock-Lead. **1829** *Glover's Hist. Derby* I. 84 Mock lead is the native sulphuret of zinc. **1757** tr. *Henckel's Pyritol* 6 These fissures..be often *mock-leady. **1624** FLETCHER *Wife for Month* I. i, I would first take to me, for my lust, a Moore, One of your Gally-slaves, that cold and hunger, Decrepid misery, had made a *mock-man, Then be your Queene. **1636** MASSINGER *Bashf. Lover* v. i, What a Mock-man property, in thy intent, Wouldst thou have made me? **1738** [see CHIMPANZEE]. **1654** VILVAIN *Epit. Ess.* v. l, Three *mock-Moons at once reflex'd hav bin. **1889** *Pall Mall G.* 27 Oct. 7/1 Occasionally for a few minutes one or other of the mock-moons was very bright. **1681** GREW *Musæum* III. §ii. iii. 338 Mundick Ore, and Black Daze, mixed with a Vein of White and Green Spar... These Ores, by some are called *Mock-Ores. **1786** WHITEHURST *Orig. St. Earth* (ed. 2) 230 This mineral has been usually known by the names of black-jack, and mock-ore. **1829** *Glover's Hist. Derby* I. 84 Mock ore, or sulphuret of zinc. **1890** B. D. JACKSON *Gloss. Bot. Terms*, **Mock-plums*. **1725** POPE *Wks. Shaks.* I. Pref. 2 Each picture like a *mock-rainbow is but the reflexion of a reflexion. **1665-6** *Mock-sun [see PARHELION]. **1671** MARTEN *Voy. into Spitzbergen* in *Acc. Sev. Late Voy.* II. (1694) 50 A Parelion or Mock-sun. **1878** BROWNING *Poets Croisic* xxxix, Let France adore No longer an illusive mock sun. **1886** *Pall Mall G.* 2 Apr. 7/2 Four mock suns were seen in the neighbourhood of Greenwich. *a* **1613** OVERBURY *New Charac., Fellow of House* (1615) L 3, His meanes will not suffer him to come too nigh [the fashion]: they afford him *Mock-velvet or Satinisco. **1845** ELIZA ACTON *Mod. Cookery* 225 *Mock Venison. Hang a plump and finely-grained leg of mutton in a cool place [etc.].

b. In popular or book names of plants, as **mock acacia**, *Robinia Pseud-Acacia* (see ACACIA[1] 2); **mock-apple**, Canadian name for *Echinocystis lobata* (*Treas. Bot.* Suppl. 1874); **mock bishop('s)-weed**, American name for the genus *Discopleura*; **mock-chervil**, (*a*) Cow parsley, *Anthriscus sylvestris*; (*b*) Shepherd's needle, *Scandix Pecten*; **mock gillyflower** (see GILLYFLOWER 3); **mock liquorice**, Goat's rue, *Galega officinalis*; † **mock-mustard**, [tr. mod.L. *sinapistrum*], ? *Salvadora indica*; **mock myrtle**, ? bog-myrtle, *Myrica Gale*; **mock-olive**, an Australian jasmine, *Notelæa longifolia* (Maiden *Native Pl. Australia* 1889); **mock-orange**, (*a*) the common syringa, *Philadelphus coronarius*; (*b*) the Carolina cherry-laurel, *Prunus caroliniana*; (*c*) the Australian native laurel, *Pittosporum undulatum* (ibid.); **mock penny-royal**, the genus *Hedeoma*; **mock plane(-tree)**, the sycamore, *Acer Pseudo-Platanus*; **mock privet**, the genus *Phillyrea*; **mock saffron**, *Carthamus tinctorius*; **mock willow**, *Spiræa salicifolia*.

1754 *Catal. Seeds* in *Fam. Rose Kilravock* (Spald. Club) 428 *Mock acacia. **1860** GRAY *Man. Bot.* 156 *Discopleura*. *Mock Bishop-weed. **1548** TURNER *Names Herbes* (E.D.S.) 54 Myrrhis is called in Cambrygeshyre casshes, in other places *mockecheruel. **1597** GERARDE *Herbal* II. cccc. 884 *Pecten Veneris*.. Shepheards Needle, wilde Cheruill, Mock-Cheruill. **1548** TURNER *Names Herbes* (E.D.S.) 86 Regalicum is also named Ruta cararia, Galega, & Gaiarda... It maye be called in englishe *mocke Licores. **1698** J. PETIVER in *Phil. Trans.* XX. 316 Five leaved *Mock-Mustard. **1837** ELLISON *Kirkstead* 26 Thickets..Of sweet *Mock-myrtle and of purple Ling. **1731** MILLER *Gard. Dict.*, *Syringa*..The *Mock-Orange; *vulgo*. **1812** BRACKENRIDGE *Views Louisiana* (1814) 59 There is particularly one very beautiful, *bois jaune*, or yellow wood: by some called the mock orange. **1903** QUILLER-COUCH *Adv. H. Revel* 139 A bush of mock-orange at the end of the verandah. **1860** GRAY *Man. Bot.* 308 *Hedeoma*. *Mock Pennyroyal. **1797-1804** MARTYN *Miller's Gard. Dict.* (1807) s.v. *Acer*, With us it [the Great Maple] is vulgarly called the Sycomore-tree and by some *Mock-plane. **1887** BENTLEY *Man. Bot.* (ed. 5) 521 The latter [*Acer Pseudo-platanus*] is generally known under the names of the Sycamore, Greater Maple, and Mock-plane. **1597** GERARDE *Herbal* III. liv. 1209 Of *mocke Priuet. 1 *Phillyrea angustifolia*. **1731** MILLER *Gard. Dict.*, *Philyrea*, Mock-Privet. **1548** TURNER *Names Herbes* (E.D.S.) 29 Cnecus or cnicus is called..in englishe Bastarde saffron or *mocke-saffron. **1633** JOHNSON *Gerarde's Herbal* App. 1601 This Willow leaued Shrub..I have named in English *Mocke willow.

c. in names of birds, as **mock-nightingale**, (*a*) the BLACKCAP, *Sylvia atricapilla*; (*b*) the Garden warbler, *Sylvia salicaria*; (*c*) the White-throat, *Sylvia rufa* (or *Motacilla sylvia*); (*d*) the Sedge warbler, *Acrocephalus schœnobænus*; **mock regent-bird**, an Australian Honey-eater, *Meliphaga phrygia*; **mock-thrush** *U.S.* = MOCKING THRUSH.

1768 PENNANT *Zool.* II. 262 It [the blackcap]..is called in Norfolk the *mock-nightingale. **1831** *Montagu's Ornith. Dict.* (ed. 2) 42 It does not appear to me that the provincial names of Mock-nightingale, Nettle-creeper, Nettle-monger, are ever applied to the Blackcap, but to the White-throat and the Fauvette. **1878** NEWTON in *Encycl. Brit.* XVI. 541/1 The name..Mock-Nightingale is in England occasionally given to some of the Warblers, especially the Blackcap..and the Sedge-bird. **1848** GOULD *Birds Austral.* IV. 48 Warty-faced Honey-eater... *Mock Regent-Bird, [of the] Colonists of New South Wales. **1890** *Century Dict.*, **Mock-thrush*.

3. *Comb.* **a.** with adjs. and advs. with the sense 'in a counterfeit manner', 'simulatedly'. Chiefly implying humorous or ludicrous simulation, as in MOCK-HEROIC.

a **1711** KEN *Edmund* Poet. Wks. 1721 II. 178 Seven mock-bright Angels on the Deck appear'd. **1836-48** B. D. WALSH *Aristoph.* 44 *note*, A mock-serious tone. **1858** GEN. P. THOMPSON *Audi Alt.* I. xliv. 173 The men, pompous, mouthing, and mock-dignified. **1864** G. MEREDITH *Emilia* xxxvi, 'It is done, sometimes', she said, mock-sadly. **1871** —— *H. Richmond* xlvii, I told her mock-loftily that I did not believe in serious illnesses coming to godlike youth. **1880** SWINBURNE *Stud. Shaks.* (ed. 2) 198 A pseudocritical and mock-historic society. **1893** *Outing* (U.S.) May 120/1 'Thank you..Mr. Smith!' she said, with a mock-offended air. **1900** G. SWIFT *Somerley* 117 Prudishly mock-modest. **1931** *Times Lit. Suppl.* 18 June 479/1 The sumptuous mock-Tudor mansion. **1933** L. BLOOMFIELD *Lang.* xxiii. 421 Mock-learned words, like *scrumptious*, *rambunctious*, *absquatulate*. **1936** *Discovery* Oct. 321/2 The short 'Brutus' curls of regency mock-classical beauties. **1949** KOESTLER

Insight & Outlook vii. 105 His facial expression and whole attitude must be mock-aggressive. **1951** W. DE LA MARE *Winged Chariot* 58 Mock-solemn creatures, with our jackdaw airs. **1952** S. KAUFFMANN *Philanderer* (1953) iii. 38 Russell inquired, in customary mock-religious tones, about the state of the Street [*sc.* Wall Street] and cotton futures. **1958** *Spectator* 8 Aug. 193/1 The viewer who is sitting proudly in mock-antique splendour. **1968** *Listener* 18 July 92/3 A baron who mock-diffidently invites him to dinner. **1969** *Ibid.* 9 Jan. 43/3 We all went off to the pub: mock Tudor, phoney like the rest of us. **1975** J. HOWLETT *Christmas Spy* II. ii. 42 Her mock-Jacobean entrance hall.

b. with a verb, with the humorous sense 'pretendingly'; also with a ppl. adj., as †**mock-made** *a.*, made as a counterfeit.

a **1619** FLETCHER *Bonduca* IV. ii, I defie thee, thou mock-made man of mat! *a* **1661** FULLER *Worthies, Somerset* (1662) III. 31 Other mens mock-commending verses thereon [*sc.* Coryat's Crudities]. **1889** J. CORBETT *Monk* xi. 158 He [*i.e.* Monk's butler] was a wag whom Charles the First had mock-knighted one evening at supper with his table-knife.

mock (mɒk), *v.* Forms: 5 **mokken, moke, mocque, 5–6 mokkyn, mok, 5–7 mocke, 6– mock.** [ME. *mokken*, *mocque*, ad. OF. *mocquer* (F. *moquer*) to deride, jeer, a northern dialect form corresp. to the synonymous Pr. *mochar*, It. *moccare*.

According to some scholars, the word represents a popular L. **muccāre* to wipe the nose (whence F. *moucher*, It. *moccare*), f. **mucc-us* (class. L. *mūcus*: see MUCUS). With the OF. (whence the Eng.) transitive use, cf. L. *ēmungĕre* to wipe the nose, to cheat. The reflexive use (the only one in mod.Fr.) *se moquer de quelqu'un*, may originally have denoted the derisive gesture imitative of the movement of wiping the nose. In mod. Provençal, according to Mistral, *mouca* means 'to wipe the nose', 'to strike on the nose', while *se mouca* = F. *se moquer*, and *moucado* means 'a blow on the nose', 'a humiliation'.

Another hypothesis, less plausible semasiologically, would connect the word with Ger. dial. *mucken* to growl, grumble, OHG. *irmuccazan* 'mutire' (mod.G. *mucksen* to grumble).]

1. a. *trans.* To hold up to ridicule; to deride; to assail with scornful words or gestures.

a **1450** *Knt. de la Tour* 64 Thei were mocked and scorned of alle folke for her leudnesse. *c* **1450** *Mankind* 371 in *Macro Plays* 14 Haue ʒe non other man to moke, but euer me? **1484** CAXTON *Fables of Poge* vii, Alle the sallary or payment of them that mokken other is for to be mocqued at the last. **1530** PALSGR. 639/2 He mocketh hym at every worde and yet the foole perceyveth it nat. *Ibid.* 663/1, I potte, I mocke one with makyng a potte in the syde of my mouth. **1610** SHAKS. *Temp.* III. ii. 34 Loe, how he mockes me, wilt thou let him my Lord? **1642** FULLER *Holy & Prof. St.* III. ii. 156 Mock not a Cobler for his black thumbes. **1781** W. CAMERON in *Sc. Paraphr.* XVII. vi, Mock not my name with honours vain, but keep my holy laws. **1812** J. WILSON *Isle of Palms* II. 273 Art thou a fiend.. Come here to mock.. My dying agony. **1869** M. ARNOLD *Urania* vii, With smiles, till then, Coldly she mocks the sons of men.

b. With *adv.* or *phrase* as complement: To bring to a certain condition by mockery. Now *rare.* Also, †*to mock out*: (*a*) to evade (an argument, etc.) by mockery or trifling; (*b*) to gain by mocking or buffoonery.

1533 [TINDALE] *Supper of the Lord* E vj, And as for M. More, whom the verite most offendeth, & doth but mocke it out when he can not sole it. **1591** SPENSER *M. Hubberd* 509 For there [at court] thou needs must learne to laugh, to lie, ..to be a beetle-stock Of thy great Masters will, to scorne, or mock. So maist thou chaunce mock out a Benefice. **1599** SHAKS. *Hen. V*, I. ii. 285 Many a thousand widows Shall this his Mocke, mocke out of their deer husbands; Mocke mothers from their sonnes, mocke Castles downe. **1625** JACKSON *Creed* v. xxiv. §4 He would.. be mocked out of his skin by Courtiers. **1655** FULLER *Ch. Hist.* IX. vii. §18 It was no solœcisme to the gravity of Eliah to mock Baals priests out of their superstition. *a* **1863** WOOLNER *My Beautiful Lady* 60 Some gigantic bell, Whose thunder laughing through my brain Mocked me back to flesh again.

c. To defy; to set at nought.

1558 KNOX *First Blast* (Arb.) 38, I thinke likewise this reason shuld be mocked. **1596** SHAKS. *Merch. V.* II. i. 30, I would ore-stare the sternest eies that looke... Yea, mocke the Lion when he rores for pray To win the Ladie. **1606** —— *Ant. & Cl.* III. xiii. 185 Fill our Bowles once more: Let's mocke the midnight Bell. **1877** C. GEIKIE *Christ* lxi. (1879) 746 The hierarchy.. know how to honor the appearance of justice while mocking the reality.

d. *fig.* of impersonal things.

1667 MILTON *P.L.* IV. 628 Our walks at noon, with branches overgrown, That mock our scant manuring. **1741–2** GRAY *Agrippina* 156 These hated walls that seem to mock my shame. **1764** GOLDSM. *Trav.* 248 Though my harsh touch, falt'ring still, But mock'd all tune, And marr'd the dancer's skill. **1788** T. WARTON *On H. M. Birth-day* 51 And many a fane he rear'd, that still sublime In massy pomp has mock'd the stealth of time. **1807** WORDSW. *White Doe* VII. 28 A perishing That mocks the gladness of the Spring. **1821** SHELLEY *Adonais* 17 Melodies, With which, like flowers that mock the corse beneath, He had adorned and hid the coming bulk of Death. **1847** A. R. C. DALLAS *Look to Jerus.* (ed. 4) 84 Australasia and Polynesia have arisen to mock our arithmetic. **1879** 'E. GARRETT' *House by Works* I. 13 Their artless sport did not seem to mock her, as did the sunshine and the breeze.

2. a. *intr.* To use or give utterance to ridicule; to act or speak in derision; to jeer, scoff; to flout. Const. *at*, †*with*.

c **1450** *Mankind* 358 in *Macro Plays* 14 We xall bargen with yow, & noþer moke nor scorne. **1502** *Ord. Crysten Men* (W. de W. 1506) II. viii. 107 Also those the whyche mocketh with these auncyentes. **1561** T. NORTON *Calvin's Inst.* III. 202 This forsooth is not to mocke with the Scriptures. **1581** MULCASTER *Positions* xli. (1887) 239 Some.. do vse to abase them, and to mocke at mathematicall heades. **1604** E. G[RIMSTONE] *D'Acosta's Hist. Indies* I. vii. 21 Lactantius Firmian, and S. Augustine mocke at such as hold there be any Antipodes. **1611** BIBLE *Prov.* i. 26, I also will laugh at your calamitie, I wil mocke when your feare commeth. **1784** COWPER *Task* v. 122 Thus Nature works as if to mock at Art. **1810** SCOTT *Lady of L.* III. v. Fleet limbs that mocked at time. **1822** SHELLEY *Chas. I*, ii. 386 If fear were made for kings, the Fool mocks wisely. **1884** TENNYSON *Becket* IV. ii, Will he not mock at me?

†**b.** To jest, trifle; to make sport. *Obs.*

c **1440** *Promp. Parv.* 341/2 Mokkyn, or iapyn, or tryfelyn, *ludifico*. *c* **1460** *Wisdom* 826 in *Macro Plays* 62 *Mynde*... On a soper I wyll.. Set a noble with goode chere redyly to spende. *Wndyrstondynge*. And I tweyn be þis feer, To moque at a goode dyner. **1537** SIR J. DUDLEY in Froude *Hist. Eng.* III. 253 He.. mocked not with me, for he brake down a part of the decks of my ship. **1611** BIBLE *Gen.* xix. 14 Lot.. said,.. the Lord wil destroy this citie: but hee seemed as one that mocked, vnto his sonnes in law.

3. a. *trans.* To deceive or impose upon; to delude, befool; to tantalize, disappoint.

c **1470** HENRY *Wallace* VIII. 1412 In spech off luff suttell ye Sotheroun ar; Ye can ws mok, suppos ye se no mar. **1538** CROMWELL in Merriman *Life & Lett.* (1902) II. 141 He dothe but to dyvise to mocke al the world by practises with faire wordes for his owne purpose. **1561** T. NORTON *Calvin's Inst.* III. 246 Let us not wilfully mocke our selues to our own destruction. **1597** SHAKS. *2 Hen. IV*, v. ii. 126 My Father is gone wilde into his Graue,.. And with his Spirits, sadly I suruiue, To mocke the expectation of the World; To frustrate Prophesies. **1611** BIBLE *Judg.* xvi. 10 Behold, thou hast mocked me, and told mee lies. **1648** BP. HALL *Breathings Devout Soul* (1851) 201 What would it avail me, O Lord, to mock the eyes of all the world with a semblance of holiness? **1667** MILTON *P.L.* x. 773 Why am I mockt with death, and length'nd out To deathless pain? **1812** H. & J. SMITH *Rej. Addr.* iii. (1873) 17 What stately vision mocks my waking sense? **1819** SHELLEY *Fragm. Tale Untold* 4 Empty cups.. Which mock the lips with air, when they are thirsting. **1847** EMERSON *Repr. Men, Napoleon* Wks. (Bohn) I. 381 As long as our civilization is essentially one of property,.. it will be mocked by delusions. **1852** M. ARNOLD *Empedocles on Etna* I. 15 Mind is a light which the Gods mock us with, To lead those false who trust it.

†**b.** To disappoint *of* something promised. *Obs.*

1541 in I. S. Leadam *Sel. Cas. Crt. Requests* (Selden) 61 Your sayd servant and subiet was.. dissapoynted and mocked of suche bandoges as he shold have had.

4. a. To ridicule by imitation of speech or action. (The current colloquial use, and presumably as old as the 16th c., but not evidenced in literature.) Hence, to imitate or resemble closely; to mimic, counterfeit. (Cf. MOCKING-BIRD.)

1595 SHAKS. *John* v. ii. 173 Another [*sc.* drum] shall.. rattle the Welkins eare, And mocke the deepe mouth'd Thunder. **1611** —— *Wint. T.* v. iii. 19–20 Prepare To see the Life as liuely mock'd, as euer Still Sleepe mock'd Death. *a* **1700** B. E. *Dict. Cant. Crew, To Mock*, or mimick another. **1742** YOUNG *Nt. Th.* III. 335 For what live ever here?.. to bid each wretched day The former mock? **1817** SHELLEY *Rev. Islam* VI. xlv. 7 He [a horse] would spread His nostrils to the blast, and joyously Mock the fierce peal with neighings. **1822** —— *Chas. I*, ii. 98 He mocks and mimics all he sees and hears. **1827–44** WILLIS *Lazarus & Mary* 16 Like life well mock'd in marble. **1843** RUSKIN *Mod. Paint.* II. IV. 311 Not one of Stansfield's lines is like another. Every one of Salvator's mocks all the rest. **1867** G. G. MCCRAE *Balladeadro* 30 (Morris) There the proud lyre-bird spreads his tail, And mocks the notes of hill and dale.

†**b.** To simulate, make a false pretence of. *Obs.*

1593 SHAKS. *3 Hen. VI*, III. iii. 255, I long till Edward fall by Warres mischance, For mocking Marriage with a Dame of France. **1606** —— *Ant. & Cl.* v. i. 2 Go to him Dollabella, bid him yeeld, Being so frustrate, tell him, He mockes the pawses that he makes.

c. *to mock up*: to make a mock-up of (see MOCK-UP); also, to counterfeit, simulate, imitate; to contrive or improvise; freq. **mocked-up** *ppl. a.*

1911 *Encycl. Brit.* XXIV. 971/2 The shapes and sizes of the armour plates are sometimes obtained by the 'mocking up' process, in which the surface of the armour is represented in three dimensions. **1914** in W. S. Churchill *World Crisis 1911–14* (1923) 527 It is necessary to construct without delay a dummy fleet... They are then to be mocked up to represent particular battleships of the 1st and 2nd Battle Squadrons. *Ibid.* 528 The utmost secrecy must be observed, and special measures taken to banish all foreigners from the districts where the mocking-up [of the battleships] is being done. **1950** *Jrnl. R. Aeronaut. Soc.* LIV. 305/1 The first type should be used.. provided that certain sections, as for example the engine installation, are mocked up accurately, if necessary as a separate mock-up. **1952** *Archit. Rev.* CXII. 55 It consisted of fabrics and prototype furniture by Terence Conran, arranged in a room cunningly mocked-up with a couple of venetian blinds and a bamboo ceiling. **1955** A. H. N. GREEN-ARMYTAGE *Portrait St. Luke* vii. 121 Mocked-up discourses in the biography of a man whose trade it was to deliver discourses of his own. **1959** *Observer* 5 April 18/4 The fuddy-duddy diplomat whose mocked-up vicissitudes make the story. **1961** *Listener* 12 Oct. 576/3 Denis Mitchell mocked up a couple of glimpses of America. **1967** *Ibid.* 2 Feb. 175/3 Not a very good play, perhaps, with some mocked-up dialogue and sex brought in as a perfunctory afterthought.

†**5.** In the 17th c. the verb-stem was prefixed to a few sbs., forming compound sbs. with the sense 'one who or something which mocks ...': **mock-beggar**, (*a*) applied to a house that has an appearance of wealth, but is either deserted or else inhabited by miserly or poor persons; also as quasi-proper name, ***Mock-Beggar*('s *Hall*, etc.**; (*b*) used by Florio (? erroneously) for BULL-BEGGAR; **mock-clown** *nonce-wd.*, a trick that deludes rustics; **mock-guest**, one who disappoints his guests of the liberal entertainment which he has led them to expect; in quot. *fig.* Also MOCK-GOD.

1611 FLORIO, *Beffana*, a bug-beare, a scarcrow, a *mock-begger, a toy to mocke an ape. **1615** *Cupids Whirligig* C 4, Whats this, A shirt that ye weare, Else 'tis a mock-beggar with stripes. **1616** *Rich Cabinet* 52 A Gentleman without meanes, is like a faire house without furniture, or any inhabitant,.. whose rearing was chargeable to the owner, and painfull to the builder, and all ill-bestowed, to make a mock-begger, that hath no goode morrowe for his next neighbour. **1622** J. TAYLOR (Water-P.) *Water-Cormorant* C 2 b, The poore receiue their answer from the Dawes, Who in their caaing language call it plaine Mockbegger Manour, for they came in vaine. *a* **1825** FORBY *Voc. E. Anglia, Mock-Beggar-Hall.* **1835** HORSFIELD *Sussex* I. 136 Some old buildings in a place called the Mock-beggars. **1840** *Gentl. Mag.* Oct. 338 Both places.. bear the name of Mock-Beggar's Hall. The one is an insulated rock near Bakewell.. presenting from the road the semblance of a house... The other is a Tudor.. mansion in the parish of Claydon.. which ..remained so long unoccupied as to be the cause of numerous disappointments to those travellers who had never been taken in before. **1598** FLORIO, *Ingannauillano*, the name of a leape or sault so called in Italian, as we should say *mock-clowne. **1642** FULLER *Holy St.* I. i. 3 Some women which hang out signes of strangers.. will not lodge strangers; yet these *mock-guests are guilty in tempting others to tempt them.

mockable ('mɒkəb(ə)l), *a.* [f. MOCK *v.* + -ABLE. Cf. F. *moquable.*] Deserving of or exposed to derision.

1600 SHAKS. *A.Y.L.* III. ii. 49 Those that are good maners at the Court, are as ridiculous in the Countrey, as the behauiour of the Countrie is most mockeable at the Court. **1837** CARLYLE *Fr. Rev.* (1872) III. I. vii. 41 This huge Moon-calf of Sansculottism,.. is not mockable only, and soft like another calf. **1892** PEYTON *Mem. Jesus* iii. 63 The Primates.. mock us unconsciously. We encounter the mockable element in man, just at the junction where flesh is passing into mind, animality into mentality.

mockadam, variant of MOKADDAM.

†**mockado** (mɒ'kɑːdəʊ). *Obs.* Forms: 6 **mockeado, mochadoo, mockadoo, -adowe, makadowe, moccadowe, 6–7 mocado, mockadoe, 6–8 moccado, 7 moccadoe, -dow, mocadoe, mochado, muckado, 8 mockade(e, 6– mockado.** [app. a corruption of It. *mocajardo* (see MOHAIR) or some variant.

Cotgrave (1611) gives 'mockado' as the rendering of F. *moucade* (not found elsewhere) and *mocayart*, and he renders *moncaiart* by 'silk moccadoe'; a Fr. form *mouquayat* occurs in 1580 as the name of a material for curtains. Florio (1611) has It. *moccaiaro*, and *moccaiorro*, 'mokado stuffe'.]

1. A kind of cloth much used for clothing in the 16th and 17th centuries. Also *attrib.*, as ***mockado cassock, doublet***, etc.; ***mockado ends, fringe*** (mentioned as a commodity sold by weight). ***tuft mockado***, a peculiar kind of mockado decorated with small tufts of wool.

It was made in Flanders and (first by Flemish refugees) at Norwich; it is usually mentioned as an inferior material (of wool) in contrast with silk and velvet, but a 'silk mockado' is also spoken of. Quot. 1638 exceptionally refers to *mockado* as a costly fabric; but the word by that time may have ceased to be generally understood.

1543 *Richmond Wills* (Surtees) 51 One night gowne of mockeado with one paire of hoase of the same. **1571–2** A. WHITFELD in *Durham Depos.* (Surtees) 246 Mochadoo for the cote, coller, and hands, with sylk boottons. **1579** DEE *Diary* (Camden) 6 Some kinde of tuft mockado, with crosses blew and red. **1587** HARRISON *England* II. v. (1877) I. 132 Mockadoes tufted and plaine. *Ibid.* III. i. (1878) II. 6 Now by meanes of strangers succoured here from domesticall persecution, the same [*sc.* wool] hath beene imploied vnto sundrie other vses, as mockados, baies, vellures [etc.]. **1589** PUTTENHAM *Eng. Poesie* III. xxiv. (Arb.) 290 Who would not thinke it a ridiculous thing to see a Lady in her milke-house with a veluet gowne, and at a bridall in her cassock of mockado. **1590** *Acc. Bk. W. Wray* in *Antiquary* XXXII. 374, 1[li] black moccado fringe, iiis. viijd. **1594** LODGE & GREENE *Looking-glass* (1598) C 3 b, When I.. saw.. what a faire mockado Cape it had. **1596** LODGE *Wits Miserie* 14 The farmer that was contented in times past with his Russet Frocke & Mockado sleeues, now sels a Cow against Easter to buy him silken geere for his credit. **1605** *Lond. Prodigal* III. i, Why she went in a fringed gown, a single ruff, and a white cap; and my father in a mocado coat. **1617** in Heath *Grocers' Comp.* (1869) 427 Crimson mochados to make sleeves for the poore men. **1620** in *Naworth Househ. Bks.* (Surtees) 123 A pound of black moccadow ends, ij[s]. viij[d]. **1638** FORD *Lady's Trial* ii. i, Imagine first our rich mockado doublet. **1660** *Act 12 Chas. II*, c. 4 Rates Inward, Mocado ends the dozen pound, iiij *li.*

b. *fig.* as the type of an inferior material. Also *attrib.* or *adj.*: Trumpery, inferior.

(In quot. 1741 used, probably by etymological misapprehension, in the sense of 'mockery'. Cf. -ADO 2.)

1577 FULKE *Confut. Purg.* 287 Mockadoe miracles, narrations, and relations. **1589** R. HARVEY *Pl. Perc.* 8, I will nicke-name no bodie: I am none of these tuft mockadoo mak-a-dooes. **1619** J. TAYLOR (Water-P.) *Kicksey Winsey* B 8 b, I muse of what stuff these men framed be, Most of them seeme Muckado vnto me. **1621** —— *Motto* D, I want that high esteemed excellence Of fustian, or mockado Eloquence. **1741** RICHARDSON *Pamela* II. 37 What Mockado is this to such a poor Soul as I?

2. (See quot.)

1738 in *6th Rep. Dep. Kpr.* App. II. 120 A new Invention of making Carpetting called French Carpets or Moccadoes.

'mockage. Now *rare* or *Obs.* [f. MOCK *sb.* + -AGE.]
Very common in the 16th and 17th centuries.

1. a. The action or an act of mocking; mockery, ridicule, derision; a derisive utterance or action.

1470–85 MALORY *Arthur* IX. i. 338 In mockage ye shalle be called la cote male tayle. **1494** FABYAN *Chron.* VII. 608 The Frenshe Gaguyne bryngeth in a matier of game, as he rehersith, to the mockage of Englisshmen. **1535** COVERDALE *Isa.* xiv. 4 Then shalt thou vse this mockage vpon yᵉ kinge of Babilon. **1548** GEST *Pr. Masse* D ij, What an vnsufferable mockedge is this aswel of god as of our soueraygne lord yᵉ king. **1561** T. NORTON *Calvin's Inst.* IV. xx. (1634) 743 Christians ought truly to bee a kinde of men..open to the malice, deceits, and mockages, of naughty men. **1577** HANMER *Anc. Eccl. Hist.* (1663) 38 In a mockage they tried the sharpnesse of their swords upon the dead bodies. **1607** R. C[AREW] tr. *Estienne's World of Wonders* 347 Turned into a matter of merriment and mockage of poore Saint Peter. *a* **1677** MANTON *Serm. Ps.* cxix. 52 (1681) 347 Their Derision and Mockage of Godliness ceaseth. *a* **1916** A. R. MACEWEN *Hist. Church in Scotl.* (1918) II. xxvii. 176 In their mockage they termed every thing that repugned to their corrupt affections 'devout imagination'. **1922** E. A. PARRY *What Judge Thought* viii. 133 It is interesting to remember that in Lewis Carroll, an ironist of a different type from Maule, we have another example of a deeply scientific mathematician revelling in the expression of ludicrous antiphrasis and quaint ridicule and mockage of commonplace humanity.

b. The fact or condition of being mocked.

1534 LD. BERNERS *Gold. Bk. M. Aurel.* (1546) G ij, The woorkes of the peple ar holden in mockage with wyse men. **1580** LYLY *Euphues* (Arb.) 344 Which then brought youth into a fooles Paradise, and hath now cast age into an open mockage. *a* **1656** HALES *Gold. Rem.* III. (1673) 36 It is but an errour to think that God is a party capable of mockage and illusion; no art, no fineness can circumvent or abuse him.

2. An object of mockery.

1535 COVERDALE *Jer.* xxv. 9, I will make of them a wildernesse a mockage and a continuall deserte. **1628** WITHER *Brit. Rememb.* Concl. 53 Nay, Law is made a mockage, and a scorne. **1657** REEVE *God's Plea* 23 Man.. was the spoil of time, the mockage of fortune, and image of consistency. *a* **1677** MANTON *Serm. Ps.* cxix. 83 (1681) 553 Though scorned and made a mockage [1725 mock] by those that..lived in pomp and splendor, yet his zeal was not abated.

3. Mimicry, close imitation; *concr.* something that mocks or resembles, a counterfeit.

1615 J. STEPHENS *Ess. & Char., A Ranke Observer* (1857) 160 Whilst he meanes to purge himself by observing other humours, he practises them by a shadow of mockage. **1686** GOAD *Celest. Bodies* III. i. 397, I can believe..that there are such Mockages of Humane Nature by Sea, as an Ape is on the Mountain.

mockaire, obs. form of MOHAIR.

'mockaniste. *nonce-wd.* [f. MOCK *v.* after the words in the context.] A mocker.

a **1550** *Image Ipocr.* III. in *Skelton's Wks.* (1843) II. 435/2 He is no Acquiniste, Nor non Occanist, But a mockaniste.

mockaseen, -a(s)sin, -ason, obs. ff. MOCCASIN.

mock-beggar: see MOCK *v.* 5.

'mock-bird. [f. MOCK *sb.*¹ + BIRD *sb.*] The American MOCKING-BIRD, *Mimus polyglottus.*

1649 *Perf. Descr. Virginia* (1837) 15 One Bird we call the Mock-bird; for he will imitate all other Birds Notes. **1709** STEELE *Tatler* No. 51 ¶4 The Indian Fowl, called the Mock-Bird, who has no Note of his own. **1774** GOLDSM. *Nat. Hist.* (1824) II. 337 The American Mock-bird. *Ibid.* 338 The mock-bird is ever surest to please when it is most itself. **1809** CAMPBELL *Gertr. Wyom.* I. iii, From merry mock-bird's song. *a* **1854** CAROLINE A. SOUTHEY *Poet. Wks.* (1867) 13 The pretty mockbird with his borrowed notes Tells thee sweet truth.

b. Applied to the Sedge-warbler and the Blackcap (cf. MOCKING-BIRD 2).

1831 *G. Montagu's Ornith. Dict.* 326 *Mock Bird,* a name applied to the Sedge Bird. **1894** NEWTON *Dict. Birds* 582.

c. *fig.*

1800 SOUTHEY *Let. to Coleridge* 8 Jan., Moses will be a very mock-bird as to languages. **1823** BYRON *Island* II. xiii, Sweep these mere mock-birds of the despot's song From the tall bough where they have perch'd so long.

mock-clown: see MOCK *v.* 5.

mocke, mockeado, var. ff. MUCK, MOCKADO.

mocked (mɒkt), *a.* [f. MOCK *v.* + -ED¹.] Imitated (in quot. *absol.*).

186. DARWIN *Orig. Spec.* xiii. (1866) 507 When the mockers and the mocked are caught and compared they are found to be totally different in essential structure.

mockedar, obs. form of MUCKENDER.

mocker¹ ('mɒkə(r)). Forms: 5 moker(e, 6 *Sc.* mokkar, mockar, 6– mocker. [f. MOCK *v.* + -ER¹. Cf. F. *moqueur.*]

1. a. One who mocks, derides, or scoffs.

1477 EARL RIVERS (Caxton) *Dictes* 14 b, Ware that ye be no mokers for that engendreth hattered. *c* **1500** *Young Childr. Bk.* 59 in *Babees Bk.,* Be no glosere nor no mokere. **1570** BUCHANAN *Ane Admonitioun* Wks. (1892) 24 Mokkaris of all religioun and vertew. **1634** CANNE *Necess. Separ.* (1849) 221 How can he prove that these were outwardly wicked and irreligious, known to be idolaters, drunkards, sorcerers, mockers,..&c. **1683** BURNET tr. *More's Utopia* 39 If the many Mockers of Elisha,..felt the Effect of his Zeal, What will become of one Mocker of so many Friars? **1688** SOUTH *Serm.* (1697) II. viii. 347 An Ordinance, in which God is so seldom mocked, but it is to the Mocker's confusion. **1750** BYROM *Rem. Middleton's Exam.* 525 What these Mockers call'd a drunken Fit, Was God's Performance of what Joel writ. **1849** MACAULAY *Hist. Eng.* ii. I. 163 The peculiarities of the Puritan..had been..favourite subjects with mockers. **1903** *Speaker* 10 Oct. 29/1 The enthusiast was a happy man, the mocker was a miserable man.

b. One who deceives or illudes.

1600 SHAKS. *A.Y.L.* II. vi. 13 If thou diest Before I come, thou art a mocker of my labour.

c. *transf.*

1611 BIBLE *Prov.* xx. 1 Wine *is* a mocker, strong drink is raging. **1972** N. MARSH *Tied up in Tinsel* vii. 177 'He was a wine-bibber,' Nigel shouted. 'Wine is a mocker.'

d. Slang phr. ***to put the mocker(s) on:*** to thwart or bring bad luck to (a person, enterprise, etc.), to deride, mock, denigrate. Also ***to have (got) the mockers on, to give*** (one) ***the mockers,*** etc. Cf. MOCK *sb.*¹ 1 b.

1923 C. DREW *Rogues & Ruses* 115 They'll ave to race without me to-morrow. I've got a mocker hung on me. **1949** L. GLASSOP *Luck Palmer* vii. 62 It's that sheila... She's put the mocker on us. **1970** 'B. MATHER' *Break in Line* v. 61 'He isn't bad at all.' 'Then what did you put the mockers on him for?' **1970** J. PORTER *Dover strikes Again* ii. 36 This investigation had got the mockers on it from the start. **1974** 'J. ROSS' *Burning of Billy Toober* xi. 102, I tailed him... Not to do anything. Just to let him see he was being tailed. To give him the mockers.

2. One who imitates in speech or gesture.

3. A mocking-bird.

1773 BARRINGTON in *Phil. Trans.* LXIII. 286 From the attention which the mocker pays to any other sort of.. noises. **1859** BAIRD *Catal. N. Amer. Birds* 253 a, Var. *Mimus caudatus* Baird Long-Tailed Mocker. **1860** —— *Birds N. Amer.* 353 *Harporhynchus rufus*..Thrasher; Sandy Mocker.

4. *Nat. Hist.* A mimetic animal.

186. DARWIN *Orig. Spec.* xiii. (1866) 507 The mockers are almost invariably rare insects.

mocker² ('mɒkə(r)). *Austral.* and *N.Z. slang.* Also **mokker.** [Origin obscure.] Clothes; a dress. So **'mockered-up** *a.,* dressed up.

1938 PARTRIDGE *Dict. Slang* (ed. 2) 1014/2 *Mockered up,* dressed in one's best. **1945** BAKER *Austral. Lang.* vi. 119 *All laired up* and its synonym *all mockered up* may also be noted. **1953** —— *Australia Speaks* iv. 106 *Mocker,* clothes in general. **1959** G. SLATTER *Gun in my Hand* 51 Gives us a hand sometimes on the mixer or labourin about. Gets into his old mocker and gets stuck in. **1965** M. SHADBOLT *Among Cinders* xxv. 250 She was mockered up to the nines.

mockere, obs. form of MUCKER.

'mocker-nut. *U.S.* The fruit of the North American White-heart Hickory, *Carya tomentosa.* Also, the tree itself.

1814 F. PURSH *Flora Americæ Septentrionalis* II. 638 *Juglans tomentosa*... This is known under the name of Mocker Nut, White-heart Hickory or Common Hickory. **1832** D. J. BROWNE *Sylva Amer.* 187 In the part of New Jersey which lies on the river Hudson, this species is known by the name of Mockernut Hickory. **1846–50** A. WOOD *Class-bk. Bot.* 491 Mocker-nut Hickory. **1859** J. G. COOPER in *Ann. Rep. Smithson. Inst.* 255 *Carya tomentosa* Nutt., Mocker-nut. **1860** GRAY *Man. Bot. North. U.S.* 402 Mocker-nut. White-heart Hickory. **1926** E. M. ROBERTS *Time of Man* 364, I see you dance under the mockernut tree. **1947** COLLINGWOOD & BRUSH *Knowing your Trees* 152/1 Attaining maturity at 250 to 300 years, mockernut hickory sometimes reaches a height of ninety or a hundred feet. **1969** T. H. EVERETT *Living Trees of World* 98/2 The mockernut.. forms a handsome specimen that grows up to 90 feet high with a trunk up to 3 feet in diameter... Its nuts have thick, hard shells that contain a very small amount of sweet meat.

mockery ('mɒkərı). Forms: 5 **moquerye, mokkery, 5–6 mockerye, mocquery,** 6 **mockeri,** *Sc.* **mokrie, mockrie,** 6–7 **mockerie,** 6– **mockery.** [a. F. *moquerie* (13th c.), f. *moquer* to MOCK.]

1. Derision, ridicule; a derisive utterance or action.

1426 LYDG. *De Guil. Pilgr.* 13020 They be no thyng off myn allye; I haue off hem but moquerye. **1481** CAXTON *Reynard* (Arb.) 11 Reynart..shal thynke how he may begyle deceyue and brynge yow to some mockerye. *a* **1533** LD. BERNERS *Huon* liv. 182 Yᵉ paynym dyd gyue it to Huon in a mockery. *a* **1548** HALL *Chron., Hen. VIII* 101 b, All our saiynges were by the Frenche kyng turned into mocquery. **1560** DAUS. tr. *Sleidane's Comm.* 193 b, This was the third mockeri of fortune that chaunced in Fraunce. **1563** WINȜET *Wks.* (S.T.S.) II. 81 Studiing to thraw be his mokrie and bairding the mekle vertew and honor of his father to be a vyce [etc.]. **1590** SPENSER *F.Q.* I. vii. 43 The forlorne Maiden, whom your eies have seene The laughing stocke of fortunes mockeries, Am th' onely daughter of a King and Queene. **1590** SHAKS. *Mids. N.* II. ii. 123 Wherefore was I to this keene mockery borne? *a* **1656** BP. HALL *Rem. Wks.* (1660) 270 Should a man be bidden to..walk steddily on his head, this would justly sound as a mockery. *a* **1719** ADDISON *Chr. Relig.* vii. Wks. 1766 III. 317 The insults and mockeries of a crouded Amphitheatre. **1838** THIRLWALL *Greece* III. xx. 163 The heralds of Darius had been put to death with cruel mockery. **1860** MRS. CARLYLE *Lett.* III. 61 'Mrs. Prudence', as Mr. Barnes calls me in mockery. **1869** FREEMAN *Norm. Conq.* (1875) III. xii. 238 Laying himself open to the jeers and mockeries of his rebellious subjects. **1884** GLADSTONE in *West. Daily Press* 2 July 3/4 He was sorry that gentlemen with no knowledge of the subject should receive this remark with mockery.

b. A subject or occasion of derision; a person, thing, or action that deserves or occasions ridicule.

1560 DAUS tr. *Sleidane's Comm.* 38 Which thinges are doubtles to all that wise be, a very mockerye. **1590** SIR J. SMYTH *Disc. Weapons* 13, I conclude, that such fortifications in England are verie skornes and mockeries. **1596** SHAKS. *Tam. Shr.* III. ii. 4 What will be said, what mockery will it be? To want the Bride-groome when the Priest attends To speake the ceremoniall rites of marriage? **1820** HAZLITT *Lect. Dram. Lit.* 314 When the name of Jeremy Taylor is no longer remembered with reverence, genius will have become a mockery, and virtue an empty shade. **1849** JAMES *Woodman* vii, As if he made a mockery of the very acquirements he boasted of. **1870** BRYANT *Iliad* I. x. 311 Let no one yield to sleep, Lest we become the mockery of the foe.

2. Mimicry, imitation; a counterfeit representation; an unreal appearance. Now only in indignant use, a contemptible and impudent simulation.

1599 SHAKS. *Hen. V,* IV. Chor. 53 Yet sit and see, Minding true things, by what their Mock'ries bee. **1605** —— *Macb.* III. iv. 107 Hence horrible shadow, Vnreal mock'ry hence. **1717** POPE *Elegy Unfort. Lady* 57 And bear about the mockery of woe To midnight dances, and the public show. **1853** KANE *Grinnell Exp.* xxvii. (1856) 225 It was a mockery of warmth, however, scarcely worthy the unpretending sincerity of the great planet. **1872** YEATS *Growth Comm.* 189 The unhappy monarch then went through the mockery of a trial for concealing his treasures.

3. Ludicrously futile action; something insultingly unfitting.

1602 SHAKS. *Ham.* I. i. 146 It is as the Ayre, invulnerable, And our vaine blowes, malicious Mockery. **1634** W. TIRWHYT tr. *Balzac's Lett.* (vol. I.) 398 It were a mockery to make choyce of sicke folkes, and..to put sovereign power into their hands, to the end onely to have them leave it to others. **1798** *Monthly Mag.* VI. 397 Although suffered to perish almost for the common necessaries, his body was ostentatiously carried to the grave in a hearse, accompanied by the mockery of a mourning-coach. **1852** ROBERTSON *Serm.* Ser. III. xvii. 215 It is mockery, brethren, for a man to speak lightly of that which he cannot know. **1863** GEO. ELIOT *Romola* xxxvi, In her bitterness she felt that all rejoicing was mockery.

4. *attrib.*

1593 SHAKS. *Rich. II,* IV. i. 260 Oh, that I were a Mockerie, King [*read* Mockerie-king] of Snow, Standing before the Sunne of Bullingbrooke, To melt my selfe away in Water-drops. **1634** FORD *Perkin Warbeck* I. i, Still to be frighted with false apparitions Of pageant Majestie, and new-coynd greatnesse, As if wee were a mockery King in state. **1834** *Tait's Mag.* 131/1 Legitimacy is a mockery word in such a case. **1898** WATTS-DUNTON *Aylwin* xi, A monstrous mountainous representation of an awful mockery-goddess.

mockeson, obs. form of MOCCASIN.

'mocket. Now *dial.* [Shortened from *mocketer,* MUCKENDER. Cf. Anglo-Irish *muckie, mocky,* in the same sense (H. C. Hart).] A bib or handkerchief; also, ? a kerchief.

1537 *Irish Act Hen. VIII,* c. 15 Or use or weare any shirt, smock..mocket, or linnen cappe, coloured or dyed with Saffron. **1611** COTGR., *Baverette,* a bib, mocket, or mocketer to put before the bosome of a (slauering) child. *Ibid.,* s.v. *Embavété.* **1880** *W. Cornw. Gloss., Mocket,* a bib attached to an apron to keep the front of the dress clean.

†'mocket-'head. *Obs.* [Origin obscure.] See quot., and cf. ANCONY.

1686 PLOT *Staffordsh.* iv. 163 They work it [*sc.* the iron] into a bloom, which is a square barr in the middle, and two square knobs at the ends, one much less then the other, the smaller being called the Ancony end, and the greater the Mocket head.

mocketto, quasi-It. form of MOQUETTE.

†'mockful, *a. Obs.* [f. MOCK *sb.* + -FUL.] Full of mockery.

1805 *Public Characters* 256 The merry maid in mockful play. **1820** C. R. MATURIN *Melmoth* (1892) III. xxxi. 253 Those whose mockful persecution, or whose vacant pity, might be equally torturing to her feelings.

Hence **'mockfully** *adv.,* in a 'mockful' manner.

1834 *Fraser's Mag.* X. 426 He was impetuous, daring, and mockfully defiant.

†'mock-God. *Obs.* [f. MOCK *v.* + GOD *sb.*] One who mocks, derides, or defies God. Also *attrib.* and forming adjs. as ***mock-God-like.*** (Very common in the 17th c.)

1601 DENT *Pathw. Heaven* 128 Now the earth is full of ranke Atheists and mocke-Gods: which scoffe at the Gospell. **1612** W. SCLATER *Ministers Portion* 49 A pretty mocke-God answere it will bee,..to tell him [*sc.* God]: for matter of tithing, thou hadst a custome to the contrary. **1618** S. WARD *Iethro's Iustice* (1627) 42 What shall I say to such mocke-god-like Esaus? **1677** W. HUGHES *Man of Sin* I. x. 45 This Impudent Mock-God dares to make Laws to bind the Conscience immediately, where God Almighty hath left it free.

mock-guest: see MOCK *v.* 5.

,mock-he'roic, *a.* and *sb.* [f. MOCK *a.*]

A. *adj.* Imitating in a derisive or burlesque manner the heroic character or style; burlesquing heroic action.

1711–12 ADDISON *Spect.* No. 273 ¶8 We find in Mock-Heroic Poems, particularly in the *Dispensary,* and the *Lutrin,* several Allegorical Persons. **1765** COLMAN tr. *Terence, Eunuch* I. iii. 123 *note,* The poet in a kind of mock heroick manner invokes the muse to teach him to draw the character of his heroine. **1839** *Penny Cycl.* XV. 296/1 Tassoni's mock-heroic poem, 'La Secchia Rapita'. **1847** TENNYSON *Princess* Concl. 11 The men required that I should give throughout The sort of mock-heroic gigantesque. **1876** BLACK *Madcap V.* v, 'I am not to go down to the foot of the lane?' said she, with mock-heroic sadness. **1889** SWINBURNE *Stud. B. Jonson* 73 The passage is a really superb example of tragicomic or mock-heroic blank verse.

absol. **1756–82** J. WARTON *Ess. Pope* (ed. 4) I. iv. 255 Cervantes; who is the father and unrivalled model of the true mock-heroic.

B. *sb.* A burlesque imitation of the heroic style or manner.

1728 *Gulliver Decypher'd* 7 Peter abused the Wittlings of the Town for not having Sense enough to taste his Mock-Heroicks. **1847** TENNYSON *Princess* Concl. 64 In mock heroics stranger than our own. **1864** W. SMITH *T. B. Shaw's Hist. Eng. Lit.* xv. (1865) 294 The famous mock-heroic of Boileau. **1879** FROUDE *Cæsar* viii. 83 He [Cæsar] had no sentimental passion about him; no Byronic mock heroics.

So **mock-he'roical** *a.* = MOCK-HEROIC *a.* Also **mock-he'roically** *adv.*, in a mock-heroic manner.

1850 L. HUNT *Autobiog.* xxiii. (1860) 370 An article which I wrote, with the mock-heroical title of The Graces and Anxieties of Pig Driving. **1905** *Daily Chron.* 27 Dec. 4/7 The 'Argonaut' mock-heroically challenges anyone to point to a single case of a college man having bitten off another player's nose or ear.

† **mock-holiday.** *Obs.* [MOCK *a.*] Only in phrase: *to play mock-holiday*, to act deceitfully. Const. *with*.

15.. *Catal. Anc. Deeds* (1906) V. 498 As it seme he plaieth mock halliday with me. *c* **1561** VERON *Free-will* 50 b, God dothe playe mocke holy daye wyth us, if he promysethe thynges, that it lyeth not in us to obtayne. **1604** *Meeting of Gallants* 21 The stirrup plaide mock-holy-day with him, and made a foole of his foote. *a* **1607** BRIGHTMAN *Revelation* (1615) 230 The Iesuites doe not interprete the Scriptures, but play mocke haliday with them.

mocking ('mɒkɪŋ), *vbl. sb.* [f. MOCK *v.* + -ING[1].] The action of the verb MOCK; the utterance of derision or scorn; imitation, mimicry. Now only *gerundial*. Also occas. †an object of derision.

c **1440** *Boctus* (*Laud MS.* 559 lf. 5 b), This came to Boctus the kyng All in scorne and in mokkyng. **1539** TONSTALL *Serm. Palm Sund.* (1823) 12 He was obediente to suffre the mockynge of the people of Jewes. **1607** SHAKS. *Timon* I. i. 35 It is a pretty mocking of the life. **1611** BIBLE *Ezek.* xxii. 4 Therfore haue I made thee..a mocking to all countries. **1656** EARL MONM. tr. *Boccalini's Advts. fr. Parnass.* I. i. (1674) 1 These false Cheaters..mind only mocking and cosenage.

† **b. mocking-stock**, a laughing-stock. *Obs.*

Very common in 16–17th c.

1526 TINDALE 2 *Pet.* ii. 13 Off you they make a mockyng-stoke. **1534** MORE *Comf. agst. Trib.* II. Wks. 1192/2 The Philisties..vsing Sampson for their mocking stocke in scorne of God. **1639** S. DU VERGER tr. *Camus' Admir. Events* 208 The wisest persons made but a mocking-stocke of his vanity. **1791** WALKER, *Mocking-stock*, a butt for merriment. **1833** HT. MARTINEAU *Charmed Sea* viii. 122 How should you bear to be made..a mocking-stock while you were full of gloomy wrath?

mocking ('mɒkɪŋ), *ppl. a.* [-ING[2].] That mocks, ridicules, deludes, or mimics.

1530 PALSGR. 720/1, I skorne one with mockynge wordes, *je raffarde*. **1588** SHAKS. *L. L. L.* II. i. 52 Some merry mocking Lord belike, ist so? **1592** DAVIES *Immort. Soul* Introd. xx, The great mocking Master mock'd not then, When he said, Truth was bury'd here below. **1634** CANNE *Necess. Separ.* (1849) 286 A mocking contradiction of Mr. Johnson. **1720** J. HUGHES *Siege Damascus* II. ii, I am dar'd to it, with mocking scorn. **186.** DARWIN *Orig. Spec.* xiii. (1866) 507 But if we proceed from a district where one Leptalis imitates an Ithomia, another mocking and mocked species belonging to the same genera, equally close in their resemblance, will be found. **1871** FREEMAN *Norm. Conq.* (1876) IV. xviii. 187 The savages, as the mocking tongues of the Normans called them.

'mocking-bird. [f. MOCKING *ppl. a.* Cf. MOCK-BIRD.]

1. An American passerine song-bird of the genus *Mimus*, esp. *Mimus polyglottus*, characterized by its habit of mimicking the notes of other birds.

1676 T. GLOVER in *Phil. Trans.* XI. 631 There are also divers kinds of small Birds, whereof the Mocking-bird, the Red-bird, and Humming-bird, are the most remarkable. **1688** J. CLAYTON *Let. to Roy. Soc.* 12 May (1844) 30 Their mocking Birds may be compared to our singing Thrushes. *Ibid.* 32 The red Mocking is of a duskish red, or rather brown; it sings very well, but has not so soft a Note as the grey mocking Bird. **1741** E. LUCAS *Jrnls. & Lett.* (1850) 11, I promised to tell you when the mocking bird began to sing. **1802** BINGLEY *Anim. Biog.* (1813) II. 155 The Mocking Bird seems to have a singular pleasure in leading other birds astray. **1855** W. S. DALLAS in *Syst. Nat. Hist.* II. 296 The hunters in the Southern States know that the moon is rising when they hear the Mocking Bird begin to sing.

2. Applied to other birds having a similar aptitude for mimicry: **a.** the Sedge-warbler, *Acrocephalus schœnobænus*; **b.** = BUTCHER-BIRD; **c.** the Blackcap, *Sylvia atricapilla*; **d.** = MOCKING-WREN; **e.** the Lyre-bird, *Menura superba*; **f.** = PARSON-BIRD 1; **g.** the Bhim-raj, *Edolius paradiseus* (Balfour *Cycl. Ind.* 1857, p. 133); **h.** *French mocking-bird* (U.S.), the Thrasher (*Harporhynchus*).

a **1779** J. COOK *Voy. Pacific* (1784) I. 151 [In New Zealand] A small greenish bird... One would imagine he was surrounded by a hundred different sorts of birds, when the little warbler is near. From this circumstance we named it the mocking bird. **1835** W. YATE *Acc. N. Zealand* ii. (ed. 2) 52 *Tui.* This remarkable bird, from the versatility of its talents for imitation, has by some been called 'the Mocking Bird'. **1846** G. H. HAYDON *Five Yrs. in Austral. Felix* vi. 131 Numerous pheasants (*menura superba*). These birds are the mocking birds of Australia. **1860** BAIRD *Birds N. Amer.* 353 *Harporhynchus rufus*..French Mocking Bird. **1883** NEWTON in *Encycl. Brit.* XVI. 541/1 The name Mocking-Bird,..is in England occasionally given to some of the Warblers, especially the Blackcap (*Sylvia atricapilla*) and the Sedge-bird (*Acrocephalus schœnobænus*). **1894** —— *Dict. Birds* 582 In North America two Wrens, *Thryothorus ludovicianus* and *T. bewicki*, seem to be widely known as 'Mocking-birds'.

mockingly ('mɒkɪŋlɪ), *adv.* [f. MOCKING *ppl. a.* + -LY[2].] In a mocking manner.

1545 ELYOT *Dict.*, *Nasute*, wyttyly, mockyngly. **1602** WARNER *Alb. Eng.* IX. xlvi. (1612) 215 And, he saying, Let vs meete, 'Let's meete', quoth Echo mockingly. **1863** GEO. ELIOT *Romola* xxx, Whispers which died out mockingly as he strained his ear after them.

mocking-stock: see MOCKING *vbl. sb.*

mocking thrush. [Cf. *mock-thrush*, MOCK *a.* 2 c.] The Thrasher, *Harporhynchus fuscus* or *rufus*.

1839 AUDUBON *Ornith. Biog.* V. 336 Townsend's Mocking Thrush. **1847** EMERSON *Poems, Musketaquid* Wks. (Bohn) I. 485 A mocking thrush, A wild rose, a rock-loving columbine, Salve my worst wounds. **1876** GENTRY *Life-Hist. Birds E. Pennsylv.* I. 26 The Mocking Thrushes as a group are chiefly southern.

mocking wren. An American wren of the genus *Thryothorus*, esp. *T. ludovicianus*.

1874 BAIRD, etc. *N. Amer. Land Birds* I. 142 The great Carolina or Mocking Wren, is found in all the South-eastern and Southern States from Florida to Maryland. **1876** GENTRY *Life-Hist. Birds E. Pennsylv.* I. 74 *Thryothorus ludovicianus*,..is commonly surnamed the Mocking Wren from its remarkable powers of mimicry.

† **'mockish,** *a. Obs.* [f. MOCK *v.* + -ISH.] Mocking, derisive; also, mock, sham.

1494 FABYAN *Chron.* VII. 398 In derysyon of the Kynge, they made this mokkysshe ryme folowyng. **1513** MORE *Rich. III*, Wks. 67/1 After this mockishe eleccion, than was he Crowned [etc.]. **1631** WEEVER *Anc. Funeral Mon.* 457 This mockish rime doggerell.

b. Of animals: Skittish.

a **1529** SKELTON *Col. Cloute* 181 Let se who that dare Sho the mockyshe mare.

Hence † **'mockishly** *adv.*, in a 'mockish' manner.

1530 PALSGR. 839/2 Mockysshly, *par mocquerie*. **1532** MORE *Confut. Tindale* Wks. 392/1 Els could he neuer finde in his heart to speke so mockyshlye of such a matter.

† **mock-shade, mog-shade.** *dial. Obs. rare*[−0]. [Original form and etymology uncertain; the first element may be MOCK *a.* or possibly MOCK *sb.*[2], tree-stump; if the correct form be *mog-*, it may be connected with MUGGY.] (See quots.) Also **mock-shadow**, twilight (Halliwell 1847).

1669 WORLIDGE *Syst. Agric.* (1681) 329 *Mogshade*, the shadows of Trees, or such like. **1681** BLOUNT *Glossogr.* (ed. 5), *Day-lights-gate*, i.e. the going down of day light; otherwise called the *Mock-shade*.

mock-sign: see MOCK *sb.*[1] 4.

mock turtle. [MOCK *a.*]

1. A dish consisting of calf's head dressed with sauces and condiments so as to resemble turtle.

1763 MRS. GLASSE *Cookery* (1767) 340 To dress a mock turtle. Take a calf's head [etc.]. **1783** J. FARLEY *Lond. Art of Cookery* (1789) I. iii. 32. **1826** MRS. DODS *Cook & Housew. Man.* 225 Mock Turtle, or Calf's Head.

2. (In full, *mock turtle soup*.) A soup made (usually of calf's head) in imitation of turtle soup.

1783 J. FARLEY *Lond. Art of Cookery* (1789) I. xiii. 158 Mock-Turtle Soup. **1789** MRS. PIOZZI *Journ. France* II. 196 The cold mock turtle soups..which London pastry-cooks keep in their shops. **1826** MRS. DODS *Cook & Housew. Man.* 83 Mock Turtle Soup. Procure the head of a middle-sized, well-fed cow calf [etc.]. **1833** MARRYAT *P. Simple* xxvii, As the midshipmen prophesied, there was plenty of pork—mock-turtle soup, made out of a pig's head [etc.]. **1855** DELAMER *Kitch. Gard.* (1861) 122 Cooks say that it [*i.e.* Sweet basil]..is a grand secret in the composition of good mock-turtle soup.

fig. **1890** W. CORY *Lett. & Jrnls.* (1897) 553 Anglo-Catholics started vestments, and a whole lot of 'mock turtle'.

mock-up ('mɒkʌp). [f. MOCK *v.* 4 c.] **a.** An experimental model (often full-sized) of a projected aircraft, ship, apparatus, etc., used esp. for study, testing, practice, or display. Also *attrib.*

1920 *Flight* 19 Feb. 218/1 If the dimensions of such parts are difficult to determine on paper, the use of 'mock-ups' should be resorted to for this purpose. **1933** *Jrnl. R. Aeronaut. Soc.* XXXVII. 759 A mock-up of the eventual design was built to full scale with every instrument, lever, and fitting installed. **1944** U. SINCLAIR *Presidential Agent* (1945) IV. xv. 292 At the moment the Germans had the fastest fighter [plane], but Robbie had a new one in the 'mock-up' stage that was going to knock them all cold. **1944** [see CONSOLE *sb.* 3 b]. **1951** R. BRADBURY *Illustr. Man* (1952) 106 It's only a mockup... When they plan a rocket they build a full-scale model first, of aluminium. **1966** T. PYNCHON *Crying of Lot 49* iv. 84 She was gazing at a mockup of a space capsule. **1968** *Daily Tel.* (Colour Suppl.) 8 Nov. 23 (*caption*) This instrument panel mock-up..resembles as closely as possible the eventual airliner. **1971** *Sunday Australian* 8 Aug. 3/3 A 747 training mock-up at Sydney Airport.

b. *transf.* and *fig.* A plan, model, conception; an imitation.

1954 G. SMITH *Flaw in Crystal* xvi. 163 These coloured sheets..were mock-ups for a new children's magazine. **1957** J. F. HORNER *Summary of Scientology* 79 Because they do not immediately alter to fit his mock-up, he is constantly failing. **1959** J. CARY *Captive & Free* xiii. 68 'What I want to know,' she said, 'is when we're going to see the mock-up of the new front page.' **1959** *Guardian* 4 Dec. 13/5 The thing is written in a half-bantering Anglicised mock-up of the Spanish idiom. **1961** L. MUMFORD *City in Hist.* Note to plate 38, 'All under one roof' may prove just a mock-up for the terminal form of the anti-city.

mock-word: see MOCK *sb.*[1] 4.

mocky ('mɒkɪ). *U.S. slang.* Also **mockey, mockie.** [Origin uncertain; perh. f. Yiddish *makeh* a boil, sore.] A Jew. Also *attrib.* or as *adj.*

1931 D. RUNYON in *Collier's* 10 Jan. 10/3, I consider this ..disrespectful, like calling Jewish people mockies, or Heebs, or geese. **1937** E. H. SUTHERLAND *Professional Thief* i. 12, I was over on the East Side and there saw this Jew who was pointed out to me as one of their best mocky cannons. **1943** I. WOLFERT *Tucker's People* xxix. 481 Love thy neighbor if he's not..a mockie or a slicked-up greaseball from the Argentine. **1955** *Publ. Amer. Dial. Soc.* XXIV. 90 Jewish organizations are referred to as *mocky mobs* or *mocky jew mobs*. 'Mocky is not a Jew. It's a Sixth Avenue Jew.'

moc-main ('mɒkmeɪn). *Surg.* [a. Chinese *muh-mien* 'cotton-tree, *Bombax Ceiba*' (Williams *Syllabic Dict. Chinese Lang.*).

Loureiro *Flora Cochin-chinensis* (1793) gives *mo-mien-hoa* as the Chinese name for *Bombax pentandra*.]

A white shining fibre of great lightness and elasticity, the produce of the seed-pod of the silk cotton-tree, *Bombax heptaphyllum*, native of Cochin China and Cambodia.

moc-main truss, a specially designed truss padded with this elastic fibre.

1856 in MAYNE *Expos. Lex.* **1866** *Treas. Bot.* 748/1 *Moc-main*, a Chinese name for *Bombax Ceiba*. **1866** *Chambers's Encycl.* s.v. *Silk-cotton*. **1881** *Syd. Soc. Lex.*, *Bombax heptaphyllum*,..a tree which affords the substance called moc-main.

‖ **moco** ('məʊkəʊ). [Tupi *mocó*.] A kind of cavy, esp. the Rock cavy, *Cavia* (or *Kerodon*) *rupestris*, a South American rodent rather larger than the Guinea-pig.

1834 *Cuvier's Anim. Kingd.* I. 139 The Mocos have rather simpler grinders than the Cobayes. **1869** R. F. BURTON *Highl. Brazil* II. 313 The brown Moco peeped out of its home. **1898** *Nat. Science* June 376 The moco is..sometimes called the rock-cavy.

moco, obs. form of MOCHA[1].

† **mocoa.** *Obs.* [Of obscure origin; perh. a use of MOCHA[1].] Some kind of 'clouded cane'.

1762 FOOTE *Orators* I. (1780) 13 To drop a hint that I may occasionally use him as a walking stick; a kind of an elegantly clouded Mocoa, or an airy Anamaboo: yet, that it is by no means my intention to depend upon him as a support.

mocoa, mocoe, obs. forms of MOCHA[1].

mocock, mococo, obs. forms of MACACO[2].

mocock (məʊ'kɒk). *N. Amer.* Also **makak, makuk, mocuck, mohcock, mokuk, muccuck.** [American Indian.] (See quot. 1827.)

1779 J. LONG *Jrnl.* (1904) II. 155 We were reduced to a few fish and some wild rice, or *menomon* (which are kept in *muccucks*, or bark boxes). **1827** T. L. MCKENNEY *Sk. Tour to Lakes* 194 A mocock is a little receptacle of a basket form, and oval, though without a handle, made of birch bark, with a top sewed on with *wattap* (the fine roots of the red cedar, split,) the smaller ones are ornamented with porcupines' quills, died red, yellow, and green. **1839** C. M. KIRKLAND *New Home* xx. 138 The Indians bring in immense quantities [of whortle-berries] slung in panniers or mococks of bark on the sides of their wild-looking ponies. **1859** P. KANE *Wanderings among Indians N. Amer.* 32 My companion was cooking some fish in a moh-cock, Indian fashion (for we had lost our kettle). **1905** *N.Y. Even. Post* 6 May, An old squaw stopped to offer a small mocock, a birch-bark box, holding perhaps a pound of maple sugar. **1931** G. L. NUTE *Voyageur* 80 In the spring maple sugar was also bought by the *makuk* (a birch-bark vessel) from the squaws. **1959** E. TUNIS *Indians* iii. 53/1 By far the commonest birch-bark container was the mocuck, with a square bottom larger than its round top, that served as box or basket at need.

‖ **moco-moco** (,məʊkəʊ'məʊkəʊ). Also 8 **mucco-mucco**, 9 **moccomocco, mocamoca, moka-moka.** [Carib.: '*moucou-moucou*, espèce de pied-de-veau' (*Dictionarium Galibi*, 1763).] A variety of arum, *Arum arborescens*, growing in Guyana, etc.

1769 E. BANCROFT *Guiana* 104 The Muccomucco always grows in water... It usually grows eight or ten feet in height and is jointed every few inches. **1825** WATERTON *Wand. S. Amer.* (1882) 25 The mocamoca trees on the banks of the Demerara. **1855** H. G. DALTON *Hist. Brit. Guiana* II. 201 Mocco-mocco, *Arum arborescens*. **1901** A. H. KEANE *Central Amer.* II. 441 The large leaved Mocomoco. **1903** DES VŒUX *Col. Service* I. 26 Moka-moka a tall arum with bare stalks.

moconer, obs. variant of MOTIONER.

mocque, mocquery, obs. ff. MOCK, MOCKERY.

mocuddum, obs. form of MOKADDAM.

mocus, mocyon, obs. ff. MOCHA[1], MOTION.

‖**Mod** (moːd), *sb.*[1] [Gael. *mòd* an assembly, court, a. ON. *mót*: see MOOT *sb.*] The yearly meeting of the Highland Association, for literary and musical competitions.

1893 *Daily News* 21 July 5/3 The Highland Association' are going to hold their second 'Mod'..at Oban. **1901** *Scotsman* 20 Sept. 4/2 The annual Gaelic Mod was held yesterday in Glasgow.

mod (mɒd), *sb.*[2] and *v.* Colloq. abbrev. of MODIFICATION and occas. abbrev. of MODIFY *v.*

1943 C. H. WARD-JACKSON *Piece of Cake* 43 Has this Wimpey got the new escape gear mod? **1958** 'N. SHUTE' *Rainbow & Rose* i. 17 Captain Pascoe had it modded, special. **1967** *Autocar* 5 Oct. 24/1 This Healey had all the works racing mods which brought the engine power up to 210 b.h.p. **1967** *New Scientist* 14 Dec. 654/2 If the 'mods' are minor, the production line could absorb them without much interruption. **1974** *Publishers' Weekly* 12 Aug. 54/2 A rising generation of behavioral psychologists..is fanning out into our society to do its 'behavior mod' thing... These lab-trained mod squads have begun infiltrating schools, American family life, [etc.].

mod (mɒd), *sb.*[3] and *a.* Also with capital initial. [Abbrev. of MODERN *a.* and *sb.* or MODERNIST.] **A.** *sb.* A teenager who is characterized by his sophistication and tidiness; freq. contrasted with ROCKER[1]. Also *attrib.* **B.** *adj.* Modern, sophisticated, stylish, esp. in dress.

1960 *New Left Rev.* Sept.–Oct. 4/2 Teds and Mods, Beatniks and Ravers. **1963** *Guardian* 13 May 18/1 Fights between the 'mods' and the 'rockers'. **1964** *Observer* 24 May 12/2 Mods and Rockers have co-existed comparatively well for a year or so—the Mods, neatly dressed and on scooters, the Rockers in studded leather jackets and on motor-bikes. **1964** *Punch* 3 June 815/1 (*heading*) Modgirl. **1965** *Granta* Summer 10 Student activists..have taken more account of the mod image cultivated by some universities. **1966** *Punch* 5 Oct. 505/2 He is naturally anxious that your furnishings should include what that enlightened store now calls 'Mod Gear'. **1968** J. IRONSIDE *Fashion Alphabet* 22 The Mods, both girls and boys, were very clean and neat and both wore close cut hair. *Ibid.* 194 The 'Mod' hair-cut, as opposed to long-haired 'Rockers', is short, neat and cut close to the head. **1970** G. JACKSON *Let.* 4 Apr. in *Soledad Brother* (1971) 207 This running dog..was transmitting the credo of the slave to our youth, the mod version of the old house nigger. **1972** *Daily Colonist* (Victoria, B.C.) 25 Feb. 4/2 The operation by the Metropolitan Police..of a 'mod squad'.. whose members stroll the streets in 'mod' dress and unshorn hair. **1973** E. BULLINS *Theme is Blackness* 167 Everybody in our integrated circle of mod people is with it, man. We're the Now Crowd. **1975** *Islander* (Victoria, B.C.) 3 Aug. 4/3 Jerry, a mod young priest from San Diego.

mod (mɒd; *also read as* 'modulo'), *prep. Math.* Also **mod.** (with point). Abbrev. of MODULO *prep.*

The notation $b \equiv c$ (mod. a) ('b is congruent to c modulo a') was introduced by Gauss (*Disquisitiones Arithmeticae* (1801) I. 2).

1854 *Cambr. & Dublin Math. Jrnl.* IX. 85 Each of these quantities must be congruent to zero, that is $A_0 \equiv 0$, $A_1 \equiv 0, \ldots A_{p-2} \equiv 0$ (mod. p). **1860** *Rep. Brit. Assoc. Adv. Sci. 1859* I. 230 The congruence $\phi(x) \equiv 0$, mod P, is said to be solved, when all the integral values of x are assigned which make the left hand number of the congruence divisible by P. **1949** USPENSKY & HEASLET *Elem. Number Theory* vi. 128 Two congruences with the same moduli can be added or subtracted, member by member, like equalities. In other words, from two congruences $A \equiv a$ (mod m), $B \equiv b$ (mod m) it follows that $A \pm B \equiv a \pm b$ (mod m). **1949** W. LEDERMANN *Introd. Theory Finite Groups* i. 17, $ax \equiv bx$ (mod. m) implies that $a \equiv b$ (mod. m). **1971** D. GORENSTEIN in Powell & Higman *Finite Simple Groups* ii. 67, q is an odd prime power congruent to -1 (mod 4).

mod, obs. form of MOOD.

mod., abbreviation for MODERN, MODERATO.

modacrylic (mɒdəˈkrɪlɪk). [f. MOD(IFIED *ppl. a.* + ACRYLIC *sb.*] A type of synthetic fibre consisting of molecules with between 35 and 85 per cent by mass of $-CH_2CH(CN)-$ units (derived from acrylonitrile), which is used for children's nightwear, dresses, and household textiles.

1959 *Federal Register* (U.S.) 10 Feb. 981/2 The following generic names for manufactured fibers..are hereby established... Modacrylic. **1964** *Which?* Aug. 253/1 Fabrics made from modacrylic are easy to wash in warm water, and require little or no ironing. **1973** *Materials & Technol.* VI. vii. 495 Materials such as Saran and modacrylics do not burn but shrink away from the flame. **1974** *Encycl. Brit. Micropædia* VI. 958/2 Wigs made of modacrylics have had good acceptance.

modal (ˈməʊdəl), *a.* and *sb.* Also (sense 4) 6 moodal. [ad. med.L. *modālis*, f. L. *mod-us*: see MODE and -AL[1]. Cf. F. *modal.*] **A.** *adj.*

1. Pertaining to mode or form as contrasted with substance.

1625 LAUD *Serm.* (*Ps.* cxxii. 3–5) 18 There must be..a paring off of foolish and vnlearned Questions, yea, and of many Modal too. **1678** GALE *Crt. Gentiles* III. 6 Moral Bonitie and Vitiositie are differences of human acts merely accidental or modal. **1782** PRIESTLEY *Corrupt. Chr.* I. I. 148 Dr. Wallis thought the distinction..was only modal. **1852** ROBERTSON *Serm.* Ser. IV. xi. (1876) 104 A heresy, known in old times by the name of Sabellianism or modal Trinity. **1876** E. MELLOR *Priesth.* iv. 172 To discount from the teaching of Christ the words 'eat' and 'drink', as modal terms enjoining modal operations..is to relinquish the literal interpretation.

2. *Law.* Of a legacy, contract, etc.: Containing provisions defining the manner in which it is to take effect.

1590 SWINBURNE *Testaments* 135 Excepte the condition be not conditionall but modall, for (*conditio*) and (*modus*) doo greatlie differ. *Ibid.* 290 When the legacy is not conditional, but modall. **1726** AYLIFFE *Parergon* 336 Some think it to be a modal Legacy;..and consequently a Legacy of this kind ought to be paid before the Mode is fulfilled. **1860** WHARTON *Law Lex.* (ed. 2), *Modal legacy*, a bequest with a direction as to the mode in which it is to be applied to the legatee's benefit.

3. *Mus.* Pertaining to mode.

1597 MORLEY *Introd. Mus.* Annot., To this daie could I neuer see..a Long set for 3 briefes, with that signe, except it had either a figure of three, or then [*read* three] modal restes sette before it. **1777** SIR W. JONES *Ess. Imit. Arts* Poems, etc. 198 Each of them has a peculiar character, arising from the position of the modal note. **1880** W. S. ROCKSTRO in Grove *Dict. Mus.* II. 340 The Modal Sign is usually placed after the Clef, like the Time Signature in modern music. **1903** *Westm. Gaz.* 27 Nov. 10/2 A great many genuine old ballads, some so old as to be modal in form—that is, pre-existent to the time of the major and minor scale.

4. *Logic.* Of a proposition: Involving the affirmation of possibility, impossibility, necessity, or contingency. By some writers used in a wider sense, so as to be applicable to any proposition in which the predicate is affirmed or denied of the subject with any kind of qualification, or which contains an adverb or adverbial phrase. Of a syllogism: Containing a modal proposition as a premiss. Esp. in various collocations, as ***modal logic***, that branch of logic which is concerned with the study of modal propositions (see also quots.).

1569 J. SANFORD tr. *Agrippa's Van. Artes* 22b, And of these doo onely approue eight Moodes and laugh at Moodal propositions. **1697** tr. *Burgersdicius his Logic* I. xxviii. 113 These Enunciations..are Modal; because they not only denounce the Predicate to agree or disagree with the Subject, but also declare the Manner how they both agree and disagree. **1774** REID *Aristotle's Logic* iv. §6 (1788) 95 In a modal proposition the affirmation or negation is modified. **1827** WHATLEY *Logic* ii. III. (ed. 2) 106 A Modal Proposition may be stated as a pure one, by attaching the Mode to one of the Terms. **1870** JEVONS *Elem. Logic* vii. 69 It has long been usual to distinguish propositions as they are pure or modal. **1932** LEWIS & LANGFORD *Symbolic Logic* vi. 153 (*heading*) Consistency and the modal functions. **1943** *Mind* LII. 265 The ideal textbook in mathematical logic would include extensive discussion of the intensional and modal logics. **1957** *Jrnl. Symbolic Logic* XXII. 176 (*title*) New foundations for Lewis modal systems. **1957** A. N. PRIOR *Time & Modality* 133 There are some modal logicians who feel that statements containing sequences of modal operators like *MM, MML*,..are one and all 'meaningless'. **1962** W. & M. KNEALE *Devel. of Logic* x. 613 We turn to consider the possibility of using quantifiers to operate across modal signs. **1968** HUGHES & CRESSWELL *Introd. Modal Logic* p. xi, Modal logic can be described briefly as the logic of necessity and possibility, of 'must be' and 'may be'. *Ibid.* ii. 25 Because of the non-truth-functionality of modal operators..the initial account does not lead to any obvious formal definition of validity for modal formulae. **1970** J. N. FINDLAY tr. *Husserl's Logical Investigations* I. 32 Modal distinctions play a central part in phenomenological theory, and Husserl is now contributing importantly to their own phenomenology.

5. *Gram.* **a.** Of or pertaining to the mood of a verb. *Esp.* in phr. ***modal auxiliary***. **b.** Of a particle: Denoting manner or modality.

1798 TOOKE *Purley* II. (1805) 467 Our language has made but small progress compared either with the Greek or with the Latin..even in this Modal and Temporal abbreviation. **1845** JELF *Grk. Gram.* I. §184 The Modal vowel, which signifies the modal relations of the verb, and varies accordingly. **1880** *Expositor* XII. 289 Those conjunctive and modal particles in which the Greek language is so incomparably rich. **1933** E. H. GROUT *Stand. Eng.* v. 122 The modal auxiliaries *may, might, can, could, must, ought*,.. give a cast to the whole sentence in which they are. **1961** R. B. LONG *Sentence & its Parts* vi. 138 A category of modal auxiliaries is often set up for modern English, to include various verbs expressing ideas of possibility, constraint, and desire.

6. **a.** *Statistics.* Of or pertaining to a mode (sense 7c); occurring most frequently in a sample or population.

1897 *Proc. R. Soc.* LXII. 175 Probable error of modal frequency y_0. **1900** K. PEARSON *Gram. Sci.* (ed. 2) 383 The average value of the character is very frequently taken as determining the type instead of the modal value. **1938** A. E. WAUGH *Elem. Statistical Method* iv. 46 In the first place it is necessary to locate the modal class. By this we mean the class which contains the most items. **1954** M. BERESFORD *Lost Villages* ix. 288 In the receipts of 1377 we have only the constables' names to add flesh and blood to the averages, modal ranges and medians of statistical calculations. **1968** *Listener* 25 July 101/1 The administrators we saw..had averaged only 2·8 years in all their completed jobs in the class; in fact, the modal (most frequently occurring) period in completed jobs was two years. **1973** *Jrnl. Genetic Psychol.* CXXII. 248 The modal age of the youngsters was 13.

b. Representative, typical; ***modal personality***, an imaginary personality in which each component trait or characteristic is present to an extent equal to the modal value of a particular society or group or, more widely, which is taken as in some way representative of it.

1944 C. DU BOIS *People of Alor* I. i. 3 Modal personality, then, is the product of the interplay of fundamental, physiologically and neurologically determined tendencies and experiences common to all human beings acted upon by the cultural milieu. *Ibid.* 5 On such a base line data will show central tendencies that constitute the modal personality for any particular culture. **1948** K. DAVIS *Human Society* xv. 427 The modal divorce now occurs in the third year of marriage. **1949** R. K. MERTON *Social Theory* i. 57 The characteristic (modal) pattern for handling a standardized problem. **1954** INKELES & LEVINSON in G. Lindzey *Handbk. Social Psychol.* II. xxvi. 980/2 In our opinion, 'national character' ought to be equated with modal personality structure. **1956** W. H. WHYTE *Organization Man* (1957) 281 What might be called the modal man, however, is a twenty-five-to-thirty-five-year-old white-collar organization man. **1968** *McGraw-Hill Yearbk. Sci. & Technol.* 50/1 Examples of these typical motor patterns are the deep cooing and bowing of the domestic pigeon, the butting of a billy goat, [etc.]... These motor patterns have been given a wide variety of names, such as modal action patterns..and instinctive movements. **1968** J. O. ELLEFSON in E. Norbeck et al. *Study of Personality* ix. 142 Field primatologists report impressions of the existence of modal personalities, often designated as temperament, that characterize species. **1970** E. MCGINNIES *Social Behavior* iii. 70 Linton (1945) has conceived of national character as a modal personality structure, or configuration that appears with considerable frequency in a society. *Ibid.* 71 Identification of such modal behavior configurations makes it possible to arrive at certain generalizations about any given society and to describe more succinctly the differences between one society and another.

7. *Petrol.* Of or pertaining to the mode (sense 5b) of a rock; as indicated by a mode.

1902 W. CROSS et al. in *Jrnl. Geol.* X. 609 A Modal Variety ..may be defined as a rock having a mode with a slightly different development of the quite subordinate component minerals. **1938** *Nature* 17 Sept. 495/2 The second volume includes all the rocks with more than 5 per cent of modal quartz. **1962** A. E. J. & C. G. ENGEL in A. E. J. Engel et al. *Petrologic Stud.* 48 The thin sections used for modal analyses of two-pyroxene amphibolites were slightly thicker than is conventional, to accentuate the color difference.

B. *sb.* **1.** *Logic.* A modal proposition (see A. 4).

1725 WATTS *Logic* II. ii. §4 There is no great need of making modals a distinct sort [*sc.* of proposition]. **1827** WHATELY *Logic* II. III. (ed. 2) 108 When a hypothetical Conclusion is inferred from a hypothetical Premiss,..then the hypothesis (as in Modals) must be considered as part of one of the Terms. **1878** S. H. HODGSON *Philos. Refl.* I. 368 It has the advantage of exhibiting the derivation of the Modals, as they are called, from the reflective mode of consciousness [etc.].

2. *Gram.* A modal verb (see A. 5).

1959 *Rep. 10th Ann. Round Table Meeting Ling. & Lang. Stud.* (Georgetown Univ. Inst. Lang.) IV. 112 Parallel rules apply to most of the modals and conjugators. **1965** N. CHOMSKY *Aspects of Theory of Syntax* ii. 63 *May* is a verbal auxiliary..and..a Modal. **1971** J. ANDERSON in A. J. Aitken et al. *Edin. Stud. Eng. & Scots* 69 These phenomena are often well documented in grammars purporting to give an account of the modals.

modalism (ˈməʊdəlɪz(ə)m). [f. MODAL + -ISM.] The Sabellian doctrine that the distinction in the Trinity is 'modal' only, i.e. that the Father, the Son, and the Holy Spirit are merely three different modes of manifestation of the Divine nature.

1859 SCHAFF *Hist. Chr. Ch.* (an. 1–311) 292 Sabellian modalism. **1905** W. SANDAY *Crit. 4th Gospel* viii. 244 The language of Ignatius tends to Modalism.

modalist (ˈməʊdəlɪst). [f. MODAL + -IST.] **a.** *sb.* One who holds or professes Modalism. **b.** quasi-*adj.* = MODALISTIC.

1832 I. TAYLOR *Saturday Even.* xxviii. 469 The error of the Modalists and Sabellians. **1897** *Expositor* Dec. 408 Passages..could be understood in a distinctly modalist sense.

Hence **modaˈlistic** *a.*, of or pertaining to the tenets of a Modalist.

1878 J. COOK *Boston Lect. Orthodoxy* ii. 40 The definition given here is not modalistic. **1882–3** *Schaff's Encycl. Relig. Knowl.* II. 1549 The old and generally accepted division into dynamic and modalistic Monarchianism.

modality (məʊˈdælɪtɪ). [ad. med.L. *modālitās*, f. *modālis*: see MODAL and -ITY. Cf. F. *modalité.*]

1. **a.** The quality or fact of being modal. Also, a modal quality or circumstance; the modal attributes of something; †a question or point relating to mode, manner, or method, and not to substance. Now *rare*.

a **1617** BAYNE *On Eph.* (1658) 144 Liberty in this sense,.. contingency, necessity, these are modalities agreeing to effects, as effects are in order to their second causes. **1647** M. HUDSON *Div. Right Govt.* II. iii. 87 Even the temporal part of that promise..was performed exactly in the reality, though not in the Modality thereof. **1656** *Burton's Diary* (1828) I. 44 Shall punctilios and modalities and forms, bind and tie up a Parliament? **1704** NORRIS *Ideal World* II. x. 401 We cannot conceive the modality of any substance as a Being distinct from that substance... We cannot conceive a circle as a being distinct from extension whose modality it is. **1825** *New Monthly Mag.* XIV. 474 The resemblance takes its colour from the modalities of thought and feeling of the artist by whom it is sketched.

b. In diplomacy, politics, etc.: a procedure or method; a means for the attainment of a desired end.

1957 G. F. KENNAN in *Listener* 28 Nov. 868/1 The modalities of German unification must flow from the will of the German people, expressed in free elections. **1960** *Guardian* 23 Aug. 7/6 He did hear nine members of the Council praise his statesmanship and the procedures ('modalities' is the new and foolish word) he had adopted. **1970** *New Yorker* 17 Oct. 162/2 The new word that is constantly being heard here is 'modalities'. Everyone

involved in the peace talks agrees that the military modalities of a cease-fire are more easily negotiated than the political modalities.

2. *Logic.* **a.** In the scholastic logic, the fact of being a modal proposition or syllogism. Also, the particular qualification by the presence of which a proposition is rendered modal.

1628 T. SPENCER *Logick* To Rdr., The modalitie of propositions doth explicate the subject or predicate of the proposition wherein it is. **1725** WATTS *Logic* II. ii. §4 But whether the modality be natural, moral, &c. yet in all these propositions it is the mode is the proper predicate. **1843** MILL *Logic* I. iv. §2 Those distinctions among propositions which are said to have reference to their modality. **1870** JEVONS *Elem. Logic* vii. 70 All these assertions are made with a different degree of certainty or modality.

b. In Kantian and subsequent use, that feature of a judgement which is defined by the class in which it is placed when judgements are classified into problematic, assertory, and apodictic.

This is a development of the older sense 2 a; the distinctive features of 'problematical' and 'apodictic' judgements being 'modalities' in the earlier sense, the term was extended to apply also to that of 'assertory' judgements. In Kant's classification 'the Categories of modality' are those of possibility and impossibility, existence and non-existence, necessity and contingency; the term is coordinate with Quantity, Quality, and Relation.

1836 *Penny Cycl.* VI. 368/1 These Categories consist of four primordial classes: 1. quantity, 2. quality, 3. relation, 4. modality; each class containing three Categories. **1884** tr. *Lotze's Logic* 53 What modality have such sentences as these, '*S* will be *P*', '*S* ought to be *P*', '*S* may be *P*', '*S* has been *P*'? No one of them affirms reality, but the unreal which is past in the last is something quite different from that which is permitted, enjoined, or future in the others... If all these shades of meaning had been taken into account, the forms of modality might have been correspondingly increased in number. **1949** HUTTEN & REICHENBACH tr. *H. Reichenbach's Theory of Probability* x. §80. 404 Like probabilities, the modalities must be regarded as properties not of individual propositions but of propositional sequences. **1951** G. H. VON WRIGHT *Ess. Modal Logic* 3 Related to the problems of mixed modalities are the problems of super-imposed or higher order modalities.

3. *Civil Law.* 'The quality of being limited as to time or place of performance, or, more loosely, of being suspended by a condition: said of a promise' (*Cent. Dict.* 1890).

4. *Psychol.* **a.** (See quot. 1909.)

1895 *Amer. Jrnl. Psychol.* VII. 84 *Sinn*, sense, sensibility, modality. **1909** *Cent. Dict.* Suppl., *Modality*, in Psychol.: (*a*) the nature or character of sensation or stimulus as determined by the sense-department to which it belongs or appeals: a term proposed by Helmholtz, to avoid a confusing use of *quality*... Hence (*b*) the sense-department itself: as, the sensations of different *modalities*. **1925** G. B. PHELAN (*title*) Feeling experience and its modalities. **1951** G. HUMPHREY *Thinking* ii. 57 Sensory presentations of various modalities—auditory, kinaesthetic, and so on. **1971** tr. *H. von Helmholtz's Sel. Writings* xiv. 369 The most fundamental [distinction] is that among sensations which belong to different senses, such as the differences among blue, warm, sweet, and high-pitched. In an earlier work I referred to these differences in the *modality* of the sensations. **1972** D. R. KENSHALO in Kling & Riggs *Woodworth & Schlosberg's Exper. Psychol.* (ed. 3) v. 119/1 If we insist that each primary sensory modality has its own nerve pathway, the tactile, pain, and temperature senses fail to qualify as different modalities because their nerves are intermingled.

b. A term used to denote qualitatively different attributes or traits of personality.

1946 R. B. CATTELL in *Brit. Jrnl. Psychol.* May 159 Three classes or 'modalities' of traits: (1) Dynamic traits, e.g. dispositions, sentiments, neurotic symptoms, ergs; (2) Temperament traits, e.g. general emotionality, surgency, preservation, hyperthyroidism, personal tempo; (3) Abilities or cognitive traits, e.g. native general intelligence, acquired perceptual and executive skills. **1962** E. R. HILGARD *Introd. Psychol.* (ed. 3) xvi. 452/2 Guilford.. writes of seven 'modalities of traits', indicating that the kind of trait we see depends upon the direction from which we view personality. **1964** L. J. BISCHOF *Interpreting Personality Theories* xiv. 594 Formally, Cattell proceeds to divide traits into three *modalities*: temperament, dynamics, and ability. **1972** *Jrnl. Social Psychol.* LXXXVII. 52 The conditioning events taking place during this phase leave an indelible imprint on the psychological modalities referred to as personality.

modalize ('məʊdəlaɪz), *v.* [f. MODAL *a.* + -IZE.] *trans.* To render modal. Hence **moda'lizable** *a.*, **modali'zation**; **'modalized** *ppl. a.*

1857 A. B. WILSON in *Oxford Ess.* 115 All dogmatic statements must be held to be modalized by greater or less probability. **1955** A. N. PRIOR *Formal Logic* III. i. 202 'Modalization' here plays a part. *Ibid.*, Provided that no propositional variable occurring in β occurs in α unless it is 'modalized', i.e. is either immediately preceded by '*M*' or '*L*' or occurs as part of a propositional formula which as a whole is preceded by '*M*' or '*L*'. *Ibid.* 209 A similar hexagon ..could be constructed for modalized conjunctive and alternative forms. **1957** —— *Time & Modality* 137 The only modalizable forms are single variables with or without a preceding sequence of N's. **1963** A. KENNY *Action, Emotion & Will* ix. 189 Descriptions of formal objects can be formed trivially simply by modalizing the relevant verbs. **1973** J. J. ZEMAN *Modal Logic* v. 80 Systems containing only a finite number of non-equivalent modalities will..be called 'systems of complete modalization'. *Ibid.*, A formula is completely modalized if the prefixing of modal operators to it does not change its 'modal quality'.

modally ('məʊdəlɪ), *adv.* [f. MODAL + -LY².] In a modal respect; with reference to mode or manner.

1647 M. HUDSON *Div. Right Govt.* II. ix. 130 Gods honour and the Kings are not really but onely modally and circumstantially different. **1704** NORRIS *Ideal World* II. i. 21 Things that are modally distinct, or distinct by a modal abstraction, that is, whose distinction is owing [etc.]. **1867** FROUDE *Short Stud.*, *Spinoza* (ed. 2) 232 Therefore because things modally distinguished do not quâ substance differ from one another there cannot be more than one substance of the same attribute.

mod. con. ('mɒd 'kɒn). Also **mod. cons.** Colloq. abbrev. of *modern convenience(s)* (see MODERN *a.* 3 a). Also *transf.*

1934 *Punch* 24 Jan. 86/2 An advertisement..describing just such a house as we wanted. Just the right number of rooms, 'five minutes from the station, h. & c. in all bedrooms, all mod. cons.' **1952** A. HOCKING *Best Laid Plans* ix. 135 Four bedrooms, two sitting-rooms, k. and b., as the house agents say; every mod. con. **1963** *Times* 13 Feb. 11/4 Such a sophisticated 'mod. con.', the equivalent of a hot bath to splash in, is, generally speaking, beyond the ambition of the normal duck. **1966** 'H. MACDIARMID' *Company I've Kept* xiii. 188 We had no 'mod cons', and were getting too old to put up with really primitive conditions. **1972** G. DURRELL *Catch me a Colobus* v. 99 It's a modest little place..but it's got all mod. con. and that sort of thing.

modd(e, obs. forms of MOOD, MUD.

moddam, moddom, moddum: see MODOM.

moddel, -der, obs. forms of MODEL, MAUTHER.

moddley-coddle, variant of MOLLY CODDLE.

mode (məʊd), *sb.* Also 4 **moede**; and see MOOD *sb.*² [In branch I, a. L. *modus* measure, size, limit of quantity, manner, method, musical 'mode' (in late Latin also 'mood' in grammar and logic), f. W. Indogermanic **mod*- (:**med*-: see METE *v.*). In branch II, a. F. *mode* fem., ad. L. *modus* (with change of gender due to the final *e*); the Fr. word had in the 16th c. developed the sense of 'fashion', and this was adopted into Eng. in the 17th c.

The F. *mode* (15th c. in Hatz-Darm.) remained fem. in all uses until the 17th c., when the masc. gender was adopted for the uses, chiefly technical, that belonged to L. *modus*. For the sense 'fashion' the fem. gender was retained. Sp., Pg., and It. have *modo* (from Latin) manner, etc., *moda* (from Fr.) fashion; the Fr. word in the latter sense has been adopted as G. *mode*, Da. *mode*, Sw. *mod.*]

I. In senses derived directly from the Latin.

1. *Mus.* **a.** A kind or form of scale; a particular scheme or system of sounds. (*a*) In ancient Greek music: Each of the scales or sets of sounds, according to one or other of which a piece of music in the diatonic style was composed; denoted by special names (Dorian, Phrygian, Lydian, etc.) and each having a special character attributed to it. Sometimes also applied to the scales used in other (e.g. Oriental) systems of music.

c **1374** CHAUCER *Boeth.* II. pr. i. 20 (Camb. MS.), Musyce A damysel of oure hows þat syngeth now lyhtere moedes or probasyons now heuyere [orig. *nunc leviores, nunc graviores modos*]. **1674** PLAYFORD *Skill Mus.* I. xi. 57 That which the Grecians called Mode or Mood, the Latins termed Tone or Tune. *a* **1727** NEWTON *Chronol. Amended* i. (1728) 59 He [Terpander] was the first who distinguished the modes of Lyric music by several names. **1841** ELPHINSTONE *Hist. Ind.* III. vii. I. 297 The Hindú music appears..to be systematic and refined. They have eighty-four modes, of which thirty-six are in general use, and each of which, it appears, has a peculiar expression. **1867** MACFARREN *Harmony* i. 8 In the diatonic genus, the Greeks had several modes.

(*b*) In mediæval church music: Each of the scales (***ecclesiastical*** or ***Gregorian modes***) in which PLAINSONG was composed (derived from and named after, but not always corresponding to, the ancient Greek ones); beginning on different notes of the natural scale, and thus having the intervals (tones and semitones) differently arranged. AUTHENTIC *modes*, PLAGAL *modes*: see these words.

1721 A. MALCOLM *Treat. Mus.* ix. 563 Authentick and.. plagal Modes. **1782** BURNEY *Hist. Mus.* II. 14 The Eight Tones or Ecclesiastical Modes. **1839** *Penny Cycl.* XV. 296/1 In what is called the Gregorian Chant there are eight modes, or tones... The Authentic modes are the Dorian, Phrygian, Lydian, and Mixo-Lydian of the antients. **1881** MACFARREN *Counterp.* iii. 6 A mode in the mediæval church was a distribution of..notes..which varied in the order of the tones and semitones according to what note was chosen for the key-note.

(*c*) In modern music: Each of the two species or classes (***major*** and ***minor***) of keys, having the intervals differently arranged: corresponding respectively to the Ionian and Æolian ecclesiastical modes. Formerly sometimes = KEY *sb.*¹ 7 b.

1721 A. MALCOLM *Treat. Mus.* ix. 274, I would propose the Word *Mode*, to express the melodious Constitution of the Octave..; and because there are Two Species, let us call that with a *3d g* the *greater Mode*, and that with a *3d l* the *lesser Mode*. *Ibid.* 277 The *3d* and *5th* of any Mode or Key deserve the Name of *essential Notes*. **1777** SIR W. JONES *Ess. Imit. Arts* Poems, etc. 198 Now a series of sounds relating to one leading note is called a mode, or a tone, and, as there are twelve semitones in the scale, each of which may be made in its turn the leader of a mode, it follows that there are twelve modes. **1797** *Encycl. Brit.* (ed. 3) IX. 285/1 Major or minor intervals, as they prevail, characterize the major or minor mode. **1880** C. H. H. PARRY in Grove *Dict. Mus.* II. 460 The Dominant major ninth is only used in the major mode, the minor ninth in both.

b. The proportion of a long to a large and to a breve; = MOOD *sb.*² 3. *Obs.* exc. *Hist.*

1667 SIMPSON *Compend. Pract. Mus.* 14 In former times they had four Moods or Modes of measuring Notes. **1782** BURNEY *Hist. Mus.* II. 421 The Circle with a point of perfection in the center, thus ⊙, was the Sign for the *great Mode perfect*, in which all long notes were equal in duration to *three* of the next shorter in degree. **1880** W. S. ROCKSTRO in Grove *Dict. Mus.* II. 340 In the Great Mode Perfect, the Large is equal to three Longs. In the Great Mode Imperfect, it is equal to two only. In the Lesser Mode Perfect, the Long is equal to three Breves. In the Lesser Mode Imperfect it is equal to two.

2. a. *Gram.* = MOOD *sb.*² 2. Also freq. *attrib.*

1520 WHITINTON *Vulg.* (1527) 3 Somtyme of the infinytyve mode folowynge. **1581** FULKE in *Confer.* II. (1584) M iij, The wordes..are both the imperatiue mode in the Greeke text. **1751** HARRIS *Hermes* Wks. (1841) 159 Thus have we established a variety of modes: the indicative or declarative,..the potential [etc.]. **1843** *Penny Cycl.* XXVI. 252/2 The term Verb comprehends those words in a language which are used to indicate the relations of mode or mood. **1933** L. BLOOMFIELD *Lang.* xvi. 273 In English..the unreal appears only in clauses introduced by *if* or *though*, or in combination with the phrasal mode-forms (*he would help us*, unreal of *he will help us*). **1946** H. HOIJER et al. *Ling. Struct. Native Amer.* 97 The forms of the verb [in Algonquian] fall into five *orders*. Each order consists of one or more *modes*, each with a full set of forms. **1946** C. MORRIS *Signs, Lang. & Behavior* v. 125 A third possibility..may be called the *mode-use classification*. **1961** R. B. LONG *Sentence & its Parts* 495 Five modes are recognized here: common (or 'indicative'), subjunctive, infinitival, gerundial, participial. **1965** *Canad. Jrnl. Ling.* Spring 175 We have now considered all the verb prefixes except those for mode-aspect. The Eyak mode-aspect system is relatively well-proportioned and clear-cut.

b. *Linguistics.* (See quots.)

1954 K. L. PIKE *Lang. in Rel. Human Behavior* I. iii. 35/2 On any level of focus each..emic unit..is divided structurally into three specific kinds of complex overlapping components which I shall call *modes*. **1967** W. A. COOK *On Tagmemes & Transforms* i. 9 Every linguistic sign is defined by its meaning, form and distribution... These are included in Pike's three modes: the manifestation mode, the feature mode, and the distribution mode. *Ibid.* 10 The tagmeme can be fully defined, parallel to the phoneme and morpheme, with its own peculiar feature, manifestation, and distribution modes.

3. *Logic.* [= med.L. *modus*, a rendering of Gr. τρόπος, introduced by the early commentators on Aristotle.] **a.** = MOOD *sb.*² 1.

1532 MORE *Confut. Tindale* III. 290 And thys syllogysme yf Tyndale wolde fayne wyt in what fygure it is made: he shall fynde it in yᵉ fyrst fygure, & the thyrd mode. **1699** T. BAKER *Refl. Learning* v. 51 To reduce our..loose reasonings to certain Rules, and make them conclude in Mode and Figure. **1774** REID *Aristotle's Logic* iii. §2 Wks. II. 694/2 The Mode of a syllogism is determined by the Quality and Quantity of the propositions of which it consists. **1843** MILL *Logic* II. ii. §1 Each figure is subdivided into modes, according to what are called the quantity and quality of the propositions.

b. The character of a modal proposition as either necessary, contingent, possible, or impossible; each of the four kinds into which modal propositions are divided as having one or another of these qualities. Also in wider use (see quots.).

1852 MANSEL *Aldrich's Logic* (ed. 2) 45. **1937** A. SMEATON tr. *Carnap's Logical Syntax of Lang.* IV. §68. 247 Some of the known examples of intensional sentences belong to the autonymous mode of speech. **1941** O. HELMER tr. *Tarski's Introd. Logic* viii. 175 The proof of Theorem 1—like any other indirect mode of inference—can be brought under the schema sketched above. **1946** C. I. LEWIS *Analysis of Knowl.* I. iii. 39 It is desirable to recognize two further modes also, which will here be called, respectively, comprehension and signification. **1965** J. O. URMSON *Philos. Analysis* 37 'Xs are logical constructions' is in the material mode of speech. **1966** W. V. QUINE *Ways of Paradox* xiii. 156 Whatever may be said about necessity may be said also, with easy and obvious adjustments, about the other modes. **1970** A. E. BLUMBERG tr. *Stegmüller's Main Currents Contemp. Germ., Brit. & Amer. Philos.* vi. 234 Two modes may *exclude* each other (necessity and impossibility). *Ibid.* vii. 308 Put in the formal mode his thesis simply states that all thing-statements can be translated into a sense-data language (a phenomenalistic language).

4. a. A way or manner in which something is done or takes place; a method of procedure in any activity, business, etc.

a **1667** JER. TAYLOR *Gold. Grove, Guide Penit.* (1836) 156 The duty itself being once resolved upon, the mode of doing it may easily be found. **1798** WELLINGTON in Gurw. *Desp.* (1837) I. 5 A regular mode of bringing to an amicable adjustment..any questions which might hereafter arise. **1794** PALEY *Evid.* (1825) II. 239 A good man will prefer that mode, by which he can produce the greatest effect. **1818** CRUISE *Digest* (ed. 2) III. 310 The mode in which a seisin of a rent may be acquired, has been already stated. **1825** WATERTON *Wand. S. Amer.* I. i. 88 The only mode then that remains is to proceed by water. **1884** F. TEMPLE *Relat. Relig. & Sci.* vi. (1885) 183 The writer made use of a mode of teaching used commonly enough in the Bible. **1900** L. H. BAILEY *Bot.* 152 When the compartments split in the middle between the partitions, the mode is loculicidal dehiscence.

†**b.** Used for 'mode of expression'. *Obs.*

1779–81 JOHNSON *L. P., Dryden* Wks. II. 385 He who writes much will not easily escape a manner, such a recurrence of particular modes as may be easily noted.

c. *Physics.* Any of the distinct kinds or patterns of vibration that an oscillatory system can sustain.

1867 J. TYNDALL *Sound* v. 188 When we make the same passage [from a fundamental tone to the first overtone] in a stopped pipe, we obtain a note a fifth above the octave. No intermediate modes of vibration are..possible. **1877** RAYLEIGH *Theory of Sound* I. vi. 141 When a string vibrates in its gravest normal mode, the excursion is at any moment proportional to sin $\pi x/l$. *Ibid.*, The production of 'harmonics' by lightly touching the string at the points of aliquot division is a well-known resource of the violinist. All component modes are excluded which have not a node at the point touched. **1911** *Encycl. Brit.* XXV. 454/1 In fig. 34 the stationary wave systems of the first four modes are represented. **1949** H. E. PENROSE *Princ. & Pract. Radar* 626 Energy may be propagated in a wave-guide in a doubly infinite series of modes analogous, to a small extent, to a singly infinite series of modes represented by a fundamental note and its harmonics. The modes are distinguished by the patterns of the lines of force traversing the fields. **1950** STEPHENS & BATE *Wave Motion & Sound* 386 In the theory of the specific heats of a solid the thermal vibrations are supposed to result from many simultaneous modes, whose phases have a random distribution. **1962** *Newnes Conc. Encycl. Electr. Engin.* 883/2 The various higher-order modes travel [along a waveguide] with different velocities. **1969** L. ALLEN *Essent. Lasers* ii. 13 The large number of modes at infrared or optical frequencies which are present in any cavity of reasonable size poses problems. This is because of the need for a high level of spontaneous emission to ensure that sufficient photons go into any one particular mode, to maintain the rate of stimulated emission.

5. a. A particular form, manner, or variety (of some quality, process, or condition). Now *rare* exc. in uses (e.g. in ***mode of life***) in which it approaches sense 4.

1661 GLANVILL *Van. Dogm.* iii. 23 If they finde a determinate intellection of any Modes of Being, which were never in the least hinted by their externall or internall senses. **1732** POPE *Ess. Man* I. 211 What modes of sight betwixt each wide extreme, The mole's dim curtain, and the lynx's beam. *Ibid.* II. 83 Modes of Self-love the Passions we may call. **1758** JOHNSON *Idler* No. 1 ¶2 Every mode of life has its conveniences. **1781** GIBBON *Decl. & F.* xvii. II. 22 *note*, The mode of superstition which prevailed in their own times. **1791** BOSWELL *Johnson* Mar. an. 1781, Condescending to trifle in the same mode of conceit. *a* **1858** DE QUINCEY *Lang.* Wks. IX. 89 The French language possesses the very highest degree of merit, though not in the very highest mode of merit. **1863** TYNDALL (*title*) Heat considered as a Mode of Motion. **1888** MISS BRADDON *Fatal Three* I. i, She considered her mode of life intensely domestic.

b. *Petrol.* The quantitative mineral (as distinct from chemical) composition of a rock sample. Cf. NORM 2.

1902 W. CROSS et al. in *Jrnl. Geol.* X. 604 We introduce two terms..as substitutes for the cumbrous and oft-repeated expressions, standard mineral composition (that calculated from the rock analysis) and actual mineral composition. For the first we propose the word norm, and for the second the word mode. **1932** A. JOHANNSEN *Descr. Petrogr. Igneous Rocks* II. III (*heading*) Table 63. Modes of sodaclase-granites. **1962** H. R. CORNWALL in A. E. J. Engel et al. *Petrologic Stud.* 361 In ash flows in cooling unit 3 of the Bullfrog Hills caldera..lithologic differences between the lower and upper parts indicate quite certainly that more than one flow is present. The differences are shown by variations in the mode. **1974** *Nature* 16 Aug. 562/2 The Clare Castle gneisses are coarse grained and weakly banded. .. Modes vary within the range: garnet 20–30%, sillimanite 5–20%, plagioclase 25–30%, potash feldspar 10–20% and quartz 10–40%.

6. *Philos.* **a.** A manner or state of being of a thing; a thing considered as possessing certain attributes that do not belong to its essence, and may be changed without destroying its identity. **b.** An attribute or quality of a substance; 'an accidental determination' (J.). **c.** In Locke's use: A 'complex idea' which denotes neither a substance nor a relation. ***mixed mode***: a 'mode' formed by the combination of different simple ideas; opposed to ***simple mode***, a mode formed by the repetition of the same simple idea. *Obs.*

1677 GALE *Crt. Gentiles* II. IV. Proem 5 Finite Ens or Being may be distributed into substance or Mode... Mode is not a complete ens or being, neither is it a mere nonentitie or nothing. **1678** *Ibid.* III. 6 Moralitie is a mode not physically or intrinsecally inherent in human acts. **1681** GLANVILL *Sadducismus* 143 That a Spirit is not an Accident or Mode of Substance, all in a manner profess. **1690** LOCKE *Hum. Und.* II. xii. §4 Modes, I call such complex Ideas, which, however compounded, contain not in them the supposition of subsisting by themselves, but are consider'd as Dependances on, or Affections of Substances; such are the Ideas signify'd by the Words Triangle, Gratitude, Murder. **1704** CLARKE *Being & Attributes of God* Wks. 1738 II. 527 To suppose that there is no Being, no Substance in the Universe, to which these Attributes or Modes of Existence are necessarily inherent, is a Contradiction in the very Terms. For Modes and Attributes exist only by the Existence of the Substance to which they belong. **1725** WATTS *Logic* I. ii. §3 The next sort of objects which are represented in our ideas, are called modes, or manners of being. **1727–52** CHAMBERS *Cycl.* s.v. *Spinozism* (end), Since the mode is not really distinct from the substance modified. **1781** COWPER *Anti-Thelyph.* 42 That substances and modes of every kind Are mere impressions on the passive mind.

II. A direct adoption of mod.F. *mode* in the sense of fashion, prevailing fashion or custom.

7. a. A prevailing fashion or conventional custom, practice or style; *esp.* one characteristic of a particular place or period.

c **1645** HOWELL *Lett.* v. xxxviii. (1655) I. 233 He is also good at Larding of meat after the mode of France. **1645** EVELYN *Diary* 8 Feb., Some of our company were flouted at for wearing red cloakes, as the mode then was. **1665** SIR T. HERBERT *Trav.* (1677) 45 The Bannyan and other Indian Females after the Oriental Mode are seldom visible. **1667** MILTON *P.L.* I. 474 Gods Altar to disparage and displace For one of Syrian mode. **1716** LADY M. W. MONTAGU *Let. to C'tess of Mar* 21 Nov., They are..dressed after the French and English modes. **1745** *De Foe's Eng. Tradesman* (1841) I. x. 75 It is the mode to live high, to spend more than we get. **1837** CARLYLE *Fr. Rev.* (1872) III. II. i. 59 There are modes wherever there are men. **1841** CATLIN *N. Amer. Ind.* (1844) II. lviii. 249 These people..have much in their modes as well as in their manners to enlist the attention. **1884** W. C. SMITH *Kildrostan* 69 We are grown To be a sort of dandies in religion, Affecting the last mode.

b. ? Something fashionable.

1841 LADY BLESSINGTON *Idler in France* I. v. 66 Oh, the misery of trying on a new *mode* for the first time, and before a stranger!

c. *Statistics.* The value or range of values of a variate for which there is a maximum number of instances in a given population.

1895 K. PEARSON in *Phil. Trans. R. Soc.* A. CLXXXVI. 345, I have found it convenient to use the term *mode* for the abscissa corresponding to the ordinate of maximum frequency. Thus the 'mean', the 'mode', and the 'median' have all distinct characters. **1906** R. H. LOCK *Rec. Progress in Study of Variations* 89 When dealing with a symmetrical curve the position of the mode is identical with that of the median. **1947** O. L. DAVIES *Statistical Methods in Res. & Production* iii. 27 In most industrial applications, however, distributions with more than one mode (multimodal) are, or should be, rare. The presence of two or more modes usually means that the sample is not homogeneous, i.e. that two or more distinct distributions have been combined. **1948** L. D. & A. CROW *Educ. Psychol.* xx. 393 The score in a given set of data that appears most frequently is called the mode. **1973** *Jrnl. Genetic Psychol.* CXXIII. 87 The Kuhlman–Anderson scores for the one group of *S*s from a fifth-grade class yielded a mean of 93·91, a range of 46, a median of 93, and a mode of 92.

d. [Shortened form of F. *gris mode* fashion grey.] The name given to a variety of shades of grey (see quot. 1930).

1895 *Montgomery Ward Catal.* 125/3 Kid gloves... Colors: Black, brown, tan, mode, slate. **1930** MAERZ & PAUL *Dict. Color* 167/1 Mode..was a term used in the nineteenth century to indicate a *class* of colors..usually on the pale order, running from neutral grays to strongly tinted greys of all hues... The old pattern books contain hundreds of samples of different colors, of every conceivable hue, all called 'Mode'. **1957** M. B. PICKEN *Fashion Dict.* 224/2 *Mode* .., pale, bluish-gray color, sometimes drab.

8. a. Conventional usage in dress, manners, habit of life, etc., *esp.* as observed amongst persons 'of fashion'.

1692 R. L'ESTRANGE *Fables* i. 2 We are to prefer..the Blessings of Providence before..the splendid Curiosities of Mode and Imagination. **1711** STEELE *Spect.* No. 6 ¶4 Is there anything so just, as that Mode and Gallantry should be built upon exerting ourselves in what is proper and agreeable to the Institutions of Justice and Piety among us? **1789** JEFFERSON *Writ.* (1859) II. 554 These sentiments became a matter of mode. **1827** CARLYLE *Misc.* (1857) I. 19 Over which the vicissitudes of mode have no sway. **1894** A. C. HILLIER in *2nd Bk. Rhymers' Club* 80 We know that way they have of old, For it is mode in Opera-land.

†**b.** (***man, people***) ***of mode*** = *man* etc. *of fashion* (see FASHION *sb.* 12 b). *Obs.*

1676 ETHEREDGE (*title*) The Man of Mode, or Sir Fopling Flutter. **1693** *Humours Town* 28 The man of Mode here in Town. **1711** ADDISON *Spect.* No. 119 ¶3 If after this we look on the People of Mode in the Country, we find in them the Manners of the last Age. **1711** STEELE *ibid.* No. 182 ¶3, I..had the Satisfaction to see my Man of Mode put into the Round-House. **1749** BOLINGBROKE *Patriot King* 181 The choice spirits of these days, the men of mode in politics.

†**c.** One who or that which sets or displays the fashion. *Obs.*

1712 STEELE *Spect.* No. 478 ¶9 Every one who is considerable enough to be a Mode. **1818** LADY MORGAN *Autobiog.* (1859) 48, I shall send two dressed dolls for the two babies, as modes.

9. ***the mode***: the fashion or custom in dress, manners, speech, and the like adopted in society for the time being. *arch.*

1649 DK. NEWCASTLE *Country Capt.* I. 11 Wee are governd by the mode, as waters by the moone. **1672** DRYDEN *Assignation* Prol., But, gentlemen, you overdo the mode. **1697** —— *Virgil, Life* *4 b, The Devotion..was their Interest, and, which sometimes avails more, it was the Mode. **1706** ADDISON *Rosamond* III. iv, It suits a person in my station T' observe the mode, and be in fashion. **1728** YOUNG *Love Fame* v, The mode she fixes by the gown she wears. **1849** SAXE *Poems, Times* 303 Slaves to the Mode, who pinch the aching waist And mend God's image to the Gallic taste. **1898** HENLEY *Lond. Types, Barmaid*, Cheaply the mode she shadows.

†**10.** In phrases: ***in, out of (the) mode***, in, out of fashion or customary use, esp. in 'polite' society; ***all, much the mode***, said of the object of a general but usually temporary popularity. *Obs.*

1664 EVELYN *Kal. Hort.* 25 This Tree is now all the mode for the Avenues to their Countrey palaces in France. **1669** WORLIDGE *Syst. Agric.* (1681) 175 The white Shock-Rabbit of Turkie is..now become the most in Mode. **1672** J. CRESSET in *N. Eng. Hist. & Gen. Reg.* (1868) XXII. 83 When they have come to Town, they must presently be in the mode, get fine clothes. **1673** *Remarques Humours Town* 3 These things are set formalities, and out of Mode. *a* **1680** BUTLER *Rem.* (1759) I. 101 Nothing can be bad or good, But as 'tis in or out of Mode. **1738** SWIFT *Pol. Conversat.* 117 Why Tom, you are high in the Mode. **1760** FRANKLIN *Lett.* Wks. 1840 VI. 230 If I would finish my letter in the mode, I should yet add something that means nothing. **1766** *Ann. Reg., Charac.* 5/2 Monsieur de Belleisle was then much the mode, being spoken of both at court and at Paris. **1773** GOLDSM. *Stoops to Conq.* II. i, What do you take to be the most fashionable age about town? Some time ago, forty was all the mode. **1849** MACAULAY *Hist. Eng.* iii. I. 408 In a few months experimental science became all the mode.

†**11. a.** = ALAMODE 4. Also *attrib.*

1751 *MacSparran Diary* (1899) 407 A la mode (or mode) was a thin, glossy silk, used for hoods, scarfs, &c. **1766** W. GORDON *Gen. Counting-ho.* 429, 33¾ yards figured mode. **1777** *Ann. Reg., Chron.* 213/1 A black silk mode cloak and other apparel. **1795** *Edin. Advert.* 6 Jan. 15/1 A Variety of Articles in the Haberdashery line..consisting of Modes,.. Vellum Modes,..Sattins, &c. **1796** *Hist. Ned Evans* I. 156, I will lay my mode cloak to a brass pin. **1819** J. H. VAUX *Mem.* I. 119, I began my depredations by taking a piece of elegant black mode. **1826** MISS MITFORD *Village* Ser. II. 55 Her close black bonnet of that silk which once..was fashionable, since it is still called mode. **1864** *Cornh. Mag.* Aug. 136 She had on a black mode cloak that had been her mother's. **1900** *Academy* 21 July 41/1 Her train of soft mode silk, she held up at the back as she walked.

b. ? An article made of this material.

1847 C. BRONTË *J. Eyre* xviii, Brocaded and hooped petticoats, satin sacques, black modes, lace lappets, &c.

12. *pl. Lace-making*: (See second quot.).

1882 COLE in *Encycl. Brit.* XIV. 185/2 The use of meshed grounds extended [1650–1720], and grounds composed entirely of varieties of modes were made. **1882** CAULFEILD & SAWARD *Dict. Needlework*, *Modes*, a term used in Lace making to denote the open work Fillings between the thick parts of the design.

†**13.** (See quot.) *Obs.*

1688 R. HOLME *Armoury* II. 117/1 Modes, or self coloured flowers.

III. 14. *attrib.*, as **mode-book**, a fashion-book; **mode-locking** *Physics*, a technique by which the phase of each mode of oscillation in a laser is 'locked' to those of the two adjacent modes (so that a fixed phase relationship arises between all the modes), resulting in the emission at intervals of about a nanosecond of short trains of extremely short pulses whose duration is of the order of picoseconds; so **mode-locked** *a.*, applied to a laser in which this technique is employed and to the resulting pulses; (as a back-formation) **mode-lock** *v. trans.*, to subject (a laser) to mode-locking.

1861 MRS. H. WOOD *East Lynne* vii, Her head-dress..was like nothing in the mode-book or out of it. **1966** *Appl. Physics Lett.* VIII. 182/1 The YAIG:Nd laser was mode locked over a frequency width of order 12·6 Gc/sec (42 × 300 Mc/sec). **1971** *Physics Bull.* Dec. 718/2 Flashlamp pumped dye lasers have been successfully modelocked to produce high power pulses of transform-limited durations of 2–3 ps. **1965** *IEEE Jrnl. Quantum Electronics* I. 16/2 The light pulses from a mode-locked laser were observed with a magnetically focussed photo-multiplier tube. **1971** *Sci. Amer.* June 24/1 As the energy in the laser cavity is built up and then decays, a string of such mode-locked pulses emerges from the partially transmitting mirror in the front of the cavity. **1965** *IEEE Jrnl. Quantum Electronics* I. 16/1 (*heading*) Effect of mode-locking. **1967** *Science* 23 June 1558/3 In the first experimental demonstration of 'mode-locking', helium-neon and argon lasers were used.

†**mode**, *v. Obs. rare.* [f. MODE *sb.*]

1. *trans.* or quasi-*trans.* **a.** To put (a person) *into* fashionable clothing. **b.** ***to mode it***, to follow the fashion.

1656 BLOUNT *Glossogr.* To Rdr. A ij b, In London many of the Tradesmen have new Dialects... The Taylor is ready to mode you into a Rochet, Mandillion [etc.]. *a* **1661** FULLER *Worthies, Sussex* (1662) III. 102 He was accounted.. somewhat Clownish,..partly, because he could not mode it with the Italians. *Ibid., Warwick* III. 119 He could not Mode it, or comport, either with French ficleness, or Italian pride.

2. *intr.* To be or become 'the mode'.

1663 *Cup of Coffee* 5 Pure English Apes! ye may, for aught I know, Would it but mode, learn to eat spiders too.

modee, obs. form of MOODY.

modefy(e, -fyshe, obs. ff. MODIFY, MUDFISH.

model ('mɒdəl), *sb.* Forms: 6 **modill, moddell**, 6–7 **moddel**, 6–8 **modell, modle**, 7 **modil**, 7–8 **modelle**, 6– **model**. [a. OF. *modelle* (mod.F. *modèle*), ad. It. *modello*, dim. of *modo*, ad. L. *modus*: see MODE *sb.* From It. or Fr. the word has passed into other langs.: Ger. and Sw. *modell*, Du. and Da. *model*. Cf. MODULE *sb.*]

I. Representation of structure.

†**1. a.** An architect's set of designs (plans, elevations, sections, etc.) for a projected building; hence, a similar set of drawings made to scale and representing the proportions and arrangement of an existing building. Also occas. a delineation of a ground-plan (*e.g.* of a town, a garden, etc.) *Obs.*

1575 GASCOIGNE *Posies, Herbes* 173 And I shall well my sillie selfe content, To come alone vnto my louely Lorde, And vnto him..To tel some..reasonable worde, Of Hollandes state, the which I will present, In Cartes, in Mappes, and eke in Models made. **1579–80** NORTH *Plutarch, Pompeius* (1595) 695 Pompey liked exceedingly

well the Theater..and drew a modell or platforme of it to make a statelyer then that in Rome. **1581** SIDNEY *Apol. Poetrie* (Arb.) 33 The same man, as soone as hee might see those beasts well painted, or the house wel in moddel, should straightwaies grow without need of any description, to a iudicial comprehending of them. *c* **1582** T. DIGGES in *Archæologia* XI. 228 The proportion of the fludgates and capestainds..shall in modell bee allsoe sett downe. **1597** SHAKS. *2 Hen. IV*, I. iii. 142 When we meane to build, We first suruey the Plot, then draw the Modell. **1601** SIR W. CORNWALLIS *Ess.* II. xl. (1631) 166 Cottages may be built without modelles, not pallaces. **1617–18** W. LAWSON *New Orch. & Gard.* (1623) Pref., The Stationer hath..bestowed much cost and care in hauing the Knots and Models by the best Artizan cut in great varietie. **1625** BACON *Ess., Gardens* (end), So I haue made a Platforme of a Princely Garden, Partly by Precept, Partly by Drawing, not a Modell, but some generall Lines of it. **1639** [see PLATFORM 2]. **1714** SWIFT *Pres. St. Affairs* Wks. 1755 II. I. 205 When a building is to be erected, the model may be the contrivance only of one head.

fig. **1599** SHAKS. *Much Ado* I. iii. 48 Will it serue for any Modell to build mischiefe on? **1611** TOURNEUR *Ath. Trag.* II. ii, My plot still rises According to the Modell of mine owne desires.

b. *transf.* A summary, epitome, or abstract; the 'argument' of a literary work. *Obs.*

a **1626** BACON *Let. to T. Matthew* in Spedding *Life & Lett.* (1870) IV. 133 Of this, when you were here, I shewed you some model. *a* **1627** MIDDLETON *Wom. Beware Wom.* V. i. 107 The actors that this model here discovers Are only four. *a* **1649** WINTHROP *New Eng.* (1826) II. 231 That treatise about arbitrary government, which he first tendered to the deputies in a model, and finding it approved by some, and silence in others, he drew it up more at large. **1760–72** H. BROOKE *Fool of Qual.* (1809) III. 45, I have now..given you the..unformed rudiments of our Britannic constitution. And here I deliver to you my little model of the finished construction thereof.

†**c.** A description of structure. *Obs.*

1578 T. DIGGES in L. Digges *Progn. Everlasting* To Rdr. M, I founde a description or Modill of the world and situation of Spheres Cœlestial and Elementare according to the doctrine of Ptolome. *Ibid.*, But in this our age one rare witte..hath by long studie,..deliuered a new Theoricke, or model of the world, shewing that the earth resteth not in the Center of the whole world, but only in the Center of thys our mortal world.

2. a. A representation in three dimensions of some projected or existing structure, or of some material object artificial or natural, showing the proportions and arrangement of its component parts. ***working model***, one so constructed as to imitate the movements of the machine which it represents.

1615 G. SANDYS *Trav.* 221 Menelaus with fiftie ships, sent him only one, with the models of the other in clay, to colour his perjury. **1662** PEPYS *Diary* 30 July, Cooper..begun his lecture upon the body of a ship, which my having of a modell in the office is of great use to me, and very pleasant and useful it is. **1665** MOXON tr. *Vignola* (1702) 76 If they were all cut out, and placed one above another..you would..have the Model of a true pair of Stairs. **1676** T. MILLER *Compl. Modellist* 1 When you go to raise the Model of any Ship or Vessel, you must in the first place know the Length of her Keel [etc.]. **1697** BP. PATRICK *Comm. Exod.* XXV. 9. 483 The Hebrew word *Tabnit*..signifies a Structure, or Building; which cannot be better expressed than by the word Model, which he now saw of the House he was to erect. **1727** DE FOE *Syst. Magic* I. i. (1840) 30 Prometheus, who..is feigned by the poets to have first formed Man; that is to say, formed the Model of a Man by the help of water and earth, and then stole fire from the sun to animate the Model. **1766** tr. *Hasselquist's Voy. Levant* 149 They..force them to buy..models of the grave of Christ. **1824** R. STUART *Hist. Steam Engine* 96 The university's collection of mechanical and philosophical models. **1832** G. DOWNES *Lett. Cont. Countries* I. 192 A model of William Tell stands opposite another of his son. They are formed of wood. **1847** TENNYSON *Princess* Prol. 73 A dozen angry models jetted steam. **1850** MRS. JAMESON *Leg. Monast. Ord.* (1863) 149 At his feet is a small model of a hill. **1875** *Encycl. Brit.* III. 833/2 Mr. Brunel had completed a working model of certain machines for constructing..blocks.

b. *fig.* Something that accurately resembles something else; a person or thing that is the likeness or 'image' of another; *esp.* in ***little model***, a thing that represents on a small scale the structure or qualities of something greater. *Obs.* exc. *colloq.* or *dial.* in ***the*** (***very***) ***model of***.

1593 SHAKS. *Rich. II*, I. ii. 28 Thou dost consent In some large measure to thy Fathers death, In that thou seest thy wretched brother dye, Who was the modell of thy Fathers life. **1602** —— *Ham.* V. ii. 50, I had my fathers Signet in my Purse, Which was the Modell of that Danish Seale. **1603** DRAYTON *Bar. Wars* IV. xxxiv, Seeing Lundy that so faire doth stand,..This little modell of his banish'd Land. **1613** PURCHAS *Pilgrimage* (1614) 21 Delighted (as the Father in his Childe) in this new modell of himselfe. **1663** BP. PATRICK *Parab. Pilgr.* xv. (1687) 131 These quiet places are the resemblances of the serene regions above, and little models of Heaven. **1824** HOGG *Conf. Sinner* 138 The likeness to my late hapless young master is so striking, that I can hardly believe it to be a chance model. **1899** CROCKETT *Little Anna Mark* lii. (1900) 438 He minds me of Sir James—the very model of Sir James.

c. An archetypal image or pattern.

1742 YOUNG *Nt. Th.* IX. 1337 When shall I..Gaze on creation's model in thy breast Unveil'd, nor wonder at the transcript more? **1785** REID *Intell. Powers* 421 Every work of art has its model framed in the imagination.

d. *Dentistry.* A positive copy of the teeth or oral cavity, which is cast in metal, plaster, etc., from an impression (sense 2 e) and which may be used to construct dental appliances.

1839 C. A. HARRIS *Dental Art* xxi. 348 The obtaining of a model of the alveolar ridge, or ridges, when one for each jaw is required, though apparently very easy, is nevertheless often attended with some difficulty. **1857** *Brit. Jrnl. Dental Sci.* I. 579/1 Mr. Saunders thought that the plan of bending down the front part of the model could be fatal to a correct impression. **1917** F. A. PEESO *Crown & Bridge-Work* vii. 140 When the plaster for the impression has been tinted, the impression and model are easily distinguished by the difference in coloring. **1938** *Dental Rec.* LVIII. 14, I think, from a study of the original models, that there had probably been pyorrhœa for some years. **1940** [see IMPRESSION *sb.* 2 e]. **1973** D. H. ROBERTS *Fixed Bridge Prostheses* v. 66 Only one model can be poured from each impression.

e. A simplified or idealized description or conception of a particular system, situation, or process (often in mathematical terms: so ***mathematical model***) that is put forward as a basis for calculations, predictions, or further investigation.

Cf. sense 1 c.

1913 N. BOHR in *Phil. Mag.* XXVI. 1 To explain the results of experiments on scattering of α rays by matter Prof. Rutherford has given a theory of the structure of atoms. According to this theory, the atoms consist of a positively charged nucleus surrounded by a system of electrons [etc.]. .. Great interest is to be attributed to this atom-model. **1923** [see BOHR]. **1938** R. W. LAWSON tr. *Hevesy & Paneth's Man. Radioactivity* (ed. 2) viii. 89 These and other fundamental facts were responsible for the introduction of the model of the atom already described. In spite of these facts, however, it was later necessary to replace the atomic model by conceptions of a less concrete nature..in order to be able to interpret more complicated spectra. **1939** H. LEVY *Mod. Sci.* xxx. 515 Models of the universe have been erected that enable us with varying degrees of definiteness to picture these earlier stages. **1940** *Econ. Jrnl.* L. 91 Previous models of the Trade Cycle..have thus mostly been based on the assumption of statically stable situations, where equilibrium would persist if once reached. **1949** *Econometrica* XVII. 193 The Mathematical Model discussed here..is a generalization of the Leontief Inter-Industry Model. **1958** *Listener* 11 Dec. 972/1, I want to discuss the cosmological theories which are generally classed as the evolutionary models of the universe. **1969** J. ARGENTI *Managem. Techniques* 170 *Any* set of mathematical equations, linking together a complexity of factors and used to study the effects of change, is a Model. **1969** *Sci. Jrnl.* Dec. 27/1 Mathematical models of the global atmosphere..can now be constructed with the aid of large, fast computers to handle the enormous quantities of data and the complex equations that represent the movements and heat balance of the atmosphere. **1970** *Nature* 21 Nov. 719/2 The equivalence of the corpuscular and wave models in the theory of optics. **1971** *Daily Tel.* (Colour Suppl.) 3 Dec. 24/3 Forrester has designed a model of the world system to try to discover the long term effects of pollution and overpopulation. The model, processed through a computer, predicts a variety of different futures. **1972** G. H. A. COLE in Cox & Dyson *20th-Cent. Mind* I. viii. 250 A system of physical concepts and quantities that describes the main features of a situation is known as a model. **1973** *Sci. Amer.* Dec. 117/1 There are many other varieties of speech error. All of them must be accounted for in a model of speech production.

f. *spec.* in *Mathematical Logic.* A set of entities that satisfies all the formulas of a given formal or axiomatic system.

1940 W. V. QUINE *Math. Logic* vi. 271 The fact that such classes constitute a model of the traditional real number system was pointed out by Dedekind. **1948** *Jrnl. Symbolic Logic* XIII. 16 (*heading*) Models of logical systems. **1952** S. C. KLEENE *Introd. Metamath.* ii. 25 When the objects of the system are known only through the relationships of the system, the system is abstract... Then any further specification of what the objects are gives a representation (or model) of the abstract system, i.e. a system of objects which satisfy the relationships of the abstract system and have some further status as well. These objects are not necessarily more concrete, as they may be chosen from some other abstract system (or even from the same one under a reinterpretation of the relationships). **1963** W. V. QUINE *Set Theory* vi. 135 We have provided a model of arithmetic in set theory when we have provided a way of so reinterpreting arithmetical notations in set-theoretic terms as to carry the truths of arithmetic into truths of set theory. **1974** *Encycl. Brit. Macropædia* XI. 639/2 By Gödel's completeness theorem of 1930, if a formal system based on the first-order functional calculus *F* is consistent, there is a model in which the objects are the natural numbers.

†**3.** A mould; something that envelops closely.

1593 SHAKS. *Rich. II*, III. ii. 153 Nothing can we call our own but Death, And that small Modell of the barren Earth, which serues as Paste and Couer to our Bones. **1599** —— *Hen. V*, II. Prol. 16 O England: Modell to thy inward Greatnesse, Like little Body with a mightie Heart.

†**4.** A small portrait. Hence confused with MEDAL. *Obs.*

1622 MALYNES *Anc. Law-Merch.* 356 Modells or Medalia to be worne by the said hundreth persons of the societie, and the Masters of counting houses. **1626** BOYLE in *Lismore Papers* (1886) II. 190, I receaved..a chayn, and the kings picture or modull of gowld fastened to the chayn of gold. **1658** WALTON *Life Donne* (ed. 2) 91 That model of Gold of the Synod of Dort, with which the States presented him at his last being at the Hague.

5. An object or figure made in clay, wax, or the like, and intended to be reproduced in a more durable material. †Also, *rarely*, a sketch or study made for a painting.

1686 AGLIONBY *Painting Illustr.* Explan. Terms, Model. Is any Object that a Painter works by, either after Nature, or otherwise; but most commonly it signifies that which Sculptors, Painters, and Architects make to Govern themselves by in their Design. **1695** DRYDEN *Dufresnoy's Art Painting* Pref. 44 To make a Sketch, or a more perfect Model of a Picture, is in the language of Poets, to draw up the Scenary of a Play. **1845** *Encycl. Metrop.* VIII. 456/1 He [*i.e.* the mould maker] then pours the semi-fluid around and over the [clay] model until the upper part has the designed thickness. **1856** *Eng. Cycl., Biogr.* II. 929 (*Flaxman*), The contents of his studio included nearly all his working models, casts of all his chief works, &c.

6. *Plastering.* A tool for moulding a cornice, having a pattern in profile which is impressed upon the plaster by working the tool backwards and forwards. Cf. MOULD.

1825 J. NICHOLSON *Operat. Mechanic* 606 Plastering. The tools of the plasterer consist of..rules called straight-edges; and wood models. *Ibid.*, The models or moulds are for running plain mouldings, cornices, &c. **1842** GWILT *Archit.* §2233.

II. Type of design.

7. Design, structural type; style of structure or form; pattern, build, make. **a.** of material structures.

1597 HOOKER *Eccl. Pol.* v. xiv. §1 A fault no lesse grieuous, ..then if some King should build his mansion house by the modell of Salomons palace. **1660** F. BROOKE tr. *Le Blanc's Trav.* 46 This Town is..built very stately at the Italian model. **1698** FRYER *Acc. E. India & P.* 107 These Vessels that are for this Voyage are huge unshapen things, and bear both the Name and Model of their old Junks. **1778** *Eng. Gazetteer* (ed. 2), Putney..has a church after the same model with that of Fulham. **1829** I. TAYLOR *Enthus.* iii. (1867) 55 Each of his works is perfect, both in model and in movement.

b. of immaterial things, systems, institutions, etc.

In the 17th and 18th c. often in ***new model***, denoting a remodelling of some institution, etc.

1593 G. HARVEY *Pierces Super.* Wks. (Grosart) II. 43 Such a new-devised modell, as neuer Sun saw before... Old Archilochus and Theon were but botchers in their rayling faculty. **1647** CLARENDON *Hist. Reb.* II. §10 It was now easy ..to suggest..that here was an entire new Model of Government in Church and State. **1678** CUDWORTH *Intell. Syst.* I. i. §45. 53 That new Modle of Ethicks, which hath been obtruded upon the world..is no Ethicks at all. **1725** DE FOE *Compl. Eng. Gent.* (1890) 22 Exactly after the modelle of the Common-wealth of Rome. **1747** W. HORSLEY *Fool* (1748) II. 331 This new Modelle of Things has quite corrupted the very Soul of Naval Affairs. **1759** ROBERTSON *Hist. Scot.* VIII. Wks. 1851 II. 239 Such acts as..paved the way for a full and legal establishment of the presbyterian model. **1764** FOOTE *Mayor of G.* II. Wks. 1799 I. 176 He will put us into the model of the thing at once. **1874** GREEN *Short. Hist.* viii. §5. 508 The new faith..borrowed from Calvin its model of Church government. **1875** JOWETT *Plato* (ed. 2) III. 51 Limited in size, after the traditional model of a Greek state.

c. ***the*** (***New***) ***Model*** (Hist.): the plan for the reorganization of the Parliamentary army, passed by the House of Commons in 1644–5.

1645 CROMWELL *Let. to Fairfax* 4 June in Carlyle *Lett. & Sp.*, That you would be pleased to make Captain Rawlins.. a Captain of Horse. He has been so before; was nominated to the Model. **1645** WHITELOCKE *Mem.* 10 Jan., The commons..debated about the new model of the army. *Ibid.* 5 Feb., Debate about the ordinance for the new model. *Ibid.* 2 Apr., The new model was by them [*sc.* the king's party] in scorn called the new noddle.

d. An article of apparel of a particular design; a specified type or design of clothing; freq. with defining word prefixed.

1880 *Queen* 12 June (Advt.), Messrs Jay import from the first houses in Paris. Models of every style. **1906** *Bazaar, Exchange & Mart* Suppl. 3 Oct. 1308/1 Great bargains in ladies' wearing apparel, new and equal to new. Paris models. **1912** *Tatler* 23 Oct. 105 The forthcoming models are more than usually extravagant and..the latest creations all seem to have been designed 'regardless of cost'. **1933** N. COWARD *Design for Living* I. 22 A silly pride made me show off to you, parade my attraction for you, like a mannequin. New spring model, with a few extra flounces! **1958** [see CASUALNESS]. **1975** *Times* 29 July 8/5 The Valentino collection is untypically small... Strikes..have dogged the production of the models.

e. A motor vehicle of a particular design; a vehicle produced in a specified year; also *transf.*, one of a series of varying designs of the same type of object; also *fig.* ***Model T***, an early type of car produced by the American Ford Company; also allusively, of a person or thing that is outmoded, mass-produced, etc. Also *attrib.* or as *adj.*

1900 *Automobile Topics* 22 Dec. 366/1 For sale. Two-passenger Winton, 1900 model, in first-class condition. **1901** *Ibid.* 21 Sept. 848 Type No. 2. Model 'C'—12 HP. Double Cylinder Gasoline Engine. **1909** *Automobile* 7 Jan. 9/1 Henry Ford made a name for himself which will cling for all time when he handed out a replica of a full-fledged automobile of the four-cylinder type at the price of a runabout—nay, at the price of the cheapest runabouts. Model T of the Ford line is in the same class, in that it is all automobile and no price. **1909** *Westm. Gaz.* 2 Nov. 5/1 The engine of the 20-h.p. model..is of the monobloc order. **1910** *Ibid.* 4 Jan. 5/2 Mr. Huff pays a visit to Europe..to inspect the new models at Olympia. **1912** V. W. PAGÉ *Mod. Gasoline Automobile* xii. 618 The Ford car is one of the most popular of moderate-priced automobiles and over 100,000 of the Model 'T' are now on the road. *Ibid.* 619 (*caption*) Outlining the distinctive control system of Ford Model 'T' automobile. **1927** *Motor Cycling* 7 Dec. 102 (*heading*) Road tests of 1928 models. **1930** L. MUMFORD *City Devel.* (1946) 62 One might call this the model T dilemma. Mass-production..suffers..from rigidity. **1930** H. CRANE *Let.* 29 Dec. (1965) 360 The middle west business man, approved panic model of 1931. **1932** A. HUXLEY *Brave New World* ii. 27 Twenty-three years after Our Ford's first T-Model was put on the market. **1942** E. PAUL *Narrow St.* ii. 17 Mary drew from somewhere inside her waist a dog-eared American passport of a model no longer in vogue. **1945** *Amer. Speech* XX. 148/1 *Model T*, non-com technician.

1947 *Reader's Digest* Jan. 119/1 Such simple demands as wages, hours and working conditions are strictly Model T. **1955** W. GADDIS *Recognitions* III. ii. 752 The minute you get used to the goddam thing some bastard puts out a new model. **1963** R. WOLFF *I, Keturah* (1964) I. vii. 47 The Model T chugged up the hill. **1966** *Economist* 26 Mar. 1251/2 A return to the one-off, custom-built job, is playing right back into Britain's hands and away from the undeveloped nations churning out marine model-Ts. **1968** *Listener* 23 May 670/1 There are still 405-line-only models, which cannot be converted, on sale. **1970** *Globe & Mail* (Toronto) 26 Sept. B 1/5 During the past model year, the trend was accelerated by the.. fact that the car companies had concentrated in their Canadian plants production of the models that happened to be most successful in the marketplace.

†**8. a.** Scale of construction; allotted measure; the measure of a person's ability or capacity. *Obs.* (Cf. MODULE *sb.* 1, 1 b.)

1605 BACON *Adv. Learn.* I. vii. §19 An Errour ordinarie with Counsellors of Princes, that they counsell their Maisters according to the modell of their owne mind and fortune. **1620** R. CARPENTER *Conscionable Christian* (1623) 39 Hauing.. spoken.. (according to the modell of time allotted for me to speake, and you to heare) of the reall religious practice [etc.]. **1624** F. WHITE *Repl. Fisher* 301 We are farre from appointing ignorant persons to be Iudges of that which exceedeth their modill and skill. **1625** BACON *Unity in Relig.* (Arb.) 427 Of this I may giue onely this Aduice, according to my small Modell. **1651** HOBBES, *Leviath.* II. xxiv. 130 Thus much (considering the modell of the whole worke) is sufficient. **1662** HIBBERT *Body Div.* I. 206 Shall any reduce and shrink up the thoughts and wayes of God to their narrow and straitned model? **1675** BAXTER *Cath. Theol.* II. i. 278, I tell you the Ignorant and Carnal sort of Priests and Fryers did each man talk according to his Model, and so do all Sects.

†**b.** Compass, extent of space. *Obs.*

?*a* **1600** in *Lyly's Wks.* (1902) III. 493 The thundringe God whose all-embracinge powre Circles ye modell of this spatious rounde.

9. Of a violin, viol, etc.: Curvature of surface.

1836 DUBOURG *Violin* ix. (1878) 266 The instruments by the three Amati are rather higher, or less flat, in the model, than those of Straduarius. **1848** J. BISHOP *Otto's Violin* i. (1875) 4 The even side [of the wood for the violin's back or belly] is then smoothed and the model traced on it.

III. An object of imitation.

10. a. A person, or a work, that is proposed or adopted for imitation; an exemplar.

1639 N. N. tr. *Du Bosq's Compl. Woman* I. E iv b, The desire we have to become like to some goodly model. **1693-4** GIBSON in *Lett. Lit. Men* (Camden) 217, I had a letter last night from Dr. Parsons, with a fresh request to send him down a [*sc.* history of a] Countie finished, from whence he might take a model to adjust his own materials. **1714** GAY *Let. to Lady* 31, I then resolved some model to pursue, Perused French critics, and began anew. **1734** tr. *Rollin's Anc. Hist.* (1827) VIII. XIX. v. 156 Which young officers should propose to themselves as a model. **1837** LYTTON *E. Maltrav.* III. ii, Models may form our taste as critics, but do not excite us to be authors. **1838** EMERSON *Addr., Cambridge, Mass.* Wks. (Bohn) II. 202 Imitation cannot go above its model. **1839** THIRLWALL *Greece* VI. 213 The system.. served.. as a model for the policy of Rome under the emperors. **1871** FREEMAN *Norm. Conq.* (1876) IV. xix. 419 [The Church] of Rouen, we are told being his special and immediate model.

b. *Biol.* An animal or plant to which another bears a mimetic resemblance.

1877 *Encycl. Brit.* VI. 127/1 Probably this beetle shared in the immunity from attack accorded to its model. **1907** *Nature* 31 Oct. 673/2 An insect thus resembled by another is spoken of as its 'model', the imitating insect is called a 'mimic'. **1930** R. A. FISHER *Genetical Theory Nat. Selection* 148 The resemblance which is favourable to the mimic will be for the same reason disadvantageous to the model. **1968** R. D. MARTIN tr. *Wickler's Mimicry in Plants & Animals* i. 16 (*caption*) Leaf beetles.. serve as models for roaches.. , which are palatable and resemble their models so closely that they are also avoided by predators. *Ibid.* iv. 43 This weed [*sc.* rye-weed].. is less demanding and tougher than its model, the wheat plant.

11. a. A person, or, less frequently, a thing, that serves as the artist's pattern for a work of painting or sculpture, or for some portion of such a work; *spec.* a person whose profession it is to pose for artists and art-students.

1691 *Emilianne's Frauds Rom. Monks* (ed. 3) 391 [She] commonly serv'd for a Model to the Limners of the Academy. **1727-41** CHAMBERS *Cycl.* s.v., In the academies, they give the term model to a naked man, disposed in several postures. **1860** HAWTHORNE *Marb. Faun* ii, One of those living models.. whom artists convert into saints or assassins, according as their pictorial purposes demand. **1891** KIPLING *Light that Failed* vii. (1900) 159 But remember, old man, she isn't a woman; she's my model; and be careful.

b. *transf.* A person, freq. a woman, who is employed to display clothes by wearing them, or to appear in displays of other goods.

1904 *Books of to-day* May 3 One of the models of the establishment came gracefully towards me. *a* **1911** D. G. PHILLIPS *Susan Lenox* (1917) II. i. 7 She was dressed in the sleek tight-fitting trying-on robe of the professional model. **1958** *Woman's Own* 5 Feb. 16/2 The first lesson every model learns is to stand and walk correctly. **1959** *Guardian* 26 Oct. 7/7 If the men were only going to become part-time models, they would need to go on doing one or two lessons a fortnight. **1962**, **1970** [see *fashion-model* s.v. FASHION *sb.* 13]. **1971** B. PATTEN *Irrelevant Song* 55 Their beauty more awkward than even the topmost models.

c. A euphemism for 'prostitute'.

1963 [see *company director* s.v. COMPANY *sb.* 10]. **1968** J. LOCK *Lady Policeman* ii. 19 There had been an increase of newsagents' notice-board ads for 'Models'. **1970** G. GREER *Female Eunuch* 195 Working as hostesses in high-class clubs, as 'models' or simply walking the streets.

12. A person or thing eminently worthy of imitation; a perfect exemplar *of* some excellence.

1788 ANNA SEWARD *Lett.* (1811) II. 104 A man [*sc.* Johnson] who, hating dissenters of all denominations, held up the writings of Clarke and the life of Watts as models of perfection. **1794** PALEY *Evid.* II. ii. (1817) 60 The Lord's Prayer is a model of calm devotion. **1805** N. NICHOLLS *Remin.* in *Corr. w. Gray* (1843) 43 Mr. Gray thought the narrative of Thucydides the model of history. **1868** SWINBURNE *Blake* 16 Their vivid and vigorous style is often a model in its kind. **1871** E. F. BURR *Ad Fidem* xi. 211 Models of pure and noble conduct.

13. a. *colloq.* in *pl.* = 'model dwellings' (see 15 a).

1887 *Pall Mall G.* 5 Oct. 4/2 The parish has gone down.. and the building of the 'models' has not made it better. **1896** *Daily Chron.* 25 Aug. 5/6 The ordinary streets and the smaller models, which make up the bulk of the Ghetto, as we find it in Whitechapel [etc.]. **1900** *Daily News* 25 Oct. 3/4 The overcrowding per acre caused by 'models' was just as unhealthy as overcrowding per room.

b. *Sc. colloq.* A model lodging-house (see sense 15 a).

1899 'J. FLYNT' *Tramping with Tramps* II. 233 The price.. is threepence a night, and this is the common price all over Great Britain, except in the so-called 'Models', where a penny more is charged simply for the very deceitful name. **1927** [see *flop-house* s.v. FLOP *sb.* 5]. **1935** MACARTHUR & LONG *No Mean City* xix. 282 'A model' in Gallowgate—one of those buildings which are ironically termed 'Working Men's Hotels'.

IV. 14. †**a.** = MODULE 1. *Obs.*

1598 HAYDOCKE tr. *Lomatius* I. 89 But because Vitruvius measureth this order by models,.. I purpose likewise to keepe the same course, making the diameter of this columne at the base, to consist of two models, whose height with the base and Capitell shal be fourteene models. **1665** MOXON tr. *Vignola* (1702) To Rdr., Our Author to avoid that.. certain uncertainty hath reduc'd all his measure, to a convenient and universal measure, which is called by the Name of a Model [It. *modulo*]: The invention whereof hath made the whole Art of Architecture very easie. **1706** in PHILLIPS (ed. Kersey).

b. = MODILLION. *Obs.*

1663 GERBIER *Counsel* 39 The Models in the Cornishes may be just over the middle of the Column.

V. 15. *attrib.* and *Comb.* **a.** appositive, passing into *adj.*: Serving or intended to serve as a model; suited to be a model, exemplary, ideally perfect, 'pattern'.

model lodging-house: originally, one of a number of lodging-houses, established *c* 1840-5 by various philanthropists and placed under regulations intended to secure the comfort and the orderly conduct of the inmates; the designation was afterwards applied by the proprietors of large lodging-houses to their own establishments, often of a very low class. ***model dwellings***: in London and elsewhere, certain large buildings divided into flats for working-class tenants, intended to supply better arrangements for sanitation and comfort than are obtainable at equally low rent in the same neighbourhoods.

1844 MARG. FULLER *Wom. 19th C.* (1862) 31 Lectures on some model-woman of bride-like beauty and gentleness. **1847** *Illustr. Lond. News* 23 Jan. 61 Model Lodging House in St. Giles's. **1849** J. S. BUCKINGHAM *National Evils* 25 My thoughts were thus.. directed to.. the desirability of forming at least one Model Town. **1856** EMERSON *Eng. Traits, Ability* Wks. (Bohn) II. 35 Sir Kenelm Digby.. was a model Englishman. **1857** KINGSLEY *Two Years Ago* Introd. (1881) I. 22 There's my lord's.. model cottages, with more comforts in them, saving the size, than my father's house had. **1857** GEO. ELIOT *Scenes Clerical Life* (1858) I. 109 What a hobby farming is with Lord Watling! .. It is really a model farm. **1860** *All Year Round* No. 57. 161 A mill-owner, whose mill, I was assured, was a model one. **1885** *Public Opinion* 9 Jan. 32/1 A model Bishop of London is.. more easily imagined than discovered. **1891** *Tablet* 2 May 694 How did so model a youth get on at the University? **1891** M. WILLIAMS *Later Leaves* 369 In the case of many cleared areas,.. model dwellings have been erected for the accommodation of the persons displaced. **1898** E. HOWARD *To-Morrow* iv. 41 Another site for a model city could be purchased. **1909** *Chambers's Jrnl.* Feb. 87/1 It [*sc.* Kinlochleven] is built on the model-town system. **1967** *Boston Globe* 18 May 14/1 The new Congress.. almost stopped the Model Cities program. **1970** G. E. EVANS *Where Beards wag All* xi. 117 A horseman applied for a job with a farmer who had a few years before built himself a *model* farm with the most up-to-date farm buildings and all the latest equipment.

b. simple attrib., chiefly with reference to the life-models employed by artists, as in ***model-day***, ***-stand***, ***-throne***. Also objective, as ***model maker***; ***-building***, ***-making***. Also freq. attrib. in sense 2 a, as ***model aeroplane***, ***aircraft***, ***boat***, ***engine***, ***railway***, ***soldier***, ***train***, ***yacht***.

1920 Model aeroplane [see *model-making* below]. **1973** *Times* 27 July (Suppl.) p. iv/4 Thousands of different hobbies and recreations: toy soldiers, model aeroplanes, cigarette cards. **1951** *Catal. of Exhibits, South Bank Exhib., Festival of Britain* 126/2 Model aircraft. **1974** *Times* 8 Feb. 15/5 Pursuits such as whippet racing and model aircraft flying. **1912** W. OWEN *Let.* 2 July (1967) 147 Bournemouth Cliffs.. and especially the Model-Boat-Canal were.. familiar to me. **1974** *Country Life* 3-10 Jan. 56/4 Model boats wanted... Cased or uncased. **1957** B. F. SKINNER in Saporta & Bastian *Psycholinguistics* (1961) 235/2 Model-building has a special status in the field of verbal behavior. **1972** *Computers & Humanities* VII. 79 His study is one of the richest we have for its methodological innovation, its model-building, and its attempt to treat the political culture of the time both as a system and as a block of evidence for larger concerns. **1873** W. MORRIS in Mackail *Life* (1899) I. 301, I keep it up, dreading the model day like I used to dread Sunday. **1906** E. NESBIT *Railway Children* i. 3 Peter had a birthday—his tenth. Among his other presents he had a model engine. **1598** FLORIO *Worlde of Wordes* 106/2 *Disegnante*, a map or modle maker. **1881** *Instr. Census Clerks* (1885) 55 Figure, Image-Maker... Model Maker. **1946** *Nature* 28 Dec. 928/2 He obtained a job as a model-maker to a firm of instrument manufacturers. **1965** *Math. in Biol. & Med.* (Med. Res. Council) IV. 132 Friendly model-makers from the physical sciences are tempted to construct theories of 'how the brain works' on the basis of a few isolated and easily mathematized facts. **1920** *Glasgow Herald* 29 Oct. 9 The Prince of Wales.. accepted from him a model aeroplane with which he won first prize in the junior section of a model-making competition. **1946** *Nature* 14 Sept. 361/2 The two tanks and propeller-testing tunnel were in operation, and it was possible to see every stage in the process of model-making and testing. **1963** L. LOEVINGER in H. W. Baade *Jurimetrics* 32 The basic elements that these procedures have in common are explication, model-making (or operational organization or programming), and the production of a testable conclusion. **1974** *Country Life* 12 Dec. 1869/1 The exhibition is divided into several sections each dealing with a different aspect of model-making. **1909** (*title of periodical*) Model railways and locomotives. **1972** *Times* 7 Aug. 2/4 A branch from an elm tree fell on to a model railway at Blenheim Palace. **1938** *Daily Herald* 21 Dec. 6/1 The collecting of model soldiers is a nursery pastime elevated into the dignity of an adult occupation by the word 'research'. **1973** *Country Life* 17 May 1385/1 Model soldiers have gone far beyond the realm of child's play and toy soldiers. **1899** MORROW *Bohem. Paris* 43 They placed the helpless M. Haidor on the model-stand. **1898** WATTS-DUNTON *Aylwin* VIII. ii, A.. burly woman,.. standing on the model-throne between two lay figures. **1969** D. E. WESTLAKE *Up your Banners* (1970) xxxviii. 274 [He] never had a model train set when he was young. **1903** A. BENNETT *Truth about Author* ii. 16 He sailed model yachts for us on the foulest canal in Europe. **1967** M. WADDELL *Otley Pursued* viii. 64 A solitary soul wore gumboots and carried a large white model yacht.

c. Special comb.: **model agency**, an agency that supplies models (sense 11 or 11 b); **model-drawing**, in art-teaching, that branch or stage of study which consists in drawing in perspective from solid figures; **model girl** = sense 11 b; also *attrib.*; **model-room**, a room for the storage or exhibition of models of machinery and the like; **model school**, (*a*) a school intended to be a model in organization, teaching methods, etc.; (*b*) a school where models (sense 11 b) are trained; **model theory**, the theory of models (sense 2 e or, esp., 2 f), dealing with their construction, the conditions of their validity, etc.; so ***model-theoretic***, ***-theoretical*** adjs., ***model-theoretically*** adv.

1945 *Glamour* Nov. 166/2 First, you have an interview with one of the leading model agencies, such as Conover or Powers. *Ibid.* 260/2 The model agency rarely selects girls for a given assignment. Invariably, the photographer calls for the girls he wants. **1950** J. D. MACDONALD *Brass Cupcake* (1955) iv. 41, I went down to New York City... A model agency took me on. **1956** S. BELLOW *Seize the Day* (1957) i. 27, I got hold of the artist and he gave me the number of the model agency. **1972** A. MACVICAR *Golden Venus Affair* vi. 62 He got me work with this model agency. **1973** *Guardian* 25 May 5/5, I mentioned reports that a model agency apparently puts men in touch with call girls. **1843** J. B. WILLIAMS (*title*) A manual for teaching model-drawing from solid forms. **1962** *John o' London's* 4 Jan. 20/1 Witches who are model girls gone macabre. **1973** A. PRICE *October Men* vii. 92 A woman in a big hat, slender like a model-girl. **1974** R. HARRIS *Double Snare* iii. 19 Her figure.. must once have been willowy in the model girl fashion. **1829** in Willis & Clark *Cambridge* (1886) III. 103 A Model Room for the Jacksonian Professor. **1854** DICKENS *Hard T.* I. iii. 15 To think of these vagabonds.. attracting the young rabble from a model school. **1935** *Discovery* Nov. 342/1 The prime cause of the excavation was the announcement that a new model school was to be built on a field.. which.. covered part of the site of Camulodunum. **1966** A. PRIOR *Operators* iv. 40 Robin.. said he knew some people in modelling who could help her... He had not been able to afford the so-called Model School. **1957** *Bull. Amer. Math. Soc.* LXIII. 289 (*heading*) Model-theoretic and decidability theorems concerning generalized products. **1963** A. ROBINSON *Introd. Model Theory* p. vi, The model-theoretic approach to set theory. **1958** *Notices Amer. Math. Soc.* V. 673 (*heading*) Some model-theoretical results concerning weak second-order logic. **1973** J. J. ZEMAN *Modal Logic* p. vi. The systems are studied model-theoretically. **1960** *McGraw-Hill Encycl. Sci. & Technol.* VIII. 525/2 On the basis of model theory, a small, readily modified model can be built and tested at low relative cost and the results applied to the full-scale device. **1967** S. C. KLEENE *Math. Logic* §23. 117 In the predicate calculus, proof theory has the advantage over model theory. **1969** W. A. J. LUXEMBURG (*title*) Applications of model theory to algebra, analysis and probability.

model ('mɒdəl), *v.* [f. prec. sb. Cf. F. *modeler*, Sp., Pg. *modelar*, It. *modellare*.]

†**1. a.** *trans.* To present as in a model or outline; to portray or describe in detail. Also with *forth*, *out*. *Obs.*

1604 DRAYTON *Moses in Map of Miracles* II. 57 Afflicted London,.. When thy affliction seru'd me for a booke, Whereby to modell Egipts miserie. *a* **1649** DRUMM. OF HAWTH. *Poems* (1656) 185 Cease dreames,.. To modell forth the passions of to morrow. *a* **1652** J. SMITH *Sel. Disc.* VII. iii. (1821) 327 Our Saviour, when he models out religion to them, points them out to something fuller of inward life and spirit.

†**b.** To frame a model or theory of the structure of. *Obs.*

1667 MILTON *P.L.* VIII. 79 When they come to model Heav'n And calculate the Starrs.

2. a. To produce or fashion in clay, wax, or the like (a figure or imitation of anything).

1665 *Phil. Trans.* I. 99 Having an extraordinary address in modelling the Figures. **1762–71** H. WALPOLE *Vertue's Anecd. Paint.* (1786) IV. 205 Michael..began by modelling small figures in clay, to show his skill. **1771** BP. HORNE *Disc. Creat. Man* Wks. 1818 II. 9 He moulded or modelled him [*sc.* man] as a potter doth. **1847** EMERSON *Poems, To Rhea* Wks. (Bohn) I. 403, I make this maiden an ensample To Nature,..Whereby to model newer races, Statelier forms, and fairer faces.

absol. **1858** O. W. HOLMES *Aut. Breakf.-t.* ii. (1859) 24, I rough out my thoughts in talk as an artist models in clay.

fig. **1641** MILTON *Reform.* ii. 45 But by what example can they shew that the form of Church Discipline must be minted and modell'd out to secular pretences?

b. [after MODEL *sb.* 2e.] To devise a (usu. mathematical) model of (a phenomenon, system, etc.).

1965 C. H. SPRINGER et al. *Adv. Methods & Models* ii. 57 We 'modeled' a business process with the aid of a ready-made algebraic model. **1971** *Nature* 18 June 425/1 The first attempts to model the urban system were made by traffic engineers. **1972** *Physics Bull.* Feb. 84/3 The UKAEA has modelled the diffusion of particles in a fluid acted on by buoyancy, winds, currents and turbulence. **1972** *Sci. Amer.* May 97/3 Our hope is that the maps will..eventually be of aid to meteorologists who are modeling the present circulation in the atmosphere. **1974** *McGraw-Hill Yearbk. Sci. & Technol.* 250/2 All models [of land use] seek to allocate land-absorbing activities on some type of spatial network of subareas. The size of the subareas will, of course, vary depending on the total area being modeled.

3. a. To give shape to; to frame, fashion (usually, an immaterial object, or a document, argument, etc.). †*to model out*: to produce (an expression of countenance) by studied effort.

1625 PURCHAS *Pilgrims* II. x. xiv. 1848 The Mother..played a womans part, shed teares,..modeld out a deiected Countenance, and..made an impression in them of her innocencie. **1768** STERNE *Sent. Journ.* (1778) I. 53, I forthwith began to model a different conversation for the lady, thinking..that I had been mistaken in her character. **1818** CRUISE *Digest* (ed. 2) IV. 382 Articles were only minutes..and ought to be so modelled..as to make them effectual. **1885** *Manch. Exam.* 16 June 5/3 Budgets..modelled too much on..free-trade principles.

†**b.** To plan out, put into preliminary shape. *Obs.*

1683 DRYDEN *Life Plutarch* 71 Having model'd but not finish'd them [*sc.* the 'Lives'] at Rome he afterwards resum'd the work in his own country.

c. To mould or assimilate in form *to*.

1683 *Brit. Spec.* 39 The Words which they received..seem much to be modelled to that Dialect. **1903** *Contemp. Rev.* Mar. 357 The sea-shell models to its form the wandering fish that dwells therein by choice.

†**d.** *to model into*, to bring into (a particular shape). *Obs.*

a **1704** T. BROWN *Sat. Antients* Wks. 1730 I. 16 Some modell'd them [*i.e.* Satires] into a purposed form to act at the end of their Comedies. *a* **1817** T. DWIGHT *Trav. New Eng.*, etc. (1821) II. 149 It is impossible for a brook of this size to be modelled into more diversified, or more delightful, forms.

e. To form (something) after a particular model. Usually const. *after, on, upon*.

1730 *Hist. Litteraria* I. 437 He was ordered either to suppress them, or to model them according to the Plan that was prescribed to him. **1841** D'ISRAELI *Amen. Lit.* (1867) 130 The earliest writers of France had modelled their taste by the Greek. **1841** ELPHINSTONE *Hist. Ind.* XII. iii. II. 655 He modelled his court on that of Nádir Sháh. **1882** HINSDALE *Garfield & Educ.* II. 302 Each new college is modelled after the older ones. **1898** BODLEY *France* II. III. iv. 181 Parliamentary institutions primarily modelled on the English pattern.

†**4. a.** To organize (a body of men, a community, a government, etc.). *Obs.*

1654 FULLER *Two Serm.* 12 Were they all connected into one Body,..summed up and modelled in one Corporation. *a* **1661** —— *Worthies, Wales* (1662) IV. 8 Wales..was not modelled into Shires..till the raign of K. Henry the eighth. **1674** BAKER *Chron., Chas. II* (an. 1659) 660 They propose first, to have the Army setled and modelled in a way of Unity before they determined upon the Government. **1678** SIR G. MACKENZIE *Crim. Laws Scot.* II. xvi. §2 (1699) 215 They having been modelled in an Army, and taken in the Field fighting..they behoved to be judged by the Military Law. **1693** *Humours Town* 41 There's not a Trader..but has his share in Modelling the Government. *a* **1715** BURNET *Own Time* (1724) I. 421 The design was to keep up and model the army now raised. **1724** R. FIDDES *Morality* Pref. 63 God, who founded human society, may model it as he pleases. **1770** LANGHORNE *Plutarch* (1879) I. 101/2 Solon..being asked, What city was best modeled? he answered, That, where those who are not injured are no less ready to prosecute..offenders than those who are. **1842** J. AITON *Domest. Econ.* (1857) 323 The whole power of instituting and modelling parishes was at one time entirely ecclesiastical.

†**b.** To classify, arrange in a system. *Obs.*

1727 THRELKELD *Stirpes Hibernicæ* Pref., He [Boerhaave] has concisely modelled plants according to method.

†**5.** To train or mould (a person) to a particular mode of life or living; also, to make a tool of. *Obs.*

1665 BOYLE *Occas. Refl.* v. v. (1848) 316 Those whom their nearness to Him, or their Employments, make the conspicuous and exemplary Persons, being thus model'd, their Relations and Dependants will quickly be so too. **1666** in *10th Rep. Hist. MSS. Comm.* App. v. 24 By their too powerfull perswasions to modell him to their designes. **1673** O. WALKER *Educ.* I. ii. 24 One..who may continually attend the Child,..model his manners, and preserve him from danger. **1701** FARQUHAR *Sir H. Wildair* II. i, 'Tis an insupportable toil, though, for women of quality to model their husbands to good breeding. **1734** tr. *Rollin's Anc. Hist.* (1827) IX. 203 He modelled him, and instructed him fully in all that it was necessary to do or say.

†**6.** To plan, machinate. *Obs. rare*$^{-1}$.

1725 POPE *Odyss.* x. 339 Each friend you seek in yon enclosure lies,..Think'st thou by wit to model their escape?

7. *intr.* Of the portions of a drawing in progress: To assume the appearance of natural relief.

18.. F. FOWLER *Charcoal Drawing* 44 (Cent.), The face now begins to model and look round.

8. *trans.* and *intr.* To act as a model (MODEL *sb.* 11 and 11 b); to display (clothes) as a model.

1915 W. B. YEATS *Reveries* (1916) 153 A pretty gentle-looking girl was modelling in the middle of the room. **1927** *Cleveland Press* 4 Mar., Vivian..will model Saturday in the shoe section of the Bailey Co. **1931** *Durant* (Okla.) *Daily Democrat* 29 Oct. 3/2 See them [*sc.* coats] modeled during style promenade tomorrow. **1948** 'J. TEY' *Franchise Affair* xxii. 260 A natural blonde with the clothes and figure of a girl who has 'modelled' clothes. **1957** M. SUMMERTON *Sunset Hour* iv. 61 Lolly..had modelled bikinis and gossamer underwear before blasé camera crews. **1969** *Guardian* 30 June 7/1, I was watching this Negro modelling sleepwear.

modeless ('məʊdlɪs), *a.* Also 6 moodelesse. [f. MODE *sb.* + -LESS.]

†**1.** Unmeasured. *Obs.* (Frequent in Greene).

1580–3 GREENE *Mamillia* I. Wks. (Grosart) II. 17 Nor to shewe himselfe such a moodelesse Aminius, to say all were Criples, because he found one halting. **1587** —— *Carde of Fancie* ibid. IV. 11 Vsing suche mercilesse crueltie to his forraine enimies, & such modelesse [1593, A 4, moodlesse] rigour to his natiue citizens.

2. In mystical use: Having no 'mode' or specific determination.

1856 R. A. VAUGHAN *Mystics* (1860) I. VI. viii. 325 *note*, The sons are utterly dead to self, in bare modeless love. **1865** T. F. KNOX tr. *Life H. Suso* 31 The modeless abyss of the divine essence.

Hence '**modelessness**.

1856 R. A. VAUGHAN *Mystics* (1860) II. x. i. 150 The contrast lies, with her, not between Finite and Infinite..between mode and modelessness,..but simply between God and Self.

‖**modeliar** (məʊ'dɛljɑː(r)). *Ceylon.* [Tamil *mudaliyār*, 'an honorific plural from *mudali* a chief' (Yule).] A head-man, chief; a chief military officer. ***grand modeliar***, a commander in chief.

1662 J. DAVIES tr. *Mandelslo's Trav.* 112 The Portuguez..made no difficulty to confer upon him the office of Grand Modeliar of Candy... Grand Modeliar, that is, Constable of the Kingdome of Candy. **1840** J. FORBES *11 Yrs. in Ceylon* 116 On our arrival at Avisavellé, the Modeliar informed us that [etc.]. **1845** *Encycl. Metrop.* XVI. 451/1 The chief military officer in each Désáveny was the Modelyár. *Ibid.* 452/1 The frequent collision of the civil and military authorities, the Korâles and Modelyárs.

modelist ('mɒdəlɪst). In quots. **modellist**. [f. MODEL *sb.* + -IST] A maker of models.

1676 T. MILLER (*title*) The Compleat Modellist: shewing The true and exact way of Raising the Model of any Ship or Vessel, small or great, either in Proportion, or out of Proportion. **1825** HOGG *Q. Hynde* I. 28 Come, modellist, thy toil renew—Such scene shall never meet thy view!

†'**modelize**, *v. Obs.* [f. MODEL *sb.* + -IZE. Cf. MODULIZE.]

1. *trans.* To frame or construct according to a model; to give a particular shape to; to model, frame; to organize. Also *refl.*

1605 SHELTON in Verstegan *Dec. Intell.* To Author, Thy curious nation..all that was rare or strange In forrain lands, at home did modellize. **1639** G. DANIEL *Ecclus.* xxiii. 86 He who ere Time was, yet Knew all things, and now Modellized fitt, Sees with a carefull Eye. **1650** *Merchant Adv. of Newcastle* (Surtees) 162 To modilise an acte for restraynige of the bretheren from taking apprentices. **1659** GAUDEN *Tears Ch.* IV. v. 426 Which..some silly Saints and devout bunglers will undertake to manage and modelize beyond their line and measure. **1660** F. BROOKE tr. *Le Blanc's Trav.* 387 Some amongst them..civilized the rest, and modelized the government. **1716** M. DAVIES *Athen. Brit.* III. *Diss. Physick* 30 The learned Protestant Antiquarian Bochard, and the erudite Popish Bishop Dan. Huetius,..agree entirely, that Apollo was modeliz'd by the Ethnicks upon the Platform of Phut. **1771** LUCKOMBE *Hist. Print.* 400 The Germans have a ragged r, ..which, in modelizing their letters to the present shape, they have castrated. **1810** *Splendid Follies* II. 196 Her impatient husband was reproving her stupidity..; for Milford would fain have modelized her.

2. To symbolize.

1625 C. BROOKE *On Sir Arthur Chichester* Poems (1872) 237 Her outward actions modelized her minde.

Hence '**modelized** *ppl. a.*, modelled, shaped; '**modelizing** *ppl. a.*, formative.

1599 B. JONSON *Ev. Man out of Hum.* III. i, For the more modelizing or enamelling, or rather diamondizing of your subiect. **1688** R. HOLME *Armory* IV. xii. (Roxb.) 475/2 Their gods, made of little Modellized stones or mettle. **1716** M. DAVIES *Athen. Brit.* II. 18 He had a Modellizing,..or an Approving Hand in all his Royal Letters, Commissions [etc.]. **1810** *Splendid Follies* III. 87 The enlightened Christian, who, but for the modelizing hand of science, which fashioned him in his cradle, had been thy [the negro's] equal.

modelled ('mɒdəld), *ppl. a.* [f. MODEL *v.* + -ED[1].]

1. Shaped or organized after a particular or desirable model: frequently with qualifying adverb.

1621 G. SANDYS *Ovid's Met.* I. (1632) 9 O would I could my Father's cunning vse! And soules into well-modul'd Clay infuse! **1670** PENN *Case Liberty Consc.* 30 We are not such model'd Christians, as they coercively would have us. **1679** in Wodrow *Hist. Suff. Ch. Scot.* (1722) II. 60 The Lord Macdonald, a professed Papist, with a modelled Army..hath remained in Armes. **1700** S. L. tr. *Fryke's Voy. E. Ind.* 177 Their vigilant, and wisely Model'd Government. **1704** J. BLAIR in W. S. Perry *Hist. Coll. Amer. Col. Ch.* I. 108 He..would keep a Standing modell'd militia in constant pay. **1863** 'OUIDA' *Held in Bondage* (1870) 3 Broad chest, and splendidly modelled arm. **1887** RUSKIN *Præterita* II. 60 A beautifully modelled forehead. **1895** MRS. B. M. CROKER *Village Tales* (1896) 21 Her two modelled arms, jingling with copper bangles.

2. Executed in relief.

1875 KNIGHT *Dict. Mech.* 1458/1 A modeled map of a country 200 miles square.

modeller ('mɒdələ(r)). [f. MODEL *v.* + -ER[1].] One who models (in any sense of the vb.) or makes models, esp. one who forms models in clay, plaster, wax, or the like. Also *fig.*

1603 FLORIO *Montaigne* I. xxv. (1632) 79 Philosophy (as a former of judgements, and modeler of customes) shall be his principall lesson. **1692** WOOD *Ath. Oxon.* II. 101 He..became..a great proposal maker, and modeller of state, and publisher of several seditious Pamphlets. **1712** ADDISON *Spect.* No. 414 ¶5 Our great Modellers of Gardens have their Magazines of Plants to dispose of. **1791** SMEATON *Edystone L.* §69 A competent draughtsman and an excellent modeller. **1825** J. NICHOLSON *Operat. Mechanic* 465 The modeller and the mould-maker, whose occupations are very distinct branches of the art. The modeller has great scope for the exertion of natural and acquired ability, taste, and ingenuity. **1837** *Rep. Roy. Mint* App. 6 The office of a modeller should be established, and I should humbly submit that he might be chosen from among the most celebrated of our Royal Academicians. **1846** *Penny Cycl.* Suppl. II. 313/1 The..formative skill of the modeller [in clay].

‖**modelletto** (model'letto). Pl. **modelletti**. [It., dim. of MODELLO.] = MODELLO.

1937 *Burlington Mag.* Mar. 133/1 The other collectors..added the bozzetti and modelletti to their bronzes and sculptures. **1938** *Ibid.* Oct. 141/2 Tiepolo has developed his theme in masterly fashion, perhaps as a 'modelletto' for an altar-piece. **1962** R. G. HAGGAR *Dict. Art Terms* 215/1 *Modello*... Another name is *modelletto*.

modelling ('mɒdəlɪŋ), *vbl. sb.* [f. MODEL *v.* + -ING[1].]

†**1.** The action of drawing or projecting plans. *Obs. rare*$^{-1}$. (The word may possibly be the ppl. adj. used *absol.* = 'modellers'.)

1581 MULCASTER *Positions* v. (1887) 35 Whose vse [*sc.* of Drawing] all modelling, all mathematikes, all manuaries do finde and confesse to be so notorious and so needefull.

2. *fig.* The action of bringing (anything) to a desired or desirable form or condition.

a **1653** BINNING *Serm.* (1845) 486 That constant..rule, which the Lord gives concerning the modelling and carriage of the armies of His people in all their wars. **1671** MILTON *Samson, Of Tragedy*, In the modelling..of this Poem..the Antients and Italians are..follow'd, as of much more authority. **1676** TOWERSON *Decalogue* 431 He who invests another person..should have the modelling of his own grant. **1722** WODROW *Hist. Suff. Ch. Scotl.* II. 277 The Council's Letter..contains some other Things anent the Modelling of the Justices of the Peace. **1749** MRS. DELANY in *Life & Corr.* (1861) II. 513 She is a fine lively girl, but wants a good deal of modelling.

3. a. The action or art of making models; the art of constructing representations of things in clay, wax, plaster, or the like; *spec.* the art of making a model in clay or wax to be copied in more permanent materials by the sculptor or founder.

1799 G. SMITH *Laboratory* II. 84 They are very expert in carving and modeling. **1856** *Eng. Cycl., Biogr.* II. 163 Chantrey..therefore turned his attention to modelling in clay. **1860** *Our Eng. Home* 167 These beautiful modellings and arboresque chasings. **1872** J. YEATS *Techn. Hist. Comm.* 351 Associated with and dependent upon casting is another new handicraft, called modelling. **1875** KNIGHT *Dict. Mech.* 1458/1 The largest attempt at geographical modeling was by Mr. Wyld.

b. *transf.*

1888 *Encycl. Brit.* XXIII. 90/2 A new school of taxidermists, with new methods, whose aim is to combine a knowledge of anatomy and modelling with taxidermic technique, are now coming to the front, and the next generation will discard all processes of 'stuffing' in favour of modelling.

c. The action of MODEL *v.* 8; the work of a fashion-model. Also *attrib.*

1949 *Chicago Tribune* 17 Feb. 10/3, I never thought of modeling as a career. **1959** 'J. CHRISTOPHER' *Scent of White Poppies* iv. 55, I did do some modelling there. **1963** G. MARX *Let.* 11 Apr. (1967) 63 She is abandoning the modeling school and plans to embark upon..settlement work. **1964** [see *fashion-modelling* vbl. sb. s.v. FASHION *sb.* 13a]. **1973** *Sun* 25 May 3 She started her modelling career when a fashion photographer spotted her on a beach near Rimini.

d. The devising or use of abstract or mathematical models (MODEL *sb.* 2e).

1965 C. H. SPRINGER et al. *Adv. Methods & Models* i. 4 The best way to untangle the confusion which many people have about mathematical modeling as a method for solving

important business problems is to untangle the whole idea of model building as a way of thinking about the world we live in. **1971** J. Howlett in B. de Ferranti *Living with Computer* ii. 13 The computer has..made it possible to apply this method—mathematical modelling followed by numerical solution of the resulting equations—to problems that would be quite intractable without its aid. **1974** *Nature* 2 Aug. 450/3 It also gives the reader some feel for the vast problems involved in any worth-while quantitative modelling of climatic change.

4. *Art.* The representation of solid form in sculpture; *transf.* the representation of material relief and solidity in painting.

1874 Symonds *Sk. Italy & Greece* (1898) I. viii. 134 An ideal Roman head, with the powerful square modelling. **1884** H. Wallis in *Athenæum* 8 Nov. 599/2 The drapery also has all his careful elaboration and accurate modelling. **1889** *Academy* 25 May 365/1 The modelling in the numerous portraits..is painstaking rather than really firm or expressive of the structure beneath.

5. *attrib.*, as ***modelling-clay***, ***-wax***; **modelling-board**, a board used in loam-moulding to give shape to the mould (Knight *Dict. Mech.* 1875); **modelling loft** = *mould-loft* (Ogilvie 1882); **modelling-plane**, a short plane used in planing rounded surfaces (Knight); **modelling-stick**, **-tool**, tools used by modellers in clay or wax.

1886 *Encycl. Brit.* XXI. 571/1 Over this iron skeleton well-tempered *modelling-clay is laid and is modelled into shape. **1807** Anna M. Porter *Hungar. Bro.* iv. (1832) 40 She plied the *modelling-sticks, or the chisel, with equal vileness. **1846** *Penny Cycl.* Suppl. II. 313/1 *Modelling tools, are made of wood and wire. **1845** *Encycl. Metrop.* VIII. 790/1 To make the best *modelling-wax, take two cakes of virgin wax [etc.]. **1866** Brande & Cox *Dict. Sci.*, etc. II. 551/1 Modelling wax consists of bees-wax melted with a small quantity of Venice turpentine, with which a little flake white in powder, or other powdered colour is mixed. **1891** Kipling *Light that Failed* x. (1900) 201 A piece of red modelling-wax.

modellion, variant form of MODILLION.

modellist, obs. variant of MODELIST.

‖**modello** (mo'dello). Pl. modelli, modellos. [It., see MODEL *sb.*] A sketch, often executed in detail, for a larger painting which is prepared for a patron's approval; also, a small model for a larger sculpture. Cf. BOZZETTO, MAQUETTE.

1937 *Burlington Mag.* Oct. 188/1 We find the more finished *modello* replaced by the quick colour sketch. **1959** *Times Lit. Suppl.* 20 Mar. 154/5 The relation of genuine *modelli* to 'engraver's copies' is left in a state of confusion. **1964** *Listener* 12 Nov. 767/2 Vasari, on his visit to Titian's house in 1566, noticed many of these modellos propped against the wall. **1967** W. Gaunt *Compan. Painting* 63 The more detailed *modello*..gave the full conception of the painting. *Ibid.* 67 The *modelli* of the Italians. **1972** *Country Life* 6 Apr. 857/1 It is possible that the picture is a modello for a larger work, intended for a church or chapel. **1974** *Daily Tel.* 29 July 8/6 The recently acquired picture..is the modello for the painting of 'The Senators of Florence swearing allegiance to the Grand Duke Ferdinand II'.

modelly ('mɒdəlɪ), *a.* [f. MODEL *sb.* + -Y^1.] Resembling a model (MODEL *sb.* 11 b); having the characteristics of a fashion-model.

1961 I. Jefferies *It wasn't Me!* vi. 70 Ghislaine was a bit too modelly to be true. **1965** *Observer* (Colour Suppl.) 5 Sept. 6/2 They wanted actresses because they thought models were too modelly.

'model-wood. The hard pale-coloured wood of the Indian rubiaceous tree *Adina* (or *Nauclea*) *cordifolia*.

1857 E. Balfour *Cycl. India*, Model or Putcha Ootoo Wood. **1866** *Treas. Bot.* 748/1 Model-wood. *Nauclea cordifolia*.

modem ('məʊdɛm). [f. MO(DULATOR + DEM(ODULATOR.] A combined modulator and demodulator (such as is used in connecting a computer to a telephone line) for converting outgoing signals from one form to another and converting incoming signals back again.

1958 *Proc. Inst. Electr. Engineers* CV. B. 450/2 Following carrier system terminology, it can be called a 'modem'. **1961** G. L. Evans et al. in *Convention Rec. 5th National Symposium Global Communications* 100 A recent study of wireline data communications..has underlined the need for advancement in the field of data modulators-demodulators (modems). **1963** *Daily Tel.* 16 Dec. 15/2 The direct current (DC) signals which flow through a computer cannot be transmitted over telephone lines, so it is necessary to convert them... The black box which does this conversion at either end of the line is called a modem. **1971** *New Scientist* 7 Jan. 18/1 It is around 3:30 pm in the communications control room of Time Sharing Ltd, in London's West End. The modems are silent... Power has been off for half an hour. **1975** *Daily Colonist* (Victoria, B.C.) 13 May 27/1 They communicated over regular telephone lines, using teletypewriters connected to the lines by electronic devices known as modems.

modena ('mɒdɪnə). [Name of an Italian city.] **1.** A deep purple colour. Also *attrib.*

1822–34 *Good's Study Med.* (ed. 4) I. 394 The modena hue is produced by the carbon with which the blood is loaded. *Ibid.* 400 [A cause which] converts it from a deep purple or modena, into a rich scarlet. *Ibid.* II. 114 The fauces present a Modena-red colour. **1888** W. Williams *Princ. Vet. Med.* (ed. 5) 219 The conjunctiva varies in shade from a bright scarlet to a modena red.

2. In full, ***Modena pigeon***. A pigeon of the variety so called, distinguished by its stocky build and red legs.

1879 L. Wright *Pract. Pigeon Keeper* xix. 220 (*heading*) Modena flying pigeons. **1936** W. A. Dalley in *Pigeons of Today* 105 When once here the Modena..became an exhibition or fancy pigeon pure and simple. **1965** W. M. Levi *Encycl. Pigeon Breeds* 247 The Modena is one of the most popular breeds in the United States. **1969** H. H. Shrives *Fancy Pigeons* 81 Modena pigeons are divided in Gazzi or Pied, Schietti or Self-coloured, and Magnani or Harlequin.

modenature. *Arch.* [a. F. *modénature*, ad. It. *modanatura*, f. *modano* moulding.] The mouldings decorating a cornice.

1664 Evelyn tr. *Freart's Archit.* II. i. 90 Its proportion.. requires an enrichment of handsome Modenatures. **1953** *Archit. Rev.* CXIV. 91 The two outstanding features of the doctrine of Auguste Perret are the insistence on modenature—the profiling and management of projecting features—and the philosophy of the concrete frame. **1959** P. Collins *Concrete* ix. 197 The only modifications to this structural composition [in Greek architecture] consisted of surface modulations intended to make the forms more pleasing to the eye (namely *modé-nature* or profiling), and optical corrections.

Modenese (mɒdɪ'ni:z), *a.* and *sb.* [f. MODENA + -ESE.] **A.** *adj.* Of or pertaining to Modena or its inhabitants. **B.** *sb.* A native or inhabitant of Modena.

1813 J. C. Eustace *Tour through Italy* I. vi. 131 The important 'Bucket'..was carried off from a well in one of the streets of Bologna, by a party of Modenese troops. **1839** K. H. Digby *Mores Catholici* IX. iii. 80 Peace was then made between all the Modenese,..more than twenty thousand of the Modenese went to Reggio and Parma; and those two cities made peace with each other. **1936** G. F.-H. & J. Berkeley *Italy in Making* II. xvi. 245 At Fivizzano, the Modenese soldiers fired on the crowd. **1957** *Encycl. Brit.* XV. 633/2 The wooden bucket captured by the Modenese from the Bolognese in the affray at Zappolino.

†**'moder**, *v.* *Obs.* Also 5 modre, 5–6 modere. [ad. OF. *moderer* (F. *modérer*), ad. L. *moderārī*: see MODERATE *v.*] = MODERATE *v.* in various senses: To restrain, hold in check; to temper, mitigate; to regulate, settle; to modify. (Frequent in 15th c.) Hence **'modering** *vbl. sb.*, a diminishing, attenuation.

1414 in *Proc. Privy Council* (1834) II. 141 Eny..offre that were moderyngge of youre hoole title or of eny of youre claymes beyonde the see. *c* **1430** *Rolls of Parlt.* V. 417/1 Moderyng aleway the nombre of the Persones and Estates of the Parlement,..and of other Officers, as the necessite and service of the Kyng..requireth. *c* **1450** tr. *De Imitatione* III. xii, That þe desires of þe herte must be examyned & moderid. **1481** Botoner *Tulle Old Age* (Caxton) d 3 b, Yf every man will tempre & modre his strength..he shal have grete desyre and plesire in his strength. **1495** *Act 11 Hen. VII*, c. 2 §1 In modring of the seid estatute..it be ordeyned. **1533** More *Apol.* xxii. Wks. 882/2 If this pacifier would moder and measure his sufficiencie by the wordes of S. Paule [etc.]. **1533** J. Heywood *Play Weather* (1903) 688 As we se the wynde in hys estate, We moder our saylys after the same rate. **1534** Whitinton *Tullyes Offices* III. (1540) 135 One referreth al to the opinyons of Socrates schole, the other modereth all after custome of men and lawe ciuyle.

moder, obs. form of MAUTHER, MOTHER.

†**'moderable**, *a.* *Obs.*$^{-0}$ [ad. L. *moderābil-is*, f. *moderārī* to moderate: see MODERATE *v.* and -ABLE.] Moderate; temperate.

1623 Cockeram, *Moderable*, temperate, measurable.

†**'moderacy.** *Obs.* [f. MODERATE *a.*: see -ACY.] Moderation.

1601 in *Archpriest Controv.* (Camden) I. 193 They did it wth muche more moderacie and shewe of peace..than these did.

†**'moderance.** *Obs.* [ad. med.L. *moderantia* (Du Cange), f. L. *moderant-em*: see next and -ANCE.] Moderation.

1481 Botoner *Tulle Old Age* (Caxton) b 5 b, Fabius..had in himsilf a good dispocicion of a moderaunce medlyd with curtesye. **1534** Whitinton *Tullyes Offices* I. (1540) 21 Endued with this slendrer vertues, as moderaunce, temperaunce and..justyce. *a* **1578** Lindesay (Pitscottie) *Chron. Scot.* (S.T.S.) I. 111 He wald wse sic moderance heirin and deill witht thame as gentill as he could.

moderant ('mɒdərənt). [ad. L. *moderant-em*, pr. pple. of *moderārī* to MODERATE: see -ANT. Cf. F. *modérant*.] Something that moderates.

1897 *Daily News* 9 Feb. 7/4 He added a moderant in the form of castor-oil.

moderantism ('mɒdərəntɪz(ə)m). *Obs.* exc. *Hist.* [F. *modérantisme*, f. *modérant*, pr. pple. of *modérer* to moderate: see MODER *v.* and -ISM.] In France, during the Revolution, and later, the doctrines and spirit of the Moderate party in politics.

1793 Burke *Policy of Allies* Wks. VII. 134 They [*sc.* the Jacobin Clubs] too have been lately subjected to an expurgatory scrutiny, to drive out from them every thing savouring of what they call the crime of moderantism. **1795** Hel. M. Williams *Lett. France* I. 139 (Jod.) The revolutionary tribunal..was denounced for its moderantism.

So **'moderantist**, one professing moderantism.

1877 Morley *Crit. Misc.* Ser. II. 95 Other prominent members of the party whom they loved to stigmatise by the deadly names of Indulgent and Moderantist.

moderate ('mɒdərət), *a.* and *sb.* Also 5 *Sc.* modreth, 5–7 moderat. [ad. L. *moderāt-us*, pa. pple. of *moderārī*: see MODERATE *v.* Cf. F. *modéré*.]

A. *adj.*

1. Of persons, their attributes, actions, etc.: Observing, exhibiting, or acting with moderation; avoiding extremes; characterized by temperance of conduct or expression.

moderate drinker: one who does not drink to excess, but is not a teetotaller. So ***moderate drinking***.

c **1412** Hoccleve *De Reg. Princ.* 2436 Moderat speche engendrith reste, and makith. **1432–50** tr. *Higden* (Rolls) IV. 309 A man lyke to a god, happy in batelle and moderate in peace. **1560** Daus tr. *Sleidane's Comm.* 175 They must bring with them a mynd neyther ambitious nor covetous, but godly and moderat. **1596** Shaks. *Merch. V.* III. ii. 112 O loue be moderate, allay thy extasie. **1611** Bible *Ecclus.* xxxi. 20 Sound sleepe commeth of moderate eating. **1634** *Documents agst. Prynne* (Camden) 53 Methinkes it should make you more moderate, just, and compassionate towardes others. **1680** Titus *Sp. Ho. of Comm.* 26 Oct. in *Collect. Poems* 186 The moderatest and meekest Man that ever was,..Slew the Egyptian. **1788** Gibbon *Decl. & F.* V. xlix. 97 In the reformation of religion, his first steps were moderate and cautious. **1849** Macaulay *Hist. Eng.* vi. II. 64 Rochester's moderate counsels. **1887** *Poor Nellie* (1888) 76 You are such a very moderate man, Octavius, that you might just as well take the pledge as not.

2. a. Of opinions and their supporters: Not extreme; not strongly partisan. **b.** Hence (now usually with initial capital) used as the designation of various political and ecclesiastical parties and their views: see B. below.

a. 1644 Heylin *Brief Relat. Laud* 4 Some of the more moderate (or rather the lesse violent) Lords..gave out that they intended onely to remove him from his Majesties eare. **1654** Gataker *Disc. Apol.* 26, I maintained a good correspondence..with the moderater sort on either side. **1705** (*title*) The New Association of those called Moderate-Church-Men. By a True-Church-Man. *a* **1715** Burnet *Own Time* IV. (1753) III. 137 He slackened all the laws made against the moderate Presbyterians. **1770** *Junius Lett.* xxxviii. (1788) 203 They have lost or renounced the moderate principles of their government. **1889** *Spectator* 28 Dec., The temptation to a Prime Minister is to appoint only 'moderate' men.

b. 1753 Witherspoon *Eccl. Characteristics* Wks. 1804 II. 299 The moderate party commonly set up on a pretence of being more learned than their adversaries. **1842** *Mem. J. Halley* 37 There are two contending principles within the Church of Scotland, the supporters of which are called respectively Evangelical and Moderate. **1848** Struthers *Rise Relief Ch.* 193 The Moderate clergy..were very unpopular. **1875** McCrie *Story Scott. Ch.* 505 In 1763, Dr. Robertson became the avowed leader of the Moderate party. **1924** J. T. Gwynn *Indian Politics* iii. 18 The Moderate or Co-operating party is to-day so unpopular that it takes some strength of mind to remain a Co-operator. **1954** B. & R. North tr. *Duverger's Pol. Parties* I. i. 46 In the nineteenth century parties were based upon the caucus and weak articulation; today most Conservative, Moderate, and 'Liberal' parties in Europe still display these two essential characteristics. **1973** *Perthshire Advertiser* 17 Feb. 1/1 Another member of the Moderate-Independent Association of Perth town councillors, Councillor Henry Giulianotti, has resigned from the association. **1973** T. K. Derry *Hist. Mod. Norway* x. 325 In the summer of 1934 Hjort had failed to put through a scheme for linking the Agrarian Party with the Moderate Liberals.

3. a. Of medium or middling quantity, quality, size, or extent; fairly large or good; 'tolerable'. Now often (esp. in phr. ***very moderate***) in depreciative sense: Mediocre, scanty.

c **1420** Lydg. *Assembly of Gods* 885 The remenaunt Of pety capteyns that with Vertu were, Moderat Dyete, & Wysdom auenaunt [etc.]. *c* **1430** —— *Min. Poems* (Percy Soc.) 69 Moderat foode [1487 in *Camb. MS.* modreth fuode] gevith to man his helthe. *a* **1547** Surrey *Ecclesiastes* v. 30 The cheif blisse that in earth to liuing man is lent, Is moderat welth. **1607** Shaks. *Timon* III. iv. 117 There's not so much left to furnish out a moderate Table. **1711** Shaftesb. *Charac.*, *Misc.* v. ii. (1737) III. 283 A good Bargain it were, cou'd we get rid of every moderate Performance in this kind [*sc.* Poetry or Essay]. **1711** Swift *Jrnl. to Stella* 10 Nov., Have you got the whalebone petticoats among you yet? I hate them; a woman here may hide a moderate gallant under them. **1748** *Anson's Voy.* III. vi. 350 It is a rock of a small circumference, but of a moderate height. **1796** Morse *Amer. Geog.* II. 73 (*Russia*), They put a very moderate faggot into them [*sc.* stoves]. **1825** J. Nicholson *Operat. Mechanic* 69 Where great quantities of water are discharged from moderate heads, the actual head of water, and the virtual head,..will nearly agree. **1828** Pusey *Hist. Enq.* I. 38 The rest are very moderate productions. **1889** *Sat. Rev.* 16 Mar. 326/1 He [*sc.* the horse Monarque] looks long in the back and has very moderate loins. **1897** *Allbutt's Syst. Med.* IV. 162 The skin assumes a moderate icteroid hue.

b. Of physical processes, conditions, or agencies: Not intense, violent, or rigorous. Of the voice: Neither excessively loud nor excessively low.

1398 Trevisa *Barth. De P.R.* XI. ii. (1495) 384 Winde that is moderate and not contraryouse to Shypmen. **1590** Spenser *F.Q.* II. xii. 51 The milde ayre with season moderate Gently attempred. **1598** *Epulario* L j b, Make a moderate fire as to a Tarte. **1704** J. Cuningham in *Phil. Trans.* XXV. 1649 Grey cloudy Weather, with moderate Gales from NW to W. **1769** Mrs. Raffald *Eng. Housekpr.*

(1778) 299 Bake them in a moderate oven. **1802** *Med. Jrnl.* VIII. 314 A second case..terminated..in a moderate sweat. **1863** Joyce *Sch. Management* 75 The monitors must be trained to speak, when teaching, in a moderate voice. **1949** J. D. B. Wilson *Southern Highlands* 175 Further east are two ribs beyond a shallow gully which give defined climbs.. of moderate standard. **1956** A. J. J. Moulam *Tryfan & Glyder Fach* 85 Ordinary route. About 200 feet. Moderate. **1966** M. Woodhouse *Tree Frog* xv. 122 If the climb had reached any level of difficulty higher than Moderate, which is the Climbers' Club's polite way of labelling a gumshoe doddle, we'd have died. **1971** N. Tennent *Islands of Scotl.* i. 32 Arran rock offers little choice between easy to moderate scrambles and hard, strenuous routes. *Ibid.* iv. 78 *Broad Buttress*, 450 ft., Moderate.

c. Of prices, charges, etc.: not excessive, reasonable, low.

1904 *Punch* 6 Apr. p. ii (Advt.), Hotel..standing high in its own beautiful park... Moderate tariff or inclusive terms. **1923–4** *Guide to Oxf.* 19 (Advt.), Norfolk Hotel,..Central Position. Moderate Terms. **1971** *Bibliotheck* VI. 57 The New Aldis..at the moderate price of £4.50 and with more than 1600 additional entries..will be especially welcome. **1973** *Michelin: France* 40 Good meals at moderate prices.

4. *Comb.*, as **moderate-minded, -priced, -sized** adjs.

1819 Byron *Juan* I. cxviii, I'm a *moderate-minded bard. **1905** *Westm. Gaz.* 22 Sept. 2/3 Extensive and *moderate-priced hotels. **1765** *Museum Rust.* III. 157, I pass a *moderate-sized roller over the field. **1925** V. Woolf *Common Reader* 134 Six moderate-sized volumes. **1959** *Guardian* 9 July 5/3 The play..has a moderate-sized cast.

B. *sb.* **a.** One who holds moderate opinions in politics, religion, or any subject of controversy. Hence (now usually with initial capital), a member of any of the various parties of which 'Moderate' has been the official or customary designation; e.g. in the French Revolution (transl. of F. *modéré*) applied to the Girondins, later to the Dantonists and others.

1794 Burke *Corr.* (1844) IV. 213, I take it for granted he will come to the moderates, and by thus reuniting the party, put himself [etc.]. **1803** Jefferson *Writ.* (ed. Ford) VIII. 222 A schism was taking place in Pennsylvania between the moderates and the high-flyers. **1831** A. W. Fonblanque *Eng. Under 7 Administr.* (1837) II. 81 The vast majority of society, Whig, Tory, and Moderates, acknowledge the necessity of Parliamentary Reform. **1833** Alison *Hist. Europe* X. II. 62 *note*, Those who..frequent the society of.. Feuillants, Moderates, or Aristocrats. **1877** Morley *Crit. Misc.* Ser. II. 98 The execution of the Anarchists only preceded by a week the arrest of the Moderates. **1882–3** *Schaff's Encycl. Relig. Knowl.* I. 659 The Moderates hastened to elect him [*sc.* Cæcilianus, bishop of Carthage]. **1920** H. V. Lovett *Hist. Indian Nationalist Movement* iii. 69 The Moderates were pushed out of a hall and assailed with stones and mud. **1924** J. T. Gwynn *Indian Politics* iii. 18 It used to be..the fashion to decry the Moderates and Co-operators as if they were a party of weak men and time-servers. **1969** *Listener* 28 Aug. 268/3 'Moderates' (who include men with a very militant record) are at present containing the extremists and hot-heads. **1975** *Times* 6 Jan. 2/3 The moderates should exercise their overwhelming strength in the trade union movement.

b. In the Church of Scotland during the greater part of the 18th and the former half of the 19th century: A member of that party which (in opposition to the 'Evangelical' party) held lax views on doctrine and discipline, and opposed the abolition of lay patronage.

About 1843 the abbreviated forms *Mods* and *Nons* were familiarly used for 'Moderates' and 'Non-intrusionists'.

1842 *Mem. J. Halley* 40 One of the facts illustrative of the principles and practice of the Moderates which made a deep impression on Halley's mind. **1848** Struthers *Rise Relief Ch.* 191 The Moderates, about the year 1735, allowed them [*sc.* the popular party] to have their own way. **1854** H. Miller *Sch. & Schm.* xxii. (1860) 239 The younger men were staunch Liberals, but great Moderates, the elder, sound Evangelicals, but decidedly Conservative in their leanings.

c. In late 19th-c. municipal politics (opposed to *Progressive*): A member of the party hostile to undertakings involving large expenditure of public money.

1894 *Times* 19 Dec. 6/1 A Progressive headed the poll, followed by six Moderates, at the election of guardians.

moderate ('mɒdəreɪt), *v.* Also 6–7 **moderat**; *pa. pple.* 5–6 **moderate**, 6 *Sc.* **moderat**. [f. L. *moderāt-, ppl. stem of *moderārī* (pre-classical and late L. *moderāre*), f. *moder-:—*modes- (whence *modestus* MODEST), a noun-stem parallel with *modo-*, *modus* measure, MODE *sb.* Cf. L. *operārī* to work, f. *oper-*, *opus* work.]

1. **a.** *trans.* To abate the excessiveness of; to render less violent, intense, rigorous, or burdensome; †to reduce the amount of (a fine, charge, financial burden).

1432–50 tr. *Higden* (Rolls) V. 31 This Marcus Antonius.. moderate grevous lawes and constitutions with other of gretter moderacion. *c* **1489** Caxton *Blanchardyn* xx. 64 The maystres..dyd perceyue..that her Indygnacion..was moderat in her herte. **1526** *Pilgr. Perf.* (W. de W. 1531) 51 These outrageous mocyons be moderate & rectifyed by the cardinall vertue temperaunce. **1541** *Act 33 Hen. VIII*, c. 22 The saide maister..shall haue..auctoritie to moderate such recognisances as be..forfaited. **1590** Spenser *F.Q.* II. ii. 38 With equall measure she did moderate The strong extremities of their outrage. **1604** E. G[rimstone] *D'Acosta's Hist. Indies* II. xiii. 111 The coolenesse of the night then is not sufficient to moderate and to correct the violent heate of the Sunne. **1606** Shaks. *Tr. & Cr.* IV. iv. 5 The griefe is fine, full perfect that I taste... How can I moderate it? **1632** Pory in Ellis *Orig. Lett.* Ser. II. III. 272 His Grace by his dyet hath so moderated his gout, as it is [etc.]. **1656** *Providence (R.I.) Rec.* (1893) II. 92 Ordered that ye Attournies fee is moderated from 6:^{s} 8^d to 3:^{s} 4^d. **1732** Lediard *Sethos* II. IX. 308, I..advise you to moderate your demands. **1731** Arbuthnot *Aliments* (1735) 146 By its astringent Quality it [*sc.* Tea] moderates the relaxing Quality of warm Water. **1765** Blackstone *Comm.* I. viii. 319 All the hopes we can entertain of ever discharging or moderating our incumbrances. **1885** *Manch. Exam.* 29 June 5/1 Mr. Balfour must moderate at once any hope he derives from the supposition. **1903** G. Matheson *Repr. Men Bible* Ser. II. 36 Lot should have remembered this, and should have moderated his desires.

b. *intr.* for *refl.* To become less violent, severe, or rigorous.

1678 Butler *Hud.* III. ii. 463 Yet when his profit moderated, The fury of his heart abated. **1819** Baron de Bonstetten in *Lady Morgan's Autobiog.* (1859) 310 As the heavens have moderated, I propose..to pay you a visit. **1897** J. Chalmers in *Life* xi. (1902) 443 Fortunately the weather moderated.

†**c.** *trans.* To simplify. *Obs.*

1557 N.T. (Genev.) To Rdr. **iij, I haue so moderat them [the arguments of Scriptures] with playnenes and breuitie, that the verie ignorant may easely vnderstande them.

d. *Nuclear Sci.* To slow down (a neutron); also, to provide (a reactor) with a moderator.

1945 H. D. Smyth *Gen. Acct. Devel. Atomic Energy Mil. Purposes* viii. 89 It would take two years to produce enough heavy water to 'moderate' a fair-sized pile for plutonium production. **1956** H. Seligman in A. Pryce-Jones *New Outl. Mod. Knowl.* 158 There are very few substances which can be used for this slowing-down process. There is carbon in pure form, or water which, instead of the normal hydrogen, has the 'heavy' hydrogen atom in its molecule. These substances are called moderators, as they are moderating the neutrons. **1958** O. R. Frisch *Nucl. Handbk.* x. 4 The type of thermal neutron spectrum obtained from a reactor depends upon the conditions under which the neutrons are moderated. **1959** *Listener* 19 Nov. 873/1 They [*sc.* the reactors]..are cooled by carbon dioxide and moderated with graphite. **1966** *New Scientist* 24 Feb. 484/3 In a fast-reactor system, so called because the neutrons causing fission are not slowed down or 'moderated' but react at high energies, it is possible in theory to consume all the uranium. **1973** *Nature* 2 Feb. 317/1 In the reactors cooled and moderated by water, the reactor vessel must also be at this pressure.

†**2.** **a.** *trans.* To exercise a controlling influence over; to regulate, restrain, control, rule. *Obs.*

1534 More *Treat. Passion* Wks. 1311/1 This coulde none do but he, that..was able..to moderate and measure theyr pacys hym selfe, in suche wyse as them selfe wyste not why. **1538** Starkey *England* I. iv. 104 By hys royal powar..he myght moderat al thyng accordyng to hys plesure and wyl. **1555** Eden *Decades* 304 A collar or rayne wherwith he moderateth the course of the hartes. **1612** Brinsley *Lud. Lit.* xx. (1627) 238 The Interlineall translation may be a worthy helpe for a man..who can so moderate his eye, as to keepe it fixed upon either Greek or Latine alone. **1615** Crooke *Body of Man* 274 The woman was ordayned..to gouerne and moderate the house at home. **1641** *Mass. Body of Liberties* 95 in *Col. Laws Mass.* (1889) 59 Provided that the whole action be guided and moderated by the Elders of the Church where the Assemblie is helde. **1742** Young *Nt. Th.* VII. 533 But these..When reason moderates the rein aright, Shall re-ascend. **1781** Gibbon *Decl. & F.* xvii. (1788) II. 33 Whatever could interest the public prosperity, was moderated by the authority of the Prætorian præfects. **1808** Barclay *Muscular Motions* 324 On what grounds are we to imagine that these two muscles shall..moderate one another with accuracy and precision?

refl. **1638** Baker tr. *Balzac's Lett.* (vol. II.) 209 Yet moderate your selfe a little at first, and be reserved in a strange country. **1673** Sir L. Jenkins *Let. to Earl of Arlington* in W. Wynne *Life* (1724) I. 128 The two Bishops have moderated themselves as much as can be desired.

†**b.** To adjust, arrange, adapt; to modify; to proportion the quantity of. *Obs.*

1477 Earl Rivers (Caxton) *Dictes* 18 He moderated so his mete and his drinke that he was at noo tyme fatter nor leener than other. **1523** Fitzherb. *Husb.* §44 And he that hath but a fewe shepe moderate this medicyne accordynge. *c* **1570** *Schort Somme 1st Bk. Discipline* §6 The ministeris stipend sould be moderated that neither [etc.]. **1630** *R. Johnson's Kingd. & Commw.* 243 Not only his orders and decrees are broken and moderated by the Councell, but also sometimes rejected and contemned.

3. **a.** In academic and Eccl. use: To preside over (a deliberative body) or at (a debate, etc.).

to moderate a call (Sc.) = 'to moderate in a call' (see 3 b).

1577 Hanmer *Anc. Eccl. Hist.* 84 There moderated there at that time the schoole of the faithfull, a famous learned man called Pantanus. **1593** Bilson *Govt. Chr. Ch.* xiv. 291 The Churches of Christ before that time were guided by certaine chiefe Pastours, that moderated as well the Presbyters as the rest of the flocke. **1630** W. Scot *Apol. Narr.* (1846) 17 The General assemblies were not moderated by Superintendents. **1638** *Act Gen. Assemb. Ch. Scotl.* 17 Dec. (1682) 51 No Minister, moderating his Session, shall usurpe a negative voice over the members of his Session. **1708** S. Sewall *Diary* 4 Feb., He expounded the first of Matthew yesterday; Moderated the Bachelours Dispute to day. **1748** *Whitehall Even. Post* No. 363 A Call was moderated for the Rev. John Edmonston, Minister at Cadross. **1809** Kendall *Trav.* I. vii. 68 The governor or some one chosen to moderate the court. **1816** Scott *Old Mort.* xxxi, Others were moderating a harmonious call, as they somewhat improperly termed it, to new officers. **1848** G. Struthers *Hist. Relief Ch.* ii. 201 A call was moderated. .. The people had set their affections upon Mr. William Adam... For him they moderated a kind of irregular call among themselves. **1968** *N.Y. Times* 26 June 1/5 Being shown live at the time was a panel discussion on the 'underground press' moderated by Steven V. Roberts, a reporter for The New York Times. **1975** *Listener* 9 Jan. 39/1 The closed circuit at the University of Kent at Canterbury was used recently to televise a meeting whose potential participants promised to be too numerous for any of the available halls... There were two 'teams' moderated by the chaplain.

b. *intr.* To act as moderator; to preside. Now chiefly *Sc.*, to act as president of a Presbyterian church court or of a synodical or congregational meeting.

In the Scottish Presbyterian churches, the 'call' or formal invitation to a minister-elect is signed by the members of the congregation at a meeting attended by the presbytery, and presided over by its moderator. On such an occasion the presbytery (or its moderator) is said ***to moderate in a call***.

1581 *Confer.* III. (1584) O j b, Any learned man present might moderate. **1614** B. Jonson *Bart. Fair* I. iii, A question of Predestination..put to 'hem by the Matron, your Spouse; who moderates with a cup of wine, euer and anone, and a Sentence out of Knoxe between. **1635** Pagitt *Christianogr.* 21 Stachis was the first Bishop of Bizantium.. who hath had a continued Succession to the Patriarch now moderating. **1647** N. Bacon *Disc. Govt. Eng.* I. xiii. (1739) 23 In the National and Provincial [Synods], sometimes Kings moderated alone, sometimes the Archbishop alone. **1707** E. Chamberlayne *Pres. St. Eng.* III. xii. (ed. 22) 468 The Regius Professors of Divinity, Law, and Physick, are obliged to moderate at every Doctors and Batchellors Act, in their several Faculties. **1766** T. Clap *Ann. Yale-Coll.* 15 Mr. Andrew moderated at the Commencements. **1778** E. Stiles *Lit. Diary* (1901) II. 311 The first Commencements were private. Rector Pierson moderated and gave Degrees till his Death. **1795** T. Hutchinson *Hist. Mass.* (ed. 3) I. 161 *note*, Mr. Mather..moderated at the masters disputations, and conferred the degrees at the commencement in 1681. **1803** *Gradus ad Cantabr.* 89 To *Moderate*, to perform the office of Moderator in the schools. **1869** A. Macdonald *Story Disputed Settlement* (1877) 69 (E.D.D.), I must go over and see him one of these days, before his call is moderated in. **1898** N. R. Johnston *Looking Back fr. Sunset Land* 150 He had moderated in a unanimous call for me in Topsham congregation.

†**4.** **a.** *trans.* To decide (a question) as an arbitrator; to settle by bringing about a compromise.

1602 Carew *Cornwall* I. 26 b, It passeth mine abilitie to moderate the question. **1603** Sir C. Heydon *Jud. Astrol.* xii. 276, I will require no other arbitrators, to moderate the controuersie beetwene vs. **1726** Leoni *Alberti's Archit.* I. 23 b, Cato moderates the matter thus. **1744** Warburton *Remarks* I. Wks. 1811 XI. 327 But St. Paul himself has long ago moderated this question for us, and declared for the negative.

†**b.** *absol.* or *intr.* To act as mediator or arbitrator. Also, to take a mediating view. *Obs.*

1597–8 Bacon *Ess., Discourse* (Arb.) 14 The honourablest part of talke is to giue the occasion, and againe to moderate and passe to somewhat else. **1612** Brinsley *Lud. Lit.* xiii. (1627) 184 When one taketh the affirmative part, another the Negative, and it may be a third moderateth or determineth betwene both. **1634** Sir T. Herbert *Trav.* 160 Elgazzuli.. moderated twixt the Cadies and his owne Reformatists. **1708** Swift *Sentim. Ch. of Eng. Man* i. Wks. 1751 IV. 65 Endeavouring to moderate between the rival Powers. **1713** Addison *Guard.* No. 122 ¶6 There were however a few select judges who moderated between both these extremes. **1756** *Connoisseur* No. 130 ¶1, I shall not pretend to moderate in family disputes of so important a nature.

moderated ('mɒdəreɪtɪd), *ppl. a.* [-ED^1.]

†**1.** **a.** Reasonably restricted and limited. *Obs.*

1643 Prynne *Sov. Power Parl.* App. 14 Theopompus left it [*sc.* the kingly power] more moderated to his successours. **1665** Manley *Grotius' Low C. Wars* 496 They say, the Netherlanders were never enslaved, but had alwayes a moderated Empire bounded by Laws. **1690** Locke *Govt.* II. xiv. (Rtldg.) 159 Moderated monarchies and well-framed governments. **1790** Burke *Fr. Rev.* Wks. 1808 V. 333 If the present project of a republick should fail, all securities to a moderated freedom fail along with it.

†**b.** ***well moderated***: well-conducted. *Obs.*

1660 Waterhouse *Arms & Arm.* 178 Abounding in rich, stout, grave, and well moderated Citizens.

2. Rendered moderate; reduced to a moderate amount or degree; duly regulated.

1814 D'Israeli *Quarrels Auth.* (1867) 261 [He] grudgingly bestows a moderated praise on this exquisite satire. **1857** Bp. Wilberforce in *Life* (1881) II. x. 345 Lord Aberdeen thinks that anything but a carefully moderated course..will come in too strong contrast with your past silence. **1878** Dowden *Stud. in Lit.* 45 Those who possess a moderated but steadfast confidence in the beneficent tendencies of the laws of the world.

3. *Nuclear Sci.* Of a reactor: provided with a moderator. Of a neutron: slowed down by a moderator.

1945 [see GRAPHITE b]. **1950** F. Gaynor *Encycl. Atomic Energy* 114 In a moderated reactor there remain more free neutrons to sustain and propagate the fission chain reaction of U^{235}. **1962** *Newnes Conc. Encycl. Nucl. Energy* 244/2 Most of the fissions [in a thermal reactor] are produced by these moderated neutrons.

moderately ('mɒdərətlɪ), *adv.* [f. MODERATE *a.* + -LY^2.] In a moderate manner, degree, extent, or amount; in or with moderation.

1398 Trevisa *Barth. De P.R.* XIX. xliii. (1495) 886 Swetnesse layed to the tonge openyth moderatly and hetyth moderatly and moysteth moderatly. *c* **1489** Caxton *Blanchardyn* i. 13 Blanchardyn..right moderatly and manerly mayntened hym self. **1560** Daus tr. *Sleidane's Comm.* 226 b, He wyll so moderately use thys victory, that no man shall nede to feare hys vyolence. **1592** Shaks. *Rom. & Jul.* II. vi. 14 Therefore Loue moderately, long Loue doth so, Too swift arriues as tardie as too slow. **1631** R. Bolton *Comf. Affl. Consc.* ii. (1635) 155 If Hee be but moderately, and not every day drunk. **1731** Arbuthnot *Aliments* (1735) 146 Tea is an Infusion of a Plant acescent, and moderately

astringent in warm Water. *a* **1763** SHENSTONE *Ess.* Wks. 1777 II. 7, I think, moderately speaking, the vulgar are generally in the wrong. **1831** J. FOSTER in *Life & Corr.* (1846) II. 193 Never more than very moderately good. **1880** *Responsib. Opium Trade* 22 The Chinaman who smokes moderately.

b. *Comb.*, as ***moderately-gifted, lighted*** adjs.

Combinations of the adv. with adjs. in -ED[2] are often incorrectly substituted for parasynthetic derivatives containing *moderate* adj., e.g. *moderately-sized* for *moderate-sized.*

1807–8 SYD. SMITH *Plymley's Lett.* Wks. 1859 II. 167/2 A set of worthy and moderately-gifted men. **1860–61** FLOR. NIGHTINGALE *Nursing* (ed. 2) 9 A moderately-sized bed-room. **1872** HUXLEY *Physiol.* ix. 220 A moderately-lighted surface.

moderateness ('mɒdərətnɪs). [f. MODERATE *a.* + -NESS.] The state or condition of being moderate.

1571 GOLDING *Calvin on Ps.* xlvi. 11 When men ronne a head without advisement, there is no roome for moderatenesse. **1658** A. FOX tr. *Wurtz' Surg.* II. iii. 52 A true moderateness in eating and drinking. **1781** JUSTAMOND *Priv. Life Lewis XV*, II. 144, I am surprized at the moderateness of the sum. **1872** BAGEHOT *Physics & Pol.* (1876) 203 A vigorous moderateness in mind and body. **1894** W. WALKER *Hist. Congregat. Ch. U.S.* 361 A moderateness of cost which should put it within the reach of the most needy.

moderater, -érateur: see MODERATOR.

moderating ('mɒdəreɪtɪŋ), *ppl. a.* [f. MODERATE *v.* + -ING[2].] That moderates.

1673 R. LEIGH *Transp. Reh.* 22 Alack, Alack, said I, that was upon the moderating part. **1714** SWIFT *Pres. St. Affairs* Wks. 1755 II. I. 207 Acting for the future upon a moderating scheme in order to reconcile both parties. **1887** *Athenæum* 26 Nov. 705/3 His moderating influence was especially valuable.

moderation (mɒdə'reɪʃən). [a. F. *modération* (14th c. in Hatz.-Darm.), ad. L. *moderātiōn-em*, f. *moderārī* to MODERATE: see -ATION.]

1. The action or an act of moderating.

†**a.** Limitation, restriction; a fixed limit; a restricting provision or clause. *Obs.*

1437 *Rolls of Parlt.* IV. 508/1 For ye reste of the saide Wolles and Wollefell, over the moderation aforesaid. **1461** *Ibid.* V. 467/1 The Kyng..assenteth to this Petition, and hit accepteth, with certeyn moderacions, provisions and exceptions. *a* **1646** J. GREGORY *Posthuma* (1650) 12 This Moderation of the words, though it hath not so much evidence as would bee required, yet it hath a notable pretens. **1700** C. DAVENANT *Disc. Grants*, etc. §111. 192 The Moderations or Savings put in writing as afore are in Number Forty Two.

†**b.** Control, rule, governance. Also, a system or method of government. *Obs.*

1526 *Pilgr. Perf.* (W. de W. 1531) 89 Whan holy persones ..seeth them selfe to profyte greatly and encrease in prosperite in maner by a moderacyon of the heuenly dispensacyons. **1531** ELYOT *Gov.* I. i, A body lyuyng, compacte or made of sondry astates and degrees of men, whiche is..gouerned by the rule and moderation of reason. **1568** GRAFTON *Chron.* II. 706 For surely he [*sc.* Humfrey Duke of Gloucester]..beyng a lyue, and hauing the moderation and gouernaunce of the common welth, king Henry had neuer wauered in so many hasardes. **1593** BILSON *Govt. Chr. Ch.* ix. 111 It cannot be doubted, but the moderation of the keies, and imposition of hands were at first setled in the Apostles and exercised by them. **1612** T. TAYLOR *Comm. Titus* i. 7 He hath lost all the bridle and moderation of himself. **1633** BP. HALL *Hard Texts, N.T.* 130 My righteous judgements in the moderation of the world and ordering all the affaires of my Church. **1726** LEONI *Alberti's Archit.* I. 77 Those who are entrusted with the supream authority and moderation in publick Affairs.

†**c.** Settlement by arbitration or compromise; an arrangement, a compromise. *Obs.*

1560 DAUS tr. *Sleidane's Comm.* 47b, Wherin not withstandyng to use this moderation, that suche as be in possession already, be permitted to enjoye the rente. **1568** GRAFTON *Chron.* II. 731 If it might please the king of Englande to appoint certayne of the yomen..to appoint not onely who should enter, but also the number of them, he thought that this moderation should be both suretie and pleasure to both the parties.

d. Abatement of severity or rigour; restriction within moderate limits. Now *rare.* Also, †reduction (of expenditure), abatement or lowering (of pecuniary charges).

1598 GRENEWEY *Tacitus' Ann.* III. v. (1622) 71 They debated the matter concerning the moderation of the law *Papia poppæa.* **1601** F. GODWIN *Bps. of Eng.* 515 [He] went about by course of law to stay him and force him to a moderation of expence. **1621** ELSING *Debates Ho. Lords* (Camden) 110 Moved, whether a generall jubelee shalbe for the debtes, or whether a moderacion? **1629** MASSINGER *Picture* IV. i, In extreames Of this condition, can it be in man To vse a moderation? **1692** DRYDEN *St. Euremont's Ess.* 202, I find but two things that may render it [*sc.* Life] happy. The Moderation of a Man's Desires, and the good use of his Fortune. **1709** STRYPE *Ann. Ref.* I. xlvii. 475 It would be with some Moderation only for Strangers. *a* **1716** SOUTH *Serm.* (1727) VI. i. 31 What is all Virtue but a Moderation of Excesses?

e. *Nuclear Sci.* The action or process of slowing down neutrons by the use of a moderator.

1945 H. D. SMYTH *Gen. Acct. Devel. Atomic Energy Mil. Purposes* ii. 20 The process of slowing down or moderation is simply one of elastic collisions between high-speed particles and particles practically at rest. **1958** O. R. FRISCH *Nucl. Handbk.* v. 17 The moderation of fast neutrons to thermal velocities occurs by transfer of energy on elastic collision. **1969** *New Scientist* 25 Sept. 639/2 The three essential functions of a blanket are neutron moderation, tritium breeding, and heat-transfer.

2. a. The quality of being moderate, in various senses; now only with reference to conduct, opinions, demands, desires, or their indulgence; avoidance of extremes; self-control, temperance; occasionally, †avoidance of severity or rigour, lenity, clemency.

1432–50 tr. *Higden* (Rolls) V. 31 This Marcus Antonius.. moderate grevous lawes and constitutions with other of gretter moderacion. **1509** HAWES *Past. Pleas.* xii. (Percy Soc.) 49 But moderacyon in theyr myndes is had, So that outrage may them not overtake. **1561** T. NORTON *Calvin's Inst.* I. 63 A pacience and quiet moderation of hart. *a* **1628** PRESTON *Breastpl. Love* (1631) 212 The moderation that keepeth from actions wherein is excesse, is good. **1702** STEELE *Funeral* v. (1734) 79 Oh! grant me, Heav'n, grant me Moderation! **1725** DE FOE *Voy. round World* (1840) 209 He admired much the moderation I had used. **1782** V. KNOX *Ess.* (1819) I. ii. 12 Moderation is the law of enjoyment. **1796** LAMB *Let. to Coleridge* 5 July, Can you write with sufficient moderation, as 'tis called, when one suppresses the one half of what one feels or could say on a subject? **1827** DISRAELI *Viv. Grey* VI. i, There is moderation even in excess. **1855** BREWSTER *Newton* II. xxiv. 346 Constantius..in place of persecuting the Athanasians, treated them with the greatest moderation. **1875** JOWETT *Plato* (ed. 2) V. 68 He is sensible that moderation is better than total abstinence.

b. Phr. ***in moderation***: in a moderate manner or proportion.

1867 *Chambers' Encycl.* IX. 350/2 The habitual use of alcoholic drinks in moderation. **1903** *Pilot* 17 Oct. 375/1 How about that cruel bearing rein? In strict moderation it may do no harm..but then in moderation it does not produce the effect aimed at by those who use it.

c. *Sc.* Applied to the views and policy of the 'Moderate' party in the Church of Scotland (see MODERATE B. b). Hence occas. ***the Moderation*** = 'the party of moderation', the 'Moderates'.

[**1735** ERSKINE *Serm.* Wks. 1871 II. 357 There is a generation of Gallios and Laodiceans who under the name of moderation, falsely so called, will look upon you as madmen.] **1753** WITHERSPOON (*title*) Ecclesiastical Characteristics..being an humble Attempt to open the Mystery of Moderation. **1801** T. BROWN in D. Welsh *Life* v. (1825) 165 The governing churchmen have persuaded the Dundases that it is absolutely necessary to secure the interest of moderation. **1831** J. M. CAMPBELL in *Mem.* (1877) I. 78 The Moderation was not half so excited against me as the Evangelicals... The 'Moderation' in my presbytery are not better than the rest.

3. *Sc.* The action of 'moderating in a call' (see MODERATE *v.* 3 b); a meeting of a congregation together with the presbytery, for the purpose of signing a 'call' to a minister-elect. See also quot. 1808.

1782 *Acts Gen. Assemb. Ch. Scotl.* (1843) 811 The resolution of Assembly respecting the moderation of calls. **1808** JAMIESON s.v. *Moderation*, When a minister is appointed to preside in this business [*sc.* of electing a pastor], it is said that the Presbytery *grant a moderation* to the people. **1867** A. DUNCAN in D. Duncan *Discourses* Memoir 5 The moderation was delayed till the month of June, when he received a unanimous call. **1875** JAS. GRANT *One of the '600'* v. I. 72 The provost and minister gabbled about presbyteries and synods, the moderation of calls, elders, deacons [etc.]. **1904** R. SMALL *Hist. U.P. Congregat.* I. 125 A moderation was applied for, £100 of stipend being promised.

4. *pl.* In the University of Oxford, the 'First Public Examination' for the degree of B.A., conducted by the Moderators (see MODERATOR 5 b). Colloquially shortened to MODS.

1858 J. C. THOMSON *Almæ Matres* 224 The next compulsory examination is called 'moderations'. **1883** *A. Barratt's Phys. Metempiric* Pref. 13 When he was reading for double Honours in Moderations.

5. *Comb.*, as (sense 2) ***moderation-monger***; (sense 3 *Sc.*) ***moderation day***.

a **1716** SOUTH *Serm.* (1727) VI. 80 No Moderation-monger under Heaven shall ever persuade me that St. Paul would have took such a Course with such Persons. **1904** R. SMALL *Hist. U.P. Congregat.* I. 353 His rejection on the moderation day was the last straw that broke the camel's back.

moderationism (mɒdə'reɪʃənɪz(ə)m). [f. MODERATION 2 + -ISM.] A policy or doctrine of being moderate or acting with moderation.

1960 [see CENTRISM].

moderationist (mɒdə'reɪʃənɪst). [f. MODERATION + -IST.] An advocate of moderation; *spec.*, one who supports the views of the 'moderate drinker' as opposed to the total abstainer.

1846 G. McCULLOCH *Sobriety contrasted w. Intemp.* 131 From the last resting place of every Moderationist arises a Voice..'Beware of Moderation'. **1883** *League Jrnl.* 20 Oct. 657/3 This is the new line of defence behind which some moderationists [*sc.* on the drink question] are disposed to shelter themselves.

moderatism ('mɒdərətɪz(ə)m). [f. MODERATE *a.* and *sb.* + -ISM.] The doctrines or policy of any of the parties known as 'Moderate'; addiction to moderate views or courses of action.

1795 *Hist.* in *Ann. Reg.* 83 It was common..with the more violent Jacobins..to make charges against those who were less so, or insinuate suspicions of Moderatism! **1835** PUSEY in *Newman's Lett.* (1891) II. 134 But I fear those persons have too far committed themselves, and are too ingrained with moderatism. **1842** *Mem. J. Halley* 38 The principles of Moderatism in the Scottish Church. **1894** *Westm. Gaz.* 2 Apr. 2/2 Moderatism, then, has made no way in Rotherhithe; but a certain number of Progressives who voted in 1892 did not take the trouble to go to the poll. **1923** G. M. TREVELYAN *Manin & Venetian Revolution* iii. 49 The event resounded through Italy and Europe. It shook the somewhat self-complacent 'moderatism' of Giobertian waiters on opportunity. **1970** *Guardian* 1 Oct. 19/4 Mr. Crouch's apologia for 'moderatism'..is as unexciting in print as it was ineffective in the worst university crises.

moderatist ('mɒdərətɪst). [f. MODERATE *a.* + -IST.] One who professes or is characterized by moderatism or moderation.

1716 M. DAVIES *Athen. Brit.* II. 337 That solid Moderatist Mr. Talents. **1817** BENTHAM *Parl. Reform* Introd. 331 The Honourable Gentleman in question, who of all moderatists..seems to be least remote from Radicalism.

‖**moderato** (mode'rato, mɒdə'rɑːtəʊ), *adv. Mus.* [It.: cf. MODERATE.] Moderately; at a moderate pace or tempo. Abbreviated *Mod.*

1724 *Explic. For. Words in Mus. Bks.*, *Moderato*, is with Moderation. **1762** STERNE *Tr. Shandy* VI. xi. **1811** BUSBY *Dict. Mus.* (ed. 3), *Moderato*, a word used adjectively to signify a time of a moderate degree of quickness.

moderator ('mɒdəreɪtə(r)). Also 4, 6 **moderatoure**, 6 **moderater**, 6–7 **moderatour**. [a. F. *modérateur* 15th c. in Hatz.-Darm. (cf. OF. *modereur*), a. L. *moderātor*, agent-n. f. *moderārī*: see MODERATE *v.*]

†**1.** A ruler, governor, director. Also *fig. Obs.*

1398 TREVISA *Barth. De P.R.* VIII. xvi. (1495) 322 The sonne is moderatoure of the fyrmament. **1563–83** FOXE *A. & M.* I. 578/1 You..take vppon you so cockishly..to be a controller and maister moderatour of other mens matters. **1579** FENTON *Guicciard.* I. (1618) 27 There were ioyned with him (as moderators of his youth) Iohn Iacques Triuulce, .. and the Count Petillane..both Captaines of great experience. **1641** PRYNNE *Antip.* Epist. 17 The great Moderator of the Universe, who hath..wrought wondrous things..for the honour and safety of his Majesty, and his Realmes. **1640** BP. HALL *Chr. Moder.* I. vii. 66 Custome of the place, care of health, regard to our ability, are fit moderators of every mans palate. **1658** J. HARRINGTON *Prerog. Pop. Govt.* II. xi. (1700) 334 The Romans having conquer'd Antiochus, became Moderators of Asia. **1680** H. MORE *Apocal. Apoc.* 102 The works of Righteousness [were numbered] by dayes, of which the Sun is moderator. **1682** GREW *Anat. Plants* I. ii. 16 The Cortical [Body] is the Moderator of that [*sc.* Motion] in the Lignous. **1705** S. SEWALL *Lett.-Bk.* 11 Sept., Storms and Tempests which Christ makes great use of in Governing the World; and in this He is only Moderator. **1808** BARCLAY *Muscular Motions* 370 The same muscles..when acting in any capacity as motors, have..at all times the same moderators and the same directors. **1867** FREEMAN *Norm. Conq.* (1877) I. iv. 209 Competent to act in his name as moderator of the Western realm.

†**2.** *nonce-use.* One who keeps a middle course.

1565 T. STAPLETON *Fortr. Faith* 158* These meane moderatours, and half halters.

3. One who acts as an arbitrator between disputants; an arbiter, umpire, judge. Also, a mediator.

c **1560** tr. *Calvin's Comm. Prayer Bk.* in *Phenix* (1708) II. 213 If so be any Contention rise, then such as are appointed Moderators either satisfy the Party, or else..exhort him to keep silence. **1578** SIDNEY *May Lady* in Nichols *Progr. Q. Eliz.* II. 99 Between whom the schoolemaster Rombus came in as a moderator. **1646** CRASHAW *Musicks Duell* 52 The high-percht treble chirps at this, and chides, Vntill his finger (Moderatour) hides And closes the sweet quarrell. **1657** TRAPP *Comm. Job.* xxxii. 279 He..takes the boldnesse to interpose as an Arbiter, or Moderator, blaming both sides [etc.]. **1712** ADDISON *Spect.* No. 309 ¶8 He acts as a kind of Moderator between the two opposite Parties. **1826** DISRAELI *Viv. Grey* II. xiv, He was earnestly requested by the contending theorists to assume the office of moderator. **1847** GROTE *Greece* II. xxvii. (1862) III. 37 They were directed.. to invite from Mantinea a moderator. **1863** H. COX *Instit.* III. iii. 633 The Sovereign is a moderator between the several political parties in the State. **1884** *Manch. Exam.* 12 Sept. 5/1 In Syria he was the moderator between two sets of fanatics.

4. a. A person chosen to preside over a meeting or assembly and conduct its business; a presiding officer or president, esp. *U.S.*, one elected to preside over a 'town meeting'.

1573 CARTWRIGHT *Reply to Answ. Whitgift* 29 What is it then that is sayde in Exodus that Moises..sate as it were moderatoure in that election? **1580** LYLY *Euphues* (Arb.) 421 The Ladie Flauia, .. as moderater commaunded them both to silence, willing Euphues as vmper in these matters, briefly to speake his minde. **1641** in *Col. Laws Mass.* (1889) 49 So shal the presedent or moderator have [a casting voice] in all Civill Courts or Assemblies. **1649** in *Rec. Muddy River & Brookline, Mass.* (1875) 36 *note*, It is ordered yt there be a Moderator chosen annually to regulate publicke towne meetings. **1766** M. CUTLER in *Life*, etc. (1888) I. 13 There should be a President appointed, to act as Moderator, to propose all matters to the Club. **1799** S. FREEMAN *Town Off.* 194 Having first chosen a Moderator to manage and regulate the business of the meeting. **1850** MARSDEN *Early Purit.* (1853) 107 A presiding moderator always concluded the exercise, which lasted from nine to eleven o'clock. **1882** *Mass. Public Stat.* 232 At every town meeting..a moderator shall be first chosen.

b. *spec.* A chairman of a television discussion (also in extended use). *N. Amer.*

1952 in A. Rothe *Current Biogr.* 433/2 Since 1946 he [*sc.* Senator Blair Moody] has also been moderator of the radio and television program *Meet Your Congress.* **1972** *Village Voice* (N.Y.) 1 June 28/3 She kept qualifying her aggression with apologies and withdrawals and cancellations..and

maintaining the good will of the moderator. **1972** *Evening Telegram* (St John's, Newfoundland) 24 June 1/2 Ron Pumphrey, moderator of an open-line program on St. John's radio station VOCM. **1973** *Guardian* 17 Oct. 12/4 The present moderators..were picked by London broadcasting to do a specific job, that of answering the phone and referring the questions to a guest expert. **1974** R. Thomas *Porkchoppers* xxv. 212 The program's moderator..was..the syndicated political columnist who specialized in political muckraking.

5. In academic use: **a.** A public officer formerly appointed to preside over the disputations or exercises prescribed in the University schools for candidates for degrees. Now (*a*) at Cambridge, one of two officers, appointed annually, who preside over and are responsible for the proper conduct of the examination for the Mathematical Tripos; (*b*) at Oxford, an examiner for Moderations.

1573 G. Harvey *Letter-bk.* (Camden) 51 As he was abroad in the schooles, so wuld neds seme a moderator at home too in the haul. **1615** Crooke *Body of Man* 132 That occulate Anatomist Petrus Pauius of Leydon..my first Maister & Moderator in Anatomie. **1674** Hickman *Hist. Quinquart.* Epist. (ed. 2) a iij b, The main work of the Moderator is, to keep the Disputants to form. **1766** Clap *Ann. Yale* 27 The Rev. Mr. Woodbridge acted as Moderator; and he and Mr. Buckingham and other Ministers present signed Certificates, that they judged them to be worthy of the Degree of Bachelor of Arts. **1797** *Cambr. Univ. Cal.* 142 Moderators are appointed and paid by the proctors. **1850** *Abstracts New Exam. Stat. Oxf.* (1851) 1 The 'First Examination' under Moderators will take place for the first time in Easter Term 1852. **1906** *Oxford Univ. Cal.* 176 Honour lists issued by Moderators from 1891.

b. At Dublin, a candidate for the degree of Bachelor of Arts who passes out first (Senior) or second (Junior) in honours.

1838 *Dublin Univ. Cal.* 15 Of the successful candidates in each department [*sc.* Physics and mathematics, Classics, Ethics and logics] there are two grades, called Senior and Junior Moderators. **1845** W. B. S. Taylor *Hist. Univ. Dubl.* 155 [List of] Works examined in for moderators in mathematics and physics. **1882** *Society* 16 Dec. 18/2 Mr. Maunsell graduated..as a Moderator and Silver Medallist.

6. In the Presbyterian churches: A minister elected to preside over any one of the ecclesiastical bodies, *e.g.* the congregation, the presbytery, the synod, the general assembly.

1563 *Min. Gen. Assembly* in Peterkin *Bk. Univ. Kirk Scotl.* (1839) 17 It was propone be the haill Assemblie that ane Moderator should be appointed for avoiding confusion in reasoning. **1582** *Reg. Privy Council Scot.* III. 476 Maister Nicholl Dalgleische, as moderatour of the haill synodal assemblie,..Patrik Gillespie, moderatour of the haill presbiterie of Striveling. **1641** 'Smectymnuus' *Answ.* xiv. (1653) 61 The Moderator in Geneva is not of a Superior order to his Brethren. **1692** Luttrell *Brief Rel.* (1857) II. 362 The moderator [of the generall assembly of the kirk] adjourned them till August 12 months. **1727** Swift *Further Acc. E. Curll* Wks. 1755 III. i. 161 Some deceased moderator of the general assembly in Scotland. **1846** McCulloch *Acc. Brit. Empire* iv. viii. (1854) II. 287 The Assembly chooses a moderator for every meeting, who, in recent times, has been always a clergyman.

7. a. One who or that which mitigates or makes moderate.

1621 Burton *Anat. Mel.* III. iv. II. ii. (1624) 535 Hope, that sweet moderator of passions as Simonides calls it. **1696** Tryon *Misc.* i. 6 This Essential Powder or pure Life, is the Moderator or Friendly Quality in all Minerals. **1817** J. Scott *Paris Revisit.* (ed. 4) 323 It was known to be..her [Russia's] policy, to recommend herself to France as the magnanimous moderator of the severity of her Allies.

b. *Hist.* A member of a band of persons opposed to the violent methods of the 'Regulators' who professed to supply the want of the regular administration of justice in the Carolinas *c* 1767–71.

1767 Ld. Montagu in A. Gregg *Hist. Old Cheraws* (1867) 182 A new set of people, who call themselves Moderators, have appeared against the Regulators. **1847** *Desperadoes of South-West* in *Harbinger* 7 Aug. 136/1 The regulators..soon find that their foes organize also; arm themselves, and prepare for systematic resistance, under the denomination of 'moderators'.

c. (Occas. in Fr. form *modérateur*.) Short for ***moderator-lamp*** (see 8 b). Also, the mechanical contrivance by which the supply of oil to the wick of such a lamp is regulated.

1851 *Pract. Mechanics' Jrnl.* Mar. 273 It is however in the mode adopted for the adjustment of the oil supply to the burner that the improvement for which the inventor claims the name 'Moderator' consists. **1859** W. G. Wills *Life's Foreshad.* II. xii. 161 He put out the modérateur. **1864** *Chamb. Encycl.* VI. 23/2 The greatest improvement ever effected in oil-lamps was in the so-called French moderator. **1875** *Ure's Dict. Arts*, etc. (ed. 7) III. 35 As the pressure employed is so great, the oil would, but for the 'moderator', flow over with too much rapidity. This moderator, or regulator, is a tapering rod of iron-wire.

d. *Nuclear Sci.* A substance that slows down neutrons passing through it; *spec.* one used in a reactor to reduce the speed of fast neutrons so that they cause fission more readily.

1945 H. D. Smyth *Gen. Acct. Devel. Atomic Energy Mil. Purposes* ii. 20 The light elements are most effective as 'moderators', i.e., slowing-down agents, for neutrons. **1958** W. K. Mansfield *Elem. Nucl. Physics* iv. 38 If the U^{235} content exceeds about 50 per cent it is possible to achieve a chain reaction without the use of a moderator. **1961** G. R. Choppin *Exper. Nucl. Chem.* viii. 115 Since it is desirable to increase the probability of capture by slowing the neutrons down, a moderator containing a low Z element with a low capture cross section surrounds the source. **1962** *Newnes Conc. Encycl. Nucl. Energy* 509/1 The most common moderators are: light water (H_2O), heavy water (D_2O), graphite, beryllium, beryllia and organic liquids. **1966** C. R. Tottle *Sci. Engin. Materials* x. 236 In nuclear reactors..a moderator, or slowing-down material, is used to decrease the energy of fast neutrons produced in fission until they are more readily captured in the fissile material at lower energies. **1969** Bennison & Wright *Geol. Hist. Brit. Isles* i. 18 Since carbon is a good moderator of neutrons, carbonaceous rocks are liable to give a spurious indication of porosity.

8. *attrib.* **a.** *Anat.* and *Phys.* in names of certain structures exercising a regulating action, as ***moderator-band, -centre, -ligament, -nerve, -ring*** (see *Syd. Soc. Lex.* 1891).

1898 *Allbutt's Syst. Med.* V. 849 The apparent provision against this distension [of the heart] in ungulates by the *moderator band, demonstrated by the late Professor Rolleston. **1782** A. Monro *Compar. Anat.* (ed. 3) 76 Each lateral or *moderator ligament of the head. **1753** Chambers *Cycl. Supp.* s.v., *Moderator-ring*..that ring which the muscles of the eye make round the optic nerve.

b. ***moderator-*** (occas. ***modérateur***) ***lamp***, a lamp in which, by a mechanical contrivance, the passage of the oil from the reservoir to the burner is regulated or moderated to a uniform flow.

1851 *Pract. Mechanics' Jrnl.* Mar. 273 Hadrot's Moderator Lamp. **1857** *Union* 23 Jan. 63 (Advt.), Moderateur lamps..just received from Paris. **1904** *Blackw. Mag.* Apr. 469/1 New lampshades..decorated the globes of the moderator-lamps.

moderatorial (mɒdərəˈtɔərɪəl), *a.* [f. Moderator + -ial.] Of, pertaining to, or characteristic of a moderator or chairman.

1867 'T. Lackland' *Homespun* II. 155 This moderatorial edict is echoed up in the bell-tower. **1926** *Scots Observer* 13 Nov. 4/4 There was a moderatorial flavour in the eloquence of the evening. **1968** *Guardian* 19 Mar. 16/1 In his moderatorial address to the council last night, the Rev. Edward Rogers, a former president of the Methodist Church, said the ecumenical movement had reached the point where it presented a challenge. **1975** *Church Times* 27 June 14/4 The most excitingly growing church I found during my Moderatorial year was such a union.

moderatorship (ˈmɒdəreɪtəʃɪp). [See -ship.] The function, office, or position of a moderator.

1641 'Smectymnuus' *Vind. Answ.* xiv. 182 From whose Moderators our Bishops differ onely in perpetuitie of Moderatorship. **1656** Heylin *Extraneus Vapulans* 153 Passed from one to another in their severall turns like the Moderatorship in the generall Assembly of the Kirk of Scotland. **1754** Richardson *Grandison* (1781) I. xiii. 76 Mr. Reeves..said he would, by way of moderatorship in the present debate, read them a passage. **1838** *Dubl. Univ. Cal.* 15 Those candidates for degrees who have obtained honors in the preceding part of the College Course, are entitled to offer themselves as candidates for Moderatorships. **1901** *Daily Chron.* 25 Dec. 6/4 Moderatorship of the Free Church of Scotland... A letter was read from the Rev. Dr. Marcus Dods, declining to be nominated to the Moderatorship of the next Assembly.

† **moderatress.** *Obs.* [f. Moderator + -ess.] A female moderator. (Only in 17th c.)

1602 Dolman *La Primaud. Fr. Acad.* (1618) III. 664 The maker of the matter and moderatresse of all nature. *a* **1661** Fuller *Worthies, Yorksh.* (1662) III. 191 Hilda..being a kind of Moderatresse in a Saxon Synod. **1686** Goad *Celest. Bodies* I. xii. 47 Those who allow the Lunar Influence to be Moderatress of the Tides.

† **modeˈratrix.** *Obs.* Also 6 **moderatrice.** [a. L. *moderātrix*, F. *modératrice*: see Moderator.] A female moderator.

1531 Elyot *Gov.* II. ix, Temperance..is the moderatrice as well of all motions of the minde, called affectes, as of all actis procedyng of man. **1577** Timme *Calvin on 1 Cor.* 64 b (*margin*), Loue the moderatrix of contention. *a* **1614** Cope in Gutch *Coll. Cur.* I. 120 He loved equity, as the true umpress between them both, as moderatrix of extremes. **1651** C. Cartwright *Cert. Relig.* I. 63 Your Church hath..practised it a long time, for a woman to be head or supreme moderatrix in the Church. **1673** *Ess. Educ. Gentlewom.* 13 She is ordinarily a Moderatrix in the Academy at the Disputation amongst learned Wits. **1741** Middleton *Cicero* II. x. 386 He had given up all his resentments to the Republic; made her the Moderatrix of all his acts. **1753** Richardson *Grandison* (1781) VI. lv. 356 The debate was closed, and referred to Mrs. Shirley, as Moderatrix.

† **ˈmoderature.** *Obs. rare*$^{-1}$. [f. Moderate *v.*: see -ure.] Moderation, temperance.

1574 Newton *Health Mag.* 77 Aristotle..referreth all the cause of prosperous health unto temperate moderature of meate and drinke, and [etc.].

modere, obs. form of Moder, Mother.

modereid, (? *erron.*) variant of Midred *Obs.*

moderhed(e, -les(se, -ly, obs. ff. Motherhead, -less, -ly.

modern (ˈmɒdən), *a.* and *sb.* Also 6–7 **moderne.** [ad. late L. *modern-us* (6th c.), f. *modo* just now (on the analogy of *hodiernus* that is of to-day, f. *hodiē* to-day). Cf. F. *moderne*, Sp., Pg., It. *moderno*, G. *modern*.]

A. *adj.*

† **1.** Being at this time; now existing. *Obs. rare.*

1500–20 Dunbar *Poems* lxxxv. 5 Hodiern, modern, sempitern, Angelicall regyne! **1555** *Extracts Aberdeen Reg.* (1844) I. 285 The next parliament, to be haldin..in name of our maist gracious quene moderne. **1597** *Burgh Rec. Glasgow* (1876) I. 185 Hew, erle of Eglingtoune moderne. **1700** *Pennsylv. Archives* I. 127 Being obliged to it by thy former as well as modern kindness. **1752** *Charter Soc. Antiq. Lond.* 7 Wee have nominated..Martin Folkes, Esquire, to be the first and modern President of the said Society.

2. a. Of or pertaining to the present and recent times, as distinguished from the remote past; pertaining to or originating in the current age or period. spec. ***(the) modern Babylon***: London; ***modern Greats***: at Oxford University, the school of Philosophy, Politics, and Economics.

In Historical use commonly applied (in contradistinction to *ancient* and *mediæval*) to the time subsequent to the Middle Ages, and the events, personages, writers, etc. of that time. So ***modern history***: see History 3 b.

1585 T. Washington tr. *Nicholay's Voy.* I. xv. 16 b, The writings of the auncient and moderne Geographers and Historiographers. **162.** Bacon *Let. to T. Matthew* in Spedding *Lett.* VII. 429 For these modern languages will at one time or other play the bank-rowtes with books. **1656** Earl Monm. tr. *Boccalini's Advts. fr. Parnass.* II. xxviii. (1674) 177 The women of this Modern Age had..need of amendment. **1676** Ray *Corr.* (1848) 122 Much also he hath..taken out of some modern writer it hath not been my hap to see. **1687** A. Lovell tr. *Thevenot's Trav.* I. 275 There is another Aqueduct somewhat older, yet still modern. **1706** Phillips (ed. Kersey) Pref., Our English Tongue..may be said to equal, if not surpass all other Modern Languages. **1713** Pope *Guard.* No. 4 ¶2 The authoress of a famous modern romance. **1757** J. H. Grose *Voy. E. Indies* 74 These last are of moderner date. **1757** tr. *Keysler's Trav.* (1760) III. 400 Their country appears to have been situated..at a great distance from the modern Padua. **1774** Mitford *Ess. Harmony Lang.* 260 The most admired modern masters. **1810** E. D. Clarke *Trav. Russia* xxv. (1839) 120/1 Perhaps we are not authorised in considering the modern Greeks as legitimate descendants of the Getæ. **1835** J. M. Wilson *Tales of Borders* I. 356, I proceeded to London... Months passed away, and I was still a wanderer upon the streets of the modern Babylon. **1847** Disraeli *Tancred* III. v. v. 77 London is a modern Babylon. **1850** Dickens *Dav. Copp.* xxxvi. 374 Bidding adieu to the modern Babylon. **1864** Kirk *Chas. Bold* II. iv. i. 170 The close of the 15th century is universally recognized as..the starting-point..of Modern, in distinction from Mediæval, history. **1904** A. Bennett *Great Man* viii. 79 The human tide which beats for ever on the shores of modern Babylon. [**1909** *Wanted! A New School at Oxf.* 4 It is a plan for, as it were, a modern-side Greats, based on Philosophy, but also..containing an admixture of certain other subjects.] **1922** Joyce *Ulysses* 611 The sights of the great metropolis, the spectacle of our modern Babylon. **1925** *Times* 15 July 19/3 The examiners in the Final Honour School of Philosophy, Politics, and Economics ('Modern Greats') issued the following class list. **1935** N. Mitchison *We have been Warned* II. 146 He was..thinking what a rotten school Modern Greats was. **1971** D. Scott *A. D. Lindsay* iii. 50 A new School of Politics, Philosophy and Economics—'Modern Greats'.

b. *Geol.* and *Zool.* Belonging to a comparatively recent period in the life-history of the world.

1823 Buckland *Reliq. Diluv.* 21 The modern hyæna is an inhabitant exclusively of hot climates. **1830** Lyell *Princ. Geol.* I. 114 If such species be termed modern, in comparison to races which preceded them, their remains, nevertheless, enter into submarine deposits many hundred miles in length. **1873** Dawson *Earth & Man* x. 248 The Modern Damans or Conies.

c. Prefixed to the name of a language to form a designation for that form of the language that is now in use, in contrast to any earlier form. In recent philology used technically to denote the last of the three periods into which it is customary to divide the history of living languages; distinguished from *Old* and *Middle.* ***modern English***: see English *sb.* 1 b.

1699 M. Lister *Journey to Paris* 108 Another Book overwritten in a small Modern Greek Hand, about 150 years ago. **1748** Smollett *R. Random* I. xxx. 275, I asserted that the modern Greek was as different from that spoke and written by the ancients, as the English used now from the old Saxon spoke in the time of Hengist. **1841** Borrow *Zincali* I. II. i. 235 The number of Persian, Sclavonian, and modern Greek words with which it [*sc.* the language of the 'Gitános of Estremadura'] is chequered. **1900** Clarke & Murray *Dent's School Gram. Mod. French* p. v, An attempt has been made to make this a grammar of modern French. **1927** S. Jónsson *Primer Mod. Icelandic* p. v, The first suggestion that I should write a text book of modern Icelandic was made to me in 1917. **1971** B. S. J. Isserlin *Hebrew Word-Bk.* 1 Grammatically modern Hebrew differs less from Biblical Hebrew than Old English does from Modern English. **1971** N. Fisher *Rise at Dawn* x. 169 He was in Corfu and he speaks good modern Greek.

d. ***modern languages***: as the designation of a department of study, ordinarily taken to include only the better-known living literary languages of Europe (sometimes merely French and German). Also *attrib.* in ***modern language master, school, tripos.*** Cf. quots. 162. and 1706 under sense 2 a.

1821 H. C. Robinson *Diary* 3 Oct. (1967) 70 Sara Coleridge..has taught herself modern languages, and is said to have great talent. **1838** *Dubl. Univ. Cal.* 55 Medals for Modern Languages. **1862** *Rep. Publ. Schools Comm.* (1864) III. 257 (Eton) With respect to modern languages, they are not cared for much, are they? **1932** Auden *Orators* I. i. 19 The really disgusted—the teacher of modern languages. **1961** R. B. Long *Sentence & its Parts* xvii. 377 In *modern-language teaching* what is modern is the languages; in *modern language teaching* what is modern..is the teaching of languages.

e. With reference to secondary education, applied (in contradistinction to *classical*) to subjects of school instruction other than the ancient languages and literature. ***modern school***, (*a*) in some English public schools, a separately organized division of the school in which 'modern subjects' form nearly the whole curriculum, Greek (and, usually, advanced Latin) not being taught; (*b*) a secondary modern school. ***modern side*** = *modern school* (a).

1862 *Rep. Publ. Schools Comm.* (1864) IV. 281 There would be this danger;..that idle and incapable boys would wish to enter this modern school to get off Latin composition and Greek. **1881** F. E. Hulme *Town, Coll., & Neighb. Marlborough* 91 In the modern school the subjects of instruction are mathematics [etc.]. **1887** *Pall Mall G.* 7 Nov. 2/2 'Modern sides' are either effective (as they all ought to be) or non-effective. If the former, there are scholarships in 'modern subjects' for them to win. **1905** *Macm. Mag.* Nov. 78 [At Harrow] the Modern Side is not self-contained in the sense of having a separate staff. It has been thought that any attempt to group Modern Side boys together and apart under separate masters and tutors would be unwise. **1944** *Ann. Reg. 1943* 62 Three main types of secondary schools—grammar, modern, and technical. **1957** *Listener* 13 June 951/1 The 1944 [Education] Act had brought the modern school into being. **1975** *Times* 29 Aug. 10/4 When university entrance is considered there is a 47 per cent advantage of the combined grammar and modern schools over the comprehensives.

f. *absol.* That which is modern. †***upon the modern***: ? peculiar to modern times.

1760–72 H. Brooke *Fool of Qual.* (1809) I. 165, I apprehend that this character is pretty much upon the modern. In all ancient or dead languages we have no term any way adequate, whereby we may express it. **1905** *Daily Chron.* 21 Jan. 4/6 He rejoices in that inability to depict the modern which is the most convincing sign of the contemporary.

g. *Typogr.* Used to designate a group of type-faces developed in the late eighteenth and early nineteenth centuries, distinguished by flat serifs, increased contrast between the thick and thin parts of the letters, and an effect of greater precision and vertical emphasis in use. Also ***modern-cut, -face(d)*** adjs.

1808 C. Stower *Printer's Gram.* Specimens of Printing Types, (*heading*) Specimens of modern-cut printing types, from the founderies of Messrs. Fry and Steele, and Messrs. Caslon and Catherwood. **1819** R. Austin in A. F. Johnson *Type Designs* (1934) iii. 97 The modern or new fashioned faced printing-type at present in use was introduced by the French, about 20 years ago. **1874** G. Simpson in Geo. Eliot *Lett.* (1956) VI. 44 Tinted paper ought never to be used with modern faced type. It suits ancient face only. **1894** *Amer. Dict. Printing & Bookmaking* 379/2 *Modern faces*, these are those kinds of Romans which have been cut since the beginning of the century. **1902** T. L. De Vinne *Pract. Typogr.: Treat. Title-Pages* 234 Of modern-cut types we have many varieties. **1926** S. Morison *Type Designs* 31 The main distinguishing characteristic of the modern-face is that the serif is thinner, longer and more refined than in the old-face. The difference as between the stem and the hair-line is more marked, and the general note of 'modern' is that of extreme precision and a certain perpendicularity. **1934** A. F. Johnson *Type Designs* iii. 73 During the eighteenth century the design of our roman types underwent a radical change, resulting in the style which we know as modern face, the type of the nineteenth century and still the type used in our newspapers and most of our books. **1972** P. Gaskell *New Introd. Bibliogr.* 210 By the second decade of the nineteenth century English printers were using modern face almost exclusively.

h. Of a movement in art and architecture, or the works produced by such a movement: characterized by a departure from or a repudiation of accepted or traditional styles and values. Cf. abstract A. 4 d.

[**1849** *Art Jrnl.* XI. 69/3 Between this society and one begun some years ago for the encouragement of modern Art and native artists, there should be no rivalry.] **1895** R. Muther *Hist. Mod. Painting* I. 10 Because this distinction between the eclectic and the personal, the derived and the independent, has not yet been carried out with sufficient strictness..it has hitherto..been found so difficult to discover the distinctive *style* of modern art. **1927** C. Bell *Landmarks 19th-Cent. Painting* 5 Géricault and then Delacroix were the new influences in France; in England the innovator was Constable. From these points of departure you can trace the whole glorious history of modern art. **1929** H. R. Hitchcock *Mod. Archit.* xvii. 201 There is..little to compare with the unconsciously 'modern' work of those architects who continued the English tradition. **1938** O. Lancaster *Pillar to Post* 74 When, shortly after the War, the Modern Movement..was first brought to public notice it led to a natural and healthy reaction against the excessive ornament..of the previous generation. **1958** S. W. Cheney *Story Mod. Art* (rev. ed.) p. v, I have accepted here the broadest traditional usage of the term 'modern art' as covering the course of creative invention since 1800. **1972** P. M. Dardi *Archit. xiii.* 117/1 The flight of refugees from the Nazis..scattered the pioneers of the Modern movement across western Europe and America. **1973** *Times* 19 June 14/4 *A Child of Six Could Do It*, [an exhibition of] cartoons about modern art at the Tate.

i. In full, ***modern first*** (***edition***). A bookseller's term for the first edition of a book published after about 1900. Also *absol.* or as *sb.*

1922 M. Sadleir *Excursions in Victorian Bibliogr.* 7 The dapper expert in ingenious moderns with his prefaces, his cancel-titles, [etc.]. **1952** J. Carter *ABC for Bk.-Collectors* 122 *Modern firsts*, a category widely employed but.. impossible to define with any precision, since its use among antiquarian booksellers is, and probably always will be, quite unstandardised. At present (1951) it commonly extends as far back as 1900, and will often include books published before that date if their author's hey-day was after it. **1968** *Bertram Rota Ltd. Catal.* No. 158 (verso front cover), We are always pleased to receive offers of modern first editions and private press books in fine state. **1973** *Directory of Dealers Secondhand & Antiquarian Bks. Brit. Isles 1973–75* 240 E. H. Bucknall..modern first editions. **1975** *Bibliognost* Aug. 5 The chance that someone will find a simple first edition of a modern author is slim, because [John F.] Fleming's firsts are very special... Each would be priced well above the average cost of 'moderns'.

3. a. Characteristic of the present and recent times; new-fashioned; not antiquated or obsolete. In spec. phrases: ***modern convenience***, an amenity, device, fitting, etc., such as is usual in a modern house; freq. *pl.*; cf. mod. con.; ***modern dance***, a free expressive style of dancing distinct from classical ballet (see quots.); hence ***modern dancer, dancing*** vbl. sb.; ***modern jazz***, jazz of a type which originated during and after the war of 1939–45.

1590 Sir J. Smyth *Disc. Weapons* 8 b, Without composing them of diuers sorts of weapons, according to the moderne vse. **1598** Barret *Theor. Warres* Gloss. 251 Moderne warre, is the new order of warre vsed in our age. **1605** B. Jonson *Volpone* iii. iv, He has so moderne, and facile a veine, Fitting the time, and catching the court-eare. **1676** Etheredge *Man of Mode* i. i, *Bell.* He thinks himself the Pattern of modern Gallantry. *Dor.* He is indeed the Pattern of modern Foppery. **1701** De Foe *True-born Eng.* 24 But England, Modern to the last degree Borrows or makes her own Nobility. **1859** [see *dish-lift* s.v. dish *sb.* 10]. **1872** Howells *Wedd. Journ.* (1892) 79 They conjectured..flavours of Tennyson and Browning in his verse, with a moderner tint from Morris. **1885** *Academy* 24 Jan. 53/1 Perhaps Gray is at his modernest in the 'Ode on Vicissitude',..if not most modern of all in that final quatrain of the Elegy which Gray's feeling for unity expunged. **1885** J. Payn *Talk of Town* I. 130 A writing on the wall, which, albeit it was not in modern characters, needed..no interpreter. **1898** *Westm. Gaz.* 26 Jan. 3/2 Against such foes, men with the modernest artillery and highest explosives are utterly powerless. **1912** E. L. Urlin *Dancing Anc. & Mod.* p. xv, Modern dances..[are] derived from some primary human instinct, such as Worship, Mimicry, Love, or War... Modern dancing begins where..the art survives solely on account of the pleasure it gives to the performer, or to the spectator. **1926** *Times* 6 May 1/6 (Advt.), Superior accommodation in lady's quiet house..all modern conveniences. **1933** J. Martin *Mod. Dance* 2 There are as many methods and systems of modern dancing as there are dancers. *Ibid.* 3 By the modern dance we..imply by a method of negation those types of dancing which are neither classic nor romantic. **1937** E. St. V. Millay *Conversation at Midnight* i. 15 Peace and Quiet poured down the sink, In exchange for a houseful of 'modern conveniences'. **1955** D. Gillespie in Shapiro & Hentoff *Hear Me Talkin' to Ya* xix. 300 No one man or group of men started modern jazz. **1957** G. B. L. Wilson *Dict. Ballet* 188 *Modern dance*, the term used to designate a variety of styles which are not founded on the *danse d'école* (i.e. the Classical ballet). *Ibid.* 189 Modern Dance claims to make much use of 'natural movements' and it is also a reflexion of a state of mind. **1961** *Metronome* Apr. 12 By the 1950's 'modern' jazz, as the more advanced developments were termed, had to free itself both from esoteric tendencies within jazz itself and from over-dependence on Western European classical traditions. **1968** J. Winearls *Mod. Dance* (ed. 2) 9 The title 'Modern Dance' distinguishes those kinds which have been invented, developed, or adapted from various sources during the past half-century and which are clearly marked by an expressive style quite different from that of other forms such as National, Folk, Musical Comedy or Ballet. *Ibid.*, Modern Dancers consider that Ballet cannot deal satisfactorily with all possible dance-subjects.

b. in disparaging use.

1753 Richardson *Grandison* (1811) V. xiii. 83 You..are not a modern woman; have neither wings to your shoulders, nor gad-fly in your cap: you love home.

c. *Her.* in ***France modern***: see quot. 1893.

1889 P. O. Hutchinson in *Notes & Gleanings* (Exeter) II. 50/2 The French arms are represented as 'France Modern'. **1893** Cussans *Her.* (ed. 4) 223 Henry the Fourth:..three Fleurs-de-lys were substituted for a field *semé*, for the Arms of France. This alteration..constituted what is commonly known as France modern.

†4. Every-day, ordinary, commonplace. (Frequent in Shaks.) *Obs.*

1591 Lodge *Catharos* H 3, It..maketh him blinde and inconsiderate in matters aswell moderne, as necessarie to his saluation. **1595** Shaks. *John* iii. iv. 42 Then..would I.. rowze from sleepe that fell Anatomy..Which scornes a moderne Inuocation! **1600** —— *A. Y. L.* ii. vii. 156 The Justice, With eyes seuere and beard of formall cut, Full of wise sawes and moderne instances. **1610** B. Jonson *Alch.* iv. i, Why, this is yet A kind of moderne happinesse, to haue Dol Common for a great lady.

5. *Comb.* with adjs. and pa. pples., as ***modern-bred, -built, -looking, -made, -minded, -practised, -sounding***. Also ***modern-day, -dress, -style*** (attrib.).

1808 Han. More *Cœlebs* I. i. 9 The mind of a true *modern-bred lady. **1811** Jane Austen *Sense & Sens.* III. vi. 111 Cleveland was a spacious, *modern-built house. **1905** *Daily Chron.* 28 Dec. 4/4 Most of these furnaces are modern built. **1909** *Westm. Gaz.* 5 July 2/3 No one can fail to be impressed by the seriousness of *modern-day cricket. **1965** *Times Lit. Suppl.* 25 Nov. 1075/4 Philip Bummidge is a modern-day Hamlet. **1885** J. K. Jerome *On the Stage* 64 For ordinary *modern-dress parts, we had to use our own things entirely. **1849** J. Forbes *Physician's Holiday* vi. (1850) 58 The church is..more *modern-looking than the rest of the town. **1899** *Daily News* 27 Mar. 2/7 The allegation was that the punches had been forged and used upon *modern-made silver-plate to represent antique goods. **1907** *Dublin Rev.* July 191 The author is at times betrayed into making Neri almost impossibly *modern-minded. **1970** *Guardian* 15 Jan. 12 Nigeria needs to prove that it is stable, modern-minded and representative. **1754** A. Murphy *Gray's-Inn Jrnl.* No. 86 Many of his Turns did not allude to *modern-practised Life. **1903** *Daily Chron.* 10 June 7/1 A piece with the more *modern-sounding title of 'The Court of Comfort'. **1883** 'Mark Twain' *Life on Mississippi* 427 Inviting *modern-style pleasure resorts. **1927** *Melody Maker* Aug. 781/2 The voice again is heard together with trumpet and saxophones alternating in a modern-style extemporisation. **1975** *Guardian* 20 Jan. 8/3 Modern-style choreography.

B. *sb.* (Chiefly in *plural.*)

1. a. One who lives in or belongs to the present time; one who belongs to a modern as contrasted with an ancient period or epoch.

1585 T. Washington tr. *Nicholay's Voy.* i. ii. 2 b, The Iles Baleares, so aunciently called: but by the modernes Maiorque and Minorque. **1609** B. Jonson *Silent Wom.* iv. ii, He must have Seneca read to him, and Plutarch, and the ancients; the moderns are not for this disease. **1717** Prior *Alma* i. 520 Some in ancient books delight; Others prefer what moderns write. **1784** *Europ. Mag.* May 366/2 No modern has been heard to play an adagio with greater taste and feeling. **1812** T. Taylor *Diss. Philos. Aristotle* (title-p.), The insufficiency also of the Philosophy that has been substituted by the Moderns for that of Aristotle is demonstrated. **1840** *Penny Cycl.* XVII. 2/1 (*Organ*), In point of touch, and mechanism generally, the moderns are far superior to their predecessors. **1888** W. Cory *Lett. & Jrnls.* (1897) 539 The old moderns, say Chaucer, Spenser and Le Sage.

b. *transf.* applied to a thing.

1735 J. Price *Stone-Br. Thames* 14 Description of many fine Bridges..in Italy wherein the finest among the Moderns is the Farnesian. **1975** *Country Life* 2 Jan. 37/2 In the visual arts the Walker Art Centre houses a world-famous collection of moderns.

2. One whose tastes or opinions are modern; a member of the modern school of thought in relation to any subject.

1897 *Mag. of Art* 283 It will be deemed old-fashioned by the latest of moderns. **1905** J. Orr *Probl. O.T.* xii. 453 *note*, Most of the moderns deny the supernatural character of prophecy.

†moˈdernal, *a.* *Obs.* [f. late L. *modern-us* (see prec.) + -al[1].] Of or belonging to the present day.

1542 Boorde *Dyetary* A iij, Y^e which [flowery language] in all wrytynges is vsed these modernall dayes.

ˈmoderner. [f. modern *a.* + -er[1].] = modern *sb.*

1592 Nashe *P. Penilesse* 21 Report (which our moderners clepe flundring Fame) puts mee in memorye of a notable iest I heard long agoe. **1926** *Brit. Weekly* 29 July 356/1 With a moderner's contempt of ailments. **1971** *Ceylon Daily News* 17 Sept. 4/6 It is psychologically impossible for a moderner to live in the same world that his predecessors lived.

†modernicide. *nonce-wd.* [f. modern *sb.* + -cide 1.] One who kills 'moderns'.

a **1774** Goldsm. *Ess., Visit to Elysium* Misc. Wks. 1837 I. 213, I should certainly have fallen beneath the hands of this company of men, who gloried in the title of Modernicides.

modernism (ˈmɒdənɪz(ə)m). [f. modern *a.* + -ism.]

1. A usage, mode of expression, or peculiarity of style or workmanship, characteristic of modern times.

1737 Swift *Let. to Pope* 23 July in P.'s Wks. 1757 IX. 218 b, The corruption of English by those Scribblers, who send us over their trash in Prose and Verse, with abominable curtailings and quaint modernisms. **1853** *Blackw. Mag.* LXXIV. 314 Shakespeare's archaism is exchanged for this modernism. *a* **1864** Hawthorne *Amer. Note-bks.* (1879) II. 77 Such modernisms as astral lamps. **1871** Earle *Philol. Eng. Tongue* §481 The last of these [*viz.* 'its'] is a comparative modernism in the language. **1897** D. C. Tovey *Rev. & Ess.* viii. 143 The published specimen contained.. some imperfections and modernisms.

2. Modern character or quality of thought, expression, style of workmanship, etc.; sympathy with or affinity to what is modern.

1830 H. N. Coleridge *Grk. Poets* (1834) 274 The women of the Odyssey discover occasionally a modernism and a want of heroic simplicity. **1844** Lingard *Anglo-Sax. Ch.* (1858) I. ii. 65 *note*, The modernism of its language. **1861** F. Metcalfe *Oxonian in Iceland* iv. (1867) 57 And somehow this very modernism begets a desire for reverting now and then to old things, old people [etc.]. **1887** *Westm. Rev.* June 348 The Roman Church and the American Republic... The one typifying mediævalism, the other illustrating with tolerable fidelity the spirit of modernism.

3. *Theol.* A tendency or movement towards modifying traditional beliefs and doctrines in accordance with the findings of modern criticism and research, esp. a movement of this kind in the Roman Catholic Church at the beginning of the twentieth century.

1901 G. Tyrell *Let.* 18 Aug. in M. D. Petre *Autobiogr. & Life Geo. Tyrell* (1912) II. ii. 52 He [*sc.* Kegan Paul] simply rants against Modernism, and glories in what ought to be our shame. **1903** —— *Let.* 19 Nov. (1920) vii. 132, I hope that the Catholicism in which we may eventually unite will be one in which all that is good and true in Modernism will be saved and sanctified. **1907** tr. *Pius X's Encyclical Let. Doctrines Modernists* 15 If we..seek to know how the believer, according to Modernism, is marked off from the Philosopher, it must be observed [etc.]. **1913** A. Fawkes *Stud. Modernism* 373 The name Modernism was given to the present phase of the liberalising movement in the Church of Rome by the *Civiltà Cattolica.* **1915** *Hastings' Encycl. Relig. & Ethics* VIII. 763/1 Modernism is the name

given by the papal encyclical which condemned it to a complex of movements within the Roman Communion, all alike inspired by a desire to bring the tradition of Christian belief and practice into closer relation with the intellectual habits and social aspirations of our own time. **1923** *Edin. Rev.* Jan. 62 Between English Modernism and the now discredited Roman Modernism there is a deep cleavage. **1927** H. D. A. MAJOR *Eng. Modernism* 18 In the Roman Church Modernism is opposed to Mediævalism; in the English Church, Modernism, as in Holland, is opposed to Traditionalism; in America Modernism is opposed to Fundamentalism. **1955** *Times* 17 Aug. 9/5 The mistake of modernism is to try to force a supernatural revelation into the mould of natural science and scholarship. **1972** L. F. BARMANN *Baron F. von Hügel & Modernist Crisis in Eng.* p. ix, In the sixty years following that conflict much has been written about modernism, though mostly from partisan standpoints.

4. The methods, style, or attitude of modern artists (MODERN *a.* 2 h); *spec.* a style of painting in which the artist deliberately breaks away from classical and traditional methods of expression; hence, a similar style or movement in architecture, literature, music, etc.

1929 H. R. HITCHCOCK *Mod. Archit.* xvii. 205 A city [*sc.* New York], whose 'modernism' consists in copying the poorest French models of the New Tradition. **1934** R. BLOMFIELD *Modernismus* viii. 145, I have already called attention to the disastrous effect of Modernism on architecture, painting, and sculpture... I find the same insidious and repulsive influence at work in a good deal of contemporary music. **1946** R. WELLEK in W. S. Knickerbocker *20th Cent. Eng.* 69 The fine arts themselves and the art of literature reacted against realism and naturalism in the direction of symbolism and other 'modernism'. **1955** *Times* 1 June 8/7 Professor A. E. Richardson.. foresaw a revival of the Hellenic influence in art and the decline of 'modernism'. **1961** *Listener* 23 Nov. 848/1 The American modernism introduced by Mr. T. S. Eliot, following Mr. Ezra Pound. **1971** *New Society* 25 Mar. 496/3 'Vision in Motion'.. a brilliant manual, or compendium, of modernism. **1973** *Observer* 5 Aug. 28/3 Sassoon became.. increasingly embittered at his neglect by the new pundits of 'modernism'. **1973** *Black World* Sept. 19/1 During the Twenties, Jorge de Lima became an important member of the literary movement known as Modernism. **1974** *New Yorker* 25 Feb. 122/1 Modernism, we are told, is passé; the Harvard English Department lists a course, 'American Modernism', that treats of 'American writing from 1900 to 1930'.

‖**modernismus** (ˌmɒdəˈnɪzməs). [G.] = MODERNISM 4.

1934 R. BLOMFIELD *Modernismus* p. v, Since the war, Modernism, or 'Modernismus', as it should be called on the German precedent, has invaded this country like an epidemic. **1934** C. LAMBERT *Music Ho!* iv. 248 Listening to his [*sc.* Hindemith's] firmly wrought works we seem to see ourselves in a block of hygienic and efficient workman's flats built in the best modernismus manner. **1948** WYNDHAM LEWIS *Let.* 18 Oct. (1963) 464 'The Waste Land', which bit of modernismus appeared a few years before. **1958** *Listener* 17 July 102/1 A city that was to be the last word in *modernismus*, a technician's 'New Jerusalem'. **1970** *Daily Tel.* (Colour Suppl.) 9 Oct. 65/2 A bale of soft material, patterned in that modernismus which was so big in the Thirties, and now survives mainly in British Rail.

modernist (ˈmɒdənɪst), *sb.* and *a.* [f. MODERN *a.* + -IST[1]. Cf. mod.L. *modernista* (Luther), F. *moderniste.*]

†**1.** A modern. *Obs.*

1588 J. HARVEY *Disc. Probl.* 106 Likewise.. of sundry other neotericall mathematicians and modernists. **1592** G. HARVEY *Pierce's Super.* 182 The witt of this, & that odd Modernist, is their owne.

2. a. A supporter or follower of modern ways or methods; in the 18th c., a maintainer of the superiority of modern over ancient literature.

1704 SWIFT *T. Tub* ix. Wks. 1751 I. 138 That his [Mr. Wotton's] Brain hath undergone an unlucky shake; which even his Brother Modernists themselves, like Ungrates, do whisper so loud, that it reaches up to the very Garret I am now writing in. **1864** *Daily Tel.* 8 June, Those Guelphs and Ghibellines of art, the modernists and the mediævalists. **1874** RUSKIN *Val D' Arno* (1886) 9 Behold, the Christians despising the Dunce Greeks, as the Infidel modernists despise the Dunce Christians.

b. *attrib.* (quasi-*adj.*)

1848 KINGSLEY *Yeast* v, That vile modernist naturalism is creeping back even into our painted glass.

3. In education, one who advocates the teaching of modern subjects (including modern languages) rather than that of the ancient classics.

1856 J. GROTE in *Camb. Ess.* 99 Let us survey the state of the attack upon it [*sc.* classical study] first by Patriots, and then by Modernists. **1905** *Jrnl. Educ.* Apr. 266/1 The presumption that the pure classicist would be degraded or contaminated by admixture with the modernist unregenerated by Greek.

4. *Theol.* One who inclines to, supports, or advocates theological modernism. Also *attrib.* or as *adj.*

1907 tr. *Pius X's Encyclical Let. Doctrines Modernists* 6 It is one of the cleverest devices of the Modernists (as they are commonly and rightly called) to present their doctrines without order and systematic arrangement. **1918** M. D. PETRE *Modernism* v. 101 These words are not written in a spirit of hostility to the Catholic modernist position. **1920** W. SANDAY *Divine Overruling* 67, I do not disclaim the name of Modernist. The name describes justly what I aim at being. I aim at thinking the thoughts and speaking the language of my own day, and yet at the same time keeping all that is essential in the religion of the past. **1923** *Edin. Rev.* Jan. 62 Roman Modernists took Newman's doctrine of development. **1931** J. S. HUXLEY *What dare I Think?* vii. 228 Accounts of God which are as modernist as could be desired. **1970** *Times* 19 Aug. 10/8 The appointment of another avowed Modernist with a strong sense of the Church and a flair for knowing men, proved to be the eirenic answer. **1972** L. F. BARMANN *Baron F. von Hügel & Modernist Crisis in Eng.* p. ix, Modernists have been concerned to defend themselves and their aims, and anti-modernists have been equally concerned to justify the conduct of the Roman authorities and the positions of Roman theologians.

5. An artist, architect, writer, etc., whose work is characterized by modernism (see MODERNISM 4). Also *attrib.* or as *adj.*

1927 F. J. MATHER *Hist. Mod. Painting* 372 Modernist pictures are becoming discreet, almost cautiously monotonous in colour. *Ibid.* 373 In comparison the Modernists have attained nothing of the coherence or authority of a school. **1934** R. BLOMFIELD *Modernismus* vii. 125 The Modernist seems to glory in his own obscurity. *Ibid.* 132 In these Modernist works there is no brushwork worth looking at. **1935** H. G. WELLS *Things to Come* xii. 99 One sits on a chair of modernist form. (All furniture is metallic.) **1937** S. W. CHENEY *World Hist. Art* (1938) xxviii. 862 This wing of modernists—with Cézanne as their prime exhibit—brought in the familiar studio talk about *form* as the indispensable creative force in painting. **1961** *Listener* 23 Nov. 863/1 Rosenberg, unlike the modernists, does not go in for phanopoeia or free association. **1963** *Ibid.* 21 Mar. 518/1 The writers were, in a sense, traitors in the modernist camp.

6. One who plays, appreciates, or supports modern jazz (see MODERN *a.* 3 a). Also *attrib.* or as *adj.*

1955 J. PRENTICE in A. J. McCarthy *Jazzbook 1955* 105 As I understand that the traditional field will be covered in another article I will confine myself to the modernists. **1958** V. BELLERBY in P. Gammond *Duke Ellington* II. 143 Such extensions and developments only lead to a destruction of its [*sc.* Jazz's] real and lasting value, as has unquestionably happened with some of the more involved modernist experiments. **1962** *Sunday Times* (Colour Suppl.) 10 June 3 The strange division between the extrovert 'traditionalists'.. and the very different *avant garde* 'modernists' (whose idol is the revolutionary Charlie Parker).

modernistic (mɒdəˈnɪstɪk), *a.* [f. MODERNIST + -IC.] Of, pertaining to, or suggestive of modernism or modernists; having affinity to or sympathy with what is modern. Hence as *sb. pl.*, examples of modernistic art, music, etc.

1909 *Daily Chron.* 12 June 1/3 'L'Unione' is denounced as reeking with modernistic and kindred ideas opposed to the principles and dogmas of the Roman Church. **1924** *Public Opinion* 17 Oct. 383/1 The New Testament in relation to its own time is essentially and boldly modernistic. **1927** *Sunday Times* 13 Feb. 20/4 The audience liked its florid style as a change from more modernistic music. **1935** *Archit. Rev.* LXXVII. 82 The beautiful new dance-hall, with its modernistic sofas and lalique panels. **1958** P. GAMMOND *Decca Bk. Jazz* xv. 190 George Shearing will be remembered for his very accomplished playing in the 1940s, not for his more recent vapid modernistics. **1960** *Times* 29 Sept. 16/7 There is much to admire in this farrago of 'modernistics'. **1973** A. BEHREND *Samarai Affair* iii. 30 A modernistic portrait in oils of the latest pilot boat.

modernity (məˈdɜːnɪtɪ). [ad. med.L. *modernitāt-em*, noun of quality f. *modern-us*: see MODERN and -ITY. Cf. F. *modernité* (Littré).]

1. The quality or condition of being modern; modernness of character.

1627 HAKEWILL *Apol.* v. (1635) 192 Yea but I vilifie the present times, you say, whiles I expect a more flourishing State to succeed; bee it so, yet this is not to vilifie modernity, as you pretend. **1782** H. WALPOLE *Let. to Cole* 22 Feb. (1858) VIII. 161 Now that the poems [*sc.* Chatterton's] have been so much examined, nobody (that has an ear) can get over the modernity of the modulations. **1796** PEGGE *Anonym.* (1809) 429 Macrobius is no good author to follow in point of Latinity, partly on account of his modernity, and partly of his foreign extraction. **1888** *Athenæum* 31 Mar. 401/3 Those unlucky stumblings into modernity which some archaizing translators do not avoid. **1904** MAY SINCLAIR *Div. Fire* 415 My dear fellow, modernity simply means democracy. And when once democracy has been forced on us there's no good protesting any longer.

2. Something that is modern.

1753 H. WALPOLE *Let. to Bentley* Sept. (1857) II. 355 But here is a modernity, which beats all antiquities for curiosity. **1884** *Harper's Mag.* Dec. 80/1 After he had.. arranged himself in these modernities.

modernization (ˌmɒdənaɪˈzeɪʃən). [f. MODERNIZE *v.* + -ATION.] The action or an act of modernizing; the state of being modernized. Also, a modernized version.

1770 GOUGH in *Lett. to Granger* 263 The Marquis of Winchester's noble house at Englefield has suffered by some late modernizations. **1818** HALLAM *Mid. Ages* (1872) I. 150 We cannot always judge by the modernisation of a proper name. **1830** W. TAYLOR *Hist. Surv. Germ. Poetry* III. 317 The *Birds* is an abridgement, or modernization, of the comedy of *Aristophanes* so entitled. **1895** C. R. B. BARRETT *Surrey* iv. 101 The town of Bletchingley.. is, despite some modernization, an old-world spot.

modernize (ˈmɒdənaɪz), *v.* [ad. F. *moderniser*, f. *moderne*: see MODERN *a.* and -IZE.]

1. *trans.* To make or render modern; to give a modern character or appearance to; esp. (*a*) to rewrite (an old text) in modern spelling or language; to change (obsolete words, language, spelling) for modern equivalents; (*b*) to remodel and refashion an ancient building.

1748 [implied in MODERNIZED *ppl. a.*]. **1752** FIELDING *Covent Gard. Jrnl.* 11 July, I have taken the liberty to modernize the language. **1802** *Brookes' Gazetteer* (ed. 12) s.v. *Russia*, The young generation are modernizing these antic [= antique] vestments. **1818** *Brathwait's Barnabees Jrnl.* Introd. 9 The text was modernized throughout. **1880** DIXON *Windsor* III. xii. 116 No one ever dreamt of modernising Surrey's lines. **1901** *Daily Express* 28 Feb. 5/3 The King has decided to have Windsor Castle thoroughly modernised.

b. To bring about modern conditions in.

1860 THACKERAY *Round. Papers, De Juventute*, Gunpowder and printing tended to modernise the world.

2. *intr.* To adopt modern customs, habits, ways, or the like. *rare.*

1753 RICHARDSON *Grandison* (1811) II. ii. 10 He scruples not to modernize a little; but then you see, that it is in compliance with the fashion, and to avoid singularity. **1802** MRS. J. WEST *Infidel Father* I. 27 Muggleton had modernized so far as to have a chitterlin tacked into his holland shirt. *a* **1853** W. JAY *Autobiog.* xviii. (1855) 172 Several new schools also, or to modernize—'colleges', for the sons of the prophets, have been established.

Hence **ˈmodernized** *ppl. a.*; **ˈmodernizing** *vbl. sb.* and *ppl. a.*

1748 H. WALPOLE *Let. to Montagu* 25 July (1857) II. 119 The rest of the house is all modernised. **1824** J. WINTERBOTTOM *Observ. Two Fr. Words* 29 A very good modernized edition of the Essays. **1869** FARRAR *Fam. Speech* ii. (1873) 77 The Lettish, spoken in Courland and Livonia, is only a modernised form of Lithuanian. **1885** *Athenæum* 25 Apr. 533/2 Capt. Burton is justly severe on the unwarrantable modernizing of Camoëns. **1904** *Blackw. Mag.* Feb. 309/1 The modernising spirit has taken hold of the Statistical Department. **1905** *Athenæum* 19 Aug. 249/3 The Gatehouse which gave entrance to the now modernized Council House.

modernizer (ˈmɒdənaɪzə(r)). [f. MODERNIZE *v.* + -ER[1].] One who modernizes.

1739 G. WHITEFIELD in *Life*, etc. (1756) 225 The Generality of our Modernizers of Christianity. **1805** SOUTHEY in *Ann. Rev.* III. 563 Not only the style, but the morals of the original,.. are vitiated by the French modernizers. **1886** POSNETT *Compar. Lit.* 47 We expect the old harmony between earlier sounds and ideas to be kept up by the modernizer.

b. One who desires to modernize education by the elimination of 'classics'.

1889 A. SIDGWICK in *Jrnl. Educ.* Feb. 116 Before it was the modernisers, asking, in view of needful modern subjects, Is there time for classics?

modernly (ˈmɒdənlɪ), *adv.* [f. MODERN *a.* + -LY[2].]

1. In modern times. Now *rare.*

1605 VERSTEGAN *Dec. Intell.* ii. (1628) 54 The honour as well antiently as modernely of that great and noble nation. **1632** LITHGOW *Trav.* III. 87 Mount Ida, of old was called Phelorita,.. but modernely Madura. **1756** TOLDERVY *Hist. 2 Orphans* II. 69 With deliberations, shorter than those modernly used by the States General, a treaty of peace was agreed upon. **1856** *Ulster Jrnl. Archæol.* IV. 244 Bonaght.. was specially due on land modernly held by sorren tenure.

2. In a modern manner; after the fashion of modern times.

1743 *Lond. Mag.* 35 To be modernly polite, introduces Extravagance. **1868** *Morn. Star* 29 June, The Latin original reads to-day most modernly. **1887** *Harper's Mag.* July 315 Most modernly American as it is, it has a flavor one tastes in travels of old times.

3. *Comb.*, as ***modernly-armed, written*** adjs.

1894 *Westm. Gaz.* 15 Oct. 5/1 The well-drilled and modernly-armed force which China can put in the field. **1905** *Daily Chron.* 28 Dec. 8/3 A modernly-written play.

modernness (ˈmɒdənnɪs). [f. MODERN *a.* + -NESS.] The quality or state of being modern; conformity to modern conditions or ideas.

1731 BAILEY vol. II, *Modernness*, newness, the being of late days. **1825** W. COBBETT *Rur. Rides* (1885) II. 19 The Bridewell, which from the modernness of its structure, appears to be [etc.]. **1835** *Fraser's Mag.* XII. 650 Though he should.. outlive his modernness as much as George Coleman the Younger has outlived his youth. **1874** MAHAFFY *Soc. Life Greece* ix. 278 The fact remains a very curious monument of the modernness of Attic life. **1905** *Athenæum* 16 Sept. 362/3 The 'modernness' of thought shown in Jevons's mode of handling his subject.

‖**modernus** (məˈdɜːnəs). Pl. moderni. [L.] A modern person; someone who is characterized by, or notable for, his modernity.

1953 W. R. TRASK tr. *Curtius's European Lit.* II. xiii. 490 He is a *modernus* and considers that the ancients had loaded down their poetic narratives with a superfluity of similes, rhetorical figures, and digressions... These *moderni* of 1175 .. either consciously break with the theory of *imitatio* or restrict it very considerably. **1962** M. MCLUHAN *Gutenberg Galaxy* 183 Francis Bacon, PR voice for the *moderni*, had both his feet in the Middle Ages.

moderschypp, -ship, obs. var. MOTHERSHIP.

moderwort, obs. form of MOTHERWORT.

modest (ˈmɒdɪst), *a.* [ad. F. *modeste*, ad. L. *modest-us* keeping due measure, moderate, modest, f. **modes-* a synonymous variant of *modo-*, *modus* measure: see MODE *sb.* Cf. Sp., Pg., It. *modesto.*]

†**1.** Well-conducted, orderly; not harsh or domineering. *Obs.*

1574 HELLOWES *Gueuara's Fam. Ep.* (1577) 158 Your Lordship ought to.. commaund your ministers of iustice.. that they be milde, modest, and manerly: for sometimes the sorrowful Sutor doth more feele a rough word they speake, then the iustice they dilate. **1611** BIBLE *2 Macc.* iv. 37 The

sober and modest behauiour [τὴν σωφροσύνην καὶ πολλὴν εὐταξίαν] of him that was dead. **1652** SIR E. NICHOLAS in *N. Papers* (Camden) I. 320 He seems to be indeed a very modest and discreet person.

2. Having a moderate or humble estimate of one's own abilities or merits; disinclined to bring oneself into notice; becomingly diffident or unassuming; unobtrusive, retiring, bashful; not bold or forward. Hence of actions and attributes: Proceeding from or indicating these qualities.

1565 COOPER *Thesaurus* s.v. *Modestus, Adolescentia modestissima*, very modest & sober youth. *Ibid., Modestus vultu*, of modest and sobre countenance. **1605** SHAKS. *Lear* II. iv. 25 Resolue me with all modest haste, which way Thou might'st deserue, or they impose this vsage? **1653** WALTON *Angler* ii. 51 You are so modest, that me thinks I may promise to grant it before it is asked. *a* **1680** BUTLER *Rem.* (1759) II. 213 Nothing renders Men modest, but a just Knowledge how to compare themselves with others. **1710** PALMER *Proverbs* 187 Tho' the modestest are not always sure to be paid first, yet an impertinent dun is very odious. **1712** BUDGELL *Spect.* No. 373 ⁋12 When they are thus mixed and blended together, they compose what we endeavour to express when we say *a modest Assurance*; by which we understand the just Mean between Bashfulness and Impudence. **1748** CHESTERF. *Let. to Son* 22 Feb., The more you know, the modester you should be. **1781** COWPER *Truth* 68 He, Christian-like, retreats with modest mien. **1781** GIBBON *Decl. & F.* xxxi. III. 223 In a modest and suppliant tone. **1816** SCOTT *Antiq.* vi, A light and modest tap was heard at the parlour door. **1859** TENNYSON *Idylls* Ded. 17 We see him as he moved, How modest, kindly, all-accomplish'd, wise. **1899** 'MARK TWAIN' *Man that Corrupted Hadleyburg*, etc. (1900) 105 A little book, merely a little book—could words be modester? **1901** J. WATSON *Life of Master* xxii. 202 Nathanael was a quiet, modest, diffident, questioning person.

b. *fig.* Of things, sometimes with semi-personification: Apparently retiring from observation, not obtrusively conspicuous.

1786 BURNS *To Mountain Daisy*, Wee, modest, crimson-tipped flow'r, Thou's met me in an evil hour. **1830** J. G. STRUTT *Sylva Brit.* 73 Their delicate green changing to modest brown. *a* **1832** BRYANT *Yellow Violet* 3 The yellow violet's modest bell Peeps from the last year's leaves below.

3. Of women, their attributes and behaviour: Governed by the proprieties of the sex; decorous in manner and conduct; not forward, impudent, or lewd; 'shamefast'. Hence (in later use also of men), scrupulously chaste in feeling, language, and conduct; shrinking from coarse or impure suggestion.

a **1591** H. SMITH *Prepar. Mariage* 32 He sayd not that she was the wisest,..nor the modestest wife in the world, but the fittest wife for him in the world. *a* **1586** MONTGOMERIE *Misc. Poems* li. 9 The myildest may; the mekest, and modest. **1596** SPENSER *F.Q.* IV. ii. 35 She modest was in all her deedes and words, And wondrous chast of life. **1607** BEAUM. & FL. *Woman-Hater* v. v, Thou woman which wert borne to teach men vertue, Faire, sweet, and modest maid forgiue my thoughts. **1667** MILTON *P.L.* IV. 310 And by her yeilded, by him best receivd, Yeilded with coy submission, modest pride, And sweet reluctant amorous delay. **1697** DRYDEN *Virg. Georg.* IV. 288 Their modest Appetites, Averse from Venus, fly the Nuptial Rites. **1711** STEELE *Spect.* No. 154 ⁋1, I am apt to believe (begging your Pardon) that you are still what I my self was once, a queer modest Fellow. *Ibid.* ⁋2, I found a sober modest Man was always looked upon by both Sexes as a precise unfashioned Fellow of no Life or Spirit. **1742** RICHARDSON *Pamela* IV. 120 Every one that can give himself the Liberty to say Things that shock a modester Person,..mistakes Courage for Wit. **1764** GOLDSM. *Trav.* 408 The modest matron, and the blushing maid. **1781** COWPER *Expost.* 48 Her women..Forgot the blush that virgin fears impart To modest cheeks, and borrow'd one from art. **1818** SCOTT *Hrt. Midl.* xxxv, A young woman.. whose countenance might be termed very modest and pleasing in expression.

b. Of female attire: Decent, not meretricious.

1611 BIBLE *1 Tim.* ii. 9 That women adorne themselues in modest apparell [Gr. ἐν καταστολῇ κοσμίῳ].

†**c.** Inoffensive to decency. *Obs.*

1638 SIR T. HERBERT *Trav.* (ed. 2) 301 Their waist is circled with a peece of Callico, which makes them modest.

†**d.** ***modest part***: that part of the body which modesty requires to be covered. *Obs.*

1634 SIR T. HERBERT *Trav.* 15 As a cover to their modest parts, they gird themselves with a piece of raw leather, and fasten a square piece..to it. **1693** DRYDEN *Persius* iv. (1697) 460 The depilation of thy modest part.

4. Of or with reference to demands, statements, estimates: Not excessive; free from exaggeration, moderate; not unduly exacting or importunate.

1601 R. JOHNSON *Kingd. & Commw.* (1603) 153 Some more modest in writing affirme, that the Moscouite could leuie 150 thousand horse. *c* **1616** FLETCHER *Thierry & Theod.* II. i, I haue in the relation of my wrongs Bene modest. **1623** T. SCOT *Highw. God* 35 There is nothing practised in our Church, but that which finds allowance and approbation from the modestest and learnedest of their side. **1652** BOYLE *Wks.* (1772) I. p. l, In less than a year, of which not the least part was usurped by frequent sicknesses and journies, by furnaces, and by (which is none of the modestest thieves of time) the conversation of young ladies. **1708** ADDISON *Pres. St. War* 5 During the last four Years, by a modest Computation there have been brought into Brest above six Millions Sterling in Bullion. **1781** COWPER *Conversat.* 889 Held within modest bounds, the tide of speech Pursues the course that truth and nature teach. **1792** BURKE *Corr.* (1844) III. 370 This is not the less modest and peaceable for being clear, open, and manly.

5. Of things: Unpretentious in appearance, style, magnitude, or amount.

1770 GOLDSM. *Des. Vill.* 140 There..The village preacher's modest mansion rose. **1823** RUTTER *Fonthill* 7 Surprised by the modest pretensions of the entrance. **1840** [see QUENCHER b]. **1842** MRS. GORE *Fasin.* 18 Dominique boasted a modest annuity of about fifty pistoles. **1856** THACKERAY *Christmas Bks.* (1872) 66 They set up a carriage—the modestest little vehicle conceivable. **1870** DICKENS *E. Drood* viii, And then I step into my modest share in the concern. **1886** *Pall Mall G.* 31 July 3/1 For the modest sum of 6*d.* **1887** RUSKIN *Præterita* II. 147 Modest gardens, and farm-dwelling houses.

6. *Comb.*, as ***modest-like, -looked, -looking, -seeming*** adjs.

1621 LADY M. WROTH *Urania* 517 Her *modest-like bashfulnes. **1654** GAYTON *Pleas. Notes* III. i. 68 Never trust a *modest-lookt Stallion. **1818** SCOTT *Hrt. Midl.* v, A *modest-looking, fair-haired girl. **1864** A. MCKAY *Hist. Kilmarnock* 191 A plain, modest-looking structure. **1728–46** THOMSON *Spring* 989 The enticing smile, the *modest-seeming eye.

modestines, erron. variant of MODESTNESS.

†**mo'destious.** *Obs. rare*$^{-1}$. [f. MODESTY + -OUS.] Modest, chaste in habits.

1547 BOORDE *Introd. Knowl.* ix. Eiij b, The women be modestiouse & in the townes & church they couer them self.

†**'modestless,** *a. Obs. rare*$^{-1}$. [f. MODEST *a.* + -LESS.] Destitute of modesty.

1591 SYLVESTER *Du Bartas* I. i. 410 Alas! how faithlesse and how modest-lesse Are you.

modestly ('mɒdɪstlɪ), *adv.* [f. MODEST *a.* + -LY^2.] In a modest manner.

†**1.** Without exaggeration, excess, or importunity; with due measure, moderately; with reserve.

1561 DAUS tr. *Bullinger on Apoc.* (1573) 36 After he [the Lord] speaketh modestly, least by exasperating ouer much the sinne and errour in the faythfull, he should trouble their myndes and discourage them vtterly. **1579** GOSSON *Sch. Abuse* Ded. (Arb.) 17 Euery man fedde modestly on that whiche stoode before him. **1581** PETTIE tr. *Guazzo's Civ. Conv.* II. (1586) 99 A prince..must use his authoritie modestlie. **1606** SHAKS. *Tr. & Cr.* IV. v. 222 Modestly I thinke, The fall of euery Phrygian stone will cost A drop of Grecian blood. **1674** TEMPLE *Let. Ld. Chamberlain* Wks. 1720 II. 317 He believes the Point of Predestination the firmest that ever any body did, and laughs at any of them, that speak modestly of it. **1712** STEELE *Spect.* No. 280 ⁋3 Shewing how forcible it was to speak Modestly of your own Wants. **1735** SWIFT *Let. to Dk. Dorset* 30 Dec., I desired you would bestow a preferment of one hundred and fifty pounds a year to a certain clergyman. Your answer was, that I asked modestly.

2. Without self-conceit or presumption; not arrogantly or obtrusively.

1568 GRAFTON *Chron.* II. 738 He modestly aunswered, most noble and redoubted Lorde, this [etc.]. **1599** SHAKS. *Much Ado* II. iii. 216, I could wish he would modestly examine himselfe, to see how much he is vnworthy to haue so good a Lady. **1638** MAYNE *Lucian* (1664) 335 Yet these speak much modestlyer then the Thebans, who derive themselves from a serpents tooth sown. **1690** DRYDEN *Don Sebast.* Pref. (1692) 23, I think I may modestly conclude, that whatever errors there may be,..they are not those which have been objected to it. **1781** COWPER *Conversat.* 485 Know then, and modestly let fall your eyes,..That air of insolence affronts your God. **1837** MARRYAT *Perc. Keene* x, He hoped I was a good boy, which being compelled to be my own trumpeter, I very modestly declared I was. **1853** J. H. NEWMAN *Hist. Sk.* (1873) II. II. ii. 92 Togrul kissed the ground, and waited modestly, till he was led to the throne.

3. With womanly modesty; decently.

1585 T. WASHINGTON tr. *Nicholay's Voy.* II. xxv. 66 The women being..richly apparrelled, yet doe weare the same modestly. **1593** SHAKS. *1 Hen. VI*, v. iii. 179 *Mar.* Such commendations as becomes a Maide, A Virgin, and his Seruant, say to him. *Suf.* Words sweetly plac'd and modest[l]ie directed. **1847** C. BRONTË *J. Eyre* vii, The hair to be arranged closely, modestly, plainly.

4. *Comb.* (cf. MODERATELY b).

1870 RUSKIN *Lect. Art* ii. (1875) 41 No modestly-tempered..thinker would now take upon himself to decide.

modestness ('mɒdɪstnɪs). Now *rare*. Also 6 **modestines.** [f. MODEST *a.* + -NESS.] Modesty.

1546 LANGLEY *Pol. Verg. De Invent.* II. ii. 36 b, A Kynge ..which attained to that dignitie by no ambicion or favour but by a singular wyt & sober modestines. **1548** R. HUTTEN *Sum of Diuinitie* Biij b, Thys precept conteineth excellent vertues, y^t is to saye diligence in obeyng, doinge our vocacion, modestnes, pitie toward our parentes ye common welth & such like vertues. **1638** H. RIDER *Horace's Epodes* xi, Then my modestness shall give o'er to strive.

modesty ('mɒdɪstɪ). Also 6–7 **modestie.** [a. F. *modestie* or ad. L. *modestia*, f. *modestus* MODEST *a.*]

†**1.** Moderation; freedom from excess or exaggeration; self-control; clemency, mildness of rule.

1531 ELYOT *Gov.* I. xxv, Modestie; whiche worde nat beinge knowen in the englisshe tongue, ne of al them which under stode latin, except they had radde good autours, they improprely named this vertue discretion. **1585** T. WASHINGTON tr. *Nicholay's Voy.* I. xviii. 21 He gouerned with all modestie to the great contentment of the inhabitauntes. **1596** SHAKS. *Tam. Shrew* Induct. i. 94, I am doubtfull of your modesties, Least..You break into some merry passion. **1601** —— *Jul. C.* III. i. 213 The Enemies of Cæsar, shall say this: Then, in a Friend, it is cold Modestie. **1639** FULLER *Holy War* III. vii. (1647) 120 Richard refused ..to strip poore mariners out of those rags of their estates wch the mercie and modestie of the waves and winds had left them. **1756** BURKE *Vind. Nat. Soc.* Wks. 1842 I. 20 Thus are we running in a circle, without modesty, and without end, and making one errour and extravagance an excuse for the other. **1781** GIBBON *Decl. & F.* xxxi. III. 192 The modesty of Alaric was interpreted..as a sure evidence of his weakness and fear.

ironical. **1839** SOUTHEY *Lett.* 18 Feb., I am likely to recover something from Baldwin and Cradock. The trustees of their affairs had the modesty to expect that I should receive a dividend of one shilling in the pound [etc.].

2. a. The quality of being modest, or having a moderate opinion of oneself; reserve springing from an unexaggerated estimate of one's qualities; freedom from presumption, ostentation, arrogance, or impudence. †***on a modesty***: from a feeling of modesty.

1553 T. WILSON *Rhet.* 19 b, Modestie is an honest shamefastnesse. **1601** HOLLAND *Pliny* I. 172 Augustus Cæsar.. expressely forbad that the Poeme of Virgil should be burned, notwithstanding that he by his last wil and testament on a modesty [orig. *contra testamenti eius verecundiam*], gaue order to the contrary. **1602** SHAKS. *Ham.* II. ii. 289 There is a kinde [of] confession in your lookes; which your modesties haue not craft enough to color. **1681** LUTTRELL *Brief Rel.* (1857) I. 62 They would trust to his own modesty. **1711** ADDISON *Spect.* No. 231 ⁋4 An Excess of Modesty obstructs the Tongue. **1712** STEELE *ibid.* No. 350 ⁋2 Modesty is the certain Indication of a great Spirit. **1779–81** JOHNSON *L. P., Addison* Wks. III. 46 By the influence of Mr. Montague, concurring,..with his natural modesty, he was diverted from..entering into holy orders. **1802** *Med. Jrnl.* VIII. 366 A desire which perhaps proceeds from too much modesty, and a mistaken deference for others. **1827** HARE *Guesses* (1859) 6 True modesty does not consist in an ignorance of our merits, but in a due estimate of them.

†**b.** Humility (towards God). *Obs. rare.*

1557 N. T. (Geneva) *Acts* xx. 19 Seruyng the Lord with all modestie [Gr. μετὰ πάσης ταπεινοφροσύνης].

†**c.** Deferential feeling. *Obs.*

1598 B. JONSON *Ev. Man in Hum.* I. i, There is a way of winning more by loue And vrging of the modestie, then feare. **1663** J. SPENCER *Prodigies* (1665) 77 Arguments from Humane Authority generally shew better in Rhetorick then Logick, and press the modesties of men more then their judgments.

†**d.** Shame, confusion. *Obs.*

1594 LYLY *Moth. Bomb.* III. i, I can neither without danger smother the fire, nor without modestie disclose my furie.

3. a. Womanly propriety of behaviour; scrupulous chastity of thought, speech, and conduct (in men or women); reserve or sense of shame proceeding from instinctive aversion to impure or coarse suggestions.

1565 COOPER *Thesaurus* s.v., *Modestia,..Virginalis modestia*, Maydenly modestie & shamefastnes. **1591** SHAKS. *Two Gent.* I. ii. 55 Maides, in modesty, say no, to that, Which they would haue the profferer construe, I. **1610** —— *Temp.* III. i. 53 By my modestie (The iewell in my dower) I would not wish Any Companion in the world but you. **1632** MASSINGER & FIELD *Fatal Dowry* I. i, To gaine their fauors, Our chastest dames put off their modesties. **1671** CLARENDON *Dial.* Tracts (1727) 288 You talk of modesty: there hath been no man seen to blush in the court since the king's return. **1691** HARTCLIFFE *Virtues* 201 In the case therefore of Conversation in general, and especially of that, which is mixt, Male and Female together, we must put on such a Modesty, as may guard our Virtue. **1699** ADDISON in *Lett. Lit. Men* (Camden) 294 A place..where Modesty is so very scarce that I think I have not seen a Blush since my first landing at Calais. **1711** STEELE *Spect.* No. 6 ⁋3 When Modesty ceases to be the chief Ornament of one Sex, and Integrity of the other, Society is upon a wrong Basis. *Ibid.* No. 154 ⁋2 My character for Modesty was so notorious.. that I resolved to shew my new Face in new Quarters. **1727–46** THOMSON *Summer* 1334 Check'd, at last, By love's respectful modesty. **1869** LECKY *Europ. Mor.* (1877) II. 319 The sister of St. Gregory of Nyssa was afflicted with cancer in her breast, but could not bear that a surgeon should see it, and was rewarded for her modesty by a miraculous cure. **1895** *Outing* (U.S.) XXVI. 8/2 They have no conception of the western idea of modesty, and go freely about in their 'nude simplicity'.

b. A kind of veil for the concealment of the bosom (see quots.). In full ***modesty-bit, -piece.***

1713 ADDISON *Guard.* No. 118 ⁋3 A narrow Lace..which runs along the upper part of the Stays before..and being as it were a part of the Tucker,..is therefore..called the Modesty-Piece. **1731** *Gentl. Mag.* I. 289 Sometimes the Stomacher rises almost to the chin, and a modesty-bit serves the purpose of a ruff; at other times but half way, and the modesty is but a transparent shade to the beauties beneath. **1789** *Loiterer* No. 32. 11 Their handkerchief opened on either side, and left between it a space of at least eight inches, which was occupied, not covered, by a bit of narrow lace, a part of the Ladies dress which I have since heard called a Modesty piece. *c* **1800** *Songs Costume* (Percy Soc.) 207 A modesty they all must have, If ne'er a smock they wear, O. **1910** *Westm. Gaz.* 21 Mar. 5/3 The 'modesty' and the edge of the sleeves are of golden lace.

transf. **1783** *Ann. Reg.* II. 14 The females [of Sumatra], before they are of an age to be clothed have what may not be inaptly termed a modesty-piece, being a plate of silver in the shape of a heart hung before.

4. Unpretentious character (of things). *rare.*

1906 *Blackw. Mag.* Apr. 494/1 The straitness of their surroundings, the modesty of their homes may better be imagined than described.

Hence †**'modesty** *v.* (*nonce-wd.*), to throw *away* by prudery.

1748 RICHARDSON *Clarissa* IV. 42 Twice already have you, my dear, if not ofterer, modesty'd away such opportunities as you ought not to have slipt. *Ibid.* 55 You..have accused me of having modesty'd away, as you phrase it, several opportunities of being—Being what, my dear?

modi, obs. form of MOODY.

modiˈation. *Hist.* [ad. late L. *modiātiōn-em* a measuring by the MODIUS.] A toll or tax on wine.

1661 BLOUNT *Glossogr.* (ed. 2), *Modiation*, a measuring by the Bushel; Also a measuring of liquid things. **1738** TOVEY *Anglia Jud.* 63 That they shou'd be free throughout England and Normandy, of all Custom, Tolls, and Modiations of Wine.

modicity (məʊˈdɪsɪtɪ). *rare.* [a. F. *modicité*, ad. med.L. *modicitāt-em*, f. L. *modicus* moderate: see next.] Moderateness.

1611 COTGR., *Modicité*, modicitie, moderatenesse, meannesse, littlenesse. **1623** tr. *Favine's Theat. Hon.* III. iv. 362 And those Iewels or Gifts..were not set down in the Inuentarie, after the Husbands decease, according to the modicitie of the price, or small value of the things then giuen. **1881** H. JAMES *Portr. Lady* II. iv. 53 Mrs. Touchett ..found compensation for the darkness of her frontage in the modicity of her rent.

modicum (ˈmɒdɪkəm). Also 7 mod(d)icom(e. [a. L., neut. sing. of *modicus* moderate, f. *mod-us* measure: see MODE *sb.*]

1. A small quantity or portion; a moderate or limited amount. (Often qualified by *little* or *small.*) **a.** of food and the like.

In quot. 1609 app. a slang term for 'something eaten in order to provoke thirst'.

c **1470** HENRYSON *Mor. Fab.* II. (*Town & C. Mouse*) xi, Ane modicum is mair for till allow, Sua that gude will be caruer at the dais, Than thrawin vult and mony spycit mais. **1580** LYLY *Euphues* (Arb.) 252 Age seeketh rather a Modicum for sustenaunce, then feastes for surfets. **1605** ARMIN *Foole upon F.* (1880) 24 There was no boote to bid runne for drams to driue downe this vndisguested moddicome. **1609** DEKKER *Gvls Horne-bke.* Prœm. 4 Lay open all thy secrets, & yͤ mystical Hieroglyphick of Rashers ath coales, Modicums & Shooing hornes. *a* **1670** HACKET *Abp. Williams* I. (1693) 74 Eat it up all, or not a whit, for a Modicum will Gripe the Belly. **1725** BRADLEY *Fam. Dict.* s.v. *Treacle*, Drink a small Modicum of good Wine upon it. **1859** TROLLOPE *West Indies* iii. (1860) 42 With the cup of coffee comes a small modicum of dry toast. **1875** H. C. WOOD *Therap.* (1879) 306 It is probable that but a modicum of the poison was absorbed.

b. of money or other property.

1604 DEKKER *Honest Wh.* Wks. 1873 II. 8 There's a little modicum more, porter, for making thee stay. **1628** BURTON *Anat. Mel.* II. iii. v. (ed. 3) 316 As Alcumists spend that small modicum [ed. 2, 1624 that little] they haue to get gold. **1647** LILLY *Chr. Astrol.* clxxxv. 784 It may also import some parcell of Land or acquisition of some modicum by the decease of a Kinsman. *a* **1734** NORTH *Exam.* I. iii. §123 (1740) 203 Upon Search of his Pockets, there was found his ordinary Modicum of Guineas. **1749** FIELDING *Tom Jones* v. viii, St. Paul hath taught me to be content with the little I have. Had the modicum been less, I should have known my duty. **1875** McLAREN *Serm.* Ser. II. i. 14 A true, lofty life may be lived with a very small modicum.

c. *gen.*

1606 SHAKS. *Tr. & Cr.* II. i. 74 What *modicums* of wit he vtters. **1606** HIERON *Wks.* I. 59 So you must euen giue all, euen tor one little modicum of hearty obedience to the truth. **1620** VENNER *Via Recta* vii. 115 They are also cooling, notwithstanding the modicum of heate in them. **1675** EVELYN *Terra* (1676) 30 Such [Earth] as having a modicum of Loam naturally rising with it, to entertain the moisture, does neither defile the Fingers, nor cleave much to the Spade. **1781** COWPER *Conversat.* 2 Though nature weigh our talents, and dispense To ev'ry man his modicum of sense. **1858** BRIGHT *Sp. Reform* 27 Oct. (1868) II. 22 And no law can pass, not the smallest modicum of freedom or of justice come to you, until [etc.]. **1874** W. E. HALL *Rights & Duties Neutrals* II. ii. 64 To possess any force at all, it must possess a modicum of armament. **1878** STUBBS *Const. Hist.* III. xix. 371 The monastic and other schools placed some modicum of learning within reach of all.

†**2.** Jocularly applied to a person of small stature. Also, more or less disparagingly, to a woman (cf. *piece, bit*). *Obs.*

1611 MIDDLETON & DEKKER *Roaring Girl* I. (*init.*), I haue culled out for him..a daintier bit or modicome then any lay vpon his trencher at dinner. **1623** MASSINGER *Dk. Milan* II. i, *Marc.* Where are you? You Modicum, you Dwarfe? *Mari.* Here, Giantesse, here. **1632** SHIRLEY *Love in Maze* v. iv, Heaven bless your worship, and the sweet-faced modicum in your company.

modifiability (ˌmɒdɪfaɪəˈbɪlɪtɪ). [f. next: see -ITY.] Capability of being modified.

1840 J. H. GREEN *Vital Dynamics* 57 The principle of organic modifiability and unity of composition. **1856** LYELL in *Darwin's Life & Lett.* (1887) II. 83, I foresee that many will go over to the indefinite modifiability doctrine. **1862** H. SPENCER *First Princ.* II. xiii. §104 (1875) 302 The structural modifiability of a child is greater than that of an adult man.

modifiable (ˈmɒdɪfaɪəb(ə)l), *a.* [f. MODIFY *v.* + -ABLE.] That can be modified.

1611 COTGR., *Modifiable*, modifiable, qualifiable. *a* **1704** LOCKE *Exam. Malebranche* §10 Wks. 1714 III. 432 It appears to me more difficult to conceive a distinct visible Image in the uniform unvariable Essence of God, than in variously modifiable Matter. **1840** J. H. GREEN *Vital Dynamics* 76 Man has the most modifiable organs of motion. **1889** *Scottish Leader* 16 Feb. 5/3 The whole case may have been modifiable by the decisions of the Commission now sitting.

Hence **ˈmodifiableness.**

1873 MORLEY *Rousseau* I. 145 This belief..of the easy modifiableness of a society in the hands of an energetic lawgiver. **1888** *Pop. Sci. Monthly* May 117 Buffon, who contended for the modifiableness of species.

modificaˈbility. *rare.* [Formed as next + -ITY.] Modifiability.

1827 COLERIDGE *Table-t.* 12 Mar., Internal or mental energy and external or corporeal modificability are in inverse proportions. **1883** ROMANES *Ment. Evol. Anim.* xviii. 281 An argument against the modificability of instinct by natural selection.

modificable, *a.* *rare*⁻⁰. [ad. L. type **modificābil-is*, f. *modificāre* to MODIFY: see -ABLE.] Modifiable.

1721 in BAILEY. **1755** JOHNSON, *Modificable*, diversifiable by various modes.

modificand (ˈmɒdɪfɪkænd). *rare*⁻¹. [ad. L. *modificand-us*, gerundive of *modificāre* to MODIFY.] Something that is to be modified.

a **1832** BENTHAM *Language* Wks. 1843 VIII. 317/2 In this way, modificative clauses in any number may be made to precede, and by that means exclusively attach upon one and the same modificand.

†**modificate,** *v.* *Obs.* [f. L. *modificāt-*, ppl. stem of *modificāre* to MODIFY.] *trans.* To modify; to limit, restrict; to distinguish with a specific mode of being or specific characteristics; to differentiate into various 'modes' or forms of existence.

1625 N. CARPENTER *Geog. Del.* I. iii. (1635) 48 A Philosopher ought to distinguish betwixt that which giues them a power to moue, and that which limits and modificates the action. **1660** R. SHERINGHAM *King's Suprem. Asserted* viii. (1682) 73 Although they do not diminish Majesty,..yet they do diversly qualifie and modificate it.

Hence †**modificated** *ppl. a.*

1646 H. LAWRENCE *Comm. Angells* 29 To see God.. evidently, clearely,..without a straitened and modificated vision. **1659** PEARSON *Creed* vi. (1662) 312 *And he shall reign for ever and ever*, not only to the modificated eternity of his Mediatorship,..but also to the complete eternity of the duration of his humanity. **1678** CUDWORTH *Intell. Syst.* I. v. §35. 870 The modificated Lives of animals and men, as such, according to them [are] accidental things.

modification (mɒdɪfɪˈkeɪʃən). [a. F. *modification* (14th c. in Hatz.-Darm.), or ad. L. *modificātiōnem*, n. of action f. *modificāre*, *-ārī* to MODIFY.]

1. a. The action of limiting, qualifying, or 'toning down' (a statement, etc.); a limitation, restriction, or qualification. (Tends to merge in sense 3.)

1603 FLORIO *Montaigne* III. iii. (1632) 459 So that it is naturally a paine unto mee, to communicate my selfe by halves, and with modification. **1626** DONNE *Serm.* lxviii. (1640) 691 He that beleeves not every Article of the Christian faith,..*Damnabitur* (no modification, no mollification, no going lesse), He shal be damned. **1657** HAWKE *Killing is M.* 49 Mariana..approves the killing of Princes by poison..yet always with this modification, that it is better to poison a Tyrant in his chair, or in his habit,.. then to poison his drink. **1660** R. COKE *Power & Subj.* 221 The Commissions and Bulls of the Popes Legate are..to be ..published with such cautions and modifications as that Court shall judge expedient for the good of the Kingdom. **1769** *Junius Lett.* xxi, This proposition they have uniformly maintained, without any condition or modification whatsoever. **1881** LOCKYER in *Nature* No. 616. 367 We find that the general statement requires a very considerable amount of modification.

†**b.** ? Appeasing, mollifying. *Obs.*

1656 FINETT *For. Ambass.* 48 The French Ambassador [having taken offence]..was entertained by one or two Lords of the Bed-Chamber..with as satisfactory reasons as they could frame for diversion, but with little effect, though Sir Thomas Edmons..were (together with the Master of the Ceremonies) sent to him immediately after to the same purpose of modification.

†**2.** *Philos.* **a.** The bringing of a thing into a particular mode of existence; determination of a substance into a particular mode or modes of being; differentiation into a variety of forms or 'modes'. *Obs.* (merged in 3).

1502 *Ord. Crysten Men* (W. de W. 1506) IV. xvii. 217 After the cyrcumstaunces and modyfycacyon of mortall synne. **1678** GALE *Crt. Gentiles* IV. III. vi. 191 If men contend about the terme *specification*..I can..substitute in the room thereof a terme equivalent thereto in point of efficace, namely, *modification*, which is used by our acute Dr. Sam. Ward. **1692** BENTLEY *Boyle Lect.* ii. 14 If these powers of Cogitation, and Volition, and Sensation, are neither inherent in Matter as such, nor acquirable to Matter by any motion and modification of it. **1701** GREW *Cosm. Sacra* II. ii. §26. 40 The Use hereof [*sc.* of Sense], being only to minister to the Modification of Life in the Vital Principle, wherein the Essence of Sense doth consist. **1836–7** SIR W. HAMILTON *Metaph.* viii. (1859) I. 150 The word *modification* is properly the bringing a thing into a certain mode of existence, but it is very commonly employed for the mode of existence itself.

†**b.** The form of existence which belongs to a particular object considered as a determination of some wider entity or substance; one of the particular or concrete forms into which a substance or entity is differentiated; a 'mode' or variety of being (cf. MODE *sb.* 6). *Obs.*

The philosophical conception having lost currency, the expression is obsolete both in philosophical and in general use, or is merged in sense 4.

1664 H. MORE *Myst. Iniq.*, *Apol.* 498 There is no Specifical change in the most contrary modifications of Matter imaginable, but onely Accidental. **1665** GLANVILL *Def. Van. Dogm.* 21 There is no way then of defending the assertion of the souls being matter, or any modification of it. **1690** LOCKE *Hum. Und.* II. xiii. §4 Each different distance is a different modification of space. **1768–74** TUCKER *Lt. Nat.* (1834) I. 17 Disposition, configuration, and motion, are not substances, but accidents in ancient dialect, or modifications according to modern philosophers. **1779–81** JOHNSON *L.P.*, *Pope* Wks. IV. 72 His *Characters of Men*, written with close attention to the operations of the mind and modifications of life. **1836–7** [see 2]. **1841** D'ISRAELI *Amen. Lit.* (1867) 128 New modifications of thought create new modes of expression.

3. a. The action of making changes in an object without altering its essential nature or character; the state of being thus changed; partial alteration.

1774 BURKE *Amer. Tax.* Wks. II. 402 Sir, a partial repeal, or, as the *bon ton* of the court then was, a *modification*, would have satisfied a timid, unsystematic, procrastinating Ministry. **1835** SOUTHEY *Doctor* ciii. III. 305 It is a curious instance of the modification which words undergo in different countries. **1853** J. H. NEWMAN *Hist. Sk.* (1873) II. II. i. 71 Here again was a very powerful instrument in modification of their national character. **1859** DARWIN *Orig. Spec.* i. (1873) 5 Our oldest domesticated animals are still capable of rapid improvement or modification. **1860** TYNDALL *Glac.* I. i. 7 It required but a slight modification of our plans.

b. *Biol.* The development of non-heritable changes in an organism; cf. sense 4 b.

1896 *Natural Sci.* IX. 288 In the life of a single individual it is obvious that no modification can affect variation, since this is necessarily antecedent. **1908** *Encycl. Relig. & Ethics* I. 66/2 Individuals are born different by variation; they become different during their lives by modification. **1960** N. POLUNIN *Introd. Plant Geogr.* viii. 214 (*heading*) Modification and distributions of crops (and weeds).

4. a. The result of such alteration; a modified form, a variety. (Cf. sense 2 b.)

1669 HOLDER *Elem. Speech* 6 The chief..of all signes is.. Humane voice, and the several modifications thereof by the Organs of Speech, viz. the Letters of the Alphabet. **1704** NEWTON *Opticks* (1721) 103 And therefore these Colours are to be derived from some other Cause than the new Modifications of Light by Refractions and Shadows. **1821** CRAIG *Lect. Drawing* iii. 142 Together with blue, red, yellow, and their modifications and combinations. **1823** J. BADCOCK *Dom. Amusem.* 24 The acid of wood in its original state, or the acetate of lime, which is its next modification. **1823** H. J. BROOKE *Introd. Crystallogr.* 96 The secondary forms of crystals have been explained to consist of modifications of the primary, occasioned by decrements on some of their edges or angles. **1857** MILLER *Elem. Chem.*, *Org.* (1862) iv. §1. 265 Stearin may exist in three modifications, each of which has a different fusing point. **1867** H. MACMILLAN *Bible Teach.* vii. (1870) 130 All the parts of a plant, from the seed to the blossom, are mere modifications of a leaf.

b. *Biol.* The non-heritable changes produced in an organism in response to a particular environment.

1896 *Natural Sci.* IX. 287 In a lucid paper he [*sc.* Lloyd Morgan] brought forward his useful distinction between variations, which are of germinal origin and congenital, and modifications, which are impressed on the organism by its environment. **1918** *Trans. Brit. Mycol. Soc.* VI. 221 If the organisms and their descendants when transplanted again into the original medium are again found to be red, then the change (loss of colour) is a modification. **1926** J. S. HUXLEY *Ess. Pop. Sci.* ii. 21 We can now..distinguish definitely between 'mutations', which are due to changes in the constitution of the animal—in the hereditary factors themselves—and 'modifications', which are due to changes in the environment. **1965** BELL & COOMBE tr. *Strasburger's Textbk. Bot.* 353 The modifications induced in the alpine plant [of *Taraxacum officinale*], probably due principally to the increased amount of ultra-violet light it receives, are not inherited.

5. a. *Scots Law.* The action of assessing or awarding a legal payment; *esp.* the determination of the amount of a parish minister's stipend. (Cf. MODIFY *v.* 5.)

1569 *Reg. Privy Council Scot.* I. 665 That he sall satisfie, content and pay all personis skaythit or hurt in thair gudis be him..at the jugement, sicht, discretioun, and modificatioun of Johnne Erskin of Dun. **1578** *Ibid.* III. 30 The ordinar assignationis of the stependis of the ministre contenit in the yeirlie buke of the modificatioun. **1595** *Extracts Aberdeen Reg.* (1848) II. 109 For payment of his vnlaw according to the modificatioun of the consall. **1838** W. BELL *Dict. Law Scot.* s.v. *Locality*, The decree of the Teind Court, modifying a stipend to a minister from the teinds of the parish, is called a decree of modification.

b. *Law.* A limitation or conditioning of the holding of property.

1818 CRUISE *Digest* (ed. 2) IV. 13 An agreement to make some future disposition or modification of real property.

6. *Gram.* **a.** Qualification or limitation of the sense of one word, phrase, etc. by another; an instance or result of this.

1727–41 CHAMBERS *Cycl.* s.v. *Modificative*, Nouns, and verbs..are susceptible of divers circumstances or modifications. **1845** *Encycl. Metrop.* I. 70/2 In all these instances, it is obvious, that the attribute expressed by the adjective undergoes some modification from the adverb.

b. Alteration of a vowel by 'umlaut'; an instance or result of this.

1845 J. M. KEMBLE in *Proc. Philol. Soc.* II. 136 This operation, for which we have no name, is known in Germany by that of Umlaut..: we must content ourselves with the very insufficient rendering 'modification'. *Ibid.*, These modifications remain, even though the vowel that caused them should have perished by lapse of time. *Ibid.* 141 The long *u*, and its modification *ý*. **1889** *Pall Mall G.* 22 Jan. 1/3 Why..cannot the 'reader' of the *Revue* look after the correct spelling of the German text? The signs of the modification are wanting in almost every case.

7. *Mus.* ? = *meantone temperament* (see MEAN TONE).

1811 BUSBY *Dict. Mus.* (ed. 3), *Modification*, a term applied to that temperament of the sounds of instruments whose tones are fixed, which gives a greater degree of perfection to one key than another, and produces between them a characteristic difference, as in organs, harpsichords, and piano-fortes.

modificational (mɒdɪfɪˈkeɪʃənəl), *a.* [f. MODIFICATION + -AL.] Having the nature of, or arising from, modification. So **modifiˈcationally** *adv.*

1908 *Athenæum* 11 July 47/2 Many of the unfit are only *modificationally* unfit. **1924** J. A. THOMPSON in *Glasgow Herald* 19 July 4 When we put aside these parasitic diseases and modificational diseases, there remain those that may be called constitutional.

modificative (ˈmɒdɪfɪkeɪtɪv), *a.* and *sb.* [ad. med.L. *modificātīv-us*, f. ppl. stem of L. *modificāre* to MODIFY: see -ATIVE. Cf. F. *modificatif, -ive* (18th c.).] **a.** *adj.* That has the property of modifying. **b.** *sb.* Something that modifies; a modifying word or clause.

a **1661** FULLER *Worthies, Gen.* (1662) I. 59 The Spirit of Truth it self, where Numbers and Measures are concerned, useth the aforesaid Modificatives ['almost', 'very nigh']. **1685** H. MORE *Paralip. Prophet.* 487 And though it be true that the Settlement of the Reformation is a further Perfection added thereto, yet that is but a modificative Addition to it, but that which is the main, the form and substance of the Reformation was before. **1727–41** CHAMBERS *Cycl.*, *Modificative*, something that *modifies*, or gives a thing a certain manner of being. *Ibid.*, This last kind of words, which serve to *modify* nouns and verbs, since they have no general name in the common grammars, he [Buffier] chuses to call *modificatives*. *a* **1832** BENTHAM *Language* Wks. 1843 VIII. 317/2 In this case put the modificative clause before the clause intended to be modified.

modificator (ˈmɒdɪfɪkeɪtə(r)). *rare.* [a. L. *modificātor*, agent-n. f. *modificāre* to MODIFY.] = MODIFIER. Also (repr. Sp. *modificador*) a member of a political party in Spain *c* 1823 which advocated the modification as opposed to the abolition of the constitution.

1824 *Westm. Rev.* Apr. 325 The drift of this gross policy was too obvious; yet with it he aimed to satisfy the modificators. **1889** *Science* 8 Nov. 318/1 Sulphuretted hydrogen, a modificator of the skin and of mucous membranes.

modificatory (ˈmɒdɪfɪkeɪtərɪ), *a.* [f. prec. + -ORY[2].] Modifying; tending to modify.

1824 *Westm. Rev.* Apr. 318 The modificatory party in Spain believed that the epoch of triumph was now at hand. **1861** MAX MÜLLER *Sci. Lang.* Ser. I. viii. 297 In Turkish.. all modificatory syllables are placed at the end of the root. **1864** *Ibid.* Ser. II. vii. (1868) 326 Here 'j' and 'dh' are clearly modificatory letters.

modified (ˈmɒdɪfaɪd), *ppl. a.* [f. MODIFY *v.* + -ED[1].] In senses of the verb: Limited, altered, qualified, etc. ***modified logic***: see quot 1837–8. ***Modified Standard (English)***: see quot. 1934.

1456 SIR G. HAYE *Law Arms* (S.T.S.) 126 Vassallis ar behaldyn to thair baroun in speciale jurisdicciоun modifyit, and to the king in generale. **1668** *Min. Baron Crt. Stitchill* (1905) 53 Three punds sevin shillings for the modified pryce thereof. **1690** LOCKE *Hum. Und.* II. xviii. §7 The names, which in several arts have been.. applied to several complex ideas of modified actions. **1837** DISRAELI *Venetia* II. ii, An uncertain light, or rather modified darkness, that seemed the sky. **1837–8** SIR W. HAMILTON *Logic* iv. (1860) I. 60 What I have called Modified Logic is identical with what Kant and other philosophers have denominated Applied Logic (*Angewandte Logik, Logica applicata*). **1845** *Proc. Philol. Soc.* II. 166 The modified word is not, as with us, the predicate or qualifying noun, but the subject or leading one. **1845** MCCULLOCH *Taxation* I. i. (1852) 61 Proprietors of estates subject to a variable land-tax have, in fact, only a modified right of property in them. **1868** OUSELEY *Harmony* xv. 175 We may also take the third below,.. and thus get a new bass, or as it is called, a *modified* bass. **1866** HUXLEY *Physiol.* xii. (1869) 314 The crystalline lens is composed of fibres which are the modified cells of the epidermis. **1913** H. C. WYLD in *Mod. Lang. Teaching* IX. 262/2 London English is a totally different thing from Received Standard: it is merely one of the many provincialisms, such as are heard in large cities, which fall under the designation of Modified Standard. **1914** —— *Short Hist. English* ix. 236 It seems probable that the influence of *Modified Standard*, that is, of forms of English differentiated out of *Received Standard* by factors of social isolation, will have to be admitted and studied in the future. **1934** —— in *S.P.E. Tract* XXXIX. 604 Thousands of persons speak a form of English which is neither a local dialect, nor what some would call 'good English'. For this latter type,.. I proposed the term *Modified Standard*.. to cover all the various types of English .. which.. while they adhere, on the whole, to the Standard, especially in accidence and syntax, are nevertheless more or less deeply affected, either by *provincialism*, or by .. *vulgarism*, in pronunciation. **1940** J. H. JAGGER *English in Future* i. 15 Changes [in Standard English].. have been mainly due to the influence of the various forms of Modified Standard—to accept Professor Wyld's terms—upon each other and upon Received Standard.

modifier (ˈmɒdɪfaɪə(r)). [f. MODIFY *v.* + -ER[1].]

1. a. One who or a thing which modifies (see the vb.).

1583 *Acts Gen. Assemb. Ch. Scotl.* (Maitland Cl.) II. 636 A request sall be made to the modifiers for that effect. **1587** *Ibid.* 726 The brethren agreeth, that certane of their number be adjoyned with the Lords Modifyers, to perfyte the assignations of this present year. **1682** H. MORE *Annot. Glanvill's Lux O.* 198 That universal Spirit of Nature is most certainly the Mover of the Matter of the World, and the Modifier thereof. **1757** HUME *Nat. Hist. Relig.* vi. in *Four Diss.* 47 That a limited deity.. should in the end be represented as sovereign maker and modifier of the universe. **1860** MAURY *Phys. Geog.* (Low) xxi. 474 A powerful modifier of climate is the latent heat of vapour in the air. **1868** G. MACDONALD *R. Falconer* I. 243 We shall have.. more modifiers and completers, and fewer inventors. **1890** *Anthony's Photogr. Bull.* III. 372 Colored media recommended as screens or modifiers of the light.

b. *Genetics.* Any gene which modifies the phenotypic expression of a gene at another locus.

1915 T. H. MORGAN et al. *Mechanism Mendelian Heredity* viii. 203 The F_2 from the crosses to self-color indicate that such modifiers are really present in the rats. **1919** *Jrnl. Exper. Zool.* XXVIII. 337 (*heading*) Specific modifiers of eosin eye color in *Drosophila melanogaster*. **1931** E. B. FORD *Mendelism & Evolution* II. iii. 49 If, however, another mutation controlling similar characters were to arise, such an old and ineffective gene might show itself as a 'specific modifier'. **1968** R. D. MARTIN tr. *Wickler's Mimicry in Plants & Animals* ii. 33 Such modifier genes can switch the other genes on or off or alter their functional level so as to improve the correspondence of the mimic with the model. **1971** LEVITAN & MONTAGU *Textbk. Human Genetics* xvi. 595 This [*sc.* gene interaction] is a very broad term and covers everything from genes whose interaction.. is so intimate that they must be considered part of the same operating unit, to genes whose activities impinge only in a most indirect manner (and so are thought of as vague 'modifiers').

2. *spec.* in *Gram.* (see MODIFY *v.* 6). **a.** A word, phrase, or clause which modifies another.

1865 TYLOR *Early Hist. Man.* ii. 26 A third construction [*sc.* of sentences] is common..; the modifier after the modified. **1924** H. E. PALMER *Gram. Spoken Eng.* II. 68 Possessives used as Modifiers. (Generally known as 'possessive adjectives'.) **1933** L. BLOOMFIELD *Lang.* xii. 194 A prepositional expression and an accusative expression.. appearing in entirely different syntactic positions (e.g. as a modifier of verbs: *sit beside John*, or of nouns: *the boy beside John*). **1961** R. B. LONG *Sentence & its Parts* 490 In the commonest type of syntactic combination, a word-or-multiword unit, a head, combines with another or others, a modifier or modifiers, and determines the syntactic character of the total combination. **1970** G. C. LEPSCHY *Survey Structural Ling.* vi. 107 Modifiers.. such as grammatical number, or article, which are centripetal.. indicate the value—singular or plural, definite or indefinite —of the particular element to which they are attached.

b. A phonetic sign or symbol which modifies a character.

1899 H. SWEET *Practical Study of Languages* iii. 21 Thus, if there is a special mark or modifier to express voice, the absence of that modifier necessarily implies breath. **1911** *Encycl. Brit.* XXI. 462/1 The Organic Alphabet especially makes a large use of 'modifiers'—characters which are added to the other symbols to indicate nasal, palatal, &c., modifications of the sounds represented by italic letters in the Narrow Romic transcription; thus (l*n*) = nasalized (l).

modify (ˈmɒdɪfaɪ), *v.* Also 4–7 modefie, -fy(e. [a. F. *modifier* (14th c.), ad. L. *modificāre, -ārī* to limit, moderate, f. *mod-us* MODE: see -FY.]

†**1.** *trans.* To limit, restrain, keep within bounds and measure. *Obs.*

1390 GOWER *Conf.* III. 157 A king after the reule is holde To modifie and to adresce Hise yiftes upon such largesce That he mesure noght excede. *Ibid.* 233 The reule of Policie, Wherof a king schal modefie The fleisschly lustes of nature. *c* **1440** *Promp. Parv.* 341/1 Modyfyyn, or settyn yn mene cowrse of resone.

†**b.** To appease, assuage. *Obs.*

1430–40 LYDG. *Bochas* IX. xxxi[i]. (1494) G iij b, Tyrauntys hertis thys vertue doth appese, Modefyeth their cruell fell wodenesse. **1433** —— *St. Edmund* II. 857 Thus kan the lord.. The rage of beestis appese and modifie. **1546** LANGLEY *Pol. Verg. De Invent.* I. xi. 21 b, [Orpheus] by the swetenes of his armony delited and modefied the grosse hartis and rude myndes of men.

†**c.** *refl.* To control one's feelings. *Obs.*

1530 PALSGR. 639/2, I modyfye, I temperate, *je me modifie*. ..What thoughe he speke a hastye worde you muste modyfye your selfe.

2. To alter in the direction of moderation or lenity; to make less severe, rigorous, or decided; to qualify, tone down, moderate. (Tends to merge in the wider sense 4.)

c **1386** CHAUCER *Knt.'s T.* 1684 Wherfore to shapen þat they shal nat dye He wolde his firste purpos modifye. **1426** LYDG. *De Guil. Pilgr.* 24376, I.. prayed hym.. that he wold ..modefyen his vengeaunce, and to with-drawe his lugement. *c* **1480** HENRYSON *Test. Cress.* 299 The pane of Cresseid for to modify. **1509** HAWES *Past. Pleas.* XXXIV. (Percy Soc.) 174 Your hasty dome loke that ye modefy. **1610** DONNE *Pseudo-martyr* 184 For so Mariana modefies his Doctrine, that the Prince should not execute any Clergy man, though hee deserue it. **1756** BURKE *Subl. & B.* IV. xxv, The great has terrour for its basis; which, when it is modified, causes that emotion in the mind, which I have called astonishment. **1813** WELLINGTON in *Gurw. Desp.* (1837) X. 382 Upon the whole I conceive that it would be best for the court to modify their sentence. **1819** BYRON *Juan* II. lxiii, They did their best to modify their case. **1859** LANG *Wand. India* 402 There is generally a light breeze to modify the heat. **1869** TOZER *Highl. Turkey* II. 264 In fairy tales.. inconsistencies are.. modified and softened down. **1873** MISS BRADDON *Milly Darrell* xii, I suppose that medicine was intended to modify those attacks of sickness from which she has suffered so much.

3. a. *Philos.* To determine (a substance or other entity) into a particular 'mode' or modes; to give (an object) its particular modality or form of being.

a **1643** S. WARD in Gale *Crt. Gentiles* IV. III. vi. 191 That the previous Concurse of God, as the first cause, doth according to its mode modifie and determine al the actions of second causes. **1678** GALE *Crt. Gentiles* IV. III. vi. 190 He doth by a particular efficacious concurse so modifie and determine the entitative act, as that the natural specification and individuation thereof may be ascribed to him as the God of Nature. **1706** PHILLIPS (ed. Kersey), *Modify*,.. In Philosophy, to give the Modality or manner of Existence. **1727–41** CHAMBERS *Cycl.* s.v. *Spinozism*, Whence it follows, that the substance modified by the square figure cannot be the same substance with that modified by the round figure.

†**b.** *gen.* To differentiate into a variety of forms; to distinguish or diversify by investing with specific characteristics. *Obs.* (merged in 4).

1669 HOLDER *Elem. Speech* 32 They ['letters'] modify and discriminate the Voice without appearing to discontinue it. **1690** LOCKE *Hum. Und.* II. xviii. §3 Sounds.. are modified by diversity of notes of different length put together, which make that complex idea called a tune. *Ibid.* §6 Some others of the simple ideas.. have been thus modified to a great variety of complex ideas. **1698** FRYER *Acc. E. India & P.* 278 More than twice Seven Plates are differently Modified to invite the Palate to Luxury. **1704** NEWTON *Opticks* (1721) 101 And therefore the differences of these Colours from one another do not arise from the different Confines of Shadow, whereby Light is variously modified, as has hitherto been the Opinion of Philosophers. **1777** SIR W. JONES *Ess. Imit. Arts* Poems, etc. 207 As the passions are differently modified in different men.

4. To make partial changes in; to change (an object) in respect of some of its qualities; to alter or vary without radical transformation.

1780 BURKE *Corr.* (1844) II. 387, I confess I see no cause to change, or to modify, my opinion on that subject. **1791** FEARNE *Cont. Remainders* (ed. 4) I. 108 Words of limitation operate by reference to or connection with other words, and extend or modify the estate given by those other words. **1798** MALTHUS *Popul.* III. vii. (1806) II. 211 Others employ themselves in modifying the raw materials of nature into the forms best suited to the gratification of man. **1834** *Tait's Mag.* I. 184/1 Measures of improvement so often mutilated, or, as the word is, 'modified' [by the House of Lords]. **1849** MACAULAY *Hist. Eng.* iii. I. 321 There are, however, some important parts of his character still to be noted, which will greatly modify this estimate. **1863** H. COX *Instit.* I. iv. 18 The Crown must either assent to or reject bills in Parliament, but cannot modify them. **1878** HUXLEY *Physiogr.* xvii. 273 The agents which are now at work in modifying the crust of the earth.

b. To alter so as to adapt (*to*). *rare.*

1800 *Med. Jrnl.* III. 514 Every medical man.. will know how to modify its dose and formula to the existing circumstances of his patient.

5. *Scots Law.* To assess, decree (a payment of money, a fine, costs); to award (a payment) *to* a person; *esp.* to determine the amount of a parish minister's stipend. †Also *absol.*

1457 *Sc. Acts Jas. II* (1814) II. 51/1 Vnder sik payne and vnlawe as þe barone or lorde sall modify. **1524** *Extracts Aberdeen Reg.* (1844) I. 108 To pass and modefy the provest and Johne Colisonis expensis. **1539** *Ibid.* 160 The provest and bailzeis.. modifit ane mendis for the said myspersonyng, as efter followis. **1569** *Acts Gen. Assemb. Ch. Scotl.* (Maitland Cl.) I. 164 Every Superintendent.. shall modifie the stipends, augment or diminish the same, as occasione shall serve. **1583** *Reg. Privy Council Scot.* III. 598 [The Lords of Council therefore] modifiis to hir the sowme of twentie schillingis to be paid to hir. **1632** LITHGOW *Trav.* VIII. 351, I receiued in compensation of my abuses.. fifty Florentine Crownes of gold, being modified by the Duke him selfe. **1752** J. LOUTHIAN *Form of Process* (ed. 2) 118 May it therefore please your Lordship.. to modify the Sum for which your Petitioners are to find Bail. **1754** ERSKINE *Princ. Sc. Law* (1809) 53 A commission of Parliament was appointed.. for.. modifying stipends to ministers out of the teinds. **1833** *Act 3 & 4 Will. IV* c. 46 §117 Such penalty.. may be recovered by summary complaint to the sheriff.. with such expences therefor as shall be modified by him. **1838** W. BELL *Dict. Law Scot.* s.v. *Modification*, The stipend ..must be modified in grain or victual, and paid in money.

6. *Gram.* **a.** To limit or qualify the sense of (a word, phrase, or sentence).

1727–41 [see MODIFICATIVE *sb.*]. **1797** *Encycl. Brit.* (ed. 3) VIII. 72/1 The usual effect of adjectives.. is to modify or particularise a general term. **1845** *Encycl. Metrop.* I. 70/1 The adverb.. is used to modify an adjective, or a verb, or another adverb.

b. To change (a vowel) by 'umlaut'.

1845 J. M. KEMBLE in *Proc. Philol. Soc.* II. 138 The short *u* continues to represent the Gothic *u*.. where it has not been dulled into *o*, or modifed by a following *i* or *ë* into *y*.

7. *Cryst.* (See quot.)

1823 H. J. BROOKE *Introd. Crystallogr.* 24 The new planes produced by decrements are denominated *secondary* planes, and the primary form, when altered in shape by the interference of secondary planes, is said to be *modified* on the edges or angles on which the secondary planes have been produced. *Ibid.* 96 Crystals rarely present themselves under their respective primary forms; they are usually modified by new planes, producing secondary crystals.

modifying (ˈmɒdɪfaɪɪŋ), *vbl. sb.* [-ING[1].] The action of the verb MODIFY.

1643 in *Dundee Charters* (1880) 86 The said Provest.. shall compeir.. and thair Judicialie consent to the modefying of the forsaid sowmes as ane constant yeirly stipend to thair persone. **1692** R. L'ESTRANGE *Fables* CCXV. 188 All this Descanting, and Modifying upon the Matter. *a* **1853** W. JAY *Autobiog.* xvii. (1855) 163 General principles of church-government, which will admit.. of considerable modifyings in their application.

ˈmodifying, *ppl. a.* [-ING[2].] That modifies.

1793 BEDDOES *Math. Evid.* 145 Indeed, except as to the sound of a language, it is indifferent whether these modifying words are prefixed or suffixed. **1823** H. J. BROOKE *Introd. Crystallogr.* 113 When the modifying planes first

touch each other on the edges of the tetrahedron, a regular octahedron is produced. **1843** BORROW *Bible in Spain* liii, There is many a cave of nature's forming..which nevertheless exhibits indications that man has turned it to some account, and that it has been subjected more or less to his modifying power. **1845** J. M. KEMBLE in *Proc. Philol. Soc.* II. 136 Where the modifying vowel has only been introduced in the process of conjugation. **1883** H. DRUMMOND *Nat. Law in Spir. W.* viii. (1884) 259 Changes of food..exert a powerful modifying influence upon living organisms.

modilich(e, -like, obs. forms of MOODILY.

modillion (məʊˈdɪljən). *Arch.* Forms: 6-8 **modiglion,** 6-8 **modilion,** 8-9 **modillon,** 7- **modillion.** [ad. It. *modiglione*; cf. F. *modillon* (in 16th c. also *modiglion*).

The ultimate etymology is not clear; the resemblance of sense would suggest connexion with L. *mutulus* MUTULE.]

A projecting bracket placed in series under the corona of the cornice in the Corinthian, Composite and Roman Ionic orders. Also applied to similar ornaments in modern building. †In 17th c. sometimes = MUTULE.

1563 SHUTE *Archit.* D iv b, Mutili, whiche is also named Modiglions. **1598** R. HAYDOCKE tr. *Lomazzo* I. xxvi. 95 Being diuided into 6 parts, one giues *denticuli*; an other *cymatium* which supporteth the modilions. **1664** EVELYN tr. *Freart's Archit.* 136 Modilions, being certain supports in the form of Corbells. **1665** MOXON tr. *Vignola* (1702) 36 The Modillion..or Underprop to bear up the Cornice. **1732** BERKELEY *Alciphr.* III. §9 The Entablature and all its Parts and Ornaments..Triglyphs, Metopes, Modiglions, and the rest. **1838** BRITTON *Dict. Archit.*, *Modillion*,..Less ornamented, they are sometimes used in the Ionic entablature. **1839** *Civil Eng. & Arch. Jrnl.* II. 82/1 On the ends of the joists, an iron capping, forming a modillion. **1845** PETRIE *Round Towers Irel.* II. iii. 233 The mouldings which cap the Corinthian modillions in the palace of Dioclesian at Spalatro. **1855** REINNEL *Masons*, etc. *Assist.* 62 Manner of fixing Modillions, &c. on Soffits.

attrib. **1737** SALMON *Country Build. Estim.* (ed. 2) 29 Modillion Cornishes, Cove-Eaves, and Dentil Cornishes, are generally measured and valued by the Foot superficial. **1817** RICKMAN *Styles Archit. Eng.* (1848) 30 This modillion cornice is, in fact..rather Italian than Roman.

modinesse, obs. form of MOODINESS.

‖**modiola** (məʊˈdaɪələ). *Nat. Hist.* [mod.L., alteration of L. *modiolus* MODIOLUS.]

1. *Zool.* A genus of mussels (Lamarck); a mussel of this genus. Cf. MODIOLUS 2.

1826 CROUCH *Introd. Lamarck's Conchol.* 18. **1839** SOWERBY *Conch. Man.* **1841** H. MILLER *O.R. Sandst.* xiv. (1842) 294 We may find the ancient modiola of the Lias in habitats analogous to those of its modern representative the muscle. **1876** *Beneden's Anim. Parasites* 16 We have opened hundreds of these modiolæ, and we have never met with any without their crabs.

2. *Bot.* A genus of *Malvaceæ* (Mönch 1794).

Named from the whorled position of the carpels, resembling the nave of a wheel.

1846 LINDLEY *Veg. Kingd.* 370. *a* **1865** PAXTON *Bot. Dict.* (1868), *Modiola*, from Modiolus, the nave of a wheel, whorled position of carpels... Nat. or. Malvaceæ.

modiolar (məʊˈdaɪələ(r)), *a. Anat.* [ad. mod.L. *modiolār-is*, f. MODIOLUS.] Belonging to the modiolus of the ear.

1856 in MAYNE *Expos. Lex.* **1868** OWEN *Vertebr. Anim.* III. 220 The inner or modiolar wall of the turns.

moˈdioliform, *a. Bot. rare*$^{-0}$. [ad. mod.L. *modioliform-is*, f. L. *modiol-us*: see MODIOLUS and -FORM.] (See quot. 1866.)

[**1839** LINDLEY *Introd. Bot.* III. i. (ed. 3) 454 Nave-shaped (*modioliformis*).] **1856** in MAYNE *Expos. Lex.* **1866** *Treas. Bot.*, *Modioliform*, shaped like the nave of a wheel, round, depressed, with a very narrow orifice; as the ripe fruit of *Gaultheria*, or the carpels in *Modiola*.

‖**modiolus** (məʊˈdaɪələs). [L. *modiolus* bucket on water-wheel, nave of wheel, trepan, etc., dim. of *modius* MODIUS.]

1. *Surg.* The crown of a trepan. *rare*$^{-0}$.

1693 tr. *Blancard's Phys. Dict.* (ed. 2), *Modiolus, Trepanum*, or *Anabaptiston*, an Instrument which they use in..Contusions, Cuts, and Fractures of Bone. **1706** PHILLIPS (ed. Kersey), *Modiolus*..Also a Trepan. **1891** *Syd. Soc. Lex.*, *Modiolus*..Also, the crown of a trephine.

2. *Zool.* Earlier name for the genus of mussels *Modiola* (see MODIOLA 1); = *Mytilus modiolus* Linn.

[**1797** *Encycl. Brit.* (ed. 3) XII. 610/1, Art. *Mytilus*, The modiolus, or great mussel.]

3. *Anat.* The conical axis around which the cochlea of the ear winds.

1823 in CRABB *Technol. Dict.* **1840** E. WILSON *Anat. Vade M.* (1842) 469 The central axis or modiolus is large near its base, where it corresponds with the first turn of the cochlea.

modir, obs. form of MOTHER.

modish (ˈməʊdɪʃ), *a.* [f. MODE *sb.* + -ISH.]

1. According to the mode or prevailing fashion. (Very common in 17-18 c.; now somewhat *arch.*) **a.** Of persons: Observant of or following the mode (usually with suggestion of disparagement).

1660 INGELO *Bentiv. & Ur.* II. (1682) 155 Such Manners as were scorned by the Modish World. **1664** PEPYS *Diary* 26 Aug., Mr. Pen, Sir William's son, is come back from France, and come to visit my wife. A most modish person grown, she says, a fine gentleman. **1712** ADDISON *Spect.* No. 399 ¶1 The modish Hypocrite endeavours to appear more vicious than he really is, the other kind of Hypocrite more virtuous. **1725** WODROW *Corr.* (1843) III. 188 All our modish writers. **1803** MAR. EDGEWORTH *Belinda* (1832) II. xxviii. 269 A very pretty, modish, affected young lady. **1885** AGNES M. CLERKE *Pop. Hist. Astron.* 14 The most brilliant and modish society in England was at that time to be met at Bath.

absol. **1675** E. PHILLIPS *Theat. Poet.* Pref. ** 3 For Cloths I leave them to the discretion of the Modish. **1902** *Westm. Gaz.* 16 Jan. 3/1 One still sees the modish clutching their skirts when they walk abroad.

b. Of things: Conforming to the mode; in accordance with the prevailing fashion; also, followed or sought after by people of fashion, fashionable.

1663 PEPYS *Diary* 21 Oct., A good velvet cloak..and other things modish. **1672** WYCHERLEY *Love in Wood* IV. ii, Besides, they say he has the modish distemper. *a* **1706** EVELYN *Sylva* (1776) 319 The Swedish Juniper, now so frequent in our modish gardens. **1743** *Lond. & Country Brew.* II. (ed. 2) 112, I believe the greatest Evil is on the Side of this destructive modish extraordinary Incorporation of the Yeast with the Beer. **1745** *De Foe's Eng. Tradesman* (1841) II. xliv. 156 Houses built thirty or forty years ago, are now old-fashioned, and must be pulled down, to build more modish apartments. **1810** S. GREEN *Reformist* I. 220 Her modish effrontery was evidently constrained by habitual puritanism. **1852** MRS. SMYTHIES *Bride Elect* xxi, Her mother's elegant and modish little abode. **1894** *Daily News* 9 Feb. 3/1 Till then [*i.e.* Easter], no one is supposed to wish for modish raiment.

¶**2.** *nonce-use.* Pertaining to 'mode' in the metaphysical sense.

1697 J. SERGEANT *Solid Philos.* 102 Whence the Notions signify'd by such Words are..Modish (as we may term it) or expressing some Manner [How] the Thing is.

modishly (ˈməʊdɪʃlɪ), *adv.* Somewhat *arch.* [-LY[2].] In a modish manner; fashionably.

1665 SIR T. HERBERT *Trav.* (1677) 144 His sleeve is either carelesly or modishly thrown over his arm. **1710** *Lond. Gaz.* No. 4642/3 A Brick Building new and modishly built. **1776** FOOTE *Bankrupt* Prol., Wks. 1799 II. 97 Unless, indeed, I modishly apply, For leave to sell my works by lottery. **1821** J. BUNTING in Treffry *Mem. J. Benson* (1840) 344 His ministry was scriptural; not metaphysically subtile, nor modishly sentimental. **1882** B. HARTE *Flip* iii, The slight..figure of a young woman modishly attired.

modishness (ˈməʊdɪʃnɪs). [f. MODISH + -NESS.] The state or quality of being modish; conformity to the fashion; affectation of the fashion.

1676 GLANVILL *Seasonable Reflect.* 30 [They] do not Scoff at Religion out of enmity or malice, but out of modishness and compliance. **1712** M. HENRY *Life P. Henry* Wks. 1857 II. 744/2 We must..not affect singularity, nor affect modishness. **1894** A. BIRRELL *Ess.* ix. 101 Wit of that genuine kind which is free from modishness.

modist (ˈməʊdɪst). *rare.* [f. MODE *sb.* + -IST.] A follower of the fashion.

1837 *Q. Rev.* LIX. 414 The announcement of a new poem by Byron never excited a greater sensation amongst the men of letters—than the description of a new dress worn by a certain beautiful English duchess, periodically excites amongst the modists of the continent. **1846** WORCESTER (citing *Q. Rev.*). Hence in later Dicts.

‖**modistæ** (məʊˈdɪstaɪ), *sb. pl.* Also **Modistæ.** [L.] The collective name given to a number of later medieval grammarians who developed and expounded a system of Latin grammar wherein Priscian's word classes and categories were integrated into the framework of scholastic philosophy.

1903 J. E. SANDYS *Hist. Classical Scholarship* I. xxxii. 642 The work in which this philosophy of grammar was first laid down was entitled *De Modis Significandi*, and its teachers were called *Modistae*. **1951** R. H. ROBINS *Ancient & Mediaeval Grammatical Theory in Europe* iii. 77 Later writers of Grammaticae Speculativae..are often referred to as a group by the name 'Modistae'. **1963** *Canad. Jrnl. Linguistics* IX. 41 This short paper will attempt to draw attention to some of the grammarians of the Middle Ages.., in particular to the group..now known as the Modistae. **1968** J. LYONS *Introd. Theoretical Linguistics* i. 15 So many works were produced with the title 'The Modes of Signifying' (*De modis significandi*) that the grammarians of the period are often referred to collectively as 'modistae'. **1971** G. L. BURSILL-HALL *Speculative Grammars of Middle Ages* 11 Martin of Dacia..was probably the first of the Modistae. **1973** *Canad. Jrnl. Linguistics* XVIII. 177 The *modistae*, linguists of the fourteenth century who developed the *grammatica speculativa* by relating the grammatical theories current during the early part of the Middle Ages to an Aristotelian framework. **1974** *Encycl. Brit. Macropædia* VIII. 267/2 Before the *modistae*, grammar had not been viewed as a separate discipline but had been considered in conjunction with other studies or skills (such as criticism, preservation of valued texts, foreign-language learning).

‖**modiste** (mɒdist). [Fr., f. *mode* fashion: see MODE *sb.*] One who makes, invents, or deals in articles of fashion; esp. a maker of ladies robes, millinery, etc.; a milliner, dress-maker.

c **1840** LADY WILTON *Art of Needlework* xiii. 188 Mercers and milliners, haberdashers and modistes. **1852** SMEDLEY *L. Arundel* xxxvi, Fashioned..by an ingenious Parisian modiste. **1880** DISRAELI *Endym.* xvi, The days of the great modistes, when an English lady might absolutely be dressed in London. **1903** *Speaker* 7 Feb. 465/2 The modiste and the governess had fallen foul of each other. **1936** G. GREENE *Gun For Sale* i. 13 He leant his face against a modiste's window and jeered silently through the glass.

modistic (məʊˈdɪstɪk), *a.*[1] [f. MODISTE + -IC.] Relating to fashion or fashions.

1907 *Times* 16 Nov. 9/6 The sleeves of this dress show the trend of modistic thought in this direction. **1915** *Queen* 6 Nov. 855/3 The modistic information it contains is of the most enlightening description.

modistic (məʊˈdɪstɪk), *a.*[2] [f. MODIST(Æ *sb. pl.* + -IC.] Of or pertaining to the modistæ.

1963 G. L. BURSILL-HALL in *Canadian Jrnl. Linguistics* IX. 51 The modus essendi is the thing itself with its various properties; the thing is perceived in the mind and in the Modistic scheme this is the modus intelligendi. **1967** R. H. ROBINS *Short Hist. Ling.* iv. 77 The same distinction between form and matter recurs at various points in modistic speculative grammar. **1971** G. L. BURSILL-HALL *Speculative Grammars of Middle Ages* ii. 40 Modistic grammatical theory rests on the study of words and the properties of these words as the 'signs of things'. **1972** *Times Lit. Suppl.* 29 Sept. 1164/2 The late medieval 'modistic' grammars, which attempted to relate the traditional 'parts of speech' to postulated categories of reality. **1974** *Lang. Sciences* XXXII. 27 Moreover, special doctrines of Thomas of Erfurt are assumed to be general features of modistic theory.

‖**modius** (ˈməʊdɪəs). *Antiq.* Pl. modii (ˈməʊdɪaɪ). [L. *modius*, whence F. *muid.*]

1. A Roman corn-measure, equal to about a peck. Also, in the Middle Ages, a measure of capacity, dry and liquid (= F. *muid*) of varying size, commonly rendered by 'bushel'.

1398 TREVISA *Barth. De P.R.* XIX. cxxviii. (1495) 932 The mesure *Modius* hathe that name for it is perfyte of his manere. **1609** HOLLAND *Amm. Marcell.* XXV. xii. 278 So grievous and extreame was the famine..that if in any place there was but one Modius or pecke of meale found..it was exchanged for ten pieces of gold. **1693** tr. *Blancard's Phys. Dict.* (ed. 2). **1706** PHILLIPS (ed. Kersey). **1802** RANKEN *Hist. France* II. v. i. 312 A modius, probably a bushel of corn, sold at Mayence for ten shekels of silver.

2. A tall cylindrical head-dress with which certain deities are represented in ancient art.

1800 J. DALLAWAY *Anecd. Arts Eng.* 245 Both [Jupiter and Pluto] have frequently the cap called 'modius', from its resemblance to a bushel. **1850** LEITCH tr. *C. O. Müller's Anc. Art* §357 (ed. 2) 437 In terracottas from Magna Græcia ..Demeter has the modius on her head.

modiwarp, -wart, obs. forms of MOULDWARP.

modle, obs. f. MODEL.

modo: see MODU.

modoc (ˈməʊdɒk). *U.S. slang.* Also **modock.** [Origin unknown.] (See quots.)

1936 ALLEN & LYMAN *Wonder Bk. Air* 312 A *modoc*, the derivation of which is obscure, is a flashy chap who goes around wearing helmet and goggles, and more than likely, leather boots and riding breeches, too, and talking about the big things he is going to do for aviation. **1942** BERREY & VAN DEN BARK *Amer. Thes. Slang* §756/2 *Modock*, one who has taken up aviation for publicity, social, or similar reasons. **1960** WENTWORTH & FLEXNER *Dict. Amer. Slang* 341/2 *Modoc*, one who becomes an Air Force flier for publicity, social prestige, or similar reasons.

modom (ˈmɒdəm). *colloq.* Also **moddam, moddom, moddum.** An alteration of MADAM *sb.*, in imitation of affectedly refined pronunciation.

1920 GALSWORTHY *In Chancery* II. xiii. 223 Very new, modom; quite the latest thing. **1932** 'E. M. DELAFIELD' *Thank Heaven Fasting* I. i. 9 Madame Myrtle..was full of assurances about knowing exactly what Moddam meant. *Ibid.* 11, I only wished Moddam to judge the general style. **1932** WODEHOUSE *Doctor Sally* iii. 29 Did you call, moddom? **1934** H. G. WELLS *Exper. Autobiogr.* I. iv. 153 We are showing some very pretty sunshades just now Moddum. *Ibid.* 155 You haven't shown the lady the gingham at six-three! The young man has made a mistake Moddum. **1944** A. THIRKELL *Headmistress* ix. 200 A very handsome afternoon dress..but, as the dressmaker said, almost with tears, making moddom look her age. **1961** *Punch* 1 Mar. 372/1 The saleslady coughed delicately... 'It's up to you, Modom,' she said.

modre, obs. form of MOTHER *sb.*

Mods (mɒdz), colloquial abbreviation of *Moderations*: see MODERATION 4. Also *attrib.*

1858 J. C. THOMSON *Almæ Matres* 226 Between the 'little-go' and 'mods' he learns nothing new. **1876** O. WILDE *Let.* 5 July (1962) 15 Tonight the Mods list comes out. **1893** BEATRICE WHITBY *In Suntime of Youth* I. ii. 26 Neither the attainment of the Balliol scholarship, nor a 'first in Mods', elicited a word of congratulation. **1952** V. GOLLANCZ *My Dear Timothy* I. xix. 221 The Schools in question were Mods—Classical Moderations—..Mods were for the language and literature of Greece and Rome. **1955** *Times* 11 Aug. 9/2, I make a point of asking them how often they take down Aeschylus or Catullus and the usual answer is that they have scarcely opened a classical text since they got their first in Mods or won the Ireland.

†**ˈModu, ˈModo.** *Obs.* The name of a devil (see quots.).

1603 HARSNET *Pop. Impost.* x. 48 Modu, Ma: Maynies deuill, was a graund Commaunder, Muster-maister ouer the Captaines of the seauen deadly sinnes..: so saith Sara Williams. *Ibid.* xxii. 148 Maho, and Modu (the two Generals of the infernal furies). **1605** Modo [see MAHU].

†**moduˈlaminous,** *a. Obs. rare*[-1]. [ad. L. type *modulāminōsus, f. L. *modulāmen* melody, f. *modulārī* to MODULATE: see -OUS.] Melodious.

1637 SYDENHAM *Serm.* 25 By a kinde of modulaminous and delightfull ayre.

modulant (ˈmɒdjʊlənt). *rare*⁻¹. [ad. L. *modulant-em*, pres. pple. of *modulārī* to MODULATE.] A modulating agent.

1869 E. WADHAM *Eng. Versification* xvi. 119 In modern English verse alliteration only plays the subordinate part of a modulant, not to be unduly decried where not overdone.

modular (ˈmɒdjʊlə(r)), *a.* [ad. mod.L. *modulār-is* (or F. *modulaire*), f. L. *modul-us*: see MODULUS and -AR¹.]

1. a. *Arch.* Of or pertaining to a module or modulus (see MODULE 4).

1842 GWILT *Archit.* Gloss., *Modular Proportion*, that which is regulated by a module.

b. Employing or involving a module or modules (MODULE *sb.* 4 d, e, f) as the basis of design or construction; designed as part of such a system.

1936 BEMIS & BURCHARD *Evolving House* III. iv. 64 Cubical modular design..simply requires that all parts of the house..be proportioned to the same module in all three dimensions. **1945** *Archit. Rec.* Jan. 102/2 The modular system does not necessarily involve making every product come out to even multiples of 4 inches... The system does suggest, however, that the 4-in. unit be considered as an increment wherever possible. **1956** W. H. WHYTE *Organization Man* (1957) 398 Modular construction is a condition of moderate-cost housing. **1960** *House & Garden* Dec. 31/1 As the houses are based on modular units, it is relatively simple to add a wing. **1966** B. J. KARAFIN in Kuo & Kaiser *System Analysis by Digital Computer* viii. 306 Modular programming makes it possible to build a library of simulation modules in much the same way as a library of numerical function subroutines is built. **1967** M. GOLDRING *Modular Directory Building Components* p. ix, The term 'modular components' covers those components that have at least two of their co-ordinating dimensions, such as length and width, in whole multiples of the basic 4 in/100 mm module. **1969** W. V. TIPPING *Introd. Mech. Assembly* ix. 217 The length of the machine obviously could, by the modular construction, be varied to within 30 in. Making the machine one sided only was considered but finally it was agreed to use a double sided module to keep down the length of the machine. **1970** *Washington Post* 30 Sept. B.1/1 The adjustable, modular-unit, wall-hung bookcase systems. **1970** [see MODULE *sb.* 4 d]. **1971** *Engineering* Apr. 71/1 Based on a modular construction, Denco floor consists of timber panels supported by jacks.. at 610 mm or 600 mm..centres over the sub-floor... A..steel Tee section is screwed to the perimeters of the underside of each module to fix and support it on the jackheads. **1972** *House & Garden* June 76/1 So-called portable houses—modular prefabs—which come on a truck and get erected within several hours. **1973** *Computers & Humanities* VII. 144 This program is modular in design, that is, it consists of several steps each doing a simple task.

c. *spec.* Of an educational course: designed as a series of units or discrete sections. Cf. MODULE *sb.* 4 g.

1968 *Economist* 25 May 18/2 The board has developed proposals both for the retraining of adults for skilled jobs, and for a so-called 'modular' scheme of training for young entrants to industry. **1972** *Timber Trades Jrnl.* 3 June 41/1 The courses would be modular, so that a company could send people in to be trained in any particular aspect. **1972** *Accountant* 19 Oct. 483/1 Much ingenuity has, however, been used by public sector institutions, and they have succeeded wherever possible in providing oral tuition on a modular basis, so that students of different bodies are able to share studies.

2. *Math.* Of or pertaining to a modulus.

1798 HUTTON *Course Math.* (1828) II. 415 If W were the greatest load which a modular wall, or column, could carry. **1815** —— *Philos. & Math. Dict.* (new ed.) II. 60 *Modular Ratio*, a term invented by Mr. Cotes, to denote the ratio or number whose logarithm is what he calls the modulus [tr. *ratio modularis*, R. Cotes *Harmonia Mensurarum* (1722) p. 5]. **1843** MACCULLAGH in *Proc. R. Irish Acad.* II. 453-4 It may happen that only one of them [*sc.* the curves] can be used in the generation of the surface by the *modular method*, as the method of which we are treating may be called, from its employment of the modulus. A focal curve which can be so used shall be distinguished as a *modular focal.* **1845** DE MORGAN in *Encycl. Metrop.* II. 385/1 Taking, therefore, ϕ a solution of the modular equation, which makes the above-mentioned equations consistent. **1862** SALMON *Anal. Geom. Three Dimens.* 109 Professor MacCullagh calls the ratio of the focal distance to that from the directrix, the modulus of the surface, and the foci having imaginary planes of contact he calls modular foci. *a* **1883** H. J. S. SMITH *Collect. Math. Papers* (1894) II. 560 The Modular Curves of an Uneven Order. **1894** FORSYTH *Theory of Functions* 633 The general definition of a modular function is that it is a uniform function such that an algebraical equation subsists between $\psi\left(\frac{\alpha\omega + \beta}{\gamma\omega + \delta}\right)$ and $\psi(\omega)$, where $\alpha, \beta, \gamma, \delta$, are integers subject to the relation $\alpha\delta - \beta\gamma = 1$.

modularity (mɒdjʊˈlærɪtɪ). [f. MODULAR *a.* + -ITY.] The property of being modular; use of modules in design or construction.

1937 *Architectural Forum* Apr. 252/2 The unit used in this kind of modular design may be defined as the 'multiple module'. Modularity of this kind has much greater potentialities as an integrating factor for building as a whole. **1964** FISHER & SWINDLE *Computer Programming Syst.* iv. 219 A growing trend in the design and implementation of input/output control systems is the concept of modularity. **1966** L. B. ANDERSON in G. Kepes *Module, Symmetry, Proportion* 112 Modularity in architecture is no respecter of scales. **1968** *Brit. Med. Bull.* XXIV. 192/1 In 1965–66 the manufacturers introduced the so-called 'third generation computers', whose principal feature was their modularity. **1970** *Times* 7 May 35 These [digital transmitters] will be of more complex construction..and impose the need for modularity in design to ease servicing. **1975** *Sci. Amer.* Jan. 50/2 (Advt.), Pop-in modularity makes it easy to replace logic boards when needed, without tools.

modularize (ˈmɒdjʊləraɪz), *v.* [f. MODULAR *a.* + -IZE.] *trans.* To construct on modular principles. So **ˈmodularized** *ppl. a.* Also **modulariˈzation**.

1959 *Res. Highlights Nat. Bureau of Standards Misc. Publ.* 229 (U.S.) 18 These tubes are compatible with the modularized electronic circuitry developed as part of the Project Tinkertoy program. **1962** *Maintainability Design Criteria Handbk. for Designers of Shipboard Electronic Equipment* (Federal Electr. Corp., U.S.) IV. i. 1 Modularization usually results in a decrease in fault isolation time. **1966** L. B. ANDERSON in G. Kepes *Module, Symmetry, Proportion* 110 Later Medieval architecture did not fail to provide a more disciplined modularization. *Ibid.* 111 In the end it is space itself which is modularized. **1968** F. F. MARTIN *Computer Modeling* ix. 193 We have applied modularization to the logical flow chart of a hypothetical air traffic control model. **1971** *New Scientist* 28 Jan. 196/2 Apollo 14 will also carry a modularised equipment transporter. **1973** *McGraw-Hill Yearbk. Sci. & Technol.* 357/1 Design and construction improvements, ranging from perfection of wire-winding techniques for the prestressed concrete reactor vessel to modularization of auxiliary systems, have decreased costs significantly.

modularly (ˈmɒdjʊləlɪ), *adv.* [f. MODULAR *a.* + -LY².] On modular principles.

1943 J. M. WOLFE *First Course Cryptanalysis* (rev. ed.) II. 19 The Vigenere operates on a modular addition while the Nihilist substitution does not. If the Nihilist addition were performed modularly, then all cipher numbers would be within the range of 4 from each other. **1972** *Sci. Amer.* Mar. 121/1 We live..in a world modularly constructed on the strictest rules; every atom is a storehouse of natural units.

ˈmodulate, *pa. pple. rare*⁻¹. [ad. L. *modulāt-us*, pa. pple. of *modulārī* to MODULATE.] Modulated.

1814 CARY *Dante, Par.* xx. 23 As sound Of cittern, at the fret-board, or of pipe, Is, at the wind-hole, modulate and tun'd.

modulate (ˈmɒdjʊleɪt), *v.* [f. L. *modulāt-*, ppl. stem of *modulārī* to measure, adjust to rhythm, make melody, etc., f. *modulus*: see MODULUS. Cf. F. *moduler.*]

1. *trans.* To set or regulate in a certain measure and proportion; to adjust, temper, vary conformably *to*; to soften, temper, tone down. (This general sense tends to be coloured by those that follow.)

1623 COCKERAM II, Done by measure, *modulated.* **1783** BURKE *Sp. E. India Bill* Wks. IV. 43, I shall certainly endeavour to modulate myself to this temper. **1797** MRS. RADCLIFFE *Italian* ii, She determined to modulate that nature to her own views. **1832** TENNYSON *Eleänore* iv, Motions flow To one another, even as tho' They were modulated so To an unheard melody. **1858** BUSHNELL *Serm. New Life* xii. (1869) 168 He learns how to modulate and operate his will. **1904** *Blackw. Mag.* Mar. 345/2 His glance ..travelled from the walls lined with well-bound books to the lamps modulated to the proper light.

2. *spec.* **a.** To attune (the voice, sounds, etc.) to a certain pitch or key; to vary or inflect in tone, adapt to a new tune; to give tune or melody to. Const. *to*, †*unto*.

1615 CROOKE *Body of Man* 911 The second vse [of the tongue] is to breake the ayer that is driuen out of the Lungs and to Modulate the voyce. **1701** GREW *Cosm. Sacra* I. v. §21. 28 The Nose, Lips, Teeth, Palate, Jaw, Tongue,..All serving to make, or to modulate the Sound. **1725** BROOME *Notes on Pope's Odyss.* IV. I. 261 Is it credible that any person could modulate her voice so artfully as to resemble so many voices? **1746** H. WALPOLE *Let. to Mann* 28 Mar., Gluck..is to play on a set of drinking-glasses, which he modulates with water. **1762** STERNE *Tr. Shandy* V. iii, He listened to the voice of nature, and modulated his own unto it. **1788** GIBBON *Decl. & F.* lii. V. 443 The songs of triumph were modulated to psalms and litanies. **1872** SPURGEON *Treas. David* Ps. lxvi. 2 The noise is to be modulated with tune and time.

fig. **1805** SURR *Winter in Lond.* (1806) III. 184 To modulate by counsels resulting from experience, the sweetest chords of the human heart; which thus regulated constitute the harmony of life. **1830** DE QUINCEY *Bentley* Wks. 1863 VI. 174 Bentley's English style was less meritorious... He took no pains with it... He would not stop to modulate a tuneless sentence. **1845** CRAIK *Sk. Lit. & Learn.* III. 100 A soul of nobleness..modulates every cadence [of Spenser's poetry].

b. *intr.* of a song: To be sung in varying cadence or harmony (*with*).

1815 SHELLEY *Alastor* 46, I wait thy breath, Great Parent, that my strain May modulate with murmurs of the air,.. And voice of living beings.

3. a. *trans.* To sing, intone (a song). **b.** *intr.* To play, make melody (*on* an instrument). *rare.*

c **1557** ABP. PARKER *Ps.* xcii. 1 To thy good name, O God so hye, Due laudes to modulate. **1698** FRYER *Acc. E. India & P.* 174 Who hearing one sweetly modulating on an Ismean Pipe, swore he would rather hear the neighing of an Horse. **1889** *Harper's Mag.* Oct. 680 We are conscious of a murmuring humble voice: it is a beggar, who is modulating a prayer for alms.

4. *Mus.* †**a.** *trans.* To pass to (a particular note) in the course of a composition. *Obs.*

1797 *Encycl. Brit.* (ed. 3) XII. 512/1 After having sung the tone *ut*, we naturally modulate the third *mi*, and the fifth *sol*, instead of the double octave of *mi*, and the octave of *sol.*

†**b.** *intr.* To pass, in accordance with the laws of melody, *from* one note *to* another; to compose music correctly. *Obs.*

1782 BURNEY *Hist. Mus.* II. 19 *note*, The Greeks more frequently modulated from the key note to its fifth below, than to the fifth above. **1797** *Encycl. Brit.* (ed. 3) XII. 192/1 To modulate properly in the same tone, it is necessary, 1. To run through all the sounds of it in an agreeable air [etc.].

c. To pass from one key *to* or *into* another; to change the key. (Also said of the key.) †*to modulate upon* (a particular note): to introduce (it) as a transition to another key.

1721 A MALCOLM *Treat. Mus.* xiii. 441 To modulate into and make Cadences upon several other Keys. *Ibid.* 446 It now remains to shew, how to modulate from one Key to another, so that the Transitions may be easy and natural. **1797** *Encycl. Brit.* (ed. 3) XII. 193/1 Issuing from the major mode of *ut*, to modulate upon its mediant. **1889** PROUT *Harmony* x. (ed. 3) 104 A minor key most often modulates to one of the related major keys. **1890** A. B. BACH *Art Ballad* 128 Loewe here modulates..from G minor into E flat minor.

transf. **1885** S. COX *Expos.* xi. 131 In the middle of verse 5, the invocation of a divine advent modulates into a sorrowful and pathetic confession of sin.

5. *trans.* Chiefly *Telecommunications.* **a.** To vary the amplitude or some other characteristic of (a wave or oscillatory signal, or a beam of particles) in accordance with the variations of a second signal, usu. a wave of lower frequency; also used with the property that is varied as obj.

1908 *Trans. Amer. Inst. Electr. Engin.* XXVII. 575 For wireless telephony three things are necessary:..2. Means for modulating this stream of waves in accordance with sound waves. **1921** J. SCOTT-TAGGART *Thermionic Tubes* xiii. 354 In wireless telephony, a steady stream of waves (usually termed the carrier wave) is usually modulated by means of a microphone. **1941** *Electronic Engin.* XIV. 485/1 The direct transmission and reception of speech or music over long distances..is impractical and propagation of audio frequencies is usually accomplished by using them to modulate an R.F. wave acting as carrier. **1952** R. W. DITCHBURN *Light* x. 299 It is not possible to observe the progress of a continuous beam of light without marking or 'modulating' it in some way. Three main methods of modulation have been used: (*a*) the toothed-wheel method, (*b*) the rotating-mirror method, and (*c*) the electronic shutter. In any of these methods the transit time is derived from a measurement of the frequency of the modulator. **1959** *Chambers's Encycl.* II. 591/2 In broadcasting on long, medium and short waves it is normally the amplitude which is modulated. **1962** *Newnes Conc. Encycl. Electr. Engin.* 428/2 In the klystron..the single cavity both modulates the beam [of electrons] to provide bunching, and abstracts energy from the beam on its return. **1965** *Science* 8 Oct. 153/3 The simplest way to modulate a beam of light—that is, the simplest way to make it carry a message—is to turn the generator of light on and off. **1972** *Sci. Amer.* Sept. 132/2 The received signal is decoded into its components and used to modulate three independent electron beams, each of which is allowed to strike only the red, green or blue phosphor dots.

b. To apply a signal to (a device) that modulates its output signal.

1920 P. E. EDELMAN *Exper. Wireless Stations* (rev. ed.) xv. 238 Starting with a telephone transmitter, this may be used to grid modulate one vacuum tube which in turn is cascaded to several others. **1953** W. A. EDSON *Vacuum-Tube Oscillators* xvi. 391 Magnetrons are ordinarily modulated by applying a large negative pulse to the cathode. **1973** *Sci. Amer.* Nov. 33/2 These diodes can be modulated rapidly by simply modulating the electric current that powers them.

c. To impress (a signal) *on to* a carrier wave by modulation.

1962 A. NISBETT *Technique Sound Studio* 267 A system for distributing audio information by modulating it on to a high frequency carrier..which is then amplified..and broadcast. **1970** J. EARL *Tuners & Amplifiers* v. 118 This [signal] cannot be added direct to the L + R information fed to the transmitter. First it has to be modulated on to a subcarrier of 38kHz. **1975** *Gramophone* Jan. 1412/3, CD-4 employs a carrier tone at supersonic frequency..on to which is [*sic*] modulated the difference signals.

d. *transf.* To exert a modifying or controlling influence on; to regulate.

1964 *Science* 15 May 819/3 This explanation..places some restriction on the details of any model involving regulation by modulating transfer RNA. **1971** *Sci. Amer.* July 55/3 It seems certain that the brain can modulate the transmission of olfactory information as early as the level of the first synapse of the olfactory pathway. **1971** *Nature* 20 Aug. 550/2 Thus we conclude that magnetism may modulate climate to some degree by the ability of the Earth's magnetic field somehow to provide a shield against solar corpuscular radiation. **1973** *Ibid.* 16 Nov. 154/1 Although strychnine had no effect in our system, actin-like proteins may form structures that modulate the mobility of lymphocyte receptors. **1974** *Sci. Amer.* Nov. 39/1 The steam flow is modulated by a control valve actuated by a speed governor on the rotor.

6. *Biol.* Of a cell: to undergo modulation *into* (see MODULATION 8).

1956 C. H. WADDINGTON *Princ. Embryol.* xvi. 361 When differentiated vertebrate cells are grown in tissue culture.., they 'modulate' into less-specialised forms which may appear to be dedifferentiated, but they do not re-acquire the ability to develop into some tissue other than the one from which they were originally derived. **1964** N. T. SPRATT *Introd. Cell Differentiation* vi. 68 Although cells of cultured tissues may undergo temporary dedifferentiation (that is, may modulate), permanent loss of basic properties which distinguish the cells as to type seems to be rare.

Hence **ˈmodulated, ˈmodulating** *ppl. adjs.*

1735 SOMERVILLE *Chase* III. 73 When The Master's Hand, in modulated Air, Bids the loud Organ breathe. **1751** W. THOMPSON *Sickness* v. 230 May the nightly Pow'r, Which whispers on my Slumbers, cease to breathe Her modulating Impulse through my Soul. *a* **1806** H. K. WHITE *Rem.* (1837) 359 The pleasure we derive from tragedy is a pleasing sorrow, a modulated pain. **1874** SYMONDS *Sk. Italy & Greece* (1898) I. ix. 173 Clear waves bathed in modulated azure. **1880** *Expositor* XII. 291 A number of phrases follow each other asyndetically, without conjunctive or modulating

particles. **1919** *Proc. IRE* VII. 193 The modulated output is therefore proportional to the curvature of the characteristic. **1920** M. B. SLEEPER *Wireless Design & Pract.* viii. 133 A modulated vacuum-tube transmitter can be divided into.. the radiating, oscillating, reaction, and modulation circuits. **1921** *Electrician* 21 Jan. 95/2 In modulated wave signalling it has been proposed to leave out one of the essential modulating effects.

modulation (mɒdjuːˈleɪʃən). [a. F. *modulation* (14th c. in Hatz.-Darm.) or ad. L. *modulātiōn-em*, n. of action f. *modulārī* to MODULATE.]

1. The action of forming, regulating, or varying according to due measure and proportion; †measured or rhythmical movement; variation (of light, line, form, etc.) with regard to artistic effect; a softening, tempering, or toning down.

1531 ELYOT *Gov.* I. xx, More ouer the emperours that were moste noble, delited in daunsyng, perceyuing therin to be a perfecte measure, whiche maye be called modulation. **1674** *Govt. Tongue* i. 3 To this purpose the infinite wisdom of God ordained Speech, which as it is a sound resulting from the modulation of the Air, has most affinity to the spirit. **1695** WOODWARD *Nat. Hist. Earth* IV. (1723) 195 The Matter of two or more Kinds being mix'd together, and, by the different Proportion and Modulation of that Matter, variously.. diversify'd. **1753** HOGARTH *Anal. Beauty* xii. 95 Different kinds of softnings and modulations of the rays of light. **1883** C. C. PERKINS *Ital. Sculpture* II. ii. 124 That delicate modulation of surface treatment which gives high value to the best Florentine metal work. **1888** *Scribner's Mag.* III. 424 It is not the firmness of a line in drawing or sculpture that makes it forbidding; it is the stiffness or poor quality of its modulation.

2. The action of inflecting the voice or an instrument musically; variation of tone or pitch; regulated variety of inflexion in the voice; a particular inflexion or intonation.

1543 TRAHERON *Vigo's Chirurg.* II. III. xv. 60 That it [*sc.* the uvula] myght gyve modulation or tunynge to the voice. **1646** SIR T. BROWNE *Pseud. Ep.* VII. xiv. 368 Although the weazon, throtle and tongue be the instruments of voice, and by their agitations doe chiefly concurre unto these delightfull modulations. **1701** GREW *Cosm. Sacra* I. v. §10. 25 The Rings of the Wind-pipe, are fitted for the Modulation of the Voice. **1756–7** tr. *Keysler's Trav.* (1760) IV. 14 Among the singers in Italy.. Farinelli indisputably makes the greatest figure for the fineness and modulation of his voice. **1797** MRS. RADCLIFFE *Italian* i, All the sensibility of character that the modulation of her tones indicated. **1824** L. MURRAY *Eng. Gram.* (ed. 5) I. 361 By modulation is meant that pleasing variety of voice, which is perceived in uttering a sentence, and which, in its nature, is perfectly distinct from emphasis, and the tones of emotion and passion. **1859** GEO. ELIOT *A. Bede* i With the same gentle modulation of voice as when he spoke to Seth. **1866** HUXLEY *Physiol.* vii. (1869) 205 The modulation of the voice into speech is effected by [etc.].

3. The action of singing or making music; an air or melody; *pl.* musical notes or sounds. Now *rare.*

1398 TREVISA *Barth. De P.R.* XIX. cxxxi. (1495) 941 Symphonia is temperate modulacion accordynge in sownes highe and lowe. *c* **1425** *St. Mary of Oignies* II. xi. in *Anglia* VIII. 178/14 Oure lorde.. fillid hir herte wiþ myrþe, and hir lippys wiþ modulacyone. **1616** BULLOKAR *Eng. Expos.*, *Modulation*, a pleasant tuning or sweete singing. **1624** DONNE *Serm.* ii. (1640) 12, I will sing of thy mercy and judgement, sayes David; when we fixe our selves upon the meditation and modulation of the mercy of God, even his judgements cannot put us out of tune. **1656** BLOUNT *Glossogr.*, *Modulation*,.. a pleasant tuning, a singing or playing by number or measure. **1728–46** THOMSON *Spring* 608 Innumerous songsters, in the freshening shade Of new-sprung leaves, their modulations mix Mellifluous. **1816** T. L. PEACOCK *Headlong Hall* xi, To ring to the profaner but more lively modulation of *Voulez vous danser*, *Mademoiselle*!

4. *Mus.* **a.** *Hist.* In the ecclesiastical modes: Each of certain notes in each mode, on which a phrase of melody must begin and end (see quot.).

1880 *Grove's Dict. Mus.* II. 351/2 The intermediate phrases can only begin, or end, on one of another set of notes, called its Modulations. Of these Modulations, four —the Final, Dominant, Mediant, and Participant—are of more importance than the rest, and are therefore called Regular. But as the constant reiteration of these four notes would prove intolerably monotonous, in a Melody consisting of very numerous phrases, other notes, called Conceded Modulations, are added to them.

†**b.** Composition or performance of music, management of melody and harmony, in a particular 'mode' or key. Also, a chord or succession of notes, an air or melody (cf. 3). *Obs.*

1721 A. MALCOLM *Treat. Mus.* xiii. 441 Under the Term of Modulation may be comprehended the regular Progression of the several Parts thro' the Sounds that are in the Harmony of any particular Key as well as the proceeding naturally and regularly with the Harmony from one Key to another. **1782** BURNEY *Hist. Mus.* II. 412 As to the Modulation, it is so monotonous, that little more than two chords are used throughout the Canon ['Sumer is i-cumen in']. **1797** *Encycl. Brit.* (ed. 3) XII. 191/2 Modulation.. frequently means no more than an air, or a number of musical sounds properly connected and arranged. *Ibid.* 511/2 The modulation formed by *ut* with the octave of *sol* and the double octave of *mi*, sung one after the other. *Ibid.* 512/2 This modulation or chord *ut, miþ, sol, ut.*

c. In modern use: The action or process of passing from one key to another in the course of a piece; the result of this, as an element in the harmony of the piece; a change of key.

1696 PHILLIPS, *Modulation*, a carrying on a Song in the same Key, sometimes passing out of it, then getting into it again, without offending the Ears. **1721** A. MALCOLM *Treat. Mus.* xiii. 450 Having thus explained the Nature of Modulation from one Key to another. **1782** BURNEY *Hist. Mus.* II. 163 *note*, The modulation from D major to C is rarely found in modern music. *Ibid.* 164 The following specimens of Chromatic Modulation, ascending and descending. **1839** *Penny Cycl.* XV. 296/2 Modulation may be divided into Simple, Chromatic (or extraneous), and Enharmonic. **1889** PROUT *Harmony* (ed. 10) xiv. §371 By.. enharmonically changing one or more of its notes it [the chord of the Diminished Seventh] can be used for modulation between any two keys.

5. *transf.* Melodious composition in prose or verse; harmonious treatment of language.

1759 JOHNSON *Idler* No. 63 ¶7 Then begin the arts of rhetoric and poetry, the regulation of figures, the selection of words, the modulation of periods. **1779–81** —— *L.P.*, *Waller* Wks. II. 269 The Poets of Elizabeth had attained an art of modulation, which was afterwards.. forgotten. **1841** D'ISRAELI *Amen. Lit.* (1867) 476 A master in the art of versification was struck by our poet's modulation.

6. *Arch.* The proportioning or regulating of the parts of an order by the module (see MODULE 4).

1665 J. WEBB *Stone-Heng* (1725) 62 Ornaments made from the Rule of the Dorick Modulation. **1842** GWILT *Archit.* Gloss., *Modulation*, the proportion of the different parts of an order.

7. a. Chiefly *Telecommunications.* The process of modulating a wave or beam (see MODULATE *v.* 5 a) in order to impress a signal upon it; the extent to which a modulated carrier wave is varied; also, the wave-form or signal so impressed. Cf. DEMODULATION.

Freq. preceded by a sb. denoting either (*a*) the characteristic of the carrier wave that is varied (as in FREQUENCY MODULATION), or (*b*) the method by which the modulation is applied (as in *grid modulation*).

1919 *Proc. IRE* VII. 193 (*heading*) Modulation. **1921** J. SCOTT-TAGGART *Thermionic Tubes* xiii. 355 Two general methods of modulation are used at present; either the amplitude of the continuous waves is varied by the microphone, or the wave-length is altered... Sometimes both wave-length and amplitude modulation occur at the same time. **1924** W. JAMES *Wireless Valve Transmitters* ix. 200 The strength of the note received is dependent.. on the degree of modulation—that is, on the extent to which the amplitude of the oscillations vary. **1931** *Proc. IRE* XIX. 2146 Amplitude modulation by means of vacuum tubes can be effected in two different ways: as plate modulation or grid modulation. **1932** LADNER & STONER *Short Wave Wireless Communication* v. 73 Rectification is essential at the receiver, for the purpose of extracting the modulation. **1943** F. E. TERMAN *Radio Engineers' Handbk.* VII. 581 In phase modulation, intelligence is transmitted by varying the phase of the transmitted wave. **1949** H. E. PENROSE *Princ. & Pract. Radar* xvi. 310 The klystron and the reflex klystron depend for their action primarily upon velocity modulation of the electron stream. **1952** [see MODULATE *v.* 5 a]. **1953** W. A. EDSON *Vacuum-Tube Oscillators* xvi. 386 The presence or absence of an output signal, in conjunction with an appropriate code, permits the communication of information. Such keying represents the simplest possible form of modulation, and is applicable to all kinds of oscillators. **1962** A. NISBETT *Technique Sound Studio* vi. 107 The equipment is lined up on a standard 1,000 c/s tone sent from the studio. The standard used is 1 milliwatt in 600 ohms.. and is equivalent to 40% modulation at the transmitter. **1968** *Radio Communication Handbk.* (ed. 4) ix. 5/2 Choke modulation employs a choke as the coupling impedance between the modulator and the r.f. stage. **1972** *Sci. Amer.* Sept. 101/2 The most widely used processes of modulation are amplitude modulation (AM), frequency modulation (FM), pulse amplitude modulation (PAM) and pulse code modulation (PCM).

b. *transf.* The action or result of varying the magnitude, degree, etc., of something.

1964 *Science* 15 May 816 Modulation of transfer RNA species can provide a workable model of an operator-less operon. **1970** R. W. MCGILVERY *Biochem.* xxiii. 543 (*heading*) Regulation [of metabolism] by modulation of enzyme activity. **1971** *Physics Bull.* July 388/1 An acoustic wave produces a periodic modulation of the density of the medium. **1973** *Sci. Amer.* Aug. 50/2 The conduction between them can be controlled by the modulation of the charge in a channel between them.

c. *attrib.*, as **modulation envelope**, the envelope of an amplitude-modulated carrier wave; **modulation factor** = *modulation index*; **modulation frequency**, the frequency of a wave used to modulate another wave; **modulation index**, a coefficient representing the degree of modulation of a carrier wave; *spec.* the ratio of the difference between the maximum and minimum frequencies of a frequency-modulated carrier to the frequency of the modulating signal.

1930 *Proc. IRE* XVIII. 2161 If this leakage is slower than the rate at which the modulation envelope decreases, then the condenser voltage cannot follow the modulation envelope. **1950** P. PARKER *Electronics* x. 301 In the radio frequency stages of a receiver, distortion is important only in so far as it makes the modulation envelope of the signal voltage different from the wave-form of the modulating sound. **1970** J. EARL *Tuners & Amplifiers* ii. 47 To the centre-tap.. is fed the mono and subcarrier stereo components, and the action of the switching transistors.. is such that a 'modulation envelope' is formed, one side carrying the left-channel information and the other side the right-channel information. **1939** *Amat. Radio Handbk.* vi. 93/1 When using a continuous pure tone (sine wave) for modulating.. the percentage modulation can be obtained by the Heising formula:—If I_O = R.M.S. value of unmodulated aerial current.. I_M = ditto when modulated. m = modulation factor. Then $I_M = I_O\sqrt{(1 + m^2/2)}$. **1930** *Proc. IRE* XVIII. 2162 The rate of decrease of the modulation envelope depends upon the modulation frequency *f* and the degree of modulation *m* of the signal. **1962** SIMPSON & RICHARDS *Physical Princ. Junction Transistors* xviii. 453 The carrier and modulation frequencies are applied to one or both of the input electrodes. **1930** B. VAN DER POL in *Proc. IRE* XVIII. 1200 The whole practical problem of the amount of disturbance arising from frequency modulation depends therefore upon the value of the ratio $m = \Delta\omega/p$ of the absolute frequency deviation to the imposed audio frequency *p*. Owing to the importance of this parameter *m*.. it may be found useful to designate it by a special name for which we suggest the expression 'frequency modulation index'. **1931** H. RODER in *Ibid.* XIX. 2151 B. van der Pol has introduced the expression 'modulation index' for m_f. We shall use this term for both m_p and m_f [where m_p represents the degree of phase modulation in a wave $i = A_0 \sin (\omega_0 t + m_p \sin \mu t)$]. **1974** *Encycl. Brit. Macropædia* XVIII. 91/2 The larger the modulation index (and hence the wider the bandwidth required for transmission), the more effectively FM performs.

8. *Biol.* Reversible variation in the activity or form of a cell in response to a changing environment.

1939 P. WEISS *Princ. Devel.* I. 94 This physiological, strictly nonprogressive fluctuation of a cell in response to its environmental conditions may be called modulation. It provides for a certain latitude within which a cell can comply adequately with certain variable functional demands of the developed body. **1964** N. T. SPRATT *Introd. Cell Differentiation* ii. 20 We.. cannot accurately draw a line between differentiations and modulations. **1970** AMBROSE & EASTY *Cell Biol.* xiii. 441 Hormones are known to affect the synthetic function and the size of certain organs. This is an example of what Weiss has called 'modulation'.

modulative (ˈmɒdjʊleɪtɪv), *a. rare.* [ad. L. type **modulātīv-us*: see -IVE.] Serving to modulate (the voice or intonation).

1888 SWEET *Hist. Eng. Sounds* 71 Our punctuation-marks seem to have been originally modulative.

modulator (ˈmɒdjʊleɪtə(r)). [a. L. *modulātor*, agent-n. f. *modulārī* to MODULATE.]

1. a. One who, or a thing which, modulates.

c **1500** *Proverbis* in *Antiq. Rep.* (1809) IV. 408 A perfyte modulatour makithe his songe trew. **1654** WHITLOCK *Zootomia* 477 Poetry.. is a most musicall Modulator of all Intelligibles by her inventive Variations. **1713** DERHAM *Phys.-Theol.* v. v. (1727) 295 The Tongue.. the artful Modulator of our Voice. **1834** DE QUINCEY *Autobiogr. Sk.* vi. Wks. 1862 XIV. 171 Thus, in a musical metaphor, the great man is the sole modulator and determiner of the key in which the conversation proceeds. **1896** MRS. CAFFYN *Quaker Grandmother* 145 The haze was a modulator of all things—a balancer.

b. *spec.* A device that produces modulation of a wave (MODULATION 7). Also *transf.*, a regulator, a controlling mechanism.

1919 *Proc. IRE* VII. 193 The curvature of the characteristic.. makes possible its employment as a modulator and detector. **1930** *Discovery* Dec. 398/2 The output from the subscriber's telephone is amplified in the transmitting voice frequency amplifier and passes to the low frequency modulator. **1952** [see MODULATE *v.* 5 a]. **1964** M. BROTHERTON *Masers & Lasers* xv. 182 If we feed into a modulator a voice frequency of 256 cps along with a carrier frequency of 50,000 cps, the modulator reacts by producing two new frequencies—one the difference frequency at 49,744 cps and the other the sum frequency at 50,256 cps. **1970** R. W. MCGILVERY *Biochem.* xxiii. 547 The deoxycytidine phosphates are not modulators of any of the reductions. **1970** *Sci. Amer.* Nov. 120/1 The use of the laser for mass communication.. awaits the development of a practical modulator: an apparatus for impressing multiple signals on the light beam. **1972** *Jazz & Blues* Nov. 21/1, I .. checked out this new modulator which a lot of people.. are now using. You put in your voice and you get another sound on it. **1974** *Nature* 17 May 250/1 Such a test might assess the role of putrescine as a potential modulator of growth in normal and neoplastic tissue.

2. A chart used in the 'tonic sol-fa' system, showing the relations of tones and scales.

1862 *Catal. Internat. Exhib.* II. xxiv. 35 The Modulator, or pointing board for teaching tunes.

modulatory (ˈmɒdjʊlətərɪ), *a.* [ad. L. type **modulātōri-us*, f. *modulārī* to MODULATE: see -ORY.] Pertaining to or serving for modulation.

1880 PARRY in Grove *Dict. Mus.* II. 348/2 [Bach's] more wonderful modulatory devices must have fallen upon utterly deaf ears.

module (ˈmɒdjuːl), *sb.* [a. F. *module* (1547 in Godefr. *Compl.*), or directly ad. L. *modul-us* small measure, limit or standard of measure, machine for measuring water, module in architecture, also rhythmic measure, dim. of *modus* measure: see MODE *sb.* (Cf. MOULD *sb.*[2], a. OF. *molde, modle*:—L *modulum.*) The earliest uses in Eng. seem to be based directly on Latin senses not found in Fr., and also to show confusion of the word with MODEL. The architectural sense appears to have been introduced from Fr. in the 17th c.]

†**1.** Allotted measure, compass, or scale; one's allotted power or capabilities. Cf. MODEL *sb.* 8. *Obs.*

1586 A. DAY *Eng. Secretary* II. (1625) 122 To repose a foundation consonant to the module or compasse of this my present intendment. **1587** FLEMING *Contn. Holinshed* III. 1369/2 His counterfet so naturallie conveied into coloures, with his white beard, the hollownesses of his cheekes,.. and all within a module the circumference whereof exceedeth

not six inches. **1607** WALKINGTON *Opt. Glass.* Ep. Ded. 3 Yet for that module of these habiliments in me I have ever bent my judgement so far as in it lay to limit [etc.]. **1628** COKE *On Litt.* Pref., The module of a preface cannot express the observations that are made in the work. **1640** G. WATTS tr. *Bacon's Adv. Learn.* IX. i. 471 That the mind for its Module [orig. *pro modulo*] be dilated to the amplitude of the Mysteries. **1663** CHARLETON *Chor. Gigant.* 41 Whose picture, though in too small a module, is taken also by our Author. **1681** WITTIE *Surv. Heavens* 70, I have reasoned with modesty according to my module.

2. †**a.** The plan or design in little of some large work. Cf. MODEL *sb.* 1. *Obs.*

1589 *Acts Privy Council* (1898) XVII. 455 Send unto us a plat forme or module of the situation of the said mylne upon the river. **1611** R. BADLEY *To Author* in Coryat *Crudities* k, Yet in thy booke the module is descried Of many a Citie, and Castle fortified. **1622** HAKEWILL *David's Vow* vi. 222 Man.. himselfe, a little map or module as it were of the great world. **1636** EARL CORK *Diary* in *Lismore Papers* Ser. I. (1886) IV. 210, I sent [them]..to tak a module of the L. presidents howse..to make the lyke by ffor my son. **1695** WOODWARD *Nat. Hist. Earth* II. 107 That's the Business of the Larger Work, of which this is only the Module or Platform.

†**b.** A plastic or graphic representation (usually on a small scale) of some material object. Cf. MODEL *sb.* 2.

1591 SYLVESTER *Du Bartas* I. vi. 1015 You that have seen within this ample Table, Among so many Modules admirable [orig. *parmy tant de pourtraits*], Th' admired beauties of the King of Creatures. **1609** HEYWOOD *Brit. Troy* XII. lxxxvii, The Pummel..rarely wrought With artful Modules. *a* **1661** FELTHAM *Resolves*, etc. *Let.* x. 74 By this weeks Carrier you shall receive the Module of the World in a box.

†**c.** *poet.* A mere image or counterfeit. *Obs.*

1595 SHAKS. *John* v. vii. 58 And then all this thou seest, is but a clod, And module of confounded royalty. **1601** —— *All's Well* IV. iii. 114 Come, bring forth this counterfet module. **1608** SYLVESTER *Du Bartas* II. iv. III. *Schisme* 492 This Childe (no Man, but Mans pale Module now).

†**d.** *poet.* A model for imitation; a type or pattern of excellence, a perfect exemplar (*of*); = MODEL *sb.* 10. *Obs.*

1609 DANIEL *Civ. Wars* IV. lxxxii, That vertuous Prince.. borne to bee The module of a glorious Monarch. **1598** SYLVESTER *Du Bartas* II. Ded., From Thee (rare Module of Heroik minds). *Ibid.* II. i. I. *Eden* 94 Ye Pagan Poets..; from henceforth still be dum Your fabled prayses of Elysium; Which by this goodly Module you have wrought.

†**e.** A regularly formulated plan or scheme (of government, etc.); = MODEL *sb.* 7 b. *Obs.*

1650 NEEDHAM *Case of Commw.* II. 50 Notwithstanding all the Reasons to the Contrary the Scottish Module was still pressed.

3. A standard or unit for measuring.

a **1628** F. GREVIL *Cælica* vi, Measure of all ioyes stay to phansie traces Module of pleasure. **1685** BERNARD *Let. to Author* in Pococke *Comm. Hosea* (a), Many of the ancients serv'd themselves with ordinary grains of corne (which module hath also entred our English Laws) for the Measures both of length and capacity. **1712** *H. More's Antid. Ath.* I. v. Schol. 145 They are not made..by measure or module, which should limit, and, as it were, design and determine them. **1845** R. W. HAMILTON *Pop. Educ.* vi. (ed. 2) 128 A precise proposition is already adjusted, a module of the truth. **1863** HERSCHEL *Fam. Lect. Sci.* (1868) 450 The only new measure I would legalize would be a 'module' (or some other name at present unoccupied) of 50 geometrical inches.

4. a. *Arch.* In the classic orders, the unit of length by which the proportions of the parts are expressed; usually the semidiameter of the column at the base of the shaft.

[**1563**: see MODULUS I.] **1664** EVELYN tr. *Freart's Archit.* I. xxvii. 66 The Chapter contains two Modules and a third. **1760** RAPER in *Phil. Trans.* LI. 814 The shafts of the columns are so nearly 16 modules, that they seem to have been designed for that proportion. **1823** P. NICHOLSON *Pract. Build.* 480 The height given to the column is fourteen modules, or seven diameters.

b. *Numism.* The diameter of a coin or medal.

1887 *Athenæum* 24 Sept. 411/3 There are thirty plates, many of them containing coins of the smallest module.

c. A length chosen as a basis for the dimensions of parts of a building, items of furniture, etc., to facilitate their coordination, so that all lengths are an integral multiple of it; *spec.* one of 4 inches (101·6 millimetres). Also *attrib.*

1936 BEMIS & BURCHARD *Evolving House* III. iv. 64 A dimension of 4″ for the module..is selected because it is the nominal greatest common divisor of the wood-frame house, which represents the bulk of American housing. **1945** *Archit. Record* Jan. 103/1 The architect can best realize the advantage of the coordination of masonry and metal window dimensions by doing preliminary building layouts on the familiar cross section paper of the module system, each grid line representing 4 inches. **1946** *Industr. Standardization* XVII. 269/1 'Module' furniture is designed on a coordinated 6-inch scale so that all pieces are interchangeable. **1949** *Architects' Jrnl.* 20 Oct. 432/1 The planning grid on which the Hertfordshire County Council structure is based was an 8 ft. 3 in. module. **1955** *Sci. News Let.* 1 Jan. 13/1 Houses of the future may all be built using a four-inch cube called a module as the structural 'atom'. **1966** L. B. ANDERSON in G. Kepes *Module, Symmetry, Proportion* 117 Now the idea of the module is again asserted, with emphasis on its ability to encompass growth and change.

d. One of a series of production units or component parts that are standardized to facilitate assembly or replacement and are usu. prefabricated as self-contained structures.

1955 *Sci. Amer.* Aug. 30 (*caption*) Assembled module consists of a stack of wafers coated with opaque plastic. Vertical wires through notches in the wafers provide electrical connections between the parts. **1959** HORSEY & SHERGAUS *Proc. Symposium Microminiaturization of Electronic Assemblies 1958* I. iv. 44 The electronic 'module'..is an individually fabricated subassembly that may be replaced *in toto* when repair becomes necessary. **1964** R. F. FICCHI *Electr. Interference* iii. 23 For circuits and components that can be grouped together, e.g., modules (a group of components mounted on a nonconducting board and wired together), and chassis drawers (groups of modules mounted in a rack), the following wiring rules should be followed. **1969** W. V. TIPPING *Introd. Mech. Assembly* ix. 240 The modules are bolted together to form a full machine ready for final trouble-shooting. **1970** J. EARL *Tuners & Amplifiers* vi. 141 The vast majority of tuner-amplifiers are now transistored, the designs being based on printed circuit boards or 'modules'. **1970** *New Yorker* 3 Oct. 28/1 In prefabrication, flat pieces of a house are built in a plant and assembled on a site. Plumbing, electrical wiring, and heating are then installed by conventional methods. Modules are larger, three-dimensional units, which are completely finished in the factory and then bolted together at the site in a much shorter time. Modular housing gives you more control in the plant. **1971** [see MODULAR *a.* 1 b]. **1971** *Real Estate Rev.* Fall 48/2 Our housing needs in the next nine years must be met with factory-built modules, assembled on site.

e. *Astronautics.* A separable section of a spacecraft that can operate as an independent unit.

1961 *New Scientist* 4 May 241/3 To deal with its dual function the *Apollo* craft will have three separate sections, or modules: first, a command centre module..; secondly, a propulsion module..; and finally, a so-called 'mission' module. **1963** *Ann. Reg. 1962* 400 A capsule was to be fired from the earth into orbit round the moon, when a special part of it, christened the lunar excursion module, would detach itself. **1969** *Listener* 24 July 123/1 The ITV audience was being guided..towards the first climax of the night, the landing of the module on the Moon's surface. **1970** *Sci. Jrnl.* Aug. 35/2 As additional modules are placed in orbit and docked with the first module, some could be devoted to specialized activities.

f. One of a number of distinct, well-defined units from which a computer program may be built up or into which any complex process or activity is analysed (usu. for computer simulation), each of which is complete in itself but bears a definite relationship to the other units.

1963 L. SCHULTZ *Digital Processing* xv. 340 Ideally, the total program system could be segmented into completely independent parts (called modules) that exhibit interdependence only through a central communication pool. **1964** FISHER & SWINDLE *Computer Programming Syst.* iv. 220 Because of such varying input/output requirements among programs and among machine configurations, it is now possible with many of the new IOCS packages to specify which modules of an IOCS [*sc.* an input/output control system, a set of routines for reading input and writing output data] are necessary for the most efficient processing of input/output requirements. **1965** *Economist* 17 July 272/2 This network is split up into sections or 'modules' that can be used in block form whenever a similar network is required. Shell used the example of the construction of chemical plant which the company put up around the world. The 'modules' in this instance are the particular items of plant, such as pressure vessels, which are standard. **1968** F. F. MARTIN *Computer Modeling* ix. 193 Modules are of two types: system or auxiliary. System modules simulate a specific function in system (or operation) logic... For example, a detection routine in a radar model is a system module that simulates the detection function of the radar... Auxiliary modules are nonsystem modules and are not necessarily unique to any given model. For example, a random statistical variates generator routine is an auxiliary module that may be applied in any stochastic model to generate random numbers. **1971** B. DE FERRANTI *Living with Computer* ix. 82 The computer programmer breaks his problem down into modules and gives the modules names so that they can be handled. **1973** R. M. ARMSTRONG *Modular Programming in COBOL* v. 60 The components of an operational control information system may be delineated as follows. Logistics: 1. Raw materials. 2. Production. 3. Salable product. Physical assets: 1. Property and equipment. 2. Capital projects... Manpower: 1. Payroll. 2. Benefits. 3. Personnel administration. We might describe these components as applicational modules at the systems level. *Ibid.* 63 In applying the above [characteristics] to a module in a computer system, a more precise definition is necessary. 1. The functions of input and output are well defined. 2. The module has a single entry point and a single exit point. 3. It exits to a standard return point in the module from which it was executed.

g. A unit or period of training or education. Cf. MODULAR *a.*, 1 c.

1966 *Economist* 3 Dec. 1005/1 Eventually the sort of retraining envisaged could fit in with the notion..of periodic training 'modules', whereby skilled men would take repeated periods off productive work to renew their perhaps rusty skills and learn new ones. **1968** *Daily Tel.* 12 Nov. 19/5 A training manual for a module course on 'Repairs and Restoration' has been produced.

5. *Math.* **a.** = MODULUS 2.

a **1883** H. J. S. SMITH *Collect. Math. Papers* (1894) II. 545 The squared modules resulting from the σ′ (*n*) primitive and primary transformations of *n*.

b. *Math.* [ad. G. *modul* (R. Dedekind in P. G. L. Dirichlet *Vorlesungen über Zahlentheorie* (ed. 2, 1871) Suppl. x. 442).] Orig., a set that is a subset of a ring and is closed under addition and subtraction; now usu. defined as a commutative additive group whose elements may be multiplied by those of a ring (usu. a ring with an identity element), the product being in the group and the multiplication obeying the associative and distributive laws; ***left, right module*** (see quot. 1970[1]). Formerly also **modul**.

1927 *Amer. Math. Monthly* XXXIV. 64 The class concept was introduced by Dedekind as follows. A set *M* of elements of *I*(α) which is closed under subtraction, and hence under addition and subtraction, is called a module. If *M* be such that, if β is any element of *M*, and γ is any element of *I*(α), then βγ is an element of *M*, the module *M* is called an ideal. **1937** A. A. ALBERT *Mod. Higher Algebra* i. 9 An additive abelian group is frequently called a modul. *Ibid.* xi. 252 A set $\mathfrak{M}$ of elements of a ring $\mathfrak{A}$ is called a modul of $\mathfrak{A}$ if $a - b$ is in $\mathfrak{M}$ for every *a* and *b* of $\mathfrak{M}$... Thus a modul is simply an additive subgroup of the additive abelian group $\mathfrak{A}$. **1948** O. ORE *Number Theory* vii. 159 The integers 0, ±1, ±2, ... form a modul, but the natural numbers 1, 2, 3, ... do not. *Ibid.* 161 A ring is a modul that is closed under multiplication. **1970** HARTLEY & HAWKES *Rings, Modules & Linear Algebra* v. 70 A module over a ring *R* (or *R*-module) is an Abelian group *M* (almost always written additively) together with a map $(r,m) \to rm$ from $R \times M$ to *M* satisfying the conditions $r(m_1 + m_2) = rm_1 + rm_2$, $(r_1 + r_2)m = r_1m + r_2m$, $(r_1r_2)m = r_1(r_2m)$, $1m = m$, for all $r, r_1, r_2 \in R$ and all $m, m_1, m_2 \in M$. It would be more accurate to call what we have just defined a left *R*-module. There is a similar definition of a right *R*-module in which the elements of *R* are written on the right. *Ibid.* 69 A module is a construct of great versatility. It turns up in many seemingly unlikely guises and has the knack of manifesting some of the quintessential features of a wide variety of mathematical structures. **1970** *Nature* 19 Dec. 1234/2 A vector space is built up linearly by means of 'scalar' multipliers from a number field. The more general concept of a module replaces the field by an arbitrary ring (with unity) related to an Abelian group so that a 'product' is defined satisfying the usual distributive and associative laws.

6. An apparatus for measuring or regulating a supply or flow of water. [= It. *modulo*.]

1875 L. D'A. JACKSON *Hydraulic Man.* (ed. 3) 136 Hydraulic engineers not having yet arrived at a perfect module for measuring the amount of water drawn off in an open channel for irrigation. *Ibid.* 147 This module discharges one cubic metre..per hour.

¶**7.** ? The capital of a pillar (cf. MUTULE). *Obs.*

1585 J. HIGGINS tr. *Junius' Nomenclator* 204/1 *Epistylium*, Vitru[vius], capitulum, modulus... The head or chapter of the piller: the module. **1610** HOLLAND *Camden's Brit.* I. 411 What a sort of modules or Chapters of pillars [orig. *quot epistylia*]..haue beene digged up.

8. *Engin.* The pitch diameter of a gear wheel in millimetres (or inches) divided by the number of teeth.

1909 in WEBSTER. **1912** G. T. WHITE *Toothed Gearing* ii. 17 Module = D^{mm}/N = ..25·4/diametral pitch = circular pitch″ × 8·085. **1964** MORRISON & CROSSLAND *Introd. Mech. Machines* ii. 142 One set of standard proportions is that the addendum should be equal to the module *m* (or the reciprocal of the diametral pitch) and the dedendum.. greater than this by an amount of one-twentieth of the circular pitch or 0·157*m*.

†ˈ**module**, *v. Obs.* [In sense 1, a. F. *module-r*, ad. L. *modulāre* to MODULATE. In sense 2, alteration of MODEL *v.* after MODULE *sb.*]

1. *trans.* To sing, perform (music).

1610 G. FLETCHER *Christ's Vict.* II. xviii, Soon the old Palmer his devotions sung, Like pleasing anthems moduled in time. **1612** DRAYTON *Poly-olb.* xiii. 70 That Charmer of the Night..That moduleth her tunes so admirably rare.

2. To MODEL, mould, form.

1598 SYLVESTER *Du Bartas* II. i. II. *Imposture* Argt., Justice and Mercy modul'd in their kinde. **1621** G. SANDYS *Ovid's Met.* I. (1632) 9 O would I could my Father's cunning vse! And soules into well-modul'd Clay infuse! **1695** WOODWARD *Nat. Hist. Earth* II. (1723) 95 Men..which were to inhabit this Earth, thus moduled anew.

†ˈ**modulet.** *Obs. rare.* [f. MODULE *sb.* + -ET[1].] A little model.

1591 SYLVESTER *Du Bartas* I. vii. 747 But, soft my Muse: what? wilt thou re-repeat The Little-World's admired modulet? **1610** W. FOLKINGHAM *Art of Survey* I. iii. 6 The Crassitude of the Soale is diuersified in seuerall Plots, and particular Modulets. *Ibid.* II. iv. 52 Proportion consists in the generall Modell and particular Modulets of the Plot.

†ˈ**modulize**, *v. Obs.* [f. MODULE *sb.* + -IZE. Cf. OF. *moduliser* to make melody, and MODELIZE.] *trans.* To model, form a model of; to organize.

1605 SYLVESTER *Du Bartas* II. iii. III. *Law* 1115 While with the Duke [Moses], th' Eternall did devise, And to his inward sight did modulize His Tabernacle's admirable Form. **1679** EVERARD *Prot. Princes Europe* 40 They who have the.. dexterity to modulize or conquer Sovereign Estates know better than any other by what Maxims their Successours may be enabled to maintain themselves therein.

modull, obs. form of MODEL.

modulo (ˈmɒdjʊləʊ), *prep. Math.* [abl. of L. *modulus*.] With respect to a modulus of. Also *attrib.*, = modular.

1897 *Bull. Amer. Math. Soc.* III. 381 Congruences irreducible modulo *p* (*p* = prime). **1903** J. BOWDEN *Elem. Theory Integers* x. 148 The statement of congruence is written $\alpha \equiv \beta$ (mod. μ), which is read 'α is congruent with β, modulo μ.' **1939** L. E. DICKSON *Mod. Elem. Theory Numbers* i. 8 Any positive integer *n* is congruent modulo 9 to the sum *s* of its digits. **1966** OGILVY & ANDERSON *Excursions in Number Theory* iv. 43 Since 8, 15, 22, 29, etc., and also −6, −13, etc. are all congruent to 1 (mod 7), they are members of the same residue class modulo 7... In arithmetic modulo 7, 8 is equivalent to 1 in many senses. *Ibid.* 44 In number theory one must often work with very large numbers. If these can be reduced to equivalent smaller numbers, much time-consuming labor can be avoided. Herein lies one of the great contributions of modulo arithmetic. **1971** J. H. SMITH *Digital Logic* vi. 115 Modulo-7 counters count normally up to six (110). The next count must reset the counter to zero.

1973 *Nature* 20 Apr. 541/3 A sufficiently dense integer sequence is well distributed in most arithmetic progressions modulo most (small enough) primes.

modulor ('mɒdjuːlə(r)). [Fr.] A scale with initial dimensions of 7 feet 5 inches (226 cm.) and 3 feet 9 inches (114·3 cm.), devised by the French architect Charles-Edouard Jeanneret, called Le Corbusier (1887–1965), based on the proportions of a human figure six feet tall, and intended to be used for the co-ordinated design of buildings, their contents, and their surroundings. Also *attrib.*

1948 M. GHYKA in *Archit. Rev.* Feb. 39 Le Corbusier's Modulor, and the concept of the Golden Mean... The Modulor is a linear scale in the form of a tape. Its object is to provide a means by which practical realization may be given to the need for efficiency and harmony in the dimensioning of objects and their containers, in architectural design and in town-planning... The Modulor differs from such a [conventional] scale in that the markings on it are related to each other by the principle of the Golden Mean. **1954** DE FRANCIA & BOSTOCK tr. *Le Corbusier's Modulor* 55 The necessities of language demanded that the golden rule should be given a name. Of several possible words, the MODULOR was chosen... The 'Modulor' is a measuring tool based on the human body and on mathematics. **1962** *Listener* 27 Sept. 472/1 The modulor which he [*sc.* Le Corbusier] invented..seemed to have served this purpose. It..forced him to develop the shell from the inside in several stages, starting with the modulor as the smallest unit. *Ibid.* 472/2 His faithful students soon learned to assemble their modulor units to very much the same buildings they had designed before. **1964** J. SUMMERSON *Classical Lang. Archit.* vi. 46 It was not till the early years of World War II that le Corbusier created the system..which he has called the 'Modulor'. **1972** *Times* 30 Nov. (Books Suppl.) p. ii/5 Furneaux Jordan quotes the story of how Corbusier's six foot 'modulor' was chosen because he had heard that the 'good-looking man' in English detective novels..is always six feet tall.

‖**modulus** ('mɒdjʊləs). Pl. moduli ('mɒdjʊlaɪ), moduluses. [L.: see MODULE.]

†**1.** *Arch.* = MODULE *sb.* 4. *Obs.*

1563 SHUTE *Archit.* C j, A Modulus, or half the thicknes of the pillor.

2. *Math.* **a.** A number by which Napierian logarithms must be multiplied in order to obtain the corresponding logarithms in another system (usually that with base 10).

[**1722** R. COTES *Harm. Mensur.* 4 Pro diversa magnitudine quantitatis assumptae M, quae adeo vocetur Systematis *Modulus*.] **1753** CHAMBERS *Cycl. Supp.* s.v. *Logarithm*, The line *oe* is what Mr. Cotes calls the *modulus* of the system. **1798** HUTTON *Course Math.* (1828) II. 306 Multiply the result by the modulus of the system of logarithms. **1897** *Chambers' Math. Tables* (ed. Pryde) 454 Modulus of common logarithms = M = 0·4342944819.

b. A constant multiplier, coefficient, or parameter involved in a given function of a variable.

For the specific applications see Greenhill *Elliptic Functions* (1892) 4, 53, and Forsyth *Theory of Functions* (1893) 377.

1843 MACCULLAGH in *Proc. R. Irish Acad.* II. 448 The given plane may be called a *directive plane*, and the constant ratio may be termed the *modulus*. **1865** BRANDE & COX *Dict. Sci.*, etc. I. 768 Any trigonometrical function of ϕ is termed an *elliptic function*, having the *argument u* and *modulus k*. **1873** MAXWELL *Electr. & Magn.* (1881) I. 217 We may call k and k′ the two complementary moduli of the confocal system. *a* **1883** H. J. S. SMITH *Collect. Math. Papers* (1894) II. 570 Geometrical Construction of the Transformed Modulus by means of the Modular Curve.

c. A measure of a quantity which depends upon two or more other quantities. In recent use chiefly, the absolute value of a complex quantity.

1845 DE MORGAN *Calculus of Functions* in *Encycl. Metrop.* II. 375/1 By the *modulus* of α (*x*, *y*) we mean the function α (*x*, *x*) considered as of a single subject. The moduli of the sum, difference, product, &c. of two functions are the sum, difference, &c. of the moduli. **1846** CAYLEY *Coll. Math. Papers* I. 238 The square of the secant of the semi-angle of resultant rotation will be the modulus of the rotation. **1891** HOBSON *Trigonom.* 255 The modulus of the sum of a number of complex quantities is less than, or equal to, the sum of their moduli.

d. *Theory of Numbers.* A number in respect of which other numbers are congruent. [Introduced in this sense by Gauss in *Disquisitiones Arithmeticae* (1801) I. I.]

1845 *Encycl. Metrop.* I. 642/2 Numbers of the same form with respect to any modulus, are all those which can be represented by the same formula. Thus, 13, 17, 21, &c. are all of the form $4n + 1$; and 19, 25, 31, &c. of the form $6n + 1$; 4 and 6 being the moduli. **1888** C. SMITH *Treat. Algebra* xxviii. 487 If two numbers *a* and *b* leave the same remainder when divided by a third number *c*, they are said to be congruent with respect to the modulus *c*. **1892** G. B. MATHEWS *Theory Numbers* 7. **1949** [see MOD *prep.*]. **1967** J. E. SHOCKLEY *Introd. Number Theory* iii. 48 Corollary 6.2 furnishes the most efficient method for solving several systems of congruences when the same sets of moduli appear in each system.

3. *Physics* and *Mech.* A constant indicating the relation between the amount of a physical effect and that of the force producing it.

modulus of elasticity: originally applied by Young to the quantity by means of which the amount of longitudinal extension or contraction of a bar of a given material, and the amount of the tension or pressure causing it, may be stated in terms of each other. Now used in a wider sense (see quot. 1877).

1807 T. YOUNG *Lect. Philos.* xiii. I. 137 According to this analogy, we may express the elasticity of any substance by the weight of a certain column of the same substance, which may be denominated the modulus of its elasticity. *Ibid.* II. 66 It may be shown that every small change of form is propagated along an extended chord with a velocity equal to that of a heavy body falling through a height equal to half the length of a portion of the chord, of which the weight is equivalent to a force producing the tension, and which may be called the modulus of the tension. **1824** TREDGOLD *Strength Cast Iron* 251 The measure of the power of a body to resist impulsion, that is, the modulus of resilience. **1843** MOSELEY *Mech. Princ. Engin.* 162 The modulus of a machine..is the relation between the work constantly done upon it by the moving power, and that constantly yielded at the working points [etc.]. **1846** MALLET in *Trans. R. Irish Acad.* (1848) XXI. 93 If we take the modulus of elasticity for the following rocks from the preceding table, and, comparing these with the modulus of cast iron, suppose the time of wave transit in each to be proportionate roughly to the square roots of their respective moduli, we get the following table of results. **1877** SIR W. THOMSON in *Encycl. Brit.* VII. 804 *Moduluses of Elasticity*. A modulus of elasticity is the number obtained by dividing the number expressing a stress by the number expressing the strain which it produces... An isotropic solid has two principal moduluses—a *modulus of compression* and a *rigidity*.

4. A unit of payment (see quot.).

1882 *Cambr. Stat., Trin. Coll.* (1883) 590 The Council shall fix for the year the amount being not more than..250*l.* to be called a *modulus*. And there shall be paid to each Fellow ..his proper dividend fixed as hereinafter mentioned by reference to the amount of the *modulus*. There shall be paid to the Master seven *moduli*, and to each of the Chaplains and to the Librarian one half of a *modulus*.

5. *gen.* A norm or standard. Cf. MODULE 3. *rare*.

1864 *Reader* 30 Apr. 544/3 He sometimes deviates from the strict modulus of the sonnet.

modur(e, obs. forms of MOTHER.

‖**modus** ('məʊdəs). Pl. (*rare*) modi ('məʊdaɪ); (in sense 4) moduses. [L. *modus*: see MODE *sb.*]

†**1.** *Old Law.* The qualification of the terms of a conveyance or other instrument; the consideration of a conveyance.

1590 SWINBURNE *Testaments* 137 *Modus* is a moderation, whereby a charge or burthen is imposed, in respecte of a commoditie... The meane or moderation is knowen by this worde (*that*) as I make A. B. my executor or giue him a hundred pound, that he maie erect a monument. **1850** BURRILL *Law Dict.*, *Modus*,..in old conveyancing. A consideration; the consideration of a conveyance, technically expressed by the word *ut*.

2. *gen.* The way in which anything is done; mode or manner of operation.

Sometimes short for *m. operandi* or *m. agendi* (see 5).

1648 EVELYN *Corr.* (1852) III. 23 Touching the reports of this day..as that Rochester was entered by stratagem, or Canterbury (for none of the relators agree either in the place or modus). *a* **1686** T. WATSON *Body Div.* (1692) 239 What shall be the modus or manner of Trial? **1780** in I. Allen *Hist. Vermont* (1798) 141 That either party should establish the modus, or rules to be pursued in determining disputes. **1846** in *Proc. Amer. Phil. Soc.* IV. 259 The modus in which the electric charge passes along the wires. **1898** A. LANG *Making Relig.* viii. 143 Because..psychologists are unable to explain, or give the *modus* of a set of phenomena.

†**3.** *Philos.* = MODE *sb.* 6. *Obs.* In full **modus essendi** or **existendi**.

1675 HOWE *Living Temple* II. i. Wks. 1724 I. 126 [Criticism of Spinoza.] And if the Essence of Substance contains the inexisting Modi, the Essence of the Modi doth equally contain their inexistence in Substance. *a* **1679** T. GOODWIN *Christ Mediator* II. v. (1692) 48 One and the same thing is differenced from it self by a different *modus*, or manner of existing. *a* **1679** —— *Man's Restaur. Grace* iii. 9 The distinction of their personality (if abstractly considered from the essence) being but *modus essendi*.

4. A money payment in lieu of tithe. In full ***modus decimandi***.

1618 SELDEN *Hist. Tithes* x. 288 Where any..Prescription or Custome hath setled a *Modus Decimandi* or certain quantitie payable, though never so little, for the Tithe. **1669** WORLIDGE *Syst. Agric.* (1681) 111 It is to be wish'd that there were some more certain Modus in lieu of that troublesome way of Tything. **1687** *Assur. Abb. Lands* 31 Also Modus of Tithes was another Infringement of the Canons. **1747** *Gentl. Mag.* 57/1 The ancient *Modusses* and compositions for tythes. **1763** BURN *Eccl. Law* II. 388 Of modus's, or exemptions from payment of tithes in kind. **1766** BLACKSTONE *Comm.* II. iii. 29–30. **1843** *Meeson & Welsby's Excheq. Rep.* (1844) XI. 676 The plaintiff was.. employed in maintaining and upholding the said moduses. **1866** GEO. ELIOT *F. Holt* vi. I. 137 The spiritual person who still took his tithe-pig or his *modus*.

5. In mod.L. phrases: **a. modus agendi**, the mode in which a thing acts or operates.

1849 NOAD *Electricity* (ed. 3) 29 Scientific men are not agreed as to the *modus agendi* of the amalgam applied to the rubber.

b. modus operandi, mode of operating: (*a*) the way in which a thing, cause, etc., operates; (*b*) in more recent use, the way in which a person goes to work.

1654 WHITLOCK *Zootomia* 222 Because their Causes, or their *modus operandi* (which is but the Application of the Cause to the Effect) doth not fall under Demonstration. **1835** *Edin. Rev.* LXI. 85 We are still ignorant of the nature ..of this force, and of its *modus operandi*. **1843** MILL *Logic* III. x. §8 I. 529 We must make entire abstraction of all knowledge of the simpler tendencies, the *modi operandi* of mercury in detail. **1874** W. ARCHER in *Q. Jrnl. Microsc. Sci.* XIV. 130 The following will show the *modus operandi*. **1894** K. GRAHAME *Pagan P.* 86 It would hardly be in the public interest to disclose his *modus operandi*. **1935** G. POOLE *Haulage & Winding* xiii. 324 Assuming that an overwind has taken place,..the *modus operandi* is as follows:—The engine-driver at once closes his throttle and immediately he has to call an assistant to go to the overwinding device; [etc.]. **1947** *Sci. News* V. 14 The *modus operandi* of insulin was, in Sakel's original theory, upon the nerve cells and the hormones which, he believed, excited their activity especially in the 'vegetative centres'. **1949** [see HOW *sb.*[3] 2]. **1955** *Bull. Atomic Sci.* Feb. 58/3 Their *modus operandi* against limited aggression would be simple. **1972** *Mod. Law Rev.* XXXV. 28 The modus operandi of a small claims judge should approximate more closely to that of a police detective.

c. modus vivendi, 'a mode of living'; a working arrangement between contending parties, pending the settlement of matters in debate.

1879 *N. & Q.* Ser. v. XI. 109 'Modus Vivendi'—This formula is in daily use to express a practical compromise. **1882** *Standard* 27 Dec. 4/7 The Russian Government and the Pope have arranged a *modus vivendi*. **1884** *Manch. Exam.* 9 Dec. 5/5 He hoped to establish a *modus vivendi* pending the conclusion of a Treaty.

d. modus ponens (*Logic*), 'mood that affirms'; the rule that from *if p then q* together with *p*, *q* may be inferred; an argument of this form. In full **modus ponendo ponens**.

a **1856** W. HAMILTON *Lect. Metaphysics & Logic* (1860) I. 344 We can always easily convert an hypothetical syllogism of one form into another,—the *modus ponens* into the *modus tollens*. **1870** W. S. JEVONS *Elem. Lessons Logic* xix. 161 The argument is said to be of the *modus ponens*, or mood which posits or affirms. **1916** H. W. B. JOSEPH *Introd. Logic* (ed. 2) xv. 335 The argument is said to be in the *modus ponens*. **1957** P. SUPPES *Introd. Logic* ii. 32 The Latin name for the Law of Detachment is *modus ponendo ponens*. **1972** *Computer Jrnl.* XV. 230/2 Applying the rule of modus ponens on the above instance.

e. modus tollens (*Logic*), 'mood that denies'; the rule that from *if p then q* together with *not-q*, *not-p* may be inferred; an argument of this form. In full **modus tollendo tollens**.

a **1856** [see *modus ponens*]. **1881** MAX MÜLLER tr. *Kant's Critique Pure Reason* II. II. i. 678 The *modus tollens* of reasoning, from consequences to their grounds, is not only perfectly strict, but also extremely easy. **1916** H. W. B. JOSEPH *Introd. Logic* (ed. 2) xv. 337 The *modus tollens* is of the form [etc.]. **1940** *Mind* XLIX. 208 An inference in the *modus tollendo tollens*..yields the contrary of the original contrary hypothesis. **1965** E. J. LEMMON *Beginning Logic* ii. 61 *Modus tollendo tollens* is the principle that, if a conditional holds and also the negation of its consequent, then the negation of its antecedent holds.

†'**modwall.** *Obs.* Also 7–8 mud-, 8 mid-. A variant or corruption, in old Dictionaries, for WOODWALL or WITWALL.

1572 HULOET, Modwall a byrde which destroyeth bees, *apiastra*. **1657** C. BECK *Univ. Char.* I ij, A mudwall or wood pecker bird. **1658** ROWLAND tr. *Moufet's Theat. Ins.* 901 The nests of Swallowes, Modwals [orig. *apiastrorum*], Owls, or Wood-peckers. **1706** PHILLIPS (ed. Kersey), *Midwall*... *Modwall*. **1736** AINSWORTH *Lat. Dict.* I, Modwall (bird), *picus*... Mud wall (bird), *apiaster*. *Ibid.* II, *Apiastra*,.. midwal.

†'**mody**, *a.* *Obs.* [f. MODE *sb.* + -Y.] Fashionable, modish.

1701 F. MANNING *Poems* 67, I am o'erjoyed, says one, that we shall see Of Mody Fans so great variety. **1741** RICHARDSON *Pamela* I. xxxii. 125, I said, O dear Mr. Longman, you make me too rich, and too mody. **1771** T. HULL *Sir W. Harrington* (1797) III. 42 These [dresses] were entirely new for the wedding..mine the mody coloured crimson, edged with ermine.

mody, obs. form of MOODY.

modyngstrete, var. or corrupt f. MIDDENSTEAD.

c **1475** *Pict. Voc.* in Wr.-Wülcker 798/4 *Hoc senum* [= *cœnum*], a modyngstrete.

modyr(e, obs. forms of MOTHER *sb.*

moe, var. MO more; obs. f. MOW *sb.* and *v.*

Mœbius ('møːbɪəs). The name of Bernhard *Mœbius* (fl. 1884 in Mexico as a German subject), used *attrib.* to designate an electrolytic process that he devised for parting gold and silver (*Brit. Pat. 16,554* (1884)), in which anodes of bullion and cathodes of silver or stainless steel are placed in a solution of silver nitrate, so that base metals go into solution and silver is deposited on the cathode, leaving behind the gold.

1902 *Encycl. Brit.* XXVIII. 110/1 Alloy scrap containing chiefly copper with, say 5 or 6 per cent. of gold, and other metals, and up to 40 to 50 per cent. of silver, is often treated electrolytically. Obviously, with modifications, the Mœbius process could be applied. **1970** *Materials & Technol.* III. iv. 295 Electrolytic refining [of doré metal] is now widely employed. In the Moebius process the impure silver is cast into anodes which are enclosed in cotton or linen bags and dissolved electrolytically in acid silver nitrate solution.

Moebius, var. MÖBIUS.

moeble, obs. f. MOBILE *a.* and *sb.*[1]; var. MOBLE.

moed(e, moeder, obs. ff. MOOD, MOTHER.

‖**moederkappie** ('mʊdəkapɪ). *S. Afr.* Also muttercap. [Afrikaans, f. Du. *moeder* mother +

kap, kapje hood, in reference to the shape of the flower.] Either of two South African orchids, *Pterygodium catholicum* or *Disperis capensis*, which bear bonnet-shaped flowers.

1887 J. MACKINNON *S. Afr. Traits* 124 Here is the Pride of Table Mountain and the Muttercap, two of the twenty-five species of orchids that exist in South Africa. **1910** D. FAIRBRIDGE *That which hath Been* xxiii. 284 Orchids in inexhaustible variety, from scarlet disas to yellow moederkapjes..are still left to us. **1952** *Cape Times* 8 May 14/1 Pine trees..together with humans, have been too much for the nerines, the *moederkappies* and other veld things which used to flower there. **1971** U. VAN DER SPUY *Wild Flowers S. Afr.* 209/2 *(caption)* Moederkappie (*Pterygodium catholicum*) bears its flowers of subtle colours in spring. **1973** *Stand. Encycl. S. Afr.* VIII. 382/1 Moederkappie. Oumakappie... These names are borne by two quite distinct species: *Pterygodium catholicum*..is usually about 20 cm high, with two or three leaves sheathing the somewhat fleshy stem. The few sulphur-yellow flowers are borne in a lax spike. As the flowers fade they turn dull red. They have a strong scent... *Disperis capensis.* Common orchid, sometimes called 'granny bonnet', with magenta, greenish or cream-coloured flowers... The leaves are rather small and clasp the stem. The flowers are usually solitary.

moedor(e, moehair, see MOIDORE, MOHAIR.

moekul, var. MOGGEL.

moelline (ˈməʊɪlɪn). [f. F. *moelle* marrow + -IN[1].] A kind of unguent for the hair.

1851 *Official Catal. Gt. Exhib.* II. 790 'Moelline', a peculiar oleaginous compound. **1860** in WORCESTER. **1864–1897** in WEBSTER.

‖**moellon**[1] (mwalɔ̃). *Arch.* [Fr., altered form (? assimilated to *moelle* marrow) of OF. *moilon, meulon, moiron*, of obscure origin.] Rubble used in masonry; = RAG *sb.*[2]

[**1836**: as Fr. in PARKER *Gloss. Archit.* (1850) s.v. *Ragstone.* **1858** SIMMONDS *Dict. Trade*, *Moellon* (French), rough stones fit for building.] **1875** in KNIGHT *Dict. Mech.*

moellon[2] (ˈmwɛlɒn). [Presumably Fr., and perh. identical with MOELLON.] The fluid obtained when fish-oils are rubbed into hides and recovered by expression, as in the manufacture of chamois leather (cf. DEGRAS, DÉGRAS a); also, a product made in imitation of this (see quot. 1969). Also called ***moellon degras***.

1897 C. T. DAVIS *Manuf. Leather* (ed. 2) 227 French moellon oil, strictly speaking, is an expressed oil from chamois tannage, French degras being a mixture of moellon and oil obtained from washing the skins in an alkaline solution. **1922**, etc. [see DEGRAS, DÉGRAS a]. **1939** *Thorpe's Dict. Appl. Chem.* (ed. 4) III. 552 *(heading)* Analysis of moëllon-dégras. **1969** T. C. THORSTENSEN *Pract. Leather Technol.* xii. 202 Natural moellon is produced by the oxidation of raw cod liver oil in the tanning of sheep and goat chamois skins. Synthetic moellon is produced by the controlled aeration of raw cod liver oil to the desired oxidation fatty acid value; it results in more hydrophilic properties.

moerdre, moerdrer, moerdrice, obs. ff. MURDER, -ER, -ESS.

Mœritherium (mɪərɪˈθɪərɪəm). [mod.L. (C. W. Andrews 1902, in *Verhandlungen V. Internat. Zool.-Congress* VI. 528), f. Gr. *Μοῖρις* the name of a lake in Egypt + *θηρίον* wild beast.] An extinct proboscidean mammal of the genus so called, known from remains found in late Eocene beds of the province of Fayum in Upper Egypt.

1902 *Encycl. Brit.* XXX. 510/2 Most remarkable is a primitive proboscidean (*Mœritherium*) with a nearly full series of front- and cheek-teeth. **1924** J. A. THOMSON *Sci. Old & New* xli. 236 Millions of years ago, in the Eocene epoch..there lived in North Africa a primitive hoofed animal called Mœritherium. **1968** A. S. ROMER *Procession of Life* xvi. 265 *Moeritherium* was still a relatively small animal, of about pig size, and, except for a rather long body, of pig-like proportions.

moes, obs. form of MOSS.

Mœso-Goth (ˈmiːsəʊgɒθ). Also **Mæso-**. [ad. late L. *Mœsogothī* pl., f. L. *Mœsī* the people of the country (from them called *Mœsia*), corresponding to the modern Bulgaria and Servia + *Gothī*: see GOTH.] A member of the Gothic tribe that inhabited Mœsia in the 4th and 5th c. after Christ.

1818 T. H. HORNE *Introd. Study Script* I. 302 Ulphilas, a celebrated bishop of the Mæso-Goths. **1864** *Chamb. Encycl., Mœso-Goths*, the name given to the Goths who in the 3d c. settled in Lower Mœsia at the mouth of the Danube.

Mœso-Gothic (miːsəʊˈgɒθɪk), *a.* and *sb.* Also **Mæso-**. [ad. late L. *Mœsogothic-us*, f. *Mœsogothī*: see prec. and -IC.] **a.** *adj.* Of or pertaining to the Mœso-Goths or their language. **b.** *sb.* The language of the Mœso-Goths.

Formerly applied to the language of the extant Gothic version of portions of the Scriptures, which is doubtless the work of the Mœso-Gothic bishop Wulfila (Ulphilas). But as the language does not differ materially from that of other remains of Gothic, and there is no evidence that such differences as exist belonged to the dialect of Wulfila himself, philologists now usually speak of 'Gothic' simply.

[**1689** HICKES *(title)* Institutiones Grammaticæ Anglo-Saxonicæ et Mœso-Gothicæ.] **1818** T. H. HORNE *Introd. Study Script.* I. 304 The Mæso-Gothic translation of the thirteen Epistles of Saint Paul made by Ulphilas. *Ibid.*, A complete set of Mæso-Gothic types has been cast. **1831** CARLYLE *Sart. Res.* III. vii, Had there been no Mœso-gothic Ulfila, there had been no English Shakespeare, or a different one. **1845** STODDART *Grammar* in *Encycl. Metrop.* I. 138/1 In Mæso-Gothic the verb *beon* or *bion* is not found. *a* **1886** J. KER *Lect. Hist. Preaching* vi. (1888) 93 The New Testament and the Septuagint..found their way into Western tongues, through the Vulgate and the Moesogothic.

Moët (moɛ). [From the name of the firm, *Moët et Chandon* of Rheims, which sells it.] The name of a class of champagne.

1841 THACKERAY *St. Philip's Day at Paris* Wks. 1900 XIII. 554 A bottle of soda-water, which all the pit takes to be real moët. **1883** MISS BRADDON *Golden Calf* III. iv. 91, I can have a bottle of Moët there.

moether, obs. form of MOTHER.

‖**mœurs** (mœrs, mœr), *sb. pl.* [Fr.:—L. *mōrēs*, pl. of *mos* custom.] The behaviour, customs, or habits of a people or a group of people.

1922 BLUNDEN *Bonadventure* xxi. 136 So strongly did I feel that in his hours of leisure and coallessness he was a critic of verse and *mœurs* that I almost asked him his name. **1940** H. G. WELLS *Babes in Darkling Wood* II. i. 145, I am a student of human behaviour. I am—how shall I call it?—an experimentalist in *mœurs*. **1954** I. MURDOCH *Under Net* xiv. 192, I sat..reflecting on the difference between French and English literary *mœurs*. **1957** L. DURRELL *Bitter Lemons* 34 Yet side by side with this crude and graceless world the true Mediterranean *moeurs* lingered. **1965** *New Statesman* 14 May 774/2 Mr. Baker's evident ambition was to present us with an authentic portrait of fleeting teenage *moeurs*.

moevable, etc.: see MOVABLE, etc.

mofe, obs. form of MOVE *v.*

‖**mofette** (mɔfɛt). Also **moffette**. [F., ad. It. (Naples) *mofetta* = Sp. *mofeta*.]

a. An exhalation of mephitic gas escaping from a fissure. **b.** An opening or fissure in the earth from which such exhalations escape.

1822–34 *Good's Study Med.* (ed. 4) III. 433 The first, formerly denominated phlogistic air, and sometimes mofette, is thrown forth largely during the decomposition of animal matter. **1823** CRABB *Technol. Dict.*, *Mofette* (*Chem.*) another name for Nitrogen. **1849** OTTÉ tr. *Humboldt's Cosmos* I. 209 Various substances have been ejected during the earthquake, as hot water,..*Mofettes* [*gloss.* exhalations of carbonic acid gas]..; mud, black smoke [etc.]. **1887** *Our Earth & its Story* I. 225 The amount of carbonic acid which is discharged by these moffettes must be enormous.

moff[1], **moph** (mɒf). [See quot. 1885.] An instrument consisting of a pair of compasses, one leg of which is fashioned like the leg of a pair of callipers.

1885 *Let.* 28 Nov. (MS.), It is a cross, in fact, between compass and calliper; and its character of cross breed got it originally the name of hermaphrodite, which was corrupted into mophrodite, which has been shortened into 'moff'. **1902** MARSHALL *Metal Tools* 12 A useful form of calipers for marking off..is known by various names, such as 'odd-leg calipers', 'scribing calipers', 'hermaphrodite calipers', 'mophs', or 'jennies'.

‖**moff**[2] (mɒf). See quot.

1851 *Official Catal. Gt. Exhib.* III. 1373 Caucasian silk stuff (called *moff*). **1858** SIMMONDS *Dict. Trade.*

moffe, obs. form of MOVE *v.*

moffel(l, moffle, obs. forms of MUFFLE *v.*

moffette, variant of MOFETTE.

moffie (ˈmɒfɪ). *slang* (esp. *S. Afr.*). Also **mophy**. [? ad. colloq. shortening and mispronunciation of HERMAPHRODITE *sb.* and *a.*; cf. Afrikaans *moffiedaai*, dial. var. *hermafrodiet*.] An effeminate man.

1929 F. C. BOWEN *Sea Slang* 92 *Mophy*, a term of contempt among seamen for delicate, well-groomed youngsters. **1960** D. LYTTON *Goddam White Man* i. 27 Moffies. They don't like women but they like women's clothes... But Achmed was not a proper moffie; he just liked fooling with boys. He didn't have the moffie voice. **1971** *Post* (S. Afr.) 23 May 18 The life of Edward Shadi—described as a beautiful, sexy moffie with a sweet soprano voice—was a strange affair.

‖**Mofussil** (məʊˈfʌsɪl). *Anglo-Ind.* Also 8 Mofussel, 8–9 -ul, 9 Mofusil. [Hindustani *mufaççil*, ad. Arab. *mufaççal*, pa. pple. of *faççala* to divide, separate.]

1. In India, the country as distinguished from the 'Presidency'; the rural localities of a district as distinguished from the chief station.

1781 *Hicky's Bengal Gaz.* 31 Mar. (Yule), A gentleman lately arrived from the Mo[f]ussel. *Ibid.* 30 June (*Ibid.*), A gentleman in the Mofussil, Mr. P., fell out of his chaise and broke his leg. **1878** *(title)* Life in the Mofussil; or the Civilian in Lower Bengal. **1886** YULE & BURNELL *Gloss. Anglo-Ind.* s.v., Thus if, in Calcutta, one talks of the Mofussil, he means anywhere in Bengal out of Calcutta; if one at Benares talks of going into the Mofussil he means going anywhere in the Benares division or district (as the case might be) out of the city of Benares. And so over India.

2. *attrib.* Of, pertaining to, belonging to, or living in the Mofussil; rural, provincial.

c **1836** MACAULAY in Trevelyan *Life* (1876) I. 395 The Mofussil newspapers..have spoken favourably of this measure. **1860** *Rural Life in Bengal* 105 Characteristic of Mofussil life. **1878** *Life in Mofussil* I. 58 The natural dulness of a wet Sunday in a Mofussil bungalow. **1906** *Advice Note, Office of Superintendent of Govt. Printing, India* Voucher No. 5656 When cheques on mofussil banks are sent, they must include the amount of discount.

Hence **Moˈfussilite**, one residing in the Mofussil; **Moˈfussilize** *v. intr.*, to live away from a town or residency (*nonce-wd.*).

1845 *(title of newspaper)* The Mofussilite. **1863** SALA *Qualk the Circumnavigator* 64 Bankrupt scholars, whose parents had been mofussilising in an inordinate degree. **1888** *Bookseller's Catal.* (*Bombay*) To Purchasers, Mofussilites should always send the price and postage of the books beforehand.

mog (mɒg), *v.*[1] *dial.* and *U.S.* Also 7–8 mogg, 9 mug, maug.

†**1.** *intr. Cards.* To exchange cards in the obsolete game of 'costly colours'. *Obs.*

1674 COTTON *Compl. Gamester* (1680) 89 You must deal off three a piece, and turn up the next Card following; then the Eldest is to take his choice whether he will Mogg (this is a changing a Card or no). **1734** SEYMOUR *Compl. Gamester* (ed. 5) II. 32.

2. To move on, depart, decamp. Chiefly with *off* or *on*.

1764 T. BRYDGES *Homer Travest.* (1797) II. 128 Get on board thy rotten ship; The rest, I hope, will scorn to mog off And dim my daylights if I jog off. **1862** C. C. ROBINSON *Dial. Leeds* 363 'Mug on!' 'Wean't mug a bit'. **1880** *Antrim & Down Gloss., Maug*, to walk away. 'Maug off with you'.

3. To walk *along* slowly but steadily; to jog *on*, move gently (E.D.D.).

1857 J. T. STATON *Bobby & Shuttle* 5 (E.D.D.) Aw mogged up eawt oth loom-shop into th' heawse. **1873** W. CARLETON *Farm Ball., Out o' the Fire* 52 He..mogged along to the door-way, with never a word of row. **1894** REMINGTON in *Harper's Mag.* Feb. 359 As our horses were thirsty and footsore, we 'mogged along'.

4. *trans.* (See quots.)

1879 MISS JACKSON *Shropshire Word-bk.*, *Mog*, to move from one place to another... 'Tell John to mog the cows i' the mornin'. **1887** *S. Cheshire Gloss.*, *Mog*,..(2) to make to go, remove. Speaking of some one who had honestly restored to her some belongings, a woman said, 'Many a one 'ud ha' mogged 'em off'.

mog, *v.*[2], dial. variant of MUG *v.*

mog (mɒg), *sb. slang.* [Abbrev. MOGGY 3.] A cat; also *transf.*, fur or a fur coat.

1927 W. E. COLLINSON *Contemp. Eng.* 26 As school-boys ..Tike for *dog*, moke for *donkey*..mog for *cat* were quite usual. **1934** P. HESELTINE in C. Gray *Peter Warlock* III. i. 253 Such lovely mogs you can't imagine—including the best cat in the world, surely. **1937** *Scrutiny* V. 391 Surrounded by vast quantities of cats and mistresses, now engaged in some fantastic quest for the Ideal Mog. **1950** PARTRIDGE *Slang To-day & Yesterday* (ed. 3) III. iii. 247 Annuvver 'orse comes up, an' it's..a new mog fer the missus.

Mogadon (ˈmɒgədɒn). *Pharm.* A proprietary name for nitrazepam.

1956 *Trade Marks Jrnl.* 22 Feb. 180/2 Mogadon... All goods included in class 5 [*sc.* pharmaceutical, veterinary and sanitary substances]. Roche Products Limited,..Welwyn Garden City, Hertfordshire; manufacturing chemists. **1965** *Brit. Med. Jrnl.* 6 Nov. 1093/2 They received 15 mg. of Mogadon (nitrazepam, an analogue of chlordiazepoxide), an effective new non-barbiturate hypnotic. **1972** D. MARLOWE *Do you remember England?* ii. 32 She took a sleeping tablet (Mogadon). **1973** *Guardian* 31 May 8/5 Police found a total of 156 drug tablets including a bottle of Mogadon.

Mogador (ˈmɒgədɔː(r)). Also **-ore**. The name of a seaport in Morocco; used *attrib.* to designate certain of its products or exports; as ***Mogador colocynth, gum***; also *absol.* (see quot. 1866).

1861–87 BENTLEY *Man. Bot.* II. iii. (ed. 5) 538 Morocco, Mogadore, or Brown Barbary Gum [is derived] from *Acacia arabica*. *Ibid.* 567 Mogador or Unpeeled Colocynth..is obtained from Mogador. **1866** R. S. CHARNOCK *Verba Nom.*, *Mogadore*, a bees'-wax from Mogador.

mogasheen, -ason, -erson, obs. ff. MOCCASIN.

Mogen David, var. MAGEN DAVID.

mogera, obs. form of MOGRA.

moget, var. MUGGET *Obs.* exc. *dial.*

mogey: see MOKI[2].

moggadored (ˈmɒgədɔːd), *a. slang.* Also mogodored. [Orig. uncertain.] Confused, 'at a loss'.

Moggadored could just possibly be Irish. The element *-adore-* looks very like the Irish agent ending *-adóir*, and *moggadore* would be the natural anglicization of an Irish **magadóir*. This is not in any of the dictionaries, but it would be a regular formation from the verbal noun *magadh* 'mock, jeer, make fun of, laugh at, etc.' (A. J. Bliss).

1936 G. INGRAM *Muffled Man* ix. 146 'I don't know,' Charlie said hopelessly, 'it's got me all ''mogodored''.' **1945** B. NAUGHTON in C. Madge *Pilot Papers* 105 He got some of these blokes moggadored: didn't know what to think, or do.

moggan ('mɒgən). *Sc.* and *dial.* Also 9 **moggen, -in, mogan, muggin, moogan.** [Of obscure origin; the Gael. *mogan* is believed by Celtic philologists to be adopted from Sc. Cf. *mokins* dial. (Hants) 'gaiters made of coarse sacking' (E.D.D.); also (though the sense is more remote), *moggins* (Cheshire) shoes with wooden soles, clogs.]

1. A long footless stocking; a stocking used as a purse; also 'long sleeves for a woman's arms, wrought like stockings' (Jam.).

1742 R. FORBES *Jrnl.* in *Ajax' Sp.* (1755) 31 I'm seer some o' them wat the sma' end o' their moggan. **1789** ROSS *Helenore*, etc. 134 Had I won the length but of ae pair of sleeves,..And on my twa gardies like moggans wad draw? **1832–53** D. S. BUCHAN in *Whistle-binkie* Ser. III. 72 He..prepared for to dee: And left..his lang neckit moggin to me. **1897** *Blackw. Mag.* Nov. 613/1 They came into the place in their mogans at night, quiet as ghosts.

†2. *pl.* The legs. *Obs.*

1780 W. FORBES *Dominie Deposed* 9 Wae to the night I first began To mix my moggans wi' thee, man.

moggel ('mɒgəl). Also **moekul.** [Afrikaans; see quot. 1902.] A South African freshwater fish of the genus *Labeo*, esp. *L. capensis*, belonging to the family Cyprinidæ.

1838 J. E. ALEXANDER *Expedition Interior Africa* I. vi. 144 My people came back in the evening with two or three large moekul or flat heads. **1902** *Trans. S. Afr. Philos. Soc.* XI. 214 It [sc. *Barbus capensis*] is now, however, called by the Dutch 'Moggel'—a word which..may be a corruption of the Latin *Mugil*, a generic name which has been applied to this fish, or it may refer to the general appearance and shape of this fish, 'moggel' in Dutch signifying a clumsy child. **1913** [see BAARDMAN]. **1947** K. H. BARNARD *Pict. Guide S. Afr. Fishes* 52 The Sandfish or Moggel..has a more cylindrical body-shape... Its chief character is the mouth with its thick fleshy lips; these form a sucking disc with which the fish browses on the algae and weeds on the rocks. The barbels are not prominent.

moggie: see MOKI[2].

moggi(n)son, obs. forms of MOCCASIN.

moggy ('mɒgɪ). [Possibly a variant of MAGGIE.] 1. *dial.* (West Midland: see E.D.D.) A pet-name for a calf or cow.

c **1825** *Houlston Tracts* II. xlviii. 4 Skelton's kine..lowed so, 'twas pitiful to hear them. For all they were dumb creatures, I knew their meaning, as well as if they had said, 'Give us a mouthful of dry food...' 'No', says I, 'poor moggies, I cannot do that..'.

2. *dial.* and *slang.* An untidily dressed woman.

1886 *S.W. Linc. Gloss.*, *Moggy*, a slattern, dressed out untidily: 'She did look a moggy'. **1896** FARMER & HENLEY *Slang*, *Moggy* (old) a badly-dressed woman; a guy.

3. *slang.* Also **moggie.** A cat. Also *attrib.*

1911 J. W. HORSLEY *I Remember* xi. 254 Cockney slang ..'moggies' for cats. **1966** *New Statesman* 27 May 788/2 He dries his hands on a moggie and uses a kitten to blot a false death certificate; 'just a fur ball, it's nothing,' he says. **1966** *New Scientist* 15 Dec. 613/3 Humans, to moggies, are but bloodheated places to sit on. **1967** *Ibid.* 4 May 257/2 In the desert, there are several little wild cats superficially indistinguishable from domestic moggies. **1972** M. BABSON *Murder on Show* v. 64 We're concentrating on the nice pretty little moggies, remember? **1973** *People's Jrnl.* (Inverness & Northern Counties ed.) 4 Aug. 4/3 Oh, and before I leave this topic of pussies, my neighbour across the lane also had a good laugh from the moggie next door to her. **1975** *Times* 7 July 5 Dodd came on wearing a shaggy red overcoat and..saying that it was genuine moggyskin and that he wore moggyskin longjohns.

Moghal, variant of MOGUL.

moghe, obs. form of MOTH, MOW *sb.*

moghet, var. MUGGET *Obs.* exc. *dial.*

Moghol, moghra: see MOGUL, MOGRA.

Moghrabbin, variant of MAUGRABIN.
1906 *Athenæum* 8 Dec. 735/2.

moght, obs. form of MOTH.

moght(e, moȝ(e, obs. ff. *might* pa. pple. of MAY *v.*[1]

Moghul, variant form of MOGUL.

‖**mogi-** (mɒdʒɪ, mɒgɪ). Combining form of Gr. μόγι-ς with toil and pain, f. μόγος toil, used in a few mod.L. pathological terms, as **mogi'graphia** [Gr. -γραφία, -GRAPHY; cf. F. *mogigraphie*], difficult or cramped writing, writer's cramp; also in anglicized form **mo'gigraphy**; hence **mogi'graphic** *a.* **mogi'lalia** [f. Gr. μογιλάλ-ος that speaks with difficulty], stammering; **mo'gilalism** = prec. (*Syd. Soc. Lex.* 1891). **mogi'phonia** [Gr. φωνή sound], 'a difficulty in producing loud vocal sounds with the larynx, ordinary speech remaining unaffected' (*Syd. Soc. Lex.*).

1856 MAYNE *Expos. Lex.*, *Mogigraphia*, term for difficult or cramped writing: mogigraphy. *Ibid.*, *Mogigraphicus*,.. mogigraphic. **1878** tr. *von Ziemssen's Cycl. Med.* XIV. 873 He distinguishes two varieties of defective speech, paraphonia and mogilalia. **1897** *Allbutt's Syst. Med.* IV. 850 The cases described by B. Fränkel under the name mogiphonia.

mogi(n)son, -issin, -nesan, obs. ff. MOCCASIN.

mognion, obs. variant of MONION.

‖**mogo** ('məʊgəʊ). [Native Australian.] The stone hatchet used by the aborigines of New South Wales.

1823 CRABB *Technol. Dict.*, *Mogo*, an Indian tomahawk. **1838** T. L. MITCHELL *Three Exped.* I. 204, I heard..the mogo of a native at work on some tree close by. **1868** W. CARLETON *Australian Nts.* 20 One mute memorial, by his bier His mogo, boomerang, and spear. **1876** *Forest & Stream* 13 July 375/2 With the head of the mogo [they] will crack the bones of animals for marrow.

mogodored, var. MOGGADORED *a.*

Mogol(l, Mogor, obs. forms of MOGUL.

mogoson, obs. form of MOCCASIN.

mogote (mə'gəʊtiː). *Physical Geogr.* [Sp. *mogote* hillock, heap, haystack.] One of the tall, steep-sided hills, approximately circular in cross-section, that occur in karstic regions in Cuba and elsewhere.

1928 *Geogr. Rev.* XVIII. 67 The Guaniguanico Mountains..rise from a smoothly undulating plain in the form of huge blocks and mesas, known as mogotes, to a maximum height of about a thousand or twelve hundred feet above the supporting floor. **1954** W. D. THORNBURY *Princ. Geomorphol.* xiii. 335 The pepino hills of Puerto Rico are much smaller than the mogotes of Cuba and hence more commonly rise to peaks rather than have flat summits. **1972** J. ROGLIĆ in Herak & Stringfield *Karst* i. 11 The karst..is characterized by isolated steep hills ('mogotes' in Cuba).

‖**mogra** ('moːgraː). Forms: 7 **mogera**, 8–9 **mogree**, 9 **mohra, moogree, morgree, moghra, mogra.** [Hindī *mogrā*.] The Arabian jasmine, *Jasminum Sambac.* Also *attrib.*

1662 J. DAVIES tr. *Mandelslo's Trav.* 86 There is almost no Flower but is sought after more for its colour then scent: for though those they call Mogera and Scampi have a good smell, yet [etc.]. **1757** J. H. GROSE *Voy. E. Indies* 229 A necklace..composed of flowers strung together, they call mogrees, something resembling Spanish double jessamy. **1813** J. FORBES *Oriental Mem.* III. 268 A sofa..adorned with wreathes of mogrees. **1834** MEDWIN *Angler in Wales* II. 317 The mogra-wreaths about his neck entwined, Those flowers the emblems of as pure a mind. **1879** E. ARNOLD *Lt. Asia* IV. 107 The Suddha Devas..Plucked the red mohra-flowers. **1891** *Syd. Soc. Lex.*, *Moogree flowers.* **1893** *Pall Mall G.* 23 Dec. 2/1 They are morgree flowers. The nautch girls wear them in their hair. **1902** MISS W. DOUGHTY *Afoot through Kashmir Valleys* xi. 143 From off the island bowers Come scents of moghra trees in bloom.

Mograbi(a)n, Mogrebbin: see MAUGRABIN.

1837 *Pop. Encycl.* V. 10/2 *Mogrebbins*; Arabs of the western part of Egypt.

Mogrebee, variant of MAUGRABEE.

moguey: see MOKI[2].

Mogul (məʊ'gʌl, 'məʊgəl), *sb.*[1] and *a.* Forms: α. 6–7 **Magoll**, 7 **Mogol(l, -ull**, 8–9 **Moghul, -hol**, 9 **Mog-, Mughal**, 7– **Mogul**; β. 6–7 (9 from Pg.) **Mogor**, 7 **Maghoore, Magor(e.** [a. Pers. and Arab. *muγal*, *muγul*, a mispronunciation of the native name MONGOL. The β-forms represent the Sp. and Pg. corruption *Mogor*.]

A. *sb.*

1. A Mongol or Mongolian; *spec.* in *Hist.* (*a*) A follower of Baber (a descendant of Tamerlane) who founded the Mongol empire in Hindustan in 1526; (*b*) a follower of Jenghis Khan in the 13th c.

α. **1625** PURCHAS *Pilgrims* I. 267 The Gouernour of Surat and the Gouernours brother of Cambaya, sent a Mogoll vnto me with a present of refreshing. **1662** J. DAVIES tr. *Mandelslo's Trav.* 82 The Mogul's..who came out of great Tartary, are good Natur'd, mild, discreet, civil [etc.]. **1841** ELPHINSTONE *Hist. Ind.* I. App. II. 433 There were Scythian irruptions into India before those of the Moguls under Chengiz Khán. **1842** W. MILES tr. *Hist. Hydur Naik* 317 The besieged Naik..had killed a great many of the Moghuls. **1874** L. J. TROTTER *Hist. Ind.* III. vii. 160 Driven out of the province he had hoped to reconquer for the Moghals, Abhi Singh..retired into his own country. **1886** YULE & BURNELL *Gloss. Anglo-Ind.* s.v., Among the Mahommedans of S. India the *Moguls* or *Mughals* constitute a strongly marked caste.

β. **1601** R. JOHNSON *Kingd. & Commw.* (1603) 179 In Cambaia it selfe, where the Mogors are of such fearefull puissance, liue the Resbuti.

†b. *Mogul's breeches*: ? a sort of long drawers or pyjamas. *Obs.*

a **1625** FLETCHER, etc. *Fair Maid Inn* IV. ii, Oh let him have his shirt on, and his Mogols breeches, here are women ith' house.

2. *the Great* or *Grand Mogul*, also shortened to *the Mogul*: the common designation among Europeans of the emperor of Delhi, whose empire at one time included most of Hindustan; the last nominal emperor was dethroned in 1857.

α. **1588** HICKOCK tr. *Frederick's Voy.* 6 Twelue yeares agoe the great Magoll a More king of Agray and Delay..became the gouernour of all..Cambaia. **1613** PURCHAS *Pilgrimage* (1614) 542 The Mogol or Mogor. **1634** SIR T. HERBERT *Trav.* 29 These Moguls or Emperours of East India. **1710** ADDISON *Whig Exam.* No. 5 ¶4 Turks and Indians, who have no laws above the Will of a Grand Signior or a Mogul. *c* **1796** T. TWINING *Trav. Amer.* (1894) 92 When I was at Dehli the Great Moghol..allowed me..to have his name and the date of my reception at his Court engraved on some personal ornament. **1840** DICKENS *Barn. Rudge* iii, But then he awoke out of a dream about picking a lock in the stomach of the Great Mogul. **1876** BANCROFT *Hist. U.S.* III. i. 11 The empire of the Great Mogul.

β. **1588** PARKE tr. *Mendoza's Hist. China* 407 The grand Tartar, or Mogor. *c* **1591** FITCH in Hakluyt *Voy.* (1599) II. I. 254 The people..call him The great Mogor. **1615** *Stow's Ann.* 945 The great Maghoore whome some corruptly call Mogall. *c* **1645** HOWELL *Lett.*, *The Vote* (1650) II. 128 That she may prize his royall favour more Than all the wares fetch'd from the Great Mogor! **1880** R. F. BURTON tr. *Camoens' Lusiad* x. II. 384 The Grand Mogor.

b. *transf.* Also **mogul.** A great personage; an autocratic ruler.

1678 DRYDEN *Kind Keeper* IV. i, Mr. Limberham is the Mogol of the next Mansion. **1754** R. WALL in *Trans. R. Hist. Soc.* (1932) XV. 29 Wen you wil read this scrape, the mogol will bee five or six leagues of going to Granad. **1877** *N.Y. Daily Tribune* 16 Feb. 4/4 John A. Logan is the Head Center, the Hub, the King Pin, the Main Spring, Mogul, and Mugwump of the final plot. **1902** 'MARK TWAIN' in *Harper's Weekly* 6 Dec. 1824/2 My old friend, the great mogul..the station-master, you know. **1928** *Dialect Notes* V. I. 69 *Mogul*, an aristocrat. 'They think they are the *moguls* of this town.' New Mexico. **1957** *Times Lit. Suppl.* 10 May 285/2 Rich but decadent, moguls and hangers-on of the film industry. **1966** T. PYNCHON *Crying of Lot 49* i. 9 One Pierce Inverarity, a California real estate mogul. **1973** *Canad. N. & Q.* Nov. 12 Those who have examined the career of Canada's first 'movie mogul', have not been able to uncover the final chapters of his life. **1974** *Times* 14 Mar. 14/7 A group of cinema moguls asked how she [*sc.* Gertrude Stein] managed to get so much publicity. 'By having a small audience' was the reply.

3. The name of a kind of plum.

1718 MRS. EALES *Receipts* 29 The great white Mogul makes a fine black Plum. **1731** MILLER *Gard. Dict.* s.v. *Prunus*, White Imperial, Bonum Magnum; white Holland or Mogul Plum. **1845** MISS ACTON *Mod. Cookery* 483 Preserve of the Magnum Bonum, or Mogul plum.

4. In full *Mogul engine*, *locomotive*: A locomotive of a peculiar type built for hauling heavy trains.

1884 KNIGHT *Dict. Mech.* Suppl. s.v., The *Mogul* is generally accepted as a type of engine especially adapted to the economical working of heavy-freight traffic. *Ibid.* fig. 1756 Mogul Locomotive. **1885** *Iron* 25 Sept. 281/3 The 'Mogul' engine.

5. *pl.* Playing cards of the best quality (see quots.).

1842 *Bradshaw's Jrnl.* 16 Apr. 371/2 The best cards are called Moguls. **1866** *Stationer & Fancy Trades Reg.* 1 Sept. 939 The different qualities of cards are distinguished as Moguls, Harry's, Highlanders, and Merry Andrews. **1867** *Philol. Soc. Trans.* 71 *Moguls*, so called from the device on the wrappers used for this particular sort of cards; the device being a fancy sketch or picture of the Great Mogul.

B. *adj.* 1. Of, pertaining or relating to, the Moguls, or the Mongol empire in India.

1617 PURCHAS *Pilgrimage* (ed. 3) 609 Wee might seeme to haue spoken sufficiently of the Cambayans alreadie, in our former Mogoll-Relations. **1719** DE FOE *Crusoe* II. (Globe) 568 We thought our selves a Match for the whole ten thousand Mogul Tartars. **1722** tr. *Petis de la Croix's Hist. Genghiz Khan* I. i. 7 Every Mogul Family..were accustom'd the first Day of the Year to celebrate a Feast. **1788** GIBBON *Decl. & F.* lxv. VI. 332 Memorials in the Mogul or Persian language. *Ibid.* 337 In the Mogul empire of the north. **1858** J. B. NORTON *Topics* 38 The old Mogul dynasty. **1903** *Blackw. Mag.* Mar. 317/2 It was here that the later Moghul emperors held their daily court.

2. Denoting works of art, jewels, etc., noted for their richness, produced in India at the time of the Mogul empire.

1921 C. H. SMITH in C. S. Clarke *Indian Drawings* Pref., The other very important Mogul drawings bequeathed to the Museum by Lady Wantage. **1931** A. U. DILLEY *Oriental Rugs & Carpets* v. 140 The Mogul animal rugs of India, equally with the flower rugs, are photographic. **1958** A. RIDLER in C. Williams *Image of City* p. xxi, He seemed so full of the energy of thought that even the most lack lustre of his listeners felt themselves, for the time being, 'mogul diamonds'. **1963** S. C. WELCH *Art Mughal India* 12 We know dozens of Mughal Old Masters by name and style... Several of the qualities we find in Mughal art (romanticism, Indian-ness, and poetry) have frequently been denied it by critics. **1963** *Times* 20 Apr. 10/4 A sabre set with emeralds, the hilt carved in seventeenth-century Moghul jade. **1969** *Cultural News from India* Nov. 30 She illustrated her theory with slides of Moghul and Rajasthani miniature painting. **1969** *Times* 25 Nov. 14/6 (Advt.), Four 17th century Mughal carpets. **1973** *New Society* 10 May 292/1 Western art influenced mughal artists.

Hence †**Mogulish** *a.* = MOGUL *a.*; '**Mogulship**, used ironically.

1719 J. T. PHILIPPS tr. *Thirty-four Confer.* 331 His two Sons..undertook to defeat all the Mogulish Army. **1851** H. MELVILLE *Moby Dick* III. xxii. 148 Before I saw it off..I must call his old Mogulship, and see whether the length will be all right. **1876** C. M. YONGE *Womankind* xxiii. 197 The mistress..viewing their summons to a parent's sick-bed..as an injury to her own Great Mogulship.

mogul ('məʊgəl), *sb.*[2] [? ad. S. German dial. *mugel*, *mugl* in same sense.] A bump on a ski-slope. Also *attrib.* Hence '**moguled** *a.*

1961 R. SKEPPER *Tackle Ski-ing this Way* iii. 45 Moguls are large bumps, and occur most frequently in couloirs, on shoulders, in gullies, or very steep hills. They are usually caused by the piste skier's steep complex... There is usually a mogul passage on every difficult run. **1965** *Daily*

Express 26 Oct. 23/6 Crowded pistes and modern technique (a series of closely linked turns near the fall-line) results [*sic*] in large areas of bumps, or moguls, on the steeper portions of the piste. **1969** M. HELLER *Ski* xv. 199 Closely related to mogul slopes is the heavily rutted traverse. **1970** *Times* 18 Dec. 20/2 At the crack of dawn the snowmobiles would be at work, compacting new snow and planing off exaggerated moguls (bumps). **1972** DEAN & SMITH *Wisconsin* 161/1 Every Wisconsin ski area has something unique to offer... Some even boast of 'friendly moguls'. **1975** *Friends* (U.S.) Mar. 25 'Hot' skiing over steep and moguled terrain.

Moguntine (məʊˈgʌntɪn), *a.* [f. L. *Moguntia*, ancient name of Mainz.] Of or pertaining to the city of Mainz in Germany (see quots.).

1641 (*title*) Looke about You.—The Plot of Contzen, the Moguntine Jesuite, to cheate a Church of the Religion established therein. **1656** BLOUNT *Glossogr.*, *Moguntine*, belonging to Moguntia or Mentz a City in Germany, where Printing was first invented by John Gutenburg an. 1440. **1775** ASH, *Moguntine*,.. belonging to the art of printing. [In recent Dicts.]

Moh: see MOHS.

‖**moha** (ˈməʊhə). Also **mohar**. [Of obscure origin; in Fr. *moha de Hongrie*.] A variety of Italian millet.

1855 OGILVIE Suppl., *Moha*. **1864** *Chamb. Encycl.* VI. 461/1 German Millet, or Mohar (*Setaria Germanica*). **1866** *Treas. Bot.*, Moha, *Setaria italica*.

mohair (ˈməʊhɛə(r)), *sb.* (and *a.*) Forms: 6 **mocayare, moochary, mockaire**, 7 **mohaire, moher, moehair, mowhayre**, 7–8 **moyhair, mowhair**, 7– **mohair**. [Ultimately a. Arabic *muχayyar* cloth of goats' hair (lit. 'select, choice', pa. pple. of *χayyara* to choose). The history of the forms is obscure, the word having come into Eng. by more than one channel. The present form is prob. due to association with *hair*.

The It. *moccaiaro* (*moccaiorro, moccaiardo*) and F. *mocayart, moncayart*, which come nearest of the European forms to the Arabic original, were early applied to textile fabrics of different material (see MOCKADO). In the 17th c. the Eng. word was adopted in Fr. as *mouaire*, now spelt *moire* (see MOIRE); the Sp. *moarre, muer*, It. *moarro*, G. *mohr*, seem to be adoptions from Fr.]

1. Properly, a kind of fine camlet made from the hair of the Angora goat, sometimes watered. Also, yarn made from this hair. In modern use often applied to a fabric in imitation of the true mohair, in the 18th c. wholly of silk, but now usually of a mixture of wool and cotton. ***mohair glacé***: see quot. 1884.

1570 G. CAMPION in *Hakluyt's Voy.* (1599) II. I. 127 There is also cotten wooll,.. chamlets, mocayares. **1584** W. BARRET *Ibid.* 273 Cloth of Wooll, Karsies, Mockaires, Chamlets, and all sortes of Silke. **1588** T. HICKOCK tr. *C. Frederick's Voy.* 6 b, Gerdles of wooll and bumbast black and red like to Moocharies. **1619** PURCHAS *Microcosmus* xxvii. 269 The new devised names of Stuffes and Colours,.. Veletato, Philizello,.. Mohaire. **1640** in Noorthouck *London* (1773) 840/2 Yarn, grogram or moyhair, the cwt. gt. five score 1*s.* 6*d.* **1641** Silke-mohers [see DURETTO]. **1668** T. ROKEBY *Let.* 28 Sept. in *Mem.* (Surtees) 16 A mohaire with a small weale [for a gown]. **1702–3** in Willis & Clark *Cambridge* (1886) II. 211 Crimson Morella mohair for the Curtains. **1727** W. MATHER *Yng. Man's Comp.* 409 They import.. Camblets, Grograms, Grogram Yarn, Mohairs of Angor. **1735** POPE *Ep. Lady* 170 She.. Observes how much a Chintz exceeds Mohair. **1742–3** MRS. DELANY in *Life & Corr.* (1861) II. 204 Let my room be hung with mohair instead of paper. **1831** A. S. MACKENZIE *Year in Spain* II. 214 A petticoat of mohair. **1884** KNIGHT *Dict. Mech.* Suppl., *Mohair Glacé*, a goat's-hair and cotton French dress goods. **1884** *West. Daily Press* 13 June 7/6 Mohair is a more ordinary material, serving for early morning outdoor wear.

2. A garment made of such material.

1673 LD. FOUNTAINHALL in M. P. Brown *Suppl. Decis.* (1826) III. 3, I have observed the most part of people to have ventured upon moyhairs. **1751** CHESTERF. *Lett.* (1792) III. 166, I could find no mohairs in London, that exactly answered that description. **1861** *Eng. Wom. Dom. Mag.* III. 69/1 A grey mohair is very pretty made with two fluted flounces at the bottom of the skirt.

3. The hair of the Angora goat.

1753 HANWAY *Trav.* I. v. lxx. 317 *note*, Mohair from turkey.. is from 2*s.* 6*d.* to 12*s.* the pound. **1878** *Encycl. Brit.* XVI. 544/2 The first importation of mohair from the Cape [of Good Hope], made in 1862, amounted to 1036 lb. **1879** *Cassell's Techn. Educ.* IV. 261/2 The woolly hair called mohair, which forms the fleece of the Angora goat.

4. *slang.* A soldier's nickname for a civilian.

1785 GROSE *Dict. Vulgar T.*, *Mohair*, a man in the civil line, a townsman, or tradesman, a military term, from the mohair buttons worn by persons of those descriptions or any others not in the army; the buttons of military men being always of metal. [**1822** SCOTT *Nigel* xii, 'I need not speak of it, my lord,' said the man of war; 'the world knows it—all, perhaps, but the men of mohair—the poor sneaking citizens of London.']

5. a. *attrib.* or *adj.* Composed or consisting of mohair.

1640 GLAPTHORNE *Hollander* III. Wks. 1874 I. 113 Moehair peticoates. **1642** *Rates Merchandize* 59 Camel or Mo-hair yarne. **1674** WOOD *Life* (O.H.S.) II. 300 License was given to gent. commoners and commoners to weare silk and mo-haire round caps. *a* **1756** MRS. HAYWOOD *New Present* (1771) 259 Mohair-stuffs may be managed in the same way. **1778** *Eng. Gazetteer* (ed. 2) s.v. *Macclesfield*, Its chief manufacture is mohair buttons. **1861** W. FAIRBAIRN *Addr. to Brit. Assoc.* p. lxi, Fancy or mixed goods from alpaca and mohair wool.

b. *spec. Comb.*: **mohair braid**, 'worsted braid used for binding garments' (*Cent. Dict.* 1890); **mohair goat**, the Angora goat; **mohair lustre** (see quot.); **mohair-shell** (see quot.).

1882 CAULFEILD & SAWARD *Dict. Needlework* 350 *Mohair or Russian Braids. **1880** *Daily News* 17 Sept. 6/2 The Angora or *mohair goat. **1884** KNIGHT *Dict. Mech.* Suppl., **Mohair Luster*, a black dress goods, resembling alpaca, consisting of mohair woven with cotton warp. **1753** CHAMBERS *Cycl. Supp.*, *Moire*,.. the *mohair shell,.. a peculiar species of voluta, which seems of a closely and finely reticulated texture, and resembles on the surface a piece of mohair.

Also **ˈmohaired, ˈmohairy** *adjs.*

1873 L. TROUBRIDGE *Jrnl.* 2 Oct. in *Life amongst Troubridges* (1966) viii. 63 An ancient mohairy sort of dress. **1965** *New Statesman* 15 Oct. 576/2 Part of the Piccadilly's audience.. mohaired, razor-cut and agog.

Mohammed, Mohammedan, etc.: see MUHAMMAD, MUHAMMADAN, and related words.

Mohaque, mohar: see MOHAWK, MOHA.

‖**moharra** (məʊˈhærə). Also **mojarra**. [American Sp. *mojarra*.] **a.** Any fish of the family *Gerridæ*, common on the coasts of the Southern United States. **b.** A Californian surf-fish, *Hypsurus caryi*. **c.** The cow-pilot, *Pomacentrus saxatilis*.

1845 STORER *Synopsis Fishes N. Amer.* in *Mem. Amer. Acad.* II. 336 Gerres Brasilianus, Cuv... Called, at Porto Rico, 'Moharra'. **1882** JORDAN & GILBERT *Synopsis Fishes N. Amer.* 611 *Pomacentrus saxatilis*.. Cow-pilot; Mojarra. **1884** JORDAN in Goode, etc. *Nat. Hist. Aquat. Anim.* 276 The names 'Minny', 'Sparada', and 'Moharra', are also applied to the smaller species [of 'perches'] northward. *Ibid.* 278 *Hypsurus Caryi*.. is known as 'Moharra' to the Portuguese at Monterey; elsewhere it is a 'Perch'. *Ibid.* 279 The Moharra Family—*Gerridæ*.

‖**Moharram** (məʊˈhʌrəm). Also 7 **muharam**, 8 **muharrem**, 8–9 **mohurrum**, 9 **moharran, muharram**. [Arab. *muḥarram* (lit. 'sacred').]

a. The first month of the Muslim year, containing thirty days. **b.** An annual celebration in this month; originally a period of mourning observed by the Shiites in memory of the 'martyrdom' of Hasan and Husain; in India the ceremonies are now rather of a festal than a mournful character, and are shared in not only by Muslims generally, but even by many Hindus.

[**1615** BEDWELL *Arab. Trudg.* N 1 b, *Moharram, Muharam*,.. the name of the first moneth of the Arabian Kalendar, containing 30 daies.] **1861** J. T. WHEELER *Madras in Olden Time* II. 347 The time came round for the Mussulman feast called 'Hossein Jossen'.. better known as the Mohurrum. **1882** FLOYER *Unexpl. Baluchistan* 80 The preparations for the Moharram were extensive.

mohaut, variant of MAHOE[1], MAHOUT.

Mohave (məʊˈhɑːvɪ). Also **Mohawa, Mojave**. [Native name, f. *aha* water + *makave* beside.]

A. *sb.* A Yuman Indian people along the Colorado river; a member of this people; also, their language. **B.** *adj.* Of or pertaining to this people.

1831 J. O. PATTIE *Personal Narr.* 93 We resumed our march, and on the 6th arrived at another village of Indians called Mohawa. **1853** L. SITGREAVES *Rep. Expedition Zuñi & Colorado Rivers* 18 The appearance of the Mohaves is striking, from their unusual stature, the men averaging at least six feet in height. **1858** *Harper's Mag.* Sept. 463/1 When the trading was concluded, the Mojave people sauntered about the camp. **1877** *Mag. Amer. Hist.* I. 153 Languages, with a sonorous, sweet, soft, and vocalic utterance,.. are the Mohave, Hualapai, [etc.]. **1949** M. MEAD *Male & Female* vi. 129 The conspicuous transvestitism of the Mohave Indians. **1949** *Word* V. 268 (*title*) Mohave voice and speech mannerisms. **1955** W. GADDIS *Recognitions* I. i. 45 The sermon, meanwhile, had progressed from vivisection to the Mojave Indians. *Ibid.* 46 Among the Mojaves, it is believed that everyone dead under the doctor's hand falls under his power in the next life. **1963** ERVIN & MILLER in J. A. Fishman *Readings Sociol. of Lang.* (1968) 85 The Mohave claim newborn children can understand speech. **1965** *Language* XLI. 305 Yuman shows various reflexes: Mohave, Cocopa, and Kiliwa have /i/. **1970** *Ibid.* XLVI. 538 There is some evidence in Mohave for contrastive pitch.

Mohawk (ˈməʊhɔːk). Also 7–8 **Mohock, Mohauk**; and in various forms purporting to represent the native pronunciation, as 7 **Mowha(w)ke, Mohaque, Mauquawog, Maquaw, Moqua**, 7–8 **Maqua**. [North American Indian. The spelling MOHOCK, q.v., is now appropriated to a transferred use that survives only *Hist.*]

1. One of a tribe of North American Indians, formerly supposed to be cannibals.

The Mohawks originally inhabited the neighbourhood of the Mohawk River, in what is now the State of New York. They were the most powerful of the Six Nations or Iroquois.

1638 P. VINCENT *True Relat.* in *Mass. Hist. Coll.* Ser. III. (1837) VI. 40 He went with forty men to the Mohocks, which are cruel, bloody cannibals. **1651** *Plymouth Col. Rec.* (1855) II. 169 A request was made the last winter by a messenger from the French at Canada to assist them against the Mowhakes. **1676** I. MATHER *K. Philip's War* (1862) 168 The Indian affirmed, that those Indians who are known by the name of *Mauquawogs* (or *Mohawks*, i.e. Man eaters) had lately fallen upon Philip. **1693** (*title*) A Narrative of an Attempt made by the French of Canada upon the Mohaque's Country. **1709** S. SEWALL *Diary* 9 Aug., Col. Hobbey's Regiment musters, and the Govr. orders the Maquas to be there and see them. **1778** WOLCOT (P. Pindar) *Poetic Epist. Reviewers* Wks. 1816 I. 3 With hatchets, scalping knives in shape of pens, To bid, like Mohocks, hapless authors die. **1819** REES *Cycl.* XXIII, *Mohawks*, an Indian Nation, acknowledged by the other tribes of the Six Nations to be the true old heads of the confederacy. **1845** *Encycl. Metrop.* XXI. 114/2 The appearance of a single Mohawk on the hills was sufficient to throw into alarm the Indian villages in New England.

b. ***Mohawks' corn***: a variety of maize.

1678 WINTHROP in *Phil. Trans.* XII. 1065 In the pure Northerly parts, they have a peculiar kind called Mohauks Corn, which though planted in June, will be ripe in season.

2. The language of the Mohawks.

1754 EDWARDS *Freed. Will* IV. xiii. (1831) 404 The question is not whether what is said be.. Latin, French, English or Mohawk. **1787** *Mohawk Prayer Bk.* (title-p.), A new edition, to which is added the Gospel according to St. Mark, translated into Mohawk by Captn. Joseph Brant, an Indian of the Mohawk Nation. **1873** R. BROWN *Races Mankind* I. 243 Mr. Jones expresses his belief that in Canada there are only two distinct Indian languages—the Ojebway and the Mohawk.

¶ **3.** Used by mistake for AMOK 1. *Obs.*

1772–84 *Cook's Voy.* (1790) I. 288 Most of our readers must have heard of the Mohawks, and these [the Indians of Batavia] are the people who are so denominated, from a corruption of the word amock. **1797** *Encycl. Brit.* (ed. 3) XII. 439/1 If the officer takes one of these *amocks* or *mohawks*.. alive, he has a considerable reward.

4. *Skating.* (See quot. 1892.)

1880 VANDERVELL & WITHAM *Figure-Skating* (ed. 3) 80 This change.. was last year introduced into the Club figures on ice, and christened by the name of 'Mohawk'. **1892** MONIER-WILLIAMS, etc. *Figure-Skating* 60 A Mohawk is simply a step or stroke from any edge in one direction to the same edge on the other foot in an opposite direction... To make an Inside forward Mohawk, the skater must [etc.].

5. *attrib.* and *adj.*, as in ***Mohawk language, nation***, etc. **Mohawk tassel** (see quot. 1891).

1753 CHAMBERS *Cycl. Supp.* s.v. *Mohauks corn*, This Mokauk kind [of maiz] need not bee sown before June. **1763** WHITAKER *Serm.* 30 June (1767) 44 This Joseph is a Chief of the Mohawk Nation. **1797** *Encycl. Brit.* (ed. 3) I. 562/1 He ..spoke well the Mohock language. **1878** (*title*) Mohawk minstrels' annual of dramas, dialogues, and drolleries. **1891** *Syd. Soc. Lex.*, *Mohawk-tassel*, the *Eupatorium purpureum*.

Mohawk, mohdi: see MOHOCK, MAHDI.

mohcock, var. MOCOCK.

mohe, obs. f. MAY *v.*[1]; var. MOWE *Obs.*

mohel (ˈməʊ(h)əl). Also **Mohel**. [Heb. *mōhēl*.] A Jewish official who performs the rite of circumcision.

1650 E. CHILMEAD tr. *Leon Modena's Hist. Rites of Jews* IV. viii. 203 They also use to make choice of a Circumciser, which they call.. Mohel. **1676** L. ADDISON *Present State of Jews* (ed. 2) 59 The chief Officer at Circumcision is the Mohel. **1753** *Jewish Ritual* 19 The Operator (called the Mohel) makes use of a sharp, double edged knife... To assist the Mohel or Circumciser, is counted a meritorious Office. **1903** *Jewish Encycl.* IV. 95/2 As a rule, the wife of the godfather carries the child in and hands it to the mohel. **1932** A. Z. IDELSOHN *Jewish Liturgy* xiii. 166 The *Mohel*—Circumciser—places the child upon the 'chair of Elijah' and recites. *Ibid.* 167 Then the Mohel recites the benediction over wine and another benediction. **1973** *Jewish Chron.* 19 Jan. 11/2 [Al Jolson's] father was the local mohel and he circumcised me. **1974** *Observer* (Colour Suppl.) 10 Nov. 34/1 By Jewish law, a boy should be circumcised on the eighth day after birth... The devout treat it as a religious ceremony, with a *mohel* officiating and giving a blessing. A *mohel* is a trained and registered circumciser and there are a few score of them in Britain.

moher, obs. form of MOHAIR; variant of MOHUR.

Mohican, Mohegan (məʊˈhiːkən, -gən), *a.* and *sb.* Also 8 **Mohigon, Mohickon**, 9 **Mohiccon, Mohigan, Moheecan**; also in renderings of the native form, 8 **Muhhekaneew**, 9 **Mahicanni, Mo-hee-con-neugh**. [From the native name.]

A. *adj.* **a.** Of or pertaining to the Mohicans.

1643 *Mass. Bay Rec.* (1853) II. 46 Concerning any advice ..about the Nariganset or Mohegen sachems and their people. **1648** T. SHEPARD *Clear Sun-Shine of Gospel upon Indians New-Eng.* 26 The Mohegen Counseller.. is counted the wisest Indian in the Country. **1766** C. BEATTY *Two Months' Tour* (1768) 109 Thirty or forty of the Mohigon Indians. **1778** T. HUTCHINS *Topogr. Descr. Virginia* etc. 66 Mohickons. **1788** J. EDWARDS (*title*) Observations on the Language of the Muhhekaneew Indians. *Ibid.* 6 The analogy between the Mohegan, the Shawanee, and the Chippewau languages. **1881** *Encycl. Brit.* XII. 831/1 The Pequod and Mohegan tribes were amongst the largest and most powerful. **1884** G. SMITH *Short Hist. Chr. Missions* II. xii. 136 In 1661–63 the Moheecan Bible, the first Bible printed in America, was printed by him [*sc.* John Eliot].

b. Of a hairstyle, resembling that worn by the Mohicans, in which the head is shaved except for a strip of hair from the middle of the forehead to the back of the neck.

1960 *News Chron.* 25 Mar. 7/5 James Greenwood, of York,.. had his hair cut in Mohican style for his thirteenth birthday. **1960** *Guardian* 27 Sept. 2/4 A Lowestoft boy.. had a 'Mohican' haircut on Saturday and then went back to the barber to have the remaining strip of hair cut. **1965**

Evening Standard 29 Oct. 6/6 A man with a Mohican hair-cut.

B. *sb.*

1. One of a warlike tribe of North American Indians of the Algonquin stock, formerly occupying the western part of Connecticut and Massachusetts. (See also quot. 1819). Also, the language of this tribe.

1788 J. Edwards *Observ. Lang. Muhhekaneew Indians* 5 They are by the Anglo-Americans called Mohegans. *Ibid.* 11 The Mohegans have no adjectives in all their language. **1819** Rees *Cycl.* XXIII, *Mohiccons*, a tribe of Indians whose habitations lie on a branch of the Susquehannah... Also an Indian tribe in the N.W. territory, which inhabits near Sandusky. **1826** J. F. Cooper (*title*) The Last of the Mohicans. **1836** *Pop. Encycl.* IV. 73/2 *note*, The word *kthuwhunin*, in Mohegan. **1873** R. Brown *Races Mankind* I. 225 The Mo-hee-con-neughs (or Mohicans) are now almost extinct.

†**2.** (See quot.) *Obs.*

1848 *Tait's Mag.* May 309 A Mohican, in Cadonian phraseology, is a tremendously heavy man, who rides five or six miles [in an omnibus] for sixpence.

3. Phr. ***the last of the Mohicans***, the title of a novel (1826) by J. F. Cooper (1789–1851), used allusively to designate the sole survivors of a noble class or race. Also *fig.*

1832 *Boston Transcript* 3 Apr. 2/1 We have seen the last of the Mohigans and the last of the cocked-hats, and we pray that we may be able to say, on the morrow we have seen the last of the snow-storms. **1894** A. Lang *Cock Lane* 136 A hundred years after the blue stockings looked on Johnson as the last survivor, the last of the Mohicans of superstition, the Psychical Society can collect some 400 cases of haunted houses in England. **1922** Joyce *Ulysses* 644 Fourpence (the amount he deposited unobtrusively in four coppers, literally the last of the Mohicans). **1946** H. Howe *We Happy Few* 7 You can't pay attention to a thing that John Calcott says because he is the perfect product of the school—our own special Last of the Mohicans.

Mohini-attam (məʊ'hiːniːætæm). Also (as one word) **Mohiniattam**. [f. *Mohini* the name of the supreme seductress of Hindu mythology (f. Skr. *muh* confuse, bewilder) + Tamil *attam* dance.] The name of an Indian dance for women showing the influence of the Kathakali school and noted for its gentle and graceful style.

1948 G. Venkatachalam *Dance in India* xii. 109 Mohini Attam.. has its own style and technique, its peculiar idioms and expressions, coloured considerably by Kathakali. **1950** K. Ambrose *Classical Dance & Costumes India* 11 *Mohiniattam*.. was prevalent in Malabar right up to the late 'twenties, and it is very largely composed of a fusion of the Tanjore temple-dance and the *Kathakali* dance style of Malabar. **1953** F. Bowers *Dance in India* 69 Mohini Attam was performed exclusively by women and was largely used by prostitutes to attract patrons. Because of its immoral associations, Mohini Attam fell into great disfavor and declined. **1967** Singha & Massey *Indian Dances* xii. 115 Mohini came to be synonymous with the essence of feminine beauty and allurement, and Mohini Attam is a dance which displays just such qualities. It is a solo dance, reserved exclusively for women... Mohini Attam is for the most part nritta although abhinaya is by no means absent. **1969** *Cultural News from India* Nov. 13 Kanak Rele.. has done deep research into South Indian dance... Her repertoire consists of three major items: Mohini-attam; Kansa-natakam and pure Kathakali. **1971** *Femina* (Bombay) 2 Apr. 11/1 She was also one of the very first women in our time to learn Kathakali and Mohini Attam.

‖**moho**¹ ('məhə). [Maori.] A ralline bird, *Notornis Mantelli*, of New Zealand. See also notornis and takahe.

1848 R. Taylor in *Proc. Zool. Soc.* (1850) xviii. 211 *Moho* Rail, colour black, said to be a wingless bird as large as a fowl ..; it is nearly exterminated by the cat. **1850** Mantell in *Proc. Zool. Soc.* xviii. 211 According to the native traditions, a large Rail was contemporary with the Moa... It was known to the North Islanders by the name of 'Moho'. **1865** Gould *Handbk. Birds Austral.* II. 576 *Notornis Mantelli* Owen. Moho.

‖**moho**² ('məʊhəʊ). [Hawaiian.] A genus of meliphagine birds peculiar to the Sandwich Islands, named in 1831 by Lesson; a bird of this genus.

[**1782** W. Ellis *Voy. Capts. Cook & Clerke* 1776–80 II. 156 A black and yellow bird called mohò.] **1890** in *Century Dict.* **1904** *Blackw. Mag.* Feb. 245 This moho feeds much also on the nectar of flowers.

Moho³ ('məʊhəʊ). *Geol.* Also **moho**. [Abbrev. of *Mohorovičić*.] = Mohorovičić discontinuity.

1956 *Adv. Geophysics* III. 118 The boundary.. is now called the Mohorovičić discontinuity (vulgarly 'The Moho'). **1959** *Daily Tel.* 21 Apr. 13/1 The bore must itself be several miles deep to penetrate to the mysterious 'moho' and find out what the bulk of the world is really made of. **1960** *New Scientist* 19 May 1278/3 It is.. generally accepted that both the density and the seismic wave velocities change at the Moho. **1972** *Nature* 15 Dec. 383/3 The graben gives clear Moho refractions with normal upper mantle velocities.

moho, variant of mahoe¹.

Mohock ('məʊhɒk). *Hist.* Also 8 **mohack**, 9 **mohawk**. [Transferred use of *mohock* Mohawk; now differentiated in spelling.]

1. One of a class of aristocratic ruffians who infested the streets of London at night in the early years of the 18th century.

1711–12 Swift *Jrnl. to Stella* 8 Mar., Did I tell you of a race of rakes, called the Mohocks, that play the devil about this town every night, slit people's noses, and beat them, etc. **1711–12** Hearne *Collect.* 30 Mar. (O.H.S.) III. 326 A certain barbarous Sect of Persons arose lately in London who distinguish themselves by the Name of Mohocks. **1717** Prior *Alma* iii. 231 But give him Port, and potent Sack; From Milk-sop He starts up Mohack. **1758** Chesterf. *Let.* 23 May *Misc. Wks.* (1777) II. 499 The other [lie] that Prince Eugene intended to murder lord Oxford, by employing a set of people called Mohocks, which society, by the way, never existed. **1789** M. Madan tr. *Persius* (1795) 111 *note*, Nero.. was a kind of Mohock in his diversions. **1829** Lytton *Devereux* ii. xi, A large band of those young men, who, under the name of Mohawks scoured the town nightly. **1894** J. Knight *Garrick* vii. 111 Garrick [had] an experience of stage mohocks.

†**2.** (Meaning unknown.)

1772 Graves *Spir. Quix.* x. xxiv, Bob Tench.. had always a little phial of Fryar's Balsam in his pocket, some.. court-plaister, as well as his cork-screw and mohock.

3. *attrib.* and *adj.*

1712 Steele *Spect.* No. 324 ¶1 A Set of Men.. who have lately erected themselves into a Nocturnal Fraternity, under the Title of the *Mohock Club*. **1882** *Punch* 18 Feb. 83/2 The Mohock Revival.

Hence '**Mohock** *v. trans.*, to assail or maltreat in the manner of Mohocks; '**Mohockism**, the practices or the spirit of the Mohocks.

1718 *Entertainer* No. 12. 76 We love Mischief for Mischief's sake, and can.. break windows,.. knock down Old Women,.. and Mohock the Tories. **1882** *Punch* 18 Feb. 83/2 That ancient form of ruffianism known as Mohockism appears to have broken out with more than ancient severity in various parts of London. **1883** L. S. Wingfield *A. Rowe* I. ii. 40 He exceeded in luxury and Mohockism that pair of immortal rowdies.

Mohock, obs. form of Mohawk.

mohoe, variant of mahoe¹.

mohogena, -g(g)on(e)y, obs. ff. mahogany.

mohol(l, obs. variant forms of mahal.

mohonono (məʊhəʊ'nəʊnəʊ). *S. Afr.* [ad. Lozi *muHonono*.] An evergreen tree with grey-green leaves, *Terminalia sericea*, of the family Combretaceæ, native to southern Africa; also called Transvaal silver leaf and vaalboom.

1864 T. Baines *Explor. S.-W. Afr.* xx. 441 Passing through a thick mopane and mohonono forest, [we] out-spanned about 7 p.m. in a more open flat. **1878** K. Johnston *Africa* xxiv. 427 The silvery mohonono.. is in form like the cedar of Lebanon. **1949** K. L. Simms *Sun-Drenched Veld* iii. 33 There is.. the cedar-spread of the mohonono.

mohoohoo (mə'huːhuː). Also **mahoohoo, mohohoo, mohohu, muhuhu, monooho(o), muchocho**. [Sechuana.] The white rhinoceros, *Ceratotherium simus*, found in central Africa and Zululand.

1835 A. Smith *Diary* 11 July (1940) II. 107 The Baquana say that two kinds [of rhinoceros] are only in this country. The black, which they call *muchli* and the white *mohohoo*. **1842** R. Moffat *Missionary Labours & Scenes S. Afr.* xxvii. 461 The mohohu, the largest species [of rhinoceros], has been known even to kill the elephant, by thrusting the horn into its ribs. **1849** A. Smith *Illustr. Zool. S. Afr.: Mammalia* plate 19 Localities abounding in grass are therefore the haunts of the Mohoohoo. **1850** R. G. Cumming *Five Yrs. Hunter's Life S. Afr.* xii. 77/2 With considerable difficulty we separated the horn of the muchocho from the skin by means of a long sharp knife. **1856** C. J. Andersson *Lake Ngami* xxx. 387 The common white rhinoceros.. called Monoohoo by the Bechuanas. **1866** *Chambers's Encycl.* VIII. 236/2 The White R[hinoceros].. or Muchuco, or Monooho, is the largest of the well-ascertained African species. **1875** W. H. Drummond *Large Game & Nat. Hist. S. & S.-E. Afr.* 84 *Rhinoceros simus*, the mohohu of the Bechuanas. **1879** E. P. Wright *Animal Life* 141 It [*sc.* the white rhinoceros] is called by the Bechuanans, Mahoohoo, and is considered by them to be one of the original animals of their country. **1884** J. Mackenzie *Day-Dawn in Dark Places* 189 It is said the flesh of the mohuhu, or white rhinoceros is very good. **1894** R. Lydekker *Royal Nat. Hist.* II. 480 The individuals exhibiting this form being known to the Bechuanas by the name of mohohu.

mohor, mohout, var. ff. mhorr, mahout.

Mohorovičić discontinuity (məʊhəʊ'rəʊvɪtʃɪtʃ). *Geol.* Also **Mohorovicic discontinuity**. [f. the name of A. *Mohorovičić* (1857–1936), Yugoslav seismologist.] The discontinuity between the earth's crust and the mantle which is believed to exist at a depth of about 10–12 kilometres under the ocean beds and 40–50 kilometres under the continents.

1936 J. B. Macelwane in Macelwane & Sohon *Introd. Theoret. Seismol.* I. viii. 204 We shall speak of this major boundary above which the various surficial layers lie as the Mohorovičić discontinuity, after A. Mohorovičić who discovered it. **1956** [see Moho³]. **1958** [see mantle *sb.* 11]. **1971** I. G. Gass et al. *Understanding Earth* iii. 58/2 On the basis of seismic velocities, the mantle is usually divided into three regions—from the Mohorovicic discontinuity down to 400 km, from 400 to 1000 km, and from 1000 km to the core boundary.

mohr, variant of mhorr.

mohr, mohra, var. forms of mohur, mogra.

Mohs (məʊz). The name of Friedrich *Mohs* (see mohsine), used *attrib.* and in the possessive (chiefly in ***Mohs('s) scale***) with reference to a scale of hardness he devised in which ten reference minerals that include very soft and very hard ones are assigned values of one to ten in order of increasing hardness.

The ten minerals of the scale are: 1, talc; 2, gypsum; 3, calcite; 4, fluor-spar; 5, apatite; 6, orthoclase; 7, quartz; 8, topaz; 9, corundum; 10, diamond.

1879 *Mineral Mag.* II. 265 Its density is 1·0025; hardness between 1 and 2 of Mohs's scale. **1897** *Amer. Jrnl. Sci.* CLIV. 409 We shall describe only a preliminary series of tests with the minerals of the Mohs scale. **1951** D. Tabor *Hardness of Metals* i. 2 The Mohs hardness scale has been widely used by mineralogists and lapidaries. **1962** R. Webster *Gems* I. iv. 74 The hardness of beryl is $7\frac{1}{2}$ on Mohs's scale. **1974** *Sci. Amer.* Aug. 64 Each material in the Mohs scale, up to Mohs 9 (corundum), is about 1·2 times as hard as the preceding material. Thus the scale is almost logarithmic from Mohs 1 through Mohs 9, a range that includes all but a few substances.

¶ Erron. written as *Moh* (or *moh*).

1903 J. E. Marr *Agric. Geol.* ii. 28 Moh's scale of hardness. **1934** J. A. Perry *Chem. Engineers' Handbk.* xvi. 1558 The hardness of a material as measured by the moh scale is not always a criterion of its resistance to crushing. **1969** B. R. Schlenker *Introd. Materials Sci.* iv. 69 A Moh's hardness determination set of minerals.

mohsine ('məʊsaɪn). *Min.* [Named after Friedrich *Mohs* a German mineralogist (1773–1839): see -ine⁴.] = löllingite.

1843 E. J. Chapman *Pract. Min.* 138 Mohsine... This substance having no general name, I have bestowed upon it that of the able and celebrated Mineralogist by whom it was first distinguished.

mohsite ('məʊsaɪt). *Min.* [Formed as prec. + -ite.] = ilmenite.

1827 A. Levy in *Phil. Mag.* Ser. ii. I. 221 Some crystals belonging.. to a new species, which.. I propose to call Mohsite, in honour of Professor Mohs. **1837** Dana *Min.* 385 Mohsite.. is supposed to have come from Dauphiny.

moht, obs. form of *might*, pa. pple. of may *v.*¹

mohua, mohur, var. mahwa.

mohuhu, var. mohoohoo.

Mohummadan, variant of Muhammadan.

‖**mohur** ('məʊhə(r)). Forms: 7 **moor**, 8 **muhr, mohr**, 9 **moher, more, muhar**, 8– **mohur**. [Pers. *muhr*, primarily seal, seal ring, cogn. w. Skr. *mudrā* seal.] A gold coin, originally Persian, but used in India from the 16th c. onward. Subsequently, 'the official name of the chief gold coin of British India' (Yule), weighing 180 grains troy, and containing 165 grains of pure gold; its value was 15 rupees. Usually ***gold mohur***.

1696 Ovington *Voy. Suratt* 219 The Gold Moor, or Gold Roupie, is valued generally at 14 of Silver; and the Silver Roupie at Two Shillings Three Pence. **1753** Hanway *Trav.* (1762) I. v. lxiv. 293 Muhr ashressie, or treble ducat of 6 mildenaer Value 6 [English crowns]. **1763** Scrafton *Indostan* (1770) 218 The Colonel.. sent.. a present of five hundred gold mohurs [*foot-note*, about £1000 sterling]. **1776** *Trial Jos. Fowke*, etc. *Depos.* 17/1, 15000 rupees in mohurs. **1796** Jane Austen *Sense & Sens.* (1879) 42 Nabobs, gold mohrs, and palanquins. **1801** *Encycl. Brit.* (ed. 3) Suppl. II. 265/1 *Moher*, in Bengal, a gold coin, worth about 33 shillings. **1827** D. Johnson *Ind. Field Sports* 175 A Gold Mohur (value two pounds). **1831** Trelawny *Adv. Younger Son* lxvii, I contrived to realize a few bags of gold mores, and rupees. **1849** E. B. Eastwick *Dry Leaves* 201 An offering of one hundred gold muhars (one hundred and fifty pounds).

attrib. **1859** Lang *Wand. India* 9 The good players are playing high. Gold mohur points.

Mohurrum, variant of Moharram.

mohw, obs. variant of maugh (a male relative).

mohwa, variant of mahwa.

Moi ('məʊiː), *a.* and *sb.* [Native name.] **A.** *adj.* Of or pertaining to a people of Indo-Australoid origin who were among the original inhabitants of Vietnam and are now found in the Southern mountain region (see quot. 1959). **B.** *sb.* **a.** The name of this people. **b.** A member of this people. **c.** The name of their language. Cf. Montagnard 1 b.

1845 *Encycl. Metrop.* XVI. 780/2 The southern branches of those mountains, and the long ridge which divides Annam from Kambója are inhabited by the Múóng and Moï, or Ké-moïs tribes, whose language also differs from that of the lowlanders. **1853** J. R. Logan in *Jrnl. Indian Archipelago* VII. 36 The Moi or Ka-moi.. on the opposite side of the Mekong occupy the broad expansion of the Anam chain towards Kamboja. **1911** *Encycl. Brit.* XIV. 491/1 The population of French Indo-China falls into five chief divisions—the Annamese.. the Khmers.. the Chams.. the Thais.. and the autochthonous tribes classed by the other inhabitants as Mois or Khas ('savages'). **1928** H. Hervey *Trav. French Indo-China* 248 Here the Moi, aboriginal tribes of ancient Chiampa, mingle with the Laotians and the Annamites. **1957** J. Oliver tr. *Riesen's Jungle Mission* i. 14 With her to interpret, I could understand and express the most varied ideas, increasing my French-Moï vocabulary. **1959** E. Brockett tr. *Bertrand's Jungle People* 11 The rather

vague term 'Moi Plateau' is applied to the area bounded to the north by the River Mekong, to the west by the Cambodian jungle and to the east by the mountain range of Annam. *Ibid.* 20 On the floor..a square sod of earth placed on a tin slab formed the traditional Moï hearth. **1961** D. LANCASTER *Emancipation French Indochina* 4 The Mois.. are a handsome, bronze-skinned people akin to the Dyaks of Borneo and the Bataks of Sumatra. **1965** B. NEWMAN *Background to Viet-Nam* vii. 73 Clever French philologists had adapted the Moïs languages to the Latin alphabet, so that reading and writing could be taught. **1968** *Listener* 13 June 760/3 Hill tribes..whom..the Vietnamese call *Moi* ..practise a primitive agriculture, live in thatched long-houses..and are much addicted to gongs, rice wine and animal sacrifice.

moich, see MOCH *a.* Sc.

moicher, obs. variant of MICHER.

moide, obs. form of MUID.

moider ('mɔɪdə(r)), *v. dial.* Also 7- **moyder, moidher**, 8 **moyther**, 9 **moither, moidur, -ar, mither, myther, meyther, meither.** [Of obscure origin; possibly related to MUDDLE *v.*]

1. *trans.* 'To confuse, perplex, bewilder; to worry, bother, fatigue' (E.D.D.). Chiefly *pass.* and *refl.* Also in *passive*, to be overcome or stupefied with heat.

1674 RAY *N.C. Words* 33 Welly *Moyder'd*: almost Distracted. *Cheshire.* **1705** [T. WALKER] *Wit of a Woman* III. 29, I've been strangely moyder'd e're sin 'bout this same News oth' French King. I conno believe 'tis true. **1787** GROSE *Provinc. Gloss.*, *Moider*, to puzzle, perplex. N. *Ibid.*, *Moytherd*, confounded, tired out. Glouc. **1794** J. WILLIAMS *Crying Epistle*, etc. 20 Sure Common Sense is moider'd. **1824** MACTAGGART *Gallovid. Encycl.* 349 One whose intellects are rendered useless, by being in the habit of taking spirituous liquors to excess, is said to be *moidert*. **1848** MRS. GASKELL *Mary Barton* vi. I. 90 Don't mither your mammy for bread, here's a chap as has got some for you. **1860** GEO. ELIOT *Mill on Fl.* III. viii, Scolding her for 'moithering' herself and going about all day without changing her cap. **1863** MRS. GASKELL *Sylvia's L.* II. ix. 156 She's fairly moithered wi' heat an' noise. **1880** MISS BROUGHTON *Sec. Th.* II. v, Moidering his brain with temperance meetings,..temperance papers, and such trash. **1900** M. O'NEILL *Songs Glens Antrim* 4 This livin' air is moithered wi' the bummin' o' the bees.

b. (See quots.)

1847 HALLIWELL, *Mither*, to muffle up; to smother; to encumber. *Northampt.* **1888** *Sheffield Gloss.* s.v., A Derbyshire woman said that a child was 'mythered up in clothing' when it was too much wrapped up.

2. *intr.* 'To talk incoherently or foolishly; to be delirious, to wander or ramble in one's mind'; also, 'to wander *about* aimlessly or confusedly' (E.D.D.).

1839 *Hereford. Gloss.*, *Moither*,..to be weak in mind. **1879** MISS JACKSON *Shropshire Word-bk.*, *Moither, mither*,.. to talk incoherently—to ramble, as in feverish sleep, or delirium. Com. 'I thought the poor child wuz gwein to 'ave a faiver, fur 'er burnt like a coal, an' moithered all night'.

3. *intr.* 'To labour very hard' (Halliwell). Also quasi-*trans.* with *away*.

1828 [CARR] *Craven Gloss.* I. 328 *Moider*,..to labour hard, to toil. **1846** BROCKETT *N.C. Words.* **18..** *Cornh. Mag.* (Ogilvie 1882), She lived only to scrape and hoard, moidering away her loveless life in the futile energies and sordid aims of a miser's wretched pleasure.

Hence '**moidered** *ppl. a.*, confused, stupefied; '**moidering** *ppl. a.*, stupefying, bewildering.

1674 Moidered [cf. MOIDER *v.*]. **1796** MARY LAMB *Let. to Coleridge* 17 Oct. in *Final Mem. C. Lamb* ii. 205 Polly, what are those poor crazy moythered brains of yours thinking of always? **1839** *Hereford. Gloss.*, *Moithering* or *Moithered*, confused, silly; also lightheaded or delirious. **1859** R. F. BURTON *Centr. Afr.* in *Jrnl. Geog. Soc.* XXIX. 163 After midday it would be difficult..to find a chief without the thick voice,..and the moidered manners, which prove that he is either drinking or drunk. **1896** J. K. SNOWDEN *Web of old Weaver* vii. (1897) 78 It was out of these moidering talks with my mother that I gathered nerve enough [etc.]. *a* **1894** J. SHAW in R. Wallace *Country Schoolm.* (1899) 350 *Moidart*, stupid.

moidore ('mɔɪdɔə(r)). Also 8 **moyodore, moedor(e, moydor(e, moider, moidor.** [Corruptly a. Pg. *moeda d'ouro* lit. 'gold coin' (*moeda* MONEY, *ouro*:—L. *aurum* gold).] A gold coin of Portugal, current in England in the first half of the 18th century (see quot. 1717). In later use, the word survived as a name for the sum of 27*s.*, which was approximately the value of the coin.

[**1702** in W. A. Shaw *Sel. Tracts Eng. Monet. Hist.* (1896) 166 In Portugal the Moeda is recconed at ten Crusados or 28*s.* 7.1*d.*] **1711-12** NEWTON *Ibid.* 178 The Moydores of Portugal, one with another, as they are brought hither by the Merchant..in England are worth 27*s.* 8*d.* Half penny. **1717** —— in Ld. Aldenham *Colloq. on Currency* (1900) 442 Some years ago the Portugal moedors were received in the west of England at 28*s.* apiece; upon notice from the mint that they were worth only about 27*s.* 7*d.*, the Lords Commissioners of the Treasury ordered their receivers of taxes to take them at no more than 27*s.* 6*d.* **1727-41** CHAMBERS *Cycl.*, *Moidore*, *Moedore*, or *Moeda*, a gold coin, struck, and current in Portugal. **1731** MRS. DELANY in *Life & Corr.* (1861) I. 325 The gentlemen subscribed two moiders a piece, and each have two tickets each night to dispose of to ladies. **1749** FRANKLIN *Let.* Wks. 1887 II. 153, I send you also a moidore enclosed, which please to accept towards chaise hire. **1775** *Mass. Spy* (U.S.) 17 Mar. 4/3 Lost, a Sum of Money, all in Gold, viz. 3 Moidores, 1 Four Pistol piece, and 1 Half Guinea. **1860** TROLLOPE *Framley P.* viii, To pay back the dowager's hard moidores. **1874** L. STEPHEN *Hours in Library* I. 30 Tangible subjects which he can weigh and measure and reduce to moidores and pistoles.

moien, obs. form of MOYEN.

moienaunt, variant of MOYENANT *Obs.*

moienne: see MOYEN (kind of cannon).

moiet, dial. variant of MOTE *sb.*[1]

moiety ('mɔɪətɪ). Forms: 4-5 **moite**, 5 **moitee**, 5-6 **moyte(e**, 5-7 **moytie**, 6 **moyity**, 6-7 **moitie, moyetie, moietie**, 6-8 **moity**, 7 **moyitie, moyety, mojety**, 6- **moiety.** [ME. *moite, moitie*, a. OF. *moité, moitié*, earlier *meité, meitiet* (mod.F. *moitié*) = Pr. *meitat-z, mitat-z* (Gascon *maytat*), Sp. *mitad*, Pg. *mitade*, It. *metà* (and in learned form *medietà*):—L. *medietātem* middle point, in late L. half, f. *medius* middle: see MEDIUM. Cf. MEDIETY.]

1. A half, one of two equal parts: **a.** in legal or quasi-legal use.

1444 *Rolls of Parlt.* V. 104/2 Ye to have the oone moite yerof, and he that espieth..hit forfaitable, to have the oyer moite. **1545** *Test. Ebor.* VI. 224 The moitie or half pairte of the mannor. **1592** KYD *Sp. Trag.* II. iii. 16 She is daughter and halfe heire Vnto our brother heere, Don Ciprian, And shall enioy the moitie of his land. **1603** HOLLAND *Plutarch's Mor.* 497 Mandron..offered him the one moitie of his country and city. *a* **1674** CLARENDON *Hist. Reb.* XI. §176 To submit others to pay..a full moiety of all they were worth. *a* **1715** BURNET *Own Time* II. (1724) I. 214 All..were required to bring in one moiety of their fines: But the other moiety was forgiven those who took the Declaration. **1838** W. BELL *Dict. Law Scot.* s.v., A sum payable in moieties is payable in two equal shares, though sometimes, erroneously, the term is applied to a sum payable in two or three different parts or instalments.

b. *gen.*

c **1475** *Partenay* 5936 Thys monstre with teeth the swerd ther taking, In moitees to Forthwith it breking. **1590** SPENSER *F.Q.* II. xii. 31 They..were depriv'd Of their proud beautie, and th'one moyity Transformd to fish for their bold surquedry. **1601** HOLLAND *Pliny* I. 164 A man at three yeares of age, is come to one moitie of his growth and height. **1641** MILTON *Reform.* II. Wks. 1851 III. 57, I know they will not turn the beame or equall Judgement the moity of a scruple. **1672** MARVELL *Reh. Transp.* I. 119 Let half of them be School-Divines and the other moity Systematical. **1776** GIBSON *Decl. & F.* x. *ad fin.*, We might suspect, that war, pestilence, and famine, had consumed, in a few years, the moiety of the human species. **1799** WASHINGTON *Lett.* Writ. 1893 XIV. 196 On this Estate I have more working negros by a full moiety, than can be employed to any advantage in the farming system. **1835-6** *Todd's Cycl. Anat.* I. 172/2 An earthworm cut in two..will continue to live, and each moiety will become..a perfect animal. **1897** *Allbutt's Syst. Med.* II. 850 Hereditary taint may be traced in a very large proportion of alcoholic cases—it is said in nearly a moiety.

2. a. *loosely.* One of two (occasionally more) parts (not necessarily equal) into which something is divided; †one's share or portion.

1596 SHAKS. *1 Hen. IV*, III. i. 96 Me thinks my Moity, North from Burton here, In quantitie equals not one of yours. **1597** HOOKER *Eccl. Pol.* V. lxxvii. §2 Saint Paul him selfe dividing the body of the Church of Christ into two moieties nameth the one part ἰδιώτας. *c* **1600** SHAKS. *Sonn.* xlvi, By their verdict is determined The cleere eyes moyitie and the deare hearts part. **1655** FULLER *Ch. Hist.* II. iv. §5 Crowned Monarch of the Southern and greater Moiety of this Island. *a* **1674** CLARENDON *Surv. Leviath.* (1676) 261 The greater moiety of the world being..mere Heathen men and Pagans. **1838** [see 1]. **1854** HUXLEY *Lay Serm.* v. (1870) 98 Physiological Science..Its subject-matter is a large moiety of the universe.

†**b.** *contextually.* A small part; a lesser share, portion, or quantity. *Obs.*

1593 SHAKS. *Lucr.* Ded., The loue I dedicate to your Lordship is without end: wherof this Pamphlet without beginning is but a superfluous Moity. **1605** *1st Pt. Ieronimo* III. i, Methinks no moyetie, not one little thought Of them ..But should raise spleens big as a cannon bullet Within your bosomes. **1611** SHAKS. *Wint. T.* II. iii. 8 Say that she were gone,..a moity of my rest Might come to me againe. **1650** H. MORE *Observ.* in *Enthus. Tri.*, etc. (1656) 144 All that will be left of this learned discourse of yours, will prove such a small moitie of knowledge your presumptuous mind conceited to be in her self, that [etc.]. **1650** FULLER *Pisgah* I. xii. 39 Who knows not, but that the word Moity.. importeth the just midst, and true half of a thing, though *small moity* in ordinary discourse is taken for any Canton, or small portion.

c. Chiefly *Biochem.* and *Pharm.* A group of atoms forming part of a molecule.

1935 DORLAND & MILLER *Med. Dict.* (ed. 17) 842/1 *Carbohydrate moiety*, the non-nitrogenous residue of the amino acids resulting from deamination. **1945** *Jrnl. Biol. Chem.* CLIX. 311 The lactone moiety [of pantothenic acid] can replace pantothenic acid for growth of the above organisms. **1954** A. WHITE et al. *Princ. Biochem.* xii. 265 The other penicillins have the same type of structure but have different side chains replacing the benzyl ($C_6H_5CH_2$—) moiety. **1962** *Lancet* 29 Dec. 1381/1 A.I.C. has been shown to be a key intermediate..in the biosynthesis of the purine moiety of inosinic acid. **1970** PASSMORE & ROBSON *Compan. Med. Stud.* II. xxxii. 9/2 Species differences may vary strikingly when the compound under examination is not itself toxic but becomes metabolized to release the toxic moiety. **1974** *Nature* 13 Dec. 586/2 Its molecular structure (containing both an indole and a phenylethylamine moiety) suggests the possibility of an interaction with brain monoamines.

3. *jocularly.* One's 'better half', i.e. a wife (rarely, a husband). (So F. *moitié.*) ? *Obs.*

1737 [S. BERINGTON] *G. de Lucca's Mem.* (1738) 212 It was to deprive the Husband of the voluntary Love of his Moiety. **1770** *Lady's Mag.* I. 228/2 Among the grievances against which Mr. Bustle exclaims abroad, is the excessive neatness of his notable moiety. **1829** LAMB in *Gem* 25 The Lady with a skeleton moiety in the old print.

4. *Anthropology.* Each of the two primary classes into which an Australian tribe is divided. Also a type of social division found in varying forms amongst tribes in other parts of the world, though rarely in Africa. Also *attrib.*

1888 HOWITT in *Jrnl. Anthrop. Inst.* XVIII. 39 There are in such cases totems which each apply to one moiety of the tribe. **1899** B. SPENCER & GILLEN *Native Tribes Centr. Austral.* ii. 70 The four [sub-classes] are Panunga and Bulthara, Purula and Kumara; the first two forming one moiety of the tribe, and the latter two forming another. **1914** W. H. R. RIVERS *Kinship & Social Organisation* iii. 72 The dual system in which there are only two social groups or moieties. **1934** R. H. LOWIE *Introd. Cultural Anthropol.* xiv. 261 The moiety system can not explain why the Murngin and Miwok permit only one kind of cross-cousin to be married, when both belong to the proper moiety. **1936** R. LINTON *Study of Man* xii. 207 Where both moieties and clans occur, the former are ordinarily more limited in their functions and of less social importance, possibly because the larger size of the moiety makes the establishment of well-defined attitudes..more difficult. **1937** R. H. LOWIE *Hist. Ethnol. Theory* xi. 182 Some Melanesians..have totemic moieties. **1938** G. A. REICHARD in F. Boas *Gen. Anthropol.* ix. 431 One of the Toda moieties considers itself superior to the other and has definite and important religious functions. **1944** B. MALINOWSKI *Sci. Theory of Culture* vi. 162 The family, an extended kinship group, a clan, or a moiety, constitute one type. **1949** M. MEAD *Male & Female* 422 Three different forms of marriage, and several types of age-grading and moiety systems, resulted in a rich and complex form of social organization. **1952** A. R. RADCLIFFE-BROWN *Struct. & Function Primitive Society* vi. 118 Such moiety totemism..is found in a number of different varieties in Australia, and still other varieties are found in Melanesia and in North America.

moif(f, obs. Sc. forms of MOVE.

moighte, obs. form of MITE[1] (an insect).

moignon, variant of MONION *Obs.*

moil (mɔɪl), *sb.*[1] *arch.* and *dial.* Also 7 **moyle**, 7, 9 **moile**, 9 **mooil, mwoil, mwile.** [f. MOIL *v.*]

1. Toil, labour, drudgery; freq. in *toil and moil.*

1612 AINSWORTH *Annot. Ps.* vii. 15 Molestation [*note*] or moyle, miserie. **1642** ROGERS *Naaman* 318 When Masters care not what excesse of toile and moile servants undergoe. **1659** HAMMOND *On Ps.* xc. 10 Their life for that space was ..hard travail or moyle. **1785** BURNS *Cotter's Saturday Nt.* ii, This night his weekly moil is at an end. **1856** BRIMLEY *Ess.*, *Angel in Ho.* 219 Enduring moil and toil in the trenches before Troy. **1881** DUFFIELD *Don Quix.* II. xliii. 284 It is for love of me that he comes on foot and with all that moil.

2. Turmoil, confusion, tangle; hence *fig.* 'trouble, vexation, concern. Also in *pl.*' (E.D.D.).

1855 BAILEY *Mystic* 47 So fierce a storm, That with the madding moil the waves themselves Inflamed. *a* **1864** HAWTHORNE *Amer. Note-bks.* (1868) II. 111 When I flounder into the midst of bushes, which..intertwine themselves about my legs, and brush my face [etc.].. It is laughable, after I have got out of the moil, to think how miserably it affected me for the moment. **1885** STEVENSON *Child's Gard.*, *Keepsake Mill* iii, Deaf are his ears with the moil of the mill.

3. 'Mud, mire; sticky, wet dirt' (E.D.D.); a spot, taint; damage caused by touch.

[**1818** TODD (citing *Upton*), *Moil*, a spot.] **1842** AKERMAN *Wiltsh. Gloss.* 36 'To get into the mwoile', to get into the mud. **1856** MRS. BROWNING *Aur. Leigh* IV. 552 A finished generation, dead of plague, Swept outward from their graves into the sun, The moil of death upon them. **1888** *Berksh. Gloss.*, *Mwile*, mire. 'A's a-gettin' vurder in the mwile', i.e. he's going from bad to worse.

†**moil**, *sb.*[2] *Obs.* Forms: 7-8 **moyle**, 8 **moyl, moile**, 8-9 **moil.** [? var. of MULE in the sense of hybrid; see quot. 1823. Cf. GENET-MOIL.

1823 J. BADCOCK *Dom. Amusem.* 47 The farina of the pippin was introduced to the flower of the Siberian crab, whereby a mule was produced.]

A variety of apple; also cider produced from this.

1657 AUSTEN *Fruit Trees* i. Ep. Ded. a iij, Cider that is made of the best Fruits, as Pearemaines, Pippins, Moyles,.. is much stronger and better than that which is made of ordinary fruits. **1708** J. PHILIPS *Cyder* I. 27 Pregnant with the Dregs Of Moyle, or Mum, or Treacle's viscous Juice. *Ibid.* 29 The Moile Of sweetest hony'd taste. **1813** SIR H. DAVY *Agric. Chem.* (1814) 254 The golden pippin, the red streak, and the moil, so excellent in the beginning of the last century, are now in the extremest stage of their decay.

moil (mɔɪl), *a.* and *sb.*[3] *dial.* (Anglo-Irish and Welsh border.) Also **moyle, muil, mweeal, miel.** (See E.D.D.) [a. Ir. *maol*, and the equivalent Welsh *moel*, lit. 'bald'.] **a.** *adj.* Of cattle: Hornless. **b.** *sb.* A hornless cow.

1847 *Gloss. Heraldry*, *Moile*, a provincial word signifying an ox without horns. **1855** *Morton's Cycl. Agric.* II. 724 *Muil* (Irish), cow without horns. **1887** HAVERGAL *Hereford. Gloss.*, *Moyle*, a hornless cow or bullock.

moil (mɔɪl), *v.* Forms: 5-7 **moile**, 6-7 **moyle**, 7-9 **moyl**, (9 *dial.* **myle, mile, mwoil, mwile**), 7- **moil.**

[a. OF. *moillier* (:—popular L. **molliāre*, f. L. *mollis* soft) to wet, moisten, also *intr.* to paddle in mud (mod.F. *mouiller* to wet).]

1. *trans.* To wet, moisten; to soil, bedaub, make dirty, chiefly in *passive*. *Obs.* exc. *dial.* and *arch.*

c **1400** *Beryn* 138 A monk that toke the spryngill,..And did right as the manner is, moillid al hir patis. **1575** TURBERV. *Venerie* 33 If they go to kenell wette and moyled with dyrt. **1653–4** WHITELOCKE *Jrnl. Swed. Emb.* (1772) I. 447 Though the streets were very dirty, and their robes very long,..yett they did not hold them up, butt were pitifully moyled. **1706** PHILLIPS (ed. Kersey), *To Moil*,..to dawb with Dirt. **1735** SOMERVILLE *Chase* I. 262 Moil'd in the clogging Clay, panting they lag Behind inglorious. **1841** C. H. HARTSHORNE *Salopia Antiqua* 508 Moiled from yed to fut. *a* **1861** MRS. BROWNING *Mother & Poet* vii, Letters moiled With my kisses.

†**b.** *fig.* To defile. *Obs. rare.*

1596 SPENSER *Hymn. Heav. Love* 220 Rouze thyself..out of thy soyle, In which thou wallowest..And doest thy mynd in durty pleasures moyle. **1647** TRAPP *Comm. Rev.* xiv. 4 Which have not moiled themselves with fornication corporall or spirituall. **1650** —— *Comm. Lev.* xviii. 20 As David, how did hee moil himself with Bathsheba.

†**2.** *intr.* To make oneself wet and muddy; to wallow in mire. *Obs.*

a **1566** R. EDWARDS *Damon & Pith.* (1571) fiii, All day I moyle in dourte. **1575** GASCOIGNE *Flowers, Fruite of Foes* Poems 1869 I. 94 A serpent..Which (almost dead for colde) lay moyling in the myre. **1577** B. GOOGE *Heresbach's Husb.* II. (1586) 51 b, The Frogge continually doth crie while in the stincking Lakes he still doth moile. **1599** *Sir Clyomon* Prol. A 2, Filthy Swine which in the mire doth moile.

3. To toil, work hard, drudge. Sometimes with some trace of the etymological sense 2: To work in wet and mire. Often coupled with verbs of similar meaning, esp. in to *toil and moil*. Very common *dial.*: see E.D.D.

1548–9 LATIMER *Serm. Ploughers* (Arb.) 26 They [*sc.* vnpreaching prelates] are so troubeled wyth Lordelye lyuynge,..mounchyng in their maungers, and moylynge in their gaye manoures and mansions, and so troubeled with loyterynge in theyr Lordeshyppes. **1559** *Mirr. Mag., Fall R. Tresilian* viii, And moyleth for no more then for his needfull hyre. **1580** H. GIFFORD *Gilloflowers* Poems (Grosart) 55 To toyle and moyle for worldly drosse. **1593** NASHE *Christ's T.* 44 b, Heere we labour, drudge and moyle. **1625** BACON *Ess., Plantations*, But moile not too much under Ground: For the Hope of Mines is very Uncertaine. **1629** H. BURTON *Truth's Triumph* 250 Vega hath spent..20 chapters..wherin he moyles in sweate and dust. *c* **1680** BEVERIDGE *Serm.* (1729) I. 387 He moils and toils..to come at them [*sc.* riches]. **1687** MRS. BEHN *Lucky Chance* II. i, I must moil on in the damn'd dirty road, And sure such pay will make the journey easie. **1714** GAY *Sheph. Week* II. 50 With thee 'twas Marian's dear Delight, To moil all day, and merry make at Night. **1830** GALT *Lawrie T.* II. xi, Who toil and moil in stores and factories. **1849** LONGF. *Kavanagh* i. 8 They saw him daily moiling and delving in the common path like a beetle. **1858** SEARS *Athan.* II. v. 205 The commentators are signally at fault in moiling at this passage. **1880** BROWNING *Dram. Idylls* Ser. II. Dr. —— 34 A lawyer wins repute Having to toil and moil.

†**4.** *trans.* To weary, fatigue; harass, torment, worry. Chiefly *passive*. *Obs.*

1582 STANYHURST *Æneis* I. (Arb.) 27 Iuno fel harted, Thee seas, thee regions, thee skies so spightfulye moyling [orig. I. 280 *quae mare nunc terrasque metu caelumque fatigat*]. **1600** HOLLAND *Livy* XL. xxii. 1074 Much moiled they were all, and sore toiled in this untoward way. **1604** T. WRIGHT *Passions* I. ix. 33 Who is moyled with heavinesse..and perceiveth not his heart to bee coarcted? **1640** tr. *Verdere's Rom. Rom.* III. 205 This while Alcidamant and Griolanis..were no lesse moiled, for the great Knight of the Sun..so stoutly withstood them. **1653** H. COGAN tr. *Pinto's Trav.* iv. 8 We had been..miserably moiled, and our hurts, that were great, but ill looked unto. **1823** *Spirit Publ. Jrnls.* (1825) 408 He seemed sadly moiled with his matrimonial miseries.

b. *refl.*

a **1560** BECON *Sich Mans Salve* Pref., We moile and tormoile oure selues in studying and deuising howe we maye come by the giftes of glassy fortune. **1581** MULCASTER *Positions* iv. (1887) 15 They [*sc.* the ancient writers] moile themselues sore, with the maners and conditions of the nurse. **1600** HAKLUYT *Voy.* (1810) III. 401 To moyle themselves thus with abiect and base worke. *c* **1611** CHAPMAN *Iliad* XXIII. 637 No more tug one another thus, nor moyle yourselues [τρίβεσθε κακοῖσι]. **1673** MARVELL *Reh. Transp.* II. 115, I only threw it out like empty Cask to amuze him..; he runs away with it as a very serious business and so moyles himself with tumbling and tossing it, that he is in danger of melting his Sperma Ceti. **1869** TENNYSON *North. Farmer, New Style* xiii, But 'e tued an' moil'd 'issen deäd.

c. *intr.* for *refl.* To distress oneself. *Obs.* exc. *dial.*, to worry, be fidgety or restless.

1567 GOLDING *Ovid's Met.* IX. 502 They moyled why others myght not geve like gift as wele as shee [orig. *Et, cur non aliis eadem dare dona liceret, Murmur erat*]. **1889** *N.W. Linc. Gloss., Moil*,..(2) To be fidgetty or restless. 'Theäre's noä gettin' noä rest wi' him at neets; he's tewin' an' moilin' aboot for iver'.

5. *trans.* To root *up*; to burrow in (the ground) like a pig, badger, etc.; 'to draw potatoes with the hand from under the growing plant' (E.D.D.). *Obs.* exc. *dial.*

1581 J. BELL *Haddon's Answ. Osor.* 101 b, Like a wilde Boare, to moyle up by the rootes, the florishyng and most plentyfull Vyncarde. *Ibid.* 325 b, It is apparaunt enough what thinges are moyled uppe by the Rootes, but what is planted in that place, he confesseth he cannot as yet discerne.

†**b.** *intr.* To burrow. *Obs.*

15.. EDGEWORTH *Serm.* i. 6 b, Couetous men be..euerlike wantes or Moles moiling in the grounde. [**1625**: cf. 3.] **1658** A. FOX *Würtz' Surg.* I. vi. 23 Why do they then molest the Patient with seeking, pressing,..and moiling in the Wound.

†**6.** *trans.* ? To maul, mangle. *Obs.*

1698 FRYER *Acc. E. India & P.* 118 Trampling a Man to Death, or Moiling him to Pieces with their Foreheads.

moil: see MOILES, MOYLE, MULE[1] and [2].

[**moile**, 'a dish made of Marrow and grated bread', in Speght's glossary to *Chaucer's Works* 1598 (copied in Blount *Glossogr.* 1656 and in later Dicts.) is due to misunderstanding of *franch moile* (see FRANCHEMYLE) in Lydgate's *Thebes* ibid. 370 b/1.]

moile: see MULE *sb.*[1] and *sb.*[2]

moiled (mɔɪld), *a. dial.* [f. MOIL *a.* or *sb.*[3] + -ED[2].] Of cattle: Hornless.

1839 *Hereford. Gloss.* s.v., 'A moiled sheep' is a sheep without horns. **1855** *Morton's Cycl. Agric.* II. 724 *Moiled* (Heref., Irish), without horns. **1879** MISS JACKSON *Shropsh. Word-bk.* s.v. *Moilled*, My pretty mwoilled 'eifer.

moiled (mɔɪld), *ppl. a.* [f. MOIL *v.* + -ED[1].]

1. Hard worked; exhausted; oppressed with labour and toil.

1617–18 W. LAWSON *Orch. & Gard.* (1623) 48 The Horse and moiled Oxe wrought to an vntimely death. **1793** *Gentl. Mag.* Dec. 1084 *Moiled*, troubled, fatigued. Sedgemoor. **1820** CLARE *Poems Rural Life* (ed. 2) 136 The rough rude ploughman,..While moil'd and sweating, by some pasture's side, Will often [etc.].

2. Made dirty or foul; soiled. *dial.*

1632 SHERWOOD, Moiled in the mire, *Enfangé*. *Ibid.*, Moyled, *Souillé*. **1839** *Hereford. Gloss.*, *Moiled*, dirty with wet mud. **1882** *W. Worcs. Gloss.*

moiler ('mɔɪlə(r)). *rare.* [f. MOIL *v.* + -ER[1].] One who moils or labours; a toiler.

1563–87 FOXE *A. & M.* (1596) 184/1 As for your Cardinals, we shut them out both of churches and cities, for that we see them not preachers but prollers;..not pillers and upholders of the church, but..moilers of monie and gold. **1568** GRAFTON *Chron.* (1809) I. 3 This Cain was a great toyler and moyler in the earth. **1880** MRS. RIDDELL *Myst. Palace Gard.* xxiii, Excepting a few millions of toilers and moilers.

moilere, obs. form of MULIER.

moiles (mɔɪlz). *Glass-blowing.* Also (in Dicts.) moil. [Cf. F. *meule* 'se dit, dans les verreries, des morceaux de verre qui s'attachent aux cannes', (Littré).] (See quot.)

1875 KNIGHT *Dict. Mech.*, *Moiles*, the metallic oxide adhering to the glass which is knocked from the end of the blow-pipe.

moiley ('mɔɪlɪ). *Sc.* and *Anglo-Irish*. Also moylie, moilya. [f. MOIL *a.*] A hornless cow or bullock; also *transf.* applied to a person; also *attrib.* or *adj.*

1824 MACTAGGART *Gallovid. Encycl.*, *Moylie*, a mild, good-natured person: an *auld moylie*, a tame person, even to sillyness; a *moylie*, is also a bullock wanting horns. **1880** *Antrim & Down Gloss.*, *Moily*, *Moilya*, a hornless cow. *Moily*, hornless.

moiling ('mɔɪlɪŋ), *vbl. sb.* [-ING[1].] The action of the verb MOIL in various senses.

c **1560** [RICHARDES] *Misogonus* II. ii. 80 (Brandl) Or to what end shoulde we here spende Our dayes in vrksome moylinge? **1575** *Gamm. Gurton* IV. iii. (Manly), Why, makes the knaue any moyling? **1581** J. BELL *Haddon's Answ. Osor.* 326 These men have..undertaken much fruitlesse labour in that lamentable moilyng of things which they have subverted. **1604** T. WRIGHT *Passions* VI. 327 What brought first hunger and thirst,..toyling and moyling into this world? **1691** WOOD *Ath. Oxon.* II. 205 After a great deal of moyling, turmoyling, perfidiousness, and I know not what, he laid down his head and died. **1885–6** SPURGEON *Treas. Dav.* Ps. cxxvii. 2 Blesses them more in their resting than others in their moiling and toiling.

moiling ('mɔɪlɪŋ), *ppl. a.* [f. MOIL *v.* + -ING[2].] That moils; labouring, toiling; fatiguing, toilsome.

1603 KNOLLES *Hist. Turks* (1621) 1198 Such moiling labor. **1608** *Merry Devil of Edmonton* (1617) F 2, We haue had the moylingst night of it that euer we had in our liues. **1692** R. L'ESTRANGE *Fables* cccv. 266 Oh the Endless Misery of the Life I Lead! crys the Moiling Husbandman, to spend all my Days in Ploughing [etc.]. *a* **1711** KEN *Edmund* Poet. Wks. 1721 II. 81 That moyling Swain who ploughs the fertile clod, Looks rarely to his Benefactor God. **1840** DICKENS *Barn. Rudge* lxxi, I am an abject slave, and a toiling, moiling..potter's wessel. **1879** MISS JACKSON *Shropsh. Word-bk.*, *Miling*, dirty and laborious—'A milin' job'. **1897** *Daily News* 14 July 7/3 A good sprinkling of real moiling workers in their best.

Hence '**moilingly** *adv.*, in a moiling manner.

1621 T. WILLIAMSON tr. *Goulart's Wise Vieillard* 7 He runnes and moylingly trots vp and downe.

moill(i)er(e, -ie, -ye, moilre, obs. ff. MULIER.

moilsome ('mɔɪlsəm), *a.* [f. MOIL *v.* = -SOME.] Involving toil = LABORIOUS 2.

1877 BLACKMORE *Erema* i, A dark, narrow gorge departed from the moilsome mountain track.

Moine (mɔɪn). *Geol.* [f. *the Moine* (Gael. *A'Mhòine*), name of an area east of Loch Eriboll in northern Sutherland where rocks of the series are exposed.] Used *attrib.* and as ***the Moine(s)*** to denote a highly folded series of metamorphic rocks, chiefly granulites and schists, in NW. Scotland and western Ireland which are thought to have been deposited in Pre-Cambrian (possibly Torridonian) times and metamorphosed later.

1888 *Q. Jrnl. Geol. Soc.* XLIV. 425 The various stages in the production of the Moine schists. *Ibid.* 438 Other intrusive igneous rocks pierce the micaceous flagstones of the Moine series. **1931** GREGORY & BARRETT *Gen. Stratigr.* i. 27 The lower part corresponds to the British Lewisian and Moine. **1934** *Geol. Mag.* LXXI. 303 The view that the Moines are Torridonian metamorphosed in post-Cambrian time is associated with the name of Peach. **1953** *Q. Jrnl. Geol. Soc.* CVIII. 100 The problems of the age of the Moine Series, and of the relations of the series with the other Highland formations, have been a source of controversy for more than a century and the metamorphism of the series has been assigned to periods ranging from early Pre-Cambrian to Lower Palæozoic. **1961** *Science Progress* XLIX. 715 Younger Dalradian rocks..overlie the Moines and separate the Scottish and Irish outcrops. The Moines rest on a Lewisian basement and cannot accordingly be older than 1600 million years. *Ibid.* 716 The Moine Series is the last great formation of sedimentary origin in the British Isles whose stratigraphical relations remain to be established. **1969** BENNISON & WRIGHT *Geol. Hist. Brit. Isles* iii. 53 The unmetamorphosed equivalent of the lower part of the Moine may be the Greywacke Group of the Torridonian of Islay and Oronsay.

moine, obs. form of MINE *sb.*

‖**moineau** ('mɔɪnəʊ, ‖mwano). *Fortif.* Also 8 **moyeneau.** [Fr.; regarded by Littré and Hatz.-Darm. as a use of *moineau* sparrow.] (See quot.)

1704 J. HARRIS *Lex. Techn.* I, *Moyeneau*..is a small flat Bastion, commonly placed in the middle of an over-long Curtain, by which the Bastions at the Extremities are not well defended from the Small-shot, by reason of their Distance; so that this Work is proper for placing in it a Body of Musqueteers to fire upon the Enemy from all sides. *Ibid.*, *Moineau* [with similar explanation]. **1802** in C. JAMES *Milit. Dict.* And in mod. Dicts.

†'**moines.** *Obs. rare.* Also **moynes.** [ad. OF. (early 14th c.) *moinesse, moynesse, moignesse*, f. *moine*: see MONK and -ESS.] A nun.

1513 BRADSHAW *St. Werburge* I. 413 The other hyght saynt Erkengode a moynes serene. *Ibid.* 3519 Blessed pure virgin moines and abbasse, O venerable werburge.

moines, obs. form of *means*: see MEAN *sb.*

1449 *Verulam MSS.* (Hist. MSS. Comm., 1906) 3 *note.*

moiniall, variant of MONIAL *sb. Obs.*

Moinian ('mɔɪnɪən), *a. Geol.* [f. MOINE + -IAN.] Of, pertaining to, or designating the Moine series of rocks (see MOINE). Also *absol.*, the Moine series.

1938 A. K. WELLS *Outl. Hist. Geol.* vi. 50 There is nothing inherently impossible in the suggestion that the Moinian rocks may be metamorphosed Torridonian. *Ibid.*, It is as well to remind ourselves that the great overthrusts separate an area where the succession is Lower Palæozoic rocks, on Torridonian, on Lewisian, from one..in which the succession is: Dalradian, on Moinian, on Lewisian. **1954** *Q. Jrnl. Geol. Soc.* CX. 46 Many bodies of Lewisian gneiss are marked on the Geological Survey maps of the Moine area of Ross-shire. Preliminary studies..suggest that some at least of these bodies resemble the so-called inliers of Scardroy and Fannich in being of Moinian age. **1969** BENNISON & WRIGHT *Geol. Hist. Brit. Isles* iii. 46 The Lewisian also forms the basement to the Moinian Series, a dominantly arenaceous sedimentary sequence but everywhere separated from the Torridonian by the Moine thrust. **1971** *Geol. Mag.* CVIII. 193 Moinian and Dalradian metamorphic rocks occur in the north-east extension of the Ox Mountains [in Eire]. The petrology and migmatization of the Moinian are discussed and Dalradian rocks are described for the first time from this area.

moir, obs. form of MORE *a.* and *adv.*

‖**moire** (mwar, mwɔː(r), mɔə(r)). Also 7 moyre. [F. *moire*, according to Fr. lexicographers an adoption of some form of Eng. MOHAIR.

The OF. *moire*, the name of some textile fabric mentioned by Chrestien of Troyes (12th c.), is believed to be unconnected with the modern word.]

Originally a kind of watered mohair; afterwards, any textile fabric (but usually silk) to which a watered appearance is given in the process of calendering; a watered or clouded silk.

moire antique, explained by Fr. lexicographers to mean a watered silk of large pattern, is in Eng. use practically synonymous with *moire*, which is apprehended as a shortened form.

1660 PEPYS *Diary* 21 Nov., We bought some greene-watered moyre, for a morning wastecoate. **1664** *Ibid.*, 8 May, A new black cloth suit and cloak lined with silk moyre. **1751** CHESTERF. *Let. to Son* 22 Apr. (1774) II. 136 Talk *pompons, moires*, &c., with Madame de Blot. **1855** MRS. CARLYLE *Lett.* II. 268 [*Dressmaker loq.*] I don't think I ever saw so trashy a moire. **1858** HOMANS *Cycl. Comm.* s.v. *Moire Antique*, If good silk be wrapped tightly and carelessly round a roller, it may become moire much against the inclination of the possessor. **1860** TROLLOPE *Framley P.* (1861) III. xvii. 316, 'I suppose Jane can put her hand at once on the moire antique when we reach Dover?' **1866** MISS BRADDON *Lady's Mile* 191 The heap of silk and moire. **1869** 'MARK TWAIN' *Innoc. Abr.* xxiii. (1872) 166 Velvets and moire antiques.

‖**moiré** (mware, 'mɔːreɪ), *a.* and *sb.* [Fr., pa. pple. of *moirer*, to give the appearance of moire to, f. *moire* MOIRE.]

A. *adj.* **a.** Of silk: Watered. Also applied to other materials (as paper, linoleum) having an appearance resembling watered silk. Of metals: Having a 'watered' or clouded appearance.

1823 J. BADCOCK *Dom. Amusem.* 140 Moiré Watering, by other Methods. **1856** MRS. BROWNING *Aur. Leigh* IV. 565 Those passed the salts, with confidence of eyes And simultaneous shiver of moiré silk. **1868** JOYNSON *Metals* iv. 104 Giving the plates [of galvanised iron] the well-known moiré appearance. **1873** *Young Englishwoman* Apr. 199/2 The bottom is covered with moiré-paper. **1893** G. EGERTON *Keynotes* (1894) 33 The lap of her moiré gown. **1947** D. HUNTER *Papermaking* (ed. 2) 528, 1806... The commencement of the use of moiré papers, embossed by heated cylinders, used in bookbindings. **1972** J. K. P. EDWARDS *Floors* v. 69 Linoleum can be manufactured to give many different patterns and a wide variety of types, including plain, jaspé, moiré, marble and others.

b. Applied to the wavy or geometrical pattern of light and dark stripes ('fringes') that is observed when one pattern of lines, dots, etc., is visually superimposed on another similar pattern, or on an identical one that is slightly out of alignment with the first; chiefly in ***moiré fringe, pattern***.

1940 *Chambers's Techn. Dict.* 553/1 *Moiré effect* (Photog.), a 'watered-silk' pattern..arising from interference between two line-screens; a defect for which occasional uses are found. **1950** *Proc. R. Soc.* A. CCI. 189 With the [diffraction] gratings made in the manner described above the moiré pattern consisted of a very complicated wavy pattern which repeated itself with great uniformity every quarter of an inch, this being the pitch of the lead-screw. **1953** H. A. CHINN *Television Broadcasting* ii. 70 The problem of a moiré pattern caused by 'beating' of the scanning lines with the lines of the target mesh does exist. **1956** J. GUILD *Interference Syst. Crossed Diffraction Gratings* p. v, Though attention was called to them by Lord Rayleigh as long ago as 1874 the fringes produced by crossed diffraction gratings, now usually termed moiré fringes, have somehow escaped mention in the textbooks of physical optics. **1963** *Sci. Amer.* May 54/3 The only general requirement for a moiré pattern is that the interacting figures have some sort of solid and open regions. The solid regions can be lines (straight, curved or wiggly), dots or any other geometric form... In the typical moiré pattern the moiré effect materializes when two sets of straight lines are superposed so that they intersect at a small angle. *Ibid.* 63/1 Moiré patterns sometimes plague the printer whenever he is obliged to print two or more halftone impressions one atop the other, which he must do in making multicolored reproductions. **1971** J. H. SMITH *Digital Logic* i. 3 Automatic programmed machines are..made to an extremely high accuracy, e.g. 5 000 steps (digits) per inch are easily realised using moiré fringe devices. **1973** *Sci. Amer.* Oct. 120/2 Two sets of concentric circles that overlap generate moiré patterns in the form of radial lines. Concentric circles that overlap a grid of comparable spacing generate ellipses, parabolas or hyperbolas, depending on the angle of inclination between the plane of the concentric circles and the plane of the grid.

B. *sb.*

1. A variegated or clouded appearance resembling that of watered silk; *esp.* as imparted to metals for the purpose of ornament. Also a moiré pattern or effect.

1818 *Jrnl. Sci. & Arts* V. 368 On the Moiré Metallique, or Fer blanc moiré. *Ibid.*, The moiré has of late been much improved by employing the blow pipe... When the moiré has been formed, the plate is to be varnished and polished, the varnish being tinted with any glazing colour, and thus the red, blue, green, yellow, and pearl coloured moirés are manufactured. **1839** URE *Dict. Arts* s.v., *Moirée métallique*, called in this country crystallized tin-plate, is a variegated primrose appearance, produced upon the surface of tin-plate, by applying to it in a heated state some dilute nitro-muriatic acid for a few seconds, then washing it with water, drying, and coating it with lacquer. **1888** TEALL *Brit. Petrogr.* 440 *Moiré*, the name given to the wavy appearance, comparable to that of watered silk, presented by thin plates of mica under crossed nicols. **1953** H. A. CHINN *Television Broadcasting* i. 27 The most objectionable moiré is probably that produced by the blanking pulses because they usually represent the greatest possible black-to-white contrast ratio. **1963** *Sci. Amer.* May 55 (*caption*) Moiré composed of beats is produced from nonintersecting parallel lines when the spacing of one set differs from that of another. **1967** E. CHAMBERS *Photolitho-Offset* xi. 160 The Agfa-Gevaert Diffusing Diaphragm is also a most useful asset in eliminating undesirable moiré and avoiding the need for excessive retouching. **1967** V. STRAUSS *Printing Industry* iv. 194/2 Moiré can also be introduced in presswork by defective overprinting.

¶ **2.** Erroneously used for MOIRE.

1851 *Official Catal. Gt. Exhib.* II. 504 'Moiré antique', for garments, various colours. **1851** *Repts. Juries Gt. Exhib.* (1852) 368 Gros-de-Naples, glacé, and checked moiré, and satin. **1862** *London Soc.* II. 40 Costly Moirés. **1862** *Catal. Internat. Exhib.* II. xx. 24 Moiré antiques. **1883** MISS BRADDON *Gold. Calf* I. ii. 43 Miss Pew..went rustling up and down the terrace..in her armour of apple-green moiré. **1885** MABEL COLLINS *Prettiest Woman* xxxi, He wore a coat of white moiré antique, embroidered with gold.

moiré, moire, *v.* [f. MOIRÉ *sb.* and MOIRE. Cf. F. *moirer.*] *trans.* To give a moiré or watered appearance to. Also **'moiring** *vbl. sb.*

1823 *New Monthly Mag.* IX. 551/2 The means which I had employed for moiring tin-plates. **1884** W. H. WAHL *Galvanopl. Manip.* 521 (Cent.) The solution [salt, or sal ammoniac] may be applied to the surfaces to be moiréed with the aid of a sponge.

moireen, obs. form of MOREEN.

moirette (mwa'rɛt). [f. MOIRE + -ETTE.] A textile fabric made to imitate moire.

1895 *Price List*, Moirette for lining. **1900** *Daily News* 1 Sept. 6/7 A nut-brown cloth dress..has a petticoat of nut-brown moirette to match it.

moirneing, obs. form of MORNING.

moirologist (mɔɪ'rɒlədʒɪst). *rare*⁻¹. [f. late Gr. *μοιρολόγος* (corruptly written *μυρολόγος*, mod. Gr. *μυριολόγος*, whence MYRIOLOGUE), f. Gr. *μοῖρα* fate, death + *-λόγος* speaker, discourser: see -LOGIST.] A hired mourner in modern Greece.

1886 *Q. Rev.* July 215 There may be found traces, too, of Lethe..in the death ballads sung by the hired mourners... The moirologists will sing of the loneliness of the living, of the horrors of death [etc.].

†**mois.** *Obs.* Also **moys(e.** [a. F. *mois* month.] Only in ***mois of Easter*** or ***Pasch*** (= OF. *mois de Pasques*, med.L. *mensis Paschæ*): **a.** the month or the fortnight ending on Low Sunday; hence Low Sunday itself; **b.** the Easter dues, payable on or before Low Sunday.

1426 *Coventry Leet Bk.* (E.E.T.S.) 104 Ric. Joy reseyved the moyse of Ester of Ric. Crosseby,..C marc'. **1442** *Rolls of Parlt.* V. 60/1 At the moys of Estre next comyng. **1449** *Ibid.* 169/1 Afore the Kyng in his Benche, atte the Moys of Pasche, that shall be in the yere of our Lorde MCCCCXLVI. **1491** *Ibid.* VI. 443/2 To be certified on this side the Mois of Ester then next folowing.

moise (mɔɪz), *v. dial.* Also 8 **moys.** *intr.* To thrive; to increase, improve, mend.

1787 W. MARSHALL *Norfolk* (1795) II. 384 To *Moys*, to thrive; spoken of crops and stock: also in a general sense, as 'he muddles on but does not moys'. **1791** *Gentl. Mag.* LXI. II. 1022 It is a common saying among the common people of this place [Norwich] when a person does not seem to recruit after a fit of illness, or when he does not thrive in the world, that such an one does not *moise*. *a* **1825** FORBY *Voc. E. Anglia*, *Moise* v. to mend, improve, increase, &c. **1860** E. GILLETT *Song Sol. in Norf. Dial.* vi. 11 To see wuther the wine-trees moised, and the pomegranates blowed.

†**moison.** *Obs. rare.* Forms: 4-5 **moysoun, muso(u)n, muyson,** 4-6 **moyson.** [a. OF. *moison*, *muison*, AF. *mewson* (1406 in Riley *Mem. Lond.* 563), early mod.F. *moison*, *moyson* (Cotgr.):—L. *mēnsiōn-em* act of measuring, f. *mēns-*, *mētīrī* to measure.] **a.** A 'measure' in music. **b.** Size, dimension.

c **1325** [see G-SOL-RE-UT]. **1362** LANGL. *P. Pl.* A. XI. 128 And alle Musons [*v.rr.* musonys, musouns, muysones] In Musyk I made hire to knowe. ? *a* **1366** CHAUCER *Rom. Rose* 1677 And some ther been of other moysoun, That drowe nigh to hir sesoun, And spedde hem faste for to sprede. **1545** RAYNOLD *Byrth Mankynde* I. xv. (1552) 49 Vaynes..the which in moyson & notable biggenesse moch surmount the quantite of yᵉ aboue named descendinge brest vaynes.

moisron, obs. form of MUSHROOM.

moissanite ('mɔɪs-, 'mwasənaɪt). *Min.* [f. the name of H. *Moissan* (1852-1907), French chemist: see -ITE¹.] A green (sometimes black or bluish) silicon carbide, SiC, with metallic lustre, which is known only from the meteoric iron of Canyon Diablo, Arizona, and is made artificially as CARBORUNDUM.

1905 G. F. KUNZ in *Amer. Jrnl. Sci.* XIX. 397 As this is the first instance in which this compound [*sc.* carborundum] has been proved to occur in nature, and therefore, as a mineral, is entitled to a distinct mineralogical name, it would seem that the name of Professor Moissan himself should be associated with it. I would, therefore, propose for it the name of Moissanite. **1968** I. KOSTOV *Mineral.* 105 Artificial moissanite is called carborundum.

moist (mɔɪst), *a.* and *sb.* Also 4-5 **moiste,** 4-6 **moyste,** 4-7 **moyst,** 5 **moste,** 6 **mowest.** [a. OF. *moiste* (mod.F. *moite*).

The ulterior etymology is disputed. By most scholars OF. *moiste* is believed to represent late L. *muccidus*, an altered form of L. *mūcidus* mouldy, related to *mūcēre* to be mouldy, *mūcor* mouldiness, *mūcus* MUCUS. Cf. F. *moisir* to grow mouldy:-popular Latin **mūcīre*, class. L. *mūcēre*; also Rumonsch *musch* wet, Friuli *moscid* doughy, It. *moscio* limp. Some, however, following Diez, consider it to represent L. *musteus* like new wine, also fresh, new (said, e.g. of cheese, pepper, etc.), f. *mustum* new wine, MUST. It is possible that the two Latin words have coalesced in Fr.]

A. *adj.*

1. a. Slightly imbued with wetness; containing liquid in a state of suspension or absorption; not dry; damp, humid.

Now differing from *damp* in having no tendency to imply either an undesirable or a merely temporary or casual condition. In early use the word had a wider application.

1398 TREVISA *Barth. De P.R.* v. xix. (1495) 123 Kynde makyth the mouth moyste wythin to tempre and chaunge the eselyar the dryenes of the mete. *c* **1400** MAUNDEV. (1839) ix. 100 ȝiff the Erthe were made moyst and weet with that Watre, it wolde nevere bere Fruyt. *Ibid.* xiv. 160 ȝif Venym or Poysoun be broughte in presence of the Dyamand, anon it begynnethe to wexe moyst and for to swete. *c* **1420** LYDG. *Assembly of Gods* 258 With her moyst clothes with teares all be spreynt. **1483** *Cath. Angl.* 244/1 To make moste, *liquidare, & cetera, vbi* to wete. **1529** WOLSEY in *Four C. Eng. Lett.* (1880) 10 This mowest & corupt ayer. **1555** EDEN *Decades* 137 The confynes of the chiefe citie are moister then is necessary. **1611** BIBLE *Song 3 Child.* 26 As it had bene a moist whistling wind. **1667** MILTON *P.L.* XI. 741 The Hills to their supplie Vapour, and Exhalation dusk and moist, Sent up amain. **1726** LEONI *Alberti's Archit.* I. 30/1 The moistest part of the Quarry. **1727-46** THOMSON *Summer* 1587 Like the red-rose bud moist with morning-dew. **1789** W. BUCHAN *Dom. Med.* (1790) 207 The skin grows moister, and the sweat..begins to have a peculiar fœtid smell. **1796** C. MARSHALL *Garden.* xviii. (1813) 311 Let spring sown seeds be watered occasionally, according to the weather, to keep them moist. **1797** COLERIDGE *Christabel* I. 218 The lady wiped her moist cold brow. **1815** ELPHINSTONE *Acc. Caubul* (1842) II. 91 The Gurmseer itself is moist, and sometimes even marshy. **1862** H. SPENCER *First Princ.* II. x. §84 (1875) 258 Moist winds..lose so much heat when they reach the cold mountain peaks, that condensation rapidly takes place. **1866** TATE *Brit. Mollusks* iv. 159 The variety inhabits moist places. **1884** F. M. CRAWFORD *Rom. Singer* I. 22 You are oppressed with a moist heat.

b. Of the eyes: Wet with tears, ready to shed tears. In 16-17th c. also, Watery, 'rheumy' (as one of the signs of old age).

c **1386** CHAUCER *Melib.* ¶26 Whan that thy frend is deed quod he lat nat thyne eyen to moyste been of teeris. **1597** SHAKS. *2 Hen. IV*, I. ii. 203 Haue you not a moist eye? a dry hand?..a white beard?..and wil you cal your selfe yong? **1609** B. JONSON *Sil. Wom.* I. i, Weake hammes, moist eyes, and shrunke members. **1807** WORDSW. *White Doe* II. 68 On the banner..He glanced a look of holy pride, And his moist eyes were glorified. **1817** SHELLEY *Rev. Islam* V. iv, Thoughts which make the moist eyes overbrim. **1859** TENNYSON *Enid.* 1199 The tender sound..Made his eye moist. **1897** 'H. S. MERRIMAN' *In Kedar's Tents* vi, A round-faced, chubby little man, with a tender mouth and moist dark eyes looking kindly out upon the world.

c. Of a season, climate, etc.: Wet; rainy; having some rain; having a considerable rainfall.

1481 CAXTON *Myrr.* III. viii. 147 One somer is softe and moyste, And another is drye and wyndy. **1545** RAYNOLD *Byrth Mankynde* 89 The hote & moyste whether. **1604** E. G[RIMSTONE] *D'Acosta's Hist. Indies* II. ii. 84 The night being colder then the day, is likewise more moist. **1697** DRYDEN *Virg. Georg.* I. 146 Ye Swains, invoke the Pow'rs who rule the Sky, For a moist Summer, and a Winter dry. **1815** ELPHINSTONE *Acc. Caubul* (1842) I. 175 Some places are refreshed in summer by breezes from moister countries. **1865** DICKENS *Mut. Fr.* I. vii, The weather is moist and raw. **1878** JEVONS *Prim. Pol. Econ.* iii. 30 In England we have good soil and a moist climate fitted for growing grass.

†**d.** In mediæval physiology, said of elements, humours, planets, etc. (= HUMID b); opposed to DRY. (See COLD *a.* 6.) *Obs.*

c **1381** CHAUCER *Parl. Foules* 380 Nature..That hot, cold, heuy, lyght, moyst, & dreye Hath knyt with euene noumberis of a-cord In esy voys gan for to speke & seye [etc.]. **1390** GOWER *Conf.* III. 120 [Cancer] of himself is moiste and cold. *c* **1400** *Lanfranc's Cirurg.* 12 Oon of þe men is of an hoot complexioun & a moist, þat oþer of a cold complexioun & a drie. **1509** HAWES *Past. Pleas.* XVI. (Percy Soc.) 73 Youth is..Hote, and moyste, and full of lustines. *c* **1550** LLOYD *Treas. Health* A j, It shal do good to moyst persons and women. **1604** SHAKS. *Ham.* I. i. 118 (2nd Qo.), And the moist starre, Vpon whose influence Neptunes Empier stands, Was sicke almost to doomesday with eclipse. **1707** FLOYER *Physic. Pulse-Watch* 71 In Children and Women the cooler and moister Diet is most agreeable to preserve their natural Pulses. **1774** GOLDSM. *Nat. Hist.* (1776) VI. 183 They [*sc.* fish] are cold and moist, and must needs, say they, produce juices of the same kind.

†**2. a.** Of plants, fruits, etc.: 'Juicy, succulent' (J.); not withered or dry; fresh as opposed to dried. *Obs.*

1377 LANGL. *P. Pl.* B. XVI. 68 Matrymonye I may nyme a moiste fruit with-alle. **1382** WYCLIF *Job* viii. 16 Moiste semeth the resshe befor the Sunne come. **1567** MAPLET *Gr. Forest* 41 b, It is then best of all riuen, clouen and cut in sunder when it is moyst and greene. **1607** SHAKS. *Timon* IV. iii. 223 Will these moyst Trees..page thy heeles And skip when thou point'st out? **1611** BIBLE *Num.* vi. 3 Nor [shall he] eate moist grapes, or dried. **1611** COTGR., *Succulent*, succulent, sappie, moist, full of iuice.

†**b.** Of liquor: New, not stale. *Obs.*

c **1386** CHAUCER *Sir Thopas* 53 Notemuge to putte in Ale, Wheither it be moyste or stale. —— *Pard. Prol.* 29 A draughte of moyste and corny Ale.

†**c.** New, not worn, 'green'. *Obs.*

c **1386** CHAUCER *Prol.* 457 Hir hosen weren of fyn scarlet reed ful streite yteyd and shoes ful moyste and newe.

†**3.** Yielding moisture or water; bringing or that brings rain or moisture; containing water (or other liquid). *Obs.*

1390 GOWER *Conf.* I. 264 Thilke blod which scholde have ese To regne among the moiste veines. **1590** SPENSER *F. Q.* III. i. 57 The moist daughters of huge Atlas strove Into the Ocean deepe to drive their weary drove. **1601** SHAKS. *All's Well* II. i. 167 Ere twice in murke and occidentall dampe Moist Hesperus hath quench'd her sleepy Lampe. **1602** *2nd Pt. Return fr. Parnass.* I. ii. 167 Plaine Meteors, bred of the exhalation of Tobacco, and the vapors of a moyst pot, that soare vp into the open ayre. **1704** POPE *Windsor For.* 119 Moist Arcturus clouds the sky.

†**4.** Liquid; watery. *Obs.*

c **1374** CHAUCER *Boeth.* v. met. v. 132 (Camb. MS.) Oother beestis by the wandrynge lyhtnesse of hir wyngis betyn the wyndes and ouerswymmyn the spaces of the longe eyr by moyst fleeynge [orig. *liquido volatu*]. **1388** WYCLIF *Jer.* xliv. 25 Offre to it moist sacrifices [1382 *Ibid.* sacryfises of licoures]. **1390** GOWER *Conf.* III. 94 The moiste dropes of the reyn Descenden into Middilerthe. **1530** PALSGR. 744/2, I swalowe downe any medycyne or lycour that is moyste, *je assorbys*. **1597** SHAKS. *2 Hen. IV*, IV. v. 140 (1600 Qo.) But for my teares, The moist impediments vnto my speech, I had forestald this deere and deep rebuke. *c* **1611** CHAPMAN *Iliad* I. 308 The moist waies of the sea they saild [Gr. *ἐπέπλεον ὑγρὰ κέλευθα*].

5. Associated or connected with liquid. *spec.* **a.** *poet.* Tearful; accompanied with tears. **b.** Said of a process or apparatus in which liquid is used. †***moist measure***: liquid measure. **c.** Of diseases,

etc.: Marked by a discharge of matter, phlegm, etc.

1562 TURNER *Baths* 13 A ciath..holdeth after moyste measure an unce and an halfe. **1605** *1st Pt. Ieronimo* I. ii. 61 Tis as common To weepe at parting as to be a woman..play not this moyst prize. **1637** MILTON *Lycidas* 159 Where ere thy bones are hurld, Whether beyond the stormy Hebrides, ..Or whether thou to our moist vows deny'd, Sleep'st by the fable of Bellerus old. **1796** KIRWAN *Elem. Min.* (ed. 2) II. 395 No effectual method of analyzing this ore [Tui stone], in the moist way has as yet been discovered. **1839** URE *Dict. Arts* 812 The assay of ores, comprehending the mechanical part: that is, by washing; the chemical part, or assays by the dry way; and the assays by the moist way. **1876** BRISTOWE *Th. & Pract. Med.* (1878) 86 When..the gangrene is what is usually called 'moist'. **1891** *Syd. Soc. Lex.*, *Moist tetter*. *Ibid.*, *Moist wart*, the *Condyloma acuminatum*. **1899** *Allbutt's Syst. Med.* VIII. 511 It [*sc.* eczema of the fingers] may be dry or moist. *Ibid.* 524 The healing of a chronic moist eczema may be indefinitely delayed by washing.

d. *Med.* Of sounds heard in auscultation: Suggesting the presence of liquid.

1843 R. J. GRAVES *Syst. Clin. Med.* xx. 230 The only stethoscopic phenomena observed were extensive minute and moist bronchial râles. **1898** *Allbutt's Syst. Med.* V. 10 Two great classes of the dry and of the moist sounds.

†**6.** Addicted to drink. (Cf. DRY *a.* 3.) *Obs. rare*$^{-1}$.

1619 R. HARRIS *Drunkard's Cup* 8 By the testimony of the loosest and moystest naturalists, the very Poets.

7. Special collocations: **moist chamber**, a 'chamber' in which microscopic objects may be kept moist; **moist colour**, a water-colour pigment in the form of a soft paste; **moist gum** = DEXTRIN (*Cent. Dict.* 1890); **moist stove**, a hot-house heated with a moist heat; **moist sugar**, unrefined or partially refined sugar; also *attrib.* and *Comb.*, as ***moist sugar-coloured*** adj.; ***moist sugar bowl, spoon***, etc.

1869 DALLINGER & DRYSDALE in *Monthly Microsc. Jrnl.* (1874) XI. 97 Recklinghausen's '*moist chamber' only enables us to arrest for a short time the dissipation of the fluid under examination. **1876** RUTHERFORD *Outl. Histol.* (ed. 2) 150 Schultze's modification of Recklinghausen's moist chamber. **1885** *Encycl. Brit.* XIX. 86/1 For water colours the pigments are prepared..as '*moist colours' contained in small porcelain dishes. **1824** LOUDON *Encycl. Gard.* (ed. 2) §6177 The bark or *moist stove..having a pit for bark or other fermenting matter instead of a stage. **1845** *Florist's Jrnl.* 124, I then place them..in a moist stove or forcing house. [**1657** R. LIGON *Barbadoes* (1673) 85 The Sugars they made, were but bare Muscavadoes,..so *moist, and full of molasses, and so ill cur'd.] **1826** KIRBY & SP. *Entomol.* xliv. IV. 202 Of a granular appearance, much resembling fine moist sugar. **1835** *Court Mag.* VI. 169/1 The two Misses Larkin..wore their own sevenpenny-moist-sugar coloured hair. **1847** A. & H. MAYHEW *Greatest Plague of Life* iii. 30 She could not for the life of her lay her hands upon the lump-sugar, and we were obliged to put up with moist. **1886** W. H. ST. JOHN HOPE in *Archæologia* L. 150 This mazer was formerly used in the family as a moist-sugar bowl.

8. *Comb.*, chiefly parasynthetic, as ***moist-brained, -eyed, -lipped, -natured, -nosed, -skinned, -tinged*** adjs; also ***moist-striking*** adj.

1606 *Sir G. Goosecappe* I. i. in Bullen *O. Pl.*, III. 9, I..know him to be a dull *moist-braind Asse. **1847** WEBSTER (citing Coleridge), **Moist-eyed*. **1962** I. MURDOCH *Unofficial Rose* xxix. 284 She was, as he looked down at her, tense, *moist-lipped. **1669** WORLIDGE *Syst. Agric.* (1681) 71 A very excellent Soil for a cold *moist-natured Land. **1934** DYLAN THOMAS *Let.* 9 May (1966) 120, I would have introduced a..paragraph all about her nasty little *moist-nosed muse. **1957** J. S. HUXLEY *Relig. without Revelation* (rev. ed.) ix. 216 The reptiles replaced the *moist-skinned amphibians. **1816** L. HUNT *Rimini* IV. 177 Then issue forth in this *moist-striking air. **1943** D. GASCOYNE *Poems 1937–42* 55 Obscurely still beneath a *moist-tinged blank Sky like the inside of a deaf mute's mouth.

†**B.** *absol.* and *sb.* That which is moist; moisture. Also, moist quality, moistness.

?*a* **1366** CHAUCER *Rom. Rose* 1564 Abouten it is gras springing, For moiste so thikke and wel lyking, That it ne may in winter dye. **1390** GOWER *Conf.* III. 97 The fyr..is withoute moist al drye. *c* **1470** HENRYSON *Mor. Fab.* i. (*Cock & Jasp*) xi, Riches..Quhilk maith, nor moist, nor vther rust can screit. **1562** TURNER *Baths* 3 b, It is good for the crampe and for all colde diseases and moyste of the synewes. **1592** DAVIES *Immort. Soul* XXXI. v, She lodgeth Heat, and Cold, and Moist, and Dry, And Life, and Death, and Peace, and War together. **1606** SYLVESTER *Du Bartas* II. iv. III. *Schisme* 419 Myrtles and Bays for want of moist grew wan. **1615** CHAPMAN *Odyss.* VIII. 67 The deepe moist then They further reacht. **1667** MILTON *P.L.* III. 652 Who..Bear his swift errands over moist and dry, O're Sea and Land. **1742** YOUNG *Nt. Th.* IX. 99 The moist of human frame the sun exhales; Winds scatter, thro' the mighty void, the dry.

moist, *v.* Forms: 4–6 **moyste, moiste,** 6–7 **moyst** (pa. pple. **moist**), 6– **moist.** [f. MOIST *a.*]

1. a. *trans.* To render moist, impart moisture to; to moisten, wet. *Obs.* exc. *dial.* (see E.D.D.).

1382 WYCLIF *Job* xxi. 24 And the bones of hym ben moistid with marȝ [Vulg. *irrigantur*]. —— *Luke* vii. 38 Sche ..bigan to moiste his feet with teeris. **1398** TREVISA *Barth. De P.R.* VI. xxii. (Tollem. MS.), Constantyn sayeþ þat drynke is nedful for many maner cause: ffor hit moysteþ þe drie body. *Ibid.* XIV. xlvi. (1495) 483 Valeyes ben moysted with stremes that come out of mountaynes. **1447** BOKENHAM *Seyntys* (Roxb.) 248 Blak brede..In hote watyr mostyd..she eet. *c* **1530** T. PRIDIOXE in Collier *Hist. Dram. Poetry* (1831) II. 384 Beholde myne eyes whose teres do moyst my paled face. **1533** ELYOT *Cast. Helthe* (1541) 32 b, Wyne heateth and moysteth the bodye. **1570–6** LAMBARDE *Peramb. Kent* (1826) 174 Moisting womens breastes that before were drie and wanted milke. **1590** C'TESS PEMBROKE *Antonie* 600 His sworde Alreadie moisted is in his warme bloude. **1655** in Hartlib *Ref. Commw. Bees* 18 Rye..need not..be dryed, but beaten and moisted with its own liquor. **1821** CLARE *Vill. Minstr.* II. 145 As evening moists the daisy by thy side.

b. To slake or quench (one's) thirst. ***to moist one's lip***: to drink very little; also (slang) ***to moist one's clay***. (Cf. MOISTEN *v.* 1 b.) Now *dial.*

1377 LANGL. *P. Pl.* B. XVIII. 366 May no drynke me moiste ne my thruste slake, Tyl [etc.]. **1530** PALSGR. 639/2, I dyd nat drinke to day, I dyd but moyste my lyppes with a quarter of wine. *a* **1562** G. CAVENDISH *Wolsey* (1893) 241 Thus passed he forthe his dynner in great lamentacion and hevynes, whiche was more fed and moystyd with sorowe & teares, than with owther pleasant mets or dylicate drynks. **1579–80** NORTH *Plutarch, Lycurgus* (1595) 45 So they al dranke hartely except himself, who..did no more but a litle moyste his mouth without, and so refreshed himself. **1602** *2nd Pt. Return fr. Parnass.* I. ii. 339 Meete me an houre hence, at the signe of the Pegasus in Cheapside, and Ile moyst thy temples with a cuppe of Claret. **1606** SHAKS. *Ant. & Cl.* V. ii. 285 Now no more The iuyce of Egypts Grape shall moyst this lip. **1834** A. SMART *Rambling Rhymes* 120 When he used to moist his clay An' lay his corn in.

†**c.** *fig.* Chiefly, To soften (the heart, etc.). *Obs.*

13.. *Propr. Sanct.* (Vernon MS.) in *Archiv Stud. neu. Spr.* LXXXI. 317/57 Þe wȝuche techers dude Moyste wel þe hertes of trewe men eueridel. **1435** MISYN *Fire of Love* II. v. 80 Froo qwhens he byrnys with lufe swetist & with a draght of heuenly passage he is moystid & vmbesett & truly is transformyd with heit of happis to-cum. **1557** *Sarum Primer* I Good Lorde Jesu Christe,..moiste my minde with thy most precious bloude. **1578** G. WHETSTONE *2nd Pt. Promos & Cassandra* v. ii, Stormes of teares did showre As myght, with rueth, haue moyst a stony hart. **1598** ROWLANDS *Betraying of Christ* 27 And let my teares be flouds to moist my heart.

†**2.** *absol.*

a **1548** HALL *Chron., Hen. V* 37 b, Sprinkle a vessell of water and it moisteth not, but cast it out wholy together and it bothe washeth and norisheth. **1562** BULLEYN *Bulwark, Bk. Simples* 5 Waxe is good for plasters..it moisteth and is used for outwarde Medicines. **1581** MULCASTER *Positions* XX. (1887) 87 Walking in the dew moystes and harmes. **1624** DONNE *Devotions*, etc. (ed. 2) 162 As thy water moysts, so it cooles too.

3. *intr.* To rain slightly, to drizzle. *U.S. rare.*

1916 H. L. WILSON *Somewhere in Red Gap* iii. 117 It was moisting when we started, and pretty soon it clouded up. *Ibid.* 118 It wasn't moisting any more—it was raining for fair.

Hence †'**moisted** *ppl. a.*; †'**moisting** *vbl. sb.* and *ppl. a.*

1382 WYCLIF *Deut.* xi. 10 Moystynge watrys [Vulg. *aquæ irriguæ*]. **1398** TREVISA *Barth. De P.R.* XIII. v. (Bodl. MS.), After thee moistinge of þe londe þe h[epes of] grauel toschedeþ. **1541** R. COPLAND *Galyen's Terap.* 2 A iv, Sease yᵉ bathynge & moystynge. **1549–62** STERNHOLD & H. *Ps.* cxvi. 8 Thou hast deliuered..my moisted eien from mourneful teares. *a* **1562** G. CAVENDISH *Wolsey* in Wordsw. *Eccl. Biog.* (1818) I. 456 After he had..dried his moisted cheekes, he spake to them in this sorte. **1586** BRIGHT *Melanch.* xl. 268 All which purgers are to be..mingled with some moysting decoction. **1612** DRAYTON *Poly-olb.* ii. 40 Upon whose moisted skirt, with sea-weed fring'd about, The bastard Corall breeds.

moist, obs. Sc. f. MOST; MUST *sb.* (musk) and *v.*

moisten ('mɔɪs(ə)n), *v.* Also 6–7 **moysten.** [f. MOIST *a.* + -EN[5].]

1. *trans.* To make or render moist, damp, or wet; to wet superficially or moderately. Also *absol.*

1580 [implied in MOISTENED, MOISTENING *ppl. adjs.*]. **1590** SPENSER *F.Q.* III. vi. 34 Ne doe they need with water of the ford..to moysten their roots dry. **1610** MARKHAM *Masterp.* II. clxxiii. 483 It looseth and scattereth humors, warmeth and moisteneth. **1611** BIBLE *Job* xxi. 24 His breasts are full of milke, and his bones are moistened with marrow. **1626** BACON *Sylva* §230 A Pipe a little moistned on the inside.. maketh a more solemne Sound, than if the Pipe were dry. *a* **1680** CHARNOCK *Chief of Sinners Obj. Mercy* Wks. (1847) 16 Water cannot but moisten, fire cannot but burn. **1727** BRADLEY *Fam. Dict.* s.v. *Apricock*, Moisten them [*sc.* the apricocks] with a Spoonful of Water or Vinegar. **1758** JOHNSON *Idler* No. 17 ¶1 By fatal confidence in these fallacious promises [of fine weather]..many curls have been moistened to flaccidity. **1799** G. SMITH *Laboratory* I. 21 Mealed powder moistened with brandy. **1850** O. WINSLOW *Inner Life* iii. 88 No tears of repentance have ever moistened the eyes.

b. In expressions relating to the satisfaction of thirst. ***to moisten the lips, throat***, etc.: to refresh oneself with liquor. ***to moisten one's clay***: see CLAY *sb.* 4 b. (Cf. MOIST *v.* 1 b.)

In quot. 1821 *moisten the lips* is used = 'make the mouth water'.

1603 DEKKER *Batchelor's Banq.* iii. B 4 b, And halfe a dosen times [they have] moystned their lips with the sweet ioyce of the purpled grape. **1741** tr. *D'Argens' Chinese Lett.* xl. 313 This same Priest..takes care to moisten his Prayers by drinking every now and then a large Glass of Wine. **1819** SHELLEY *Cyclops* 583 *Ulysses*. If you drink much after a mighty feast, Moistening your thirsty maw, you will sleep well. **1821** LAMB *Elia* Ser. I. *Grace before Meat*, The savoury soup and messes steaming up the nostrils, and moistening the lips of the guests with desire. **1826** SCOTT *Woodst.* v, You have been moistening your own throat to some purpose. **1840** DICKENS *Old C. Shop* xlviii, Mr. Swiveller..chanced at the moment..to be moistening his clay, as the phrase goes, rather copiously. **1842** A. COMBE *Physiol. Digestion* (ed. 4) 37 The generous self-denial of him who passed the cup to his wounded neighbour, without stopping even to moisten his own lips.

†**c.** *fig.* = MOIST *v.* 1 c. *Obs. rare.*

1582 [implied in MOISTENED *ppl. a.* 2]. ?*a* **1661** FULLER (Webster 1864), It moistened not his executioner's heart with any pity.

2. *intr.* To become moist.

1859 TENNYSON *Enid* 520 Nor let her..blue eye Moisten, till she had lighted on his wound. **1880** G. MEREDITH *Tragic Com.* (1881) 71 The burning eyes of her Indian Bacchus fixed on her till their brightness moistened and flashed.

moistened ('mɔɪs(ə)nd), *ppl. a.* Also 6 **moistned.** [f. MOISTEN *v.* + -ED[1].]

1. Rendered moist.

moistened chicken (nonce-phrase), a literal rendering of F. *poule mouillée*, applied to a person excessively afraid of incurring any discomfort.

1580 SIDNEY *Ps.* VI. v, My moistned bed proofes of my sorrow showeth: My bed..With my teares floweth. **1591** SHAKS. *1 Hen. VI*, I. i. 49 When at their Mothers moistned eyes, Babes shall suck, Our Ile be made a Nourish of salt Teares. **1697** DRYDEN *Virg. Georg.* III. 652 The Southern Air And dropping Heav'ns the moisten'd Earth repair. **1749** FIELDING *Tom Jones* XIII. i, All those strong energies of a good mind, which fill the moistened eyes with tears. **1825** *Greenhouse Comp.* I. 247 Any dirt or dust [should be] carefully wiped off with a moistened sponge. **1859** THACKERAY *Virgin.* II. xvii. 139 The story about the French is, that their governor, the Duke of Aiguillon, was rather what you call a *moistened chicken*. **1860** TYNDALL *Glac.* II. xxiii. 351 When two pieces of ice, with moistened surfaces, were placed in contact, they became cemented together. **1902** *Daily Chron.* 8 Jan. 5/1 A moistened finger..may be recommended in an emergency.

†**2.** Softened, made tender. (Cf. MOISTEN *v.* 1 c.)

1582 T. WATSON *Centurie of Loue* xxi. Poems (Arb.) 57 Theire beames drawe forth by great attractiue power My moistned hart.

moistener ('mɔɪs(ə)nə(r)). Also 7 **moystner, moistner.** [f. MOISTEN *v.* + -ER[1].] One who or something which moistens.

1611 COTGR., *Trempeur*, a dipper; wetter, moistener; soaker, steeper; seasoner, temperer. **1632** tr. *Bruel's Praxis Med.* 103 His diet must be liquid broths, and moystners of the body. **1755** JOHNSON, *Moistener*, the person or thing that moistens. **1867** *Contemp. Rev.* V. 34 The ocean, that great moistener and softening equalizer of the atmosphere.

moistening ('mɔɪs(ə)nɪŋ), *vbl. sb.* [-ING[1].] The action of the verb MOISTEN; also *concr.*

1611 BIBLE *Prov.* iii. 8 It shalbe health to thy nauill, and marrow [*marg.* Hebr. watring, or moystning] to thy bones. **1611** COTGR., *Mouillement*, a wetting, or moistening. **1627** HAKEWILL *Apol.* I. v. §3. 52 It pleased God to open the windowes of Heauen for the moistning and nourishing of their seedes. **1854** RONALDS & RICHARDSON *Chem. Technol.* (ed. 2) I. 321 A moderate moistening of small coal has..the advantage of preventing its falling through the grate-bars and creating dust.

'**moistening,** *ppl. a.* [-ING[2].] That moistens; rendering or becoming moist.

1580 SIDNEY *Ps.* XXII. ix, My moistning strength is like a pottsheard dried. **1597** A. M. tr. *Guillemeau's Fr. Chirurg.* 10 b/1 With moysteninge medicamentes must it be cured and helped. **1683** SALMON *Doron Med.* I. 51 Moistning medicines. **1700** DRYDEN *Sigism. & Guiscardo* 504 When the World began, One common Mass compos'd the Mould of Man; One Paste of Flesh on all Degrees bestow'd, And kneaded up alike with moistning Blood. **1880** MISS BRADDON *Just as I am* iv, 'God bless you, Sir Everard', said Vargas, with moistening eyes.

moister, obs. form of MOISTURE *sb.* and *v.*

moistful ('mɔɪstfʊl), *a. rare.* [f. MOIST *a.* + -FUL 1.] Full of moisture; moist.

1591 SYLVESTER *Du Bartas* I. iv. 94 Moistfull matter. **1612** DRAYTON *Poly-olb.* xviii. 28 Her moystfull Temples bound, with wreaths of quiuering Reeds. **1855** SINGLETON tr. *Virgil* I. 347 The next Aurora..Was scanning earth, and moistful shade from heaven Had chased away. **1892** *Punch* 17 Sept. 132/2 When it has to play quick It is moistful and thick, For the trombone is fond of beer.

moistify ('mɔɪstɪfaɪ), *v.* [f. MOIST *a.* + -FY.] *trans.* To moisten; used humorously of 'topers'.

1786 BURNS *Earn. Cry* Postscr. vii, Tho' whyles ye moistify your leather. **1840** MRS. F. TROLLOPE *Widow Married* xxix, The ladies taught her how to arrange a 'spit-curl', so as to defy the moistifying effects of the climate. **1882** J. WALKER *Jaunt to Auld Reekie* 87 [They] moistified their drouthy clay Wi rousin brandy-whitters O' punch.

moistish ('mɔɪstɪʃ), *a.* [f. MOIST *a.* + -ISH.] Somewhat moist or damp. Hence '**moistishness.**

1576 NEWTON *Lemnie's Complex.* II. iii. 109 b. This humour..is a certayne vliginous moystishnes..which ought..to be sent out and purged. **1610** W. FOLKINGHAM *Art of Survey* I. xi. 36 A..moistish earth. **1776–96** WITHERING *Brit. Plants* (ed. 3) III. 684 Moistish mountainous situations.

moistless ('mɔɪstlɪs), *a.* [f. MOIST *sb.* + -LESS.] Devoid of or free from moisture; dry.

1592 WARNER *Alb. Eng.* VIII. xxxix. 174 Some Cloudes giue Snow, that lights and lyes a moysture moystles. **1634** SIR T. HERBERT *Trav.* 183 A rinde moystlesse hard and scaly. **1827** CAPT. G. BEAUCLERK *Journ. to Marocco* xii. 141 The moistless tongue rattled as it essayed to speak. **1884** J. PURVES in *Gd. Words* Nov. 768 The subterranean galleries.. leave the seed dry and moistless.

'**moistly,** *adv.* [f. MOIST *a.* + -LY[2].] In a moist manner (in quot. 1602, drunkenly).

1602 *2nd Pt. Return fr. Parnass.* IV. iii. 1921 Swaggering full moistly on a tauernes bench. **1905** H. G. WELLS *Kipps*

II. iii. 197 The bull really came at them..opened a mouth below his moistly glistening nose, and booed. **1906** B. von Hutten *What became of Pam* 78 March had moistly melted into April. **1927** H. V. Morton *In Search of England* x. 180 Three of those prim, sallow, enthusiastic, middle-aged lovers of England..were..regarding moistly the bare rooms in which Brewster and the 'Pilgrim Fathers' were imprisoned. **1939** L. M. Montgomery *Anne of Ingleside* vii. 50 Walter hated to be kissed moistly on the forehead. **1957** R. A. Heinlein *Door into Summer* (1960) i. 14 He shook hands moistly, sat me down,..and attempted to take my bag.

moistness ('mɔɪstnɪs). [f. moist *a.* + -ness.] The quality or state of being moist; in early use also †*concr.*, moisture.

1398 Trevisa *Barth. De P.R.* iv. iv. (1495) 85 Yf moystnes be shedde in to the vtter partes of a thynge, it fyllyth alle the voyde place therof. *c* **1400** tr. *Secreta Secret., Gov. Lordsh.* 80 Whos grape..ys noght..gedryd or..þe moystnesse of his stok sty vp to þe crope and þe braunches. **1526** Tindale *Luke* viii. 6 Some [of the seed] fell on ston and as sone as yt was spronge vp yt widdred awaye because yt lacked moystnes. **1565** Cooper *Thesaurus, Alopecurus*,..an hearbe like a foxe's taile: full of mostnesse. **1591** Florio *2nd Fruites* 159 Looke that they [*sc.* the sheets] be drie, and without moistnesse. **1662** Gerbier *Princ.* 25 The moistnesse of this Clime. **1725** Bradley *Fam. Dict.* s.v. *Sweetmeats*, Which proceeds from the Moistness of the Fruit. **1825** J. Nicholson *Operat. Mechanic* 722 Cotton wool is generally used..to take the [gold] leaf up..on account of its..slight moistness. **1885** *Manch. Exam.* 23 Feb. 5/4 A hybrid much better adapted to..the moistness of our climate.

†**b.** *transf.* and *fig. Obs.*

c **1425** *St. Mary of Oignies* i. vi. in *Anglia* VIII. 139/19 Whanne she [was] comen to hirselfe ageyne as after a moystnesse of mynde, rekenyd & countid streitly atte euene alle hir deedys. **1551** Bible (Matthew) *Job* xv. *notes*, Out of whiche procedeth suche false doctryne as drieth vp the moistnes of the soule in trifling out yᵉ truth. **1576** Woolton *Chr. Manual* B iv, He hath the name of a christian, because he is ingraffed in Christ, as the branche in the stocke,..& so to receyue of his moystnesse and lyfe.

moistre, obs. form of moisture *v.*

moisture ('mɔɪstjʊə(r), 'mɔɪstʃə(r)), *sb.* Also 4-7 **moysture**, 5 **mostour**, 5-6 **moystour**, **-er**, 6 **moistur**, **-er**. [a. OF. *moistour* (mod.F. *moiteur*), f. *moiste* moist *a.*]

†**1.** Moistness; the quality or state of being moist or damp. *Obs.*

1398 Trevisa *Barth. De P.R.* v. xxiv. (Bodl. MS.) lf. 13 b/1 Hoossenes of þe voice comeþ of the moisture of þe wosen and of þe lunges. **1477** Norton *Ord. Alch.* v. in Ashm. (1652) 54 Moisture, and Drines, be qualityes Passive. **1575** Laneham *Let.* (1871) 20 The weather enclynde too sum moyster & wynde. **1597** A. M. tr. *Guillemeau's Fr. Chirurg.* 42 b/2 Through the humiditye or moyster therof, it may soacke through the Escara. **1604** E. G[rimstone] *D'Acosta's Hist. Indies* v. xviii. 379 At such time as the fountaines, springs, and rivers, did increase by the moistures of the weather. **1625** N. Carpenter *Geog. Del.* ii. ii. (1635) 22 In the Earth are ingendred the foure ferst qualities of Heate, Cold, Drouth, and Moisture. **1774** Goldsm. *Nat. Hist.* (1776) VII. 94 Seldom venturing out, except when the moisture of a summer's evening invites them abroad. **1777** Watson *Philip II* (1839) 247 Alva had..applied to Philip for liberty to leave the Low Countries, on account of the bad state of his health, occasioned by the moisture of the climate. **1794** S. Williams *Vermont* 61 Another remarkable effect is an alteration in the moisture or wetness of the earth.

2. a. Water or other liquid diffused in small quantity through air as vapour, or through a solid substance, or condensed upon a surface.

? *a* **1366** Chaucer *Rom. Rose* 1424 Through moisture of the welle swete Sprange up the sote grene gras. *c* **1386** —— *Pars. T.* ¶ 146 God shal destroie the fruyt of the erthe as fro hem; ne water ne shal yeve hem no moisture, ne the Eyr no refresshyng, ne fyr no light. *c* **1400** Maundev. (Roxb.) vii. 23 Þai hafe na moisture bot þat þe forsaid ryuer ministers. **1412-20** Lydg. *Chron. Troy* (E.E.T.S) ii. 990 It [ebony] wil..nat corrupte with water nor moysture. **1483** *Cath. Angl.* 244/1 A Mostour, *fluor, humor*. **1599** Davies *Immort. Soul* xxx. xviii. (1714) 94 The Moisture, which the thirsty Earth Sucks from the Sea. **1611** Bible *Luke* viii. 6 Some fell vpon a rocke, and assoone as it was sprung vp, it withered away, because it lacked moisture. **1697** Dryden *Virg. Georg.* i. 387 For Moisture then abounds, and Pearly Rains Descend in silence to refresh the Plains. **1719** De Foe *Crusoe* i. 123 The Earth having had no Rain after the Seed was sown, it had no Moisture to assist its Growth. **1783** Burke *Sp. Fox's E. India Bill* Wks. IV. 78 In that country the moisture..is given but at a certain season. **1803** *Med. Jrnl.* IX. 231 Oxydated muriatic gas mixed with different other gasses..is easily changed into acid by the moisture of the flesh. **1843** Borrow *Bible in Spain* xxx, No moisture was wrung from his tanned countenance. **1878** Huxley *Physiogr.* 64 Snow is not the only solid form in which atmospheric moisture is precipitated. **1885** *Manch. Exam.* 6 Apr. 5/2 The breeze is more balmy, with a touch of moisture in the air.

b. with reference to tears.

1597 Shaks. *Lover's Compl.* 323 That infected moysture of his eye. **1838** Dickens *Nich. Nick.* vii, Nicholas Nickleby's eyes were dimmed with a moisture that might have been taken for tears. **1897** 'H. S. Merriman' *In Kedar's Tents* vi, With, as it were, a small solution of sympathy, indicated by a moisture of the eye, for the family..in their bereavement.

†**c.** The liquid part or constituent of a body. In Mediæval philosophy, the humours or humid property, naturally inherent in all plants and animals. Also ***radical moisture***: see radical *a.* 1. *Obs.*

1398 Trevisa *Barth. De P.R.* vii. xxxi. (1495) 245 A Feuer Etyk..wastith the substancyall moisture of the body. *c* **1450** Lydg. *Secrees* 1259 Yif purgacyons Be necessarye..Solve flewm brennyng or moysture To kepe a mene. **1471** Radical moisture [see radical *a.* 1]. **1521** Fisher *Serm. agst. Luther* ii. Wks. (1876) 323 The trees whan they be wydred..and all the moystour shronke into the rote & no lust of grenenes nor of lyfe appereth outwardly. **1547** Boorde *Brev. Health* cclxxxiv. 94 This matter [*sc.* spittle] doth come of the humiditie or moisters of bloude. **1593** Shaks. *3 Hen. VI*, ii. i. 79, I cannot weepe: for all my bodies moysture Scarce serues to quench my Furnace-burning hart. **1732** Arbuthnot *Rules of Diet* in *Aliments*, etc. i. 406 When the worms are large they will consume the moisture.

d. *transf.* and *fig.*

1426 Lydg. *De Guil. Pilgr.* 2618 The soule..may profyt neuer a dele To bere frut..Of vertu,..ffor that yt lakketh moysture Off grace. **1622** Malynes *Anc. Law-Merch.* 64 Gaine was the radicall moisture of commerce. **1871** Morley *Crit. Misc.* Ser. i. *Carlyle* (1878) 173 A cloud of sedulous ephemera still suck a little spiritual moisture.

†**e.** A noxious exhalation or humidity. *Obs.*

1542 Boorde *Dyetary* iv. (1870) 239 To drye up the contagyous moysters of the walles. **1542-5** Brinklow *Lament.* (1874) 81 Oh Lorde God,..when they be in troble or plaged rightfullye of the, eyther be drught, moysture, or pestilence, or anye suche like.

†**3.** Liquid in general. *Obs.*

1530 Palsgr. 585/1, I hysse,..as a hote thyng whan one putteth to any moysture. **1555** [see bulwark *sb.* 1 b]. **1592** Kyd *Sol. & Pers.* i. iii. 80 The earth is my Countrey, As..the marine moisture To the red guild fish. **1697** Dryden *Virg. Past.* iii. 172 Now dam the Ditches, and the Floods restrain: Their Moisture has already drench'd the Plain. **1713** Addison *Cato* iii. v, When you..offer'd the full helmet up to Cato, Did he not dash th' untasted moisture from him? **1741** J. Martyn *Virg. Georg.* i. (1811) 80 Their wives..boil away the moisture of the sweet must over the fire.

4. *attrib.* and *Comb.*, as ***moisture-seal***, ***supply***; ***moisture-bearing***, ***-charged***, ***-holding***, ***-laden***, ***-loving***, ***-proof*** (hence ***-proofness***) adjs.; ***moisture-proofing*** vbl. sb.; **moisture content**, the proportional amount of moisture in any substance; **moisture cream**, a cosmetic cream which keeps the skin moist; a type of face-cream; cf. moisturizer; **moisture lotion**, a liquid preparation for moisturizing the skin; **moisture meter**, an instrument for indicating the moisture content of a substance (commonly by measuring its electrical resistivity).

1922 W. G. Kendrew *Climates of Continents* 290 The rainfall increases steadily towards the east and south. An irregularity is caused by the Appalachians,..within range of the moisture-bearing winds from both the Gulf and the Atlantic. **1895** Swettenham *Malay Sk.* 281 Plains and slopes of green on which the moisture-charged clouds unceasingly pour fatness. **1923** H. M. Bunbury *Destructive Distillation of Wood* iii. 20 The moisture content of the limbs or branches is also greater than that of the trunk. **1936** *Burlington Mag.* Nov. 229/2 It was necessary to bring the panels to the agreed moisture-content before these repairs were put in hand. **1952** L. M. Thompson *Soils & Soil Fertility* x. 159 Increasing the moisture content of soils increases the up-take of phosphorus. **1971** *Materials & Technol.* II. 601 The moisture content of coke may..be high because of its high porosity. **1957** *New Yorker* 2 Nov. 61/2 (Advt.), Tussy Moisture Cream and Lotion..won't let your skin dry out. **1961** *Which?* Mar. 58/1 Basically, like other types of face cream moisture creams are emulsions of oils, fats or waxes, with water. **1952** A. G. L. Hellyer *Sanders' Encycl. Gardening* (ed. 22) 407 Culture of Pears: Soil, well drained and well supplied with humus to improve moisture-holding capacity. **1959** *Times* 7 Dec. (Agric. Suppl.) p. viii/5 The moisture-holding properties of old clay wastings. **1896** *Allbutt's Syst. Med.* I. 252 The moisture-laden monsoon. **1957** Moisture lotion [see *moisture cream* above]. **1974** *Country Life* 28 Nov. 1694/3 Their own products include moisture lotion..eye shadow and lipsticks. **1827-35** Willis *May* 19 Dews for the moisture-loving flowers. **1911** E. M. Clowes *On Wallaby* x. 272 A thick grove of moisture-loving palms. **1949** V. G. Childe *Prehist. Communities Brit. Isles* (ed. 3) viii. 135 The land molluscs of this period are..no longer the moisture-loving woodland species found in the neolithic camps. **1974** *Country Life* 28 Feb. 443/2 The moisture-loving hydrangeas. **1952** *Sci. Amer.* Sept. 61 (*caption*) Moisture meter..senses moisture in textile yarn by electrical conductivity and controls the speed of the drying drum by feedback. **1970** *Harrods Catal.* May 20/2 Moisture meter indicates condition of soil... 47/-. **1904** *Electr. Rev.* (N.Y.) XLV. 422/1 These transformers are mounted in moistureproof iron cases and may be operated either dry or with oil. **1929** *U.S. Patent 1,737,187* 4/1 By the term 'moistureproof'..we mean the ability to resist the diffusion of water vapor to an extent at least as great as..that displayed by ordinary waxed papers..and functioning to resist the penetration of water vapor therethrough. **1960** *Farmer & Stockbreeder* 19 Jan. (Suppl.) 27/1 The birds being vacuum packed in moisture-proof bags. **1975** *Sci. Amer.* July 123/1 The cell that supports the mirror is also made of moistureproof plywood. **1929** *U.S. Pat. 1,737,187* 4/1 A sheet or film of regenerated cellulose combined with a moisture-proofing composition. **1971** J. F. Hanlon *Handbk. Package Engin.* x. 8 For moisture protection a layer of asphalt between two layers of paper is generally used. It is the least expensive moistureproofing, but in cold weather it becomes stiff. **1929** *U.S. Pat. 1,737,187* 4/1 The product..is one which has all of the desired properties of moistureproofness, flexibility,..and lack of odor. **1962** *Punch* 22 Aug. 256/1 We have improved on the moisture-proofness of Cellophane. **1960** Moisture-seal [see crisper b]. **1878** K. Johnston *Africa* ii. 26 There is naturally a marked difference in the moisture supply north and south of the Atlas.

†'**moisture**, *v. Obs.* Forms: 5-7 **moysture**, 6 **moster**, **moystre**, 6 **moisture**, 6-7 **moister**. [f. moisture *sb.*]

1. *trans.* To moisten; to water, make wet or damp.

1471 Ripley *Comp. Alch.* iii. viii. in Ashm. (1652) 141 Therwith dyd Hermes moysture hys Tre. **1545** Raynold *Byrth Mankynde* i. xi. (1552) 24 b, Moystrynge al that parte, as it were wyth a dewe. ? **1554** Coverdale *Hope Faithf.* xxxi. (1574) 221 They water and moisture all things, and make them fruteful. **1584** Lyly *Sappho* iii. iii. 18 Will you haue any of this Syrope, to moysture your mouth? **1610** Markham *Masterp.* i. xxxi. 60 It proceedeth only from flegme, cold and grosse, which moysturing the braine too much, causeth heauinesse.

2. *intr.* **a.** *to moisture away*: to decay from damp. **b.** To shed moisture.

1519 in *Fabric Rolls York Minster* (Surtees) 268 Item the amendynge of the dalmatykes for ye Advent & Septuagesym myghte be done wᵗ a litile cost, which nowe mosters away & not occupied. Item the lettron wherupon the gospell is red is moistered away & faullyn downe. **1610** G. Fletcher *Chr. Vict.* i. xl, Heau'n stole it selfe from earth by clouds that moisterd vnder.

'**moistureless**, *a.* Also *dial.* **moisterless.** [-less.] Lacking, or destitute of, moisture.

1828 J. Ruddiman *Tales & Sk.* 241 Some aged female, whose dry and moisterless eyes can best withstand the pungent fumes of the operation. **1847** in Webster. **1872** Jefferies *Wild Life in S.C.* 20 The chalk is moistureless, and nothing can grow on it.

moisturize ('mɔɪstjʊəraɪz, -stʃər-). *v.* [f. moisture *sb.* + -ize.] To render moist, used esp. of a cosmetic cream applied to the skin. Hence '**moisturized** *ppl. a.*; '**moisturizing** *vbl. sb.* and *ppl. a.*

1945 Mencken *Amer. Lang.* Suppl. I. 402 Verbs made of common nouns:..to moistureize. **1958** *Inside the ACD* (Amer. College Dict.) X. ii. 1/1 *Moisturize*: Television advertisers have been giving this word hard use. Creams and lotions now moisturize the skin and scalp. **1958** *Times* 22 Sept. 13/5 Intended for all types of skin, it [*sc.* a cream] is said to have balancing qualities which include moisturizing and mild stimulating action. **1958** *Vogue* July 5 This make-up..is moisturized to help guard your skin against the sun's chief danger, dryness. Wear it over..exquisite moisturised foundation. **1959** *News Chron.* 14 July 6/3 A very light type of fluid foundation..with a moisturising content. **1963** *Word Study* Dec. 6/2 The word *to moisturize*, currently fashionable in cosmetic and beauty-care advertising and attacked by some linguists as superfluous and barbaric. **1965** M. Frayn *Tin Men* i. 5 Tropical plants..perpetually watered by invisible built-in moisturising systems. **1966** *Harper's Bazaar* Sept. 73/2, I cover my face, lips too, with Veiled Radiance—it's essential that I use a moisturised base. **1971** *Homes & Gardens* Sept. 99/2 So much for the face, but the rest of the body will appreciate a little bit of moisturising as well. **1973** *Country Life* 26 Apr. 1194/4 The creamy moisturised lipsticks are available in pinks, browns, red and tawny tones. **1974** *She* Jan. 5 Skin Tone..moisturises and conditions your skin.

moisturizer ('mɔɪstjʊəraɪzə(r), -stʃər-). [f. moisturize *v.* + -er¹.] A preparation that renders or keeps the skin moist; a cosmetic cream.

1957 *Daily Mail* 17 Oct. 10/3 If the face then feels uncomfortably taut use a skin moisturiser before applying a foundation. **1966** J. S. Cox *Illustr. Dict. Hairdressing* 99/2 Moisturizer permanent wave. **1967** *Times* 17 Jan. 13/1 A moisturiser under the foundation is essential if the skin is dry. **1972** *Guardian* 7 Nov. 11/3 The Vichy preparations include complete ranges of cleansers, toners, moisturisers, night creams.

moisty ('mɔɪstɪ), *a.* [f. moist *a.* + -y¹.]

†**1.** Of ale: New. (= moist *a.* 2 b.) *Obs.*

c **1386** Chaucer *Manciple's Prol.* 60 For were it wyn or oold or moysty Ale That he hath dronke he speketh in his nose.

2. Moist, damp, wet. Now *rare.*

1422 tr. *Secreta Secret., Priv. Priv.* 219 The bloode Is hotte and moysti. **1561** Hollybush *Hom. Apoth.* 27 b, The Lyuerworte that groweth in moystye marishes or standinge waters. **1590** C'tess Pembroke *Antonie* 1317 Nor yet the cruell murth'ring blade Warm in the moistie bowells made Of people pell mell dieng. **1603** Drayton *Bar. Wars* ii. xxxv, Amongst the Ayre-bred moystie Vapours throwne. **1632** Lithgow *Trav.* ix. 404 The moysty and choaking heat. *c* **1666** Sir J. Lauder (Fountainhall) *Jrnls.* (S.H.S.) 76 Upright poddock stools..grow in humid, moisty places. **1889** F. R. Stockton *Ardis Claverden* (1890) 372 Tossed out upon the moisty air.

b. of a day, season, country, etc.

1545 Ascham *Toxoph.* ii. (Arb.) 156 A little winde in a moystie day, stoppeth a shafte more than a good whiskynge wynde in a clere daye. **1596** Spenser *F.Q.* vi. ix. 13 The moystie night..Her deawy humour gan on th' earth to shed. **1856** Lowell *Lett.* (1894) I. 301 A misty, moisty morning. **1861** Miss Yonge *Yng. Step-mother* ii, It is not doing the place justice to study it on a misty, moisty morning. **1894** P. Collier in *Forum* (U.S.) Aug. 731 A misty, moisty island [*sc.* England].

†**3.** Given to drink. *Obs. rare*⁻¹.

1593 'P. Foulface' *Bacchus Bountie* C 2, Which beeing once tasted, dooth maruellously encrease a moystie appetite.

moit (mɔɪt). *dial.* and *Austral.* [var. mote *sb.*¹] A particle of wood, stick, or some other substance caught in the wool of a sheep. Hence '**moiting** *vbl. sb.* (see quot. 1862), '**moity** *a.*

1862 C. C. Robinson *Dial. Leeds* 359 *Moiting*, a process in the manufacture of cloth, by which the wool, subsequent to being scoured..and preparatory to its passing through the 'willey', is cleansed from 'moits' or shivs. **1878** *Yorkshireman* 17 Aug. 97/2 I've a splendid lot [of wool] in just now—..not moity, and free from burr. **1878** 'R. Boldrewood' *Ups & Downs* viii. 83 The 'heavy and moity' parcels were not touched by the cautious operators at any price. **1903** *Eng. Dial. Dict.* IV. 144/2 T'sliver's full o' moits an' as rough as a bear's back. **1945** Baker *Austral. Lang.* iii.

67 Many terms used by Australian wool-traders come from old English dialect, including..*moits*, short pieces of stick and scrub, principally found in neck wool. **1959** —— *Drum* 127 *Moity* (of wool), carrying vegetable matter other than burr. **1965** J. S. Gunn *Terminol. Shearing Industry* II. 4 *Moit(s)*, pieces of stick and rubbish matted in wool, especially the neck wool.

moit, obs. Sc. form of MOAT *sb.*[1], MOTE.

moite(e, obs. form of MOIETY.

moither, moithern, var. ff. MOIDER, MATHERN.

moitie, -y, moitive, obs. ff. MOIETY, MOTIVE.

mojarra, variant of MOHARRA.

Mojave, var. MOHAVE.

mojo[1] ('məʊdʒəʊ). *local U.S.* [Prob. of Afr. orig.: cf. Gullah *moco* witchcraft, magic, Fula *moco'o* medicine man.] Magic, the art of casting spells; a charm or amulet used in such spells. Also *attrib.* and as *vb.*

1926 N. N. Puckett *Folk Beliefs Southern Negro* i. 19 The term *mojo* is often used by the Mississippi Negroes to mean 'charms, amulets, or tricks', as 'to work mojo' on a person or 'to carry a mojo'. **1930** R. Bass in A. Dundes *Mother Wit* (1973) 382/2 There are a few signs that are more or less common to all mojo-workers. *Ibid.* 384/2 [Of the deepest South] Their mojo is not fakery. It is not trickery. It is magic... Mojo is making its last stand. It has retreated to the swamp-lands. **1934** B. A. Botkin in W. T. Couch *Culture in South* xxvi. 585 Fragments of hoodoo and conjuration, whose spells,..mojos,..goofer bags are the special province of the Negro 'root doctor' or 'hoodoo man'. **1962** N. E. Whitten in A. Dundes *Mother Wit* (1973) 406/1 Local names for amulets are 'mojo', 'monjo', 'lucky hand'.. and 'jomo'. **1966** *Crescendo* Aug. 3/2 With his weather mojo working overtime he got four hot sunny days. **1970** R. Welburn in A. Chapman *New Black Voices* (1972) 356 It is overdue time To mojo the demons... Now it is time for mojo. **1971** *Black World* Apr. 81 A Mojo..a Mojo workin for you. **1973** C. Himes *Black on Black* 18 *Slick* (in a whining voice): You got the best go and the mojo.

mojo[2] ('məʊdʒəʊ). *U.S.* [Orig. unknown: see quot. 1955.] An addict's name for any narcotic drug, esp. morphine.

1935 A. J. Pollock *Underworld Speaks* 77/1 *Mojo*, any of the poisonous habit forming narcotics (dope). **1955** *Amer. Speech* XXX. 87 *Mojo* (probably from Sp. *mojar*, 'to celebrate by drinking')..a euphemism for morphine. **1963** R. I. McDavid *Mencken's Amer. Lang.* 725 An addict well supplied is *on the mojo* and is said to be *in high*. **1971** E. E. Landy *Underground Dict.* 134 *Mojo*,..morphine.

mok, obs. form of MOCK, MUCK *sb.* and *v.*

Moka, variant of MOCHA[2].

‖**mokaddam** (mɒ'kʌdʌm). *India.* Also 7 **mockadam, mocadan,** 9 **muccudum, mucuddum, mokaddam, mokhad(d)am, -em, mocuddim, -um, mukaddim, muquaddam.** [Arab. *muqaddam*, pa. pple. of *qaddama* to place in front.] = HEADMAN 1.

1634 Sir T. Herbert *Trav.* 36 The better sort [of the Banian priests of Surat] are called Mockadams, or Masters. **1653** H. Cogan tr. *Pinto's Trav.* iv. 8 The Jaylor, which in their language is called Mocadan [etc.]. **1801** R. Patton *Asiat. Mon.* 118 The subordinate collectors have been denominated choudries, and those who collected in villages, mocuddims. **1803** Wellington *Let.* 16 Sept. in Gurw. *Desp.* (1844) I. 712 It has more than once happened that soubahdars and muccudums, and between 60 and 100 drivers, have deserted in one night. **1870** Sir G. Campbell in *Syst. Land Tenure* (Cobden Club) 158 This headman was called the Mokaddum in the more northern and eastern provinces. **1891** *Blackw. Mag.* Mar. 371 The 'muqaddam of Spins' in Anglo-Indian parlance only means the chief of Spinsters. **1901** *Ibid.* Oct. 551 The minor sheikhs..have certain limited powers in nominating the Mokaddems or lesser officials.

mokado(u)r, variant forms of MUCKENDER.

moka-moka, variant of MOKO-MOKO.

moke[1] (məʊk). *dial.* Also 7 *pl.* **mockes.** [Assumed sing. of *mokes*:—OE. *máx* net: see MESH.] A mesh of a net. Also *pl.* wicker-work.

1604 *Hastings Corpor. Rec.* 4 Aug., in Cooper *Sussex Gloss.* (1853) 61 Any trawl-net, whereof the moak holdeth not five inches size throughout. **1669** Worlidge *Syst. Agric., Dict. Rust.*, The *Mocks* of a net, the mashes of a net. **1674** Ray *S. & E. C. Words* 72 The *Mokes* of a net. **1787** Grose *Provinc. Gloss.*, *Moke*, the mesh of a net. Also wicker-work, perhaps from the resemblance to the meshes of a net. Norf.

moke[2] (məʊk). *slang* and *dial.* [Of unknown origin. Cf. dial. *mokus* donkey (Hampshire, Devon).

In the 16th c. proverbial phrase 'Mocke (or Mok) hath lost her shoe' (Skelton *Why Nat to Courte*, 83, *Garlande of Laurell* 1396) it is possible that *Mocke* is a name for a donkey or a mare (cf. Skelton's use of MOCKISH *a.*), but connexion with the modern *moke* is unlikely. Senses 4 and 5 may be etymologically distinct.]

1. A donkey.

1848 [J. L. Tupper] in *Art & Poetry* No. 3 (1850) 131 They might live like gods, have infinite *smokes*, Drink infinite rum, drive infinite *mokes*. **1851** Mayhew *Lond. Labour* II. 85/1, I had a good moke (donkey), and a tidyish box ov a cart. **1854** Thackeray *Newcomes* xxx, Miss Chummey..inclines to the one [*sc.* of the costermongers] who rides from market on a moke rather than to the gentleman who sells his greens from a hand-basket. **1863** Kingsley *Water-Bab.* viii. 305 But he saw the end of such fellows, when he came to the island of the Golden Asses... For they were all turned into mokes with ears a yard long, for meddling with matters which they do not understand. **1871** J. R. Green *Lett.* (1901) 286 At last I have resumed my donkey... Never was such a moke. She rushes at the steepest hillside.

2. *transf.* 'A stupid fellow, a dolt' (*Cent. Dict.* 1890); = DONKEY 2.

1855 D. G. Rossetti *Let.* 25 Nov. (1965) I. 282 He has an irreconcilable grudge against a poor moke of a fellow called Archer Gurney. **1873** J. A. Mair *Handbk. Proverbs* 459 *Moke*, an old person, disrespectfully spoken to. **1915** *Dialect Notes* IV. 199 Terms of disparagement..*moke* about the same meaning and usage as *mutt*, or *boob*.

3. *Australian slang.* A very inferior horse.

1879 in L. A. Smith *Music of Waters* (1888) 356 For many a long time he tried a Derby to win, But I was the moke to carry him in. **1888** 'R. Boldrewood' *Robbery under Arms* I. viii. 105, I am regular shook on this old moke. **1891** *Argus* (Melbourne) 12 May 6/3, I have exchanged my hired moke for a fine black horse. **1898** in M. Davitt *Life & Progr. Australia* xxxv. 191 And a bosom friend's a 'cobber' And a horse a 'prad' or 'moke'. **1901** M. Franklin *My Brilliant Career* xxvi. 220 My old moke flung a shoe and went dead lame. **1928** 'Brent of Bin Bin' *Up Country* xiii. 210 If I lend you my mokes, the bridles are mine if you win. **1943** 'W. Hatfield' *I find Austral.* 53 He's an old quiet moke these days.

4. *U.S.* A Negro.

1856 C. White *Oh, Hush!* 9 Rose, don't you interfere, I'll show dis moke a sight. **1871**, **1879** in Schele de Vere *Americanisms*. **1882** G. W. Peck *Peck's Sunshine* 53 They want to hear old fashioned negro melodies, and yet these mokes will tackle Italian opera. **1901** *Cosmopolitan* Sept. 637/2 Across the stage have paraded long processions of 'musical mokes', 'knock-abouts' and 'monologists'. **1945** Mencken *Amer. Lang.* Suppl. I. 635 *Moke* was thrown into competition with *coon* in 1899 by the success of 'Smokey *Mokes*', a popular song by Holzmann and Lind.

5. *Theatrical slang.* 'A variety performer who plays on several instruments' (*Cent. Dict.* 1890).

moke[3]. *dial.* Also **moak.** [Of obscure origin. Cf. *Sc.* MOCH *a.* and MUGGY *a.*; also Sw. dial. *moket* cloudy (Rietz).] A mist, fog.

1866 J. E. Brogden *Lincoln. Gloss.*, *Moke*,..a mist, foggy thick weather. **1876** *Mid-Yorksh. Gloss.*, *Moke*,..cloud and dampness together.

Hence **'moky** *a. dial.* (See quots.)

1706 Phillips (ed. Kersey), *Moky*, (old Word) cloudy; as *Moky Weather*. **1736** Ainsworth *Lat. Dict.*, Moky weather, *tempestas caliginosa*. **1866** J. E. Brogden *Lincoln. Gloss.*, *Moaky*, hazy, dull, dark, weather.

Moke[4] (məʊk). = *Mini-Moke* (see MINI- b).

1963 *Daily Tel.* 8 Jan. 11/1 BMC believes the twin-engine Moke could be useful to farmers and for military and industrial use. **1967** *Guardian* 26 June 5/2 The Moke, a risky, insolent-looking little vehicle..has the minute quality of a 'Dinky' car. **1969** [see FADE *sb.*[1] 1]. **1974** A. Williams *Gentleman Traitor* ix. 135 Keys to Thackeray Mansions and the Moke.

moke, obs. form of MOCK, MUCK *sb.* and *v.*

mokedore, variant of MUCKENDER.

mokel(l, moker, obs. ff. MICKLE, MOCKER[1].

mok-e-mok, var. MOKI-MOKI.

†**mokerard.** *Obs.* [See -ARD.] = MUCKERER, miser.

1303 R. Brunne *Handl. Synne* 6230 Auaryce, ryche and harde, ys a þefe, a mokerad [*v. r.* mokerard].

mokere, mokerer, obs. ff. MUCKER, MUCKERER.

mokhad(d)am, variant of MOKADDAM.

‖**moki**[1] ('mɔki). [Maori.] Either of two New Zealand marine fishes, *Latridopsis ciliaris*, which is blue-grey and white, or the red moki, *Chironemus spectabilis*, which is reddish-brown, with dark brown bars on its sides; also, formerly, the blue cod, *Parapercis colias*.

[**1820** *Gram. & Voc. Lang. N. Zealand* (C.M.S.) 182 *Moki*, *s.* A fish so called.] **1845** E. J. Wakefield *Adventure in N.Z.* I. iv. 93 The *moki* is also a well-flavoured fish, weighing 10 lbs. or 12 lbs. **1851** E. Ward *Jrnl.* 14 Feb. (1951) 129 A Maori brought us a fish today which he called 'Moko'—it was a very fair fish. **1857** Hursthouse *N. Zealand* I. 122 Sea fish are more plentiful: the best are the Hapuka,..the Moki, the Wharehou [etc.]. **1893** *Star* 25 May 2/8 The fish in question was New Zealand 'Moki', or blue cod, as it is called there, though it has less affinity with cod than with our own gray mullet. **1960** Doogue & Moreland *N.Z. Sea Anglers' Guide* 235 Red Moki... Belongs to the same family [*sc.* the Chironemidæ] as tarakihi and porae, but the stouter body form and colour distinguish it immediately. **1968** *N.Z. Listener* 15 Mar. 6/1 I've left a moki and a feed of crayfish in the outside safe. **1971** *N.Z. News* 3 Feb. 3/2 A member of the Whangarei Underwater Club..shot a six-pound red moki.

‖**moki**[2] ('mɔki). Also **mogey, moggie, mokihi, moguey.** [Maori.] A kind of Maori raft. (See quots.)

1835 J. A. Wilson *Jrnl.* 25 Aug. in *Missionary Life & Work N.Z.* (1889) ii. 25 The moki only carries one person at a time. You sit as on horseback. **1840** J. S. Polack *Manners & Cust. New Zealanders* I. 226 In the absence of canoes, a quantity of dried bulrushes are fastened together, on which the native is enabled to cross a stream..; these humble conveyances are called moki. **1858** *Jrnl. Ho. Represent. N. Zealand* App. iii. 18 (Morris), We crossed the river on mokis. **1860** W. C. *Let.* 16 Apr. in J. H. Beattie *Pioneers explore Otago* (1947) vii. 45 He started in the dead of winter, on a moggie by himself... He crossed and re-crossed the lake several times. **1871** C. L. Money *Knocking About in N. Zealand* 52 (ibid.), Moguey, a Maori name for a raupo or flax-stick raft. **1884** R. C. Reid *Rambles on Golden Coast N.Z.* 53 It had been used by the diggers as the keel of their 'mogey'. **1889** V. Pyke *Wild Will Enderby* 115 From amongst the bushes he drew forth a 'mokihi', on which he crossed the river in safety. **1963** *Evening Post* (Wellington, N.Z.) 9 Dec., He made the journey from Kingston to Queenstown on a mokihi.

attrib. **1858** *Jrnl. Ho. Represent. N. Zealand* App. iii. 18 (Morris), Moki navigation.

moki, var. MOKI-MOKI.

‖**mokihana** (moki'hana). Also **mokehana.** [Hawaiian.] A Hawaiian tree, *Pelea anisata*, of the family Rutaceæ.

1888 W. Hillebrand *Flora Hawaiian Islands* 64 *P[elea] anisata*... Nat[ive] name: 'Mokehana'.—All parts of the tree, but particularly the capsules, when bruised, emit a strong spicy odor of anise. **1915** W. A. Bryan *Nat. Hist. Hawaii* xv. 221 The most highly scented of all are the seed pods of the mokihana used in making leis. **1954** *Ellery Queen's Mystery Mag.* Oct. 45/1 She..hung around her neck a *lei* of *mokihana* and *maile*.

‖**moki-moki** ('mɒkɪmɒkɪ). *N.Z.* Also **mok-e-mok, moki, moki-mok, mokky.** [Maori.] = MAKOMAKO[1]; MOKO-MOKO 2.

1928 *Daily Express* 6 June 3 What is the moki-moki? **1935** E. Hodgkinson in A. E. Currie *Cent. Treas. Otago Verse* (1949) 33 The forest rings with tuis' and mokis' chiming. **1940** N. Marsh *Surfeit of Lampreys* (1941) xiv. 218 English birdsong there was pierced by the colder and deeper notes of bell-birds and mok-e-moks. *a* **1948** L. G. D. Acland *Early Canterbury Runs* (1951) 361 Bell-bird.—Mako-mako, or Moki-mok... The name is still sometimes used; but the bird is now generally called a 'Mokky'.

mokkar, mokkery, obs. ff. MOCKER[1], MOCKERY.

‖**moko**[1] ('mɔkɔ). [Maori.] The system of tattooing practised by the Maoris; also, any particular pattern of tattooing.

[**1769** J. Banks *Jrnl.* 22 Nov. (1896) 203 The people.. were browner..and they had a much larger quantity of *amoca* or black stains upon their bodies and faces... In this particular, I mean the use of *amoca*, almost every tribe seems to have a different custom. **1823** Cruise *Jrnl. Resid. N. Zealand* 310 The lines upon the faces and persons of the New Zealanders are universally designated amoco.] **1855** R. Taylor *Te Ika a Maui* 150 The grand ornament of all was the moko or tattoo. **1896** Robley (*title*) Moko; or Maori Tattooing. **1896** —— *Moko* 13 Fig. 8. —— Moko signature on a deed. *Ibid.* 16 He drew for Dr. Traill the mokos of his brother and of his son.

Hence **'moko** *v. trans.*, to tattoo in the Maori manner. Hence **'mokoed** *ppl. a.*

1896 Robley *Moko* 183 Mokoed heads in museums and collections. **1902** Webster Suppl., *Moko*, *v. t.*

moko[2] ('məʊkəʊ). *slang.* (See quot.)

1860 *Hotten's Slang Dict.* (ed. 2), *Moko*, a name given by sportsmen to pheasants killed by mistake in partridge shooting during September, before the pheasant shooting comes in. They pull out their tails and roundly assert they are no pheasants at all, but mokos.

‖**moko-moko** ('mɔkɔ'mɔkɔ). Also **mako-mako, moka-moka.** [Maori.]

1. A New Zealand species of lizard (*Lygosoma ornatum* or *L. moko*).

[**1820** *Gram. & Voc. Lang. N. Zealand* (C.M.S.) 182 *Moko moko*, a small lizard.] **1902** in Webster *Suppl.*

2. The Bell-bird, *Anthornis melanura*.

a **1888** A. W. Bathgate in Sladen *Australian Ball.* 22 (*title*) To the Moko-Moko, or Bell-Bird. **1889** Parker *Catal. N. Zealand Exhib.* 119 (Morris s.v. Bell-bird), Bell-bird,..or Mako-mako (*Anthornis melanura*), is still common in many parts of the South Island. **1900** *Longm. Mag.* Jan. 231 The tuis and moka-mokas vie with each other to see who can sing the sweetest.

moksha ('mɒkʃə). *Hinduism* and *Jainism.* Also 8 **moksh,** 9- **moksa.** [Skr. *moksha* liberation, emancipation, f. *muc* to loose, release.] The final liberation of the soul when it is exempted from further transmigration; the bliss attained by this liberation. Also called MUKTI.

1785 C. Wilkins tr. *Bhăgvăt-Geetā* xvi. 115 The divine destiny is for *Mōksh*, or eternal absorption in the divine nature. **1828** H. H. Wilson in *Asiatick Res.* XVI. 104 An important consequence of this doctrine is the denial of *Moksha*, in its more generally received sense, that of absorption into the universal spirit. **1831** V. Kennedy *Res. Anc. & Hindu Mythol.* vi. 185 The terms employed for final beatitude, that is identification with the supreme Being.. are *kaivalyam*, *moksha*, or *jivanmukti*. **1840** H. H. Wilson *Two Lect. Relig. Pract. Hindus* ii. 64 All the philosophical schools propose for their object the ascertainment of those means by which the wanderings of the soul may be arrested, ..its emancipation from bodily imprisonment and degradation be effected for ever. This is what is termed *Moksha*, or *Muktî*. **1875** M. Williams *Indian Wisdom* vii. 131 There are three 'gems' which together effect the soul's *Moksha*..right intuition..right knowledge..right conduct. **1915** *Encycl. Relig. & Ethics* VIII. 772/1 *Mokṣa* as the supreme aspiration runs through that best known portion of the *Mahābhārata* epic called the *Bhagavad-Gītā*. **1933** J. Baillie *And Life Everlasting* (1934) v. 118 In the concurrent tendency to regard *nirvana*—or *moksha*..as a state not of utter annihilation but of (unconscious) blissful union with the divine, we may surely find a foreshadowing..of a positive doctrine of eternal life. **1962** A. Huxley *Island* ix.

136 Murugan calls it dope... We, on the contrary, give the stuff good names—the *moksha*-medicine, the reality-revealer, the truth-and-beauty pill. **1971** *Illustr. Weekly India* 11 Apr. 9/2 They are the Tirthankaras, the Finders of the ford by which to cross the Ocean of Rebirth, or the Guides that show the way to *moksha*.

mokuk, var. MOCOCK.

mokum (ˈməʊkəm). [a. Japanese *moku-me*.] An alloy used in metal-work.

[**1884** C. G. W. LOCK *Workshop Receipts* Ser. III. 38/2 Attention should be called to the so-called moku-me, a word which might be rendered by 'veins of the wood'.] **1889** BRANNT *Krupp & Wildberger's Metallic Alloys* 322 The so-called 'mokum', an alloy..introduced from Japan... Chiefly used for decorations upon gold and silver articles.

mol, variant form of MAIL *sb.*², MULL.

mol: see MOLE *sb.*⁷

‖**mola**¹ (ˈməʊlə). [L. *mola* (1) millstone; (2) salt cake; (3) a false conception (after Gr. μύλη). Senses 2 and 3 below are mod.Latin.]

1. A fleshy mass occurring in the womb; a false conception; = MOLE *sb.*⁵ Also *transf.* and *fig.*

1601 HOLLAND *Pliny* I. 163 A false conception called Mola, *i.* a moone calfe. **1636** JAMES *Iter Lanc.* (Chetham Soc.) 9, I hope no sisters did of molaes dye. **1646** SIR T. BROWNE *Pseud. Ep.* II. vi. 93 Many Mola's and false conceptions there are of Mandrakes. **1649** G. DANIEL *Trinarch., Hen. IV*, cccxlix, The Age (it seemes) after soe great a Birth In Treason, as his owne, broke in the Cell; Slipt her Rebellions, like rude Molaes forth. **1671** GREW *Anat. Plants* iv. App. §1 These Thorns [have their origin], from the outer, and less fecund Part; and so produceth no Leaves, but is, as it were, the Mola of a Bud. **1753** N. TORRIANO *Midwifry* 39 Mola's and false Conceptions. **1822–34** *Good's Study Med.* (ed. 4) IV. 196 The human mola sometimes attains considerable developement without either brain or spinal cord.

†**2.** A fish; = MOLE *sb.*⁶ 1, MOLEBUT.

The Latin word is in Carpentier's additions to Du Cange, with a quotation from an anonymous MS. of the 16th c.; the passage is in Rondelet *De Pisc. Mar.* (1554) 425: see MOLEBUT.

1678 PHILLIPS (ed. 4), *Mola*, a Fish found in the Adriatick Sea.

3. *Ent.* The grinding surface of the broad basal projection of the mandible of certain insects.

1826 KIRBY & SP. *Entomol.* III. 437 These mandibles.. are furnished with..miniature mill-stones to grind it [*i.e.* food]. The part here alluded to I call the *Mola*.

mola² (ˈməʊlə). [Native name.] A square of brightly coloured, appliquéd cloth worn as a blouse by Cuna Indian women of the San Blas Islands, Panama. Also *attrib.*

1941 *Nat. Geogr. Mag.* Feb. 217 With the skirt is worn a short-sleeved waist called a *mola*. The mola is of true Indian manufacture. **1964** I. SALEM tr. *M. & H. Larsen's Forests Panama* viii. 99 These *molas*..are perhaps the only really interesting things produced by the Cuna. Layers of different-coloured materials are cut into various shapes and superimposed one on another to produce a very colourful raised design. *Ibid.*, Some of these *molas* still depict the rather naïve, stylized animals portrayed on pre-Columbian pottery. **1966** J. M. KELLY *Cuna* i. 26 The 'Mola' tops had been introduced by the Spaniards who didn't like the women walking around with their breasts showing. **1972** *Islander* (Victoria, B.C.) 23 July 7/3 The women are known for their 'molas'. A mola is a square of five layers of material, and each piece is cut to show the colors of the different layers underneath. **1973** M. MACKINTOSH *King & Two Queens* v. 79 'These are original Cuna Indian molas,' said Rodger, 'and the most modern things in this upper hall.' **1974** *Daily Colonist* (Victoria, B.C.) 10 July 18/5 Molas are worn by women and girls of the Cuna tribe. The rectangular panels, approximately 16 by 24 inches, are worn in matched sets on the front and back of the blouse atop wrap-around print skirts.

†**molair.** *Obs. rare. Anat.* Used in pl. as rendering of L. *molaria* in the early editions of Vegetius IV. i; mod. editors read *malaria*, but the meaning is not clear. Topsell 1607, rendering the same passage, has 'grinding bones'; Markham 1610, copying Blundevil, has *molairs*, which in ed. 1675 becomes *molars*.

1580 BLUNDEVIL *Diet. Horses* viii. 4b, Then there is a great bone in his [the horse's] breast wherevnto are fastened .xxxvi. ribbes. And to the Columell behind be two bones, and from the molairs to the ioints other two.

molal (ˈməʊləl), *a. Physical Chem.* [f. MOLE *sb.*⁷ + -AL.] **a.** = MOLAR *a.*³ a, MOLECULAR *a.* 1 a.

1908 GOODWIN & MAILEY in *Physical Rev.* XXVI. 49 In the fifth column we have computed the values of the fluidity F divided by the corresponding molecular volume ϕ of the liquid; this we have denoted by f and called the molal fluidity. **1923** LEWIS & RANDALL *Thermodynamics* iii. 22 If w is the molal mass of a substance (also known as molal weight or molecular weight), a mol of the substance in question is defined as w grams. **1972** *Science* 2 June 1011/2 Carbon dioxide..has a molecular weight M of 44 and a partial molal volume of 34·8 ml/mole.

b. Of a solution: containing one mole, or a specified number of moles, of solute per kilogramme of solvent or (now *rare*) per litre of solution. Of a concentration: expressed in terms of these quantities. Cf. MOLAR *a.*³ b.

1923 LEWIS & RANDALL *Thermodynamics* iv. 33 When we speak of a molal or tenth molal aqueous solution.., we shall refer, not to the concentration, but to the number of mols of solute in 1000 grams of water, which we may call the molality. **1924** J. C. W. FRAZER in H. S. Taylor *Treat. Physical Chem.* I. vii. 236 Concentrations expressed in terms of 1000 cc. of solution and using the above methods of expressing the amounts of substances are known as molal, formal or normal concentrations. **1930** W. T. HALL *Textbk. Quantitative Analysis* iii. 26 A solution is said to be molal in hydrogen ions if it contains 1·008 g of H^+ per liter. **1938** LUNDELL & HOFFMAN *Outl. Methods Chem. Analysis* xxxv. 127 One author will regard a solution containing one mole of solute per liter of solution as molal, whereas another calls such a solution molar. **1965** PHILLIPS & WILLIAMS *Inorg. Chem.* I. vii. 250 The activity coefficient is then around 10^{-14} for molal solutions of these ions. **1970** [see MOLALITY below].

Hence **moˈlality**, the molal concentration of a solution.

1923 [see sense b above]. **1931** [see MOLARITY]. **1963** W. J. MOORE *Physical Chem.* (ed. 4) v. 117 One advantage of molality is that it is easy to prepare a solution of given molality by accurate weighing procedures. **1970** *Man. Symbols & Terminol. Physicochem. Quantities & Units* (I.U.P.A.C.) 12 A solution having a molality equal to 0·1 mol kg^{-1} is sometimes called a 0·1 molal solution. **1973** [see MOLARITY].

Molale (məʊˈlɑːliː). Also **Molele**. [Native name.] A Penutian Indian people of Oregon; a member of this people; also, their language. Also *attrib.*

1846 H. HALE in *U.S. Exploring Expedition 1838–42: Ethnogr. & Philol.* 561 The Waiilatpu family [of languages]. .. Waiilatpu... Moléle. **1848** *Trans. Amer. Ethnol. Soc.* II. i. 15 These Indians [*sc.* the Waiilatpu] include two tribes, the Cayuse..: and the Molele, west of the Cayuse..in the mountainous territory about Mounts Hood and Vancouver ..; probably extinct. *Ibid.* 77 Waiilatpu,..*Language*.. Molele. **1891** *7th Ann. Rep. U.S. Bureau Amer. Ethnol. 1885–86* 127 Hale established this family and placed under it the Cailloux or Cayuse or Willetpoos, and the Molele... The Molále were a mountain tribe and occupied a belt of mountain country south of the Columbia River. *Ibid.* 128 There are 31 Molále now on the Grande Ronde Reservation, Oregon. **1965** *Canad. Jrnl. Ling.* Spring 124 Inland, no.. Molale, or Cayuse were found. **1966** C. F. & F. M. VOEGELIN *Map N. Amer. Indian Lang.* (*caption*) Molale language isolate. **1972** *Language* XLVIII. 380 A Molale myth.

†**molan.** *Obs.* Also 4 **molayne**, 5 **molane**, **mulan**. [Of obscure origin: cf. MOLLET.] A bit for a horse.

13.. *Gaw. & Gr. Knt.* 169 His molaynes, & alle þe metail anamayld was þenne, þe steropes þat he stod on, stayned of þe same. **1483** *Cath. Angl.* 242/2 A molan [*MS. M. erron.* mokan, *MS. A.* molane] of a brydelle, *lorale, mordaculum, salmares*. *Ibid.* 246/1 A Mulan, *vbi* Molan (A.).

molar (ˈməʊlə(r)), *a.*¹ and *sb.* Also 7 **molare**, and 7–8 *pl.* in L. form **molares**. [ad. L. *molār-is* belonging to a mill (*sb.* millstone, grinder tooth), f. *mola* a millstone: see -AR¹. Cf. F. *molaire* (16th c.); also AF. *dentz moellers* (Britton).]

A. *adj.*

1. Grinding, serving to grind. **a.** *spec.* Applied to the back-teeth or grinders of mammals, and the flat or rounded grinding teeth of certain fishes.

1626 BACON *Sylva* §752 The Back-Teeth, which we call the Molar-Teeth, or Grinders. *a* **1661** FULLER *Worthies, Cheshire* (1662) I. 172 How necessary these [mill stones] are for mans sustenance, is proved by the painful experience of such aged persons, who wanting their Molare Teeth must make use of their Gums for Grinders. **1728** BAILEY, *Molar Teeth* (*i.e.* Grinders), the five outmost Teeth on either side of the Mouth. **1871** DARWIN *Desc. Man.* I. i. 36 It appears as if the posterior molar or wisdom-teeth were tending to become rudimentary in the more civilised races of man. **1888** ROLLESTON & JACKSON *Anim. Life* 12 The number of molar teeth is greater in the Hare and Rabbit than in any other Rodents.

fig. **1831** SYD. SMITH *Wks.* (1859) II. 219/2 The majority of the new members will be landed gentlemen: their genus is utterly distinct from the revolutionary tribe; they have Molar teeth; they are destitute of the carnivorous and incisive jaws of political adventurers.

b. *gen.*

1844 *Civil Engin. & Arch. Jrnl.* VII. 401/2 The peculiar mechanical power which streams employ in forming their channels by the operation of cataracts,..the molar or grinding process, most common in mountainous countries.

2. Of or pertaining to a molar-tooth. ***molar forceps*** (see quot. 1884).

1831 R. KNOX *Cloquet's Anat.* 599 At the back part, between the masseter and buccinator muscles, are two small bodies formed of the assemblage of these follicles. They are designated by the name of *Molar Glands*, because the orifice of their excretory duct is situated opposite the last molar tooth. **1884** KNIGHT *Dict. Mech.* Suppl. 613/2 *Molar Forceps*, heavy forceps for extracting the molars; or cowhorn forceps for eradicating roots when the crowns have decayed below the alveolar process. **1891** *Syd. Soc. Lex.*, *Molar glands*.

3. *Ent.* Of or pertaining to a mola.

1879 WOOD-MASON in *Trans. Ent. Soc. Lond.* 152 In.. other 'Rove-beetles',..no molar process is developed. *Ibid.*, The molar branch of the jaws in *Blatta* and *Machilis*.

4. *Path.* Of the nature of a mola or false conception.

1822–34 *Good's Study Med.* (ed. 4) IV. 186 Simulating pregnancy, from molar concretions. **1891** in *Syd. Soc. Lex.*

B. *sb.*

1. A molar or grinding tooth; a grinder; spec., a ***true molar***, a molar tooth in the adult which is not preceded by a deciduous or milk-molar. ***false molar***, a pre-molar; a molar tooth which has replaced a deciduous or milk-tooth.

1541 [see DUAL *sb.* 2]. **1671** J. WEBSTER *Metallogr.* ix. 140 Two or three of the molares or grinding teeth of an old Cow. **1767** *Phil. Trans.* LVII. 465 None of the molares, or grinding teeth of elephants, are discovered with these tusks. **1834** MCMURTRIE *Cuvier's Anim. Kingd.* 50 The canini have two roots, which causes them to partake of the nature of false molars. **1855** W. S. DALLAS in *Syst. Nat. Hist.* II. 494 The true molars are furnished with sharply tubercular crowns. **1881** MIVART *Cat* 29 Behind the third premolar is an exceedingly small tooth, which is called a true molar.

2. *Ichthyology.* A tooth which has a rounded or convex or a flat surface.

1880 GÜNTHER *Fishes* 344 In all the species [*sc.* of *Myliobatidæ*] the dentition consists of perfectly flat molars, forming a kind of mosaic pavement. *Ibid.* 406 Jaws [*sc.* of *Sargina*] with a single series of incisors in front, and with several series of rounded molars on the side.

3. *Ent.* One of the thick internal processes with a grinding surface found on and near the base of the mandibles of many insects.

1892 J. B. SMITH in *Trans. Amer. Entom. Soc.* XIX. 84 Another of the basal pieces,..I propose to call the *molar*, or grinder... In the present species the molars are ridged and dissimilar.

molar (ˈməʊlə(r)), *a.*² [f. L. *mōlēs* mass; see -AR¹; cf. MOLE *sb.*³] **a.** Pertaining to mass; acting on or by means of large masses of matter. Often contrasted with *molecular*.

1862 H. SPENCER *First Princ.* II. v. §55 (1875) 181 The molar motion which disappears when a bell is struck by its clapper, reappears in the bell's vibrations. **1871** TYNDALL *Fragm. Sci.* (1879) I. xii. 360 This cleavage is..molar, not molecular. **1903** F. W. H. MYERS *Human Personality* II. 509 This apparently molar world consists..of at least two interpenetrating environments, molecular and etherial.

b. *Psychol.* (See quot. 1932.)

1925 C. D. BROAD *Mind & its Place* xiv. 616, I will lump together all such changes under the name of 'molar behaviour', as contrasted with 'molecular behaviour'. **1932** E. C. TOLMAN *Purposive Behavior* I. i. 7 On the one hand, he [*sc.* J. B. Watson] has defined behavior in terms of its strict physical and physiological details, i.e., in terms of receptor-process, conductor-process, and effector-process per se. We shall designate this as the molecular definition of behavior. And on the other hand, he has come to recognize ..that behavior..is more than and different from the sum of its physiological parts. Behavior..has descriptive and defining properties of its own. And we shall designate this latter as the molar definition of behavior. **1946** C. MORRIS *Signs, Lang. & Behavior* ii. 55 Behavioristics naturally attempts to supplement its description of behavior in molar or macroscopic terms. **1971** *Jrnl. Gen. Psychol.* LXXXIV. 157 Attention has been concentrated on those papers which do not support the notion that single cell behavior is reflected in molar behavior.

molar (ˈməʊlə(r)), *a.*³ *Physical Chem.* [f. MOL(E *sb.*⁷ + -AR¹.] **a.** Of or pertaining to one mole of a substance; = MOLAL *a.* a, MOLECULAR *a.* 1 a.

1902 A. FINDLAY tr. *Ostwald's Princ. Inorg. Chem.* vi. 89 The ratio of the weight of a given gas to that of an equal volume of the normal gas under the same conditions, is called its molecular weight or its molar weight. Since the former name has been derived from certain hypothetical notions regarding the constitution of the gases, notions which are not essential to the actual facts, we shall give preference to the name molar weight although, at present, the other is still the one most used. **1906** [see *gramme-molecular* adj. s.v. GRAM² b]. **1946** J. R. PARTINGTON *Gen. & Inorg. Chem.* i. 7 This is called the molar volume V_m, and Avogadro's hypothesis shows that it is the same for all substances. **1962** P. J. & B. DURRANT *Introd. Adv. Inorg. Chem.* xi. 303 If both sides of the equation are multiplied by the molecular weight M and divided by the density ρ, $(k-1)M/(k+2)\rho = \frac{4}{3}\pi N\alpha = P_M$ where N is Avogadro's number and P_M is known as the molar polarisation. *Ibid.* 307 A quantity R known as the molar refraction. **1967** *Oceanogr. & Marine Biol.* V. 154 Some normal calcite and a small amount of dolomite with a molar ratio of $CaCO_3$:$MgCO_3$ of 1·1:1 were also present.

b. Of a solution: containing one mole, or a specified number of moles, of solute per litre of solution. Of a concentration: expressed in terms of these quantities. Cf. MOLAL *a.* b.

1927 C. J. ENGELDER *Textbk. Elem. Qualitative Analysis* I. 4 Thus 34·468 grams of HCl or 58·46 grams of NaCl, dissolved and diluted to one liter, are molar solutions of these compounds. **1946** *Nature* 26 Oct. 585/1 The molar concentration required to produce a given effect is approximately one third that of the preceding member [of a homologous series]. **1970** *Man. Symbols & Terminol. Physicochem. Quantities & Units* (I.U.P.A.C.) 12 A solution with a concentration of 0·1 mol dm^{-3} is often called a 0·1 molar solution. **1971** G. D. CHRISTIAN *Analytical Chem.* i. 9 A one-molar solution of silver nitrate and a one-molar solution of sodium chloride will react on an equal-volume basis.

Hence **moˈlarity**, the molar concentration of a solution.

1931 J. C. WARE *Analytical Chem.* I. i. 3 Where the solubility is very small, the molarity and the molality of the solution will be approximately the same. **1951** M. A. PAUL *Princ. Chem. Thermodynamics* vii. 388 The molarity of a given solution evidently varies in general with temperature. **1970** *Man. Symbols & Terminol. Physiochem. Quantities & Units* (I.U.P.A.C.) 12 Concentration is sometimes called 'molarity' but this name is both unnecessary and liable to cause confusion with molality and is therefore not recommended. **1973** BLOCK & HOLLIDAY *Mod. Physical Chem.* ix. 203 In general, molarities cannot easily be related either to mole fraction or to molality, unless the changes in volume on dissolution are either negligible or can be allowed for.

molariform (məʊ'lærɪfɔːm), *a. Bot.* and *Zool.* [ad. mod.L. *mŏlāriform-is*, f. L. *molār-is*: see -FORM.] Having the form of a molar tooth.

1856 in MAYNE *Expos. Lex.* **1888** O. THOMAS *Catal. Marsupialia Brit. Mus.* 4 The milk-premolar well developed and long-persistent, molariform. **1903** *Amer. Jrnl. Sci.* XV. 176 The premolars rarely become molariform.

molarization (məʊləraɪ'zeɪʃən). *Zool.* [f. MOLAR *a.*[1] and *sb.* + -IZATION.] The assumption, during the course of evolution, of the characteristics of a molar tooth by a non-molar tooth (usu. a premolar).

1937 *Proc. Zool. Soc.* B. CVII. 104 The molarization of the premolars is a case of convergent evolution. **1953** J. S. HUXLEY *Evolution In Action* ii. 56 The so-called molarization of the pre-molars.—The gradual conversion of the front grinders, which have milk-teeth predecessors, so as to resemble the true molars, which develop later and have no 'milk' fore-runners. **1972** *Nature* 24 Nov. 236/1 A morphological complex characterizes the earliest hominids. This complex..includes..lowering of the molar cusps, molarization of the premolars, [etc.].

So **'molarized** *ppl. a.*, showing the consequences of molarization.

1971 A. A. DAHLBERG *Dental Morphol. & Evolution* viii. 99 The more distant from the canine, the more molarized or cuspidate the tooth. **1973** *Nature* 14 Sept. 106/1 In other cretaceous eutherians P^4 is always three-rooted and partly molarized.

molary ('məʊlərɪ), *a.* [ad. F. *molaire* MOLAR *a.*: see -ARY[2].] Adapted for grinding or pulverizing food; = MOLAR *a.*[1] 1.

1826 KIRBY & SP. *Entomol.* III. xxxiv. 435 He [Marcel de Serres]..divides them [*sc.* the teeth of the Orthoptera] into *incisive* or cutting, *laniary* or canine, and *molary* or grinding teeth. **1835** KIRBY *Hab. & Inst. Anim.* II. xxi. 381 Their laniary, incisive, and molary teeth. **1884** *Sunday at Home* Jan. 28/2 It is this unequal wearing surface of the elephant's grinders which makes them truly 'molary' or 'mill-stony'.

†**mo'lass.** *Sc. Obs.* Also molash. [Assumed sing. form from MOLASSES.] = MOLASSES 2.

1773 FERGUSSON in Herd *Songs* (1904) 48 The ignorant ass Who drinks all the evening at burning molass. *a* **1779** D. GRAHAM *Coalm. Crtship.* Writ. 1883 II. 51 Spout ye a mutchkin o' molash in her cheek, ye'll get her mind an' speed the better. **1813** G. BRUCE *Poems* 25 The only guid molass has dune, Some drouthie wives it's sent hame soon.

Hence **mo'lassed** *ppl. a.*, drunk with 'molass'.

1789 W. BUCHAN *Dom. Med.* (1790) 98 *note*, The common people have got so universally into the habit of drinking this base spirit, that when a porter or labourer is seen reeling along the streets, they say, *he has got molassed.*

‖**molasse** (mɔlas). *Geol.* Also 8 mollasse. [F. *molasse.*] A soft coherent greenish sandstone of Miocene age, esp. that peculiar to the region between the Alps and the Jura.

1796 KIRWAN *Elem. Min.* (ed. 2) I. 99 *Mollasse*, a grey or yellowish grey stone, found in the neighbourhood of Lausanne, and various parts of France. **1827** R. JAMESON tr. *Cuvier's Theory Earth* 97 Certain lignites and molasses do in fact contain them [*i.e.* fossil remains of terrestrial mammifera]. **1886** J. GEIKIE *Outl. Geol.* 351 The lower portions of this Molasse pertain to the Oligocene.

molasses (mə'læsɪz). Forms: 6 melasus, molassos, 6–7 malasso(e)s, 7 molosso(e)s, malosses, mallassus, mellasses, mullasses, 7–8 molosses, -us, 8 molossa's, mollossus, 7–9 melasses, 7– molasses. [a. Pg. *melaço* = It. *melazzo*:—late L. *mellāceum* must, neut. of **mellāceus* of the nature of honey, f. *mell-*, *mel* honey. A fem. form (:—late L. **mellācea*) occurs in Sp. *melaza*, F. *mélasse* (whence It. *melassa*), which may be the source of some of the Eng. forms.

The word was adopted in the plural form, and this has remained constant in Eng. exc. in the application to an alcoholic spirit (see MOLASS); the word is however construed as a sing. In the Western U.S. (according to Bartlett *Dict. Americanisms* 275) it is treated as a plural.]

1. a. The uncrystallized syrup drained from raw sugar; also, the syrup obtained from sugar in the process of refining.

The word is now rare in British use, but in the U.S. is commonly used promiscuously with *treacle.* In technical language, *molasses* is applied to the drainings of raw sugar and *treacle* to the syrup from sugar in the process of refining.

1582 N. LICHEFIELD tr. *Castanheda's Conq. E. Ind.* I. xxiv. 61 b, There was nothing els but Cocos and Melasus, which is a certeine kinde of Sugar made of Palmes or Date trees. **1588** N. H. *Voy. Cavendish* in Hakluyt *Voy.* (1589) 810 One was laden with..molassos or sirrope of sugar, beanes [etc.]. **1599** HAKLUYT *Voy.* II. II. 8 We spent here very neere three moneths before we could get in our lading, which was Sugar, Dates, Almonds, and Malassos or sugar Syrrope. **1663** BOYLE *Usef. Exp. Nat. Philos.* II. iv. 105 Which, together with Rice and Molossos (or black course Suger) they put into a quantity of Water, and distil it in an Alimbick. **1694** WESTMACOT *Script. Herb.* (1695) 6 Good store of Molossus or common Treacle to sweeten it. **1731** P. SHAW *Three Ess. Artif. Philos.* 31 An Inquiry into a Method of converting Melasses or Treacle into tolerable Sugars. **1764** *Museum Rust.* II. iii. 17 Whatever saccharine particles touch the greatly-heated boiler are turned black, and form what is called molasses. **1864** GLADSTONE *Sp. on Budget* 7 Apr., There was also liquid sugar under the class of melasses or molasses.

b. *fig.*

1925 T. DREISER *American Tragedy* (1926) I. I. xvii. 127 'You're the cutest thing here,' whispered Clyde, hugging her fondly. 'Gee, but you can pour on the molasses, kid, when you want to,' she called out loud. **1972** *N.Y. Times Book Review* 26 Nov. 1/1 The mournful molasses of his [*sc.* Eisenhower's] prose.

†**2.** *Sc.* A spirit distilled from this: see MOLASS.

1789 W. BUCHAN *Dom. Med.* (1790) 98 *note*, Above two thousand private stills [in Edinburgh] are constantly employed in preparing a poisonous liquor called Molasses.

3. *attrib.* and *Comb.*, as ***molasses barrel, cake, candy, cask, cookie, gingerbread, hogshead, jug, scone, taffy, tierce***; **molasses acid** = MELASSIC ACID; **molasses beer**, a fermented liquor flavoured with molasses (cf. *treacle beer*); **molasses bird** (see quot.); **molasses cistern**, a tank which receives the molasses; **molasses-gate** (see quot. 1875); **molasses spirit** = sense 2.

1838 T. THOMSON *Chem. Org. Bodies* 624 The nature of the *melasses acid is not better known than that of the herbaceous matter. **1846** D. CORCORAN *Pickings* 29 Isn't that cotton bale dancing a quadrille with the *molasses barrel? **1742** *Lond. & Country Brew.* I. (ed. 4) 31 Of Brewing *Molosses Beer. **1839** URE *Dict. Arts* 91 Molasses beer. **1878** *Proc. U.S. Nat. Mus.* (1879) I. 190 [Birds of St. Vincent] *Certhiola saccharina*... Called the '*Molasses bird'. **1836** W. G. SIMMS *Mellichampe* II. xxiv. 192 The negro broke his *molasses-cake evenly between himself and the soldier. **1863** B. TAYLOR *H. Thurston* i. 19 The distribution of wedges of molasses-cake. **1869** *Harper's Mag.* Oct. 753/1 With that penny he bought a 'bolivar'—as the huge molasses-cake was called in those days. **1809** 'D. KNICKERBOCKER' *Hist. N.Y.* II. VII. iii. 195 Each..he patted on the head..and gave him a penny to buy *molasses candy. **1850** N. KINGSLEY *Diary* (1914) 103 [We] are privately enjoying ourselves over a dish of molasses candy. **1945** *This Week Mag.* 15 Dec. 2/2 Cookies, molasses candy, popcorn balls and cider were brought out. **1834** H. J. NOTT *Novellettes* I. 79 He was in a *molasses cask. **1851** A. O. HALL *Manhattaner* 5 It was a modest commercial plain.. with..molasses casks, and corn sacks. **1845** *Encycl. Metrop.* VIII. 503/2 The curing-house is a large airy building provided with a capacious *molasses cistern. **1887** I. ALDEN *Little Fishers* xxi. 373 Dough-nuts, *molasses cookies, and soft gingerbread. **1974** 'D. SHANNON' *Crime File* (1975) iv. 66 She asked for my recipe for molasses cookies. **1875** KNIGHT *Dict. Mech.*, **Molasses-gate*, a faucet with a sliding lip at the discharge end, to cut off the flow positively and prevent drip. **1884** PHIN *Dict. Apicult.* 44 Beekeepers have adopted the 'molasses-gate'. **1832** L. M. CHILD *Amer. Frugal Housewife* 70 A very good way to make *molasses gingerbread. **1864** T. L. NICHOLS *40 Yrs. Amer. Life* I. 36 The spectators..ate molasses-gingerbread. **1849** THOREAU *Week Concord River* 198 An 'unteameable fly' buzzed at my elbow with the same non-chalance as on a *molasses hogshead. **1863** 'G. HAMILTON' *Gala-Days* 76 He..came back with a molasses hogshead. **1839** *Southern Lit. Messenger* V. 65/2 Behind the bar were..a *molasses jug, a bottle of vinegar, and..decanters. **1906** F. LYNDE *Quickening* 111 She went..to fill the molasses jug. **1927** M. DE LA ROCHE *Jalna* xxii. 275, I am bringing you a *molasses scone to stay you, Mamma. **1731** P. SHAW *Three Ess. Artif. Philos.* 123 History of *Melasses spirit. **1753** CHAMBERS *Cycl. Supp.* s.v. *Sugar spirit*, The manner of preparing it is the same with that used for malt and melasses spirits. **1928** S. V. BENÉT *John Brown's Body* 113 An awful *molasses-taffy voice Behind them yelled 'Halt!' **1946** PARTRIDGE & BETTMANN *As We Were* 13 Molasses taffy was cooked in a kettle on top of the kitchen stove and when ready for pulling was served out in gobs. **1910** *Chambers's Jrnl.* Feb. 88/2 A few rusty *molasses-tanks. **1851** H. MELVILLE *Moby Dick* I. xxii. 168 Have an eye to the *molasses tierce, Mr. Stubb.

Hence **mo'lassed** *a.* = MOLASSIED *a.*; **mo'lassied, mo'lassy** *adjs.*, charged with molasses.

1839 URE *Dict. Arts* 1209 The liquor..can dissolve none of the crystalline sugar, but only the coloured molassy matter. **1866** BLACKMORE *C. Nowell* vii, A glass of first-rate brown sherry—not the vile molassied stuff, thick as the sack of Falstaff, but the genuine thing. **1941** *Nature* 3 May 532/2 Nehring & Schramm also tested the effect..of molassed bran plus urea [on sheep]. **1960** *Farmer & Stockbreeder* 16 Feb. 128/3 Dried molassed beet pulp can replace an equal weight of oats in rations for store cattle and calves.

molat, variant of MOLET *Obs.*

molata, -atto, obs. forms of MULATTO.

molavee, -vie, obs. forms of MOOLVEE.

molayne, obs. form of MOLAN, MULLEIN.

molberi, -bery(e, obs. forms of MULBERRY.

mold, obs. form of MOLE *sb.*[2] and *sb.*[3]

mold, mold-: see MOULD, MOULD-.

†**moldave.** *Obs.* [f. *Moldavia*: see next.]

1. A long outer garment worn by ladies during the first half of the 19th cent.

1800 [MRS. ST. GEORGE] *Jrnl. Visit Germany* (1861) 95 She [the Queen of Prussia] wore..a moldave (simply a body, train, and short sleeves) of pale pink silk.

2. With capital initial. = MOLDAVIAN *sb.*

1851 BORROW *Lavengro* xlvii, 'He is a Moldave', said the Armenian.

Moldavian (mɒl'deɪvɪən), *a.* and *sb.* [f. *Moldavia*, formerly a province of northern Turkey, now part of Romania: see -IAN.]

A. *adj.* Of or pertaining to Moldavia or its inhabitants. ***Moldavian balm, mint***, the plant *Dracocephalum moldavicum*. ***Moldavian cloak*** = MOLDAVE 1.

1760 J. LEE *Introd. Bot.* App. 319 Moldavian Baulm, *Dracocephalum*. **1821** SHELLEY *Hellas* 289 The false Moldavian serfs fled. **1890** *Century Dict.* s.v., *Moldavian cloak*. **1891** *Syd. Soc. Lex.*, *Moldavian mint*, the *Dracocephalum moldavicum*.

B. *sb.* **a.** An inhabitant of Moldavia. **b.** The Moldavian language.

1603 [see MISS *v.* 23 f]. **1847** W. C. L. MARTIN *Ox* i. 8/1 The names of this animal in the present day are as follow:—*bison*,..in Polish *tur*,..in Moldavian *zimbr* [etc.]. **1851** BORROW *Lavengro* xlviii, The cuffs which I had seen him bestow upon the Moldavian. **1904** *Speaker* 24 Dec. 320/1 Translations from the Turkish, Arabic,..or Moldavian.

moldavite ('mɒldəvaɪt). [ad. G. *moldawit*, f. *Moldau*, G. name of the Vltava River in western Czechoslovakia: see -ITE[1].] A tektite from the tektite field of Czechoslovakia; formerly, the substance (considered a local variety of obsidian) of which such tektites consist.

1896 A. H. CHESTER *Dict. Names Minerals* 179 *Moldawite*, an obs. syn. of obsidian. **1909** [see BILLITONITE]. **1915** *Bull. Geol. Soc. Amer.* XXVI. 281 The moldavites occur here and there, but never in any manner indicative of their origin. **1935** *Times* 28 Jan. 15/4 'Tektites' from Bohemia and Moravia have for more than 150 years been cut as gem stones under the names 'obsidian', 'water chrysolite' and 'moldavite'. **1964** *New Scientist* 16 Jan. 160/2 The moldavites from Bohemia and Moravia, about 14·8 million years old (Miocene). **1972** *Science* 11 Aug. 519/2 In 1970 and 1971, two noteworthy finds of double moldavites were made in the fields of southern Bohemia.

molde, obs. var. MOLE *sb.*[2], MOULD.

Moldo-Wallachian (ˌmɒldəʊwə'leɪkɪən), *a.* Also **Moldavo-Wallachian**. [f. MOLD(AVIAN *a.* and *sb.* + -O + WALACHIAN *a.*] Of or pertaining to both Moldavia and Wallachia, principalities of Romania united in 1859. Also as *sb.*

1848 [see ANARCHIAL *a.*]. **1869** *Bradshaw's Railway Manual* XXI. 358 A promise that the whole of the Moldo-Wallachian network should be under one supervision. **1929** W. G. EAST *Union Moldavia & Wallachia* iii. 54 The alleged desire of the Moldo-Wallachians to form one national state. *Ibid.* 58 Napoleon was secretly planning a war with Austria during his advocacy of Moldo-Wallachian union. **1971** P. CLINCA tr. *Giurescu's Making of Romanian Unitary State* 117 The twin Moldavo-Wallachian town of Focsani lying on the former border.

mole (məʊl), *sb.*[1] Forms: 1 maal, mál, 5 mool, 6 moole, 6–7 moll, moale, 7 molle, moal, 9 *Sc. dial.* maele, mail, 4– mole. [OE. *mál* ? neut., corresp. to OHG. *meil* neut., *meila* str. and wk. fem. (MHG. *meil* neut., *meile* str. and wk. fem.), Goth. *mail* neut.]

†**1.** A discoloured spot, esp. on cloth, linen, etc. ***iron-mole***: see the corrupted form IRON-MOULD. *Obs.*

c **1000** ÆLFRIC *Gloss.* in Wr.-Wülcker 125/19 *Stigmentum*, tul maal on rægel. *c* **1050** *Voc.* ibid. 446/10, 523/15 *Maculam*, mal. **1377** LANGL. *P. Pl.* B. XIII. 315 Þi best cote, haukyn, Hath many moles and spottes. **14..** in *Rel. Ant.* I. 108 To done away mool or spoot from clothe. *a* **1535** FISHER *Serm.* Wks. (1876) 402 Any moole in your kerchiues. **1579** LYLY *Euphues* (Arb.) 39 One yron mole defaceth the whole peece of Lawne. **1588** L. M. tr. *Bk. Dyeing* 6 Weat it still againe, till ye see the moll go forth. **1807** HOGG *Mount. Bard* Poet. Wks. 1838 II. 262 That mantle bears the purple dye. And all the waters in Liddisdale,..Can ne'er wash out the wondrous maele! **1825–80** JAMIESON, *Mail*, a spot in cloth, especially what is caused by iron; often, *an irne mail*.

2. *spec.* A spot or blemish on the human skin; in mod. use, an abnormal pigmented prominence on the skin, sometimes accompanied by a close hairy growth.

1398 TREVISA *Barth. De P.R.* VII. xvi. (1495) 235 Whan a mole of the eye is fresshe and lytyl redde popy sede suffyceth to helpe it. **1571** HYLL *Physiognomie* (title-p.), A little Treatise of Moles, seen on any part eyther of man or woman. **1588** GREENE *Pandosto* (1843) 15 One moale staineth the whole face. **1598** BARCKLEY *Felic. Man* III. (1603) 203 His wife had a little blacke spot (a mole some call it) behind in her necke. **1601** SHAKS. *Twel. N.* v. i. 249 My father had a moale vpon his brow. **1601** HOLLAND *Pliny* II. 76 Pimples, wems, and molls that be eye-sores. *Ibid.* 299 The haire growing in any molle or wert vpon the face. *a* **1618** RALEIGH *Mahomet* (1637) 74 An hairy moale as big as a pease. **1672** SIR T. BROWNE *Let. Friend* §10 In consumptive Diseases some eye the complexion of Moals. **1693** [see NÆVUS]. **1711** ADDISON *Spect.* No. 130 ¶4 The several Moles and Marks by which the Mother used to describe the Child. **1835** J. GREEN *Dis. Skin* 335 A small mole upon the cheek is sometimes held rather as a heightener of female beauty than otherwise. **1899** *Allbutt's Syst. Med.* VIII. 819 It is very difficult to discriminate warts from moles. **1900** EL. GLYN *Visits Elizabeth* (1906) 32 We saw a..family of elderly girls ..and they all had moustaches or moles on the cheek.

†**b.** An ulcerated sore on an animal. *Obs.*

1522 SKELTON *Why not to Court* 243 A mayny of marefoles, That occupy theyr holys, Full of pocky molys.

†**c.** *fig.* (*a*) A blemish, fault; (*b*) a distinguishing or identifying mark. *Obs.*

1644 BULWER *Chiron.* 103 Reckoned by Quintilian among the moales of Rhetoricke. **1651** N. BACON *Disc. Govt. Eng.* II. xxxvii. (1739) 167 A Mole in the fair Face of Church-government. **1660** SHARROCK *Vegetables* 9 There is a great controversie..whether this be a seed, or onely particular mole, and character of Plants of that nature. **1699** BENTLEY *Phal.* 393 A few particular marks and moles in the Letters. **1715** POPE *Iliad* I. Pref. E 4, There are two Peculiarities in Homer's Diction that are a sort of Marks or Moles, by which every common Eye distinguishes him at first sight. **1743**

WHITEHEAD *On Ridicule* 217 The random pencil haply hit the mole; Ev'n from their prying foes such specks retreat.

3. *attrib.* and *Comb.*, as ***mole-like***, ***-marked*** adjs.

1876 *Trans. Clinical Soc.* IX. 45 On the arms and hands were several mole-like specks of discoloration. **1906** *Blackw. Mag.* May 637/1 Such masculine flotsam as our mole-marked friend.

mole (məʊl), *sb.*² Forms: α. 4–7 molle, 5 mooll, mulle, 6 moal, mowl, mol, 6–7 moale, moole, moule, mowle, 6–7 moll, 7 moul, 4– mole; β. 5–6 molde, 5–7 mold, mould, 6 moold. [ME. *mulle*, *molle*, corresponding to MDu. *mol*, *moll(e*, MLG., LG. *mol*, *mul* masc.; an early Frankish form (? 7th c.) appears in the Reichenau glosses in latinized form: 'talpas, *muli* qui terram fodiunt'.

Some scholars regard the word as a shortening of OTeut. **moldowerpon-*, *-worpon-* MOULDWARP; according to others it is an independent derivative from the root of MOULD *sb.*, MULL. The word resembles in form a WGer. word for 'lizard': OS., OHG. *mol*, MHG. *mol*, *molm*, *molch*, mod.G. *molch*; the two can hardly be identical, but they may be from the same root, or they may be hypocoristic shortenings of different compounds of **moldâ* mould, earth.]

1. a. Any one of the small mammals of the family *Talpidæ*; esp. the common mole of the Old World, *Talpa europæa*, a small animal about six inches in length, having a velvety fur, usually blackish, exceedingly small but not blind eyes, and very short strong fossorial fore-limbs with which to burrow in the earth in search of earthworms and to excavate the galleried chambers in which it dwells.

α. **1398** TREVISA *Barth. De P.R.* XVIII. i. (1495) 739 The molle that hathe eyen closyd wythin a webbe. **14..** *Stockh. Med. MS.* I. 411 in *Anglia* XVIII. 305 Take & fle a mole owte of þe skynne. **1426** LYDG. *De Guil. Pilgr.* 18390 For low in erthe, on euery syde, Lyche a molle, they abyde. **1481–90** *Howard Househ. Bks.* (Roxb.) 359 My Lady gaff Braby for takynge of mulles xij.d. **1486** [see LABOUR *sb.* 1 d]. **1530** PALSGR. 246/1 Mole a beest, *talpe*. **1573** TUSSER *Husb.* (1878) 86 Go strike off the nowles of deluing mowles. **1584** LYLY *Sappho* II. 131 Talke [not] with any neere the hill of a mowle. **1611** BIBLE *Lev.* xi. 30 These also shalbe vncleane vnto you, ..the Lyzard, and the Snaile, and the Molle. **1714** GAY *Sheph. Week, Friday* 157 While Moles the crumbled Earth in Hillocks raise. **1819** WARDEN *United States* I. 194 The Red mole of Seba, *Talpa rubra Americana*. **1886** J. DALLAS in *Jrnl. Anthrop. Inst.* XV. 323 The distribution of the moles is also noteworthy. **1898** *Daily News* 21 Sept. 6/6 That leader, instead of burrowing underground like the mole, should appear on the surface.

β. *c* **1420** *Pallad. on Husb.* IV. 130 The molde & other suche as diggeth lowe Anoy hem not, in hard lond yf they growe. **1570** LEVINS *Manip.* 160/21 A Mold, *talpa*. *Ibid.* 218/40 A Mould, *talpa*. **1576** *Nottingham Rec.* IV. 164 Payd to Bacon ..for takyng of mouldes in the felde xiijs. **1592** LYLY *Entertainm.* Wks. 1902 I. 478 Me he terrified..saying that he would turne me..to a molde.

b. In allusion to the blindness attributed to the European mole in classic and later times.

1563 *Mirr. Mag.*, *Rivers* lxiv, Blynde as molles. **1598** F. ROUS *Thule* L 4 b, Like blinde Moles into our bane we goe. **1598** SYLVESTER *Du Bartas* II. i. II. *Imposture* 376 In heav'nly things ye are more blinde then Moals. **1697** DRYDEN *Virg. Georg.* I. 266 The blind laborious Mole In winding Mazes works her hidden Hole. **1713** BENTLEY *Rem. Disc. Freethink.* II. xlix. 269 In the whole Compass and last Tendency of Passages he is as blind as a mole.

2. *transf.* and *fig.* **a.** One who works in darkness.

1601 DENT *Pathw. Heaven* 76, I woonder..that these Moules and Mucke-wormes of this earth, should so minde these shadowish things [*sc.* riches]. **1602** SHAKS. *Ham.* I. v. 161 Well said old Mole, can'st worke i'th' ground so fast? A worthy Pioner. **1742** YOUNG *Nt. Th.* IX. 949 The miser earths his treasure; and the thief, Watching the mole, half-beggars him ere morn. **1855** J. R. LEIFCHILD *Cornwall Mines* 151 The miners there must have been generations of human moles pursuing their slow but certain advances in mysterious candlelight.

b. One whose (physical or mental) vision is deemed defective.

1610 SHAKS. *Temp.* IV. i. 194 Pray you tread softly, that the blinde Mole may not heare a foot fall. **1677** W. HUGHES *Man of Sin* I. iii. 11 A very mole must see, and Papist can't gainsay the Truth propounded.

c. *colloq.* A secret intelligence agent who gradually achieves a position deep within the security defences of a country or organization. Also *loosely*, anyone within an organization or in a position of trust who betrays confidential information. Cf. SLEEPER 2 d, MOLE *v.*² 2.

[**1925** J. BUCHAN *House of Four Winds* xi. 234, I also have certain moles at my command... When the Cirque Doré mobilizes itself it has many eyes and ears. **1960** G. BAILEY *Conspirators* (1961) vi. 124 [In 1935] Fedossenko traveled at Magdenko's invitation to Berlin, where he was introduced to this 'Ivanov'. The latter displayed such a disconcerting knowledge of the innermost workings of the White military organizations that Fedossenko decided to join his network.. in order to discover the source of his information. He was recruited under the alias of 'The Mole'.] **1974** 'J. LE CARRÉ' *Tinker, Tailor, Soldier, Spy* viii. 62 Ivlov's task was to service a mole. A mole is a deep penetration agent so called because he burrows deep into the fabric of Western imperialism. **1976** —— in *Listener* 22 Jan. 90 A 'mole' is, I think, a genuine KGB term for somebody who burrows into the fabric of a bourgeois society and undermines it from within. **1977** *Time* 11 July 10/3 He also introduced a secret computer system to ferret out even 'sleepers' and 'moles', deepcover agents whose meticulous disguises are planned for long-term use. **1979** *Daily Tel.* 3 Dec. 20 Brown says his men are searching for the 'mole' who betrayed their 1900 catalogue into the hands of foreign scientists. They are also checking on the patent. **1979** A. BOYLE *Climate of Treason* viii. 242 There were no 'moles' at large in Washington: 'Indifference, not treachery, was at the root of America's attitude to the [German] conspiracy.' **1980** *National Times* (Austral.) 10 Aug. 3/2 The death has sparked off speculation that Paisley was the mole long suspected of penetrating the CIA. **1984** *Times* 30 Nov. 3/8 Clearly therefore, we suggest, this points to a 'mole' within British Telecom Prestel headquarters.

3. a. Applied, usually with defining prefix, to other animals, as **Cape mole**, (*a*) the mole-rat *Bathyergus maritimus* (*Cent. Dict.* 1890); (*b*) the golden mole; **duck-mole** (see DUCK *sb.*¹ 12 b); **gold-, golden mole**, the Cape chrysochlore, *Chrysochloris aureus*; **marsupial mole**, a small pouched burrowing animal, *Notoryctes typhlops*, native of Australia; **radiated** or **star-nosed mole**, *Condylura cristata*. See also SHREW-MOLE, WATER-MOLE.

1731 MEDLEY *Kolben's Cape G. Hope* II. 123 Moles..are pretty numerous at the Cape. **1781** PENNANT *Hist. Quad.* II. 487 Linnæus places this [Brown Mole] and our radiated Mole, in his class of Sorex or Shrew. **1855** W. S. DALLAS in *Syst. Nat. Hist.* II. 490 The peculiar metallic lustre of their coats, which has given rise to the name of Golden Mole (*Chrysochloris aurea*), applied to the best known species. **1859** WOOD *Illustr. Nat. Hist.* I. 429 Radiated Mole, or Star-nosed Mole.—*Astromyctes cristatus*. **1898** *Guide Mammalia* 113 Marsupial Mole (*Notoryctes typhlops*). **1904** *Q. Rev.* Oct. 470 The golden moles, recognisable by the iridescent sheen of their fur.

†**b.** Short for *mole-cricket* (see 9 b). *Obs.*

1714 DERHAM *Phys.-Theol.* IV. xiii. (ed. 2) 234 *note*, Their two Fore-legs are formed somewhat like those of the ordinary Moles, or *Gryllotalpa*. **1761** *Ann. Reg.* 113 The gardeners round Lambeth are pestered with vermin called flying moles.

†**4.** ***French mole***: app. a translation of F. *taupe*, 'a sort of tumour formed under the integuments of the head, which are raised like the earth mined by the mole' (Littré). *Obs.*

1607 C. TOURNEUR *Rev. Trag.* Wks. 1878 II. 10 Ile hold her by the fore-top fast enough, Or like the French moale heave up hair and all.

5. The borer of a MOLE-PLOUGH.

1805 R. W. DICKSON *Pract. Agric.* I. Plate xlvii, Fig. 1. is the beam, 2. the mole, to which segments for lengthening it screw on at 3. **1834** *Brit. Husb.* I. 453 The mole, or borer, is a well-tempered cast-iron conical share, of about three inches diameter at the largest end.

6. *pl.* Moleskin trousers. Also ***mole trousers***.

1881 H. W. NESFIELD *Chequered Career* vii. 75 We..met men in rough flannels and dirty soil-stained moles. **1888** G. O. PRESHAW *Banking under Difficulties* xxvi. 163 These moles are 12s. a pair. **1890** *Times* 16 Sept. 10/4 The missing man..was wearing..dark gray waistcoat, white mole trousers. **1900** H. LAWSON *Over Shiprails* 164 Tom stood up in his clean, white moles and white flannel shirt.

7. A shade of grey. Also as *adj.*

1908 *Westm. Gaz.* 29 Aug. 13/2 Mole has always been recognised..as a shade universally harmonious. *Ibid.* 26 Sept. 13/2 How charming with a mole suit is a mole hat, massed with roses! **1914** [see BEAVER¹ 2 c]. **1923** [see BRICK *sb.*¹ 4 c]. **1971** *Vogue* 15 Sept. 49 Rich autumn colours like wine, mole and teak.

8. *attrib.* and *Comb.* **a.** Simple attrib., as ***mole-earth***, ***-heap***, ***-hillock***, ***-hole***, ***-run***, ***-track*** (†***-tract***); also ***mole-grains***, ***-spade***, ***-spear***, ***-staff***, †***-tine***, ***-trap***, implements used in the destruction of moles.

1904 *Westm. Gaz.* 26 Nov. 16/1 There are some interesting diagrams of *mole-earths. **1658** EVELYN *Fr. Gard.* (1675) 100 They are destroyed likewise with *mole-graines, which is a set of sharp iron-points, skrewed upon a staff. **1617** MINSHEU *Ductor*, Mole-hill, or *Mole-heape. **1879** G. MACDONALD *P. Faber* II. xii. 234 Some mere moleheap, of which her lovelily sensitive organization,.. made a mountain. **1523** FITZHERB. *Surv.* xxvii. (1539) 50 The moss wyll rotte, and the *moll hyllockes wyll amende the ground wel. **1824** SCOTT *Redgauntlet* ch. viii, A stumble ..over an obstacle so inconsiderable as a mole-hillock, cost the haughty rider his life. **1579** LANGHAM *Gard. Health* (1633) 350 Put Leekes into the *moldholes to make them come forth. **1613–16** W. BROWNE *Brit. Past.* II. v. 86 Or in the bancke the water hauing got Some Mole-hole, runs, where he expected not. **1844** H. STEPHENS *Bk. Farm* I. 604 A small opening in the soil..in the form of a *mole-run. **1587** MASCALL *Govt. Cattle* (1596) 291 Then take your *mole-spade and cast her vp. **1589** GREENE *Menaphon* (Arb.) 33 Poore Menaphon neither asked his swaynes for his sheepe, nor tooke his mole-spade on his necke to see his pastures. **1573** TUSSER *Husb.* (1878) 38 Sharp *moul-spare with barbs, that the mowles do so rue. **1617–18** W. LAWSON *Orch. & Gard.* xiii. (1623) 47 You must watch her well with a Mole-speare. **1587** MASCALL *Govt. Cattle* (1596) 289 Be readie with your *mole-staffe to strike at the first..putting up the earth. **1676** T. GLOVER in *Phil. Trans.* XI. 633 They strike with an Instrument of Iron somewhat like *Mole-tines. **1707** MORTIMER *Husb.* (1721) I. 318 A deep Earthen Vessel set in the ground, with the brim even with the bottom of the *Mole-tracts. **1712** J. JAMES tr. *Le Blond's Gardening* 174 Traps should be laid about half a Foot deep in the Mole-Tracks. **1651** R. CHILD in *Hartlib's Legacy* (1655) 91 A *Mole-trap which the Gardiners frequently use about London. **1712** J. JAMES tr. *Le Blond's Gardening* 174 The surest way to catch them, is by..Boxes, or Cases, called Mole-Traps, made of Elder-Boughs slit in two.

b. Similative, as ***mole-colour***, ***-eye***; ***mole-blind***, ***-eyed***, ***-grey***, ***-like***, ***-sighted*** adjs.; ***mole-blindedly***, ***-like***, ***-wise*** adverbs.

a **1660** *Contemp. Hist. Irel.* (Ir. Archæol. Soc.) II. 98 How are the Irish soe *mould-blinde that they cannot see those abuses. **1820** A. RODGER *Poems & Songs* (1838) 246 Scores o' mole-blind fools forby. **1882** CON. F. WOOLSON *Anne* 502 As the prosecution *mole-blindedly averred. **1906** *Westm. Gaz.* 13 Oct. 13/1 The neutral tones, *mole-colour and grey. **1629** N. CARPENTER *Achitophel* III. (1640) 149 The child of nature, whose *mole eyes..can hardly pierce so farre as its own spheare. **1610** HEALEY *St. Aug. Citie of God* 149 But farre mistaken was hee, and *mole-eid in this matter. **1897** E. K. CHAMBERS in *Bookman* Jan. 113/1 The German dissertation..has..the narrowness of mole-eyed outlook. **1906** *Daily Chron.* 15 Oct. 8/2 A simple skirt in *mole-grey velveteen. **1662** HIBBERT *Body Div.* I. 262 They are sharp-sighted abroad..but *mole-like blind at home. **1837–9** HALLAM *Hist. Lit.* (1847) III. v. §23. 472 A purblind mole-like pedantry. **1891** *Daily News* 18 June 5/8 The blind mole-like marsupial recently discovered in South Australia. **1813** J. QUINCY in *Life* (1867) 285 It is now apparent to the most *mole-sighted. **1833** CARLYLE *Diderot* Misc. Ess. (1872) V. 30 He digs unweariedly, *molewise, in the Encyclopaedic field.

c. Objective, as ***mole-seeker***, ***-taker***.

c **1515** *Cocke Lorell's B.* 10 Harde ware-men, *mole sekers, and ratte takers. *Ibid.* 5 With Ielyan Ioly at sygne of the bokeler, And mores *moule taker. **1541** in *Vicary's Anat.* (1888) App. ii. 109 Item, for John Whatson, molletaker, ix s. iiijd.

9. a. Special combinations: **mole-cast**, a mole-hill; **mole-catcher**, (*a*) one whose business it is to catch moles; †(*b*) used as a vague term of abuse or contempt; so also **mole-catching** *a.*; **mole ditch** = *mole drain*; so ***mole-ditching*** vbl. sb.; **mole-diver**, the Little Grebe, *Tachybaptes fluviatilis*; **mole drain** *v.*, to make drainage courses with the MOLE-PLOUGH; a drain made by a mole-plough; **mole-drainer** = MOLE-PLOUGH; **mole-plant** = *mole-tree*; **mole-stone**, a stone of a particular character regarded as an amulet (cf. TOADSTONE); **mole-tree**, the caper-spurge, *Euphorbia Lathyris*; **molewort**, the genus *Arabis* or wall-cress. Also MOLE-HILL.

1707 MORTIMER *Husb.* (1721) I. 330 An Instrument much used in the West Country for the spreading of *Mole casts. **1880** *Daily Tel.* 9 Dec., A fresh mole-cast, apparently just thrown up. **1573** TUSSER *Husb.* (1878) 90 Get *mowle catcher cunninglie mowle for to kill. **1603** DEKKER *Wonderfull Year* D 2 That God would blesse the labors of those mole-catchers [sextons]. **1629** SHIRLEY *Wedding* III. G, Whorson mole-catcher. **1851** D. JERROLD *St. Giles* xiv. 138 A mole-catcher of tolerable parts. *a* **1693** *Urquhart's Rabelais* III. xlviii. 391 The *Mole-catching *Symmysts* have been..incensed. **1868** *Rep. Comm. Agric. 1867* (U.S. Dept. Agric.) 232 *Under draining* wet, heavy places, with '*mole ditches', or blind drains. **1868** *Rep. Iowa Agric. Soc. 1867* 154 Under-draining by *mole-ditching has been tried. **1887** A. C. SMITH *Birds Wilts.* 505 In Sussex it [*sc.* the Little Grebe] is called the '*Mole Diver'. **1939** WEBSTER Add., *Mole drain. **1950** *N.Z. Jrnl. Agric.* June 534/1 A number of standard mole drains was drawn with the 3 in. plug at depths of 18 to 20 in. **1957** E. BLUNDEN *Poems of Many Years* 280 Waters drawn together From gully and moledrain by contour, chance and weather. **1844** H. STEPHENS *Bk. Farm* I. 606 An acre of ground can be *mole-drained for 13s. 6d. **1859** *Trans. Ill. Agric. Soc.* III. 361 Dragging the *mole drainer all over our lands. **1842** *Encycl. Brit.* (ed. 7) VIII. 139/2 The drain thus made is like a large mole gallery, and hence it is called *mole-draining. **1700** E. LHWYD *Let.* 12 Mar. in Rowlands *Mona Antiqua* (1723) 338 Besides, the Snake-Stones..the Highlanders have their Snail-Stones, Paddoc-Stones, *Mole-Stones..and to all which they attribute their several Virtues. **1846–50** A. WOOD *Class-bk. Bot.* 487 *Euphorbia Lathyris*. *Mole-tree. Caper Spurge. **1770** J. HILL *Herb. Brit.* II. 269 Genus iv. Arabis. *Mole-wort.

b. In the names of animals, as **mole-cricket** [cf. Du. *molkrekel*], any one of the fossorial orthopterous insects of the genus *Gryllotalpa*, esp. *G. vulgaris*; **mole hog-louse**, a cheliferous crustacean, *Apseudes talpa*; **mole-rat**, (*a*) any one of the myomorphic rodents of the family *Spalacidæ*, esp. *Spalax typhlus*; (*b*) *dial.*, the common mole; **mole shrew**, (*a*) the American genus *Blarina* of *Soricidæ*; (*b*) the genus *Urotrichus* of *Myogalinæ*; **mole snake**, a non-venomous colubrid snake, *Pseudaspis cana*, native to Southern and E. Africa, and feeding on rats and mice.

1714 DERHAM *Phys.-Theol.* IV. xiii. (ed. 3) 233 *note*, The *Mole-Cricket (*Gryllotalpa*). **1879** TODHUNTER *Alcestis* 18 In the glowing leas The shy mole-cricket shrilled. **1850** A. WHITE *List Crustacea Brit. Mus.* 67 *Apseudes talpa*, *Mole Hog-louse. **1781** PENNANT *Hist. Quad.* II. 469 Blind *Mole-Rat. **1836–9** *Todd's Cycl. Anat.* II. 176/2 The mole-rat (*Aspalax zemni*). **1849** *Sk. Nat. Hist.*, *Mammalia* IV. 89 The Mole-Rat..*Spalax typhlus* [etc.]. **1855** W. S. DALLAS in *Syst. Nat. Hist.* II. 463 The *Georhychidæ*, or Mole-Rats, form another family nearly allied to the Muridæ. **1885** *Riverside Nat. Hist.* (1888) V. 101 The Mole-rats, or family *Spalacidæ*. *Ibid.* 102 There are some half-dozen species of the latter [*sc.* *Bathyergus*], all of South Africa, among them the Strand Mole-rat (*B. maritimus*). **187.** *Cassell's Nat. Hist.* I. 376 The Hairy-tailed *Mole-shrew *Urotrichus talpoides*. **1885** *Riverside Nat. Hist.* (1888) V. 148 The typical species, called the Mole-shrew, *Blarina brevicauda*. **1893** J. NOBLE *Illustr. Official Handbk. Cape & S. Afr.* 84 The Colubrinæ include the large and abundant 'black' or '*mole' snake. **1911** *East London* (Cape Province) *Dispatch* 1 Sept. 7 When alarmed the mole snake is very pugnacious. **1931** *Discovery* Mar. 74/2 The South African mole snake is a non-poisonous species. It constricts its prey and swallows it whole. **1951** R. CAMPBELL *Light on Dark Horse* ii. 36 A mole-snake has not only an apparent immunity [to bites from other snakes] but also the power to strangle other snakes. **1966** E. PALMER

Plains of Camdeboo xiii. 220 Sometimes we see a long, graceful, chinless snake in the veld, with a dark muscular body shining as if carefully polished. This is the mole snake and is harmless to man, killing its prey by constriction. **1970** [see BOOMSLANG].

Hence **ˈmoleism** *nonce-wd.*, mole-like character.

1787 ANNA SEWARD *Lett.* (1811) I. 378 Darwin is a mole to Milton, and that you will say is indeed a molism. **1796** *Ibid.* IV. 189 She, not aware of his moleism, relied upon it that all was well.

mole (məʊl), *sb.*³ Also 6 molle, 7–8 (in sense 2) **mould, mold**; 7 in Latin form **moles**. [In sense 1, ad L. *mōlēs* fem., mass; cf. OF. *mole*. In senses 2 and 3, a. F. *môle* masc., ad. L. *mōlēs*. It. and Sp. have *mole* fem., (from the Latin) in the sense 'mass'; the sense 'pier, breakwater' (= 2 below) is expressed by Sp. *muelle*, Pg. *molhe*, It. *molo* (whence G. *molo*, beside *mole* from Fr.), the relation of which to L. *mōlēs* is uncertain.]

†**1.** A great mass, large piece; the collective mass of any object.

a **1552** LELAND *Itin.* (1769) VII. 52 Kent Ryver is of a good Depthe not wel to be occupied with Botes for rowllyng Stones and other Moles. **1555** EDEN *Decades* 27 When they sawe soo greate a mole to moue as it were by it selfe without ores. **1578** BANISTER *Hist. Man* I. 1, If he note..how the whole mole, and pack of members are sustayned by them [*sc.* bones]. **1596** F. SABIE *Adam's Compl.*, etc. G2, O mightie Founder of the earthly mole. **1607** TOPSELL *Four-f. Beasts* (1658) 153 The very mole and quantity of his [*i.e.* the elephant's] body is sufficient to arme him against the fear of death. **1611** CORYAT *Crudities* 486 That Superlatiue moles vnto which I now bend my Speech. **1637** HEYWOOD *Royal Ship* 27 How else could such a mighty Mole be rais'd? **1657** TOMLINSON *Renou's Disp.* 549 Whole roots..should be condited, for their mole hinders not. **1677** HALE *Contempl.* II. 92 The Guilt grows to such a *moles*, that a Man is desperately given over to all kind of Villany. **1711** G. HICKES *Two Treat. Chr. Priesth.* (1847) II. 108 The victim to be slain was brought to the mole (or bulk) of the altar.

2. A massive structure, esp. of stone, serving as a pier or breakwater, or as a junction between two places separated from each other by water. Hence metonymically, the water-area contained within the mole; an artificial harbour, a port.

a **1548** HALL *Chron., Hen. VIII* 204 The Turkeiplier with .vi. English Knyghtes were appoynted to defende the Molle or Peere at the hauen mouthe. **1579** FENTON *Guicciard.* VI. (1599) 231 The other..retired to the mole of Naples. **1615** G. SANDYS *Trav.* 12 The sea-ruined wall of the Mould. *Ibid.* 255 The Mole, that from the South windes defendeth the hauen. **1632** LITHGOW *Trav.* x. 448 A French ship..that was lying in the Mould. **1695** BLACKMORE *Pr. Arth.* IV. 483 As when a Mold repels th' Invading Seas. *a* **1674** CLARENDON *Hist. Reb.* xv. §12 He anchored in their very mole. **1727** A. HAMILTON *New Acc. E. Ind.* I. vi. 53 It has ..a pretty good Mould, or Bason, for the Easterly [monsoons]. **1773** BRYDONE *Sicily* vii. (1809) 69 A stream of lava running into the sea, formed a mole, which no expence could have furnished them. **1791** W. BARTRAM *Carolina* 253 A long point of flat rocks, which defended the mole from the surf. **1840** *Civil Eng. & Arch. Jrnl.* III. 265/2 The extremity of the mole, called the chop, in which the sea made a large breach. **1847** E. CRESY *Encycl. Civil Engineer.* I. 67 The Mole, which united Chalcis in the island of Eubœa with Aulis in Bœotia. **1862** MERIVALE *Rom. Emp.* (1865) VI. xlviii. 64 A complete mole or break-water. **1872** YEATS *Growth Comm.* 42 Democrates..connected Pharos with the mainland by a jetty or mole. **1893** SLOANE-STANLEY *Remin. Midshipm. Life* xx. 264 We took up our position off the New Mole. *Ibid.* 267 Landing at the Old Mole..we emerged into Warport Street.

†**3.** *Antiq.* A Roman form of mausoleum. *Obs.*

1700 J. MONRO in *Misc. Cur.* (1708) III. 401 D.M. at the head of an Inscription, argues the Moles, the Sepulchre, the Monument, &c. was in the primary intention made for and dedicated to the Soul. **1715** POPE *Ep. Addison* 21 Huge Moles, whose shadow stretch'd from shore to shore, Their ruins perish'd, and their place no more! **1726** LEONI *Alberti's Archit.* II. 56/1 The Sepulchres of the Ancients are ..in several other forms, as Moles and the like. **1818** BYRON *Ch. Har.* IV. clii, Turn to the Mole which Hadrian rear'd on high. **1842** GWILT *Archit.* 1005 The mole of Adrian.

†**mole,** *sb.*⁴ *Antiq. Obs.* [ad. L. *mola* (Gr. μύλη): see MOLA¹.] A cake made of grains of spelt coarsely ground and mixed with salt (*mola salsa*) which was customarily strewn on the victims at sacrifices.

a **1547** SURREY *Æneid* IV. 694 She with the mole all in her handes devout Stode neare the aulter. **1621** MOLLE *Camerar. Liv. Libr.* III. xviii. 206 This mole, lumpe, or seasoned dough. **1697** DRYDEN *Virg. Past.* VIII. 115 Crumble the sacred Mole of Salt and Corn.

mole (məʊl), *sb.*⁵ *Path.* Also 7 moale. [a. F. *môle*, ad. L. *mola* (Gr. μύλη): see MOLA¹.] A false conception; = MOLA¹ 1.

1611 COTGR. s.v. *Frere, Freres des Lombards*, Moles, or Mooncalues. **1615** CROOKE *Body of Man* 298 The Coagmentation therefore of the Mole is neuer made without copulation. *a* **1617** BAYNE *Lect.* (1634) 117 Living births are strangers here, moales and abortives are otherwise. **1770** HEWSON in *Phil. Trans.* LX. 382 Those large clots which.. have often been called moles or false conceptions. *c* **1850** *Arab. Nts.* (Rtldg.) 721 They showed a piece of wood, which they falsely affirmed to be a mole, of which the sultana had been delivered. **1881** *Trans. Obstet. Soc. Lond.* XXII. 44 The patient..had not menstruated..A fortnight afterwards the mole..was expelled.

†**mole,** *sb.*⁶ *Obs.* [a. F. *mole*. See MOLA¹ 2 and MOLEBUT.]

1. The sunfish, *Orthagoriscus mola.* (Cf. MOLEBUT.)

1601 HOLLAND *Pliny* I. 249 The Mole or Lepo called Phycis, doth alter her hue. **1661** LOVELL *Hist. Anim. & Min.* 233 Mole. *Mola*...The whole Fish is of a ferine savour, and very unpleasant.

2. *dial.* [Perh. a different word.] The rock goby, *Gobius niger*.

1880 in *Cornwall Gloss.*

mole (məʊl), *sb.*⁷ *Physical Chem.* Also **mol** (formerly as an alternative spelling, now usu. as an abbrev.). [a. G. *mol* (W. Ostwald *Grundlinien d. anorg. Chem.* (1900) viii. 163), f. *mol-ekül* MOLECULE.] That amount of any particular substance having a mass in grammes numerically the same as its molecular or atomic weight; now defined equivalently in the International System of Units as the quantity of specified elementary entities (molecules, ions, electrons, or the like) that in number equals the number of atoms in 0·012 kilogramme of carbon 12.

1902 A. FINDLAY tr. *Ostwald's Princ. Inorg. Chem.* viii. 156 When one gram-molecule or one mole (the molar or molecular weight of a substance expressed in grams) of any substance is dissolved in a litre or 1000 gm. of water, the solution produced freezes at −1·850°. **1923** LEWIS & RANDALL *Thermodynamics* iii. 22 The mol is not defined unless the chemical formula is established by universal usage or is definitely stated. **1954** *Physiol. Rev.* XXXIV. 342 Estimations of the molar concentration (mols per kilogram of water or osmols if the salts are known..). **1959** N. FEATHER *Introd. Physics Mass, Length & Time* xv. 282 A mass equal to 'the molecular weight in grammes', which we define as 1 mole of a substance, contains the same number of molecules (Avogadro's constant), whatever the substance. **1963** W. J. MOORE *Physical Chem.* (ed. 4) ix. 326 One mole of electrons would be one faraday of electrical charge. **1970** [see MOLALITY]. **1971** G. D. CHRISTIAN *Analytical Chem.* i. 8 Each mole of silver ion will react with one mole of chloride ion. **1972** *Physics Bull.* Jan. 40/1 The 14th General conference of Weights and Measures (CGPM) met in Paris on 4–7 October 1971... Amongst the main decisions taken by the conference were the final adoption of the 'mole' (mol) as an SI base unit. **1973** BLOCK & HOLLIDAY *Mod. Physical Chem.* xi. 256 In the chemical reaction occurring in the Daniell cell..two moles of electrons are required to convert one mole of copper (II) to one mole of zinc (II).

2. *Comb.* **mole fraction**, the ratio of the number of moles of a component in a solution to the total number of moles of all components present.

1923 LEWIS & RANDALL *Thermodynamics* xxii. 261 The mol fraction of bromine in a solution containing 160 grams bromine and 154 grams carbon tetrachloride is ½ if we are considering the formula Br_2. **1973** A. W. ADAMSON *Textbk. Physical Chem.* ix. 345 The partial pressure of a component becomes proportional to its mole fraction in the limit of zero concentration.

‖**mole** (ˈməʊliː), *sb.*⁸ [Mexican Sp., ad. Nahuatl *mulli, molli* sauce, stew.] A highly spiced sauce made chiefly from chilli and chocolate and served with various meats.

1932 H. W. BENTLEY *Dict. Sp. Terms in Eng.* 169 *Mole*.., a sauce used in Mexican cookery in connection with the serving of meats. **1948** *Sat. Even. Post* 2 Oct. 52/3 Señora Gonzalez does her stuff on such fabulous and sustaining dishes as chicken mole—boiled chicken bathed in a sauce of exotic Mexican spices, cinnamon, chili, mashed-up peanuts and even a dash of chocolate [etc.]. **1957** 'B. BUCKINGHAM' *Boiled Alive* xviii. 121 Turkey swimming in *mole*, a hot sauce made of chilli and chocolate, stuffed sweet peppers and mounds of pink-brown beans. **1966** *Punch* 9 Mar. 364/2 We were..sated with rich turkey *mole*.

†**mole,** *v.*¹ *Obs.* Chiefly *dial.* 7–9 **male**, 9 **mail.** [f. MOLE *sb.*¹] *trans.* To spot, stain, discolour.

1377 LANGL. *P. Pl.* B. XIII. 275 He hadde a cote..Ac it was moled in many places with many sondri plottes. **1677** W. NICOLSON *Gloss. Brigantinum* in *Trans. Roy. Soc. Lit.* Ser. II. (1870) IX. 315 *Male*, to stain. **1691** RAY *Collect. Words* 145 To Mäle, *decolorare*. *c* **1700** KENNETT *MS. Lansd.* 1033 (Halliwell), To male, to discolour, to spot, *Northumb.* **1808–18** JAMIESON, To *Mail, Male*, to stain. **1818** SCOTT *Hrt. Midl.* xvii, A bit rag we hae at hame that was mailed wi' the bluid of a bit skirling wean that was hurt some gate.

mole (məʊl), *v.*² [f. MOLE *sb.*²]

1. *trans.* To free from mole-hills (Webster 1832) or moles (*Cassell's Encycl. Dict.* 1885).

a **1800** PEGGE *Suppl. to Grose* (1814), *Moling*, clearing the ground from mole-hills. York. **1827** MACKENZIE *Hist. Newcastle* II. 713 The two noltherds are..also required to scale, mole, and dress the Cow-hill, Moor, and Leazes.

2. a. To burrow or form holes in, as a mole (Ogilvie 1882). ***to mole** (something) **out***, to grope darkly in order to find (something); also, to elicit, bring to light.

1855 DICKENS *Dorrit* I. xxxv, He had felt his way inch by inch and 'Moled it out, sir' (that was Mr. Pancks's expression), grain by grain. **1924** W. M. RAINE *Troubled Waters* vii. 70 Tait would mole out quite enough evidence against him without any additional data supplied by indiscretion. **1932** L. C. DOUGLAS *Forgive us our Trespasses* (1937) xiii. 251 Maybe I'll ask you to mole out further data.

b. *intr.* To behave in the manner of a mole.

1856 W. G. SIMMS *Eutaw* xii. 129 How he snaked, and moled, and cooned,..we need not undertake to narrate.

3. *intr.* To destroy moles (*Cent. Dict.* 1890).

ˈmolebut. *Obs. rare.* Forms: 6–7 **molebout**; in Dicts. 7 **moleboute, -baut, -but(t**, *erron.* **-pout**, 8 **-bat.** [a. F. *molebout*.

Said by Rondelet (*De Pisc. Mar.* 1554) to be a compound of the Provençal (Marseilles) name *mole* (which he says is from the L. *mola*, millstone, with allusion to the shape of the fish) and the Spanish synonym *bout*. Cf. MOLA¹ 2 and MOLE *sb.*⁶; with the second element, which cannot be Sp. or even Cat., cf. OF. (12th c.) *tourbout* TURBOT, and BUTT *sb.*¹]

The sun-fish, *Orthagoriscus mola*; = MOLE *sb.*⁶ 1.

1598 FLORIO, *Bota*, a fish that grunteth called a Molebout. **1601** HOLLAND *Pliny* II. 429 The greatest of all other fishes is the Mole-bout. **1659** TORRIANO, *Bóta*, a..Mole-pout. **1668** CHARLETON *Onomasticon* 129 *Mola*..the Molebut. **1672** JOSSELYN *New Eng. Rarities* 29 Porpuise or Porpiss, Molebut, Sea Hog, Sus Marinus, Tursion. **1678** PHILLIPS (ed. 4), *Mole-butt.* See Porpus. **1736** AINSWORTH *Lat. Dict.*, A molebat (fish) *Orthragoriscus*.

‖**moˈlecula.** *Obs.* [mod.L.: see MOLECULE.] = MOLECULE.

1678 CUDWORTH *Intell. Syst.* I. i. §16. 16 Asclepiades.. supposed all the Corporeal world to be made..of Dissimilar and inconcinn Moleculæ, i.e. Atoms of different Magnitude and Figures. **1796** BURKE *Regic. Peace* i. Wks. VIII. 191 All these particular *moleculæ* united, form the great mass of what is truly the body politick. **1800** tr. *Lagrange's Chem.* I. 14 The moleculæ, which first unite themselves to a body, adhere with much greater force than the last.

b. In etymological sense: A small mass or aggregation.

1713 CHESELDEN *Anat.* III. x. (1726) 227 In such persons as have their blood too thin, the Globuli cohere and form Moleculæ or polypuses.

molecular (məʊˈlɛkjʊlə(r)) *a.* [f. mod.L. *mōlēcula* (see MOLECULE) + -AR¹. Cf. F. *moléculaire*.]

1. a. Pertaining to, consisting of, or concerned with molecules; acting or inherent in the molecules of a substance. *spec.* applied to numerous physical quantities that involve the molecular weight of the substance concerned in their calculation (for most of which *molar* is a more appropriate designation; see MOLAR *a.*³ a). ***molecular heat, weight***: see the sbs.

1823 H. J. BROOKE *Introd. Crystallogr.* 51 Parallelopipeds, whose least molecular attraction is in the direction of their diagonal planes. **1826** KIRBY & SP. *Entomol.* IV. xxxvii. 3 Comparative anatomists have considered the nervous system of animals as formed upon three primary types, which may be called the *molecular*, the *ganglionic*, and *cerebro-spinal*. **1841–4** EMERSON *Ess., Experience* Wks. (Bohn) I. 181 The new molecular philosophy shows astronomical interspaces betwixt atom and atom. **1855** H. SPENCER *Princ. Psychol.* (1872) I. I. iii. 51 Each portion, while passing on the wave of molecular motion, adds the molecular motion given out during its own transformation. **1859** DARWIN *Orig. Spec.* iv. (1878) 100 The shape of a crystal is determined solely by the molecular forces. **1867** C. L. BLOXAM *Chem.* 515 One equivalent of each of these hydrocarbons in the state of vapour occupies four volumes. [*Indexed, p.* 660, *as*] Molecular volumes of olefines. **1879** THOMSON & TAIT *Nat. Phil.* I. I. §385 The ultimate, or molecular, constitution of the bodies. **1880** *Jrnl. Chem. Soc.* XXXVIII. 294 For every substance, therefore, $(A - 1)/d$ is a constant... If this constant be multiplied by the molecular weight P of any body, then $P.(A - 1)/d$, referred to chemically comparable quantities, is the molecular refractive index, called in the rest of this paper the molecular refraction of the body. **1884** J. TAIT *Mind in Matter* 100 Molecular movements are not identical with thought and feeling. **1886** *Jrnl. Chem. Soc.* L. 294 The author [*sc.* W. Ostwald] in continuing his researches on 'Electrical Conductivity'..has examined about 130 different inorganic and organic acids in different states of dilution (gram-molecules in *n*-litres). He..expresses his results in terms of molecular conductivity. **1921** HOOD & CARPENTER *Text-bk. Pract. Chem.* VI. x. 489 The molecular conductivity is that of a solution containing 1 gram-molecule of the substance, as above [*sc.* when placed between electrodes of indefinite size and 1 cm. apart]. **1938** H. A. PERKINS *Course of Physics* xlvii. 624 The number of gram molecules per liter, or moles per liter, is called molecular concentration. **1959** N. FEATHER *Introd. Physics Mass, Length & Time* xv. 283 Equation (126) is now the equation of state for a mass *m* of an ideal gas of molecular weight, or, strictly, of molar mass, *M*. **1966** GUCKER & SEIFERT *Physical Chem.* (1967) xiii. 346 One molecular weight of the salt contains *N* ions of *each* element in the molecular volume *V*, equal to the molecular weight divided by the density.

b. Applied to the name of a science to denote a branch of it that deals with phenomena at the molecular level.

1880 *Sci. Amer. Suppl.* 10 Jan. 3342/2 Their favourite study is molecular physics. **1950**, etc. [see MOLECULAR BIOLOGY]. **1960** *N.Y. Times* 3 Jan. 1F/2 The chief executive officer..disclosed that Westinghouse was actively engaged in 'molecular electronics'. **1961** R. D. BAKER *Essent. Path.* i. 6 With the electron microscope we are entering an era of molecular pathology. **1963** *Adv. Computers* IV. 141 'Integrated' circuits fabricated using 'molecular electronics' techniques. **1963** *Listener* 17 Jan. 121/2 It seemed to me that soon what Russian biology will mean will not be Lysenko, but some first-class molecular genetics. **1966** *McGraw-Hill Yearbk. Sci. & Technol.* 43/1 This view of the gene has changed considerably in molecular genetics, since the gene is now recognized as the information necessary to assemble a protein molecule. **1970** *Sci. News Yearbk.* 225 Molecular astronomy is a science only a few years old. Its purpose is to determine what chemical molecules can be found in interstellar space and, if possible, how they got there and what their being there means for theories of galactic and stellar evolution and of cosmology. **1973** *Sci. Amer.* Apr. 52/3 That was more or less the picture of the interstellar

medium in 1968, the year marking the birth of molecular astronomy as we now know it. **1974** *Nature* 23 Aug. 685/1 Now it is the turn of immunochemistry, or as some would have it, molecular immunology.

†**2.** *Biol.* Of tissue: consisting, or assumed to consist, of molecules (sense 3); finely granular. *Obs.* (but the use survives in *molecular layer* (see 5)).

1826, **1851** [see MOLECULE 3]. **1856** *Quain's Elem. Anat.* (ed. 6) III. 26 The intermediate portion, *f*, has a longitudinally-striped appearance, and is formed by the fine fibres of Müller.., which intervene between the two parts of the granular layer, together with a homogeneous molecular uniting material.

3. *Philos.* Designating a proposition, sentence, etc., consisting of simpler propositions, sentences, etc. connected by a conjunction. Also *ellipt.* as *sb.*

1892 *Mind* I. 237 The molecular proposition—which cannot be expressed as a synthesis of more elementary propositions—involves a single (absolute or relative) predication and a number of interconnected individual subjects. *Ibid.* 239 The synthesis of moleculars having the same subject is represented by a synthesis of the predications. **1914** B. RUSSELL *Our Knowl. External World* ii. 54 'Molecular' propositions are such as contain conjunctions—*if*, *or*, *and*, *unless*, etc.—and such words are the marks of a molecular proposition. **1933** [see ATOMIC *a.* 2 a]. **1937** A. SMEATON tr. *Carnap's Logical Syntax of Lang.* III. §28. 88 $\mathfrak{S}_1$ is called a *molecular sentence* when $\mathfrak{S}_1$ is either an atomic sentence itself, or is formed from one or more such by means of symbols of negation and junction (and brackets). **1965** B. MATES *Elem. Logic* iii. 44 A formula that is not an atomic formula is called *general* if it begins with a universal or existential quantifier; otherwise it is called *molecular*.

4. *Psychol.* Concerned with or pertaining to an elementary unit of behaviour such as a physiological response. Cf. MOLAR *a.*[2] b.

1925, **1932** [see MOLAR *a.*[2] b]. **1970** F. A. LOGAN in W. S. Sahakian *Psychol. of Learning* xvi. 307 The molar response 'bar depression' includes a number of responses distinguishable at a more molecular level, such as depression with the right paw, left paw, etc. **1973** *Jrnl. Genetic Psychol.* CXXIII. 99 The continuous-recording technique did.. yield a more molecular analysis in that incidence of behaviors could be subdivided into frequency and duration.

5. Special collocations: ***molecular fossil***, a molecular species found in ancient rock that is regarded as evidence of the early development of life; ***molecular layer*** Anat., (*a*) either of the two plexiform layers of the retina; (*b*) the outermost layer of the cortex of the cerebellum and cerebrum, containing a mass of nerve fibres with many synapses but relatively few cells; ***molecular orbital***, an orbital in a molecule; ***molecular sieve***, a substance containing in its crystal structure pores and channels of molecular dimensions that permit the entry of certain small molecules but are impervious to others; *esp.* a zeolite used as a selective adsorbent.

1965 M. CALVIN in *Proc. R. Soc.* A. CCLXXXVIII. 443 We are going to spend much of our time tracing organic evolution back in so far as we can trace it back in terms of 'molecular fossils' from the earliest well recognized fossils of morphological form. **1969** *Sci. Jrnl.* Apr. 36 The exciting studies of Calvin, who has attempted to prove the existence of what he calls 'molecular fossils', have not, however, firmly established the biogenic nature of these substances. **1971** *Nature* 30 July 325/2 The search for geological evidence about the origin and evolution of life on Earth has led to detailed searches for morphological and molecular fossils in Early Precambrian sedimentary rocks. [**1856** Molecular layer: cf. sense 2 above]. **1867** *Quain's Elem. Anat.* (ed. 7) III. 726 The retina.. exhibits a series of dissimilar strata, together with structures not confined to one stratum. (1st) Externally is the columnar layer; (2nd), in the middle is the granular layer, comprising the external nuclear, the internuclear, the internal nuclear, and the molecular layers; and (3rd) internally is the nervous layer. **1874** A. E. J. BARKER tr. *Frey's Histol. & Histochem. of Man* 593 Externally—that is, directed towards the surface of the cerebellum—these large ganglion cells send off several (generally two) characteristic protoplasm processes through the so-called 'molecular layer of Hess'. **1955** P. D. TREVOR-ROPER *Ophthalm.* i. 19 The outer molecular layer is a reticular layer in which the end-knobs of the axons of the rod and cone cells arborise with the dendrites of the bipolar cells. *Ibid.* 20 The inner molecular layer consists of the arborisations of the axes of the bipolar cells with the dendrites of the ganglion cells. **1968** PASSMORE & ROBSON *Compan. Med. Stud.* I. xxiv. 46/1 In the older parts of the [cerebral] cortex, such as the rhinencephalon, only three layers of cells may be distinguished: the superficial molecular layer of fibres, the intermediate granular layer and a deep layer of pyramidal cells. **1932** R. S. MULLIKEN in *Physical Rev.* XLI. 50 The method followed here will be to describe unshared electrons always in terms of atomic orbitals but to use molecular orbitals for shared electrons. **1965** PHILLIPS & WILLIAMS *Inorg. Chem.* I. iii. 67 The problem will be introduced by a summary of the two important wave-mechanical approximation methods, the L.C.A.O. (linear combination of atomic orbitals) molecular-orbital method and the valence-bond method. **1926** *Colloid Symp. Monogr.* IV. 11 Collander's work on the sieve structure of semipermeable membranes of copper ferrocyanide has shown that the interstices between the micelles or aggregates are about 4 Ångstrom units in diameter. I would suggest a better molecular sieve, namely such crystals as dehydrated zeolites, etc. **1949** *Discussions Faraday Soc.* VII. 135 By cation interchange and by burning out interstitial ammonium ions a diversity of modified molecular-sieve sorbents can be produced. *Ibid.*, Some natural crystalline zeolites fall into three classes of molecular-sieve sorbent each capable of separating mixtures by selective occlusion. **1965** PHILLIPS & WILLIAMS *Inorg. Chem.* I. xiv. 544 The molecular-sieve zeolites, sodium and calcium aluminosilicates, are used to fractionate noble gases and low molecular weight molecules generally. **1966** *McGraw-Hill Encycl. Sci. & Technol.* VIII. 547/1 Molecular sieves are capable of drying gases and liquids to extremely low residual water concentrations.

molecular biology. [f. MOLECULAR *a.* + BIOLOGY.] Biology at the molecular level, esp. that branch of biology which is concerned with the formation, organization, and activity of macromolecules essential to life (i.e. nucleic acids, proteins, etc.).

1950 *Harvey Lectures* XLVI. 3 The name 'molecular biology' seems to be passing now into fairly common use... It implies.. an approach from the viewpoint of the so-called basic sciences with the leading idea of searching below the large-scale manifestations of classical biology for the corresponding molecular plan. It is concerned particularly with the forms of biological molecules, and with the evolution, exploitation and ramification of those forms in the ascent to higher and higher levels of organization. **1963** *Listener* 17 Jan. 121/2 The newest and most refined field of genetics, which deals with definite chemical substances and is known as molecular biology. **1964** G. H. HAGGIS et al. *Introd. Molecular Biol.* p. x, We may say that molecular biology is primarily concerned with the structure of proteins, nucleic acids and other large biological molecules, and with the detailed structure of myofilaments, chromosomes, ribosomes, membranes and other cell components. But the study of structure cannot be divorced from the study of function. **1970** *Nature* 4 July 13/1 The synthesis of genes *de novo* has been an aim of molecular biology since its very inception. **1974** *Daily Tel.* 3 Sept. 6 Molecular biology and genetic engineering have reached the stage where results of research could plunge the world into far deeper problems that those raised by the atom bomb.

mo'lecularist. *rare.* [f. MOLECULAR *a.* + -IST.] One who investigates the properties of molecules.

1869 J. H. STIRLING *As regards Protoplasm*, etc. 61 Neither molecularists nor Darwinians, then, are able to level out the difference between organic and inorganic.

molecularity (məʊlɛkjʊ'lærɪtɪ). [f. MOLECULAR *a.* + -ITY.] **1.** The quality or state of being molecular; also, molecular agencies generally.

1842 *Penny Cycl.* XXIV. 335/2 Theories of molecularity. **1871** H. MARSHALL *For very Life* I. I. xvii. 123 Human will has knit particles together as close and tight as molecularity could.

2. *Chem.* The number of reacting molecules involved in a (real or postulated) single step of a chemical reaction.

1939 FOWLER & GUGGENHEIM *Statist. Thermodynamics* xii. 500 In general there is no simple connection between the molecularity of the mechanism.. and the order of the reaction. **1950** K. J. LAIDLER *Chem. Kinetics* iii. 56 Whereas the order of a reaction is deduced directly from the experimental results, the molecularity can be determined only on the basis of additional arguments about which there is sometimes some uncertainty. **1970** PRETTRE & CLAUDEL *Elem. Chem. Kinetics* v. 64 If we accept that the reaction $I_2 + H_2 \rightarrow 2HI$ is a simple one, this means that it involves a molecule of iodine and a molecule of hydrogen and that consequently its molecularity is two.

molecularly (məʊ'lɛkjʊləlɪ), *adv.* [f. MOLECULAR *a.* + -LY[2].] In a molecular manner; as regards molecules. Also, on a molecular scale.

1850 GROVE *Corr. Phys. Forces* (ed. 2) 16 All matter.. is ever in movement, not merely in masses,.. but also molecularly, or throughout its most intimate structure. **1873** ROBERTS *Handbk. Med.* 132 The tongue becomes moist, and cleans from the edges, either in patches or molecularly. **1927** L. B. LOEB *Kinetic Theory Gases* vii. 273 The surfaces are not completely molecularly rough. **1969** *Physics Bull.* June 227/1 Muscovite mica.. gives molecularly smooth surfaces on cleavage.

molecule ('mɒlɪkjuːl, 'məʊlɪkjuːl). [a. F. *molécule* (1678 in Hatz.-Darm.), ad. mod.L. *mōlēcula*, dim. of L. *mōlēs* mass.

The word seems to have arisen in the 17th c. in the discussions initiated by the physical speculations of Descartes.]

1. a. *Physics* and *Chem.* One of the extremely minute discrete particles of which material substances are conceived to consist. In early use the term was employed somewhat vaguely; in modern chemistry the molecules of any element or compound are assumed to be of uniform size and mass, representing the smallest portions into which the substance can be divided without losing its chemical identity. (Cf. the earlier MOLECULA.)

organic molecules: Buffon's term for the indestructible and unchangeable minute particles, endowed with life, of which he supposed all animal and vegetable bodies to consist.

1794 G. ADAMS *Nat. & Exp. Philos.* I. iii. 79 Fermentation disengages a great quantity of air, that is disseminated among the fluid molecules. **1796** KIRWAN *Elem. Min.* (ed. 2) I. 20 The shape of the crystal will be determined by that of the first molecule formed. **1802** PALEY *Nat. Theol.* xxiii. (ed. 2) 459 For instance, I could never see the difference between the antiquated system of atoms, and Buffon's organic molecules. **1804** *Phil. Trans.* XCIV. 286 The word molecule.. is understood to represent the peculiar solids, of definite composition and invariable form, the accumulation of which forms the crystals of mineral substances. **1869** ROSCOE *Elem. Chem.* (1871) 169 The smallest particle of an element in the free state is, however, not a single atom, but a group of atoms mechanically indivisible, or a molecule. **1882** TYNDALL in *Longm. Mag.* I. 30 A group of atoms drawn and held together by what chemists term affinity, is called a molecule.

b. *transf.* and *fig.*

1838–9 HALLAM *Hist. Lit.* II. II. i. 19 Language is always a mosaic work, made up of associated fragments, not of separate molecules. **1879** GEO. ELIOT *Theo. Such* vii. 134 He was a political molecule of the most gentlemanlike appearance.

c. Occasionally used for: A chemical equivalent (usually, of a compound).

1867 C. L. BLOXAM *Chem.* 515 One equivalent of each of these hydrocarbons in the state of vapour occupies four volumes. [*Note*] Or one molecule occupies two volumes (H = 1 vol.). **1878** A. CRUM BROWN in *Encycl. Brit.* XVI. 621/1 When a chemist speaks of acting on a molecule of succinic acid with two molecules of pentachloride of phosphorus, he means that he mixes them in the proportion of 118 parts of the former to 2 × 177·5 of the latter. For the sake of precision we sometimes speak of a molecule of water (or other substance) in grammes, or even of a gramme-molecule, a grain-molecule, &c.

2. In popular or loose use: A small particle.

1799 KIRWAN *Geol. Ess.* 478 The molecules of soil abraded and carried from some spots are often annually recruited by vegetation. **1835** KIRBY *Hab. & Inst. Anim.* I. iv. 162 The first plants and the first animals are scarcely more than animated molecules. **1859** J. R. GREENE *Man. Anim. Kingd.*, *Protozoa* Introd. 12 Both alike [plants and animals] spring from germs, *i.e.* minute independent living molecules. **1878** GEO. ELIOT *Coll. Breakf. P.* 33 Feeding on molecules of floral breath.

†**3.** *Biol.* A minute but functional particle of animal tissue that is invisible or barely visible under the light microscope. *Obs.*

1826 KIRBY & SPENCE *Introd. Entomol.* IV. xxxvii. 3 Comparative anatomists have considered the nervous system of animals as formed upon three primary types, which may be called the molecular, the ganglionic, and cerebrospinal. The first is where invisible nervous molecules are dispersed in a gelatinous body, the existence of which has only been ascertained by the nervous irritability of such bodies, [etc.]. **1841** T. R. JONES *Gen. Outl. Animal Kingdom* 6 In animals belonging to this division, no nervous filaments or masses have been discovered... The contractile molecules of their bodies are not yet aggregated into muscular fibre. **1851** W. WILKINSON *Outl. Physiol.* 9 Molecular and granular matter consists of particles that vary in size from immeasureable minuteness to 1·10,000th of an inch in diameter; and these particles are called molecules or granules, according to the appearance they present when examined with a magnifying power of 300 diameters. *Ibid.*, Molecules are merely indistinct granules; but under a higher magnifying power molecules become granules, and new molecules appear.

mole-head. [f. MOLE *sb.*[3] + HEAD *sb.*[1] 18 b.] = PIER-HEAD.

1585 T. WASHINGTON tr. *Nicholay's Voy.* I. vi. 4 b, All the people.. runne to the mole head to see vs enter into the port. *Ibid.* vii. 6 b, We saw al along the mollehead the people with the souldiers. **1587** FLEMING *Contn. Holinshed* III. 1536/2 The pierre was not finished by 350 foot so far as the foundation thereof (which he called the Molehead) was laid. *c* **1710** *Torrington Mem.* (1889) 141 To the southward of the mould head. **1802** *Eng. Encycl.* VIII. 431/1 Ports—formed by throwing a strong mound.. across the harbour's mouth to some island or rock—called mole-heads. **1836** MARRYAT *Midsh. Easy* xxxiii, Was he to be thrown over the molehead to the fishes?

'mole-hill, molehill. [f. MOLE *sb.*[2]]

1. A small mound, or occas. a ridge, of earth thrown up by moles in burrowing near the surface of the ground.

c **1430** *Pilgr. Lyf Manhode* III. xxx. (1869) 152 At a molle hille j stumblede and fil doun. **1485–6** in *Durham Rolls* (Surtees) 98 Pro aspercione lez modhylles. **1492–3** *Ibid.* 652 Lez moldhillez. **1531** *MS. Acc. St. John's Hosp., Canterb.*, Paid for castyng a brode of moll hillys. **1610** G. FLETCHER *Christ's Vict.* I. lv, Like a sort of busie ants, that crawle About some molehill. **1726** SWIFT *Gulliver* II. v, Walking to the top of a fresh Mole-hill, I fell to my Neck in the Hole. **1855** W. S. DALLAS in *Syst. Nat. Hist.* II. 489 The little heaps well known as Mole-hills. **1878** *Encycl. Brit.* XVI. 609/1 Passages.. along which the animal hunts its prey, throwing out the soil in the form of mole-hills.

2. In allusions to the smallness of a mole-hill; chiefly antithetic with *mountain*. ***to make a mountain*** (*out*) ***of a mole-hill***: to attribute great importance to something (esp. a difficulty or grievance) which is really insignificant.

1570 FOXE *A. & M.* (ed. 2) II. 1361/1 To much amplifying things y[t] be but small, makyng mountaines of Molehils. **1576** FLEMING *Panopl. Epist.* 237 *margin*, To whome you are as much comparable as a mole hill to a mountaine. **1592** LYLY *Entert.* Wks. 1902 I. 489 Among my ioies, there is one griefe, that my daughter, the Mistris of a Moole hil, hath so much forgotten.. duetie. **1594** *Battle of Alcazar* II. ii. King of a mole-hill had I rather be, Than the richest subiect of a monarchie. **1609** SHAKS. *Cor.* v. iii. 30. **1631** *Celestina* 282 Thou promisest mountaines, but performest Mole-hils. *a* **1680** CHARNOCK *Mercy for Chief Sinners* Wks. (1846) 58 Can mole-hills stand against him who has levelled mountains? **1778** T. HUTCHINSON *Diary* 5 May, I told him his nerves were affected: every mole-hill was a mountain. **1892** J. TAIT *Mind in Matter* (ed. 2) 53 [This is] like making mountains out of molehills.

attrib. **1679** DRYDEN & LEE *Œdipus* IV. i, Each mole-hill thought swells to a huge Olympus. **1802–12** BENTHAM *Ration. Judic. Evid.* (1827) V. 738 Of the mountain of their nonsense the magnitude may be measured by the molehill dimensions of.. their.. sense.

3. A small eruption or excrescence. *nonce-use.*

1650 BULWER *Anthropomet.* 157 Whose heaving phantsies fill their Faces full of such artificial Mole-hils.

Hence (*nonce-wds.*) **'molehillish** *a.*, like a mole-hill: **'mole-hilly** *a.*, abounding in mole-hills.

1830 *Blackw. Mag.* XXVIII. 888 Obstacles.. we smile at the idea of surmounting, so molehillish do they *kythe*. **1835** CLARE *Rural Muse* 111 When I stroll o'er the mole-hilly green. **1891** 'ANNIE THOMAS' *That Affair* I. xii. 201 A rather mole-hilly piece of grass.

moleine, obs. form of MULLEIN.

moleism: see MOLE *sb.*²

†**molen.** *Obs.* ? Shortening of MIRAMOLIN.

1538 *Bury Wills* (Camden) 136, vj sylver sponys wyth the molens heddes.

molen, obs. form of MULLEIN.

†**molen'darious**, *a. Obs. rare*⁻⁰. [f. med.L. *molendāri-us*, f. *molend-us*: see MOLENDINAR.] Of or pertaining to a mill.

1656 in BLOUNT *Glossogr.*: whence in later Dicts.

molendinaceous (məʊlɛndɪˈneɪʃəs), *a. Bot.* [f. med.L. *molendīn-um* mill (see next) + -ACEOUS.] Of vegetable fruits or seeds: Resembling the sails of a windmill, i.e. having many 'wings'.

1840 SMART, *Molendinaceous*, shaped as the sail of a mill. **1856** in MAYNE *Expos. Lex.* **1900** B. D. JACKSON *Gloss. Bot. Terms* 160 *Molendinaceous*, furnished with large wing-like expansions. In mod. Dicts.

molendinar, *a.* and *sb. nonce-wd.* (*humorously pedantic*). [ad. med.L. *molendinār-ius* (pertaining to a mill, f. *molendīnum* mill, f. *molend-us* (*frumentum molendum* corn to be ground) gerundive of *molĕre* to grind. (A brook at Glasgow is called the *Molendinar Burn*; the local pronunciation is (molənˈdiːnər).)] **a.** *adj.* Of or concerning a mill or miller. **b.** *sb.* A molar tooth.

1820 SCOTT *Monast.* xxviii, O most Molendinar beauty. **1824** —— *St. Ronan's* xiii, The extraction of a carious molendinar. **1827** —— *Diary* 10 Feb. in Lockhart *Life*, The stories of the Miller of Thirlstane, and similar molendinar tragedies.

So **mo'lendinary** *a.*, belonging to a mill; *sb.*, a mill.

1820 SCOTT *Monast.* xxix, The house of thy molendinary father. **1822** —— *Pirate* xi, Can a man.. look at that thing there, which they have the impudence to call a corn-mill, without trembling to think that corn should be intrusted to such a miserable molendinary?

molendi'narious, *a. Obs.*⁻⁰ [Formed as prec. + -OUS.] Of or pertaining to a mill.

1656 BLOUNT *Glossogr.*, *Molendinarious*, of or pertaining to a Mill. **1728** in BAILEY.

mole-plough. [f. MOLE *sb.*² + PLOUGH *sb.*] A plough in which a pointed iron shoe attached to a standard is drawn along beneath the surface, making a hollow channel resembling the track of a mole, which serves as a deep drain.

1798 J. MIDDLETON *View Agric. Midsx.* 289 A mole plough, invented by Mr. Adam Scott, for the purpose of making hollow-drains. **1879** SIR T. WRIGHTSON in *Cassell's Techn. Educ.* IV. 219 First we have the mole-plough forcing its way through a tenacious clay, and leaving a hollow channel.

moler¹ (ˈməʊlə(r)). [f. MOLE *v.*² + -ER¹.] A mole-catcher.

1893 BARING GOULD *Cheap-Jack Z.* II. 39 Artisans out of humour because trade was slack, gangers.. millers, molers, gozzards. **1902** C. G. HARPER *Cambr., Ely & King's Lynn Road* 206 The moles.. caught by the molers.

moler² (ˈməʊlə(r)). Also **Moler**. [a. Da. *moler*, f. northern Da. dial. *mo* loose chalky soil (= Norw., Sw. *mo* sandy heath) + *ler* loam, clay (= Norw., Sw. *ler* clay).] (See quot. 1923.) (A proprietary name.)

1910 *Chem. Abstr.* IV. 2363 'Moler' is an argillaceous diatomaceous earth found in a limited region in the fiords of Denmark. **1923** A. B. SEARLE *Sands & Crushed Rocks* I. iii. 127 Moler is a sandy material somewhat resembling kieselguhr or diatomaceous earth.., but it is less refractory and contains a considerable proportion of clay and volcanic ash, for which reason it is self-binding and can be made into bricks without any other bond. **1932** A. G. GEESON *Gen. Building Repairs* (ed. 2) I. i. 48 Plaster, terra cotta, moler and breeze slabs have the advantage that they can be sawn to size. **1936** *Times* 9 Nov. 20/1 (Advt.), An extensive deposit of Diatomite of a high quality, known as 'Moler', which is suitable for many of the above purposes, exists on the Island of Für in Denmark. **1948** *Archit. Rev.* CIV. 57 The remaining blocks will be finished in a 4½ in. external concrete-brick cladding with an internal 4 in. skin of molar [*sic*] blocks with a 2 in. cavity. **1963** *Trade Marks Jrnl.* 6 June 766/1 Moler... Insulators and insulating materials. Aktieselskabet Skarrehage Molervaerk.., Nykbøing Mors, Denmark; manufacturers; and Refractulation Limited,.. London,.. merchants.

Moler, var. MALER *sb.* and *a.*

moleskin (ˈməʊlskɪn). [f. MOLE *sb.*² + SKIN.]

1. The skin of the mole used as a fur. Also other skins sheared so as to resemble this.

1668 R. L'ESTRANGE *Vis. Quev.* (1708) 14 The Impositions now to be set on foot, are upon Bare-neck'd Ladies, Patches, Mole-skins, Spanish Paper, and all the Mundus Muliebris more than what is necessary and decent. **1903** *Edin. Even. News* 17 Apr. 6 There is just now an exceptional demand for moleskins,.. due to a report that the King recently had a waistcoat made of moleskins. **1906** *Westm. Gaz.* 3 Nov. 13/1 The moleskin that is produced by shearing musquash.

2. A strong, soft, fine-piled cotton fustian the surface of which is 'shaved' before dyeing.

1803 *Ann. Reg.* 830 A patent, dated June 28th, to Joseph Everett, clothier, for an article.. which he denominates Salisbury Angola Moleskin. **1831** *Lincoln Herald* 9 Sept. 3/6 The trowsers are of stout moleskin. **1873** BLACK *Adv. Phaeton* xviii, The loafer in moleskin stood at some little distance.

3. *pl.* Outer garments, esp. trousers, made of moleskin (in sense 2).

1836 J. STRUTHERS *Poet. Wks.* (1850) II. 113 Our moleskins are every way as capable as their blouses. **1858** *Times* 20 Nov. 8/5 Our agricultural labourers who wear corduroys, or moleskins. **1893** MRS. C. PRAED *Outlaw & Lawmaker* I. 238 Bushmen in immaculate moleskins and flaring ties.

4. *attrib.* and *Comb.*, as ***moleskin breeches***, ***clothes***, ***coat***, ***colour***, ***trousers***; ***moleskin-breeched***, ***-coloured*** adjs.; **moleskin shaver**, a workman who 'shaves' or crops the surface of moleskin; **moleskin squatter** *Austral.* and *N.Z.* (see quot. 1941).

1896 *Daily News* 25 July 8/1 Plodding old labourers, *moleskin-breeched. **1899** QUILLER-COUCH *Ship of Stars* xii, Taffy went forth to work in *moleskin breeches. **1854** H. MILLER *Sch. & Schm.* viii. 146 A suit of strong *moleskin clothes. **1903** *Westm. Gaz.* 10 Sept. 4/2 There is *moleskin colour, a term born of the mania for *moleskin coats, which.. will result in *moleskin-coloured cloths of many kinds. **1881** *Instr. Census Clerks* 71 Fustian Manufacturer.. *Moleskin Shaver. **1941** BAKER *N.Z. Slang* v. 40 Among other terms we have derived from farm life and sheep stations are **moleskin squatter*, 'a working man who has come to own a small sheep run.' *a* **1948** L. G. D. ACLAND *Early Canterbury Runs* (1951) 387 *Moleskin squatter*... A correspondent writes: 'The last time I heard it was when the Government cut up Cheviot in 1893... Since then *m.ss.* have become too numerous to attract attention.' **1873** TROLLOPE *Harry Heathcote* (1874) i. 3 The young man.. had on a flannel shirt, a pair of *moleskin trousers, and an old straw hat. **1900** H. LAWSON *On Track* 57 The scrub steamed—and stunk like a new pair of moleskin trousers.

mo'lest, *sb. Obs.*, exc. *arch.* [a. OF. *moleste*, ad. L. *molestia* trouble, f. *molest-us*: see next.] Trouble, hardship; molestation, injury.

13.. *K. Alis.* 5443 The kyng thereof hadde molest. *Ibid.* 5811 Bot of bestes and wormes felle, And of the wederes stronge, and tempestes, That hem duden grete molestes. ?*a* **1412** LYDG. *Two Merch.* 577 What grevous molest and what heuynesse With many assaut in dreed doth vs to doute! *c* **1489** CAXTON *Blanchardyn* xviii. 58 Neuertheles, they lefte not to lodge hem self there, what for daunger nor moleste that men coude do to them. **1590** GREENE *Mourn. Garment* (1616) K 2, Thus clogg'd with loue, with passions and with griefe, I saw the country life had least molest. **1647** LILLY *Chr. Astrol.* clxxxv. 821 You have victory,.. and acquire what you desired.. even out of these molests. **1865** W. J. LINTON *Claribel*, etc. 53 Alfred.. Sat down to keep the feast of Epiphany Within his walls, secure from all molest.

†**mo'lest**, *a. Obs. rare.* [a. OF. *moleste*, ad. L. *molest-us*: see next.] Troublesome, vexatious.

1539 TAVERNER *Erasm. Prov.* (1552) 64 Many ther be which while they studie to do a man good do hym much harme, or otherwise be molest and greuouse unto him.

molest (məʊˈlɛst), *v.* [a. OF. *molester* (12–13th c. in Hatz.-Darm.) = Sp. *molestar*, It. *molestare*, ad. L. *molestāre* to trouble, annoy, f. *molest-us* troublesome, burdensome, annoying, f. **moles-*, perh. cogn. w. *mōlēs* mass, burden.]

†**1.** *trans.* To cause trouble, grief, or vexation to; to vex, annoy, put to inconvenience. *Obs.*

c **1374** CHAUCER *Troylus* IV. 852 (880) But how this cas doth Troilus moleste, That may non erthely mannes tonge seye. *c* **1400** *Rom. Rose* 5274 If he do not his requeste, He shal as mochel him moleste As his felow. **1490** CAXTON *Eneydos* vi. 26 Elysse faynynge that she ne myghte no lenger duelle in the hous of Acerbe late her husbonde, bycause that she was overmoche moleste and greved by [etc.]. **1541** *Act 33 Hen. VIII*, c. 35 For lacke of the saide water [they] shall be muche greeued annoyed and molested. **1549** *Compl. Scot.* xv. 134 ȝour gudscheir molestit the pepil victht intollerabil exactions. **1568** GRAFTON *Chron.* II. 645 Neither will I molest you with the recitall of all the perticulers thereof. **1617–18** W. LAWSON *New Orch. & Gard.* (1623) 4 If ouerflowing molest you after one day, auoid it then by deepe trenching. *a* **1667** COWLEY *Ess. in Verse & Prose, Liberty* i, These are the small uneasie things Which about Greatness still are found, And rather it Molest than Wound. **1705** ADDISON *Italy* (1733) 51 The Colds of Winter, and the Heats of Summer, are equally incapable of molesting you. **1726** LEONI *Alberti's Archit.* I. 4/1 The Western.. Reflections of the Sun.. molest us most of all: because they double the Heat.

†**b.** Of disease: To afflict, affect. Also *fig. Obs.*

1576 FLEMING *Panopl. Epist.* 268 If he be molested still, with that mischiefous maladie, yet [etc.]. **1600** J. PORY tr. *Leo's Africa* VIII. 299 With the French poxe I think that no other countrie vnder heauen is so molested. **1604** T. WRIGHT *Passions* I. iv. 17 If the passions of the Mynde bee not moderated according to reason.. immediately the Soule is molested with some maladie. **1646** SIR T. BROWNE *Pseud. Ep.* v. xiii. 253 Using continuall riding, they were generally molested with the Sciatica or hippegowte. **1696** *Phil. Trans.* XIX. 252 He has been.. generally molested with a Diarrhœa for some years past.

2. To interfere or meddle with (a person) injuriously or with hostile intent. Now almost exclusively in negative contexts.

1494 FABYAN *Chron.* VII. 469 Certayne men of the duchie of Burgoyne.. gaue vnto hym, to the entent he shulde nat molest or hurte that countre, CC. M. floryns of golde. **1553** EDEN *Treat. Newe Ind.* (Arb.) 34 Their chiefe studie is in no case to moleste their neyghboures. **1598** BARCKLEY *Felic. Man* (1631) 458 Another companie of Mice joyned with these and molested them more then before. **1659** MILTON *Civ. Power* 34 No protestant.. ought, by the common doctrine of protestants, to be forc'd or molested for religion. **1660** R. COKE *Power & Subj.* 231 No person shall be molested for any offences abovesaid. **1695** KEN *Hymn, 'Glory to thee, my God'* v, Let.. No powers of darkness me molest. **1769** BLACKSTONE *Comm.* IV. 115 By the statute 1 & 2 Ph. & Mar. c. 8. to molest the possessors of abbey lands granted by parliament to Henry the eighth, and Edward the sixth, is a *praemunire*. **1861** HURLSTONE & NORMAN *Excheq. Rep.* VI. 450 He the plaintiff should not nor would molest or disturb the said Ann Thomas in her person or in her manner of living. **1864** CARLYLE *Fredk. Gt.* xv. ii. (1872) V. 278 Prussians, under strict discipline, molest no private person. **1884** *Law Rep.*, 14 *Q.B.D.* 796 The Countess.. 'molested' the defendant contrary to the covenant contained in the separation deed. **1902** A. LANG *Hist. Scot.* II. vii. 156 It does not seem.. to follow that she intended to persecute or molest Protestants.

†**b.** To tamper with (a thing). *Obs.*

1603 T. M. *True Narrat. Ent. Jas. I* E 4 b, A great common (which as the people there-about complaine, sir I. Spenser of London hath very vncharitable molested). **1774** T. WEST *Antiq. Furness* (1805) 366 When it was first molested, some of the tomb stones were removed.

†**3.** *intr.* To cause annoyance or vexation. *Obs.*

1580 LYLY *Euphues* (Arb.) 421 Your pardons obteyned, if I offend in sharpnesse, and your patience graunted, if molest in length, I thus beginne to conclude against you all [etc.].

†**mo'lestance.** *Obs.* [f. MOLEST *v.* + -ANCE.] Molestation.

1693 LYDE *True Acc. Retaking 'Friend's Adventure'* 14 Being uncapable of making any further resistance, he went out upon Deck staggering to and fro, without any further Molestance from the Boy.

†**molestate**, *v. Obs.* [f. ppl. stem of L. *molestāre* MOLEST *v.*] trans. To harass, trouble.

1543 GRAFTON *Cont. Harding* 573 He desired the kyng yᵗ he would not molestate his realme herafter with suche cruel tormentyng and fieryng.

molestation (mɒlɪˈsteɪʃən, ˌməʊ-). [a. OF. *molestation*, ad. L. *molestātiōn-em*, n. of action f. *molestāre* to trouble: see MOLEST *v.*]

1. The action of molesting, or the condition of being molested; annoyance, hostile or vexatious interference; †vexation, distress.

c **1400** *Beryn* 1599 Wee have no nede to dout werr, ne molestacioun. **1513** DOUGLAS *Æneis* II. ii. 28 With this regrate our hartis sterit to petie, All molestatioun cessit and lattin be. **1578** T. N. tr. *Conq. W. India* 28 Neyther his person, nor none of his countrey should receyve anye molestation of him. **1597** A. M. tr. *Guillemeau's Fr. Chirurg.* 2 There are some of the Plates (vnto my great molestatione and sorrowe) lost. **1604** SHAKS. *Oth.* II. i. 16, I neuer did like mollestation view On the enchafed Flood. **1611** FLORIO, *Asa*,.. Also molestation, lazines, or anxiety of mind. *a* **1661** FULLER *Worthies, Westminster* (1662) II. 239 Such his hazarding his person (really worth ten thousand of them) to the great molestation of his true friends. *a* **1691** BOYLE *Hist. Air* (1692) 180 Having in great veneration the bodies of their ancestors, being most extreamly against any molestation of the dead. **1708** MRS. CENTLIVRE *Busy Body* I. i, You are.. to move your suit to Miranda.. without let or molestation. *a* **1720** SEWEL *Hist. Quakers* (1722) Pref. b 2, The People called Quakers at length obtained Liberty to perform their publick Worship without Molestation. **1777** WATSON *Philip II* XXII. (1839) 483 He arrived in a few weeks without receiving any molestation by the way. **1878** BOSW. SMITH *Carthage* 97 He would be safe from Roman molestation.

b. *Scots Law.* The harassing of a person in his possession or occupation of lands. **c.** *Eng. Law.* (See quots. 1884.)

1456 SIR G. HAYE *Law Arms* (S.T.S.) 106 The pape.. may tak fra thame thair foresaid jurisdictioun.. gif thai mak ony molestacioun to cristyn that is in thair jurisdictioun. **1497** *Extracts Aberdeen Reg.* (1844) I. 65 Or yit, that ye or thai mak ony arrestment, molestatioun, tribule, or injur to the saide Nicholl. **1547** *Reg. Privy Council Scot.* I. 72 He sall desist and cese fra all stop, molestatioun, lett, and impediment making to the said Schir George Douglas. **1564** *Ibid.* 275 The partie makand the invasioun, persute, and molestatioun sall pay.. the soum of fyve thousand markis. **1597** SKENE *De Verb. Sign.* s.v. *Assisa*, In sundrie civil causes, sik as perambulations, cognitions, molestations,.. serving of brieves, and in all and sundrie criminal causes. **1627** *Burgh Rec. Glasgow* (1876) I. 359 Sik as beis imprissonet for capitall crymes, truble, molestatioun or ryett done within the said burghe. **1861** HURLSTONE & NORMAN *Excheq. Rep.* VI. 453 The words 'molest or disturb', in that convenant, mean personal molestation or disturbance. **1884** *Law Rep.*, 12 *Q.B.D.* 543 It amounted to substantial molestation, using the word 'molestation' in the sense of injury knowingly and without lawful excuse inflicted upon another in his person, character, social position, or property. **1884** *Law Rep.*, 14 *Q.B.D.* 796 The molestation may be of different kinds: adultery and the birth of an illegitimate child as a consequence of that adultery are sufficient evidence of molestation. **1885** *Law Times Rep.* LIII. 306/1 The trustees covenanted to indemnify the husband from the debts of and molestation by the wife.

2. With *a* and in *pl.*: A trouble, annoyance, vexation; *concr.* a cause of annoyance. Now *rare.*

c **1400** *Beryn* 1101 For a molestacioune Ther was noon othir remedy, but a consolacioune. **1474** CAXTON *Chesse* 111 There cometh of glotonye riottes wronges and molestacions. **1555** EDEN *Decades* 359 Such greefes & molestations as they

otherwyse receaue. **1576** FLEMING *Panopl. Epist.* 62, I wil withdraw me selfe from al molestations and perplexities. **1604** T. WRIGHT *Passions* I. iv. 16 If the inferior appetite or passions obey and concurre with the will..they take away the molestations and tediousnesse that occurre in the practise of good woorks. **1629** J. COLE *Of Death* 93 The molestations of trade, or worldly affaires. **1642** FULLER *Holy & Prof. St.* III. xxii. 213 All the molestations of Marriage are abundantly recompenced with other comforts. **1863** GEO. ELIOT *Romola* lxxi, The man who was as great a molestation to vicious citizens..as to a corrupt clergy.

mo'lested, *ppl. a.* [f. MOLEST *v.* + -ED[1].] In senses of the vb.; in quot., †harassed.

1597 A. M. tr. *Guillemeau's Fr. Chirurg.* 2 Throughe the iniuryes of this most disturbede and molestede time, there are some of the Plates lost.

molester (məʊ'lɛstə(r)). [f. MOLEST *v.* + -ER[1].] One who molests or disturbs.

1579 W. WILKINSON *Confut. Family of Loue, Brief Descr.* A j, God make him to be a member, not a molester of the Church. *c* **1670** COTTON *Voy. Irel.* II. Poems (1689) 178 Till the Bells, that had been my morning molesters, Now wak'd me again, chiming all in to Vespers. **1725** KIRKPATRICK *Relig. Ord. Norwich* (1845) 10 To restrain all such molesters by ecclesiastical censure. **1895** *Pop. Sci. Monthly* July 118, It has no offensive odors to warn off molesters.

molestful (məʊ'lɛstfʊl), *a.* Now *rare.* [f. MOLEST *sb.* or *v.* + -FUL.] Troublesome, annoying, painful.

1596 DALRYMPLE tr. *Leslie's Hist. Scot.* I. 94 In tyme of weir quhen..to karie..kitchine veshels thay thoᵗ hauie and molestful. *Ibid.* VII. 13 Quha suspectet this kuir thairfor to be committit to him that he war nocht molestful to his ȝoung sone Dauid. **1604** T. WRIGHT *Passions* I. ii. 9 Wee have a continuall and molestfull battell with Carnall vices. **1621** T. WILLIAMSON tr. *Goulart's Wise Vieillard* 57 Thou oughtest not..to hold it grieuous or molestfull to haue lost thy sight. **1675** WOODHEAD, etc. *Paraphr. St. Paul* 116 The wicked also shall have a resurrection..to all manner of molestful passibility. **1891** C. E. NORTON *Dante's Hell* x. 47 That noble fatherland to which perchance I was too molestful.

Hence † **mo'lestfully** *adv.* (Minsheu *Sp. Dict.* II. 1599.)

† **molestie.** *Obs. rare*⁻¹. [a. OF. *molestie*, ad. L. *molestia*: see MOLESTIOUS.] Trouble.

1532 *Chaucer's Boeth.* III. pr. ix. (Skeat) l. 77 He ne geteth him nat suffisaunce that power forleteth, and that molestie [*Camb. & Addit. MSS.* moleste] prikketh..and that derkenesse hydeth.

mo'lesting, *vbl. sb.* [f. MOLEST *v.* + -ING[1].] The action of MOLEST *v.*; †annoyance, injury.

1523 CROMWELL in Merriman *Life & Lett.* (1902) I. 33 The grete molestyng and trowbelyng of all the nacions abowte theym. **1561** DAUS tr. *Bullinger on Apoc.* (1573) 211 b, If Christ will come to iudgement, why doth he differre it so long, and to so great molestyng of his? **1577** HANMER *Anc. Eccl. Hist.* (1585) 394 Againe he fell a molesting of yᵉ Nouations.

† **mo'lesting,** *ppl. a. Obs. rare.* [f. MOLEST *v.* + -ING[2].] Troublesome, interfering.

1597 A. M. tr. *Guillemeau's Fr. Chirurg.* 10 b/2 The fracture of the bone, with the molestinge and troublesome accidentes thereof. **1604** T. WRIGHT *Passions* I. iv. 16 If our heartes..reioyce in God, then paine is turned into pleasure, and a molesting service into a delightfull obsequie. **1822** GALT *Provost* xl, In nothing, however, did his molesting temper cause so much disturbance, as when [etc.].

† **mo'lestious,** *a. Obs.* [f. L. *molestia* (n. of quality f. *molestus* troublesome) + -OUS.] Troublesome.

1524 PACE in Strype *Eccl. Mem.* (1721) I. App. xi. 20 Tediousnes of heats, thirst and hunger with molestious passage of baggage. **1597** A. M. tr. *Guillemeau's Fr. Chirurg.* 34 b/1 They weare too intollerable and molestiouse vnto the patient. **1611** SPEED *Hist. Gt. Brit.* VI. xxiii. §14.114 Here in Britaine, the most vnquiet and molestious Prouince of all. **1620** VENNER *Via Recta* ii. 32 If the time be very hot, and the thirst molestious,..foure parts of water may be mingled with one of wine.

Hence **mo'lestiousness,** troublesomeness.

a **1670** HACKET *Cent. Serm.* (1675) 895 They come upon us with some molestiousness and torment.

molestive (məʊ'lɛstɪv), *a.* [f. MOLEST *v.* + -IVE.] Tending to annoy; troublesome, interfering.

1905 *North Amer. Rev.* Nov. 657, I suppose that the stranger always finds the patriotism of a country molestive. **1929** W. DEEPING *Roper's Row* vi. 58 If the young Prossers had persecuted the son, Mrs. Prosser had been equally molestive to the mother.

† **mo'lestous,** *a. Obs. rare.* [f. L. *molest-us* troublesome + -OUS.] = MOLESTIOUS.

1555 EDEN *Decades* 90 It is a warlyke nation and hath byn euer hetherto molestous to theyr bortherers. *Ibid.* 150 They seemed to bee molestous to thinhabitantes. **1657** W. MORICE *Coena quasi Κοινὴ* Pref. 18 Humors which were neither discerned, nor were molestous.

† **mo'lestuous,** *a. Obs.* [erron. f. L. *molest-us* troublesome; after *tempestuous*, etc.] Troublesome; troublous.

a **1572** KNOX *Bk. Common Order* (1602) 129 Afflictions are molestuous [*ed.* 1575 molestsome], noysome and hard to be borne with. **1611** MUNDAY *Briefe Chron.* 239 Pompilius..appointed his seate in another City..but finding it too mollestuous he transferred the State to another Citty. **1657** TRAPP *Comm. Job* iii. 17 Vexatious persons,..molestuous and mischievous.

molet, obs. form of MOLLET *Obs.*, MULLET.

moletta, molette, obs. ff. MULATTO, MULLET.

molewarp, obs. form of MOULDWARP.

moley ('məʊlɪ), *sb. slang.* [Origin obscure.] (See quot. 1950.)

1950 J. D. CARR *Below Suspicion* xi. 132 'Use the moleys when you catch 'im.' The moley was an ordinary potato, its surface jagged with the edges of safety-razor blades. They ground it into your face, twisted it, and... **1959** *Spectator* 6 Mar. 314/1, I suppose if I go on criticising him I shall end up by having the boys with the moleys call on me one dark night.

moley ('məʊlɪ), *a. rare*⁻¹. [f. MOLE *sb.*[2] + -Y.] Of the nature of a mole.

1758 GOLDSM. *Hist. Our Own Lang.* ii. Wks. (Bohn) IV. 449, I am far from saying that Parker was a fine..writer of the English language, but he certainly did it infinite service in discouraging..the moley, creeping style, which, at that time, infected all the ranks both of the laity and clergy.

moleyne, molhah, obs. ff. MULLEIN, MULLAH.

moliable, obs. variant of MOLLIABLE.

‖ **molimen** (məʊ'laɪmɛn). *Phys.* and *Path.* Pl. **molimina** (məʊ'lɪmɪnə). [L. *mōlīmen* effort, f. *mōlīrī* to make an effort, undertake, attempt.] An effort by which the system endeavours to perform any natural function, esp. ***menstrual molimen***, the straining to bring about the catamenia.

1865 T. H. TANNER *Pract. Med.* (ed. 5) 670 The effect of the menstrual molimen is felt by the whole system. **1878** A. HAMILTON *Nerv. Dis.* 220 She never had had her catamenia nor noticed any molimina. **1889** J. M. DUNCAN *Lect. Dis. Women* xvii. (ed. 4) 133 There may be a molimen, or no molimen. When there is said to be a molimen or attempt, the girl expects the flow.

† **mo'liminous,** *a. Obs.* [f. L. *mōlīmin-* MOLIMEN + -OUS.]

1. Characterized by great effort or endeavour; laborious.

1656 BLOUNT *Glossogr.*, *Moliminous*, that hath force, or useth endeavor to do any thing; difficult. **1686** H. MORE *Real Pres.* viii. 62 All which things to repeat here would be too moliminous and inconsistent with the Brevity I intend. **1722** WOLLASTON *Relig. Nat.* v. 93 If the genius of the language..were well understood, some labord and moliminous attempts to account for it [the flood] might have been prevented.

2. a. Massive, cumbrous. **b.** Weighty, momentous.

c **1643** *Observ. on his Majesty's late Answ. & Expresses* 11 Some way was invented to regulate the motions of the peoples moliminous body. **1660** H. MORE *Myst. Godl.* VII. i. 281 Some Prophecies are not conditional but absolute, as certainly all those are that are of so vast and Moliminous Concernment to the World as the appearing of the Messias is. **1684** —— *Answ.*, etc. 176 In this place it was impertinent, and too moliminous, nor sutable to the accustomed brevity and succinctness of the Apocalyptick style.

Hence † **mo'liminously** *adv.*, laboriously.

1678 CUDWORTH *Intell. Syst.* I. ii. §19. 82 If this Deity must needs go about moliminously to make a world.., what Tools and Instruments could he have to work withall?

molin obs. form of MULLEIN.

molinary ('məʊlɪnərɪ), *a. rare.* [f. late L. *molīnāri-us*, f. *molīna* mill: see -ARY[1].] Of or pertaining to the grinding of corn.

1774 PENNANT *Tour Scot. in 1772*, 280 All the molinary operations are done at home. **1876** RUSKIN *Fors Clav.* VI. 161 The 'Lead', a stream 'led' from the Tay into the town for molinary purposes.

moline (məʊ'laɪn). *a.* and *sb. Her.* [Prob. repr. AF. **moliné*, f. *molin* (mod.F. *moulin*) mill: see MILL *sb.*[1] and -EE.]

A. *adj.* Of or resembling the expanded and curved extremities of a mill-rind; esp. in ***cross moline***, a cross each of the arms of which terminates in two expanded and curved branches resembling the extremities of a mill-rind.

1562 LEIGH *Armorie* 188 b, He beareth ermin a crosse moline Or. **1610** GUILLIM *Heraldry* II. vii. 70 The Field is Azure, a Crosse Moline Pierced Losenge-waies. **1688** R. HOLME *Armoury* III. xvi. (Roxb.) 90/1 A cleever with a moline cutting end. **1761** *Brit. Mag.* II. 532 Azure, a cross moline, argent. **1868** CUSSANS *Her.* (1893) 118 There are twelve families of Miller who bear Crosses-Moline..and none who bear Millstones or Mill-rinds.

ellipt. **1864** BOUTELL *Her., Hist. & Pop.* vi. 29 The Cross Patonce..expands more widely than the Moline.

B. *sb.* **1.** = *cross moline.*

1777 PORNY *Elem. Heraldry*, Dict., *Moline*..is used in Heraldry to denote a Cross which turns round both ways at all the extremities. **1823** CRABB *Technol. Dict.*, *Molines.*

2. = MILL-RIND (Ogilvie 1882).

Hence † **molined** *a. rare* = MOLINE *a.*

1688 R. HOLME *Armoury* III. 342/1 Let it be called a Mill Rinde molined, because the ends turn like the Cross Moline.

† **molinet.** *Obs.* Also 8 **molionet.** [ad. F. *moulinet*, dim. of *moulin* a mill: see -ET[1].]

a. A little mill, a small grinding apparatus. **b.** A stick for whipping chocolate.

1648 GAGE *West Ind.* xvi. 106 The Chocolatte..is stirred in a cup by an instrument called a Molinet, or Molinillo. **1676** WORLIDGE *Cyder* (1691) 176 This kernel being ground fine by a molinet. **1690** [EVELYN] *Mundus Muliebris* 11 A Tea and Chocolate Pot, With Molionet and Caudle Cup. *a* **1700** B. E. *Dict. Cant. Crew*, *Molinet*, a Chocolate Stick, or little Mill. **1728** BAILEY, *Mollinet*, a small Muller to grind Colours.

‖ **molinete** (moli'nete). Also **molinet.** [a. Sp. *molinete*, lit. (toy) windmill, little mill.] In *Bullfighting*, a decorative pass made by a matador (see quot. 1959[2]).

1932 [see FAROL]. **1959** V. J. KEHOE *Aficionado!* 19 Manolo then did a *derechazo*,..ending the series with a *molinete* on his knees. *Ibid.* 208 The *molinete.* Performed with either hand, this pass is started by the matador citing the toro as for a cambiado, then spinning out of the pass in the opposite direction of the toro's charge. **1971** J. LEIBOLD *This is Bullfight* xvii. 202 The molinete can be executed with either the right or left hand... Timing, grace and elegance of execution are of prime importance in accomplishing the molinete.

Molinism[1] ('mɒlɪnɪz(ə)m). [f. the name of the Spanish Jesuit Luis *Molina* (1535–1600) + -ISM. Cf. F. *molinisme.*] The doctrine propounded in 1588 by Molina, that the efficacy of grace depends simply on the will which freely accepts it.

1669 GALE *True Idea Jansenisme* 107 The subversion of Molinisme.

Molinism[2] ('mɒlɪnɪz(ə)m). [f. the name of Miguel de *Molinos* (1627–96) a Spanish priest.] The doctrine of Molinos; quietism.

1720 *Lond. Gaz.* No. 5863/1 [Auto da Fé] There were 43 Criminals brought out of the Prison of the Inquisition on this Occasion,..most of them accused of Molinism or Judaism. **1868** BROWNING *Ring & Bk.* VI. 152, I heard..what is priest's-duty—labour to pluck tares And weed the corn of Molinism.

Molinist[1] ('mɒlɪnɪst). [f. *Molina* + -IST.] One who holds the doctrine of Molinism; a follower of the Jesuit Molina. Also *attrib.*

1655 J. OWEN *Vind. Evang.* xxxi. 646 The Molinists and Jesuits on the one side, with the Jansenians, or Bayans on the other. **1859** *All Year Round* No. 30. 82 The Molinists, were ..analogous to our High-Church party.

attrib. **1768** HUME *Ess. & Treat.* (1809) II. 481 The Molinist party had tried to discredit these miracles.

Hence † **Moli'nistic** *a.*

1669 GALE *True Idea Jansenisme* 54 They publisht this *Cartel of Defiance* to the whole Molinistick Partie.

Molinist[2] ('mɒlɪnɪst). [Formed as MOLINISM[2] + -IST.] A follower of Molinos.

1868 BROWNING *Ring & Bk.* V. 1838.

† **Molinosist.** *Obs.*⁻⁰ [a. F. *molinosiste*, f. the name *Molinos*: see prec.] = prec.

1727–52 CHAMBERS *Cycl.*, *Molinosists*..the same with what are otherwise called *Quietists.* **1797** *Encycl. Brit.* (ed. 3) s.v.

molionet, erron. form of MOLINET.

† **mo'lition**[1]. *Obs.* [a. F. *molition* (Rabelais), ad. L. *mōlītiōn-em*, n. of action f. *mōlīrī* to make exertions, to build, construct.] **a.** An endeavour, effort **b.** A contrivance, apparatus.

1597 A. M. tr. *Guillemeau's Fr. Chirurg.* iv b, This treasure house of Engines, Molitiones, and of other Chyrurgicall Instrumentes. **1642** M. NEWCOMEN *Craft Church's Adversaries* (1643) 24 You that have bin now these two yeares wrastling with them, you know what their Molitions have bin. **1678** CUDWORTH *Intell. Syst.* I. ii. §22. 86 Infinite Atoms..after many Convolutions and Evolutions, Molitions and Essays..chanced..to settle into this form and system of things.

† **mo'lition**[2]. *Obs. rare*⁻⁰. [a. med.L. *molitiōn-em*, n. of action from L. *molĕre* to grind: see -ITION.] The action of grinding.

1731 BAILEY vol. II, *Molitions*, grindings.

† **moliture.** *Obs. rare*⁻¹. [ad. med.L. *molitūra*, f. L. *molĕre* to grind: see -TURE.] = MULTURE.

1656 BRAMHALL *Replic. Bp. Chalcedon* v. 204 This claim of universall power and authority doth bring more moliture to their mill.

molkasin, obs. form of MOCCASIN.

moll (mɒl), *sb.* Also 6–7 **Mall.** [A familiar diminutive of *Mary.* Cf. MOLLY.]

1. A female personal name. ***Moll Cut-purse***, the nickname of a notorious female of the first half of the 17th c., introduced by Middleton and Dekker into their *Roaring Girl* and by Field into his *Amends for Ladies.* † ***Moll Thomson's mark*** (slang): see quot. 1785.

1567 WAGER *Marie Magdalene* 1194 (Carpenter) Conscience? how doth thy conscience, little Mall? **1611** MIDDLETON & DEKKER (*title*) The Roaring Girle. Or Moll Cut-Purse. As it hath lately beene Acted on the Fortune-stage by the Prince his Players. *Ibid.*, Dramatis Personæ..Mol the Roaring Girle. **1662** *Womans Champion* (title-p.) A true Relation of the mad Pranks..and most unheard of Stratagems of Mrs. Mary Frith, commonly called Mall Cutpurse. **1663** BUTLER *Hud.* I. ii. 368 A bold Virago, stout and tall, As Joan of France, or English Mall. **1711** BUDGELL *Spect.* No. 67 ¶9 At last an impudent young Dog bid the Fidlers play a Dance called Mol Patley. **1785** GROSE *Dict.*

Vulg. T., *Moll Thompson's Mark*, M. T. i.e. empty; take away this bottle, it has Moll Thompson's mark upon it.

b. ***Moll Blood***, the gallows.

1818 SCOTT *Hrt. Midl.* xx, Three words of your mouth would give the girl the chance to nick Moll Blood.

c. In names of animals and plants, as **moll-blob** = MARSH-MARIGOLD; **moll-hern (-heron, -yern)**, the heron, *Ardea cinerea*; **moll-washer**, the pied wagtail, *Motacilla lugubris*.

1847–78 HALLIWELL, *Moll-washer*, the water-wagtail. **1848** *Zoologist* VI. 2191 Herons are not only very commonly called 'cranes'..but also 'moll-herons', or rather 'moll-yerns'. **1854** MISS BAKER *Northampt. Gloss.*, *Moll-blobs*, or *Molly-blobs*. **1880** JEFFERIES *Gt. Estate* iv. 78 'A moll ern flod away.' **1939** F. THOMPSON *Lark Rise* v. 97 All legs and wings, like a moll-heron.

2. a. A prostitute. gen., a girl, woman; a girl-friend or sweetheart, esp. of a criminal; the unmarried female companion of a professional thief or vagrant; a female pickpocket or thief. See also *gun moll*. *slang*.

1604 MIDDLETON *Father Hubburd's T.* Wks. (Bullen) VIII. 78 None of these common Molls neither, but discontented and unfortunate gentlewomen. **1753** J. POULTER *Discoveries* (ed. 2) 34 To nap the Slangs from the Cull or Moll; that is, . . to take the Things from the Man or Woman. **1785** GROSE *Dict. Vulg. T.*, *Moll*, a whore. **1819** T. THOMPSON in *Collect. Songs Newcastle Dial.* 10 When the Malls began their reels. **1823** 'J. BEE' *Dict. Turf*, *Molls* are the female companions of low thieves, at bed, board, and business. **1840** H. D. MILES *Dick Turpin* xxi. 250 You might ha' knowed his moll, a spicy, swellish sort of a bit o'muslin. **1872** G. P. BURNHAM *Mem. U.S. Secret Service* 190 Doctor Blake and his 'moll' visited the town of Toms River. **1877** *Five Yrs. Penal Serv.* iii. 242 Once, when he was speaking of 'his old woman' for the time being, I asked if she was a 'crooked' one too. 'Oh, yes', he replied; 'I never had nothin' to do with any "moll" who couldn't cut her own grass.' **1891** J. BARON *Blegburn Dickshonary* 44 'Aw'm gooin' to meet mi Moll to-neet' is a varra common sayin' wi' factory lads: some o' th' better soort say 'woman' i' th' place o' Moll, but nooan so mony. **1923** [see DAME 2 c]. **1931** *Amer. Speech* VII. 111 *Moll.* 1. A gangster's sweetheart or mistress. 2. Any girl whether associated with the underworld or not. **1934** DYLAN THOMAS *18 Poems* 22 In this our age the gunman and his moll, Two one-dimensioned ghosts, love on a reel. **1946** K. TENNANT *Lost Haven* (1968) i. 20 He went off with that bloody moll whose name I wouldn't speak. **1955** *Publ. Amer. Dial. Soc.* xxiv. 99 A woman pickpocket is..a *moll*. **1962** N. MARSH *Hand in Glove* iii. 90, I can see you're in a fever lest slick Ben and his moll should get back..before you make your getaway. **1975** C. FREMLIN *Long Shadow* xxvi. 190 The Psychopath's Moll. I'm doing it again, thought Imogen..saving him from the consequences of his follies.

b. *attrib.* and *Comb.*, as **moll-shop** *slang*, a brothel; **moll-tooler** *slang*, a female pickpocket.

1923 J. MANCHON *Le Slang* 196 Moll-shop. **1957** M. K. JOSEPH *I'll soldier no More* (1958) 181 Pretty faces..peered shyly into the street. 'Looks like a moll-shop,' said Connolly. **1859** HOTTEN *Dict. Slang* 63 *Moll tooler*, a female pickpocket.

†**3.** ? A ramrod (sense uncertain; perh. a distinct word). *Obs.*

1596 *Acc. Winsford* in *Proc. Somerset Archæol. Soc.* 1900, 194 One muskett with his flaxe, twich boxe, moll, and rest.

Hence **moll** *v.* (see quot. 1851); **molled** *ppl. a.*, associating with or accompanied by a woman.

1851 MAYHEW *Lond. Labour* I. 310/2 'There is a great many furnished cribs, let to needys (nightly lodgers) that are molled up' (that is to say, associated with women in the sleeping-rooms). **1882** *Sydney Slang Dict.* 6/1, I see yer the other night when yer was Molled up and too proud to speak. **1935** *Flynn's* 19 Jan. 87/2 With each man molled, and his moll posing as his wife, they would not attract the suspicion which would be directed against a mob of men living together.

†**moll**, *a.* *Obs. rare.* Forms: 5 **mole**, 6–7 **molle**, 7 **moll**. [a. OF. *mol* (mod.F. *mou*, *mol*, fem. *molle*):—L. *moll-em* soft.]

1. Soft.

1474 CAXTON *Chesse* III. v. G viij, Hit happeth ofte tymes that the nature of them that ben softe and mole taketh soner Impressyon than the nature of men that be rude & stronge.

2. *Mus.* In ***B moll***, ***♭ moll*** = flat. (Also BEMOL.)

1597 MORLEY *Introd. Mus.* 5 *Phi.* What is ♭ *molle?* *Ma.* It is a propertie of singing, wherein *fa* must alwaies be song in ♭ *fa* ♭ *mi*, and is when the *vt* is in *F fa vt*. *a* **1600** MONTGOMERIE *Misc. Poems* iii. 14 Sing sho tua notis, the one is out of tone, As B acre lau and B moll far abone. **1667** C. SIMPSON *Compend. Pract. Mus.* 113 *B Molle* was when they sung *fa* in *B*.

moll, obs. f. MOLE *sb.*[1] and *sb.*[2], MOULD, MULL.

molla, variant of MULLAH.

mollag ('mɒləg). *Manx dial.* [Manx.] 'A dog's skin blown up as a bladder, and used to float the herring-nets' (Kelly *Manx Dict.* 1866). ***as empty as a mollag***, quite empty; ***as full as a mollag***, dead drunk.

1883 *Fisheries Exhib. Catal.* (ed. 4) 132 One Balk or long line for cod-fishing, . . with 'mollag' or buoy. **1894** HALL CAINE *Manxman* 151 Your head's as empty as a mollag.

mollah, variant of MULLAH.

'**molland.** *Obs.* exc. *Hist.* Also 3 **mollond**, 4–6 **moland**. [f. *mōl*, southern ME. form of MAIL *sb.*[2] + LAND.] Land for which rent was paid in commutation of servile customs.

The explanation in quot. 1607 is erroneous; the term apparently continued to be traditionally applied to certain lands, but its import was matter of conjecture.

1290 *Reg. Bury St. Edmunds* in Vinogradoff *Villainage* (1892) 183 Omnes tenentes de mollond solebant esse custumarii. ? *a* **1300** *Reg. Eye Priory* ibid. 184 Si tota terra fuerit mollond primogenitus debet eam retinere. [**1399** in *Essex Rev.* July (1904) 131 John Pyg was admitted to tenure of four acres of molond.] **1505** *Will of Gyrden* (Somerset Ho.), v. acres molland. **1507** *Ibid.*, Molland Werkland Freeland Worland. [**1563** in *Essex Rev.* July (1904) 131 Richard and Clemence Everard..held Sayer's molond, a quarter of molond belonging to it.] **1607** NORDEN *Surv. Dial.* IV. 183 *Molland* is up-land, or high ground, and the contrary is *Fenland*, low ground.

†'**mollart.** *Obs.* [F. (*poire de*) *mollart*, f. *mol*, *molle* soft + *-art*: see -ARD.] A kind of pear.

1600 SURFLET *Country Farm* III. xlix. 537 Delicate peares, such as are..the roset, hasting, rimolt, mollart, greening [orig. *de renoult, de mollart, de verdelet*].

mollasse, variant of MOLASSE.

mollat, variant of MOLLET *Obs.*

moll-'buzzer. *Thieves' slang.* [f. MOLL *sb.* + BUZZER.] So **moll-buzzing** *vbl. sb.* (see quots.).

1859 MATSELL *Voc.* (Farmer), s.v. *Moll*, . . Moll-buzzer, a thief that devotes himself to picking the pockets of women. **1900** 'FLYNT' & WALTON *Powers that Prey* 225 Her gift for mathematics made it clear that 'moll-buzzing' was much more remunerative than sleeping in cellars and peddling Park Row literature. **1903** Moll-buzzing [see GRAFT *sb.*[5]]. **1904** *Speaker* 11 June 256/2 He made a lot of money by 'moll-buzzing' or picking women's pockets in the streets. **1910** *N.Y. Even. Post* 25 Aug., To have the country cousin clutch his arm and enquire whether that rough-looking customer coming out of a Chatham Square saloon is a dip, a yegg, a stall, a moll-buzzer, a Fagin, or a gun. **1912** A. BERKMAN *Prison Mem. Anarchist* II. xxii. 278 The 'gun'.. gathers messages for their 'moll buzzers' [*f.n.* women thieves]. **1912** *Collier's* 23 Nov. 12/2 When he came out he began as a 'moll buzzer', which, you understand, means a pickpocket who specializes on the fair sex; he buzzes the 'molls'. **1936** *Evening News* 9 Dec. 8/5 Buzzers are male pickpockets who specialise in opening women's handbags; moll buzzers are the females of the species. **1955** *Publ. Amer. Dial. Soc.* XXIV. 169 The *moll buzzer* (male or female) is not strictly speaking a pickpocket... But the thief takes money from the purses or handbags..carried by women. *Ibid.*, There's a reason for moll buzzing.

moll-caudle, -coddle, var. ff. MOLLY-CODDLE.

†**molle.** *Obs.* [a. Sp. *molle*, a. Quichua *mulli*; cf. F. *molle* 'an Indian tree' (Cotgr.).] The Peruvian mastic-tree, *Schinus molle*, native of tropical America.

1604 E. G[RIMSTONE] *D'Acosta's Hist. Indies* IV. xxx. 292 Molle is a tree of many vertues, which casteth foorth small boughes, whereof the Indians make wine. **1640** PARKINSON *Theat. Bot.* 1524 *Lentisci Pecuani* [? read *Peruani*] *similis Molle dicta*. The Indians Molle. **1753** CHAMBERS *Cycl. Supp.* App. s.v., Indian Mastic, the name by which the Molle, or Peruvian Lentisk is sometimes called.

molle, mollee, obs. ff. MOLE, MULL, MALI *sb.*[1]

mollefye, obs. form of MOLLIFY.

mollemoke, obs. form of MOLLYMAWK.

mollen, obs. form of MULLEIN.

mollescent (mɒ'lɛsənt). *Med.* [ad. L. *mollēscent-em*, pr. pple. of *mollēscĕre*, f. *mollis* soft: see -ESCENT.] Tending to become soft. Hence **mo'llescence**, tendency towards softness; = MOLLITIES b.

1822–34 *Good's Study Med.* (ed. 4) III. 26 The brain..has been found in a mollescent or pulpy state. *Ibid.* 240 There is always to the touch a mollescence in their structure. **1855** DUNGLISON *Med. Lex.* (ed. 12), *Mollescence*, Mollities.

mollestuous, variant of MOLESTIOUS.

†'**mollet**, *sb.* *Sc. Obs.* Also 6 **molet**, **mol(l)at**. [a. OF. *molete* spur-rowel, also an ornamental stud imitating this: see MULLET. Cf. MOLAN.] (? Originally, a boss or stud on a bridle-bit. Hence:) A studded or toothed bit for a horse; also ***mollet bit***. Also **mollet-bridle**, a bridle having a bit of this kind (rendering L. *frenum lupatum*).

1503 in *Ld. Treas. Acc. Scotl.* (1900) II. 206 Item, for ane molat bridill and ane tee, xij s. *Ibid.* 396 And for mollat bit, small bittis [etc.]. **1505** *Ibid.* (1901) III. 135 Item, for ane gret mollet bit to the King, xiiij s. **1508** DUNBAR *Tua Mariit Wemen* 349 Thar myght na molet [*v.r.* mollat] mak me moy, na hald my mouth in. **1513** DOUGLAS *Æneis* VII. v. 196 Thair harnyssing of gold rycht deyrly dycht, Thai runge the goldin mollettis burneist brycht. **1536** BELLENDEN *Cron. Scot.* (1821) II. 269 Makbeth..said, 'This man wil not obey my chargis, quhill he be riddin with ane mollet bridil; nochtheles I sall gar him draw like ane avir in ane cart'.

†'**mollet**, *v.* *Obs.* ? *nonce-wd.* [f. prec.] intr. To ride.

1529 LYNDESAY *Complaynt* 333 Bot, geue thay can play at the cairtis, And mollet moylie on ane Mule, Thocht thay had neuer sene the scule, 3it..Wyll be maid sic ane spirituall man. [Cf. quot. 1508 under prec. sb.]

mollet, obs. form of MULLET.

molleton ('mɒlɪtɒn). [f. F. *molleton* f. *mollet*, dim. of *mol* (*mou*), *molle* soft.] = SWANSKIN.

1858 SIMMONDS *Dict. Trade*, *Molleton* (French) swanskin; a kind of blanket or flannel. **1896** *Allbutt's Syst. Med.* I. 744 Some close, soft material ('molleton' is suitable).

b. The rags of closely woven white flannels (*Eng. Dial. Dict.* 1903).

mollewell, variant of MULVEL.

molley, variant of MALI *sb.*[1]; obs. f. MOLLY *sb.*[1]

1852 *Life in Bombay* 23 There must be from one to six Molleys, or gardeners.

†'**molliable**, *a.* *Obs.* [Badly f. L. *mollīre* to soften + -ABLE.] Capable of being softened.

1688 R. HOLME *Armoury* II. 85/2 Tar, a compounded Rosin, or Rosin made molliable. *Ibid.* 119/3 Gums..Liquid or more moliable, as Liquidambra [etc.]. **1766** *Compl. Farmer* s.v. *Stone*, a hard solid body, neither molliable, fusible by fire, nor soluble in water.

†'**molliate**, *v.* *Obs.* *rare*$^{-1}$. [Formed as prec. + -ATE[3].] *trans.* To make soft or easy.

1702 *Poet* (*Ovid*) *Bantered* (ed. 2) 23 Soon will she molliate your way, Charm'd with the Magick of a Fee.

†'**mollicine**, *a.* *Obs.*$^{-0}$ [ad. mod.L. *mollicīnus* (in *mollicinum emplastrum* soothing plaster, Phillips, ed. Kersey, 1706), inferred from late L. *mollicina* a kind of soft garment.] Mollifying.

1856 MAYNE *Expos. Lex.* s.v. *Mollicinus*.

†**mollicinous**, *a.* *Obs.* [f. prec. + -OUS.] Softening, mollifying (*Syd. Soc. Lex.* 1891).

mollie: see MALI *sb.*[1] and MOLLY.

mollient ('mɒlɪənt), *a.* and *sb.* [f. L. *mollient-em*, pr. pple. of *mollīre* to soften, f. *molli-s* soft: see -ENT.] **a.** *adj.* Softening. *rare*$^{-0}$. †**b.** *sb.* *Med.* A softening application. *Obs.*

1612 *Enchiridion Med.* 92, I apply mollients and resolutiues. **1721** BAILEY, *Mollient*, softening, mollifying. **1736** AINSWORTH *Lat. Dict.*, Mollient, *molliens, deliniens*.

Hence '**molliently** *adv.*, soothingly, assuagingly.

1847 in WEBSTER; and in later Dicts.

†**molli'faction.** *Obs.* *rare*$^{-1}$. [f. MOLLIFY *v.*: see -FACTION.] = MOLLIFICATION.

1822–34 *Good's Study Med.* (ed. 4) III. 460 There is a considerable difference in explaining upon the same principle the mollifaction of the diseased area.

mollifiable ('mɒlɪfaɪəb(ə)l), *a.* [f. MOLLIFY *v.* + -ABLE.] Capable of being mollified.

1611 SPEED *Hist. Gt. Brit.* IX. vi. §14. 488 The King.. perceiuing Beckets stiffenesse..to be no way mollifiable by whatsoeuer his old fauours [etc.]. **1755** in JOHNSON. In mod. Dicts.

mollification (mɒlɪfɪ'keɪʃən). [a. OF. *mollificacion* (F. *mollification*), ad. L. *mollificātiōn-em* f. *mollificāre*: see MOLLIFY *v.* and -ATION.] The action of the verb MOLLIFY; an appeasing, appeasement, pacification. Also, †something that softens (a substance) or mitigates the harshness of (an action or quality); †a softening expression, a qualifying clause.

c **1386** CHAUCER *Can. Yeom. Prol. & T.* 301 Yet forgat I to maken rehersaille Of watres corosif and of lymaille And of bodies mollificacion. **1541** R. COPLAND *Guydon's Form.* S j b, The dylygent workman..ought to wyt to whiche resolucyon is due, and to which mollyfycacyon. **1562** BULLEYN *Bulwark, Dial. Soarnes & Chir.* 13 You muste use mollifications, and softenyng medicenes. **1590** BARROUGH *Meth. Physick* II. xi. (1596) 91 If it [*sc.* matter] creepe into the belly, you must minister most of all mollifications. *a* **1619** FOTHERBY *Atheom.* II. viii. §5 (1622) 290 There is a mollification vsed, to reduce the..Deification, within the compasse of this sense. **1626** DONNE *Serm.* lxviii. (1640) 691 *Damnabitur* (no modification, no mollification, no going lesse) He shall be damned. **1698** NORRIS *Pract. Disc.* (1707) IV. 226 A Truth, which may be represented nakedly as it is, or with some tenderness and mollification. **1716** M. DAVIES *Athen. Brit.* II. 184 In return of all his reciprocal Mollifications and Meliorations of some uncouth Points. **1881** *Daily News* 7 Feb., We close the book with some feeling of mollification toward its faults. **1886** G. ALLEN *Maimie's Sake* xvii, With some faint show of mollification in his softened tone.

†**mollificative**, *a.* and *sb.* *Obs.* Also 5 **molyficatyffe**, **mollificatif(e**, 6 **molificative**. [a. F. *mollificatif*, *-ive*, ad. med.L. **mollificātīv-us*, f. *mollificāre* to MOLLIFY.] **a.** *adj.* That causes mollification or softening. **b.** *sb.* A medicine or application that softens.

c **1400** *Lanfranc's Cirurg.* 47 Þe chapitle of medicyns mollificatyues [*v.r.* molyficatyffes]. *Ibid.* 211 Þis is a mollificatif þat rasis made. **1590** BARROUGH *Meth. Physick* VII. iv. (1596) 388 If you will make a clyster mollificatiue lacking the things aforesayd, doe thus. *Ibid.*, Then make a clyster partly of mollificatiues & partly of expulsiues. **1612** WOODALL *Surg. Mate* Wks. (1653) 32 This unguent is..of temperament cold..mollificative, and attractive. **1656–74** in BLOUNT *Glossogr.* **1775** in ASH.

mollified ('mɒlɪfaɪd), *ppl. a.* [f. MOLLIFY *v.* + -ED[1].] In senses of the vb.: †Softened, rendered

soft or supple (*obs.*); †rendered less severe; mitigated (*obs.*); appeased, conciliated.

1696 A. M. tr. *Guillemeau's Chirurg.* 37/1 The fleshe and all the other mollifyed parts of the ioyncte. **1682** DRYDEN *Relig. Laici* Pref., Wks. (Globe) 187 Those texts may receive a kinder and more mollified interpretation. **1764** HARMER *Observ.* XII. i. 35 [When] the sacred writer . . says Ægypt has no rain he must be understood in the same mollified sense that Maillet, or rather the Abbot Muscrier, puts upon Pliny. **1849** THACKERAY *Pendennis* I. xxix. 284 'Boys will be boys', the mollified uncle thought to himself. **1860** HOLLAND *Miss Gilbert* x, 'We are disappointed here again, Fanny', said the doctor with a mollified tone.

Hence **'mollifiedly** *adv.*

1626 W. FENNER *Hidden Manna* (1652) 72 The bloud of Christ is of a sufficient value to redeeme them all *à toto*: Secondly, mollifiedly, *à tanto*.

mollifier ('mɒlɪfaɪə(r)). [f. next + -ER[1]; cf. F. *mollifieur* (Cotgr.).] One who or something which mollifies.

1592 in *Misc. Hist. & Philol.* (1703) 169 The Lord Treasurer . . ever secretly feigned himself to be a Moderator and Mollifier of the Catholicks Afflictions. **1610** MARKHAM *Masterp.* II. clxxiii. 485 Branckvrsin is a wonderfull great mollifier. **1710** T. FULLER *Pharm. Extemp.* 317 Vinegar . . is itself a prime Corrector and Mollifyer.

mollify ('mɒlɪfaɪ), *v.* Also 5–8 molify, 5–6 mol(l)yfy(e, -efy(e. [ad. F. *mollifier*, ad. L. *mollificāre*, f. *molli-s* soft + *-ficāre*: see -FY.]

1. *trans.* To render soft or supple; to make tender; to reduce the hardness of. Also *absol.* Now *rare.*

1426 LYDG. *De Guil. Pilgr.* 8399 Han a leche . . Thy synwes harde to mollefye With oynementys, to make hem plye. *Ibid.* 10982 Dyamaunt, I trowe, ys noon, Nor noon other maner ston So indurat, to mollefye, As he. **1490** CAXTON *Eneydos* xv. 59 The erth . . was alle made fatte and molyfyed wyth the blode of the bestes that were there Immolated. **1555** EDEN *Decades* 220 These skynnes being made verye harde, they hunge them . . in the sea . . to mollifie them. **1610** MARKHAM *Masterp.* II. clxxiii. 493 Manna is of equall temper hote and dry; it openeth, it mollifieth, and incarnateth. **1638** WILKINS *New World* xiv. (1707) 119 Metals are not rarify'd by melting, but mollify'd. **1707** *Curios. in Husb. & Gard.* 300 One of the . . Plants is that which so mollifies the Bones, that . . we cannot stand upon our Legs. **1832** W. IRVING *Tales Alhambra, Moor's Legacy* (1875) 161 Pedrillo Pedrugo . . put a basin of hot water under his chin, and began to mollify his beard with his fingers. *fig.* **1624** DONNE *Devotions* 306 Thou rainest vpon vs and yet doest not alwayes mollifie all our hardnes.

†**b.** *to mollify the fist* (? nonce-use): a jocular substitution for 'to grease the palm'.

1698 FRYER *Acc. E. India & P.* 98 Making the Merchant dance attendance till a right understanding be created betwixt the Shawbunder and them, which commonly follows when the Fist is mollified.

†**c.** *to mollify the belly*: to relax the bowels. *Obs.*

1533 ELYOT *Cast. Helthe* (1539) 21 Quynces . . taken after meate . . mollifieth the bealy. **1631** WIDDOWES *Nat. Philos.* 45 It mollifieth the belly, and cureth hardnesse of the backe and belly.

†**d.** *intr.* To become soft or tender. *Obs.*

1528 PAYNEL *Salerne's Regim.* O ij b, Tyll tyme the meate of them mollifie, and waxe tender.

2. *trans.* To soften in temper or disposition; to allay the anger or indignation of; to render less obdurate; to calm, pacify, or appease. From the 15th to the 17th c. very common in the phrase †*to mollify* (*one's*) *heart. Obs.*

c **1412** HOCCLEVE *De Reg. Princ.* 2638 Lat vs mollifie Our hertes stoute to his genterie. **1560** DAUS tr. *Sleidane's Comm.* 408 b, Ambassadours, whiche might mollifie their myndes and perswade them to peace. **1667** DRYDEN & DK. NEWCASTLE *Sir M. Mar-all* III. (middle), I must mollify him with money. *a* **1715** BURNET *Own Time* (1724) I. 213 Even the Presbyterians were much mollified . . by his mild and heavenly course of life. **1754** HUME *Hist. Gt. Brit.* I. *Chas. I*, v. 271 To mollify, by these indulgences, the rage of his most furious persecutors. **1872** BLACK *Adv. Phaeton* xxvii, 'Oh, as you please', said the young man, a trifle mollified.

†**b.** *intr.* To become softened in temper or disposition; to grow more kindly or genial; to relax one's severity, to become less angry or obdurate, to relent. *Obs.*

1526 *Pilgr. Perf.* (W. de W. 1531) 246 Shall make the most harde herted persone that is, to mollify & melte. *c* **1533** TINDALE *Answ. More* Wks. (1573) 330/2 The hart here beginneth to mollifie and waxe soft. *a* **1586** SIDNEY *Arcadia* IV. (1598) 413 Philinax feeling his hart more & more mollifying vnto her, renewed [etc.]. **1694** DRYDEN *Love Triumphant* v. i, She has a delicious tongue of her own, and I begin to mollify. **1741** H. WALPOLE *Lett. to Mann* 23 Nov., He . . owned his father had mollified, but hoped she would excuse him. **1823** *Examiner* 268/2 The father mollifies and is reconciled to the marriage.

†**3.** To enervate, enfeeble. *Obs.*

1490 CAXTON *Eneydos* xii. 42 This man onely hath molyfyed my wyttes, and perturbed the corage of myn opynyon firste. **1577** NORTHBROOKE *Dicing* (1843) 165 Whose mind is so well ordered . . that these wanton dauncings . . woulde not corrupt, ouercome, and vtterlye molifie?

†**4.** To abate the violence or intensity of (passions; also heat, cold, tempests, etc.); to relieve (care). *Obs.*

c **1495** *Epitaffe*, etc. in *Skelton's Wks.* (1843) II. 390 To mollyfy oure monys. **1542–5** BRINKLOW *Lament* 10 Their absence shulde not quenche nor mollifye your loue towardes your brethren. **1577** B. GOOGE *Heresbach's Husb.* II. (1586) 85 The extreeme heate of the sunne, is somthing mollified with the cold blastes of the winde. **1612** DRAYTON *Poly-olb.* xii. 186 Refresh you in my bathes, and mollifie your care With comfortable wines and meats. **1653** LD. VAUX tr. *Godeau's St. Paul* 238 His great courage could not be mollified. *a* **1833** R. WATSON in Spurgeon *Treas. Dav.* Ps. cxiii. 7 What sources of comfort does it [*sc.* Christianity] open to mollify the troubles of life!

5. To lessen the harshness or severity of (expressions, laws, etc.); abate the rigour of (demands); also, to represent in favourable terms, to euphemize. Now *rare.*

1523 LD. BERNERS *Froiss.* (1812) I. ccccxxiv. 741 The erle of Flaunders . . molefyed the mater as moche as he might. **1549** COVERDALE, etc. *Erasm. Par. 2 Cor.* Argt., He mollifieth the sharpenes vsed in his former epistle. *a* **1674** CLARENDON *Hist. Reb.* VIII. §203 They would, by yielding to some things when they refused others, sooner prevail with the Houses to mollify their demands. **1681** DRYDEN *Sp. Friar* v. ii. 75 Now mince the Sin, And mollifie Damnation with a Phrase. **1785** SARAH FIELDING *Ophelia* xiii, He had not mollified the term of Savage. **1798** JEFFERSON *Writ.* (1859) IV. 249 Our alien bill struggles hard for a passage. It has been considerably mollified. **1880** *Expositor* XI. 469 The Apostle . . could easily and euphoniously have modified and mollified his expression.

†**6.** To impart a tender beauty to. *Obs.* or *nonce-use.*

c **1750** SHENSTONE *Ruin'd Abbey* 20 The vocal flute . . Crowns his delight and mollifies the scene.

mollifying ('mɒlɪfaɪɪŋ), *vbl. sb.* [f. prec. + -ING[1].] The action of the verb MOLLIFY.

c **1532** DU WES *Introd. Fr.* in Palsgr. 1040 Molifiyng of angre. *a* **1540** BARNES *Wks.* (1573) 274/1 Duns saith, that there is a mollifieng, that precedeth grace, which hee calleth attrition. **1643** STEER tr. *Exp. Chyrurg.* xiv. 55 They [*sc.* scars] require greater mollifying.

mollifying ('mɒlɪfaɪɪŋ), *ppl. a.* [f. as prec. + -ING[2].] That mollifies (in senses of the vb.).

1590 BARROUGH *Meth. Physick* III. xxxvii. (1596) 163 It profiteth greatly to discend into a bath made of mollifying herbs. **1611** BIBLE *Wisd.* xvi. 12 It was neither herbe, nor mollifying plaister that restored them to health. **1622** T. SCOTT *Belg. Pismire* 31 The Nobilitie liue idlely, acquainting themselues with all effeminate fashions, and mollifying pleasures. **1713** M. HENRY *Meekness & Quietness of Spirit* (1822) 163 Could any thought be more mollifying than that? *a* **1797** H. WALPOLE *Mem. Geo. II* (1847) II. ii. 41 The face of Lord Kildare, one of the mollifying demagogues, was blackened on sign-posts. **1906** *Outlook* 24 Mar. 403/2 We should not embrace the mollifying delusion of security in private or in national life.

mollifyingly ('mɒlɪfaɪɪŋlɪ), *adv.* [f. MOLLIFYING *ppl. a.* + -LY[2].] In a mollifying manner.

1920 E. O'NEILL *Beyond the Horizon* I. ii. 44 *Mayo* (*mollifyingly*). Of course I will, boy, and be glad to. **1928** 'S. S. VAN DINE' *Greene Murder Case* ii. 25 'You understand, of course,' he added mollifyingly, 'that I shall not interfere with your activities in any way.' *a* **1953** E. O'NEILL *Long Day's Journey* (1956) 30 *Tyrone* (*impressed—mollifyingly*). I know you may have thought it was for the best.

molligut ('mɒlɪgʌt). *U.S. dial.* The angler, *Lophius piscatorius.*

1884 G. B. GOODE, etc. *Nat. Hist. Aquatic Anim.* 173 The Goose Fish or Monk Fish *Lophius piscatorius*. . . The names of the fish are many; . . In Eastern Connecticut [it is called] 'Molligut'.

mollimock, variant of MOLLYMAWK.

mollin, obs. form of MULLEIN.

molline ('mɒlɪn). *Med.* Also -in. [A trade name; ? f. L. *moll-is* soft + -INE.] A yellowish-white saponaceous preparation used as a base for ointments in the treatment of skin diseases.

1889 *Lancet* 6 Apr. 698/1 A saponaceous preparation which is known under the name of 'molline'. **1891** *Syd. Soc. Lex.*, *Mollin.*

mollinet, obs. variant of MOLINET.

mollipilose (mɒlɪ'paɪləʊs), *a.* [f. L. *mollis* soft: see PILOSE.] Having soft pilage or plumage (*Cent. Dict.* 1890). Hence **mollipi'losity** (*Ibid.*).

mollipuff, variant of MULLIPUFF.

mollisher ('mɒlɪʃə(r)). *slang.* A woman.

1812 J. H. VAUX *Flash Dict.*, *Mollisher*, a woman. **1851** MAYHEW *Lond. Labour* I. 424 One old mollesher (woman) . . brought out 8 lbs. of white rags.

mollitie, variant of MOLLITY.

‖**mollities** (mɒ'lɪʃɪiːz). Also 7 mollicies. [L. *mollitiēs*, f. *molli-s* soft.] †**a.** *fig.* Effeminacy (*obs.*). **b.** *Med.* Softening, softness. ***mollities cerebri***, softening of the brain (*Syd. Soc. Lex.* 1891); ***mollities ossium***, softening of the bones.

1604 JAS. I *Counterbl.* (Arb.) 110 Mollicies and delicacie were the wracke and ouerthrow . . of the Romane Empire. **1835–6** *Todd's Cycl. Anat.* I. 437/1 The phenomena of mollities . . and . . other morbid actions. **1876** BRISTOWE *Th. & Pract. Med.* (1878) 923 Mollities ossium is characterised anatomically by progressive softening of the bones.

†**mo'llition.** *Obs. rare*[−1]. [ad. L. **mollītiōn-em*, f. *mollīre* to soften: see -ION[1].] Softening.

1657 TOMLINSON *Renou's Disp.* 75 Mollition is the beginning of Liquation.

mollitious (mɒ'lɪʃəs), *a. rare.* [f. L. *molliti-ēs* softness + -OUS.] Luxurious, sensuous.

1646 QUARLES *Barnabas & B.* (1651) 79 Can lusty diet, and mollicious rest bring forth no other fruits, but faint desires, rigid thoughts, and Phlegmatick conceits? **1840** BROWNING *Sordello* III. 129 Mollitious alcoves gilt Superb as Byzant-domes the devils built.

†**'mollitude.** *Obs.* [ad. L. *mollitūdo*, f. *molli-s* soft: see -TUDE.] Softness, effeminacy.

1656 BLOUNT *Glossogr.*, *Mollitude*, softness, niceness, tenderness, effeminateness, wantonness. **1767** A. CAMPBELL *Lexiph.* 11 A perennial mollitude of manners. In mod. Dicts.

†**'mollity.** *Obs.* In 7 mollitie. [ad. L. *mollitiē-s* softness: see MOLLITIES.] Gentleness.

1655 *Marrow of Complements* 2 If that tenderness and mollitie inherent and predominant in your soft sex sway its scepter in you.

mollotto, obs. form of MULATTO.

mollusc, mollusk ('mɒləsk). *Nat. Hist.* Also 9 **mollusque.** [ad. F. *mollusque*, ad. mod.L. MOLLUSCA.] An animal belonging to the Mollusca.

1783 BARBUT *Genera Vermium* p. xvii, *Ascidia.* The Bladder Shaped Mollusque. *Holothuria.* The Tentaculated Mollusque. *Medusa.* The Snake-lock Mollusque. **1808** HOME in *Phil. Trans.* XCVI. 286 All the mollusques which creep on their bellies. **1839** *Penny Cycl.* XIV. 321/2 Terrestrial and fluviatile Mollusks. **1867** F. FRANCIS *Angling* vii. (1880) 259 These molluscs took well to the lake. **1898** R. MUNRO *Preh. Scot.* 81 This mollusc is now extinct in the Clyde.

Mollusca (mə'lʌskə), *sb. pl. Zool.* [mod.L. *mollusca* (Jonston 1650), neut. pl. of L. *molluscus* (occurring in *mollusca nux*, a soft kind of nut), also ellipt. as sb., and *molluscum* neut., used subst. as the name of a kind of fungus.]

a. Applied by Linnæus in 1758 to a heterogeneous group of invertebrates, forming the second order of his class Vermes, and comprising the Echinoderms, Hydroids, Annelids, and naked Mollusca. To these the shell-bearing Mollusca were added by later naturalists. **b.** In present use (mainly following the classification proposed by Cuvier in 1788–1800), a phylum or sub-kingdom of animals, comprising the four classes Gastropoda (limpets, snails, etc.), Scaphopoda (tooth-shells), Cephalopoda (cuttlefish, etc.), and Lamellibranchia (oyster, mussel, etc.); the classes Cirrhopoda, Tunicata, and Brachiopoda, included by Cuvier among the Mollusca, are now placed elsewhere, and the Polyzoa have since Cuvier's time been added to the phylum and again removed.

1797 *Encycl. Brit.* (ed. 3) XII. 204/1 *Mollusca*, in the Linnæan system, is the denomination of the second genus of vermes or worms. These are simple naked animals, not included in a shell, but furnished with limbs. **1806** TURTON tr. *Linn. Syst. Nat.* IV. 3 Class VI. Worms. . . They are divided into five Orders. I. Intestina. . . II. Mollusca. Are naked, furnished with tentacula or arms, for the most part inhabitants of the sea; and [etc.]. **1828** FLEMING *Brit. Anim.* 224 It is my intention to proceed to the consideration of the species [of Radiata] . . immediately after the enumeration of the Mollusca. **1896** KIRKALDY & POLLARD tr. *Boas' Text-bk. Zool.* 289 *note*, In many Mollusca . . certain parts of the epithelial covering of the pericardium are glandular.

molluscan (mə'lʌskən), *a.* and *sb. Zool.* [f. prec. + -AN.] **a.** *adj.* Of, pertaining to, or having the characters of the Mollusca. **b.** *sb.* One of the Mollusca; a mollusc.

1828–32 in WEBSTER. **1835** KIRBY *Hab. & Inst. Anim.* I. viii. 236 The Cirripedes . . seem to have little to do with the bivalve Molluscans. *Ibid.* 255 The superiority of the Insect over the Molluscan tribes. **1883** *Gd. Words* Aug. 531/2 The molluscan population of our British shores.

molluscicide (mə'lʌskɪsaɪd). Also **molluscacide.** [*molluscicide* f. MOLLUSC + -I- + -CIDE; *molluscacide* f. MOLLUSCA *sb. pl.* + -CIDE.] Any substance used to kill molluscs.

1947 DORLAND & MILLER *Med. Dict.* (ed. 21) Molluscacide. **1948** *Jrnl. Parasitol.* XXXIV. Suppl. 33 (*heading*) Results of screening tests on chemicals as molluscicides. **1949** *Ibid.* XXV. 475 (*heading*) Influence of some potential molluscacides on the oxygen consumption of *Australorbis glabratus.* **1965** *New Scientist* 22 Apr. 229/2 No efforts had previously been made to wipe out the snails with molluscicides. **1972** *Country Life* 2 Mar. 527/3 A new molluscicide spray is now being used . . to eradicate the pest. **1974** *Nature* 22 Mar. 363/1 The widely used molluscicide sodium pentachlorophenate is a repellant to snails.

Hence **mollusci'cidal** *a.*

1950 *Jrnl. Parasitol.* XXXVI. 152 The molluscacidal activity of a series of 42 organic compounds has been studied. **1950** *Biol. Abstr.* XXIV. 3249/2 In this series of tests alpha-chloro-esters and amides of aliphatic monobasic acids showed a more marked molluscicidal activity than the unchlorinated derivatives. **1968** *New Scientist* 4 Jan. 24/3 Chlorinated hydrocarbons and organo-phosphates were found to have no molluscicidal activity.

molluscigerous (mɒlə'sɪdʒərəs), *a.* Also **molluskigerous.** [f. MOLLUSC + -GEROUS.] Bearing or producing molluscs.

1877 HUXLEY *Anat. Inv. Anim.* viii. 513 In some few of the *Synaptæ* . . elongated tubular molluskigerous sacs are found attached . . to one of the intestinal vessels.

molluscoid (mə'lʌskɔɪd), *a.* and *sb.* [f. as prec. + -OID.] A. *adj.*

1. *Zool.* **a.** Belonging to or resembling the Mollusca; **b.** Of or belonging to the Molluscoidea.

1855 *Eng. Cycl., Nat. Hist.* III. 858 The Molluscoid subdivision of the neural forms. **1877** LE CONTE *Elem. Geol.* I. (1879) 296 Their affinities [*i.e.* those of the Polyzoa] are probably molluscoid.

2. *Path.* Of the nature of molluscum.

1899 *Allbutt's Syst. Med.* VIII. 926 Molluscoid acne.

B. *sb.*

1. One of the Molluscoidea.

1855 W. S. DALLAS in *Syst. Nat. Hist.* I. 416 The *Bryozoa* and the *Tunicata*..have been formed into a separate subdivision, the Molluscoids. **1879** VERRILL in *Bull. U.S. Nat. Mus.* No. 15. 147 Molluscoids.

2. = MOLLUSCUM 1 (*Syd. Soc. Lex.* 1891).

molluscoidal (mɒlə'skɔɪdəl), *a.* [f. MOLLUSCOID + -AL[1].] = MOLLUSCOID *a.*

1872 DARWIN *Orig. Spec.* xi. (ed. 6) 309 At an ancient epoch the highest and lowest molluscoidal animals [ed. 5 (1869) x. 412 molluscs]..swarmed in numbers.

So **mollu'scoidan** *a.* (*Cent. Dict.* 1890).

molluscoidea (mɒlə'skɔɪdɪə). *Zool.* Also -oida. [mod.L. (Milne-Edwards 1844), f. MOLLUSC-A: see -OID.] A division of invertebrates comprising the Polyzoa and the Brachiopoda, and formerly also the Tunicata.

1855 *Engl. Cycl., Nat. Hist.* III. 858 Milne-Edwards has proposed a division of the *Mollusca* into the *Mollusca* proper, and the *Molluscoida* (*Molluscoides*), including under the latter class those Polype-like forms, the *Polyzoa* and the *Ascidioida*. **1869** HUXLEY *Introd. Classif. Anim.* iv. 82 The Ascidioida, Brachiopoda and Polyzoa..may be conveniently denominated *Molluscoida*. **1875** NICHOLSON *Man. Zool.* (ed. 4) 330 Distribution of Molluscoida in Time.

molluscoidean (mɒlə'skɔɪdɪən), *a.* and *sb.* [f. MOLLUSCOIDEA: see -AN.] = MOLLUSCOID *a.* and *sb.* (*Cent. Dict.* 1890).

molluscous (mə'lʌskəs), *a.* [f. L. *mollusc-us* (see MOLLUSCA, MOLLUSCUM) + -OUS.]

1. Of or belonging to the Mollusca.

1813 BAKEWELL *Introd. Geol.* 179 Moluscous animals of a particular species. **1816** BINGLEY *Useful Knowl.* III. 13 Molluscous Worms are simple animals, without shell, and furnished with limbs, as the cuttle fish, medusæ, star-fish, and sea-urchins. **1840** *Chamb. Jrnl.* No. 438. 174/3 The snail belongs to the Molluscous division of the animal kingdom. **1886** *Gentl. Mag.* Apr. 407 Now that oysters are so dear..we should look around for some molluscous substitute.

2. *fig.* esp. in the sense of 'flabby', 'invertebrate'.

1873 W. S. MAYO *Never Again* xxix, Reclining in molluscous languor upon a mother-of-pearl reading-lounge, she seemed [etc.]. **1884** *Chr. World* 28 Aug. 648/4 The molluscous might of China. **1886** *Manch. Exam.* 9 Nov. 5/2 We may regard him as a fair type of Toryism in its present molluscous condition.

3. *Path.* Of, pertaining to, or of the nature of molluscum.

1837 *London Med. Gaz.* XIX. 860/2 The structure of the molluscous tubercles. **1885-8** FAGGE & PYE-SMITH *Princ. Med.* (ed. 2) I. 112 The peculiar discoid shape of molluscous growths. **1899** *Allbutt's Syst. Med.* VIII. 824 Molluscous tumours.

Hence **mo'lluscousness**.

1870 *Contemp. Rev.* XIV. 408 That 'moral molluscousness' which my Lord Elcho has had the good fortune to make into a proverb.

‖**molluscum** (mə'lʌskəm). [mod.L., neut. of L. *molluscus*: see MOLLUSCA.]

1. *Path.* **a.** Any of various disorders characterized by soft rounded tumours or nodules on the skin, *spec.* (and orig.) molluscum contagiosum. Freq. in mod.L. collocations, as **molluscum contagiosum**, a viral disorder characterized by small, smooth, pinkish nodules with a central depression, that are painless, yield a milky fluid when squeezed, and usu. occur in groups; **molluscum sebaceum**, (*a*) molluscum contagiosum (? *Obs.*); (*b*) = *kerato-acanthoma* s.v. KERATO-.

This use is thought to derive from the adjectival use in quot. 1793.

[**1793** C. F. LUDWIG in W. G. Tilesius *Historia Pathologica Singularis Cutis Turpitudinis* 6/1 Verum enim vero Rheinhardi visu foedum corpus tectum est verrucis mollibus sive molluscis et madidis sive myrmeciis.] **1813** T. BATEMAN *Pract. Synopsis Cutaneous Dis.* 268 Molluscum. This form of tubercular disease is noticed rather as a singularity, which occasionally occurs, and of which a few instances are recorded, than as an object of medical treatment. **1817** —— *Delineations of Cutaneous Dis.* Explan. of Plate LXI, Molluscum contagiosum. This singular eruption had not been noticed by Dr. Willan, and was unknown to myself till after the publication of two editions of my Synopsis. **1818-20** E. THOMPSON *Cullen's Nosol. Method.* (ed. 3) 332 Molluscum; Small soft wen. **1837** *London Med. Gaz.* XIX. 860/1 (*heading*) A few remarks on molluscum; with two cases of molluscum non-contagiosum. *Ibid.* 860/2 The non-contagious molluscum is characterized by tumors of various sizes, some of them as large as a hen's egg. **1868** *Jrnl. Cutaneous Med.* I. 53 (*heading*) On molluscum sebaceum. **1870** *Med.-Chirurgical Trans.* XXXV. 225 The definition of Plenck could hardly be applied to any disease but Molluscum Contagiosum; the case recorded by Tilesius appears certainly to have been one of Molluscum Fibrosum. *Ibid.* 230 The patient was covered with the tumours of Molluscum, or, as he [*sc.* Virchow] prefers to term it, Fibroma Molluscum. **1899** *Allbutt's Syst. Med.* VIII. 874 The molluscum tumours. **1932** R. L. SUTTON *Introd. Dermatol.* xv. 280 Molluscum contagiosum. Synonyms.—Molluscum sebaceum; Molluscum epitheliale; [etc.]. **1936** MACCORMAC & SCARFF in *Brit. Jrnl. Dermatol.* XLVIII. 625 The microscopic architecture bears a resemblance to molluscum contagiosum, and it is possible that some of the recorded cases of giant molluscum contagiosum are examples of this tumour. We suggest the name 'molluscum sebaceum' as a convenient label. **1950** Molluscum sebaceum [see *kerato-acanthoma* s.v. KERATO-]. **1960** J. MARSHALL *Dis. Skin* xxvi. 684 Molluscum sebaceum presents as a solitary lesion usually on the centre face, sometimes..elsewhere. **1961** D. M. PILLSBURY et al. *Man. Cutaneous Med.* ix. 205 Molluscum is of no more than cosmetic importance, except when the conjunctivae are involved. **1967** H. MONTGOMERY *Dermatopathology* II. xxxiv. 1036/2 Cutaneous tags or papillomas have been given many different names in the older literature, including acrochordon, fibroma molluscum, molluscum fibrosum, and soft warts. **1970** PASSMORE & ROBSON *Compan. Med. Stud.* II. xviii, 116/2 Cowpox may develop after contact with infected animals... In contrast, molluscum contagiosum is contracted only from human cases.

b. A soft nodule characteristic of molluscum.

1841 *Edin. Med. & Surg. Jrnl.* LVI. 216 In the 2d and 3d Figures are represented the free and attached surfaces of a tubercle, consisting of three mollusca, each with its proper aperture. **1890** J. L. MILTON *On Path. & Treatm. Dis. Skin* (ed. 3) ix. 449 A boy, twenty-two months old, was brought to St. John's Hospital with several molluscum spots on the left side of the face and neck... His mother, who had suckled him, had now a molluscum on her breast. **1960** J. MARSHALL *Dis. Skin* xv. 336 When they appear the papules [of molluscum contagiosum] are 1 to 2 mm. in diameter and the fully developed lesions are usually 5 to 10 mm.; but much larger 'giant mollusca' are sometimes seen.

c. *attrib.*, as ***molluscum tumour***; **molluscum body**, †**corpuscle**, one of the characteristic ovoid bodies that are found in the core of the nodules of molluscum contagiosum and are thought to be degenerate epidermal cells; also, a cytoplasmic inclusion in a cell that is in the early stages of degeneration.

1892 *Edin. Med. Jrnl.* XXXVIII. 283 The so-called molluscum bodies..are not independent animal organisms. **1937** E. H. MOLESWORTH *Introd. Dermatol.* vii. 228 The so-called molluscum bodies are degenerate and deformed cells contained in the core of the lesion. They are not the infective agents. **1966** WRIGHT & SYMMERS *Systemic Path.* II. xxxix. 1571/2 The epidermal cells that are infected by the virus [of molluscum contagiosum] undergo premature keratinization and form the so-called molluscum bodies, which contain the virus inclusions. **1974** PASSMORE & ROBSON *Compan. Med. Stud.* III. II. xxxi. 58/1 Cytoplasmic inclusions (molluscum bodies) form in the cells of the stratum spinosum. **1886** C. H. FAGGE *Princ. & Pract. Med.* II. 688 The white material seems to be made up almost entirely of characteristic oval transparent bodies..without a nucleus... These have been described as molluscum corpuscles. *Ibid.*, A molluscum tumour resembles an ordinary sebaceous cyst or steatoma, but the contents are white instead of yellow.

†2. *Zool.* = MOLLUSC. *Obs.*

1832 JOHNSTON in *Proc. Berw. Nat. Club* I. No. i. 9 The *Eolis rufibranchialis* [is] a molluscum new to naturalists.

mollusk, -sque, variant forms of MOLLUSC.

Mollweide ('mɒlvaɪdə). The name of Karl B. *Mollweide* (d. 1825), German mathematician and astronomer, used in the possessive, *attrib.*, and *absol.* to designate a homalographic map projection in which the surface of the globe is represented by an ellipse, with lines of latitude represented by the major axis and straight lines parallel to it (spaced more closely towards the poles) and meridians represented by the minor axis and equally spaced elliptical curves.

1901 C. F. CLOSE *Map Projections* II. 22 (*heading*) Homalographic equal-area (Mollweide's). Sometimes called Babinet's. **1912** A. R. HINKS *Map Projections* vii. 73 For the whole world on a single sheet we have Mollweide, which is useful for distribution diagrams, but can scarcely be called a map. **1937** F. DEBENHAM *Exercises in Cartography* x. 118 Draw an interrupted Mollweide projection to show continental areas with the least distortion. *Ibid.*, Make an approximate graticule on the Oblique Mollweide suitable for showing the British Empire Seas. **1947** H. D. THOMPSON *Fundamentals Earth Sci.* v. 52 Mollweide's Homalographic equal-area projection (1805) shows the entire surface of the earth inside an ellipse, the major, or equatorial axis of which is twice as long as the minor axis. **1960** F. LAND *Lang. Math.* vi. 70 Mollweide's map..is an equal-area map, preserving area relations at the expense of shapes. **1971** R. W. PURTON *Let's look at Maps & Mapmaking* 14 Mollweide's projection can be drawn with any line of longitude as its centre and can be used to draw attention to one particular part of the world.

molly ('mɒlɪ), *sb.*[1] Also 8 molley, 8– mollie. [f. MOLL *sb.*[1] 1 + -Y.]

1. (With capital M.) A familiar pet-form of the name *Mary*; often applied contemptuously to a 'lass', 'wench', and occas. to a prostitute. (Cf. MOLL.)

1719 D'URFEY *Pills* I. 5 Town follies and Cullies, And Molleys and Dolleys, For ever adieu. **1819** SHELLEY *Peter Bell 3rd* VI. xxxii, 'Twould make George Colman melancholy To have heard him, like a male Molly, Chanting those stupid staves. **1890** *Gloucester Gloss.* 97 The men and girls [at a hiring-fair] are called 'Johnnies and Mollies'.

2. An effeminate man or boy; a milksop. ***Miss Molly***, in the same sense (cf. *Miss Nancy*, MISS *sb.*[2] 3 b); hence ***Miss Mollyism***. Cf. MOLLY-CODDLE.

1754 W. WHITEHEAD *World* No. 58 ¶1 If he goes to school, he will be perpetually teized by the nick-name of Miss Molly. **1785** GROSE *Dict. Vulg. T.*, *Molly*, a miss Molly, an effeminate fellow, a sodomite. **1816** 'QUIZ' *Grand Master* I. 19 In fact, a specimen of folly, A *semi-ver* [sic], a mere Miss Molly. **1834** J. WILSON in *Blackw. Mag.* XXXVI. 843 It would be sad..if John Bull were to be emasculated by Miss-Mollyism. **1879** L. B. WALFORD *Cousins* III. 172 Simon is not a molly, whatever he may be. **1884** *Illustr. Lond. News* 18 Oct. 363/3 When a man makes a 'molly' of himself by describing the work of the housemaid. **1901** 'R. CONNOR' *Man fr. Glengarry* vii, The Langfords are regular Mollies.

3. A large basket used for packing fruit, etc.

1883 *Newspaper*, Pears, 2*s.* to 4*s.* per molley;..walnuts, 3*s.* 6*d.* to 4*s.* 6*d.* per molley. **1885** *Standard* 11 Sept., Innumerable 'mollies' (big baskets) of plums. **1898** *Gard. Mag.* 3 Sept. 581/1 Dutch [pears], 2*s.* to 2*s.* 6*d.* per molly.

4. Special combinations: **Molly cotton-tail** *U.S.* = *cotton-tail*; **Molly dancer** *dial.* (see quots.); **molly-head** *slang*, a 'soft-head', simpleton; **molly-mop**, an effeminate man; **Molly washdish**, the pied wagtail, *Motacilla lugubris*.

1859 BARTLETT *Dict. Amer.*, *Molly Cotton-tail, a rabbit. **1885** *Riverside Nat. Hist.* (1888) V. 78 Molly Cotton-tail. **1959** I. & P. OPIE *Lore & Lang. Schoolch.* xii. 261 In north Manchester, gangs of boys calling themselves '*Molly Dancers' wear old clothes, mostly women's, and make-up their faces, and go around singing..'Spare a copper for the Molly dancers'. **1971** *Jrnl. Lancs. Dial. Soc.* xx. 8 *Molly Dancers*, performers of a traditional folk play, of which a number survived in North Staffordshire into the 1930's. I assume the phrase to be a popular etymology for *Morris Dancers*. **1902** *Munsey's Mag.* XXVI. 492/1 Stephens is in it to pass the stuff to the *mollyheads that can't be got at without him. **1829** MARRYAT *F. Mildmay* xvi, I'll disrate you,..you d—d *molly mop. **1885** SWAINSON *Prov. Names Birds* 44 Pied Wagtail (*Motacilla lugubris*)... *Molly washdish.

Hence †**'mollyish** *a.*

1801 DIBDIN *Frisk, Jack at the Opera* iii, If it wasn't for the petticoat gear, With their squeaking, so mollyish, tender, and soft, One should scarcely know ma'am from mounseer.

molly *sb.*[2], **mollie** ('mɒlɪ). *dial.* [Alleged to be an abbreviated form of MOLLYMAWK.]

1. = FULMAR. Cf. MAW (*mall*).

1857 F. O. MORRIS *Hist. Eng. Birds* VI. 237 Fulmar.. Mallemoke. Molly. **1874** A. H. MARKHAM *Whaling Cruise to Baffin's B.* 144 The voracity of the 'mollies' swarming round the ship is perfectly astonishing. **1882** *Nature* XXVI. 387 Other birds were..seen, including..the molly.

2. A meeting of ship-captains held on board one of several ice-bound ships in company.

1874 A. H. MARKHAM *Whaling Cruise to Baffin's B.* 112 In the evening..I got some little insight into the mysteries of a 'mollie', though on a small scale. In whaling parlance, a 'mollie' means having a night of it. **1885** SCHLEY & SOLEY *Rescue of Greely* 183 These interviews are called 'Mollies', and are announced by a bucket hoisted as a signal at the fore-royal masthead... Generally speaking, a 'Mollie' means making a night of it.

molly ('mɒlɪ), *v.* [f. MOLLY[1] or MOLLY-CODDLE *v.*] 1. *intr.* (See quot.) *dial.*

1884 R. LAWSON *Upton-on-Severn Words* 23 *Molly*, to do woman's work indoors, being a man. ''E were a good un to molly for 'isself, were old Joe.'

2. *trans.* = MOLLY-CODDLE *v.*

1907 M. C. HARRIS *Tents of Wickedness* II. ii. 138 Paul hasn't been mollied, and I hope he's a nice fellow.

molly, var. MALI *sb.*[1]

molly-coddle ('mɒlɪkɒd(ə)l), *sb.* Also 9 moll caudle, -coddle. [f. MOLLY *sb.*[1] + CODDLE *v.*[2]]

a. One who coddles himself or is coddled; one who takes excessive care of his health; an effeminate man. Also *attrib.* **b.** *dial.* = MOLLYCOT.

1833 SIR C. NAPIER *Colonies* 209 A 'moll caudle' spirit that reigned supreme through all the acts of this government. **1849** THACKERAY *Pendennis* I. xxxii. 310 You have been bred up as a molly-coddle, Pen, and spoilt by the women. **1851** —— *Eng. Hum.* v. (1853) 257 He couldn't do otherwise than ..hold him up to scorn as a moll-coddle and a milksop. **1894** WILKINS & VIVIAN *Green Bay Tree* I. 24 This desperately molly-coddle age. **1895** *Times* 12 Nov. 14/2 They..come.. from well-meaning but molly-coddle friends. **1903** *Eng. Dial. Dict.*, *Mollycoddle*,..2. A man who does household work; one who interferes with women's business.

molly-coddle ('mɒlɪkɒd(ə)l), *v.* Also 9 moddle-coddle, moddley-coddley. [f. prec.] *trans.* To coddle or cocker up.

1870 DICKENS *E. Drood* ii, Don't moddley-coddley, there's a good fellow. I like anything better than being moddley-coddleyed. **1880** MRS. FORRESTER *Roy & V.* I. 264, I am not going to have the child molly-coddled in that way. **1883** MISS BRADDON *Gold. Calf* III. vii. 227 Look here, mother dear: I'm as well as ever I was, and I'm not going to be mollicoddled any more. **1898** *Cath. News* 21 May 8/3 This is very much like appealing to a householder to molly coddle a burglar who had invaded his premises rather than bring in the police.

Hence **'molly-coddling** *vbl. sb.* and *ppl. a.*

1881 'RITA' *My Lady Coquette* xv, Fresh air is a thousand times better for her than molly-coddling and medicines. **1885** *Times* 2 Jan. 10 A hypersensitive and mollycoddling regard for our finer feelings. **1893** *Westm. Gaz.* 6 Feb. 10/2 Moddle-coddling is the curse of missions.

molly-coddler (ˈmɒlɪˌkɒdlə(r)). [f. MOLLY-CODDLE *v.* + -ER[1].] One who molly-coddles.

1863 A. J. MUNBY *Diary* 31 Aug. (1972) 172 It keeps up a wholesome protest against the Mollycoddlers, to see a whole countryful of stout lasses devoted to field-labour only. **1933** J. CARY *Amer. Visitor* 213 Minnie was a molly coddler, in Bewsher's phrase, and liked to take temperatures.

mollycot (ˈmɒlɪkɒt). *dial.* [f. MOLLY *sb.*[1] + COT *sb.*[5]] One who 'fusses' about domestic concerns; a man who performs a woman's domestic duties.

1826 *Blackw. Mag.* XX. 846/2 What in vulgar English is called a Molly-cot. **1837** MISS MITFORD *Country Stories* (1850) 99 He's a worse mollycot than a woman. *c* **1861** J. T. STATON *Rays fro' Loominary* (1867) 63 If ever aw contentedly turn Mollycot, there'll ha to be some very different noshuns oth whole duty o man.

molly-dook (ˌmɒlɪˈduːk), *a.* *Austral. slang.* [f. MOLLY[1] (or perh. MAULEY) + DUKE *sb.* 7.] Left-handed. So **molly-dooker, -hander**, a left-handed person; **molly-duked** *a.*, left-handed.

[**1926** 'J. V. MARSHALL' *Timely Tips to New Australians*, *Mauldy*, left-handed.] **1934** *Bulletin* (Sydney) 21 Mar. 11/3 Hence the trade is taboo to the molly-hander. **1941** BAKER *Dict. Austral. Slang* 47 *Mollydooker*, a left-handed person. Whence, 'mollydook' (adj.): left-handed. **1969** *Southerly* XXIX. 8 It could be being written by someone else with the same absurdly decorous aim, someone molly-duked, atheist, over-educated.

mollyhawk (ˈmɒlɪhɔːk). Erron. form of MOLLYMAWK.

1880 L. V. BRIGGS *Jrnl.* 19 Oct. in *Around Cape Horn on Bark 'Amy Turner'* (1926) 105, I caught and skinned two mollyhawks, or mollymoke, as some sailors call them. **1884** SPURGEON in *Sword & Trowel* Apr. 167 The Mollyhawks, and Cape-pigeons.. followed faithfully in our wake. **1888** *Daily News* 10 Sept. 2/4 Molly-hawks. **1917** [see *John Down* (JOHN 4)]. **1923** D. H. LAWRENCE *Kangaroo* viii. 169 A big albatross swung slowly down the surf: albatross or mollyhawk, with wide, waving wings. **1927** M. M. BENNETT *Christison of Lammermoor* i. 16 The mollyhawks and albatrosses planed and circled, keeping up with the ship with scarcely a movement of their great wings. **1969** *Landfall* XXIII. 103 In front of his house a mollyhawk was patiently taking up and dropping a pipi to break it on the hard sand by the water.

Molly Maguire (ˈmɒlɪ məˈgwaɪə(r)). Now *Hist.* [A female name (see MOLLY *sb.*[1]; *Maguire* is a common Irish surname) assumed together with the female disguise: see quot.] **a.** A member of a secret society formed in Ireland in 1843 for the purpose of resisting the payment of rent.

1868 W. S. TRENCH *Realities Irish Life* vi. 82 These 'Molly Maguires' were generally stout active young men, dressed up in women's clothes... The 'Molly Maguires' became the terror of all our officials. **1908** L. H. DAWSON *Nicknames & Pseudonyms* 202 *Molly Maguires*, young men, usually dressed in women's clothes, who formed an Irish association to resist distraint for rent in 1843. Their name was derived from Connor.. Maguire, 2nd Baron of Enniskillen, who in 1641 took a prominent part in the Catholic conspiracy. **1909** *Westm. Gaz.* 19 Feb. 2/3 There were Molly Maguires in Ireland.. long before the time of Mr. William O'Brien. **1971** E. NORMAN *Hist Mod. Ireland* iii. 57 The secret societies formed to stimulate local violence on behalf of individual tenant claims;.. societies which adopted the awful names of 'Whiteboys', 'Rockites', 'Levellers', 'Whitefeet', 'Molly Maguires', 'Ribbonmen', and so on.

b. *transf.* A similar society formed in the mining districts of Pennsylvania for purposes of intimidation, but suppressed in 1876.

1867 DIXON *New Amer.* II. 299 The judge who tried this murderer was elected by the Molly Maguires; the jurors who assisted him were themselves Molly Maguires. **1886** P. STAPLETON *Major's Christmas* 86 There come among us some men that belonged to a band of murderers that called themselves Molly Maguires. **1970** *Guardian* 14 May 10/1 The Molly Maguires were a group of rebel miners who fought a brave and reckless losing battle with employers who stopped at nothing to destroy them.

mollymawk, mollymauk. Also 7–8 **mallemucke**, 8 **mallemuck**, 9 **mallemak, -muk(ke, -maulk, mallemoke, -mock, -muk, malmock, mollemoke, mollimock.** [a. Du. *mallemok*, f. *mal* foolish + *mok* gull; cf. the synonymous *mallemeeuw*. Hence G. *mallemuck* (1675), F. *malamoque*.] The fulmar, *Fulmarus glacialis*; also applied to other similar or nearly related birds. Cf. MOLLYHAWK.

1694 tr. *Marten's Voy. Spitzb.* (1711) 100 Of the Mallemucke. *a* **1705** RAY *Syn. method. Avium* (1713) 130 Wagellus Cornubiensium.. Mallemuck. **1776** PENNANT *Zool.* II. 464. **1815** J. LAING *Voy. Spitzbergen* (1822) 81 The Greenlanders account the flesh of the Mallemukke good food. **1832** GOODRIDGE *Voy. South Seas* 20 Various birds.. such as the Albatross, Nellys, Peeos, Mollimocks [etc.]. **1835** SIR J. ROSS *Narr. 2nd Voy.* iii. 38 There were some shearwaters and mollemokes about the ship. **1880** *Standard* 20 May 3 Flocks of mallemokes. **1892** E. REEVES *Homeward Bound* 103 Cape pigeons and mollymawks. **1898** *Spectator* 13 Aug. 208 The 'mallymoke', which comes nearest to the albatross in size and beauty. **1913** H. K. SWANN *Dict. Eng. & Folk-Names Brit. Birds* 153 *Mallemuck*, an old Dutch-mariner's name for the Fulmar. Now corrupted into 'Molly-mawk', and applied to various other species such as the Black-browed Albatross. **1933** *Geogr. Jrnl.* LXXXI. 217 The mollymauk is a wild sea-bird which inhabits the regions of Cape Horn. **1959** D. A. BANNERMAN *Birds Brit. Isles* VIII. 193 Dr Cushman Murphy describes this mollymauk [*sc.* the black-browed albatross, *Diomedea melanophrys*] as 'the commonest albatross in the southern hemisphere, the most sociable and the most fearless of man while at sea'. **1972** M. F. SOPER *N.Z. Birds* 181 Albatrosses and mollymawks are tube-nosed birds.. that, except for a few species inhabiting the North Pacific, are confined to the Southern Hemisphere. In New Zealand waters the term 'molly-mawk' is conveniently applied to the smaller forms, all of which have black backs, and the term 'albatross' to the two 'great' albatrosses, the Wandering and the Royal, the adults of which have white backs.

ˈmolman. *Obs.* exc. *Hist.* Pl. **molmen.** [late OE. ****málman***, f. *mál* MAIL *sb.*[1] + MAN. Cf. Sc. *mail-man*.] A holder of MOLLAND; one who held land for which he paid rent in commutation of servile customs.

1277 *Ely Survey* in Vinogradoff *Villainage* 442 De consuetudinariis qui vocantur Molmen. **1291** *Inquisition* 19 *Edw. I* (Rec. Office) *ibid.* 186 Liberi tenentes per cartam. Liberi tenentes qui vocantur fresokemen. Sokemanni qui vocantur molmen. Custumarii qui vocantur werkmen. **1892** VINOGRADOFF *Villainage in Engl.* 184 The word mal-men or mol-men is commonly used in the feudal period for villains who have been released from most of their services by the lord on condition of paying certain rents.

Moloch (ˈməʊlɒk). [a. L. *Moloch* (Vulg.), Gr. *Μόλοχ*, *Μολόχ* (LXX), repr. Heb. *ˈmōlek*. It is believed that the true form of the name (or rather title) was *ˈMelek* king (cf. the name of the Tyrian god Melcarth, 'king of the city'), but that the Jews after the Captivity pronounced it with the vowels of *ˈbōsheth* shame, in order to mark their horror of idolatry.

The Bible of 1611 has the name always as *Molech*, exc. in Amos v. 26, where it has 'your Moloch', though the Masoretic reading of the Heb. is *malkᵉkem* 'your king'. The earlier Eng. versions spell the name *Moloch* after the Vulgate.]

1. The name of a Canaanite idol, to whom children were sacrificed as burnt-offerings (Lev. xviii. 21); represented by Milton as one of the devils. Hence (as appellative, but now always with capital M), applied to an object to which horrible sacrifices are made. Also *attrib.*

The Rabbinical story that children were burnt *alive* (being placed in the arms of the image, whence they fell into the flames) appears to be unfounded, but is popularly well-known, and has influenced the transferred use.

1667 MILTON *P.L.* I. 392 Moloch, horrid King besmear'd with blood Of human sacrifice, and parents tears. **1794** COLERIDGE *Relig. Musings* 185 Thee to defend the Moloch Priest prefers The prayer of hate. **1799** *Sporting Mag.* XII. 332 The moloch to whom her honour and happiness had been sacrificed. **1817** COLERIDGE *Statesm. Man.* App. 10 The Molocks [*sic*] of human nature. **1838** *Civil Eng. & Arch. Jrnl.* I. 394/2 More lives have been sacrificed to the Moloch of high pressure steam, than [etc.]. **1882** BARLOW *Ultim. Pessimism* 49 The trouble of rearing new victims for the Moloch of culture. **1868** W. CORY *Lett. & Jrnls.* (1897) 237 This holocaust, this human incense, this Moloch-squeezing of innocents [a hot Sunday in school chapel].

2. The thorn-lizard or thorn-devil, *Moloch horridus*, native of Australia, one of the most grotesque and hideous of existing reptiles. Also *attrib.*, as ***moloch-lizard*** (Ogilvie *Suppl.* 1855).

[The mod.L. *Moloch horridus* (Gray 1841) was suggested by Milton's expression: see quot. 1667, sense 1.]

1845 J. E. GRAY *Catal. Specim. Lizards Brit. Mus.* 263 The Moloch, Moloch horridus, Gray. **1893** *Daily News* 22 Dec. 5/4 Australia produces many curiosities.. but few are greater oddities in.. appearance than the Moloch lizard. *Ibid.*, The Moloch is decidedly the most remarkable of recent additions to the Reptile House.

3. A Brazilian monkey, *Callithrix moloch*.

1875 *Encycl. Brit.* II. 155 The Moloch Callithrix. **1893** *Roy. Nat. Hist.* I. 173 Another Brazilian species is the Moloch titi (*Callithrix moloch*).

Hence **ˈMolochship** *nonce-wd.*

1661 COWLEY *Govt. Cromwell* Wks. (1688) 57 To set himself up as an Idol,.. and make the very Streets of London like the Valley of Hinnom, by burning the bowels of men as a Sacrifice to his Moloch-ship.

‖**molochine** (ˈmɒləkɪn), *a.* and *sb.* *Zool.* [f. mod.L. *Moloch* (generic name of the moloch lizard) + -INE[1].] **a.** *adj.* Pertaining to or connected with the reptilian sub-family *Molochinæ*, represented only by the MOLOCH (*Cent. Dict.* 1890). **b.** *sb.* A molochine lizard (*Ibid.*).

molochite(s, obs. forms of MALACHITE.

Molochize (ˈməʊləkaɪz), *v.* [f. MOLOCH + -IZE.] *trans.* in *nonce-uses*. **a.** To imbue with the cruelty characteristic of the worship of Moloch. **b.** To immolate, to sacrifice as to Moloch.

1825 HONE *Every-day Bk.* I. 295 Humanity was dead, for superstition Molochized the heart. **1877** TENNYSON *Harold* I. i, I think that they would Molochize them [*sc.* their babies] too, To have the heavens clear.

Hence **ˈMolochizing** *ppl. a.*

1878 P. W. WYATT *Hardrada* 44 The Molochizing fire that sears the germ Of kindness in man's soul.

moloker (ˈmɒləkə(r)). *slang.* Also **molocker.** A renovated silk hat. So **ˈmoloker** *v.* (see quot.).

1863 SALA *Breakf. in Bed.* v. 105 'Tis like an old hat that has been 'molokered', or ironed and greased into a simulacrum of its pristine freshness. **1893** *Westm. Gaz.* 18 July 3/3 A good Molocker (Molocker, it appears, is the trade term for renovated old *chapeaux*). *Ibid.*, We came across one shop where Molockers were sold.

moloss(e (məʊˈlɒs). *rare.* [ad.L. *molossus*.]

†**1.** = MOLOSSUS 1. *Obs.*

1731 BLACKWALL *Sacr. Classicks def. & illustr.* II. 100 The smaller Alcaic verse with a Molosse interpos'd.

2. = MOLOSSUS 2.

1842 DE QUINCEY *Mod. Greece* Wks. 1863 XIII. 460 Out bounds.. a horrid infuriated ruffian of a dog—oftentimes a huge *moloss*, big as an English cow.

3. A mastiff-bat (see MOLOSSINE).

1845 *Encycl. Metrop.* XXII. 249 Molosses of the Old World... Collared Molosse.. Plaited Molosse.

molossa's, obs. form of MOLASSES.

molosses, obs. form of MOLASSES.

Molossian (məʊˈlɒsɪən), *a.* and *sb.* *Hist.* [f. L. *Molossia* (= Gr. *Μολοσσία*) a country in Epirus, f. Gr. *Μολοσσός* MOLOSSUS: see -AN, -IAN.]

A. *adj.* Of or pertaining to Molossia; esp. ***Molossian dog, hound***, a kind of mastiff.

1649 OGILBY *Virg. Georg.* (1684) III. 434 But feed Fleet Spartan Whelps, and thy Molossian Breed. **1837** *Penny Cycl.* IX. 481/1 Alexander was the first of the Molossian princes who bore the title of king of Epirus. **1879** FARRAR *St. Paul* (1883) 460 The carcase of a Molossian hound.

B. *sb.* An inhabitant of Molossia.

a **1592** GREENE *Mamillia* II. (1593) G 3 Sarcas the king of the Molossians. **1878** *Encycl. Brit.* VIII. 483/2 The Molossians [inhabited] the inland district of which the lake of Pambotis or Yannina may be regarded as the centre.

molossic (məʊˈlɒsɪk), *a.* *Prosody.* [f. MOLOSS-US + -IC.] Of or pertaining to a molossus.

1864 H. BUSHNELL *Work & Play* i. 34 You distinguish.. the solemn, religious spondee, the swift trochaic run of eagerness or fear, the heavy molossic tread of grief or sorrow. **1890** in *Century Dict.*

molossine (məʊˈlɒsaɪn), *a.* and *sb.* *Zool.* [f. mod.L. *Molossinæ* a family of bats (f. *Moloss-us*: see MOLOSSUS 2): see -INE.]

A. *adj.* Relating to the *Molossinæ*.

1891 FLOWER & LYDEKKER *Mammals* xiii. 669 The Molossine division is characterised by [etc.].

B. *sb.* One of the *Molossinæ* or mastiff-bats.

1840 *Cuvier's Anim. Kingd.* 69 The Molossines... These have the muzzle simple [etc.].

molossoid (məʊˈlɒsɔɪd), *a.* and *sb.* [Formed as prec.: see -OID.] = MOLOSSINE.

1864 H. ALLEN *Bats N. Amer.* (*Smithsonian Misc. Collect.* VII.) 6 The Molossoid group of the Noctilionidæ.

molossus (məʊˈlɒsəs). [a. L. *Molossus* = Gr. *Μολοσσός* Molossian, used subst. as below.]

1. *Prosody.* A metrical foot consisting of three long syllables.

1585 W. WEBBE *Eng. Poetrie* (Arb.) 69 Molossus, that is [a foot] of three long, as - - - *forgiuenes*. **1879** J. W. WHITE tr. *Schmidt's Rhythmic & Metric* 33 The Molossus, like the spondee, was used in solemn religious melodies.

2. A Molossian dog.

1882 'OUIDA' *Maremma* I. 54 She was afraid of the white Molossus dog.

molossus, -otto, obs. ff. MOLASSES, MULATTO.

Molotov (ˈmɒlətɒf). Also **Molotoff**, and with lower-case initial. The name of Vyacheslav Mikhailovich *Molotov* (1890–1986), U.S.S.R. Minister for Foreign Affairs from 1939 to 1949, used *attrib.* in **Molotov bread-basket**, a container carrying high explosive and scattering incendiary bombs; **Molotov cocktail**, a make-shift incendiary hand-grenade, consisting of a breakable container filled with inflammable liquid, and a means of ignition; also *ellipt.* as *Molotov*.

1940 *Illustr. London News* 6 Apr. 446/2 The 'Molotov Breadbasket'.. appeared to consist of two types. **1940** *Hutchinson's Pict. Hist. War* 7 Aug.–1 Oct. 91 Used with success in the Finnish war, the so-called 'Molotov cocktails' are considered an effective weapon against armoured divisions and have been adopted by the Home Guard. **1940** *Flight* 26 Sept. 244/1 A Molotoff bread basket dropped some 50 incendiary bombs in a S.E. district of London. **1942** J. T. GORMAN *Mod. Weapons of War* ix. 147 Stationary tanks can be disabled by dropping grenades or Molotov cocktails through the ventilating openings. **1943** T. W. LAWSON *Thirty Seconds over Tokyo* 32 A 500-pound incendiary, something like the old Russian Molotov Breadbasket. **1951** J. CARSWELL in A. Somerville *Autobiogr. Working Man* p. xiv, Feargus O'Connor was trying to popularize the ginger-beer bottle filled with inflammable mixture (a version of the Molotov Cocktail to which Englishmen seem to turn when ammunition is short). **1969** *Oz* Apr. 5/1 Issue number three carried instructions on how to make a molotov with diagram and said where in the university to strike with same. **1970** R. JOHNSTON *Black Camels* vi. 90 Sulaiman was on the last bottle. Half fill it with petrol, drop in one end of the wick, plug the neck of the bottle and, hey presto, a Molotov Cocktail... Select a target, light the wick, throw the bottle. Bottle hits target, bottle smashes, petrol spills out, flame from wick ignites petrol. **1972** R. K. SMITH *Ransom* IV. 168 Thirty cars zooming out of the night loaded with molotovs.

molour, -owre, obs. forms of MULLER.

†**molrowing** (ˈmɒlraʊɪŋ). *Obs. slang.* Also **moll-rowing.** [Perh. f. MOLL *sb.* + ROW *v.*[3] + -ING[1].] **a.** (See quot. 1860.) So **ˈmolrower**, a wencher or whoremonger. **b.** Caterwauling, row, noise.

1860 HOTTEN *Dict. Slang* (ed. 2) 174 *Molrowing*, 'out on the spree', in company with so-called 'gay women'. In

allusion to the amatory serenadings of the London cats. **1892** E. J. MILLIKEN *'Arry Ballads* 42 A pootily piped 'Blooming Lavender',..as meller as blackbirds in June, Beats 'Andel's molrowings a buster. **1894** G. A. SALA *Things I have Seen* II. xiii. 121 The scene wound up with a great concert of practical cats on the roof, whose diabolical mollrowings still ring in my ears. **1896** FARMER & HENLEY *Slang* IV. 332/1 *Molrower*, a whoremonger.

molsh, obs. form of MULCH.

mol stick, obs. form of MAULSTICK.

molt: see MELT *v.*; obs. form of MOULT.

†**'moltable**, *a. Obs. rare*$^{-0}$. [f. *molt*, obs. form of MELT *v.* + -ABLE.] Capable of being melted, meltable.

1552 HULOET, Moltenable [**1572** (ed. Higgins), Molteable], *fusilis*.

molte, molted: see MELT *v.*

molten ('məʊlt(ə)n), *ppl. a.* Forms: see MELT *v.* [strong pa. pple. of MELT *v.*]

1. Liquefied by heat; in a state of fusion.

Now said only of metals or other bodies that require great heat to melt them; not, e.g., of wax or ice. Cf. MELTED.

*c*1375 *Sc. Leg. Saints* xlviii. (*Juliana*) 39 þar men þane dang hir sare,..& moltyne led he gert ȝet a-pone hir hed. **1500-20** DUNBAR *Poems* xxvi. 62 Out of thair throttis thay schot on vdder Hett moltin gold. **1526** *Pilgr. Perf.* (W. de W. 1531) 135 To some the boylynge oyle or molte leed hath ben no more payne, than the pleasaunt warme water. *Ibid.* 192 b, Goddes of metall molten. **1596** SHAKS. *1 Hen. IV*, v. iii. 34, I am as hot as molten Lead, and as heauy too. **1611** BARREY *Ram-Alley* IV. i, It lies, As heauy in my belly as moult lead. **1697** DRYDEN *Virg. Georg.* III. 686 Scum that on the molten Silver swims. **1784** COWPER *Task* I. 170 The stream, That, as with molten glass, inlays the vale. **1884** C. G. W. LOCK *Workshop Receipts* Ser. III. 249/2 Malleable iron is iron which has been 'decarburized'..by the action of air upon it in a molten state.

b. *fig.*

1824 LANDOR *Imag. Conv., Demosth. & Eub.* Wks. 1853 I. 86/2 He leaves them in the quiet possession of all their moulten arguments. **1871** SWINBURNE *Songs bef. Sunrise, Tenebræ* 27 In the manifold sound remote, In the molten murmur of song. **1884** F. HARRISON *Choice Bks.* (1886) 253 The molten passion of Burke. **1885** *Times* (weekly ed.) 15 May 5/3 The molten material of his mind too abundant for the capacity of the mould, overflowed it in gushes of fiery excess.

†**c.** ***molten grease*** (see quot. 1754). *Obs.*

1706 PHILLIPS (ed. Kersey), *Molten Grease*, a Disease in Horses. **1754** BARTLET *Farriery* (ed. 2) 166 By molten-grease is meant a fat or oily discharge with the dung, and arises from a colliquation or melting down of the fat of the horse's body, by violent exercise in very hot weather.

2. a. Of metal or other substance: That has been melted (and again solidified). **b.** Of an image, etc.: Made or produced by melting and running into a mould; = CAST *ppl. a.* 8.

*c*1290 *S. Eng. Leg.* I. 316/580 þei he of molten bras were. **1428** *Surtees Misc.* (1888) 2 Ȝai fand certein smale peces multen tyn menged with other metall. **1535** COVERDALE *Exod.* xxxii. 4 They made a molten calf. **1641** BEST *Farm. Bks.* (Surtees) 29 Wee buy our molten tallowe..of the hucksters and tripe-wives. **1718** PRIOR *Solomon* II. 327 His Mystic Form the Artizans of Greece In wounded Stone, or molten Gold, express.

†**3.** Dissolved (in a liquid); also, *loosely*, reduced to a partially liquid condition, e.g. by putrefaction.

*a*1300 *Cursor M.* 22791 It semis al again kind þan man es molten flexs and banes, fra time þat þai be roten anes ha pith and lijf als þai had ar. *c*1420 *Pallad. on Husb.* II. 284 And summe hem kepe Thre nyght in molten [L. *liquide*] donge.

4. *Comb.*, as ***molten-blue***, ***-crystal***, ***-golden*** adjs.

1862 G. M. HOPKINS *Poems* (1930) 132 As though some sapphire molten-blue Were vein'd and streak'd with dusk-deep lazuli. **1950** D. GASCOYNE *Vagrant* 27 Moulting molten-crystal plumes of birds of paradise. **1849** POE *Bells* in *Sartain's Union Mag.* Nov. 304/1 From the molten-golden notes,..What a liquid ditty floats.

Hence **'moltenly** *adv.*, like what is molten.

1870 LOWELL *Among my Bks.* Ser. I. iii. (1870) 149 A..language..that is still hot from the hearts and brains of a people, not hardened yet, but moltenly ductile to new shapes of sharp and clear relief in the moulds of new thought.

molter, obs. form of MOULDER, MULTURE.

moltid, obs. pa. t. and pa. pple. of MELT *v.*

moltlong, variant of MALTLONG, MATLONG.

‖**molto** ('molto, 'mɒltəʊ), *a.* and *adv.* [It.] (See quot. 1801.)

1801 T. BUSBY *Dict. Mus.*, *Molto*, very or much. A word used in conjunction with some other, by way of augmentation; as *Molto Allegro*, very quick, *Molto Adagio*, very slow. **1889** G. B. SHAW *London Music 1888-89* (1937) 148 The *molto sostenuto* indicated by Gounod, which is the characteristic effect of the movement, was quite lost. **1928** [see MARTELLATO *a.*] **1959** *Times* 15 Jan. 12/6 Mr. Buckley did not play them *molto dramatico* in octaves as Rachmaninov used to do. **1970** *Times* 23 Feb. 12/3 That striking but rarely heard effect, *molto pianissimo* from a large choral body.

†**'molton.** *Obs.* [f. the name South *Molton*, a town in North Devon.

The word appears as in Ger. use (but with Fr. pronunciation, and said to be from Fr.) in Flügel's *Ger.-Eng. Dict.* 1893. (? Confused with MOLLETON.)]

A kind of coarse woollen cloth.

1545 *Rates Custom Ho.* d vij b, Tauestockes tawntons moltons. [**1759** BRICE *Grand Gazetteer* 1208 *South-Moulton*. .. As the chief Manufactures are Serges, Shalloons, and Felts, great Quantities of Wool are brought here to Market.] **1809** A. HENRY *Trav.* 34 A molton, or blanket coat. *Ibid.* 139 The lock..I had carried under my molton coat.

molton, obs. pa. pple. of MELT *v.*

moltoun, obs. form of MUTTON.

moltring, obs. form of MOULDERING *a.*

moltyn(e, -tynnyd, obs. pa. pple. of MELT *v.*

Molucca (mə'lʌkə). Also 7 **Molluca, Molucco.** [Appears in Fr. (1522) as *Isles Moluques*, in It. (1598) as *Isole Moluche*, and in 17th c. Sp. and Pg. as *Maluco*, *islas Malucas* and *Molucas*.] The name (*the Moluccas, the Molucca Islands*) of a group of islands (also called the Spice Islands) situated in the Eastern Archipelago; used *attrib.* in **Molucca balm**, a cultivated labiate plant, *Moluccella lævis*, native of the Eastern Mediterranean region; **Molucca bat**, the Harpy bat, *Harpyia cephalotes*, native of the islands of Celebes and Amboyna; **Molucca bean**, the fruit of a species of BONDUC, *Guilandina Bonducella*; **Molucca berry**, the fruit of a large tiliaceous tree, *Elæocarpus serratus*, native of India; **Molucca crab**, a name for species of the genus *Limulus*; the king-crab; **Molucca deer**, a species of deer, *Cervus moluccensis*, found in the Moluccas; **Molucca grains**, the seeds of the East Indian tree *Croton Tiglium*, from which croton oil is extracted; **Molucca nut**, the BONDUC nut (Mayne *Expos. Lex.* 1856).

1731 MILLER *Gard. Dict.* s.v. *Molucca*, *Molucca Balm. **1789** W. AITON *Hortus Kewensis* II. 310 *Moluccella lævis*... Smooth Molucca Balm... *Moluccella spinosa*... Prickly Molucca Balm. **1781** PENNANT *Hist. Quad.* II. 558 *Molucca Bat. *a*1688 J. WALLACE *Descr. Orkney* (1693) 14 Upon the Rocks you will find..very oft these pretty Nutts [*marg.* *Molluca Beans], of which they use to make Snuff Boxes. **1700** J. WALLACE Jr. *Acc. Orkney* ii. 36 After Storms of Westerly Wind, amongst the Sea-weed, they find commonly in places expos'd to the Western-Ocean these *Phaseoli*, that, I know not for what reason, go under the Name of Molucca Beans. [Cf. SLOANE in *Phil. Trans.* (1696) XIX. 398, where the name *Phaseoli Molucani* is cited from Sibbald *Prodr. Hist. Nat. Scot.* p. 55 part 2.] **1753** CHAMBERS *Cycl. Supp.*, *Anacardium*, the Portuguese denominate it *Fava de Molaqua*, the Molucca bean, by which title it is also known in England. **1887** BENTLEY *Man. Bot.* (ed. 5) 484 *Elæocarpus* (*Ganitrus*) *serratus*.—The fruits are commonly known under the name of *Molucca Berries. **1681** GREW *Musæum* I. §v. iv. 120 The *Molucca-Crab. *Cancer Molucensis*. **1902** KROPOTKIN *Mutual Aid* 11 The big Molucca crab (*Limulus*). **1893** LYDEKKER *Horns & Hoofs* 299 The *Molucca deer. **1837** *Penny Cycl.* VIII. 179/2 The seeds of the *Croton Tiglii* were formerly used as a drastic purgative medicine, under the name of grains of Tilly, or *Molucca grains. **1696** SLOANE *Catal. Plant. Jamaica* 225 *Molucco Nuts of med. cur.

molwarp, obs. form of MOULDWARP.

moly[1] ('məʊlı). [a. L. *mōly*, a. Gr. *μῶλυ*.]

1. *Mythology.* A fabulous herb having a white flower and a black root, endowed with magic properties, and said by Homer to have been given by Hermes to Odysseus as a charm against the sorceries of Circe.

The Homeric moly is by some modern writers identified with the mandrake, but Theophrastus and Dioscorides apply the name to some species of garlic (*Allium*).

1567 GOLDING *Ovid's Met.* Ep. Ded. a iv b, And what is else herbe Moly than the gift of stayednesse And temperance? **1579** GOSSON *Sch. Abuse* (Arb.) 42 It shall preuayle as much against these abuses, as Homers Moly against Witchcraft. **1580** LYLY *Euphues* Wks. 1902 II. 19 But as ye hearb Moly hath a floure as white as snow, & a roote as blacke as incke: so age hath a white head, showing pietie, but a black hart swelling w^{t} mischiefe. **1634** MILTON *Comus* 636 And yet more med'cinal is it then that Moly That Hermes once to wise Ulysses gave. **1725** POPE *Odyss.* x. 365 Black was the root, but milky white the flower, Moly the name, to mortals hard to find. **1884** A. LANG *Custom & Myth* 154 Homer's moly, whatever plant he meant by that name.

fig. **1593** LODGE *Phillis*, *Compl. Elstred* (1875) 68 He had Loues Moly growing on my pappes, To charme a hell of sorrow and mishappes.

2. Applied to various plants that have been supposed to be identical with the moly of Homer.

a. The liliaceous genus *Allium*, esp. the wild garlic, *Allium Moly*. Also with prefixed word, applied to various species of this genus, as ***civet***, ***Dioscorides'***, ***dwarf***, ***Homer's***, ***Indian***, ***Montpellier***, ***pine-apple***, ***serpent's***, ***yellow moly***.

1629 PARKINSON *Paradisus* 141 Moly. Wilde Garlicke. **1660** SHARROCK *Vegetables* 105 The late Pine-apple Moly, the Civet Moly of Monspelier..are well preserved many yeares. **1664** EVELYN *Kal. Hort.*, *May* (1679) 17 Flowers in Prime, or yet Lasting... Bugloss, Homers Moly, and the white of Dioscorides [etc.]. *Ibid.*, *Sept.* 25 Flowers in Prime, or yet lasting... Moly, Monspeliens [etc.]. **1682** WHELER *Journ. Greece* I. 7, I should have taken it for a Moly, but that it had no smell. **1688** R. HOLME *Armoury* II. 55/2 Serpents Moly..the small green leaves twine and crawl, from whence it took its name. **1721** MORTIMER *Husb.* (ed. 5) II. 231 Moly, or Wild Garlick, is of several Sorts or Kinds, as the Great Moly of Homer, the Indian Moly, the Moly of Hungary, Serpents Moly, the Yellow Moly, Spanish Purple Moly, Spanish Silver-capped Moly, Dioscorides's Moly, the Sweet Moly of Montpelier, &c. **1789** W. AITON *Hortus Kewensis* I. 422 *Allium subhirsutum*... Hairy Garlick or Dioscorides's Moly. *Ibid.* 423 *Allium magicum*... Homer's Garlick, or Moly. *Ibid.* 428 *Allium Moly*... Yellow Garlick, or Moly. **1856** J. H. NEWMAN *Callista* (1890) 126 The stately lily, the royal carnation, the golden moly. **1899** *Westm. Gaz.* 4 Oct. 2/1 Moly, however, can be identified. It is a common bulb of Southern Europe,..covering the ground with sheets of brilliant yellow.

†**b.** App. identified with Thrift, *Armeria vulgaris*. *Obs. rare*$^{-1}$.

1578 LYTE *Dodoens* IV. l. 508 You may also reckon amongst the kindes of Moly, a sort of grasse growing alongst the sea coast..and..bearing flowers..tuft fashion, of a white purple, or skie colour.

moly[2] ('mɒlı), colloq. abbrev. of MOLYBDENUM. Also used for *molybdenum disulphide* (a lubricant).

1961 in WEBSTER. **1963** R. F. WEBB *Motorists' Dict.* 155 The [lubricating] action of 'moly' has been likened to a pack of cards resting on a table. **1970** *Financial Times* 13 Apr. 27/8 Not that Amax is remaining dormant on the moly front. The bringing in of the Henderson mine..will nigh on double production capacity.

molybdate (məʊ'lıbdət). *Chem.* Also 8-9 **molybdat.** [mod., formed as MOLYBDIC *a.*: see -ATE[1]. Cf. F. *molybdate.*] A salt of molybdic acid.

1794 G. ADAMS *Nat. & Exp. Philos.* I. App. 546 Molybdats, soluble in water..but little known. **1796** HATCHETT in *Phil. Trans.* LXXXVI. 288 The acidulous molybdate of pot-ash. *Ibid.* 292 Molybdate of lead. **1861** BRISTOW *Gloss. Min.*, *Molybdate of Iron*, occurs in subfibrous or in tufted crystals of a deep yellow colour; also pulverulent. **1899** CAGNEY tr. *Jaksch's Clin. Diagn.* v. (ed. 4) 185 Molybdate of soda.

molybdena (mɒlıb'diːnə). ? *Obs.* Also 7-9 **-dæna**, and 9 in anglicized or Ger. form **molybden.** [a. L. *molybdæna*, a. Gr. *μολύβδαινα*, f. *μόλυβδος* lead. For the history of the application of the word, see PLUMBAGO (note at end of article).]

a. Applied vaguely to various ores or salts of lead. **b.** An older name for MOLYBDENITE, by early mineralogists confused with graphite and with various ores of lead. **c.** From *c* 1790 to *c* 1820 sometimes used for MOLYBDENUM.

1693 tr. *Blancard's Phys. Dict.* (ed. 2), *Molybdæna*, native and factitious, the native is only a mixture of Lead and Silver Mine; the Factitious is a sort of Litharge. **1783** WITHERING tr. *Bergman's Outl. Min.* 65 The acid of molybdæna has never yet been obtained quite free from phlogiston. **1786** BEDDOES tr. *Scheele's Chem. Ess.* 227 Experiments upon Molybdæna 1778. **1796** KIRWAN *Elem. Min.* (ed. 2) II. 4 The Molybdenous acid has been extracted from Molybdena. *Ibid.* 215 The Molybden seems to me to be only in the state of a Calx. **1798** *Phil. Trans.* LXXXVIII. 123, I evaporated it to dryness, without perceiving any vestige of oxide of molybdæna. **1816** P. CLEAVELAND *Min.* 403 The Graphite and sulphuret of molybdena often strongly resemble each other.

d. *attrib.*: †**molybdena acid**, molybdic acid; **molybdena ochre** = MOLYBDITE.

1783 WITHERING tr. *Bergman's Outl. Min.* 18 Molybdæna acid. **1854** DANA *Syst. Min.* (ed. 4) II. 144 Molybdena Ochre.

Hence †**molyb'denic**, †**mo'lybdenous** *adjs.*, obtained from or pertaining to molybdena (cf. MOLYBDIC). **molybde'niferous** *a.*, containing molybdenum (*Cent. Dict.* 1890).

1790 WEDGWOOD in *Phil. Trans.* LXXX. 317 The molybdænic acid, discovered by Scheele. **1796** Molybdenous acid [see MOLYBDENA]. **1796** KIRWAN *Elem. Min.* (ed. 2) II. 216 The molybdenic Calx is known to communicate a yellow colour to Lead. *Ibid.* 478 A pure Molybdenic acid. **1815** J. SMITH *Panorama Sci. & Art* II. 431 This is the molybdenous acid.

†**mo'lybdenated,** *a.* *Chem. Obs.* [f. MOLYBDEN-A + -ATE[2] + -ED[1].] Combined with molybdenum.

1796 KIRWAN *Elem. Min.* (ed. 2) II. 212 Yellow Molybdenated Lead Ore. *Ibid.* 322 Molybdenated Barytes is soluble in cold water.

molybdenian (mɒlıb'diːnıən), *a.* *Min.* [f. MOLYBDEN(UM + -IAN 2.] Of a mineral: having a (small) proportion of a constituent element replaced by molybdenum.

1930 W. T. SCHALLER in *Amer. Mineralogist* XV. 571 Molybdenum—molybdenian. **1953** *Amer. Mineralogist* XXXVIII. 904 Prior to oxidation the rock contained..a few grains of molybdenian scheelite.

molybdenite (məʊ'lıbdənaıt). [f. MOLYBDEN-A + -ITE. Cf. F. *molybdénite.*] †**a.** *Chem.* An artificial sulphide of molybdenum (*obs.*). **b.** *Min.* Disulphide of molybdenum occurring in tabular bluish-grey crystals.

1796 KIRWAN *Elem. Min.* (ed. 2) II. 319 Molybdenite... By this name I distinguish the Regulus produced from Molybdena. **1837** DANA *Min.* 426 Molybdenite generally occurs imbedded in..granite..and other primitive rocks. **1901** *Scotsman* 4 Nov. 5/8 Molybdenite in Queensland.

molybdenum (mə'lɪbdənəm, mɒlɪb'diːnəm). *Chem.* [mod.L., alteration of MOLYBDENA.]

a. A metallic element (symbol Mo) occurring in combination, as in molybdenite, wulfenite, etc.

When separated it is a brittle, almost infusible silver-white metal, permanent at ordinary temperatures, but rapidly oxidized by heat. ***molybdenum oxide*** = MOLYBDITE (Cassell 1885). ***molybdenum sulphide*** = MOLYBDENITE (*Ibid.*).

1816 J. SMITH *Panorama Sci. & Art* II. 408 The ore containing molybdenum has almost the appearance of plumbago. **1873** WATTS *Fownes' Chem.* (ed. 11) 512 Molybdenum occurs in small quantity as sulphide.

b. molybdenum blue, a complex oxide or mixture of oxides of pentavalent or hexavalent molybdenum with a strong blue colour that is produced, usu. as a colloidal solution, when an acidic solution of a molybdate is reduced, and is used in chemical analysis and occas. as a dye; also, the colour of this substance.

1901 *Jrnl. Chem. Soc.* LXXX. II. 163 Molybdenum blue does not appear to contain the dioxide, MoO_2, .. but the semipentoxide, Mo_2O_5. **1920** F. A. MASON tr. *G. von Georgievics's Text-bk. Dye Chem.* 542 Molybdenum blue.. was used experimentally for a certain time on silk and cotton materials. **1951** *Amer. Mineralogist* XXXVI. 610 Ilsemannite is soluble in water, first producing a greenish blue solution which later deepens to a typical molybdenum blue. **1952** KIRK & OTHMER *Encycl. Chem. Technol.* IX. 203 The present importance of molybdenum blue rests on the fact that several colorimetric methods depend upon it: (*1*) the determination of trace quantities of phosphorus or phosphates by the preferential reduction of phosphomolybdic acid; and (*2*) a number of other methods employing phosphomolybdic acid as a reagent (for phenols, tyrosine, tryptophan, etc.) for reducing compounds. **1965** D. ABBOTT *Inorg. Chem.* xii. 642 Molybdenum 'blue' is an oxide formed when an acidified molybdate solution is greatly reduced. It has variable composition, usually about 67–68 per cent Mo.

molybdian (mə'lɪbdɪən), *a. Min.* [alteration of MOLYBDENIAN *a.*] = MOLYBDENIAN *a.*

1951 C. PALACHE et al. *Dana's Syst. Min.* (ed. 7) II. 1078 Seyrigite... A molybdian scheelite, with MoO_3 24·01 per cent.

molybdic (məʊ'lɪbdɪk), *a.* [f. MOLYBD-ENA + -IC. Cf. F. *molybdique*.] **a.** *Min.* Containing or derived from molybdenum. ***molybdic ochre*** = MOLYBDITE. ***molybdic silver*** = WEHRLITE. **b.** *Chem.* Applied to compounds containing molybdenum in its higher valency; esp. in ***molybdic acid***.

1796 HATCHETT in *Phil. Trans.* LXXXVI. 317 The yellow molybdic acid. **1807** T. THOMSON *Chem.* (ed. 3) II. 247 The molybdic acid precipitates in the state of a fine white powder. **1823** W. PHILLIPS *Introd. Min.* (ed. 3) 287 Molybdic Silver. **1854** DANA *Syst. Min.* (ed. 4) II. 527 (Index) Molybdic ochre. **1873** WATTS *Fownes' Chem.* (ed. 11) 514 Solutions of molybdic salts have a reddish-brown colour.

molybdine (məʊ'lɪbdɪn). *Min.* Also **-in.** [f. MOLYBD-ENA + -INE[5].] = MOLYBDITE.

1854 DANA *Syst. Min.* (ed. 4) II. 144 Molybdine... An earthy yellow powder... Occurs with molybdenite.

molybdite (məʊ'lɪbdaɪt). *Min.* [f. MOLYBD-ENA + -ITE. Cf. F. *molybdite*.] Trioxide of molybdenum occurring in yellow capillary crystals or incrustations.

1868 DANA *Syst. Min.* (ed. 5) 185.

molybdo- (məʊ'lɪbdəʊ), prefix.

1. *Path.* [repr. Gr. μόλυβδος lead]. Used in the names of certain diseases to indicate that they are caused by the presence of lead as ***molybdo-colic***, ***molybdo-dyspepsy***, ***molybdo-paresis***, etc.

2. *Chem.* [Taken as combining form of MOLYBDENUM.] Prefixed to names of salts, to indicate the presence of molybdenum.

1836–41 BRANDE *Chem.* (ed. 5) 905 Tersulphuret of molybdenum.. combines with the sulphurets of the electropositive metals.. and forms a class of sulphur-salts, which may be called molybdo-tersulphurets.

molybdomancy (məʊ'lɪbdəmænsɪ). *rare*[−1]. [f. MOLYBDO- + -MANCY.] (See quot.)

[**1753** CHAMBERS *Cycl. Supp.*, Molybdomantia, Μολυβδομαντεία (citing Potter *Archæol. Gr.* II. xviii).] **1895** ELWORTHY *Evil Eye* 445 Molybdomancy, [divination] by noting motions and figures in molten lead.

molybdomenite (ˌməʊlɪbdə'miːnaɪt). *Min.* [f. Gr. μόλυβδος lead + μήνη moon: see -ITE.] Selenite of lead occurring in thin fragile white lamellæ (*Cassell's Encycl. Dict.* 1885).

molybdophyllite (ˌmɒlɪbdəʊ'fɪlaɪt). *Min.* [ad. G. *molybdophyllit* (G. Flink 1901, in *Bull. Geol. Inst. Univ. Upsala* V. I. 91), f. Gr. μόλυβδο-ς lead + φύλλ-ον leaf: see -ITE[1].] A hydrous silicate of lead and magnesium.

1901 *Jrnl. Chem. Soc.* LXXX. II. 664 Molybdophyllite.—This new mineral is of rare occurrence with hausmannite in granular limestone or dolomite at Långbanshyttan, in Wermland, Sweden. **1968** I. KOSTOV *Mineral.* 327 Perfect cleavage in one direction is displayed by molybdophyllite.

molybdous (məʊ'lɪbdəs), *a. Chem.* [f. MOLYBD-ENA + -OUS.] Applied to compounds into which molybdenum enters in its lower valency, as opp. to MOLYBDIC: esp. in ***molybdous acid***.

1796 HATCHETT in *Phil. Trans.* LXXXVI. 336 The green oxyde, which.. I am inclined to call molybdous acid. **1826** HENRY *Elem. Chem.* II. 59 When one part of powdered molybdenum, and two parts of molybdic acid, are triturated in boiling water;.. we obtain a fine blue powder, which is molybdous acid. **1873** WATTS *Fownes' Chem.* (ed. 11) 514 Molybdous salts in acids, are opaque and almost black.

molysite ('mɒlɪsaɪt). *Min.* [said by Dana, the coiner of the name, to be f. Gr. μόλυσις stain, which was app. taken (in error for μόλυσμα) as the sb. corresp. to μολύνειν to stain, perh. by confusion with μώλυσις scalding (f. μωλύ(ν)ειν to scald, parboil): see -ITE[1].

The statement in quot. 1935 as to the origin of the name is incorrect. In *Atti d. R. Accad. d. Sci. fis. e matem.* (1874) VI. IX. 43, Scacchi attributes the name *molysite* to Dana (in *Syst. Min.* (ed. 5)), and renders it in It. as *molisite* so as to make it conform to It. orthography (as he explains in *Lo Spettatore del Vesuviano* (1887)).]

Natural ferric chloride, $FeCl_3$, formed as a sublimation product on lavas surrounding fumaroles and occurring (before being hydrated by the air) as a yellow to red film or incrustation.

1868 DANA *Syst. Min.* (ed. 5) 118 Molysite. **1935** J. W. MELLOR *Comprehensive Treat. Inorg. & Theoret. Chem.* XIV. lxvi. 41 A. Scacchi observed in recent eruptions a yellowish or brownish-red incrustation associated with the lavas of fumaroles or steam holes. The coloration was attributed to the presence of ferric chloride, $FeCl_3$, and A. Scacchi called the mineral molisite, which J. D. Dana altered to molysite—from μόλυσις, a stain. **1968** I. KOSTOV *Mineral.* II. iii. 195 Molysite $FeCl_3$.

mom (mɒm). Also **Mom.** Colloq. abbrev. (chiefly *U.S.*) of MAMMA[1], MAMA; *spec.* the typical American matriarchal mother. Also *attrib.* and *Comb.*, as ***mom cult***, ***culture***; ***mom-bashing***, ***-like***, etc.; *spec.* **mom-and-pop** *U.S.*, used *attrib.* to denote a small shop or store, etc., of a type often run by a married couple.

1894 *Dialect Notes* I. 332 *Mam*, *mom*, *mæ*, for mamma or mother. **1911** R. W. CHAMBERS *Common Law* v. 156 City-wearied fathers of youngsters who called their parents 'pop' and 'mom'. **1950** *Brit. Jrnl. Psychol.* June 230 The 'mom' culture in which American adolescents are often said to live. **1951** Mom-and-Pop [see HOLE *sb.* 7b]. **1957** *Economist* 28 Dec. 1121/2 Tin Pan Alley, Fundamentalism, and the Mom cult had it coming to them. **1958** *Manch. Guardian* 7 June 4/6 Three leading serious comedies are studies in parent-hating or mom-bashing. **1961** J. HELLER *Catch-22* (1962) i. 9 The hot dog, the Brooklyn Dodgers. Mom's apple pie. That's what everyone's fighting for. **1961** J. MCCABE *Mr. Laurel & Mr. Hardy* (1962) v. 102 The troubles of the boys in their continuing endeavour to get away from their domineering, Mom-like wives. **1962** *Listener* 20 Dec. 1053/1 These 'mom and pop' stores and the somewhat larger ones certainly have no love for the supermarkets. **1966** *Economist* 9 July p. xxi/3 'Mom-and-pop' dealers in smaller communities and suburban fringes. **1968** *Globe & Mail* (Toronto) 17 Feb. 46/8 (Advt.), A family kitchen with mom in mind boasts a.. built-in range and oven. **1972** *New Yorker* 21 Oct. 30/1 The mom-and-pop grocery store was the New York State headquarters of the McGovern campaign. **1975** *Ibid.* 13 Jan. 36/2 'Of course we will, Mom,' I said, and I patted her hand and laid it aside.

mom, momble, obs. ff. MUM, MUMBLE.

mombin (məm'biːn). [Amer. Sp. *mombín*, f. Caribbean native name.] A West Indian tree of the genus *Spondias*, esp. *S. lutea*, of the family Anacardiaceæ, or its yellow or purplish fruit, resembling a small plum; = HOG-PLUM a.

1837 J. MACFADYEN *Flora of Jamaica* I. 228 The fruit [of *Spondias graveolens*] is called Mombin by the French colonists. **1920** W. POPENOE *Man. Tropical & Subtropical Fruits* iv. 156 The red mombin is a small tree, often spreading in habit. *Ibid.* 158 The red mombin is abundant in Mexico and Central America. *Ibid.* 159 The Yellow Mombin.. is generally considered inferior in quality to the red mombin. **1972** A. F. SIMMONS *Growing Unusual Fruit* 201 Mombin fruit... Spondias species. *Ibid.* 202 Yellow mombin or hog plum (*Spondias mombin*). The egg-shaped yellow fruits are about 1 in long and sub-acid to sweet.

[**momblishness.** Explained as: Muttering talk. Error for *moubliemies* in *ne moubliemies* forget-me-nots.

[*a* **1500** *Assemb. Ladies* 61 (Addit. MS.) Ne moubliemies and souenez also.] **1532** *Chaucer's Wks.* 294 Ne momblysnesse and souenesse. **1721** BAILEY, *Momblishness*, talk, muttering. *O*[*ld word*]. **1837** RICHARDSON s.v. *Mumble*, 'Ne *momblisnesse* ne sonenesse.'—No *mumbling* talk nor noisy sound. *Chaucer.* **1890** *Century Dict.*, *Momblishness*, muttering talk. *Bailey*.]

mombu: see MAMBU.

mombyll, momchaunce, obs. ff. MUMBLE, MUMCHANCE.

†**mome,** *sb.*[1] *Obs.* [Corresponds to MLG. *môme*, OHG. *muoma* (MHG, *muome*, mod.G. *muhme*), prob. a reduplication of the first syll. of OTeut. **mōdar* MOTHER. A probably related formation is represented by ON. *móna* 'mammy', MDu. (rare) *mône* aunt (and perh. ME. MONE *sb.*[2], crone).] An aunt.

c **1440** *Promp. Parv.* 342/1 Mome, or awnte [*Pynson* faders suster. Mome, or aunte, moders syster].

mome (məʊm), *sb.*[2] *Obs.* exc. *arch.* [Of obscure origin: possibly related to MUM. Some have compared Fr. (Norman dial.) *môme* 'little child' (Moisy).] 'A dull blockish fellow' (Phillips, ed. Kersey 1706): a blockhead, dolt, fool.

1553 *Respublica* I. iv. 348 An honest mome; ah, ye dolt, ye lowte, ye Nodye. **1560** INGELEND *Disob. Child* G iij b, And me her husbande as a starke mome, With knockyng and mockynge she wyll handell. **1573** TUSSER *Husb.* (1878) 139 Ill husbandrie spendeth abrode like a mome. **1584** R. SCOT *Discov. Witchcr.* VII. xii. (1886) 118 Saule saw nothing, but stood without like a mome. **1590** SHAKS. *Com. Err.* III. i. 32 Mome, Malthorse, Capon, Coxcombe, Idiot, Patch. **1609** DEKKER *Gvlls Horne-bk.* 5 Grout-nowles and Moames will in swarmes fly buzzing about thee. **1656** S. H. *Gold. Law* 23 And yet like senseless Momes, sit still. **1719** D'URFEY *Pills* I. 147 Joan lisping her Liquor scatters, And Nelly hiccoupping calls her Mome. **1721** —— *Two Queens Brentford* IV. i, At this the Knight look'd like a Mome. **1881** DUFFIELD *Don Quix.* I. p. cxix, But if thou cook a kind of fare That not for every mome is fit, Be sure that fools will nibble there. **1923** E. SITWELL *Bucolic Comedies* 17 An old dull mome With a head like a pome.

transf. **1736** in Lediard *Life Marlborough* III. 438 But let their molten Mome of Triumph stand, And blush, tho' Brass, at Marlbro's mighty Hand.

mome (məʊm), *sb.*[3] [Anglicized form of MOMUS.] †**a.** A carping critic (*obs.*). **b.** *nonce-use.* A buffoon, jester.

1563 *Mirr. Mag.*, *Wilful Fall Blacksmith* xiv, I dare be bolde a while to play the mome, Out of my sacke some others faultes to lease, And let my owne behinde my backe to peyse. **1652** A. ROSS *Hist. World* Pref. 4 [It is] farre more easie to play the Mome then the Mime, to reprehend, then to imitate. **1652** —— *View all Religions* (1655) To Rdr., These censorious Momes. **1676** MOXON *Print Lett.* 4 My Pains and Endeavours may lie under the Censure of Detracting Momes. **1902** *Q. Rev.* Oct. 465 Samuel Rogers.. could still describe the Italian mome as one 'Who speaks not, stirs not, but we laugh;.. Arlecchino'.

mome (məʊm), *a.* A factitious word introduced by 'Lewis Carroll' (see quot. 1855).

Also occurs in *Through the Looking-Glass* (1871) i. 21.

1855 'L. CARROLL' *Rectory Umbrella & Mischmasch* (1932) 139 All mimsy were the borogoves; And the mome raths outgrabe. *Ibid.* 140 *Mome* (hence *solemome*, *solemone* and *solemn*), 'grave'. **1960** M. GARDNER *Annotated Alice* 195/1 'Mome' has a number of obsolete meanings such as mother, a blockhead,.. none of which, judging from Humpty Dumpty's interpretation, Carroll had in mind. **1970** R. D. SUTHERLAND *Lang. & Lewis Carroll* vii. 149 Humpty Dumpty is reporting the generally accepted meanings... The information he imparts is 'as sensible as a dictionary'... He admits some difficulty with *mome*.

mome, variant of MALM *a. dial.*, soft.

momele, -ell, -elyng, obs. ff. MUMBLE, -BLING.

momene, variant of MALMENY *Obs.*

moment ('məʊmənt), *sb.* Also 5 **momentt**, 6 **momente**; *Sc.* 6 **mamunt**, 9 **mament**. [ad. L. *mōmentum* movement, moving power (hence, importance, consequence), moment of time, particle, f. *mō-*, *movēre* to MOVE. Cf. F. *moment* (from 12th c.), Sp., Pg., It. *momento*, MHG. *momente* fem., moment of time, mod.G. *moment* masc. (from Fr.), moment of time, *moment* neut. (from Latin) momentum, decisive consideration, essential factor.]

1. a. A portion of time too brief for its duration to be taken into account; a point of time, an instant. Also in the same sense, †***moment of an hour***, ***of a minute*** (prob. originally used with reference to sense 2).

1340 HAMPOLE *Pr. Consc.* 5650 A moment of tyme es nan othir thyng, Bot a short space als of a eghe twynklyng. *c* **1386** CHAUCER *Knt.'s T.* 1726 In that selue moment Palamon Is vnder Venus. **1471** CAXTON *Recuyell* (Sommer) I. 236 And than the same moment & tyme þt she had so doo Alcumena ..began [etc.]. **1483** *Cath. Angl.* 242/2 A Momentt, *articulus*, *momentum*, *momentulum*. **1526** TINDALE 1 *Cor.* xv. 52 We shall all be chaunged and that in a moment and in the twincklynge of an eye. *a* **1548** HALL *Chron.*, *Edw. IV*, 201 In a moment of an houre, the Welshemen wer clene discomfited. **1590** SHAKS. *Mids. N.* III. ii. 33 When in that moment (so it came to passe) Tytania waked, and straightway lou'd an Asse. **1596** DALRYMPLE tr. *Leslie's Hist. Scot.* v. 300 In the verie selfe mamunt quhen thay war to Joyne battell, Bischope ffothadie.. cumis betueine thame. **1627** FELTHAM *Resolves* II. [I.] xlix. (1628) 143 Wee are curdled to the fashion of a life, by time, and set successions; when all again is lost, and in the moment of a minute, gone. **1690** LOCKE *Hum. Und.* II. xv. (1695) 103 Such a small part in Duration, may be called a Moment, and is the time of one Idea in our Minds, in the train of their ordinary Succession there. **1748** CHESTERF. *Let. to Son* 16 Feb., The value of moments, when cast up, is immense, if well employed... Every moment may be put to some use. *a* **1774** GOLDSM. *Surv. Exp. Philos.* (1776) II. 295 As the sun is every moment altering its situation, so is the landskip every moment varying its shade. **1856** SIR B. BRODIE *Psychol. Inq.* I. iv. 125 The mind is often active even at the very moment of death. **1863** GEO. ELIOT *Romola* xxii, It seemed a long while to them—it was but a moment. **1871** FREEMAN *Norm. Conq.* (1876) IV. xvii. 78 Eadgar, the King of a moment. **1891** E. PEACOCK *N. Brendon* II. 10 At this moment a servant entered.

†*personified.* **1642** FULLER *Holy & Prof. St.* IV. xiii. 304 She remembreth how suddenly the Scene in the Masque was altered (almost before moment it self could take notice of it).

b. ***the moment***: occas. in pregnant sense, the fitting moment, the momentary conjunction of circumstances that affords an opportunity.

1781 WASHINGTON in Bancroft *Hist. Const.* (1882) I. 21 The moment should be improved; if suffered to pass away it may never return. **1865** M. ARNOLD *Ess. Crit.* i. 5 The man is not enough without the moment.

c. Phrases. †***at a moment***: at a moment's notice; (***at this***) ***moment in time***: now, the present instant; ***for a moment***: (*a*) predicatively, destined to last but a moment; (*b*) *adv.*, during a moment; ***not for a moment***: emphatically not; ***for the moment***: so far as the immediate future is concerned; also, temporarily during the brief space referred to; ***to have one's*** (or ***its***) ***moments***: to be impressive, etc., on occasions; ***to live for*** (or ***in***) ***the moment***: to live without concern for the future; ***of the moment***: of importance at the time in question; esp. ***man of the moment***; ***never a dull moment***: a catch-phrase designating constant variety; ***one moment***: elliptically for 'wait one moment', 'listen for one moment'; ***on the spur of the moment***: see SPUR; ***on, upon the moment*** (now *rare*): immediately, instantly; ***the moment***: elliptically for 'the moment when' or 'that', as soon as ever; ***this moment***: used advb. for (*a*) without a moment's delay, immediately; (*b*) just now, hardly a moment ago; ***to the moment***: with exact punctuality; also, for the exact time required.

1585 T. WASHINGTON tr. *Nicholay's Voy.* II. xviii. 51 b, The other..being kept & reserued as at a moment to succour & supply the instant necessities which might happen. **1607** SHAKS. *Timon* I. i. 79 All those which were his Fellowes but of late, Some better then his valew; on the moment Follow his strides. **1611** BIBLE *Prov.* xii. 19 The lip of trueth shall bee established for euer; but a lying tongue is but for a moment. *a* **1763** SHENSTONE *Ess.* Wks. 1765 II. 206 The best time to frame an answer to the letters of a friend, is the moment you receive them. **1800** LAMB *Let. to Manning* 13 Dec., I have received your letter this moment, not having been at the office. **1840** DICKENS *Old C. Shop* i, I rose to go:..'One moment, Sir,' he said. **1871** R. ELLIS tr. *Catullus* x. 3 She a lady, methought upon the moment, Of some quality. **1871** BROWNING *Pr. Hohenst.* 28 Well, that's my mission, so I serve the world, Figure as man o' the moment. **1871** M. COLLINS *Mrq. & Merch.* III. i. 24 A cook who could roast a joint..to the moment. **1878** TENNYSON *Revenge* ii, You fly them for a moment to fight with them again. **1889** J. K. JEROME *Three Men in Boat* ix. 85 There is never a dull moment in the boat while girls are towing it. **1890** *Spectator* 18 Oct. 509/1 The political crisis in Portugal ended for the moment on Monday. **1926** I. MACKAY *Blencarrow* xxiii. 207 With the proper sort of company the situation might have had its moments. **1927** *Sat. Even. Post* 9 Apr. 119 Even a mailman has his moments. **1932** *Weekend Rev.* 14 May 617/1 There is never a dull moment. **1935** E. CARR *Jrnl.* in *Hundreds & Thousands* (1966) 185 The three dogs lie on the bed,..trusting me to attend to their wants, living for the moment. **1935** *Discovery* Aug. 220/1 Land utilisation is the problem of the moment. *Ibid.* 221/1 This is the need dictated by world economic conditions *of the moment*. **1936** *Punch* 12 Aug. 170/2, I don't suggest for a moment that these are finished ideas. They are no more than artists' roughs. **1950** L. KAUFMAN *Jubel's Children* xx. 223 Jubel says there's never a dull moment. **1963** W. H. MISSILDINE *Your Inner Child of Past* xii. 127 Because they 'live in the moment', they actually tend to be blindly unaware of the feelings of others. **1970** O. NORTON *Dead on Prediction* vii. 137 That's something I *didn't* know... You have your moments! **1972** G. BROMLEY *In Absence of Body* iii. 30 What can we actually do to help at this moment in time? **1972** 'T. COE' *Don't lie to Me* (1974) xxii. 169 Hargerson had his moments; happily this was one of them. **1972** R. ADAMS *Watership Down* xx. 126 'No one hurt?' 'Oh, several have been hurt, one way and another.' 'Never a dull moment, really,' said Bigwig. **1973** *Guardian* 12 Mar. 11/2 The usual stuff about meaningful confrontations taking place..at this moment in time. **1974** C. EGLETON *October Plot* i. 11 There were five similar [flak] towers..but at this moment in time, they were only of passing interest. **1974** V. BROME *Day of Destruction* xv. 153 Here's our man of the moment... Hail the conquering hero comes.

d. ***moment of truth***: the time of the final sword-thrust in a bull-fight (Sp. *el momento de la verdad*); *transf.*, a crisis or turning-point; a testing situation.

1932 E. HEMINGWAY *Death in Afternoon* vii. 68 The whole end of the bullfight was the final sword thrust, the actual encounter between the man and the animal, what the Spanish call the moment of truth. **1949** *New Statesman* 15 Jan. 61/1 A good detective story should be like a good bull-fight... The author plunges the unexpected explanation into him like a sword—the moment of truth, as the Spaniards call it. **1954** H. CASTEEL *Running of Bulls* v. 106 The Spanish call the kill the hora de la verdad (the hour (moment) of truth)...this is still the climactic second to which the whole fight has been dedicated. **1956** I. BROMIGE *Enchanted Garden* III. iii. 140 This, thought Fiona, was the moment of truth. **1957** 'D. RUTHERFORD' *Long Echo* viii. 150 This was his Moment of Truth, but there was no arena packed with spectators to give him vicarious courage. **1959** *Listener* 6 Aug. 215/2 Now comes 'the moment of truth'... The matador causes the bull to stand square..and plunges his sword between its shoulder-blades. **1965** H. I. ANSOFF *Corporate Strategy* (1968) i. 16 We shall have..very little [to say]..about the utility function applied at the ultimate 'moment of truth' in selecting the preferred alternative. **1972** H. MACINNES *Message From Malaga* i. 9 You've become a self-centred bastard, he told himself... He blamed this moment of truth on the combination of guitar, scent of flowers, night sky.

†**2.** As the name of a definite measure of time. **a.** In mediæval reckoning, the tenth part of a 'point' (see POINT *sb.*[1] A. 10), the fortieth or the fiftieth part of an hour. **b.** With reference to Rabbinical modes of computation (repr. Heb. *'ḥēleq*): see quot. 1625. **c.** In the 17–18th c. occas. used for SECOND. *Obs.*

a. **1398** TREVISA *Barth. De P.R.* IX. ix. (1495), And a day [contains] foure quadrantes. And a quadrant conteynyth syxe houres. And an houre foure poyntes. And a poynt .x. momentes. And a moment twelue vnces. And an vnce seuen and fourty attomos. *c* **1532** DU WES *Introd. Fr.* in *Palsgr.* 1078 Of atmos ben made the momentes, of momentes ben made the mynutes. **1621** BRATHWAIT *Nat. Embassie* 15 Who gouernes thee, point, moment, minute, houre.

b. **1625** T. GODWIN *Moses & Aaron* III. 155 Not before the ninth houre, and the 204. moment of an houre... Note in the last place, that 1080. moments make an houre.

c. **1642** H. MORE *Song of Soul* Notes 163/1, I understand, ..by a moment one second of a minute. **1767** LADY MARY COKE *Jrnl.* 23 Aug., The Clock has three hands, one for the hours, one for the minutes, and a third for the moments.

d. *Geol.* [a. F. *moment* (proposed in this sense by E. Renevier 1882, in *Congrès géol. internat.: Compt. Rend. de la 2me Session, 1881* 540).] A period of geological time corresponding to a stratigraphical zone (as defined by its fossil content).

1933 W. J. ARKELL *Jurassic Syst. Gr. Brit.* i. 21 Strictly speaking,..'moment' should take priority over secule, and Diener adopts it, with the variations time-moment and zone-moment. **1958** *Bull. Geol. Soc. Amer.* LXIX. 113/2 At the Congress in Bologna in 1881..the only concrete suggestion came from the Swiss delegation (Renevier, 1882), which formally proposed 'moment' for the time equivalent of a zone. *Ibid.*, The term 'moment' has priority, as was..recognized at an early date by Diener (1919). **1969** BENNISON & WRIGHT *Geol. Hist. Brit. Isles* ii. 23 A zone is defined as strata deposited during an interval of time (known as a secule or moment, though these terms are not widely used) throughout which a particular faunal or floral assemblage existed.

†**3. a.** A small particle. ***to the moment***: to the smallest detail.

moment of a balance: lit. from the Vulg. *momentum steræ*, which is a mere Hebraism, and therefore has not, as is sometimes supposed, any share in the sense-development of the Latin word.

1382 WYCLIF *Isa.* xl. 15 Lo! Ientiles as a drope of a boket, and as a moment of a balaunce ben holden. **1594** BLUNDEVIL *Exerc.* III. I. xvii. (1636) 316 For to every severall place, yea to every little moment of the earth in an oblique Spheare, belongeth his proper Horizon. **1638** JUNIUS *Paint. Ancients* 77 Examining therein every little moment of Art with such infatigable..care that it is easie to be perceived they do not acknowledg any greater pleasure. **1642** H. MORE *Song of Soul* I. Ep. to Rdr. *note*, This opinion, though it have its moments of reason, yet [etc.]. **1691** NORRIS *Pract. Disc.* 23 One of the Scales may and will receive some moments of Advantage more than the other. **1754** RICHARDSON *Grandison* VI. xvi. 58 Be good, and write me every-thing how and about it; and write to the moment. You cannot be too minute.

†**b.** *Math.* An infinitesimal increment or decrement of a varying quantity. *Obs.*

[**1704** NEWTON *De Quadratura Curvarum*, Momenta id est incrementa momentanea synchrona.] **1706** PHILLIPS (ed. Kersey) s.v., *Moments* are such indeterminate and uncertain Parts of Quantity, as are supposed to be in a perpetual Flux. **1743** EMERSON *Fluxions* 3 The Moments and Fluxions ought not to be confounded together, since the Moments..are as different from the Fluxions, as any Effect is different from its Cause.

4. Importance, 'weight'. Now only in the adjectival phrase *of* (***great, little, any,*** etc.) ***moment***.

1522 CLERK in Ellis *Orig. Lett.* Ser. III. I. 310 He said the kyngs Highnes lettres if they had comme in season shulde have been of no smale momente. **1591** SHAKS. *1 Hen. VI*, I. ii. 5 What Townes of any moment, but we haue? **1617–18** W. LAWSON *New Orchard* i. (1623) 2 The Gardner had not need be an idle, or lazie Lubber, for so your Orchard being a matter of such moment, will not prosper. **1647** CLARENDON *Hist. Reb.* I. §152 The Crown well knowing the moment of keeping Those the objects of reverence, and veneration with the People. **1709** *Tatler* No. 67 ¶11 A Matter of too great Moment for any one Person to determine. **1772** JOHNSON in *Boswell* (1811) II. 203 The great moment of his authority makes it necessary to examine his position. **1790** BURKE *Fr. Rev.* 90 Things which appear at first view of little moment. **1823** SCOTT *Peveril* xxiii, The affairs of moment which have called me hither. **1874** GREEN *Short Hist.* vi. §3. 290 He [Caxton] printed all the English poetry of any moment which was then in existence.

†**5.** Cause or motive of action; determining influence; determining argument or consideration.

1606 SHAKS. *Ant. & Cl.* I. ii. 147, I haue seene her dye twenty times vppon farre poorer moment. **1611** B. JONSON *Catiline* IV. v, Can these, or such, be any aydes to vs? Looke they, as they were built to shake the world, Or be a moment to our enterprise? **1627** MAY *Lucan* v. 389 Thinke ye that such as ye Can any moment to my fortunes be? **1632** LITHGOW *Trav.* III. 117 The diuine Maiestie doth swey the moments of things, and sorteth them..to strange and vnlooked for effects. **1663** JER. TAYLOR *Funeral Serm. Bramhall* 36 He so press'd the former arguments..and added so many moments and weights to his discourse, that [etc.]. **1691** NORRIS *Pract. Disc.* 59 This is a certain sign that we are not determined by the Moments of Truth,..but by some other By-Consideration and partial Inducement.

†**6.** Motion, movement. *Obs.*

1641 MILTON *Ch. Govt.* i. Wks. 1851 III. 97 All the moments and turnings of humane occasions are mov'd to and fro as upon the axle of discipline.

7. A definite stage, period, or turning-point in a course of events.

This sense now tends to be apprehended as an application of sense 1, 'point of time'.

1666 SANCROFT *Lex Ignea* 6 A threefold Song [*sc.* Isa. xxiv–xxvii]..tun'd, and fitted to the three great Moments of the Event. The first, to the time of the Ruine itself... The second..fitted to a time of their Return... The third.. belongs to the whole middle Interval. **1906** C. BIGG *Wayside Sk.* p. v, These Lectures..might have been called Essays on the Development of the Church. They refer to three great moments in that fateful process—the making of the mediæval system, the decay of the mediæval system, and the beginnings of modern Christianity.

8. *Mech.* †**a.** = MOMENTUM 4. *Obs.*

1706 W. JONES *Syn. Palmar. Matheseos* 282 Moment..is compounded of Velocity..and..Weight. **1727–52** CHAMBERS *Cycl.*, *Moment*, *Momentum*, in mechanics, is the same with *impetus*.

b. Applied, with qualifying words, to certain functions serving as the measure of some mechanical effect the quantity of which depends on two different factors.

Thus the ***moment of a force or a velocity*** about a point is the product of the length of the directed line representing the force or the velocity, multiplied by the length of the perpendicular from the point. The ***moment of a couple*** is the product of either of the two equal forces into the length of the arm. The ***moment of inertia*** of a body about any axis is the sum of the products of the mass of each particle of the body into the square of its least distance from the axis. ***moment of momentum*** of a rotating body is the product of momentum into the distance from the axis.

1830 KATER & LARDNER *Mech.* x. 135 The moment of a force is therefore found by multiplying the force by its leverage. *Ibid.* 137 The product of the numerical expressions for the mass of the body and the square of the radius of gyration..has been called the moment of inertia. **1858** RANKINE *Man. Appl. Mechanics* 22 The *moment* of a couple means the product of the magnitude of its force by the length of its arm. *Ibid.* 308 This is called the *bending moment* or *moment of flexure* of the beam at the vertical section in question.

c. *Physics.* The distance between the two poles of a simple bar magnet, or the two charges of an electric dipole, multiplied by the strength of either of them (called more fully the ***magnetic*** and the ***electric moment***, respectively); more widely, the maximum torque that any given system of poles, or charges, can experience in a uniform magnetic, or electric, field (respectively) of unit strength; more fully called (***magnetic*** or ***electric***) ***dipole moment***. Similarly the moment of order 2 (***quadrupole moment***) is a certain tensor of rank 2, whose components are quadratic functions of the spatial co-ordinates of the poles or charges; so ***octupole moment*** (moment of order 3), etc. Cf. MULTIPOLE *sb.*

1865 *Phil. Mag.* XXIX. 441 The product of the strength of the poles into the length between them is called the magnetic moment of the magnet. **1884** J. T. SPRAGUE *Electricity* (ed. 2) iii. 110 The magnetic moment of any uniformly magnetized substance is proportional to its volume. **1892** O. LODGE *Mod. Views Electricity* 445 A circuit conveying a current exactly imitates a magnet of definite moment, the equivalent moment being..μnAC where A is the mean area of the coil, *n* the number of turns of wire, C the current, and μ a constant characteristic of the medium inside the coil. **1903** S. J. BARNETT *Elements of Electromagnetic Theory* xi. 282 The quantity $M = mL = T/H \sin \theta$ is called the magnetic moment of the magnet (analogous to the electric moment of an electret). **1916**, etc. [see MULTIPOLE *sb.*]. **1920** *Chem. Abstr.* XIV. 3014 Assuming the mol. to be a dipole it is possible to obtain the distance between the 2 charges from the moment of inertia and from this in turn to calc. the elec. moment by application of the quantum theory. **1934** *Physical Rev.* XLV. 761/1 We derived the magnetic moment of the deuton in the same way as the magnetic moment of the proton. **1942** J. D. STRANATHAN *'Particles' of Mod. Physics* x. 401 The magnetic moment of a neutron must be regarded as a fundamental property of the particle. **1953** *Sci. News* XXX. 7 The magnetization [of a piece of iron] is the magnetic moment per unit volume, or the pole strength per unit cross-sectional area. **1958** CONDON & ODISHAW *Handbk. Physics* IV. ii. 19/2 A quadrupole term is related to the second-order moments of the charge distribution... (Various slightly different definitions of the quadrupole moment are to be found in the literature.) *Ibid.* 20/1 The spherical-harmonic addition theorem..permits the writing of $V_\kappa(\mathbf{R})$ in the form

$$V_k(\mathbf{R}) = \frac{1}{R^{k+1}} \sum_{m=-k}^{+k} Q_{km} F_{km}(\Theta) e^{-\mathrm{i}m\phi}$$

where the 2^κ-pole moment is fully described by the $2k + 1$ quantities,

$$Q_{\kappa m} = \frac{4\pi}{2k+1} \int \rho(\mathbf{r}) F_{\kappa m}(\theta) e^{im\phi} dv.$$

1962 CORSON & LORRAIN *Introd. Electromagn. Fields & Waves* v. 210 We set $\mathbf{m} = I\mathbf{S}$ as the dipole moment of the current loop, where **S** is a vector whose magnitude is equal to the area of the loop. It is perpendicular to the loop. *Ibid.*, It is possible to generalize the concept of magnetic dipole moment to any distribution of current in space... For a current distribution **J** in a volume τ, $\mathbf{m} = ..\frac{1}{2}\int \mathbf{r} \times \mathbf{J} d\tau$. **1970** G. K. WOODGATE *Elem. Atomic Struct.* ix. 177 In order to be able to discuss departures of the nuclear charge distribution from spherical symmetry we should like to attribute to the nucleus electric multipole moments. *Ibid.* 180 The quadrupole moment Q is positive if the nuclear charge distribution is elongated along the direction of **I** [*sc.* the nuclear spin] (prolate) and negative if the distribution is flattened (oblate).

d. *Statistics.* Each of a series of quantities (***first, second,*** etc., ***moment***) that express the

average or expected value of the first, second, etc., powers of the deviation of each component of a frequency distribution from some given value, usu. the mean (giving a ***central moment***) or zero.

1893 K. PEARSON in *Nature* 26 Oct. 615/2 Now the centre of gravity of the observation curve is found at once, also its area and its first four moments by easy calculation. **1925** R. A. FISHER *Statistical Methods for Research Workers* iii. 70 The standard error of the variance is $\sqrt{[(\mu_4 - \mu_2^2)/N]}$, where N is the number of samples, and μ_2 and μ_4 are the second and fourth moments of the theoretical distribution. **1938** A. E. WAUGH *Elem. Statistical Method* vi. 114 The formula for the first moment about the mean involves Σx and..it reduces to zero, since $\Sigma x = 0$. We can thus say some things about the moments of all curves in advance: (1) $v_0 = 1$, (2) $v_1 = 0$, (3) $v_2 = \sigma^2$. *Ibid.*, In any symmetrical curve the odd moments, being based on the sums of odd powers of deviations, will equal zero. **1959** G. & R. C. JAMES *Math. Dict.* 257/2 $\mu_r = \int_{-\infty}^{\infty} (x - a)^r f(x)dx$ is the *r*th moment of *x* around the point *a*, where *x* is a random variable with frequency function *f*(*x*). **1961** D. V. HUNTSBERGER *Elem. Statistical Inference* v. 102 The first moment about the origin is the mean μ of the theoretical distribution... The variance σ^2 of a random variable *Y* is defined as the second moment about the mean, the average value of $(Y - \mu)^2$.

9. One of the elements of a complex conceptual entity. (After Ger. use.) Cf. MOMENTUM 5.

1863 J. G. MURPHY *Comm. Gen.* xxv. 1–11 These are all moments, potent elements in the memory of man, foundation-stones of his history and philosophy. *a* **1864** FERRIER *Grk. Philos.* (1866) I. v. 125 Being and not-Being are the elements or moments of Becoming. **1869** *Jrnl. Specul. Philos.* III. 351 The moments of the Comprehension are Universality, Particularity, and Individuality. **1879** J. VEITCH tr. *Descartes' Method* (1880) Introd. 79 It is a complete mistake historically to assume that the moment of Cartesianism is consciousness. **1906** E. F. SCOTT *4th Gospel* iii. 96 The ethical moment is thus markedly absent.

10. *attrib.* and *Comb.*, as †***moment-space***; ***moment-lived***, ***-living*** adjs.; **moment-axis** *Physics*, a line indicating by its length and direction respectively the moment and the direction of a couple; †**moment-hand**, the seconds-hand of a time-piece; **moment-to-moment** *attrib. phr.*, of an immediate requirement, necessity, etc.

1865 BRANDE & COX *Dict. Sci.*, etc. I. 575 Such a line is called the *moment-axis of the couple. **1809** T. DONALDSON *Poems* 67 On Seeing a Clock; the hour and *moment-hands of which were going in contrary directions. **1833** LAMB *To Moxon* 24 July, *Life*, etc. (1876) I. 143 She takes it [*sc.* her watch] out every moment to look at the moment-hand. **1654** WHITLOCK *Zootomia* 404 All mans Creations (his Actions) are vanity; (but what he doth for his Creatour) and his Creatures, (the Effects of those Actions) but Abortives, or *moment-lived. **1826** W. ELLIOT *Nun* 20 *Moment-living flowers that blow, Full of fragrance, soon to perish. **1508** DUNBAR *Goldyn Targe* 210 Than was I woundit to the deth wele nere, And yoldyn as a wofull prisonnere To lady Beautee, in a *moment space. **1934** T. S. ELIOT *Elizabethan Essays* 8 Contemporary literature, like contemporary politics, is confused by the *moment-to-moment struggle for existence. **1957** A. MILLER *Coll. Plays* (1958) Introd. 23 It wanted..a kind of moment-to-moment wildness in addition to its organic wholeness.

†**moment**, *v. Obs. rare*$^{-1}$. [f. MOMENT *sb.*] *trans.* To determine to the moment the time or occurrence of; to time precisely.

a **1661** FULLER *Worthies, Suffolk* (1662) III. 62 All Accidents are minuted and momented by Divine Providence.

momenta, pl. of MOMENTUM.

momental (məʊ'mɛntəl), *a.* [a. F. *momental*, ad. late L. **mōmentāl-is* (implied in *mōmentāliter*, adv.) f. *mōmentum*: see MOMENT *sb.* and -AL[1].]

†**1.** Having only the duration of a moment; momentary. *Obs.*

1606 BRETON *Sidney's Ourania* D, Not one momentall minute doth she swerue. **1632** LITHGOW *Trav.* IV. 133 Mahomet the second..liuing in a discontented humour, to behold..this famous Citie, that so flourished in his eyes, by momentall circumstances, collected his cruel intentions, to the full height of ambition. **1646** SIR T. BROWNE *Pseud. Ep.* V. v. 240 For holding no dependence on any preceding efficient but God, in the act of his production there may be conceived some connexion, and Adam to have been in a momentall Navell with his Maker.

†**2.** 'Important; valuable; of moment'. *Obs.*

1818 in TODD, but with quot. 1606 as in sense 1 above.

3. *Math.* Of or pertaining to momentum, esp. in ***momental ellipse***, ***ellipsoid***.

1877 B. WILLIAMSON *Integr. Calculus* (ed. 2) x. §207 The boundary of an elliptical lamina may be regarded as the momental ellipse of the lamina.

†**mo'mentally**, *adv. Obs.* [f. prec. + -LY[2].]

1. From moment to moment.

1612 tr. *Benvenuto's Passenger* I. i. 31 The bodies of liuing creatures remayning in a daily ebbing and flowing, so that momentally the corporall spirits are dissolued.

2. For a moment.

1646 SIR T. BROWNE *Pseud. Ep.* III. xxi. 160 Ayre but momentally remaining in our bodies, it hath no proportionable space for its conversion.

†**momentane**, *a.* and *sb. Obs.* Also 6 -tain, -tayne, 6–7 -taine. [a. OF. *momentain*, ad. L. *mōmentāneus* momentary, f. *mōment-um*: see MOMENT *sb.* Cf. MOMENTANY *a.*]

A. *adj.* Lasting for a moment, momentary.

1510 *Hours Bl. Virg.* 102 This life that is momentaine. **1555** L. SAUNDERS in Coverdale *Lett. Mart.* (1564) 182 Our tribulation, which is momentane and light, prepareth an exceding & an eternal weight of glory vnto vs. **1619** DONNE *Serm.* (1661) III. 271 Present any of the prophecies of the Revelation concerning Antichrist and a Papist will understand it of a single, and momentane, and transitory man, that must last but three yeer and a half. **1630** BRATHWAIT *Eng. Gentlem.* (1641) 375 Promising them..for this momentaine sorrow, an incessant joy in Sion.

B. *sb. Math.* = MOMENT 3 b.

1708 *Misc. Curiosa* II. 129 The Momentane of any Power.

Hence †**momentanely** *adv.* = MOMENTARILY 2.

a **1631** DONNE *Serm.* (1661) III. 405 For the mercies of God work momentanely in minuts.

†**momen'taneal**, *a. Obs.* [f. L. *mōmentāne-us* (see MOMENTANE) + -AL[1].] Lasting but a moment. So †**momen'tanean** *a.*

a **1598** ROLLOCK *Serm.* Wks. (Wodrow Soc.) II. 300 The momentanean lichtness of afflictioun wirkis into us ane everlasting wecht of glorie. *c* **1610** *Women Saints* 4 That which by nature..is..transitorie, and momentaneall. **1654** WHITLOCK *Zootomia* 283 He scarce affordeth the uncheckt Current of the Affaires of the wicked, so much as to be a delay, but onely in the apprehension of us Momentanean Ephemeri, and span-long-lived Accountants.

momentaneity (məʊməntə'niːɪtɪ, -'eɪɪtɪ). [f. MOMENTANE(OUS *a.* + -ITY, after SPONTANEITY.] Transitory character; momentariness.

1921 D. H. LAWRENCE *Sea & Sardinia* viii. 314, I felt my sound Sardinian soul melting off me, I felt myself evaporating into the real Italian uncertainty and momentaneity. **1923** —— *Kangaroo* vii. 157 All her high moments would have this Bacchic, weapon-like momentaneity.

†**momen'taneous**, *a.* [f. L. *mōmentāne-us* (see MOMENTANE) + -OUS.]

Very common in the 17th c.

1. Lasting but a moment; momentary.

c **1610** *Women Saints* 78 Contemning vile pleasure and momentaneous delighte. *a* **1711** KEN *Preparatives* Poet. Wks. 1721 IV. 41 Or on this Momentaneous Stage, In a short Time to live an Age? **1801** FUSELI *Lect. Paint.* iii. (1848) 407 Form displayed in space, and momentaneous energy, are the element of painting. **1921** H. POUTSMA *Characters of Eng. Vb. & Expanded Form* i. 2 The actions expressed by verbs..may be..momentaneous, i.e. covering only one moment, or comprised between two closely contiguous moments, so that the beginning and the end practically synchronize. **1921** E. SAPIR *Language* v. 108 'Cry out every now and then' or 'cry in fits and starts' is momentaneous-iterative. **1923** D. H. LAWRENCE *Kangaroo* vii. 163 Do I want this curious transparent blood of the antipodes, with its momentaneous feelings? **1926** H. POUTSMA *Gram. Late Mod. Eng.* II. §2. 545 When distinctly verbal in nature, the attributive past participle mostly has a momentaneous or resultative aspect.

2. Occurring in a moment, instantaneous.

1657 W. MORICE *Coena quasi Κοινὴ* xv. 231 Though the previous dispositions were precedent, yet the introduction of the form is momentaneous. **1670** W. CLARKE *Nat. Hist. Nitre* 88 In which momentaneous explosion of the whole quantity all the force consists. **1692** RAY *Disc.* III. vi. (1732) 391 Shall this Dissolution be gradual and successive or momentaneous and sudden? **1793** HOLCROFT tr. *Lavater's Physiog.* xxvii. 130 Creation of every kind is momentaneous.

†**3.** Pertaining to an infinitesimal division of time. Cf. MOMENT 3 b. *Obs.*

1708 *Misc. Curiosa* II. 128, I make use here, of what the celebrated Mr. Newton has demonstrated..concerning the Momentaneous Increments or Decrements of Quantities that Increase or Decrease by a continual Flux.

Hence †**momen'taneously** *adv.*, in a moment, also, every moment; **momen'taneousness**.

1727 BAILEY vol. II, *Instantaneousness*, Momentaneousness, or happening in the Nick of Time. **1753** N. TORRIANO *Gangr. Sore Throat* 8 Bad Humours, which when once formed, increase momentaneously, and that too with great Velocity. **1782** ELIZ. BLOWER *George Bateman* I. 225 Hassell, staggered by this application to his hinder part,..turned momentaneously round. **1921** H. POUTSMA *Characters of Eng. Vb. & Expanded Form* i. 5 [Actions expressed by verbs may be] momentaneously iterative, which may be graphically represented by a succession of dots.

†**momentaniness**. *Obs.* [f. next + -NESS.] Momentariness.

1634 BP. HALL *Char. Man* (1635) 35 How doth the momentaninesse of this misery adde to the misery. *a* **1653** GOUGE *Comm. Hebr.* x. 25 (1655) II. 484 As great a difference as is..betwixt momentaninesse and everlastingnesse.

†**momentany**, *a. Obs.* [ad. F. *momentané*, ad. L. *mōmentāne-us*: see MOMENTANE.]

Very common in the 16th and 17th c.

Pertaining to the moment, momentary; transitory; evanescent.

1508 FISHER *7 Penit. Ps.* cii. Wks. (1876) 196 Euery thynge in this worlde is caduke, transytory & momentany. **1600** HOLLAND *Livy* XLV. i. 1201 The momentanie joy of some vaine and uncertein occurrence. **1644** HEYLIN *Brief Relat. Laud* 26 His death was glorious, the paines whereof were short and momentany to himselfe, the benefit like to be perpetuall [etc.]. **1726** HUXHAM in *Phil. Trans.* XXXIV. 140 Vivid Coruscations..which..formed by their Collision momentany Arches of a Circle.

momen'tarian. *nonce-wd.* [f. MOMENT *sb.* + -ARIAN.] One who believes in 'moments' (see MOMENT *sb.* 3 b).

1863 DE MORGAN in Graves *Life Sir W. R. Hamilton* (1889) III. 598 Cotes was an infinitesimalist; so was Newton, till he abjured in 1706. But he continued a momentarian—which I take to be a $(dx)^{\infty}$-man—all his life.

momentarily ('məʊməntərɪlɪ), *adv.* [f. MOMENTARY *a.* + -LY[2].]

1. For a moment.

1654–66 EARL ORRERY *Parthen.* (1676) 519 The offended god, to make those Sentinels sleep eternally, that would not momentarily, sends down Mercury. **1799** in *Spirit Publ. Jrnls.* (ed. 2) I. 72 It may be momentarily palliated by a connection with a more wholesome family. **1878** F. A. WALKER *Money* xiii. 266 The price of gold..mounted..from 15·63 to 17·77, rising momentarily even to 20·17. **1891** T. HARDY *Tess* xxix, He released her momentarily-imprisoned waist, and withheld the kiss. **1928** 'S. S. VAN DINE' *Greene Murder Case* iii. 39 The situation probably drove everything momentarily from their minds except the two victims of the shooting. **1975** *Times* 8 Sept. 12/3 One MP..was 'growled down'... He wondered momentarily if he had wandered into the Lords by mistake.

2. At every moment; moment by moment. *rare.*

1800 SOUTHEY *Let. to Coleridge* 1 May in *Life* (1850) II. 64, I am interrupted momentarily by visitors, like fleas, infesting a new-comer! **1895** J. G. MILLAIS *Breath fr. Veldt* (1899) 34 The light was also momentarily getting worse.

3. At the moment, instantly.

1799 SICKELMORE *Agnes & Leonora* I. 8 This was momentarily agreed to. **1801** ELIZ. HELME *St. Marg. Cave* II. 60 The friar groaned, but almost momentarily recovered his emotion. **1899** W. J. LOCKE *White Dove* (1900) iii. 43 Sylvester.., having done all that was momentarily possible, was at last able to reflect.

4. At any moment. *N. Amer.*

1928 *Sun* (Baltimore) 13 Aug. 1/2 Arrests were expected momentarily as police continued their investigation of the fantastic murder mill. **1944** *Musical America* 25 Mar. 7/4 An addition to the family..is expected momentarily. **1970** *New Yorker* 3 Oct. 30/3 Miss Loren had been delayed in traffic but would arrive momentarily. **1970** *Daily Tel.* 22 Oct. 18 The [Canadian] captain came on the intercom. 'Please fasten your seat belts,' he said. 'We shall be taking off momentarily.' **1972** *New York* 8 May 6/2 We are expecting our first child momentarily. **1975** *Publishers Weekly* 10 Feb. 52/1 There is one woman who imagines she is in a motel and that her deceased husband will momentarily arrive to pick her up.

momentariness ('məʊməntərɪnɪs). [f. MOMENTARY + -NESS.] The quality or condition of being momentary or transitory. Also *fig.*

1827 HARE *Guesses* (1874) 510 One of those paradoxes.. for which..their momentariness and unpremeditatedness are mostly a sufficient excuse. **1872** MORLEY *Voltaire* v. (ed. 2) 266 The momentariness of guilt and eternity of remorse.

momentary ('məʊməntərɪ), *a.* Also 6 -tarry, -arye, 6–7 -arie. [ad. L. *mōmentāri-us*, f. *mōment-um*: see MOMENT *sb.* and -ARY[2].]

1. Lasting but a moment; of but a moment's duration; transitory.

1526 TINDALE *2 Cor.* iv. 17 Tribulacion, which is momentarry and light. **1592** GREENE *Groat's W. Wit* (1617) 2 All mortall things are momentarie. **1641** MAISTERTON *Serm.* 17 A momentary dalliance. **1711** STEELE *Spect.* No. 75 ¶8 His Griefs are Momentary, and his Joys Immortal. **1791** *Gentl. Mag.* 32/1 This error seems to have arisen from a momentary forgetfulness. **1856** KANE *Arct. Expl.* II. xxii. 220 We availed ourselves of a momentary lull to shoulder the sledge. **1903** W. H. GRAY *Our Divine Sheph.* 55 The liar may get some momentary benefit..from his falsehood.

2. Of living beings: Short-lived; ephemeral.

1587 GREENE *Penelopes Web* C 2 b, Men are..the true disciples of tyme, and therefore momentarie. **1640** QUARLES *Enchirid.* II. c, How full of death is the miserable life of momentary Man. **1692** DRYDEN *Cleomenes* IV. i. 47, I wou'd have swopp'd Youth for old Age, and all my Life behind, To have been then a momentary Man. *a* **1762** LLOYD *Genius, Envy & T.* 99 Born like a momentary fly, To flutter, buzz about, and die. **1873** M. ARNOLD *Lit. & Dogma* (1876) p. xxxi, Truth more complete than the parcel of truth any momentary individual can seize.

3. *nonce-use.* Ready at the moment.

1725 POPE *Odyss.* XIV. 552 Hardly waking yet, Sprung in his mind the momentary wit.

4. Recurring or operative at every moment. Now *rare.*

1745 T. WARTON *Pleas. Melancholy* 210 Attentive mark The due clock swinging slow.., Measuring time's flight with momentary sound. **1799** E. DU BOIS *Piece Family Biog.* II. 112 A dealer in the fine arts in momentary fear of a spunging-house. **1806–7** J. BERESFORD *Miseries Hum. Life* (1826) I. Introd., What..are the senses but five yawning inlets to hourly and momentary molestations? **1869** GOULBURN *Purs. Holiness* viii. 92 God is not only the ground, but the momentary support, of all existence.

†**5.** Instant, instantaneous. *Obs.*

1799 E. DU BOIS *Piece Family Biog.* I. 21 An affair that demands a momentary decision. **1847** DISRAELI *Tancred* II. xi, I settled..that you were not to go away if anything occurred which required my momentary attention.

†**6.** *Math.* Pertaining to an infinitesimal portion of time. *Obs.*

1812–16 PLAYFAIR *Nat. Phil.* (1819) I. 23 The change which any variable quantity undergoes in an infinitely small portion of time, is called the Momentary Increment of that quantity. **1833** HERSCHEL *Astron.* xi. 323 Between the momentary change of inclination, and the momentary recess of the node there exists an intimate relation.

7. quasi-*adv.*: = MOMENTARILY 3.

1725 POPE *Odyss.* VIII. 227 She spoke; and momentary mounts the sky: The friendly voice Ulysses hears with joy.

†**'momentless,** *a. Obs. rare.* [f. MOMENT *sb.* + -LESS.] Having no foundation (see MOMENT *sb.* 5).

1633 AMES *Agst. Cerem.* II. 61 The Rejoynder forgetteth himself muche, when upon this uncertaine and momentlesse conjecture, he compareth the Replier to a hungrie creature.

momently ('məʊməntlɪ), *a. rare.* [f. MOMENT *sb.* + -LY[1].]

1. Occurring at every moment.

1641 J. JACKSON *True Evang. T.* II. 152 Moderne Christians, whose very lives are, in short, a dayly, horary, momently breaking of that great Euangelicall precept. **1867** MRS. WHITNEY *L. Goldthwaite* xii, He told them of God's momently thought and care.

2. Enduring for a moment.

1817 COLERIDGE *Satyrane's Lett.* i. in *Biog. Lit.*, etc. (1882) 245 A beautiful white cloud of foam at momently intervals coursed by the side of the vessel with a roar.

momently ('məʊməntlɪ), *adv.* [f. MOMENT *sb.* + -LY[2].]

1. From moment to moment; every moment.

1676 W. ROW *Contn. Blair's Autobiog.* ix. (1848) 144 Take up the sweet cross of Christ daily, hourly, yea momently. **1747** *Mem. Nutrebian Crt.* II. 79 Who was dearer to him than the vital blood that momently circulated in his heart. **1892** ZANGWILL *Childr. Ghetto* I. vii, Reb Shemuel's tone became momently more sing-song.

Comb. **1848** H. AINSWORTH *Lanc. Witches* I. ix, He.. whirled on with momently-increased velocity.

2. At any moment; on the instant.

1775 PRICE in *Phil. Trans.* LXVI. 113, I will next state the different values.. of life-annuities, according as they are supposed to be payable yearly, half-yearly, quarterly, or momently. *a* **1822** SHELLEY *Pericles* Ess. & Lett. (1886) 139 In the act of watching an event momently to arrive.

3. *nonce-use.* Instantly.

1824 HOGG *Conf. Sinner* 357, I was momently surrounded by a number of hideous fiends.

4. For the moment; for a single moment.

1868 GEO. ELIOT *Sp. Gipsy* 265 Thoughts.. look at me With awful faces, from the vanishing haze That momently had hidden them. **1892** *Spectator* 2 Apr. 451/1 The fall in the price of Silver, which this week momently touched 39*d.* an oz.,.. is creating genuine alarm. **1895** CROCKETT *Sweeth. Trav.* 157 The rain comes in furious dashes, and a chill blue blink looks momently through between.

momento (mə'mɛntəʊ), ? var. MEMENTO 3.

1871 GEO. ELIOT *Jrnl.* 19 Mar. in J. W. Cross *George Eliot's Life* (1885) III. xvi. 129 My present fear is that I have too much matter—too many *momenti.* **1951** DYLAN THOMAS *Let.* 12 Apr. (1966) 356 And the London frowsty Casino, a momento of which I enclose.

momentous (məʊ'mɛntəs), *a.* [f. MOMENT *sb.* + -OUS.]

†**1.** Having motive force. *Obs.*

1652 L. S. *People's Liberty* x. 18 In such particulars.., as are not momentous to the impairing of the publick welfare.

2. Of moment; of great weight, consequence, or importance; important, weighty.

1656 JEANES *Mixt. Schol. Div.* 15 There remaineth a second objection, which is the more momentous. *a* **1761** CAWTHORN *Poems* (1771) 202 Who.. could decide whene'er they met Momentous truths without a bett. **1844** THIRLWALL *Greece* VIII. lx. 77 His death forms a momentous epoch in Grecian history. **1874** GREEN *Short Hist.* vi. §6. 325 The ten years which follow the fall of Wolsey are among the most momentous in our history.

3. Of persons: Having influence or importance. Now *rare.*

1667 J. CORBET *Disc. Relig. Eng.* 2 The Roman-Catholicks in England,.. being Rich and Powerful,.. are very momentous, and seem to be capable of great Designs. **1824-9** LANDOR *Imag. Conv.* Wks. 1846 I. 464 Epaminondas was undoubtedly a momentous man, and formidable to Lacedæmon. **1898** G. B. SHAW *Plays* I. *Widower's Ho.* 13 Cokane, hardly less momentous than Sartorius himself, contemplates Trench with the severity of a judge.

†**4.** Pertaining to momentum. *Obs.*

1775 WHITEHURST in *Phil. Trans.* LXV. 278 It seems reasonable to infer, that the momentous force is much superior to the simple pressure of the column IK.

Hence **mo'mentously** *adv.*

1748 J. LIND *Lett. Navy* ii (1757) 73 A person may offend very notoriously and momentuously [*sic*]. **1880** KINGLAKE *Crimea* VI. ix. 250 Two or more courses of action momentously different.

momentousness (məʊ'mɛntəsnɪs). [-NESS.] The state or quality of being momentous.

1672 DODWELL in Baxter *Answ. Dodwell* (1681) 72 It may put them in mind of the greater momentousness of good Government and peace than many of their differences. **1752** CARTE *Hist. Eng.* III. 89 The momentousness of the affair. **1870** J. H. NEWMAN *Gram. Assent* II. x. 412 A conviction.. of the reality and momentousness of the unseen world. **1884** *Daily News* 11 Feb. 5/5 A matter of a momentousness so stupendous.

†**mo'mentual,** *a. Obs.* [irreg. f. MOMENT *sb.*, after *actual*, etc.] Having 'moment' or significance.

1613 SHERLEY *Trav. Persia* 53 Hauing gathered his intentions by very momentuall circumstances, hee gaue the King, from time to time, notice of them.

momentum (məʊ'mɛntəm). Pl. **-ta.** [a. L. *mōmentum*: see MOMENT *sb.*]

†**1.** = MOMENT 3 b. *Obs.*

1735 B. ROBINS *Disc. Newton's Meth. Fluxions* 75 Sir Isaac Newton's definition of momenta, That they are the momentaneous increments or decrements of varying quantities, may possibly be thought obscure.

†**2.** 'Impulsive weight' (J., s.v. *Moment*); force of movement. *Obs.*

1740 CHEYNE *Regimen* 109 The Particles of Mercury have the greatest Momentum and Force. **1754-64** SMELLIE *Midwif.* I. 107 In young people the Momentum of the circulating fluid is greater than the resisting force of the Solids. **1817** COLERIDGE '*Blessed are ye*' 84 The short interruptions may be well represented as a few steps backward, that it might leap forward with an additional momentum.

†**3.** *Mech.* = MOMENT *sb.* 8 b. *Obs.*

1839 *Penny Cycl.* XV. 311 *Momentum*, or *Moment, of Inertia.*

4. a. *Mech.* The 'quantity of motion' of a moving body; the product of the mass by the velocity of a body. ***angular momentum*** (see quot. 1870).

1699 KEILL *Exam. Refl. Th. Earth* 10 According to the Laws of motion, the momentum or quantity of motion of both bodies taken together would remain the same. **1727-41** CHAMBERS *Cycl.* s.v. *Moment*, In comparing the motions of bodies, the ratio of their momenta is always compounded of the quantity of matter, and the celerity of the moving body. **1870** EVERETT *Deschanel's Nat. Philos.* 75 The *angular momentum* of a rotating body is a name given to the product of the moment of inertia and the angular velocity. **1882** MINCHIN *Unipl. Kinemat.* 106 The momentum of a moving particle in any direction is defined to be the product of the number of units of mass in the particle and the number of units of velocity in its component of velocity in that direction.

b. Hence, in popular use, applied to the effect of inertia in the continuance of motion after the impulse has ceased; impetus gained by movement.

1860 TYNDALL *Glac.* I. xxvii. 216 His momentum rolled him over and over down the incline. **1874** H. R. REYNOLDS *John Bapt.* III. iii. 189 Every drop of the Nile or the Ganges has been.. lifted by the sunbeam to the height, the fall from which give the momentum of its onward passage to the sea.

Comb. **1880** C. & F. DARWIN *Movem. Pl.* 508 This momentum-like movement probably results from the accumulated effects of apogeotropism.

c. *fig.*

1782 V. KNOX *Ess.* I. lviii. 257 Such genius.. makes itself felt by its own native force, and bears all before it by an irresistible momentum. **1790** BURKE *Fr. Rev.* Wks. V. 100 That momentum of ignorance,.. presumption, and lust of plunder, which nothing has been able to resist. **1868** KINGLAKE *Crimea* (1877) III. i. §44. 308 Ambition lends strength and momentum to the purposes of a general. **1902** A. B. DAVIDSON *Bibl. & Lit. Ess.* vii. 188 Faustus Socinus gave a new momentum to the exposition of the Epistle.

5. = MOMENT *sb.* 9.

1829 SIR W. HAMILTON *Discuss.* (1852) 31 You have all the *momenta* whose relation and notion constitute the reality of knowledge. **1874** MORRIS tr. *Ueberweg's Hist. Philos.* II. 232 The momenta of Quantity are: pure quantity, quantum, and degree. **1903** A. B. DAVIDSON *O.T. Prophecy* viii. 114 Revelation.. was in all cases part of the life of the individual, a momentum in the spiritual relations of him and God.

6. Special Comb.: **momentum space** *Physics*, a three-dimensional space in which each particle of a physical system is represented by a point whose three Cartesian co-ordinates are numerically equal to the components of its momentum in the directions of the three co-ordinate axes.

1948 W. HUME-ROTHERY *Electrons, Atoms, Metals & Alloys* xx. 143 The momentum space is divided into little cells of side h/L, and volume h^3/L^3. **1970** I. E. MCCARTHY *Nuclear Reactions* I. v. 111 We consider the matrix element in momentum space. **1970** G. K. WOODGATE *Elem. Atomic Struct.* vi. 98 Under this assumption the electrons are moving freely, with no forces acting on them, and their translational momenta can be taken to be directed isotropically in momentum space.

momerie, -ry, obs. forms of MUMMERY.

momia, etc., obs. forms of MUMMY.

momie-cloth: see MUMMY-CLOTH 2.

momin, obs. variant of MAMMEE.

momiology (məʊmɪ'ɒlədʒɪ). [f. F. *momie* MUMMY: see -LOGY.] The science of mummies.

1894 *Athenæum* 3 Mar. 283/2 Even the history of the Egyptian dynasties is a department of momiology.

†**'momish,** *a. Obs.* [f. MOME *sb.*[2] + -ISH.] Resembling a 'mome' or fool.

1546 PHAER *Bk. Childr.* (1553) A ij, Snuffing at all that offendeth the noses of their momishe affections. **1592** BABINGTON *Comf. Notes Gen.* xii. §8 Cutting thereby and therein the combes of all such momish Monkes that [etc.].

†**'momism**[1]. *Obs. rare*—0. [f. MOM-US + -ISM.] Carping; fault-finding.

1611 COTGR., *Momerie*, momerie, momisme, carping, fault-finding. **1625** in MINSHEU *Ductor* (ed. 2) 471.

momism[2] ('mɒmɪz(ə)m). *U.S.* Also **Momism.** [f. MOM + -ISM.] Excessive attachment to, or domination by, the mother.

1942 P. WYLIE *Generation of Vipers* xi. 185 Hitherto.. man has shown a considerable qui vive to the dangers which arise from momism and freely perceived that his 'old wives' were often vixens, dragons, and xanthippes. *Ibid.* 197 The mealy look of men today is the result of momism and so is the pinched and baffled fury in the eyes of womankind. **1947** *Sat. Rev.* (U.S.) 18 Jan. 19/2 Philip Wylie's latest diatribe about momism is welcome since it frankly implies that men have relinquished their duties as fathers. **1958** *Times Lit. Suppl.* 17 Oct. 595/1 The great *condottiere* of the lodes was a victim of 'momism'. His mother, it seems, made marriage impossible. **1962** R. E. FITCH *Odyssey of Self-Centred Self* iv. 129 We reject the Father God, and turn to Mother Nature. This is metaphysical Momism. **1968** 'E. V. CUNNINGHAM' *Cynthia* (1969) ix. 117 You never made a real pass at me. You suffer from reverse Momism.

†**'momist.** *Obs.* [f. MOM-US + -IST.] A fault-finder.

1597 MORLEY *Introd. Mus.* Ded., Insulting momistes who think nothing true but what they doo themselues. **1619** HUTTON *Follie's Anat.* Epil. D 2 b, What Momists censure, or the roring sect; Be what it will, tis but their dialect. **1626** L. OWEN *Spec. Jesuit.* Ded. (1629) A ij b, All malignant Zoilysts, and biting Momists.

†**'momize,** *v. Obs.* [f. MOM-US + -IZE.] *intr.* To play the part of Momus; to cavil.

1654 WHITLOCK *Zootomia* Pref. a vj b, If Authors Carp (were not my Principle of Character otherwise) I could momize and cavil at Matter or Form.. of their Labours.

momlyng, obs. form of MUMBLING *sb.*

momma ('mɒmə). Also **Momma.** Chiefly U.S. var. of MAMMA (see the etym. note there). Also *attrib.* and *Comb.* Cf. MOM.

1884 *Century Mag.* Apr. 859/1 This incident.. illustrates the position of the 'momma' or 'mammy' in a Southern family in the olden time. **1895** *Harper's Mag.* Nov. 841/2 Do you think you'd catch anybody reading a contract wrong to old Meakum? Oh, momma! Why, he's king round here. **1929** *Amer. Speech* IV. 476 A final note may be added on the word *momma* 'negro nurse'... The term is associated with the negroes.. but is not an example of negro dialect, but rather of American English. **1939** L. M. MONTGOMERY *Anne of Ingleside* viii. 58 You're nothing but a sweet little girl. Momma's Pet! **1947** AUDEN *Age of Anxiety* (1948) v. 116 I've made their magic but their Momma Earth is His stone still. **1951** 'J. WYNDHAM' *Day of Triffids* ii. 43 How'd that be, Momma? **1960** G. W. TARGET *Teachers* 223 A real nice Yiddisher Momma. **1961** *John o' London's* 9 Nov. 519/2 Mommy is the all-American Momma-figure. **1970** G. GREER *Female Eunuch* 158 Baby-talk, even to the extent of calling.. the wife 'momma'. **1972** M. J. BOSSE *Incident at Naha* iii. 128 A real live trollop.. the last of the red-hot mommas. **1972** *Times* 29 Sept. 20/6 How well we have seen the result of this [price-] battle in the position of the small retailer, affectionately known as the 'Momma and Poppa shop'. **1973** *Black World* Apr. 57 My momma always set more places than there was folks to eat.

‖**momme** (mɒm, 'mɒmeɪ). Also 8 **mome, momi.** A Japanese measure of weight equal to 3·75 grammes.

1727 J. G. SCHEUCHZER tr. *Kæmpfer's Hist. Japan* I. IV. vii. 349 The yearly value of the *Cobanj*.. is from 55 to 59 *Mome*, or *Maas* in silver. *Ibid.* viii. 362 The highest value of the *Cobang*, as current in the country, is of sixty *Momi*, or *Maas*, of silver. **1868** in Seyd *Bullion* 265 The quantity of silver being coined daily.. was 50,000 momme. **1898** *Echo* 20 Jan. 1/6 Heyl gives the mommes as equal to 1.75 grammes, while the correct equivalent is 3.75 grammes. **1902** L. HEARN *Kottō* vii. 58, I have already been able to put by about one hundred *mommé* of silver. **1965** *Economist* 25 Dec. 1432/1 We buy gold by the—tael in Shanghai; momme in Tokyo; tola in Karachi; hong ping tael in Macao; and kilogram in Kabul. **1974** S. MARCUS *Minding the Store* (1975) ix. 184 This select 5% are not.. our best customers, but.. our most exacting ones. They know.. the difference between a silk scarf made of twelve-momme weight and one made of sixteen-momme.

momme chance, obs. form of MUMCHANCE.

mommer, mommet, mommie, -y: see MUMMER *sb.*, MAUMET, MUMMY.

mommy[1] ('mɒmɪ). *U.S. dial.* The long-tailed duck, *Harelda glacialis* (*Cent. Dict.* 1890).

Mommy, mommy[2] ('mɒmɪ). Chiefly *U.S.* Var. MAMMY and MUMMY *sb.*[2] Cf. MOM, MOMMA.

1902 in *Dialect Notes* II. 239. **1974** HAWKEY & BINGHAM *Wild Card* vi. 59 Mommy'll bring you a glass of water. **1975** *Listener* 18 Sept. 386/2 'You and Mommy are always with people,' she complains.

mommyng(e, obs. forms of MUMMING *sb.*

momordicin (məʊ'mɔːdɪsɪn). *Chem.* Also **-ine.** [f. mod.L. *Momordica* the balsam-apple (C. Durante *Herb. nov.*, 1585, ed. 1602 p. 59), now the name of a cucurbitaceous genus (Tournefort 1700) + -IN.] = ELATERIN.

1865 WATTS *Dict. Chem.* III. 1046. **1874** GARROD & BAXTER *Mat. Med.* (1880) 260 Elaterium contains an active principle, elaterine or momordicine.

†**mo'morsion.** *Obs. rare.* [Badly f. L. *momordī*, perfect of *mordēre* to bite, after MORSION.] = CORROSION 1 a.

1597 A. M. tr. *Guillemeau's Fr. Chirurg.* 51/1 As we have sayed of the momorsions or Bittes. **1599** —— tr. *Gabelhouer's Bk. Physicke* 20/1 They sensiblye perceave a momorsion, and corrosion in their Wombe.

momot, variant of MOTMOT.

‖**mompei, mompe** ('mɒmpeɪ). [Jap.] Baggy working trousers worn in Japan.

1947 J. MORRIS *Phoenix Cup* II. 24 Most of the women wear *mompei*, rather ugly baggy trousers normally worn only

when working in the fields. **1959** R. K. Beardsley et al. *Village Japan* v. 101 For field work, women wear a surplice-cut blouse of dark cotton work cloth tucked into roomy, gathered-ankle field trousers (*mompei*) of similar material. **1960** B. Leach *Potter in Japan* v. 109 To keep moderately clean, I wear a pair of Hamada's 'mompei' (baggy overall trousers) and rubber boots. **1965** W. Swaan *Jap. Lantern* xix. 224 The bending figures in their *mompe* or baggy trousers. **1972** *Nat. Geographic* May 672/2 Groups of women in *mompe*, the traditional baggy work trousers worn in rural areas, shifted the seaweed by hand.

mompyn, obs. variant of MUMPING *sb.*[1]

†**'mompyns**, *sb. pl. Obs.* Also **mone pynnes**. [f. **mone*, MUN mouth + PIN.] The teeth.

c **1430** Lydg. *Min. Poems* (Percy Soc.) 30 Thy mone pynnes bene lyche old yvory. *c* **1460** *Towneley Myst.* xii. 210 Syrs, let vs cryb furst for oone thyng or oder, That thise wordis be purst, and let vs go foder Oure mompyns.

momser, momza, momzer, varr. MAMZER.

†**'momurdotes**, *sb. pl. Obs.* [f. ME. **momur* = MAMMER *v.* + DOTE *sb.* (cf. DORT *sb.* and *cankerdort* Chaucer *Troil. & Cr.* II. 1572).] Sulks.

c **1400** *Destr. Troy* 9089 (*heading*), The Solempnite of The Obit of Ector, And How Achilles Fell in þe Momurdotes for Luff.

‖**Momus** ('məʊməs). *Myth.* Occas. *pl.* 7 **Momi**, **Momusses**, 8 **Momus's**. [L. *Mōmus*, Gr. Μῶμος, personification of μῶμος ridicule.] A Greek divinity, the god of ridicule, who for his censures upon the gods was banished from heaven; hence, a fault-finder, a captious critic. ***a daughter, disciple, son of Momus***, a facetious or humorously disagreeable person; a wag, a buffoon.

Often in allusions to the story (Lucian *Herm.* xx, Babrius lix) that when Hephaistos (or Zeus) had made a man, Momus blamed him for not having put a window in his breast.

1563 J. Hall in T. Gale *Enchirid.* A iiij, But maugre nowe the malice great of Momus and his sect. **1579** Fulke *Refut. Rastel* 710 The sentence is wel inough placed, if Momus could let any thing alone. *a* **1586** Sidney *Apol. Poetrie* (Arb.) 72 If you.. by a certaine rusticall disdaine, will become such a Mome, as to be a *Momus* of Poetry. **1601** Holland *Pliny* Pref. to Rdr., Certes, such *Momi* as these.. thinke not so honourably of their native countrey and mother tongue as they ought. **1605** Bacon *Adv. Learn.* II. xxiii. 14 That window which Momus did require. **1624** Sanderson *Serm.* (1674) I. 223 A fault more pardonable, if our censures stayed at the works of men, like our selves; and Momus-like, we did not quarrel the works of God also. **1669** Sturmy *Mariner's Mag.* a ij, The Rules.. in the following Treatise, are most exact.., though much more abused by ignorant Momus and his Mates..; I say, such Momusses will have their.. Tails lash'd by the Devils. **1709** Swift *Trit. Ess.* Wks. 1751 IV. 180 Those carping Momus's, whom Authors worship as the Indians do the Devil, for fear. **1822** Byron *Werner* III. i, Were Momus' lattice in your breasts, My soul might brook to open it more widely Than theirs. **1835** *Court Mag.* VI. 184/1 Th——e H—k, the momus of the social, the literary and the political world! **1848** Dickens *Dombey* viii, 'I do not think.. that Wickam is a person of very cheerful spirits, or what one would call a——' 'A daughter of Momus', Miss Tox softly suggested. **1860** Ruskin *Mod. Paint.* V. IX. x. §7. 306 'Momus', the Spirit of Blame.

momy, momyan: see MUMMY.

‖**mon** (mɒn), *sb.*[1] [Japanese.] A family crest or badge. (Frequently used in decorative design.)

1878 Mrs. B. Palliser tr. *Jacquemart's Hist. Furniture* 457 Of these princely [Japanese] families we shall give the 'mon' or arms most frequently occurring.

Mon (məʊn), *sb.*[2] and *a.* Also **Moan, Mun, Mwun**. [Native name.] **A.** *sb.* A people of Indo-Chinese origin, also called TALAING, now inhabiting eastern Burma and western Thailand but having their ancient capital at Pegu in southern Burma; a member of this people. Also, their language. **B.** *adj.* Of or pertaining to the Mon. Cf. MON-KHMER.

1798 F. Buchanan in *Asiatick Researches* V. 235 To the kingdom, the natives of which call themselves Moan, we have given the name of Pegu, a corruption of the vulgar appellation of its capital city Bagoo. **1828** J. Crawfurd *Jrnl. Embassy to Siam & Cochin China* xv. 448 Of the Mon, or Pegu, race, although the Siamese be in possession of no part of their territory, there are a considerable number in Siam. **1854** F. Mason in *Jrnl. Amer. Oriental Soc.* IV. 284 *Moan*, the name by which the Talaings now call themselves. **1873** *Jrnl. Asiatic Soc. Bengal* XLII. 34 The people of Pegu.. call themselves Mun, Mwun, or Mon... The Burmese, since the conquest of Pegu.. in 1757–58, had strongly discouraged the use of the Mun language. **1877** [see ANNAMITE *a.* and *sb.*]. **1881** C. J. F. S. Forbes *Compar Gram. Languages of Further India* iv. 49 In three savage and more primitive dialects we find further traces of affinity with the Mon. **1907** V. C. S. O'Connor *Mandalay* IV. ii. 400 Under Binya Dala a strenuous effort was made by the Môn people to recover their ancient ascendency in Burma, and restore the glories of Pegu. **1939** L. H. Gray *Foundations of Lang.* xii. 393 *Mōn-Khmēr* has six sub-divisions: Central (Mōn or Talaing, Khmēr or Cambodian, Bahuar, etc.). *Ibid.* 394 The earliest Mōn inscription is of 1084 (?). **1948** D. Diringer *Alphabet* vii. 410 The early Mon character was not only the ancestor of the modern Mon script, but also of the Burmese and some Shan characters. **1962** *Listener* 25 Oct. 646/2 U Nu proposed to.. create separate states for the Mon and Arakanese peoples. **1971** *National Geographic* Mar. 356 Masterpieces of lacquer ware... The craft may have originated in China and spread across Southeast Asia to the Mons, who brought the technique to the capital. **1972** W. B. Lockwood *Panorama Indo-Europ. Lang.* 228 The group [*sc.* Mon-Khmer] takes its name from two of its members: Mon, the vernacular of the coastal districts round the Gulf of Martaban between Rangoon and Moulmein, and Khmer or Cambodian, the state language of Cambodia.

mon, mun (mʌn), *sb.*[3] Colloq. abbrev. of MONEY *sb.*

1895 W. C. Gore in *Inlander* Nov. 64 *Mon*,.. money. **1896** W. C. Gore *Student Slang* 7 *Mun*,.. money. *a* **1911** D. G. Phillips *Susan Lenox* (1917) II. v. 119 In little old New York.. you've got to have the mon. or you get.. the swift, hard, kick. **1958** A. Wilson *Middle Age of Mrs. Eliot* II. 122 *I'm* only going because she's got lots of lovely 'mon' and might leave it to me. **1959** M. Steen *Tower* II. i. 147 You'll adore Kendall—American—tons and tons of lovely *mun*! **1963** 'J. Bell' *Flat Tyre in Fulham* iii. 30 All that good 'mon' down the drain. **1968** J. N. Chance *Rogue Aunt* v. 86 'You should write little tabs, and tie them on,' said Clara... 'Tabs corsts mun,' said Barnskin. **1974** *Sunday Times* 22 Dec. 12/7 They were in this gambling club and he won lots and lots of lovely mun.

mon: see MAN *sb.*[1], MAN *indef. pron. Obs.*, MOAN, MONE *sb.* and *v. Obs.*, MOON, MUN *v.*

mona ('məʊnə). [a. Sp., Pg., It. *mona* monkey (whence the mod.L. specific name).] A small, long-tailed African monkey, *Cercopithecus mona*.

1774 Goldsm. *Nat. Hist.* (1824) II. 157 The fifth [of M. Buffon's species of African monkeys] is the Mona..: it is distinguished by its colour, which is variegated with black and red; and its tail is of an ash colour, with two white spots on each side at its insertion. **1874** Wood *Nat. Hist.* i. 47 All the long-tailed African monkeys are termed Monas by the Moors. **1897** H. O. Forbes *Handbk. Primates* II. 66 The Mona Guenon. *Cercopithecus mona*.

monacal: see MONACHAL.

monacanthid (mɒnə'kænθɪd), *a. Zool.* [f. Gr. μονάκανθος (f. μόνο-ς MONO- + ἄκανθα spine) + -ID.] Of a starfish: Having the ambulacral spines in a single row.

1890 *Century Dict.*

monacetin (mɒ'næsɪtɪn). *Chem.* Also **monoacetin**. [MONO- 2.] (See ACETIN.)

1856 *Fownes' Chem.* (ed. 6) 607 With acetic acid.. it [glycerin] forms three combinations,—monacetin, diacetin, and triacetin. **1869** Roscoe *Chem.* (1874) 386 Mono-acetin.

†**monach(e**. *Obs. rare.* [ad. L. *monach-us* MONK.] An affected substitute for 'monk'.

c **1540** tr. *Pol. Verg. Eng. Hist.* (Camden) 129 Augustine and Miletus, two monaches of sownde livinge. **1611** H. Broughton *Require of Agreement* 62 Fuller of eyes then all the Bridge-maker monaches to this day.

monachal, monacal ('mɒnəkəl), *a.* Forms: 7 **monac(h)all**, 7– **monachal**, 8– **monacal**. [ad. eccl.L. *monachāl-is*, f. *monach-us* MONK. Cf. F. *monacal* (16th c. Hatz.-Darm.).] Of, pertaining to, or characteristic of a monk or of monastic life; monastic; monkish.

1587 T. Rogers 39 *Art.* (1625) 166 Papists, who.. make the vowe and profession of the Monachall, or life of a Monck, as good a token of Christians, as Baptisme. **1632** Lithgow *Trav.* II. 76 This monachall and licentious life. **1685** Lovell *Gen. Hist. Relig.* 159 There are no Monachal Constitutions that so much oblige Monks to obey their Superiour, as [etc.]. **1726** Ayliffe *Parergon* 368 If a child.. has taken on himself the Monachal or Monkish Tonsure. **1841** *Blackw. Mag.* XLIX. 374 Under every creed, monachal austerity and seclusion had been attempted. **1889** Farrar *Lives Fathers* II. xvi. 237 Jerome seems to have had the monacal feelings which led him wholly to avoid the society of women.

monachate ('mɒnəkət). *rare*[−1]. [ad. L. *monachāt-us*, f. *monachus*: see MONK and -ATE[1].] The period of life passed as a monk.

1819 Dugdale *Monast. Angl.* II. 94/1 Abbat Turketul.. died, in his sixty-eighth year, and the twenty-seventh of his monachate.

monachism ('mɒnəkɪz(ə)m). [f. L. *monach-us* MONK + -ISM. Cf. F. *monachisme*.]

1. The mode or rule of life distinctive of monks and nuns; the monastic system or principle; monasticism.

1577 Holinshed *Descr. Brit.* vii. 11/2 Augustine.. thinking this sufficient for.. the stablishment of hys monachisme. **1615** W. Hull *Mirr. Maiestie* 41 Popish Monachisme desineth and confineth profession of religion, to bare contemplation and meditation. **1726** Ayliffe *Parergon* 375 From the time of King Edgar, to the Reign of Henry viii, Monachism had been growing here in England. **1862** *Macm. Mag.* Sept. 370 Monachism.. separates the duty of charity from domestic duty, making the one the task of the nun alone, and the other of the wife and mother. **1876** J. H. Newman *Hist. Sk.* II. I. v. 97 Monachism became.. nothing else than a peculiar department of the Christian ministry.

†**2.** A monkish characteristic. *Obs.*

1670 Milton *Hist. Brit.* Wks. 1738 II. 70 Florence of Worcester, Huntingdon, Simeon of Durham,.. with all their Monachisms.

monachist ('mɒnəkɪst), *a.* [f. eccl.L. *monach-us* MONK + -IST.] Favouring monachism.

1860 Ruskin *Mod. Paint.* V. IX. ix. §11. 295, I do not find in Giorgione's work any of the early Venetian monachist element.

monachi'zation. *rare*[−1]. [f. next + -ATION.] The action or event of becoming a monk.

1813 J. Forsyth *Rem. Excurs. Italy* 260 A sonnet ready for every occasion, such as births,.. monachization, death.

monachize ('mɒnəkaɪz), *v.* [f. L. *monach-us* MONK + -IZE.] **a.** *intr.* To live the life of a monk; to become a monk. **b.** *trans.* To make (persons) monks.

1884 Ornsby *Mem. Hope-Scott* I. 179 Individuals.. were soon attempting to monachize, and to live as they thought that men in their places would have lived in the olden days. **1896** *Dublin Rev.* July 222 The large share taken by Teuton women in the works of conversion and monachising.

Monacholite, blundered form of MONOTHELITE.

monacid (mɒ'næsɪd), *a. Chem.* Also **monoacid**. [MONO- 2.] Having the power of saturating one molecule of a monobasic acid.

1862 Hofmann in *Proc. Roy. Soc.* XII. 7 Water decomposes them with reproduction of the monacid compound. **1863** *Fownes' Chem.* (ed. 9) 494 The mono-acid ethers. **1866** Frankland in *Jrnl. Chem. Soc.* XIX. 385 The monacid alcohols.

monack: see MOONACK.

monacord(e, obs. forms of MONOCHORD.

monact (mɒ'nækt), *a.* and *sb.* [Shortened from MONACTINE.] **a.** *adj.* = next. **b.** *sb.* A sponge-spicule consisting of only one ray (*Cent. Dict.* 1890).

1885 tr. F. E. Schulze in *Rep. Sci. Results Voy. H.M.S. Challenger, Zool.* XXI. 29 It seems to me, however, that those spicules, called by Carter 'Clavulæ'.. are really monacts. *Ibid.* 37 The derived nature of a monact spicule is in many cases determinable.

monactinal (mɒ'næktɪnəl), *a.* [Formed as next + -AL[1].] Of a sponge-spicule: That has only one ray.

1887 S. O. Ridley in *Rep. Voy. Challenger* XX. Introd. 6 The chief spicules of the group are 'monactinal', that is to say, consisting of only a single ray.

monactine (mɒ'næktɪn), *a.* [f. (mod.L. type **monactin-us*) Gr. μόνο-ς (see MONO-) + ἀκτιν-, ἀκτίς ray.] = MONACTINAL *a.*

1887 W. J. Sollas in *Encycl. Brit.* XXII. 416 (Fig. 12), Typical megascleres. *a*, rhabdus (monaxon diactine); *b*, stylus (monaxon monactine).

monactinellid (mɒnæktɪ'nɛlɪd), *sb.* and *a.* [ad. mod.L. *Monactinellidæ* sb. pl. (see below), formed as MONACTINE + *-ella* dim. suffix + *idæ*: see -ID.] **a.** *sb.* A sponge of the sub-order or group *Monactinellidæ*, characterized by the presence of uni-axial spicules. **b.** *adj.* Of or pertaining to this sub-order or group. So **monacti'nellidan** *a.* = prec. adj.

1883 Carter in *Ann. Nat. Hist.* Ser. v. XI. 32 The great number of existing Monactinellid sponges. **1884** *Riverside Nat. Hist.* (1888) I. 67 The Monactinellidan forms in the palæozoic rocks are uncertain. **1885** Hinde in *Phil. Trans.* CLXXVI. 434 Those monactinellids whose skeletons are exclusively composed of uniaxial spicules.

monad ('mɒnæd). Also 7 **monade**. [a. L. *monad-*, *monas* unit, ad. Gr. μονάς unit, f. μόνος alone. Cf. F. *monade*, Sp., Pg. *monada*, It. *monade*.]

1. a. The number one, unity; an arithmetical unit. Now only *Hist.* with reference to the Pythagorean or other Greek philosophies, in which numbers were regarded as real entities, and as the primordial principles of existence.

1615 G. Sandys *Trav.* 144 [tr. *Sibyl. Orac.* I. i.] Eight monads, decads eight, eight hecatons Declare his name [*sc.* ΙΗΣΟΥΣ = 888]. **1649** G. Daniel *Trinarch., Hen. V*, cclv, Numbers carrie Their Preiudice, but Monads never varie. **1660** Stanley *Hist. Philos.* IX. (1687) 523/2 They make a difference betwixt the Monad and One, conceiving the Monad to be that which exists in Intellectuals; One in numbers. *Ibid.* 525/1 The Monad is a quantity, which in the decrease of multitude, receiveth mansion and station; for below Quantity, Monad [*read* below Monad, Quantity] cannot retreat. **1678** Cudworth *Intell. Syst.* I. iv. 372 The Cause of that Sympathy, Harmony, and Agreement, which is in things,.. was by Pythagoras called Vnity or a Monade. **1706** J. Matthews *Forgiveness* To Rdr., They fram'd up a whole decad of frivolous depositions, without one entire monad of truth. **1875** Jowett *Plato* (ed. 2) I. 485 Instead of saying that oddness is the cause of odd numbers, you will say that the monad is the cause of them.

b. applied to the Deity.

1642 H. More *Song of Soul* II. iii. III. xii, One steddy Good, centre of essencies, Unmoved Monad, that Apollo hight. **1678** Cudworth *Intell. Syst.* I. iv. 225 That which was called by them [*sc.* the Platonists and Pythagoreans] the τὸ ἓν or μονὰς, Unity itself or a Monad—that is, one most simple Deity. **1841** D'Israeli *Amen. Lit.* III. 233 He [Robert Fludd] reveals the nature of the Divine Being, as 'a pure monad, including in itself all numbers'. **1850** Daubeny *Atom. Th.* xiv. (ed. 2) 451 The monad is used to signify the

Deity, as being the first great Cause, one and the same, throughout all space, and in all time. **1870** J. H. NEWMAN *Gram. Assent* I. iv. 49 But of the Supreme Being it is safer to use the word 'monad' than unit.

2. An ultimate unit of being; an absolutely simple entity. Also *attrib.*

Chiefly used with reference to the philosophy of Leibniz (1646–1716), according to which the universe of existence consists of entities without parts, extension, or figure, and possessing, in infinitely various degrees, the power of perception. Those among these 'monads' which have the perceptive power in the higher degrees are souls; the rest are formed in the view of the percipient mind into aggregates, which constitute bodies. The term was adopted by Leibniz from Giordano Bruno (*d.* 1600), with whom the 'monad' has the twofold aspect of a material atom and an ultimate element of psychical existence.

1748 HARTLEY *Observ. Man* II. i. 27 No Sensation can be a Monad, inasmuch as the most simple are infinitely divisible in respect of Time. **1785** REID *Intell. Powers* III. iv. 345 A person is something indivisible, and is what Leibnitz calls a monad. **1856** SIR B. BRODIE *Psychol. Inq.* I. ii. 38 The conscious indivisible monad which I feel myself to be. **1874** MORRIS tr. *Ueberweg's Hist. Philos.* §111 II. 27 Bruno opposes the doctrine of a dualism of matter and form... The elementary parts of all that exists are the minima or monads, ..they are at once psychical and material. The soul is a monad... God is the monad of monads. **1879** HUXLEY *Hume* iii. 81 The possibility that the mind is a Leibnitzian monad. *a* **1914** C. S. PEIRCE *Coll. Papers* (1931) I. 146, I therefore divide all objects into monads, dyads, and triads; and the first step in the present inquiry is to ascertain what are the conceptions of the pure monad, free from all dyadic and triadic admixtures. *Ibid.* ii. 149 Now in order to convert that psychological or logical conception into a metaphysical one, we must think of a metaphysical monad as a pure nature, or quality, in itself without parts or features, and without embodiment. **1929** R. BRIDGES *Test. Beauty* i. 19 It was no flaw In Leibnitz to endow his monad-atoms with Mind. **1937** [see ACTIO IN DISTANS]. **1965** *New Statesman* 18 June 942/2, I had been very impressed, wandering around housing estates, at the growth of what..seemed 'monad' politics... People didn't connect, except through mass media, but found images difficult to accept as reality.

transf. **1862** *Q. Rev.* Apr. 402 The wealth, the might..of the British empire are due not to the mere aggregation and activity of monads or units of mankind [etc.].

3. *Biol.* A hypothetical simple organism, assumed in evolutionary speculations as the first term in the genealogy of living beings, or regarded as associated with a multitude of similar organisms to form an animal or vegetable body.

1835 KIRBY *Hab. & Inst. Anim.* I. Introd. 24 Thus [according to Lamarck], by consequence, in the lapse of ages a monad becomes a man!!! **1847** TULK tr. *Oken's Physiophilos.* 570 Decomposition is a separation into Monads, a retrogression into the primary mass of the animal kingdom. **1851** H. SPENCER *Soc. Stat.* xxx. 451 We are warranted in considering the body as a commonwealth of monads, each of which has independent powers of life, growth, and reproduction. **1880** BASTIAN *Brain* 10 The encysted mass of living matter may after a time divide into a swarm of smaller though most active monads.

4. *Zool.* A protozoon of the genus *Monas*, or, more widely, of the older *Monadidea* or the class *Flagellata*.

1836–9 R. OWEN *Entozoa* in *Todd's Cycl. Anat.* II. 133/2 Some species of the Trematode Entozoa are infested by parasitic *Polygastrica* which belong to the Monads. **1846** MANTELL *Th. Animalcules* 38 The monads we have just examined are single, free animalcules. **1847–9** R. JONES *Polygastria* in *Todd's Cycl. Anat.* IV. 7/1 The genus *Uvella* ..somewhat resembles a transparent mulberry rolling itself about at will, whence the name 'grape monad', which these animalcules bear.

5. *Chem.* An element or radical which has the combining power of one atom of hydrogen.

1869 ROSCOE *Elem. Chem.* (1874) 172 The elements of the first group combine atom for atom with hydrogen, they are monovalent elements or monads. *Ibid.* 264 Thallium is a monad in the thallious compounds.

6. *attrib.* and *Comb.* **a.** *Biol.*, as ***monad-deme*** (see DEME² 2), ***-form***; ***monad-like*** adj. **b.** *Chem.*, as ***monad atom, element, radical***.

a. 1842 PRITCHARD *Hist. Infusoria* 89 Separate Monad-like bodies. **1846** DANA *Zooph.* i. (1848) 7 *note*, Monad-like in their motions. **1874** *Monthly Jrnl. Microsc. Soc.* XII. 261 The minute monad-forms found in macerations of fish.

b. 1869 ROSCOE *Elem. Chem.* (1874) 172 Each atom.. requires two monad atoms for saturation. *Ibid.* 175 The monad elements unite amongst themselves to form only few and simple compounds. **1873** RALFE *Phys. Chem.* Introd. 26 From all dibasic acids a monad as well as a diad radical may be derived.

7. quasi-*adj.* = MONADIC. **a.** Of or pertaining to the monadic constitution of matter; **b.** *Chem.* That has the atomic constitution of a monad.

1846 DANA *Zooph.* vii. (1848) 107 These remarks are intended to support no monad or Lamarckian theory. **1866** ODLING *Anim. Chem.* 16 Monad, dyad, and triad combinations. **1878** LOCKYER *Spect. Anal.* (ed. 2) 124 Many monad metals give us their line spectra at a low degree of heat.

monadary ('mɒnədərɪ). [ad. mod.L. *monadārium*, f. *monas*: see MONAD and -ARY¹ B. 2.] The outer covering or envelope of an assemblage of monads. So also **mo'nadiary**, in the same sense.

1847–9 R. JONES *Polygastria* in *Todd's Cycl. Anat.* IV. 7/2 Several genera composed of numerous Monads, associated together and connected by a common envelope, which constitutes a kind of compound polypary or monadary, as it has been recently called. **1880** PASCOE *Zool. Classif.* (ed. 2) 283 *Monadiary*.

‖**Monadelphia** (mɒnə'dɛlfɪə). *Bot.* [mod.L. (Linnæus 1735), f. Gr. μόνος one + ἀδελφ-ός brother + -IA¹.] The sixteenth class in the Linnæan Sexual System, comprising plants with hermaphroditic flowers having the stamens united in one bundle.

1753 CHAMBERS *Cycl. Supp.*, *Monadelphia*,..a class of plants whose stamina or male parts, by reason of their filaments running in among one another, are all formed into one body. **1785** MARTYN *Rousseau's Bot.* ix. (1794) 92 In the sixteenth class, called *monadelphia*, the filaments are united so as to form one regular membrane at bottom.

Hence **'monadelph**, a plant of this class; **mona'delphian** *a.* = next. (1828–32 Webster.)

monadelphous (mɒnə'dɛlfəs), *a. Bot.* [Formed as prec. + -OUS.] **a.** Of stamens: Having the filaments united so as to form one bundle. **b.** Of plants: Having the stamens monadelphous; belonging to the *Monadelphia*.

1806 GALPINE *Brit. Bot.* §321 Stam[ina] all connected, or monadelphous. **1830** LINDLEY *Nat. Syst. Bot.* Introd. 28 The stamens..are monadelphous in Malvaceæ and Meliaceæ. **1870** HOOKER *Stud. Flora* 397.

monadiary, variant of MONADARY.

monadic (mɒ'nædɪk), *a.* [ad. Gr. μοναδικός composed of units, f. μοναδ-, μονάς MONAD.]

1. a. Composed of monads or units; pertaining to or of the nature of a monad; existing singly. Also quasi-*sb.*, that which is composed of units.

1788 T. TAYLOR *Proclus* I. Diss. 14 The monadic, or that which is composed from certain units, they justly considered as nothing more than the image of essential number. **1839** BAILEY *Festus* xxvii. (1852) 467 In this fatal life There is no real union. All things here Seem of monadic nature. **1858** J. HADLEY *Ess.* (1873) 342 So, too, we have the seven openings of the head, the three twin pairs of eyes, ears, and nostrils, with the monadic mouth to make the seventh. **1872** BROWNING *Fifine* xlviii, What does it give for germ, monadic mere intent Of mind in face? **1873** *Contemp. Rev.* XXII. 45 Personality, self-consciousness, and freedom of the will, is rather the power of breaking through the limits of relative monadic existence, of expanding into the infinite by consciousness and will. **1875** J. H. NEWMAN *Let. Dk. Norfolk* 27 We cannot take as much as we please, and no more, of an institution which has a monadic existence.

b. *Philos.* Of a proposition, fact, function, etc., or the predicate contained therein, when the predicate is non-relational and applies to only one subject term.

1897 C. S. PEIRCE in *Monist* VII. 167 A non-relative name with a substantive verb, as '—is a man',..has one blank; it is a *monad*, or *monadic relative*. **1921** W. E. JOHNSON *Logic* I. 203 The number of substantival references are respectively one, two, three and four, and the corresponding adjectives or propositions may be called monadic, diadic, triadic and tetradic. **1939** *Mind* XLVIII. 486 It appears sometimes to be assumed that the elementary statement must be monadic, *i.e.*, must have the form of a one-termed predicate, ϕx. **1946** C. MORRIS *Signs, Language & Behavior* iii. 78 'Black' is in this sense *monadic*... 'Deer' and 'black' are both monadic... But it would often be added that 'deer' designates an object and 'black' a quality of an object. **1956** J. O. URMSON *Philos. Analysis* ii. 17 A fact in which a particular has some absolutely simple and determinate characteristic was known as a monadic fact. **1963** W. W. LAMBERT in S. Koch *Psychol.* VI. 177 Most studies in general experimental psychology are carried out in terms of a monadic rather than a dyadic character. **1965** HUGHES & LONDEY *Elem. of Formal Logic* xxxix. 274 Such a schema might contain only monadic predicate variables (e.g. 'fx ⊃ gy').

2. *Chem.* Of the nature of a monad; univalent.

1877 WATTS *Fownes' Chem.* (ed. 12) I. 262 Potassium forms only one chloride, KCl, and is therefore univalent or monadic.

3. Relating to monadism.

1862 MAURICE *Mor. & Met. Philos.* IV. viii. §72. 517 Leibnitz, whose monadic tendencies may have placed him ..at no very great distance from his opponent. **1874** MORRIS tr. *Ueberweg's Hist. Philos.* §121 II. 145 Kant..brings the monadic nearer to the atomistic doctrine.

monadical (mɒ'nædɪkəl), *a.* [f. prec. + -AL¹.] Of the nature of a monad; pertaining to a monad or monads.

1642 H. MORE *Song of Soul* II. i. III. xxiv, All here depend on the Orb Unitive, Which also hight Nature Monadicall. **1678** CUDWORTH *Intell. Syst.* I. iv. 556 Henadical (or Monadical) Gods, and Intellectual Gods. **1875** McCOSH *Scott. Philos.* xl. 282 The monadical theory of Leibnitz.

Hence **mo'nadically** *adv.*

1794 T. TAYLOR tr. *Plotinus* Introd. 39 It is said..that.. every number subsists monadically in unity. **1934** *Proc. Brit. Acad.* XIX. 71 Thus, Carnap holds, if we insist that protocol propositions must refer to content, then each protocol-language can be used only *monadically*. **1950** W. V. QUINE *Methods of Logic* (1952) §23. 130 A capital letter occurs monadically, i.e., with variables attached singly.

monadiform (mɒ'nædɪfɔːm), *a. Biol.* [f. MONAD: see -FORM.] Having the form of a monad.

1862 G. KEARLEY *Links in Chain* i. 9 The *Gonium pectorale*, commonly called the High Priest's Breast-plate.. consists of a combination of sixteen monadiform bodies, disposed regularly in a four-cornered tablet. **1866** [see next]. **1877** HUXLEY *Anat. Inv. Anim.* ii. 96 In Bicosœca..a fixed monadiform body is enclosed within a structureless and transparent calyx. **1885** E. R. LANKESTER in *Encycl. Brit.* XIX. 837/2 A very large number of Gymnomyxa produce spores which are termed 'monadiform', that is, have a single or sometimes two filaments of vibratile protoplasm extended from their otherwise structureless bodies.

monadigerous (mɒnə'dɪdʒərəs), *a. Zool.* Bearing or composed of monads.

1866 JAMES-CLARK in *Mem. Boston Soc. Nat. Hist.* I. 325 The monadigerous layer lines the cavity of the body... This layer is composed of monadiform animalcules packed closely side by side in a vast colony.

monadine ('mɒnədɪn), *a.* and *sb.* [ad. mod. L. *monadīnus* (Ehrenberg), f. *monad-* MONAD.]

a. *adj.* Of or pertaining to the monads or *Flagellata*. **b.** *sb.* A protozoon belonging to this class.

1847–9 R. JONES *Polygastria* in *Todd's Cycl. Anat.* IV. 7/2 The..group of animalcules belonging to the Monadine type. *Ibid.* 9/2 A proboscidiform mouth similar to that possessed by the Monadines of Volvox. **1881** CARPENTER *Microsc. & Rev.* (ed. 6) §418 Monadine forms.

So **mona'dinic** *a.*, of or belonging to the monadine family.

1885 CUNNINGHAM in *Sci. Mem. Med. Officers India* I. 11 Crowded with infusorial, monadinic, and schizomycete forms. *Ibid.* 29 The development..of some Monadinic organism.

monadism ('mɒnədɪz(ə)m). [f. MONAD + -ISM.] The theory of the monadic nature of matter or of substance generally; the philosophical doctrine of monads, esp. as formulated by Leibniz.

1875 J. CLERK MAXWELL in *Encycl. Brit.* III. 37/2 Of the different forms of the atomic theory, that of Boscovich may be taken as an example of the purest monadism. **1877** E. CAIRD *Philos. Kant* Introd. v. 81 We must free Monadism from the slough of ordinary Atomism, which, with Leibnitz, it never completely cast off. **1886** SYMONDS *Renaiss. It., Cath. React.* (1898) VII. ix. 78 [Bruno] supplied..Leibnitz with his theory of monadism.

monadist ('mɒnədɪst). Also **Monadist**. [f. MONAD + -IST.] A follower of monadism; Leibniz himself.

1855 J. M. D. MEIKLEJOHN tr. *Kant's Critique Pure Reason* 274/2 Against the assertion of the infinite sub-divisibility of matter..objections have been alleged by the Monadists. **1900** B. RUSSELL *Crit. Exposition Leibniz* §78. 136 A Monadist must, with Leibniz, maintain the mutual independence of substances. **1932** *Mind* XLI. 518 Leibniz ..the great Monadist.

monadistic (mɒnə'dɪstɪk), *a.* [f. MONAD + -ISTIC.] Pertaining to monadism.

1891 in *Syd. Soc. Lex.* **1903** B. RUSSELL *Princ. Math.* IV. xxvi. 221 Given, say, the proposition *aRb*, where *R* is some relation, the monadistic view will analyse this into two propositions..ar_1 and br_2. **1906** *Hibbert Jrnl.* Oct. 197 The theory of monadistic idealism. **1917** A. S. PRINGLE-PATTISON *Idea of God* ix. 179 On this monadistic theory, the organic vesture of the spirit and its environmental conditions are both resolved into innumerable quasi-spiritual centres. **1937** *Mind* XLVI. 275 He rejects a pantheist version of the Absolute in favour of a monadistic one. **1941** D. H. PARKER *Experience & Substance* xvii. 348 The merits of a monadistic as opposed to a holistic interpretation of the 'wisdom of the body'.

monadite ('mɒnədaɪt). *rare*⁻¹. [f. MONAD + -ITE.] One who believes in monadism.

1753 tr. *Genard's School of Man* 38, I close with the Monadites, and with them affirm that matter cannot absolutely think.

monadity (mɒ'nædɪtɪ). *rare*⁻¹. [f. MONAD + -ITY.] Monadic state or condition.

1844 MRS. BROWNING *Lett. to Horne* II. 31 All truth is assimilative, and perhaps even reducible to that monadity of which Parmenides discoursed.

monadnock (mə'nædnɒk). *Geomorphol.* [The name of a mountain in New Hampshire, U.S.A., having this character.] A hill or mountain of erosion-resistant rock rising above a peneplain.

The place-name appears in Melville's *Moby Dick* (1851), 'his great, Monadnock hump'.

1893 W. M. DAVIS in *Nat. Geogr. Mag.* V. 70 The continuity of the plateau-like uplands [of New England] is interrupted in two ways; isolated mountains rise above it, and branching valleys sink below it. Mount Monadnock is a typical example of the former, with its bold summit more than a thousand feet above the surrounding plateau... It is simply an unconsumed remnant of the greater mass of unknown dimensions and form, from which the old lowland was carved... In my teaching, Monadnock has come to be recognized as an example of a distinct group of forms, and its name is used as having a generic value. A long paragraph of explanation is packed away when describing some other mountain as a 'monadnock' of greater or less height. **1900** J. E. MARR *Sci. Study Scenery* 147 The peneplain will be cut up by denudation, which may give rise to new hills, carved out of the plain, and marked at first by the possession of flat tops; to these Davis gives the name 'monadnocks'. **1935** *Geogr. Jrnl.* LXXXVI. 268 Only here and there a monadnock stands out distinctly, as for instance the Umanak Rifkol, which forms a landmark 900 feet high. **1947** AUDEN *Age of Anxiety* (1948) v. 108 O stiffly stand, a staid monadnock, On her peneplain. **1968** R. W. FAIRBRIDGE *Encycl. Geomorphol.* 709/1 Monadnocks may take the form of hills, ridges or ranges.

monadological (ˌmɒnədəʊ'lɒdʒɪkəl), *a.* [ad. G. *monadologisch*, F. *monadologique*: see -AL.] Of or pertaining to monadology. So **monado'logically** *adv.*

1895 A. C. ARMSTRONG tr. *Falckenberg's Hist. Mod. Philos.* vii. 278 Leibnitz's..monadological and harmonistic

principles. **1897** C. H. JUDD tr. *Wundt's Outl. Psychol.* 313 Matter is thought of as made up of similar [mental] atoms of a lower order (monistic, or monado-logical spiritualism). **1937** *Mind* XLVI. 503 Must we think, monadologically, of as many object worlds as there are knowing minds, though these many object worlds may have common features, in the sense of numerically diverse instances of the same universals? **1938** *Jrnl. Theol. Stud.* XXXIX. 427 It must be a matter for consideration how far it is of any profit to be familiar with (e.g.) Leibniz's monadological religious metaphysic without his doctrine of the judgement. **1943** M. FARBER *Found. Phenomenology* xvi. 533 The objective world is 'innate' in the monado-logical world. **1957** R. MANHEIM tr. *Cassirer's Philos. Symbolic Forms* III. II. iv. 170 'Monadological' time is the πρότερον τῇ φύσει, and..we can only thence arrive at mathematical-physical time.

monadology (mɒnəˈdɒlədʒɪ). [a. F. *monadologie* (Leibniz), f. *monade*: see MONAD and -LOGY.] The philosophical doctrine of monads.

1732 *Hist. Litteraria* IV. 193 The second Argument is borrow'd from Leibniz's Monadology. **1847** LEWES *Hist. Philos.* (1867) II. 271 When that reasoning conducts him to such hypotheses as the pre-established Harmony and the Monadology. **1867** *Contemp. Rev.* VI. 60 He is developing ..his monadology like a disciple of Leibnitz. **1902** *Encycl. Brit.* XXX. 651/1 His [*sc.* Leibniz's] monadology, or half-Pythagorean, half-Brunistic analysis of bodies into monads.

†**ˈmonady.** *Obs. rare.* [irreg. f. MONAD.] The number one.

1637 HEYWOOD *London's Mirr.* B4b, [The Pythagorean school reasoned that] all nations..can tell no farther than to the Denary, which is Ten, and then returne in their account unto the Monady, that is one. **1659** tr. *Fludd's Mos. Philos.* 132 God..is understood to be that absolute Monady or Unity, which onely was in it self.

monal, variant of MONAUL.

Monalechite, blundered form of MONOTHELITE.

Mona Lisa (ˈməʊnə ˈliːzə). [It.] The name of a portrait painted by Leonardo da Vinci (1452–1519), used allusively and *attrib.* of an enigmatic smile or expression such as that of the woman in this painting. Also *fig.* See also GIOCONDA.

1923 D. H. LAWRENCE *Birds, Beasts & Flowers* 162 She, smiling with goaty munch-mouth, Mona Lisa, arranges it so. **1930** J. COLLIER *His Monkey Wife* xiv. 197 She eyed Emily with what had been called, in her last year at school, her Mona Lisa smile. **1934** T. S. ELIOT *Elizabethan Essays* 60 It [*sc. Hamlet*] is the 'Mona Lisa' of literature. **1950** A. WILSON *Such Darling Dodos* 59 She twisted her face into what she felt to be a more than usually Mona Lisa smile. **1967** J. CREASEY *Famine* xii. 113 She stood in front of him with that half-smile, a Mona Lisa kind of inscrutability. **1975** G. LYALL *Judas Country* xxx. 215 Mitzi was looking at me with a little mousey Mona Lisa smile.

Mona marble (ˈməʊnə). [f. *Mona*, Roman name for Anglesey + MARBLE *sb.*] A serpentine limestone from the metamorphic beds of the island of Anglesey, off the N. coast of Wales.

1816 *Repository of Arts* (Ackermann) Oct. 243 (*heading*) Mona marble chimney-piece. *Ibid.* 244/2 The beautifully variegated tints of the mona marble. **1911** *Encycl. Brit.* XVII. 677/1 Mona marble is an ophicalcite from the metamorphic series of the Isle of Anglesey. **1971** *Country Life* 6 May 1089/1 'A chaste and elegant structure of Mona Marble', inscribed in Latin and Welsh.

‖**mon ami** (mɔn ami). Also fem. **mon amie.** [Fr.] 'My friend', as a term of address.

1786 W. COWPER *Let.* 31 Aug. (1904) III. 93 Adieu, *mon ami*, yours faithfully, W. C. **1856** *Newsp. & Gen. Reader's Pocket Compan.* II. §1564 All in good time *mon ami*—all in good time. *Ibid.* §1788 Throughout the journal she is designated emphatically as *mon amie*. **1896** C. M. YONGE *Release* II. ii. 95 'Are you speaking of Beaudésert, *mon amie*?' said M. de Nidemerle. **1911** 'I. HAY' *Safety Match* xv. 236 Flirtation is a crooked business, and you are straight, *mon amie*. **1966** A. CHRISTIE *Third Girl* xxi. 216 'I was quite sure she *wouldn't* walk out on me.' 'Ah yes. And then, *mon ami*, she did.' **1973** 'A. HALL' *Tango Briefing* vi. 72 The desert is different from other places, *mon ami*.

monamide (ˈmɒnəmaɪd). *Chem.* [f. MON(O)- + AMIDE.] An amide formed by the displacement of one of the three hydrogen atoms of ammonia. See AMIDE 2 *note*.

1861 *Fownes' Chem.* (ed. 8) 734 Organic derivatives of ammonia—monamines, and monamides. **1869** ROSCOE *Elem. Chem.* (1871) 368 Lactic monamide is obtained by the action of ammonia on lactide.

monamine (ˈmɒnəmaɪn). *Chem.* [f. MON(O)- + AMINE.] = MONOAMINE.

1859 HOFMANN in *Proc. Roy. Soc.* IX. 293 Contributions towards the History of the Monamines. **1878** KINGZETT *Anim. Chem.* 35 The amines..may be grouped into 3 classes, namely monamines, diamines, and triamines. **1943** SUMNER & SOMERS *Chem. & Methods of Enzymes* xv. 269 It is probable that all of these enzymes are one and the same... The most suitable name for the enzyme would be 'monamine oxidase'. **1969** *Times* 21 Feb. 10/7 The patients were receiving anti-depressant drugs known as monamine oxidase inhibitors. **1973** *Sci. Amer.* Sept. 121/1 It was also discovered that iproniazid acted to inhibit the enzyme monamine oxidase. (Monamines, such as serotonin, norepinephrine and dopamine, are believed to act as chemical transmitters between nerve cells in the brain.)

monanaˈpæstic, *a. Pros. rare*⁻⁰. In Dicts. **-anapestic.** [f. MON(O)- + ANAPÆSTIC.] Containing but one anapæst.

1890 *Century Dict.*

monanday, Sc. variant of MONDAY.

‖**Monandria** (mɒˈnændrɪə). *Bot.* [mod.L. (Linnæus 1735), f. Gr. μόνανδρος having one husband (f. μόνος MONO- + ἀνδρ- man, male).] The first class in the Linnæan Sexual System, comprising all plants having hermaphrodite flowers with but one stamen or male organ.

1753 CHAMBERS *Cycl. Supp.*, *Monandria*,..a class of plants which have hermaphrodite flowers, with only one stamen in each. **1760** J. LEE *Introd. Bot.* II. ii. (1765) 73. **1785** MARTYN *Rousseau's Bot.* ix. (1794) 87.

attrib. **1797** *Encycl. Brit.* (ed. 3) XVI. 80/2 A genus.. belonging to the monandria class of plants.

Hence **moˈnander** (*rare*⁻⁰), a plant belonging to the class *Monandria*; **moˈnandrian, moˈnandric** *adjs.* (*rare*⁻⁰) = MONANDROUS.

1828–32 WEBSTER, *Monander. Ibid., Monandrian.* **1891** *Syd. Soc. Lex., Monandric.*

monandrous (mɒˈnændrəs), *a.* [f. Gr. μόνανδρ-ος (see MONANDRIA) + -OUS.]

1. *Bot.* Belonging to the class Monandria; of a flower, having a single stamen.

1806 GALPINE *Brit. Bot.* §15 F[lowers] monandrous. **1849** BALFOUR *Man. Bot.* §394. **1881** *Jrnl. Linn. Soc.* XVIII. 365 Surrounded by 2 or more monandrous male flowers.

2. Having but one husband. *nonce-use.*

1866 SHUCKARD *Brit. Bees* 323 The queen is monandrous or single-spoused.

monandry (mɒˈnændrɪ). Also **mono-andry.** [ad. Gr. *μονανδρία, f. μόνανδρος: see MONANDRIA and -Y.]

1. The custom of having only one husband at a time.

1855 MISS COBBE *Intuit. Mor.* 155 Monogamy and Monoandry are general rules conducive to the Happiness of mankind. **1880** WEBSTER *Suppl.*, *Monandry.* **1882** A. MACFARLANE *Consanguin.* 8 In countries where monandry is established. **1904** *Contemp. Rev.* Oct. 486 From promiscuity ..to..monogamy and monandry, every possible phase and form of the institution [of marriage] can be studied outside of the human species.

2. *Bot.* The condition of having but one perfect stamen.

1900 in B. D. JACKSON *Gloss. Bot. Terms* App.

monanthous (mɒˈnænθəs), *a. Bot.* [f. Gr. μόν-ος MON(O)- + ἄνθ-ος flower + -OUS.] Bearing a single flower (on each stalk).

1858 A. GRAY *Bot. Gloss.*, *Monanthous*, one-flowered.

monapsal (mɒˈnæpsəl), *a.* [f. MON(O)- + APSE + -AL¹.] Having a single apse.

1884 A. J. BUTLER *Coptic Ch.* I. i. 33 Mr. Freshfield's canon that a Greek triapsal church is later, and a monapsal church earlier, than the time of Justin II.

monarch (ˈmɒnək) *sb.*¹ Also 5 **monarcha**, 6–7 **monark(e**, 6 **monarche**. [ad. L. *monarcha*, ad. Gr. μονάρχης (more commonly μόναρχος), f. μόν-ος alone + ἄρχ-ειν to rule. Cf. F. *monarque* (14th c. Hatz.-Darm.), Sp., It. *monarca*, Pg. *monarcha*.]

1. a. In early use, a sole and absolute ruler of a state. In modern use, a sovereign bearing the title of king, queen, emperor, or empress, or the equivalent of one of these. (Ordinarily, a more or less rhetorical substitute for the specific designation of the person referred to.)

c **1450** LYDG. *Secrees* 299 Souereyn of Renoun, Which as monarcha of euery Regioun, Gaff me this Charge. **1538** ELYOT *Dict.*, *Monarcha*, a prynce, whiche reuleth alone without peire or companyon, monarche. **1572** H. MIDDELMORE in Ellis *Orig. Lett.* Ser. II. III. 5 His deseign ..is to make himselfe monarche of Christendome. **1587** GOLDING *De Mornay* viii. (1592) 96 From the great Monarkes we come to the Kings of seuerall Nations, and from them to vnderkings of Prouinces. **1596** SHAKS. *Merch. V.* IV. i. 189 The quality of mercy..becomes The throned Monarch better then his Crowne. **1638** SIR T. HERBERT *Trav.* (ed. 2) 312 He is reputed as absolute a monark as any other in India. **1783** WATSON *Philip III*, III. (1839) 183 The French and English monarchs, in whose name this proposal had been made. **1875** MAINE *Hist. Inst.* xii. 350 According to..Austin, the Sovereign, if a single person, is or should be called a Monarch.

b. *transf.* and *fig.*

1581 SIDNEY *Apol. Poetrie* (Arb.) 40 To be moued to doe that which we know, or to be mooued with desire to knowe, *Hoc opus: Hic labor est.* Nowe therein of all Sciences..is our Poet the Monarch. **1606** SHAKS. *Ant. & Cl.* II. vii. 120 Come thou Monarch of the Vine, Plumpie Bacchus, with pinke eyne. **1609** C. BUTLER *Fem. Mon.* i. A2, And al this vnder the government of one Monarch, of whom aboue al things they [*sc.* the bees] haue a principal care. **1640** H. KING *Serm.* 15 The Sunne..who is the Prince and Monarch of the Skie. **1698** FRYER *Acc. E. India & P.* 91 Unless the Seamen or Soldiers get Drunk,..then are they Monarchs, and it is Madness to oppose them. **1742** YOUNG *Nt. Th.* IX. 1617 How far, how wide, The matchless monarch [*sc.* the sun], from his flaming throne..throws his beams about him. **1782** COWPER *Alex. Selkirk* 1, I am monarch of all I survey. **1807** P. GASS *Jrnl.* 105 Most of the corps crossed over to an island, to attack and rout its monarch, a large brown bear. **1817** BYRON *Manfred* I. i, Mont Blanc is the monarch of mountains. **1872** MORLEY *Voltaire* (1886) 7 In the realm of mere letters, Voltaire is one of the little band of great monarchs.

2. *slang.* The coin called a sovereign.

1851 MAYHEW *Lond. Labour* I. 52/1 Upper Benjamins, built on a downey plan, a monarch to half a finnuf... Pair of long sleeve Moleskin..half a monarch.

3. A very large red and black butterfly (*Danaus Plexippus*). In full, ***monarch butterfly***.

1890 HYATT & ARMS *Insecta* 186 The monarch or milk-weed butterfly..is abundant during July and August wherever the milk-weed grows. **1893** MORRIS *Brit. Butterfl.* 71 The Monarch..is one of the commonest species throughout a great part of North America. **1945** E. B. FORD *Butterflies* i. 23 The Milkweed, Monarch, or Black-veined Brown Butterfly, *Danaus plexippus*... The first specimen [in Britain] was caught by Mr. J. Stafford at Neath, South Wales, on September 6th, 1876. **1974** A. DILLARD *Pilgrim at Tinker Creek* xiv. 252 Each monarch butterfly had a brittle black body and deep orange wings limned and looped in black bands. A monarch at rest looks like a fleck of tiger. **1975** *Country Life* 20 Feb. 450/1 The magnificent black-veined brown or monarch butterfly, that rare migrant to Britain.

4. *attrib.* and *Comb.*: **a.** simple attrib., as ***monarch-like*** adj. and adv., ***monarch-wise***.

c **1586** C'TESS PEMBROKE *Ps.* XCIII. i, *Monarck-like Iehova raignes. **1662** GERBIER *Princ.* 12 The Monarchlike Staires of the Pallace of Darius. **1839** BAILEY *Festus* xviii. (1852) 252 The lion, monarchlike, alone Hath sympathies with no race but his own. **1586** T. B. *La Primaud. Fr. Acad.* lv. 561 If a citie be assembled in *Monarch-wise [orig. *si monarchiquement*], it is to bee defended against strangers.

b. appositive, as ***monarch-bee, -dead, -god, -judge, -love, -martyr, -mind, -monster, -oak, -pope, -reason, -savage, -spirit, -swain, -victor***.

1766 *Compl. Farmer* s.v. *Queen-bee*, This was giving great talents to the *monarch-bee. **1864** NEALE *Seaton. Poems* 131 The monarch, midst the *monarch-dead Reposes in his glory. **1870** BRYANT *Iliad* I. I. 3 The *monarch-god, Apollo. **1837–9** HALLAM *Hist. Lit.* II. iv. §61 Reasons..in favour of a *monarch-judge. **1647** COWLEY *Mistr.*, *Heart-breaking* v, Thus have I chang'd with evil Fate My *Monarch-Love into a Tyrant-State. **1842** SIR A. DE VERE *Song of Faith* 259 Mid wild revelry..Should thus the *Monarch-martyr's son appear. **1812** CRABBE *Tales* i. 67 And now, into the vale of years declined, He hides too little of the *monarch-mind. **1593** NASHE *Christ's T.* Wks. (Grosart) IV. 114 Vengeance on your soules..for thus mirrouring mee for the *Monarch-monster of Mothers. **1682** DRYDEN *Mac Fl.* 28 *Monarch oaks that shade the plain And, spread in solemn state, supinely reign. **1904** A. LANG *Hist. Scotl.* III. II. 28 Charles I was acting on the example of four English *monarch-popes. **1700** DRYDEN *Cock & Fox* 326 Dreams are but interludes, which fancy makes; When *monarch reason sleeps, this mimic wakes. **1725** POPE *Odyss.* IV. 454 The *monarch-savage [*sc.* a lion] rends the trembling prey. **1800** COLERIDGE *Piccolom.* III. iii, This great *monarch-spirit, if he fall, Will drag a world into the ruin with him. **1727–46** THOMSON *Summer* 494 Amid his subjects safe, Slumbers the *monarch swain. **1821** MRS. HEMANS *Dartmoor* Poems (1875) 145 The trophied car Wheeling the *monarch-victor fast and far.

c. objective, instrumental, etc., as ***monarch-murderer***; ***monarch-murdered*** adj.

1611 FLORIO, *Monarcacida*, a Monarch-murtherer. **1795** COLERIDGE *To Author of Poems* 28 There for the monarch-murder'd Soldier's tomb You wove th'unfinish'd wreath of saddest hues.

Hence **ˈmonarch** *v. intr.*, to act the monarch; also ***to monarch it***.

a **1653** G. DANIEL *Idyll., Illustr.* 4 The Tirrannous High-Preist Once but a Man, now Monarchs o're the Rest. **1737** *Common Sense* I. 11 While he monarchs it in his own closet, [he] becomes contemptible in the Eyes of the World. **1839** *Fraser's Mag.* XX. 126 So be it known, We monarch it by rule of two, and not of one.

†**ˈmonarch,** *sb.*² *Obs.* [a. OF. *monarche*, *monarque* fem., semi-popular ad. late L. type *moˈnarchia*.] = MONARCHY.

1483 *Chron. Eng.* III. f vj b, The Monarch of Rome a bowt this time mightili encresed. **1572** J. JONES *Bathes of Bath* Ep. Ded. aiij, Bladud..a Brittayn the ix King of this Monarch after Brute. **1588** A. MARTEN *Exhort. Faithf. Subjects* D2b, The Roman Monarch..was one hundred times greater then ours. **1602** WARNER *Alb. Eng.* x. lvii. 250 It..was Aduisde a Monarch absolute in France to bring to pas. Aristocratick gouernment, nor Democratick pleasd.

monarch (ˈmɒnɑːk), *a. Bot.* [f. Gr. μόν-ος one, single + ἀρχ-ή beginning, origin: cf. DIARCH.] Arising from only one point of origin, as the woody tissue of a root. ***monarch-bundle***, a xylem-bundle in which there is only one strand.

1884 BOWER & SCOTT *De Bary's Phaner.* 350 In the heptarch or octarch examples of Lycopodium clavatum investigated, I almost always found one of the concave plates larger,..the other smaller..with a separate..vascular strand (in itself monarch), lying in front of its..outer surface. *Ibid.* 363 The monarch bundles of some species of Trichomanes.

monarch, var. MONIKER *slang*, name.

monarchal (məˈnɑːkəl), *a.* Also 6–7 **-all.** [f. MONARCH *sb.* + -AL¹. Cf. OF. *monarchal*.]

1. Of, belonging to, or characteristic of a monarch; befitting a monarch.

1592 *Nobody & Someb.* F3, My kinglie browes itch for a stately Crowne, This hand to beare a round Monarchall Globe. **1610** GUILLIM *Heraldry* VI. vii. 280 The Blazon of these his Maiesties most Roiall and Monarchal Ensignes. **1667** MILTON *P.L.* II. 428 Satan, whom now transcendent glory rais'd Above his fellows, with Monarchal pride..thus spake. **1825** LAMB *Elia* Ser. II. *Convalescent*, To be sick is to enjoy monarchal prerogatives. **1826** G. S. FABER *Diffic.*

Romanism (1853) 60 The Bishops of Rome have legitimately inherited the alleged monarchal prerogatives of Peter. **1845** *Blackw. Mag.* LVII. 783 The royal harangue..has..a certain monarchal tone. **1886** *Belgravia Mag.* LX. 43 A bastard, crowned, Aped manners of monarchal state.

fig. **1612** DRAYTON *Poly-olb.* iii. 371 By whose monarchal sway, She fortifies herself.

2. Having the status of a monarch; that exercises the functions of a monarch.

1586 FERNE *Blaz. Gentrie* II. 26 This is that fashioned Crowne which appertaineth to kinges onely monarchall. **1620** DEKKER *Dreame* (1860) 41 Hee [Adam]..was sole monarchall lord O're the whole globe. **1656** FINETT *For. Ambass.* 3 He..would never allow (he sayd) so much as a question or thought of competition betweene him a monarchall soveraigne and a meane Republique. **1678** MARVELL *Growth Popery* 12 The king..was more Generous and Monarchal than to assign Cause..for his Actions. **1826** G. S. FABER *Diffic. Romanism* (1853) 217 Christ's Monarchal Vicar might send two of his dependant suffragans..upon an ecclesiastical errand.

3. Of a state, etc.: That is ruled by a monarch. Of government or institutions: Monarchical. Now *rare* or *Obs.*

a **1586** SIDNEY *Arcadia* v. (1613) 451 The Princes persons; being in all monarchall gouernements the very knot of the peoples welfare. **1635** J. HAYWARD tr. *Biondi's Banish'd Virg.* Pref. verse, The ware..by thee in-brought To this Monarchall Ile. **1640** H. KING *Serm.* 41 Look..upon Kingdomes governed by formes Monarchall and Absolute as yours. **1836** LANDOR *Peric. & Asp.* clvii. Wks. 1853 II. 419/1 Nations monarchal and aristocratical. **1846** HARE *Mission Comf.* (1850) 15 [Such a change] would have overthrown the legitimate monarchal constitution of your being, to set up the ochlocracy within you in its stead.

Hence **mo'narchally** *adv.*, as a monarch.

1838 G. S. FABER *Inquiry* 392 Antichrist..hath already appeared in his true character, seated monarchally in the seven-hilled city.

monarchess ('mɒnəkɪs). Now *rare.* [f. MONARCH *sb.* + -ESS.] A female monarch.

1595 MARKHAM *Sir R. Grinvile, To the fayrest* ix, Thou.. Onelie immatchlesse Monarchesse of harts. **1596** FITZ-GEFFRAY *Sir F. Drake* (1881) 74 Death-scorning Gilbert.. To Englands Monarchesse did force to yeeld The savage land. **1616** CAPT. SMITH *Descr. New Eng.* 32 For example: Rome, What made her such a Monarchesse, but onely the adventures of her youth..in dangers abroade. **1642** BROME *Queens Exch.* v. i, Were I sole monarchess of this Island. **1843** J. NICHOLSON *Hist. & Tradit. T.* 92 Meg Merrilies or the monarchess of tinkers and gipsies.

monarchial (mə'nɑːkɪəl), *a.* [f. L. *monarchia* MONARCHY + -AL[1]. Cf. OF. *monarchial.*]

1. Of, pertaining to, or of the nature of a monarchy; that is under the dominion of a monarch. Cf. MONARCHAL *a.* 3.

1600 W. WATSON *Decacordon* (1602) 39 When these Realmes of England, Wales and Scotland, shal be all one Monarchiall Ile of Iesuits. **1642** BRIDGE *Wounded Consc. Cured* iii. 56 The nature of Monarchiall government, we shall come to consider..in that which followes. **1680** AUBREY in *Lett. Eminent Persons* (1813) III. 447 The Liberty of Mankind, wch he thought would be greater under a free state than under a monarchiall government. **1737** *Common Sense* I. 119 The ancient Form of government, which was Kingly or Monarchial. *a* **1806** C. J. FOX *Reign Jas. II* (1808) 232 To promise, therefore, the continuance of a monarchial establishment, and to designate the future monarch, seemed to be necessary. **1869** RAWLINSON *Anc. Hist.* 339 The form of government was monarchial.

2. = MONARCHAL *a.* 1.

1788 ANNA SEWARD *Lett.* (1811) II. 104 A man..who worshipped the monarchial claims and despised the parental ones. **1841** *Blackw. Mag.* XLIX. 368 The authoritative sentiment of duty is upheld..in all its absolute and monarchial rights. **1850** R. G. CUMMING *Hunter's Life S. Afr.* (1902) 47/2 The dignified and truly monarchial appearance of the lion. **1870** BALDW. BROWN *Eccl. Truth* 273 The growth of the monarchial power.

†**3.** = MONARCHAL *a.* 2. *Obs. rare.*

1600 W. WATSON *Decacordon* (1602) 319 He shall haue the title in words of a king monarchiall. *Ibid.* 324 One Iesuite Pope and prince Monarchiall. **1661** BAXTER *Mor. Prognost.* (1680) 65 A Visible Constitutive, or Governing-Head; whether Monarchial,..or Aristocratical or Democratical.

Monarchian (mə'nɑːkɪən), *sb.* and *a. Eccl. Hist.* [ad. late L. *monarchiānī* pl., f. *monarchia*: see MONARCHY and -AN.

The term *monarchiani* is merely a nickname applied by Tertullian (*Adv. Prax.* x) to certain opponents of the doctrine of the Trinity, in derision of their unintelligent use of the word *monarchia* ('Monarchiam, inquiunt, tenemus', *ibid.* ii). In early apologetics, ἡ μοναρχία τοῦ Θεοῦ ('the monarchy of God') was a current designation for Christian monotheism, and these heretics regarded themselves as the defenders of this cardinal doctrine against the Trinitarians.]

A. *sb.* One of those heretics in the 2nd and 3rd centuries who denied the doctrine of the Trinity.

Modern historians distinguish between 'Dynamistic' or 'Adoptionist' Monarchians, who regarded Christ as a man endowed with Divine power, and 'Modalistic' Monarchians, who maintained that He was an incarnation of God the Father.

1765 A. MACLAINE tr. *Mosheim's Eccl. Hist.* II. v. §20 (1833) 64/1 His [*sc.* Praxeas'] followers were called Monarchians, because of their denying a plurality of persons in the Deity. **1841** H. J. ROSE tr. *Neander's Hist. Relig.* II. 283 The Monarchians who reduced the whole Trias (or Trinity) only to different conceptions and relations under which the One Divine Being is viewed. **1872** MORRIS tr. *Ueberweg's Hist. Philos.* §82 I. 308 The Monarchian, Praxeas,..appears..to have taught that the Father descended into the Virgin.

B. *adj.* Of or belonging to the Monarchians or to Monarchianism.

1847 J. TORREY tr. *Neander's Hist. Relig.* II. 333 The founder of this Monarchian party in Rome. *Ibid.*, There arose..another Monarchian sect in Rome. **1853** W. E. TAYLER *Hippolytus* II. i. 75 The leaders of the Monarchian heretics. **1872** MORRIS tr. *Ueberweg's Hist. Philos.* §94 I. 387 He [Abelard] gives to the doctrine of the Trinity a Monarchian interpretation. **1899** A. E. GARVIE *Ritschlian Theol.* IV. vi. 122 In spite of the opposition of the monarchian schools, whether adoptionist or modalist.

Hence **Mo'narchianism**, the antitrinitarian doctrine of the Monarchians. **Mo'narchianist** = MONARCHIAN *sb.* **Monarchia'nistic** *a.* = MONARCHIAN *a.*

1841 H. J. ROSE tr. *Neander's Hist. Relig.* II. 259 The others..were still more strongly opposed to this class of Monarchianism. **1858** J. MARTINEAU *Stud. Chr.* 246 This shows the yet powerful influence of the Judaic Monarchianism. **1872** MORRIS tr. *Ueberweg's Hist. Philos.* §82 I. 308 In the teachings of these Monarchianists the Logos-conception is not found. *Ibid.* §94. 394 He [Abelard] often employs..the almost Monarchianistic comparisons of Augustine. **1888** HATCH *Infl. Greek Ideas* vii. (1890) 207 The two schools of Monarchianism, in one of which Christ was conceived as a mode of God, and in the other as His exalted creature.

monarchic (mə'nɑːkɪk), *a.* Also 7 -ique, 7–8 -icke. [a. F. *monarchique*, ad. Gr. μοναρχικ-ός, f. μόναρχ-ος: see MONARCH and -IC.]

1. Of a government: Having the characteristics of monarchy. Now *rare*; usually replaced by MONARCHICAL.

1624 *Brief Inform. Affairs Palatinate* 24 The Empire is not an Estate Monarchique, where the Prince ruleth absolutely. **1647** CLARENDON *Hist. Reb.* VI. §120 That the Parliament only aimed at taking his majesty's regal rights from him, to the prejudice of monarchic government, without any thought of reforming religion. **1727** WARBURTON *Eng. Causes of Prodigies* 119 He [*sc.* Sallust] first wrote under the Consular, and the other [*sc.* Tacitus] under the Monarchic State. **1864** CARLYLE *Fredk. Gt.* IV. 492 'What form of government do you reckon best?' inquired he..'The monarchic, if the king is just and enlightened'.

2. Of or belonging to a monarchy; pertaining to or favouring monarchy as a form of government.

1647 CLARENDON *Hist. Reb.* III. §80 In that [bill]..there were some clauses very derogatory to monarchic principles, as, giving the people authority to assemble together if the King failed to call them. *a* **1668** DAVENANT *Epithal.* Wks. (1673) 312 For Hymens common-weale cannot dispence In private with Monarchick excellence. **1756** BURKE *Vind. Nat. Soc.* 67 The Monarchick, Aristocratical, and Popular Partizans have been jointly laying their Axes to the Root of all Government. **1851** GALLENGA *Italy* 159 Mazzini.. blames the Milanese for throwing themselves into the arms of an Italian, however monarchic, confederate. **1867** FREEMAN *Norm. Conq.* (1877) I. iii. 74 The monarchic, the aristocratic, and the democratic branches of our constitution.

3. Of or pertaining to a monarch or monarchs. Now *rare* or *Obs.*

1612 SELDEN *Drayton's Poly-olb.* Author of Illustr. to Rdr., The Author, in Passages of first Inhabitants, Name, State, and Monarchique succession in this Isle, followes [etc.]. **1676** NEEDHAM *Packet of Adv.* 15 The conteining of Monarchick Power in its just bounds. **17..** *Addit. Pope's Wks.* (1776) I. 107 In vain was ministerial breath, In vain monarchic folly. **1807** J. BARLOW *Columb.* IV. 420 A new creation waits the western shore, And moral triumphs o'er monarchic power.

†**4.** = MONARCHICAL 4. (In quot. *transf.*) *Obs.*

1632 LITHGOW *Trav.* v. 185 Cyprus, Candy, and Sicily, are the onely Monarchicke Queenes of the Mediterranean Seas. *Ibid.* 191 The Cedars of Libanon,..like Monarchick Lyons to wild beasts,..become the chiefe Champions of Forrests.

monarchical (mə'nɑːrkɪkəl), *a.* Also 6–7 -all. [f. MONARCHIC *a.* + -AL[1].]

1. Of the nature of or having the characteristics of a monarchy; *esp.* of government, vested in a monarch.

1589 *Hay any Work* (1844) 48 Such is the civil governement..Monarchicall in her Maiesties person. **1602** FULBECKE *Pandects* 32 Thus in the end they came to a Monarchicall estate. And these Nations..do create a Duke or Capitaine, who may gouerne the rest. *a* **1618** RALEIGH *Prince* (1642) 13 That a Kingdome be not too Monarchicall. **1771** *Junius Lett.* lix. (1820) 305, I hope the English constitution will for ever preserve its original monarchical form. **1850** PRESCOTT *Peru* II. ii. 19 With the Aztecs..it [the form of government] was monarchical and nearly absolute. **1869** LECKY *Europ. Mor.* II. iv. 286 The monarchical.. institutions of feudalism. **1888** SCHAFF *Chr. Church* VI. I. x. 44 Every little principality in monarchical Germany..has its own church establishment.

transf. **1615** CROOKE *Body of Man* 39 It is more honourable (say they [*sc.* the Peripatetics]) and monarchical, that there should be one principle [*e.g.* the Heart] then many.

2. Of or pertaining to monarchy; that advocates monarchy as a form of government.

1628 WITHER *Brit. Rememb.* VIII. 1530 Ev'n what the son of Hannah told the Jewes, Should be their scourge (because they..were so vaine To aske a King..) that curse they shall Affirm to be a Law Monarchicall. **1658** SIR T. BROWNE *Gard. Cyrus* iii. 143 More in the edificial Palaces of Bees and Monarchical spirits; who make their combs six-cornered, declining a circle. **1833** ALISON *Hist. Europe* (1849) I. iv. §38. 474 The remains of monarchical attachment yet lingered. **1865** MAFFEI *Brigand Life* I. 90 Men representing all varieties of opinion..appeared in Naples..Mazzinians, monarchical democrats, &c. **1869** LECKY *Europ. Mor.* II. iv. 287 When the course of events has been to glorify.. monarchical..spirit, a great..sovereign..will arise.

3. Of, pertaining to, or characteristic of a monarch; befitting a monarch; monarchal.

1576 FLEMING *Panopl. Epist.* 198, I am content with my Monarchicall maiestie or title royall. **1622** DONNE *Serm. 2 Cor.* iv. 6 Serm. 1660–1 III. 377 There is not so Regal, so Soveraign, so Monarchical a Prerogative, as to have [etc.]. **1647** COWLEY *Mistress, Vain Love* 12 Your brave and haughty scorn of all Was stately, and Monarchical. **1649** MILTON *Eikon.* xv. 144 That his Monarchical foot might have the setting it upon thir heads. **1772** FOOTE *Nabob* I. (1778) 7 A very monarchical address. **1865** DICKENS *Mut. Fr.* I. viii, When..the bees worry themselves..about their sovereign and become perfectly distracted touching the slightest monarchical movement.

4. Having the power or functions of a monarch; having undivided rule; †autocratic.

a **1618** RALEIGH *Prince* (1642) 6 So that a Monarch bee not to Monarchicall,..as the Russe Kings. **1641** J. JACKSON *True Evang. T.* III. 173 The Messias where he is Monarchicall, and rules, is also Eirenarchicall, and atones. **1906** D. W. FORREST *Authority of Christ* vii. 409 In the churches of Egypt, as we have seen, there was no monarchical bishop.

Hence **mo'narchically** *adv.*, in a monarchical form or manner.

1586 T. B. *La Primaud. Fr. Acad.* I. 587 Who can denie, that it is not a great deale better for great and mightie nations to be governed monarchically. **1651** HOBBES *Leviath.* II. xix. 98 Nor are those Provinces..Democratically, or Aristocratically governed, but Monarchically. **1656** J. HARRINGTON *Oceana* (1700) 70 To plant it Nationally, it must be..either Monarchically in part,..or Monarchically in the whole. **1839** *Fraser's Mag.* XIX. 127 He lived..with Kings, monarchically; with the people, democratically. **1882–3** *Schaff's Encycl. Relig. Knowl.* II. 987/1 The Roman church..organized monarchically, the whole power centring in the Pope.

mo'narchico-aristo'cratic(al, *a.* That combines the monarchic and aristocratic principles.

1817 BENTHAM *Parl. Reform* Introd. 120 The monarchico-aristocratical theory. **1874** BLACKIE *Self-Cult.* 7, I once heard..that all the miseries of this country arise from its monarchico-aristocratic government.

monarchism ('mɒnəkɪz(ə)m). [a. F. *monarchisme*, f. *monarchie*: see MONARCHY and -ISM.]

1. The principles of monarchical government; attachment to monarchy or the monarchical principle.

1838 *Fraser's Mag.* XVII. 213 The object..is to combine republicanism with monarchism. **1848** *Tait's Mag.* XV. 340 A president of a civil tribunal, and a president of a tribunal of commerce, were suspended for no act save their former monarchism. **1898** *Atlantic Monthly* LXXXII. 564/1 His [Bismarck's] monarchism rested not only on his personal allegiance to the hereditary dynasty [etc.].

2. Belief in a sole ruler (among the gods).

1877 J. E. CARPENTER *Tiele's Hist. Relig.* 215 All the gods [in the Homeric theology] are little else than representatives of Zeus, each in his own realm... Thus, monarchism has touched the borders of monotheism.

monarchist ('mɒnəkɪst). [f. MONARCH-Y + -IST. Cf. F. *monarchiste.*]

1. An advocate or supporter of monarchy. Also in ***Fifth-Monarchist*** (see FIFTH MONARCHY).

1647 M. HUDSON *Div. Right Govt.* II. ii. 83 This Relative blessing of Monarchie,..the *Relatum* or Monarch, and the *Correlatum* or Monarchists and subjects. **1660** in *Brit. Mag.* (1833) IV. 147 Ye widowes of those slaine &c., by 5th Monarchists. *a* **1677** BARROW *Pope's Suprem.* ii. (1687) 76 The..Supposition of the Church Monarchists..That Saint Peter's Primacy..was not personal but derivable to his Successours. *a* **1734** NORTH *Lives* (1826) I. 118 For the principles of the former being demagogical, could not allow much favour to one who rose a Monarchist declared. **1823** BENTHAM *Not Paul* 203 Monarchists and Aristocrats! mark well! **1872** *Echo* Oct. 5 The Monarchists pretend that 'the beginning of the end of the Republic' has commenced. **1882–3** *Schaff's Encycl. Relig. Knowl.* III. 2449 Constitutional monarchists and absolute monarchists.

2. One who believes in monarchy among the gods.

1678 CUDWORTH *Intell. Syst.* I. iv. §23. 403 Plato acknowledged and worshiped many gods yet..he was no polyarchist, but a Monarchist, an assertor of One Supreme God. **1893** R. C. JEBB *Growth Class. Grk. Poetry* 200 Aeschylus..is no monotheist, yet he might be described as a monarchist in religion.

3. = MONARCHIAN *sb. rare.*

1876 A. PLUMMER tr. *Döllinger's Hippolytus & C.* IV. i. 188 It is now no longer possible to define exactly what Sabellius himself or other later Monarchists contributed to the development of this view.

monarchistic (mɒnə'kɪstɪk), *a.* [f. prec. + -IC.] Of or pertaining to monarchism; in quot. = MONARCHIAN *a.*

1833 J. H. NEWMAN *Arians* I. v. (1876) 120 To confess that God was, in such sense, one Person with Christ, as (on their Monarchistic principle) to be in no sense distinct from Him.

monarchize ('mɒnəkaɪz), *v.* [f. MONARCH *sb.* + -IZE. Cf. F. *monarchiser.*]

1. *intr.* To perform the office of monarch; to rule as a monarch; to rule absolutely. Also *to monarchize it.*

1592 [see MONARCHIZING *ppl. a.* below]. **1593** SHAKS. *Rich. II*, III. ii. 165 Allowing him a breath, a little Scene, To

Monarchize, be fear'd, and kill with lookes. **1649** HOWELL *Pre-em. Parlt.* 11 That King hath an advantage hereby one way, to monarchize more absolutely, and never want money. **1656** S. H. *Gold. Law* 62 He was necessitated to Monarchize it, and self-ly manage all. **1822** SHELLEY *Tri. Life* 504 The delegated power, Arrayed in which those worms did monarchize, Who made this earth their charnel.

b. of personified agencies.

1592 NASHE *Four Lett. Confut.* K, Shee [*sc.* Art] a banisht Queene into this barraine soile, hauing monarchizd it so long amongst the Greeks and Romanes. **1600** DEKKER *Old Fortunatus* Wks. 1873 I. 105 Vice..in euery land doth monarchize. **1849** J. WILSON in *Blackw. Mag.* LXVI. 25 The enthusiast adores Greece—not knowing that Greece monarchises over him.

2. *trans.* †**a.** To make subservient to one monarch; to rule over as a monarch. *Obs.*

1606 WARNER *Alb. Eng.* XV. xciii. 375 King Rodericke, surnamd the great, did monarchize at last Wales, that had neere as many Kings as Cantrefes in times past. **1612** DRAYTON *Poly-olb.* v. 68 By whom three sever'd Realms in one shall firmly stand, As Britain-founding Brute first Monarchiz'd the Land. **1621** LADY M. WROTH *Urania* 189 Raise vp your spirit, that which is worthy to Monarchise the world.

b. To make a monarchy of.

1660 MILTON *Free Commw.* Wks. 1851 V. 453 So far shall we be from mending our condition by monarchizing our Government. **1794** J. COURTENAY *Pres. St. Manners*, etc. *France & It.* 102 Let's boldly advance To hang the Convention, and Monarchise France. **1800** JEFFERSON *Writ.* (1896) VII. 451 Principles which go..to sink the state governments, consolidate them into one, and to monarchize that.

Hence **'monarchizing** *vbl. sb.* and *ppl. a.* Also **'monarchizer**, one who monarchizes.

1592 NASHE *P. Penilesse* (ed. 2) 34 b, Such a monarchizing spirite it was, that sayd vnto Christ, If thou wilt fall down [etc.]. **1593** —— *Christ's T.* Wks. (Grosart) IV. 137 The spyrite of monarchizing in pryuate men is the spyrite of Lucifer. **1608** HEYWOOD *Rape Lucrece* I. ii, Let the pride Of these our irreligious monarkisers Be Crown'd in blood. *a* **1610** PARSONS *Leicester's Ghost* (1641) 10 Or like as Cæsars Monarchising spright Pursued false Brutus at Phillippos field.

†**Mo'narcho.** *Obs.* Also **Monarcha, Monarko.** [repr. It. *monarca* MONARCH.]

1. The title assumed by an insane Italian who fancied himself emperor of the world; hence *transf.* applied to one who is the object of general ridicule for his absurd pretensions.

1588 SHAKS. *L.L.L.* IV. i. 101 This Armado is a Spaniard that keeps here in court A Phantasime, a Monarcho, and one that makes sport To the Prince and his Booke-mates. **1596** NASHE *Saffron Walden* M 2 b, But now he was an insulting Monarch aboue Monarcha the Italian, that ware crownes on his shooes. **1634** MERES *Wits Commw.* 390 They [*sc.* braggers] gape after..vaine prayse and glory. As..in our age Peter Shakerly of Pauls, Monarcho that liued about the Court.

2. Used derisively for MONARCH.

1598 MARSTON *Sat.* IV. F 2, This thunderer..Is now the great Monarko of the earth, Whose awfull nod,..Shakes Europs ground-worke.

monarcho- (mə'nɑːkəʊ), comb. f. MONARCHIC *a.*, esp. in ***monarcho-fascist***, in Communist phraseology, of a fascist form of government with a king as titular head of state, such as that established in Greece after the war of 1939–45.

1947 *Times* 10 May 3/5 Marcos speaks of the 'Monarcho-Fascist régime of the British occupation'... He refers further to the 'Greek Monarcho-Fascist forces' who collaborated with the occupation forces. **1950** R. LEEPER *When Greek meets Greek* xii. 195 Our critics on the Left had got so much into the habit of denouncing us as reactionaries (I myself was generally dubbed a monarcho-fascist) that perhaps they had come to believe it. **1966** *Economist* 27 Aug. 809 Aeschylus expounds what would sound today like 'monarcho-fascist' theories. **1971** W. H. MCNEILL in A. Bullock *20th Century* 51/2 A new guerilla movement.. claimed to represent the democratic will of the Greek people against the 'monarcho-fascist' regime.

†**monar'chomachist.** *Obs.* [f. mod.L. *monarchomach-us* (see below) + -IST.] One who fights against monarchy; an anti-monarchist.

[**1600** (*title*) G. Barclaii..de Regno et regali Potestate adversus Buchananum, Brutum, Boucherium, & reliquos Monarchomachos.] **1639** J. CORBET *Ungird. Scot. Armour* 30 That assertion of the Monarchomachists is not alwaies true. *a* **1649** DRUMM. OF HAWTH. *Sp.* Wks. (1711) 219 The history which I have written, of the lives of the five kings of Scotland, may, by some monarchomachists, be challenged as scandalous. **1816** *Edin. Rev.* Sept. 221 The monarchom[ach]ists of the sixteenth century.

monarchy ('mɒnəkɪ). Forms: *α.* 4–7 **monarchie**, 5–6 **-ye**, 6–7 **monarkie, -ky**, 5– **monarchy**; *β.* 6–7 **monarchia.** [a. F. *monarchie* (13th c.), ad. L. *monarchia*, Gr. μοναρχία rule of one, f. μόναρχ-ος MONARCH.]

†**1.** Undivided rule by a single person; sole rule or sovereignty; absolute power. *Obs.*

α. **1390** GOWER *Conf.* I. 26 The Monarchie Of al the world in that partie To Babiloyne was soubgit. *Ibid.* I. 27, 67. **1432–50** tr. *Higden* (Rolls) III. 33 And then the monarchye off men of Assiria, whiche contynuede from Belus other Ninus to the laste tymes of Sardanapallus..failede. **1561** NORTON & SACKV. *Gorboduc* Dumb Show bef. 1st Act, Gorboduc deuidinge his Lande to his two Sonnes, which he before held in Monarchie. **1729** BUTLER *Serm.* Wks. 1874 II. 200 The monarchy of the universe is a dominion unlimited in extent, and everlasting in duration. **1845** LINGARD *Anglo-Sax. Ch.* I. iii. 114 [St. Peter] whose happy lot it had been to receive..the power of binding and the monarchy of loosing [orig. *potestatem ligandi et monarchiam solvendi*] both in heaven and on earth. **1876** MOZLEY *Univ. Serm.* i. 1 Gregory VII..claimed the monarchy of the world.

β. **1535** STEWART *Cron. Scot.* (Rolls) II. 425 Kenethus.. was the first..that had monarchia Of tua kinrikis. **1602** WARNER *Alb. Eng.* x. lvii. (1612) 251 Discourst of his Experience thus, he then descends to it, Whereby of Monarchia might himselfe the French King fit.

¶**b.** *loosely.* Exclusive dominion (of a body of persons). *Obs.*

1600 W. WATSON *Decacordon* (1602) 324 The Iesuits aspire to the whole and absolute monarchie of the world.

2. A state having a form of government in which the supreme power is vested in a single person. Formerly, also, a nation or state having dominating power over all other states.

absolute or ***despotic m.***, a government by the absolute will of the monarch. ***constitutional m.*** (see CONSTITUTIONAL *a.* 4 b). ***elective m.***, one in which the monarch is determined by election as opposed to heredity. ***hereditary m.***, one in which the sovereign power descends by hereditary right. ***limited m.*** (see LIMITED 2).

c **1430** LYDG. *Min. Poems* (Percy Soc.) 128 The realmes and the monarchyes, Of erthely princes. **1494** FABYAN *Chron.* v. xci. 67 [Egbert] hadde subdued the more partie of the Kyngdomes of Saxons, and made of all but one Monarchy. **1552** LYNDESAY *Monarche* 1979 As, quhen one Prouince..Had hole power Imperiall,.. Abufe all Kyngis and Nationis, One Monarchie that men doith call. **1560** DAUS tr. *Sleidane's Comm.* 392 b, That the same Monarchye, that hath ben now so many yeares in framinge, maye at the lengthe be established. **1599** SHAKS. *Hen. V*, II. iv. 73 Good my Soueraigne..let them know Of what a Monarchie you are the Head. *a* **1618** RALEIGH *Prince* (1642) 2 Monarchies.. are of 3 sorts touching the right or possession of them; *viz.* 1. Hereditary,..2. Elective,..3. Mixt... Monarchies are of 2 sorts touching their power or authority; *viz.* 1. Intier... 2. Limited. **1651** HOBBES *Leviath.* II. xxvi. 140 It is.. necessary to consider in this place..what is the will of the Soveraign, as well in Monarchies, as in other formes of government. **1776** GIBBON *Decl. & F.* vii. (1782) I. 204 Of the various forms of government,..an hereditary monarchy seems to present the fairest scope for ridicule. **1874** BANCROFT *Footpr. Time* i. 47 The Chaldean Monarchy was the first in order of time.

3. In the abstract: Monarchical rule.

1638 *Hamilton Papers* (Camden) 40 It is chiflie monarchie uhich is intended by them to be destroyed. **1651** HOBBES *Leviath.* II. xix. 95 For they that are discontented under Monarchy, call it Tyranny. **1681** DRYDEN *Abs. & Achit.* II. 904 Who once at such a gentle reign repine, The fall of monarchy itself design. **1742** HUME *Ess.* I. vii. (1777) 33 Absolute monarchy, therefore, is the easiest death, the true Euthanasia of the British constitution. *a* **1862** BUCKLE *Civiliz.* (1873) III. iii. 156 The very institution of monarchy was repulsive to them.

†**4.** The territory of a monarch. *Obs. rare.*

c **1550** BALE *K. Johan* (Camden) 91 Than shall never Pope rule more in thys monarchie. **1699** BENTLEY *Phal.* 403 Crouds of those that would have come to Court from the furthest parts of the Monarchy.

5. *transf.* and *fig.* (From senses 1–3.)

1609 C. BUTLER (*title*) The Feminine Monarchie Or A Treatise concerning Bees. **1695** CONGREVE *Love for L.* Ded., Nobody can dispute Your Lordship's Monarchy in Poetry. **1713** STEELE *Englishman* No. 7. 44 Liberty is checked by the Restraints of Truth, and the Monarchy of right Reason. **1791** BENTHAM *Panopt.* II. 205 A prison, a sort of monarchy which has never yet been noted for plans of conquest. **1884** J. PARKER *Apost. Life* III. 133 The only monarchy that is not tinsel is the monarchy of holiness.

‖**monarda** (məʊ'nɑːdə). Also 8 **monardus.** [mod.L. (Linnæus *Hortus Cliffortianus* (1737) 11), f. the name of Nicolas Monardes (1493–1588), Spanish physician and botanist, one of the earliest writers on American plants.] An aromatic herb of the North American genus so called, belonging to the family Labiatæ, esp. *Monarda didyma*, which has bright red flowers and is also called bergamot, bee balm, or Oswego tea.

1712 tr. *Pomet's Hist. Drugs* I. 179 This was doubtless the gum Monardus us'd against the gout. **1789** W. AITON *Hortus Kewensis* I. 36 Scarlet Monarda or Oswego-tea. **1865** WATTS *Dict. Chem.* s.v., Oil of Monarda. The essential oil of an American Labiate plant, the *Monarda punctata*. It easily separates into a liquid oil and a camphor. **1931** M. GRIEVE *Modern Herbal* I. 95/1 Another American swamp plant... *M*[*onarda*] *didyma*, the Scarlet Monarda, is said to yield an oil of similar composition [to that of thymol]. **1970** C. LLOYD *Well-Tempered Garden* i. 45 For plants of an intricately branching habit like *Aster acris*, *Salvia superba*, or monardas, peasticks are ideal [support]. **1974** A. SCOTT-JAMES *Sissinghurst* xiv. 149 A charming lilac-pink monarda called Beauty of Cobham.

monardin (məʊ'nɑːdɪn). *Chem.* [f. prec. + -IN.] A crystalline solid, isomeric with thymol, which separates from monarda oil.

1890 BILLINGS *Med. Dict.*, *Monardin*, a crystalline stearopten, isomeric with thymol, obtained from oil of horsemint.

monarsenous (mɒ'nɑːsənəs), *a.* *Zool.* [f. MON(O)- + Gr. ἀρσεν-, ἄρσην male + -OUS.] Having only one male for several females.

In some recent Dicts.

monarthritis (mɒnɑː'θraɪtɪs). *Path.* [f. MON(O)- + ARTHRITIS.] 'Articular rheumatism of one joint only' (*Syd. Soc. Lex.* 1891).

1893 in DUNGLISON *Dict. Med.* (ed. 21).

monarticular (mɒnɑː'tɪkjʊlə(r)), *a.* *Path.* Also **mono-**. [f. MON(O)- + ARTICULAR.] Of a disease: Affecting a single joint (of the body).

1874 VAN BUREN *Dis. Genit. Organs* 82 This form is generally mono-articular. **1897** *Allbutt's Syst. Med.* III. 78 The partial or monarticular form of rheumatoid arthritis is Charcot's third division. **1898** *Ibid.* V. 862 Occasionally endocarditis may follow monarticular rheumatism.

‖**monas** ('mɒnæs). Pl. **monades** ('mɒnədiːz). [Gr. μονάς: see MONAD.]

1. = MONAD in various senses.

1568 J. DEE in Ashm. (1652) 334 Our Monas trewe thus use by natures Law. **1656** BLOUNT *Glossogr.*, *Monas* (Gr.), the number one, unity. **1768–74** TUCKER *Lt. Nat.* (1834) I. 472 Though He be a monas and we are monades, yet [etc.]. **1865** GROTE *Plato* I. i. 11 The first principle or beginning of Number was the One or Monas. **1870** J. H. NEWMAN *Gram. Assent* I. v. 121 The One Personal God, who is not a logical or physical Unity, but a living Monas. **1872** MORRIS tr. *Ueberweg's Hist. Philos.* §82 I. 309 So the divine Logos, after its hypostatization in Christ, returned again to the Father or Monas.

†**2.** *Arith.* (See quot.) *Obs. rare*$^{-1}$.

1674 JEAKE *Arith.* (1696) 5 Digits are sometimes called Monades. **1704** in J. HARRIS *Lex. Techn.* I.

-monas [a. Gr. μονάς: see MONAD], an ending of some mod.L. names of genera of simple organisms (chiefly bacteria, protozoa, and algæ): cf. CHLAMYDOMONAS, LEPTOMONAS.

monast, obs. form of MONISH *v.*

monaster (mɒ'næstə(r)). *Biol.* [f. MON(O)- + Gr. ἀστήρ star.] The single-star figure which occurs between the rosette and diaster stages in cell-division.

1889 BENHAM tr. *Waldeyer* in *Q. Jrnl. Microsc. Sci.* XXX. 177 The stage [of cell division] which is termed the 'mother star', 'aster', or 'monaster'. **1889** KLEIN *Elem. Histol.* 10.

monasterial (mɒnə'stɪərɪəl), *a.* Now *rare.* [f. L. *monastēri-um* (see MONASTERY) + -AL[1].] Belonging to or of the nature of a monastery.

c **1420** LYDG. *Assembly of Gods* 913 Monasteriall monks. **1632** LITHGOW *Trav.* I. 19 Idle monasteriall Loyterers. *Ibid.* v. 219 False miracles, first inuented partly by monasteriall pouerty. **1670** WALTON *Lives* II. 134 [He declared] himself for the Church of Rome;..betaking himself to a monasterial life. **1845** LINGARD *Anglo-Sax. Ch.* I. 250 Motives which led to the first monasterial establishments. **1846** CARD. WISEMAN *Fate of Sacrilege* Ess. 1853 I. 370 Sir Edward Dodsworth..possessed the monasterial property of Newland.

Hence **mona'sterially** *adv.*, like a monk.

1653 URQUHART *Rabelais* I. Prol. 3 It is not the habit makes the Monk, many being Monasterially accoutred, who inwardly are nothing lesse then monachal.

Monasterian (mɒnə'stɪərɪən), *a.* and *sb.* *Eccl.* [f. med.L. *Monastēri-um* Münster (Westphalia) + -AN.] The designation of a fanatical sect of Anabaptists who, early in the 16th c., settled themselves at Münster under the style of 'the New Jerusalem'.

1641 T. HAYNE *Luther* 93 Luther wrote..a Preface to Vrbanus Rhegius book against the Monasterians [etc.]. **1650** TRAPP *Comm. Exod.* ii. 12 The like madness is reported of the Monasterian Anabaptists.

†**mona'sterical**, *a.* *Obs. rare*$^{-1}$. [f. L. *monastēr-ium* (see MONASTERY) + -IC + -AL[1].] Of or pertaining to a monastery; monastic.

1651 *Fuller's Abel Rediv.*, *Musculus* 250 The Prior.. demanded of him how he liked a Monasterical life.

monastery ('mɒnəstərɪ). Forms: *α.* 5–7 **monasterie**, (5 **-eri**, 8 **-try**, 6 **monnestarie**), 5– **monastery**; *β.* 5–6 **monaster**, (6 **-tre**), 5 **monestre**, 6 **-tar**, 6–7 **-ter.** [ad. eccl. L. *monastēri-um*, a. late Gr. μοναστήριον, f. μονάζειν to live alone, f. μόν-ος alone. The *β*-forms are from OF. *monastere*. Cf. MINSTER.] A place of residence of a community of persons living secluded from the world under religious vows; a monastic establishment. Chiefly, and now almost exclusively, applied to a house for monks; but applicable also to the house of any religious order, male or female.

1432–50 tr. *Higden* (Rolls) II. 27 The monastery of Wynneburne [1387 *Trevisa* mynistre, L. *monasterium*]. *Ibid.* 129 The monastery of Seynte Hilda [*Trevisa* abbay]. *c* **1440** *Gesta Rom.* xliv. 364 (Add. MS.) Sir, why purpose ye to distroye þis monestre? **1451** *Rolls of Parlt.* V. 221/1 Th' abbesse and covent of oure Monasterie of Saint Saviour. **1483** CAXTON *Gold. Leg.* 386/1 What monaster is yonder that I see? **1539** PERY in Ellis *Orig. Lett.* Ser. II. II. 141 He sainge what a goode Crysten is yowre Kinge of Ynglande to pwte downe the Monesterys. **1596** DALRYMPLE tr. *Leslie's Hist. Scot.* x. 310 A certane monestar not far fra the place quhair tha lay. *c* **1610** *Women Saints* 21 By her example, many monasteries of Virgins and monks were founded at Rome. *a* **1660** *Contemp. Hist. Irel.* (Ir. Archæol. Soc.) I. 255 Captain Con Oneylle did guarde the monester of the fryers preachers of S. Dominicks Order. **1759** B. MARTIN *Nat. Hist. Eng.* I. *Somerset* 73 Its Church..was at first a Monastry. **1828** SCOTT *F.M. Perth* xi, There arose that great tumult at the outward gate of the Monastery. **1841** ELPHINSTONE *Hist. Ind.* I. 201 They have nothing of the freedom of the Hindú monastic orders..and seem never allowed to leave the monastery. **1872** YEATS *Techn. Hist. Comm.* 143 Each monastery was a luminous point, whence the light of civilisation radiated into the darkness around.

b. *attrib.* and *Comb.*

1591 HORSEY *Trav.* (Hakl. Soc.) 264 A yonge bishop of Rostove..who had a sonn before he was exposed to that monnestarie liff. **1828** MOORE *Mem.* (1854) V. 254 A most monastery-like state of gloom and cheerlessness.

monastic (mə'næstɪk), *a.* and *sb.* [ad. med.L. *monastic-us*, a. late Gr. μοναστικός (lit. 'pertaining to solitary life'), f. μονάζειν to live alone: see MONASTERY. Cf. F. *monastique* (14th c.), Sp. *monástico*, Pg., It. *monastico*.] **A.** *adj.*

†**1.** See quot. (prob. a misapprehended use).

c **1449** PECOCK *Repr.* I. xviii. 107 In lengthe of tyme ful greet chaunge is alwey maad in..the circumstauncis of politik gouernauncis, ȝhe, and of monastik gouernauncis (that is to seie, of gouernauncis bi whiche oon man gouerneth him silf aloon).

2. Pertaining to or characteristic of persons living in seclusion from the world under religious vows and subject to a fixed rule, as monks, nuns, friars, etc.; pertaining to monasteries.

1600 SHAKS. *A.Y.L.* III. ii. 441 To forsweare the ful stream of yᵉ world, and to liue in a nooke meerly Monastick. **1622** DRAYTON *Poly-olb.* xxiv. 444 He [Saint Gregory] at Myniard led A strict monastic life, a Saint alive and dead. *a* **1631** DONNE *Elegy Mris. Boulstred* 69 He sinkes the deepe Where harmelesse fish monastique silence keepe. **1664** H. MORE *Myst. Iniq.* 447 Out of which luckless Representation ..this Monastick Legend seems to be framed. **1769** ROBERTSON *Chas. V*, VI. Wks. 1851 IV. 147 The three vows of poverty, of chastity, and of monastic obedience, which are common to all the orders of regulars. *Ibid.* 148 The primary object of almost all the monastic orders is to separate men from the world. **1806** *Gazetteer Scotl.* (ed. 2) 250 Ruins of monastic buildings. **1861** M. PATTISON *Ess.* (1889) I. 47 The inmates..were submitted to an almost monastic discipline. **1872** YEATS *Growth Comm.* 333 Monastic lands..yielded a scanty produce.

3. *Bookbinding.* The distinctive epithet of a method of finishing by tooling without gold. More commonly called 'antique'.

1880 ZAEHNSDORF *Bookbinding* xxii. 111 Finishing is divided into two classes—blind or antique, or as it is sometimes called, monastic and gold-finished. **1885** W. J. E. CRANE *Bookbinding for Amateurs* xx. 162.

B. *sb.* A member of a monastic order; a monk.

1632 LITHGOW *Trav.* x. 474 Your order..by all the other Monasticks, is hated. **1721** R. KEITH tr. *T. à Kempis Vall. Lillies* Pref. 7 The pious Author having been a Monastick or Brother of the Order of St. Augustine. **1860** HOOK *Lives Abps.* I. v. 226 [They] are warned not to give to seculars or monastics an example of..wicked conversation.

transf. **1864** LOWELL *Fireside Trav.* 26 His pie-plants.., compulsory monastics, blanched under barrels, each in his little hermitage, a vegetable Certosa.

Hence †**mo'nasticly** *adv.*, in a monastic manner.

1596 DALRYMPLE tr. *Leslie's Hist. Scot.* IV. 227 Quhair, quhen thair lyfe he monastiklie had informed, a Magnifik Monasterie..he erected.

monastical (mə'næstɪkəl), *a.* Forms: 5 monasticale, -alle, 6–7 -all, 6 *Sc.* monestycall, 6– monastical. [f. med.L. *monastic-us* MONASTIC *a.* + -AL¹.] Pertaining to or characteristic of the monastic life; in early use = MONASTIC *a.* 1.

1401 *Pol. Poems* (Rolls) II. 65 The thridde degree..off sich as ben gaderid in coventis togidere;..the which for worldly combraunce kepen in cloistris,..and this clepe we monasticale. **1432–50** tr. *Higden* (Rolls) IV. 327 The.. Essei, exercisede and usede allemoste in alle thynges a life monasticalle. *a* **1548** HALL *Chron., Hen. IV* 11 These monasticall persones..toke on them to write..the noble actes..of kynges and princes. **1593** R. HARVEY *Philad.* 51 A monasticall liuer..hath no partes of time for such young childish studies. *c* **1610** *Women Saints* 79 Her monasterie was at Derham, which she herself built, and in it receiued her monasticall weede. *a* **1626** BACON *Ch. Controv.* Wks. 1879 I. 347 The idle and monastical continuance within the universities. **1641** MILTON *Animadv.* Wks. 1851 III. 232 Their liking of doltish and monasticall Schoolemen daily increast. **1686** AGLIONBY *Painting Illustr.* 131 One of the first Founders of the Monastical Orders. **1774** T. WEST *Antiq. Furness* 61 [transl. of papal document] We will, that monastical discipline be there observed at all times. **1859** C. BARKER *Assoc. Princ.* i. 9 The gradual departure from primitive monastical austerity.

Hence **mo'nastically** *adv.*, in a monastic manner.

1600 SURFLET *Countrie Farme* II. xlvi. 294 The Spaniards ..did erect and set vp a Couent of Friers Cordeliers, liuing monastically. *a* **1652** J. SMITH *Sel. Disc.* ix. 452 To confine the soul thus monastically to its own home. **1729** SWIFT *Let. to Bolingbroke* 31 Oct., Years..monastically passed in this Country of liberty and delight, and money, and good company! **1867** *Contemp. Rev.* IV. 377 A monastically organised community of ascetics.

monasticism (mə'næstɪsɪz(ə)m). [f. MONASTIC + -ISM.] The monastic system or mode of life.

1795 MILNER *Hist. Ch. Christ* IV. xix. (1812) II. 243 Monasticism continued to make a rapid progress through this whole century. **1845** H. ROGERS *Ess.* (1874) I. iii. 144 The church would soon have fallen back, like the purified forms of monasticism, into its ancient corruptions. **1868** FREEMAN *Norm. Conq.* (1877) II. x. 452 Monasticism, in one form or another, was dominant for some ages. **1883** *Contemp. Rev.* Dec. 806 No one can question the services rendered to civilization by western monasticism.

monasticize (mə'næstɪsaɪz), *v.* [Formed as prec. + -IZE.] *trans.* To make monastic in character; to convert to monasticism. Hence **mo'nasticized** *ppl. a.*

1854 *Fraser's Mag.* L. 321 Subjects..belonging to the Romish, or, to speak more truly, to any monasticised church. **1854** MILMAN *Lat. Chr.* III. vi. (1864) II. 80 The institutions, which were hereafter to send forth S. Columban to convert and monasticise the German forests. **1893** *Edin. Rev.* July 256 A married clergy monasticised in vain by Dunstan.

Monastral (mɒ'næstrəl). The proprietary name of two groups of pigments having exceptional fastness: (*a*) blue and green pigments that are derivatives of phthalocyanine and are widely used esp. in paints, printing inks, and plastics; *spec.* copper phthalocyanine (Monastral Fast Blue B, or BS); (*b*) red and violet pigments that are derivatives of quinacridone.

1936 *Trade Marks Jrnl.* 2 Jan. 2/2 Monastral... All goods included in Class 1, but not including chemical photographic developers and not including any goods of a like kind to chemical photographic developers. British Dyestuffs Corporation Limited, Imperial Chemical House, ..London,.. manufacturers. **1936** *Discovery* Jan. 2/1 A new blue pigment, which combines fastness to light, heat, acids and alkalis with tinctorial strength, has recently been introduced by Imperial Chemical Industries, Ltd. Known as Monastral Fast Blue BS. **1952** K. VENKATARAMAN *Chem. Synthetic Dyes* II. xxxvii. 1133 There are only three [phthalocyanine derivatives] which are extensively used for coloring printing inks, paints, varnishes, enamels, plastics, and other materials. These are metal-free phthalocyanine (Monastral Fast Blue G, ICI), copper phthalocyanine (Monastral Fast Blue B) and highly chlorinated copper phthalocyanine (Monastral Fast Green G). **1958** *Times* 4 Dec. 3/2 Some series of squares [of mosaic] were made to order in a precise shade of colour indicated by Mr. Piper himself, a rich monastral blue and a delicate pale yellow being examples. **1961** H. F. PAYNE *Org. Coating Technol.* II. xx. 904 At present a family of three distinctly different pigment colors is commercially available, namely: Monastral Red B: a dark, transparent, blue-shade red toner; Monastral Red Y: a yellow-shade red toner, lighter and more opaque in mass tone than red B; Monastral Violet R: a dark, transparent, red-shade violet toner. **1970** *Sunday Times* (Colour Suppl.) 22 Nov. 69/4 Monastral Blue, an incredibly powerful synthetic pigment of fairly recent origin ..is sold under..different names: Windsor Blue, Phthalocyanine Blue.

monatomic (mɒnə'tɒmɪk), *a.* *Chem.* Also **mono-**. [f. MON(O)- + ATOM *sb.* + -IC.] Containing one atom; consisting of molecules each containing one atom. Also used for: Univalent.

1848 WATTS tr. *Gmelin's Handbk. Chem.* I. 53 Monatomic gases. **1866** ODLING *Anim. Chem.* 32 Monatomic alcohol. **1871** TYNDALL *Fragm. Sci.* (1879) I. iv. 105 Chlorine itself is molecular and not monatomic. **1874** J. P. COOKE *New Chem.* 278 Such hydrates are said to be mono-atomic. *Ibid.*, A hydrate is..monatomic, diatomic, triatomic, etc. according as it contains one, two, three, or more hydroxyl groups.

monatomism (mɒ'nætəmɪz(ə)m). [Formed as prec. + -ISM.] The quality or condition of being monatomic.

1854 J. SCOFFERN in *Orr's Circ. Sci., Chem.* 46 The proof of monatomism would be capability of electric decomposition.

monaul (mɒ'nɔːl). Also **monal, minaul, -al, moonaul, menall.** ['Hind. *munāl* or *monāl* (it seems to be in no dictionary)' (Yule).] The Anglo-Indian name for the Impeyan pheasant (*Lophophorus Impeyanus*). (See also quot. 1864.)

1787 LATHAM *Synopsis Birds* Suppl. 209 Impeyan Pheasant... Sir Elijah [Impey] informs me, that these birds are known in India by the name of Monaul. **1858–9** RUSSELL *Diary India* (1860) II. 164 They had only killed a few splendid minaul (monal, menall—*les trois se disent*), and another kind of pheasant called coqplass. **1864** JERDON *Birds of India* III. (II. II.) 510 *Lophophorus Impeyanus* Latham... The Monaul Pheasant. *Ibid.* 516 *Ceriornis satyra*, Linnæus. ..'Monaul' popularly by Europeans at Darjeeling, or Argus Pheasant. **1895** KIPLING *2nd Jungle Bk.* 39 The villagers.. saw the *minaul*, the Himalayan pheasant, blazing in her best colours.

‖**monaulos** (mɒ'nɔːlɒs). [L., f. Gr. μόναυλος single flute, flute with a single pipe, f. μόνο-ς single + αὐλός pipe.] An ancient Greek flute with one pipe.

1797 *Encycl. Brit.* (ed. 3) XII. 487/2 The monaulos, or single flute. **1864** ENGEL *Mus. Anc. Nat.* 155.

monaural (mɒn'ɔːrəl), *a.* [f. MON(O)- + AURAL.] **1.** Of or pertaining to the use of one ear only.

1888 *Pop. Sci. Monthly* XXXIII. 87 Direction cannot be appreciated by monaural observation. **1935** *Brit. Jrnl. Psychol.* XXV. 270 Differences in the time of arrival of sounds from a single source at the two ears, or differences in intensity,..are far smaller than the monaural or binaural thresholds for such time or intensity differences. **1955** *Sci. News Let.* 24 Sept. 204/3 Splitting sounds so that one ear hears it first is known as 'monaural delay'. Its use by the Air Force and airlines promises better and clearer communications in the air. **1972** L. A. JEFFRESS in J. V. Tobias *Found. Mod. Auditory Theory* II. ix. 360 The case where the noise is binaural and in phase at the ears and the signal is monaural..is an interesting one.

2. = MONOPHONIC *a.* 2.

1931 *Jrnl. Acoustical Soc. Amer.* Apr. 483 The fundamental difficulty is that we are at present restricted to monaural recording. **1948** *Electronics* Aug. 88/2 A person listening to sound through a binaural system has the illusion that the sound originates in the room rather than in the [head]phones. The effect is striking to anyone used to hearing monaural sound from a headset. **1951** *Wireless World* Mar. 85/1 Current radio broadcast and recording techniques are almost exclusively monaural, using a single microphone and transmission channel. **1959** *Sci. News* LIII. 57 A discerning listener could never be deceived into believing that even the best monaural reproduction was an original performance. **1964** P. J. GUY *Disc Recording* x. 148 Two loudspeakers are better than one, even for monaural reproduction. **1968** *Times* 29 Nov. p. iv/7 In July, 1967, E.M.I. ceased to produce new classical recordings in the monaural form. **1970** [see MONOPHONIC *a.* 2]. **1971** M. MCCARTHY *Birds of America* 212 Their gramophone and scratched monaural-78 records. **1974** *Encycl. Brit. Macropædia* XVII. 53/2 Stereophonic systems..produce a far greater sense of realism than single-channel (or monaural) systems.

monaurally (mən'ɔːrəlɪ), *adv.* [f. prec. + -LY².] **a.** With or to one ear.

1933 *Jrnl. Acoustical Soc. Amer.* IV. 288 The observer is placed in a sound field which is substantially that of a plane progressive wave, facing the source and listening monaurally. **1948** *Psychol. Bull.* XLV. 194 He observed that a sound heard binaurally was always louder than the same sound heard monaurally. **1972** N. I. DURLACH in J. V. Tobias *Found. Mod. Auditory Theory* II. x. 385 The tone is presented monaurally.

b. In a monaural (monophonic) manner; = MONOPHONICALLY *adv.* b.

1958 *Manch. Guardian* 30 June 5/3 Dvořák's Fourth Symphony is first played through one speaker, then monaurally through both, and finally stereophonically through both. **1964** P. J. GUY *Disc Recording* x. 147 It was the original aim of the record manufacturers to make stereophonic records playable monaurally with an ordinary pickup.

monax: see MOONACK.

monaxial (mɒ'næksɪəl), *a.* *Bot.* and *Zool.* [f. MON(O)- + L. *axi-s* + -AL¹, after AXIAL.] Having only one axis; developing along a single line.

1880 *Nature* XXI. 449 In many cases it [the central capsule] is monaxial, in others dipleuric. **1880** PASCOE *Zool. Classif.* (ed. 2) 283 *Monaxial*, when the axis is in one direction only. **1888** *Athenæum* 31 Mar. 406/2 Sponges with monaxial spicules. **1902** *Encycl. Brit.* XXV. 433/2 If this be the primary, or relatively primary axis [of flower] the plant is monaxial; the majority of plants are, however, pluriaxial.

monaxile (mɒ'næksɪl), *a.* and *sb.* *Zool.* [f. MON(O)- + L. *ax-is* + -ILE.] **a.** *adj.* Of a sponge-spicule: Having only one axis. **b.** *sb.* A monaxile spicule.

1888 ROLLESTON & JACKSON *Anim. Life* 810 Monaxile spicules. *Ibid.*, Spicules to a great extent tetraxile; large monaxiles common..spicules for the most part monaxiles.

monaxon (mɒ'næksɒn), *a.* *Zool.* [f. Gr. μόν-ος (see MONO-) + ἄξον-, ἄξων axis. Cf. mod.L. *Monaxona* neut. pl., the name of an order of sponges.] Having only one axis. So **mona'xonic** *a.*

1885 E. R. LANKESTER in *Encycl. Brit.* XIX. 849/2 A spherical (homaxonic) or a cone-shaped (monaxonic) perforated shell. **1887** SOLLAS *Ibid.* XXII. 416/1 Monaxon Biradiate Type (rhabdus). *Ibid.* 416/2 Modifications of monaxon type.

monaxonid (mɒ'næksənɪd), *a.* and *sb.* *Zool.* [ad. mod.L. *Monaxonida* neut. pl., formed as prec.: see -ID.] **a.** *adj.* Belonging to the sub-order *Monaxonida* of sponges. Of a sponge or sponge-spicule: Having only one axis. **b.** *sb.* A monaxonid sponge.

1887 S. O. RIDLEY in *Rep. Voy. Challenger* XX. Introd. 5 Monaxonid sponges. *Ibid.* 6 Both these forms of spicule are ..'monaxonid'. **1887** SOLLAS in *Encycl. Brit.* XXII. 422/1 The scleres are moulded on a Monaxonid base. *Ibid.* 427/2 The *Choristida*..are commoner than the Monaxonids.

monazite ('mɒnəzaɪt). *Min.* [Named by Breithaupt, 1829 (Ger. *monazit*), f. Gr. μονάζειν, to be solitary, on account of its rarity.] Phosphate of the cerium metals, found in small, reddish or brownish crystals (A. H. Chester).

1836 T. THOMSON *Min., Geol.*, etc. I. 672 Monazite... This name was given by Breithaupt to a mineral brought by Fielder from the Uralian mountains. **1865** WATTS *Dict. Chem.*, *Monazite*. Edwardsite, Mengite, Eremite. A phosphate of cerium and lanthanum, also containing thorinum according to some authorities. **1903** *Edin. Rev.* Oct. 388 The North Carolinian monazite.

monbar, var. MIMBAR.

Monbazillac (‖mɔ̃bazijak, mɒn'bæzɪlæk). Also **Mont Bazillac, Montbazillac.** [Name of a village south of Bergerac in the Dordogne department of S.W. France.] A sweet, white dessert wine, similar to Sauternes.

[**1833** C. REDDING *Mod. Wines* v. 158 The best wines are produced on the hills, upon the left bank of the Dordogne, in the communes of St. Laurent and Monbazillac.] *Ibid.* 404/2 (*index of wines*) Mont Basillac, 158. **1926** P. M. SHAND *Bk. Wine* v. 66 Montbazillac..is a label still met, which prepares one for a rich, sweet white wine that is made from the Sémillon grape. **1935** C. W. BERRY *In Search of Wine* viii. 186 We then had a bottle of 1918 Monbazillac—a trifle

sweet for me. **1955** J. THOMAS *No Banners* v. 39 A bottle of Montbazillac stood on the little table between their chairs. **1967** A. LICHINE *Encycl. Wines* 131/2 With one exception —sweet, white Monbazillac—the wines of Bergerac are simply not in the same class [as those of Bordeaux]. **1975** *Times* 17 May 11 Montbazillac is made with grapes that have been subjected to the action of *botrytis cinerea* or 'noble rot'.

monchaunce, variant of MUMCHANCE.

monche, obs. form of MUNCH *v.*

monchen, -ioun, -on, -yn, var. ff. MINCHEN.

‖**mon cher** (mɔ̃ ʃɛr). [Fr.] 'My dear fellow', as a term of address.

1680 ROCHESTER *Poems* 24 But now Moncher, dear Pug, says she, adieu. **1888** 'RITA' *Vivienne* I. ii. 23 Good bye, *mon cher*, and don't overwork yourself. **1920** F. M. FORD *Let.* 30 May (1965) 100 You see, mon cher, there are plenty of other people.. with the temperament of poets. **1975** A. CHRISTIE *Poirot's Last Case* xv. 162 So far, *mon cher*, this X has operated with so much ability that he has defeated me, Hercule Poirot!

monchiquite (mɒn'tʃiːkwaɪt). *Petrogr.* [a. G. *monchiquite* (Hunter & Rosenbusch 1890, in *Tschermak's mineral. u. petrograph. Mittheilungen* XI. 447), f. Serra de *Monchique*, name of a mountain range in southern Portugal where such a rock is found: see -ITE[1].] A lamprophyre containing small phenocrysts of olivine and augite, and usu. also biotite or an amphibole, in a glassy ground-mass consisting of or containing analcite.

1891 *Ann. Rep. Arkansas Geol. Survey 1890* II. iv. 110 The Brazilian dikes.. form an olivine-free class of the rock that Rosenbusch calls monchiquite. **1896** *Jrnl. Geol.* IV. 679 (*heading*) On the monchiquites or analcite group of igneous rocks. **1961** [see CAMPTONITE]. **1965** [see FERROAN *a.*].

monck, -ely, -ery: see MONK, MONKLY, etc.

moncorne, obs. form of MONGCORN.

Mond (mɒnd). The name of Ludwig *Mond* (1839–1909), German-born British chemist, used *attrib.* to designate processes devised by him and the plant and products of these processes, esp. (*a*) a method of manufacturing producer gas by passing air and an excess of steam into a gas producer so that most of the nitrogen of the coal is converted into ammonia and can be recovered; (*b*) a process for obtaining high-purity nickel by decomposing by heat the volatile nickel carbonyl, which is obtained from crude nickel oxide by reduction with hydrogen followed by reaction with carbon monoxide.

1887 *Encycl. Brit.* XXII. 244/1 The Mond process, of all the many sulphur-recovery processes yet introduced, is the best. **1903** *Jrnl. Franklin Inst.* CLV. 390 The success of the Mond nickel process, as carried on in England, has been seriously hindered by the discovery that the process is dangerous to the health of the men employed. **1907** E. L. RHEAD *Metallurgy* (new ed.) vi. 76 Mond gas is generated by passing into the producer air containing the maximum amount of water vapour that the heat produced is capable of decomposing. **1936** BONE & HIMUS *Coal* xxiv. 424 The trades using Mond Gas are diverse, including.. manufacture of motor cars and component parts, foundries .., chemical works, [etc.]. **1946** J. R. PARTINGTON *Gen. & Inorg. Chem.* xvii. 485 Mond gas is formed with a large excess of steam which keeps the temperature low. **1947** G. W. HIMUS *Elements Fuel Technol.* xv. 324 A number of Mond plants were installed and found to be economic. **1969** H. T. EVANS tr. *Hägg's Gen. & Inorg. Chem.* xxxiv. 727 In the so-called Mond process a very fine powder is desired, and the reduction is done with water gas at 350–400°C.

mond, obs. form of MOUND, world, orb.

mondain, obs. form of MUNDANE.

‖**mondaine** (mɔ̃dɛn), *sb.* (and *a.*) [F. *mondaine*, f. *mondain* worldly, ad. L. *mundānus*, f. *mundus* world: cf. MUNDANE *a.* (*sb.*)] A woman belonging to fashionable society. Also **mondain** (mɔ̃dæ̃), a man belonging to fashionable society.

1888 MRS. H. WARD *R. Elsmere* II. IV. xxvi. 285 He was in a mood to be impatient with a *mondaine's* languid inquiries into clerical work. **1889** E. DOWSON *Let.* 24 Mar. (1967) 55 Here you have the refinement of the mondaine with the independence of the cocotte. **1902** [see ETIQUETTE 4]. **1906** B. VON HUTTEN *What became of Pam* xii. 192 He was a dandy and a *mondain*, who.. had never done anything noteworthy. **1908** *Westm. Gaz.* 3 Oct. 13/2 The bold attempt of the milliners to coax mondaines to the smaller hat will be watched with interest. **1912** *Tatler* 23 Oct. p. vi (Advt.), Not only have the requirements of the smart mondaine been carefully considered but [etc.]. **1920** A. HUXLEY *Let.* 4 May (1969) 185 Cocteau is a man of fabulous cleverness, but not serious—He is just a mondain. **1920** *Q. Rev.* July 38 The provocative elegance of the Flavian *mondaines.* **1924** *Public Opinion* 7 Nov. 458/2 She was in point of fact a most accomplished mondaine. **1970** G. GREER *Female Eunuch* 266 Flatly contemptuous words like *kept-woman* and *call-girl* have taken over.. from.. *courtesan, mondaine.*

b. *adj.* Attached to things of the world; worldly.

1889 E. DOWSON *Let.* c 11 Jan. (1967) 23, I will free myself from the intolerable *corvée* of the *mondain* dinner. **1896** C. M. YONGE *Release* II. viii. 144 Ah! you are *mondaine*, you are Protestant, madame. **1927** H. NICHOLSON *Some People* 88 When I got to bed I realised that by 'worldly' he had meant 'mondaine'. **1929** L. REA *Six Mrs. Greenes* II. 58 Lavinia, mondaine, vivid, with a delicate certainty of touch that enabled her [etc.]. **1962** *Listener* 24 May 920/3 His pleasure in the company of children and simple people—as opposed to *mondain* people.

mondanity, var. MUNDANITY.

Monday ('mʌndeɪ, -dɪ). Forms: 1–2 **Mónan dæȝ**, 2 **Monendæiȝ, Móndæȝ**, 3 **Monen dai, Munendai**, 3–4 **Monenday, Monedai**, (3 **-dæi**, 5 **-day**), 5–7 **Munday**, (6 **-day(e)**, 5 **Monnyn day, Monunday**, 8 **Mooneday**, 4– **Monday**; *Sc.* 5 **Monoundai, Monynday, Monnunda**, 6 **Mon(o)unday**, 6–9 **Mononday**, (7 **Moonday**), 8 **Mununday**, 9 **Munan-, Mona(n)-, Munonday.** [OE. *Mónandæȝ*, f. *mónan* genit. of *móna* MOON *sb.*[1] + *dæȝ* DAY; a translation of late L. *Lūnæ diēs*, whence F. *lundi*, It. *lunedì*, etc. Equivalent forms in the other Teut. langs. are OFris. *mônendei, mônedei*, MLG. *mânendach, mândach*, MDu. *manendach, maendach* (Du. *maandag*), OHG. *mânetag* (MHG. *mântac, mæntac, môntac*, mod.G. *Montag*), ON. *mánadag-r* (Sw. *måndag*, Da. *mandag*).]

1. The second day of the week.

c **1000** *Ags. Gosp.* John vii. 32 *rubric*, Ðys sceal on monan dæȝ on þære fyftan wucan innan lenctene. *c* **1050** *Byrhtferth's Handboc* in *Anglia* (1885) VIII. 321 þæs sunnandæȝes nama wæs of þære sunnan, & þæs monandæȝes of þæs monan. *c* **1060–1125** *Rect. Singul. Person.* §3 in Liebermann *Gesetze* 445 Kotesetlan riht be ðam ðe on lande stent: on sumor he sceal ælce Mondæȝe ofer ȝeares fyrst his laforde wyrcan. **1129** *O.E. Chron.* an. 1129, þa began þæt mot on Monendæiȝ & heold on an to ðe Fridæiȝ. *c* **1200** *Winteney Rule St. Benet* (1888) 49 þæt is asunnandæȝe & on monan dæȝ. *c* **1250** *Gen. & Ex.* 72 He fel out on ðe munendai. *c* **1290** *Beket* 900 in *S. Eng. Leg.*, And þe Monenday sore syk þe bischop thomas lay. **1387** TREVISA *Higden* (Rolls) II. 25 From Saturday at none for to Monday. **1422** *Rolls of Parlt.* IV. 173/2 The Monunday next before the fest of Seint Martyn. *a* **1557** *Diurn. Occur.* (Bannatyne Cl.) 24 The Inglismen come on Scottis ground, and lay still fra Monunday to Sattirday. **1562** WINȜET *Cert. Tractates* iii. Wks. (S.T.S.) I. 23 On Pasche Monunday last passit. **1592** SHAKS. *Rom. & Jul.* III. iv. 17 *Cap.* But soft, What day is this? *Par.* Monday, my Lord. **1624** LAUD *Diary* 29 Mar., Wks. 1853 III. 151 Easter Monday. **1638** BRATHWAIT *Barnabees Jrnl.* (1818) 15 Banbery.. Where I saw a Puritane-one Hanging of his cat on Monday, For killing of a mouse on Sonday. *c* **1713** H. CAREY *Ballad, Sally in our alley* iv, And that's the day that comes betwixt A Saturday and Monday. *a* **1810** TANNAHILL *Poems* (1846) 145, I see I maun quat takin' Mununday's yill. **1896** A. E. HOUSMAN *Shropshire Lad* iii, Or come you home of Monday When Ludlow market hums.

2. With specific epithet. **Black Monday**, (*a*) a name for Easter Monday (the historical explanations in the quots. are untrustworthy; for the unlucky character ascribed to Mondays generally, and esp. to one or more Mondays in April, see *Leechdoms* III. 76 and 162, Brand's *Pop. Antiq.* ed. Ellis 1813 I. 466 ff., and quot. 1700; the common notion that rejoicing is naturally followed by calamity may have caused the day after Easter day to be regarded as even more perilous than other Mondays); (*b*) *school slang*, the first school-day after a vacation. †**Bloody Monday** *school slang*, the first day of vacation, a day of punishment for offenders. †**Fat Monday** [= F. *lundi gras*], the Monday before Shrove Tuesday. **Saint Monday**, used with reference to the practice among workmen of being idle on Monday, as a consequence of drunkenness on the Sunday; chiefly in phrase ***to keep Saint Monday***. ***Collop Monday***: see COLLOP[1] 1 c. ***Handsel Monday***: see HANDSEL 5. Also HOCK-MONDAY, PLOUGH-MONDAY.

? **1359** (MS. ? **1389**) *E.E. Gilds* (1870) 97 Yis gilde schal haue, by ȝere, foure mornspeches.. ye secunde schal be on blake monunday. *c* **1435** *Chron. London* (Kingsford 1905) 13 In the same yere [1360] the xiiij day off April and the morwe after Ester Day, Kyng Edward with his Oost lay byfore the Citee off Parys; the which was a ffoule Derke day.. so bytter colde, that syttyng on horse bak men dyed. Wherefore, vnto this day yt ys called blak Monday. **1449** BOWER *Fordun's Scotichron.* XIV. xvii. 358–9 [Relates that the army of the Black Prince sustained terrible losses from a storm on Easter-Monday 1357.] Propter hoc hucusque in Anglia feria secunda Paschæ Blak-mononday vulgariter nuncupatur. **1491** *Acc. Ld. High Treas. Scot.* I. 176 Item, on Blak Monnunda, to the Freris of Edinburgh, ix s. **1596** SHAKS. *Merch. V.* II. v. 25 It was not for nothing that my nose fell a bleeding on blacke monday last. **1601** *Nottingham Rec.* (1889) IV. 256 Itt ys ordered, that the Aldermen.. shall wayte on Maister Maior on Blake Monday yearely. *a* **1604** HANMER *Chron. Irel.* (1633) 186 Anno 1209, the occasion of blacke Munday, and the originall remembrance thereof rose at Dublin. [A massacre of the English settlers of Dublin by the Irish on Easter-Monday.] **1700** *Poor Robin* Feb., I find not by the Stars we shall have ever a Black-Monday this Month, which we are very glad of, because such days are very prejudicial to the Credit of Astrology. **1735** *Ibid.* Jan., But after Twelfth day Christmass is visibly eclips'd and beclouded; then comes Black monday for the School boys, and they as well as the rest must go to their daily Labour. **1749** FIELDING *Tom Jones* VIII. xi, My mother.. made home so disagreeable to me, that what is called by school-boys Black Monday, was to me the whitest in the whole year. **1829** BROCKETT *N.C. Words* (ed. 2), *Black-Monday*, the first day of going to school after the vacation. **1682** R. VERNEY *Let. to Father* Winchester College 18 May, We shall breack up on the Whensday before holy Thursday: And S[r]. I would desire you to let your horses be here on the Satterday following that I may be going on Bloddy Munday, upon which day all the Children.. Goe home & after that day noebody stays but some of the Children which the Warden makes stay here for some notorious action they have committed. **1765** GARRICK in *Univ. Mag.* XXXVII. 326/1, I, like a boy who long has truant play'd.. On bloody Monday take my fearful stand And often eye the birchen-scepter'd hand. **1585** T. WASHINGTON tr. *Nicholay's Voy.* IV. xxxvi. 159 b, They doe obserue two Lents.. wherof the first beginneth on the fat munday, being ix. dayes before the lent of the Latins. **1753** *Scots Mag.* Apr. 208/1 (*title*) St. Monday; or, the tipling tradesmen. **1804** MAR. EDGEWORTH *Popular T., Tomorrow* vii. (1856) 408 *note*, It is a custom in Ireland among shoemakers, if they intoxicate themselves on Sunday, to do no work on Monday; and this they call making a Saint Monday. **1857** GEN. P. THOMPSON *Audi Alt.* I. vii. 22 An assemblage of artisans keeping Saint Monday. **1890** E. ROPER *By Track & Trail* xvii. (1891) 255 Ah Sin loses no time in holiday.. he has no St. Mondays.

3. *attrib.*, as ***Monday night, pop***, etc. Also **Monday Club**, a right-wing Conservative club (cf. CLUB *sb.* 13) that originally held its meetings on Mondays; so **Monday-clubber**, a member of this club; **Monday-morning** *attrib.*, suggestive of lethargy or disinclination after a busy or eventful weekend.

1596 SHAKS. *1 Hen. IV*, I. ii. 39 A purse of Gold most resolutely snatch'd on Monday night. **1602** —— *Ham.* II. ii. 406 A Monday morning 'twas so indeed. **1676** LADY CHAWORTH in *12th Rep. Hist. MSS. Comm.* App. v. 33, I shall send your Lordship the peck of chesnuts.. by the Munday carrier. **1862** Monday pop [see POP *sb.*[4]]. **1880** W. S. GILBERT *Patience* II, Who thinks suburban 'hops', More fun than 'Monday Pops'. **1884** J. QUINCY *Figures of Past* 198 Here we were, Monday evening, actually dining in New York. **1892** KIPLING *Barrack-r. Ballads, Snarleyow*, An' if one wheel was juicy, you may lay your Monday head 'Twas juicier for the niggers. **1897** MARY KINGSLEY *W. Africa* 142 This morning the French official seems sad and melancholy. I fancy he has got a Monday head (Kipling). **1921** D. H. LAWRENCE *Sea & Sardinia* 261 The rather inert, narrow, Monday-morning street. **1938** R. G. COLLINGWOOD *Princ. Art* v. 95, I get back to my book with that Monday-morning feeling. **1962** *Evening Standard* 12 Feb. 6 (*caption to cartoon*), Lord Salisbury has become patron of the 'Monday Club', a new group of Young Conservatives formed to 'keep the Conservative Party Conservative'. **1966** *Observer* 16 Oct. 12/5 To dismiss them simply as acts of political vengeance or as another example of 'African savagery' is Monday Club mumbo-jumbo. **1970** G. K. ROBERTS *Political Parties & Pressure Groups in Britain* i. 9 Pressure-groups *within* political parties... Recent examples in Britain are:.. the Monday Club, which tries to maintain what it chooses to regard as the basic principles of Conservatism. **1972** R. COPPING *Story of Monday Club* 5 Rebelling against Macmillan's 'Winds of Change' speech a tiny group of young conservative dissentients formed the Monday Club on 1st January 1961. **1972** *Times* 21 July 12/1 His successful conservative opponent, the Monday Clubber, Harold Soref. **1973** *Times* 20 June 4/3 The executive of the Monday Club, the right-wing Conservative pressure group, decided last night.. to expel the Essex branch of the club for its associations with the National Front. **1973** *Guardian* 27 June 1/3 Mr Enoch Powell.. banned reporters from a Monday Club meeting last night.

Mondayish ('mʌndeɪɪʃ), *a.* [f. prec. + -ISH.] Affected with the indisposition, often felt by clergymen on Monday, resulting from the work of Sunday. Hence '**Mondayishness**.

1804 W. BULL in *Mem.* (1864) 313, I quite forgot it was Monday, and I dare say I am Mondayish. **1850** GILFILLAN in Watson *G.'s Lett. & Jrnls.* (1892) 145 Your letter has cheered my 'Mondayishness'. **1884** *Congregationalist* Apr. 320 There is a disease, only known among ministers, of Mondayishness. **1884** *Guardian* 10 Sept. 1350/2 It might be read.. even by the Mondayish clergyman.

mondayn(e, obs. forms of MUNDANE *a.*

‖**monde** (mɔ̃d). [Fr.: lit. 'world'. Cf. BEAU MONDE.] The 'world' of fashionable or aristocratic persons; 'society'. Also, a person's particular 'world' or circle; the 'set' in which one moves.

1765 H. WALPOLE *Lett.* 26 Sept., When the *monde* returns to Paris, I shall probably be more dissipated. **1774** *Ibid.* 23 Apr., I.. expect you will think no personages of less *monde* fit to invite to our *partie quarrée.* **1823** BYRON *Juan* XIV. xix, 'Tis said.. That no one has succeeded in describing The monde, exactly as they ought to paint. **1862** THACKERAY *Philip* iv, Unless you are of the very great *monde. Ibid.*, You come home late, and you don't live in a proper *monde*, sir! **1872** E. BRADDON *Life in India* v. 167 Bills have been left at the houses of the *monde.*

monde, obs. pa. t. of MUN *v.*

mondeyne, obs. form of MUNDANE.

mondglorye, variant of MANDGLORYE *Obs.*

'**mondial**, *a.* In 5 **-all**. [a. OF. *mondial*, ad. late L. *mundiālis*, f. L. *mund-us* world: see MUNDANE *a.*] †**1.** Wordly, mundane. *Obs.*

c **1475** *Partenay* 18 And wel at ease of goodes mondiall.

2. [ad. mod.F. *mondial.*] Pertaining to, affecting, or involving the whole world; world-wide, universal. Hence **mondiali'zation**.

[**1918** A. GRAY tr. *Grelling's Crime* II. iii. 175 While in this question Germany could accept the system *individuel* she could not accept the system *mondial.*] **1919** S. HUDDLESTON *Peace Making at Paris* i. 10 Chaos threatened, with the black

night of a mondial revolution. **1920** *Glasgow Herald* 28 June 8 The codification of mondial commercial laws is also aimed at. **1924** *Blackw. Mag.* Aug. 280/2 They were resolved to create their 'mondial situation', and to strengthen it.. against the English. **1960** R. CARPENTER *Greek Sculpture* viii. 213 Be it hoped without consequent detriment to its mondial reputation. **1961** *Economist* 11 Nov. 528/1 A vast extension of the common market—a '*mondialisation*' to use the latest jargon. **1962** *Spectator* 5 Oct. 495 Chiding the French for their fear of *mondialisation*. **1965** *New Scientist* 2 Sept. 544/1 Perhaps this capitalist-sounding manœuvre towards the 'mondialization' of a natural resource will appeal to the Afro-Asian bloc at the UN.

mondic, obs. form of MUNDIC.

‖**mon Dieu** (mɔ̃ djø). [Fr.] = *my God!* (cf. GOD 7).

1768 STERNE *Sent. Journey* I. 57 The poor monk blush'd ..*Mon Dieu!* said he.. you never used me unkindly. **1849** THACKERAY *Pendennis* I. viii. 80 'You may come and live down here—down here, *mon Dieu!* for ever' (said the Major, with a dreary shrug, as he thought.. of Pall Mall). **1861** G. MEREDITH *Let.* 19 Nov. (1970) I. 113, I had, the truth is, a miserable walking companion; to wit, Buonaparte Wyse (son of the Minister at Athens, who will hardly own him), and of Mde Bon[aparte] Wyse (Lucien's daughter), whom he will hardly own... Mon Dieu! **1945** 'O. MALET' *My Bird Sings* I. vi. 43 *Mon dieu!* But nobody answers. **1964** *Guardian* 10 Oct. 5/4 We eat, *mon dieu*, how we eat! **1974** P. HIGHSMITH *Ripley's Game* ii. 17 *Mon dieu!*—Well, where did *he* hear it from?

Mondism (ˈmɒndɪz(ə)m). [f. the name of Alfred *Mond* (1868–1930), British politician.] The views of A. Mond, especially his advocacy of co-ordination and co-operation as bases of industrial enterprise.

1917 F. M. FORD *Let.* 5 Jan. (1965) 82 What a Ministry! Everything one has fought against all one's life. Northcliffism,.. Mondism, Balliolism! **1928** *Daily Tel.* 10 July 10 After further disorder Mr. Cook was called upon. He attacked 'Mondism', which he declared was the infant of Fascism and should be killed at birth. **1962** T. L. JOHNSTON *Collective Bargaining in Sweden* vii. 169 This labour peace conference is usually referred to as the Swedish attempt at Mondism.

‖**mondo** (ˈmɒndəʊ). [Jap., f. *mon* asking + *do* answering.] An instructional technique of Zen Buddhism consisting of rapid dialogue of questions and answers between master and pupil.

1927 D. T. SUZUKI *Essays in Zen Buddhism* I. vi. 256 The following 'mondo' or dialogue (literally questioning and answering) will give us a glimpse into the ways of Zen. **1960** KOESTLER *Lotus & Robot* x. 233 In its mondos and koans, Japanese ambiguity reaches its metaphysical peak. **1961** *Times Lit. Suppl.* 17 Feb. 8/3 Perhaps the most significant part of its [*sc.* a book's] contribution consists in its argument ..that the zen *mondo* are full of direct, coherent, systematic and intelligible communication.

mondongas, obs. form of MUNDUNGUS.

‖**mondongo** (mɒnˈdɒŋgəʊ). [Sp. *mondongo*. Cf. MUNDUNGUS.] A dish composed of tripe.

1622 MABBE tr. *Aleman's Guzman d'Alf.* II. 274 On the Saturdayes, we alwaies made our meales of Mondongo's [*marg.* The tripes or intrals of any beast]. **1884** *Health Exhib. Catal.* 159/2 Mondongo (a soup-like dish; a favourite preparation in the country) [Venezuela].

mondoyne, obs. form of MUNDANE.

Mondrian (ˈmɒndrɪən), *a.* [f. the name of P.C. ('Piet') *Mondrian*, *Mondriaan* (1872–1944), Dutch painter.] Resembling the geometrical abstract style of Mondrian.

1958 *Listener* 27 Nov. 888/1 A Mondrian scheme of simple primary colors. **1963** *Times* 30 Apr. 15/5 The Mondriaan-like luminous coloured panels.

†**mone**, *sb.*¹ *Obs.* Forms: 1 ȝemána, 3 ymone, imone, man, 3–4 mone. [OE. *ȝemána* wk. masc.:—OTeut. type **gamainon-*, cogn. w. **gamainjo-* common: see MEAN *a.*¹]

1. Companionship; sexual intercourse. Cf. MENE.

a **900** tr. *Bæda's Hist.* II. viii. [ix.] (1890) 120 þa he ærest his ærendwrecan sende.. & þisse fæmnan ȝemanan bæd. *c* **1205** LAY. 25916 Ne mihte þat maiden his mone i-þolien. *a* **1225** *St. Marher.* 13 Ant heom i folhi neodelukest þæt cunnið to beon cleane wiðuten monnes man ant fleoð flesches fulðen. **1297** R. GLOUC. (Rolls) 6359 So nis it noȝt quaþ þe king uor mi kinedom is ymone [*v.r.* in mone] Vor an felawe ich abbe þer to. *c* **1315** SHOREHAM I. 1690 And ȝif hys make mone craueþ. *Ibid.* 1763 Bot ȝif þer ulesches y-mone be Folȝynde. **1387** TREVISA *Higden* (Rolls) VI. 29 He was i-bore of þe mayde Marie by vertu of God wiþ oute mannys mone [L. *non humano semine*].

2. A companion.

1297 R. GLOUC. (Rolls) 6436 þo he was of al engelond king wiþoute mone. *a* **1300** *K. Horn* 560 (Camb. MS.) Aþulf was his mone.

†**mone**, *sb.*² *Obs. rare*⁻¹. [? a. ON. *móna* 'mammy'.] An old woman, a crone.

1390 GOWER *Conf.* I. 97 He sende up for the lady sone, And forth sche cam, that olde Mone.

mone (məʊn), *sb.*³ [ad. mod.L. *mona*, the specific name, or its source Pg. *mona*: see MONA. Cf. F. *mone* (Buffon).] = MONA.

1868 *Museum Nat. Hist.* I. 30 The mone.. is usually brought to Europe from Senegal.

†**mone**, *v. Obs.* Forms: 3 mune-n, 3–4 mun, 3 mon, 4 monne, 3–5 mone. [a. ON. *muna* to remember (a preterite-present, 1 and 3 sing. *man*, 1 pl. *munom*, pa. t. *munða*, *munda*), etymologically identical, and in most of its forms coincident, with *munu* to intend (see MUN *v.*).

The equivalent OE. *munan* to think, consider, is rare exc. in the compounds *ȝemunan* (see I-MUNE *v.*), *ofmunan* to recollect, *onmunan* to consider; it is unlikely that the ME. verb is of native origin, as the examples are all from dialects with Scandinavian admixture. For the root and the cognates in other Teut. and Indogermanic langs., see MIND *sb.*¹]

1. *trans.* To remember, bear in mind. Also *intr.* (const. *of*).

c **1220** *Bestiary* 370 in *OE. Misc.* 12 Đe hertes costes we oȝen to munen [*rime* sunen = *shun*]. *c* **1250** *Gen. & Ex.* 558 Noe and hise ðre sunen, Sem, Cam, Iaphet, if we riȝt munen, And here foure wifes woren hem wið. *Ibid.* 2409 So ðinked euerilc wis man.. ðe of adames gilte muneð. *a* **1300** *E.E. Psalter* lxv. 5 Comes and sees, goddes werkes mones. *a* **1300** *Cursor M.* 8384 Bot if þou þar-of wil mone, sir king Will i wat þat þou me hight. *Ibid.* 23927 Leuedi [Mary].. giue me grace.. Mi sinnes to bete.. þi suns ded to mon on ai. **1303** R. BRUNNE *Handl. Synne* 7673 Yn a prouerbe of olde Englys.. þat ȝougþe wones, yn age mones. *c* **1320** *Sir Tristr.* 657 Child.. How were þou fram rohand lorn? Monestow neuer in lede? *c* **1330** R. BRUNNE *Chron. Wace* (Rolls) 4811 [Androcheus] preied hym 'þat he wolde mone þat he was his broþer sone'. **1375** BARBOUR *Bruce* XIX. 526 But othir dedis nane war donne That gretly is apone till monne.

b. *intr.* To make remembrance. Const. *on*, *for*.

a **1425** *Cursor M.* 8252 (Trin.) Of cercles þat he toke awey Offringe he made to mone on ay. *a* **1440** *Sir Eglam.* 1008 (Lincoln MS.) He gafe thame [lands] for to lyfe appone, For Cristabelle saule to mone.

2. To mention, tell of. Also *absol.* and *intr.* const. *of*.

a **1300** *Cursor M.* 9233 Iechonias ȝe herd me mun [*other texts* mone], Salatiel he had to sun. *a* **1300** *Ibid.* 9519 þis ilk king þat i of mon He had an anlepe son. *a* **1310** in Wright *Lyric P.* xxxii. 92, Y wole mone my song on wham that hit ys on y-long. *c* **1330** R. BRUNNE *Chron. Wace* (Rolls) 214 Bot Noe & his þre sones And þeir wyues—þe bible hit mones —Were none worthi in Godes sight. *Ibid.* 14823 Myster Edmond seis, as me mones. þat þe Engle hadde nynetene sones. **13..** *Propr. Sanct.* (Vernon MS.) in *Archiv Stud. neu. Spr.* LXXXI. 106/99 Bariona, þat we of mone, hit is to mene 'a coluer sone'.

b. const. *dat.* of person.

a **1300** *Cursor M.* 20325 [Mary *loq.*] I sal mon mi suet sun, He sal te [*sc.* John] do til him com. *Ibid.* 24758 Quat time ..þat þis bitidd þat sco was geten.. I sal yow mon widvten mis. **1303** R. BRUNNE *Handl. Synne* 11888 Now haue ȝe herde þe poyntes twelue.. Prestes oghte hem alle to kunne Lewed men to teche and monne. *c* **1325** *Body & Soul* in *Map's Poems* (Camden) 336 Ȝwanne thouȝ me tauȝtist on untiȝth, an me gan ther offe mone. *a* **1400** *Relig. Pieces fr. Thornton MS.* ix. 239 'What may þis mene', quod these men, 'mone it vs mare'.

mone, obs. f. MANY, MOAN, MONEY, MOON, MUN.

monechen, -on(e, -yn, var. ff. MINCHEN *Obs.*

monecian, obs. form of MONŒCIAN.

Monéddo, variant of MANITOU.

1845 HIRST *Com. Mammoth*, etc. 17 We deemed Monéddo's will Had given us to these sons of Flame.

Monégasque (mɒnegask), *sb.* and *a.* Also **Monegasque**. [Fr.] **A.** *sb.* A native or inhabitant of Monaco. **B.** *adj.* Belonging to or characteristic of Monaco or its inhabitants.

1882 T. H. PICKERING *Monaco* i. 11 That which may be, and is, done in Riviera towns,.. is impossible in the Monégasque metropolis on the Mediterranean. *Ibid.* vi. 96 Three harvests of four different products make up a total, according to Monégasque arithmatic, of twelve crops. *Ibid.* iii. 59 The Monégasques enjoy the privilege of being governed—and well governed—without being called upon to contribute in any way towards the expenses. **1926** MUIRHEAD & MONMARCHÉ *Southern France* 196 The inhabitants ('Monégasques') are forbidden access to the gaming tables. **1938** H. G. WELLS *Apropos of Dolores* iii. 88 She was really Monégasque. **1962** *Listener* 3 May 761/1 The population [of Monaco] is 23,000, but only 3,000 of them are real Monégasques. **1966** G. GREENE *Comedians* iii. 64, I am uncertain whether she was French—perhaps she was a rare Monegasque. **1966** S. ROSSITER *South of France* 162 The inhabitants ('Monégasques').. enjoy immunity from taxation. *Ibid.* 167 A joint-stock company, which pays an annual tribute to the Monégasque government for its 'concession' of the gambling monopoly. **1968** *Guardian* 5 Jan. 6/6 Installed as manager is Georges Penna, a Monegasque of Italian parentage. **1973** *Daily Tel.* 19 Mar. 3/2 In 1958 there was more publicity when Prince Rainier banned them from Monaco after Lady Docker tore up a paper Monégasque flag.

monek(e, obs. forms of MONK.

monekeer, monekur, varr. MONIKER.

Monel (ˈməʊnəl). Also **monel**. [(Altered form of) the name of Ambrose *Monell* (d. 1921), president of the International Nickel Company when that firm introduced the alloys.] Used as a proprietary name (usu. *attrib.*) to denote alloys composed of about 68 per cent nickel and 30 per cent copper with small amounts of other elements, which have a high tensile strength and good resistance to corrosion, particularly towards sea-water.

1909 *Trade Marks Jrnl.* 17 Feb. 286 Monel Metal... Metal alloy. International Nickel Company.., Manhattan, New York, U.S.A. **1918** *Chambers's Jrnl.* Mar. 207/1 These discs are made of monel metal. **1945** *Electronic Engin.* XVII. 384 Electrodes on the instrument consist of Monel metal cores which do not corrode in saline solution. **1970** *Motor Boat & Yachting* 16 Oct. 49/2 The original iron fastenings have been superseded by monel fastenings. **1970** W. J. PATTON *Mod. Manufacturing Processes* iv. 54 Nickel and the monels are too soft and ductile to be readily machinable, but a more machinable monel is available in R Monel (Monel R-405), containing 66% nickel, 31·5% copper, and 0·05% sulfur. **1972** T. P. McMAHON *Issue of Bishop's Blood* (1973) xiii. 191, I was shuddering at what Meredith was going to charge. He's got a thing about always using Monel metal on what he calls 'furnishings'.

monellin (ˈmɒnəlɪn). *Chem.* [f. the name of the *Monell* Chemical Senses Center, in Philadelphia, U.S.A., where it was first isolated + -IN¹.] A protein with a sweet taste isolated from the berries of the tropical plant *Dioscoreophyllum cumminsii*.

1972 MORRIS & CAGAN in *Biochim. & Biophys. Acta* CCLXI. 114 We propose the name 'monellin' for the sweet material we have isolated. **1972** *Daily Colonist* (Victoria, B.C.) 27 Feb. 25/6 [Scientists] had isolated a new, low-calorie sweetener said to be 3,000 times more intense by weight than sugar. Named 'Monellin' the product is derived from a wild red berry that grows abundantly in tropical West Africa. **1973** *Nature* 27 July 196/3 Both thaumatin and monellin exhibit sweetness to a prodigious degree.

monembryony (mɒˈnɛmbrɪənɪ). Also **mono-**. [f. MON(O)- + EMBRYON + -Y.] The condition of producing but one embryo. Hence **monembryˈonic** *a.*, having a single embryo.

1849 BALFOUR *Man. Bot.* §586 In general, one embryo is produced [in fertilization], constituting what is denominated monembryony. **1879** STORMONTH *Man. Sci. Terms, Monembrionic*.

moneme (ˈmɒniːm). *Linguistics.* [a. F. *monème*, f. MON(O- + -EME.] In the terminology of some linguists, the smallest meaningful unit of language: = MORPHEME.

1953 C. E. BAZELL *Linguistic Form* i. 9 In the modern school of Geneva,.. there is a tendency to use the otherwise unknown term *moneme* for the American *morph*. **1960** H. MARCHAND *Categories Present-Day Eng. Word-Formation* x. 367 The result of blending is, indeed, always a moneme, i.e. an unanalysable, simple word, not a motivated syntagma. **1960** A. MARTINET in *Word* XVI. 4 Minimal meaningful units.. have sometimes been called 'morphemes'... I will rather use.. *moneme*, which has been used with that meaning by some linguists of the Geneva school. **1968** J. W. F. MULDER *Sets & Relations in Phonology* i. 47 The phonological features.. do not represent moneme expressions, i.e. they are.. not distinctive on the grammatical level. **1970** *English Studies* LI. 446 It is noteworthy that Anglian *ald* often becomes *old* (in *o*-areas) in ME nicknames like *Oldman* but not in Christian names like *Aldith*, *Aldred* etc. which are somewhat fossilized and no longer associated with the moneme. **1970** G. C. LEPSCHY *Survey of Structural Linguistics* vi. 106 A linguistic utterance undergoes a first articulation into monemes, which are the elementary grammatical units corresponding to what American linguists call morphemes.

monemerous: see MONOHEMEROUS.

†**monen-**. *Obs. rare.* [ME. *Monen* in *Monenday*, Monday. Cf. OE. *Mónan æfen*, *niht*, Sunday night.] ***monen morrow***, Monday morning.

a **1300** *Vision of Paul* (MS. Laud 108) in *Archiv Stud. neu. Spr.* LII. 38 Fram saturday non to þe monen moruwe.

monenergist, monenergistic, *a.*: the more correct forms of MONERGIST, MONERGISTIC *a.* (see s.v. MONERGISM).

1915 *Encycl. Relig. & Ethics* VIII. 821/2 The Monenergistic or Monothelete controversy seems at first glance to be a mere sequel to the Monophysite conflict. *Ibid.* 822/1 The Monenergists were possessed with the idea that the redemptive activity of the God-man emanated wholly and solely from His divine nature.

‖ˈ**moneo.** *Oxford Univ. Obs.* [L., = 'I warn'.] A formal reminder of a University function. So ˈ**moneo** *v. trans.*, to serve with a 'moneo' or reminder.

1715 HEARNE *Collect.* (O.H.S.) V. 83 This Morning preached Mʳ. Mear.. at Sᵗ. Marie's... It was about half an hour after ten er'e he came to Church... He excused himself by saying he was moneo'd for yᵉ Afternoon. *Ibid.* 128 This Morning preached at Xᵗ Church Dʳ. Potter... Mʳ. Taylor of Xᵗ Ch. was put in the Note, there having been a Mistake in delivering the Moneo.

moneour, obs. form of MONEYER.

monepic (mɒˈnɛpɪk), *a. rare.* Also **monoepic**. [f. MON(O)- + Gr. ἔπ-ος word + IC.] Composed of a single word or of sentences consisting of a single word.

a **1832** BENTHAM *Lang.* Wks. 1843 VIII. 333/1 This proposition will consist of one word only, or of divers words, —will be either monoepic or polyepic. **1895** *Pop. Sci. Monthly* Feb. 440 A child's first imitative talk, which might be described as monepic or single-worded—as 'wow-wow', 'dow' (down)—is essentially vague. *Ibid.* Apr. 781 His speech is monepic.

monepiscopacy (mɒnɪˈpɪskəpəsɪ). [f. MON(O)- + EPISCOPACY.] Government of the Church by bishops endowed with monarchical authority.

1889 GORE *Ministry Chr. Ch.* ii. 73 No one..can maintain that the existence of what may be called, for lack of a distinctive term, monepiscopacy is essential to the continuity of the Church. **1903** *Dublin Rev.* Jan. 84 St. Peter is commonly said by the Fathers to be the type of monepiscopacy.

So **moneˈpiscopal** *a.*, pertaining to or of the nature of a monepiscopacy; ‖**moneˈpiscopus** (quasi-Latin), a monepiscopal bishop.

1891 G. G. FINDLAY tr. *Sabatier's Apostle Paul* App. 396 The mon-episcopal *régime* of Ignatius. *Ibid.* 399 The failure of Baur's attempt to identify the bishop of the Pastorals with the mon-episcopus (or monarchical bishop) of the second century.

moner (ˈməʊnə(r)). *Biol.* Also **monere**. Anglicized form of *moneron*, sing. MONERA.

1868 HUXLEY in *Q. Jrnl. Microsc. Sci.* VIII. 210, I propose to confer upon this new 'Moner' the generic name of *Bathybius*. **1869** tr. *Haeckel* ibid. IX. 219 Detaching themselves..from the periphery of the Moner-colony. *Ibid.*, This Moner-form would be intimately allied to Protogenes. **1873** MAX MÜLLER in *Fraser's Mag.* July 5 The physiologist..sees in the lowest Moneres the living proof of an independent beginning of life. **1882** COUES *Biogen.* (1884) 33 The chain of life is unbroken from moner to man.

moner, obs. form of MANNER.

‖**monera** (mɒˈnɪərə), *sb. pl.* [mod.L., badly f. Gr. μονήρης single.] Haeckel's name for a group of protozoa composed of organisms of the simplest form. Also sing. **moˈneron**, one of the monera.

1869 tr. *Haeckel* in *Q. Jrnl. Microsc. Sci.* IX. 28, I have called those forms of life standing at the lowest grade of organization Monera. *Ibid.* 35 A Protozoan organism of the Monera group. **1876** tr. *Haeckel's Hist. Creat.* I. 184 The first complete observations on the natural history of a Moneron..were made by me..in 1864. **1894** E. CLODD in *Academy* 7 July 14/1 The theory of the continuity of life from moneron to man.

Hence **moˈneral, moˈneric** *adjs.* = MONERAN *a.* **moˈneran** *a.*, of or belonging to the monera; *sb.* a moneron.

1877 HUXLEY *Anat. Inv. Anim.* ii. 95 An endoplastic repetition of the moneran Protomonas. **1881** CARPENTER *Microsc. & Rev.* (ed. 6) §394 Another very interesting 'moneric' type is the *Vampyrella*. **1891** *Q. Jrnl. Microsc. Sci.* XXXII. 611 Haeckel was mistaken in assuming their disappearance in a 'moneran stage'.

monergism (ˈmɒnədʒɪz(ə)m). *Theol.* [ad. mod.L. (and Ger.) *monergismus*, f. Gr. μόνος (see MONO-) + ἔργον work: see -ISM.] **a.** The doctrine of some Lutherans that regeneration is entirely the work of the Holy Spirit; opposed to SYNERGISM. **b.** Applied by some mod. writers to the doctrine (closely akin to Monothelitism) that the two natures in Christ have only 'one operation' (μία ἐνέργεια). (In this sense some Ger. writers have, more correctly, *monenergismus*.) Hence **ˈmonergist** *sb.*, one who professes monergism; also *adj.* = next. **monerˈgistic** *a.*, of or pertaining to monergism. See also MONENERGIST(IC *adjs.*

1867–80 M'CLINTOCK & STRONG *Cycl. Bibl. Lit.* VII. 481 (Cassell *Suppl.*) It is held by monergists that the will of sinful man has not the least inclination towards holiness.. until it has been acted upon by divine grace. **1893** E. K. MITCHELL tr. *Harnack's Outl. Hist. Dogma* 300 The Monergistic and Monotheletic Controversies. **1898** SPEIRS & MILLAR tr. *Harnack's Hist. Dogma* IV. 252 The Monergist and Monothelite Controversies.

‖**monerozoa** (mɒnɪərəʊˈzəʊə), *sb. pl. Zool.* [mod.L., f. Gr. μονήρης single + ζῷον animal.] An alternative name for MONERA.

1881 CARPENTER *Microsc. & Rev.* (ed. 6) §392 Monerozoa (as they have been designated by Prof. Haeckel, who first drew attention to them).

Hence **moneroˈzoan** *a.*, of, belonging to, or characteristic of the monerozoa; *sb.* one of the monerozoa; **moneroˈzoic** *a.* = prec. adj.

1879 CARPENTER in *Encycl. Brit.* IX. 375/1 Living organisms of the simplest possible 'monerozoic' type.

mones, monesche, obs. forms of MONISH *v.*

monesia (məʊˈniːʃ(ɪ)ə). [Origin unknown.] An astringent substance obtained from the bark of a Brazilian tree, *Chrysophyllum Buranhem* (*C. glycyphlœum*). Hence **monesin** (mɒˈniːsɪn) *Chem.*, an acrid principle obtained from monesia.

1843 *Pharm. Jrnl.* III. 292 Dr. G. Martin St. Ange..says: 'A vegetable substance, called *monesia*, has lately been imported from South America, in the form of hard thick cakes... M. Bernard Derosne, the druggist, who introduced it, informs me that some travellers call the monesia bark, *goharem*; and others, *buranhem*'. **1858** HOGG *Veg. Kingd.* 500 An acid [*read* acrid] principle, analogous to saponin, called *monesin*.

monest, obs. form of MONISH *v.*

monestar, -er, -re, obs. forms of MONASTERY.

monestycall, obs. Sc. form of MONASTICAL.

monetain, obs. form of MOUNTAIN.

†**moneˈtarian**, *a. Obs. rare*⁻¹. [f. L. *monētāri-us* (see MONETARY *a.*) + -AN.] Of or pertaining to money or coins; numismatic.

1716 M. DAVIES *Athen. Brit.* III. 80 The last of all the Medal-kind Authors and Monetarian Writings.

monetarism (ˈmɒn-, ˈmʌnɪtərɪz(ə)m). [f. MONETARY *a.* + -ISM.] The economic doctrine or theory of a monetarist or of monetarists.

1969 *Newsweek* 6 Jan. 48 The combination of Stansian horse-and-buggy finance with Friedmanian go-go monetarism. **1970** *Times* 13 Mar. 10 The lecture was a full-blooded onslaught on 'the new monetarism', the doctrines of the Chicago school of economists led by the celebrated Professor Milton Friedman. **1971** *Times* 2 Aug. 13/4 Professor Paul Samuelson..describes monetarism as a disease and defines it as a 'pathological belief..that only the rate of growth of the money supply can affect significantly the rate of inflation or the level of unemployment'. **1971** *Sunday Times* 8 Aug. 4 Monetarism, the belief that the state of the economy can be decisively manipulated through regulating the flow of money, became an accepted cult in the White House after Dr Burns had left it to assume the chairmanship of the Federal Reserve Board. **1975** *Times* 28 Aug. 24/5 The Treasury['s]..distrust of 'monetarism' arises from a belief that it has only one equation, that which links the money supply and the money national income.

monetarist (ˈmɒn-, ˈmʌnɪtərɪst), *a.* and *sb.* [f. MONETARY *a.* + -IST.] **A.** *adj.* Of a monetary character or having a monetary basis.

1914 GEDDES & THOMSON *Sex* x. 239 This order of things —avowedly mechanical, militarist, and monetarist at best,.. seems to many of us..the only possible form of industrial civilisation. **1971** *Times* 2 Aug. 13/4 The father of the current monetarist school of economic thought. **1972** *Times* 6 Dec. 22/8 The distinctive monetarist assertion is that inflation is attributable solely to increase in the money supply. **1973** *Times* 16 Aug. 15/2 It is not..true—even in terms of the monetarist theories on which Mr Powell relies —that the Government deficit uniquely determines the money supply. **1974** *Financial Times* 21 Oct. 16/8 The basic argument of the sadly mislabelled 'monetarist' school is that attempts by monetary and fiscal stimulation to lower the level of unemployment below a sustainable minimum, determined by underlying forces, will not bring about a lasting drop in the level of unemployment.

B. *sb.* One who places emphasis on monetary matters, *spec.* one who advocates tighter control of the money supply as an important remedy for inflation.

1963 *Economist* 27 Apr. 299/2 To control inflation by curtailment, as prescribed by the 'monetarists'. **1965** *Ibid.* 25 Sept. p. xxiv/1 The main battle was between the 'monetarists' (who..believe that screwing down the money supply is always the answer to inflations of any sort) and the 'structuralists'. **1971** *Daily Tel.* 25 Jan. 12/2 It is argued by monetarists that lower rates of interest would contribute to inflation. **1971** *Times* 2 Aug. 13/4 In a highly controversial article in today's *Washington Post* influential monetarists in the United States are compared to water diviners.

Hence **monetaˈristic** *a.*

1972 *Publisher's Weekly* 6 Mar. 60/1 Nixon's two-and-a-half-year dalliance with laissez-faire and the monetaristic theories of Milton Friedman.

monetary (ˈmɒn-, ˈmʌnɪtərɪ), *a.* [ad. L. *monētāri-us* of or belonging to the mint, f. *monēta* mint: see MONEY.]

1. Of or pertaining to the coinage or currency. ***monetary unit***, the standard unit of value of a country's coinage.

1802–12 BENTHAM *Ration. Judic. Evid.* (1827) I. 148 Monetary forgery—forgery in relation to the current coin. **1830** GEN. P. THOMPSON *Exerc.* (1842) I. 208 The principles of what he terms monetary value. **1832** tr. *Sismondi's Ital. Rep.* iv. 85 The whole monetary system of Europe was.. abandoned to the depredations of sovereigns, who continually varied the title and weight of coins. **1853** HUMPHREYS *Coin Coll. Man.* vi. 56 The effigy of Pan was adopted as a monetary type by the Panticapeans. **1874** GREEN *Short Hist.* i. §6. 53 Laws which regulated the monetary standard.

2. Pertaining to or concerned with money, pecuniary.

1860 RUSKIN *Mod. Paint.* V. IX. xi. 330 Monetary asceticism, consisting in the refusal of pleasure and knowledge for the sake of money. **1865** BRIGHT *Sp. Canada* 13 Mar. (1876) 67/1 Men who are deep in great monetary transactions. **1866** CRUMP *Banking* iii. 74 The person who introduces a customer to a bank is expected to have some knowledge..of his friend's monetary affairs. **1872** J. H. GLADSTONE *Faraday* ii. 76 But it was not in monetary gifts alone that his kindness to the distressed was shown. **1936** J. M. KEYNES *Gen. Theory Employment* xv. 203 A monetary policy which strikes public opinion as being experimental in character or easily liable to change may fail in its objective. **1944**, etc. [see *International Monetary Fund* s.v. INTERNATIONAL *a.* 2]. **1951** R. FIRTH *Elements of Social Organization* iv. 142 Even where monetary rewards for labour are largely current, he has noted that work may be undertaken for other than money symbols. **1961** *Ann. Reg. 1960* 475 The measures ranged from the traditional restraints to a new and previously untried monetary instrument. **1973** *Times* 6 July 17/1 The 'Smithsonian' agreement, which President Nixon characterized..as 'the most significant monetary agreement in the history of the world'.

moneth(e, obs. forms of MONTH.

monethyl (mɒˈneθɪl). *Chem.* Also **mono-**. [f. MON(O)- + ETHYL.] An organic compound in which one atom of hydrogen is replaced by one molecule of ethyl. Hence **moˈnethylic** *a.*

1868 *Fownes' Chem.* (ed. 10) 615 Monethylic borate $C_2H_5BO_2$. **1869** ROSCOE *Elem. Chem.* 339 Monœthyl [*sic*] phosphine. **1881** *Academy* 14 May 360/2 An ethylether malic acid isomeric with the monethyl malate of Desmondisir.

ˈmonetism. *nonce-wd.* [f. L. *monēta* (see MONEY) + -ISM.] The worship of money. So also **ˈmonetist**, one who practises monetism.

1707 J. STEVENS tr. *Quevedo's Com. Wks.* (1709) 488 For founding the new Sect of Monetism, changing the Name of Atheists into that of Money-mongers, or Monetists [translating Sp. *dinerismos* and *dineristas*].

monetite (ˈməʊnɪtaɪt). *Min.* [f. *Moneta*, name of a small island near Puerto Rico: see -ITE[1].] A hydrogen phosphate of calcium, $CaH(PO_4)$, occurring as translucent, pale yellowish white crystals.

1882 C. U. SHEPARD in *Amer. Jrnl. Sci.* CXXIII. 400 The Moneta mineral, which we call monetite from its locality, is accompanied by two other species. **1968** I. KOSTOV *Mineral.* 458 Monetite and stercorite are triclinic.

monetization (ˌmɒn-, ˌmʌnɪtaɪˈzeɪʃən). [f. next + -ATION. Cf. mod.F. *monétisation*.] The action of monetizing.

1864 in WEBSTER. **1890** G. B. SHAW *Fabian Ess. Socialism* 191 Monetization of silver, import duties.

monetize (ˈmɒn-, ˈmʌnɪtaɪz), *v.* [f. L. *monēt-a* MONEY + -IZE. Cf. F. *monétiser*.] *trans.* To give a standard value to (a metal) in the coinage of a country; to put into circulation as money.

1880 in WEBSTER, Suppl. **1903** *Speaker* 10 Oct. 52/1 He demonetised silver in Germany and monetised gold.

Moneto, obs. variant of MANITOU.

1773 *Hist. Brit. Domin. N. Amer.* XIII. xi. 241 They assert, there are two monetoes or spirits; that the one sends all the good things they have, and the other all the bad.

moneur, obs. form of MONEYER.

money (ˈmʌnɪ), *sb.* Pl. **moneys**. Forms: 3–6 **moneye**, 4–5 **monoie, -oye, moone**, 4–6 **monay(e, monei(e, mone(e, monye**, 4–8 **mony**, 5–7 **monny**, 6–7 **monie**, 4– **money**. [a. OF. *moneie, mon(n)oie* (mod.F. *monnaie*) = Pr., Sp. *moneda*, Pg. *moeda*, It. *moneta*:—L. *monēta* (?f. *monēre* to warn, remind): orig. the name of a goddess (in classical times regarded as identical with Juno), in whose temple at Rome money was coined, hence, a mint, money. Cf. MINT *sb.*[1]

For the plural the irregular spelling *monies* is still not uncommonly met with, esp. in sense 4.]

1. a. Current coin; metal stamped in pieces of portable form as a medium of exchange and measure of value. ***piece of money***: see PIECE *sb.* 3 c.

c **1330** R. BRUNNE *Chron.* (1725) 238 Edward..wille wite certeyn, who schent has his mone. Of clippers, of roungers, of suilk takes he questis. **1340** *Ayenb.* 26 Of guod metal hy makeþ ualse moneye. **1377** LANGL. *P. Pl.* B. xv. 343 Þe merke of þat mone is good, ac þe metal is fieble. **1611** BIBLE *1 Kings* xxi. 2, I will giue thee the worth of it in money. **1680** MORDEN *Geog. Rect., Asiat. Tartaria* (1685) 396 The Mony of this kingdom is of a good Alloy. **1711** ADDISON *Spect.* No. 3 ⁋5 Behind the Throne was a prodigious Heap of Bags of Mony. **1859** GEO. ELIOT *A. Bede* ix, It's no use filling your pocket full of money if you've got a hole in the corner.

fig. **1651** HOBBES *Leviath.* I. iv. 15 Words are wise mens counters, they do but reckon by them: but they are the mony of fooles.

b. Applied occas. by extension to any objects, or any material, serving the same purposes as coin.

c **1400** MAUNDEV. (1839) xxii. 239 He [the great Khan].. makethe no Money, but of Lether emprented, or of Papyre. **1553** EDEN *Treat. Newe Ind.* (Arb.) 24 The monie which they vse, is made of a certayne paper..with ye kinges ymage printed theron. **1600** J. PORY tr. *Leo's Africa* Introd. 22 Salt is the principall thing which runneth currant for money throughout all the emperours dominions. **1807** ROBINSON *Archæol. Græca* II. xix. 177 In cases of emergency..the Spartans were allowed the use of money made from the skins of beasts.

c. In mod. use commonly applied indifferently to coin and to such promissory documents representing coin (esp. government and bank notes) as are currently accepted as a medium of exchange. See PAPER MONEY.

1819 *Noble's Instr. Emigr. U.S.* 107 The best money to take to the United States, is either guineas or Spanish milled dollars;..Bank of England notes will not do. **1864** *Chamb. Encycl.* VI. 529/2 No one hesitates in counting a £5 Bank of England note as money. **1880** BON. PRICE in *Fraser's Mag.* May 675 Only 3*l.* in each 100*l.* were cash—that is, coin and bank notes, true money. **1903** *Westm. Gaz.* 18 June 2/1 In international commerce the form of money most used is a bill of exchange, and a good bill is good money.

†**d.** ***black money*** (= med.L. *moneta nigra*), copper coinage; ? also, debased silver coin. ***white money***, standard silver coin. *Obs.*

[**1335** *Act 9 Edw. III*, stat 2, c. 1 §4 Que totes maneres de noire monoie, que courent ja communalment en notre roialme..soient tote oultrement ostez.] **1423** *Rolls of Parlt.* IV. 256/2 For as muche as gret scarcite of Whit money is wyth inne this land, because that silver is bought. **1469** *Sc. Acts Jas. III* (1597) §40 That there be na Deniers of France,

..nor nane vther counterfaictes of black money, be tane in payment in the Realme, bot our soveraine Lords awin black money. **1567** HARMAN *Caveat* 42 He plucked oute viii. shyllinges in whyte money. **1607** MIDDLETON *Phœnix* I. vi, He had so much grace before he died to turn his white money into gold, a great ease to his executor. **1642** FULLER *Holy & Prof. St.* IV. v. 264 Receiving black money from cheatours, he payes them in good silver.

2. (With *pl.*) A particular coin or coinage. Also, a denomination of value representing a fraction or a multiple of the value of some coin; in full, ***money of account*** (see ACCOUNT *sb.* 1).

1426 LYDG. *De Guil. Pilgr.* 17614 Thys hand in frenshe.. Ys callyd 'Poitevyneresse', For yt forgeth.. A monye callyd Poytevyn. **1481** CAXTON *Myrr.* III. xiv. 165 The monoyes were establisshed first; for as moche as they had not of alle thinges necessarye to gydre. **1588** J. READ tr. *Arcæus' Compend. Meth.* 69, I made an orifice with the Trepan, to the greatnes of a siluer mony called a Roiall. **1617** MORYSON *Itin.* I. 285 Now I will set downe the divers moneys of Germany with the severall values of them. *c* **1630** MUN *Eng. Treas.* (1664) 4 He ought to know the Measures, Weights, and Monies of all forraign Countries. *a* **1637** B. JONSON *Discov. Consuetudo* etc. (1640), Custome is the most certaine Mistresse of Language, as the publicke stampe makes the current money. **1648** C. WALKER *Hist. Independ.* I. 169 Francis Allen a poor Goldsmith... In honour of whom Clipped moneys are now called (Allens). **1756** NUGENT *Gr. Tour, Germany* II. 62 At Cologne, the most remarkable money is the rixdollar. **1837** *Penny Cycl.* VIII. 328/1 Constantine I. introduced the milliarensis, worth somewhere about a shilling of our money. **1839** *Ibid.* XV. 322/1 The denominations.. of the different moneys current among the chief nations of antiquity. **1885** *Athenæum* 30 May 690/1 The reasons for these changes in coinage, the intentions of those who issued moneys..are often almost unknown.

3. a. Coin considered in reference to its value or purchasing power; hence, property or possessions of any kind viewed as convertible into money or having value expressible in terms of money.

c **1290** *S. Eng. Leg.* I. 262/41 Non oþur Moneye, heo seide, ich ne habbe bote mi-self her. **1377** LANGL. *P. Pl.* B. XIII. 394 To marchaunden with monoye [*v.r.* moneie] and maken her eschaunges. *c* **1386** CHAUCER *Prol.* 705 Up-on a day he gat him more moneye Than that the person gat in monthes tweye. *c* **1430** LYDG. *London Lyckpeny* i, But for lack of mony I cold not spede. **1529** MORE *Suppl. Soulys* Wks. 325/2 Then were he very cruell in that he deliuereth them not without monei. **1539** BIBLE *1 Tim.* vi. 10 For couetousnes of money is the rote of all euyll. **1651** HOBBES *Leviath.* II. xxii. 122 Sometimes Iustice cannot be had without mony. **1718** LADY M. W. MONTAGU *Lett.* (1887) II. 237 'Tis his business to get money, and hers to spend it. **1753** HANWAY *Trav.* II. I. iii. 15 They have introduced the custom of giving money to servants. **1776** ADAM SMITH *W. N.* IV. i. ¶1 Wealth and money..are, in common language, considered as in every respect synonymous. **1879** FROUDE *Cæsar* xviii. 301 He already owed half a million of money. **1890** *Murray's Mag.* June 764 He'll come into a lot of money some fine day.

b. with demonstrative or possessive adj., designating a sum applied to a particular purpose or in the possession of a particular person.

a **1300** *Cursor M.* 16475 Here i yeld yow yur mone, ges me a-gain mi war. *c* **1330** R. BRUNNE *Chron.* (1725) 308 þat tyme no þing he wrouht, bot spendid his mone. **1463** *Bury Wills* (Camden) 27 This mony not to be delyuerid to noon of hem. **1590** SHAKS. *Com. Err.* IV. i. 63 The monie that you owe me for the Chaine. *c* **1645** [see FOOL *sb.*^{1} 1 d]. **1684** BUNYAN *Pilgr.* II. (1862) 351 Then said one of them, I will pay you when I take my Mony. **1818** CRUISE *Digest* (ed. 2) I. 477 Notwithstanding the father paid the whole money. **1838** D. JERROLD *Men of Character* (1851) 320 The highway laconism of 'your money or your life!' **1891** KIPLING *Light that Failed* iii, Come back when your money's spent.

c. considered as a commodity in the market (for loan, etc.).

a **1687** PETTY *Pol. Arith.* vi. (1691) 100 It is certain that mony which payeth those Rents, and driveth on Trade, must have increased also. **1691** SIR D. NORTH *Disc. Trade* Pref. B 2, Money is a Merchandize, whereof there may be a glut, as well as a scarcity. **1776** ADAM SMITH *W. N.* IV. i, It is not any scarcity of gold and silver, but the difficulty which such people find in borrowing, and which their creditors find in getting payment, that occasions the general complaint of the scarcity of money. **1797** BURKE *Regic. Peace* iii. Sel. Wks. III. 208 The value of money must be judged, like every thing else, from it's rate at market. **1878** *Encycl. Brit.* XVI. 721/1 In mercantile phraseology the value of money means the interest charged for the use of loanable capital. Thus, when the market rate of interest is high money is said to be dear, when it is low money is regarded as cheap.

¶ **d.** ***a certain money*** (see CERTAIN *sb.* 5 b).

c **1380** *Antecrist* in Todd 3 *Treat. Wyclif* 149 To sett þereon her syngnet for a certeyne moneye. **1556** *Chron. Gr. Friars* (Camden) 70 [She] gave hare husbande a sartyne mony a yere dureynge hys lyffe.

e. Wages, salary; one's pay.

1887 PARISH & SHAW *Dict. Kentish Dial.* 103 He's getting good money, I reckon. **1916** G. B. SHAW *Pygmalion* II. 143 His proper trade's a navvy; and he works at it sometimes.. and earns good money at it. **1920** E. O'NEILL *Beyond the Horizon* II. i. 85 If that's the case, you can go to the devil... You'll get your money tomorrow when I get back from town. **1963** H. GARNER in R. Weaver *Canad. Short Stories* (1968) 2nd Ser. 45 Nobody really liked working for Malloy-Harrison, but the money was better than most places.

4. *pl.* Properly = 'sums of money', but often indistinguishable from the sing. (sense 3). Now chiefly in legal and quasi-legal parlance, or as an archaism.

1382 WYCLIF *2 Macc.* iii. 6 And tolde to hym the tresorie in Jerusalem for to be ful with moneys [Vulg. *pecuniis*] vnnoumbreable. **1625** BACON *Ess., Usury* (end), No Man will Lend his Moneyes farre off, nor put them into Vnknown Hands. **1632** LITHGOW *Trav.* IV. 140 [He] furnished him with great moneys, and other necessaries. **1734** tr. *Rollin's Anc. Hist.* XIX. v. (1827) VIII. 163 To make him a present of the monies arising from that sale. **1822** BYRON *Werner* II. ii, But to steal The moneys of a slumbering man! **1865** *Morn. Star* 3 Feb., A young woman, was charged..with stealing from the person of Robert Tharston,..7*s.* 6*d.*, his moneys. **1866** CRUMP *Banking* v. 118 An agreement to pay the bill when certain monies were realised. **1871** R. ELLIS tr. *Catullus* xxix. 22 Is not all his act To swallow monies, empty purses heap on heap?

¶ From Shakspere onwards, the use of the pl. for the sing. has been commonly attributed to Jews, whose supposed pronunciation is sometimes ridiculed by the spelling 'monish'.

1596 SHAKS. *Merch. V.* I. iii. 117 You come to me, and you say, Shylocke, we would haue moneyes. **1794** CUMBERLAND *Jew* II. ii, *Sheva.* Why truly, monies is a goot thing. **1819** SCOTT *Ivanhoe* xi, 'O', said the Jew, 'you are come to pay moneys... And from whom dost thou bring it?'

5. With defining word, forming specific phrases, as **big money**: see BIG *a.* B. 2; † **chief money** = capital; **dirty money**: see DIRTY *a.* 6 b; **even money**, equal betting, also *attrib.*; † **present**, † **real money** = READY MONEY; † **single, small money**, small change; † **Spanish money** *slang* (see quot. 1700).

For *hard, soft money* see HARD *a.* 2, SOFT *a.* Freq. with prefixed sb., denoting the reason or purpose for which money is expended, as *beer-money* (BEER *sb.*^{1} 4), BLOOD-MONEY, *card-money* (CARD *sb.*^{2} 14), *conscience-money* (CONSCIENCE 16 c), †COPY-MONEY, *gate-money* (GATE *sb.*^{1} 13), HUSH-MONEY, POCKET-MONEY, SMART-MONEY, etc.

a **1380** *St. Bernard* 738 in Horstm. *Altengl. Leg.* (1878) 53 Ȝif i take þe þe chef moneye [L. *capitale*] Wiþ to pleye. **1553** *Stanford Churchw. Acc.* in *Antiquary* XVII. 117 It. of ye parisheoners for crowche monay or paschull monay iiijs. vij*d.* **1590** SHAKS. *Com. Err.* IV. i. 34, I am not furnish'd with the present monie. **1591** GREENE *2nd Pt. Conny-c.* (1592) D 2, [There] came another and bought a knife and should haue single money again. **1611** DONNE *Anat. World, 1st Anniv.* 234 And that rich Indie which doth gold interre, Is but as single money coyn'd from her. **1685** PETTY *Last Will* p. v, Which..raised me an estate of about 13000*l.* in ready and real money. *a* **1700** B. E. *Dict. Cant. Crew, Spanish-money*, fair Words and Compliments. **1722** DE FOE *Plague* (1884) 106 Small Money to make up any odd Sum. **1903** *Daily News* 8 Aug. 4/5 If number five wins the bank collects all the even-money bets.

6. Phrases, etc.

a. Proverbs. ***money makes the mare*** (or †***horse***) ***to go***; ***money is the sinews*** (or †***nerves***) ***of war*** (cf. Cicero *Phil.* v. ii. 5 'nervos belli, pecuniam infinitam'); ***time is money***; etc.

c **1450** *Cov. Myst.* (Shaks. Soc.) 268 In old termys I have herde seyde That mony makyth Schapman. **1573** J. SANDFORD *Hours Recreat.* (1576) 213 Money makes the horsse to goe. **1605** BACON *Adv. Learn.* II. xxiii. §38 But that opinion I may condemne with like reason as Macchiauell doth that other: that monies were the sinewes of the warres. **1611** BIBLE *1 Tim.* vi. 10 The loue of money is the root of all euill. **1638** [see NERVE *sb.* 2]. *c* **1645** [see FOOL *sb.*^{1} 1 d]. **1660** T. M. *C. Walker's Hist. Independ.* IV. 65 The Army could not subsist without money (which is the Nerve of War). **1659, 1698** [see MARE^1 1 b]. **1681** A. BEHN *Rover* II. III. i. 43 Money speaks sense in a Language all Nations understand. **1748** B. FRANKLIN *Advice to Young Tradesman* in *Writings* (1905) II. 371 Remember that *time* is money. **1792** WOLCOT (P. Pindar) *More Money, Odes to Mr. Pitt* iv, 'Tis money makes the old mare trot. **1845** C. LEVER *Let.* in L. Stevenson *Dr. Quicksilver* (1939) ix. 149 You have paid your money, and you may take your choice. **1846** *Punch* 3 Jan. 17 *(caption)* You pays your money, and you takes your choice. **1853** T. T. LYNCH *Lect. Self Improvement* v. 113 Money is power—power for bread and power for tinsel. **1861** TRAFFORD *City & Suburb* xiv, Money makes money, it is said. **1886** BARING-GOULD *Court Royal* xliii, Time was money to Mr. Cheek. He did not allow the grass to grow under his feet. **1898** G. B. SHAW *Arms & Man* II. III. 57 A twenty leva bill! Sergius gave me that, out of pure swagger. A fool and his money are soon parted. **1903** *Sat. Even. Post* 5 Sept. 12/1 When money talks it often merely remarks 'Good-by'. **1905** 'O. HENRY' in *N.Y. World Mag.* 12 Nov. 8/1 Money talks. But you may think that the conversation of a little old ten-dollar bill in New York would be nothing more than a whisper. **1927** E. O'NEILL *Marco Millions* I. ii. 36 He'll have time enough for that, but with us time is money. *Ibid.* iii. 44 Money isn't everything, not always. **1930** G. B. MEANS *Strange Death of President Harding* IV. 72 One can do nothing—be nothing, without money, not even in the White House. Money is power. **1952** W. G. HARDY *Unfulfilled* 199 Money isn't everything. **1956** A. WILSON *Anglo-Saxon Attitudes* II. ii. 277 Yeah, he's on the Market. .. You know the sort of stuff. Money talks and so on. **1965** *Times* 14 July 8/4 In the Government today were known supporters of C.N.D. Why? Because the Prime Minister put them there. Why? Because he shared their views? Because it was expedient to do so? Because he was practising some duplicity? Why? 'You pays your money and you takes your choice.'

b. ***for money***: in return or exchange for money. ***for*** or ***at the money***: at the price paid. ***for love or money***: see LOVE *sb.*^{1} 7 c. ***(so and so) for my money***, a colloq. expression of approbation = '..is what I desire or like', '..is my choice', 'give me..'; ***for my money***: also = in my opinion. †***to take eggs for (one's) money***: see EGG *sb.* 4. ***to have a run for one's money***: see RUN *sb.*^{1} 1 d.

c **1330** R. BRUNNE *Chron.* (1725) 246 þei wer out of þe tour delyuerd for mone. *c* **1380** WYCLIF *Wks.* (1880) 241 Whanne prelatis..fauouren hem in synne for moneye. **1513** BRADSHAW *St. Werburge* I. 1677 There was habundaunce Of all-maner pleasures to be had for monye. **1549** [see GO *v.* 24 b]. **1566** E. H. tr. *Erasmus's Diuersoria* sig. B2^v This behauiour doth well beseme Frenchmen peraduenture, how be it the fashions of Duche lande shall go for my monye when all is done. **1589** [see GO *v.* 24 b]. **1599** SHAKS. *Much Ado* II. iii. 63 Well, a horne for my money when all's done. **1616** W. HAUGHTON (*title*) English-Men for my Money. **1667** DRYDEN & DK. NEWCASTLE *Sir M. Mar-All* v. i, They may talk what they will of Oxford for an university, but Cambridge for my money. **1700** [see GIVE *v.* 3 c]. *a* **1734** NORTH *Life Dudley North* (1744) 181 It is certain the Pamphlet is..utterly sunk, and a Copy not to be had for Money. **1802–12** BENTHAM *Ration. Judic. Evid.* (1827) IV. 93 The higher you pay for your dispatch, the more delay you have for your money. **1840** *Spirit of Times* 21 Nov. 447/3 Give me the gall, I say, that *has an eye for dirt*, for she is the gall for my money. **1842** S. LOVER *Handy Andy* x, 'You're right', said Dick, 'Murphy is the very man for our money'. **1882** *Daily Tel.* 30 Jan., Khamseen, who cost 570 guineas at Mr. Vyner's sale, is reckoned a bargain..at the money. **1932** D. L. SAYERS *Have his Carcase* xi. 138 Peter's the man for my money. He won't see a hardworking man lose a job for want of a good news story. **1943** *N.Y. Times* 9 May II. 5/5 Glenn was, and for my money is still tops. **1954** J. SYMONS *Narrowing Circle* xiv. 59 For my money, Marian was responsible..for the trouble we'd had. **1969** D. CLARK *Death after Evensong* iv. 97, I wouldn't mind not finding who did Parseloe in. For my money he deserved it.

c. ***to make money***: to acquire or earn money; also, to get money by the sale *of*, make a profit *out of*. ***to coin money***: to acquire wealth rapidly (see COIN *v.*^{1} 1 c). ***to cost money***: see COST *v.* 1 d.

1457 *Paston Lett.* I. 416 He..resseyvyth but chaffr and waare for hys cornys and wollys, &c. and then most abyde along day to make money. **1472–1632** [see MAKE *v.* 29]. **1828** W. McDOWALL *Poems Galloway Dial.* 25 When Buonaparte in splendour shone, 'Twas then I made the money. **1901** *Spectator* 20 July 82/1 The War Office ought not to make money out of, any more than they should subsidise, the rifle clubs.

d. (*it is*) ***everybody's*** or ***every man's money***: in early use, what everybody prefers to buy; also, what everybody can afford to buy; now (mainly in negative context) what everybody would find worth its price. (Also in analogous phrases: see quots. 1625, 1712, 1851.) ***to be*** (***good, bad,*** etc.) ***money***: to be a (good or bad) investment, to 'pay'. ***there is money in*** (***something***): money can be made out of it.

1601 HOLLAND *Pliny* I. 381 The ointment of Saffron confected at Soli in Cilicia, imported for a good while and caried the praise alone: but soone after that of Rhodes was every mans money. **1625** BACON *Ess., Riches*, When a Mans Stocke is come to that, that he can expect the Prime of Markets, and ouercome those Bargaines, which for their greatnesse are few Mens Money. **1653** GATAKER *Vind. Annot. Jer.* 29 The whole work..consists of two great volumes, and the price consequently correspondent, not every mans money, and in fewer hands therefore. **1712** ADDISON *Spect.* No. 482 ¶1 Such a Discourse is of general Use, and every married Man's Money. **1851** MAYHEW *Lond. Lab.* I. 91/1, I sell dry fruit, sir, in February and March, because I must be doing something, and green fruit's not my money then. *Ibid.* 139/1 Mignonette's everybody's money. Dahlias didn't go off so well. *Ibid.* (1861) III. 103, I reckon Astley's is the worst money for any man. *Ibid.* 130 Richardson's used..to be more money, but now it's as bad as the rest of 'em. **1887** *Pall Mall G.* 1 Mar. 14/1 There is undoubtedly money in guns.

e. ***money burns (a hole) (in) one's pocket*** (or †***purse***) (and similar phrases): one is impatient to spend one's money. Cf. BURN *v.*^{1} 16.

1529 MORE *Dyaloge of Ymagys* II. x. f.lxi, Hauyng a lytell wanton money whyche hym thought brennyd out the botom of hys purs. **1702** FARQUHAR *Inconstant* v. iii. 77 My time lyes heavy on my hands, and my Money burns in my Pocket. **1875** S. SMILES *Thrift* viii. 125 A man who has more money about him than he requires..is tempted to spend it... It is apt to 'burn a hole in his pocket'. **1943** M. LASSWELL *Suds in your Eye* xiv. 103 Her money was burning a hole in her pocket. **1958** L. DURRELL *Balthazar* xiii. 227 I've scraped a dowry together over the years... The money burns my pocket. **1972** A. S. NEILL *Neill! Neill! Orange Peel!* II. 238 Today, I don't see the young..saving money. It burns a hole in their pockets.

f. ***your money or your life***: a formula used by highwaymen, etc., in threatening to kill a person if he does not hand over money.

1841 F. A. BURNEY *Jrnl.* 23 Feb. (1926) 321 Mr. Dixon attempted expostulation, upon which the Highwayman drew out a Pistol,..exclaiming, with an oath, 'Your money or your life!' **1848** J. A. FROUDE *Let.* 16 May in W. H. Dunn *Froude* (1961) I. 118 Nothing will open rich John Bull's understanding but a hand at his throat and 'Your money or your life'. **1864** J. PAYN *Lost Sir Massingberd* II. xiii. 212 A pistol, was protruded into the carriage. 'Your money or your life!..,' said a rough voice.

g. ***in the money***: among the prize-winners in a competition, show, or the like; amply or sufficiently supplied with money; rich.

1902 'D. DIX' *Fables of Elite* 48 It is True that when the Spurt is over I am generally in the Money. **1928** *Morning Post* 20 Oct. 6/1 One of them is to-day a full champion, the other three all winners, and 'in the money', as the fanciers say, whenever shown. **1945** G. CASEY in *Coast to Coast 1944* 3 Shift her round like you was doin' yesterday and you'll be in the money. **1946** L. BROMFIELD *World we live In* 325 Being in the money at the moment, I said that of course I'd lend her any reasonable amount. **1969** T. PARKER *Twisting Lane* 200 She said we could stay there rent free until I was in the money again.

h. ***money for jam, money for old rope*** (and similar phrases): a profitable return for little or

no trouble; a very easy job; someone or something easy to profit from, beat, etc.

1919 *Athenæum* 8 Aug. 727/2 The great use of jam in the Army..originated a number of phrases, such as 'money for jam' (money for nothing). **1927** T. E. LAWRENCE *Let.* 22 Sept. (1938) 540 Recently I made nearly ten pounds out of reviewing eleven books. Money for jam, as the airman says. **1936** J. CURTIS *Gilt Kid* xiii. 134 He would spin her a fanny about the marriage laws, tie the poor kid up. It ought to be money for old rope. **1942** E. WAUGH *Put out More Flags* 150 At the moment there were no mortars and he was given instead a light and easily manageable counterfeit of wood which was slung on the back of his haversack, relieving him of a rifle. At present it was money for old rope. **1958** 'A. GILBERT' *Death against Clock* iv. 47 If he saw the wallet it must have seemed money for jam. **1966** 'L. LANE' *ABZ of Scouse* 70 *Money fer owd rope*, something for nothing. Other similar phrases are *money fer dirt*; *money fer raggety kecks*; *money fer jam*, etc., etc. **1973** A. HUNTER *Gently French* iii. 24 Wasn't no risk, it was money for jam. **1974** N. BENTLEY *Inside Information* v. 52 I'll advance you another two hundred. Christ, that's money for old rope.

i. ***not everybody's money***: not to everybody's liking.

1923 J. MANCHON *Le Slang* 196 *You ain't everybody's money*, vous ne pouvez pas plaire à tout le monde. **1933** 'G. ORWELL' *Let.* c 10 Dec. in *Coll. Ess.* (1968) I. 128 As to the actual writing in *Ulysses*, it isn't everybody's money, but personally I think it is superb in places.

j. ***to put one's money on***: to bet on (a horse, etc.); also *fig.*, to favour or depend on; to expect the success of.

1931 T. R. G. LYELL *Slang, Phrase & Idiom* 528 If you've got any sense, you'll put your money on that horse I told you of. **1963** *Listener* 21 Feb. 341/3 She does not put all her money on love. **1969** *Ibid.* 8 May 636/1 A century hence, prophesied one critic, it would be only 'the careless glance of curiosity, or the student's all-ranging eye' that would turn upon the Little Nells and Paul Dombeys; he put his money instead on Dickens's humour.

k. ***to put*** (or ***get***) ***one's money where one's mouth is***: to produce, bet, or pay out money to support one's statements or opinions. orig. *N. Amer.*

1942 Z. N. HURSTON in A. Dundes *Mother Wit* (1973) 224/1 'Put your money where your mouth is!' he challenged. **1951** *Amer. Speech* XXVI. 99/1 *Get your money where your mouth is*, a phrase [in poker] which means, 'put up or shut up'. **1970** *Globe & Mail* (Toronto) 26 Sept. 7/3 Eventually it got to the point when he suggested that maybe I was the guy who should take it on. Sort of put your money where your mouth is. **1975** A. PRICE *Our Man in Camelot* v. 95 The squadron betting book the barman keeps..for guys who are ready to put their money where their mouth is.

l. ***to have money to burn***: see BURN *v.*[1] 8 d.

7. *attrib.* and *Comb.* **a.** simple attrib., as ***money-affair***, ***-bond***, ***-chest***, ***†-codger*** (= miser), ***-coffer***, ***-controversy***, ***-debt***, ***-draught***, ***-drawer***, ***-economy***, ***-fear***, ***-fine***, ***-flow***, ***-god***, ***-hunger***, ***-lust***, ***-market***, ***†-means***, ***†-miser***, ***-mulct***, ***-payment***, ***-price***, ***-purse***, ***-rent***, ***†-sack***, ***-safe***, ***-sense***, ***-slave***, ***-standard***, ***-supply***, ***-system***, ***-till***, ***-token***, ***-transaction***, ***-valuation***, ***-value***, ***-wages***.

1702 STEELE *Funeral* II. i, Your Lordship will send for Him, when you are at Leisure to look upon *Money-affairs. **1837** CARLYLE *Fr. Rev.* I. III. viii, Rich if Court-titles and *Money-bonds can enrich him. **1836** PUSEY in Liddon *Life* (1893) I. xvii. 393 To put a canker into the *money-chests of the Protestant landlords. **1818** *Blackw. Mag.* III. 402 Musty, frousy, stingy, *money-codger. **1525–6** *Rec. St. Mary at Hill* 331 For..mendyng of the lock of the *money cofur within the plate chest. **1597** BEARD *Theatre God's Judgem.* (1612) 490 If there were anie *money-controuersies to be decided. **1711** M. HENRY *Forgiv. Sin* Wks. 1853 II. 319/2 Our Saviour in his parables alludes to *money-debts. **1890** SIR G. F. DUCKETT *Visit. Eng. Cluniac Found.* 31 He found the house with a money-debt of 935. marks. **1758** *M. P.'s Let. on Navy* 19 These assigned Tickets would be equal to *Money-draughts upon any responsible Banker. **1880** W. NEWTON *Serm. for Boys & Girls* (1881) 372 She had lost the key of her *money-drawer. **1942** L. B. NAMIER *Conflicts* 50 It is not easy to translate into exact figures this barter business, which is..contrasted with the *money-economy and transactions of the Western Powers. **1962** H. R. LOYN *Anglo-Saxon Eng.* iv. 159 The earliest law-codes give evidence..of the importance of a money-economy. **1927** *Money-fear [see *money-lust* below]. **1875** STUBBS *Const. Hist.* I. iii. 47 Such are the proportions of the wer-gild and the *money-fines. **1953** C. F. HOCKETT in Saporta & Bastian *Psycholinguistics* (1961) 64/1 *Money-flow (at least in one direction) is *income*. **1590** SPENSER *F. Q.* II. vii. 39 'Suffise it then, thou *Money God,' (quoth hee) 'That all thine ydle offers I refuse'. **1891** STEVENSON & OSBOURNE *Wrecker* (1892) vii. 120 Far from the *money-hunger of the West. **1965** *Times Lit. Suppl.* 25 Nov. 1047 (Advt.), A young manhood of scheming and money-hunger in Chicago. **1927** D. H. LAWRENCE *Let.* 18 Dec. (1962) II. 1027 They must first overthrow in themselves the money-fear and *money-lust. **1930** E. POUND *XXX Cantos* xiv. 61 The perverts, who have set money lust Before the pleasures of the senses. **1600–12** ROWLANDS *Four Knaves* (Percy Soc.) 63 A knight.. Intreates his father..Some *mony-means to help him he would make. **1586** A. DAY *Eng. Secretary* I. (1625) 45 A wretched ending of such *money-misers. **1650** TRAPP *Comm. Exod.* xx. 17 Violence offered to a woman..if shee were not quick, it was onely a *monie-mulct. **1799** *Hull Advertiser* 15 June 1/2 The house is..subject to a *money payment in lieu of tithes. **1776** ADAM SMITH *W. N.* I. v. (1869) I. 49 Six shillings and eight pence..in the time of Edward I, I consider as the same *money-price with a pound sterling in the present time. **1861** MAINE *Anc. Law* v. 157 The husband..pays a money-price to her relations for the tutelage which they surrender to him. *c* **1821** J. W. MASTERS in *Eng. Dial. Dict.* (1903) IV. 149/2 He brought our Jack a leather cap An' Sal a *money-puss. **1878** B. F. TAYLOR *Between Gates* 273 We stood under fig-trees hung with money-purses filled with seeds. **1966** A. R. SCAMMELL *My Newfoundland* 33, I kept mine [*sc.* a dollar bill] for weeks in my little money-purse (we never called them purses). **1792** A. YOUNG *Trav. France* I. iv. 340 Much the greater part of the lands of France are not let at a *money-rent, but at one-half or one-third produce. **1848** MILL *Pol. Econ.* I. II. viii. 366 An attempt to introduce..a system of money rents and capitalist farmers. **1603** DAVIES *Microcosm.* 153 The *Money-Sacke best kept the Land from sack. **1799** *Hull Advertiser* 6 Oct. 3/3 Charged..with having broken open..the *money-safe within the said dwelling-house. **1865** D. G. ROSSETTI *Let.* 14 Sept. (1965) II. 571 This might have been..executed..more profitably in a *money-sense than what I did do. **1963** *Times Lit. Suppl.* 25 Jan. 62/3 Their hair-dressing or their money-sense. **1929** D. H. LAWRENCE *Pansies* 116 He can't help being a slave, a wage-slave, A *money-slave. **1771** RAPER in *Phil. Trans.* LXI. 468, I discovered the Eginean Talent to have been the *money-standard of Macedon. **1878** F. A. WALKER *Money* iv. 76 (*heading*) The importance of the *money supply. **1975** *Times* 18 June 29/7 For this year a 15 per cent rise in the money supply and a 12½ per cent rise in gnp..would be the right interim targets. **1929** D. H. LAWRENCE *Pansies* 109 Why don't we do something about the *money system? **1857** *Quinland* I. II. ii. 289 If the stars were extinguished, it would not disturb him, unless his *money-till were upset. **1937** C. M. ARENSBERG *Irish Countryman* 175 His or her remittances would eventually reach his money-till. **1875** JOWETT *Plato* (ed. 2) III. 242 They will need a market-place, and a *money-token for purposes of exchange. **1858** LD. ST. LEONARDS *Handy-Bk. Prop. Law* xviii. 133 Looking at this as a simple *money transaction. **1848** MILL *Pol. Econ.*, Prel. Remarks, I. 5 He accepted these [goods] at a *money valuation. **1870** EMERSON *Soc. & Solit.*, *Eloquence* Wks. (Bohn) III. 32 In old countries, a high *money-value is set on the service of men who have achieved a personal distinction. **1817** MALTHUS *Popul.* (ed. 5) I. 31 An increased number of labourers receiving the same *money-wages will necessarily, by their competition, increase the money price of corn.

b. objective and objective genitive, as ***money-borrower***, ***-catcher***, ***-clipper***, ***-coiner***, ***-getter***, ***-grabber***, ***-hoarder***, ***-loser***, ***-lover***, ***-raiser***, ***-spender***, ***-teller***, ***†-thirster***; ***money-breeding***, ***-catching***, ***-changing***, ***-clipping***, ***-earning***, ***-getting***, ***-grabbing***, ***-grasping***, ***-losing***, ***-loving***, ***-meditating***, ***-raising***, ***-saving***, ***-spending***, ***-sucking*** vbl. sbs. and ppl. adjs.; ***money-conscious***, ***-directed*** adjs.; **c.** advb. and instrumental, as ***money-bloated***, ***-distressed***, ***-mad***, ***-minded***, ***-mouthed***, ***†spelled*** (= spellbound) adjs.

a **1845** SYD. SMITH *Ballot* Wks. 1859 II. 306/1 The *money-bloated blockhead. **1766** GOLDSM. *Vic. W.* iii, Though he was a *money-borrower. **1796** MRS. M. ROBINSON *Angelina* I. 71 The blustering,..*money-breeding savage, her father. **1702** C. MATHER *Magn. Chr.* VII. 33 The Disciples of this *Money-catcher became so Exceeding Fierce. **1841** EMERSON *Lect.*, *Man the Reformer* Wks. (Bohn) II. 236 The most bronzed and sharpened money-catcher. **1737** (*title*) The Pleasant Art of *Money-Catching. **1938** G. GREENE *Nineteen Stories* (1947) 76 Mr. Calloway sat on his usual seat staring out over the *money-changing booths at the United States. **1759** B. MARTIN *Nat. Hist. Eng.* I. *Somerset* 68 A notorious shelter for Robbers and *Money-clippers. **1563–87** FOXE *A. & M.* (1596) 311/1 About which time also,..Iewes for *monie clipping were put to execution. **1715** LEONI *Palladio's Archit.* (1742) II. 78 The *Mensarii* had the inspection over *Money-Coiners, and Bankers. **1933** *Money-conscious [see CONSCIOUS *a.* 12]. **1963** *Times* 1 May 15/4 The parties being money-conscious to the highest degree. **1970** T. HILTON *Pre-Raphaelites* vi. 171 The destructiveness of capitalist society, its callous and *money-directed disregard of culture. **1852** THACKERAY *Esmond* I. xiv, Few fond women feel *money-distressed. **1912** J. LONDON *Let.* 7 Sept. (1966) 364 My long stuff is pretty good at *money-earning. **1813** L. HUNT in *Examiner* 26 Apr. 257/2 An assembly of jobbers and *money-getters. **1653** WALTON *Angler* i. 5 *Money-getting men. **1836** J. H. NEWMAN *Par. Serm.* (ed. 2) II. xxviii. 395 A life of money-getting is a life of care. **1875** JOWETT *Plato* (ed. 2) I. 190 Socrates makes a playful allusion to his money-getting habits. **1903** *Eng. Dial. Dict.* s.v., He's a regular *money grabber. **1933** *Times Lit. Suppl.* 27 Apr. 283/3 A money-grabber, notorious in a money-grabbing age. **1920** D. H. LAWRENCE *Touch & Go* 9 We say it is a mere material struggle, a *money-grabbing affair. **1789** WOLCOT (P. Pindar) *Expost. Odes* iii, Perdition catch the *money-grasping wretch. **1643** TRAPP *Comm. Gen.* xxiii. 16 It may well be said of *money-hoarders, they have no quick-silver, no currant money. **1795** LD. AUCKLAND *Corr.* (1862) III. 301 The *money-holders know..that the whole continental system is involved in calamity. **1928** *Weekly Dispatch* 6 May 15 About 30 [musical comedies] prove to be *money-losers. **1963** E. HUMPHREYS *Gift* II. iv. 239 If a reputation for being a money-loser had reached as far as Barrot's ears, there was very little hope of him ever making a film again. **1870** J. K. MEDBERY *Men & Myst. Wall St.* 200 It is the greatest money-making and *money-losing spot on the globe. **1960** *Farmer & Stockbreeder* 16 Feb. 87/2 All your life you have heard that farming is a money-losing proposition. **1832** MRS. GRANT *Mem.* (1844) III. 214 He is no *money-lover, and is kind-hearted. **1703** ROWE *Fair Penit.* I. i. 54 Sour, unrelenting, *Mony-loving Villains. **1768** *Woman of Honor* III. 219 That *money-mad avarice. **1929** D. H. LAWRENCE *Pansies* 79 Fear of my money-mad fellow-men. **1965** G. JACKSON *Let.* 16 Mar. in *Soledad Brother* (1971) 69 The shocks and strains of this money-mad society are enough to ruin the purest of minds. **1974** A. ROSS *Bradford Business* 169 Money-mad property developers. **1749** FIELDING *Tom Jones* XI. ix, Not so travels the *money-meditating tradesman. **1588** W. KEMPE *Educ. Children* sig. C3 One of these *money minded parents. **1957** *Times Lit. Suppl.* 20 Dec. 769/4 The insistence of the more money-minded directors on its premature exploration. **1604** PRICKET *Honors Fame* (1881) 4 Some golden *mony mouthed eloquence, that vseth a detractors Oratory. **1909** *Westm. Gaz.* 11 Aug. 1/3 This remarkable man began his career as a *money-raiser fifteen years ago with an £8,000 collection. **1955** W. DEAN in H. Van Thal *Fanfare for E. Newman* v. 61 *Don Giovanni* in Trianon's version and Nicolai's *Merry Wives of Windsor* had to be put on as money-raisers. **1960** *Farmer & Stockbreeder* 29 Mar. 105/3 The huge success of *money-raising efforts. **1826** E. IRVING *Babylon* I. IV. 311 Legislation upon any principle but that of money-making, or *money-saving, hath gone to sleep. **1615** T. ADAMS *White Devil* 42 A mercenary tongue and a *money-spel'd conscience. **1920** *Edin. Rev.* July 163 Meleager was always a *money spender rather than a money maker. **1900** J. LONDON *Let.* 1 Mar. (1966) 97 The habit of *money spending. **1911** H. GRANVILLE BARKER *Madras House* III. 91 The Middle Class Women of England form one of the greatest Money Spending Machines the world has ever seen. **1921** GALSWORTHY *To Let* II. v. 162 A lot of slow-fly *money-sucking officials. **1594** R. ASHLEY tr. *Loys le Roy* 29 b, *Money-tellers, and changers. **1651** FRENCH *Distill.* Pref. *3 b, Did you never heare of a vapouring fellow..that ..was..caught aside by *money-thirsters?

8. Special combinations: **money-back** *a.*, designating a system, agreement, etc., whereby a customer will be refunded the money he pays, if he is not satisfied with the goods or service provided; **†money-bank** = BANK *sb.*[3] 2 or 7; so **†money-banker**; **†money-batterer**, a clipper or sweater of coin; **†money-bawd**, derisive name for a userer; **money-belt** orig. *U.S.*, a belt designed for carrying money; **money-bill**, a bill in Parliament for granting supplies; **money-broker**, a money-dealer; **money bug** *U.S. slang*, a person having great wealth or financial power; **money centre** *U.S.*, a place of pre-eminent importance in the financial affairs of a region or country; *spec.* New York; **money-clause**, a clause (in a Parliamentary bill) for granting supplies; **money-column**, (*a*) a portion of an account-book page or the like, marked off by vertically ruled lines for the reception of figures denoting sums of money; (*b*) the column of a newspaper devoted to the money-market; **money-cowrie** = COWRIE 1 a; **money crop** *U.S.*, a crop that is grown mainly for selling and not for the grower's consumption; = *cash-crop*; **money-dealer**, one who deals in money in the way of exchange, banking, lending, etc.; so **money-dealing** *vbl. sb.*; **†money-dropper**, a sharper who drops a piece of money and then pretends to have found it, in order to obtain the confidence of his intended dupe; **money-flower**, the plant Honesty, *Lunaria biennis*; **†money-gentleman**, a 'money-man' (see below) of good position; **money-gold** *rare*, gold coin; **money illusion** (orig. *U.S.*), the illusion that money has a fixed value in terms of its purchasing power; **money-jobber**, a dealer in money or coin; so **money-jobbing** *vbl. sb.*; **money king** *U.S.*, a magnate in finance; a person of great wealth; **money-letter**, a letter containing money; **money-man**, a financier; also (*nonce-use*) one who desires money; **money market**, (*a*) the sphere of operation of the dealers in loans, stocks and shares, etc.; (*b*) a place in which the financial activity of a region is centred; **†money-master**, one who possesses large funds with which he does business, a capitalist; **†money-merchant**, a trader in money, money-dealer; **money-order**, an order for payment of a specified sum, issued at one post-office and payable at another (in British official use restricted to what is popularly called a *post-office order*, in which the name of the payee does not appear on the order, but is transmitted from the issuing to the paying office in a 'letter of advice'; thus distinguished from the *postal order*); **money-player**, (*a*) *U.S.*, a type of gambler (see quot. 1935); (*b*) a professional, as opposed to an amateur; **money-pot**, an earthenware money-box from which coins can be taken only by breaking the vessel; **money-power**, (*a*) the power to coin money, regulate its use, etc.; (*b*) the power exercised by money or by wealthy people, firms, etc.; **money-quake**, a financial smash of seismic magnitude; **†money-scrivener**, one whose business it is to raise loans, put money out at interest, etc., on behalf of his clients (see SCRIVENER); **money-shark** orig. *U.S.*, an avaricious money-dealer; **money shop**, a shop where money can be obtained; *spec.* an establishment which performs more conveniently many of the functions of a bank, and specializes in arranging loans; **money-spider** = next (*a*); also, a spider of the genus *Salticus*; **money-spinner**, (*a*) a small spider, *Aranea scenica*, supposed to bring good luck in money or other matters to the person over whom it crawls; (*b*) one who makes great profits by speculation or usury; also, a person who, or thing which, makes a lot of money;

something that is very profitable; hence **money-spinning** *vbl. sb.* and *ppl. a.*; **money-taker**, †(*a*) one who takes bribes; (*b*) one who is appointed to receive payments of money, *esp.* one who is set at the entrance of a place of entertainment to receive the money for admission.

1922 *Weekly Dispatch* 12 Nov. 4 (Advt.), All our business is conducted on the '*Moneyback' principle; that is to say, if you are not perfectly satisfied with your purchase return it to us within seven days and we will refund your money in full by return of post. **1955** *Radio Times* 22 Apr. 2/3 Sisco paints are sold on a 'money back' guarantee. **1972** *Farm & Country* 19 Dec. 13/3 We are certain that you will be satisfied and offer a money back guarantee. *a***1628** F. GREVIL *Sidney* (1652) 230 That provident Lady..made his credit swell through all the *money-banks of Europe. **1677** YARRANTON *Eng. Improv.* 18 All persons that have designs to get considerable Sums of Moneys into their hands for intended designs, or hazardous adventures, apply themselves to the *Money-Bankers. *c***1515** *Cocke Lorell's B.* (Percy Soc.) 11 Players, purse cutters, *money bateres, Golde washers. **1626** B. JONSON *Staple of N.* 2nd Intermeane, Old Couetousnesse,..the *Money-bawd, who is a flesh-bawd too, they say. **1846** *St. Louis* (Missouri) *Reveille* 9 Sept. 3/2 The stock consists, in part, of Shirts, Collars,..*Money Belts. **1923** *Outward Bound* Mar. 408/2 Among cowboys.. one might..leave one's money-belt full of gold and notes beside the fire. **1958** P. KEMP *No Colours or Crest* viii. 174, I had a hundred gold sovereigns in my money belt. *a***1715** BURNET *Own Time* III. (1724) I. 439 The House of Commons gave a *money bill for this. **1827** HALLAM *Const. Hist.* (1876) III. xiii. 27 The long agitated question of the right of the lords to make alterations in money-bills. **1616** B. JONSON in *Browne's Past.* II. To Author, Or, like our *Money-Brokers, take vp names On credit, and are cossen'd. **1833** J. HOLLAND *Manuf. Metal* II. v. 113 Mr. Rothschild, the eminent capitalist and money-broker. **1898** *People* 20 Mar. 4/4 The happiness or the misery of 3 millions of people wholly dependent on the whims and caprices of, say, half a dozen '*money bugs', as they are called in the States. **1922** *Public Opinion* 11 Aug. 132/2 The profiteering class, money bugs as the Americans call them. **1838** D. D. BARNARD *Speeches & Rep.* 36 Composed of twenty-six local sovereignties, of all which New-York is the *money centre, as London is the money centre of half the world. **1900** *Congress. Rec.* 17 Feb. 1897/2 Gilt-edged paper can be placed in the money-centers at a small per cent. **1844** LD. BROUGHAM *Brit. Const.* xvii. (1862) 266 The assent of the Lords to a *money-clause is just as necessary as to any other part of a Bill. **1727–51** CHAMBERS *Cycl.* s.v. *Book-keeping*, They may keep the debt and credit both on one side, by double *money-columns. **1861** *Chamb. Encycl.* II. 227/2 The first money-column on each page is for the discount, and the second for the cash. **1906** *Daily Chron.* 23 May 6/4 A keen eye intent on the money-column [of a newspaper]. **1839** SOWERBY *Conch. Man.* 65 *Money Cowry, *Cypræa Moneta.* **1881** *Harper's Mag.* Oct. 723/1 Cotton is the *money crop. **1904** T. WATSON *Bethany* 5 They never failed to make it their object to produce on the farm the necessary supplies, tobacco or cotton being merely the surplus crop, the money crop. **1974** S. MARCUS *Minding the Store* (1975) xii. 243 Until about 1932, Texas had essentially an agriculturally based economy. By 1905 cotton was the money crop. **1787** HAWKINS *Life Johnson* 423 A company of *money-dealers, who, in their time, held the balance of the Antwerp exchange. **1866** CRUMP *Banking* i. 1 Some authorities assert that the Lombard merchants commenced the business of *money-dealing. **1748** SMOLLETT *Rod. Rand.* xv, A rascally *money-dropper, who made it his business to decoy strangers in that manner to one of his own haunts. **1578** *Mony floure, **1597** money flower [see *penny-flower*, PENNY 12]. **1665** PEPYS *Diary* 7 Apr., Unless the King can get some nobleman or rich *money-gentleman to lend him money. **1841** *N.Z. Jrnl.* No. 32. 92 Natives talk about *money-gold. **1842** *Lett. Settlers in Wellington, Nelson & New Plymouth* (1843) 137 We can get them [*sc.* pigs] from the natives for blankets, or for 'money gold' as they call it, which we call sovereigns. **1925** J. GREGORY *Bab of Backwoods* xxiii. 283 Gold that had..been dull bits of ore dug from rocky hillsides; that men had taken and made into money-gold. **1928** I. FISHER *Money Illusion* (1929) i. 4 The '*Money Illusion'.., the failure to perceive that the dollar, or any other unit of money, expands or shrinks in value. **1975** *Times* 30 June 12/8 Money illusion is, as in Germany, dying..as people spend indexed wages rather than save. **1696** J. CARY *Ess. Coyn* 9 The People were again furnish'd by the *Money-Jobbers, with new Arguments against the Government. **1798** BP. WATSON *Address People Gt. Brit.* 5 Money-jobbers, who deal in large speculations on credit. **1790** BURKE *Fr. Rev.* 277 By this means the spirit of *money-jobbing and speculation goes into the mass of land itself. **1838** D. D. BARNARD *Speeches & Rep.* 106 To see him [*sc.* the President] sit as a great *money king over the nation. **1900** *Congress. Rec.* 7 Feb. 1610/1 Where ought control of the currency to rest?.. At present the banks and the money kings wield this power. **1886** W. J. TUCKER *E. Europe* 85 As to those with the parcels, or *money letters, ask them to wait. **1575–85** ABP. SANDYS *Serm.* i. 5 As before he exhorted vs to come and buie freely, without monie; because God is no *monie man. **1662** PEPYS *Diary* 18 Sept., To dinner to Sheriff Maynell's, the great money-man. **1928** Money man [see DATE *v.* 2 d]. **1958** Money-man [see CACKLE *sb.* 3 a]. **1973** *Times* 2 Feb. 14/7 New York money men have been known to quake in the knowledge that they have on deposit $1,000m of overnight money. **1791** A. HAMILTON *Establishment of Mint* in *Wks.* (1810) I. 291 In Holland, the greatest **money* market of Europe, gold was to silver..as 1 to 14·88. **1816** SCOTT *Antiquary* II. vii. 190 In the present state of the money-market. **1861** GOSCHEN *For. Exch.* 10 The power which foreign capitalists, holders of bills of exchange upon England, may exert over our money-market. **1883** *Century Mag.* Sept. 691/2 Wall Street..is the money market of the whole country. **1964** *Financial Times* 12 Mar. 10/2 South Africa has developed a money market which, in relation to national income, handles a larger volume of funds than the traditional London discount market. **1604** T. M. *Black Bk.* in *Middleton's Wks.* (Bullen) VIII. 28 An hoary *money-master..his only recreation was but to hop about the Burse. **1630** *R. Johnson's Kingd. & Commw.* 339 They are great Bankers and money Masters. **1647** TRAPP *Comm. Matt.* xxi. 12 Christ is everyday casting out of his Church all these *money merchants. *a***1656** HALES *Gold. Rem.* III. *Serm.*, etc. (1673) 26 Augustinus Chiessius, a Banker, a Money-merchant at Rome. **1802** in H. Joyce *Hist. Post Office* (1893) 438 At Sight pay..one Pound..and place the same to the Account of the *Money Order Office. *a***1861** A. H. CLOUGH *Mari Magno* in *Poems* (1871) 320 The money-order had been cashed. **1893** in H. Joyce *Hist. Post Office* (1893) 420 The Money Order Office had been established in 1792. **1972** *Post Office Guide* 590 Inland money orders are issued by and payable at all money order offices. **1935** A. J. POLLOCK *Underworld Speaks* 77/1 **Money player*, the tougher the game, this particular gambler excels on account of having lots of nerve. **1944** *Gen* 11 Mar. 30 It is one of the die-hard notions that no money-player is fit to lead an England team. **1681** GREW *Musæum* IV. §iv. 381 A Roman *Money-Pot..fashion'd almost like a Pint Jug without a Neck. Closed at the top, and having a Notch on one side, as in a Christmas-Box. **1829** *H. R. Doc. 21st U.S. Congress 1 Sess.* No. 6. 12 The application of the *money power of the Government to regulate the unequal action. **1831** T. H. BENTON in *Reg. Deb. Congress U.S.* 2 Feb. 50/2 The money power of the bank is both direct and indirect. **1840** J. S. MILL in *Edin. Rev.* LXXII. 11 The additions to the 'money-power' of the higher ranks, consist of the riches of the *novi homines* who are continually aggregated to that class from among the merchants and manufacturers. **1926** R. H. TAWNEY *Religion & Rise of Capitalism* ii. 89 When he [*sc.* Luther] looks at German social life, he finds it ridden by a conscienceless money-power, which incidentally ministers ..to the avarice and corruption of Rome. **1959** *Ann. Reg. 1958* 90 The United Party was pictured as being.. dominated by jingoes and in the hands of the money-power. **1841** HOR. SMITH *Moneyed Man* III. iii. 67 A **money-quake*, whose explosion should hurl all their fortunes into the air. **1852** MUNDY *Our Antipodes* (1857) 20 At the time of the general money-quake he fell like the rest—failing for an immense sum. **1704** LUTTRELL *Brief Rel.* (1857) V. 414 Mr. Adams, an eminent *money scrivener of this citty,..is gone aside (as tis said) for 50,000*l.* *a***1784** JOHNSON in Boswell *Life* (1816) III. 20 Jack Ellis, a money scrivener behind the Royal Exchange. **1844** *Congress. Globe* 28th Congress 2 Sess. App. 37/2 Banks..managed..by a set of irresponsible *money sharks. **1972** G. F. NEWMAN *You Nice Bastard* 347 *Moneyshark*, unlicenced money-lender (operating at especially high rates of interest). **1816** SCOTT *Let.* 23 July (1932) I. 502 You had better be looking out & inquiring after some *money-shop, as we shall have enough of bills. **1972** *Guardian* 9 June 11 The new 'money shop' branches which are sprouting up in the High Streets... Money shops are not really banks at all... 'Loan shop'..is still the best shorthand description. **1875** MELLISS *St. Helena* 217 *Salticus nigrolimbatus*, Cambr.—The large black and white 'Fly-catcher' or '*Money-spider', as it is commonly called. **1879** *N. & Q.* Ser. v. XII. 229 The superstition in connexion with so-called 'money-spiders'. **1756** MRS. F. BROOKE *Old Maid* No. 36. 289 Last night you were more pleased than a wise woman ought to have been, at seeing a *money-spinner upon your handkerchief. **1859** G. A. SALA *Twice round Clock* 69 The clown, the dunderheaded moneyspinner who votes that books are 'rubbish'. **1862** SALA *Seven Sons* I. x. 253 The son of a city money-spinner of mushroom extraction. *c***1880** A. W. PINERO *Money Spinner* (1890) 22 Have you forgotten my father's [gaming] house... Have you forgotten what they called me then, because of my never-failing good fortune—because of my *luck*. They called me the *Money Spinner*! **1952** W. GRANVILLE *Dict. Theatr. Terms* 119 *Money-spinner*, a successful play or artiste. **1954** G. SMITH *Flaw in Crystal* 87 He found he had a pretty knack of writing so that ordinary men and women could understand and feel something of the beauty he saw around him. And he turned that touch into a money-spinner. **1958** A. WILSON *Middle Age of Mrs Eliot* II. 237 If he publishes anything it'll have every chance of being a money spinner. **1970** *Times* 23 Jan. 25/5 (Advt.), Their products range from fertilizers and basic heavy chemicals to..complex petro-chemicals..big money-spinners for Britain's export. **1855** CHAMIER *My Travels* III. iv. 95 *Money-spinning defies even a sirocco or a pestilence. **1936** J. BUCHAN *Island of Sheep* vi. 105 He's a stockbroker—a one-man firm which he founded himself. His interests? Not financial exclusively—indeed, he professes to despise the whole money-spinning business. **1973** *Courier & Advertiser* (Dundee) 1 Mar. 2/2 The money spinning lager boom already accounts for some 12 per cent. of the beer drunk in Britain. **1616** R. C. *Times' Whistle* IV. 1442 Sayth master *mony-taker, greasd i' th' fist, 'And if thou comst in danger, for a noble I'le stand thy friend'. **1825** HONE *Every-day Bk.* 5 Nov. I. 1185, I paid my penny to the money-taker.

money ('mʌnɪ), *v.* [In sense 1, ad. F. *monnayer*; in the other senses, f. MONEY *sb.*]

1. *trans.* To coin or mint (money). *rare.*

*c***1430** *Pilgr. Lyf Manhode* I. cxii. (1869) 59 And therfore on him was forged and moneyed thi ransoum; the wikkede smithes forgeden him on his bak and moneyden [orig. Fr. *monnoyerent*] him. **1691** LOCKE *Lower. Interest* Wks. 1727 II. 44 If your Exportation will not balance your Importation ..away must your Silver go again, whether Monied or not Monied. **1865** SALA *Amer. in War* I. 136 The American.. double-eagle..is perhaps the most beautiful and splendid coin ever moneyed in any mint.

†**2.** To supply with money, bestow money upon. In bad sense, to bribe. *Obs.*

1528 TINDALE *Obed. Chr. Man.* D ij b, How many yeres they will prolonge the sentence with cavillacions & suttelte, if they be well monyed on both parties. **1530** —— *Pract. Prel.* G j, Then come in the embassadours of Fraunce and monye a fewe prelates..to betraye both the kynge and the royalme to. **1611** SPEED *Hist. Gt. Brit.* IX. xi. (1623) 674 Some perfidious English, whom King Robert had monyed. **1624** HEYWOOD *Captives* I. i. in Bullen *O. Pl.* IV, Thou hast monied me in this, Nay landed me. *a***1625** FLETCHER & MASS. *Laws of Candy* I. i, He out of his own store Hath monied Cassilanes the General.

†**b.** To furnish money for (an undertaking).

*a***1697** AUBREY *Lives*, *Ingelbert* (1898) II. 1 He was a poore-man, but Sir Hugh Middleton..moneyed the businesse.

3. To dispose of for money. *rare.*

*c***1611** CHAPMAN *Iliad* XI. 590 Our prey was rich and great; Twice fiue and twentie flockes of sheepe [etc.];..And these soone-monied wares We draue into Neileus towne. **1895** *Funk's Stand. Dict.*, *Money v*...2. (Rare.) To dispose of for money; as, to money a cargo.

4. ***to money out***: to state in detail the prices of; to 'price out' or 'figure out' (a tender or estimate). *Sc.*

1833 LOUDON *Encycl. Archit.* §1059 (Scottish Specification) A detailed bill of every article contained in the estimate, together with the price at which each article was monied out, must accompany such tender. **1893** *Westm. Gaz.* 1 Nov. 7/3 The high prices at which they moneyed out their tenders.

'moneyage. *Hist.* [a. OF. *monneage* (mod.F. *monnayage*), mint, tax upon money, f. *monnayer* MONEY *v.* Cf. med.L. *monētāgium* and *monētāticum*.] 'A payment by the moneyers for the privilege of coining; otherwise explained as a payment by the subjects to prevent loss by the depreciation or change of coinage' (Stubbs *Sel. Charters* Gloss. s.v. *Monetagium*).

1747 CARTE *Hist. Eng.* I. 482 Moneyage was a duty of twelve pence paid every third year in Normandie to the Duke for not altering the coin. **1762** HUME *Hist. Eng. to Hen. VII*, I. App. II. 414 Moneyage was also a general land-tax.. levied by the two first Norman kings, and abolished by the charter of Henry I.

'money-bag.

1. A bag for holding money. Often used jocularly in pl. to denote 'wealth'.

1565 COOPER *Thesaurus* s.v. *Numarius*, *Theca numaria*, a money bagge. **1596** SHAKS. *Merch. V.* II. v. 18, I did dreame of money bags to night. **1713** ADDISON *Guard.* No. 106 ⁋4, I found my place taken up by an ill-bred, aukward puppy, with a money-bag under each arm. **1825** LAMB *Elia* II. *Stage Illusion*, The insecure tenure by which he [*sc.* the miser] holds his money bags and parchments? **1884** *St. James's Gaz.* 9 July 6/1 The elder had possession of the money-bags; and so Prince Victor was forced to eat the leek.

2. *transf.* (*pl.*) A person who is chiefly remarkable as a possessor or lover of money.

1818 KEATS *Isabella* xviii, How could these money-bags see east and west? **1898** J. ARCH *Story of Life* 378 Though squarsons and squires, landlords and money-bags leagued together against me, I was returned by a majority of 34.

money-bound, *a. jocular.* [after *weather-bound*.] Detained by want of money.

1825 MOORE *Mem. Sheridan* II. 488 His letters to the treasurer of the theatre on these occasions were generally headed with the words 'Money-bound'. **1863** JEAFFRESON *Sir Everard's Dau.* 85 When you were often money-bound for a month at a time at a manor-house, because you hadn't the requisite amount of cash wherewith to tip the servants on leaving. **1867** SMYTH *Sailor's Word-bk.*, *Money-bound*, a phrase expressive of such passengers as are detained on board till a remittance arrives for paying the passage made.

'money-box. A box in which money is kept; *esp.* a closed box into which savings or contributions are dropped through a slit.

1585 HIGINS tr. *Junius' Nomencl.* 249 *Capsella fictilis*..a mony box made of potters clay, wherein boyes put their mony to keepe, such as they hang in shops, &c. towards Christmas. **1611** COTGR., *Cachemaille*, a money box. **1755** JOHNSON, *Moneybox*, a till. **1848** DICKENS *Dombey* xviii, The juggler's wife is active with the money-box in another quarter of the town. **1858** O. W. HOLMES *Aut. Breakf.-t.* vii. (1895) 169 The brains also are shaken up [by riding] like coppers in a money-box.

'money-changer. One whose business it is to change money at a fixed or authorized rate.

1382 WYCLIF *John* ii. 14 And he fond in the temple men sellinge scheep, and oxen, and culueris, and chaungeris [*v.r.* money chaungeris] sittinge. *c***1440** *York Myst.* xxvi. 73 In oure temple..Where tabillis full of tresoure lay..Of oure cheffe mony-changers. **1526** TINDALE *Matt.* xxi. 12 And overthrew the tables of the mony chaungers. **1727** ARBUTHNOT *Coins*, etc. 212 The Usurers or Money-changers being a sort of a scandalous employment at Rome. **1827** MACAULAY *Ess.*, *Machiavelli* ⁋13 The tables of Italian money-changers were set in every city.

moneyche, obs. form of MONISH.

moneyed ('mʌnɪd), *a.* Forms: 5–7 **monyed**, 6 **monide**, 6–9 **monied**, 6– **moneyed**. [f. MONEY *sb.* + -ED[2].]

1. Having or possessing money, rich in money. ***moneyed man*** often *spec.* = CAPITALIST.

1457 *Paston Lett.* I. 416 Of such chaffr takyng he shall nevere be monyed. **1573** L. LLOYD *Pilgr. Princes* 104 Hee should bee the most monyed Prince that euer shoulde raigne in India. *c***1592** MARLOWE *Jew of Malta* I. (1633) C, Thou art a Merchant and a monied man. **1597** BACON *Ess.*, *Colours* v. (Arb.) 143 When a great moneyed man hath deuided his chests and coines and bags. **1625** *Ibid.*, *Usury* ⁋4 To inuite Moneyed Men, to lend to the Merchants, for the Continuing and Quickning of Trade. **1647** CLARENDON *Hist. Reb.* VI. §288 The Marquis of Worcester was generally reputed the greatest monied man of the kingdom. **1712** SWIFT *Cond. Allies* Wks. 1751 VIII. 119 That Set of People, who are called the Monied Men; such as had raised vast Sums by trading with Stocks and Funds and lending Money upon great Interest. **1727** A. HAMILTON *New Acc. E. Ind.* I. xii. 139 The Insolence of the Portugueze makes it unsafe for money'd strangers to dwell among them. **1803** WORDSW. *Poems Nat. Indep.* I. xx. *Sonnet*, These times strike monied worldlings with dismay. **1822** J. FLINT *Lett. Amer.* 108 To appropriate to themselves the labour of less moneyed citizens. **1844** STANLEY *Arnold* (1858) I. vi. 237 The landed aristocracy and moneyed aristocracy. **1868** RUSKIN *Time & Tide* (1872) 154 The monied men and leaders of commerce.

1871 M. COLLINS *Mrq. & Merch.* III. ix. 226 So moneyed a man deserves better treatment.

†**b.** With qualifying adv.: (*well*, *plenteously*, etc.) supplied with money. *Obs.*

1471 RIPLEY *Comp. Alch.* v. xxxix. in Ashm. (1652) 157 For they can tech hys Monkys to leve in poverte, And to go clothyd and monyed relygyously. **1479** *Paston Lett.* III. 254, I was nott weell monyed, ffor I hadde nott paste x. marke. **1556** J. HEYWOOD *Spider & F.* lxxiii. 3 Had he bene an ant plenteouslie monide. **1688** FAIRFAX in *Magd. Coll. & Jas. II* (O.H.S.) 245 Ye best monyed was best qualifyed.

2. Consisting of money, derived from money.

1790 BURKE *Fr. Rev.* Sel. Wks. II. 129 The monied property was long looked on with rather an evil eye by the people. **1798** MALTHUS *Popul.* (1817) II. 398 The clear monied rent yielded to a certain number of proprietors [etc.]. **1812** COMBE *Picturesque* XIX, 'Tis a proud scene of monied strife Forms this magnificence of life. **1825** W. IRVING in *Life & Lett.* (1864) II. 233 The moneyed influence of the man of wealth. **1835** *Penny Cycl.* III. 475/2 Trade revived, and the monied resources of the State were improved. **1856** LEVER *Martins of Cro' M.* 346 For these, we want power from you and some present moneyed assistance.

3. ***moneyed interest***: interest or concern in money as a possession; a class or body of persons having such interest. (Cf. *landed interest*.)

1711 [see LANDED *a.* 2]. **1757** J. H. GROSE *Voy. E. Indies* 407 A class of men called the moneyed interest. **1776** ADAM SMITH *W.N.* II. iv. (1869) I. 355 As such capitals are commonly lent out and paid back in money, they constitute what is called the monied interest. **1790** BURKE *Fr. Rev.* 164 The monied interest is in its nature more ready for any adventure; and its possessors more disposed to new enterprizes of any kind. **1793** A. YOUNG *Example France* 81 The monied interest..have some advantages from the more portable nature of their wealth. **1865** J. BRIGHT *Sp. Canada* 13 Mar. (1869) 67 We know what 'the City' means... It means that the people who deal in shares..'the moneyed interest' of the City, are alarmed.

4. *U.S.* Of a company or corporation: Having power to deal in money.

1872 SCHELE DE VERE *Americanisms* 301 A Moneyed Institution, as chartered companies are generally called, like banks, insurance companies, and the like. **1889** *Century Dict.* s.v. *Corporation, Moneyed corporation*, a corporation having banking powers, or power to make loans on pledges or deposits, or authorized by law to make insurances.

moneyer (ˈmʌnɪə(r)). Forms: 4 **moneur**, 4–5 **monyour, moneyere**, 4–7 **monyer**, 5 **moneyour, monyowre, moneour, moniour**, 6–8 **monier**, 4– **moneyer**. [a. OF. *mon(n)ier*, *mon(n)oier*:—L. *monētārius* coiner, minter.]

1. †**a.** A money-changer. *Obs.*

a **1300** *Cursor M.* 14727 Þair ox, þair cu, þair scepe þai sald, And moneurs [*Fairf.* moneyers] þair mone tald. *c* **1380** WYCLIF *Sel. Wks.* II. 49 Jesus..turnede up so doun þe bordis of monyeris. *c* **1400** *Rom. Rose* 6811 But see what gold han usurers, And silver eek in garners, Taylagiers, and these monyours.

b. A money-dealer, banker, capitalist. ? *Obs.*

1706 PHILLIPS (ed. Kersey), *Moneyers*... Also Bankers that make it their Trade, to deal in Monies upon Return. **1755** JOHNSON, *Moneyer* 1. One that deals in money; a banker. **1855** THACKERAY *Newcomes* lxiv, F. B., sir, has a station in the world; F. B. moves among moneyers and City nobs.

2. One who coins money; a coiner, minter. Now chiefly *Hist.*

Formerly used as an official designation at the Mint; the 'Company of Moneyers' was abolished in 1837.

1421–2 HOCCLEVE *Dialogue* 174 Ye cursed men, ye false moneyours. **1469** in *Archæologia* XV. 175 The seid moniours to coyne and to make it. *a* **1577** SIR T. SMITH *Commw. Eng.* II. xxi. (1589) 91 To enquire of all heretiques ..false moniers, extortioners [etc.]. **1631** BEDWELL *Descr. Tottenham* E 3 b, A House..sometime in the tenure and occupation of Simon Bolton, monyer. **1668** *Lond. Gaz.* No. 294/4 The Provost and Company of Moneyers. **1670** PETTUS *Fodinæ Reg.* 41 The Master-worker, who receiveth the Silver from the Warden,..and delivereth it to the Moniers. **1697** EVELYN *Numism.* i. 4 Coin'd by certain Florentine moneyers. **1815** *Ann. Reg., Chron.* 84 The moneyers' hall and offices also escaped with little injury. **1874** STUBBS *Const. Hist.* I. x. 314 The general depreciation of the coinage, caused by the dishonesty of the moneyers.

†**ˈmoneyfied**, *pa. pple. Obs. rare*⁻¹. In quot. **monifide, -fi'd**. [f. MONEY *sb.*: see -FY.] Endowed with money.

1641 *Witt's Recreat.* M 8, Nature did well in giving poore men wit, That fooles well monifide [**1663** *Ibid.* I 5 b, monifi'd] may pay for it.

ˈmoneyful, *a. rare*⁻¹. [-FUL.] Abounding in money.

1604 BROUGHTON *Corrupt. in Handl. Relig.* 52 The Iewes ..looke for a moneyfull King.

ˈmoney-grub. [See GRUB *sb.* 2 c.] One who is sordidly intent on amassing money.

1768 *Woman of Honor* III. 235 Vanity is seen capable of erecting the very dirtiest money-grubs into Peers. **1816** T. L. PEACOCK *Gryll Gr.* (1861) 128 He has been chosen as the most conspicuous grub among the moneygrubs of his borough.

ˈmoney-grubber. [See GRUBBER 3.] = prec.

1840 *Bentley's Miscellany* VIII. 449 The money-grubber, pent up in a close city. **1851** D. JERROLD *St. Giles* xxxii. 333 And so, they've turned you over..to the old money-grubber. **1862** THORNBURY *Turner* II. 258 Was this..the mere money-grubber and sordid Harpagon? **1932** A. HUXLEY *Lett.* (1969) 361 It's terrifying what can be done by people who have a monopoly of means of propaganda—private money-grubbers.

So **ˈmoney-grubbing** *vbl. sb.* and *ppl. a.*

1848 THACKERAY *Van. Fair* xx, The whole pack of money-grubbing vulgarians. **1870** DISRAELI *Lothair* xxxii, They have become absorbed in money-grubbing and what they call industry.

ˈmoney-lender. One whose business is lending money at interest.

178. BURKE *Sp. Durat. Parl.* Wks. 1812 V. 378 In every district of the kingdom, there is some leading man,..some active attorney, some popular preacher, some moneylender, &c. &c. who is followed by the whole flock. **1835** DICKENS *Sk. Boz, Pawnbroker's Shop*, The better sort of pawnbroker calls himself a silversmith,..while the more humble money-lender boldly advertises his calling, and invites observation. **1878** STUBBS *Const. Hist.* III. xviii. 91 The odium which has been heaped upon him as a money-lender.

So **ˈmoney-lending** *vbl. sb.* and *ppl. a.*

1765 FOOTE *Commissary* I. Wks. 1799 II. 7 That canting, couzening, money-lending, match-making, pawnbroking ——. **1818** T. L. PEACOCK *Nightmare Abbey* 118 A money-lending Jew. **1866** CRUMP *Banking* i. 8 Money-lending was carried on very extensively after the return from captivity.

moneyless (ˈmʌnɪlɪs), *a.* [-LESS.] Without money, having no money.

1362 LANGL. *P. Pl.* A. VIII. 130 Meteles and Moneyeles on Maluerne hulles. **1509** BARCLAY *Shyp of Folys* (1570) 5 That poore men and monyles may her once see. **1641** MILTON *Ch. Govt.* II. iii. Wks. 1851 III. 173 Where bribery and corruption solicits, paltring the free and monilesse power of discipline with a carnall satisfaction by the purse. **1712** *Spect.* No. 437 ¶1 She marries..a Moneyless Girl to a Man of Fortune. **1841** EMERSON *Lect., Man the Reformer* Wks. (Bohn) II. 242 We are first thoughtless, and then find that we are moneyless. **1841** R. OASTLER *Fleet Papers* I. xxxvii. 289 Her public coffers are moneyless.

ˈmoney-maker.

†**1. a.** One who coins money; a minter, moneyer.

c **1400** *Destr. Troy* 1590 Marchandes, Monymakers, Mongers of fyche. **1431** *Test. Ebor.* (Surtees) II. 16 Ego Johannes Esyngwald de Eboraco, monymakerr. **1523** LD. BERNERS *Froiss.* I. cxxxvi. 163 Two hundred money makers, that forged there the Money for the french kyng.

†**b.** A maker of counterfeit coin. *Obs.*

c **1440** in Hearne *R. Glouc.* (1724) 587 Another [statute] he made a none ryghte That monye makers shuld lesse hure syghte. **14..** *Agst. Friars* in *Pol. Poems* (Rolls) II. 250 Mony-makers I trow thei be, *regis proditores*. *a* **1734** J. COMER in *Rhode Island Hist. Soc. Coll.* (1893) VIII. 65 This day came up ye case of ye money makers to trial. **1777** in *New Hampsh. Hist. Soc. Coll.* (1863) VII. 93 To pay Col. Sam'l Folson nineteen pounds eleven shillings for.. apprehending Money makers. **1778** in *Ibid.* 149 Jnᵒ Mac Glauglin, a money maker.

2. a. One who gains and accumulates money; one who is skilled in, or intent on, getting money.

1864 G. MEREDITH *Sandra Belloni* i, The fact of his being a money-maker was redeemed in their sight by his devotion to music. **1899** R. WALLACE *G. Buchanan* ii. 41 He was no money-maker.

b. A thing which yields pecuniary profit.

1899 ADE *Doc' Horne* 22, I expect to have an interest in the Neapolitan Dental Parlors, where I'm working now. It's a sure money-maker. **1901** *Munsey's Mag.* XXV. 748/2 Some wells have been great money-makers for their owners. **1940** E. FERGUSSON *Our Southwest* xix. 349 He has instead snapped up his dances as money-makers.

So **ˈmoney-making** *vbl. sb.*, acquisition of wealth; *ppl. a.*, occupied in, or intent on, acquiring wealth; also (of things), yielding money, lucrative.

1739 CIBBER *Apol.* (1740) 58 These Shares of the Patentees were promiscuously sold out to Mony-making Persons, call'd Adventurers. **1855** MILMAN *Lat. Chr.* XI. viii. V. 187 The Jews were the first; their strange obstinacy in money-making made them his perpetual victims. *a* **1862** BUCKLE *Civiliz.* (1869) III. iii. 171 A mercantile and money-making spirit. **1887** JESSOPP *Arcady* ii. 63 Farming never has been a money-making pursuit.

money matter. [See MATTER *sb.*¹ 21.] An affair turning upon money. Chiefly *pl.*, the financial side of things.

1552 LATIMER *Serm. 2nd Sund. Adv.* (1584) 252 b, It is not a triflyng matter, it is not a money matter. **1560** DAUS tr. *Sleidane's Comm.* 74 A money matter can not breake their frendshyp. **1618** *Barnevelt's Apol.* C iv b, I settled the money-matters of the Prouinces. **1712** ARBUTHNOT *John Bull* IV. ii, What if You and I, Nic., should inquire how Money-matters stand between us? **1855** MACAULAY *Hist. Eng.* xii. III. 203 He had been a principal agent of the Order of Jesuits in money matters. **1887** RUSKIN *Præterita* II. 247 Anxiety about money matters.

ˈmoney-monger. A dealer in money, esp. in the way of lending it.

1571 GOLDING *Calvin on Ps.* xv. 5 For it is a very vnmeet thing, that..only the monymongers sitting stil shuld take tribute of euery mans labors. **1639** MASSINGER *Unnat. Combat* IV. ii, My pay..The citie cormorants, my monie-mongers, Have swallow'd downe already. **1755** J. SHEBBEARE *Lydia* (1769) II. 32 The 'Change-alley jobbers, who can no more suffer a story to lie still without improving, than these money-mongers can their cash without interest. **1844** KINGLAKE *Eöthen* (1845) 102 Rothschild (the late money-monger). **1877** RUSKIN *Fors Clav.* lxxxii. 325 Given ..not by God..but only by the Jew money-monger in twenty per cent.

appos. *c* **1613** ROWLANDS *Paire of Spy-Knaves* 14 The sonnes of Mammon, mony-monger slaues.

Hence **ˈmoney-mongering** *vbl. sb.* and *ppl. a.* Also †**ˈmoney-monging** (cf. *mass-monging*, etc.).

1594 R. WILSON *Cobler's Proph.* I. ii. 140 The money monging mate with all his knauerie. *c* **1600** *Timon* V. v. (Shaks. Soc.) 90 Away, thou mony-monging cormorant. **1816** KEATS *Sonn. to Haydon*, A money mong'ring, pitiable brood. **1848** KINGSLEY *Yeast* xv. (1881) 304 The last place in which he will look for the cause of his misery is in that very money-mongering to which he now clings as frantically as ever. **1874** FARRAR *Christ* xiii. (1881) 88 These money-mongering Jews.

moneyocracy (mʌnɪˈɒkrəsɪ). *jocular.* [See -CRACY.] The moneyed class as a ruling power.

1834 *Blackw. Mag.* XXXV. 339 Which has at last precipitated the nation, bound hand and foot into the bonds of the shopocracy and moneyocracy. **1859** SALA *Gas-light & D.* xxvi, The flower of the British aristocracy and moneyocracy.

moneyour, obs. form of MONEYER.

money's-worth. [WORTH *sb.*]

1. Something that is worth money, or is recognized as equivalent to money. Often in phr. ***money or money's worth***. Cf. the older MONEY-WORTH.

a **1604** HANMER *Chron. Irel.* (1633) 160 Laden with gold, silver, money, and monies worth. **1674** ALLEN *Danger Enthu.* 90 To take mony, or moneys-worth, whereby to live. **1760** FOOTE *Minor* II. (1767) 40 Tho' money is not to be had, money's worth may, and that's the same thing. **1845** STEPHEN *Comm. Laws Eng.* (1874) II. 174 An obligation to pay money or money's worth on the breach of any covenant.

2. An equivalent for the sum of money paid or to be paid; full value. (Now chiefly with poss. pron.)

1588 SHAKS. *L.L.L.* II. i. 137 In surety of the which, One part of Aquitaine is bound to vs, Although not valued to the moneys worth. **1875** JOWETT *Plato* (ed. 2) I. 141, I give my pupils their money's-worth.

ˈmoneywort. [Suggested by the old L. name *Nummularia*.] The plant *Lysimachia Nummularia* or Herb Twopence, which has roundish glossy leaves. Also, a book-name for *Anagallis tenella*, *Sibthorpia europæa* (Bastard or Cornish Moneywort), and other plants.

1578 LYTE *Dodoens* I. liii. 78 Monyworte hath small slender stalkes..vpon euery side whereof groweth small rounde leaues..almost like to a penny. **1597** GERARDE *Herbal* II. clxxxix. 505. **1756** WATSON in *Phil. Trans.* XLIX. 815 The purple-flowered Moneywort. **1787** WITHERING *Brit. Plants* (1796) II. 239 *Anagallis tenella*... Purple-flowered Money-wort. Bog Pimpernel. *Ibid.* III. 557 *Sibthorpia europæa*. Bastard Moneywort. **1848** C. A. JOHNS *Week at Lizard* 287 *Sibthorpia Europæa*, Cornish Moneywort,..clothes the sides of every..rill.

ˈmoney-worth, *sb.* [WORTH *sb.*]

1. = MONEY'S-WORTH 1. ? *Obs.*

c **1380** WYCLIF *Wks.* (1880) 67 Alle syche as taken money or money worþ for gostly offices. *c* **1394** *P. Pl. Crede* 715 Þat þey may kachen Money oþer money-worthe and mede to fonge. **1526** *Pilgr. Perf.* (W. de W. 1531) 275 Yf they be founde to haue ony money or money worth, contrary to theyr rule. **1545** BRINKLOW *Compl.* xxiv. (1874) 71 And if thei..geue no mony nor mony worth, thei shal be cownted heretyckes. **1668** CLARENDON *Vindic.* Tracts (1727) 23, I do positively deny that ever I received..the least sum of mony or mony-worth for any lease made by his Majesty of his customs. **1800** *Chron.* in *Asiat. Ann. Reg.* 101/1 To dispose of his patronage for money, for money-worth, or for any thing convertible into money.

2. Worth in money, money-value.

1903 *Expositor* Apr. 271 The value of a gift is independent of its money-worth. **1904** *Quaritch's Catal.*, It is.. equivalent in intrinsic value to an early Quarto, and ought to be equivalent in money-worth likewise.

†**ˈmoney-worth**, *a. Obs.* [WORTH *a.*] Worth money, valuable.

In examples like quot. 1611, the word may be the prec. sb. used predicatively.

1611 COTGR. s.v. *Argent, C'est argent qu'argent vaut*: Prov. Nothing but money is money-worth. **1645** USSHER *Body Div.* (1647) 294 Whether it be Cattell, money, or any thing that is money-worth. **1649** BP. HALL *Cases Consc.* (1650) 24 There is no great difference between this case, and that of loane..; save that there money is let, here commodities money-worth.

monful, obs. form of MANFUL *a.*

mong (mʌŋ), *sb.*¹ Also 8–9 **mung**, 9 **mang**. [Aphetic form of YMONG *sb.* (OE. *ȝemang*).]

1. A mingling, mixture. *Obs.* exc. *dial.*

a **1225** *Ancr. R.* 384 Þis mong woreð so þe eien of þe heorte þet heo ne mei iknowen God. *a* **1240** *Sawles Warde* in *Cott. Hom.* 251 For eider is unþolelich ant iþis ferliche mong þe leatere þurh þe earre derueð þe mare. **1848** A. B. EVANS *Leicestersh. Words* s.v., 'All of a mang loike': i.e. all, as it were, mashed or jumbled together.

†**b.** Intercourse, commerce. *Obs.*

a **1240** *Ureisun* in *Cott. Hom.* 185 Ich nabbe no mong, ne felawscipe, ne priuete wiþ þe world. *c* **1330** R. BRUNNE *Chron. Wace* (Rolls) 7384 Wyþ false Godes ȝe make monge.

2. Applied to mixtures of different kinds of meal (the precise application varying according to locality).

[**1380** in *Essex Rev.* July (1904) 146, 3 acres of peasemong & 3 of benemong.] *c* **1475** *Pict. Voc.* in Wr.-Wülcker 785/12 *Hec mixtilio*, mo[n]ge. **1787** GROSE *Provinc. Gloss.*, *Mung*, food for chickens. *a* **1825** FORBY *Voc. E. Anglia*, *Mung*, a

mixture of coarse meal with milk or pot-liquor for the food of dogs, pigs, or poultry. **1888** *Sheffield Gloss.*, *Mung*, a mixed food for horses.

3. A crowd. *dial.*

1877 E. LEIGH *Cheshire Gloss.*, *Mung*, a crowd, a rabble. **1883** C. F. SMITH *Southernisms* in *Trans. Amer. Philol. Soc.* 51 A student..(from West Tennessee) was heard to say recently: 'Well, if I fail on my examination, I'll have the consolation that I am in the *mang*' [i.e. 'the crowd'].

4. *attrib.* See quot. 1872.

1849 *N.Y. Express* 17 Feb. (Bartlett), As many of our citizens who intend to go to California may base their arrangements upon the mung news of some of the papers, we conceive it to be our duty to state that most of these letters are fictions. **1872** SCHELE DE VERE *Americanisms* 618 *Mung* news means confused news; statements which seem contradictory are, in like manner, called *mung*.

mong (mʌŋ), *sb.*[2] Austral. slang abbrev. of MONGREL *sb.*

1933 *Bulletin* (Sydney) 16 Aug. 39/1 And the mong fired him! **1934** *Ibid.* 30 May 20/3 The silliest dogs for miles around live in Warrnambool; these mongs crouch down when a car approaches and spring at the front wheels with snappy barks. **1956** G. CASEY in *Coast to Coast 1955–6* 80 Reckon Charlie Spend's having trouble with that mong of his. **1966** [see HEEL *v.*[1] 4]. **1967** [see BLUDGE *v.*]. **1967** PARTRIDGE *Dict. Slang* Suppl., *Mong*, a mongrel dog... 2. Hence, pejorative for any dog, even of the best pedigree. **1970** J. CLEARY *Helga's Web* v. 77, I can't *lose*. I backed a mong last night that had only three legs..and it finished up beating the bunny home.

†**mong**, *v.*[1] *Obs.* Forms: 1 **mangian**, 3 **mang**, 7 **mung**. [OE. *mangian* = OS. *mangôn*, ON. *manga*:—OTeut. **maŋgôjan*, f. L. *mango* dealer, trader. In quot. 1606 a back-formation from MONGER *sb.*[1] (which Holland spells *munger*).]

a. *intr.* To traffic (*with*). **b.** *trans.* To barter.

*c*897 K. ÆLFRED *Gregory's Past. C.* xliv. 333 Hwæt forstent ænizum menn ðæt, ðeah he mangize ðæt he ealne ðisne middanzeard aze, zif he his saule forspildt? *c* **1000** ÆLFRIC *Hom.* (Th.) I. 412 Mid sceapum he mangað. *a* **1225** *Ancr. R.* 146 Seint Gregorie awundreð him, & seið þet men beoð wode þet treoweð so vuele [*v.r.* mangen swa uuele]. *Ibid.* 407 Vndeore he makeð God..þet for eni worldliche luue his luue trukie [*v.r.* manges]. *a* **1300** *E.E. Psalter* ci. 27 And als hilinge wende saltou þa, And þai sal be turned [*v.r.* manged, Vulg. *mutabuntur*] swa. **1606** HOLLAND *Sueton.* 68 He was none of these that lie in the winde to mung and catch at Inheritances.

mong, *v.*[2] *dial.* Also **mung**. [app. f. MONG *sb.*[1]]

†**1.** *intr.* ? To mingle (*with*). *Obs.*

a **1310** in Wright *Lyric P.* xvi. 52 With murthes monie mote heo monge, that brid so breme in boure.

2. *trans.* To mix; also, to knead.

1790 GROSE *Provinc. Gloss.* (ed. 2), *Mung*, to mix. Worcest. **1810** MARSHALL *Rev. Rep. Agric., West.* 334 *note*, The term in use, for this mixed mongrel crop,..is..mong corn; doubtless from the obsolete verb *mong* to mix. **1893** *Broad Norfolk* 17 To *mung* is used as meaning to knead dough.

mong (mʌŋ), *prep.* Now always written **'mong** (*Sc.* **'mang**). Also 3–4 **mang**. [In ME. an aphetic form of *amang*, *among*, or *imong* (OE. *zemang*) YMONG *prep.*; since the 16th c. only poetical shortening of AMONG.] Among.

c **1200** ORMIN 239 þatt icc ne beo mang wimmannkinn Till hæþinng butenn childre. *c* **1205** LAY. 10292, & mong [*c* 1275 a-mong] heom seoluen vnimete seorzen. *a* **1300** *Cursor M.* 10274 þe tre þat bers na fruit to hand, Mang oþer tres aght not to stand. **1596** SHAKS. *Merch. V.* III. v. 94 How som ere thou speakst 'mong other things, I shall digest it? **1640** HABINGTON *Q. Arragon* II. i. C 2 b, Tis that will make thee held a potent Peere, Mong men oth' Pike, of buffe, and bandeliere. **1678** BUTLER *Hud.* III. ii. 351 'Mong these there was a Politician, With more Heads than a Beast in Vision. **1786** BURNS *Vision* II. v, 'Mong swelling floods of reeking gore. **1796** MACNEILL *Waes o' War* II. 60 Thrice frae aff the ground he started,..Thrice..Sigh'd—and sank 'mang heaps o' slain. **1858** W. T. MATSON *Poems* 3 The breeze that 'mong the branches makes a stir Of leaves.

mongan (ˈmɒŋgən). *Austral.* [Native name.] A species of ring-tailed opossum, *Pseudocheirus herbertensis*, found in the rain forest of north-eastern Queensland.

1890 C. LUMHOLTZ *Among Cannibals* 173 (Morris), Jimmy..had..found mongan.., a new and very pretty mammal, whose habitat is exclusively the highest tops of the scrubs in the Coast Mountains. **1970** W. D. L. RIDE *Guide to Native Mammals of Australia* 76 Mongan, Herbert River Ringtail, *Pseudocheirus herbertensis*... Very dark brown with white under-surface; tip of tail white.

mongcorn (ˈmʌŋkɔːn). *Obs.* exc. *dial.* Forms: 3 **mancorn**, 5 **mongorne**, 5–6 **mong(e)corne**, 6 **mon-, muncorne**, 7 **mun(c)k-corn**, **mungcorne**, 7, 9 **muncorn**, 8 (in Dicts.) **mangcorn**, 8–9 **mungcorn**, (9 **monk-corn**). [f. MONG *sb.*[1] + CORN *sb.*[1]] 'Mixed corn'; a mixture of two kinds of grain (usually wheat and rye) sown together; = MASLIN[2].

1263 *Muniment Magd. Coll. Oxf.* (1882) 144 Mancorn. *c* **1440** *Promp. Parv.* 334/2 Mestlyone, or monge corne..(*S.* mongorne), *mixtilio.* **1552** HULOET, Beere corne, barley bygge, or moncorne. **1572** J. JONES *Bathes Buckstone* 9 b, Some [make bread] of Miscelling, or Muncorne, as in Worcester Shyre. **1620** MARKHAM *Farew. Husb.* 117 Masline, or as some call it Munck-corne or Blend-corne, being part Rye, and part Wheate mixed together. **1686** PLOT *Staffordsh.* 341 They sow it with Muncorn or Miscellane in the place of wheat. **1805** DUNCUMB *Agric. Heref.* 66 Rye, which with an equal proportion of wheat, constituted the bread-corn used in religious houses before their suppression, is now sown but sparingly, but grain thus mixed in flour during a time of scarcity, or dearness, still retains the name of monk-corn, from the circumstances above-mentioned. **1855** *Morton's Cycl. Agric.* II. 724 *Muncorn* (Herefords.), a mixture of different seeds sown to come up as one crop.

b. *attrib.*, as ***mongcorn bread***, ***heap***; also as adj. = mingled, mixed, in ***mongcorn team***.

c **1394** *P. Pl. Crede* 786 And mene mong-corn bred to her mete fongen. **1598** BP. HALL *Sat.* v. ii. 116 A jolly rounding of a whole foote broad From of the mong-corne heape shall Trebius loade. **1655** MOUFET & BENNET *Health's Impr.* xxv. 239 Misslin or Munckcorn-bread, made of Rye and Wheate together. **1839** *Hereford. Gloss.* 128 A 'muncorn team' means a team of horses and oxen mixed. **1879** MISS JACKSON *Shropsh. Word-bk.* s.v., Muncorn bread's very..good, but theer's nuthin' like a bit o' good w'eaten flour.

monge presawnte, var. MAUNCH PRESENT *Obs.*

monger (ˈmʌŋgə(r)), *sb.*[1] Forms: 1 **man(c)gere**, 2 **mangare**, 3–5 **mongere**, 5 **mounger**, 6–7 **munger**, 3– **monger**. [OE. *mangere* (= OHG., ON. *mangari*), agent-n. of *mangian* MONG *v.*[1]]

1. A dealer, trader, trafficker. From the 16th c. onwards, chiefly, one who carries on a petty or disreputable 'traffic'; also, in recent use, in conscious analyses of words like *cheesemonger*.

a **975** *Canons K. Edgar* §14 in Thorpe *Laws* II. 246 We læraþ þæt preosta zehwilc tilize him rihtlice & ne beo ænig mangere mid unrihte. *c* **1000** *Ags. Gosp.* Matt. xiii. 45 Eft is heofena rice zelic þam mangere þe sohte þ gode mere-grot. *c* **1150** *Voc.* in Wr.-Wülcker 539/31 *Mercator, uel negociator*, mangare. *c* **1400** *Destr. Troy* 1590 Marchandes, Monymakers, Mongers of fyche. **1567–9** JEWEL *Def. Apol.* (1611) 615 Against these Mongers of Miracles, my God hath armed me. **1601** HOLLAND *Pliny* II. 485 One rich munger or other, buying vp a commodity,..for to haue the Monopoly of it, raiseth the market. **1639** FORD *Lady's Trial* I. i, *Fvt.* I am..no monopolist Of forged Corantos, monger of Gazets. *Pie.* Monger of courtezans, fine Futelli. **1654** GAYTON *Pleas. Notes* III. vii. 111 Their [the Barbers'] shops are..the Magazines of all Newes..All the Mongers of that kinde come thither for matter and Inspiration. **1812** *Religionism* 23 Cheese-mongers not more like, nor beans, each other; For every monger is a monger's brother. **1841** SYD. SMITH in Lady Holland *Mem.* (1855) II. 445 Mongers who have lived in the midst of cheese. **1874** RUSKIN *Fors Clav.* xxxviii. 33 He would be..more reverend to mortals..as a true monger of sweet fish. **1881** DUFFIELD *Don Quix.* I. Pref. 32 Official guardians of the faith and mongers of prayers.

†**b.** Used for: WHOREMONGER. *Obs.*

1706 BAYNARD in Sir J. Floyer *Hot & Cold Bath.* II. (1709) 282 Some strong young Mongers of good Constitutions, have brushed through such Misfortunes.

2. Used as a second element in compounds, as ***cheesemonger***, ***costermonger***, ***fishmonger***, ***fleshmonger***, ***ironmonger***. In formations dating from the middle of the 16th c. onwards *-monger* nearly always implies one who carries on a contemptible or discreditable 'trade' or 'traffic' in what is denoted by the first element of the compound, as ***ceremony-monger***, ***fashion-monger***, ***mass-monger***, ***merit-monger***, ***news-monger***, ***pardon-monger***, ***scandal-monger***. The more important compounds of this kind are given as main words or under their first element; the following are examples of the occasional formations, the number of which is unlimited.

1297 *Coram Rege Roll* m. 22 *dorso* (1898) 143 Willelmum le Heymonger. *c* **1475** *Plumpton Corr.* (Camden) 30, I fand one which hath bene of old a supersedias mounger. **1550** BALE *Image Both Ch.* xviii. Bb vj, Foule priestes,..and holy water mongers dayly peruerting the ignorant people. **1678** BUTLER *Hud.* III. ii. 999 The impatient States-Monger Could now contain himself no longer. **1748** CHESTERF. *Let. to Son* 6 Dec., The numerous..tribe of insect-mongers, shell-mongers, and pursuers and driers of butterflies. **1761** CHURCHILL *Rosciad* 509 The nice punctilio-mongers of this age. **1829** SOUTHEY *Sir T. More* I. v. 109 The humanity-mongers, who deny the necessity and lawfulness of inflicting capital punishment in any case. **1837** HAWTHORNE *Twice-told T.* (1851) I. xix. 276, I must be content to bear the stigma of a fiction monger. **1858** *Eclectic Rev.* Ser. VI. III. 411 The latter qualification..is notoriously complied with by most of our recent word-mongers. **1863** KINGSLEY *Lett.*, etc. (1877) II. 181 My only fear is that people will fancy me a verbal-inspiration-monger. **1900** *Academy* 28 July 73/2 Ah, Mr. Haggard, what an incorrigible hero-monger you are!

†**'monger**, *sb.*[2] *Obs.* [Origin obscure; perh. a use of prec.] A kind of fishing vessel.

1561 EDEN *Arte Nauig.* Pref. Ciiv b, Fyshermen that go a trawlyng for fyshe in Catches or mongers. **1570** *Act 13 Eliz.* c. 11 §3 The Catches, Mongers and Picardes pretendyng to buy fressh Herrynges.

monger (ˈmʌŋgə(r)), *v.* [f. MONGER *sb.*[1]] *trans.* To deal or traffic in.

1928 *Observer* 5 Feb. 15/1 Both American and British opinion is laughing out of court those who monger their scares about the United States Navy. **1962** *Times Lit. Suppl.* 10 Aug. 570/3, I laughed at her and told her, that she cannot monger any money out of my pocket.

mongerell, obs. form of MONGREL.

mongering (ˈmʌŋgərɪŋ), *vbl. sb.* [f. MONGER *sb.*[1] + -ING[1]. Cf. *soldiering*.] Trading, trafficking. Chiefly used, like *monger*, as a second element in compounds, with a like implication.

1846 THORPE *Ælfric's Hom.* II. 95 Let none of them undertake any reeveship or mongering. **1867** H. C. LEA *Sacerdotal Celibacy* xxv. (1884) 413 The salvation mongering of Tetzel. **1892** STEVENSON *Across the Plains* 314 All these..militant mongerings of moral half-truths.

So **'mongering** *ppl. a.*, as in ***borough-mongering***.

mongery (ˈmʌŋgərɪ). [f. MONGER *sb.*[1] + -Y.] = MONGERING *vbl. sb.*, only as second element in compounds, as ***book-mongery***, IRON-MONGERY, etc.

1876 BLACKIE *Lang. & Lit. Highl. Scot.* ii. 68 These days of widespread prose and bookmongery.

Monghol, Mongholian, var. ff. MONGOL, -IAN.

†**Mongibel.** *Obs.* [ad. *Mongibello* (for *Monte Gibello*: from Arab. *jabal* mountain), the mod. Sicilian name.] Mount Ætna: in quots. *transf.*

1660 HOWELL *Parly of Beasts* 134 Within us we felt too often..such furnaces or Mongibells of fires. **1674** T. FLATMAN *On Death Dk. Albemarle* vi. 8 The City turn'd into one Mongibel.

†**'monging**, *vbl. sb.* *Obs.* Also 1 **mang(g)ung**, 3 **manging(e**. [OE. *mangung*, f. *mangian* MONG *v.*[1]] Trading, trafficking. In mod. use only as a second element in compounds, as ***mass-monging***, ***scandal-monging***.

c **1000** *Ags. Gosp.* Matt. xxii. 5 Đa forzymdon hiz þæt & ferdun, sum to his tune, sum to hys manggunge. *c* **1000** ÆLFRIC *Hom.* (Th.) I. 524 Se færð embe his mangunge. *a* **1300** *E.E. Psalter* xliii. 14 þou salde þi folke with-out waringe, And noght was mikelhede in þair manginge. **1560** W. BALDWIN *Funeralles Edw. VI*, C ij (Roxb. Club), Repent you, marchantes, your straunge marchandises Of personages, prebends [etc.]..Your monging of vitayles, corne, butter, and cheese.

So †**monging** *ppl. a.*, as in ***fashion-monging***, ***mass-monging***, ***merit-monging***.

mongke, obs. form of MONK.

†**'mongle**, *v.* *Obs.* [? freq. of root *mong-*, *mang-* to mix (cf. MONG *sb.*[1]). Cf. the much later MINGLE.] To mingle. Hence †**'mongling** *vbl. sb.* and *ppl. a.*

a **1225** *Ancr. R.* 6 þeos riwle..is euer on & schal beon, wiðute monglunge & wiðute chaungunge. *Ibid.* 116, Ich am stille of þe more, nout one monglinde honden, auh puten honden utward. *Ibid.* 338 þus euer sum vuel mongleð him mit mine gode. *Ibid.* 384 þe heorte schir..þet non ne mei habben mid monglunge of unðeauwes.

Mongo[1] (ˈmɒŋgəʊ). Also **Lomongo**. [Native name.] A Bantu people living in Zaïre (formerly the Belgian Congo); a member of this people; the language of this people. Also *attrib.*

1906 VISCT. MOUNTMORRES *Congo Independent State* 45 East of the Launoa..the Mongo, perhaps on account of their contact with the Arabised tribes..appear to have advanced to a much higher state of civilisation than in other parts. **1910** *Encycl. Brit.* VI. 925/1 Farther north and largely occupying the valley of the Ruki are the Mongo, a large forest tribe. **1919** A. WERNER *Introd. Sketch Bantu Lang.* 314 *Congo*,..the languages included under this heading are ..*Lolo* (Mongo, Lunkundu)—on the Equator within the great northern bend of the Congo. **1928** E. A. & L. RUSKIN *Dict. Lomongo Lang.* Introd., Lomongo belongs to the Bantu group of languages and is spoken by at least 300,000 people, dwelling in Middle Belgian Congo, north and south of the equator. **1946** *Nature* 6 July 14/2 Important monographs were produced on the Mongo, Basongo, and Bakongo. **1961** G. GREENE *Burnt-Out Case* VI. i. 178 She remembered..her father teaching her the Mongo for 'bread' and 'coffee' and 'jam'. They were still the only three words in Mongo that she knew. **1961** *Listener* 16 Nov. 831/1 If the Mongo tribes had been contained within a single province..the prospect of maintaining an independent Congo as a single state would hardly have been worth considering.

mongo[2] (ˈmɒŋgəʊ). [Mongolian.] A monetary unit of Mongolia, one hundred of which are equal to one tugrik.

1935 *Statesman's Year Bk.* 774 The *Tukhrik*, a silver coin equivalent to half an American gold dollar, and divided into 100 *Mongo*. **1968** C. NARBETH *Coin Collector's Encycl.* 145 The Mongolian People's Republic..first minted coins in copper and silver of Mung and Tugrik denominations. **1969** *Whitaker's Almanack 1970* 984 Mongolia (Outer), Tugrik of 100 Mongo. **1972** *Statesman's Year-Bk.* 1165, 100 *möngö* = 1 *tugrik*.

mongoe, variant of MUNGO.

mongoes, obs. form of MONGOOSE.

Mongol (ˈmɒŋgɒl), *sb.* and *a.* Also 8 **Mungul**, **-al**, 8–9 **Mongul**, 9 **-ghol**, **-gole**. [The native name, said to be f. *mong* 'brave'. Cf. MOGUL.]

A. *sb.* **1.** One of an Asiatic race now chiefly inhabiting Mongolia, a large territory situated between China proper and Siberia, but formerly extending into eastern Europe; also more widely, one of the Mongolian race, a Mongolian.

1738 tr. *Strahlenberg's Descr. Russ.*, etc. 138 Those few Mungals of King Ill-chan's Army, who [etc.]. **1788** GIBBON *Decl. & F.* lxv. VI. 358 Timour dispatched..a numerous army..to subdue the Pagan Calmucks and Mungals. **1837** *Pop. Encycl.* V. 33/1 Having subjugated Russia, the

Monguls entered Poland in 1240. **1883** *Encycl. Brit.* XVI. 744/1 Lamaism has always had a great attraction in the eyes of the Mongols.

2. (Also with lower-case initial.) A person afflicted with mongolism.

[**1866**: see MONGOLIAN *a.* and *sb.* A. 3.] **1896** *Brit. Med. Jrnl.* 12 Sept. 617/1 There is probably in the Mongol a more profound and general condition of intrauterine failure of development than in the cretin. **1913** *Jrnl. Nerv. & Mental Dis.* XL. 338 Mentally, mongols are as a rule quiet, good tempered, and easily amused. **1926** *Lancet* 23 Jan. 190/2 The resemblance between the Mongol and the cretin has naturally produced an endocrine theory. **1932** [see B. 2 below]. **1960** *Guardian* 29 Apr. 6/5 The number of adult mongols was likely to increase fairly steadily. **1970** PASSMORE & ROBSON *Compan. Med. Stud.* II. xxxi. 17/1 A variety of cytogenetic aberrations have been found amongst the 2–5 per cent of mongols who are neither simple trisomics nor trisomic/normal mosaics.

B. *adj.* **1.** Pertaining to or characteristic of the Mongols, their country, or language; Mongolian.

1763 SCRAFTON *Indostan* (1770) 18 The Tartars, or the Mungul Tartars..are commonly called Moguls. **1799** *Monthly Rev.* XXX. 489 The Nogais still bear..in their countenance the marks of their Mongul descent. **1845** *Encycl. Metrop.* XXV. 867/1 The Monghol and Manchu languages. **1857** DUFFERIN *Lett. High Lat.* (ed. 3) 254 Oblique Mongol eyes. **1883** *Encycl. Brit.* XVI. 741/2 An expedition into Syria, by which the country was made tributary to the Great Mongol Empire. **1883** *Ibid.* 749/2 The Mongol tongue is a member of the great stock which recent scholars designate as Finno-Tataric or Ural-Altaic.

2. (Also with lower-case initial.) Pertaining to or affected with mongolism; = MONGOLIAN *a.* and *sb.* A. 3.

1896 *Brit. Med. Jrnl.* 12 Sept. 617/1 There are at present in the Royal Albert Asylum 19 Mongol idiots in a population of 560. **1932** SHRUBSALL & WILLIAMS *Mental Deficiency Pract.* xiii. 206 In mongols, laxity of the joints is very characteristic, and mongol imbeciles tend in sitting naturally, to take up the crossed position of the Buddha in contemplation. **1965** [see DOWN'S SYNDROME]. **1970** PASSMORE & ROBSON *Compan. Med. Stud.* II. xxxi. 18/1 The greatly increased risk of having mongol offspring is the reason why every effort should be made to discover translocation carriers so that appropriate genetic advice may be given. **1974** G. F. NEWMAN *Price* ii. 68 He made contributions to the maintenance of his ex-wife and her mongol son.

Mongolfier, variant of MONTGOLFIER.

Mongolian (mɒŋ'gəʊlɪən), *a.* and *sb.* Also 8 **Mungalian,** 9 **Mongholian.** [f. MONGOL + -IAN.]

A. *adj.*

1. a. Pertaining to the Mongols, their country, language, etc.; = MONGOL *a.* Also ***Mongolian lamb.***

1738 tr. *Strahlenberg's Descr. Russ.*, etc. (title-p.), A Vocabulary of the Kalmuck-Mungalian Tongue. *Ibid.* 139 After the Tartars had totally defeated the Mungalian Army. **1836** H. MURRAY, etc. *Hist. & Descr. Acc. China* I. ii. 39 The opinion which assigns to the Chinese a Tartar, or rather Mongolian lineage. **1862** *Chamb. Encycl.* IV. 692/1 The Mongolian goat. **1878** *Encycl. Brit.* XVI. 750/1 The Mongolian characters..are written perpendicularly from above downward. **1893** LYDEKKER *Horns & Hoofs* 182 The tseain or Mongolian gazelle. **1963** *Sunday Express* 27 Jan. 9/5 A Mongolian lamb hat. **1970** *Vogue* Jan. 22/3 A helmet of white Mongolian lamb.

b. ***Mongolian hot-pot*** (see quot. 1971).

1967 E. HUNT *Danger Game* viii. 152 He ate oysters at Lo Fan Shan and Mongolian Hotpot. **1968** *Times* 6 Jan. 20/5 The New Hong Kong..are serving a speciality called 'bin lo'..a cross between Mongolian hotpot and Japanese *sukiyaki*. **1971** *Good Food Guide* 421 Mongolian hot-pot (a kind of Mandarin fondue bourguignonne, for which you do your own cooking at the table).

2. *Anthropology.* **a.** Belonging to the yellow-skinned straight-haired type of mankind (according to Blumenbach's classification). Cf. MONGOLOID.

1828 STARK *Elem. Nat. Hist.* I. 38 The Mongolian variety inhabits eastern Asia, Finland, and Lapland in Europe, and includes the Esquimaux of North America. **1834** *Penny Cycl.* II. 473/1 The white (or Caucasian), the yellow (or Mongolian), and the black (or Ethiopian). **1903** *Blackw. Mag.* Mar. 372 Their features are decidedly Mongolian.

b. ***Mongolian fold*** = EPICANTHUS; so ***Mongolian eye,*** one with an epicanthus.

1913 [see EPICANTHUS]. **1926** H. H. WILDER *Pedigree of Human Race* v. 298 It follows that it is not the Mongolian eye that is racial. **1927** PEAKE & FLEURE *Priests & Kings* xii. 192 The head is..relatively low and rounded with, in many individuals, flattened features and the additional or 'Mongolian' fold of the eyelid. **1935** HUXLEY & HADDON *We Europeans* iv. 117 A fold of skin, the 'epicanthic fold', covers the inner angle of the eye. This gives the effect known as the 'Mongolian eye'. **1964** *New Statesman* 10 Apr. 559/1 A quick and painless operation will..remove the young lady's Mongolian fold.

3. Applied to a person born with the condition known as MONGOLISM. Also with lower-case initial.

1866 J. L. H. DOWN in *Clin. Lect. & Rep.* (London Hospital) III. 260, I have for some time had my attention directed to the possibility of making a classification of the feeble-minded, by arranging them around various ethnic standards... The great Mongolian family has numerous representatives, and it is to this division, I wish..to call special attention. A very large number of congenital idiots are typical Mongols. *Ibid.* 261 The Mongolian type of idiocy occurs in more than ten per cent. of the cases which are presented to me. **1890** *Jrnl. Mental Sci.* XXXVI. 189 Mongolian imbeciles. **1892** J. L. DOWN in Tuke *Dict. Psychol. Med.* II. 644 Ten per cent. of all cases of idiocy arrange themselves around a highly characteristic type which the writer has proposed to call the Mongolian variety. **1904** *Brit. Med. Jrnl.* 17 Sept. 679 The histological examination of two brains of Mongolian idiots. **1965** [see DOWN'S SYNDROME].

4. ***Mongolian pheasant,*** a variety of pheasant, *Phasianus colchicus mongolicus*, native to southern Russia and Mongolia, introduced to other countries early in the twentieth century; also called the Kirghiz pheasant; also *ellipt.*; ***Mongolian spot,*** a bluish or brownish spot found, usu. singly, in the sacral region of nearly all new-born babies of Oriental races (and occas. in other races), and which usu. disappears in two or three years.

1903 W. ROTHSCHILD in *Field* 20 June 1033/3 The bird known in America as the Mongolian pheasant is not the *Phasianus mongolicus* of Brandt, but the *Phasianus colchicus*, *var. mongolicus* of Pallas, otherwise our common Chinese ring-necked pheasant (*Phasianus torquatus*) Linné. *Ibid.* 1033/6, I have had a number of the true Mongolian pheasant (*Phasianus mongolicus*) alive at Tring for two years. **1909** J. G. MILLAIS *Nat. Hist. Brit. Game Birds* 104 If the pure and cross-bred Mongolians have a fault it is a tendency to stray more than other pheasants. **1921** *Daily Colonist* (Victoria, B.C.) 23 Oct. 18/1 This boy [*sc.* an old cock pheasant] looked like a Mongolian, seemed too dark for an ordinary ringneck. **1963** D. A. BANNERMAN *Birds Brit. Isles* XII. 338 The Kirghiz pheasant *Phasianus mongolicus* Brandt. Commonly (but incorrectly) named the Mongolian pheasant, is distinguished by the broad white-ring around the neck interrupted in front, having the mantle, chest and breast bronzy orange-red... Introduced into England for Lord Rothschild in 1900. **1965** *Observer* (Colour Suppl.) 10 Oct. 33/2 There's a Mongolian there..a fine ring neck... That old bird he always roosts in that apple tree there. **1907** *Arch. Pediatrics* XXIV. 428 His findings led him..to a special study of the morphology of the 'Mongolian' spot. **1966** WRIGHT & SYMMERS *Systemic Path.* II. xxxix. 1507/1 The blue naevus..is analogous to the 'Mongolian spot', but may occur in any race and on any part of the body. **1969** *Beaver* Spring 49/1 A baby's pale Mongolian spots are patted lovingly.

B. *sb.* **a.** A native of Mongolia; a Mongol. **b.** One of the Mongolian race of mankind (see A. 2). **c.** The language of the Mongols.

1846 *J. Bell's Geog., Asiat. Russ.* iii. IV. 176 They speak a very rude dialect of Mongolian. **1854** R. G. LATHAM in *Orr's Circ. Sci., Org. Nat.* I. 316 The Mongolians are the most nomadic of populations. *Ibid.* 317 Zingis-Khan was a Mongolian and not a Turk. **1905** *Blackw. Mag.* Mar. 341/1 The white officers bade the chattering Mongolians cease their clavers.

Mongolianize (mɒŋ'gəʊlɪənaɪz), *v.* [f. MONGOLIAN *a.* + -IZE.] *trans.* To render Mongolian in character or quality.

1923 *Contemp. Rev.* Mar. 299 The Bolshevik, striving originally to make Russia Western, has succeeded merely in Mongolianising her.

Mongolic (mɒŋ'gɒlɪk), *a.* and *sb.* [f. MONGOL + -IC.] **a.** *adj.* Mongolian. **b.** *sb.* The Mongolian language.

1834 *Penny Cycl.* II. 473/2 The Bhots, or inhabitants of Bhotan and Tibet, are Mongolic. **1884** G. SMITH *Short Hist. Chr. Missions* xvii. (1904) 212 The Negritic or Black, the Mongolic or yellow, and the Caucasic or white. **1888** A. H. KEANE in *Encycl. Brit.* XXIV. 2/2 Many Turkic forms and words can be explained only by reference to Mongolic.

Mongoliform (mɒŋ'gəʊlɪfɔːm), *a.* [f. MONGOL + -(I)FORM.] Having the form characteristic of the Mongolians.

1849–52 *Todd's Cycl. Anat.* IV. 1355 The cranium is Mongoliform and brachycephalic.

Mon'golioid, *a.* and *sb.* *rare*$^{-0}$. = MONGOLOID.
1882 in OGILVIE. **1891** in *Syd. Soc. Lex.*

mongolism ('mɒŋgəlɪz(ə)m). *Med.* Also **Mongolism.** [f. MONGOL *sb.* and *a.* + -ISM. Cf. MONGOLIAN *a.* and *sb.* A. 3.] A relatively common congenital form of mental deficiency which is associated with a low expectation of life, is always accompanied by a chromosomal abnormality (usually trisomy for chromosome 21), and is marked by numerous signs, including short stature, short thick hands and feet, a large tongue, a flat face with features somewhat similar to those of Mongolians, and a friendly and cheerful disposition; Mongolian idiocy. Cf. DOWN'S SYNDROME.

1900 *Lancet* 6 Jan. 23/1 (*heading*) The differential diagnosis of Mongolism and cretinism in infancy. **1924** *Psyche* V. 1 It is..well known that a certain type of mental and physical backwardness has long been described, under the name of 'Mongolism'. **1960** *News Chron.* 1 July 5/4 From a medical dictionary he learned that mongolism was a type of congenital idiocy. **1961** R. D. BAKER *Essent. Path.* xxii. 615 Cases of..spina bifida and meningocele, mongolism, and cerebral palsy occur at the rate of 1 or 2 of each of these conditions per 1000 births. **1961** [see DOWN'S SYNDROME]. **1971** *Brit. Med. Bull.* XXVII. 47/1 The epidemicity of mongolism has also been studied.

Mongolize ('mɒŋgəlaɪz), *v.* [f. MONGOL + -IZE.] *trans.* To render (a people) Mongolian in character, customs, etc.; to introduce a large Mongolian element into. Hence **Mongoli'zation.**

1814 tr. *Klaproth's Trav.* 10 They perhaps belong to the most ancient branches of Mongolized Tartars. **1887** *Amer. Missionary* (N.Y.) Sept. 270 The Mongolization of America. **1906** *Daily News* 2 July 6/2 Australia was determined..not to Mongolise its dominions.

'Mongolo- ('mɒŋgələʊ), used as combining form of MONGOL or MONGOLIAN, to denote 'partly Mongolian and partly..'

1888 A. H. KEANE in *Encycl. Brit.* XXIV. 2/2 Mongolo-Turkic and Finno-Ugro-Samoyedo-Tungusic. **1903** *Contemp. Rev.* Aug. 190 The Mongolo-Manchurian question.

Mongoloid ('mɒŋgəlɔɪd), *a.* and *sb.* [f. MONGOL + -OID. Cf. F. *mongoloïde.*] **A.** *adj.*

1. a. Belonging to that one of the five principal races of mankind (according to Huxley's division), which prevails over the vast region lying east of a line drawn from Lapland to Thailand.

1868 HUXLEY in *Trans. Intern. Congr. Preh. Archæol.* (1869) 93 In the Mongoloid race the complexion ranges from brownish-yellow to olive. **1934** WEBSTER & WESTLEY *World Civilization* ii. 22 These three races are generally called Negroid, Mongoloid, and Caucasian. *Ibid.* 23 The Malays, Polynesians, and American Indians are included among Mongoloid peoples. **1939** C. S. COON *Races of Europe* i. 2 From a branch of this hyperborean group there evolved, in northern Asia, the ancestral strain of the entire specialized mongoloid family. **1967** E. A. HOEBEL in Rapport & Wright *Anthropol.* 70 The most outstanding Mongoloid physical trait is the slant eye, more elegantly known to anthropologists as the internal epicanthic fold.

b. ***Mongoloid eye, fold*** = *Mongolian eye, Mongolian fold.*

1931 E. A. HOOTON *Up from Ape* v. 420 The Mongoloid eye characteristically fills the orbit and protrudes slightly. *Ibid.* 421 A common modification..is the inner or internal epicanthic fold, often referred to as the 'Mongoloid fold'. **1960** J. COMAS *Man. Physical Anthropol.* v. 271 Generally, the eyelid opening is horizontal, but in many groups of Asia and America the so-called Mongoloid fold is found.

2. (Also with lower-case initial.) = MONGOLIAN *a.* 3; characteristic of or resembling a mongol or mongolism.

1899 *Allbutt's Syst. Med.* VIII. 236 Dr. A. E. Garrod mentions six cases of mongoloid idiots. **1949** S. S. SARASON *Psychol. Probl. Mental Deficiency* viii. 210 Ages of the mother and father at the birth of the Mongoloid child are relatively advanced. **1961** *Lancet* 13 May 1028/2 (*heading*) 21-Trisomy/normal mosaicism in an intelligent child with some mongoloid characters. **1962** [see B. 2 below]. **1965** ROSEN & GREGORY *Abnormal Psychol.* xxi. 462/1 She was mongoloid in appearance, good natured, cheerful and cooperative. **1973** *Times Lit. Suppl.* 19 Oct. 1269/5 The bereaved mother peopling her flat with 'friends' via spiritualist contact with a mongoloid daughter.

B. *sb.* **1.** One of the Mongoloid race.

1868 HUXLEY in *Trans. Intern. Congr. Preh. Archæol.* (1869) 95 The Xanthochroi inhabit a far smaller area of the earth's surface than the Mongoloids. **1964** R. T. ANDERSON in M. F. A. Montagu *Concept of Race* 62 The second [interpretation] holds that the Lapps represent a remnant of an ur-race that was the ancestor of both modern Mongoloids and modern Caucasoids. **1971** *National Geographic* Mar. 323/1 Like the majorities, they are virtually all Mongoloids, and often hard to tell apart.

2. (Also with lower-case initial.) = MONGOL *sb.* and *a.* A. 2.

1949 *Amer. Jrnl. Mental Deficiency* LIV. 204 (*heading*) Case report: reproduction in a mongoloid. **1962** *Amer. Jrnl. Human Genetics* XIV. 125 Trisomy of a short acrocentric chromosome in the human complement has come to be recognized as such a common etiologic factor in mongolism ..that the discovery of a forty-seven chromosome mongoloid is no longer worthy of note. Only a few cases have been described in which the mongoloid patient had forty-six chromosomes. **1974** E. TIDYMAN *Dummy* vi. 87 Its ..inmates..were mongoloids and schizoids, the emotionally disturbed and the mentally incompetent.

mongoose, mungoose ('mɒŋguːs, 'mʌŋguːs). Forms: 8 **mongoes, -goos, mungos,** 8–9 **mungoos, mongooz, -goz,** 9 **mongous, mungoose,** (*pl.* ?erron. **mungoes**), 7– **mongoose;** *β.* 8–9 **mangoust,** (**-oost**). [a. (?through Pg. *mangus*) Marathi *mangūs* (Telugu *mangīsi*, Konkani *mungasa*, Canarese *mungisi*). The *β*-forms are from F. *mangouste.*]

1. An ichneumon, *Herpestes griseus*, common in India, and well known for its ability to kill venomous snakes unharmed. Also applied to other ichneumons (subfamily *Herpestinæ*); in the form *Mungos* the word has been used in zoological Latin as the name of a genus (now *Crossarchus*) of this subfamily. The proper plural form is **mongooses**, but ***mongoose, mongeese,*** and other variants are occasionally used.

1698 FRYER *Acc. E. India & P.* 116 A Mongoose is a-kin to a Ferret. **1764** GRAINGER *Sugar Cane* II. 95 *note*, A species of East India animal, called a Mongoes, which bears a natural antipathy to rats. **1800** *Asiat. Ann. Reg., Misc. Tracts* 3/2 The *viverra ichneumon*, which, by the Europeans, is called mongoos. **1827** D. JOHNSON *Ind. Field Sports* 204 A cat withstood the poison better than any other animal, excepting the Mungoose (Ichneumon). **1859** BOWRING *Vis. Philippine Isl.* xvi. 274 Oxen, swine, buffaloes, deer, goats.. flying squirrels, dogs, rats, mungoes and other quadrupeds,

are found in various stages of domesiticity and wildness. **1881** *Encycl. Brit.* XII. 629/1 The Indian ichneumon or mungoos..is considerably smaller than the Egyptian form. **1893–4** *Roy. Nat. Hist.* I. 474 The thick-tailed mungoose (*Cynictis penicillata*)..inhabits the Cape Colony, and is of medium size. **1894** KIPLING *Jungle Bk.* 124 It is the hardest thing in the world to frighten a mongoose. **1896** R. LYDEKKER *Hand-bk. Carnivora* 244 (*heading*) The mungooses. Genus Herpestes. **1927** L. GASK *All about Animals* 158 Mongooses..are well known in Africa and in the warmer parts of Asia. **1927** G. JENNISON *Nat. Hist.: Animals* 82 Mongoose saved the West Indian sugar plantations from total destruction by rats. **1960** G. DURRELL *Zoo in my Luggage* 109 Young pigmy mongooses flatly refuse to feed from bottle or from fountain pen filler. **1971** F. COLLYMORE in J. Figueroa *Caribbean Voices* I. 81 The mongoose..is a troublesome sort of creature... For nobody seems to know with any degree of certainty which to choose of his plural forms—mongooses, mongeese, mongoose or mongooze.

β. **1774** GOLDSM. *Nat. Hist.* II. 304 The Weasil kind.. comprehends..the Ferrit, the Mangoust [etc.]. **1785** G. FORSTER tr. *Sparrman's Voy. Cape G.H.* (1786) II. 246 The *viverra ichneumon*, or the mangoust. **1840** tr. *Cuvier's Anim. Kingd.* 93 The *Urva* of Mr. Hodgson appears also to be a Mangouste, with incomplete orbits.

2. A species of lemur or maki, *Lemur mongoz*.

[Possibly a distinct word; but no source has been found for it in Malagasy or any other language of the Indian Ocean, and it may be a transferred use of the name of the ichneumon.]

1758 EDWARDS *Glean. Nat. Hist.* I. 12 The Mongooz. [The Fr. version, in parallel columns, has *Le Mongous.*] These animals are brought from Madagascar, and many of the smaller islands between that and the East Indies; they seem to be one remove from the direct Monkey. **1774** GOLDSM. *Nat. Hist.* IV. 240 A second of this kind [*sc.* the Maki], which is also a native of Madagascar, is the Mongooz. **1797** *Encycl. Brit.* (ed. 3) IX. 785/2 The mongooz, or woolly maucauco, inhabits Madagascar. **1828** STARK *Elem. Nat. Hist.* I. 60 *L. mongoz*... The Mongooz... The Mongous pass a considerable portion of the day in sleep. **1839** *Penny Cycl.* XV. 331/2 Mongoose, or Mongooz, one of the names of a species of Macauco, *Lemur Mongoz*, Linn. **1868** *Museum Nat. Hist.* I. 43 The Mongous (*Lemur Mongoz*).. is a little larger than the ring-tailed lemur.

mongorne, obs. form of MONG-CORN.

mongrel (ˈmʌŋgrəl), *sb.* and *a.* Forms: 5 **mengrell**, 6 **mon-**, **mungerell**, 6–7 **mangrel(l**, **·mo(u)ngrel**, **-ell**, 6–8 **mungrel**, **-il**, **mongrell**, **-il**, 7 **mungrill**, 7– **mongrel**. [app. f. root *meng-*, *mang-*, *mong-*, to mix (see MENG *v.*, MONG *sb.*¹ and *v.*²) + -REL.] **A.** *sb.*

1. The offspring of two different breeds of dog. Chiefly, and now only, a dog of no definable breed, resulting from various crossings.

1486 *Bk. St. Albans* f iij b, A Grehownd, a Bastard, a Mengrell, a Mastyfe. **1573** TUSSER *Husb.* (1878) 98 Of mastiues and mungrels. **1576** FLEMING tr. *Caius' Dogs* 43 Of mungrels or rascalls [L. *degeneres*] somwhat is to be spoken. And among these, yᵉ Wappe or Turnespet. **1607** TOPSELL *Four-f. Beasts* 154 Of the mixt kind of Dogs called in English Mangrels or Mongrels. Those we call Mangrels which though they be on both sides, propagated by Dogges, yet are they not of one kind. *a* **1613** OVERBURY *A Wife*, etc. (1638) 111 Like a true mongrell, he neither bites nor barks, but when your back is towards him. **1674** *Lond. Gaz.* No. 945/4 A great old Indian Spaniel, or Mongrel, as big as a Mastiff. **1697** DRYDEN *Virg. Past.* III. 25 His Mungril bark'd, I ran to his relief. **1704** *Lond. Gaz.* No. 4079/4 A..Greyhound,.. with..a brushy Stern like a Mongrel. **1766** GOLDSM. *Mad Dog* iv, Both mongrel, puppy, whelp, and hound, And curs of low degree. **1827** HOOD *Mids. Fairies* xx, A flock of panick'd sheep..Watching the warning mongrel here and there. **1862** CALVERLEY *Verses & Transl.* (ed. 2) 48 A long-backed fancy-mongrel. **1882** MISS BRADDON *Mt. Royal* III. vi. 106 'What kind of dogs did you see in your travels?'.. 'Two or three very fine breeds of mongrels'.

†**b.** Applied to persons as a term of contempt or abuse. (Cf. *cur.*) *Obs.*

a **1585** MONTGOMERIE *Flyting* 772 Gleyd gangrell, auld mangrell! to the hangrell, and sa pyne. **1601** B. JONSON *Poetaster* III. iv, You mungrels, you curres, you ban-dogs, wee are Captaine Tvcca, that talke to you. **1620** MIDDLETON *Chaste Maid* II. ii, How did the mongrels hear my wife lies in? **1647** WHARTON *Bellum Hybern.* Wks. (1683) 227 To the intent that this barking mungrel may not delude the ignorant with his pedling trash. **1764** FOOTE *Mayor of G.* I. Wks. 1799 I. 171 Is that your manners, you mongrel?

2. In wider use: An animal or plant resulting from the crossing of different breeds or kinds; restricted by some scientists to the result of the crossing of varieties (opp. to *hybrid*).

1677 CHARLETON *Exercit. de Differ. et Nom. Anim.* (ed. 2) 26 *Canis*..*Lyciscus*, a Mongrel, engendered of a Wolf and a Bitch. **1706** PHILLIPS (ed. Kersey), *Mongrel*, a Creature got by two kinds. **1796** MORSE *Amer. Geog.* I. 197 Mongrels, the offspring of the wolf and dog. **1828** WEBSTER, *Hybrid*, a mongrel or mule. **1859** DARWIN *Orig. Spec.* iv. 99 A large majority..of the seedlings thus raised will turn out mongrels. *Ibid.* viii. 273 The parents of mongrels are varieties, and mostly domestic varieties. **1879** tr. *De Quatrefages' Hum. Species* I. vii. 63 This crossing itself is differently named according to whether it takes place between different races or different species. In the first case it produces a mongrel, in the second a hybrid.

3. A person not of pure race; the offspring of parents of different nationalities, or †of high and low birth. Chiefly in disparaging use.

1542 UDALL *Erasm. Apoph.* 15 By the waie of reuilyng or despite, laiyng to the charge of the same Antisthenes that he was a moungreell, and had to his father a citezen of Athenes, but to his mother a woman of a barbarous or saluage countree. **1577** HANMER *Anc. Eccl. Hist.* (1619) 356 Selenas, ..a mungrell, by father a Gotth, by mother a Phrygian. **1600** HOLLAND *Livy* IV. ii. 140 Being a mungrell, as it were, the one halfe a Noble, the other a Commoner. **1622** FLETCHER *Sea Voy.* IV. ii, *Cla.* Of what sort are they? *Jul.* They say they are Gentlemen. But they shew Mungrels. **1708** WILSON, etc. tr. *Petronius Arbiter* 62 He's of a right Breed both by Father and Mother, no Mungril. **1870** EDGAR *Runnymede* xxii, Men..of every race, mongrels almost to a man. **1898** F. T. BULLEN *Cruise of Cachalot* 115 Neither do the Arab mongrels..bear any too good a reputation.

fig. **1632** LITHGOW *Trav.* I. 2, I being..borne to the Muses, as to the World, a mungrell to both.

4. In transferred applications, more or less contemptuous.

†**a.** A person of mixed or undefined opinions, or who leans to both sides (in religion or politics). Also (*rare*), a person of undefined official position.

1554 T. SAMPSON in Strype *Eccl. Mem.* (1721) III. App. xviii. 53 A weak brother seeth you, as mungrels mingling yourselves with the Papists in their idolatry. **1561** DAUS tr. *Bullinger on Apoc.* (1573) 58 It were better thou were a Sinner or an Heathen, than an hypocrite and a mongerell. **1632** LITHGOW *Trav.* VIII. 361 Our seuerall Ambassadours ..at Constantinople, who rather stay there as Mungrels than absolute Ambassadours. *a* **1638** MEDE *Wks.* IV. (1672) 819 You desired but to know what I thought of *Genuflexio versus Altare*, and I think I have told you; and you see hereby what a mungrel I am. **1645** *King's Cabinet Opened* 48 The King..despiseth you by the name of Mungrells, as not altogether firme enough to his owne designe. *a* **1677** BARROW *Serm.* (1686) III. 89 If thou wilt be brave, be brave indeed; singly and thoroughly; be not a double-hearted mongrel. **1713** ADDISON *Cato* III. vi, Mongrils in faction, poor faint-hearted traitors!

b. A 'cross' (*between*).

1613 PURCHAS *Pilgrimage* (1614) 586 Whose Religion was a mungrell of the Greekish, Egyptian, and their own. **1645** MILTON *Colast.* Wks. 1851 IV. 377 Though his two faculties of Serving-man and Solliciter, should compound into one mongrel. **1863** COWDEN CLARKE *Shaks. Char.* xvi. 411 In character he is a sort of mongrel between the thoroughbred jester-clown and the cur errand-boy. **1864** CARLYLE *Fredk. Gt.* XVII. v. (1872) VII. 56 Some cart, or dilapidated mongrel between cart and basket.

B. *adj.* (appositive and attributive uses of the sb.)

1. Of dogs: That is a mongrel or of mixed breed.

1576 FLEMING tr. *Caius' Dogs* 33 It remaineth that we deliuer vnto you the Dogges of a mungrell or currishe kind. **1679** BLOUNT *Anc. Tenures* 10 A Mungrel Hound, for the Chase of the wild Boar. **1688** J. CLAYTON in *Phil. Trans.* XVIII. 133 There followed them two or three Mungrel Curs. **1773–83** HOOLE *Orl. Fur.* XVII. 629 When th' exerting voice of village-swains A mungrel cur against the wolf constrains. **1890** C. L. MORGAN *Anim. Life & Intell.* (1891) 168 The bitch retains the influence of the mongrel puppies ..and therefore mongrelizes subsequent litters.

b. As an abusive epithet for a person.

1605 SHAKS. *Lear* II. ii. 24 A Knaue, a Rascall,..and the Sonne and Heire of a Mungrill Bitch. **1606** —— *Tr. & Cr.* V. iv. 14 That mungrill curre Aiax. **1720** J. HUGHES *Siege Damascus* V. ii. (1777) 63 Perfidious mungrel slave!

2. In wider use, of animals and plants. (Cf. A 2.)

1635 SWAN *Spec. M.* (1670) 355 The Tassel [or male] of the Saker is called a Hobbie, or Mongrel Hawk. *c* **1645** HOWELL *Lett.* III. 54 The Welsh nag..is right and of no mongrill race. **1768** BOSWELL *Corsica* i. (ed. 2) 40 Their sheep being of a mongrel race. **1770–4** A. HUNTER *Georg. Ess.* (1803) I. 489 Care should be taken that the cabbage tribe..should be cultivated at as great a distance from each other as possible, to prevent the ill consequences of a mongrel produce. **1871** DARWIN *Desc. Man* II. xv. 156 The result would..be the production..of a mongrel piebald lot [of pigeons].

3. Of persons: Of mixed race or nationality; having parents of different races. Chiefly in disparaging use.

1606 HOLLAND *Sueton.* 30 Diuers mungrell Gaules no better than halfe Barbarians. **1670** DRYDEN *Conq. Granada* I. i, Their Mungril Race is mix'd with Christian Breed. **1728** MORGAN *Algiers* I. i. 10 A mungrel breed of Tyrians and old Africans. **1805** SOUTHEY *Madoc in W.* xv, To learn that law from Norman or from Dane, Saxon, Jute, Angle, or whatever name Suit best your mongrel race! **1861** *Lond. Rev.* 16 Feb. 187 We Englishmen may be proud of the results to which a mongrel breed and a hybrid race have led us. **1871** DARWIN *Desc. Man* I. vii. 225 An immense mongrel population of Negroes and Portuguese. **1879** FARRAR *St. Paul* (1883) 354 Men..unsophisticated by the debilitating Hellenism of a mongrel population.

4. *transf.* Of persons, things, classes: Of mixed origin, nature, or character; not referable to any definite species or type; that is 'neither one thing nor the other'. Chiefly in contemptuous use.

1581 SIDNEY *Apol. Poetrie* (Arb.) 65 Neither the admiration and commiseration, nor the right sportfulnes, is by their mungrell Tragy-comedie obtained. **1600** SURFLET *Country Farm* VI. xxii. 792 Such wines are called mungrell or bastard wines, which (betwixt the sweete and astringent ones) haue neither manifest sweetenes, nor manifest astriction. **1632** *High Commission Cases* (Camden) 319 What is betweene Adam and Christ, halfe a new creature and halfe an ould, a mongrell Christian. **1645** *King's Cabinet Opened* 47 He [the king] calls those, who have deserted their trust in Parliament,..by the name of a base, mutinous, and mungrell Parliament. *a* **1661** FULLER *Worthies, Wilts* (1662) III. 158 These Mungrell Pamphlets (part true, part false) doe most mischief. **1663** BUTLER *Hud.* I. iii. 1225 This zealot Is of a mungrel, divers kind, Cleric before, and Lay behind. **1691** WOOD *Ath. Oxon.* I. 186 About that time King Hen. 8 [was] setting up a mongrel Religion in the Land. **1702** in Somers *Tracts* 4th Collect. (1751) III. 21 A Sort of mungril Church-goers, whose Conformity was not the Result of Principle, but of a luke-warm Compliance with the Humour of the Times. **1762–71** H. WALPOLE *Vertue's Anecd. Paint.* (1786) IV. 84 His imitators, without his taste, compounded a mungrel species, that had no boldness, no lightness, and no system. *a* **1764** LLOYD *Law Student* Poet. Wks. 1774 I. 24 That mungrel, half-form'd thing, a Temple-Beau? **1826** HOOD *Irish Schoolm.* viii, A mongrel tint, that is ne brown ne blue. **1833–5** J. H. NEWMAN *Hist. Sk.* (1876) III. I. iii. 51 [He] had been brought up..a mongrel sort of religionist, part Jew, part Pagan. **1884** W. ST. J. BRODRICK in *Fortn. Rev.* June 755 A subservient peerage, elastic principles, and a mongrel policy.

b. Applied to a word formed of elements from different languages, or to a dialect made up of different languages.

1610 HOLLAND *Camden's Brit.* I. 486 A mungrell name halfe Saxon and halfe Latin. **1652–62** HEYLIN *Cosmogr.* II. (1682) 180 A mungrel Language, composed of Italian, French, and some Spanish words. **1715** tr. *Pancirollus' Rerum Mem.* I. I. viii. 21 Aurichalcum..is a mungrel Word derived from both those languages [Greek and Latin]. **1867** DEUTSCH in *Q. Rev.* CXXIII. 450 The Aramaic..had become in the hands of the people a mongrel idiom. **1871** FARRAR *Witn. Hist.* iii. 93 If they spoke their own language, it betrayed them by its mongrel dialect.

Hence (*nonce-words*) **ˈmongreldom**, **monˈgrelity**, the condition of being a mongrel; **ˈmongrelish** *a.*, **ˈmongrelly** *a.*, resembling a mongrel.

18.. MOORE *On Hunt* in *Byron's Wks.* (1846) 526/1 They suffer small mongrelly curs in their kitchen. **1859** F. FRANCIS *Newton Dogvane* (1888) 40 A mongrelish-looking, coarse-sterned pointer. **1859** SALA *Gas-light & D.* xxi, A brown dog of an uncertain shade of mongrelity. **1884** BLACKMORE *Tommy Upm.* II. ii. 17 What marvel, that we have sold our birth-right to an acephalous mollusk, when the simple use of the tongue has passed into such headless mongreldom? **1889** *Pall Mall G.* 9 Jan. 2/1 [The dog] began to develop undoubted signs of mongreldom.

†**ˈmongrel**, *v. Obs. rare.* In 7 **moun-**, **mun-**. [f. prec.] *trans.* To make mongrel or hybrid.

1602 MARSTON *Ant. & Mel.* I. Induct., Millane being halfe Spanish, half high Dutch, and halfe Italians, the blood of the chifest houses is corrupt and mungrel'd. **1607** —— *What you Will* I. i, Shall our blood be moungreld with the corruption of a stragling French?

mongrelism (ˈmʌŋgrəlɪz(ə)m). [f. MONGREL *sb.* + -ISM.] The condition or quality of being mongrel or hybrid.

1598 FLORIO, *Bastardume*, bastardise, mungrelism. **1831** *Examiner* 274/2 [He] has passed from rank Toryism to the mongrelism of 'moderate reformer'. **1849** D. T. BROWNE *Amer. Poultry Yd.* (1855) 66 There is no breed of fowls more disfigured by mongrelism than this. **1871** GALTON in *Proc. Roy. Soc.* XIX. 396 The variations to which the breed is liable, and which might at first be thought due to mongrelism.

mongrelize (ˈmʌŋgrəlaɪz), *v.* [f. MONGREL *sb.* + -IZE.] *trans.* To make mongrel in race, composition, or character.

1629 MAXWELL tr. *Herodian* (1635) 256 It was not fit that either of their Races should be Mungreliz'd in that manner. **1859** DARWIN *Orig. Spec.* iv. 99 How..comes it that such a vast number of the seedlings are mongrelized? **1871** GALTON in *Proc. Roy. Soc.* XIX. 396 The breed of rabbits which I endeavoured to mongrelize was the 'Silver-Grey'. **1890** [see MONGREL *a.* 1].

Hence **mongreliˈzation**.

1889 H. CAMPBELL *Caus. Dis.* x. 76 Hybridization or mongrelization of disease.

ˈmongrelizing, *vbl. sb.* [-ING¹.] The action of the verb MONGRELIZE.

1922 *Edin. Rev.* July 36 Unchecked mongrelising destroys the symmetry of a national type.

ˈmongst (mʌŋst), *prep. poet.* Aphetic form of AMONGST.

c **1590** MARLOWE *Faustus* vii, Faustus is feasted mongst his noblemen. **1601** SHAKS. *Phœnix & Turtle* 20 Mongst our mourners shalt thou go. **1632** MILTON *L'Allegro* 4 'Mongst horrid shapes, and shreiks, and sights unholy. **1707** WATTS *Hymns & Spir. Songs* I. xxxix. (1751) 28 And 'mongst a thousand tender Thoughts [can] Her Suckling have no Room? **1871** PALGRAVE *Lyr. Poems* 38 'Mongst all perfections the most perfect wife.

†**ˈmongster.** *Obs.* [f. MONG-ER *sb.*¹: see -STER.] A female trader; only as the second element in comb., as ***flour-mongster***.

1281 in *Cal. Pat. Rolls Edw. I* 462 Agathe le Flurmongester.

monguba, variant of MUNGUBA.

Mongul, obs. form of MONGOL.

monhad, -heade, obs. ff. MANHOOD, -HEAD.

monhydride (mɒnˈhaɪdraɪd). *Chem.* [f. MON(O)- + HYDRIDE.] A compound of one atom of hydrogen with an element or radical.

1866 ODLING *Anim. Chem.* 1 Monhydrides, dihydrides, and trihydrides..and their derived chlorides.

moni, obs. form of MANY.

ˈmonial, *a.* and *sb.*¹ *Obs.* Also 4 **-yale**, 4–6 **-yal(l**, 6 **-iale**, **moiniall**. [a. OF. *monial*, *moinal* (*moniale* sb. fem.), f. F. *moine* MONK; or ad. med.L. *moniāl-is*.] **A.** *adj.* Monastic. *rare*⁻⁰.

1656 BLOUNT *Glossogr.*, *Monial* or *Monachal*.

B. *sb.* A nun.

1377 LANGL. *P. Pl.* B. x. 319 þere shal come a kyng and confesse ȝow religiouses,..And amende monyales monkes and chanouns. **1513** BRADSHAW *St. Werburge* II. 319 Virgin and moiniall of mycle excellence. *c***1550** BALE *K. Johan* (Camden) 18 Canons of S. Marke, Vestals and Monyals. **1587** FLEMING *Contn. Holinshed* III. 1027/1 The first was a house for women called moniales or nuns.

monial ('məʊnɪəl), *sb.*[2] *Arch.* Now *Antiq.* Forms: 4 **moniel, monyele, moyniele,** 4–6 **moynel(l,** 5 **munell,** 6 **monyelle, -al, mun(y)iall, moinel, mynell,** 9 **monial.** [a. OF. *moinel, moynel, monial* (also *meigneaul, mayneau, maineau,* mod.F. *meneau*), of unknown origin. Cf. MULLION, MUNNION.]

1. A mullion.

1330 in J. T. SMITH *Antiq. Westminster* (1807) 185 [For the purpose of strengthening and keeping in their places the] moynells [in the east gable]. **1379** *Mem. Ripon* (Surtees) III. 102 Et in j moniel lapid. figend. cum plumbo in prædictis aluris. *a***1440** *Sir Degrev.* 1459 Square wyndowus of glas, The rechest that ever was Tho moynelus was off bras. **1426–7** *Rec. St. Mary at Hill* 64 For iiij munell for wyndowes. *a***1548** HALL *Chron., Hen. VIII* 73 The postes or monyelles of euery wyndow was gylte. **1569** in *Pension Bk. Gray's Inn* (1901) 464 Munialls in the said windowes. **1846** *Ecclesiologist* V. 164 The west window of the north aisle, of three lights with simply intersecting monials. **1856** J. ALLEN *Liskeard* viii. 119 Three small square-headed lights..the openings separated by monials. **1878** MCVITTIE *Christ Church Cathedral* 28 *note*, In all these old walls were found ..annulated monials and cusped tracery.

†**2.** One of the plates of gold on the back of a bishop's or abbot's glove. *Obs.*

*c***1540** *Inv. Westm. Abbey* in *Trans. Lond. & Mdsx. Archæol. Soc.* IV. 317 The best payre of Pasturall Gloves, with parells of brodered work and small perells haveyng on them ij monyals of gold garnyshed with vj stones and xxiiij gret perles.

moniast, obs. Sc. superl. of MANY.

monic ('mɒnɪk), *a. Math.* [f. MON(O- + -IC.] Of a polynomial: having the coefficient of the term of highest degree equal to one.

1937 A. A. ALBERT *Mod. Higher Algebra* ii. 24 The coefficient a_n is called the leading coefficient of f and we shall call f a monic polynomial when $a_n = 1$. [*Note*] This notion occurs so frequently in algebra that the author believes it would be wise to adopt the above term. **1963** BEAUMONT & PIERCE *Algebraic Found. Math.* ix. 328 Thus, for any nonzero polynomial $g(x)$, there is a unique monic polynomial $f(x)$ which is a multiple of $g(x)$ by a nonzero element of F.

monica, monick(er, varr. MONIKER.

monide, obs. f. MONEYED.

monie, obs. f. MANY, MONEY.

monied, var. MONEYED.

moniefauld, moniel, obs. ff. MANIFOLD, MONIAL.

monier, var. MONEYER.

monies, irreg. pl. of MONEY *sb.*

monies cunnes, kinnes, kunnes: see MANYKIN.

moniest, obs. f. superl. of MANY.

monifald, -fold, obs. ff. MANIFOLD.

monifide: see MONEYFIED.

moniker ('mɒnɪkə(r)). *slang.* Also **monarch, monekeer, monica, monick(er, monniker,** etc. [Origin unknown.] A name, a nick-name. Also (*rare*) as *v. trans.*, to apply a name to (a person).

1851 MAYHEW *Lond. Labour* I. 218/2 'What is your "monekeer" (name)?'—Perhaps it turns out that one is 'White-headed Bob', and the other 'Plymouth Ned'. **1851** [see REAM *a.*]. **1879** *Macm. Mag.* Oct. 502/1 While at the station they asked me what my monarch (name) was. **1882** *Sydney Slang Dict.* 6/1 *Monniker*, a person's name (often assumed). *Ibid.* 10/1 The padding ken of Sally Hicks, who's got a new moniker, which is Lushing Loo. **1885** M. DAVITT *Prison Diary* I. xvi. 151 Many of them having a fresh 'monicker' (name) each conviction. **1895** *Times* 11 Nov. 3/4 The van is alright; I have had the 'monnick' (slang word for name) taken off it. **1903** 'J. FLYNT' *Rise Ruderick Clowd* i. 46 In the—Ward 'monakers', or nicknames, mean more than they do in uptown communities. **1907** J. LONDON *Road* (1914) 169 His 'monica' was Skysail Jack. **1926** J. BLACK *You can't Win* ix. 111 Whether it was his appearance or his careful manner of speech that got him his monoger, 'The Sanctimonious Kid', I never knew. **1936** J. CURTIS *Gilt Kid* v. 50 Eileen, or something, that was the sister's monick. **1936** M. FRANKLIN *All that Swagger* iii. 488 'I thought it was mimosa.' 'That's its trade moniker; it's home name is wattle.' **1938** *Amer. Speech* XIII. 195, I monikered him (gave him his moniker, or tramp name). **1944** *Sun* (Baltimore) 7 Aug. 2/7 He came by the name of Omar N. (the N being for Nelson) through his father's searching for a 'distinctive' moniker for his offspring. **1959** *Times Lit. Suppl.* 13 Feb. 84/1 Henry Handel Richardson herself..was able to hide behind the male signature on her books (her maiden name wedded to two favourite family monikers). **1960** *Melody Maker* 31 Dec. 6/3 Oliver Cool is the pseudonym of singer Larry Ellis, who found he won more success when he adopted the 'far-out' monniker. **1964** *Punch* 2 Dec. 826/1 Mildly bitter moniker given to Swiss-based moneymen. **1968** L. MORTON *Long Wake* i. 18 The documents came to Jack Roberts for my 'Monica'. **1972** *Village Voice* (N.Y.) 1 June 78/3 Slim and his brother helped bail the pilot out. The Airplane Kid moniker followed.

monilated ('mɒnɪleɪtɪd), *ppl. a. Anat.* [f. L. *monile* necklace + -ATE[2] + -ED[1].] Moniliform.

1877 HUXLEY *Anat. Inv. Anim.* vii. 416 An accessory gland composed of dichotomous monilated tubes. **1898** P. MANSON *Trop. Diseases* xxvi. 393 The individual hairs become white, or downy, or splintered or monillated [*sic*].

moniless(e, obs. forms of MONEYLESS.

monilia (mə'nɪlɪə). *Bot.* and *Med.* Also **Monilia.** Pl. **monilia, -iæ, -ias.** [mod.L., f. L. *monile*, necklace, in allusion to the chains of spores.] A fungus belonging to the genus *Monilia*, which now (properly) consists only of imperfect forms of *Sclerotinia* and *Neurospora*, several of which cause plant diseases, but formerly included some species (now assigned to *Candida*) which are important human pathogens. Also *attrib.*

1751 J. HILL *Gen. Nat. Hist.* II. 69 Monilia is a genus of Fungi, consisting of a pedicle supporting a number of naked seeds, arranged in series like the beads of a necklace. The Monilia all produce distinct male and female flowers... [Micheli] has..divided this genus into two, under the names of Botrytis and Aspergillus; but the differences, this division are founded upon, are rather specific than generical; we have therefore arranged them all together under one genus. **1916** *Jrnl. Trop. Med. & Hygiene* XIX. 89/1 White, creamy, roundish colonies, characteristic of a monilia, developed within twenty-four hours. **1920** *Lancet* 17 Apr. 851/2 The 20°C. incubator in which the collection of monilias was kept. **1932** *Jrnl. Infectious Dis.* L. 75 Various types of moniliae. **1950** *Jrnl. Amer. Med. Assoc.* 13 May 215/2 A pyoderma in which Monilia may be present merely as saprophytes. **1968** J. H. BURN *Lect. Notes Pharmacol.* (ed. 9) 112 In extreme cases there may be a fatal septicaemia due to monilia. **1975** C. A. THOROLD *Diseases of Cocoa* iii. 27 Monilia disease is confined to the north-west of South America and the adjacent part of Central America.

So **mo'nilial** *a.*, of, caused by, or pertaining to a monilia or moniliæ; **mo'nilioid** *a.*, resembling a fungus of this type.

1928 *Mycologia* XX. 127 (*title*) The monilioid species of *Sclerotinia*. **1947** *Jrnl. Amer. Med. Assoc.* 20 Sept. 192/2 (*heading*) Iodine treatment in monilial infections. **1951** *Ibid.* 27 Jan. 207/1 (*heading*) Monilial infections complicating the therapeutic use of antibiotics. *Ibid.* 208/1 A severe monilial esophagitis. **1973** *Nature* 28 Sept. 214/1 Specimens of clinically uninflamed gingiva were cultured with the addition of nystatin..to prevent monilial over-growth. **1974** PASSMORE & ROBSON *Compan. Med. Studies* III. xiii. 13/1 Trichomonal and monilial infections should be excluded by the examination of smears of vaginal exudate [in the treatment of vulvovaginitis].

moniliasis (mɒnɪ'laɪəsɪs). *Path.* Pl. **-ases.** [f. MONIL(IA + -IASIS.] Infection with or a disease caused by a fungus of the genus *Candida*.

1920 *Lancet* 24 Apr. 898/2 It is probable therefore that the so-called tea-taster's cough is a moniliasis. **1925** *Jrnl. Obstetr. & Gynæcol.* XXXII. 69 (*heading*) Vaginal monilias and vaginal moniliases. **1947** *Jrnl. Amer. Med. Assoc.* 27 Dec. 1186/2 The moniliases form a group of infections. **1958** *New Biol.* XXVII. 62 Moniliasis, which is a disease or complex of diseases with diverse manifestations caused by several yeast-like fungi of which *Candida albicans* is the most important, has a world-wide distribution... The most familiar aspect of moniliasis is thrush in infants. **1964** WINNER & HURLEY *Candida Albicans* p. v, We refer to these diseases as candidosis, this being the term, which..we have preferred to 'candidiasis', 'candidasis' and 'moniliasis'. 'Moniliasis' was the correct term when the causative organism was known as Monilia, but its continued use today leads to confusion. **1974** PASSMORE & ROBSON *Compan. Med. Studies* III. xix. 9/2 (*heading*) Candidiasis (thrush, moniliasis).

moniliform (mɒ'nɪlɪfɔːm), *a.* [a. F. *moniliforme*, or mod.L. *monīliformis*, f. *monīle* necklace: see -FORM.] Of the form of or resembling a necklace; necklace-shaped; having contractions at regular intervals; consisting of or characterized by a series of globular or oval protuberances suggesting a string of beads.

1802–3 tr. *Pallas' Trav.* (1812) II. 195 Moniliform iron-ore, and pudding-stone, are still more common in the schistous beds. **1819** SAMOUELLE *Entomol. Compend.* 260 Antennæ as long or shorter than the body, with moniliform joints. **1826** KIRBY & SP. *Entomol.* III. 146 *note*, That [*sc.* the horn on the tail] of *Sphinx Iatrophæ*..is moniliform. **1874** COOKE *Fungi* 38 The spores are..generated in a moniliform manner, and afterwards separating at the joints. **1899** *Allbutt's Syst. Med.* VI. 582 Portions of the veins on the back of the hand become quite moniliform, that is to say, there was an alternation of small dark swellings with narrow almost colourless intervals between them.

Hence **mo'niliformly** *adv.*, so as to resemble a necklace.

1848 E. FORBES *Naked-eyed Medusæ* 59 From the four bulbs spring as many pale yellow, moniliformly-granulated, slender, coiling tentacula. **1882** J. M. CROMBIE in *Encycl. Brit.* XIV. 553/2 In *Ephebacei* they [*sc.* the gonidial granules] are not moniliformly arranged.

moniment, obs. form of MONUMENT.

monimolimnion (,mɒnɪməʊ'lɪmnɪən). Pl. **-limnia.** [a. G. *monimolimnion* (I. Findenegg 1935, in *Internat. Rev. d. ges. Hydrobiol. u. Hydrographie* XXXII. 377), f. Gr. μόνιμο-ς stable + *-limnion*, after EPILIMNION, HYPOLIMNION.] The lower, denser, non-circulating layer of a meromictic lake. Cf. MIXOLIMNION.

1937 [see MIXOLIMNION]. **1957** G. E. HUTCHINSON *Treat. Limnol.* I. vii. 464 These lakes have never fully circulated in the ordinary way, since they developed large monimolimnia. **1968** [see MIXOLIMNION].

monimolite (mɒ'nɪməlaɪt). *Min.* [Named by L. J. Igelström, 1865 (*monimolit*), f. Gr. μόνιμο-ς stable, because it is decomposed with great difficulty: see -LITE.] Antimonate of lead and iron, found in yellowish or brownish crystals.

1868 DANA *Syst. Min.* (ed. 5) 546.

†**'monion.** *Mil. Obs.* Also 7 **mougnon,** 7–9 **mognion,** 8 **moignon.** [a. F. *moignon*, in 17th c. †*mougnon*, of obscure origin: cf. Sp. *muñon* muscle of the arm.] (See quots. 1658, 1706.)

1652 LOVEDAY tr. *Calprenède's Cassandra* I. 47 His sleeve which issuing forth of a Mougnon of gold, in the forme of a Lions Jawes, cover'd his Arme to the elbow, was of the same. **1658** PHILLIPS, *Mougnon*, (French) the brawny part of the arm, also the brassel, or that part of a Coat of Armour, that covereth the Arms. **1659** HOWELL *Lex., Partic. Vocab.* xliv, Monions for the shoulders, *gli spalacci, Les moignons, Espaldares.* **1706** PHILLIPS (ed. Kersey), *Moignon*, the Stump of a Leg or Arm that is cut off; also Armour for the Arms. **1802** JAMES *Milit. Dict., Mognions.*

monion, moniour, obs. ff. MUNNION, MONEYER.

moniplies, variant of MANYPLIES.

monipolical: see MONOPOLICAL.

monish ('mɒnɪʃ), *v.* Forms: α. 4–5 **monast, -yst, moonest,** 4–6 **monest(e;** β. 4 **mones, moneyche,** 5 **-ys(s)ch(e, -esche, -yche,** 5–6 **monysh(e, -ysshe,** 6 **monis(s)h(e,** *Sc.* **monis, -ys,** 6– **monish.** *Pa. t.* and *pa. pple.* in *-st*. 4–5 **monyst,** 4–6 **monest,** 6 **-ist.** [a. OF. *monester*:—popular L. *monestāre*, an unexplained derivative of *monēre* to advise, warn. For the change of termination in English, see ADMONISH.]

1. *trans.* To ADMONISH (a person), in various senses. (Also *absol.*) *arch.*

α. *a***1300** *Cursor M.* 27330 And for to monest [*Fairf.* monast] him ful gerne, if he can noght, for to lerne. *c***1380** WYCLIF *Sel. Wks.* III. 6 Here he monestiþ ech man to lyve wel. *c***1400** *Rom. Rose* 3579 For I you pray, and eek moneste, Nought to refusen our requeste. *c***1449** PECOCK *Repr.* IV. iv. 445 Poul bade him [*sc.* Titus]..forto correcte defautis as weel as forto moneste. **1494** FABYAN *Chron.* VI. cliii. 140 Monesting hym..that he shuld exchew and forbere suche doynge.

β. *a***1300** *Cursor M.* 26828 We moneyche [*Fairf.* monest] biscops preistes bath,..þat þai thol na sauls for to be lend vnto þe feinddes hand. **1375** BARBOUR *Bruce* XII. 383 Thai may weill monyss [*Camb. MS.* monast] as thai will. *c***1440** *Gesta Rom.* xlviii. 216 (Add. MS.), Whan Ioseph was monysshed and bidden by the aungell, that he shuld flee into Egipte. **1483** *Chron. Eng.* g vij, He monyschyd all cristen men that prestes shuld be worsshipped a bown all other men. **1513** DOUGLAS *Æneis* x. viii. 5 The haly nymphe..Hyr brother Turnus did monys and exhort To succur Lawsus. *a***1533** FRITH *Answ. More* (1829) 175 And so are we monished by Isaiah, in the 8th chapter, that we believe no such fantasies. *a***1568** ASCHAM *Scholem.* I. (Arb.) 31 Chide not hastelie:..but monish him gentelie. **1606** G. W[OODCOCKE] *Lives Emperors* in *Hist. Ivstine* Hh iij, Men say that his parents were monished in a dreame to cal him Theodosius. **16..** SWINBURNE *Spousals* (1686) 91 Yet is he rather to be monished than compelled to marry this Woman. **1839** BAILEY *Festus* iv. (1848) 31 Were thou and I To monish them. **1856** MISS WINKWORTH tr. *Tauler's Life & Serm.* xxi. (1857) 360 Each doing as he is inwardly monished by the Holy Ghost. **1866** T. N. HARPER *Peace thro. Truth* Ser. I. 15 The Apostle then, as Pacian monishes us, speaks of a visible unity.

¶ Pa. t. and pple. in *-st*.

*a***1300** *Cursor M.* 29292 He þat aght..fra hali kirk has laght, and he þar-for es monest thrise [etc.]. **1375** BARBOUR *Bruce* XII. 379 Tharfor thai monyst thame to be Of gret vorschip. *a***1400–50** *Alexander* 3127 (Ashm. MS.) Þus monest he þe messangers þaire maistir to say. *c***1450** *St. Cuthbert* (Surtees) 6400 Of þis wyse monest was he. **1513** DOUGLAS *Æneis* III. iii. 77 Lat ws obey Phebus..As we bene monest. **1536** BELLENDEN *Cron. Scot.* (1821) I. 231 Reule monist be this visioun, come with the said reliquies.

b. In ecclesiastical use. (Cf. MONITION 3 b.)

*c***1440** *Jacob's Well* 56 Alle þo þat..kepin or defendyn an opyn theef, after þe tyme þey be thryes monestyd of here ordinarye, in specyal or in general [etc.]. **1533** *Acc. Ld. High Treas. Scot.* VI. 152 To monis the priores..for nonpayment of thair taxt of the Beltane terme. **1607** in W. H. Hale *Prec. in Causes of Office* (1841) 10 He is now monished to appeare in the Consistorie the first court day of Easter next. **1633** *Acts Durham High Commission Crt.* 36 Hath heard the late Lord Bishopp Neile..monish and require Vaux to give over the profession of casting of figures. **1847** COOTE *Pract. Eccl. Courts* 257 [Form of Monition.] We do therefore hereby authorize..you..peremptorily to monish, or cause to be monished, the said Alexander McMath, that he shall [etc.]. **1872** O. SHIPLEY *Gloss. Eccl. Terms* s.v. *Monition*, an order monishing the party complained against to obey. **1885** *Law Times* LXXIX. 438/1 Whether the clergyman..had sufficiently monished him or any other erring parishioner.

†**2.** With thing as obj. (chiefly in translations): To exhort to; to give warning of; to call to mind.

1382 WYCLIF *Luke* iii. 18 He monestinge manye othere thingis [Vulg. *Multa quidem et alia exhortans*]. **1382** —— *John* iii. 10 If I shal come, I shal moneste [Vulg. *commonebo*] his werkes, whiche he doith. **1388** —— *Eccles.* vii. 3 The ende of alle men is monestid [Vulg. *finis cunctorum admonetur hominum*]. *a***1533** FRITH *Disput. Purgat.* Pref.

(1829) 83 Let them remember what Paul monisheth 1 Tim. 4. **1540** PALSGR. *Acolastus* D iij b, Surely he is a stoute and a hartye monysher, if he monysh any thynge well.

Hence **'monishing** *vbl. sb.* Also **'monisher**, one who admonishes.

1382 WYCLIF *Isa.* xxx. 21 Thin eres shuln heren the wrd bihinde the bac of the monestere. **1388** —— *Deut.* xxi. 20 He dispisith to here oure monestyngis. *c* **1440** *Gesta Rom.* II. xxix. 370 And the voice of monysshyng is this. **1483** *Cath. Angl.* 243/1 A Monyschere, *hortator, monitor.* **1513** DOUGLAS *Æneis* IV. viii. 115 Eik bygane the feirfull sawis seir Off the devynis, with terrible monysingis. **1540** Monysher [see MONISH *v.* 2]. *a* **1600** *Ballad* in T. James *Corrupt. Scripture* (1611) III. 44 In his monestings he forsaketh despisings. **1624** GEE *Hold fast* 33, I should seeme rather to be an accuser..then a monisher in..dutie to my Countrey.

monish ('mʌnɪʃ), *sb.* [See MONEY *sb.* 4 ¶.]

1846 *Swell's Night Guide* 125/2 *Monish, tip us the,* give me the money. **1848** *Sinks of London laid Open* 116/1 *Monish, tip us the,* give me the money.

'monishment. *arch.* Also 5 monestement. [f. MONISH *v.* + -MENT. In Caxton, a. OF. *monestement.*] Admonition, warning. Also, †a reminder.

1483 CAXTON *Gold. Leg.* 265/2 Gerard..refused alwey his monestementes and techynges. **1494** FABYAN *Chron.* VII. ccxliv. 286 Kynge John came not at ye day appoynted.. accordyng to ye monysshement to hym gyuen. **1563** FOXE *A. & M.* 853 b, Monkes, friers, and nonnes..forgat that their ceremonies wer monishmentes to put them in mynd of theyr profession. **1565** COOPER *Thesaurus, Commonitio*..a monishment: an aduertisement. **1896** SNOWDEN *Web of Weaver* xix. (1897) 212, I was fairly plagued with it till I had shaved my beard, to spite her monishments.

monism ('mɒnɪz(ə)m). [ad. mod.L. *monism-us*, f. Gr. μόνος single: see -ISM.]

1. *Philos.* A metaphysical system based on the assumption of a single ultimate principle or kind of being instead of two or more: opposed to DUALISM and PLURALISM in various applications.

a. The doctrine that only one being exists.

1862 F. HALL *Hindu Philos. Syst.* 160 To the Vedântins the establishment of monism, or non-duality, is most essential. They wish to make out the soul to be Brahma, and the world to be false; whence it would follow, that Brahma solely is true, and that nought but him exists.

b. A general name for those theories which deny the duality (i.e. the existence as two ultimate kinds of substance) of matter and mind.

Thus materialism and idealism or spiritualism are both species of monism; the name, however, is often applied specifically to a third variety, viz. the doctrine that physical and psychical phenomena are alike manifestations of a reality which cannot be identified with either matter or mind.

1876 tr. *Haeckel's Hist. Creat.* I. ii. 35 The Monism here maintained by us is often considered identical with Materialism. **1887** *Encycl. Brit.* XXII. 564/1 Until dualism had been thought out, as in the Peripatetic school, it was impossible that monism (or at any rate materialistic monism) should be definitely and consciously maintained. **1898** ILLINGWORTH *Div. Imman.* iii. 71 Monism..started from the physical side, from analysis of the cerebral conditions of thought.

c. The doctrine that there is only one Supreme Being, as opposed to the belief in a Good and an Evil Principle as co-ordinate powers.

1872 MORRIS tr. *Ueberweg's Hist. Philos.* I. 334 Against the dualism of the Manichæans..Augustine defends the monism of the good principle.

d. In various uses indicating a theory or doctrine of a single force, source, or system from which all particular instances devolve.

1890 W. JAMES *Princ. Psychol.* I. x. 366 The contrast between the Monism thus reached and our own psychological point of view can be exhibited schematically. **1903** B. RUSSELL *Princ. Math.* I. iv. 43 The subject is important, since the issues between monism and monadism, between idealism and empiricism..all depend, in whole or in part, upon the theory we adopt in regard to the present question. *Ibid.* 44 Numerical identity and diversity are the source of unity and plurality; and thus the admission of many terms destroys monism. **1949** P. A. SCHILPP *Albert Einstein* xxiii. 591 The question is still open whether it is possible thereby to arrive at a real monism; for the conversion of Joule into *mkg* does not prove that the two forms of energy are in essence the same. **1964** GOULD & KOLB *Dict. Soc. Sci.* 440/1 Monism is the notion..that in any society there must be one supreme power or authority and this must be lodged in the state. **1970** G. A. & A. G. THEODORSON *Mod. Dict. Sociol.* 93 *Cultural monism*, a doctrine that advocates the assimilation of ethnic minorities into the dominant culture of a society to attain cultural uniformity. **1971** R. F. C. HULL tr. *Jung's Psychol. Types* in *Coll. Wks.* VI. viii. 318 The idea-oriented attitude must tend towards monism.

2. (See quot.: perh. a misapprehension.)

1880 PASCOE *Zool. Classif.* (ed. 2) 283 *Monism*, the descent of all organic beings from one primitive stock.

monist ('mɒnɪst). [f. Gr. μόνος single + -IST.] One who holds a doctrine of monism (in any sense).

1836-7 SIR W. HAMILTON *Metaph.* xvi. (1859) I. 295 The Realists or Substantialists are again divided into Dualists, and into Unitarians or Monists, according as they [etc.]. **1862** F. HALL *Hindu Philos. Syst.* 267 Can monism be established by simply showing, that two things are different in kind? If so, the Naiyâyikas, no less than you, are monists. **1934** F. W. COKER *Recent Political Thought* xviii. 504 The pluralist charges the monists with the error of regarding all non-political associations created by the state as dependent for their continued existence upon the will of the State. **1960** L. LIPSON *Great Issues of Politics* (ed. 2) vi. 153 The monist, too, has his problems. Desiring to provide society with an integrating focus, he must designate what this should be. **1964** GOULD & KOLB *Dict. Soc. Sci.* 439/2 In international law the monists are those who believe that international and municipal law are both parts of a single system of law. *Ibid.* 563/2 Politically, public opinion is regarded by the monists as simply the manifested general will.

Also *attrib.* or as *adj.*, of or pertaining to the doctrine of monism.

1931 *Times Lit. Suppl.* 5 Mar. 164/2 Ramanuja fought against the monist view with as intense spiritual passion as any Christian critic could have shown. **1960** L. LIPSON *Great Issues of Politics* (ed. 2) vi. 152 Both philosophies stand unequivocally against something: the pluralist, against organized unity; the monist, against anarchic diversity.

monist: see MONISH *v.*

monistic (mə'nɪstɪk), *a.* [f. MONIST + -IC.] Pertaining to, involving, or holding monism.

1862 F. HALL *Hindu Philos. Syst.* 251 The belief, that the internal organ, &c., the whole world, are false, is the very life of the monistic doctrine. **1866** J. MARTINEAU *Ess.* I. 158 Mind, to think out its problems..cannot be monistic. **1872** *Contemp. Rev.* XX. 393 Eleaticism was monistic, did not intend to recognise any distinction between matter and spirit. **1880** PASCOE *Zool. Classif.* (ed. 2) 283 *Monistic* theory holds that creation was the product of natural forces. **1886** MYERS in Gurney, etc. *Phantasms of Living* I. Introd. 50 A monistic scheme of the universe. **1890** W. JAMES *Princ. Psychol.* I. x. 367 For *us* it is an unpardonable logical sin,.. to change the terms without warning... For monistic idealism, this is the very enfranchisement of philosophy. **1903** B. RUSSELL *Princ. Math.* IV. xxvi. 221 The monistic view..regards the relation as a property of the whole composed of *a* and *b*, and as thus equivalent to a proposition which we may denote by (*at*)r. **1926** J. C. SMUTS *Holism & Evolution* v. 108 The fundamental concept of Holism will bring us nearer to that unitary or monistic conception of the universe which is the immanent ideal of all scientific and philosophic explanation. **1957** S. AUROBINDO in Radhakrishnan & Moore *Sourcebk. in Indian Philos.* xvi. 586 In the monistic view the individual soul is one with the Supreme. **1960** L. LIPSON *Great Issues of Politics* (ed. 2) xiv. 417 There are classic instances of a monistic state combined with a controllable government. *Ibid.*, A monistic state like Britain, therefore, has its powers both centralized and integrated. **1964** GOULD & KOLB *Dict. Soc. Sci.* 563/2 The divisions..can be roughly classified as being between advocates of a monistic, organic view and holders of a pluralistic, numerical theory of public opinion. **1971** J. Z. YOUNG *Introd. Study Man* x. 124 Others [committed by] their addiction to a monistic science, try to find a system that avoids the separation of mind and matter. **1971** R. F. C. HULL tr. *Jung's Psychol. Types* in *Coll. Wks.* VI. viii. 301 Intellectualism is always monistic.

So **mo'nistical** *a.* (*Cent. Dict.* 1890); hence **mo'nistically** *adv.*, from a monistic point of view.

1880 *Athenæum* 25 Dec. 851/3 [Bahnsen's] philosophy.. defines the 'Ding an sich' of Schopenhauer, the Will, pluralistically, and not, as Hartmann does, monistically.

†'monit. *Obs.* [ad. L. *monit-us.*] A reminder.

1692 THORESBY *Diary* (ed. Hunter) I. 227 Lord, sanctify all monits of mortality!

monition (mə'nɪʃən), *sb.* [a. OF. *monition* (from 13th c.), or ad. L. *monitiōn-em*, n. of action f. *monit-*, *monēre* to admonish.]

1. †**a.** Instruction, direction (*obs.*). **b.** Warning; admonitory counsel. Also in particularized sense, an admonition, a warning.

c **1375** *Sc. Leg. Saints* iii. (*Andreas*) 655 Andro mad þame monicione, þat þai suld nocht his passione let. *Ibid.* vi. (*Thomas*) 49 þe kinge..gerte mak gret monicione, þat, al þat euire vare in þe tovne Suld..cume to þat feste. **1421-2** HOCCLEVE *Dialog* 234 To do this labour..at the excitynge and monicion of a devout man. **1471** CAXTON *Recuyell* (Sommer) II. 527 But neuer for..the monyssions ne warnynges of cassandra the kyng wold not change his purpoos. **1494** FABYAN *Chron.* II. xlvii. 32 The kynge disdeynynge this demeanure of Andragius, after dyuers monycions to hym gyuen, gatheryd his knyghtes & made warre vpon Andragius. **1516** *Joseph Arim.* 34 By monycion of the Archaungell gabryell they made a Churche..of our Lady. **1529** MORE *Dyaloge* III. Wks. 245/2 With a good monicion & fatherly counsell to vse it reuerently. **1552** *Bk. Com. Prayer, Coll. 1st Sund. Lent*, O Lord..geue us grace to use such abstinence, that..we may euer obey thy godly monicions. **1636** JACKSON *Creed* VIII. xii. §4 That peremptory monition to his Apostles. 'Pray that yee enter not into temptation'. **1682** SIR T. BROWNE *Chr. Mor.* II. §11 The capital sufferings of others are rather our monitions than acquitments. **1692** R. L'ESTRANGE *Fables* ccxx. 193 Deaf..to the Councels and Monitions of the very Spirit of Reason it self. **1713** SWIFT *On Himself* Wks. 1755 IV. I. 11 Sage monitions from his friends His talents to employ for nobler ends. **1843** CARLYLE *Past & Pr.* III. xiii, To them the voice of Prophecy, of heavenly monition, is quite ended. **1879** GREEN *Read. Eng. Hist.* xxiii. 117 Turning the deafest of all deaf ears to the monitions which he received to stay.

2. A warning or intimation of the presence or imminence of something (now only, of some impending danger).

1398 TREVISA *Barth. De P.R.* XVI. xlviii. (1495) 569 Blacke gete gyuyth monycyon of them that haue fendys wythin theym. **1432-50** tr. *Higden* (Rolls) II. 229 In that he ȝafe not to hym a monicion þer of. **1694** W. HOLDER *On Time* vi. 72 We have no visible Monition of the Returns of any other Periods, such as we have of the Day, by Successive Light and Darkness. **1839** *Penny Cycl.* XV. 332/1 These Monitory Lizards..obtained credit for this monition solely from the accident of their haunts. **1906** *Daily News* 10 Apr. 6 The first monitions of the impending catastrophe occurred in 63 A.D., when..Campania was shaken by an earthquake.

3. An official or legal intimation or notice, esp. one calling on a person to do something specified.

c **1460** *Oseney Reg.* 92 After thre monicions or warnynges (by þ^e^ vicare of Cudelynton or his stedys beryng to þem to be paide) [etc.]. **1467** in *Eng. Gilds* (1870) 406 That they appere in the yeld halle..vpon monicion to them yeven by eny seriaunt, vppon the peyn of xij d. **1492** *Bury Wills* (Camden) 78 That than the seyd aldyrman..shall after resonable warnyng and ther monycion avoyde hym. **1512** *Act 4 Hen. VIII*, c. 4 *Preamble*, Of the which outlaries..the partie defendaunt..had never knowlege ne monycion. **1540-1** ELYOT *Image Gov.* (1549) 142 Onely hearyng that he was chosen Pretor, before that he had monicion thereof, he fled. **1615** *Act 12 Jas. I*, c. 8 in Bolton *Stat. Irel.* (1621) 434 That every person should have lawfull knowledge and monition of such actions as hereafter bee to be..sued against him. **1863** JOWETT in *Life & Lett.* (1897) I. x. 311, I hear that this monition is to be issued at the V.-C. Court next week.

b. A formal notice from a bishop or an ecclesiastical court admonishing the person complained of to refrain from a specified offence.

1509 BARCLAY *Shyp of Folys* (1570) 236 To thy monition my Bishop I assent. **1610** BP. CARLETON *Jurisd.* 275 That all Translations of Prelates, all depriuations, reuocations, monitions, Ecclesiasticall censures..shall be voide, vaine, and of none effect. **1696** PHILLIPS (ed. 5), *Monition*,..a warning given by Ecclesiastical Authority to a Clerk to reform his Manners, upon Intimation of his Scandalous Life. **1725** tr. *Dupin's Eccl. Hist. 17th C.* I. III. i. 77 What Monitions soever, Excommunications or Interdicts he [the Pope] may make. **1827** HALLAM *Const. Hist.* I. ii. 77 *note*, A severe monition from Archbishop Morton to the abbot of St. Alban's, imputing all kinds of scandalous vices to him and his monks. **1847** COOTE *Pract. Eccl. Courts* 255 [Form of] Monition to Refrain. **1906** [see MONITION *v.*].

c. In those courts which use the civil law process (as the court of admiralty), a process in the nature of a summons. (Bouvier *Law Dict.* 1856.)

1840 HAGGARD *Cases Admiralty* III. 300 The Court.. further decreed a monition against Matthew Russell. **1854** *Act 17 & 18 Vict.* c. 78 §13 It shall be competent to him to proceed by way of Monition, citing the Owner or Owners of such Ship [etc.]..to appear and defend the Suit.

mo'nition, *v. Eccl. Law.* [f. prec. sb.] *trans.* To warn by a monition.

1883 *Q. Rev.* CLVI. 530 The offending clergymen had been solemnly monitioned. **1906** SIR L. DIBDIN in *Guardian* 28 Feb. 347/2, I suspend Mr. F. from office and benefice for two years. I monition him not to offend again... Disobedience to the monition which I have decreed..can be ..dealt with by the infliction of an even severer sentence.

monition, obs. form of MUNITION.

†mo'nitioner. *Obs.* [f. MONITION *v.* + -ER^1^.] One who or that which gives admonition or warning.

1556 OLDE *Antichrist* 199 b, As many as considre not so faithfull a monicionar. **1597** J. KING *On Jonas* (1618) 595 Wretched is the man, whom the Lord correcteth not; whose first messenger and monitioner is the first borne of death.

†'monitive, *a.* and *sb. Obs. rare.* [f. L. *monit-*, ppl. stem of *monē-re* to admonish + -IVE.]

a. *adj.* Warning, admonitory. **b.** *sb.* A warning or reminder.

a **1638** MEDE *Wks.* (1672) 326 Ignatius..urges the Vnity of the Altar for a monitive to the Congregation to agree together in one. *a* **1677** BARROW *Serm.* Wks. 1716 II. 140 Considering the usefulness of them..as they are exemplary and monitive.

monitor ('mɒnɪtə(r)), *sb.* Also 7-8 -our. [a. L. *monitor*, agent-n. f. *monēre* to advise, warn, admonish: see -OR.]

1. a. One who admonishes or gives advice or warning to another as to his conduct. Now somewhat *arch.* †Also (*rare*), one who advises another to do some particular action, an instigator.

1596 BACON *Max. & Use Com. Law* I. xvi. (1636) 61 When a man is author and monitor to another to commit an unlawfull act. **1616** —— *Adv. Villiers* in *Cabala* (1663) 42 In this [*sc.* religion] you need not be a Monitor to the King; the chiefest of his imperiall titles, is, to be The Defender of the Faith. **1630** BRATHWAIT *Eng. Gentlem.* (1641) 116 Though reason like a discreet Monitor advise them to Moderate their passions. **1630** BP. HALL *Occas. Medit.* xc. (1633) 229 O God, thou art still equally mercifull... Let the sound of thy faithfull monitors smite my eares. **1692** DRYDEN *Cleomenes* I. i, *Panth.* You promis'd Patience, Sir. *Cleom.* Thou art a Scurvy Monitor, I am Patient. **1751** JOHNSON *Rambler* No. 155 ⁋5 The officious monitor is persecuted with hatred.. because he assumes that superiority which we are not willing to grant him. **1771** BURKE *Corr.* (1844) I. 278 Strict and faithful monitors, that keep watch on every action of my life. **1830** CUNNINGHAM *Brit. Paint.* II. 231 'George', said his monitor, 'you must have reasons for keeping such company.' **1855** THACKERAY *Newcomes* II. i. 7 'You boast of its being over. You see it is not over', says Clive's monitor and companion.

b. *transf.* of things more or less personified. (Often of conscience.)

1651 JER. TAYLOR *Serm. Gold. Grove, Summer* xiii. 162 A final judgement is no good monitor to him, to whom it is a severe executioner. **1759** STERNE *Tr. Shandy* II. xvii, Conscience, this once able monitor,—placed on high as a judge within us. **1824** HOGG *Conf. Sinner* 1 Of the matter furnished by the latter of these powerful monitors [*sc.* history and tradition], I have no reason to complain.

2. A senior pupil in a school, or (formerly in England and still in America) a student in a college, who has special duties assigned to him, esp. that of keeping order, and who may occasionally (as in some elementary schools) act as a teacher to a junior class.

1546 in Peacock *Stat. Cambr.* (1841) 123 Let them [*sc.* the deans] appoint six monitors, two for public worship and four for speaking Latin [i.e. to enforce the speaking of Latin]. **1607** *Stat.* in *Hist. Wakefield Gram. Sch.* (1892) 65 Theire severall absences, negligencies and misbehaviours.. given up by the monitours in their bille. **1612** Brinsley *Lud. Lit.* 295 The Monitours of that weeke. *a* **1656** Bp. Hall *Rem. Wks.* (1660) 248 Even the most carelesse boyes will be affraid to offend in the face of the monitor. **1764** *Mem. G. Psalmanazar* 75 This mark of distinction [*sc.* a large riband] did moreover entitle me to be head monitor and marshal of that whole school. **1841** Elphinstone *Hist. Ind.* I. 353 They are taught, with the aid of monitors, in the manner introduced from Madras into England. **1848** *Stat. & Laws Harvard* (1854) 11 Monitors are appointed, and their duties and compensation fixed, by the Faculty. **1875** A. R. Hope *My Schoolboy Fr.* 76 We looked to see that none of the monitors were in sight. **1882** *New Educ. Code* (ed. J. Russell) 23 Temporary monitors employed in place of the teachers causing the vacancies are recognised as part of the school staff.

3. a. Something that reminds or gives warning.

1655 Fuller *Ch. Hist.* v. i. §32 That picture was placed there by the Cardinals own appointment, to be to him a monitour of humility. **1675** Traherne *Chr. Ethics* 202 All our enjoyments.. are daily monitors of mercy to us, because they are purchased by the blood of Christ. **169.** Locke *Educ.* §107 The Pains that come from the Necessities of Nature, are Monitors to us to beware of greater Mischiefs, which they are the Fore-runners of. **1760** Gray *Corr. w. Nicholls* (1843) 205, I sympathise with your gout: it would be strange if I did not, with so many internal monitors as I carry about me, that hourly bid me expect it myself this autumn. **1791** W. Bartram *Carolina* 100 At the reanimating appearance of the rising sun, nature again revives; and I obey the chearful summons of the gentle monitors of the meads and groves. **1840** Bp. Jolly *Observ. Sunday Serv.* 219 Such emblematical rites.. cleared of superstition, are useful helps and monitors to our weak minds.

b. One who is appointed to listen to and report on radio broadcasts, esp. from a foreign country.

1939 *Times* 2 Nov. 5/3 The material, after it is taken down and translated by the monitors, is summarized by an editorial staff. **1945** *Times* 26 May 2/4 In another room monitors were listening to Morse signals. **1974** *Daily Tel.* 16 July 1/2 Radio monitors heard what purported to be a 20-second reading by the Archbishop.

c. *Broadcasting.* A device for indicating or ascertaining the technical quality of a transmission without disturbing the transmission itself; esp. (also ***monitor screen, tube***) a television screen for displaying the picture from a particular camera or that being transmitted. Freq. *attrib.*

1931 A. Nadell *Projecting Sound Pictures* ii. 36 The projectionist has only to listen to the sound in his monitor and adjust the guides until the disturbance disappears. **1934** *Proc. IRE* XXII. 450 The monitors are designed for continuous operation, giving a continuous indication of the radio transmitter's frequency, and enabling the radio station operator to tell at a glance whether the transmitter is within the assigned limits. **1944** R. E. Lee *Television* 155 The video engineer clamps down one of the 'pots' on his control panel, draining the light from the monitor screen. **1958** M. Dickens *Man Overboard* x. 155 He caught sight of himself on the small monitor screen at one side of the cameras. *Ibid.* 160, I saw myself on the monitor. **1959** *Listener* 13 Aug. 238/1 In their monitors the searchers could see the boxes televised by the camera 200 feet down beneath the surface of the lake. **1961** G. Millerson *Technique Telev. Production* i. 16 Above each camera's control unit is a monitor-tube on which its picture is displayed. **1961** K. R. Sturley *Sound & Television Broadcasting* v. 338 Equipment known as a 'transmitter executive monitor' may be installed at a station to keep a watch on distortion due to overload and noise such as hum. **1969** *Times* 22 July (Moon Suppl.) p. i/1 There's a great deal of contrast in it and currently it's upside down on our monitor but we can make out a fair amount of detail. **1971** H. E. Ennes *Television Broadcasting* i. 32 On the monitor panel are located adjustments for the kinescope focus and brightness.., oscilloscope (waveform monitor) focus and brightness, and a switch to accommodate monitoring either the line waveform.. or the field waveform.. on the oscilloscope tube.

d. Any instrument or device for monitoring some process or quantity; *spec.* one for detecting or measuring radioactivity.

1948 *Nucl. Sci. Abstr.* I. 282 The different types of radiation distribution.. and detecting devices, such as air monitors.. are briefly explained. **1958** O. R. Frisch *Nucl. Handbk.* ii. 9 A special monitor.. has been designed for the use of persons leaving a laboratory; this counts α- or β-activity on both sides of the two hands. **1961** *Rev. Sci. Instruments* XXXII. 1098 (*heading*) Transmission current monitor for high energy electron beams. **1962** *IRE Trans. Audio* X. 132/1 The audio-radar monitor recorder is designed to continuously monitor and record 16 audio channels and one radar display on a single reel of magnetic tape. **1966** P. J. O'Higgins *Basic Instrumentation* x. 289 A monitor is an instrument that is used to measure continuously or at intervals a quantity or condition that must be kept within a prescribed limit. An example is the oil gauge in an automobile. **1973** *Biomed. Engin.* VIII. 255/3 There are situations in which a portable monitor can with advantage be replaced by a permanently-installed instrument which performs a 'watch-dog' function and gives warning if the radiation level rises above a pre-set value (or alternatively warns if any radiation is present at times when none should exist). **1973** *Daily Tel.* 10 Aug. 3 (Advt.), A foetal heart monitor.. enables medical staff to tune in to the heart-beat of an unborn baby. **1974** *Rev. Sci. Instruments* XLV. viii. p. xi (Advt.), Continuous liquid helium level monitor.

†**4.** = back-board 4. *Obs.*

1784 Cowper *Task* ii. 585 A Monitor is wood—plank shaven thin. We wear it at our backs. **1828** *Lights & Shades* I. 315 In one corner of the room may be seen Miss Jenny choaking in a monitor. **1831** Britton *Irishmen & Irishwom.* (ed. 3) 67 Every real young lady she averred ought to wear monitors and steel collars.

5. A large lizard of the family Varanidæ, found in Africa, Asia, and Australia; so called from being supposed to give warning of the vicinity of crocodiles.

1826 Prichard *Research. Phys. Hist. Man* (ed. 2) I. 73 Africa possesses the Monitors. **1832** Lyell *Princ. Geol.* II. 103 The monitor of New Holland is specifically distinct from the Indian species; these latter again from the African. **1884** *American* VIII. 218 Large monitors and many smaller lizards abound. **1900** *Westm. Gaz.* 19 Apr. 1/3 Among the latest arrivals at the Zoo is a Bengal monitor. **1958** [see agamid]. **1965** R. McKie *Company of Animals* i. 3 Not twenty paces away was a six-foot Malayan lizard, a monitor, grey against the shingle.

6. a. An ironclad having a very low free-board and one or more revolving turrets containing great guns, built on the model of the vessel invented by Captain Ericsson (see quot. 1862).

1862 Ericsson *Let.* 20 Jan. in Church *Life* (1890) I. 255 The iron-clad intruder will thus prove a severe monitor to those leaders [*sc.* of the Southern Rebellion]... On these and many similar grounds I propose to name the new battery Monitor. **1864** *Ibid.* II. 49 The ability of a dozen monitors to take Charleston. **1862** [see ironclad *sb.*]. **1887** *Westm. Rev.* June 368 It is stated that the United States possesses fourteen monitors twenty years old, and five in process of construction.

attrib. **1864** H. Draper in *Q. Jrnl. Sci.* I. 520 When a person enters a Monitor turret, he cannot fail to feel a sensation of absolute protection, surrounded as he is on all sides by 11 inches of iron.

b. An ironclad railway truck carrying a big gun.

1885 W. W. Burns in *Century Mag.* July 460 General Lee's famous railroad monitor was approaching.

7. *U.S.* (In full ***monitor roof*** or ***top***.) A raised part of a roof (e.g. in a railway-carriage or omnibus), with openings for light and ventilation. Hence ***monitor-car***.

1871 Snow *Pathfinder* 2 'The roofs [of certain railway passenger cars] are of the monitor pattern', meaning slightly elevated along the centre, to make the car airy. **1875** Knight *Dict. Mech.*, *Monitor-car.*

8. A jointed nozzle used in hydraulic mining, which may be turned in any direction.

1881 Raymond *Mining Gloss.* **1883** *Century Mag.* Jan. 324 Pipes from fifteen to thirty inches in diameter.. may be seen winding through a hydraulic mine. These pipes terminate in monitors, each discharging a gleaming shaft of water so powerful as to toss about rocks, tons in weight. **1891** *Engineer* LXXII. 217 The monitor.. has a ball joint that permits it to be slung in any direction. **1898** [see hydraulic *a.* 1].

9. *attrib.* (see also 3 c), as ***monitor man, room, speaker***; **monitor lizard** = sense 5.

1869 P. Gillmore tr. *Figuier's Reptiles & Birds* (1870) 13 In the Crocodiles and *Monitor Lizards.. a mutilated part is not renewed. **1908** E. J. Banfield *Confessions of Beachcomber* i. iii. 99 There is.. no iguana (rather, monitor lizard), though a fair variety of other reptiles. **1947** I. L. Idriess *Isles of Despair* xiv. 92 The great carved head of Kodal the crocodile, of Karum the monitor lizard. **1966** D. Forbes *Heart of Malaya* viii. 93 The only creature we saw was a six-foot long monitor lizard slithering across the road. **1929** *Photoplay* (Chicago) Apr. 31/2 **Monitor man*, the person who operates the volume control on talking picture production, modulating sounds as they come through the microphone so as to get a more even and natural tone. **1931** *Star* 8 May 12/1 The '*monitor room' where the sound experts listen to the conversation was moved 50 feet away. **1960** O. Skilbeck *ABC of Film & TV* 86 **Monitor speaker*, loudspeaker used as a check in dubbing, or as an alternative to headphones by recordists. **1975** *Independent Broadcasting* Aug. 11/1 The technical area with two mixing desks.. and two monitor speakers.

'monitor, *v.* [f. prec. sb.] **1.** *trans.* To guide as a monitor. *nonce-word.*

1818 Keats *Endym.* iv. 884 In that same void white Chastity shall sit, And monitor me nightly to lone slumber.

2. a. To check or regulate the technical quality of (a radio transmission, television signal, etc.).

1924 [implied in monitoring *vbl. sb.*]. **1929** G. Allighan *Romance of Talkies* 64 During the recording, the mixer operator monitors the record through the light valves, thereby assuring himself that no record is lost. **1930** *Bell System Techn. Jrnl.* IX. 273 The.. control desk provides facilities by which the attendant can monitor the incoming voice currents and the outgoing radio signal. **1934** *Electronics* May 139/2 Methods of monitoring program transmission both visually and aurally. **1958** *Times Rev. Industry* Aug. 9/3 The output from the analyser can be monitored with headphones. **1962** A. Nisbett *Technique Sound Studio* 258 The signal is monitored by the limiter and any wave which exceeds a certain volume causes a corresponding increase in feedback, which reduces the signal.

b. To listen to and report on (radio broadcasts, esp. from a foreign country); also, to eavesdrop on (a telephone conversation).

1939 *Times* 2 Nov. 5/3 About 150 news bulletins alone, in many different languages, are monitored each day. **1948** *Amer. Speech* XXIII. 219 From secret radios, constructed and hidden by British prisoners, the B.B.C.'s broadcasts were monitored. **1955** F. Swinnerton *Sumner Intrigue* xi. 85 A telephonist had illegitimately monitored a conversation. **1958** 'N. Shute' *Rainbow & Rose* i. 7 We've been monitoring their frequency. *Ibid.* 22 The constable sat down to monitor the conversations. **1971** R. Dentry *Encounter at Kharmel* v. 92 If I were running Ziauddin's operation, I'd be monitoring every newscast in Asia. **1972** D. Haston *In High Places* vi. 74 We sat for three weeks in Kleine Scheidegg, monitoring weather forecasts twice a day.

c. In more general use: to observe, supervise, or keep under review; to measure or test at intervals, esp. for the purpose of regulation or control.

1944 *Times* 20 Mar. 5/7 American and British control officers work at the same desks throughout the 24 hours, 'monitoring' the aircraft as they travel across the 3,000 miles of ocean. **1947** C. Goodman *Sci. & Engin. Nuclear Power* I. 255 We must monitor the cooling water to be sure that it contains no dangerous activities. **1957** *Listener* 3 Oct. 501/2 The Royal Observer Corps have been given the vital job of monitoring the extent of fall-out all over the country. **1958** *Observer* 9 Nov. 17/5 The phonocardiograph is useful in monitoring the [unborn] child's heart when the mother is sleeping or is over-anxious. **1959** *Daily Tel.* 14 Apr. 1/6 The committee was set up in November, 1956, to initiate and monitor a programme of research design. **1961** *New Scientist* 21 Dec. 744/1 The principle is now used.. to monitor (while in service) the thickness of boiler shell and pipe walls that are subject to corrosion. **1966** *Lancet* 24 Dec. 1387/1 Pulse-rate and blood-pressure were closely monitored. **1967** S. Woodgate in Wills & Yearsley *Handbk. Management Technol.* 94 These work schedules give supervision and management the ability to monitor progress and to detect immediately if delays to schedules are occurring. **1972** *Sci. Amer.* Aug. 110/3 The radius of the mirror was monitored frequently during the grinding operation by a center-of-curvature test. **1974** *Nature* 17 May 204/2 Thirty-five inspectors monitor the 2,000-odd works registered under the Alkali Act. **1974** *Physics Bull.* Nov. 533/1 Traces of metals in air and water as low as 0·01 parts per million can be monitored with the latest instrument.

So **'monitored** *ppl. a.*; **'monitoring** *vbl. sb.* and *ppl. a.*

1924 *Proc. IRE* XII. 561 A third requirement relates to monitoring facilities. **1929** G. Allighan *Romance of Talkies* 64 Acoustic treatment of the walls of the monitoring room secures the reverberation characteristic of the theatre. **1933** *Electronics* June 160 A monitoring panel and a two-way communication system so that the operator may keep in constant communication with the pilot of a landing aircraft. **1937** *Discovery* Nov. 330/2 At the side of the studio there is a 'monitoring' television receiving set, so that the floor directors and the announcers can see the outgoing programme. **1939** *Times* 2 Nov. 5/3 Monitoring consists of listening to and recording information contained in programmes broadcast by other countries. *Ibid.*, The monitoring service [of the B.B.C.] deals with some 250,000 words every 24 hours. **1945** *Times* 7 Apr. 4/7 The Japanese Government intended to continue its efforts.. according to a monitored report from the United States Office of War Information. **1949** *Atomic Energy & Life Sci.* (U.S. Atomic Energy Comm.) 61 Automatic monitoring equipment, measuring radioactivity of water.. would stop flow if radiation were above safe limit. **1961** *Lancet* 22 July 187/2 Continuous monitoring of the atrial pressure would provide early warning of a dangerous rise. **1962** *B.S.I. News* Mar. 24/2 Two types of plug are dealt with in B.S. 196: two-pole and two-pole and pilot contact, the latter being chiefly required for use with electrical interlocks or with 'monitored earth' circuits. **1971** *Hi-Fi Sound* Feb. 66/1 Systems of this standard are, or can be, of 'monitoring' class—the sort of equipment *Hi-Fi Sound* would use for examining the qualities of new recordings or evaluating new cartridges or other components. **1972** *Accountant* 17 Aug. 214/1 A period of.. regulated and monitored practical training.

monitorial (mɒnɪ'tɔərɪəl), *a.* [f. L. *monitōri-us* (see monitory) + -al¹, or ad. F. *monitorial.*]

1. = monitory *a.* 1, 1 b.

1725 tr. *Dupin's Eccl. Hist. 17th C.* I. ii. i. 17 The Senate being inform'd that the Monitorial Bull was publish'd. *a* **1754** Carte *Hist. Eng.* (1755) IV. 63 The Emperor.. issued on the 30th of that month monitorial letters requiring him to lay down his arms. **1816** F. H. Naylor *Hist. Germany* I. i. iv. 128 They resolved to preface hostilities with a monitorial address to the Palatine. **1858** Carlyle *Fredk. Gt.* viii. v. II. 342 His Majesty even honours him by expecting he should quietly keep a monitorial eye upon the Crown-Prince.

2. Of, pertaining to, connected with, or performed by monitors in schools.

1845 R. W. Hamilton *Pop. Educ.* iv. (ed. 2) 81 Bell and Lancaster introduced the reciprocal and monitorial system. **1864** *Edin. Rev.* July 185 The 'monitorial' system, or the system of governing the younger boys through the elder. **1888** W. Hunt in *Dict. Nat. Biog.* XVI. 57/1 He [Drury, headmaster of Harrow] disliked flogging, and the system of monitorial caning seems to have grown up in his time.

3. Belonging to the monitors (monitor *sb.* 5).

1878 *Ann. & Mag. Nat. Hist.* July 92 In one special dental modification they are Iguanian, in another Monitorial.

Hence **moni'torially** *adv.*, in a monitorial manner (1847 Webster).

'monitorship. [-ship.] The office or position of a monitor; also, the period during which any one holds the office of monitor.

1641 'Smectymnuus' *Vind. Answ.* §15. 187 Those.. who ..might be fit Monitors.. were designed to that office of Monitorship. **1847** *Tait's Mag.* XIV. 292 They not only pay the boys and girls for acquiring a knowledge of the business, but they also pay the person who, during their monitorship and apprenticeship, is to have the benefit of their assistance, for teaching them. **1851** R. Nesbit in Mitchell *Mem.* xii. (1858) 301 The Government Institution has such advantages over us.. in monitorships and teacherships, &c. **1866** *Harvard Mem. Biog.*, *C. B. Brown* I. 359 He met his expenses by keeping school during the winter and with the aid furnished by the college monitorship.

monitory ('mɒnɪtərɪ), *a.* and *sb.* Also 5 **manyterye.** [ad. L. *monitōri-us*, f. *monitor*: see MONITOR and -ORY. Cf. F. *monitoire*.]

A. *adj.*

1. Giving or conveying a warning; serving to admonish; admonitory.

c **1450** *Mankind* 872 in *Macro Plays* 33 Mankend, ȝe were obliuyows of my doctrine manyterye. **1586** A. DAY *Eng. Secretary* I. (1625) 3 Sundry Epistles, the titles whereof are ..Monitorie, Accusatorie..and such like. **1622** BACON *Hen. VII*, 75 The King also made a Statute in that Parliament, Monitory and Minatory, towards Iustices of Peace, that they should duly execute their office. *a* **1652** J. SMITH *Sel. Disc.* vi. 199 The general difference between prophetical dreams and those that are merely nouthetical or monitory. **1692** R. L'ESTRANGE *Fables* xxxi. 31 That which was Rudeness, and Ill Nature in the Aggressor, was only a Monitory Justice, and a Discreet Sharpness in the Other. **1783** BURKE *Sp. Fox's E. India Bill* Wks. 1842 I. 298 These were the sole object of the monitory resolution of this house. **1819** WORDSW. *Waggoner* II. 154 He heard the monitory growl [of a mastiff]. **1834** *Tracts for Times* No. 22. 10 'The Warning Clauses', or 'The Monitory Clauses' [of the *Quicunque vult*]. **1856** EMERSON *Eng. Traits, Truth* Wks. (Bohn) II. 52 The mottoes of their families are monitory proverbs. **1885** *Manch. Exam.* 26 June 5/3 Lord Brabourne had to say a few monitory words to bring the preachers back to their forgotten text.

Const. *of.* *a* **1854** H. REED *Lect. Eng. Lit.* v. (1855) 157 William Caxton—whose life is to be thought of..as monitory of 'perpetual industry'.

b. ***monitory letter*** = B. 2.

1696 PHILLIPS (ed. 5), *Monitory Letters*, Letters from an Ecclesiastical Judge, upon Information of Scandals and Abuses within Cognizance of his Court. **1699** C. MATHER in Quincy *Hist. Harvard Univ.* (1840) I. 487, I have already written a large monitory letter to those innovators. **1769** ROBERTSON *Chas. V*, x. III. 211 The Pope..immediately issued monitory letters. **1839** JAMES *Louis XIV*, II. 23 Judging that the monitory letters he received were rather from the hands of enemies than of friends, he displayed a calm countenance.

2. ***monitory lizard*** = MONITOR *sb.* 5.

1810 *Naval Chron.* XXIII. 59 That extraordinary animal called the Monitory Lizard, from its faculty of warning persons of the approach of any venomous animal. **1839** *Penny Cycl.* XV. 332/1 The warning of these Monitory Lizards was said to be a hissing or whistling.

B. *sb.*

†**1.** An admonition; something that serves as a warning. *Obs.*

c **1557** ABP. PARKER *Ps.* lxxviii. 118 Argt., This hye profound oration A monitorie is To God to turne. **1613** PURCHAS *Pilgrimage* I. iv. 19, I see not why these should denie God that libertie to impose, or man that necessitie to need such monitories. *a* **1677** BARROW *Serm.* (1686) III. iii. 31 Monitories, encouragements and excitements to our duty.

2. A letter containing an admonition or warning, *esp.* one issued by a bishop or pope.

1624 BACON *Apothegm* 70 in *Resuscitatio* (1661) 303 There was a King of Hungary, took a Bishop in Battel,.. Whereupon the Pope writ a Monitory to him; For that he had broken the priviledge of Holy Church. **1707** *Lond. Gaz.* No. 4360/1 There are Three Monitories printed, and affix'd in the most frequented Places of that City. **1790** GIBBON *Misc. Wks.* (1814) III. 458 A monitory, or summons, to appear in fifteen days, was affixed on the church doors. **1816** F. H. NAYLOR *Hist. Germany* I. II. xi. 479 Ferdinand..in a thundering monitory, annulled their proceedings. **1872** MORLEY *Voltaire* 219 This testimony, given with a vagueness that ought to have proved it legally valueless, was the fruit of the episcopal monitory.

monitress ('mɒnɪtrɪs). [f. MONITOR *sb.* + -ESS.]

1. A female monitor or admonisher.

1748 RICHARDSON *Clarissa* IV. 54 His divine monitress, he called me! **1813** SCOTT *Rokeby* IV. xii, She..Assumes a monitress's pride, Her Redmond's dangerous sports to chide. **1859** THACKERAY *Virgin.* xvi, Harry..corrected the faulty intonation, under his English monitresses. **1897** 'OUIDA' *Massarenes* xv. 187 It must be very annoying to have a perpetual monitress in one's own daughter.

attrib. **1887** RUSKIN *Præterita* II. 422 Lady Trevelyan.. became at once a monitress-friend in whom I wholly trusted.

2. In a girls' school, a pupil having special duties assigned to her (cf. MONITOR *sb.* 2).

1844 *Yng. Communicant* (1848) 12 As head monitress I know them both very well. **1868** *Regul. & Ord. Army* §465 The training of School Mistresses, pupil teachers and Monitresses. **1884** *Cassell's Fam. Mag.* Mar. 216/2 The monitress..moves towards the three culprits, and tells them,..that talking is not allowed.

monitrix ('mɒnɪtrɪks). *rare*⁻¹. [fem. in Latin form of MONITOR: see -TRIX.] = prec.

1727 SOMERVILLE *Hor. Epist.* I. x. 42 In vain from Nature's rules we blindly stray, And push th' uneasy monitrix away.

moniwhat, variant of MANYWHAT *Obs.*

monk (mʌŋk), *sb.*¹ Forms: 1–3 munuc, (munec-), 2–3 munec, -ek, 3 munuch, 3–4 monek(e, 4 monok, munc, mun(c)k, 4–6 monke, munke, 5 mongke, 6 moonke, *Sc.* mounche, moun(c)k(e, mwn(c)k(e, 5–6 monck, 3– monk. [OE. *munuc*:—pre-historic **muniko-*, ad. popular L. **monicus* for *monachus*, a. late Gr. μοναχός, subst. use of Gr. μοναχός adj., single, solitary, f. μόν-ος alone. Cf. OFris. *munek*, *-ik*, *monik* (MDu. *monic*, *monc*. *mun(i)c*, Du. *monnik*, *munnik*), MLG. *mon(n)ik*, *monk*, OHG. *munih* (MHG. *mun(i)ch*, *mün(e)ch*, G. *mönch*), ON. *múnkr* (Da., Sw., *munk*); also the Rom. forms, F. *moine*, Pr. *monge-s*, Sp. *monje*, Pg. *monge* (:—Rom. type **monio*), It. *monaco*.

In accordance with its etymology, *monachus* originally meant a religious hermit or solitary, but was from an early period applied to cœnobites, and this eventually became the ordinary use.]

1. a. A member of a community or brotherhood of men living apart from the world under the vows of poverty, chastity, and obedience, according to a rule (characteristic of the particular order), and devoted chiefly to the performance of religious duties and the contemplative life. The different orders of monks are distinguished by habits of various shapes and colours (cf. b).

In England, before the Reformation, the term was not applied to the members of the mendicant orders, who were always called *friars*. From the 16th c. to the 19th c., however, it was usual to speak of the friars as a class of monks. In recent times the distinction between the terms has been carefully observed by well-informed writers. In Fr. and Ger. the equivalent of *monk* is applied equally to 'monks' and 'friars'.

The word properly belongs to Christian use, but is sometimes applied to persons of other religions (e.g. Muslims, Buddhists).

a **900** tr. *Bæda's Hist.* v. xii. [xi.] (1890) 434 Wæs sum munuc & mæssepreost in nehnesse his cetan eardiȝende, þæs noma wæs Hamgels. *c* **961** ÆTHELWOLD *Rule St. Benet* i. (1885) 9 Feower synt muneca cyn..Ðæt forme is mynstermonna..Oþer cyn is ancrena [etc.]. *c* **1122** *O.E. Chron.* an. 675 (Laud MS.) Hwilc abbot þe beþ þær coren of þe munecan. *c* **1175** *Lamb. Hom.* 143 þe treowe men, þe munckes, þe meidene, þe weddede wiues..sculen beon icleoped on þe fader riht halue. *c* **1205** LAY. 12906 þæt child munec wes inne Winchæstre. *a* **1225** *Ancr. R.* 318 Munuch, preost, oðer clerk. **1297** R. GLOUC. (Rolls) 11478 Sir alein was ek inome in monekene wede In þe priorie. *a* **1300** *Cursor M.* 22002 Quatkin man sum euer it es,..or clerc, or munk [*Gött.* monk], or canun. **1377** LANGL. *P. Pl.* B. xx. 262 Monkes and monyals and alle men of Religioun. *c* **1400** MAUNDEV. (Roxb.) ii. 5 Ane abbay of munkes. **1518** WRIOTHESLEY *Chron.* (Camden) I. 12 All the orders of friers channons, moncks of Stratforde and Tower Hill. **1530** PALSGR. 246/1 Monk of the charterhouse, *chartrevx*. **1560** DAUS tr. *Sleidane's Comm.* 371 The common people named him Monke, because he was of thordre of Paule, the first Hermit. **1567** *Gude & Godlie B.* (S.T.S.) 206 The Monkis of Melros maid gude kaill, On Frydayis quhen they fastit. **1596** DALRYMPLE tr. *Leslie's Hist. Scot.* x. 436 A Dominican mounck. **1603** KNOLLES *Hist. Turks* (1638) 251 Bajazet.. there executed Torlac Keman another seditious Turkish Monk. **1649** EVELYN *Diary* 19 May, A Monk at his beades. **1788** GIBBON *Decl. & F.* lx. VI. 129 The priests and monks were the loudest and most active in the destruction of the schismatics. **1846** GREENER *Sci. Gunnery* 18 Many ascribe the discovery [of gunpowder] to Roger Bacon, the monk. **1849** KEMBLE *Saxons in Eng.* II. ix. II. 448 Although monks are not necessarily clergymen..many of the body in this country took holy orders. **1889** *Ch. Times* 992/1 That the object of a monk was to make a good man of himself, the object of a friar was to do a good work among others.

b. Preceded by defining adj. having reference to the colour of the habit: **black monk**, a Benedictine; also, a Black or Augustinian Canon; †**gray monk, white monk**, a Cistercian monk.

c **1290** *S. Eng. Leg.* I. 20/42 A faire Abbeye he let þare a-rere..Of blake Monekes. *c* **1290**–*c* **1300** [see GREY *a.* 2]. *c* **1305** *Edmund Conf.* 184 in *E.E.P.* (1862) 76 Blake monekes he seȝ. *c* **1400** *Rom. Rose* 6695 As these chanouns regulers, Or white monkes, or these blake. *c* **1450** HOLLAND *Howlat* 178 The Se Mawis war monkis, the blak and the quhyte. *c* **1500** *Lytell Geste Robin Hood* iv. 35 (Ritson) Than were they ware of two blacke monkes, Eche on a good palferay. *c* **1630** RISDON *Surv. Devon* §204 (1810) 213 Which monastery he replenished with black monks, Augustines. **1700** TYRRELL *Hist. Eng.* II. 744 The White Monks..were forced to pay..40000*l.* of Silver. **1766** ENTICK *London* IV. 237 This parliament was adjourned to Westminster, amongst the black monks.

c. Proverbs.

1340 *Ayenb.* 165 Vor þe cloþinge ne makeþ naȝt þane monek. **1546** HEYWOOD *Prov.* (1867) 62 Ye make hir a cook-queane, and consume her good. And she must syt like a beane in a moonkis hood. **1613** SHAKS. *Hen. VIII*, III. i. 23 But All Hoods, make not Monkes. **1678** RAY *Prov.* (ed. 2) 296 The Devill was sick, the Devill a monk would be, The Devill was well, the devill a monk was he.

†**2.** *pl.* The house of a particular order. (Cf. FRIAR 2 c, quot. 1375.) *Obs. rare.*

1556 *Chron. Gr. Friars* (Camden) 3 Whane he [*sc.* King John] had raynyd xvij. yeres he dyde, & is burryd there in the monkes before the hye auter.

3. As the name of certain animals whose form suggests the costume of a monk, esp. with reference to the cowl or hood; see also quots. and SEA-MONK. (Cf. G. *mönch*.)

1789 BROWNE *Jamaica* 430 *Buprestis* I. *Fusca minima rugosa*. The Monk. This Insect is smaller than the Wevil. **1815** S. BROOKES *Conch.* 156 Monk, *Conus monachus*. **1831** *G. Montagu's Ornith. Dict.* 326 Monck, a name for the Bullfinch. **1840** tr. *Cuvier's Anim. Kingd.* 99 [Seals] The Monk (*Pelagius*). **1848** J. GOULD *Birds Australia* IV. pl. 58 *Tropidorhynchus Corniculatus*... Its bare head and neck have also suggested the names of 'Friar Bird', 'Monk', 'Leather Head', etc. **1848** *Zoologist* VI. 1976 Angel Fish, *Squatina angelus*. This strange fish..is frequently called a 'monk'. **1851** MAYHEW *Lond. Labour* (1861) II. 64 His pigeon-cote..is no longer stocked with carriers, dragoons, horsemen, jacobins, monks. **1863** *Cassell's Pop. Nat. Hist.* I. 116 The Monk, *Pithecia monachus* [a monkey].

4. As the name of various objects in certain arts and crafts (see quots.) Cf. F. *moine*, G. *mönch*. Also *spec.* in *Printing*, a blotch or area where the ink is excessive.

1683 MOXON *Mech. Exerc., Printing* 385 When the Press-man has not Destributed his Balls, some splotches of Inck may lye on..them, which..he delivers upon the Form; so that the Sheet Printed on has a black blotch on it: Which Blotch is called a Monk. **1683** PETTUS *Fleta Min.* I. 15 When the Loam is prepared you must then have a Frame, in which you may beat the Proof-Test and Crucibles:..then..grease also the upper part of the Frame which is called the Monk. **1763** W. LEWIS *Comm. Phil.-Techn.* 130 A round-faced pestle, called a Monk. **1771** P. LUCKOMBE *Hist. & Art of Printing* 500 *Monk*, when the Press-man has not distributed his balls and the ink lies in blotches, it is called a Monk. **1834–47** J. S. MACAULAY *Field Fortif.* (1851) 207 The piece of agarick used to communicate the fire to the powder is called the monk. **1876** VOYLE & STEVENSON *Milit. Dict.*, *Monk*, a piece of junk or touch-wood laid over the priming of a mine to give the miner time to retire. **1892** A. POWELL *Southward's Pract. Printing* (ed. 4) xliv. 409 Be very careful not to let the roller 'run into the ink'.., or the roller will be 'smothered'.. If not perceived, and the roller is applied to the type, there will be great blotches of ink in different places, perhaps filling it up and causing 'monks', or black patches, in the impression. **1915** *Southward's Mod. Printing* (ed. 3) II. i. 4 This is called rolling the forme... If inefficiently performed there will be too much ink on the impression, or even blotches, technically, 'monks'. **1938** *Amer. Speech* XIII. 272 A dark spot on a page is a *monk*. **1956** *Collins's Authors' & Printers' Dict.* (ed. 10) 265/2 *Monk*,..a patch of letterpress with too much ink.

5. a. *attrib.* and *Comb.*, as ***monk-artist***, ***-bishop***, ***-land***; ***monk-like*** adj. and adv., ***monk-educated***, ***-made***, ***-ridden***, ***-taught*** adjs.

1855 MILMAN *Lat. Chr.* XIV. x. (1864) IX. 321 No doubt ..many *monk-artists fled from the sacrilegious East to practise their holy art in the safe and quiet West. **1861** tr. *Montalembert's Monks of West* II. 19 St. Martin, the great *monk-bishop whose ascetic and priestly virtues had edified Gaul. **1633** *Sc. Acts Chas. I* (1817) V. 26/1 Any church lands fryer lands *monk lands or comoun lands. **1611** FLORIO, *Monacale*, *Munke or Nun-like. **1818** COBBETT *Pol. Reg.* XXXIII. 691 But, monk-like, whenever it deviates from downright dullness, it is only to discover its malignity towards toleration and freedom. **1895** *Westm. Gaz.* 23 Oct. 7/3 With a monk-like girdle round his waist. **1865** KINGSLEY *Herew.* xx, The French look on us English *monk-made knights as spurious and adulterine. **1848** LYTTON *Harold* VI. v, He concealed his disdain of the monks and *monk-ridden. **1868** MILMAN *St. Paul's* 246 The shouts of a rabble of monks, of *monk-taught men, and boys *monk-educated.

b. Special comb.: **monk-bat**, the *Molossus nasutus* of Jamaica, etc.; **monk bond** *Building* (see quot. 1936); †**monk-child**, a boy who is being brought up to be a monk; **monk-craft** (after *priestcraft*), monkish practice or policy based upon unworthy motives; **monk-flower**, a name for the supposed genus *Monachanthus*, to which the orchids of the genus *Catasetum* have been sometimes referred; †**monk-house**, a monastery; **Monk-Latin**, the corrupt Latin used by monks; **monk-monger**, a favourer of monks or monasticism; **monk parrot** (see quot.); **monk's bench** = *monk's table*; **monk's cloth**, 'a kind of worsted' (Halliwell 1847); †**monk's cowl** = MONKSHOOD; **monk-seal**, a white-bellied seal inhabiting the Mediterranean and neighbouring ocean; **monk's gun, harquebus** *Antiq.* [= G. *mönchsbüchse*], a name given to the wheel-lock gun of the 16th c., from the fancy that it was invented by the monk Schwarz, the alleged inventor of gun-powder; **monk's-head**, †(*a*) ? = *monk-seal*; (*b*) = MONKSHOOD; (*c*) the plant *Leontodon Taraxacum*; †**monk's peason**, woodlice (cf. *monkey-pease*); **monk('s)-seam** *Naut.*, (*a*) a seam in which the selvages of sails are sewn flat one over the other; (*b*) 'the fash left at the junction of the moulds when a ball is cast' (Smyth *Sailor's Word-bk.*); **monk('s) shoe** (see quot. 1969); also *ellipt.* as *monk*; **monk's table**, a convertible wooden seat, the back of which is hinged to swing over and rest horizontally on the arms, thus forming a table; †**monk-swan** (see quot.).

1851 GOSSE *Nat. Sojourn Jamaica* 294 The habit so strongly reminded me of a herd of monks shutting themselves up in a convent, that I thought the species might well be designated as the *Monk Bat. **1936** *Archit. Rev.* LXXIX. 241/3 *Monk bond, which is a better ordered arrangement than Yorkshire or Flying bond, is popular in the North of Europe. Two stretchers are followed by one header in every course, the headers being so disposed that verticality of their axial lines is little apparent, and a striking result is obtained of diagonal lines of stretchers, which look like a series of corbels or cantilevers embedded in the wall. **1952** *Ibid.* CXII. 87 A double monk bond was adopted, the whole of the façade being set out to a large scale to ensure that the pattern over them was an even one. *c* **1000** ÆLFRIC *Hom.* (Th.) II. 174 Sum *munuc-cild drohtnode on his mynstre. *c* **1205** LAY. 13251 Nime þane munec child & makien Brutlondes king. **1691** *D'Emilianne's Frauds Rom. Monks* (ed. 3) 242 They were only the effects of Priest and *Monk-Craft to get Mony. **1848** LYTTON *Harold* VI. iv, I shall need no mediator between nature and monk-craft. **1483** *Cath. Angl.* 247/1 (MS. A) A *Munke howse, *cenobium* & cetera; vbi Abbey. **1694** MOTTEUX *Rabelais* v. xxvii. (1737) 123 The Prior of the Monk-House. **1843** CARLYLE *Past & Pr.* II. vi, Some of us can preach, in English-Saxon, in Norman-French, and even in *Monk-Latin. **1873** LELAND *Egypt. Sketch Bk.* 3 A Monk-Latin chronicle. **1655** FULLER *Ch. Hist.* II. v. §24 Oswald (a great *monk-monger..) held

York and Worcester. 1865 KINGSLEY *Herew.* xxiii, Are you a monk-monger into the bargain? 1878 *Daily News* 16 Sept. 3/1 '*Monk' parrots are sickly parrots, which have caught cold on their passage to the wholesale dealers in Liverpool, London, &c. 1925 BRODHURST & LAYTON *Gloss. Eng. Furnit.* 110 Sometimes settles were treated in a similar manner and called *Monks' Benches. 1950 S. HOWARD *Our Furnit. through Ages* viii. 162 A table-settle..was of Cromwellian inspiration and was in consequence most uninspiring; it is sometimes called a 'Monk's Bench'. 1441–2 *Act. 20 Hen. VI*, c. 10 Draps appellez *monkes clothes. 1950 '*Mercury' Dict. Textile Terms* 352/2 **Monks' cloth*, a heavy all-cotton fabric woven in a basket weave from coarse and rough yarns. 1972 P. MARKS *Collector's Choice* i. 26 The yards of monk's cloth and fawn-colored carpet lining his galley. 1548 TURNER *Names Herbes* (E.D.S.) 9 It is called muench kappen in duche, and it maye be called in englishe *monkes coule or blewe wolfsbaine. 1841 *Penny Cycl.* XXI. 158/1 The skull of the *Monk Seal (*Phoca Monachus*). 1855 W. S. DALLAS in *Syst. Nat. Hist.* II. 470 The Monk Seal (*Stenorynchus monachus*), which inhabits the Mediterranean. 1894 *Nature* 26 July 307 A Monk Seal (*Monachus albiventer*) from Madeira. 1881 GREENER *Gun* 47 In the Dresden Museum there is an example of this [wheel-lock] system in the celebrated '*Monk's Gun'. 1870 BLACK tr. *Demmin's Weapons of War* 69 The flock of compilers still continue to call this little hand-cannon 'Moenchs-büchse', or *monk's arquebus. 1666 J. DAVIES *Hist. Caribby Isles* 101 There is another kind of Porposes which have the snout round and hollow,..some call them *Monks-heads, and Sea-Monks. 1682 WHELER *Journ. Greece* I. 25 *Aconitum Lycoctinum* [sic]..which I took to be a kind of monks-head. 1760 J. LEE *Introd. Bot.* App. 319 Monk's-head, *Leontodon*. 1845 BURNETT *Plantæ Util.* II. Pl. lx, From the receptacle looking bald, after the flower and seeds are gone, it [*sc.* Leontodon Taraxacum] is sometimes called Monkshead. 1558 WARDE tr. *Alexis' Secr.* (1568) 24 The little beastes called *Monkes peason or sowes. 1626 CAPT. SMITH *Accid. Yng. Seamen* 17 A *munke seame, a round seame. 1750 BLANCKLEY *Nav. Expositor, Monk Seam*—Sewing the Edges or Selvedges of Sails together, over one another on both Sides to make it the Stronger. 1938 L. MACNEICE *I crossed Minch* vii. 92 Ginger-coloured *monk suede shoes. 1953 J. KORN *Boot & Shoe Production* xxv. 142 The Monk Shoe... Like the Cromwell, this was formerly a quarter-over shoe. 1968 *Times* 6 Dec. 10/6 The best-selling shoes are..boots and monks (almost boots). 1969 R. T. WILCOX *Dict. Costume* (1970) 217/1 *Monk's shoe*, a low shoe of soft but heavy leather with heel and plain toe and a strap passing over the instep and buckled at the side. 1907 *Yesterday's Shopping* (1969) 130/4 Bamboo *Monks' Table... This can be used either as a seat or table, the top being made so that it will slide off to form back of seat. 1972 *Country Life* 23 Mar. 723/3 The so-called monk's table, serving as seat and table..was developed during the 17th century... In shape it was a low-backed box-chair with a solid round or rectangular back, wider than the seat, and with horizontal arms. 1668 CHARLETON *Onomasticon* 114 *Dodo Lusitanorum, Cygnus Cucullatus*,..the Dodo or *Monk-swan of S. Maurice's Iland.

monk (mʌŋk), *sb.*² Colloq. abbrev. of MONKEY *sb.*

1843 *Spirit of Times* 1 Apr. 54/1 P. Fowler..is one and identical with the celebrated jockey of Miss Foote, in stable parlance, ycleped Monk... The word Monk in this case..is in fact an abbreviation of a noun substantive by which a certain animal is recognised, the countenance of which is said strongly to resemble that of the very jockey in question. 1901 GREENOUGH & KITTREDGE *Words & their Ways* (1902) vi. 61 Slang is fond of clipped words: as, *monk* for *monkey*. 1903 A. M. BINSTEAD *Pitcher in Paradise* xii. 285 He swore at the monkey freely, and the monk retaliated in cordial but vehement dumbshow with every bitter curse that was known to the forest. 1958 G. BARKER *Two Plays* 70 That's the one. His little monk's dead.

†**monk**, *v. Obs. rare.* [f. MONK *sb.*¹]

1. *trans.* **a.** To make a monk of. **b.** *nonce-use.* ? To cause to look like a monk.

a 1000 *Ecgberti Confess.* xxvii. in Thorpe *Laws* II. 152 He hine mot munecian. *c* 1205 LAY. 12904 þa þis child wes iwaxen þæt hit cuðe riden, þa lette his fader hit munekien [*c* 1275 monaki]. 1738 LD. S. MANNERS in *Fam. Rose Kilravock* (Spald. Club) 448, I don't care twopence what I wear, provided he [*sc.* Ramsay, the painter] does not monk me.

2. *to monk it*: to be a monk.

1756 AMORY *Buncle* (1770) III. 63 It pleased me so much to see these monks march off with their smiling partners.. It is really a fine thing to monk it on this plan.

monk-corn, variant of MONGCORN.

monkdom (ˈmʌŋkdəm). [f. MONK *sb.*¹ + -DOM.] The condition of a monk; monks collectively; the domain of monks.

1862 HOOK *Lives Abps.* II. iv. 281 Throwing off the restraints of monkdom..he travelled as a visitor from one monastery to another. 1883 FROUDE *Luther* in *Contemp. Rev.* XLIV. 5 Hans..was bitterly disappointed, knowing, perhaps, more of monks and monkdom than his son. 1890 E. JOHNSON *Rise Christendom* 485 Monkdom passed under the ..condemnation of the world some 400 years ago.

monke, obs. form of MONKEY.

monkery (ˈmʌŋkərɪ). Chiefly *contemptuous*. Also 6–7 monk(e)rye, -erie, monckery, 7 munk(e)ry. [f. MONK *sb.*¹ + -ERY. Cf. MDu. *monikerie*.]

1. The state, condition, or profession of monks (or religious orders in general); monastic life, monasticism.

?1536 LATIMER in *Lett. Suppress. Monast.* (Camden) 149 For the upstandynge of his forsayd howsse, and contynuance of the same to many good purpasesse, natt in monkrye. 1581 J. BELL *Haddon's Answ. Osor.* 349 But Monckery was then a sequestration & departyng from the world, not a profession in the world. 1601 F. GODWIN *Bps. of Eng.* 17 For the space of 90 yeeres after, monkerie ceased throughout the realme. 1635 PAGITT *Christianogr.* 34 Oswald one of the greatest setters up of Monkery, begat Oswald the Monke. 1749 WESLEY *Wks.* (1872) X. 8 You quote not one line from any Father in the third century, in favour of monkery. 1818 HALLAM *Mid. Ages* (1872) III. 274 After the introduction of monkery, and its unsocial theory of duties. 1844 STANLEY *Arnold* (1858) I. ii. 65 Monkery seems flourishing there in great force. 1874 H. R. REYNOLDS *John Bapt.* iii. §2. 181 The..modern eulogists of monkery.

2. a. A body or community of monks; an establishment of monks; a monastery.

1549 LATIMER *4th Serm. bef. Edw. VI* (Arb.) 118 If he dye in the state of dampnation, he shal rise in the same. Yea, thoughe he haue a whole Monkerye to synge for hym. 1581 *Sc. Acts Jas. VI* (1814) III. 276/1 The monkreis ar altogidder abolishit, and thair places and abbayis ar for þe maist pairt left waist. 1581 J. BELL *Haddon's Answ. Osor.* 302 b, Whom the Pope deposed from his kingdome, and thrust into a monkery. 1600 SURFLET *Country Farm* II. liv. 367 In many countries it [*Agnus Castus*] is seene planted almost in all the monkeries. 1716 M. DAVIES *Athen. Brit.* III. *Diss. Drama* 24 For refusing to submit to the Union of the Spanish and Italian Monkeries into one Congregation. 1740 H. WALPOLE *Ep. to T. Ashton* 22 To woods and caves she never bade retreat, Nor fix'd in cloister'd monkeries her seat. 1852 R. KNOX *Gt. Artists & Gt. Anat.* 168 A long residence..in courts, monkeries, and barracks. 1866 *Lond. Rev.* 28 Apr. 470/2 Brother Ignatius has quite as much right to set up a monkery at Norwich as the Irvingites have to set up a temple in Gordon Square. 1898 W. WHITE *Jrnls.* 244 To Shulbred farm, an old monkery.

b. Monks collectively; also, the monks (of a particular place).

1552 LYNDESAY *Monarche* 4669 All Monkrye, ȝe may heir and se, Ar callit Denis, for dignite. 1552 LATIMER *Serm. 5th Sund. Epiph.* (1584) 322 Do not as the fondness of the Monkery first did. 1837 LANDOR *Pentameron, 5th Day's Interview* Wks. 1853 II. 346/2 The clergy and monkery at Certaldo had never been cordial with Messer Giovanni. 1878 E. C. G. MURRAY *Russians of To-day* 141 It was the custom to recruit the ranks of monkery by..impressing some of the worst-behaved pupils in the four ecclesiastical academies of St. Petersburg, Moscow, Kiew and Kazan. 1880 SWINBURNE *Stud. Shaks.* iii. (ed. 2) 214 And of such here is enough to glut the gorge of all the monks in monkery.

3. *pl.* Monkish practices, appurtenances, or paraphernalia.

1624 DARCIE *Birth of Heresies* xv. 62 The principall Monkeries are celebrated on the left side of the Altar. 1873 MRS. H. KING *Disciples, Ugo Bassi* v. (1877) 179 It likes me ill To see..thy bright face above the monkeries Of the black habit of the Barnabites. 1878 MORLEY *Diderot* I. iii. 59 The ..confused theological wilderness of sin, asceticism, miracle, and the other monkeries.

4. Conduct or practice characteristic of monks (esp. those of the Middle Ages); a system of life or conduct marked by the alleged faults or abuses of monasticism.

1649 BP. HALL *Cases Consc.* IV. i. (1654) 290 Although those Casuists doe sufficiently doat upon their Monkery. 1695 KENNETT *Par. Antiq.* vii. 26 If we renounce all the monkery of this tale. 1846 HARE *Mission Comf.* (1850) 425 This righteousness lies not..in human service, monkery, pilgrimages [etc.]. 1854 MILMAN *Lat. Chr.* I. i. (1864) I. 57 A second marriage..was revolting to the incipient monkery of the Church. 1872 CREIGHTON *Hist. Ess.* ii. (1902) 61 A reaction against..the monkery and bigotry of the Middle Ages. 1884 TENNYSON *Becket* IV. ii, I, that thro' the Pope divorced King Louis, Scorning his monkery.

5. *slang.* The practice of going on tramp; also, the country districts frequented by tramps.

a 1790 POTTER *Dict. Cant* (1795), *Monkery*, the country. 1812 J. H. VAUX *Flash Dict.*, *Monkery*, the country parts of England are called *The Monkery*. 1851 MAYHEW *Lond. Labour* I. 244 He had followed the 'monkry' from a child. *Ibid.* 247 The writer of this account was himself two whole years on the 'monkry', before he saw a lodging-house for tramps. *Ibid.* 248 'Well', said he, 'I don't know what this 'ere monkry will come to, after a bit'.

ˈ**monkess.** *rare.* [f. MONK *sb.*¹ + -ESS.] A nun.

1729 T. CONSETT *State of Russia* 167 Monkesses to knitt, sow, or weave lace. 1861 tr. *Montalembert's Monks of West* I. 426 How little she desired to be a monkess [orig. F. *moinesse*, rendering Jerome's *monacha*].

monkey (ˈmʌŋkɪ), *sb.* Forms: 6 munckey, munkkey, munkye, monke, 6–7 munkey, 7 monkeye, -eie, 7–8 monkie, 6– monkey. *Pl.* 6–9 monkies, 7– monkeys. [Of uncertain origin.

The MLG. version of *Reynard the Fox* (1498) has (only once, l. 6161) *Moneke* as the name of the son of Martin the Ape; and early in the 14th c. the same character is mentioned as *Monnekin* (v.r. *Monnequin*) by the Hainaulter Jean de Condé in *Li Dis d'Entendement* (Scheler) 853 (the passage is also printed by Chabaille as a 'branche' of the *Roman du Renart*). As the name does not occur in any other version of *Reynard*, the Eng. word can hardly be derived from the story. But it is not unlikely that the proper name may represent an otherwise unrecorded MLG. **moneke*, MDu. **monnekijn*, a colloquial word for monkey, and that this may have been brought to England by showmen from the continent. The MLG. and MDu. word would appear to be a dim. (with suffix *-ke*, *-kijn*: see -KIN) of some form of the Rom. word which appears as early mod.F. *monne* (16–17th c.), It. *monna* (earlier *mona*), Sp., Pg. *mona*, mod.Pr. *mouno* female ape (a masc. *mono* occurs in Sp. and Pg.), whence the diminutive forms, early mod.F. *monine*, It. *monnino* and †*monicchio* (Florio). The origin of the Rom. word has not been discovered.]

I. The simian animal, and transferred uses.

1. a. In its widest application, an animal of any species of the group of mammals closely allied to and resembling man, and ranging from the anthropoid apes to the marmosets; any animal of the order *Primates* except man and the lemurs. In a more restricted sense, the term is taken to exclude the anthropoid apes, and the baboons; in popular use associated chiefly with the greenish long-tailed species having cheek-pouches, often kept as pets.

By some writers, the word *ape* is used to express the wider of the two senses above explained, and *monkey* is confined to its narrower application. Others employ *monkey* as the wider term, restricting *ape* to the tailless and especially the anthropoid 'monkeys'.

1530 PALSGR. 246/1 Monkey a beest, *brouticque, marmot*. ?1533 in Ellis *Orig. Lett.* Ser. III. II. 242, ij Muske Catts, iij lytyll Munkkeys, a Marmazat [etc.]. 1570 B. GOOGE *Pop. Kingd.* II. 16 b, Besides at home they Parots keepe, and Apes and Munekeys store. *a* 1585 MONTGOMERIE *Flyting* 483 Manie monkes and marmaisits came with the mother. 1600 SHAKS. *A.Y.L.* IV. i. 154 More giddy in my desires, then a monkey. 1622 BACON *Hen. VII* 243 His Monkie..tore his Principall Note-Booke all to pieces, when by chance it lay forth. 1664 WOOD *Life* 21 Dec. (O.H.S.) II. 25 His person ridiculous, like a monkey rather than a Xtian. 1706–7 FARQUHAR *Beaux Strat.* II. ii, She reads Plays, keeps a Monkey, and is troubled with Vapours. 1727 *Philip Quarll* (1816) 26 The greener sort of monkies. 1796 MORSE *Amer. Geog.* II. 562 They sit on their hams, with their legs and arms disposed in the manner of monkeys. 1810 SOUTHEY *Kehama* XIII. xii, The antic Monkies, whose wild gambols late,..Shook the whole wood. 1820 SHELLEY *Witch Atl.* lxxiv, The chatterings of the monkey. 1880 HAUGHTON *Phys. Geog.* vi. 273 The American monkeys differ widely.. from all the apes and monkeys of the Old World.

b. With qualifying word: see quots.

howling monkey: a monkey of the genus *Mycetes*. See also CAPUCHIN, MOUSTACHE, PROBOSCIS, SQUIRREL, SPIDER, VERVET *monkey*.

1607 [see MARTIN²]. 1802 BINGLEY *Anim. Biog.* (1813) I. 86 The howling monkey. 1863 BATES *Nat. Amazon* ix. (1864) 255 The nocturnal Owl-faced Monkey (*Nyctipithecus Trivirgatus*). *Ibid.* xii. 391 The Scarlet-faced Monkey. 1905 *Westm. Gaz.* 14 Sept. 4/1 *Cercopithecus albigularis*. Sykes's Monkey, as it is called after its discoverer, who brought the first specimen home more than seventy years ago, is a handsomely marked species.

c. ***monkey up*** (or ***on***) ***a stick***: a toy consisting of the figure of a monkey attached to a stick so that it can be moved up and down it on a sliding ring. Also *transf.* and *fig.*

1863 *Tyneside Songs* 18 In these days he was a regular brick, When he seld the munkeys up the stick. 1874 'MAX ADELER' *Out of Hurly-burly* viii. 96 Willie had a purple monkey climbing on a yellow stick. 1890 KIPLING *Let.* in C. E. Carrington *Rudyard Kipling* (1955) v. 157 The blandishments of the people to whom a new writer-man is as a new purple monkey on a yellow stick. 1926 W. DE LA MARE *Connoisseur* 317, I went bobbing over its boulders and chasms like a jack-in-a-box or a monkey-on-a-stick. 1927 W. E. COLLINSON *Contemp. Eng.* 8 The monkey on a stick, often used to indicate someone very fidgety and restless. 1966 G. BUTLER *Nameless Coffin* xii. 192 A 'monkey' is a man who has never been in prison..but is the known associate of criminals. He is a monkey on a stick and it is usually only a matter of time before his stick breaks and he's down there with his friends.

d. ***three*** (***wise***) ***monkeys***: a conventional sculptured group of three monkeys, one with its paws over its mouth ('speak no evil'), one with its paws over its eyes ('see no evil'), and one with its paws over its ears ('hear no evil'); hence used allusively.

1926 *Army & Navy Stores Catal.* 197/3 The three wise monkeys. 'Speak no evil, see no evil, hear no evil.' Per group of three Monkeys -/4. 1969 B. KNOX *Tallyman* v. 89 The three wise monkeys would be non-starters against those people. 1969 G. MITCHELL *Dance to your Daddy* x. 119 Perhaps there are three other wise monkeys in this house besides yourselves. 1970 A. DRAPER *Swansong for Rare Bird* viii. 66, I know the score. I'm like the three monkeys. 1974 J. STUBBS *Painted Face* vii. 108 He was like those three monkeys... Neither heard, saw nor spoke evil.

2. *transf.* **a.** One who resembles a monkey in appearance or behaviour; esp. a mimic, or one who performs comical antics.

1589 NASHE *Martins Months Minde* 34 See how like the old Ape this young Munkey pattereth. 1607 TOPSELL *Four-f. Beasts* 7 The Englishmen call any man vsing such Histrionical actours [*sic*] 'a Munkey'. *a* 1716 SOUTH *Serm.* (1842) IV. 106 In a word, no man can be exact and perfect in this way of flattery, without being a monkey and a mimic. 1791–1823 D'ISRAELI *Cur. Lit.* (1866) 25/2 Imitation by which an inferior mind becomes the monkey of an original writer. 1809 MALKIN *Gil Blas* IV. viii. ¶10 If she is stark mad for such a monkey as this. 1873 SYMONDS *Grk. Poets* viii. 256 Grote clearly thinks that Aristophanes was a meddling monkey.

b. Used as a term of playful contempt, chiefly of young people. Also *spec.* in various *slang* uses (see quots.).

1604 SHAKS. *Oth.* IV. i. 131 This is the Monkeys owne giuing out: She is perswaded I will marry her [etc.]. 1605 —— *Macb.* IV. ii. 59 Now God helpe thee, poore Monkie: But how wilt thou do for a Father? 1616 B. JONSON *Devil an Ass* II. viii, I cannot get my wife To part with a ring, on any termes: and yet The sollen Monkey has two. 1710 SWIFT *Jrnl. to Stella* 2 Nov., Well, little monkeys mine, I must go write; and so good-night. 1715 DE FOE *Fam. Instruct.* II. i. (1841) I. 170 Our master's son..is such a religious monkey. 1819 BYRON *Juan* I. xxv, A little curly-headed, good-for-nothing, And mischief-making monkey from his birth. 1849 THACKERAY *Pendennis* iii, The young monkey used to ride out..in quest of Dulcinea. 1876 RUSKIN *Let. to Yng. Girls* 8 Serve the poor, but, for your lives, you little monkeys, don't preach to them. 1895 'EDNA LYALL' *How Children raised Wind* i, Go to sleep, you monkeys, and don't worry your brains at this time of night. 1912 A. H. LEWIS *Apaches of N.Y.* xi. 225 'Did youse lobsters hear me handin' it to th'

monkeys?' he asked... 'That chink, Low Foo, snakes two of me shirts. I sends him five, an' he on'y sends back three. So I caves in his block wit' a flatiron.' **1914** JACKSON & HELLYER *Vocab. Criminal Slang* 59 *Monkey*, a man, used in the mildly indifferent sense of a stranger... Sometimes used to signify a 'boob'. **1928** *Amer. Mercury* Aug. 399/2 Several chorus girls from a Broadway show entered the room against the vigorous protests of the head waiter. One of the monkies, as they are called, sang and did an infinitely torrid dance. **1941** J. SMILEY *Hash House Lingo* 38 *Monkey*, dish washer. **1942** BERREY & VAN DEN BARK *Amer. Thes. Slang* §451/2 Plebeian,..*monkey*. *Ibid.* §460/5 *Monkey*,..a Chinese. *Ibid.* §511/3 (*Bridge*) *monkey*, a bridge builder. *Ibid.* §576/22 Orchestra leader,..*monkey*. **1966** [see sense 1 c above]. **1967** G. JACKSON *Let.* 2 Nov. in *Soledad Brother* (1971) 137, I am the object of the severest ridicule (coon, monkey, shoe..). **1970** P. LAURIE *Scotland Yard* 291 *Monkey*, *a*, an unpleasant person.

c. Slang phr. ***to make a monkey (out) of***: to make a fool of (someone); to deceive, dupe; to ridicule. orig. *U.S.*

1900 ADE *Fables in Slang* 164 His friends would stand and watch him make Monkeys of these anaemic Amateurs. **1900** F. P. DUNNE *Mr. Dooley's Philos.* 192 'Willum Waldorf Asthor has busted th' laws iv hospitality, an' made a monkey iv a lile subjick iv th' queen,' he says. **1931** M. ALLINGHAM *Police at Funeral* viii. 101, I don't want to put up any idea that isn't useful, and if I'm making a monkey of myself you mention it. **1932** KAUFMAN & RYSKIND *Of Thee I Sing* II. i. in *Famous Plays* (1933) 668 The man who ought to love me Tried to make a monkey of me. **1934** J. O'HARA *Appt. in Samarra* (1935) vii. 211 So then you turn around and pay him back by..making a monkey out of him right in his own spot. **1938** E. BOWEN *Death of Heart* I. v. 97 You make a monkey of me. **1952** [see AGIT-PROP]. **1973** 'M. INNES' *Appleby's Answer* xxi. 180 The plain fact was that Bulkington had..made a monkey of her. It was all very mortifying.

d. orig. *U.S.* A modern dance.

1964 [see DISCOTHÈQUE]. **1965** [see FRUG]. **1969** N. COHN *AWopBopaLooBop* (1970) ix. 85 Dance-crazes bossed pop right up until the Beatles broke. There was the Hully Gully, the Madison,..the Monkey. **1975** *Time* (Canadian ed.) 25 Aug. 49/1 The frug, the boogaloo, the monkey and similar 'hang-loose' mating rituals.

3. In Australia: = *monkey-bear* (see 18).

1847 CARPENTER *Zool.* §314 (1857) I. 352 The Phascolarctos or Koala..by the colonists..is usually termed the native Bear or Monkey.

4. a. *dial.* A young hare. **b.** *Australian.* A sheep.

1881 A. C. GRANT *Bush Life Queensland* vii. (1882) 66 No one felt better pleased than he did to see the last lot of 'monkeys', as the shearers usually denominated sheep, leave the head-station. **1889** *Fishing Gaz.* 7 Sept. 147/3 A young hare (or monkey, as they are called here [*sc.* on the Wye] at this time of the year). **1893** F. ADAMS *Austral.* 137 Now and then..you lit upon a 'mob' of the wild, timid, yet inquisitive 'monkeys' (sheep).

II. Applied to various machines or implements.

†**5.** A kind of gun or cannon. *Obs.*

1650 *Art. Rendition Edinb. Castle* 4, 28 Short Brasse Munkeys *alias* Dogs. 10 Iron Munkeys. **1663** *Flagellum, or O. Cromwell* (1672) 103 Twenty-eight Brass Drakes called Monkeys.

6. a. A machine consisting of a heavy hammer or ram working vertically in a groove and used in anchor-making and in driving bolts and piles. Also applied to the ram itself and to the hook by which it is raised.

1750 BLANCKLEY *Nav. Expositor*, *Monkey*, a Block made of Iron with a Catch, made use of in Ginns for driving Piles. **1794** *Rigging & Seamanship* I. 80 The *Monkey* is a machine for setting the arms, &c. It consists of a weight of about 200 lb.,..and a long iron shank suspended by an iron chain to a crane. **1823** CRABB *Technol. Dict.*, Monkey (*Mil.*), a machine which is used for driving large piles of wood into the earth. **1839** URE *Dict. Arts* 44 The junction, or shutting on, as the workmen call it, of the several members of an anchor, is effected by an instrument called a monkey. **1847** *Illustr. Lond. News* 16 Oct. 252/3 A pointed iron rod..took 46 blows of a monkey. **1855** OGILVIE, The monkey of a pile-driving machine is the double hook which takes up the ram. **1874** THEARLE *Naval Archit.* 135 The bolt is driven with an iron sliding ram, termed a 'monkey', an operation usually requiring four men. **1902** *Engineer* 19 Sept. 285 The snatch hook of the pile driver is the monkey whilst the falling weight is the ram.

b. *Mil.* The instrument which drives a rocket.

1885 in CASSELL. **1896** in FARMER *Slang*.

c. Short for *monkey-block* (see 18).

1833 MARRYAT *P. Simple* vi, 'What blocks have we below?'..I have a couple of *monkeys* down in the store-room.

7. Applied to various receptacles for liquor. (Cf. the phrase in 12 below.) **a.** A kind of wooden kid for grog. (Adm. Smyth.)

b. ? A hunting flask. *Obs.*

1852 R. S. SURTEES *Sponge's Sp. Tour* (1893) 309 Having ..filled his 'monkey' full of sherry, our friend Jog slipped out the back way to loosen old Ponto.

c. A globular earthenware water-vessel with a straight upright neck. Cf. MONKEY-POT 2.

1834 M. SCOTT *Cruise Midge* xvi. (1842) 301 That claret, Brail—and the monkey of cool water—thank you. **1875** KNIGHT *Dict. Mech.* 1166/2 The water-jars, or monkeys, used in tropical countries. These are merely unglazed earthenware jugs having a small neck and a spout. **1883** OLIVE SCHREINER *African Farm* II. viii, In the front room a monkey and two tumblers stood on the centre table.

8. a. A bricklayer's hod. (1885 in *Cassell's Encycl. Dict.*) **b.** (See quot.)

1886 *Good Words* 530 [Lucifer-match making.] The splints..are received in large cases and are transferred in batches of 20,000 or so on to trays, technically known as 'monkeys'.

9. *Mining.* (See quots.)

1883 GRESLEY *Gloss. Coal-mining* 170 *Monkey* (Lei.), an iron catch or scotch fixed in the floor of a way. **1888** W. E. NICHOLSON *Coal Trade Gloss.* (E.D.D.), *Monkey*, an arrangement placed between the rails at the head of an incline, which allows the wagons to pass over it in going up, but prevents them from running back.

10. A solution of zinc chloride, used as a flux in soldering.

1890 in *Century Dict.*

11. *Austral.* and *N.Z.* (See quots.)

1933 *Press* (Christchurch, N.Z.) 4 Nov. 15/7 *Monkey*, a handle made by putting a strap between two dees on a saddle and rolling it round itself. It is to hold on to when riding a bucking horse. **1945** BAKER *Austral. Lang.* iii. 71 A *monkey* or *monkey-strap*, a looped strap on the offside of a saddle pommel, used by inferior 'rough-riders'.

III. Colloquial and slang uses.

12. ***to suck*** (or ***sup***) ***the monkey***: (*a*) to drink from the bottle; hence, to tipple; (*b*) to drink out of a cocoa-nut emptied of milk and filled with spirit; (*c*) to drink spirits from a cask through a straw or tube inserted in a small hole.

1797 MRS. A. M. BENNETT *Beggar Girl* (1813) III. 253 Thee hast been sucking the monkey. *Ibid.* 270 A goodish wench in the main, if one keeps a sharp look-out after her, else she will sup the monkey. **1822** SCOTT *Pirate* xxxix, 'Why, he has sucked the monkey so long and so often', said the Boatswain, 'that the best of him is buffed'. **1833** MARRYAT *P. Simple* xxx, Do you know what 'sucking the monkey' means?.. It is a term used among seamen, for drinking rum out of cocoa-nuts, the milk having been poured out. **1842** BARHAM *Ingol. Leg.* Ser. II. *Black Mousquetaire*, Besides, what the vulgar call 'sucking the monkey' Has much less effect on a man when he's funky. **1868** *Star* 27 Mar., Three men..were charged with an offence called 'sucking the monkey', but in legal phraseology feloniously stealing, taking, and carrying away brandy from a cask in the London Dock. **1894** *Westm. Gaz.* 10 Dec. 5/3 'Sucking the Monkey'..was the cause of the death of a dock labourer... He had driven in the bung of a cask of brandy, and having had a good draught of the liquor, became unconscious.

13. a. ***monkey's allowance*** (see quots.).

1785 GROSE *Dict. Vulg. Tongue* s.v., *Monkey's allowance*; more kicks than halfpence. **1833** MARRYAT *P. Simple* ii, You'll find monkey's allowance—more kicks than halfpence.

b. Slang phr. ***cold enough to freeze the balls off a brass monkey***: extremely cold. Also in similar and allusive phrases.

[**1835** F. CHAMIER *Unfortunate Man* I. iv. 117 He was told to be silent, in a tone of voice which set me shaking like a monkey in frosty weather.] **1928** *Amer. Speech* IV. 123 Cold enough to freeze the tail off a brass monkey. **1937** PARTRIDGE *Dict. Slang* 528/2 Cold enough to freeze the balls off a brass monkey. **1972** *Evening Telegram* (St. John's, Newfoundland) 5 Aug. 3/1 Here's Smallwood still putting up a brass-monkey face right to the bitter end. **1973** *Guardian* 20 July 9 (*headline*) Brass monkey weather. *Ibid.*, You ought to buy yourself a brass monkey and then you will know what a freeze is.

c. ***I'll be*** (or ***I am***) ***a monkey's uncle***: a colloquial expression of surprise.

1926 MAINES & GRANT *Wise-Crack Dict.* 5/2 *Be a monkey's uncle*, be surprised. **1961** PARTRIDGE *Dict. Slang* Suppl. 1142/2 I'll be a monkey's uncle!

d. Slang phr. ***not to give*** (or ***care***) ***a monkey's*** (***fuck***, etc.): not to care at all; to be completely indifferent or unconcerned.

Even without the last bracketed word a fairly coarse expression.

1960 G. W. TARGET *Teachers* 100 The Old Man's door opened and the pair of them came out, Stillwell not seeming to give a monkey's, but too casual, and poor Jimmy Taylor with his hands clenched before him like the broken forelegs of a ginned rabbit. **1961** PARTRIDGE *Dict. Slang* Suppl. 1188/1 *Monkey's f*ck, not to care a*, not to care a rap; low (esp. Naval). **1968** M. WOODHOUSE *Rock Baby* xii. 116, I don't give a monkey's knee if he was with the Resistance or the Mafia. **1970** *Observer* 10 May 33/5 Tony Martin has booked himself a vasectomy... 'I was brought up a Catholic,' he said, 'but I don't give a monkey's; you've got to be practical.' **1972** J. BROWN *Chancer* iii. 44, I don't give a monkey's if you drop down dead. **1975** J. WAINWRIGHT *Square Dance* 26 'Not,' snarled Sugden, 'that I give a solitary monkey's toss what you wear.'

e. ***a barrel*** (***wagon-load***, etc.) ***of monkeys***: a type of something extremely cunning, mischievous, jolly, or disorderly, esp. in phr. ***as artful as a wagon-load of monkeys*** (and varr.). *colloq.*

1895 W. C. GORE in *Inlander* Dec. 115 *Barrel of monkeys*, or bushel of monkeys, *to have more fun than*, to have an exceedingly jolly time. **1930** G. GOODCHILD *McLean Investigates* xvi. 310 If once we lose touch with Feeny—good-bye to the Rajah's ruby. He is as clever as a cartload of monkeys. **1933** H. SIMPSON in 'A. Berkeley' et al. *Ask a Policeman* II. i. 106 Didn't I say you could never be up to Fate? Not if you were as clever as a wagon-load of monkeys with their tails burnt off. **1937** WODEHOUSE *Summer Moonshine* xvii. 194 His brother-in-law..was..as artful as a barrel load of monkeys. **1958** *Times* 14 Aug. 9/4 A wagon-load of monkeys is, as everyone knows, a conveyance filled to the brim with a superabundance of high spirits, artfulness, and mischief. **1968** A. POWELL *Mil. Philosophers* 155 They're as artful as a cartload of monkeys when it comes to breaking the rules. **1978** G. VIDAL *Kalki* ii. 24 Christianity was never exactly a barrel of monkeys when it came to the here and now. **1986** *Times* 28 Apr. 31/6 Plot-wise, it is as mischievous as a wagon-load of monkeys.

14. a. ***my monkey's up***: I am angry or enraged. So ***to get one's m. up***, ***to put*** (a person's) ***m. up***.

1833 B. WEBSTER *Golden Farmer* II. ii. 40 The Golden Farmer,..ven his monkey's up, vould go through me like a flash of lightning through a gooseberry bush. *c* **1852** J. R. PLANCHÉ *Good Woman in Wood* II. ii. 27 I'm short in stature —that I don't deny, But put my monkey up, I'm six feet high! **1863** *Tyneside Songs* 25 For when maw mungky's up aw gan The yell hog or nyen. **1873** *Routledge's Yng. Gentl. Mag.* June 433/2 My ole massa's monkey up, and no mistake. **1889** 'F. ANSTEY' *Pariah* II. iv, I always get my monkey up when I hear these swells laying down the law about indigo. **1880** 'OUIDA' *Moths* II. 91 I'm glad that girl put my monkey up about the coals.

b. ***to have a*** (or ***the***) ***monkey on one's back***: (*a*) to be angry or enraged (*obs.*); (*b*) orig. *U.S.*, to be a drug-addict (see also quot. 1942); hence ***monkey*** = addiction to, or habitual use of, drugs. *slang.*

1860 HOTTEN *Dict. Slang* (ed. 2) 174 A man is said to have his monkey up, or the monkey on his back, when he is 'riled', or out of temper. **1942** BERREY & VAN DEN BARK *Amer. Thes. Slang.* §509/28 *Have a Chinaman* or *monkey on one's back*, to manifest withdrawal distress. **1949** N. ALGREN *Man with Golden Arm* 60 He *wants* to carry the monkey, he's punishin' hisself..'n don't even know it. *Ibid.*, Then I got forty grains 'n went up to the room 'n went from monkey to nothin' in twenny-eight days 'n that's nine-ten years ago 'n the monkey's dead. **1960** C. L. COOPER *Scene* xii. 168 We're just little kids with the monkey and a couple bucks. Well, *our* monkey weighs just as much as yours, and it hurts just as much, and it takes the same stuff to get it off as it does yours! **1970** E. R. JOHNSON *God Keepers* (1971) vi. 61 An addict's greatest worry would not be his, since Vito would feed his monkey. *Ibid.* 68 Having a monkey on your back..always worked out logically to be the first purpose in a junkie's life. **1972** H. C. RAE *Shooting Gallery* iii. 204, I didn't have the monkey then. That's how I got started.

15. £500; in America, $500. *slang.*

The explanation in quot. 1832 is prob. erroneous; the German original has 'five pounds', but this sense is equally unauthenticated.

1832 tr. *Pueckler-Muskau's Tour of German Prince* III. xiv. 372, I won eight rubbers and two 'Monkeys'. What is a 'Monkey'? you ask... One for twenty-five pounds is called a Poney; and one for fifty, a 'Monkey'. **1861** WHYTE MELVILLE *Gd. for Nothing* xxviii. II. 31 A 'monkey' at least to the credit-side of your own book landed in about a minute and a half. **1881** *Standard* 23 Mar. 3/7 Dourance..was decidedly favourite, and after 500 to 45 had been noted to her name, nearly a monkey went on at 10 to 1. **1922** E. WALLACE *Flying Fifty-Five* x. 57, I lost a monkey on the last race, and a monkey on the Coventry. That's a thousand, isn't it? **1972** *Sunday Sun* (Brisbane) 9 Jan. 18/4 Lady from pub A told lady from pub B that the boss had given her a monkey as a bonus. Lady from pub B interpreted monkey as the slang term for $500 and immediately attacked her boss for his stinginess in only handing out $100. **1973** *Times* 9 Jan. 4/8 It looks like you are going to be roped into that theft from the pub but it will be all right. It will cost you a monkey (£500).

16. ***to have a monkey on a house***, etc.: to have a mortgage on it.

Common in northern and midland dialects: see E.D.D. Presumably suggested by the initial *m* of *mortgage*.

1877 *N. & Q.* ser. v. VIII. 289 A Monkey on the House. **1886** *Graphic* 10 Apr. 399/2 To a lawyer..a mortgage is a 'monkey with a long tail'.

IV. 17. *attrib.* and *Comb.*, as ***monkey appendage***, ***fur***, ***-god***, ***-kind***, ***-mimic***, ***-mischief***, ***-people***, ***-skin***, ***-tribe***; ***monkey-faced***, ***-led***, ***-looking***, ***-tailed*** adjs.; ***monkey-like*** adj. and adv.; ***monkey-fashion*** adv.

1795 SOUTHEY *Lett. fr. Spain* (1799) 6 The little boys wear the *monkey appendage of a tail. *a* **1864** HAWTHORNE *Amer. Note-bks.* (1879) I. 39 With something of the *monkey aspect inseparable from a little Frenchman. **1868** A. J. MUNBY *Diary* 7 Sept. (1972) 245 She sprang or climbed, *monkeyfashion. **1895** KIPLING *2nd Jungle Bk.* 218 When he tired of ground-going he threw up his hands monkey-fashion to the creeper. **1920** in C. W. Cunnington *Eng. Women's Clothing* (1952) v. 160 Afternoon frock..with..fringe of *monkey fur. **1960** *Sunday Express* 23 Oct. 14/5 The latest fur coat for cult-clothes addicts is in monkey fur. **1883, 1886** *Monkey-god [see HANUMAN 1]. **1962** *Listener* 22 Feb. 350/2 The monkey-gods of Stupidity, Mediocrity, and Servility to be always defied. **1774** GOLDSM. *Nat. Hist.* (1776) II. 101 Man's head..is differently formed from that of all other animals, the *monkey-kind only excepted. *a* **1843** SOUTHEY *Comm.-pl. Bk.* III. 809 Mankind at the lowest point where monkey-kind is at its highest. **1775** SHERIDAN *Rivals* II. i, But country dances!..to be *monkey-led for a night! **1611** COTGR., *Pierre du Coignet*, a *Monkie-like Image of stone in our Ladies Church at Paris. **1856** MACAULAY *Biog.*, *Johnson* (1860) 99 The master was often provoked by the monkey-like impertinence of the pupil. **1884** *Pall Mall Budget* 22 Aug. 14/2 Brown urchins swarm up trees monkeylike. **1834** M. SCOTT *Cruise Midge* xviii. (1842) 341 The *Monkey-looking paws. **1728** POPE *Dunc.* II. 236 The *monkey-mimics rush discordant in. **1778** P. THICKNESSE *Year's Journey* (ed. 2) II. xlv. 103 All [negroes] have a degree of monkey cunning, and even *monkey mischief. **1886** C. M. YONGE *Chantry House* I. xv. 142 He made no secret of his contempt for the insufferable dulness of the country, enlivening it by various acts of monkey-mischief. **1895** KIPLING *2nd Jungle Bk.* 140 Ere Mor the Peacock flutters, ere the *Monkey-People cry. **1910** W. DE LA MARE *Three Mulla-Mulgars* viii. 105 Mishcha and Môha..wouldn't touch *monkey-skin. **1962** E. E. EVANS-PRITCHARD *Ess. Soc. Anthropol.* v. 112 His head was covered with a monkey-skin cap. **1733** *Harmony in Uproar* in *Arbuthnot's Misc. Wks.* (1751) II. 25 The taunting Reproaches of this foul-mouth'd *monkey-tail'd Railer. **1728** POPE *Dunc.* II. 232 Three Cat-calls be the bribe Of him, whose chatt'ring shames the *monkey-tribe.

18. a. Special comb.: **monkey bag** (see quot.); **monkey band** = *monkey orchestra*; **monkey-bear**, the koala or native bear of Australia; **monkey-bird** (see quots.); **monkey-block**, 'a

small single block strapped with a swivel; also, those nailed on the topsail-yards of some merchantmen, to lead the buntlines through' (Smyth *Sailor's Word-bk.* 1867); **monkey-board**, a footboard at the back of a vehicle for a footman or conductor to stand on; **monkey-boat**, (*a*) and (*b*) see quots. 1858, 1867; (*c*) a long narrow canal boat; **monkey bridge** *Naut.* (see quots.); **monkey business** orig. *U.S.*, foolish, trifling, or deceitful conduct (cf. MONKEY *v.* 2); **monkey-chaser** *U.S. slang*, (*a*) a Negro from the West Indies or other tropical regions; (*b*) (see quot. 1952); **monkey coat** = *monkey-jacket*; **monkey-doodle business** *U.S. slang* = *monkey business*; **monkey-drift**, 'small prospecting drift' (Raymond *Mining Gloss.* 1881); **monkey-eating eagle**, also **monkey eagle**, the largest eagle found in the Philippine Islands, *Pithecophaga jefferyi*; **monkey-engine**, a form of pile-driver having a monkey or ram moving in a wooden frame (Knight *Dict. Mech.* 1875); **monkey forecastle** *Naut.* (see quot. 1948); **monkey-gaff** ? *U.S.*, a small gaff on some large merchant-vessels, placed above the spanker-gaff; **monkey gland**, a gland or testicle from a monkey, grafted on to a man as a possible means of rejuvenation; also *attrib.*; **monkey-hammer**, a jeweller's drop-press; **monkey-house**, a building in which monkeys are kept for show, as at zoological gardens; also *transf.* and *fig.*; **monkey-hurdler** *U.S. slang* (see quots.); **monkey island** *Naut. slang*, a small bridge above the pilot-house; **monkey-jacket**, a short close-fitting jacket, such as is worn by sailors; **monkey-man**, (*a*) *U.S. slang*, a weak and servile husband; (*b*) a man resembling a monkey; **monkey meat** *U.S. Army slang*, tinned meat; *spec.* tinned beef-and-potato hash; **monkey orchestra**, a group of Meissen or other porcelain figures representing monkeys playing musical instruments; **monkey** (or **monkey's, monkeys'**) **parade** *slang* (see quots.); also **monkey-parading** *vbl. sb.* and *ppl. a.*; †**monkey-pease**, wood-lice (cf. *monk's-peason*); **monkey poop** *Naut. slang* (see quot. 1929); **monkey pox**, a virus disease of monkeys (and of human beings), similar to smallpox; **monkey-press** = *monkey-hammer*; **monkey-pump**, 'straws or quills for sucking the liquid from a cask, through a gimlet-hole made for the purpose' (Smyth 1867); **monkey-rail**, a supplementary rail above the quarter rail; **monkey-rigged** *a.*, rigged with 'monkey-spars' (in quot. used for 'not full-rigged'); **monkey-rope**, a rope fastened to a sailor's waist-belt when he is working in a dangerous position; (see also 18 b below); **monkey's fist**, a thick knot made at the end of a rope to give it weight when it is thrown; **monkey shaft** *Austral.* and *N.Z. colloq.*, a small trial shaft; **monkey-shines** *pl.*, *U.S. slang*, monkey-like tricks or antics; also *sing.*; **monkey's island** *Naut. slang* = *monkey island*; **monkey-spars**, 'reduced masts and yards for a vessel devoted to the instruction and exercise of boys' (Smyth); **monkey('s)-tail**, a short hand-spike; 'a lever for training a carronade' (Smyth); **monkey strap** = sense 11 above; **monkey suit**, †(*a*) a type of child's suit (see quot. *a* 1901); (*b*) *slang* (orig. *U.S.*), a uniform; a formal dress suit, evening dress; **monkey's wedding** *S. Afr. colloq.*, a situation of alternating or simultaneous sunshine and rain; **monkey-trap** *colloq.* or *dial.*, something decorative worn by women to make themselves attractive to men; **monkey trial**, the trial in 1925 of a Tennessee school-teacher, J. T. Scopes, for teaching evolutionary theories; also *transf.* and *attrib.*; **monkey trick**, a mischievous, foolish, or underhand trick or act; an antic; usu. *pl.*; †**monkey-waist**, a waist resembling a monkey's; **monkey-wrench**, a wrench or spanner having a movable jaw; also *fig.*, esp. in colloq. phr. ***to throw*** (or ***hurl***) ***a monkey-wrench into the machinery***, etc.: to act as an obstruction or hindrance; to 'throw a spanner into the works'; hence as *v. trans.*, to turn with a monkey-wrench.

1847 H. MELVILLE *Omoo* xxxiv. 134 A small leather wallet—a '*monkey bag' (so called by sailors)—usually worn as a purse about the neck. **1934** W. B. HONEY *Dresden China* iv. 118 Some of the best known of all Meissen figures are the *Monkey Band.., an assemblage of more than twenty separate figures with a conductor, which is said to have been modelled in ridicule of Count Brühl's orchestra. **1891** 'ADA CAMBRIDGE' *Three Miss Kings* ii. 9 A little *monkey-bear came cautiously down from the only gum tree that grew on the premises. **1848** SCHOMBURGK *Hist. Barbados* 681 *Vireo olivacea* Wilson. The *Monkey Bird. **1861** DU CHAILLU *Equat. Afr.* xvi. 306 This little monkey is also a great favourite with the monkey-birds (*Buceros albocrystatus*), which I often saw playing with it. **1794** *Rigging & Seamanship* I. 156 *Monkey-blocks*...* This sort of blocks is sometimes used on the lower yards of small merchant ships, to lead (into the mast or down upon deck) the running rigging belonging to the sails. **1842** MRS. F. TROLLOPE *Vis. Italy* II. xxii. 366 The almost grotesque effect occasioned by..four laquais crowded on the *monkey-board. **1865** *Morn. Star* 11 Feb., The man..pursued the omnibus and again jumped on the step and endeavoured to get on the spare monkey-board. **1884** *Law Rep.* 12 Q.B. Div. 201 In consequence of a defect in the ironwork by which the 'monkey-board'..was supported, the plaintiff fell. **1858** SIMMONDS *Dict. Trade*, **Monkey-boat*, a boat employed in the docks. **1867** SMYTH *Sailor's Word-bk.*, *Monkey-boat*, a half-decked boat above-bridge on the Thames. **1882** *Standard* 26 Sept. 6/4 They had to cross a 'monkey-boat' to get to the barge. **1885** *Harper's Mag.* May 859/1 [On Regent's Canal]. We are in the midst of a little fleet of monkey-boats, deep down in the water with bricks and sand. **1927** G. BRADFORD *Gloss. Sea Terms* 115/2 **Monkey bridge*, usually above the pilot or chart house where the standard compass is commonly set. Sometimes the fore and aft bridge on a sailing ship. **1967** C. JOKSTAD *Captain & Sea* 100 We placed the body on the monkey bridge, which is the very after end or stern of the vessel. **1883** G. W. PECK *Peck's Bad Boy* 109 There must be no *monkey business going on. **1902** H. HAPGOOD *Spirit of Ghetto* vii. 209 The 'monkey business' of learning had ruined the child. **1934** C. DAY LEWIS *Hope for Poetry* vi. 29 A pandemonium of slogans, national anthems, headlines..manifestos, monkey business. **1972** 'H. CARMICHAEL' *Naked to Grave* vi. 79 Because I've seen her talking with one of the neighbours isn't to say there was any monkey-business between them. **1926** C. VAN VECHTEN *Nigger Heaven* 286 **Monkey-chaser*, a Negro from the British West Indies. **1952** *New Yorker* 30 Aug. 15/3 Monkey chasers are gin and ice, with a little sugar and a trace of water. That term 'monkey chaser' comes from Georgia. **1859** *Times* 27 Jan. 9/4 Jones was at the time dressed not as he now is, but in what they call a '*monkey coat'. **1928** *Sat. Even. Post* 12 May 41/2 They ought not to go abroad with such *monkey-doodle business. **1909** *Westm. Gaz.* 6 Sept. 5/3 The general plumage of the *Monkey Eagle is a rich brown above and creamy white in the under parts. **1909** R. C. MCGREGOR *Man. Philippine Birds* I. 226 (*heading*) *Pithecophaga jefferyi* Grant. *Monkey-eating eagle. **1966** R. & D. MORRIS *Men & Apes* vi. 204 The heavy-billed, shaggy-crested *Pithecophaga* eagle of the Philippines is popularly called the monkey-eating eagle. **1971** J. E. DUPONT *Philippine Birds* 47 (*heading*) Monkey-eating Eagle. **1873** *Rep. R. Comm. Unseaworthy Ships* 808/1 in *Parl. Papers* (C. 853) XXXVI. 315 Has a half poop and *monkey forecastle. **1948** R. DE KERCHOVE *Internat. Maritime Dict.* 473/1 *Monkey forecastle*, a short low forecastle open on the after side and used solely for anchor gear (windlass, and so on). **1883** *Century Mag.* Oct. 946/2 An answering pennant flying from her *monkey-gaff. **1924** G. B. SHAW *St. Joan* p. xix, Fortified..against old age by..weekly doses of *monkey gland. *Ibid.* p. xx, Which is the healthier mind? the saintly mind or the monkey gland mind? **1929** *Encycl. Brit.* XI. 747/2 The grafting into men of testicles from apes (the so-called 'monkey glands') has been practised by Voronoff and others with resulting rejuvenation. **1971** R. DENTRY *Encounter at Kharmel* iv. 72 Stop talking like Noel Coward after a shot of monkey glands! **1869** *Routledge's Ev. Boy's Ann.* 308 An instrument something like what in engineering is called a *monkey-hammer, but is known in the goldsmith's trade as a 'drop-down' or monkey press. **1854** *Zoologist* XII. 4283 The *monkey-house has been subjected to a course of cleansing. **1914** 'I. HAY' *Knight on Wheels* (ed. 2) xxiii. 221 The rooms..were described by the agent and Timothy as 'a lovely little bachelor suite' and 'a self-contained monkey-house' respectively. **1923** A. HUXLEY *Antic Hay* xvii. 246 The world would soon be a..bear-garden..and a monkey-house. **1924** J. BUCHAN *Three Hostages* ix. 131 It's up to the few sahibs like him in that damned monkey-house at Westminster to make a row about it. **1966** J. B. PRIESTLEY *Salt is Leaving* iv. 49 'Why do you have this window thing—here along the wall?' 'So I can see what's happening in my club... Come in later one night—..when it's all lit up down there—and you're looking through a window at a monkey house.' **1936** *Amer. Mercury* May p. x/2 *Monkey hurdler, organist. **1951** W. MORUM *Gabriel* II. ix. 250 Nelson's a monkey hurdler... He plays one of those Wurlitzer organs at the talkies. **1912** 'AURORA' *Jock Scott* xix. 243, I was on *Monkey Island (a pet name for the upper bridge) for hours. **1963** P. J. ABRAHAM *Last Hours* xi. 134 Up on the monkey island he had realized there would be no power for the lights. **1830** N. AMES *Mariner's Sk.* 187 My wardrobe consisted of a '*monkey' jacket, bought in Gravesend, [etc.]. **1840** R. H. DANA *Bef. Mast* xxiii, We always took our monkey-jackets with us. **1894** C. N. ROBINSON *Brit. Fleet* 515 In 1889 a monkey jacket took the place of the blue tunic. **1968** J. IRONSIDE *Fashion Alphabet* 37 *Monkey-jacket*. This was originally a warm, heavy, thick, jacket worn by sailors... But more usually now it refers to a shorter waist-length jacket similar to a bell-boy, middy or mess jacket. **1924** J. E. & L. MARTIN (*song-title*) *Monkey man. **1927** S. A. BROWN in C. Cullen *Caroling Dusk* 132 Had a stovepipe blonde in Macon Yaller gal in Marylan In Richmond had a choklit brown Called me huh monkey man—Huh big fool monkey man. **1928** *Collier's* 5 May 36/3 A money man is a contemptuous thing among Negroes, friendless, distrusted, and generally despised. But a monkey man! Well, there's nothing lower than a monkey man. **1935** E. R. BURROUGHS *Pirates of Venus* iii. 54 Venus was inhabited! But by what?.. Were they a species of monkey-man? **1960** P. OLIVER *Blues fell this Morning* 117 The man who is proud of his sexual prowess, real or imaginary, takes pleasure in ridiculing the 'monkey men': the West Indians and other Negroes that he despises whom he compares with the apes. **1966** *Southern Folklore Q.* XXX. 230 The Monkey Man is the servile mate who without protest turns over his hard-earned money to a woman... The husband who stayed and put up with it all became a Monkey Man and a standing joke. **1968** P. OLIVER *Screening Blues* vi. 258 The 'creeping man' and the 'monkey man' are objects of contempt in the blues, but they are the lovers who succeed when the singer fails. **1918** in Cowing & Cooper *Dear Folks at Home* (1919) x. 87 He was crying pitifully, and we gave him cigarettes and some of our *monkey meat and hardtack. **1919** *Red Cross Mag.* Feb. 37/1 When you hear the soldier's side of the story, his mess in camp and on the line consists of 'monkey meat' (canned beef-and-potato hash). **1929** *Papers Mich. Acad. Sci. & Arts* X. 309 *Monkey meat*, canned beef and potato-hash. **1906** R. L. HOBSON *Porcelain* xiii. 122 A Frenchman named Acier..worked at Meissen from 1764 till he was pensioned off in 1799, and modelled the celebrated Cries of Paris..and the *Monkey Orchestra. **1960** R. G. HAGGAR *Conc. Encycl. Continental Pott. & Porc.* 22/2 Monkey orchestra: a series of twenty-one porcelain figures of monkeys playing instruments with a conductor, modelled by Kändler at Meissen in 1747. **1910** H. G. WELLS *New Machiavelli* (1911) I. iii. 66 These twilight parades of young people, youngsters chiefly of the lower middle-class, are one of the odd social developments of the great suburban growths—unkindly critics..call them, I believe, *Monkeys' Parades. **1914** E. PUGH *Cockney at Home* 116 If you don't know what a monkey parade is ask Anderson here... 'It's a place where the elite of the beau monde of Suburbia meet nightly, for purposes of flirtation.' **1934** J. B. PRIESTLEY *Eng. Journey* iv. 183 Elderly citizens have been protesting against this practice of promenading on Sunday nights [in Bradford]. They have always been disgusted by the sight of young people *monkey-parading in this fashion... They could easily do it in a much more civilised fashion than this of monkey-parading. *Ibid.* 185 A Sabbatarian town of this kind, which could offer its young folk nothing on Sunday night but a choice between monkey-parading and dubious pubs. **1682** HARTMAN *Preserver & Restorer of Health* 47 Take a hundred *Monkey-pease, or Hoglice, those that roul themselves round when they are touched. **1929** F. C. BOWEN *Sea Slang* 92 **Monkey poop* [misprinted *poor*], the half deck of a flush decked ship. **1959** P. VON MAGNUS et al. in *Acta Path. & Microbiol. Scand.* XLVI. 156 The isolation of a virus from the diseased animals will also be described as well as some studies on the properties of the agent which in this paper will be referred to as *monkey pox virus. **1960** *Ann. N.Y. Acad. Sci.* LXXXV. 957 The etiological agent of monkey pox has been isolated from naturally infected animals by using both embryonated chicken eggs and tissue cultures. **1971** *Daily Colonist* (Victoria, B.C.) 25 Aug. 5/1 Monkey-pox, a disease very like smallpox, has been discovered for the first time in human beings in Africa. What caused the outbreak is a mystery. **1869** *Monkey-press [see *monkey-hammer*]. **1840** R. H. DANA *Bef. Mast* xxxv, [We] painted..the *monkey-rail, black, white, and yellow. **1900** *Scribner's Mag.* Sept. 290/1 Hanging over the monkey-rail in order to see as well as feel the quick answer of the vessel to her helm. **1882** *Daily Tel.* 12 Sept. 2/1 Most of the steamers nowadays are *monkey-rigged. **1851** H. MELVILLE *Whale* lxxii, The *monkey-rope was fast at both ends. **1927** G. BRADFORD *Gloss. Sea Terms* 115/2 **Monkey's fist*, a complicated knot with weight enclosed, used at the end of a heaving line. **1961** K. VONNEGUT *Sirens of Titan* (1967) i. 21 The hard, ball-like knot known as a *monkey's fist*. **1974** *Islander* (Victoria, B.C.) 29 Sept. 10/2 They were so high above us that we had to crane back our necks to look at them, waiting for the lethal lead-filled monkey's fists at the end of their lines to come whistling down. **1880** G. SUTHERLAND *Tales of Goldfields* 69 They began to think they might be already too deep for it, and a small '*monkey'-shaft was therefore driven upwards from the end of the tunnel. *c* **1832** T. D. RICE *Jim Crow* iii, I cut so many *munky shines, I dance de gallopade. **1847** 'H. FRANCO' *Trippings of Tom Pepper* I. vi. 43 Let me catch him cutting up any monkey shines in this house, and I'll bea[n] him! **1878** A. R. GROTE in *Pop. Sci. Monthly* XIII. 435 You may have noticed barefooted boys cutting up 'monkey shines' on trees with entire safety to themselves. **1894** F. R. STOCKTON *Pomona's Trav.* 76 Most of them played and cut up monkey-shines on the hay. **1932** R. FROST *Let.* 13 Dec. (1964) 231 In a way it was a monkey-shine and he needn't have minded poetry's having a little the best of it for once. **1945** Monkey-shines [see CUT *v.* 60 o]. **1973** 'H. HOWARD' *Highway to Murder* xi. 141 Why all the monkeyshines to get rid of Lucy? He'd been divorced before and he could be divorced again. **1917** 'TAFFRAIL' *Sub* iv. 110 He kept watch on the '*monkey's island'. **1919** W. LANG *Sea-Lawyers' Log* iii. 33 Now this 'ere is called the forebridge, and that little platform above it is the Compass Platform. Monkey's island, they calls it. **1833** MARRYAT *P. Simple* vi, Hand me that *monkey's tail. **1929** W. SMYTH *Bonzer Jones* i. 13 Put a *monkey strap on [the buck-jumper for riding]! **1886** C. M. YONGE *Chantry House* I. i. 9 Mrs. Gooch had only to thrust her hand into the little pocket of his *monkey suit to convict him on the spot. *a* **1901** —— *Autobiogr.* in C. Coleridge *C. M. Yonge* (1903) ii. 66 'Monkey suits', with jacket and waistcoat all in one, and trousers fastened over. **1920** R. LARDNER in *Sat. Even. Post* 27 Nov. 42/4, I and the Mrs. and Kate was the only ones there in evening clothes. The others had attended these functions before and knew that they wouldn't be enough suckers on hand to make any difference whether you wore a monkey suit or rompers. **1928** *Daily Mail* 7 May 6/4 *Monkey suit*, flying suit. **1950** DYLAN THOMAS *Let.* 10 Jan. (1966) 343, I..demothed my monkey-suit and borrowed some proper shoes. **1974** A. FOWLES *Pastime* v. 46 He could..hire one of those monkey-suits from Moss Bros. **1949** *Cape Times* 29 Nov. 16/3 The Peninsula had a '*monkey's wedding' rainfall yesterday with the sun shining at intervals and rain falling intermittently. **1961** *Ibid.* 8 Aug. 7 The weather was not exactly 'monkey's wedding' weather last week, sunshine alternating with a drizzle. **1931** W. DE LA MARE *Seven Short Stories* 85, I take you for an honest man's daughter with not a ha'penny to spare on fal-lals and *monkey-traps. **1925** *Evening Sun* (Baltimore) 26 June 17/3 Washington is getting the reflex of increasing European interest in the so-called *monkey trial. **1963** *Times* 30 Apr. 11/6 The student teachers, Miss Dori Doss and Miss Martha Powell, are apparently prepared for a second 'monkey trial' if necessary, though they realize that their determination could cost them their careers. **1969** D. F. HORROBIN *Science is God* ii. 15 It is associated more with the summer heat of the monkey-trial country of Tennessee rather than with the coolness of the dreaming spires of Oxford. **1653** W. DENTON *Let.* 13 Mar. in M. M. Verney *Memoirs* (1894) III. vi. 203 Bringe it [*sc.* a colt] with you in your coach, and then she will teach it all her *Monkey tricks. **1742** RICHARDSON *Pamela* (ed. 3) III. xxxiv. 408 Hold him fast, and play over all thy monkey tricks with him, with all my heart. **1809** MALKIN *Gil Blas* v. i. ¶90 Playing a hundred monkey tricks. **1864** BURTON *Scot Abr.* I. v. 315 Imitating by divers monkey-tricks, the holy ceremonies of the Mass. **1910** G. K. CHESTERTON *G. B. Shaw* 152 Shaw treats vengeance as something too small for man—a monkey trick

he ought to have outlived. **1951** Monkey trick [see DOT *v.*[1] 5]. **1958** C. ACHEBE *Things fall Apart* III. xxv. 184 He had warned Obierika that if he and his men played any monkey tricks they would be shot. **1604** ROWLANDS *Looke to it* (1872) 28 You with the Hood, the Falling-band, the Ruffe, The *Moncky-wast, the breeching like a Beare. **1858** SIMMONDS *Dict. Trade*, *Monkey-wrench. **1894** *Outing* (U.S.) XXIV. 132/2, I luckily had a pair of gas pliers in my valise which I used as a monkey wrench. **1904** W. N. HARBEN *Georgians* 267 He..dug down in the road whar his pipe j'ined the main, till he got to it, an' then he monkey-wrenched it off. **1920** *Everybody's Mag.* May 36/3 Don't throw a monkey-wrench into the machinery! **1931** *Daily Express* 16 Oct. 1/2 Mr. Lloyd George hurled a monkey wrench last night into the creaking and decrepit machinery of Liberalism. **1966** D. VARADAY *Gara-Yaka's Domain* xi. 126 Just as I was about to squeeze the trigger an ebb wind threw the monkey wrench into the works. The rising ill-wind struck the back of our necks, carrying our scent down to the elephant. **1971** *Black Scholar* Apr.–May 30/2 It is the black inmate who throws the monkey wrench into the works. **1975** *Jewish Chron.* 16 May 2/3 Mr Eban has thrown a monkey-wrench into the Israeli information campaign in the United States.

b. In names of fruits and plants: **monkey apple, apple-tree** (see quots.); **monkey-cup**, the pitcher-plant, genus *Nepenthes*; **monkey fiddle**, a West Indian tree or shrub, *Pedilanthus tithymaloides* or *P. angustifolius*, of the family Euphorbiaceæ; **monkey-flower**, the genus *Mimulus*; **monkey grass**, the fibre of *Attalea funifera*; **monkey guava**, *Diospsyos mespiliformis*; **monkey nut**, a name for the pea-nut, *Arachis hypogæa*; **monkey orchis**, *Orchis tephrosanthos*; **monkey-pod (tree)** = GUANGO; **monkey-puzzle**, a large, evergreen tree, *Araucaria araucana*, native to Chile and belonging to the family Pinaceæ, whose leaves are densely arranged to cover the whorled branches; also *fig.*; **monkey-puzzler** = *monkey-puzzle*; **monkey-rope** *S. Afr.*, one of several climbing plants, esp. *Secamone alpinii*, of the family Asclepiadaceæ; **monkey's dinner-bell**, the sandbox tree, *Hura crepitans*; **monkey-vine**, *Ipomea Nil*. Also MONKEY-BREAD, -FACE, -POT.

1823 *Trans. Hort. Soc.* (1824) V. 446 [Sierra Leone] *Monkey Apple. *Anisophyllea laurina.* **1833** *Penny Cycl.* I. 187/1 The monkey apple (*Anisophyllea laurina*) the drupe of which is, in flavour and size, between a nectarine and a plum. **1857** HENFREY *Bot.* §427 *Clusia flava* is called the Wild Mango, or Monkey-apple, in Jamaica. **1750** G. HUGHES *Barbados* 129 The *Monkey Apple-tree... The Fruit hath its Name from its being eaten by Monkeys. **1848** SCHOMBURGK *Hist. Barbados* 599 *Anona palustris* Linn. Monkey Apple Tree *Hughes.* **1845–50** MRS. LINCOLN *Lect. Bot.* 54 The pitcher-plant is a native of Ceylon, where it is called *monkey-cup. **1913** *Publ. Field Columbian Museum Bot. Ser.* II. 360 The peculiar silicious ridges of the stems and branches [of *Pedilanthus bahamensis*] produce a high squeak when they are rubbed together—children play at fiddling with them, hence the local name '*Monkey-fiddle'. **1954** *Caribbean Quarterly* III. I. 6 The duppy fiddle (more often called monkey fiddle) makes a grotesque squeaking when two sticks of it are rubbed together. **1789** W. AITON *Hortus Kewensis* II. 361 Mimulus... *Monkey-flower. **1796** C. MARSHALL *Garden.* xix. (1798) 344 Monkey flower, or American fox glove, blue. **1882** *Garden* 24 June 437/3 The ..dull *cupreus* section of Monkey flowers. **1858** *Monkey grass [see PIASSABA]. **1887** MOLONEY *Forestry W. Afr.* 522 *Monkey Guava. **1880** *Encycl. Brit.* XI. 221/2 Even in England large quantities of these '*monkey nuts' are consumed by the poorer children. **1892** ZANGWILL *Childr. Ghetto* I. iii, There was brisk traffic in toffy and gray peas and monkey-nuts. **1896** H. L. TANGYE *New S. Afr.* iv. 297 He brings a whole heap of sweet potatoes..and monkey nuts, the latter being sometimes known as ground, or pea-nuts. **1916** [see ARACHIS]. **1950** T. S. ELIOT *Cocktail Party* III. 142 *Alex.* Three of us have been out on a tour of inspection Of local conditions. *Julia.* What about? Monkey nuts? **1855** MISS PRATT *Flower Pl.* V. 209 *Monkey Orchis. **1888** W. HILLEBRAND *Flora Hawaiian Islands* 115 *Pithecolobium Sumang*, the Samang or *Monkey-pod tree, enjoys great favour as a shade tree. **1937** D. & H. TEILHET *Feather Cloak Murders* ix. 156 They drove down the scented street, overshadowed by the great leafy monkey pod trees which rustled in the night breeze. **1969** T. H. EVERETT *Living Trees of World* 203/1 The rain tree, monkey pod or saman.., an evergreen or deciduous native of the West Indies and Central America now planted in many other tropical regions ...has a wide-spreading, dome-shaped crown and grows up to 100 feet in height. **1866** *Reader* 9 June 566 Mr. Carruthers calls attention to the singular genus *Araucaria* (the '*monkey-puzzle' of ignorant gardeners). **1891** *Times* 7 Oct. 10/6 Cones of the monkey puzzle. **1923** DALLIMORE & JACKSON *Handbk. Coniferæ* II. 160 The common name of *Monkey Puzzle* is said to have originated in Cornwall... On one occasion when the owner of a plant was exhibiting it to friends a remark was passed to the effect that 'it would puzzle a monkey to climb that tree', and the owner forthwith adopted the name 'monkey puzzle'. **1938** *Times Lit. Suppl.* 14 May 342/2 The multitudinous little Careys of the future will have to be trained in mental agility on this veritable monkey-puzzle of a pedigree. **1940** [see CHILE]. **1969** T. H. EVERETT *Living Trees of World* 24/2 The dark green leaves of the monkey puzzle are broad, stiff, leathery and sharp-pointed. They overlap each other and clothe the curious, rather brittle snakelike branches closely. **1906** J. GALSWORTHY *Man of Property* III. iii. 298 In the shade of a *monkey-puzzler or in the lee of some india-rubber plant. **1936** E. WAUGH *Mr. Loveday's Little Outing* 9 The weather ..had suddenly blackened into a squall. There had been a scuttle for cover;..a table-cloth lofted to the boughs of the monkey-puzzler, fluttering in the rain. **1838** W. H. HARVEY *Genera S. Afr. Plants* 221 S[ecamone] *Thunbergii*... known by the colonial name of 'Babianstouw' or '*Monkey-rope', is a voluble [*sic*] climbing shrub, not uncommon in our woods. **1849** E. E. NAPIER *Excurs. S. Afr.* II. 369 Noble forest-trees, mostly connected together by various lianes and creepers —here called '*monkey ropes'. **1876** H. BROOKS *Natal* 125 The festooned stems of evergreen twiners hang down as 'monkey ropes'. **1907** T. R. SIM *Forests & Forest Flora Cape of Good Hope* 177 Both [species of *Vitis*] form 'Monkey-ropes', which, split up, are much used by the natives for tying down the thatch on hut-roofs. **1972** *Stand. Encycl. Southern Africa* VII. 515/1 Monkey-rope... (*Secamone alpinii.*) Plant of the family *Asclepiadaceæ*, a scrambler on bushes and trees. When it grows in a forest its old stems form the well-known 'monkey-ropes' hanging down from the trees. *Ibid.* 515/2 Other climbers, also called monkey- or bush-rope, are *Rhoicissus capensis* (monkey grapes), *Cynachum obtusifolium*, and *Dalbergia* spp. ('doringtou'). The runners of most of these plants are particularly strong and are therefore used by baboons and monkeys for climbing. **1849** BALFOUR *Man. Bot.* 495 The juice of *Hura crepitans*, Sandbox-tree, or *Monkey's dinner-bell, is also very acrid. **1750** G. HUGHES *Barbados* 168 *Monkey-Vine. **1848** SCHOMBURGK *Hist. Barbados* 612 *Ipomea Nil*, Pers. Monkey Vine *Hughes.* Blue Ipomea.

'monkey, *v.* [f. MONKEY *sb.*]

1. *trans.* **a.** To ape the manners of, mimic. **b.** To mock, make a jest of.

1859 MRS. BROWNING *Villafranca* viii, All cursed the Doer for an evil Called here, enlarging on the Devil,— There, monkeying the Lord! **1875** BROWNING *Aristoph. Apol.* Wks. 1896 I. 674/1 Then marched the Three who.. Monkeyed our Great and Dead to heart's content That morning in Athenai. **1892** PEYTON *Mem. Jesus* iii. 63 If man allows vanity, lust, vulgarity in his nature, he delivers himself to be mocked and monkeyed.

2. *intr.* To play mischievous or foolish tricks. Also, to fool or mess *about* or *around*; to waste time, or spend time aimlessly; to tamper *with*. So **'monkeying** *vbl. sb.* orig. *U.S.*

1881 I. M. RITTENHOUSE *Jrnl.* in *Maud* (1939) ii. 39 What with talking, running back and forth and general monkeying Clara slipped and fell. **1884** E. W. NYE *Baled Hay* 38 The young coyote may come and monkey o'er his grave. **1884** *Canon City* (Colo.) *Mercury* 22 Aug. 4/1 This reminds us of a sign in a Michigan planing mill, 'Dont Munkey with the Buz Saw.' **1886** *Chicago Advance* 9 Sept. 565 There can be no 'monkeying' with the issue. **1887** F. FRANCIS *Saddle & Mocassin* 143 It is just possible that I may have been monkeying with the cards a little. **1889** *Anthony's Photogr. Bull.* II. 188 His time is too fully occupied in 'monkeying' about his boat, sails and rigging. **1891** KIPLING & BALESTIER *Naulahka* vi, I don't see how you fellows have the time to monkey around here. **1916** *Dialect Notes* IV. 277 'What did you do after supper?' 'We just monkeyed around.' **1932** E. WAUGH *Black Mischief* v. 168 I'm not going to have any monkeying about with my men. You'll lame the whole army in a day if you try to make 'em wear boots. **1939** G. B. SHAW *Geneva* III. 98 A frontier is a frontier; and there must be no monkeying with it. **1955** *Times* 27 June 2/7 Any attempt to 'monkey about' with the powers or composition of the Upper House would destroy the balance of the constitution. **1957** *Times* 23 Sept. 11/1 Any departure from tradition form or colour would be as serious as monkeying about with the colour of an old school tie. **1972** J. W. THOMPSON in W. King *Black Short Story Anthol.* 257 Muhdear [*sc.* Mother] monkeyed with my collar again. And for what must have been the twentieth time, she smoothed my tie.

3. To dance the 'monkey': see MONKEY *sb.* 2 d. *U.S.*

1969 *New Yorker* 11 Oct. 50/3 Gamely they tried to Frug (or was it Monkey?) to the plangent anthems of a younger generation.

'monkey-bread. Also monkey's bread. The fruit of the baobab tree; the tree itself.

1789 W. AITON *Hortus Kewensis* II. 439 *Adansonia digitata*... Ethiopian Sour Gourd, or Monkies-bread. **1849** BALFOUR *Man. Bot.* §784 The Baobab tree of Senegal, or monkey-bread. **1897** MARY KINGSLEY *W. Africa* 149 Dr. Pélessier then insists on banging down monkey bread-fruit with a stick, to show me their inside.

'monkeyed, *ppl. a.* [f. MONKEY *sb.* + -ED[2].] Made like a monkey.

1790 J. WILLIAMS *Shrove Tuesday* in *A Cabinet*, etc. (1794) 29 Champanze humanis'd, and monkey'd man.

'monkey-face.

1. a. A face like a monkey's. Also *attrib.* Also, a person with a monkey-like or funny face.

1598 FLORIO, *Mona*, an ape, a munkie, a pug, a kittin, a munkie face. **1660** F. BROOKE tr. *Le Blanc's Trav.* 333 One ..made us good laughing, with his mows and monkey faces. **1681** T. FLATMAN *Heraclitus Ridens* No. 33 (1713) I. 214 Harry will..have his little Monkey-face mounted to adorn the top of the Amsterdam-Coffee-house. **1765** FOOTE *Commissary* I. Wks. 1799 II. 17 Doctor Catgut, the meagre musician; that sick monkey-face maker of crotchets. **1936** C. SANDBURG *People, Yes* lvi. 130 Where did ja cop dat monkeyface. *Ibid.* 131 Gwan monkeyface peddle yer papers. **1946** E. O'NEILL *Iceman Cometh* (1947) I. 17 Hello, leedle Rocky! Leedle monkey-face! I did not recognise you. *Ibid.*, Laugh, leedle monkey-faces! Laugh like fools, leedle stupid peoples! **1959** I. & P. OPIE *Lore & Lang. Schoolch.* ix. 171 A funny-faced person may also be called..'Monkey Face'.

b. A grimace. *West Indies colloq.*

1943 L. BENNETT *Jamaican Humour in Dialect* 3 For wen she laugh it like she Dah meck up monkey face. **1946** E. N. BURKE *Stories told by Uncle Newton* I. 31 The boys make monkey faces at me and I return the compliment with interest. **1952** S. SELVON *Brighter Sun* iv. 58 'Pewee, come an' go to school!' but Pewee made them a 'monkey face' and ran into the shop.

†**2.** The betel-nut. *Obs.*

1700 PLUKENET *Opera Bot.* (1769) III. 145 Palma Arecifera fructu compresso [etc.]. Hujus fructus Nucis..ex Angola allatus est, & à nostratibus *Monkey-face*, ibi dictus.

3. The monkey-faced owl. *U.S. colloq.* or *dial.*

1955 *Amer. Speech* XXX. 180 The barn owl is very generally called *monkey-faced owl*, a designation often shortened to *monkey face*.

So **'monkey-faced** *a.*: spec. *U.S.*, ***monkey-faced owl***, the barn-owl, *Tyto alba.*

1803 *Lett. Miss Riversdale* II. 284, I shall be so much my own enemy, as to take up with any monkey-faced battered rake. **1850** R. G. CUMMING *Hunter's Life S. Afr.* (1902) 14/1 This is a common failing among this monkey-faced race. **1915** J. BUCHAN *Thirty-Nine Steps* i. 12, I went home, dressed, dined at the Café Royal, and turned into a music-hall. It was a silly show, all capering women and monkey-faced men. **1917** *Dialect Notes* IV. 426 *Hibou paille*, the American barn owl (Aluco pratincolo): also called *monkey-faced owl*. **1955** [see MONKEY-FACE 3]. **1961** O. L. AUSTIN *Birds of World* 154/1 Barn owls differ from the typical owls in their heart-shaped facial disk, which is so simian in aspect that the birds are often called 'monkey-faced owls'.

monkeyfy ('mʌŋkɪfaɪ), *v.* Also 8 monkify. [f. MONKEY *sb.* + -FY.] *trans.* To make like a monkey; to make ridiculous-looking. Hence **'monkeyfied, 'monkeyfying** *ppl. adjs.*

1761 *Chron.* in *Ann. Reg.* 126 A parcel of prentice boys monkified in the same manner [*i.e.* 'frenchified up in the new mode']. **1834** M. SCOTT *Cruise Midge* x. (1842) 174 The people have so monkeyfied him that he is scarcely presentable on the quarterdeck. **1836** E. HOWARD *R. Reefer* xix, His features were compressed into a small monkeyfied compass. **1862** D. WILSON *Preh. Man* vii. 121 The very monkeyfying process to which some of the illustrations of inferior human types have been subjected in this pictorial chorography.

monkeyhood ('mʌŋkɪhʊd). [f. MONKEY *sb.* + -HOOD.] The condition or state of being a monkey; also monkeys collectively.

1846 G. MOORE *Power of Soul over Body* (1852) 9 The first man, was luckily evolved after passing through all the variety of monkeyhood, into a being fit to produce others like himself. **1873** L. STEPHEN *Ess. Freethinking* 266 The upright posture appeared at a certain period in the course of his development from monkeyhood.

monkeyish ('mʌŋkɪɪʃ), *a.* [f. MONKEY *sb.* + -ISH.] Like a monkey; resembling a monkey in imitativeness or mischievousness.

1621 BP. MONTAGU *Diatribæ* 11 Some Apish and Munkeyish as well as Lion-like diuels. **1830** ARNOLD in *Life & Corr.* (1844) II. App. C. 388 But monkeyish imitation will do no good. **1852** DICKENS *Bleak Ho.* xx, He drinks, and smokes, in a monkeyish way. **1882** 'F. ANSTEY' *Vice Versa* iv, Their [*sc.* boys'] monkeyish mischief.

Hence **'monkeyishness.**

1824 *Blackw. Mag.* XV. 263 This is the great excellence of Talma in tragedy—that he has little or none of the monkeyishness of his country. **1890** BARING-GOULD *In Troub. Land* iv, The Germans have a saying that the higher a monkey climbs the more he exposes his monkeyishness.

monkeyism ('mʌŋkɪɪz(ə)m). [f. MONKEY *sb.* + -ISM.] Monkey-like nature or character; behaviour characteristic of a monkey.

1845 *Blackw. Mag.* LVII. 51 The chattering and capering monkeyism of the Parisian exquisite. **1867** GOLDW. SMITH *Three Eng. Statesmen* (1882) 207 The religious middle classes were soon repelled by the impieties of the [French] revolution..all men of sense by its monkeyism and its madness.

'monkey-pot. Also monkey's pot.

1. The woody seed-vessel of the Brazilian tree *Lecythis ollaria*; the tree itself.

1849 BALFOUR *Man. Bot.* §867 *Lecythis ollaria*, a large Brazilian tree, yields the woody capsules called Monkey-pots. **1855** DALTON *Hist. Brit. Guiana* II. 201 Monkey's pot, *Lecythis grandiflora.* **1861** BENTLEY *Man. Bot.* 310 Pyxis of the Monkey-pot..with transverse dehiscence. **1871** KINGSLEY *At Last* xi, If nature has played the poor monkeys a somewhat tantalizing trick about Brazil nuts, she has been more generous to them in the case of some other Lecythids, which go by the name of monkey-pots.

2. A vessel used in tropical countries for cooling drinking-water. Cf. MONKEY *sb.* 7 c.

1897 GUNTER *Susan Turnbull* xxi. 265 Let him [the butler] remember that the rain-water for our drinking is to be well chilled in monkey-pots.

†**monkey'rony.** *Obs.* Alteration of MACARONI (in sense 2) by association with *monkey*.

1775 SHERIDAN *Rivals* III. iv, An' we've any luck we shall see the Devon monkeyrony in all the print-shops in Bath! **1786** MRS. A. M. BENNETT *Juvenile Indiscr.* III. 5 The sneaking crew of monkeyronies.

monkeyry ('mʌnkɪrɪ). *rare*[−1]. [f. MONKEY *sb.* + -RY.] A place where monkeys abound.

1826 H. N. COLERIDGE *West Indies* (1832) 201 The froggeries of France, the crabberies of Antigua, or the monkeries of Trinidad.

'monk-fish. [f. MONK *sb.*[1] Cf. Ger. *mönch.*]

1. The Angel-fish, *Squatina angelus.*

1610 GUILLIM *Heraldry* III. xxvi. (1611) 183 To these must be added Mantegres, Satyrs, Monk-fishes. **1672** JOSSELYN *New Eng. Rarities* 96 *Munk Fish*, a flat Fish like scate, having a hood like a Fryers Cowl. **1769** HEWSON in *Phil. Trans.* LIX. 205, I next went to Brighthelmstone, where I found kingston, or monk-fish, a species of skate. **1836** YARRELL *Brit. Fishes* II. 407 The Angel-fish..is also called Monk-fish, because its rounded head looks as if enveloped in a monk's hood. **1883** *Fisheries Exhib. Catal.* (ed. 4) 108 Monk Fish or Angel Shark, caught at Lynn, Norfolk.

2. The Angler, *Lophius piscatorius.*

1666 MERRETT *Pinax* 186 *Rana piscatrix*, the Monk, Toad, Nass, or Devil fish. **1880–4** DAY *Fishes Gt. Brit.* I. 74. **1884** [see MOLLIGUT].

Mon-Khmer (ˈməʊnk(ə)mɛə(r)). [f. MON *sb.*² and *a.* + KHMER *sb.* and *a.*] The designation of a group of Indo-Chinese languages, of which the most important are Mon and Khmer, spoken in south-east Asia and considered by some philologists to belong to the Austroasian family. Also *attrib.*, with reference to the peoples who speak these languages.

1887 *Trans. Philol. Soc. 1885–86* 428 The.. Indo-Chinese division and its two branches Mōn-Khmer, and Taï-Shan. *Ibid.* 435 The numerals and many words belong to the Mōn-Khmer family. **1904** G. A. GRIERSON *Linguistic Survey of India* II. 1 The Mōn-Khmēr languages are monosyllabic. **1932** [see KHMER *sb.* and *a.*]. **1933** [see AUSTRIC *a.*]. **1936** [see AUSTRO-²]. **1964** S. WAVELL *Naga King's Daughter* ii. 36 The Semelairs, whose unique language is Mon-Khmer, had lived on the lake as long as they could remember.

monkhood (ˈmʌŋkhʊd). [f. MONK *sb.*¹ + -HOOD.] The state, condition, or profession of a monk; the monastic life, monasticism. Also, monks collectively. So †**monkhede** [-HEAD].

a **900** tr. *Bæda's Hist.* v. xiii. [xii.] (1890) 434 þæt he in ðæt ȝemyndȝade mynster mid his bene innȝedon wæs & inn munuchade bescoren. *c* **1000** ÆLFRIC *Hom.* (Th.) II. 126 Æȝðer ȝe preosthades ȝe munuchades menn. **1303** R. BRUNNE *Handl. Synne* 201 Þat he forsake.. God of heuene and hys bapteme And alle þe godenesse of hys munkhede. *c* **1449** PECOCK *Repr.* IV. vii. 460 Dynys.. makith mensioun that the grete dukis of the chirche.. ordeyneden the religioun of monkehode to be had and vsid in the chirche. *c* **1450** *St. Cuthbert* (Surtees) 6410 He left all and to monkhede he pas. **1687** ATTERBURY *Answ. Consid. Spirit Luther* 25 He had left off his Monkhood too. **1740** HOR. WALPOLE *Ep. fr. Florence* 189 Nor the dark cloister's mystick rites display, Whence num'rous brawny Monkhoods waste away. **1839** LONGF. *Hyperion* I. vii. (1853) 47, I think the name of Martin Luther, the monk of Wittemburg, alone sufficient to redeem all monkhood from the reproach of laziness. **1854** MILMAN *Lat. Chr.* IV. vii. (1864) II. 344 Image worship in the mass of the people, of the whole monkhood. **1888** H. C. LEA *Hist. Inquis.* I. 252 The council had forbidden the formation of new orders of monkhood.

monkie, obs. form of MONKEY.

†**ˈmonking**, *ppl. a. Obs.* [f. MONK *sb.*¹ + -ING².] **a.** Living like monks. **b.** ? Harbouring monks.

1537 tr. *Latimer's Serm. bef. Convoc.* 8 Neither these be solitary, how religious, how mocking, how muncking, I would say; so euever they be. **1650** FULLER *Pisgah* II. xiii. 286 Behold here the large difference betwixt him [*sc.* John the Baptist] and monking Eremites. **1834** COLERIDGE *Table-t.* 31 May, The old cœnobitic establishments.. were converted.. into monasteries and other monking receptacles.

monkish (ˈmʌŋkɪʃ), *a.* [f. MONK *sb.*¹ + -ISH.]

1. Of or belonging to monks; monastic.

1546 BALE *Eng. Votaries* I. (1548) 42 b, Those .ii. hornes of that earthly Beast were here in Englande, the .ii. monkysh sectes that in those dayes fyrst entered. **1560** DAUS tr. *Sleidane's Comm.* 59 Men must be warned that they suffre not them selves to be bounden to Monkish vowes. **1587** *T. Norton's Calvin's Inst.* IV. xiii. 422 b, Only monkish life [is] termed perfection in the Papacie. **1617** MORYSON *Itin.* III. 212 Monkish vowes being against the word of God. **1781** COWPER *Charity* 43 Where wast thou then, sweet Charity?.. Wast thou in monkish cells and nunn'ries found? **1840** DICKENS *Old C. Shop* i, Fantastic carvings brought from monkish cloisters. **1843** BORROW *Bible in Spain* iii, Most of these men spoke of priestcraft and the monkish system with the utmost abhorrence. **1869** MCLAREN *Serm.* Ser. II. vi. 104 Sometimes you will find in an old monkish library the fair vellum that [etc.].

b. That is a monk.

1697 T. SMITH in *Lett. Lit. Men* (Camden) 243 The life of this Great Saint, written by an old Monkish author. **1859** C. BARKER *Assoc. Princ.* iii. 72 A Latin history.. written.. by a monkish historian, known as Geoffrey of Monmouth. **1881** WARREN *Celtic Liturgy* 56 A monkish pilgrim from the city of Constantinople.

c. Used, executed, or performed by monks.

1612 SELDEN *Illustr. Drayton's Poly-olb.* ix. 147 He.. is affirmed the same with Ine K. of Westsex in our Monkish Chronicles. **1646** EVELYN *Mem.* (1819) I. 229 A MS. in yᵉ old Monkish character. *a* **1761** CAWTHORN *Antiquarians* 62 Wrapp'd in a leaf of monkish Latin. **1833** CHALMERS in *Mem.* (1851) III. 410 Mr. Sparke.. invited me to the palace to see an old monkish painting. **1838** *Murray's Hand-bk. N. Germ.* etc. 63 [Utrecht is] in monkish Latin Ultra Trajectum, whence comes its modern name.

d. Suited to an establishment of monks.

1791 W. GILPIN *Forest Scenery* II. 144 The situation of Beaulieu-abbey is.. perhaps more monkish, than could easily have been found in the neighbourhood.

2. Resembling a monk or what pertains to a monk.

1577 tr. *Bullinger's Decades* (1592) 884 The greatest part of these monkish priests, doe nothing else but sing in the Church, and mumble masse. **1581** HANMER *Answ. Jesuit's Challenge* To Rdr. 2 In weede monkish, frierish, priestly and Pharisaicall. **1602** MARSTON *Ant. & Mel.* I. Wks. 1856 I. 14 A thinne lippe, and a little monkish eye. **1645** MILTON *Colast.* Wks. 1851 IV. 365 The exposition.. is the receav'd Exposition by all lerned men, unless it bee a Monkish Papist heer and there. **1849** DICKENS *Dav. Copp.* xxiii, 'What *is* a proctor, Steerforth?'.. 'Why, he is a sort of monkish attorney'. **1882–3** *Schaff's Encycl. Relig. Knowl.* II. 917 He lived like a monk... He was not monkish, though.

3. Characteristic of monks or the monastic system; chiefly in depreciatory sense, having the evil characteristics, features, or tendencies attributed to monasticism.

1570–6 LAMBARDE *Peramb. Kent* (1826) 231 By this and such other Monkish partes of theirs, you may see *Quid otium & cibus faciat alienus*. **1591** *Troub. Raigne K. John* (1611) To Gentlem. Rdrs. 70 Fond rashnesse murdreth first a Prince, And Monkish falsenesse poysneth last a King. **1625** N. CARPENTER *Geog. Del.* II. vii. (1635) 126 In such a Monkish age.—the most petty Inuentions were admired for great matters. **1641** MILTON *Animadv.* Wks. 1851 III. 190 Your Monkish prohibitions, and expurgatorious indexes. **1695** KENNETT *Par. Antiq.* Pref. (end), There be some, who slight and despise this sort of Learning, and represent it to be a dry, barren, Monkish studie. **1790** BURKE *Fr. Rev.* 149 This Gothic and monkish education. **1813** SHELLEY *Notes to Q. Mab* Poet. Wks. (1891) 44/1 Chastity is a monkish and evangelical superstition. **1863** RUSKIN *Munera Pulv.* Wks. 1872 II. 4 The monkish doctrine of the opposition of body to soul. **1864** BURTON *Scot. Abr.* II. i. 68 He.. is a monkish, bookish person, who meddles with nothing but literature.

Hence **ˈmonkishness**.

1882 in OGILVIE. **1900** *Daily News* 27 July 4/6 The monkishness of Henry the Sixth's portrait.

monkism (ˈmʌŋkɪz(ə)m). [f. MONK *sb.*¹ + -ISM.] The monkish system.

1716 M. DAVIES *Athen. Brit.* II. 272 Back again.. into their unavoidable Mahometanism, and consequentially Monkism, and judaical Papism. **1807** G. CHALMERS *Caledonia* I. II. vii. 318 The merit of Monkism now found its way into Western Europe. **1848** *Blackw. Mag.* Sept. 328 They have been sunk in the mire of their monkism.

monkly (ˈmʌŋklɪ), *a.* Now *rare.* [f. MONK *sb.*¹ + -LY¹.] Of or pertaining to a monk or monks; monastic.

a **900** tr. *Bæda's Hist.* V. xix. *title* (Schipper) 652 Ðætte Cynred Mercna cyning & Offa Eastseaxna cyning on munuclicum hadum to Rome becom. *c* **1375** *Sc. Leg. Saints* xviii. (*Egipciane*) 29 For sa ennornyt þat man was in monklyke vorke, vord, & dede,.. þat [etc.]. **1532** MORE *Confut. Tindale* Wks. 397/2 As Otho did in Almain which ranne oute of the charterhouse, &.. toke a wyfe for sobrenes and chastisyng of hys munkelye membres. **1548** G. WISHART tr. *Swiss Conf. Fayth* in *Wodrow Soc. Misc.* (1844) 22 We reject and refuse this monckely chastite. **1652** EARL MONM. tr. *Bentivoglio's Hist. Relat.* 73 But to return to the Monkly Order. **1893** *Month* Dec. 574 No longer monkly garbs, but dainty muslins or frilled confections, flit hither and thither.

Hence **ˈmonkliness**.

1887 I. TAYLOR in *Pall Mall G.* 8 Oct. 11/2 Islam.. replaced monkliness by manliness.

monkrie, -ry(e, obs. forms of MONKERY.

monkship (ˈmʌŋkʃɪp). [f. MONK *sb.*¹ + -SHIP.] **a.** The monastic system; monks collectively. **b.** With *poss. pron.* The personality of a monk.

1620 BRENT tr. *Sarpi's Counc. Trent* (1676) 634 All Catholick Writers do condemn Luther.. of Heresy, for saying that Monkship is a humane invention. **1716** M. DAVIES *Athen. Brit.* II. 159 For 'tis truly said of Mathew Paris, that his Monkship is at every body that comes in his way. **1861** BERESF. HOPE *Eng. Cathedr. 19th C.* v. 168 As society and monkship drew more apart from each other [etc.].

monk's-hood, monkshood (ˈmʌŋkshʊd). [Named from resemblance of form.]

1. A plant of the genus *Aconitum*, esp. *Aconitum Napellus*.

[Cf. Du. *monnikskap* (early mod.Du. '*Munckskappekens*, aconitum, hecatheis, vulgo cappa vel cucullus monachi', Kilian), Ger. *mönchskappe*.]

1578 LYTE *Dodoens* III. lxxix. 427 Blew Woolfs bane, or Monkes Hoode,.. is small... The flowers be as litle hoodes. **1597** GERARDE *Herbal* II. ccclx. 823 This kind of Woolfs bane, called *Napellus verus*, in English, Helmet flower, or the great Munks hood. **1629** PARKINSON *Parad.* 215 *Napellus verus flore cæruleo*, Blew Helmet flower or Monkes hood. **1634** T. JOHNSON tr. *Parey's Wks.* 805 The juice, fruit, and substance of *Napellus* [*marg.* or Monks-hood] taken inwardly, killeth a man the same day. **1845–50** MRS. LINCOLN *Lect. Bot.* 31 Such plants as have horned or hooded nectaries, as the Columbine and Monk's-hood, are mostly poisonous. **1872** OLIVER *Elem. Bot.* II. 130 Monkshood is very poisonous, and the root has been mistaken for Horse-radish,.. with fatal result.

2. Applied to species of the genus *Delphinium* (Larkspur); also, to *Dielytra Cucullaria* (Treas. Bot. 1866).

1597 GERARDE *Herbal* II. ccccxxvi. 924 In English Larkes spur.. and Munkes hoode. **1629** PARKINSON *Parad.* Table, Monkes hoode, or Larkes spurs. **1678** PHILLIPS, *Monkeshood*, a kind of flower called in Latin *Consolida Regalis*.

†**3.** *Anat.* The trapezius muscle. *Obs.*

1615 CROOKE *Body of Man* 773 The second is called *Cucullaris* or the Monkes-hood.. *Galen* calleth it *Trapezius* or the Table-muscle. **1683** SNAPE *Anat. Horse* IV. xxii. (1686) 193 The *Cucullaris* or Monk's Hood.

4. monkshood moth, book-name for *Plusia moneta*, which lives on the plant monkshood.

1882 W. F. KIRBY *Europ. Butterfl. & M.* (1903) Plate xli.

monk's rhubarb. [trans. med.L. *Rheubarbarum* (or *Rha barbarum*) *Monachorum*; cf. F. *rhubarbe des moines*.] A name for species of dock, *esp. Rumex Patientia* and *R. alpinus*.

1578 LANGHAM *Gard. Health* 197 Drinke one dramme of the roote of the garden Docke, or Monkes rubarb to purge withall. **1597** GERARDE *Herbal* II. lxxviii. 314 The Monkes Rubarbe is called.. of some *Rhubarbarum Monachorum*, or Monkes Rubarbe: because as it should seeme some Monke or other haue used the roote heereof in steed of Rubarbe. **1707** *Curios. in Husb. & Gard.* 280 *Hippolapathum* or Monks-Rhubarb. **1731** MILLER *Gard. Dict.* s.v. *Lapathum*, Round-leav'd Alpine Dock, by some call'd Monks Rhubarb. **1866** *Treas. Bot.* 998/1 s.v. *Rumex*. **1895** J. SHAW in R. Wallace *Country Schoolm.* (1899) 22 Plants, such as Monks' rhubarb and masterwort, of no value now, but formerly used in poor people's broth.

¶ Erroneously applied to the garden rhubarb, *Rheum Rhaponticum*.

1737 BRACKEN *Farriery Impr.* xxv. (1749) 216 *Rhaponticum* or Monk's Rheubarb. **1832** *Veg. Subst. Food* 310 Monk Rhubarb.. is.. a native of Asia..; we find it mentioned by Tusser as early as 1573, as being then cultivated in England.

Monmouth (ˈmʌn-, ˈmɒnməθ). *Hist.* Also 7 **Munmoth**. The name of a town in Gwent, Wales (formerly the county town of Monmouthshire), used *attrib.*

1. ***Monmouth cap***: a flat round cap formerly worn by soldiers and sailors.

1599 SHAKS. *Hen. V*, IV. vii. 104 The Welchmen.. wearing Leekes in their Monmouth caps. **1605** CHAPMAN, etc. *Eastw. Hoe* IV. F 3, Hurle away a browne dozen of Monmouth capps or so, in sea-ceremony to your bone voyage. **1640** HOWELL *Dodona's Gr.* 13 Sometimes you shall not see in the whole atmosphere from morning to night as much cloud as would line a Monmoth Cappe. **1641** *Arminian Nunnery* 6 They came to Church in round Monmouth Capps. **1644** SYMONDS *Diary* (Camden) 14 Bewdley. The onely manufacture of this towne is making of capps called Monmouth capps. **16..** *Song of Caps* in J. P. Collier *Roxb. Ball.* (1847) 173 The souldiers that the Monmouth wear. **1713** *Lond. Gaz.* No. 5182/4 The Caps that the Dutch Seafaring Men do generally wear, formerly called Monmouth Caps. **1777** *Maryland Jrnl.* 22 July (Th.), [He had on a] Monmouth cap, and old coarse shoes. **1938** A. L. MAYCOCK *Nicholas Ferrar* viii. 204 The three masters in their black gowns and Monmouth caps followed by the boys, two and two.

2. ***Monmouth cock***: a military 'cock' of the hat in vogue towards the end of the 17th century.

[Prob. named after James Duke of Monmouth, natural son of Charles II.]

1711 ADDISON *Spect.* No 129 ¶10 The smartest of the Country Squires appear still in the Monmouth-Cock. **1769** GRANGER *Biog. Hist. Eng.* II. 470 The Monmouth, or military cock of the hat, was much worn in this reign [*sc.* Charles II].

monn, variant of MUN *v.*, must.

monnestarie, obs. form of MONASTERY.

†**monnet.** *Obs. rare.* (See quot.)

1653 R. SANDERS *Physiognomie* 176 Little ears denote a good understanding, but they must not be of those ears which being little, are withall deformed, which happens to men as well as cattel, which for this reason they call Monnets; for such ears signifie nothing but mischief and malice.

monnick, monniker, varr. MONIKER.

monnyplies, variant of MANYPLIES.

‖**mono** (ˈmono), *sb.*¹ [Sp.] A boiler-suit, workman's overalls (see also quot. 1937).

1937 F. BORKENAU *Spanish Cockpit* ii. 123 The streets and cafés are full of militia, all of them dressed in their *monos*, the new dark-blue uniforms. **1965** C. D. EBY *Siege of Alcázar* (1966) i. 28 Many of them wore their regular overalls—loose-fitting blue boiler-suits called *monos*.

mono (ˈmɒnəʊ), *sb.*² and *a.* [The prefix MONO- abstracted from compounds in which it occurs.]

1. Colloq. abbrev. of MONOPHONIC *a.* 2; also as *sb.*, monophonic recording or reproduction.

1959 *Manch. Guardian* 4 Aug. 3/2 For the benefit of non-stereo collectors, most of these records have appeared also in mono. **1961** *Times* 1 July 11/5 The mono recording is fair enough. **1963** *Which?* Jan. 3/1 When a mono orchestral record.. is reproduced, the sound from any one instrument generally appears to come from much the same direction as all the other instruments. **1971** M. MCCARTHY *Birds of America* 24 'Did it *have* to be stereo?' Peter groaned, homesick for their old mono set. **1972** K. BONFIGLIOLI *Don't point that Thing at Me* ii. 16 The Flying Scotsman whooped stereophonically... I competed in mono. **1974** *Listener* 14 Feb. 219/2 A radio play with a surplus of stereo trickery is not likely to be well received by listeners on mono sets.

2. Colloq. abbrev. of MONONUCLEOSIS.

1964 *Amer. Speech* XXXIX. 120 The general student preoccupation with internal disorders and other forms of illness, especially around examination time (cf. the frequent references among students to *mono* for 'mononucleosis'). **1970** *New Yorker* 9 May 45/3 After three sleepless, cold nights.. he came down with something resembling mono. **1972** F. KNEBEL *Dark Horse* (1973) vi. 88, I had a chance to meet the Yugoslav ambassador last summer, but then I came down with mono.

mono: see MONOSABIO.

mono- (mɒnəʊ, məˈnɒ), before a vowel often **mon-**, repr. Gr. μονο-, combining form of μόνος, alone, only, sole, single, occurring in a number of words adopted from existing Greek compounds (as MONARCH, MONODY, MONOGAMY, MONOGRAM, MONOLOGUE, MONOPOLY), and hence used to form words, mostly scientific and technical, independently of a Greek original. The second element of these words is normally of Greek origin, but in recent formations *mono-* is often combined (instead of

UNI-) with a Latin element (as *monocellular*: see also 2 below), and occas. prefixed to an English word (as MONOLINE, MONO-RAIL). Many of these words have correlatives in *di-* (see DI- *pref.*²), *tri-*, *poly-*, etc. The more important will be found as Main words; others of less importance follow here.

1. General words: **monoalpha'betic** *a.*, denoting a cipher in which each letter corresponds to one letter of the normal alphabet. ‖**mon(o)anæs'thesia** *Path.*, anæsthesia of a single part. **mono'anthropism**, belief in the unity or indivisibility of mankind. **'monoblast** *Biol.* [a. G. *monoblast* (O. Naegeli *Blutkrankheiten und Blutdiagnostik* (ed. 3, 1923) 143): see -BLAST], a cell that develops into a monocyte. **mono'blastic** *a. Biol.* [Gr. βλαστ-ός sprout, bud], having a single germinal layer (*Cent. Dict.* 1890). ‖**mono'blepsia, -'blepsis** *Path.* [Gr. βλέψις vision], a state of vision in which objects are distinct only when one eye is used (Mayne *Expos. Lex.* 1856). **mono'branchiate** *a.*, having only one set of branchiæ or gills (*Syd. Soc. Lex.* 1891). **'monocable**, an aerial ropeway in which a single endless rope is used both to support the loads and to move them; usu. *attrib.* **mono'cardian** *a.* [Gr. καρδία heart], 'having a single heart, as fishes and reptiles' (Webster 1847). **mono'causal** *a.*, in terms of a sole cause. **mono'cellular** *a. Biol.* = UNICELLULAR; so **mono'cellule**, a unicellular organism (*Cent. Dict.*). **mono'centric** *a. Biol.*, having a single centre, as a cell; *Anat.* = UNIPOLAR. **mono'cercous** *a. Zool.* [Gr. κέρκ-ος tail] = *monomastigate* (*Cent. Dict.*). **monoci'stronic** *a. Genetics*, containing as much genetic information as is carried by a single cistron. ‖**monocho'rea** *Path.*, 'chorea limited to one area, as an arm' (*Syd. Soc. Lex.*). **monociliate, -'ciliated** *adjs. Zool.*, having a single cilium, uniciliate. **mono'clonal** *Biol.* and *Med.*, forming a single clone; derived asexually from a single individual or cell. **mono'cœlian** *a.* (and *sb.*) *Zool.* [Gr. κοιλία cavity], having the encephalocœle single; pertaining to the class *Monocœlia*, otherwise called *Leptocardii* (*Cent. Dict.*); so **mono'cœlic** (*-celic*), 'having a single cavity' (Mayne). **mono'colour** = MONOCHROME *sb.* 2 c. **mono-coloured** *a. rare*, having only one colour; also *fig.* **mono'condylar, -con'dylian, -con'dylic** *adjs. Zool.* [Gr. μονοκόνδυλ-ος single-knuckled, f. κόνδυλος knuckle], having one occipital condyle, as the skull of birds and reptiles; distinguished from DICONDYLIAN. **monoconso'nantal** *a.*, containing a single consonant. **mono'cormic** *a. Bot.* [Gr. κορμ-ός tree-trunk], having a single main axis of growth. **mono'crotic, mo'nocrotous** *adjs. Phys.* [Gr. κρότ-ος beat], of a pulse, having a single beat, not DICROTIC. **'monocrystal**, a single crystal; so **mono'crystalline** *a.*, consisting of or constituting a monocrystal. **mono'dentate** *a. Chem.* [L. *dentātus*: see DENTATE *a.*], (of a ligand) having only one point of attachment to a central atom. **mono'dermic** *a.* [Gr. δέρμα skin], having, or consisting of, a single dermal layer. **monodi'abolism** (*nonce-wd.*), belief in a single devil; cf *polydiabolism* (POLY- 1). **monodia'lectal** *a.*, speaking only one dialect; hence **monodia'lectally** *adv.* **monodi'ametral** *a. Math.*, term proposed for quartan curves with a single diameter. **monodichla'mydeous** *a. Bot.* [cf. MONOCHLAMYDEOUS], 'having indifferently either a calyx only, or both calyx and corolla' (*Treas. Bot.* 1866). **'monodiet**, a diet confined to one type of food. **monodi'mensional** *a.*, existing in or having only one dimension; linear. **monodi'metric** *a. Cryst.* = DIMETRIC. **monodi'sperse** *a. Physical Chem.*, (of a dispersed phase) present as particles all of the same mass; (of a sol) containing such a phase. **mono'distich** (*nonce-wd.*), a distich forming a complete poem. **mono'dynamous** *a. Bot.* [Gr. δύναμις power; after DIDYNAMOUS], having one stamen much longer than the rest (Mayne). **monoener'getic** *a. Physics*, (consisting of particles) of the same energy; emitting radiation all of one energy. **mo'nœstrous** *a. Zool.* [ŒSTRUM 2 b, ŒSTRUS 2 b] (see quot.). **'monofil, 'monofilament**, a single strand of man-made fibre; freq. *attrib.* **mono'flagellate** *a. Zool.* = *monomastigate*. **mono'functional** *a. Chem.*, having or corresponding to a single functional group per molecule. **mono'ganglial** *a. Path.* [see GANGLION 1], epithet of a bubo affecting only one gland. **monogangli'onic** *a.*, having a single ganglion (*Cent. Dict.*). **'monogerm** *a. Agric.*, (of a sugar-beet variety or seed produced by it) having or consisting of only one seed in each seed ball; (cf. *multigerm* s.v. MULTI- 3). **mono'glacial** *a.*, applied to the theory that there was only one ice age; so **mono'glacialism**, the monoglacial theory. **mono'glacialist** *sb.* and *a.*, (of or pertaining to) a supporter of this theory. **monogo'neutic** *a. Ent.* [Gr. γονεύ-ειν to beget], having only one brood a year (*Syd. Soc. Lex.*). **monogono'poric, -go'noporous** *adjs. Zool.* [Gr. γόν-ος generation + πόρ-ος passage], having only one sexual aperture or generative pore, as certain dendrocœle worms (*Cent. Dict.*); **mo'nolobite**, a trilobite in which the division into three lobes is not distinctly marked (*Ibid.*). **mono'lobular** *a. Path.*, having a single lobule or lobe. **mono'locular** *a. Bot.* and *Path.*, having a single cavity or cell, unilocular (Mayne). **'monolog** *Linguistics* (see quots.). **mono'mastigate** *a. Zool.* [Gr. μαστīγ-, μάστιξ whip], of infusorians, having a single flagellum, uniflagellate (*Cent. Dict.*). **monomero'somatous** *a. Zool.* [Gr. μονομερ-ής consisting of one part (μέρ-ος part) + σωματ-, σῶμα body], having the body formed of one segment, as the order *Monomerosomata* of *Arachnida* in Leach's classification (Mayne). **mono'mictic** *a.* [Gr. μικτός mixed], applied to a lake in which there is only one overturn each year. **monomine'ralic** *a. Petrol.*, composed of a single mineral. **mono'neuran** [Gr. νεῦρ-ον nerve], a member of Rudolphi's division *Mononeura* of animals with only a ganglionic nervous system (Brande 1842); so **mono'neurous** *a.*, belonging to this division (Mayne). **mono'personal** *a.*, having but one person (Worcester 1860, citing Meadows). **'monophane** *Min.* [Gr. μονοφαν-ής visible alone], obs. synonym of EPISTILBITE, prob. so named because it has one very distinct and brilliant cleavage (Chester). **mo'nophanous** *a.* [see prec.], 'similar in appearance' (Maunder 1830). **'monoplacid** *a. Zool.* [Gr. πλακ-οῦς flat cake], having but one madreporic plate, as a star-fish (*Cent. Dict.*). **mono'pleurid** [PLEURA], one of the family *Monopleuridæ* of bivalves. **mono'pleurobranch** *a.*, belonging to the sub-order *Monopleurobranchiata* of gastropods, which have gills only on one side; *sb.*, a member of this sub-order (*Cent. Dict.*); so **monopleuro'branchian** (Brande 1842), **monopleuro'branchiate** (*Cent. Dict.*). **monopneu'monian** *a.* (and *sb.*) *Zool.* [Gr. πνεύμων lung], belonging to the *Monopneumona* or fishes with one lung; so **mono'pneumonous** *a.* (*Cent. Dict.*). **mono'prostyle** *a.*, of a colonnade, consisting of a single row of columns placed in advance of the wall of a building. **monopte'rygian** *a.* (and *sb.*) *Zool.* [Gr. πτερυγ-, πτέρυξ wing, fin], belonging to the order *Monopterygii* or fishes with one fin (*Cent. Dict.*); so **monopte'rygious** *a.* (Mayne). **'monopulse**, used *attrib.* and *absol.* to designate (the mode of operation of) radar in which the direction (and usu. also the range) of a target is precisely determined from a single echo pulse that is detected using two or more adjacent aerials. **mono'pylean** *a.* (and *sb.*) *Zool.* [Gr. πύλη gate], belonging to the group *Monopyleæ* of radiolarians, which have a single pseudopodal opening (*Cent. Dict.*). **mono'schemic** *a. Pros.* [Gr. μονόσχημ-ος of but one form, f. σχῆμα form], consisting of one form of foot throughout (*Ibid.*). **'mono-sentence** *nonce-wd.*, a brief or insufficient sentence. **monoso'matic** *a. Cryst.* [Gr. σωματ-, σῶμα body] (see quot.). **mono'somatous** *a. Zool.* [see prec.], having a single body or cell, as a rhizopod (*Cent. Dict.*). **'mono-sound** *rare*⁻¹, an abrupt single sound. **'monospasm**, spasm confined to one side. **mono-spe'cific** *a. Biol.*, affecting or containing only one species. **'monostach, mo'nostachous, mono'stachyous** *adjs. Bot.* [mod.L. *monostachyus*, Gr. στάχυ-ς ear of corn], bearing a single spike. **mono'static** *a.*, (of radar) having a single aerial as both transmitter and receiver. **mono'stigmatous** *a. Bot.*, having but one stigma (Mayne). **'monostylous** *a. Bot.*, having but one style (Mayne). **monosympto'matic** *a. Med.*, having a single dominant symptom; also in *Psychol.* and more general use. **mono'telephone**, a telephone adapted for transmitting sounds of definite pitch; hence **monotele'phonic** *a.* (*Cent. Dict.*). **mono'thelious** *a. Zool.* [Gr. θῆλ-υς female], applied to species in which several males serve to fecundate a single female; polyandrous (*Ibid.*). **mono'thetic** *a.*, (*a*) *Philos.* [Gr. θετικ-ός positing, pertaining to a thesis], 'positing or supposing a single essential element' (*Ibid.*); (*b*) *Taxonomy*, (of a classification) having groups formed on the basis of a single characteristic, or a series of single characteristics; hence **mono'thetically** *adv.* **mo'notomous** *a. Min.* [Gr. τομ-ή cutting, section], having a cleavage distinct only in a single direction. **'monotower**, used *attrib.* and *absol.* to designate a crane whose jib is mounted on a single tower. **mono-un'saturated** *a. Chem.*, (of a compound) saturated except for one multiple bond (usu. between carbon atoms) at which addition can normally occur. **mono'xenic** *a. Parasitology* [Gr. ξένος stranger], applied to a culture, or the cultivation, of a parasitic organism in the presence of a single other species. **mono'xenous** *a. Parasitology* [a. G. *monoxen* (A. de Bary 1867, in *Bot. Zeitung* XXV. 264/1), f. Gr. ξένος stranger], of a parasitic plant or animal: restricted to a single host species during its entire life-cycle.

1927 *Daily Express* 24 Nov. 13 The most simple code is the '*monoalphabetic', in which a letter is always represented by the same sign, letter, or numeral. **1893** DUNGLISON *Med. Lex.* (ed. 21) *Monanæsthesia. **1899** *Allbutt's Syst. Med.* VII. 302 The co-existence of brachial monoplegia with brachial monoanæsthesia. **1950** A. HUXLEY *Themes & Variations* 259 The best antidote to nationalistic idolatry is a monotheism with its corollary (since God's fatherhood implies men's brotherhood) of *monoanthropism. **1925** *Contrib. Embryol. Carnegie Inst. Washington* XVI. 241 Naegeli.. derives the monocyte from the myeloblast of the bone-marrow.. and terms this young cell the '*monoblast'. **1938** H. DOWNEY *Handbk. Hematol.* I. v. 386 Ehrich has taken.. exception to Bloom's conclusion that monoblasts other than lymphocytes and myeloblasts do not exist. **1968** PASSMORE & ROBSON *Compan. Med. Stud.* I. xxvi. 12/2 These cells [*sc.* monocytes] are produced mainly in the spleen and lymph nodes. The parent cell, the monoblast, is like the myeloblast and lymphoblast, a cell of about 15 μm in diameter with a large nucleus, containing 2–3 nucleoli, filling much of the cell cytoplasm. **1926** H. BLYTH *Mod. Telpherage & Ropeways* xiii. 111 The *mono-cable system has been developed very extensively in this country, and although formerly considered as being suitable only for light duty and small gradients, has now proved to be quite suitable for capacities up to 150 tons per hour and gradients of 1 in 2½. **1958** I. C. F. STATHAM *Coal Mining Pract.* II. vii. 509 The Mono-Cable is the oldest and simplest, being first used in Dantzig in 1644. **1964** *Economist* 14 Nov. 745/2 Using [for bridges] a mono-cable instead of dual cable suspension. **1973** *Gloss. Terms Materials Handling* (*B.S.I.*) VII 8 *Mono-cable trestle*, a structure supporting a mono-cable ropeway between the ropeway stations. **1957** C. HUNT *Guide to Communist Jargon* xxiv. 86 Lenin's doctrine illustrates the weakness of *monocausal explanations of highly complex phenomena. **1972** R. PLANT in Cox & Dyson *20th Cent. Mind.* I. v. 161 Weber conceded that an economic interpretation of history and social life was possible, but he was not willing to accept any monocausal view in its entirety. *Ibid.* 165 Against the Marxist monocausal view of history therefore, Weber poses a far more complex picture. **1859** *Todd's Cycl. Anat.* V. [129/2] The simpler and *monocellular Algæ. **1880** W. S. KENT *Infusoria* I. 99 The monocellular unimpregnated ovum. **1878** tr. *Gegenbaur's Comp. Anat.* 597 If the rete remains broken up, then it is known as a diffuse, unipolar, or *monocentric rete mirabile. **1887** H. M. WARD in *Nature* 27 Jan. 301/2 A complexity is introduced as soon as the sap-vacuoles appear, in many cases making the cells not monocentric but polycentric. **1866** H. J. CLARK in *Amer. Jrnl. Sci.* XLII. 324 The *monociliate *Flagellata.* **1857** *Ann. Nat. Hist.* Ser. II. XIX. 260 A group of *monociliated Monads. **1880** W. S. KENT *Infusoria* I. 145 The normal, small, monociliated and uniciliated sponge-cells. **1965** *Proc. Nat. Acad. Sci.* LIV. 1193 For these purposes, one would prefer a *monocistronic message containing information for only one protein. **1972** *Nature* 21 Jan. 131/2 Each segment is transcribed into a single messenger RNA and at least eight of these ten molecules are translated as monocistronic messengers. **1914** W. E. AGAR in *Phil. Trans. R. Soc.* B. CCV. 422 When a population is known to have been descended asexually from a single common ancestor, it consists of a single clone and may be described as *monoclonal. *Ibid.* 442 The monoclonal population was descended from 70 original ancestors, themselves all descended parthenogenetically from a single known female. **1973** *Sci. Amer.* Aug. 44/1 Are the plaque cells transformed cells, in which the genetic material has somehow become changed from that of the normal cell population? If so, the plaque cells could be expected to be monoclonal: a homogeneous population derived from a single cell, rather than a mixed population of cells as in normal human tissue. **1963** *Listener* 31 Jan. 220/2 The idea of using full orchestra was avoided... To paint a picture which should have universality of expression.. the *monocolour of strings seemed the only possible medium. **1798** *Trans. Soc. Arts* XVI. 284 A *mono-coloured substance. **1955** *Times* 25 June 5/6 The parties of the extreme left and those of the right favour a 'mono-coloured' Government.. since such a one-party Government.. would be more or less permanently at the mercy of right or left. **1890** *Century Dict.*, **Monocondylar*, **Monocondylian*. **1891** FLOWER & LYDEKKER *Mammals* iii. 83 The former [the Anomodontia] have become *monocondylic by [etc.]. **1948** D. DIRINGER *Alphabet* x. 161 The consonantal principle and the selected symbols to represent *mono-consonantal words were used by the Egyptians at the beginning of the third millennium B.C. **1965** *Canad. Jrnl. Linguistics* Spring 154 In other cases we find monoconsonantal roots in one language cognate with biconsonantal forms in the other.

1899 *Nature* 9 Nov. 28/1 Following Vöchtung, the author recognises two principal types—the *monocormic and polycormic respectively... The common spruce fir is an example of a monocormic conifer. 1891 *Syd. Soc. Lex.*, **Monocrotic*, a term applied to the pulse in which the dicrotic wave is absent. 1877 ROBERTS *Handbk. Med.* (ed. 3) II. 22 Among the principal dangerous signs are a marked dicrotous or *mono-crotous pulse. 1934 *Rev. Sci. Instr.* V. 402/2 *Monocrystals with dimensions of the order of 10 cm were readily produced. 1946 *Nature* 10 Aug. 199/2 The X-ray density must be related to monocrystals, and if indeed the starch grain were a monocrystal the numbers found might be considered as a proof. 1973 *Ibid.* 16 Nov. 124/1 Of future plans perhaps the most striking was V. Braginsky's.. idea of using a massive monocrystal instead of an aluminium bar with a resultant very high quality factor to look for the sort of signals astronomers expect from nearby galaxies. 1934 *Rev. Sci. Instr.* V. 402/2 The test showed the main body of the growth to be *monocrystalline with the seed. 1946 *Nature* 24 Aug. 261/1 An extensive study was made by R. Jacquersson on the effect of torsion on a monocrystalline rod. 1968 C. G. KUPER *Introd. Theory Superconductivity* vi. 97 Pippard..made measurements with a number of monocrystalline cylindrical specimens of tin. 1949 KIRK & OTHMER *Encycl. Chem. Technol.* IV. 382 Monofunctional ligand groups..are sometimes known as unidentate or *monodentate groups. 1974 *Jrnl. Inorg. & Nuclear Chem.* XXXVI. 1221/1 The behaviour of ethylenediamine as a monodentate ligand has also been reported in a few other cobalt..and chromium..complexes. 1891 *Syd. Soc. Lex.*, **Monodermic*, having an envelope or skin consisting of one layer only. 1897 *Nature* 7 Oct. 555/2 The elements which constitute the mono-dermic outer wall of the cœlom. 1880 SPALDING *Eliz. Demonology* 17 *Monodiabolism being as impossible as monotheism. 1972 J. L. DILLARD *Black English* iii. 85 Reading and writing almost pre-suppose a certain degree of mastery of Standard English, since nothing was written for the *monodialectal speaker of Plantation Creole. 1964 *Archivum Linguisticum* XVI. 73 Martinet ..[distinguishes] two senses of the term *dialect*: dialect$_1$, a variety of a language..used *monodialectally within a whole language area,..and *dialect*$_2$, a local dialect within a larger dialect$_1$ area. 1872 *Brit. Assoc. Rep.* II. 23 On *Monodiametral Quartan Curves. By F. W. Newman. 1920 *Chambers's Jrnl.* 1 May 349/2 No matter what the advocate of a mixed-food diet may say to the contrary, there is no disputing the fact that the nearer one gets to the *mono-diet the better the health will be. 1953 'I. DEVI' *Forever Young Forever Healthy* v. 61 The mono-diet..is the kind of diet where you eat only *one* type of food. It makes no difference whether it is only milk,..or anything else. 1952 *New Biol.* XII. 100 Besides such two-dimensional layers of more or less loosely fixed molecules there certainly must exist some analogous linear phenomena along the edges of crystals, and this would make *monodimensional strings or chains of adsorbed particles. 1959 *Brno Studies in English* I. 31 The monodimensional character of spoken utterances..as opposed to the..polydimensional character of written utterances. 1854 *Pereira's Polarized Light* (ed. 2) 196 The pyramidal, the tetragonal, or the *monodimetric system. 1925 G. BARGER tr. *H. Freundlich's Elements Colloid Chem.* 132 The preparation of colloidal solutions containing particles of uniform size—so-called unidisperse (*monodisperse) sols—is mostly very difficult. 1940 GLASSTONE *Text-bk. Physical Chem.* xiv. 1232 By means of the ultracentrifuge it has been found that many protein solutions are monodisperse. 1971 *Europ. Jrnl. Biochem.* XXIII. 575 The binding of human serum albumin by monodisperse latex particles was studied. 1825 CARLYLE *Schiller* III. (1845) 154 The plan was that it [the *Xenien*] should comprise an immense multitude of detached couplets, each conveying a complete thought... It was at first intended to provide about a thousand of these pointed *monodistichs. 1950 GLASSTONE *Sourcebk. Atomic Energy* xi. 310/1 Another source of *monoenergetic neutrons is the $Li^7(p,n)Be^7$ reaction, the energy of the incident protons being carefully controlled. 1954 *Sci. News* XXXIII. 41 If, therefore, we bombard a nucleus of a particular element with a monoenergetic beam of particles, the nuclei which are excited as a result of the collisions taking place will have a wide range of excitation energies. 1971 *Nature* 3 Dec. 261/1 This factor can be experimentally determined through the use of mono-energetic gamma-ray sources. 1900 HEAPE in *Q. Jrnl. Microsc. Sci.* Nov. 16 There are two forms of sexual season evident in female mammals; the *monœstrous, in which there is only a single œstrus at one or more particular times of the year (bitch), and the polyœstrous, in which there are two or more concurrent diœstrous cycles at a particular time of the year (mare). 1916 CROSS & BEVAN *Text-bk. Paper-Making* (ed. 4) i. 10 The [cellulose] solution has been extensively applied to the production of artificial threads of high lustre, so-called 'artificial silk', and various grades of *Monofil (*Crin, Crinole*). 1940 *Times* 21 Mar. 5/5 The other two factories will convert the raw material into intermediate products—monofil at the works of I.C.I. [etc.]. 1972 *Trout & Salmon* June 58/2 Nylon monofil slips more easily through the rod-rings. 1949 *Mod. Plastics* Nov. 69/1 Nylon *monofilaments are well established as a material for bristles. 1960 *Aeroplane* XCVIII. 43/3 The chafer covering the bead is of monofilament nylon, as in the case of all other Firestone tubeless tyres, to prevent capillary action of the air and so assist in the maintenance of pressure. 1960 M. SHARCOTT *Place of Many Winds* vii. 115 These lures..are attached to nylon monofilament lines in varying lengths. 1973 *Sci. Amer.* Dec. 134/1 New forms of nylon rope without stretch (a braided sheath around a monofilament core) are used for the long, dark climb. 1880 W. S. KENT *Infusoria* I. 310 A simple *monoflagellate organism. 1898 SEDGWICK *Student's Text-bk. Zool.* I. 36 Monoflagellate forms. 1946 *Jrnl. Amer. Chem. Soc.* LXVIII. 360/2 The *monofunctional trimethylchlorosilane acts as a growth terminating agent or 'chain-stopper'. 1949 [see *monodentate* adj. above]. 1964 *Brit. Med. Bull.* XX. 91/1 The carcinogenic action of a series of monofunctional ethyleneimines. 1971 *Nature* 10 Dec. 324/1 When the number of bonds was anything less than twelve, the bifunctional reagent was able to react with only a monofunctional stoichiometry. 1974 *Analytical Chem.* XLVI. 344 (*heading*) Potentiometric titration of monofunctional bases in ion exchanger-aqueous solution medium. 1861 BUMSTEAD *Ven. Dis.* (1879) 401 It is very rare for more than a single gland on one or both sides to suppurate specifically; and hence the virulent bubo is said to be '*monoganglial'. 1950 *Proc. Amer. Soc. Sugar Beet Technologists* VI. 156 *Monogerm sugar beet varieties have not been developed in either Europe or America. Failure to develop such varieties is due to difficulties in detecting monogerm plants. 1971 *Farmers Weekly* 19 Mar. 38/3 Modern monogerm varieties mean there is less worry about bolting than before. 1972 *Nature* 21 Jan. 136/2 Larks still destroy young seedlings, spaced scientifically and grown from monogerm seeds. 1914 W. B. WRIGHT *Quaternary Ice Age* vi. 125 We are bound to take our stand on the comparatively simple *monoglacial hypothesis until we can prove at least one interglacial period. 1961 L. D. STAMP *Gloss. Geogr. Terms* 323/1 The monoglacial theory considers the Pleistocene ice-sheet to have expanded and contracted in only one general movement without any substantial 'interglacial periods' of recession followed by advance. 1957 J. K. CHARLESWORTH *Quaternary Era* II. xxxvi. 920 Upholders of *monoglacialism are becoming fewer, and discussion is turning more and more upon the number of the epochs rather than upon the question of their existence. 1959 F. E. ZEUNER *Pleistocene Period* ii. 54 (*heading*) Monoglacialism. 1914 W. B. WRIGHT *Quaternary Ice Age* vi. 125 The Cyprina Clays of Denmark..were referred by Geikie..to one of the interglacial periods, but..it was very justly held by the *monoglacialists that they might easily be of preglacial age. 1946 *Antiquity* XX. 10 Controversy raged with considerable acrimony between the monoglacialist and polyglacialist exponents of Pleistocene geology. 1968 R. W. FAIRBRIDGE *Encycl. Geomorphol.* 458/2 For a long time, a considerable controversy persisted between monoglacialists and polyglacialists, eventually to be conclusively won by the latter. *Ibid.* 913/1 For a long time, there was a minority belief in only one glacial epoch, the so-called monoglacialist school, and a few representatives still survive. 1888 *Lancet* 26 May 1043 The cirrhosis is at first *monolobular. 1929 H. E. PALMER *Rep. Res. Activities 1928–9 Inst. Res. Eng. Teaching* (Tokyo) 9 Each of these white spots is a word, that which is contained in a ring is not a *word* but a *word-family*. .. I propose to call the spots *monologons* and the rings *monologemes* (the termination *on* suggests the individual unit, and the termination *eme* suggests the group unit..). There are times however when..instead of the cumbrous 'monologons or monologemes' we may use the convenient common form **monologs*. 1947 H. BONGERS *Hist. & Princ. Vocab. Control* I. iii. 56 The vocabulary of a language consists of:..Units neither more nor less than single words written without a break... These have been conveniently termed '*monologs*'. 1956 *Proc. Nat. Acad. Sci.* XLII. 84 For the three categories of Forel's classification [*sc.* polar, temperate, and tropical] the terms cold *monomictic, dimictic, and warm monomictic have been used by one of us [*sc.* Hutchinson]..in a forthcoming extensive work on limnology. 1957 G. E. HUTCHINSON *Treat. Limnol.* I. vii. 438 It is..proposed to use the term dimictic for any lake circulating twice a year; warm monomictic will be employed as a substitute for tropical, implying winter circulation above 4°C; and cold monomictic as a substitute for polar, implying summer circulation below 4°C. 1968 R. W. FAIRBRIDGE *Encycl. Geomorphol.* 603/2 The monomictic lake waters [of Lake Atitlán, in Guatemala] appear to be fully circulating in the dry season, but Deevey (1957) found that in August the temperature at the surface is 24°C versus 20°C at the bottom. 1917 *Jrnl. Geol.* XXV. 243 The inquiry gives considerable support to the belief that the *monomineralic rocks..are generated by the process of collection of crystals under the action of gravity. 1956 *Mineral. Mag.* XXXI. 120 Specimens (24) to (28) inclusive are practically monomineralic rock specimens from which small, platey single crystals may be obtained. 1970 *Nature* 17 Oct. 258/2 The extreme composition range of the lunar sprays can be most readily explained by solar flares melting minute, essentially monomineralic particles on the lunar surface. 1865 WATTS *Dict. Chem.* III. 1047 **Monophane*. 1903 GEIKIE *Text-bk. Geol.* VI. III. iii. (ed. 4) 1170 The families of *Monopleurids..and Hippuritids. 1843 *Civil Eng. & Arch. Jrnl.* VI. 330/2 The advanced or *monoprostyle colonnade in the centre is 200 feet in length. 1955 *IRE Convention Record* VIII. 132/2 A third method for generating both positive and negative errors simultaneously..is known as *monopulse radar, since all information on range and angle errors is generated from each single pulse. This very satisfactory name was proposed by Bell Telephone Laboratories engineers. 1965 D. K. BARTON in R. S. Berkowitz *Mod. Radar* vii. 603 (*heading*) Operation of amplitude-comparison monopulse. *Ibid.* 598 In return for the added complexity in the receiving and antenna system, the monopulse radar offers reduction in tracking errors caused by target scintillation, an improved data rate.., and efficiency in overcoming thermal noise errors on distant targets. 1966 *McGraw-Hill Encycl. Sci. & Technol.* VIII. 577/2 An additional advantage of monopulse tracking as compared to conical scan is that no mechanical action is required in monopulse. 1970 *Sci. Jrnl.* May 46/1 Modern radars, such as those of the chirp or monopulse types, need compression filters to convert long shallow pulses into tall brief ones and expansion filters to do the opposite. 1817 KEATS *Let.* Mar. (1931) I. 13 Your kindness affects me so sensibly that I can merely put down a few *mono-sentences. 1888 TEALL *Brit. Petrogr.* 440 **Monosomatic*, a term applied to crystals and their inclusions when both belong to the same mineral species. 1875 *Gentl. Mag.* XV. 445 His laugh—with an abrupt, short, *monosound—more like a short gasp or snort than a laugh. 1899 *Allbutt's Syst. Med.* VII. 291 The *monospasms or protospasms of Jacksonian epilepsy. 1951 WHITBY & HYNES *Med. Bacteriol.* (ed. 5) xvii. 293 One such *mono-specific serum thus appropriately prepared will only agglutinate *Br*[*ucella*] *melitensis*. 1964 A. L. THOMSON *New Dict. Birds* 309/2 Flocks may be mono-specific or composed of several species. 1970 *Nature* 22 Aug. 779 (*caption*) *Digenea subarticulata*..belongs to a genus formerly thought to be monospecific. 1974 *Ibid.* 1 Nov. 78/2 The reactivity of the DeV reagent was abolished by previous incubation with a monospecific rabbit anti-human IgG serum. 1819 *Pantologia*, **Monostach caulis*, in botany, a stem bearing a single spike. 1850 OGILVIE, **Monostachous*. 1775 J. JENKINSON tr. *Linnæus' Brit. Plants* 254 **Monostachyous* [wrongly explained, 'consisting of but one range or order']. 1856 MAYNE *Expos. Lex.*, *Monostachyous*. 1957 R. WATSON-WATT *Three Steps to Victory* xxii. 128 We had already erected a direction-finding hut so close to the others as to show that we were..confidently counting on wholly *monostatic working. That is to say we would obtain all the information required from a sector of our front by observations made at a single site accommodating both transmitter and receiver. 1973 *Nature* 9 Mar. 109/2 Some work has been reported in which a steerable monostatic radar has been pointed obliquely in several directions successively, so as to measure more than one velocity component. 1899 *Allbutt's Syst. Med.* VIII. 119 Charcot thinks..that in children the usual stigmata [of hysteria] are often absent and the disease is '*monosymptomatic'. 1937 G. W. ALLPORT *Personality* (1938) p. ix, Cultural determinism is one of the monosymptomatic approaches; it has a blind spot for the internal balancing factors and structural tenacity within personality. 1965 Monosymptomatic [see *conversion hysteria*]. 1972 H. J. EYSENCK *Psychol. is about People* iii. 111 Her patients were all..suffering from serious and complex phobic anxieties; there were no monosymptomatic cases. 1962 P. H. A. SNEATH in Ainsworth & Sneath *Microbial Classification* 291 Special classifications are usually based on single characters, or on a series of single characters... Beckner..calls such groups monotypic, because the defining set of features is unique, but since monotypic has other meanings, *monothetic is a better term. 1965 *Math. in Biol. & Med.* (Med. Res. Council) III. 82 (*caption*) Group Y is monothetic, and is subdivided monothetically. 1969 E. MAYR *Princ. Systematic Zool.* iv. 83 When the definition of the logicians—'individuals sharing common characters'—was replaced by 'members of a group having descended from a common ancestor', a monothetic characterization of a taxon was no longer necessary. 1835 SHEPARD *Min.* I. p. xxxi, Pearl Kerate..1 Hexahedral..2 Pyramidal..3 *Monotomous. 1938 *Engineer* 3 June 615/1 Messrs. Butters Brothers are showing..a '*Monotower' electric crane. 1953 *Dock & Harbour Authority* XXXIV. 88/2 The design of the mast for the monotower crane. 1963 *Engineering* 19 Apr. 532 During erection as a monotower up to 90 ft, the crane grows from the bottom. 1971 B. SCHARF *Engin. & Its Lang.* xvi. 230 Monotower cranes..consist of a latticed tower surmounted by a derrick crane. 1972 J. R. ILLINGWORTH *Movement & Distribution Concrete* vi. 84 With monotowers, full circle slewing is obtained, but static base operation limits coverage to the area swept out by a particular jib length. 1939 *Thorpe's Dict. Appl. Chem.* III. 241 (*table*) Fully saturated triglycerides... *Mono-unsaturated-di-saturated glycerides. 1950 *Analytical Chem.* XXII. 1261/1 Extinction coefficients..are reported for seventeen pure cis and trans mono-unsaturated and saturated acids, esters, and alcohols. 1965 E. D. WILSON et al. *Princ. Nutrition* (ed. 2) v. 35 The quantity of the monounsaturated fatty acids in the average American diet matches that of the saturated ones, about 40 per cent. 1953 E. C. DOUGHERTY in *Parasitology* XLII. 259/2 Such an expression as 'two-membered culture' becomes '*monoxenic culture'. 1969 *Oikos* XX. 287 (*heading*) The monoxenic cultivation of some rhabditid nematodes. *Ibid.* 288/1 Some nematode species were studied under controlled conditions on monoxenic agar cultures. 1940 B. G. CHITWOOD in J. R. Christie *Introd. Nematology* II. iv. 243/2 Parasites of animals may also be classified according to the number of hosts necessary for completion of the life cycle. Species in which there is a single host are termed *monoxenous. 1962 W. P. ROGERS *Nature of Parasitism* x. 219 A specific parasite (sometimes called species-specific or monoxenous) can live on or in one species of host only. 1973 N. D. LEVINE *Protozoan Parasites* (ed. 2) i. 5/1 A monoxenous parasite has only one type of host—the definitive host. *Ibid.* 5/2 The term monoxenous parasite is used by some authors for a parasite which is restricted to a single host species.

2. *Chem.* Used in the names of compounds to signify the presence of a single atom or combining equivalent of the element or radical indicated by the word to which *mono-* is prefixed. Also used to indicate monomeric compounds (e.g. *mononucleotide* below). **monoetha'nolamine**, 2-aminoethanol $H_2NCH_2CH_2OH$, a viscous high-boiling liquid used in making detergents; **mono'glyceride**, any compound consisting of glycerol esterified at only one of its hydroxyl groups; **mono'nucleotide** [ad. G. *mononucleotid* (Levene & Mandel 1908, in *Ber. d. Deut. Chem. Ges.* XLI. 1906)], any of the compounds whose molecules are formed from a single molecule each of phosphoric acid, a sugar, and a heterocyclic base, and are the units of which nucleic acids are composed; a monomeric nucleotide.

PROTO- has also been used with the same meaning. The nomenclature is regularly continued in the series *di-*, *tri-*, *tetra-*, *penta-*, *hexa-* (see HEXA- and HEX-), *hepta-*.

The more important of these names are treated as main-words: see MONACETIN, MONAMIDE, MONETHYL, MONOCHLORIDE, MONOXIDE, etc.; also MONOBROMO-, MONONITRO-, etc. With a like sense are formed MONACID, MONATOMIC, MONOBASIC, MONOVALENT. A free use of the prefix is illustrated here in **mono-compound** (see quot.); **mono-substitution**, substitution affecting only one of the elements or radicals in a compound; **mono-substituted** *a.*, formed by mono-substitution.

1865 WATTS *Dict. Chem.* III. 1047 **Mono-compounds*. This term is applied to compounds containing 1 at. of the element specified. 1929 *Chem. Abstr.* XXIII. 3232 If 352 parts of ethylene oxide is added to 3400 parts of 25% aq. NH_3 at 10°, *monoethanolamine is obtained. 1959 *Times Rev Industry* Jan. 67/1 The CO_2 removed by scrubbing with monoethanolamine is used as a purge gas. 1972 *Materials & Technol.* IV. xv. 516 Since monoethanolamine reacts more readily with ethylene oxide than does ammonia, excess of the latter and careful control of the ethylene oxide concentration is essential for appreciable amounts of the mono-alcohol to be formed. 1860 H. DEBUS in *Q. Jrnl. Chem. Soc.* XII. 243 (*heading*) *Monoglycerides. 1926 G. D. ELSDON *Edible Oils & Fats* iv. 17 The β monoglycerides

have been prepared by using dichlorhydrin. **1954** E. W. Eckey *Veg. Fats & Oils* iv. 143 An important practical application of alcoholysis of fats is the preparation of monoglycerides which are used in shortenings to improve their cake-making properties and as emulsifiers... Monoglyceride mixtures are prepared also as a first step in the manufacture of oil-modified alkyd resins, and in the preparation of certain detergents. **1972** *Lipids* VII. 433/1 Palmitic, stearic and oleic acids were the predominant fatty acids present in the monoglycerides. **1908** *Jrnl. Chem. Soc.* XCIV. I. 587 The composition of the thyminglucophosphoric acid is almost identical with that of heminucleic acid.., and may be considered to be a *mononucleotide. **1956** *Nature* 11 Feb. 271/1 Preparations or fractions of ribonucleic acid were hydrolysed in *N* potassium hydroxide to mononucleotides. **1968** H. Harris *Nucleus & Cytoplasm* iii. 55 The mononucleotides released from this material by alkali hydrolysis are contaminated with other compounds. **1974** *Nature* 1 Nov. 75/2 The data show total ^{32}P c.p.m. in the RNA and in the triphosphate termini as mononucleotides and pppNps released by KOH hydrolysis of that RNA. **1889** *Nature* 26 Sept. 539/2 On the constitution of *monosubstituted derivatives of camphor, by M. P. Cazeneuve. **1881** Watts in *Nature* 15 Dec. 148/1 The saturated hydro-carbons..are first described; next their *mono-substitution derivatives. **1885** Remsen *Org. Chem.* (1888) 131 The lactic acids..will be shown to be mono-substitution products of propionic acid.

mono-acetin, -acid: see MONACETIN, -ACID.

monoamine (mɒnəʊˈeɪmiːn). *Biochem.* [f. MONO- 2 + AMINE.] **a.** Any compound having a single (primary, secondary, or tertiary) amine group in its molecule, *spec.* one which is a neurohormone; = MONAMINE.

1951 I. L. Finar *Org. Chem.* I. xiii. 260 Diamines may be prepared by methods similar to those for the monoamines, using alkylene halides instead of alkyl halides. **1965** J. Pollitt *Depression & its Treatment* iv. 53 Monoamines are neurohormones regarded as essential for normal activity of the brain. **1972** *Nature* 31 Mar. 225/2 There is much evidence pointing to changes in monoamine metabolism in mental illnesses characterized by alterations in mood.

b. *Comb.* **monoamine oxidase**, the enzyme or group of enzymes that brings about the oxidation (and consequent inactivity) of monoamines in the body; **monoamine oxidase inhibitor**, any of a class of drugs which inhibit the functioning of monoamine oxidase (so allowing accumulation of serotonin and noradrenaline in the brain), some of which are used as antidepressants.

[**1943**: cf. MONAMINE.] **1951** *Proc. Soc. Exper. Biol. & Med.* LXXVIII. 157/1 Despite numerous investigations of its enzymatic function, monoamine oxidase has not been significantly purified. **1962** *Lancet* 29 Dec. 1343/1 There is a strong impression that iproniazid is clinically more effective in relieving depression than other monoamine-oxidase inhibitors. **1965** J. Pollitt *Depression & its Treatment* iv. 47 Methedrine and other amphetamines are incompatible with monoamine oxidase inhibitors. **1973** *Nature* 6 Apr. 417/1 Roulston, studying the action of chlordimeform and related compounds on the southern cattle tick, suggested that inhibition of monoamine oxidase (MAO) could be involved.

monoanæsthesia: see MONO- 1.

monoao, var. MANOAO.

mono-articular: see MONARTICULAR.

monoaxal (mɒnəʊˈæksəl), *a. Physics.* [f. MONO- + AX-IS + -AL[1].] (See quot.)

1890 *Century Dict.*, *Monoaxal*, pertaining to a single axis. *Monoaxal isotropy*, the case in which the homotatic coefficients are completely isotropic round one axis only.

monobasic (mɒnəʊˈbeɪsɪk), *a. Chem.* [f. MONO- + BASE *sb.*[1] + -IC.] Having one base, or one atom of a base. Of an acid: Containing one atom of replaceable hydrogen. Also = MONATOMIC.

1842 T. Graham *Elem. Chem.* 167 Monobasic salts. **1849** D. Campbell *Inorg. Chem.* 140 Solutions of bibasic or mono-basic phosphate of soda. **1862** Miller *Elem. Chem.* (ed. 2) III. 52 Monatomic or monobasic elements, one atom of which is in combination equivalent to..one atom of hydrogen. **1869** Roscoe *Elem. Chem.* (1871) 349 Formic acid is monobasic.

monoblastic, -blepsia, -blepsis: see MONO- 1.

monobloc (ˈmɒnəʊblɒk), *a.* (*sb.*) [Fr. (1906 in Robert); cf. MONO- 1 and BLOC(K *sb.*] Made as, or contained within, a single casting. Also as *sb.*, a monobloc engine.

1909 *Westm. Gaz.* 2 Nov. 5/1 The engine of the 20-h.p. model..is of the monobloc order. **1929** *Radio Times* 8 Nov. 448 (Advt.), Batteries beyond present standards... Above is the LDG, 2v. 60 a.h... Below: the monobloc 10v. DMHG with special elements. **1930** *Engineering* 26 Sept. 401/3 The cylinders form a monobloc casting. **1944** *Jrnl. R. Aeronaut. Soc.* XLVIII. 365 In liquid-cooled engines, separate steel cylinders were generally abandoned in favour of monobloc light alloy castings. *Ibid.*, At the outbreak of the present war the monoblocs in use were still not entirely satisfactory. **1963** *Engineering* 2 Aug. 140/3 Of monobloc construction, the new pump is available in cast iron. **1972** *Shooting Times & Country Mag.* 24 June 14/2, I must confess to being disappointed that our top-flight English gunmakers..do not offer an alternative. I visualise a self-opening boxlock, with monobloc barrels, [etc.].

monobranchiate: see MONO- 1.

monobromated (mɒnəʊˈbrəʊmeɪtɪd), *a. Chem.* [See MONO- 2 and BROMATE.] Said of organic compounds in which one atom of bromine has been substituted or added in each molecule.

1889 *Cent. Dict.* s.v. *Camphor*, Monobromated Camphor.

monobromide (mɒnəʊˈbrəʊmaɪd, -mɪd). *Chem.* [f. MONO- 2 + BROMIDE.] A compound of one atom of bromine with a monad element or radical.

1875 in *Family Herald* 4 Dec. 78/2 The monobromide of camphor produced the most extraordinary effect. **1881** *Syd. Soc. Lex.* s.v. *Camphor*.

monoˈbrominated, monoˈbromized, *adjs. Chem.* [MONO- 2.] = MONOBROMATED.

1862 Oppenheim in *Jrnl. Chem. Soc.* XV. 29 Monobrominated menthene. **1862** Miller *Elem. Chem.* (ed. 2) III. 243 Monobrominated ethylene. **1878** Kingzett *Anim. Chem.* 104 A monobrominated product. **1889** *Nature* 26 Sept. 539/2 On a new monobromized camphor.

monobromo- (mɒnəʊbrəʊməʊ). *Chem.* Also (esp. before a vowel or *h*) **monobrom-**. [See MONO- 2 and BROMO-.] Combining form, expressing the presence in a compound of one atom of bromine, as ***monobromacetic acid, monobromobenzene***.

1858 *Fownes' Chem.* (ed. 7) 464 Monobromacetic acid. **1862** Miller *Elem. Chem.* (ed. 2) III. 370 Monobromosuccinic Acid. **1869** Roscoe *Elem. Chem.* (1871) 369 Monobromsuccinic acid. **1873** *Fownes' Chem.* (ed. 11) 759 Monobromobenzene is a liquid boiling above 150°.

monocalcic (mɒnəʊˈkælsɪk), *a. Chem.* [MONO- 2.] Containing one atom or equivalent of calcium.

1897 *Allbutt's Syst. Med.* IV. 299 Two molecules of dicalcic phosphate and one of monocalcic phosphate.

monocarbon (mɒnəʊˈkɑːbən), *a. Chem.* [MONO- 2.] Containing or derived from one atom of carbon.

1866 Odling *Anim. Chem.* 49 The most stable monocarbon compound known to chemists, namely, carbonic anhydride. **1869** Roscoe *Elem. Chem.* (1874) 317 Monocarbon or methyl series.

monocarbonate (mɒnəʊˈkɑːbənət). *Chem.* [MONO- 2.] A neutral salt of carbonic acid (H_2CO_3) in which both atoms of hydrogen are replaced by a metal: see CARBONATE *sb.* 1.

1854 J. Scoffern in *Orr's Circ. Sci., Chem.* 457 It is a true neutral, or mono-carbonate. **1876** Harley *Mat. Med.* (ed. 6) 152 By continued boiling it is further reduced to mono-carbonate.

monocardian: see MONO- 1.

monocarp (ˈmɒnəʊkɑːp). *Bot.* [a. F. *monocarpe* (De Candolle), f. Gr. μόνο-ς MONO- + καρπ-ός fruit; in mod.L. *monocarpus*.] A monocarpic plant.

1846 Smart, *Monocarp*, a plant that bears fruit but once.

monocarpellary (ˌmɒnəʊˈkɑːpəlɛrɪ), *a. Bot.* [MONO-.] Having or consisting of a single carpel.

1863 Bentham *Flora Austral.* I. Introd. 17 Where a more precise nomenclature is adopted, the flower is *monocarpellary* when the pistil consists of a single simple carpel. **1873** Oliver *Less. Bot.* 30 Garden pea..pistil superior, apocarpous, monocarpellary. **1875** Bennett & Dyer *Sachs' Bot.* 492 A whorl of monocarpellary ovaries.

monoˈcarpian, *a. Bot. rare*[−0]. Also **-ean.** [Formed as next (or f. mod.L. *monocarpe-us*) + -IAN. Cf. F. *monocarpien*.] = next.

1856 Henslow *Dict. Bot. Terms*, Monocarpean, Monocarpous, [L.] *Monocarpeus*. **1891** *Syd. Soc. Lex.*, Monocarpian.

monocarpic (mɒnəʊˈkɑːpɪk), *a. Bot.* [Formed as MONOCARPOUS + -IC.] Of a plant: Bearing fruit only once (and then dying).

1849 Balfour *Man. Bot.* §634 Annuals and biennials, which flower the first or second year and die, as well as the Agave, and some Palms which flower only once in forty or fifty years, are monocarpic. **1857** Henfrey *Elem. Bot.* 548 Monocarpic perennials. **1875** Bennett & Dyer *Sachs' Bot.* 519.

monocarpous (mɒnəʊˈkɑːpəs), *a.* [f. mod.L. *monocarp-us*: see MONOCARP and -OUS.]

1. *Bot.* = MONOCARPELLARY.

1731 Bailey vol. II, *Monocarpous*, a term apply'd to such plants as bear but one single fruit. **1856** Mayne *Expos. Lex.* **1876** Harley *Mat. Med.* (ed. 6) 603 Fruit monocarpous. **1882** Vines *Sachs' Bot.* 560 When the gynæceum of a flower consists of a single ovary only one fruit is formed, and the flower is said to be monocarpous.

2. *Bot.* = MONOCARPIC.

1830 Lindley *Introd. Bot.* III. i. (1839) 475 *Monocarpous*: bearing fruit but once, and dying after fructification, as Wheat. **1842** Brande *Dict. Sci.*, etc., *Monocarpons* [read *Monocarpous*]..is a term invented by De Candolle to designate what gardeners call annual plants. **1875** Bennett & Dyer *Sachs' Bot.* 806 The plant itself is also completely exhausted, all its disposable formative substances are given up to the seed and the fruit, and it dies off (monocarpous plants).

3. *Path.* (See quot.)

1891 *Syd. Soc. Lex.*, *Monocarpous*... In Medicine, formerly used to describe an eruption the spots of which were not close to each other but discrete.

monocaryon, -caryotic, varr. MONOKARYON, -KARYOTIC *a.*

monocellular, -cellule, -centric: see MONO- 1.

monocephalous (mɒnəʊˈsɛfələs), *a.* [f. mod.L. *monocephal-us*, Gr. μονοκέφαλ-ος one-headed (f. μόνο-ς MONO- + κεφαλ-ή head) + -OUS.] Having only one head.

1. *Bot.* **a.** A term applied to a fruit or ovary which has but one head or summit. **b.** Applied to a plant which has its flowers disposed in a single head or umbel.

1845–50 Mrs. Lincoln *Lect. Bot.* xv. 90 They [*sc.* the capsules] are monocephalous, as in the lily, or polycephalous, as in Nigella. **1856** Henslow *Dict. Bot. Terms*, *Monocephalous*, where flowers are disposed in single heads or umbels, &c. Also, where the ovary is surmounted by a solitary style or stigma.

2. Having the character of a monocephalus.

1885 in *Cassell's Encycl. Dict.*; and in mod. Dicts.

‖**monocephalus** (mɒnəʊˈsɛfələs). *Teratology.* [mod.L., see prec. Cf. F. *monocéphalien* (Littré).] A double monster having one head and two bodies more or less completely blended together.

1882 in Ogilvie; and in later Dicts.

So **monoˈcephaly** (see quot.).

1891 *Syd. Soc. Lex.*, *Monocephaly*, the condition of a *Monocephalus*.

monocercous: see MONO- 1.

monoceros (məˈnɒsərɒs). Also 4–5 **monoceron,** 7 **-cerot.** [a. OF. *monoceros*, *monoceron*, a. L. *monoceros*, med.L. also *monoceron*, a. Gr. μονόκερως, -κερωτ-, f. μόνο-ς MONO- + κέρας horn.]

†**1.** The UNICORN. *Obs.*

13.. *K. Alis.* 6539 A best ther is..That is y-cleped Monoceros. **1398** Trevisa *Barth. De P. R.* XVIII. xc. (1495) 839 Monoceron is a wyld beest moste shape like to the horse in bodi. **1601** Holland *Pliny* I. 206 The Licorne or Monoceros. **1621** Burton *Anat. Mel.* II. iv. I. iv. (1624) 303 A Monocerots horne. **1656** Trapp *Comm. James* iii. 7 Some creatures indeed may be taken, but not tamed, as the tiger, panther, monoceros. **1684** tr. *Bonet's Merc. Compit.* VI. 239 [He] cured several of the Plague, onely by applying a piece of the Monocerot's horn. **1749** Pointer *Oxon. Acad.* 160 [In the Musæum] Monoceros and Rhinoceros Horns.

†**2.** A fish having a 'horn', as the saw-fish, sword-fish, or narwhal. *Obs.*

1590 Spenser *F.Q.* II. xii. 23 Bright Scolopendraes arm'd with silver scales; Mighty Monoceros with immeasured tayles. **1635** Swan *Spec. M.* (1670) 329 The Monoceros or a fish with one horn may fitly be called the Sea-Unicorn. **1706** Phillips (ed. Kersey), *Monoceros*... Also the Saw-fish. **1825** G. Paxton *Illustr. Holy Script.* (ed. 2) I. 89 The Monoceros is a native of the Indian seas.

3. *Astron.* The zodiacal constellation of the Unicorn, lying between Canis Major and Canis Minor.

1797 *Encycl. Brit.* (ed. 3) XII. 239/2. **1839** *Penny Cycl.* XV. 340/1.

4. A genus of prosobranchiate gasteropods (Lamarck 1809), so called from the prominent spine on the outer lip; the unicorn-shell.

1828 J. Fleming *Hist. Brit. Anim.* 342. **1851–6** Woodward *Mollusca* 113.

monocerous (məˈnɒsərəs), *a.* [f. Gr. μονόκερ-ως (cf. prec.) + -OUS.] Having a single horn or horn-like process. (In recent Dicts.)

‖**monochasium** (mɒnəʊˈkeɪzɪəm). *Bot.* Pl. **-ia.** Also anglicized **moˈnochasy.** [mod.L., f. μόνο-ς MONO- + χάσι-ς chasm, separation. Cf. DICHASIUM.] Eichler's name for that form of cymose inflorescence in which the main axis produces only a single branch; a uniparous cyme.

1890 in *Century Dict.* **1891** in *Syd. Soc. Lex.* **1898** tr. *Strasburger's Text-bk. Bot.* (1903) 436 A monochasium is termed a *helicoid cyme* or *bostryx* when the lateral branches always arise on the same side of the pseudaxis. **1900** B. D. Jackson *Gloss. Bot. Terms*, *Monochasy*, a uniparous cyme, either pure, or resulting from the reduction of cymes.

Hence **monoˈchasial** *a.*, of the nature of or pertaining to a monochasium.

1887 Bentley *Man. Bot.* (ed. 5) I. iv. §1. 215 The same form of unilateral, monochasial, or uniparous cyme.

monochlamydeous (mɒnəʊkləˈmɪdɪəs), *a. Bot.* [f. mod.L. *Monochlamydeæ*, f. Gr. μόνο-ς MONO- + χλαμυδ-, χλαμύς cloak: see -EOUS.] Having only one floral envelope; having a single perianth; belonging to the division *Monochlamydeæ*.

1830 Lindley *Nat. Syst. Bot.* Introd. 24 If it [*sc.* the calyx] is unaccompanied by the corolla, plants are said to be Monochlamydeous. **1845** *Encycl. Metrop.* VII. 47/2 The Great Nightshade and many other monochlamydeous flowers. **1882** G. Allen *Colours of Flowers* vi. 111 There would be no reason why flowers with petals should not appear sporadically among monochlamydeous families.

monochloride (mɒnəʊˈklɔəraɪd, -rɪd). *Chem.* [MONO- 2.] A compound of one equivalent of chlorine with an element or radical.

1866 ODLING *Anim. Chem.* I Analogous mono-, di-, and trichlorides of metals. **1873** *Fownes' Chem.* (ed. 11) 194 Iodine unites directly with chlorine, forming a monochloride and a trichloride.

monochlorinated (mɒnəʊˈklɔərɪneɪtɪd), *a. Chem.* [MONO- 2.] Having one equivalent of chlorine added or substituted in each molecule.

1852 WATTS tr. *Gmelin's Handbk. Chem.* VII. 289 Monochlorinated Methyl-Ether. **1873** *Fownes' Chem.* (ed. 11) 555 A mono-chlorinated or monobrominated olefine. **1876** *Encycl. Brit.* V. 676/2 Monochlorinated ethylic ether.

monochloro- (mɒnəʊklɔərəʊ). *Chem.* Also (esp. before vowel or *h*) monochlor-. [See MONO- 2 and CHLORO-.] Combining form, expressing the presence in a compound of one equivalent of chlorine, as *monochloracetic acid*, *monochlorhydrin*, etc.

1855 WATTS tr. *Gmelin's Handbk. Chem.* IX. 192 Monochloracetic Acid. $C^4H^3ClO^4$. *Ibid.* 498 Monochlorhydrine. **1858** *Ibid.* XII. 540 Monochloracetate of Ethyl. **1857** MILLER *Elem. Chem.* III. 380 Monochlorhydrin. **1862** *Ibid.* (ed. 2) III. 373 Glycolic Acid ..has also been procured by heating monochloracetate of potash for some time [etc.]. **1869** ROSCOE *Elem. Chem.* (1871) 367 Monochlor propionic acid. *Ibid.* 409 Monochlorbenzol. **1873** *Fownes' Chem.* (ed. 11) 759 Monochlorobenzene.

monochord (ˈmɒnəkɔːd). Forms: 5-6 monacord(e, monocorde, 5 *Sc.* mony-, monicord, 7- monochord. [a. F. *monocorde* (from 14th c.), ad. med.L. *monochordos, -on*, a. Gr. μονόχορδον, neut. of μονόχορδος adj., having a single string, f. μόνο-ς MONO- + χορδή string (see CHORD *sb.*). Cf. MANICHORD.]

1. A musical instrument composed of a soundboard with a single string; in the 11th c. used in singing-schools to teach the intervals of plain-song; in later use, an instrument for the mathematical determination of musical intervals.

1432-50 tr. *Higden* (Rolls) III. 211 As hit may be schewed in the monocorde [orig. *in monochordo* (v.r. *monacordo*)], when the wire extendede on a holowe body is distreynede diametrally. **1609** DOULAND *Ornith. Microl.* 23 A Monochord..is a long square peece of wood hollow within, with a string drawne ouer it. **1642** FULLER *Holy & Prof. St.* II. vii. 72 His mother tongue was like the dull musick of a monochord, which by study he turns into the harmony of severall instruments. **1652** WHARTON tr. *Rothman's Art Divining* 157 That the Soule of the World..may..be as a Monochord sounding out by the threefold kinds of Creatures, Intellectuall, Celestiall, and Corruptible, at one Blast, one only Life. **1694** HOLDER *Harmony* (1731) 50 These Rations are more certainly found upon the Measures of a Monochord. **1782** BURNEY *Hist. Mus.* (1789) II. ii. 78 The method Guido pursued in teaching boys to sing was by making them practice with the monochord. **1880** GROVE *Dict. Mus.* II. 354 *Monochord*..an instrument consisting of a long box of thin wood with a bridge fixed at each end, over which is stretched a wire or catgut string. **1881** BROADHOUSE *Mus. Acoustics* 101 Thompson's monochord is a method of demonstrating the pitch by adding different weights to a stretched string.

2. A mediæval musical instrument with several strings and bridges for the production of a combination of sounds. *Obs.* exc. *Hist.*

c **1407** LYDG. *Reson & Sens.* 5583 And Instrumentys.. Many moo than I kan telle:..Orgnys, cytolys, monacordys. *c* **1450** HOLLAND *Howlat* 758 The crovde, and the monycordis, the gittyrnis gay. **1497** *Acc. Ld. High Treas. Scotl.* I. 116 Item, to Johne Hert, for bering a pare of Monicordis of þe Kingis fra Abirdene. **1885** A. J. HIPKINS *Pianoforte* in *Encycl. Brit.* XIX. 65/2 We attribute the adaptation of the narrow regal keyboard to what was still called the monochord, but was now a complex of monochords over one resonance board, to the latter half of the 14th century.

3. A harmonious combination of sound; hence *fig.* harmony, agreement. Now *rare.*

c **1420** LYDG. *Assembly of Gods* 7 Musyng..how that I myght make Reason & Sensualyte in oon to acorde; but I cowde nat bryng about that monacorde. *Ibid.* 2016. *c* **1500** in Grose *Antiq. Rep.* (1809) IV. 408 Purenes in the margent makithe a trew monacorde. **1509** HAWES *Past. Pleas.* XVI. (Percy Soc.) 62 The vii. scyences in one monacorde, Eche upon other do full well depende. *a* **1548** HALL *Chron., Hen. IV* Introd., By the whiche you shal..bryng vs into an vnitie and monacorde. *Ibid., Hen. VII* 3 There lacked a wrest to the harpe to set all the strynges in a monacorde and tune. *a* **1550** *Image Ipocr.* III. 471 in *Skelton's Wks.* (1843) II. 439 For of that monocorde The scripture doth recorde. **1644** BULWER *Chirol.* 105 Their cunning mannaging of the Hand in time and tone, I have sometimes call'd the Horse-Rhetorique of Smithfield, which by calculation I have found to differ from the Fish Dialect of Billingsgate, in the monochord of motion. **1880** SWINBURNE *Stud. Shaks.* iii. (ed. 2) 210 We hear a sound of sacred and spiritual music as solemn as the central monochord of the inner main itself. **1880** —— *Stud. Song* 91 The sense of thy golden Great harp's monochord Was the joy in the soul of the singers that hailed thee for master and lord.

Hence †**monochordize** *v.* [tr. F. *monochordiser*], *intr.* to perform on the monochord; **monochordist**, a writer who treats of the monochord. Also †**monochordical** *a.*, pertaining to the science of the monochord. **monochordous** *a.* (see quot. 1856).

1653 URQUHART *Rabelais* I. vii. (Rtldg.) 35 He..would nod his head, monochordizing with his fingers. **1687** SETTLE *Refl. Dryden* 95 To answer him in Trigonometrical, Metaphysical, and Monochordical Fustian is not to the purpose. **1834** *Westm. Rev.* XX. 81 The monochordists from Euclid downwards. **1856** MAYNE *Expos. Lex.*, *Monochordus*, having only one string: monochordous.

monochorea: see MONO- 1.

monochroic (mɒnəʊˈkrəʊɪk), *a. rare.* [f. Gr. μονόχρο-ος of one colour (f. μόνο-ς MONO- + χρό-α colour) + -IC.] Having or showing only one colour.

1890 in *Century Dict.* **1899** CAGNEY tr. *Jaksch's Clin. Diagn.* i. 1 Arterial blood is monochroic.

monochromasy (mɒnəʊˈkrəʊməsɪ). *Ophthalm.* Also -chromacy. [f. MONO- + Gr. χρῶμα colour: see -Y[3].] = MONOCHROMATISM b.

1900 *Stud. Yale Psychol. Lab.* VIII. 15 Still another form of color-vision is found in monochromasy. All the visible objects are seen as shades of one color. What this color is, it has as yet been impossible to say. **1922** W. PEDDIE *Colour Vision* ii. 16 The most extreme condition is that of total colour blindness in which every colour in the spectrum can be matched with grey. It is not inconceivable that a case of this kind may be one of true monochromasy, the one colour extending throughout the whole spectrum. **1957** *Jrnl. Optical Soc. Amer.* XLVII. 338/2 (*heading*) 'Blue monocone monochromacy': a new color vision defect. **1971** *Jrnl. Physiol.* CCXII. 211 (*heading*) Colour vision in blue cone 'monochromacy'.

monochromat (mɒnəʊˈkrəʊmæt), **-chromate** (-krəʊmeɪt), *sb. Ophthalm.* [ad. L. *monochrōmat-us*, Gr. μονοχρώματ-ος: see -ATE[1].] A person who suffers from monochromatism (sense b).

1902 J. M. BALDWIN *Dict. Philos. & Psychol.* II. 793/2 König affirmed that the vision of the faint-light 'monochromates' was in quality blue. **1915** J. H. PARSONS *Introd. Study Colour Vision* II. i. 159 Differing from all these groups there are people who apparently see all parts of the spectrum of one hue... These are the total colour-blind or monochromats. **1956** *Brit. Jrnl. Ophthalm.* XL. 463 This female 'cone monochromate' would thus have to be a compound heterozygote for protanopia and deuteranopia. **1971** *Nature* 9 Apr. 395/1 The recovery of the rod sensitivity after a long full bleach can be followed for a wider than normal range when an area of the monochromat's retina which has few cones is tested.

monochromate (mɒnəʊˈkrəʊmeɪt), *v.* [Backformation from MONOCHROMATOR.] *trans.* = MONOCHROMATIZE *v.* So **'monochromated, -chromating** *ppl. adjs.*

1955 G. E. BACON *Neutron Diffraction* iv. 80 For any position *XY* of the monochromating crystal there will be some particular wavelength which is at the right glancing angle θ to the crystal to undergo Bragg reflection when it is incident along *PB*. **1955** *Rev. Sci. Instruments* XXVI. 564 A bent crystal monochromator..was constructed to monochromate the specimen-reflected x-ray beam. *Ibid.*, X-ray diffraction laboratories are making increasing use of single crystal monochromated radiation for various types of investigations. **1961** J. THEWLIS et al. *Encycl. Dict. Physics* IV. 827/2 Normally, the monochromating crystal is used in conjunction with a neutron spectrometer. **1971** *Nature* 16 Apr. 436/1 The aim of our experiments was..to check that there was no large disparity between the observed and calculated flux of monochromated synchrotron radiation.

monochromatic (mɒnəkrəʊˈmætɪk), *a.* [f. Gr. μόνο-ς MONO- + χρωματικός CHROMATIC (f. χρῶμα colour); Gr. has μονοχρώματος of one colour.]

1. Of or presenting one colour only; applied *spec.* to light of one wave-length. Also applied to other radiation that is (nominally) of a single wavelength or energy throughout.

monochromatic lamp, a lamp which produces such a light.

1822 BREWSTER in *Trans. Roy. Soc. Edin.* IX. 437 The Monochromatic Lamp being thus completed, I lost no time in applying it to the illumination of Microscopic objects. **1827** *Q. Jrnl. Sci.* XXII. 374 Talbot on Monochromatic Light. **1854** DE QUINCEY *Autob. Sk.* i. §2 Wks. 1854 II. 36 *note*, Porphyry is far from being so monochromatic as Gibbon's argument would presume. **1854** *Pereira's Polarized Light* (ed. 2) 27 The component prismatic colours are simple or homogeneous lights. Each of these may be termed a monochromatic light. **1874** T. HARDY *Far fr. Mad. Crowd* II. iii. 30 Under a monochromatic Lammas sky. **1923** GLAZEBROOK *Dict. Appl. Physics* IV. 22/2 The crystal is pulverised and the powder compressed into a rod, placed in the axis of a cylindrical photographic film and subjected to 'monochromatic' X-rays. **1955** C. R. N. STROUTS et al. *Analytical Chem.* II. xxvi. 942 It is desirable to use essentially monochromatic radiation for most analytical applications of X-ray diffraction. **1967** R. CASTAING et al. in A. Septier *Focusing Charged Particles* II. iv. 289 An incident monochromatic electron beam.

2. a. Executed in monochrome.

1823 J. BADCOCK *Dom. Amusem.* 52 Mr. Gilpin's mode of monochromatic painting and printing. **1828** *Edin. Rev.* Sept. 75 The Monochromatic works were highly esteemed. **1879** ROOD *Chromatics* xviii. 310 In monochromatic designs the small interval is very frequently employed.

b. *sb. pl.* = studies in monochrome.

1893 *Athenæum* 27 May 676/2 There are examples of all sorts of styles..[including] the monochromatics and subtle tone-studies of Mr. Whistler.

3. *Ophthalm.* Exhibiting or affected with monochromatism (sense b); completely colour-blind.

1902 J. M. BALDWIN *Dict. Philos. & Psychol.* II. 793/2 The sensations of those individuals whom they named 'monochromatic'..were dogmatically affirmed to be vision under the form of red or blue or green, it was uncertain which. **1956** *Brit. Jrnl. Ophthalm.* XL. 470 His vision is monochromatic when examined in the colour apparatus. **1974** *Sci. Amer.* Dec. 25/3 The ophthalmologist testified that the witness was actually monochromatic, which meant he could perceive no colors at all.

Hence **monochro'matically** *adv.*, also *fig.*; **monochroma'ticity**, the condition of being monochromatic; the extent to which any radiation is concentrated at one wavelength or frequency; †**mono'chromatist**, a painter in monochrome.

1784 J. BARRY in *Lect. Paint.* i. (1848) 81 The old method of those they called monochromatists. **1880** W. SEVERN in *Macm. Mag.* No. 245. 376 Nothing is more puzzling to beginners than to determine between two very opposite colours as to which is the darkest in tone, or, to use a long word monochromatically. **1890** *Anthony's Photogr. Bull.* III. 408 For development, a monochromatically lighted room is still a necessity. **1960** S. TOLANSKY *Surface Microtopography* i. 5 For two-beam work the Wratten 77A didymium glass filter gives excellent monochromaticity. **1963** G. TROUP *Masers & Lasers* (ed. 2) vii. 113 The advantages of maser optical sources are: the extreme monochromaticity, resulting in huge spectral energy-densities; [etc.]. **1972** *Daily Tel.* 31 May 10/3 Janacek's Sonata '1905'..was massively though rather monochromatically delivered. **1972** *Nature* 22 Dec. 483/1 The intensity, coherence and monochromaticity of laser light have made it an ideal radiation source for selective alteration of cell organelles.

monochromatism (mɒnəʊˈkrəʊmətɪz(ə)m). [f. MONOCHROMAT(IC *a.* + -ISM.]

a. The monochromatic condition.

c **1865** J. WYLDE in *Circ. Sci.* I. 54/1 A series of.. phenomena connected with mono-chromatism.

b. *Ophthalm.* Complete colour-blindness, in which all colours appear as shades of one colour, probably grey.

1934 in WEBSTER. **1946** W. D. WRIGHT *Res. Normal & Defective Colour Vision* xxiv. 297 In monochromatism, all qualitative differences in stimuli disappear, so that colour matching is reduced to brightness matching. **1956** *Brit. Jrnl. Ophthalm.* XL. 462 There exist rare cases of monochromatism in which the characteristic symptoms accompanying typical total colour blindness are lacking. **1966** *Arch. Internal Med.* CXVIII. 491/2 This report describes a family with atypical congenital monochromatism.

monochromatize (mɒnəʊˈkrəʊmətaɪz), *v.* [f. MONOCHROMAT(IC *a.* + -IZE.] *trans.* To make monochromatic. So **mono'chromatized, mono'chromatizing** *ppl. adjs.*

1951 *Jrnl. de Physique* XII. 268/1 It is..necessary to 'monochromatize' the beam. *Ibid.* 268/2 The monochromatized neutrons..had de Broglie wavelengths 1·06 Å and hence velocities approximately three times thermal. **1955** G. E. BACON *Neutron Diffraction* iv. 102 Two methods of making diffraction measurements have..been described using a neutron beam direct from the pile, without first monochromatizing. **1962** *Rev. Sci. Instruments* XXXIII. 875/1 (*heading*) Preparation of bent crystals for monochromatizing x rays. **1974** *Nature* 19 Apr. 671/2 Both structure analyses were based on diffractometer data taken with monochromatised Cu radiation. **1974** *Physics Bull.* Oct. 443/2 The three essential components of a neutron scattering spectrometer: monochromatizing crystal, material sample and crystal for analysis of the scattered beam.

Also **,monochromati'zation**, the process of making monochromatic.

1955 C. B. WALKER tr. *Guinier & Fournet's Small-Angle Scattering X-Rays* iii. 104 It might be thought that the double monochromatization and the large distance from X-ray tube to film would require a prohibitive increase in the exposure time. **1955** *Rev. Sci. Instruments* XXVI. 564 The usual method of monochromatization consists of inserting (at the required Bragg angle) a single crystal between the x-ray source and the specimen. **1967** J. LECIEJEWICZ tr. *Auleytner's X-Ray Methods in Study of Defects in Single Crystals* ii. 76 The only disadvantage of the method is the very long exposure time caused by the low intensity due to precise monochromatization of the beam.

monochromator (ˈmɒnəkrəmeɪtə(r), mɒnəʊˈkrəʊmeɪtə(r)). *Physics.* [f. MONOCHROMAT(IC *a.* + -OR.] Any device used to select radiation of a single wavelength or energy (or, in practice, a very narrow range of wavelengths or energies).

1909 *Chem. Abstr.* III. 2074 The monochromator is a spectrometer arrangement of the Pellin and Broca or Hilger type with constant deviation of 90°, in which the eyepiece can be replaced by a second slit. **1924** E. C. C. BALY *Spectroscopy* (ed. 3) I. iv. 109 Any fixed arm spectrometer can be converted into a monochromator by replacing the eyepiece by a slit placed in the focus of the telescope lens or mirror. **1955** C. B. WALKER tr. *Guinier & Fournet's Small-Angle Scattering X-Rays* iii. 100 Bent crystals were originally introduced in X-ray spectroscopy, serving as analyzers capable of producing intense spectra; they can serve equally well as monochromators. **1969** *Nature* 11 Oct. 146/1 Changes in diffraction geometry, and more especially the use of focusing monochromators, should yield a considerably higher neutron flux, permitting the use of smaller crystals.

monochrome (ˈmɒnəʊ-, mɒnəʊˈkrəʊm), *sb.* and *a.* Forms: 7-9 monochrom, 8 monocrome, 9- monochrome. [In sense 1, ad. med.L. *monochrōma, -chrōmat-*, evolved from Gr.

μονοχρώματος adj.; in the other uses a. F. *monochrome* or ad. Gr. *μονόχρωμος, -ον*, of one colour, a by-form of *μονοχρώματος* (see MONOCHROMATIC).] **A.** *sb.*

1. a. A painting executed in different tints of one colour, with representation of light and shade.

1662 EVELYN *Chalcogr.* iv. 35 Those wretched gravings.. where the Devil is but one great blot..and the rest of the Figures Monochroms as ridiculous. **1760** *Ann. Reg.* III. ii. 164/1 Four monocromes which stand first in the catalogue of pictures [from Herculaneum]. **1801** FUSELI *Lect. Paint.* i. (1848) 350 Monochrom, or paintings of a single colour. **1848** *Ibid.* 351 *note*, There appears to be no example of the perfect monochrom (μονοχρώματον) on the ancient vases. **1849** RUSKIN *Sev. Lamps* iv. §41. 132 The Elgin frieze is a monochrom in a state of transition to sculpture. **1861** THORNBURY *Turner* I. 105 His earliest works being mere monochromes in sepia. **1866** BRANDE & COX *Dict. Sci.* s.v., A drawing in chiaro-scuro is a monochrome, whether in black and white or in any colour and white... The skiagram or silhouette is not a monochrome, though executed in a single colour.

b. *transf.*, esp. in *Photogr.* (see quots.).

1940 *Chambers's Techn. Dict.* 555/2 *Monochrome*, a photographic print in one colour of varying brightness. **1968** *Gloss. Terms Offset Lithogr. Printing* (*B.S.I.*) 8 *Monochrome*, an original or print in a single colour. **1973** D. A. SPENCER *Focal Dict. Photographic Technologies* 394 *Monochrome*, an image or picture in a single colour which is usually (but need not be) black.

2. a. Representation in one colour; *esp.* in phr. (to paint, etc.) ***in monochrome***. Hence occas., the state of being in one colour; a tract of one colour.

1851 *Illustr. Lond. News* 31 May 493/1 Messrs. Hullmandel, who produce effects in monochrome. **1858** BIRCH *Anc. Pottery* I. 259 A great improvement..was the use of incised lines cut through the colour to relieve the monochrome. **1861** J. BELL *Colour on Statues* in *Jrnl. Soc. Arts* IX. 424/1 The wonderful groups of the Medici monuments, have come down to us in their native monochrome, untouched by change of tint. **1874** FERGUSSON in *Contemp. Rev.* Oct. 759 No architect ever proposed to line the whole..with one cold, monotonous monochrome of gray. **1876** T. HARDY *Ethelberta* II. 47 Here grassed hills rose like knuckles gloved in dark olive, and little plantations between them formed a still deeper and sadder monochrome. **1902** *Encycl. Brit.* XXXI. 685/1 If a coloured object were illuminated solely by a paraffin light, a print from the negative would give a fair representation of the object in monochrome.

b. *Cinemat.* and *Television.* Reproduction in black and white.

1918 H. CROY *How Motion Pictures are Made* 294 Relieving the monotony of the monochrome. **1957** *Encycl. Brit.* XV. 859/2 Monochrome.—For black-and-white photography the principal problem is to make a reasonable compromise between film grain and film speed. **1961** G. MILLERSON *Technique Television Production* 128 Colour media can employ both tonal and colour separation, to distinguish between planes. Colour separation may mean nothing when transformed into monochrome.

c. *fig.*

1962 *Listener* 10 May 828/3 A dramatic exaggeration, associated with Verdi and Puccini, inevitably crept into the gentle monochrome.

3. A paint or glaze of a single colour.

1906 S. W. BUSHELL *Chinese Art* II. viii. 40 Some of the most brilliant monochromes of the time are plain washes of one of the enamel colours used in polychrome decoration. **1933** *Burlington Mag.* Nov. 203/1 Monochromes, which may be divided into celadons and semi-celadons, brown-glazed, white-glazed, and black-glazed wares.

B. *adj.* **a.** Having only one colour; executed in one colour. Also *fig.*

1849 RUSKIN *Sev. Lamps* iv. §41. 133, I have an intense love for these monochrom figures. **1850** LEITCH tr. *C.O. Müller's Anc. Art* §74 Outline drawing and monochrome painting. **1861** THORNBURY *Turner* II. 89 Some almost monochrome but powerful water-colour Swiss scenes. **1902** *Encycl. Brit.* XXXI. 685/1 This light-filter..will render all coloured objects in correct monochrome luminosity. **1906** S. W. BUSHELL *Chinese Art* II. viii. 35 All the new monochrome glazes introduced under his rule. **1957** *Encycl. Brit.* II. 540/1 At Mersin, the burnished and incised monochrome pottery of the Neolithic period was almost entirely replaced by the painted wares. **1959** [see BICHROME *a.* and *sb.*[2]]. **1970** *Daily Tel.* 13 Jan. 16 One must have balanced communities; there is nothing worse for society than a monochrome area. **1972** C. STEPHENSON *Merrily on High* xii. 181 As a curate in Cowley St. John I worked in a completely monochrome district as far as the church was concerned.

b. *Photogr.* and *Television.* Reproducing all colours as shades of grey; 'black and white'; pertaining to such reproduction.

1918 H. CROY *How Motion Pictures are Made* 290 A strip of Priezma negative differs but slightly from a monochrome film. *Ibid.* 294 Monochrome effect on the screen is varied successfully by a different process. **1958** *Newnes Compl. Amat. Photogr.* 144 The monochrome photographer who turns to colour is rather apt to think his old principles still apply. **1961** G. MILLERSON *Technique Telev. Production* 128 A further variation can arise through distinctions between techniques when making colour and monochrome motion pictures. *Ibid.* Although colourful design may delight those in the studio, it has no significance to the viewer in monochrome television. **1972** *Sci. Amer.* Feb. 117/1 Intended largely for paramedical students, nurses and technicians, it presents both in sharp monochrome and strong color photographs, all blood red and fat yellow, a review of the general structure of the body.

Hence **mono'chromic, mono'chromical** *adjs.* = MONOCHROME *a.* **'mono,chromist**, a painter in monochrome; also (quot. 1861[1]), one who advocates the use of monochrome. **mono'chromous** *a.* = MONOCHROME *a.* **'mono,chromy**, the art of painting in monochrome.

1839 *Civil Eng. & Arch. Jrnl.* II. 368/1 These kinds of sculpture..were held in greater estimation than *monochromic sculpture. **1854** *Blackw. Mag.* LXXVI. 556 These gentlemen..wear a monochromic or one-coloured suit. **1901** in *N. & Q.* 9th Ser. VIII. 503/2 These *bacini*.. are sometimes monochromic..others show a number of fantastic designs. **1890** *Century Dict.*, *Monochromical. **1662** EVELYN *Chalcogr.* v. 127 Heredices the Corinthian, and Thelophanes the Sicyonian, who were both of them but *Monochromists. **1861** J. BELL *Colour on Statues* in *Jrnl. Soc. Arts* IX. 424/1 Is the addition of coloring to statues to be looked upon as an advance in art, or a retrogression? The polychromists will, of course, hold it to be the former, while the monochromist in sculpture will represent that [etc.]. **1861** THORNBURY *Turner* I. 99 Girtin was at first little more than a monochromist. *a* **1878** SIR G. SCOTT *Lect. Archit.* (1879) I. 180 The churches..of one unvaried stone colour.. have been made over periodically to the tender mercies of the monochromist. **1856** MAYNE *Expos. Lex.*, *Monochromus* ..*monochromous. **1880** SALA in *Daily Tel.* 26 Feb. 5/8 The general monochromous dinginess of the disestablished hotel. **1855** HYDE CLARKE *Dict.*, *Monochromy,..painting in one colour. **1879** ROOD *Chromatics* xviii. 310 We return now to a brief consideration of monochromy, or decoration in a single colour.

monochronic (mɒnəʊ'krɒnɪk), *a.* [Formed as next + -IC.] Relating to a single period of time.

1840 SMART, *Monochronic*, existing at one and the same geological period. **1882** OGILVIE, *Monochronic*, in *geol.* applied to organic remains which seem to have been deposited at the same period. [Similarly in later Dicts.] **1905** F. E. CLEMENTS *Research Methods in Ecology* 319 *Monochronic*, arising but once. **1967** *Philos.* XLII. 140 Geography was at one time in danger of running into a dead monochronic alley by limiting itself to the visible present.

monochronous (mə'nɒkrənəs), *a. Pros.* [f. Gr. μονόχρον-ος (f. μόνος MONO- + χρόνος time) + -OUS.] Consisting of one 'time' or mora; monosemic.

1890 in *Century Dict.*

monochroous (mə'nɒkrəʊəs), *a.* [f. Gr. μονόχροος (see MONOCHROIC) + -OUS.] = MONOCHROIC.

1856 MAYNE *Expos. Lex.*, *Monochroüs*,..monochroous. **1891** in *Syd. Soc. Lex.*

monociliated: see MONO- 1.

monocle ('mɒnək(ə)l), *sb.* [a. F. *monocle* (in OF. as adj. = one-eyed), ad. L. *monoculus*: see MONOCULOUS.]

1. A single eye-glass.

1858 SIMMONDS *Dict. Trade*, *Monocle* (French), a reading-glass for one eye. **1886** W. J. TUCKER *E. Europe* 46 'He has..a glass in his eye'. 'A binocle or a monocle?' **1889** D. C. MURRAY *Dang. Catspaw* xiv. (1890) 247 A great monocle which the old gentleman used for the critical examination of his work lay near at hand. **1894** *Idler* Sept. 175 The young man screwed a monocle into his right eye.

2. = MONOCULE (*Cent. Dict.* 1890).

'monocle, *v.* [f. the sb.] *trans.* To provide with a monocle. So **'monocled** *a.*

1922 M. B. HOUSTON *Witch Man* xii. 154 Major Coberton monocled his eye. **1926** L. P. GREENE *Major—Diamond Buyer* 18 The monocled one coughed deprecatingly. **1940** *Horizon* Mar. 185 The monocled idiot who made good on the fields of Mons and Le Cateau. **1965** *Listener* 30 Dec. 1063/1 Colonel Creighton, monocled, and seated bolt upright in his rickshaw as though it were a Daimler. **1974** *Times* 26 Apr. 18/6 It is ironical that youth and the new guard should be represented by a 63 year old monocled cavalry officer.

monocleid(e ('mɒnəklaɪd). [f. Gr. μόνο-ς MONO- + κλειδ-, κλείς key.] A cabinet locked by a single key.

c **1840** (*title*) Description of the Monocleid Writing-cabinets..invented by Thomas Sopwith. **1885** *Newcastle Chron.* 25 May, Superior Oak Monocleide.

monoclinal (mɒnəʊ'klaɪnəl), *a.* and *sb. Geol.* [f. Gr. μόνο-ς MONO- + κλῑν-ειν to bend + -AL[1]. Cf. *anti-*, *iso-*, *synclinal*.]

A. *adj.* **a.** Consisting of strata that slope in the same direction and at the same angle throughout.

In quot. 1876 the word appears to have been used with a slightly different meaning, perh. because 'direction' was interpreted as referring to directions in a horizontal plane rather than a vertical one.

1843 W. B. & H. D. ROGERS in *Rep. 1st, 2nd & 3rd Meetings Assoc. Amer. Geologists & Naturalists* 485 While the phrases, *anticlinal dip*, and *synclinal dip*, sufficiently express the directions of the beds, due to concave and convex flexures, we propose the term *monoclinal*, to signify a sameness in the direction of the dip, and shall term a mountain or valley, in which such sameness prevails, a *monoclinal* mountain, or *monoclinal* valley. **1858** H. D. ROGERS *Geol. Pennsylv.* I. 10 The ridges..are of three orders... In geological language they are of anticlinal, synclinal, and monoclinal structure. *Ibid.* 18 Monoclinal Valleys. **1875** J. W. POWELL *Explor. Colorado River* xi. 160 Monoclinal valleys..run in the direction of the strike between the axes of the fold—one side of the valley formed of the summits of the beds, the other composed of the cut edges of the formation. **1876** PAGE *Adv. Text-bk. Geol.* iv. 83 The strata of a district, though lying at different angles, may all slope in the same way, and in such a case they are said to be monoclinal or dipping in one main direction. **1930** *Compt. Rend. 15th Internat. Geol. Congress 1929* II. vi. 361, I shall consider only four major types of blocks included between bounding faults: 1. Tilted or monoclinal blocks; [etc.]. **1942** O. D. VON ENGELN *Geomorphology* xv. 327 Monoclinal ridges, alternating with monoclinal valleys, appear where a series of resistant and weak beds all dip in the same direction. **1957** G. E. HUTCHINSON *Treat. Limnol.* I. i. 111 The channel containing Lenore Lake lies in a zone of fractured basalt on a monoclinal slope.

b. Applied to a fold consisting of a single slope connecting strata that are parallel and more or less horizontal but at different levels.

1877 LE CONTE *Elem. Geol.* (1879) 178 Such a bend is called a monoclinal fold or axis. **1880** C. E. DUTTON *Rep. Geol. High Plateaus Utah* ii. 25 The great structural features of the High Plateaus are the faults and monoclinal flexures. **1940** E. S. HILLS *Outl. Struct. Geol.* v. 111 An individual normal fault may pass either laterally or vertically into a monoclinal flexure. **1969** J. BUNDRED *Basic Geol. for Engineers* iv. 115 A monoclinal fold..has basically a single undulation.

B. *sb.* **a.** A monoclinal fold.

1880 C. E. DUTTON *Rep. Geol. High Plateaus Utah* ii. 26 So close is the homology that we are justified in calling a monoclinal in some of its aspects a modified fault. The only difference for structural purposes is that in the case of a typical fault of the simplest form the shearing is along one plane, while in the monoclinal the shearing lies between two planes. **1886** T. M. READE *Orig. Mount. Ranges* xx. 250 The Water-Pocket flexure, one of the grandest monoclinals of the west. **1914** J. PARK *Text-bk. Geol.* ix. 140 In sharply bent monoclinals, the strata in the middle limb are generally drawn out, compressed, or deformed.

b. A monoclinal set of strata; = HOMOCLINE.

1916 *Bull. Geol. Soc. Amer.* XXVII. 92, I welcome the suggestion of the term homocline. The need of a term for this structure has long been felt in the United States Geological Survey, where confusion has been avoided in editing by using *monoclinal* for the homocline as distinct from *monocline* or monoclinal fold.

Hence **mono'clinally** *adv.*

1858 H. D. ROGERS *Geol. Pennsylv.* I. 10 Dipping only in one direction, or monoclinally. **1880** C. E. DUTTON *Rep. Geol. High Plateaus Utah* ii. 31 At East Fork Cañon the thrown beds..are turned up monoclinally. **1968** R. W. FAIRBRIDGE *Encycl. Geomorphol.* 483/2 At coastlines the same ancient cyclic landsurface may be monoclinally warped down to pass beneath marine sequences of Jurassic or Cretaceous rocks.

monoclinate (mɒnəʊ'klaɪnət), *a. Cryst.* [Formed as MONOCLIN-AL + -ATE[2].] = MONOCLINIC.

1847 in WEBSTER; and in later Dicts.

monocline ('mɒnəklaɪn). *Geol.* [Formed as MONOCLIN-AL; cf. *anti-*, *iso-*, *syncline*.]

a. A monoclinal fold.

1879 GEIKIE in *Encycl. Brit.* X. 300/1 The strata are thus bent up and continue on the other side of the tilt at a higher level. Such bends are called *monoclines* or *monoclinal folds*, because they present only one fold, or one half of a fold, instead of the two which we see in an arch or trough. **1898** MILNE *Seismol.* iii. 33 The bases of monoclines are tracts where faults are frequent. **1916** [see MONOCLINAL *a.* and *sb.* B. b]. **1940** E. S. HILLS *Outl. Struct. Geol.* iv. 70 A monocline is a local steepening of an otherwise uniformly dipping or horizontal series, and is composed of an anticlinal bend above, followed by a synclinal bend at a lower level... In oil-field geology, however, the term is used for formations in which the dip is more or less uniform in one direction. **1942** M. P. BILLINGS *Struct. Geol.* iii. 41 In plateau areas..the strata may locally assume a steeper dip. .. Such a fold is a monocline. The beds in a monocline may dip at angles ranging from a few degrees to ninety degrees. **1962** READ & WATSON *Introd. Geol.* I. viii. 487 In this way monoclines may be formed and may grade into zones of normal faulting.

b. = HOMOCLINE.

1912 E. H. C. CRAIG *Oil-Finding* v. 74 Oil may be obtained from monoclines, often in great quantity. In such cases the more gentle the dip, the better. **1925** A. B. THOMPSON *Oil-Field Exploration* I. v. 186 The term 'monocline' is here retained in its customary oil-field phraseology as representing a series of uniformly dipping beds, irrespective of the relationship they may bear to the general structure of the district. **1951** E. N. TIRATSOO *Petroleum Geol.* iv. 79 The monocline can be considered as virtually one limb of an anticline up which the migrating fluids pass, leaving well-marked layers of dynamically separated gas, oil and water.

monoclinian (mɒnəʊ'klɪnɪən), *a. Bot.* [Formed as MONOCLIN-OUS + -IAN.] = MONOCLINOUS.

1900 B. D. JACKSON *Gloss. Bot. Terms.*

monoclinic (mɒnəʊ'klɪnɪk), *a. Cryst.* [Formed as MONOCLIN-AL + -IC. Cf. F. *monoclinique*.] Having three unequal axes, two of which intersect each other at right angles and the third or principal axis intersects one at right angles and the other obliquely.

1869 PHILLIPS *Vesuv.* x. 275 The fifth, or oblique, or monoclinic system, has one of its axes perpendicular to the other two. **1869** ROSCOE *Elem. Chem.* xix. (1874) 215 Yielding the salt, $(NH_4)_2HPO_4$, which crystallizes in the monoclinic system. **1879** GEIKIE in *Encycl. Brit.* X. 227/2 The Monoclinic or Orthoclase felspars.

So **monoclino'hedral, monoclino'hedric, monoclino'metric** *adjs.* [see HEDRAL, CLINOHEDRIC s.v. CLINO- 2, METRIC *a.*[1]] (in the same sense).

1888 TEALL *Brit. Petrogr.* 440 *Monoclinohedral. **1854** *Pereira's Polarized Light* (ed. 2) 229 The *monoklinohedric system. **1862** J. B. JORDAN *Const. Models Crystallogr.* 20 Fifth System. The Monoclinohedric. **1858** THUDICHUM

Urine 123 Creatinine crystallizes in the *monoclinometric system.

monoclinous (mɒnəʊˈklaɪnəs), *a.* [f. F. *monocline* (1799), or mod.L. *monoclīnus*, f. Gr. μόνο-ς MONO- + κλίνη bed, couch: see -OUS.]

1. *Bot.* Having both stamens and pistils in the same flower, hermaphrodite.

1828 STARK *Elem. Nat. Hist.* II. 466 Those vegetables where the male and female organs occur on the same plant are called Monoclinous; and the others Diclinous. **1849** BALFOUR *Man. Bot.* §648 The flower is hermaphrodite, or monoclinous. **1888** VINES in *Encycl. Brit.* XXIV. 131/2 Series 2. *Polypetalæ*: usually monoclinous.

2. *Geol.* = MONOCLINAL *a.*

1882 in OGILVIE; and in later Dicts.

monocœlian, -cœlic, -coloured: see MONO 1.

monoˈcolous, *a. nonce-wd.* [f. Gr. μονόκωλ-ος (f. μόνο-ς MONO- + κῶλον limb) + -OUS.] (See quot.)

1798 FERRIAR *Illustr. Sterne, Varieties of Man* 200 The people were monocolous, that is, having only one leg, or sciapodous, having feet so large as to shelter the whole body, in a supine posture.

mono-compound: see MONO- 2.

monocondylar, etc.: see MONO- 1.

monocoque (ˈmɒnəʊkɒk). [a. F. *monocoque*, f. *mono-* MONO- + *coque* egg-shell.] **a.** *Aeronaut.* A fuselage or other structure having an outer covering in the form of a rigid skin or shell designed to bear all or most of the stresses that arise; now esp. one without longerons or stringers (see quot. 1948). Also *transf.* Usu. *attrib.*

1914 *Sphere* 3 Oct. p. ii/1 The very speedy monocoques of the French. **1919** A. W. JUDGE *Elem. Princ. Aeroplane Design* vi. 98 The Monocoque Type of Body. This type of body..consists of a single shell, conforming with the outside shape of the body, and..so constructed that it can withstand all the stresses which it is called upon to bear, without the necessity for longerons or cross bracing members. **1935** C. G. BURGE *Compl. Bk. Aviation* 595/1 The 'monocoque' is becoming increasingly popular for both military and commercial aeroplanes. **1938** E. W. C. WILKINS *Aeroplane Design* vii. 171 The monocoque fuselage ..consists of a thin shell..built around a number of transverse rings or formers... These formers are placed at intervals of about 2 ft. or more in the case of a wooden monocoque, but are very much closer together in the case of the metal monocoque. **1948** C. E. CHAPEL *Aircraft Basic Sci.* ii. 84/2 Monocoques may be divided into three classes (monocoque, semimonocoque, and reinforced shell), and different portions of the fuselage may belong to any of these classes. The true monocoque has as its only reinforcement vertical bulkheads formed of structural members... All stresses are carried by the shell or skin. **1951** *Engineering* 2 Nov. 573/1 A wing of the thin-walled monocoque type. **1969** K. MUNSON *Pioneer Aircraft 1903–14* 123/2 Late in 1911 the ideas of the Swedish engineer Ruchonnet, for a monocoque fuselage shell of moulded plywood, were applied by Armand Deperdussin's designer, Louis Béchereau. **1970** *New Scientist* 12 Nov. 329/2 No longer would an airship need to have a metal fabric-covered skelton. Instead it could have a 'monocoque' structure—the strength would be in a stiff lightweight outer shell. **1971** *Daily Colonist* (Victoria, B.C.) 6 June 25/6 Launched four years ago, she is of monocoque design—one shell, no ribs, no frame, smooth inside and out.

b. In a motor vehicle, an underframe and body built as a single rigid structure (or in racing cars as a number of box-like sections) throughout which the stresses are distributed. Usu. *attrib.*

1956 MOLLOY & LANCHESTER *Automobile Engineer's Ref. Bk.* XVIII. 2 All-metal bodies fall into two main categories, firstly those which are used in conjunction with a separate chassis frame and secondly which are of the type known as monocoque or unit construction. The former naturally require only body structure panels, whereas the latter, in addition, require many pressings to form a unit (underframe or subframe), which although ultimately part of the body, is [a] substitute for the chassis frame and has provision made for all necessary attachment points for the various mechanical units. **1961** COSTIN & PHIPPS *Racing & Sports Car Chassis Design* v. 43 All these, plus the single transverse torsion bar and the telescopic dampers, pick up on the rear bulkhead of the monocoque. **1963** *Engineering* 1 Feb. 181/1 GT cars featuring monocoque construction of laminated wooden box sections. **1968** *Daily Tel.* (Colour Suppl.) 15 Nov. 29/2 Despite the terrible force of the impact, the integrity of the cockpit area was preserved by the immensely strong monocoque chassis of his car. **1969** 'D. RUTHERFORD' *Gilt-Edged Cockpit* i. 15 With the whole of his body encased in the monocoque shell and no part of his face visible he was an anonymous figure... Already other cars were flashing past. **1973** TERRY & BAKER *Racing Car Design & Devel.* vi. 129 Although the basic space-frame is a comparatively light structure, it requires a separate body and fuel containers, all of which are integral parts of a monocoque, so this tends to nullify any hoped-for weight advantage.

monocorde, obs. form of MONOCHORD.

monocormic: see MONO- 1.

monocot, monocotyl, shortened forms of MONOCOTYLEDON.

1877 LE CONTE *Elem. Geol.* I. (1879) 354 Types..of the monocotyls on the one hand, and of the Dicotyls on the other. **1890** *Athenæum* 22 Nov. 702/1 Angiosperms are divided [by Dr. D. H. Campbell] into two 'sub-classes', thus placing the monocots and dicots on a lower level than the cycads.

monoˈcotyle, *a. Bot. rare*⁻⁰. [See prec. and cf. MONOCOTYLOUS 2.] = MONOCOTYLEDONOUS.

1828–32 in WEBSTER; and in some later Dicts.

monocotyledon (ˌmɒnəʊkɒtɪˈliːdən). *Bot.* [ad. mod.L. *monocotylēdōn*, f. Gr. μόνο-ς MONO- + κοτυληδών cup-shaped cavity: see COTYLEDON.

The term *Monocotyledones* was employed by Ray, but its practical introduction into botanical classification dates from Jussieu 1779.]

A flowering plant having one cotyledon or seed-leaf in the embryo. The Monocotyledons (in Bot. Lat. *Monocotyledones*), or Endogens, constitute one of the two great classes of flowering plants.

[**1703** RAY *Methodus Plant.* 2 Monocotyledones, quæ nec folia seminalia bina efferunt, nec lobos binos condunt.] **1727** BAILEY (vol. II.), *Monocotyledon*, which springs from the Seed with a single Leaf at first, as Corn, Tulips, Onions, &c. **1800** tr. *Lagrange's Chem.* II. 261 It is chiefly from the seeds of the monocotyledons..that the greater part of the feculæ are extracted. **1857** HENFREY *Elem. Bot.* §750 The stems of Monocotyledons are very generally herbaceous.

monocotyledonous (ˌmɒnəʊkɒtɪˈliːdənəs), *a. Bot.* [f. prec. + -OUS.] Having a single cotyledon; belonging to the class of Monocotyledons.

1770 C. MILNE *Bot. Dict.* s.v. *Cotyledones*, some seeds, however, have only one seminal leaf; in which case, the plants, by botanists, are termed Monocotyledonous. **1785** MARTYN *Rousseau's Bot.* xiii. (1794) 131 *note.* **1845** DARWIN *Voy. Nat.* xi. (1873) 244 Stately trees..loaded by parasitical monocotyledonous plants. **1851** RICHARDSON *Geol.* vii. (1855) 164 The monocotyledonous, or endogenous classes.

b. Of or belonging to a monocotyledon.

1849 BALFOUR *Man. Bot.* §91 Endogenous or Monocotyledonous Stem. **1876** PAGE *Adv. Text-bk. Geol.* ix. 185 The parallel venation of a monocotyledonous leaf.

monocotylous (mɒnəʊˈkɒtɪləs), *a.* [In sense 1 f. mod.L. *monocotyl-us*, f. Gr. μόνο-ς MONO- + κοτύλ-η cup, cavity: see -OUS. Cf. F. *monocotyle*.]

1. *Zool.* Having one vent or mouth (see quot.).

1856 MAYNE *Expos. Lex.*, *Monocotylus*, applied by Blainville to a Family (*Monocotyla*) of the *Entozoa myzocephala*, comprehending those of which the body has but one vent: monocotylous.

2. *Bot.* Used for MONOCOTYLEDONOUS.

1905 BALFOUR *Goebel's Organogr. Plants* II. 327 The seedlings..have the ordinary leaf-form of monocotylous plants.

monocracy (məˈnɒkrəsɪ). [ad. assumed Gr. type *μονοκρατία: see next and -CRACY.] Government by a single person, autocracy.

1651 BIGGS *New Disp.* ⁋34 The Monocracy and single-sol'd intemperature of the Liver. **1754** A. MURPHY *Gray's Inn Jrnl.* No. 95 Monocracy, Aristocracy, and Democracy. **1839** SYD. SMITH *Ballot* (ed. 2) 29 A scene of wholesale bacchanalian fraud,..which would disgust any man with a free government, and make him sigh for the monocracy of Constantinople. **1893** GOLDW. SMITH *United States* 160 Jefferson's jeremiads over the encroachments and corruptions of monocracy under the first two Presidents.

monocrat (ˈmɒnəkræt). [ad. Gr. μονοκρατ-ής ruling alone, f. μόνο-ς MONO- + κρατ-εῖν to rule: see -CRAT.] **a.** One who rules alone; an autocrat. (In Dicts.) **b.** A partisan of monocracy or monarchy; a political nickname given *circa* 1790 by Jefferson to members of the Federalist party, because they sided with England as against France.

1792 JEFFERSON *Writ.* (1859) III. 494 The doctrines of the Monocrats. **1793** *Ibid.* IV. 9 The war between France and England has brought forward the Republicans and Monocrats in every State. **1883** J. T. MORSE jr. *Jefferson* xv. (1885) 251 Here was an act, done by the great Republican doctrinaire-president,..monarchical, beyond what any 'monocrat' had ever dared to dream of.

appos. **179.** JEFFERSON in W. Irving *Washington* (1863) V. 148 (Funk) Even the monocrat papers are obliged to publish the most furious philippics against England.

Hence **monoˈcratic** *a.*, relating to monocracy.

1890 LOWELL *Milton's Areop.* Latest Lit. Ess. (1891) 101 His experience of Cromwell apparently having made any monocratic devices distasteful to him.

monocrotic, -crotous: see MONO- 1.

monocular (məˈnɒkjʊlə(r)), *a.* Also (in sense 2) **mono-ocular.** [f. late L. *monocul-us* (see MONOCULUS) + -AR. Cf. F. *monoculaire*.]

1. a. Having only one eye, or the use of only one eye. Now *rare.*

1640 HOWELL *Dodona's Gr.* 86 Who going to cut downe an ancient white Hauthorne-Tree..had some of the prickles flew into his eye, and made him Monocular. **1664** POWER *Exp. Philos.* I. 82, I could never find any Animal that was monocular. **1696** E. LHWYD in *Phil. Trans.* XXVII. 464 He had..catch'd Monocular Trouts. **1767** BARRINGTON *ibid.* LVII. 207 Monocular fish, which are said by Giraldus Cambrensis to be found in the lakes of Snowden. **1886** R. F. BURTON *Arab. Nts.* (abr. ed.) I. 90 Had we escaped the mortification of those monocular Kalandars. **1887** *Brit. Med. Jrnl.* 7 May 995 A small monocular fœtus.

b. quasi-*sb.* A one-eyed person.

1886 R. F. BURTON *Arab. Nts.* (abr. ed.) I. 82 [She] returned with three monoculars.

2. a. Of or pertaining to one eye only; adapted to one eye.

1858 *Edin. Rev.* CVIII. 439 Monocular vision, or vision with a single eye. **1874** VAN BUREN *Dis. Genit. Org.* 87 These varieties of ophthalmia..are rarely mono-ocular. **1878** CARPENTER in *Encycl. Brit.* XVI. 274/1 By the insertion of a suitably constructed binocular eye-piece into the body of any ordinary monocular microscope. **1891** *Syd. Soc. Lex.*, *Monocular bandage*, a bandage applied to one eye only. **1902** *19th Cent.* Apr. 605 It is still more rare for it [*sc.* colour-blindness] to be monocular.

fig. **1890** J. MARTINEAU *Seat Author. Relig.* 163 Such a monocular phenomenon is the orthodoxy of the Church. **1923** *Public Opinion* 8 June 542/3 The bane of cancer research has been its monocular myopia.

b. Wearing a monocle. *rare.*

1903 G. B. SHAW *Man & Superman* p. xxiii, These college passmen, these well groomed monocular Algys and Bobbies.

c. quasi-*sb.* A glass, esp. a field-glass, in the use of which only one eye is employed in viewing an object.

1936 *British Birds* XXX. 39 It was only when I turned my monocular on the bird in the water that I realized it was a Red-legged Partridge. **1959** *Chambers's Encycl.* IX. 385/2 The modern microscope usually has interchangeable bodies, making it possible to use the same stand with monocular or binocular. **1971** D. WHILLANS in C. Bonington *Annapurna South Face* v. 58 There was a monocular in the tent which I focused on the dark, moving shape.

Hence **monocuˈlarity**, monocular condition; **moˈnocularly** *adv.*, with the use of one eye only.

1857 *Nat. Mag.* II. 276 Thieving may not unnaturally be assigned to a mental strabismus or monocularity. **1880** W. JAMES *Coll. Ess. & Rev.* (1920) 177 If under these circumstances the object thus monocularly seen were translocated outwardly, we should have a complete verification. **1881** CARPENTER *Microsc.* §36 (ed. 6) 39 No one who has only thus worked monocularly can appreciate the guidance derivable from binocular vision. **1972** *Sci. Amer.* Aug. 86/3 An insect disguised as a leaf may be invisible monocularly but stand out in a different depth plane from real leaves when it is viewed stereoscopically.

†**moˈnoculate**, *a. Obs. rare*⁻¹. [f. late L. *monocul-us* (see MONOCULUS) + -ATE², after L. *oculātus* OCULATE *a.*] One-eyed.

1618 T. ADAMS *Spir. Eye-salve* Wks. (1629) 664 Philosophy (vnbaptized with grace) is said to be monoculate, to haue but one eye, and that is of naturall Reason.

monocule (ˈmɒnəʊkjuːl). *rare.* [a. F. *monocule*, or ad. L. *monocul-us* MONOCULUS.] A creature with only one eye (e.g. the Cyclops). Also, a member of the Linnæan genus MONOCULUS.

1771 J. R. FORSTER *Catal. Anim. N. Amer.* 33 Monocule, King's Crab, Monoculus Polyphemus. **1829** *Blackw. Mag.* XXVI. 285 Little moving things, no bigger than mites, were bustling about, and now and then I could perceive one or two of these diminutive monocules venturing [etc.]. **1832** *Ibid.* XXXII. 667 The orifice in the forehead of the Monocule abhorr'd.

monoculist (məˈnɒkjʊlɪst). *rare.* [f. late L. *monocul-us* (see MONOCULUS) + -IST. Cf. F. *monoculiste*.] A monoculous person.

1622 MISSELDEN *Free Trade* 114 Some Monoculists, by the sharpnesse of the sence drawne to one Eie, see better with that, then both. **1659** 'HODG TURBERVIL' *Walk knaves, walk* in Morgan *Phoenix Brit.* (1732) I. 262 Our Learned Monoculist and Noble Commander, Col. Hewson. **1866** *North Brit. Mail* 26 Sept., O'Baldwin had the valuable assistance of a..not over-refined monoculist, and another equally objectionable member of pugilistic society.

monoculite (məˈnɒkjʊlaɪt). *rare.* [Formed as prec. + -ITE¹.]

†**1.** ? = MONOCULIST. *Obs.*

1718 *Entertainer* No. 14. 95 Are there no Deputies of oak or Monoculites?

2. 'A fossil animal that appears to have but one eye' (*Cent. Dict.* 1890).

monoculous (məˈnɒkjʊləs), *a.* [f. L. *monocul-us* (see MONOCULUS) + -OUS.] One-eyed.

1656 BLOUNT *Glossogr.*, *Monocular, Monosculous* [sic], that hath but one eye, one ey'd. *a* **1661** FULLER *Worthies*, *Carnarvonsh.* (1662) IV. 30 He telleth us also of Monoculous Fishes. **1661** GLANVILL *Van. Dogm.* 129 We judge truth to be circumscrib'd by the confines of our belief,..and.. repute all the rest of the world Monoculous. **1785** *Gent. Mag.* LV. I. 267 *note*, But Polypheme surely was monoculous. **1861** F. HALL in *Jrnl. Asiatic Soc. Bengal* XXX. 206 *note*, Every one-eyed man, in these parts, [is now known] as Holkar, from the monoculous Marāthā chieftain of that name. **1887** O. W. HOLMES in *Atlantic Monthly* LIX. 638 Dr. Knox was the monoculous Waterloo surgeon, with whom I remember breakfasting.

fig. **1845** NAPIER *Conq. Scinde* II. ii. 283 Outram's monoculous diplomacy.

monoculture (ˈmɒnəʊkʌltjʊə(r)). [irreg. f. MONO- + CULTURE *sb.* Cf. F. *monoculture* (1842 in Robert).] **a.** The cultivation or exploitation of a single crop, to the exclusion of others that are possible. Also *fig.*

1915 C. R. ENOCK *Tropics* xxxiii. 373 The decline of sugar 'monoculture' may have proved a blessing in disguise. Cotton and many food-stuffs are now produced. **1925** E. F. ROW tr. *Demangeon's Brit. Empire* 134 This plantation system, this exploiting to the uttermost of a single valuable product, involves the dangers of all monoculture. **1948** *Times* 17 June 5 The name [*sc.* groundnut scheme] is too suggestive of monoculture and dustbowls. **1961** J. RUSSELL tr. *Lévi-Strauss's World on Wane* iv. 39 Humanity has taken to monoculture, once and for all, and is preparing to produce civilization in bulk, as if it were sugar-beet. **1962** *Economist*

7 July 60/1 A 'monoculture' economy dependent on only one resource for most of its income. **1970** J. ARDAGH *New France* vi. 206 The monoculture of cheap wine was dangerous for the region's economy. **1974** *Country Life* 28 Mar. 710/1 The replacement of broad-leaved woodland with conifer and increasing monoculture.

b. An area in which monoculture is practised or a single kind of (higher) animal maintained.

1951 *New Biol.* X. 56 Nature abhors a monoculture, and the most carefully tended orchards soon become ecological associations with distinctive flora and fauna. **1970** *New Scientist* 21 May 372/1 The transformation of habitats from virgin forests to cultivated woods, vast crop monocultures, industrial areas and big cities is the most radical change of nature that has struck Europe since the last glaciation. **1974** *Environmental Conservation* I. 17/2 Huge areas are turned into monocultures. **1974** *Nature* 24 May 307/3 One is towards the establishment of monocultures of eland, wildebeest, gazelle or kob.

c. An area in which all the inhabitants share a common culture or way of life.

1968 *Listener* 5 Sept. 298/1 Los Angeles's least endearing characteristic: the tendency to fragment into self-contained, specialised areas—social monocultures. Functional monocultures, too: in Los Angeles you tend to go to a particular place to do a particular thing.

Hence **mono'cultural** *a.*; **mono'culturist**, one who practises or advocates monoculture.

1915 C. R. ENOCK *Tropics* xl. 442 Events in some tropical lands have laid bare the unwisdom of monocultural methods. **1928** E. R. JOHNSON et al. *Princ. Transportation* xxi. 243 The South from earliest colonial days has been agricultural and primarily monocultural. **1964** GOULD & KOLB *Dict. Soc. Sci.* 583/1 The 'Deep South' region of U.S.A. exhibits specialized cultural, political, and economic (monocultural) features. **1965** *New Scientist* 23 July 199/1 Monocultural crop planting on totally cleared areas. **1968** W. E. LAMBERT et al. in J. A. Fishman *Readings Sociol. of Lang.* (1968) 479 It is of special interest to note a basically similar pattern appearing in all three of the American settings, two bicultural and one monocultural. **1973** *Country Life* 30 Aug. 586/2 The monoculturists' ideas of good yields being likely to cause any self-respecting rotational farmer to blush with shame.

‖**monoculus** (mə'nɒkjʊləs). [late L., irreg. f. Gr. *μόν-ος* MON(O)- + L. *oculus* eye.]

1. A one-eyed being.

c **1440** *Alphabet of Tales* 389 When he had þurgh raklesnes loste ane of his een and was made monoculus. **1597** BACON *Coulers Gd. & Euill* Ess. (Arb.) 152 As to a monoculos [*sic*] it is more to loose one eye, than to a man that hath two eyes. **1638** SIR T. HERBERT *Trav.* (ed. 2) 20 The Arimaspi (who from wincking when they shoot are said to be *Monoculi*). **1709** *Tatler* No. 36 ¶5. *Ibid.* No. 56 ¶1. [Used as a proper name.] **1722** QUINCY *Lex. Physico-Med.* (ed. 2), *Monoculus*, is used for a Person having but one Eye. **1819** *Pantologia*, *Monoculus*,.. *Monopia*. A very uncommon species of monstrosity, in which there is but one eye, and that mostly above the root of the nose.

2. A Linnæan genus of 'insects' or minute crustaceans; a member of this genus.

1752 J. HILL *Hist. Anim.* 22, 23. **1774** GOLDSM. *Nat. Hist.* VII. 288 The Monoculus or Arborescent Water-Flea. **1797** *Encycl. Brit.* (ed. 3) XII. 240/2 The quadricornis, or four-horned monoculus, a very small species about half a line in length. **1848** E. FORBES *Naked-eyed Medusæ* 60 So wrote Otho Frederic Müller—filled, by his studies of minute life, with a deep spirit of reverence and admiration of his monoculi. **1880** HUXLEY *Crayfish* v. 279 The water-fleas or the monoculi of the ponds.

3. a. A bandage for one eye.

1849 in CRAIG. **1875** in KNIGHT *Dict. Mech.*

b. A single eye-glass (*Syd. Soc. Lex.* 1891).

monocycle ('mɒnəsaɪk(ə)l). [f. Gr. *μόνο-ς* MONO- *κύκλος* wheel, CYCLE. Cf. Gr. *μονόκυκλος* with one circle.] A velocipede having only one wheel.

'In one form the rider is seated inside the wheel' (Webster *Suppl.* 1902).

1869 *The Velocipede* (N.Y.) Apr. 79 A New York mechanic has devised a monocycle or single machine. **1869** *Sci. Amer.* 22 May 330 The machine is evidently a monocycle. **1902** *Speaker* 15 Feb. 564/1 Monocycles progressing at eighty miles an hour.

monocyclic (mɒnəʊ'sɪklɪk, -'saɪklɪk), *a.* [Formed as prec. + -IC.] Having a single circle or cycle.

1. *Zool.* **a.** Of or pertaining to the *Monocyclica*, a subclass of crinoid Echinoderms having only a single circlet of basal plates. **b.** Of or pertaining to the *Monocyclia*, a division of Holothurians having the tentacles in a single circle or series.

1882 F. H. CARPENTER in *Q. Jrnl. Microsc. Sci.* XXII. 377 The monocyclic *Comatulæ*. **1888** ROLLESTON & JACKSON *Anim. Life* 545 When they [*sc.* underbasals] are present the base of the apical system is said to be dicyclic, when absent monocyclic. **1900** *Lankester's Treat. Zool.* III. 111 Monocyclic and dicyclic genera should not be placed in the same line of descent.

2. *Bot.* **a.** Having the members of a floral series disposed in a single whorl. **b.** Annual (B. D. Jackson *Gloss. Bot. Terms* 1900).

1882 S. H. VINES tr. *Sachs' Text-bk. Bot.* 601 When the members of a series (calyx, corolla, etc.) are in one whorl, the series is said to be monocyclic. **1891** *Syd. Soc. Lex.*, *Monocyclic*, having the members of a series all in one whorl. **1895** S. H. VINES *Students' Text-bk. Bot.* II. iii. 501 The simplest case is that in which each series of floral organs.. occupies a single whorl, or is monocyclic.

3. *Electr.* 'Designating a certain system or arrangement of armature windings and transmission lines for the utilization of currents in a combined lighting and power service' (Webster *Suppl.* 1902).

4. *Chem.* Having a molecular structure with a single ring.

1910 *Jrnl. Chem. Soc.* XCVII. 1616 From this glycol we could obtain a monocyclic terpene. **1939** *Nature* 26 Aug. 349/1 The detailed consideration of monocyclic compounds is then taken up. **1967** M. E. HALE *Biol. Lichens* viii. 105 Free monocyclic phenolic substances.

5. *Geol.* Having undergone a single cycle of erosion or (quot. 1969) of mountain-building.

1952 *Jrnl. Geol.* LX. 188/1 Four general types of landscapes, suggested by Bryan's (1943, pp. 472–473) classification of soils: (1) simple, monocyclic landscapes which can be fitted to the idealized cycle; (2) complex, multicyclic landscapes which require historical interpretation; (3) compound landscapes..; (4) exhumed landscapes. **1954** W. D. THORNBURY *Princ. Geomorphol.* ii. 23 Monocyclic landscapes are less common than multicyclic and are in general restricted to such newly created land surfaces as a recently uplifted portion of the ocean floor. **1968** R. W. FAIRBRIDGE *Encycl. Geomorphol.* 286/2 Monocyclic landscapes are rarely found except in very recently formed land surfaces. **1969** BENNISON & WRIGHT *Geol. Hist. Brit. Isles* iii. 36 Within both the Caledonian and Lewisian belts there is evidence of several periods of folding and metamorphism and neither represents a simple monocyclic unit.

monocyclous (mɒnəʊ'sɪkləs), *a. Conch. rare*$^{-0}$. [f. mod.L. *monocycl-us* (formed as MONOCYCLE) + -OUS.] (See quot.)

1856 MAYNE *Expos. Lex.*, *Monocyclus*, applied to the *Scalaria monocycla*, because its last turn is circumscribed at the base by a transversal filament: monocyclous.

monocyst ('mɒnəsɪst). *Path.* [f. MONO- + CYST.] A tumour consisting of a single cyst.

1869 T. G. THOMAS *Dis. Women* (ed. 2) 553 The monocyst ..develops the power of cysto-genesis and becomes polycystic. **1897** *Allbutt's Syst. Med.* II. 1110 The hydatid bladder.. consists of a single simple sac or mono-cyst.

monocysted ('mɒnəsɪstɪd), *a.* [Formed as prec. + -ED².] = next.

1885 T. GILL in *Smithsonian Rep.* (1886) I. 765 The monocysted Gregorines [*read* Gregarines].

monocystic (mɒnəʊ'sɪstɪk), *a.* [Formed as prec. + -IC.] Having or consisting of a single cyst.

1872 T. G. THOMAS *Dis. Women* (ed. 3) 652 Unilocular or monocystic tumors rarely attain a great size as such. **1885** E. R. LANKESTER in *Encycl. Brit.* XIX. 853/2 The sporulation ..of the various monocystic Gregarinides.

Hence **mono'cystically** *adv.*

1872 PEASLEE *Ovar. Tumors* 31 The distinction..of the monocystically inclined and the polycystic..cystoma.

monocystid (mɒnəʊ'sɪstɪd). *Zool.* [ad. mod.L. *Monocystid-ea* (neut. pl.), f. Gr. *μόνο-ς* MONO- + *κύστ-ις* bladder, CYST: see -ID.] A member of the order *Monocystidea* of Gregarines, having the body simple, i.e. not segmented.

1882 E. R. LANKESTER in *Q. Jrnl. Microsc. Sci.* XXII. 58 The Monocystid *Adelia ovata.* **1888** ROLLESTON & JACKSON *Anim. Life* 859 The Monocystids of the Earthworm.

So **monocy'stidean** *a.* and *sb.* (in recent Dicts.).

monocyte ('mɒnəsaɪt). *Biol.* [ad. G. *monozyt* (Pappenheim & Ferrata 1910, in *Folia Haematologica* X. I. 81): see MONO- and -CYTE.] A kind of large leucocyte which has a single oval or indented nucleus and no coarse granulation in the cytoplasm, constitutes 3–8 per cent of the total leucocytes in human blood, and is the circulating form of the macrophage.

1913 STEDMAN *Med. Dict.* (ed. 2) 556/1 Monocyte. **1927** A. PINEY *Rec. Adv. Hæmatol.* ii. 16 The large hyaline leucocyte or monocyte is not easy to place with certainty into either the granular or the non-granular group. **1970** T. S. & C. R. LEESON *Histology* (ed. 2) viii. 140/1 Monocytes migrate readily through vessel walls and develop into phagocytic cells which cannot be distinguished from macrophages already present within the connective tissues. They are effective in combating tubercle bacilli. **1974** PASSMORE & ROBSON *Compan. Med. Stud.* III. xxi. 5/1 Absence of monocytes or basophils from the blood film or reduction in their number does not have clinical significance.

Hence **mono'cytic** *a.*; **monocy'tosis** [-OSIS], an abnormal increase in the number of monocytes in the blood.

1914 STEDMAN *Med. Dict.* (ed. 3) 576/1 Monocytosis. **1934** WEBSTER, Monocytic. **1935** WHITBY & BRITTON *Disorders Blood* i. 18 The origin of the monocytic cells has been and still is, the subject of much controversy. **1938** H. DOWNEY *Handbk. Hematol.* I. v. 389 Monocytes may appear in large numbers in the peripheral blood in the monocytic leucemias. *Ibid.* II. xv. 1067 In chronic malaria, the irritation of the reticulo-endothelium often leads to a monocytosis in the peripheral blood. **1972** *Nature* 4 Feb. 275/1 Cells of the monocytic series. **1974** PASSMORE & ROBSON *Compan. Med. Stud.* III. xxi. 5/1 Monocytosis is seen in the course of infectious mononucleosis and in some bacterial infections, notably tuberculosis.

monocyttarian (mɒnəʊsɪ'tɛərɪən), *a.* and *sb. Zool.* [f. mod.L. *Monocyttaria* neut. pl. (f. Gr. *μόνο-ς* MONO- + *κύτταρ-ος* cell) + -AN.]

a. *adj.* Belonging to the group *Monocyttaria* of Radiolarians, which have a single central capsule; unicapsular. **b.** *sb.* A member of this group.

1890 in *Century Dict.*

monodactyl, -yle (mɒnəʊ'dæktɪl), *a. Zool.* [ad. Gr. *μονοδάκτυλ-ος* one-fingered, f. *μόνο-ς* MONO- + *δάκτυλ-ος* finger. Cf. F. *monodactyle.*] = MONODACTYLOUS.

1819 G. SAMOUELLE *Entomol. Compend.* 177 Monodactyle claws. **1826** KIRBY & SP. *Entomol.* III. xxviii. 48 The foot or *Tarsus* [of the *Diptera*], is almost universally monodactyle. **1852** DANA *Crust.* II. 1036 A monodactyle hand. **1870** FLOWER *Osteol. Mamm.* xix. (1876) 319 The monodactyle foot of the Horse.

monodac'tylic, *a. Pros. rare*$^{-0}$. [f. MONO- + DACTYLIC.] Containing but one dactyl.

1890 in *Century Dict.*

monodactylous (mɒnəʊ'dæktɪləs), *a. Zool.* [f. MONODACTYL + -OUS.] Having only one finger, toe, or claw. In Crustacea = SUBCHELATE.

1828–32 in WEBSTER. **1841** *Penny Cycl.* 421/1 The last three pairs [of feet] are monodactylous. **1856–8** W. CLARK *Van der Hoeven's Zool.* I. 671 Hippoidea.—First pair of feet monodactylous or subchelate. **1881** *Nature* 29 Sept. 527/2 A link..between our modern monodactylous horse and its three-toed ancestor.

mono'dactyly. [f. MONODACTYL + -Y.] The condition of being monodactyl.

1897 *Amer. Naturalist* Feb. 161 The monodactyly, observed in the pig by Aristotle.

monodelph ('mɒnədɛlf). *Zool.* [ad. F. *Monodelphe* (De Blainville), f. mod.L. *Monodelph-ia*, f. Gr. *μόνο-ς* MONO- + *δελφύς* womb.] A mammal belonging to the subclass *Monodelphia* of mammals, characterized by a single uterus and vagina, and comprising all mammals except the monotremes and marsupials.

1842 BRANDE *Dict. Sci.* etc., *Monodelphs*.., a name given by De Blainville to the first sub-class in his binary division of Mammalia. **1878** BARTLEY tr. *Topinard's Anthrop.* 22 The Monodelphs include (1) The *Cetacea* and *Amphibia*. (2) The Pachydermata [etc.].

So **mono'delphian**, (*a*) *adj.* of, belonging to, or characteristic of the *Monodelphia*; (*b*) *sb.* a member of this subclass; **mono'delphic**, **mono'delphous** *adjs.*

1856 MAYNE *Expos. Lex.*, *Monodelphus*,..monodelphous. **1869** HUXLEY *Introd. Classif. Anim.* 90 In this manner.. the Monodelphian fœtus is supplied with nourishment. *Ibid.* 98 The type of a distinct order of deciduate Monodelphous *Mammalia.* **1870** FLOWER *Osteol. Mamm.* i. (1876) 3 The remaining Monodelphian Mammals are:—1. Primates. **1881** MIVART *Cat* 469 The Cat, as a monodelphous mammal, of course shares the characters which distinguish that subclass from both the others. **1882** OGILVIE, *Monodelph*, *Monodelphian*, *sb.* a mammal belonging to the sub-class Monodelphia. *Ibid.*, *Monodelphic.*

monodelph, etc., erron. ff. MONADELPH, etc.

monodermic: see MONO- 1.

‖**mo'nodia.** *Mus.* [It. or L.: see MONODY.] (See quot.)

1880 ROCKSTRO in Grove *Dict. Mus.* II. 354/1 *Monodia.* A term applied, by modern critics, to music written in what is sometimes called the Homophonic Style: that is to say, music, in which the Melody is confined to a single part, instead of being equally distributed between all the Voices employed, as in the Polyphonic Schools.

monodiabolism, -diametral: see MONO- 1.

monodic (mə'nɒdɪk), *a.* [ad. Gr. *μονῳδικ-ός* f. *μονῳδ-ός*: see MONODY and -IC.] Pertaining to or of the nature of monody. In *Music*, characterized by the predominance of one part or melody, to which the other parts merely furnish harmonies.

1818 BUSBY *Gram. Mus.* 99 *note*, The first of these styles of melody they term *monodic*, the second *polyodic*. **1879** GROVE *Dict. Mus.* I. 746/1 Homophone..is sometimes applied to music written in what was formerly called the Monodic style. **1883** ROCKSTRO *ibid.* III. 278/2 The Monodic School of Florence. **1896** J. A. F. MAITLAND in *Dict. Nat. Biog.* XLVII. 42/2 The new art of monodic writing, as opposed to the elaborate involutions of the madrigalian period. **1900** H. W. SMYTH *Greek Melic Poets* p. xxi, Monodic melic, or that which is sung by a single voice, is represented in the earliest stage of Greek song by the nome.

So **mo'nodical** *a.*; **mo'nodically** *adv.*

1656 BLOUNT *Glossogr.*, *Monodical.* **1890** *Century Dict.*, *Monodically.*

monodichlamydeous, etc.: see MONO- 1.

monodist ('mɒnədɪst). [f. MONOD(Y + -IST.]

1. One who writes or sings a monody.

1751 RICHARDSON *Corr.* (1804) III. 183 Think you, Madam, that a certain monodist did not imagine himself possessed by this purer flame. **1825** HONE *Every-day Bk.* 13 Aug. I. 1106 The monodist [*sc.* Huddesford, who wrote a 'Monody on the Death of Dick, an Academical Cat'] connects him with cats of great renown in the annals of witchcraft.

2. One who composes in the monodic style; opposed to *contrapuntist* (Cent. Dict. 1890).

1916 STANFORD & FORSYTH *Hist. Mus.* vii. 148 There is no sudden revolution in the method of handling the musical material such as the monodists engineered in 1600. **1974** *Country Life* 14 Mar. 590/3 In the early-17th century..the Italian Monodists..sought to find a new expressive force by abandoning the use of the contrapuntal device.

monodistich: see MONO- 1.

'monodize, *v. nonce-wd.* [f. MONOD(Y + -IZE.] *trans.* To make the subject of a monody.
1796 COLERIDGE *Let.* Aug. in *Biog. Lit.* (1847) II. 370, I was at Matlock, the place monodized by Bowles.

‖**monodon** ('mɒnədɒn). *Zool.* [mod.L., f. Gr. *μονοδοντ-, μονόδους*, f. *μόν-ος* MON(O)- + *ὀδοντ-, ὀδούς* tooth.] A genus of delphinoid cetaceans, containing only the narwhal (*M. monoceros*); also, a member of this genus.
1752 J. HILL *Hist. Anim.* 314 *Monodon*, the Unicorn-fish, or Nar-wal. **1753** CHAMBERS *Cycl. Supp.* *c* **1865** LETHEBY in *Wylde's Circ. Sci.* I. 103/2 Even the Monodons or narwhales may be made to yield train-oil.

monodont ('mɒnədɒnt), *a. rare*$^{-0}$. [Formed as prec.] Having only one tooth. Also **mono'dontal** *a.*, of the nature of an 'only tooth'; also, pertaining to the genus *Monodon*.
1853 KANE *Grinnell Exp.* xxxvii. (1856) 340 The horn, that monodontal process which gives them their name of sea-unicorn. **1891** *Syd. Soc. Lex.*, *Monodont*.

monodrama ('mɒnəʊdrɑːmə, mɒnəʊ'drɑːmə). Also 9 **monodram(e**. [f. MONO- + DRAMA.] A dramatic piece for a single performer. Now esp. an opera for one singer.
1793 SOUTHEY *Let. to G. C. Bedford* 26 Oct. in *Life* (1849) I. 185 Monodramas, comodramas, tragodramas, all sorts of dramas. **1803** in *Spirit Publ. Jrnls.* (1804) VII. 170 He [an actor] is assisting to get up the Monodram, in which he takes a principal part. **1823** *Edin. Rev.* XXXVIII. 183 The first attempt at dramatic writing would naturally be in the form of a monodrame. **1829** *Examiner* 275/2 The puns and drollery of Mathews in his new mono-drama *At Home*. **1849** *Eclectic Rev.* XXVI. 211 The entire sum of his [Browning's] poetry may be said to be dramatic, though much of it..simple monodrama. **1904** *Athenæum* 18 June 776/1 Tennyson intended 'Maud' to be a pure monodrama, yet it was taken for a portrait of himself. **1954** *Grove's Dict. Mus.* (ed. 5) V. 666/2 The title part of Berlioz's 'Lélio'.., in which a single actor appears, may also be called a 'monodrama'. *Ibid.*, A work like Schoenberg's 'Erwartung', in which a single acting singer appears, is also in the nature of 'monodrama'. **1966** *Listener* 19 May 736/3 *Erwartung*,.. a monodrama or 'prose opera' (Stravinsky)... This fragmentary half-hour composition..is scored for soprano (no supporting cast) and large orchestra. **1974** *New Yorker* 29 Apr. 129/1 An extravagant monodrama for singer, pianist, and orchestra.
fig. **1824** *New Monthly Mag.* X. 41 Friendship is with them a *mono-drama*, in which they play the principal and sole part.
Hence ˌ**monodra'matic** *a.*, pertaining to or characteristic of a monodrama; **mono'dramatist**, one who writes a monodrama.
1801 *Monthly Mirror* Aug. 136 A German..has lately appeared on this stage, in an Italian mono-dramatic interlude, called Il Cazolaro. **1803** in *Spirit Publ. Jrnls.* (1805) VIII. 178 Hint to a Mono-dramatist, how to avoid damnation. **1825** *Blackw. Mag.* XVII. 731 These great performers..have retired into a dignified and limited range of mono-dramatic parts. **1897** TENNYSON *Mem. Ld. Tennyson* I. 402 'Maud' and other monodramatic poems.

monodromic (mɒnəʊ'drɒmɪk), *a. Math.* [f. Gr. *μόνο-ς* MONO- + *δρόμ-ος* course + -IC, after F. *monodrome* (Cauchy).] Of a function: Having a single value for one value of the variable.
1890 in *Century Dict.* **1893** FORSYTH *Theory of Functions* 15 *note*.

monodromy (mə'nɒdrəmɪ). *Math.* [f. as MONODROMIC *a.* + -Y³.] (See quot. 1909.)
1897 B. RUSSELL *Essay on Foundations of Geometry* i. 24 As regards independence of rotation in rigid bodies (Monodromy). If $(n-1)$ points of a body remain fixed, so that every other point can only describe a certain curve, then that curve is closed. **1903** *Nature* 19 Feb. 382/2 It is pointed out that in the non-Pythagorean geometries devised by Hilbert, Helmholtz's axiom of monodromy is not verified, inasmuch as it is possible by rotation through four right angles, to bring the points of a line into positions which they do not occupy before the rotation. **1909** *Cent. Dict.* Suppl., *Monodromy*, (*a*) the characteristic property that, if the argument returns by any path to its original value, the function also returns to its original value. (*b*) The property that the curves described by a revolution or rotation through four right angles are closed. **1949** G. & R. C. JAMES *Math. Dict.* 237/1 *Monodromy theorem.* The theorem states that, if the function $f(z)$ of the complex variable z is analytic at the point z_0 and can be continued analytically along every curve issuing from z_0 in a finite simply connected domain D, then $f(z)$ is a function-element of an analytic function which is single valued in D; in other words, analytic continuation around any closed curve in D leads to the original function element.

monody ('mɒnədɪ). [ad. L. *monōdia, monōdium*, a. Gr. *μονῳδία* solo, lament, f. *μονῳδ-ός* singing alone, f. *μόν-ος* MONO- + *ᾠδ-* contracted form of *ἀοιδ-* ablaut-var. of *ἀείδ-ειν* to sing: cf. *ᾠδή* ODE. Cf. F. *monodie*, It. *monodia*.]
1. In Greek literature: **a.** A lyric ode sung by a single voice; an ode sung by one of the actors in a tragedy (as distinct from the chorus); hence, a mournful song or dirge.
[**1589** PUTTENHAM *Eng. Poesie* I. xxiv. (Arb.) 63 Such funerall songs were called *Epicedia* if they were song by many, and *Monodia* if they were vttered by one alone.] **1623** COCKERAM, *Monodies*, mournefull songs. **1656** BLOUNT *Glossogr.*, *Monodie*, a lamentable or funeral song, where one sings alone. **1751** JOHNSON *Rambler* No. 156 ⁋7 Tragedy was a monody or solitary song in honour of Bacchus, improved afterwards into a dialogue. **1760** FAWKES tr. *Sappho* Introd., She wrote nine Books of Odes, besides Elegies, Epigrams, Iambics, Monodies and other Pieces. **1896** HAIGH *Greek Drama* 363 The monodies form one of the most salient features in the tragedy of Euripides. **1900** H. W. SMYTH *Greek Melic Poets* p. xxi, The chief representatives of the monody are the Aiolians and the Ionic Anakreon.
b. A funeral oration. [So in late Gr.]
1781 GIBBON *Decl. & F.* xviii. II. 110 *note*, The monody pronounced on the death of Constantine, might have been very instructive; but prudence and false taste engaged the orator to involve himself in vague declamation.
2. A poem in which a mourner bewails some one's death.
1637 MILTON *Lycidas* Argt., In this Monody the Author bewails a learned Friend, unfortunately drown'd. **1691** WOOD *Ath. Oxon.* I. 590 Soon after was a tomb erected.. whereon was insculp'd a Monodie made by Dr. Laur. Humphrey. **1790** COLERIDGE (*title*) Monody on the Death of Chatterton. **1809** BYRON *Bards & Rev.* 747 Let monodies on Fox regale your crew. **1866** M. ARNOLD (*title*) Thyrsis. A Monody, to commemorate the author's friend, Arthur Hugh Clough.
3. *Mus.* The homophonic style of composition (see MONODIA). Also, a composition in this style.
1887 *Daily News* 3 May 6/1 Songs for a single voice were not known in art music until Vincenzo Galilei..composed solos with instrumental accompaniments. On the invention of these 'monodies', as they were called, the three above-named [Italian] masters..founded their dramatic attempts. **1890** in *Century Dict.*
4. 'Monotonous sound; monotonousness of sound' (*Cent. Dict.*).
a **1849** POE *Bells* iv, Hear the tolling of the bells—Iron bells! What a world of solemn thought their monody compels! **1885** MISS MURFREE *Prophet Gt. Smoky Mts.* i. 30 The vague, sighing voice of the woods rose and fell with a melancholy monody.

monodynamic (ˌmɒnəʊdaɪ'næmɪk, -dɪn-), *a. rare.* [f. Gr. *μόνο-ς* MONO- + *δύναμ-ις* power + -IC.]
1. Having only one power or talent. *nonce-use.*
1823 DE QUINCEY *Herder* Wks. 1862 XII. 128 Monodynamic men, men of a single talent.
2. *Chem.* = MONOVALENT.
1872 THUDICHUM *Chem. Phys.* 23 Butyryl..is a monodynamic radical.

monodynamism (mɒnəʊ'daɪnəmɪz(ə)m). *rare.* [f. Gr. *μόνο-ς* MONO- + *δύναμ-ις* power, force + -ISM.] The doctrine that all forms of activity in nature are only various manifestations of one force.
1867 LEWES *Hist. Philos.* (ed. 3) I. 3 Side by side with this tentative..monotheism there is a bold and unhesitating monodynamism, the efforts of all the early thinkers being to reduce all the powers of nature to one principle.

monodynamous: see MONO- 1.

‖**Monœcia** (mɒ'niːʃɪə). *Bot.* [mod.L. (Linnæus 1735), f. Gr. *μόνο-ς* MONO- + *οἶκ-ος* house: cf. DIŒCIA.] The twenty-first class in the Sexual System of Linnæus, comprising plants which have the stamens and pistils, or male and female organs, in separate flowers, but on the same plant.
1753 CHAMBERS *Cycl. Supp.*, *Monœcia*, in botany, a class of plants which have not the male and female parts,..in the same, but in different flowers; and those on the same root. **1785** MARTYN *Rousseau's Bot.* ix. (1794) 95. **1862** DARWIN in *Life & Lett.* (1887) III. 304 About one-third of the British genera of aquatic plants belong to the Linnean classes of Mono- and Diœcia.
Hence **mo'nœcian** *a.* = MONŒCIOUS; *sb.* a monœcious plant or animal.
1828–32 WEBSTER, *Monecian* [*a.* and *sb.*]; and in mod. Dicts.

monœcious (mɒ'niːʃ(ɪ)əs), *a.* Also **monecious**. [f. MONŒCI-A + -OUS.]
1. *Bot.* **a.** Of phanerogams: Having unisexual male and female flowers on the same plant; belonging to the Linnæan class MONŒCIA. (Cf. MONOICOUS *a.*)
1761 STILES in *Phil. Trans.* IV. 259 Not only in the Diœcious plants, but in the Monœcious and Polygamious also. **1822** *Hortus Anglicus* II. 545 With flowers monœcious. **1877** DARWIN *Forms of Fl.* Introd. 9 We now come to our second Class, that of monœcious species, or those which have their sexes separated but borne on the same plant. **1900** B. D. JACKSON *Gloss. Bot. Terms*, *Monœcious homogamy*, fertilization from another inflorescence of the same plant (Delpino).
b. Of cryptogams: Having both male and female organs on the same individual.
1861 BENTLEY *Man. Bot.* 393 When conceptacles of both kinds [*sc.* with antheridia and sporangia] occur on the same plant, this is termed *monœcious*, if on different plants, they are *diœcious*. **1887** *Ibid.* (ed. 5) 396 Some species, as *Fucus platycarpus*, are monœcious, i.e. contain both antheridia and oogonia in the same conceptacle.
2. *Zool.* [Cf. MONOIC *a.*] Having the two sexes in one individual; hermaphrodite.
1826 KIRBY & SP. *Entomol.* IV. xlvii. 401 The first of these purposes was best promoted by creating things 'according to their kind', with sexes monœcious or diœcious. **1880** PASCOE *Zool. Classif.* (ed. 2) 283 *Monœcious.* When the male and female are associated in one organism. **1888** ROLLESTON & JACKSON *Anim. Life* Introd. 25 The testis may co-exist with the ovary in the same animal, which is then said to be monoecious or hermaphrodite.
Hence **mo'nœciously** *adv.*
1847 W. DARLINGTON *Amer. Weeds* Gloss. (1860) 424/2 *Monœciously* or *monoiciously polygamous*; having perfect and imperfect flowers on the same plant. **1890** in *Century Dict.*; and in later Dicts.

monœcism (mɒ'niːsɪz(ə)m). [ad. mod.L. *monœcismus*, f. Gr. **μόνοικ-ος* (see MONŒCIA) + -ISM.] The condition of being monœcious.
1875 BENNETT & DYER *Sachs' Bot.* III. vi. 807 If the plant which produces both kinds of sexual organs is large or at least strongly differentiated, distance in the relationship of the two kinds of reproductive cells is still attained by the male and female organs being produced on different branches; and this phenomenon, which is in general termed *Monœcism*, is also common in the vegetable kingdom. **1966** AINSWORTH & SUSSMAN *Fungi* II. xx. 661 Monoecism and dioecism..are defined on a physiological basis according to whether an organism contributes one or two nuclei to the sexual process.

monœcy (mɒ'niːsɪ). *Biol.* [f. MONŒC(ISM + -Y³.] = MONŒCISM.
1949 DARLINGTON & MATHER *Elem. Genetics* xii. 242 Dioecy ensures outbreeding. Monoecy only favours it. **1970** [see DIŒCY].

monoeidic (mɒnəʊ'aɪdɪk), *a. rare*$^{-1}$. [f. Gr. *μονοειδ-ής* of one form or kind (f. *μόνο-ς* MONO- + *εἶδ-ος* form) + -IC.] Of one form or nature.
a **1822** SHELLEY *Ess. & Lett.* (1840) I. 145 A beauty wonderful in its nature... It is eternally uniform and consistent and monoeidic with itself. *Ibid.* 146 The divine, the original, the supreme, the monoeidic beautiful itself.

monoembryony: see MONEMBRYONY.

monoepic: see MONEPIC.

monœstrous, monoflagellate: see MONO- 1.

monoethyl: see MONETHYL.

monogam ('mɒnəgæm). *Bot.* [a. F. *monogame*, ad. mod.L. *monogamæ*, fem. pl. of *monogamus* MONOGAMOUS.] A plant of the order MONOGAMIA.
1828–32 WEBSTER, *Monogam*, *in botany*, a plant that has a simple flower, though the anthers are united. [citing] *Lee*. In mod. Dicts.

‖**Monogamia** (mɒnəʊ'geɪmɪə, -'gæmɪə). *Bot.* [mod.L. (Linnæus) use of late L. *monogamia* 'single marriage', MONOGAMY.] The sixth order in the nineteenth class (*Syngenesia*) in the Linnæan Sexual System, comprising species which bear solitary flowers (not collected in a capitulum) in which the anthers are united. Not now recognized as an order in any system.
1760 J. LEE *Introd. Bot.* II. iii. (1765) 81 *Monogamia*. **1807** J. E. SMITH *Phys. Bot.* 400 Linnæus has a 6th Order in this [*sc.* the 19th] Class, named Monogamia, consisting of simple flowers with united anthers; but this I have presumed to disuse, because [etc.].
Hence **mono'gamian** *a.*¹, pertaining to this order.
1828–32 in WEBSTER.

monogamian (mɒnəʊ'geɪmɪən), *a.*² *rare.* [f. MONOGAMY + -AN.] Of or pertaining to monogamy; monogamous.
1876 L. H. MORGAN in *N. Amer. Rev.* CXXIII. 62 It was founded upon marriage between single pairs, but it fell below the monogamian family of civilized society. **1881** —— *Contrib. N. Amer. Ethnol.* IV. 5 As the syndyasmian family of the period began to assume monogamian characteristics.
b. *Zool.* 'Mating with but one of the opposite sex' (Funk's *Stand. Dict.*).

monogamic (mɒnəʊ'gæmɪk), *a.* [f. Gr. *μονόγαμ-ος* (see MONOGAMOUS) + -IC. So F. *monogamique*.]
1. Of or pertaining to monogamy; (less correctly) practising monogamy, monogamous.
1840 *Fraser's Mag.* XXI. 391 All trace of the monogamic pillar of orthodoxy therefore disappears. **1860** J. M. LUDLOW in *Macm. Mag.* II. 46 If M. Michelet has satisfied himself by means of physiology that man is a monogamic animal, so much the better. **1876** in Ruskin *Fors Clav.* VI. 376 A Home should minister to all the needs of its members. This, ordinary monogamic homes cannot do. **1882–3** SCHAFF *Encycl. Relig. Knowl.* III. 2549/1 The institution of monogamic marriage in Genesis.
2. *Bot.* = MONOGAMOUS *a.* 3.
1856 MAYNE *Expos. Lex.*, *Monogamicus*, *Monogamus*. The latter of these two terms is applied by H. Cassini to the *calathidia* of the *Synanthereæ* when they contain flowers which are of the same sex, as in the *Lactuca*: monogamic: monogamous. **1866** *Treas. Bot.*, *Monogamia* (adj. *Monogamic*), having flowers distinct from each other, and not collected in a capitulum.
Hence **mono'gamically** *adv.*, in a monogamic manner.

1911 G. B. Shaw *Getting Married* 140 In our population there are about a million monogamically superfluous women.

mono'gamious, *a. Bot.* [f. MONOGAMI-A + -OUS.] Belonging to the Linnæan order *Monogamia*.

1856 in MAYNE *Expos. Lex.*

monogamist (mɒ'nɒgəmɪst). [f. Gr. μονόγαμ-ος (see MONOGAMOUS) + -IST.]

1. 'One who disallows second marriages' (J.); also, one who by custom or law is debarred from second marriage after the death of the first spouse; opposed to *digamist*.

1651 C. CARTWRIGHT *Cert. Relig.* I. 49 Hierom [was] a Monogamist. **1766** GOLDSM. *Vic. W.* ii, I maintained..that it was unlawful for a priest of the church of England, after the death of his first wife, to take a second; or, to express it in one word, I valued myself upon being a strict monogamist.

2. One who has but one living and undivorced spouse, as opposed to *bigamist* or *polygamist*.

1731 BAILEY (vol. II.), *Monogamist*, one who is of single marriage. **1861** *Sat. Rev.* 21 Dec. 637 Polygamy is forbidden by the Gospel, and..consequently, on becoming a Christian, a man must..become a monogamist. **1862** MAX MÜLLER *Chips* (1867) I. 168 The Parsis are monogamists.

3. quasi-*adj.* = MONOGAMISTIC.

1875 POSTE *Gaius* IV. (ed. 2) 545 A monogamist forum will not enforce polygamistic laws. **1906** *The Christian* 1 Nov. 9/2 Christianity, the only absolute monogamist religion.

Hence **monoga'mistic**, *a*, of or pertaining to monogamists (sense 2) or monogamy; favouring monogamy.

1890 in *Century Dict.*

mo'nogamize, *v.* [Formed as prec. + -IZE.]

†1. *intr.* To hold the opinion of the 'monogamists' (see MONOGAMIST 1). *Obs.*

1605 T. BELL *Motives Rom. Faith* Ded., If Tertullian.. erred montanizing; ..if Hyeronimus monogamizing.

2. *trans.* To make monogamous in character.

1911 H. S. HARRISON *Queed* xxiii. 297 Since, however, the church and the law allowed him but one [wife], he must more drastically monogamize his heart.

monogamous (mɒ'nɒgəməs), *a.* [f. eccl.L. *monogam-us* (a. Gr. μονόγαμος marrying only once, f. μόνο-ς MONO- + γάμος marriage) + -OUS. Cf. F. *monogame*.]

1. Of persons: Practising monogamy.

a. Having or permitted to have only one living and undivorced husband or wife at one time: opposed to *bigamous* or *polygamous*. b. Refraining or debarred from remarriage after the death of the first spouse: opposed to *digamous*.

1798 MALTHUS *Popul.* (1817) I. 216 The number of people increased in a fourfold ratio by polygamy, to what it is in those countries that are monogamous. **1828-32** WEBSTER, *Monogamous*, having one wife only and not permitted to marry a second. **1865** W. G. PALGRAVE *Arabia* I. 295 A faithful and (though wealthy) a monogamous husband.

2. *Zool.* Of animals, esp. applied to birds: Pairing with only one male or female, either for the breeding season, or for life.

1770 G. WHITE *Selborne*, *To Pennant* xxix, Among the monogamous birds several are to be found, after pairing-time, single, and of each sex. **1830** 'B. MOUBRAY' *Dom. Poultry* (ed. 6) 141 The pigeon is monogamous, that is, the male attaches and confines himself to one female, and the attachment is reciprocal. **1835** KIRBY *Hab. & Inst. Anim.* xxi. II. 384 Both sexes [of these fishes], for they are monogamous, watch and defend them [*sc.* their eggs] till the young come forth. **1835-6** OWEN in *Todd's Cycl. Anat.* I. 267/1 All the Birds of Prey..are monogamous. **1871** DARWIN *Desc. Man.* II. xx. 361 Several kinds, as some of the Indian and American monkeys, are strictly monogamous, and associate all the year round with their wives. **1880** GÜNTHER *Fishes* xii. 178 Some Teleostei.. are monogamous.

3. *Bot.* Belonging to the Linnæan order *Monogamia*.

1821 tr. *Decandolle & Sprengel's Elem. Philos. Plants* II. ii. 94 The Linnæan Monogamous plants. **1856** [see MONOGAMIC *a.* 2]. **1891** in *Syd. Soc. Lex.*

4. Of or pertaining to monogamy.

1882 BABER in *Roy. Geog. Soc., Suppl. Papers* I. I. 97 A European..whose personal conviction..is strictly monogamous. **1878** LECKY *Eng. in 18th C.* (1883) I. 495 Perpetual monogamous attachments would always be the most common. **1884** *Century Mag.* XXVIII. 621 The monogamous family, formed by the union of one woman with one man. **1885** J. G. BERTRAM *British Alm. Comp.* 77 The grouse..[is] a bird of strictly monogamous habits. **1895** 'G. PASTON' *Stud. Prejudices* vii, Monogamous marriage.

Hence **mo'nogamously** *adv.*; **mo'nogamousness**.

1875 *Echo* 3 July 1/3 There are in this country..500,000 women who cannot possibly be monogamously married. **1946** KOESTLER *Thieves in Night* II. iv. 170 There remains the tyranny of monogamousness.

monogamy (mɒ'nɒgəmɪ). Also 7 *monogamie*. [ad. F. *monogamie*, ad. eccl.L. *monogamia*, Gr. μονογαμία, f. μονόγαμ-ος (see MONOGAMOUS).]

1. The practice or principle of marrying only once, or of not remarrying after the death of the first spouse: opposed to *digamy*. Now *rare*.

1612 T. TAYLOR *Comm. Titus* i. 6 The marriage of the wiues sister is forbidden by proportion euen in monogamie.

1620 BP. HALL *Hon. Marr. Clergy* I. xix. 106 If hee had euer read the Booke following, of Monogamie, he might have found [etc.]. **1656** BLOUNT *Glossogr.*, *Monogamie*, a marrying of one onely wife all the life time. **1727-51** [see 2] **1856** MACAULAY *Biog., Goldsm.* (1860) 62 Moses and his spectacles, the Vicar and his monogamy..have caused.. much harmless mirth.

2. The condition, rule, or custom of being married to only one person at a time (opposed to *polygamy* or *bigamy*); chiefly applied to the rule or custom (more explicitly called *monogyny*) by which a man can have only one wife, but also including *monandry*, the rule or custom by which a woman can have only one husband.

1708 *Brit. Apollo* No. 82. 1/1 Monogamy is Agreeable to the Primary Intention of a Marriage-state. **1727-51** CHAMBERS *Cycl., Monogamy*, the state or condition of those who have only married once, or are restrained to a single wife. **1788** REID *Active Powers* III. III. vi, Suppose again, that we reason for monogamy from the intention of nature. **1869** LECKY *Europ. Mor.* I. 107 In Rome..monogamy was firmly established. **1878** K. JOHNSTON *Africa* iii. 41 In Marocco Monogamy is the rule both amongst the Arabs and the Berbers. **1886** *Law Times* LXXX. 335/2 A country where monogamy is the only legal form of marriage.

3. *Zool.* The habit of living in pairs, or having only one mate.

1785 G. FORSTER tr. *Sparrman's Voy. Cape G. H.* II. 120 Thevenot is right when he asserts, that the ostrich lives in monogamy, or with one female. **1828** STARK *Elem. Nat. Hist.* I. 51 These apes..live in monogamy.

monoganglial, -ganglionic: see MONO- 1.

monogastric (mɒnəʊ'gæstrɪk), *a.* [ad. F. *monogastrique*: see MONO- and GASTRIC.]

1. *Anat.* (See quots.)

1753 CHAMBERS *Cycl. Supp.*, *Monogastric*, in anatomy, a name given by Vieussens, and some French writers, to one of the muscles of the ear, called by Cowper, the *internus auris*, and more properly by Albinus, the *tensor tympani*. **1904** *Appleton's Med. Dict.*, *Monogastric*,..2. having a single belly (said of muscles).

2. Having only one stomach or digestive cavity.

1814 *Edin. Rev.* XXIII. 289 The one [i.e. Avarice] is a monogastric bloodsucker. **1849** HUXLEY in *Phil. Trans.* CXXXIX. 426 The stomach of a monogastric Diphyes. **1855** DUNGLISON *Med. Lex.* (ed. 12) s.v., Man is monogastric; ruminating animals, on the contrary, are polygastric. **1875** H. C. WOOD *Therap.* (1879) 547 Youatt states that..both with monogastric animals and ruminants, he has never known the drug to fail.

monogen ('mɒnədʒɛn). *Chem.* [See MONO- 2 and -GEN I.] An element which combines in one proportion only.

1873 [see POLYGENIC *a.* 2].

monogenean (mɒnəʊ'dʒɛniːən), *sb.* and *a.* [f. mod.L. name of order *Monogenea* (J. V. Carus in W. C. H. Peters et al. *Handbuch der Zoologie* (1863) II. 477), f. MONO- + Gr. γενεά race, generation: see AN.] A. *sb.* A trematode parasite of the order Monogenea, which passes its entire life cycle in one host, esp. an ectoparasitic fluke of fishes; a monogenetic trematode. B. *adj.* Of or pertaining to this group of parasites.

1960 *Parasitology* L. 51 (*title*) The attachment of the monogenean *Discotyle sagittata* Leuckart. **1963** J. LLEWELLYN in *Adv. Parasitol.* I. 287 (*title*) Larvae and larval development of monogeneans. *Ibid.*, The two studies were based on samples of monogenean larvae. **1971** *Nature* 23 July 225/1 The targets of the larvae of monogenean flukes are mostly fish of much greater size. **1972** D. A. ERASMUS *Biol. Trematodes* vii. 166 Within their hosts, monogeneans generally occur on the fins, skin, gills, gill chamber and buccal cavity.

monogeneity (mɒnədʒɪ'niːɪtɪ). *Math.* [Formed as next + -ITY.] The state or condition of being monogeneous.

1906 *Athenæum* 20 Jan. 83/3 The following papers were communicated [on Jan. 11]: 'On the Monogeneity of an Algebraic Function', by Dr. H. F. Baker, [etc.].

monogeneous (mɒnə'dʒiːniːəs), *a.* [f. mod.L. *monogene-us*, f. Gr. μονογεν-ής (f. μόνο-ς MONO- + γέν-ος kind, race) + -OUS. Cf. F. *monogéné*.]

1. Of one race or family.

1856 in MAYNE *Expos. Lex.*

2. *Biol.* Generated in the same form as that of the parents.

1890 *Century Dict.* s.v. **1891** *Ibid.* s.v. *Trematoda*, The monogeneous and digeneous suborders [of *Trematoda*].

3. *Math.* Having a single differential coefficient. Cf. MONOGENOUS *a.* 7.

1888 B. WILLIAMSON in *Encycl. Brit.* XXIV. 72/1 (*Variable*) The function is monogeneous.

monogenesis (mɒnəʊ'dʒɛnɪsɪs). [a. mod.L.: see MONO- and GENESIS. Cf. F. *monogénèse*.]

1. *Geol.* Oneness of origin.

1864 WEBSTER (cites Dana).

2. *Biol.* in various uses (see quots.).

1866 BRANDE & COX *Dict. Sci.*, etc., *Monogenesis*. Professor van Beneden understands this term as applied to the direct development, e.g. of an Entozoon from a parent resembling itself. Prof. A. Thomson uses it as applied to descent of an individual from one parent form, containing both the sperm cell and germ cell, or male or female parent principles. **1866** *Chamb. Encycl.* VIII. 195/2 The terms

---

Monogenesis and *Homogenesis* have been..applied to the cases in which non-sexual reproduction takes place by fission or gemmation. **1882** OGILVIE, *Monogenesis*..(*c*) Defined by Haeckel to mean development of all the beings in the universe from a single cell. **1891** *Syd. Soc. Lex.*, *Monogenesis*,..the doctrine of the descent of the members of a species from an original single pair. *Ibid.*, *Monogenesis*,.. the same as *Monogeny*.

3. *Linguistics.* The theory that all languages have one common origin.

[**1905** A. TROMBETTI *L'Unità d' Origine del Linguaggio* 56 Noi dunque consideriamo la monogenesi del linguaggio per lo meno come un argomento assai forte in favore della monogenesi dell' uomo.] **1936** *Science & Society* I. 23 At various times scholars have raised the question of monogenesis as opposed to polygenesis of human speech: whether it had a single origin at a given time and place, whence it spread over the rest of the earth, or whether it was independently evolved by different branches of the human family. **1949** *Archivum Linguisticum* I. 76 The issue of monogenesis *versus* polygenesis is likewise evaded, although a critical appraisal of Trombetti's arguments might have been useful. **1949** M. PEI *Story of Lang.* (1952) vii. 357 A few daring linguists, like the Italian Trombetti, have strenuously asserted the thesis of the 'monogenesis', or single common origin, of all the world's tongues. **1966** H. LANDAR *Lang. & Culture* xx. 153 His guess implicates a monogenesis of the world's languages, much as the Italian duck-hunter Trombetti supposed, but a monogenesis which occurred as recently as 30,000 years ago.

Hence **mono'genesist** = MONOGENIST.

1862 *Temple Bar* V. 215 The theory of gradual climatic changes must..be abandoned, and the mongenesists must ..fall back upon a new line of defences... This quarrel of the mono- and polygenesists..is a very pretty one.

monogenesy (mɒnəʊ'dʒɛnɪsɪ). [f. Gr. μόνο-ς single + -γενεσία, f. γένεσις: cf. MONOGENESIS.]

1. = MONOGENISM.

1885 in *Cassell's Encycl. Dict.*, and in later Dicts.

2. = MONOGONY.

1890 in *Century Dict.*

monogenetic (ˌmɒnədʒɪ'nɛtɪk), *a.* [Formed as MONOGENESIS: see -GENETIC.]

1. *Geol.* Of or pertaining to monogenesis; 'resulting from one continued process of formation' (Webster *Suppl.* 1880).

1873 [see POLYGENETIC *a.* 2]. **1880** DANA *Man. Geol.* (ed. 3) 776 The Appalachians..constitute one individual among mountains, because a result of one genetic process, or in a word, monogenetic.

2. *Biol.* Of or pertaining to monogenesis or monogenism.

1873 MAX MÜLLER in *Fraser's Mag.* July 2 There are, indeed, two schools of physiologists, the polygenetic and monogenetic, the former admitting from the beginning a variety of primitive cells, the latter postulating but one cell, as the source of all being. **1886** *Science* VII. 169/1 The monogenetic theory which believes in the original common origin of all mankind from one pair. **1896** F. B. JEVONS *Introd. Hist. Relig.* i. 7 Man's origin was monogenetic.

3. *Zool.* (See quot. 1903.)

1888 ROLLESTON & JACKSON *Anim. Life* 649 In the monogenetic Trematoda it [the ovum] is always laid; in the digenetic it may, or may not commence its development in the oviduct. **1903** MINCHIN *Sporozoa* in E. R. Lankester *Treat. Zool.* I. 166 In *Monocystis* the whole life-history is a single cycle,..it is, in fact, monogenetic... But in many other Sporozoa..the life-cycle becomes digenetic, that is to say, it is differentiated into two distinct generations.

4. *Bot.* (See quot.)

1900 B. D. JACKSON *Gloss. Bot. Terms, Monogenetic Reproduction*, asexual reproduction.

monogenic (mɒnəʊ'dʒɛnɪk), *a.* [f. Gr. μόνο-ς MONO- + γέν-ος kind, origin (cf. -GEN) + -IC.]

1. *Geol.* (See quot.) So F. *monogénique*.

1856 MAYNE *Expos. Lex.*, *Monogenicus*, applied to a rock of which all the parts are of the same nature; thus the monogenic gompholite is a calcareous rock in a calcareous cement, more or less pure: monogenic.

2. *Chem.* Combining with an element in only one form; forming only one compound with a monovalent element.

1873 FOWNES' *Chem.* (ed. 11) 231 There are a few other monogenic elements.

3. *Math. monogenic function*: a function which has a differential coefficient; i.e. one whose rate of variation in any direction is independent of that direction by being independent of the mode of change of the variable.

1893 FORSYTH *Theory of Functions* 14 The idea of a monogenic function of a complex variable and the idea of dependence expressible by arithmetical operations are not coextensive. **1902** H. F. BAKER in *Encycl. Brit.* XXVIII. 539/1 A monogenic analytical function; the word monogenic having reference to the fact that various series, in x-c, x-c_1, x-c_{11},..., which represent the function in different parts of the plane, have a single origin, namely, the series $f(x)$, all the properties of the function being virtually continued in this one series.

4. *Biol.* a. 'Of or pertaining to monogenesis' (Webster 1897). b. (See quot.)

1894-1900 G. M. GOULD *Dict. Med.* (ed. 5), *Monogenic*, in biology, producing but one sort of embryo, as distinguished from *diphygenic*.

5. 'Having a single origin;—applied to the human species' (Webster *Suppl.* 1902).

6. *Biol.* [cf. GENIC *a.*] Involving or controlled by a single gene.

1939 *Jrnl. Genetics* XXXVIII. 420 These results indicate that the asynaptic condition in *N. sylvestris* is determined by a difference which behaves as a monogenic recessive. **1960** *Phytopathology* L. 766 (*heading*) Dominance of avirulence and monogenic control of virulence in race hybrids of *Ustilago avenae*. **1971** *Brit. Med. Bull.* XXVII. 40/2 Conventional measurements of blood pressure are too variable to distinguish between monogenic and polygenic models of heredity.

Hence **mono'genically** *adv.*

1970 *Plant Disease Rep.* LVI. 696 A true resistance mechanism which is monogenically controlled.

monogenism (mə'nɒdʒɪnɪz(ə)m). [f. MONO- + -GEN + -ISM. So F. *monogénisme.*]

1. The doctrine of monogeny; the theory that the human races have all descended from a common ancestry, or from a single pair.

1865 HUXLEY in *Fortn. Rev.* I. 273 Five-sixths of the public are taught this Adamitic Monogenism, as if it were an established truth, and believe it. **1878** *N. Amer. Rev.* CXXVI. 471 But the church doctrine as to man's moral condition does not depend at all upon monogenism. **1880** A. H. KEANE in *Nature* 30 Dec. 199/1 Unorthodox monogenism, that is monogenism not starting from a created pair, . . seems [etc.].

2. 'Lamarck's term for the doctrine that all animal types actually living have derived their origin from the same anatomical element' (*Syd. Soc. Lex.* 1891).

monogenist (mə'nɒdʒɪnɪst). [f. MONO- + -GEN + -IST. So F. *monogéniste.*]

1. One who believes or maintains the theory of the origin of mankind from a single pair.

1857 GLIDDON in Nott & G. *Indig. Races* 402 The Monogenists and the Polygenists: being an exposition of the doctrines of schools professing to sustain dogmatically the Unity or the Diversity of human races. **1865** HUXLEY in *Fortn. Rev.* I. 273 According to the Monogenists, all mankind have sprung from a single pair. **1875** TYLOR in *Encycl. Brit.* II. 114/1 The monogenist has claimed all mankind to be descended from one original stock, and generally from a single pair.

attrib. **1865** HUXLEY in *Fortn. Rev.* I. 273 The Monogenist hypotheses. **1883** TYLOR in *Nature* 3 May 8/2 Prichard, the leader of the monogenist school forty years ago. **1888** CAVE *Inspir. O. Test.* ii. 103 A monogenist argument.

2. One who maintains the unity of origin of living beings.

1868 OWEN *Anat.* III. 817 To meet the inevitable question of 'Whence the first organic matter?' the Monogenist is reduced to enumerate the existing elements into which the simplest living jelly . . or sarcode . . is resolvable.

Hence **monoge'nistic** *a.*, pertaining to monogenists or monogenism.

1865 *Reader* 11 Feb. 162/3 A consideration of the monogenistic and polygenistic theories of the origin of man. **1865** HUXLEY in *Fortn. Rev.* I. 275 Combining all that is good in the Monogenistic and Polygenistic schools. **1890** — in *19th Cent.* July 754 Their judgment was often unconsciously warped by strong monogenistic proclivities.

monogenous (mə'nɒdʒɪnəs), *a.* [f. Gr. μόνο-ς MONO- + γέν-ος kind, origin, γεν- to grow, produce (see -GEN) + -OUS.]

1. *Bot.* (See quot. 1856.)

1856 MAYNE *Expos. Lex.*, *Monogenus, Bot.*, applied by Lessing to monocotyledonous plants, because they have but one surface of increase, which is central: monogenous. **1891** in *Syd. Soc. Lex.* **1900** B. D. JACKSON *Gloss. Bot. Terms*, *Monogenous = Endogenous.*

2. = MONOGENEOUS *a.* 1.

1866 *Reader* 15 Sept. 796 One wild bird may have been the ancestor of all the fantails, another of all the carriers, and so on. Thus domestic pigeons may be said to be 'monogenous' as to their origin from one wild species, 'polygenous' as to the individual ancestor of each variety. **1891** in *Syd. Soc. Lex.*

3. *Chem.* = MONOGENIC 2.

1870 *Eng. Mech.* 11 Feb. 524/1 Chlorine forms only one compound with hydrogen. . . Chlorine may, for this reason, be called a monogenous element.

4. *Geol.* (See quot.) Cf. MONOGENIC 1.

1888 TEALL *Brit. Petrogr.* 440 *Monogenous*, a word applied by some authors to clastic rocks the fragments of which are derived solely from one rock.

5. *Biol.* Used as a general designation for gemmation, or sporulation, as modes of asexual reproduction involving but one parent.

1884 SEDGWICK tr. *Claus' Zool.* I. 96 Reproduction by fission, which, with that by budding and spore-formation, is included under the term monogenous asexual reproduction.

6. 'Of or pertaining to monogenism' (*Cent. Dict.*).

7. *Math.* 'Having a single differential coefficient considered as a rule of generation' (*Cent. Dict.*), = MONOGENIC 3.

monogeny (mə'nɒdʒɪnɪ). [f. Gr. μόνο-ς MONO- + -GENY. Cf. F. *monogénie.*]

1. The (theoretical) origination of mankind from one common pair of ancestors; also *loosely*, the theory of such origination, monogenism.

1865 *Anthrop. Rev.* Oct. 362 This paper was entitled, 'On Monogeny and Polygeny'. **1893** S. LAING *Hum. Origins* 405 As the old orthodox argument for monogeny faded into oblivion, a new and more powerful one was furnished by the doctrine of Evolution, as expounded by Darwin.

2. Monogenesis; monogenous reproduction.

1856 MAYNE *Expos. Lex. Monogenia, Physiol.*, applied by Burdach to the mode of generation which consists in the production, by an organised body, of a part which separates at some period and becomes by its growth a new individual, similar to that which has produced it: monogeny.

monoger, var. MONIKER.

monoglot ('mɒnəglɒt), *a.* and *sb.* [ad. Gr. μονόγλωττ-ος, f. μόνο-ς MONO- + γλῶττα, γλῶσσα tongue, language.] A. *adj.*

1. Of a person: That speaks, writes, or understands only one language.

1830 SOUTHEY *Let.* 19 June in *Life* (1850) VI. 106 Lamentable experience makes me know how much is lost by a monoglot traveller. **1905** *Schoolmaster* 15 Apr. 774/1 'Monoglot' Welsh maidens are few in these days.

2. Written in only one language.

1890 in *Century Dict.* **1895** *Funk's Stand. Dict.* s.v., A monoglot dictionary.

B. *sb.* One who knows only one language.

1894 *Times* 11 Jan. 7/4 Whether monoglots only are reckoned, or [etc.]. **1895** *Westm. Gaz.* 8 May 2/3 Four or five of them [*sc.* the jurors] . . are Welsh monoglots, and do not know a word of English. **1896** *Blackw. Mag.* 717 Sour and Saxon-hating monoglots.

monogoneutic: see MONO- 1.

monogonic (mɒnəʊ'gɒnɪk), *a. Biol.* [f. Gr. μόνο-ς MONO- + γονικός parental, f. γον-, γεν- to bear, produce.] Of the nature of monogony; non-sexual. So **mo'nogonous** *a.*

1876 tr. *Haeckel's Hist. Creat.* I. 183 The phenomena of non-sexual or monogonic propagation. *Ibid.* Contents p. viii, Nonsexual or Monogonous Propagation.

monogonoporic, -gonoporous: see MONO- 1.

monogony (mə'nɒgənɪ). *Biol.* [f. Gr. μόνο-ς MONO- + -γονια begetting. Cf. MONOGONIC.] Reproduction by fission or gemmation; non-sexual propagation.

1873 MAX MÜLLER in *Fraser's Mag.* July 4 Cells . . capable of producing by the processes of monogony . . and amphigony, the endless variety of living creatures. **1876** [see AMPHIGONY]. **1900** B. D. JACKSON *Gloss. Bot. Terms* Add.

monogram ('mɒnəgræm). Also 7 **monogramme**. [Two formations. (1) In sense 1, ad. L. *monogrammus* adj., a. Gr. *μονόγραμμος, f. μόνο-ς single, only + γραμμ-ή line. Cicero attributes to Epicurus the use of this word (app. with the virtual sense 'unsubstantial') as descriptive of the gods according to his conception of them, and Lucilius uses *monogrammus* for a thin and colourless person, a 'mere shadow'. Nonius (*c* 280) who has preserved the passage of Lucilius, explains the word as designating a picture drawn in line only, before the colour is applied. (2) In sense 2, ad. late L. *monogramma* neut. (5th c.), irregularly formed after late Gr. μονόγραμμον, neut. of μονόγραμμος, f. μόνο-ς single + γράμμα letter. Both the late L. and the late Gr. words were applied to the 'monogram' (in the modern sense) which represented the signature of the Byzantine emperors. In med.L. *monogramma* was common. Cf. F. *monogramme* masc. (1633 in Hatz.-Darm.).]

†1. A picture drawn in lines without shading or colour; a sketch. *Obs.*

1610 HEALEY *St. Aug. Citie of God* II. xxi. *Vives' Comm.* (1620) 84 Painters . . first doe onely delineate and line forth the figure they will draw: which is called a Monogramme. *a* **1637** B. JONSON *Underwoods, Poet to Painter* 11 You were . . To . . draw My Superficies: . . Which if in compasse of no Art it came To be described by a Monogram, With one great blot, yo' had formed me as I am. *a* **1660** HAMMOND *Serm.* ii. Wks. 1684 IV. 571 A kind of first draught, or ground colours only, and monogram of life. **1675** COCKER *Morals* 66 You here, our choicest Monograms may scan, Where man is fairly pictur'd forth to Man. **1801** FUSELI *Lect. Paint.* i. (1848) 350 The next step of the art was the monogram: outlines of figures without light or shade, but with some addition of the parts within the outline. **1843** [see MONOCHROME *sb.*].

2. A character composed of two or more letters interwoven together, the letters being usually the initials of a person's name; now often, such a character stamped or otherwise made on notepaper, seals, etc.

the Christian monogram or ***monogram of Christ***, the combination (☧) of the first two letters of Χριστός (Christ).

1696 in PHILLIPS (ed. 5). **1697** EVELYN *Numism.* v. 186 A monogram oftentimes served their turn. **1727–52** CHAMBERS *Cycl.* s.v., The Roman labarum bore the monogram of Jesus Christ. **1761** *Phil. Trans.* LII. 31 The fourth letter is succeeded by a monogram, or complex character, formed of E and the aforesaid accented I. **1781** GIBBON *Decl. & F.* xx. (1787) II. 194 The mysterious monogram, at once expressive of the figure of the cross, and the initial letters of the name of Christ. **1839** *Penny Cycl.* XV. 341/1 The monograms used by the German and Italian engravers. The French artists rarely used monograms. **1845** *Encycl. Metrop.* XXIII. 568/2 Most of the ancient Printers made use of monograms or ciphers, containing the initial letters of their names, or other devices curiously interwoven. **1847** LD. LINDSAY *Sk. Hist. Chr. Art* I. 102 A cross . . supporting the monogram of Christ. **1865** DICKENS *Mut. Fr.* I. x, Twemlow received a highly-perfumed cocked-hat and monogram from Mrs. Veneering. **1883** ANNA K. GREEN *Hand & Ring* viii, I have read the Monogram upon your handkerchief. **1900** A. LANG *Hist. Scot.* I. ii. 24 On these stone pillars is found the Christian monogram, surrounded by a circle.

†3. (See quot.) *Obs. rare*$^{-0}$.

1656 BLOUNT *Glossogr.*, *Monogram*, . . a sentence in one line, or an Epigram in one verse. As *Pauper videri Cinna vult, & est pauper*, Mart. **1658–1706** PHILLIPS. **1721** BAILEY.

†4. (See quot.) *Obs. rare.*

1801 J. HAGER *Babylon. Inscr.* 53 Some arbitrary sign, figure or character, destined to express complete words, and which I therefore call monograms. *Ibid.* 56 The characters on the Babylonian bricks being . . monograms . . designed to express either whole sentences or whole words.

5. *attrib.*

1871 'M. LEGRAND' *Cambr. Freshm.* 364 With gorgeous monogram buttons. **1884** KNIGHT *Dict. Mech.*, Suppl., *Monogram Machine*, a foot press for stamping monograms, initials, sizes, etc., on paper or manufactured articles. **1919** T. WRIGHT *Romance of Lace Pillow* xvi. 223 Monogram Lace, in the form of medallions—the sacred monogram I.H.S. from an antique pattern being most in demand—has been made for Mr. George Smith at Olney during the last thirty years, and sent to the Continent for ecclesiastical purposes.

Hence **'monogram** *v. trans.*, to decorate with a monogram; **'monogrammed** *a.*, bearing a monogram; **'monogrammist**, one who applies a monogram.

1868 E. YATES *Rock Ahead* I. vii, The much monogrammed note. **1884** *Harper's Mag.* Jan. 299/2 Its monogrammed coupés. **1890** 'L. FALCONER' *Mlle. Ixe* vi, The . . monogrammed envelopes. **1939** 'A. BRIDGE' *Four-Part Setting* vi. 64 I took those new pillow-cases round to be monogrammed. **1939** *Burlington Mag.* Jan. 40/2 No 'monogrammist' was too petty . . to be scrutinised with the same minute and untiring precision. **1951** *Good Housek. Home Encycl.* 139/2 Monogrammed handkerchiefs must be ironed on the wrong side. **1971** *Daily Tel.* 27 Jan. 11 (*caption*) Red wool suit, . . monogrammed in red with Balmain initials. **1974** *Ibid.* 30 Sept. 12 Young Conservatives have their shirts monogrammed 'Y.C.' **1974** *Ashmolean Mus. Rep. Visitors 1972–3* 38 A 19th-century woodcut by the monogrammist *H. Ch.*, *Rothenburg ob der Tauber, Rathaus.* **1975** 'E. LATHEN' *By Hook or by Crook* xvii. 160 Lois . . instructed Cartier to monogram a demitasse set.

†**mono'grammal**, *a. Obs. rare.* [f. L. *monogramm-us* (see prec.) + -AL^{1}.] Drawn in line only, without colour.

a **1619** FOTHERBY *Atheom.* II. x. §4 (1622) 306 And as I shewed before, of Punctum in Geometry; that it hath diuers lines, as monogrammall draughts of the image of God: so may the same be shewed in *Arithmeticall vnity*. *Ibid.* xiv. §2. 355 A monogrammal description, and a kind of rude draught, as it were with a Cole.

monogrammatic (ˌmɒnəgrə'mætɪk), *a.* [f. late L. *monogrammat-*, *monogramma*, MONOGRAM + -IC. So F. *monogrammatique.*] Of, pertaining to, or in the style of, a monogram.

1773 SWINTON in *Phil. Trans.* LXIV. 322 It will follow, that the Romans borrowed the monogrammatic way of writing rather from the Etruscans than the Greeks. **1820** *Gentl. Mag.* XC. I. 431 As far as Roman Capitals can express this Inscription which is partly monogrammatic, it stands thus [etc.]. **1874** W. H. WITHROW *Catacombs of Rome* (1877) 401 They frequently abound also in . . monogrammatic abbreviations. **1905** *Athenæum* 11 Nov. 654/1 The monogrammatic cross belongs to the third century after Christ.

So **monogra'mmatical** *a.*, concerned with monograms.

1871 *Athenæum* 16 Sept. 374 Mr. Richard Redgrave joins his two 'R's' back to back, and triumphs as a monogrammatical artist.

mono'grammatize, *v.* [Formed as prec. + -IZE.] *intr.* To use monogrammatic characters in writing.

1818 *Edin. Rev.* XXXI. 108 In their inscriptions . . the Spanish Goths . . were fond of using combined capitals—of monogrammatizing.

monogrammic (mɒnəʊ'græmɪk), *a. rare.* [f. MONOGRAM + -IC.]

†1. = MONOGRAMMAL. *Obs.*

1721 BAILEY, *Monogrammick Picture*, a Picture only drawn in Lines without Colours.

2. Pertaining to or of the nature of a monogram.

1851 D. WILSON *Preh. Ann.* (1863) II. IV. iv. 286 A species of Monogrammic Runic writing.

†**mono'grammical**, *a. Obs.* [Formed as prec. + -ICAL.] = prec. 1.

1685–6 H. MORE in Norris *Theory Love* (1688) 219 No Attention is sufficient to make us rightly discern the beauty of Holiness, but onely a shadowy Notion or Meager Monogrammical Picture thereof.

†**mono'grammous**, *a. Obs. rare*$^{-1}$. [f. L. *monogramm-us* adj. (see MONOGRAM) + -OUS.] In outline; indistinct.

1678 CUDWORTH *Intell. Syst.* I. ii. §2. 61 As for those Romantick Monogrammous Gods of Epicurus, had they been seriously believed by him, they could have been nothing else but a certain kind of Aerial and spectrous men.

monograph ('mɒnəgrɑːf, -græf), *sb.* [f. MONO- + -GRAPH.

The earlier word with this meaning was MONOGRAPHY (= Fr. and Ger. *monographie*, still in use), which was discarded prob. because its formation suggested an abstract sense. (Cf. Eng. *photograph* and F. *photographie.*) Fr. has *monographe*

sb., writer of a monograph, and adj. (of a book) treating of one subject.]

1. Originally, in Natural History, a separate treatise on a single species, genus, or larger group of plants, animals, or minerals. (In this use often with const. *of* instead of the more usual *on*.) Hence, in later use, *gen.* a separate treatise on a single object or class of objects: in contradistinction to the general treatises in which this is dealt with as part of a wider subject.

1821 tr. *Decandolle & Sprengel's Elem. Philos. Plants* III. i. §6. 163 By a Monograph we understand a complete account of any one family, tribe, or genus, nothing being neglected which is necessary for a perfect knowledge of it. **1827** *Q. Jrnl. Sci.* XXII. 39 By the frequent publication of monographs,.. the science of natural history cannot but be essentially promoted. **1828–32** WEBSTER s.v., A monograph of violets in botany; a monograph of an Egyptian mummy. **1839** G. BIRD *Nat. Philos.* 77 On the subjects treated of, in the preceding five chapters, the student may consult.. the monographs in Sir David Brewster's Encyclopædia. **1847** HARDY in *Proc. Berw. Nat. Club* II. No. 5. 234 A Monograph of the Scottish species. **1862** ANSTED *Channel Isl.* Pref. (ed. 2) 7 The Channel Islands.. deserve and require a monograph. **1876** PAGE *Adv. Text-bk. Geol.* xiii. 237 Mr. Woodward's Monograph of Fossil Crustacea. **1880** *Athenæum* 12 June 762 Monographs on Poe, Hawthorne [etc.].

¶ **2.** Misused for MONOGRAM 2.

1849 ALB. SMITH *Pottleton Legacy* (1854) 24 A steel key.. with some initials worked in a monograph in the handle. **1876** FREEMAN *Hist. & Arch. Sk.* 49 On one of which [pillars] is a monograph out of which ingenious men have spelled the word 'Theodoricus'.

monograph (ˈmɒnəgrɑːf, -æ-), *v.* [f. MONOGRAPH *sb.*] *trans.* To write or produce a monograph on; to treat or discuss in a monograph.

1876 T. GILL in *Harper's Mag.* Jan. 229/2 Dr. H. Wood has monographed our fresh-water algæ. **1881** DARWIN *Veg. Mould* i. 8 The British species of Lumbricus have never been carefully monographed. *a* **1887** HOOKER in *Darwin's Life & Lett.* I. 347 It was monographing the Barnacles that brought it about. **1890** MISS A. M. CLERKE *Syst. Stars* 277 This extraordinary object.. has been monographed, mapped, measured, figured and photographed.

monographer (məˈnɒgrəfə(r)). [f. mod.L. *monograph-us* (see MONOGRAPHY) + -ER¹.] One who writes or has written a monograph.

1770 G. WHITE *Selborne, To Barrington* 8 Oct., Every kingdom, every province, should have it's own monographer. **1826** KIRBY & SP. *Entomol.* xlviii. IV. 425 Apollodorus.. was the first monographer of insects. **1880** NEWTON in *Encycl. Brit.* XIII. 825/2 Few existing birds offer a better subject for a monographer [than the kakapo]. **1905** *Speaker* 11 Mar. 565/1 It is impossible to imagine two subjects more attractive to the intending monographer than Matthew Arnold and Sidney Smith.

monographic (mɒnəʊˈgræfɪk), *a.* and *sb.* [f. MONO- + -GRAPHIC; in senses 1 and 2 after MONOGRAM; in sense 4 after MONOGRAPHY; cf. F. *monographique*.] **A.** *adj.*

†**1.** = MONOGRAMMIC 1. *Obs.*

1731 BAILEY, *Monographick Picture*, a Picture only drawn in Lines without Colours. **1859** GULLICK & TIMBS *Paint.* 38 The monographic style [of painting in Greece] consisted also of lines, but the inner lines or markings were given as well as the exterior outline.

2. = MONOGRAMMIC 2.

1888 *Harper's Mag.* Apr. 746 A monographic combination of the letters A and P. **1890** in *Century Dict.*

3. Representing a sphere in a single diagram.

1855 *Rep. Brit. Assoc., Sections* 148 On Improved Monographic Projections of the World. By James Gall.

4. Pertaining to or of the nature of a monograph.

1825 GOOD *Study Med.* (ed. 2) II. 547 The monographic and clinical writers of our own country. **1869** W. S. DALLAS tr. *Müller's Facts for Darwin* x. 106 A Monographic Memoir. **1899** *Allbutt's Syst. Med.* VI. 205 Material for.. monographic treatment. **1959** C. SINGER *Short Hist. Sci. Ideas* vii. 274 The earliest modern scientific works of a monographic character, the great books of Belon, Rondelet, Vesalius, Gesner, are exclusively biological. **1970** *Daily Tel.* 12 Sept. 8/5 There is Waterhouse's monograph on Gainsborough.. and some exhibition catalogues that are monographic in their range. **1974** *Nature* 18 Jan. 165/3 The book as a whole usefully fills an important gap in the monographic literature.

†**B.** *sb. pl.* Writings treating a subject monographically. *Obs.*

1768 PENNANT *Zool.* (1776) I. 342 The curious monographics on the swallow tribe of that worthy correspondent.

monoˈgraphical, *a. rare.* [Formed as prec. + -ICAL.] = MONOGRAPHIC *a.* 3.

1709 *Med. Jrnl.* I. 305 This valuable monographical book is divided into four distinct parts. **1828–32** in WEBSTER. **1904** *Edin. Rev.* July 152 The monographical method has been much discussed.

monoˈgraphically, *adv.* [f. prec. + -LY².] In the manner or form of a monograph.

1838 V. THOMAS *Addr. B'ham Roy. Sch. Med. & Surg.* 29 Aug., To write monographically, is to write profoundly, it is to write professionally. **1874** COUES *Birds N.W.* Introd. 7 Three families.. are treated monographically. **1964** R. H. GERHARD in D. Abercrombie et al. *Daniel Jones* 281 The idea of representing monographically the vowels of *go* and *gay*.

monographist (məˈnɒgrəfɪst). [f. MONOGRAPH or MONOGRAPHY + -IST.] A monographer.

1822 GOOD *Study Med.* III. 198 The ophthalmic monographists, by making every variety of affection a distinct disease, have most unmercifully enlarged the list under this genus. **1847** WEBSTER, *Monographist*, one who writes a monograph [cites *Keith*].

monography (məˈnɒgrəfɪ). [f. Gr. μόνο-ς MONO- + γράφ-ειν to write: see -GRAPHY. In sense 1, it represents mod.L *monographia* (18th c.), f. *monograph-us* (Linnæus), one who writes a treatise on a single genus or species. Cf. F. *monographie* (1807 in Littré).]

1. = MONOGRAPH 1. (*Obs.* in Natural History applications; but still occasionally applied to a treatise on some special subject in other departments of knowledge.)

1773 G. WHITE *Selborne, To Barrington* 20 Nov., My monography of this little domestic and familiar bird. **1777** *Ibid.* 20 May, A good monography of worms would afford much entertainment and information. **1785** SIR J. E. SMITH in *Mem.* (1832) I. 133 Schreber is writing a monography on the genus *Aster*. **1819** W. LAWRENCE *Lect. Physiol. Zool.* (1822) 22 The best monography we possess in the class Mammalia. **1838** J. G. DOWLING *Eccl. Hist.* iii. §3. 208 Monographies (if I may be allowed to naturalize an useful word) or treatises on particular branches, have been still more abundant [in Germany] than works on the general history of the church. **1849** R. A. VAUGHAN in *Brit. Q. Rev.* May 307 Schleiermacher.. wrote also monographies on Anaximander.. and Socrates. **1866** MERIVALE *Sallust* Introd. (ed. 2) 15 The *Catilina* and *Jugurtha* are what are denominated in modern times Monographies; i.e. narratives of a detached series of connected events. **1876** FERGUSSON *Hist. Ind. & East. Archit.* III. i. 294 In order to write a complete monography of the Kashmiri style, we ought to be able to trace it very much further back than anything in the previous pages enables us to do.

†**2.** (See quot.) *Obs.*⁻⁰

1828–32 WEBSTER, *Monography*, a description drawn in lines without colors. Qu. should not this be *monogram*?

monogyn (ˈmɒnədʒɪn). *Bot.* [ad. mod.L. *monogyn-us*: see MONOGYNIA.] (See quot.)

1828–32 WEBSTER, *Monogyn*, in *botany*, a plant having only one style or stigma [cites *Smith*]. **1860** WORCESTER, *Monogyn* [cites *Lindley*].

‖**Monogynia** (mɒnəʊˈdʒɪnɪə). *Bot.* [mod.L. (Linnæus), f. *monogyn-us* monogynous (f. Gr. μόνο-ς MONO- + γυν-ή woman, taken in the sense 'pistil'): see -IA.] The first order in each of the first thirteen classes of the Linnæan Sexual System, comprising plants having flowers with only one pistil or stigma. Also used *attrib.* or *adj.*

1760 J. LEE *Introd. Bot.* II. iii. (1765) 78. **1785** MARTYN *Rousseau's Bot.* x. (1794) 99. **1845** *Encycl. Metrop.* XXV. 7/1.

Hence **monoˈgynian**, **monoˈgynic**, **monoˈgynious** *adjs.* = MONOGYNOUS *a.* 1.

a **1794** SIR W. JONES *Enchanted Fruit* Wks. 1799 VI. 182 Taught.. To class by pistil and by stamen, Produce from nature's rich dominion Flow'rs Polyandrian Monogynian. **1891** *Syd. Soc. Lex.*, *Monogynic*, same as *Monogynous*. **1856** MAYNE *Expos. Lex.*, *Monogynius*, having one pistil, or one style;.. monogynious.

monogynist (məˈnɒdʒɪnɪst). [f. MONOGYN-Y + -IST.] One who practises or is in favour of monogyny.

1895 in *Funk's Stand. Dict.* **1902** in *Cassell's Suppl.*

monogynœcial (ˌmɒnəʊdʒaɪˈniːʃ(ɪ)əl), *a. Bot.* [f. MONO- + GYNŒCI-UM + -AL¹.] Applied to a simple fruit formed by the gynœcium of a single flower.

1876 H. J. BALFOUR in *Encycl. Brit.* IV. 150/2 Simple fruits are hence sometimes denominated monogynœcial, as being formed by one gynœcium.

monogynous (məˈnɒdʒɪnəs), *a.* [f. mod.L. *monogyn-us* (see MONOGYNIA) + -OUS.]

1. *Bot.* Having only one pistil, style, or stigma; belonging to the order *Monogynia*.

1816 P. KEITH *Syst. Phys. Bot.* I. 117 Sometimes the pistil is single or solitary.. the flower is [then] said to be monogynous. **1837** —— *Bot. Lex.* s.v., Flowers having but a single style are said to be monogynous, as in Primula. **1861** BENTLEY *Man. Bot.* I. iv. §4. 274.

2. Of or pertaining to monogyny; living in monogyny.

1890 in *Century Dict.* **1906** *19th Cent.* Feb. 223 The Report [on the decline of the birth-rate in N.S.W.].. stigmatises the married state of those who practise it [*sc.* limitation of offspring] as one of 'monogynous prostitution'.

3. *Zool.* 'Having only one female mate' (*Cent. Dict.*).

monogyny (məˈnɒdʒɪnɪ). [f. MONO- + Gr. γυνή woman, wife.] The practice of mating with only one female, or of marrying only one wife. (Corresp. to MONANDRY.)

1876 H. SPENCER *Princ. Sociol.* (1877) I. 698 Monogyny does not fully express the union of one man with one woman.. since the feminine unity is alone indicated by it.. Hence monogamy, expressing the singleness of the marriage, may be fitly retained.

monohalogen (mɒnəʊˈhælədʒɛn), *a.* [f. MONO- + HALOGEN.] Containing one equivalent of a halogen.

1893 *Proc. Royal Soc.* LIV. 101 On the Ratio of the Specific Heats of the Paraffins and their Monohalogen Derivatives, by J. W. Capstick.

monohemerous (mɒnəʊˈhiːmərəs), *a. Med.* Also 9 **monemerous.** [f. mod.L. *monohēmer-a* neut. pl. (ad. Gr. μονοήμερος, var. of μονήμερος lasting one day only, f. μόνο-ς MONO- + ἡμέρ-α day) + -OUS.] Lasting or existing only one day.

[**1693** tr. *Blancard's Phys. Dict.* (ed. 2), *Monohemera*, Diseases that are cured in one Day.] **1731** BAILEY, *Monohemerous Diseases*, such as last but one Day, or are cured in a Day. **1856** MAYNE *Expos. Lex.*, *Monemeros*,.. lasting or enduring one day..: monemerous.

monohull (ˈmɒnəʊhʌl). [f. MONO- + HULL *sb.*²] A boat with a single hull. Also *attrib.* or as *adj.* Cf. MULTIHULL.

1967 *Motor Boating* Oct. 135 This year the race was split into two divisions, caused by the catamaran show of superiority: one for monohulls, the other for cats. **1968** *Observer* 9 June 23/5, I would like to see two separate [single-handed Atlantic crossing] races in future,..—one for monohulls and one for multihulls. **1969** *Sunday Times* 2 Feb. 50 The design of the monohull can be improved—there is constant experiment with materials. **1971** *New Scientist* 4 Feb. 265/2 The superiority of the Planesail concept over the conventional monohull or multihull arrangement had already been amply demonstrated. **1972** *Observer* 11 June 18/7, I am confident that Three Cheers, and certainly a multihull, will win—with the radical monohull Strongbow our only serious competitor. **1973** 'A. YORK' *Captivator* iii. 44 She's all but thirty feet long.. and being a cat, she's fourteen feet wide. That means she has about the same accommodation as a monohull.

monohybrid (mɒnəʊˈhaɪbrɪd), *sb.* and *a. Biol.* [f. MONO- + HYBRID *sb.* and *a.*] **A.** *sb.* A hybrid that is heterozygous with respect to a single gene. **B.** *adj.* Of, pertaining to, or characteristic of such a hybrid, or a cross resulting in such a hybrid. So **monoˈhybridism** (*rare*).

1904 *Rep. Evolution Comm. R. Soc.* No. 2. 126 Unresolved characters in ordinary mono-hybrids. **1907** R. C. PUNNETT *Mendelism* (ed. 2) 34 The cases.. concern only a single pair of differentiating characters, that is to say, are cases of monohybridism. **1910** *Amer. Naturalist* XLIV. 67 The crosses have all given a simple mono-hybrid ratio. **1911** FARMER & DARBISHIRE tr. *H. de Vries's Mutation Theory* II. 585 We have given the name of monohybrids to those mongrels whose parents differ from one another in a single elementary character only. **1931** A. F. SHULL *Heredity* (ed. 2) vii. 52 Offspring produced by two parents which differ in only one inherited feature are known as monohybrids. **1964** M. CRITCHLEY *Developmental Dyslexia* x. 64 The author concluded that developmental dyslexia follows a monohybrid autosomal dominant mode of inheritance. **1967** A. MÜNTZING *Genetics: Basic & Applied* v. 46/2 Heterozygotes for one gene pair, monohybrids,.. display monohybrid segregation in the ratio of 3:1.

monohydrate (mɒnəʊˈhaɪdrət). *Chem.* [See MONO- 2 and HYDRATE.] A hydrate containing one equivalent of water. So **monoˈhydrated** *a.*, compounded with one equivalent of water.

1853 URE *Dict. Arts* I. 987 Monohydrated nitric acid. **1854** J. SCOFFERN in *Orr's Circ. Sci.*, *Chem.* 315 Monohydrate of nitric acid. **1857** MILLER *Elem. Chem.* (1862) III. 309 The normal or monohydrated monobasic organic acids. **1876** HARLEY *Mat. Med.* (ed. 6) 69 The acid thus obtained is the Monohydrate (HNO_3).

monohydric (mɒnəʊˈhaɪdrɪk), *a. Chem.* [See MONO- 2 and HYDRIC.] **a.** Having one equivalent of hydrogen in combination.

1856 in MAYNE *Expos. Lex.*

b. Of an alcohol or phenol: containing a single hydroxyl group.

1880 *Jrnl. Chem. Soc.* XXXVIII. 28 (*heading*) Sulphates of mono- and poly-hydric alcohols. **1926** J. READ *Text-bk. Org. Chem.* xxiv. 541 Ordinary phenol, or carbolic acid,.. is a monohydric phenol. **1937** *Jrnl. R. Aeronaut. Soc.* XLI. 737 Fuels containing monohydric alcohols are rendered harmless to magnesium and its alloys by saturating such fuels with complex alkali fluorides soluble in them. **1967** I. L. FINAR *Org. Chem.* (ed. 5) I. vi. 144 The monohydric alcohols form an homologous series with the general formula $C_nH_{2n+2}O$.

monoˈhydrogen. [MONO- 2.] Used *attrib.* to denote compounds with one equivalent of hydrogen.

1869 ROSCOE *Elem. Chem.* xv. (1871) 160 Monohydrogen phosphate.

monoic (məˈnɒɪk), *a. Zool. rare.* [ad. mod.L. *monoica* (neut. pl., De Blainville 1825), a. Gr. type *μόνοικος: see MONŒCIA.] = MONŒCIOUS 2.

1856 MAYNE *Expos. Lex.*, *Monoïcus*... *Zool.* Applied by Blainville to a sub-Class (*Monoïca*, nom. pl. n.) of the *Paracephalophora*, comprehending those which have the sexes distinct, but in the same individual: monoic animals. **1882** *Entom. Mag.* Mar. 226 The.. evolution of monoic insects.

monoicous (məˈnɔɪkəs), *a. Bot.* [f. mod.L. *monoic-us*, F. *monoïque*, irreg. ad. Gr. type *μόνοικος (see MONŒCIA) + -OUS.] **a.** = MONŒCIOUS 1. Now *rare* or *Obs.* **b.** Applied by Darwin to those 'polygamous' plants which

have the three sexual varieties together on the same individual: opposed to *trioicous*.

1822 GOOD *Study Med.* IV. 5 Monoicous plants. **1831** J. DAVIES *Manual Mat. Med.* 154 Flowers greenish, small, monoicous, disposed in spikes. **1863** BERKELEY *Brit. Mosses* 65 Cryphæa, Mohr. Monoicous. **1877** DARWIN *Forms of Fl.* Introd. 12 Of the other or monoicous sub-group of polygamous plants, or those which bear hermaphrodite, male and female flowers on the same individual, the Common Maple (*Acer campestre*) offers a good instance.

Hence **mo'noicously** *adv.*

1847 [see MONŒCIOUSLY].

monoid ('mɒnɔɪd), *a.* (and *sb.*) [ad. Gr. μονοειδ-ής of one form, uniform, f. μόνο-ς MONO- + εἶδ-ος form: see -OID.]

1. *Anc. Prosody.* Composed of feet of one kind.

1890 in *Century Dict.*

2. *Math.* Applied to a surface which possesses a conical point of the highest possible $(n - 1)$th order. Also *absol.* or *sb.* = *monoid surface*.

1862 CAYLEY in *Proc. Brit. Assoc., Sections* 3 A cone.. and a monoid surface with the same vertex. **1866** BRANDE & COX *Dict. Sci.* s.v., The cones P and Q are called respectively the superior and inferior cones of the monoid.

monoideal (mɒnəʊaɪ'diːəl), *a.* *rare*$^{-1}$. [f. MONO- + IDEAL *a.* 3 b.] Expressing or conveying only one idea.

1922 JOYCE *Ulysses* 667 The infinite possibilities hitherto unexploited of the modern art of advertisement if condensed in triliteral monoideal symbols.

monoïdeism (ˌmɒnəʊaɪ'diːɪz(ə)m). Also **monoideism**. [f. MONO- + IDE-A + -ISM.] Concentration of the mind, or fixation of the attention, upon one idea; *esp.* as a form of monomania or a hypnotic condition.

1860 FOWLER *Med. Voc., Mono-ideism*, that artificially induced condition in which the acts of the mind, sensation, and motion, may be completely governed by means of suggestive ideas—the individual being conscious.—*Braid.* **1885** GURNEY & MYERS in *Proc. Soc. Psych. Research* III. 407 It is observed that the mental condition of hypnotised 'subjects' is often one of marked mono-ideism—of strong and one-sided attention. **1890** tr. *T. Ribot's Psychol. of Attention* iii. 96 This higher form of ecstasy may at times reach the state of complete, absolute monoideism, that is, the state of perfect unity of consciousness. **1891** W. J. GREENSTREET tr. *Guyau's Educ. & Heredity* i. 14 This state has been called monoideism, and is found in somnambulists. **1891** *Syd. Soc. Lex., Monoïdeism*, Braid's term for the condition in which mental conditions in one person are governed by ideas suggested by another. **1892** SULLY in Tuke *Dict. Psych. Med.* I. 110/2 Narrowness of interest with its accompanying tendency to monoideism is one fertile source of danger in an age when subdivision and specialisation of work has been carried to an extreme point. **1907** *Athenæum* 2 Mar. 258/1 Monoïdeism in science is always a present peril. **1966** D. W. ABSE *Hysteria* viii. 116 It was essentially a narrowing of the attention, or a 'monoideism'.. that ushered in the hypnotic trance.

Hence **monoide'istic** *a.*, pertaining to or characterized by monoideism.

1902 W. JAMES *Var. Relig. Exper.* 525 Philosophy, with its passion for unity, and mysticism with its monoideistic bent, both 'pass to the limit' and identify the something with a unique God who is the all-inclusive soul of the world. **1904** G. S. HALL *Adolescence* II. 50 The history of philosophy shows that the mono-ideistic thinkers.. were the victims of an environment or an age itself overwrought, one-sided and extreme.

mono-'iodo-. *Chem.* [See MONO- 2 and IODO-.] Combining form, denoting the presence in a compound of one atom of iodine.

1873 *Fownes' Chem.* (ed. 11) 802 Oxyphenols are formed from the corresponding monoiodophenols. **1891** *Syd. Soc. Lex., Monoiodopentane*, same as *Amyl iodide*.

monok, obs. form of MONK.

monokaryon (mɒnəʊ'kærɪɒn). *Bot.* Also **monocaryon**. [f. MONO- after DIKARYON.] A mononuclear cell, spore, or mycelium in higher fungi that have a dikaryotic stage of the life cycle. Hence **monokary'otic** *a.*, containing or characteristic of a monokaryon.

1935 E. A. BESSEY *Text-bk. Mycol.* xii. 323 The secondary mycelium (dicaryon phase) is of far greater importance in the life cycle, the primary mycelium (monocaryon phase) occupying but a short period of the life of the fungus. **1936** *Amer. Jrnl. Bot.* XXIII. 310/1 Throughout this paper the terms *monocaryon mycelium* and *dicaryon mycelium* will be employed instead of the older terms *haploid* and *diploid*. **1941** *Bot. Rev.* VII. 412 These give rise either to dikaryotic diploid oidia or to monokaryotic haploid oidia. **1947** F. A. & F. T. WOLF *Fungi* II. xiv. 334 The complete cycle from the monocaryotic to the dicaryotic condition. **1968** R. RIEGER et al. *Gloss. Genetics & Cytogenetics* 299 *Monokaryon*, a uninucleate cell, a spore, or a tissue consisting of such cells, as opposed to a dikaryon. **1972** E. MOORE-LANDECKER *Fund. Fungi* iv. 91 The monokaryon is at first nonseptate. *Ibid.* 92 When the monokaryotic hyphae fuse, the nuclei of one hypha flow into the other.

monokini (mɒnəʊ'kiːnɪ). [f. MONO- after BIKINI b, with reference to BI- *pref.*[2]] A one-piece beach garment, usu. one equivalent to the lower half of a bikini and worn by women.

1964 *Daily Mirror* (Brisbane) 6 July 6 Monokinis are selling in Paris like iceboxes in Alaska. **1964** *Time* 7 Aug. 36/3 Sunbathing.., she in a bikini.., he in a monokini. **1965** *New Yorker* 10 Apr. 92 He works wearing only a jet monokini, a trained canary perched on his shoulder. **1966** B. E. WALLACE *Murder in Touraine* xi. 96 She was standing there near naked in her brief monokini. **1966** *N.Y. Times* 30 May 20 Hand-loomed Orlon yarn 'monokini' has top and bottom joined by a band. **1968** B. FOSTER *Changing Eng. Lang.* iii. 121 In France in the year 1964.. there was much talk of a topless bathing suit, immediately known as the *monokini*. **1971** *Observer* (Colour Suppl.) 9 May (recto front cover), This monokini is not a tattered pair of cut-down jeans but the latest smart, expensive one-piece swimsuit made of disguised suede. **1974** *Guardian* 4 July 2/7 The monokini is no longer the rage only at St-Tropez. French girls usually go topless in Paris open-air swimming pools.

monoklinohedric, var. MONOCLINOHEDRIC.

monolater (mə'nɒlətə(r)). [f. MONOLATRY, after *idolater*.] A worshipper of one god. So **mo'nolatrist**.

1900 *Dublin Rev.* July 210 He.. declares them to have been 'monolatrists', *i.e.* to have believed in many gods, and worshipped but one, Jehovah. **1905** J. ORR *Problem O.T.* iv. 86 Israel emerges from the dim past as a loose aggregate of polytheists or at least monolaters.

mo'nolatrous, *a.* [f. MONOLATRY, after *idolatrous*.] Of or pertaining to monolatry.

1892 MONTEFIORE *Hibbert Lect.* i. 18 A conscious infraction of a known monolatrous law. **1897** R. L. OTTLEY *Aspects O.T.* ii. 69 In its earlier stages the worship of the ordinary Hebrew was not monotheistic but monolatrous.

monolatry (mə'nɒlətrɪ). [f. Gr. μόνο-ς MONO- + λατρεία worship, -LATRY.] The worship of one god, where other gods may be supposed to exist.

1881 W. R. SMITH *Old Test. In Jew. Ch.* x. 273 The religion of the Old Testament is no mere natural variety of Semitic monolatry. **1886** HUXLEY in *19th Cent.* Apr. 495 A worship of one God—monolatry as Wellhausen calls it—which is very different from genuine monotheism. **1892** MONTEFIORE *Hibbert Lect.* i. 11 Monolatry is the worship of one god; monotheism, of the one and only God.

monolayer ('mɒnəleɪə(r)). [f. MONO- + LAYER *sb.*] **a.** A layer or film one molecule thick.

1933 *Biochem. Jrnl.* XXVII. 1581 The structure of proteins in bulk solution is different from that which exists when the protein is extended as a monolayer in a film. **1950** W. J. MOORE *Physical Chem.* xvi. 496 The ordinary three-dimensional states of aggregation have many counterparts in the two-dimensional world of monolayers. **1972** R. G. KAZMANN *Mod. Hydrol.* (ed. 2) iii. 62 Ideally this would form a film one molecule thick on the water surface—a monolayer. **1973** *Nature* 10 Aug. 328/2 In these severe conditions of lack of water (a few monolayers of water adsorbed on soil particles) some growth and metabolic activity of bacteria.. does occur.

b. *Biol.* and *Med.* A culture consisting of a layer of cells one cell thick.

1952 *Proc. Nat. Acad. Sci.* XXXVIII. 748 The virus of Western Equine Encephalomyelitis, adapted to chicken embryo, will produce plaques when it is grown on a monolayer of cells obtainable from chicken embryos. **1961** *Nature* 22 Apr. 370/2 The vaccina virus was grown in monolayer cultures of monkey kidney tissue. **1973** *Ibid.* 6 Apr. 399/2 The division of most 'normal' cells in culture is inhibited after they have grown to a confluent monolayer.

monolein (mə'nəʊlɪn). *Chem.* [MONO- 2.] An OLEIN containing one equivalent of oleic acid.

1857 MILLER *Elem. Chem.* (1862) III. 278 Monolein... Diolein... Triolein. **1873** RALFE *Phys. Chem.* 49.

monoline ('mɒnəlaɪn). [f. MONO- + LINE *sb.*]

1. (With capital initial.) The inventor's name for one of the printing machines which cast a line at a time. Cf. LINOTYPE.

1902 *Encycl. Brit.* XXXIII. 522/2 The former class [of type-setting and type-casting machines] is exemplified by the Linotype, the Typograph, and the Monoline machines.

2. = MONO-RAIL.

1902 *Westm. Gaz.* 1 Feb. 10/2 A project for constructing a railway between Edinburgh and Glasgow on the monoline principle.

monolingual (mɒnəʊ'lɪŋgwəl), *a.* and *sb.* [f. MONO- + LINGUAL *a.* 4 b.] **A.** *adj.* Speaking only one language; written in a single language.

1953 *Use of Vernacular Lang. in Educ.* (Unesco) ii. 50 It cannot be denied that the business of government is easier in a monolingual than in a multilingual nation. However, it does not follow that legislation or school policy requiring the use of the official language at all times will give the same results as actual monolingualism. **1954** L. MACNEICE *Autumn Sequel* 54 At times she is monolingual, monotone, At others mistress of the Tower of Babel. **1968** *Amer. N. & Q.* Mar. 109/1 As a monolingual dictionary and a ready reference work.. the Larousse has no parallel in any other language. **1972** *Language* XLVIII 910 The English translations do not, I think, allow the monolingual speaker of English to get any sense of how a speaker of Japanese feels when he is addressed with *-san*.

B. *sb.* One who speaks only one language.

1956 E. HAUGEN *Bilingualism in Americas* iv. 77 Any kind of sampling test which adequately measures monolingual skill can be used to make comparisons between monolinguals and bilinguals speaking the same language. **1971** G. ANSRE in J. Spencer *Eng. Lang. W. Afr.* 147 Essentially,.. in cases of both monolinguals and bilinguals incorporating loans, the results seem similar. **1972** H. KURATH *Studies Area Linguistics* vii. 112 A few of them have even been adopted by English monolinguals of Pennsylvania.

Hence **mono'lingualism**, the ability to speak only one language; **mono'linguist** = MONOLINGUAL *sb.*; **monolin'guistic** *a.* = MONOLINGUAL *a.*

1928 *Observer* 8 Apr. 14/3 There is no one living.. speaking only Manx and no English. Ten years before that the monolinguists had dwindled to under half a dozen. **1942** L. B. NAMIER *Conflicts* 3 Union.. in monolinguistic national States became in the nineteenth century the political aim of the educated, and in time of the semi-educated, classes in Europe. **1960** J. LODWICK *Asparagus Trench* 66 All the monolinguists who.. would opt for Indian tea in Pekin. **1968** Y. MALKIEL *Essays on Linguistic Themes* i. 6 It is.. held that bilingualism and even trilingualism are more widely disseminated the world over than is strict monolingualism. **1972** H. KURATH *Studies in Area Linguistics* 124 Monolingualism prevails in large parts of the world.

monolith ('mɒnəlɪθ), *sb.* and *a.* Also **monolithe.** [a. F. *monolithe* adj. and sb., or ad. L. *monolith-us* adj., a. Gr. μονόλιθος made out of one stone, f. μόνο-ς MONO- + λίθος stone.]

A. *sb.* **1.** A single block of stone, *esp.* one of notable size, shaped into a pillar or monument.

[**1827** G. HIGGINS *Celtic Druids* 214 The monolithoi or single stones.] **1848** *Chamb. Inform. People* I. 433/2 Twenty-four colossal monolithes, representing Indian gods, are placed in separate divisions. **1851** D. WILSON *Preh. Ann.* (1863) I. v. 166 The giant monoliths of Salisbury plain. **1862** R. H. PATTERSON *Ess. Hist. & Art* 411 Several remarkable monoliths, or temples carved out of single rocks. **1875** *Encycl. Brit.* II. 390/2 The obelisks of Egypt are generally huge monoliths of red granite or syenite.

2. *transf.* and *fig.* A person or thing resembling a monolith; *esp.* (after Russ. *monolít*; cf. *monolítnost'* monolithic unity of the party) a political or social structure presenting an indivisible or unbroken unity.

1934 H. NICOLSON *Curzon: Last Phase* xi. 323 M. Stamboliisky, the peasant Prime Minister of Bulgaria, was also granted an audience... Curzon was attracted towards this solid, somewhat helpless, monolith. He always felt at his ease with entirely self-made people. **1940** AUDEN *Another Time* 117 The monolith Of State. **1953** *Manch. Guardian* 6 Apr. 4/1 The 'monolith' of Soviet power is stirring. **1957** *Economist* 7 Sept. 766/2 A growing diversity in the economic scene is liable to lead to cracks in the political monolith. **1959** P. H. JOHNSON *Unspeakable Skipton* xxiii. 203 If the Commissioners of Inland Revenue ever caught up with her, she would undoubtedly bring tears to their eyes, reducing them from monoliths to simple, sentimental men with mothers of their own. **1962** J. WAIN *Strike Father Dead* 115 She was a woman of few words, as thick round the middle as an oak, with strong limbs and a big head and shoulders. She wasn't talkative, but.. you just wouldn't expect to get a flow of words out of a monolith like that. **1966** *Listener* 12 May 700/3 His [*sc.* Bruckner's] symphonies are towering monoliths. **1975** *Times* 4 Jan. 13/3 State run monoliths whose inspiration would owe more to the opportunism of Benito Mussolini than to idealism.

B. *adj.* **1.** = MONOLITHIC 1.

1850 LEITCH tr. *C. O. Müller's Anc. Art* §310 (ed. 2) 352 Monolith colossal statues. **1864** PUSEY *Lect. Daniel* i. (1876) 32 Monarchs who transported a monolith obelisk from Armenia. *a* **1878** SIR G. G. SCOTT *Lect. Archit.* (1879) II. 48 The side doorways were found to have monolith jambs.

2. *fig.* = MONOLITHIC *a.* 4.

1922 E. BLUNDEN *Shepherd* 53 Between great monolith trees.

monolithal ('mɒnəlɪθəl), *a.* *rare.* [f. MONOLITH + -AL[1].] = MONOLITHIC *a.* 1.

1830 MAUNDER *Treas. Knowl.* I. **1847** SMEATON *Builder's Man.* 215 The principal Egyptian buildings were the pyramids, obelisks, labyrinths, monolithal chambers, sphinxes, and temples. **1859** W. H. GREGORY *Egypt* I. 190 The image of the god in his monolithal (made of a single stone) shrine.

monolithic (mɒnəʊ'lɪθɪk), *a.* [f. MONOLITH + -IC.]

1. a. Formed of a single block of stone; of the nature of a monolith.

1825 FOSBROOKE *Encycl. Antiq.* I. 12 These sanctuaries often consisted of a single excavated block. They are called Monolithic temples. **1849** FREEMAN *Archit.* 101 The Greek column, which, in idea at least, is so essentially monolithic. **1859** TENNENT *Ceylon* II. x. ii. 622 Rows of monolithic pillars, each twenty-six feet high. **1876** FERGUSSON *Hist. Ind. & East. Archit.* IV. ii. 338 There is no doubt that their monolithic character is the principal source of the awe and wonder with which they have been regarded.

b. *Electronics.* Of a solid-state circuit: composed of active and passive components formed in a single chip (or thin film: see quot. 1967).

1963 E. KEONJIAN *Microelectronics* i. 8 (*heading*) Monolithic circuits. *Ibid.* 9 A monolithic piece of material is treated in such a way as to possess an electronic circuit function. **1965** *New Scientist* 20 May 510/2 The multi-chip assembly has some advantages over the monolithic circuit—for example, the various chips can be tested before assembly. **1967** *Encycl. Dict. Physics* Suppl. II. 173/1 *Monolithic circuit*, an integrated circuit which uses either thin film or silicon chip techniques for both active and passive devices but not a mixture of these techniques. Since true monolithic thin film circuits are not commercially available the term is more usually applied to silicon chip construction, where it implies, in particular, that any circuit capacitors do not use evaporated dielectrics. However, monolithic silicon chip circuits may use a deposited pattern of connectors between circuit elements. **1970** [see INTEGRATED *ppl. a.* b]. **1971** *Physics Bull.* Jan. 45/1 The new computer has a main memory constructed entirely of monolithic circuits and uses silicon memory chips instead of magnetic cores for storage.

2. Composed or consisting of monoliths; relating to or characterized by monoliths.

1851 D. WILSON *Preh. Ann.* v. 100 The remarkable monolithic group called The Stones of Stennis. *Ibid.* 103 What may be styled the monolithic era of art.

3. (See quot. 1881.)

1881 YOUNG *Ev. Man his own Mech.* §1232 It is intended to build the walls in 'monolithic' concrete, that is to say, a wall composed of concrete built up piece-meal which hardens into a solid unbroken mass. **1885** [see BETON]. **1898** *Engineering Mag.* XVI. 131/1 A Large Monolithic Concrete Building. *Ibid*, A large Monolithic Factory Building.

4. *transf.* and *fig.* Resembling a monolith, having one or more of the qualities of a monolith; great, massive; immovable, unwavering, unemotional; unified, homogeneous, unchallenged. *Esp.* applied to organizations, parties, governments, etc., which are autocratic or monopolistic (freq. in derogatory use).

1920 D. H. LAWRENCE *England, my England* (1922) 87 Maurice had a curious monolithic way of sitting in a chair, erect and distant. **1923** A. HUXLEY *Antic Hay* xiii. 192 His appearance is monolithic and grim. **1937** *Nation* (N.Y.) 10 July 32/1 The monolithic corporation talks loudly to the workers. **1942** *New Republic* 9 Nov. 598/2 The monolithic power structure of the totalitarian state. **1945** A. L. ROWSE *West-Country Stories* 26 The Fourth Symphony of Sibelius, the most monolithic of them all. **1948** J. TOWSTER *Polit. Power in U.S.S.R.* p. ix, The peculiarities of the monolithic Communist Party. **1952** *Economist* 22 Mar. 702/1 Herr Grotewohl and his monolithic Socialist Unity Party are democratic. **1953** *Times* 11 Apr. 7/2 Wherever there is monolithic rule the autocrat is bound to repress all views that are not his own. **1959** *Listener* 5 Mar. 423/1 There were many contradictory elements in her, but they and she were static, immovable, almost monolithic. **1971** *Nature* 7 May 2/2 But would not the merging of the research councils create too monolithic a central sponsor? **1974** E. AMBLER *Dr. Frigo* II. 124 We were never a monolithic party.

mono'lithically, *adv.* [f. MONOLITHIC *a.*; see -ICALLY.] In a monolithic form or manner (see senses 3 and 4 of MONOLITHIC *a.*).

1905 C. S. HILL in Buel & Hill *Reinforced Concrete Constr.* vi. 138 The readiness..with which they may be bonded monolithically. **1932** KIPLING *Limits & Renewals* 80, I was monolithically military. **1952** SPARKES & SMITH *Concrete Roads* xvii. 398 Integral kerbs are those which are constructed monolithically with the slab. **1960** *Times* 17 Feb. 5/6 Insulating concrete can be cast monolithically. **1960** *Sunday Times* 22 May 17/5 Greedy for praise and monolithically uncharitable. **1962** *Friend* 14 Sept. 1116/1 A row of intent figures... Sometimes the families, the lovers and the photographers got mixed up with these still figures. But they monolithically stood on, for three full hours. **1966** *New Statesman* 27 May 762/3 The church [in Spain] can no longer be regarded as an institution monolithically in support of the *status quo*, opposed to change at all costs. **1975** *Times* 11 July 15/4 The contention that the Liberal Party is monolithically moderate.

monolithism (ˈmɒnəlɪθɪz(ə)m). [f. MONOLITH *sb.* + -ISM.] The quality or fact of being monolithic (see MONOLITHIC *a.* 4); the principle of totalitarian rule.

1927 *Nation* 21 Dec. 703 The tactics..constituted a danger to the 'monolithism' of the party. **1948** J. TOWSTER *Polit. Power in U.S.S.R.* II. vi. 132 Cutting across both the monopoly and monolithism power principles, this act was.. condemned as 'open counter-revolution'. **1957** T. KILMARTIN tr. *Aron's Opium of Intellectuals* 129 The Bolsheviks have always had two slogans, one which insisted on monolithism, the other which encouraged conflicts of ideas and tendencies to sustain the vigour of the Party.

monolobite, -lobular, -locular: see MONO- 1.

mono'logian. *rare.* [Formed as next + -IAN.] = MONOLOGIST.

1625 MINSHEU *Ductor* (ed. 2) 474 A Monologian, or a Monologue, one that will haue all the talke to himselfe, or one that loues to heare himselfe talke. **1835** *Tait's Mag.* II. 18 Pierre [is] a monologian well worth the listening to.

monologic (mɒnəʊˈlɒdʒɪk), *a. rare.* [f. Gr. μονόλογ-ος (see MONOLOGUE) + -IC. Cf. F. *monologique*.] Pertaining to, or of the nature of, a monologue.

1852 BLACKIE *Stud. Lang.* 27 You will thus make for yourself a sort of speaking practice in the monologic form. **1866** BLACKMORE *Cradock Nowell* liii, A page and a half of monologic dialogue. **1886** *Academy* 16 Oct. 253/3 A record of her [*sc.* Miss F. Marryat's] 'musical, dramatic, and monologic' triumphs.

monological (mɒnəʊˈlɒdʒɪkəl), *a.* [Formed as prec. + -ICAL.] = MONOLOGIC. Also of a person: Given to monologue or soliloquy.

1823 *New Monthly Mag.* IX. 394/2 [He] appeared not only in his monological entertainments, but also in the drama. **1829** CARLYLE *Misc., Ger. Playw.* (1840) II. 55 Plays, which..are essentially monological. **1834** BECKFORD *Italy* II. 228 In return for the honour of being admitted to this monological dialogue I kept nodding and bowing. **1842** J. STERLING *Ess.* (1848) I. 453 [Tennyson's] *St. Simeon Stylites*, a kind of monological personation of a..mad ascetic. **1872** O. W. HOLMES *Poet Breakf.-t.* x. 281 King Thomas [*sc.* Carlyle], the last of the monological succession.

monologist (məˈnɒlədʒɪst). [f. Gr. μονόλογ-ος (see MONOLOGUE) + -IST.] One who talks in monologue, one who soliloquizes; also, one who monopolizes the conversation. See also MONOLOGUIST.

1711 SHAFTESB. *Charac.* (1737) III. Misc. III. ii. 185 Thus our Monologist, or Self-discoursing Author, in his usual Strain. **1727** BAILEY (vol. II), *Monologist*, one that loves to have all the Talk to himself. **1848** GILFILLAN in *Tait's Mag.* XV. 279 A lecturer, in the common sense of the term, he is not; call him rather a public monologist, talking rather to himself than to his audience. **1882** *Athenæum* No. 2841. 435 When monologist meets monologist mutual admiration rarely results. **1885** E. C. STEDMAN in *Century Mag.* XXIX. 509 The Autocrat..is always acute,—the liveliest of monologists.

b. One who performs monologues.

1858 *Sat. Rev.* 7 Aug. 133 An indifferent troupe of actors can produce an excitement far beyond that which is caused by the pert song or flippant anecdote of the most accomplished monologist. **1892** *Speaker* 30 July 141/2 One prominent comedian and monologist of the Comédie Française.

monologize (məˈnɒlədʒaɪz), *v. intr.* [Formed as prec. + -IZE.] *intr.* To talk in monologue.

1826 DISRAELI *Viv. Grey* I. i, 'Now who could have told the child that?' monologised mamma, with all a mamma's admiration. **1890** SYMONDS *Mem. C. Gozzi* I. 128 Celio monologised against his mortal foe Morgana. **1899** *Speaker* 2 Dec. 237/2 The characters seem to monologise abstractedly.

monologue (ˈmɒnəlɒg), *sb.* [a. F. *monologue*, 'one that loues to heare himselfe talke; or talkes very much about very little' (Cotgr.), ad. Gr. μονόλογος speaking alone, f. μόνο-ς MONO- + -λογος speaker, speaking. See -LOGUE.]

†**1.** One who does all the talking. *Obs.*$^{-0}$

1625 [see MONOLOGIAN].

2. a. 'A scene in which a person of the drama speaks by himself' (J.); contrasted with *chorus* and *dialogue*. Also, in modern use, a dramatic composition for a single performer; a kind of dramatic entertainment performed throughout by one person.

1668 DRYDEN *Ess. Dram. Poesy* (Ker) I. 78, I can show.. in *Catiline* and *Sejanus* sometimes thirty or forty lines [of rhyme together], I mean besides the Chorus, or the monologues. **1696** PHILLIPS (ed. 5), *Monologue*, a Dramatick Scene, where only one Actor speaks. **1739** CIBBER *Apol.* (1756) II. 164 The monologues and pageants drawn from place to place on wheels answer exactly to the cart of Thespis. **1845** E. HOLMES *Mozart* 200 The opera began with a monologue. **1872** LIDDON *Elem. Relig.* iv. 132 The true sense of the monologue in Hamlet may be thus summed up. **1883** S. C. HALL *Retrospect* II. 254 It was in monologues that he [Mathews] surpassed all competitors.

transf. **1849** LYTTON *Caxtons* VI. i, Life is a drama, not a monologue.

b. In generalized sense: Literary composition of this nature.

1668 DRYDEN *Ess. Dram. Poesy* (Ker) I. 50 He also gives you an account of himself..in monologue; to which unnatural way of narration Terence is subject in all his plays.

c. A poem, or other non-dramatic composition, in the form of a soliloquy. Used *spec.* of Old English verse.

1866 *Athenæum* 3 Feb. 175/1 Mr. Robert Buchanan's new volume of poems, 'London Idyls', will consist principally of monologues. **1902** W. W. LAWRENCE in *Jrnl. Eng. & Gmc. Philol.* IV. 462 Ebert expressed the opinion that the Seafarer should be interpreted as a monologue from beginning to end. **1905** E. RICKERT in *Mod. Philol.* II. 372 They are specimens of the *giedd* or short monologue arising from a dramatic situation, such as occurs frequently in *Beowulf*. **1935** A. C. BARTLETT *Larger Rhet. Patterns Anglo-Saxon Poetry* 106 Monologue and duologue, direct and indirect discourse, all are undramatic. **1943** B. F. HUPPÉ in *Jrnl. Eng. & Gmc. Philol.* XLII. 529 The basic outline [of the *Wanderer*] has already been set, with the two contrasting and complementary pagan monologues, framed and bound together by the expository Christian introduction, conclusion and 'bridge passage'.

3. A long speech or harangue delivered by one person who is in company or conversation with others; talk or discourse of the nature of a soliloquy.

1859 HELPS *Friends in C.* Ser. II. II. v. 115 Notice the self-contained talker, whose talk is a monologue. **1873** BLACK *Pr. Thule* iii, He was pleasing himself with a series of monologues, interrupted only by his cigar. **1905** A. C. BENSON *Upton Lett.* (1906) 310 He will plunge into a fiery monologue about his ambitions.

'monologue, *v.* [f. prec.] *intr.* To MONOLOGIZE. Hence **'monologuing** *vbl. sb.*

1834 *Tait's Mag.* I. 367/1 'What, the rectory of——, if I'll change my coat?' monologues the vicar. **1863** *Not an Angel* I. 140 Miss Mary..monologued the while, after her manner. **1892** *Blackw. Mag.* Aug. 205 Holmes..goes on with his monologuing—if we may coin a word. **1894** G. MOORE *Esther Waters* 41 Feeling that he had secured an appreciative listener, he continued to monologue regarding the wealth and rank his family had formerly held.

monologuist (ˈmɒnəlɒgɪst). Also -logueist. [f. MONOLOGUE + -IST.] One who talks or performs in monologue; one who delivers monologues.

1865 *Athenæum* 29 July 151/3 The newest of the monologuists is Mr. McCabe. **1866** *Ibid.* 3 Feb. 175/1 Such subjects as 'The Murder Idyl', in which the monologuist is a woman whose husband has been hanged. **1874** W. MATHEWS *Gt. Conversers*, etc. i. 30 The name..would imply that he [Ld. Macaulay] was a monologueist, not a converser. **1901** *Dict. Nat. Biog.* Suppl. I. 317/2 Browning was, as a writer, largely a psychological monologuist.

monologuize (ˈmɒnəlɒgaɪz), *v.* [Formed as prec. + -IZE.] = MONOLOGIZE.

1870 READE *Put yourself*, etc. II. xiii. 185 He kept the ball always going, but did not monologuize. **1885** G. MEREDITH *Diana* xvii, Finding Redworth beside him, he monologuized in his depths. **1886** BESANT *Childr. Gibeon* Prol. I, Her lips had a habit of silently monologuising.

monology (məˈnɒlədʒɪ). [ad. Gr. μονολογία (f. μονόλογος: see MONOLOGUE).]

†**a.** A monologue. *Obs.* **b.** The habit of monologizing.

1608 CHAPMAN *Byron's Conspir.* E 3 b, Which the Welch Herrald of their praise, the Cucko Would scarce haue put, in his monology, In iest, and said with reuerence to his merits. **1616** BULLOKAR *Eng. Expos.*, *Monologie*, a speaking still of one thing, a long tale of one matter. **1625** MINSHEU *Ductor* (ed. 2) 474 Monologie, a long tale of little matter, only speech without substance. *a* **1859** DE QUINCEY *Convers.* Wks. 1860 XIV. 171 Coleridge persisted in monology through his whole life.

mono'machic, *a. rare*$^{-1}$. [ad. Gr. μονομαχικός, f. μονομάχος: see MONOMACHY.] Of the nature of single combat.

a **1610** SIR J. SEMPLE in *Sempill Ballatis* (1872) 246 Thes monomachicke [*printed* -th-] Jarris betuix my selff and the.

monomachist (məˈnɒməkɪst). *rare.* [f. Gr. μονομάχ-ος + -IST.] One who fights in single combat.

1846 DE QUINCEY *Notes Gilfillan's Lit. Portraits* Wks. 1859 XII. 281 With the air of some Titan slinger or Monomachist from Thebes and Troy.

monomachy (məˈnɒməkɪ). [a. F. *monomachie* or ad. L. *monomachia*, a. Gr. μονομαχία, f. μονομάχ-ος, that fights alone, f. μόνο-ς MONO- + μαχ-, μάχεσθαι to fight.] A single combat; a contest between two; a duel.

1582 A. FLEMING (*title*) A Monomachie of Motives in the mind of man. *a* **1586** SIDNEY *Arcadia* II. xix. *heading*, The monomachie betweene Anaxius and Pyrocles. **1618** T. ADAMS *Crucifix* Wks. (1629) 823 Christ after his monomachie or single combate with the Deuill in the Desart, had Angels to attend him. **1624** HEYWOOD *Gunaik.* II. 62 All the monsters and terrours of the earth in single monomachy to overcome. **1649** BP. HALL *Cases Consc.* II. ii. (1650) 83 A monomachie of twelve single combatants on either part. *a* **1770** SMART *Duellist* 38 The morning came —and man to man, The grand monomachy began. **1822** BYRON *Let. to Kinnaird* 6 Feb., The duello, or monomachie. **1885** R. F. BURTON in *Academy* 1 Aug. 69/1 The other [kind of combat] is the monomachy for especial purpose..to decide an important question without shedding the blood of the general.

b. In Latin form.

1624 HEYWOOD *Gunaik.* II. 110 He died in a single monomachia valiantlie by the hand of Achilles. **1845** FORD *Handbk. Spain* II. 604 This monomachia is evidently Oriental. **1903** A. LANG in *Blackw. Mag.* July 46/2 These were the first wounds he received either in battle, siege or the monomachia.

'monomane. [a. F. *monomane*: see next and -MANE.] A monomaniac.

1846 WORCESTER cites *Month. Rev.*

monomania (mɒnəʊˈmeɪnɪə). [a. mod.L. *monomania*, f. Gr. μόνο-ς MONO- + μανία MANIA; after F. *monomanie* (Esquirol).] A form of insanity in which the patient is irrational on one subject only.

1823 *Quart. Jrnl. For. & Brit. Med.* V. 311 [M. Esquirol's Account of Colony of Maniacs, at Gheel, near Brussels]. Monomania is sometimes successfully treated with neutral salts in aqua graminis. **1833** PRICHARD in *Cycl. Pract. Med.* II. 833 The term monomania, meaning madness affecting one train of thought..has generally been adopted of late times instead of melancholia. **1877** L. O. PIKE in *Encycl. Brit.* VI. 584/2 Kleptomania and homicidal monomania are asserted by medical theorists to be forms of mental aberration. **1883** T. S. CLOUSTON *Clin. Lect. Mental Dis.* 17 The fixed delusional states without excitement or depression come next, the Monomanias.

b. *transf.* in popular use: An exaggerated enthusiasm for or devotion to one subject: a craze (*for*).

1834 *Edin. Rev.* LIX. 43 The epidemic monomania which infected the world so largely during the sixteenth and seventeenth centuries. **1849** DICKENS *Dav. Copp.* xvi, I call it quite my monomania, it is such a subject of mine. **1864** KINGSLEY *Rom. & Teut.* iii. (1875) 72 A virtuous youth whose monomania was shooting. **1866** MISS BRADDON *Lady's Mile* xxxiii, That sort of thing is a monomania with very rich people.

monomaniac (mɒnəʊˈmeɪnɪæk), *sb.* (*a.*) [f. MONOMANIA: see -MANIAC.] **a.** One who suffers from monomania; one who has a monomania or craze.

1833 *Athenæum* 23 Nov. 792 In the year 1793, there was, at Besançon, an idiot—a mono-maniac—a fool. **1838** *Penny Cycl.* XII. 484/2 It is rarely that the mind of the monomaniac is otherwise perfectly sound; there is generally combined with the delusion a morbid state of the moral feelings. **1862** H. AÏDÉ *Carr of Carrlyon* I. 167 The old gentleman is a monomaniac on the subject of society. **1889** JESSOPP *Coming of Friars* vii. 322 A small army of wandering monomaniacs..were roaming about London.

b. *adj.* = next.

1836 SIR J. PAGET *Let.* 29 Nov. in *Mem.* v. (1901) 93 He is certainly a sharp fellow, but I should think rather monomaniac on the reflections. **1849** GEO. ELIOT *Let.* 24 Oct. (1954) I. 318 How does she manage to endure her life with that poor monomaniac husband.

monomaniacal (ˌmɒnəʊməˈnaɪəkəl), *a.* [f. MONOMANIA, after *maniacal*.] Pertaining to, characterized by, or afflicted with monomania.
1833 *Blackw. Mag.* XXXIV. 452 He is transformed at the beck of our Monomaniacal Necromancer into a fish. **1845** R. W. HAMILTON *Pop. Educ.* x. (ed. 2) 327 These are the fanatics to whom this subject [*sc.* education] is a monomaniacal idea. **1857** DICKENS *Lett.* 13 July, He retired from the stage early in life (having a monomaniacal delusion that he was old). **1897** S. S. SPRIGGE *Life T. Wakley* xxv. 230 Wakley was not monomaniacal on medical reform. **1971** *Eng. Studies* LII. 249 He is, in short, a soulless creature set apart from the rest of humanity by his monomaniacal devotion to pure avarice.
Hence **monomaˈniacally** *adv.*
1856 DICKENS *Dorrit* (1857) I. xxi. 186 Young Sparkler hovering about the rooms, monomaniacally seeking any sufficiently ineligible young lady. **1972** *New York* 3 Apr. 65 Her voice adheres monomaniacally to the same pitch.

monoˈmanious, *a. rare*$^{-0}$. [f. MONOMANIA + -OUS.] Monomaniacal.
1872 LATHAM, *Monomanious*, monomaniacal. *Colloquially* it is, probably, the commoner word, though avoided by writers who study purity.

Monomark (ˈmɒnəʊmɑːk). Also **monomark**. [f. MONO- + MARK *sb.*[1]] A combination of letters and/or figures used as an identification mark for goods or personal property. Also *transf.* Hence **ˈmonomark** *v. trans.*, to apply a monomark to; **ˈmonomarking** *vbl. sb.*
1925 *Westm. Gaz.* 10 July, The Monomark system was explained by its inventor, Mr. William Morris, at a luncheon yesterday in London. A monomark, said Mr. Morris, is the shortest officially recognised postal name and address. **1925** *Glasgow Herald* 10 July 11 The idea..is to set up an international system whereby firms may be granted a 'monomark', consisting of a combination of symbols preceded by B.C.M. (British Commercial Monomark). *Ibid.*, Any individual, child or adult, who cares to pay a modest fee will be entitled to be 'monomarked'. *Ibid.*, The eternal enigma of the identity of Smith—in England alone there are 530,000 bearers of the name—could be kept from business intercourse by the 'monomarking' of each number of the clan. **1926** *Ibid.* 27 Feb. 10 The persistency of the Scot's mental monomarks applied also to the vocal expression of them. **1928** *Daily Mail* 14 Aug. 9/7 Bench yesterday held that a monomark on a dog's collar did not fulfil the requirements of the law in respect of the address of the animal's owner. **1975** *Times* 18 Sept. 2/1 (Advt.), A Telex at your disposal for £25 p.a...British Monomarks (Est. 1926).

monomastigate: see MONO- 1.

monome (ˈmɒnəʊm), *sb.* and *a.* ? *Obs.* [a. F. *monôme*. f. MONO- in imitation of *binôme*: see BINOMIAL.] = MONOMIAL.
a **1719** HARRIS (J.). **1829** SANG in *Philos. Mag.* VI. 262 The Primitives and Derivatives of the Product of two Monome Functions. **1845** LARDNER in *Encycl. Metrop.* I. 527/1 Monomes are said to be homogeneous when they are of the same degree.

monomeniscous (mɒnəʊmɪˈnɪskəs), *a.* [f. MONO- + MENISCUS + -OUS.] Applied to those eyes, in invertebrates, that have only one lens.
1883 LANKESTER & BOURNE in *Q. Jrnl. Microsc. Sci.* XXIII. 196 The closely-set groups of monomeniscous eyes of Myriapods. **1888** ROLLESTON & JACKSON *Anim. Life* 525 With the exception of the lateral eyes of *Limulus*,.. Arachnidan eyes are always monomeniscous.

monoment, obs. form of MONUMENT *sb.*

monomer (ˈmɒnəmə(r)). *Chem.* [f. MONO- + -MER.] Any compound from which a polymer might be formed by the combining together of its molecules (sometimes with the molecules of another compound).
1914 *Chem. Abstr.* VIII. 1037 If released from this combination, it [*sc.* chromic acid] gives at once a polychromic acid, which goes back to the monomer only in the presence of strong bases. **1942** *Electronic Engin.* XIV. 668/3 Impurities in the monomer styrene can have a very serious effect in the electrical properties of the finished polystyrene. **1957** *Technology* July 176/2 Will these catalysts polymerize monomers other than ethylene? **1974** *Guardian* 31 Jan. 6/2 Plastics manufacturers are now mounting health hazard investigations of vinyl chloride monomer.
Hence **monoˈmeric** *a.*, existing in the form of a monomer.
1929 [see DIMERIC *a.* 2]. **1944** *Electronic Engin.* XVI. 348/3 This 'frost'..was caused by volatile impurities and residual monomeric styrene. **1969** *Nature* 13 Dec. 1060/2 The process by which the monomeric constituents of DNA are produced from their ribose analogues is now recognized to constitute a biochemical control mechanism of the greatest importance.

monomerosomatous: see MONO- 1.

monomerous (məˈnɒmərəs), *a.* [f. mod.L. *monomer-us* (ad. Gr. μονομερής, f. μόνο-ς MONO- + μέρ-ος part) + -OUS.] **a.** *Ent.* Consisting of only one member or joint. **b.** *Bot.* Applied to flowers having one member in each whorl.
1826 KIRBY & SP. *Entomol.* IV. 326 Monomerous (*Monomerus*). When the trunk has no suture or segment. *Ibid.* 378 *Tarsi* mostly trimerous, rarely dimerous or monomerous. **1880** GRAY *Struct. Bot.* vi. §2. 176 Terms.. composed of the Greek numerals prefixed to the word meaning parts or members, as *Monomerous*, for the case of a flower of one member of each.

monometallic (mɒnəʊmɪˈtælɪk), *a.* [f. MONO- + METALLIC, after *bimetallic*.]
1. Pertaining to, involving, or using a standard of currency based upon one metal.
1877 [see BIMETALLIC]. **1878** *N. Amer. Rev.* CXXVII. 130 A mono-metallic basis of gold. **1879** *Sussex Daily News* 14 June 5/1 England is what is called monometallic, that is, she bases her currency on one metal, gold. **1890** *Times* 4 Jan. 9/2 If the world became monometallic on a silver basis.
2. *Chem.* (See quot.)
1905 G. M. GOULD *Dict. New Med. Terms, Monometallic*, 1. containing one atom of a metal in a molecule. 2. capable of replacing one atom of hydrogen in an acid. 3. consisting of one metal.

monometallism (mɒnəʊˈmɛtəlɪz(ə)m). [f. prec.: see -ISM.] The monometallic system or standard of currency.
1879 *Blackw. Mag.* Aug. 232 British statesmen of all parties..have united in extolling the advantages of 'monometallism' in the form of a single gold standard. **1881** *World* 11 May 6/1 The only alternatives were universal monometallism by the adoption of gold, or a convention among the nations binding each other to use silver and gold equally at certain fixed values.
Hence **monoˈmetallist**, one who advocates or favours monometallism. Also *attrib.*
1876 *N. Amer. Rev.* CXXVI. 163 The mono-metalists denounce it for demonetizing the best of the two metals. **1885** *Atlantic Monthly* Apr. 448/2 Monometallists and bimetallists, business men and bankers, are assaulting the dangerous silver legislation. **1886** *Contemp. Rev.* May 622 The ever-growing scarcity of gold..was remarked..also by the monometallist Economist.

monometer (məˈnɒmɪtə(r)). *Pros.* [a. L. *monometer*, a. Gr. μονόμετρος, f. μόνο-ς MONO- + μέτρ-ον METRE.] A line consisting of one 'metre'.
1847 in WEBSTER. **1870** R. C. JEBB *Sophocles' Electra* (ed. 2) 141/1 Dochmiac monometer. **1900** H. W. SMYTH *Grk. Melic Poets* 248 The refrain is an iambic monometer, which was often used in exclamations.

monomethyl (mɒnəʊˈmɛθɪl). *Chem.* [MONO- 2.] Used *attrib.* to denote organic compounds in which one equivalent of methyl takes the place of one of hydrogen. Also **monoˈmethylated**, **-meˈthylic** *adjs.* in same sense.
1869 ROSCOE *Elem. Chem.* (1871) 340 Mono-methyl phosphine. **1880** FRISWELL in *Jrnl. Soc. Arts* XXVIII. 444 Dimethylaniline..free from unaltered aniline, and containing only 3 per cent. of the monomethylated compound. **1902** WEBSTER Suppl., *Monomethylic*.

monometric (mɒnəʊˈmɛtrɪk), *a.* [f. Gr. μόνο-ς MONO- + μέτρ-ον measure (see METRE *sb.*[1]) + -IC.]
1. *Cryst.* = ISOMETRIC 3.
1837 DANA *Min.* 348 Primary form: monometric. **1868** *Fownes' Chem.* (ed. 10) 288 The monometric, regular, or cubic system.—The crystals of this division have three equal axes, all placed at right angles to each other.
2. Written in one metre.
1892 *Century Mag.* June 185 Its serene verse, impressive even in the monometric dialogue.

monometrical (mɒnəʊˈmɛtrɪkəl), *a.* [f. MONOMETER + -ICAL.] Pertaining to or consisting of a monometer or monometers.
1882 in OGILVIE.

monomial (məˈnəʊmɪəl), *sb.* and *a.* [irreg. f. MONO- after *binomial*. Cf. MONOME and MONOMIAL.]
1. *Algebra.* **a.** *sb.* An expression consisting of one term only.
1706 PHILLIPS (ed. 6), *Monomial*, in *Algebra*, a Magnitude or Quantity of one Name, or of one single Term. **1854** J. R. YOUNG in *Orr's Circ. Sci., Math. Sci.* 209 The square of a monomial is itself a monomial. **1866** BRANDE & COX *Dict. Sci.* etc. s.v., Thus a, $2\ ab$, $3\ acx^2$ are monomials.
b. *adj.* Consisting of one term only.
1801 *Monthly Rev.* XXXV. 471 Formation of the powers of monomial quantities. **1854** J. R. YOUNG in *Orr's Circ. Sci., Math. Sci.* 234 When the surd..is monomial. **1902** *Encycl. Brit.* XXIX. 180/2 Sarrau's Monomial Formula is much employed, in giving the muzzle velocity.
2. Applied to a term consisting of one word only.
1884 *Jrnl. Nerv. Dis.* XI. 452 Professor Wilder urges the adoption of technical, brief, monomial terms. **1885** B. G. WILDER *Ibid.* XII. 272 Most of the names selected or introduced by me consist of a single word each; they are monomials, or better, mononyms.

monomolecular (mɒnəʊməˈlɛkjʊlə(r)), *a.* [f. MONO- 1 + MOLECULAR *a.*] **a.** Composed of or pertaining to a single molecule or single molecules.
1877 *Chem. News* 23 Mar. 124/1 (*heading*) On the monomolecular unit of volume for gases and vapours. **1915** *Jrnl. Amer. Chem. Soc.* XXXVII. 191 The anhydride of betaine, $(CH_3)_3NCH_2CO_2$, has the structure of a salt, but no one seems to have determined whether this is monomolecular or dimolecular. **1974** *Biochim. & Biophys. Acta* CCCXLVI. 79 (*heading*) A monomolecular electron transfer chain.
b. In chemical kinetics: having or pertaining to an order or a molecularity of one. Cf. UNIMOLECULAR *a.*
1899 *Jrnl. Franklin Inst.* CXLVII. 469 Another classical case of the monomolecular reaction is the decomposition of arsine. **1935** J. N. FRIEND *Text-bk. Physical Chem.* II. iii. 56 Radioactive transformations..provide the only known examples of true monomolecular reactions. *Ibid.* 81 As the solvent and catalyst molecules remain virtually constant in amount, many reactions that really are polymolecular are found to conform to the requirements of the monomolecular law. **1943** SUMNER & SOMERS *Chem. & Methods of Enzymes* i. 13 In most instances enzyme reactions classed as monomolecular are only approximately so. **1973** *Biol. Abstr.* LV. 2244/1 The monomolecular reaction equation gives a good fit to disease progress curve in the field within the primary infection period.
c. Of a film or layer: being one molecule in thickness.
1917 *Jrnl. Amer. Chem. Soc.* XXXIX. 1904 On cooling these surfaces to liquid air temperature the surfaces become covered with a monomolecular layer. **1931** *Jrnl. Physical Chem.* XXXV. 859 If a mono-molecular layer of gas is adsorbed at 300°C while the volume is kept constant the pressure increase will be about 8 mm. **1941** *Ann. Reg. 1940* 353 The remarkable properties of monomolecular films of certain organic liquids spread over water, mercury, or gallium. **1965** B. E. FREEMAN tr. *Vandel's Biospeleology* xviii. 317 It is the monomolecular waxy layer which makes the integument of terrestrial arthropods impermeable to water.

monomorphemic (mɒnəʊmɔːˈfiːmɪk), *a.* *Linguistics.* [f. MONO- + MORPHEMIC *a.*] Consisting of a single morpheme.
1936 *English Studies* XVIII. 160 Alongside his [*sc.* Trnka's] five 'monomorphemic' or simple phonemes..he is forced to set up a like series of 'dimorphemic' combinations. **1942** [see BIMORPHEMIC *a.*]. **1953** C. E. BAZELL *Linguistic Form* i. 5 Neither *John start-* nor *start-ed* can be replaced by a monomorphemic constituent. **1971** B. MAFENI in J. Spencer *Eng. Lang. W. Afr.* 110 By far the greater majority of Nigerian Pidgin words are invariable in form and are usually monomorphemic—that is, not divisible into smaller meaningful units. **1973** R. HARRIS *Synonymy & Linguistic Analysis* iii. 66 English *older* consists of two morphemes,.. while *sister* is monomorphemic, since neither *sist-er* nor any other division gives units which can plausibly be identified as having 'reasonable similarity of meaning' with phonemically comparable units in other utterances.

monomorphic (mɒnəʊˈmɔːfɪk), *a.* [Formed as MONOMORPHOUS *a.* + -IC.] = MONOMORPHOUS *a.* Now *spec.* in *Genetics*, identical as regards genotype, a particular chromosome, or a part of a chromosome.
1880 WEBSTER Suppl. **1894–1900** G. M. GOULD *Dict. Med.* (ed. 5), *Monomorphic*, in biology: (*a*) applied to a collection of individuals, exhibiting similarity or identity of form; (*b*) applied to species in which the same forms recur one after another with comparatively insignificant individual character. **1894** W. BATESON *Materials for Study of Varieties* 37 The..case in which the whole community, grouped according to the degrees in which they display a given character, forms one Curve of Error, may conveniently be called monomorphic in respect of that character. **1895** *Cambr. Nat. Hist.* V. 498 This species [of Hymenoptera] is said to be monomorphic. **1957** *Cold Spring Harbor Symp. Quantitative Biol.* XXII. 397/2 A highly polymorphic population..will be able..to leave progeny of some sort in a wider range of environment than could a monomorphic one. **1960** *Proc. Nat. Acad. Sci.* XLVI. 41 The population fails to reach the level of adaptedness which it would have if it were monomorphic for a genotype with an adaptive value equal to that of the A_1A_2 heterozygotes. Suppose, then, that a mutation produces an allele A_3 such that the fitness of the homozygote A_3A_3 is equal to that of the heterozygote A_1A_2. Natural selection is expected to lead to gradual elimination of A_1 and A_2, and to establishment of a population monomorphic and homozygous for A_3A_3. **1971** *Nature* 17 Sept. 190/2 *D. simulans* is one of the three widespread species of *Drosophila* considered to be monomorphic with regard to chromosome structure. **1973** *Ibid.* 31 Aug. 574/2 Of the thirty-one loci examined eight are monomorphic in all eleven populations. **1974** *Ibid.* 11 Oct. 514/1 *T. vivax* is generally considered monomorphic, although evidence of morphological variation between strains has been reviewed recently.

monoˈmorphism. [f. as prec. + -ISM.] **1.** The condition of being monomorphous. Cf. MONOMORPHIC *a.*
1863 WALSH in *Proc. Entom. Soc. Philad.* II. 223 Monomorphism is the rule; Dimorphism is the exception. **1957** *Cold Spring Harbor Symp. Quantitative Biol.* XXII. 399/1 In nature..it is unlikely that..a reversion to monomorphism will often occur. **1960** *Proc. Nat. Acad. Sci.* XLVI. 45 The replacement of the balanced polymorphisms present in the parental races by chromosomal monomorphisms certainly proves that acquisition in evolution of a balanced polymorphic condition need not be irreversible. **1973** *Nature* 31 Aug. 575/1 Most loci tend to monomorphism in reproductively as well as geographically isolated populations.
2. *Math.* A one-to-one homomorphism.
1956 C. CHEVALLEY *Fund. Concepts Algebra* i. 11 A homomorphism which is injective is called a monomorphism; a homomorphism which is surjective is called an epimorphism. **1969** F. M. HALL *Introd. Abstr. Algebra* II. ii. 39 In a monomorphism different objects always have different images. **1971** E. C. DADE in Powell & Higman *Finite Simple Groups* viii. 252 The diagonal map $\sigma \to \sigma \times \sigma$ is a natural monomorphism of G into $G \times G$.

monomorphous (mɒnəʊˈmɔːfəs), *a.* [f. Gr. μόνο-ς MONO- + μορφ-ή form + -OUS.] Having only one form; exhibiting similarity of form throughout its various stages of development.
1839 WESTWOOD *Mod. Classif. Insects* I. 17 In the Monomorphous division..the pupa continues active. **1874** LUBBOCK *Wild Flowers* ii. 37 We find monomorphous and heteromorphous species in the same genus. **1899** *Allbutt's Syst. Med.* VIII. 472 The features of the eruption, whether monomorphous or polymorphous..are..all characteristic.

Monomoy ('mɒnəʊmɔɪ). The name of a peninsula (Monomoy Point) in Mass., U.S.A., used *attrib.* or *absol.* to denote a type of surfboat (see quot. 1966).
1908 *Ann. Rep. U.S. Life-Saving Service 1907* 65 The keeper..returned to the station..to..attempt to reach the steamer in the *Monomoy* surfboat. **1966** *Random House Dict., Monomoy surfboat,* a double-ended surfboat having rather full lines with high carrying capacity and seaworthiness, used by the U.S. Coast Guard. **1967** *Proc. U.S. Merchant Marine Council* Jan. 19/2 The transfer was accomplished by the *Rockaway's* boat, a 26-foot Monomoy, with a crew of 12 men.

monomyarian (ˌmɒnəʊmaɪ'ɛərɪən), *a.* and *sb.* [f. mod.L. *Monomyari-a* n. pl. (f. Gr. μόνο-ς MONO- + μῦ-ς muscle) + -AN.] **A.** *adj.* = MONOMYARY *a.*
1840 *Penny Cycl.* XVII. 111/1 Oysters, or Ostraceans, a family of monomyiairian [*sic!*] conchifers. **1851** WOODWARD *Mollusca* 48 The monomyarian bivalves lie habitually on one side. **1862** BURTON *Bk. Hunter* (1863) 2 If you make an allusion to monomyarian malacology, it will not naturally be supposed to have reference to the cooking of oyster sauce.
B. *sb.* = MONOMYARY *sb.*
1837 *Penny Cycl.* VII. 433/2 The common oyster will serve as an example of the Monomyarians. **1881** *Cassell's Nat. Hist.* V. 232 We may..notice in the valve of the Monomyarian a simple unbroken line.
So **monomy'arious** *a.*
1852 FORBES in *Edin. New Philos. Jrnl.* LII. 72 Monomyarious Lamellibranchiata.

monomyary (mɒnəʊ'maɪərɪ), *a.* and *sb.* [See prec. and -ARY.]
A. *adj.* Belonging to the group *Monomyaria* of bivalves, having only one adductor muscle.
1835-6 *Todd's Cycl. Anat.* I. 695/2 The family of monomyary Conchifers. **1872** NICHOLSON *Palæont.* 218 In the Monomyary Bivalves it is the posterior adductor which remains, and the anterior adductor is absent.
B. *sb.* A bivalve of the group *Monomyaria.*
1842 BRANDE *Dict. Sci.* etc., *Monomyaries,* all those bivalves or conchifers which have only one adductor muscle. **1851** WOODWARD *Mollusca* 26 The valves of the oyster (and other monomyaries) are connected by a single muscle.

mono'neirist. [f. Gr. μόν-ος MON(O)- + ὄνειρος dream.] A person who has never dreamed but once.
1762-71 WALPOLE *Vertue's Anecd. Paint.* (1786) V. 100 It seems he had never dreamed before, and Thoresby quotes Mr. Locke for another mononeirist.

mononeuran, -neurous: see MONO- 1.

Monongahela. *U.S.* (See quot. 1859.)
1805 *Mississippi Messenger* (Natchez) 1 July 3/1 *From Pittsburgh*..a Quantity of best Monongahela Whiskey for sale by the barrel. **1831** J. J. AUDUBON *Ornith. Biogr.* I. 504 The women..soon found my flask filled with *monongahela* (that is, reader, strong whisky). **1834** W. G. SIMMS *Guy Rivers* I. 76 Having cleared his throat with the contents of a tumbler of Monongahela which seemed to stand permanently full by his side. **1847** W. I. PAULDING *Madmen All* in J. K. & W. I. Paulding *Amer. Comedies* 192 May I never taste Monongahela again! **1859** BARTLETT *Dict. Amer., Monongahela.* A river of Pennsylvania, so called, gave its name to the rye whiskey of which large quantities were produced in its neighbourhood, and indeed to American whiskey in general. **1863** DICEY *Federal St.* I. 157 Where the cigar-case was always ready, and the flask of monongahela was always full.

mononitrate (mɒnəʊ'naɪtrət). *Chem.* [MONO- 2.]
1856 G. GORE in *Orr's Circ. Sci., Pract. Chem.* 56 The mononitrate is formed by dissolving bismuth to saturation in warm dilute nitric acid.

mononitro- (mɒnəʊ'naɪtrəʊ). *Chem.* [See MONO- 2 and NITRO-.] Used to denote organic compounds in which one equivalent of the radical NO_2 takes the place of one atom of hydrogen.
1869 ROSCOE *Elem. Chem.* (1871) 421 Mononitro-naphthalin. **1873** *Fownes' Chem.* (ed. 11) 765 Mononitrotoluene. *Ibid.* 766 The mononitroxylenes are heavy oils. **1891** *Syd. Soc. Lex., Mononitrocellulose,* $C_6H_9(NO_2)O_5$, the chief result of the action of cold nitric acid of moderate strength on cotton.

mononomial (mɒnəʊ'nəʊmɪəl), *a.* and *sb.* Intended as a more correct form of MONOMIAL.
1844 DE QUINCEY *Logic Pol. Ec.* Pref. 9 Consequently, whilst 'natural price' (the contradiction of 'market price') is always a mononomial, price, founded on the relation of Supply to Demand, must always be a binomial. **1873** F. HALL *Mod. Eng.* vi. 175 *note,* Then there is *dynameter,* with the *monomial* of the mathematicians,..slavishly copied from the French, for *dynamometer* and *mononomial.*

mono'nomian, *a.* [f. MONO- after *antinomian.*] Recognizing or based upon one law.
c **1810** COLERIDGE *Lit. Rem.* (1838) III. 307 When Jeremy Taylor escapes from the Mononomian Romaism, which netted him in his too eager recoil from the Antinomian boar.

mononuclear (mɒnəʊ'njuːklɪə(r)), *a.* (*sb.*) [f. MONO- + NUCLEUS + -AR.] **a.** Having one nucleus. **b.** *sb.* A mononuclear cell; *spec.* a monocyte.
1886 tr. *Hueppe's Bact. Investig.* 68 Large mononuclear cells. **1896** *Allbutt's Syst. Med.* I. 818 The large mononuclear leucocytes. **1904** *Brit. Med. Jrnl.* 10 Sept. 583 These cells are supposed to be transitional between the large mononuclear and the polymorphonuclear neutrophiles. **1908** *Jrnl. Infectious Dis.* V. 175 In the experiments recorded subsequently.. + + [indicates] destruction of the large mononuclears with degeneration of the lymphocytes. **1928** *Amer. Jrnl. Physiol.* LXXXV. 490 There are many forms of large mononuclears which are hard to distinguish from lymphocytes by the ordinary Wright stain. **1956** *Nature* 21 Jan. 138/2 The total leucocyte count was about double.., the mononuclears being increased by about 10,000 and the polymorphonuclears by about 6,500. **1974** PARK & GOOD *Princ. Mod. Immunobiol.* xiii. 171 Other chemotactic substances..derive from the complement components and these influence the mononuclears, as well as polymorphonuclears.
So **mono'nucleated** *a.* = MONONUCLEAR; *spec.* (see quot. 1930).
1890 *Q. Jrnl. Microsc. Sci.* XXX. 490 Large mononucleated cells are seen lying scattered between the lymphocytes. **1896** *Allbutt's Syst. Med.* I. 117 Round mononucleated cells with fairly abundant protoplasm. **1930** W. S. THOMPSON *Population Problems* xvi. 279 The modern city..always has one nucleus which is far more important than any of the others and indeed as a rule it has a 'downtown' area in which are congregated most of the important offices, stores, hotels, amusements, and public buildings... Why have our modern large cities assumed this mononucleated form? **1938** L. MUMFORD *Culture of Cities* vii. 489 Under this mode of design, the planner proposes to replace the 'mono-nucleated city', as Professor Warren Thompson has called it, with a new type of 'poly-nucleated city', in which a cluster of communities, adequately spaced and bounded, shall do duty for the badly organized mass city. **1971** *Nature* 10 Sept. 105/1 Attached cells..were mostly mononucleated, though sometimes binucleated.

mononucleate (mɒnəʊ'njuːklɪət), *a. Biol.* [f. MONO- + NUCLEATE *a.*] = MONONUCLEAR *a.*
1957 *New Biol.* XXIV. 30 In the primitive type, *Iridia* studied by le Calvez, there is no visible difference between the sexual and the asexual individuals until they begin to reproduce. Both are mono-nucleate. **1971** *New Scientist* 8 July 90/1, I shall be concerned with the mononucleate hybrid cells that are produced when the nuclei of two cells (and occasionally three) fuse together.

mononucleosis (ˌmɒnəʊnjuːklɪ'əʊsɪs). *Med.* [f. MONONUCLE(AR *a.* (*sb.*) + -OSIS.] An abnormally high proportion of mononuclear leucocytes (monocytes or lymphocytes), or of monocytes alone, in the blood; esp. = *infectious mononucleosis* (see INFECTIOUS *a.* 2c).
1920, etc. [see *infectious mononucleosis* s.v. INFECTIOUS *a.* 2c]. **1928** *Amer. Jrnl. Physiol.* LXXXV. 497 The spleen is an important factor in the production of an emotional relative mononucleosis. **1950** *Biol. Abstr.* XXIV. 1776/1 (*heading*) Exceptional hematological reactions in chronic benzene poisoning. Neutrophilic granulocytosis, lymphocytosis, and mononucleosis. **1968** *New Scientist* 25 Jan. 203/2 Suspecting that the presence of the EB virus and the girl's glandular fever were connected, the Henles..started testing blood samples from other patients who had contracted mononucleosis. **1972** T. P. MCMAHON *Issue of Bishop's Blood* (1973) vii. 88 I'm not too sure that mononucleosis isn't a modern-day version of the megrims of our Victorian ancestors. **1974** J. HELLER *Something Happened* 333 Even people who've been out awhile with hepatitis or mononucleosis have a hard time making their way back. They lack pep.

mononym ('mɒnənɪm). [f. Gr. μόνο-ς MONO- + ὄνυμα name.] A term consisting of one word only.
1884 COUES in *Auk* Oct. 321 **1889** [see POLYONYM 3]. **1895** B. G. WILDER in *Buck's Handbk. Med. Sci.* IX. 100/1 It has now become a serious question which of these short mononyms shall be employed.
Hence **mononymic** (mɒnəʊ'nɪmɪk) *a.*, consisting of a mononym or mononyms; **mononymy** (mə'nɒnɪmɪ), a mononymic system; **mononymize** (mə'nɒnɪmaɪz) *v.*, to convert into a mononym; whence **mononymi'zation.**
1872 J. W. DUNNING in *Entom. Monthly Mag.* VIII. 274 In a mononymic system, we should require as many separate names as there are objects to be named. **1885** B. G. WILDER in *Jrnl. Nerv. Dis.* XII. 272 This feature of mononymy particularly characterizes the terms which [etc.]. **1889** *Buck's Handbk. Med. Sci.* VIII. 525/1 *note,* A polyonymic adjective..may be mononymized, by selecting a main adjective and combining it with a prefix. *Ibid.* 525/2 *note,* The desired mononymization is best attained by simply dropping the superfluous genitive [in *torcular Herophili*].

monooho(o), varr. MOHOOHOO.

mono'ousian, -ious, *adjs. rare.* [f. eccl. Gr. μονοούσι-ος (f. μόνο-ς MONO- + οὐσί-α essence) + -AN, -OUS.] Of one substance.
1678 CUDWORTH *Intell. Syst.* I. iv. §36. 611 Athanasius..disclaimeth a monoousian Trinity, as Epiphanius did before a tautoousian. *Ibid.* 620 According to Athanasius, the Three divine Hypostases, though not monoousious, but homoousious only, are really but one God.

mono-oxy-: see MONOXY-.

mono'palmitin. *Chem.* [MONO- 2.] The lowest in the series of palmitates of glyceryl: see PALMITIN.
1857 MILLER *Elem. Chem.* III. 278 Monopalmitin..Dipalmitin..Tripalmitin. **1873** RALFE *Phys. Chem.* 48.

monopathic (mɒnəʊ'pæθɪk), *a.* [f. next + -IC.] Affecting one organ or function.
[**1856** MAYNE *Expos. Lex., Monopathia,* term for a single suffering of disease. *Monopathicus,* of or belonging to *Monopathia*: monopathic.] **1890** *Century Dict.* **1891** *Syd. Soc. Lex.*

monopathy (mə'nɒpəθɪ). [ad. mod.L. *monopathia* or Gr. μονοπάθεια (in sense 2): see MONO- and -PATHY.]
†**1.** Solitary suffering. *Obs.*
1654 WHITLOCK *Zootomia* 31 Every one calculateth his Nativity..by crying at his Birth, not comming only from the Bodies Monopathy, or sole suffering by change of its warme Quarters; but..from Sympathy with the divining Soule.
2. A disease or disorder affecting only one organ or function (Ogilvie 1882).

monoped ('mɒnəpɛd). Also **-pede.** [f. MONO- + L. *ped-, pēs* foot.] A creature having only one foot. Also *adj.*
1827 J. WILSON *Noct. Ambr.* Wks. 1855 I. 319 Any one single thing in this world.., rational or irrational, monoped, biped, or quadruped. **18..** *Even. Star* 24 Dec., The apparent monoped. **1891** *Syd. Soc. Lex., Monopede,* a monstrosity in which the two lower limbs are fused into one.

monopersonal: see MONO- 1.

monopetalous (mɒnəʊ'pɛtələs), *a.* Also 7 **-ose.** [f. mod.L. *monopetal-us* + -OUS: see MONO- and PETAL *sb.*] Of a flower: Having the corolla in one piece or the petals united so as to form a tube. (Called also *gamopetalous* and *sympetalous.*)
1693 *Phil. Trans.* XVII. 762 The Flowers come out in Clusters, are monopetalose, with five *Laciniæ* or Incisures. **1704** J. HARRIS *Lex. Techn.* I, *Monopetalous Flowers*..are..all of one piece. **1783** DAVIDSON in *Phil. Trans.* LXXIV. 455 The corolla is monopetalous. **1839** LINDLEY *Introd. Bot.* I. ii. 167. **1877-84** F. E. HULME *Wild Fl.* p. vi, Corolla rotate, monopetalous, five-cleft, tube very short.

monophagize (mə'nɒfədʒaɪz), *v.* [f. Gr. μονοφάγ-ος (see next) + -IZE.] *intr.* To eat alone.
1854 BADHAM *Halieut.* 518 Whereas the glutton might sometimes munch and monophagize in solitude.

monophagous (mə'nɒfəgəs), *a.* [f. Gr. μονοφάγος that eats alone: see MONO- and -PHAGOUS.] Eating only one kind of food.
1868 BREWER *Dict. Phrase & Fable, Monophagous,* the eater of one sort of food only. **1879** tr. *Semper's Anim. Life* 51 A very conspicuous contrast exists..between Monophagous animals..and Polyphagous creatures. **1881** E. R. LANKESTER in *Nature* 3 Mar. 406/1 Monophagous and polyphagous animals are distinguished.
So †**mono'phagian,** †**'monophague** (see quot.).
1625 MINSHEU *Ductor* (ed. 2) 474 A Monophagian, or Monophague, one that eats his meat alone without companie, or eats only of one kinde of meat.

monophagy (mə'nɒfədʒɪ). [ad. Gr. μονοφαγία eating alone: see MONO- and -PHAGY.]
1. Eating alone.
1658 PHILLIPS, *Monophagy,* an eating alone, or of one kind of meat. **1872** DASENT *Three to One* II. 250 Monophagy makes a man melancholy and unsocial.
2. The eating of only one kind of food.
1625 MINSHEU *Ductor* (ed. 2) 474 Monophagie, a meale made with one kinde of meat. **1656** BLOUNT *Glossogr., Monophagie,* a meal made of, or a living alwayes with, one kind of meat. **1879** tr. *Semper's Anim. Life* 56 Monophagy in animals is often connected with the occurrence of special organs.

monophane, -phanous: see MONO- 1.

monophase ('mɒnəʊfeɪz), *a. Electr.* [f. MONO- + PHASE *sb.* 3.] Exhibiting a single phase: cf. *polyphase.*
1902 L. BELL in *Encycl. Brit.* XXXI. 888/2 Monophase Induction Motors closely resemble the polyphase motors in construction, but have only a single-phase winding in the primary.

mono'phasic, *a.* [f. prec. + -IC.] **a.** *Electr.* = prec. Hence, **b.** Applied to (a record of) a nerve impulse that is of the same sign throughout, and to experimental arrangements devised to give such records.
1883 *Phil. Trans. R. Soc.* CLXXIII. 35 (*table*) Character of variation. Monophasic, −39·1. Diphasic, +11·7, −21·2. **1900** *Nature* 26 July 290/2 So producing a monophasic variation of considerable E.M.F. **1915** W. M. BAYLISS *Princ. Gen. Physiol.* xii. 380 If electrode B is on a spot [of the nerve] which has been killed, the wave of negativity..disappears in the killed area, so that the only electrical effect seen is that due to the becoming negative of spot A and consists, therefore, of only the first half..of the diphasic response; it is..'monophasic'. **1932** *Jrnl. Cellular & Compar. Physiol.* I. 177 Local asphyxia at one of the leading-off electrodes renders a nerve potential record monophasic even more effectively than crushing does. **1950** *Jrnl. Gen. Physiol.* XXXIII. 654 The problem of obtaining a monophasic lead, by which is meant one in which no membrane changes at the distal electrode are recorded, is one of great importance in view of the complexity of the potentials to be analyzed. Crushing or heating was so unsatisfactory that keeping the distal lead on intact nerve was a preferable arrangement. **1967** L. A. GEDDES in C. C. Brown *Methods in Psychophysiol.* xv. 441 As a result of the intermittent activity of a variety of cells and organs, short duration, asymmetrical (with respect to the time axis) or completely monophasic pulses are presented to the reproducing apparatus.

Hence **mono'phasically** *adv.*, by a technique yielding a monophasic record; **monopha'sicity**, the property of being monophasic.

1928 *Amer. Jrnl. Physiol.* LXXXVI. 187 The size of response was measured by the action current led off monophasically..from the peroneal nerve. **1932** *Jrnl. Cellular & Compar. Physiol.* I. 178 Gerard argues that monophasicity results because the asphyxiated region of the nerve is completely depolarized, while a killed region, if supplied with oxygen, may partially repolarize to give a diphasic record. **1941** S. H. BARTLEY *Vision* xii. 286 The monophasically recorded optic-nerve pattern produced by a flash of light on the retina, is a complex series of oscillations. **1950** *Jrnl. Gen. Physiol.* XXXIII. 654 By the time at which the equilibrium period was completed the fibers were fully blocked. Monophasicity continued without further difficulty to the end of the experiment. **1972** *Science* 2 June 1044/1 The excitability of primary afferent terminals was tested by stimulating the fibers through a low-resistance, glass microelectrode.., and the conducted antidromic volley was recorded monophasically.

monophone ('mɒnəʊfəʊn). *rare.* [f. Gr. μόνο-ς MONO- + φωνή sound.]

1. (See quot.)

1891 R. L. GARNER in *New Rev.* Nov. 429, I have found it necessary to coin a new word to describe the character of their [*sc.* monkeys'] speech, and as each idea seems to be couched in a single word of one syllable and nearly, indeed of one letter, I have called it a monophone.

2. = HOMOPHONE.

1891 *Teachers' Aid* 27 Jan. 311 A list of spelling, prefixes, affixes, and roots, with a few monophones, is all it contains.

monophonematic (ˌmɒnəʊfəʊnɪ'mætɪk), *a. Linguistics.* [f. MONO- + PHONEMATIC *a.*] = MONOPHONEMIC *a.*

1940 *Language* XVI. 249 The argument for the monophonematic character of Dutch *ei*,..(and the same applies to the English sounds in *bite*..) can be shown not to hold if the total structure of the syllable and the behavior of the..diphthongs are examined. **1952** A. COHEN *Phonemes of Eng.* ii. 24 The problem of how to decide whether we have to do with one or more phonemes (monophonematic or polyphonematic interpretation). **1961** *Brno Studies in English* III. 68 It is..in this medium section of the concerned sound trace that this most essential quality of the monophonematic diphthong must obtain the most obvious prominence.

Hence **monophone'matically** *adv.*, **monophonema'ticity**.

1953 C. E. BAZELL *Linguistic Form* iv. 47 The absence of possibility of being on a morph-boundary..may be a criterion of monophonematicity. **1961** *Brno Studies in English* III. 68 What matters..is..the direction and the zonal extent of the monophonematically evaluated 'gliding diphthong'. **1961** F. W. HOUSEHOLDER in Saporta & Bastian *Psycho-linguistics* 18/1 The chief metaphysical bones hassled over..concern such points as 'biuniqueness', 'monophonematicity' [etc.].

monophonemic (mɒnəʊfəʊ'niːmɪk), *a. Linguistics.* [f. MONO- + PHONEMIC *a.*] Of or pertaining to a single phoneme; consisting of a single phoneme.

1936 *Amer. Speech* XI. 206 Over against the monophonemic words cited above are to be set the pleiophonemic words made up of two or more phonemes each. **1955** *Archivum Linguisticum* VII. 154 A distinction is drawn between monophonemic short-vowel and polyphonemic long-vowel diphthongs. **1957** S. POTTER *Mod. Linguistics* ii. 42 The simplest instances of the commutation test are provided by such monophonemic forms as occur in most languages.

monophonic (mɒnəʊ'fɒnɪk), *a. Mus.* [Formed as MONOPHONE + -IC.] **1.** = HOMOPHONIC 1, 2.

1885 *Cassell's Encycl. Dict.* **1895** *Funk's Stand. Dict.* **1920** E. WALKER in F. S. Marvin *Recent Devel. Europ. Thought* 286 If we exclude some monophonic conceptions that have still their value for us, it [*sc.* music] is barely five hundred years old. **1942** *Scrutiny* XI. I. 7 The monophonic work of Léonin and Perotin. **1972** *Harper's Dict. Mus.* 206/1 Monophonic vocal music has existed since ancient times.

2. Of sound broadcasts, gramophone records, etc.: involving only one channel, so that there is only one output signal and all the sound appears to the listener to come from a single source; = MONAURAL *a.* 2. Opp. STEREOPHONIC *a.*

1958 *Newsweek* 13 Oct. 102/2 Bending an ear to a single-track (monophonic, to hi-fi devotees) record is 'like listening to a concert through a crack in the door'. **1959** *Proc. Inst. Electr. Engin.* CVI. B. Suppl. No. 14. 257/1 The monophonic reproduction on two loudspeakers appears to issue from a very small source situated between them but, when operating in a stereophonic manner, the ambient studio sound appears to fill the whole space between the loudspeakers with positional accent on the individual sound sources. **1960** *New Scientist* 4 Feb. 262/2 Such a stereo system may not be 'compatible' with ordinary monophonic receivers. **1962** A. NISBETT *Technique Sound Studio* 240 In a monophonic recording..noise at a natural level will generally sound excessive. **1968** *Consumer Reports* Sept. 502/1 Only stereo discs are reviewed, since record companies have all but stopped producing classical monophonic discs. **1968** *Times* 29 Nov. (Sound of Leisure Suppl.) p. vi/4 The sound was still monophonic: that is, it still came from a single track or radio signal and could never give us any sensation of listening to real musicians spread naturally across an audio stage. **1970** *Jrnl. Gen. Psychol.* LXXXIII. 256 The pure tones..were..recorded on magnetic tapes by a single-track monophonic Tandberg tape recorder. Subsequently, these magnetic tapes were played back to *S* through a pair of Sharpe monaural liquid-filled headphones. **1974** *Nature* 13 Dec. 535/1 Monophonic reproduction gave no explicit directional information, even when reproduced from more than one loudspeaker.

monophonically (mɒnəʊ'fɒnɪkəlɪ). *adv.* [f. prec. + -AL + -LY[2].] **a.** *Mus.* As regards monophony.

1942 *Scrutiny* XI. 12 It is well that we should understand how in 'progressing' music lost much, polyphonically as well as monophonically.

b. In a monophonic (monaural) manner; as regards monophonic reproduction; = MONAURALLY *adv.* b.

1959 *N.Y. Times* 8 Feb. 14X/3 The disks are available stereophonically and monophonically. **1959** *Proc. Inst. Electr. Engin.* CVI. B. Suppl. No. 14. 207/1 If coincident directional microphones are employed and we add left A to right B..the resultant may well be unsuitable monophonically. **1963** *Which?* Jan. 8/2 Both these could play stereo records, without conversion, though the sound was reproduced monophonically. **1974** *Encycl. Brit. Macropædia* XVII. 53/2 A record that can be played stereophonically over stereophonic equipment or monophonically over monophonic equipment is called a compatible recording.

monophonous (mə'nɒfənəs), *a. rare.* [Formed as MONOPHONE + -OUS.]

1. Of a musical instrument: Producing only one note at a time.

1878 J. HULLAH in *Grove's Dict. Mus.* I. 47 An air is a composition for a single voice or any monophonous instrument.

2. = HOMOPHONOUS.

1869 J. L. NEVINS *China* xiv. 197 In our language, these monophonous words are so few that the other words in the sentence clearly fix the meaning.

monophony (mə'nɒfənɪ). *Mus.* [Formed as MONOPHONE + -Y.] **1.** = MONODY.

1890 *Century Dict.* **1964** W. LOVELOCK *Student's Dict. Mus.* 56/2 *Monophony*, music which consists simply of a melodic line without any form of accompaniment. **1968** *Encycl. Brit.* XV. 745/2 *Monody*,..a musical term that in England is often used to describe music for a single melodic line, though in the U.S. monophony is preferred for this meaning.

2. Monophonic recording or reproduction.

1959 *Proc. Inst. Electr. Engin.* CVI. B. Suppl. No. 14. 201/1 The best microphone positions for monophony and stereophony frequently differ considerably and are often quite incompatible. **1961** *Atlantic Monthly* Jan. 146/3, I am sure their transients, meaning the quick high overtones of fiddles and trumpets, are as hard to handle in monophony as in stereo.

monophote ('mɒnəʊfəʊt), *a.* [f. Gr. μόνο-ς MONO + φωτ-, φῶς light.]

1. Epithet of an electric arc-lamp regulator (see quot.). Also **monophotal** *a.* (Funk's *Stand. Dict.* 1895).

1884 KNIGHT *Dict. Mech.* Suppl., *Monophote Regulator*, a voltaic-arc regulator adapted to but a single light on a circuit: as distinguished from *polyphote* regulator.

2. ***monophote lamp*** = HOLOPHOTE.

1893 SLOANE *Electr. Dict.* 321 *Lamp, Holophote*... Synonym—Monophote Lamp.

Monophoto (mɒnəʊ'fəʊtəʊ). [f. MONO(TYPE *sb.* and *a.* + PHOTO.] The proprietary name of a photo-composing machine which uses a perforated paper tape produced by a keyboard unit to control filmsetting by a second unit which replaces the type-caster of a Monotype machine. Also *attrib.*

1954 [see FILMSET *v.*]. **1958** *Times Lit. Suppl.* 18 Apr. 209/3 How important the correction factor is may be seen from the history of the Monophoto..which is likely to become one of the more successful photo-composing machines. **1967** COX & GROSE *Organiz. Bibliogr. Rec. by Computer* II. 27 (*caption*) These [*sc.* trial galley proofs] were produced on a Monophoto composing machine. **1973** S. JENNETT *Making of Books* (ed. 5) v. 85 The mechanical Monophoto may be called a first-generation photo-composing machine.

monophthalmic (mɒnɒf'θælmɪk), *a.* [f. Gr. μονόφθαλμ-ος (f. μόνο-ς MONO- + ὀφθαλμός eye) + -IC.] One-eyed.

1857 J. W. DONALDSON *Chr. Orthod.* 356 The belief in Cyclopian or monophthalmic deities. **1865** *Sat. Rev.* 16 Sept. 355/2 St. Jerome was equally explicit about the existence of the Phœnix and monophthalmic men.

monophthong ('mɒnəfθɒŋ). [ad. Gr. μονόφθογγ-ος adj., f. μόνο-ς MONO- + φθόγγος sound.] A single vowel sound. Also *attrib.*

1620 T. GRANGER *Div. Logike* 303 Syllables of one letter, that is, euery vowell, Monophthongues. **1776** CAMPBELL *Philos. Rhet.* (1801) I. 219 An equal mixture of consonants with soft and monophthong vowels. **1783** J. BEATTIE *Diss.* 266 *Eau* in *beau* is as truly a monophthong as the interjection O. **1885** E. SIEVERS in *Encycl. Brit.* XVIII. 782/2 The sound of the so-called long *a* in *make, paper*, &c., although once a monophthong, is now pronounced as a diphthong. **1888** SWEET *Eng. Sounds* 22 The levelling of the two elements of a diphthong under a monophthong.

Hence **monophthongal** (mɒnəf'θɒŋgəl) *a.*, consisting of a monophthong; **monoph'thonging** *vbl. sb.* = MONOPHTHONGIZATION.

1783 J. BEATTIE *Diss.* 266 Grammarians..speak of tripthongs, or three monophthongal sounds coalescing in one syllable. **1863** A. M. BELL *Princ. Speech* 123 The Scottish dialect, in which the monophthongal A is a very common vowel. **1894** G. DUNN in *Class Rev.* Mar. 94 In general.. diphthongs have two monophthongal correlates. Thus: eu: ū: ŭ. **1894** F. J. CURTIS *Invest. Rimes Clariodus* 52 The monophthonging of *ai* was of too old a date to allow us to suppose that [etc.].

monophthongize (mɒnəf'θɒŋgaɪz), *v.* [f. MONOPHTHONG + -IZE.] *trans.* To convert into a monophthong. Also *intr.* Hence **monophthongi'zation**.

1880 SWEET in *Trans. Philol. Soc.* 158 That unaccented (æi) underwent a gradual approximation of its elements, ending in monophthongization and shortening. **1885** *Amer. Jrnl. Philol.* VI. 420 Cases claimed as examples of the monophthongization of ει. *Ibid.* 435 A monophthongized diphthong. **1904** *Expositor* Apr. 313 That Boeotian monophthongizing of the diphthongs. **1914** H. C. WYLD *Short Hist. Eng.* vi. 107 In W.S. the *ēa* which resulted from *æ* preceded by a front consonant was monophthongized in L.O.E. itself, and became *e*. **1927** J. J. HOGAN *Eng. Lang. in Ireland* 69 *M.E. ai, ei*. These were levelled under *ai* in M.E. This was monophthongized, and converged with M.E. *ā*. **1965** W. S. ALLEN *Vox Latina* ii. 62 Although French has monophthongized to *o*, the *au* diphthong must have survived long enough to cause the change of *c* to *ch* in..*chose* from *causam*. **1968** —— *Vox Graeca* ii. 71 The [ẹ̄] of Boeotian was the result of monophthongizing the diphthong [ai]. **1970** B. M. H. STRANG *Hist. Eng.* ii. 111 The diphthong, in either form, began to monophthongise.

monophyletic (mɒnəʊfaɪ'lɛtɪk), *a.* [f. Gr. μόνο-ς MONO- + φυλετικ-ός, f. φυλέτης tribesman, f. φυλή tribe.] Pertaining to one family or race or to descent from a single prototypal form. Hence **mo'nophyly** (see quot. 1961).

1874 *Q. Jrnl. Microsc. Sci.* XIV. 247 Monophyletic stem-structure of the Animal Kingdom. **1875** tr. *Schmidt's Desc. & Darw.* 325 The so-called monophyletic hypothesis, according to which the different families of organisms are derived from a single primordial form. **1879** tr. *Haeckel's Evol. Man* I. 247 My Gastraea Theory, on which I base the monophyletic genealogy of the animal kingdom. **1927** N. P. WILLIAMS *Ideas of Fall* viii. 516 The 'monophyletic' theory of the origin of humanity (that is, the view which regards the whole of mankind as descended from a single pair of ancestors). **1945** G. G. SIMPSON in *Bull. Amer. Mus. Nat. Hist.* LXXXV. 17/1 It is not useful to set up a classification in which groups with different names cannot be distinguished morphologically, but this does happen if theoretical monophyly is too strictly demanded. **1946** *Nature* 16 Nov. 719/1 This clear distinction between the genera at so deep a level in the Palæocene is not suggestive of a monophyletic origin for the family. **1953** E. MAYR et al. *Methods & Princ. Systematic Zool.* iii. 41 One of the objects of taxonomists in the post-Darwinian period was to construct a classification of animals composed of monophyletic groups. **1961** G. G. SIMPSON *Princ. Animal Taxonomy* iv. 124 Monophyly is the derivation of a taxon through one or more lineages (temporal successions of ancestral-descendant populations) from one immediately ancestral taxon of the same or lower rank. **1963** DAVIS & HEYWOOD *Princ. Angio-sperm Taxonomy* ii. 46 It is a widely expressed principle that taxonomic groups (at least above the species level) should be monophyletic. **1969** E. MAYR *Princ. Systematic Zool.* iv. 75 The issue of monophyly has been confounded by various confusions.

monophyllous (mɒnəʊ'fɪləs), *a.* [f. Gr. μονόφυλλ-ος (f. μόνο-ς MONO- + φύλλον leaf) + -OUS.] Of a calyx: Consisting of one leaf.

1746 HILL in *Phil. Trans.* XLIV. 63 This Ring is truly a monophyllous undulated Calyx. **1830** LINDLEY *Nat. Syst. Bot.* 216 Calyx monophyllous, divided.

monophyodont (mɒnəʊ'faɪəʊdɒnt), *a.* (*sb.*) *Zool.* [f. Gr. μόνο-ς MONO- + φύ-ειν to generate + ὀδοντ-, ὀδούς tooth.] **a.** *adj.* Having only one set of teeth. Said also of the teeth.

1849–52 OWEN in *Todd's Cycl. Anat.* IV. 901/2 The Monophyodont character of the Cetacea. **1875** BLAKE *Zool.* 47 The Cetacea are either toothless or monophyodont. **1890** FOTHERGILL *Zool. Types & Classif.* 179 Edentata. Teeth.. are monophyodont, rootless, and without enamel.

b. *sb.* A monophyodont animal.

1849–52 OWEN in *Todd's Cycl. Anat.* IV. 901/2 The 'Monophyodonts', or those that generate a single set of teeth. **1888** ROLLESTON & JACKSON *Anim. Life* 363.

Monophysite (mə'nɒfɪsaɪt), *sb.* (*a.*) *Eccl. Hist.* [ad. eccl.L. *Monophysīta*, a. eccl.Gr. Μονοφυσίτης, f. μόνο-ς MONO- + φύσ-ις nature: see -ITE[1] 1 a.] A heretic who believes that there is only one nature in the person of Jesus Christ.

The bodies of Christians now professing this belief are the Coptic, Armenian, Abyssinian, and Jacobite churches.

1698 FRYER *Acc. E. India & P.* 272 The Acephali and Monosyphites [*sic*]. **1727–41** CHAMBERS *Cycl.*, *Monophysites*, a general name given to all those sectaries in the Levant, who only own one nature in Jesus Christ. The Monophysites, however, properly so called, are the followers of Severus, and Petrus Fullensis. **1788** GIBBON *Decl. & F.* xlvii. IV. 591 Under the rod of persecution, the Nestorians and Monophysites degenerated into rebels and fugitives. **1861** J. G. SHEPPARD *Fall Rome* xi. 587 Pernicious heresies, like that of the Monophysites in Egypt. **1875** BOULTBEE *Theol. Ch. Eng.* 20 Nor can the human nature be converted into the divine, as the Eutychians and other monophysites taught.

b. *attrib.* or *adj.* = next.

1788 GIBBON *Decl. & F.* xlvii. IV. 563 The *monophysite* doctrine (one incarnate nature) was rigorously preached in the churches of Egypt and the monasteries of the East. *Ibid.* 608 Severus, the Monophysite patriarch of Antioch. **1861** J. G. SHEPPARD *Fall Rome* xi. 608 The Monophysite heretics ..were cruelly persecuted by the orthodox Greeks. **1882** *Century Mag.* XXIII. 851 Those old fears about lapsing into the Monophysite heresy. **1905** *Expositor* Apr. 261 Christianity in its Nestorian or Monophysite form.

monophysitic (mɒnəʊfɪˈsɪtɪk), *a.* [f. prec. + -IC.] That is a Monophysite; pertaining to or characteristic of Monophysites or their heresy. So **monophyˈsitical** *a.* (Ogilvie *Suppl.* 1855).

1823 ROSCOE tr. *Sismondi's Lit. Eur.* (1846) I. ii. 51 The Nestorians..massacred seven or eight thousand of their orthodox or monophysitic adversaries. **1893** E. K. MITCHELL tr. *Harnack's Outl. Hist. Dogma* 299 Origen, who had many sympathizers among the monophysitic monks.

monophysitism (məˈnɒfɪsaɪtɪz(ə)m). [f. MONOPHYSITE + -ISM.] The belief of the Monophysites.

1837 *Pop. Encycl.* V. 37/1 In 483, the Acephali..had already seceded, and formed the real strength of Monophysitism. **1899** *Dublin Rev.* Jan. 83 The extension of the Coptic Rite in Egypt favoured the spread of monophysitism.

monopitch (ˈmɒnəʊpɪtʃ), *sb.* and *a.* [f. MONO- + PITCH *sb.*²] **A.** *sb.* Uniformity of pitch in speaking or singing.

1939 in WEBSTER Add. **1942** A. T. WEAVER *Speech Forms & Princ.* x. 243 Monopitch, frequently miscalled monotone, results first, from unemotional speaking and, second, from a dull or inactive mind which fails to see distinctions in the meanings of the language which is being spoken. **1964** CRYSTAL & QUIRK *Systems Prosodic & Paralinguistic Features in Eng.* ii. 16 These deficiencies also mar his discussion of..pitch (including 'monopitch', step up and down, and slide).

B. *adj.* Of a roof: consisting of a single uniformly sloping surface. Of a building: having such a roof.

1941 *Archit. Rev.* LXXXIX. 47 The mono-pitch roof was employed for simplicity and to enable all the rain-water to be collected at the front of the house owing to the limited fall available for the drains. **1961** *Guardian* 25 Mar. 5/5 A simple and comely monopitch building. **1971** *Daily Tel.* 14 Aug. 7/3 The crematorium's group of mono-pitch grey slate roofs appear to form a large pyramid.

monoplacid: see MONO- 1.

monoplane (ˈmɒnəʊpleɪn). [f. MONO- + PLANE *sb.*³] An aeroplane or glider having only one 'plane' or main supporting surface on either side of the fuselage (so called because in the earliest monoplanes the wing on each side was part of a single structure extending across the fuselage); †the wing itself. Also *attrib.* or as *adj.*

1907 *Sci. Amer.* 16 Nov. 358/1 (*heading*) The latest French aeroplanes and their records. The Pelterie monoplane. *Ibid.* 358/3 One end of the monoplane (which is made in two halves) was broken. *Ibid.*, The Pelterie aeroplane resembles the monoplane machine with which M. Bleriot experimented unsuccessfully last spring. **1907** *Nature* 5 Dec. 106/2 Another aëroplane which is also attracting considerable attention at Paris is the 'monoplane' of M. Robert Esnault Pelterie. This, unlike most recent types, has only a single transverse supporting surface. **1908** *Times* 20 May 7/6 A monoplane aeroplane..made some successful evolutions yesterday. **1908** *Sci. Amer.* 18 July 44/1 The rear half of the monoplane, at its outer ends, has movable planes for correcting the transverse stability. **1910** *Blackw. Mag.* July 4/1 The aeroplane, whether monoplane, biplane, or other. *a* **1918** J. T. B. MCCUDDEN *Five Yrs. in R. Flying Corps* (1919) 63 Two Taube monoplanes came over St. Omer. **1922** *Glasgow Herald* 8 Aug. 8 A Swiss pilot on a motorless monoplane succeeded in making a flight lasting 45 seconds. **1935** C. G. BURGE *Compl. Bk. Aviation* 123/1 Gliders are usually of monoplane type, though biplane constructions have been used. **1960** C. H. GIBBS-SMITH *Aeroplane* x. 54 The year 1907 saw the crystallisation of the two basic forms of early aeroplane—the pusher biplane and the tractor monoplane. **1969** K. MUNSON *Pioneer Aircraft 1903–14* 98/1 Levasseur's first full-size aeroplane, a bird-like monoplane tested in 1903, was an utter failure. **1973** J. DI MONA *Last Man at Arlington* (1974) xi. 84 A single engine monoplane thundering toward an ammunition ship.

monoplast (ˈmɒnəʊplæst). *Biol.* [f. MONO- + -PLAST.] An organism consisting of a single cell. Hence **monoˈplastic** *a.*

1877 E. R. LANKESTER in *Q. Jrnl. Microsc. Sci.* XVII. 403 The Monoplast = Ovum. *Ibid.* The monoplastic phase of individual development. **1879** STORMONTH *Man. Sci. Terms, Monoplast*, a naked non-vesicular body; an animal cell destitute of envelope. *Monoplastic*, having one primary form.

monoplastid (mɒnəʊˈplæstɪd). [f. MONO- + PLASTID.] = MONOPLAST. Also *attrib.*

1889 VINES in *Nature* 24 Oct. 621 Weissmann appears to have fully established, that the body of unicellular organisms (monoplastides)..is immortal at any rate potentially. **1894–1900** G. M. GOULD *Dict. Med.* (ed. 5), *Monoplastid.* **1895** MOORE in *Sci. Progress* June 323 There are many monoplastid forms with affinities among the polyplastids.

‖**monoplegia** (mɒnəʊˈpliːdʒ(ɪ)ə). *Path.* [mod.L., f. Gr. μόνο-ς MONO- + -πληγία, πληγή stroke.] Paralysis of one part or limb only. Hence **monoˈplegic** *a.*, pertaining to or affected with monoplegia.

1890 *Century Dict.* **1893** W. R. GOWERS *Man. Dis. Nerv. Syst.* (ed. 2) II. 437 A monoplegia affecting the leg only. **1896** *Allbutt's Syst. Med.* I. 666 Paralyses of the limbs in epidemic cerebro-spinal meningitis..may be of very various type (hemiplegic, paraplegic, monoplegic).

monopleurid, -pleurobranch, -pneumonian, etc.: see MONO- 1.

monoploid (ˈmɒnəplɔɪd), *a.* (and *sb.*) *Biol.* [a. G. *monoploid* (O. F. I. Langlet 1927, in *Svensk Bot. Tidskr.* XXI. 1): see MONO- and -PLOID.] = HAPLOID *a.* (and *sb.*) (see quot. 1968). Hence **ˈmonoploidy**, the state or condition of being monoploid.

1928 *Jrnl. Genetics* XIX. 138, I do not think it necessary to replace haploid with monoploid as Langlet (1927) proposes. **1943** L. W. SHARP *Fund. Cytol.* xiv. 211 In the sporophytes of plants true monoploidy occurs very rarely. **1944** *Genetics* XXIX. 232, 16 monosomes and five trisomes were found in the 11 aberrant offspring of a monoploid pollinated by a diploid. **1952** SRB & OWEN *Gen. Genetics* xi. 215 Doubling the chromosomes of a monoploid can give rise to diploid individuals homozygous for all the gene pairs in the organism. **1955** G. F. SPRAGUE *Corn & Corn Improvement* iv. 131 Monoploid or haploid plants, which have one set of chromosomes, arise spontaneously by the parthenogenetic development of unfertilized eggs. Much less frequent are the androgenetic monoploids. *Ibid.* Genes for a high incidence of monoploidy. **1968** R. REIGER *Gloss. Genetics & Cytogenetics* 299 *Monoploid*, of cells or individuals (monoploids) having one chromosome set with the basic number of chromosomes, i.e., the lowest haploid number of chromosomes in a polyploid series.

monopode (ˈmɒnəʊpəʊd), *sb.* and *a.* Also **-pod.** [ad. L. *monopodius*, a. Gr. *μονοπόδιος = μονόπους (-ποδ-), f. μόνο-ς MONO- + πούς foot. Cf. F. *monopode.*]

1. A creature having only one foot; *spec.* one of a race of men fabled to have only one foot, with which they shaded themselves from the heat of the sun (see Pliny *Nat. Hist.* VII. ii). Also *transf.*

1816 KIRBY & SP. *Entomol.* xxii. (1818) II. 277 Some [larvæ], a kind of monopods, have only one of such [pediform] prominences. **1864** LOWELL *Fireside Trav.*, *At Sea* 172 The monopodes, sheltering themselves from the sun beneath their single umbrella-like foot. *a* **1963** C. S. LEWIS *Poems* (1964) 43 Ran till the sunrise shone upon the bouncing Monopods at their heels. **1971** C. BONINGTON *Annapurna South Face* App. F. 286 Each member of the team was also issued with a special clamp to fit on the head of an ice axe with a ball-and-socket attachment for the camera, which made a very useful and compact monopod. **1972** QUICK & LABAU *Handbk. Film Production* xiii. 100 A 'monopod' is a single fixed leg terminating in a screw base that matches the bottom of the camera.

2. = MONOPODIUM.

1890 in *Century Dict.*

3. As *adj.* Having only one foot.

(Cf. L. *monopodium* one-footed table.)

1890 in *Century Dict.* **1896** *Archæol.* (*Inst.*) *Jrnl.* LIII. 42 Monopode tables for the reception of oblations.

monopodial (mɒnəʊˈpəʊdɪəl), *a.* [f. MONOPODIUM + -AL¹.] Pertaining to or of the nature of a monopodium; characterized by having a single and continuous axis from which lateral shoots are produced. Hence **monoˈpodially** *adv.*

1876 BALFOUR in *Encycl. Brit.* IV. 93/2 In monopodial branchings the primary axis may continue to develop more strongly than its lateral axes. *Ibid.* 125/1 In Myosotis (Forget-me-not) the axis is not a sympodium, but the branching takes place monopodially. **1880** GRAY *Struct. Bot.* iii. §3. 55 *note*, A stem formed by the continued development of a terminal bud is monopodial or a monopodium.

‖**monopodium** (mɒnəʊˈpəʊdɪəm). [mod.L., f. Gr. μόνο-ς MONO- + ποδ-, πούς foot.]

1. *Bot.* A single axis which extends at the apex producing in succession lateral structures beneath it.

1875 BENNETT & DYER tr. *Sachs' Bot.* 156. **1876** BALFOUR in *Encycl. Brit.* IV. 93/2.

2. (See quot. 1970.) Also, the support for an early 19th-century table, sideboard, etc., comprising an animal's head with a single foot. (Cf. MONOPODE *sb.* 1.)

1807 T. HOPE *Househ. Furnit.* 36 Little round monopodium or stand, of which the top..is capable of being raised or lowered at pleasure. **1948** M. JOURDAIN *Regency Furnit. 1795–1820* (ed. 2) 105 Console table supported by carved gilt lion monopodia. **1959** G. SAVAGE *Antique Collector's Handbk.* 195 The monopodium, or single leg surmounted by a human or animal head and torso, is peculiarly Regency. **1970** —— *Dict. Antiques* 275/2 *Monopodium*..is applied to certain small tables of the Regency and Empire period which have a three-sided support usually terminating in brass claws at the bottom corners. **1971** *Country Life* 22 July 225/3 From about 1815 the marble top of a console table might be supported at each front corner by an eagle monopodium with boldly outcurving breast and widespread wings.

monopodous (məˈnɒpədəs), *a. rare.* [f. Gr. μόνο-ς MONO- + ποδ-, πούς foot + -OUS.] One-footed.

1884 *Harper's Mag.* Jan. 307/1 Monopodous storks and impossible parrots.

monopody (məˈnɒpədɪ). *Pros.* [ad. mod.L. **monopodia*, a. Gr. μονοποδία, f. μόνο-ς MONO- + ποδ-, πούς foot.] A measure consisting of a single foot.

1844 [see DIPODY].

Hence **monopodic** (mɒnəʊˈpɒdɪk) *a.*, consisting of or constituting a monopody.

1890 in *Century Dict.*

monopolar (mɒnəʊˈpəʊlə(r)), *a.* [f. MONO- + POLAR *a.*] **a.** Of, having, or using a single electrode; applied esp. to techniques and apparatus (*a*) for passing electric currents through the body using two electrodes of different sizes or natures, one being usually much larger than the other, and (*b*) for measuring electric potentials in the body, where one electrode is inserted in the region to be studied and the other acts as a reference electrode.

1906 *Practitioner* Dec. 772 The patient, if the monopolar bath had to be administered, grasped a metal bar, suspended from the ceiling, and in connection with the battery swung over the bath, the other electrode remaining in the water. **1936** H. H. U. CROSS *Electr. in Therapeutics* xiii. 296 In the spark-gap system the patient may be connected to the solenoid in monopolar or bipolar fashion. **1956** S. LICHT *Some Clin. Applic. Electroneurophysiol.* i. 8 Chauveau.. introduced the monopolar method of stimulation into physiology. **1962** BLAKE & TROTT *Periodontology* xiii. 135 Monopolar diathermy of this type is particularly suitable for minor oral surgery. **1973** M. SCHWARTZ *Physiol. Psychol.* i. 20 In monopolar recordings, one electrode is placed on some relatively neutral or 'indifferent' location, such as the ear, for the EEG, while the other is placed on the scalp.

b. Of or pertaining to a MONOPOLE³.

1971 I. G. GASS et al. *Understanding Earth* xvi. 239/2 The dipolar rather than monopolar nature of the Earth's magnetic field.

ˈmonopole¹. Also 6 **money polde, monopolle, monapole,** 7 **monopol.** [a. OF. *monopole* or ad. late L. *monopōlium* MONOPOLY.]

†**1.** = MONOPOLY. *Obs.*

a **1548** HALL *Chron., Hen. VI* 158 Diuers other crymes were layde to his charge, as..gathering together and making a money polde of offices, fees, wardes, and fermes. **1596** BP. W. BARLOW *Three Serm.* ii. 49 The intollerable licenses of Monopoles and Solesales. **1596** HARINGTON *Metam. Ajax* 97 Now for my monapole, I would aske but this trifling sute. **1609** J. DAVIES *Humour's Heav. on Earth* (Grosart) 35 Some to gaine Some Monopole, which then could not be got.

†**2.** An emporium. *lit.* and *fig. Obs.*

(Cf. Gr. μονοπώλιον trading mart enjoying a monopoly.)

1600 W. WATSON *Decacordon* (1602) 61 Merchants.. trafficke..from one Mart, hauen, promontorie, or Monopole to another. *Ibid.* 237 [Father Parsons is] a Monopole of all mischiefe. **1610** BOYS *Wks.* (1629) 454 The deuill..begat insolent pride, which is a monopol of mischiefe.

†**3.** An unlawful convention; a conspiracy. *Obs.*

1549 *Compl. Scot.* xvi. 140 The ciuil lauis deffendis & forbiddis al monopoles and conuentions of the comont pepil. **1587–8** *Reg. Privy Council Scot.* IV. 253 It becomes alwayes his majestie..to repres and stay all monopolles and factiounes.

4. [Fr., monopoly.] (See quot. 1967.)

1883 *Daily News* 31 Aug. 6/2 The familiar pop of the champagne cork being very rarely heard. Perhaps those learned authorities, Dr. Oliver and Dr. Myrtle..have 'shut down' on 'monopole' and 'extra dry'. **1885** *Christie's Catal. Wines* 14 Apr. 9 Three Dozens of Champagne, Heidsieck's Dry Monopole, 1874. **1886** *St. Stephen's Rev.* 13 Mar. 12/1 The pint of dry Monopole, with which he sustained exhausted nature. **1915** T. BURKE *Nights in Town* 399 He shouted for a half-of-bitter with the solemnity of one who commands that two bottles of dry Monopole be put on the ice. **1967** A. LICHINE *Encycl. Wines* 356 *Monopole.* This designation, frequently found on wine labels, literally means 'an exclusive'. Blank Monopole would be the proprietary brand of the wine shipper whose name would occupy the blank.

†**ˈmonopole².** *Obs.*—⁰ [ad. Gr. μονοπώλης, f. μόνο-ς MONO- + πώλης seller.] A monopolist.

1648–60 HEXHAM *Dutch Dict., Een Focker*, a Monopole, or an Engrosser of Wares and Commodities.

monopole³ (ˈmɒnəpəʊl). [f. MONO- + POLE *sb.*²]

1. A single electric charge or, esp., a single magnetic pole, having a spherically symmetric field. Freq. *attrib.* or as *adj.*

1937 J. W. T. SPINKS tr. *G. Herzberg's Atomic Spectra & Atomic Struct.* i. 63 The system gives an external electric field, which..falls off more rapidly with increasing distance that that of the dipole, which itself falls off more rapidly than that of the monopole. **1950** D. HALLIDAY *Introd. Nuclear Physics* ii. 59 A single charge at the origin is a simple monopole, with no higher moments. **1951** *Proc. Cambr. Philos. Soc.* XLVII. 196 Dirac has suggested that the quantization of electric charge could be explained by the existence of magnetic monopoles. *Ibid.* 206 The main difference of behaviour between electric particles and monopoles lies in the greater ionizing power per centimetre of the monopole, except near the end of the path. **1958** CONDON & ODISHAW *Handbk. Physics* VII. iv. 59/1 The first term of Eq. (4.6) corresponds to a monopole or simple charge, the second to the electric-dipole moment, the third to the electric-quadrupole moment, the fourth to the electric-octupole moment, etc. A similar multipole expansion is possible with magnetic interactions..leading to magnetic-dipole terms, etc. **1962** CORSON & LORRAIN *Introd. Electromagn. Fields* ii. 54 The first term is merely the potential which we would have at P if the whole charge were concentrated at the origin. It is called the monopole term and is zero only if the net charge is zero. **1967** W. R. HINDMARSH *Atomic Spectra* v. 49 We must extend the concept of the nucleus by attributing to it magnetic and electric moments (in addition to the electric monopole or nuclear charge) and a finite volume. **1969** *Physical Rev.* CLXXXIV. 1393 (*heading*) Search for magnetic monopoles in deep ocean deposits. *Ibid.* 1401/2 This work would indicate that there is less than one monopole/4000 m³ of the earth. **1973** *Nature* 20 Apr. 527/1 The scheme..ignores all

other atomic monopoles (including those on the methyl carbons and hydrogens which closely approach the negative charge) as well as all higher moments. **1974** *Ibid.* 3 May 15/1 Searches for quarks, magnetic monopoles and intermediate vector bosons have all so far proved negative. **1975** *Physical Rev. Lett.* XXXV. 489/2 We conclude that we have detected a magnetic monopole of strength $g = 137e$.

2. *Radio.* An aerial consisting of a single conducting rod with the electrical connection made at one end, the length of which is usually about a quarter of the wavelength to be transmitted or received.

1950 *Proc. IRE* XXXVIII. 1040 (*heading*) Measured directivity induced by a conducting cylinder of arbitrary length and spacing parallel to a monopole antenna. **1966** L. V. BLAKE *Antennas* iv. 176 When the quarter-wave vertical antenna (monopole) is fed at its base with the other side of the feed line connected to ground, its radiation resistance and input impedance are just half the values for the half-wave dipole in free space. **1974** *Nature* 5 Apr. 493/1 The transmitter antenna was a vertical monopole lifted to 1,000 to 1,500 m by balloon.

† **monopoled**, *ppl. a.* *Obs.*$^{-0}$ (See quot.)

1611 [see MONOPOLIZE *v.* 1].

† **mo'nopoler**. *Obs.* Also 6-7 -ier. [a. OF. *monopolier*: see MONOPOLE[1] and -IER.] A monopolist.

1589 G. FLETCHER in *Lett. Lit. Men* (Camden) 81 The said Companie..having reduced themselves to the number of xij, and so beeing now more notable Monopoliers than they weare beefore. **1601** J. WHEELER *Treat. Comm.* 102 The said companie by no sound reason..can be charged to bee anie such Monopoliers. **1611** COTGR., *Monopolier*, a monopoler, or monopolizer. **1640** [see POLLER 2]. **1641** *Frogs of Egypt* 5 By Thee our base Monopolers doe fall.

† **mono'polian**. *Obs.* [f. MONOPOLE[1] or MONOPOLY + -AN.] A monopolist.

1601 J. WHEELER *Treat. Comm.* 66 The said M. M. Aduenturers were now in his town of Embden no more to be accounted Monopolians, then they were here tofore in Antwerp. **1622** E. MISSELDEN *Free Trade* (ed. 2) 57 The setling of the price at the pleasure of the Monopolian to his priuate benefit, and the preiudice of the publique.

† **mono'polical**, *a.* *Obs.* (In quot. 7 moni-.) [f. MONOPOLE[1] + -ICAL.] Monopolistic.

1624 CAPT. SMITH *Virginia* 139 Whosoeuer..seeketh either by getting monipolicall patens, or by forging vniust tales to hinder our welfare.

† **monopolish**, *a.* *Obs.* [f. MONOPOLE[1] or MONOPOLY + -ISH.] Monopolistic.

1580 in *Cal. St. Papers, Foreign* 366 There is no such 'monopolish' trade used at Emden. **1601** J. WHEELER *Treat. Comm.* 105 The aboue said slander of Monopolie, and monopolish trade vsed in Embden. **1613** —— in *Buccleuch MSS.* (Hist. MSS. Comm.) I. 122 A monopolish passport granted to Verstegan.

monopolism (mə'nɒpəlɪz(ə)m). [f. MONOPOLY + -ISM.] The system of monopolies.

1881 *Nature* 27 Oct. 602/1 A land of strong tendencies toward monopolism and conservatism. **1888** BRYCE *Amer. Commw.* III. v. xciv. 318 The two great national parties..denounce monopolism in the abstract.

monopolist (mə'nɒpəlɪst). [f. MONOPOLE[1] or MONOPOLY + -IST. Cf. It. *monopolista*, G. *monopolist*.]

1. One who monopolizes or possesses a monopoly; one who favours monopoly.

1601 J. WHEELER *Treat. Comm.* 72 By this means..the Hanses should..possesse the whole trade of the realme, as Monopolists of the whole kingdom. **1648** GAGE *West Ind.* xii. 61 The Marquesse of Serralvo..was the best Monopolist of salt that ever those parts knew. **1671** W. PERWICH *Despatches* (R. Hist. Soc.) 148 The army has been sickly, & the monopolist that undertook the furnishing them with provision is much blamed. **1775** BURKE *Sp. Concil. Amer.* Wks. III. 63 To raise the value of the possessions in the hands of the great private monopolists. **1866** GEO. ELIOT *F. Holt* xxx, We know what monopolists are: men who want to keep a trade all to themselves, under the pretence that they'll furnish the public with a better article. **1885** *Law Times* LXXVIII. 222/1 An absolute right to refuse to supply a prime necessary of life is a dangerous weapon indeed with which to arm a monopolist.

2. *transf.* One who obtains, assumes, or occupies anything to the exclusion of others.

1742 YOUNG *Nt. Th.* II. 508 Joy is an import; joy is an exchange; Joy flies monopolists; It calls for two. **1781** COWPER *Conversat.* 627 When some green heads..Suppose themselves monopolists of sense. **1813** BYRON *Corsair* III. vi, The life thou leav'st below, denied above By kind monopolists of heavenly love. **1817** KEATS *Wks.* (1889) III. 5 He feels his being as deeply as Wordsworth, or any other of our intellectual monopolists. **1866** BRIGHT *Sp., Reform* 4 Dec. (1876) 392 The monopolists of political power.

3. *attrib.* passing into *adj.*

1844 COBDEN in *Pall Mall G.* (1891) 16 Oct. 3/1 Those monopolist humbugs, who are ready to hurrah for free trade in China, and vote against it in England. **1879** G. ALLEN *Col. Sense* i. 1 The pleasure of colour is one which raises itself above the common level of monopolist gratification, and attains to the higher plane of æsthetic delight. **1887** *Westm. Rev.* June 327 The immunities..conceded to the members of that monopolist corporation.

monopolistic (mɒnəpə'lɪstɪk), *a.* [f. prec. + -IC.] Relating to, or connected with, a monopoly or a system of monopolies. Spec. ***monopolistic competition***, a type of imperfect competition characterized by monopolistic trading.

1883 *N. York Chr. Union* Aug. 30 The monopolistic 'railroad trunk-line fare-agreement'. **1891** *Review of Rev.* 15 Aug. 171/1 Associated press franchises are a monopolistic possession that gives some newspapers an advantage over others. **1892** *Nation* (N.Y.) 25 Aug. 138/1 The spirit of trades unionism is essentially monopolistic and prescriptive. **1903** R. T. ELY *Studies in Evolution of Industrial Soc.* iv. 196 Private favoritism monopolies are businesses not naturally monopolistic. **1933** E. CHAMBERLIN *Theory of Monopolistic Competition* iv. 69 Monopolistic competition..concerns itself not only with the problem of an *individual* equilibrium (the ordinary theory of monopoly), but also with that of a *group* equilibrium (the adjustment of economic forces within a group of competing monopolists, ordinarily regarded merely as a group of competitors). **1937** [see IMPERFECT *a.* 11]. **1938** E. W. SHANAHAN *Mod. Econ. Organisation* x. 235 The movement towards combination..has been successful in establishing monopolistic enterprises. **1942** W. B. TAYLOR *Financial Policies of Business Enterprise* xxxi. 750 The warp and woof of business enterprise are interwoven with ever-changing threads of competition and monopoly; and when both are found co-existing in a given enterprise, that business is said to be carrying on its functions under conditions of monopolistic competition. **1962** *Daily Tel.* 31 Jan. 10/2 The Monopolies Commission can report on monopolistic practices referred to it. **1964** GOULD & KOLB *Dict. Social Sci.* 441/1 Monopolistic competition denotes a condition of partial market control due to the exclusive possession of the trade in some commodity on the part of a seller and limited by the fact that one commodity may be substituted for another with varying degrees of ease. **1969** *Times* 27 Jan. 10/7 It is starting to match monopolistic selling power against monopolistic buying power in the grain market. **1969** D. C. HAGUE *Managerial Econ.* II. iv. 87 The first of these [kinds of imperfect competition] can be dealt with quite briefly. It is known as monopolistic competition, though the originator of the term, the American economist Professor E. H. Chamberlin intended this to be used in a slightly different sense.

Hence **monopo'listically** *adv.*

1923 *Glasgow Herald* 30 July 6 We need no longer cry out to obstructive departmental control and monopolistically inclined private enterprise—'A plague on both your houses.' **1957** K. A. WITTFOGEL *Oriental Despotism* ii. 45 They [*sc.* industries] were for the most part either directly managed or monopolistically controlled by the hydraulic governments. **1966** *Economist* 26 Feb. 774/1 Rises in dividends are determined individually, not monopolistically.

† **mono'politan**. *Obs.* [Formed as MONOPOLITE + -AN.] A monopolist.

1601 MARTIN in D'Ewes *Jrnls. Parl. Eliz.* (1682) 646 The Monopolitans of Starch, Tinn, Fish,..Salt, and I know not what. **1607** COKE *Charge at Norwich Assizes* 41 Unto whom is rightly ioyned a Promooter, a Monopolitan, and an Alcumist. **1630** J. TAYLOR (Water P.) *Wks.* II. 342/1 Hee was no diuing Politician, Or proiect-seeking Monopolitan.

Hence † **monopoli'tanian**, in the same sense.

1630 J. TAYLOR (Water P.) *Navy of Landships* Wks. I. 78/1 It serues for the Dyet of Project-mongers, Monopolitanians and diligent Sute-joggers.

† **mo'nopolite**. *Obs.* [f. MONOPOLE[1] or MONOPOLY + -ITE[1] 1.] A monopolist.

1591 SYLVESTER *Du Bartas* I. iii. 522 You Marchant Mercers, and Monopolites. **1599** T. M[OUFET] *Silkwormes* 58 To keepe out fell and black Monopolites, The Myrmedonian crue [referring to ants]. **1616** R. CARPENTER *Christ's Larum bell* 58 Monopolites, ingrossers, regraters.

So **monopolitical** *a.* (*nonce-wd.*), interested in monopolies.

1860 W. H. RUSSELL *Diary in India* I. 7 'The confounded public', as that large and respectable body is frequently styled in the privacies of official and monopolitical life.

monopolizable (mə'nɒpəlaɪzəb(ə)l), *a.* [f. MONOPOLIZE *v.* + -ABLE.] That can be monopolized.

1898 W. J. LOCKE *Idols* xxii. I'm not a monopolisable woman.

monopolization (mə,nɒpəlaɪ'zeɪʃən). [f. next + -ATION.] The action of the verb MONOPOLIZE; the process of monopolizing or the condition of being monopolized.

1727 A. HAMILTON *New Acc. E. Ind.* II. xlvi. 155, I advised him to take Protection from the Dutch, and allow them the Monopolization of the Trade of his Country. **1791** NEWTE *Tour Eng. & Scot.* 391 The immoderate extension of sheep walks, and that spirit of territorial monopolization which prevails..in..Scotland. **1878** *N. Amer. Rev.* CXXVI. 524 The swarm of Chinese..and their monopolization of many branches of industry. **1879** H. GEORGE *Progr. & Pov.* v. ii. (1881) 261 The monopolization of land that went on in England during the reign of Henry VIII.

monopolize (mə'nɒpəlaɪz), *v.* [f. MONOPOLE[1] or MONOPOLY + -IZE. Cf. F. *monopoliser*.]

1. *trans.* With reference to commerce: To get into one's hands the whole stock of (a particular commodity); to gain or hold exclusive possession of (a trade); to engross.

Now tending to be felt as merely a contextual application of sense 2; the use with a saleable commodity as obj. is consequently almost obsolete. In early use often, †*to monopolize into* (one's) *hands*; also †const. *from*.

1611 COTGR., *Monopolé*, Monopoled, or monopolized;..ingrossed, as a commoditie, into one, or a few mens hands. **1615** in *Buccleuch MSS.* (Hist. MSS. Comm.) I. 169 The Hollanders would engross this..merchandise, and monopolise it from all mankind. **1626** BERNARD *Isle of Man* (1627) 173 Covetousnesse..hath monopolized commodities into his hands, inhanced the prices of things [etc.]. **1653** in Rymer *Fœdera* (1735) XX. 644 To endeavour thereby to Monopolize all Trade into your Hands, and to exclude all other Nations. *a* **1704** T. BROWN *Walk round Lond.*, *Upon Compters* Wks. 1709 III. III. 54 Another [man]..marches from one side of the Ward to another, as if he was just going to the Exchange, to monopolize the Commodities of both the Indies. **1783** JUSTAMOND tr. *Raynal's Hist. Indies* I. 144 The Arabians..repaired in crowds to these celebrated islands, the productions of which they had already monopolized. **1817** JAS. MILL *Brit. India* II. IV. vii. 254 If the trade was..monopolized and engrossed by a combination. **1854** BADHAM *Halieut.* 470 The Emperor of all the Russias used to monopolize the acipenser helops..to supply himself..with..caviare. **1878** BOSW. SMITH *Carthage* 27 Those who monopolised the commerce of the countries where alone the citron tree grows. **1879** H. GEORGE *Progr. & Pov.* VI. ii. (1881) 295 Land..the source of all wealth and the field of all labor, is monopolized.

† **b.** *absol.* or *intr.* To have a monopoly. *Obs.*

1622 BACON *Hen. VII* 163 There passed a Law..for Monopolizing and exacting vpon the Trade. **1714** C. JOHNSON *Country Lasses* I. i, London,..Satan's chief residence: he picks up a vagabond soul or two now and then with us, but he monopolizes there.

2. *transf.* and *fig.* To obtain exclusive possession or control of; to get or keep entirely to oneself. †Const. *to* (oneself), *from* (another).

1628 PRYNNE *Brief Surv.* Epist., The enuious..cauils of some peevish Diuines, who would monopolize Diuinity to themselues alone. **1656** COWLEY *Anacr.* vii, Gold alone does Passion move, Gold monopolizes Love. **1659** T. PECKE *Parnassi Puerp.* 38 Nor shall mute Fish, the Sea Monopolize. **1668** R. STEELE *Husbandman's Calling* x. (1672) 250 When you suffer the world to monopolize your hearts from God, then the right use of the world is perverted. *a* **1714** M. HENRY *Layman's Reasons* Wks. 1853 II. 549/1, I cannot monopolize the Church; it is narrow enough, I dare not make it narrower. **1762** H. WALPOLE *Vertue's Anecd. Paint.* (1765) III. 44 *note*, Descamps says, that Lely growing jealous of Roestraten, proposed to him a partition of the art; portraits were to be monopolized by Lely. **1778** MISS BURNEY *Evelina* vi, She is a little angel! I cannot wonder that you sought to monopolize her. **1838** DICKENS *Nich. Nick.* xix, This fellow, Hawk, is monopolising your niece. **1861** F. METCALFE *Oxonian in Iceland* vii. (1867) 114 A title now monopolized in England by Knights and Baronets. **1886** *Sk. fr. Acad. Life* 62 Dr. Johnson was allowed to monopolise conversation as he did, because his sagacity was admitted to be enormous. **1889** A. R. WALLACE *Darwinism* 27 The progeny of any one species would, if allowed to increase unchecked, alone monopolise the land.

Hence **mo'nopolized** *ppl. a.*

1788 JEFFERSON *Writ.* (1859) II. 540 We participate now of a monopolized, instead on an open market. **1845** *Encycl. Metrop.* VI. 172/1 Any..monopolized commodity. **1894** C. N. ROBINSON *Brit. Fleet* 18 The advantages of monopolized commerce.

monopolizer (mə'nɒpəlaɪzə(r)). Also **monopoliser**. [f. MONOPOLIZE *v.* + -ER[1].] One who monopolizes.

1629 GAULE *Holy Madn.* 389 Now an Ingrosser..now an Haberdasher of small wares..nay worse than these..a Monopolizer. **1651** G. W. tr. *Cowel's Inst.* 283 Monopolizers, who were called Ingrossers, Fore-stallers, and Regrators,..and many others who are punishable by Imprisonment and the Pillory. **1668** CHARLETON, etc. *Ephes. & Cimm. Matrons* II. Pref., I am no Monopolizer of such Commodities. **1734** FIELDING *Univ. Gallant* IV. Wks. 1882 X. 95, I wonder he escapes being destroyed by the men as a monopolizer [of the women]. **1760** *Chron.* in *Ann. Reg.* 96 Some Armenians..bought up great quantities of grain...Several monopolizers have been put to death. **1769** MRS. F. BROOKE *Hist. Emily Montague* cxcv. (1784) IV. 47, I am a most intolerable monopolizer of the sex; in short, I have very little relish for any conversation but theirs. **1779** W. SMITH in *15th Rep. R. Comm. Hist. Manuscripts* App. VI. 429 in *Parl. Papers 1897* (C. 8551) LI. 1 The common people sick of the War, and think they are made a prey of by commissaries, quarter-masters, forage-masters, monopolisers, schemers, &c., &c. **1812** *Examiner* 25 May 327/1 The..avarice of an hard-hearted monopolizer. *a* **1862** BUCKLE *Civiliz.* (1869) III. ii. 88 The nobles..were, at that period, the monopolizers of political power. **1877** F. A. S. HEWITT in Raymond *Statist. Mines & Mining* 372 It is the fashion to denounce these corporations as monopolizers. **1879** H. GEORGE *Progr. & Pov.* v. ii. (1881) 259 The extent to which the monopolizers of land, can, in rent, levy tribute upon the earnings of labor.

mo'nopolizing, *vbl. sb.* [f. MONOPOLIZE *v.* + -ING[1].] The action of the vb. MONOPOLIZE; monopolization.

a **1617** HIERON *Wks.* (1619) II. 487 An opinion will be had that that man seekes the raysing of his owne esteeme out of others blemishes, and the engrossing and monopolizing of all respect and reuerence to himselfe. **1622** MISSELDEN *Free Trade* (ed. 2) 54 Some thinke that the reducing of trade into Order and Gouernment, is a kind of Monopolizing and restraint of trade. **1712** M. HENRY *Life P. Henry* Wks. 1853 II. 714/1 This monopolizing of the great ordinance of baptism. **1747** MRS. DELANY in *Life & Corr.* (1861) II. 473 She has many friends that wish to have a share of her company, and as I am no friend to monopolizing, I can't and must not murmur at their enjoying a pleasure I am so sensible of. **1902** S. SMITH *Life Work* xvi. 149 All poverty and suffering arose from the monopolizing of land by private owners.

attrib. **1792** A. YOUNG *Trav. France* 73 These people have the true monopolizing ideas. **1818** HALLAM *Mid. Ages* ix. II. (1819) III. 380 The discontents..resulted from the monopolizing spirit of their corporations, who oppressed all artisans without the pale of their community. **1837** —— *Hist. Lit.* I. I. iii. §56 With that true love of letters which scorns the monopolising spirit of possession, Lorenzo permitted his manuscripts to be freely copied for the use of other parts of Europe.

mo'nopolizing, *ppl. a.* [-ING².] That monopolizes; having a monopoly.

1797 BURKE *Let. Affairs Irel.* Wks. IX. 460 A small monopolizing junto. **1825** COBBETT *Rur. Rides* 407 This canting son of the monopolizing sect. **1854** H. MILLER *Sch. & Schm.* (1858) 75 A wall erected by some monopolizing proprietor of the neighbouring lands. **1869** LANDRETH *Life A. Thomson* i. 17 The stir has been diverted to the monopolising railway. **1891** *Athenæum* 24 Oct. 545/2 [Prof. Marshall pleads] for the collective good against the too pertinacious individualism of monopolizing capitalists.

†**mo'nopolous,** *a. Obs. rare*⁻¹. [f. MONOPOLE¹ + -OUS.] Monopolistic.

a **1628** F. GREVIL *Sidney* xv. (1652) 203 She never was.. overloaden with any such excesses in her Person, or defects in her Government, as might constraine her to support, or be supported by a monopolous use of favourites.

monopoly (mə'nɒpəlɪ). [ad. late L. *monopōlium*, a. Gr. μονοπώλιον (also -πωλία), f. μόνο-ς MONO- + πωλ-εῖν to sell. Cf. MONOPOLE *sb.*]

1. a. Exclusive possession of the trade in some article of merchandise; the condition of having no competitor in the sale of some commodity, or in the exercise of some trade or business. In U.K. law, a situation in which one supplier or producer controls over one third of the market.

1534 MORE *Treat. Passion* Wks. 1303/2 He knoweth.. that of all the dyscibles, there woulde none bee so false a traytour.. but him selfe alone. And therefore is thys ware Judas all in thyne owne hande. Thou haste a monopoly thereof. **1551** ROBINSON tr. *More's Utop.* I. (1895) 58 Suffer not thies ryche men to bye vp all, to ingrosse and forstalle, and with theyr monopolye to kepe the market alone as please them. **1625** BACON *Ess., Riches* (Arb.) 239 Monopolies, and Coemption of Wares for Resale,.. are great Meanes to enrich: especially, if the Partie haue intelligence, what Things are like to come into Request, and so store Himselfe before hand. **1648–58** HEXHAM, *Fockerie*, a Monopolie, or an Engrossement of all sorts of Wares and Commodities. **1774** BURKE *Sp. Amer. Tax.* Sel. Wks. I. 102 You have, in this kingdom, an advantage in Lead, that amounts to a monopoly. *a* **1850** CALHOUN *Wks.* (1874) III. 112 This hostility terminated in breaking down the exclusive monopoly of the Bank of England, and narrowing greatly the specie basis of its circulation. **1861** M. PATTISON *Ess.* (1889) I. 41 In the reign of Edward III [German traders] had a practical monopoly of the carrying trade. **1948** *Act 11 & 12 Geo. VI* c. 66 Prelim. Note, This Act sets up a permanent Commission to investigate conditions in industry and trade which tend towards a monopoly. **1964** *Times Rev. Industry* Mar. 16/1 The Act also laid down the definition of a monopoly that is still operative: a situation in which one company or group of companies acting together control one third of an industry. **1970** *Daily Tel.* 15 July 17/5 By law, over a third of the market is defined as monopoly.

b. In generalized sense. (In 17th c. often, †the crime of 'engrossing'.)

1601 J. WHEELER *Treat. Comm.* 65 Setting also price before hand of that which they sell, and of that which they will buy, and so committing open Monopoly. **1606** HOLLAND *Sueton.* Annot. 24/2 Who knoweth not that Monopoly is, when one engrosseth some commoditie into his owne handes, that none may sell the same but himselfe or from him? **1622** MISSELDEN *Free Trade* 57 Monopoly is a kind of Commerce, in buying, selling, changing or bartering, vsurped by a few, and sometimes but by one person, and forestalled from all others, to the gaine of the Monopolist, and to the Detriment of other men. **1727–41** CHAMBERS *Cycl., Monopoly*,.. an unlawful kind of traffic, when one or more persons make themselves sole masters of any commodity, trade, manufacture, or the like, with design to enhance its price; those who have occasion for it being obliged to purchase it at their hands, and on their own terms. **1793** BENTHAM *Emancipate your Colonies* Wks. 1843 IV. 412 Monopoly, that is, exclusion of customers, has certainly no tendency to produce increase of the number of traders.

2. An exclusive privilege (conferred by the sovereign or the state) of selling some commodity or trading with a particular place or country.

1596 DRAYTON *Legends* iii. 517 Then daily beg'd I great Monopolies. **1601** B. JONSON *Poetaster* v. iii, Thou [*sc.* an actor] shalt haue a monopoly of playing, confirm'd to thee and thy couey, vnder the Emperours broad scale, for this seruice. **1604** R. CAWDREY *Table Alph., Monopolie*, a licence that none shall buy or sell a thing, but one alone. *c* **1605** ROWLEY *Birth Merl.* v. ii, Take her hence.. To be shown up and down at fairs and markets, Two pence apiece. To see so foul a monster Will be a fair monopoly and worth the begging. **1620** MIDDLETON *Chaste Maid* v. iii, I would not have my cruelty so talk'd on To any child of mine for a monopoly. **1640** HABINGTON *Queen of Arragon* IV. F 2 b, 'Cause one of Oberons Groomes had got from her The Monopoly of transporting gnats. **1641** *Remonstr. State Kingd.* 9 The Monopolies of Sope, Salt, Wine, Leather, Sea-Cole, and, in a manner, of all things of most common and necessary use. **1753** HANWAY *Trav.* (1762) I. v. lxxi. 320 Monopolies, or exclusive privileges, are generally ungrateful to the people of a free state. **1831** SIR J. SINCLAIR *Corr.* II. 249 The Public Revenue [of Russia].. is likely to increase, particularly the customs, and the farm, or monopoly of brandy. **1831** MACAULAY *Ess., Bacon* (1897) 361 Raleigh held a monopoly of cards, Essex a monopoly of sweet wines. **1845** STOCQUELER *Handbk. Brit. India* (1854) 269 The finest salt in India is manufactured on the coast of Cuttack, yielding the Government a revenue little short of eighteen lacs of rupees, when the East-India Company possessed a monopoly of the manufacture of that necessary of Hindoo life. **1872** YEATS *Growth Comm.* 214 They [the Dutch] secured a monopoly of trade with Japan which lasted throughout the modern period. **1875** *Encycl. Brit.* III. 650/2 The monopoly of the right to print the Bible in England is still possessed by the Universities of Oxford and Cambridge, and her Majesty's printer for England. **1878** LECKY *Eng. in 18th C.* I. i. 122 The Assiento treaty, by which England obtained the monopoly of the slave-trade to the Spanish Colonies.

3. *transf.* and *fig.* (often with conscious metaphor). **a.** Exclusive possession, control, or exercise of something.

1643 SIR T. BROWNE *Relig. Med.* II. §3, I make not my head a grave, but a treasure of knowledge. I intend no Monopoly, but a Community in learning. **1653** MILTON *Hirelings* Pref., Till which greevances be remov'd and religion set free from the monopolie of hirelings. **1712** HENLEY *Spect.* No. 396 ¶2 The monopoly of Punns.. has been an immemorial privilege of the Johnians. **1787** BENTHAM *Def. Usury* xii. 123 Wealth has indeed the monopoly of justice against poverty. **1823** SCOTT *Peveril* vii, Do you think you have a monopoly of rebellion, and that we have not a right to show a trick of disobedience in our turn? **1861** FREEMAN *Hist. Ess.* Ser. I. ix. (1871) 268 Neither side has a monopoly of right or.. wrong. **1878** H. S. WILSON *Alp. Ascents* ii. 45 Peter has almost a monopoly now of the Matterhorn.

b. In generalized sense.

1804 J. GRAHAME *Sabbath* (1839) 8/1 Thy children, Scotia, in the desert land, Driven from their homes by fell Monopoly, Keep holy to the Lord the seventh day. **1813** J. THOMSON *Lect. Inflam.* Introd. 29 That spirit of domination, exclusion, and monopoly, by which most of her [*sc.* the church of Rome's] institutions at that period were actuated.

4. *to make a monopoly of*: **a.** *lit.* to obtain the exclusive sale of (a commodity); **b.** *fig.* to 'monopolize', keep to oneself (a possession).

1576 GASCOIGNE *Steele Gl.* 753 Master Merchant.. Can finde the meane, to make Monopolyes Of euery ware, that is accompted strange. **1595** DANIEL *Civ. Wars* (1609) v. xcviii, He.. makes a Monopoly of offices. **1629** H. BURTON *Truth's Triumph* 231 The iniquity of the Pontificians in making a monopoly of Gods grace. **1693** DRYDEN *Juvenal* Ded. (1726) p. v, Johnson [= Ben Jonson].. had been acquainted with the Rules, yet seemed to envy to Posterity that Knowledge, and like an Inventer of some useful Art, to make a Monopoly of his Learning. **1710** ADDISON *Whig Exam* No. 1 ¶1 The Kitcat have pretended to make a Monopoly of our sense. **1745** P. THOMAS *Jrnl. Anson's Voy.* 10 A certain Honourable Gentleman.. is.. Endeavouring to make a Monopoly of this Voyage, and to that end designs to publish by Authority. **1769** BURKE *Late St. Nat.* Wks. II. 87 Government in France has made a monopoly of that great article of salt.

5. A thing which is the subject of a monopoly (in senses 1–3).

1838–9 HALLAM *Hist. Lit.* IV. IV. vii. §7 It is one of those happy ideas which have been privileged monopolies of the first inventor. **1845** MCCULLOCH *Taxation* II. v. (1852) 206 The culture of opium.. is a government monopoly, being confined to the provinces of Bahar and Benares... Every one who chooses may raise opium within the prescribed limits. **1868** G. DUFF *Pol. Surv.* 186 The culture.. of tobacco was made a Crown monopoly. **1878** *Print. Trades Jrnl.* XXIII. 22 Printing the Holy Scriptures is a monopoly. **1902** W. M. ALEXANDER *Demonic Possession in N.T.* ii. 25 Such traits are not the monopoly of the Babylonian spirits.

6. A trading company that has a monopoly.

[*a* **1692** POLLEXFEN *Disc. Trade* (1697) 125 If Corporations in Trade with Joint-Stocks, should appear to be.. to all intents and purposes Monopolies, mischievous to Trade.] **1871** *Q. Rev.* Oct. 461 Other enterprises with enormous capitals, e.g. banks,.. are not monopolies. **1887** E. BELLAMY *Looking Backward* v. (1890) 41 Without being.. checked by the clamour against it, the absorption of business by ever larger monopolies continued.

7. (With capital initial.) The proprietary name of a game (invented by Mr. Charles Darrow) in which the players use imitation money to engage in simulated financial dealings. Also *attrib.* **Monopoly money**, money that is not 'real', valueless currency.

1935 *N.Y. Times* 24 Nov. x. 6/2 Heading all other 'board games'.. is the season's craze, 'Monopoly', the game of real estate. **1938** C. BEATON *Diary* 1 Aug. in *Wandering Years* (1961) 344 The game of 'Monopoly' wasn't very enjoyable this morning. **1939** G. GREENE *Lawless Roads* Prol. 5 A game called 'Monopoly' played with a picture-board and dice and little counters. *Ibid.*, There were 'Monopoly' parties. **1954** *Trade Marks Jrnl.* 23 June 634/2 *Monopoly*.. Board games John Waddington Limited.. Leeds. **1960** *Guardian* 9 Dec. 9/7 My knowledge of the world of big business.. I gained entirely from playing Monopoly. **1972** K. BONFIGLIOLI *Don't point that Thing at Me* xiii. 110 Martland's word was as good as his bond, but his bond was mere Monopoly money. **1972** *Times* 8 Apr. 1/3 Private tenants in rented flats are banding together.. against property speculators whom they accuse of ruthlessly playing Monopoly with their homes. **1974** *Times* 27 Apr. 10/7, I think they are playing with Monopoly money because some people say things like 'I have lost £10,000'.

8. *attrib.*, as ***monopoly licence, price, problem, profits, -trend***; **monopoly capitalism**, a capitalist system typified by trade monopolies in the hands of a few people; **monopoly value**, the value of anything the supply of which is controlled by the holders of a monopoly; *spec.* applied to licensed premises.

1937 C. DAY LEWIS *Mind in Chains* 13 The quality of intellectual production is inevitably debased under *monopoly-capitalism. **1943** H. READ *Politics of Unpolitical* i. 6 It [*sc.* the oligarchy of trade unions] is now openly merging itself with the ascendant oligarchy of monopoly capitalism, to form what James Burnham has called 'the managerial class'. **1955** —— *Grass Roots of Art* (rev. ed.) vii. 139, I feel fairly sure that that barrack-room will have more amenities under monopoly capitalism than in the totalitarian State. **1964** GOULD & KOLB *Dict. Social Sci.* 442/2 Monopoly capitalism in Marxist terminology is the stage of capitalism in which control over means of production and distribution has become highly concentrated in the hands of a small group of capitalists. **1625** BACON *Apophth.* xxix. Resusc. (1671) I. 227 The Lord Keeper, Sir Nicholas Bacon, was asked his Opinion by Queen Elizabeth, of one of these *Monopoly licenses. **1905** J. J. COCKSHOTT *Licensing Act 1904* 3 The State, in conferring upon me a monopoly license, had also granted me a commercial asset of great value. **1776** ADAM SMITH *W.N.* I. xi. (1869) I. 153 The rent of land,.. considered as the price paid for the use of the land, is naturally a *monopoly price. **1807** *Edin. Rev.* X. 347 They still fight for the impossibility of driving a distant traffic, without encouragement of monopoly-prices. **1955** *Times* 15 June 5/4 The *monopoly problem is discussed usually in terms of a single seller or a small group of sellers acting in concert, who are able to restrict supplies. **1931** *Economist* 26 Dec. 1222/1 The 'ring', producing a sectionalised product, will be able to exaggerate the *monopoly profits already exacted from the helpless consumer. **1964** GOULD & KOLB *Dict. Social Sci.* 543/1 Profits include.. permanent monopoly profits, more properly termed monopoly rents. **1944** *Horizon* Jan. 67 What is valid.. is no more than the good old perception of *monopoly-trends in finance and industrial organization. **1883** F. A. WALKER *Polit. Econ.* III. i. 90 Here is a high degree of value.. where yet no labor has been... This is an instance of what may be called '*monopoly-value', or as some prefer to call it, scarcity-value. **1904** *Hansard Commons* 20 Apr. 735 We think that when any new licence is granted the monopoly value should go to the public. **1905** J. J. COCKSHOTT *Licensing Act 1904* 6 The monopoly value will be secured to the public instead of being 'handed over to wealthy brewery companies for the mere asking'. **1934** DUMMEIER & HEFLEBOWER *Econ. with Applications to Agric.* viii. 166 Monopoly value refers to exchange value for any commodity of which the supply is sufficiently under one control that the exchange value or price which prevails for it is different.. than it would be under ordinary competitive conditions. **1936** JATHAR & BERI *Introd. Econ.* ix. 170 In all cases of monopoly value, the monopolist must carefully weigh.. the nature of the demand, and.. the expenses of production per unit. **1953** B. SPILLER *Innkeeping* x. 190 On the grant of a new licence the justices must exact the payment of a *monopoly value*, i.e. the difference between the value of the premises licensed and unlicensed.

monopo'lylogist. [f. next + -IST.] One who performs a MONOPOLYLOGUE.

1830 *Examiner* 278/1 The Monopolologist [*sic*] startled his audience. **1832** *Ibid.* 294/2 Mathews made his first appearance as a Monopolylogist.

monopolylogue (mɒnəʊ'pɒlɪlɒg). [f. Gr. μόνο-ς MONO- + πόλυ-ς POLY- + -λογος -LOGUE.] An entertainment in which a single performer sustains many characters. Also *fig.*

1824 in *Spirit Publ. Jrnls.* (1825) 333 Like Mathews in a Monopolylogue. **1834** T. H. LISTER in *M. Napier's Corr.* (1879) 153 The Duke of Wellington lays aside his mysterious monopolylogue. **1838** *New Monthly Mag.* LII. 76 The third part was another Monopolylogue, called 'All well at Natchitoches'—all the characters by Mr. Mathews. *a* **1845** HOOD *To Lady on Dep. India* v, Go where with human notes the Parrot dealeth In mono-*polly*-logue. **1848** J. H. NEWMAN *Loss & Gain* x. 68 The conversation, or rather mono-polylogue, as some great performer calls it, ran in somewhat of the following strain. **1860** *Sat. Rev.* X. 273/1 Last week we gave a view of a distinguished religious actor in a monopolylogue and domestic performance—Spurgeon at Home.

monopo'tassic, *a. Chem.* [See MONO- 2.] Containing one equivalent of potassium.

1873 *Fownes' Chem.* (ed. 11) 325 Monopotassic sulphate, is commonly called bisulphate of potash.

monopous (mɒ'nəʊpəs), *a. nonce-wd.* [f. Gr. μονωπ- (μονώψ) or μονώπ-ος one-eyed (f. μόν-ος MONO- + ὤψ eye) + -OUS.] One-eyed.

1798 in *Spirit Publ. Jrnls.* (1799) II. 327 That a great many gentlemen.. never had more than one eye..; that their progeny also were like themselves monopous.

monoprionidian (,mɒnəʊpraɪəʊ'nɪdɪən), *a. Palæont.* [f. Gr. μόνο-ς MONO- + πρίων saw.] Having serrations on one side of the stem only: said of graptolites. Also **mono'prionid** *a.*

1870 NICHOLSON *Man. Zool.* 95 Besides the simple forms of Graptolites with a row of cellules on one side (monoprionidian), there are others with a row of cellules on each side (diprionidian). **1888** ROLLESTON & JACKSON *Anim. Life* 769 A typical or monoprionid Graptolite.

Monoprix ('mɒnəʊpriː). [Fr., lit. 'one price'.] One of a chain of multiple stores (in France) in which a cheap class of goods is sold (orig. all at the same price).

1937 W. FORTESCUE *Sunset House* ix. 164 Bulky goods hastily thrust into bags at the Monoprix. **1965** V. CANNING *Whip Hand* v. 48, I bought six pairs of pants at a Monoprix. **1966** G. GREENE *Comedians* I. i. 23 Cynicism is cheap—you can buy it at any Monoprix store. **1973** D. ORGILL *Jasius Pursuit* i. 8 She had seen *Mademoiselle* in the Monoprix down in Cannes.

monopropellant (mɒnəʊprə'pɛlənt), *sb.* and *a.* [f. MONO- + PROPELLANT *a.* and *sb.*]

A. *sb.* A substance which can be used as a rocket fuel without needing an additional oxidizing agent.

1949 G. P. SUTTON *Rocket Propulsion Elements* v. 115 Monopropellants are stable at ordinary atmospheric conditions, but decompose and yield hot combustion gases when heated and pressurized. **1958** C. C. ADAMS et al. *Space Flight* iii. 79 A monopropellant is generally unstable and delivers energy through its own decomposition, which is generally induced by a catalytic agent such as potassium permanganate (with hydrogen peroxide). **1972** *Materials & Technol.* IV. xix. 741 Hydrogen peroxide was employed as a monopropellant to provide power for the turbine-driven pumps [in the V2 rocket].

B. *adj.* Employing a monopropellant.
1949 G. P. SUTTON *Rocket Propulsion Elements* v. 115 The feed system of monopropellant units is usually simple, because only one liquid needs to be supplied. **1954** K. W. GATLAND *Devel. Guided Missiles* (ed. 2) i. 23 Rockets can be classified into two main types: (*a*) Bi-propellant, in which the fuel and oxygen supplies are..injected separately into the combustion chamber, and (*b*) mono-propellant, in which the fuel and oxygen are combined in a single substance. **1967** *Technology Week* 23 Jan. 28/2 Anhydrous hydrazine will fuel the liquid monopropellant engine.

monoprostyle: see MONO- 1.

monops (ˈmɒnɒps), *a.* and *sb.* [f. Gr. μόν-ος MONO- + ὤψ eye.] †**A.** *adj.* One-eyed. *Obs. rare*$^{-0}$. **B.** *sb.* A one-eyed individual. *rare*$^{-1}$.
1857 R. G. MAYNE *Expos. Lex. Med. Sci.* (1860) 716/2 *Monops*, having but one eye: one-eyed. **1876** G. MEREDITH *Beauch. Career* III. ix. 155 He would have been a Nelson of politics, if he had been a monops, with an excuse for not seeing. **1900** DORLAND *Med. Dict.* 396/1 *Monops*, a fetus having but a single eye. [And in later med. dicts.]

monopsony (məˈnɒpsənɪ). *Econ.* [f. MON(O- + Gr. ὀψων-εῖν to buy provisions + -Y^3.] A condition in which there is only one buyer for the product of a large number of sellers; cf. MONOPOLY. Also in extended use (see quot. 1971). Hence **moˈnopsonist; monopsoˈnistic** *a.*
1933 J. ROBINSON *Econ. Imperfect Competition* xviii. 219 When the market changes..to a single buying agency..this may be described as monopsony buying. *Ibid.* 224 Just as we have price discrimination for a monopolist, so we may have price discrimination for a monopsonist. *Ibid.* xxvi. 296 Monopsonistic exploitation can also arise where..the supply of labour to each firm is less than perfectly elastic. **1941** R. TRIFFIN *Monopolistic Competition & General Equilibrium Theory* iii. 113 Other types of interrelationships, intermediate between monopsony and pure competition, can be distinguished. **1948** *Commerce & Industry* (Pretoria) Mar. 280 The supplying of sawlogs on a contract term of 20 years..may place the sawmiller in a monopsonistic position in a particular forest region. *Ibid.* Bargaining power will be fairly evenly divided between the two parties. The dangers of monopsony..will thus be limited. **1955** *Times* 15 June 5/4 The term 'monopsonist' for a monopoly buyer was coined in the thirties—but has got little foothold in popular discussion. **1964** *Economist* 1 Feb. 434/1 Bargaining between a monopsony buyer and a suppliers' ring. **1968** *Internat. Encycl. Social Sci.* X. 464 Analogous to a seller's monopoly power, a buyer is said to have 'monopsony' power when he can significantly affect the price of what he buys by varying the quantity bought. **1969** D. C. HAGUE *Managerial Econ.* II. iv. 98 When there is a single buyer in any market, he is often described as a *monopsonist*. **1971** M. COOPER in *Royal Soc. Health Jrnl.* XCI. 220/2 The main risks of the B.M.A. scheme however are not of this type. Rather they lie in breaking up the State monopsony. *Ibid.* 221/2 A monopsony is a consumer so large that it can exert pressure on price merely by the threat of withdrawing its custom. **1973** *Times Lit. Suppl.* 9 Mar. 255/2 The granting of monopsonistic concessions to wholesale merchants.

monopsychism (mɒnəʊˈsaɪkɪz(ə)m). [f. Gr. μόνο-ς MONO- + ψῡχ-ή soul + -ISM.] The theory that all souls (or the souls of all mankind) are one; the unity of souls asserted by this theory.
1864 W. HEELEY in *Calcutta Rev.* XXXIX. 383 Some of his expressions point clearly to the middle-age notion of monopsychism—that all mankind had but one soul. *a* **1894** ROMANES *Th. on Relig.* (1895) 50 Wherein all causation is gathered up into the monopsychism of a single personality.

‖**monopsychosis** (ˌmɒnəʊsaɪˈkəʊsɪs). [mod.L., see MONO- and PSYCHOSIS.] = MONOMANIA.
1883 T. S. CLOUSTON *Clin. Lect. Mental Dis.* 18 A true impression from a nerve of common sensibility may be misinterpreted, as when a man has cancer of his stomach that causes him real gnawing pain, and he says he has rats inside him that are eating his vitals. It might help you to understand this condition better if it were called Monopsychosis. **1902** *Baldwin's Dict. Philos. & Psychol.* s.v. *Mono-, Monomania* (..also termed, by Clouston, monopsychosis).

†**monopter.** *Arch. Obs. rare*$^{-0}$. Also 8 monoptere. [ad. F. *monoptère*, ad. med.L. *monopteros*: see MONOPTEROS.] = MONOPTEROS.
1696 PHILLIPS (ed. 5), *Monopter*, was a sort of a round Temple, whose Roof was supported by one Pillar only. **1727–41** CHAMBERS *Cycl.*, *Monoptere*,..a kind of temple among the antients, round, and without walls; having its dome supported by columns. **1775** in ASH.

monopteral (məˈnɒptərəl), *a.* and *sb.* [f. late L. *monopter-os* (Vitruvius, in sense 1 below), mod.L. *monopter-us* (in sense 2), a. Gr. *μονόπτερος, lit. 'having one wing or fin', f. μόνο-ς MONO- + πτερ-όν wing, fin, row or circle of columns: see -AL^1.]
A. *adj.*
1. *Arch.* Of a temple: Consisting of a single circle of columns supporting a roof.
1823 P. NICHOLSON *Pract. Build.* Gloss. 588 *Monopteron*, or *Monopt[e]ral Temple*, an edifice consisting of a circular colonnade, supporting a dome, without any inclosing wall. **1841** *Civil Eng. & Arch. Jrnl.* IV. 118/2 The uppermost is a Corinthian rotunda, forming an open or monopteral temple (i.e. without any cella).
2. *Zool.* Having a single fin, wing, or alate part [Cf. F. *monoptère* (1798 in Hatz.-Darm.).]
1887 SOLLAS in *Encycl. Brit.* XXII. 417/2 (Fig. 17) *K*, monopteral cymba.
B. *sb.* A monopteral temple; a monopteros.
1845 PARKER *Gloss. Archit.* (ed. 4) I. 243 *Monopteros, Monopteral*,..a circular temple consisting of a roof supported on columns, without any cell.

‖**monopteros** (məˈnɒptərɒs). *Arch.* Also 8–9 monopteron. [subst. use of late L. *monopteros* adj.: see MONOPTERAL.] A monopteral temple.
1706 PHILLIPS (ed. Kersey), *Monopteron*, a sort of round Temple, whose Roof was only supported by Pillars; so call'd, from its having but one Wing or Isle. **1823** [see MONOPTERAL *a.* 1]. **1850** LEITCH tr. *C. O. Müller's Anc. Art* §190 (ed. 2) 171 Temple..of Mars Ultor on the capitol, a small monopteros, which we still see on coins. **1883** tr. *Reber's Hist. Anc. Art* 476 *Monopteros*, a circular structure of outstanding columns, commonly without a cella enclosed by walls.

monopterous (məˈnɒptərəs), *a. Bot.* [f. mod.L. *monopter-us* (see MONOPTERAL) + -OUS.] Of certain seeds: Having but one wing.
1856 MAYNE *Expos. Lex.*, *Monopterus*, having but one wing, as the *carcerula* of the *Fraxinus*: monopterous. **1866** in *Treas. Bot.*

monopterygian, -ious: see MONO- 1.

monoptic, *a.* [f. Gr. μόν-ος MONO- + ὀπτικ-ός of or pertaining to sight (see OPTIC).] One-eyed. Also, pertaining to or involving vision with one eye. Also *absol.*
1656 BLOUNT *Glossogr.*, *Monoptick*, that seeth onely with one eye. **1730** BAILEY (fol.), *Monoptick*. **1960** KOLERS & ROSNER in *Amer. Jrnl. Psychol.* LXXIII. 4 One may distinguish at least three modes of viewing: monocular, binocular, and a third which we shall call 'dichoptic'. [*Note*] Consistency of usage would require that the first two be called 'monoptic' and 'dioptic' respectively. **1968** *Perception & Psychophysics* III. 237/2 Under the monoptic condition, both disk and ring were presented to the same eye, half the time to the left eye and half the time to the right eye. **1971** *Jrnl. Gen. Psychol.* LXXXIV. 163 Dichoptic masking was nearly as strong as under monoptic and binocular conditions.
Hence **moˈnoptically** *adv.*, with one eye.
1965 *Jrnl. Exper. Psychol.* LXIX. 199/1 The extent of masking by pattern was slightly less dichoptically than monoptically. **1972** *Nature* 22 Dec. 480/1 The observer perceives a pattern which approximates very closely a square-wave distribution, just as if the two components were superimposed physically and viewed monoptically.

monoptical (məˈnɒptɪkəl), *a. humorously pedantic.* [Formed as prec. + -AL^1.] One-eyed.
1821 *Blackw. Mag.* IX. 61 Monoptical Squire Polyphemus. *c* **1842** M. J. HIGGINS *Ess.* (1875) 74 He was a rugged veteran, white-haired, bloated, lame, and monoptical.

monoptote (ˈmɒnəptəʊt). Also 7–8 -tot. [ad. late L. *monoptōt-us*, a. late Gr. μονόπτωτ-ος, f. Gr. μόνο-ς MONO- + πτωτός falling, cogn. w. πτῶσις case, f. πί-πτ-ειν to fall. So F. *monoptote.*] A noun occurring in a single oblique case (as L. *astu*).
1612 BRINSLEY *Pos. Parts* (1669) 101 *Q.* Which call you Monoptots? *A.* Such words as are found in one oblique case. **1656** BLOUNT *Glossogr.*, *Monoptote*, a word having but one Case. **1751** WESLEY *Wks.* (1872) XIV. 40 Monoptots, which have but one Case; as, *astu*. **1854** ANDREWS & STODDARD *Lat. Gram.* §94. 36 Monoptote.
Hence **monopˈtotic** *a.*, having only one case.
1872 LATHAM s.v. *Monoptote*, A word that appears in one form only is, on the first view, equally aptotic and monoptotic—both or either.

monopylean: see MONO- 1.

monopyrenous (mɒnəʊpaɪˈriːnəs), *a. Bot.* [f. Gr. μόνο-ς MONO- + πυρήν fruit-stone + -OUS. Cf. F. *monopyrène.*] Having but one stone or kernel: said of fruits.
1706 PHILLIPS (ed. Kersey), *Monopyrenous Fruit*, such Fruit of a Plant, as contains in it only one Kernel, or Seed. **1866** *Treas. Bot.*, *Monopyrenous*, containing one stone.

mono-rail (ˈmɒnəʊreɪl). Also **monorail.** [f. MONO- + RAIL *sb.*^{2}] **a.** A single rail astride which or suspended from which railway vehicles or the like run; also, a vehicle that travels in this way. Also *attrib.* Hence **ˈmono-railer; ˈmonorailing** *vbl. sb.* **mono-railway.**
1897 *Westm. Gaz.* 9 Apr. 4/2 Patent electric express railway..built on the mono-rail system. **1901** *Daily News* 14 Mar. 3/2 The Proposed Monorail between Liverpool and Manchester. **1902** *Westm. Gaz.* 16 May 5/3 A scheme..for the construction of a mono-railway. **1902** *Encycl. Brit.* XXXII. 143/2 In the Langen mono-rail the car is hung from a single overhead rail; a line on this system is worked between Barmen and Elberfeld, a distance of about 9 miles. **1949** *Sun* (Baltimore) 3 Oct. 2/7 These chutes will pull the guns out of the rear clam shell doors of the C-82 along monorails attached to the roof of the fuselage. **1958** *Daily Mail* 17 Jan. 9/4 A trip on the world's first monorail. **1960** *Farmer & Stockbreeder* 16 Feb. (Suppl.) 35/1 One is an overhead monorail down the centre feeding passage to carry a food container from which the rations may be semi-automatically fed into the troughs. **1962** R. B. FULLER *Epic Poem on Industrialization* 44 Their 1929 failure With world monopoly 'Mono-railing' Was only caused by the fact that Their first trial section of single rail Was not long enough. **1963** *Punch* 7 Aug. 194/2 The monorailer slid to a halt. **1964** *Daily Tel.* 7 Jan. 15/1 A free monorail system may be built in North Buckinghamshire. **1971** *Ibid.* 16 Apr. 6/7 A French demonstration hovertrain has been running for 18 months on an 11-mile stretch of elevated monorail outside Orléans. **1973** R. KERROD *First Look at Railways Today* 45 It is called a monorail, for it moves along a single rail.

b. monorail camera, a technical camera having as part of its stand a bar or monorail which allows considerable adjustment of the apparatus and may support additional components.
1958 D. CHARLES *Commercial & Industr. Photogr.* i. 10 Monorail camera..a recent, mainly metal, engineer-built construction, with a full array of 'movements'. **1971** P. D. JAMES *Shroud for Nightingale* iii. 52 The Yard photographer manœuvred his tripod and camera—a new Cambo monorail.

monorchid (mɒˈnɔːkɪd), *a.* and *sb.* [f. mod.L. *monorchis, monorchid-*: see MONORCHIS. Cf. F. *monorchide.*] **a.** *adj.* Having only one testicle; characterized by or exhibiting monorchism. **b.** *sb.* A monorchid person; = MONORCHIS.
1822–34 *Good's Study Med.* (ed. 4) IV. 6 There is a set of barbarians at the back of the Cape of Good Hope, who appear to be very generally monorchid, or possessed of only a single testis. **1874** VAN BUREN *Dis. Genit. Org.* 390 A Monorchid has only one testicle in the scrotum. **1885** *Lancet* 18 July 141/2 The question as to the possible..inconvenience to which monorchids are liable falls under two heads.

monorchidism (mɒˈnɔːkɪdɪz(ə)m). [f. prec. + -ISM.] = MONORCHISM.
1860 *New Syd. Soc. Year-bk. Med.* 304 Researches in Monorchidism and Cryptorchidism in Man. **1874** VAN BUREN *Dis. Genit. Org.* 392 Occasionally monorchidism is acquired.

‖**monorchis** (mɒˈnɔːkɪs). Pl. **monorchides** (-ˈɔːkɪdiːz). [mod.L. *monorchis*, pl. (incorrectly) *-ides*, a. Gr. μόνορχις adj., f. μόν-ος MONO- + ὄρχις testicle.] A person or animal with only one testicle.
1722 QUINCY *Lex. Physico-Med.* (ed. 2), *Monorchis*. **1843** CURLING *Dis. Testis* 52 Many instances of monorchides, or persons having only a single testis, are also mentioned by the old authors. **1865** A. S. TAYLOR *Princ. & Pract. Med. Jurispr.* 866 Monorchides..have been known to be prolific.

monorchism (mɒˈnɔːkɪz(ə)m). [Formed as MONORCHIS + -ISM.] The condition of having only one testicle.
1876 in DUNGLISON *Med. Lex.*

monorganic (mɒnɔːˈgænɪk), *a.* [f. MON(O)- + ORGAN + -IC.]
1. *Med.* Of a disease: Affecting a single organ.
1880 in WEBSTER *Suppl.*
2. Having only one organ.
1887 *Science* 3 June 534 In the natural world some beings are monorganic, others are polyorganic.

monorheme (ˈmɒnəʊriːm), *sb. Linguistics.* Also **monorrheme.** [f. MONO- + RHEME.] A single element or word with a phrasal meaning. So **monoˈrrhemic** *a.*
1937 J. ORR tr. *Iordan's Introd. Romance Linguistics* iv. 379 Bally proceeds to view the sentence in its genetic and psychological aspects, its development from the 'monorheme' to the 'dirheme' by a process of integration or 'condensation' of two originally independent units. **1939** L. H. GRAY *Foundations of Lang.* viii. 229 Another type of monorrhemic verbal sentence is seen in verbs expressing meteorological conditions, such as Latin *pluit*. *Ibid.* 230 A verb is the sole part of speech which can form a complete sentence, i.e., which can contain both a subject and a predicate in a single monorrheme. **1950** *Archivum Linguisticum* II. 186 The nature of the 'monorhemes' varies between a wish or request, a questioning attitude,..and..a mere report of something perceived. **1969** tr. *Akhmanova & Mikael'an's Theory of Syntax in Mod. Linguistics* iii. 55 Phrases are called 'monorhemes' when they consist of a single element, and 'dirhemes' when the number of elements is two. **1970** *Language* XLVI. 923 In these apparent monorhemes a hic-et-nunc adverb has been deleted.

monorhine (ˈmɒnɒraɪn), *a.* and *sb. Zool.* Also **monorrhine.** [f. mod.L. *Monorhīna*, f. Gr. μόνο-ς MONO- + ῥῑν-, ῥίς nose.] **A.** *adj.* Having a single nasal passage only; *spec.* applied to the *Monorhina*, a group of skulled vertebrates, having only one nasal passage, and comprising the lampreys and hags. Also **monorhinal** (ˈmɒnɒraɪnəl), **monorhinous** (ˈmɒnɒraɪnəs), *adjs.* in the same sense.
1890 *Century Dict.*, *Monorhinal*. *Ibid.*, *Monorhine*. **1897** E. R. LANKESTER in *Nat. Science* July 47 To assume..that these fishes were monorrhine, is surely illegitimate and arbitrary. **1900** *Nature* 20 Sept. 504/2 There is no evidence whatever that any of the creatures classed together as Ostracodermi were monorhinal like the Lampreys. **1902** *Webster's Dict., Suppl.*, *Monorhinous*.
B. *sb.* A monorhinal vertebrate.
1890 in *Century Dict.*; and in later Dicts.

†**monorhythm.** *Obs.*$^{-0}$ [f. Gr. μόνο-ς MONO- + ῥυθμ-ός RHYTHM.] = MONORIME.
Etymologically the word should mean 'having one rhythm'; but prob. it was intended as a more correct form to be substituted for the hybrid *monorhyme* (*-rime*), the word *rhyme* being regarded as a derivative of ῥυθμός.
1775 ASH, *Monorhythme*, a poetical composition in which all the verses end with the same rhyme.

monoˈrhythmic, *a. rare Pros.* [Formed as prec. + -IC.] = MONORIME *a.* (Cf. prec.)
1833 LONGF. *Anc. Span. Ball.* Prose Wks. 1886 I. 162 They [old Spanish ballads] are all monorhythmic, with full

consonant rhymes. **1833** —— *Drift-Wood* ibid. 296 In these old romances.. the verse is monorhythmic.

monorime, -rhyme (ˈmɒnɒraɪm), *sb.* and *a.* [a. F. *monorime* (1690 in Hatz.-Darm.), f. Gr. μόνο-ς MONO- + *rime* RIME, RHYME.]

A. *sb.* **a.** A poetical composition or passage in which all the lines have the same rime. **b.** *pl.* Lines forming a 'tirade' with one rime.

1731 BAILEY (vol. II.), *Monorhyme*, a poetical composition, all the verses whereof end with the same rhyme. **1868** T. WRIGHT *Pref. to Langtoft's Chron.* (Rolls) II. p. xi, In this manuscript each new set of monorimes is headed by a title in Latin. **1886** POSNETT *Compar. Lit.* 46 *note*, The rudeness of this versification, says M. Géruzez.. is marked by monorimes, of indeterminate length.

B. *adj.* Having a single rime. So also **ˈmonorimed** *ppl. a.* [see -ED[2]].

1833 LONGF. *Drift-Wood* Prose Wks. 1886 I. 299 The old romances were sung; and.. hence there was a good reason for dividing them into monorhyme stanzas. **1898** SAINTSBURY *Short Hist. Eng. Lit.* (1905) 737 These rolling quatrains, rhymed as a rule *a a b a*,.. but sometimes monorhymed throughout. **1902** H. LYNCH *G. Paris' Med. Fr. Lit.* 90 A little poem.. in monorhymed quatrains.

‖**monosabio** (monoˈsabjo). [Sp., f. *mono* monkey + *sabio* wise, trained.] A picador's assistant in the bullring. Also *ellipt.* as **mono**.

1897 *Encycl. Sport* I. 158/2 *Monos sabios*, boys and men employed in the service of the bull fight. **1924** E. HEMINGWAY *In our Time* xii. 22 The horse's entrails hung down in a blue bunch.. the *monos* whacking him on the back of his legs with the rods. **1927** —— *Men without Women* 38 The monos were leading a horse out by the bridle toward the bull. **1928** *Daily Tel.* 17 July 9/3 In another bull-ring at Vista Allegre.. the matador Albageno and a 'monosabio' were dangerously wounded by bulls yesterday. **1932** E. HEMINGWAY *Death in Afternoon* vi. 58 You will see.. the picadors arriving on the horses they have ridden in from town, these horses having been ridden from the bull ring by the red-bloused monos or bullring servants. *Ibid.* xvi. 187 [The] San Sebastian monosabios should be, by rights, policemen... They carry.. puntillas, broad-headed knives. **1959** V. J. KEHOE *Aficionado!* 37 The *monosabios*.. handle the picadores' horses and aid them in getting into the correct position for the charge of the toro. *Ibid.* 53 The areneros and monosabios generally wear a red shirt, and dark blue pants. **1973** J. M. WHITE *Garden Game* 61 An image from the *corrida de toros*.. the *monosabios* smoothing the cruelly trampled area.

monosaccharide (mɒnəʊˈsækəraɪd). *Chem.* Also †**-saccharid**. [f. MONO- + SACCHARIDE.] Any sugar which cannot be hydrolysed to give simpler sugars.

1896 W. D. HALLIBURTON *Essent. Chem. Physiol.* (ed. 2) i. 10 (*table*) Monosaccharides or glucoses. **1902** *Encycl. Brit.* XXXI. 723/2 The simplest carbohydrates constitute the group of monosaccharids, of which dextrose.. is the most important. **1936** C. S. GIBSON *Essent. Princ. Org. Chem.* xv. 445 The production of a ketohexose from the preliminary aldohexose may be due to the usual interconversion of monosaccharides in the presence of alkalis in aqueous solution. **1968** *Punch* 11 Sept. 356/3 'Oh, ah,' said Walter Gabriel, 'especially considering that, at the same time, she'm also producing monosaccharides, trisaccharides, and a whole perishing range of they oligosaccharides.' **1972** *Sci. Amer.* Oct. 71/1 Lactose is a disaccharide composed of the monosaccharides glucose and galactose.

monosaccharose (mɒnəʊˈsækərəʊz, -s). *Chem.* [f. MONO- + SACCHAROSE.] = MONOSACCHARIDE.

1902 J. B. COHEN *Theoret. Org. Chem.* xx. 276 The monosaccharoses possess strong reducing properties. **1919** S. B. SCHRYVER *Introd. Study Biol. Chem.* v. 199 All the native monosaccharoses are optically active. **1951** I. L. FINAR *Org. Chem.* I. xviii. 357 Monosaccharides (monosaccharoses).

monoschemic: see MONO- 1.

monoscope (ˈmɒnəskəʊp). *Television.* [f. MONO- + -SCOPE.] (See quot. 1953.)

1938 C. E. BURNETT in *RCA Rev.* II. 414 'Monoscope' is the name which has been given to a developmental type of tube designed to produce a video signal of a test picture or pattern enclosed in the tube. Since the picture must be enclosed in the tube, the Monoscope is not suitable for developing a video signal which represents action. **1953** AMOS & BIRKINSHAW *Television Engin.* I. iv. 79 A monoscope is a camera tube containing a target on which a pattern or photograph is printed and which, by scanning the target, generates a picture signal corresponding to the printed image. **1955** G. M. GLASFORD *Fund. Television Engin.* xv. 480 A useful device for generating a video test signal is the monoscope.

monose (ˈmɒnəʊz, -s). *Chem.* [f. MON(O + -OSE[2].] = MONOSACCHARIDE; (see also quot. 1948).

1892, 1903 [see BIOSE]. **1935** TIPSON & STILLER in Harrow & Sherwin *Textbk. Biochem.* ii. 77 (*heading*) The action of alkalis on monoses. **1948** [see DIOSE].

monoˈselenide. *Chem.* [MONO- 2.] A selenide containing one equivalent of selenium.

1873 *Fownes' Chem.* (ed. 11) 228 The mono, tri, and pentaselenides.

monosemantic (mɒnəʊsiːˈmæntɪk), *a.* [f. MONO- + SEMANTIC *a.*] Of a word or phrase, having only one meaning. Also **monosemanˈtemic** *a.*

1957 S. POTTER *Mod. Linguistics* vii. 147 The simplest words are manifestly those which symbolize single things or concepts, like proper names. These may be described as *monosemantemic*, and therefore unambiguous. **1960** E. DELAVENAY *Introd. Machine Translation* vi. 97 The vocabulary is classified into monosemantic and polysemantic grammatical words. **1966** *English Studies* XLVII. 56 Such case-forms are not strictly monosemantic, but can vary in their function according to the context.

monoseme (ˈmɒnəʊsiːm), *a.* *Pros.* [ad. Gr. μονόσημ-ος: see next.] = next.

1902 in *Webster's Dict., Suppl.*

monosemic (mɒnəʊˈsiːmɪk), *a.* [f. Gr. μονόσημ-ος cited in sense 'having only one signification' (f. μονό-ς MONO- + σῆμα sign, mark) + -IC.]

a. *Pros.* Consisting of or equal to a single mora. (Cf. *disemic, trisemic.*)

1890 in *Century Dict.*

b. *Linguistics.* = MONOSEMANTIC *a.*

1969 *Computers & Humanities* III. 251 The verses contain a very high proportion of monosemic words and polysemic words used in their primary meaning. **1971** O. A. WOJTASIEWICZ tr. *Pelc's Studies in Functional Logical Semiotics of Natural Lang.* 23 The English word 'bay' has more usages... 'Orchid', on the other hand, is a monosemic word.

monosemy (ˈmɒnəʊsiːmɪ). [f. MONO- + SEM(ANTIC *a.* + -Y[3].] Of a word or phrase, the quality of having only one meaning. Cf. POLYSEMY.

1951 S. ULLMANN *Princ. Semantics* ii. 107 Multiple meaning—which includes a number of non-lexical elements—comprises everything running counter to 'monosemy' in the language system. **1969** S. HOOK *Lang. & Philosophy* III. 255 Now on to the comments concerning polysemy and monosemy. **1972** HARTMANN & STORK *Dict. Lang. & Linguistics* 144/1 *Monosemy*, when a word or phrase has only one semantic meaning, e.g. *ball-point pen*, as opposed to polysemy or multiple meaning.

monosepalous (mɒnəʊˈsɛpələs), *a.* *Bot.* [f. MONO- + mod.L. *sepal-um* SEPAL + -OUS. In F. *monosépale.*] Properly, Having one lateral sepal only; but commonly misused for *gamosepalous*.

1830 LINDLEY *Nat. Syst. Bot.* Introd. 24 In Scleranthеæ the calyx is always monosepalous. **1837** P. KEITH *Bot. Lex.* s.v., If the calyx of any flower consists merely of a single piece, or sepal, or of several sepals united, it is said to be monosepalous, as in Primula. **1861** BENTLEY *Man. Bot.* 225 When a monosepalous calyx is entire, the number of sepals can then only be ascertained by the venation.

monosexual (mɒnəʊˈsɛksjuːəl), *a.* [f. MONO- + SEXUAL *a.*] Of one sex, or with the attribute of being either male or female; pertaining to one sex exclusively. (See also quot. 1970.)

1964 *Oceanogr. & Marine Biol.* II. 209 Peripheral cells of the adult thallus undergo meiosis and give rise to attached haploid leafy appendages which are monosexual and produce anisogamous male and female gametes respectively. **1966** *Listener* 23 June 918/3 A film whose monosexual character is emphasized by a sound-track which contains only three words.. spoken by a female voice. **1969** *Sunday Times* 31 Aug. 4/7 The £1.8 million belonging to well over half the university's monosexual seats of collegiate learning. **1970** *Diogenes* LXXII. 61 Mono-sexual, in need of no deep or lasting relation with a partner of the opposite sex. **1971** *Guardian* 2 June 9/4 The Edwardian situation in which half the bachelor population were always off doing monosexual Empire-building.

So **ˌmonosexuˈality**, the property or state of being monosexual.

1910 A. A. BRILL tr. *Freud's Three Contributions to Sexual Theory* 7 The conception which we gather from this long known anatomical fact is the original predisposition to bisexuality, which in the course of development has changed to monosexuality, leaving slight remnants of the stunted sex. **1958** B. MAGEE *Go West Young Man* ii. 43 Yale has female graduate students, but no female teachers or undergraduates. This monosexuality is Yale's biggest fault. **1970** *Diogenes* LXXII. 61 In Roman times this monosexuality took the form of imperialistic sex.

monosign (ˈmɒnəʊsaɪn). [f. MONO- + SIGN *sb.*] A 'sign' or word used with only one meaning at a time: opp. PLURISIGN. Hence **monosigˈnation**, **monoˈsignative** *a.*

1940 *Kenyon Rev.* II. 266 The atomic ingredient of literal language is the monosign (called in logic the 'term'); the atomic ingredient of poetic language tends to be the plurisign. *Ibid.*, I am not inquiring whether the ideal of monosignation is ever perfectly realized. *Ibid.* 267 A logician.. requires monosignative clarity. **1949** WELLEK & WARREN *Theory of Lit.* xv. 190 Instead of aiming at a system of abstractions consistently expressed by a system of monosigns, poetry organizes a unique, unrepeatable pattern of words, each an object as well as a sign. **1954** P. WHEELWRIGHT *Burning Fountain* 378 The plurisign is.. distinguished from the monosign, or steno-term. **1965** *Encycl. Poetry* 760/1 The depth symbol.. defies any adequate analysis into monosignative components.

monosigˈnificant, *a.* [f. MONO- + SIGNIFICANT *a.*] Having only one meaning. Also **monosigˈnificance**.

1940 *Kenyon Rev.* II. 503 *Monosignificance*. Mr. Wheelwright uses.. in two ways, as formal logical abstraction.. and as a useful temporarily consistent selection. *Ibid.* 505 If.. words are not statically and isolatedly monosignificant in the prose of science and instruction, what better sense can be made of.. the realm of poetry—connotation—plurisignification. **1947** H. JACOB *Planned Auxiliary Lang.* 20 A high degree of precision.. can be attained by assigning to each element one invariable meaning, *i.e.*, each element is monosignificant. *Ibid.*, No language.. has so far achieved absolute monosignificance... The principle of monosignificance is.. understood to apply to the smallest but complete unit of thought, the sentence.

monoˈsilicate. *Chem.* [MONO- 2.] A silicate containing one equivalent of silicic anhydride.

1857 MILLER *Elem. Chem.* (1862) III. 198 Monosilicate of ethyl.

monosiphonous (mɒnəʊˈsaɪfənəs), *a.* *Bot.* [f. Gr. μόνο-ς MONO- + σίφων tube, pipe (SIPHON) + -OUS.] Having a single siphon; applied to certain Algæ (*Florideæ*) in which a transverse section of the frond shows only a single large, elongated central cell or siphon not surrounded by smaller similar cells. So **monosiphonic** (-saɪˈfɒnɪk) *a.*

1853 HARVEY *Nereis Boreali-Amer.* II. 8, IX. Wrangeliaceæ. Frond filiform, monosiphonous. **1857** BERKELEY *Cryptog. Bot.* §133 Of those green Algae which are masked by calcareous matter, there are two series distinguished by their monosiphonous or polysiphonous stems. **1888** VINES in *Encycl. Brit.* XXIV. 126/2 The filaments [of the *Phæosporeæ*] may consist of single rows of cells (*monosiphonous*), as in most *Ectocarpeæ*, or of several rows of cells (*polysiphonous*), as in the *Mesoglæaceæ*. **1900** B. D. JACKSON *Gloss. Bot. Terms, Monosiphonic.*

‖**monosis** (mɒˈnəʊsɪs). *Bot.* [mod.L., a. Gr. μόνωσις solitariness, singleness, f. μονοῦν to make single or solitary, f. μόνο-ς single.] The isolation of an organ from the rest. (Cf. MONOSY.)

1873 COOKE *Man. Bot. Terms* (ed. 2) 73. **1874** R. BROWN *Man. Bot.* 609.

mono-ski (ˈmɒnəʊskiː). [f. MONO- + SKI *sb.*] A ski on which a person can stand with both feet. Hence as *v. intr.*, to use mono-skis; **ˈmono-skier**, one who uses mono-skis.

1953 *Austrian Information* (U.S.) 3 Jan. 9/2 Monoskis are at present being displayed in Viennese sporting goods stores. They are single skis on which beginners or below-average skiers can stand with both feet. **1963** *Water Skier* Spring 12/2 Carry out series of connected virages across wakes on mono ski (feet on front and rear bindings). **1966** *Ibid.* Sept.–Oct. 15/2 Anne and Pat are confident mono-skiers. **1968** A. DIMENT *Gt. Spy Race* viii. 129 It looked.. pretty amateur from the beach. Round here if you can't mono-ski you're not worth watching. **1971** 'D. HALLIDAY' *Dolly & Doctor Bird* xiv. 201 Dolly's launch passed with a man and a girl on monoskis.

monosodic (mɒnəʊˈsəʊdɪk). *a.* *Chem.* [MONO- 2.] Containing one equivalent of sodium.

1873 *Fownes' Chem.* (ed. 11) 333 Monosodic Carbonate. *Ibid.* 340 Monosodic orthophosphate.

So **ˌmono-ˈsodium**, used *attrib.*

1857 MILLER *Elem. Chem.* (1862) III. 250 Mono-sodium glycol. **1929**, etc. [see GLUTAMATE]. **1954** A. WHITE et al. *Princ. Biochem.* xx. 588 Guanine gout has been reported in this species [*sc.* the pig]; this is.. analogous to human gout, in which monosodium urate may accumulate in the cartilages. **1975** *Listener* 14 Aug. 205/1 Cargoes of factory food, bound for the supermarket shelves... 'The Taste of Monosodium Glutamate.'

monosomatic, -ous: see MONO- 1.

monosome (ˈmɒnəsəʊm). *Cytology.* [f. MONO- + -SOME[4].] **1.** A chromosome in a diploid chromosome complement which lacks its homologous partner; a diploid individual having such a chromosome in its complement.

1921 [see *hexasome* s.v. HEXA-]. **1944** *Genetics* XXIX. 232, 16 monosomes and five trisomes were found in the 11 aberrant offspring. **1970** *Caryologia* XXIII. 359 In this paper, we report on the rates of transmission of disomes (21 II), monosomes (20 II + 1 I), double monosomes (19 II + 2 I) and plants carrying isochromosomes and telocentric chromosomes in two aneuploid series of wheat.

2. A single ribosome attached to a molecule of messenger RNA.

1964 HASELKORN & FRIED in *Proc. Nat. Acad. Sci.* LI. 308 In a previous communication we presented evidence indicating that the addition of RNA from turnip yellow mosaic virus (TYMV) to purified *E. coli* ribosomes results in the formation of a complex containing one 70s ribosome and one molecule of RNA. We shall call such complexes monosomes. **1971** *Nature* 10 Sept. 107/2 Most ribosomes appeared as 'free' monosomes, while in the reticular cells most of them were attached to membranes in typical 'polysome' patterns. **1972** *Ibid.* 31 Mar. 237/2 Fig. 1 shows a typical distribution of monosomes and polysomes isolated from non-infected and infected Proctor barley leaves.

monosomic (mɒnəʊˈsəʊmɪk), *a.* (*sb.*) *Cytology.* [f. MONOSOM(E + -IC.] Having or being a diploid chromosome complement in which one (or occas. more than one) chromosome lacks its homologous partner. Hence as *sb.*, a monosomic individual.

1926 *Univ. Calif. Publ. Bot.* XI. 61 This paper is devoted to a second form called 'fluted', which has been found on cytological examination to be a monosomic ($2n - 1$). *Ibid.* 67 Monosomic forms may be used advantageously for a determination of linkage groups. **1932** *Genetics* XVII. 689 Comparatively few investigations have been concerned with a study of monosomics ($2n - 1$ types) and their mode of inheritance. **1957** C. P. SWANSON *Cytol. & Cytogenetics* (1958) vi. 190 Probably the best known monosomic type is the haplo-IV Drosophila. **1961** *Lancet* 23 Sept. 723/2 The normal male is naturally monosomic for the X, and the XO-female can reach maturity in reasonably good health. **1972** *Hereditas* LXX. 132/1 A number of monosomic lines of Chinese Spring were used as pollen parents. **1974** *Nature* 19 Apr. 714/3 Monosomics and trisomics have seldom been developed in the same species.

So ˈ**monosomy**, the character or condition of having a monosomic chromosome complement.
1948 *Nature* 5 June 873/1 Genetical experience shows that, like polyploidy, monosomy and polysomy in a wide range of plants and animals can characterize whole individuals. **1961** *Lancet* 16 Sept. 625/1 Both cases show monosomy and trisomy involving the X chromosome or an autosome of similar size and morphology. **1972** *Science* 5 May 518/3 Not so well documented.. are the occasional observations of monosomy, trisomy and other aneuploidies.

monospasm: see MONO- 1.

monosperm (ˈmɒnəʊspɜːm). *Bot. rare*$^{-0}$. [f. Gr. μόνο-ς MONO- + σπέρμ-α seed, SPERM. Cf. F. *monosperme* (adj.).] A plant having but one seed.
1879 in STORMONTH *Man. Sci. Terms*; and in later Dicts.

monospermal (mɒnəʊˈspɜːməl), *a. Bot. rare.* [Formed as prec. + -AL^{1}.] Having only one seed; monospermous. Also **monoˈspermatous** *a.* [Cf. F. *monospermatique.*]
1856 MAYNE *Expos. Lex., Monospermal, Monospermatous,* having only one seed: one-seeded; both of these terms are used, but the second is the more correct one. **1876** J. H. BALFOUR in *Encycl. Brit.* IV. 151/2 The drupe is a.. monospermal and unilocular indehiscent fruit.

monoˈspermic, *a.* [Formed as prec. + -IC.]
1. *Bot.* = MONOSPERMOUS.
[**1856** MAYNE *Expos. Lex., Monospermicus,* the same as *Monospermus.*] **1891** *Syd. Soc. Lex., Monospermic,* the same as *Monospermatous.*
2. *Phys.* Pertaining to, or affected with, monospermy.
1902 *Webster's Dict., Suppl.* s.v., Monospermic eggs.

monospermous (mɒnəʊˈspɜːməs), *a. Bot.* [Formed as prec. + -OUS.] Having only one seed.
1727 BAILEY (vol. II), *Monospermos* [**1737** *Ibid., Monospermous*], which bears a single Seed to each Flower, as in Valerian, the Marvel of Peru, &c. **1760** J. LEE *Introd. Bot.* I. xv. (1765) 39. **1797** *Encycl. Brit.* (ed. 3) XI. 388/2 There are eight barren stamina, and two monospermous berries [in *Menispermum*]. **1830** LINDLEY *Nat. Syst. Bot.* 8 Bocconia has.. a monospermous capsule. **1861** BENTLEY *Man. Bot.* 336 The pericarp is monospermous.

monospermy (ˈmɒnəʊspɜːmɪ). *Phys.* [After POLYSPERMY (Gr. πολυσπερμία), f. Gr. μόνο-ς MONO- + σπέρμα seed. Cf. F. *monospermie.*] Impregnation of an ovum by a single spermatozoon; opposed to *polyspermy.*
1902 in *Webster's Dict., Suppl.*

monospherical (mɒnəʊˈsfɛrɪkəl), *a. rare*$^{-0}$. [f. Gr. μόνο-ς MONO- + σφαῖρ-α sphere + -ICAL.] Consisting of or having a single sphere.
1775 in ASH. **1836** in SMART; and in recent Dicts.

monospondylic (ˌmɒnəʊspɒnˈdɪlɪk), *a.* [f. Gr. μόνο-ς MONO- + σπόνδυλ-ος (Attic σφόνδυλος) vertebra + -IC: see SPONDYLE.] Having a single centrum, as a vertebra; without intercentra, as a vertebral column.
1884 RYDER in *Rep. U.S. Fish. Comm.* 983 The caudal part of the axial column may be perfectly monospondylic.

‖**monosporangium** (ˌmɒnəʊspɒˈrændʒɪəm). *Bot.* [mod.L., f. MONO- + SPORANGIUM.] A sporangium containing or bearing monospores.
1892 *Jrnl. Quekett Microsc. Club* July 25 The monosporangia are terminal, on one- or two-celled branches. **1900** B. D. JACKSON *Gloss. Bot. Terms, Monosporangium,* used by Sauvageau for the organ which produces monospores.

monospore (ˈmɒnəʊspɔə(r)). *Bot.* [f. MONO- + SPORE.] An undivided spore, as in some of the lower Algæ.
1892 *Jrnl. Quekett Microsc. Club* July 24 Their neutral organs are undivided, *i.e.* they are monospores. **1900** B. D. JACKSON *Gloss. Bot. Terms, Monospore,* a special spore in *Ectocarpus,* by Sauvageau considered to be a *Gemma.*

monospored (ˈmɒnəʊspɔəd), *a. Bot.* [f. MONO- + SPORE + ED^{2}. Cf. F. *monosporé.*] = MONOSPOROUS.
1882 J. M. CROMBIE in *Encycl. Brit.* XIV. 555/1 Monospored species.

monosporiferous (ˌmɒnəʊspɒˈrɪfərəs), *a. Bot.* [f. MONOSPORE + -(I)FEROUS.] Bearing monospores.
1892 *Jrnl. Quekett Microsc. Club* July 24 There was ample material for learning the true characters of the epiphyte in all stages of the neutral or monosporiferous state.

monosporogony (ˌmɒnəʊspɒˈrɒgənɪ). [f. Gr. μόνο-ς MONO- + σπόρο-ς sowing, seed + -γονία begetting.] (See quot.)
1891 *Syd. Soc. Lex., Monosporogony,* the form of asexual reproduction in which a single cell detaches itself from the adjoining cells of an organism, increases by division, and forms a multicellular organism.

monosporous (mɒnəʊˈspɔərəs, məˈnɒspərəs), *a. Bot.* [f. Gr. μόνο-ς MONO- + σπόρ-ος SPORE + -OUS.] Having but a single spore.
1856 MAYNE *Expos. Lex., Monosporus,* applied to any concepticle of a cryptogamious plant which contains but a single sporule: monosporous. **1874** COOKE *Fungi* 26 M. Sévéillé was of opinion that the basidia of the Tremelli were monosporous. *Ibid.* 145 Each of them [*sc.* these tubes] very soon emits four monosporous spicules.

monostable (ˈmɒnəʊsteɪb(ə)l), *a. Electronics.* [f. MONO- + STABLE *a.*] Stable in one position or state only; characteristic of a device with this property.
1952 [see ASTABLE *a.*]. **1966** *McGraw-Hill Encycl. Sci. & Technol.* VIII. 631/2 The monostable multivibrator has frequent application in electronic circuits where timing and gating operations are required. **1974** LONG & EVANS *Electronic Princ. & Circuits* xiii. 346 Monostable and bi-stable circuits require a triggering source in order for switching to take place.

monostach, etc.: see MONO- 1.

monostearin (mɒnəʊˈstiːərɪn). *Chem.* [MONO- 2.] That species of stearine formed from glycerin by the replacement by stearyl of one only of the three OH groups.
1854 *Fownes' Chem.* (ed. 5) 599 Three compounds of stearic acid with glycerin have been thus produced, which M. Berthelot distinguishes as monostearin, bistearin, and tetrastearin. **1879** C. R. A. WRIGHT in *Encycl. Brit.* X. 697/2 The process of saponification may be viewed as the gradual progressive transformation of tristearin.. into distearin, monostearin, and glycerin.

monostele (ˈmɒnəʊstiːl). *Bot.* [f. Gr. μόνο-ς MONO- + στήλη block of stone, slab: see STELE.] A single axial cylinder of tissue in certain plants. So **monoˈstelic** *a.* Also **monoˈstely** (see quot.) and **monoˈstelous** *a.*
1900 B. D. JACKSON *Gloss. Bot. Terms, Monostelic,* having a single axial cylinder of tissue, in which the vascular tissue is developed. *Ibid., Monostely,* the state of having a single stele; adj. *monostelous.* **1902** *Encycl. Brit.* XXV. 412/2 *margin,* Arrangement in strands: the cylinder or monostele.

monostich (ˈmɒnəʊstɪk), *sb. Pros.* Forms: 7–8 **monostick**, 7– **monostich**. Also 6, 8 in Gr. form **monostichon**. [ad. late L. *monostich-um, monostich-ium* (Ausonius), a. Gr. μονόστιχον, neut. of μονόστιχος adj. consisting of one verse, f. μόνο-ς MONO- + στίχος row, line, or verse. Cf. F. *monostique* adj. (*a* 1382 in Du Cange) and sb.] A poem or epigram consisting of but one metrical line.
1577 KENDALL *Flowers of Epigr.* 104 b, This Monostichon here followyng, was written vpon the gate of the Monestarie of the Benedictines. **1607** J. CARPENTER *Plaine Mans Plough* 38 [The seven works of mercy] aptly comprehended in this Monostich. *Visito, poto, cibo, redimo, tego, colligo, condo.* **1693** J. H. tr. *Juvenal* x. Ep. Ded. 3, I know not whether you have ever met with the following Monostick. **1708** *Brit. Apollo* No. 47. 1/1 That Celebrated Monostick, The Bashful Water saw her God, and Blusht. **1721** BAILEY, *Monostichon,* an Epigram consisting of one single Verse. **1871** BROWNING *Balaust.* 169 Who could speak A chorus to the end, or prologize,.. Or thrust and parry in bright monostich. **1891** DRIVER *Introd. Lit. O.T.* (1892) 342 Single lines or monostichs: these are found but rarely.

monostich (ˈmɒnəʊstɪk), *a.* Also 7 **monostick**, 9 (sense 2) **monostic**. [a. Gr. μονόστιχος (see prec.); in sense 2 a. F. *monostique* (Haüy).]
1. *Pros.* Consisting of a single line of verse.
1656 BLOUNT *Glossogr., Monostick, (monostichon)* that which consists of one onely verse. **1895** W. R. W. STEPHENS *Life & Lett. Freeman* I. 37 It contains monostich passages.
†**2.** *Min.* = MONOSTICHOUS 1. *Obs.*
1805–17 R. JAMESON *Char. Min.* (ed. 3) 211 Monostic topaz.. is a slightly oblique eight sided prism, in which two and two lateral planes meet under very obtuse angles.

monostichous (məˈnɒstɪkəs), *a.* [f. Gr. μόνο-ς MONO- + στίχ-ος row, line + -OUS.]
1. *Min.* (See quot.) Cf. MONOSTICH *a.* 2.
1856 MAYNE *Expos. Lex., Monostichous,* applied by Haüy to a variety of the prism, the base of which is surrounded with facets which have different inclinations, as the *Yenites monosticha*: monostichous.
2. *Bot.* Arranged in a single vertical row, rank, or series, on one side of an axis, as the flowers in certain grasses. (Opposed to *distichous.*)
1866 *Treas. Bot., Monostichous,* arranged in one row. **1900** B. D. JACKSON *Gloss. Bot. Terms.*
3. *Zool.* Consisting of a single layer or row.
1883 LANKESTER & BOURNE in *Q. Jrnl. Microsc. Sci.* XXIII. 195 These may be called respectively Monostichous and Diplostichous eyes. **1888** ROLLESTON & JACKSON *Anim. Life* 492 (*Arthropoda*) The hypodermic cells beneath the thickened cuticle constitute the *ommateum,* and remain either in a single or form a double layer; hence mono- or diplo-stichous. The monostichous ommateum is said to be apostatic when cup-shaped. *Ibid.* 525 All the eyes of *Limulus* are monostichous. **1902** E. R. LANKESTER in *Encycl. Brit.* XXV. 697/2 The monomeniscous eye is rarely provided with a single layer of cells beneath its lens, when it is so, it is called monostichous.

monostigmatous: see MONO- 1.

monostomatous (mɒnəʊˈstɒmətəs), *a. Zool.* [f. Gr. μόνο-ς MONO- + στοματ-, στόμα mouth + -OUS: cf. next.] Having only one mouth or sucker; *spec.* of or pertaining to the *Monostomata,* the higher of the two main divisions of the *Metazoa,* including all metazoans (with a single oral aperture) except the sponges or *Polystomata.* Opposed to *polystomatous.*
In recent Dicts.

monostome (ˈmɒnəʊstəʊm), *a.* and *sb.* [a. F. *monostome* (Littré), ad. Gr. μονόστομ-ος with one mouth, f. μόνο-ς MONO- + στόμα mouth.]
a. *adj.* Having only one mouth or sucker. **b.** *sb.* An animal having only one mouth or sucker, as a metazoan, or a parasitic trematode worm of the genus *Monostomum* or family *Monostomidæ.* So **moˈnostomous** *a.* [f. Gr. μονόστομ-ος + -OUS], having only one mouth; monostomatous.
1848 E. FORBES *Naked-eyed Medusæ* 80 Brandt.. divided the *Discophoræ* into Monostomous and Polystomous. **1849** HUXLEY in *Phil. Trans.* CXXXIX. 426 The stomachal membrane of the Monostome Medusæ. **1856** MAYNE *Expos. Lex., Monostomus,* having but one mouth, or opening: monostomous. **1860** COBBOLD in *Jrnl. Linn. Soc.* (1861) V. 38 The absence, however, of a ventral sucker.. points to a closer alliance with the Monostomes.

monostrophe (ˈmɒnəʊstrəʊf). *Pros.* [ad. Gr. μονόστροφ-ος adj., f. μόνο-ς MONO- + στροφ-ή recurring metrical scheme, STROPHE.] A poem in which one strophic arrangement is repeated throughout.
1890 in *Century Dict.*

monostrophic (mɒnəʊˈstrɒfɪk), *a.* (and *sb.*) *Pros.* [ad. Gr. μονοστροφικ-ός, f. μονόστροφ-ος: see MONOSTROPHE and -IC.] **A.** *adj.* Consisting of repetitions of one and the same strophic arrangement.
1671 MILTON *Samson* Pref., The measure of Verse us'd in the Chorus is of all sorts, call'd by the Greeks Monostrophic, or rather Apolelymenon, without regard had to Strophe, Antistrophe or Epod. **1788** [CUMBERLAND] *Observer* No. 111. IV. 158 By making his Chorus monostrophic, he has robbed it of that lyric beauty, which [etc.]. **1847** GROTE *Greece* II. xxix. (1862) IV. 119 Until this time [600 B C.] the song had been monostrophic, consisting of nothing more than one uniform stanza, repeated from the beginning to the end of the composition. **1849** J. W. DONALDSON *Theat. Grks.* I. ii. (ed. 6) 27 The Dithyramb of Lasus eventually became monostrophic.
B. *sb. pl.* Monostrophic verses.
1784 G. I. HUNTINGFORD (*title*) An Apology for the Monostrophics which were published in 1782. With a second collection of Monostrophics. **1785** COWPER *Let. to Unwin* 22 Oct., Wks. 1836 V. 169 Huntingford's Monostrophics.

monostyle (ˈmɒnəʊstaɪl), *a.*^{1} *Arch.* [f. MONO- + STYLE^{1}.] Built in one style throughout.
1850 PARKER *Gloss. Archit.* (ed. 5) I. 308.

ˈ**monostyle**, *a.*^{2} *Arch.* [f. Gr. μόνο-ς MONO- + στῦλ-ος pillar: see STYLE^{2}.] Having or consisting of a single shaft, pillar, or column. So **monoˈstylar** *a.*
1844 *Civil Eng. & Arch. Jrnl.* VII. 10/1 We question whether any more monostylar monuments, supporting nothing, will be erected for some time. **1850** PARKER *Gloss. Archit.* (ed. 5) I. 308 Monostyle.

monostylous: see MONO- 1.

mono-substitution: see MONO- 2.

monosulphide (mɒnəʊˈsʌlfaɪd). *Chem.* [MONO- 2.] A sulphide containing one equivalent of sulphur. Also †**monoˈsulphuret**, in the same sense. Also **monoˈsulphite**, a sulphite containing one equivalent of sulphurous acid.
1854 J. SCOFFERN in *Orr's Circ. Sci., Chem.* 408 Two compounds of sulphurous acid with soda are known—the monosulphite and the bisulphite. *Ibid.* 411 The monosulphuret or monosulphide of potassium.

‖**monosy** (ˈmɒnəʊsɪ). *Bot.* [a. F. *monosie* (Morren), f. Gr. μόνωσις: see MONOSIS.] (See quots.)
1869 M. T. MASTERS *Veget. Terat.* 58 The late Professor Morren proposed the general term Monosy for all these cases of abnormal isolation. **1900** B. D. JACKSON *Gloss. Bot. Terms, Monosy,* Morren's term for the abnormal isolation of parts due to (*a*) *Adesmy* or (*b*) *Dialysis.*

†**monosyllabe**. *Obs.* [a. F. *monosyllabe* or ad. late L. MONOSYLLABON.] = MONOSYLLABLE *sb.*
1585 JAS. I *Ess. Poesie* (Arb.) 59 Gif ȝour Sectioun be nocht.. a monosyllabe.

monosyllabic (ˌmɒnəʊsɪˈlæbɪk), *a.* [ad. med.L. *monosyllabic-us* (R. Bacon 1271), f. late L. *monosyllab-us* = Gr. μονοσύλλαβος: see MONOSYLLABON. Cf. F. *monosyllabique* (1752 in Hatz.-Darm.).]
1. Of a word: Consisting of one syllable.
1828–32 WEBSTER, *Monosyllabic,* 1. Consisting of one syllable; as, a monosyllabic word. **1845** STODDART *Gram.* in *Encycl. Metrop.* I. 151/1 A short monosyllabic preposition. **1906** *Athenæum* 12 May 575/1 Monosyllabic roots.
2. Consisting of monosyllables or of a monosyllable. (Cf. MONOSYLLABLE *sb.* c.)
1828–32 WEBSTER, *Monosyllabic,*.. 2. Consisting of words of one syllable; as, a monosyllabic verse. **1838** DICKENS *Nich. Nick.* xvi, The same gentleman.. again made a monosyllabic demonstration, by growling out 'Resign!' **1866** GEO. ELIOT *F. Holt* Introd., Throwing out a monosyllabic hint to his cattle. **1872** ATKINSON tr. *Ganot's*

Nat. Philos. §161 A person speaking with a loud voice in front of a reflecting surface at the distance of 112·5 feet can only distinguish the last reflected syllable: such an echo is said to be monosyllabic. **1877** DOWDEN *Shaks. Prim.* iv. 41 The appearance in Shakespere's verse of weak monosyllabic endings. **1899** *Allbutt's Syst. Med.* VIII. 367 The speech is often monosyllabic, a whispered monotone.

b. *Philol.* Used as the distinctive epithet of those languages (e.g. Chinese) which have a vocabulary wholly composed of monosyllables.

1824 *Crit. Res. in Philol. & Geol.* 172 The Chinese, and other monosyllabic tongues. **1875** WHITNEY *Life Lang.* xii. 239 If we met with monosyllabic tongues in different parts of the earth, we should have no right to infer their connection.

3. Of a person: Uttering only monosyllables.

1870 DISRAELI *Lothair* viii, Lothair was somewhat monosyllabic and absent. **1892** MRS. H. WARD *D. Grieve* I. viii, Mr. Ancrum..had been cheered a little during his last days at Clough End by the appearance of David, very red and monosyllabic, on his doorstep.

†**monosy'llabical**, *a. Obs. rare.* [Formed as prec. + -AL[1].] = MONOSYLLABIC.

1686 *Phil. Trans.* XVI. 63 A Monosyllabical Name. **1755** JOHNSON, *Monosyllabical*, consisting of words of one syllable. **1776** —— in Boswell *Life* 22 Mar., He is quite unsocial; his conversation is quite monosyllabical.

monosyllabically (ˌmɒnəʊsɪ'læbɪkəlɪ), *adv.* [f. MONOSYLLABICAL + -LY[2].] In a monosyllable or monosyllables.

1816 COLERIDGE *Lett.* (1895) 664 Which I know to be (monosyllabically speaking) a lie. **1821** LAMB *Elia* Ser. I. *My First Play, Vice versâ*..in his own peculiar pronunciation monosyllabically elaborated, or Anglicised, into something like *verse verse*. **1882** SALA *Amer. Revis.* ix. (1885) 118 He became responsive, but only monosyllabically so. **1904** *Daily Chron.* 1 June 6/7 Hone wrote of 'cabs' monosyllabically in 1827.

monosyllabicity (mɒnəʊsɪlə'bɪsɪtɪ). [f. MONOSYLLAB(LE *sb.* + -ICITY.]

= MONOSYLLABISM. Also **monosyllabi'cation**.

1951 N. C. BODMAN in *Language* XXVII. 205 There has been no change..in the monosyllabicity of the Chinese morpheme from the most ancient times that we know of to the present. **1956** J. WHATMOUGH *Language* iii. 42 The ideal seems to be..somewhere between the extremes of monosyllabication and polysynthesis. **1957** *Archivum Linguisticum* IX. 73 Grappin might have mentioned..the monosyllabicity of *bóbr*. **1968** *Language* XLIV. 131 The simultaneous trend toward polysyllabic creations in pseudo-scientific language and monosyllabicity (*the mods, the frug*).

monosyllabism (mɒnəʊ'sɪləbɪz(ə)m). [Formed as MONOSYLLABE + -ISM. Cf. F. *monosyllabisme*.] Addiction to the use of monosyllables; the quality of being monosyllabic.

1804 MITFORD *Inquiry* 414 In the spirited and easy flow of that line thus, its monosyllabism is apt to escape the ear's notice. **1824** *New Monthly Mag.* XII. 198 The rounded and sonorous Italian enunciation does not admit of being despatched in the snip-snap articulation compatible with the monosyllabism of our own language. **1885** *Encycl. Brit.* XVIII. 774/2 Which..brought back so considerable a part of the vocabulary to monosyllabism.

b. *spec.* in *Philology.* (See MONOSYLLABIC 2 b.)

1846 WORCESTER (cites *Ec. Rev.*). **1860** FARRAR *Orig. Lang.* 183 It should be observed that triliteralism is not necessarily incompatible with monosyllabism. **1896** A. H. KEANE *Ethnol.* 208 Monosyllabism is thus shown to be, not the first but the last stage in the evolution of human speech.

monosyllabize (mɒnəʊ'sɪləbaɪz), *v.* [Formed as prec. + -IZE.] *trans.* To render monosyllabic. Hence **mono'syllabizing** *vbl. sb.*

1857 *Zoologist* Ser. I. XV. 5692 The English love for monosyllabizing. **1904** *Speaker* 4 June 229/1 This monosyllabising of the language.

monosyllable (mɒnəʊ'sɪləb(ə)l), *sb.* and *a.* Also 6 monosillable, 6–7 **monasyllable, -sillable,** 7 **monesyllable, -sillible.** [ad. late L. *monosyllabus* (see MONOSYLLABON) after SYLLABLE.]

A. *sb.* A word of one syllable.

1533 MORE *Debell. Salem* Wks. 956/1 He forgetteth thys lyttle shorte woorde, thys monasyllable, Such, which he rehearsed first. **1589** PUTTENHAM *Eng. Poesie* II. v[i]. (Arb.) 90 For this purpose serue the monosillables of our English Saxons excellently well. **1607** TOPSELL *Four-f. Beasts* (1658) 324 The French men call it 'furchette'; which word our farriers.. do make it a monosyllable, and pronounce it the 'frush'. **1620** DONNE *Serm.* lxxiv. (1640) 753 This one little particle, this monasyllable, So. **1638** SIR T. HERBERT *Trav.* (ed. 2) 339 Their language is most part of monosyllables. **1647** WARD *Simp. Cobler* (1843) 86 Some are raking in old musty Charnel books, for old mouldy monesyllables. **1680** MORDEN *Geog. Rect., China* (1685) 418 They have above 60,000 Letters but not above 300 Words, which are, for the most part, all Monasillables. **1692** DRYDEN *Cleomenes* II. i. 14 By Heav'n, I'll change it [my name] into Jove or Mars! Or any other civil Monosyllable, That will not tire my Hand. **1711** J. GREENWOOD *Eng. Gram.* 181 Almost all the Original Words of our Language are Monosyllables. **1751** JOHNSON *Rambler* No. 88 ¶4 It is pronounced by Dryden, that a line of monosyllables is almost always harsh. **1906** J. OMAN *Probl. Faith & Freedom* iii. 101 To perpetrate ten monosyllables in succession was a high offence.

b. Phrase, ***in monosyllables***, †***in monosyllable***.

1570–6 LAMBARDE *Peramb. Kent* (1826) 233 Erasmus compareth the English toong to a Dog's barking that soundeth nothing els but Baw waw waw in Monosillable. **1888** C. MORRIS *Aryan Race* viii. 190 Philologists are generally satisfied that man first spoke in monosyllables, each of which conveyed some generalized information.

c. Often used to indicate some emphatic word (esp. *yes* or *no*), which is sometimes intentionally left unnamed. ***to speak*** **(*answer*,** etc.) ***in monosyllables***: to speak with intentional curtness; to answer little but 'yes' or 'no'.

1608 DEKKER *Lanth. & Candle-Lt.* i. A, She dealt in nothing but in Monosyllables, (as if to haue spoken words of greater length would haue crackt her Voice). **1679** DRYDEN *Tr. & Cr.* II. iii, *Achil.* I can brook no comparisons. *Ajax.* Nor I. *Achil.* Well, Ajax. *Ajax.* Well, Achilles. *Thers.* So, now they quarrel in monosyllables. **1824** MISS MITFORD *Village* Ser. I. 20 A low soft voice, sweet even in its monosyllables. **1833** L. RITCHIE *Wand. by Loire* 165 Her reply was conveyed in a monosyllable. **1865** TROLLOPE *Belton Est.* v, 'No'. She pronounced the monosyllable alone. **1885** 'E. GARRETT' *At Any Cost* vi. 104 He..remembered her only as a gaunt, black-eyed girl, who answered in monosyllables. **1903** *Longm. Mag.* Sept. 291 Juliet leant back in her corner responding by an occasional monosyllable.

B. *adj.* **1.** = MONOSYLLABIC *a.* 1. Now *rare.*

1589 PUTTENHAM *Eng. Poesie* II. vi[i]. (Arb.) 92 Words monosillable which be for the more part our naturall Saxon English. **1640** TORRIANO *Ital. Tutor* title-p., A display of the monasillable particles of the Language, by way of Alphabet. **1656** BLOUNT *Glossogr.*, *Monasyllable*, that hath but one syllable. **1658** PHILLIPS Pref., Pronouns, and Monosyllable Verbs, as *Mine, Thine, This, What, Love, Give.* **1676** MARVELL *Mr. Smirke* 43 The Gentleman's name..is the Monosyllable voice with which Cats do usually address themselves to us. *c* **1790** COWPER *Wks.* (1837) XV. 320 [He] would think the line improved by a monosyllable epithet, which would make it run more smoothly.

2. = MONOSYLLABIC *a.* 2. *rare.*

1697 DRYDEN *Æneid* Ded. (e) 4 b, It seldom happens but a Monosyllable Line turns Verse to Prose. **1706** POPE *Let. to Walsh* 22 Oct., Monosyllable-lines, unless artfully managed, are stiff or languishing; but may be beautiful to express Melancholy. **1821** BYRON *Juan* v. liii, Others in monosyllable talk chatted.

mono'syllable, *v. rare.* [f. MONOSYLLABLE *sb.*] *trans.* To reduce to a monosyllable.

a **1647** CLEVELAND *Smectymnuus* 46 Like to nine Taylors, who if rightly spell'd, Into one man are monosyllabled.

mono'syllabled, *a. rare.* [f. MONOSYLLABLE *sb.* + -ED[2].] = MONOSYLLABIC *a.* 3.

1838 I. TAYLOR *Home Educ.* 131 A monosyllabled stanza.

‖**mono'syllabon.** *Obs.* Pl. **-syllaba.** [L. *monosyllabon*, a. Gr. *μονοσύλλαβον*, neuter of *μονοσύλλαβος* adj., f. *μόνο-ς* MONO- + *συλλαβ-ή* SYLLABLE.] A monosyllable.

1576 GASCOIGNE *Steele Gl.* (Arb.) 77 That Grammer grudge not at our English tong, Bycause it stands by Monosyllaba, And cannot be declined as others are. **1580** G. HARVEY *Three Proper Lett.* 55 You shal as well..heare *fayer* as *faire*,..wyth an infinyte companye of the same sort: sometime Monosyllaba, sometime Polysyllaba. **1608** MIDDLETON *Fam. Love* V. iii, I will onely in Monosillaba aunswere for my selfe. **1672** H. MORE *Brief Reply* 102 It was a great oversight..to leave out that Monosyllabon which was of such principal signification in the sentence. **1716** M. DAVIES *Athen. Brit.* II. 299 No Laconick Monosyllabon.

monosyllogism (mɒnəʊ'sɪlədʒɪz(ə)m). [f. MONO- + SYLLOGISM.] (See quot.) So **monosyllo'gistic** *a.*

1838 SIR W. HAMILTON *Logic* xix. (1860) I. 363 A syllogism, viewed as an isolated and independent whole, is called a Monosyllogism, that is, a single reasoning. *Ibid.* xxvi. II. 44 In respect to the External Form, Probations are Simple or Monosyllogistic, if they consist of a single reasoning.

monosymmetric ('mɒnəʊsɪ'mɛtrɪk), *a.* [f. MONO- + SYMMETRIC.]

a. *Cryst.* = MONOCLINIC.

1880 in WEBSTER *Suppl.* **1887** *Athenæum* 10 Sept. 345/2 [Graphite occurs] in tabular crystals so indistinctly formed as to render it uncertain whether they belong to the hexagonal or monosymmetric system.

b. *Bot.* = next.

1890 in *Century Dict.*

monosy'mmetrical, *a. Bot.* [f. MONO- + SYMMETRICAL.] Of flowers, fruits, etc.: Divisible into exactly similar halves in one plane only.

1875 BENNETT & DYER *Sachs' Bot.* 184 A shoot with alternating leaves in two rows is also simply bilateral without being monosymmetrical. *Ibid.* 533 The happy expression *zygomorphic* already used by Braun may be applied equally to monosymmetrical flowers. **1898** tr. *Strasburger's Text-bk. Bot.* (1903) 16 When..a division into two similar halves is only possible in one plane, the degree of symmetry is indicated by the terms *simply symmetrical, monosymmetrical,* or *zygomorphic.*

Hence **monosy'mmetrically** *adv.*

1875 [see POLYSYMMETRICALLY].

monosymmetry (mɒnəʊ'sɪmɪtrɪ). *Bot.* [f. MONO- + SYMMETRY.] The condition of being monosymmetrical.

1875 BENNETT & DYER *Sachs' Bot.* 183 Monosymmetry is ..a particular case of the ordinary bilateral structure.

monosymptomatic: see MONO- I.

monosystemic (mɒnəʊsɪ'stɛmɪk), *a. Linguistics.* [f. MONO- + SYSTEMIC *a.* 2.] Based on a single system of language analysis.

1949 *Trans. Philol. Soc. 1948* 127 Such studies I should describe as paradigmatic and monosystemic in principle. **1951** *Archivum Linguisticum* III. 130 The structural method still tends to concern itself with units evolved by a monosystemic analysis at the word-level. **1958** J. BERRY in J. A. Fishman *Readings Sociol. of Lang.* (1968) 739 The initial consonant in the Kikuyu word for 'book'..in terms of a monosystemic analysis at any rate is a phoneme contrasting with other ('original') b-sounds..but relatively rare. **1964** R. H. ROBINS *Gen. Linguistics* iv. 158 In this sense phonemic analysis is monosystemic. **1967** F. P. DINNEEN *Introd. Gen. Linguistics* x. 319 The American structuralist approach [is] 'monosystemic', whereas Firth's approach is designed to be 'polysystemic'.

‖**monota** (mɒ'nəʊtə). *Antiq.* Pl. **-tæ.** [mod.L., f. Gr. *μόνωτος* (also *μονούατος*) one-eared, with one handle, f. *μόνο-ς* MONO- + *ὠτ-, οὐατ-, οὖς* ear, handle.] A one-handled vase.

1887 B. V. HEAD *Hist. Numorum* 521 Amphora with small monota beside it.

monotechnic (mɒnəʊ'tɛknɪk), *a.* [f. MONO- + TECHNIC *a.*: after POLYTECHNIC *a.* and *sb.*] Dealing with or providing instruction in a single technical subject; also designating an educational institution providing such instruction. Also *ellipt.* as *sb.*, an institution of this kind.

1904 *Jrnl. Inst. Electr. Engin.* 25 Feb. 458 Many of the American schools of engineering are practically monotechnic institutes in contradistinction to the polytechnics here. **1904** G. S. HALL *Adolescence* I. 170 Thousands of our youth of late have been diverted from secondary schools to the monotechnic or trade classes. **1931** *Times Educ. Suppl.* 15 Aug. 319/4 Some of these schools are in universities, some in schools of art, some in technical colleges and polytechnics, while one forms a monotechnic. **1962** *Technology* Dec. 276 Furniture. Monotechnic... The local College of Further Education is one of only two centres offering a complete course in furniture manufacture. **1967** *Times Rev. Industry* July 82/1 Monotechnic education, all the rage 20 years ago, is out. *Ibid.* 82/3 A comparatively small monotechnic cannot keep pace with all these developments.

monotelephone, -phonic: see MONO- I.

Monotessaron (mɒnəʊ'tɛsərən). [a. med.L. *monotessaron*, f. (erron. after *diatessaron*) Gr. *μόνο-ς* single + *τέσσαρ-ες* four.] A continuous scriptural narrative prepared from a collation of the four Gospels; = DIATESSARON 3.

1831 *T. H. Horne's Introd. to Bible* (U.S. ed.) II. I. xi. 478 (Funk) The importance..of..obtaining the clear amount of their various narratives, has..suggested the plan of digesting the Gospels into..a connected history..termed.. a Monotessaron. **1862** F. BARHAM (*title*) Improved Monotessaron;..combining the words of the Four Gospels. **1882** in OGILVIE.

monothalamic (mɒnəʊθə'læmɪk), *a.* Also incorrectly **-thalmic.** [Formed as next + -IC.]

1. = MONOTHALAMOUS 2.

1845 J. PHILLIPS *Geol.* in *Encycl. Metrop.* VI. 608/2 Monothalamic cephalopoda.

2. *Bot.* Of fruits: Formed from one pistil or flower.

1870 *Henfrey's Elem. Bot.* §255 Fruits may be divided into *free* or *monothalamic fruits*, formed from single flowers, and *confluent fruits*. **1871** MASTERS in *Nature* 2 Nov. 6/2 Classification of Monothalamic Fruits. **1874** R. BROWN *Man. Bot.* 483 Monothalmic Fruits.

b. (See quot.)

1900 B. D. JACKSON *Gloss. Bot. Terms, Monothalamic, monothalamous*, (1) applied to apothecia consisting of a single chamber; (2) when galls consist of only one interior chamber.

monothalamous (mɒnəʊ'θæləməs), *a.* [f. Gr. *μόνο-ς* MONO- + *θάλαμ-ος* bed-chamber (see THALAMUS) + -OUS.] Having only one chamber.

1. *Ent.* (See quot.)

1816 KIRBY & SP. *Entomol.* xiv. (1818) I. 456 The majority of galls are what entomologists have denominated mono-thalamous, or consisting of only one chamber or cell.

2. Applied to the chambered shells of foraminifers and gasteropodous molluscs.

1834 ROGET *Anim. & Veg. Physiol.* I. 265 Some,..as the Argonaut, or Paper Nautilus, have shells undivided by partitions; and are accordingly termed *unilocular* or *monothalamous*. **1835–6** *Todd's Cycl. Anat.* I. 114/1 The surface of the body is..covered with a shell, which is..rarely monothalamous. **1880** W. S. KENT *Infusoria* I. 328 Some Monothalamous Foraminifer such as *Lagena* or *Miliola*. **1888** ROLLESTON & JACKSON *Anim. Life* 875 (*Radiolaria*) The cyrtoid skeleton may be monothalamous..or.. polythalamous.

3. *Bot.* Applied to the apothecia of certain lichens.

a **1886** E. TUCKERMAN (Cent.). **1900** [see MONOTHALAMIC 2 b].

monothallious (mɒnəʊ'θælɪəs), *a. Chem.* [MONO- 2.] Applied to thallious salts which contain one equivalent of thallium.

1868 WATTS *Dict. Chem.* V. 755 The monothallious salt TlH^2PO^4, is formed on mixing the dithallious salt with [etc.]. **1873** *Fownes' Chem.* (ed. 11) 413 Monothallious orthophosphate.

monothalloid (mɒnəʊ'θælɔɪd), *a. Bot.* [f. Gr. *μόνο-ς* MONO- + *θαλλ-ός* (see THALLUS) + -OID.] Having a single or undivided thallus.

1891 in *Syd. Soc. Lex.*

monothamnoid (mɒnəʊˈθæmnɔɪd), *a. Bot.* [f. Gr. μόνο-ς MONO- + θάμν-ος bush, shrub, + -OID.] = MONOTHALLOID.
1891 in *Syd. Soc. Lex.*

monothecal (mɒnəʊˈθiːkəl), *a. Bot.* [f. Gr. μόνο-ς MONO- + θήκ-η case, box + -AL¹.] Having only one loculament or cell: applied to anthers.
1849 BALFOUR *Man. Bot.* §405 Sometimes the anther has a single cavity, and becomes unilocular.., or monothecal. **1880** in WEBSTER *Suppl.*; and in recent Dicts.

monotheism (ˈmɒnəʊθiːɪz(ə)m). [f. Gr. μόνο-ς MONO- + θε-ός god + -ISM. Cf. F. *monothéisme.*] The doctrine or belief that there is only one God.
1660 H. MORE *Myst. Godl.* III. ii. 62 But thus to make the World God, it to make all; and therefore this Kinde of Monotheisme of the Heathen is as rank Atheisme as their Polytheisme was proved to be before. **1736** BAILEY (folio) Pref. (end), *Monotheism*, the Doctrine or Principles of the Unitarians. **1812** COGAN *Jewish Disp.* ii. §7. 322 [The Jews] have continued firm..in their adherence to pure Monotheism, under every persecution. **1865** LECKY *Ration.* (1878) II. 277 A race whose pure monotheism formed a marked contrast to the scarcely disguised polytheism of the Spanish Catholics. **1876** GLADSTONE in *Contemp. Rev.* June 18 The only large monotheism known to historic times is that of Mahomet.

monotheist (ˈmɒnəʊθiːɪst), *sb.* (*a.*) [Formed as prec. + -IST. Cf. F. *monothéiste.*] One who believes in only one God; an adherent of monotheism.
1680 H. MORE *Apocal. Apoc.* 84 They destroy the worship of the Son of God under an ignorant pretence of Monotheisme; whereas the more distinct knowledge of that one God does not make us less Monotheists than they. **1812** COGAN *Jewish Disp.* ii. §7. 321 The general propensity to the worship of Idols was totally subdued; and they became Monotheists in the strictest sense of the term. **1874** MAHAFFY *Soc. Life Greece* xi. 334 Their literary monuments were composed by the cultivated monotheists.
b. *attrib.* or *adj.* = next.
1825 *Gentl. Mag.* XCV. I. 235 Abury..might be a temple of the first, or Monotheist Druids. **1872** BAGEHOT *Physics & Pol.* ii. (1880) 77 The Jews, who were monotheist, were conquered by the Romans who were polytheist. **1875** [see POLYTHEIST b].

monotheistic (ˌmɒnəʊθiːˈɪstɪk), *a.* [f. prec. + -IC: see -ISTIC.] Of, pertaining to, believing in, or characterized by monotheism.
1846 TRENCH *Miracles* Introd. 58 The monotheistic religion of the Jews. **1871** C. HODGE *Syst. Theol.* I. I. iii. 243 There are monotheistic hymns in the Vedas. **1900** SAYCE *Babylon. & Assyr.* xi. 262 A monotheistic school actually existed in one of the literary circles of Babylonia.
So **monotheˈistical** *a.* = MONOTHEISTIC; hence **monotheˈistically** *adv.*, in a monotheistic manner.
1877 T. SINCLAIR *Mount* (1878) 81 The severe monotheistical spirit. **1905** J. ORR *Probl. O.T.* iv. 93 They [the patriarchs] thought and spoke monotheistically.

Monothelete (məˈnɒθɪliːt). *Theol.* A more correctly etymological form of MONOTHELITE. So ˌ**Monotheˈletian**, **Monotheˈletic** *adjs.*; **Monoˈtheletism**.
1850 NEALE *Hymns East. Ch.* 33 He [S. Germanus] might be the more favourably disposed to Monotheletism, because he had been so deeply injured by its great opponent, Pogonatus. **1880** T. M. LINDSAY in *Encycl. Brit.* XI. 156/1 The Monotheletes refused to submit. **1887** HEARD *Russian Ch.* i. 2 The monotheletian patriarchs and the dyotheletian popes mutually anathematized each other. **1885** SCHAFF *Hist. Church, Mediæval Christ.* §110. 490 The Monotheletic or one-will controversy.

monothelious: see MONO- I.

Monothelism (məˈnɒθɪlɪz(ə)m). *rare.* [f. MONOTHEL(ITE) + -ISM. Cf. F. *monothélisme.*] = MONOTHELITISM.
1685 LOVELL *Gen. Hist. Relig.* 132 They who look upon Monothelism as an Heresie, ought [etc.]. **1856** J. C. ROBERTSON *Hist. Chr. Ch., 2nd Period* 39 He..agreed with him..in a personal profession of Monothelism.

Monothelite (məˈnɒθɪlaɪt), *sb.* and *a.* Also 6, 8 -it; in blundered forms 5 **Monachalite, Monalechite, 7 Monotholite**; cf. MONOTHELETE. [ad. med.L. *monothelīta*, ad. (with assimilation to *-īta* -ITE¹) late Gr. μονοθελήτης (7th c.), f. Gr. μόνο-ς single + θελητής, agent-n. from θέλ-ειν to will. Cf. F. *monothélite.*] **A.** *sb.* An adherent of the heretical sect (founded in the 7th c.) which maintained that Christ has only one will.
1430–40 LYDG. *Bochas* IX. iv. (1558) 23 Of a secte called Monacholites. **1460** CAPGRAVE *Chron.* (Rolls) 96 His [*sc.* Eraclius] heresie, whech thei clepid Monalechites. *c* **1559** R. HALL *Life Fisher* in *F.'s Wks.* (E.E.T.S.) II. 135 Agatho against the monothelits. **1597** HOOKER *Eccl. Pol.* v. xlviii. §9 The Church hath of old condemned Monothelites as Heretiques, for holding that Christ had but one will. **1615** SIR E. HOBY *Curry-combe* iv. 174 You haue heard that Honorius the first was a Monotholite. **1638** SIR T. HERBERT *Trav.* (ed. 2) 161 They professe Christianity taught them erroniously by Jacobus the Syrian Monothelite. **1716** Monothelit [see MONOTHELITIC *a.*]. **1856** J. C. ROBERTSON *Hist. Chr. Ch., 2nd Period* 67 Wilfrid.. was invited to take a place in the council against the Monothelites.
allusively. **1652** *Observ. Forms Govt.* 16 It is nothing else but a Monarchy of Monothelites, or of many men of one will most commonly in one point onely.
B. *adj.* Of or pertaining to the Monothelites or their doctrine.
1619 PURCHAS *Microcosmus* lxix. 695 The Maronites.. maintaine the Monothelite Heresie. **1680** BAXTER *Answ. Stillingfl.* xxxviii. 64 So were the Orthodox under the Nestorian, Eutychian, Monothelite,..Princes. **1788** GIBBON *Decl. & F.* xlvii. IV. 589 *note*, The Monothelite monk. **1840** W. PALMER *Eccl. Hist.* vii. 73 Honorius [bishop] of Rome sanctioned the Monothelite heresy. **1856** J. C. ROBERTSON *Hist. Chr. Ch., 2nd Period* 55 The Monothelite controversy for a time weakened the influence of Rome.

Monothelitic (mɒnɒθɪˈlɪtɪk), *a.* Cf. MONOTHELETIC. [f. prec. + -IC.] = MONOTHELITE *a.*
1716 M. DAVIES *Athen. Brit.* II. 290 The Emperor Constans the 2d, that he might the better execute his Monothelitick Principles of Arian Prosecution, he pretended to impose Silence on the Heterodox Monothelits. **1854** MILMAN *Lat. Chr.* II. 126 Severinus..repudiated the Monothelitic doctrine. **1882–3** *Schaff's Encycl. Relig. Knowl.* II. 1192 The Monothelitic confession of the Patriarch Sergius.

Monothelitism (məˈnɒθɪlaɪtɪz(ə)m). See also MONOTHELETISM. [f. MONOTHELITE + -ISM.] The doctrine of the Monothelites.
1765 MACLAINE tr. *Mosheim's Eccl. Hist.* VII. II v. §5 The doctrine of Monothelitism. *a* **1861** CUNNINGHAM *Hist. Theol.* (1864) I. xi. 328 Honorius advocated Monothelitism. **1882–3** *Schaff's Encycl. Relig. Knowl.* I. 457 Monothelitism continued among the Maronites on Mount Lebanon.

monothematic (mɒnəʊθɪˈmætɪk), *a.* [f. MONO- + THEMATIC *a.*] Having a single dominant theme or element, *spec.* in *Mus.* So **monoˈthematism**.
1886 F. PRAEGER tr. *Naumann's Hist. Mus.* II. 1188 The employment of *leit-motiv*..is nothing but a return to monothematism. **1907** R. BOUGHTON *Bach* 15 Monothematic music in polyphonic style was bound to result in a fugue. **1934** C. LAMBERT *Music Ho!* v. 326 The work is entirely monothematic, and..should be regarded as a continuation of the formal principles first evolved by Liszt. **1958** *Times* 13 Sept. 10/4 The basically monothematic nature of the opening movement is unusual in a symphony. **1961** *Times* 2 Nov. 16/3 Edwin Muir, a dour, almost monothematic poet. **1962** H. R. LOYN *Anglo-Saxon Eng.* iii. 125 These names are often..dithematic such as Wulfbold, Wulfhere, Leofric, and the like rather than monothematic.

monothetic: see MONO- I.

monothionic (mɒnəʊθaɪˈɒnɪk), *a. Chem.* [See MONO- 2 and DITHIONIC.] In ***monothionic acid***, a very unstable fluid, H_2SO_2, obtained by the action of diluted sulphuric acid on iron or zinc, with exclusion of air.
1891 in *Syd. Soc. Lex.*

monotint (ˈmɒnəʊtɪnt). [f. MONO- + TINT.] Representation in a single colour or tint; also a picture in only one colour. Chiefly in phr. ***in monotint***. Cf. MONOCHROME.
1886 *Contemp. Rev.* Sept. 405 To borrow the language of painting, the characters are mere studies in mono-tint. **1886** *Athenæum* 28 Aug. 273/3 The list of books..includes..'All round the Clock', from original drawings in colour and monotint by Harriett M. Bennett. **1887** *Ibid.* 24 Sept. 413/2 Books illustrated in colour and monotint.

monotocardian (mɒnəʊtəʊˈkɑːdɪən). [f. mod.L. name of suborder *Monotocardia*, f. MON(O- + Gk. ὠτό-ς gen. of οὖς auricle + καρδία heart.] A prosobranch mollusc having only one auricle and one row of gill leaflets, belonging to the suborder Pectinibranchia, formerly called Monotocardia. Also as *adj.* So **monotoˈcardiac** *a.*
1901 *Q. Jrnl. Microsc. Sci.* XLIV. 258 It is fairly easy to derive the Monotocardian type of nervous system, radula, gill, and reproductive system from the corresponding organs of existing Diotocardia. *Ibid.* 259 In the adult Monotocardian a single kidney alone is present. *Ibid.* 261 The monotocardian kidney. **1902** *Rep. Brit. Assoc. Adv. Sci.* 630 Recent research..has resulted in proof that the dextral torsion which leads to the monotocardiac condition, does not affect all organs lying primitively to the left of the rectum. **1958** G. A. KERKUT *Borradaile & Potts's Invertebrata* (ed. 3) xv. 613 (*caption*) Heteropods..are pelagic monotocardians. **1971** *Oxf. Bk. Invertebrates* 36 Some archaeogastropods show the primitive features of paired gills within the mantle cavity... But others, the 'monotocardians',..have lost the second gill.

monotocous (məˈnɒtəkəs), *a.* [f. Gr. μονοτόκ-ος bearing but one at a time (f. μόνο-ς MONO- + τοκ-, τίκτειν to bring forth) + -OUS.] **a.** *Zool.* Bearing only one or normally only one at a birth; uniparous. **b.** *Ornith.* Laying only one egg before incubating. **c.** *Bot.* Bearing fruit only once: a term proposed instead of MONOCARPIC.
1880 GRAY *Struct. Bot.* 33 *note*, *Monotocous* (bearing progeny once)..would be more appropriate [than monocarpic]. **1890** [all three uses] in *Century Dict.* **1936** *Nature* 12 Sept. (Suppl.) 451/2 Conceptual thought could only have arisen in a monotocous mammalian type with an arboreal ancestry. **1937** A. HUXLEY *Ends & Means* xiv. 264 After achieving a stable inner environment, placental and, in some cases, monotocous birth, highly developed sense organs, and a well co-ordinated nervous system, all but one [*sc.* mammal] proceeded to specialize. **1968** *Economist* 15 June 49/2 The rest of us, monotocous individuals that we are, certainly ought to be fascinated by all the bizarre phenomena involved in multiple births.

monotome (ˈmɒnəʊtəʊm), *a. rare.* [f. Gr. μόνο-ς MONO- + τόμος TOME.] Comprised in one volume.
1872 F. HALL *Recent Exempl.* 55 *note*, It is used by Southey, in *The Doctor* (monotome ed.), p. 32. **1873** —— *Mod. Eng.* iii. 56 *note*, The monotome edition of Gibbon's *Miscellaneous Works*, in 1837.

monotomous: see MONO- I.

monotone (ˈmɒnəʊtəʊn), *a.* and *sb.* [ad. mod.L. **monoton-us* adj., a. late Gr. μονότονος, f. Gr. μόνο-ς MONO- + τόνος TONE. Cf. F. *monoton* adj. Sp. *monó tono*, It. *monotono*, G. *monoton* adjs. The use of the word as a sb. is peculiar to Eng.]
A. *adj.* **1.** = MONOTONOUS *a.* I (*rarely* 2).
1769 *Phil. Trans.* LIX. 494 The Europeans conclude.. the Chinese tongue..is barren, monotone, and hard to understand. **1862** C. P. SMYTH *Three Cities in Russia* II. 195 The dark figure of a watchman soldier pacing his weary round through the monotone snow, appeared the only living object. **1872** O. SHIPLEY *Gloss. Eccl. Terms* 6 The accent being either plain, i.e. monotone; or *medius* [etc.]. **1875** KINGLAKE *Crimea* (1877) V. i. 51 As lulling as the monotone waves. **1901** R. BRIDGES *Milton's Prosody* 78 The monotone recitation of the prayers in cathedrals.
2. *Math.* [ad. G. *monoton* (C. Neumann *Ueber die nach Kreis-, Kugel- und Cylinderfunctionen fortschreitenden Entwickelungen* (1881) ii. 26).] = MONOTONIC *a.* 2, MONOTONOUS *a.* 3.
1905 J. PIERPONT *Lect. Theory of Functions of Real Variables* I. ii. 68 A sequence $A = a_1, a_2, \ldots$, whose elements satisfy the relations $a_n < a_{n+1}$, $n = 1, 2, \ldots$ is called an increasing sequence... If, on the other hand, $a_n \leqslant a_{n+1}$, $n = 1, 2, \ldots$ *A* is said to be a monotone increasing sequence. **1937** *Duke Math. Jrnl.* III. 489 We assume that $\phi(\rho)$ is completely monotone in $0 \leqq \rho < \infty$. **1948** [see MONOTONICITY a.]. **1968** P. A. P. MORAN *Introd. Probability Theory* iv. 186 We say that a sequence, A_i, is monotone if we always have $A_1 \subset A_2 \subset A_3 \subset \ldots$, or $A_1 \supset A_2 \supset A_3 \supset \ldots$ [Etc.] **1970** R. B. ASH *Basic Probability Theory* viii. 255 ϕ has a monotone nondecreasing power function.
B. *sb.*
1. a. A continuance or uninterrupted repetition of the same tone; the utterance, in speech or singing, of a number of successive syllables without change of pitch.
1644 BULWER *Chiron.* 136 Shun similitude of gesture; for as a monotone in the voyce, so a continued similitude of gesture. **1768** PENNANT *Brit. Zool.* I. 224 The pigeon kind excepted, whose slow plaintive continued monotone has something sweetly soothing in it. **1870–74** J. THOMSON *City Dreadf. Nt.* x. xv, He murmured thus and thus in monotone. **1899** *Allbutt's Syst. Med.* VIII. 367 The speech is often monosyllabic, a whispered monotone. **1906** H. BLACK *Edin. Serm.* 184 There is no music in a monotone.
b. *transf.*
a **1849** POE *Bells* Poems (1859) 77 Tolling, tolling, tolling In that muffled monotone. **1850** ALLINGHAM *Goblin Child of Ballyshannon* vii, The monotone Of the river flowing down Through the arches of the bridge. **1863** WOOLNER *My Beautiful Lady* 76 Drearily solemn runs a monotone, Heard through breathless hush. **1878** H. S. WILSON *Alp. Ascents* i. 15 A monotone of murmur from the river.
2. Monotony or sameness of style in composition or writing; something composed in such a style.
1871 T. W. HIGGINSON *Atlantic Ess., Let. to Yng. Contrib.* 78 An essay may be thoroughly delightful without a single witticism, while a monotone of jokes soon grows tedious. **1875** STEDMAN *Vict. Poets* v. (1887) 169 'In Memoriam'.. although a monotone, [is] no more monotonous than the sounds of nature,—the murmur of ocean [etc.]. **18..** BLACKIE (Ogilvie 1882), The sentimental monotone of Macpherson's *Ossian*. **1903** *Edin. Rev.* Jan. 65 The whole story is a miracle in monotone.
3. *fig.* A monotonous continuance or recurrence *of* something.
1856 RUSKIN *Mod. Paint.* IV. 172 Its [*sc.* science's] history is a monotone of endurance and destruction. **1901** HENLEY *Hawthorn & Lavender* 61 In a dull dense monotone of pain.
4. One tone or colour; cf. MONOTINT.
1896 *Boston* (Mass.) *Youth's Companion* 3 Dec. Advt., Single and double-page engravings in monotone.
Hence **ˈmonotonely** *adv.* = MONOTONICALLY *adv.* 2.
1948 BOCHNER & MARTIN *Several Complex Variables* vii. 135 If a sequence of (real) harmonic functions which are collectively bounded from above are monotonely decreasing, then either they converge uniformly to a harmonic function proper, or they diverge 'uniformly' to $-\infty$.

monotone (ˈmɒnəʊtəʊn), *v.* [f. MONOTONE *sb.*] *trans.* To recite, speak, or sing in one unvaried tone; to chant or intone on a single note.
1864 J. W. BROOKS & J. PLACE (*title*) On monotoning Prayer. **1880** F. G. LEE *Ch. under Q. Eliz.* I. 313 The parish clerk..was duly authorized by the Primate of England..to monotone the Psalms at Mattins and Evensong. **1890** *Tablet* 25 Oct. 655 He knelt while the Litany was monotoned. **1899** *Eclectic Mag.* Feb. 184 He generally seized the opportunity ..to monotone long extracts. **1899** *Daily News* 7 Feb. 6/3 The choir monotone the service.
Hence **ˈmonotoning** *vbl. sb.* and *ppl. a.*
1883 SIR H. OAKELEY *Bible Psalter* Pref. 6 The recited portion ought to approach as nearly as possible to good

monotoning. **1897** F. THOMPSON *New Poems* 159 The wind and I keep both one monotoning tongue.

monotoned (ˈmɒnəʊtəʊnd), *a. rare.* [f. MONO- + TONE *sb.* + -ED².] Having only one tone.

1890 'R. BOLDREWOOD' *Miner's Right* xxxvi, The monotoned wastes of the great Gold Desert. **1890** —— *Col. Reformer* (1891) 394 Sandy spaces, already flushed with green, had succeeded to the pale, dusty, monotoned landscape.

monotonic (mɒnəʊˈtɒnɪk), *a. Mus.* [f. MONOTONE *sb.* + -IC.] **1.** Relating to or uttered in a monotone; 'also capable of producing but a single tone, as a drum' (*Cent. Dict.* 1890).

1797 *Encycl. Brit.* (ed. 3) XII. 538/2 The fundamental bass which in itself is monotonic and little suited for singing [etc.]. **1828–32** WEBSTER, *Monotonic*, monotonous (*little used*). **1850** HELMORE *Man. Plain Song* 227 Monotonic mediation. **1880** ROCKSTRO in Grove *Dict. Mus.* II. 355/1 The use of Monotonic Recitation is of extreme antiquity.

2. Of a function or quantity: varying in such a way that it either never increases or never decreases. Of a sequence: consisting of terms that vary in this way. = MONOTONE *a.* and *sb.* A. 2, MONOTONOUS *a.* 3.

1901 *Ann. Math.* II. 116 It follows that $f(s)$ is a monotonic function that actually decreases in parts of the interval $0 \leq s \leq l$. **1908** T. J. I'A. BROMWICH *Introd. Theory Infinite Series* i. 5 A sequence in which $a_{n+1} \geq a_n$ for all values of n is called an increasing sequence; and similarly if $a_{n+1} \leq a_n$ for all values of n, the sequence is called decreasing. Both increasing and decreasing sequences are included in the term monotonic sequences. **1923** *Proc. Cambr. Philos. Soc.* XXI. 633 Z shall be monotonic considered as a function of ρ. **1957** G. E. HUTCHINSON *Treat. Limnol.* I. v. 251 The velocity at any point in a fluid could be expressed as a continuous monotonic or regularly oscillating function of time. **1968** E. T. COPSON *Metric Spaces* i. 16 Every bounded monotonic sequence of real numbers is convergent. **1970** *Nature* 3 Oct. 36/2 The rate of uptake of calcium by the isolated reticulum . . also displayed monotonic dependence on the concentration of free Ca^{2+} in the medium. **1973** *Jrnl. Genetic Psychol.* CXXII. 327 Young-adult responses were . . even more clearly a monotonic function of actual figure age than were preschool responses.

So **monoˈtonical** *a.*

1752 CHESTERF. *Let. Son* 23 Jan., A play, in which one should not be lulled to sleep by the length of a monotonical declamation.

monoˈtonically, *adv.* [f. prec. + -AL¹ + -LY².]

1. In the manner of a monotone.

1890 *Lippincott's Mag.* Jan. 100 Hear'st thou that rush of homeward-hurrying things, And word-calls monotonically harsh?

2. In the manner of a monotonic function, i.e. either without ever increasing or without ever decreasing.

1904 E. R. HEDRICK tr. *Goursat's Course in Math. Analysis* I. iv. 148 A function $f(x)$ is said to increase monotonically in a given interval (a, b) if for any two values x', x'' in that interval $f(x') \geq f(x'')$ whenever $x' > x''$. **1934** *Amer. Math Monthly* XLI. 421 Equation (13) defines Y as a single-valued, continuous, monotonically decreasing function of X. **1958** *Jrnl. Geol.* LXVI. 164/2 The rate of solution should increase monotonically as the fresh solvent is brought up at ever increasing rate. **1974** *Nature* 2 Aug. 451/3 These provided the dramatic highlight of the programme, which declined monotonically in interest for its final hour.

monotonicity (mɒnətəˈnɪsɪtɪ). [f. MONOTONIC *a.* + -ITY.] The property or state of being monotonic. **a.** Of a function or variable (see MONOTONIC *a.* 2).

1948 *Duke Math. Jrnl.* XV. 313 (*heading*) The complete monotonicity of certain functions derived from completely monotone functions. **1961** [see ENTROPY 2 b]. **1972** *Computer Jrnl.* XV. 218/2 We now derive a monotonicity relation which will be used in Section 5 to prove convergence.

b. Of sounds (see MONOTONIC *a.*).

1971 *Nature* 23 Apr. 524/2 Speech remained unaffected except for slight slowing and slurring of words and the presence of some monotonicity.

monotonist (məˈnɒtənɪst). [f. MONOTONE *sb.* or MONOTONY + -IST.] In various nonce-uses: One who speaks monotonously; one who constantly 'harps on' one subject; one whose style is monotonous; one who loves or advocates monotony.

1748 RICHARDSON *Clarissa* (1768) IV. 125 If I ruin such a Virtue, sayest thou! Eternal monotonist! **1785** TRUSLER *Mod. Times* I. 139 To others, who do not like to be taught by boys, . . and who go to church more to keep up appearances, than from any spirit of devotion, he would provide a monotonist of sixty. **1848** GILFILLAN in *Tait's Mag.* XV. 521 To avoid insipidity of excellence in his seraphs, and insipidity of horror in his fiends, . . was a problem requiring . . dramatic as well as epic powers. No mere monotonist could have succeeded in it. **1905** *Westm. Gaz.* 30 Sept. 4/2 The Imperialist or monotonist who likes to see as many people as possible under a Government of the same pattern.

monotonize (məˈnɒtənaɪz), *v.* [f. MONOTONOUS + -IZE.] *trans.* To render monotonous.

1804 SOUTHEY *Lett.* (1856) I. 257 The very snow, which you would perhaps think must monotonise the mountains, gives new varieties. **1824** *Examiner* 199/2 Madame Rossini has languished through *Zelmira*, and Madame Vestris monotonized *Rosina*, till every frequenter of the opera must be completely wearied. **1889** *Blackw. Mag.* July 93 This destroys individuality and monotonises character.

monotonous (məˈnɒtənəs), *a.* [f. Gr. μονότονος (see MONOTONE *a.*) + -OUS.]

1. a. Of sound or utterance: Continuing on one and the same note; usually in modified sense, having little variation in tone or cadence. **b.** (See quot. 1811.)

1778 WARTON *Hist. Eng. Poetry* II. Emend. a 4, Every line was perhaps uniformly recited to the same monotonous modulation with a pause in the midst. **1795** SEWARD *Anecd.* (ed. 2) II. 367 Lord Chatham's eloquence . . was neither the rounded and the monotonous declamation, . . that we have seen admired in our times. **1811** BUSBY *Dict. Mus.* (ed. 3), *Monotonous*, an epithet applied to any instrument which produces but one tone or note: as the drum, the tamborine, &c. **1814** SCOTT *Wav.* xvii, The monotonous and murmured chant of a Gaelic song. **1839** FR. A. KEMBLE *Resid. in Georgia* (1863) 61 A melancholy, monotonous boat horn. **1854** BUSHNAN in *Circ. Sci.* (1865) I. 285/2 The successive notes have nearly all the same pitch. This kind of succession . . is properly termed the monotonous. **1859** TENNYSON *Guinevere* 417 A voice, Monotonous and hollow like a Ghost's Denouncing judgment. **1863** MARY HOWITT tr. *F. Bremer's Greece* II. xii. 42 The owl of Minerva lets us hear in the evening his monotonous cry.

2. *transf.* and *fig.* Lacking in variety; uninteresting or wearisome through continued sameness: said e.g. of occupations, scenery, literary style, etc.

1791–1823 D'ISRAELI *Cur. Lit.* (1859) II. 208 The national character retained more originality and individuality than our monotonous habits now admit. **1827** STEUART *Planter's G.* (1828) 60 The Lime, a Tree, which, unless on the foreground, is always formal and monotonous in landscape. **1831** MACAULAY *Ess., Byron* (1897) 154 The monotonous smoothness of Byron's versification. **1873** HAMERTON *Intell. Life* XII. i. (1875) 434 The monotonous character of the Midland scenery. **1876** MISS BRADDON *J. Haggard's Dau.* II. 23 The life is somewhat monotonous, . . but I hope you will not grow weary of it. **1876** GREEN *Stray Stud.* 6 Dull straight streets of monotonous houses. **1895** RIDER HAGGARD *Heart of World* i, These men proved to be half-breeds of the lowest class, living in an atmosphere of monotonous vice.

quasi-*adv.* **1845** BROWNING *Pictor Ignotus* 58 As monotonous I paint These endless cloisters and eternal aisles With the same series, Virgin, Babe and Saint.

3. *Math.* Of a function (see quot.).

[= Ger. *monoton*, introduced by C. Neumann 1881.]

1890 in *Century Dict.* **1902** LOVE in *Encycl. Brit.* (ed. 10) XXVIII. 547 A function which never increases or never diminishes throughout an interval is said to be 'monotonous throughout' the interval. **1935** T. CHAUNDY *Differential Calculus* iii. 51 Over the whole domain we may call the function 'monotonous'.

Hence **moˈnotonousness**.

1839 *Fraser's Mag.* XIX. 158 Rhymed alexandrines . . produce a wearisome monotonousness. **1881** *Times* 15 Mar. 12 The weary monotonousness of Russian life. **1889** 'MARK TWAIN' *Yankee at Crt. K. Arthur* xxvi. 303 There is a profound monotonousness about its facts.

moˈnotonously, *adv.* [f. MONOTONOUS *a.* + -LY².] **1.** In a monotonous manner; with tiresome uniformity or lack of variation.

1828–32 WEBSTER, *Monotonously*, with one uniform tone; without inflection of voice [*citing* Nares]. **1871** L. STEPHEN *Playgr. Eur* xiii. (1894) 327 Wreaths of mist . . chased each other monotonously along the rocky ribs. **1872** LIDDON *Elem. Relig.* iv. 143 A man in whom disease had never been latent, and whose constitution had been even monotonously free from its assaults.

2. = MONOTONICALLY *adv.* 2.

1938 *Physical Rev.* LIV. 948/1 $F(a)$ is a monotonously decreasing function. **1954** D. TER HAAR *Elem. Statistical Mech.* 444, In x is a monotonously increasing function of x. **1970** *Internat. Jrnl. Quantum Chem.* IV. 611 E decreases monotonously from $R = 10a_H$ to $R = 2a_H$. **1974** *Nature* 17 May 243/2 The torque might have been expected to decrease monotonously as the polymer dissolved.

monotony (məˈnɒtənɪ). [f. late Gr. μονοτονία sameness of tone, monotony, f. μονότονος MONOTONE *a.* Cf. F. *monotonie* (1690 in Hatz.-Darm.).] The quality of being monotonous.

1. Sameness of tone or pitch; want of variety in cadence or inflection; occas. quasi-*concr.* a monotonous sound, a monotone.

[Cf. **1706** in sense 2.] **1724** BAILEY (ed. 2), *Monotony*, the having but one Tone. [**1731** *Ibid.* (vol. II.), *Monotonia*, the having but one tone; also a want of inflection or variation of voice, or a pronunciation, where a long series of words are delivered with one unvaried tone.] **1748** J. MASON *Elocut.* 19 To avoid a Monotony in Pronunciation, or a dull, set, uniform Tone of Voice. **1749** *Power Pros. Numbers* 15 For though its [*sc.* the drum's] Sound be only a Monotony, yet [etc.]. **1761** STERNE *Tr. Shandy* IV. xix, It is in vain longer, said my father, in the most querulous monotony imaginable, to struggle as I have done. **1774** WARTON *Hist. Eng. Poetry* I. 21 Our earliest poets . . were fond of multiplying the same final sound to the most tedious monotony. **1818** SHELLEY *Stanzas written in Dejection* iv, I might . . hear the sea Breathe o'er my dying brain its last monotony. **1831** W. GODWIN *Thoughts Man* 22 A sheepish . . schoolboy, that hung his head, and replied with inarticulated monotony. **1866** GEO. ELIOT *F. Holt* i, The soft monotony of running water. **1896** 'H. S. MERRIMAN' *Flotsam* ii, The sleepy monotony of the rattling block-sheaves.

2. *transf.* and *fig.* Wearisome sameness of effect; tedious recurrence of the same objects, actions, etc.; lack of interesting variety in occupation, scenery, literary style, etc.

1706 POPE *Let. to Walsh* 22 Oct., I could equally object to the Repetition of the same Rhimes within four or six lines of each other, as tiresome to the ear thro' their Monotony. **1783** BLAIR *Lect. Rhet.* xiii. 261 Monotony is the great fault into which writers are apt to fall, who are fond of harmonious arrangement. **1820** W. IRVING *Sketch Bk.* I. 13 At sea, everything that breaks the monotony of the surrounding expanse, attracts attention. **1831** MACAULAY *Ess., Byron* (1807) 158 Never was there such variety in monotony as that of Byron. **1843** BORROW *Bible in Spain* vii. 46 A tower—the only object which broke the monotony of the waste. **1883** GILMOUR *Mongols* xxiv. 295 The monotony of prison life.

monotremal (mɒnəʊˈtriːməl), *a. rare*⁻¹. [f. MONOTREME + -AL¹.] = MONOTREMATOUS.

1866 *Reader* No. 163. 152/2 Monotremal mammalians.

‖**Monotremata** (mɒnəʊˈtriːmətə), *sb. pl. Zool.* [mod.L., neut. pl. of *monotrēmatus* adj., f. Gr. μόνο-ς MONO- + τρηματ-, τρῆμα perforation, hole, f. τρᾱ- root of τετραίνειν to bore through, perforate.] The lowest Order of Mammalia, containing mammals which have only one opening or vent for the genital, urinary, and digestive organs.

The Order comprises the duck-billed platypus (*Ornithorhynchus paradoxus*) and several species of spiny ant-eaters of the genera *Tachyglossus* (or *Echidna*) and *Zaglossus* or *Acanthoglossus*. They are native to Australia and New Guinea, and are oviparous.

1833 *Proc. Zool. Soc.* 12 Mar. 29 [tr. of Geoffroy St. Hilaire], The Monotremata. **1839–47** OWEN in *Todd's Cycl. Anat.* III. 368/1 The skull in both genera of Monotremata is long and depressed.

monotremate (mɒnəʊˈtriːmət), *a.* and *sb. Zool.* [ad. mod.L. *monotrēmatus*: see prec.]

a. *adj.* = MONOTREMATOUS. **b.** *sb.* in *pl.* = MONOTREMATA.

1846 SMART, *Monotremates.*

monotrematous (mɒnəʊˈtriːmətəs), *a. Zool.* [f. MONOTREMATA + -OUS.] Pertaining to or characteristic of the *Monotremata.*

1835–6 *Todd's Cycl. Anat.* I. 174/2 The monotrematous animals . . form a complete exception to this statement. **1886** *Fortn. Rev.* Apr. 527, I am by no means convinced that all mammals had monotrematous progenitors.

monotreme (ˈmɒnəʊtriːm), *sb.* and *a. Zool.* [f. Gr. μόνο-ς MONO- + τρῆμ-α: see MONOTREMATA. Cf. F. *monotrème.*]

A. *sb.* A member of the *Monotremata.*

1835 KIRBY *Hab. & Inst. Anim.* II. xxiv. 483 This Subclass is divided into two Orders, Monotremes, and Marsupians. **1884** *Rep. Brit. Assoc.* 777 Mr. Caldwell . . had discovered that the Monotremes were oviparous.

B. *adj.* = MONOTREMATOUS.

1890 *Century Dict.* s.v., Monotreme mammals; a monotreme egg.

Hence ˌ**monoˈtremous** *a.* = MONOTREMATOUS.

1890 in *Century Dict.*

monotriglyph (mɒnəʊˈtraɪglɪf), *a.* and *sb. Arch.* [ad. L. *monotriglyph-os* (Vitruvius), a. Gr. *μονοτρίγλυφος adj., f. Gr. μόνο-ς MONO- + τρίγλυφος TRIGLYPH. Cf. F. *monotriglyphe* sb. and adj.]

A. *adj.* Having only one triglyph in the space over an intercolumniation.

1797 *Encycl. Brit.* (ed. 3) II. 239/1 [The Doric intercolumniations] were either systyle, monotriglyph . . ; diastyle . . ; or aræostyle. **1823** P. NICHOLSON *Pract. Build.* 588 *Monotriglyph*; having only one trigliph between two adjoining columns: the general practice in the Grecian Doric. **1842** GWILT *Archit.* §2605, A is the systyle monotriglyph intercolumniation of 3 modules.

B. *sb.* (See quot. 1850.)

1706 PHILLIPS (ed. Kersey), *Monotriglyph.* **1734** *Builder's Dict.* **1823** CRABB *Technol. Dict.*, *Monotriglyph* (*Archit.*), monotriglyphon; the space of one triglyph between two pilasters or columns. **1850** PARKER *Gloss. Archit.* (ed. 5) I. 308 *Monotriglyph*, . . the intercolumniation in the Doric order which embraces one triglyph and two metopes in the entablature.

So **monotriˈglyphic** *a.* = MONOTRIGLYPH *a.*

1837 *Penny Cycl.* VII. 218/2 Monotriglyphic intercolumniation.

†**ˈmonotroch.** *Obs.* Also -troche. [ad. Gr. μονότροχ-ος one-wheeled (car), f. μόνο-ς MONO- + τροχός wheel.] A vehicle with only one wheel.

1807 *Sporting Mag.* XXIX 66 A most curious sort of gig called a Monotroche from its having only one wheel was exhibited in Bond Street, the 24th inst. **1825** MOORE *Sheridan* I. 22 Ixion . . instead of being fixed to a torturing wheel, was to have been fixed to a vagrant monotroche, as knife-grinder. **1828** SCOTT *My Aunt Margaret's Mirr.* (*Init.*), These monotrochs [*jocularly* = wheelbarrows].

monotrochal (məˈnɒtrəkəl), *a. Zool.* [f. mod.L. *monotroch-us* (Ehrenberg, a. Gr. μονό-τροχος: see prec.) + -AL¹.] **a.** Belonging to the division *Monotrocha* of rotifers, in which the trochal disk or 'wheel' is single. **b.** Having a single band of cilia, as the larva of a polychæte worm. **c.** Belonging or pertaining to the division *Monotrocha* of *Hymenoptera*, in which the trochanter has but one joint. So **monoˈtrochian** *a.* (*sb.* a monotrochal rotifer), **moˈnotrochous** *a.*

1845 *Encycl. Metrop.* VII. 266/1 The Wheel Organs are either *Monotrochous*, i.e. have a simple connected ring of cilia, or [etc.]. **1854** ADAMS, etc. *Man. Nat. Hist.* 341 Rotifers . . I Order.—Monotrochians (Monotrocha). **1886** A. G. BOURNE in *Encycl. Brit.* XXI. 8/1 A monotrochal

polychætous larva. **1890** *Century Dict.*, *Monotrochian* [*a.* and *sb.*]. **1895** *Cambr. Nat. Hist.* V. 494 In the stinging Hymenoptera the trochanters are usually of a single piece, and these Insects are called monotrochous.

‖**monotropa** (məˈnəʊtrəpə). *Bot.* [mod.L. (Linnæus 1737), f. Gr. μονότροπος living alone, solitary, f. μόνο-ς MONO- + τρόπος turn, direction, way, manner (f. τρέπειν to turn).] A genus of dicotyledonous plants, the type of the N.O. *Monotropeæ*, characterized by a solitary flower with separate petals. *M. uniflora* (the only species) is the Indian-pipe or corpse-plant. Also this plant.

[**1753** CHAMBERS *Cycl. Supp.*, *Monotropa*, in botany, the name of a genus of plants, called by Tournefort, *orobanchoides*, and by Dillenius, *hypopitis*.] **1778** G. WHITE *Selborne, To Barrington* 3 July, *Monotropa hypopithys*, yellow monotropa, or birds' nest. **1845–50** MRS. LINCOLN *Lect. Bot.* x. 61 The *Monotropa*, or Indian pipe, is of pure white, resembling wax-work. **1905** *Longm. Mag.* Jan. 257 The uncanny yellow monotropa abounds as of old.

monotropaceous (ˌmɒnəʊtrəʊˈpeɪʃəs), *a.* *Bot.* [f. mod.L. *Monotropāce-æ* (Lindley 1836) + -OUS.] Of or pertaining to the *Monotropaceæ* (or *Monotropeæ*), an order of gamopetalous herbs, having the *Monotropa* as typical genus.

In recent Dicts.

monotropeous (mɒnəʊˈtrəʊpiːəs), *a.* *Bot.* [f. mod.L. *Monotrope-æ* (Nuttal 1818) + -OUS.] = MONOTROPACEOUS.

1856 MAYNE *Expos. Lex.*, *Monotropeus*, applied to a Family..of plants established by Nuttal, having the Monotropa for their type: monotropeous.

monotrophic (mɒnəʊˈtrɒfɪk), *a.* *Zool.* [f. Gr. *μονότροφ-ος (f. μόνο-ς MONO- + τρέφειν to feed) + -IC. Cf. μονοτροφεῖν (Strabo) to eat but one kind of food.] Of a parasitic organism: Infesting only one host; feeding on one kind of food.

1900 A. C. JONES tr. *Fischer's Struct. Bacteria* 49, I. Prototrophic Bacteria..occur only in the open in nature, never parasitic, always monotrophic. II. Metatrophic Bacteria,..(facultative parasites), monotrophic or polytrophic.

monotropic (mɒnəʊˈtrɒpɪk), *a.* [f. Gr. μόνο-ς single, MONO- + τρόπ-ος turn + -IC.]

1. *Math.* = MONODROMIC (opp. to *polytropic*).

1891 tr. *Harnack's Diff. & Int. Calc.* 128 The total course of a one-valued (monotropic) function is realised by help of two planes.

2. (See quot.) [? Error for *monotrophic*.]

1900 B. D. JACKSON *Gloss. Bot. Terms*, *Monotropic*, applied to bees which visit only one species of flower.

3. *Physical Chem.* Exhibiting monotropy.

1897 W. D. BANCROFT *Phase Rule* iii. 32 It is probable that the substances classified as 'monotropic' by Lehmann..are analogous to phosphorus. **1924** A. E. HILL in H. S. Taylor *Treat. Physical Chem.* I. ix. 390 In other cases it is not easy to determine whether a given form is monotropic or enantiotropic. **1955** J. ZERNIKE *Chem. Phase Theory* ii. 29 Cubic and hexagonal white phosphorus..are monotropic with respect to the violet form. **1964** G. I. BROWN *Introd. Physical Chem.* xx. 217 In monotropic substances there is no definite transition temperature, and one form of the substance is more stable than the other.

monotropism (məˈnɒtrəpɪz(ə)m). *Physical Chem.* [f. MONOTROP(IC *a.* 3 + -ISM.] = next.

1924 A. E. HILL in H. S. Taylor *Treat. Physical Chem.* I. ix. 390 An example of monotropism is found in the case of phosphorus. **1950** W. J. MOORE *Physical Chem.* v. 109 (*heading*) Enantiotropism and monotropism.

monotropy (məˈnɒtrəpɪ). *Physical Chem.* [ad. G. *monotropie* (O. Lehmann *Molekularphysik* (1888) I. 119), f. Gr. μονο- MONO- + τροπή turning.] The existence of two polymorphs of a substance, one of which is stable and the other metastable over the whole range of their existence, so that conversion of the latter into the former can occur but not *vice versa*.

1902 A. FINDLAY tr. *Ostwald's Princ. Inorg. Chem.* 255 (*heading*) Enantiotropy and monotropy. **1932** J. N. FRIEND *Text-bk. Physical Chem.* I. xi. 181 It may..so happen that, in certain cases of presumed monotropy, the transition point lies very much below the melting point and has not been realised experimentally for this reason. **1970** CHAKRAVARTI & MITRA *Textbk. Physical Chem.* I. vi. 232 Examples of monotropy are white and violet phosphorus, diamond and graphite, silica, iodine monochloride [and] α- and β-benzophenone.

monotypal (ˈmɒnəʊtaɪpəl), *a.* [f. MONOTYPE + -AL[1].] = MONOTYPIC.

1890 in *Century Dict.* And in later Dicts.

monotype (ˈmɒnəʊtaɪp), *sb.* and *a.* [f. MONO- + TYPE; in sense 1 repr. mod.L. *monotypus*.]

A. *sb.* **1.** 'The only or sole type; especially, a sole species which constitutes a genus, family, or the like' (Ogilvie *Suppl.* 1882).

1881 BENTHAM in *Jrnl. Linn. Soc.* XVIII. 345 Macodes, Blume, and Hyophila, Lindley, are both monotypes from the Malayan Archipelago.

2. In graphic art, a print taken from oil-colour or printer's ink painted on a sheet of glass or metal, the process being such that prints are produced singly. Also, the method of producing such a print. Also *attrib.*

1882 *Artist* 1 Feb. 60/1 A very interesting collection of monotypes executed by Mr. Charles A. Walker of Boston. Though Mr. Walker did not invent the monotype still to him is due the credit of developing this process. **1902** E. BALE in *Encycl. Brit.* XXXII. 18/1 The monotype is not a new, but a revival of a somewhat old, method of reproducing on paper a painting by an artist. **1926** L. BINYON *Engraved Designs of W. Blake* ii. 13 Out of such experiments may have come the idea of the 'monotype' which Blake was to use to such good purpose. **1954** *Oxford Mag.* 21 Jan., Anyone who does not know what Monotypes are can spend a profitable twenty minutes at his exhibition at Black Hall in deducing the nature of Mr. Baynes's technique. **1955** P. HERON *Changing Forms of Art* xi. 174 No English artist living excels him in this medium, especially where it involves the process known as 'monotype'. **1962** *Listener* 18 Oct. 624/2 An exhibition of monotypes and off-set drawings completed by Robert Colquhoun just before he died. **1970** *Oxf. Compan. Art* 736/1 G. B. Castiglione made monotypes on etching plates in the 17th c., William Blake's monotypes were apparently done on pieces of card.

3. (With capital initial.) The proprietary name of a composing machine consisting of two units, a keyboard which produces the perforated paper tape used to control the caster, which produces type in individual characters.

1893 *Official Directory World's Columbian Exposition* (Chicago) 459/1 Lanston Monotype Machine Co., Washington, D.C. Monotype Machine. **1895** *Current Hist.* (Buffalo) V. 961 The Lanston Monotype..invented by Tolbert Lanston, of Washington, D.C. marks an important advance in the development of typographical art..both a type-setting and a type-casting machine. **1897** *Daily News* 15 Oct. 6/2 The monotype machine. **1906** *Daily Chron.* 15 Sept. 6/5 The machinery..included a couple of Monotypes. **1931** A. ESDAILE *Student's Man. Bibliogr.* iii. 58 The monotype method..involves two machines. **1959** [see INTERTYPE]. **1965** J. MORAN *Composition of Reading Matter* vi. 65 The Monotype machine consists of two units—the keyboard and the caster. By operation of the keyboard a paper ribbon is perforated by means of compressed air. The ribbon is fed into a caster which carries a matrix-case. This moves to different positions in accordance with the perforated ribbon and molten metal is pumped into the appropriate matrix. Cast types are ejected singly and assembled in a channel until a line is completed. **1973** S. JENNETT *Making of Books* (ed. 5) iv. 79 The type produced by the Monotype is of excellent quality, and in use is indistinguishable from founders' type.

B. *adj.* = MONOTYPIC [cf. F. *monotype* adj.]. Cf. also MONOTYPE 2 and 3.

1885 in *Cassell's Encycl. Dict.* And in later Dicts.

monotypic (mɒnəʊˈtɪpɪk), *a.* [f. mod.L. *monotyp-us* (see next) + -IC.]

1. Having or containing only one type or representative.

1878 T. GILL in *Proc. U.S. Nat. Mus.* 231 All the genera are monotypic except *Malthe*. **1881** BENTHAM in *Jrnl. Linn. Soc.* XVII. 322 Paradisanthus, Kegelia [etc.]..are all monotypic genera. **1888** J. T. GULICK *ibid.*, *Zool.* XX. 201 Monotypic Evolution is any transformation of a species that does not destroy its unity of type. *a* **1894** ROMANES *Darwin & after D.* (1897) III. 75 The all-important distinction between monotypic and polytypic evolution.

2. That is a monotype; that is the sole representative of a genus or a higher group.

1886 P. L. SCLATER *Catal. Birds Brit. Mus.* XI. 17 *Hemidacnis*... This is again a monotypic form.

So **monoˈtypical** *a.* = MONOTYPIC.

1890 in *Century Dict.* And in later Dicts.

monotypous (məˈnɒtɪpəs), *a.* [f. mod.L. *monotyp-us* (f. Gr. μόνο-ς MONO- + τύπ-ος TYPE) + -OUS.] = MONOTYPIC 1. (See quots.)

1856 MAYNE *Expos. Lex.*, *Monotypus*, applied by Mirbel to *genera*, as the *Rosa*, and to Families, as the *Labieæ*, composed of one union of objects intimately joined by a multitude of relations perceptible at first glance; applied by De Candolle to *genera* which contain but a single species: monotypous. **1891** *Syd. Soc. Lex.*, *Monotypous*, of one type. Applied to genera the species of which are very similar, and form a distinct type.

monoundai, -day, obs. forms of MONDAY.

monovalent (mɒnəʊˈveɪlənt, məˈnɒvələnt), *a.* [Hybrid f. MONO- + VALENT.] **1.** *Chem.* = UNIVALENT.

1869 ROSCOE *Elem. Chem.* (1871) 172 The elements of the first group combine atom for atom with hydrogen, they are monovalent elements or monads. **1881** tr. *A. Strecker's Org. Chem.* 114 The Monovalent Alcohol Radicals.

2. *Med.* **a.** Containing or being an antigen from a single strain of a micro-organism.

1930 H. CHILD tr. *Besredka's Immunity in Infectious Dis.* iii. 44 The same conclusion,..that the streptococcus is unique, because the monovalent serum acts against all the human streptococci. **1960** *Jrnl. Amer. Med. Assoc.* 19 Mar. 1230/1 The influenza pandemic which occurred in the United States in 1957–1958 provided an excellent opportunity to determine the efficacy of monovalent vaccines. **1968** *Amer. Jrnl. Epidemiol.* LXXXVIII. 149/1 Group B received monovalent vaccine containing 400 CCA units of B/Maryland/1/59 antigen. **1972** *Clin. Sci.* XLIII. 871 The monovalent influenzal antigen used was the strain AO/Swine (Shope) vaccine treated with desoxycholate to eliminate possible toxic effects.

b. Of an antigen or antibody: having only one site at which it can become attached to antibody or antigen, respectively.

1960 *Jrnl. Immunol.* LXXXIV. 409 The studies..were carried out with antibodies specific for two haptenic groups of dissimilar nature... It was essential for the experiments involving hapten-antibody combination *in vivo* that the haptens be molecularly dispersed, since aggregation of hapten *in vivo* would result in the hapten no longer being monovalent. **1966** *Jrnl. Exper. Med.* CXXIII. 229 Hapten-specific delayed hypersensitivity was only transiently suppressed by intravenous injections of monovalent conjugates of arsanilic acid and *N*-acetyl-tyrosine. **1970** J. T. BARRETT *Textbk. Immunol.* vi. 127/2 Monovalent (incomplete) Rh antibodies can be responsible for erythroblastosis. **1972** *McGraw-Hill Yearbk. Sci. & Technol.* 142/2 The agglutinin used in this experiment was a monovalent rather than a divalent agglutinin, that is, a molecule which binds to the cell surface with its one remaining active site but which cannot cause agglutination because it lacks a second active site.

3. *Cytology.* = UNIVALENT *a.*

1906 *Rep. Brit. Assoc. Adv. Sci.* 1905 570 Whether each half of the chromosome is to be regarded as a monovalent chromosome is doubtful.

Hence **monovalence**, **monovalency**, the character of being monovalent.

1890 in *Century Dict.* And in later Dicts.

monovular (məˈnɒv-, məˈnəʊvjuːlə(r)), *a.* *Biol.* [f. MON(O- + OVULAR *a.*] = MONOZYGOTIC *a.*

1936 *Yale Jrnl. Biol. & Med.* VIII. 589 We think of human monovular twins as having identically the same inheritance and as being so similar in height, weight, build, appearance, and mentality as to confuse relatives and friends. **1962** *Biol. Abstr.* XL. 1726/1 While neonatal polycythemia in monovular twins is obviously due to intrauterine transfer of blood.., the postnatal polycythemia in single newborn infants remains unexplained. **1966** *Arch. Surg.* XCII. 865/1 The occurrence of Hashimoto's thyroiditis in a mother and her three daughters, two of whom are monovular twins.

monoxide (mɒˈnɒksaɪd, -ˈɒksɪd). *Chem.* [f. MONO- 2 + OXIDE.] An oxide containing one equivalent of oxygen.

The term is used where several oxides of the same element are to be distinguished, as carbon monoxide CO, to be distinguished from carbon dioxide CO_2.

1869 ROSCOE *Elem. Chem.* (1871) 69 The salt decomposes on heating into nitrogen mon-oxide and water. **1873** *Fownes' Chem.* (ed. 11) 129 Equal weights of oxygen, nitrogen, and carbon monoxide are transpired in equal times. **1891** *Lancet* 2 May 993/2 Small quantities of carbon monoxide.

b. *attrib.*

1900 *Lancet* 25 Aug. 607/2 Deaths from carbon monoxide poisoning. **1904** *Athenæum* 31 Dec. 909/2 The oxygen.. combines with a portion of the carbon to form carbon monoxide gas.

monoxy-, monox-. *Chem.* Also **mono-oxy-**. [f. MONO- 2 + OXY(GEN).] Combining form, expressing the presence in a compound of one equivalent of oxygen.

1863 *Fownes' Chem.* (ed. 9). 494 Monoxethylenamine $C_4H_4O_2$, NH_3. Dioxethylenamine $(C_4H_4O_2)_2$, NH_3. *Ibid.* 578 Monooxysalicylic-acid. **1881** *Nature* 14 Apr. 566/1 Benzene, when acted on by..nitrogen tetroxide—N_2O_4—yields..monoxy-benzene—C_6H_4O—an isomer or metamer of quinone. **1891** *Syd. Soc. Lex.*, *Monoöxybenzol*. *Ibid.*, *Monoxybenzol*, the same as *Carbonic acid*.

monoxyle (məʊˈnɒksɪl). Also **-xyl**. [a. F. *monoxyle* adj. (Littré), ad. Gr. μονόξυλον: see MONOXYLON.] = MONOXYLON.

1774 *Misc.* in *Ann. Reg.* 169/2 To these succeeded trunks of trees cut hollow, termed by the Greeks monoxyles. **1840** KEIGHTLEY *Rom. Emp.* III. v. 376 The Goths embarked their warriors in three thousand monoxyls or canoes. **1885** R. F. BURTON *Arab. Nts.* IV. 168 *note*, Here it [*sc.* the Arab word] refers to the canoe..pop. 'dug-out' and classically 'monoxyle'.

monoxylic (mɒnɒkˈsɪlɪk), *a.* [Formed as MONOXYLOUS + -IC.] = MONOXYLOUS.

1863 D. WILSON *Preh. Ann.* III. vi. (ed. 2) II. 160 The rude oaken coffin, or monoxylic cist. **1878** MILLER & SKERTCHLY *Fenland* ii. 28 Monoxylic canoes could not have conveyed a large number of men. **1882** C. ELTON *Orig. Eng. Hist.* 168 Buried in the canoe-shaped chests of oak which are known as the 'monoxylic coffins'.

‖**monoxylon** (mɒˈnɒksɪlən). Pl. **monoxyla**. Also 7–8 in mod. Gr. form **monoxylo** (sing.). [a. Gr. μονόξυλον, neut. of μονόξυλος: see next.] A canoe or boat made from one piece of timber.

1555 EDEN *Decades* 78 Theyr canoas whiche we may well caule Monoxyla, bycause they are made of one hole tree. **1682** WHELER *Journ. Greece* I. 37 The Fortress..neither can be approached to by Land, nor Sea, except in those Monoxylo's, or little Barques, which draw not above a foot of water. **1776** R. CHANDLER *Trav. Greece* 281 A man waded to it [*sc.* a hut] and procured us a monoxylo or tray. *Ibid.*, The monoxyla or skiffs carry every thing to and fro. **1800** *Naval Chron.* III. 478 There you may see the Monoxylon, built exactly upon the model of the ancient Greek vessel; whose name it likewise retains. **1863** D. WILSON *Preh. Ann.* I. ii. (ed. 2) I. 57 The rude British monoxyla, shaped and hollowed out by stone axes, with the help of fire.

¶**b.** Erroneously explained.

1867 SMYTH *Sailor's Word-bk.*, *Monoxylon*, boats in the Ionian Isles propelled with one oar. [Hence in recent Dicts.]

monoxylous (mɒˈnɒksɪləs), *a.* [ad. L. *monoxyl-us* (a. Gr. μονόξυλος made from a solid trunk, f. μόνο-ς MONO- + ξύλ-ον wood, timber, piece of wood) + -OUS.] Formed or made out of a single piece of wood; also, using one piece of wood to make a boat or coffin, etc.

1863 D. WILSON *Preh. Ann.* I. ii. (ed. 2) I. 47 The monoxylous artificers of Britain's prehistoric times. *Ibid.* ix.

229 The monoxylous boat-builders of the Forth. **1875** —— in *Encycl. Brit.* II. 338/2 The monoxylous oaken canoes dug up from time to time in the valley of the Clyde.

mono'zoan, *a. Zool.* [Formed as next + -AN.] = MONOZOIC 1.

1890 in *Century Dict.*

monozoic (mɒnəʊ'zəʊɪk), *a. Zool.* [f. mod.L. *Monozō-a* neut. pl. (f. Gr. μόνο-ς MONO- + ζῷον animal) + -IC.]

1. Belonging to the division *Monozoa* of radiolarians; = MONOCYTTARIAN.

1890 in *Century Dict.*

2. Applied to a spore which produces one sporozoite (see quot.).

1901 [see POLYZOIC 1 b]. **1903** MINCHIN *Sporozoa* in E. R. Lankester *Zool.* I. 165 The spores are distinguished as *monozoic, dizoic, tetrazoic, polyzoic*, and so forth, according as they contain one, two, four, or many sporozoites. In the monozoic condition there is no secondary multiplication within the sporocyst.

monozygotic (mɒnəʊzaɪ'gɒtɪk), *a.* (*sb.*) *Biol.* [f. MONO- + ZYGOT(E + -IC.] Of twins (also *rarely* of triplets, etc.): derived from a single ovum (and therefore identical). Also as *sb.*, such an individual.

1917 H. H. NEWMAN *Biol. of Twins* 3 Such twins, quadruplets, or larger sets of offspring are known as monozygotic. **1930**, etc. [see DIZYGOTIC *a.*] **1957** *Ann. N.Y. Acad. Sci.* LXIV. 759 Because the twins were believed to be probable monozygotics, excess skin was taken from the less extensively burned twin and cross-transplanted to her sister. **1965** *Listener* 24 June 930/2 We have learnt, too, the significance of a natural freak—the monozygotic or identical twin. **1968** [see MONOZYGOSITY below]. **1970** *Sci. Jrnl.* June 30/2 Such monozygotic twins..form only a small proportion of all twins.

Hence **monozy'gosity**, the property of being monozygotic.

1928 *Biol. Abstr.* II. 685/2 (*heading*) Value of dactyloscopic and dermatologic methods in diagnosing monozygosity in twins. **1952** *New Biol.* XII. 28 The only method at present available for diagnosing monozygosity involves comparison of as many morphological and physiological characters as possible. **1968** *Obstetr. & Gynecol. Survey* XXIII. 940 Two-thirds of monozygotic twins have a single placenta with a single chorion, and the diagnosis of monozygosity can be definitely established in this two-thirds.

monra(d)dene, variant forms of MANRED *Obs.*

monradite ('mɒnrædaɪt). *Min.* [a. G. *monradit* (A. Erdmann 1842), f. the name of Dr. *Monrad* of Bergen: see -ITE.] A massive granular variety of pyroxene found at Bergen in Norway.

1846 *Penny Cycl.* Suppl. II. 308/2. **1849** J. NICOL *Man. Min.* 190. **1852** BROOKE & MILLER *Phillips' Min.* 662.

monræidene, monreden, var. ff. MANRED.

Monroeism (mən'rəʊɪz(ə)m). [f. name of James *Monroe*, president of the United States 1817–1825.] The 'Monroe doctrine' (see DOCTRINE 2 c). So **Mon'roeist**, a supporter of the Monroe doctrine.

1896 *Westm. Gaz.* 18 Jan. 5/1 It is stated..that the report ..in its definition of Monroeism, declares that the acquisition by purchase, aggression, or otherwise, of territory on the American Continent by a foreign Power will be construed as an unfriendly act. **1901** *Ibid.* 17 Sept. 2/2 He was a determined Monroeist. **1904** *Speaker* 1 Oct. 6/2 Monroism before the advent of Mr. Roosevelt has always been confined to enforcing a 'hands off' policy.

monrolite ('mʌnrəʊlaɪt). *Min.* [f. *Monroe* the name of its locality in New York State + -LITE.] = FIBROLITE.

1849 SILLIMAN in *Amer. Jrnl. Sci.* VIII. 385 On Monrolite. **1852** BROOKE & MILLER *Phillips' Min.* 662.

Monrovia (mən'rəʊvɪə). The name of the capital city of Liberia used *attrib.* with reference to the political grouping of African states resulting from a conference which took place there in May 1961.

1962 *Ann. Reg. 1961* 304 The Monrovia Powers, which included the heirs of *Afrique noire d'expression française*, ..were more disposed to co-operate with Europe. **1962** *Listener* 18 Oct. 594/2 It [*sc.* Nigeria] is one of the leading countries of the so-called Monrovia group of African states who have sought to maintain a realistic course on international problems. **1963** HAILE SELASSIE in *Jrnl. Mod. African Studies* Sept. 285 The commentators of 1963 speak, in discussing Africa, of the Monrovia States, the Brazzaville Group, the Casablanca Powers... Let us put an end to these terms. **1965** H. LAND in C. Legum *Africa* (rev. ed.) 217 It [*sc.* Nigeria] played a major rôle in helping to eliminate the friction between the Casablanca and Monrovia groups, and in establishing the Organization of African Unity. **1971** W. LAQUEUR *Dict. Politics* 313 Tubman..sponsored the Monrovia Conference of 1961.

‖**mons** (mɒnz). Pl. **montes** ('mɒntiːz). [L. *mons* mountain.] The Latin word for 'mount', 'mountain', used in certain phrases.

a. *Palmistry.* **mons area**, the sensitive area of the *mons veneris*. **mons Jovis, mercurii, saturni, veneris** (see quot. 1678). **b.** *Anat.* **mons pubis**, the more or less prominent fatty eminence covering the pubic symphysis of the human male. **mons Veneris**, the similar eminence in the woman; also (usu. in phr.) **mons**.

1621 B. JONSON *Gipsies Metam.* Wks. (Rtldg.) 620/2 You are no great Wencher, I see by your table, Although your *Mons Veneris* sayes you are able. **1678** PHILLIPS (ed. 4), *Tubercula*, in Chiromancy are those more eminent Muscles, or protuberant parts under the Fingers; they are otherwise called *Montes*; that under the Thumb, *Tuberculum*, or *Mons Veneris*; that in the Root of the Fore-finger, is called *Mons Jovis*, of the Middle-finger, *Mons Saturni*, of the Ring-finger, *Mons Solis*, of the Little-finger, *Mons Mercurii*. **1693** tr. *Blancard's Phys. Dict.* (ed. 2), *Mons Veneris*, the upper part of a Womans Secrets, something higher than the rest. **1797** *Encycl. Brit.* (ed. 3) I. 740/1 The *mons veneris*..is internally composed of adipose membranes. **1857** BULLOCK tr. *Cazeaux' Midwif.* 39 The Mons Veneris is a rounded eminence..situated in front of the pubis, and surmounting the vulva. **1965** MASTERS & JOHNSON in J. Money *Sex Research* iv. 109 The concept of manipulating only the clitoris rather than the entire mons area is grossly in error. **1968** T. LIDZ *Person* xiv. 427 Stimulation of the mons area or perineal region in general can rapidly revive the arousal. **1969** 'J' *Sensuous Woman* (1970) iii. 32 It takes longer to come to orgasm with mons manipulation, but it is just as satiating an experience as direct clitoral shaft massage.

mons., erroneous abbreviation of MONSIEUR.

monsc(h)ipe, obs. forms of MANSHIP.

monse, obs. form of MANSE *v.*

‖**monseigneur** (mɔ̃sɛnjœr). Pl. **messeigneurs** (mɛsɛnjœr). Forms: 7 **montseigneur, -senior, mount-segnior, -senior, mons(e)igneur**, 7– **monseigneur**. [F., f. *mon* my + *seigneur* lord. Cf. SEIGNEUR.]

1. A French title of honour given to persons of eminence, esp. to princes, cardinals, archbishops, and bishops. Abbreviated *Mgr.* †In absolute use: The title conferred since the time of Louis XIV upon the Dauphin of France. *Obs.*

1610 *Histrio-m.* E ij, Every Pedlers French is term'd Monsigneur. **1698** M. LISTER *Journ. Paris* (1699) 195 The chief of the Blood Royal are lodged here, *viz.* the King, Monseigneur the Dauphin, and the 3 Grandsons [etc.]. *Ibid.* 201 Monseigneur had been but lately possessed of it [*sc.* Meudon]. **1727–41** CHAMBERS *Cycl.*, *Monseigneur*, in the plural Messeigneurs, a title of honour and respect used by the French. *Ibid.*, *Monseigneur*..is a quality now restrained to the dauphin of France. **1859** DICKENS *T. Two Cities* II. vii, Monseigneur, one of the great lords in power at the Court, held his fortnightly reception. **1871** E. C. G. MURRAY *Member for Paris* III. 331, 'I drink to the health of Monseigneur le Duc de Hautbourg', cried M. Ballanchu.

†**2.** Used for MONSIGNOR. *Obs.*

1600 W. WATSON *Decacordon* (1602) 96 First he [Doctor Lewis] was made Montseigneur. **1601** *Imp. Consid. Sec. Priests* (1675) 55 And when was that, our great Monseigneurs? **1660** FISHER *Rusticks Alarm* Wks. (1679) 589 The Pope, and his Cardinals Mount Seniors, Jesuits [etc.].

‖**monsieur** (‖məsjø, mə'sjɜː). Forms: 6 **monsure, -sire, -sieú, mounsire, -syre**, *Sc.* **monsour**, 6–7 **mouns(i)er, -sieur**, 7 **mouncer, -seur, monser, monnsieur, meunsier**, 6– **monsieur**. Also *jocularly* 8–9 MOUNSEER, 9 MOSSOO. [F.; originally two words, *mon* my, *sieur* lord. Cf. MESSIRE and MONSEIGNEUR.

Cf. Sp. *monsiur*, It. *monsù*, used in speaking to or of a Frenchman.]

1. The title of courtesy prefixed to the name, surname, or nobiliary title of a Frenchman; originally restricted to men of high station, but now equivalent to the Eng. 'Mr.', exc. that it is applied to the bearer of any title of rank as well as to others. In English often used in speaking of (European) foreigners of other than Fr. nationality, instead of the equivalent prefix (as *Herr*, *Signor*, *Señor*) used by the particular nation. Abbreviated *M.* (the forms *Mons.*, *Monsr.*, often occurring in Eng. writings, are not now current in France). See also the plural MESSIEURS.

1512 in *Acc. Ld. High Treas. Scotl.* (1902) IV. 399 Monsure Lamote servitouris, that dansit ane moris to the King. **1523** *St. Papers Hen. VIII*, VI. 194 Monsr. de Rokyndolfff off thAllmains. **1533** in *Acc. Ld. High Treas. Scotl.* (1905) VI. 133 Writtingis send furth of Ingland to Monsieur Bewis. **1616** SIR C. MOUNTAGU in *Buccleuch MSS.* (Hist. MSS. Comm.) I. 248 Mouncer Shamburgh when he is in town I hear lies near me. **1643** EVELYN *Diary* 5 Dec., The palace of Mons. de Bassompiere. **1670** COTTON *Espernon* I. I. 3 Monsieur de la Valette was he that would take upon him to execute this design. **1759** GOLDSM. (*title*) Memoirs of M. de Voltaire. **1763** *Ann. Reg.* 86 When M. Rousseau published his Emilius... The following letter from mons. Rousseau... To accept of Mons. Rousseau's resignation. **1798** (*title*) Stella. Translated from the German of M. Goethe. **1848** JULIA KAVANAGH *Madeleine* viii. 99 Monsieur Bignon was a hale..little man, on the verge of fifty. **1871** E. C. G. MURRAY *Member for Paris* III. 332 M. le Duc de Hautbourg.

†**b.** *transf.* and *jocular*. Often with reference to the French custom of prefixing the title to designations of office. *Obs.*

1553 *Respublica* I. iv. 395 Sayde not I he sholde be called Mounsier Authoritye? *a* **1553** UDALL *Royster D.* IV. viii. (Arb.) 77, I my selfe will mounsire graunde captaine vndertake. **1556** J. HEYWOOD *Spider & F.* lvii. 246 With this mounser graund captayne the great bragger: Was much a mased. **1563** PILKINGTON, etc. *Burn. Paules* D j b, But that a man may not be wiser than Mounser Pope, I would interprete this greate miracle thus. **1590** SHAKS. *Mids. N.* IV. i. 10 Mounsieur Cobweb, good Mounsier get your weapons in your hand. **1678** DRYDEN *All for Love* Pref., He has.. transformed the Hippolytus of Euripides into Monsieur Hippolyte. **1792** WOLCOT (P. Pindar) *Solomon & Mousetrap* ii, To catch that vile free-booter, Monsieur Mouse.

c. ***Monsieur (de) Paris***, a euphemistic title conferred in France upon the public executioner.

1859 DICKENS *T. Two Cities* II. vii, At the gallows and the wheel..Monsieur Paris..presided.

2. Used (vocatively or otherwise) as a title of courtesy substituted for the name of the person addressed or referred to: (*a*) in speaking to or of a Frenchman; (*b*) in literal renderings of the mode of speech of Frenchmen.

1588 SHAKS. *L.L.L.* V. i. 47 Mounsier, are you not lettred? **1601** —— *All's Well* II. v. 94 Where are my other men? Monsieur, farwell. **1713** SWIFT *Salamander* Wks. 1755 III. II. 75 We say monsieur to an ape Without offence to human shape. **1768–74** TUCKER *Lt. Nat.* (1834) II. 595 The French carpenter cannot saw his boards without..calling to his fellow, 'Monsieur, have the goodness to reach me that file'. **1873** HOWELLS *Chance Acquaint.* viii, 'Monsieur heaps me with benefits;—monsieur'—began the bewildered cooper.

†**b.** Used for: The French people. *Obs.*

1673 *Remarques Humours Town* 95 When they are witty, they are alwaies beholding to Monsieur. **1695** *Roxb. Ball.* (1887) VI. 446 Now Monsieur bring out all you can, We'll fight yon ship or man to man. **1701** T. BROWN *Advice* in *Collect. Poems* 106 That, that's the sure way to Mortifie France: For Monsieur our Nation will always be Gulling. [**1755**: see MOUNSEER.]

3. *Hist.* A title given to the second son or to the next younger brother of the King of France.

1572 MIDDELMORE in Ellis *Orig. Lett.* Ser. II. III. 8 The motion that was made to the Quene your mistris for Monsieur. **1608** MIDDLETON *Mad World* IV. F 3, It was suspected much in Mounsiers dayes. *a* **1635** NAUNTON *Fragm. Reg.* (Arb.) 36 The same time that Mounsier was here a Suitor to the Queen. **1670** COTTON *Espernon* III. ix. 445 The King, the Queens, the Monsieur, and Madame, with all the other Princes, and Princesses. **1798** R. C. DALLAS tr. *Cléry's Jrnl. Occur. Louis XVI* 159 Monsieur, and the Count d'Artois, were again assembling all the emigrants. **1821** JEFFERSON *Autobiog. & Writ.* (1892) I. 128 They procured a committee to be held..to which Monsieur and the Count d'Artois should be admitted.

4. A person who is addressed as 'Monsieur'; in early use, a Frenchman of rank; in later use, a Frenchman generally. Now *rare* or *Obs.*: see MOSSOO, MOUNSEER.

1500–20 DUNBAR *Poems* lxiii. 42 Monsouris of France, gud clarat-cunnaris. **1613** SHAKS. *Hen. VIII*, I. iii. 21 Now I would pray our Monsieurs To thinke an English Courtier may be wise, And neuer see the Louure. **1627** DRAYTON *Agincourt* 59 A shoolesse Souldier there a man might meete, Leading his Mounsier by the armes fast bound. **1640** T. RAWLINS *Rebell.* II. i. D, And I..onely surviv'd to threat defiance In the Mounsiers teeth, and stand Defendant For my Countries cause. **1644** MILTON *Educ.* 8 Nor shall we then need the Mounsieurs of Paris to take our hopefull youth into thir..custodies, and send them over back again transform'd into mimics. **1659** HOWELL *Lexicon, Ital. Prov.*, The Counts of Germany, the Dons of Spain, the Monnsieurs of France, the Cadets of England, the Nobles of Scotland,..make a poor company. **1698** FRYER *Acc. E. India & P.* 88 The French..whose Factory is better stor'd with Monsieurs than with Cash. **1705** LUTTRELL *Brief Rel.* (1857) V. 580 At last the monsieurs struck, and are brought into Plymouth. **1756** *Rhode Island Col. Rec.* (1860) V. 472, I do not doubt if the monsieurs should think proper to attack us, we should be able to give them a good flogging. **1846** H. MELVILLE *Typee* (rev. ed.) Sequel 304 Jimmy..had a talk about the 'Wee-Wees', as the people of Nukukeva call the Monsieurs.

5. Monsieur John, Jean, a kind of pear.

[**1664** EVELYN *Kal. Hort.* Nov. 78 Pears. Messire Jean.] **1731** MILLER *Gard. Dict.* s.v. *Pyrus*, Messire-Jean blanc & gris, *i.e.* The White and Grey Monsieur John. **1741** *Compl. Fam.-Piece* II. iii. 400 These Pears. [Oct.] Green Sugar,.. Monsieur Jean,..and others. **1860** R. HOGG *Fruit Manual* 200 [Pears] Messire Jean (..Monsieur John).

6. (See quot.) ? *Obs.*

1760 MRS. GLASSE *Cookery* (1767) 331 To dress a turtle the West Indian way... Then take from the back-shell all the meat and entrails, except the monsieur, which is the fat, and looks green. **1769** ELIZ. RAFFALD *Eng. Housekpr.* (1805) 15. **1785** FARLEY *Lond. Art Cookery* (1789) 30.

†**7.** *attrib.* and *Comb.*, as **Monsieur-land**, France; **Monsieur-like** *adv.*, after the manner of a Frenchman; **Monsieur's pear**, ? = 5; **Monsieur('s) plum**, a large yellow plum. *Obs.*

1668 DRYDEN *Evening's Love* I. ii, They were of your wild English.., a kind of Northern Beast, that is taught its feats of activity in *Monsieur-land. **1679** G. R. tr. *Boaystuau's Theat. World* III. 245 And dressing of themselves *Monsieur-like. **1658** EVELYN *Fr. Gard.* (1675) 114 *Monsieurs Pear. *Ibid.* 128 *Monsieurs Plum. **1706** LONDON & WISE *Retir'd Gard.* I. 40 The Monsieur Plum is large, round, and of a Violet Colour. **1731** MILLER *Gard. Dict.* s.v. *Prunus*, Prune de Monsieur, *i.e.* the Monsieur Plum.

†**Monsieurship.** *Obs.* [f. MONSIEUR + -SHIP.] **a.** The personality of a 'monsieur'. **b.** The condition of being a 'monsieur'.

1579 G. HARVEY *Letter-bk.* (Camden) 66 Hath your Monsieurshipp so soone forgottin. **1607** DEKKER *Knt.'s Conjur.* (1842) 36 Practising all the foolish tricks of fashions after their Mounsieur-ships. **1673** WYCHERLEY *Gentl.*

Dancing-Master IV. i, You have sworn..he shall never have me if he does not leave off his Monsieurship.

monsignor, -nore (mɒnsiːˈnjɔː(r), -ˈnjɔːreɪ, mɒnˈsiːnjə(r)). Pl. **monsignori** (-ˈnjɔːriː). [It. *Monsignore* (shortened -*signor*), formed after Fr. MONSEIGNEUR: see SIGNOR.] An honorific title bestowed upon prelates, officers of the Papal court and household, and others. Also *absol.*

1641 MILTON *Ch. Govt.* II. i. 43 Bilson hath decipher'd us all the galanteries of Signore and Monsignore, and Monsieur. **1670** G. H. *Hist. Cardinals* II. I. 130, I have encharged Monsignor Burlemont to wait upon you. **1768** BARETTI *Acc. Manners & Cust. Italy* II. 168 Their cardinals and principal monsignori's seem in general to have a greater turn for the science of politics than for any other. **1813** C. O'CONOR *Columbanus ad Hibernos* No. 6. 116 The thunders of scarlet Cardinals and purple Monsignores. **1870** DISRAELI *Lothair* lxiii, There were some cardinals in the apartment and several monsignori. **1884** *Men of Time* (ed. 11) 218/2 Monsignor Capel..was named private chamberlain to Pope Pius IX., in 1868. **1896** *Century Mag.* Feb. 595 'Monsignori' are not necessarily bishops, nor even consecrated priests, the title being really a secular one.

Hence **monsiˈgnorial** *a.*, possessing this title.

1876 *Tinsley's Mag.* XIX. 342 [He] was not a cardinal archbishop, a monsignorial prelate, or Loyolite.

monslæht, -slauȝt, etc.: see MANSLAUGHT, etc.

monsoon (mɒnˈsuːn). Forms: 6 **monssoyn**, 6–8 **monson**, 7 **monzoon(e**, **-sone**, **-coin**, **-zoin**, **monthsoune**, **mon(e)thsone**, **moonsoon**, **mounson**, **-soun(e**, **munso(o)n**, **manson**, **-sound**, **mossoon**, **mous(s)on**, 8 **mounsoon**, **mous(s)oon**, 6– **monsoon**. [a. early mod.Du. *monssoen*, *-soyn* (Linschoten 1596), a. Pg. *monção*, in 16th c. also *moução* (Yule), believed to be a. Arab. *mausim* lit. season, hence monsoon, f. *wasama* to mark.

The word is found in all the Rom. langs.: F. *mousson* (in 17th c. also *monson*, *muesson*), Sp. *monzon*, It. *monsone* (in 16th c. *moson*).]

1. a. A seasonal wind prevailing in southern Asia and especially in the Indian Ocean, which during the period from April to October blows approximately from the south-west, and from October to April from the north-east, the direction being dependent upon periodic changes of temperature in the surrounding land-surfaces.

The south-west or summer monsoon is commonly accompanied by heavy and continuous rainfall, and is therefore often referred to as the ***wet*** or ***rainy monsoon***, the north-east or winter monsoon being known as the ***dry monsoon***.

1584 BARRET in *Hakluyt's Voy.* (1599) II. i. 278 The times or seasonable windes called Monsons. *Ibid.* 280 The monson from India for Portugall. **1598** W. PHILLIP tr. *Linschoten* I. xcii. 143 In Goa they stayed till the Monson, or time of the windes came in to sayle for China. **1615** in Danvers & Foster *Corresp.* III. 268, I departed for Bantam having..the opportunity of the Monethsone. **1615** SIR T. ROE *Embassy* (Hakl. Soc.) I. 36 The Monthsone will here also be spent. **1687** A. LOVELL tr. *Thevenot's Trav.* III. i. i. 1 The proper season for Sailing on the Indian-Sea is called *Mousson* or *Monson*, by corruption of *Moussem*. **1757** J. H. GROSE *Voy. E. Indies* 365 The winter monsoon. **1778** ORME *Hist. Milit. Trans. in Indostan* II. 533 The monsoon..warned Admiral Pococke to quit the coast. **1779** FORREST *Voy. N. Guinea* 182 During the north east monsoon, the highest tide is in the night. **1783** JUSTAMOND tr. *Raynal's Hist. Indies* I. 47 The dry and rainy monsoons. **1804** C. B. BROWN tr. *Volney's View Soil U.S.* 205 The current called the summer monsoon. **1815** ELPHINSTONE *Acc. Caubul* (1842) I. 167 The most remarkable rainy season, is that called in India the south-west monsoon. **1873** H. F. BLANFORD *Winds N. India* 12 North-east winds are more than twice as frequent in the so-called south-west monsoon as at the opposite season, when the north-east monsoon prevails at sea. *Ibid.* 23 While the average direction of the summer monsoon is less easterly, that of the winter monsoon is less westerly.

b. ***the breaking up, change of the monsoon***: the period of tempestuous weather which frequently prevails between the north-east and the south-west monsoons.

1693 SIR T. P. BLOUNT *Nat. Hist.* 418 The Tempestuous Months about Autumn, or at the change of the Monsoons. **1698** FRYER *Acc. E. Ind. & P.* 48 The breaking up of the Munsoons. **1761** *Ann. Reg., Charac.* 7/1 Toward the end of October, the rainy season, which they term the change of the monsoon, begins on the coast of Coromandel. **1898** F. T. BULLEN *Cruise Cachalot* 99 The change of the monsoon in the Bay of Bengal is beastliness unadulterated.

c. The rainfall which accompanies the south-west monsoon; the rainy season.

1747 *Scheme Equip. Men of War* 23 Like Monsoons or Water-Spouts, the higher they rise, the more they are contracted. **1800** WELLINGTON in Gurw. *Desp.* (1837) I. 77, I doubt whether that will be sufficiently early to enable us to conclude matters before the setting in of the monsoon. **1838** *Lett. fr. Madras* (1843) 224 There is a great deal of distress among the natives, owing to the failure of the monsoon. **1869** E. A. PARKES *Pract. Hygiene* (ed. 3) 82 The floods of the excessive monsoon which prevails there [*i.e.* Burmah]. **1877** C. GEIKIE *Christ* xlix. (1879) 589 The early rains were longed for as the monsoons in India after the summer heat.

2. *transf.* Any wind which has periodic alternations of direction and velocity, caused by variations of temperature between the land surfaces and the surrounding ocean, or by the difference of temperature between the polar and equatorial regions. Cf. TRADE WIND.

1691 RAY *Creation* I. (1692) 79 That the Monsoons and Trade Winds should be so constant and periodical even to the thirtieth Degree of Latitude all round the Globe..is a Subject worthy of the Thoughts of the greatest Philosophers. **1796** MORSE *Amer. Geog.* II. 560 Easterly and westerly monsoons..prevail in this country. *c* **1796** T. TWINING *Trav. Amer.* (1894) 8 The northwest monsoon was now prevailing. **1855** MAURY *Phys. Geog. Sea* xiv. §787 Monsoons are, for the most part, formed of trade-winds. When at stated seasons of the year a trade-wind is deflected in its regular course..it is regarded as a monsoon. **1889** W. FERREL *Treat. Winds* 199 All the great monsoons..are found in countries and on oceans adjacent to high mountain ranges.

3. *fig.* and in figurative context.

1785 BURKE *Nabob of Arcot* Wks. IV. 320 Those who have seen their friends sink in the tornado which raged during the late shift of the monsoon. **1831** CARLYLE *Sart. Res.* III. viii, Such a minnow is Man;..his Ocean the immeasurable All; his Monsoons and periodic Currents the mysterious Course of Providence. **1846** DE QUINCEY *Antigone of Sophocles* Wks. 1862 XIII. 212 In the very monsoon of his raving misery.

4. *attrib.* and *Comb.* **monsoon forest** [tr. G. *monsunwälder* (A. F. W. Schimper *Pflanzengeographie* (1898) III. iii. 281)], a deciduous forest found in regions of heavy seasonal rainfall.

1662 J. DAVIES tr. *Mandelslo's Trav.* 245 Which put us in hope, we should soon have the Manson-wind. **1804** ANNA SEWARD *Mem. Darwin* 186 The monsoon winds. **1883** ELIOT in *Ind. Meteorol. Mem.* II. 2 These characteristics of the monsoon rains of that year. *Ibid.* 3 Cyclonic or South-west Monsoon Storm of..July 1878. **1903** W. R. FISHER tr. *Schimper's Plant-Geography* III. iii. 260 The monsoon forest is more or less leafless during the dry season,..is tropophilous in character, usually less lofty than the rain-forest, rich in woody lianes, rich in herbaceous but poor in woody epiphytes. **1926** TANSLEY & CHIPP *Study of Vegetation* xv. 291 Monsoon forest occurs in regions where the rainfall exceeds 180 cm..but where there is a prolonged dry season during which the forest is more or less leafless. **1960** N. POLUNIN *Introd. Plant Geogr.* xiv. 439 Widespread though variable are the monsoon forests or similar 'seasonal' forests, developed in regions enjoying abundant rainfall during the wet season, but having this alternating with a pronounced drought lasting from four to six months or sometimes longer.

Hence **monˈsoonal** *a.*, of or relating to a monsoon; **monˈsoonish** *a.*, suggestive or characteristic of a monsoon; **monˈsoonishly** *adv.*, as in a monsoon.

1878 *Encycl. Brit.* XVI. 148/2 The heavy monsoonal rains fairly set in. *Ibid.*, The winds of Australia are also strictly monsoonal. **1886** KIPLING *Plain Tales from Hills* (1888) 118 Not a mere hill-shower but a good, tepid, monsoonish downpour. **1900** —— in *Academy* 17 Mar. 219/1 It rained monsoonishly. **1913** J. MURRAY *Ocean* iv. 83 The monsoonal deflection of the tradewinds, for some distance out to sea, out of their course to westward. **1936** *Geogr. Jrnl.* LXXXVIII. 297 The arrival of the deep mass of monsoonal air. **1961** *Aeroplane* CI. 504/1 Hundreds of these birds had made their way to Australia by soaring in front of 'monsoonal fronts'. **1972** *Kent Life* July 82/2 Under the equatorial sun and monsoonal rains, two crops of rice are easily obtained. **1975** *Bangladesh Observer* 22 July 5/3 Two friends from Dacca and I were enjoying a monsoonish evening in Delhi. It had rained not torrentially but heavily enough to flood some areas and bring the temperature down.

monster (ˈmɒnstə(r)), *sb.* and *a.* Forms: 3–6 **monstre**, 5–6 *Sc.* **monstir**, **-tour**, 6 **mounster**, **monstur(e**, **-tuire**, *Sc.* **-toure**, 5– **monster**. [OF. *monstre* (= Pg., It. *monstro*), ad. L. *monstrum* monster, something marvellous; orig. a divine portent or warning, f. root of *monēre* to warn.]

A. *sb.*

†**1.** Something extraordinary or unnatural; a prodigy, a marvel. *Obs.*

c **1374** CHAUCER *Boeth.* II. pr. i. 20 (Camb. MS.) Thilke meruayles Monstre [L. *illius prodigii*] fortune. **1382** WYCLIF *2 Macc.* v. 4 Alle men preyeden, the monstris, or wondres, ..for to be turned in to good. *c* **1412** HOCCLEVE *De Reg. Princ.* 344 Was it not eek a monstre as in nature þat god I-borë was of a virgine? *c* **1430** LYDG. *Min. Poems* (Percy Soc.) 119 It were a monstre geyne nature, as I fynde, That a grete mastyfe shuld a lyoun bynde. **1533** BELLENDEN *Livy* IV. viii. (S.T.S.) II. 74 Is it nocht ane huge monstoure,..þat It [*sc.* the city] suld haue made him king. **1537** in *Lett. Suppress. Monast.* (Camden) 160 The vicar off Mendyllsham..hath.. brought home hys woman and chyldern into hys vicarage. Thys acte by hym done is in thys countre a monster, and many do growge at it. **1558** KNOX *First Blast* (Arb.) 20 He that iudgeth it a monstre in nature, that a woman shall exercise weapons. **1562** WINȜET *Last Blast* Wks. (S.T.S.) I. 44 Ingratitude and vtheris deuyllische monstres of vice. **1614** BUDDEN tr. *Ærodius' Disc. Parents' Hon.* (1616) 5 Contempt, impiety, murdering of parents, were therefore ordinary monsters among the Greekes. **1641** *Vind. Smectymnuus* vii. 91 That power, which was a stranger and a monster to former times. **1702** *Eng. Theophrast.* 43 'Tis the rarity that makes the monster. **1710** SHAFTESB. *Adv. Author* III. iii. 183 Monsters and Monster-Lands were never more in request.

2. a. An animal or plant deviating in one or more of its parts from the normal type; *spec.*, an animal afflicted with some congenital malformation; a misshapen birth, an abortion. Cf. MONSTROSITY.

a **1300** *Cursor M.* 9846 If þou fand..A barn..þat had thre fete and handes thre, And if þou siþen a-noiþer fand þat wanted oiþer fote or hand,..monstres moght man call þam like. *c* **1400** MAUNDEV. (1839) v. 47 A monstre is a thing difformed aȝen Kynde both of Man or of Best. **1481** CAXTON *Myrr.* I. xiv. 44 Or it hath a membre lasse than he ought to haue,..and may be called therfor a monstre. **1556** *Chron. Gr. Friars* (Camden) 57 A monstre, a calfe wyth ij. heddes, iiij. eres, iiij. eyne, viij. f[eete] and ij. taylles. **1607** TOPSELL *Four-f. Beasts* 337 A horsse-keeper which broght..an infant, or rather a monster, which he had got vpon a Mare. **1614** B. JONSON *Bart. Fair* III. i, Then you met the man with the monsters, and I could not get you from him. *a* **1680** BUTLER *Rem.* (1759) II. 72 His Parts are disproportionate to the whole, and like a Monster he has more of some, and less of others than he should have. **1717** LADY M. W. MONTAGU *Let. to C'tess Mar* 16 Jan., The princes keep favourite dwarfs. The Emperor and Empress have two of these little Monsters. **1727–41** CHAMBERS *Cycl.* s.v. *Mule*, Mules, among gardeners, denote a sort of vegetable monsters. **1754–64** SMELLIE *Midwif.* I. 123 When two children are distinct they are called twins; and monsters, when they are joined together. *a* **1793** J. HUNTER *Ess. & Observ.* (1861) I. 240 The vegetable kingdom abounds with monsters. **1840** POE *1002nd Tale* Wks. 1864 I. 141 The term 'monster' is equally applicable to small abnormal things and to great. **1897** *Allbutt's Syst. Med.* IV. 528 It [*i.e.* congenital absence of spleen] has been noted in monsters.

b. *transf.* and *fig.*

1604 SHAKS. *Oth.* III. iii. 107 Thou ecchos't me; As if there were some Monster in thy thought Too hideous to be shewne. **1821** SCOTT *Kenilw.* xxx, Varney was one of the few—the very few moral monsters, who contrive to lull to sleep the remorse of their own bosoms. **1837** EMERSON *Address, Amer. Schol.* Wks. (Bohn) II. 175 The state of society is one in which the members have suffered amputation from the trunk, and strut about so many walking monsters. **1873** M. ARNOLD *Lit. & Dogma* (1876) 356 The non-Christian religions are not to the wise man mere monsters.

3. a. An imaginary animal (such as the centaur, sphinx, minotaur, or the heraldic griffin, wyvern, etc.) having a form either partly brute and partly human, or compounded of elements from two or more animal forms.

Except in heraldic use, the word usually suggests the additional notion of great size and ferocity, being specifically associated with the 'monsters' victoriously encountered by various mythical heroes.

c **1385** CHAUCER *L.G.W.* 1928 (*Ariadne*) This Minos hath a monstre, a wikked beste, That was so cruel that..he wolde him [*i.e.* a man] ete. **1390** GOWER *Conf.* III. 123 A Monstre [*i.e.* Sagittarius] with a bowe on honde: On whom that sondri sterres stonde. *c* **1420** *Pallad. on Husb.* I. 935 For eddris, spritis, monstris, thyng of drede. To make a smoke and stynk is good in dede. **1490** CAXTON *Eneydos* xv. 58 Wherof was made a monstre fulle terrible, that hath as many eyen in her hede..as she hathe fedders vpon her. **1500–20** DUNBAR *Poems* xxxv. 28 He sall ascend as ane horrebble grephoun, Him meit sall in the air ane scho dragoun; Thir terrible monsteris sall togidder thrist. **1567** *Gude & Godlie Ball.* (S.T.S.) 214 Thocht Hercules, for Exionie, A mychtie monster did subdew, Zit endit he in miserie. **1586** MARLOWE *1st Pt. Tamburl.* IV. iii, A monster of fiue hundred thousand heades, Compact of Rapine, Pyracie, and spoile. **1610** SHAKS. *Temp.* II. ii. 69 This is some Monster of the Isle, with foure legs. **1613** PURCHAS *Pilgrimage* (1614) 54 Annedotus a Monster (otherwhere like a fish, his head, feet and hands like a Man). **1737** POPE *Hor. Epist.* II. i. 18 The great Alcides, ev'ry Labour past, Had still this Monster [*sc.* Death] to subdue at last. **1821** BYRON *Sardan.* I. ii, A sort of semi-glorious human monster. **1874** PAPWORTH & MORANT *Brit. Armorials* Introd. 7 How difficult it often is to determine what species of beast, bird,..monster,..or tree, a charge was intended to represent. **1875** JOWETT *Plato* (ed. 2) V. 13 The book of the Laws if left incomplete is compared to a monster wandering about without a head. **1893** CUSSANS *Her.* (ed. 4) 98 The Dragon is a winged monster.

b. *transf.* and *fig.*

1500–20 DUNBAR *Poems* xxvi. 91 The fowll monstir Glutteny. **1515** BARCLAY *Egloges* iv. (1570) C vj b, Fearefull is labour,..Dreadfull of visage, a monster intreatable. **1560** DAUS tr. *Sleidane's Comm.* 17 b, He would wishe that all learned men woulde set on with touch and nayle to overcome that Monstre. **1666** DRYDEN *Ann. Mirab.* ccxviii, The infant monster [*i.e.* the fire of London], with devouring strong, Walk'd boldly upright with exalted head. **1702** ROWE *Tamerl.* I. i. 96 Oh thou fell Monster, War. **1825** LYTTON *Zicci* i, The monster that lives and dies in a drop of water—carnivorous—insatiable. **1856** EMERSON *Eng. Traits, Wealth* Wks. (Bohn) II. 75 Engineers and firemen without number have been sacrificed in learning to tame and guide the monster [*sc.* Steam].

¶ In collocations like 'faultless monster', 'monster of perfection', connoting an incredible or repulsively unnatural degree of excellence.

1682 SHEFFIELD (Dk. Buckhm.) *Ess. Poetry* 235 Reject that vulgar error which appears So fair, of making perfect characters, There's no such thing in Nature, and you'l draw A faultless Monster which the world ne'r saw.

4. A person of inhuman and horrible cruelty or wickedness; a monstrous example *of* (wickedness, or some particular vice).

1556 J. HEYWOOD *Spider & F.* liv. 22 Which deede: if we do, wheare are our like monsturs? **1598** B. JONSON *Ev. Man in Hum.* III. iii, And he to turne monster of ingratitude, and strike his lawfull host. **1605** SHAKS. *Lear* I. ii. 102 He cannot bee such a Monster. **1613** PURCHAS *Pilgrimage* (1614) 51 That Monster of irreligion, Mahomet. **1642** D. ROGERS *Naaman* 14 Open monsters and odious livers. **1683** EVELYN *Diary* 5 Dec., That monster of a man, Lord Howard of Escrick. **1707** WATTS *Hymns & Spir. Songs* I. xxxix. (1751) 28 Should Nature change, And Mothers Monsters prove. **1713** ADDISON *Guard.* No. 105 ⁋5 These monsters of inhumanity. *a* **1715** BURNET *Own Time* II. (1724) I. 269 Dryden..being a monster of immodesty. **1783** JUSTAMOND tr. *Raynal's Hist. Indies* VI. 293 They were no sooner landed at Barbadoes, but the monster sold her who had saved his life. **1847** EMERSON *Repr. Men, Montaigne* Wks. (Bohn) I. 336 The correspondence of Pope and Swift describes mankind around them as monsters. **1877** MRS. OLIPHANT *Makers Flor.* xii. 297 Alexander VI was a monster of iniquity. **1887** BOWEN *Æneid* I. 347 Pygmalion, monster unrivalled in hellish deed.

5. An animal of huge size; hence, anything of vast and unwieldy proportions.

1530 PALSGR. 744/2 A monster of the see. *a* **1533** LD. BERNERS *Huon* I. 167, I condempne thee to be .xxviii. yeres a monster in yᵉ see. **1613** PURCHAS *Pilgrimage* (1614) 839 A great beast..(a Crocodile or some other monster). **1738** WESLEY *Ps.* CXLVII. vii, Monsters sporting on the Flood, In scaly Silver shine. **1759** GOLDSM. *Pres. St. Polite Learn.* (Globe) 432/2 From these inauspicious combinations proceed those monsters of learning, the Trevoux, Encyclopédies, and Bibliothèques of the age. **1832** TENNYSON *Lotos-eaters* 152 The wallowing monster spouted his foam-fountains in the sea. **1966** K. MARTIN *Father Figures* i. 20 Buying from the all-purposes shop bullseyes and, for a penny, 'monsters', which were big bottles of fizzy lemonade.

6. *attrib.* and *Comb.* **a.** simple attrib., as ***monster-brood, -bulk, -land, -market, -spite***; ***monster-like*** adj. and adv.; ***monster-browed, -headed*** adjs.; **b.** objective, as ***monster-master, -monger, -queller, -slayer, -tamer; monster-bearing, -breeding, -killing, -quelling, -slaying, -taming, -teeming*** adjs.; **c.** instrumental, as ***monster-guarded, -spouted*** adjs.; **d.** appositive, as ***monster-cloud, -crew, -god, -lord, -machine, -man, -mask, -master, -paddock, -people.***

1648 FANSHAWE *Il Pastor Fido* I. v. 9 The *monster-bearing earth Did never teem such a prodigious birth. **1728** POPE *Dunc.* I. 108 In each she marks her Image full exprest, But chief, in Tibbalds *monster-breeding breast. **1738** GRAY *Propertius* ii. 41 Earth's *monster-brood stretch'd on their iron-bed. **1929** BLUNDEN *Near & Far* 49 Though the full cloud Frowns *monster-browed. **1697** DRYDEN *Æneid* IX. 959 Down sunk the *Monster-Bulk, and press'd the Ground. **1934** BLUNDEN *Mind's Eye* 16 A sky of freakish *monster-clouds. **1697** DRYDEN *Æneid* VIII. 395 Thy Hands, unconquer'd Heroe, cou'd subdue The Cloud-born Centaurs, and the *Monster Crew. **1716** POPE *Iliad* v. 954 To tame the *Monster-God Minerva knows, And oft' afflicts his Brutal Breast with Woes. **1594** *Selimus* K 2, Thou hast trode The *monster-garded [*printed* monster-garden] paths, that lead to crownes. **1869** 'MARK TWAIN' *Innoc. Abr.* xx. 147 The more immediate scenery consisted of fields and farm-houses outside the car, and a *monster-headed dwarf and a moustached woman inside it. These latter were not show-people. **1966** *English Studies* XLVII. 141 Digressions ..thrown in by the poet..as the fair means by which an experienced teller of long stories overcomes the monotony of a series of *monster-killings. **1710** SHAFTESB. *Adv. Author* III. iii. 183 Monsters and *Monster-Lands were never more in request. **1736** THOMSON *Liberty* v. 676 Vanish'd Monster-land. **1561** T. NORTON *Calvin's Inst.* III. xxii. (1634) 456 It was a *monsterlike change that the honour of first birth was removed to Jacob. **1606** SHAKS. *Ant. & Cl.* IV. xii. 36 Monster-like. **1610** GUILLIM *Her.* III. xxvi. 183 Animals, which being duly shaped, doe neuerthelesse monster-like degenerate from their kind. **1655** H. L'ESTRANGE *Chas. I*, 119 In the same moneth..wherein this *Monster-Lord [Audley] was sentenced. **1970** G. JACKSON *Let.* 4 Apr. in *Soledad Brother* (1971) 211 He was giving to us all of the life force and activity that the *monster-machine had left to him. **1598** SYLVESTER *Du Bartas* II. i. II. *Imposture* 638 Which, like the vaunting *Monster-man of Gath, Have stirr'd against us little David's wrath. **1690** DRYDEN *Amphitryon* v. i, Monsters and monster men he shall engage. **1638** JUNIUS *Paint. Ancients* 43 A man may find them always upon the *monster-market, where they stand and stare upon such maimed creatures. **1969** L. J. CHIARAMONTE in Halpert & Story *Christmas Mumming in Newfoundland* 89 They are great favourites with little children, who beg their parents for money to buy a new *monster mask. **1598** SYLVESTER *Du Bartas* II. ii. II. *Babylon* 85 This *monster-master stout, This Hercules..they tender. **1634** SIR T. HERBERT *Trav.* 5 Guiding their Monster-masters to a prey. **1704** SWIFT *T. Tub* v, I have always looked upon it as a high Point of Indiscretion in *Monster-mongers, and other Retailers of strange Sights, to hang out a fair large Picture over the Door, drawn after the Life. **1634** MASSINGER *Very Woman* III. i, A March Frog kept thy mother; Thou art but a *monster Paddock. **1680** OTWAY *Caius Marius* I. i, The *Monster-people roar'd aloud for joy. **1751** *Pope's Dunciad* IV. 492 *Scribl. note*, It becomes a doubt, which of the two Hercules's was the *Monster-queller. **1959** A. G. BRODEUR *Art of Beowulf* 81 Outside the climate of mutual love.., Beowulf would be little more than the monster-queller and marvelous swimmer of folk-tale. **1948** K. MALONE in *English Studies* XXIX. 167 Beowulf's mention of sea-monsters..takes us back to the swimming match with Breca, one detail of which is precisely this monster quelling on the part of the hero. **1948** L. SPITZER *Linguistics & Literary Hist.* iii. 98 She must ask Hippolyte to resemble his father, the *monster-slayer, by slaying the monster that *she* has become. *Ibid.* 95 We learn that Hippolyte has not, to his regret, equaled his father in his feats of *monster-slaying. **1797** *College* 26 How to mitigate their *monster-spite. **1942** BLUNDEN *Romantic Poetry & Fine Arts* 17 *Monster-spouted fountain. ? **1606** DRAYTON *Eglog* iv. *Poems* D 7 b, Such *monster-tamers who would take in hand? **1648** FANSHAWE *Il Pastor Fido* I. i. 155 That *monster-taming King..Had never grown so valiant..If first the monster Love he had not tam'd. **1819** SHELLEY *Prometh. Unb.* I. 447 Never yet there came Phantasms so foul through *monster-teeming Hell.

7. Special Comb., as † **monster-little-man**, a dwarf monstrosity; † **monster-love**, a deformed or aborted love.

1607 TOPSELL *Four-f. Beasts* 12 The most parte thought him to be some Monster-little-man. **1633** FORD *Broken H.* I. i, This thought Begets a kind of monster-love.

B. *adj.* [developed from the attrib. and appositive use of the sb.]

1. Of extraordinary size or extent; gigantic, huge, monstrous. Cf. MONSTRE *a.*

1837 (*title of play*) The elements—earth, air, fire water; or, The monster ballroom of 1837 (R.A.M. 15/5/1837). **1839** *Spirit Metrop. Conserv. Press* (1840) II. 152 This monster product of our time. *c* **1842** F. ROGERS (Ld. Blachford) *Lett.* (1896) 113 The phrase 'monster meeting' was due to me. An immense balloon..had been popularly christened the 'monster balloon', and I applied the phrase contumeliously to one of O'Connell's immense..meetings. **1843** BORROW *Bible in Spain* xxxvi, The monster bell of Moscow. **1843** *Ann. Reg.* 227 The assemblage of immense masses of people ..denominated 'Monster Meetings'. **1844** LINGARD *Anglo-Sax. Ch.* (1858) II. App. C. 344 In the old church..was a monster organ. **1853** KANE *Grinnell Exp.* xlvi. (1856) 423 The port of Pröven is securely sheltered by its monster hills. **1868** DISRAELI *Let. to Mrq. Abercorn* 8 June (in *Davey's Catal.* (1895) 21), I have to receive this morning a monster deputation of your Excellency's subjects. **1901** *Oxford Times* 16 Mar. 4/2 This monster liner, will..be the biggest vessel afloat. **1952** 'R. CROMPTON' *William & Tramp* ii. 83 Their jaws never ceased to move rhythmically around a couple of Monster Humbugs. **1961** *Guardian* 27 Sept. 8/3 Many older housewives..find great satisfaction in a monster weekly 'bake'.

2. *Comb.* with advb. force = 'like a monster', as ***monster†-eating, -neighing*** adjs. *rare.*

1607 TOPSELL *Four-f. Beasts* 261 Their..liuely vgly figure, represented in this monster-eating-beast. **1886** KIPLING *Departm. Ditties*, etc. (1888) 82 An incarnation of the local God, Mounted upon a monster-neighing horse.

Hence † **'monsterful** *a.*, marvellous, extraordinary. † **'monsterfy** *v.*, to make monstrous. **'monsterhood**, the state of being a monster. **'monstership**, a mock title for a monster.

c **1400** *Beryn* 2767 These monstrefulle thingis, I devise to the Be-cause þow shuldist nat of hem a-basshid be. **1597** WARNER *Syrinx* N iv, These Monsters [abusers of women] woulde monsterfie the Manners and beautifull Ornaments of Women. **1598** B. JONSON *Ev. Man in Hum.* III. ii, Let who will make hungrie meales for your monster-ship, it shall not bee I. *a* **1745** SWIFT *Dr. Delany's Reply* 10 'Tis so strange, that your monstership's crany Should be envied by him, much less by Delany. **1852** *Fraser's Mag.* XLV. 90 It was a Behemoth of puffs..standing alone in solitary monsterhood.

monster ('mɒnstə(r)), *v. rare.* [f. MONSTER *sb.*]

1. *trans.* To make a monster of.

1605 SHAKS. *Lear* I. i. 223 Sure her offence Must be of such vnnaturall degree, That monsters it.

2. To exhibit as a monster; to point out as something wonderful.

1607 SHAKS. *Cor.* II. ii. 81, I had rather haue one scratch my Head i' th' Sun, When the Alarum were strucke, then idly sit To heare my Nothings monster'd. **1833** LAMB *Elia* Ser. II. *Productions Mod. Art*, Were the 'fine frenzies', which possessed the brain of thy own Quixote, a fit subject..to be monstered, and shown up at the heartless banquets of great men? **1873** E. FITZGERALD *Lett.* (1889) I. 352 He [Béranger] hated Paris,..hated being monstered himself as a Great Man, as he proved by flying from it.

3. *to monster it*: to play the monster, assume the appearance of greatness. *nonce-use.*

1646 BUCK *Rich. III* Ded., They will haunte the noblest merits and endeavors to their Sun-set, then they monster it.

Hence **'monstered** *a.*, rendered monstrous, abnormally great. Also **'monsterer**, one who makes great in a remarkable degree, an exaggerator. (Echoing Shaks.: see MONSTER *v.* 2, 1607.)

1877 BLACKIE *Wise Men* 95 You worship your own selves, and make your gods A monstered self. **1840** MRS. GORE in *New Monthly Mag.* LX. 52 The political Lady Patroness;.. the accredited monsterer of nothings inaudible in the gallery.

monster: see MONSTRE *sb.*¹ *Obs.*

† **'monstrable**, *a. Obs. rare*⁻¹. [ad. L. *monstrābil-is*, f. *monstrāre*: see MONSTRATE *v.* and -ABLE.] Capable of being shown or demonstrated.

c **1450** *Mirour Saluacioun* 1694 Thre thinges notable The whilk be thre figures of olde tyme ware monstrable. **1656** in BLOUNT *Glossogr.*

† **monstral.** *Obs. rare*⁻¹. [Perh. some error; cf. MONSTRATE.] = MONSTRANCE 2.

1532 CRANMER *Let. to Hen. VIII* in *Misc. Writ.* (Parker Soc.) 233 Spoiling and robbing all the countries of Austria, Stiria, and Carinthia..as well churches as other houses, not leaving Monstral nor the Sacrament.

monstrance ('mɒnstrəns). Also 3–4 **mustrance**, 4 **munstrance**, 6 **monstrans**. [a. OF. *monstrance* (AF. *moustraunce*: Britton *c* 1290), ad. med.L. *monstrant-ia*, f. L. *monstrant-em*: see MONSTRANT *a.* and -ANCE.]

†**1.** Demonstration, proof. *Obs.*

a **1300** *Cursor M.* 21796 In constantinopil and in france, Godd had mad mani mustrance. *c* **1400** *Ibid.* 22298 (Edinb.) Antecriste..in þe tempil sale he site..þare sale he do him circumsise, and munstrance make of his maistris.

†**b.** *Law.* In ***monstrance of right***, translating AF. *monstrance* (*moustrance*) *de droit*, a writ issuing out of Chancery, for restoring a person to lands or tenements legally belonging to him, though found in possession of another lately deceased. *Obs.*

1651 tr. *Kitchin's Courts Leet* (1675) 421 He shall have Traverse or Monstrans of Right to the same. **1668** HALE *Pref. to Rolle's Abridgm.* a ij b, Offices post Mortem, Traverses interpleder, and Monstrans of Right in relation thereunto.

2. *R.C. Ch.* **a.** An open or transparent vessel of gold or silver, in which the host is exposed.

1506 in *Brit. Mag.* (1833) III. 39 Itm paid for the hyre of A Monstrans at corpus xpe tyde viij d. **1552** *Inv. Ch. Goods Surrey* 84 A monstrance of sylver. **1851** J. H. NEWMAN *Cath. in Eng.* 244 One of them [*i.e.* the priests]..takes out the Blessed Sacrament, inserts it upright in a Monstrance of precious metal. **1872** O. SHIPLEY *Gloss. Eccl. Terms* s.v. *Benediction*, The priest..turns and blesses the people with the monstrance which contains the blessed Sacrament.

b. A receptacle used for the exhibition of relics.

1522 in Nichols *Mann. Anc. Times* (1797) 272 Item, a monstrans, wᵗ a relike of Sent Marten. **1876** C. M. DAVIES *Unorth. Lond.* 233 The chapel of St. Paul..exhibited in a monstrance the relics of the saint.

† **monstrant**, *sb. Obs. rare.* In 6 **monstraunt.** [app. ad. L. *monstrant-em* (see MONSTRANT *a.*) in subst. use. Cf. MONSTRAL, MONSTRATE *sb.*] = MONSTRANCE 2.

1509 FISHER *Serm. in St. Pauls* Wks. (1876) 274 He.. kyssed not the selfe place where the blessyd body of our lorde was conteyned, but..the fote of the monstraunt.

† **'monstrant**, *a. Obs. rare*⁻⁰. [ad. L. *monstrant-em*, pr. pple. of *monstrāre*: see MONSTRATE *v.*] Showing or declaring.

1727 in BAILEY vol. II.

† **monstrate**, *sb. Obs. rare*⁻¹. [Perh. some error; cf. MONSTRAL, MONSTRANT *sb.*] = MONSTRANCE 2.

1524 in G. Oliver *Hist. Coll.* (1841) App. 16 A Monstrate, siluer, hole gilte with..a crucifix in the topp.

† **monstrate**, *v. Obs.* [f. L. *monstrāt-*, ppl. stem of *monstrāre* to show, f. *monstr-um*: see MONSTER *sb.*] *trans.* To prove, demonstrate.

1647 M. HUDSON *Div. Right Govt.* II. x. 166 The light of nature is sufficient to monstrate the..impiety thereof.

† **mon'stration.** *Obs.* [ad. L. *monstrātiōn-em*, f. *monstrāre*: see prec.] A demonstration.

1568 GRAFTON *Chron.* II. 82 The blood burst incontinent out of the nose of the dead king at the comming of his sonne, geuing thereby as a certaine monstracion, howe he was the author of his death.

† **'monstrative**, *a. Logic. Obs. rare*⁻¹. [ad. L. type **monstrātīvus*, f. *monstrāre* to show: see -IVE.] (See quot.)

1653 Z. COKE *Logick* (1657) 164 A necessary Syllogism is either Monstrative [or] Demonstrative. Monstrative is, whose Mean is taken from a monstrative place, that is, from every place of necessary invention, except the efficient cause, the end, and the effect.

† **mon'strator.** *Obs.* [L., f. *monstrāre*: see MONSTRATE *v.*] A demonstrator, exhibitor.

1852 SIR W. HAMILTON *Discuss. Philos.* etc. 689 This exhibition a University ought to supply; and at the same time, as a necessary concomitant, a competent monstrator.

† **'monstre**, *sb.*¹ *Obs.* Also **monster, monstyr, monestere.** [ad. med.L. *monstrum*, app. ad. OF. *monstre* fem. (mod.F. *montre*), vbl. sb. f. *monstrer* to show.] = MONSTRANCE.

c **1480** *Acc. St. Andrew Hubbard* in *Rec. St. Mary at Hill* p. lxi, The crose of the monestere. **1498–9** *Rec. St. Mary at Hill* 233 Item, for mendyng of the monstyr for the Sacrament xvj d. **1519** *Churchw. Acc. St. Margaret's, Westm.* (Nichols 1797) 8 A monstre of siluer and gilt to bear in the Sacrament on Corpus Christi day. **1548** in *Archæologia* (1869) XLII. 89 Item a monster of silver and gilt.

‖ **monstre** (mɔ̃str), *sb.*² [Fr.] In phr. **monstre sacré** (lit. sacred monster), a striking and eccentric public figure; a false idol, esp. in the world of entertainment.

[**1940** J. COCTEAU (*title*) Les monstres sacrés.] **1959** *Manch. Guardian* 17 July 4/3 Unlike Mlle Sagan she seems vulnerable, and capable of development, not a born 'monstre sacré'. **1965** *Listener* 10 June 870/1 We must forgive Mailer because he is both exceptional *and* typical —the paradigm who is also a *monstre sacré*. **1969** *Ibid.* 9 Jan. 62/1 Compare her with the late Edith Piaf, a *monstre sacré* of a different order. **1969** *Times* 26 Nov. 9/4 That most fabulous of *monstres sacrés*, Sarah Bernhardt. **1975** *Times* 30 Oct. 8/5 Half saint, half satyr, wholly *monstre sacré*, the face [of Bertrand Russell] looks out upon us from the photographs.

‖ **monstre** (mɔ̃str), *a.* [Fr.; adjectival use of *monstre* MONSTER *sb.*] A frequent journalistic substitute for MONSTER *a.*, esp. as applied to meetings, 'demonstrations', etc.

1840 BARHAM *Ingol. Leg.* Ser. I. *Monstre Balloon* (*ad fin.*), Three cheers for the 'Monstre' Balloon. **1893** PEEL *Spen Valley* 352 He..helped..to organise the monstre gathering on Peep Green.

monstre, obs. form of MONSTER.

'monstricide. *nonce-wd.* [f. L. *monstr-um*: see -CIDE 2.] The slaughter of monsters.

1859 THACKERAY *Virgin.* xxv, If Perseus had cut the latter's [*i.e.* the Dragon's] cruel head off he would have committed not unjustifiable monstricide.

† **mon'striferous**, *a. Obs.* [f. L. *monstr-um*: see -FEROUS.] Producing or bearing monsters.

1558 KNOX *First Blast* (Arb.) 7 This monstriferouse empire of women. **1716** M. DAVIES *Athen. Brit.* II. 379 Not to be able to stand the Brunt or Medusæan Aspect of his own Monstriferous Bantling. **1891** in *Syd. Soc. Lex.*

monstrifi'cation. *nonce-wd.* [Formed as next: see -FICATION.] The action of making monstrous.

1849 RUSKIN *Sev. Lamps* iv. §3. 96 Many forms of so called decoration..ought in truth to be set down in the architect's contract, as 'For *monstrification*'.

†**'monstrify,** *v. Obs.* [f. L. *monstr-um*: see -FY.] *trans.* To render monstrous; to pervert.

1617 COLLINS *Def. Bp. Ely* To Rdr. 12 How punctuall he is in his recitings, marring and monstrifying anothers directest meaning, with his..prodigious interpunctions.

†**monstrison.** *Obs. rare*⁻¹. [OF. *monstraison, -treson, -trison*, repr. L. *monstrātiōn-em*: see MONSTRATION.] A parade.

1422 tr. *Secreta Secret., Priv. Priv.* 139 Ther was a fayre custome amonge the Iues, for onys a yere the kynge sholde haue of his Pepill and his hoste a monstrison.

monstrosity (mɒn'strɒsɪtɪ). [ad. late L. *monstrōsitās*, f. *monstrōs-us* MONSTROUS: see -ITY.]

1. An abnormality of growth, esp. in an animal or plant; *concr.* a part or organ that is abnormally developed; also occas. = MONSTER *sb.* 2.

1555 EDEN *Decades* To Rdr. (Arb.) 53 So that the monstrositie growth owt of the body. **1652–62** HEYLIN *Cosmogr.* IV. (1682) 138 Amongst these there are some Rarities, if not monstrosities, in nature. **1793** CLARKE in *Phil. Trans.* LXXXIII. 161 The defect of heart (not an uncommon kind of monstrosity) proves, that [etc.]. **1797** M. BAILLIE *Morb. Anat.* (1807) 38 The person to whom this monstrosity belonged, lived to near fourteen years of age. **1859** DARWIN *Orig. Spec.* ii. (1878) 33 By a monstrosity, I presume is meant some considerable deviation of structure, generally injurious, or not useful to the species. **1884** J. TAIT *Mind in Matter* (1892) 49 It is because nature refuses to propagate monstrosities that hybrids are sterile.

b. *transf.* and *fig.*

1639 FULLER *Holy War* II. xxxiv. (1647) 89 The body of their state being a very monstrosity, and a grievance of mankind. **1664** POWER *Exp. Philos.* Concl. 184 This numerous piece of Monstrosity (the Multitude). **1701** NORRIS *Ideal World* I. ii. 48 Those few defects,.. monstrositys or whatever you please to call them, which are to be found in the world, and seem to disfigure the face of nature. **1831** [see MOON-CALF 1 b]. **1858** GREENER *Gunnery* 113 Such a monstrosity [*sc.* as the 'Lancaster gun'] would have been buried soon after its birth. **1886** C. A. BRIGGS *Messianic Proph.* Pref. 11 The word Jehovah..is a linguistic monstrosity.

2. = MONSTER *sb.* 3. Also *fig.*

1643 SIR T. BROWNE *Relig. Med.* II. §1 The Multitude.. confused together, make but one great beast, and a monstrosity more prodigious then Hydra. **1646** —— *Pseud. Ep.* v. xix. 262 We shall tolerate flying Horses,..Harpies and Satyres; for these are monstrosities, rarities, or else Poeticall fancies. **1665** GLANVIL *Scepsis Sci.* xiv. 95 Education..can lick us into shapes beyond the monstrosities of Africa.

3. The condition or fact of being monstrous, or formed contrary to the ordinary course of nature.

1656 BLOUNT *Glossogr., Monstrosity*,..monstrousness. *c***1714** ARBUTHNOT, etc. *Mem. M. Scribl.* I. xv. (1741) 56 'Monstrosity could not incapacitate from Marriage', witness the Case of Hermaphrodites. **1766** *Compl. Farmer* s.v. *Smut*, Wolfius was of opinion that the smut of corn proceeds from a monstrosity of the embryo. **1873** MIVART *Elem. Anat.* ix. 389 The optic structure is never single and median except by monstrosity.

b. *transf.* and *fig.*

1651 BINNING *Serm.* (1847) 530 What a monstrosity is it for one member to seek its own things..as if it were a distinct body. **1662** GURNALL *Chr. in Arm.* verse 18. I. lv. §2 (1669) 425/1 Sin being a brat of hell, comes not to its full complexion and monstrositie, till it be sent back to the place it came from. *a***1697** SOUTH *Serm.* II. v. 224 We sometimes read..of Monstrous Births, but we may often see a greater Monstrosity in Educations. **1826** SOUTHEY *Vind. Eccl. Angl.* 246 The statement of his contemporary biographer confuted itself by its monstrosity. **1856** HORT *Coleridge* in *Cambr. Ess.* 327 The moral monstrosity of supposing that God can have given us lying faculties. **1902** A. B. DAVIDSON *Called of God* xi. 282 To be lost..does not imply any uncommonness of vice, or monstrosity of wickedness.

monstrous ('mɒnstrəs), *a.* Forms: 5 monstrows, 6 monstrowis, -terus, -trose, -t(e)rouse, monstreous, 6–7 monsterous, 6– monstrous. [ad. OF. *monstreux, -tereux*, ad. late L. *monstrōsus*, f. L. *monstrum* MONSTER: see -OUS and cf. MONSTRUOUS.]

†**1. a.** Of things, material and immaterial: Deviating from the natural order; unnatural. *Obs.*

1460 CAPGRAVE *Chron.* (Rolls) 26 Zoroastes, whan he was bore, low as no child ded but he, and this lawhing was no tokne of good, for it was monstrows, that is to seyn, ageyn course of kyndc. **1508** DUNBAR *Tua Mariit Wemen* 57 God gif matrimony were made to mell for ane ȝeir! It war bot monstrous to be mair, but gif our myndis pleisit. **1577** VAUTROUILLIER *Luther on Ep. Gal.* 83 It seemeth a very straunge and a monstrous maner of speaking thus to say: I liue, I liue not: I am dead, I am not dead [etc.]. **1625** BACON *Ess., Unity in Relig.* (Arb.) 433 It is a thing monstrous, to put it [*i.e.* the temporal sword] into the hands of the Common People. **1648** BEAUMONT *Psyche* I. xv, His Diadem was neither brass nor rust, But monstrous Metal of them both begot. **1682** SIR T. BROWNE *Chr. Mor.* I. §9 That Vice may be uneasy and even monstrous unto thee, let iterated good Acts..make Virtue..a second nature in thee. **1701** ROWE *Amb. Step-Moth.* II. ii. 924 More monstrous Tales have oft amus'd the Vulgar. **1736** BUTLER *Anal.* I. iii. Wks. 1874 I. 60 That there are instances of an approbation of vice..for its own sake..is evidently monstrous.

†**b.** Of persons: Strange or unnatural in conduct or disposition. *Obs.*

1568 BIBLE (Bishops') *Zech.* iii. 8 They are monstrous persons. **1579** LYLY *Euphues* (Arb.) 108 Pasiphae so monstrous to love a Bull. *Ibid.* 158 An atheist, a man in my opinion monstrous. **1627** DRAYTON *Moone-calfe, Aginc.* etc. 165 And in her fashion she is likewise thus, In euery thing she must be monstrous. **1607** SHAKS. *Timon* IV. ii. 46 Hee's flung in Rage from this ingratefull Seate Of monstrous Friends. **1654** tr. *Scudery's Curia Pol.* 137, I must appear to them..uncivill and monstrous.

2. a. Of animals and plants: Abnormally formed; deviating congenitally from the normal type; malformed.

1597 GERARDE *Herbal* I. lxxxix. 143 A degenerate Garlick growen monstrous. **1638** JUNIUS *Paint. Ancients* 23 They are as little brought forth after the nature of man, as prodigious and monstrous bodies. *a***1697** SOUTH *Serm.* II. v. 224 We sometimes read and hear of Monstrous Births. **1790** HORNE in *Phil. Trans.* LXXX. 296 The..double skull of a monstrous child. **1830** R. KNOX *Béclard's Anat.* 307 Certain monstrous fœtuses, acephalous and others, have been seen destitute of all the muscles. **1859** DARWIN *Orig. Spec.* v. (1873) 115 This is often seen in monstrous plants.

fig. **1742** YOUNG *Nt. Th.* v. 489 A sensual, unreflecting life is big With monstrous births. **1875** E. WHITE *Life in Christ* III. xviii. (1878) 233 It was a mingling of the law and the gospel; which, like all unnatural unions, produced a monstrous birth.

†**b.** said of human beings. *Obs.*

[**1500–20**: see 4.] **1586** MARLOWE *1st Pt. Tamburl.* IV. (1590) D 2 b, Were that tamburlaine As monstrous as Gorgon, prince of Hell, The Souldane would not start a foot from him. **1615** CHAPMAN *Odyss.* IX. 268 In which kept house A man in shape, immane, and monsterous. **1688** in *Wood's Life* 28 July (O.H.S.) III. 273 A monstrous young woman,..whose shapes is very wonderful.

transf. and *fig.* **1538** STARKEY *England* I. iii. 84 The partys in proportyon not agreyng..make in thys polytyke body grete and monstrose deformyte. **1575–85** ABP. SANDYS *Serm.* xx. 349 Those are ougly paternes of monstrous mindes.

3. a. Having the nature or appearance of a monster (see MONSTER *sb.* 3).

*c***1540** *Pilgr. T.* 325 in *Thynne's Animadv.* (1863) App. 86 This is the woman..whom Iohn saw..syting apon a monsterus best. **1547** BOORDE *Introd. Knowl.* vi. (1870) 141 Castours and whyte beares, & other monstrous beastes. **1581** MARBECK *Bk. of Notes* 924 The Sea of the monsterous beast Antichrist. **1615** G. SANDYS *Trav.* 113 Adorned with the statues of gods and men; with other monstrous resemblances. **1667** MILTON *P.L.* II. 625 Nature breeds, Perverse, all monstrous, all prodigious things..Gorgons and Hydra's, and Chimera's dire. **1697** DRYDEN *Virg. Past.* VII. 62 Such and so monstrous let thy Swain appear, If one Day's Absence looks not like a Year. **1719** DE FOE *Crusoe* II. (Globe) 580 Their monstrous Idol. **1835** THIRLWALL *Greece* I. vi. 210 On its confines are the haunts of the monstrous Chimæra, and the territory of the Amazons. **1870** MORRIS *Earthly Par.* I. I. 418 Long-necked dragons..And many another monstrous nameless thing.

b. Abounding in monsters. ? *Obs.*

1637 MILTON *Lycidas* 158 Where thou..under the whelming tide Visit'st the bottom of the monstrous world. **1725** POPE *Odyss.* IV. 658 Must I the warriors weep, Whelm'd in the bottom of the monstrous deep?

4. a. Of unnaturally or extraordinarily huge dimensions; gigantic; immense; enormous.

1500–20 DUNBAR *Poems* xviii. 29 Be I bot littill of stature, Thay call me catyve createure; And be I grit of quantetie Thay call me monstrowis of nature. **1553** EDEN *Treat. Newe Ind.* (Arb.) 29 They haue serpentes of monstrous greatnes. **1568** GRAFTON *Chron.* II. 379 This man..in his Mairaltie had made great and monstreous stockes to emprison men in. **1582** T. WATSON *Centurie of Love* lviii, There is a monstrous hill in Sicill soyle. **1600** J. PORY tr. *Leo's Africa* IX. 349 Of locustes there are..such monstrous swarmes..that [etc.]. **1667** MILTON *P.L.* I. 197 Thus Satan..Lay floating..in bulk as huge As whom the Fables name of monstrous size, Titanian,..Briarios,..or that Sea-beast Leviathan. **1711** ADDISON *Spect.* No. 129 ¶7 Dressed in a most monstrous Flaxen Periwig. **1726** SWIFT *Gulliver* II. viii, I was equally confounded at the Sight of so many Pigmies..after having so long accustomed mine Eyes to the monstrous Objects I had left. **1818** CREEVEY in *C. Papers* (1904) I. 277 Dined at Lord Hill's with my young ladies..and a monstrous party. **1848** W. H. BARTLETT *Egypt to Pal.* xxi. (1879) 452 The soil revealed its singular fertility in noble grain-crops and weeds of monstrous growth.

b. of immaterial things.

1601 SHAKS. *All's Well* II. ii. 34 It must be an answere of most monstrous size, that must fit all demands. **1867** J. G. ROGERS *Priests & Sacram.* v. 103 The power, indeed, is too monstrous for any man under heaven to exercise.

†**c.** Excessively difficult. *Obs. nonce-use.*

1664 POWER *Exp. Philos.* I. 81 The right figures of both which Crystallines are monstrous, if not impossible, to find out.

5. With emotional sense, expressing indignation or wondering contempt: Outrageously wrong or absurd.

1573–80 BARET *Alv.* E. lf. 1 What a monstrous absurditie is this that E...should haue neither sound nor signification. **1588** *Marprel. Epist.* (Arb.) 31 Nay saies my L. of winchester (like a monstrous hypocrite, for he is a very duns). **1588** SHAKS. *Tit. A.* IV. iv. 51 Shall I endure this monstrous villany? **1610** —— *Temp.* III. ii. 33 Wilt thou tell a monstrous lie? **1662** STILLINGFL. *Orig. Sacræ* III. i. §15 What monstrous arrogancy would it be in any man to think there is a mind and reason in himself and that there is none in the world? **1682** DRYDEN & LEE *Dk. of Guise* III. i, To spread your monstrous Lyes and sow Sedition. **1715** ADDISON *Freeholder* No. 7 ¶4 So many absurd and monstrous falshoods. **1836** J. GILBERT *Chr. Atonem.* viii. (1852) 221 Monstrous would be the supposition that an injury could be repaired by a compensation provided at the cost of Him who had been injured. **1850** ROBERTSON *Serm.* Ser. III. i. (1872) 4 The monstrous fact of Christian persecution. **1878** R. W. DALE *Lect. Preach.* ix. 285 It seems monstrous for us to sing about God's goodness to the Jews and never to sing about his goodness to ourselves. **1888** BRYCE *Amer. Commw.* I. xxv. 371 A monstrous system of bribery.

6. Like or befitting a 'monster' of wickedness; atrocious, horrible.

1560 DAUS tr. *Sleidane's Comm.* 336 Monstrouse and pestiferous persones. **1567** *Ballad on Murder Darnley* in *Fraser's Mag.* LXX. 221 His cruell murther ye will call monsterous. **1595** SHAKS. *John* ii. i. 173 *Qu.* Thou monstrous slanderer of heauen and earth. *Con.* Thou monstrous Iniurer of heauen and earth. **1608** *Yorksh. Trag.* I. ix, What made you show such monstrous cruelty? *a***1661** HOLYDAY *Juvenal* (1673) 22 No man at first is monstrous. **1858** HOLLAND *Titcomb's Lett.* viii. 159 So I say that a godless woman is a monstrous woman.

absol. **1898** G. MEREDITH *Odes Fr. Hist.* 15 Nor would he shun her sullen look, nor monstrous hold The doer of the monstrous.

†**7.** As an exclamation, in the sense 'greatly to be marvelled at', 'astounding'. *Obs.*

1590 SHAKS. *Mids. N.* III. i. 107 O monstrous. O strange. We are hanted. **1596** —— *1 Hen. IV*, II. iv. 243 O monstrous! eleuen Buckrom men growne out of two? *Ibid.* 591 O monstrous, but one halfe penny-worth of Bread to this intollerable deale of Sacke? **1605** —— *Lear* v. iii. 159 Most monstrous! O, know'st thou this paper? **1693** CONGREVE *Old Bach.* IV. xxi, O bless me! O monstrous! A Prayerbook?

†**8. a.** Used as a colloquial or affected intensive. *Obs.* Cf. 4.

1710–11 SWIFT *Jrnl. to Stella* 7 Feb., We have a monstrous deal of snow. **1717** LADY M. W. MONTAGU *Let. to Abbé Conti* 29 May, The Greeks have a most monstrous taste in their pictures..drawn upon a gold ground. **1782** MISS BURNEY *Cecilia* I. iii, After all this monstrous fatigue, I was forced to have my hair dressed by my own maid. **1782** WOLCOT in J. J. Rogers *Opie & his Wks.* (1878) 22 West the famous painter, a monstrous favourite of George's. **1825** COBBETT *Rur. Rides* (1885) II. 38 Here is a monstrous deal of vanity and egotism.

b. quasi-*adv.* in the sense: Exceedingly, wonderfully, 'mighty'. Now mainly *U.S.*

1590 SHAKS. *Mids. N.* I. ii. 54 Ile speake in a monstrous little voyce. **1608** ROWLANDS *Humors Looking Glasse* 14 A Gentleman..Hath a young wife and she is monstrous fine. **1655** in *Nicholas' Papers* (Camden) II. 262, I cannot but feare he may doe this monstrous vnhappy act. **1710** SWIFT *Jrnl. to Stella* 6 Dec., It is such monstrous rainy weather, that there is no doing with it. **1782** MISS BURNEY *Cecilia* I. v, She's a monstrous shocking dresser. **1801** tr. *Gabrielli's Myst. Husb.* III. 84 She had a prettyish face and monstrous nice hair. **1826** DISRAELI *Viv. Grey* II. xiii, The most monstrous clever young man. **1840** MRS. F. TROLLOPE *Widow Married* xii, I think we shall be monstrous good friends. **1848** W. T. THOMPSON *Major Jones's Sketches of Travel* iii. 23 Augusty's a monstrous pretty city; but it ain't the place it used to was, not by a grate sight. It seems like it was rottin off at both eends, and ain't growin much in the middle. **1884** 'MARK TWAIN' *Huck. Finn* 134 Behind a monstrous long raft. **1907** *Dialect Notes* III. 233 'Yes'm, I'se *monstrous* hungry.' **1942** BERREY & VAN DEN BARK *Amer. Thes. Slang* §20/14 *Very; exceedingly*,..mighty, monstrous.

9. *Comb.*, as †*monstrous-kinded* adj.; **monstrous craws**, a form of elephantiasis common in the West Indies; **monstrous pippin, rennet**, large kinds of apple.

1787 H. WALPOLE *Let. to C'tess Ossory* 6 Sept., The principal babe put me in mind of what I read so often, but have not seen, the *monstrous craws. **1558** PHAER *Æneid* VIII. (1562) Cc ij b, All *monstrous kynded gods. **1860** R. HOGG *Fruit Manual* 9 (Apples), *Gloria Mundi*, ..*Monstrous Pippin. **1731** MILLER *Gard. Dict.* s.v. *Apple*, A List of such Apples as are preferr'd for Kitchen Use ..*Monstrous Reinette. **1797** *Encycl. Brit.* (ed. 3) XV. 721/1 Monstrous rennet.

monstrously ('mɒnstrəslɪ), *adv.* [-LY².]

†**1.** In the manner of a monster; with congenital malformation. *Obs.*

1532 MORE *Confut. Barnes* VIII. Wks. 741/2 A man myght haue seene frere Barns when he came laste into the lande.. and yet myght happely..haue taken him for a monstre, he had so monstrously dressed himself because he would be wondred on. **1604** T. WRIGHT *Passions* I. x. 44, I might declare, what Passions they are subiect vnto, whom Nature monstrously hath signed.

2. †**a.** In an unnatural or extraordinary manner.

1555 EDEN *Decades* To Rdr. (Arb.) 53 Vicious behauoures which monstrously deforme the myndes of men. **1588** J. UDALL *Diotrephes* (Arb.) 17 My flesh trembleth to heare you speake so monstrously. **1646** SIR T. BROWNE *Pseud. Ep.* I. iii. 10 They melted down their stolen ear-rings into a calf, and monstrously cryed out: These are thy gods O Israel! that brought thee out of the land of Egypt. **1797** *Encycl. Brit.* (ed. 3) XII. 330/1 Virtues..of the same nature as those which the Basilians [*sic*] attributed to their monstrously cut stones.

b. To a monstrous degree; in later use often as a mere intensive, 'hugely', 'vastly'.

*a***1674** CLARENDON *Surv. Leviath.* (1676) 301 We are monstrously in the fault. **1709** STEELE *Tatler* No. 48 ¶1 Heels to his Shoes so monstrously high, that he had three or four Times fallen down, had he not [etc.]. **1782** MISS BURNEY *Cecilia* I. v, She had been..so monstrously engaged, I could never find her at home. **1826** DISRAELI *Viv. Grey* IV. ii, In life, surely man is not always as monstrously busy as he appears to be in novels and romances. **1861** HUGHES *Tom Brown at Oxf.* ii, In monstrously short time the pursuing skiff showed round the corner. **1904** 'ANTHONY HOPE' *Double Harness* i. 4 She's monstrously fat.

monstrousness ('mɒnstrəsnɪs). [Formed as prec. + -NESS.] The quality of being monstrous,

in various senses of the adj.; esp. unnaturalness, hugeness; enormity.

1574 *Brieff Disc. Troub. Frankford* 211 All monstrousnes off errors, and whiche Satan newlie sekethe to bring into the churche againe [being] driuen awaie. **1606** *Proc. agst. Late Traitors* 22 The monstrousnesse and continuall horrour of this so desperate a cause. **1625** K. LONG tr. *Barclay's Argenis* v. vii. 350 The monstrousnesse of his knavery. *a* **1734** NORTH *Exam.* III. vii. §33 (1740) 527 Let none start at the Monstrousness of this supposition. **1818** HALLAM *Mid. Ages* (1872) I. 138 The apparent incredibility of the charges from their monstrousness.

b. as a mock-title. *nonce-use.*

1726 in *Hist. Norfolk* (1829) II. 1202 The two dick fools will be new dressed to attend to his monstrousness [*sc.* the Norwich Guild Snap Dragon].

†**monstru'osity.** *Obs.* [ad. F. *monstruosité*: see MONSTRUOUS and -ITY.] = MONSTROSITY.

1402 *Repl. Friar Daw Topias* in *Pol. Poems* (Rolls) II. 106 Kynde hath determyned the noumbre of thi fyngris, and if it passe noumbre, it is clepid monstruosité. **1601** HOLLAND *Pliny* I. 359 Ouer and aboue those monstruosities which Italy hath deuised of it selfe, we haue remaining..those also of strange..nations abroad. **1604** T. WRIGHT *Passions* v. 265 If his Parents were..marked by any monstruositie of Nature. **1606** SHAKS. *Tr. & Cr.* III. ii. 87 This is the monstruositie in loue Lady, that the will is infinite, and the execution confin'd. **1650** GENTILIS *Considerations* 84 That of one member bigger than another, hath nothing to doe with goodness, but with Monstruosity. **1724** WARBURTON *Tracts* (1789) 2 If the Monstruosity of their Crimes exceed even imaginary ones. **1797** *Encycl. Brit.* (ed. 3) XII. 247/2 M. Fabri arranges..compressions of the cranium, and many other deformities of this kind in the class of morbific monstruosities. *Ibid.* 248/2 Monstruosities which are perpetuated exist in the original organization of the seed of the plant.

†**'monstruous,** *a. Obs.* Also 4 -ruos, 5-6 -ruus, -rowous, 6 -ruows, 6-7 -ruouse. [ad. L. *monstruōs-us*, irreg. f. *monstrum* MONSTER: see -OUS. Cf. F. *monstrueux*, Sp., Pg., It. *monstruoso*.] = MONSTROUS in various senses.

Very common in the 16th c.

c **1374** CHAUCER *Boeth.* IV. met. iii. 95 (Camb. MS.) Hem ..þat..byweyleth the Monstruos chaungynge þat they suffren. **1432-50** tr. *Higden* (Rolls) VII. 133 This pope Benedicte appered to a man after his dethe, in a monstruous similitude. **1471** CAXTON *Recuyell* (Sommer) 17 The fiers dragons, the dedely griffons, the monstrowous bestes. *c* **1495** *Epitaffe*, etc. in *Skelton's Wks.* (1843) II. 392 O murtherer vnmesurable..Monstruus of entrayle, aborryd in kynde. **1542** BECON *Pathw. Prayer* xlvii. R iv b, All the monasticall sectes haue put of theyr cowles & monstruous garmentes. **1562** WIN3ET *Cert. Tractates* (S.T.S.) I. 12 The monstruus ydoll of auarice. **1609** BIBLE (Douay) *Numb.* xxii. Comm., Being accustomed to such monstruous thinges, he replied familiarly, nothing therwith astonished. **1668** CULPEPPER & COLE *Barthol. Anat.* I. xvii. 45 Tis monstruous, when both the kidneys are joyned into one beneath, and cleave together. **1692** LUTTRELL *Brief Rel.* (1857) II. 332 A monstruous fish of an ell long, having the parts and shape of a dog..was shot in the Thames. **1700** W. KING *Transactioneer* 55 A Monstruous Birth. **1724** WARBURTON *Tracts* (1789) 3 Revenge is monstruous. **1727** *Philip Quarll* 238 Several Rarities, which they said did belong to a monstruous English Hermit.

Hence †**'monstruously** *adv.*, **'monstruousness** = MONSTROUSLY, MONSTROUSNESS.

1545 ASCHAM *Toxoph.* I. (Arb.) 53 If I woulde enter, to descrybe the monstruousenes of it, I shoulde rather wander in it, it is so brode. **1561** T. NORTON *Calvin's Inst.* IV. 125 They that vomite out such monstruousnesse, are so not ashamed of their own shame, that [etc.]. **1563** *Homilies* II. *Agst. Idol.* III. 56 Some spake more monstruously then euer did Balams Asse. **1653** R. SANDERS *Physiogn.* 159 Malice is represented in a man by some deformity or monstruousness. **1690** CHILD *Disc. Trade* (1694) 206 It is evident they do monstruously increase. **1708** *Brit. Apollo* No. 38. 1/2 Two children.., who are so monstruously conjoyn'd.

monstuire, -tur(e, obs. ff. MONSTER.

monsware, variant of MANSWEAR *sb. Obs.*

mont, obs. form of MOUNT.

montabanke, obs. form of MOUNTEBANK.

montage ('mɒntɑːʒ). [Fr., f. *monter* to MOUNT.]

1. *Cinemat.* and *Television.* **a.** The selection and arrangement of separate cinematographic shots as a consecutive whole; the blending (by superimposition) of separate shots to form a single picture; the sequence or picture resulting from such a process.

1929 I. MONTAGU tr. *Pudovkin's On Film Technique* 179 It is important to gain a clear conception of the activities embraced here by the word *Editing.* The word used by Pudovkin, the German and French word, is *montage.* Its only possible English equivalent is *editing.* **1930** *Observer* 5 Oct. 20/4 Montage, or constructive cutting..is simply the method of building up a film from broken and isolated strips of celluloid. **1936** *World Film News* July 48/3, I recall the fate of *montage* when it was adopted in England. **1939** H. G. WELLS *Holy Terror* IV. ii. 398 Using the cinema in the schools to display the rapid development of the new life of mankind..with a montage in which the Beethovenised head of Rud, the ruler and guide, was displayed in such a manner as to evoke and sustain a world-wide enthusiasm. **1959** *Punch* 10 June 787/2 Very good photography..and montage, or editing..in the jazz-club scene behind the credit titles. **1961** *Listener* 10 Aug. 217/1 The programme opened with a *montage* of newspapers cascading from the presses. **1974** *Some Technical Terms & Slang* (Granada Television), *Montage*, a sequence of film images cut together, usually to music.

b. *attrib.* passing into *adj.*

1948 A. HUXLEY *Ape & Essence* (1949) 125 A series of montage shots exhibits, in twenty seconds, the slow, hour-long advance of Loola and Dr. Poole. **1949** *Here & Now* (N.Z.) Oct. 29/3 It doesn't matter if it's [*sc.* a film is] documentary, expressionist, montage, poetic, or just plain cinematic. **1961** K. REISZ *Technique Film-Editing* (ed. 9) II. vi. 112 The term *montage sequence*..refers to the quick impressionistic sequence of disconnected images, usually linked by dissolves, superimpositions or wipes, and used to convey passages of time, changes of place, or any other scenes of transition. **1962** *Listener* 4 Oct. 536/2 An edgy.. musical score, perfectly geared to the montage shots of computers, drawing-boards, teleprinters. *Ibid.* 29 Nov. 909/2 The rows of cells and their inhabitants are arranged like a montage sequence from a Russian silent film. **1963** *Movie* Jan. 5/3 Montage sequence of individual crows attacking each child.

2. The act or process of producing a composite picture by combining several different pictures or pictorial elements so that they blend with or into one another; a picture so produced.

1938 A. COOPER *Making a Poster* 34 Used as 'montage' in conjunction with blue skies, or green fields, photographs of human beings appear singularly unattractive. **1938** *Times* 26 Feb. 10/3 The colours, photographs, and lettering which in the ordinary poster are brought into an effect of unity by skilful 'montage'. **1941** A. HUXLEY *Let.* 27 May (1969) 467 Use either the portrait of Father Joseph..or else a montage made of the various illustrations in the book. **1958** *Observer* 18 May 16/5 They see, upon the pink and gold jacket [of a book], a *montage* of representative faces of the period. **1972** *Islander* (Victoria, B.C.) 16 July 10/2 This art [*sc.* découpage] is not, however, to be confused with either collage or montage, both of which are used as pictures rather than as a decoration for furniture.

3. *transf.* and *fig.* (The process of making) a mixture, blend, or medley of various elements; a pastiche; a sequence, miscellany.

1934 C. LAMBERT *Music Ho!* v. 329 The montage or pastiche of the neo-classicists. **1941** B. SCHULBERG *What Makes Sammy Run?* iii. 45 It [*sc.* a night club] was a montage of hot music, drunken laughter, loud wisecracks and hostesses like lollypops in red, green and yellow wrappers. *Ibid.* ix. 172 It was flashing through my mind like a montage nightmare. **1961** *Listener* 23 Nov. 863/1 It [*sc.* a poem] is certainly not modernist, if by modernist one thinks of a play of images, a montage in free verse. **1963** T. A. SEBEOK in J. A. Fishman *Readings in Sociol. of Lang.* (1968) 19 When describing speech phenomena, many linguists,..continue to employ a mixed nomenclature, drawing for their technical vocabulary now on articulatory, now on acoustic, and sometimes on perceptual phonetics; the resulting montage may show seams, but the total picture makes sense. **1973** *Guardian* 21 Apr. 10/2 She has used a montage of sound, from the throbbing..[of] your own heart beat to various street sounds, even a street musician.

Montagnais (mɔ̃taɲe), *sb.* and *a.* Also **Montagnois, Mountaine(e)r, Mountainier.** [a. F. *montagnais* mountaineer; hence, member of a mountain tribe.] **A.** *sb.* An Algonquian Indian people of eastern Canada; a member of this people; also, their language. **B.** *adj.* Of or pertaining to this people.

1625 PURCHAS *Pilgrimes* IV. VIII. vi. 1607 They were three Nations when they went to war; the *Estechemins, Algoumequins,* and *Mountainers.* **1703** tr. *Lahontan's New Voy. N.-America* I. 207 He deals with the other Savage Nations, namely, the *Montagnois*, and the *Papipanachois* in Arms and Ammunition. **1792** G. CARTWRIGHT *Jrnl.* I. Explanation of frontispiece, His jacket.., sash, and rackets are Mountaineer. **1800** *Mass. Hist. Soc. Coll.* VI. 16 The ensuing vocabulary I transcribed *viva voce* from Gabriel, a young Mountaineer Indian. *Ibid.* 17 There is evidently a great resemblance between the Skoffie and Mountaineer. **1863** H. Y. HIND *Explor. Labrador Peninsula* II. xxvii. 101 The Nasquapees, like their friends and allies the Montagnais, hate the Esquimaux. **1894** *11th Ann. Rep. U.S. Bureau Amer. Ethnol. 1889-90* 267 The Indians of the Ungava district are locally known as Naskopie, a term of reproach applied to them by the mountaineers (the Montagnais of the early Jesuit missionaries). **1916** *Trans. R. Soc. Canada* X. I. 314 It..is possibly a transition between the Ojibwa and Montagnais snowshoe. **1933** [see CREE *sb.* and *a.*]. **1934** D. JENNESS *Indians of Canada* (ed. 2) xviii. 271 The Montagnais country was a well-wooded area abounding in moose. **1941** *Beaver* Mar. 27 The Montagnais shoe is the commonest form used throughout the Labrador Peninsula. **1966** C. F. & F. M. VOEGELIN *Map of N. Amer. Indian Lang.* (*caption*) Algonquian Family. 1. Cree—Montagnais—Naskapi. **1973** HOWAT & TAYLOR *Dict. World Hist.* 1013/1 *Montagnais Indians*, group of Canadian Algonquian tribes, discovered (1603) at the mouth of the Saguenay by Champlain, who enlisted them in an expedition (1609) against the Iroquois.

‖**montagnard** (mɔ̃taɲar). [Fr., f. *montagne*: see MOUNTAIN and -ARD.]

1. An inhabitant of a mountain region; a highlander, mountaineer. Also *attrib.*

1842 MRS. F. TROLLOPE *Vis. Italy* I. i. 10 A montagnard population is always better worth looking at, than any other.

b. An aboriginal people living in the highlands of South Vietnam; a member of this people; also *attrib.* or as *adj.* Cf. MOI *a.* and *sb.*

1962 *Courier-Mail* (Brisbane) 1 Aug. 2/6 Montagnard scouts report that they have seen elephants carrying artillery pieces. *Ibid.*, Whether a montagnard could distinguish between a mortar and a field piece [etc.]. **1966** *Listener* 29 Dec. 949/2 Next..the mountains and the high plateaux where the Montagnard tribesman lives. **1968** *Ibid.* 13 June 760/3 The Highlands take up half the physical area of South Vietnam but they contain less than one tenth of its people. Moreover most of these are not ethnic Vietnamese but hill tribes of South Seas descent whom the French called Montagnards and the Vietnamese call *Moi*, meaning savages. **1972** *Times* 31 May 5/4 (*caption*) A Montagnard woman comforts her husband as he lies in Kontum hospital. **1972** *Guardian* 3 June 11/1 The name Montagnard was first given to the hill tribes of Vietnam by the French colonisers —it means simply 'the mountain people'. **1974** *Nature* 15 Mar. 186/3 The Montagnards (the highlanders) conduct much of their agriculture in cleared areas of forests, and so their fields were often sprayed during attacks on the inland forests.

2. *Hist.* A member of the 'Mountain' or extreme democratic party in the legislatures of the first French revolution.

1879 *Encycl. Brit.* IX. 602/2 The Montagnards alone.. opposed a declaration of war.

‖**montagne russe** (mɔ̃taɲ rys). *Canad.* [F. *montagnes russes* switchback.] A switchback, scenic railway, roller coaster.

1838 *United Service Jrnl.* July 302 Wherever there is a hill or declivity, a '*montagne Russe*' is speedily prepared. **1885** [see CUL-DE-SAC 2]. **1947** *Horizon* July 32 Political excitement..'ran high', but..it seems like a switchback, a *montagne russe* compared with Mount Everest.

Montagu[1] ('mɒntəgjuː). The name of George *Montagu* (1751-1815), British naturalist, used *attrib.* or in the possessive to designate animals first described by him, as **Montagu's blenny,** a small marine fish, *Coryphoblennius galerita*; **Montagu's harrier,** *Circus pygargus*, the smallest British harrier; also *ellipt.*; **Montagu's sea-snail,** a small marine fish, *Liparis montagui*; **Montagu shell,** the shell of a small marine bivalve of the genus *Montacuta* which lives as a commensal with an echinoderm; **Montagu's sucker, sucking-fish** = *Montagu's sea-snail*; **Montagu's Venus,** the shell of the marine bivalve *Venerupis pullastra.*

1836 W. YARRELL *Hist. Brit. Fishes* I. 219 (*heading*) Montagu's Blenny. **1969** A. WHEELER *Fishes Brit. Is. & N.-W. Europe* 439/1 Montagu's blenny has a very restricted distribution in the British Isles, being found only on rocky shores on the south-western coasts. **1843** W. YARRELL *Hist. Brit. Birds* I. 101 It will..be an advantage, as well as a gratification, to call this bird in future Montagu's Harrier and *Circus Montagui.* **1880** *Encycl. Brit.* XI. 492/1 This was called by him the Ash-coloured Falcon, but it now generally bears his name, and is known as Montagu's Harrier. **1930** J. S. HUXLEY *Bird Watching* ii. 27, I could take a map and mark down just where I saw my first dartford warbler, my first smew, Montagu's harrier, and so on. **1954** A. W. P. ROBERTSON *Bird Pageant* ii. 38 While hunting, the montagu usually flies into the wind. **1971** *Country Life* 20 May 1245/3 The old, wild, undrained Fens..where the Montagu's harrier still nests in the reed-beds. **1835** L. JENYNS *Man. Brit. Vertebr. Anim.* 473 Montagu's Sea-Snail... Discovered by Montagu, at Milton, on the south coast of Devon. **1925** J. T. JENKINS *Fishes Brit. Is.* 106 The illustration shows eggs of Montagu's Sea Snail. **1969** A. WHEELER *Fishes Brit. Is. & N.-W. Europe* 505/1 Montagu's sea snail is a more littoral species, found on the shore up to mid-tide level. **1901** E. STEP *Shell Life* 101 The rusty Montagu-shell (*M*[*ontacuta*] *ferruginosa*) is more oblong, greyish white in hue, but this is hidden by a rusty-looking incrustation. **1961** P. STREET *Shell Life on Seashore* viii. 122 The Montagu shells attach themselves near the mouth of the urchin so that they can extract food particles. **1836** W. YARRELL *Hist. Brit. Fishes* II. 277 (*heading*) Montagu's Sucking-fish. *Ibid.* 278 Montagu's Sucker, in the adult state, is from two inches and a half to three inches long. **1925** J. T. JENKINS *Fishes Brit. Is.* 106 Montagu's Sucker is common from the north of Norway to the Channel. **1819** W. TURTON *Conchol. Dict. Brit. Is.* 243 *Venus Montacuti.* Montagu's Venus.

Montagu[2] ('mɒntəgjuː). *Naut.* [The name of Rear-Admiral Victor Alexander *Montagu* (1841-1915): see quot. 1974.] Used to designate a rig used for small boats in the Royal Navy. Hence **Montagu whaler,** a whaler carrying this rig.

1925 A. MOORE *Last Days Mast & Sail* vii. 228 The Montagu whalers recently introduced into the Navy carry a standing lug. **1939** A. S. BENNETT *June of Rochester* i. 12 *Hecla* was only a converted Montagu whaler with barely sitting headroom in the tiny cabin. **1948** R. DE KERCHOVE *Internat. Maritime Dict.* 473/2 *Montagu rig*, a two-mast fore-and-aft service rig for ship's boats in the British Navy. The sail plan includes a stay foresail, standing lug mainsail, and jib-headed mizen. A centerboard is fitted to boats with Montagu rig. **1974** W. E. MAY in *Maritime Monogr. & Rep.* (Nat. Maritime Museum) No. 15, 18 It was not until the early years of the present century that the Montagu whaler appeared. This boat, partially following the proposals of Rear-Admiral Victor Alexander Montagu, had a fuller body aft and was rigged with a standing-lug mainsail, triangular foresail and small triangular mizen.

Montague ('mɒntəgjuː). *Hairdressing.* Also **Montague curl.** [Origin unknown.] A flat curl, several of which were used to dress the front of the hair, often forming a fringe.

1881 *Mme. Demorest's 'What to Wear' 1881-82* Autumn & Winter 68/1 The flat Montague curls and *crève-cœur* locks are being affected. **1882** *Mme. Demorest's 'What to Wear' 1882* Spring & Summer 80/1 Montagues continue, as formerly, to please the fancy. They may be flattened or combed up; the latter is preferred. **1905** A. B. MOLER *Man. Barbering* 86 Artificial curls... Montagues are made by fastening a strand of hair to a style of hairpin for this purpose. *Ibid.* 90 Montagues, or short curls, for the front of the face,..are usually dressed on a wig block. **1960** CUNNINGTON & BEARD *Dict. Eng. Costume* 138/1 *Montague Curls*,..an evening dress coiffure, the front hair arranged in a crescent-shaped fringe of curls gummed to the forehead.

1966 J. S. Cox *Illustr. Dict. Hairdressing* 99 *Montague*,.. a pin curl mounted on a hairpin.

monta(i)gne, obs. forms of MOUNTAIN.

Montaignesque (mɔ̃teɪˈnɛsk), *a.* [See -ESQUE.] Characteristic of or relating to the French philosopher and essayist, Michel de *Montaigne* (1533–92), or his writings. Also **Monˈtaignian** (-ɪən), **Monˈtaignish** (-ɪʃ) *adjs.* So **Monˈtaignism**, the theories or ideas of Montaigne.

1831 DISRAELI *Young Duke* III. v. vi. 175 In the Lords, I admire the Duke... There is a gruff, husky sort of a downright Montaignish *naïveté* about him. **1917** J. STRAHAN *Andrew Bruce Davidson* iv. 65 One cannot but be struck by the curiously Montaignesque style. **1959** *Jrnl. Philos.* LVI. 544 Hume.. has also affinities to the Montaignian sceptical tradition. **1964** *Philos.* XXXIX. 205 He.. found it necessary to refute Montaignism. **1965** *Amer. Philos. Q.* II. 19/1 The same scepticism, with the same Montaignian arguments.

montan, obs. form of MOUNTAIN, MUNTIN.

‖**Montaña**[1] (mɒnˈtaɲa). [Sp.: see MOUNTAIN.] **1.** *pl.* As the proper name of certain mountain districts in Spain.

1842 *Penny Cycl.* XXII. 291/1 The Montañas of Asturias.

2. In Spanish-American countries: A forest of considerable extent; *spec.* the name of the part of Peru east of the Andes. Cf. MONTE[2].

1840 *Penny Cycl.* XVIII. 3/2 [Peru], The Mountain Region, or *Montaña*, runs parallel to the Pacific. **1856** I. F. HOLTON *New Granada* 436 (Cent.) All land covered with thicket is called monte if it be but a few miles through, and montaña if more. **1878** H. W. BATES *Central Amer.*, etc. 210 The traveller.. finds himself in the Montaña of Peru, a.. little-known region on the eastern slopes of the Andes. *Ibid.* 339 The Ecuador Montaña is.. more abundantly watered. **1888** GUILLAUME *Amazon Prov. Peru* 3 The Montaña or forest country—is that immense region lying along the slopes of the.. eastern range of the Andes.

Montana[2] (mɒnˈtɑːnə, -ˈtænə). The name of a state in the north-west of the U.S.A. used *attrib.* in **Montana tree**, a type of saddle or saddle-tree.

1891 *Harper's Mag.* June 7/2 Their saddle is what is known as the Montana tree.

Montanan (mɒnˈtɑːnən, -ˈtæn-), *a.* Also **Montanian**. [f. MONTANA[2] + -AN or -IAN.] A native or inhabitant of Montana.

1870 *Montana Pick & Plow* (Bozeman) 29 July 2/2 That desire to know, so prominently a characteristic of our countrymen, is perhaps enhanced among Montanians, by reason of their comparative isolation. **1894** *Harper's Mag.* Aug. 482/1 (*caption*) The unterrified Montanians. **1932** *Frontier* (Missoula, Montana) Mar. 206/2 The better Montanan you are.. the better American. **1972** *Fairbanks* (Alaska) *Daily News-Miner* 3 Nov. 2/4 Montanans struggled for years with the question of whether to have a convention.

montance, obs. variant of MOUNTANCE.

montane (ˈmɒnteɪn), *a. Nat. Hist.* [ad. L. *montān-us*, f. *mont-*, *mons*: see MOUNT *sb.* and -ANE. So F. *montane.*] Pertaining to or inhabiting mountainous country.

1863 J. G. BAKER *N. Yorks. Stud. Bot.*, etc. 211 One of the most frequent of the characteristically montane species. **1881** *Gardeners' Chron.* 15 Oct. 503/2 A single species restricted to elevated montane localities in Tasmania. **1885** J. G. BAKER *Lake Dist. Flora* 238 Parsley Fern.. one of the most universal of the montane Lakeland plants.

montane, obs. form of MOUNTAIN.

†**monˈtanic**, *a. Obs. rare.* [f. L. *montān-us* (see MONTANE) + -IC.] Of or pertaining to mountains; consisting of mountains.

1799 KIRWAN *Geol. Ess.* 161 The most extensive montanic ranges commonly consist of three chains.

†**Monˈtanical**, *a. Obs. rare*$^{-1}$. [f. *Montan-us* (see MONTANISM) + -ICAL.] = MONTANISTIC.

1607 *Schol. Disc. agst. Antichr.* I. i. 39 It was superstitious and neere Montanicall.

Montanism (ˈmɒntənɪz(ə)m). [f. *Montān-us* (see below) + -ISM.] The tenets of a heretical Christian sect, founded in Phrygia by Montanus about the middle of the 2nd century.

Montanus claimed for himself and two female associates prophetic inspiration. The tenets of the sect were millenarian and severely ascetic, but otherwise did not differ appreciably from those of the Catholic church.

1597 HOOKER *Eccl. Pol.* v. lxxii. §11 Tertullian proclayming euen open warre to the Church maintained Montanisme. **1649** JER. TAYLOR *Gt. Exemp.* III. Disc. xvi. 57 If by such austerities I lead others to a good opinion of Montanism I must.. alter my dyet. **1902** T. M. LINDSAY *Ch. & Ministry in Early Cent.* vi. 215 *note*, Prophecy lasted until it was finally discredited by Montanism.

Montanist (ˈmɒntənɪst), *sb.* (and *a.*) [f. *Montān-us* (see prec.) + -IST.] A believer in Montanism. Also as *adj.* = MONTANISTIC.

1577 HANMER *Anc. Eccl. Hist.* 89 *margin*, Apollonius against the Montanistes. **1579** FULKE *Heskins' Parl.* 439 Other heresies of yᵉ Montanistes. **1653** BAXTER *Chr. Concord* 69 Some Arians, Nestorians, Monothelites, Montanists, denied the souls immortality. **1702** ECHARD *Eccl. Hist.* (1710) 546 Tertullian.. began to incline towards the errors of the Montanists. **1833** MOORE *Trav. Irish Gentl. in Search Relig.* I. 263 The Montanists.. took it on the word of their founder that he was the very Paraclete promised by the Redeemer. **1859** SCHAFF *Hist. Chr. Ch.* (an. 1–311) 300 The Montanist prophets. *Ibid.* 301 The Montanist Proclus.

Hence **Montaˈnistic**, †**Montaˈnistical** *adjs.*, of or relating to Montanism.

1629 BP. HALL *Hon. Marr. Clergy* II. xvi, The Montanisticall vaunt of virginitie. **1645** PAGITT *Heresiogr.* (1647) 89 A fourth hold Antinomian, Montanisticke, and Familisticke Tenets. **1660** STILLINGFL. *Iren.* II. ii. (1662) 160 Setting aside the Montanistical spirit.. the first-rise of this Ignis fatuus was from the bogs of Popery. **1833** J. H. NEWMAN *Arians* I. i. (1876) 17 The perverse spirit.. which we have been tracing in its Montanistic and Novatian varieties, still lurked in those parts.

montanite (ˈmɒntənaɪt). *Min.* [f. the name of *Montana*, one of the States of the American Union: see -ITE.] A hydrous telluride of bismuth occurring in yellowish earthy incrustations.

1868 GENTH in *Amer. Jrnl. Sci.* Ser. II. XLV. 317 A tellurate of bismuth, for which I propose the name 'Montanite'.

Montanize (ˈmɒntənaɪz), *v.* [f. *Montān-us* (see MONTANISM) + -IZE.] *intr.* To follow the doctrines of the Montanists.

1594 HOOKER *Eccl. Pol.* IV. vii. §4 Tertullian.. iudged all them who did not Montanize to be but carnally minded. **1620** BP. HALL *Hon. Marr. Clergy* I. xix, Hee might haue found his Tertullian, then Montanizing, to vpbraid the true and catholike Church. **1840** MILMAN *Hist. Chr.* III. 363 *note*, Tertullian evidently Montanises in this treatise.

†**montanous**, *a. Obs. rare*$^{-1}$. [ad. L. *montān-us* (f. *mont-*, *mons*: see MOUNT) + -OUS.] 'Belonging to Mountains, mountainous' (Bailey 1721).

1658 ROWLAND tr. *Moufet's Theat. Ins.* 947 *Bombilophagus*, is a Fly, montanous, big, very black.

montant[1] (ˈmɒntənt). ? *Obs.* In 5 **mountaunt.** [a. F. *montant*, pres. pple. of *monter* to rise, MOUNT, used subst.] = MUNTIN. Also *attrib.*

1449 in *Cal. Proc. Chanc. Q. Eliz.* (1830) II. Pref. 55 Beames, mountaunts,.. rafturs. **1723** CHAMBERS tr. *Le Clerc's Treat. Archit.* I. 108 Without the Chambranle is a Plat-Band.. called a Montant or Window-post. **1823** P. NICHOLSON *Pract. Build.* 228 Muntins or Montants. **1838** *Civ. Eng. & Arch. Jrnl.* I. 150/1 They [*i.e.* the piles] were driven in panels (montants) of sixteen feet. *Ibid.*, Two other similar pieces were then placed near the top of the 'montant' piles. *Ibid.* 150/2 Additional ties.. were notched on to the 'montant' pieces.

†**montant**[2]. *Obs. rare.* Also 6 **montanto.** [a. F. *montant* 'an upright blow, or thrust' (Cotgr.), subst. use of *montant* pr. pple.: see prec. The form *montanto* is fictitious It. or Sp.; Prof. Skeat compares Sp. *montante* 'two-handed sword' (Minsheu).] A 'downright' blow or thrust.

1598 B. JONSON *Ev. Man in Hum.* IV. v, I would teach these nineteene [gentlemen], the speciall rules, as your *Punto*,.. your *Passada*, your *Montanto*: till they could all play very neare.. as well as my selfe. **1598** SHAKS. *Merry W.* II. iii. 27 To see thee fight,.. to see thee passe thy puncto,.. thy distance, thy montant. [**1599** —— *Much Ado* I. i. 30, I pray you, is Signior Mountanto return'd from the warres?]

montan wax (ˈmɒntən wæks). Also **Montan wax.** [f. L. *montān-us* of or belonging to a mountain + WAX *sb.*[1]] A hard, brittle substance that is extracted from lignite by means of benzene or other solvents, consists mainly of higher fatty acids and their esters, and is used in making polishes and as an electrical insulator.

1908 *Chem. Abstr.* II. 2875 Montan wax is obtained by extracting brown-coal by benzene and purifying the product by repeated distillation with superheated steam. **1920** *Times* 4 Feb. 11/3 Another by-product recovered from this particular lignite.. is Montan wax.... This mineral is very valuable on account of its high melting point, and for this reason it is unequalled in the manufacture of high-grade boot polishes, gramophone records, and other articles. **1936** BONE & HIMUS *Coal* v. 55 The raw coals contain.. anything up to about 7·5 per cent. of 'Montan wax' (m.p. usually 78° to 88°). **1947** *Times* 23 June 2/7 The shortage of mined coal, together with the value of montan wax, has given added value to lignite. **1969** R. F. LANG tr. *Henglein's Chem. Technol.* 411 Montan wax is obtained from strongly bituminous, dry coal by extraction with benzene or benzene-alcohol.

‖**montaría** (montaˈria). [Pg.] A dugout canoe used in the Amazon region.

1933 P. FLEMING *Brazilian Adventure* I. xvi. 132 The other two boats belonged to smaller and faster types. One was a *montaria*, also clinker-built and actually I think a more finished and substantial bit of work than the true montaria of the Amazon. **1936** *Discovery* Dec. 382/2 Whole families, with their *montarias*, the hire of which was included in the daily wage, were recruited near the collecting-grounds.

montayn(e, obs. forms of MOUNTAIN.

Mont Bazillac, Montbazillac, varr. MONBAZILLAC.

‖**montbretia** (mɒntˈbriːʃ(ɪ)ə). [mod.L. (De Candolle), named after A. F. E. Coquebert de *Montbret*, a French botanist (1780–1801).] A genus of iridaceous plants, bearing bright orange-coloured flowers; a plant of this genus.

[**1845** LINDLEY *Veg. Kingd.* (1846) 161.] **1899** *Daily News* 22 July 4/4 Nasturtiums, montbretias, etc. **1900** *Book of Gardening* 352 Those [Tritonias] usually catalogued as Montbretias are the most popular.

‖**mont de piété** (mɔ̃ də pjete). [Fr.] = *mount of piety* (see MOUNT *sb.*[1] 5 b).

1854 THACKERAY *Newcomes* I. xxviii. 265, I saw his grandeur when I went lately to Strasbourg, on my last pilgrimage to the Mont de Piété. **1890** W. BOOTH *In Darkest England* II. vi. 215 There would be no difficulty.. of instituting a private Mont de Piété. **1923** WODEHOUSE *Inimitable Jeeves* iv. 43 The idea of—er—pledging the pearls at the local Mont de Pieté was, you will readily understand, repugnant to us. **1967** S. PAKENHAM *Sixty Miles from England* ii. 31 The Mont de Piété was full of gold earrings, pawned by fishwives, for the price of fish was low. **1969** [see HOCK *sb.*[7] b].

monte[1] (ˈmɒnteɪ). Also **monty.** [a. Sp. *monte* mountain; heap or stock of cards left after each player has his share.] **1. a.** A Spanish and Spanish-American game of chance, played with a pack of forty-five cards. ***three-card monte***, a game of Mexican origin, played with three cards only of which one is usually a court-card.

1824 J. R. POINSETT *Notes on Mexico* (1825) iii. 37 We found a numerous assembly of men gambling deeply, at a game called *monte*. **1850** B. TAYLOR *Eldorado* I. xii. 80 They are playing monte, the favorite game in California. **1876** BESANT & RICE *Gold. Butterfly* Prol. ii, I thought we should find a choice hotel, with a little monty or poker afterwards. **1877** BLACK *Green Past.* xiii, Five-Ace Jack received a liberal percentage from the three card-monte men who entertained these innocent folks. **1887** F. FRANCIS *Saddle & Mocassin* 66 'Do you want to play monte?' he asked. *Ibid.* 144 He.. was eight hundred [dollars] ahead once. But he played it off at monté.

b. *attrib.* and *Comb.*, as ***monte-banker***, ***blanket***, ***card***, ***game***, ***operator***, ***table***, etc.; **monte-bank**, a monte table; also used as the name of the game itself.

a **1861** T. WINTHROP *Life in Open Air* (1863) 128 A background of mustangs, monte-banks, and lynch-law. **1939** T. KING *21 Games to play for Money* 27 To take its [*sc.* Faro's] place, Monte Bank has come into being. **1855** F. S. MARRYAT *Mts. & Molehills* xiv. 267, I was soon asleep, notwithstanding.. the clinkings of the monté-bankers, and the noise of the crowd below. **1898** H. S. CANFIELD *Maid of Frontier* 78 His long and angular shadow fell across the monte blanket spread flat upon the ground. **1897** *Sears, Roebuck Catal.* 356/3 'Spanish Monte Cards', 48 cards in pack, assortment of black and colors. **1899** T. W. HALL *Tales* 276 Judge Leander Quinn was lured away from a monte game with a couple of buck Indians. **1961** J. SCARNE *Compl. Guide to Gambling* xix. 520 Countless Monte operators plied their trade on the steamboats of the Ohio and Mississippi.. in the 1850s. **1873** J. H. BEADLE *Undevel. West* iv. 92 We take our stand near the monte table, where a considerable crowd gathers. **1889** K. MUNROE *Golden Days* ii. 15 This influx of gold caused monte-tables, and other gambling layouts, to spring up.

2. (See MONTY.)

‖**monte**[2] (ˈmonte). [Sp.: lit. 'mountain'.] In Spanish-American countries: A more or less wooded tract; a small forest.

1856 [see MONTAÑA[1]]. **1879** *Encycl. Brit.* IX. 406/2 The montes of Uruguay are of no commercial value.

Monte[3] (ˈmɒntiː). Colloq. shortening of MONTE CARLO. Also = *Monte Carlo rally.*

1928 P. DE KETCHIVA *Confessions of Croupier* xvi. 194 After her extraordinary luck at Monte,.. she had lost all her winnings the following night at the Cannes Casino. **1956** R. BAXTER in M. Couper *Rallying to Monte Carlo* p. v, 'Doing the Monte' is like being a dog owner. Once you start, it's difficult to stop. **1968** *Autocar* 25 Jan. 35/3 Driving genius helps, but Montes are finally won by masterly planning.

monte, obs. form of MOUNT.

montebank(e, obs. forms of MOUNTEBANK *sb.*

montebrasite (mɒntɪˈbrɑːzaɪt). *Min.* [f. the name of *Montebras* in France (A. Des Cloizeaux 1871): see -ITE] A variety of AMBLYGONITE.

1873 J. NICOL *Elem. Min.* (ed. 2) 124 Amblygonite... *Montebrasite*, with no soda, is perhaps distinct. **1882** C. ELTON *Orig. Eng. Hist.* 9 The newly described mineral 'montebrasite', a phosphate of alumina.

Monte Carlo (ˌmɒntɪ ˈkɑːləʊ). [Name of a resort in Monaco famous for its gambling casino.]

1. a. Used *attrib.* to designate methods of estimating the solution to numerical problems that involve the random (or pseudo-random) sampling of numbers with some chosen frequency distribution.

1949 *Math. Tables & Other Aids to Computation* III. 546 This method of solution of problems in mathematical physics by sampling techniques based on random walk models constitutes what is known as the 'Monte Carlo' method. The method as well as the name for it were apparently first suggested by John von Neumann and S. M. Ulam. **1950** *Nucleonics* May 27 (*heading*) Random sampling (Monte Carlo) techniques in neutron attenuation problems. **1955** *Sci. Amer.* May 90/3 The accuracy of a Monte Carlo approximation improves only as the square of the number of trials. **1961** *New Scientist* 16 Mar. 678/3 This method of imitating the apparently random fluctuation of events in the real world which it is unnecessary or impossible to study in detail, is the crux of the Monte Carlo simulation technique. **1964** *Guardian* 19 June 6/6 (Advt.), Familiarity with Monte Carlo methods and computer programming would be an advantage. **1970** O. DOPPING *Computers & Data Processing* xx. 328 An important field of application of random numbers is in the Monte Carlo methods. They are based on

the repetition of a computation in a great number of cases, where one or more parameters are allowed to vary in a random fashion from one computation to the next. *Ibid.*, Monte Carlo methods can also be used for computing determined results. For instance, we can, in principle, calculate an approximation of π/4 by investigating which fraction of a number of points, chosen at random in a square, are inside the inscribed circle. **1972** *Computers & Humanities* VII. 39 Monte Carlo methods of simulation were applied to a population model for Paleolithic human populations.

b. *absol.*

1951 *Nat. Bureau of Standards Appl. Math. Ser.* (U.S.) XII. iii. 6/1 In some instances..a judicious combination of Monte Carlo applied to the physical model with analysis of the equations is indicated. **1962** D. SLAYTON in *Into Orbit* 23 A branch of probability mathematics which the scientists call 'Monte Carlo'—because it boils down, really to nothing more than a complex way of figuring the odds. **1969** *Nature* 15 Mar. 999/2 Monte Carlo involves, essentially, a sequence of operations on a sequence of random numbers $\{u_i\}$, where, ideally, the $\{u_i\}$ are independent and identically distributed. **1969** J. ARGENTI *Managem. Techniques* 172 Monte Carlo is a form of simulation..and both often require the use of a computer. It is possible, however, to use Monte Carlo with pencil and paper.

c. ***Monte Carlo fallacy***: the fallacy that the probability of any particular outcome to one of a series of repeated but independent events of chance is inversely dependent upon the previous outcomes (so that, e.g., a succession of failures is thought to increase the probability of success on the next occasion).

1957 *Sci. Amer.* Nov. 136/2 In our studies of the manifestations of subjective probability in gambling we have given particular attention to the Monte Carlo fallacy; the well-nigh unanimous belief that after a run of successes a failure is inevitable, and *vice versa.* **1973** A. J. AYER *Central Questions of Philos.* viii. 164 The notorious Monte Carlo fallacy consists in assuming that because the odds against an even number's coming up ten times in succession are over a thousand to one, there is equally little chance of the tenth spin yielding an even number, if the previous nine have done so.

2. ***Monte Carlo rally***: an annual international car rally, first held in 1911, of which the final stages take place in Monte Carlo (also shortened to *Monte Carlo*).

1950 R. LOWRY *Monte Carlo Rally* ix. 76 There are Rallies ideally suited to such tastes but the Monte Carlo is not one of them. **1973** *Guardian* 26 Jan. 13/1 Irate Monte Carlo Rally drivers..complained about speed traps set up by the French police... On the Monte Carlo, two reports of excessive speeding mean automatic disqualification.

montecule, variant of MONTICULE.

‖**monte di pietà** ('monte di pjeta). Also **monte de pietà**. Pl. **monti di pietà**. [It.] = *mount of piety* (see MOUNT *sb.*[1] 5 b).

1654 J. HOWELL *Parthenopoeia* Epistle to Reader sig. A1v *Monte de pietà*, an Hospital of 60000. Duckets of yeerly Revenue. **1805** P. BECKFORD *Familiar Lett. from Italy* I. 231 The *Monte di Pietà* was established first at Florence, in the year 1496, to restrain the usury of the Jews. **1883** *Athenæum* 18 Aug. 218/1 The..186 first-class pictures from the Monte di Pietà, where they had been pawned ages ago by destitute aristocratic families. **1973** *Listener* 18 Jan. 81/2 These Christian pawnshops, still in existence in Italy today, were known as *Monti di Pieta* or 'funds of charity'. When they were first founded, in Umbrian towns of the mid-15th century, they charged low interest rates.

monteere, obs. form of MONTERO.

montéff, variant of MONTEITH *Obs.*

Montefiascone (montefia'skone). Also **Monte Fiascone**. The name of a town in Latium, central Italy, used (freq. *attrib.*) to designate the sweet white wine made there.

1673 J. RAY *Observations Journey Low-Countries* 363 Heer [*sc.* in Rome] is great variety of Wines..: as Greco, Lagrime of Naples..Monte Pulciano, di Monte fiascone. **1803** C. WILMOT *Let.* 1 Jan. in *Irish Peer* (1920) 136 The Montefiascone wine is celebrated; we found it excellent. **1833** C. REDDING *Hist. Mod. Wines* ix. 240 Of the home growths..another is the Monte Fiascone, of a fine aroma, and intoxicating. It is grown near the Lake Bolsena. **1966** H. JOHNSON *Wine* 136 Fugger went no further, but ended his days drinking Montefiascone, and no doubt boring his boon-companions to death with the story of Est Est Est. **1967** A. LICHINE *Encycl. Wines* 356 *Montefiascone*, white wine grown in the foothills of the Volsini Mountains, Italy.

montegre, variant of MANTIGER.

monteigh, erron. form of MONTEITH.

monteigne, -ir(o, obs. ff. MOUNTAIN, MONTERO.

monteith[1] (mən'ti:θ). *Antiq.* Also 7 **monteigh**, 8 **montéff**, 7–9 **monteth**. (See quot. 1683.)

1683 WOOD *Life* Dec. (O.H.S.) III. 84 This year..came up a vessel or bason notched at the brims to let drinking glasses hang there by the foot so that the body or drinking place might hang in the water to coole them. Such a bason was called a 'Monteigh', from a fantastical Scot called 'Monsieur Monteigh', who at that time or a little before wore the bottome of his cloake or coate so notched ∪∪∪∪. **1689** *Lond. Gaz.* No. 2453/4 Stolen..; a large Monteth. **1699** FARQUHAR *Constant Couple* Epil., The poet merits an ignoble death, Who fears to fall over a brave Monteth. **1728** *Ann. Barber-Surg. Lond.* (1890) 489 An earthen monteth. **1721** BAILEY, *Monteth*, a scollop'd Bason to cool Glasses in. **1773** *Lond. Chron.* 7 Sept. 248/3 The following articles.. were assayed and marked;..montéffs, mazareens. **1901** *Athenæum* 10 Aug. 197/2 A monteth, containing thirteen silver beakers, given to the town [*i.e.* Nottingham] in 1689.

Monteith[2] (mən'ti:θ). A type of coloured cotton handkerchief with a white design (see quots.).

1882 CAULFIELD & SAWARD *Dict. Needlework* 350 *Monteiths*, a description of Cotton Handkerchiefs, which are dyed of one uniform colour, but have a pattern of white spots occurring at regular distances... These goods are known by the name of the manufacturers, at Glasgow. **1957** M. B. PICKEN *Fashion Dict.* 226/1 *Monteith*.., cotton handkerchief, having colored background with white design, made by discharging dye. **1958** A. & N. L. CLOW in C. Singer et al. *Hist. Technol.* IV. viii. 249, 5000 looms were employed in 1796 in the neighbourhood of Glasgow making pullicates for the Turkey-red dyers. These became known throughout Europe as monteiths, after Henry Monteith, who acquired Dalmarnock from Macintosh.

monte-jus (mɔ̃t(ə)ʒys). Also **-juice**. [Fr., f. *monter* to raise + *jus* juice, liquid.] In the making of sugar, an apparatus for raising the level of the liquid by means of air or steam pressure.

1872 P. SOAMES *Manuf. Sugar* 133 The cane-juice runs along the gutter to the monte-jus C, where it is elevated into the clarifiers, D. **1921** *Dict. Occup. Terms* (1927) §449 *Montejuice attendant, montejuice boy*: stands by valves of montejus apparatus. **1924** A. J. WALLIS-TAYLER *Sugar Machinery* viii. 147 This monte-jus should be sunk in the ground, and enclosed with brickwork or masonry in a sort of well. **1950** N. DEERR *Hist. Sugar* II. xxxiii. 578 The montejus was introduced into the industry in 1819 by Dubrunfaut.

Montelian (mɒn'ti:lɪən), *a. Archæol.* [f. the name of the Swedish archæologist, Oscar *Montelius* (1843–1921) + -AN or -I)AN.] Applied to a system of classification and nomenclature devised by Montelius.

1937 G. E. DANIEL in *Antiquity* XI. 185 The implications of the Montelian theory of the dolmen are fivefold. **1938** —— in *Ibid.* XII. 302 These modifications are not enough to make the Montelian classification a really workable typology. *Ibid.* 303, I use the word dolmen throughout here in the Montelian sense of a small single chamber. **1941** *Proc. Prehistoric Soc.* VII. 21 Archaeologists who neglect the B-Dolmens of northern Europe are destroying..any case they might make for the defence of the Montelian sequence. **1950** G. E. DANIEL *Hundred Yrs. Archaeol.* xii. 235 The Montelian periods were rendered difficult to use because of their very close linkage in typology and name with the various classes of collective tombs.

Montélimar (mɒn'teɪlɪmɑ:(r)). The name of a town in the department of Drôme in S.E. France used *attrib.* and *absol.* to designate a type of nougat orig. made there.

1908 J. KIRKLAND *Mod. Baker* IV. 16 *Nougat Montélimar* is another kind of mixture in which almonds are used. **1923** R. WHYMPER *Manuf. Confectionery* 139 Montélimar nougat for chocolate coating should not be as hard as that which is sold in blocks. **1968** W. J. FANCE *International Confectioner* 569/1 Nougat Montélimar which is very well known, originally came from the East. **1972** 'J. MELVILLE' *Ironwood* iii. 50, I wanted to cheer him up. I had some bags of montelimar and marchpane.

Montem ('mɒntɛm). *Obs.* exc. *Hist.* In 8 **montain**. [From the L. *ad montem*, 'to the Hill'.] A festival (originally annual, latterly triennial) formerly celebrated by the scholars of Eton, who in fancy costumes went in procession to 'Salt Hill', a mound near Slough, and there collected money from the bystanders. The money collected was applied to defray the expenses of the senior colleger (the 'Captain of the Montem') at King's College, Cambridge. The last celebration was in 1844.

1743 DOD in *Phil. Trans.* XLII. 561 This young Gentleman had..over-heated himself..by performing a Part at the Montain, near Eton, where he was a Scholar. **1745** R. CUST in Maxwell-Lyte *Eton Coll.* (1899) 511 It was never Mr. Cook's intention to let us have a Montem this year. **1777** SHERIDAN *Sch. Scand.* v. ii, Mr. Surface, it seems, had come home the night before late from Salthill, where he had been to see the Montem with a friend, who has a son at Eton. **1817** J. EVANS *Excurs. Windsor*, etc. 353 The ancient custom of the Montem is celebrated at Eton every third year on Whit-Tuesday. **1899** SIR A. WEST *Recoll.* I. i. 60, I took part in the last 'montem'.

b. *attrib.* and *Comb.*, as ***montem day, dinner, dress, pole, procession***; **montem-sure-night**, the night of the twentieth day before the montem, when it became 'sure' that the senior colleger could not receive a twenty-day summons to present himself for a vacancy in King's College, Cambridge, and so would be Captain of the Montem.

a **1769** HUGGETT in *Brand's Pop. Antiq.* (1813) I. 345 The Montem day used to be fixed for the first Tuesday in Hilary Term. **1817** *Gentl. Mag.* June 559/2 The young Gentlemen walked..in grand procession, to Frogmore, in their full Montem dresses. **1865** W. L. C. *Etoniana* 153 The night which followed the twentieth day before the Montem was called *Montem-sure-night.* **1886** DOWDEN *Shelley* I. i. 25 The years 1805 and 1808 were made glorious by the Montem processions. **1893** A. G. GRINNAN in *Will. & Mary Coll. Quarterly* II. 118 Mrs. Young..paid the bills of tailors,..cost of montem poles and the montem dinner, and all manner of expenses incident to their position.

montenance, variant of MOUNTENANCE.

†**Monte'negrian,** *a. Obs. rare.* = next.

1845 *Blackw. Mag.* Jan. 45/1.

Montenegrin(e (mɒntɪ'ni:grɪn), *a.* and *sb.* Also **Montenegran**. [f. *Montenegro* (Venetian It., = Tuscan *monte nero*, black mountain, a literal translation of the local Slavonic name *Crnagora*) + -IN.]

A. *adj.* Relating to Montenegro (a republic of Yugoslavia, formerly a Slavonic principality, on the east of the Adriatic) or to its inhabitants, language, etc.

1840 *Brit. & For. Rev.* XI. 136 The Montenegrine mode of making war. **1849** PATON *Highl. Adriatic* I. 105 The idea of a Montenegrine port on the Adriatic was at once negatived. **1883** *Encycl. Brit.* XVI. 781/2 The first Montenegrin newspaper..began to appear in 1870. **1939** W. B. YEATS *Statesman's Holiday* in *Last Poems & Plays* (1940) 77 Here's a Montenegrin lute, And its old sole string Makes me sweet music And I delight to sing. **1942** *R.A.F. Jrnl.* 13 June 24 The Montenegrin guerrillas attacked the hotel. **1958** P. KEMP *No Colours or Crest* x. 220 The German and Albanian forces..had started an offensive against the Montenegrin Partisans. **1970** *Internat. & Compar. Law Q.* XIX. 334 The Montenegran Code of Property. **1972** *Times* 20 Oct. 9/7 Montenegran officials and a guard of honour awaited the Queen's arrival.

B. *sb.*

1. A native or inhabitant of Montenegro.

1840 *Brit. & For. Rev.* XI. 136 A Montenegrine is always armed. **1887** L. OLIPHANT *Episodes* (1888) 181 A stalwart Montenegrin, looking magnificent in his national costume.

2. A close-fitting woman's garment resembling some Oriental military costumes, and ornamented with braid-work and embroidery (*Cent. Dict.* 1890).

Montepulciano (montepul'tʃano). The name of a town in southern Tuscany, Italy, used to designate the red wine made there.

1673 [see MONTEFIASCONE]. **1702** LADY VERNEY *Let.* 25 Aug. in M. M. Verney *Verney Lett.* (1930) I. vii. 114 Mr. Cheret..has sent you a hamper of Montepunchana [*sic*]... A dozen bottles. **1817** T. JEFFERSON *Let.* in A. Lichine *Encycl. Wines* (1967) i. 5 There is still another wine to be named to you, which is the wine of Florence called Montepulciano. **1958** A. L. SIMON *Dict. Wines* 112 *Montepulciano*, one of the better red table wines of Tuscany. **1966** C. RAY *Wines of Italy* xiv. 135 *Marsicano*..lighter in colour and in alcohol than Montepulciano and fresh to the taste when drunk young.

‖**montera** (mɒn'tera). [Sp.: see MONTERO.] The black hat worn by a bullfighter.

1838 *Quarterly Rev.* LXII. 416 He [*sc.* the matador] then throws his cap, 'montera', on the ground with peculiar action. **1932** E. HEMINGWAY *Death in Afternoon* vi. 62 As the matadors come in front of the president's box they bow low and remove their black hats or monteras. **1967** MCCORMICK & MASCAREÑAS *Compl. Aficionado* iv. 130 With a single traje de luces costing the equivalent of $225, a good montera costing $30, and all the other equipment in that ratio, to launch a novillero requires capital such as Ayala does not have. **1969** A. ARENT *Laying on of Hands* (1971) xi. 125 He yanked off the sombrero and replaced it with the *montera*, the black bullfighter's hat.

Monterey (mɒnteɪ'reɪ, mɒntə-). The name of a city in California. Used *attrib.* in **Monterey cypress** (= MACROCARPA), **halibut, mackerel, pine** (= INSIGNIS) (see quots.).

1873 J. LESTER *Atlantic to Pacific* 92 Beneath the shade of a *Monterey Cypress, is the sarcophagus which holds the cherished dust of Starr King. **1884** *Sargent Rep. Forests N. Amer.* (10th Census IX) 179 *Cupressus macrocarpa* Hartweg. .. Monterey Cypress. **1969** T. H. EVERETT *Living Trees of World* 35/2 The Monterey cypress.., restricted to a very small area on the coast of central California,..sometimes is as much as 90 feet tall. **1882** JORDAN & GILBERT *Synopsis Fishes N. Amer.* 821 *Paralichthys californicus*..*Monterey halibut; Bastard Halibut. **1884** G. B. GOODE *Nat. Hist. Aquatic Anim.* 316 The *Monterey Mackerel—*Scomberomorus concolor.* **1834** SARGENT *Rep. Forests N. Amer.* (10th Census IX) 196 *Pinus insignis* Douglas ..*Monterey Pine. **1874** J. S. HITTELL *Resources of Calif.* (ed. 6) xi. 358 The Monterey pine (*Pinus insignis*) is extensively cultivated as an ornamental tree. **1935** *Discovery* Mar. 82/1 The Monterey Pine (*Pinus radiata*) is the tree that has proved most successful in Australia as a forestry product. **1957** [see INSIGNIS]. **1971** *Countryman* LXXVI. iv. 184 The collared dove has..one stronghold in the Monterey pines on the west side of Porthcressa. **1974** HAWKEY & BINGHAM *Wild Card* xxi. 168 The patio overlooked a large garden planted with mature Monterey pines.

‖**montero** (mɒn'tɛərəʊ). Also 7 **muntiro**, **mountera, -re, -ro**, 7, 9 **montera**, 9 **monteiro**; 7 *anglicized* **mountire, monte(e)re, mounteer, montier**. [Sp. *montera*, f. *montero* hunter, lit. 'mountaineer', f. *monte*: see MOUNT *sb.*] A Spanish hunter's cap, having a spherical crown and a flap capable of being drawn over the ears. Also ***montero cap***. (Common in the 17th cent.)

1622 R. HAWKINS *Voy. S. Sea* xiii. 28 Upon their heads they weare a Night-capp, vpon it a Montero, and a Hat over that. *a* **1626** BACON *New Atl.* (1900) 32 His Hatt was like a Helmett, or Spanish Montera. *a* **1642** BEDELL *Erasmus* in Fuller *Abel Rediv.* (1867) I. 83 Another..sent him..a muntiro lined with rich sables. **1652** URQUHART *Jewel* Wks. (1834) 230 A mountera-cap on his head. **1659–60** PEPYS *Diary* 20 Mar., Two monteeres for me to take my choice of. **1665** J. FRASER *Polichron.* (S.H.S.) 164 The fellow..shot an arrow at him, which stuck fast in the tippet of his mountire cape which hung behind his back. *Ibid.* 354 A Montier cape

called Magirky on his [Montross's] head. *a* **1674** CLARENDON *Hist. Reb.* IX. §55 [He] was taken in his Journey, having a Mountero on his head. **1694** MOTTEUX *Rabelais* IV. xxx. (1737) 124 The *Midriff*, like a Mounteer-Cap. *a* **1713** ELLWOOD *Autobiog.* (1765) 74 A large Montier-cap of Black Velvet, the Skirt of which being turned up in Folds [etc.]. **1762** STERNE *Tr. Shandy* VI. xxiv, The Montero-cap was scarlet..mounted all round with furr, except [etc.]. **1823** SCOTT *Peveril* xxxv, A large montero cap, that enveloped his head. **1826** J. WILSON *Noct. Ambr.* Wks. 1855 I. 98 Now all these old heroes Of helms and monteros. **1833** LONGF. *Outre Mer* Prose Wks. 1886 I. 146 A peasant woman..with a montera cocked up in front.

transf. **1820** W. IRVING *Sketch Bk.* II. 382 The cedar bird, with..its little monteiro cap of feathers.

Montessori (mɒntɪˈsɔːrɪ). The name of the Italian physician and educationalist, Dr. Maria *Montessori* (1870–1952), used to designate her educational system or ideas for the individual development of young children through free but guided play with apparatus designed specially to encourage sense perception and mental interest; also *ellipt.* Hence **Monteˈssorian** *a.* and *sb.*, **Monteˈssorianism**.

1912 A. E. GEORGE tr. M. Montessori (*title*) The Montessori method. **1917** A. S. NEILL *Dominie Dismissed* vii. 96 'But I thought that was your line..Montessori and all that kind of thing!' 'I don't know what Montessorianism is,' I said; 'I have forgotten everything I ever read about Froebel and Pestalozzi.' **1929** J. VAN DRUTEN *After All* III. ii. 114 Even if you do succeed in turning our kids' home into a sort of..Montessori school of confidence. **1934** WEBSTER Montessorian, adj. & n. **1949** G. B. SHAW *Let.* in *To Young Actress* (1960) 188 Montessori is all right while the children are under six, but no use afterwards. **1958** *Times Lit. Suppl.* 31 Jan. 59/4 From the first three of these it is possible to distil the essence of the Montessorian doctrine. **1958** *Times* 20 Mar. 13/4 The question is why all teachers are not Montessorians. *Ibid.*, Montessorianism is sometimes presented more like a religious cult than an educational method. **1972** 'E. LATHEN' *The Longer the Thread* viii. 81, I was thinking of something much more ambitious—with preschool training, possibly Montessori teachers.

monteth, variant of MONTEITH.

Monteverdian (mɒntɪˈvɜːdɪən), *a.* [See -AN.] Of, pertaining to, or resembling the Italian composer Claudio *Monteverdi* (1567–1643) or his music.

1947 M. F. BUKOFZER *Music in Baroque Era* (1948) iii. 98 Schein adopted here the airy dialogue of the Monteverdian continuo canzonetta. **1952** K. DALE tr. *Redlich's Claudio Monteverdi* IV. 160 The realization of the Monteverdian Basso Continuo has at all times been a rock upon which many editors have foundered. **1959** *Times* 20 Mar. 16/2 The Monteverdian recitative should be compulsory training for all second-year operatic students. **1963** D. ARNOLD *Monteverdi* vii. 138 Whereas no one could find anything Monteverdian in the 'Gombert Mass', the vespers bear the imprint of his style.

monteyne, obs. form of MOUNTAIN.

Montezuma's revenge (mɒntɪˈzuːməz rɪˈvɛndʒ). *slang.* [f. the name of *Montezuma* II (1466–1520), Aztec ruler at the time of the Spanish conquest of Mexico + REVENGE *sb.*] Diarrhœa suffered by visitors to Mexico.

1962 *Western Folklore* XXI. 28 The North American in Mexico has coined a number of names for the inevitable dysentery and diarrhea: 'Mexican two-step', 'Mexican fox-trot', 'Mexican toothache', and, less directly if more colorfully, 'Montezuma's revenge', the 'Curse of Montezuma' and the 'Aztec hop'. **1969** *Daily Tel.* 11 Apr. 28/5 Prevent gippy tummy. Also known as Delhi belly, Rangoon runs, Tokyo trots, Montezuma revenge. **1970** *New Scientist* 8 Jan. 47/1 An intestinal attack known as gyppy tummy..in the Middle East;..Montezuma's revenge in Mexico. **1970** *Times* 8 May 9/3 England's World Cup football squad suffered their first casualty in Mexico on Wednesday, when 20-year-old Brian Kidd was struck down by what is known as 'Montezuma's Revenge'—a stomach complaint.

Montgolfier (mɒntˈgɒlfɪə(r); Fr. mɔ̃gɔlfje). Also *erron.* **mongolfier**. [The name of the brothers J. M. and J. E. *Montgolfier* of Annonay (Ardèche), France, who invented the apparatus. In Fr. the Montgolfier balloon is called by the derivative name *montgolfière* fem., which has sometimes been adopted by Eng. writers.] A balloon raised by heated air instead of gas; a 'fire-balloon'. (More fully ***Montgolfier balloon***.)

The first voyage made in a Montgolfier balloon was by Pilatre de Rozier, 21 Nov. 1783.

1784–5 *Ann. Reg.* 329 He made a small balloon filled with inflammable air..suspended to which was an enormous Montgolfier (a balloon of rarified air). **1785** *Ibid.*, *Principal Occur.* 39/1 A Montgolfier, or fire-balloon. **1849** SIR G. HEAD *Rome* I. 46 A huge paper 'Montgolfier', or fire balloon. **1860** *Chamb. Encycl.* I. 646/2 The longest voyage ever executed in a Montgolfière. **1866** BRANDE & COX *Dict. Sci.* etc., *Mongolfier Balloon*, a balloon filled with atmospheric air..dilated by heat.

montgomeryite (mɒntˈgɒmərɪaɪt). *Min.* [f. the name of Arthur *Montgomery* (b. 1909), U.S. geologist + -ITE[1].] A hydrated basic phosphate of calcium and aluminium, $Ca_4Al_5(PO_4)_6(OH)_5.11H_2O$, which is found as green monoclinic crystals at Fairfield, Utah, U.S.A.

1940 E. S. LARSEN in *Amer. Mineralogist* XXV. 321 The name montgomeryite is proposed for this mineral after Mr. Arthur Montgomery of New York City, who..collected the material. **1964** *Ibid.* XLIX. 1119 This apparently represents the first reported occurrence of montgomeryite from a pegmatite.

month[1] (mʌnθ). Forms: 1 **mónað, -oð, -eð, mónð**, 3 **monð**, 2–5 **moneð**, 3 **moneþþ**(*Orm.*), 3–4 **monþe, monthe, monet**, 3–7 **monethe**, 4 **munth, mooneþ, monyþ, mooneth, mounthe**, 4–5 **moneþe**, 4–6 **monyth**, 4–7 **moneth**, 5 **munethe**, 5–6 **monythe**, 6 **monneth**, *Sc.* **monecht**, 3– **month**. [Common Teut.: OE. *mónað* masc., = OFris. *mônath*, *môn(a)d*, masc., OS. *mânoth* masc. (in glosses: MLG. *mânet*, MDu. *maent*, Du. *maand* fem.), OHG. *mânôa* (MHG. *mânôt*. mod.G. *monat*) masc., ON. *mánuð-r* masc. (Sw. *månad*, Da. *maaned*), Goth. *mēnōþ-s*:—OTeut. **mǣnōþ-*, related to **mǣnon-* MOON *sb.*[1]

In the 16–17th c. the spelling *moneth* was almost universal.]

A measure of time corresponding to the period of revolution of the moon.

1. a. Any one of the twelve portions into which the conventional year is divided. (When not otherwise determined by the context, the reference is to the 'months' inherited by Western civilized nations from the Romans, and known by the names January, February, etc.) More explicitly ***calendar month***, less commonly †***calendary***, ***civil***, ***political***, ***usual month*** (for illustrations of these designations see under the adjs.).

The primitive calendar month of ancient nations began on the day of new moon or the day after, and thus coincided (except for fractions of a day) with the synodical month (see 2). Among many peoples of antiquity, however, it was from a very early period found desirable that the calendar year should contain an integral number of the smaller periods used in ordinary reckoning. Hence the true 'months' were superseded by a series of twelve periods each having a fixed number of days (on the average one-twelfth of the number in the calendar year), and thus having no relation to the changes of the moon; but this artificial period continued to bear the name of 'month'. The systems according to which the reckoning by months was brought into relation with that by years were very various. In the Julian calendar, the months in leap year had alternately 31 and 30 days, while in other years February had only 29 instead of 30. This symmetrical arrangement was under Augustus broken up by the transference of a day from February to August, and of a day from September and November to October and December respectively, producing the system now in use.

c **888** K. ÆLFRED *Boeth.* v. §2 þonne ðære sunnan scima on Agustes monðe hatost scinð ðonne dyseȝað se ðe þonne wile hwelc sæd oðfæstan þæm dryȝum furum. *c* **1000** ÆLFRIC *Gen.* vii. 11 On þam oðrum monðe on þone seofenteoðan dæȝ þas monðes. *a* **1123** *O.E. Chron.* an. 1110 On þære fiftan nihte on Maies monðe. *c* **1205** LAY. 7220 He [Julius Cæsar] makede þane kalender þe dihteð þane moneð & þe ȝer. *c* **1386** CHAUCER *Prol.* 92 He was as fresh as is the month of May. **1477** EARL RIVERS (Caxton) *Dictes* 1 In the moneth of Iuyll the said yere. **1535** COVERDALE *Exod.* xiii. 4 This daye are ye gone out, euen in yͤ moneth of Abib. **1615** BEDWELL *Arab. Trudg.*, *Alkoran*, This moneth they call *Ramadhan*, which also is their Lent. **1678** SIR G. MACKENZIE *Crim. Laws Scot.* II. iv. §1 (1699) 185 Registrat in the Books of Secret Council, the 15. day of that Moneth. **1681** W. ROBERTSON *Phraseol. Gen.* (1693) 868 The Moneth of March. **1775** S. J. PRATT *Liberal Opin.* lxiv. (1783) II. 236 The arid month of July. **1794** CRUDEN *Concord.* (ed. 5) s.v. *Month*, The names and order of the months in the [Hebrew] Civil year are the same as in the preceding table, only beginning the year with Tisri or September. **1807** ROBINSON *Archæol. Græca* III. xxv. 332 The Roman January, which was their first month, was in the depth of winter. The Macedonians reckoned Dius their first month from the autumnal equinox. **1861** M. PATTISON *Ess.* (1889) I. 36 Dr. Pauli..more than once gives the day and the month, without remembering to add the year of an event.

b. An emblematic representation of this.

1644 EVELYN *Diary* 7 Nov., The Temple of Janus quadrifrontis, having 4 arches importing the 4 Seasons, and on each side niches for the Monethes. **1712** BUDGELL *Spect.* No 425 ¶4 Then came up the three Months which belong to this season. *Ibid.*, Then came the Attendant Months.

2. *Astr.* **a.** (In full ***lunar month***.) The period in which the moon makes a complete revolution relatively to some point, either fixed or moveable.

There are thus several species of lunar month, as the time of the revolution is different according to the point with regard to which it is reckoned. Usually the term denotes the *synodical month*, i.e. the period from one new moon to the next, the length of which is 29 days, 12 hours, 44 minutes, 2·7 seconds. The other kinds of lunar month (the lengths of which are all between 27 and 28 days) are the *anomalistic*, *sidereal*, *tropical*, and *nodical month*: see those adjs.

c **1000** *Sax. Leechd.* III. 248 On ðam monðe synd ȝetealde niȝon & twentiȝ daȝa & twelf tida, þis is se monelica monað. *c* **1250** *Gen. & Ex.* 145 Ðe mones liȝt is moneð met. **1398** TREVISA *Barth. De P.R.* IX. ix. (1495) 354 The month of the mone is that space in the whyche the mone passyth from one poynt in the fyrmament and comyth ayen to the same.. conteynyth xxvij dayes and viij houres. **1483** *Cath. Angl.* 246/2 A munethe, *interlunium*. **1551** RECORDE *Cast. Knowl.* (1556) 14 A Moneth is the iuste time of the propre course of the Moone, from chaunge to chaunge. **1715** tr. *Gregory's Astron.* (1726) I. 241 Tho' a Month be properly that space of time wherein the Moon goes thro' the Zodiac; yet [etc.]. **1875** *Encycl. Brit.* II. 800/1 We have as many different species of months as there are different motions with which that of the moon can be compared. *Ibid.* 800/2 The different lunar months. Synodical month, Sidereal month, Tropical month [etc.].

†**b.** ***month of apparition***, ***illuminative month***: that part of the lunation during which the moon is actually visible. (The length of this was variously stated.) *Obs.*

1594 BLUNDEVIL *Exerc.* III. I. xlvi. (1636) 360 The month of Apparition consisteth of eight and twenty daies. **1658** PHILLIPS s.v., A moneth of Apparition, *i.* the space of 26 dayes and 12 hours, wherein the Moon appears, the other three days being deducted wherein it is obscured by the Sun.

c. ***solar month***: the twelfth part of the solar year; the time occupied by the sun in passing through one of the signs of the zodiac.

c **1000** *Sax. Leechd.* III. 244 Ðære sunnan ȝear is þæt heo beyrne þone miclan circul zodiacum... Ælce monðe heo yrnð under an þæra tacna. **1398** TREVISA *Barth. De P.R.* IX. ix. (1495) 354 The monthe of the sonne duryth as longe as the sonne abydyth in one sygne in his course. **1715** tr. *Gregory's Astron.* (1726) I. 241 That space of time..wherein the Sun runs thro' one Sign of the Zodiac, is call'd a Solar Month.

3. a. A space of time, reckoned from any moment, and either (*a*) extending to the corresponding day of the next calendar month (in which case the space of time is called 'a calendar month'), or (*b*) containing 28 days (often miscalled a 'lunar month').

a **900** tr. *Bæda's Hist.* v. xvii. [xix.] (1890) 454 He þa fela monþa þær ȝesæliȝum ȝ elesum ȝeornlice abyseȝad wæs. *c* **1000** ÆLFRIC *Gen.* xxix. 14 Ða an monuð aȝan wæs. *c* **1205** LAY. 7771 þreottene monðes wunede Julius in Oðeres. *c* **1250** *Gen. & Ex.* 2592 Ðre moneð haueð ȝhe him hid. *c* **1350** *Will. Palerne* 5074 þe fest of þat mariage a moneþ fulle lasted. **1362** LANGL. *P. Pl.* A. III. 140 Heo may as muche do In a Mooneþ ones, As [ȝoure] secre seal In Seuen score dayes. *c* **1400** MAUNDEV. (1839) v. 49 At the ende of 3 Wekes or of a Monethe, thei comen aȝen. **1481** CAXTON *Godeffroy* cxxi. 183 The siege had thenne endured nygh ix. monethes. **1579** LYLY *Euphues* (Arb.) 46 A quicke vnderstanding, is able to attaine to more in a moment..then a dull and blockish head in a month. **1599** *Acts Privy Council* XXIX. 591 Allowance..at x.li. the monneth, accompting xxviij daies to the monethe, is yearlie cxxx.li. **1628** COKE *On Litt.* 135 b, A month *mensis* is regularly accounted in Law 28. dayes, and not according to the Solar moneth, nor according to the Kalender, vnlesse it bee for the account of the laps in a *quare impedit*. **1683** TRYON *Way to Health* 134 Which comes to pass in six, eight or twelve Moneths, more or less. **1747** W. HORSLEY *Fool* (1748) II. 248 The hurricane Months begin about the Twelfth of July, and continue to the Nineteenth of October. **1766** BLACKSTONE *Comm.* II. ix. 141 A month in law is a lunar month, or twenty-eight days, unless otherwise expressed. **1842** J. AITON *Domest. Econ.* (1857) 303 In Scotland, we are said to enjoy nine months of winter and three months of very bad weather. **1850** *Act 13–14 Vict.* c. 21 (An Act for shortening the Language used in Acts of Parliament) §4 The Word 'Month' to mean Calendar Month, unless words be added showing Lunar Month to be intended. **1886** LUCY *Gladstone Parl.* 372 That plank bed, every square inch of which is as well known in the House of Commons as if members had passed upon it a month of all-night sittings.

b. *sing.* for *pl.* after a numeral. *Obs.* exc. *dial.*

c **1175** *Lamb. Hom.* 3 þe mon þe leie xii moneð in ane prisune. *a* **1225** *Ancr. R.* 218 Sum ancre is þet weneð þet heo schule beon stronglukest iuonded iðe uormeste tweolf moneð þet heo bigon ancre lif. *a* **1300** *Cursor M.* 11127 Mare þan thre monet duelld he In his aghen kindli contre. *c* **1300** *Harrow. Hell* 208 Twelue moneþ is agon, þat I þolede martirdom. *c* **1400** *Destr. Troy* 8373 Sex moneth & no more. *c* **1470** HENRY *Wallace* III. 334 Till x moneth war gayne.

c. *spec.* One of the 'nine months' commonly accounted to make up the period of pregnancy in women (about 270–80 days). So ***seven months' child***, one born about 30 weeks after conception.

c **950** *Lindisf. Gosp.* Luke i. 36 Ðis moneð [*Rushw. MS.* monoð] is ðe seista ðær ðiu ȝe-ceiȝed is un-berend. **1834** *Cycl. Pract. Med.* III. 471/2 Both mother and daughter.. were in the habit of menstruating up to the seventh month.

d. Used as an indefinite measure of time, esp. in *pl.*, a long while.

1601 SHAKS. *All's Well* IV. iii. 99, I haue to night dispatch'd sixteene businesses, a moneths length a peece. **1819** SHELLEY *Cenci* III. i. 330 What you in one night squander were enough For months! **1891** MEREDITH *One of our Conq.* xxv, 'Is there anything of Dartrey's wife?' 'Dead', he answered. 'When?' 'Months back'. **1897** *Allbutt's Syst. Med.* II. 455 Beriberi often originates in ships miles and months away from the land.

e. *ellipt.* for a month's leave, duty, absence, etc.; also for the amount of wages corresponding to a month's service.

1787 CHARLOTTE SMITH *Romance Real Life* I. 211 Here Beaulieu put the infant to nurse with Gabriella Niviniot, to whom he paid a month before-hand. **1793** SMEATON *Edystone L.* §330 The present third man, who was at this time taking his month on shore.

f. Phrases. †***month about***: during alternate months. ***month by month***: in each successive month (without suggestion of cessation). ***month after month***: each month as a sequel to the preceding (without suggestion of continuity). ***from month to month***: continuously from one month to the next. ***from the month***: from the period when the lying-in mother is left by the monthly nurse. ***month of Sundays*** (colloq.): an

indefinitely prolonged period. *this day month*: at a time a month after the day indicated.

1611 BIBLE *1 Chron.* xxvii. 1 Nowe the children of Israel ..which came in, and went out moneth by moneth, throughout all the moneths of the yeare. **1656** H. PHILLIPS *Purch. Patt.* (1676) 89 Moneth by moneth, nay, day by day. **1668** PEPYS *Diary* 11 Mar., About four o'clock the House rises, and hath put off the debate to this day month. **1749** *Hist. Pelham, Mass.* (1898) 224 Said Scole is to be Keept, Month about at each Plase. **1771** GOLDSM. *Hist. Eng.* II. 74 Entrusted with the charge of guarding him month about. **1808** *Times* 26 Feb. 4/4 A Widow..[wants] to take the Care of a Child from the month. **1818** SHELLEY *Marenghi* xiii. 3 He hid himself, and hunger, toil, and cold, Month after month endured. **1832** MARRYAT *N. Forster* v, It may last a month of Sundays. **1864** TENNYSON *Aylmer's Field* 488 So month by month the noise about their doors..made The nightly wirer of their innocent hare Falter before he took it. **1884** H. COLLINGWOOD *Under Meteor Flag* 269 Don't be a month of Sundays about it. **1894** OWEN & BOULGER (*title*) The Country Month by Month.

†**4.** Applied (as the name of the nearest recognized division of time) to certain measures of duration supposed to be important in particular sciences. ***philosophical month*** (old Chem.): see quot. 1727-41. ***medical*** or ***medicinal, decretory*** or ***decretorial month***: the space of 26 days 22 hours, formerly supposed by physicians to represent the interval between the crises of disease. *Obs.*

1646 [see MEDICAL *a.* 1 d]. **1727-41** CHAMBERS *Cycl.* s.v. *Month*, Philosophical Month, amongst chymists, is the space of 40 days and nights.

†**5.** *pl.* = MENSES. *Obs.*

1578 LYTE *Dodoens* II lxxi. 241 The wilde Basill.. stoppeth..the inordinate course of the Moneths. **1664** PEPYS *Diary* 27 Sept., My wife having..her months upon her is gone to bed. **1694** WESTMACOTT *Script. Herb.* 183 Saffron..expelleth the Months and Child.

6. Attributive uses and combinations.

a. *attrib.*, as ***month-brother, -end; month-old*** adj.; ***month-long*** adj. and adv.; †**month book**, an account book intended to serve a month; **month clock**, a clock which goes for a month between windings; †**month courses** = MENSES; †**month-day**, (*a*) a stipulated or allowed period of a month's duration, chiefly in phr. ***within a month day*** (cf. DAY *sb.* 11); (*b*) the corresponding day of the following calendar month; **month-man** *dial.* = *month's man* (see b); **month-name**, the name of any one of the calendar months; †**month-nurse** = ***monthly nurse***.

1557 *Order of Hospitalls* F vj, You shall kepe xiij *Moneth-Bookes. Every Booke shall containe all your receipts and Paiments receued and paid in euery Moneth. *a* **1889** G. M. HOPKINS *Poems* (1967) 37 A sister, born for each strong *month-brother. **1799** *Times* 1 June 4/4 Turkey carpets, a *month clock, a quantity of old china. **1884** F. J. BRITTEN *Watch & Clockmaker's Handbk.* 268 Month Clocks have an intermediate wheel and pinion between the great and centre wheels. **1962** E. BRUTON *Dict. Clocks & Watches* plate 7 (*caption*) French month clock with skeleton frame. **1563** HYLL *Art Garden.* (1593) 100 The same water drunk.. doth stay the excesse of the *month courses. **1390** GOWER *Conf.* II. 27 He his trowthe leith to borwe To come, if that he live may, Ayein withinne a *Monthe day. *Ibid.* 100 Withinne..tuo Monthe day. *c* **1440** *Generydes* 1890 To muster withynne a moneth day. *c* **1470** [see DAY *sb.* 11]. **1546** LANGLEY *Pol. Verg. De Invent.* V. iv. 103 b, Thei vse commonly not to be purified afore the moneth day. **1929** *Times* 30 Oct. 14/2 The corporations would..withdraw funds from the call money market to meet their *month-end requirements. **1843** PUSEY *Serm. Holy Euch.* 28 All but a *month-long fast from our 'daily Bread'. **1887** MORRIS *Odyss.* x. 14 And me month-long there he cherished. **1794** *Annals of Agric.* XXII. 212 Harvest-men, (month-men) 4l. per month. **1906** *Athenæum* 8 Sept. 280/3 The old dislike of Quakers to the ordinary *month names. **1828** *Lights & Shades* II. 312, I was boxed up with a market-gardener, a *month-nurse [etc.]. **1909** R. BROOKE *Let.* Jan. (1968) 155 On Thursday..I go..to our filthy academy in the Fens ..(by a *month-old engagement) with a pack of women. **1940** W. FAULKNER *Hamlet* IV. 292 The month-old corn-silk beard which concealed most of his abraded face. **1960** *Farmer & Stockbreeder* 1 Mar. 150/3 Day-old pullets.. chicks as hatched..month-old pullets.

b. Possessive genitive, as †**month's day** = *month day* (see a); also = MONTH'S MIND; **month's end** *dial.*, a religious celebration held after the expiration of a month from the date of a funeral (cf. MONTH'S MIND); **month's man**, a man employed at enhanced wages for one month's labour during harvest.

c **1526** *Plumpton Corr.* (Camden) 226 As I understand, ye are contented to bide the order of me & others,..so that an end wear maid before *months day next. **1542** in *Suss. Arch. Coll.* (1869) XXI. 201 [Will of T. Delve: At his burial x masses... At his month's day a cast of bread, two pounds of beef, and a penny]. **1863** *Monthly Packet* Dec. 683 In many a parish, the only occasions on which the church is well filled is when one of these '*Month's Ends' (as they are called, whatever time may have elapsed since the funeral) gathers together a train of mourners. **1750** W. ELLIS *Mod. Husbandm.* V. ii. 8 He commonly employed six *Months-Men every Harvest. **1804** CHARLOTTE SMITH *Conversations*, etc. I. 191 But what is a monthsman?.. One who is hired by the farmer, to work for him for a month, during harvest.

month[2] (mʌnθ). *Obs.* exc. *Hist.* Also 5 **monthe**, 5, 9 *Hist.* **mounth.** [ad. Gael. *monadh* until 13th c. pronounced (monað). Cf. place-names such as *Month Blair.*] A high hill, mountain. Applied *spec.* to the Grampians, esp. towards their eastern extremity (Jamieson).

1375 BARBOUR *Bruce* II. 494 Dreand in the month thar pyne. *c* **1425** WYNTOUN *Cron.* VII. v. 634 þe bak þai turnyt richt son, and flede, And oure þe Monthe richt son þaim spede. *c* **1470** HARDING *Chron.* (1543) 236 Betwixt the mounthes and the water of Tay, Which some do call mountaignes in our language. **1520** *Sc. Acts Parl.* (1814) I. 201 All kynd of monthis..hes mercheis thre, Heidrowm, watter, and monthis bord. **1561** *Reg. Privy Council Scot.* I. 193 The benefices on this syde of the Month..and beyond the Month. *c* **1600** *Battell of Balrinness* in *Scot. Poems 16th C.* (1801) II. 347 On Towie Mounth I mett a man. **1640** in *Rose of Kilravock* (Spalding Club) 333 [Twelve tenants of the] Twa Culmores were peacefully leading peats..from the Month of Mulbuy.

†**'monthish**, *a.* *Obs.* *rare*$^{-1}$. [f. MONTH *sb.*[1] + -ISH.] Of or pertaining to a month, monthly.

1540 PALSGR. *Acolastus* Q iij, A monthyshe vytayle...i. as moche vitayles, as wolde serue vs for a hole monethe.

monthling ('mʌnθlɪŋ). *rare*$^{-1}$. [f. MONTH[1] + -LING.] A child a month old, or whose age can be counted only by months.

1804 WORDSW. *To my Infant Daughter* 16 Frail, feeble Monthling!—by that name methinks, Thy scanty breathing time is portioned out Not idly.

monthly ('mʌnθlɪ), *a.* and *sb.* [f. MONTH[1] + -LY[1]. OE. had *món(a)þlic*: cf. OS. *mânothlic*, OHG. *mânôdlîh* (G. *monatlich*).] **A.** *adj.*

1. a. Done or recurring once a month or every month.

1647 FULLER *Good Th. in Worse T.* (1841) 125 We have.. not care enough to keep one monthly day of humiliation. **1661** COWLEY *Prop. Adv. Exp. Philos.* Verses & Ess. (1669) 46 Two of the Professors by daily, weekly or Monethly turns shall teach the publick Schools. **1783** BURKE *Ind. Comm. Rep.* Wks. II. 260 Mr. Hastings..urges the necessity of the monthly payment of the Nabob's stipend being regularly made. **1838** LYTTON *Alice* I. iii. 26 She saw Evelyn opening the monthly parcel from London. **1889** H. CAMPBELL *Causat. Disease* viii. 54 Monthly migraine.

b. = MENSTRUAL *a.* 2.

1612 WOODALL *Surg. Mate* Wks. (1653) 68 Anise-seed.. moveth urine and monethly termes. *Ibid.* 71 *Amoniacum*.. provoketh the monethly courses and urine. **1806** *Med. Jrnl.* XV. 29 About five years ago the monthly period ceased, and since that time the head-ach became universal. **1889** J. M. DUNCAN *Clin. Lect. Diseases Wom.* xix. (ed 4) 152 The woman has this violent disease during her monthly time.

2. Pertaining or relating to a month; payable every month.

1572 WALSINGHAM in Digges *Compl. Ambass.* (1655) 213 My monethly charges [are] drawning now to two hundred pounds the moneth. **1573** *Reg. Privy Council Scot.* II. 219 Dalie, owlklie, or monethlie wageis. **1843** BORROW *Bible in Spain* xli, An offer of a monthly salary. **1848** GLAISHER in *Phil. Trans.* CXXXVIII. 125 On the Corrections to be applied to the Monthly Means of Meteorological Observations taken at any hour, to convert them into Mean Monthly values. **1902** T. M. LINDSAY *Ch. & Ministry in Early Cent.* iv. 125 They paid a monthly subscription to the common fund (*stips menstrua*).

3. Continued or enduring for a month. Now *rare* exc. as applied to the revolution of the moon, where the sense blends with sense 1.

1589 GREENE *Menaphon* (Arb.) 26 Minutes ioyes are monthlie woes. **1605** SHAKS. *Lear* I. i. 134 Our selfe by Monthly course..Shall our abode Make with you by due turne. **1667** MILTON *P.L.* III. 728 The neighbouring Moon ..her aide Timely interposes, and her monthly round Still ending,..in her pale dominion checks the night. **1692** BENTLEY *Boyle Lect.* vi. 24 The monthly Revolutions of the Moon. **1825** A. R. C. DALLAS *Prelim. Statem.* in R. C. Dallas *Corr. Byron* I. p. lxxx, It is truly absurd to see how all Lord Byron's *monthly* friends prostitute the word *intimacy*.

4. Special combinations, as **monthly bird**, the fieldfare (Swainson *Prov. Names Birds* 1885); **monthly boat, ship**, a ship on a long voyage on which the crew is paid by the month; †**monthly mind** = MONTH'S MIND; **monthly nurse**, a sick-nurse who attends a woman lying in during the first month after her accouchement; **monthly rose (tree)**, the Indian or China rose, erroneously supposed to flower every month.

1898 *Nautical Mag.* Dec. 827 She passed the ship *Libertas*, evidently a good *monthly boat, jogging along the same way under close-reef topsails. **1649, 1660** Monthly mind [see MIND *sb.* 5 b]. **1798** E. WYNNE *Diary* 9 Mar. (1952) 294 These ladies say I shall very soon be brought to bed. I am exceedingly well, had the *monthly nurse in the house. **1840** DICKENS *Sk. Young Couples* 21 If one of a friend's children die, the formal couple are..punctual in sending to the house..if a friend's family be increased the monthly nurse is not more attentive than they. **1844** DICKENS *Mart. Chuz.* xix, A monthly-nurse, or, as her sign-board boldly had it, 'Midwife'. **1664** EVELYN *Kal. Hort., Mar.* (1699) 31 Cut away some Branches of the *Monthly Rose-tree close. **1664** *Ibid.* in *Sylva* 75 September... Flowers in Prime, or yet lasting... Muske Rose, and Monethly Rose. **1688** R. HOLME *Amoury* II. 62/2 The Monthly Rose [is] of the purple colour, it bears three times in the year. **1707** MORTIMER *Husb.* (1721) II. 164 The Monthly Rose bearing Flowers only three Months in England. **1866** *Chamb. Encycl.* VIII. 335/2 The name Monthly Rose is often given to it from the notion that it flowers every month. **1955** G. S. THOMAS *Old Shrub Roses* ix. 60 There was one ancient Rose which under favourable conditions of high culture and special pruning often produced a second crop of flowers in the autumn. This Rose was known in England as the Monthly Rose. **1893** E. I. BARRA *Tale Two Oceans* 20 She was what the sailors called a good old *monthly ship. **1903** H. HOLMES *Life & Adventures on Oceans* 34 'I like a good monthly ship,' remarks a seaman standing by. 'In these racehorses a fellow's dead horse is hardly worked out before you think of getting into port again.'

B. *sb.*

1. *pl.* = MENSES. Now *colloq.*

1872 J. G. MURPHY *Comm. Lev.* xv. 25 The issue is not at the usual time of the monthlies. **1922** JOYCE *Ulysses* 361 That squinty one is delicate. Near her monthlies, I expect, makes them feel ticklish. **1960** C. MACINNES *Mr. Love & Justice* 30 'Don't go,' she said. 'I'm sorry—I'm wrought up. I always am a bit just after my monthlies.' **1963** *Observer* 29 Sept. 31/5 One mother..said she had told him most of them [*sc.* the facts of life]—'even about girls and the monthlies'.

2. A literary periodical magazine or review published once in each month.

1833 *Knickerbocker* I. 185 We have articles on Political Economy in the monthlys, the weeklys, and the dailys. **1849** C. BRONTË *Let.* 15 Nov. in C. Shorter *Brontës: Life & Lett.* (1908) II. 83, I feel that the fiat for which I wait does not depend on newspapers... The monthlies and quarterlies will pronounce it. **1856** *Gentl. Mag.* July 7 All the monthlies above named had passed away before Cave started The Gentleman's Magazine. **1904** *Daily Chron.* 12 Mar. 4/7 'Can you get me a copy of the Apocrypha?' he asked... 'I can't quite remember, sir', she replied; 'is it a weekly—or a monthly?' **1973** *Nation Rev.* (Melbourne) 31 Aug. 1464/1 The emphasis in the early days of the new monthlies and quarterlies was on strong opinion.

3. Short for *monthly rose* (see A 4).

1852 MOTLEY *Corr.* (1889) I. v. 130 Our gardener has dug up his half-hardy roses, multifloras, and monthlies.

monthly ('mʌnθlɪ), *adv.* [f. MONTH[1] + -LY[2].]

1. Once a month; in each or every month; month by month.

1533-4 *Act 25 Hen. VIII*, c. 8 The poore cariers.. repairynge wekely and monthely to your citee of London. **1569** *Reg. Privy Council Scot.* II. 23 And sua furth monethlie upoun the first day of everie moneth. **1603** OWEN *Pembrokeshire* (1892) 10 He held Sessions and a Countye Courte monethlie. **1664** EVELYN (*title*) Kalendarium Hortense, or Gard'ner's Almanack, directing what he is to do monthly throughout the Year. **1744** BERKELEY *Let. to Prior* 3 Sept., Wks. 1871 IV. 300 Two pamphlets that come out monthly. **1878** JEVONS *Prim. Pol. Econ.* 53 Clerks receive their salaries monthly.

†**2.** After the manner of a lunatic. *Obs.* *rare*$^{-1}$.

1611 MIDDLETON & DEKKER *Roaring Girl* v. ii, The man talkes monthly:..I see hee'l be starke mad at our next meeting.

month's mind. Also 5-7 **month mind.**

1. *Eccl.* In England before the Reformation, and still in Ireland among Roman Catholics: The commemoration of a deceased person by the celebration of masses, etc., on a day one month from the date of his death.

There seems to be no authority for applying the term to the commemoration *throughout* the month following the funeral. The notion that it meant a commemoration recurring every month is baseless. For an English rustic survival of the 'month's mind' custom, see *month's end* in MONTH *sb.* 6 b.

1466 in *Somerset Medieval Wills* (1901) 210, I will that there be at my dirige mass and moneth mynde noon other tapers ne candelstikkes but such as be of the same chirch. **1487** in *Paston Lett.* III. 463 Every weke folowing unto my monthes mynde oon trentall, and iij. trentalles at my monthes mynde biside the solempne dirige and masse that is to be requyred for me at that tyme. **1530** in *N. & Q.* (1900) 9th Ser. VI. 414/1, I will that my executors cause an hole trigintall of masses to be saide..upon the day of my buryall ..and likewise as manny at the moneths mynde and asmany at my yeres day. **1546** LANGLEY *Pol. Verg. De Invent.* VI. viii. 128 In England the custome is to kepe the thirty daie or moneth mynde with like Obites, as wer dooen on the buriall daies. [Orig. *Apud Anglos hoc fit vigesimo nono die postquam mortuus est sepultus.*] **1565** COOPER *Thesaurus*, *Cenotaphium*, a monument of one dead where the body is not, as the herse at the monthes minde. **1721** STRYPE *Eccl. Mem.* II. iv. 281 The month's mind for the two Dukes of Suffolk late deceased was kept September 22: so the more solemn celebration of the funerals of great persons about a month more or less after their interments used to be callid. **1830** W. CARLETON *Traits Irish Peas.* (1843) I. 163 He hadn't even a Month's mind! *Ibid. note*, A Month's Mind is the repetition of one or more masses, at the expiration of a month after death, for the repose of the departed soul. **1884** *Weekly Reg.* 11 Oct. 452/2 The month's mind of the late Marchioness of Londonderry was celebrated in the Catholic Church of Newtownards.

b. *transf.* and *fig.*

1598 TOFTE *Alba* (1880) 18 Loe here the Months Mind of my deare bought loue Which (once a Month) I vowd to memorise. **1601** HOLLAND *Pliny* II. 522 They doe offer sacrifice euery 20 day of the Moone, and these moneth-mindes they keep as holy-daies. **1613** PURCHAS *Pilgrimage* VIII. vi. 763 They vse to solemnize certaine months-mindes in their Sauage manner for any great personage dead.

2. Used allusively as a more or less playful synonym for MIND *sb.*[1] 13; an inclination, a fancy, a liking. Also (rarely) ***to be in a month's mind***, to have a strong expectation. *Obs.* exc. *dial.*

1580 LYLY *Euphues* (Arb.) 464 Determininge to ende his lyfe in Athens, although he hadde a moneths minde to England. **1598** BP. HALL *Sat.* IV. iv. 116 He thaw's like Chaucers frosty Ianiuere; And sets a Months minde vpon smyling May. **1611** COTGR. s.v. *Engrand*, *Tu es bien engrand de trotter*..thou hast a moneths mind to be gone. **1621** BP. MOUNTAGU *Diatribæ* 382 You bend toward them in the parting, and beare a moneths mind still vnto them. **1660** PEPYS *Diary* 20 May, In another bed there was a pretty Dutch woman, but though I had a month's mind I had not the boldness to go to her. **1700** CONGREVE *Way of World* III.

i, She has a Month's mind; but I know Mr. Mirabell can't abide her. **1755** J. Shebbeare *Lydia* (1769) II. 76 This baronet then had a month's mind to the Dowager Viscountess. **1809** Malkin *Gil Blas* VI. ii. ⁋2 If you once leave us, we are in a month's mind that we shall not see you again. **1815** *Hist. J. Decastro & his bro. Bat* IV. 224 Now her ladyship felt malice enough against the men to have a month's mind to another husband. **1826** Scott *Jrnl.* 8 July, He [a lion] was lying like a prince in a large cage, where you might be admitted if you wish. I had a month's mind—but was afraid of the newspapers.

Montian ('mɒntɪən), *a. Geol.* [ad. F. *montien* (G. J. G. Dewalque *Prodrome d'une Descr. géol. de la Belg.* (1868) x. 185), f. *Mons* (L. *mons, mont-* mountain), name of a town in SW. Belgium: see -IAN.] Of, pertaining to, or designating a stage of the Palæocene series that lies above the Danian (and like it is not represented in Britain) and below the Landenian. Also *absol.*

[**1882** A. Geikie *Text-bk. Geol.* 848 The most ancient Tertiary deposit of the west of Europe appears to be the limestone of Mons (Système Montien).] **1896** J. W. Judd *Student's Lyell* xv. 220 Paleocene Beds ('Montian').—In the coarse limestone of Mons in Belgium and in the Marls of Meudon in the Paris basin we have strata which are perhaps older than any in the British Islands. **1914** J. Park *Textbk. Geol.* xxx. 416 The concretionary limestone of the upper division, representing the Montian sub-stage of the Cretaceous system, has yielded..the very characteristic Danian cephalopod, *Nautilus danicus*. **1921** *Geol. Mag.* LVIII. 146 The Montian (Calcaire pisolitique) is now only found in a few isolated patches and seems to have been deposited in certain areas rather than over the whole Paris region. **1955** G. G. Woodford tr. *Gignoux's Stratigr. Geol.* ix. 473 Far from being localized in narrow grooves, the Montian sea was widespread in a large gulf bounded on the north by the Pays de Bray and Chateau-Thierry and in the south reaching Mantes..and Vertus. **1960** [see Danian *a.*]. **1969** Bennison & Wright *Geol. Hist. Brit. Isles* xv. 336 The earliest Tertiary beds found on the continent of Europe, the Danian and Montian which together form the Palaeocene (though some authors consider the Danian late Cretaceous), were never deposited in the British area.

monticellite (mɒntɪ'sɛlaɪt). *Min.* [f. the name of T. *Monticelli* (1758-1846) an Italian mineralogist: see -ITE.] A yellowish chrysolitic silicate of magnesium, calcium, and iron.

1831 H. J. Brooke in *Philos. Mag.* X. 265 Monticellite... On the supposition of its being an undescribed mineral, and from Vesuvius, I have named it after Mr. Monticelli, who has published a work in illustration of the minerals found in the neighbourhood of that mountain. **1845** *Encycl. Metrop.* VI. 509/1 *Monticellite*... A Mineral from Vesuvius. **1896** in Chester *Dict. Min.*

monticle ('mɒntɪk(ə)l). Also 5 mo(u)ntycle. [ad. F. *monticule*: see MONTICULE.] A small mountain or hill.

1490 Caxton *Eneydos* i. 13 Vpon whom was so moche sonde layde, that vpon polydorus semed to be a lityl hille or montycle. *Ibid.* iii. 17 In whiche place there hadde be accumyled, or heped, of sonde a lytyl hylle or mountycle. **1721** Bailey, *Monticles*, little Mountains. **1842** Borrow *Lavengro* xxv, He stood on the top of a steep monticle. **1877** Lytteil *Landmarks* II. ii. 51 A moated hillock,..the learned-men's monticle or moated camp.

monticoline (mɒn'tɪkəʊlaɪn), *a. Nat. Hist. rare*$^{-0}$. [f. L. *monticol-a* mountaineer (f. *monti-, mons* mountain + *col-ĕre* to inhabit) + -INE.] Inhabiting mountains (*Cent. Dict.* 1890).

monticolous (mɒn'tɪkələs), *a. rare*$^{-0}$. [Formed as prec. + -OUS.] Living or growing on mountains.

1856 Mayne *Expos. Lex.* **1891** *Syd. Soc. Lex.*

† **mon'ticulate**, *a. Obs. rare*$^{-0}$. [f. MONTICULE + -ATE[2] 2.] (See quot.)

1840 Smart s.v. *Montanic*, Monticulate means, having many little projections.

monticule ('mɒntɪkju:l). Also *erron.* 9 monticole. [a. F. *monticule* (whence the earlier MONTICLE), ad. late L. *monticulus*, dim. of *monti-, mons* mountain: see -CULE.]

1. = MONTICLE. Also *fig.*

1799 *Hist. Europe* in *Ann. Reg.* 46/2 Five sources contribute to form these fountains, which send up to the top little monticules of sand. **1818** J. Mitford in *Observer* 15 Nov., Mount Ida (a small monticole so named). **1864** M. Eyre *Lady's Walks in S. France* xxi. (1865) 236 On a high monticule frowns the grim old ruin. **1904** *Speaker* 19 Mar. 592/2 An amphitheatre of abrupt monticules.

b. *spec.* A small conical mound produced by volcanic eruption.

1833 Lyell *Princ. Geol.* III. 100 If we could strip off from Etna all the lateral monticules now visible..the diminution of the entire mass would be extremely slight! **1883** Burton & Cameron *To Gold Coast for Gold* I. ii. 41 The lower monticules and parasitic craters.

2. *Anat.* and *Zool.* A minute eminence (on the surface of an animal or organ).

1874 H. A. Nicholson in *Q. Jrnl. Geol. Soc.* XXX. 501 The presence of 'monticules' or 'mamelons' from which the name *Monticulipora* was derived, cannot be relied upon. **1890** *Century Dict.*, *Monticulus*, in *anat.*, a little elevation, a monticule.

monticuliporoid (,mɒntɪkju:'lɪpərɔɪd), *a.* and *sb. Zool.* [f. mod.L. *Monticulipora*, a genus of corals (f. L. *monticul-us* + mod.L. *-pora*: see MADREPORE) + -OID.] **a.** *adj.* Of or pertaining to the genus *Monticulipora*. **b.** *sb.* A coral of the genus *Monticulipora*.

1881 H. A. Nicholson *Genus Monticulipora* 12 Some other Monticuliporoid type. *Ibid.*, This character being common to many Monticuliporoids. **1883** —— in *Ann. Nat. Hist.* Ser. v. XIII. 117 The Monticuliporoid Corals of the Wenlock Limestone. *Ibid.*, Some of the commoner Wenlock Monticuliporoids.

monticulose (mɒn'tɪkju:ləʊs), *a.* [Formed as next: see -OSE.] Covered with small eminences.

1846 Dana *Zooph.* (1848) 562 With an uneven or monticulose surface.

monticulous (mɒn'tɪkjʊləs), *a. rare*$^{-0}$. [ad. med.L. *monticulōsus*, f. L. *monticul-us*: see MONTICULE.] Having little projections or hills.

1656 Blount *Glossogr.*, *Monticulous*, full of hills or mountains. (In mod. Dicts.)

montiform ('mɒntɪfɔ:m), *a.* [f. L. *monti-, mons* mountain + -FORM.] Mountain-like; having the shape of a mountain.

1816 G. S. Faber *Orig. Pagan Idol.* II. 289 Like the montiform pagodas of Buddha. **1819** *Blackw. Mag.* V. 583 The earliest montiform edifice, which the sons of men reared as a studious copy of Mount Meru.

montigenous (mɒn'tɪdʒɪnəs), *a. rare*$^{-0}$. [f. late L. *montigen-a* native of the mountains (f. *monti-, mons* mountain + *gen-* root of *gignĕre* to beget) + -OUS.] Native of mountain localities.

1721 Bailey, *Montigenous*, born on the hills.

Montilla (mɒn'tɪljə). [Name of a town in Southern Spain.] A dry sherry-type wine made in the vicinity of Montilla.

1793 D. McBride *Gen. Instructions for Choice of Wines* i. 29. Montilla is a light white wine, the chief beverage at Seville. [**1846** R. Ford *Gatherings from Spain* xiv. 155 The name of amontillado..has been given to it from its resemblance in dryness and quality to the wines of Montilla, near Cordova.] **1851** C. Redding *Hist. Mod. Wines* (ed. 3) xii. 208 At Montilla, near Cordova, they have a very fine-flavoured dry wine, called Montilla, which is generally consumed in that place. **1876** H. Vizetelly *Facts about Sherry* viii. 86 With these wines we tasted some choice Montilla of a fabulous age. **1935** Schoonmaker & Marvel *Complete Wine Bk.* iv. 96 Montilla..is, in every way, an admirable wine. **1961** *Spectator* 21 Apr. 582 Montilla is fairly rare in this country..and is not, in the very strictest sense of the word, really a 'sherry' at all for it doesn't come from the delimited area around Jerez, but from near Cordoba. **1967** A. Lichine *Encycl. Wines* 358/1 In Spain, Montillas are usually sold from the barrel and in their first year.

montipore ('mɒntɪpɔə(r)). *Zool.* [ad. mod.L. *montipora* a genus of perforate corals, f. L. *monti-, mons* mountain + mod.L. *-pora*: see MADREPORE.] A perforate coral of the genus *Montipora*.

1899 Bernard in *Jrnl. Linn. Soc., Zool.* XXVII. 129 A heterogeneous group consisting of Montipores [etc.].

So **mon'tiporine** *a.*, related to the Montipores.

1899 Bernard in *Jrnl. Linn. Soc., Zool.* XXVII. 147 *Psammocora*, Dana, is the last genus which Milne-Edwards and Haime placed in their Montiporine subfamily of the Poritidæ.

montit, obs. pa. t. of MOUNT *v.*

† **mon'tivagant**, *a. Obs. rare*$^{-0}$. [f. L. *monti-, mons* mountain + *vagant-em*, pres. pple. of *vagārī* to roam (cf. *montivagus*): see -ANT[1].] (See quot.)

1656 Blount *Glossogr.*, *Montivagant*, that wandreth on the mountains.

So † **mon'tivagous** *a.* [f. L. *montivag-us* + -OUS.]

1658 Phillips, *Montivagous*, wandering up and down the hills and mountains.

† **montjoy.** *Obs. rare*$^{-1}$. [a. F. *mont joie*, a commemorative cairn, f. *mont* hill + *joie* joy.] See quot. 1727; also *transf.*

1653 Urquhart *Rabelais* II. xxxiii. 218 Finally they found a montjoy or heap of ordure and filth. **1727** Bailey vol. II, *Mont-joye*, a Name by which they call Heaps of Stones, laid together by Pilgrims, in which they stick Crosses [etc.].

montmartrite (mɒnt'mɑ:traɪt). *Min.* [Named by Delamétherie 1806 after *Montmartre*, near Paris, its locality: see -ITE.] A variety of gypsum containing calcium carbonate.

1821 Ure *Dict. Chem.*, *Montmartrite*.

montmorillonite (mɒntmɒ'rɪlənaɪt). [Named 1847 after *Montmorillon* in France: see -ITE.]

a. A massive rose-red silicate of aluminium. Also, any of the montmorillonoids, or these minerals collectively (see quots. 1954, 1966[2]).

1854 [see DELANOVITE]. **1865** Watts *Dict. Chem.*, *Montmorillonite*, a rose-red, fragile, argillaceous substance found at Montmorillon. **1866** in Brande & Cox *Dict. Sci.*, etc. II. 534/3 s.v. *Mineralogy*. **1934** [see DELANOVITE]. **1935** *Amer. Mineralogist* XX. 482 Montmorillonite, beidellite, and nontronite form an isomorphous completely miscible series. **1949** P. C. Carman *Chem. Constitution & Properties Engin. Materials* xiii. 383 The main constituent is a mineral of the montmorillonite group, either montmorillonite or beidellite. **1954** H. Williams et al. *Petrogr.* xvii. 327 By substitution of magnesium or iron for aluminum, especially in montmorillonite, the composition of clay minerals may vary considerably from the formulas given. Beidellite, for example, is essentially a magnesian montmorillonite, and nontronite is one rich in iron. **1962** *Amer. Mineralogist* XLVII. 145 Beidellites and montmorillonites should be divided at the composition at which the lattice charges from octahedral and tetrahedral substitution equal one another. *Ibid.*, The term beidellite should be used for the aluminium-rich members of the montmorillonite-beidellite series of minerals. **1966** *McGraw-Hill Encycl. Sci. & Technol.* VIII. 587/2 Montmorillonite clays have wide commercial use. The high colloidal, plastic, and binding properties make them especially in demand for bonding molding sands and for oil-well drilling muds. They are also widely used to decolorize oils and as a source of petroleum cracking catalysts. **1966** W. A. Deer et al. *Introd. Rock-Forming Min.* III. 264 The name montmorillonite..was originally applied to a clay mineral with composition similar to that of pyrophyllite except for the presence of excess water, $Al_4Si_8O_{20}(OH)_4{\cdot}nH_2O$. Chemical variation of this basic formula yields a group of clay minerals which are related by a common structure and by similarity of chemical and physical properties, and are therefore classed as the 'montmorillonite group'. According to present usage one member of this group is itself called montmorillonite and has the formula $(Na)_{0.7}(Al_{3.3}Mg_{0.7})Si_8O_{20}(OH)_4{\cdot}nH_2O$. An alternative term once used for this type of clay is 'smectite', and this has now been revived to describe the group as a whole (Mackenzie, 1957a), which contains the following principal members: montmorillonite, beidellite, nontronite, saponite, hectorite and sauconite. **1971** *Nature* 15 Jan. 157/2 Montmorillonite, a silicate mineral with typical expanding layers, consists of mica-like sheets that are normally separated by one or two layers of water molecules.

b. *attrib.* **montmorillonite group**, the group of clay minerals (of which montmorillonite is the type) otherwise known as montmorillonoids.

1938 *Mineral. Mag.* XXV. 153 The montmorillonite group is shown to have three end-members, montmorillonite, $Al_2Si_4O_{11}$, nontronite, $Fe_2Si_4O_{11}$, magnesium-beidellite, $Mg_3Si_4O_{11}$. **1946** *Amer. Mineralogist* XXXI. 423 The minerals of the montmorillonite group are characterized by a very wide range in the ions which can proxy Si or Al within the crystal lattice. **1949**, etc. [see above].

montmorillonitic (,mɒntmɒrɪlə'nɪtɪk), *a. Min.* [f. prec. + -IC.] Resembling or containing montmorillonite.

1943 *Proc. Soil Sci. Soc. Amer.* VII. 134 (*heading*) The adsorption of phosphate by kaolinitic, and montmorillonitic clays. **1958** *Nature* 6 Dec. 1596/1 The montmorillonitic nature of this mineral. **1970** *New Scientist* 15 Jan. 98/1 In Mexico..the remarkable natural montmorillonitic clay itself provides the mud.

montmorillonoid (mɒntmɒ'rɪlənɔɪd). *Min.* [f. as prec. + -OID.] Any of a group of clay minerals that comprises montmorillonite together with some chemically related minerals that likewise undergo a reversible expansion on absorbing water and have a characteristic structure in which water molecules are situated between sheets composed of two layers of silicon atoms sandwiching one nominally of aluminium, the differences between the minerals consisting in the extent and nature of the replacement of silicon and aluminium by other elements. Also *attrib.* or as *adj.*

1951 *Clay Minerals Bull.* I. 195 To avoid this confusion and also the lengthy term 'minerals of the montmorillonoid group'..the term 'montmorillonoid' was suggested [by D. M. C. MacEwan] for this group of minerals. **1951** D. M. C. MacEwan in G. W. Brindley *X-Ray Identification & Crystal Struct. Clay Minerals* iv. 86 (*heading*) The montmorillonite minerals (montmorillonoids). **1953** *Jrnl. Soil Sci.* IV. 233 It is fairly simple to detect by X-ray diffraction the presence of montmorillonoids in clays using glycerol..or ethylene glycol. **1955** *Trans. Faraday Soc.* LI. 582 Considerable attention has been paid in recent years to the retention of organic molecules by clays of the montmorillonoid group. **1959** *Clay Minerals Bull.* IV. 67 The name montmorillonoid is understood as covering a continuous isomorphous series extending from montmorillonite, with ideal formula $Al_2Si_4O_{10}(OH)_2$, to beidellite, with ideal formula $(R_1H_3O)Al_2(Si_3Al)O_{10}(OH)_2$. **1966** *Canad. Jrnl. Soil Sci.* XLVI. 235 Montmorillonoid minerals are sometimes more abundant in the lower horizons of soils in which other clay minerals are more uniformly distributed. **1971** *Clay Minerals* IX. 107 Results of..analyses confirm the general montmorillonoid character of the mineral.

‖ **montoir.** *Obs.* [Fr., f. *mont-er* to MOUNT.]

1. A horse-block.

1727 Bailey vol. II, *Montoir*, a stone as high as the Stirrups, which Italian Riding Masters mount their Horses from. **1755** in Johnson. In mod. Dicts.

2. (See quot.)

1727 Bailey vol. II., *Montoir*, the Poise or Rest of the Foot on the left Stirrup.

† **monton**[1]. *Obs.* [a. OF. *monton*, var. of *mouton* sheep: see MUTTON.] A battering-ram.

a **1533** Ld. Berners *Huon* cv. 348 Themperour..dressed vp his engyns and montons to breke the walles.

‖ **monton**[2] ('mɒntɒn). *Mining.* [Sp. *monton* heap, pile, f. *monte* MOUNT *sb.*]

1. (See quots.)

1858 Simmonds *Dict. Trade*, *Monton* (Spanish), a miner's name for a heap of ore; a batch under the process of amalgamation, varying in quantity in different localities, from 15 to 32 quintals. **1880** D. C. Davies *Metall. Minerals*

414 *Monton*..a pile of ore, the weight of which varies in the various mining districts of South America.

2. A unit of weight employed in Mexico chiefly for ore under the process of amalgamation (*Cent. Dict.* 1890, citing Duport).

Montpellier (‖ mɔ̃pɛlje, mɒnt'pɛlɪeɪ). The name of a town in the department of Hérault in Southern France used *attrib.*, as **Montpellier butter**, a sauce made from butter coloured green and flavoured with herbs and anchovies; **Montpellier green** = *verdigris green* [VERDIGRIS 2]; **Montpellier yellow** = *Cassel yellow* [CASSEL], also called *mineral yellow* [MINERAL *a.* 5 b].

1889 Montpellier butter [see *green butter* (GREEN *a.* 13)]. **1960** E. DAVID *French Provincial Cooking* 117 Montpellier butter is usually served with salmon and the chef's way of doing it is to have a fine piece of middle cut of cold salmon with the skin removed, and the fish thickly spread with the green butter. **1930** MAERZ & PAUL *Dict. Color* 185/2 An old synonym for Verdigris is 'Montpellier Green', from the name of the French city, which was a center for the color trade in the Middle Ages and during the Renaissance. **1969** R. MAYER *Dict. Art Terms & Techniques* 420/1 Other names for verdigris are Montpellier green, viride aeris..and vederame. **1835** G. FIELD *Chromatogr.* ix. 77 Patent Yellow, Turner's Yellow, or Montpellier Yellow..has an excellent body, and works well in oil and water, but is soon injured both by the sun's light and impure air. **1969** R. MAYER *Dict. Art Terms & Techniques* 406/2 Turner's yellow... Among its many names are..Montpellier yellow, [etc.].

†**'montra.** *slang. Obs.* [a. F. *montre* watch: cf. MUNTER *Sc.*] A watch.

1812 J. H. VAUX *Flash Dict.*, *Montra*, a watch.

Montrachet (mɔ̃traʃe, mɔ̃raʃe). Name of a wine-growing district of the Côte d'Or, France, used to designate the white wine produced there.

1833 C. REDDING *Hist. Mod. Wines* v. 99 The situation to the south-west of Meursault, where it joins Puligny, is noted for the delicious white wine called Mont-Rachet, of exquisite perfume, and deemed the most perfect white wine of Burgundy, and even of France. **1839** URE *Dict. Arts* 1300 The insulated part towards the top furnishes the wine called *Chevalier Montrachet*, which is less esteemed..than the delicious wine grown on the middle height, called *true Montrachet*. Beneath this district, and in the surrounding plains, the vines afford a far inferior article, called *bastard Montrachet*. **1841** *Fraser's Mag.* June 533 A bottle of Montrachet, similarly poured out to us, was very fair. **1875** H. VIZETELLY *Wines of World* II. 24 The distinguishing characteristics of Montrachet are *finesse*, fulness, absolute homogeneity, and softness, combined with a powerful yet delicate flavour and immense richness. **1903** A. CONAN DOYLE *Adventures Gerard* vi. 218 But there are times when Montrachet is better than the wine of Bordeaux. **1938** W. S. MAUGHAM *Summing Up* 310 A dozen oysters and a pint of Montrachet. **1965** O. A. MENDELSOHN *Dict. Drink* 228 Dumas has said that Le Montrachet should be drunk bareheaded, on one's knees.

‖**montre** (mɔ̃tr). *Organ-building.* [F. *montre* sample, show, f. *montre-r* to show.] (See quots.)

1876 STAINER & BARRETT *Dict. Mus. Terms*, *Montre*, mounted diapason. An organ stop whose pipes form part of the case or are placed away from the soundboard. **1888** tr. *Locher's Explan. Organ Stops* 40 *Montre* is the name given by the French to the visible, or front, Principals.

Montrealer (mɒntrɪ'ɔːlə(r)). [f. *Montreal* + -ER¹.] A native or inhabitant of the city of Montreal in Canada.

1888 [see SEIGNEUR]. **1909** *Westm. Gaz.* 1 Apr. 9/3 Dr. Macnamara..is always claimed as a Montrealer, because he was born in this city while his father..was quartered here. **1963** *Guardian* 13 Mar. 13/5 Most Montrealers find London in winter..marrow-freezing. **1967** *Times* 28 Feb. (Canada Suppl.) 31 Two out of three Montrealers speak French.

montross, montt, obs. ff. MATROSS, MOUNT.

montroydite (mɒn'trɔɪdaɪt). *Min.* [f. the name of *Montroyd* Sharpe (see quot. 1930) + -ITE¹.] Mercuric oxide, HgO, which is found as deep red orthorhombic crystals.

1903 A. J. MOSES in *Amer. Jrnl. Sci.* XVI. 262 The name Montroydite is suggested in honor of Mr. Montroyd Sharpe, one of the owners of the mines at Terlingua [in Brewster County, Texas]. **1932** *Amer. Mineralogist* XVII. 541 The mineral [*sc.* mosesite] was found in association with eglestonite, terlinguaite, montroydite and kleinite in the quick-silver mining district [of Texas]. **1958** *Prof. Papers U.S. Geol. Survey* No. 312. 71/1 Montroydite occurs as hairs and growths and as needlelike crystals along the cleavage planes of calcite. **1968** I. KOSTOV *Mineralogy* II. iv. 257 Montroydite is also red but has very strong birefringence.

montuno (mɒn'tuːnəʊ). [Amer.-Sp. *montuno* native to mountains, wild, rustic, untamed.] An improvised passage in a rumba.

1951 *Sat. Rev. Lit.* 24 Nov. 75 His modernisms grow logically from an amalgam of influences that includes Tatum, Wilson, Hines, Gillespie, and the Cuban *montuno* masters. **1956** M. STEARNS *Story of Jazz* (1957) xix. 248 The *montuno*, or *ad lib* passage,..is often based on just one, or sometimes two, chords. **1957** J. KEROUAC *On Road* (1958) IV. v. 287 The piano montunos showered down on us from the speaker. **1958** E. BORNEMAN in P. Gammond *Decca Bk. Jazz* xxi. 270 Whereas the themes of the sones were usually lilting tunes of obviously Spanish descent, the montunos were unmistakably African.

montuous, variant of MOUNTUOUS *Obs.*

monture ('mɒntjʊə(r)). [a. F. *monture*, f. *monter* to MOUNT: see -URE.]

1. 'A mounting, setting, or frame; the manner in which anything is set or mounted: as, the monture of a diamond. ***shaft-monture***, a kind of mounting for the heddles of looms in figure-weaving'. (*Cent. Dict.* 1890.)

1831 G. R. PORTER *Silk Manuf.* 245 The carefulness and skill..required in preparing the various arrangements of the harness in the loom or, to use the technical phrase, in *building the monture*. **1882** OGILVIE, *Monture*, a setting, mounting, frame, or the like.

‖**2.** [As Fr. (mɔ̃tyr).] Something mounted or 'set up'.

1886 *York Herald* 10 Aug. 3/2 Flower Department... A quantity of French Montures.

monture: see MOUNTURE.

monty ('mɒntɪ). *Austral.* and *N.Z. colloq.* Also **monte.** [Prob. the same word as MONTE¹.] A certainty: used esp. of a horse considered certain to win a race.

1894 H. LAWSON *Martin Farrell* in *Coll. Verse* (1967) I. 269 Chaps, I've got a vote for Hughie—but it ain't no monte yet. **1901** *Bulletin Reciter* (Sydney) 182 It's the biggest bloomin' monte Dat 'as ever come our way. **1908** E. S. SORENSON *Squatter's Ward* xii. 122 It's a monty the little squib would let out a yell jest as I was gettin' clear. **1910** O'BRIEN & STEPHENS *Material for Dict. Austral. Slang 1900-10* (typescript), *Monte*, a take-down game of cards—a sure thing. **1930** K. S. PRICHARD *Haxby's Circus* iii. 41 She's the chance of a life-time... The biggest bloomin' monty ever started on a racecourse. **1933** *Bulletin* (Sydney) 29 Nov. 10/1 'And they'll take, it's a monty, an ell,' said Pat, 'if we give them an inch.' **1946** *Coast to Coast 1945* 27 He's a monty! We always were lucky. **1947** D. M. DAVIN *For Rest of our Lives* 297 From Christchurch this chap Sloan, for a monty, with that particular brand of New Zealand English. **1970** *N.Z. Listener* 12 Oct. 12/1 Old Jerry wouldn't think of looking for me over this way. That's for a monty. To keep going's the right thing.

monty, variant of MONTE¹.

monument ('mɒnjʊmənt), *sb.* Forms: 4-5 **monyment**, 4-6 **monumente**, 6-7 **moniment**, 3- **monument.** [ad. L. *monu-*, *moniment-um* something that reminds, a memorial, monument, f. *monēre* to remind: see -MENT. Cf. F. *monument*, Sp., Pg., It. *monumento*.]

†**1.** A sepulchre, place of sepulture. *Obs.*

[The earliest recorded sense in Eng.; repr. a late L. development of the sense as in 5 b, which was adopted later. Cf. Welsh *mynwent* (a. L. *monumentum*), graveyard.]

a **1300** *Cursor M.* 16904 Þe prince o preistes o þair lagh went to þat monument, And sperd it wit a mikel stan. **13..** *Evang. Nicod.* 723 in *Archiv Stud. neu. Spr.* LIII. 404 He wand þat cors..And layd it in his monument. *c* **1450** *Mirour Saluacioun* 3403 The dore of the monument was stopped with a grete stone. **1526** *Pilgr. Perf.* (W. de W. 1531) 228 All yᵗ be in theyr monumentes, or graues, shall heare the voyce of the sone of god. **1592** SHAKS. *Rom. & Jul.* III. v. 203 In that dim Monument where Tybalt lies. **1611** BIBLE *Isa.* lxv. 4 A people..Which remaine among the graues, and lodge in the monuments. **1658** SIR T. BROWNE *Hydriot.* ii. (1736) 31 The Saints we observe arose from Graves and Monuments. [Echoing Vulg. Matt. xxvii. 53.]

fig. *c* **1380** WYCLIF *Wks.* (1880) 299 Wo be to you, pharisies,..þat ben but hud monumentis.

2. a. A written document, record; a legal instrument. (App. sometimes confused with *muniment*.)

c **1440** *Promp. Parv.* 342/2 Monyment, or charterys, or oþer lyke, *munimentum*. **1559** MORWYNG *Evonym.* 332 Leaninge to the moniments and sayings of Paulus Ægineta. **1563** FOXE (*title*) Acts and Monuments of these latter and perillous Dayes. **1631** GOUGE *God's Arrows* III. §65. 303 Their rolles in which they recorded their monuments. **1685** STILLINGFL. *Orig. Brit.* i. 4 Gildas..sadly laments the want of any Domestick Monuments, to give him certain information. **1709** STRYPE *Ann. Ref.* I. iv. 84 This discourse of Guest..I have transcribed from the original, and put in among the monuments in the end of the book. ? **1757** BURKE *Abridgm. Eng. Hist.* III. ix. Wks. 1812 V. 727 All our monuments bear a strong evidence to this change [in the laws]. **1868** M. PATTISON *Academ. Org.* v. 184 The critical study of the monuments of Roman and Feudal Law may justly claim no inconsiderable share in our endowments.

†**b.** A piece of information given in writing.

†*monuments of letters* (= Renaissance Latin *monumenta litterarum*): information furnished by documents.

1555 EDEN *Decades* 283 But when Demetrius was demaunded whether eyther by the monumentes of letters or by fame lefte theym of theyr predecessours they hadde any knowleage of the gothes. *c* **1560** R. MORICE in *Lett. Lit. Men* (Camden) 24 Suche papers of monuments as I hadd in my custodie concernyng the furnyture of your Ecclesiasticall storye. **1650** STAPYLTON *Strada's Low C. Warres* VII. 40, I can promise many Animadversions concerning them, out of the Monuments of Letters in my hands.

3. a. An indication, evidence, or token (of some fact). Now *rare*.

1605 ROWLANDS *Hell's Broke Loose* 4 For Fatus the Gouernour of Iury ouertooke Theudas, and sent his head as a monument to Ierusalem. **1672** PETTY *Pol. Anat.* (1691) 25 There is at this Day no Monument or real Argument that, when the Irish were first invaded, they had any Stone-Housing at all. **1711** WALLIS in *J. Greenwood's Eng. Gram.* Pref. 4 Other Books..where may be found many Monuments of uncommon Learning. **1903** MATHESON *Repr. Men of Bible* 93 They came to Aaron to ask a sign—a visible monument of the Divine Presence.

†**b.** Something serving to identify; a mark, indication; something that gives warning, a portent.

1590 SPENSER *F.Q.* I. v. 38 His goodly corps..Was quite dismembred, and his members chast Scattered on every mountaine as he went, That of Hippolytus was lefte no moniment. *Ibid.* II. xii. 80 His brave shield, full of old moniments, Was fowly ras't, that none the signes might see. **1596** SHAKS. *Tam. Shr.* III. ii. 97 Wherefore gaze this goodly company, As if they saw some wondrous monument, Some Commet, or vnusuall prodigie? **1656** tr. *Hobbes' Elem. Phil.* (1839) 13 For acquiring of philosophy, some sensible moniments are necessary, by which our past thoughts may be not only reduced, but also registered every one in its own order. **1657** THORNLEY tr. *Longus' Daphnis & Chloe* 205 Laius has shewed the monuments [*orig.* γνωρίσματα] thou hadst about thee.

c. *U.S. Law.* Any object, natural or artificial, fixed permanently in the soil and referred to in a document as a means of ascertaining the location of a tract of land or any part of its boundaries.

1828-32 in WEBSTER. **1858** J. KENT *Comm. Amer. Law* (ed. 9) IV. 546 In the description of the land conveyed, the rule is, that known and fixed monuments control courses and distances.

4. a. Anything that by its survival commemorates a person, action, period, or event.

c **1530** TINDALE *Answ. More* Wks. (1573) 283/1 For our false fayth in visityng the monumentes of Christ, therefore hath God also destroyed them. **1596** SPENSER *State Irel.* Wks. (Globe) 628/1 Is there any token, denomination, or monument of the Gaules yet remaynyng in Ireland? **1618** BOLTON *Florus* (1636) 92 He razed Saguntus to the ground, an ancient rich City of Spaine, and a great, but grievous moniment of her truth, and faith to the Romans. **1769** *De Foe's Tour Gt. Brit.* IV. 130 Many Monuments of this Battle are still to be seen here. **1837** J. PHILLIPS *Geol.* 5 It is not certain that monuments remain of all the changes which have occured. **1876** E. MELLOR *Priesth.* vi. 280 The Supper becomes thus a historic objective monument.

b. An enduring evidence or example.

1675 *Strange News from Oakingham* 5 We..do deserve, no more mercie at his hands than other the Monuments of his Exemplary Justice. **1713** ADDISON *Cato* III. ii, One..Who pants for breath, and stiffens, yet alive, In dreadful looks: a monument of wrath! **1789** GIBBON *Autobiog.* (1896) 154, I wished to have observed a country, the monument of freedom and industry. **1820** HAZLITT *Lect. Dram. Lit.* 40 It may be considered as a monument of the taste and skill of the authors. **1853** KANE *Grinnell Exp.* xxxiv. (1856) 299 They [ice-bergs] were beautiful objects, monuments of power.

c. Applied, like mod.F. *monument*, to outstanding survivals of an early literature.

1852 E. A. ANDREWS *Copious Latin-Eng. Lex.* App. A. 1653 (*title*) Specimens of the oldest monuments of the Latin language. **1897** W. P. KER *Epic & Romance* ii. 183 *Beowulf* is, at any rate, the specimen by which the Teutonic epic poetry must be judged. It is the largest monument extant. **1949** G. K. ANDERSON *Lit. Anglo-Saxons* iii. 63 Unquestionably the most important monument of Old English epic literature..is the poem *Beowulf*.

5. a. A structure, edifice, or erection intended to commemorate a notable person, action, or event.

the Monument: a Doric column 202 feet in height, built in the City of London (1671-77) after the design of Sir C. Wren, to commemorate the great fire of London, 1666, which originated in a house 202 feet from the site of the column.

1602 WARNER *Alb. Eng.* Epit. (1612) 365 Their edifying and sumptuous Erections of all our chiefe Minsters, Monasteries, and Monuments. **1645** EVELYN *Diary* 26 Feb., This monument [*i.e.* the Forum Trajanum] being at first set up on a rising ground. **1685** *Ibid.* 17 June, At this time the words engraved on the monument in London, intimating that the Papists fir'd the Citty, were erased and cut out. **1701** *Lond. Gaz.* No. 3718/4 Mr. Jer. Wayte, Fishmonger, near the Monument in New Fish street, London. **1842** BARHAM *Ingol. Leg.* Ser. II. *Misadv. Margate*, And now I'm here, from this here pier it is my fixed intent To jump, as Mister Levi did from off the Monu-ment! **1864** BRYCE *Holy Rom. Emp.* xvi. (1875) 284 Over all rose those two monuments of the best of the heathen Emperors..the columns of Marcus Aurelius and Trajan.

b. A structure of stone or other lasting material erected in memory of the dead, either over the grave or in some part of a sacred edifice. (Cf. 1.)

1588 SHAKS. *Tit. A.* I. i. 350 Traytors away, he rest's not in this Tombe: This Monument fiue hundreth yeares hath stood, Which I haue Sumptuously re-edified. **1683-4** in SWAYNE *Sarum Churchw. Acc.* (1896) 346 Setting up yᵉ monument of Mrs. Ray. **1771** *Junius' Lett.* liv. (1820) 286 Honours shall gather round his monument. **1860** WARTER *Sea-board* II. 183 Sometimes the dead were buried in haste, and Monuments were erected..on the sides of the public roads. **1903** MORLEY *Gladstone* II. v. ix. 157 He found the speech for a monument to Lord Palmerston in the Abbey 'a delicate and difficult duty'.

†**c.** A carved figure, statue, effigy. *Obs.* (Often in Shaks.)

1593 SHAKS. *Lucr.* 391 Where, like a vertuous Monument shee lies, To be admir'd of lewd vnhallowed eyes. **1601** —— *All's Well* IV. ii. 5 If the quicke fire of youth light not your minde, You are no Maiden but a monument. **1601** HOLLAND *Pliny* II. 567 At Rome there bee divers peeces of Praxiteles his making..standing among the monuments and bookes within the librarie of Asinius Pollio. **1611** SHAKS. *Cymb.* II. ii. 32 O sleepe, thou Ape of death, lye dull vpon her, And be her Sense but as a Monument, Thus in a Chappell lying.

†**6.** abstr. ***in monument of***: in commemoration of.

1613 PURCHAS *Pilgrimage* (1614) 695 At the foot thereof was a great heape of Elephants teeth,..vpon them were set

the skulls of dead men, which they had slaine in the warres, in monument of their victorie.

7. *attrib.* and *Comb.*, as ***monument-builder***, ***-maker***; ***monument-like*** adj.; †**monument candlestick**, a candlestick fashioned after the model of the Monument (see 5 above); **Monument City** = MONUMENTAL CITY; †**monument-money**, money collected from visitors to Westminster Abbey who were shown the monuments.

1654 WHITLOCK *Zootomia* 409 All more or lesse strive at a Perpetuity of their Names; though let me say in a more Preposterous way, than these *Monument-Builders do. **1688** *Lond. Gaz.* No. 2316/4 A pair of *Monument Candlesticks. **1856** *Life Illustrated* 31 May 33/4 Baltimore is the '*Monument City', from the great battle monument, and several others of note, within its limits. **1906** *Springfield* (Mass.) *Weekly Republ.* 8 Mar. 4 Baltimore has been known for years as the 'Monument City', and some of these monuments are in reality works of art. **1886** A. WINCHELL *Walks Geol. Field* 42 A striking *monument-like remnant of a formation that once covered the whole of this high plateau. *Ibid.* 55 Many a monument-like outlier. **1665** J. WEBB *Stone-Heng* (1725) 86 These were..their barbarous *Monument-makers. **1655–6** in *Athenæum* 9 Aug. (1884) 187/1 The Counsell was moved this day,..that those who have the..disposing of the *monument money at Westmr, may be directed to dispose the same..to the maintainance of five Masters of Musicke.

monument (ˈmɒnjʊmənt), *v.* [f. prec. Cf. F. *monumenté* placed on official record.] *trans.* In various nonce-uses: To cause to be perpetually remembered; to record on a monument; to furnish with a monument.

1606 FORD *Honor Tri.* (Shaks. Soc.) 24 Unspotted Lucrece who..monumented her rape with extremity of death. **1660** WATERHOUSE *Arms & Arm.* 36 They had their *Arcus Triumphales*, in which..were monumented the Victories of those to whose memory those piles of fame were erected. **1756** H. WALPOLE *Let. to Bentley* Aug., The poor woman..passed her whole widowhood..in collecting and monumenting the portraits and relics of all the great families from which she descended. **1856** HAWTHORNE *Eng. Note-bks.* (1870) II. 86 The ecclesiastical dignitaries bury themselves and monument themselves to the exclusion of almost everybody else.

monumental (mɒnjuːˈmɛntəl), *a.* [ad. late L. *monumentalis*, f. L. *monument-um* MONUMENT *sb.*: see -AL¹. Cf. F. *monumental.*] **A.** *adj.*

1. Pertaining to a monument or memorial structure, or to monuments in general. †In early use (cf. MONUMENT *sb.* 1), pertaining to the tomb, sepulchral.

1604 SHAKS. *Oth.* v. ii. 5 Skin..smooth as Monumentall Alabaster. *c* **1647** CRASHAW *Upon Death of most desired Mr. Herrys* 68 Softly may he be possest, Of his monumentall rest! **1715–20** POPE *Iliad* VI. 591 Press'd with a Load of Monumental Clay! **1728** —— *Dunc.* II. 313 And Monumental brass this record bears. **1760–72** H. BROOKE *Fool of Qual.* (1809) III. 143 Marbled effigies and monumental deposits of the renowned. **1769** THORPE (*title*) Registrum Roffense: or, a Collection of..Instruments of divers kinds... Together with the Monumental Inscriptions in the several Churches and Chapels. **1856** *Eng. Cycl., Biogr.* II. 163 Chantrey's career for the last twenty years of his life, as a monumental sculptor, was unrivalled. **1890** *John Bull* 5 Apr. 228/1 When the light of monumental history first dawned upon Assyria, the land was found to be inhabited by a Semitic race.

fig. **1837** J. PHILLIPS *Geol.* 6 The general rules of geology contribute continually to fill up the void spaces in its monumental history.

2. Serving as a monument or memorial.

1632 BROME *Northern Lasse* III. ii. Wks. 1873 III. 55, I will now bestow my wealth in Monumental good deeds. **1784** COWPER *Task* i. 276 The Mole..Toils much to earn a monumental pile, That may record the mischiefs he has done. **1785** BURKE *Sp. Nabob of Arcot's Debts* Wks. IV. 30 A name that will be well remembered as..long as the monumental debt of England shall endure. **1817** RICKMAN *Archit.* 108 The monumental chapels of this style are peculiarly deserving attention.

†**b.** Serving as a memento; also, serving as a proof of identity. *Obs.*

1601 SHAKS. *All's Well* IV. iii. 20 Hee hath giuen her his monumentall Ring. **1657** THORNLEY tr. *Longus' Daphnis & Chloe* 207, I exposed her with these monumentall toyes.

3. Having the aspect of a monument; like a monument.

1606 SHAKS. *Tr. & Cr.* III. iii. 153 Perseuerance, deere my Lord, Keepes honor bright, to haue done, is to hang Quite out of fashion, like a rustie male, In monumentall mockrie. **1632** MILTON *Penseroso* 135 Shadows brown that Sylvan loves Of Pine, or monumental Oake. **1740** BAYNARD *Health* (ed. 6) 25 Lot's sad monumental wife. **1839** *Fraser's Mag.* XX. 710 It has really an air quite *monumental*, as our French neighbours phrase it. **1874** MICKLETHWAITE *Mod. Par. Churches* 18 A monumental building, such as a church should be. **1879** SALA in *Daily Tel.* 8 May, The monumental fourpost bed has been taken down.

4. *transf.* Comparable to a monument in massiveness and permanence. Often said of literary works. Also, *loosely*, vast, stupendous.

a **1658** CLEVELAND *Gen. Poems*, etc. (1677) 77 Defend my Rump, great Iove, allay my grief, O spare me this, this Monumental Beef! **1864** SALA in *Daily Tel.* 18 Nov., The public began to doubt the veracity of that monumental liar. **1876** GEO. ELIOT *Dan. Der.* xxii, His monumental obtuseness. **1894** J. T. FOWLER *Adamnan* Pref. 11 Dr. Reeve's original edition of Adamnan, a truly monumental work. **1901** *Weekly Reg.* 6 Dec. 714 Manuals of etiquette..embodying monumental snobbery and priggishness.

5. Historically prominent and significant; remaining conspicuous to posterity.

1844 MRS. BROWNING *Drama of Exile* 36 Thou shalt be an Idea to all souls;—A monumental melancholy gloom Seen down all ages. **1870** SWINBURNE *Ess. & Stud.* (1875) 313 That gallery of monumental men and mighty memories. **1876** LOWELL *Among my Bks.* Ser. II. 94 The relation of Dante to literature is monumental, and marks the era at which the modern begins.

†**B.** *sb.* in *pl.* **a.** Identifying tokens. **b.** Monumental erections. *Obs. rare.*

1657 THORNLEY tr. *Longus' Daphnis & Chloe* 203 Now it seem'd best..to view the monumentals. *a* **1687** COTTON *Martial* VIII. iii. 5 When raz'd Messalla's Monumentals must Lye with Licinus's lofty Tomb in dust.

Hence **monumen'tality**, the quality of being monumental.

1888 G. B. SHAW *Let.* 9 Feb. (1965) 184 If I had..physical monumentality, I should bring London up to the mark. **1890** *Scott. Leader* 11 Nov. 7 Art, in spite of a number of good artists, lacks monumentality. **1934** J. J. SWEENEY *Plastic Redirections in 20th Cent. Painting* 60 A genuinely new 'archaism'—an extreme simplicity and monumentality of form, with no necessary naturalistic association. **1937** *Archit. Rev.* LXXXII. 49/1 The proposed King George V Memorial in Old Palace Yard..epitomizes all that is implied by the hideous word 'Monumental'. And the chosen site admits of very little monumentality. **1963** *Times Lit. Suppl.* 4 Jan. 2/3 The sculptor Ivan Schadr..who among many other monumentalities has been responsible for the large moveable pink rose. **1969** R. BANHAM in Jencks & Baird *Meaning in Archit.* 108 According to Baird, the Thinkbelt's avoidance of showy monumentality..will lead to practically every fashionable evil in the book. **1974** *Impressionism* (R. Acad.) 37/1 The strong contrasts between simple planes of colour, and the vigorous forms of tree and house, give the painting a great monumentality.

Monumental City. *U.S.* The city of Baltimore, Md. Cf. *Monument City* above.

1827 *National Gaz.* (Philadelphia) 20 Nov. 213 The brave sons of Cincinnatus at the festal board in the 'monumental city'. **1853** F. W. THOMAS *John Randolph* 178 In 'the monumental city' I read law. **1882** *Harper's Mag.* June 20/2 No women..equal the fair daughters of the Monumental City. **1904** *Baltimore American* 5 Dec. 14 Detectives..of the Baltimore force, have been working there during the past week, and it is probable that they will return to the Monumental City today. **1949** *Business Week* 24 Sept. 101 'The Monumental City' is the nation's second largest seaport.

monumentalism (mɒnjuːˈmɛntəlɪz(ə)m). [f. MONUMENTAL *a.* + -ISM.] A monumental style; building on a grand scale.

1902 *Encycl. Brit.* XXVIII. 451/2 The plain lessons of the Crimean War were unheeded, and monumentalism became the ideal of coast defences. **1970** H. BRAUN *Parish Churches* xiv. 174 A tower..supplies its church with the element of monumentalism, the dimension of which is height.

monumentalize (mɒnjuːˈmɛntəlaɪz). *v.* [f. MONUMENTAL + -IZE.] *trans.* To make permanent record of; to record or commemorate as by a monument.

1857 G. J. WIGLEY *Borromeo's Instr. Eccl. Building* Pref. 1 Christianity has dwelt and monumentalized itself. **1874** C. P. SMYTH *Our Inher. in Gt. Pyramid* III. xi. (ed. 2) 223 Our ancient measures..had been monumentalized there..before history began. **1881** *Athenæum* 20 Aug. 229/3 Who are..impelled to monumentalize their impressions in rhyme. **1885** 'HELEN FAUCIT' in *Blackw. Mag.* 758 Looks and gestures, which it is, or it is not, the business of the artist to monumentalise.

Hence **monu,mentali'zation**, the act of making or state of being monumental. **monu'mentalizing** *vbl. sb.*, a placing on record, commemoration.

1877 C. P. SMYTH *Our Inherit. in Gt. Pyramid* (ed. 3) 32 This monumentalisation of superhuman contemporary knowledge. **1881** *Athenæum* No. 2811. 328/2 The sonnet as a poetic form for the monumentalizing of a single thought or phase of emotion..is already high in favour.

monumentally (mɒnjuːˈmɛntəlɪ), *adv.* [f. MONUMENTAL *a.* + -LY².]

†**1. a.** By means of a monument. *Obs. rare*⁻¹.

a **1619** FLETCHER, etc. *Knt. Malta* v. i, Thy memory..in brazen Characters, Shall monumentally be register'd To ages consequent.

b. As regards monuments.

1882–3 M. R. VINCENT in *Schaff's Encycl. Relig. Knowl.* 2000 Monumentally, the city [Ravenna] falls into the line of ecclesiastical history with the era of the Theodosian family.

2. By way of a monument or memorial; like a monument.

1654 GAYTON *Pleas. Notes* I. 2 Like Pauls Scaffolds, Monumentally standing, because none dare take them down. **1705** PENN in *Pa. Hist. Soc. Mem.* X. 15, I would have the said county to be marked northerly by trees or stones monumentally. **1891** *Harper's Mag.* July 275/1 Embodied monumentally in stone.

3. a. In a 'monumental' degree.

1888 LOWELL in *Daily News* 26 July 6/3, There is something especially—I might almost use a cant word and say monumentally—interesting in a meeting like this. **1955** *Sci. Amer.* Oct. 118/2 The authors deserve admiration for their persistence and energy in carrying out a monumentally tedious series of experiments.

b. In a monumental way (cf. MONUMENTAL *a.* 4).

1918 E. POUND *Let. c* Apr. (1971) 134 Frazer has of course done the whole job monumentally, BUT good god how slowly, in how many volumes.

monumentary (ˌmɒnjuːˈmɛntərɪ), *a.* [f. MONUMENT *sb.* + -ARY. Cf. late L. *monumentarius.*] Of the nature of a monument.

1810 *Sporting Mag.* XXXVI. 153 The remains of this once celebrated character are permitted to remain without any monumentary token of respect.

monumented (ˈmɒnjʊməntɪd), *ppl. a.* [f. MONUMENT *v.* + -ED¹.] Monumentally commemorated.

1774 S. WESLEY in *Westm. Mag.* II. 654 When..lies desert the monumented clay. **1844** R. CHAMBERS *Vest. Creation, Early Hist. Man.* (1850) 249 The dimly monumented Toltecans.

monumenter (ˈmɒnjʊməntə(r)). [f. MONUMENT *v.* + -ER¹.] One who erects monuments.

1890 E. L. ARNOLD *Phra* viii, Nor did I think I was marble, or even the plaster of more frugal monumenters.

'monumentless, *a.* [f. MONUMENT *sb.* + -LESS.] Without monuments or memorials.

1843 CARD. WISEMAN *Ess., Superficial Trav.* (1853) III. 441 The mushroom growth of a monumentless people.

‖**mon vieux** (mɔ̃ vjø). [Fr.] An affectionate form of address: old friend, old man.

1913 BARONESS ORCZY *Eldorado* I. vii. 55 If you are not satisfied, *mon vieux*..you can send in your resignation when you like. **1917** F. M. FORD *Let.* 5 Jan. (1965) 83 Well, God bless you, mon vieux! **1919** C. MACKENZIE *Sylvia & Michael* i. 12 It has been a thoroughly third-class adventure, *mon vieux*. **1924** E. HEMINGWAY *In our Time* i. 9 I'm drunk, I tell you, mon vieux. **1959** L. DURRELL in *Spirit of Place* (1969) 360 Wait till you see the menu—it is pure trigonometry, *mon vieux*.

mony, obs. form of MANY.

mony-: see MONI-.

-mony, *suffix*, occurring only in sbs. adopted from Latin; in *acrimony*, *ceremony*, *querimony*, *sanctimony*, it represents L. *-mōnia*, and in *matrimony*, *parsimony*, *patrimony*, *testimony*, it represents L. *-mōnium*; for *alimony* there are two L. forms *alimōnia*, *-mōnium*, the former being ante- and post-classical. The *-mōn-* of the two L. suffixes is related by ablaut to the suffix *-men* of object-nouns, of which *-mentum* -MENT is an extended form.

monyal(e, monyall, var. ff. MONIAL.

monycion, obs. variant of MUNITION.

monye, monyel(l, obs. ff. MANY, MULLION.

monyer, obs. form of MONEYER.

monyfa(u)ld(e, -ffold, obs. ff. MANIFOLD.

1509 *Sel. Cas. Crt. Star Chamber* (Selden) 198 The monyffold rightes oppressions & wranges don to him.

monykin: see MANYKIN.

monyment, obs. form of MUNIMENT.

monyon, obs. form of MULLION.

monyour, -owre, obs. forms of MONEYER.

monyple: see MANYPLIES.

monys, -y(s)ch, obs. forms of MONISH.

monyssh, obs. form of MANNISH, MOONISH.

monyst: see MONISH.

monyth(e, obs. forms of MONTH.

†**monzie.** *rare.* Sc. corruption of MONSIEUR.

a **1686** PEDEN in *Biogr. Presbyt.* (1838) I. 79 Oh the Monzies, the French Monzies, see how they run.

monzonite (mɒnˈzəʊnaɪt). [Named after Mt. Monzoni, Tyrol, its locality: see -ITE¹.]

1. *Min.* [F. v. Kobell (*monzonit*), 1871.] A silicate of aluminium, iron, etc., resembling green hornstone.

1882 *1st App. to 5th ed. Dana* 11.

2. *Petrogr.* [a. F. *monzonite* (de Lapparent 1864, in *Ann. des Mines* VI. 259).] A granular igneous rock with a composition intermediate between syenite and diorite, *spec.* one containing approximately equal amounts of orthoclase and plagioclase.

1895 A. HARKER *Petrol.* iii. 44 A special type of augite-syenite is presented by the Triassic intrusions of Monzoni in the southern Tirol (monzonite of authors). **1925** *Jrnl. Geol.* XXXIII. 506 The term 'monzonite' properly will apply only to the rocks with a mixture of andesine and orthoclase. **1956** E. W. HEINRICH *Microscopic Petrogr.* iii. 53 Monzonites occur as stocks, laccoliths, dikes, sills, and small plutons. **1974** *Encycl. Brit. Macropædia* IX. 222/2 In general appearance and in field relations monzonites resemble granitic rocks; they differ from granites by reason of their lower quartz content.

Hence **monzo'nitic** *a.*, (composed) of monzonite or monzonites.

1932 F. F. GROUT *Petrogr. & Petrol.* 85 The plagioclase of monzonites crystallized before orthoclase, and the resulting mixture of euhedral and anhedral crystals is the typical

'monzonitic' texture. **1936** A. Johannsen *Descr. Petrogr. Igneous Rocks* III. 96 The relations between the orthoclase rocks, the plagioclase rocks, and the monzonitic series. **1974** W. C. Luth in H. Sørensen *Alkaline Rocks* vii. 514/1 The greatest effects, in terms of producing alkaline magmas would be expected of dioritic, monzonitic and andesitic magmas.

moo (muː), *sb.*[1] [f. moo *v.*] The low of a cow; an act of lowing.

1789 D. Davidson *Seasons* 46 Thou rangest o'er thy food, among the queys, A' fearless o' thy moo, or cap'ring tail. **1902** *Contemp. Rev.* Dec. 840 The cows utter long 'moos' of excitement.

moo (muː), *sb.*[2] Shortened f. moola.

1945 F. Fay *How to be Poor* i. 3 In the vernacular of those in the know, you have the 'moola' (sometimes abbreviated 'moo', meaning 'money'). *Ibid.* xi. 45 What Are We Gonna Do, To Get Rid of All Our 'Moo'? Catchy, isn't it?.. Later on I shall give and teach you—for free—..the lyrics and music for this our battle cry of freedom, using my well-known 'Dum-De-De-Um-Dum' method. After you have mastered 'What Are We Gonna Do, To Get Rid of All Our "Moo"?', I shall expect to hear you full-throatedly singing this chant of Truth from the housetops. **1949** W. R. Burnett *Asphalt Jungle* (1950) vii. 56 After all, as far as she knew, he was still loaded with what the boys vulgarly referred to as moo! **1975** D. Bloodworth *Clients of Omega* ix. 84 Most of my nurses..don't work for moo... But local stuff I pay.

moo (muː), *v.* Also 6 mo, (9 mue). [Echoic.] *intr.* Of a cow or ox: To low. **b.** Of a person: To utter the sound represented by 'moo'.

1549 *Compl. Scot.* vi. 39 The calfis began tyl mo. **1565** Golding *Ovid's Met.* i. (1593) 21 Thou [*sc.* Io]..dolefullie dost moo Unto my talke. **1607** *Barley-Breake* (1877) 25 Whose dolefull Sounds the Eccho did receiue, That to his moanes the syluan beasts did moo. **1818** Todd, To *Mue*,.. 2. To low as a cow; usually pronounced *moo*, though *mue* should seem to be the orthography. **1855** Thackeray *Newcomes* II. 174 Blessed darling crows, moos, jumps in his nurse's arms. **1892** J. S. Fletcher *When Chas. I was King* ii, I used to wonder..if that were Farmer Denby's roan cow that mooed so loudly under the western window.

Hence **'mooing** *vbl. sb.*

1844 Thackeray *Little Trav.* i, A huge penful of Durham oxen..maintain an incessant mooing and bellowing. *transf.* **1888** *Harper's Mag.* Apr. 738 The mooing of the waters seemed to deepen.

moo, obs. f. mo, more; obs. and dial. f. mow.

mooch (muːtʃ), *sb. slang* and *dial.* Also mouch. [f. mooch *v.*]

1. *slang.* The action of mooching; esp. in phr. *on the mooch.*

1867 *Lond. Herald* 23 Mar. 221 (Farmer s.v. *Moocher*) If ..asked..what he was doing, he would have said he was on the mouch. **1889** J. K. Jerome *Three Men in Boat* iv, You are doing a mouch round the town.

2. *dial.* The fruit of the blackberry.

1839 *Hereford. Gloss.* 69 In the Forest of Dean 'to mooche blackberries', or simply 'to mooch', means to pick blackberries; and blackberries have thus obtained their name of 'mooches'. **1886** Britten & Holland *Eng. Plant-n.*

3. *slang.* = moocher 4.

1914 Jackson & Hellyer *Vocab. Criminal Slang* 60 *Mooch*,..current amongst beggars. A mendicant, an alms solicitor. **1953** W. Burroughs *Junkie* (1972) xiv. 146 Cash was a junk mooch on wheels. He made it difficult to refuse.

mooch, mouch (muːtʃ), *v.* Now *slang* and *dial.* Forms: 5 mowche, 7, 9 mouche, 7 mootch, 9 mooche, moach, moche, modge, 7- mouch, 8- mooch. [In 15th and 17th c. *mowche, mouche*; the senses, closely similar to those of mitch *v.*, suggest that it was adopted from the source of that word (OF. *muchier* to hide, skulk, etc.) with some dialectal variety of pronunciation.]

†**1.** *intr.* ? To act the miser, pretend poverty; = mitch *v.* 3 b. *Obs. rare*[−1].

c **1460** *Towneley Myst.* xxx. 571 The pennys thai powchid and held thaym still; The negons thai mowchid and had no will ffor hart fare.

2. To play truant; *esp.*, in later use, to play truant in order to pick blackberries; hence *trans.* to pick (blackberries).

1622 Mabbe tr. *Aleman's Guzman d'Alf.* ii. 289 Wee.. runne a-mouching eyther to our Aunts house, or our grandfathers, where wee are made much of. **1655** tr. *Com. Hist. Francion* vi. 9 The Eagle more mindfull of Prey than Honour, did one day mootch from the Thunder which lame Vulcan had made..for Almighty Iupiter. **1787** Grose *Provinc. Gloss.*, *Mooch*, to play the truant. **1839** [see mooch *sb.* 2]. **1887** F. T. Havergal *Herefordsh. Gloss.* 23 'Where is ——?' 'Oh, he's gone mouching'.

3. *intr.* To loaf, skulk, sneak, loiter, or hang *about*; to slouch *along*.

1851 Mayhew *Lond. Labour* I. 424/1 These hedge fellows are slow and dull; they go mouching along as if they were croaking themselves. **1879** Miss Jackson *Shropsh. Word-bk.* 285 ''E's no good, 'e does nuthin' but moach about from mornin' tell neet'. **1882** Ogilvie, *Mouch*,..to live a sort of semi-vagabond life, selling water-cresses and other wild produce, and without a fixed place of abode. **1888** 'R. Boldrewood' *Robbery under arms* xxii. II. 15 And I don't see but what bushranging..ain't as safe a game,..as mooching about cattle duffing. **1889** J. K. Jerome *Three Men in Boat* vii, All the inhabitants..come out and mouch round the lock with their dogs, and flirt, and smoke.

transf. **1881** *Daily Tel.* 20 Oct., They found the vessel able to do little more than drift. After mooching along in barge-fashion awhile, they sighted a steamer.

4. *trans.* To pilfer, steal.

1862 Mayhew *Lond. Labour* [IV.] 418/2, I don't mean to say that if I see anything laying about handy that I don't mouch it (*i.e.* steal it). **1880** Jefferies *Hodge & M.* II. 178 To mouch a good armful of fresh-cut clover. **1888** *Daily Tel.* 27 Nov. 5/2 They..would hotly assert that they never mouched a penny from anybody.

5. *intr.* 'To sponge, to slink away and allow others to pay for your entertainment' (Barrère & Leland *Dict. Slang*).

1857 'Ducange Anglicus' *Vulgar Tongue* 13 *Mouch, v.*, to go about sponging on your friends. **1975** D. Ramsay *Descent into Dark* ii. 69, I mooch these days because I've given it [*sc.* smoking] up.

6. *trans.* To beg, cadge, scrounge.

1899 'J. Flynt' *Tramping with Tramps* iv. 395 *Mooch*, to beg. **1914** *Sat. Even. Post* 4 Apr. 10/2 And State Street, Chicago, 60. He sure mooched that stem. No nickels. Dimes, buddie... He can beg coin. **1931** 'D. Stiff' *Milk & Honey Route* iii. 33 Loan your safety razor to a bum and he will mooch you for half your blades. **1933** 'G. Orwell' *Down & Out* xxxiv. 254 Every night I mooched tanners for my kip off of the students. **1953** W. Burroughs *Junkie* (1972) xiv. 147 He would mooch junk off Old Ike, who couldn't turn down anyone sick. **1954** G. Kersh in D. Knight *100 Yrs. Sci. Fiction* (1969) 228, I came across a student, mooching drinks, an educated man with no place to sleep. **1972** D. Morrell *First Blood* i. iii. 17 First thing I know, a bunch of your friends will show up, mooching food, maybe stealing, maybe pushing drugs.

moocha ('muːtʃə). Also moochi(e), muchi, mutsha, mutshi, umutsha. [Bantu.] A short skirt worn as a loin-cloth by the aboriginal inhabitants of eastern South Africa before the introduction of European dress.

1878 H. A. Roche *On Trek in Transvaal* xv. 325 A wee little Kafir boy with nothing upon him but his 'moochie', or tails, drives by a herd of calves. **1885** R. Haggard *King Solomon's Mines* x. 153 He slipped off the 'moocha' or girdle round his middle, and stood naked before us. **1898** *Chambers's Jrnl.* 8 Jan. 95/2 His only dress consisted of a monkey skin *muchi*, or apron, and in his hand he carried a rifle. **1909** N. Paul *Child in Midst* 139 Presently he appeared, a tall thin native, with no clothing except a cow-hide mutshi, with flaps around his waist. **1923** *Chambers's Jrnl.* Apr. 222/1 The native kilt or *moocha* composed of strips of raw hide. **1936** *Blackw. Mag.* Mar. 304/1 All the bravery of the Zulu war-dress was there:..the leopard-skin karosses, the embroidered *moochas*, the white goat-hide garters. **1936** Williams & May *I am Black* xviii. 181 There came before his eyes a boy of fourteen years wearing only a *moochi* of cowhide polished with pig's fat. **1948** O. Walker *Kaffirs are Lively* 30 The menfolk stride along bare-thighed, in swinging *umutshas* of monkey-tails. **1967** E. M. Slatter *My Leaves are Green* 1 He wore only his 'mutsha' of monkey-skin tails. **1970** *Rand Daily Mail* 29 Oct. 12 (*caption*) Beaded 'muchi'.

moochary, obs. form of mohair.

moocher, moucher ('muːtʃə(r)). Now *slang* and *dial.* Forms: (9 mochar, mutcher, mocher), 7, 9- moucher, 9- moocher. [f. mooch *v.* + -er[1].]

†**1.** ? An offender *against*. *Obs. rare*[−1].

1671 J. Brydall *Law Eng. relating to Nobility & Gent.* (1675) Pref., If High-Shoon Common-wealths-men, and other Mouchers against Honor, Decency, and Order should continue as they were wont before the Re-Erecting of this Honorable Court, I should be sorry.

2. *dial.* One who 'mooches' or plays truant from school, *esp.* in order to gather blackberries; hence a gatherer of blackberries.

1870 Lady Verney *Lettice Lisle* x. 117 What a moucher you are, David! Allays after them blackberries. **1876** Mrs. Ewing *Jan of Windmill* vi, 'I played moocher', he continued —by which he meant truant.

3. *slang.* One who loiters about, a loafer; also in various specific applications (see quots.).

1862 Mayhew *Lond. Labour* [IV.] 282/1 They loiter about the streets and public-houses to steal from drunken persons, and are called 'Bug-hunters' and 'mutchers'. **1878** Jefferies *Gamekeeper at H.* vii. 142 There are three kinds of poachers, the local men, the raiders,..and the 'mouchers'—fellows.. who occasionally loiter along the roads and hedges, picking up whatever they can lay hands on. **1880** —— *Gt. Estate* 89 Broad burdock leaves, which the mouchers put on the top of their baskets to shield their freshly gathered watercresses from the sunshine. **1905** J. K. Jerome *Idle Ideas* xi, The Whitechapel hawker or the moocher of the Paris boulevard. **1906** *Daily News* 17 Dec. 6 The moucher—the man who lives by gathering watercress, blackberries, nuts, mushrooms [etc.].

4. *slang.* A beggar, a cadger; one who begs or scrounges. Cf. mooch *sb.* 3, *v.* 6.

1857 'Ducange Anglicus' *Vulgar Tongue* 13 *Moucher*, beggar. **1899** 'J. Flynt' *Tramping with Tramps* iv. 395 *Moocher*, a beggar. This word is the generic term for tramps in England. **1925** *Amer. Speech* I. 152/1 'Mooch' is a gem of a word, with its expressive agent-noun 'moocher', the name for a person who sponges on another. **1931** 'D. Stiff' *Milk & Honey Route* ix. 96 A moocher may do all the things a panhandler does, only he draws smaller dividends because he lacks the salesman's poise. **1933** 'G. Orwell' *Down & Out* xxxii. 236 Some of the cant words now used in London. .. A moocher—one who begs outright, without pretence of doing a trade. **1962** K. Orvis *Damned & Destroyed* xi. 75 You moocher, you—don't you respect a lady's natural curiosity? Be nice to me. After all, I'm paying for this party.

moocherus, variant of mochras.

moochi(e), varr. moocha.

moochin ('muːxɪn). *Anglo-Welsh colloq.* Also mwchin. Anglicized form of Welsh *mochyn* pig. (cf. Ir. *muc*), applied to a person, esp. a child, as a term of reproach or opprobrium. Cf. pig *sb.*[1] 5.

1940 Dylan Thomas *Portrait of Artist as Young Dog* 58 He sat down in the road. 'I'm on a sledge,' he said, 'pull me, Patricia, pull me like an Eskimo.' 'Up you get, you moochin, or I'll take you home.' **1945** —— *Let.* 30 July (1966) 280 He said, 'Look, what they did, the moochin.' **1953** —— *Under Milk Wood* (1954) 12 Saw him in the bushes..Playing mwchins..Send him to bed without any supper.

mooching, mouching ('muːtʃɪŋ), *ppl. a.* [f. mooch *v.* + -ing[2].] That 'mooches'.

1862 Hughes in *Macm. Mag.* V. 250/1 And the yuckle did scraam, 'Let us peck out his eyes' 'Zich a girt mouchin wosbird deserves to be caddled'. **1888** *Bury Times* 28 Jan. 7/5 The Mouching Fraternity.—James Thompson..and John Sullivan..were charged with begging at Walmersley.

moochulka, variant of muchulka.

‖**moochy** ('muːtʃɪ). *Anglo-Ind.* Also mochee. [Hindī *močī.*] One of the caste of leather-workers.

1837 *Lett. fr. Madras* (1843) 123 The Bramins and merchant boys all sat together; there was another row of the Moochy or workman caste. **1850** *Benares Mag.* IV. 380 Mild indeed we thought such a penalty for a vile mochee's infringement of the great budmash's dustoor.

moock, dial. variant of muck *sb.*

moo-cow ('muːkaʊ). [f. moo *v.* + cow.] A childish name for a cow.

1812 Combe *Picturesque* xiv. *ad fin.*, The sheep all baa'd, the asses bray'd, The moo-cows low'd, and Grizzle neigh'd! **1841** Thackeray *Charac. Sk.*, *Artists* (1869) 428 Can they design so much as a horse, or a dog, or a 'moo-cow', for little Jack who bawls out for them? not they.

mood (muːd), *sb.*[1] Forms: 1 mód, 3-5 mod, 3 modd, 4-5 *Sc.* mud, mwde, 5 modde, moed(e, 4-6 mode, *north.* and *Sc.* mude, 5 *north.* moyde, 6 moud, *Sc.* moyd, muyd, 5-7 moode, 3- mood. [Com. Teut.: OE. *mód* neut. = OFris. *môd* neut., mind, thought, intention, OS. *môd* masc., mind, courage (MDu. *moet, moed-*, Du. *moed* masc.), OHG. *muot* masc., mind, thought, courage (MLG. *muot*, mod.G. *mut*), ON. *móð-r* masc., anger, grief (Sw. *mod* neut., Da. *mod* courage), Goth. *môþ-s*, *môd-* anger, emotion:—OTeut. **mōdo-*, f. pre-Teut. root **mō-*: *mē-*: *mə-* (in Doric Gr. *μῶ-σθαι* to seek after, OSl. *sŭ-měti* to venture, Gr. *μα-τεύειν* to seek).]

†**1.** Mind. heart, thought, feeling. *Obs.*

a **900** tr. *Bæda's Hist.* iv. xxx. (1890) 374 God onsende in ðara broðra mod, þæt heo woldan his ban ȝeneoman. *c* **1205** Lay. 11 Hit com him on mode & on his mern þonke þet he wolde of Engle þa æðelæn tellen. *Ibid.* 4489 Heo hauede enne leoue-mon..þe leof hire weis on mode [*c* 1275 on heorte]. *a* **1225** *Ancr. R.* 240 Nim ofte iðine mode þene grime dom of domesdei. *c* **1275** *Wom. Samaria* 22 in *O.E. Misc.* 84 Wymmon, if þu vnderstode Hwo hit is þat drynke byd, þu woldest beon of oþer mode. *c* **1290** *S. Eng. Leg.* I. 103/85 Nov ich wot, quath þe Iustise, ȝware-to þou tornest þi mod. *c* **1300** *Seyn Julian* 103 (Ashm. MS.) Vor we nabbeþ power no mon to bringe in sunne aȝen is mode. **1390** Gower *Conf.* III. 163 If thou wolt take into thi mod Reson, thou myht be reson deeme That [etc.]. *c* **1400** *Destr. Troy* 515 For to mele with þat maidyn & hir mode here.

2. With specific colouring.

†**a.** Fierce courage; spirit, stoutness, pride.

Beowulf 1167 He hæfde mod micel. *c* **1205** Lay. 25476 Ah cniht he wes wunder god & he hafde swiðe muchel mod. *c* **1290** *Beket* 1838 in *S. Eng. Leg.* I. 159 Heo bi-leueden al heore grete mod and heore þretningue al-so. *a* **1330** *Otuel* 1123 þo was otuwel fol of mood, & fauȝt as he were wood. **13** .. *E.E. Allit. P.* A. 401 Maysterful mod & hyȝe pryde. **1375** Barbour *Bruce* xix. 622 The erll, that wes of meikill mude. *a* **1500** *Syr Peny* 117 in Hazl. *E.P.P.* I. 166 Peny wyll mayster be, Prove nowe man of mode. [**1579** Fenton *Guicciard.* xiii. (1599) 604 Not weighing in their glorious moodes, how farre the daunger exceeded the attempt.]

†**b.** Anger. *to peck, pick mood*: to take offence, become angry. *Obs.*

c **1175** *Pater Noster* 215 in *Lamb. Hom.* 67 For-ȝif þi wreððe and þi mod, for þenne is þi bode god. *c* **1205** Lay. 8792 þat mines æmes muchele mod swa milde is iwurðen. **13** .. *Seuyn Sag.* (W.) 262 And sone sche gan to pekke mod. *c* **1320** R. Brunne *Medit.* 345 To turne a waye from hem, fadyr, þy mode. *c* **1380** *Sir Ferumb.* 3635 His herte wax angry & ful of mod. *c* **1386** Chaucer *Knt.'s T.* 902 Til at the laste aslaked was his mood. *c* **1412** Hoccleve *De Reg. Princ.* 4347 But or þey twynned þens, þei pekkid moode. **1513** Skelton *Agst. Scottes, Vnto diuers people* 21 Who so therat pyketh mood, The tokens are not good To be true Englysh blood. *c* **1535** Redforde *Play Wit & Sci.* etc. (Shaks. Soc.) 101 Lord let thy mercye fall, And mytygate thy moode. **1591** Shaks. *Two Gent.* iv. i. 51 Who, in my moode, I stab'd vnto the heart. **1600** Holland *Livy* i. x. 9 Mood without might is vain and bootlesse [orig. *vanam sine viribus iram esse*]. [**1819** Scott *Ivanhoe* xxix, And now my father in his mood may slay this poor bondsman. **1855** Tennyson *Maud* i. i. xiv, What! am I raging alone as my father raged in his mood?]

†**c.** Passionate grief. *Obs.*

a **1300** *K. Horn* 1519 (Cambr. MS.) Rymenhild was ful of mode; He wep teres of blode. **13**.. *Guy Warw.* (A.) 1549 Neyȝe his hert brast for mode, & for sorwe ȝede ner wode. *c* **1430** *Syr Gener.* (Roxb.) 1259 She wept, she sobbed, for grete moode.

3. a. A frame of mind or state of feelings; one's humour, temper, or disposition at a particular time.

In early use not always distinguishable from sense 1.

Beowulf 50 Him wæs ȝeomor sefa, murnende mod. **971** *Blickl. Hom.* 7, & bliþe mode heo sang on þæm cantice. *c* **1200** ORMIN 8945 Witt hafenn sohht te widewhar..Wiþþ serrhfull hertte & sariȝ mod. *a* **1250** *Owl & Night.* 8 And eyþer ayeyn oþer swal And let þat vuele mod vt al. *c* **1250** *Gen. & Ex.* 3577 So wurð he wroð, o mode sarp. *a* **1300** *Cursor M.* 7701 Dauid. þat was mild o mode. *c* **1300** *Havelok* 1703 Þo was Ubbe bliþe of mod, þat he saw him so fayr and hende. **1481** CAXTON *Reynard* iv. (Arb.) 7 Tho spack Grymbart the dasse..with an angrey moed. **1590** SPENSER *F.Q.* I. iii. 8 With pittie calmd downe fell his angry mood. **1601** SHAKS. *Jul. C.* III. ii. 272 Fortune is merry, And in this mood will giue vs any thing. **1638** R. BAILLIE *Lett.* (Bann. Cl.) I. 37 Thir reasones make the multitude in a high moode to flock to the Counsell-house. **1660** F. BROOKE tr. *Le Blanc's Trav.* 382 But like mules they [sheep] are humoursome, and one must..expect their good mood before they will travail. *a* **1703** BURKITT *On N.T.* Luke ii. 38 Nature will have her good moods, but grace is steady. **1807** *Med. Jrnl.* XVII. 8 The self-dubbed Doctor retired in an angry mood. **1839** KEIGHTLEY *Hist. Eng.* II. 52 Assailing him with a virulence of scurrility hardly exceeded by Luther in his worst moods. **1852** MRS. STOWE *Uncle Tom's C.* xix, Miss Ophelia had never seen him in this mood before, and she sat perfectly silent. **1887** BOWEN *Virg. Æneid* IV. 424 Only to thee were his moods and his hours of tenderness known.

transf. **1816** BYRON *Siege Cor.* xvi, Wildest of waves, in their angriest mood. **1872** LIDDON *Elem. Relig.* ii. 58 Men talked about..the moods of Nature, the religion of Nature.

b. *to change* (†*turn*) *one's mood*: to change one's state of mind. Also, *one's mood changes*. (Cf. MIND *sb.*[1] 13.)

a **1300** *Siriz* 109 Dame, dame, torn thi mod. **13..** *K. Alis.* 102 Y-chaunged was al his mod. *c* **1375** *Sc. Leg. Saints* I. (*Katerine*) 485 The emprioure þan changit his mud. ? *a* **1440** *Morte Arth.* 3222 Bot be ane aftyre mydnyghte alle his mode changede. **1551** CROWLEY *Pleas. & Payne* 19 No fende, therefore, shall chaynge your mode. **1860** TYNDALL *Glac.* I. xxiv. 170 His mood was entirely changed.

c. *in a mood* (*for* something), *in the mood* (*to do* something): disposed, inclined. Also † *in the mood* (*of* doing something).

1589 [see MOOD *sb.*[2] 1 b]. **1613** FLETCHER, etc. *Captain* V. iii, You'r pleasant, but Fabritio know I am not in the mood [*printed* wood] of Suffering jest. **1838** THIRLWALL *Greece* III. xxv. 393 But the Council was not in a mood for such reflections. **1840** DICKENS *Barn. Rudge* ix, She was in no mood for sleep. **1880** MCCARTHY *Own Times* III. xlvii. 426 He saw what men were in the mood to do.

d. *pl.* Fits of variable or unaccountable temper; esp. melancholy, gloomy, or bad-tempered fits.

1859 TENNYSON *Elaine* 795 Then turn'd Sir Torre, and being in his moods Left them. **1863** 'HOLME LEE' *A. Warleigh* II. 307 When first he asked me to marry him did I not say 'No'..? Have I not told him since I should be dead with moods in a month?

e. *attrib.* and as quasi-*adj.* That is intended to suggest, induce, recall, or depict a particular mood or frame of mind.

1898 G. B. SHAW *Perfect Wagnerite* 124 Beethoven had shown how those inarticulate mood-poems which surge through men who have..no exceptional command of words, can be written down in music as symphonies. **1927** *Observer* 14 Aug. 8 On the last side of 86 is Joseph Speaight's expressive little mood-picture for quartet, 'The Lonely Shepherd'. **1940** A. OBOLER *Fourteen Radio Plays* 257 *Mood music*, music as background to plant mood of scene. **1946** R. HULL in A. L. Bacharach *Brit. Music* xviii. 230 First-rate powers of argument are to the fore..but the variations themselves admit of mood-contrasts which keep the music free from any danger of dry impersonality. **1948** L. LEVY *Music for Movies* x. 111 The slicker, more expressive phrase, 'mood music', which has been imported from the United States. **1955** D. KEENE *Who was Wilma Lathrop?* ii. 19 'Would you prefer mood music?'.. Wilma stacked the spindle with records. **1957** MANVELL & HUNTLEY *Technique Film Music* i. 22 To help them in this task, volumes of classified 'mood' music began to appear as early as 1913, when the Sam Fox Moving Picture Music Volumes by J. S. Zamecnik were published. **1960** *Times* 28 Sept. 15/4 The *Moon of the Caribbees* hardly more than a mood piece. **1962** *Listener* 27 Dec. 1102/2 They seem to me to be mood-poetry in a pejorative sense. **1969** J. BURMEISTER *Hot & Copper Sky* ii. 39 'What did you sing?'.. 'Oldies, "Body and Soul". "Smoke Gets In Your Eyes". "Blue Moon". Strictly mood.' **1970** *Daily Tel.* 20 May 16/8 It says much for Mr Wesker's delicate mood-piece that it nevertheless made an effect. **1972** H. KEMELMAN *Monday the Rabbi Took Off* xiv. 99 The organ had been playing mood music, a series of mournful cadenzas in a minor key.

f. *Comb.* **mood swing** *Psychol.*, an abrupt change of mood without apparent cause which is associated with some forms of mental instability.

1942 *Amer. Jrnl. Orthopsychiatry* IV. 715 Present methods of examining candidates for the air service are good so far as they go since they inquire into the presence of such symptoms as enuresis, somnambulism, mood swings, or phobias. **1943** J. W. MACFARLANE in R. Barker et al. *Child Behavior & Devel.* xviii. 316/1 At year five, four clusters were apparent. The first included quarrelsomeness, mood swings, negativism,..and competitiveness. **1965** J. POLLITT *Depression & its Treatment* i. 5 Manic-depressive type... Commoner among those with a family history of mood swings or similar illness. **1970** H. P. LAUGHLIN *Ego & Defenses* xiii. 201 An interesting..application of the principles of Inversion is encountered in the area of mood and mood swings.

4. Formerly used in many alliterative collocations: **a.** with verbs, as *to mend, amend, mese one's mood*; *to mar, meng, meve* (= move) *one's mood*; also *marred, meved*, etc., *in one's mood*. Also *to mourn in mood, to mean one's mood* (MEAN *v.*[2]), *mean oneself of one's mood*.

c **1205** LAY. 3407 His mod him gon mengen, he morȝnede swiðe. *a* **1225** [see MENG *v.* 3]. *a* **1300** *Cursor M.* 2259 Bot sua he mengud þam þair mode, þat naman oþer vndirstode O his spece wat he wald sai. *Ibid.* 3059 Quils sco hir mened of hir mode Comfort had sco son ful gode. *a* **1300-1400** [see MEAN *v.*[2] 1 b]. *a* **1300** [see MEND *v.* 2]. *c* **1325** *Spec. Gy de Warewyke* 123 Hit is a derne mourni[n]g in mod. **13..** [see MESE *v.*]. **1377** LANGL. *P. Pl.* B. x. 263 Why meuestow þi mode for a mote in þi brotheres eye. ? *a* **1400** *Morte Arth.* 3454 Mane, amende thy mode, or thow myshappene. *c* **1440** *York Myst.* xxii. 43 He has fastid, þat marris his mode, Ther fourty dayes with-owten foode. *c* **1470** HENRY *Wallace* VII. 1099 Als Inglismen sair murnyt in thar mude. *a* **1510** DOUGLAS *K. Hart* I. 170 Out of mesour marrit in thair mude. **1513** —— *Æneis* I. ii. 13 Witht sceptour in hand thair muyd to meis and still. *a* **1518** SKELTON *Magnyf.* 2394 He may mende your mode. *a* **1529** —— *Bowge of Courte* 317 Meuyd all in moode.

† **b.** (*with*) *mood and main, main and mood, mood and might.* (Cf. MAIN *sb.*[1] 2, MIGHT *sb.* 5.)

Cf. OS. *môd endi meginkraft* (Hel. 156).

a **900** tr. *Bæda's Hist.* I. xvi. (1890) 54 Ða ongunnon heo sticce mælum mod & mæȝen monian. **971** *Blickl. Hom.* 97 Forðon we sceolan mid ealle mod & mæȝene to Gode ȝecyrran. *c* **1300** *Cursor M.* 2624 Þou sal hir serue wit mode and mayn. *Ibid.* 23584 To wirscip þat godd þam had fordight, Þai graid þam bath mode and might. *a* **1352** MINOT *Poems* (ed. Hall) vi. 77 God..Strenkith him main & mode His reght in France to win. *c* **1450** *St. Cuthbert* (Surtees) 555 Þai þat loues god with mayne and mode. *c* **1460** *Towneley Myst.* xix. 157 With moyde and mayn. **1560** [see MENG *v.* 3].

mood (muːd), *sb.*[2] [An alteration of MODE *sb.*, due to association with MOOD *sb.*[1]]

1. *Logic.* **a.** (= MODE *sb.* 3 a.) Any one of the classes into which each of the four 'figures' (see FIGURE *sb.* 23) of valid categorical syllogisms is subdivided on the ground of the several ways in which syllogisms differ with regard to the quality and quantity of their constituent propositions.

The moods have mnemonic names (BARBARA, CELARENT, etc.), in which the three vowels represent the quality and quantity of the three propositions: A = universal affirmative, E = universal negative, I = particular affirmative, O = particular negative. (Some of the consonants also have significant functions.) The number of recognized moods is 19, viz. four in the first figure, four in the second, six in the third, and five in the fourth.

A different, probably a historically older, sense of the word occurs in some writers (e.g. Aldrich and Whately) alongside the sense above explained, and without being expressly distinguished from it. In this sense the mood of a syllogism is the type of structure to which it belongs in respect of quality and quantity alone, without regard to the figure; so that, e.g. Celarent in the first figure and Cesare in the second would be not two moods but two varieties of the same mood. (See quot. 1906, where this sense is definitely adopted to the exclusion of the other.)

[**1532**: see MODE *sb.* 3 a.] **1569** J. SANFORD tr. *Agrippa's Van. Arts* 21 b, A Syllogisme..which ought to be in one of the .xix. Moodes. **1589** *Marprel. Epit.* E iv b, The moode answereth unto Celarent, elder daughter to Barbara. **1638** CHILLINGW. *Relig. Prot.* I. iii. §29. 142 In what mood or figure, would this conclusion follow out of these Premises? **1870** JEVONS *Elem. Logic* xvi. 136 We call each of these triplets of propositions a mood or form of the syllogism. **1884** tr. *Lotze's Logic* 88 The above rule, which, where both premisses are affirmative, requires one to be universal, prescribes a particular affirmative conclusion, and admits the moods *Darapti, Datisi*, and *Disamis*. **1906** JOSEPH *Logic* xii. 240 The difference of mood depends on the quantity and quality of the propositions composing the syllogism. This may be the same in different figures, or different in the same figure... The different moods have received distinct names in the various figures wherein they occur; and hence what are called the 'mood-names'..indicate both figure and mood.

b. *in mood and figure*: in due logical form.

1589 *Pappe w. Hatchet* B b j, Tis neither in moode nor figure. [**1699**: see MODE *sb.* 3 a.]

attrib. **1693** DRYDEN *Juvenal* vi. (1697) 146 O what a midnight Curse has he, whose side Is pester'd with a Mood and Figure-Bride! [*Note*] A Mood and Figure-Bride, a woman who has learn'd Logick.

2. *Gram.* **a.** Any one of the several groups of forms in the conjugation of a verb which serve to indicate the function in which the verb is used, i.e. whether it expresses a predication, a command, a wish, or the like; that quality of a verb which depends on the question to which of these groups its form belongs.

1573 GOLDING in Baret *Alv.* To Rdr. viii, How shall men directly fynde The Coniugation, Nomber, Person, Tence, And Moode of Verbes togither in their kynde? **1669** MILTON *Acced. Grammar* 17 There be four Moods which express the manner of doing; the Indicative, the Imperative, the Potential or Subjunctive, and the Infinitive. **1751** HARRIS *Hermes* I. viii. (1765) 140 Hence..the variety of Modes or Moods. **1824** L. MURRAY *Eng. Gram.* (ed. 5) I. 111 Mood is a particular form or state of the verb, showing the manner in which the being, action, or passion, is represented. **1869** J. MARTINEAU *Ess.* II. 69 A mere grammatical metamorphosis from mood to mood.

¶ **b.** with punning reference to MOOD *sb.*[1]

1621 B. JONSON *Gipsies Metam.* (1641) 52 All your fortunes we can tell yee,..In the Moodes too, and the Tenses, That may fit your fine five senses. **1682** N. O. *Boileau's Lutrin* II. 14 This Baggage once in her mad Moods and Tenses Had Lombard read, the Master o' th' Sentences. **1818** SCOTT *Rob Roy* xvii, You are, of course, jealous, in all the tenses and moods of that amiable passion? **1905** *Westm. Gaz.* 1 July 13/1 The things that were momentous to FitzGerald were the moods and tenses of himself, of nature, and his friends.

c. *attrib.*

1928 H. POUTSMA *Gram. Late Mod. Eng.* (ed. 2) I. i. 31 Some of these verbs..are also used as modal auxiliaries, i.e. as substitutes for actually existing mood-forms. **1931** M. CALLAWAY *Temporal Subjunctive in Old Eng.* 19 The use of the Subjunctive of Antecedent Action, in dependent clauses introduced by particles meaning 'after'..is to be accounted for..by the nature of the main clause... This theory is substantially identical with that advocated by Oskar Erdmann..and by Ernst Bernhardt.., hereafter referred to by me as the Erdmann-Bernhardt theory of mood-syntax. **1962** F. BEHRE *Contrib. Eng. Syntax* 59 Certain uses of the indicative that have not earlier been duly considered by writers on mood-syntax. **1965** —— in *English Studies* XLVI. 90 In both the Old English and Middle English examples the mood-form is indeterminate.

3. Musical senses. † **a.** In mediæval music, a term used to indicate the relative duration or time-value of certain notes to each other in the rhythm of a piece; = MODE *sb.* 1 b. *Obs.*

The *great mood* determined the relation of the 'long' to the 'large', the *lesser mood* that of the 'breve' to the 'long'; each of these was called *perfect* when the greater note was equal to three of the smaller, *imperfect* when it was equal to two. (Cf. PROLATION, TIME.)

1597 MORLEY *Introd. Mus.* 12 *Ma.* Degrees of musicke they made three, Moode: Time and Prolation. *Phi.* What did they tearme a Moode? *Ma.* The dew measuring of Longes and Larges, and was either greater or lesser. *Ibid.* 18 There be foure Moodes now in common vse: Perfect of the more prolation, Perfect of the lesse prolation. Imperfect of the more prolation. And Imperfect of the lesse prolation. *Ibid., Annot.* ¶ 4 b, If a plainsong consisted al of Longes, it was called the first mood: if of a Long & a Briefe successiuely, it was called the second mood, &c. **1609** DOULAND *Ornith. Microl.* 42 A Moode..is the measure of Longs in Larges, or of Breefes in Longs. **1609** C. BUTLER *Fem. Mon.* v. (1623) K iij, Now and then she beginneth in duple time some two or three Semibriefes, but alwaies endeth with Minims of the triple Moode. **1782** BURNEY *Hist. Mus.* II. 183 As all Discant moves in some particular Measure, Mode, or *Mood*, he [Franco] first defines a Mood. ..'A *Mood* is the representation of the time of measured sounds, expressed by Longs or Breves.'

† **b.** A written symbol used to indicate 'mood' (in the above sense). *retorted mood*: see RETORTED *ppl. a.*

1597 MORLEY *Introd. Mus.* 2.

† **c.** = MODE *sb.* 1 a (in the various applications).

1597 MORLEY *Introd. Mus., Annot.* ¶ 4 b, By the name of Mood, were signified many things in Musicke. First those which the learned call moodes, which afterwards were tearmed by the name of tunes. **1667** C. SIMPSON *Compend. Pract. Mus.* 112 That which the Grecians called Mode or Mood, the Latins termed Tone or Tune. **1667** MILTON *P.L.* I. 550 Anon they move In perfect Phalanx to the Dorian mood Of Flutes and soft Recorders. **1694** HOLDER *Harmony* 138 The several Moods (some call'd them Tones) of Music. **1706** A. BEDFORD *Temple Mus.* iii. 57 Their [*sc.* the Greeks'] Seven Moods,..were no more than the Seven different Methods of altering their Tunes, by Flats and Sharps placed at the Beginning of a Lesson. **1788** CAVALLO in *Phil. Trans.* LXXVIII. 252 The best keys to be played in are the keys of C, of F, of E flat, of B flat, of G and of D in the major mood, and the keys of C, of D, of A, and of B, in the minor mood. **1844** BECK & FELTON tr. *Munk's Metres* 59 Poems of the Doric mood.

d. *transf.* (from c, associated with MOOD *sb.*[1]).

1597 SHAKS. *2 Hen. IV*, IV. v. 200 And now my death Changes the Moode: For what in me, was purchas'd, Falles vpon thee, in a more Fayrer sort. **1637** MILTON *Lycidas* 87 That strain I heard was of a higher mood. **1671** —— *Samson* 662 But with th' afflicted in his pangs thir sound..seems a tune, Harsh, and of dissonant mood from his complaint.

† **4.** = MODE *sb.* 6. *Obs. rare*$^{-1}$.

1666 BOYLE *Orig. Formes & Qual.* 10 Whether these Accidents may not conveniently enough be call'd the Moods or primary affections of Bodies.

† **5.** = MODE *sb.* 9. *Obs. rare*$^{-1}$.

1646 SHIRLEY *Poems* II. 48 Others, that have..fashionably observ'd the English Scene, Say (but with lesse hope to be understood) Such titles unto Playes are now the mood.

† **mood**, *v. Obs. rare*$^{-1}$. [? f. MOOD *sb.*[1] (if not an error for *brood*.] *intr.* To reflect moodily.

1796 SIR J. DUCKWORTH in *Corr. Adm. J. Markham* (1904) 81 We returned to Port au Prince to mood upon our absurd indigested and blundering plan.

mood, dial. (Sheffield) variant of MOULD *sb.* and *v.*, adopted in certain technical uses.

1833 J. HOLLAND *Manuf. Metal* II. 23 In this state it [*sc.* the fork] is called, in common with all articles after the first formation by the hammer, a *mood*. **1860** TOMLINSON *Arts & Manuf.* Ser. II. *Cutlery* 49 This *mood* or *mould*, as it is called, is shown in the annexed cut. **1875** KNIGHT *Dict. Mech.* 1233/1 A length is cut off, and the forger speedily *moods* this, that is, shapes it roughly into the form of a pocket-knife blade.

mood(e, moodal, obs. ff. MUD, MODAL.

mooddin, variant of MUEZZIN.

mooded (ˈmuːdɪd), *a. rare.* [f. MOOD *sb.*[1] + -ED[2].] Formed to convey or reflect different moods.

1868 G. M. HOPKINS *Jrnls. & Papers* (1959) 166 Fine, with gracefully mooded clouding.

mooder, obs. form of MOTHER *sb.*

moodie, variant of MOUDIE (mole).

moodily (ˈmuːdɪlɪ), *adv.* Forms: 1 módelíce, 3 modi(ȝ)liȝ, modi(ȝ)like, 4 modilich, 4-5

mo(o)diliche, 7– moodily. [OE. **módiȝlíce* (for the actual form *módelíce* cf. the parallels cited s.v. MIGHTLY *adv.*), f. *mód* MOOD *sb.*[1]: see -LY[2].]

†**1.** Bravely, boldly; haughtily, angrily. *Obs.*

993 *Battle of Maldon* 200 þær modelice maneȝa spræcon. *c* **1200** ORMIN 1296 Forr bule lateþþ modiliȝ, & bereþþ upp hiss hæfedd. *Ibid.* 2041 þuss mihhte ȝho full modiȝliȝ Off hire sinne ȝellpenn. *c* **1250** *Gen. & Ex.* 2584 Ðo bad ðis king al opelike, In alle burȝes modilike, Euerilc knape child of ðat kin ben a-non don ðe flod wið-in. **1377** LANGL. *P. Pl.* B. IV. 173 And modilich [C. v. 167 *v. rr.* modiliche, moodiliche] vppon Mede with myȝte þe kynge loked. **1603** FLORIO *Montaigne* I. xlvii. (1632) 152 If the fervor of Monsieur de Foix had not drewne him over rashly and moodily to pursue the straglers.

2. In a moody or sullen manner.

1611 COTGR., *Mornement*, sadly, pensiuely; moodily, lumpishly. **1833** MARRYAT *P. Simple* xxxviii, 'I can do nothing for you, Peter; I have no interest whatever', replied he moodily. **1872** TENNYSON *Last Tourn.* 647 Pacing moodily up and down. **1876** LOWELL *Among my Bks.* Ser. II. 306 When his mother died, in 1810, [he] was moodily inconsolable. **1906** *Blackw. Mag.* Jan. 104/1 Thirlstone.. was staring moodily into the fire.

moodiness ('muːdɪnɪs). [OE. *módiȝnes*, f. *módiȝ*: see MOODY and -NESS.]

†**1.** Pride, passion, anger. *Obs.*

c **1000** ÆLFRIC *Hom.* (Th.) I. 360 Ða heofenlican myrhðe beȝytan, ðe ða heofenlican englas ðurh modiȝnysse forluron. *a* **1175** *Cott. Hom.* 219 Hi wolde mid modinesse beon betere þonne he ȝesceapen were. *c* **1200** ORMIN 4979 þiss mahhte tredeþþ unnderrfot All modiȝnessess strenncþe. *a* **1250** *Owl & Night.* 1405 þe gost.. styhþ on heyh þur modynesse. *c* **1275** *Sinners Beware* 79 in *O.E. Misc.* 74 Prude and modynesse. **1530** PALSGR. 246/1 Modynesse angre, *attayne, ire.* **1571** GOLDING *Calvin on Ps.* lv. 16 This wish proceeded not of a trubbled or unadvysed head, or of moodynesse. **1626** tr. *Boccalini's New-found Politicke* III. ii. 179 Such was the naturall hatreed of the sheepe towards the Dogs, and the implacable moodinesse which they conceiued to be hurried vp and downe, that [etc.].

2. The state or condition of being moody, sullen, or abstracted.

1858 CARLYLE *Fredk. Gt.* (1872) I. I. iii. 29 Whiffs of jealousy.. the product of accidental moodinesses in him. **1861** J. NICHOL in *Mem.* (1896) 75 His kindness was often tried by my moodiness and eccentricity. **1891** WEYMAN *Story F. Cludde* x, In the general silence and moodiness I escaped notice.

†'**mooding.** *dial. Obs.* [f. **mood* a. Welsh *mwd* arch + -ING[1].] Vaulting, an arched ceiling.

1749 in D. R. Thomas *Hist. Dioc. St. Asaph* (1870) 701 The mooding of the chancel.

moodir, moodirieh, var. ff. MUDIR, MUDIRIEH.

moodish ('muːdɪʃ), *a. rare*⁻⁰. [f. MOOD *sb.*[1] + -ISH.] Characterized by moods; fitful, capricious. Hence '**moodishly** *adv.*, '**moodishness**.

Davies, followed by recent Dicts., quotes an example of *moodishly* from Richardson's *Grandison*; but in the passage quoted (I. let xxii) all early editions have *moodily*.

1876 H. GARDNER *Leone* II. in *Sunflowers* 122 Lay aside this rustic moodishness. **1898** *Academy* 29 Oct. 173 The turbulent neurotic moodishness of the Italian poet.

moodle ('muːd(ə)l), *v.* [Origin unknown.] *intr.* To dawdle aimlessly, to idle time away. Const. *about, on.*

1893 G. B. SHAW *Music in London 1890–94* (1932) 116 The literary man.. hardly able to believe that the conductor can be serious in keeping the band moodling on for forty-five mortal minutes before the singers get to business. **1921** —— *Back to Methuselah* v. 223 That old one who saw you out of your shell has gone off to moodle about doing nothing. **1928** —— *Intelligent Woman's Guide Socialism* lxix. 328 Napoleon often moodled about for a week at a time doing nothing but play with his children or read trash or waste his time helplessly.

‖**moodooga** (muː'duːgə). [a. Telegu *moduga.*] The East Indian tree *Butea frondosa* or *monosperma*; only *attrib.* in **moodooga oil**, a clear oil obtained from the seeds of this tree.

1866 *Treas. Bot.* s.v. *Butea*, The seeds [of *Butea frondosa*] yield a small quantity of oil, called moodooga oil, which the native doctors consider to possess anthelmintic properties. **1887** BENTLEY *Man. Bot.* (ed. 5) 532. **1890** in *Century Dict.* **1891** in *Syd. Soc. Lex.*

moodur, obs. form of MOTHER.

moody ('muːdɪ), *a.* Forms: 1 *módiȝ*, *-eȝ*, 2–3 modiȝ, 1–5 modi, 3–6 mody, 4 modey, *Sc.* mwdy, 4–5 mode, 4, 6 *Sc.* mudy, 5 modee, 6 modye, 6–7 (8 *Sc.*) moodie, (7 muddy), 8 *Sc.* mudie, 6– moody. [OE. *módiȝ* = OS. *môdag, -ig* (MDu. *moedich*, Du. *moedig*), OHG. **muotag* implied in *muotigî* courage (MHG. *muotec, -ig*, mod.G. *mutig*), ON. *móðug-r* (Sw., Da. *modig*), Goth. *môdag-s* angry:—OTeut. *mōdago-*, f. **mōdo-* MOOD *sb.*[1]]

†**1.** Brave, bold, proud, high-spirited. (Often applied vaguely as an epithet of praise.) *Obs.*

Beowulf 1812 þæt wæs modiȝ secg. *c* **1205** LAY. 23698 Muche cniht & strong mon and modi on heorten. *a* **1250** *Owl & Night.* 500 þu art wel modi & wel breme. **1375** BARBOUR *Bruce* IX. 659 Thretten Castellis with strynth he wan, And ourcom mony a mody man. *a* **1400–50** *Alexander* 215 þe mode kynge of Messedone. *Ibid.* 3327 þe mody men of Messedone. **1606** BIRNIE *Kirk-Buriall* xvii. (1833) E 3 b, *Πολυάνδριον*, sometyme the name of Gehenna, for the boulkes of many muddy men that fell in that greene. **1755** *Capt. Car* xxvii. in Child *Ballads* III. 434/2 But mony were the mudie men Lay gasping on the grien.

†**2.** Proud, haughty, arrogant; headstrong, stubborn, wilful, obstinate. *Obs.*

c **1000** ÆLFRIC *Deut.* xxi. 18 ȝif æniȝ man hæbbe modiȝne sunu and rancne [Vulg. *filium contumacem et protervum*]. *a* **1100** *Voc.* in Wr.-Wülcker 316/17 *Superbus*, modiȝ. *c* **1200** ORMIN 9613 Forr Drihhtin hateþþ modiȝ mann, & lufeþþ alle meoke. *Ibid.* 11852 To ȝeornenn affterr laferrddom & affterr modiȝ wikenn. *a* **1225** *Leg. Kath.* 418 Ʒef ha þeos modi motild [L. *hanc contionatricem temerariam*] ouercumen mahten. **1362** LANGL. *P. Pl.* A. x. 212 And so comeþ Dobest aboute and bringeþ a-doun Modi, And þat is wikkede wil. *c* **1460** *Towneley Myst.* xxiii. 86 Yee, for as modee as he can loke, he wold haue turnyd an othere croke Myght he haue had the rake.

†**3.** Angry, given to anger, wrathful. *Obs.*

c **1200** ORMIN 8263 Forr þatt he wass modiȝ mann & grimme wiþþ his leode. *c* **1250** *Gen. & Ex.* 2712 A modi stiward he ðor fond, Betende a man wid hise wond. **13..** *Guy Warw.* (A.) 906 þe douke Reyner seye þat cas Of Sessoine: wel modi [*Caius MS.* full angry] he was. *c* **1440** *Promp. Parv.* 341/1 Mody or angry. **1544** BALE *Brief Chron. Cobham* B vij, In his modye madnesse without iust profe ded he openlye excommunicate him. **1567** GOLDING *Ovid's Met.* VI. 43 Hir countnance did bewray Hir moodie minde [orig. *confessaque vultibus iram*]. **1589** WARNER *Alb. Eng.* VI. xxxiii. (1612) 162 When, like a Lion thirsting bloud, did moodie Richard range. **1608** SYLVESTER *Du Bartas* II. iv. IV. *Decay* 1190 O ragefull Tyrants! moody Monsters, see, See here my Case. **1649** MILTON *Eikon.* 240 There be a sort of moodie, hot-brain'd, and always unedify'd consciences. **1697** DRYDEN *Æneid* XII. 1233 Angry Jove.. the moody sire.

4. Subject to, or indulging in, moods of ill-humour, depression, or the like; ill-humoured, gloomy, sullen, melancholy.

1593 SHAKS. *Lucr.* 553 And moodie Pluto winks while Orpheus playes. **1632** SHERWOOD, Moodie, *morne, triste.* **1658** *Witty Apophth.* 147 A young maid having married an old man, was observed on the day of marriage to be somewhat moody. **1681** DRYDEN *Abs. & Achit.* 45 The Iews, a headstrong, moody, murmuring race. **1805** WORDSW. *Waggoner* iv. 134 It rather hath Stirred him up to livelier wrath; Which he stifles, moody man! With all the patience that he can. **1815** BYRON *Hebr. Melodies* x. ii, Those smiles unto the moodiest mind Their own pure joy impart. **1846** TRENCH *Mirac.* xx. (1862) 327 Her sickness.. had brought her into a moody melancholic state. **1887** T. HARDY *Woodlanders* I. iv. 64 Even among the moodiest, the tendency to be cheered is stronger than the tendency to be cast down.

b. Applied to humour, thought, action, etc.

1593 SHAKS. *Lucr.* 1602 Unmaske deare deare, this moodie heauinesse. *a* **1649** DRUMM. OF HAWTH. *Poems* (1656) 178 Those Soules which vices moody Mists most blind. **1742** GRAY *Eton Coll.* 79 Moody Madness laughing wild. **1785** BURKE *Sp. Nabob of Arcot's Debts* Wks. IV. 215 It may be said that this letter was written by the nabob of Arcot in a moody humour, under the influence of some chagrin. **1829** HOOD *Eugene Aram* 38 Then leaping on his feet upright Some moody turns he took. **1850** PRESCOTT *Peru* II. 48 The cavaliers rode back to Caxamalca, with many moody speculations on what they had seen.

c. Expressive of moodiness or ill-humour.

1596 SHAKS. *1 Hen. IV*, I. iii. 19 Maiestie might neuer yet endure The moody Frontier of a seruant brow. **1800** COLERIDGE *Death of Wallenstein* III. vii, What! meet such news with such a moody face? **1814** WORDSW. *Excursion* IV. 482 Cleave not so fondly to your moody cell. **1820** BYRON *Mar. Fal.* I. ii, A moody brow and mutter'd threats.

Hence **modiȝleȝȝc** (Orm.) [see -LAIK], pride.

c **1200** ORMIN 73 Acc þurrh þatt laþe modiȝleȝȝc þatt comm all off hemm sellfenn. *Ibid.* 2633 Ne toc ȝho þohh nan modiȝleȝȝc Off hire miccle sellþe.

moody ('muːdɪ), *sb. slang.* [f. the adj.] A persuasive and insidious approach adopted in order to gain confidence; any flattery or lies intended to suggest compliance. Hence, nonsense, twaddle, 'rubbish', esp. in phr. (*a lot of*) *old moody*. Also as *vb.*, to bluff or deceive by means of flattery, etc.

1934 P. ALLINGHAM *Cheapjack* xii. 148 'Moody' meant a bit of humbug. It is a very common word among the grafters. They would say, 'We'd better moody the landlady a bit,' when they meant that they would pay her a few compliments; and when they did not believe something you were saying they would tell you to 'cut out the moody'. **1958** F. NORMAN *Bang to Rights* I. 37 'I don't think that you are as bad as you are painted, I would like you if you would to tell me a little about yourself.' This aproch [*sic*] is known as the old moody. **1960** *News Chron.* 16 Feb. 6 You trying to give me the old moody? **1962** R. COOK *Crust on its Uppers* i. 21 Trying to moody through to the royal enclosure on the knock. **1966** A. PRIOR *Operators* x. 142 Emmie was always giving me a lot of old moody about you having some money stashed. **1970** R. BUSBY *Frighteners* x. 93 The same old moody he'd heard a thousand times before.

moody, variant of MOUDIE (mole).

mooe, obs. form of MO, more.

mooey ('muːɪ), *sb. slang.* Also moey, mooe. [f. Romany *mooi* mouth, face; cf. MOW *sb.*[2]] A mouth; a face.

1859 HOTTEN *Dict. Slang* 64 Mooe. **1896** FARMER & HENLEY *Slang* IV. 328/1 Moey. **1955** P. WILDEBLOOD *Against Law* iii. 148 All nylons and high-heeled shoes and paint an inch thick on their mooeys.

mooftee, -ti, variant forms of MUFTI.

Moog (məʊg, muːg). Also **moog.** [f. the name of R. A. *Moog*, an American engineer, its inventor.] In full, **Moog synthesizer.** An electronic musical instrument (see quots. 1969 and 1971).

The word *Moog* is a registered proprietary term.

1969 *Punch* 5 Feb. 193/3 A moog synthesiser.. is an electronic musical instrument capable of generating all kinds of weird sounds. **1970** *Melody Maker* 31 Oct. 9/4 'Switched-On Bach'.. gave a lot of people the idea to throw Moog records on the market very quickly. **1971** *Playboy* Feb. 156/2 Says drummer Graeme Edge: 'We've got a Moog synthesizer that gives us complete control of any sound frequency that the human ear can hear, and we plan to use it to make tapes for the Mellotron. We'll use the two combined and the Mellotron will eventually be a playback machine for the Moog.' **1971** *Guardian* 5 Mar. 9/4 A Moog synthesiser.. is a computer that can provide any thing from electronic drum beats against a background of flashing psychedelic lights, to bird song.. complete with country scenes. **1971** *Melody Maker* 13 Nov. 39/1 The Moog is basically a collection of electrical modules, some of which you would find in any good recording studio. **1973** *Observer* 21 Jan. 30/3 Jesus Christ Superstar: The music from the show given the full studio treatment (including moog) by an Australian line-up. **1974** *Official Gaz.: Trademarks* (U.S. Patent Office) 5 Feb. TM 21/1 Moog Music Inc., Williamsville, N.Y. Filed Dec. 1, 1972 Moog. For Electronic Musical Instruments.. First use Jan. 1, 1954.

moogan, moogree, var. ff. MOGGAN, MOGRA.

Moohummudam, variant of MUHAMMADAN.

mooil, dial. variant of MOIL *sb.*[1]

mooktee, var. MUKTI.

mool (muːl), *sb. Sc.* and *north. dial.* Forms: 6–9 **mule**, 6 **mull**, 7 **mole**, 7, 9 **mowle**, 8–9 **mooil**, 9 **moul, muil, mowl, mee(a)l** (see E.D.D.), 8– **mool.** [app. a dial. variant of MOULD *sb.*[1]; for the form cf. *gool* GOLD *sb.*[2] Some of the forms coincide with those of MULL *sb.*, and it is occasionally difficult to distinguish the two words.]

1. Mould, earth, soil; also in *pl.* 'dry earth in a pulverized state; earth for working' (*Eng. Dial. Dict.*); a small lump or clod of earth. (In the first quot. used *fig.*)

a **1578** LINDESAY (Pitscottie) *Chron. Scot.* (S.T.S.) I. 369 Quhen scho come on Scottis ground scho.. inclynnit hir self to the earth and tuik the mullis thairof and kissit. **1641** BEST *Farm. Bks.* (Surtees) 107 They.. rake it all over with hey-rakes.. till the mowles bee indifferent small. *Ibid.*, Another hath a showle and showleth the mowles into the hole. **1775** J. WATSON *Hist. Halifax* 543 *Mooil*, Mold or Earth. **1788** W. MARSHALL *Yorks.* II. 341 Gloss., *Meals*, mould, earth soil. **1802** A. SCOTT *Poems* (1808) 48 Now fields, convuls'd like dashin' waves, Wild row alang, An' out the ripen'd treasure laves The mools amang. **1834** J. WILSON *Noct. Ambr.* Wks. 1856 IV. 72 Men ca' the wee sleek mole blind because he has nae een they can see, and leeves darklin in the moul. **1889** FENN *Cure of Souls* 52 (E.D.D.) Good leafy mowles for nex year's blubs [bulbs].

2. The soil for a grave; the grave. Also *pl.* grave-clods.

1596 DALRYMPLE tr. *Leslie's Hist. Scot.* I. 69 The rest I pas ouer, of quhilkes mony now vndir ane mule and lumpe of clay ly togither. **1645** RUTHERFORD *Tryal & Tri. Faith* xx. (1845) 258 The mules of the holy grave. **1728** RAMSAY *Robt., Richy, & Sandy* 22 Ah, heavens! did e'er this lyart head of mine Think to have seen the cauldrife mools on thine. **1789** BURNS *Addr. to Toothache* iv, Or worthy friends rak'd i' the mools, Sad sight to see! **1816** SCOTT *Antiq.* xxxiv, When ye laid his head in the grave.. ye saw the mools laid on an honest lad that likit you weel. **1885** RUNCIMAN *Skippers & Sh.* 260 Aw'll be putten away and happed up amang the mouls afore maw bonny lad comes hyem ony mair. **1894** CROCKETT *Lilac Sunbonnet* ix. 75 Ye smell o' the muils. **1903** J. LUMSDEN *Toozle* IV. i. 74 Guid auld Younger's i' the mools.

3. *Comb.*, **mool-board**: see MOULD-BOARD.

mool (muːl), *v. Sc.* Forms: 6, 9 **mule**, 9 **moul**, 6– **mool.** [f. MOOL *sb.*]

1. *trans.* To crumble; esp. to crumble (bread) into a bowl in order to soak it in liquid.

1595 DUNCAN *App. Etymol.* (E.D.S.) 70 *Intero*, to mule in. **1737** RAMSAY *Sc. Prov.* (1797) 95 Ye ken naithing but milk and bread when it is mool'd in to you. **1824** MACTAGGART *Gallovid. Encycl.* 413 The bairnies them daigh did mool.

2. *intr.* To associate intimately *with.*

17.. *Blythsome Bridal* iii. in Herd *Coll. Scot. Songs* (1776) II. 24 And there will be Alaster Sibbie Wha in wi' black Betsy did mool. **1808–80** JAMIESON, *To mule in with one*, to have intimacy with one, as those who crumble their bread into one vessel; q. to eat out of the same dish. *I wadna mule in with him*, I would have no intimate fellowship with him. **1818** HOGG *Brownie of Bodsbeck* I. xi. 219 Though I ken I'll soon be in a warld o' spirits, an' that I maun mingle an' mool wi' them for ages.

3. *trans.* To bury (cf. MOOL *sb.* 2 and 3).

1818 HOGG *Brownie of Bodsbeck* I. xi. 208 But where are they now? A' mouldet! a' mouled!

mool, obs. f. MOLE, MULE, var. MOUL.

moola ('muːlə). *slang* (orig. *U.S.*). Also **moolah.** [Origin unknown.] Money.

1939 J. O'HARA *Pal Joey* (1940) 97, I never saw the day wherein no matter how much moola I had I could not use some more. **1944** *Penguin New Writing* 20 111 You don't like it, but you like the moola all right. **1951** *People* (Austral.) 1 Aug. 20/3 She left there, too. 'Not enough moolah.' **1968** BUSBY & HOLTHAM *Main Line Kill* v. 44 Expensive though. You blokes must spend a lot of moola on that stuff. **1970** *New Yorker* 5 Sept. 40 (*caption*) Gentlemen, nothing stands in the way of a final accord except that management wants profit maximization and the union wants more moola. **1973**

J. WAINWRIGHT *High-Class Kill* 154 What did he do for a living?.. Where did the moolah come from? **1975** J. SYMONS *Three Pipe Problem* xiv. 113 Then the only thing to be settled is the lolly, the moolah.

moola(e, -lah, obs. forms of MULLAH.

moolavee, variant of MOOLVEE.

moolberye, obs. form of MULBERRY.

moold, obs. form of MOLE^2; MOULD.

moole, obs. form of MOLE, MULE.

mooley: see MULEY, MOOLEY *sb.* and *a.*^{1}

'moolin(g)s, *sb. pl. Sc.* Also mu(i)lin, moulin. [f. MOOL *v.* + -ING^1.] Crumbs.

1828 MOIR *Mansie Wauch* vii. 60 The laddie's girn set with moolings of bread. **1895** CROCKETT *Men of Moss-Hags* ii. 18, I fed him with crumblings out of my jacket pocket—'moolings' Maisie Lennox called them.

mooll, obs. f. MOLE^2.

moollah, var. f. MULLAH.

moollen, obs. form of MULLEIN.

†**moolowe**, *a. Obs. rare*$^{-1}$. ? Variant of or error for MELLOW *a.*

1574 R. SCOT *Hop Gard.* 6 If your grounde be grassye, roughe, or styffe, it should be first sowen with Hempe, or Beanes, which naturally maketh the grounde moolowe, destroyeth weedes [etc.].

‖**moolvee** ('mu:lvi:). Forms: α. 7 meuleuee, 8 moulewy, molavie, -vee, moulavie, 9 moolavee, 9 moulavie, maulavi; β. (7 *erron.* moolevelee), 9 moulvi(e, -vee, maulvie, moolvee. [Urdū *mulvī*, a. Arab. *maulawiyy*, properly an adj., judicial, but used as sb., = *maulā* MULLAH, of which it is a derivative.] A Muslim doctor of the law; in India, a complimentary designation among Muslims for a teacher of Arabic, or a learned man generally.

1625 PURCHAS *Pilgrims* II. IX. xv. 1611 Amongst the Turkes..the Meuleuees..are an order of Derueeshes, that turne round with Musike in their Diuine Seruice. **1772** *Order of Council of H.E.I.C.* in *Claim of Roy Rader Churn* 13/2 (Stanf.) The Cauree and Muftee of the district, and two Moulewys, shall sit to expound the Law. **1784** N. B. HALHED in *Calcutta Rev.* (1856) XXVI. 79 A Pundit in Bengal, or Molavee May daily see a carcase burn. **1788** BURKE *Sp. agst. W. Hastings* Wks. XVI. 103 These women have Mr. Middleton's..guarantee..for their having a law officer of high rank, or moulavie (*printed* moulavre) of their own. **1834** *Baboo* II. xii. 253 The holy Moolavee was sent on board the ship. **1841** ELPHINSTONE *Hist. Ind.* II. VIII. iii. 235 Though there was no organised body of clergy, there was a class (called moulavis or mullahs) from which judges, lawyers, and ministers of religion were..taken. **1862** BEVERIDGE *Hist. Ind.* III. IX. vi. 677 The Moulvie of Lucknow. **1864** J. A. GRANT *Walk across Afr.* xi. 239 The Seedees, though knowing nothing of the Mohammedan religion, the majority not being circumcised, were much more particular on those occasions, and offered more opinions than a 'moulvie', or Mussulman priest, would. **1891** *Daily Chron.* 4 Sept. 5/5 Mohammedan moulvis. **1904** G. SMITH *Short Hist. Chr. Missions* 106 The Maulvies or Mohammedan doctors of Tunis. **1972** *Guardian* 1 Dec. 14/3 The great bulk of [Guyanese] Indians are Hindus or Moslems, and pundits, moulvis and parents always viewed such [Christian] schools with suspicion.

Hence **moolvee-ship**, the office of the moolvee formerly appointed as assessor in certain courts.

a **1886** SIR G. YULE in Yule & Burnell *Anglo-Ind. Gloss.* Suppl. (1886) s.v. *Law-officer*, The Moulvee-ship..must have been abolished before I became a judge (I think), which was 2 or 3 years before the Mutiny; for I have no recollection of ever sitting with a Moulvee.

mooly, Sc. variant of MOULY *a.*^{1} and ^{2}.

moomba ('mu:mbə). *Austral.* [Aboriginal word.] An annual carnival or pre-Lent festival held in Melbourne.

1963 *Times* 26 Feb. 9/1 A procession of floats to mark the beginning of Melbourne's curious Moomba festival. **1965** *Austral. Encycl.* IV. 55/1 Melbourne followed in March 1954 with a fortnight of carnival that was termed Moomba. **1967** *Australian* 18 Mar. 11/1, I recall the early Moombas very well: parts of them, at least.

Moomin ('mu:mɪn). In the children's tales of the Finnish writer Tove Jansson (b. 1914), one of an imaginary race of small, shy, fat, hibernating creatures that live in the forests of Finland. Also *attrib.* and *Comb.* So **Moomin-like** *a.*, resembling or characteristic of a Moomin.

1950 E. PORTCH tr. *Jansson's Finn Family Moomintroll* i. 14 One spring morning at four o'clock the first cuckoo arrived in the Valley of the Moomins. *Ibid.* 22 Moomintroll ..threw his eggshell into the waste-paper basket, for he was (sometimes) a well brought up Moomin. *Ibid.* vii. 162 Now you can all have a wish—the Moomin family first! **1957** M. ALLINGHAM in T. Jansson *Moomin* 1 On the Moomins themselves I find myself uncharacteristically reticent. Their appeal is so personal and so intricate that I feel chatter about them is like gossip in public about friends... When Moomin fans discover each other they..are..likely to sit down trustingly together. **1965** G. MITCHELL *Pageant of Murder* iii. 29 Kitty made an unseemly grimace behind the massive, Moomin-like back. **1967** B. W. ALDERSON tr. *Hürlimann's Three Centuries Children's Bks. in Europe* vi. 81 Nonsense.. is perhaps found at its best in the Moomin books of this author. The Moomins..conquered children in a trice. **1971** K. HART tr. *Jansson's Moominvalley in Nov.* xviii. 136 Let us observe half-a-minute's silence to show our appreciation of the Moomin family.

moon (mu:n), *sb.*^{1} Forms: 1 móna, 2–7 mone, (4 mon, mowne), 4–7 moone; *north.* 4–6 moyn(e, 5–6 mwne, 8 mune, 8–9 muin, 6– moon. [Com. Teut.: OE. *móna* wk. masc. = OFris. *môna*, OS. *mâno* masc. (MLG. *mâne* masc., MDu. *mâne* masc., fem., Du. *maan* fem.), OHG. *mâno* masc. (MHG. *mâne*, *mône*, *môn* masc., rarely fem.; also *mânt*, *mônt*, *mônde*, mod.G. *mond* masc.), ON. *máne* masc. (Sw. *måne*, Da. *maane*), Goth. *mêna* masc.:—OTeut. **mǣnon-*.

According to Brugmann this form has arisen by substitution of suffix, from the *t*-stem **mǣnōþ-* MONTH, as OTeut. **nefon-* NEPHEW from Indogermanic **nepōt-* (cf. L. *nepōt-em*). Cognate words for 'moon' and 'month' are found in all branches of the Indogermanic family; outside Teut. the following types occur: **mēnā* (Gr. μήνη moon), **mēnon-* (Lith. *mēnů* moon), **mēne-s*, *-os-* (Lith. *mėnesis*, dial. *mėnas*, month), and with reduced grade of stem-suffix **mēns-* (Skr. *mās*, *māsa*, Zend *mâŋha*, OSl. *měsęcĭ*, moon, month, Gr. μήν, Ion. μείς, L. *mēnsis*, Irish *mī*, month). The prevailing view that the root is **mē-*, to measure (the moon having, it is supposed, been named from its function as a measurer of time) is plausible, but cannot be considered certainly true.]

1. a. The satellite of the earth; a secondary planet, whose light, derived from the sun, is reflected to the earth and serves to dispel the darkness of night.

The moon's constantly recurring changes and phases (see 1 c and NEW MOON, FULL MOON, HALF-MOON, HARVEST MOON, and cf. CRESCENT, QUARTER) have caused it to be taken as a common type of changeableness or fickleness. They are popularly supposed to influence the health of body and mind, and to cause lunacy (cf. LUNATIC). The moon's appearance to the eye of being diversified with light and dark patches gave rise to the fanciful comparison of its disc to a man's face (see 1 f and MAN-IN-THE-MOON). It has been worshipped as a deity by many races; in classical mythology it was identified with various goddesses (see 1 b). Its white or silvery light is taken as emblematical of coldness or chastity.

The moon's attraction is the chief cause of the tides. The period in which the moon completes her series of changes, or in which her orbital revolution brings her back to the same apparent position with regard to the sun, is called a month; in astronomical use this term is applied in a wider sense (see MONTH *sb.*^{1} 2 a).

c **888** K. ÆLFRED *Boeth.* xxi, Sio sunne bringð leohte dæʒas, & se mona liht on niht. *c* **1205** LAY. 17861 þa a þan auen time þe mone gon to scine. *c* **1250** *Gen. & Ex.* 145 Ðe mones liȝt is moneð met. *a* **1300** *Cursor M.* 17288 + 59 He wald for vus marterd bee, þat time when þe moyn wor ful. *c* **1384** CHAUCER *H. Fame* III. 1026 To wexe and wane..As dooth the faire whyte mone. *c* **1460** *Towneley Myst.* xiv. 177 It gyfys more light..Then any son..Or moone, when he of son has ton his light. **1486** *Bk. St. Albans* c vj, Take hony at the chaungyng of the moon. **1577** B. GOOGE *Heresbach's Husb.* I. (1586) 20 Looke that the winde be Westerly, and the moon in the wane. **1588** SHAKS. *L.L.L.* IV. iii. 30 The siluer Moone. **1649** FULLER *Just Man's Funeral* 13 The moon would have shined without any spots. **1774** GOLDSM. *Nat. Hist.* (1776) I. 253 The waters of the sea, running from all parts, to attend the motions of the moon, produce the flowing of the tide. **1850** TENNYSON *In Mem.* xxviii, The moon is hid; the night is still. **1873** DAWSON *Earth & Man* i. 9 The moon seems to be a body which has had time to complete the whole history of geological change, and to become a dry, dead, and withered world.

b. Since the disappearance of the grammatical genders of OE., in which *móna* was masc., the feminine pronoun has commonly been used in referring to the moon, even when no personification is intended (the neuter pronoun occurs, but less frequently); in poetry the moon is often personified, always as a female, and sometimes, after classical example, identified with various goddesses, as Cynthia, Diana, Phœbe.

c **1290** *St. Michael* 451 in *S. Eng. Leg.* I. 312 Ase man may bi þe Mone i-seo þe ȝwyle heo is neowe riȝt. **13..** *E.E. Allit. P.* A. 1069 The mone may þer-of acroche no myȝte, To spotty ho is, of body to grym. **1382** WYCLIF *Isa.* xiii. 10 The moone shal not shyne in his [1388 hir] lyȝt. —— *Matt.* xxiv. 29 The sunne schal be maad derk, and the mone schal not ȝyue hir liȝt. **1390** GOWER *Conf.* III. 108 Benethe alle othre stant the Mone..: Of flodes hihe and ebbes lowe Upon his change it schal be knowe. **1591** SPENSER *Virg. Gnat* 508 And eke the Moone her hastie steedes did stay. **1784** COWPER *Tiroc.* 38 And, when descending he [*sc.* the sun] resigns the skies, Why takes the gentler moon her turn to rise? **1842** TENNYSON *Love & Duty* 22 The Sun will run his orbit, and the Moon Her circle.

c. With reference to the moon's changes or phases, its influences, etc.

c **1374** CHAUCER *Compl. Mars* 235 He that hath with love to done Hath ofter wo then changed is the mone. **1393** LANGL. *P. Pl.* C. x. 108 Lunatik lollers and leperes a-boute, And mad as þe mone sitt more oþer lasse. **1509** HAWES *Past. Pleas.* XVIII. (Percy Soc.) 83 The minde of men chaungeth as the mone. **1603** SHAKS. *Meas. for M.* III. i. 25 Thou art not certaine, For thy complexion shifts to strange effects, After the Moone. *a* **1668** DAVENANT *Law agst. Lovers* III. i, That were a sudden change, and would shew More of the Moon in him, than is in a mad-woman. **1784** COWPER *Task* II. 599 Our habits..change with ev'ry moon. **1803** *Med. Jrnl.* IX. 138 This periodical increase and decrease of the fever he was inclined to ascribe to the changes of the moon.

d. ***mean moon*** (Astr.): an imaginary moon supposed for purposes of calculation to move uniformly in the ecliptic, completing its circuit in the same time as the actual moon. ***calendar, ecclesiastical moon***: an imaginary moon used in determining the date of Easter.

1712 *Rule for Finding Easter* p. vii, In the Year 1664, the Astronomical Moon, viz. the Moon in the Heavens; and the Ecclesiastical one, viz. that found by the Column of Golden Numbers, happening to differ from each other, this Rule became matter of great Dissention. **1877** *Encycl. Brit.* VII. 615/1 This calendar moon is not the moon of the heavens, nor the mean moon of the astronomers. **1878** *Bk. Com. Prayer acc. to Use Ch. Irel.*, The Moon referred to in the definition of Easter-Day is not the actual Moon of the Heavens, but the Calendar Moon, or Moon of the Lunar Cycle, which is counted as full on its fourteenth day.

e. Proverb. ***to believe that the moon is made of*** **(†*a*) *green cheese*** (or ***cream cheese***): to believe an absurdity. Similarly, †***to say that the moon is blue***. See also CHEESE *sb.*^{1} 2 a.

1528 ROY *Rede Me* (Arb.) 114 Yf they saye the mone is belewe, We must beleve that it is true. **1529** FRITH *Antith.* Wks. (1573) 105/1 They woulde make men beleue..that ye Moone is made of grene chese. **1611, 1638, 1783** [see CHEESE *sb.*^{1} 2]. **1752** MRS. LENNOX *Fem. Quix.* IV. i, You may as well persuade me the Moon is made of a Cream Cheese, as that [etc.]. **1768–74** [see CREAM-CHEESE].

f. with allusion to the MAN-IN-THE-MOON.

a **1310** in Wright *Lyric P.* xxxix. 110 This ilke mon upon heh when er he were, wher he were ythe mone boren ant y-fed. *c* **1374** CHAUCER *Troylus* I. 1024 Þou hast a ful grete care Lest þat þe Cherl wole falle out of þe mone. *c* **1449** PECOCK *Repr.* II. iv. (Rolls) 155 A man which stale sumtyme a birthan of thornis was sett in to the moone, there forto abide for euere. **1588** SHAKS. *L.L.L.* V. ii. 214 *Rosa.* You tooke the Moone at full, but now shee's changed? *Kin.* Yet still she is the Moone, and I the Man. **1597** LYLY (*title*) The Woman in the Moone.

†**g.** ***moon's man***: a man who is under the moon's influence. (See also MOON-MAN.) ***minion of the moon*** = MOON-MAN 1. ***moon's minion*** (pseudo-arch.): a night-watchman.

1596 SHAKS. *1 Hen. IV*, I. ii. 30 Let vs be Dianaes Forresters, Gentlemen of the Shade, Minions of the Moone. [Cf. I. ii. 15.] *Ibid.* 35 The fortune of vs that are the Moones men, dooth ebbe and flow like the Sea. **1609** [DEKKER] *Ravens Alm.* B, At the beginning of every Almanack, it is the fashion to haue the body of a man..bitten and shot at by wild beasts and monsters. And this fellow, they..call the man of the moon, or the moons man. **1623** CAMDEN *Rem.*, *Apparel* (1636) 237 To what cause our mutability..may be referred, I know not, vnlesse that we..are *Lunares* or the Moones men. **1827** LYTTON *Pelham* xlix, In an instant two of the moon's minions, staffs, lanterns, and all, were measuring their length at the foot of their name-sake of royal memory.

h. *fig.* (esp. associated with the sun or the stars).

c **1586** ROYDON *Elegie Sir P. Sidney* Spenser's Wks. (Globe) 569/2 Tis likely they acquainted soone; He was a Sun, and she a Moone. **1588** SHAKS. *L.L.L.* IV. iii. 230 My Loue (her Mistres) is a gracious Moone, Shee (an attending Starre) scarce seene a light. **1668** R. STEELE *Husbandman's Calling* v. (1672) 70 The moon of the world doth interpose and hide from him the sight and beams of the Sun of Righteousness. **1778** JOHNSON 29 Apr. in *Boswell*, Modern writers are the moons of literature; they shine with reflected light, with light borrowed from the ancients.

2. The moon as visible during one (lunar) month is in popular language spoken of as a distinct object from that of another month; its 'age' being the number of days that have elapsed since new moon. Similarly, the sb. is used with qualifying words for: The moon as shining or visible at some particular time or place, or as presenting some particular appearance. (See also NEW MOON, FULL MOON, HARVEST MOON, etc.)

there is a moon, there is no moon = the moon is visible (not visible) at the time and in the place indicated or implied. ***the old moon in the new moon's arms*** (or ***lap***): the appearance of the moon during the first quarter in which the dark portion of the orb is made faintly luminous by earth-light.

c **1000** *Sax. Leechd.* III. 182 On anre nihte ealdne monan. *Ibid.* 252 Se winterlica mona gæð norðor þonne seo sunne ga on sumera. **1154** *O.E. Chron.* an. 1135 Als it uuare threniht ald mone an sterres abuten him at mid dæi. *c* **1386** CHAUCER *Prol.* 403 But of his craft to rekene wel his tydes,.. His herberwe and his moone,..Ther nas noon swich. **1556** WITHALS *Dict.* (1568) 1/2 The time betweene the olde Moone and the newe. **1602** SHAKS. *Ham.* III. ii. 167 And thirtie dozen Moones with borrowed sheene, About the World haue times twelue thirties beene. **1661** EVELYN *Tyrannus* (ed. 2) 13 When the State it self was as seldome above the Age of a Moon without a new face. **17..** *Sir Patrick Spens* vi, I saw the new moon..Wi' the auld moone in her arme. **1802** COLERIDGE *Dejection* 13 Lo! the New-moon winter-bright!.. I see the old Moon in her lap, fortelling The coming-on of rain and squally blast. **1820** KEATS *Hyperion* I. 83 One moon, with alteration slow, had shed Her silver seasons four upon the night. **1823** F. CLISSOLD *Ascent Mt. Blanc* 22 The sun being now near his setting, and there being no moon. **1837** *Penny Cycl.* IX. 253/1 If the paschal moon fall on a Sunday, the next Sunday is Easter Sunday. **1860** TYNDALL *Glac.* I. xxv. 185 The night being without a moon, we carried three lanterns. **1884** *Harper's Mag.* Nov. 906/2 The young moon hung in the west. **1894** H. NISBET *Bush Girl's Rom.* 17 The moon was divine as it bathed everything with its silver lustre, as only Australian moons can do.

3. a. With reference to the moon's position above the earth, or its conspicuousness in the sky; often quasi-personified, e.g. as the witness

of terrestrial doings, the 'queen of the night', or the like.

Shakspere has many passages containing such allusions. *c* **1220** *Bestiary* 598 He sweren bi ðe rode, bi ðe sunne and bi ðe mone. **1484** CAXTON *Fables of Æsop* IV. x. (1889) 115 God kepe.. the mone fro the wulues. [Cf. Cotgr. s.v. *Lune, Garder la lune des loups*, and Rabelais I. xi.] **1553** *Respublica* III. iv. 759, I will couche youe all vp soone, where ye shalnot bee spied neither of Sonne nor Mone. **1597** MORLEY *Introd. Mus.* 183 Making as little account of them as the moone doth of the barking of a dog. **1600** SHAKS. *A.Y.L.* v. ii. 119 Pray you no more of this, 'tis like the howling of Irish Wolues against the Moone. **1667** MILTON *P.L.* I. 784 While over head the Moon Sits Arbitress. **1807** COLERIDGE *To Wordsw.* 101 A tranquil sea, Outspread and bright, yet swelling to the moon.

b. Phrases. † ***under the moon, anunder moon***: in this sublunary sphere, on earth; contrariwise † ***above, beyond the moon***. † ***below the moon***: sublunary, earthly. († ***to praise, boast) above*** or ***beyond the moon***: extravagantly. † ***to cast, go beyond the moon***: to go to extravagant lengths. ***to be*** (or ***jump***) ***over the moon***: to be very happy or delighted.

a **1300** *Cursor M.* 15610 Of his soru mai naman tell þat liues vnder þe mone. **13..** *E.E. Allit. P.* A. 1092 His lyf wer loste an-vnder mone. *c* **1380** WYCLIF *Wks.* (1880) 192 Trewe seruyce of god is lettid & þis veyn knackynge.. is preised abouen þe mone. *c* **1425** *Cast. Persev.* 2691 in *Macro Plays* 154 Mary! þi sone a-bouyn þe mone, as make Mankynde trewe & sad, In grace for to gon. *a* **1518** SKELTON *Magnyf.* 226 All is without measure, and fer beyonde the mone. *a* **1533** FRITH *Another Bk. agst. Rastell* (1829) 220 Rastell thinketh that I stand well in my own conceit, and boast myself above the moon. **1559**, etc. [see CAST *v.* 41]. **1586** A. DAY *Eng. Secretary* I. (1625) 80 You reckon too wide, you goe beyond the Moone. **1602** SHAKS. *Ham.* IV. vii. 146 All Simples that haue Vertue Vnder the Moone. **1613** —— *Hen. VIII*, III. ii. 134 His Thinkings are below the Moone, not worth His serious considering. **1625** BACON *Ess., Ceremonies* (Arb.) 27 The Dwelling vpon them, and Exalting them aboue the Moone, is.. Tedious. **1724** RAMSAY *Vision* xii, Far abuve the mune, We watching beings do convene. [*c* **1765** in *Oxf. Dict. Nursery Rhymes* (1951) 205 High diddle, diddle, The Cat and the Fiddle, The Cow jump'd over the Moon.] **1833** S. SMITH *Life & Writings J. Downing* 18, I could have jumped over the moon. **1840** T. C. HALIBURTON *Clockmaker* 3rd Ser. viii. 109 Ready to jump over the moon for delight. **1936** M. KENNEDY *Together & Apart* III. 189 She didn't know she had a brother and she's over the moon. **1944** N. COWARD *Middle East Diary* 116 The Captain.. is.. absolutely over the moon with pleasure at having this command. **1972** J. BROWN *Chancer* iv. 53 He goes back there. She's over the moon, of course, and off they go to parties.

c. Typifying a place impossible to reach or a thing impossible to get. Esp. in phr. ***to ask*** (***cry, wish***) ***for the moon***: to ask or wish for the unattainable.

[**1550** N. UDALL *Answer to Commoners of Devonshire & Cornwall* in N. Pocock *Troubles connected with Prayer Bk. of 1549* (1884) 178 They will cry to have a piece of the moon.] **1593** SHAKS. *2 Hen. VI*, III. i. 158 And dogged Yorke, that reaches at the Moone, Whose ouer-weening Arme I haue pluckt back. **1777** PRIESTLEY *Matt. & Spir.* (1782) I. Pref. 7 My mind is no more in my body, than it is in the moon. **1813** WELLINGTON in Gurw. *Desp.* (1838) XI. 86 If I had been at any time capable of doing what these gentlemen expected, I should now I believe have been in the Moon. **1847** TENNYSON *Princess* IV. 408, I babbled for you, as babies for the moon. **1852** DICKENS *Bleak Ho.* vi, He was a mere child in the world, but he didn't cry for the moon. **1860** THACKERAY *Lovel* v. (1861) 196, I might as well wish for the moon as hope to get her. **1928** E. O. WINSTEDT tr. *Cicero's Lett. to Atticus* II. x. 293 You are asking for the moon. **1930** J. B. PRIESTLEY *Angel Pavement* vi. 307 That was not asking much, and yet.. he could not help thinking it was really like asking for the moon. **1946** V. S. PRITCHETT *Living Novel* 44 They are grown up. They do not cry for the moon. **1965** *Listener* 16 Sept. 431/1 To turn on the telly every night for a week and expect to see what you yourself would choose to see is little short of asking for the moon. **1972** *Accountant* 5 Oct. 410/1 To hope for equity or justice in any such scheme is to cry for the moon.

† **d.** In various phrases expressing ineffectual or useless action or attempt. *Obs.*

a **1529** SKELTON *Bouge of Court* 383 Thou mayste not studye, or muse on the mone. **1590** SIR J. SMYTH *Disc. Weapons* 15 Their bullets doo worke as much effect against the Moone, as against the Enemie that they shoote at. **1655** [see BARK *v.*[1] 2]. **1705** tr. *Bosman's Guinea* 433 To think of forcing any thing from them, is to dispute with the Moon.

e. ***to shoot*** (†***bolt***, †***shove***) ***the moon*** (slang): to make a 'moonlight flit'.

1823 *Grose's Dict. Vulgar T.* (ed. Egan), *Shoving the Moon*, moving goods by moonlight to prevent their being seized by the landlord. *Cant. a* **1825** *Universal Songster* I. 70 She wish'd to gammon her landlord, and likewise bolt the moon. **1837** COL. HAWKER *Diary* (1893) II. 123 He having just 'shot the moon', I had to follow him to a cockloft in St. Giles's. **1892** ZANGWILL *Bow Mystery* 10 It is well for the landlord to be about his own estate in Bow, where poachers often shoot the moon.

4. An appearance in the sky resembling a moon. (Cf. *mock-moon*.)

a **1123** *O.E. Chron.* an. 1106 (MS. E) On þa niht þe on morȝen wæs Cena Domini.. wæron ȝesewen tweȝen monan. **1500–20** DUNBAR *Poems* xxxv. 50 Full weill I wist to me wald nevir cum thrift, Quhill that twa monis were sene vp in the lift. **1595** SHAKS. *John* IV. ii. 182 They say fiue Moones were seene to night: Foure fixed, and the fift did whirle about The other foure, in wondrous motion. **1784** COWPER *Task* v. 152 A wat'ry light.. that seem'd Another moon new risen, or meteor fall'n From heav'n to earth.

5. A figure or representation of the moon, either crescent-shaped (cf. HALF-MOON) or circular (like the full moon); a moon-shaped ornament or vessel.

Specific uses are: (*a*) a gas-globe (cf. MOON-SHADE); (*b*) *U.S. slang*, a large circular biscuit.

1431 *Rec. St. Mary at Hill* (1905) 26 A hole vestement of blu veluet with sterres & mones of golde. **1520–1** *Fabric Rolls York Minster* (Surtees) 305 Too corporax casis.. the one wth a moone, & the other of cloth of tusshew blake of the owt side. **1594** ? PEELE *Alcazar* I. i, Our Moores haue seen the siluer moons to wane, In banners brauely spreading ouer the plaine. **1642** R. CARPENTER *Experience* v. xix. 326 Your arguments are like your invincible Armado's which in their first appearance make a mighty Moone, but are burnt and confounded in the end. **1821** [see MAHOMET]. **1832** TENNYSON *Pal. Art* 188 And pure quintessences of precious oils In hollow'd moons of gems. **1883** 'MARK TWAIN' *Life on Missis.* lii. 460, I spent my last 10 cts. for 2 moons (large round sea-biscuit) & cheese. **1883** *B'ham Daily Post* 11 Oct., Tumblers and Gas Moons.

b. *slang.* The buttocks. (Used in *sing.* and *pl.*)

1756 *Life & Mem. E. T. Bates* iii. 31 But his Moon shall never be covered by me or Buck..'till they put down the Ready—and no Brummagums. **1922** JOYCE *Ulysses* 82 Or their skirt behind, placket unhooked. Glimpses of the moon. **1938** S. BECKETT *Murphy* 220 Placing her hands upon her moons, plump and plain.

c. A moon-shaped mark or area; *spec.* a small area of greater translucency observable by transmitted light in some early porcelains such as Chelsea.

1855 *Poultry Chron.* III. 57 Breast. The best spangled and clearest from tipping with white at the end of the moon. **1865** *Chambers's Encycl.* VII. 535/2 An artificial fly.. adorned with two moons from a peacock's tail. **1909** *Chambers's Jrnl.* Sept. 586/2 Chelsea [porcelain].. may be distinguished by.. greasy-looking discs known as 'moons' in the paste. **1935** *Amer. Speech* X. 159/1 *Moons*, crescent-shaped nicks which agates [*sc.* marbles] receive from hard hits. The belief was that soaking an agate in vinegar would take out the moons. **1948** W. B. HONEY *Old Eng. Porc.* (new ed.) ii. 53 The exceptionally beautiful porcelain of the red-anchor period has a very soft paste of fine grain, often showing by transmitted light the round spots of higher translucency known to collectors as 'moons'. **1959** G. SAVAGE *Antique Collector's Handbk.* 79 From 1750 to 1753 a body noted for its 'moons', or patches of greater translucency, was employed.

6. The disc, plate, or orifice representing the moon in a clock which exhibits the moon's phases.

1546–7 *Burgh Rec. Stirling* (1887) 45 Ane orlege and mone with all necessaris tharof, kepand just cours fra xij houris to xij houris. **1628** *Burgh Rec. Glasgow* (1876) I. 366 For.. vpputting of the horolog brodis, mones, bunkis and roweris. **17..** FERGUSON in J. Nicholson *Operat. Mechanic* (1825) 493 The plate that carries the moon, that is a round hole *m*, through which the phase or appearance of the moon is seen on the sun's plate.

7. The satellite of a planet.

1665 *Phil. Trans.* I. 72 If these two Planets have Moons wheeling about them. **1667** MILTON *P.L.* VIII. 149 And other Suns.. With thir attendant Moons. **1784** COWPER *Tiroc.* 634 The moons of Jove. **1838** J. P. NICHOL *Solar Syst.* 139 Jupiter has four moons, each larger than ours.

8. a. *poet.* = MOONLIGHT.

1390 GOWER *Conf.* I. 327 Piramus cam after sone Unto the welle, and be the Mone He fond hire wimpel blodi there. **1667** MILTON *P.L.* I. 440 To whose bright Image nightly by the Moon Sidonian Virgins paid their Vows. **1833** TENNYSON *Lady of Shalott* I. 33 And by the moon the reaper weary, Piling sheaves in uplands airy. **1896** A. E. HOUSEMAN *Shropshire Lad* xxxvi, White in the moon the long road lies.

b. *U.S. colloq.* = MOONSHINE 4; *spec.* whisky.

1928 *Collier's* 29 Dec. 8/2 Wherever you go in Colorado a bootlegger.. says to you 'Mister, this is good stuff. It's Leadville "moon".' *Ibid.* 8/3 The art of producing sugar 'moon' and aging it in charred casks. **1950** *Sat. Even. Post* 27 May 20/1, I would buy a couple of pints of moon.

† **9.** With ordinal numeral, denoting a particular day after a new moon. *Obs.*

Cf. L. *luna tertia, quarta*, etc.

c **1000** *Sax. Leechd.* III. 184 Mona se forma on eallum þingum dondum nytlic ys.. & blod lætan oððe wanian ealne dæȝ mona god ys. *Ibid.*, Mona se oðer.. Mona se ðridda. **1709** *Rule for finding Easter* 8 By fixing Easter-Day upon the Lord's-Day following the 14th Moon.

10. a. The period from one new moon to the next; a lunation, lunar month; *gen.* a month. † ***twelve moons*** = twelvemonth. Until recently, common in ***the —th*** (***day***) ***of the moon***; now chiefly *poet.* and in renderings of the speech of primitive or uncivilized peoples.

c **1375** *Cursor M.* 9152 (Fairf.) Helias þat prophete.. þat stint þe rayne þorou his praier, hit lasted vj. mones [*Cott.* monet, *Gött.* monethes] & iij. ȝere. *a* **1400** *Med. Receipts* in *Rel. Ant.* I. 52 The .ix. day in that ilk mone. *c* **1400** *Destr. Troy* 1064 At Mid Aprille, the mone when myrthes begyn. **1523** FITZHERB. *Husb.* §20 Terre.. neuer dothe appere, tyll the moneth of Iune, and specyallye whanne there is great wete in that mone. **1608** SHAKS. *Per.* II. v. 10 One twelue Moones more shee'le weare Dianas liuerie. **1618** J. DYKE *Caveat Archippus* (1619) 20 Who may not soone be sufficient to reade.. the Church-seruice, and once in a Moone to bestow a mornings blessing vpon his people? **1653** H. COGAN tr. *Pinto's Trav.* ii. (1663) 33 The last assault, that was given on the thirteenth day of the Moon. **1716** GAY *Trivia* II. 360 When hoary Thames.. Was three long moons in icy fetters bound. **1756** WASHINGTON *Lett.* Writ. 1889 I. 393 They proposed.. to stay only one moon, and then to start for their nation. **1822** LAMB *Elia* Ser. I. *Roast Pig*, A young and tender suckling—under a moon old. **1876** *Encycl. Brit.* IV. 675/1 The 14th of the paschal moon. **1877** W. MATTHEWS *Ethnogr. Hidatsa* 60 A land where the summer was but three moons long. **1901** HENLEY *Hawthorn & Lavender* 40 This is the moon of roses, The lovely and flowerful time.

b. *slang.* A month's imprisonment. Freq. with *pl.* as *moon*.

1830 MONCRIEFF *Hrt. London* II. i. (Farmer), They've lumbered him for a few moons, that's all. **1894** A. MORRISON *Mean Streets* 259 So Scuddy's life went on, with occasional misfortunes in the way of a moon, or another drag. **1928** E. WALLACE *Gunner* vi. 50 Gunner's got three moon for bein' a suspected. **1936** J. CURTIS *Gilt Kid* iv. 39, I was doing nine moon for screwing. **1953** K. TENNANT *Joyful Condemned* xviii. 167, I got a twelve moon.

c. = HONEYMOON.

[**1709** MRS. MANLEY *Secret Mem.* (1736) I. 28 Tho' it survives not the Hymenæan moon.] **1859** G. MEREDITH *R. Feverel* xxxii, Where may these lunatics have gone to spend the Moon?

11. The time during which the moon is visible. *Obs.* or *poet.*

1375 BARBOUR *Bruce* IV. 617 And als soyn as the moyn wes past, Hym thoucht weill that he saw a fyre. **1832** TENNYSON *Eleanore* 124 The.. odorous wind Breathes low between the sunset and the moon.

† **12.** ***the moon*. a.** *Alch.* Silver. **b.** *Her.* Argent.

1572 BOSSEWELL *Armorie* II. 119b, His fielde is Saturne, an hande dextre in fesse, of the moone. **1610** B. JONSON *Alch.* II. i, The great med'cine! Of which one part proiected on a hundred Of.. Venus, or the Moone, Shall turne it to as many of the Sunne. **1651** FRENCH *Distill.* vi. 197 It will resolve the bodies of the Sunne, and Moone.

† **13.** A fit of frenzy; = LUNE 2. *Obs.*

1607 TOURNEUR *Rev. Trag.* II. E 2, I know 'twas but some peeuish Moone in him. **1642** SIR E. DERING *Sp. on Relig.* 94 A new Moon did take these men, I did begin to finde a different greeting.

14. = MOON-EYE 1. ? *Obs.*

1726 W. GIBSON *Dict. Horses* (ed. 2) 213 Other Infirmities.. such as Moons and Defluxions in the Eyes.

15. *attrib.* and *Comb.* **a.** Simple attrib. = 'of or pertaining to the moon, existing in or made by the moon or moonlight', as ***moon-base, -blasting, -cloud, -dawn, -dew, -dust, -folk, -gleam, -glimpse, -haze, -land, -lander, -landing, -landscape, -maid, -mist, -mountain, -path, -pull, -ray, -rising, -rock, -setting, -shadow, -sky, -stuff, -tide, -track, -wake***; **b.** objective, as ***moon-gazing*** adj.; **c.** instrumental or locative = 'by the moon or moonlight, in the moonlight, under the influence of the moon', as ***moon-bathed, -blanched, -blasted, -bright, -brightened, -chained, -charmed, -chequered, -crazed, -dappled, -dazzled, -drawn, -drenched, -flecked, -flooded, -freezing, -gathered, -glittering, -haunted, -horned, -led, -locked, -loved, -mad, -made, -mellowed, -misted, -parched, -raised, -rich, -shadowed, -soaked, -tanned, -taught, -trodden, -warmed, washed, -whitened*** adjs.; also (sense 5) ***moon-crowned*** adj.; **d.** similative, as ***moon-arched, browed, -faced*** ppl. adjs.; also = 'moon-shaped', as ***moon-head***; **e.** ***moon-blue, -cold, -coloured, -cool, -grey, -pale, -white, -yellow*** adjs.

1776 MICKLE tr. *Camoens' Lusiad* II. 77 Stern warriors with the quivering lance, Or *moon-arch'd bow. **1961** *Economist* 18 Nov. 676/2 Commercial services.. between New York and *Moonbase Alpha in one day. **1969** *Guardian* 15 July 6/6 One of the things we shall be doing in those early lunar flights is to find a good place for a moon base. **1909** *Daily Chron.* 4 Sept. 7/4 He was looking up at the *moon-bathed cliff with a rapt intense look. **1939** SPENDER & GILI tr. *Lorca's Poems* 51 To the sound of cold tambourines And moon-bathed cithars. **1852** M. ARNOLD *Summer Night* 1 In the deserted *moon-blanched street. **1794** COLERIDGE *Relig. Musings* 338 Ghastlier shapings than surround *Moon-blasted Madness when he yells at midnight. **1642** MILTON *Apol. Smect.* Wks. 1851 III. 314 Those thanks in the womans Churching for her delivery from Sunburning and *Moonblasting. **1918** D. H. LAWRENCE *New Poems* 33 A *moon-blue moth goes flittering by. **1922** JOYCE *Ulysses* 438 Her moonblue satin slipper. **1806** MOORE *Epist.* I. iv, How we should feel, and gaze with bliss Upon the *moon-bright scenery here! **1911** *Moon brightened [see *image crowded* adj. (IMAGE *sb.* 8)]. **1855** BAILEY *Mystic*, etc. 90 *Moon-browed maids. **1946** DYLAN THOMAS *Deaths & Entrances* 63 The *moon-chained and water-wound Metropolis of fishes. **1855** M. ARNOLD *Southern Night* xxx, Down to the brimm'd *moon-charmed Main. **1910** W. DE LA MARE *Three Mulla-Mulgars* vii. 95 The deep shadows of the *moon-chequered forest. **1813** HOGG *Queen's Wake* II. Wks. (1876) 19 His cap the *moon-clouds silver gray. **1933** W. DE LA MARE *Fleeting* 119 The autumnal night Hung starry and radiant.. O'er *moon-cold hills. **1944** E. SITWELL *Green Song* I Till the fire of that sun The heart and the moon-cold bone are one. **1922** W. DE LA MARE *Down-adown-Derry* 20 A beaming of *moon-coloured light. **1930** R. LEHMANN *Note in Music* 98 The grass.. foamed with the moon-coloured profusion of the flower which she called milkwort or Star-of-Bethlehem. **1969** G. MACBETH *War Quartet* 29 Staled Of heat, now *moon-cool. **1921** W. B. YEATS *Four Plays for Dancers* 72 The *moon-crazed heron Would be but fishes' diet soon. **1776** MICKLE tr. *Camoens' Lusiad* IV. 168 And *moon-crown'd mosques lay smoaking in the dust. **1910** W. DE LA MARE *Three Mulla-Mulgars* xix. 252 The *moon-dappled forest through which they had so heavily ascended. **1895** F. M. CRAWFORD *Casa Braccio* xiii, The *moon-dawn sending up its soft radiance to the sky. **1940** C. DAY LEWIS *Poems in Wartime* 10 All over the countryside *Moon-dazzled men are peering out for invaders. **1927** JOYCE *Simples* in *Pomes Penyeach*, A *moondew stars her hanging hair. **1844** EMERSON *Essays* 2nd Ser. viii. 243 In countless upward-striving waves The *moon-drawn tide-wave strives. **1922** JOYCE *Ulysses* 48 A tide westering, moondrawn, in her wake. **1929** C. MACKENZIE *Gallipoli Memories* xi. 189 The grillos shrilling far and wide across that *moon-drenched island.

1959 *Britannica Bk. of Year* (U.S.) 753/1 *Moon dust, meteoric particles on the surface of the moon. **1969** Guardian 30 July 1/7 The first experiments of exposing germ-free mice to moon dust. **1619** *Pasquil's Palm.* (1877) 131 To comfort *Moone-fac'd Cuckolds, that were sad. **1806–7** J. Beresford *Miseries Hum. Life* 304 The necessity of borrowing the spectacles of a moon-faced friend. **1855** Tennyson *Maud* I. I. xviii, Maud the beloved of my mother, the moon-faced darling of all. **1913** W. de la Mare *Peacock Pie* 98 Those wallowing, *moon-flecked waves. **1945** C. Mann in Murdoch & Drake-Brockman *Austral. Short Stories* (1951) 262 Nights... *moon-flooded, starlit. **1901** H. G. Wells *First Men in Moon* xviii. 218 We have shown these *moon folk violence. **1819** Shelley *Prometh. Unb.* I. 32 The spears Of their *moon-freezing crystals. **1834** Lytton *Pompeii* III. xi, These old hags, with.. their *moon-gathered herbs. **1828** *Lights & Shades* II. 274 This ominous ramble of the *moon-gazing 'thrice illustrious'. **1870–4** J. Thomson *City Dreadf. Nt.* xiv. i, With tinted *moongleams slanting here and there. **1821** Shelley *Hellas* 633 In the faint *moon-glimpse He saw.. the Turkish admiral. **1794** Coleridge *Relig. Musings* 274 Where by night,.. The lion couches.. Or serpent plants his vast *moon-glittering bulk. **1927** J. Joyce *She weeps over Rahoon* in *Pomes Penyeach*, His sad heart has lain Under the *moon-grey nettles. **1934** L. B. Lyon *White Hare* 34 The moon-grey barn. **1930** Blunden *Summer's Fancy* 42 Whispering their vows below *moon-haunted trees. **1891** Kipling *Light that Failed* (1900) 103 A faint beating like that of a muffled drum came out of the *moon-haze. **1837** Carlyle *Fr. Rev.* I. III. vi, The rubicund *moonhead goes wagging; darker beams the copper visage. **1894** O. Wilde *Sphinx*, And did you talk with Thoth, and did you hear the *moon-horned Io weep? **1960** T. Hughes *Lupercal* 60 And has shorn Summarily the moon-horned river From my bed. **1922** J. A. Dunn *Man Trap* xv. 207 Death cold the nights in this dead land that looks like *moonland. **1970** *Sci. Jrnl.* May 7/1 Neil Armstrong climbing down those few fragile steps of his *moonlander's ladder to the craggy lunar surface. **1962** *Daily Tel.* 5 July 26/6 A small *Moon-landing capsule. **1969** *Guardian* 16 July 17/4 An American moon landing does not constitute an unchallenged lead over Russia. **1954** Koestler *Invisible Writing* iii. 43 Certain scenes.. have the rugged and hostile greatness of a *moon-landscape. **1832** Tennyson *Pal. Art* 252 A still salt pool.. that hears.. The plunging seas draw backward from the land Their *moon-led waters white. **1943** C. Day Lewis *Word over All* 42 The earth is buoyed in *Moon-locked oblivion. **1629** Milton *Hymn Nativ.* xxvi, The yellow-skirted Fayes.. leaving their *Moon-lov'd maze. **1869** W. Barnes *Early England & Saxon-English* 103/2 *Moon-mad. **1920** Blunden *Waggoner* 31 To hear the moon-mad gypsy rave. **1880** W. Watson *Prince's Quest* Poems (1905) II. 178 As steals The *moon-made shadow at some traveller's heels. **1928** Blunden *Retreat* 14 Or mist-veil brushed thee, fine as yet was wove For *moonmaid's clothing. ?**1795** Coleridge *To Nightingale* 10 Within whose mild *moon-mellow'd foliage hid. **1910** W. de la Mare *Three Mulla-Mulgars* i. 4 Mutta-matutta's father died from sleeping in the *moon-mist. **1913** D. H. Lawrence *Love Poems* 13 The moon-mist is over the village. **1936** L. B. Lyon *Bright Feather Fading* 17 Yet parishes *moon-misted, Yet Avon, Severn, Humber His name remember. *a***1821** Keats *Sonnet: To Nile* in *Compl. Poetical Wks.* (1907) 305 Son of the old *moon-mountains African! **1927** F. B. Young *Portrait of Clare* 129 An orchard.. in which *moon-pale apples lay where they had fallen. **1914** C. Mackenzie *Sinister Street* II. III. vii. 637 Most people.. would obtain the finest thrill that Oxford could offer from the sudden sight of.. the *moon-parched High Street in frost. **1897** Kipling *Captains Courageous* iv. 103 She sat down in the *moon-path on the water. **1922** D. H. Lawrence *Fantasia of Unconscious* xv. 279 Her [woman's] deep positivity is in the downward flow, the *moon-pull. **1818** Scott *Hrt. Midl.* xxix, Haud your tongue, ye *moon-raised b——! **1844** Ld. Houghton *Palm Leaves* 202 A picture by *moon-rays designed. **1925** C. Day Lewis *Beechen Vigil* 30 In a *moon-rich garden. **1927** *Observer* 11 Sept. 8 A.. short interval between successive *moonrisings being favourable for late harvest work. **1969** *Guardian* 15 July 7/2 On July 24, if all goes well, 50 kilogrammes of *moonrock will arrive on earth. **1971** *New Scientist* 24 June 766/1 The exchange in Moscow recently of a minute quantity of Apollo moonrock for an even more minute quantity of Luna 16 moonrock. **1905** E. F. Benson *Image in Sand* xviii. 290 The sublimities of the sun-rises and *moon-settings were gone from her. **1925** E., O., & S. Sitwell *Poor Young People* 28 The *moon-shadows Palely pass and re-pass. **1958** J. Betjeman *Coll. Poems* 270 Near your curious mausoleum *Moonshadowed on the grass. **1934** Blunden *Choice or Chance* 55 To silence too that speaks angelic tongues From *moon-skies and the sun's November gleam. **1892** Ld. Lytton *King Poppy* Epil. 133 Herbs *moon-soak'd on Hecate's altars. **1929** E. H. Visiak *Medusa* (1963) xviii. 226 They are too apt already to be taken with such *moonstuff. **1969** *New Scientist* 18 Dec. 607/1 We should not go 'up there'.. merely to bring back a few pounds of 'moonstuff'. **1648** Herrick *Hesper., Oberon's Pal.*, And now he finds His *Moon-tann'd Mab. **1850** Mrs. Browning *Sea-side Walk* ii, The water grey Swang in its *moon-taught way. —— *Early Rose* xii, Singing gladly all the *moontide Never waiting for the suntide. **1858** Lytton *What will he do with It?* (1859) III. vi. x. 196 They were to his eyes the *moon track in the ocean of history. **1899** Kipling *Five Nations* (1903) 9 The moon-track a-quiver bewilders our eyes. **1865** Swinburne *Atalanta* 41 Making sweet.. *moon-trodden ways And breathless gates and extreme hills of heaven. **1876** Morris *Sigurd* II. 137 The *moonwake over the waters. **1959** R. Graves *Coll. Poems* 316 A *moon-warmed world of discontinuance. **1902** W. D. Howells *Literature & Life* 62 A few *moon-washed stars pierce the vast vault with their keen points. **1967** *Coast to Coast 1965–66* 131 Vicky sat staring into the mysterious moon-washed night. **1885** W. B. Yeats *Island of Statues* I. ii, in *Dublin Univ. Rev.* May 82/2 Some say that all who touch the island lone Are changed for ever into *moon-white stone. **1916** Blunden *Harbingers* 5 Through the moonwhite sea. **1957** C. Day Lewis *Pegasus* 12 O moon-white brow and milky way of flesh! *a***1963** S. Plath *Crossing Water* (1971) 38 The moth-face of her husband, moonwhite and ill, Circles her like a prey. **1892** Ld. Lytton *King Poppy* vii. 187 Their *moon-whiten'd wings. **1961** R. Graves *More Poems* 29 And in my dreams went chasing here and there A fugitive beacon—your *moon-yellow hair.

16. Special combinations: **moon-blink** (see quot.); **moon-blow**, injury to the body produced by the moon's rays; **moon-born** *ppl. a.*, (*a*) born under the moon's influence; (*b*) born in the moon; **moon-bounce**, the use of the moon as a reflector of radio waves (chiefly in the UHF band) aimed at it from one ground station and detected by another; **moonbound** *a.* (orig. *U.S.*), directed or moving towards the moon; **moon-bow**, a lunar rainbow; **moon-box**, a device for exhibiting the moon on the stage of a theatre (*Cent. Dict.*); **moonbug** *colloq.*, a lunar module; **moon buggy** = *moon-car*; †**moon-burnt** *ppl. a.*, moonstruck; **moon-cake**, a round Chinese cake eaten during mid-Autumn festivities; **moon-car**, a vehicle designed for use on the moon; **moon-clock**, a clock showing the changes and phases of the moon; †**moon-clover** = *moon-trefoil*; **mooncraft**, a spacecraft for travel to the moon; also = *moon-car*; **moon crawler** = *moon-car*; **moon-creeper** = MOON-FLOWER 2 (*Cent. Dict.*); **moon-culminating** *ppl. a.*, applied to such stars (used in calculating longitude) as culminate with the moon and are near its parallel of declination; so **moon-culmination**, the culmination of certain stars with the moon (*Cent. Dict.*); **moon-culminator**, a moon-culminating star; **moon-cutter**, one who cuts gas globes (see sense 5); **moon-daisy**, the ox-eye daisy, *Chrysanthemum Leucanthemum*; **moon-dog**, a dog that bays the moon; †in early use = MOONER 1; **moon-down** *N. Amer.*, the time when the moon goes down or sets; †**moon-drake** (fancifully modelled on FIRE-DRAKE), a fiery moon; **moon-face**, a moon-shaped face; *spec.* a rounded swollen face characteristic of individuals with excessive amounts of glucocorticoids in the body, e.g. in cases of Cushing's syndrome; †**moon-flaw**, a defect attributed to the moon's influence; **moon-flight**, a flight to the moon; **moon-glade** *U.S.*, the track made by moonlight on water; **moonglow**, glowing moonlight; **moon-god**, the god of the moon; a deity associated with the moon; so **moon-goddess**; **moon-knife**, a crescent-shaped knife used by leather-workers; **moon-lily** = MOON-FLOWER 2; **moon-madness**, lunacy (cf. sense 1 c); **moonmark** (see quots.); **moon milk** = *milk of the moon* (see MILK *sb.* 6); **moon-month**, a lunar month (Ogilvie 1882); **moon-penny**, *Chrysanthemum Leucanthemum* (Treas. Bot. 1866); **moon-plant**, the plant SOMA; **moonport** [after AIRPORT], (*a*) a place from which rockets are launched to the moon; (*b*) a landing-place for rockets on the moon; **moon probe** *Astronautics*, an exploratory space flight made towards the moon by an unmanned vehicle; also, the vehicle itself; **moon-proof** *a.*, proof against the moon's light or influence; **moon race**, competition between nations to be the first to effect a landing on the moon; **moon-rainbow**, a lunar rainbow; **moon-rocket**, (*a*) a ride at a fun-fair consisting of rocket-shaped cars travelling round an inclined circular track; (*b*) a rocket designed for flight to the moon; **moon-sail, -sheered** *ppl. a.* (see quots.); **moon-shaft**, a ray of moonlight; **moon-ship**, a spaceship designed to travel to or towards the moon; **moon-shoot** = *moon-shot* sb.; **moon-shooter** *slang*, one who makes a 'moonlight flit'; **moon-shot** (orig. *U.S.*), the launching of a spacecraft to or towards the moon; **moon-shot** *ppl. a.*, accompanied by fitful moonlight; **moon-slave** *poet.*, applied to the tide as dependent upon the moon; **moon-sted** *ppl. a.*, ? occupied by the moon; **moon-suit**, a suit designed to be worn on the moon; **moon-trefoil**, *Medicago arborea*; **moon-walk**, the action of walking on the moon; so as *v. intr.*, to walk on the moon; **moonwalker**, one who walks on the moon (see also quot. 1950); **moon-walking** *vbl. sb.*; **moon-wise** *a.*, learned in the moon's movements, etc.; †**moon-wiser**, an instrument for finding the position of the moon; †**moon-work** (see quot.); **moon-year** [cf. G. *mondjahr*], a lunar year (Webster 1864).

1867 Smyth *Sailor's Word-bk.*, *Moon-blink, a temporary evening blindness occasioned by sleeping in the moonshine in tropical climates. **1851** R. F. Burton *Scinde* I. ii. 12 It took his countenance a year or two to recover from the effects of the *moonblow. **1691** Dryden *K. Arthur* II. i, A *moon-born elf. **1857** W. Smith *Thorndale* IV. ii, There would be no end to the astonishment of your moon-born traveller. **1892** Ld. Lytton *King Poppy* vii. 69 The moon-born music of the nightingale. **1960** *Aeroplane* XCVIII. 320/1 The *Moon-bounce technique was a form of long-distance radio communication which could be carried out on wavelengths which were not susceptible to ionospheric or other terrestrial disturbances. **1968** *Radio Communication Handbk.* (ed. 4) xii. 20/2 Typical ground station equipment for moonbounce requires a transmitter output power exceeding 100 watts, net aerial gains of the order of 15–20 db, and receivers of 500 c/s bandwidth. **1975** *Nature* 4 Sept. 36/1 On July 7, 1974 while using a Moon Bounce technique on 1,296 MHz I observed the appearance of strange, delayed echoes. **1965** *NASA Facts* III. I. 4 The *moonbound Apollo's space navigation system includes two relatively conventional units. **1968** *Guardian* 23 Dec. 1 The world last night saw.. life on board the moonbound capsule. **1871** G. Macdonald *Ode to Light* in *Organ Songs*, All the colours.. In rainbow, *moon-bow, or in opal gem. **1963** *Britannica Bk. of Year* (U.S.) 856/1 *Moon bug, the LEM [*i.e.* lunar excursion module]. **1969** *Daily Tel.* (Colour Suppl.) 10 Jan. 21 (*caption*) Parent spacecraft (command and service modules) separates leaving lunar module ('moonbug') attached to rocket stage. **1971** *Guardian* 23 July 11 The astronauts will have a powered *moon buggy called Rover. *c***1560** A. Scott *Poems* (S.T.S.) iv. 65 Sum *monebrunt madynis myld, At nonetyd of the nicht, Ar chappit vp with chyld. **1938** Chiang Yee *Silent Traveller in London* 38 At this time [*sc.* mid-September] all the sweet-shops produce a great variety of seasonable cakes, which we call '*Moon-Cake', and those especially which are made in Canton in South China are very famous. **1952** D. Yen Hung Feng *Joy Chinese Cooking* xii. 211 Moon cakes are seldom made at home, for the genuine type are difficult to make and require a long list of hard-to-prepare ingredients as well as special wooden forms and cooking implements. **1966** 'Han Suyin' *Mortal Flower* viii. 174 In all the markets, the mooncakes.. parade their roundness in all the foodshops, light, feathery, moon-white. **1971** *Nat. Geographic* Oct. 556 (*caption*) Golden yolks,.. salted and dried in the sun.. are steamed with rice or cooked in Cantonese moon cakes, served at festival time. **1965** *Sci. World* 28 Oct. 8 Would a sticky coating of dust block the window of an astronaut's '*moon car'? **1973** *Daily Tel.* 13 Mar. 19/4 The Lunokhod 2 robot mooncar has.. resumed studies of Moon soil and rock and taking photographs. **1800** *Gentl. Mag.* 1226/2 Under the West tower is a *moon-clock. **1713** J. Petiver in *Phil. Trans.* XXVIII. 47 Camerarius his *Moon Claver. **1962** F. I. Ordway et al. *Basic Astronautics* v. 216 Evidence derived from stationary and mobile *mooncraft will doubtless support the belief that any manned bases or outposts on the Moon will have to be underground. **1963** *Times* 31 May 19/7 Two gigantic crawler transport vehicles for use in the Apollo mooncraft launching. **1971** *Daily Tel.* 3 Aug. 1/6 Falcon, the Apollo 15 mooncraft, blasted off yesterday from the lunar surface. **1970** *Guardian* 18 Nov. 1/2 Russia is likely to try to bring its *moon crawler Lunokod-I back to earth. **1827** *Philos. Mag.* I. 47 A List of *Moon-culminating Stars for 1827. **1867** Smyth *Sailor's Word-bk.*, *Moon-culminators, certain stars near the same parallel of declination as the moon [etc.]. **1883** *B'ham Daily Post* 11 Oct., Flint-glass Trade.—*Moon Cutter wanted. **1855** Miss Pratt *Flower. Pl.* (1861) III. 311 Ox-eye or *Moon Daisy. *a***1887** Jefferies *Toilers of Field* (1892) 310 The broad moon-daisies stand in the grass. **1668** Evelyn *Corr.* 24 June, Let the *Moon-dogs bark on, 'till their throats are drie. **1688** R. Holme *Armoury* II. 184/1 The Mooner, or Moon-Dog which continually is Barking at the Moon. **1832** J. Bree *St. Herbert's Isle* 163 'Tween the screech of the owl and the moon dog's moan. **1797** B. Hawkins *Let.* 23 Dec. in *Georgia Hist. Soc. Coll.* (1916) IX. 276 Last evening, just before *moon down, his camp had been fired on. **1863** W. B. Cheadle *Jrnl. Trip across Canada* (1931) 125 Camp at moondown in wood close to our lake. **1938** C. H. Matschat *Suwanee River* 68 Five hours till moondown. *a***1635** Corbet *A non sequitur* Poems (1807) 218 See where a *moon-drake 'gins to rise. **1855** Thackeray *Newcomes* liii, He.. surveyed the beauties of his time as the Caliph the *moonfaces of his harem. **1944** J. Hoffman *Female Endocrinology* xxxv. 574 The facial adiposity may materially alter the normal features and is responsible for the 'moon face' and 'pig-eyed' expression of the classical case. **1958** *Spectator* 11 July 60/3 Swelling of the face—'moon-face' after cortisone. **1959** J. Fleming *Miss Bones* xii. 136 Her large moon-face remained quite expressionless. *a***1652** Brome *Queen & Conc.* IV. vii, I fear she has a *Moonflaw in her brains. **1963** *Daily Tel.* 28 Oct. 12 The Soviet Union, he says, is planning no manned *moon-flights. **1975** S. Johnson *Urbane Guerilla* v. 182 The famous moonflight of Apollo 11. **1866** Lowell *Biglow P.* Ser. II. Introd., *Moonglade: a beautiful word: for the track of moonlight on the water. **1893** *Westm. Gaz.* 8 Nov. 3/1 The gondolas and launches pass like dark shadows in a moon-glade. **1926** *Blackw. Mag.* Oct. 530/2 She could no longer see the moving shape presently lost among the vague masses of *moonglow and darkling shadow which veiled the moor. **1934** W. Hudson et al. (*song-title*) Moonglow. **1965** M. West *Ambassador* viii. 181, I.. woke.. to a room full of moonglow. **1862** Rawlinson *Anc. Mon., Chald.* viii. I. 200 The temple at Mugheir was built in honour of the *moon-god, Sin or Hurki. **1831** Keightley *Myth. Gr. & It.* 194 From their confounding her with their own Artemis, it would seem that they regarded her as the *moon-goddess. **1882** J. Paton in *Encycl. Brit.* XIV. 389/2 The dyed leather is.. grounded with a curious *moon knife. **1888** Clark Russell *Death Ship* III. 129 The *moon-lily when it hangs down its white beauty and contracts its milky petals. **1817** Shelley *Rev. Islam* VI. xvii. 2 Want, and *Moon-madness, and the pest's swift Bane. **1879** G. M. Hopkins *Poems* (1967) 80 Only I'll Have an eye to the sakes of him, quaint *moonmarks, to his pelted plumage under Wings. **1879** —— *Lett. to R. Bridges* (1955) 83 By *moonmarks* I mean crescent shaped markings on the quill-feathers, either in the colouring of the feather or made by the overlapping of one on another. **1885** *Encycl. Dict.*, *Moon-milk. **1965** *New Scientist* 3 June 666/2 These crystals form a colloid in water to give the substance that, in British caves, is called moonmilk. **1973** P. O'Donnell *Silver Mistress* ix. 161 They reached a huge stalactite chamber. Around the perimeter shimmered white patches of the calcite deposit called moonmilk. **1866** Lindley & Moore *Treas. Bot.* II. 754/1 *Moon-penny. *Chrysanthemum leucanthemum.* **1940** F. Kitchen *Brother to Ox* ix. 152 The grass-reaper.. cuts through life, sweeping down the slender moon-pennies and toppling them over. *a***1843** Southey *Comm.-pl. Bk.* IV. 634 A seller of *moonplant. **1862** R. H. Patterson *Ess. Hist. & Art* 475 The soma or moon-plant is a round smooth twining plant, peculiar to the Aravalli Hills [etc.]. **1963** *New Scientist* 18 Apr. 138/3 NASA has acquired 87,000 acres just

north of Cape Canaveral, Florida, as the site for its '*Moonport'. **1965** *New Statesman* 16 July 74/1 To have two Moonports is extravagance enough. **1967** *Britannica Bk. of Year* (U.S.) 803/3 *Moonport*, a place on the surface of the earth equipped for sending spacecraft to the moon. **1958** *Oxford Mail* 16 Aug. 1/8 Engineers are making final checks on the multiple rocket which is expected to be launched tomorrow on America's first '*Moon probe'. **1972** *Guardian* 22 Feb. 2/4 The unmanned Soviet moon probe Luna 20 made a soft landing on the moon's surface last night. **1616** B. JONSON *Masque of Oberon* Wks. 979 Be your eyes, yet *Moone-proofe? **1817** SHELLEY *Rev. Islam* VI. xxvii. 9 A hanging dome of leaves, a canopy moon-proof. **1835** J. P. KENNEDY *Horse Shoe R.* vi, Your thick skull is moon-proof. **1963** *Guardian* 17 July 1/5 It is now intended to have the whole question of the '*moon race' brought up in the International Astronomical Union. **1971** S. CAVELL *World Viewed* 63 We lash ourselves to these ideas with burning coils of containment, massive retaliation, moon races, yellow perils. **1850** BROWNING *Christmas Eve* VI. 11 'Twas a *moon-rainbow, vast and perfect. **1946** G. TYRWHITT-DRAKE *English Circus & Fair Ground* xvii. 202 There were many..rides, such as Airways, Autodrome Aeroplanes, and *Moon Rocket. **1953** POHL & KORNBLUTH *Space Merchants* (1955) i. 5 The slim V-2s and stubby Moon rockets of the past. **1954** 'R. CROMPTON' *William & Moon Rocket* i. 20 A fair ain't a fair these days without a Moon Rocket. **1841** R. H. DANA *Seaman's Man.* 116 **Moon-sail*, a small sail sometimes carried in light winds, above a skysail. **1896** E. PHILLPOTTS *Down Dartmoor Way* 201 They turned intu the black wudes all laced wi' *mune-shafts. **1930** E. POUND *XXX Cantos* xxi. 98 Yellow wing, pale in the moon shaft. **1867** SMYTH *Sailor's Word-bk.*, **Moon-sheered*, a ship the upper works of which rise very high, fore and aft. **1949** *Moonship [see GRAVITY 5]. **1963** *Wall St. Jrnl.* 19 Aug. 20 North American Aviation awarded $934.4 million job... Order is for Apollo Moonship. **1970** *Universe* 30 Jan. 9/5 The horror of some future manned moonship being marooned in space is something we don't like to think about. **1958** *Oxford Mail* 14 Aug. 1/9 The United States first '*moon-shoot' has about a one-in-ten chance of success. **1892** *Globe* 2 Apr. 1/5 The *moon-shooters sometimes have lodgers in their abodes. **1958** *Washington Post* 18 Aug. A. 8/4 Yesterday's *moon shot blew up 50,000 feet and 77 seconds after the launching at Cape Canaveral. **1969** *New Scientist* 9 Jan. 56/3 Much heartened by the success of the three-man Moon shot, the National Aeronautics and Space Administration is unveiling ambitious plans for the mid-1970s. **1971** R. NESBITT *Evolution & Existence of God* 10 If the Universe were in fact a chaos, Apollo moonshots would be inconceivable. **1902** *Contemp. Rev.* Dec. 842 The gusty *moon-shot night. **1839** BAILEY *Festus* viii. (1852) 93 Where tide, the *moonslave, sleeps. **1591** *Troub. Raigne K. John* II. (1611) 75 Could I..Remoue the Sunne from our Meridian, Vnto the *moonested circle of th' antipodes. **1953** POHL & KORNBLUTH *Space Merchants* (1955) xii. 131 *Moon suits rented '50 Years Without a Blowout'. **1731** MILLER *Gard. Dict.*, *Medicago*; *Moon-Trefoil... It hath..a..Fruit, shap'd somewhat like a Half-Moon. **1966** WEBSTER Add., *Moonwalk, Moonwalker. **1969** *Daily Tel.* 16 July 22/2 While on the moon, the astronauts will..only moon-walk for about 3½ to four hours. **1969** *Observer* 20 July 1/2 Hints that the 'moonwalk' will also be brought forward were strengthened when the astronauts' physician, Dr Charles Berry, said that he did not now expect the two men to go to sleep on the moon. **1971** *New Scientist* 11 Feb. 286/2 Physical activity exacerbated this condition and contributed to the unusually high heart-rates seen on the moonwalk. **1973** J. WAINWRIGHT *Touch of Malice* 31 It was a little like a moon-walk. A slow deliberate progression from point 'A' to point 'B'. **1950** WEBSTER Add., *Moonwalking*, sleepwalking outdoors in bright moonlight.—**Moonwalker*. **1969** *Times* 3 June (Suppl.) p. iii/1 The two moon-walkers will be in the lunar module's upper, or ascent stage. **1966** *Punch* 31 Aug. 336/3 Machines with metal boots are being constructed for *moon-walking. **1582** STANYHURST *Æneis* III. (Arb.) 74 And *moonewise Coribants on brasse their od harmonie tinckling. **1674** FLAMSTEED in *Phil. Trans.* IX. 219, I fell to peruse Mr. Street's Discourse, and to consider the Contrivance of his *Moon-wiser. **1679** C. NESSE *Antichrist* 201 His work is Idolatry, a work of darkness, *moon or night-work.

Moon (mu:n), *sb.*² The name of Dr. William Moon (1818–94), of Brighton, used *attrib.*, *absol.*, or in the possessive to designate the embossed type which he invented to enable blind people to read.

1859 *3rd Rep. Soc. of Supplying Books in Moon's Type* 7 The plan of teaching the Blind..to read by Books embossed in Moon's type has been tested. **1859** M. FISON *Darkness & Light* 19 Moon's System of Embossed Books... Moon's Alphabet consists of the common letters simplified, and therefore is easily learnt... By Moon's method of Stereotyping, the letters are thrown up with such sharpness and prominence, as to be felt even by fingers become dull through age. **1910** *Encycl. Brit.* IV. 63/1 A society was instituted in 1847 by Dr. W. Moon for stereotyping and embossing the Scriptures and other books in 'Moon' type. **1959** *Listener* 14 May 868/3 Books in Braille and Moon. **1973** *Times* 28 Feb. (Victoria Centre, Nottingham, Suppl.) p. ii/1 (Advt.), [Blind people] may prefer to develop a particular handcraft as a hobby, or to concentrate on mobility, braille, Moon type reading, typing. **1973** *Times Lit. Suppl.* 7 Dec. 1511/4 (Advt.), Books in Braille and Moon that are specially prepared for the Blind of all ages.

moon (mu:n), *v.* [f. MOON *sb.*¹]

1. In various nonce-uses. **a.** *trans.* To expose to the rays of the moon; *refl.* to 'bask' in the moonlight (cf. SUN *v.*); to give *out* (a light) as a moon. **b.** *intr.* To shine as a moon; to move as a satellite.

1601 HOLLAND *Pliny* II. 96 If they would haue it [*sc.* wax] to be exceeding white indeed, they seeth it yet once more, after it hath bin thus sunned and mooned. *a* **1850** MRS. BROWNING *Night & Merry Man* i, Where be all thy laughters clear?.. Where thy festive companies, Mooned o'er with ladies' eyes? **1854** DE QUINCEY *Autobiog. Sk.* vi. Wks. II. 337 The huge man..not sunning, but mooning himself—apricating himself in the occasional moonbeams. **1871** G. MACDONALD *Wks. Fancy & Imag.* IV. *Parables, Love's Ordeal*, An earthen lamp whose faint light Mooned out a tiny halo. **1886** R. F. BURTON *Arab. Nts.* (abr. ed.) III. 99 White as a full moon when it mooneth on its fourteenth night. *a* **1903** H. S. MERRIMAN *Tommaso's Fortune*, etc. (1904) 64 The more curious of the President's guests, who were now mooning innocently around them as they sat.

c. *intr.* and *trans.* To expose one's buttocks to (someone). Cf. MOON *sb.*¹ 5 b. *slang.*

1968–70 *Current Slang* (Univ. S. Dakota) III–IV. 84 *Moon*,..to display one's bare buttocks as a taunt. **1974** *News & Reporter* (Chester, S. Carolina) 24 Apr. 3-A/1 The convention..was to last through Saturday afternoon, and we imagine that it did although we did hear a wild rumor that a cut-up named Fannie might pull her own version of 'the streak' during the Sunday breakfast..just to get the Sunday session off to a good start if the session started getting dull. But, Fannie has assured us that she didn't 'moon' anybody.

2. *intr.* To move or look listlessly or aimlessly (as if moonstruck); to go *about*, *along*, *around* (etc.) in a moonstruck or listless manner. *colloq.*

1848 ALB. SMITH *Idler upon Town* 46 A mooner is an individual who moons about without any object, half absent, half contemplative. **1861** HUGHES *Tom Brown at Oxf.* i, I mooned up and down the High-street, staring at all the young faces. **1867** MISS BRADDON *Run to Earth* I. ii. 40 'What are you standing mooning there for?' asked the man. 'Why don't you go to bed?' **1886** J. K. JEROME *Idle Thoughts* (1889) 44, I..did nothing whatever, except moon about the house and gardens.

b. *trans.* To pass *away* (the time) in an aimless or listless manner; also *occas.* to utter mooningly.

1836 T. HOOK *G. Gurney* III. 179, I 'mooned' out, that my sympathetic ignorance of the object of our dialogue had wounded her feelings. **1876** BESANT & RICE *Gold. Butterfly* xvi, I might have mooned away the afternoon in the Park. **1878** W. C. SMITH *Hilda among Broken Gods* (1879) 235 Why had I mooned away the night, when there was that to do Which still might heal our sorrow?

3. To hunt by moonlight.

1898 *Encycl. Sport* II. 64 All the excitement of the expedition may be said..to lie in this 'mooning'. If the dark object which the hunter fondly imagines to be an opossum lie higher than the line of the moon, he must perforce fix his eyes on it and walk steadily backwards until the moon is directly behind it... The beast can obviously be mooned from one spot only at any given moment.

moon, rare obs. f. MAN *sb.*¹; obs. f. MOAN.

moonack ('mu:næk). Also 7–8 **monack**, 8 **monax**, 9 **moonax**. [a. Lenape *monachgeu* (f. *monham* to dig); the mod.L. form is *monax*.] The ground-hog or woodchuck, *Arctomys monax*.

Among Blacks, the name is applied to a mythical animal supposed to have a baneful influence.

1676 T. GLOVER *Virginia* in *Phil. Trans.* XI. 630 There are also several sorts of ravenous Beasts, as Wolves, Racoons,..Monacks, Flying Squirrels. **1740** P. COLLINSON *Mem. Bartram* (1849) 140 A harmless land-animal, about the size of the large gray Fox-Squirrel, called a Monack. **1747** G. EDWARDS *Nat. Hist. Birds* II. 104 The Monax, or Marmotte, of America. **1814** LEWIS & CLARK *Trav. Missouri River* (1893) III. 966 We observed in our route no animals except..a moonax. **1872** SCHELE DE VERE *Americanisms* 152 The poor negro who meets it..is doomed... Experienced negroes say when they look at him: 'He gwine to die; he seed the moonack'.

moonaul, variant of MONAUL.

'moonbeam. A ray of moonlight. Also *fig.*

1590 SHAKS. *Mids. N.* III. i. 176 And plucke the wings from painted Butterflies, To fan the Moone-beames from his sleeping eies. **1626** BACON *Sylva* §113 As the Moone-Beames playing vpon a Waue. **1737** POPE *Hor. Sat.* II. vi. 189 Tell how the Moon-beam trembling falls, And tips with Silver all the walls. **1793** COLERIDGE *Imit. Ossian* 19 But I..shall..dwell, the Moon-beam of thy soul, In Slumber's nightly hour. **1817** WOLFE *Burial Sir J. Moore* ii, By the struggling moonbeams' misty light.

'moon-blind, *a.* [Cf. Du. *maanblind*, G. *mondblind*.]

1. Of horses: Suffering from 'moon-eye'; moon-eyed. Also used *sb.* as the name of the disease.

1668 *Phil. Trans.* III. 731, I had a very narrow escape from an excellent Horse which had that only defect, which they call Moon-blind. **1689** O. HEYWOOD *Diaries*, etc. (1885) IV. 134 [The mare] was a very likely beast, but proved moon-blind. *c* **1720** W. GIBSON in *Compl. Farmer* (1766) s.v. *Blind* Q 3/2 Most..foreign writers,..in treating the diseases of horses, have..reckoned the moon-blind symptoms as a peculiar disease of the eyes, without having any relation to a cataract. **1905** *Blackw. Mag.* Jan. 66/1 Another horse..which was..moonblind—that is to say, he was more blind at certain times than at others.

2. *fig.* Of intellect: Purblind. ? *Obs.*

1711 SHAFTESB. *Charac.* (1737) III. 211 We have to deal with a sort of moon-blind wits, who..may be said to renounce day-light, and extinguish..the bright visible outward world. **1738** WARBURTON *Div. Legat.* I. 39 The Professors of them [*sc.* metaphysics and logic] are Moon-blind Wits. **1757** —— *Let. to Hurd* 8 June (1809) 244 In full ..confidence of the publick's being more than moon-blind, you gave them a key to the secret.

3. Suffering from blindness brought on by sleeping exposed to the moon's rays. Also used as *sb.* (see quot. 1877).

1830 MARRYAT *King's Own* xxii, It would be as well..to request the officer of the watch not to permit the men to sleep on the upper deck. We shall have many of them moon-blind. **1846** MRS. R. LEE *Afr. Wanderers* xviii. (1854) 314 Soldiers who have been moon-blind for life. **1877** R. I. DODGE *Plains Gt. West* v. 67 There is said to be [a] plains malady, which, however, I cannot vouch for. It is called 'moon-blind'. The idea is that the full rays of the moon affect the eyes of a man sleeping exposed to them, so that he cannot see at night.

Hence **'moon-blindness.**

c **1720** W. GIBSON in *Compl. Farmer* (1766) s.v. *Blind* Q 4/1 Another kind of moon-blindness, which is also the fore-runners of cataracts. **1857** LIVINGSTONE *Trav.* vi. 133 You may sleep out at night, looking up to the moon till you fall asleep, without a thought or sign of moon-blindness. **1894** HAYES *Among Men & Horses* i. (ed. 2) 9.

'moon-calf. [Cf. G. *mondkalb* (Luther); also *mondkind*, MLG. *maanenkind* (*kind* = child).]

†**1. a.** An abortive shapeless fleshy mass in the womb; a false conception. *Obs.*

Regarded as being produced by the influence of the moon.

1565 COOPER *Thesaurus*, *Mola*,..a moone calfe (in the womans woumbe). **1594** T. B. *La Primaud. Fr. Acad.* II. 387 The moone calfes in the womb, which fall out often. **1615** CROOKE *Body of Man* 193 The signes of the Mola or Moon-calfe. **1658** tr. *Porta's Nat. Magic* II. ii. 29 A certain woman ..brought forth in stead of a child, four Creatures like to frogs... But this was a kind of a Moon-calf.

fig. **1623** *Poems on Aff. State* (1703) II. 106 And then Democracy's Production shall A Moon-calf be. **1644** *Prerogative Anatomized* 12 The Parliament is in labour of a Moon-Calfe.

b. A misshapen birth, a monstrosity. *Obs.* or *arch.*

1610 SHAKS. *Temp.* II. ii. 139 How now Moone-Calfe. **1831** CARLYLE *Sart. Res.* III. x. (1858) 168 England..offers precisely the elements..in which such moon-calves and monstrosities are best generated. **1837** —— *Fr. Rev.* (1872) III. I. vii. 41 This huge mooncalf of Sansculottism.

c. One born with undeveloped brain; a congenital idiot; a born fool.

[**1620** B. JONSON *News fr. New World*, *Pr*... Moone Calves! what Monster is that..? 2 *Her*. Monster? none at all; a very familiar thing, like our foole here on earth] **1627** DRAYTON (*title*) The Moone-Calfe. *Stultorum plena sunt omnia.* **1693** DRYDEN *Juvenal* vi. (1697) 158 The Potion..turns his Brain, and stupifies his Mind. The sotted Moon-Calf gapes. **1765** BEATTIE *To Churchill* 4 Fame,..What half-made moon-calf can mistake for good? **1818** SCOTT *Hrt. Midl.* xxx, If he is as you say, d'ye think he'll ever marry a moon-calf like Madge? **1886** STEVENSON *Kidnapped* v, 'No', said the poor moon-calf, changing his tune at once.

2. In allusive or misapprehended senses.

a. One who gazes at the moon; a 'mooning', absent-minded person. (Cf. CALF¹ 1 c.)

c **1613** MIDDLETON *No Wit like Woman's* I. i. 112 One Weatherwise,..Observes the full and change, an arrant moon-calf. **1826** DISRAELI *Viv. Grey* III. vi, I have been playing, I fear, the mooncalf tonight; and find that, though I am a late watcher, I am not a solitary one. **1840** DICKENS *Barn. Rudge* vi, Instead of standing gaping at her, like an old mooncalf as I am.

†**b.** A child of the moon; a fickle, unstable person. *Obs. rare.*

1607 CHAPMAN *Bussy d' Ambois* IV, Women..Are the most perfect images of the Moone (Or still-vnweand sweet Moon-calues with white faces). **1647** TRAPP *Comm. Acts* xxii. 19, I shall be counted a Moon-calf; a *Retraxit* shall be entred against me. **1656** —— *1 Tim.* iii. 8 Ministers must neither be Sea-calves, nor Moon-calves; double-tongued, nor unstable, or double-minded.

3. An animal imagined to inhabit the moon.

1901 H. G. WELLS *First Men in Moon* xi. 116 We saw..the mooncalf's shining sides... First of all impressions was its enormous size; the girth of its body was some fourscore feet, its length perhaps two hundred. *Ibid.* 120 We came upon another drove of mooncalves bellowing up a ravine. **1955** *Times* 11 Aug. 7/4 It will be nice if, when we make our landfall on the moon, we find the mooncalves prodding their craters with a noiseless drill.

'moon-curser. †**a.** *Old Cant.* (See quot. 1673.) **b.** *dial.* A wrecker.

1673 R. HEAD *Canting Acad.* 101 The Moon Curser is generally taken for any Link-Boy; but particularly he is one that waits at some Corner of Lincolns-Inn-Fields with a Link in his hand, who under the pretence of Lighting you over the Fields..shal light you into a Pack of Rogues. **17..** in J. Ashton *18th Cent. Waifs* (1887) 234 One Volly Vance, otherwise call'd Glym Jack from his having been a Moon Curser, or Link Boy. **1770** C. BIDDLE *Autobiog.* (1883) 51 A ship from Jamaica..the crew of which had left her, and gone to Providence in what was called one of the Mooncursers or wreckers. **1813** R. B. THOMAS *Farmer's Almanack* (Boston, U.S.) Dec., All the village moon-cursers came in for their portion of the wreck.

'moon-dial. A dial for showing the hours of the night by the moon.

1686 GOAD *Celest. Bodies* I. vi. 17 Some pretious Stones are Natural Moon-dials; the Selenite [etc.]. **1727–52** CHAMBERS *Cycl.* s.v. *Dial*. *a* **1849** POE *Fairyland* 11 About twelve by the moon-dial. **1877** *Encycl. Brit.* VII. 154 *note*, In one of the Courts of Queens' College, Cambridge, there is an elaborate sun-dial..and around it a series of numbers which make it available as a moon-dial when the moon's age is known.

moondoggle ('mu:ndɒg(ə)l). *slang* (chiefly *U.S.*). [Blend of MOON *sb.*¹ and BOONDOGGLE *sb.*] Lunar exploration regarded as a 'boondoggle' (see BOONDOGGLE *sb.* b). Hence **'moondoggling** *vbl. sb.*

1962 *Economist* 1 Sept. 780/1 The.. taunts of 'moondoggle'..when Mr Kennedy first outlined his plans for exploring the moon. **1963** *Punch* 1 May 620/2 The vast expense of the crash programme to put a man on the moon

is.. open to the charge of being.. economic moondoggling. **1967** *Britannica Bk. of Year* (U.S.) 803/2 *Moondoggle*, useless exploration of the moon that is wasteful of time and money.

moone, obs. form of MOAN, MOON.

mooned (muːnd, *poet.* 'muːnɪd), *ppl. a.* [f. MOON *sb.*[1] or *v.* + -ED.]

†**1.** Lunatic. *Obs. rare*$^{-1}$.

c **1550** CHEKE *Matt.* iv. 24 Al yᵗ weer.. other sprited, or moond, or palseid.

2. a. Shaped like the (crescent) moon; crescent-shaped. **b.** Ornamented with moons or crescents; having moon-shaped markings.

1607 DEKKER *Whore of Babylon* Wks. 1873 II. 258 Goe; cut the salt fome with your mooned keeles. *a* **1618** SYLVESTER *Mirac. Peace* Sonn. xxxviii, The Mahomite.. in Vienna plaine His mooned Standards hath already pight. **1630** DRAYTON *Noah's Flood* 381 When with his mooned traine The strutting Peacock.. Flutters into the Arke. **1667** MILTON *P.L.* IV. 978 Th' Angelic Squadron.. sharpning in mooned hornes Thir Phalanx. **1776** MICKLE tr. *Camoens' Lusiad* I. (1778) 20 Their bowsprits pointing to the shore, (A safe moon'd bay). **1817** SHELLEY *Rev. Islam* XII. xiii. 6 The brazen rein she flung Upon his neck, and kissed his mooned brow. **1868** TEGETMEIER *Pigeons* xxi. 174 The Swiss and Mooned pigeons have a crescent-shaped coloured mark on the breast. **1885–94** R. BRIDGES *Eros & Psyche* Nov. v, 'Twas then he wrought this work.. Emboss'd with rich design, a moonèd car.

3. †**a.** *mooned man* = MAN-IN-THE-MOON. *Obs.* **b.** Accompanied or attended by the moon, or moonlight. Also applied to a moon-goddess.

1605 DRAYTON *Man in the Moon* ad fin., And oftentimes the Mooned man outspies the Eauedropper. **1629** MILTON *Hymn Nativ.* xxii, Mooned Ashtaroth, Heav'ns Queen and Mother both. *c* **1825** BEDDOES *Apotheosis* Poems (1851) 96 Be pale, thou mooned midnight!

4. Moonlit. *rare.*

1831 LYTTON *Milton* I. ii, Dreams he of nymph half hid in sparry cave, Or Naiad rising from her mooned wave?

mooner ('muːnə(r)). [f. MOON *sb.*[1] or *v.* + -ER[1]. In first sense rendering mod.L. *lūnārius.*]

†**1.** A kind of watch-dog (see quots.). *Obs.*

1576 FLEMING tr. *Caius' Dogs* 29 This kinde of dogge is likewise called.. the Mooner: Because he doth nothing else but watch and warde.. bawing and wawing at the Moone. **1589** L. WRIGHT *Hunting of Antichrist* 16 The dogge called Lunarius, the Mooner, whose nature is continually to barke at the Moone-shine in the water. **1688** R. HOLME *Armoury* II. 184/1.

2. One who moons about.

1848 [see MOON *v.* 3]. **1866** SALA *From Waterloo to Peninsula* II. 102 A 'Mooner' is an idle, listless, friendlessly inquisitive person, of street-wandering habits. **1884** *Punch* 5 July 1/1 The ancient grey Bridge is delightful to moon on, For ne'er such a spot for the mooner was made.

3. One who moons (sense 1 c).

1974 [see MOONING *vbl. sb.* 3].

moonery ('muːnərɪ). [f. MOON *v.* + -ERY.] = MOONING *vbl. sb.* 1.

a **1834** COLERIDGE in *Blackw. Mag.* CXXXI. 119/2 The most fantastic yet maudlin moonery.

moonest: see MONISH *v.*

†'**moonet.** *Obs. rare*$^{-1}$. [f. MOON *sb.*[1] + -ET[1].] A small moon, satellite.

1642 BP. HALL *Free Prisoner* ii. Three Tract. (1646) 112 Some lesser Planets moving round about the Sun, and the Moonets about Saturn and Jupiter.

'**moon-eye.** [f. MOON *sb.*[1] + EYE *sb.*; in sense 1 transl. of L. *oculus lunaticus* (Vegetius).]

1. *Farriery.* (Usually *pl.*) An eye affected with intermittent blindness (attributed to the moon's influence); also, the disease itself, moon-blindness.

1607 TOPSELL *Four-f. Beasts* (1658) 280 Of Lunatick or Moon-eyes. **1639** T. DE GRAY *Compl. Horsem.* 6 Be you.. marvellous carefull that neither your stallion or mare have.. moon-eyes, watry eyes, or bloud-shotten eyes. **1748** tr. *Vegetius' Distemp. Horses* 152 There is another Distemper.. the Ancients called it a Moon-eye.

2. a. A North American fish, *Hyodon tergisus*. **b.** The cisco, *Coregonus hoyi*.

1845 STORER *Synopsis Fishes N. Amer.* in *Mem. Amer. Acad.* II. 462 Hyodon tergisus.. Called 'Moon-eye', 'Shiner', 'Lake Herring' at Buffalo. **1884** G. B. GOODE *Nat. Hist. Aquatic Anim.* 541 The Moon-eye or Cisco.

'**moon-eyed,** *ppl. a.* [f. MOON-EYE + -ED[2]. Cf. G. *mondäugig*.]

1. a. *Farriery.* Affected with the disease of 'moon-eyes'; moon-blind.

1610 MARKHAM *Masterp.* II. xii. 239, I haue seene many a slothfull and heauy horse brought to be moone eyed by the folly of his rider. **1792** A. YOUNG *Trav. France* 75 The English mare that carries me.. is going rapidly blind. She is moon-eyed. **1821** *Sporting Mag.* VIII. 202 George Parker on his examination found that she was 'moon-eyed'. **1889** 'C. E. CRADDOCK' *Despot of Broomsedge Cove* vi. 105 Do ye know ennything 'bout'n a horse's eyes? I be sort'n 'feard he's moon-eyed, or suthin'. **1905** A. ADAMS *Outlet* 21 Tolleston took the only blind horse in the herd... At the time of his purchase, no one could see anything in the eyeball which would indicate he was moon-eyed.

b. Purblind; squint-eyed. *Obs.* exc. *dial.*

1688 DRYDEN *Brit. Red.* 94 So manifest, that even the moon-eyed sects See whom and what this Providence protects. **1736** AINSWORTH *Lat. Dict.*, Moon eyed, *lusciosus, luscitiosus.* **1785** GROSE *Dict. Vulg. T.*, *Moon-eyed hen*, a squinting wench. **1886** R. E. G. COLE *Gloss. Words S.-W. Lincs.* 93 Old Jane, his first wife, was moon-eyed. When folks are moon-eyed, they have to gleg at you (look askance) out of the corner of the eye. **1912** *Dialect Notes* III. 583 *Moon-eyed*, half-blind.

†**2.** Having eyes adapted for seeing at night. *Obs.*

1699 WAFER in *Phil. Trans.* LV. 51 From their seeing so clear as they do in a moon-shiny night, we used to call them moon-eyed. **1706** PHILLIPS (ed. 6), *Moon-eyed* or *Owl-eyed*, that can see better at Night, than by Day. **1796** *New Ann. Reg.* 166 Or whether blinded by the solar glare, The moon-ey'd Indian.. to balsam groves repair. **1817** G. FIELD *Chromatics* (1845) §335. 165 That kind of nyctalophia [*sic*] called moon-eyed, which is common to the Bushmen of Southern Africa, who sleep out the day, and are blind when the sun shines, but.. see well in seeming darkness.

3. Having round, wide-open eyes, as a terrified person.

1790 WOLCOT (P. Pindar) *Compl. Ep. to J. Bruce* Wks. 1812 II. 358 Moon-eyed Wonder opes her lap to thee. **1799** CAMPBELL *Pleas. Hope* II. 265 Fly, like the moon-ey'd herald of Dismay, Chased on his night-steed by the star of day.

4. Drunk; intoxicated. *U.S. slang.*

1737 *Pennsylvania Gaz.* 6–13 Jan. 2/1 He sees two Moons, Merry, Middling, Moon-Ey'd, Muddled, [etc.]. **1940** *Amer. Speech* XV. 447/2 Sid gits moon-eyed every Saturday night.

'**moon-fern.** [Cf. G. *mondfarn.*] = MOON-WORT 1.

1671 in SKINNER *Etymol. Ling. Angl., Bot.* **1813** HOGG *Queen's Wake* I. iii. (1814) 68 We saddled ouir naigis wi' the moon-fern leif, And rode fra Kilmerrin kirk. **1840** BROWNING *Sordello* III. 2 Braid moonfern now with mystic trifoly.

'**moon-fish.** A name used for several pale-coloured marine fishes having thin, moon-shaped bodies, esp. the OPAH, *Lampris guttatus*, a sunfish, *Mola mola*, or a North American fish of the genera *Selene* or *Vomer*.

1646 SIR T. BROWNE *Pseud. Ep.* III. xxiv. 169 The Moone fish, or Orthragoriscus. **1681** GREW *Musæum* I. 102 Moon-fish, *Mola Salviani Luna*; Because the Tail-fin is shaped like a Half-Moon. **1810** *Nat. Hist.* in *Ann. Reg.* 631/2 The moon-fish (tetraodon mola). **1845** STORER *Synopsis Fishes N. Amer.* in *Mem. Amer. Acad.* II. 339 Ephippus gigas, Parkinson... Called 'Moon-fish' in the Antilles. **1873** [see ANGEL-FISH]. **1878** *Proc. U.S. Nat. Museum* I. 376 *Argyriosus vomer.*—Moon-fish. *Ibid.*, *Selena argentea.*—Moon-fish... Not common. *Ibid.*, *Vomer setipinnis.*—Moon-fish; Sun-fish. **1883** GOODE *Fish. Indust. U.S.* 17 (Fish. Exhib. Publ.) Moon-fish *Chætodipterus faber.* **1884** —— *Nat. Hist. Aquatic Anim.* 322 *Selene setipinnis*.. known .. in North Carolina as the 'Moonfish' or 'Sunfish'. *Ibid.* 323 The Silver Moonfish—*Selene argentea.* **1896** JORDAN & EVERMANN *Check-List Fishes N. & Mid. Amer.* 350 *Lampris luna*... Mariposa; Opah;.. Gudlax; Moonfish. **1959** A. HARDY *Fish & Fisheries* II. iv. 75 Another wanderer from warmer waters, coming right into the North Sea and occasionally being taken off the Yorkshire coast, is the most brilliantly coloured of all our fishes, the opah or moon-fish, *Lampris guttatus* (which has in turn also been called the sun-fish). **1963** P. H. GREENWOOD *Norman's Hist. Fishes* (ed. 2) xviii. 329 The order [*sc.* Lampridiformes] includes the large oceanic Opah or Moon-fish (*Lampris*). **1965** A. J. MCCLANE *Standard Fishing Encycl.* 499/1 The moonfish (*Vomer*) have a head profile that is only moderately high. *Ibid.* 499/2 Both the lookdowns and the moonfish grow to about 10–12 inches.

'**moon-flower.**

1. The ox-eye daisy, *Chrysanthemum Leucanthemum*; also *C. segetum* (Treas. Bot.).

1787 WITHERING *Brit. Plants* (ed. 2) II. 929 Greater Daisy. Ox-eye. Moon-flower. **1861** DORA GREENWELL *Poems* 268 The Sun-flowers and the Moon-flowers.

2. A tropical climbing plant, *Ipomœa alba*, of the family Convolvulaceæ, which bears fragrant, white, trumpet-shaped flowers opening at night; also, other closely-related plants of the genera *Ipomœa* and *Quamoclit*.

1859 TENNENT *Ceylon* II. VII. iii. 162 One most interesting flower.. is a night-blowing convolvulus, the moon-flower of Europeans. **1887** MISS E. MONEY *Dutch Maiden* (1888) 23 The odorous moon-flower gave out a rich perfume. **1939** A. H. WOOD *Grow them Indoors* 102 Morning glory, moon flower, dawn flower—there are numerous common names for different members of this group of woody climbers. **1963** W. BLUNT *Of Flowers & Village* 110 My cobaeas and moonflowers have both already germinated. **1969** G. MACBETH *War Quartet* 28 Split tins.. Leafed into fronds of moon-flowers.

3. A name used in Africa for *Datura arborea* or *D. suaveolens*, shrubs native to Central America and belonging to the family Solanaceæ, bearing fragrant, white, trumpet-shaped flowers; also called moon-lily or angel's trumpet.

1913 C. PETTMAN *Africanderisms* 325 Moon lily or Moon flower, *Datura Knightii*, which has long, pendulous, strongly scented white flowers. **1973** PALMER & PITMAN *Trees S. Afr.* III. 1976 It [*sc.* the potato family] yields foods .. flowers.. shrubs—such as the moonflower, *Datura arborea* L., and *Cestrum* species.

moong: see MUNG, MOONG.

moonge, variant of MUNGE *dial.*

Moonie ('muːnɪ). *slang.* [f. the name of Sun Myung *Moon* (see *Unification Church* s.v. UNIFICATION 2) + -IE.] A nickname for a member of the Unification Church. Chiefly in *pl.*

1974 *Washington Monthly* Feb. 55/2 The Moonies.. are extremely media-conscious. **1976** *Fiji Times* 10 Jan. 12 Last year, two of their children left home to cast their lot in with 'the Moonies'. **1977** *Observer* 20 Feb. 6/4 Some of Mr Patrick's deconverted youngsters told the conference of life with Sun Myung's 'Moonies'. **1979** *N.Y. Rev. Bks.* 25 Oct. 8/3 Chris has been transferred to 'city work' and is a full-time Moonie. **1984** S. TOWNSEND *Growing Pains A. Mole* 75, I don't care if he's a Moonie or a Divine Light Missionary so long as he is far away from me.

†'**moonified,** *ppl. a. Obs. rare*$^{-1}$. [f. MOON *sb.*[1] + -IFY + -ED[1].] Shaped like a moon.

1795 *Jemima* I. 143 [A peacock's] moonified tail.

moonily ('muːnɪlɪ), *adv.* [f. MOONY *a.* + -LY[2].] **a.** ? Like a moon. **b.** In a mooning manner.

a **1849** BEDDOES *Song on Water* ii, So our sails in the bubbles Ghostily Are mirrored, and hover Moonily. **1887** *Punch* 10 Sept. 110 'Far worse!' he moonily muttered.

mooniness ('muːnɪnɪs). [f. MOONY *a.* + -NESS.] The quality or condition of being moony.

1895 G. MEREDITH *Amazing Marriage* I. xix. 216 Contact with her spirited him out of his mooniness. **1929** W. DEEPING *Roper's Row* xiv. 149 The other girls at Fogson and George's observed her 'mooniness'. **1929** A. HUXLEY *Do what you Will* 55 The human countenance.. of pallid mooniness.

'**mooning,** *vbl. sb.* [f. MOON *v.* + -ING[1].]

1. The action of the verb MOON; listless or aimless wandering about or contemplation.

1857 KINGSLEY *Two Y. Ago* i, John Briggs.. neglected alike work and amusement for lazy mooning over books. **1882** L. STEPHEN *Swift* ix. 195 The knight used, it seems, to lose himself in metaphysical moonings.

attrib. **1859** MEREDITH *R. Feverel* xii, Lady Blandish likewise hinted at his mooning propensities. **1862** SALA *Acc. Addresses* 214 It may have been on a mooning excursion.. when I had.. nothing to do.

2. Hunting by moonlight. (See MOON *v.* 3.)

3. The action of exposing one's buttocks (MOON *v.* 1 c).

1974 *Guardian* 22 Mar. 17/8 Streaking.. seems to be the mainly male equivalent of the mainly female practice that cropped up in campuses across the United States in the late fifties and early sixties. This was known as 'mooning'... Mooning consisted.. of exposing the bottom in the general direction of whoever the mooner wanted to impress, protest to, or affront.

'**mooning,** *ppl. a.* [-ING[2].] Listless, aimless. Hence '**mooningly** *adv.*

1893 MAX PEMBERTON *Iron Pirate* 177 Chinese mooningly silent. **1905** *Athenæum* 19 Aug. 232/2 The Celt of 'the Forty-five' was not a mooning misanthrope.

moonish ('muːnɪʃ), *a. Obs.* or *arch.* Also 5 **monyssh.** [f. MOON *sb.*[1] + -ISH.] Resembling or characteristic of the moon; influenced by the moon; acting as if under the moon's influence; changeable, fickle.

c **1407** LYDG. *Reson & Sens.* 6183 God forbade That ther sholde in womanhede Ben any Monyssh tache at al, But stedfaster than ys a wal. **1581** MULCASTER *Positions* xxxviii. (1887) 176 As for bodies the maidens be more weake, most commonly euen by nature, as of a moonish influence. **1600** SHAKS. *A.Y.L.* III. ii. 430 At which time would I, being but a moonish youth, greeue, be effeminate, changeable. **1612** WEBSTER *White Devil* K 3, These are but Moonish shades of greifes or feares. **1834** SIR H. TAYLOR *2nd Pt. Artevelde* IV. ii, 'Tis moonish madness.

'**moonite.** [f. as prec. + -ITE.] A dweller in the moon.

1762 STERNE *Tr. Shandy* V. xxxiii.

‖**moonjah, munjah** ('mundʒa, 'mʌndʒa). Also moon-, munja, moonyah. [Hindī *munj*, Skr. *munja.*] A name for certain Indian plants yielding fibres used for making ropes.

1855 ROYLE *Fibr. Plants India* 32. **1864** *Chamb. Encycl.* VI. 559/1 *Moonjah, Munjah*, or *Moonyah* (*Saccharum Munja*), a grass of the same genus as the sugar-cane. **1866** *Treas. Bot.*, *Moonyah*, an Indian name for the fibre of *Arundo Karka.* **1879** E. ARNOLD *Lt. Asia* v. 130 Its head bound back With munja grass.

moonke, -rie, obs. forms of MONK, MONKERY.

moonless ('muːnlɪs), *a.* [f. MOON *sb.*[1] + -LESS.] Without a moon; not lit up by the moon.

1508 DUNBAR *Flyting* 92 Eolus full woid, and Neptunus, Mirk and moneless. **1535** STEWART *Cron. Scot.* (Rolls) III. 53 But saill or rythur in the mirk midnycht, And mvneles als withoutin ony licht. **1653** H. MORE *Conject. Cabbal.* (1713) 3 Moonless and starless nights. **1750** CARTE *Hist. Eng.* II. 393 It was.. in a dark moonless night that the Scots before midnight.. marched under cover of the adjoining wood. **1894** K. GRAHAME *Pagan Papers* 104 The moonless night has a touch of frost, and is steely-clear.

moonlet ('muːnlɪt). [f. MOON *sb.*[1] + -LET.] A little moon. Also, an artificial satellite.

1832 MOTHERWELL *Poems* 47, I pledge thee in the silver horn Of yonder moonlet bright. **1891** *Cassell's Fam. Mag.* Dec. 55/1 The satellites of satellites, the little moonlets of the moons. **1895** [see *impact crater*]. **1955** *Sci. News Let.* 13 Aug. 107/2 The man-made moonlets will circle the earth many times every day, appearing to rise in the west and set in the east, reversing other sky phenomena. **1965** J. BLISH *Mission to Heart Stars* ii. 27 Since Phobos always kept the same face turned towards Mars, there would be no need to

bother stumbling around on the dark side of the moonlet. **1971** *Sci. Amer.* Jan. 47/1 Was the heat provided by the impact of meteorites or of a larger celestial body, or by the collision of 'moonlets' to form the present moon?

Hence †'**moonleted** *a. Bot.* = LUNATE.

1787 tr. *Linnæus' Fam. Pl.* 385 *Isopyrum*... Capsules many, moonletted, recurved, one-cell'd.

moonlight ('mu:nlaɪt), *sb.* [f. MOON *sb.*¹ + LIGHT *sb.*¹ Cf. Du. *maanlicht*, Ger. *mondlicht*.]

1. a. The light of the moon.

?*a* **1366** CHAUCER *Rom. Rose* 1010 Ne she was derk ne broun, but bright, And cleer as [is] the mone-light. *c* **1440** *Jacob's Well* 166 In þe nyȝt folwyng, be þe moneylyȝt, a knyȝt ..cam rydyng homwarde. **1596** SHAKS. *Merch. V.* v. i. 54 How sweet the moone-light sleepes vpon this banke. **1666** DRYDEN *Ann. Mirab.* lxviii, Till the last streaks of dying day withdrew And doubtful moonlight did our rage deceive. **1765** MATY in *Phil. Trans.* LV. 311, I saw the comet, but could form no judgment as to its appearances, because of the moon-light. **1883** STEVENSON *Silverado Sq.* 4 A tall ship lying anchored in the moonlight.

b. *transf.* and *fig.*

a **1450** *Tourn. Tottenham* 153 The cheefe was a plowmell, And the shadow of a bell, Quartered with the Moone-light. **1868** FARRAR *Silence & V.* ii. (1875) 30 This pale moonlight of a utilitarian or rational morality. **1873** BLACK *Pr. Thule* iii, If you asked him what Sheila was like, he would have answered by saying that there was moonlight in her face.

c. The colour of the light of the moon, as a shade in fabrics.

1922 *Daily Mail* 18 Dec. 1 (Advt.), In the following colours: Turquoise, Mastic, Moonlight, Silver, [etc.]. **1927** *Daily Tel.* 26 Apr. 13 (Advt.), Following shades: Sapphire, Moonlight, Bois de Rose, [etc.].

d. ***moonlight and roses***: used allusively of a situation, atmosphere, etc., characterized by sentimentality or romance.

1925 BLACK & MORET (*song-title*) Moonlight and roses. **1942** *Amer. Speech* XVII. 58 The moonlight-and-roses kind of Civil War play. **1959** *Encounter* Apr. 79/1 In *Look Homeward Angel* we have the romanticised figure of Laura James, the moonlight-and-roses woven about her.

†**2.** A moonlight scene or landscape. *Obs.*

1753 *Scots Mag.* May 263/2 A moon-light, from Van Bosman. **1762–71** H. WALPOLE *Vertue's Anecd. Paint.* (1786) III. 243 A small moon-light. **1778** SIR J. REYNOLDS *Disc.* viii. (1876) 457 A picture which I have of Rubens: it is a representation of a moonlight.

3. = MOONSHINE *sb.* 4. ? *Obs.*

1809 SCOTT *Poacher* 81 Yon cask holds moonlight, run when moon was none. **1824** —— *Redgauntlet* ch. xviii, A cask of moonlight. **1829** [see MOONSHINE *sb.* 4].

4. *U.S.* An excursion made by moonlight. Ellipt. for *moonlight flit*. *colloq.*

1886 *Boston* (Mass.) *Jrnl.* 13 Aug. 3/7 To-night the fourth in the series of moonlights will be made. **1958** G. BELLAIRS *Corpse at Carnival* ix. 131 His bags has gone... He's packed up... Done a moonlight as likely as not. **1971** R. PARKES *Line of Fire* xvi. 149 It's no good him trying to find 'em... Done a moonlight, they did.

5. *Amer. Univ. slang.* (See quots.)

1851 B. H. HALL *College Words* 210 *Moonlight*. At Williams College, the prize rhetorical exercise is called by this name; the reason is not given. The students speak of 'making a rush for moonlight', i.e. of attempting to gain the prize for elocution. **1860** C. DURFEE *Hist. Williams College* 104 Those who receive the appointment to speak for the prize have always..been called 'Moonlights'.

6. *attrib.* as *adj.* **a.** Accompanied by, bathed in moonlight; lit up by the moon, moonlit; performed by the light of the moon.

1584 R. SCOT *Discov. Witchcr.* x. ix. (1886) 150 Riding in a moone light night. **1590** SHAKS. *Mids. N.* II. i. 141 If you will..see our Moone-light reuels, goe with vs. **1797** MRS. RADCLIFFE *Italian* xii, The gate opened at once upon the moonlight mountains. **1819** KEATS *Eve St. Agnes* xiii, A little moonlight room, Pale, latticed, chill. **1829** COLERIDGE *Monody Chatterton* (later vers.) 135 Dancing to the moonlight roundelay.

b. ***moonlight flit, flitting***: the removal of household goods by night to avoid paying rent. Also, the action of leaving rented accommodation without paying the rent; a stealthy, usu. nocturnal, departure. So *moonlight wanderer*. (*colloq.* or *slang*.)

1721 [see FLITTING *vbl. sb.*]. **1821** J. GALT *Ann. Parish* xxxi. 263 He was fain to make a moonlight flitting, leaving his wife for a time to manage his affairs. **1823** 'J. BEE' *Dict. Turf* 120 Moonlight wanderers, or 'fly-by-night' persons, who cheat their landlords and run away by night. **1824** *Craven Gloss.* 93 Moon-light flit. **1855** [see FLIT *sb.* a]. **1866** *Athenæum* 13 Oct. 474 Probably Walkden wished to have his rent before it was due, that he might be safe against 'a moonlight flit'. **1892** STEVENSON & OSBOURNE *Wrecker* v. 79 In the excellent Scots' phrase, I made a moonlight flitting, a thing never dignified. **1924** M. ARGO in *Sc. Nat. Dict.* (1965) VI. 364/1 Takkin' a meenlichty flittin', are ye? **1969** *Listener* 27 Mar. 424/3 Very often we were living somewhere and couldn't pay the rent, so we had to indulge in what was known as a moonlight flit with what furniture and goods were available.

c. **moonlight lustre**, a lustre glaze with a marbled effect used on porcelain in the early 19th century, *spec.* by the Wedgwood factory.

1924 H. BARNARD *Chats on Wedgwood Ware* ix. 236 Lustre ware was not made until the beginning of the nineteenth century, when some very beautiful effects were produced, including the one which has since been called 'Moonlight'. **1966** G. A. GODDEN *Illustr. Encycl. Brit. Pott. & Porc.* p. xxiv, Messrs Wedgwood introduced a decorative type of marbled pink or purple 'gold' lustre called 'Moonlight Lustre'. **1970** *Times* 7 Oct. 10/6 This type of service was first made around 1820 and only the early examples, like that sold yesterday, are splashed in a pink glaze known as moonlight lustre.

7. *Comb.*

1762 WARTON *On Birth Pr. Wales* 48 The cloister's moonlight-chequer'd floor. **1820** SHELLEY *Sensitive Plant* I. 34 The wand-like lily..lifted up..its moonlight-coloured cup.

moonlight ('mu:nlaɪt), *v.* [Back-formation f. MOONLIGHTER.] **1. a.** *pass.* To be attacked by moonlighters. **b.** *intr.* To engage in moonlighting.

1887 *Spectator* 15 Oct. 1376 An Irish tenant pays this rather than be moonlighted. **1887** *Times* 26 Feb. 8/3 Eight men were..charged with moonlighting... The accused were not moonlighting.

2. To do a 'moonlight flit'. *dial.* and *colloq.*

1903 in *Eng. Dial. Dict.* **1971** A. NIXON *Attack on Vienna* vii. 71 He moonlit out of his luxury flat..and moved into a boarding-house.

3. To do paid work, usu. at night, in addition to one's regular employment. *colloq.* (orig. *U.S.*).

1957 [implied in MOONLIGHTING *vbl. sb.* 3]. **1960** *Economist* 12 Nov. 657/1 The firemen and police have long been supplementing their pay..by 'moonlighting', that is, by taking outside paid work. **1965** *Daily Tel.* (Colour Suppl.) 7 May 19/1 Some manage to 'moonlight' with two or three jobs—though jobs are harder to find. **1970** P. CARLON *Death by Demonstration* xvi. 175 You think I moonlight? Believe me, one job's enough. **1974** *Times Lit. Suppl.* 15 Feb. 157/4 He..—naturally for one who moonlights as the *Financial Times's* gardening correspondent when not otherwise engaged as a Fellow of Magdalen—never misses a turn on botanical or horticultural matters.

moonlighted ('mu:nlaɪtɪd), *ppl. a.* [f. MOON *sb.*¹ + LIGHTED *ppl. a.* after MOONLIGHT *sb.* Cf. MOONLIT.] Moonlit.

1829 JAMES *Richelieu* xxviii, The thunder-clouds passed away, and left the sky clear and moonlighted. **1859** MEREDITH *R. Feverel* xx, The moon-lighted valley.

moonlighter ('mu:nlaɪtə(r)). [Formed as next: see -ER¹.] **1.** One who engages in moonlighting or commits a moonlighting outrage.

1882 *Leeds Merc.* 27 Mar., A 'moonlighter' shot by the police. **1893** VIZETELLY *Glances Back* II. xxxv. 275 Irish landlords driven abroad..by the fear of moonlighters.

2. One who does a 'moonlight flit'. *dial.* and *colloq.*

1903 in *Eng. Dial. Dict.* **1964** *Sunday Mail* (Brisbane) 15 Nov. 12 Brisbane flat owners..estimate that moonlighters —tenants who slip away overnight without paying the rent —are costing them £100,000 a year.

3. One who 'moonlights' (MOONLIGHT *v.* 3). *colloq.*

1957 *Times* 12 Nov. (Canada Suppl.) p. ix/4 'Moonlighters' take a second job after hours; married women take advantage of modern kitchens to do the same. **1964** *Observer* 9 Aug. 9/2 Even in America, an estimated four million workers are 'moonlighters'—that is, they take on a part-time job on top of their full-time one. **1973** C. EGLETON *Seven Days to Killing* v. 61, I employ a lot of moonlighters, blokes who take a second job at nights.

moonlighting ('mu:nlaɪtɪŋ), *vbl. sb.* [f. MOONLIGHT *sb.* + -ING¹.]

1. The performance by night of an expedition, or of an illicit action.

1881 *Gentl. Mag.* Jan. 67 The exciting occupation of moonlighting... The object is to capture the cattle that have gone wild [etc.]. **1883** *Century Mag.* July 330/2 Sometimes well owners 'torpedo' their wells stealthily by night to avoid paying the high price charged by the company. This operation is called 'moonlighting'.

2. *spec.* In Ireland, the perpetration by night of outrages on the persons or property of tenants who incurred the hostility of the Land League.

1882 *Pall Mall G.* 20 June 2/1 As Boycotting is preferable to 'Moonlighting', so is parliamentary obstruction to physical force. **1892** *Times* 9 Dec. 9/1 A gross 'moonlighting' outrage is reported from Kerry, where..a party of ten men entered the house of a farmer..and treated him so brutally that he is not expected to recover. *fig.* **1886** HUXLEY in *Life* (1900) II. ix. 144 All good men and true should combine to stop this system of literary moonlighting.

3. The act or practice of MOONLIGHT *v.* 3. *colloq.* (orig. *U.S.*).

1957 *Reporter* (N.Y.) 8 Aug. 11/3 He takes two or three hours off and then..departs for a second job... The practice is known as 'moonlighting'. **1961** *Economist* 16 Dec. 1145/2 Several attempts have been made to ban moonlighting on the ground that it robs the unemployed of jobs. **1972** *Times* 8 Jan. 21/2 What about moonlighting? This is not the distilling of illicit liquor but the taking of a second job to keep body and soul together, or to finance one's own personal brand of extravagance.

So '**moonlighting** *ppl. a.*

1886 *Pall Mall G.* 26 Aug. 8/2 Small Moonlighting gangs. **1887** *Spectator* 8 Oct. 1330 One of the moonlighting party that attacked Sexton's house.

moonlighty ('mu:nlaɪtɪ), *a.* [f. MOONLIGHT *sb.* + -Y.] Resembling moonlight.

1876 MRS. OLIPHANT *Curate in Charge* vii, A sort of moonlighty blue.

'**moon-like**, *a.* and *adv.* [f. MOON *sb.*¹ + -LIKE.] Like or resembling a moon; having the characteristics of the moon; after the manner of the moon.

1596 SPENSER *F.Q.* v. vii. 13 She saw transfigured Her.. Moone-like Mitre to a Crowne of gold. **1642** H. MORE *Song of Soul* II. iii. III. lxii, Venus Moon-like grows corniculate. **1810** SOUTHEY *Kehama* VIII. iv, The multitude behind close up the rear With moon-like bend. **1865** G. MACDONALD *A. Forbes* 5 A pale face, on which a faint moon-like smile was glimmering.

†'**moonling.** *Obs.* [f. MOON *sb.*¹ + -LING¹.] A simpleton; an idiot.

1616 B. JONSON *Devil an Ass* I. vi, I haue a husband,..But such a moon-ling, as no wit of man Or roses can redeeme from being an Asse.

moonlit ('mu:nlɪt), *a.* [f. MOON *sb.*¹ + LIT *ppl. a.*] Lit up by the moon; bathed in or flooded with moonlight.

1830 TENNYSON *Arab. Nts.* 27 The sloping of the moonlit sward. **1883** *Gd. Words* 112 She stood on deck, watching the moonlit sea.

'**moon-litten**, *a. poet.* [See LITTEN *ppl. a.*] = prec.

1845 HIRST *Poems* 74 Under a lattice encircled with flowers Dim with the dew of the moon-litten hours. **1870** MORRIS *Earthly Par.* II. III. 105 A piece of fair moonlitten snow.

'**moon-man.** [Cf. MOON *sb.*¹ 1 g.]

†**1.** One whose occupation is pursued by moonlight; a 'night-walker'; one who robs by night. *Obs.*

Cf. 'the moones men', Shaks. *1 Hen. IV*, I. ii. 35. **1632** SHERWOOD, Moone-men, *brigands*.

†**2.** A gipsy. *Obs.*

1608 DEKKER *Lanth. & Candle Lt.* G 2 b, A Moone-man signifies in English a mad-man..By a by name they are called Gipsies, they call themselues Egiptians, others in mockery call them Moone-men. **1621** B. JONSON *Gipsies Metam.* Wks. (1641) 65 They are Gipsies o' this yeare, o' this Moone... *Cl.* Oh they are called the Moone men I remember now! *a* **1700** B. E. *Dict. Cant. Crew*, *Moon-men*, Gipsies.

3. A dweller in the moon. Also *fig.*

a **1625** FLETCHER, etc. *Fair Maid Inn* IV. ii, *Tay.* Shall I be a moon-man? *Foro.* I am of opinion, the people of that world ..do vary the fashion of their cloathes oftner then any Quick-silver'd nation in Europe. **1847** EMERSON *Poems* (1857) 104 Beauty of a richer vein..Unto men these moonmen lend, And our shrinking sky extend. **1958** *Spectator* 5 Sept. 305 An electronic sideshow starred Gygan, the Man from the Moon, a seven-foot creature of steel with a sixty-inch chest to keep all the transistors in. He walked spastic fashion with that curious whirring noise which all Moonmen seem to affect. **1962** A. WESKER *Chips with Everything* I. iii. 19 All right you creepy crawly nig-nogs, moon men that's what you are, moon men.

4. An astronaut who travels to the moon.

1965 *N.Y. Jrnl.-American* 21 Feb. 11/1 The spot where America's Moonmen are most likely to land. **1968** *Daily Tel.* 30 Dec. 1/3 (*headline*) Moonmen greeted by wives. **1970** *Observer* 19 Apr. 8/4 They were virile men, these astronauts. They were patriots, but they were moonmen.

moonquake ('mu:nkweɪk). *Astr.* [f. MOON *sb.*¹ after EARTHQUAKE.] A tremor of the moon's surface. (In quot. 1940 a *poet. nonce-use*.)

1940 R. GRAVES *No More Ghosts* 41 The pallid sky heaved with a moon-quake. **1953** *Jrnl. Brit. Interplanetary Soc.* XII. 66 The work which such an expedition could do is then described: amongst other things, artificial 'moon-quakes' would be set off by explosives, so that seismic records could be made. **1961** *Flight* LXXIX. 427/2 Other scientific instruments aboard the Surveyor will include a sensitive seismometer to record moonquakes or meteorite impacts. **1968** *Observer* 29 Dec. 17/3 The astronauts will place on the surface an instrument to register moonquakes. **1970** *Nature* 5 Dec. 906/1 It is now clear..that tidal strain is causing moonquakes when the Moon is at its nearest to the Earth. **1973** *Telegraph* (Brisbane) 13 Mar. 14/1 A seismologist has said that for some mysterious reason almost all moonquakes occur only in two separate belts on the moon.

moonraker ('mu:nreɪkə(r)). [f. MOON *sb.*¹ + RAKER¹.]

1. A native of Wiltshire.

See quot. 1787. In Wiltshire a more complimentary turn is given to the story: the men were caught raking a pond for kegs of smuggled brandy, and put off the revenue men by pretending folly.

1787 GROSE *Provinc. Gloss.*, *Prov.* R vij b, Wiltshire Moon-rakers. Some Wiltshire rusticks, as the story goes, seeing the figure of the moon in a pond, attempted to rake it out. **1819** J. C. HOBHOUSE *Let.* in Smiles *J. Murray* (1891) I. xvi. 409, I have been..immersed in the miserable provincial politics of my brother moon-rakers of this county. **1881** SLOW *Wiltsh. Rhymes* 1 The Wiltshire Moonrakers.

2. *Naut.* A sail above the sky-sail; cf. *moonsail*.

c **1829** D. JERROLD in M. R. Booth *Eng. Plays of 19th Cent.* (1969) I. 173 Now she makes more sail..mounts her royals, moon-rakers and sky-scrapers. **1867** SMYTH *Sailor's Word-bk.* **1890** W. J. GORDON *Foundry* 37 Now all the old canvas has gone, with its snowy wings from the watersails to the moonrakers.

Hence '**moon-raking** *vbl. sb.*, 'raking the moon'; *fig.* pursuing vain thoughts.

1869 BLACKMORE *Lorna D.* xvii, As soon as ever it was known that my wits were gone moonraking. **1894** HALL CAINE *Manxman* I. ix. 43 Have the lad's wits gone moonraking, I wonder?

'**moonrise.** [f. MOON *sb.*¹ + RISE *sb.*] The rise of the moon. Also used for: The east. Also (*U.S.*), the time at which the moon rises.

1728 *Phil. Trans.* XXXV. 454 A luminous Arch..which extended it self almost from Sun-set to Moon-rise. **1817** SHELLEY *Rev. Islam* II. x, O'er the still sea and jagged islets

darted The light of moonrise. **1868** LOCKYER *Elem. Astron.* 172 The time between two successive moonrises varies considerably. **1877** in BARTLETT *Dict. Amer.* (ed. 4). **1884** 'MARK TWAIN' *Huck. Finn.* viii. 63 When it was good and dark, I slid out from shore about moonrise. **1913** D. H. LAWRENCE *Love Poems & Others* 26 (*title*) Red moon-rise. **1926** E. M. ROBERTS *Time of Man* (1927) x. 379 I'll be gone at moonrise. **1931** E. O'NEILL *Mourning becomes Electra* I. i. 191 You dasn't stay there till moonrise at ten o'clock. **1975** *Sci. Amer.* Feb. 70/2 A lunar day is 24·8 hours in length, the interval between successive moonrises.

moonscape ('muːnskeɪp). [f. MOON *sb.*[1] + SCAPE *sb.*[3]] The surface or landscape of the moon, or a scene resembling this. Also *fig.*

1926 *World's Work* May 5 It embodies all the scientific facts known to-day, and the 'moonscape' in the foreground is an actual scene as viewed through the telescope. **1960** *20th Cent.* June 509, I..took..off..on a mightly leap across the moonscape. **1961** I. FLEMING *Thunderball* xvi. 173 Now the pale moonscape changed. **1969** *Sun* 22 July 1/3 Armstrong, the first to walk, looked at the desolate moonscape and told the world: 'It has a beauty of its own.. it's very pretty up here.' **1971** D. LEES *Rainbow Conspiracy* vi. 89 The deserted moonscape terrain of Pike's Scar. **1974** V. CANNING *Mask of Memory* ii. 23 His thin, drawn face a moonscape of chalky white.

moonseed ('muːnsiːd). [f. MOON *sb.*[1] + SEED *sb.*, after mod.L. *mēnispermum* (badly f. Gr. μήν moon, σπέρμα seed).] A plant of the genus *Menispermum* (having lunate seeds).

1739 MILLER *Gard. Dict.* II, *Menispermum*, Moon-seed. **1822** *Hortus Anglicus* II. 547 *Menispermum Canadense*. Canadian Moon Seed... *M. Virginicum*. Virginian Moon Seed. **1857** GRAY *First Less. Bot.* (1866) 95 The rudiments of pistils are often found in the sterile blossom, and rudimentary stamens in the fertile blossom, as in Moonseed.

attrib. **1849** BALFOUR *Man. Bot.* §746 *Menispermaceæ*, the Moon-seed Family.

moonset ('muːnsɛt). *poet.* [f. MOON *sb.*[1], after *sunset.*] The setting of the moon.

1845 BROWNING *Good News* iii, 'Twas moonset at starting. **1870** MORRIS *Earthly Par.* III. IV. 280 In the darkling tide Betwixt the moonset and the dawn of day.

'moon-shade. [Cf. G. *mondschatte* in sense 3.]

†**1.** The plant nightshade. *Obs.*

1626 BACON *Sylva* §975 Soporiferous Medicines.. Hemlocke, Mandrake, Mooneshade.

2. A circular lamp-shade. (Cf. MOON *sb.*[1] 5.)

1830 GALT *Lawrie T.* IX. vii, A table-lamp with a moon-shade. **1841** *Civil Eng. & Arch. Jrnl.* IV. 195/1 No moon-shades should ever be used, as, besides intercepting a considerable portion of the light, they [etc.].

3. Shadow occurring between spells of moonlight.

1905 H. HUNT. *Pre-Raphaelitism* II. 19 Like palled shapes in a heavy dream, detached by moonlight and moonshade.

'moon-shaped, *a.* Shaped like the moon, *esp.* crescent-shaped, lunate.

1709 *Lond. Gaz.* No. 4510/7 The Hoy Burthen 9 or 10 Tun,.. Moon shap'd in her Sleir. **1763** MILLS *Pract. Husb.* III. 282 Compressed moon-shaped pods. **1868** W. K. PARKER *Shoulder-girdle Vertebr.* 32 The moon-shaped 'glenoid' spaces of the coraco-scapular cartilage.

‖**moonshee, munshi** ('muːnʃiː). Also 8 munchee, 8–9 moonshi, -shy, 9 munshee. [Urdū *munshī*, a. Arab. *munshi'*, pres. pple. of *ansha'a* to compose, causative of *nasha'a* to grow up.] A native secretary or language-teacher in India.

1776 N. B. HALHED *Code Gentoo Laws* I. 17 *Moonshī*, a Writer or Secretary. **1782** J. PRICE *Tracts* I. 89 (Y.) The young gentlemen..reason and dispute with the *munchees* (tutors) in Persian and Moors. **1788** BURKE *Sp. agst. W. Hastings* Wks. XVI. 223 There was a Persian moonshee in a secret, of which Cantoo Baboo was ignorant. **1800** WELLESLEY in Owen *Desp.* (1877) 743 An establishment of Moonshies and native teachers.. will be attached to the new College. **1849** E. B. EASTWICK *Dry Leaves* 40, I made my old Muhammadan Munshi..compute the date. **1865** *Spectator* 11 Feb. 164 The Queen read Persian like a moonshi. **1947** R. O. WINSTEDT *Malays* 152 His father was *munshi* to William Marsden. **1968** D. DUFF *Victoria in Highlands* 360 Abdul Karim advanced to become the Queen's India Secretary and was thereafter known as the Munshi Hafiz Abdul Karim... The Munshi's privileged position led to much opposition. **1975** *Times* 26 July 7/6 The language teacher, or munshi.. was larger than I expected.

moonshine ('muːnʃaɪn), *sb.* Also 5 -shone (?). [f. MOON *sb.*[1] + SHINE *sb.* Cf. OHG. *mânschîn* (mod.G. *mondschein*), Du. *maneschijn*, ON. *mánaskin.*]

1. a. = MOONLIGHT *sb.*[1] 1. Now *rare* or *poet.*

c **1500** *Melusine* 22 Here shall we abyde tyl it be mone shyn. **1598** SHAKS. *Merry W.* v. v. 106 Pinch him, and burne him, and turne him about, Till Candles, and Star-light, and Moone-shine be out. **1633** EARL MANCH. *Al Mondo* (1636) 130 His dayes..passe as a shadow by Moone-shine. **1798** COLERIDGE *Anc. Mar.* I. 78 Whiles all the night, through fog-smoke white, Glimmered the white moon-shine. **1814** SCOTT *Wav.* xxxvii, The twilight had given place to moonshine when the party halted upon the brink of a precipitous glen. **1884** W. C. SMITH *Kildrostan* 45 Every.. gleam of moonshine..mocked and laughed at him.

b. *fig.* and *allusive.*

1607 CHAPMAN *Bussy d'Ambois* IV. i, Women..as the tender Moon-shine of their beauties Cleeres, or is cloudy, make men glad or sad. **1839** BAILEY *Festus* xvi. (1852) 186 The lap-dog dreams, as round he lies, In moonshine of his mistress' eyes.

†**c.** The time when the moon begins to shine.

1690 *Gt. Scanderberg* 19 We went together, at the Moon-Shine, upon the Sea Shore.

†**d.** *transf.* (*jocular*). A month. *nonce-use.*

1605 SHAKS. *Lear* I. ii. 5 For that I am some twelue, or fourteene Moonshines Lag of a Brother?

2. a. Taken as the type of: An appearance without substance; something unsubstantial or unreal; now *esp.* foolish or visionary talk, ideas, plans, etc.; orig. in phr. †***moonshine in the water***, later simply ***moonshine***. Also ***a matter of moonshine*** (?*obs.*).

1468 *Paston Lett.* II. 326 If Sir Thomas Howys wer.. made byleve and put in hope of the moone shone in the water and I wot nat what. **1530** PALSGR. 865/1 For moone shyne in the water *pour vne chose de riens.* **1588** SHAKS. *L.L.L.* v. ii. 208 **1617** MORYSON *Itin.* III. 6 Their continuall brawlings about Moone shine in the water. **1624** BEDELL *Lett.* ii. 49 Our dissentions are about Moone-shine. **1658** R. FRANCK *North. Mem.* (1821) 33 Their..delectable morsels will melt into moonshines. **1785** GROSE *Dict. Vulg. T.* s.v., A matter or mouthful of moonshine, a trifle, nothing. **1822–56** DE QUINCEY *Confess.* (1862) 7 Coleridge's entire statement upon that subject is perfect moonshine. **1841** B. HALL *Patchwork* II. viii. 155, I found the whole affair..a matter of moonshine. **1874** L. STEPHEN *Hours in Library* (1892) I. vii. 261 A science, and not a mere edifice of moonshine. **1887** *Spectator* 3 Sept. 1173 As for all this talk about Federalism, it is moonshine. It means nothing practical at all.

†**b.** ***to hang by the moonshine***: to be baseless.

1532 MORE *Confut. Tindale* Wks. 564/2 Ye may wel perceiue..that the profe of al his whole conclusion.. hangeth all by the moneshyne.

c. *slang.* ***gilded moonshine***: see quot. ? *Obs.*

1823 'J. BEE' *Dict. Turf* 121 *Gilded Moonshine*, sham bills of exchange: 'no effects'. **1824** *Hist. Gaming* 19 To borrow money on his own notes of hand, which they call 'gilded moonshine'.

†**3.** *Cookery.* **a.** ***eggs in moonshine***: a preparation of eggs used in the 16th and 17th c. Also *allusively* (with reference to sense 2). **b.** A dish in which a 'sky' of blancmange or custard was diversified with a half-moon and stars in clear jelly. (Mrs. Glasse *Cookery*, 1767, p. 289.)

1576 in *Hakluyt's Voy.* (1600) III. 23 It is to be thought that the King of Portugall would not have given to the Emperor such summes of money for egges in mooneshine. **1593** G. HARVEY *Pierce's Super.* 24 You may discourse of.. I wott not what marueilous egges in mooneshine. **1605** SHAKS. *Lear* II. ii. 35 Ile make a sop oth' Moonshine of you. *c* **1645** HOWELL *Lett.* (1655) II. xxii. 34 Could I those whitely Stars go nigh,.. I'd poach them, and as Moon-shine dress, To make my Delia a curious mess. **1660** MAY *Accompl. Cook* (1665) 437 Eggs in Moon-shine.

4. Smuggled or illicit spirit. Cf. MOONLIGHT *sb.* 3. In the U.S., illicitly distilled liquor, esp. whisky.

(The precise application varies with the locality.)

1785 GROSE *Dict. Vulg. T.* s.v., The white brandy smuggled on the coasts of Kent and Sussex, is [ed. 1796 and the gin in the north of Yorkshire are] called moonshine. **1829** BROCKETT *N.C. Gloss.* (ed. 2), *Moon-light, Moon-shine*, ..smuggled whiskey. **1841** J. T. HEWLETT *Parish Clerk* I. 9 A glass of real Hollands—genuine moonshine. **1875** E. KING *Southern States N. Amer.* 479 Would we have some more 'moonshine'? No? **1957** M. MCCARTHY *Memories Catholic Girlhood* vii. 157 It did not smell like the whisky my grandfather drank. It was moonshine, they said; corn whisky. **1960** A. LOMAX *Folk Songs N. Amer.* 257 I'll eat when I'm hungry and drink when I'm dry, If moonshine don't kill me, I'll live till I die. **1973** 'B. MATHER' *Snowline* i. 16 All liquor is either bootleg—smuggled—or moonshine, distilled from anything and everything.

attrib. **1875** E. KING *Southern States N. Amer.* 478 Producing from his pocket a flask of 'moonshine' whiskey, [he] invited us to drink. **1886** *Century Mag.* XXXI. 432/1 He had a moonshine apparatus over on Sweetwater. **1901** *Munsey's Mag.* XXV. 428/1 Georgia and Arkansas have the greatest number of moonshine stills. *Ibid.* 430/2 Moonshine whisky.

†**5.** *attrib.* or as *adj.* **a.** Illuminated by the moon; moonlit; (of persons) active by moonlight or at night. Cf. MOONLIGHT *sb.* 6. *Obs.*

1587 HARRISON *England* I. xxiv. 129 A spirit that would of custome in a moone shine night..run at tilt and turneie in complet armor with anie knight..in that place. **1598** SHAKS. *Merry W.* v. v. 42 You Moone-shine reuellers. **1626** BACON *Sylva* §866 Starre-Light Nights, yea, and bright Moone-shine Nights, are Colder than Cloudy Nights. **1726** SWIFT *Gulliver* I. v, It being likewise a Moon-shine Night. **1820** *Sporting Mag.* VII. 97 Moonshine sportsmen, familiarly termed poachers. **1831** BREWSTER *Nat. Magic* xiii. (1833) 327 During the clear moonshine nights of November.

†**b.** Vain, empty. *Obs.*

1668 H. MORE *Div. Dial.* III. xxvi. (1713) 242 They are weak, abortive, Moonshine Conceptions.

moonshine ('muːnʃaɪn), *v.* [f. the sb.]

1. *trans.* To cheat or deceive by means of 'moonshine' (MOONSHINE 2 a). *rare*[−1].

1824 E. WEETON *Let.* 6 July in *Jrnl. of Governess* (1969) II. 298, I visited the Diorama... I was too much gratified to think I was moon-shined out of my money.

2. *intr.* To make liquor, esp. whisky, illicitly. *U.S. colloq.*

1883 [implied in MOONSHINING *vbl. sb.*]. **1902** W. N. HARBEN *Abner Daniel* 209 We moonshined it together two year, though he never knowed my chief hidin'-place. **1910** 'O. HENRY' *Whirligigs* xv. 173 He acknowledged no occupation save that of a squirrel hunter, but he 'moonshined' occasionally by way of diversion. **1949** *Times-Picayune Mag.* (New Orleans) 13 Feb. 6/2 Even a small operator can make fair living moonshining.

moonshiner ('muːnʃaɪnə(r)). [f. MOONSHINE *sb.* + -ER[1].] **a.** A smuggler. **b.** *U.S.* A distiller of 'moonshine' (MOONSHINE 4).

1860 AGNES STRICKLAND *Old Friends* 31 The moonshiners had no cargo to defend. **1877** *N.Y. Even. Post* 16 June, Nelson County, Kentucky, is the home of the Moonshiner; that is, the manufacturer of illicit whiskey. **1892** *Pall Mall G.* 8 Mar. 7/3 A Knoxville (Tenn.) telegram..says:—A desperate fight has occurred between a party of 'moonshiners' and a sheriff's posse. **1927** [see FEUDIST 3]. **1970** N. ARMSTRONG et al. *First on Moon* iv. 77 Some seven hundred people had to be moved, including quite a few moonshiners. **1973** *Guardian* 12 Oct. 1/8 Senator Sam Ervin ..has made a long-playing record of his homespun Southern philosophy. The record features stories about moonshiners. **1973** *Globe & Mail* (Toronto) 9 Nov. 31/4 That same gallon, he says, costs the moonshiner only $2 to $3 to manufacture, and—if he isn't making it for his own use —he usually sells it for around $30.

So **'moonshining** *vbl. sb.*, illicit distilling.

1883 'S. BONNER' *Dialect Tales* 183 You can't stop moonshinin' 's long's there's an honest man in Old Hickory's State. **1895** *Chicago Advance* 6 June 1285/3 A young man speaking at a temperance meeting while his brother is in the penitentiary for 'moonshining'. **1946** G. WILSON *Fidelity Folks* 54 He stoutly maintained that a regulated open saloon was to be preferred to the evils of moonshining and boot-legging.

†**'moonshining,** *ppl. a. Obs.* [f. MOONSHINE *sb.* + -ING[2].] = MOONSHINY 1.

1710 R. WARD *Life H. More* 134 Lying one Moon-shining Night in the Cradle awake, he was taken up thence. **1786** MRS. INCHBALD *I'll tell you what* IV. i, It was a fine moon-shining night, last night. **1828** *Lights & Shades* II. 231 Jack and myself went thither on a moonshining Monday.

moonshiny ('muːnʃaɪnɪ), *a.* [f. MOONSHINE *sb.* + -Y.]

1. Illuminated by the moon; moonlight.

1602 CAREW *Cornwall* 136b, In a faire Moone-shinie night, he hyeth to dig it up. **1717** POPE in *Lady M. W. Montagu's Lett.* Oct., I lie dreaming of you in moonshiny nights. **1886** P. S. ROBINSON *Valley Teetotum Trees* 140 Every one who likes to do so may still believe that on moon-shiny nights the elves and fays come out into the meadows.

2. White as moonlight; resembling moonlight.

? **1825** COLERIDGE *Alice du Clos* 18 As spotless fair, as airy light As that moon-shiny doe. **1837** CARLYLE *Fr. Rev.* I. IV. iv, Thy serenely beautiful Philosophising, with its soft moonshiny clearness.

3. Of the nature of 'moonshine'; vain, unreal.

1857 H. MELVILLE *Confidence Man* xli. 312 And moon-shiny as it in theory may be, yet a very practical philosophy. **1880** *Sat. Rev.* No. 1291. 122 There is a good deal of moon-shiny sentiment in it, especially in the conversation of the lovers. **1884** A. MACLAREN in *Chr. Commw.* 11 Dec. 111/2 Unsubstantial emptinesses and moonshiny illusions.. which men chase after.

†**'moonsick,** *a. Obs.* [f. MOON *sb.*[1] + SICK *a.* In OE. *mónsék* (Northumb.), **mónséoc* = MDu. *maensiec* (Du. *maanziek*).] Lunatic.

c **975** *Rushw. Gosp.* Matt. iv. 24 þa þe dioful hæfdun & mon-sekæ [*lunaticos*] & loman. **1562** J. HEYWOOD *Prov. & Epigr.* (1867) 205 Wyfe, I weene thou art dronke or Leunitike. Nay husband: women are neuer moone sicke. **1616** T. ADAMS *Soul's Sickness* Wks. (1629) 473 If his Itch proceed from a Moone-sicke head, the chiefe intention is to settle his braines.

‖**moonsif(f, munsif** ('muːnsɪf). [Urdū, a. Arab. *munçif* just, honest (pres. pple. of *ançafa* to be bisected, be impartial, from *niçf* half).] A native judge in India.

1812 *Gloss. to 5th Rep. Sel. Comm. E. Ind. Comp.* 31 *Munsiff*. **1835** MACAULAY in Trevelyan *Compet. Wallah* (1866) 327 The Shasters and the Hedeya will be useless to a Moonsiff or Sudder Ameen. **1844** H. H. WILSON *Brit. India* II. 519 It was provided, that the Heads of villages should be Munsifs in their respective villages. **1876** GRANT *Hist. India* I. ci. 556/2 Moonsifs, who were at first restricted to hearing cases valued at fifty rupees, were made competent to deal with those of 150.

moonstone ('muːnstəʊn). [f. MOON *sb.*[1] + STONE *sb.*, after L. *selēnītēs*, Gr. σεληνίτης (λίθος) SELENITE.] 'A popular name, alluding to the lustre, for some varieties of adularia and albite. The moonstone of the ancients was probably selenite' (Chester *Dict. Min.* 1896).

1632 SHERWOOD, A moone-stone, *pierre de la lune.* **1681** W. ROBERTSON *Phraseol. Gen.* (1693) 893 A moon-stone; *Selenites.* **1778** *Eng. Gazetteer* (ed. 2), *Hanborough*, Oxf. near Woodstock, is noted only for the selenites, or moon-stone. **1802** *Phil. Trans.* XCII. 289 Moonstone of Ceylon. **1839** BAILEY *Festus* xix. (1852) 311 The moonstone's changing light. **1877** STREETER *Prec. Stones* 210, 211.

attrib. **1898** G. MEREDITH *Odes Fr. Hist.* 24 She gazed With eyes, the moonstone portals to her heart. **1898** *Westm. Gaz.* 5 May 3/2 The coat was of Parma violet velvet and the skirt moonstone-grey.

'moon-stricken, *ppl. a.* = MOONSTRUCK.

1820 SCOTT *Abbot* xxxi, Like some moon-stricken knight in a Spanish romance. **1844** LD. BROUGHAM *Brit. Const.* xvi. (1862) 248 The moonstricken Prince.

moonstruck ('muːnstrʌk), *ppl. a.* [f. MOON *sb.*[1] + *struck*, pa. pple. of STRIKE *v.* Cf. *Ps.* cxxi. 6 and late Gr. σεληνόβλητος, -πληκτος.]

1. Affected in mind or deranged in conduct (through the supposed influence of the moon); in early use and *arch.* = lunatic; now implying a

distracted or dazed condition apparently due to some mental obsession.

1674 MILTON *P.L.* XI. 486 And Moon struck madness, pining Atrophie. **1742** POPE *Dunc.* IV. 12 The moon-struck Prophet felt the madding hour. **1849** DICKENS *Dav. Copp.* xxxiii, I, the moon-struck slave of Dora, perambulated round and round the house and garden for two hours. **1852** M. ARNOLD *Tristr. & Iseult* I. 209 'Up, Tristram, up!' ..'thou moonstruck knight! What foul fiend rides thee?' **1885–94** R. BRIDGES *Eros & Psyche* Mar. xxii, Deform'd in body, and of moonstruck mind.

2. (See quots. and cf. MOON-BLIND 2.)

1846 MRS. R. LEE *Afr. Wanderers* xviii, I was afraid I was moon-struck [*note*, by sleeping in the open air]. **1867** SMYTH *Sailor's Word-bk.*, *Moon-struck*, an influence imputed to the moon in the tropics, by which fish..though recently taken, become intenerated, and even spoiled... Human beings are also said to be injured by sleeping in the moon's rays.

moontan, obs. form of MUNTIN.

moon-up ('mu:nʌp). *U.S. dial.* [f. MOON *sb.*[1] + UP *adv.* Cf. SUN-UP.] Moonrise.

1907 S. E. WHITE *Arizona Nights* I. v. 90 'Didn't git in till moon-up last night,' he growled. **1941** *Sat. Even. Post* 1 Mar. 84/2 They'd come between first dark and moon-up.

moonward(s ('mu:nwəd(z), *adv.* [f. MOON *sb.*[1] + -WARD(S.] Towards the moon.

1855 BAILEY *Mystic* 35 From the immoveable star-plane to the prime Conceptacle of motion, moonwards, through All spheres in graded order. **1879** G. MACDONALD *Hist. Photogen & Nycteris* xiv, in *Graphic* Christmas No. 8/2 The fountain kept rushing moon-ward. **1900** O. WILDE *Let.* 21 Apr. (1962) 823 He really bayed for boots, as a dog moonwards. **1918** C. W. BEEBE *Jungle Peace* (1919) xi. 270 Here and there in the jungle on each side, where a tree had fallen, or a flue of clear space led moonwards, the effect was of cold electric light seen through trees in city parks. **1959** C. MACKENZIE *Lunatic Republic* i. 21 Every sound without was so muted that the explosion which started the rocket moonwards sounded no more than the noise of one of the old railway trains of my youth.

moonwort ('mu:nwɜ:t). [f. MOON *sb.*[1] + WORT *sb.*, after med.L. *lūnāria* LUNARY *sb.*[1], Du. *maankruid*, G. *mondkraut*.]

1. The fern *Botrychium Lunaria* = LUNARY *sb.* b. Also ***small*** or ***lesser moonwort*** (=old Bot. name *Lunaria minor*).

1578 LYTE *Dodoens* I. xciv. 136 This herbe is now called in Latine *Lunaria*, and *Lunaria minor*..in English Lunarie, or Moonewort. **1591** SYLVESTER *Du Bartas* I. iii. 763 Horse, that..Tread upon Moon-wort with their hollow heels; Though lately shod, at night goe bare-foot home. **1597** GERARDE *Herbal* II. lxxxv. 329 *Lunaria* or small Moonewoort groweth vpon dire and barren mountaines and heathes. **1651** FRENCH *Distill.* ii. 46 The leaves of..the lesser Moon-wort. **1785** MARTYN *Rousseau's Bot.* xxxii. (1794) 489 Moon-wort, which grows on dry pastures, has one naked stem, and one pinnate frond. **1854** S. THOMSON *Wild Fl.* III. (ed. 4) 138 The curious little fern moonwort.

2. The plant Honesty, *Lunaria biennis*; = LUNARY *sb.* a. Also ***great moonwort***. ? *Obs.*

1611 COTGR., *Lunaire majeur*, ou *grande lunaire*. Great Moonewort, Pennie-flower... Honestie. **1656** W. COLES *Art of Simpling* 37 The seed of Bulbonack resembles the Moon, which is therefore called Great Moonwort. **1785** MARTYN *Rousseau's Bot.* xxiii. (1794) 320 The brilliant whiteness of these silicles has occasioned this plant [*sc.* Honesty] to be called White Sattin: and from the shape of them it is named Lunaria and Moonwort.

†**3.** = MADWORT, *Marrubium Alysson*. *Obs.*

1597, 1611 [see MADWORT 1]. **1635** SWAN *Spec. M.* (1670) 216 Mad-wort or Moon-wort...in Latine *Alyssum* or *Lunaria*.

4. The tree-sorrel, *Rumex Lunaria*.

1697 *Phil. Trans.* XIX. 435 A Tree-Sorrel from the Canaries, which is no other than the Magicians Moon-wort of the Arabians in Lobel. **1866** *Treas. Bot.*

†**5.** ***blue moonwort***: a plant of Switzerland, *Soldanella alpina*, having circular leaves. *Obs.*

1629 PARKINSON *Parad.* 234 *Soldanella Alpina*. Mountaine Soldanella or blew Moonewort.

moony ('mu:nɪ), *a.* [f. MOON *sb.*[1] and *v.* + -Y.]

1. Of or belonging to the moon; resembling or characteristic of the moon; like that of the moon.

a **1586** SIDNEY *Arcadia* III. (1622) 257 What mou'd me to inuite Your presence (sister deare) first to my Moony sphere. **1789** BLAKE *Songs Innoc., Cradle Song* 4 Sweet dreams of pleasant streams By happy, silent, moony beams! **1875** G. MACDONALD *Malcolm* III. x. 148 The cave shone silvery gray, with a faint moony sparkle.

2. Moon-shaped. †**a.** Crescent-shaped, lunate; hence, having the crescent as an emblem or ensign, belonging to the Turkish or Muslim power.

1591 SYLVESTER *Du Bartas* I. ii. 467 The Moony Standards of proud Ottoman. **1697** DRYDEN *Æneid* XI. 963 They clash with manly force their Moony Shields. **1716** FENTON *Poems* 227 The miscreant Moony Host, Before the Victor-Cross shall fly. **1814** SOUTHEY *Roderick* XIII, One.. aim'd against his neck The moony falchion's point.

b. Round, circular.

1836 *Blackw. Mag.* XXXIX. 670 He was large and stout with a very red face, full and moony. **1865** DICKENS *Mut. Fr.* I. x, An oilcake-fed style of business-gentleman with mooney spectacles.

3. Illuminated by the moon; also, resembling moonlight.

1648 HERRICK *Hesper.*, *Oberon's Pal.*, Mildly disparkling, ..like those mites Of Candi'd dew in Moony nights. **1830** W. TAYLOR *Hist. Surv. Germ. Poetry* I. 292 The scenery of Klopstock is always illuminated by a moony twilight, a misty glory. **1883** G. MACDONALD *D. Grant* II. xvii. 187 On the moony side [of the street] people..could recognize each other two houses away.

4. Inclined to moon or act in a listless, aimless manner; given to mooning; stupidly dreamy.

1848 THACKERAY *Bk. Snobs* xliii, Casting upon the reflection of his white neckcloth a pleased moony smile. **1865** DICKENS *Mut. Fr.* III. ii, What a mooney godmother you are, after all. **1879** MCCARTHY *Own Times* II. xxiii. 170 It was agreed..that he [*sc.* Louis Napoleon] was a fatuous, dreamy, moony, impracticable, stupid young man.

b. Slightly intoxicated. *slang.*

1854 N. I. LUCAS *Eng.-Germ. Dict.* 1125. **1867** SMYTH *Sailor's Word-bk.*, *Mooney*, not quite intoxicated, but unfitted for duty. **1872** LATHAM, *Moony*..3 Tipsy. *Colloquial.*

moony, obs. form of MANY.

c **1460** *Oseney Reg.* 139 John Duke..and moony other þenne þere Beyng present.

moop, variant of Sc. MOUP, to nibble, etc.

moope, mooped, obs. ff. MOPE *sb.*, MOPED.

moopoo, variant of MOPOKE.

moor (mʊə(r), mɔə(r)), *sb.*[1] Forms: 1 mór, 3–5 mor, 3–8 more, 4–5 mur, *Sc.* mwr(e, 4–6 mure, 5–7 moore, 8–9 *Sc.* muir, 7– moor. [OE. *mór* masc. = MDu., Du. *moer* neut., MLG. *môr*, *moor* (whence mod.G. *moor* neut., Da. *mor*), OHG. *muor* neut.:—OTeut. **môro-*, whence **môrjâ* fem., represented in OHG. *muorra* str. fem., ON *mǿr-r* fem., moorland.

ON. had *mó-r* in the same sense; but this must be wholly unconnected, unless the *-ro* of OTeut. **môro-* be a suffix, the pre-Teut. root being **mō-* (: *mə-*, as possibly in **mə-ri* MERE *sb.*[1]). Most scholars, however, regard the *r* as belonging to the root, which they consider to be an ablaut variant of **mer-*, *mr̥-* to die, so that the primitive sense of the sb. would be 'dead' or barren land.]

1. a. A tract of unenclosed waste ground; now usually, uncultivated ground covered with heather; a heath. Also, a tract of ground strictly preserved for shooting.

Beowulf 103 Se þe moras heold, fen and fæsten. *Ibid.* 1405 Ofer myrcan mor. *c* **1205** LAY. 4817 Meduwen and mores & þa hæȝe muntes. *a* **1340** HAMPOLE *Psalter* lxxvii. 18 He brake þe stane in þe more [Vulg. *in eremo*]. **1375** BARBOUR *Bruce* VII. 108 Syne in a mwre thai enterit ar, That wes bath hee & lang & braid. **1390** GOWER *Conf.* II. 95 The Ro, which renneth on the Mor, Is thanne noght so lyht as I. **14..** *Customs of Multon* in *Surtees Misc.* (1888) 58 It was grauntyd..pastur' to all þe bestes in þe feyldes and in þe more. *c* **1470** HENRY *Wallace* III. 60 Wyth thar serwandis fra Ricardtoun thai raid To Mawchtlyne mur. **1596** DALRYMPLE tr. *Leslie's Hist. Scotl.* I. 17 Heir I say is ane gold mynde in Craufurde mure. **1602** SHAKS. *Ham.* III. iv. 67 Could you on this faire Mountaine leaue to feed, And batten on this Moore? **1776** ADAM SMITH *W.N.* I. xi. (1869) I. 155 The most desert moors in Norway and Scotland produce some sort of pasture. **1785** BURNS *Holy Fair* i, The risin' sun owre Galston muirs, Wi' glorious light was glintin. **1846** MCCULLOCH *Acc. Brit. Empire* (1854) I. 16 The Yorkshire moors are by far the most extensive and important of any in the kingdom. **1860** EMERSON *Cond. Life, Culture* Wks. (Bohn) II. 371 In the country he can find.. moors for game, hills for geology, and groves for devotion. **1886** *Times* (weekly ed.) 6 Aug. 13/3 The moors thrown on the market for the year hung heavily on hand at first.

b. *spec.* (Usu. with capital initial.) Dartmoor Prison (cf. DARTMOOR b).

1869 F. HENDERSON *Six Yrs. in Prisons Eng.* xix. 228 'How long were you at the Moor, Dick?' 'Three years.' **1924** E. WALLACE *Room 13* vii. 69, I was on the 'moor' with him. **1939** [see ISLAND *sb.* 1 d]. **1958** F. NORMAN *Bang to Rights* I. 22 I'm doing a bleeding neves. I'll be going down the Moor soon that will be the third poxy time. **1962** D. WARNER *Death of Bogey* IV. iii. 146 A stretch in the Ville or on the Moor. **1967** C. DRUMMOND *Death at Furlong Post* xvi. 192 There's nothing like the Moor, T.B. more or less guaranteed after fifteen years. **1968** *Guardian* 3 Jan. 5/3 One more stretch for GBH, then down to the Moor.

2. †A marsh (*obs.*); also *dial.* (see quot. 1883).

1441 *Tintinhull Churchw. Acc.* (Som. Rec. Soc.) 180 Et de segitibus venditis in le more hoc anno [etc.]..xs. *c* **1475** *Pict. Voc.* in Wr.-Wülcker 797/9 *Hec Palis*, a more. **1591** SPENSER *Virg. Gnat* 230 Therto the frogs, bred in the slimie scowring Of the moist moores, their jarring voices bent. **1701** A. DE LA PRYME in *Phil. Trans.* XXII. 982 Acorns have frequently been found at the bottom of the Soil of those Levels and Mores. **1706** PHILLIPS (ed. Kersey), *Moor*..is now commonly taken for a Marsh, or Fen. **1787** WINTER *Syst. Husb.* 25 Moors and Bogs generally consist of rotten trees, roots of weeds, and other half dissolved vegetable substances. **1883** GRANT ALLEN *Colin Clout's Calendar* xxxviii. 228 In Yorkshire a moor means a high stretch of undulating heath-covered rock; whereas in Somerset it means a low flat level of former marshland, reclaimed and drained by means of numerous 'rhines'.

3. *dial.* The soil of which moorland consists; peat.

1596 DALRYMPLE tr. *Leslie's Hist. Scot.* I. 9 Ruch, scharpe and hard hillis full of mosse, more and marrase. **1610** W. FOLKINGHAM *Art of Survey* 3 The vulgar [species of the earth] is either simple as Clay, Moulde, Moor, Gravell, Sande. **1799** J. ROBERTSON *Agric. Perth* 25 A thin stratum of moss, where the subsoil is gravel or sand, is called Moor. **1877** SKERTCHLY *Geol. Fenland* 138 The word *peat* is quite unknown among the agricultural population of the fens. The substance is called *turf*, and where thin, or so weathered as to be unfit for fuel, the term *moor* is applied.

4. *Cornwall.* **a.** A moor or waste land where tin is found; hence ***moor-house, -tin, -works*** (see quots. 1602, 1778). **b.** (See quots. 1778, 1860.)

1602 CAREW *Cornwall* 8 Under this title [Streamworke], they comprise also the Moore workes. *Ibid.* 15 b, A foote of good Moore-tyn (which is counted the best sort) will way about fourescore pound. *Ibid.* 18 The Tynners of the whole shire are deuided into foure quarters, two called Moores, of the places where the Tynne is wrought, viz. Foy moore, and Black moore: the other Tiwarnaill and Penwith. **1778** PRYCE *Min. Cornub.* 316 But if the place or Mine lies low, it is usual to say, 'He is gone to Moor;' if in the valley, they say, 'He is gone to Coomb.' *Ibid.* 324 *Moor*... This word signifies a root or a quantity of Ore in a particular part of the Lode; as 'A Moor of Ore'. 'A Moor of Tin'. *Ibid.*, *Moorhouse*, a hovel built with turf for workmen to change cloaths in. A Coe, Derby. **1860** *Eng. & For. Min. Gloss.* (Cornw. Terms), *More*, a quantity of ore in a particular part of a lode, as a 'more' of tin.

5. *attrib.* and *Comb.*, as ***moor-dike, -keeper, -owner, -side, -wind***; ***moor-bred, -haunting*** adjs.

1603 DRAYTON *Barons Wars* VI. lxiv. 147 The *more-bred Mallard. **1579** *Mem. St. Giles, Durham* (Surtees) 1 Payde to Rycharde gylson for sixe dayes..at the *more dycke for layinge up earthe to yᵉ whicke. **1871** W. MORRIS in Mackail *Life* (1899) I. 234 With a wild musical note, like all the *moor-haunting birds. **1891** *Pall Mall G.* 1 July 5/1 The *moor-keepers state that searches for grouse-nests during April proved most successful. **1915** R. LANKESTER *Diversions of Naturalist* v. 47 One *moor-owner was able to boast that he had on several occasions killed over 500 head of grouse in a single day. **1971** *Country Life* 12 Aug. 396/1 For the moor-owner grouse soon became more profitable than sheep. *c* **1470** HENRY *Wallace* v. 131 At the *mur syde. **1813** VANCOUVER *Agric. Devon* 282 Those cold and blighting vapours carried by the *moor-winds through all the country below. **1902** R. W. CHAMBERS *Maids of Paradise* xvii, To my numbed ears the moor-winds bore a sound coming from a great distance.

6. Special comb.: **moor-band**, a hard substratum of the soil found in moorland, consisting of clay, iron ore, and small stones, and impervious to moisture; called also **moor-band pan**; **moor-bath** [after G. *moorbad*], a therapeutic procedure in which the patient is buried up to the neck in peat taken from a bog; **moor-coal**, †(*a*) ? peat used for burning (*obs.*); (*b*) a friable variety of lignite [after G. *moorkohle* (Werner)]; †**moor-earth**, peaty soil; **moor-evil**, a kind of dysentery in sheep and cattle; †**moor-fen**, a marsh; †**moor grieve**, an overseer of a moor; **moor-hag**, broken ground from which peats have been dug; = *peat hag* (see PEAT[1] 4 d); **moor-head**, the highest part of a moor; **moor-house** (see 4); **moor-ill** = *moor evil*; **moor-master**, †(*a*) an officer of the corporation of York; (*b*) in Cumberland 'the superintendent (not captain) of a mine' (Linton *Lake Country*, 1864, p. 308); **moor-pan** = *moor-band*; **moor peat**, peat derived chiefly from varieties of sphagnum or moss (*Cent. Dict.*); **moor planter** (see quots.); **moor-sick** *a.*, affected with moor-sickness; **moor-sickness**, a disease of sheep = *moor-evil*; **moor-tin, -works** (see 4).

1800 TUKE *Agric. N. Riding* 10 There is some cold thin clay upon what is here called a *moorband. **1844** STEPHENS *Bk. Farm* I. 670 Moor-band pan belongs to a class of bodies known to chemists under the name of *ochrey deposites*. **1882** GEIKIE *Text-bk. Geol.* III. II. ii. §2. 354 A dark ferruginous layer known to Scottish farmers as 'moorband-pan'. **1878** tr. *von Ziemssen's Cycl. Med.* XIII. 170 *Moor-Baths and Mud Baths, so-called form a separate class. **1562** *Act 5 Eliz.* c. 4 §6 Woorking..of any..Stone Sea Cole, Stone Cole, *Moore Cole or Cherk Cole. **1816** JAMESON *Syst. Min.* (ed. 2) II. 378 Moor-Coal or Trapezoidal Coal. **1607** NORDEN *Surv. Dial.* IV. 229 Many fetch *Moore-earth or Murgion from the river betweene Colebrooke and Uxbridge, and carry it to their barren grounds. **1749** W. ELLIS *Compl. Syst. Sheep*, etc. III. v. 321 What they call Wood-Evil in some other Parts, they call it here the *Moor-Evil, because they conceive it is bred in a Sheep or Lamb, by its lying on moory, cold Ground. **1787** A. CROKE *Short View Otmoor* 8 The larger cattle are frequently visited by an epidemical distemper called the Moor-evil. **1847** W. C. MARTIN *Ox* 151 Wood-evil, moor-evil, or pantas. *c* **1205** LAY. 20164 Swa doð þe wilde cron i þan *moruenne [*c* **1275** mor-fenne]. **1590** *Reg. Privy Council Scot.* IV. 499 Thomas Strauchane, his *mure greiff. **1814** W. NICHOLSON *Tales in Verse* 241 The *moor-haggs were wide—but he sten'd them. **1637–50** ROW *Hist. Kirk* (Wodrow Soc.) 557, I hope if I may rule my familie on a *moorhead, may my neighbours in a citie robbe me of my priviledge because I have nighbours? **1798** R. DOUGLAS *Agric. Roxb.* 150 Cattle..are seized frequently with a serious and alarming disease called the *wood-ill*, and sometimes the **moor-ill*. **1816** SCOTT *Bl. Dwarf* x. Though he helped Lambside's cow weel out o' the moor-ill. **1785** *Hist. & Antiq. York* (1788) I. 249 The chamberlains..had two assistants, called bridge-masters, and *mure-masters. **1846** J. BAXTER *Libr. Pract. Agric.* (ed. 4) II. 306 The sub-soil plough was used for breaking the *moor-pan. **1832** *Planting* 35 in *Libr. Usef. Knowl., Husb.* III, Slit planting.. is performed..by the *moor planter. *Ibid.*, The moor planter is a heavy instrument, consisting of a wooden shaft and handle two feet nine inches in length, terminated by a single slightly curved prong of well tempered iron or steel. **1811** in W. Marshall *Rev. South. Rep. to Board Agric.* 532 Sheep pastured on these moors..become what is called *moor-sick. **1814** SHIRREFF *Agric. Surv. Shetl.* 66 A pining, or wasting, called provincially the *moor-sickness, affects sheep, chiefly in autumn.

b. In names of plants: **moor-ball**, a sponge-like ball formed by the threads of a fresh-water alga, *Conferva ægagropila*; **moor-berry**, any plant of the genus *Vaccinium*, esp. the bog

bilberry (*Vaccinium uliginosum*) and the cranberry (*V. oxycoccos*); **moor myrtle**, *Myrica Gale* (Britten & Holland *Plant-n.*); **moor-palm**, (*a*) the flower of the *Carex* or sedge tribe; (*b*) the flower of the *Eriophorum* or cotton-rush; (*c*) the catkin of the dwarf sallow, *Salix aurita*; **moor-silk** = *moor-palm* (b); **moor-wort**, † (*a*) in OE., some unidentified plant, conjectured by some to be the sundew; (*b*) *Andromeda polifolia*.

1777 ROBSON *Brit. Flora* 318 *Conferva ægrogropila* ..*Moor-balls. **1866** *Treas. Bot.* s.v., Moorballs are sometimes used as pen-wipers. **1760** J. LEE *Introd. Bot.* App. 319 *Moor Berries, *Vaccinium*. **1777** ROBSON *Brit. Flora* 56 *Vaccinium Oxycoccus*..Cranberry,..Moorberry. **1788** W. MARSHALL *Yorksh.* II. 342 *Moor-pawms (that is, Moor-Palms), the flowers of the *carex* tribe [ed. 2, 1796, II. 333, the flowers of *eriophorum*, the cotton rush]. **1849** *Sidonia Sorc.* II. 46 From the quantity of moor-palms (*Eriophorum Vaginatum*) which grow in their numerous rich meadows. **1888** F. A. LEES *Flora W. Yorks.* 406 *Salix aurita* L. Dwarf Sallow. 'Moor-palm'. *Ibid.* 470 *Carex binervis* Sm. 'Seggs'. 'Moor Palms'—the polliniferous catkins in bloom. *c* **1882** J. LUCAS *Stud. Nidderdale* 10 In the spring the sheep feed greedily on the flowers of the *moor-silk (cotton-grass). *c* **1000** *Sax. Leechd.* II. 128 Of pæne smalan *mor-wyrte. **1776** WITHERING *Brit. Plants* (1796) II. 373 *Andromeda Daboecia*. Linn. Irish Wort, or Moorwort.

c. In names of animals: **moor-bird**, a bird that nests in the moors, esp. the common grouse, *Tetrao lagopus*; **moor blackbird** (see quot.); **moor-buzzard**, the marsh harrier, *Circus æruginosus*; **moor coot**, the common gallinule or water hen, *Gallinula chloropus*; **moor-fly**, a fly used by anglers; cf. *moorish fly*; **moor game**, the red grouse, *Lagopus scoticus*; also rarely, the black grouse, *Tetrao tetrix*; **moor harrier**, the marsh harrier; **moor hawk** = *moor buzzard* (Swainson 1885); **moor-tetter, -tit, titling**, (*a*) the stone-chat, *Pratincola rubicola*; (*b*) the meadow-pipit, *Anthus pratensis*.

1812 ANNE PLUMPTRE tr. *Lichtenstein's Trav. S. Afr.* I. 224 Woods and level green valleys, with ponds in them, in which were large flocks of *moor-birds. **1900** H. SUTCLIFFE *Shameless Wayne* v, Moor-birds were clamorous up above her head. **1839** MACGILLIVRAY *Brit. Birds* II. 100 *Turdus torquatus*. The Ringed Thrush, or Ring Ouzel... *Moor Blackbird. **1678** RAY *Willughby's Ornith.* 75 The *More-Buzzard: *Milvus Æruginosus*..common to be seen in Heaths and Wasts. **1605** DRAYTON *Man in Moone* 186 The Teale and *Morecoot raking in the Weed. **1831** *G. Montagu's Ornith. Dict.* 327 Moor coot and Moor hen, names for the Gallinule. **1653** WALTON *Angler* iv. 97 The *moor flie. **1611** COTGR., *Poule griesche*,..the henne of the Grice, or *Mooregame. **1769** MRS. RAFFALD *Eng. Housekpr.* (1805) 52 To pot red and black Moor Game. **1846** J. BAXTER *Libr. Pract. Agric.* (ed. 4) I. 333 The red grouse, or moor game, is found upon most of the mountainous districts in the United Kingdom. **1840** MACGILLIVRAY *Brit. Birds* III. 382 *Circus æruginosus*. The Marsh Harrier... *Moor Harrier. Moor Buzzard. **1544** TURNER *Avium Præcip.* I 1 b, Qualis est avicula Anglis stonechattera aut *mortettera dicta. **1668** CHARLETON *Onomasticon* 91 *Rubetra, Rubicola*..the Stone-chatter... Mortetter, or Black Cap. **1885** SWAINSON *Prov. Names Birds* 45 Meadow Pipit (*Anthus pratensis*)... *Moor tit. **1900** H. SUTCLIFFE *Shameless Wayne* iii, Thou look'st scared as a moor-tit. *a* **1672** WILLUGHBY *Ornithol.* II. xv. (1676) 169 The *Moor-Titling: The Stone-smich or Stone-chatter. **1855** *Eng. Cycl., Nat. Hist.* III. 894 *Moor-titling*, one of the names of the..Stone-Chat,..*Saxicola rubicola*.

Moor (mʊə(r), mɔə(r)), *sb.*[2] Forms: 4 **Maur**, 4–7 **More**, 5 **Moure**, **Mowre**, 6, 8 **Maure**, 6–7 **Moore**, 7– **Moor**. [ME. *More*, a. F. *More* (13th c.), *Maure*, ad. L. *Maurus* (med.L. *Mōrus*), Gr. *Μαῦρος*. Cf. Sp., Pg., It. *Moro*; MDu. *Moor*, *Moer* (Du. *Moor*), OHG. *Môr*, pl. *Môrî* (MHG. *Môr*, *Mœr*, mod.G. *Mohr*).

The L. *Maurus*, Gr. *Μαῦρος* may possibly be from some ancient North African language. Some believe the word to be merely a use of Gr. *μαῦρος* black (which on this view is aphetic from *ἀμαυρός* blind); but this adj. (or at least this sense of it) is confined to late Gr., and may even be derived from the ethnic name.]

1. In *Ancient History*, a native of *Mauretania*, a region of Northern Africa corresponding to parts of Morocco and Algeria. In later times, one belonging to the people of mixed Berber and Arab race, Muslim in religion, who constitute the bulk of the population of North-western Africa, and who in the 8th c. conquered Spain. In the Middle Ages, and as late as the 17th c., the Moors were commonly supposed to be mostly black or very swarthy (though the existence of 'white Moors' was recognized), and hence the word was often used for 'Negro'; cf. BLACKAMOOR.

1390 GOWER *Conf.* I. 98 Ther was no grace in the visage, ..Sche loketh forth as doth a More. **1398** TREVISA *Barth. De P. R.* XIX. ix. (1495) 869 Also men of the nacyon of Maurys theyr blacke colour comyth of the inner partyes. *c* **1400** MAUNDEV. (1839) xiv 156 Ethiope is departed in 2 princypalle parties;..the..partie meridionelle is clept Moretane. And the folk of that Contree ben blake..and thei ben clept Mowres. *c* **1489** CAXTON *Sonnes of Aymon* xxvi. 565 He was soo angry for it, that he became as blacke as a moure. **1512** in *Acc. Ld. High Treas. Scotl.* (1902) IV. 338 Item,..to the Bischop of Murrais more, at brocht ane present to the King..xiiijs. **1547** BOORDE *Introd. Knowl.* xxxvi. (1870) 212 Barbary..the inhabytours be Called the Mores: ther be whyte mores and black moors. *a* **1548** HALL *Chron., Hen. VII* 23 b, Granado, which many yeres had bene possessed of the Moores or Mawritane nacion. **1555** W. WATREMAN *Fardle Facions* I. iv. 48 The reste of the people of Libia westward..are called Maures, or Moores. **1555** EDEN *Decades* 355 Ethiopes, which we nowe caule Moores, Moorens, or Negros. **1596** SHAKS. *Merch. V.* III. v. 42, I shall answere that better to the Commonwealth, than you can the getting vp of the Negroes bellie: the Moore is with childe by you Launcelet? **1609** RO. C. *Muley Hamets Rising* title p., The Religion and Policie of the More, or Barbarian. **1613** MIDDLETON *Triumphs of Truth* C 1, I being a Moore; then in Opinions lightnesse As far from Sanctity as my Face from whitenesse. **1613** PURCHAS *Pilgrimage* (1614) 687 The Sea coast-Moores, called by a general name Baduini. **1632** LITHGOW *Trav.* v. 232 A Towne inhabited by Christians, Arabs, and Moores: not blacke Moores, as the Affricans be, but..a kinde of Egyptians. **1647** COWLEY *Mistr., Not Fair*, A very Moor (methinks) plac'd near to Thee, White as his Teeth, would seem to be. **1706** PHILLIPS (ed. Kersey), *Moor*, or *Black-moor*, a native of Mauritania, in Africa. **1707** M. HENRY *Expos. Exod.* ii. 5, etc., Pity so fair a Child should suck the Brest of a Tawny-more. **1728** ELIZA HEYWOOD tr. *Mme. de Gomez's Belle A.* (1732) II. 121 Mezemorte was extremely diverted at the recital, in what manner the Maure had been entertain'd. **1776** J. RICHARDSON *Arab. Gram.* 4 The Mauritanick [hand], which is used by the Moors of Morocco and Barbary. **1849** JAMES *Woodman* iv, A tawny Moor with silver bracelets on his arms, and a turban on his head. **1904** *Athenæum* 2 July 20/1 Another discussion has arisen on the origin..of the term 'Moor'... M. Bloch finds the expression used in five different senses, as applying to the mixed race inhabiting the towns of Algeria and Tunisia, the mountain tribes of Morocco on the Algerian frontier, and the nomadic tribes of Western Sahara... M. Delisle..thinks that those called Moors have never been either black or the descendants of black races.

2. A Muslim, esp. a Muslim inhabitant of India. (Cf. MOORS.)

1588 HICKOCK tr. *Frederick's Voy.* 23 And wheras I speak of Moores I meane Mahomets sect. **1607** TOPSELL *Four-f. Beasts* 462, I haue heard a story of an Englishman in Barbary which turned Moore. **1697** DAMPIER *Voy.* I. 507 A Town of the Moors; which name our Seamen give to all Subjects of the great Mogul, but especially his Mahometan Subjects. **1763** SCRAFTON *Indostan* (1770) 18 The word Moors is used by us to express the Mahometans of all sects and countries who are settled in India. **1864** TREVELYAN *Compet. Wallah* (1866) 251 In those days the rank and file of our army always spoke of the inhabitants of India by the appellation of 'Moors'.

3. *attrib.* and *Comb.*, as *Moor-lass*, *-tabroner*; **Moor bridle**, a kind of bridle used by Moors; **Moor dance** (see quot.); **Moor-lipped** *a.*, having thick lips like those of a Moor; **Moor macaque**, monkey, the black macaque, *Macacus maurus*; **Moor saddle**, a Moorish saddle.

1704 *Lond. Gaz.* No. 4056/8 A *Moor Bridle and Saddle. **1801** STRUTT *Sports & Past.* III. v. 171 The Morisco or *Moor dance is exceedingly different from the morris-dance,..being performed with the castanets, or rattles, at the end of the fingers, and not with bells attached to various parts of the dress. **1504** in *Acc. Ld. High Treas. Scotl.* (1900) II. 465 Item, for hors to the *More lasses. *Ibid.* 469 Quhen the More las wes cristinit. **1639** MASSINGER *Unnat. Combat* IV. i, *Moore lip'd, flat nos'd, dimme ey'd [etc.]. **1906** *Westm. Gaz.* 26 Oct. 8/3 The *Moor Macaque, a stump-tailed Indian monkey. **1885** *Cassell's Encycl. Dict.*, *Moor-monkey. **1504** in *Acc. Ld. High Treas. Scotl.* (1900) II. 430 Item,..to the *More taubronar, to his expens maid be the Morienis, viij Franch crounis.

moor (mʊə(r), mɔə(r)), *sb.*[3] *Naut.* [f. MOOR *v.*[1]] An act of mooring. ***flying*** (or ***running***) ***moor*** (see quot. 1883).

1750 BLANCKLEY *Nav. Expositor*, *Moar*, signifies the laying out the Anchors of a Ship so, as is best and safest for her Riding. **1883** CLARK RUSSELL *Sailors' Lang.*, *Flying moor*, letting go a weather anchor whilst the ship has way, and then, when the cable range is nearly out, letting go the other anchor. **1893** SLOANE-STANLEY *Remin. Midshipm. Life* xxxii. 437 The *Queen*..ran into Beikos, and there made a running moor, which was well performed.

attrib. **1906** *Daily Chron.* 19 Nov. 5/5 In being cast out of the boat they actually fell upon the moor rope.

moor (mʊə(r), mɔə(r)), *v.*[1] Also 5, 7 **more**, 6–8 **moore**, 7 **moar**. [Early mod.E. *more*; prob., in spite of its late occurrence, repr. OE. **márian*, corresponding to MDu. (according to Kluyver originally Frisian, which accounts for the vowel) *mâren* to moor (a vessel), tie up (an animal):—WG. **mairôjan*, a parallel formation with **mairjan*, whence OE. **mǽran* (not recorded, but implied by the derivative *mǽrels* mooring-rope), MDu. *mêren* (mod.Du. *meren*) to moor (a vessel). The word passed from Teut. into Fr. as *amarrer* (13th c.), for which the simple *marer* occurs in OF.

The MDu. *merren, marren* to moor (whence MARLINE) resulted from a confusion of this vb. with *merren, marren* to delay, hinder (mod.Du. only *marren* intr., to loiter, delay, hesitate), cogn. w. MAR *v.*]

1. *trans.* To secure (a ship, boat, or other floating object) in a particular place by means of chains or ropes, which are either fastened to the shore or to anchors.

[**1495**: see MOORING *vbl. sb.*] **1497** *Naval Acc. Hen. VII* (1896) 239 Yron chaynes..that the seid Ship was mored & Rode by in Portesmouth haven. **1540** in R. G. Marsden *Sel. Pl. Crt. Adm.* (1894) I. 91 The said shippe..being not moryd came rydyng with thee floode by force. **1577** NORTHBROOKE *Dicing* (1843) 64 If it bee lawfull (as Christ sayth)..to moore a ship faster that is ready to runne against the rockes. **1653** H. COGAN tr. *Pinto's Trav.* v. 12 They had moored up the Galley. **1769** FALCONER *Dict. Marine* (1780) Cc 3, A ship may be either moored by the head..or by the head and stern. **1793** SMEATON *Edystone L.* § 102 A transport buoy..was moored with chains at the distance of about fifty fathoms directly North from the Gut. **1810** SCOTT *Lady of L.* I. xxiv, Until the rocky isle they reach, And moor their shallop on the beach. **1840** R. H. DANA *Bef. Mast* xv, Until night, we were employed in getting out the boats and mooring ship. **1896** MRS. CAFFYN *Quaker Grandmother* 301 I'll..moor up the boat at our landing-place.

†**b.** ***to moor anchor***, to anchor. *Obs.*

1600 HAKLUYT *Voy.* III. 66 The Michael mored ancker vpon this great yce. **1621**, **1647** [see d].

c. *refl.* or in *passive* with personal subject.

1614 RALEIGH *Hist. World* v. i. § 4. 331 They therefore not only mored themselues strongly by their Anchors, but chained the sides of their Gallies together. **1748** *Anson's Voy.* II. i. 112 We carried our hawsers on board her, in order to moor ourselves nearer in shore. **1877** C. W. THOMSON *Voy. Challenger* I. ii. 109 About mid-day we were moored in the Tagus off the town.

d. *transf.* and *fig.*

1621 T. WILLIAMSON tr. *Goulart's Wise Vieillard* 179 Who hath commaunded you to moore your ancher of hope in such a little lump of dust as man is? **1647** WARD *Simp. Cobler* (1843) 20 Those men never Moored their Anchors well in the firme soile of Heaven, that are weather-waft up and down with every eddy-wind of every new doctrine. **1742** YOUNG *Nt. Th.* IX. 597 Thou, whose heart, Whose little heart, is moor'd within a nook Of this obscure Terrestrial. **1856** STANLEY *Sinai & Pal.* i. (1858) 65 The camels as they lie, like stranded ships, moored round the tents. **1860** TYNDALL *Glac.* I. xxv. 185 Moored to the rock on two sides, the cabin stood firm.

2. *absol.* and *intr.* **a.** To secure one's ship (etc.) in a particular place; to anchor.

1627 CAPT. SMITH *Seaman's Gram.* ix. 45 More Crosse. To More a crosse is to lay one anchor to one side of the streame, and the other to the other right against one another, and so they beare equally ebbe and flood. *Ibid.*, More Prouiso. To more a Prouiso, is to haue one anchor in the riuer, and a hawser a shore, which is mored with her head a shore. *Ibid.*, Two cables is the least, and foure cables the best to more by. **1667** MILTON *P.L.* I. 207 The Pilot of some small night-founder'd Skiff,..With fixed Anchor in his skaly rind Moors by his side under the Lee. **1678** PHILLIPS (ed. 4), To *Moor alongst*, is to lay an Anchor amidst the stream, a Head, and another a Stern, when you fear driving ashore. **1688** R. HOLME *Armoury* III. 165/1 Mooring Water-shot, that is quartering between both [anchors]. **1748** *Anson's Voy.* II. i. 114 Cumberland Bay, where we moored. **1877** A. B. EDWARDS *Up Nile* xxi. 641 Most travellers moor for a day or two at Karnak.

b. Of a ship: To be made secure by means of anchors; to take up a particular position at anchor.

1697 DRYDEN *Æneid* VI. 1246 At length on Oozy ground his Gallies moor. **1701** in Picton *L'pool Munic. Rec.* (1883) I. 308 Such ships..shall moore West Nor-west and East Southeast. **1875** J. H. BENNET *Winter Medit.* II. xi. 364 A solid granite quay, that enables small vessels to moor close to land.

c. With *up*: to secure a seaplane; of a seaplane, to be made secure.

1936 [see GRABBIT (BOAT) HOOK]. **1942** *Times* 3 Sept. 5/7 Night was slowly mastering daylight as we..landed, to moor up near some naval patrol boats.

Hence **moored** *ppl. a.*

1867 JEAN INGELOW *Christ's Resurrect.* x, Swaying on a purple sea, The many moored galleys clustering at her quay. **1900** *Daily News* 24 Sept. 8/7 A violent collision with the moored barges followed.

moor (mʊə(r), mɔə(r)), *v.*[2] [Prob. f. MOOR *sb.*[1] Cf. *moor-evil*.] *intr.* Of cattle: To evacuate sanguineous urine. Hence '**mooring** *vbl. sb.*

1737 BRACKEN *Farriery Impr.* (1756) I. 257 Cattle which piss Blood, or have the Mooring, as they call it. **1775** J. WATSON *Hist. Halifax* 543 Moor, as a cow does, when her water is mixed with blood. **1824-8** *Craven Dial.* s.v., When cattle are inflicted with a disease which occasions bloody urine, they are said to be moored... Some attribute it to coarse grass in marshy grounds.

moor: see MOAR, MOHUR, MORE, MORT.

moorad, variant of MOORIT.

moorage ('mʊərɪdʒ, 'mɔərɪdʒ). [f. MOOR *v.*[1] + -AGE.]

1. The action or process of mooring; the condition of being moored; also a place for mooring.

1648 EARL OF WESTMORLAND *Otia Sacra* 162 She's come to Moorage, and there fast, To lie aside untill carin'd. **1682** WHELER *Journ. Greece* I. 25 It hath good Moorage, and is deep enough for Ships of any rate. **1887** HALL CAINE *Deemster* xl, Since my coming to moorage there no boat had crossed its water. **1892** *Daily News* 30 May 2/3 There are spots where you may pay for moorage.

2. Money paid for the use of moorings.

a **1676** HALE *Narr. Customes* iv. in S. A. Moore *Foreshore* (1888) 344 Morage for ships, terrage, wharfage. **1868** *Rep. Trial Appledore Harbour* in *Exeter & Plymouth Gaz.* 13 Mar., The only custom he had proved was the right to come in, paying a certain moorage or postage.

moorat, variant of MOORIT.

'**moor-burn**. *Sc.* Forms: see MOOR *sb.*[1] [f. MOOR *sb.*[1] + BURN *sb.*[3]] The burning of the heather on a moor, which is unlawful between April 11 and Nov. 1. So **moor-burner**, one who sets fire to heather; also **moor-burning** *vbl. sb.*

14.. *Ordo Justiciarie* in *Sc. Acts* (1814) I. 342/1 All..mur burnaris in forbodin tyme. **1424** *Sc. Acts Jas. I* (1814) II. 6/1 It is ordanyt þ[t] na man mak murbyrn eftir þe monethe of

marche..vnder þe payne of xls. **1499** *Exch. Rolls Scotl.* XI. 395 That thair be na murcburne. **1610** *Act 7 Jas. I*, An Acte against burning of Lingard Heath and other Moor Burning. **1678** SIR G. MACKENZIE *Crim. Laws Scot.* II. xiv. §1 (1699) 210 They have power to punish.. Makers of Moor-burn, Keepers of Crooves, wilful Beggers. **1773** *Act 13 Geo. III* c. 54 §4 Every Person who shall make Muir-burn, or set fire to any Heath or Muir, in..Scotland,..shall [etc.]. **1851** STEPHENS *Bk. Farm* 3736 As heath constitutes a principal food of the mountain sheep, muir-burning improves the heath for food. **1894** CROCKETT *Raiders* 218 We were now among the burnt heather..kicking up the ashy dust of the March muirburn.

fig. **1839** in J. MacKerrow *Hist. Secession Ch.* (1841) 647, I was afraid of raising a *muir burn* that might not be easily quenched.

'moor-cock. [f. MOOR *sb.*[1] + COCK *sb.*[1]] The male of the red grouse, *Lagopus scoticus.* Also occas. the blackcock, *Tetrao tetrix.*

1329-30 *Durham Acc. Rolls* (Surtees) 16 In..xij Murkokes emptis. In..vij Murkokes. **1427** *Sc. Acts Jas. I* (1814) II. 16/2 Blak cokes gra hennys and mur cokes. **1567** GOLDING *Ovid's Met.* VIII. (1593) 201 Now it is a meare And moorecockes, cootes, and cormorants do breed and nestle there. *a* **1695** WOOD *Oxford* (O.H.S.) III. 157 Arms.. argent, a chevron between 3 more-cocks sable. **1731** ALBIN *Nat. Hist. Birds* I. 23 The Red Game, or More-Cock *Lagopus altera.* **1780** EDMONDSON *Her.*, *Moor cock*, the male of the black game, or large black grouse. **1850** J. STRUTHERS *Life* Poet. Wks. I. p. xiv, The Scraigh of the paitrick, the birr of the muircock. **1899** CROCKETT *Kit Kennedy* 298 Moor-cocks were crowing in the hollows.

Moorcroft ('mʊəkrɒft). The name of William *Moorcroft* (1872–1945) used *attrib.* and *ellipt.* to designate pottery produced by him at his workshop in Cobridge, north Staffordshire, and noted for its powdered blue effects and flambé glazes.

1910 *Pottery Gaz.* May 551/2, I cannot now do more than mention the most interesting developments in glaze effects and wonderful colour schemes revealed in the latest examples of 'Moorcroft Faïence'. **1918** *Pottery & Glass Record* Nov. p. i (Advt.), Moorcroft ware, hand-made decorative objects..W. Moorcroft, Ltd., Potters, Burslem. .. Works adjoining Cobridge Station. **1923** *Pottery Gaz. & Glass Trade Rev.* 2 Apr. 660/1 Baron Hayashi, the Japanese Ambassador, on purchasing two flambé vases, expressed the opinion that the Moorcroft vases were so like early Chinese work that had Mr. Moorcroft's name not been on them experts would have found it difficult to distinguish the difference. **1939** *Times* 8 Mar. 12/4 Moorcroft pottery has for some years been recognized abroad as standing in a class by itself among the modern products of ceramic art. **1946** *Pottery & Glass* June 33/1 Several American museums possess representative collections of Moorcroft ware. **1956** C. G. E. BUNT *Brit. Potters & Pottery Today* 41 The rich and generous decoration is..all hand work. To this is largely due the distinctiveness, the individuality of Moorcroft Pottery. **1972** F. MACCARTHY *All Things Bright & Beautiful* 85 Blue Moorcroft Pottery and Cornish Ware were endlessly in favour [in the 1920s]. **1974** M. KELLY *That Girl in Alley* iii. 40 The Moorcroft vases, the Lalique bowl, the silk runner on top of the piano. **1975** *Times* 17 Jan. 3 Sotheby's Belgravia sale of studio ceramics..underlined the tremendous new collector interest in the art potters of about 1880–1950... Minor Moorcroft was selling like hot cakes.

moord(e)re, obs. forms of MURDER.

Moore (mʊə(r), mɔə(r)). Designating an almanac, the first edition of which, compiled by Francis *Moore* (1657–*c* 1715), was issued in 1700 under the title of *Vox Stellarum*, and which was later known as *Old Moore's Almanac.* Also *ellipt.* Hence (nonce-wd.) **Old Moore's Almanac** *v. absol.*, to engage in predictions of the future.

1817 KEATS *Let.* 10 Sept. (1931) I. 39, I know not whether you prefer..Cinderella and her glass slipper to Moor's Almanack. *a* **1821** —— *Cap & Bells* lvi, in *Compl. Poetical Works* (1907) 476 Look in the Almanack—*Moore* never lies. **1855** GEO. ELIOT in *Westm. Rev.* Oct. 437 Let him..rival Moore's Almanack in the prediction of political events. **1873** C. M. YONGE *Pillars of House* IV. xl. 170 The mysteries of Moore's Almanac on the wall. **1896** G. B. SHAW *Our Theatres in Nineties* (1932) II. 124 As devoutly as any superstitious washerwoman ever read Zadkiel or Old Moore. **1916** D. H. LAWRENCE *Let.* 24 May (1962) I. 452 But I am afraid I bore you Old-Moore's Almanacking. **1936** *Discovery* Dec. 389/1 He published a sort of Old Moore's Almanac and told people's fortunes, and generally practised the acts of the astrologer. **1975** *Broadcast* 15 Sept. 16/3 Throw the net wide and don't always toss back the little 'uns are old Moore's words of wisdom.

moore, obs. form of MOOR, MORE.

mooreash, obs. form of MOORISH *a.*[1]

mooreed, var. MURID.

mooreite ('mʊəraɪt, 'mɔəraɪt). *Min.* [f. the name of Gideon *Moore* (1842–1895), U.S. chemist + -ITE[1].] A hydrated basic sulphate of magnesium, manganese, and zinc, $(Mg,Mn,Zn)_8SO_4(OH)_{14}.4H_2O$, found as colourless monoclinic crystals.

1929 BAUER & BERMAN in *Amer. Mineralogist* XIV. 165 The cavities in the pyrochroite are lined, and some of the crevices are filled, with glassy white tabular crystals which, upon investigation, proved to be a new mineral, for which the name mooreite is here proposed, in honor of Dr. Gideon E. Moore, an early investigator of Sterling Hill and Franklin minerals. **1951** *Mineral. Abstr.* XI. 384 The action of salt water on the minerals of this vein in the August Victoria mine at Hüls, Westphalia, has produced the following secondary minerals:..mooreite, dickite, sericite, and blödite. **1969** *Amer. Mineralogist* LIV. 973 Mooreite..is monoclinic although the space group is not $P2_1/m$ as previously reported but rather $P2_1/a$.

Mooren, variant of MORIAN.

Moorery ('mʊərərɪ, 'mɔərərɪ). *nonce-wd.* [f. MOOR *sb.*[2] + -ERY. Cf. *Jewry.*] A Moorish quarter.

1808 SOUTHEY *Chron. Cid* App. 386 They arose and entered the Moorery, and slew many Moors.

Mooress ('mʊərɪs, 'mɔərɪs). [f. MOOR *sb.*[2] + -ESS.] A female Moor.

1611 COTGR., *Moresque*, a Mooresse, a shee Moore, a blacke woman. **1677** T. HOLYOKE *Eng.-Lat. Dict.*, A shee moor, or mooress, *morula.* **1835** CAMPBELL *Epistle fr. Algiers to Hor. Smith* 25 The Mooresses, shrouded in white. **1891** HALL CAINE *Scapegoat* xxii, A matronly Mooress.

mooret, variant of MOORIT.

'moor-fowl. [f. MOOR *sb.*[1] + FOWL.]

1. *Sc.* The red grouse, *Lagopus scoticus.*

1506 in *Acc. Ld. High Treas. Scotl.* (1901) III. 191 Tua wild geis and xij mure fowlis. **1632** LITHGOW *Trav.* III. 106 Abundance of Geese,..Pigeons, Partridges, Moore-Fowle. **1773** *Act 13 Geo. III* c. 54 §3 Pheasants, Muir Fowl, Tarmagans, Heath Fowl [etc.]. **1787** BURNS *Tam Samson's Elegy* xiii, Perhaps upon his mould'ring breast Some spitefu' muirfowl bigs her nest, To hatch an' breed. **1881** J. GRANT *Cameronians* I. iv. 56 Muirfowl, ptarmigan [etc.].

Comb. **1816** SCOTT *Old Mort.* i, The moor-fowl shooter has been often surprised to find him busied in cleaning the moss from the grey stones.

2. *South Carolina.* The ruffed grouse.

1791 W. BARTRAM *Trav. Carolina*, etc. (1792) 329 The wary moor fowl thundering in the distant echoing hills.

3. *Sc.* **moorfowl('s egg**, a variety of pear.

1705 *Lease* in W. Hector *Select. Judic. Rec. Renfrew* (1876) 42 That pear tree called the Muirfowl Egg. **1817** NEILL *Hortic.* in *Edin. Encycl.* (1830) XI. 212 The Muirfowl egg is another pear of good qualities, said to be originally Scottish. **1860** HOGG *Fruit Man.* 202 Muirfowl's Egg.

'moor-grass. [f. MOOR *sb.*[1] + GRASS.]

1. Sundew, *Drosera rotundifolia.*

1597 GERARDE *Herbal* III. clv. 1366 It is called in English Sunne deaw,..in the North parts Red rot,..and in Yorkeshire Moore grass. **1674** JOSSELYN *Voy. New Eng.* 80 *Rosa-solis*, Sun-dew, moor-grass. **1749** W. ELLIS *Compl. Syst. Sheep*, etc. III. v. 321 Now this Moor-Grass, in the Parish of Wing [Buckinghamshire], they call *Rosa-Solis*, as it is distinguished by Shepherds from other Grasses.

2. *Sc.* Silver-weed, *Potentilla anserina.*

1777 LIGHTFOOT *Flora Scot.* I. 268 *Potentilla anserina*.. Moor-Grass. Scotis.

3. A grass of the genus *Molinia*, esp. *M. cærulea*, blue moor-grass.

1749 W. ELLIS *Compl. Syst. Sheep* 321 This moor-grass.. they call *Rosa-Solis*, as it is distinguished by Shepherds from other Grasses, which know it by its three-square Leaf, Rapier-like. **1799** J. HULL *Brit. Flora* I. 21 *Sesleria cærulea*, ..Blue Moor-grass. **1866** *Treas. Bot.* s.v. Grass. **1950** W. H. PEARSALL *Mountains & Moorlands* ix. 179 The moor-grass may be found growing on oxygen-poor peats with a moderately high salt content and low acidity. **1972** *Country Life* 13 Jan. 104/1 There was a telling use of..a cultivated form of the extremely common purple moor grass.

4. The cotton-grass, *Eriophorum angustifolium* (Britten & Holland).

5. *gen.* A grass growing on a moor.

1900 *Archæol. Æliana* XXII. 80 Black-faced sheep, which maintain a spare existence on the heather and moor-grasses.

Moor-head: see MOOR'S-HEAD.

'moor-hen. [f. MOOR *sb.*[1] + HEN.]

1. The Water-hen, *Gallinula chloropus.*

c **1300** *Pol. Songs* (Camden) 158 Heo cometh by-modered ase a mor-hen. **14..** *Voc.* in Wr.-Wülcker 599/43 *Palestris*, a morhen. **1575** TURBERV. *Falconrie* 137 Some hold opinion, that the bones and bloud of a Bargander, Moorehen, and such like, may be giuen to an hauke. **1655** MOUFET & BENNET *Health's Impr.* (1746) 205 Some Birds are sodden or roasted without their Skins, because they are black and bitter, as Rooks, Daws, Coots, and Moor-hens. **1705** DALE *Pharmacol.* Suppl. 359 *A. Gallina aquatica*... The Common Water-Hen, or Moor-Hen. **1883** *Encycl. Brit.* XVI. 808/2 In winter, when the inland waters are frozen, the majority of Moor-hens betake themselves to the tidal rivers.

2. The female of the red grouse, *Lagopus scoticus.*

1347 *Durham Acc. Rolls* (Surtees) 42 In..vj Morehennes empt. **1530** PALSGR. 246/1 Morehen, *poulle griache.* **1553** *Burgh Rec. Edin.* (1871) II. 185 The best mure hen vjd. **1611** COTGR., *Poule griesche*, a Moorehenne, the henne of the Grice, or Mooregame. *a* **1796** BURNS *'The Heather was blooming'* 4 At length they discovered a bonie moor-hen. **1837** MACGILLIVRAY *Brit. Birds* I. 169 *Lagopus Scoticus*... Moor-fowl. Moor-cock, Moor-hen.

3. A bird of the Australian genus *Tribonyx.*

1860 G. BENNETT *Gatherings Nat. in Australasia* viii. 169 The Rail-like bird, the Black-tailed Tribonyx, or Moor Hen of the colonists.

4. The American coot, *Fulica americana.*

1888 TRUMBULL *Names of Birds* 117.

Moorian, variant of MORIAN.

mooring ('mʊərɪŋ, 'mɔərɪŋ), *vbl. sb.* [f. MOOR *v.*[1] + -ING[1].]

1. The action of the verb MOOR *v.*[1]

1485 [see *mooring-chain* below]. **1495** *Naval Acc. Hen. VII* (1896) 162 The Bryngyng the seyd Ship to the Shore And for moryng of hyre there. **1626** CAPT. SMITH *Accid. Yng. Seamen* 3 To haue..the command of the long boate, for..warping, towing, and moreing. **1797** BURKE *Regic. Peace* iii. (1892) 251 There is much want of room for the safe and convenient mooring of vessels, and constant access to them. **1886** *Encycl. Brit.* XXI. 598/1 One of the objections made to slack mooring is that turns are formed below water where they are not visible.

2. *concr.* Something (*e.g.* a rope, chain, etc.) by which a floating object is made fast; also the object to which it is moored. **a.** *sing.* (Somewhat *rare.*)

1775 FALCK *Day's Diving Vessel* 51 Slacking a little of the mooring. **1809** BYRON *Lines to Mr. Hodgson* 17 Now our boatmen quit their mooring, And all hands must ply the oar. **1820** SCORESBY *Acc. Arctic Reg.* I. 256 Wrecked by the fall of their icy mooring. **1843** *Penny Cycl.* XXVI. 451/1 To one end of the line a chain-shot was attached by way of mooring. **1894** *Outing* (U.S.) XXIII. 401/1 Mainsail, foresail and gaff-topsail were hoisted, and her jib ready to hoist as soon as the mooring was dropped.

fig. *a* **1854** H. REED *Lect. Brit. Poets* xiv. (1857) II. 184 The tempest which had driven him from his domestic mooring was followed by a fitful calm.

b. *pl.*

1744 J. PHILIPS *Jrnl. Anson's Exped.* 192 The Prize drove off from her Moorings. **1750** BLANCKLEY *Nav. Expositor*, *Moarings*, are laid out in Harbour, and consists of Claws, Pendant Chains, Cables [etc.]. **1858** LYTTON *What will he do* I. v, Vance loosened the boat from its moorings, stepped in, and took up the oars. **1875** *Encycl. Brit.* II. 8/2 Mushroom anchors first proposed for ships, are now only used for moorings. **1889** *Cath. News* 27 July 8/6 The huge Rodney fouled a lightship the other day and broke her moorings.

transf. and *fig.* **1836** J. GILBERT *Chr. Atonem.* (1852) 116 Having broken from all moral moorings, he will find himself adrift. **1897** *Allbutt's Syst. Med.* III. 507 When..the pylorus is dragged from its moorings.

3. *pl.* The place in a river or harbour where a vessel can be moored.

1758 J. BLAKE *Plan Mar. Syst.* 65 Nearly the same time will be elapsed before the..ship..can be secured at her moorings. **1849** MACAULAY *Hist. Eng.* iii. I. 300 Some of the new men of war, indeed, were so rotten that, unless speedily repaired, they would go down at their moorings. **1860** LONGF. *Wayside Inn*, *P. Revere's Ride* 18 Where swinging wide at her moorings lay The Somerset.

fig. **1851** CARLYLE *Sterling* II. iv. (1872) 118 When once the household was settled in its new moorings..he returned to his employments and pursuits.

4. *attrib.* and *Comb.*, as *mooring bridle, boat, buoy, cable, chain, -ground, hook, -port, -stone*; **mooring anchor**, one of the fixed anchors placed at the bottom of a harbour, to which vessels are moored; **mooring-block** (see quot. 1815); **mooring mast**, a strong upright structure to which an airship is moored; **mooring-out**, used *attrib.* to denote a site at which an airship may be moored; **mooring-post**, (*a*) a strong upright post fixed into the ground for securing vessels to the landing-place by hawsers or chains; (*b*) one of the strong pieces of oak inserted into the deck of a large ship for fastening the moorings to when alongside a quay (Adm. Smyth); **mooring swivel**, a swivel used in mooring a ship to shackle two chains together so that they may not become twisted.

1820 SCORESBY *Acc. Arctic Reg.* I. 257 For the purpose of placing a *mooring anchor. **1875** *Encycl. Brit.* II. 8/1 Mooring anchors are not limited by considerations of weight, &c., as other anchors are... Mooring anchors may therefore be of stone..or of cast iron. **1809** in *Trans. Soc. Arts* (1811) XXVIII. 173 Many of the line-of-battle ships.. are moored with Mr. Hemman's cast-iron *mooring-blocks. **1815** *Falconer's Dict. Marine* (ed. Burney), *Mooring-block* is a sort of cast iron anchor of about 150 cwt. used in some of his Majesty's ports for riding ships by. **1957** D. G. O. BAILLIE *Sea Affair* xii. 227 The Arab *mooring-boat crews were ready at the buoys to cast off our lines. **1967** S. WATERS *Indentures Indorsed* xxvi. 153 The two ships were almost alongside each other with only a small mooring boat containing five men between them. *a* **1865** SMYTH *Sailor's Word-Bk.* (1867) 484 **Mooring-bridle*, the fasts attached to moorings, one taken into each hawse-hole, or bridle-port. **1919** *Gloss. Aeronaut. Terms* (R. Aeronaut. Soc.) 58 *Mooring bridle*, a rigging passing between two points from a fitting in the length of which the mooring rope is attached. **1948** R. DE KERCHOVE *Internat. Maritime Dict.* 474/2 *Mooring bridle*, the chains or fasts attached to permanent moorings and taken into the hawse holes. **1809** *Naval Chron.* XXIV. 23 She ran against one of the *mooring buoys. **1875** *Encycl. Brit.* II. 8/1 A large buoy is attached to the end of a *mooring cable. **1485** *Naval Acc. Hen. VII* (1896) 38 Chenes for the Loves..j, *Moryng chenes..ij. **1812** *Dramatic Censor 1811* 223 The monopoly of the East-India Company, Lord Gwydir's mooring-chain monopoly, should be all abolished. **1888** KIPLING *Departmental Ditties* (1890) 68 Through the mooring-chains The wide-eyed corpse rolled free. **1856** LEVER *Martins of Cro' M.* 576 Can you not see..that where one drags the anchor so easily, the *mooring-ground was never good? **1907** J. MASEFIELD *Tarpaulin Muster* viii. 97, I..cast the painter around the *mooring-hook. **1919** *Gloss. Aeronaut. Terms* (R. Aeronaut. Soc.) 59 **Mooring mast*, a mast to the head of which an airship may be moored. **1929** *Times* 2 Nov. 9/4, R 101..was walked over to the mast at dawn..in 20 minutes, was at once coupled up to the mooring-mast cable and then waited patiently..for the actual mooring. **1972** *Daily Tel.* 26 June 5/1 Europa was in the air for the first time since its mooring mast snapped and the airship careered for threequarters of a mile. **1769** FALCONER *Dict. Marine* (1780) Cc 3 b, Bridles ..whose upper ends are drawn into the ship at the *mooring-ports. **1864** MRS. LLOYD *Ladies Polc.* 41 Two or three hardy fellows, who held on for life to the *mooring-posts. **1803** *Chron.* in *Ann. Reg.* 468/2 The *mooring-stones remained perfectly steady as did all the ships that were

properly moored. *c* **1860** H. STUART *Seaman's Catech.* 54 What is the use of a *mooring swivel? It is put on when the ship has two anchors down, to keep the turns out of the cables. **1934** J. A. SINCLAIR *Airships in Peace & War* 190 The *mooring-out station was more of a war measure. **1971** *Country Life* 6 May 1087/1 On flying from our base in Anglesey, or our mooring-out ground at Malahide, [etc.].

moorish (ˈmʊərɪʃ, ˈmɔərɪʃ), *a.*[1] Forms: 4 **moorysshe**, 4–5 **moryssh(e**, 5–6 **moresch**, **-isch**, 6 **moarish(e**, **morishe**, **-ysh**, 6–7 **morish**, 7 **mooreash**, 9 *Sc.* **muirish**, 6– **moorish**. [f. MOOR *sb.*[1] + -ISH.]

†**1.** Of soil: Boggy, swampy. *Obs.*

1491 CAXTON *Vitas Patr.* (W. de W. 1495) I. xxxiii. 28 The grounde was soo softe and moryssh, that they entred up to the raynes. **1538** LELAND *Itin.* V. 81 It is to be supposid that thes Pooles for the most part in Morisch [*v.r.* Moresch] Groundes, and lying sumwhat in low Groundes dreane the moist Places about them. **1591** SPENSER *Ruines of Time* 140 There now no rivers course is to be seene, But moorish fennes, and marshes ever greene. **1634** MILTON *Comus* 432 By lake, or moorish fen. **1641** WITHER *Hallelujah* II. xx. (1879) 292 Moorish Grounds are now so hard, That, on them we safe may ride. **1766** ENTICK *London* IV. 199 A thousand loads..were..laid in a moorish place. **1820** SCORESBY *Acc. Arctic Reg.* I. 120 This swamp had a moorish look, and consisted apparently of black alluvial soil.

fig. **1601** B. JONSON *Poetaster* v. i, They be path-lesse, moorish minds That..sinke Beneath the steps of any villanie.

†**b.** *transf.* ? Spongy, soft. *Obs.*

1398 TREVISA *Barth. De P.R.* XVIII. xci. (1495) 840 The frogge is watry and moorysshe. *Ibid.* XIX. ix. 869 Moryssh thynges dooth growe in erthe. **1750** E. SMITH *Compl. Housew.* 8 If their noses are snotty, and their throats moorish and muddy, they are bad.

†**c.** Of water: Such as is found in bogs. *Obs.*

1496 *Fysshynge w. Angle* (1883) 11 Those waters that ben hethy or morysshe. **1596** SPENSER *F.Q.* IV. xi. 29 The chaulky Kenet,..The morish Cole. *a* **1640** DAY *Parl. Bees* xii. (1881) 75 The moorish pooles stand emptie, left By water.

d. ***moorish mallow*** = MARSH MALLOW.

1597 GERARDE *Herbal* II. cccxxxviii. 789 In English marsh Mallow, Moorish Mallowe, and white Mallowe.

e. moorish brown, moorish fly, the names of an artificial fly for fishing.

1635 MARKHAM *Pleas. Princes* 26 The Moorish-fly is made of fine flocks, shorne from a freese-gray russet, and the wings of the blackest male of a Drake. **1799** G. SMITH *Laboratory* II. 309 March... Flies proper..3. Moorish-brown.

2. Of or pertaining to a moor; abounding in moors or moorland; having the characteristics of a moor; belonging to a moor.

1546 *Yorks. Chantry Surv.* (Surtees) II. 413 In a wyld and morishe contree. *c* **1600** NORDEN *Spec. Brit., Cornw.* (1728) 63 A church standinge amonge the moarishe hills. **1744** PRESTON in *Phil. Trans.* XLIII. 61 The Land is mountainous and moorish, abounding with Moss and Heather. **1787** BURNS in Cunningham *Life* (1850) 55/1 A romantic, but rather moorish place, on the banks of the Poole. **1802** WORDSW. *Resol. & Independ.* xi, Upon the margin of that moorish flood. **1853** G. JOHNSTON *Nat. Hist. E. Bord.* I. 104 Common in muirish pastures. **1887** RUSKIN *Præterita* II. 177 Moorish Skiddaw and far-sweeping Saddleback.

3. Inhabiting a moor; growing on moors.

1612 DRAYTON *Poly-olb.* xii. 580 Or'e-gone with loue of Hanse, a dapper More-land Lad..the wanton hart of that delicious mayd..was turn'd so much from being coy That shee might seeme to doat vpon the Morish boy. **1844** STEPHENS *Bk. Farm* II. 474 The disease..is there called the muir-ill, as if it were the consequence of cows eating muirish plants.

Moorish (ˈmʊərɪʃ, ˈmɔərɪʃ), *a.*[2] Also 5 **morys**, 7 **morish**. [f. MOOR *sb.*[2] + -ISH.]

1. Of or pertaining to the Moors. Now often used with reference to the style of furniture and architecture, popular in England in the nineteenth century, characteristic of that made by the Moors in Spain (8th–15th c.) and in Northern Africa (cf. MORESQUE).

1434 in *Privy Purse Exp. Eliz. of York* (1830) 242/2 Her hullyng of black, red and green, with morys letters, with cushions. **1600** E. BLOUNT tr. *Conestaggio* 323 For that a moorish slaue, who hoped by that meanes to saue himselfe, discouered him to a Prouost marshall. **1709** STEELE *Tatler* No. 112 ¶3 Augustus..is said to have passed many of his Hours with little Moorish Boys at a Game of Marbles. **1797** *Encycl. Brit.* (ed. 3) II. 223/1 The greatest peculiarity in the Moorish architecture is the horse-shoe arch. **1843** BORROW *Bible in Spain* vii, A large ancient and seemingly Moorish castle. **1885** *Encycl. Brit.* XIX. 622/2 A fine dish, now in the British Museum..; though Moorish in style, it has a Spanish inscription. **1903** *Edin. Rev.* Apr. 278 The Moorish peasantry..fought for their masters. **1903** A. BENNETT *Leonora* iii. 80 Bessie..set a Moorish stool before the Chesterfield. **1912** —— *Matador* 49 They were having tea at a little Moorish table in..the lounge. **1965** J. ARONSON *Encycl. Furnit.* (1966) 410/1 The X-type chair was common .., a light Moorish type of repeated slats with inlay. **1969** M. ALLINGHAM *Case-Book* 101 Towards the [sea] port..the architecture veers towards Victorian Moorish. **1972** E. JOY *Furniture* vii. 188 Of completely different character was the imported..Moorish furniture which first made Liberty's reputation when they began in business in 1875 as an 'Oriental Warehouse'. **1975** R. BUTLER *Where all Girls are Sweeter* iv. 30 'Four Winds' was all Moorish, Bauschule and Odeon but it stood back in at least five acres.

b. Befitting a Moor, barbarous. *nonce-use.*

1795 COLERIDGE *Plot Discovered* 28 And if by the wanton and moorish exercise of this privilege he can ensnare the assembly into marks of indignation, then [etc.].

2. Muslim. Now only *colloq.* (chiefly in uneducated use) in Southern India and Sri Lanka (Ceylon). †Formerly also used (*adj.* and quasi-*sb.*) as a name of the Urdū or Hindustānī language: see MOORS.

1613 PURCHAS *Pilgrimage* (1614) 482 The Religion in Cambaia is partly Moorish, partly Heathenish. **1763** ORME *Milit. Trans. Hindostan* I. 276 The centinel was sitting at the top of the gate, singing a moorish song. **1784** in Seton Karr & Sandeman *Select. fr. Calcutta Gaz.* (1864) I. 15 Lieutenants Speediman and Rutledge..were bound, circumcised, and clothed in Moorish garments. **1804** WELLINGTON in Gurw. *Desp.* (1837) III. 290 She had a Moorish woman interpreter, and as I heard her give orders to her interpreter in the Moorish language [etc.]. **1889** *Ceylon Observer* 11 June, From Weligama comes the news that another alexandrite has just been discovered by the Moorish priest (Moulana) weighing 6 lb. and 8 rupees.

†ˈ**moorishly**, *adv.* *Obs.*[−1] [f. MOORISH *a.*[1] + -LY[2].] In a marshy manner.

1622 DRAYTON *Poly-olb.* xxv. 332 Shee in her foggy Fennes so moorishly doth feed.

†ˈ**moorishness.** *Obs.* [f. MOORISH *a.*[1] + -NESS.] Marshy or peaty quality.

1649 BLITHE *Eng. Improv. Impr.* (1653) 59 If this be not.. steeped so wth constant corrupt water, that it is turned into a moorishness,..this very Land may prove your best Land in a little time. **1692** R. L'ESTRANGE *Josephus, Wars of Jews* III. xviii. (1733) 686 The Water sweet and potable, without any thing of Moorishness either in the Taste or Colour.

†ˈ**Moorism.** *Obs.* [f. MOOR *sb.*[2] + -ISM.]

a. The polity or religion of the Moors; Islam. **b.** Moors collectively. **c.** Conduct befitting Moors, barbarism.

1620 SHELTON *Quix.* II. xxvi. 174 Don Quixote seeing and hearing such a deale of Moorisme, and such a coyle, he thought fit to succour those that fled. *Ibid.*, He began to raine strokes vpon the Puppetish Moorisme, ouerthrowing some, and beheading others. **1627** R. ASHLEY *Almansor* 1 The great Caliph, the sustayner of Morisme. **1681** RYCAUT tr. *Gracian's Critick* 148 Banishing not only her, but her devoted Worshippers from the extent of their Dominions, with which barbarous Morism, not yet fully satisfied [etc.].

moorit (ˈmurət), *a.* and *sb.* *Shetland dial.* Also **moorad**, **-at**, **-et**, **murid**, **murrit**. [a. ON. *móráuð-r*, f. *mó-r* moor, heath + *rauð-r* red.]

a. *adj.* Heather-brown, reddish brown: *esp.* of sheep and wool. **b.** *sb.* A reddish brown colour.

1809 EDMONDSTON *Zetland* II. 210 The sheep..are of different colours; as white, grey, black, speckled, and of a dusky brown called moorit. **1871** R. COWIE *Shetland* ix. 162 Sheep..of a peculiar brownish shade, termed by the natives murid. **1884** RAMPINI in *Gd. Words* Nov. 746/2 A herd of native sheep, black, white, grey, and moorat. **1895** *Spectator* 31 Aug. 278/1 It is sometimes difficult to convince people that our moorad is not dyed.

moorland (ˈmʊələnd, ˈmɔələnd), *sb.* [f. MOOR *sb.*[1] + LAND *sb.*[1]]

1. Uncultivated land; in early use chiefly fenland; in mod. use, country consisting of moors; land abounding in heather; a moor.

c **950** *Lindisf. Gosp.* Luke i. 65 Ofer alle mor-londa iudæes. *c* **1250** *Gen. & Ex.* 2968 And aaron held up his hond, to ðe water and ðe more lond. *c* **1450** *Godstow Reg.* 288, j half acre in the morelond. **1773** *Act 13 Geo. III* c. 54 §6 Every Proprietor of high and wet Muir Lands. **1851** D. JERROLD *St. Giles* xi. 103 The road opened into a patch of moor-land. **1896** 'Q' (Quiller Couch) *Ia* 94 They stood in the heart of a moorland.

b. *spec.* (See quot. 1845.)

1612 DRAYTON *Poly-olb.* xii. 531 But Muse, thou seem'st to leaue the Morelands too too long. **1845** *Encycl. Metrop.* XXV. 10/1 The Northern part [of Staffordshire] bordering upon Derbyshire, contains a great portion of waste, devoted to feeding sheep, and enclosed with stone walls, denominated the Moorlands.

2. (See quot.)

1753 CHAMBERS *Cycl. Supp.*, *Moor-land* or *Moory-land*, in agriculture is a black, light and soft earth, very loose, and without any admixture of stones; and with very little clay, or sand. The uppermost stratum of fen-lands is usually of this earth.

3. *attrib.* passing into *adj.* Of the nature of or pertaining to moorland; inhabiting moorland.

[**1500–20** DUNBAR *Poems* xiii. 1 Ane morlandis man of vplandis mak At hame thus to his nychbour spak.] **1612** DRAYTON *Poly-olb.* xii. 576 Or'e-gone with loue of Hanse, a dapper More-land Lad. **1785** BURNS *To William Simpson* 104 While moorlan' herds like guid, fat braxies. **1799** J. ROBERTSON *Agric. Perth* 306 In the moorland parts of the county, the attention of the farmer is mostly confined to his cattle. **1810** SCOTT *Lady of L.* I. xxxiii, But vainly did the heath-flower sped Its moor-land fragrance round his head. **1902** R. W. CHAMBERS *Maids of Paradise* x, The moorland wind rose and tossed her elf-locks in her eyes.

moorlander (ˈmʊələndə(r), ˈmɔələndə(r)). [f. MOORLAND + -ER[1].] One who lives in a moorland; *spec.* one who lives in the Moorlands of Staffordshire.

c **1646** *True Relat.*, etc. in *Glover's Hist. Derby* (1829) I. App. 62 The moorlanders in Staffordshire came to him, entreating him for assistance. **1660** *Leyborne-Popham MSS.* (Hist. MSS. Comm. 1899) 139 The county [Stafford] is apt to fly into arms, the northern inhabitants being 'moorlanders' and the southern parts abounding with 'ironmen'. **1667** COTTON *Scarron.* IV. 69 Rascals as false as Moorlanders.

†ˈ**moorlandish**, *a.* *Obs.*[−1] [f. as prec. + -ISH.] Characteristic of the inhabitants of the moorlands.

1686 PLOT *Staffordsh.* 109 To prevent these little country Moorelandish cheats,..the Factors keep a Surveyor all the summer here.

ˈ**moorlog.** Also **-logg.** [app. f. MOOR *sb.*[1] + LOG *sb.*] (See quots.)

1651 R. CHILD in *Hartlib's Legacy* (1655) 141 This is in briefe my Philosophy concerning Moorlog. **1721** PERRY *Daggenh. Breach* 72 *note*, Moorlogg, is a vein of divers sorts of rotten Wood..which lyes about 3 Foot and a half.. underneath the Surface of the Marsh Ground. **1840** *Civil Eng. & Arch. Jrnl.* III. 106/1 Moorlogg is described as a vein of matted brushwood, with nuts and pieces of rotten wood interspersed. **1933** *Antiquity* VII. 38 In the summer of 1932 the skipper of the steam drifter *Colinda* procured another bone harpoon of Maglemose type in a sample of 'moorlog' (peat) brought up by the trawl. **1939** G. CLARK *Archæol. & Society* ii. 20 Over many parts of the North Sea bed..fishermen have found the remains of a great freshwater fen in the form of lumps of 'moor log'.

moorman[1] (ˈmʊə-, ˈmɔəmən). [f. MOOR *sb.*[1] + MAN *sb.* Cf. MOORSMAN.]

1. One who lives on a moor.

c **1790** SIR M. HUNTER *Jrnl.* (1894) 74 The Moormen fight cocks, and are very fond of the diversion. **1836** MRS. BRAY *Tamar & Tavy* I. 23 The moormen most commonly convey their peat, and all things else, on what is called a crook. **1872** M. COLLINS *Two Plunges for Pearl* I. vi. 123 The best pedestrian upon ordinary roads will find himself tried by the swinging step of the moorman on his native soil.

2. An official who has charge of a moor.

1687 in Croke *Case of Otmoor* (1831) 38 Every man that keeps cattle upon the More, shall bring his cattle to the Moor-man to be branded. **1885** *Sat. Rev.* 5 Sept. 322 Dartmoor is divided into four quarters,..and there is a functionary called *par excellence* a Moorman, who has charge of each quarter on behalf of the Duchy.

ˈ**Moorman**[2]. [f. MOOR *sb.*[2] + MAN.] = MOOR *sb.*[2]; in India, a Muslim.

1698 FRYER *Acc. E. India & P.* 55 These Moormen.. never set their hands to do any Labour, but that they sing a Psalm, or Prayer. **1763** SCRAFTON *Indostan* (1770) 26 The Moormen..make them, of whom they have no jealousy, the ministers of their oppression. **1836** *Lett. fr. Madras* (1843) 41, I gave some embroidery to be done by a Moorman recommended by my tailor. **1850** WHITTIER *Derne* 113 Men speak the praise of him who gave Deliverance to the Moorman's slave. **1889** *Ceylon Observer* 4 May, The gem was bought in by the owner. I hear since that some of the Moormen who came for the sale have made offers. **1897** *Tablet* 16 Oct. 606 Whether the man be a Christian, Jew, Agnostic, Buddhist, Mormon or Moorman.

moorn(e, obs. forms of MORN, MOURN.

ˈ**Moor-**ˈ**park.** [Use of *Moor Park*, the name of the house of Sir W. Temple (*d.* 1699), by whom this fruit was cultivated.] A variety of apricot.

1788 *Brompton Park Catal.* in Hogg *Fruit Man.* (1875) 177. **1797** W. NICOL *Sc. Forcing Gardener* 156 Apricots... More Park. **1812** *Trans. Hortic. Soc.* (1817) II. 19 On the proper Stock for the Moor Park Apricot. **1881** *Encycl. Brit.* XII. 270/1 The Moorpark is undoubtedly the best apricot in cultivation.

moor-pout (ˈmʊəpaʊt, ˈmɔəpaʊt). Also 7 **moore poult**, **-pout**, **moorpoot**, **-poult**, **-powte**, **more pout**, 8 **moor powt**, 9 *Sc.* **muir poot**, *dial.* **moor-pot**, 7– **moor-pout.** [f. MOOR *sb.*[1] + *pout*: see POULT *sb.*[1]] A young grouse.

1506 in *Acc. Ld. High Treas. Scotl.* (1901) III. 333 Item, to ane man brocht quyk mure powtis to the King..iijs. **1677** N. COX *Gentl. Recreat.* III. 45 How to take Rails, Quails, Morepoots, &c. **1684** E. CHAMBERLAYNE *Pres. St. Eng.* I. (ed. 15) 6 What abundance of..heath-cocks, more-pouts, or grouse-thrushes. **1728** RAMSAY *Lure* 12 Peartricks, teals, moor-powts, and plivers. **1816** SCOTT *Old Mort.* Introd., The Laird accused our Landlord, deceased, of having encouraged..the destruction of hares,..moor-pouts [etc.]. *a* **1835** HOGG *Siege Roxb.* iv. Tales & Sk. 1837 VI. 105, I will ..smoor the transgressors like as many moor-poots.

‖**moorpunky** (mɔəˈpʌŋkɪ). *Indian.* Also **moorpungkey**, **moorpunkey**, **morpunkee.** [Hindī *morpaŋkhī*, lit. 'peacock-tailed', f. *mor* peacock + *paŋkhī* fan.] A kind of Indian pleasure-boat formerly used on the Ganges.

1767 in J. Long *Select. fr. Unpubl. Rec. Govt.* (1869) 524 (Y.) A few moorpungkeys and beauleahs for the service of Mahomed Reza Khan..25,000.0.0. **1796** ELIZA HAMILTON *Lett. Hindoo Rajah* (1811) I. 253 Moor Punky. A country vessel of a peculiar construction, used for the conveyance of cotton and other bulky articles. **1855** OGILVIE, *Morpunkee*, a native pleasure boat of the Ganges, elegantly decorated, and propelled by numerous paddles.

†**Moors**, *a.* and *sb.* *Anglo-Indian. Obs.* [Perh. a. Du. *Moorsch*, MOORISH. Yule refers to the parallel forms *Bengals* for *Bengālī*, *Indostans* for Hindustānī, and *Turks* for Turkish.] A name for the Urdū or Hindustānī language: cf. MOORISH.

1767 J. RENNELL *Let.* 10 Mar. (MS.) (Y.), The politest Language is the Moors or Mussulmans and Persian. **1784–5** *Ann. Reg.* II. 81 The Hindustanic or as it is vulgarly termed in India, the Moors language. **1796** HADLEY (*title*) A compendious Grammar of the Current Corrupt Dialect of the Jargon of Hindostan (commonly called Moors); with a Vocabulary, English and Moors, Moors and English. **1803** BEDDOES *Hygëia* x. 53 Speaking scarce any thing but *Moors*. **1883** R. N. CUST *Mod. Lang. Afr.* I. ix. 97 Forty years ago

in India in Military circles a man who knew the Vernacular of British India was said to know 'the Moors'.

†**Moor's-head.** *Obs.* Also **moor-head.** [f. MOOR *sb.*^{2} + HEAD *sb.*^{1}]

1. A representation of the head of a Moor; *spec.* in *Her.* (see quot. 1780).

1673 RAY *Journ. Low C.* 487 Vpon many of the pillars are Moors heads carved in the stone, and one or two with turbants on. **1722** NISBET *Syst. Her.* 267 John Moir of Stonniewood, Argent, three Moors Heads couped, distilling Drops of Blood proper. **1780** EDMONDSON *Heraldry* II. Gloss., *Moor's Head*..the head of a black, or negro-man, placed in profile, couped at the neck, wreathed about the temples, ar. and az. and having a pearl pendent at his ear. **1847** *Gloss. Heraldry* 160 Moor's or Blackamoor's head,

2. (See quots.) Cf. F. *téte-de-More.*

1677 tr. *Glaser's Compl. Chem.* 31 The Brass Vesica, with its Refrigeratory, or Moors head. **1678** SALMON *New Lond. Dispensatory* 816 Of the cover of the Vesica, or Moors-head. It is made of Brass, having a Neck six Inches deep [etc.]. **1706** PHILLIPS (ed. Kersey), *Moors-head*, a Copper cap, tinn'd on the inside, and made like a Head, to be set over the Chimney of a Reverberating Furnace; Also the Head of a Copper or Glass-still, which is luted on the Body, having a Beak, Nose, or Pipe, to let the raised Spirit run down into the Receiver. **1712** tr. *Pomet's Hist. Drugs* I. 8 Put green Anniseeds..in a Glass Cucurbit, which cover with its Moor-Head. **1844** T. WEBSTER *Encycl. Dom. Econ.* 1045 The Moor's head is another form of still that has been used, and is found convenient for distillation on a small scale.

3. (See quots.) Cf. F. *cheval teste de more* (Cotgr.).

1660 HOWELL *Voc.* ii, A horse that hath his head darker then his body, called the Moors head. **1726** W. GIBSON *Diet. Horses* (ed. 2) 212 The Roan well mark'd, or with a More's Head. **1753** CHAMBERS *Cycl. Supp.*, *More's-head*, in the manege, implies the colour of a Roan horse, who besides the mixture or blending of a grey and a bay, has a black head.

'**Moorship.** *nonce-wd.* [f. MOOR *sb.*^{2} + -SHIP.] ***his Moorship***, a derisive title applied to a Moor.

1604 SHAKS. *Oth.* I. i. 33 This Counter-caster, He (in good time) must his Lieutenant be, And I (blesse the marke) his Mooreships Auntient.

moorsman ('mʊəz-, 'mɔəzmən). [f. *moor's*, gen. of MOOR *sb.*^{1} + MAN. Cf. MOORMAN.] A dweller on the moors (in quot., on the 'moors' or drained marshes of Somerset). Also, one accustomed to the moors.

1889 DOYLE *Micah Clarke* xxxii, The Bussex Rhine..is not..broad, and was, therefore, unmentioned by the moorsmen. **1904** E. RICKERT *Reaper* 246 These dangers to life and limb never entered the head of the practised moorsman.

moorstone ('mʊə-, 'mɔəstəʊn). *Min.* [f. MOOR *sb.*^{1} + STONE.]

1. A kind of granite found chiefly in Cornwall.

c **1600** NORDEN *Spec. Brit., Cornw.* (1728) 18 There is a stone called a Moar-Stone, which lyeth dispersed vpon the face of the mountaynes and on the confused rockes. *c* **1630** RISDON *Surv. Devon* §215 (1810) 223 Where is a table and seats of moorstone. **1674** RAY *Collect. Words, Prep. Tin* (E.D.S.) 13 A mould made of moore-stone. **1793** SMEATON *Edystone L.* §91 Moorstone, which in reality is the true Granite. **1842** GWILT *Archit.* Gloss., *Moorstone*, a species of granite found in Cornwall and some other parts of England, and very serviceable in the coarser parts of a building. **1875** W. MCILWRAITH *Guide Wigtownshire* 105 This ancient fence [the Deil's Dyke] is built of blocks of common moorstone.

2. A slab or piece of moorstone.

1698 LISTER *Journ. Paris* (1699) 146 By reason of those Sand or Moore Stones, with which they grind their Corn. **1707** MORTIMER *Husb.* (1721) I. 104 The Sand is very white, and in Scilly glistering, which may be occasion'd from the mouldering of Moor-stones.

3. *attrib.*

c **1630** RISDON *Surv. Devon* §22 (1810) 32 Their arms are cut in the moorstone pillars. **1773** IRONSTONE in *Phil. Trans.* LXIV. 102 A globular piece of moorstone granite. **1883** F. G. HEATH in *Century Mag.* Dec. 165/1 Semicircular arches surmounting moor-stone columns.

‖**mooruk** ('mʊərʊk). [See quot. 1860.] A kind of cassowary, *Casuarius Bennetti.*

1860 G. BENNETT *Gatherings Nat. in Australasia* 244 A new species of Cassowary procured from the natives of New Britain... It utters a peculiar whistling sound, and I am informed it also emits a loud one resembling the word Mooruk, whence no doubt is derived its native name. **1876** *Encycl. Brit.* V. 186/1 The Mooruk, or Bennett's Cassowary ..approaching in the thickness of its legs to the moas.

‖**moorva** ('mʊəvə). [Skr. *mūrvā.*] Bowstring hemp (see BOW-STRING 3).

[*a* **1794** SIR W. JONES in *Asiatic Res.* IV. 271 Murva.] **1855** ROYLE *Fibrous Pl. India* 55 The Moorva fibre is employed by the natives for their bowstrings. **1884** *Imp. & Mach. Rev.* 1 Dec. 6710/2 The Glenrock Company..intend to treat on a somewhat large scale the 'moorva' or bowstring hemp.

‖**moory** ('mʊərɪ), *sb.* Also 7–9 **moree**, 8 **moore**, **mouri.** [Possibly connected with Pg. *morim*, shirting.] A kind of Indian cloth.

1696 J. F. *Merch. Wareho. laid open* 29 Morees... This is a Callico extreamly in use..to Work for Petty-Coats and Waste Coats. **1703** *Lond. Gaz.* No. 3933/4 The Cargo of the Star of the East, consisting of Long Cloth,..Betelles, Moores, Neckcloths [etc.]. **1704** *Ibid.* No. 4054/6 Lots 414, 415, Cont. 200 Moores. **1754** SEWEL *Eng.-Du. Dict.*, Morees, *mouris*, zekere Oostindische Katoenen. **1857** BALFOUR *Cycl. India, Moories, Blue.* These cloths are principally manufactured [etc.]. The trade..at Pondicherry consists of long cloths..morees, dimities [etc.]. **1858** SIMMONDS *Dict. Trade, Moory*, a brown cloth made in India. **1882** CAULFEILD & SAWARD *Dict. Needlework* 350 *Morees*, Manchester-made Muslins, much employed for the African export trade.

moory ('mʊərɪ, 'mɔərɪ), *a.*^{1} Forms: 4–5 **mory**, 6 **morey**, 6–7 **moorie**, 7 **moarie**, 8 **moary**, 9 *Sc.* **muiry**, 6– **moory**. [f. MOOR *sb.*^{1} + -Y. Cf. MDu. *môrich* (mod.Du. *moorig*), G. *moorig.*]

1. Marshy, fenny; growing in a marsh or fen. ***moory land***, ***-earth*** = MOORLAND *sb.* 2.

1387 TREVISA *Higden* (Rolls) IV. 157 Herdes fond hym among mory flagges and sprayes. ?*c* **1400** LYDG. *Æsop's Fab.* v. 118 The frosshe delyteþ to abyde in mory lakys. **1577** B. GOOGE *Heresbach's Husb.* I. (1586) 31 b, It delighteth in a watrishe moorie grounde. **1603** HOLLAND *Plutarch's Mor.* 1191 Because neither the Palme tree is a moorie plant and loving the waters,..neither [etc.]. **1612** DRAYTON *Poly-olb.* ix. 444 Guint, forth along with her Lewenny that doth draw; And next to them againe, the fat and moory Frawe. **1667** MILTON *P.L.* II. 944 As when a Gryfon through the Wilderness With winged course ore Hill or moarie Dale, Pursues the Arimaspian [etc.]. **1731** MILLER *Gard. Dict.* s.v. *Lupulus*, The Essex Planters account a moory Land the properest for Hops. **1805** R. W. DICKSON *Pract. Agric.* II. 853 On peaty or moory lands marl and other similar materials will be of advantage in rendering them more compact. **1877** SKERTCHLY *Geol. Fenland* 130 [In Lincolnshire] It is usual to speak of 'moory land', 'black land', or 'fen' where the soil is peaty.

2. Of or pertaining to a moor or heath; having the characteristics of a moor; abounding in heath.

1794 W. MARSHALL *Central Highl. Scot.* 12 On the Yorkshire hills, the moory earth, generally of greater thickness, lies on a dead sand, or an infertile rubble; without any intervening soil. **1830** COBBETT *Rur. Rides* (1885) II. 326 The moory and rocky parts in the West Riding. **1865** GEIKIE *Scen. & Geol. Scotl.* x. 267 A tract of moory heights. **1875** *Encycl. Brit.* I. 360/2 On muiry soils this crop is also not unfrequently lost.

moory ('mɔərɪ, 'mʊərɪ), *a.*^{2} [? f. MOOR *sb.*^{2} + -Y^1.] ? Dark coloured, black.

1581 J. STUDLEY *Seneca's Hercules Œtæus* II. 196 b, Him that weildes the moary mace [L. *furva sceptra*] of blacke Auerne to smoake. *Ibid.* IV. 210, I see the dumpish moary denne of glowming lady night. **1600** TOURNEUR *Transf. Metam.* vii, The skie..Is cloathed with moorie Vesperugoe's coate.

moos, obs. variant of MOSS.

moose^1 (muːs). Also 7 **mose**, **mosse**, **mus**, 7–8 **moos**, 8 **mooze**. [a. Narragansett *moos* (= Abenaki *mus*, Penobscot *muns*); according to Trumbull, from *moosu* 'he trims or cuts smooth', in allusion to the animal's habit of stripping the lower branches and bark from trees when feeding.] **a.** A cervine animal native to N. America closely allied to, or identical with, the European Elk (*Alces malchis*). Also ***moose deer***. Also used *collect.*

The moose is termed *Alces americana* by those zoologists who regard it as specifically distinct from *A. malchis.*

1613 PURCHAS *Pilgrimage* (1614) 755 Captaine Thomas Hanham sayled to the Riuer of Sagadahoc 1606. He relateth of their beasts..redde Deare, and a beast bigger, called the Mus. **1637** T. MORTON *New Eng. Canaan* II. v. 74 The Elke, which the Salvages call a Mose..is a very large Deare, with [etc.]. **1672** JOSSELYN *New Eng. Rarities* 19 The Moose Deer ..is a very goodly Creature. **1783** JUSTAMOND tr. *Raynal's Hist. Indies* VI. 494 The mooze-deer, called there Caribou. **1817** S. R. BROWN *Western Gazetteer* 202 Cabree and moose are plentiful. **1849** J. PRITTS *Mirror Border Life* 60 Their food was principally the entrails of moose, deer, bears. **1877** *Encycl. Brit.* VII. 24/1 The Elk or Moose Deer (*Alces malchis*) is the largest of living *Cervidæ.* **1879** LD. DUNRAVEN in *19th Cent.* July 50 The Moose of America is almost, if not quite, identical with the Elk of Europe, but it attains a greater size. **1903** KIPLING *5 Nations* 39 The lakeside lilies where the bull-moose waits the cow. **1957** *Listener* 14 Nov. 778/2 Large wooden corrals into which their moose were driven. **1964** *Globe & Mail* (Toronto) 12 Dec. 8/7 A few point to the slow resurgence of moose, particularly in the southwest of the province.

b. *attrib.* and *Comb.*, as ***moose-flesh***, ***-hair***, ***-hide***, ***-horn***, ***-hunt*** sb. and vb., ***-hunter***, ***-hunting***, ***-meat***, ***-path***, ***-sinew***, ***-skin***, ***-track***, ***-trail***; **moose berry** *U.S.*, the fruit of the moose-bush; **moose-bird** *N. Amer.*, a name used for several birds, esp. the Canada jay, *Perisoreus canadensis*; **moose bush** *U.S.*, the shrub *Viburnum lantanoïdes*; **moose call**, a trumpet of birch bark used by hunters in calling moose to an ambuscade or blind (*Sportsman's Gazetteer* in *Cent. Dict.*); **moose-calling** (see quot. 1879); **moose elm**, the slippery elm, *Ulmus rubra*; **moose fly**, one of several North American horse flies, esp. one of the genus *Chrysops*; **moose-head plant** *U.S.*, some river-side plant; **moose man**, a moose-hunter; **moose maple**, either of two small maples of eastern North America, *Acer spicatum* or *A. pennsylvanicum*; **moose shanks** (see quot. 1887); †**moose suit**, a suit of clothes made of moose-skin; **moose tick**, a North American tick, *Dermacentor albipictus*, which infests moose and other animals; **moose warden** *U.S.*, a person employed to protect moose; **moose-wood**, (*a*) striped maple, *Acer pennsylvanicum* or *striatum*; (*b*) leatherwood, *Dirca palustris*; **moose-yard**, an area in which the snow is trodden down by moose, where they remain together during the winter months.

1848 THOREAU *Maine W.* (1894) 79 Solomon's seal and *mooseberries. **1832** W. D. WILLIAMSON *Hist. State of Maine* I. 150 The *moose-bird..feeds on the berries of the moose brush. **1857** THOREAU *Maine W.* (1894) 293 Three large slate-colored birds of the jay genus (*Garrulus Canadensis*), the Canada jay, moose-bird, meat-bird, or what not. **1890** S. M. ST. MAUR *Impressions of Tenderfoot* 273 My friend of the woods, the moose-bird... I found his real name was the great northern shrike, *Lanius borealis.* **1941** E. .T. SETON *Trail of Artist-Naturalist* 270 Presently the wailing of the moose-bird fell on my anxious ear. **1964** *Atlantic Advocate* Oct. 67/1 This time of year there were always a pair of moosebirds on the maple. **1784** M. CUTLER in *Life*, etc. (1888) I. 102 The ground covered with an underwood of *moose bush. *a* **1817** T. DWIGHT *Trav. New Eng.*, etc. (1821) II. 418 The black-moose bush, a pretty shrub with a rich pulpy leaf and a tuft of brilliant white flowers at the end of each branch. **1838** *United Service Jrnl.* July 305 In *moose-calling, success mainly depends on the judicious selection of a station. **1879** LD. DUNRAVEN in *19th Cent.* July 52 Moose-calling..consists in imitating the cry of the female moose, and thereby calling up the male. **1956** W. R. BIRD *Off-Trail in Nova Scotia* vi. 167 The September moon is just right for moose calling. **1810** F. A. MICHAUX *Hist. Arbres Forestiers de l'Amérique Septentrionale* I. 39 Red elm,..Slippery elm,..*Moose elm,..dans le haut de l'Etat de New York. **1832** D. J. BROWNE *Sylva Amer.* 311 This species of elm..bears the name of Red Elm, Slippery Elm and Moose Elm. **1884** SARGENT *Rep. Forests N. Amer.* (10th Census IX) 122 *Ulmus fulva*,..Red Elm... Moose Elm. **1873** MISS BRADDON *L. Davoren* I. Prol. i. 4 Rare meals of buffalo or *moose flesh. **1834** J. J. AUDUBON *Ornith. Biogr.* II. 437 The musquitoes and *moose flies did their best to render us uncomfortable. **1913** *Chambers's Jrnl.* Nov. 764/1 The lordly moose finds..relief from the torturing moose-fly in the cool depths of the lakes. **1953** A. R. M. LOWER *Unconventional Voyages* 43 Further south, where they are never so numerous, they [*sc.* bulldog flies] are called horse-flies, or moose-flies. **1820** D. W. HARMON *Jrnl. Voy. & Trav. Interior N. Amer.* 317 From two points in this bow,.. two strips of leather..are suspended, at the ends of which, tassels, composed of *moose hair, are fixed. **1956** D. LEECHMAN *Native Tribes Canada* 43 Some used moose hair for embroidery. There is a tuft of pale, stiffish hair about seven inches long, between the shoulders of the moose. **1868** LOSSING *Hudson* 6 A winding and narrow river, fringed with rushes, lilies, and moose-head plants. **1708** J. OLDMIXON *Brit. Empire in Amer.* I. 395 Every Man has commonly two Wives, whom they..make 'em do all Slavery; as draw Sledds,..and dress *Moose Hides. **1858** THOREAU *Maine W.* (1894) 121 A St. Francis Indian, with his canoe and moose-hides. **1955** R. P. HOBSON *Nothing too Good for Cowboy* vii. 67, I sat up, pulled my moosehide coat over my sweater, [etc.]. **1966** *Globe & Mail* (*Toronto*) 18 May 6/2 When he is racing [on snowshoes], he wears moosehide moccasins. **1672** JOSSELYN *New Eng. Rarities* 19 *Moose Horns better for Physick use than Harts Horns. **1876** *Forest & Stream* 24 Aug. 34/2 Sebatis and Lola went off on a *moose hunt. **1837** *Penny Cycl.* VIII. 352/2 The skill of a *moose-hunter is most tried in the early part of the winter. **1857** THOREAU *Maine W.* (1894) 307 Some friends of mine ..were serenaded by wolves while *moose-hunting by moonlight. **1858** THOREAU *Maine W.* (1894) 148 *Moose-men. **1839** C. F. HOFFMAN *Wild Scenes Forest & Prairie* 38 We would come to a sort of plateau of swampy land, overgrown with *moose maple. **1904** S. E. WHITE *Blazed Trail Stories* vi. 104 He..was holding aside the screen of moose-maples. **1952** J. JENNINGS *Strange Brigade* II. iii. 128 To our left lay the woodsy thickets..beech and chokecherry and moose maple. **1797** C. CHABOILLEZ *Jrnl.* in B. C. Payette *Northwest* (1964) 163 The People returned, they brought 1 Bear skin..8 pieces *Mouse Meat half Dryed. **1857** THOREAU *Maine W.* (1894) 369 He found himself dining one day on moose-meat. **1930** L. MUNDAY *Mounty's Wife* iii. 48 We camped that night with some Indians [and] huge plates of moose meat were served, as good as any beef, and far better than most other meats. **1961** H. C. DODGE *My Childhood Canad. Wilderness* i. 27 We ate them fried, roasted, boiled, but we never grew tired of moose meat. **1969** in Halpert & Story *Christmas Mumming in Newfoundland* 84 This late supper might include a meal of 'bottled moose-meat', warmed-over soup..'pork-buns', [etc.]. **1876** *Forest & Stream* 10 Aug. 2/1, I saw the bear lying in an old well-worn *moose-path quite dead. **1887** *Harper's Mag.* Feb. 458/2 '*Moose shanks' are made by peeling the skin from the hind legs of the animal. The smaller end is then sewn up to form the toe; and thus a moose-hide stocking is formed. **1952** E. BUCKLER *Mountain & Valley* 100 The Rothesays down the road..wore moose shanks with the hair still on them. **1765** T. HUTCHINSON *Hist. Mass.* I. v. 464 Their bowstrings were made of *Moose sinews. **1637** T. MORTON *New Eng. Canaan* I. vi. 29 They make shooes of *Mose skinnes, which is the principall leather used to that purpose. **1664** *Essex County, Mass. Probate Rec.* (1916) I. 458 Moose skin sute. **1775** in *Mass. Hist. Soc. Coll.* (1822) 2nd Ser. IX. 162 Donations..1 pair moose-skin breeches. **1903** *All Nations* Mar. 73/1 Living a shivering life in moose-skin tents. **1957** C. HARRIS *Cariboo Trail* 174 The mooseskin-trousered [one] looked at him darkly. **1971** D. C. BROWN *Yukon Trophy Trails* x. 120 Lonny Johnny, a full-blood Loucheux, was building himself a moose-skin boat... Lonny used the lateral roots of a spruce tree for ribs and two large bull moose hides for the canvas. **1645** in *N. Eng. Hist. & Gen. Reg.* (1849) III. 82 The said Alexander Bradford have giuen to Robert Stowton his *Moose Suite and a musket and Sworde. **1868** *Amer. Naturalist* II. 559 The *Moose Tick... When the cow arrived in New York, her sides and back were almost covered with adult ticks. **1857** THOREAU *Maine W.* (1894) 390 There were pretty fresh *moose-tracks by the water-side. **1890** N. HIBBS in *Big Game N. Amer.* 37 Just as I passed the point..I found a *Moose-trail. **1853** *Maine Acts & Resolves* 24 The governor shall..appoint one county *moose warden for each of the counties. **1883** G. B. GOODE *Rev. Fishery Industries U.S.* 83 He had a canoe of birch, and on it he had burnt..the title 'Moose Warden', and he said he would take care of all the moose that came within the reach of his rifle. **1778** J. CARVER *Trav. N.-Amer.* 507 The *Moose Wood grows about four feet high, and is very full of

branches. **1792** BELKNAP *Hist. New Hampsh.* III. 163 He [the Moose] feeds on..a species of the maple, which is called moose-wood. **1860** A. GRAY *Man. Bot.* 84 *Acer Pennsylvanicum*.. Moose-Wood. *Ibid.* 380 *Dirca*.. Moose-wood. **1890** W. J. GORDON *Foundry* 116 His poultices will be the bark of the moose wood boiled till it is soft. **1933** D. G. CAMERON *Twigs from Oak* 129 The under-growth consisted of..moose-wood, dogwood. **1969** T. H. EVERETT *Living Trees of World* 222/2 Conspicuous in winter because of its white-striped bark, the moosewood (*A[cer] pennsylvanicum*) inhabits open woods throughout eastern North America. **1800** C. D. ROUSO D'ERES *Mem.* 117 The animals are overtaken in their retreats (for they herd together..) which is called the *Moose yard, formed by them in trampling down the snow. **1843** *Zoologist* I. 134 It will take so many days to reach the moose-yard. **1872** SCHELE DE VERE *Americanisms* 53 They [*sc.* Moose] live in families of fifteen to twenty, each one of which confines itself to a certain part of the woods; this is called a moose yard. **1946** W. R. BIRD *Sunrise for Peter* 209 Nathan plunged to join him and almost fell into a well-trodden moose-yard.

c. *transf.* and *fig.*

1925 *Dalhousie Rev.* V. 321 There is much meandering in the neighbouring woods; and..it is known as the game of 'moose'. **1941** *Amer. Speech* XVI. 187 *Moose*, a sister, notably a kid-sister, who informs her mother when her brother is playing stick-ball, shooting dice, etc. **1948** *Sat. Even. Post* 16 Oct. 130/3 Schaeffer was a moose of a man. **1963** *Amer. Speech* XXXVIII. 173 An unattractive female date:..Ugliness..ranges from such general terms as beast ..to the more specific bear, cow, goose, moose, roach.., squirrel, and wet fish. **1968** *Word Study* Dec. 3/2 *Moose* is sometimes used for any large and strong person, but it is mostly widely applied to large and strong persons of Scandinavian descent.

†**moose**[2]. *Obs. rare.* [a. Du. *moes.*] Pottage, stewed vegetables.

1568 TURNER *Herbal* III. 9 The weomen cookes in the spring time use to gather this herbe, and put it in there potages and mooses with other pot herbes. *Ibid.* 20.

moose[3] (mu:s). *U.S. Forces' slang.* [ad. Jap. *musume* daughter, girl.] A young Japanese or Korean woman; *esp.*, the wife or mistress of a serviceman stationed in Japan or Korea.

1953 in Partridge *Dict. Slang* (1961) Suppl. 1188/2 An eligible female of Japan or Korea is known as a 'moose',.. from the Japanese word 'musume'—girl. **1954** *Amer. Speech* XXIX. 302 To spell the word *mus* might be a good transcription from the Japanese but..it is the spelling *moose* that is most encountered in semiformal Army poop sheets; in signs urging Americans..to meet the best mooses in Kyoto, [etc.]. **1964** *Ibid.* XXXIX. 236 The word *moose* refers, not without some disdain, to Korean wives of Americans, often soldiers.

MOOSE[4] (mu:s). [See quot. 1968.] A contrivance for the protection of an astronaut working in outer space.

1968 *New Acronyms & Initialisms* (Gale Research Co.) 144 MOOSE, Man (or Manual) orbital operations safety equipment (Space life raft) (NASA). **1969** *Scottish Sunday Express* 14 Dec. 12/8 American engineers have designed a space 'lifeboat'..known as MOOSE, from the initial letters of Manned Orbital Operations Safety Equipment.

moosel(l, obs. forms of MUZZLE.

'moosey, *a. nonce-wd.* Suggestive of the presence of the moose.

1857 THOREAU *Maine W.* (1894) 377 It is all mossy and moosey.

moosh, var. MUSH *sb.*[1] 3 d, MUSH *sb.*[4], MUSH *sb.*[5]

mooshik, variant of MOUJIK.

moosie, variant of MOSY *a. dial.*, mossy.

moosle, moost, obs. ff. MUZZLE, MOST, MUST.

moosted, variant of MUSTED.

Moosulman, variant of MUSSULMAN.

moot (mu:t), *sb.*[1] Forms: 1 **ȝemót**, 2–3 **imot**, **mot**, 4–9 **mote**, 5–6 **mute**, 6 **mout**, 6–7 **mute**, 7 **moat**, **mott**, 5– **moot**. [Early ME. *mōt*, *imōt*, repr. OE. *mót* neut. (before 12th c. found only in compounds) and *ȝemót* neut. (with prefix *ȝe-*, Y-; the prefix in sbs. disappeared early in ME., so that the two forms became coincident); an adoption of the equivalent ON. *mót* neut., encounter, meeting, public assembly, may prob. have coalesced with the native word. The sb., OTeut. *(*ga*)*mōtom*, is found in OLow Frankish (Hildebrandsl.) *muot* encounter, MDu. *moet* neut., masc., *gemoet* neut. (mod.Du. *gemoet*), MHG. *muoz*, *môz* (and in LG. form *muot*), *gemôt* fem.; the derivative MEET *v.* appears in all branches of Teut. The ultimate etymology of OTeut. **mōtom* is unknown.]

†**1.** *gen.* Meeting, encounter. *Obs.*

a **1000** *O.E. Chron.* an. 937 Gar mittinge gumena ȝemotes wæpen ȝewrixles. *c* **1400** *Laud Troy-Bk.* 10389 Many a man was ther assoyned Off ther lyff ther at her mote. *c* **1470** HENRY *Wallace* VIII. 1529 Wallang fled our, and durst nocht bid that mute.

2. An assembly of people, *esp.* one forming a court of judicature; a meeting, also the place where a meeting is held. *Obs.* exc. *Hist.* and *arch.* Cf. GEMOT, WITENAGEMOT; also BURGH-MOTE, FOLK-MOTE, HALL-MOTE, HUNDRED-MOTE, etc.

c **950** *Lindisf. Gosp.* Matt. x. 17 Hia ȝesellas forðon Iuih in ȝemotum. **1154** *O.E. Chron.* an. 1129 Þa hi ðider comen þa be gan þæt mot on Monendæiȝ & heold on an to ðe Fridæig. *c* **1200** *Trin. Coll. Hom.* 83 Þe soðe quen shal a domes [dai] arisen, on þe michele mote, and fordemen þis frakede folc. *c* **1205** LAY. 11545 Hit wes witene-imot. *a* **1225** *Leg. Kath.* 2458 Lo! al þat meidene mot & tet hird of heouene, cumeð her aȝein þe, mid kempene crune! *c* **1275** *Passion our Lord* 280 in *O.E. Misc.* 45 Heo by-wste þe dure þer al þat mot was. **13..** *Childh. Jesus* 260 in *Archiv Stud. neu. Spr.* LXXIV. 330 Modire, one mee he [Caiphas] salle halde mote, And do bete my body all bare. **14..** *Assise Reg. Willelmi* xxv. in *Acts Parlt. Scotl.* (1845) I. 379 Þe twa hed mutis of þe Justice salbe haldin ȝerly at Edinburgh or Peblis. *a* **1641** BP. MOUNTAGU *Acts & Mon.* (1642) 416 In Common Councels, at popular mootes, they could beare no sway. *c* **1670** HOBBES *Dial. Com. Laws* (1840) 169 After the Saxons had received the faith of Christ, those bishops that were amongst them, were always at the great moots in which they made their laws. **1794** W. HUTCHINSON *Hist. Cumb.* I. 252 The whole country..seems to have been parcelled out into small districts,..in each of which there was a mote, or court of justice. **1885** *Encycl. Brit.* XVIII. 302/2 In the Anglo-Saxon moots may be discerned the first germs of popular government in England. **1903** *Contemp. Rev.* Oct. 496 Necessary results of the Customs Union would be an imperial Moot containing representatives from the various parts of the Empire.

†**3.** Litigation; an action at law; a plea; accusation. *Obs.*

c **888** K. ÆLFRED *Boeth.* xxvi. §2 Hwi bið elles ælce dæȝ swelc seofung & swelce ȝeflitu & ȝemot & domas. *a* **1240** *Lofsong* in *Cott. Hom.* 205 Nim mot for me and were me for ich am pine wurðe. *a* **1300** *Cursor M.* 16299 Þe man es noght ouertan in mote at smit him as tresun. *Ibid.* 27694 If þou bringes man in iuel blame, or mote,..of this behoues þe mak þi scrift. ? *a* **1500** *Chester Pl.* (E.E.T.S.) 438 Now is the Devill ready, I see, his moote to further agaynst me. **1566** DRANT *Horace, Sat.* I. i. A j b, Of mout or suite undreamde Of barre thou beares no kepe. *c* **1575** *Balfour's Practicks* (1754) 53 All mutes and pleyis quhilk happinis to rise within burgh, sould be pleadit and determinat within the samin. **1609** SKENE *Reg. Maj.* I. 13 The order of mute or pley in court, is alreadie exponed.

†**4.** Argument; discussion; disputation; talking.

a **1225** *Leg. Kath.* 1321 Ah nis nawt lihtliche of þis meidenes mot; for, ich soð schal seggen, in hire ne moted na mon. *c* **1250** *Owl & N.* 468 Þeos vle luste & leyde on hord Al þis mot, word after word. *a* **1300** *Cursor M.* 11949 Was þar wit him na langer mote, Bot þar he fel dun at his fote. *c* **1400** *Gamelyn* 373, I swor in that wraththe and in that grete moot, That thou schuldest be bounde bothe hand and foot. **1565** JEWEL *Repl. Harding* (1611) 457 Afterward, hee keepeth great Mootes about Qualities and Quantities. *c* **1620** A. HUME *Brit. Tongue* Ded., In the disputes of al purposes quherwith, after the exemple of the wyse in former ages, you used to season your moat. **1645** MILTON *Tetrach.* 53 But to end this moot, the Law of Moses is manifest to fixe no limit therin at all. **1676** *Doctrine of Devils* 125 When the Lord hath decided the Controversy, & setled the Question, should men's Moots, groundless Opinions, small Arguments, and wilde Winter-Tales, unsettle us?

5. *Law.* The discussion of a hypothetical case by students at the Inns of Court for practice; also a hypothetical doubtful case that may be used for discussion. Revived in the Inns of Court after falling into disuse, and introduced into universities where law is studied.

1531 ELYOT *Gov.* I. xiv, In the lernyng of the lawes of this realme, there is at this daye an exercise, wherin is a.. shadowe..of the auncient rhetorike. I meane the pleadynge used in courte and Chauncery called motes. **1539** *Magna Carta* title-p., With an Almanacke & a Calender to know the mootes. Necessarye for all yong studiers of the lawe. **1605** *Hist. Capt. Stukeley* A 4, I had as liue you had seen him in the Temple walk, confering with some learned Councelor or at the moote vpon a case in Law. *a* **1650** SIR S. D'EWES *Autobiog.* (1845) I. 232 On Thursday,..after our supper in the Middle Temple Hall ended, with another utter barrister, I argued a moot at the bench to the good satisfaction of such as heard me. **1797** *Encycl. Brit.* (ed. 3) XII. 271/2 There is a bailiff, or surveyor of the moots, annually chosen by the bench, to appoint the moot-men for the inns of chancery. **1855** *Rep. Comm. Inns of Court* 81 Mr. Lewis [*c* 1847]..also established what are called 'Moots', that is to say, discussions on points of Law? **1876** *Times* 8 Nov. 10/6 A moot was held last night in the hall of Gray's-inn on the following question. **1926** E. WEEKLEY *Words Anc. & Mod.* 70 The practice of holding at the Inns of Court moots at which law students gain experience by arguing an hypothetical case. **1962** E. MITCHELL *Business Man's Lawyer* 441/2 *Moot*, a gathering of lawyers or law students, to argue—semi-formally—interesting but academic points of law. **1973** *Univ. of Leicester Prospectus 1974–75* facing p. 33 (*caption*) A 'moot' in the Department of Law. The Department has won the national 'Observer' mooting competition twice in the last three years.

6. *attrib.* †**moot-bell**, a bell to summon people to a moot or assembly; †**moot book**, a book containing law cases to be 'mooted' by students; **moot court**, a court at which students argue imaginary cases for practice; †**moot horn**, a horn for summoning people to a moot; **moot-stow** *Hist.*, the place where a moot was held. Also MOOT HALL, -HILL, -HOUSE, -MAN.

a **1066** *Laws Edw. Conf.* c. 32 §4 Pulsatis campanis, quod Anglici uocant *motbele. **1647** N. BACON *Disc. Govt. Eng.* I. xxiv. (1739) 42 If the emergent occasions were sudden and important, by extraordinary summons of ringing the Moot-bells. **1588** FRAUNCE *Lawiers Log.* I. xvii. 61 b, Wee by a *moote-booke and a Brookes abridgement climbe to the Barre. **1788** JEFFERSON *Writ.* (1859) II. 428 He gives lectures regularly, and holds *moot courts and parliaments wherein he presides. **1899** *Law Quarterly* XV. 422 A moot-court is held there [*sc.* at Gray's Inn] six or eight times a year. **1888** BRYCE *Amer. Commw.* III. xcviii. 376 In some law schools much educational value is attributed to the moot courts in which the students are set to argue cases. **12..** *Chron. Joc. de Brakelonda* (Camden) 54 Habitaque disputatione de cujus manu cornu acciperent, quod dicitur **mot-horn*. *c* **1000** ÆLFRIC *Gloss.* in Wr.-Wülcker 145/11 *Forus, uel prorostra*, *motstow on burȝe. *Ibid.* 164/34 *Forus, uel prorostra*, motstow. **1898** MAITLAND *Township & Borough* 39 Cambridge is the right and proper moot-stow for the thegns of the shire.

moot (mu:t), *sb.*[2] *Mech.*

1. A piece of hard wood hooped with iron at each end, used in block-making.

1815 in *Falconer's Dict. Marine* (ed. Burney). **1875** in KNIGHT *Dict. Mech.*

2. a. A ring-gauge for shaping treenails cylindrically to required size. **b.** Any particular size or diameter to which a treenail is to be made.

1815 *Falconer's Dict. Marine* (ed. Burney), *Mooter*, or *Tree-Nail Mooter*, a name given to the person who turns the tree-nails by the assistance of a moot. *c* **1850** *Rudim. Navig.* (Weale) 133 *Mooting*. Making a treenail exactly cylindrical to a given size or diameter, called the *moot*. **1875** KNIGHT *Dict. Mech.*, *Moot*, a gage-ring for determining the size of tree-nails.

moot (mu:t), *sb.*[3] *dial.* Also **moote, mote, mott.** The stump of a tree.

1832 *Planting* 91 (*Libr. Usef. Knowl.*), *Moot*, in Devonshire, is the same with stool in other counties. **1862** *Blackw. Mag.* Jan. 2 There was a layer of motts, as the stumps of old trees are called in the west. **1863** J. R. WISE *New Forest* xiv. 150 Sailors..dredging..sometimes draw up great logs of wood, locally known as 'mootes'. **1872** W. CORY *Lett. & Jrnls.* (1897) 288 Old roots festooned with flowers —roots called here [Devon] 'motes'.

moot (mu:t), *a.* [Developed from the attributive use of MOOT *sb.*[1], to which some of the earlier examples should perhaps be referred.] That can be argued; debatable; not decided, doubtful.

Orig. in *moot case* (?obs.), primarily meaning a case proposed for discussion in a 'moot' of law students. See MOOT *sb.*[1] 5.

1577–87 HOLINSHED *Chron.* II. 19/2 The like question [*sc.* whether 'fish' or 'flesh'] may be mooued of the sell [= seal], and if it were well canuassed, it would be found at the leastwise a moot case. *a* **1650** SIR S. D'EWES *Autobiog.* (1845) I. 240, I was scarce come into commons, but..I was set at work, arguing a moot-point or law-case on Thursday night after supper. *a* **1652** BROME *Covent Gard.* II. i. (1658) 22 Now I'll put a plain home-spun case, as a man may say, which we call a moot-case. **1658–9** in *Burton's Diary* (1828) III. 46 Jersey is part of France; so it is a moot point whether a *habeas corpus* lies. **1732–3** SIR C. WOGAN in *Swift's Wks.* (1824) XVII. 460 'My lords and gentlemen', says he, 'it is a very moot point to which of those causes we may ascribe the universal dulness of the Irish. **1736** WEST *Let.* in *Gray's Poems* (1775) 15 An inn of court is as horrid a place as a college, and a moot case is as dear to gentle dullness as a syllogism. **1797** *Encycl. Brit.* (ed. 3) XII. 271/2 Particular times are appointed for the arguing moot-cases. **1876** A. D. MURRAY *Charnwood* 110 It remains a moot problem to be guessed at. **1899** J. HUTCHINSON in *Arch. Surg.* X. No. 38. 190 Those who are already well informed in essentials and quite prepared to discuss moot and difficult points.

moot (mu:t), *v.*[1] Forms: 1 **mótian**, 2 **motien**, 3 **motin**, 3–6 **mote**, **mot**, *Sc.* **mwt**, 3–4, 5 *Sc.* **mut**, **mwte**, 3–4, 5–7 *Sc.* **mute**, **muit**, 5 **moyte**, **moytt**, 4–7 **moote**, 7– **moot**. [OE. *mótian*, f. *mót* MOOT *sb.*[1]]

†**1. a.** *intr.* To speak, to converse. In Sc. of 16–17th c. to complain, murmur. *Obs.*

c **1000** ÆLFRIC *On N. Test.* 15 (Gr.) Man mot on eornost motian wið his drihten, se þe wyle, þæt we sprecon mid weorcum wið hine. *c* **1205** LAY. 1443 Cniht þu ært muchel sot þat þu swa motest. *a* **1300** *Cursor M.* 22550 O murthes þan es nan to mote; Vnquemfulli þan sal þai quak, þat all þe erth it sal to scak. **1375** BARBOUR *Bruce* XIII. 60 This marschall that I of mwt, That schir Robert of Keth was cald ..Quhen that he saw [etc.]. *c* **1375** *Sc. Leg. Saints* xxxiii. (*George*) 138 Quhen he It fand na but forthir þare-o for to mute, one þe morne he [etc.]. *c* **1400** *Ywaine & Gaw.* 3328 The lord saw it was na bote Obout that mater mor to mote. **1535** STEWART *Cron. Scot.* (Rolls) II. 178 In this mater heir will I mute no moir. *a* **1600** MONTGOMERIE *Misc. Poems* ix. 12 If thou be he of vhom so many moots [etc.]. **1603** *Proph. of Waldhaue* (Bannatyne) 39 Mute on if ye may for mister ye haue.

†**b.** *trans.* To say, to utter. *Obs.*

c **1375** *Sc. Leg. Saints* xxiv. (*Alexis*) 430 Þat is my bale, but ony but, for þu na word wil to me mut. *c* **1430** *Syr Tryam.* 1439 Syr Tryamoure faght on fote, What schalle we more of hym mote? **1508** KENNEDIE *Flyting w. Dunbar* 375 For thou sik malice of thy maister mutis, It is wele sett that thou sik barat brace. **1529** LYNDESAY *Compl.* 91 The first sillabis that thow did mute Was 'pa, Da Lyn, vpon the lute'. *a* **1585** MONTGOMERIE *Flyting* 294 Of this mismade mowdewart, mischeif they muit.

†**2. a.** *intr.* To argue, to plead, to discuss, dispute, esp. in a law case. In later use *esp.* to debate an imaginary case of law, as was done by students in the Inns of Court. *Obs.*

c **1000** tr. *Basil's Hexameron* iii. (1849) 6 Ðu scealt ȝelyfan on ðone lifiȝendan God, and na ofer ðine mæðe motian be him. *c* **1175** *Lamb. Hom.* 43 Ofter he walde anuppon his underlinges mid wohe motien and longe dringan þenne he walde salmes singen oðer eani oðer god don. *a* **1225** *Leg. Kath.* 587 Makien se monie clerkes to cumene & se swiðe crefti of alle clergies..to motin wið a meiden! *c* **1330** R. BRUNNE *Chron.* (1725) 58 The kyng com to London, with

lawe to mote in benke. *c* **1350** *St. Mary Magd.* 360 in Horstm. *Altengl. Leg.* (1881) 85 þe gude man saw it was no bute Ogayns hir wil more forto mote. *a* **1352** MINOT *Poems* (ed. Hall) vi. 28 Oure men sall with ȝow mote. **1362** LANGL. *P. Pl.* A. III. 155 Heo ledeþ þe lawe as hire luste and louedayes makeþ, þ e Mase for a Mene mon þauȝ he mote euere. *c* **1400** *Laud Troy Bk.* 17236 Hem is no bote A-ȝeyn Gregays more to mote. *c* **1440** *Jacob's Well* xlvii. 295 To mote in wronge causys. *c* **1460** *Towneley Myst.* xx. 298 Syr, therof let vs moyte no mare. *c* **1470** HENRY *Wallace* x. 994 The byschop Synclar agayn fled in to But; With that fals king he had no will to mut. **1483** *Cath. Angl.* 247/2 To Mute, *allegare.* **1570** LEVINS *Manip.* 178/32 To moote, *arguere, mouere dubia.* **1602** *2nd Pt. Return fr. Parnass.* IV. i. 1536 It is a plaine case, whereon I mooted in our Temple. **1621** BP. MOUNTAGU *Diatribæ* 169, I meruaile, Master Selden should moote no better. **1628** EARLE *Microcosm., Aturney* (Arb.) 66 He talkes Statutes as fiercely, as if he had mooted seuen yeers in the Inns of Court. **1637** HEYLIN *Answ. Burton* 9, I ..marveile that you have not mooted all this while in some Inne of Chancery. *a* **1652** BROME *Covent Gard.* II. i. (1658) 25 We will Cry mercy, you are busie, we will not moote to day then?

†**b.** *trans.* To argue (a point, case, etc.). *Obs.*

a **1470** in *Hist. Coll. Citizen London* (Camden) 60 Ande that yere were the plays holdyn and motyde at the Towre of London. **1531** ELYOT *Gov.* I. xiv, A case is appoynted to be moted by certayne yonge men, contaynyng some doubtefull controuersie. **1609** SKENE *Reg. Maj.* I. 106 b, Quha sa mutes any partie in Court to the third day. **1770** FOOTE *Lame Lover* I. i. 24 *Mrs. Circuit.* Lord! I wonder Mr. Circuit you would breed that boy up to the bar. *Sergeant.* Why not, chuck? He has fine steady parts, and for his time moots a point——. **1770** BURKE *Pres. Discont.* Sel. Wks. I. 22 If it were not a bad habit to moot cases on the supposed ruin of the constitution. **1796** J. ANSTEY *Pleaders' Guide* (1803) 145 Then dreams he that some point he's mooting.

3. *trans.* To raise or bring forward (a point, question, subject, etc.) for discussion.

1685 *Gracian's Courtier's Orac.* 253 Politicians now a-days moot nothing else, but that the greatest Wisedom consists in making it appear. **1817** J. GILCHRIST *Intell. Patrimony* 153 Those who chiefly moot the business. **1842** E. FITZGERALD *Lett.* (1889) I. 82, I am now awaiting the third request in confidence: if you see no symptoms of its being mooted, perhaps you will kindly propose it. **1848** J. H. NEWMAN *Loss & Gain* xix. 285 And now..the question is at least plausibly mooted again. **1902** A. LANG *Hist. Scot.* II. ix. 202 The idea of their marriage had been mooted.

moot (muːt), *v.*^{2} *Obs.* exc. *dial.* [? f. MOOT *sb.*^{3} (which, however, has not been found earlier than the 19th c.).] *trans.* To dig up, to dig up by the roots. Also, to dig out, unearth (an otter). Hence '**mooted** *ppl. a.* (Her.), '**mooting** *vbl. sb.*

1473 *Yatton Churchw. Acc.* (Somerset Rec. Soc.) 109 For motyng of the Asschys. xx^{d}. **1610** GUILLIM *Heraldry* III. vii. (1660) 131 He beareth, Gules, the Stemme or Trunk of a Tree Eradicated, or Mooted up by the roots. **1661** MORGAN *Sph. Gentry* I. iii. 23 Trees on a stock are called Trunked, which also if they are cut, they are called Couped; but if torn (as it were) it is called Irradicated, or Mooted up by the roots. **1823** *New Monthly Mag.* VIII. 500 Thrice did he 'scape us after we mooted him [*sc.* an otter] from the bank. **1847** *Gloss. Heraldry* 226 *Mooted* (or *Moulted*) *up by the roots*, eradicated. **1855** *Archæologia* XXXVI. 428 A huge portion of it [*sc.* this building] on all sides had, to use the provincial term, been 'mooted up', and carried away, for the sake of the stone for building purposes. **1867** ROCK *Jim an' Nell* lxxxiv. (E.D.S. No. 76) Moot iv'ry brack about un.

moot (muːt), *v.*^{3} [f. MOOT *sb.*^{2}] *intr.* To fashion by means of a moot. Hence '**mooted** *ppl. a.*, '**mooting** *vbl. sb.*

c **1850** *Rudim. Navig.* (Weale) 133 *Mooting.* Making a treenail exactly cylindrical to a given size or diameter, called the *moot*: hence, when so made, it is said to be *mooted.* **1865** *Navy Dockyard Expense Acc.* 6 The planed deals and board, and mooted treenails must be separated from the rough articles to admit of valuation. **1867** SMYTH *Sailor's Word-bk.*, Mooting. **1880** *Times* 2 Dec. 8/2 Several thousands rough and mooted oak treenails.

moot, obs. form of MOTE *sb.* and *v.*

mootable ('muːtəb(ə)l), *a.* [f. MOOT *v.*^{1} + -ABLE.] Capable of being mooted; open to discussion.

1533 MORE *Debell. Salem* Wks. 944/2 Much after the maner of a motable case. **1824** DIBDIN *Libr. Comp.* 526 But, surely this was a mootable point.

mootah, mooter ('muːtə). *U.S. slang.* Also **moota, mootie, mota, muta**, and other varr. [Origin unknown.] Marijuana.

1933 C. DE LENOIR *Hundredth Man* xiii. 220 This drug.. looked like chopped hay, or dried clover... In short, a 'muggles', 'weed', or 'mootie', cannabis indica. **1938** *Detective Fiction Weekly* 8 Jan. 47/2 He found plenty of marijuana... As always, it came in cigarettes, called 'reefers', 'muggles', 'moocahs', 'mus', 'grifos', 'mootas', or sometimes, playfully, 'Mary Warners'. **1943** *Time* 19 July 54/2 Marijuana may be called muggles, mooter, Mary Warner, Mary Jane, Indian hay, loco weed, love weed, bambalacha, mohasky, mu, moocah, grass, tea or blue sage. **1946** MEZZROW & WOLFE *Really Blues* (1957) 52 All the time he was in the asylum he kept waiting for a big train to pull in with a carload of muta just for him. **1950** H. E. GOLDIN *Dict. Amer. Underworld Lingo* 285/1 *Marijuana*...mota; muggles; stink-weed. **1956** 'E. MCBAIN' *Cop Hater* (1958) x. 92 One of the guys was on mootah. So he got a little high. **1971** E. E. LANDY *Underground Dict.* 128 *Marijuana*,.. moocah, mota, mutha.

mootch, obs. form of MOOCH *v.*

moote, obs. f. MOAT *sb.*^{1}, MOTE, MOULT *v.*

mooted ('muːtɪd), *ppl. a.* [f. MOOT *v.*^{1} + -ED^{2}.] Brought forward for discussion.

1650 EARL MONM. tr. *Senault's Man bec. Guilty* 147 What would you say if the crime were in a mooted case put to you. **1856** DOVE *Logic Chr. Faith* v. i. §2. 269 We must turn to the often mooted question of Idealism. **1887** *Pall Mall G.* 19 Nov. 7/1 He supposed that Sir L. Sackville West and himself..could decide any mooted point.

mooted, obs. form of MOULTED *ppl. a.*

mooter^{1} ('muːtə(r)). Forms: 1 **mótere**, 3 **motere**, 4 **mutere**, 5 **mootiere, motare, muter, mwter**, 6– **mooter**. [f. MOOT *v.*^{1} + -ER^{1}.] One who moots, in senses of the vb.

†**1.** A speaker; one who argues or discusses, a lawyer who argues cases in a court of justice, a pleader; one who discusses a moot case. *Obs.*

a **1000** *Gloss.* in Wr.-Wülcker 212/16 *Contionator*, i. *locutor*, motere, *uel* maþelere. *a* **1225** *Leg. Kath.* 725 Maxence..bed bringen biforen him þeos modi moteres. *c* **1375** *Sc. Leg. Saints* xxxvi. (*Baptista*) 968 þis alisander can so lere, þat he wes a gud mutere. *c* **1430** *Pilgr. Lyf Manhode* IV. xix. (1869) 185 And for our mootiere þou art, and our sergeantesse we [etc.]. **1483** *Cath. Angl.* 247/2 A Muter, *actor, aduocatus.* *a* **1500** *Ratis Raving* I. 990 Trow weil, It mone be swa, ore vere, Fra þow be mwter at the bare. **1580** HOLLYBAND *Treas. Fr. Tongue, Declamateur*, a Declaimer, a moocer [*read* mooter]. **1637** J. WILLIAMS *Holy Table* 72 For the Case must be taken as it is in the Letter..not as this poore Mooter doth reasonably (that is, against all the Laws of reasoning) presume it. **1706** PHILLIPS (ed. Kersey), *Mootmen* or *Mooters*, Students at Law, who argue Reader's Cases. **1827** *Mirror* II. 151/2 An expounder of the laws, an arbiter of quibble mooters.

2. One who starts or proposes a question, etc.

1844 HOOD *On a Certain Locality* 2 Of public changes, good or ill, I seldom lead the mooters. **1891** *Q. Rev.* Oct. 322 One Professor Beddoes was its mooter.

mooter^{2} ('muːtə(r)). *Ship-building.* [f. MOOT *sb.*^{2} + -ER^{1}.]

1. (See quots.)

1750 BLANCKLEY *Nav. Expositor, Mooter*, is the Person who (after the Tree-Nails which are received into Store, rough from the Merchant) makes them smooth, and of proper Sizes. **1815** [see MOOT *sb.*^{2}] In some recent Dicts.

2. A spike, bolt, treenail.

1867 SMYTH *Sailor's Word-bk.*

mooter, obs. form of MULTURE.

moot hall. Also 4 **mut halle**, 4–6 **mot(e hall(e**, 5 **moyt halle, mute hall(e**, 6 **moute hal.** [f. MOOT *sb.*^{1} + HALL^{1}.] A hall in which a moot is held.

a. A council chamber; a town hall; a judgement hall. (Now only *Hist.* and in names of buildings surviving in certain English towns.) **b.** In the inns of court, a hall where moot cases were argued.

c **1380** WYCLIF *Serm.* Sel. Wks. II. 123 þei ledden Jesus in to þe Mut-halle. *c* **1400** *Gamelyn* 717 Gamelyn com boldelich in-to the moot-halle. *c* **1440** *Alphabet of Tales* 299 Saynt Leonard apperid in myddest of þe mute-hall. **14..** *Nom.* in Wr.-Wülcker 729/22 *Hoc pretorium*, a moythalle. **1526** *Pilgr. Perf.* (W. de W. 1531) 253 He was brought forth agayn of the mote hall, & presented to the iewes. **1566** DRANT *Horace, Sat.* II. vi. H vj b, The scribes pray me, for maine affayres, to haste the moute hal fro. **1648** *Siege of Colchester* in *Antiquary* Apr. (1880) 168 Fairfax..appointed a Council of War which met at the Moot Hall. **1677** NICOLSON *Gloss. Cumb. & Westm.* in *Trans. R. Soc. Lit.* (1870) IX. 316 *Moothall*, guildhall. **1684** *Cowel's Interpr.* s.v. *Moot*, The places where Moot-Cases were argued, was anciently called a Moot-hall. **1794** W. HUTCHINSON *Hist. Cumbld.* I. 253 The hall in which the assizes are held at Carlisle, still goes by the name of the mote, or moot-hall. **1865** *Reader* 5 Aug. 144 [Hexham] A picturesque moot-hall and prison in one. **1905** *Athenæum* 23 Sept. 402/2 Kindly coastguards had stretched flags from the old Moot Hall [Aldeburgh] to the houses opposite.

moother, obs. form of MOTHER *sb.*

'**moot-hill.** *Antiq.* Also 7 *Sc.* **mute-**. [f. MOOT *sb.*^{1} + HILL *sb.*

Often confused with MOTE-HILL; but there seems to be no reason for doubting that both words are genuine.]

A hill on which 'moots' or assemblies were held.

1609 SKENE *Reg. Maj.* I. 1 King Malcolme..reserved na thing in propertie to himselfe, bot..the Mute-hill, in the Towne of Scone. **1827** *Archæologia* (1829) XXII. 200 Moot-hills were first raised for such purposes as Churches were considered unfit for. **1874** GREEN *Short Hist.* i. §2. 12 Each little village-commonwealth..had its moot hill or sacred tree as a centre. **1902** W. S. CROCKETT *Scott Country* vii. 123 The Scottish motes have been generally confounded with moot-hills or meeting places, and their military character has even been altogether denied.

†'**moot-house.** *Obs.* [OE. *móthús*: see MOOT *sb.*^{1} and HOUSE *sb.*] = MOOT HALL.

c **1050** *Suppl. Ælfric's Gloss.* in Wr.-Wülcker 184/8 *Epicausterium*, domhus, *uel* mothus. *c* **1275** *Passion our Lord* 304 in *O.E. Misc.* 46 þe Gywes..brouhten vre louerd crist to heore mothuse. **1677** THOROTON *Antiq. Nottinghamsh.* 71 A certain Pit on the top of the Hill,..near the most westerly corner of Bingham Lordship, called Moot-house Pit, where the Hundred Court, now known by the name of Moot-house Court, is, or ought to be still kept, or called.

mooti, var. MUTI.

mooting ('muːtɪŋ), *vbl. sb.* [OE. *mótung* fem., f. *mótian*: see MOOT *v.*^{1} and -ING^{1}.] The action of MOOT *v.*^{1}; an instance of this.

†**1.** Discussion, debate; in later use *esp.* forensic argument, legal contest or pleading.

a **1000** *Aldh. Glosses* 4522 in Napier *O.E. Glosses* 117/2 *Colloquio*, of motunge. *c* **1205** LAY. 30235 þer wes þa motinge bituxe þan twam kinge. *c* **1275** *Passion Our Lord* 87 in *O.E. Misc.* 39 Hi nomen heom to rede at heore motynge. **1362** LANGL. *P. Pl.* A. VIII. 61 His pardoun In purgatorie is petit, I trouwe, þat eny Meede of mene Men for Motynge receyueþ. *c* **1400** MAUNDEV. (Roxb.) xvii. 79 It giffez him grace to ouercomme his enmys, if his cause be riȝtwys, bathe in were and in motyng. **1483** *Cath. Angl.* 247/2 A Mutynge, *causa.* **1496** *Dives & Paup.* (W. de W.) III. vii. 143/1 Also pledynge, motynge, markettes, fayres,..& all the werkes that sholde lette a man from goddes seruyce. *a* **1500** *Ratis Raving* I. 978 For causs of mwtyne and of pled. *a* **1529** SKELTON *Col. Cloute* 1075 Stande sure, and take good fotyng, And let be all your motyng, Your gasyng and your totyng. **1553** T. WILSON *Rhet.* 39, I haue knowne diuers, that by familiar talkyng and moutyng together, haue come to right good learnyng. **1641** BAKER *Apol. Laymen* 43 We are no Patrons of Lay Elders: though wee give them place in Theological mootings. **1649** MILTON *Eikon.* v. Wks. 1851 III. 373 To which and other Law-tractats I referr the more Lawyerlie mooting of this point. **1848** L. HUNT *Town* iii. 138 Young men, brought up in the mooting of points.

†**b.** A deliberative meeting or body. *Obs.*

c **1275** *Passion of Our Lord* 178 in *O.E. Misc.* 42 Nedde he bute þet word iseyd iudas him com þrynge Mid Gyues and myd phariseus from heore motynge. *c* **1290** *Beket* 753 in *S. Eng. Leg.* I. 128 In þe castel sat þe motinge of þis tyraunz ech-on.

2. *spec.* Discussion of imaginary cases at law, as practised by students of the Inns of Court.

1602 *2nd Pt. Return fr. Parnass.* IV. ii. (Arb.) 52, I thinke I do remember this also at a mooting in our Temple. **1636** B. JONSON *Discov., Eloquentia*, There is a difference betweene Mooting, and Pleading, betweene Fencing, and Fighting. **1737** J. CHAMBERLAYNE *St. Gt. Brit.* I. III. x. (ed. 33) 241 There are no Mootings or Readings in the Inns of Court or Chancery at this Day. **1880** *Encycl. Brit.* XIII. 89/1 The society of Gray's Inn has revived mootings..with some success.

attrib. **1634** W. CARTWRIGHT *Ordinary* III. v. Song, A Mooting Night brings wholsome smiles When John an Okes, and John a Stiles, Doe greaze the Lawyers Satin.

3. The action of propounding for discussion.

1858 FROUDE *Hist. Eng.* III. 509 Anne herself—who, after the slight agitation which the first mooting of the matter naturally produced, had acquiesced in everything which was proposed to her,—received this intimation with placidity.

mooting ('muːtɪŋ), *ppl. a.* [f. MOOT *v.*^{1} + -ING^{2}.] Taking part in a 'moot' of an Inn of Court.

1817 J. GILCHRIST *Intell. Patrimony* 131 Probably neither the one nor the other understands what he is writing about more than a big school-boy or mooting babbler.

mooting, obs. form of MOULTING.

mootit, variant of MOULTED.

mootley, obs. form of MOTLEY.

†'**mootman.** *Obs.* [f. MOOT *v.*^{1} + MAN *sb.*^{1}]

1. A law student of an Inn of Court; a student who argues a moot case.

1602 COKE *Rep.* III. To Rdr. D iv, So in the profession of the Law, there are Mootemen, (which are those that argue Readers Cases in houses of Chauncerie..). Of Mootemen after eight yeres Studie or thereabouts, are chosen Vtter-barristers. **16..** HOWELL *Twelve Treat.* (1661) 391 In the Constitutions of England, there are two incontroulable Maximes, whereof the meanest mootman that hath but saluted Littleton cannot be ignorant. **1671** E. CHAMBERLAYNE *Pres. St. Eng.* II. (1679) 225 Out of these Mootmen are chosen Readers for the Inns of Chancery. **1707** *Ibid.* III. (ed. 22) 416 The young Student in the Common-Law..is admitted to be one of the four Inns of Court, where he is first called a Moot-man. **1797** *Encycl. Brit.* (ed. 3) XII. 271/2 There is a bailiff, or surveyor of the moots, annually chosen by the bench, to appoint the mootmen for the inns of chancery.

2. Used for: ELECTOR 3.

1654 VILVAIN *Epit. Ess.* VI. lxxvii. 149 The 7 German Princes or Mootmen, which the Pope constituted to meddle in electing the Emperor.

mootness ('muːtnɪs). *U.S. Law.* [f. MOOT *a.* + -NESS.] Of a legal case or question: the fact or condition of being hypothetical.

1946 *Univ. Pennsylvania Law Rev.* XCIV. 127 No distinction will be made between cases where only a single issue is alleged to be moot and those in which the entire case stands or falls on a determination of mootness or its absence. **1951** WOLFSON & KURLAND *Robertson & Kirkham's Jurisdiction of Supreme Court of U.S.* xxxvi. 505 The Court may request counsel to discuss an issue as to mootness. **1955** *Univ. Pennsylvania Law Rev.* CIII. 773 Since a court is deprived of jurisdiction when a case becomes moot, the fact of mootness can be raised at any time during the judicial proceeding and, once proved, will prevent decision of the case on the merits. **1960** *U.S. Supreme Court Reports* 362 U.S. §577 If..George Parker's five-year quest for justice must end ignominiously in the limbo of mootness, surely something is badly askew in our system of criminal justice. **1970** *Harvard Law Rev.* LXXXIII. 1674 This Note will explore a situation, labeled a mootness question, that has become a recurrent problem for the Supreme Court: where events subsequent to the judgment of the trial court have so affected the relations between the parties that the two conditions for justiciability relevant on appeal—adverse interest and effective remedy—have arguably been compromised. **1974** *Ibid.* LXXXVIII. 373 (*heading*) The mootness doctrine in the Supreme Court. *Ibid.* 376 Mootness questions arise only once a court has determined,

usually implicitly, that a litigant has standing to bring the action.

moove, moozheek: see MOVE *v.*, MOUJIK.

moozle, moozy: see MUZZLE, MOSY *a.*

† **mop**, *sb.*[1] *Obs.* Forms: 4 **mopp**, 4–5 **moppe**, 5 **mop**. [Of obscure origin: prob. related to MOPE *v.* and *sb.*; and perh. also related to MOP *v.*[1] Cf. Du., LG. *mop, mops*, G. *mops* poodle, LG. *mops* blockhead.]

1. A fool. Cf. MOPE *sb.* 1.

13.. *Seuyn Sages* (W.) 1414 Ther was a burgeis in this toun.. That wolde spouse no nethebours schild, But wente fram hom as a moppe wild. He let his negheboures child for a vice, And wente from hem als moppe and nice. **13..** *Evang. Nicod.* 21 in *Archiv Stud. neu. Spr.* LIII. 392 þis mopp, þat merres our men, calles him god son of heuen. *c* **1440** *York Myst.* xxxi. 196 This mop meynes þat he may marke men to þer mede.

2. A playful term for a baby; in quot. 1440 app. a rag doll. Cf. MOPPET[2] 2.

c **1440** *Promp. Parv.* 342/2 Moppe, or popyne [cf. '*Popyne*, chylde of clowtys', *ibid.* 409], *pupa, pusio*. *c* **1460** *Towneley Myst.* xiii. 724 Hayll, lytyll tyne mop! **1598** FLORIO, *Pupo* ..a daintie mop, a playing babie.

mop (mɒp), *sb.*[2] Also 5 **mappe**, 7–8 **map(p**, **mopp**, 9 *dial.* **map**. [Late 15th c. *mappe*; the relation to the earlier MAPPLE is not quite clear.

On the assumption that *mapple* is ad. L. *mappula* (dim. of *mappa* napkin) which may in monastic Latin have been used for 'mop', it would be possible that *mappe* is similarly a direct adoption of L. *mappa*. The ordinary hypothesis that the word is a. OF. *mappe*:—L. *mappa* involves the difficulty that the evidence for this OF. form is slender and doubtful, the Fr. representative of the L. word having been *nap(p)e* from the 11th c. Cf., however, mod. Walloon *map* table-cloth, *mappe* napkin (Remacle).

The form *mop* first appears in the 17th c. (cf. however MOPPET[1], which is recorded much earlier), and may have been due to association with MOP *sb.*[1] in the sense of 'rag doll'. The W. Flem. *moppe*, a ship's mop (De Bo), may possibly be adopted from Eng.]

1. a. A bundle of coarse yarn or cloth fastened at the end of a stick and arranged so as to soak up liquid easily, used in cleaning floors, etc., and nautically for laying on pitch.

1496 *Naval Acc. Hen. VII* (1896) 174 Shepeskyns bought & spent abought makyng of mappes for layng on of piche Rosyn & talow uppon the seid ship. **1614** *Vestry Bks.* (Surtees) 169 A mapp: for the pulpitt, iiij d. **1623–4** MIDDLETON & ROWLEY *Sp. Gipsy* II. ii, Not such maps as you wash houses with, but maps of countries. **1624** CAPT. SMITH *Virginia* 245 Thrums for pitch Maps. **1659** TORRIANO *Ital. Dict.*, *Pannatore*, a maulkin, a map of clouts or rags to rub or cleanse withall. **1711** TEMPEST *Cryes of London* 28 Maids buy a Mapp.

1665 BOYLE *Exp. Hist. Cold* Postscr. 678 The water that was imployed to wash them, being thinly spread with a Mop, would presently congeal. **1709** SWIFT *Morning* in *Tatler* No. 9 ¶1 Now Moll had whirl'd her Mop with dext'rous Airs. **1801** MAR. EDGEWORTH *Gd. Fr. Governess* (1831) 200 A woman was twirling a mop at the door. **1881** BESANT & RICE *Chapl. of Fleet* I. xii, She was supposed to be ..helping Molly the maid with the mop. **1884** KNIGHT *Dict. Mech.* Suppl., *Rubber Mop*. The mop-head has a plate of thick rubber which is used as a scrubber or squeezer.

b. (*to be*) ***mops and brooms***: half-drunk.

It has been conjectured that this is an allusion to the drinking that took place at the hiring fairs (see MOP *sb.*[5]), at which the maids carried mops or brooms in token of the capacity in which they wished to be hired.

1814 *Sporting Mag.* XLIV. 188 'Now Tom, you're drunk!' 'No Dame not I, I'm only mops and brooms!' **1858** S. BROOKS *Gordian Knot* xxiv. (1868) 217 If I had married a wife, I don't think I should go home to her in a state of mops and brooms. **1891** T. HARDY *Tess* xxxiv. (1892) 288 There is not much doing now, being New Year's Eve, and folks mops and brooms from what's inside 'em.

¶ **c.** (See quot.) ? *nonce-use*.

Halliwell 1847 gives '*Mop*, a napkin (Glo.)'.

1683 SNAPE *Anat. Horse* I. viii. (1686) 13 [The Caul is] called *mappa ventris*, the Map or Dish-clout of the Belly.

d. ***Mrs. Mop(p***: see MRS. 2 c.

2. *transf.* **a.** Applied to various small instruments resembling a mop, e.g. a circular pad of cloth, used in polishing silver with rouge; a brush used by gilders; a surgical instrument with a sponge or other absorbent substance at the end of a handle, for applying medicated fluids or for removing purulent matter, etc.

1869 *Eng. Mechanic* 26 Nov. 254/1 Trees..are painted in ..with a tool called a gilder's mop. **1875** H. C. WOOD *Therap.* (1879) 100 It should be applied by means of a little mop, scrupulous care being exercised to prevent any of the acid from coming in contact with parts not protected. **1898** T. B. WIGLEY *Art Goldsm. & Jeweller* xv. 136 A 'calico mop' charged with a little rouge moistened with water. **1904** *Brit. Med. Jrnl.* 17 Dec. 1647 A Uterine Mop.

b. *nonce-use.* An aspergillum.

1838 PRESCOTT *Ferd. & Is.* I. xvii. II. 231 The mop, or hyssop, with which the Roman Catholic missionaries were wont to scatter the holy drops. *Ibid.* II. vi. II. 513.

3. A thick mass (of hair, occasionally of foliage).

1847 HALLIWELL, *Mop*, a tuft of grass. West. **1874** SYMONDS *Sk. Italy & Greece* (1898) I. xiv. 307 She had..a tempestuously frizzled mop of powdered hair. **1886** MRS. F. H. BURNETT *Lit. Ld. Fauntleroy* vii, A little boy..with a splendid mop of bright waving hair. **1887** O. W. HOLMES *Hundred Days in Europe* i. 32 Trees..feathered all the way up their long slender trunks with a lop-sided mop of leaves at the top, like a wig which has slipped awry.

4. *attrib.* and *Comb.*: **a.** simple attrib., as ***mop-cloth***, † ***staff***; ***mop-haired***, ***-headed***, ***-topped*** adjs.; **b.** objective, as ***mop-maker***; **c.** special comb., as **mop-board** orig. *U.S.* (see quot. 1859); **mop brush**, a round paint-brush with a short thick head; **mop-head**, (*a*) the head of a mop; (*b*) a thick head of hair resembling a mop; also, a person having a 'mop' of hair; (*c*) a clamp for a mop-rag on the end of a handle (Knight *Dict. Mech.* 1875); **mop-nail** (see quot. 1875); **mop-squeezer** *slang*, a housemaid.

1854 *Mop-board [see *baseboard* (BASE *sb.*[1] 20)]. **1859** BARTLETT *Dict. Americanisms*, *Mop-board*, the wash-board which extends around the floor at the base of the walls in the interior of a house, is so called in New England. **1904** *Westm. Gaz.* 10 Sept. 14/2 Take a *mop brush and coat the paper quickly and evenly. **1875** KNIGHT *Dict. Mech.* s.v. *Mop-head*, The *mop-cloth is clamped between toothed jaws. **1924** L. ECKENSTEIN *Tutankh-aten* v. 46 The..*mop-haired Syrian almost daily presented himself at the gate. **17..** SHERIDAN (Hoppe), The fops at your end of the town, with *mop-heads and empty skulls. **1824** SCOTT *Redgauntlet* ch. xxiv, Benjie thrust in his mop head. **1878** H. M. STANLEY *Dark Cont.* II. xvi. 426 Many adopt the mop head. *a* **1625** FLETCHER, etc. *Fair Maid Inn* II. ii, As long as we kept the *Mop-headed butter-boxes sober. **1779** FORREST *Voy. N. Guinea* 68 The long hair'd Moors..and the mopheaded Papuas. **1862** H. MARRYAT *Year in Sweden* II. 354 Mop-headed junipers with myriads of unripe berries. **1891** *Syd. Soc. Lex.*, *Mop-headed*, a term applied to those races of men with crisp or woolly hair, which is long and bristly, and grows into a round mass on the top of the head, as in Kafirs. **1900** M. THORN in W. D. DRURY *Bk. Gardening* xi. 360 Trees that are 'mop-headed', or top-heavy, should be supported by stakes. **1926** S. T. WARNER *Lolly Willowes* II. 85 She looked at the large mop-headed blossoms [*sc.* chrysanthemums]. **1934** *Times Educ. Suppl.* 3 Feb. p. iv/4 The autumn-flowering, mop-headed group of *P[rimula] capitata*. **1966** *Gloss. Landscape Work* (*B.S.I.*) IV. 15 *Mop-headed*, having naturally or induced a compact, rounded head, small in relation to the height of stem. **1972** *Guardian* 26 Jan. 9/6 Straight Jane Ltd...are now offering a Twist-n-Wring mop..with a head of the traditional type that gave mop-headed hair-dos their name. **1974** *Sunday Express* 21 Apr. 6/8 His mop-headed adventures are told in an oddly convoluted style and some will find them decidedly gooey. **1723** *Lond. Gaz.* No. 6172/8 John Elston,..*Mopmaker. **1851** in *Illustr. Lond. News* 5 Aug. (1854) 119/2 Mop-maker. **1841** S. BAMFORD *Passages in Life of Radical* I. xxxvii. 216 Some had been grinding scythes, others..screw-drivers, rusty swords, pikels, and *mop-nails. **1875** KNIGHT *Dict. Mech.*, *Mop-nail*, a flat-headed nail, used in securing a bunch of junk or rope-ends to a handle in making a mop such as sailors use. **1876** AITKEN *Brit. Manuf. Industr.*, *Guns*, etc. 34 Gate, pipe, plate, scupper, mop nails and spikes. **1771** *Misc. Ess.* in *Ann. Reg.* XIV. 197/2 She looks like a *mop-squeezer. **1718** *Free-thinker* No. 21. 146 A Wife has been trained up to handle a Broomstick or a *Mopstaff. **1887** W. RYE *Norfolk Broads* 77 With its trimly-kept lawn, and *mop-topped rose trees.

mop (mɒp), *sb.*[3] Also 7 **mopp**. [f. MOP *v.*[1]] A grimace, esp. one made by a monkey. Chiefly in phrase ***mops and mows***.

1581 PETTIE tr. *Guazzo's Civ. Conv.* I. (1586) 32 b, The Ape..giueth himself to make vs laugh with his mops and mowes. **1621** FLETCHER *Wild Goose Chase* III. i, Heartily I hate these Travellers, These Gim-cracks, made of Mops and Motions. **1668** R. L'ESTRANGE *Vis. Quev.* (1708) 29 Others they call'd Apes (and we Mimicks), these were perpetually making of Mopps and Mowes. **1710** *Banbury Apes* (ed. 4) 8 Truly, says the Mayor, there's sufficient witness that saw him make Mops and Mows at her. **1820** *Marmaiden of Clyde* in Whitelaw *Sc. Ball.* (1857) 92/2 Wi' mop an' mowr, an' glare an' glowr, Grim faces grin ower the waves. **1893** STEVENSON *Catriona* iii, The mops and mows of the old witch.

† **mop**, *sb.*[4] *Obs.* Also 6 **moppe**, 7–8 **mopp**. [Of obscure origin: cf. MOP *sb.*[1], sense 2.] In the combinations ***whiting-mop***, ***gurnard-mop***, a young whiting or gurnard. Hence (perh. with allusion to MOP *sb.*[1]) used as a playful appellation for a girl.

1589 PUTTENHAM *Eng. Poesie* III. xix. (Arb.) 229 In our triumphals calling familiarly vpon our Muse, I called her Moppe... Vnderstanding by this word (Moppe) a litle prety Lady, or tender young thing. For so we call litle fishes, that be not come to their full growth (*moppes*,) as whiting moppes, gurnard moppes. **1597** LYLY *Wom. in Moon* v. i, Pandora..louest thou Gunophilus? *Pan.* I, if he be a fish, for fish is fine; Sweete Stesias helpe me to a whiting moppe. **1607** DEKKER & WEBSTER *Westw. Hoe* D.'s Wks. 1873 II. 302 Do you hear, the whiting mop has nibled. **1624** HEYWOOD *Captives* II. ii. in Bullen *O. Pl.* IV, Wheres my sweete? Not heare? no where? why, hoe, my whytinge mopp Late scapt from feeding haddocks. **1630** J. TAYLOR (Water P.) *Jacke-a-Lent* Wks. I. 117/1 The Whiting, Rotchet,..and the Mop. **1758** *Descr. Thames* 222 The young Fish of this Sort are called by the Londoners Whiting-Mopps.

mop (mɒp), *sb.*[5] *dial.* Also 8 **mapp**. [Perh. short for *mop-fair*, f. MOP *sb.*[2]; for the reason for the name see quot. *c* 1830.] The name in some districts for the annual fair or gathering at which servants are hired; a 'statute fair'.

1677 PLOT *Oxfordsh.* 203 In the Northern part of Oxfordshire,..it has always been the custom at set times of year, for young people to meet to be hired as servants; which meeting, at Banbury they call the Mop; at Bloxham the Statute. **1743** in Noake *Rambler in Worcs.*, A mapp will be held at the same time for the hiring of servants. **1797** EDEN *State of Poor* I. 33 *note*, In Gloucestershire..servants continue to attend the mopp or statute, as it is called (i.e. Michaelmas fair), in order to be hired. *c* **1830** MRS. SHERWOOD in *Houlston Tracts* III. No. 62. 3 It is an ancient custom..for servants out of place to assemble, once a year, in or near some great town, for the purpose of being hired. I have heard my mother say, that formerly each person carried a mop, or a broom, or a flail,..or some other badge denoting the office in which they desired to engage; but this was done away with before my time. In this assemblage, which is called a mop, persons in want of servants generally make their choice. **1859** *All Year Round* No. 29. 52 The provincial policeman had said that it was the Mop, or, as the officer pronounced it, the Mope-day. **1870** *3rd Rep. Comm. Employm. Children, etc. Agric.* 62 As many as 500 young men and women come to the great mop fair at Monmouth which takes place in May. **1894** *Westm. Gaz.* 13 Oct. 5/3 Stratford-on-Avon 'mop', said to be the largest statute fair in England, was held yesterday.

† **mop**, *sb.*[6] *Obs.*[—0] [Cf. MAUPE; R. Holme perh. mistook the application.] = COALMOUSE.

1688 R. HOLME *Armoury* II. 122/2 Crows, Pies,.. Titmouses, Mopps, &c. do much hurt in Orchards. *Ibid.* 243/1 This..we in our Countrey call Tittimous, or Mop.

mop (mɒp), *sb.*[7] and *int. U.S. slang.* [Echoic; cf. BOP *sb.*[2]] (See quots.)

1944 in R. S. Gold *Jazz Lexicon* (1964) 208 (*tune-title*) Mop mop. **1945** L. SHELLY *Jive Talk Dict.* 15 *Mop*, the finale. **1947** *Britannica Bk. of Year* 840/2 *Mop*, slang, a word connoting surprise, anguish; a mild sort of 'hubba, hubba, hubba' (1944). **1952** B. ULANOV *Hist. Jazz in Amer.* (1958) xxv. 349 Such words as 'mop!' an exclamation of wide currency in the early forties which accurately described a musical device (the final beat in a cadence of triplets, usually bringing the release of a jazz composition to an end). **1959** *Village Voice* (N.Y.) 28 Oct. 13, I wait a while, eyes closed, and I look, mop! I'm in the bathtub, all alone. **1970** C. MAJOR *Dict. Afro-Amer. Slang* 82 *Mop*, the last beat at the end of a jazz number with a cadence of triplets.

mop (mɒp), *v.*[1] Also 6 **moppe**. [Perh. imitative of movements of the lips: cf. Du. *moppen* to pout.] *intr.* To make a grimace. Chiefly in phrase ***to mop and mow*** (cf. the older *mock and mow*).

1567 GOLDING *Ovid's Met.* XIV. 174 b, Too moppe and mowe, but not too speake. **1570** LEVINS *Manip.* 169/17 To moppe, maw, *mouere labia*. **1583** GOLDING *Calvin on Deut.* xxiii. 138 Whensoeuer a Crucifix stands mopping & mowing in the Church [etc.]. **1606** RICH *Faults & nothing but F.* 7 Marke but his countenance, see how hee mops, and how he mowes. **1655** tr. *Com. Hist. Francion* IV. 17 Fremond, drawing her mouth an inch and a half wider than ordinary, and mopping at him [etc.]. **1692** R. L'ESTRANGE *Fables* x. 9 An Asse was so Hardy once, as to fall a Mopping and Braying at a Lyon. **1823** BYRON *Island* IV. vii, Fantastic faces mop'd and mow'd on high. **1858** MERIVALE *Rom. Emp.* I. (1865) VI. 206 He mops and mows, and shakes his palsied head.

mop (mɒp), *v.*[2] [f. MOP *sb.*[2]]

1. a. *trans.* To rub with a mop; to wipe or clean with or as with a mop. Also with *out*.

1755 in JOHNSON. **1812** H. & J. SMITH *Rej. Addr.*, *Baby's Debut* vii, I wiped the dust from off the top, While Molly mopp'd it with a mop, And brushed it with a broom. **1898** HENLEY *Lond. Types*, *Barmaid*, And having mopped the zinc for certain years, And faced the gas, she fades and disappears. **1898** P. MANSON *Trop. Diseases* xxiii. 375 The whole breadth of the abscess cavity, which he [i.e. Zancarol] mops out and stuffs with iodoform gauze. **1927** *Motor Cycling* 7 Dec. 104/2 With a successful chromium plate the finished surface is so hard that it cannot be buffed or mopped.

b. slang. ***to mop the floor with***: said of a combatant in whose hands his opponent is helpless.

1887 HENLEY & STEVENSON *Deacon Brodie* I. iii. 1 Newcastle Jemmy! Muck: that's my opinion of him... I'll mop the floor up with him any day. **1897** *Daily News* 2 Oct. 6/2 James I. of England, was more Popish than Protestant; and the King of Spain mopped his floor with him.

2. a. To wipe perspiration, tears, etc., from (the face, brow, etc.). Also *rarely* with *up*.

1840 THACKERAY *Paris Sk.-bk.* (1869) 67 Gambouge mopped his eyes with his handkerchief. **1852** MRS. STOWE *Uncle Tom's C.* xi, The good-natured old body..who had pulled out a great yellow silk pocket-handkerchief, and was mopping up his face with great energy. **1870** LOWELL *Study Wind.* 4 As we mopped our brows at each other. **1881** BESANT & RICE *Chapl. of Fleet* I. xii, A boy pumped the cold water over him. This done, he..mopped his poll with his silk handkerchief.

b. To wipe (perspiration, tears, etc.) *from* the face or brow.

1872 R. W. BUCHANAN *Saint Abe & his Seven Wives* i. 4 And mopping from his brow the sweat, The boy glanced round with teeth still set. **1907** *Smart Set* Apr. 18/2 She.. mopped the hot tears from her face.

3. mop up. To absorb, wipe up (water, etc.) with or as with a mop. Also *fig.* Various slang uses: To drink greedily; also with *it*; also, to eat greedily; to absorb, appropriate, get hold of (profits, etc.); to make an end of, slaughter; also *Mil.*, to complete the occupation of (a district, etc.) by capturing or killing enemy troops left there (cf. quot. 1901); also *absol.* and *transf.*

1709 [E. WARD] *Rambling Fuddle-Caps* 10 Come, mop up the Batter you've trampl'd and stood in. **1781** P. BECKFORD *Hunting* (1803) 36 If water should remain,..it should be carefully mopped up. **1811** *Lex. Balatron.*, *To Mop up*, to drink up. To empty a glass or pot. **1851–61** MAYHEW *Lond. Labour* III. 203 If I gets inside I'll mop up 1*s.* if it's good company. *Ibid.* 250, I have seen the youngest 'mop up' his half-quartern as well as I did. **1888** RIDER HAGGARD *Col. Quaritch* III. i. 2 As he mopped up the streaming blood with a sponge. **1890** 'R. BOLDREWOOD' *Miner's Right* xv, It seems they have been mopping up some rich surfacing. **1898** T.

Troubridge in W. A. Morgan '*House' on Sport* 393 The birds..come over in one's and two's, and are 'mopped up'. **1899** Rider Haggard *Farmer's Yr.* 387 Afterwards this reverend gentleman very nearly slew me also in mopping up a low pheasant. **1901** *Westm. Gaz.* 18 Dec. 7/2 It is not to be expected..that a force, however large, will be able to 'mop up'..a far smaller body of Boers in a short time. **1902** Wodehouse *Pothunters* i. 17, I hope your first man mops you up. **1915** A. Huxley *Let.* Dec. (1969) 88 It is *up to you*..to roll in the Texan subscriptions, while our agents..are..to mop up other corners of the dark continent. **1917** P. Gibbs *Battles of Somme* 295 Reserve battalions..came up behind to 'mop-up' the captured ground. **1920** M. A. Mügge *War Diary of Square Peg* 221 The second wave going over the top; it 'mops up', 'cleans up' the enemy's dug-outs. **1921** Wodehouse *Indiscretions of Archie* vii. 64 'Seacliff always had a—a tendency—a—a weakness—it was a family failing —' 'Mopping it up, do you mean? Shifting it?' **1936** —— *Laughing Gas* iii. 37, I find you here, mopping up the stuff like a vacuum cleaner. **1938** *Sun* (Baltimore) 31 Oct. 4/1 Three fires..were reported to be under control with the fire-fighters 'mopping up' today. **1940** *Times* (Weekly ed.) 10 Jan. 7/4 While mopping up the ground captured, the Zouaves took five machine-guns, 2,000 rounds of ammunition, and 12 prisoners. **1942** *R.A.F. Jrnl.* 30 May 33 The enemy was still fighting behind us but they would be mopped up in time. **1962** A. Nisbett *Technique Sound Studio* 239 Membrane and vibrating panel absorbers..readily remove sound energy from the air at their resonant frequency and this is then mopped up within the absorber by various forms of damping. **1970** *Toronto Daily Star* 24 Sept. 1/7 King's troops were pursuing the fleeing rebels, mopping up. **1971** *E. Afr. Standard* (Nairobi) 13 Apr. 1/1 Troops were reported to be mopping up remnants of the..insurgents. **1973** *Times* 30 July 18/2 He also had to mop up the ensuing threatening chaos when prices rose much further than had been predicted. **1973** *Press & Jrnl.* (Aberdeen) 7 Aug. 16/8 A perfect crossfield ball to Hay allowed the inside left to dribble to the by-line and cut it back, but Watson was on hand to mop up the danger. **1973** *Times* 27 Dec. 11/1 The Bank of England 'mopped up' a large surplus by selling Treasury bills to both houses and banks. **1974** *Times* 5 Apr. 16/4 While mopping up a Knickerbocker Glory or two we devised a new form of the old game.

Hence **mop-up** *sb.*, a state of being 'mopped up'. Also, an act of 'mopping-up'.

1900 Doyle *Gt. Boer War* xv. 263 Better six battalions safely down the hill than a mop up in the morning. **1902** *19th Cent.* June 910 He was in for a mop-up this time. **1917** P. Gibbs *Battles of Somme* 296 The honour of the new attack was given to the 'mop-up' battalions behind. **1921** *Daily Colonist* (Victoria, B.C.) 2 Oct. 1/5 Men..known among the strikers as 'mop-up gangs' have committed depredations, beaten up a few loyal employees, and threatened and intimidated other employees. **1944** *Sun* (Baltimore) 29 Apr. 2 (*caption*) Sergt. Charles H. Wolverton..prepares to throw a hand grenade into a Japanese dugout during the mop-up of the Empress Augusta Bay area after 18 days of bitter fighting.

mop, *v.*³, variant of map *v.*², to bewilder.

c **1400** *Laud Troy Bk.* 18204 The knyghtes that were In that hors stopped, Thei were nother mased ne mopped.

mopane (mɒˈpɑːniː). *S. Afr.* Also **mapani, mopanè, mopani.** [Bantu *mo-pane.*] **1.** A tree, *Colophospermum mopane*, of the family Leguminosæ, native to areas of low rainfall in southern Africa, and distinguished by rough, flaking, grey or brown bark, racemes of small, pale green flowers, and leaves formed of a pair of triangular leaflets joined at the base, which fold together during periods of intense heat. Also *attrib.*

1857 D. Livingstone *Missionary Trav. & Res. S. Afr.* 91 In some parts there are forests of mimosæ and mopane. *Ibid.* 162 Numbers of 'Baobab' and 'Mopané' trees abound all over this hard smooth surface [of calcareous tufa]. **1864** T. Baines *Explor. S.-W. Afr.* xv. 422 The palms and open grassy plain had given place to thickets of mimosa..and mopane. **1871** J. Mackenzie *Ten Years North of Orange River* viii. 140 We at length found in a large mopane forest a well-beaten path. **1881** E. E. Frewer tr. *Holub's Seven Yrs. in S. Afr.* I. 48 The mapani-tree, with its oleaginous leaves and porous brittle wood. **1893** F. C. Selous *Trav. & Adventure S.-E. Afr.* 160 The fork of a mopani tree. **1906** *Chambers's Jrnl.* Mar. 213/1 Viewed across the hazy expanse of baobab and mopane bush. **1910** J. Buchan *Prester John* iv. 87 The mopani trees with their dull green wearied me. **1932** *Discovery* July 224/1 The mopané is a resinous tree, making good fuel. **1947** J. Stevenson-Hamilton *Wild Life S. Afr.* iv. 36 The Mopani belt in its extension along the Imbabate River. **1958** L. van der Post *Lost World of Kalahari* vi. 110 We came down the side of the dunes on to a level plain covered with Mopani trees. **1973** Palmer & Pitman *Trees S. Afr.* II. 842 The mopane is the dominant tree of large parts of northern South and South West Africa where great stretches of hot, arid country..are covered with it. *Ibid.* 843 Farmers in mopane veld look upon the tree as providing valuable fodder. **1975** M. Hartmann *Game for Vultures* iii. 44 They moved..away into the black mopani bush.

2. mopane bee, beetle, fly, worm (see quots.).

1953 S. H. Skaife *African Insect Life* xxi. 357 The stingless bees, or Mopani bees, as they are often called, that are found in Africa belong to the genus *Trigona*. **1972** L. van der Post *Story like the Wind* vi. 161 At about ten in the morning..all the billions of mopani beetles, hidden behind the butterfly leaves of the trees, began to sing their Messiah to the day. **1975** M. Hartmann *Game for Vultures* i. 2 Mopani flies, little black squelches, were skitting around his eyes and ears. **1966** D. Varaday *Gara-Yaka's Domain* xvii. 182 No less a find than crawling, fat, three-inch-long worms! Mopani worms—Masonja—as the Bantu call these brightly coloured insects, are regarded by them as a great delicacy. **1973** Palmer & Pitman *Trees S. Afr.* II. 843 Large, dark, spotted caterpillars, the larvae of the moth *Gonimbrasia belina*—5 to 8 cm long and fat as a finger—feed upon the mopane leaves and are used by Africans and Bushmen as food... Mopane worms are much valued by rural Africans and are often their richest source of protein.

mope (məʊp), *sb.* Also 6 **moope.** [Related to mope *v.*, from which senses 2 and 3 are derived.]

1. A fool; = mop *sb.*¹ 1.

1540 Hyrde tr. *Vives' Instr. Chr. Wom.* (1592) I viij, Nor thou shalt not thereof be reckoned the more moope and foole but the more wise. **1638** Burton *Anat. Mel.* I. ii. iv. iv. (ed. 3) 142 They will be scoffing..till they haue made by their humoring or gulling, *ex stulto insanum*, a mope or a noddy. **1932** J. T. Farrell *Young Lonigan* vi. 259 They had a lot of pep, and weren't a bunch of mopes. **1962** E. O'Brien *Lonely Girl* i. 8 It happens to country mopes like you, as soon as you dance with a fellow.

2. One who mopes; a gloomy, listless person.

1693 *Humours Town* 125, I shou'd grow the veriest Mope in the World, if I shou'd forsake this Town. **1728** Pope *Dunc.* II. 33 A Poet's form she plac'd before their eyes, No meagre, muse-rid mope, adust and thin. **1747** W. Horsley *Fool* (1748) II. 257 All dull and disconsolate, as the Mopes in Bedlam. *a* **1766** Mrs. F. Sheridan *Sidney Bidulph* IV. 121 She is become such a mope, that she is really fit company for no one but herself. **1878** M. C. Jackson *Chaperon's Cares* xiii, She is no mope, only thoughtful and quiet.

3. pl. *the mopes*; depression of spirits.

1825 Hone *Every-day Bk.* I. 944, I have got the mopes. **1838** Thackeray *Yellowpl. Corr.* iii, Master still in the mopes. **1845** *P. Parley's Ann.* VI. 199 If I go with my eyes fixed upon the ground, they say I have got the mopes, and am going mad. **1900** *Westm. Gaz.* 29 Mar. 3/2 If you did not take exercise you fell into a state of weakness and mopes, in which you were an easy victim to enteric.

mope (məʊp), *v.* Also 6-7 **moop(e,** 7-8 **moape.** [Of obscure origin; connexion with mop *v.*¹ is doubtful. Cf. mop *sb.*¹, map *v.*², mop *v.*³

In mod. dialects (see *Eng. Dial. Dict.*) the vb. has the senses 'to wander about aimlessly', 'to grope'; among the dialectal forms are *maup*, *maap*, etc. The corresponding word is found in several Scandinavian langs.: cf. Sw. dial. *mopa* to look discontented, sulk, Da. *maabe* to be stupid or unconscious, to mope, Norw. *maapa* to lay about one wildly with a weapon, Bornholm *mâva* to stand gaping, expecting something good. (MSw. *mopa* to befool seems to be more nearly connected with mop *sb.*¹)]

1. *intr.* 'To be in a state of unconsciousness, to move and act without the impulse and guidance of thought' (Schmidt). *Obs.* exc. *dial.* (see *E.D.D.*).

1568, 1593 [see moping *ppl. a.*]. **1599** Shaks. *Hen. V*, III. vii. 143 What a wretched and peeuish fellow is this King of England, to mope with his fat-brain'd followers so farre out of his knowledge. **1602** —— *Ham.* III. iv. 81 (1604 Qo.) What deuill wast That thus hath cosund you at hodman blind; Eyes without feeling, feeling without sight... Or but a sickly part of one true sence Could not so mope. **1610** —— *Temp.* v. 240 Euen in a dreame, were we diuided from them, And were brought moaping hither.

2. a. To yield oneself up to ennui; to remain in a listless, apathetic condition, without making any effort to rouse oneself; to be dull, dejected and spiritless.

c **1590** Greene *Alphonsus* IV. Wks. (Grosart) XIII. 395 And as for Mars..He moping sits behind the kitchen-door. **1676** Etheredge *Man of Mode* v. ii, Sitting moping like Three or Four Melancholy Birds in a spacious vollary. **1709** Steele *Tatler* No. 2 ¶2 Here I sit moping all the live-long Night, Devour'd with Spleen, and Stranger to Delight. **1770** Foote *Lame Lover* II. Wks. 1799 II. 73 For this fortnight he has gone about sighing, and musing, and moping. **1865** Trollope *Belton Est.* v, He's out somewhere, thinking of what is going on, instead of moping in the house. **1882** Miss Braddon *Mt. Royal* II. iii. 31 She was still moping and regretting the discarded lover.

fig. **1795** Wolcot (P. Pindar) *Pindariana* Wks. 1812 IV 164 See yonder cloud that mopes with mournful shade.

b. quasi-*trans.* with *away*.

1791 Charlotte Smith *Celestina* II. 227 Celestina has too much spirit and too much sense to mope away her youth and beauty. *a* **1792** Horne *Disc.* (1795) IV. xii. 279 His religion..directs him not to shut himself up in a cloister alone, there to mope and moan away his life.

3. *trans.* To make dull, dejected, or melancholy. Now only *refl.* and in *passive*, to be the victim of ennui.

1602 Warner *Alb. Eng.* XII. lxxi. (1612) 297 Not moop't at home, but mapping Lands. **1621** Burton *Anat. Mel.* I. ii. iv. iv. (1624) 134 Many men are vndone by this meanes, moped, and so dejected that [etc.]. **1681-4** J. Scott *Chr. Life* I. iv. (ed. 3) 283 It is doubtless a great Disgrace to our Religion to imagine..that it is an Enemy to Mirth and Chearfulness,..that men are never serious enough till they are mope'd into Statues. **1740** J. Clarke *Educ. Youth* (ed. 3) 140 Boys of mild..Tempers, must be dispirited, and moaped..by it. **1799** Mrs. J. West *Tale of Times* II. 94 The viscountess..urged her not to mope herself at home. **1803** Jane Porter *Thaddeus* xxxvi, My father is moped to death for want of you both. **1881** Lady Herbert *Edith* 16 Gordon could not compel her to remain at home and 'mope herself to death' as she expressed it. **1903** *Longm. Mag.* Apr. 494 Any one can see you are moped to death.

4. To confine or shut *up* (in a place).

1863 A. D. Whitney *Faith Gartney's Girlhood* xvi. 140 The child shouldn't be moped up here, all winter!

moped (məʊpt), *ppl. a.* [f. mope *v.* + -ed¹.] †**a.** Stupefied, bewildered (*obs.*). **b.** Affected with ennui, dejected, melancholy, low-spirited.

1606 *Sir G. Goosecappe* I. i. in Bullen *O. Pl.* III. 8 Out, ye mopede monckies, can yee not knowe a man from a Marmasett, in theis Frenchified dayes of ours? *a* **1625** Fletcher *Hum. Lieutenant* IV. vi, He is bewitch'd or moop'd or his braines melted. **1692** Locke *Educ.* §51 Severity..often..breaking the Mind; and then in the Place of a disorderly young Fellow, you haue a low-spirited moap'd Creature. **1713** Swift *Frenzy J. Dennis* Wks. 1755 III. I. 140 Her master never read in them, but he was either quite moped, or in raving fits. **1866** Mrs. Gaskell *Wives & Dau.* xlviii, I've got quite moped and dismal. **1887** R. N. Carey *Uncle Max* i, I was moped, hipped, with all that dreary hospital work.

moped (ˈməʊpɛd), *sb.* [Sw. (1952), f. *tramp-cykel med motor och pedaler*, pedal cycle with engine and pedals; cf. also Ger. *moped.*] A motorized pedal cycle. Also *attrib.*

1956 I. Dunlop *Going to Britain* (ed. 2) 21 You must have a license to drive an autocycle ('moped'). **1957** *Times* 19 Nov. 11/3 The accompanying recommendation that the minimum age limit for riding mopeds should be reduced from sixteen to fifteen will be less readily accepted. **1960** F. Farr *Mo-Peds & Scooters* i. 14 The name 'mo-ped' originated in Sweden, was popularized in Germany and is now generally accepted here. The machines are internationally defined..as cycles fitted with engines of under 50 cubic centimetres capacity and retaining the normal characteristics of bicycles. **1971** *Guardian* 4 June 22/4 Cut the minimum age for moped riders from 16 to 14. **1973** *Times* 18 May 21/7 As the rider of a single-seater moped, I am required by law to possess insurance against claims from mythical passengers. **1974** *Guardian* 25 Mar. 21/1, I bought an electric moped. It..has a range of about 20 miles.

†ˈ**mopedness.** *Obs.* [f. moped *ppl. a.* + -ness.] The condition of being moped.

1660 H. More *Myst. Godl.* VII. x. 321 Unless Scepticism be heightned unto a disease as perfect as either Madness or down-right Mopedness. **1668** —— *Div. Dial.* II. xxiii. (1713) 161 Given over either to miserable Mopedness or Distraction.

ˈ**mope-eye.** *rare*⁻⁰. [Back formation from next.] Myopia.

1891 in *Syd. Soc. Lex.*

mope-eyed (ˈməʊpˈaɪd), *a.* Also 7 **mop(p)-eyed.** [f. stem of mope *v.* (where see sense 1).] Purblind, short-sighted.

Johnson 1755 erroneously explains it as 'blind in one eye', following Ainsworth, who renders it by L. *luscus*.

1606 Heywood *2nd Pt. You know not me* (1609) D 3, I think thou art mop-eide this morning, giue me the booke. **1607** Walkington *Opt. Glass* 36 A mope-ei'd foole he rising, first was deem'd. **1648** Herrick *Hesper., Upon Himselfe*, Mop-ey'd I am, as some have said, Because I've liv'd so long a maid. **1736** Ainsworth *Lat. Dict.* II, *Lippus*..Having dropping, or waterish eyes; mopeyed. **1768** Boyer *Dict. Eng. & Fr.* II, *Mopeyed* (dim sighted.) *Qui a la vue courte.* **1861** *Temple Bar* I. 174 He is not good-looking; he is mope-eyed and ungainly.

ˈ**mopeful,** *a.* [f. mope *v.* + -ful.] (See quot.)

1846 Worcester, *Mopeful*, drowsy; stupid; dull. *C. B. Brown.* In recent Dicts.

ˈ**moper.** [f. mope *v.* + -er¹.] One who mopes.

1876 W. Cory *Lett. & Jrnls.* (1897) 422 Am I not the same moper that heard Hallam read aloud? **1880** J. Nicoll *Poems & Songs* 169 I'll be nae permissive moper.

mopey, var. mopy *a.*

moph: see moff¹.

ˈ**mophrodite.** Also 8 **morphrodite.** A vulgar corruption of hermaphrodite.

1706 Vanbrugh *Prov. Wife* IV. iii. (ed. 2), I heard Mr. Constable say she was little better than a morphrodite. **1742** Fielding *Jos. Andrews* I. ix, You must..get a set of mophrodites to wait upon you. **1889** *N.W. Linc. Gloss.*, *Mophrodite.* (1) An hermaphrodite. (2) A waggon that can be converted into a cart. [Cf. morfrey.]

mophy, var. moffie.

mopiness (ˈməʊpɪnɪs). [f. mopy *a.* + -ness.] Mopy state or condition.

1927 *Smallholder* 26 Mar. 115/1 Ordinary Diarrhoea [in chicks]. Symptoms. Looseness of the bowels... There may or may not be mopiness but invariably there is inactivity.

moping (ˈməʊpɪŋ), *vbl. sb.* [-ing¹.] The action of the vb. mope; an instance of this.

1671 H. Foulis *Hist. Rom. Treasons* (1681) 63 One may know his meaning by his moping. **1700** Dryden *Pal. & Arc.* I. 541 Full of museful Mopings, which presage The loss of Reason, and conclude in Rage. **1850** Kingsley *Alton Locke* xxxvi, Long melancholy mopings..were periodically succeeded by wild frenzies.

attrib. **1812** Byron *Ch. Har.* I. xxviii, Again he rouses from his moping fits.

moping (ˈməʊpɪŋ), *ppl. a.* [f. mope *v.* + -ing².] That mopes; †wandering aimlessly, bewildered (*obs.*); in mod. use, dejected, dull, spiritless.

1568 *Hist. Jacob & Esau* I. i. A iij b, Nowe a mischief on all mopyng fooles for mee. **1593** Drayton *Ecl.* vi. 167 See where yon little moping Lambe of mine It selfe hath tangled in a crawling Breere. **1674** Milton *P.L.* (ed. 2) XI. 485 Moaping Melancholie. **1709-10** Steele *Tatler* No. 125 ¶2 A moaping Lover would grow a pleasant Fellow. **1750** Gray *Elegy* iii, The moping owl. **1851** Borrow *Lavengro* lxx, How sad and moping must life be in mighty Jupiter, on which no sun ever shines. **1876** T. Hardy *Ethelberta* (1890) 402 Moping sounds came from the trees and sky, as from Sorrow whispering to Night.

Hence ˈ**mopingly** *adv.*, in a moping manner.

1880 Miss Broughton *Sec. Th.* I. viii, She sits..mopingly thinking from breakfast to bed-time.

†'**mopish**, *a.*^{1} *Obs.* Also 7 **moppish**, 4 **mop(p)isch(e**. [f. MOP *sb.*^{1} + -ISH. (Sense 1 is akin to that of MOPE *v.* 1, though appearing much earlier.)]

1. Stupidly bewildered. *Obs.*

c **1300** *Beket* 78 Heo..ȝeode aboute as a best that ne couthe no wysdom, As heo were of another wordle, that folc thicke ynouȝ To biholde such a mopisch best aboute hire ther drouȝ. **13..** *St. Brandan* 115 (Trin. Coll. Camb. MS.) Hu wende aboute as moppysche [*Harl. MS.* maskede] men that nuste wer hu were.

2. Foolish.

1568 *Hist. Jacob & Esau* v. x. G iij, Yea mother, see that ye holde with that mopishe elfe. **1577** T. KENDALL *Flowers of Epigr.* 107 As mopish Monkes and foolish Friers did weare most commonly. **1608–11** BP. HALL *Medit. & Vows* II. §51, I need not be so mopish as not to beleeue rather the language of the hand than of the tongue. **1609** BP. W. BARLOW *Answ. Nameless Cath.* 315 Presenting nothing worthy view but moppish toies, in ridiculous fables.

mopish ('məʊpɪʃ), *a.*^{2} [f. MOPE *v.* + -ISH.] Given to moping; causing moping; characterized by a weak melancholy; dejected.

1621 S. WARD *Life of Faith* 16 Why are many of thy followers so dead, so mopish, so melancholy? **1675** HOWE *Liv. Temple* I. v, 'Tis a sad moapish disconsolate Temper, cuts off, and quite banishes all manly rational joy. **1716** M. DAVIES *Athen. Brit.* III. *Suppl. Diss. Drama* 18 Becoming stupid and mopish as well as sottish and foolish. **1889** CLARK RUSSELL *Marooned* (1890) 262 A woman who had been fretful and mopish.

Hence '**mopishly** *adv.*; '**mopishness**.

1598 J. DICKENSON *Greene in Conc.* (1878) 100 Tush (quoth he) thou art too scrupulous; this is not modesty, but mopishnesse. **1651** BP. HALL *Soliloq.* xxix. Wks. 1808 VI. 359 Here, one mopishly stupid, and so fixed to his posture, as if he were a breathing statue. **1707** SLOANE *Jamaica* I. p. cxiv, By degrees she fell into a perfect Mopishness or stupidity. **1859** C. S. HENRY *Dr. Oldham's Talks* xi. (1860) 93 His mopishness vanished with his wife's return. **1879** MISS BRADDON *Vixen* III. 115 You have behaved mopishly of late.

Moplah ('mɒplə). *Anglo-Indian.* Also 8–9 **mopla**, 9 **mapilla, mopilla, moplai, -lar, -lay**. [a. Malayālam *māppila*.] One of the Muslim inhabitants of Malabar, descended from Moors and Arabs who have settled on that coast, and married Malabar women.

1787 RITSON *Life & Lett.* (1833) I. 124 Your wond'rous tales..Of Moplas fierce your hand has tam'd, And monsters that your sword has maim'd. **1807** F. BUCHANAN *Journ. Madras*, etc. II. 391 No instance occurs of a Moplay having been converted. **1880** C. R. MARKHAM *Peruv. Bark* 363 The Chettis, Nairs, and Moplahs, who occupy land in Wainad, generally select elevated knolls for the sites of their dwellings.

mopoke ('məʊpəʊk), **morepork** ('mɔəpɔək). Also **maw(e)pawk, mope hawk, moopoo**. [Imitative of the bird's note; the forms *morepork*, *mope hawk* are obvious interpretative corruptions; the prevailing form in Australian use is now *mopoke*.]

1. a. A name given in New Zealand to an owl, the *Spiloglaux novæ-zealandiæ*, in Tasmania to the night-jar, *Podargus cuvieri*, and in Australia to other birds, as the *Ninox boobook*.

1827 HELLYER in Bischoff *Van Diemen's Land* (1832) 177 One of the men shot a 'more pork'. **1846** G. H. HAYDON 5 *Yrs. Austral. Felix* vi. 132 The doleful cry of the more-pork. **1848** GOULD *Birds Australia* II. pl. 1 *Ægotheles Novæ-Hollandiæ* Vig. and Horsf., Owlet Nightjar..Little Mawepawk, colonists of Van Diemen's Land. **1849** W. T. POWER *Sketches in N.Z.* ix. 74 Among the commonest birds which frequent the forest is a small owl, generally known.. by the denomination of 'More pork'. **1852** MRS. MEREDITH *My Home in Tasmania* II. xviii. 253 The Maw-pawk, More Pork, or Mope Hawk, is common in most parts of the colony. **1864** J. ROGERS *New Rush* II. 39 A Mopoke may pick out my eyes. **1866** M. A. BARKER *Let.* in *Station Life N.Z.* (1870) xiv. 100 The last cry of a very pretty little owl, called from its distinctly uttered cries, the 'more-pork'. **1874** T. H. POTTS *On Recent Changes Fauna N.Z.* 8 The name.. morepork is well-known throughout the country. Australian settlers distinguish a podargus by a similar name. **1882** —— *Out in Open* 118 *Athene Novæ Zelandiæ*, morepork, ruru rarupeho of the Maoris. **1890** *Melbourne Argus* 26 July 4/4 The shapeless moopoo seemed to cast down an evil eye as he flitted past. **1894** C. W. RICHMOND *Let.* 22 Mar. in *Richmond–Atkinson Papers* (1960) II. x. 597 Once..they had nothing to eat but a tui and a morepork. **1896** SPENCER *Through Larapinta Land* 124 In the gum trees the 'mopokes' (*Ninox boobook*) were calling to one another. **1898** M. ROBERTS *Keeper of Waters* 138 He sold a station in Victoria, and they said he was as silly as a 'morepork'. **1905** J. M. THOMSON *Bush Boys of N.Z.* iv. 59 The More-pork is the small New Zealand owl, so-called from its peculiar guttural cry. **1963** *Evening Post* (Wellington, N.Z.) 26 Oct., In the..action shots which are skilfully interwoven with Maori legends and traditions about each bird, are the morepork..fantail, bellbird, tui.

b. *transf.* A 'stupid'.

1845 R. HOWITT *Impressions Australia Felix* 233 'A more-pork kind of fellow' is a man of cut-and-dry phrases; a person remarkable for nothing new in common conversation. **1890** 'R. BOLDREWOOD' *Col. Reformer* xiii. 125 What a regular more-pork I was to be sure. **1946** *Coast to Coast 1945* 132 He was such a helpless sort of a poor mopoke.

2. The note of the mopoke.

1827 HELLYER in Bischoff *Van Diemen's Land* (1832) 177 The owl's doleful cry of 'more pork'. **1868** CARLETON *Austr. Nts.* 19 The Austral cuckoo spoke His melancholy note—'Mo-poke'. **1889** LUMHOLTZ *Cannibals* 33 We are lulled to sleep by the melancholy..voices of the night bird Podargus 'more-pork! more-pork!' **1916**, **1934** [see BOOBOOK].

'**mopper-up**. *Mil.* [f. MOP *v.*^{2} 3 + -ER^1.] A soldier who 'mops up' an enemy area (see MOP *v.*^{2} 3). Also *fig.* (perhaps in these uses owing as much to MOP *v.*^{2} 3).

1917 *London Gaz.* 26 Nov. 12330/1 Pte. Dancox was one of a party of about ten men detailed as moppers-up. **1919** W. H. DOWNING *Digger Dial.* 34 *Mopper-up*, (1) One of a party of men who follow the leading waves of an attack in order to clear the enemy from the ground behind the assaulting troops; (2) a drunkard. **1920** G. K. ROSE *2/4th Oxf. & Bucks. Lt. Infty.* x. 122 The Berks came afterwards as 'moppers-up'. **1923** KIPLING *Irish Guards in Great War* I. 230 The 'mopper-up' who dealt with the débris of attacks. **1928** *Mod. Lang. Rev.* Apr. 136 His plan of attack is described on p. 174 of his *Philosophy of Grammar*; his 'moppers up' follow in the *Modern English Grammar*. **1936** *Daily Tel.* 15 Aug. 15/5 How..fascinating to know that your goods are coming to the London market by the Mopper Up.

†'**moppet**^{1}. *Obs.* Forms: 6 **mappatt, moppat(t, moppett**. [? Alteration of *mapolt*, var. of MAPPLE.] A mop; a sponge for a cannon.

1512 *Acc. Ld. High Treas. Scotl.* IV. 454 For moppatis to the calfetouris. **1512–13** *Ibid.* 465 For iiij scheip skynnys to mak moppatis for the tallowyng of the James. **1532** *Ibid.* VI. 157 For mappattis and tappounis xxs. **1566** *Inv. R. Wardr.* (1815) 168 Item, nyne moppatis mountit, all serving to sindrie peceis. **1580** *Reg. Privy Council Scot.* III. 320 With thre moppettis to serve the saidis peces.

moppet^2 ('mɒpɪt). Also 7 **mopphet**. [f. MOP *sb.*^{1} + -ET^1.]

1. a. Used as an endearing appellation for a baby, a girl, etc.; a darling, a favourite. Also used contemptuously (? after sense 2) for a gaily dressed or frivolous woman.

1601 MUNDAY & CHETTLE *Death Earl Huntington* K 2 b, And, moppet, you were best To take their proffers. **1630** LENNARD tr. *Charron's Wisd.* III. xiv. (1670) 460 A simple instinct..according to which Parents love..their children, though deformed..and use them like moppets or little apes. **1713** ROWE *Jane Shore* IV. Wks. 1792 II. 164 A moppet made of prettiness and pride. **1746** FRANCIS tr. *Horace, Sat.* I. iii. 64 Is he of dwarfish and abortive size? 'Sweet little moppet', the fond father cries. **1782** ELIZ. BLOWER *Geo. Bateman* III. 70 I'll..tell father and mother, and Peggy, what a moppet you have made of yourself. **1796** MRS. M. ROBINSON *Angelina* II. 79, I had rather see her dead, than making such a moppet of herself, as to run about like a vagrant, play-acting. **1801** CHARLOTTE SMITH *Lett. Solit. Wand.* II. 10 While the most insipid moppet that ever looked in a glass is preferred to one of those reasoning damsels. **1973** *Houston* (Texas) *Chron. Mag. People, Places, Pleasures* 14 Oct. 6/3 Jane Withers..made a long-delayed transition from movie moppet 'heavy' to middle-aged TV pitchlady. **1975** *Time Out* 10 Jan. 45/2 Watching the well-mannered moppets and well-groomed mums roll up in taxis and Bentleys to the Theatre Royal, Haymarket, certainly helped to set the scene.

b. Contemptuously applied to a man.

1707 CIBBER *Double Gallant* 111, He'll think I don't love him else. Poor Moppet! **1766** H. WALPOLE *Lett.* 13 Nov., He went to the Lord Mayor's feast, and dragged along with him that wise moppet, Lord Lyttelton. **1781** *Ibid.* 25 Mar., A moppet in Grosvenor Square has conceived hopes from this rising storm [etc.].

†**2.** A rag doll. *Obs. rare*$^{-0}$.

[Cf. quot. *c* 1440 s.v. MOP *sb.*^{1} 2.]

1755 JOHNSON, *Moppet*, a puppet made of rags, as a mop is made.

3. A woolly variety of dog. (Cf. MOPS^2.)

1861 GEN. P. THOMPSON in *Bradford Advertiser* 7 Dec. 6/1 The curly moppet of the respectable household, whose locks are carved into some absurd suggestion of a lion.

†'**moppet**^{3}. *Obs. rare*$^{-1}$. [f. MOP *sb.*^{2} + -ET^1.] A grimace.

1693 *Urquhart's Rabelais* III. Prol. 17 And albeit we see them sometimes counterfeit Devotion, yet never did Old Age [? *read* Ape] make pretty Moppet [orig. *onques vieil singe ne fit belle mouë*].

mopp-eyed, obs. form of MOPE-EYED.

moppie ('mɒpɪ). *S. Afr.* [Afrikaans, ad. Du. *mopje* ditty.] A street-song of the Cape Malays.

1949 *Cape Times* 10 Jan. 2/6 He hoped that the Cape 'moppies' or comic songs and the *liedjies* would become a regular feature of future carnivals. **1953** DU PLESSIS & LÜCKHOFF *Malay Quarter* iii. 48 Moppies are little songs (often of doubtful content) sung in order to challenge, deride, or irritate the listener, or merely as foolery. When singing a moppie, the singer often includes a person's name, and if the person referred to cannot respond in similar vein, he is laughed at by all present. **1974** *S. Afr. Panorama* June 20 The 'moppie' is a comical song. The soloist uses gestures of the hands and other movements to illustrate it as he goes.

mopping ('mɒpɪŋ), *vbl. sb.*^{1} [f. MOP *v.*^{1} + -ING^1.] Grimacing; also, an instance of this.

1615 G. SANDYS *Trav.* 227 Administring matter of mirth with their ridiculous moppings. **1881** STEVENSON *Virg. Puerisque* 110 Such a mopping and a mowing.

mopping ('mɒpɪŋ), *vbl. sb.*^{2} [f. MOP *v.*^{3} + -ING^1.] Rubbing or wiping with or as with a mop. Also **mopping-up**, the action of the verb *mop up*, in various senses (also *fig.*). Also *attrib.*

1833 MARRYAT *P. Simple* xxxi, The heat was terrible, and the *mopping* of the ladies' faces everlasting. **1897** *Allbutt's Syst. Med.* IV. 830 A method which combines general chloroform narcosis with frequently-repeated local moppings of the pharynx and larynx of the patient. **1909** *Westm. Gaz.* 3 Sept. 9/4 Persistent 'mopping up' of London stocks [of silver] naturally restricts supplies for Continental and other requirements. **1918** E. S. FARROW *Dict. Mil. Terms* 394 *Mopping up trenches*, the crushing of hostile units which continue the resistances at certain parts of the trench, and the searching of the trenches and bombproofs with a view to making sure that none of the enemy are left in them. **1925** FRASER & GIBBONS *Soldier & Sailor Words* 158 *Mopping-up*, the term for the work allotted to special parties of men appointed to follow close in the track of advancing 'waves' of troops, in order to explore and clear the enemy lines and dug-outs of men remaining behind... The Mopping-up method was first adopted at the Battle of Arras in February, 1917. **1937** *Sun* (Baltimore) 12 July 5/1 Six flood-weary West Virginia communities began mopping-up operations..today after two surging creeks flooded homes and business houses. **1940** *Economist* 20 Apr. 717/2 We must not be diverted in Narvik, which is now..a mopping-up operation. **1940** *Ibid.* 2 Nov. 552/1 In the last war, the Excess Profits Duty proved itself an excellent 'mopping-up' tax, against an inflationary background. **1940** 'GUN BUSTER' *Return via Dunkirk* II. iv. 120 Mopping-up parties of Tommies were investigating the farmhouses. **1959** *Listener* 19 Mar. 521/1 Shakespeare is naturally drawn upon very little, since he had already been the subject of 'mopping up' in every volume of this kind. **1962** W. NOWOTTNY *Lang. Poets Use* i. 24 A mopping-up of successive problems in one area after another until the whole domain of poetic language is occupied and systematized. **1967** G. F. FIENNES *I Tried to Run a Railway* i. 4 We rounded up a few volunteers to do a mopping up operation on the permanent way. **1973** I. BUTLER *Eldest Brother* xix. 339 Mopping-up operations in Gujerat.

moppish: see MOPISH *a.*^{1}

moppit, obs. form of MOPPET.

moppy ('mɒpɪ). [f. MOP *sb.*^{2} + -Y.]

1. Of hair, foliage, etc.: Resembling a mop; having the characteristics of a mop; thick.

1725 BRADLEY *Fam. Dict.* s.v. *Orange tree*, Let him pare off two Thirds of the Earth, and prune the Fibres and moppy Roots. **1880** A. H. KEANE in *Nature* 30 Dec. 202/2 The moppy head being thoroughly Papûan. **1884** G. MOORE *Mummer's Wife* (1892) 49 His moppy black hair.

2. *slang.* Intoxicated. (Cf. MOP *sb.*^{2} 1 b.)

1823 *Grose's Dict. Vulg. T.* (ed. Egan), *Moppy*, drunk. *Cant.*

†**mops**^{1}. *Obs.* Also 7 **mopse**. [Prob. an extension of MOP *sb.*^{1}; cf. MOPPET^1, MOPSY.] A term of endearment for a young girl.

1565 GOLDING *Ovid's Met.* III. (1567) 32 b, Little bibling Phyale, and Pseke that pretie Mops. **1584** PEELE *Arraignm. Paris* IV. i, I' faith, i' faith, my gentle mops, but I do know a cast. **1588** T. THOMAS *Dict.* (1615), *Puellula*,..a little pretie girle: a little mopse. **1592** LYLY *Midas* I. ii, We are no chase (prettie mops,) for Deere we are not, neither red nor fallow. **1654** GAYTON *Pleas. Notes* II. ii. 37 Which Sancho stole from his ill favoured Mopse.

mops^2 (mɒps). *rare*$^{-0}$. [a. G. *mops* = Du. *mops*, *mop*.] A pug-dog.

1890 in *Century Dict.*

†'**mopsical**, *a. Obs. rare*$^{-1}$. [? f. MOPS^1 or MOPSY + -ICAL.] ? Like a spoiled child, pettish.

Blount *Glossogr.* 1656–61 explains it as 'that cannot see well'; connecting it with 'our phrase *mop-eyed*'. The explanation has been copied in many later Dicts.

1653 GAUDEN *Hierasp.* Pref. to Rdr. 9 Their Mopsicall humors being never satisfied, but in fancying themselves as Kings, and reigning with Christ..

mopstick ('mɒpstɪk). [f. MOP *sb.*^{3} + STICK.]

1. a. The handle of a mop.

1710 SWIFT *Jrnl. to Stella* 16 Dec., Hang it [a picture] carefully in some part of your room, where chairs and candles and mop-sticks won't spoil it. **1818** MISS MITFORD in L'Estrange *Life* (1870) II. 31 Our candidate is vastly like a mopstick, or, rather, a tall hop-pole.

†**b.** ***cry mapsticks!*** app. a vulgar jocose perversion of 'I cry you mercy'. *Obs.*

1738 SWIFT *Pol. Conversat.* I. 26 *Neverout.* Cry, Mapsticks, Madam; no Offence, I hope.

c. = COCKALORUM 3. *colloq.*

1969 I. & P. OPIE *Children's Games* viii. 257 In Warwick, 'Mollie, Mollie Mopstick, all off! all off!' In Nuneaton: Mopstick, mopstick, bear our weight, Two, four, six, eight, ten. *Ibid.* 260 'Jack upon the Mopstick' (Warwickshire, 1892),..'Johnny on the Mopstick' (Worcester, *c.* 1930), ..'Mopstick' (Kettering, *c.* 1915).

2. *Pianoforte manufacture.* (See quot. 1875.)

1870 BRINSMEAD *Hist. Pianoforte* 52 The sticker, or mop-stick,..raised the damper at the same moment that the hammer was impelled against the string. **1875** KNIGHT *Dict. Mech.*, *Mop stick*, a vertical damper-rod at the end of the key in the old piano-forte movement, single action.

attrib. **1885** HIPKINS in *Encycl. Brit.* XIX. 72/2 This defect is overcome by Zumpe's 'mopstick' damper.

3. *slang.* **a.** A stupid man. **b.** *U.S.* (See quot. 1915.)

1886 H. BAUMANN *Londinismen* 111/2. **1915** *World* (N.Y.) Sunday Suppl. 9 May 14/3 *Mopstick*, one who loafs around a cheap saloon or barrel house and cleans up the place for drinks.

mopsy ('mɒpsɪ). Also 7–8 **mopsie**, 8 **mapsie**, 9 **mopsey**. [f. MOP *sb.*^{1}; the ending *-sy* is common *dial.* in terms of endearment, as in *babsy*, *ducksy*: cf. the pet names *Betsy*, *Patsy*.]

1. Used as a term of endearment; a pretty child; a darling, a sweetheart. ? *Obs.*

1582 STANYHURST *Æneis* I. (Arb.) 41 Thee mopsy [*sc.* the infant Ascanius] her phantasye lurcheth. **1583** STUBBES *Anat. Abus.* I. (1879) 147 Borrowed for the most parte of

their pretie Mopsies & loouing Besses. **1705** VANBRUGH *Mistake* IV. i, *Jacin.* But don't expect I'll follow her Example. *San.* You would, Mopsie, if I'd let you. **1706** E. WARD *Hud. Rediv.* x. v. 10 These mix'd with Brewers, and their Mopsies.

2. A slatternly, untidy woman. Also *attrib.* or as *adj.* (Sense passing into that of MOP *sb.*⁴ in some examples.)

a **1700** B. E. *Dict. Cant. Crew, Mopsie,* a Dowdy, or Homely Woman. *c* **1785** *John Thompson's Man* 14 If you wed an old mapsie, murlie..deformed Creature to be thy Wife. **1800** LAMB *Let. to Coleridge* You encouraged that mopsey, Miss Wesley, to dance after you, in the hope of having her nonsense put into a nonsensical Anthology. **1916** A. BENNETT *These Twain* xviii. 406, I always knew that girl was a mopsy slut. **1958** J. CAREW *Wild Coast* iii. 44 He don't have juice in his back to fill up a mopsy with delight. **1958** *Times Lit. Suppl.* 14 Mar. 140/5 Poor Swann's pain and frustration..are a simpler matter, Odette de Crécy being the most commonplace of lying mopsies and a born torturer of the sensitive.

3. 'A woolly variety of dog'.

1855 OGILVIE *Suppl.*

mopus¹ ('məʊpəs). *Obs.* exc. *dial.* (see E.D.D.). [f. MOPE *sb.* (? with quasi-Latin ending).] A mope; a dull, stupid person.

a **1700** B. E. *Dict. Cant. Crew* s.v., *A meer Mopus grown,* become dispirited, dull and Stupid. **1700** CONGREVE *Way of World* III. i, Dids't thou not hear me, Mopus? **1729** SWIFT *Grand Quest. Debated* 27 I'm grown a mere mopus; no company comes But a rabble of tenants and rusty dull rums.

†'**mopus**². *Obs.* In Barbados, the local name of the Knot, *Tringa canutus.*

1750 G. HUGHES *Barbados* 78 Of the Mopuses. There are three Sorts of these..the Large, the Small, and the Hiding Mopus. **1848** in SCHOMBURGK *Hist. Barbados* 681.

mopus³ ('məʊpəs). *slang.* †**a.** 'A halfpenny or farthing' (B. E. *Dict. Cant. Crew, a* 1700). **b.** *pl.* Money in general.

1769 *Stratford Jubilee* II. i. 32 If she [a rich widow] has the mopus's, I'll have her, as snug as a bug in a rug. **1798** *Geraldina* I. 44 You have got the *mopusses, the ready.* **1840** *New Monthly Mag.* LX. 373 Without the mopuses to pay for your call, the demand will be like Owen Glendower's demand for 'spirits from the vasty deep'. **1892** M. WILLIAMS *Round Lond.* (1893) 23 They hav'nt got any mopusses.

attrib. **1848** THACKERAY *Van. Fair* vi, Look to the pewter room, Blowser. You, Mark, to the old gaff's mopus box!

mopy ('məʊpɪ), *a.* Also mopey. [f. MOPE *v.* + -Y.] Given to moping, causing moping, dull.

1827 *Sporting Mag.* XIX. 274, I am so very deaf and mopy like. **1883** MRS. LYNN LINTON *Ione* i, A dull country town like this mopy old Oakhurst! **1889** W. S. GILBERT *Gondoliers* II. 33 After you left we felt very dull and mopey.

Moqua, obs. form of MOHAWK.

moquet, obs. var. MUGGET².

moquette (mɒ'kɛt). Also 8 *quasi-It.* mocketto. [a. F. *moquette*; according to Hatz.-Darm. a corruption of *mocade* MOCKADO.] A material composed of wool and hemp or linen, chiefly used for carpeting. Also *moquette carpet.*

1762 tr. *Busching's Syst. Geog.* II. 401 In it are also made very beautiful baragons, together with mockettoes, a kind of carpets. **1852–4** *Tomlinson's Cycl. Usef. Arts* (1866) II. 867 The Wilton carpet, called *Moquette* by the French, differs from the Brussels in the form of the wire [etc.]. **1858** SIMMONDS *Dict. Trade, Moquette,* a tapestry Brussels carpet of a fine quality; a species of Wilton carpet. **1876** *Encycl. Brit.* V. 130/1 Moquette or Wilton Carpets are woven in the same manner as Brussels carpets. **1894** J. PENDLETON *Our Railways* I. 443 Its saloons..upholstered in moquette.

mor (mɔə(r)). *Soil Sci.* [Da., lit. 'humus' (adopted in this specific sense by P. E. Müller 1879, in *Tidsskrift for Skovbrug* III. 7): cf. MOOR *sb.*¹] Humus which forms a discrete layer on top of the soil with little or no mineral soil mixed with it, which is characteristic of coniferous forests and is generally strongly acid in reaction. Cf. MULL *sb.*¹⁰

1931, 1952 [see MULL *sb.*¹⁰]. **1971** *Nature* 10 Sept. 133/1 Formation of the mor type of forest litter..has been attributed to a number of factors. **1974** [see MULL *sb.*¹⁰].

mor, obs. form of MOOR, MORE.

‖**mora**¹ ('mɔərə). [L. *mora* delay.]

1. *Scots Law.* Negligent delay (see quot. 1838).

1569 *Reg. Privy Council Scot.* II. 9 Nowther the said Erll of Huntley nor yit the parteis complenaris ar in mora. **1838** W. BELL *Dict. Law Scotl., Mora,* or delay, is a general term applicable to all undue delay in the prosecution or completion of an inchoate bargain, diligence, or the like.

†**2.** A short space of time; a delay. *Obs. rare.*

a **1633** G. HERBERT *Jacula Prud.* 145 Good is the *mora* that makes all sure. *a* **1677** HALE *Prim. Orig. Man.* 76 This preparation..requires a competent *mora,* or time, antecedent to its complete and full constitution. *Ibid.* 102.

3. a. (Pl. *moræ.*) A unit of metrical time equal to the duration of a short syllable.

1832 [see TIME *sb.* 10]. **1848** DONALDSON *Gr. Gram.* 16 The shortest time in which a syllable can be pronounced is called a *mora,* or single *time.* A short syllable has one *mora*: a long syllable contains two *moræ.* **1879** J. W. WHITE tr. *Schmidt's Rhythmic & Metric* 65.

b. In linguistic analysis, the minimal unit of duration of a speech-sound. Also *attrib.*

1933 L. BLOOMFIELD *Language* vii. 110 In dealing with matters of quantity, it is often convenient to set up an arbitrary unit of relative duration, the *mora.* Thus, if we say that a short vowel lasts one mora, we may describe the long vowels of the same language as lasting, say, one and one-half morae or two morae. **1941** G. L. TRAGER in L. Spier et al. *Lang. Culture & Personality* 136 In many cases it will be found that an element smaller than the phonetic syllable functions as the accentual or prosodic unit; this unit may be called, following current practice, the mora... The term *mora*..is useful in avoiding confusion, even if it should turn out to mean merely phonemic syllable. **1964** E. PALMER tr. *Martinet's Elem. General Linguistics* iii. 80 Each of the segments characterized by one of the successive punctual tones is called a mora. **1964** K. L. PIKE in D. Abercrombie et al. *Daniel Jones* 425 A train of alternating stresses.. clashes with a different wave train keyed into a mora count beginning from the last suffixual syllable. **1968** W. S. ALLEN *Vox Graeca* ii. 81 For diphthongs in Greek cannot strictly be distinguished as 'short' and 'long'; for accentual purposes they all have the same value of 2 'morae' (time-units), as for a long simple vowel.

‖**mora**², **morra** ('mɔrə). [It. *mora,* of unknown origin. Cf. F. *mourre* in the same sense.] A popular game in Italy in which one player guesses the number of fingers held up simultaneously by another player. Also applied by Europeans to a similar game in China.

1706 PHILLIPS (ed. Kersey), *Mora,* the Italian Play of Love with the Fingers. **1797** MRS. RADCLIFFE *Italian* ii, Vivaldi heard only the quick and eager voices of some Lazaroni..as they contended at the simple game of *Morra.* **1833** LONGF. *Outre-Mer, Rome in Midsummer* ¶1 The idle facchino..plays at *mora* by the fountain. **1848** S. W. WILLIAMS *Mid. Kingd.* (1883) I. 808 The guests relieve its tedium by playing the game of *chai mei,* or morra (the *micare digitis* of the old Romans), which consists in showing the fingers to each other across the table, and mentioning a number at the same moment; as, if one opens out two fingers, and mentions the number four, the other instantly shows six fingers, and mentions that number. If he mistake in giving the complement of ten, he pays a forfeit by drinking a cup.

‖**mora**³ ('mɔərə). *Gr. Hist.* Pl. moras. [Gr. μόρα, f. μορ-, μερ- to divide.] One of the (originally six) divisions of which the Spartan army consisted.

1838 THIRLWALL *Greece* xxxviii. V. 77 Two moras had been kept at home, together with the veterans. **1850** GROTE *Greece* II. lvi. VII. 109 Every order emanated from the Spartan King..and was given to the Polemarchs, each commanding a mora, the largest military division.

‖**mora**⁴ ('mɔərə). [Shortened from Tupi *moira-tinga* 'white tree', f. *moira* tree, *tinga* white.] A lofty tree, *Mora excelsa,* found in Guyana and Trinidad. Also *attrib.,* as *mora-tree, wood.*

1825 C. WATERTON *Wanderings S. Amer.* i. 5 Heedless, and bankrupt, in all curiosity must he be, who can journey on without stopping to take a view of the towering mora. **1826** SYD. SMITH *Wks.* (1859) II. 74 Among these, pre-eminent in height rises the mora. **1840** SCHOMBURGK *Descr. Brit. Guiana* 31 The Mora (*Mora excelsa,* Benth.) may well be called the king of the forest; it towers above every other tree. **1843** HOLTZAPFFEL *Turning,* etc. I. 94 Mora-wood..is close-grained like teak, and superior to oak, esteemed for ship-building..; in colour it resembles moderately red mahogany. **1864–5** WOOD *Homes without H.* ii. (1868) 82 The Toucan..may generally be seen perched on the topmost boughs of the lofty mora-tree. **1918** C. W. BEEBE *Jungle Peace* (1919) vii. 140 A house with roof of pale pink like a giant mora in full bloom. **1949** *Caribbean Quarterly* I. III. 42 Three forest areas..could be..logged so as to yield about 3 million cubic feet of saleable timber per year, mainly Greenheart but also Mora and other hardwoods. **1956** *Handbk. of Hardwoods* (Forest Prod. Res. Lab.) 154 Mora is a dominant tree of mixed swamp forests and is found in the Guianas, Trinidad and eastern Venezuela. **1958** J. CAREW *Black Midas* vi. 109 Santos stopped under a mora tree. **1971** *Advocate-News* (Barbados) 17 Sept. Guyana Suppl. p. ii/2 Boys at work in pouring rain felling giant mora and wallaba trees.

‖**mora**⁵ ('mɔərə). *Anglo-Indian.* Also morah. [Hind. *moṛha.*] A stool, foot-stool. ('In common colloquial use', Yule.)

c **1813** MRS. SHERWOOD *Stories Ch. Catech.* vii. 45 She took her Bible and a mora, and went and sat in one corner of the room. **1845** STOCQUELER *Handbk. Brit. India* (1854) 98 One or two morahs, or stools. **1907** B. M. CROKER *Company's Servant* xviii. 195 Sitting..on a little 'morah' at her feet. **1971** *Illustr. Weekly India* 4 Apr. 22/3, I resorted to circumlocutions..which invariably produced a *mora* or a chair in the little Chandni Chowk shops.

morabit, -bot, obs. forms of MARABOUT.

‖**morai,** incorrect form of MARAE.

1772–84 COOK *Voy.* (1790) V. 1705. **1840** F. D. BENNETT *Whaling Voy.* II. 394.

morain, variant of MORION.

morainal (mɒ'reɪnəl), *a.* [f. MORAINE + -AL¹.] Of or pertaining to a moraine.

1872 C. KING *Mountain. Sierra Nev.* viii. 154 An accumulation of morainal matter deposited by ancient Merced glaciers. **1899** *Pop. Sci. Monthly* LV. 570 The flora is morainal in its general character.

moraine (mɒ'reɪn). [a. F. *moraine.*]

a. An accumulation of débris from the mountains carried down and deposited by a glacier.

lateral, terminal moraine, a deposit at the side or the extremity of a glacier respectively. ***medial moraine,*** a deposit between two conjoining glaciers.

1789 COXE *Trav. Switz.* II. xxxviii. 3 We crossed some snow..and immediately got upon the moraine, the term given to the stones and earth which the glaciers disgorge on each side. **1863** LYELL *Antiq. Man* xv. 298 The lateral, medial, and terminal moraines of great glaciers. **1878** HUXLEY *Physiogr.* 159 We generally find, across the end of the glacier, a confused heap of rubbish, known as a *terminal moraine.*

attrib. **1863** *Q. Rev.* CXIV. 410 It seems to be moraine mud. **1878** HUXLEY *Physiogr.* 163 Bergs break off and float away carrying their burden of moraine matter.

b. In rock-gardening, a bed, often raised, constructed of rubble covered with fine chippings, in an attempt to produce suitable conditions for alpine plants. Also *attrib.*

1907 R. J. FARRER *My Rock-Garden* i. 14 There..is my toy-garden, my baby moraine, the particular pet joy of my heart. **1914** H. H. THOMAS *Rock Gardening* 65 The moraine may be described as a bed or border of varying size, preferably situated on a slight slope, and consisting of broken stone, with which, however, a certain proportion of light, sifted soil is mixed. *Ibid.* 72 Favourite Moraine Plants. **1931** *Times Lit. Suppl.* 16 Apr. 297/2 This [*sc.* bad drainage] is..the cause of most failures and disappointments in moraine gardening. **1961** W. INGWERSEN in W. E. Shewell-Cooper et al. *Alpine & Rock Gardening* vi. 43 If one moraine is to be divided into limestone and lime-free compartments, then the limestone area must be at the bottom.

moraine, obs. form of MURRAIN.

morainic (mɒ'reɪnɪk), *a.* [f. MORAINE + -IC.] Of or pertaining to, or of the nature of, a moraine.

1863 LYELL *Antiq. Man* xv. 314 The ponds..consist exclusively of what M. de Mortillet has denominated morainic lakes, i.e. caused by barriers of glacier-mud and stones. **1889** G. F. WRIGHT *Ice Age N. Amer.* 478 Morainic ridges.

moral ('mɒrəl), *sb.* Also 6–7 mor(r)all. [Subst. use of MORAL *a.*; but several of the uses are wholly or in part suggested by the corresponding late L. *mōrāle* neut. sing., *mōrālia* neut. pl., F. *moral* masc., *morale* fem. (see MORALE).]

1. *pl.* (earlier †*sing.*) Used to render L. *Moralia* pl. as the title of St. Gregory the Great's work on the moral exposition of the Book of Job, and (later) as the collective title given to Plutarch's writings other than the 'Lives', to the ethical writings of Seneca, etc.

c **1380** *Antecrist* in Todd *3 Treat. Wyclif* (1851) 121 Gregor in þe two & þritti boke of hise moral. **1526** *Pilgr. Perf.* (W. de W. 1531) 22 As saynt Gregory sayth in his Moralles. **1603** HOLLAND (*title*) The Philosophie commonlie called, The Morals. Written by..Plutarch. **1678** R. L'ESTRANGE (*title*) Seneca's Morals, by way of Abstract. **1824** SCOTT *Epilogue* (init.), The sages—for authority, pray look Seneca's morals, or the copy-book.

2. a. The moral teaching or practical lesson (of a fiction or fable; sometimes, of a real occurrence); also in phr. ***to point a moral*** (cf. POINT *v.*¹ 5 b).

a **1500** *Everyman* end, This morall men may have in mynde: Ye herers take it of worth,..And forsake Pryde. **1593** SHAKS. *Rich. II,* IV. i. 290 Marke silent King, the Morall of this sport. **1602** WARNER *Alb. Eng.* x. lx. (1612) 263 The Fables Morall of the Stock and Stork. **1634** W. TIRWHYT tr. *Balzac's Lett.* (vol. I.) 282 The Morall hereof is, that you must make use of your youth, and gather Nose-gays before the roses wither. **1742** YOUNG *Nt. Th.* IX. 361 No fancy'd God..descends To solve all knots; to strike the moral home. **1748** JOHNSON *Van. Hum. Wishes* 222 To point a moral, or adorn a tale. **1848** DICKENS *Dombey* ii, There's a moral in everything. **1861** M. PATTISON *Ess.* (1889) I. 45 An inscription..in which the moral was better than the point.

b. An exposition of the moral teaching or practical lesson contained in a literary composition; that part of a composition (*e.g.* of a fable) which applies or points the moral meaning.

1560 T. H. (*title*) The Fable of Ouid treting of Narcissus, translated out of Latin into Englysh Mytre, with a moral ther vnto. **1892** R. L'ESTRANGE (*title*) Fables, of Æsop.. with Morals and Reflexions. **1752** YOUNG *Brothers* v. i, As if the Thracian queen conducted all, And wrote the moral in her children's blood.

†**c.** Import, meaning, signification. *Obs.*

1596 SHAKS. *Tam. Shr.* IV. iv. 79 *Biond.* You saw my Master winke and laugh vpon you? *Luc.* Biondello, what of that? *Biond.* Faith nothing: but has left mee here behinde to expound the meaning or morall of his signes and tokens. **1841** CATLIN *N. Amer. Ind.* (1844) I. xiv. 102 Indians,.. with their few and simple oddities, all of which have their moral or meaning.

†**3. a.** A symbolical figure. *Obs.*

1584 CONSTABLE *Sonn.* IV. iv, Fooles be they that inueigh gainst Mahomet, Who's but a morrall of loues Monarchie. **1599** SHAKS. *Hen. V,* III. vi. 40 Fortune is painted blinde.. to signifie to you, that Fortune is blinde... Fortune is an excellent Morall.

b. *vulgarly.* Counterpart, likeness. Chiefly in phr. ***the very moral of***... (Cf. MODEL *sb.* 2 b.)

1757 SMOLLETT *Reprisal* I. ii, Och! the delicate creature! —she's the very moral of my own honey. **1850** SMEDLEY *F. Fairlegh* (1894) 41 He's the very moral (as the old women call it) of Sir John. **1890** 'R. BOLDREWOOD' *Col. Reformer* (1891) 102 He's..the very moral of a horse the whipper-in ..rode.

4. = MORALITY 4 b. *Obs.* exc. *Hist.*

1578 in Cunningham *Revels at Crt.* (1842) 125 A Morrall of the marryage of Mynde and Measure shewen at Richmond. **1592** Nashe *Four Lett. Confut.* 21 You haue counterfeited the stile of the olde Vice in the Morralls. **1606** Dekker *Sev. Sinnes* vii. (Arb.) 45 Crueltie hath yet another part to play, it is acted (like the old Morralls at Maningtree) by Trades-men. **1875** A. W. Ward *Eng. Dram. Lit.* I. i. 23 Morals teach and illustrate the same religious truths.. by allegorical means.

†**5.** A moralist. *Obs. rare.*

1615 Brathwait *Strappado* 125 Nor did that Morall erre, who wisely would, Compare a Courtiers witte to th' Marigold. **1626** Breton *Fantastiques* (Cass.), That experienst morall [*i.e.* Socrates].

†**6. a.** *sing.* (A person's) moral principles or practice. *Obs.*

1688 *Answ. Talon's Plea* 6 But they continue still to upbraid 'em, that they are of the Caball;.. that their Moral is rotten. **1718** Prior *Epitaph* 17 Their Moral and Oeconomy, Most perfectly They made agree. **1733** Pope *Ess. Man* iii. 286 Twas then.. Poet or Patriot, rose but to restore The Faith and Moral Nature gave before. **1757** Mrs. Griffith *Lett. Henry & Frances* (1767) I. p. iii, This pair of polite and happy lovers seem to have used their passions as they were designed by Providence, to inspirit their reason, and to actuate their moral. **1820** Byron *Let. to Murray* 21 Feb., Their [*sc.* Italians'] moral is not your moral; their life is not your life.

‖**b.** The condition (of troops, etc.) with respect to discipline, subordination, and confidence.

[Fr.; pronounced (mɔral): see morale 2.]

1883 Eve in *Three Lect. Educ.* 18 It is not good for the *moral* of a class if [etc.]. **1900** *Westm. Gaz.* 19 Mar. 5/1 The force investing Mafeking.. is daily becoming shaken in *moral*. **1901** Henderson tr. *Sternberg's Exper. Boer War* Introd. 37 Whatever might be the percentage of casualties our battalions suffered, they never lost their *moral*.

7. *pl.* In early use: †(A person's) moral qualities or endowments (*obs.*). Now, Moral habits or conduct; habits of life in regard to right and wrong conduct; also *spec.*, sexual conduct.

1613 Fletcher, etc. *Captain* ii. i, My morals and those hidden pieces That art bestows upon me, they are such That ..I am sure will shame me. **1663** Cowley *Govt. O. Cromwell* Wks. (1669) 69 Which if you please to take notice of for the advantage of his Intellectuals, I desire you to allow me the liberty to do so too, when I am to speak of his Morals. **1697** Dryden *Georg.* Ded., 'Tis infectious even to the best Morals to live always in it [*sc.* the Court air]. **1719** Swift *To Yng. Clergyman* Wks. 1751 V. 27 The People of England are more corrupt in their Morals than any other Nation this day under the Sun. **1849** Macaulay *Hist. Eng.* vi. II. 69 The morals of Sedley were such as, even in that age, gave great scandal. **1862** Lytton *Str. Story* I. vii. 54 An earl's daughter, with a good income and an awfully bad name, of the best manners, and of the worst morals.

8. a. *pl.* Moral science; moral doctrine; ethics. Chiefly construed as *sing.* Now *rare.*

1651 Hobbes *Govt. & Soc.* Ep. Ded., For treating of Figures, tis call'd Geometry; of motion, Physick; of naturall right, Moralls. **1655** Stanley *Hist. Philos.* iii. (1687) 73/2 His [*sc.* Socrates'] Morals, consider a Man either as a single person, or as the Father of a Family, or as a member of the Commonwealth. **1785** Paley *Mor. & Polit. Philos.* Pref. ⁋1 All just principles of reasoning in morals. **1861** Mill *Utilit.* v. 92 A direct emanation from the first principle of morals. **1872** Swinburne *Ess. & Stud.* (1875) 41 In morals the action is judged by the intention.

¶*sing.* in the same sense. [? After G. *moral.*]

1828 Pusey *Hist. Enq.* I. 149 It contains a perfect system of moral.

†**b.** ***the small morals***: the 'minor moralities'; rules of behaviour in small matters. *Obs.*

1651 Hobbes *Leviathan* i. xi. *init.*, By Manners, I mean not here, Decency of behaviour; as how one man should salute another, or how a man should wash his mouth, or pick his teeth before company, and such other points of the *Small Moralls.*

9. *slang.* A 'moral certainty': see moral *a.* 11. Now chiefly *Austral.* Also quasi-*adj.*, morally certain.

1861 Whyte Melville *Mkt. Harb.* 24 A contingency which the dealer was pleased to observe amounted to what he called 'a moral'. **1887** Black *Sabina Zembra* 460 'Why, Joe,' I said, 'it's a moral, if the horse is ridden fair.' **1916** C. J. Dennis *Moods of Ginger Mick* 40 'E 'as struck it for a moral. Ginger's found 'is game at last. **1933** *Bulletin* (Sydney) 18 Jan. 20 Had been winning all over the countryside and was a moral for the big jumping event. **1934** [see *ear-biter*]. **1946** R. Franklyn in *Coast to Coast 1945* 221, I think we orta go home, Darky. We're a moral to get nabbed. **1957** 'N. Culotta' *They're a Weird Mob* (1958) v. 72 As I was sayin' this bloke says 'e's a moral. **1972** I. Hamilton *Thrill Machine* xxvii. 124 Eric said this bloke had a new film... It's a moral to be a load of bull but you never know. **1975** L. Ryan *Shearers* 79 Andy Burns rang last night ..reckons Dallas is a moral in the first.

10. *attrib.* and *Comb.*, as ***moral-directing*** adj.; ***moral-mender***.

1645 Rutherford *Tryal & Tri. Faith* xx. 196 Which condemnation.. doth go and come without hurting the essence of the Law, and its commanding and eternall Morall-directing power. **1739** Cibber *Apol.* (1756) I. 200 Collier is by profession a moral-mender himself.

moral ('mɒrəl), *a.* Also 4 **morale, -alle,** 4–7 **morall.** [ad. L. *mōrālis*, f. *mōr-*, *mōs* custom (pl. *mōrēs* manners, morals, character): see -al[1].

The Latin word was formed by Cicero (*De Fato* ii. i) as a rendering of Gr. ἠθικός ethic *a.* (*mōrēs* being the accepted Latin equivalent of ἤθη). It has passed into all the mod. Rom. and Teut. langs.: Fr., Sp., Pg. *moral*, It. *morale*; G. *moralisch*, Du. *moraal*, Sw., Da. *moral*.]

1. a. Of or pertaining to character or disposition, considered as good or bad, virtuous or vicious; of or pertaining to the distinction between right and wrong, or good and evil, in relation to the actions, volitions, or character of responsible beings; ethical.

moral virtue: a rendering of L. *virtus moralis*, Gr. ἀρετὴ ἠθική (Aristotle), (an) excellence of character or disposition, as distinguished from *intellectual virtue* (ἀρετὴ διανοητική). As in English (and in other modern languages) *virtue* is rarely used exc. as synonymous with *moral virtue*, the use of the adj. with this sb. has become infrequent.

a **1340** Hampole *Psalter* cxviii. 1 Þis psalme.. all shynys of haly lare and morale swetnes. *c* **1386** Chaucer *Prol.* 307 Sownynge in moral vertu was his speche. *c* **1449** Pecock *Repr.* ii. iv. (Rolls) 155 Sum vntrewe opinioun of men.. is leding into deedis whiche ben grete moral vicis. **1529** More *Dyaloge* i. Wks. 173/2 He called his churche out of the gentiles which els as for morall vertues and politicall.. were ..not farre vnder mani of vs. **1592** G. Harvey *Pierce's Super.* 103 An aduancement.. of that morall, and intellectuall good, that.. so forciblie emprooueth itselfe. **1601** Shaks. *All's Well* i. ii. 21 Youth, thou bear'st thy Fathers face.. Thy Fathers morall parts Maist thou inherit too. **1675** R. Burthogge *Causa Dei* 97 Since the Objection doth proceed of Moral, and not of Metaphysical and Abstract Goodness. **1698** Stillingfl. *Serm.* III. vi. 242 In Matters of Religion, Moral Difficulties are more to be regarded than Intellectual. **1699** Shaftesb. *Inq. Virtue* i. i. §1 in *Charac.* (1711) II. 8 An Author.. who dares plead for Religion and Moral Virtue. *Ibid.* 30 *margin*, Moral Beauty and Deformity. **1711** Addison *Spect.* No. 195 ⁋6, I have not here considered Temperance as it is a Moral Virtue.. but only as it is the Means of Health. **1839** Hallam *Hist. Lit.* IV. iv. 306 The theologians who went no farther than revelation, or at least than the positive law of God, for moral distinctions. **1876** Mozley *Univ. Serm.* iv. (1877) 85 It is plain that eloquence, imagination, poetical talent, are no more moral goodness than riches are. **1949** M. Fortes *Social Structure* 60 Its form derives from a paradigm.. sanctioned by.. moral values. **1951** R. Firth *Elem. Social Organiz.* vi. 200 This can be illustrated by considering the moral values attached to human personality in certain social situations. **1964** S. M. Willhelm in I. L. Horowitz *New Sociol.* 184 The scientific ideology simply places the scientist in a moral vacuum. *Ibid.* 186 Recognizing his historical obligation to impose the very moral accountability which certain scientists seek to avoid, the intellectual insists upon his right to direct the affairs of a recalcitrant scientist.

¶**b.** ***moral virtue*** occasionally occurs in contradistinction to the 'Christian virtues' (Faith, Hope, Charity), or as restricted to such virtues as may be attained without the aid of religion.

1598 Barckley *Felic. Man* (1631) 713 To pray to God... That He will endue us with vertues both Morall and Christian. *a* **1686** T. Watson *Body of Div.* (1692) 979 Moral Vertue may stand with the hatred of Godliness. **1791** Bp. Horne *Charge to Clergy* 14 Cold inanimate Lectures on moral virtue, independent of christianity.

c. Of knowledge, opinions, judgements, etc.: Relating to the nature and application of the distinction between right and wrong. (Cf. sense 2.)

1500–20 Dunbar *Poems* lxv. 2 To speik.. Off vertew, morall cwnnyng, or doctrine [etc.]. **1752** Chesterf. *Lett. to Son* 6 Jan., If the religious and moral principles of this society [*sc.* the Jesuits] are to be detested. **1817** Coleridge *Biogr. Lit.* I. x. 213 My essays contributed to introduce the practice of placing the questions and events of the day in a moral point of view. **1860** Mill *Repr. Govt.* (1865) 6/2 It was not by any change in the distribution of material interests, but by the spread of moral convictions, that negro slavery has been put an end to in the British Empire. **1879** Geo. Eliot *Theo. Such* xvi, A correct moral judgment is the strong point in woman. **1883** W. James *Let.* 23 Jan. in R. B. Perry *Tht. & Char. W. James* (1935) I. 389 Although from a moral point of view your sympathy commands my warmest thanks, from the intellectual point of view, it seems, first, to suppose that I am a bachelor [etc.]. **1951** C. Day Lewis *Poet's Task* 19 As an aesthetic judgement this is so bizarre that one can only take it for a moral judgement. **1972** *Jrnl. Social Psychol.* LXXXVI. 158 The mean moral judgment quotient for girls was slightly higher than that for boys.

d. ***moral sense***: the power of apprehending the difference between right and wrong, *esp.* when viewed as an innate and unanalysable faculty of the human mind. Similarly ***moral faculty***.

1699 Shaftesb. *Inq. Virtue* i. iii. §1 in *Charac.* (1711) II. 41 The taking away the natural Sense of Right and Wrong. *Marg.* Loss of Moral Sense. **1754** Edwards *Freed. Will* i. v. (1831) 43 To moral agency belongs a moral faculty, or sense of moral good and evil. **1827** Whately *Logic* (1837) 380 The Moral faculty.. is one of which brutes are destitute. **1885** J. Martineau *Types Eth. Th.* II. 93 Bentham describes the moral-sense-man as a sort of bully, intent on brow-beating men into accepting the verdict he wants them to pronounce. **1901** Baldwin *Dict. Philos.* s.v. *Moral Sense*, The term 'moral sense writers' is now commonly used to denote a succession of English moralists, of whom Shaftesbury and Hutcheson were the chief.

e. Of feelings: Arising from the contemplation of an action, character, etc., as good or bad.

1768 Sterne *Sent. Journ.* (1778) I. 134 (*Amiens*), With what a moral delight will it crown my journey. **1837** M. Donovan *Dom. Econ.* II. 45 To those who have got over the moral disgust of such food [*viz.* human flesh], it.. has recommendatory qualities. **1871** Morley *Voltaire* (1886) 8 Perhaps a moral relish for veritable proofs of honesty.. drives men to grasp even a crudity with fervour.

f. Of concepts or terms: Involving ethical praise or blame.

1845 Whewell *Elem. Morality* I. 238 The Supreme Standard.. is expressed by the Moral Ideas, Benevolence, Justice, Truth, Purity, and Wisdom. **1865** J. Grote *Moral Ideals* (1876) 108 Those words, like all moral words, by frequent complimentary use.. have lost much of their warmth and force. **1892** Westcott *Gospel of Life* 216 The distinctness of moral conceptions will correspond with the growth of the race.

2. a. Treating of or concerned with virtue and vice, or the rules of right conduct, as a subject of study. (Cf. 1 c.)

moral philosophy: the department of philosophy which treats of the virtues and vices, the criteria of right and wrong, the rightness or wrongness of particular classes of actions, the methods to be adopted for the formation of virtuous character, and the like; ethical philosophy, ethics. Formerly often employed in a wider sense, including psychology and metaphysics. ***moral philosopher***: one who studies or is versed in moral philosophy. ***moral science*** has in recent times been used in the same senses as 'moral philosophy'. ***the moral sciences*** is sometimes used (e.g. at Cambridge) as a comprehensive name for a branch of academic study including psychology, ethics, political and economic science, and in fact all that is now commonly understood by the term 'philosophy'. Also *attrib.* as in ***moral sciences tripos***.

1387 T. Usk *Test. Love* iii. i. (Skeat) l. 53 Philosophie, with her three speces, that is, natural, and moral, and resonable. **1398** Trevisa *Barth. De P.R.* i. (1495) 3 Deuowte doctours of Theologye.. for this consyderacyon.. rede and vse natural philosophye and morall. **1531** Elyot *Gov.* i. xi, Hit were nedefull to rede unto hym.. that parte that may enforme him unto vertuous maners, whiche parte of philosophie is called morall. **1600** J. Pory tr. *Leo's Africa* iii. 151 Certaine learned men, which will haue themselues called wizards and morall philosophers. **1606** Shaks. *Tr. & Cr.* ii. ii. 167 Young men, whom Aristotle thought Vnfit to heare Morall Philosophie. **1651** Hobbes *Leviath.* i. xv. 79 Morall philosophy is nothing else but the Science of what is Good, and Evill. **1785** Paley *Mor. Philos.* i. i. 1 Moral Philosophy, Morality, Ethics, Casuistry, Natural Law, mean all the same thing. **1791** Bp. Horne *Charge to Clergy* 14 Morality.. hath four chief virtues, which moral writers have well explained. **1828** G. Payne (*title*) Elements of Mental and Moral Science. **1830** Mackintosh *Eth. Philos.* Introd. (1862) 8 The purpose of the Moral Sciences is to answer the question *What ought to be?* *a* **1866** J. Grote *Exam. Utilit. Philos.* iv. (1870) 61 A description as complete and beautiful, I think, as is to be found in any moral writings. **1866** *Students' Guide Univ. Cambr.* 162 The establishment of a Philosophical or Moral Sciences Tripos in the year 1851. **1870** H. Spencer *First Princ.* ii. i. §36 Under the head of Moral Philosophy, we treat of human actions as right or wrong.

b. ***moral theology***: (*a*) the practical part of ethics treated as a branch of theology; the part of theological learning which is concerned with the resolution of cases of conscience; casuistry, casuistic divinity; (*b*) see quot. 1902.

1727–41 in Chambers *Cycl.* **1883** in *Catholic Dict.* **1902** Baldwin *Dict. Philos.*, *Moral Theology*, the doctrines of theology developed as postulates of the moral as distinguished from the logico-speculative reason.

c. ***moral psychology***: psychology concerned with the psychological effect of rules of conduct, esp. the sense of virtue and vice, upon behaviour. Hence ***moral-psychological*** adj.

1859 J. Martineau in *National Rev.* IX. 504 Does an author, who has so distinguished himself in Logical psychology,.. doubt that there is also a Moral psychology? *a* **1865** J. Grote *Treat. Moral Ideals* (1876) xiii. 297 Moral psychology endeavours to co-ordinate individual experiences. **1867** Mill *Exam. Hamilton's Philos.* (ed. 3) xxvi. 586 This vital truth in moral psychology, that we can improve our character if we will. **1946** *Mind* LV. 189 His interest in moral psychology and the empirical facts of the moral life remained. **1963** J. Wiesenfarth *Henry James* ii. 51 This is precisely the decision that climaxes her coming to grips with the moral-psychological problem in the novel. **1972** J. Rawls *Theory of Justice* §29. 181 The parties must consider the general facts of moral psychology.

3. a. Of a person, esp. a writer: That enunciates moral precepts. ? *Obs.* In early quots. applied to writers of allegory.

c **1374** Chaucer *Troylus* v. 1856 O moral Gower þis boke I directe To the. *c* **1430** Lydg. *Min. Poems* (Percy Soc.) 25 The tragidés diverse and unkouth Of morall Senec. **1599** Shaks. *Much Ado* v. i. 30 'Tis all mens office, to speake patience To those that wring vnder the load of sorrow: But no mans vertue nor sufficiencie To be so morall, when he shall endure The like himselfe. **1718** Prior *Picture of Seneca*, While cruel Nero only drains The moral Spaniard's ebbing Veins. **1742** Young *Nt. Th.* v. 319 Let us read Her moral stone. *Ibid.* ix. 534 The moral muse has shadow'd out a sketch.

b. Of a literary work, a pictorial or dramatic representation, etc.: That deals with or treats of the ruling of conduct; that has the teaching of morality as its motive; that conveys a moral; also, †allegorical, emblematical. **moral play** (*obs.* exc. *Hist.*) = morality 4 b.

c **1386** Chaucer *Melib.* Prol. 22 It is a moral tale vertuous. *c* **1400** tr. *Secreta Secret., Gov. Lordsh.* 48 He [Alexander] made many morales epistels to Aristotel. *a* **1500** *Everyman* (1773), Here begynneth a treatyse.. in maner of a moralle playe. **1526** *Pilgr. Perf.* (W. de W. 1531) 2 They shal haue therby a lyght to perceyue the better all moral matter, that they shall here preched or taught. **1607** Shaks. *Timon* i. i. 90 A thousand morall Paintings I can shew, That shall demonstrate these quicke blowes of Fortunes, More pregnantly then words. **1660** F. Brooke tr. *Le Blanc's Trav.* 272 We had the pleasure there to see a morall representation of the Magdalens conversion. **1726** Swift *Gulliver* ii. vii, From this way of reasoning the author drew several moral applications useful in the Conduct of Life. **1744** *Pope's Wks.* (ed. Warburton 1755) III. 105 (*title*) Moral Essays, in four epistles to Several Persons. **1784** Cowper *Tiroc.* 126 Lisping our syllables, we scramble next Through moral narrative, or sacred text. **1789** Mrs. Piozzi *Journ. France* I. 115 To what purpose then.. the moral dances, as they call them now? One word of solid instruction to the ear, conveys more knowledge to the mind at last, than all these

marionettes presented to the eye. **1831** J. P. Collier *Hist. Dram. Poetry* II. 384 John Heywood's dramatic productions ..are neither Miracle-plays nor Moral-plays. **1873** Browning *Red Cott. Nt.-cap* 171 The late death-chamber, tricked with..Skulls, cross-bones, and such moral broidery.

Comb. **1798** Edgeworth *Pract. Educ.* (1822) I. 427 A tragedy heroine..is a moral-picturesque object.

c. Of a literary work: Beneficial in moral effect.

1671 Milton *Samson* Introd., Tragedy..hath been ever held the gravest, moralest, and most profitable of all other Poems.

d. ***moral tutor***: a university tutor appointed to have a particular concern for the moral well-being of a student. Hence ***moral pupil***.

1932 *Oxf. Univ. Handbk.* i. 130 In some colleges an undergraduate is assigned for all his time to a 'moral tutor', who is often not the tutor to whom he is going for his reading, but one who undertakes to keep in touch with him during his career and to help and advise him generally in his life. **1963** J. I. M. Stewart *Last Tresilians* xiv. 106 That's Leech, the Pro-Provost. He's my moral tutor. **1966** *Rep. Comm. Inquiry Univ. Oxf.* II. 383 Plus £1 per moral pupil other than those for whom a fellow is tutorially responsible. *Ibid.*, Paid to 16 moral tutors. **1969** V. de S. Pinto *City that Shone* xi. 249 Jackie would continue to be my 'moral tutor', but..my 'English tutor' would be Mr Percy Simpson.

4. ***moral law***: the body of requirements in conformity to which right or virtuous action consists; a particular requirement of this kind. Opposed to 'positive' or 'instituted' laws, the obligation of which depends solely on the fact that they have been imposed by a rightful authority. Also ***moral code, norm, order, rule, system***.

In early use chiefly applied to that part of the Mosaic Law which enunciates moral principles, and therefore, unlike the 'ceremonial' and 'judicial' parts, remains valid under the Christian dispensation. So ***moral commandment***, etc.

c **1380** Wyclif *Wks.* (1880) 366 Siþ þat moyses lawe is moralle in þis poynte,..criste myȝte not distroy þes lawis. *a* **1450** *Wyclif's Bible* Prol. ii, The old testament is departid ..in to moral comaundementis, iudicials, and cerimonyals. **1551** [see judicial *a.* 1 b]. **1606** Shaks. *Tr. & Cr.* ii. ii. 184 If Helen then be wife to Sparta's King..these Morall Lawes Of Nature, and of Nation, speake alowd To haue her backe return'd. **1640** Bastwick *Lord Bps.* viii. H iij b, If the Prelates shall pronounce the 4th Commandement not to be Morall for the sanctifying of a Seventh day. **1645** Milton *Tetrach.* Wks. 1851 IV. 215 The firmenesse of such right to divorce as here pleads, is fetcht from the prime institution, does not stand or fall with the judiciall Law, but is as morall as what is moralest. **1667** —— *P.L.* xii. 298. **1690** Locke *Hum. Und.* i. iii. 15, I think it will be hard to instance any one moral rule. **1819** [see judicial *a.* 1 b]. **1851** H. Spencer *Soc. Stat.* i. 55 The moral law must be the law of the perfect man. **1876** L. Stephen *Eng. Th. 18th C.* II. ix. 5 Hobbes.. audaciously identified the moral with the positive law. **1927** *Amer. Jrnl. Sociol.* XXXII. 736 The same forces which co-operate to create the characteristic social organization and the accepted moral order of a given society or social group determine at the same time..the character of the individuals who compose that society. **1931** H. S. Walpole *Judith Paris* ii. ii. 240 A rather blowzy red-cheeked lady, who..had a warm heart but an uncertain moral code. **1951** R. Firth *Elem. Social Organiz.* vi. 185 The effective standard of judgement..has appeared to be the recognition of offences against a moral code of behaviour. *Ibid.* 187 The moral rules to be found in different types of society. *Ibid.* 202 Divergence from the Western moral norms is seen much more widely in infanticide. *Ibid.* 213 A moral system.. includes the idea of an elaborate interlocking set of judgements. **1957** P. Worsley *Trumpet shall Sound* 250 The role of ritual obscenity as providing an occasion for the statement and reinforcement of moral norms is well known from many societies. **1958** R. C. Angell *Free Society & Moral Crisis* ii. 16 The most basic—though not the most tangible—aspect of the moral order is the set of common values that motivates the members of a society. **1970** G. A. & A. G. Theodorson *Mod. Dict. Sociol.* 264 The various moral systems of the world may include many of the same moral ideas.

5. Of rights, obligations, responsibility, etc.: Founded on the moral law; valid according to the principles of morality. Opposed to *legal*.

1690 Locke *Hum. Und.* ii. xxviii. §3 Sometimes the foundation of considering things, with reference to one another, is some act whereby any one comes by a moral right, power, or obligation to do something. **1736** Butler *Anal.* ii. 403 Our obligation to attend to his voice is surely moral in all cases. **1818** Cruise *Digest* (ed. 2) I. 178 Dower is not only a civil, but also a moral right. *Ibid.* IV. 584 There is one case in which a conveyance, founded on a moral consideration only, has been held good against a subsequent purchaser. **1882** Morley *Cobden* xix. (1902) 71/1 Cobden thus strove to diffuse the sense of moral responsibility in connexion with the use of capital.

6. a. Of actions: Subject to the moral law; having the property of being right or wrong. ***the moral world***: the sphere or region of moral action.

1594 Hooker *Eccl. Pol.* i. xvi. §3 The axiomes of that lawe ..haue their vse in the morall, yea, euen in the spirituall actions of men. **1690** Locke *Hum. Und.* ii. xxviii. §4 There is another sort of relation, which is the conformity or disagreement men's voluntary actions have to a rule to which they are referred, and by which they are judged of; which, I think, may be called moral relation, as being that which denominates our moral actions. **1809–10** Coleridge *Friend* (1866) 278 To possess the end in the means, as it is essential to morality in the moral world, and the contra-distinction of goodness from mere prudence, so is it, in the intellectual world, the moral constituent of genius.

b. Of an agent or his attributes: Capable of moral action; capable of volition for the rightness of which he is responsible.

1736 Butler *Anal.* i. iii. Wks. 1874 I. 58 That God has given us a moral nature..[is] a proof of our being under his moral government. **1754** Edwards *Freed. Will.* i. v. (1831) 43 A moral agent is a being that is capable of those actions that have a moral quality. **1802** Paley *Nat. Theol.* xxvii. (1819) 485 The moral and accountable part of his terrestrial creation. **1868** Bain *Ment. & Mor. Sci.* 403 Every creature possessing mind is a moral agent. **1887** J. A. C. Morison *Service Man* (1889) 84 Good and bad men, whose goodness and badness depends on their moral endowment.

7. a. Pertaining to, affecting, or operating on the character or conduct, as distinguished from the intellectual or physical nature of human beings. ***moral suasion***: see suasion 1 b.

1597 Hooker *Eccl. Pol.* v. lvii. §4 Sacraments..are not physicall but morall instruments of saluation, duties of seruice and worship. **1599** Shaks. *Much Ado* i. iii. 13, I wonder that thou..goest about to apply a morall medicine to a mortifying mischiefe. **1659** H. Thorndike *Wks.* (1846) II. 539, I acknowledge the Scriptures to be an instrument of God, though a moral instrument. **1727–41** Chambers *Cycl.* s.v. *Necessity*, The schools distinguish a physical necessity, and a moral necessity... Moral Necessity is only a great difficulty; such as that arising from a long habit, a strong inclination or violent passion. **1742** Young *Nt. Th.* ii. 46 For what calls thy disease, Lorenzo? not For Esculapian, but for moral aid. *Ibid.* v. 284 I'll..gather ev'ry thought of sov'reign power To chace the moral maladies of man. *Ibid.* vi. 814 'Tis moral grandeur makes the mighty man. **1780** Cowper *Progr. Err.* 272 'Tis not alone the grape's enticing juice Unnerves the moral pow'rs, and mars their use. **1823** Cobbett *Rur. Rides* (1885) I. 291 There is now very little moral hold which the latter [the clergy] possess. **1823** D'Israeli *Cur. Lit.* Ser. ii. I. 183 The art of curing moral disorders by corporeal means has not yet been brought into general practice. **1833** J. C. Prichard in *Cycl. Pract. Med.* II. 826/2 Moral insanity, or madness consisting in a morbid perversion of the natural feelings,..and moral dispositions, without any notable lesion of the intellect. **1841** Thoreau *Jrnl.* 19 Feb. in *Writings* (1906) VII. 217 It is a moral force as well as he. **1851** *Edin. Rev.* XCIII. 225 The only effect produced was a kind of amicable splitting of the repeal party into two co-operative factions,—the moral-force men and the physical-force men. **1851** H. Spencer *Soc. Stat.* i. 58 Just so it is with a true morality... Its office is simply to expound the principles of moral health... Whether it is possible to develope scientifically a Moral Pathology and a Moral Therapeutics seems very doubtful. **1868** Bain *Ment. & Mor. Sci.* 395 Moral Inability expresses the insufficiency of ordinary motives, but not of all motives. **1913** *Act 3 & 4 Geo. V* c. 28 §1 Moral imbeciles; that is to say, persons who from an early age display some permanent mental defect coupled with strong vicious or criminal propensities. **1927** *Act 17 & 18 Geo. V* c. 33 §1 Moral defectives, that is to say, persons in whose case there exists mental defectiveness coupled with strongly vicious or criminal propensities and who require care, supervision and control for the protection of others. **1951** R. Firth *Elem. Social Organiz.* vi. 213 It is in the capacity to generate and adapt moral force that man derives one of the most potent springs to social action. **1952** R. M. Hare *Lang. Morals* i. iv. 71 If, when we did as we were told, the total effects of our so doing..were always such as we would not have chosen.. then we should..work out our own salvation or become moral defectives. **1967** D. J. West *Young Offender* v. 106 A paper..seeking to prove the moral imbecility of habitual criminals. **1968** *Listener* 26 Sept. 408/1 'Moral insanity' was superseded by 'moral imbecility'; this in turn gave way to 'psychopathic personality' (which had developed out of 'constitutional psychopathic inferiority').

†**b.** ***moral cause***: see quot. (Cf. cause *sb.* 5.)

1697 tr. *Burgersdicius his Logic* i. xvii. 63 Author, here is said to be him who proposing Reasons, persuades the principal Cause either to, or from Action: He is also call'd the Moral Cause.

c. Applied to the indirect effect of some action or event (e.g. a victory or defeat) in producing confidence or discouragement, sympathy or hostility, and the like. ***moral support***: support or help the effect of which is psychological rather than physical. ***moral victory***: applied to a defeat or an indecisive result which it is claimed will, on account of special circumstances, produce the moral effects of a victory.

1835 Alison *Hist. Europe* (1849–50) V. xxxi. §17. 310 The loss to the contending parties was nearly equal;..but all the moral advantages of a victory were on the side..of the French. **1860** Mill *Repr. Govt.* (1865) 61 The instructed minority would, in the actual voting, count only for their numbers, but as a moral power they would count for much more. **1883** C. J. Wills *Mod. Persia* 111 Armenian..scowls staggering along in secure insolence, confident in the moral protection given him by the presence of the Englishman. **1885** *Daily Chron.* 23 Jan. 4/8 Italy on her side will on all occasions offer moral support to England in her Egyptian policy. **1888** *Times* 13 June 6/1 His idea was that the moral effect of artillery fire was greater than the positive. **1896** *Daily News* 14 Nov. 7/4 One had gained an actual victory, and the other had gained a moral victory. **1921** W. S. Maugham *Circle* i. 19 You were rather scared... I thought I'd come and give you a little moral support. **1926** F. M. Ford *Man could stand Up* i. ii. 37 He needed her moral support! **1968** 'M. Carroll' *Dead Trouble* iii. 44 Where were you? Couldn't you have given me some moral support? **1973** J. Burrows *Like an Evening Gone* i. 7 She had it all worked out. All she wanted from her husband was a little moral support.

d. ***moral courage***: that kind of courage which enables a person to encounter odium, disapproval, or contempt, rather than depart from what he deems the right course: contradistinguished from *physical courage*. Similarly ***moral fibre***; esp. in phr. ***lack of moral fibre***, used *euphem.* for lack of courage. Cf. *LMF* s.v. L 7.

1822 Colton *Lacon* (1825) I. 44 Hypocrisy..sometimes neutralized his [Cromwell's] moral courage, never his physical. **1860** Fitzjames Stephen *Ess.* (1862) 175 Moral courage is readiness to expose oneself to suffering or inconvenience which does not affect the body. It arises from firmness of moral principle, and is independent of the physical constitution. **1884** *Boy's Own Paper* 11 Oct. 18/2 Fanshawe was a boy in whom bad instincts had been nourished by his training, and who, from constant lack of moral fibre, had gradually deteriorated. **1887** [see courage 4]. **1942** [see grounded *ppl. a.*[1] 8]. **1960** *Times* 11 Jan. 13/6 Fail to register for the cut-price course in foundry management and clearly you are lacking in moral fibre. **1970** L. Deighton *Events Last Flight R.A.F. Bomber* xvii. 263 The R.A.F. authorities..would stamp the words 'lack of moral fibre' across the man's documents..and send him away..an officially recognized coward. **1973** K. Royce *Spider Underground* iii. 52 She was tough all right, of high moral fibre.

e. ***moral turpitude***: conduct considered depraved; an instance of such conduct.

1879 [see turpitude 1 a]. **1931** J. P. Clark *Deportation of Aliens from U.S. to Europe* v. 165 An alien convicted of stealing $15 in Massachusetts was held subject to deportation because of conviction of a crime involving moral turpitude.

f. ***Moral Rearmament***: a religious group founded by the American evangelist Frank Buchman (1878–1961); the beliefs or practices of this group; = Buchmanism. Abbrev. *M.R.A.* (q.v.). Also *transf.* and *fig.* So ***Moral Rearmer***.

1938 *Times* 2 Nov. 6/4 Moral rearmament, which is the true basis of national fitness, is an individual responsibility. **1940** Earl of Athlone et al. *Moral Re-Armament* 3 Moral Re-Armament stands for a change of heart, for that new spirit which must animate all human relationships. **1940** N. Mitford *Pigeon Pie* iii. 55 Luke had been guided to ask a hundred people to dinner..to talk about Moral Rearmament. *Ibid.* iv. 80 If the British people had gone all out for moral rearmament and real appeasement, things need never have reached this pass. **1951** V. A. Demant *What is happening to Us?* iii. 22 The Emperor Augustus tried to save the civilization of Ancient Rome by reviving the old cults..and the poet Horace..wrote his lovely Odes to help in this older version of 'Moral Rearmament'. **1956** A. Huxley *Adonis & Alphabet* 118 For *their* campaigns, the Moral Rearmers have a whole arsenal of Christian *Oklahomas* and ethical *Cats on Hot Tin Roofs*. **1961** [see Buchmanism]. **1969** *Guardian* 20 June 10/4 Senator Ralph Vibert, an advocate and a Moral Re-Armer. **1973** *Ibid.* 11 June 11/6 We were made to confess all our weaknesses... It was like Moral Re-Armament.

8. a. Of, pertaining to, or concerned with the morals (of a person or a community). Also (*occas.*), pertaining to the 'morale' of an army.

1794 Paley *Evid.* i. v. §4 (1817) 97 The phrases which the same writer employs to describe the moral condition of Christians compared with their condition before they became Christians. **1818** Hallam *Mid. Ages* ix. (1868) 700 *note*, His standard is taken, not from Avignon, but from Edinburgh,..where the moral barometer stands at a very different altitude. **1844** H. H. Wilson *Brit. India* I. 545 He quoted largely from a memoir on the Moral State of India by Mr. Grant. **1848** W. H. Kelly tr. *L. Blanc's Hist. Ten Y.* I. 382 The moral interests of society seemed still more compromised than the material. **1889** D. Hannay *Capt. Marryat* 38 The squadron was in an indifferent moral condition, divided by sour professional factions, and impatient of its Admiral.

b. ***moral welfare***: see quot. 1965.

1927 *8th Ann. Rep. Archbishops' Advisory Board Preventive & Rescue Work* 9 The League of Nations Report on the Traffic in Women and Children..has awakened an interest in moral welfare work that is bound to help in arousing the public conscience against prostitution. **1944** A. Thirkell *Headmistress* x. 211 Doing wonders with her Moral Welfare Committee. **1965** Hall & Howes *Church in Social Work* 2 'Moral welfare' is a term which..appears to have come into general use during the inter-war period to designate the social work in relation to sex, marriage and the family.

9. a. ***moral sense*** or ***interpretation***: originally, that mode of interpreting a passage of Holy Scripture which treats of the events recorded as typical of something in the life of the Christian soul. (Now chiefly *Hist.*) †Hence *transf.* applied to the 'moral' of a fable and the like.

1503 Hawes *Examp. Virt.* ix. 10, I..lykened the wyldernes by morall scence Vnto worldely trouble by good experyence. **1572** Huloet s.v., The morall sence of a fable, *epimythium*. **1599** Shaks. *Much Ado* iii. iv. 80 Morall? no by my troth, I haue no morall meaning, I meant plaine holy thissell. **1609** Bible (Douay) *Gen.* i. 1 Comm., There are three spiritual senses besides the literal..: Allegorical.. Moral..and Anagogical.

quasi-adv. **1529** More *Supplic. Soulys* Wks. 322/1 Because som doctours do conster those wordes of the apostle in diuers other senses,..sometyme after the letter, sometime moral, & sometime otherwyse.

b. Qualifying a descriptive noun: That is such in a metaphorical sense relative to moral character or condition.

1692 R. L'Estrange *Fables* I. cccxxviii. 286 If all our Moral Wolves in Sheeps-Cloathing, were but Serv'd as This Hypocritical Wolfe was in the Fiction. **1813** Shelley *Q. Mab* ii. 163 Where Athens, Rome, and Sparta stood, There is a moral desert now. **1819** —— *Peter Bell 3rd* iv. xi, But from the first 'twas Peter's drift To be a kind of moral eunuch. **1821** Scott *Kenilw.* xxx, Varney was one of the few —the very few moral monsters, who contrive to lull to sleep the remorse of their own bosoms. **1848** Thackeray *Van. Fair* xxxvii, I mean a *moral* shepherd's dog... A dog to keep the wolves off me... A companion. **1852** Mundy *Our Antipodes* (1857) 18 Sufferers for the sins of their fathers, moral bastards. **1894** Gladstone in *Times* 9 Nov. 7/5 In my opinion..an undenominational system of religion, framed by or under the authority of the State, is a moral monster.

10. a. Of persons, their habits, conduct, etc.: Morally good; conforming to the rules of morality.

1638 SIR T. HERBERT *Trav.* (ed. 2) 233 Morall men they are, and humane in language and garbe. **1697** DRYDEN *Æneid* Ded. (a) 3 Your Essay of Poetry..I read over and over with much delight,..and, without flattering you, or making my self more Moral than I am, not without some envy. **1700** —— *Fables* Pref., My enemies..will not allow me so much as to be a Christian, or a moral man. **1781** COWPER *Conversat.* 193 A moral, sensible, and well-bred man Will not affront me. **1841** MYERS *Cath. Th.* IV. §23. 293 A man may be Moral without being Religious, but he cannot be Religious without being Moral. **1868** RUSKIN *Arrows of Chace* (1880) II. 199 A man taught to plough, row or steer well..[is] already educated in many essential moral habits.

¶**b.** with reference to 'moral' as opposed to 'evangelical' virtue (cf. 1 b).

a **1686** T. WATSON *Body of Div.* (1692) 979 A Moral Man doth as much hate Holiness as he doth Vice. **1824** HOGG *Conf. Sinner* 197 A Mr. Blanchard, who was reckoned a worthy, pious divine, but quite of the moral cast.

c. Virtuous with regard to sexual conduct. ***moral restraint***: see quot. 1803–6.

1803 MALTHUS *Popul.* IV. i. 483 The various checks to population..seem all to be resolvable into moral restraint, vice, and misery. **1806** *Ibid.* I. I. i. 19 *note*, By moral restraint I..mean a restraint from marriage, from prudential motives, with a conduct strictly moral. **1820** SHELLEY *Œd. Tyr.* I. 74 Spay those Sows That load the earth with Pigs.. Moral restraint I see has no effect. **1879** GEO. ELIOT *Theo. Such* xvi, Sir Gavial..is a thoroughly moral man... Very different from Mr. Barabbas, whose life..is most objectionable, with actresses and that sort of thing. *Ibid.*, Yet I find even respectable historians..after showing that a king was treacherous, rapacious [etc.]..end by praising him for his pure moral character.

d. Of a tale, etc.: Conforming to morality; not ribald or vicious. (Cf. 3 b.)

c **1386** CHAUCER *Pard. Prol.* 39 Nay lat hym telle vs of no ribaudye; Telle vs som moral thyng þat we may leere Som wit. **1780** COWPER *Table-t.* 599 But still, while virtue kindled his delight, The song was moral, and so far was right.

11. Used to designate that kind of probable evidence that rests on a knowledge of the general tendencies of human nature, or of the character of particular individuals or classes of men; often in looser use, applied to all evidence which is merely probable and not demonstrative. ***moral certainty***: a practical certainty resulting from moral evidence; a degree of probability so great as to admit of no reasonable doubt; also, something which is morally certain. ***moral universality***: see quot. 1727–41.

This use of the word is prob. ultimately connected with Aristotle's ἠθικὴ πίστις, which means the effect of the known personal character of an orator in producing conviction.

The currency of the terms *certitudo, evidentia moralis* appears to be due to the Cartesian logicians of the 17th c.

1646 Moral certainty [see CERTAINTY 5]. **1660** JER. TAYLOR *Duct. Dubit.* I. v. Rule i. §6 The Negative doubt is either Metaphysical or Moral, or it is only a Suspicion. *a* **1677** HALE *Prim. Orig. Man.* II. i. 128 Though the evidence be still in its own nature but moral, and not simply demonstrative or infallible. **1664** TILLOTSON *Wisdom of being Religious* 25 Conclusions in Natural Philosophy are to be proved by a sufficient Induction of experiments; things of a moral nature by moral Arguments, and matters of Fact by credible Testimony. **1692** R. L'ESTRANGE *Fables* ccxci. 254 He..so Parts with a Moral Certainty in Possession, for a Wild and a Remote Possibility in Reversion. **1725** WATTS *Logic* II. ii. §9 In Matters of Faith, an exceeding great Probability is called a moral Certainty. **1727–41** CHAMBERS *Cycl.* s.v. *Universality*, Moral Universality, is that which admits of some exception... In such-like propositions, it is enough that the thing be ordinarily so. *a* **1754** FIELDING *Conversat.* Wks. 1784 IX. 373 When your guest offers to go, there should be no solicitations to stay..farther than to give him a moral assurance of his being welcome so to do. **1864** BOWEN *Logic* xii. 378 The inference is rightly said to rest upon moral, or probable, evidence. **1868** FREEMAN *Norm. Conq.* (1877) II. ix. 430 Was the succession of Harold merely a likelihood, a moral certainty?

†**12.** In etymological sense: Pertaining to manners and customs. *Obs. rare.*

1604 E. G[RIMSTONE] *(title)* The Naturall and Morall Historie of the East and West Indies... Written in Spanish by Ioseph Acosta.

moral (ˈmɒrəl), *v.* Also 7 mor(r)all. [f. MORAL *sb.*] = MORALIZE *v.* in various senses. **a.** *intr.* To make a moral application. **b.** *trans.* To expound the moral of. **c.** To symbolize.

1600 SHAKS. *A.Y.L.* II. vii. 29 When I did heare The motley Foole, thus morall on the time. **1608** ARMIN *Nest Ninn.* (1842) 40, I would fain morrall of it, if you please. *a* **1618** J. DAVIES *Ecl. betw. Willy & Wernocke* 175 Morall thy matter so, that, tho thou smite, Thou maist with tickling her dull sence, deceiue. **1627** DRAYTON *Moon-Calf* in *Agincourt*, etc. 181 As you haue moral'd Bumbyes [*sc.* tale], I will yours. **1839** BAILEY *Festus* ix. (1852) 99 This is a snakelike world, And always hath its tail within its mouth, As if it ate itself, and moralled time.

Hence ˈ**moralling** *vbl. sb.*, moralizing.

1890 *Sat. Rev.* 26 July 110/2 Here is..'Genseric', soundest of historical morallings; and many excellent fables.

morale (mɒˈrɑːl; as Fr. mɔral). [a. F. *morale*, fem. of *moral* adj.: see MORAL *a.*]

1. Morality, morals. **a.** Moral principles or practice.

1752 CHESTERF. *Lett. to Son* 6 Jan., If you would know their [*sc.* the Jesuits'] *morale*, read Pascal's *Lettres Provinciales.* **1839** MISS PARDOE *Beauties Bosphorus* 22 Here the Frank traveller may see more of the habits and morale of the Turkish women than he can hope to do elsewhere.

b. Moral teaching; lesson of conduct.

1812 CHALMERS in Hanna *Mem.* (1849) I. xi. 280 There are two verses in the Bible which comprise the whole morale of a man's conduct in these circumstances,—'Watch ye, stand fast' [etc.]. **1824** *Ibid.* (1851) III. i. 8 You have already made full conveyance to my mind of the whole *morale* of this intended honour, and..it does not lie within the power of any *matériel* to enhance the impression of it.

c. Moral aspect.

1834 *Tait's Mag.* I. 551/1 To look at the *morale* of any case was..out of the question. He looked to his brief.

2. Moral condition; conduct, behaviour; esp. with regard to confidence, hope, zeal, submission to discipline, etc. Said of a body of persons engaged in some enterprise, esp. of troops.

[In Fr. the word used in this sense is not *morale*, but *moral*: see MORAL *sb.* 6 b.]

1831 GEN. P. THOMPSON *Exerc.* (1842) I. 342 But the greatest advantage of all, on the side of the people, is the *morale*. Every soldier knows in his heart..that he was not made to fire upon the citizens. **1860** TYNDALL *Glac.* I. xxiii. 162 The morale in my case had a physical basis. **1866** CRUMP *Banking* ii. 71 To improve the *morale* of the entire mercantile community. **1870** *Times* 8 Aug. 5/3 The *morale* of the troops is excellent.

3. *attrib.* and *Comb.* uses of sense 2, as **morale-booster**, an event, occurrence, or saying which raises one's spirits; also ***morale-boosting, -building, -raising*** vbl. sbs. and adjs.

1943 J. B. PRIESTLEY *Daylight on Saturday* xxx. 234 Grandiose and impracticable schemes of morale-building. **1946** *Nature* 30 Nov. 777/2 Being more formally educational and only indirectly a morale-raising agent, instruction in it could be given not only by officers, but also [etc.]. **1956** C. COCKBURN *In Time of Trouble* xvi. 205 The quick-firers of..controversy who..for obvious morale-building purposes prophesied that the current crisis..was the final crisis of American capitalism. **1959** *Punch* 2 Sept. 98/3 To find so many and such diverse people coming out into the open on your side is a superb morale-booster. **1960** *Harper's Bazaar* July 21/2 A beauty salon..has become a morale-boosting relaxant centre. **1961** *Sunday Express* 12 Mar. 10/3 Another morale-boosting idea for the troops. **1961** *Guardian* 3 May 8/3 The Festival..was a national morale-booster. **1970** C. KERSH *Aggravations M. Ashe* xi. 158 With that morale-boosting thought to end her day, my mother went to bed. **1970** 'B. MATHER' *Break in Line* vi. 71 Even though it was a slip of the tongue..it was quite a morale booster. And Lord knows I needed one. **1971** A. PRICE *Alamut Ambush* xiii. 155 It was immensely morale-raising to see Mary floor him.

moralism (ˈmɒrəlɪz(ə)m). [f. MORAL + -ISM.]

1. Addiction to moralizing; also (with *pl.*) an instance of this, an act of moralizing.

1828 J. WILSON in *Blackw. Mag.* XXIV. 674 A' she writes has..an endearin' mainnerism and moralism about it. **1836** *Fraser's Mag.* XIV. 703 In all their poetry..we find no romance, no fable; but familiar descriptions, and sharp and lively moralisms. **1859** FARRAR *J. Home* xx. 257 A delicious spice of worldliness..which was quite refreshing to him, accustomed as he was to the somewhat droning moralisms of his 'congenial friends'.

2. The practice of a natural system of morality; religion consisting of or reduced to merely moral practice; morality not spiritualized.

1850 H. JAMES *(title)* Moralism and Christianity. **1872** *Contemp. Rev.* XIX. 810 No mere philosophy or moralism can ever transmute itself with evangelical righteousness. **1889** BOYD CARPENTER *Permanent Elem. Relig.* vi. 210 There is in the realm of morality a shadow corresponding to that which we saw waiting on religion. This shadow we shall call Moralism. *Ibid.* 212 Thus, where inward sympathy with good is lacking, though there may be outward moralism, there can be no true morality. **1890** H. S. BOWDEN tr. *Hettinger's Nat. Relig.* 284 *note*, We describe this theory [*sc.* the moral idea as independent of religion] as 'moralism'.

moralist (ˈmɒrəlɪst). [f. MORAL + -IST. Cf. F. *moraliste.*]

1. One who practises morality.

1621 BP. HALL *Heaven upon Earth* iii. Wks. (1625) 75 The wisest and most resolute Moralist that euer was, lookt pale when he should taste of his Hemlocke. **1750** GRAY *Elegy* 84 And many a holy text around she strews, That teach the rustic moralist to die. **1836** HOR. SMITH *Tin Trump.*, *Advice*, That man must be a sturdy moralist, who does not love his own judgment better than the interest of his neighbours. **1874** H. R. REYNOLDS *John Bapt.* i. §6. 54 A certain man, good, virtuous..an uncompromising moralist, acquired great influence over the people.

2. A teacher or student of morals; a moral philosopher. ***intuitive moralist***: see INTUITIVE *a.* 6.

a **1639** WOTTON in *Reliq.* (1651) 321 Nature surely (if she be well studied) is the best Moralist. **1661** BOYLE *Style of Script.* 116 Too many of our Moralists write, as if they thought Virtue could be taught as easily..as Grammar. **1736** BUTLER *Anal.* II. v. Wks. 1874 I. 215 Heathen moralists thought the present state to be a state of punishment. **1770** GOLDSM. *Bolingbroke* Wks. (Globe) 468/2 As a moralist.. Lord Bolingbroke..seems to have done nothing; but as a political writer few can equal..him. **1821** BYRON *Juan* III. lxiv, Soft Persian sentences, in lilac letters, From poets, or the moralists, their betters. **1869** [see INTUITIVE *a.* 6]. **1876** L. STEPHEN *Eng. Th. in 18th C.* I. III. iii. 125 Clarke, though an intuitive moralist, is by no means inclined to dispense with hell. *Ibid.* II. ix. 2 Hobbes..represented the evil principle to moralists as well as to theologians.

3. One who lives by or teaches a natural system of ethics; a merely moral man.

1649 HAMMOND *Chr. Obligations*, etc. 135 The Love (in the Moralist of vertue, but in the Christian) of God himself. *a* **1716** SOUTH *Serm.* (1744) VII. 286 How severely..do they judge of Men's Hearts? Such a Man is profane, another is carnal, and a mere Moralist. **1816** A. STEWART in *Mem.* (1822) 326 Moralists fear that salvation is degraded by connecting it with faith alone.

4. *Cambridge University.* A student who is examined in the 'Moral Sciences Tripos'. ***Senior Moralist***: the head of the first class in this Tripos.

1866 *Students' Guide Univ. Cambr.* 177 *note*, [He] obtained his Fellowship on the ground of his very high distinction as a Moralist, without having taken honours either in the Classical or Mathematical Tripos.

moralistic (mɒrəˈlɪstɪk), *a.* [f. prec. + -IC.] Pertaining to or characteristic of a moralist; addicted to moralizing; characterized by moralism.

1865 J. GROTE *Moral Ideals* (1876) 108 Those words..by frequent commonplace and moralistic enlarging upon, have lost much of their warmth and force. *a* **1866** —— *Exam. Utilit. Philos.* (1870) 34 By the 'moralistic' view of life, in a sense slightly depreciatory, I mean such a view of it as is taken by Juvenal in the tenth Satire. **1876** STEDMAN *Victorian Poets* 242 Several moralistic poets date from this early period—Mitford, Trench, Alford, and others of a like religious mood. **1889** BOYD CARPENTER *Permanent Elem. Relig.* vi. 211 Such an action is moralistic rather than moral, for it has not been prompted by the sentiment of goodness.

moraˈlistically, *adv.* [f. MORALISTIC *a.*: see -ICALLY.] In a moralistic manner; by way of moral judgement.

1890 W. JAMES *Princ. Psychol.* II. xxi. 317 The perfect object of belief would be a God or 'Soul of the World', represented both optimistically and moralistically. **1965** *New Statesman* 30 Apr. 677/2 The historical development of psychoanalysis out of medicine, from which it inherited criteria of normality and health which are much more moralistically loaded when applied to psychological than to somatic therapy. **1972** E. LUCIE-SMITH *Eroticism in Western Art* iii. 66 *The Golden Age* (otherwise, and more moralistically, dubbed *The Corruption of Men Before the Deluge*).

morality (mɒˈrælɪtɪ). Also 4–5 **moralite(e**, 5 **moralte**, 5–6 **moralyte**, 6 **-ytee**, **-ytye**, 5–7 **-itie**. [a. F. *moralité* (13th c.), ad. L. *mōrālitās*, f. *mōrālis*: see MORAL *a.* and -ITY.]

†**1.** Ethical wisdom; knowledge of moral science.

c **1386** CHAUCER *Monk's T.* 507 A maister hadde this Emperour To teche hym lettrure and curteisye ffor of moralitee he [*sc.* Seneca] was the flour. **1423** JAS. I *Kingis Q.* cxcvii, Gowere and Chaucere..quhill thai were lyvand here, Superlatiue as poetis laureate In moralitee and eloquence ornate. **14..** LYDG. *Ball. Gd. Counsel* 101 And though a man..Of Tullius hadde the sugred eloquence, Or of Senek the greet moralitee,..Yet [etc.].

2. *pl.* Moral qualities or endowments.

c **1386** CHAUCER *Pars. T.* ⁋388 For sothe o manere gentrie is for to preise that apparailleth mannes corage with vertues and moralitees. **1581** CAMPION in *Confer.* IV. (1584) D d iv, The wise men of the Gentiles did alledge their moralities as a cause of their election. **1684** Z. CAWDREY *Cert. Salvation* 26 A person..of such eminent Moralities and Intellectuals. **1819** BYRON *Juan* I. xx, Neglect, indeed, requires a saint to bear it, And such, indeed, she was in her moralities.

3. a. Moral discourse or instruction; a moral lesson or exhortation. Now chiefly in disparaging sense, moralizing.

c **1386** CHAUCER *Pars. Prol.* 38 If that yow list to heere Moralitee and vertuous mateere..I wol fayn..Do yow plesaunce leefful. **1509** HAWES *Past. Pleas.* XI. (Percy Soc.) 39 They fayned no fable without reason, For reasonable is al theyr moralitie. **1526** *Pilgr. Perf.* (W. de W. 1531) 5 We haue not taken theyr errours..but all moralytees and instruccyons of good maner and pollicy. **1625** T. H[AWKINS] *(title)* Odes of Horace.., Contayning much morallity, and sweetnesse. **1648** BOYLE *Seraph. Love* xx. (1700) 125 The excellent Moralities, couched in those ingenious Emblems. *a* **1704** T. BROWN *Walk round Lond., Coffee-Houses* (1709) 37 We pop'd into *Old Man's* just as I had ended my Morality. **1837–9** HALLAM *Hist. Lit.* II. II. v. §58 (1854) 120 Too often he [Hunnis] falls into trivial morality. **1841** D'ISRAELI *Amen. Lit.* I. 285 The *Confessio Amantis*..; a singular miscellany of allegory, of morality, and of tales. **1877** MRS. OLIPHANT *Makers Flor.* iii. 68 Quaint monkish moralities and scriptural quotations. **1889** RUSKIN *Præterita* III. 147 What is only a dream in Chaucer, becomes to us, understood from Scott, a consummate historical morality and truth.

†**b.** Moral sense or interpretation (see MORAL *a.*); also, the moral (of a fable, etc.). *Obs.*

c **1386** CHAUCER *Nun's Pr. T.* 620 But ye that holden this tale a folye,..Taketh the moralite goode men. **1447** BOKENHAM *Seyntys* (Roxb.) 46 Yf yt lyke on to moralyte To draw ye names of the progenytours Of marye. *c* **1470** HENRYSON *Mor. Fab.* II. (*Town & C. Mouse*) xxx, Freindis, ye may find..In to this fabill ane gude moralitie. **1523** FITZHERB. *Husb.* Prol., But who that redeth in the boke of the moralytes of the chesse, shal therby perceyue, that [etc.]. **1622** DRAYTON *Poly-olb.* xxi. 197 Orpheus, whose sweet Harpe..Intised Trees, and Rocks, to follow him along: Th' moralitie of which, is that [etc.]. **1623** COCKERAM III. s.v. *Aglaia*, The morallity of this inuention was to expresse the cheerfull conuersation which ought to be amongst friends.

c. Moral truth or significance.

1773 GOLDSM. *Stoops to Conq.* v, *Tony.* Ecod, mother, all the parish says you have spoiled me, and so you may take the fruits on't..*Hard.* There's morality, however, in his reply.

†**4. a.** A literary composition or artistic representation inculcating a moral lesson; a moralizing commentary; a moral allegory. *Obs.*

c **1430** LYDG. *Min. Poems* (Percy Soc.) 117 The moralite of the hors, the goose, and the sheepe, translated by Dan Johne

Lidgate. **1599** THYNNE *Animadv.* (1875) 28 Molinet, the frenche auctor of the moralytye vppon the Romante of the roose. **1627** DRAYTON *Moon-Calf* in *Agincourt*, etc. 176 *margin*, The morallity of mother Bumbyes tale. *a* **1649** DRUMM. OF HAWTH. *Fam. Ep.* Wks. (1711) 140 She presented..a fair Face,..but on the other Side..was the Image of Death; by which Morality [*printed* Mortality] he surpassed the others [*i.e.* other painters of the same subject], more than they did him by Art.

b. *Hist.* Used by mod. writers as the distinctive name for the species of drama (popular in the 16th c.) in which some moral or spiritual lesson was inculcated, and in which the chief characters were personifications of abstract qualities.

App. adopted in the 18th c. from French literary historians; the F. *moralité* had this sense in the 16th c., but in English we find only *moral* and *moral play*.

1773 (*half-title to reprint of J. Skot's ed.*), Everyman. A Morality. **1801** STRUTT *Sports & Past.* III. ii. 113 When the mysteries ceased to be played, the subjects for the drama were not taken from historical facts, but consisted of moral reasonings in praise of virtue and condemnation of vice, on which account they were called moralities. **1858** R. A. VAUGHAN *Ess. & Rem.* I. 55 In one of our old English Moralities, the seven cardinal virtues are represented as besieged by the seven deadly sins.

5. a. The doctrine or system concerned with conduct and duty; moral science.

c **1449** PECOCK *Repr.* II. iv. (Rolls) 155 Sum other vntrewe opinioun of men is such that for it her conuersacioun schal not be maad the worse moralli, or ellis not aȝens notable, good, vertuose moralte. **1605** BACON *Adv. Learn.* II. xviii. §2 The end of Moralitie, is to procure the Affections to obey Reason, and not to inuade it. **1690** LOCKE *Hum. Und.* III. xi. §16 Upon this ground it is I am bold to think, that morality is capable of demonstration, as well as mathematicks. **1726** SWIFT *Gulliver* II. vii, The learning of this people.. consisting only in morality, history, poetry, and mathematics. **1841** ELPHINSTONE *Hist. Ind.* I. 237 Principles ..on which every theory in physics and every maxim in morality depends.

b. *pl.* Points of ethics, moral principles or rules.

1605 BACON *Adv. Learn.* II. xxii. §7 Wherin they ought to haue handled Custom, Exercise, Habit, Educacion [etc.]: theis as they haue determinate vse, in moralityes, from these the mind suffereth. **1712** ADDISON *Spect.* No. 447 ¶4 If we consider attentively this Property of Human Nature, it may instruct us in very fine Moralities. *a* **1854** H. REED *Lect. Eng. Lit.* xii. (1855) 405 The letters of Lord Chesterfield make a book of the minor moralities, and the major immoralities of life. **1861** MILL *Utilit.* v. 89 The moralities which protect every individual from being harmed by others.

c. A particular system of morals.

1680 BURNET *Rochester* (1692) 38 The two maxims of his morality were, that [etc.]. **1695** LOCKE *Reas. Chr.* (1696) 271 He that shall collect all the Moral Rules of the Philosophers ..will find them to come short of the Morality delivered by our Saviour. **1781** GIBBON *Decl. & F.* xxxi. III. 261 He soon experienced, that the principles of honour and integrity, which might regulate the ordinary conduct of Constantius, were superseded by the loose doctrines of political morality. **1867** FREEMAN *Norm. Conq.* (1877) I. ii. 33 The morality of the Gospel had a direct influence upon the politics of the age. **1898** *Westm. Gaz.* 26 Sept. 8/1 In these days of lying advertisements, when 'commercial morality' has become almost synonymous with ordinary immorality.

d. Ethical aspect (of a question).

1869 FREEMAN *Norm. Conq.* (1875) III. xii. 253 The morality of the question is easily summed up.

6. The quality or fact of being moral.

a. Conformity to the moral law; moral goodness or rightness; (of writings) good moral tendency. Now *rare* or *Obs.*

1592 G. HARVEY *Pierce's Super.* 104 Oh, that learning were euer married to such discretion;..contention to such moralitie. **1691–8** NORRIS *Pract. Disc.* (1711) III. 181 The Good represents the Morality of His Nature. **1715** ADDISON *Freeholder* No. 6 ¶7 Euripides..tho' famous for the morality of his plays, had introduced a person, who, being reminded of an oath he had taken, reply'd, 'I swore with my mouth, but not with my heart'. **1772** *Junius Lett.* lxviii. (1820) 338 Instances..of genius and morality united in a lawyer..are distinguished by their singularity.

†**b.** Of a Mosaic enactment: The fact of being part of the moral law (see MORAL *a.* 4). *Obs.*

1656 in *Burton's Diary* (1828) I. 25 By the Mosaic law, blasphemers were to be stoned to death. The morality of this remains. *a* **1662** HEYLIN *Laud* (1668) 124 These Doctrinal heads [of Puritanism], being ten in number, related to the indispensible morality of the Lords-day-Sabbath [etc.].

†**c.** The quality or fact of being a 'moral action' (see MORAL *a.* 6 a), i.e. of being morally either good or evil. *Obs.*

a **1716** SOUTH *Serm.* (1727) II. 326 Did Christ himself ever assume such a Power, as to alter the Morality of Actions, and to transform Vice into Virtue..by his bare Word? **1736** BUTLER *Anal.* I. iii. 72 The..advantage in this case is gained by the action itself, not by the morality, the virtuousness or viciousness of it.

7. a. Moral conduct; usually, good moral conduct; behaviour conformed to the moral law; moral virtue. (Sometimes in contradistinction to the higher excellences of the Christian character.)

1609 B. JONSON *Sil. Wom.* III. i. (1620) F 2 b, Goe to, behaue your selfe distinctly, and with good moralitie. **1658** T. WALL *Charact. Enemies Ch.* 59 It is hatred of sin makes them so malicious: It is separation from the wicked that makes them void of Christian society and common Morality. *a* **1699** STILLINGFL. *Serm.* Wks. 1710 I. viii. 117 They [*sc.* the Jews in their spiritual pride] had the purity of his ordinances,..whereas all others, they thought, served God only with their own Inventions, or placed their Religion in dull morality. **1791** BP. HORNE *Charge to Clergy of Norwich* 14 And here, by Religion is to be understood the Christian Religion; and by Morality, such good works as are independent of it. **1814** JANE AUSTEN *Mansf. Park* ix, We do not look in great cities for our best morality. **1824** HOGG *Conf. Sinner* 214 The most popular of all their preachers of morality. *Ibid.* 216 It was easy to see that the true Gospel preachers joined all on one side, and the upholders of pure morality and a blameless life on the other. **1877** E. R. CONDER *Bas. Faith* i. 19 Justice, truth, love, duty, virtue —in one word, morality. **1878** R. W. DALE *Lect. Preach.* viii. 243 There may be morality where there is no religion; but that there should be religion where there is no morality, is impossible. **1887** TENNYSON in *Mem.* (1897) II. 337 Evil must come upon us headlong, if morality tries to get on without religion.

b. Used as a nickname or a mock-title for one who assumes airs of virtue.

1672 MARVELL *Reh. Transp.* I. Wks. (Grosart) III. 98, I am resolved, instead of his *Grace*, to call him alwayes his *Morality*. **1806** SURR *Winter in Lond.* (ed. 3) III. 138, I suspect that his own son, young morality, will require a little of his parental inspection.

8. *attrib.*, as **morality squad**, in Canada, a municipal or provincial police unit dealing with infractions of legislation concerning prostitution, pornography, etc. So ***morality officer***, etc.

1963 J. N. HARRIS *Weird World Wes Beattie* (1964) x. 119 He called an acquaintance on the morality squad of the Ontario Provincial Police in order to get the low-down on the obscene film racket. **1967** *Canad. News Facts* 4 Dec. 183, 18 arrested on gambling charges... Eight of the men were arrested in Montreal by the Montreal morality squad. **1970** *Toronto Daily Star* 24 Sept. 7/5 Man appears to need some censorship to protect himself from his baser tastes. I trust the morality squad will continue its good work. **1976** *Globe & Mail* (Toronto) 17 Jan. 12/4 Pasquale Zappia..died of a heart attack Thursday while being questioned by an Ottawa police morality officer outside a restaurant.

moralizable (mɒrəˈlaɪzəb(ə)l), *a.* [f. MORALIZE *v.* + -ABLE.] That can be rendered moral or expressed in terms of morality; amenable to moralizing.

1916 F. VON HÜGEL *German Soul* ii. 64 They are not really moral, nor even moralisable. **1961** J. N. FINDLAY *Values & Intentions* ix. 399 Religion can be seen thus to be intrinsically moralizable.

moralization (mɒrəlaɪˈzeɪʃən). [ad. late L. *mōrālīzātiōn-em*, f. *mōrālīzāre* to MORALIZE. Cf. mod.F. *moralisation.*] The action of moralizing.

1. a. Moral interpretation; a moralizing commentary (*of* or *upon* a book of Scripture, etc.). **b.** Indulgence in moral reflection; a moralizing discourse.

c **1420** LYDG. *Assembly of Gods* 860 Moralizacion of Holy Scripture. **1509** HAWES *Past. Pleas.* v. (Percy Soc.) 24 Who knewe gramer wythout impediment Shoulde perfytely have intelleccion Of a lytterall sense and moralyzacion. **1531** ELYOT *Gov.* I. xxvi, If the players haue radde the moralization of the chesse. **1599** THYNNE *Animadv.* (1875) 74 The learned molinet, in his moralizatione of that Romant. **1641** BAKER *Chron.* (1674) 179/2 William Wallis.. who made a Book of Moralizations upon Ovid's Metamorphosis. **1795** R. ANDERSON *Johnson* 201 These compositions..evince..that happy art of moralization, by which he gives to well-known incidents the grace of novelty and the force of instruction. **1820** *Retrospective Rev.* II. 5 [In Sidney's *Arcadia*] there is perceptible an air..of melancholy yet not gloomy moralization. **1846** WRIGHT *Ess. Mid. Ages* II. xii. 62 In the thirteenth century these stories with moralizations were already used extensively by the monks.

2. The action of making moral or more moral; the process of becoming moral.

1848 *Tait's Mag.* XV. 325 None ever laboured more for their happiness and moralization. **1879** H. SPENCER *Data of Ethics* vii. §46. 127 The sense of duty or moral obligation.. will diminish as fast as moralization increases. **1884** *Ch. Reformer* 201 Those who would work at the moralization of our literature. **1892** MONTEFIORE *Hibbert Lect.* ii. 101 The moralization of Yahveh's character was by no means completed at the close of the pre-prophetic period.

moralize (ˈmɒrəlaɪz), *v.* [a. F. *moraliser*, ad. late L. *mōrālīzāre*, f. *mōrāl-is*: see MORAL *a.* and -IZE.]

1. *trans.* To interpret morally or symbolically; to explain the moral meaning of; to point the moral of; to make (an event, etc.) the subject of moral reflection.

c **1450** in *Lydgate's Nightingale* 1 This [fable of the nightingale] ys moralysyd vn-to Cryste. **1593** G. HARVEY *Pierce's Super.* 18 My leisure will scarsely serue to moralize Fables of Beares, Apes, and Foxes; (some men can giue a shrewd gesse at a courtly allegory). **1594** SHAKS. *Rich. III*, III. i. 83 Thus, like the formall Vice, Iniquitie, I morallize two meanings in one word. **1600** —— *A.Y.L.* II. i. 44 But what said Iaques? Did he not moralize this spectacle? **1608** WILLET *Hexapla Exod.* 465 Some doe moralize it; that by boring the eare is signified [etc.]. **1692** R. L'ESTRANGE *Fables* I. cccxxviii. 286 This Fable is Moraliz'd in the Holy Gospel it self. *a* **1711** KEN *Hymnotheo* Poet. Wks. 1721 III. 293 The Herd of Gods, which his Olympus stor'd, He mean'd, should moraliz'd be, not ador'd. **1841** TRENCH *Parables* xii. (1877) 245 Christ moralizes the whole parable ..with those solemn words, 'For many are called, but few are chosen'.

†**2.** Of an incident, event, etc.: To exemplify or instance the moral of (a fable, saying, etc.). *Obs.*

1597 J. KING *On Jonas* (1618) 119 Nay, but there shall be a king ouer vs; yet it may be, when they haue their wish, the fable will be moralized, and verefied vpon them; A storke was giuen them. **1601** BP. W. BARLOW *Eagle & Body* (1609) B ij, I speake..onely to shewe how it doth moralize this Prouerbe, That where the Body is, the Eagles will Resort. **1608–11** BP. HALL *Medit. & Vows* ii. §4 (1624) 23 That which is said of the Elephant,..we see well moralized, in men of euill conscience.

†**b.** To supply (a poem) with a moral or subject for moralizing. *Obs.*

1590 SPENSER *F.Q.* I. Induct. i, Fierce warres and faithful loves shall moralize my song. **1706** PRIOR *Ode to Queen* i, And with his Prince's Arms He moraliz'd his Song.

†**c.** To make (something) the subject of an allegory; to symbolize. *Obs.*

1652 *Persuasive to Compliance* 12 Not sparing Jupiter himselfe, whom they chalenge to have wrested the Celestiall Monarchy from his Father Saturne: (in which is morallized the unnaturalnesse of Ambition).

3. *intr.* To indulge in moral reflection; to found a moral (*on* or *upon* an event, etc.).

1649 OGILBY *Virg. Georg.* I. (1684) 51 *note*, Seneca takes occasion thus to morallize: The Land..is divided into Regions..; the Chief Good hath its place too. **1692** R. L'ESTRANGE *Fables* ccclxxxix. 362 The Pretended Criminal began now to Moralize upon the Story. **1710** STEELE *Tatler* No. 170 ¶5, I know you came Abroad only to Moralize and make Observations. **1813** SHELLEY *Q. Mab.* 22 A gloomy theme, On which the lightest heart might moralize. **1824** W. IRVING *T. Trav.* I. 343 No one can moralize better after a misfortune has taken place. **1886** KIPLING *Departm. Ditties*, etc. (1888) 82 So we said He was a victim to the Demon Drink, And moralized upon him.

b. *trans.* To change the condition or aspect of (a person or thing) by moral discourse or reflection. Const. *into*, *out of*.

1722 MITCHELL *Ep. Death Dalrymple* 9 Nor is it Rudeness for the Friendly Muse To moralize Affliction into Use. **1796** BURNEY *Mem. Metastasio* II. 274 Whom he very anxiously tries to moralize into philosophy and tranquillity. **1807–8** W. IRVING *Salmag.* (1824) 275 In a similar humour was Launcelot at present, and I knew the only way was to let him moralise himself out of it.

4. To make moral; to give a moral quality to or affect the moral quality of (actions, feelings).

1592 LYLY *Gallathea* III. iii, *Astron.* Thy thoughts shall be metamorphosed, and made haile fellowes with the Gods. *Raffe.* O fortune! I feele my very braines moralized. **1627** SANDERSON *Serm.* (1681) I. 282 God..seldom bringeth a man from the wretchedness of forlorn nature,..but..by His restraining grace..He doth correct nature, and moralize it. **1647** CUDWORTH *Serm. 1 Cor. xv.* 57 (1676) 93 Such other laws and circumstances as moralize humane actions. **1682** SIR T. BROWNE *Chr. Mor.* III. §7 Good and bad Stars moralize not our Actions. **1762** *Gentl. Mag.* 86 To raise the thoughts and moralize the mind. **1861** MILL *Utilit.* v. 77 When moralized by the social feeling it [the natural feeling of retaliation] only acts in the directions conformable to the general good.

5. To improve the morals of.

1633 PRYNNE *Histrio-m.* 106 If Stage-playes doe onely discover Vices for to make them odious, then those lascivious Pagans who most delighted in them, should have beene meliorated and morralized by them. **1647** N. BACON *Disc. Govt. Eng.* I. xlvi. (1739) 76 Henry the first..being trained up..in the English garb, moralized by Learning, and now admitted to the Throne. **1723** WELSTED *Steele's Consc. Lovers* Prol., 'Tis yours with Breeding..To Chasten Wit, and Moralize the Stage. **1817** COLERIDGE *Biog. Lit.* xxii. (1882) 217 For the communication of pleasure is the introductory means by which alone the poet must expect to moralize his readers. **1840** THACKERAY *Paris Sk.-bk.* (1869) 250 Was any man who saw the show [the execution of a murderer] deterred..or moralised in any way? **1891** W. J. GREENSTREET tr. *Guyau's Educ. & Heredity* 96 Not only individuals, but whole races are moralised or demoralised.

moralized (ˈmɒrəlaɪzd), *ppl. a.* [-ED[1].]

1. a. Morally or symbolically applied or interpreted. **b.** Made instructive in morals.

c **1412** HOCCLEVE *De Reg. Princ.* 2111 There is a booke.. That 'the Chesse moralisede' cleped is. **1498** *Lydgate's Assembly of Gods, Interpr. Names Gods* end, Thus endeth this lytell moralized treatyse. **1601** BP. W. BARLOW *Eagle & Body* (1609) D iij, These moralized Eagles. **1865** TYLOR *Early Hist. Man.* xii. 342 A story of which the European fable..might be a mere moralized remnant.

2. Of a man or his attributes: Made moral.

1647 W. LYFORD *Transl. Sinner* (1648) 4 Moralized Christians, which have a forme of knowledge and of the truth in the Law. **1648** JENKYN *Blind Guide* i. 3 Thousands of moralliz'd heathens..would blush. **1656** T. WATSON *One Thing Necessary* 70 A moraliz'd man is but a tame divell. **1677** W. HUBBARD *Narrative* II. 48 There are two principal Actors among the Indians..who are said to be..a strange kind of moralized Salvages. **1831** *Fraser's Mag.* III. 54 [His] finely moralized mind, elevated with the purest religious sentiments, is exactly fitted for such a subject. **1892** MONTEFIORE *Hibbert Lect.* i. 38 Resembling rather the insensate violence of angered nature, than the reasonable indignation of a moralized personality.

†**3.** Having morals of a specified kind. *Obs.*

1650 H. MORE *Observ.* in *Enthus. Tri.*, etc. (1656) 145 Do you think that they are..so singularly moralized, that Socrates-like, if an Asse kick they will not kick again? **1652** GAULE *Magastrom.* 15 Why God would call the Magi..to Christ? Not because they were wisemen or men well morrallized.

moralizer (ˈmɒrəlaɪzə(r)). [f. MORALIZE *v.* + -ER[1].] One who or something which moralizes.

1. One who is given to making moral reflections.

1600 NASHE *Summer's Last Will* Prol. B 2 Moralizers, you that wrest a neuer meant meaning, out of euery thing, applying all things to the present time, keepe your attention

for the common Stage. **1742** RICHARDSON *Pamela* IV. 120 But what a Moraliser am I! **1825** COLERIDGE *Aids Refl.* (1848) I. 26 There sometimes occurs an apparent play on words, which not only to the moralizer, but even to the philosophical etymologist, appears more than a mere play. **1837** HAWTHORNE *Twice-told T.* (1851) I. xvi. 248 The old man looks eastward, and (for he is a moralizer) frames a simile.

2. A moralizing agent.

1840 CHALMERS in Hanna *Mem.* (1851) IV. xi. 206 The Gospel..is the most powerful and efficient of all moralizers.

moralizing (ˈmɒrəlaɪzɪŋ), *vbl. sb.* [-ING¹.]

†**1.** The action of explaining the moral meaning of (a fable or tale); a moralization, moral. *Obs.*

c **1422** HOCCLEVE *Jereslaus' Wife* Moralization 12 Where is the moralizynge..Bycome heere-of? Was ther noon in the book Out of the which þat thow this tale took?

2. The action of making moral.

1677 GALE *Crt. Gentiles* II. III. Pref., There are many excellent Philosophemes and Notions..which..may be of great use..for the moralising of persons and republics. **1691–8** NORRIS *Pract. Disc.* (1711) III. 227 Such studies as signify little or nothing to the moralizing of their Minds.

3. Moral reflection; an instance of this.

1692 R. L'ESTRANGE *Fables* ccxcvi. 258 And let there be No Moralizing in the Pulpit upon the Fable. **1727** DE FOE *Syst. Magic* I. i. (1840) 31 But to leave moralizing,..I go on with my story. **1870** MRS. STOWE *Oldtown* xxviii, It will be seen by these edifying moralisings how eminently scriptural was the course of Sam's mind.

moralizing (ˈmɒrəlaɪzɪŋ), *ppl. a.* [-ING².] That moralizes, in the senses of the verb.

1796 COLERIDGE *To Yng. Friend* Poems (1877) I. 154 It were a lot divine To cheat our noons in moralizing mood. **1816** *Remarks Eng. Mann.* 79 A nation of moralizing, thinking people. **1825** SOUTHEY *Paraguay* III. xx, A land Which..should one day Take up from thence his moralizing lay. **1869** LECKY *Europ. Mor.* (1880) I. ii. 291 We find a society almost absolutely destitute of moralising institutions. **1902** J. H. ROSE *Napoleon* xii. 295 He [*i.e.* the legislator] will turn by preference to education as a more potent moralizing agency. **1904** *Speaker* 23 Apr. 93/1 Thackeray and the other moralizing theorists were wrong.

Hence ˈ**moralizingly** *adv.*

1782 ELIZ. BLOWER *Geo. Bateman* III. 180 They likewise moralizingly observed, that [etc.]. **1865** *Daily Tel.* 15 Dec. 5/3 Moralisingly, she added,..There were girls since the world began [etc.].

moralled (ˈmɒrəld), *ppl. a.* Also **moraled**. [f. MORAL *sb.* + -ED².] Having morals (of a specified kind, indicated by a prefixed adv. or adj.).

1614 W. B. *Philosopher's Banquet* (ed. 2) 98 The king thus morald, he was vnfit to gouern others. **1826** *Westm. Rev.* VI. 18 This vice..is well touched on by Locke, in the same finely toned and finely moraled discourse. **1863** COWDEN CLARKE *Shaks. Char.* x. 257 He is light-moraled, loose-conscienced. **1884** *Pall Mall G.* 5 Aug. 5/2 Silenus..sought consolation in wine, and thus..became the agreeable and well-informed but loosely-moralled old person who is represented in..Virgil's Eclogues.

†ˈ**moraller**. *Obs. rare*⁻¹. [f. MORAL *v.* + -ER¹.] A moralizer.

1604 SHAKS. *Oth.* II. iii. 301 Come, you are too seuere a Moraller.

moralless (ˈmɒrəllɪs), *a.* [f. MORAL *sb.* + -LESS.] Without a moral.

1884 *Mag. Art* Feb. 150/1 The artist of independent and moral-less purpose. **1898** G. A. SMITH *Drummond* vi. (1899) 140 Drummond had never treated religion..as if it were utterly without the great law of life, a moral-less magic of arbitrary formulas.

morallon: see MORILLON.

morally (ˈmɒrəlɪ), *adv.* [f. MORAL *a.* + -LY².]

†**1.** In a moral sense; with a moral meaning or purpose. *Obs. rare.*

a **1400** HYLTON *Scala Perf.* (W. de W. 1494) II. xliii, Whan Jhesu is mayster it is expowned and declared litterally: morally: mystily: and heuenly. **1509** HAWES *Past. Pleas.* xiii. (Percy Soc.) 51 They take no hede nothyng they wryte, Whyche morally dyd so nobly endyte, Reprovyng vyce.

2. In respect of moral character or conduct; from the point of view of ethics or of the moral law; with reference to moral responsibility.

c **1449** PECOCK *Repr.* II. (Rolls) 155 Sum vntrewe opinioun of men is such that for it her conuersacioun is the worse morali. **1526** *Pilgr. Perf.* (W. de W. 1531) 153 What so euer vertue enclyneth or moueth man or woman morally to moo thynges than one perteyneth to the actyue lyfe. **1634** *Documents agst. Prynne* (Camden) 40 They are all able umpyres of all vices and vertues, of things that are morally good or evill. *a* **1716** SOUTH *Serm.* (1727) II. 321 For generally speaking, to take away the Life of a Man, is neither morally Good, nor Morally Evil. **1790** BURKE *Fr. Rev.* 28 The house of lords..is not morally competent to dissolve the house of commons. **1841** MYERS *Cath. Th.* III. §9. 33 The testimony of the best men morally as to the immediate origin of their thoughts and feelings may conceivably not be trustworthy. **1859** KINGSLEY *Misc.* (1860) I. 124 A government is morally bound to keep itself in existence. **1897** MARY KINGSLEY *W. Africa* 499 Morally speaking, the African is far from being the brutal fiend he is often painted.

3. In accordance with morality; virtuously.

a **1540** BARNES *Wks.* (1573) 312/2 Those poore men that marry, be cause they would not all onely lyue vertuously beefore God, but also morally before the world. **1685** DRYDEN *Sylvæ* Pref. a2 To take away rewards and punishments, is only a pleasing prospect to a Man, who resolves before hand not to live morally.

4. On grounds of moral evidence.

1645 [see CERTAIN *a.* 4]. **1647** CLARENDON *Hist. Reb.* VI. §76 It being morally sure, that the Earl of Essex would put himself in their way. **1660** JER. TAYLOR *Duct. Dubit.* I. v. Rule ii. §5 But there is a Negative doubt which is called Morally negative; that is, when there is no way of being readily and clearly determined, but yet the doubt is founded upon some slight conjecture, and no more. **1660** R. COKE *Power & Subj.* 95 God did scarce ever leave men so destitute, but they were morally certain to whom they did owe their topical and natural obedience. **1667** in *10th Rep. Hist. MSS. Comm.* App. v. 48 The said Manley was gone for England, and, as he himselfe hath given out and is morally supposed, will not returne. **1692** LUTTRELL *Brief Rel.* (1857) II. 462 He was morally assured of success. **1782** MISS BURNEY *Cecilia* III. iv, It's quite morally impossible I should raise such a sum. **1808** LIEUT. COL. SYMES in J. Moore *Narr. Campaign Spain* (1809) 131 It is morally impossible that they can stand before a line of French infantry. **1869** *Bradshaw's Railway Manual* XXI. 174 It is morally certain that there will be enough net income at the end of next half-year to pay the full year's interest. **1966** 'R. STANDISH' *Widow Hack* ix. 97 Morally certain that I had not been seen, I returned to my car.

5. *Comb.*: **morally-given** *a.*, whose inclinations are on the side of morality.

1896 A. MORRISON *Child of the Jago* 25 So well-conducted, morally-given and respectable a gathering.

moralness (ˈmɒrəlnɪs). *rare.* [f. MORAL *a.* + -NESS.] The state of being moral; morality. Also *personified.*

1642 D. ROGERS *Naaman* 10 It is not the moralnes of any people, nor their vertuous qualities. **1889** *Univ. Rev.* Jan. 91 Go, mask of Pride and mannered Moralness!

‖**moran** (ˈmɒrən). Also **Il-moran**. [Masai.] The warrior group of the Masai tribe which comprises the younger unmarried males. Also a member of this group.

1885 J. THOMSON *Through Masăi Land* (ed. 3) x. 425 A certain rite, better known in Africa than in Europe, was performed; and..he was an El-moran—a warrior. **1902** H. H. JOHNSTON *Uganda Protectorate* II. xix. 822 In former days, before the Masai warriors, called 'El Mórran', started on an expedition, they would fortify their courage with a war medicine, which was said to be the bark of *Acacia verrugosa*. **1905** A. C. HOLLIS *Masai* 298 Their hair is allowed to grow, and as soon as it has grown long enough to plait, they are called Il-muran (warriors). **1947** *E. African Ann.* 1946–7 43/1 The 'moran' are the warrior age-grade... In the past the 'moran' constituted a free military organization within the tribe. **1960** *Times* 8 Nov. 13/2 One Kikuyu was killed and a score were injured by Masai *moran*. **1975** *Times* 9 Apr. 12/8 The *moran* system of organized adolescence.

morass (mɒˈræs). Also 7 **moras(e, morasse, morost**. [a. Du. *moeras*, earlier *moerasch*, an altered form (influenced by *moer* MOOR *sb.*¹) of MDu. *marasch*, *maras*, a. OF. *maresc*, *marais*: see MARISH. Cf. MLG. *moras*, early mod.G. *morasz*, from 17th c. *morast* (whence the Eng. form *morost*); from LG. are Sw. *moras*, Da. *morads*.

The word is now confined to literary use, exc. in some parts of the West Indies, where it survives with the pronunciation (ˈmɒrəs).]

1. A wet swampy tract, a bog, marsh; occas. in generalized sense, boggy land.

1655 FULLER *Hist. Camb.* v. 72 Athens..was seated in a Morase or Fenny place. **1657** R. LIGON *Barbadoes* (1673) 25 There remains, making a great part of that flat, a kinde of Bog or Morost. **1691** LUTTRELL *Brief Rel.* (1857) II. 199 They..are making canalls to drain the moras. **1730–46** THOMSON *Autumn* 476 Nor the deep morass Refuse, but thro' the shaking wilderness Pick your nice way. **1815** SCOTT *Guy M.* i, The sighs of the wind as it passed along the dreary morass. **1860** HOOK *Lives Abps.* (1869) I. 355 Only a small portion of the country was under cultivation, the rest was morass or impenetrable forest.

fig. **1867** MACGREGOR *Voy. Alone* (1868) 64 The east end of London—that morass of vice, and sighs and savagery. **1884** GLADSTONE *Sp.* 28 Feb. (1885) 136 Let us not wander into the morasses and fogs of doubt.

2. *West Indian.* Short for *morass-weed*, q.v. in 3.

3. *attrib.*, as ***morass ground***, ***-way***; **morass ore**, bog iron ore; **morass-weed** *West Indian*, the aquatic plant *Ceratophyllum demersum*.

1712 E. COOKE *Voy. S. Sea* 149 This *Morass Ground was full of the largest Toads I ever saw. **1804–8** JAMESON *Syst. Min.* (1816) III. 294 *Morass-ore, or Friable Bog Iron-ore. Morasterz, Werner. **1817** T. THOMSON *Chem.* (ed. 5) III. 478 Morass Ore. **1675** OGILBY *Brit.* (1698) 2 Here bear to the Left, thro' a *morass-way..to Morton in the Marsh. **1756** P. BROWNE *Jamaica* 345 The Morass or *Morass-weed is very common in all the brackish waters of Jamaica. **1864** GRISEBACH *Flora W. Ind.* 785 Morass-weed.

morassic (mɒˈræsɪk), *a.* [f. MORASS + -IC.] Of, pertaining to, or characteristic of a morass; morassy.

1897 C. MACMILLAN in *Minnesota Bot. Stud.* (1894–8) I. 995 All of these morassic formations characterize quiet shores.

morassy (mɒˈræsɪ), *a.* [f. MORASS + -Y¹. Cf. Ger. *morastig*, earlier *marassig*.] Of or pertaining to a morass; having the characteristics of a morass; consisting of wet spongy ground; found in a morass. *morassy iron ore* = *morass ore*.

1699 DAMPIER *Voy.* II. I. 160 The Land on the backside of the Town seems to be morassy. **1784** DARWIN in *Phil. Trans.* LXXV. 3 Our next operation was to build a wall of clay against the morassy sides of the well. **1801** *Encycl. Brit. Suppl.* II. 240/1 Morassy iron ore. **1881** BLACKMORE *Christowell* (1882) II. x. 219 The ground was uneven, though not bouldery, nor morassy.

Morasthite (ˈmɒrəsθaɪt). Also **Morascite, Morashite, Morashtite, Morastite**. [f. *Moresheth* in Gath, name of the home town of Micah.] Epithet of Micah, the Judæan prophet of the 8th century B.C.

a **1390** WYCLIF *Micah* i. 1. The word of the Lord..is maad to Mycheas Morastites. **1535** COVERDALE *Jer.* xxvi, Micheas the Morascite, which was a prophet vnder Ezechias kinge of Iuda, spake. *Ibid. Micah* i, This is the worde of the Lorde, that came vnto Micheas the Morastite. **1611** BIBLE *Jer.* xxvi. 18 Micah the Morashite prophecied in the dayes of Hezekiah king of Iudah. *Ibid. Micah* i. 1 The word of the Lord..came to Micah the Morasthite in the dayes of Iotham, Ahaz, and Hezekiah. **1839** *Penny Cycl.* XV. 172/1 Micah..is called in the title to his prophecy the Morasthite. **1845** J. KITTO *Cyclopedia Biblical Lit.* II. 334/1 It is stated that Micah the Morasthite foretold the destruction of Jerusalem in the reign of Hezekiah. **1904** *Jewish Encycl.* VIII. 533/1 Micah..was a Morasthite; that is to say, a native of Moreshethgath. **1944** G. B. SHAW *Everybody's Political What's What?* xxvi. 231 The noble God of Micah the Morasthite. **1963** GRANT & ROWLEY *Hasting's Dict. Bible* 674 *Morashtite*,—a gentilic used in RV to designate the prophet Micah,..(AV *Morasthite*..); probably derived from Morsheth-gath.

morat (ˈmɔərət). *Antiq.* [ad. med.L. *mōrātum*, f. L. *mōr-us* mulberry: see -ATE¹.] A drink made of honey and flavoured with mulberries.

1807 SHARON TURNER *Hist. Anglo-Saxons* II. 52 The vessels of wine, mead, ale, pigment, morat and cyder. **1809** CAMPBELL *O'Connor's Child* iv, And kneeling pages offer'd up The Mórat in a golden cup. **1819** SCOTT *Ivanhoe* iii, Place the best mead,..the richest morat,..upon the board. **1842** SIR H. TAYLOR *Edwin the Fair* III. vii, Six meals a day, With morat and spiced ale, is generous living.

morate (ˈmɔəræt), *sb. Chem.* [f. L. *mōr-us* mulberry + -ATE¹.] A salt of moric acid.

1856 in MAYNE *Expos. Lex.* **1891** in *Syd. Soc. Lex.*

†ˈ**morate**, *a. Obs.* [ad. L. *mōrāt-us*, f. *mōr-ēs*: see MORAL *a.*] Mannered; well-mannered, respectably conducted, moral.

1652 GAULE *Magastrom.* xvii. 138 To see a man well morate so seldom applauded. *a* **1677** HALE *Prim. Orig. Man.* IV. vii. 355 So that the wiser and more morate part of Mankind were forced to set up Laws and Punishments, to keep the generality of Mankind in some tolerable order.

moration (mɒˈreɪʃən). *rare.* [ad. L. *morātiōn-em*, n. of action f. *morā-rī* to delay.] Delay, tarrying.

16.. SIR T. BROWNE *Pseud. Ep.* VI. x. (1658) 400 We shall ..say he [*sc.* the sun] is more powerful in the Northern Hemisphere, and in the Apogeum; for therein his moration [1646, p. 325 motion] is slower. **1839** *New Monthly Mag.* LV. 518 The sublime Obscure still lingered—a moration which failed not to raise some misgivings.

moratorial (mɒrəˈtɔərɪəl), *a.* [f. MORATORI(UM + -AL¹.] Pertaining to or payable in respect of a moratorium.

1914 *Economist* 7 Nov. 833/1 On the debts due to them and covered by the moratorium, they are entitled to a moratorial interest of 5 per cent.

moratorium (mɒrəˈtɔərɪəm). Pl. **-ia, -iums**. [mod.L., neut. of late L. *morātōrius*: see next.]

1. *Law.* A legal authorization to a debtor to postpone payment for a certain time.

1875 *Times* 28 Sept. 5/3 The merchants of Belgrade, taking advantage of the warlike rumours, have asked for a *moratorium*. **1884** *Pall Mall G.* 27 Aug. 5/2 The Vienna sugar firm..in demanding a *moratorium*..assumes that its assets will, in a year's time, be sufficiently valuable to pay the debts which it is now unable to liquidate. **1905** (Official Receiver in) *Author* XV. 233/2 The refusal of his largest unsecured creditors to consent to a *moratorium* of sufficient length to enable him to recover his position. **1932** *Sun* (Baltimore) 7 Sept. 8/2 There is little evidence that past Farm Board 'moratoriums' on sales of its commodity holdings, or its quota schemes to sift holdings into the markets in small lots, have buoyed the market for these commodities. **1972** *Times* 27 Jan. 14/4 Those who wanted to agree to moratoria to assist businesses in financial difficulties. **1973** *Nation Rev.* (Melbourne) 31 Aug. 1434/1 Will there be resolutions to the federal or sitdown moratoria in Collins street?

2. A postponement, an agreed delay, a deliberate temporary suspension (of some activity, etc.).

1932 *Sun* (Baltimore) 5 Sept. 1/2 The moratorium on picketing ordered by Milo Reno, of Des Moines, national leader of the strike, seemed virtually achieved when only on two highways near Sioux City were farmers turning back live stock and produce trucks. **1934** W. B. WOLFE *Nervous Breakdown* i. 2 In a nervous breakdown the whole personality declares a moratorium of normal activities, and both body and soul join in a cry for help. **1944** *Word Study* May 7/2 A moratorium on 'of course' sentences. **1956** *Jrnl. Amer. Psychoanal. Assoc.* Jan. 66 Societies offer..more or less sanctioned intermediary periods between childhood and adulthood, institutionalized *psycho-social moratoria*. **1957** *Observer* 25 Aug. 8/2 Their new proposal that nuclear tests should be suspended not for ten months but for two years... Under their plan, the launching of the first year's moratorium would depend on an East-West agreement to a partial disarmament plan covering several fields. **1961** I. MURDOCH *Severed Head* xiii. 113 For me they [*sc.* words] constituted rather a kind of moratorium, a momentary neutral zone where I could..absolutely rest. **1969** *Guardian*

13 Oct. 3/2 Moratorium-day on Vietnam..has so captured the attention that Wednesday is expected to see the most wide-spread political protest in America's history. 1970 *Daily Tel.* 29 Apr. 13/4 Could we not now have a moratorium on Dylan Thomas records? 1972 *Nature* 17 Mar. 94/1 A provision calling for a five-year moratorium on the killing of all ocean mammals.

moratory (ˈmɒrətərɪ), *a. Law.* [ad. late L. *morātōr-ius* serving to delay, f. *morā-rī* to delay: see -ORY. Cf. F. *moratoire*, It. *moratorio*.] Authorizing delay in payment.

1891 CHALMERS *Bills of Exchange* 149 By a French moratory law, passed in consequence of war, the maturity of bills payable in Paris is postponed three months.

Moratta, Morattoe, obs. forms of MAHRATTA.

moratto (mɒˈrætəʊ). ? *Obs.* Also 8 **morotto**, 9 **marotta**. A kind of pea.

1731 MILLER *Gard. Dict.* s.v. *Pisum*, The Spanish Morotto Pea... The Spanish Morotto..is a great Bearer, and a hardy Sort of Pea. 1789 J. FARLEY *Lond. Art of Cookery* (ed. 6) 163 Take a quart of green Moratto peas. 1824 LOUDON *Encycl. Gard.* (ed. 2) §3599 The egg, the moratto, the Prussian blue, and the rouncivals..are all very fine eating peas in young growth. 1835 *Trans. Horticult. Soc.* Ser. II. I. 386 Varieties of the Pea..Spanish Marotta.

Moratty, obs. form of MAHRATTI.

Moravian (mɒˈreɪvɪən), *sb.*¹ and *a.*¹ [f. med.L. *Moravia* Moray (ad. Gael. *Muireibh*) + -AN.]

A. *sb.* An inhabitant of Moray (in early use, one of the great divisions of Scotland; subsequently, a county occupying part of the territory formerly so named).

1577–87 HOLINSHED *Hist. Scot.* 52/2 When they were thus assembled, Britains, Scots, Picts, & Morauians on one part, and Romans..on the other. 1791 NEWTE *Tour Eng. & Scot.* 191 A striking difference between the Moravians and Aberdonians appears. 1836 SKENE *Highlanders Scot.* (1902) II. vi. 282 He easily succeeded in exciting the Moravians once more to revolt.

B. *adj.* Of or pertaining to Moray.

1897 C. RAMPINI *Hist. Moray & Nairn* i. 43 No period of Moravian history is more obscure than that which followed the accession of Malcolm Ceannmor.

Moravian (mɒˈreɪvɪən), *sb.*² and *a.*² [f. *Moravia* (med.L., f. *Morava* the river March), the English name of a portion of the former Austro-Hungarian empire, called in Ger. *Mähren* (now part of Czechoslovakia): see -AN.] **A.** *sb.*

1. An inhabitant of Moravia.

1555 [see LUSATIAN *sb.* and *a.*]. 1611 CORYAT *Crudities* sig. B1 A Noble Scholler..George Haunschildt of Furstenfeldt, a Morauian. 1788 GIBBON *Decl. & F.* V. 554 That..land was loosely occupied by the Moravians, a Sclavonian name and tribe. 1847 [see ZECHIAN].

2. A member or adherent of the 'Unity of Moravian brethren', a Protestant sect, founded early in the 18th c. in Saxony by emigrants from Moravia, and continuing the tradition of the *Unitas Fratrum*, a body holding Hussite doctrines, which had its chief seat in Moravia and Bohemia.

The virtual founder of the body was Count Zinzendorf, who was the patron of the Moravian refugees, and embraced their doctrines. The Moravians early obtained many adherents in England and the American colonies.

1746 WESLEY *Princ. Methodist* 10 There needs a little farther Proof, that I charge any dreadful Crimes on the Body of the Moravians. 1760 *Ann. Reg.* 108 Died.., in the 60th year of his age, Count Nicholas Lewis of Zinzendorff, founder and head of the sect of Moravians. 1777 JOHNSON 28 June in Boswell *Life* (1816) III. 130 He had a Moravian with him much of his time. 1809 BYRON *Bards & Rev.* 323 Moravians rise! bestow some meet reward On dull devotion. 1838 W. BELL *Dict. Law Scotl.*, *Moravians*, a sect of dissenters, who, on account of conscientious scruples, are permitted, in lieu of an oath, to make a solemn affirmation in courts of justice. 1871 LONGF. in *Life* (1891) III. 173 Meditating a third play,..the scene to be among the Moravians at Bethlehem, Pennsylvania.

B. *adj.*

1. Of or pertaining to Moravia.

1616 B. JONSON *Epigr.* cvii. *To Captain Hungry*, Fill them full Of your Morauian horse, Venetian bull. 1837 YOUATT *Sheep* v. 139 The Moravian sheep are larger.

2. Of or belonging to the sect of Moravians.

1739 W. STEPHENS *Jrnl.* 22 Aug. in *Colonial Rec. Georgia* (1906) IV. 393 An heavy Complaint being exhibited against the Moravian Brethren. 1745 WESLEY *Answ. to Ch.* 5, I have scarce heard one Moravian Brother own his Church to be wrong in any thing. 1777 J. ADAMS in *Fam. Lett.* (1876) 236 The Moravian mills in New Jersey. 1876 L. STEPHEN *Eng. Th. in 18th C.* I. vii. 351 He [Warburton] calls the Moravian hymn book 'a heap of blasphemous and beastly nonsense'.

Hence **Moˈravianism**, the religious system of the Moravians; **Moˈravianized** *ppl. a.*, influenced by Moravianism.

1820 SOUTHEY *Wesley* I. 344 The Areopagite was a favourite book among the Moravianized members. 1829 BENTHAM *Justice & Cod. Petit.*, *Abr. Petit. Justice* 21 Of Quakerism or Moravianism declaration can no longer serve. 1888 SCHAFF *Hist. Chr. Ch.* VI. VII. xcix. 598 Frederick the Great had as little sympathy with pietism and Moravianism as with Lutheranism and Calvinism.

moray (mɒˈreɪ). *U.S.* Also 7 **moreraye**, 8–9 **muray, murrey**, 9 **maray, murry** (*Cent. Dict.*). [? a. Pg. *moreia* = Sp. *morena*:—L. *muræna*.] A name for various tropical species of eel belonging to the family *Murænidæ*.

1624 CAPT. SMITH *Virginia* v. 172 Some of them yet knowne to the Americans, as the Purgoose, the Cauallo, the Gar-fish, Flying-fish and Morerayes. 1735 MORTIMER *Nat. Hist. Carol. & Bahamas* in *Phil. Trans.* XXXIX. 112 *Muræna maculata nigra*; the black Murrey. 1754 CATESBY *Nat. Hist. Carol.* II. 20 *Muræna maculata, nigra, & viridis*. The Muray. 1884 G. B. GOODE, etc. *Nat. Hist. Aquatic Anim.* 629 The Morays—Murænidæ... The most important species is the Speckled Moray, *Sidera ocellata*. 1897 H. G. CARLETON in *Outing* XXIX. 330/1 [Fishes of Florida.] There is the murrey, which is pronounced with the accent on the final.

morayne, morbery: see MURRAIN, MULBERRY.

morbid (ˈmɔːbɪd), *a.* [ad. L. *morbid-us*, f. *morb-us* disease, f. root of *morī* to die. Cf. F. *morbide*, It., Pg. *morbido*, Sp. *mórbido*.]

1. a. Of the nature of or indicative of disease; also, †productive of disease, morbific.

1656 H. MORE *Enthus. Tri.* (1712) 51 There may be very well a sanative and healing Contagion, as well as a morbid and venomous. 1748 THOMSON *Cast. Indol.* II. 705 Of morbid hue his features, sunk and sad; His hollow eyne shook forth a sickly light. 1771 T. PERCIVAL *Ess.* (1777) I. 8 Sylvius exults in the discovery that an acid is the sole morbid principle. 1799 UNDERWOOD *Dis. Children* (ed. 4) I. 44 Under such treatment, the morbid-snuffles has been found to yield in the course of two or three weeks. 1799 *Med. Jrnl.* I. 324 The variolous matter, first inserted by the puncture, like that of other morbid poisons, is not capable of being immediately absorbed. 1845 BUDD *Dis. Liver* 335 No morbid appearance could be discovered to account for his sudden death, except that [etc.]. 1883 *Nature* XXVII. 236 Evolution of microscopic organisms..in the dead body and morbid products.

fig. 1828 MACAULAY *Ess.*, *Hallam* (1851) I. 53 It may be quickened into morbid activity. It may be reasoned into sluggishness.

b. Of persons or animals, their parts, etc.: Affected by disease, diseased, unhealthy. ? *Obs.*

1731 ARBUTHNOT *Aliments* vi. (1735) 152 Tho' every Human Constitution is morbid, yet are their Diseases consistent with the common Functions of Life. 1750 JOHNSON *Rambler* No. 43 ¶1 Every man comes into the world morbid. 1846 G. E. DAY tr. *Simon's Anim. Chem.* II. 406 Morbid Bones.

c. ***morbid anatomy***: the anatomy of diseased organs or structures.

1804 ABERNETHY *Surg. Obs.* 6 The structure of tumours is a part of morbid anatomy which deserves to be examined. 1883 *Encycl. Brit.* XV. 816/1 This increase of knowledge is therefore due, not to auscultation alone, but to auscultation combined with morbid anatomy.

fig. 1851 WILLMOTT *Pleas. Lit.* 291 Books..belong to the study of the mind's morbid anatomy.

2. Of mental conditions, ideas, etc.: Unwholesome, sickly: chiefly applied to unreasonable feelings of gloom, apprehension, or suspicion. Hence of persons: Addicted to morbid feelings or fancies.

[1777 JOHNSON in Boswell *Life* (1816) III. 210 There must be a diseased mind, where there is a failure of memory at seventy. A man's head, Sir, must be morbid, if he fails so soon.] 1834 B'NESS BUNSEN in Hare *Life* (1879) I. x. 419 But that was a morbid vision, and has given way to the actual reality of so much good. 1842 KINGSLEY *Lett.* (1878) I. 59 Pray to God to save you from the temptations of morbid melancholy and unavailing regret. 1853 HUMPHREYS *Coin-Coll. Man.* xxvi. (1876) 392 Such a morbid kind of enthusiasm in this delightful science is much less common now. 1886 HALL CAINE *Son of Hagar* III. iv, You morbid little woman, you shall be happy again. 1889 RUSKIN *Præterita* III. 145 The morbid German fancies which proved so fatal to Carlyle. 1902 W. JAMES *Var. Relig. Exper.* ii. 46 The athletic attitude tends ever to break down, and it inevitably does break down even in the most stalwart when ..morbid fears invade the mind. *Ibid.* vi. 163 It seems to me that we are bound to say that morbid-mindedness ranges over the wider scale of experience. 1907 —— *Mem. & Stud.* (1911) 248 Dr. Janet has discussed five cases of morbid impulse. 1918 KIPLING *Land & Sea Tales* (1923) 113 My Sub's a morbid-minded young animal. 1922 JOYCE *Ulysses* 413 Those who are not so intimately acquainted with the minutiae of the municipal abattoir as this morbid-minded esthete. 1935 *Discovery* Nov. 346/2 The 'misfits' and perverts of morbid psychology.

3. *Painting.* Of flesh-tints: Painted with 'morbidezza'. [After It. *morbido*.]

1727–52 CHAMBERS *Cycl.*, *Morbid*, in painting, is particularly applied to fat flesh very strongly expressed.

‖**morbidezza** (mɔrbiˈdɛtsa). *Painting.* [It., f. *morbido* MORBID *a.*] **1.** Life-like delicacy in flesh-tints.

1624 WOTTON *Archit.* II. 89 A kinde of Tendernesse, by the Italians tearmed Morbidezza. 1686 AGLIONBY *Painting Illustr.* i. 21 There is a thing which the Italians call Morbidezza; The meaning of which word, is to Express the Softness, and tender Liveliness of Flesh and Blood. 1722 J. RICHARDSON *Statues, etc., Italy* 58 But the Beauty! the Morbidezza! the Thought and Expression! Good God! 1881 *Athenæum* 19 Feb. 271 Nor does the morbidezza which distinguishes every line of its perfect contours and characterizes all of them detract from the fineness of the whole.

2. *transf.* (esp. *Mus.*): delicacy, softness, sensibility, smoothness; sometimes (degenerating into) unwholesomeness, effeminacy, sickliness.

1890 E. DOWSON *Let. c* 31 Mar. (1967) 146 As for Browning!.. The subtility, the tact of omission, the Morbidezza! 1895 *Funk's Stand. Dict.*, *Morbidezza*,..*Mus.* Extreme delicacy: a direction to the performer. 1910 G. B. SHAW *Brieux* 3 The artistic morbidezza of Byron and Victor Hugo. 1934 *Times Lit. Suppl.* 3 May 324/2 In spite of a collective morbidezza on the part of Pansy's lovers, the characterization is clean cut. 1947 C. GRAY *Contingencies* 118 In spite of its *morbidezza* and romantic sentimentality it nevertheless retains the purity of line which is the hallmark of all classic art. 1960 C. S. LEWIS *Studies in Words* vi. 160 But in Mrs Radcliffe *sensibility* perhaps implies a more universal *morbidezza*. 1974 *Times* 13 May 14/7 'E lucevan le stelle' and 'O dolci mani' had true *morbidezza*.

morbidity (mɔːˈbɪdɪtɪ). [f. MORBID *a.* + -ITY.]

1. The quality or condition of being morbid; a morbid state or symptom; *pl.* morbid characteristics or ideas.

1721 in BAILEY. 1795 ANNA SEWARD *Lett.* (1811) IV. 364 To decry episodes of sentiment, allegory, or narrative, in didactic composition, is a singular morbidity in criticism. 1821 *New Monthly Mag.* II. 300 Our feelings..lie rankling and rotting into morbidity and corruption. 1825 *Ibid.* XV. 508 We trust he will endeavour to shake off his morbidities, whether real or assumed. 1884 *Spectator* 4 Oct. 1324/1 On the whole the story is singularly free from morbidity. 1904 A. C. BRADLEY *Shakesp. Trag.* 111 It makes all his cynicism, grossness and hardness appear to us morbidities.

2. *Med.* Prevalence of disease; the extent or degree of prevalence of disease in a district: = MORBILITY.

1882 *Quain's Med. Dict.* 998/2 *Morbidity*. This term, which is of recent introduction, is employed to denote the amount of illness existing in a given community; and, as 'mortality' expresses the death-rate, so 'morbidity' indicates the sick-rate, whether the diseases be fatal or not. 1896 *Allbutt's Syst. Med.* I. 30 The table which I have constructed in order to exhibit the relative morbidities of several groups of [French] departments. 1898 P. MANSON *Trop. Diseases* i. 1 [Malaria] is the principal cause of morbidity and death in the tropics and sub-tropics.

3. *attrib.*, as ***morbidity rate, statistics***.

1939 KURTZ & EDGERTON *Statistical Dict. Terms & Symbols* 108 **Morbidity rate*, the ratio of the number of cases of a particular disease in a year to the midyear population, usually expressed per 100,000. 1964 GOULD & KOLB *Dict. Social Sci.* 445/1 Frequently suitable criteria are provided by the effects of the illness upon everyday life. This is the only possible approach to aggregating morbidity rates from all conditions. 1971 *Brit. Med. Bull.* XXVII. 11/2 The respiratory morbidity-rates were far in excess of those found in English areas with comparable levels of pollution. 1964 GOULD & KOLB *Dict. Social Sci.* 445/1 The main uses of *morbidity statistics relate to the study of particular conditions, public health work, the economic aspects of illness, the cost of medical care or social security systems.

morbidize (ˈmɔːbɪdaɪz), *v. rare.* [f. MORBID *a.* + -IZE.] *trans.* To make morbid.

1850 L. HUNT *Autobiog.* I. ii. 62 They helped to morbidize all that was weak in my temperament.

morbidly (ˈmɔːbɪdlɪ), *adv.* [f. MORBID *a.* + -LY².] In a morbid manner.

1804 *Med. Jrnl.* XII. 380 Hence the vessels will be morbidly distended with blood. 1816 J. SCOTT *Vis. Paris* (ed. 5) 7 This indifference as to the past, chiefly arises out of a morbidly quick sensibility to the present. 1873 T. H. GREEN *Introd. Pathol.* (ed. 2) 56 The morbidly fatty liver is one which contains an abnormal quantity of fat. 1883 *Harper's Mag.* Dec. 116/1 You are morbidly afraid of death.

morbidness (ˈmɔːbɪdnɪs). [f. MORBID *a.* + -NESS.] The quality or state of being morbid.

1668 H. MORE *Div. Dial.* II. iv. (1713) 95 To which he adds..the Morbidness of the Seasons of the Year, and the frequentness of untimely Death. 1681 GLANVILL *Sadducismus* I. (1726) 103 By some Weakness or Morbidness of Mind tumbling into so foul an Error. 1791 BOSWELL *Johnson* an. 1777, To consider such indifference as a failure of reason, morbidness of mind. 1883 *Harper's Mag.* Mar. 633/2 The story [is] free from any element of morbidness.

morbiferal (mɔːˈbɪfərəl), *a. rare*⁻¹. [f. L. *morbifer* (f. *morb-us* disease + *-fer* bearing) + -AL¹.] Causing disease or illness.

1848 LOWELL *Biglow P.* Poems 1890 II. 1 Certificates to the virtues of various morbiferal panaceas.

morbiferous (mɔːˈbɪfərəs), *a.* = prec.

1806 *Med. Jrnl.* XV. 23 It may well be doubted, whether more sacrifices are not annually made to the injudicious administration of mercury, than to all the combined effects of the morbiferous poisons. 1808 *Ibid.* XIX. 199 The action of it upon the body is very extensive and morbiferous.

morbific (mɔːˈbɪfɪk), *a.* Also 7 **morbiffick, morbifique**, 7–8 **morbifick**. [ad. F. *morbifique* or its source mod.L. *morbificus*, f. *morbus* disease: see -FIC.] That produces disease; causing disease.

1652 FRENCH *Yorksh. Spa* iv. 43 Winter also, and a cold, crass slimy morbifick..matter,..forbid the use of cold water. 1706 BAYNARD in Sir J. Floyer *Hot & Cold Bath.* II. 300 Impregnated with morbifick Salts. 1804 ABERNETHY *Surg. Obs.* 127 It is probable that these morbific poisons may be absorbed without any evident ulcer. 1898 *Allbutt's Syst. Med.* V. 347 Pleurisy is due to irritation of the pleural membrane by certain morbific microbes or poisons.

¶**b.** Sometimes misused for: Diseased, pertaining to or caused by disease.

1658 R. FRANCK *North. Mem.* 295 Morbifick Deformities. 1800 *Med. Jrnl.* IV. 77 A morbific bone. 1858 *London Jrnl.* 27 Feb. 408/3 What a capital green-house for the production of morbific rarities.

†**morˈbifical**, *a. Obs.* [Formed as MORBIFIC *a.* + -AL¹.] = MORBIFIC.

1620 VENNER *Via Recta* viii. 190 They..doe at length.. produce morbificall affects. 1646 SIR T. BROWNE *Pseud. Ep.*

IV. iii. 183 The vessels whereby the morbificall matter is derived unto this membrane, are [etc.]. **1694** WESTMACOTT *Script. Herb.* 40 Its [the cedar's] perfuming odor corrects the malignity..of a morbifical air.

Hence **mor'bifically** *adv.*, with regard to the production of disease.

1716 M. DAVIES *Athen. Brit.* II. 340 The Astrological Influences of the Heavens are Morbifically and Politically as well as Learnedly declar'd against.

†**mor'bificous**, *a. Obs.*⁻¹ [f. mod.L. *morbificus* MORBIFIC *a.* + -OUS.] = MORBIFIC.

1657 TOMLINSON *Renou's Disp.* 20 Medicine is not made for the Disease, but for the morbificous cause.

morbify ('mɔːbɪfaɪ), *v.* [f. L. *morb-us* disease + -IFY. Late L. had *morbificāre*.] *trans.* To make diseased.

1875 BROWNING *Aristoph. Apol.* Wks. 1896 I. 680/2 So morbifies their flesh The poison-drama of Euripides.

morbility (mɔː'bɪlɪtɪ). *Path.* [ad. G. *morbilität*, ad. mod.L. type **morbilitās*, f. **morbili-s* characterized by disease, f. *morb-us* disease: see -ILE and -ITY.] The proportion of sickness in a given locality; the sick rate. = MORBIDITY 3.

1876 tr. *Wagner's Gen. Pathol.* (1877) 70 It is, however, further necessary to know the mortality and morbility of a locality in order to proceed upon perfectly safe ground. **1885** *Med. Times* 4 July 13/1 Dr. John Williams..was able to state a very low rate of deaths and morbility.

morbillary (mɔː'bɪlərɪ), *a. Path.* [f. med.L. *morbill-us* (see next) + -ARY.] Resembling measles.

1900 *Brit. Med. Jrnl.* 5 May 1084 On the neck and chest there was..subcutaneous mottling, morbillary in character.

‖**morbilli** (mɔː'bɪlaɪ), *pl. Path.* [med.L., pl. of *morbillus*, dim. of L. *morbus* disease.] The spots characteristic of measles.

1693 tr. *Blancard's Phys. Dict.* (ed. 2), *Morbilli*, the Meazles, red Spots, which proceed from an Aerial Contagion in the Blood. **1706** in PHILLIPS (ed. Kersey).

morbilliform (mɔː'bɪlɪfɔːm), *a.* [f. med.L. *morbill-us* + -(I)FORM.] Resembling measles.

1879 *St. George's Hosp. Rep.* IX. 204 Morbilliform eruption. **1899** *Allbutt's Syst. Med.* VIII. 935 In the morbilliform variety [of antitoxin rashes] the face may be affected.

morbillous (mɔː'bɪləs), *a. Path.* [ad. med.L. *morbillōsus*, f. *morbill-us*: see MORBILLI and -OUS.] Of or pertaining to measles.

1775 J. PERCIVAL *Ess.* (1776) III. 104 The morbillous matter has since been ingrafted by means of lint. **1879** *St. George's Hosp. Rep.* IX. 64 A faint morbillous rash was still visible on admission.

‖**morbleu** (mɔrblø). Also 7 **morbleau**, 8 **mortblue**, 9 **marblue**, **mortbleu**. [Fr.; an altered form of *mort Dieu*: see MORTDIEU.] A comic oath: usually attributed to French speakers.

to sing out morbleu dial. (Cornw.), to cry out lustily, as a boy when flogged (N. & Q., 8th Ser. V. 34).

1664 ETHEREDGE *Comical Revenge* III. iv, Morbleu, see, see de insolence of de Foot-boy English. **1679** SHADWELL *True Widow* II. 30 *Stan.* Come let's in, and put it off to the Ladies as if you were friends. *Prig.* Ay, with all my heart; what care I? *Y. Mag.* Morbleau, Brutal. **1692** M. MORGAN *Late Victory* 11 Morbleus and Jernies were but common Sport, Oathes only for the Lacquies of the Court. *a* **1754** FIELDING *Fathers* Wks. (1840) 1106 A lady whom I..saw again last night with another young lady at the play; and mortblue, if I marry any other woman. **1823** SCOTT *Peveril* xxvii, He upset both horse and Frenchman,—*mortbleu*! thrilling from his tongue as he rolled on the ground. **1840** BARHAM *Ingol. Leg., Bagman's Dog*, His ear caught the sound of the word 'Morbleu!' **1888** NELLIE CORNWALL *Twice Rescued* xvii. 211 Just listen to my Johnnie—he is singing out marblue [*footn.* Making a great noise].

morbose ('mɔːbəʊs), *a.* [ad. L. *morbōsus*, f. *morb-us* disease: see -OSE.] Proceeding from disease, causing disease, unhealthy.

1691 RAY *Creation* II. (1692) 77 All Preternatural and Morbose Tumors and Excrescencies of Plants. **1765** *Ann. Reg.* II. 108/2 He philosophises..on the effect of this bath, and believes that the earth absorbs into it morbose miasmas, &c. **1891** *Syd. Soc. Lex.*, *Morbose*, sickly, unhealthy.

†**mor'bosity.** *Obs.* [f. MORBOSE + -ITY.] The condition of being morbose; also, a morbose characteristic.

1646 SIR T. BROWNE *Pseud. Ep.* VI. x. 328 Their morbosities have vigorously descended to their posterities. **1689** T. PLUNKET *Char. Gd. Commander* 2 Nor coin excuses in a time of War,..Nor counterfeit Morbosity, when well.

'morbous, *a.* Now *rare.* [ad. L. *morbōsus*: see MORBOSE and -OUS.] Causing disease; of or pertaining to disease, diseased.

1651 WITTIE tr. *Primrose's Pop. Err.* II. xv. 130 When an inward disposition lurks in the body, and a morbous preparation, which such causes do stir up. **1682** T. GIBSON *Anat.* (1697) 100 In a morbous state it is often of several other colours. **1684** tr. *Bonet's Merc. Compit.* XIV. 506 Nature..does sometimes purge out..the Morbous purulent Matter. **1922** JOYCE *Ulysses* 412 Organisms in which morbous germs have taken up their residence.

morbulent ('mɔːbjʊlənt), *a. rare*⁻⁰. [f. L. *morb-us* disease: see -ULENT.] (See quots.)

1656 BLOUNT *Glossogr.*, Morbulent (*morbulentus*), full of diseases; sickly. **1891** *Syd. Soc. Lex.*, *Morbulent*, somewhat sickly.

‖**morbus** ('mɔːbəs). [L.] A disease. Used in combination in mod. Latin names of diseases, as CHOLERA *morbus*; ***morbus Gallicus*** (see quots.).

1579 W. CLOWES (*title*) A short and profitable treatise touching the cure of the disease called Morbus Gallicus by Unctions. **1656** BLOUNT *Glossogr.*, *Morbus Galicus*, otherwise called *Morbus Indicus*, *Neopolitanus*, *Hispanicus* (in Lat. *Lues Venerea*) the French Pox or great Pox. **1663** BOYLE *Usef. Exp. Nat. Philos.* II. ii. 43 An humour, such as that which causes the cholera morbus. **1672** JOSSELYN *New Eng. Rarities* 34 They are good for the Ptisick and Consumptions, and some say the *Morbus Gallicus*. **1693** tr. *Blancard's Phys. Dict.* (ed. 2), *Icterus*, the Jaundice,..the Latins call it *Regius Morbus*, the Kingly Disease.

morbut, obs. form of MARABOUT.

1769 *Town & County Mag.* Sept. 406/1 Magic figures drawn upon paper by the morbuts or priests of the country.

‖**morceau** (mɔrso). Pl. **morceaux**. [Fr.: see MORSEL *sb.*] **a.** A short literary or musical composition.

1751 SMOLLETT *Per. Pic.* (1799) I. iii. 25 He sat down and produced the following morceau. **1767** J. BEATTIE *Let.* 8 Jan. (1820) I. 39, I dare say Metastasio despises those little *morceaux* of sing-song. **1788** 'A. PASQUIN' *Childr. Thespis* (1792) 149 She purloined the stool on which Kemble had writ, The choicest morceaus of his Jesuit wit. **1819** *Europ. Mag.* LXXVI. 161 This very laughable operatic morceau. **1839** GEO. ELIOT *Let.* 22 Nov. (1954) I. 34 What I could wish to have added to many of my favourite morceaux is an indication of less satisfaction in terrene objects. **1889** J. K. JEROME *Three Men in Boat* viii. 119 We played *morceaux* from the old German masters. **1960** *Times* 29 July 13/2 Surely it would be easy to intersperse congruent *morceaux* among lyric poems.

b. morceau de musée (də myze): a museum piece; **morceau de salon** (də salɔ̃): a well-known tune elaborated by variations, etc.

1964 *English Studies* XLV. 237 Leaving behind the artifact, the *morceau de musée, 'Medallion'. **1886** F. HUME *Mystery of Hansom Cab* (1887) viii. 41 When the gentlemen entered the drawing-room a young lady was engaged in playing one of those detestable pieces of music called **Morceau de Salon*, in which an unoffending air is taken and variations embroidered on it till it becomes a perfect agony to distinguish the tune and the perpetual rattle of quavers and demi-semi-quavers. **1906** A. BENNETT *Whom God hath Joined* v. 185 A *morceau de salon* of Chaminade's stood on the open piano... Not in Lawrence's house would such examples of the brilliant secondrate have been found conspicuous. **1947** A. EINSTEIN *Mus. Romantic Era* xv. 209 From his [*sc.* Liszt's] pen there are no 'Scenes from Childhood', though there is a series—unfortunately too extensive—of *morceaux de salon*.

morcel(e, morcell, obs. forms of MORSEL.

morcellated ('mɔːsəleɪtɪd), *ppl. a.* [f. **morcellate* vb. (formed after MORCELLEMENT) + -ED¹.] Divided into many pieces; parcelled. Also *fig.*

1888 N. S. SHALER in *9th Rep. U.S. Geol. Surv.* (1889) 585 It is probably to this morcellated character of the rock..that we owe the great erosion of the granites..of this vicinity. **1953** E. L. MASCALL *Corpus Christi* iii. 57 It is perfectly possible for the parish communion to result in a far more morcellated and fragmented conception of the Church and of the liturgy than can be produced in any number of 'private masses'. **1964** *Welsh Hist. Rev.* II. 52 The centrifugal tendencies inherent in Welsh tribal life and custom did more than anything else to perpetuate the severely-morcellated political system.

morcellation (mɔːsə'leɪʃən). *Surg.* [f. **morcellate* vb.: see prec. and -ATION.] The action of breaking up a diseased part into small pieces. Also *fig.*

1898 *Brit. Med. Jrnl.* 17 Sept. 789 Any myomatous nodules that presented in the wound were removed generally by morcellation. **1900** *Lancet* 12 May 1368/1 The method of performing vaginal ablation..and vaginal ablation with morcellation are all fully and clearly described. **1968** J. HOWKINS *Shaw's Textbk. Operative Gynæcology* (ed. 3) xvi. 306/2 The expert at vaginal hysterectomy can convert the difficult operation into a relatively easy one..by removing the obstructing myoma by morcellation and vaginal myomectomy. **1973** *Amer. Jrnl. Obstetr. & Gynecol.* CXVI. 258/2 Morcellation was, and is, done when indicated by the size and extent of uterine tumors and when malignancy does not exist. **1975** E. L. MASCALL in *Critique 'Eucharistic Agreement'* v. 70 Merely to state the question in this way..presupposes an artificial and perverse separation between Christ and his members, a morcellation or fragmentation of the body of Christ.

‖**morcellement** (mɔrsɛlmɑ̃). [Fr., f. *morceler* to break in pieces, f. OF. *morcel*, *morceau* morsel: see -MENT.] **a.** Division (*spec.* of land or property) into small portions.

1848 H. DRUMMOND in *Croker Papers* (1884) III. xxvi. 184 As a national system it [the allotment system] is again infinitesimal *morcellement*. *a* **1859** AUSTIN *Jurispr.* (1863) II. xlv. 462 The effect of this *morcellement* would be endless repetition. **1889** *Pall Mall G.* 3 July 3/1 In the South peasant proprietors own most of the land, and the morcellement is in many cases excessive.

b. *Surg.* = MORCELLATION.

1903 *Philadelphia Med. Jrnl.* 31 Jan. 199/1 Porcellini suggested morcellement, the danger of which consists in the subsequent necrosis of the stump of the cervix. **1919** F. E. LEAVITT *Operations of Obstetrics* xi. 239 When there are tumors to deal with, like the outgrowths in the region of the buttocks and neck, their removal by morcellement must be undertaken. **1954** W. SHAW *Textbk. Operative Gynæcology* vi. 63/1 By processes of morcellement and splitting of the uterus in the midline it is possible to remove relatively large myomata by the vaginal route.

morchuel: see MORHWELL.

morcok, obs. form of MOOR COCK.

mordacious (mɔː'deɪʃəs), *a.* Now *rare.* Also 9 *erron.* **mordaceous**. [f. L. *mordāc-*, *mordax* (f. *mord-ēre* to bite) + -IOUS.]

1. Biting; given to biting.

1777 G. FORSTER *Voy. round World* I. 450 They likewise assured us the bats were very mordacious. **1801** J. JONES tr. *Bygge's Trav. Fr. Rep.* xiv. 335 Serpents in general, and mordaceous ones in particular. **1829** LANDOR *Imag. Conv.*, *Galileo, Milton*, etc. Wks. 1853 II. 234/1 To begin with the horses:..all are noisy and windy, skittish and mordacious. **1875** E. J. PAYNE *Burke's Sel. Wks.* II. Introd. 59 The mordacious snarl of the cur.

†**2.** Of material substances: 'Biting', pungent, caustic. *Obs.*

1675 EVELYN *Terra* (1676) 29 All Earths abounding more or less in their peculiar Salts..; some sweet and more grateful; others bitter, mordacious or astringent. **1684** tr. *Bonet's Merc. Compit.* VI. 232 So mordacious a matter must never be carried off by vomit.

3. Of or with reference to sarcasm or invective: Biting, keen.

1650 T. B. tr. *Estienne's Art Making Devises* Catal. 71 The Earle of Carnarvan was thus mordacious in his Devise, wherein he had a Lyon depainted, and 6 Dogs bayting or baying at him. **1654** COKAINE *Dianea* IV. 315 Then..shall I neither have power nor punishment to bridle thy mordacious insolency. **1823** D'ISRAELI *Cur. Lit.* Ser. II. II. 270 Grand-duke and taxes were synonimes, according to this mordacious lexicographer! **1841** —— *Amen. Lit.* (1867) 465 A repose freed from..mordacious malignity.

Hence **mor'daciously** *adv.*

1663 WATERHOUSE *Comm. Fortescue's De Laud. Legum Angliæ* 201 Buchanan, a learned though violent Scot, has mordaciously taunted this tradition.

mordacity (mɔː'dæsɪtɪ). [ad. F. *mordacité*, ad. L. *mordācitās*, f. *mordāc-*, *mordax*: see MORDACIOUS *a.* and -ITY.]

1. Propensity to biting.

a **1677** BARROW *Serm.* v. Wks. 1687 I. 65 He hath little of the Serpent (none of..its rancorous venom, of its keen mordacity). **1824** in *Spirit Pub. Jrnls.* (1825) 406 We all know the vivacity, or mordacity, with which the veriest cur resents an outrage offered to his tail.

2. 'Biting' or mordant quality. †**a.** Of material substances: Causticity, pungency, penetrating power, etc. *Obs.*

1601 HOLLAND *Pliny* II. 83 It goeth into..collyries or eye-salues, by reason of a certain subtil mordacitie and penetratiue qualitie that it hath. **1651** BIGGS *New Disp.* §301 Most medicines do depone all their acrimony and mordacity. **1699** EVELYN *Acetaria* 57 The young..Roots..affording a very grateful mordacity. **1725** BRADLEY *Fam. Dict.* s.v. *Sallet*, The Mordacity thus allay'd, be sure to make the Mortar very clean before you stamp any thing else in it.

b. Mordancy in speech.

c **1630** C. MORE *Life Sir T. More* i. 24 He ieasteth, but without mordacitie. **1660** WATERHOUSE *Arms & Arm.* 168 But for all these speeches of anger and mordacity, London has bin and I hope yet will be London. **1823** D'ISRAELI *Cur. Lit.* Ser. II. II. 329 [*Lenglet du Fresnoy*] His mordacity, his sarcasm.., contribute to his reader's amusement more than comports with his graver tasks. **1846** POE *L. Osborn* Wks. 1864 III. 55 Its mordacity cannot be gainsaid.

mordancy ('mɔːdənsɪ). [f. MORDANT *a.*: see -ANCY.] The quality of being biting in speech; sarcastic force; incisiveness (of style).

1656 BLOUNT *Glossogr.*, *Mordancie*, biting; sharpness of speech, detraction, bitter tearms. **1871** *Echo* 26 Aug., Speeches denouncing Mr. Gladstone,..none of them equal in mordancy to the Duke of Somerset's recent jet of vitriol. **1892** *Critic* 1 Oct. 176/1 This is surprising from a man the mordancy of whose style has been heretofore so remarkable.

mordant ('mɔːdənt), *sb.* Also 4 **mourdant**, 5–6 **mordaunt**. [a. OF. *mordant*, subst. use of *mordant* adj.: see next.]

I. An instrument that 'bites' or holds fast.

†**1.** A chape or tag of metal, sometimes jewelled, at the end of the pendant of a girdle. *Obs.*

?*a* **1366** CHAUCER *Rom. Rose* 1094 The mourdant, wrought in noble wyse, Was of a stoon ful precious. *c* **1400** *Laud Troy Bk.* 8242 Eche man his coffer vnsperes And takes gerdeles of riche barres With bokeles of gold and fair pendaunt, Wel anamayled with the mordaunt. **1500** *Will of Whiting* (Somerset Ho.), A girdell of black silk..the pendaunt and the mordaunt ther of ys syluer

2. One of the nippers of a crab, lobster, etc.

1848 JOHNSTON in *Proc. Berw. Nat. Club* II. No. 6. 300 The mandibular arms have a short..pincer, with a moveable nipper (mordant) placed above.

II. 3. *Dyeing.* A substance used for fixing colouring matters on stuffs.

1791 HAMILTON *Berthollet's Dyeing* Introd. 10 Mordants [serve] to render the colour more fixed. **1826** HENRY *Elem. Chem.* II. 375 The latter class, however, may be durably attached by the mediation of what was formerly called a mordaunt, but has since been more properly termed, by the late Mr. Henry, a *basis*. **1865** LIVINGSTONE *Zambesi* i. 32 Columba root is said to be used as a mordant for certain

colours. **1887** *Manch. Courier* 13 May 8/4 Turkey purple, which is made by substituting a mordant or basis of iron. *fig.* **1809–10** COLERIDGE *Friend* (ed. 3) III. 131 The link or mordant by which philosophy becomes scientific and the sciences philosophical. **1864** LOWELL *Fireside Trav.* 124 Practical application is the only mordant which will set things in the memory.

b. *Gilding.* An adhesive compound for fixing gold-leaf.

1825 J. NICHOLSON *Operat. Mechanic* 748 Some prepare their mordants with Jew's pitch [etc.]... They employ it for gilding pale gold. **1881** YOUNG *Ev. Man his own Mechanic* §1629 The principal mordants, or sizes, used by the gilder are known as *gold size* and *fat-oil gold size*.

c. In Pathological laboratories (see quot.).

1891 *Syd. Soc. Lex.*, *Mordant.* In Pathological investigations mordants are certain substances such as anilin oil, salicylic aldehyde, turpentine, carbolic acid, and borax, which are added to the basic anilin dyes to fix them on bacteria which may be present, and so render them more or less insensitive to decolourising agents. **1899** CAGNEY tr. *Jaksch's Clin. Diagn.* x. (ed. 4) 438.

4. *Etching.* The fluid used to 'bite in' the lines on the plate.

1878 P. G. HAMERTON in *Encycl. Brit.* VIII. 443/2 The nitrous mordant widens the lines; the Dutch mordant bites in depth.

mordant ('mɔːdənt), *a.* Also 5, 9 **mordent.** [a. F. *mordant*, pres. pple. of *mordre* to bite:—popular L. **mordĕre* (= classical L. *mordēre*); the form *mordent* is assimilated to the L. pple. *mordentem*.] Biting (in various senses).

1. Of satiric utterances (hence also of speakers or writers): Caustic, incisive.

1474 CAXTON *Chesse* II. v. (1481) d viij b, They ben.. right mordent and bytyng detractours. **1858** ELLICOTT *Destiny Creature* (ed. 3) 22 A petty spirit of detraction, with unkindly words or mordant satire. **1881** *Spectator* 19 Nov. 1454/1 Lord Salisbury was, as usual, very mordant in his tone towards Mr. Gladstone. **1903** *Blackw. Mag.* July 12/2 He was endowed with a peculiarly mordant wit.

2. Corrosive. Now *rare.*

1601 HOLLAND *Pliny* I. 506 Of those marles which are found to be fat, the white is chiefe; and thereof be many sorts. The most mordant and sharpest of them all, is [etc.]. **1666** G. HARVEY *Morb. Angl.* v. 61 The consumption of the kidneys is to be imputed to.. mordant armoniack salt. *fig.* **1870** BALDW. BROWN *Eccl. Truth* 225 The mordant acid of what they were pleased to conceive of as pure reason.

3. That causes pain or smart; pungent; biting. Of pain: acute, burning.

a **1845** SYD. SMITH *Recipe for Salad* 7 in Lady Holland *Mem.* (1855) I. 373 Of mordant mustard add a single spoon. **1876** G. MEREDITH *Beauch. Career* III. xii. 218 With a shadow of an elevation of her shoulders as if in apprehension of mordant pain.

4. a. Having the property of fixing colouring matter or gold-leaf (see MORDANT *sb.* 3, 3 b).

1825 J. NICHOLSON *Operat. Mechanic* 748 Mordant Varnish for Gilding. **1836** *Penny Cycl.* VI. 156/1 [Calico-printing.] Mordant reserves, which form the *lapis lazuli* style. **1847–64** in WEBSTER.

b. Of a dye: becoming fixed on the fibre as a result of forming an insoluble compound with a mordant.

1902 *Encycl. Brit.* XXVII. 559/2 Employed by themselves, Mordant Colours are usually of little or no value as dyestuffs, because.. either they are not attracted by the fibre.. or they only yield a more or less fugitive stain. Their importance and value as dyestuffs are due to the fact that they act like weak acids and have the property of combining with metallic oxides to form insoluble compounds termed 'lakes', which vary in colour according to the metallic oxide or salt employed. **1917** FORT & LLOYD *Chem. Dyestuffs* xiii. 112 Acid mordant dyes may be first dyed on wool like acid dyes and then after-chromed. **1940** *Thorpe's Dict. Appl. Chem.* (ed. 4) IV. 127/2 Mordant dyes rank amongst the oldest dyes used by mankind for colouring purposes. **1963** [see AFTER-CHROME *a.*]. **1965** E. GURR *Rational Use of Dyes in Biol.* i. 115 Since sun yellow does not contain a hydroxyl group it cannot be classified as a mordant dye.

5. In literal sense: Given to biting. *rare.*

1891 BAX *Outlooks New Standp.* III. 174 Those who would take steps to restrain the mordant liberty of the cur, since they do not hold the doctrine of the divine right of dogs to bite. **1895** *Pop. Sci. Monthly* Sept. 652 The boy C—— was for some time vigorously mordant in his angry fits.

mordant ('mɔːdənt), *v.* *Dyeing.* [f. MORDANT *sb.*] *trans.* To impregnate with a mordant. Hence '**mordanted** *ppl. a.*, '**mordanting** *vbl. sb.* and *ppl. a.*

1836 *Penny Cycl.* VI. 153/2 The bath must be replenished with dung from time to time, as it gets exhausted by the passage of the mordanted goods. **1839** URE *Dict. Arts* 195 Such stuffs must be galled, mordanted with alum.. and cleared with a soap boil. **1877** O'NEILL in *Encycl. Brit.* VII. 574/1 The cloth is mordanted by boiling it in a solution of salt of tin. *Ibid.*, Owing to the decomposition of the mordanting salts. **1884** I. LEVINSTEIN in *Manch. Exam.* 6 Oct. 4/5 The preparing or mordanting of the stocking (before any dye whatever had been used).

mordant, variant of MORDENT.

mordantly ('mɔːdəntlı), *adv.* [f. MORDANT *a.* + -LY².] **a.** In a mordant manner; bitingly. **b.** In the manner of a mordant.

1836 *New Monthly Mag.* XLVI. 205 To lay to her heart more mordently the serpents of jealousy and despair. **1849** in CRAIG; and in later Dicts.

mordauncester, obs. f. MORT D'ANCESTOR.

mordaunt, variant of MORDANT *sb.*

mord de chien: see MORTECHIEN *Sc.*, glanders.

† '**mordell.** *Obs.* [app. repr. an OE. type **morȝendǽl*, f. *morȝen* MORN, MORROW + *dǽl* DEAL *sb.*¹ Cf. the synonymous *morrow-part.*] The share of the husband's property to which a widow was entitled, as representing her 'morning-gift'.

1552 *Will of Baldwin* (Somerset Ho.),[Mentions his wife's] mordell [part of property].

mordenite ('mɔːdənaıt). *Min.* [Named by H. How, 1864, from *Morden*, Nova Scotia, its locality. See -ITE.] A hydrous silicate of aluminium, calcium, and sodium, resembling heulandite.

1864 How in *Jrnl. Chem. Soc.* XVII. 100 On Mordenite, a New Mineral from the Trap of Nova Scotia.

mordent ('mɔːdənt). *Mus.* Also **mordant, mordente.** [a. G. *mordent*, ad. It. *mordente*, pr. pple. of *mordere* to bite. Cf. MORDANT *a.*] A grace consisting in the rapid alternation of a written note with the one immediately below it. It has two varieties, the ***short mordent*** (symbol ✛), and the ***long*** or ***double mordent*** (✛✛).

Also applied by various writers to the passing shake (G. *Pralltriller*), sometimes called ***inverted mordent***; to the ACCIACCATURA (***abbreviated mordent***); to the TURN; and to various other graces.

1806 CALLCOTT *Mus. Gram.* vi. 61 The Mordent, Beat, Slide, and Spring are peculiar to the Germans. **1818** BUSBY *Gram. Mus.* 153 The *Mordente*, or according to the Germans, the *Spring*, consists of two notes preceding the note to be graced; the first of which is the same as the principal, and the second, one note higher than the principal. **1845** GWILT in *Encycl. Metrop.* V. 775/1 *Mordente*, a grace used by the Italian School, by turning upon the note without employing the note below. **1906** *Daily Chron.* 12 Nov. 3/4 The importance of the proper interpretation of the 'upper mordant' in Beethoven's sonatas. **1907** *Grove's Dict. Mus.* (ed. 5) III. 259 The appropriateness of the term Mordent.. is found in the suddenness with which the principal note is, as it were, attacked by the dissonant note and immediately released. Walther says its effect is 'like cracking a nut with the teeth'.

mordent, morder, obs. ff. MORDANT, MURDER.

† '**mordicancy.** *Obs.* [f. next: see -ANCY.] The quality of being biting or pungent; also, a biting or acute irritation.

a **1693** *Urquhart's Rabelais* III. xxxii. 271 Their.. figging Itch, wrigling Mordicancy. **1699** EVELYN *Acetaria* 53 The Mordicancy thus allay'd, be sure to make the Mortar very clean.

mordicant ('mɔːdıkənt), *a.* and *sb.* [ad. L. *mordicant-em*, pr. pple. of *mordicāre*: see next.]

A. *adj.* Biting, sharp, pungent.

1597 A. M. tr. *Guillemeau's Fr. Chirurg.* 48/1 Accompanied with bitinge or mordicante payn. **1603** HOLLAND *Plutarch's Mor.* 669 These fruits (for the most part) carrie with them a certeine piercing and mordicant quallitie. **1675** EVELYN *Terra* (1676) 124 First be sure they [*sc.* pigeons' dung, etc.] pass their mordicant and piercing spirits, and be discreetly mixt. **1822–34** *Good's Study Med.* (ed. 4) II. 338 In the latter the itching is more mordicant and aculeate.

† **B.** *sb.* A mordant. *Obs. rare*⁻¹.

1799 *Med. Jrnl.* I. 168 The three principal mordicants in dying cotton red, are, oil, galls, and alum.

mordicate ('mɔːdıkeıt), *v.* [f. L. *mordicāt-*, ppl. stem of *mordicāre*, f. *mord-ēre* to bite.] *trans.* To bite, sting, affect with a biting pain.

1651 BIGGS *New Disp.* §150 The urine also, though salt, doth not mordicate or fret the bladder. **1656** BLOUNT *Glossogr.*, *Mordicate*.. to hurt with biting.

mordication (mɔːdı'keıʃən). [ad. L. *mordicātiōn-em*, n. of action f. *mordicāre*: see prec.]

1. A biting, burning, or gnawing sensation or pain in a part of the body. Now *rare.*

1528 PAYNEL *Salernes Regim.* P iv, Whey is.. washyng & leusynge and therin is no mordication. **1574** NEWTON *Health Mag.* 21 When throughe drinkinge of wine there is any upbraidinge and mordication in the Stomacke. **1684** tr. *Bonet's Merc. Compit.* x. 353 The Meat creates trouble and mordication, so that it cannot be retained. **1891** *Syd. Soc. Lex.*, *Mordication*, inflammation of the skin with burning and prickling.

† **2.** 'A biting or fastning the teeth deep in anything' (Phillips 1658). *Obs.*

† **mordicative,** *a.* *Obs.* [ad. late L. *mordicātīv-us*, f. *mordicāre*: see MORDICATE and -IVE.] Biting or stinging, sharp, pungent.

1603 HOLLAND *Plutarch's Mor.* 944 Whereas the conceits and jests of Aristophanes are bitter and sharpe withall, carrying with them a mordicative qualitie which [etc.]. *Ibid.* 1187 That the aire in the citie of Delphos was.. mordicative, as witnesseth the speedie concoction of meat that it causeth. *Ibid.* Explan. Words, *Mordicatiue*, that is to say, Biting and stinging: as mustard seed, Pelletary of Spaine. **1634** R. H. *Salernes Regim.* 45 The cause why this fume is mordicative is by reason that the wine that it commeth of, is mordicative.

‖ **mordida** (mɔr'dida). [Central-Amer. and Mex. Sp.] A bribe; an illegal exaction (in Mexico, etc.).

1940 *Life* 2 Dec. 102 In Mexico, and throughout Latin America, it is next to impossible to make headway with petty officials without constant applications of the *mordida*, which literally translated means 'the bite', or bribe. **1946** M. LOWRY *Let.* 15 June (1967) 101 The defection was the original defection of my failing to pay the 'mordida'. **1967** *Punch* 18 Jan. 102/1 Just go see my friend, Sr. G., at *Gobernacion*... He's such a good friend of mine that you'll not even have to pay a *mordida*.

† **mordificative,** *a.* *Obs. rare*⁻¹. [Altered form of MORDICATIVE *a.*, after *mundificative*, etc.] = MORDICATIVE *a.*

1612 *Benvenuto's Passenger* 113 Garlicke... It hath a facultie mordificatiue (as it were of the race of backbiters and slanderers). [The It. has *mordificativo.*]

† **mordi'sheen.** *Anglo-Indian.* *Obs.* Forms: 6 **mordexijn,** 7 **mordesin, mordechan, mordechine, mordisheen,** 8 **mordechin, mordyxim,** 8–9 **morxi,** 9 **mordexyn.** See also MORT-DE-CHIEN. [a. Pg. *mordexim*, a. Mahrattī *moḍachī* cholera.] The cholera.

1598 W. PHILLIP tr. *Linschoten* I. xxxiv. 67 There raigneth a sicknesse called Mordexijn, which.. weakeneth a man, and maketh him cast out all that he hath in his bodie. **1660** F. BROOKE tr. *Le Blanc's Trav.* 51 Another infection called Mordesin,.. begins with vomiting, and pains in the head, and is infectious. **1687** A. LOVELL tr. *Thevenot's Trav.* III. 108 The Portuguese call the four sorts of Cholicks that people are troubled with in the Indies.. Mordechin. **1696** OVINGTON *Voy. Suratt* 350 The Mordechine is another Disease of which some die, which is a violent Vomiting and Looseness. **1698** FRYER *Acc. E. India & P.* 114 They apply Cauteries most unmercifully in a Mordisheen, called so by the Portugals, being a Vomiting with a Loosness. **1753** CHAMBERS *Cycl. Supp.*, *Morxi*, an Indian name of a pestilential distemper, very common in Malabar. **1757** J. H. GROSE *Voy. E. Indies* 52 The mordechin.. is a fit of violent vomiting and purging, that often proves fatal. **1787** *Proc. Madras Med. Board* 29 Nov., in *Good's Study Med.* (1834) I. 219 An epidemic.. under the appearance of dysentery, cholera morbus or mordyxim. **1823** CRABB *Technol. Dict.*, *Mordexyn.*

‖ **mordoré** (mɔrdɔre). Also 8 **mortdore,** 9 **mordorés.** [Fr., in 17th c. *moredoré*, f. *more* MOOR *sb.*² + *doré* gilt.] A brown colour mixed with red.

1796 KIRWAN *Elem. Min.* (ed. 2) I. 29 Colours... Mordoré dark red of the crimson kind, mixed with brown. **1804** TINGRY *Paint. & Varnish. Guide* 240/1 Pulverulent lake of a dark mordoré colour. **1839** URE *Dict. Arts* 420 To this shade may be referred.. marigold, orange peel, *mordorés*, cinnamon, gold, &c. **1894** *Westm. Gaz.* 3 May 3/3 Another, in brown lace of the shade known as *Morderé* [*sic*].

mordre, mordrer, mordrice, obs. forms of MURDER, MURDERER, MURDERESS.

mordu, obs. variant of MORTDIEU.

Mordvin ('mɔːdvın). Also **Mordv, Mordvian, Mordvine, Mordvinian.** [Russ.] **a.** A member of a Finnish people inhabiting the region of the middle Volga. **b.** The Finno-Ugric language of this people. Also *attrib.* or as *adj.* So '**Mordva,** this people collectively.

1736 tr. *P. J. von Strahlenberg's Historico-Geogr. Descr. N. & E. Europe & Asia* xiii. 412 Morduini, Are Pagans, in Russia, who live under the Government of Nischneygorod. **1800** W. TOOKE *Hist. Russia* I. i. 19 *The Mordvines*, called by themselves Moræ, and formerly by the Russians Meren. **1802** F. W. BLAGDON tr. *Pallas's Trav. S. Provinces Russian Empire* I. 34 The Mordvines.. are more solicitous to preserve the forests in the countries they inhabit. **1879** *Encycl. Brit.* VIII. 700/1 Finnic or Ugrian represented by.. Mordvinian. *Ibid.* IX. 219/2 The Volga Finns include.. the Mordvinian, divided into small communities on both banks of the Volga. **1883** *Ibid.* XVI. 45/2 Even now part of the Mordvinians (of Finnish origin) call themselves Meschers. *Ibid.* 813/2 Mordvinians, more correctly Mordva, or Mordvs, are a people numbering about one million. **1898** R. BROWN *Semitic Influence in Hellenic Mythol.* III. iii. 89 Chaïtan (= Arabic Shaitan, Heb. Satan) appears in the Mordvinian Pantheon. **1925** P. RADIN tr. *Vendryès's Lang.* iii. 118 In Chermish and Mordvian, the *-t* forms both the plural of nouns and the third person plural of verbs. **1931** K. BRESHKOVSKAIA *Hidden Springs of Russian Revolution* xxiv. 287, I talked also to the Cheremisses and the Mordva. **1933** [see CHEREMIS(s)]. **1939** L. H. GRAY *Found. Lang.* xii. 369 The languages of the Uralic family are.. *Finnish* group: Finnish proper.., Lapp.., Cheremiss, and Mordvin. **1942** K. W. DEUTSCH in J. A. Fishman *Readings Sociol. of Lang.* (1968) 601 Of the 13 remaining nationalities, nine have formed administrative units on a national, linguistic basis with various degrees of political self-government within the European part of the U.S.S.R.: the Bashkirs, Chuvashs, Cheremiss, Mordvins, [etc.]. **1944** B. H. SUMNER *Survey Russian Hist.* i. 23 The Mordva.. centred around the junction of the Volga and the Kama. **1960** E. R. GOODMAN *Soviet Design for World State* ix. 275 Examining any one of the languages of the Soviet Union, e.g., Mordvinian, one is shocked by the discovery that it swarms with Russian words, and that only the suffixes are Mordvinian. **1971** P. LONGWORTH *Cossacks* ii. 55 There was a ruling class of semi-nomadic Tatars and the primitive Ostyaks, Voguls and Mordvins paid them tribute. **1972** W. B. LOCKWOOD *Panorama of Indo-European Lang.* 152 The chief [languages] are Estonian.., Mordvin (1 m[illion], Mordva ASSR).

mordyxim: see MORDISHEEN.

more, *sb.*[1] *Obs.* exc. *dial.* (chiefly s.w.). Also 5–7 **moore**, 6 **maure**, **moare**, 8–9 **maur**, **moor**, **moar**, 9 **mor**, **mawer**, **mawr(e**, **mar**, **moir**, **moer**. [OE. *more*, *moru* wk. fem., corresp. to OHG. *moraha*, *morach*, *morha* (MHG. *morche*, *morhe*, *more*; mod.G. *möhre* carrot, *morche* dial., carrot, mushroom:—OTeut. type **murhōn*-; cf. Lith. *mõrkas*, Russian *morkov'*, carrot.]

1. The root of a tree or plant; the fibrous roots of a tap-root; a tree-stump.

In OE., an edible root, e.g. a carrot or parsnip.

c **1000** *Sax. Leechd.* I. 354 Ete .. wælwyrte moran. *Ibid.* II. 312 Wylisc moru .. englisc moru. *a* **1100** *Ags. Voc.* in Wr.-Wülcker 301/25 *Pastinace*, moran. *c* **1200** *Trin. Coll. Hom.* 139 Moren and wilde uni was his mete. *c* **1205** LAY. 31885 Heo lufeden bi wurten, bi moren and bi roten. *c* **1290** *St. Brendan* 284 in *S. Eng. Leg.* I. 227 Ȝwite moren, ase it of herbes were, bi-fore heom he sette al-so. **1297** R. GLOUC. (Rolls) 7228 A grene wexinge tre þat is fram þe more Ismite adoun. *c* **1400** *Beryn* 1056 A man I-passid ȝowith, & is withouten lore May be wele I likened, to a tre withouten more. *c* **1470** *Build. Bodm. Ch.* in *Camden Misc.* VII, Item de Will. Androwe for olde tymber and moris xj[d]. **1486** *Bk. St. Albans* B iij, Take the Juce of percelly Moris otherwise calde percelly Rootis. **1578** LYTE *Dodoens* III. lxxxviii. 441 The roote putteth foorth many branches or moores, spread abrode here and there. **1599** T. M[OUFET] *Silkwormes* 6 Long Plantaine, Hysope, Sage, and Comfrey moares. **1725** *Lond. Gaz.* No. 6447/4 Taking up small Moors of Wood. **1787** GROSE *Provinc. Gloss.* s.v. *Maur*, *More*, or Maur, also in Gloucestershire, signifies a root; as, a strawberry-more. **1796** W. MARSHALL *W. England* I. 328 *Mores*, roots, whether of grass or trees (the ordinary name). **1885** JEFFERIES *Open Air* (1890) 211 The mars or stocks of the plants that do not die away.

†**b.** A plant. *poet. Obs.*

a **1599** SPENSER *F.Q.* VII. vii. x, And all the earth .. Was dight with flowers that voluntary grew Out of the ground, .. Tenne thousand mores of sundry sent and hew, That might delight the smell, or please the view.

†**2.** *fig.* Origin, source, 'stock'. Also ME. in certain phrases, associated with *top*. *Obs.*

c **1175** *Lamb. Hom.* 103 *Auaricia* .. heo is more of elchere wohnesse. *c* **1200** *Trin. Coll. Hom.* 217 An ȝerd sal spruten of iesse more. *a* **1250** *Owl & Night.* 1328 Ac he ne con þe bet þarvore of clerkes lore top ne more. *Ibid.* 1422 Vp to þe toppe from þe more. *c* **1305** *Pilate* in *E.E.P.* (1862) 111 Pilatus was a liþer man and com of liþer more. *c* **1374** CHAUCER *Troylus* v. 25 As she þat was þe soþfast crop and more Of al his lust or Ioyes here byfore. **14..** *Sir Beues* (MS. M.) 70 A ffeyrer child was nevure none bore, Sithe god spronge of Jesses more.

†**3.** *Comb.*: **more-loor** (see quot.). *Obs.*

1733 TULL *Horse-Hoeing Husb.* xiii. 163 Another sort of lodging Blight there is, which some call Moar-Loore, .. mostly happens on light Land; this is when the Earth sinking away from the Roots, leaves the bottom of the Stalk higher than the subsided Ground, and then the Plant .. falls down to the Earth.

†**more**, *sb.*[2] *Obs. rare.* Also 1 **mór-**, 4 **mour**, **moor(e**. [OE. *mór-(béam)*, ad. L. *mōrus*.] The mulberry tree. Also ***more-tree*** (in OE. *mórbéam*).

c **825** *Vesp. Psalter* lxxvii. 47 Ofsloᵹ in heᵹle winᵹeardes heara & marbeamas heara [L. *moros eorum*] in forste. *a* **1340** HAMPOLE *Psalter* lxxvii. 52 He sloghe .. þaire mours [**1388** WYCLIF moore trees] in ryme froist. **1382** WYCLIF *Luke* xvii. 6 Ȝe schulen seye to this more tree [*v.r.* tree moor, Vulg. *huic arbori moro*], Be thou drawun vp by the roote.

†**more**, *sb.*[3] *Obs. rare.* [ad. L. *mōrum* mulberry, used in mod.L. with this sense (Blancard *Lex. Nov. Med.* 1690).] A small swelling or tumour (resembling a mulberry); cf. MORO[1].

1547 BOORDE *Brev. Health* ccxxxix. 81 b, A More or a lytle lumpe of fleshe the whiche doth growe in the browes or eares, or in any mannes foundement or other places.

more (mɔə(r)), *a.* (*sb.*) and *adv.* Forms: 1 **mára** (*fem.* and *neut.* **máre**), 2–3, 4–6 *north.* **mare**, 4–6 *north.* **mar**, *Sc.* **maire**, **mayr**, 4– *Sc.* **mair**; 3–6 **mor** (5–6 *Sc.* **moir**), 4–6 **moor(e**, 3, 6 **moare**, 2– **more**. Also with added compar. suffix, 4 **marere**. [The adj. is Com. Teut.: OE. *mára* = OFris. *mâra*, OS. *mêro* (MLG., MDu. *mêre*; mod.Du. has the double compar. *meerder*), OHG. *mêro* (MHG. *mêre*; mod.G. has traces in the inflected *mehr-* in *mehres* neut., *mehre* pl.; cf. the double compar. forms OHG. *mêrôro*, *mêriro* greater, MHG. *mêrer*, *mêrre*, mod.G. *mehrere* pl., several), ON. *meire* (Sw. *mera*, Da. *mere*, which are the neut. adj. used advb.), Goth. *maiza*:—OTeut. **maizon-*, f. **maiz* adv., which (with normal loss of final *z*) is represented by OE. *má*: see MO. The use of the neut. adj. as quasi-sb. and as adv. occurs in OE., but rarely, as *má* (see MO) was the ordinary word in both applications.]

A. *adj.*

(In senses 1, 2, 3 the word expresses respectively the comparative of the three adjectival notions now denoted by *great*, *much*, and *many*.)

1. Greater.

†**a.** Of material objects: Greater in size, larger. Also of a city, country, etc. (with mixture of senses b and f). Of persons and animals: Taller, bigger.

c **897** K. ÆLFRED *Gregory's Past. C.* xxi 155 Ða nietenu ðonne, ðeah hie maran sien, hie beoð suiður ahæfen from eorðan. *c* **1200** *Trin. Coll. Hom.* 179 Eft-sone þe more fishes in þe se eten þe lasse. **1297** R. GLOUC. (Rolls) 999 More he [*sc.* Ireland] is þan engelond. *a* **1300** *Cursor M.* 2112 Mani contre þar-in es And dughti cites mare and lesse. *c* **1300** *Havelok* 1701 Þo stod Hauelok .. Riht al bi þe heued more Þanne ani þat þer-inne stod. *c* **1350** in *Eng. Gilds* (1870) 360 Þilke cofre w[t] þe þre heuedes shal be y-set in a more Cofre. *c* **1384** CHAUCER *H. Fame* I. 500 Hit semed moche more Then I had any Egle seyne. *c* **1400** MAUNDEV. (1839) xxi. 231 He founded the grete Cytee Iȝonge in Cathay, that is a gret del more than Rome. *c* **1440** *Alphabet of Tales* 132 Þer is with-in my body a precious stone .. and it is more þan ane egg. *c* **1460** J. RUSSELL *Bk. Nurture* 65 Looke þow haue tarrers two, a more & lasse for wyne. *c* **1540** in *Trans. Lond. & Mdsx. Archæol. Soc.* IV. 346 A more and a lesse quysshion of crymsyn velvet. **1596** DALRYMPLE tr. *Leslie's Hist. Scot.* I. 20 Another kynde of hunting dog is to sent, of quhilkes sum ar mekle mair than vthir sum.

†**b.** Greater in number, quantity, or amount.

c **1000** ÆLFRIC *Hom.* (Th.) I. 74 Ðu cwæde þæt ic anbidode, þæt ic ðe mare folc ᵹestrynde. *c* **1200** ORMIN 19566 Þatt miccle mare genge Off Lerninngcnihhtess wass att himm þann att Johan Bapptisste. *c* **1250** *Gen. & Ex.* 993 His name ðo wurð a lettre mor. **1521** *St. Papers Hen. VIII*, II. 66 Sending a more power to hym .. for his assistence. **1529** RASTELL *Pastyme, Hist. Brit.* (1811) 125 The Danis, with a more strenght, enteryd the west part of this land.

†**c.** Qualifying a sb. which expresses quantity or amount. *Obs.* exc. *arch.* (in phr. ***the more part***).

13.. *Gaw. & Gr. Knt.* 649 In þe more half of his schelde. *c* **1374** CHAUCER *Boeth.* IV. pr. ii. 116 Shrewes whiche þat contienen þe more partie of men. *c* **1380** WYCLIF *Sel. Wks.* III. 352 But more part of þis world erreþ here. **1525** LD. BERNERS *Froiss.* II. ccxxxii. [ccxxviii.] 721 Tyll the kyng had assembled toguyder more nombre of noble men. **1533** *Acc. Ld. High Treas. Scotl.* VI. 155 In part of payment of ane mair soume. **1535** COVERDALE *Acts* xxvii. 12 The more parte off them toke councell to departe thence. [Also **1611.**] **1577–82** BRETON *Flourish upon Fancie* (Grosart) 6/2, I .. learned so long there, till I prou'd more halfe a very foole. *a* **1648** LD. HERBERT *Hen. VIII* (1683) 298 The more Party of the Sutors of this Your Realm. **1871** FREEMAN *Norm. Conq.* (1876) IV. xviii. 117 The more part of them perished by falling over the rocks.

†**d.** Greater in power or importance. *Obs.*

The absol. use in the phrase *more and less* (B. 2 f) survived until Shakspere's time.

c **1175** *Lamb. Hom.* 131 Bitwuxe were and wife nes nefre mare mon þenne he. **1382** WYCLIF *John* xiii. 16 The seruaunt is not more than his lord. *c* **1430** *Hymns Virg.* 102 Of which þre noon is more ne moost, But al oon god.

†**e.** Used *spec.* to characterize the greater or superior of two things, places, etc., of the same name, as (***the***) ***more Britain***, (***the***) ***more Ind***. (Cf. LESS *a.* 3, LESSER *a.* 2, GREATER *a.* 4.) *Obs.*

1297 R. GLOUC. (Rolls) 2223 Þe more brutaine. **1340** HAMPOLE *Pr. Consc.* 1484 Þe mare world es þis world brade, And þe les es man. **1375** *Sc. Leg. Saints* iii. (*Andreas*) 13 In more Iynd Mathew prechit. **1387** [see LITANY 1]. *a* **1400–50** *Stockh. Med. MS.* 157 More morel, *solanum nigrum*. **1436** *E.E. Wills* (1882) 105 The chirche of Alhalowen the more. *c* **1460** *Oseney Reg.* 117 All the tithis (both more ande smale). **1477** *Rolls of Parlt.* VI. 168/2 The maners of Sillry Mountsorell the more, and the lesse. **1593** *Rites & Mon. Ch. Durham* (Surtees) 57 Then the Buship Aldunus dyd hallowe the more kyrk or Gret Kirke.

†**f.** Used for L. *major* = 'elder'; also in ***St. James the More***; opposed to LESS. *Obs.*

a **1300** *Cursor M.* 3486 O þir tua breþer .. þe less þe mare laght be þe fote. *Ibid.* 21009 Iohn and iacob þe mar. **1382** WYCLIF *Gen.* xxvii. 1 And he clepide Esau, his moor sone [Vulg. *filium suum majorem*]. **1555** W. WATREMAN *Fardle Facions* II. xii. 294 The firste of Maie is hallowed for Philippe and James the more. **1594** CAREW *Huarte's Exam. Wits* ix. (1596) 122 Of the same opinion was Cato the more.

g. With sbs. of quality, condition, action, and the like: Greater in degree or extent; also, having a fuller title to the designation. *Obs.*, exc. where it coincides with sense 2. The expression (***the***) ***more's the pity*** may be regarded as a historical survival.

971 *Blickl. Hom.* 35 Swa maᵹon we þe maran blisse habban þa Easterdaᵹas. **1297** R. GLOUC. (Rolls) 156 Vpe þe plein of salesbury þat oþer wonder is, Þat ston heng is icluped, non more wonder nis. **1362** LANGL. *P. Pl.* A. v. 228 For nis no gult her so gret his Merci nis wel more. *c* **1374** CHAUCER *Troylus* I. 643 Ek whit by blak .. Eche set by oþer more for other semeth. **1390** GOWER *Conf.* II. 324 His moder wiste wel sche mihte Do Tereüs no more grief Than sle this child. *a* **1440** [see PITY *sb.* 3]. **1477** *Paston Lett.* III. 191 Ye dyd it off kyndenesse, and in eschywyng off a moor yll that myght befall. **1529** MORE *Dyaloge* III. ii. Wks. 208 So is it a much more faute to be therin rechelesse & negligent. **1562** J. MOUNTGOMERY in *Archæologia* XLVII. 233, I .. dailie doe heare, of the greate decaie of parrishes in Ingland; the more ys the pittie. **1563** *Homilies* II. *Rogation Week* I. 234 Borne among the number of Christian people, and thereby in a muche more nyghnes to saluation. **1632** HEYWOOD *2nd Pt. Iron Age* IV. i. Wks. 1874 III. 413 Lets flye to some strong Cittadell, For our more safety. **1685** EVELYN *Diary* 6 Feb., That the Lords, &c. should proceede in their coaches thro' the Citty for the more solemnity of it. **1752** J. LOUTHIAN *Form of Process* (ed. 2) 102 And, for the more Verification, I and the said Witnesses have subscribed the same. **1829** SOUTHEY *Pilgr. to Compostella* Poet. Wks. 1838 VII. 267 To make the miracle the more, Of these feathers there is always store. **1859** GEO. ELIOT *A. Bede* xxxviii, There's no amends I can make ye, lad—the more's the pity.

h. Qualifying the designation of a person with the sense: Entitled to the designation in a greater degree. (Cf. GREAT *a.* 17 a.)

Surviving only in *the more fool* (*you* etc.), where *more* would now be explained as adv. (see C. 1 a).

c **1380** WYCLIF *Wks.* (1880) 190 Þus þes fonnyd ypocritis putten errour in ihū crist. But who ben more heretikis? *c* **1400** *Gamelyn* 232 Whyl thou were a yong boy a moche schrewe thou were... 'Now I am older woxe thou schalt me find a more!' **1530** PALSGR. 852/2 The more fole is he, *tant plus sot est il*. **1584** R. SCOT *Discov. Witchcr.* II. xi. 36 A more heretike than either Faustus or Donatus. **1607–12** BACON *Ess., Beauty* (Arb.) 210 A man cannot tell whether Apelles or Albert Durere were the more trifler. **1611** *Tarlton's Jests* (1638) C j, Well, said Tarlton, the more foole you. **1613–18** DANIEL *Hist. Eng.* (1621) 21 The pressing necessity of the time that required a more man to vndergo the burthen of warre. **1844** THACKERAY *B. Lyndon* iii, The more great big blundering fool you, for giving the gold piece to him. **1917** D. H. LAWRENCE *Phoenix II* (1968) 69 'What have you done now?—lost more money?' 'Three thousand marks.' She was silent in deep wrath. 'More fool you!' she said. **1971** E. FENWICK *Impeccable People* iv. 25, I had to go and feel sorry for this Iversen piece, more fool me.

†**i.** with *in* = having a greater supply of. *Obs.*

1526 TINDALE *John* xix. 11 Therfore he that delivered me vnto the is moare in synne. **1666** DRYDEN *Ann. Mirab.* lv, The Duke, less numerous, but in courage more.

2. a. Existing in greater quantity, amount, or degree; a greater quantity or amount of. Phr. ***more*** (something) ***than one cares*** (or ***likes***) ***to think about***.

Developed from the older use of mo with partitive genitive.

In many of the examples here given (where the sb. is abstract) the word would at an earlier date have been the adj. of quality = 'greater' (see 1 g).

c **1386** CHAUCER *Prol.* 703 Vp on a day he gat hym moore moneye Than þat the person gat in Monthes tweye. **1508** DUNBAR *Flyting* 133 Thow skaffis and beggis mair beir and aitis Nor ony cripill in Karrik land abowt. **1542** UDALL *Erasm. Apoph.* 38 *margin*, The more hast ye wurst speede. **1606** SHAKS. *Tr. & Cr.* III. ii. 160 Perchance my Lord, I shew more craft then loue. **1611** BIBLE *Exod.* v. 9 Let there more worke be layde vpon the men, that they may labour therein. **1640** T. CAREW *Poems* (1651) 14 Give me more Love, or more Disdaine. **1742** *Lond. & Country Brew.* I. (ed. 4) 26 So that the Brewer is capacitated .. to make more Ale. **1781** J. MOORE *View Soc. It.* (1790) I. xxxiv. 368 There is more appearance of industry. **1830** COLERIDGE *Table-t.* 11 May (1835) I. 125, I recognize more genius in the latter. **1850** M[c]COSH *Div. Govt.* IV. ii. (1855) 517 There is some truth, but there is more error, in each of these representations. **1875** JOWETT *Plato* (ed. 2) I. 405 Ten is two more than eight. **1894** SOMERVILLE & 'ROSS' *Real Charlotte* I. xi. 152 He happened to have lost more money at the Galway races than he cared to think about. **1895** R. L. DOUGLAS in *Bookman* Oct. 23/1 Had he but shown a little more firmness and astuteness. **1935** E. GLASGOW *Let.* 12 July (1958) 188 For more years than I like to think of (a silly figure of speech, for I am not afraid of the years) I have battered my nerves against human cruelty.

†**b.** with *a* (cf. *many a*). *Obs.*

1680 HICKERINGILL *Meroz* Wks. 1716 I. 250 If there be but two or three Fanaticks in a Parish, .. they shall make more a Noise, more a Disturbance, .. than all the rest.

3. a. (With sb. in *pl.*) A greater number of ... Phrs. ***more days, more dollars***; ***more ships than parish churches***.

The earlier word is *mo* (see MO *adv.*, quasi-*sb.*[1] and *a.* 2); *more* in this use is not found in the Bible of 1611 or Shakspere.

1584 LYLY *Campaspe* III. iv. 95 So in painting, the more colours, the better counterfeit. **1669** STURMY *Mariner's Mag.* I. ii. 15 There was never more lame and decrepit Fellows .. as is now adays. **1711** STEELE *Spect.* No. 17 ¶6 If there shall be two or more Competitors for the same Vacancy. **1775** BURKE *Sp. Conc. Amer.* Sel. Wks. I. 231 The more they multiply, the more friends you will have. **1785** PALEY *Mor. Philos.* III. III. vi. (1841) 146 If to one man be allowed an exclusive right to five or more women. **1836–7** SIR W. HAMILTON *Metaph.* xl. (1870) II. 409 Nature never works by more .. instruments than are necessary. **1842** TENNYSON *Morte d'Arthur* 247 More things are wrought by prayer Than this world dreams of. **1843** J. F. COOPER *Ned Myers* II. ii. 40, I knew there were more ships than parish churches. **1845** STEPHEN *Comm. Laws Eng.* (1874) I. 83 With more or less restrictions. **1898** A. J. BOYD *Shellback* xv. 258 The captain was acting on the principle of 'More days, more dollars'. **1946** W. MCFEE *In First Watch* i. 28 There were more ships than parish churches. **1962** GRANVILLE *Dict. Sailors' Slang* 78/1 *More days: more dollars!* American Merchant seamen's phrase of the Second World War, meaning that the more days they were at sea the more 'danger money' they would receive. The term was used sarcastically by British Naval-men whose pay compared unfavourably with the Americans'.

b. with ellipsis of *sb.*

1656 COWLEY *Death Sir H. Wootton* 4 Who had so many Languages in store, That onely Fame shall speak of him in More!

c. Existing in greater numbers, more numerous. *Obs.* exc. (*rarely*) in predicative use.

1565 STAPLETON tr. *Bæda's Hist.* 27 As though they had ben thrise as many more in number then they wer. **1590** SWINBURNE *Testaments* 272 The fewer and weaker presumptions giue place to the more & stronger. **1614** in Swayne *Sarum Churchw. Acc.* (1896) 164 It was agreed by the more voyces. **1885** BIBLE (R.V.) *2 Kings* vi. 16 They that be with us are more [so 1762; 1611 moe] than they that be with them.

4. a. Additional to the quantity or number specified or implied; an additional amount or number of, further. Now *rare* exc. as preceded by an indefinite or numeral adj., e.g. ***any more***, ***no more***, ***some more***; ***many more***, ***two more***, ***twenty more***; and in archaic phrases like ***without more ado***.

This use appears to have been developed from the advb. use as in *anything*, *nothing more* (see C. 4 b).

a **1300** *K. Horn* 834 Sire, ischal al one Wiþute more ymone Wiþ mi swerd wel eþe Bringe hem þre to deþe. **13..** *Sir Beues* 3541 Beues .. tok þe tresore anon riȝte: Wiþ þat and wiþ mor catel He made þe castel of Arondel. **1375** BARBOUR *Bruce* I. 142 He buskyt hym, but mar abad. *c* **1380** [see ADO 3]. *c* **1400** MAUNDEV. (1839) xxxi. 314 With outen ony more

rehercyng..of marvaylles. *a* **1400–50** *Alexander* 118 How his land suld be lost withouten lett mare. **1570** *Satir. Poems Reform.* x. 185 Quha stickit him, withouttin proces moir. **1672** C. MANNERS in *12th Rep. Hist. MSS. Comm.* App. v. 25 Wee have every day newes of more townes taken by the French in Holland. **1818** CRUISE *Digest* (ed. 2) III. 370 Then the wife received some rent for the houses; and afterwards.. the son was born, and..the widow received more rent: then the son died..and she received some more rent after his death. **1876** [see ADO 3].

b. with ellipsis of sb.

1774 GOLDSM. *Nat. Hist.* (1776) I. 237 The Dead Sea..is so exceedingly salt, that its waters seem scarce capable of dissolving any more. **1802** DOROTHY WORDSWORTH *Jrnl.* 16 Apr. (1897) I. 106 As we went along there were more, and yet more. **1838** DICKENS *O. Twist* ii, Oliver..basin and spoon in hand, said..'Please, sir, I want some more'.

B. *absol.* and quasi-*sb.*

1. Used *absol.* in the sense 'greater'.

†**a.** In the phrases ***more and less, more and min*** = persons of all ranks; all without exception.

c **1205** LAY. 31253 Nefden heo nane are of þan lasse no of þan mare, ah al þa ferde wes of-slaȝen. *a* **1300** *Assump. Virg.* (Camb. MS.) 62 Heo seruede boþe lasse and more. *c* **1330** *Arth. & Merl.* 6650 'As armes!' gred alle..Boþe þe more & þe lasse. *c* **1375** *Lay Folks Mass Bk.* (MS. B) 136 Haue mercie on vs, more & mynne. **1567** *Gude & Godlie Ball.* (S.T.S.) 43 Christ..gaif the same Till his Apostillis mair and min. **1605** SHAKS. *Macb.* v. iv. 12.

†**b.** Used to render L. *majores*, elders, ancestors. Also with plural inflexion as a *sb. Obs.*

1382 WYCLIF *Deut.* xxxii. 7 Aske thi fader, and he shal telle to thee, thi more [Vulg. *majores tuos*] and thei shulen seie to thee. —— *2 Kings* xv. 7 They birieden hym with his moris [Vulg. *cum majoribus suis*] in the cytee of Dauith.

†**c.** ***the more***: that which is greater. *Obs.*

1387–8 T. USK *Test. Love* II. ix. (Skeat) l. 74 Every cause is more and worthier than thing caused, and in that mores possession al thinges lesse ben compted. **1398** TREVISA *Barth. De P.R.* XIII. xxix. (Tollem. MS.), Some [fish] eteþ euery oþer..and þe lesse is þe more is mete, and þan þe more is his mete þat is more þan hee. **1413** *Pilgr. Sowle* (Caxton) (1859) 70 Nedes must the lesse be conteyned within the more.

2. a. Something that is more; a greater quantity, amount, degree, etc.

a **1100** *Gerefa* in *Anglia* (1886) IX. 259 Ac he mot æȝðer witan ȝe læsse ȝe mare. *c* **1175** *Lamb. Hom.* 111 Ðu gederast mare and mare [*orig.* (Ælfric) p. 300 þu gaderast ma & ma]. *a* **1225** *Leg. Kath.* 1561 Þet ha nowðer ne ete lesse ne mare tweolf dahes fulle. *a* **1300** *Cursor M.* 10219 Sum wit lesse and sum wit mare, All þair vois þai yeld ai þare. *a* **1340** HAMPOLE *Psalter* cxl. 8 Comm., My wordis myght marere þan þairs. *c* **1412** HOCCLEVE *De Reg. Princ.* 259 He wele telle al and more. **1500–20** DUNBAR *Poems* xv. 11 Sum askis mair than he deservis. **1611** BIBLE *Exod.* xvi. 17 And the children of Israel..gathered some more, some lesse. **1632** MILTON *Penseroso* 120 Where more is meant then meets the ear. **1725** WATTS *Logic* I. vi. §10 All the Parts taken collectively..must contain neither more nor less than the Whole. **1886** RUSKIN *Præterita* II. 177 The more I got, the more I asked.

b. followed by *of* partitive.

a **1225** *Ancr. R.* 308 Hwon he of hire naueð more ne lesse. **1297** R. GLOUC. (Rolls) 5951 So þat is quene deide, & of sorwe & sore Him com in ech half euere þe leng þe more. **1390** GOWER *Conf.* II. 136 The more he hath of worldes good, The more he wolde it kepe streyte. *c* **1460** FORTESCUE *Abs. & Lim. Mon.* x. (1885) 131 For in tho dayis ther was but litle more off the reaume off Fraunce in the kynges handes, but þat parte wich is callyd the Ile off Fraunce. **1693** DRYDEN *Juvenal* (1697) Ded. 15 An Heroique poem requires..as much, or more of the Active Virtue, than the Suffering. **1802–12** BENTHAM *Ration. Judic. Evid.* (1827) I. 509 The quack, that he may sell the more of his pills at one time, distributes them gratis at another. **1856** RUSKIN *Mod. Paint.* IV. v. xviii. §5 We may see more and more of it the longer we look. **1860** TYNDALL *Glac.* I. iii. 28 The more I saw of my guide the more I liked him. **1886** *Manch. Exam.* 13 Mar. 5/2 If money could be eaten or worn, the more we had of it the better.

c. Used predicatively: Something of greater importance or magnitude. ***to be more***: to count for more, to be of greater importance. (Cf. the similar use of *much.*) Also in phrases introducing a sentence or clause as expressing something more important than what has preceded, e.g. ***what is more***, †***and*** (***that***) ***more is***.

1484 CAXTON *Fables of Æsop* v. x, I shalle not ete the, For thow sholdest hurte my tendre stomak, and more is, I shall this day haue better mete. **1577** tr. *Bullinger's Decades* I. i. (1592) 6 Yea, and that more is, should by adoption make them the sonnes of God. **1600** SHAKS. *A. Y. L.* III. ii. 241 To say I and no, to these particulars, is more then to answer in a Catechisme. **1618** BOLTON *Florus* (1636) 143 There is more in it, to keepe a Province, than to make one. **1833** TENNYSON *Lady Clara Vere de V.* 55 Kind hearts are more than coronets. **1842** —— *Locksley Hall* 142 And the individual withers, and the world is more and more. **1849** MACAULAY *Hist. Eng.* ii. I. 168 Honour and shame were scarcely more to him than light and darkness to the blind. **1859** FARRAR *J. Home* xvi. 204 He'll carry all our provisions ..up to the top, which is more than most of our A.C.'s would do.

d. ***or more***: added to approximate designations of quantity, to indicate that the actual amount is probably greater than that stated. Cf. 4 e.

c **1440** *Alphabet of Tales* 249 A damysell of þe age of x yere or mor. **1800** WORDSW. *Michael* 473 Three years, or little more, did Isabel Survive her Husband.

e. ***more or less***: appended to a designation of quantity to indicate that it is merely approximative.

1589 HAKLUYT *Voy.* 560 They [*sc.* sheep]..liue together in heards, in some 500. as it happeneth, more or lesse. **1709** *Lond. Gaz.* No. 4509/3 Her Cargo of about 1000 Bushels of French Salt, more or less. **1798** *Times* 28 June 4/1 Consisting of 91 acres, more or less, of excellent..land.

f. When coupled with *less*, the word is sometimes treated as a real sb., admitting of qualifying words.

1874 MORLEY *Compromise* ii. 64 There is no discoverable law fixing precisely the more or the less of these. **1884** tr. *Lotze's Metaph.* II. vii. 327 Such effects as do not directly display a more or a less. **1902** PHILLIMORE *Sophocles* Introd. 83 The colouring of the phrase, its more or less of poetical and imaged quality.

3. (With plural construction.) A greater number *of* the class specified; also, a greater number of persons.

1629 MASSINGER *Picture* IV. ii, I must confesse The more the merier. *a* **1633** G. HERBERT *Jacula Prud.* 682 More have repented speech then silence. **1666** STILLINGFL. *Serm.* Wks. 1710 I. 11 It is hard to say whether ever any Age produced more studious and skilful to pervert the design of Laws.. than this of ours hath done. **1818** CRUISE *Digest* (ed. 2) III. 395 More of the purchaser's male ancestors have been descended from..the femes in the higher classes.

¶ The phr. ***more than one*** is followed by a verb in the sing., like Fr. *plus d'un*.

1865 OAKELEY *Hist. Notes Tract. Movemt.* 103 More than one who took a part in the more extreme developments of the work has since been conspicuous on the rationalistic side of more recent controversies.

4. An additional quantity, amount, or number.

a. Something else in addition to what is specified. Chiefly with prefixed word, *any, some, no, little, much*: for examples see those words; also NO MORE.

For the advb. use of *any more*, see C. 4 a.

c **1175** *Lamb. Hom.* 79 ȝif þu mare spenest of þine. **1611** SHAKS. *Wint. T.* II. i. 168 We neede no more of your aduice. **1697** DRYDEN *Virg. Georg.* IV. 765 This Answer Proteus gave, nor more he said. **1895** SIR E. E. KAY in *Law Times Rep.* LXXIII. 651/1 If the underwriters wanted to know more, they ought to have asked for information.

b. *ellipt.* (as obj. of an omitted verb of 'saying' or the like). Now somewhat *arch.*

c **1460–1822** [see NO MORE A. 1 b]. ? **1536** LATIMER in *Lett. Suppress. Monast.* (Camden) 149 Butt of thys my dewtye moor att moor leyser. **1580** LYLY *Euphues* (Arb.) 390 But more of this at our next meeting. **1596** SHAKS. *Merch. V.* II. vi. 20 Heere comes Lorenzo, more of this hereafter. **1863** *Chem. News* 14 Feb. 84/1 Lubricating Oils.—Some consignments to hand, of which more again.

†**c.** ***without more*** (Sc. ***but mair***, etc.): without anything further or additional; often = without more ado, without delay. ***without less, without more; but min or more***: without addition or diminution; exactly. *Obs.*

1297 R. GLOUC. (Rolls) 81 Þanne beþ þer in walis þre wiþ oute Mor. *a* **1300** *Cursor M.* 1186 To beriing þai his bodi bare Adam and eue wit-outen mare. *c* **1374** CHAUCER *Troylus* IV. 105 (133) They yaf hym Antenor withoute more. **1375** *Sc. Leg. Saints* i. (*Petrus*) 51 Na clathis he had, at ware gude, bot kirtil and clok, but mare. *Ibid.* iii. (*Andreas*) 128 Forowtine ony mare to þe bordale I wente ine hy. **1447** BOKENHAM *Seyntys* (Roxb.) 83 And anoon iulyan wyth out moor For hir to presoun hys offycers sent. **1552** LYNDESAY *Monarche* 2732 Four hundreth stageis and four score In circuit, but myn or more. **1560** ROLLAND *Crt. Venus* I. 802 Inclining law but mair this Nimph anone,..Scho said [etc.].

†**d.** ***with the mair*** (*Sc.*): ? = 'and more'. *Obs.*

1563–4 *Reg. Privy Council Scot.* I. 257 Quhairat thai remanit thir twa yeris bigane, with the mair. **1568** *Ibid.* 636 Fourty thowsand stane wecht of leid ure, with the mair.

e. ***and more***: used (chiefly after a statement of quantity or number), to indicate an indefinite or unspecified addition to what has been mentioned.

a **1225** *Ancr. R.* 54 Þer heo lei ine prisune uour þusend ȝer & moare. *a* **1300** *Cursor M.* 5056 He hint him in his armes þare And kyst him, fourti sithes and mare [*Gött.* sexti sith or mar]. *c* **1400** *Gamelyn* 205, I wold ȝeue ten pound by Iesu Crist! and more. **1450** *Paston Lett.* I. 126 Peris Brusy.. hadde x m[l]. Frenshe men and more. *c* **1470** *Gol. & Gaw.* 480 Be it wes mydmorne and mare, markit on the day. **1610** SHAKS. *Temp.* I. ii. 48 Had I not Fowre, or fiue women once, that tended me? Thou hadst; and more, Miranda. **1856** AYTOUN *Bothwell* I. xxv, They call me savage, brutal, base, And more.

f. Other persons *than* that or those mentioned.

1896 A. E. HOUSMAN *Shropshire Lad* xxx, More than I, if truth were told, Have stood and sweated hot and cold.

¶ **g.** Often rhetorically treated as a real sb. with qualifying words: The 'something more' that has been spoken of or implied in the context.

c **1600** SHAKS. *Sonn.* xl, What hast thou then more then thou hadst before?..All mine was thine before thou hadst this more. **1690** LOCKE *Hum. Und.* II. xvii. §15 He knows the depth to be so many fathoms, and more; but how much that more is, he hath no distinct notion at all. **1849** M. ARNOLD *To Indep. Preacher*, Know, man hath all which Nature hath, but more, And in that *more* lie all his hopes of good. **1849** CLOUGH *Dipsychus* II. v, Hints haunt me ever of a more beyond.

h. Phr. (***there's***) ***more where it*** (or ***that, this,*** etc.) ***came from***: eat or use freely, do not be sparing of (a food, commodity, etc.).

1810 J. PORTER *Scottish Chiefs* II. v. 92, I..told him not to spare it, it was a chilly night, and I should get more where it came from. **1854** MAYNE REID *Young Voyageurs* xix. 250 He only looks after his lost root with an air of chagrin, and then, reflecting that there is 'plenty more where it came from', kicks up his heels, and once more plunges to the bottom. **1954** R. BISSELL *High Water* xxii. 270 Plenty more where this came from.

C. *adv.*

1. In a greater degree, to a greater extent.

a. qualifying a verb, a ppl. adj., an adjectival or advb. phrase, or the whole predication.

c **1175** *Lamb. Hom.* 47 For-þi þa engles heom [*MS.* hem heõ] rested mare þenn on sum oðer dei. *c* **1200** ORMIN 4662, & mare lufesst tu þatt þing þann ohht off Godess wille. *c* **1380** WYCLIF *Sel. Wks.* III. 350 And þus þei loven more þer ordre þan Crist. **1411** *Rolls of Parlt.* III. 650/2 For as myche I am a Justice, that more than an other comun man scholde have had me more discretly and pesfully. **1431–2** in *Wills & Inv. N.C.* (Surtees) I. 70 *note*, And touching tidinges..I haue charged ye berar of this to c'tfie yow mor at large. **1538** STARKEY *England* I. ii. 27 Surely they wold mor extyme hyt then they dow. **1597** BEARD *Theatre God's Judgem.* (1612) 335 To reuenge himselfe more at full vpon the citizens. **1662** GURNALL *Chr. in Arm.* III. verse 19. iii. §4. 677 If any in the World need walk pendantly upon God, more than others, the Minister is he. **1677** EARL ORRERY *Art of War* 15 More at home, and at ease, and safety. **1694** F. BRAGGE *Disc. Parables* xi. 384 A man is never more himself, than when he exercises his reason upon the best of objects, religion. **1706** POPE *Let. to Wycherley* 10 Apr., Some [verses]..I have entirely new express'd, and turned more into Poetry. **1735** BERKELEY *Reasons for not replying Mr. Walton* §7 The more he explains, the more I am puzzled. **1742** YOUNG *Nt. Th.* II. 28 O time! than gold more sacred; more a load Than lead, to fools. **1797** GODWIN *Enquirer* I. ii. 10, I shall be..more a man and less a brute. **1797–8** JANE AUSTEN *Sense & Sens.* xxxi, Every friend must be made still more her friend by them [her sufferings]. **1836** *Lett. fr. Madras* (1843) 20 The more trifles and the less worth telling they seem to you, the more valuable to me at such a distance. **1855** WHEWELL in Todhunter *Acc. Writ.* (1876) II. 404 The notion must be followed much more into detail than he has done. **1857** BUCKLE *Civiliz.* I. ii. 112 The fine arts are addressed more to the imagination; the sciences to the intellect.

b. qualifying an adj. or adv., to form the comparative.

With most adjs. and advs. of more than one syllable, and with all of more than two syllables, this is the normal mode of forming the comparative. A few monosyllables (e.g. *right, just*) normally form their comparatives in this way instead of taking the suffix *-er*.

c **1175** *Lamb. Hom.* 5 Þes we ahte to beon þe edmoddre and þa mare imete. **1340** HAMPOLE *Pr. Consc.* 858 And what es mar horibel in stede þan a man es when he es dede? **1375** BARBOUR *Bruce* VII. 555 He beheld hir mayr ynkirly. **1711** STEELE *Spect.* No. 6 ¶2 He finds Rest more agreeable than Motion. **1788** MRS. HUGHES *Henry & Isabella* I. 180 He was ..more gallant, more generous, more everything that is agreeable in youth, than his brother. **1821** SOUTHEY in *Life* (1850) V. 106 His merits are every day more widely acknowledged. **1851** LANDOR *Popery* 30 It is more just that a bishop's salary should be reduced to a thousand a-year than an admiral's to three hundred. **1884** tr. *Lotze's Logic* 348 The true law is far more complicated.

c. Often prefixed to monosyllabic and disyllabic adjs. and advs. which have otherwise a regular comparative in *-er*; as ***more true, more busy, more often*** = *truer, busier, oftener*. Esp. in phr. ***I*** (or ***you***, etc.) ***couldn't be more*** ——: I, etc., am extremely ——.

By mod. writers this alternative form is used (1) for special emphasis or clearness; (2) to preserve a balance of phrase when other comparatives with 'more' occur in the context; (3) to qualify the whole predicate rather than the single adj. or adv.

c **1330** R. BRUNNE *Chron.* (1810) 235 Was neuer at Saynt Denys feste holden more hy. **1340** *Ayenb.* 63 Ac þe leazinges likinde byeþ more grat zenne. *c* **1400** MAUNDEV. (1839) xxx. 305 He rennethe more faste than ony of the tother. **1470–85** MALORY *Arthur* VII. vii. 222, I am a gentyl man borne and of more hyghe lygnage than thou. **1597** HOOKER *Eccl. Pol.* v. lxxx. §4 So that of the two indefinite ordination..doth come more neere th' Apostles example. **1645** *Ord. Lords & Com. Sacram.* 1 Neuer had they more high and strong engagements. *a* **1649** DRUMM. OF HAWTH. *Poems* Wks. (1711) 3 Their arms more white than milk. **1650** W. BROUGH *Sacr. Princ.* (1659) 177 Thou wilt live more wel, and dye much better. **1765** GOLDSM. *Ess.* Misc. Wks. 1837 I. 160 With a voice more rough than the Staffordshire giant's. **1798** COLERIDGE *Anc. Mar.* VI. v, Fly, brother, fly! more high, more high! **1803–5** WORDSW. *Solitary Reaper* 21 Or is it some more humble lay? **1849** MACAULAY *Hist. Eng.* ix. II. 441 He was more busy than they had ever known him. **1849** M. ARNOLD *Mycerinus* 17, I look'd for life more lasting, rule more high. **1851** WHEWELL *Grotius* I. 99 The opposite opinion, as it is the more common, so does it seem to us the more true. **1877** MORLEY *Crit. Misc.* Ser. II. 211 A clumsy collector, who more often than not knew neither how to read nor to write. **1939** N. MARSH *Overture to Death* xvii. 188 'I thought,' flashed Dinah, 'that nowadays the C.I.D. was almost a gentleman's job.' 'Oh, no!' said Alleyn. 'You couldn't be more mistaken.' **1951** —— *Opening Night* vi. 139 'I couldn't be more sorry,' Percival said weakly. **1954** 'N. BLAKE' *Whisper in Gloom* I. iii. 49 This party couldn't be more heaven, don't you think? **1971** P. D. JAMES *Shroud for Nightingale* i. 12 She could hardly have been more wrong.

d. Formerly often prefixed pleonastically to the comparative of the adj. or adv. *Obs.* exc. *arch.*

In quot. *c* 1205 the use is not pleonastic.

[*c* **1205** LAY. 4349, & þu ær muchele ahtere & ec mare hærdere.] **1340** *Ayenb.* 61 An eddre..þet yernþ more zuyþere þanne hors. *Ibid.* 64 Hi byeþ more worse þanne þe gyewes. *c* **1400** MAUNDEV. (1839) iv. 29 That Lond is meche more hottere than it is here. **1470–85** MALORY *Arthur* xx. vi. 806 Ye shold haue the same dethe or a more shamefuller dethe. **1561** T. HOBY tr. *Castiglione's Courtyer* II. (1577) K viij b, More excellent it cannot be, nor more subtiller. **1589** *Rare Tri. Love & Fort.* in *Five Old Plays* (Roxb. Club) 111 If thou escape the perrill of distresse, My feare and care is twenty times more lesse. **1598** GRENEWEY *Tacitus' Ann.* IV. i. (1622) 89 He vsed sometime largesse and lauishing; but

more oftner industrie and diligence. **1669** STURMY *Mariner's Mag.* I. ii. 15, I should be glad..to see a more equaller Balance among Sea-men, and their Imployers. **1676** WOOD *Jrnl.* in *Acc. Sev. Late Voy.* I. (1694) 166 Captain Hawes ship got clear, wearing more rounder. **1832** TENNYSON *Œnone* Poems (1833) 56 But Paris was to me More lovelier than all the world beside.

e. ***more and more***: in an increasing degree.

c **1200** ORMIN 676 He wile himm færenn, ȝiff he maȝȝ, & skerrenn mare & mare. *c* **1250** *Gen. & Ex.* 511 Chirches ben wursiped mor and mor. *a* **1300** *Cursor M.* 5865 þai rise and bredes ai mare and mare. **1567** *Gude & Godlie Ball.* (S.T.S.) 9 Greuand God ay moir and moir. **1732** BERKELEY *Alciphr.* v. §7 Men grow daily more and more wicked. **1875** JOWETT *Plato* (ed. 2) I. 46 At this he blushed more and more.

f. with ellipsis of the word or sentence qualified. Also (now more frequently) ***more so***, where *so* is substituted for the omitted part. ***the more*** = the rather, the more so (*because*, etc.).

1340 *Ayenb.* 127 He ssolde by wel perfect and yblissed ine þise wordle and more ine þe oþre. ?**1461** *Paston Lett.* II. 74 And hevery man wyl sey wel ther of, the mor cause he is a gentylman,..and in gret penur. **1561** T. HOBY tr. *Castiglione's Courtyer* II. (1577) N iij b, I wyl we defer the whole vntil to morow, the more for that I thynke it wel done wee folowe the L. Julians counsel. **1640** O. SEDGWICKE *Christs Counsell* 84 How much more, when thy crowne is losing! **1735** BERKELEY *Def. Free-think. in Math.* §28 This is so plain that nothing can be more so. **1852** M. ARNOLD *A Farewell* viii, I too have wish'd, no woman more, This starting, feverish heart away. **1862** BORROW *Wild Wales* lii, 'Are the Welsh..as clannish as the Highlanders?' said I. 'Yes', said he, 'and a good deal more'. **1876** BESANT & RICE *Gold. Butterfly* Prol. i, The English servant was dressed like his master, but 'more-so'.

g. ***any more, no more*** (dial. also ***more*** simply) are used to exclude or deny a second clause equally with a first. See NO MORE C. 4.

1838 JAS. GRANT *Sk. Lond.* 209 Faith, Sir! she did not come back again at a', mair than the ither. **1844** LINGARD *Anglo-Sax. Ch.* (1858) I. vii. 273 These..did not, any more than those.., lead to controversy. **1875** JOWETT *Plato* (ed. 2) I. 112 Poets, who ought not to be allowed, any more than flute-girls, to come into good society.

h. ***more like*** (colloq.) = nearer (a specified number or quantity). Cf. *something like*, *nothing like* (LIKE *a.* 2 f).

1902 W. HEADLAM in *Class. Rev.* XVI. 348/1 Some 200 conjectures.., among which Mr. Housman considered 4 quite certain; I gladly adopted more like 12 in my prose version.

2. a. Phr. ***more or less*** (†*less or more*, †*more or min*, etc.): in a greater or less degree; to a greater or less extent; also used *attrib.* (usu. with hyphens). Hence with negative: (Not) at all.

a **1225** *Ancr. R.* 92 Efter þet me lueð hine more oðer lesse. **1390** GOWER *Conf.* I. 107 Riht so ne mor ne lesse. *c* **1398** CHAUCER *Fortune* 61 The see may ebbe and flowen moore or lesse. ?*c* **1400** *Pety Job* 143 in 26 *Pol. Poems* 125 Though I offende more or mynne. **1526** *Pilgr. Perf.* (W. de W. 1531) 27 b, Ought to folowe hym more or lesse euery persone after his habilite. **1625** HART *Anat. Ur.* II. iv. 74 This fluxe continued lesse or more for some few dayes after. **1683** MOXON *Mech. Exerc., Printing* xix. ¶7 It will more or less job against every Letter. **1711** ADDISON *Spect.* No. 21 ¶3 Lawyers..that are more or less passionate according as they are paid for it. **1839** URE *Dict. Arts* 827 Formerly fluxes more or less compound were employed for these purposes. **1855** HT. MARTINEAU *Autobiog.* (1877) I. 39, I certainly never believed, more or less, in the 'essential doctrines' of Christianity. *Ibid.* 170, I could not afford to ride, more or less. **1863** MRS. CARLYLE *Lett.* (1883) III. 173, I had had pain more or less in my left arm for two months. **1963** *Language* XXXIX. 460 As far as the bees are concerned, it is clear that their behavior resembles that of an analog computer.., that is, a control machine of the more-or-less type, and not at all of a digital computer, of a yes-or-no type. **1964** M. A. K. HALLIDAY et al. *Linguistic Sci.* v. 124 But this, like synonymy, is a 'more or less' not a 'yes or no' relation. **1975** *Country Life* 13 Feb. 386/2 Every more-or-less sound horse was purchased for the Expeditionary Force by Civilian Re-mount Purchasing Officers.

†**b.** ***more and less*** (***more and min***): altogether, entirely, as a whole. (Cf. B. 1 a.) *Obs.*

a **1300** *Cursor M.* 13664 þair strijf he wist bath less and mare. *c* **1420** LYDG. *Assembly of Gods* 306 Clad all in purpur was she more & lesse. *c* **1560** ROLLAND *Seven Sages* 243, I sall ȝow schaw the mater mair and min. **1567** *Gude & Godlie Ball.* (S.T.S.) 29 Quhat I haif tholit les and mair.

3. Qualifying a predicate or a predicative adjunct as being applicable in greater measure or degree *than* another. Hence often used to indicate that the one predicate, etc., is more correct than the other, or (by way of euphemism or cautious statement) that the former and not the latter expresses the truth. Cf. RATHER *adv.* 5 a, b.

c **1200** *Vices & Virtues* 39 Þe soðe luue of godd, hie is mare on werkes ðanne on wordes. *c* **1375** *Sc. Leg. Saints* xiv. (*Lucas*) 40 Luke mad his ewangel syne, of thingis hard mar þan of sene. *c* **1477** CAXTON *Jason* 78 Fro day to day they apayred more than amended. **1546** HEYWOOD *Prov.* (1867) 9 He shall let fall all, And be more fraid then hurt. **1568** GRAFTON *Chron.* II. 29 Which..was done more of pride than of compassion. **1590** SPENSER *F.Q.* II. ii. 17 More huge in strength then wise in workes he was. **1616** B. JONSON *Epigrams* xxxv, A Prince that rules by example, more than sway. **1663** BUTLER *Hud.* I. i. 30 But here our Authors make a doubt, Whether he were more wise, or stout. **1834** MEDWIN *Angler in Wales* xxvi. II. 146 More dead than alive. **1857** BUCKLE *Civiliz.* I. vii. 331 The Puritans were more fanatical than superstitious. **1899** *Westm. Gaz.* 17 Aug. 2/1 The railways are laid more with a strategical purpose than with a view to [etc.].

4. Additionally, in addition. (Cf. A. 4.)

a. In negative, interrogative, or hypothetical contexts: In repetition or continuance of what has taken place up to a particular time; further, longer, again. Frequent in phrases ***ever more***, ***never more*** (see EVERMORE, NEVERMORE), ***once more*** (see ONCE 8 b). The phrase ***any more*** (freq. written as ***anymore***) (see B. 4 a), in which *more* is the absolute adj., is used *advb.* in the same sense, and has superseded the simple adv. except in rhetorical or poetic use; also *dial.* (chiefly *U.S.*) used in affirmative as well as negative contexts in the sense 'now, now-a-days, at the present time; from now on'. See also NO MORE *adv.*

c **1000** *Ags. Gosp.* Matt. xxii. 46 Ne nan ne dorste or ðam dæge hyne nan þing mare axigean. *c* **1275** *Passion our Lord* 39 in *O.E. Misc.* 38 Anon he hyne byleuede more to vondy. *c* **1330** R. BRUNNE *Chron. Wace* (Rolls) 14001 ȝyf ȝe chalange hym any mare. *c* **1400** *Gamelyn* 265 Ther was noon with Gamelyn wolde wrastle more. **1526** *Pilgr. Perf.* (W. de W. 1531) 212 But now he shall neuer dye ony more. **1610** SHAKS. *Temp.* I. ii. 294 If thou more murmur'st. **1611** BIBLE *Gen.* viii. 12 Hee..sent forth the doue, which returned not againe vnto him any more. **1709** STEELE *Tatler* No. 83 ¶3 Little did I think I should ever have Business of this Kind on my Hands more. **1712** —— *Spect.* No. 272 ¶1 She is now odious to her Mistress for having so often spoke well of me, that she dare not mention me more. **1784** COWPER *Task* v. 91 Where neither grub, nor root, nor earth-nut, now Repays their labour more. **1870** RUSKIN *Lect. Art* vii. §182 Since their day, painting has never flourished more. **1871** R. ELLIS tr. *Catullus* lxiv. 69 Not for silky tiara nor amice..Recks she at all any more. **1885–94** R. BRIDGES *Eros & Psyche* June xiv, But never call me woman more, if soon I cannot lure her from her height divine. **1898** *Eng. Dial. Dict.* I. 63/1 A servant being instructed how to act, will answer 'I will do it any more'. **1903** *McClure's Mag.* Dec. 215/1 There's just only this one any more. **1920** D. H. LAWRENCE *Women in Love* (1921) xiii. 159 'Quite absurd,' he said. 'Suffering bores me, any more.' **1938** J. STUART *Beyond Dark Hills* vi. 120 They tell me this Macey plant only hires the best of men any more. *Ibid.* x. 319 You know, Jesse, any more I don't worry a great lot. **1973** *Capital Times* (Madison, Wis.) 14 Mar. 2/1 Any more, the difference between a white collar worker and a blue collar worker is simply a matter of shirt preference.

b. In addition to what has been specified or implied; besides, moreover. Now used only after a designation of quantity or number (whether definite or indefinite), indicating an addition which swells a previous total.

c **1200** *Trin. Coll. Hom.* 3 Hit lasteð þre wuke fulle and sum del more. *a* **1225** *Ancr. R.* 426 Siggen..Pater noster & Aue Maria biuoren mete, and efter mete also, & Credo moare. **1375** BARBOUR *Bruce* XII. 314, I wat nocht quhat mar say sall I. *a* **1550** *Freiris Berwik* 395 in *Dunbar's Poems* (S.T.S.) 298 Baith breid and wyne, and vthir thingis moir. **1573** TUSSER *Husb.* (1878) 195 Of siluer, golde, of precious stones, and treasures many more. **1577–87** HOLINSHED *Hist. Scot.* 430/1 To which he more added these speeches. *c* **1578** in *Household Ord.* (1790) 241 The Lord Chauncellor..fee 419*l.* os. od. For his attendance in the Star-chamber, 200 o o. More, by the names of annuities 300 o o. **1589** *Burgh Rec. Glasgow* (1876) I. 142 Item, fyvetene schillingis for the price of ane hogheid; item, mair, twentie sex schillingis viij[d]. for ane lang courchay; item, mair, twentie schillingis for ane cod and codwair. **1616** B. JONSON *Epigrams* xxxiii, Ile not offend thee with a vaine teare more. **1707** MORTIMER *Husb.* (1721) I. 35 It will ripen in about a Month's time more. **1719** DE FOE *Crusoe* II. (Globe) 500, I won't have one Creature touch'd more, upon Pain of Death. **1766** GOLDSM. *Vic. W.* i, After an interval of twelve years, we had two sons more.

5. a. Expressions in which *more* (in sense B. 2) is followed by *than* with a designation of number or quantity admit of being used instrumentally or adverbially, as in 'more than ten years old'. The analogy of these has given rise to expressions like 'more than once' (a multiplicative corresponding to the quasi-numeral 'more than one'). Hence, from the 16th c. onwards, ***more than*** has been placed before adjs., advs., vbs., and descriptive sbs., to indicate that the word thus qualified is (in some obvious respect) inadequate to the intended meaning. **more'n, mor'n** *colloq.* (orig. *U.S.*) = more than; also *ellipt.* = no more than.

Cf. the similar uses of *plus quam* in Latin.

c **1440** *Alphabet of Tales* 196 The scriptur of þaim is mor þan ccclxxij yere old. **1553** *Respublica* I. ii. 32 (Brandl) And yonder he cometh—me thinketh more then half madde. **1572** *Reg. Privy Council Scot.* II. 168 The grit murtheris and mair then beastlie crewelteis usit..aganis the trew Christianis. **1585** T. WASHINGTON tr. *Nicholay's Voy.* I. xviii, Sheepe, which haue very long tayles more then a foote long. **1615** G. SANDYS *Trav.* 58 It is..more then conjectured, that Mahomet grounded his devised Paradise, upon the Poets invention of Elisium. *a* **1626** BACON *Ch. Controv.* Wks. 1879 I. 344 It is more than time that there were an end..made of this immodest..manner of writing. **1696** DRYDEN *Lucian* Prose Wks. 1800 III. 360 For this reason he calls himself more than once an Assyrian. **1742** YOUNG *Nt. Th.* III. 69 So frequent death, Sorrow, he more than causes, he confounds. **1777** CHATHAM *Sp. on Address* 18 Nov., These more than popish cruelties. **1818** BYRON *Mazeppa* xiii, 'Twas more than noon. **1834** MEDWIN *Angler in Wales* I. 203 Places that it was hardly safe to have descended at more than a walk. **1847** DISRAELI *Tancred* III. v, O, my more than sister, 'tis hell! **1848** J. R. LOWELL *Biglow Papers* 1st Ser. 23, I felt a thing go thru my leg,—'t wuz nothin' more'n a skeeter! **1867** RUSKIN *Time & Tide* xix. §116 My much more than disrespect for the Jamaica Committee. **1870** L'ESTRANGE *Miss Mitford* I. v. 163 The orator was more than usually brilliant. **1885** W. L. ALDEN *Adv. Jimmy Brown* 142 They say that Squire Meredith and Deacon Willets are mornhalf eaten up by mosquitoes. **1886** *Harper's Mag.* July 323/2 But he (mor'n you and I with all of our might) Could not here always remain. **1889** D. HANNAY *Capt. Marryat* 147 'The Little Savage'..ends by being more than a little tiresome. **1903** K. D. WIGGIN *Rebecca of Sunnybrook Farm* 8 We've only just started on it, ..it's more'n two hours. **1952** E. WILSON *Equations of Love* 196, I know a lot more'n I did. **1973** E. BERCKMAN *Victorian Album* 47, I don't know any more'n I've told you.

b. ***neither more nor less than***: exactly, precisely, (that) and nothing else.

So F. *ni plus ni moins que.*

c **1460** SIR R. ROS *La Belle Dame* 305 For my desire is nothir more ne lesse But my seruise to doo for your plesance. **1749** FIELDING *Tom Jones* v. i, The drama, which he will have contain neither more nor less than five acts. **1843** BORROW *Bible in Spain* xxxvi, The first step which I took.. was a very bold one. It was neither more nor less than the establishment of a shop for the sale of Testaments.

c. *Comb.* with following adj. or sb.

1923 D. H. LAWRENCE *Birds, Beasts, & Flowers* 99 Cats, and the Neapolitans, Sulphur sun-beasts, Thirst for fish as for more-than-water. *Ibid.* 141 Why do you arch your naked-set eye with a more-than-comprehensible arrogance? **1924** H. E. PALMER *Gram. Spoken Eng.* p. xxvii, The words *trees, towns, boys*, form an association-group through having the..meanings 'more-than-oneness' in common. **1938** R. GRAVES *Coll. Poems* 150 Nor could a compromise be found Between the giver's thoughtlessness And his own more-than-thanklessness. **1950** *Scott. Jrnl. Theol.* III. 367 Nyberg says it is clear from the beginning that the Servant is a more-than-individual (*överindividuell*) figure, notwithstanding that the description moves throughout on the individual plane. **1961** *Times* 24 Oct. 13/1 The Official Image of Picasso..may well be a more-than-life-size..figure.

6. Used conjunctionally to introduce a clause or sentence which is of the nature of an important addition. Now only *arch.* chiefly in ***nay more***, rarely (***and***) ***more***. Formerly also †***more above***. Cf. MAIRATOUR (*Sc.*), MOREOVER. ***more by token***: see TOKEN *sb.*

1390 GOWER *Conf.* II. 83 To tile lond..Saturnus of his oghne wit Hath founde ferst, and more yit Of Chapmanhode he fond the weie. *a* **1578** LINDESAY (Pitscottie) *Chron. Scot.* (S.T.S.) I. 85 Mair, it had bene goode for the commone weill of Scotland that [etc.]. **1591** SHAKS. *Two Gent.* II. iv. 179 We are betroathd: nay more, our mariage howre.. Determin'd of. **1602** —— *Ham.* II. ii. 126 This in Obedience hath my daughter shew'd me: And more aboue hath his soliciting..All giuen to mine eare. **1615** W. LAWSON *Country Housew. Gard.* (1626) 19 More then this, there is no tree like this for soundnesse. **1683** CREECH tr. *Lucretius* II. (ed. 3) 43 But more, 'tis nothing strange that every Mass Seems quiet and at rest. **1870** DASENT *Annals* (ed. 4) II. 15 He was industrious, and more, he was handsome. **1905** A. R. WHITHAM *Watchers by the Cross* ii. 15 Tradition..tells us that she was wealthy, influential and beautiful, and yet before her conversion living a life of worldliness,—more, a life of deadly sin.

†**7.** quasi-*prep.* = PLUS 1. *Obs.*

1545 *St. Papers Hen. VIII* (1830) I. 796 Item, 2 of the gretest hulkes that may be gotten, more the hulkes that rydeth within the havyn. **1694** HOLDER *Harmony* (plate opp. p. 120), 5 to 4 more Diesis... 5 to 3 more Diesis & comma. **1706** W. JONES *Syn. Palmar. Matheseos* 67 That Number more one.

more, *v.*[1] *Obs.* exc. *dial.* Also 7 **moare**. [f. MORE *sb.*[1]]

1. *intr.* To take root, become rooted; chiefly *fig.*

c **1200** *Trin. Coll. Hom.* 163 [Hie] sewen on þis lond godes word for sede and hit morede on here heorte and weacs and wel þeaȝh. **1607** *Schol. Disc. agst. Antichr.* I. i. 42 They gaue them scope..not only to moare but also to spread, and finally to gaine that height in which at this day we find them. **1825** JENNINGS *Obs. Dial. W. Eng.* 56 To *More*, v.n. to root; to become fixed by rooting.

†**2.** *trans.* To root, implant; to establish. *Obs.*

a **1300** *Leg. Rood* (1871) 28/126 To one hi [the three trees] were alle icome And Imored so uaste also þat hi ne miȝte awei be inome. *c* **1330** R. BRUNNE *Chron. Wace* (Rolls) 16587 Whenne..þe folk was wel y-mored. *c* **1380** *Sir Ferumb.* 2834 Hure loue ys mored on þe ful vaste. **1398** TREVISA *Barth. De P.R.* XIV. ii. (1495) 466 Noo thynge on lyue maye growe but yf he be rotyd and moryd in substaunce of erthe. *Ibid.* XV. xxxvii. (Tollem. MS.), Seuen naciones of them were of children of Canaan, in þe whiche þe curse þat was ȝeuen to them, was y moret, as it were by heritage. **1593** BILSON *Govt. Christ's Ch.* 15 The grounding vs in faith, moring vs in hope, and rooting vs in charitie.

3. To uproot, root *up*.

1297 R. GLOUC. (Rolls) 10263–4 Þe erchebissopes wodes ek þe king het echon þat me morede al clene vp, þat þer ne bileuede non. þat ech tre were vp mored, þat it ne spronge namore þere. **1890** *Gloucester Gloss.* s.v. *More* sb., *To more*, to root up.

Hence **moring-axe**, an axe for 'moring' trees.

1777 *Horæ Subsecivæ* 277 (E.D.D.). **1787** GROSE *Provinc. Gloss.*, *Moreing-ax*, an ax for grubbing up the roots of trees. **1890** *Gloucester Gloss.*

†**more**, *v.*[2] *Obs.* Also 3–4 **mare**, 5 **mooryn**. [f. MORE *a.* Cf. MDu., MLG. *mêren* (Du. *vermeeren*, *vermeerderen*), OHG. *mêrôn* (MHG. *mêren*, mod.G. *mehren*).]

1. *trans.* To increase, augment, exaggerate.

a **1300** *Cursor M.* 2354 To mare þe medes of his fai. **1340** *Ayenb.* 79 Of þe guodes þet god him ylend uor to mory. *Ibid.* 175 Efterward me ssel zigge naȝt onlepiliche þe zennes ac þe aboutestondinges alle þet moreþ þe zennes. **1390** GOWER *Conf.* III. 147 What he wol make lasse, he lasseth, What he wol make more, he moreth. **1433** LYDG. *St. Edmund* I. 891 So was he besy the tresour, that men calle Rem publicam, to moren and amende. *c* **1440** *Jacob's Well* xvi. 111 To encresyn & to moryn þi mede in blysse. *c* **1440** *Promp. Parv.*

343/1 Moryn, or make more (*H.* mooryn), *majoro.* *a* **1450** in *Eng. Gilds* (1870) 451 In moryng the pris of the liuere. **1450–1530** *Myrr. our Ladye* 209 Then the kynge of all blysse mored hys treasure puttynge in to yt a lyuynge sowle. **1483** *Vulg. abs Terentio* 15 He dredith lest thy olde angyr or hardnes be mored or incresyd.

2. *intr.* To become increased or augmented.

1412–20 LYDG. *Chron. Troy* III. xxvii. (1555) Sj, They him besought.. on their woo to rewe, That lykly was to more [ed. 1513 morne] and renewe. *c* **1430** —— *Min. Poems* (Percy Soc.) 243 For rihte as Ver ay moreth in grennesse, So doth childhood in amerows lustynesse.

‖**more** (ˈmɔəreɪ). [L., abl. of *mos* manner, custom: see MORES.] In phrases: chiefly with *poss. adjs.*, as **more suo**, in his own fashion, **more meo**, in my own fashion; and with national *adjs.*, as **more hispanico, turcesco**, in accordance with Spanish (Turkish) customs. Also **more majorum**, in traditional manner.

1600 HOLLAND tr. *Livy's Romane Hist.* XXVI. 585 Hee might proceed in the suite at his owne good pleasure, *more maiorum. i.* [according to the auncient manner used by their forefathers]. **1612** T. SHELTON tr. *Cervantes's Hist. Don Quixote* III. vi. 176 Hee spoke to his Lord with his Cap in his hand, his head bowed, and his body bended (*more Turcesco*). **1713** ADDISON in *Guardian* 3 July 2/1, I have.. been drawn in to tattle of my self, *more Majorum*, almost the length of a whole *Guardian.* **1810** SOUTHEY *Let.* 27 Sept. (1856) II. 203 The preface, *more meo*, is short and explicit. *c* **1842** H. JAMES *Let.* in R. B. Perry *Tht. & Char. W. James* (1935) I. 43 Let him try, and above all let him forgive *more suo* all my botherings. **1865** MILL *Exam. Hamilton's Philos.* xviii. 358 In a later part of his Lectures.. he, *more suo*, forgets this definition. *a* **1937** J. L. STOCKS *Reason & Intuition* (1939) xiv. 212 What Mill, *more suo*, offers us in the *Logic* is a compromise or middle position. **1943** G. BRENAN *Spanish Labyrinth* vii. 154 The workmen.. shot the offending mayor and, *more hispanico*, cut off his head and those of the police who had been killed in the fight and paraded them around the town.

more, var. MOHUR; obs. f. MOOR.

-more (mɔə(r)), *suffix*, forming advs. of place (rarely of time) in the comparative degree (most of which have given rise to adjs. of identical form). Chiefly appended to advs. having already the comparative ending *-er*, as in *backermore, downermore, farthermore, furthermore, hindermore, innermore, outermore, overmore, rathermore, uttermore*; in the 16–17th c. a few formations occur in which it is added to a positive or uncompared adv., as *hindmore, hithermore, inmore*, Sc. *yonder mair*.

The suffix is identical with MORE *adv.*; the addition of this adv. to comparatives occurs in Scandinavian, as ON. *fyrrmeir* earlier, *firrmeir* farther off, *nærmeir* nearer, OSw. *innarmer* = INNERMORE, *nithirmer* = NETHERMORE. The earliest instances in Eng. occur in the Ormulum (*furthermore*) and the Cursor Mundi (*farthermore, innermore*); it is therefore likely that the use was originally due to Scandinavian influence. But the majority of the comparatives in *-more* were formed to correspond to previously existing superlatives in -MOST, which were partly altered forms of OE. superlatives in *-m-est*, and partly new formations on the analogy of these.

Morea, Moria, varr. MURIA *sb.* and *a.*

more bery, obs. form of MULBERRY.

Moreclacke: see MORTLAKE.

†ˈ**morecrop**. *Obs. rare.* Also 6 (? *erron.*) merecrop. [? f. MORE *a.* + CRAP *sb.*[1] (sense 2).] The plant Burnet Saxifrage, *Pimpinella Saxifraga.*

a **1400–50** *Stockholm Med. MS.* 194 Pympernol or selfhol or weyewourth or morecrop: *ipia maior.* **1597** GERARDE *Herbal* App., Merecrop is Pimpernell.

moreen (mɒˈriːn). Also 8 **morine**. [Of obscure origin; possibly a fanciful formation on MOIRE. Cf. MORELLA.] A stout woollen or woollen and cotton material either plain or watered, used for curtains, etc. Also *attrib.*

a **1691** ETHEREDGE *Song of Basset* 4 Wks. (1704) 287 Let Equipage and Dress despair, Since Basset is come in; For nothing can oblige the Fair Like Mony and Morine. **1796** CHARLOTTE SMITH *Marchmont* III. 67 A high, long, old-fashion room, with a dark blue morine bed at the end of it. **1797** *Bradford Parish Acc.* (E.D.D.), Moreen and lace, 12*s.* 1*d.* Making a curtain of it before the organ, 14*s.* 1*d.* **1823** J. F. COOPER *Pioneers* vii, Her petticoat of green moreen. **1857** J. H. WALSH *Dom. Econ.* 183 Woollen damasks and moreens are sold at from 9*d.* to 1*s.* 6*d.* per yard. *a* **1864** HAWTHORNE *Dolliver Rom.* (1883) 15 The old gentleman.. pulled aside the faded moreen curtains of his ancient bed. **1905** *Longm. Mag.* July 198 She had discarded horsehair for cretonne and moreen for dimity.

b. *Comb.*: **moreen-damask, moreen-silk**.

1837 T. HOOK *Jack Brag* xx. III. 185 An unsavoury smell of pitch, moreen-damask, savoury viands, and fresh paint. **1889** *John Bull* 2 Mar. 151/2 A dress of blue moreen silk.

ˈ**morefold**, *adv. rare.* [f. MORE *a.* + -FOLD.] More times over.

1830 MARRYAT *King's Own* xli, There is no talent which returns morefold than courage.

morefound, variant of MORFOUND.

moreghen, obs. form of MORN.

†ˈ**morehand**, *adv. Obs. rare.* [f. MORE *a.* + HAND *sb.* Cf. *at least hand* (LEAST *a.* 3) and HAND *sb.* 4 c.] = MORE *adv.*

13.. *E.E. Allit. P.* A. 475 What more-hond moȝte he acheue þat hade endured [etc.].

morehen, morehen(n)e, obs. ff. MOORHEN.

morein, moreis, obs. ff. MURRAIN, MORRIS.

moreings: see MORINGS.

moreish (ˈmɔərɪʃ), *a. colloq.* Also **morish**. [f. MORE *a.* + -ISH.] That makes one desire more.

1738 SWIFT *Pol. Conversat.* 9 How do you like this Tea, Colonel? Well enough, Madam; but methinks it is a little more-ish. **1886** *Peasant* Nov. 187 The beer was the best they had ever drank in their lives and tasted so 'morish'. **1901** *Advt.*, M——'s Extra Cream Toffee is 'Moreish'. More you eat, More you want. **1905** *Dialect Notes* III. 63 That tastes morish. **1971** *Times* 3 Dec. 12/4 Home-made, thin ginger biscuits are very 'morish' they slip down so easily you cannot stop munching them.

morel (mɒˈrɛl), *sb.*[1] Forms: 3–5 **morele**, 6 **morrell**, 5 **moreole**, 5–9 **morelle**, 6–8 **morell**, 5– **morel**. [a. OF. *morele* (mod F. *morelle*) = Pr., It., med.L. *morella*; prob. the fem. of *morel* (= It. *morello*): see MOREL *a.* Cf. MDu., Du. *moreel.*]

1. A name applied to various plants also known as NIGHTSHADE; chiefly the Black Nightshade (= *petty morel*: see 2).

c **1265** *Voc. Plants* in Wr.-Wülcker 558/25 *Morella*, morele, atterlope. *c* **1400** *Lanfranc's Cirurg.* 55 Putte to þis medicyn þe ius of sum cold erbe: as morel, penywort, virge pastoris. **14..** *MS. Linc. Med.* lf. 295 (Halliw.) Tak moreoles, and the rute of everferne that waxes on the ake. **1483** *Cath. Angl.* 243/2 Morelle, *quedam herba est, solatrum.* **1519** HORMAN *Vulg.* 110 Purple veluette of Ynde: that hath the coloure of morelle, or vyolette, or rousty yron: is mooste of pryce. **1546** PHAER *Bk. Childr.* (1553) S vj, The iuyce of morel, otherwyse called nightshade. **1598** SYLVESTER *Du Bartas* II. i. II. *Imposture* 580 Thou seest, no wheat Helleborus can bring; Nor barley, from the madding Morrell spring. **1601** HOLLAND *Pliny* II. 58 Morel or Night-shade. **1707** *Curios. in Husb. & Gard.* 256 If we make use of the Juice of Poppy, of Morel,.. or of Hen-bane, we shall have Fruits of a Narcotick and Soporative Virtue. **1836** J. M. GULLY *Magendie's Formul.* (ed. 2) 144 Solania.. may be employed in all cases where the extract of the morel or the bitter-sweet is indicated.

attrib. **1544** PHAER *Regim. Lyfe* (1553) C ij b, Seeth it in nightshade or morell water.

2. petty morel. Also 6 **petermorell, petimorel, petiemorel.**

a. The black nightshade (*Solanum nigrum*).

c **1450** *ME. Med. Bk.* (Heinrich) 85 Take groundeswele, lemke, chiken mete, daysyes, reubarbe, petit morel, & herbe benet. **1548** TURNER *Names Herbes* (1881) 75 *Solanum hortense*.. is called in Englishe Nyghtshade, or pety morel.. in frenche Morel. **1578** LYTE *Dodoens* III. lxxxix. 444 The greene leaves of Petiemorel, or Nightshade, pounde with parched barley meale, is maruelous profitable.. layd to Saint Antonies fire. **1611** COTGR., *Morelle*, the hearbe Morell, pettie Morell, garden Nightshade. **1725** BRADLEY *Fam. Dict.* s.v. *Headache*, Dissolve four or five Grains of Camphire, in either Lettice, Petty-Morel, or Purslain-Water. **1879** PRIOR *Plant-n.* s.v. *Morel, Petty-Morel*, the garden nightshade, *Solanum nigrum*, L.

b. *U.S.* American spikenard, *Aralia racemosa.*

1846–50 A. WOOD *Class-bk. Bot.* 294 *Aralia racemosa* Pettymorrel. Spikenard. **1890** in *Century Dict.*

3. great morel, *Atropa Belladonna* (*Treas. Bot.* 1866).

morel (mɒˈrɛl), *sb.*[2] Also 7–8 **morell**, 9 **morelle**. [app. a. F. *morelle* (Cotgr. 1611; not in recent Dicts.): see MORELLO.] A morello cherry. Also *morel cherry.*

1611 COTGR., *Morelles*, Morell Cherries; late-ripe Cherries, dryed for Winter prouision. **1813** HOGG *Queen's Wake* III. xvii. (1814) 293 His lip like the morel when glossed with dew. **1819** *Pantologia* VIII, *Morel*, or Morella Cherry.

morel (mɒˈrɛl), *sb.*[3] Forms: 7–9 **morille**, 8 **murrel(l**, 8–9 **morell(e, morrell(e, moril**, 8– **morel**. See also MORIGLIO. [a. F. *morille* (16th c. in Hatz.-Darm.); the history of the word is obscure, but it is certainly a. some form of the Teut. word represented by OHG. *morhila* (MHG. *morchel, morel*, mod.G. *morchel*, whence the botanical L. *morchella*), dim. of *morha* MORE *sb.*[1]

In OHG. the dim., like the primary word, occurs only for 'carrot' or 'parsnip'; in MHG. both were applied also to the fungus; mod.G. *morchel* means only this.]

An edible fungus of the genus *Morchella*, esp. *Morchella esculenta.*

1672 EVELYN *Fr. Gard.* (1675) 260 Concerning Morilles and Truffs: (the first whereof is a certain delicate red Mushroom..). **1716** GAY *Trivia* III. 203 Spongy morells in strong ragousts are found, And in the soup the slimy snail is drown'd. **1761** *Ann. Reg.* IV. I. 242/2 Third service. Consisting of vegetable and made dishes.. green morrelles, green truffles. **1791** H. WALPOLE *Let. to Lady Ossory* 29 Aug., Queen Elizabeth, when shrivelled like a morel, listened with complacency to encomiums on her beauty. **1856** GRIFFITH & HENFREY *Microgr. Dict.*, *Morels*, species of *Morchella.* **1884** *Encycl. Brit.* XVII. 76 *Morel.* This delicious edible fungus, *Morchella esculenta* (Pers.), is more common in Britain than is generally supposed.

†**morel**, *a.* and *sb.*[4] *Obs.* Also 5 **morrel**, 6 **morrell(e, morrell**. [a. OF. *morel* (early mod.F. *moreau*) = It. *morello*, perh. f. L. *mōrum* mulberry. Some scholars refer the word to late Gr. *μαῦρος* black: see MOOR *sb.*[2] Sp. and Pg. have *moreno* dark complexioned, 'brunette'. The Fr. sb. appears in MDu. as *moreel* black horse.]

A. *adj.* †Of a horse: Dark-coloured. *Obs.*

c **1530** LD. BERNERS *Arth. Lyt. Bryt.* (1814) 293 He was well mounted vpon a good black morell horse.

B. *sb.* A dark-coloured horse; hence, a proper name for such a horse.

c **1425** WYNTOUN *Cron.* IV. vii. 729 Þar morel, bayerde, don and gray, Withe wondis flyngande ran away. *c* **1440** *Promp. Parv.* 343/1 Morel, horse, *morellus.* **1466** *Plumpton Corr.* (Camden) 17, I have sold both my horse, good morrel & his felow. *a* **1529** SKELTON *Agst. Garnesche* III. 13 Gup, marmeset, jast ye, morelle! *c* **1550** (*title*) The Wife lapped in Morels Skin. **1587** M. GROVE *Pelops & Hipp.* (1878) 120 For such was Morrell slayne and layde in saltish bryne.

moreland, obs. form of MOORLAND.

morele, variant of MOREL *sb.*[1]

moreling, obs. form of MORLING.

†**moˈrella.** *Obs.* Also 7 **morelly**. [Perh. a quasi-It. dim. of MOIRE: cf. MOREEN.] A kind of material used for dresses, curtains, etc. Also *morella mohair.*

1670 LADY M. BERTIE in *12th Rep. Hist. MSS. Comm.* App. v. 21 Upon the Queene's Birthday most wore.. plaine black skirts of Morella Mohair and Prunella. **1681** in *Mem. Verney Fam.* (1899) IV. 252 My Mother hath bought yᵉ Child a Morelly Coate Striped Yellow & Black. **1702–3** in Willis & Clark *Cambridge* (1886) II. 211 Crimson Morella mohair for the Curtains.

morella, morelli: see MORELLO.

morelle, variant of MOREL *sb.*[3]

†**Moˈrellian**, *a.*[1] *Obs.* [f. *Morelli-us* (see below) + -AN.] Pertaining to the opinions of Morellius (J. B. Morély of Geneva, *fl.* 1560) who advocated an extreme democratic theory of church government. Hence †**Moˈrellianism.**

1644 RATHBAND *Brief Narrat. Ch. Courses* vi. 26 They professe to condemne Morellian and popular Government, but what can be more popular than this, wherein all have equall power to decree [etc.]. **1676** W. HUBBARD *Happiness of People* 62 This [*sc.* charity] would cure all the morellianisme, and libertinisme in the Brethren of New-England Churches.

Morellian (mɒˈrɛlɪən), *a.*[2] [f. the name of Giovanni *Morelli* (1816–91), Italian patriot and art critic, + -AN.] Of, pertaining to, or characteristic of the critical method of Morelli, which introduced a new, systematic approach to art criticism, insisting esp. on the study of detail as a guide in the attribution of paintings. So **Moˈrellian** *sb.*, a follower of Morelli's critical method; **Moˈrellianism**, the technique of art criticism employed by Morelli.

1890 *Academy* 3 May 306/3 It would no more be possible.. for the art-historian to go back to a pre-Morellian state of things in criticism. **1916** B. BERENSON *Study & Criticism of Italian Art* 3rd Ser. 34 Morellianism, surgical, pitiless, iconoclastic even as it seemed, was yet inspired by the Romantic ideal of genius. *Ibid.* 35 We Morellians fought for authenticity with the uncompromising zeal of Legitimists. **1934** *Times Lit. Suppl.* 21 June p. xv/1 The persistence of Morellianism is naturally more apparent in the strictly historical literature of art than in its criticism. **1942** *Burlington Mag.* Oct. 241/1 In this country there are small conventicles, in which foregather members of the strictest sect of the Morellians, where hard-shell elders impart to neophytes the narrow precepts of the old Morellian creed. **1968** *Encycl. Brit.* XV. 835/2 The so-called 'Morellian method' was followed in this and his later *Critical Studies.*

morello (mɒˈrɛləʊ). Also 7 **morrello**, 8 **morelli**, 7–9 **morella**. [Of uncertain origin.

Usually referred to It. *morello*, fem. *morella* dark-coloured; but evidence that the fruit was so designated in It. is wanting. On the other hand the early mod. Flemish name was *marelle*, recognized by Kilian as aphetic for *amarelle*, ad. It. *amarella*, dim. of *amaro*:—L. *amārus* bitter. The Eng. name (also MOREL *sb.*[2], obs. F. *morelle*) may be an alteration of this, due to association with MOREL *a.*]

1. A kind of cherry, with a bitter taste. Also *attrib.*

a **1648** DIGBY *Closet Open.* (1669) 112 Morello Wine. **1657** AUSTEN *Fruit Trees* I. 81 The Morello Cherry and other deep-coloured pleasant Cherries no doubt would make a speciall good wine. **1664** EVELYN *Kal. Hort.* July 70 Cherries. Carnations, Morella, Great-bearer [etc.]. **1693** —— *De La Quint. Compl. Gard.* II. 89 For really those Bigarreaux, and Morello's are admirable Fruits. **1707** MORTIMER *Husb.* (1721) II. 297 Morella, or the Great Bearer, being a black Cherry fit for the Conservatory before it be through ripe, but 'tis bitter eaten raw. **1755** JOHNSON *Connoisseur* No. 80 ⁋3 One was to pickle walnuts.. another

to make Morella brandy. **1761** FITZGERALD in *Phil. Trans.* LII. 72 Several branches of a morelli cherry-tree. **1824** LOUDON *Encycl. Gard.* (ed. 2) §4583 The morello is much improved in flavor when planted against a wall of good aspect. **1882** *Garden* 21 Jan. 50/2 We should like..to know where a more beautiful flowering tree than the Morello Cherry can be found in spring.

†**2.** ***morello peach***: see quot. *Obs.*

1665 REA *Flora* 220 Morello Peach is a fair red-sided fruit, and parts from the stone.

morelly, Moren, var. ff. MORELLA, MORIAN *sb.*

moren, obs. form of MORN, MOURN, MURRAIN.

more'n: see MORE *adv.* 5 a.

‖**mo'rena**[1]. *Obs.* [Sp., fem. of *moreno*, cogn. w. It. *morello* MOREL *a.*] A brunette.

1661-2 PEPYS *Diary* 27 Jan., One Mr. Dekins, the father of my Morena. *Ibid.* 18 Dec., To church, where..I spent most of my time looking on my new Morena..an acquaintance of Pegg Penn's.

‖**morena**[2] (mɒ'reɪnə). Also **marena**. [Native name.] The title given to a chief in Lesotho; hence a respectful form of address.

1835 A. SMITH *Diary* 29 Aug. (1940) II. 186 They walked boldly in though they saw the Matabeli, saluted all the white people with '*Moron*' and then went towards the Matabeli fire. **1861** E. CASALIS *Basutos* II. xii. 214 The Basutos give to the princes who govern them the title of *Morena*... *Morena* .. signifies, He who watches over the public safety and welfare. **1912** J. C. MACGREGOR tr. *D. F. Ellenberger's Hist. Basuto* 292 One is agreeably surprised to see..so much politeness, and so many rules of etiquette..faithfully observed... The chiefs often addressed their subjects as *marena* ('chiefs'), *benghali* ('my masters'). **1923** E. A. T. DUTTON *Basuto of Basutoland* vii. 67 You meet a man on the road; he may simply say, 'Lumela, Morena' (*Good morning, Chief*), and to this the reply is a drawn-out 'Eh!' **1953** P. LANHAM *Blanket Boy's Moon* I. ii. 17 The Chief is highly respected by his subjects, who call him, *Morena*. **1974** *Sunday Times* (S. Afr.) 1 Sept. 3 If it is known, call him by his name and surname and add 'mister' (Morena), particularly if you are in his homeland.

morencite (mɔə'rɛnsaɪt). *Min.* [f. *Morenc-i*, the name of a village in Arizona, U.S.A. + -ITE[1].] A variety of nontronite with part of the ferric iron replaced by magnesium, $(Fe, Mg)_2Si_4O_{10}(OH)_2$, which occurs as brownish yellow seams in lime shale.

1904 LINDGREN & HILLEBRAND in *Amer. Jrnl. Sci.* CLXVIII. 457 Considering that the mineral is not a mixture, but optically well individualized, we have.. thought it best to designate it by the name morencite, derived from the locality in which it was found. **1928** *Ibid.* CCVIII. 12 There is no good reason for separating müllerite, morencite, and hoeferite from nontronite on account of their lower water content. **1935** *Amer. Mineralogist* XX. 475 Nontronites including morencite, pinguite, faratsihite, stilpnochloran and chloropal are like montmorillonite in structure.

‖**morendo** (mo'rendo). *Mus.* [It., lit. 'dying'; gerund of *morire* to die.] (See quot.)

1811 BUSBY *Dict. Mus.* (ed. 3), *Morendo* (Ital.), a term indicating a style of performance in which the tones of the instruments are to be gradually..made to die away.

†**morene**. *Obs. rare*⁻¹. [ad. It. *morena*:—L. *muræna*.] A kind of eel, *Muræna helena*.

1773 BRYDONE *Sicily* xviii. II. 194 The morene..is a species of eel found only in this part of the Mediterranean.

morene, -er, obs. forms of MOURN, MOURNER.

†'**moreness**. *Obs.* [f. MORE *a.* + -NESS.]

1. The condition of being greater or more than another.

c **1380** WYCLIF *Serm.* Sel. Wks. I. 386 Here we synnen doubli, deniyng þat we knowun not, and reversing Cristis sentence of morenesse þat he spake of. *Ibid.*, Gretenes of clerkes is morenesse of mekenesse and morenesse in service. **14..** in Hawkins *Hist. Mus.* (1776) II. 234 Arithmeticke [tretith] of morenesse and lassnesse of numbir.

2. The condition of being more than one; plurality.

1611 COTGR., *Pluralité*, pluralitie, or morenesse; more then one of. **1674** N. FAIRFAX *Bulk & Selv.* 187 A moreness of worlds, and a sooneness of this world, may alwayes be, and often are, grounded upon a like way of reasoning.

morening, obs. form of MOURNING *a.*

morenly, variant of MURRAINLY *Obs.*

morennyng(e, obs. forms of MORNING.

morenosite (mɒ'rɛnəʊsaɪt, mɔərɛ'nəʊzaɪt). *Min.* [ad. Sp. *morenosita* (D. A. Casares 1851, in *Revista Minera* II. 176), f. the name of *Moreno*, 19th-cent. Spaniard: see -ITE[1].] A hydrated nickel sulphate, $NiSO_4.7(or\ 6{\cdot}5)H_2O$, which occurs as green orthorhombic crystals and is formed by the oxidation of nickeliferous sulphides.

1868 J. D. DANA *Syst. Min.* (ed. 5) 648 (*heading*) Morenosite. **1901** M. F. HEDDLE *Mineral. Scotl.* I. 24 [Millerite occurs] with rosettes of brilliant green Morenosite in Mesitine Spar. **1949** *Amer. Mineralogist* XXXIV. 193 On standing in the open in dry air, crystals of morenosite generally dehydrate rapidly to the tetragonal hexahydrate, retgersite. **1962** *Mineral. Abstr.* XV. 458/2 The Valtournache morenosite with 6·5 H_2O has the same structure as $NiSO_4.7H_2O$.

morens, pl. of MORING *vbl. sb. Obs.*

Morenu (mɒ'reɪnu:). Also **morenu**. [Heb.] A title of honour conferred on rabbis and Talmudic scholars.

1650 E. CHILMEAD tr. *L. Modena's Hist. Rites of Jews* II. iii. 69 In Germany, and Italy, they are to be honoured..with the Title..of..Morenu,..that is to say, Master... These men, that is to say, the Cacham, Rab, or Morenu, decide all Controversies concerning the Things that are either Lawful or Prohibited, and all other Differences. **1733** tr. *Picart's Ceremonies & Relig. Customs.* I. II. iii. 46 The *Cacham Rau*, or *Morenu*, determines all Manner of Debates..and passes Judgement upon all Religious Concerns. **1905** *Jewish Encycl.* IX. 15/2 *Morenu*, (lit. 'our teacher'). Term used since the middle of the fourteenth century as a title for rabbis and Talmudists. *Ibid.* 16/1 It can not be determined definitely why a special title was applied to rabbis, or why the term 'morenu' was chosen. **1962** B. ABRAHAMS tr. *Life of Glückel of Hameln* ii. 18 Rabbi David Hanau, the great scholar who bore the distinguished title 'Morenu'.

moreole, variant of MOREL *sb.*[1]

Moreote ('mɔəri:əʊt), *sb.* and *a.* Also **moreot**. [ad. mod.Gr. Μορεώτης, f. Μορέα Morea, the modern name of Peloponnesus.]

A. *sb.* A native of the Morea.

1838 *Penny Cycl.* XI. 432/2 The Moreotes, on the contrary, with the exception of Maina, had completely submitted to the Turkish yoke. **1905** *Q. Rev.* July 113 The descendants of the unwarlike Moreots.

B. *adj.* Of or pertaining to the Moreotes.

1838 *Penny Cycl.* XI. 434/2 Some intrigues and dissensions between the Roumeliote chiefs, the Moreote primates, and the old Klepht Colocotroni. **1848** J. G. WILKINSON *Dalmatia & Montenegro* II. 453 The Moreote character, too, bears a far stronger resemblance to that of the ancient Greeks, than of the Slavonians.

moreover (mɔə'rəʊvə(r)), *adv.* Now only *literary* and slightly *arch.* Forms: 3-5 **more-over**, 4-7 **more over**, 5 **mare over, more ovyr**, 5-6 **morover**, 6 *Sc.* **mair over, mairovir, maiowyr, marower, moirover**, 6-7 **mairour, mairover**, 4- **moreover**. [f. MORE *adv.* + OVER *adv.*]

†**1.** In the phrase ***and yet more over*** = 'that is not all,' 'there is yet more to be said.' *Obs.*

Frequent in Chaucer, who does not otherwise use *moreover*. Here *more* is not strictly an adv., but rather an elliptical use of the absolute adj. (quasi-sb.).

c **1374** CHAUCER *Boeth.* II. Pr. iv. l. 110 And yit more ouer [orig. *ad hæc*] what man that [etc.]. *c* **1386** —— *Knt.'s T.* 1943 And yet moore ouer for in hise Armes two The vital strengthe is lost and al ago. *c* **1386** —— *Melib.* ¶415 And yet moore ouer of thilke word that Tullius clepeth consentynge, thou shalt considere if [etc.]. **1526** *Pilgr. Perf.* (W. de W. 1531) 13 b, And yet more ouer he hath not lefte vs as chyldren confortlesse.

2. Used at the beginning of a sentence or clause, or parenthetically, in order to mark the statement as additional to what has been said before; besides, further. (Often preceded by *and*; sometimes by *but*.) Cf. MAIRATOUR *Sc.*

1382 WYCLIF *Acts* xxi. 28 This is the man, that aȝens peple and lawe..techinge euery where alle men more ouer and [Vulg. *insuper et*] hath ledd yn hethen men into the temple. **1393** LANGL. *P. Pl.* C. VI. 53 And al-so more-ouer me þynkeþ..men sholde constreyne no clerke to knauene werkes. *c* **1430** LYDG. *Min. Poems* (Percy Soc.) 37 He..askid hir if she myght feithfullie Luf him of herte, and, morover, fynallye Become his wife. **1483** *Cath. Angl.* 228/1 Mare ouer, *preterea, insuper, quineciam*. **1509** FISHER *Funeral Serm. C'tess Richmond* Wks. (1876) 295 And more ouer to thentente all her werkes myght be more acceptable [etc.]. **1530** TINDALE *Num.* xx. 2 More ouer there was no water for the multitude. **1552** ABP. HAMILTON *Catech.* (1884) 50 Mairouir thow so doand, condemnis thi awin saule to panis eternal. **1654** BRAMHALL *Just Vind.* ii. (1661) 16 Some were excluded..only from the use of the Sacraments, others moreover..both from Sacraments and Prayers. **1725** DE FOE *Voy. round World* (1840) 278 And he, moreover, told me that it was next to a miracle they could keep possession of the place. **1839** KEIGHTLEY *Hist. Eng.* II. 41 And moreover, then, as at all times, the clergy had been the most lenient of landlords. **1849** MACAULAY *Hist. Eng.* ii. I. 177 He was, moreover, partial to the Roman Catholic religion. **1860** TYNDALL *Glac.* I. x. 65 Vast plates of ice moreover often stood out midway between the walls of the chasms.

†**b.** in fuller form, ***moreover than this***, etc. *Obs.*

1569 J. SANFORD tr. *Agrippa's Van. Artes* 71 b, More ouer then this, if there be any Philosophie or Doctrine of manners [etc.]. **1795** *Jemima* I. 162 But moreover than all that, he is painted up to the eyes and perfumed.

†**3.** Qualifying a predicate: Besides. *Obs. rare.*

1517 *Domesday Inclos.* (1897) I. 260 Thei say that [etc.].. thei say that [etc.]..And moreouer thei have nothing to say.

†**4.** Used prepositionally. *Obs.*

1390 GOWER *Conf.* II. 341 And if I schol more over this Declare what this vertu is [etc.].

†**b.** Governing a clause: Besides *that*. *Obs. rare.*

1602 SHAKS. *Ham.* II. ii. 2 Moreouer, that we much did long to see you, The neede we haue to vse you, did prouoke Our hastie sending.

morepork: see MOPOKE.

more pout: see MOORPOUT.

†'**morer**. *Obs.* [f. MORE *v.* + -ER[1].] One who increases.

1451 CAPGRAVE *Life St. Augustine* 2 It [Augustus] soundith in our langage as a morer of þe lordschip. *Ibid.*, A morer of þe cite a-boue, a gret encreser of þe blis of heuene.

moreraye, mores, obs. ff. MORAY, MORRIS *sb.*[1]

mores ('mɔəri:z). Normally const. as *sb. pl.* [a. L. *mores* pl. of *mos* manner, custom.] **1.** Those acquired customs and moral assumptions which give cohesion to a community or social group, the contravention or rejection of which produces a reaction of shock and outrage. Also *attrib.*

1907 W. G. SUMNER *Folkways* 30 The mores are the folkways, including the philosophical and ethical generalizations as to societal welfare which are suggested by them, and inherent in them as they grow. *Ibid.* 37 The Latin word 'mores' seems to be..convenient..as a name for the folkways with the connotation of right and truth in respect to welfare, embodied in them. **1927** J. DOWD *Negro in Amer. Life* xxi. 154 The adjustment of the South to her new educational problem is only one of the many adjustments incident to her passing from the mores of slavery to the mores of freedom; and any sociologist knows that it is impossible to change the mores of a people suddenly. **1948** *Mind* LVII. 511 It frequently happens that any individual variations from cultural traits cause great indignation. When this is so the cultural traits in question are called *mores-traits*. **1958** J. K. GALBRAITH *Affluent Soc.* xviii. 200 Television and the violent mores of Hollywood and Madison Avenue must contend with the intellectual discipline of the school. **1958** *Spectator* 1 Aug. 167/1 It is surely a mistake for a nation of independent character and traditions to ape the different and often alien *mores* of another. **1967** *Ibid.* 30 June 765/1 The law, in the shape of the jury, is the custodian of our *mores*. **1970** G. GREER *Female Eunuch* 171 Perhaps the pop revolution..has had a far-reaching effect on sexual *mores*. **1975** *Verbatim* Feb. 4/2 The fact of the matter is that mores, politics, and sentiment change.

2. *Ecology.* The habits, behaviour, etc., of a group of animals of the same kind; also, occasionally, the group itself. Cf. NICHE *sb.* 3 c. Also *attrib.*

1911 V. E. SHELFORD in *Biol. Bull.* XXI. 146 Ecological succession is based upon physiology, habits, behavior, mode of life, and the like, which I have proposed to call mores (opposed to the term form). *Ibid.* 147 It is of course recognized that within rather uncertain limits the mores of a morphological species remain, in a general way, the same throughout its geographic range. **1913** —— *Animal Communities Temperate Amer.* ii. 33 Ecology..considers physiological life histories primarily in nature, for this reason the central problem of ecology is the *mores* problem. **1954** A. M. WOODBURY *Princ. Gen. Ecol.* xi. 197 Ecologically an individual may be classified under two or more headings in which the unit is a mores. For example, an insect may pass through an egg stage, a larval stage, a pupal stage, and an adult stage, each of which would represent a mores, an ecological unit in a community. **1962** H. HANSON *Dict. Ecol.* 229 *Mores*, the general behavioural attributes of motile organisms, or groups of animals possessing particular ecological characteristics. **1973** P. A. COLINVAUX *Introd. Ecol.* viii. 117 The fish had different physiologies, habits, behavior, and modes of life, a collection of parameters which he [*sc.* Shelford] called the mores of the animals... His word mores, which has an awkward and alien sound, disappeared, but the idea he was seeking to express by it later found an outlet in Elton's 'niche' and became a central ecological concept.

moresch, obs. form of MOORISH *a.*[1]

Moresco (mɒ'rɛskəʊ), *a.* and *sb.* Also 6 **moresko**. [a. It. *moresco*, f. *Moro* MOOR *sb.*[2]: see -ESQUE. Cf. the Sp. form MORISCO.]

A. *adj.* Of or pertaining to the Moors; Moorish.

1551 W. THOMAS tr. *Barbaro's Trav.* (1873) 52 Besides him was his buckler of the Moresco facon with his scimitarra. **1584** W. BARRET in *Hakluyt's Voy.* (1599) II. I. 272 The said mamedine is of siluer, hauing the Moresco stampe on both sides. **1673** RAY *Journ. Low C.* 482 Within there is all the same kind of Moresco-work. *a* **1780** WATSON *Philip III*, III. (1783) 288 A tax..a part of which he was authorised to employ in building..a Moresco college. **1832** W. IRVING *Alhambra* II. 4 A small gallery supported by.. moresco arches.

B. *sb.*

1. A Moor, *esp.* one of the Moors in Spain.

1577-87 HOLINSHED *Chron.* III. 805/1 The torchbearers were apparelled in crimsin sattin and greene, like Moreskoes, their faces blacke. **1777** WATSON *Philip II* (1839) 65 The Morescoes in Spain. **1845** *Encycl. Metrop.* XII. 526/1 An Edict was published, forbidding the Morescoes, under pain of death, from using their native language.

†**2.** The Moorish language. *Obs.*

1615 G. SANDYS *Trav.* 110 Some in the Copticke language, vnderstood but by few; most in the Moresco. **1678** J. PHILLIPS tr. *Tavernier's Trav.* I. II. v. 76 The little Moresco or Gibbrish of the Country.

3. An Italian dance to which the English morris dance is related. Cf. MORISCA, MORISKA.

It. has the fem. *moresca* in this sense.

1625 PURCHAS *Pilgrims* II. VII. iv. 1020 According to the sound they dance and moue their feet, as it were in a Moresco, with great grauitie. [**1869** W. GILBERT *Lucrezia Borgia* I. 213 Between each act of the comedies a moresca was to be performed.] **1933** E. K. CHAMBERS *Eng. Folk-Play* 150 A *Moresca* or *Morisco* first appears in the fifteenth century used as *intermedii* in the courtly *ludi* of Italy, Burgundy, and France. **1947** A. EINSTEIN *Mus. Romantic Era* xvii. 293 Even the separate regions..began to make

themselves heard: in Italy around 1535, for example, the *Canzon villanesca alla napoletana*, or the *Moresca* in the south of the peninsula. **1959** *Collins Music Encycl.* 437/1 *Moresca*, . . a dance of the 15th and 16th cent., most often a sword dance in which a fight between Christians and Mohammedans was represented.

attrib. **1715** tr. *C'tess D'Aunoy's Wks.* 464 They exceeded all the Tumblers and Moresco-dancers in Activity.

4. Arabesque ornament.

1823 CRABB *Technol. Dict.*, *Moresque-work* (*Paint.* &c.) or *moresco.*

Moresk, -esko, obs. ff. MORESQUE, MORESCO.

morespike, -py(c)ke, obs. ff. MORRISPIKE.

Moresque (mɒ'rɛsk), *a.* and *sb.* Also 7 **moresk,** 9 **mauresque.** [a. F. *moresque*, ad. It. *moresco*: see MORESCO and -ESQUE.] **A.** *adj.*

1. Of painting, carving, architecture, etc.: Moorish in style, or ornamental design.

1611 COTGR. s.v. *Moresque, Fueillage, & Ouvrage, moresque.* Moreske worke; a rude, or anticke painting, or caruing, wherein the feet and tayles of beasts, &c., are intermingled with, or made to resemble, a kind of wild leaues, &c. **1656** in BLOUNT *Glossogr.* (citing *Cotgr.*). **1757** J. H. GROSE *Voy. E. Indies* 177 Their style of building, which is partly Gentoo and partly Moresk. **1817** MOORE *Lalla R.* (1824) 11 Between the porphyry pillars, that uphold The rich Moresque-work of the roof of gold. **1842** GWILT *Archit.* §126 The first period in the history of Moresque architecture is from the foundation of Islamism to the ninth century. **1875** *Encycl. Brit.* II. 234/1 While the genuine Arabian art, the Saracenic, was distinguished as Moresque or Moorish. **1888** *Lady* 25 Oct. 374/3 [A lady's cap] made of mauresque lace.

†**2.** ***Moresque dance***: a modern etymologizing rendering of MORRIS-DANCE. *Obs.*

1727–41 CHAMBERS *Cycl.*, *Moresque dances*, vulgarly called *morrice-dances*, are those altogether in imitation of the Moors; as sarabands, chacons, &c.

B. *sb.*

1. Arabesque ornament.

1727–52 [see MORISCO B. 3]. *a* **1843** SOUTHEY *Comm.-pl. Bk.* Ser. II. (1849) 457 Here, too, the dome is gold and azure Moresque within.

2. A Moorish woman.

1895 WORKMAN *Algerian Mem.* 18 The women, or Mauresques, cannot impress one with the idea of grace.

morethrumble, obs. variant of MIRE-DRUM.

1398 TREVISA *Barth. De P.R.* XIX. cvi. (1495) 916.

Moreton Bay ('mɔːtən beɪ). Also **Morton Bay** (only in sense b). The name of a bay in Queensland, Australia (orig. *Morton*). **a.** Used attrib. to designate several trees native to the surrounding region, esp. **Moreton Bay ash (-tree),** *Eucalyptus tessellaris*, of the family Myrtaceæ; **Moreton Bay chestnut,** an evergreen tree, *Castanospermum australe*, of the family Leguminosæ, bearing racemes of yellow flowers; **Moreton Bay fig (-tree),** *Ficus macrophylla* or *F. platypoda*, of the family Moraceæ; **Moreton Bay pine,** the hoop pine, *Araucaria cunninghamii*, of the family Pinaceæ.

1847 L. LEICHHARDT *Overland Expedition* 75 (Morris), The Moreton Bay Ash (a species of *Eucalyptus*) . . was here also very plentiful. **1908** E. J. BANFIELD *Confessions of Beachcomber* I. i. 15 Moreton Bay ash and other eucalypts. **1944** F. CLUNE *Red Heart* 64 Here he saw a Moreton Bay ash tree blazed with the letter L, made on Leichhardt's 1846 expedition. **1884** A. NILSON *Timber Trees N.S.W.* 40 *C*[*astanospermum*] *australe*—Moreton Bay Chestnut; Bean Tree.—A beautiful tree, attaining a height of 130 feet and a diameter of 5 feet. **1908** E. J. BANFIELD *Confessions of Beachcomber* II. i. 259 One of the chief vegetable foods of the blacks is the fruit of 'tindaburra' (Moreton Bay chestnut —*Castanospermum australe*). **1947** J. C. RICH *Materials & Methods of Sculpture* x. 286 *Blackbean* is an Australian wood, also referred to as Moreton Bay Chestnut. It is hard and heavy and resembles teakwood. The color is light to dark brown with lighter colored streaks. **1969** T. H. EVERETT *Living Trees of World* 193/2 Very handsome lumber, resembling walnut and esteemed for cabinet work and furniture, is obtained from the Moreton Bay chestnut. **1883** *Encycl. Brit.* XX. 173/2 The Moreton Bay fig-tree has immense wall-like abutments. **1890** 'R. BOLDREWOOD' *Miner's Right* xliv. 380 (Morris), The . . venerable church with its alleys of araucaria and Moreton Bay fig-trees. **1917** 'H. H. RICHARDSON' *Fortunes R. Mahony* IV. ix. 362 Mahony turned in and drove past exotic firs, Moreton Bay figtrees and araucarias. **1933** D. G. STEAD *Tree Bk.* xxii. 89 A species with large glossy leaves is the well-known Moreton Bay Fig, which . . is so hardy. **1943** K. TENNANT *Ride on Stranger* (1968) viii. 86 She was particularly fond of the Domain. . . Here were great avenues of Moreton Bay figs; great bulks cold as stone with loose-wrinkled grey skin for bark and roots. **1965** *Austral. Encycl.* IV. 58/2 The Moreton Bay fig (*F*[*icus*] *macrophylla*) is extensively planted as a shade and ornamental tree, but in its wild state is not very common. *Ibid.* 59/1 The small-leaved Moreton Bay fig (*F. platypoda*) is the most widely distributed of all the Australian species. **1838** J. C. LOUDON *Arboretum et Fruticetum Britannicum* IV. 2444 The Moreton Bay pine is found, as the name imports, on the shores of Moreton Bay: it has also . . a range of 900 miles . . on the eastern coast of New South Wales. **1884** [see *hoop-pine* (HOOP *sb.*[1] 13 b)]. **1911** E. M. CLOWES *On Wallaby* ix. 251 Queensland! the home of the red pine and the kauripine, the red cedar, the Moreton Bay pine, and black-bean; and nine men to guard the interests of all this wealth! **1923** DALLIMORE & JACKSON *Handbk. Coniferæ* 155 Moreton Bay Pine. . . A tree 150 ft. or occasionally 200 ft. high, with a girth up to 12 ft.

b. *slang.* (See quots.)

1953 BAKER *Australia Speaks* v. 134 *Morton Bay* (*fig*), any witness who lays an information, anyone who unwarrantably attends to or meddles in the affairs of others; by rhyme on *gig*, . . and which may be a contraction of *fiz-gig*, an informer. **1966** —— *Austral. Lang.* (ed. 2) xii. 267 *Moreton Bay*, a trickster's victim or *gay*.

morewe, moreys, obs. ff. MORROW, MORRIS *sb.*[1]

†**morfer.** ? *dial.* ? *Obs.* [? corruption of W. *morfran* cormorant.] (See quot.)

1706 PHILLIPS (ed. Kersey), *Morfer*, the lesser Puffin, a kind of Water-fowl.

morfew(e, obs. forms of MORPHEW.

†**morfound,** *sb.* *Obs.* Also 6 **morfounde,** 7–8 **morefound.** [f. MORFOUND *v.*] A disease in hawks, horses, sheep, etc., resulting from taking cold after being too hot.

1523 FITZHERB. *Husb.* §100 Morfounde is an yll sorance, and cometh of rydynge faste tyll he swete, and than sette vp sodeynely in a colde place. **1575** TURBERV. *Falconrie* 326 Morfound is the frenche worde which doth signifie in English the taking of colde. **1614** MARKHAM *Cheap Husb.* 74 (Sheep.) Of the Sturdy, Turning-euill, or More-found. **1725** BRADLEY *Fam. Dict.* s.v. *Turning Evil*, The Morefound.

†**morfound,** *v.* *Obs.* Also 5 **morefound,** 6 **morfonde,** *Sc.* pa. pple. **mortfundit.** [ad. F. *morfondre* to affect (a horse) with catarrh, to chill (a person) through; according to Hatz.-Darm. f. *morve* mucus, catarrh + *fondre* to melt: cf. FOUND *v.*[3] and *v.*[5]] *intr.*, *refl.*, and in *passive*. Of horses or other animals: To take a thorough chill, to be benumbed with cold. Hence **morfounded** *ppl. a.*; **morfounding** *vbl. sb.*

c **1410** *Master of Game* (MS. Digby 182) xii, Sometyme for þei [*sc.* hounds] more foundeth [*Royal MS.* morfoundeth] as an horse. **1525** LD. BERNERS *Froiss.* II. clxxiv. [clxx.] 516 We shal be morfounded and frosen to dethe. **1530** PALSGR. 640/2, I morfonde, as a horse dothe that waxeth styffe by taking of a sodayne colde, *je me morfons.* **1575** TURBERV. *Falconrie* 326 Sometimes it falleth out that hawkes are morfounded. **1639** T. DE GRAY *Compl. Horsem.* 38 Morfounding, which is the foundring in the body by over riding. *c* **1720** W. GIBSON *Farrier's Guide* II. xxv. (1738) 85 Of a Cold and Morfounding.

transf. **1513** DOUGLAS *Æneis* VII. Prol. 136 The dew droppis congelyt on stibyll and rynd, And scharp hailstanis, mortfundit of kynd, Hoppand on the thak.

†**morfounder,** *v.* *Obs.* Also 6–7 **marfounder.** [a. the infinitive form of F. *morfondre*: see prec.] = prec. Hence **morfoundering** *vbl. sb.*

1525 LD. BERNERS *Froiss.* II. lxxx. [lxxvi.] 241 They and theyr horses, after theyr trauayle all the daye in the hote sone, shall be morfoundred or they be ware. **1575** TURBERV. *Venerie* 24 They woulde marfounder themselues and would not fayle to become maungie. **1688** R. HOLME *Armoury* II. 188/1 Marfounder, is when a Dog is not able to run, sick, subject to Mange. **1737** BRACKEN *Farriery Impr.* (1756) I. 149 Of Colds, or what Farriers call Morfound'ring.

morfrey ('mɔːfrɪ). *dial.* Also **mophrey, morfra.** [Corruption of HERMAPHRODITE. Cf. MOFF[1], MOPHRODITE.] (See quot. 1886.)

1886 *S.W. Linc. Gloss.*, *Morphrey*, the common contraction for a so-called Hermaphrodite, that is, a Cart which may be used as a Wagon also. **1892** P. H. EMERSON *Son of Fens* 150 Make your end fast to the forerunners of the morfra. **1903** *Longm. Mag.* Oct. 519 Nockold was obliged to take the horse out of the morfrey and hook it on to the waggon.

morfu, variant of MORPHEW.

morgage, obs. form of MORTGAGE *sb.* and *v.*

†'**morgan**[1]. *Obs.* (See quot.)

1659 FULLER *App. Inj. Innoc.* I. 65 There were lately false twenty-Shilling pieces, (commonly called Morgans,) coined by a cunning and cheating Chymist.

morgan[2] ('mɔːgən). Now *dial.* (Sussex, Hants). Also 9 **margon, margin** (E.D.D.). [See MARG.] A name for various species of camomile (*Anthemis*); also applied to the Ox-eye Daisy, *Chrysanthemum Leucanthemum.*

1669 WORLIDGE *Syst. Agric.* (1681) 189 Mugwort, Morgan, Wormwood, . . or other bitter or noisome Weeds or Herbs. *a* **1722** LISLE *Husb.* (1757) 448, I filled my meads with morgan and other trumpery. **1847** HALLIWELL, *Margan*, the stinking camomile. **1886** BRITTEN & HOLLAND *Eng. Plant-n.* 341 Dutch Morgan, *Chrysanthemum Leucanthemum.* **1892** *Times* 15 Feb. 12/1 A large number of ewes are said to have aborted in one farm in Hampshire through being fed on hay containing 'morgan' or 'hay weed'.

Morgan[3] ('mɔːgən). *U.S.* The surname of Justin Morgan (1747–98), American teacher, used *attrib.* or *absol.* to designate a breed of light, thickset horse developed in New England from the progeny of a stallion owned by him.

1843 *Knickerbocker* XXI. 331 The stage generally being able to work its own way, drawn by horses of the Morgan breed. **1849** *New England Farmer* I. 314 There has never been a stock of horses in New England which has proved so generally useful as the Morgan stock of the original Morgan horse, raised by Justin Morgan, of West Springfield, Mass., in 1793. **1869** C. L. BRACE *New West* xiv. 187 Each coach well made and comfortable, with six horses, evidently picked Morgans. **1876** *Rep. Vermont Board Agric.* III. 172 You can teach a Morgan colt anything. **1884** J. HAY *Bread-Winners* v. 77 If you don't want to talk, a train of Morgan horses couldn't make you. **1906** W. CHURCHILL *Coniston* 22 The tough little Morgans of that time . . have all but disappeared. **1913** J. LONDON *Valley of Moon* xxi. 516 They call her Ramona—some Spanish name: sired by Morellita out of genuine Morgan stock. **1923** R. FROST *Selected Poems* 4 A little Morgan had one forefoot on the wall, The other curled at his breast. **1934** *Dict. Amer. Biogr.* XIII. 183/1 Before the middle of the nineteenth century Morgan horses had become a distinct type or breed, famed throughout the country for their attractive appearance and their endurance, docility, and utility as driving, riding, cavalry, stage, and general-purpose horses. **1973** *Washington Post* 13 Jan. F1/7 (Advt.), Must sell this w[ee]kend.—Dark bay Morgan gelding, 15·2 h, good temperament, excel. hunter prospect.

morgan[4] ('mɔːgən). *Genetics.* [named after Thomas Hunt *Morgan* (see MORGANISM).] A unit of the relative distance on a chromosome between two linked genes, defined in terms of the frequency of crossing-over between them so that the distance in morgans between two genes is equal to this frequency when they are close enough together for the effect of multiple crossing-over to be negligible. (Sometimes used for one hundredth of this unit.)

1919 J. B. S. HALDANE in *Jrnl. Genetics* VIII. 305 Let x be the distance between the loci of two factors, y their cross-over value, and let the unit of distance be chosen so that when y is sufficiently small x becomes equal to y. . . The value of y for a given value of x is the sum of the probabilities of all odd numbers of cross-overs. $\therefore y = \ldots \frac{1}{2}(1 - e^{-2x})\ldots$ It is suggested that the unit of distance in a chromosome as defined above be termed a 'morgan', on the analogy of the ohm, volt, etc. Morgan's unit of distance is therefore a centimorgan. *Ibid.*, The cross-over values ·412 and ·236 correspond, according to curve (*c*), . . to distances of ·549 and ·261 morgans respectively. **1965** J. A. SERRA *Mod. Genetics* I. vii. 260 Map distances between gene loci are the cross-over values expressed as percentages of recombination for small intervals. Thus, 1% of recombination is often called one cross-over unit . . or a centimorgan. . . One morgan is equal to 100 centimorgans. [*Note*] Some authors call a cross-over unit one morgan. **1971** LEVITAN & MONTAGU *Textbk. Human Genetics* ix. 376 Each morgan is divisible into 100 centimorgans, each centimorgan corresponding to the map distance between two loci showing 1 per cent crossing over between them. For close loci the crossover percentage can be translated directly into centimorgans, but this is not possible for more distant loci, especially those more than 30 centimorgans apart. **1971** *Nature* 24 Dec. 475/1 Pedigree studies by Lawler and her co-workers established a close linkage (0·03 morgans) between *Rh*, the rhesus set of blood group loci, and one of the loci, El_1, that can lead to elliptocytosis of the red cell.

morganatic (mɔːgə'nætɪk), *a.* [ad. mod.L. *morganāticus* (whence G. *morganatisch*, F. *morganatique*, It. *morganatico*, etc.) evolved from the med.L. phrase *matrimonium ad morganaticam*, where the last word is prob. synonymous with *morganāticum* MORNING-GIFT, f. OHG. *morgan* (= MORN) in **morgangeba* morning-gift (*morganegibu* in Gregory of Tours, 6th c.; MHG. *morgengâbe*). The literal meaning of the term 'morganatic marriage' (*matrimonium ad morganaticam*) is, as is explained in a 16th c. passage quoted by Du Cange, a marriage by which the wife and the children that may be born are entitled to no share in the husband's possessions beyond the 'morning-gift'.] The distinctive epithet of that kind of marriage by which a man of exalted rank takes to wife a woman of lower station, with the provision that she remains in her former rank, and that the issue of the marriage have no claim to succeed to the possessions or dignities of their father; also, occasionally, used to designate the marriage, under similar conditions, of a woman of exalted rank to a man of inferior station. Hence ***morganatic husband, wife.***

A morganatic marriage is sometimes called a 'left-handed marriage' (G. *Ehe zur linkenhand*), because in the ceremony the bridegroom gave the bride his left hand instead of his right. The latter term is sometimes used in a wider sense, for the *matrimonium inæquale* of German law, in which, though the spouse of inferior rank was not elevated, the children retained the rights of succession.

1727–41 CHAMBERS *Cycl.* s.v. *Marriage*, In Germany, they have a kind of Marriage called *morganatic*, wherein [etc.]. **1827** DISRAELI *Viv. Grey* VI. iv, His Royal Highness . . espoused the lady with his left hand . . which we . . call a morganatic marriage. **1838** *Murray's Handbk. N. Germ.* p. xxxix, A Countess of Hochberg, to whom he [the Grand Duke] was united by a left-handed, but not morganatic, marriage, an union which did not exclude the children from the succession. **1846** *Times* 10 Sept. 4/4 Maria Christina [ex-Queen of Spain] after procuring the title of 'highness' to her morganatic husband and 'grandee of the first class' to the eight children [etc.]. **1865** *Even. Stand.* 7 Feb., The Countess Danner, the morganatic wife of the late King of Denmark, is about to marry Count Silfwerstolpe.

So **morga'natical** *a.*

In recent Dicts.

morganatically (mɔːgə'nætɪkəlɪ), *adv.* [f. MORGANATICAL + -LY[2].] In a morganatic manner.

1865 *Pall Mall G.* 11 Aug. 11/1 The well-known Rosina, whom it is said he has married morganatically, . . also has her civil list. **1895** *Daily News* 29 May 6/4 Elizabeth, Princess of Saxony, who after the death in 1855 of her first husband, was morganatically married . . to the Marquis de Rapallo.

morganic (mɒr'gænɪk), *a.* [ad. mod.L. *morganicus* (Zedler 1739).] = MORGANATIC.

[**1830** *Chron.* in *Ann. Reg.* 259 The eldest of three sons of the grand-duke Charles-Frederick, by his *morganique*, or private-marriage, with Louisa-Caroline, countess of Hochberg.] **1854** *Fraser's Mag.* L. 248 Scandal to which the Queen-Mother sought to put an end by a morganic marriage.

Morganism ('mɔːgənɪz(ə)m). *Biol.* [f. the name *Morgan* + -ISM.] Mendelian genetics, incorporating a theory of the gene that came to be generally accepted, as propounded by Thomas Hunt Morgan (1866–1945), U.S. geneticist and zoologist. Hence **'Morganist** *a.*

1934 H. J. MULLER in *Pamyati V.I. Lenina* (Akad. Nauk SSSR) 572 The great bulk of the facts of real significance, subsequent to 1911, and practically all after 1913, were found by the younger workers quite independently of any guidance from him, in experiments which they had planned. .. Their results and interpretations were, however, later accepted by Morgan and presented chiefly by him to the scientific and lay public, so that these developments have sometimes been referred to, especially in circles farthest removed from contact with the original work, as 'Morganism'. **1950** A. HUXLEY *Themes & Variations* 167 The canonization of Lysenko and the anathema pronounced on 'reactionary Morganism'. **1966** E. A. CARLSON *Gene* xi. 95 The article [published by H. J. Muller in 1934].. dissociates 'Morganism' from the gene concept developed at the Columbia laboratory. *Ibid.*, The controversy.. eventually erupted into a clear cut 'Lysenkoist' camp and a formal genetics camp, disparagingly referred to as 'Morganist'.

morganite ('mɔːgənaɪt). *Min.* [f. the name of John Pierpont *Morgan* (1837–1913), U.S. financier + -ITE[1].] A pink lithian variety of beryl which is prized as a gem.

1911 *Amer. Jrnl. Sci.* CLXXXI. 81 Dr. George Kunz described some new and remarkable gems which had been cut from a rose-colored beryl found in Madagascar. He proposed the name morganite for them in honor of Mr. John Pierpont Morgan of New York City. **1955** BROWN & DEY *India's Mineral Wealth* (ed. 3) xv. 598 The lovely gem known as morganite is a pink or rose beryl which owes its colour to the presence of small amounts of lithium. **1959** [see HELIODOR]. **1968** *Rocks & Minerals* XLIII. 651/2 Morganite is a pink variety of transparent beryl. A few samples of this rare type have been found at Poona but not associated with the emerald workings.

morganize ('mɔːgənaɪz), *v. U.S.* [f. *Morgan*, proper name + -IZE.] 'To assassinate secretly, in order to prevent or punish disclosures, as the Freemasons were said to have done in the case of William Morgan in 1826' (*Cent. Dict.* 1890).

1832 *Amer. Rail Road Jrnl.* I. 165/3 Let him be *Morganized*, and his work suppressed by burning. **1923** J. MANCHON *Le Slang* 197 *Morganize*, v. (amér.), faire disparaître un témoin gênant.

Hence **morgani'zation**, the fact or process of getting rid of or destroying by secret methods.

1919 J. L. GARVIN *Econ. Foundations of Peace* 502 When there were fears about the 'Morganisation' of British vessels, he said that it would be sounder for Britain to nationalise her entire shipping.

morgan sterne: see MORGENSTERN.

morgay ('mɔːgeɪ). Also morghi. In some Dicts. *erron.* morgray. [a. Cornish (and Welsh) *morgi*, f. *môr* sea + *ci* dog.] The dog-fish, esp. the lesser spotted dog-fish.

a **1672** WILLUGHBY *Hist. Pisc.* (1686) 64 *Mustelus Stellaris tertius Bellonii.* The Rough Hound or Morgay, *Cornub.* **1752** J. HILL *Hist. Anim.* 303 We, in Cornwall, call it the rough Hound or Morgay. **1828** FLEMING *Brit. Anim.* 165 *Scyllium Catulus.* Bounce or Morgay. **1828–32** WEBSTER, *Morgray.* **1862** COUCH *Brit. Fishes* I. 16 In the West of Cornwall it [the Rough Hound] is used to make what is there valued as Morghi soup.

morgelai, -ay, variant forms of MORGLAY.

morgeline, variant form of MARGELINE.

‖**morgen** ('mɔːgən). [Du. and G. *morgen*, believed to be the same word as *morgen* MORN, with the sense 'area of land that can be ploughed in one morning'.] A measure of land in Holland and S. Africa (and hence in parts of the U.S.), equal to about two acres. Also, in Prussia, Norway, and Denmark, a measure of land now equal to about two-thirds of an acre.

1674 *New Jersey Archives* (1880) I. 151 Each is allowed a piece of land for a bouwerie, each piece 25 morgens. **1688** *Ann. of Albany* (1850) II. 101 Two flatts or plains upon both sides of ye Maquase river..containing about eleven morgen. **1845** *Encycl. Metrop.* XXII. 483/1 (*Netherlands*) Of Superficial measures, the morgen, or Dutch acre, is equal to 2 acres and a perch English. **1849** JOHNSTON *Exp. Agric.* 104 The produce from a Prussian morgen (0.631 of an imp. acre) was [etc.]. **1868** *Rep. U.S. Comm. Agric.* (1869) 151 Connected with this department of forestry are six thousand morgen of forest. **1885** RIDER HAGGARD *K. Solomon's Mines* v, This queer hill..covering at the base nearly a morgen (two acres) of ground. **1895** J. G. MILLAIS *Breath fr. Veldt* (1899) 42 With 10,000 morgen of land that he can call his own, he is indeed a happy man.

morgen, obs. form of MORN.

morgenstern ('mɔːgənstɜːn). *Antiq.* Also 7 **morgan sterne**, 9 **morgenstiern**. [a. Ger. *morgenstern*, lit. 'morning star', f. *morgen* MORN + *stern* STAR.] A club with a head set with spikes: = MORNING-STAR 2.

1637 R. MONRO *Exped.* I. 65 One of our souldiers shewing them over the worke, a Morgan sterne. **1868** *Archæol. Jrnl.* XXV. 141 As for huge two-handed swords, morgensterns, partizans,..the walls are loaded with them. **1889** DOYLE *Micah Clarke* 37 Pike or half-pike, morgenstiern, and halbert.

morgeown, morghen, obs. ff. MURGEON, MORN.

morghi, variant of MORGAY.

†**Morglay.** *Obs.* Forms: 4 **Morgelai, -ay,** 5 **Morglaye,** 5– **Morglay.** [? a. Welsh **mawrgleddyf* (or the equivalent Breton or Cornish form), f. *mawr* great + *cleddyf* sword. Cf. CLAYMORE, which contains the Gaelic equivalents of these words in reversed order.]

1. The name of the sword belonging to Sir Bevis.

13.. *Sir Beues* 956 (MS. A.) His gode swerd Morgelay [*v. rr.* Mordelay, Morglay(e)]. **1598** [see EXCALIBUR]. **1612** DRAYTON *Poly-olb.* ii. 332 Arundell his steed, And Morglay his good sword.

2. Used allusively for: A sword.

1582 STANYHURST *Æneis* II. (Arb.) 60 And bootelesse morglay to his sydes hee belted vnhable. **1592** *Nobody & Somebody* D 4 Giue me my sword, my morglay! **1644–7** CLEVELAND *Char. Lond. Diurn.*, etc. 16 The Souldier with his Morglay watch't the Mill.

morgray, morgree, erron. ff. MORGAY, MOGRA.

‖**morgue**[1] (mɔrg). [Fr., of unknown origin.] A haughty demeanour, haughty superiority, pride.

1599 JAS. I Βασιλ. Δωρον (1603) 116 Neither looking sillely, like a stupide pedant, nor vnsetledlie, with an vncouth morgue, like a new-comouer Caualier. **1614** BP. FORBES *Def. Lawf. Ministers Ref. Ch.* 65 A vaine..bravado, which to offer vs with a newe and high morgue, our adversaries have newlie bene animated, by their late supplement of fresche forces from beyond sea. **1829** SCOTT *Anne of G.* xxix, Prudence..induced him to wave the *morgue*, or haughty superiority of a knight and noble towards an inferior personage. **1863** M. ARNOLD *Lett.* 2 Dec., An amiable family, and with nothing at all of the English *morgue*. **1893** F. ADAMS *New Egypt* 59 That official *morgue*, that narrow and unsympathetic self-satisfaction which has done us such incalculable harm in our dealings with other races.

morgue[2] (mɔːg, ‖mɔrg). [a. Fr.]

1. The name given to a building in Paris, in which the bodies of persons found dead are exposed, in order to be identified. Hence (esp. in the *U.S.*), any building or room used for the same purpose.

1821 *Sporting Mag.* VIII. 69 'The Morgue' where those who die by accident or self-murder are carried—a small building in Paris. **1885** *Boston* (Mass.) *Jrnl.* 4 May 1/7 The body was taken to the morgue.

attrib. **1883** *Pall Mall G.* 28 Nov. 3/1 He was a morgue-keeper [in New York].

2. *slang.* **a.** In a newspaper office, the collection of material assembled for the future obituaries of persons still living.

1903 E. L. SHUMAN *Practical Journalism* 103 This can be done with the aid of the 'morgue' or cabinet of biographical and obituary materials that is maintained in every wide-awake newspaper office. **1925** B. BENEFIELD *Chicken-Wagon Family* 94, I have written a column of assorted obituaries after having dug up enough material in the 'Transcript's' 'morgue' for six columns. **1951** A. C. CLARKE *Sands of Mars* xi. 136 In a score of newspaper offices, the copy culled from the Morgue began to be set up in type. **1964** *Listener* 5 Nov. 732/2 *The Raker* begins in a newspaper obituary department, usually known as the Morgue. **1971** L. M. HARROD *Librarians' Glossary* (ed. 3) 433 *Morgue*, a collection of obituary notices of famous living people kept up to date in newspaper offices. **1975** J. SYMONS *Three Pipe Problem* xviii. 187 The *Banner* morgue was unusually comprehensive, and it contained some interesting material about Haynes.

b. Hence a 'library' of cuttings, photographs, and information in a newspaper office, film studio, etc., often including sense 2a. Also *attrib.*

1918 H. CROY *How Motion Pictures are Made* viii. 200 To make sure that the details are true, a studio has filed away in its morgue photographs of the life it wishes to depict. **1923** G. C. BASTIAN *Editing Day's News* 10 The person in charge of the newspaper files, clippings, and pictures [is] called the 'morgue librarian'. **1927** *Amer. Speech* II. 238/2 A 'morgue' is a necessary department of a newspaper... Here photographs and engravings of prominent men, obituaries prepared in advance, pictures of buildings, ships, and even animals, and reference clippings on every conceivable subject are filed away ready for instant use. **1937** *Nat. Geogr. Mag.* Feb. 148/2 Beside his [*sc.* Jack London's] California laurel desk, with its oil burning..lamp..is preserved his neat 'morgue', as writers call their reference library. **1942** BERREY & VAN DEN BARK *Amer. Thes. Slang* §606/2 Parts of Studio... *morgue*, the film filing room. **1962** *Listener* 12 July 57/1 Cartoonists in the United States rely for day-to-day material on newspaper morgues and wire-photographs. **1972** *Times* 16 May (Wall Street Suppl.) p. vii/2 Over to the *New York Times* for background material from their morgue: yes, the library is officially called that.

3. *Comb.* **morgue-like**, resembling a morgue (sense 1); **morgue-man**, the man in charge of a morgue (sense 2).

1913 *Cassell's Magazine of Fiction & Pop. Lit.* June 50/1 The long deserted tables, shrouded in black covers, would have seemed *morgue-like to a casual observer. **1947** G. GREENE *Nineteen Stories* 28 Her large morgue-like mouth was full of blackened teeth. **1912** *Outlook* (N.Y.) 14 Sept. 84/1 In some newspaper offices the *morgue man and his assistants..work inside of steel cages. **1935** T. E. LAWRENCE *Let.* 4 Feb. (1938) 851 Let us now pass to the epitaph. Yes, Hogarth did the morgue-men a first sketch of me in 1920, and they are right to overhaul their stocks.

†**morhwell.** *Obs.* Also 7 morchuel (? *erron.* for **morrhuel*). [ad. (after mod.L. MORRHUA) OF. *moruel* (cf. mod.F. *moruau*), dim. of *morue* cod.] A small cod.

The word (*morhuel*) is quoted as English by Rondelet *De Pisc. Mar.*, 1554, p. 280.

1611 COTGR., *Moruë*, the Cod, or Greenefish; (a lesse, and dull-eyed kind whereof is called by some, the Morhwell). **1668** CHARLETON *Onomasticon* 122 *Molva Minor, seu Morhua*, the Morchuel.

‖**moria** ('mɔərɪə). *Path.* [mod.L., a. Gr. μωρία folly, f. μωρός, μῶρος foolish.] (See quots.)

1693 tr. *Blancard's Phys. Dict.* (ed. 2), *Moria*, Dulness or Folly, or Stupidity, is a defect of Judgment and Understanding; it proceeds chiefly from lack of Imagination and Memory. **1856** MAYNE *Expos. Lex.*, *Moria*, the same as *Fatuity*... Also, a variety of *Monomania* in which the patient believes himself distinguished for talents, bravery, genius, etc.; also called *Morosis*.

moriam, obs. form of MORION.

†**'Morian**, *a.* and *sb.* *Obs.* Also α. 6 **Maurien,** 6 **Maurian;** β. 6 **Mooren, Moren, Moriane, Morien, Moryan, -en, Morryon, Murreyne, -ian, -ionn, -yen, -yon,** (7 **Moorian**). [Early mod.E. *Morien, Maurien, -an*, a. OF. *Morien, Maurien*, f. *More, Maure*, MOOR *sb.*[2]: see -IAN.]

A. *adj.* Moorish, of Moorish race; pertaining to the Moors; resembling a Moor; black, dark.

1504 in *Acc. Ld. High Treas. Scotl.* (1900) II. 427 Item,.. to the Moryen taubronar, v Franch crounis. **1570** *Satir. Poems Reform.* x. 133 Thocht he wes blak and Moriane of hew, In credite sone and gorgius clais he grew. **1595** MUNDAY *John a Kent* (Shaks. Soc.) 17 First the golden Tunne Borne by that monstrous murrian black-a-moore. **1597** J. KING *On Jonas* (1618) 493 What remaineth, but to repent? to change our Morian skinnes, to put off our stained coats, and to wash our feet from their filthinesse.

B. *sb.* A Moor, blackamoor, Negro.

1500 in *Acc. Ld. High Treas. Scotl.* (1900) II. 97 Item, to Petir the Moryen..xxviij *s.* **1509** BARCLAY *Shyp of Folys* (1570) 198 The uggly Maurians are also of this sect. *a* **1529** SKELTON *Agst. Garnesche* iii. 170 Thou murrionn, thou mawment, Thou fals stynkyng serpent. **1535** COVERDALE *Ps.* lxviii. 31 The Morians londe shal stretch out hir hondes vnto God. **1580** LYLY *Euphues* (Arb.) 315 A faire pearle in a Murrians eare cannot make him white. **1657** REEVE *God's Plea* 120 How often hath this Morian been washed, and yet he is never the whiter?

attrib. *c* **1530** in Gutch *Coll. Cur.* II. 311 Oone doson of Sponnes parcell gilte withe morryan heddes. **1559** in Jupp *Acc. Carpenters' Comp.* (1887) 52 Item payd for skarffe for morren heads ij[s] vij[d]. **1631** BRATHWAIT *Eng. Gentlew.* (1641) 354 It is incredible what rare effects were sometimes drawne from a Morian-picture being onely hung up in a ladies Chamber.

Morian, variant of MARIAN *sb.*[1]

1721 MORTIMER *Husb.* (ed. 5) II. 245 Violet Morian, or Canterbury Bells, come up the first Year.

morian, obs. form of MORION.

moribund ('mɒrɪbʌnd), *a.* and *sb.* [a. L. *moribund-us*, f. *mor-ī* to die. Cf. F. *moribond* (from 16th c.), Sp. *moribundo*, It. *moribondo*.]

A. *adj.* At the point of death; in a dying state.

1721 in BAILEY. **1835–6** *Todd's Cycl. Anat.* I. 801/1 The state of the respiration in a moribund person is extremely various. **1875** H. C. WOOD *Therap.* (1879) 354 Cases..of persons apparently moribund who have been aroused by the inhalation of nitrite. **1886** BYNNER *A. Surriage* xvi. 174 A tangle of brambles and moribund herbs.

b. *fig.* On the point of coming to an end.

1837 CARLYLE *Fr. Rev.* I. II. viii, The wail of a moribund world. **1865** EARL DERBY in Hansard *Parl. Deb.* Ser. III. CLXXVII. 22 One of just such a character as might naturally have been expected to be addressed by an aged Minister to a moribund Parliament. **1889** *Spectator* 9 Nov. 624/2 We all talk of the Turkish Empire as moribund.

B. *sb.* A person in a dying state.

1835 CAROLINE BOWLES in *Corr. w. Southey* (1881) 328 Another person was mortally wounded and his death hourly expected... Every day the moribund's door was besieged by crowds of anxious inquirers. **1852** MUNDY *Our Antipodes* (1857) 205 There will be more lawyers than litigants, more medicos than moribunds. **1890** 'R. BOLDREWOOD' *Miner's Right* xxvii, 'What's the odds?' queried the persistent moribund wearily.

moribundity (mɒrɪ'bʌndɪtɪ). *rare.* [f. MORIBUND + -ITY.] Moribund condition.

1842 SYD. SMITH in Lady Holland *Mem.* (1855) II. 471 Mrs. Sydney and I are both in fair health,—such health as is conceded to moribundity and caducity. **1900** HENLEY *Mem.* in *G. W. Steevens' Things Seen* p. xvi, The 'National Observer'..was still afoot, and though conscious of its moribundity..was keeping the bravest of fronts.

moric ('mɔərɪk), *a.* [f. L. *mōr-us* mulberry + -IC.] *moric acid*, (*a*) see quot. 1856; (*b*) = MORIN.

1856 MAYNE *Expos. Lex.*, *Moricus*, applied by Klaproth to a particular acid which he found in the bark of the *Morus*

alba: moric. **1866** BRANDE & COX *Dict. Sci.*, etc., *Moric acid, Morin*, a variety of tannic acid existing in the wood of *Morus tinctoria*, or *fustic*.

morice, obs. form of MORRIS *sb.*[1] and *v.*

moriche (mɒˈrɪtʃeɪ). *West-Indian.* [a. Carib *moriche, morichi, muriche* = Tupi *muriti, miriti.*] A South American palm of the genus *Mauritia*. Also called ***moriche palm***. ***moriche apple, nut***: names for the fruit of this palm.

1866 [see ITA]. **1871** KINGSLEY *At Last* viii, Sixty feet and more aloft, the short smooth columns of the Moriches towered around us. *Ibid.* xii, The Moriche apples floated down the stream. *Ibid.* xvii, The ripple lapped the Moriche-nuts about the roots of the Manchineel bush.

Morien, variant of MORIAN.

†**ˈmorient**, *a. Obs.* [ad. L. *morient-em*, pr. pple. of *morī* to die.] Dying.

1679 C. NESSE *Antichrist* 64 He adds a 6th period, to wit, morient.. our posterity shall see him die.

moriform (ˈmɔərɪfɔːm), *a.* [f. L. *mōr-um* mulberry + -(I)FORM.] Having the shape or form of a mulberry.

1856 in MAYNE *Expos. Lex.* **1897** *Allbutt's Syst. Med.* IV. 719 Moriform hypertrophy of the inferior turbinals.

morigerate (mɒˈrɪdʒərət), *a. rare.* [ad. L. *mōrigerātus*, pa. pple. of *mōrigerārī*: see next.] Complying, obedient.

a **1533** LD. BERNERS *Gold. Bk. M. Aurel.* (1546) Z viij b, The armies.. were as well disciplined and morigerate, as the schooles of the philosophies. **1560** ROLLAND *Crt. Venus* III. 14 Baith ald and ȝoung richt weill Morigerat. **1836** J. H. NEWMAN *Lett.* (1891) II. 199 They were morigerate, through the Exhortation and half the Confession, when they bolted.

†**morigerate**, *v. Obs.*[−0] [f. L. *morigerāt-*, ppl. stem of *mōrigerārī*, f. *mōriger-us*: see MORIGEROUS.] *intr.* (See quot.)

1623 COCKERAM, *Morigerate*, to doe as one is commanded, to obey.

morigeration (mɒrɪdʒəˈreɪʃən). [ad. L. *mōrigerātiōn-em* compliance, n. of action f. *mōrigerārī* (see prec.) + -ATION.] Obedience, compliance, deference to superiors, obsequiousness.

1605 BACON *Adv. Learn.* I. iii. §10 Not that I can taxe or condemne the morigeration or application of learned men to men in fortune. **1659** EVELYN *Let. to Boyle* 3 Sept., That fond morigeration to the mistaken customs of the age. **1903** *Edin. Rev.* Apr. 384 Morigeration served their turn during the first part of their Asiatic journey.

morigerous (mɒˈrɪdʒərəs), *a.* [f. L. *mōriger-us* (f. *mōr-*, *mōs* custom, humour + *ger-ĕre* to bear, carry; after the phr. *morem gerere* to humour or comply with the wishes of a person) + -OUS.] Obedient, compliant, submissive. Const. *to*.

c **1600** *Timon* III. v. (Shaks. Soc.) 53 Timon, thou hast a wife morigerous Shee is the onely comfort of my age. **1637** BASTWICK *Litany* I. 3 Fire, aire, water, earth, all most morigerous; the winds and the seas obey him. **1681** H. MORE *Exp. Dan.* Pref. 65 Let us.. be morigerous to the Magistrate. **1706** PHILLIPS (ed. Kersey), *Morigerous*, obedient, dutiful, complaisant. **1814** BERINGTON *Lit. Hist. Mid. Ages* v. (1846) 260 He had early acquired the character of a morigerous and well disciplined monk.

Hence †**moˈrigerousness**.

1681 H. MORE *Exp. Dan.* Pref. 77 All Decency and Order and Morigerousness to the Magistrate.

‖**moriglio.** *Obs.* Also 8 morillia. [It. = F. *morille* MOREL.] = MOREL *sb.*[3]

1698 W. KING tr. *Sorbière's Journ. Lond.* 32 As that for Champignons, and Moriglio's they were as great strangers to 'em as if they had been bred in Japan. **1699** M. LISTER *Journ. Paris* 154 The Moriglio split in two from top to bottom is all hollow and smooth. **1713** C'TESS WINCHELSEA *Misc. Poems* 35 In the plain, unstudied Sauce Nor Treufle, nor Morillia was.

moril, morille, var. forms of MOREL *sb.*[2]

moˈrilliform, *a.* [f. F. *morille* MOREL *sb.*[3] + -(I)FORM.] Having the form of a morel (fungus).

1828–32 in WEBSTER; and in recent Dicts.

†**morillion.** *Obs.* [Cf. MORILLON[1]] A kind of tulip.

1721 MORTIMER *Husb.* (ed. 5) II. 241 Morillion of Antwerp, a pale Scarlet and pale Yellow.

morillo (moˈriʎo). *Bullfighting.* Also morrillo, murillo. [Sp. *morrillo* fleshy part of the neck of an animal.] The muscle at the back of the bull's neck, one of the targets for the lances of the bullfighters.

1932 E. HEMINGWAY *Death in Afternoon* xvi. 180 The morillo, or hump of muscle that rises from the back of the bull's neck to his shoulders. **1959** V. J. KEHOE *Aficionado!* i. 34 They [*sc.* the picadors] must place a *pica* (lance) into the rear part of the toro's long hump of neck muscle, known as the *morrillo* or *cerviguillo*. **1967** [see DIVISA]. **1968** S. OAG *In Presence of Death* 261 They [*sc.* the picadors] should give it a minimum of three varas to test the bull's courage, weaken its powerful tossing muscle, the murillo, and lower its head. **1971** J. LEIBOLD *This is Bullfight* ii. 31 The throwing muscle at the back of the neck (called the *morrillo*) is remarkably developed [in the fighting bull].

morillon[1] (mɒˈrɪlən). [a. F. *morillon* (OF. *moreillon*, 13th c.), according to Hatz.-Darm. related to *morel* dark-coloured: see MOREL *a.*] A variety of the vine; also, its fruit.

1664 EVELYN *Kal. Hort., Catal.* (1699) 174 Vines.. Muscatell, Black, White, excellent, Morillon, Chassela [etc.]. **1731** MILLER *Gard. Dict.*, *Vitis; præcox Columellæ, acinis dulcibus, nigrantibus.* The black Morillon. **1824** LOUDON *Encycl. Gard.* (ed. 2) §4801 Black morillon... White morillon.

attrib. **1860** REDDING *French Wines* iii. 40 The black morillon grape.

morillon[2] (mɒˈrɪlən). [a. F. *morillon.*] A name for the female or young of the Golden-Eye, formerly mistaken for a separate species.

1678 RAY *Willughby's Ornith.* 368 The Glaucium or Morillon of Bellonius. **1768** PENNANT *Brit. Zool.* (1776) II. 498 Morillon. This species is rather less than the last [*sc.* the Golden Eye]. **1802** G. MONTAGU *Ornith. Dict.* (1831) 211 This bird [Golden-eye], in its immature state is the Morillon (*Anas glaucion*) of various authors. **1863** C. ST. JOHN *Nat. Hist. & Sport Moray* 36 There was not a single duck of any sort to be seen, with the exception of one morillon. **1883** *Encycl. Brit.* XVI. 824/2 *Morillon*, a name commonly given by fowlers to the female or immature male of the Golden-Eye.

morimal, variant of MORMAL.

morin (ˈmɔərɪn). *Chem.* [a. F. *morine*, f. L. *mōr-us* (in mod.L. the name of the genus formerly including the fustic-tree): see -IN.] A yellow colouring matter obtained from fustic.

1837 P. KEITH *Bot. Lex.* 259 The colouring matter obtained from *Morus tinctoria* has been regarded by M. Chevreul as a peculiar substance, and designated by the appellation of *morin.* **1875** *Ure's Dict. Arts* III. 365 *Morine.* This is the name given by Gerhardt to the principal colouring matter of the *Morus tinctoria* or *old fustic.*

‖**morinda** (mɒˈrɪndə). *Bot.* [mod.L., f. L. *mōr-us* mulberry tree + *Ind-us* Indian.] A cinchonaceous genus of plants, native of tropical Asia and Polynesia, the bark and roots of which yield red and yellow dyes. Also *attrib.* in ***morinda bark***.

1882 J. SMITH *Dict. Econ. Plants* 276 Morinda Bark.

morindin (mɒˈrɪndɪn). *Chem.* Also -ine. [f. mod.L. *Morind-a* (see prec.) + -IN.] (See quots.)

1848 ANDERSON in *Trans. Roy. Soc. Edin.* (1849) XVI. 438 The colouring matter of sooranjee, to which I give the name of Morindine. **1858** *Fownes' Chem.* (ed. 7) 630 Morindin.. yellow crystalline colouring matter.

morindone (mɒˈrɪndəʊn). *Chem.* Also morindon. [See prec. and -ONE.] (See quots.)

1848 ANDERSON in *Trans. Roy. Soc. Edin.* (1849) XVI. 441 Morindine, when heated, is entirely altered, a quantity of carbonaceous matter being left, and a crystallizable principle sublimed... To it I give the name of Morindone. **1858** *Fownes' Chem.* (ed. 7) 630 Morindin,.. when heated.. is converted into.. morindon.

morine, obs. form of MOREEN.

morinel (ˈmɒrɪnɛl). ?*Obs.* [ad. mod.L. *morinellus*. Cf. F. *morinelle* (Littré).

The mod.L. word is due to Caius *De rar. Anim.* (1570) 21. He says that he gave this name to the bird for two reasons: because it is common in north-eastern France (*apud Morinos*), and on account of its stupidity (Gr. μωρότης folly).]

A name for the DOTTEREL.

1828–32 in WEBSTER; and in later Dicts.

†**ˈmoring**, *vbl. sb. Obs.* Also 4 morynge, 6 *pl.* morens. [f. MORE *v.*[2] + -ING[1].]

1. The action of the vb. MORE; making greater.

c **1380** WYCLIF *Serm.* Sel. Wks. I. 65 þis was no morynge but lassing of God. *c* **1430** CAPGRAVE *Sermon* (B.M. Addit. MS. 36704 lf. 119), The xj son hite Joseph, and he is to say a moring or augmentacion.

2. *pl.* Extras.

1532 in *Househ. Ord.* (1790) 221 [Charge for] Necessaries yearly, without any further allowance for moreings or other, to be given by peticion. **1540** *Ibid.* 237 Likewise of Morens of Beefs & Muttons.

moringa (mɒˈrɪŋgə). Also 8 morunga, 9 marenga. [ad. mod.L. *Moringa*.] The Ben-nut tree (*Moringa pterygosperma*). Also *attrib.*

1753 CHAMBERS *Cycl. Supp.*, *Moringa*, in botany, the name by which some authors call the tree which produces the ben nut. **1797** *Encycl. Brit.* (ed. 3) VIII. 176/2 s.v. *Guilandina*, The moringa, or morunga nickar, is a native of the island of Ceylon, and some places on the Malabar coast. **1861** BENTLEY *Man. Bot.* 531 The Moringa or Ben-Nut Order. **1892** MAR. NORTH *Recoll. Happy Life* I. 102, I saw the two marenga-trees, from the berries of which the oil of Ben used by watch-makers is pressed.

Hence **moˈringad**, Lindley's term for a plant of the order *Moringaceæ* (Veg. Kingd. 1846, p. 336).

morintannic: see MORITANNIC.

morion[1] (ˈmɒrɪən). *Antiq.* Forms: 6 mirrioun, (morlion), morrian, mory(o)n, murreowne, murryon, 6–7 morian, murren, 6–8 morrion, murrian, -ion, 7 morioune, morryoune, mourron, murrain, murrin, 8 moriam, 6– morion. [a. F. *morion* (according to Hatz.-Darm. not found earlier than 1553, Rabelais), or the equivalent Sp. *morrion* (Pg. *morrião*) or It. *morione*. The history of the Rom. word is obscure; most etymologists regard it as originally Sp., f. *morra* crown of the head.]

1. A kind of helmet, without beaver or visor, worn by soldiers in the 16th and 17th c.

Antiquaries have distinguished certain varieties by prefixed designations, as ***cockscomb, pear-shaped morion***.

1563 *Lanc. Wills* (1857) I. 141 A shirt of mayle wth the hed peece or murren thereunto belonginge. *a* **1575** *Diurn. Occurr.* (Bannatyne Cl.) 212 Ane greit number of hagbittis, corslattis and mirriounis, togedder with some vyne [etc.]. **1582–8** *Hist. James VI* (1804) 137 In the shipp was funden ..twa hundrethe murreownes. **1590** C'TESS PEMBROKE *Antonie* 1768 The vseles morion shall On crooke hang by the wall. **1601** HOLLAND *Pliny* I. 480 The people of Thracia.. do with Ivie.. garnish the heads of their launces,.. their mourrons also and targuets. **1650** BULWER *Anthropomet.* i. 22 At Brasil.. Helmets are of little use, every one having an artificialized natural Morian of his head. **1688** R. HOLME *Armoury* III. xix. (Roxb.) 166/1 The Italians call such caps, a Morion, and we from them a Murrian. **1700** DRYDEN *Pal. & Arc.* III. 451 Polish'd Steel that cast the View aside, And Crested Morions with their Plumy Pride. **1808** SCOTT *Marm.* I. ix, The soldiers of the guard With musquet, pike, and morion. **1834** *Gentl. Mag.* CIV. I. 158 The combatants' headpieces are different in form; one has a rim like a morion, and much resembles a modern hat. **1907** *Q. Rev.* Jan. 83 It belongs to the school of poetry in which helmets are called morions.

†**2.** A kind of punishment used at sea. *Obs.*

[In Fr. the word appears to have been in military rather than naval use, and to have denoted a number of blows with a pike-staff.]

1626 CAPT. SMITH *Accid. Yng. Seamen* 4 The Marshall is ..to see Justice executed according to directions, as.. setting in the bilbowes, and to pay the Cobty or the Morryoune.

morion[2] (ˈmɒrɪən). *Min.* [a. F. *morion*, a. corrupt L. *morion*, a misreading in early edd. of Pliny for *mormorion.*] Black smoky quartz.

1748 J. HILL *Hist. Fossils* II. 470 Pramnion Morio sive Morion dictum. The Morion or Pramnion of the antients. **1796** KIRWAN *Elem. Min.* (ed. 2) I. 241 Mountain or Rock Crystal. When.. pale or dark brown, or bronze falling into black, then called morion. **1866** BRANDE & COX *Dict. Sci.*, etc., *Morion*, a lapidaries' name for black Rock Crystal.

morioplasty (ˈmɒrɪəʊplæstɪ). *Surg.* [mod. f. Gr. μόριον part + -PLASTY.] 'The restoration of lost parts of the body' (Webster's *Suppl.* 1880).

Moriori (mɒrɪˈɔərɪ). [Native word.] An early Polynesian people of New Zealand, now extinct, who preceded the Maori; associated *spec.* with the Chatham Islands, where most evidence of their culture is found; also, a member of this people.

1865 A. S. ATKINSON *Jrnl.* 9 Jan. in *Richmond-Atkinson Papers* (1960) II. iii. 145, I had a long talk with a genuine Moriori.. or real aboriginal of the Chatham islands & of some of the southern parts of New Zealand. **1874** A. BATHGATE *Colonial Experiences* xviii. 258 The Moriori population, which, at the time of the discovery of the islands, in 1791, was estimated at over 2,000, must at one time have been very large. **1882** T. H. POTTS *Out in Open* 160 The Moriori was robust in figure, tall of stature, not darker in colour, perhaps, than many a Maori, but of a dull dusky hue. **1905** W. B. *Where White Man Treads* 27 The ancient Moriori mother scooped a shallow hole in the earth, and warmed it with embers, and lined it with dry grass and well-scorched 'kohu kohu' (moss), to nestle her new-born child in. **1949** P. BUCK *Coming of Maori* (1950) I. ii. 14 The Moriori became extinct as a separate people, but their blood is present in some mixed Maori families. **1950** R. DUFF *Moa-Hunter Period of Maori Culture* 15 Moriori, like Maori, is a recent term probably coined to distinguish its bearers from Europeans, and was probably never used before the eighteen hundreds. *Ibid.* 20 The Maori invasion of 1835 [of the Chatham Islands].. marked the end of the culture which we know as Moriori. **1962** *Listener* 19 Apr. 676/2 The Moriori, now extinct, were a group of Polynesians who settled in the Chathams somewhere after the twelfth century. *Ibid.*, The Morioris carved birds on the front of their houses.

morioune, moris, obs. ff. MORION[1], MORRIS.

Moriscan (mɒˈrɪskən), *a.* [f. MORISC-O + -AN.] Moorish.

1838 LYTTON *Leila* I. iii, Gilded balconies, the super-addition of Moriscan taste.

morisch, obs. form of MOORISH *a.*[1]

Morisco (mɒˈrɪskəʊ), *a.* and *sb.* Forms: 6–8 morisko, 7 morissco, 9– moriska, 20 morisca, 6– morisco. [a. Sp. *morisco*, f. *Moro* MOOR *sb.*[2] Cf. the It. form MORESCO.]

A. *adj.* Of or pertaining to the Moors; Moorish.

1551 W. THOMAS tr. *Barbaro's Trav.* (1873) 53 Sitteng vpon carpetts aftre the Morisco maner. **1586** T. B. *La Primaud. Fr. Acad.* I. (1594) 84 The emperor Frederike the II. spake the Greeke, Latin, Hebrew, Arabian, Morisko, Almaigne, Italian and French toong. **1605** *Relat. Journ. Earl Nottingham* 27 Diuers Gypsies (as they termed them) men and women, dauncing and tumbling much after the Morisco fashion. **1612** SHELTON *Quix.* IV. xiv. (1620) 452 In the Morisco tongue. **1656** EARL MONM. tr. *Boccalini's Pol. Touchstone* (1674) 277 The chain.. being of Morisco-work. **1710** PALMER *Proverbs* 95 A true Spaniard.. is particularly proud.. that he's no heretick, has neither Jews nor Morisco

blood in his body. **1835** MARRYAT *Pirate* xiii, It was of a composite architecture, between the Morisco and the Spanish. **1847** PRESCOTT *Peru* v. i. II. 308 Fears were generally entertained of a general rising of the Morisco population.

Comb. **1834** BECKFORD *Italy* I. 48 Aldernach, an antiquated town with strange morisco-looking towers. **1885** KERRY-NICHOLLS in *Jrnl. Anthrop. Instit.* XV. 195 Many of the women of this class are remarkable for their personal beauty, which partakes somewhat of the Morisco-Spanish type.

†**b. alla Morisco** [= It. *alla moresca*]: in the Moorish fashion. *Obs.*

a **1592** GREENE *2nd Pt. Mamillia* (1593) H 1 b, Needelesse noughts, as crisps, and scarphes worne Alla Morisco.

B. *sb.*

1. A Moor, *esp.* one of the Moors in Spain.

1629 WADSWORTH *Pilgr.* v. 40 These Moriscoes came into Spaine with Iacob Almansor. **1706** tr. *Dupin's Eccl. Hist. 16th C.* II. IV. xi. 451 As he went to Montserrat, he met a Morisco upon the Road. **1838** PRESCOTT *Ferd. & Is.* II. vi. (1846) II. 390 From this period the name of Moors..gave way to the title of Moriscoes. **1903** *Edin. Rev.* Apr. 278 The Moriscos were preferred as tenants because they were tied to the soil.

†**b.** *Her.* ***Morisco's head*** = MOOR'S-HEAD 3.

a **1550** in Baring-Gould & Twigge *W. Armory* (1898) 8 Gyronny of 6 or and sab.: 3 moriscoes heads of the 2nd.

c. In Mexican use. (See quot.)

1900 DENIKER *Races Man* xiii. 542 A Mulatto woman, the offspring of a Spaniard and a negress, may give birth to a Morisco by uniting with a Spaniard.

†**2.** The Moorish language. *Obs.*

1612 SHELTON *Quix.* IV. xiv. (1620) 457 He..said in Morisco, Let none of you..stirre himselfe.

3. Arabesque ornament.

1727–52 CHAMBERS *Cycl.*, *Moresk*, or *Morisko*, a kind of painting, carving, &c. done after the manner of the Moors. **1855** OGILVIE *Suppl.*, *Morisco*, the work called *moresque*.

4. A morris dance.

1561 T. HOBY tr. *Castiglione's Courtyer* II. L iij b, To goe about the streetes daunsing the Morisco. **1600** ROWLANDS (*title*) The Letting of Hvmors Blood in the Head-Vaine. With a new Morissco, daunced by seauen Satyres, vpon the bottome of Diogines Tubbe. **1634** SIR T. HERBERT *Trav.* 113 The bride-maids..began a Morisko, their faces, hands, and feet painted with flowres. **1844** LOUISA S. COSTELLO *Béarn & Pyrenees* II. 252 The celebrated dance called the Morisco, which is reserved for great occasions. **1935** *Discovery* Sept. 265/2 Miss Violet Alford's comparative study of the relation of the Morris to other seasonal dances of Europe and to the Morisca. **1938** C. SACHS *World Hist. Dance* vii. 301 The carved figures with which Erasmus Grasser decorated the Ratssaal in Munich in 1480... These so-called *maruschka* or *moriska* dancers are..beautiful. *Ibid.* 335 In Europe..the name *morisca* covers many choral dances in double file formation. **1950** L. ARMSTRONG *Dances of Spain* II. 13 Moriscas came into being as the Moors were driven southwards.

fig. **1612** BEAUM. & FL. *Cupid's Rev.* II. iii, There's mad Morisco's in the state; but what they are, I'll tell you when I know.

†**b.** A morris-dancer. *Obs.*

1593 SHAKS. *2 Hen. VI*, III. i. 365, I haue seene Him capre vpright, like a wilde Morisco.

c. *attrib.*

1679 BLOUNT *Anc. Tenures* 149 With Musick and a Morisco Dance of Men, and another of Women. **1698** FRYER *Acc. E. India & P.* 136 He..diverted me with several Interludes of Morisco Dancing.

morise, obs. f. MORRIS.

morish, var. MOREISH *a.*

morish(e, obs. forms of MOORISH *a.*[1] and *a.*[2]

morish(e pike, pyke, obs. ff. MORRIS-PIKE.

†**Morisk**, *a.* and *sb. Obs.* Also 5 **mouryske**, 6 **morisque, moryske**, 6–7 **moriske**, 7 **maurisk(e**. [Anglicized form of MORISCO.]

A. *adj.* Of or pertaining to the Moors; Moorish.

1547 BOORDE *Introd. Knowl.* xxxvii. (1870) 216 Some dothe speake Moryske speche.

B. *sb.*

1. The Moorish language.

1485 CAXTON *Paris & V.* (1868) 69 Whan Parys coude wel speke mouryske.

2. A morris-dance.

1512 *Helyas* in Thoms *Prose Rom.* (1858) III. 31 Moriskes, comedies, daunces, interludes. **1530** PALSGR. 553/2, I foote a dance or morisque. **1613** T. GODWIN *Rom. Antiq.* (1625) 57 The former 12 being called *Salij Palatini*, from the Palatine Mount, where they did begin their mauriske. **1627** HAKEWILL *Apol.* (1630) 365 To this purpose were taken up at Rome these forraine exercises of vauting and dancing the Moriske.

attrib. **1601** HOLLAND *Pliny* I. 192 To make good sport in a kinde of Moriske dance.

3. A Moorish coin.

1525 LD. BERNERS *Froiss.* II. liii. [lii.] 187 We pray you to be our frende, and we wyll gyue you xx. moryskes of golde.

Moriska, -o, variant forms of MORISCO.

Morisonian (mɒrɪˈsəʊnɪən), *a.* and *sb.* [f. *Morison* + -IAN.] **a.** *adj.* Holding the doctrines of James Morison, who in 1841 was suspended from the office of minister of the United Secession Church at Kilmarnock for preaching against Calvinism, and founded a sect called the 'Evangelical Union'. **b.** *sb.* A follower of Morison; a member or adherent of the Evangelical Union. Hence **Moriˈsonianism**.

a **1861** CUNNINGHAM *Hist. Theol.* (1864) I. xi. 324 In the Morisonianism of our own day they have assumed a more scriptural..garb. *Ibid.* II. xxiv. 357 Those who are popularly known amongst us by the name of Morisonians. **1878** *Encycl. Brit.* VIII. 726/1 'Morisonian' doctrines.

morispike, obs. form of MORRIS-PIKE.

Morisque, variant of MORISK.

Morissco, morisse, obs. ff. MORISCO, MORRIS.

moritannic (mɒrɪˈtænɪk), *a. Chem.* Also **morintannic**. [f. MORI-N + TANNIC *a.*] Only in ***moritannic acid*** (see quots.).

1857 MILLER *Elem. Chem.* (1862) III. 602 Fustic furnishes a yellow colouring matter..termed moritannic acid. **1891** *Syd. Soc. Lex.*, *Morintannic acid*... The name given by Wagner to a powder obtained from fustic.

morituri te salutant (mɒrɪˈtʊərɪ teɪ sæˈluːtænt), *phr.* [L., lit. those about to die salute you (see Suetonius *Claudius* xxi. 6).]

a. The words addressed to the emperor by the gladiators of ancient Rome on entering the arena, in anticipation of their death. **b.** This address used allusively by anyone facing danger or difficulty. Also in third person sing., **moriturus te salutat**, and in first person sing., **moriturus te saluto**.

[**1606** HOLLAND tr. *Suetonius* 165 When he [*sc.* Claudius] was about to let out the water of the mere: Ficinus he exhibited in it a navall fight before: And as they who were to fight this battaile, cryed out to him, Ave Imperator, &c. i. All haile O Emperour; They salute thee and wish thy life who are ready to dye: and he againe made answere Avete vos.] **1704** B. KENNETT *Antiquities of Rome* (ed. 3) II. iii. 269 The Naumachiæ of Claudius which he presented on the Fucine Lake before he drain'd it, deserve to be particularly mention'd, not more for the greatness of the Show, than for the Behaviour of the Emperour: who when the Combatants pass'd before him with so melancholy a Greeting as, Ave imperator, morituri te salutant, return'd in Answer, Avete vos. **1869** S. R. HOLE *Bk. about Roses* i. 6 They may say as they enter the arena, with the gladiators of old to the emperor..*Morituri te salutant*. **1894** —— *More Memories* xix. 248 If the slightest ailment affects him, it is a case of *moriturus te salutat*. **1910** *Encycl. Brit.* XII. 65/1 The admirable picture of Gérome which bears the title, 'Ave, Caesar, morituri te salutant.' **1930** E. H. YOUNG *Miss Mole* vi. 59 I'm speaking, as it were, from my deathbed. *Moriturus te saluto*! Tomorrow..I'm moving on. **1951** N. MARSH *Opening Night* xi. 254 Moriturus, to coin as Miss G. would say, a phrase, te saluto, Caesar. **1967** M. GRANT *Gladiators* iii. 73 When the combatants arrived opposite the emperor's platform, they extended their right hands towards him and cried 'Hail, emperor, greetings from men about to die!' (*Ave, imperator, morituri te salutant!*) **1972** A. ROUDYBUSH *Sybaritic Death* (1974) xx. 166 'Ave Petersen,' Per read. 'Morituras te salutat... I killed Clare.'

†**mork**, *v. Obs. rare.* [OE. *murcian*, a formation (with *k* suffix as in *talk*, *lurk*) on the onomatopœic root *murr-* (MLG. *murren*, Du. *morren*, G. *mürren* to grumble). OE. had also *murcnian* in the same sense.] *intr.* To complain, murmur.

c **888** K. ÆLFRED *Boeth.* v. § 1 Sona swa ic þe ærest on þisse unrotnesse ʒeseah þus murciende. *a* **1300** *E.E. Psalter* cv. 24 (Horstm.) Noght leued þai to his worde oghte; And morkedene with þair thoghte.

morkin[1] (ˈmɔːkɪn). Also 5 **mortkyn**, 6 **morkyn**, 7 **morkein, morking, mortkin**. [Late ME. *mortkyn* = AF. *mortekine* (Angier, 15th c.), a distorted form (influenced by -KIN) of OF. *mortecine*, ad. L. *morticina* carrion, f. *mort-*, *mors* death.]

1. A beast that dies by disease or accident.

14.. *26 Pol. Poems* 91 As mortkyn forsaken, she let me liȝe. **1598** BP. HALL *Sat.* III. iv. 4 Could he not sacrifice Some sorry morkin that unbidden dies? **1656** BLOUNT *Glossogr.*, *Morkein* or *Morkin*..among huntsmen is a Deer that dies by some disease or mischance. **1786** *Burns's Poems* Gloss., *Braxie*, a morkin sheep.

¶**b.** *erron.* or *transf.* An abortive animal. *rare*$^{-0}$.

1530 PALSGR. 246/1 Morkyn a beest, *auortin*.

†**2.** ? The skin of a morkin sheep. *Obs.*

1582 *Rates of Custom Ho.* F v, Lamb skinnes called Morkins. **1640** in Noorthouck *London* (1773) 843/1 Skins, morkins, tawed or raw. **1660** *Act 12 Chas. II*, c. 4 Sched. 2 Lambe skins vocant Morekins.

†**3.** *Comb.*, **morkin-gnoff**, a miser.

1602 W. BAS *Sword & Buckler* B iij, A morkin-gnoffe that ..Sits carping how t'advance his shapelesse brood.

†**morkin**[2]. *Obs.* [a. MDu. *moorkijn*, MHG. *mörche(n*, dim. of *Moor* MOOR *sb.*[2]: see -KIN. Cf. med.L. *mauriculus*, OF. *morequin*.] A German coin of small value.

1547 BOORDE *Introd. Knowl.* xiv. (1870) 161 In Hygh Almayne..they haue Morkyns, Halardes, Phenyngs.

morking, variant of MORKIN[1].

Morlach (ˈmɔːlæk), *sb.* and *a.* Also **Morˈlacchi** (*pl.*), **Morˈlacchian, Morˈlacco, Morlack, Morlak**. [ad. It. *Morlacco*, pl. *-cchi* (also Croatian *Morlak*, pl. *-laci*; also *Morovlah*), ad. late L. *Morovlachus*, ad. Byzantine Gr. *Μαυρόβλαχος*, f. *μαῦρο-ς* black + *Βλάχος* Vlach: cf. VLACH.]

A. *sb.* A member of a Vlach people centred on the eastern Adriatic port of Ragusa (mod. Dubrovnik) and, from the twelfth to the fifteenth centuries, in parts of maritime Croatia and northern Dalmatia, forming the country known eventually as Morlacchia, being later incorporated with Slavic peoples. **B.** *adj.* Of, pertaining to, or characteristic of Morlacchia or its people.

1778 tr. *A. Fortis's Travels into Dalmatia* 56 The Morlacchi, in general, have little notion of domestick œconomy... Yet the Morlack is a great œconomist in the use of his wearing apparel. *Ibid.* 65 It rarely happens..that a Morlacco carries off a girl against her will... The Morlack women keep themselves somewhat neat till they get a husband. *Ibid.* 83 Simplicity, and want of order..form.. the principal character of the Morlacchian poetry. **1778** *Critical Review* Mar. 378 The Morlacchians chiefly live on milk. **1793** *Universal Mag.* Oct. 268/1 The people called Morlacks, or Morlacchi, inhabit Morlacchia, which is among the inland mountains of Dalmatia. *Ibid.* 271/2 A Morlack village. **1837** *Mirror* 9 Dec. 383/1 At the death of a Morlach..the family weep and howl... The Morlach women go every holiday to renew their lamentations. **1849** A. A. PATON *Highlands & Islands of Adriatic* II. iii. 32 The Morlack principle is to allow the man to grow as the beast of the forest. *Ibid.* 33 The Morlack is the best soldier and the worst citizen in the Austrian empire. **1877** [see *Illyric* adj. s.v. ILLYRIAN *a.* and *sb.*]. **1881** E. A. FREEMAN *Sk. Subject Lands of Venice* 184 Are we to believe that the Morlacchi used the turban as their head-dress before the Ottoman came? **1904** L. VILLARI *Republic of Ragusa* xii. 322 The Morlachs in the Venetian service made raids into Turkish territory. **1911** *Encycl. Brit.* VII. 773/2 The name of *Morlachs*, *Morlaks* or *Morlacks* commonly bestowed by English writers on the Dalmatian Slavs..is an abbreviated form of *Mavrovlachi*, meaning either 'Black Vlachs', or, less probably, 'Sea Vlachs'... In northern Dalmatia the Slavs of the interior are still called *Morlacchi*; in the south this name expresses contempt. **1920** M. E. DURHAM *Twenty Years of Balkan Tangle* i. 12 They are known as Morlachs,..and historically are in all probability descendants of the pre-Slav native population. **1922** D. H. LOW tr. *Kraljević's Ballads* p. xii, In 1775 a translation by Werthes of the Morlacchian section was published at Berne. **1957** *Encycl. Brit.* XXIII. 230/1 In the 14th century the Mavrovlachi or Morlachs extended themselves towards the Croatian borders, and a large part of maritime Croatia and northern Dalmatia began to be known as Morlacchia. *Ibid.* 230/2 The Morlachs have now become Slavonized. **1968** *Ibid.* XXIII. 93/2 There were also colonies of the Morlachs in the interior of the ancient Serbia.

morling (ˈmɔːlɪŋ). Forms: 5–6 **morlyng**, 6 **moreling**, 7 **morlin, morlinge**, 7–9 **mortling**, 5– **morling**. [App. formed after MORKIN[1] by substitution of -LING suffix for -KIN.]

1. Wool taken from the skin of a dead sheep.

Obs. exc. in the traditional language of schedules to Acts of Parliament. Opposed to *shorling*.

1448 *Act 27 Hen. VI*, c. ii, Colourant par novelles controves nouns come Morlyng & Shorlyng, &c. **1455** *Rolls of Parlt.* V. 330/2 Carie Woll and Wolfelles, Shorlyng and Morlyng, oute of this youre Reame. **1562–3** *Act 5 Eliz.* c. 22 § 2 Yt shall not bee laufull..to shippe..any maner of Shepe skynnes, Woolfelles, Shorelinges, Morelinges [etc.]. **1607** COWELL *Interpr.*, *Morlinge* seemeth to be that wolle which is taken from the skinne of a dead sheep. **1669** STURMY *Mariner's Mag.*, *Penalties & Forfeit.* 4 Wooll, Wooll-fells, Wooll-flocks, Mortlings. **1688** *Royal Proclam.* 6 Apr. in *Lond. Gaz.* No. 2338/1 Laws..Prohibiting the Transportation of Sheep Wooll, Wooll-fells, Woolen-yarn, Mortlings, Shorlings. **1819** *Mortimer's Commerc. Dict.* (ed. 2), *Morling* or *Mortling*, is that wool taken from the skin of a dead sheep, either dying of the rot, or killed, called in some counties mort-wool. **1833** *Act 3 & 4 Will. IV*, c. 56 Woolfels, Mortlings, Shortlings, Yarn.

†**2.** = MORKIN 1. *Obs.*

1636 *Fasciculus Florum* 35 A wretched witherd Mortling, and a piece Of Carrion, wrapt up in a Golden Fleece. **1753** CHAMBERS *Cycl. Supp.* s.v. *Shorling*, In some parts of England, they understand by a shorling, a sheep whose fleece is shorn off; and by a morling, a sheep that dies.

morlop (ˈmɔːlɒp). *Min.* A variety of jasper pebble found in New South Wales.

1886 *U.S. Cons. Rep.* No. 70. 319 (Cent.) Amongst the jasper pebbles are some of pale mottled tints of yellow, pink, drab,..&c. These are termed morlops by the miners.

†**ˈmormal.** *Obs.* Forms: 4–7 **mormal**, 5, 7 **morimal, mormale**, 5–7 **mormall(e**, 6 **marmoll(e, mortmale, mermole**, 6–7 **marmole**, 7 **marmall, mortmal**. [a. OF. *mortmal* (= med.L. *mortuum malum*), f. *mort* dead + *mal* evil. Cf. F. *mal de mort*, used *Hist.* to render the OF. word.]

1. An inflamed sore, esp. on the leg.

Prob. used vaguely; the description in quot. 1543 and its context seems to refer to ecthyma or impetigo.

c **1386** CHAUCER *Prol.* 386 Greet harm was it as it thoughte me That on his shyne a mormal hadde he. *c* **1400** *Lanfranc's Cirurg.* 178 Þe blood-letyng of þis veyne is good..for cancrena þat ben in þe hipis & for a mormal. *c* **1400** *Brut* (E.E.T.S.) 230/3 Also ij men haue bene helede þere of þe morimal. *c* **1483** CAXTON *Dialogues* 41/40 He can hele and cure..mormale. *a* **1518** SKELTON *Magnyf.* 1906 Some with the marmoll to halte I them make. **1533** MORE *Answ. Poysoned Bk.* Wks. 1088/1 To heale the foule marmole of theyr scabbed shynnes. **1543** TRAHERON *Vigo's Chirurg.* v. iii. 164 Of the deed euyll, or mortmale. The deed euyl..is a maligne, fylthy, and corrupt scabbe, which begynneth for yᵉ most part in yᵉ armes, thyghes, & legges, & chefly in the legges it causeth crusty pustules, ful of fylthy matter. **1579** LANGHAM *Gard. Health* (1633) 41 For Festers, Mermoles, sores of the yard, and all other sores, take Ash [etc.]. **1601**

Holland *Pliny* II. 588 Such morimals or sores as scorne ordinary cures & be full of suppuration.
fig. **14..** *Seven Deadly Sins* 109 in *Pol. Rel. & L. Poems* (1903) 247 'Luxiria' ys a lyther mormale. **1547–64** Bauldwin *Mor. Philos.* (Palfr.) 57 The festered & stinking cores of old marmoles & inueterate sores of the weale publike.

2. ? Used for AGNAIL 3.
1685 *J. Cooke's Marrow Chirurg.* I. xi. (ed. 4) 75 There are also little Marmoles, so called by some, which are little bits of the Skin that rise near to the Nails.

[**mormal**, *a.*, 'grievous, dangerous' (Webster 1864) is app. a mistaken inference from prec. sb.]

‖**mormaor** (mɔːˈmɛːə(r)). Also **maormor, mormaer,** *erron.* **maarmor.** [a. Gael. *mormaer* (Book of Deer), mod. *mòrmhaor*, app. f. *mòr* great + *maor* bailiff, steward; the form *maormor* app. originated from the notion that the word should follow the rule of placing the adj. after the sb.] In ancient Scotland, a high steward of a province.
1807 G. Chalmers *Caledonia* I. III. vii. 405 He became maormor of Moray, during the infancy of Lulach. **1882** *Blackw. Mag.* Mar. 350 The title of earl having been substituted for mormaer when Normanism and feudalism made their way across the Border. **1900** A. Lang *Hist. Scot.* I. 169 Macbeth being introduced as a king, by the English Chronicle, before he was even a mormaor.

Hence **morˈmaordom, morˈmaorship.**
1837 Skene *Highlanders Scot.* (1902) II. ix. 365 The Rikis or districts in Scotland mentioned in the Sagas.. are exactly synonymous with maormorships. **1860** W. Anderson *Scott. Nation* I. 54 Edgar had bestowed on his cousin the maormordom of Athol.

mormaset, obs. form of MARMOSET.

mormelade, obs. form of MARMALADE *sb.*

mormeluche, variant of MORMOLUKEE.

mormeracyone, obs. form of MURMURATION.

†ˈ**mormo.** *Obs.* Also 7–8 **mormoe.** [a. Gr. μορμώ, a hideous she-monster.] A kind of hobgoblin; a bugbear; an imaginary terror.
1605 Z. Jones tr. *De Loyer's Specters* 15 In like sort Mormo.. was one of those with which they terrified little children. *a* **1652** J. Smith *Sel. Disc.* ii. 37 To all which we may add the.. frightful apparitions of ghosts and mormos. **1676** [see MORPHOSIS]. **1738** Warburton *Div. Legat.* I. 335 A Mormo fit only to fright Women and Children.

†**mormolukee.** *Obs.* Also 7 **mormeluche, mormolyceue.** [ad. Gr. μορμολυκεῖον, -λύκη, f. μορμώ MORMO + λύκ-ος wolf.] = MORMO.
1621 Burton *Anat. Mel.* III. iv. II. vi. (1624) 556 Diuells and Mormeluches, noysome smells &c. **1624** Bp. Mountagu *Gagg* To Rdr. 2 Horrible affrights and mormolyceues, to put young children out of their wits. **1644** J. Goodwin *Innoc. Triumph.* (1645) 9 Hee tells his Antiquerist, that hee must renounce his oath of Allegeance [etc.].. with some such other mormolukees as these.

Mormon (ˈmɔːmən). [f. *Mormon*, the name of the pretended author of 'The Book of Mormon': see below. The earlier name was MORMONITE.]

1. A member or adherent of a religious body, calling itself 'The Church of Jesus Christ of the Latter-day Saints', founded in 1830 at Manchester, New York, by Joseph Smith, on the basis of alleged Divine revelations contained in the 'Book of Mormon', which Smith professed to have translated by special inspiration from the original written on gold plates, miraculously discovered by himself.

The feature of the sect which is popularly best known, and which is referred to in allusive uses of the name, is the practice of polygamy: but this is not countenanced by the Book of Mormon, and is now understood to have been abandoned in obedience to the law of the United States.

1830 [see CAMPBELLITE]. **1837** J. M. Peck *Gaz. Illinois* (ed. 2) I. 74 There are.. a few Mormons.. scattered through the state. **1842** Caswall *City of Mormons* 34, I begged him to inform me whether the Mormons believed in the Trinity. **1845** G. Struthers in *Ess. Chr. Union* vii. 372 Mormons, Atheists, Deists,.. and other small sects and parties. **1881** W. G. Marshall *Thro. Amer.* viii. 184 Considerable disgrace attaches to a Mormon if he lives a bachelor life. **1922** *Lit. Digest* 10 June 40/1 Because a few of the inmates of the Hollywood film colony have 'married from time to time', they are less to be censured as Mormons than pitied as morons. **1928** R. Campbell *Wayzgoose* i. 26 Muses Nine, Those strapping girls whose love, to say the least, Would make a rabid Mormon of a priest. **1963** K. S. Latourette *Christianity in Revolutionary Age* V. ii. 14 In the Rocky Mountain area and on the west coast the Mormons were prominent.
fig. **1906** *Spectator* 3 Feb. 175/2 In distinction from the barnyard duck, who is a regular Mormon, the mallard is monogamous.

2. *attrib.* passing into *adj.*
1842 Caswall *City of Mormons* 6 Houses.. occupied, I was told, by Mormon emigrants. **1843** Marryat *M. Violet* xliii, The whole of Texas becomes Mormon. **1884** J. Hall *Chr. Home* 42 We have on the one side the Mormon problem to face, and on the other the divorce problem. **1913** J. London *Valley of Moon* 430 He had been provost marshal when the Mormon trouble flared up. **1920** *Encycl. Relig. & Ethics* XI. 83/1 The first principle is set forth by the chief Mormon theologian, Parley P. Pratt. **1942** W. Stegner *Mormon Country* 65 He had sprung clear across the Great Basin deserts to locate the Mormon Station. **1948** [see *Mormon cricket*, below]. **1966** *Encycl. N.Z.* III. 64/2 The many similarities between Maori traditions and Mormon teachings. **1968** *Encycl. Brit.* XIII. 795/2 Space, time, matter and the universe in Mormon theology are limitless by nature. **1975** *Times* 20 Sept. 2/5 The fires at.. the high school and the Mormon church [in Kirkcaldy], caused little damage.

3. Special Combs.: **Mormon battalion** (now *Hist.*), a company of soldiers from Mormon communities in Iowa enlisted for service in the Mexican war; **Mormon Bible**, the Book of Mormon; **Mormon Church**, the name by which the Church of Jesus Christ of the Latter-Day Saints is commonly known; **Mormon City**, Salt Lake City, Utah; **Mormon cricket**, a longhorn grasshopper, *Anabrus simplex*; **Mormon fly**, a hesperiid butterfly, *Atrytone hobomok*; **Mormon State**, in the U.S., a State in which Mormons are predominant, usu. applied to Utah; **Mormon trail**, the trail followed by Mormon migrants to Utah in 1847; **Mormon war**, disorders arising between Mormon communities and their neighbours, and *spec.* the fighting between Utah Mormons and the federal troops in 1857–8; **Mormon weed** *U.S.*, the Indian mallow, *Abutilon theophrasti*.
1848 *Santa Fé* (New Mexico) *Republican* 27 June 1/4 Capt. Hunt of the *Mormon battalion, has left the Ciudad de Los Angelos for the Salt Lake. **1929** L. H. Creer *Utah & Nation* iii. 32 While crossing the Sierras, he met the returning members of the Mormon Battalion. **1838** Whittier in W. P. & F. J. Garrison *Life W. L. Garrison* (1885) II. 221 A discussion of the merits of animal magnetism, or of the *Mormon Bible, would have been quite as appropriate. **1845** *Southern Lit. Messenger* XI. 476/1 These facts were withheld from the world for the nine years which intervened from the first publication of the Mormon Bible. **1882** J. W. Buel *Metrop. Life Unveiled* 349 These three men have subscribed to an oath which will be found in all Mormon bibles. **1838** *Niles' Reg.* 13 Oct. 103/3 We, and all the *Mormon church,.. entertain the same feelings and fears toward the Indians. **1948** *Newsweek* 12 Jan. 38/2 Once a basic tenet of the Mormon Church, the doctrine of plural marriage was formally abandoned in 1890. **1957** W. Mulder *Homeward to Zion* xi. 289 In 1887 the Edmunds-Tucker Act.. disincorporated the Mormon Church itself. **1878** J. H. Beadle *Western Wilds* 39 We got to the *Mormon City all beat out. **1942** Berrey & Van den Bark *Amer. Thes. Slang* §46/1 *Mormon City*,.. Salt Lake City, Utah. **1896** J. B. Smith *Economic Entomology* iv. 97 At the base of the Rocky Mountains, extending up into the foothills.. the '*Mormon cricket', *Anabrus simplex*, occasionally multiplies so greatly that it migrates to the plains below, destroying everything in its path. **1934** *Sun* (Baltimore) 1 May 13/1 The devastating 'mormon' crickets, which came into prominence in 1848, when they threatened the first colonists in Utah with starvation, have appeared in a half dozen spots of Southern Idaho to carry on the destruction they started last year. Black creatures two inches long when full grown, they eat everything in sight. **1948** *U.S. Dept. Agric. Yearbk.* 274/2 The early Mormon settlers knew no satisfactory way of fighting the Mormon cricket. **1959** E. Tunis *Indians* 109/1 Grasshoppers and big mormon crickets were driven into trenches from which they could be gathered in baskets. **1972** Swan & Papp *Common Insects N. Amer.* 75 Mormon cricket: *Anabrus simplex*... Dark brown, black, or green; stout-bodied, wings absent. **1975** *Islander* (Victoria, B.C.) 26 Jan. 15/3 Densest pheasant populations occur in areas offering bonanza supplies of grasshoppers, Mormon crickets or some other.. insect. **1845** N. F. Moore *Diary* 26 Aug. (1946) 46 Our boat and everything about it is now covered with *Mormon flies as they are called, being, I am told, peculiar to this neighborhood. **1847** C. Lanman *Summer in Wilderness* v. 34 They are called the Mormon fly and I was told were found on these rapids alone. [**1909** *Cent. Dict.* Suppl. 828/3 *Mormon*... In *entom.*, an American hesperiid butterfly, *Atrytone hobomok*, which occurs from eastern Canada to the Mississippi valley.] **1882** C. M. Chase *Editor's Run in N. Mexico* 109 Axtell.. went so far as to lay plans.. to get the territory admitted into the Union as a *Mormon state. **1893** L. Wagner *More about Names* 35 Utah, otherwise The Mormon State, is called by the Mormons themselves Deseret. **1920** *Encycl. Relig. & Ethics* XI. 89/1 The economic salvation of the Mormon State arose.. from the money spent in Utah by the Forty-Niners. **1948** Mencken *Amer. Lang.* Suppl. II. 640 Utah calls itself the *Beehive State*,.. but the designation *Mormon State* is far more popular, and seems likely to stick. **1850** *Ann. Iowa* (1910) 3rd Ser. IX. 453 Here we struck the old *Mormon trail. **1868** 'Mark Twain' in *Galaxy* May 631 The post route.. changed partly to the old Mormon trail. **1949** *Kansas Hist. Q.* Feb. 39 The War Department decided.. to improve the Mormon trail from Omaha as far as New Fort Kearney. **1833** in *D.A.* s.v., The *Mormon War. **1834** *Knickerbocker* Aug. 159/2 *The Mormon War*... The war between the citizens of Jackson county, Missouri, and the disciples of the Book of Mormon. **1846** *Quincy* (Illinois) *Whig* 3 Feb. 2/4 He was a Major in the last '*Mormon War*'. **1857** *San Francisco Plaindealer* 10 Dec. 2/2 The Mormon war will furnish abundant material for Buncombe speeches. **1942** C. C. Rister *Land Hunger* 8 Upon the outbreak of the 'Mormon War', Dave and his older brother Jack, rode away.. to join the army. **1872** *Trans. Ill. Dept. Agric.* IX. p. ix, Mr. James H. McConnell.. has.. prosecuted experiments with the Indian Mallow (*Abutilon Avacennae*) variously known as 'stump weed', 'velvet leaf', 'butter print', '*Mormon weed', etc. **1907** A. B. Lyons *Plant Names* (ed. 2) 8 Abutilon... American Hemp, Indian Hemp, Mormon-weed, Pie-marker, Pie-print, Sheep-weed.

Hence ˈ**Mormondom**, Mormons collectively, the territory of the Mormons, Mormon usages; **Morˈmonic** *a.*, resembling the Mormons, polygamous; ˈ**Mormonish** *a.*, pertaining to or characteristic of Mormons or their beliefs; ˈ**Mormonry** *rare* = MORMONDOM.
1846 *Quincy* (Illinois) *Whig* 19 Mar. 3/3 It would be desirable by all quiet citizens that they should be able to discover a complete evacuation of everything Mormonish in Nauvoo, before they hazard purchases in that place. **1852** *Oregon Statesman* (Oregon City) 6 Jan. 2/6 Your course looks as Mormonish as anything I ever saw. **1860** Mayne Reid in *Chamb. Jrnl.* XIV. 359 He would not be the only parent who.. has so sacrificed upon the unhallowed altar of Mormondom. **1860** *Harper's Mag.* Nov. 857/2 We may be a trifle more fastidious than they are in Mormondom, but we have a notion that all the 'bad words' ought to be skipped when the ladies are around. **1873** Mormondom [see DIXIE[2] 2]. *a* **1886** H. S. Brown *Autobiog.* (1887) 114 Salt Lake City is the capital of Mormondom. **1904** *Blackw. Mag.* June 812/1 Other domesticated male animals are so mormonic in their ideas that they recognise no distinction of any kind between their own kittens, puppies, calves, &c., and their neighbours' children. **1920** *Encycl. Relig. & Ethics* XI. 86/2 That Joseph Smith.. was the real master of Mormondom is borne out by.. accounts of him in the height of his power. **1930** *Amer. Mercury* Jan. 6/1 The next step was an accident, one of a series that has displayed God's providence to Mormonry. **1957** W. Mulder *Homeward to Zion* xi. 289 The 'iniquitous' Cullom bill.. stirred Mormondom to its center.

Mormoness (mɔːməˈnɪs). [-ESS[1].] A female Mormon.
a **1861** T. Winthrop *John Brent* (1862) ix. 99 Selecting, perhaps, a Mormoness to kidnap to-night. **1862** C. F. Browne *A. Ward his Book* (1865) 76 'Yes,' hollered a lot of femaile Mormonesses, ceasin me by the cote tales & swingin me round very rapid. **1906** *Out West* May 305 (*title*) The Writer Lady and the Mormoness.

Mormonism (ˈmɔːmənɪz(ə)m). [f. MORMON + -ISM.] The religious doctrine of the Mormons. Also *fig.*
1831 *Niles' Reg.* 16 July 353/1 Mormonism.. a new religion. **1834** E. D. Howe (*title*) Mormonism unvailed. **1845** J. H. Newman *Ess. Developm.* iv. §1. 241 A religion, such that men look at a convert to it with a feeling which no other sect raises, except Judaism, Socialism, or Mormonism. **1855** A. L. Phillipps *Mahometanism* vi. 244 Socialism and Mormonism and infidelity taking the place of religion and social order. **1881** W. G. Marshall *Thro. Amer.* viii. 184 Mormonism does not necessarily involve polygamy. **1913** E. F. Benson *Thorley Weir* i. 33 'They can't all be serenading me.' 'I cannot imagine why not. A Mormonism of serenading young men is not illegal.' **1929** L. H. Creer *Utah & Nation* i. 3 Herein was also established the principle of modern revelation, one of the basic principles of Mormonism. **1958** Mulder & Mortensen *Among Mormons* p. v, The learned journals have discovered in Mormonism a ripe field for scholarship.

Mormonist (ˈmɔːmənɪst). [f. MORMON + -IST.] = MORMON.
1842 Dickens *Amer. Notes* I. v. 181, I should like to try the experiment on a Mormonist or two to begin with. **1890** in *Century Dict.*

Mormonite (ˈmɔːmənaɪt), *sb.* and *a.* Now *rare.* [f. the personal name *Mormon* (see MORMON) + -ITE.] **a.** *sb.* A Mormon. **b.** *adj.* Of or pertaining to the Mormons.
1831 *Columbian Reporter* (Taunton, Mass.) 24 Aug. 1/5 The Mormonites. We learn.. that this infatuated people are again in motion. **1833** T. Hamilton *Men & Manners in Amer.* II. vii. 310 We passed several parties of what were called Mormonites. **1835** C. Bradley *Jrnl.* 24 June in *Ohio Archaeol. & Hist. Q.* (1906) XV. 269 We have, too, a company of Mormanite missionaries aboard. **1859** Mill *Liberty* iv. 164 The article of the Mormonite doctrine which is the chief provocative.. is its sanction of polygamy. **1882** *Illustr. Mission. News* Mar. 28 Meetings.. to denounce Mormonite polygamy. **1947** B. De Voto *Across Wide Missouri* 185 The 'Mormonites'.. had been driven into the unsettled lands of Clay County. **1958** Mulder & Mortensen *Among Mormons* p. vi, Once the new church is founded the religious press is full of letters.. about the Mormonites and their New Jerusalem.

mormope (ˈmɔːməʊp). *Zool.* [ad. mod.L. *mormōp-*, *mormōps*, f. Gr. μορμώ MORMO + ὤψ face.] 'A bat of the genus *Mormops*' (*Cent. Dict.* 1890).

mormor, mormur, obs. forms of MURMUR.

mormosett, obs. form of MARMOSET.

‖**mormyrus** (ˈmɔːmɪrəs). *Ichth.* Also 8 **mormylus.** [mod.L., a. Gr. μορμύρος (corruptly μορμύλος).] A fish of the African genus *Mormyrus*.
1706 Phillips (ed. Kersey), *Mormyra*, or *Mormyrus*, (*Gr.*) a kind of Sea-fish of divers Colours. **1752** J. Hill *Hist. Anim.* 254 The Mormylus. This is a very singularly marked species [etc.]. **1774** Goldsm. *Nat. Hist.* (1776) VI. 315 The Mormyrus. The body oblong; the head elongated. **1887** *Amer. Naturalist* XXI. 584 G. A. Boulenger has recently described a Mormyrus from the Lower Congo.

Hence ˈ**mormyr(e, morˈmyrian, ˈmormyrid,** a fish of the family *Mormyridæ*, of which the genus *Mormyrus* is the type.
1890 *Century Dict.*, *Mormyre*, *Mormyrian*. **1898** *Proc. Zool. Soc.* 15 Nov. 778 Those possible ancestors of the Mormyrs belong to the most generalized forms of Clupeines. **1899** *Ibid.* 28 Nov. 934 The Mormyrids.

morn (mɔːn). Forms: 1 **morȝen, marȝen, mer(i)ȝen, merien** (also in oblique forms **morȝn-, morn-, marn-**), 2 **marȝan, moreȝen,** 2–3 **marȝen,** 3

mærȝen, marhen, mor(e)ghen, 2–4 morȝen, (4 moryhen); 3 marwen, morwhen, 3–5 morwen, 4 morewen, 5 morewane, morwyn, morwoun, morwynge; 3–5 morun, 4 moroun, 4–5 moren, 5 moron, moryn; 4–7 morne, 3– morn. See also MORROW. [Com. Teut.: the OE. forms represent three distinct types, each of which is represented in one or more of the other Teut. langs. (1) OE. *morȝen* (inflected also *morȝn-, morn-*) = OFris. **morgen, morn*, OS. *morgan* (MLG., MDu., Du. *morgen*), OHG. *morgan* (MHG., mod.G. *morgen*):—OTeut. **murgano-z*, represented also, with variation of suffix, by ON. *morgunn, -onn* (Sw. *morgon*, Da. *morgen*). (2) OE. *myrȝen-* (in the comb. *myrȝenlic*) = ON. *myrginn*, Goth. *maurgin-s*:—OTeut. **murgino-z*. (3) OE. *marȝen, męrȝen* = MDu. *margen, mergen*, ON. *merginn* (OSw. *marghan*):—OTeut. **margano-z, -ino-z*. The word in all forms retains the masculine gender.

The affinities outside Teut. are doubtful. Some refer the word to the pre-Teut. root **merk-* to be dark; but the absence of consonant-ablaut, as well as the inappropriateness of the sense, seems to render this view less probable than the alternative hypothesis that the root is **mergh-*, represented by Lith. *mirgu* to twinkle, *margas* parti-coloured.

The present monosyllabic form descends, partly at least, from the OE. contraction in oblique cases, *morne, mornes* for *morȝ(e)ne, morȝ(e)nes*. (The same contraction existed in ON.) But it may also in part represent the result of a process of contraction starting from ME. *morwen*, the intermediate forms being *morun, moren*, etc.

The ME. forms that retain the final *n* are for convenience placed here, though many of them might with equal propriety be referred to MORROW. In MSS. it is often doubtful whether the word is *morn* or *moru* = 'morrow'.]

1. The beginning of the day, dawn, sunrise. Only *poet.*: often *personified*.

Beowulf 1077 Syþðan morȝen com. *Ibid.* 2103 Merȝen. *c* **1400** *Destr. Troy* 9141 Hit semyt by sight of sitters aboute, As the moron mylde meltid aboue, When ho hasted with hond þe hore for to touche. **1480** CAXTON *Chron. Eng.* ccxliv. 298 The morne aroos, the day gan spryng. **1592** SHAKS. *Ven. & Ad.* 454 Like a red morne, that euer yet betokend Wracke to the sea-man, tempest to the field. **1637** MILTON *Lycidas* 187 While the still morn went out with Sandals gray. **1792** WORDSW. *Descr. Sk.* 405 'Tis morn: with gold the verdant mountain glows. **1830** TENNYSON *Ode to Mem.* 70 What time the amber morn Forth gushes from beneath a low-hung cloud. **1852** M. ARNOLD *Parting* 86 Thy high mountain platforms, Where Morn first appears.

fig. **1813** SHELLEY *Q. Mab* ix. 38 Yet slow and gradual dawned the morn of love. **1852** M. ARNOLD *Empedocles* I. ii. 167 The first faint morn Of life.

b. The east; 'the land of dawn'.

1642 H. MORE *Poems* (1647) 31 A trimly decked Close Whose grassie pavement wrought with even line Ran from the Morn upon the Evening-close. **189.** BARING-GOULD *Hymn*, '*On the Resurrection morning*' iii, For a while the wearied body Lies with feet toward the morn. **1896** A. E. HOUSMAN *Shropshire Lad* iii, And you will list the bugle That blows in lands of morn.

c. ***northern morn*** (poet. nonce-use): the aurora borealis (cf. MORNING 4 b).

1842 TENNYSON *Morte d'Arthur* 139 The great brand.. Shot like a streamer of the northern morn.

2. The early part of the day; morning. Now chiefly *poet.*

Beowulf 2450 Symble bið ȝemyndȝad morna ȝehwylce eoforan ellorsið. *c* **950** *Lindisf. Gosp.* Matt. xx. 1 Ar in merne [Vulg. *primo mane*]. *c* **1175** *Lamb. Hom.* 115 Wa þere þeode ..þer þa aldormen etað on erne marȝen ulaȝeliche [Eccl. x. 16]. *c* **1250** *Kent. Serm.* in *O.E. Misc.* 33 On good-man was þat ferst uut-yede bi þe Moreghen for to here werkmen into his winyarde. **13..** *E.E. Allit. P.* B. 493 Myryly on a fayr morn, monyth þe fyrst. **1389** in *Eng. Gilds* (1870) 4 In morun atte messe. *c* **1400** MAUNDEV. (1839) xv. 164 For sume of hem, worschipe the Sonne,.. or the first thing that thei meeten at morwen. **1567** *Satir. Poems Reform.* iii. 1 About vj. houris at morne. **1606** SHAKS. *Tr. & Cr.* IV. ii. 1 Deere trouble not your selfe: the morne is cold. **1629** MILTON *Christ's Nativ.* i, This is the Month, and this the happy morn Wherein [etc.]. **1750** GRAY *Elegy* xxviii, One morn I miss'd him on the custom'd hill. **1859** TENNYSON *Marriage Geraint* 157 But Guinevere lay late into the morn. **1896** A. E. HOUSMAN *Shropshire Lad* iv, Morns abed and daylight slumber Were not meant for man alive.

fig. **1594** SHAKS. *Rich. III*, IV. iv. 16 Say that right for right Hath dim'd your Infant morne, to Aged night. **1602** —— *Ham.* I. iii. 41 And in the Morne and liquid dew of Youth, Contagious blastments are most imminent.

b. In phrases, as ***at* (†*on*) *morn and* (*at*, †*on*) *even*** (also ***eve and morn***), etc.; ***morn by morn***, morning after morning, occurring every morning; ***from morn to*** (or ***till***) ***night***, etc., all day long; †***good morn***, a salutation (see further GOOD *a.* 10 c).

c **825** *Vesp. Psalter* liv. 18 On efenne on marne & on midne deȝ. *a* **1300** *Cursor M.* 6385 It come at morn and euening. **13..** *Gaw. & Gr. Knt.* 1208 'God moroun, sir Gawayn', sayde þat fayr lady. *a* **1400–50** *Alexander* 4769 Fra morewane to þe mydday merely þai spring. *c* **1450** HOLLAND *Howlat* 195 At euyn and at morn. **1588** SHAKS. *L.L.L.* v. ii. 660 He would fight, yea From morne till night. **1667** MILTON *P.L.* I. 742 From Morn To Noon he fell, from Noon to dewy Eve, A Summer's day. **1781** COWPER *Truth* 509 Herself, from morn to night, from night to morn, Her own abhorrence. **1816** J. WILSON *City of Plague* II. iii. 48 A morn and even, And through the dismal day, that fierce aspect Glared on the city. **1827** KEBLE *Chr. Y.*, *Even.* viii, Abide with me from morn till eve. **1847** TENNYSON *Princess* VII. 30 Morn by morn the lark Shot up and shrill'd in flickering gyres. **1896** A. E. HOUSMAN *Shropshire Lad* vi, Buy them, buy them: eve and morn Lovers' ills are all to sell.

3. The next morning. Hence, the day after to-day or the day mentioned; = MORROW 2.

[Com. Teut.: cf. Goth. *du maurgina*, G. *morgen*, etc.]

†**a.** Without article. Chiefly with prep. as ***on*** or ***upon morn***. *Obs.* exc. in TO-MORN *dial.* (See also A-MORROW 2.)

Beowulf 2484 þa ic on morȝne ȝefrægn mæȝ oðerne billes ecgum on bonan stælan. *c* **1000** ÆLFRIC *Saints' Lives* iii. 584 Se læce him cwæð to . Ne lyfastu oð æfen . þa cwæð basilius. hwæt ȝif ic bide meriȝenes. *c* **1250** *Gen. & Ex.* 1161 Abraham up on morȝen stod. *a* **1300** *Cursor M.* 3345 On morn wit godds beniscon Was mai rebecca lede o ton. *c* **1450** *St. Cuthbert* (Surtees) 7104 þai war on morne to durham boun.

†**b.** ***other morn*** (*Sc.*): the next day but one.

1572 tr. *Buchanan's Detect. Mary Q. Scot.* T ij b, He hes prayit me to remane vpoun hym quhill vther morne.

c. ***the morn***: the morrow. Now only *Sc.* and *north. dial.*

c **1175** *Lamb. Hom.* 79 A þe marȝen [the good Samaritan] bitahte him twa peneȝes to spenen on him. *a* **1300** *Cursor M.* 2917 Abraham went him, on þe morn, To þat sted. *c* **1300** *Havelok* 811 On þe morwen, hwan it was day, He stirt up sone. *a* **1440** *Sir Degrev.* 1337 Sire Degrivaunt on the morwoun Com aȝe to the thorun. **1485** CAXTON *Paris & V.* (1868) 42 Tyl on the morne at nyght. **1508** DUNBAR *Poems* v. 18 Scho slepit quhill the morne at none, et rais airly. **1544** in Tytler *Hist. Scot.* (1864) II. 401 My lord Governor tuke to be advised while the morne at even. **1887** P. M'NEILL *Blawearie* 133 Mother's away for the morn's meat. **1888** BARRIE *Auld Licht Idylls* viii. 171 Ay, Bell, the morn's the Sabbath.

d. ***the morn***: used advb. (orig. in the accus.) = to-morrow, on the morrow. Now only *Sc.*

a **1300** *Cursor M.* 11532 þe morun quen þai risen ware, ..þai tok þair leue. **1340** *Ayenb.* 46 þane morȝen huanne he zet ate gemene: his arowe vil ope þet cheker al blody. **1461** *Rolls of Parlt.* V. 476/2 And the morne, the xvi day of Decembre, my Lord Chaunceller opened..the matiers above-seid. *c* **1475** *Rauf Coilȝear* 299 Cum the morne to the Court and do my counsall. **1569** *Reg. Privy Council Scot.* I. 669 To tak jornay the morne the aucht day of this instant. **1621** *Gude & Godlie Ball.* App. i. (S.T.S.) 234 This day thow was ane King with Croun, The morne cummis deith withouttin dreid. **1788** BURNS '*There was a lass*' ii, But Duncan swoor a haly aith That Meg should be a bride the morn. **1818** SCOTT *Rob Roy* xxiii, He wad be glad if I wad eat a reisted haddock..at breakfast wi' him the morn. **1869** C. GIBBON *R. Gray* iv, I'll see how ye're getting on the morn or neist day.

†**e.** More explicitly, ***the morn after***. *Obs.*

14.. *Gregory's Chron.* in *Hist. Coll. Citizen London* (Camden) 110 The kyng sende hem worde yf they wolde delivery the towne on the morne aftyr, be the oure of mydnyght..he wolde accepte hyt [etc.]. *Ibid.* 112 Onne the morne aftyr Syn Symonnys day and Jude. **1483** *Rolls of Parlt.* VI. 253/2 From the afore written morne next after Seint Hillarie day. **1560–1** *Bk. Discipl. Ch. Scot.* I. (1621) 2 The Assembly appointed, the laird of Dunn..to conveen the morn after the preaching. *a* **1578** LINDESAY (Pitscottie) *Chron. Scot.* (S.T.S.) I. 55 The morne thairefter the gentillmen war honourabillie burieit in the kirk yaird.

f. ***the morn's morn(ing, night***, etc. = to-morrow morning, night, etc. Also used advb. *Sc.*

1816 SCOTT *Antiq.* xi, Till the morn's morning. **1822** GALT *Sir A. Wylie* lx, Your Leddyship's brother..will be here betimes the morn's morning. **1889** BARRIE *Window in Thrums* xx. 193 Jamie, I'll no hae ye to sit aside me the morn's nicht.

4. *attrib.* and *Comb.* **a.** In the sense of 'morning', as ***morn-devotion, -dew, -drink, -light, milk, -prayer, rising, sleep, -song***; †**morn-bell**, a bell rung as a call to matins or to early mass; †**morn-mass** = MORROW-MASS; †**morn-priest**, the priest celebrating early mass; also similative, instrumental, and objective, with *adjs.* and *pples.*, as ***morn-bright***, †***-dawning, -like, -loved, -waking***.

1568–9 in *Fabric Rolls York Minster* (Surtees) 115 To Nicholas Richerdson for a rope to the *morne bell, 3s. **1642** H. MORE *Song of Soul* III. III. xlv, She sees his blazing *morn-bright eye. **1645** RUTHERFORD *Tryal & Tri. Faith* (1845) 269 A glimmering of *morn-dawning light. **1600** FAIRFAX *Tasso* I. xv, Godfrey..then his *morne deuotions sed. **1606** SHAKS. *Ant. & Cl.* III. xii. 9 The *Morne-dew on the Mertle leafe. *a* **1440** *Sir Eglam.* 381 Hys *morne-drynke he had tane. *Beowulf* 917 Ða wæs *morȝenleoht scofen and scynded. *c* **1205** LAY. 17946 þat we i þan morȝen-liht mæȝen come forð riht forn at Meneue. **1593** NASHE *Christ's T.* 71 b, Your *morne-like christall countenaunces shall be netted ouer. **1606** DRAYTON *Eglog.* ii. Poems D 2, The *morn-lou'd Mary-gould. **1511** *Acc. Ld. High Treas. Scotl.* IV. 180 For offerand to tua *morne missis and at the hie miss. *a* **1310** in Wright *Lyric P.* ix. 36 Whittore then the *moren mylk. *c* **1386** CHAUCER *Prol.* 358 An Anlaas and a gipser al of silk Heeng at his girdel, whit as morne Milk. **1603** SHAKS. *Meas. for M.* II. iv. 71 If that be sin, Ile make it my *Morne-praier, To haue it added to the faults of mine, And nothing of your answere. **1466** in *Archæologia* L. I. 44 Item j nothir Riddyll be hynde the *morne preste in the quere. **1601** HOLLAND *Pliny* I. 13 [Mercurie hath] the *morne rising in Aquarius, but very seldome in Leo. *a* **1572** KNOX *Hist. Ref.* Wks. 1846 I. 175 And therefore qwyetness, after the reullis of phisick, and a *morne sleap was requisite for My Lord. **1601** DEACON & WALKER *Spirits & Divels* 339 His Euen-song and *Morne-song, they are one and the same. **1593** LODGE *Phillis* (1875) 21 And Phillis hath *morne-waking birdes, Hir risinges for to honour.

†**b.** In the sense of 'to-morrow', as ***morn-day***, MORN-WHILE. *Obs.*

971 *Blickl. Hom.* 213 Godes man ne sceolde be þan morȝendæȝe þencean, þylæs þæt wære þæt [etc.]. *c* **1375** *Sc. Leg. Saints* xl. (*Ninian*) 462 þai.. bad þare til þe morne-day. *a* **1450** *Cursor M.* 5993 (Fairf.), Moises prayed þe morne day & alle þe fleys ware a-way.

mor'n: see MORE *adv.* 5 a.

Mornay ('mɔːneɪ). Also **mornay**. [perh. f. the name of Philippe de *Mornay* (died 1623), a French Huguenot writer.] ***Mornay sauce*** (also in Fr. form ***sauce mornay***): a rich white sauce flavoured with cheese. Also *ellipt.*, a dish served with Mornay sauce.

1906 A. FILIPPINI *International Cook Bk.* 623 Fillet of sole, mornay. **1925** LEYEL & HARTLEY *Gentle Art of Cookery* 20 Sauce mornay, a cheese sauce. **1939** A. L. SIMON *Conc. Encycl. Gastron.* I. 39/1 Mornay, sauce. Heat the required amount of *Béchamel*... When ready to serve, add as much Parmesan cheese as desired. **1948** L. MARION *Be your Own Chef* xii. 230 Remove the vegetable marrow from the oven. Throw away the water..and pour the Mornay Sauce over the pieces of vegetable. **1963** R. CARRIER *Great Dishes of World* 62 Mornay sauce—for fish, vegetables, poultry, poached eggs, noodle and macaroni mixtures. **1965** *House & Garden* Dec. 84/2 *Mornay.* Just cheese, but the basis of some of the most wonderful recipes there are. **1974** I. MURDOCH *Sacred & Profane Love Machine* 311 Well, *oeufs* somehow? Mornay?

morne (mɔːn), *sb.*[1] *Antiq.* Forms: 5 **moorne**, 6–7 **mourne**, 8 **mourn**, 9– **morne**. [a. F. *morne*, vbl. sb. f. OF. *morner* to blunt (a lance), f. *morne* blunted, dull: see MORNE *a.*] The rebated head of a tilting lance; = CORONAL *sb.* 3.

The editor of Guillim (quot. 1632) gives an explanation which would make the word synonymous with MORNETTE.

1494 in *Lett. & Papers Rich. III & Hen. VII* (Rolls) I. 399 Thomas Ryder came owt of the towne and to hym was presented ij speres with moornes, where of he toke the choise and Treury toke the toder. *Ibid.* 400 And Sir Edward A Borough at that cours brac his spere well apon therll of Suffolke; and the said erll glissed on the helme of the said Sir Edward, the wiche ran with speres with moornes. *c* **1500** in *Strutt's Sports & Past.* (1801) Introd. 13 The speare hedded with the morne. *a* **1586** SIDNEY *Arcadia* II. (1622) 179 His Lances..so were they coloured with hookes neere the mourne, that they prettily represented sheep-hooks. **1632** *Guillim's Her.* IV. xiv. 342 The Iron heads of Tilt-speares.. which usually haue six or eight Mournes (for so are those little piked things called, which are on the top or head of this cronell or Coronet). **1824** MEYRICK *Anc. Armour* II. 246 Their lances have small points rebated or bent down, called mornes. **1876** *Jrnl. Brit. Archæol. Assoc.* XXXII. 125 We hear of spears, of..tilting-lances with mornes, coronels, and vamplates.

‖**morne** (mɔːn), *sb.*[2] [American-French, ? corruption of Sp. *morón*.] A small round hill.

1889 *Harper's Mag.* Nov. 846/1 The road..sinks between mornes wooded to their summits.

‖**morne** (mɔːn), *a.* [Fr.; believed to be of Teut. origin: cf. MOURN *v.*] Dismal, dreary.

1844 KINGLAKE *Eothen* xvi. 215 The chaunt was morne and doleful. **1848** AYTOUN *Danube & Euxine* 16 Rolling down my torpid waters Through a silence morne and drear. **1879** MRS. OLIPHANT *Geo. II*, I. 14 The morne monotony of the life that lingers out to its last moment.

morne, obs. form of MOURN.

‖**morné** ('mɔːneɪ), *a. Her.* Also **mornee**, *erron.* **mortne, mortné**. [Fr.; pa. pple. of *morner* to blunt.] Said of a lion rampant represented as having no tongue, teeth, or claws.

1722 NISBET *Syst. Her.* 296 The Lion of his Family was represented afterward, without Claws, and blazoned Mornee. **1725** J. COATS *Dict. Her.* (1739), Mort ne, is a term Colombiere has, and apply'd to a Lyon. **1780** EDMONDSON *Heraldry* II. Gloss., *Morné* or *Mortné*. **1868–93** CUSSANS *Handbk. Her.* viii. (ed. 4) 129 *Morné*: Disarmed.

morned (mɔːnd), *a. Her.* [f. MORNE *sb.*[1] + -ED[2].] Of a spear: Having a blunt head.

1890 in *Century Dict.*

morner, obs. form of MOURNER.

mornette (mɔː'nɛt). *Antiq.* [a. OF. *mornet* (Littré), dim. of *morne*: see MORNE *sb.*[1]] One of the points of the coronel of a tilting-spear.

1824 MEYRICK *Anc. Armour* II. 246 *note*, The points of the cronel were called mornettes, or little mornes. **1846** FAIRHOLT *Costume* (1885) II. Gloss. 289.

mornevall, obs. form of MOURNIVAL.

†'**mornif**, *a. Obs. rare*[−1]. [? f. MOURN *v.* + *-if*, -IVE; but cf. OF. *morni*, f. *morne* sad.] Mournful.

13.. *E.E. Allit. P.* A. 386 In blysse I se þe blyþely blent & I a man al mornyf mate.

morning ('mɔːnɪŋ), *sb.* (and *a.*) Forms: 3 **moreȝening(e**, 3–4 **mor(e)wening(e**, 4 **mor(e)wenyng(e**, **morennyng(e**, 4–5 **morwenyng(e**, **mor(o)wnyng(e**, **morowning**, **morowenyng**, 5 **morenyng(e**, 6 *Sc.* **moirneing**, 4–6 **mornyng(e**, 4– **morning**. [ME. *morwening*, *morning*, f. *morwen* MORN + -ING[1], on the analogy of EVENING.]

I. The simple word.

1. a. Originally, the time of the approach or beginning of 'morn'; the period extending from a little before to a little after sunrise. The word gradually became synonymous with MORN

(which is now only *poet.* and *dial.*). In modern use: The early part of the day-time, ending at noon or at the hour of the midday meal.

a **1250** *Owl & Night.* 1718 (Jesus Oxf. MS.) þe wrenne for heo cuþe singe þar com in þare moreweninge [(Cott. MS.) moreȝeninge] To helpe þare nyhtegale. *c* **1330** R. BRUNNE *Chron.* (1725) 17 Right in the mornyng in aldermost nede Com þe kynge's sonnes tuo. *c* **1380** WYCLIF *Serm.* Sel. Wks. I. 266 A nyȝt is partid in foure houres; as evenynge and mydnyȝt, cockis crowinge and morewnynge. *c* **1407** LYDG. *Reson & Sens.* 458 Herest, how the briddes synge For gladnesse of the morwenynge. *c* **1450** HOLLAND *Howlat* 157 All thus in May, as I ment in a mornyng. **1596** SHAKS. *Tam. Shr.* III. ii. 113 The morning weares, 'tis time we were at Church. **1678** R. L'ESTRANGE *Seneca's Mor.* II. xix. (1696) 282 How many precious Mornings do we spend in Consultation with Barbers, Taylors [etc.]. *a* **1707** BP. PATRICK *Autobiog.* (1839) 90 Some pious persons..had desired prayers at the hour of ten in the morning. **1728** VANBR. & CIB. *Prov. Husb.* IV. i, An hundred Pound in the Morning, and want another afore Night! **1833** TENNYSON *New-Year's Eve* vi, In the early early morning. *Mod.* My mornings are occupied with correspondence.

b. ***in the morning***, appended to an hour-date, means between midnight and noon; = *a.m.*

a **1654** SELDEN *Table-T.* (Arb.) 82 Sitting up till two of the Clock in the Morning. **1727–52** CHAMBERS *Cycl.* s.v., The astronomers reckon *morning, mane*, from the time of midnight, to that of midday.—Thus an eclipse is said to begin at eleven o'clock in the morning, &c. **1797** T. WRIGHT *Autobiog.* (1864) 194 A quarter past one o'clock in the morning. **1876** *Encycl. Brit.* V. 292/1 The Celestines were bound to say matins in the choir at two o'clock in the morning.

c. The portion of the day extending to the fashionable dinner time.

1749 FIELDING *Tom Jones* xv. ii, Past three in the morning, or to reckon by the old style, in the afternoon. **1840** *John Bull* 31 May 1 M. Liszt will give at Two o'clock on Tuesday morning, June 9, Recitals on the Pianoforte.

d. *fig.* The beginning, or early part (of anything likened to a day).

1595 W. S. *Locrine* II. vi. E, Thus in the morning of my victories, Thus in the prime of my felicitie To cut me off by such hard ouerthrow. **1613** PURCHAS *Pilgrimage* (1614) 351 Moses telleth of the reigne and power of Chederlaomer King of Elam, in that morning of the world extended to the borders of Canaan. **1786** BURNS *To James Smith* xv, O Life! how pleasant in thy morning. **1855** PRESCOTT *Philip II*, I. viii. (1857) 149 A war which hung like a dark cloud on the morning of her reign.

e. *Ellipt.* for *morning paper. colloq.*

1961 [see EVENING *sb.*[1] 2 f]. **1966** *New Statesman* 7 Oct. 503/3 Thomson already controls the *Scotsman*, three provincial mornings and nine evenings. **1970** K. GILES *Death in Church* v. 121 Did you see the mornings?.. The act of killing the clergy seems to enrage English journalists.

2. a. With qualifying adj. denoting the kind of weather, etc., prevailing, or the pleasure (or the contrary) experienced during the morning.

one or *some fine morning*, etc.: see FINE *a.* 15 b.

c **1374** CHAUCER *Compl. Mars* 151 And therfore in this lusty morwnynge As I best can I wol hit seyn and synge. *c* **1402** LYDG. *Compl. Bl. Knt.* 25 Clere and faire was the morowning. **1546** J. HEYWOOD *Prov. & Epigr.* (1867) 81 Thus cloudy mornynges turne to cleere after noones. **1678** R. L'ESTRANGE *Seneca's Mor., Epist.* vi. (1696) 503 In a Frosty Morning. **1784** COWPER *Task* VI. 58 The morning [was] sharp and clear. **1865** G. MACDONALD *A. Forbes* 11 When the morning was wet.

b. ***good morning***: see GOOD *a.* 10 c. (Cf. the earlier *good morn*, GOOD-MORROW.) In informal speech often shortened to *morning*.

1611 [see GOOD *a.* 10 c]. **1653** WALTON *Angler* i. 1 You are wel overtaken Sir, a good morning to you. **1751** ELIZA HEYWOOD *Betsy Thoughtless* I. 268 In going out, he saw Mr. Goodman in the parlour, who gave him the good morning as he passed. **1895** 'H. S. MERRIMAN' *Grey Lady* II. vii. (1899) 254 'Morning—morning!' he cried. 'Good morning', replied Luke. **1911** G. B. SHAW *Blanco Posnet* 390 Morning, Elder. (*Passing on*). Morning Strapper. (*Passing on*). Morning, Miss Evans. **1968** G. BUTLER *Coffin Following* vi. 120 'Morning,' said the ticket collector.

3. Idiomatic uses and phrases. **a.** Used advb. (in ME. rarely †*the morning*) for 'in the morning'. Now only in collocations like ***morning and evening***. Also in proverbial phrase ***morning, noon, and night*** = all the day, incessantly.

1297 R. GLOUC. (Rolls) 11676 þe tiwesday to euesham he wende þe morweninge. **1697** T. BROWN *Dispensary (ad fin.)* Wks. 1709 III. III. 90 Take one Spoonful of it Morning and Evening. **1808** E. WEETON Let. 1 Apr. in *Jrnl. of Governess* (1969) I. 80 Your praises..have operated almost like a dose of salts, and have worked me morning, noon, and night for these two days. **1864** TROLLOPE *Can you forgive Her?* I. xx. 160 Your sitting here all alone, morning, noon, and night, won't bring him back. **1891** N. GOULD *Double Event* 17 I'm sick of the name. Morning, noon, and night I hear nothing else. **1892** C. WHITAKER *Student's Aid to Prayer Bk.* Hist. Sk. p. vi, The Litany may be used morning or evening or both.

b. In certain phrases the article is omitted, as †*in morning* (obs.), *at morning* (now *rare*), *till morning, before morning; from morning till evening, to night*, etc.; also *all morning* (adv.) beside *all the morning*. Also †A-MORNING.

a **1300** *Cursor M.* 7181 On nighter-tale, or in morning. *Ibid.* 13291 Amorning fand he dan leui. **1530** PALSGR. 434/1 He applyeth his crafte from mornyng to nyght. **1596** SHAKS. *Merch. V.* III. ii. 279 He plyes the Duke at morning and at night. **1713** SWIFT *Address to Earl of Oxford, Imit. Horace, Ep.* I. vii. 78 Soon grows Domestick; seldom fails Either at Morning, or at Meals. **1788** MRS. HUGHES *Henry & Isabella* III. 17 Not having seen her all morning, she [etc.]. **1832** SOUTHEY *Lett.* (1856) IV. 261, I..very seldom employ myself upon the same [thing] at morning and in the evening. **1842** PLANCHÉ *White Cat* II. Extravaganzas 1879 II. 164 We won't go home till morning, Till day-light doth appear. **1849** M. ARNOLD *New Sirens* i, I, who in your train at morning Stroll'd and sang with joyful mind, Heard, at evening, sounds of warning. **1887** HALL CAINE *Deemster* xii, All morning she had dreamt of her husband.

c. †***on mornings***, A-MORNINGS (*obs.*), ***of mornings*** (see OF *prep.* 52 b): habitually in the morning. Also *mornings* as adv. in the same sense; now *rare* or *dial.* Also, †***of a mornings*** = 'of a morning'.

[**1377**, etc.: see A-MORNINGS]. **1523** LD. BERNERS *Froiss.* I. xxvi. 38 The scottis, on mornyngis and nyghtis, made many skryes to trouble the oste, but lytle hurt they dyd. **1575** LANEHAM *Let.* (1871) 58, I am..iolly & dry a mornings. **1620** VENNER *Via Recta* (1650) 55 Sometimes mornings fasting a small draught thereof may be profitable for them. **1652** tr. *Scudery's Ibrahim* IV. II. 174 Mornings and evenings only I took him out Lessons. **1732** MRS. WESLEY in *Wesley's Wks.* (1829) I. 388 Mornings they had always spoon-meat; sometimes at nights. *c* **1740** CHESTERF. *Lett. to Son* xlvii. (1774) I. 118 When the sun shines on either side of us (as it does mornings and evenings) the shadows are very long. **1795** COLERIDGE *Lett.* (1895) I. 137 Only amusing myself on mornings. **1849** [see OF 52 b]. **1893** H. C. O'NEILL *Told in the Dimpses* 28 Farmer Spurrier could see the plough at work ..before he got out of his bed mornings. **1936** *S.P.E. Tract* XLV. 192 A peculiar use of the plural form is illustrated in 'The operatic tenor Campanini was engaged to sing mornings'. **1938** T. WILDER *Our Town* I. 11 Quarter of nine mornings, noontimes, and three o'clock afternoon's [*sic*], the hull town can hear the yelling and screaming from those schoolyards.

d. ***this morning***: the morning of to-day. Chiefly in advb. use.

1577 C'TESS MAR in *3rd Rep. Hist. MSS. Comm.* 419/1, I rassauit this moirneing ane wreitting. **1592** SHAKS. *Rom. & Jul.* v. iii. 305 A glooming peace this morning with it brings. **1606** —— *Ant. & Cl.* IV. v. 5 The Soldier That has this morning left thee. **1703** MAUNDRELL *Journ. Jerus.* 5 May (1810) 181 This morning we pass'd by the fountain of Barrady. **1865** H. KINGSLEY *Hillyars & B.* xii, The fellows who got bailed up by young Hillyar this morning.

e. ***in*** or ***of a morning***: habitually in the morning.

1678 R. L'ESTRANGE *Seneca's Mor.* II. xvi. (1696) 264 We wonder..how any Man can..endure to rise so early in a Morning. **1798** *Monthly Mag.* VI. 171 To take a walk in the High-Street in a morning. **1824** LADY GRANVILLE *Lett.* (1894) I. 325, I am..going to receive them of a morning. **1862** MRS. H. WOOD *Channings* x, He should only have to go to the office for two hours before breakfast in a morning, to make up for the two lost in the day.

f. In genitive. Formerly often equivalent to the attrib. use. Now only in the senses 'belonging to the particular morning', 'occupying a morning'.

1588 SHAKS. *Tit. A.* II. iii. 201 Vpon whose leaues are drops of new-shed-blood, As fresh as mornings dew distil'd on flowers. **1602** F. HERING *Anat.* 8 Readie to visit his Patients at any hour, being as good an afternoones-man as a morning's-man. **1655** WALTON *Angler* v. (1661) 90 Come give my Scholer and me a Mornings-drink, and a bit of meat to breakfast. **1678** R. L'ESTRANGE *Seneca's Mor.* II. xxii. (1696) 318 He gave me a Mornings Visit. **1697** T. BROWN *Dispensary* I. Wks. 1709 III. III. 68 What will be the Charges of this Morning's Work? **1711** STEELE *Spect.* No. 134 ¶2, I constantly peruse your Paper as I smoke my Morning's Pipe. **1859** TENNYSON *Geraint & Enid* 571 So the ruffians growl'd, Fearing to lose..Their chance of booty from the morning's raid.

g. (***the***) ***morning after*** (***the night before***): a morning on which the effects of the previous night's drinking or revelry are unpleasantly felt; also *attrib.* and *absol.*, these effects or a person suffering from them; also in extended use for any unpleasant aftermath of pleasure. Also ***morning after***, applied to a contraceptive pill that is effective when taken some time after sexual intercourse.

1884 *Punch* 31 May 264/1 His method of inoculation for hydrophobia seems uncommonly like the old 'morning-after' remedy, when the chippy one who could 'strike matches on his tongue' was recommended to take 'a hair of the dog that bit him'. **1909** E. NESBIT *Daphne in Fitzroy St.* xvi. 256 'I'm all right,' said the girl... 'That's what we all of us says, when it comes to be the morning after,' said Mrs. Delarue. **1922** JOYCE *Ulysses* 231 It was blue o'clock the morning after the night before. **1927** KIPLING *Limits & Renewals* (1932) 157 There wasn't much doubt what Jimmy had been up to. He was altogether 'the morning after'. **1942** T. BAILEY *Pink Camellia* v. 28 She sat up and looked at herself in the mirror. 'The morning after! And my face looks like it.' **1946** 'BRAHMS' & 'SIMON' *Trottie True* vi. 152 'Dr. Duke's got a morning-after,' she said crisply. **1947** *Sat. Rev.* (U.S.) 12 Apr. 20/1 The nation relaxes, and only the morning-after headaches and the morning-after quarterbacks remain. **1957** A. C. CLARKE *Deep Range* iv. 43 He was not pleased to find that the entire stock of 'morning-after' pills had already been consumed. *a* **1963** S. PLATH *Crossing Water* (1971) 33 Musky as a lovebed the morning after. **1967** V. C. CLINTON-BADDELEY *Death's Bright Dart* 169 One of those aristocratic men in the advertisements whose morning-after needs are ministered to by a smiling and provident butler. **1967** *N.Y. Times* 24 Aug. 35 Dr. Chang and Dr. Pincus had been working recently on a new pill, known popularly as the 'morning-after' pill. It affects the egg after ovulation. **1969** *Daily Tel.* 3 July 23/3 Trials of a 'morning after' pill had been promising. **1973** *Express* (Trinidad & Tobago) 17 Mar. 7/1 The Food and Drug Administration will approve the use of diethylstilbestrol or DES as a 'morning after' contraceptive pill for women in emergency situations such as rape. **1973** L. MEYNELL *Thirteen Trumpeters* xiv. 215 'I felt *awful*. I didn't care whether I lived or died..' 'A classic case of the morning-after-the-night-before feeling.'

4. a. *poet.* The dawn, daybreak; the light of dawn. Often *personified*. (Cf. Ps. cxxxix. 9.)

1593 SHAKS. *3 Hen. VI*, II. i. 21 See how the Morning opes her golden Gates. **1599** —— *Hen. V*, IV. i. 88 Is not that the Morning which breaks yonder? **1611** BIBLE *Isa.* xiv. 12 O Lucifer, sonne of the morning. **1667** MILTON *P.L.* v. 20 Awake, the morning shines, and the fresh field Calls us. **1781** COWPER *Retirement* 432 While morning kindles with a windy red. **1821** SHELLEY *Adonais* xiv, Morning sought Her eastern watch-tower, and her hair unbound. **1833** TENNYSON *Œnone* 54 Far up the solitary morning smote The streaks of virgin snow. **1859** FITZGERALD tr. *Omar* i, Awake! for Morning in the Bowl of Night Has flung the Stone that puts the Stars to Flight.

fig. **1742** YOUNG *Nt. Th.* VIII. 255 The blush of morning, in his cheek, turns pale.

b. ***northern morning***: the Aurora Borealis. *rare.*

1836 *Uncle Philip's Convers. Whale Fishery* 215 The Aurora Borealis, or northern morning, as it is called. **1842** TENNYSON *Talking Oak* 275.

5. a. A morning draught, a glass of liquor taken before breakfast. Chiefly *Sc.*

1718 RAMSAY *Christ's Kirk Gr.* III. vi, Steen..Came in to get his morning. **1814** SCOTT *Wav.* xviii, Of this he took a copious dram, observing, he had already taken his *morning* with Donald Bean Lean, before his departure. **1843** LEVER *J. Hinton* iv, 'Are you ready for your morning?'.. He poured ..a brimming goblet full of some white compound, and handed it to me... I put it to my lips, and found it to be capital milk-punch. **1894** 'IAN MACLAREN' *Bonny Brier Bush* v. 187 Aifter a whilie they tak a mornin' wi' a freend and syne a gless at the public-hoose in the evenin'.

b. 'A slight repast taken at rising, some hours before what is called breakfast' (Jam.). *dial.*

1818 SCOTT *Leg. Montr.* vi, But now I must go down..and see that Gustavus [a horse] has his morning. **1861** HUGHES *Tom Brown at Oxf.* iii, I just watched the 'ed porter..across to the buttery to get his mornin'. **1897** *Shetland News* 29 May (E.D.D.), Bread for the Mason's mornings.

II. *attrib.* and *Comb.* (and quasi-*adj.*).

6. Simple *attrib.*, with various nouns of action, as in ***morning-dawn***, ***-peep***, ***-rise***, †***-spring***, ***-wake***. Chiefly *poet.*

1810 S. GREEN *Reformist* I. 28 Notwithstanding the moon lasting till *morning-dawn. *a* **1687** VILLIERS (Dk. Buckhm.) *Poems* (1775) 144 Rhime next his heart, he takes at *morning-peep, Some love-epistles at his hours of sleep. **1599** SHAKS., etc. *Pass. Pilgr.* xiv, The *morning rise Doth scite each mouing scence from Idle rest. **1535** COVERDALE *Josh.* vi. 15 Vpon the seuenth daye whan the *mornynge sprynge arose, they gat them vp early. **1678** DRYDEN & LEE *Œdipus* III. i. (1679) 44 My Soul then stole my Body out by night; And brought me back to Bed e're *Morning-wake.

7. *attrib.* passing into adj. **a.** With the sense: Existing, prevailing, or taking place in the morning.

1593 SHAKS. *Lucr.* 778 With rotten damps rauish the *morning aire. **1928** E. BLUNDEN *Retreat* 33 With friends as nimble as *morning-beams, Who sped with him to this playground. **1535** COVERDALE *Hosea* vi. 4 Youre loue is like a *mornynge cloude, & like a dew yͭ goeth early awaye. **1535** —— *Wisd.* xi. 22 Yee as a droppe of yᵉ *morninge dew, that falleth downe vpon the earth. **1590** SHAKS. *Mids. N.* IV. i. 126 Their heads are hung With eares that sweepe away the morning dew. **1590** SPENSER *F.Q.* I. ix. 41 And he, that points the Centonell his roome, Doth license him depart at sound of *morning droome. **1890** KIPLING *Barrack-Room Ballads* (1892) 163 He hewed the living rock with sweat and tears, And reared a God against the *morning-gold. **1634** MILTON *Comus* 920 And I must haste ere *morning hour To wait in Amphitrite's bowr. **1667** —— *P.L.* IX. 194 The humid Flours, that breathd Thir *morning Incense. **1593** SHAKS. *Lucr.* 745 He in his speed lookes for the *morning light. **1820** SHELLEY *Good-Nt.* iii, To hearts which near each other move From evening close to morning light, The night is good. **1930** R. CAMPBELL *Adamastor* 86 With food and drink, at morning-light, The children met me at the water-side. **1722** DE FOE *Plague* (1840) 51 The watchman..let them alone till the *morning-man, or day-watchman, as they called him, came to relieve him. **1675** HAN. WOOLLEY *Gentlewoman's Comp.* 203 Cheese, of which there are three kinds: *Morning-Milk-Cheese, Nettle-Cheese, and floaten-Milk-Cheese. **1827** T. J. DIBDIN *Reminisc.* I. 251 A large play bill from Dublin, announcing *morning performances, on account of a partial insurrection or rebellion. **1896** MARY ANDERSON *Few Mem.* vi. (ed. 2) 92 A morning performance when two young men..disturbed the actors and public with loud remarks. **1535** COVERDALE *Hosea* vi. 3 As the euenynge and *mornynge rayne vpon the earth. **1634** MILTON *Comus* 622 Every..plant..That spreds her verdant leaf to th' *morning ray. **1657** in *Shropsh. Parish Documents* (1903) 51 Published 3 severall Lords Days..at the close of *morning service. **1862** MRS. H. WOOD *Channings* xxxviii, The day was a holiday from school, but not from morning service. **1891** *Law Times* XCI. 3/1 For the two sessions 1833 and 1834 *morning sittings from twelve to three were devoted to petitions. **1894** *Daily News* 17 Jan. 5/3 There have been twenty-three morning sittings of the House of Commons since the beginning of the present session. A 'morning' sitting, as most people know, opens at two o'clock in the afternoon, and ends at seven. **1593** SHAKS. *3 Hen. VI*, IV. vii. 80 When the *Morning Sunne shall rayse his Carre Aboue the Border of this Horizon. **1632** SHERWOOD, The *morning time, *la matinée*. **1858** W. T. MATSON *Sonn.* Poems 460 In the rathe morning-time of life. **1727–52** CHAMBERS *Cycl.* s.v., **Morning twilight.* **1849** DE QUINCEY *Dream Fugue* Wks. 1890 XIII. 321 The morning twilight even then was breaking.

¶ In poetry, ***morning*** adj. often connotes vaguely the attributes possessed in the morning, or the fact that morning is the time referred to.

1590 SHAKS. *Mids. N.* IV. i. 99, I doe heare the morning Larke. **1600** —— *A.Y.L.* II. vii. 146 The Schoole-boy with his Satchell And shining morning face. **1602** —— *Ham.* I. ii.

218 The Morning Cocke crew lowd. **1833** BROWNING *Pauline* 13 The morning swallows with their songs like words. **1916** D. H. LAWRENCE *Amores* 125 It seemed that I and the morning world Were pressed cup-shape to take this reiver Bird. **1917** —— *Look! We have come Through!* 77 See, glittering on the milk-blue, morning lake They are laying the golden racing-track of the sun.

b. Of things intended to be worn in the morning.

In this use *morning* usually means early morning or forenoon; but in *morning dress, clothes, costume*, it is now used merely in contradistinction to 'evening'.

c **1620** *Roxb. Ball.* (1891) VII. 422 Casting from him his morning gown. **1700** T. BROWN *Acc. Journ. Exon.* Wks. 1709 III. II. 101, I have given you an Account of my Journey, every Part just scribbled o'er with as much Freedom as 'twas acted, wanting Leisure to put it in any other than a loose Morning-dress. **1755** JOHNSON, *Morning gown*, a loose gown worn before one is formally dressed. **1804** *Jackson's Oxford Jrnl.* Aug., Morning dress of fine cambric. **1825** J. F. COOPER *Lionel Lincoln* II. vi. 151 As the airy band of her morning cap waved aside. **1862** MRS. H. WOOD *Channings* xvii, At ten, Lady Augusta..entered the breakfast-room in a dirty morning wrapper, and rang the bell. **1867** *Harper's Mag.* Aug. 362/1 He got himself a new morning suit for shop use. **1891** T. HARDY *Tess* xxxii, A perfect morning costume. **1896** MARY ANDERSON *Few Mem.* vii. (ed. 2) 110 Her strange working costume of pale grey cloth, made like a man's morning suit. **1897** *Genealog. Mag.* Oct. 325 Ladies wore what is technically described as morning dress. **1912** 'C. F. BENTON' *Fairs & Fetes* 118 They should sell brushes and combs..and morning jackets. **1933** *Week-end Review* 21 Jan. 69/2 Black morning coat and waistcoat, grey striped trousers, grey tie and pearl pin. **1969** R. GODDEN *In this House of Brede* xix. 395 Japanese gentlemen in morning coats, grey waistcoats, striped trousers.

8. *Comb.* (similative, objective, or instrumental) with adjs. or pples., as in ***morning-blue***, ***-breathing***, ***-bright***, ***-cold***, ***-coloured***, ***-fair***, ***-gathered***, ***-grey***, ***-winged*** adjs. Usu. *poet.*

1920 D. H. LAWRENCE *Lost Girl* xvi. 366 The lovely translucent pale irises, tiny and *morning-blue, they lasted only a few hours. **1596** FITZ-GEFFRAY *Sir F. Drake* (1881) 15 Clymenes audacious boy Torne by the *morning-breathing horses rage. **1820** KEATS *Hyperion* II. 294 *Morning-bright Apollo! young Apollo! **1922** E. BLUNDEN *Shepherd* 48 Cheeks all morning-bright. **1923** D. H. LAWRENCE *Birds, Beasts & Flowers* 76 My heart which like a lark at heaven's gate singing, hovers morning-bright to Thee. **1945** J. BETJEMAN *New Bats in Old Belfries* 43 There splashed about our ankles as we waded Those intersecting wavelets *morning-cold. **1601** CHESTER *Love's Mart.* (1878) 3 Her *morning-coloured cheekes. **1938** W. DE LA MARE *Memory* 34 Eyes blue as speedwell, tranquil, *morning-fair. **1857** *Leisure Hour* 2 July 421/1 You cannot now get out of hearing of..'strawberries, *morning gathered'. **1903** *Farmer & Stockbreeder* 8 June 950/3 The vegetables mostly arrive in freight trains from distant States. They are well packed, and despatched with regularity, but nothing is absolutely fresh or 'morning gathered', as London green-grocers love to shout. **1961** *Daily Mail* 15 Mar. 8/8 'Morning gathered?' (Which morning?) **1943** C. DAY LEWIS *Word over All* 15 Children look down upon the *morning-grey Tissue of mist that veils a valley's lap. **1818** SHELLEY *Lines Written Euganean Hills* 297 The leaves unsodden Where the infant Frost has trodden With his *morning-winged feet.

9. Special comb., as **morning call**, a visit paid during the 'morning' (*i.e.* afternoon); hence **morning-calling** *ppl. a.*, that makes a morning call; **morning caller**, one who pays a formal morning call; **morning coffee**, coffee taken at mid-morning or (a less common use) at breakfast; **morning draught**, a portion of drink taken in the morning; **morning-flower** (see quot.); **morning girl**, a non-resident maid-servant employed during the morning only; **morning-gun**, a gun fired from the admiral's or senior officer's ship, or at a military post or camp, to announce day-break; **morning-hour** *U.S.*, 'in the Senate and House of Representatives of the United States, the hour after the reading of the journal, set apart for reports, motions, etc., before the taking up of unfinished business' (*Cent. Dict.* 1890); †**morning-house**, a tavern or public-house open in the early morning; **morning-killer**, one who wastes the morning by lying in bed; †**morning-knowledge** [L. *cognitio matutina*], according to St. Augustine and Aquinas the knowledge of things in their causes or Divine archetypal ideas, as opposed to 'evening knowledge', which is of things in their actual nature; **morning-land** [cf. G. *morgenland*], the East, the Orient; **morning line**, a list of probable betting odds established by the bookmaker prior to a sporting event; also *attrib.*; **morning-office**, morning-prayer; **morning paper**, a newspaper published so as to be on sale during the morning; **morning planet** = MORNING-STAR 1; **morning prayer**, (*a*) a prayer said in the morning; (*b*) the Anglican service of matins; (*c*) *Mil. slang* (see quot. 1965); **morning-red**, (*a*) (see quot. 1805–17); (*b*) the dawn (*rare*, after G. *morgenroth*); **morning room**, a room used as a sitting-room during the early part of the day; **morning-sickness**, nausea occurring in the morning, one of the earlier symptoms of pregnancy; † **morning-stead** *rare*$^{-1}$, the time of dawn; **morning tea**, tea taken either before rising or at mid-morning; **morning visit**, (*a*) a visit made in the morning; (*b*) a formal 'afternoon' visit (cf. *morning call*); so ***morning visiting, visitor***. Also MORNING-GIFT, -GLORY, etc.

1811 L. M. HAWKINS *C'tess & Gertr.* (K.O.), *Morning call. **1862** MRS. H. WOOD *Channings* xv, I am only making a morning call upon you, after the fashion of gentlefolks. **1848** GEO. ELIOT *Let.* in J. W. Cross *George Eliot's Life* (1885) I. 184 The bliss of having a very high attic in a romantic Continental town..far away from *morning-callers, dinners, and decencies. **1863** MRS. GASKELL *Dark Night's Work* viii. 128 She allowed Fletcher to..usher him into the library just like any common visitor, any morning-caller. **1941** G. HEYER *Faro's Daughter* i. 1 While the butler went to convey this message to the morning-caller, her ladyship tidied her ruffled person. **1840** GEO. ELIOT in Cross *Life* I. 65 A magazine of easily-wielded weapons for *morning-calling and evening-party controversialists. **1855** GEO. ELIOT in *Fraser's Mag.* June 705/1 The dark little bedroom, and the arm-chair where he took his *morning coffee as he read. **1917** CONRAD *Shadow-Line* iv. 131 Presently Ransome brought me the cup of morning coffee. **1959** T. S. ELIOT *Elder Statesman* II. 43 When I asked about morning coffee She said 'I'm not the one for elevens's.' **1973** A. CHRISTIE *Postern of Fate* III. xv. 231, I was just going to bring your morning coffee up. **1588** *Marprel. Epist.* (Arb.) 38 Whereunto he resorted for his *morning draught. **1667** PRIMATT *City & C. Build.* 49 Money..given to workmen for Morning-draughts. **1843** BORROW *Bible in Spain* l, Some fishermen entered, clamouring for their morning draught. **1890** *Century Dict.*, **Morning-flower*, a plant of the iris family, *Orthrosanthus multiflorus* (Australia). **1921** *Dict. Occup. Terms* (1927) §900 Daily servant,..*morning girl; a non-resident general servant. **1743** WOODROOFE in *Hanway's Trav.* (1762) I. II. xx. 91 We beat the drum and fired the *morning gun. **1867** in SMYTH *Sailor's Work-bk.* **1781** R. KING *Mod. Lond. Spy* 110 You have seen several night-houses..we shall now see a *morning-house. It is between 4 and 5. **1753** RICHARDSON *Grandison* (1811) II. vi. 109 Lady L—— is a **morning-killer*: she always loved her bed. **1621** JENISON *Height Israels Idol.* 31 This knowledge, of S. Augustine is called *scientia matutina & diurna*, *morning and day-knowledge. **1704** NORRIS *Ideal World* II. xii. 469 That morning-knowledge which they [*sc.* the Schoolmen] ascribe to the angels. **1842** MACAULAY *Prophecy of Capys* xxxi, Through the sand of *morning-land The camel bears the spice. **1935** A. J. POLLOCK *Underworld Speaks* 77/2 **Morning line*, the betting odds quoted in poolrooms on horse races. **1941** *Sun* (Baltimore) 26 Dec. 11/5 The old Louisiana Jockey Club abandoned the sport following a controversy over the..ruling eliminating the 'morning line' bookmaking. **1964** A. WYKES *Gambling* viii. 192 The day starts with the numbers of the runners in the first race posted in order, with the 'morning line' odds in lights opposite them. The morning line is the odds established by the racing officials for each horse (on the basis of its past performance) on the morning of a particular racing day. **1968** *Wall St. Jrnl.* 31 Jan. 1/1 Mr. Lewin has been track handicapper at Atlantic City, making up the 'morning line' (early odds) and picking likely winners for the official track program. **1765** H. WALPOLE *Otranto* iv. (1798) 74 It was not till late after the *morning-office, that he recollected [etc.]. **1727–41** *Morning paper [see PAPER *sb.* 8]. **1768** J. WEDGWOOD *Let.* 13 June (1965) 64 That Morning Paper which is mostly taken in by People of Fashion. **1862** MRS. H. WOOD *Channings* v, It is in all the morning papers. **1968** R. B. HEATH *Newspapers* i. 13 National daily morning papers. **1667** MILTON *P.L.* VII. 366 And hence the *Morning Planet guilds his horns. **1552** *Bk. Comm. Prayer*, An ordre for *morninge prayer dayly throughout the yeare. **1557** SEAGER *Sch. Vertue* in *Babees Bk.* 225 ¶ The mornynge prayer. 'O God, from whom al good gifts procede! [etc.]'. **1585** in *Fabric Rolls York Minster* (Surtees) 137 To Sir Hugh Hook, clerk, for saying morenynge praiers..33s. 4d. **1857** TROLLOPE *Barchester Towers* III. xv. 264 Eleanor was dressed a full hour before the time fixed in the Ullathorne household for morning prayers. **1916** JOYCE *Portrait of Artist* iii. 130 Death..is a blessed moment for him who has walked in the right path..attending to his morning and evening prayers. **1965** B. SWEET-ESCOTT *Baker St. Irreg.* viii. 250 'Morning prayers' in 12th Army headquarters, the daily briefing of the staff, began with a statement of temperature and humidity. **1805–17** R. JAMIESON *Char. Min.* (ed. 3) 71 *Aurora* or **morning red* is carmine-red mixed with much lemon yellow. *a* **1864** HAWTHORNE *Amer. Note-bks.* (1879) II. 132 The birds that..sing for us at morning-red. **1816** JANE AUSTEN *Emma* II. xiv. 260 That room was the very shape and size of the *morning-room at Maple Grove. **1822** *Magic Lantern* 4 The morning room of the female part of the family next excited my attention. **1876** T. HARDY *Ethelberta* x, The next day old Lady Petherwin..came into the morning-room, with a newspaper in her hand. **1893** ASHBY-STERRY *Naughty Girl* iii. 26 He had the morning-room [of the club] all to himself. **1879** *St. George's Hosp. Rep.* IX. 124 A fortnight's dyspepsia and *morning sickness. *a* **1618** SYLVESTER *Maiden's Blush* 1176 Toward *morning-sted To mighty Pharaoh the Almighty sent A double Dream. **1727** SWIFT *Furnit. Woman's Mind* in *Poetical Wks.* (1967) 329 Can at her *Morning Tea run o'er The Scandal of the Day before. **1923** WODEHOUSE *Inimitable Jeeves* xii. 135 Sometimes when Jeeves has brought in my morning tea and shoved it on the table beside my bed, he drifts silently from the room. **1940** Morning tea [see *evening paper*]. **1948** H. V. MORTON *In Search of South Africa* iv. 123, I saw groups of storm-bound people sitting at their morning tea. **1963** A. LUBBOCK *Austral. Roundabout* 6 The meals called 'tea'. There are three... First you have 'morning tea', which consists of cups of tea and biscuits, or savouries, at eleven o'clock. **1736** AINSWORTH *Lat. Dict.*, A *morning visit, *Matutina salutatio.* **1787** A. YOUNG *Jrnl.* 28 June in *Trav. France* (1792) I. 25 We return in time to dress for dinner, at half after twelve or one: then adjourn to the drawing-room..as the first thing done, by every person who arrives, is to pay a morning visit to each party already in the place. **1828** P. CUNNINGHAM *N.S. Wales* (ed. 3) II. 112 Morning visits, too, are made in the afternoon. **1864** TROLLOPE *Can you forgive Her?* I. ii. 9 The old lady walked into the drawing-room one morning at eleven o'clock.. these morning visits were made almost every day. **1852** C. M. YONGE *Two Guardians* xi. 195 The afternoons were less certain to be agreeable... Marian had become liable..[to] being carried forth..on a *morning visiting expedition. **1777** P. THICKNESSE *Year's Journey through France* II. 234 The French never give..any refreshment..to their *morning or evening visitors. **1831** M. EDGEWORTH *Let.* 6 Jan. (1971) 469 Scarcely had I taken up my pen and breathed when other morning visitors entered.

'morning-gift. *Antiq.* A modern rendering of OE. *morʒenʒifu* (see MORYEVE) or the equivalent form in other Teut. langs.

1597 [see MORWYNGIFT, quot. 1593]. **1597** SKENE *De Verb. Sign.* s.v. *Dos*, The Dutch word *morgengab*, morning gift, is ane kind of dowry. **1824** J. MAIDMENT *North Countrie Garland* (1884) 1 He has wooed the young Countess..An' given her for a morning gift Strathboggie and Aboyne. **1867** FREEMAN *Norm. Conq.* (1877) I. v. 306 The royal bride, like other Teutonic brides, had her morning-gift.

'morning-'glory. [f. MORNING + GLORY *sb.*]

1. A twining herb of the genus *Ipomœa* or closely related genera of the family Convolvulaceæ, esp. *Ipomœa* (or *Pharbitis*) *purpurea*, which is native to tropical America and bears large trumpet-shaped flowers; also *attrib.* and *fig.*

1814 F. PURSH *Flora Americæ Septentrionalis* I. 146 *Ipomoea Nil*... Flowers beautiful pale blue, only open early in the morning, from which it has been called Morning-glory. **1836** *Backwoods of Canada* 142 The pillars [of the verandah] are wreathed with the..'morning glory', the American name for the most splendid of major convolvuluses. **1885** G. ALLEN *Babylon* i, The morning-glories opened their great pink bells. **1892** *Harper's Mag.* May 937/1 The..little cabin that sat smiling through a cool green garment of..morning-glory vines. **1934** E. BLUNDEN *Choice or Chance* 11 And with wonder saw The morning-glory about the bucket twined. **1947** R. P. T. COFFIN *Yankee Coast* 59 The owners..have to make guitars and banjos do. And accordions, phonographs with morning-glory horns, and, latterly, radios. **1963** W. BLUNT *Of Flowers & Village* 176 I've not been very successful with morning glories. **1964** C. WILLOCK *Enormous Zoo* v. 89 We found the DC..in a morning glory-covered bungalow up on the Sudan border. **1966** *Times* 22 Mar. 5/1 The Pharmaceutical Society is carrying out laboratory investigations to determine whether any Morning Glory seeds sold in this country could be dangerous. **1968** PETERSON & MCKENNY *Field Guide to Wildflowers Northeastern & Northcentral N. Amer.* 338 Common Morning-glory. Alien. *Ipomoea purpurea*... A twining vine; the garden morning-glory with broad heart-shaped leaves. Flowers purple, pink, blue, or white. **1970** R. LOWELL *Notebk.* 101 The jellied green creepers and morning-glories of the saurian sunset.

2. *attrib.* (*U.S.*) designating a kind of stove.

1885 ROE *Driven back to Eden* Pref. 1 A morning-glory stove gave out abundant warmth.

3. *U.S. slang.* Something which fails to maintain its early achievement; *esp.* in sporting contexts.

1904 *Outing* XLV. 170/1 Didn't I tell you he was nothing but a morning glory—why that dog couldn't beat a ferry boat. **1920** *Harvey's Weekly* 15 May 15/2 You have..sent one more morning glory statesman to limbo. **1935** A. J. POLLOCK *Underworld Speaks* 77/2 *Morning glory*, race horse that works in fast time in the morning but fails to race well. **1938** *Amer. Speech* XIII. 30 Clubs which bloom luxuriantly early in the season, but which are expected to wilt ignominiously as the competition becomes hotter, are known as *Morning Glories*.

'morningless, *a. poet. rare.* [f. MORNING + -LESS.] Having no morning. Cf. MORNLESS *a.*

1866 M. ARNOLD *Thyrsis* xvii, Thine earth-forgetting eyelids keep The morningless and unawakening sleep. **1930** O. GOGARTY *Wild Apples* 15 Those resinous timbers immuned from decay By thunders ancestral and morningless storms.

morningly ('mɔːnɪŋlɪ), *adv. rare.* [f. MORNING + -LY[2].] In the morning; also, every morning.

1560 ABP. PARKER *Corr.* (Parker Soc.) 131 That cause which all your loving subjects so daily sigh for and morningly in their prayers desire to appear to their eyes. **1563** HYLL *Art Garden.* II. liv. (1593) 135 The Onion accustomed to be eaten morningly. **1844** J. T. HEWLETT *Parsons & W.* xlv, That used to be taken in morningly.

So **'morningly** *a.*, occurring every morning.

1894 CROCKETT *Lilac Sunbonnet* 148 The nightly and morningly ceremony of 'milking'.

morning star. [Cf. the earlier MORN-STAR.]

1. The planet Venus when visible in the east before sunrise; = LUCIFER 1. Also *gen.* a star or planet that is visible in the morning.

1535 COVERDALE *Job* xxxviii. 7. **1590** SPENSER *F.Q.* I. xii. 21 As bright as doth the morning starre appeare Out of the East. **1630** MILTON *On May Morning* 1 Now the bright morning Star, Dayes harbinger, Comes dancing from the East. **1812** WOODHOUSE *Astron.* xxiii. 249 Perceive Venus rising just before the Sun, and becoming the Morning Star.

b. *fig.* Applied (after Rev. xxii. 16) to Christ; also, to any person who is regarded as the precursor of a figurative 'dawn'.

1567 *Gude & Godlie B.* (S.T.S.) 145 He [Christ] is the Morning Star. **1671** MILTON *P.R.* I. 694 So spake our Morning Star then in his rise. **1720** J. HUGHES *Siege Damascus* III. (1777) 38 The great Mahomet, Arabia's morning-star. **1732** NEAL *Hist. Purit.* I. 3 John Wickliffe, the morning star of the Reformation. **1818** BYRON *Giaour* 1130 She..rose, where'er I turn'd mine eye, The Morning-star of Memory! **1833** TENNYSON *Dream of Fair Wom.* i,

'*The Legend of Good Women*', long ago Sung by the morning star of song, who made His music heard below.

2. *Antiq.* = MORGENSTERN.

1684 J. PETER tr. *Siege Vienna* 87 Our Men being provided with.. Hooks and Clubs headed with Iron, Morning Stars and the like Instruments. **1868** *Archæol. Jrnl.* XXV. 85 The acquisition by the Royal Artillery Museum..of some specimens of 'Morning Stars'. **1871** B. TAYLOR *Faust* (1875) II. IV. iii. 259 There hangs a morning-star so strong, The like of which I've wanted long.

3. *dial.* = *star-of-Bethlehem.*

1890 *Nature Notes* I. 23 (Hampshire), Morning-star ..*Ornithogalum umbellatum.*

'morningtide. Now *poet.* [f. MORNING + TIDE.] The morning, or early part of the day.

1530 PALSGR. 68 Of *matyn*, a mornyng, *matynée*, a mornynge tyde. **1611** COTGR., Matinée, a forenoone, or morning-tide. **1848** KINGSLEY *Saint's Trag.* I. i, All the gentle angels Which glance about my dreams at morning-tide. **1881** BLACKMORE *Christowell* i, But morning-tide spread all soft herbage with a silvery tissue.

'morningward. *rare.* [f. MORNING + -WARD.] *to the morningward of*: = to the east of.

1845 E. WARBURTON *Crescent & Cross* II. 48 The seas, over which the sun rises to the morningward of Malta.

morning-watch. [f. MORNING + WATCH *sb.*]

1. The last of the (three or four) watches into which the night was divided by the Jews and Romans.

1535 COVERDALE *1 Sam.* xi. 11. **1667** MILTON *P.L.* XII. 207 All night he will pursue, but his approach Darkness defends between till morning Watch.

2. *Naut.* The watch between four and eight A.M.; the men on duty at that time.

1840 R. H. DANA *Bef. Mast* iii, The larboard watch..go below until four in the morning, when they come on deck again and remain till eight, having what is called the morning watch. **1867** SMYTH *Sailor's Word-bk.*, *Morning watch*, those of the crew on watch from 4 to 8 A.M.

mornivall, obs. form of MOURNIVAL.

'mornless, *a. rare.* [f. MORN + -LESS.] Having no morn. Cf. MORNINGLESS.

1795 ANNA SEWARD *Lett.* (1811) IV. 97 Before the long and mornless night descends. **1830** J. WRIGHT *Retrospect* II. 95 One wayward step—thou sink'st in mornless night.

†**'mornly,** *adv. Obs. rare.* [f. MORN + -LY².] In the morn or morning; every morning.

1598 SYLVESTER *Du Bartas* II. ii. II. *Babylon* 327 All the winged quiers Which mornly warble, on green trembling briers, Ear-tickling tunes. **1609** HEYWOOD *Brit. Troy* XII. lxix, These faire Andromache doth mornely feed.

†**'morn-speech, 'morrow-speech.** *Obs.* Forms: see *α*. MORN; *β*. MORROW (also 4–5 morspeche); and SPEECH. [Cf. MDu. *morgensprake* in the same sense, mod.Du. *morgenspraak* discussion.] A periodical assembly of a guild held on the morrow after the guild-feast.

α. *c* **1000** in Thorpe *Charters* 613 Se ȝeȝilda ðe ne ȝesece his morgenspæce ȝilde his syster huniȝes. **1389** in *Eng. Gilds* (1870) 49 At þᵗ mornspeche, þorow on assent of all þe brethen to chesen an Aldirman. **1487** *Ann. Barber-Surgeons Lond.* (1890) 578 At the first mornspeech after he shall have taken the said apprentice.

β. **1389** in *Eng. Gilds* (1870) 49 To haue foure morspeches in þe ȝere. **1431** *Ibid.* 275 At ech of these ij. morowe spechis euery brother schall payen to yᵉ costage..ij denar. *c* **1440** *Promp. Parv.* 344/1 Morow speche [*King's Coll. MS.* and *Heber MS.* morwe speche, *Winch. MS.* morspech], *crastinum colloquium*. [**1890** GROSS *Gild Merch.* II. 143 The Gild at its meetings, which were called 'morrow-speeches'.]

'morn-star. *Obs.* exc. *poet.* [Cf. MDu., MHG. *morgensterre* (MHG. also *-sterne*, mod.G. *-stern*), Du. *morgenstar.*] = MORNING-STAR I.

c **888** K. ÆLFRED *Boeth.* iv, þone beorhtan steorran þe we hatað morȝensteorra. *c* **1440** *Promp. Parv.* 344/2 Morow sterre (morwynstere, K.), *Lucifer.* **1811** SHELLEY *To a Star* 6 More sweet Than the expiring morn-star's paly fires.

†**'morn-tide.** *Obs.* Forms: see MORN and TIDE; also MORROW-TIDE. [Cf. OS. *morgantîd*, MDu. *morgentijt*, G. *Morgenzeit.*] = MORNINGTIDE.

Beowulf 484 Ðonne wæs þeos medoheal on morȝentid, drihtsele dreorfah. *c* **1250** *Gen. & Ex.* 59 Ðat was ðe firme morȝen tid, ðat euere sprong in werld[e] wid. *a* **1300** *Cursor M.* 6333 Þar he sleped þat morntide. *c* **1440** *Bone Flor.* 114 Sche schall..in hur lovely armes me lappe Bothe evyn and morne tyde.

'mornward(s, *adv. poet. rare.* [f. MORN + -WARD, -WARDS.] Towards the morning, towards the rising sun or the east; eastward.

1850 LOWELL *New Year's Eve* i, And mornward now the starry hands move on. **1855** BAILEY *Mystic*, etc. 88 From Athabascan cape, mornwards, to where [etc.].

†**'morn-while.** *Obs.* Forms: *α*. see MORN and WHILE; *β*. 3 morȝewile, -quile. Morning; the time of morning.

α. *c* **1250** *Gen. & Ex.* 3275 God him bad helden up his hond to-ward ðis water, in a morȝen quile ðe se luked, so god it wile. ?*a* **1400** *Morte Arth.* 2001 Thise lordly knyghttez, Salle lenge on his lefte hand, wyth legyones ynewe, To meue in the morne-while.

β. *c* **1200** *Trin. Coll. Hom.* 39 Mid-niht ðe bilimpeð to frumberdligges, hanecrau þe bilimpeð þowuene men, morȝewile to alde men. *c* **1250** *Gen. & Ex.* 3461 Ðe ðridde daiȝes morȝe quile, ðunder and leuene made spile.

mornyfle, obs. form of MOURNIVAL.

mornyng(e, obs. ff. MORNING, MOURNING.

‖**moro**¹ ('mɔərəʊ). *Path. Obs.* [It. *moro* mulberry, also 'a wart in a horse called an Anburie' (Florio 1598).] (See quot. 1891.)

1823 in CRABB *Technol. Dict.* **1891** *Syd. Soc. Lex.*, *Moro*, old name for a small abscess like a mulberry. Also, a mulberry-like tumour on the genitals.

‖**Moro**² ('moro). [Sp. = MOOR *sb.*²] One of the Muslim Malays in the Philippine Islands.

1886 YULE & BURNELL *Anglo-Ind. Gloss.* Suppl., *Moro* is still applied at Manilla to the Musulman Malays. **1901** A. H. KEANE in *Chamb. Encycl.* VIII. 118/1 Nearly all Malays are either 'Indios' (i.e. Roman Catholics) or 'Moros' (i.e. Mohammedans). **1902** *Westm. Gaz.* 23 Aug. 6/1 Dealing with the situation in the Philippines, he asserted that it was imperative that the United States should chastise the Moros for their delinquencies.

‖**moro**³ ('mɔərəʊ). [f. Sp. *pájaro moro*, Moorish sparrow.] The vinous grosbeak, or stone-bird, *Carpodacus* (*Bucanetes*) *githagineus*, inhabiting the desert countries of North Africa.

1890 in *Century Dict.*; and in later Dicts.

Moroccan (mɒ'rɒkən), *a.* and *sb.* Also **Maroccan.** [f. *Morocco* (also *Marocco*, F. *Maroc*) + -AN.] **A.** *adj.* **a.** Of or pertaining to Morocco (see next).

a **1706** EVELYN *Diary* an. 1682 (1955) IV. 285 We had at this time in Lond together The Russian, Morrocan, & Indian Ambassador. **1869** 'MARK TWAIN' *Innoc. Abr.* vii. 69 The Spaniards built these watch towers on the hills to enable them to keep a sharper look out on the Moroccan speculators. **1883** BURTON & CAMERON *Gold Coast* I. i. 17 The Mersa or water-port of a Moroccan town. **1905** *Jewish Encycl.* IX. 27/2 (*Morocco*) The Moroccan Jewesses.

b. In the names of various preparations of cannabis.

1970 E. GOODE *Marijuana Smokers* i. 18 Another recipe book..has exotic Oriental dishes, such as 'Bhang Sherbet', 'Moroccan Majoon' [etc.]. **1972** J. BROWN *Chancer* iii. 38 People talk about the effects of cannabis as if there was just one kind... You smoke Moroccan Gold..you'll just feel, like, a little drunk. But you smoke Egyptian Black, that will stone you out of your head. **1972** *Times* 14 Dec. 2/3 The changes involved 'speed'..and other drugs, referred to in the hearing as..'Moroccan black'.

B. *sb.* An inhabitant of Morocco.

1860 *Chamb. Encycl.* I. 8/1 He [Abd-el-Kader] would not abandon his attached followers..to the plunder and massacre of the Maroccans. **1900** *Q. Rev.* Oct. 354 The Moroccan has a jingling rhyme which he loves to repeat.

Morocco (mɒ'rɒkəʊ), *sb.* Also 7 **morocko, maroco,** 9 **marocco, morrocco.** [The European name (= It. *Marocco*, Sp. *Marruecos*, F. *Maroc*) of the 'sultanate' or 'empire' called in Arabic *Maγrib-al-Aqçā* 'Extreme West', comprising the north-western part of Africa. The name properly belongs not to the country but to the chief city; its native form is *Marrākesh.*]

I. 1. Used *attrib.* in the sense 'of or pertaining to, or made in Morocco'; *esp.* in the names of things coming (or supposed to have originally come) from Morocco, as ***Morocco cherry, daisy, gum, grape, -leech, plum.***

1664 EVELYN *Kal. Hort., June* (1706) 78 Cherries..Great-bearer, Morocco Cherry, the Egriot [etc.]. *Ibid.*, Plums..the King's-Plum, Spanish, Morocco-Plum [etc.]. **1731** MILLER *Gard. Dict.* s.v. *Prunus* §2 The early black Damask, commonly called The Morocco Plum. **1763** MILLS *Pract. Husb.* IV. 378 The morocco, or barbarou, is a large purple grape, the bunches of which are also of an extraordinary size. **1882** *Garden* 8 July 19/3 The blue Morocco Daisy is much admired. **1887** BENTLEY *Man. Bot.* (ed. 5) 538 Morocco,..or Brown Barbary Gum [is obtained] from *Acacia arabica.* **1891** *Syd. Soc. Lex.*, *Morocco leech*, the *Sanguisuga interrupta.* **1901** *Daily Chron.* 7 Dec. 3/4 The Morocco youth has no tendency towards reform.

b. ***morocco leather***: see 3. So ***morocco hides, skins***: the skins from which morocco is made.

1716 GAY *Trivia* I. 30 Then let the prudent walker shoes provide, Not of the Spanish or Morocco hide. **1727–52** CHAMBERS *Cycl.* s.v., We have Morocco-skins brought from the Levant, Barbary, Spain, Flanders, and France.

†**2. Morocco-man:** see quots. *Obs.*

1796 COLQUHOUN *Police Metrop.* (ed. 3) 153 *note*, Fraudulent Lottery Insurances have not diminished. The Offices are numerous all over the Metropolis,..to many of which there are persons attached, called Morocco Men, who go about from house to house among their former customers, and attend in the back parlours of Public Houses, where they are met by customers who make insurances. **1798** EDGEWORTH *Pract. Educ.* (1811) I. 315 And the men who are sent about to public-houses to entice poor people into illegal lottery insurances, are called Morocco-men.

II. (Cf. MAROQUIN.)

3. (In full ***morocco-leather.***) Leather made from goatskins tanned with sumac, originally produced in Morocco (and other Barbary States), and afterwards in the Levant, Turkey, and now in Europe from skins imported from Asia and Africa; it is used particularly for bookbinding and upholstery. Also, a leather in imitation of this, made from sheepskins and lambskins, etc., and used for the same purposes, but chiefly in shoemaking.

French morocco, an inferior quality of Levant morocco, having a smaller and less prominent grain; **imitation morocco**, see above; **Levant morocco**, a high-grade morocco, with a large grain, properly made from the skin of the Angora goat; **Persian morocco**, see PERSIAN *a.* 2.

[**1600** J. PORY tr. *Leo's Africa* II. 61 Here is that excellent leather dressed, which is called leather of Maroco.] **1634** SIR T. HERBERT *Trav.* 151 Saddles of Veluet, some like the Morocko. **1695** MOTTEUX tr. *St. Olon's Morocco* 140 The Red Morocco Leather, known here by the Name of Spanish Leather, is drest in that City [Fez], and is the finest in all Barbary. **1727–52** CHAMBERS *Cycl.* s.v., The various manners of preparing Moroccos. *Ibid.*, Manner of preparing black Morocco. *Ibid.*, Red Morocco. **1743** POPE *Last Will* Wks. 1751 IX. 268 All the volumes of my Works and Translations of Homer, bound in red morocco. **1771** *Ann. Reg.* XIV. II. 88/1 When they [*sc.* skins of the sea-lions] are tanned, they have a grain almost like Morocco. **1817** DIBDIN *Bibliogr. Decam.* II. 533 For your Fifteeners..let me entreat you invariably to use morocco. **1839** *Penny Cycl.* XIV. 436/1 The marocco leather of the capital is yellow, that made in Tafilet green, and in Fez it is dyed red. **1852** MORFIT *Tanning & Currying* (1853) 363 Imitation Morocco..is prepared from sheep-skins in the same manner as true Morocco. **1870** YEATS *Nat. Hist. Comm.* 297 Deer skins are used for the finer kinds of morocco leather, and for bookbinding. **1879** *Cassell's Techn. Educ.* IV. 88/1 English, French, and Spanish moroccos all excel in their own way, either in grain or in colour. **1907** *Edin. Rev.* Apr. 431 A..parchment album bound in green morocco.

b. *attrib.* in the sense 'made of or covered with morocco'; also *Comb.*, as ***morocco-bound, -covered, -like*** adjs.

1817 DIBDIN *Bibliogr. Decam.* II. 481 Your De Thous..are almost always in morocco bindings. **1820** W. IRVING *Sketch Bk.* (1849) 141 Small morocco-bound prayerbooks. **1827** DISRAELI *Viv. Grey* VII. iv, The morocco case was unlocked, and the manuscript of Haroun Al Raschid revealed. **1849** THACKERAY *Pendennis* vii, A little morocco box, which..contained the Major's back-teeth. **1858** MRS. GORE *Heckington* II. i. 16 A morocco-housewife or pocket-book. **1873** 'MARK TWAIN' & WARNER *Gilded Age* II. ix. 97 A very official chair behind a long green morocco-covered table. **1886** A. HORNBLOW tr. *Normand's Splashes from Parisian Ink-Pot* 83 Plunged in a big green morocco-covered fauteuil, he began to scan over the 'dailies'. **1896** *Sat. Rev.* 12 Dec. 623/2 'Little Eyolf'..has been promoted into a full-blown fashionable theatrical speculation, with a 'Morocco Bound' syndicate in the background. **1899** *Allbutt's Syst. Med.* VIII. 613 In lupus erythematosus the adherent crusts and morocco-like surface are a characteristic feature. **1958** *Listener* 2 Oct. 520/2 Sentences like 'I have still to see that lofty homeland of the potato and the llama'..belong to a solid, morocco-bound tradition.

c. *local U.S.* **morocco-head,** the American merganser, *Mergus americanus*; **morocco-jaw,** the surf-scoter or surf-duck, *Œdemia perspicillata.*

1888 G. TRUMBULL *Names of Birds* 65, 103.

4. A fanciful name given to a kind of strong ale brewed at Levens Hall, Cumbria.

1792 BUDWORTH *Fortn. Rambles Lakes* 17 We were regaled by a liquor called Morocco..; it is of a high colour, and is made from malt and hops; has an acid taste, and does not ferment. **1870** M. COLLINS *Vivian* III. ix. 186 Washed down with more copious draughts of strong ale and Morocco. **1894** R. S. FERGUSON *Hist. Westmorland* 285 Levens Hall..is also famed for its 'morocco' or old ale.

5. ***red morocco***: a local name for the plant *Adonis autumnalis* or Pheasant's eye.

1771 *Encycl. Brit.* I. 27/2 The English names [of the genus *Adonis*] are, adonis-flower, pheasant's eye, red maithes, or red morocco. **1863** PRIOR *Plant-n.* 188 Red Morocco, from the colour of the petals, *Adonis autumnalis.*

6. ***in morocco***, used by Longfellow as gipsy slang for: Stripped, naked. Cf. BUFF.

1843 LONGF. *Sp. Stud.* III. v, There you are in your morocco!

mo'rocco, *v. trans. rare*⁻⁰. [f. MOROCCO *sb.*] To convert into morocco.

1890 in *Century Dict.*

morocock, variant of MARACOCK.

1706 PHILLIPS (ed. Kersey), *Morococks.*

moroder, obs. form of MARAUDER.

moro'logical. *Humorously pedantic.* [f. MOROLOGY + -ICAL.] Pertaining to 'morology'. Hence **moro'logically** *adv.*

1607 R. C[AREW] tr. *Estienne's World of Wonders* 269 The old maner [of preaching] was, to make one part Allegoricall, another Anagogicall, and a third Tropological: whereas they should haue made one part Morological, another Mythological, and a third Pseudological. **1865** STRANGFORD *Lett. & P.* (1878) 164 Morologically speaking, the production is no richer or sillier than your prize-fool from Gloucestershire. **1867** —— *Select.* (1869) I. 320 If the condition of liberalism be insisted upon, as well as the morological..conditions of mind necessary to such a question, there is but one man in the House who can put it.

morologist (mɒ'rɒlədʒɪst). *rare*⁻¹. [f. MOROLOG-Y + -IST.] **a.** One who talks foolishly. **b.** A student of 'morology'.

1727 in BAILEY (vol. II). **1894** WILKINS & VIVIAN *Green Bay Tree* I. 146 But then I am a student of fools, a morologist—to coin a word.

morology (mɒˈrɒlədʒɪ). [ad. Gr. μωρολογία foolish talking, f. μωρολόγ-ος that talks foolishly, f. μωρό-ς foolish + -λόγος that speaks: see -LOGY.] †**1.** Foolish talking. *Obs.*

1596 in *J. Melvill's Diary* (Wodrow Soc.) 350 Corrupt communication, morologie, aischrologie. **1652** W. ROWLAND *Judic. Astrol.* Title-p., Of Will. Ramsey's Morologie in his pretended Reply (called *Lux veritatis*) to Doctour Nathaniel Homes his Demonologie. **1656** in BLOUNT *Glossogr.*

2. *humorously.* The science that treats of fools.

1867, 1894 [implied in MOROLOGICAL, MOROLOGIST].

†**moromantie.** *Obs.*$^{-0}$ [F. *moromantie* (Cotgr.), f. Gr. μωρό-ς foolish + μαντεί-α -MANCY.] 'Foolish divination' (Blount *Glossogr.* 1656).

‖**moron**[1]. *Obs.* [F. *moron, mouron* (OF. *moronne*, 14th c.).] A variety of salamander.

1774 GOLDSMITH *Nat. Hist.* (1824) III. 158 With respect to the Salamander, the whole tribe, from the Moron to the Gekko, are said to be venomous to the last degree.

moron[2] (ˈmɔərən). orig. *U.S.* [f. L. *mōrus*, Gr. μωρός stupid.] **a.** One of the highest class of feeble-minded; an adult person having a mental age of between eight and twelve. Also *attrib.*

The term was first adopted and given this meaning by the American Association for the Study of the Feeble-minded in 1910.

1910 H. H. GODDARD *Let.* 29 Apr. in *Jrnl. Psycho-Asthenics* Sept.–Dec. 65 The other (suggestion) is to call them [*sc.* feeble-minded children] by the Greek word 'moron'. It is defined as one who is lacking in intelligence, one who is deficient in judgement or sense. **1912** —— *Kallikak Family* 54 The type of feeblemindedness of which we are speaking is the one to which Deborah belongs, that is, to the high grade, or moron. **1919** H. WOODROW *Brightness & Dullness in Children* iii. 45 The term *moron*..is a new term... The desirability of this new term arose from the fact that the term feeble-minded, which is used in England to designate only the highest class of mental defectives, had long been used in America to include all three classes. **1937** C. L. BURT *Subnormal Mind* (rev. ed.) ii. 102 All through their years of training, most of them [*sc.* social workers and teachers] had never, to their certain knowledge, set eyes on a moron or an imbecile. **1948** J. W. BRIDGES *Psychol.* xxiv. 352 The moron has an I.Q. of 50 to 70..and the idiot below 20. This distinction is made on the basis of intelligence test results and is consequently not very reliable. **1968** W. B. STEPHENS tr. *Inhelder's Diagnosis of Reasoning in Mentally Retarded* ii. 72 The normal child of seven, the moron of twelve, or even the imbecile assimilates an enormous number of varied experiences which are..qualitatively irreducible from one level to the other.

b. *colloq.* A stupid or slow-witted person; a fool. Also *attrib.*

1922 W. R. INGE in *Edin. Rev.* July 48 It is possible that while we are governed by high-grade 'morons' there will be no practical recognition of the dangers which threaten us. **1922** H. TITUS *Timber* iii. 37 So this backwoods moron, even, knew something about his affairs that John Taylor did not know. **1922** L. STODDARD *Revolt against Civilization* iv. 129 It is a mutilated, deformed, moron humanity which glowers or drivels at us through expressionist pictures. **1928** HECHT & MACARTHUR *Front Page* II. 91 Another one of your moron blunders. **1930** R. MACAULAY *Staying with Relations* ii. 22 'You mutt,' said young Mrs. Rickaby..'Catherine will think we're all morons.' **1959** *Punch* 10 June 780/2 It was so obvious it might have occurred to anyone but a complete moron. **1968** M. WOODHOUSE *Rock Baby* xxiii. 219 What we have here is a poxed-up, paralytic bunch of morons... They're technically incompetent..and they're pretty useless in almost every other field. **1975** G. MOFFAT *Miss Pink* xii. 169 He'd have had to be a moron not to have guessed that the killer was really after himself.

So **moˈronic** *a.*, **moˈronically** *adv.*

1926 *N.Y. Herald-Trib.* 28 Nov. VII. 4/2 A facetious account of a young girl's discovery that her brother had died of a venereal disease which has the romping moronic quality of a tabloid front page. **1931** *Churchman* 14 Feb. 15 The philosophers go home considerably enheartened when they find Socrates moronically low in his I.Q. score. **1957** R. A. HEINLEIN *Door into Summer* (1960) ii. 25 It was a moronically simple idea: don't repair, replace. **1957** *Times Lit. Suppl.* 18 Oct. 621/3 The psychopathic juvenile delinquent, moronically searching for 'the truth'. **1959** *Punch* 13 May 641/2 They interrupt Macbeth, they cackle at M. Hulot, they share their moronic comments with their escorts. **1975** D. BLOODWORTH *Clients of Omega* xxi. 204 Provoking desperate people into believing that they can only bring about unity among men by knocking their moronic heads together.

moron, obs. form of MORN.

morone, incorrect var. MAROON *sb.*[1] and *a.*[1] In some Dicts. with pseudo-etymological explanation as if from L. *mōr-um* mulberry.

1808 *Examiner* 6 Mar. 157/2 Coquelicot and morone are on the decline. **1836** SMART, *Morone*, a deep crimson, or the colour of the unripe mulberry. **1890** *Century Dict.*

moror, var. MAROR.

morose (mɒˈrəʊs), *a.*[1] Also 7 morous, moross. [ad. L. *mōrōs-us* peevish, fretful, wayward, fastidious, scrupulous (*transf.* of things, hard to manage), f. *mōr-*, *mōs* manner: see MORAL *a.* and -OSE.]

1. Of persons, their attributes and actions: Sour-tempered, sullen, gloomy, and unsocial.

1565 COOPER *Thesaurus, Morosus*, waywarde: frowarde: overthwarte: morose: diuers in condition: harde to please. [**1609** B. JONSON *Sil. Wom.* Dram. Pers. (1620), *Morose*, a Gentleman that loues no noyse.] **1620** VENNER *Via Recta* viii. 166 Neither..am I against sauces so morose as that I doe altogether deny them. **1647** CLARENDON *Hist. Reb.* I. §185 He was a man of very morose manners, and a very sowr aspect. **1694** F. BRAGGE *Disc. Parables* xiv. 458 They were ..of very morose countenances, as greatly mortified, and strangers to the world. *a* **1770** JORTIN *Serm.* (1771) VI. i. 18 A man should not give way to a morose, captious and cavilling humour and be eager to find fault. **1775** MASON *Mem. Gray* Poems 119 He was also morose, unsocial, and obstinate. **1815** J. SMITH *Panorama Sci. & Art* I. 242 There are very few so obstinately morose, as to be uninfluenced by the opinions of others. **1853** C. BRONTE *Villette* xi, She looked stony and stern, almost mortified and morose. **1849** MACAULAY *Hist. Eng.* i. I. 3 No man who is correctly informed as to the past will be disposed to take a morose or desponding view of the present. **1907** *Spectator* 5 Jan. 9/2 That great morose genius [*sc.* Swift].

absol. **1620** T. GRANGER *Div. Logike* 275 This to delight, to moue, and to allure with wiles, euen the refractory, and morose. **1762** GOLDSM. *Nash* 40 Let the morose and grave censure an attention to forms and ceremonies.

b. of opinions, principles, etc.

1791 MAXWELL in Boswell *Johnson* an. 1770, His philosophy..was by no means morose and cynical. **1838** LYTTON *Alice* II. iv, Morbid and morose philosophy, begot by a proud spirit on a lonely heart. **1861** J. A. ALEXANDER *Gospel of Christ* xiv. 194 Pleasures which a more morose religion would proscribe as dangerous.

c. *transf.*

1658 FRANCK *North. Mem.* (1821) 311 The carp is a fish complicated of a moross mixture, and a torpid motion. **1902** A. LANG *Hist. Scot.* II. v. 104 Mary's arrival was darkened by the morose climate.

†**2.** Scrupulous, painstaking. *Obs.*

1696 BENTLEY *Serm.* ix. (1724) 354 Unworthy of the most cautious and morose searcher of truth. **1695** J. EDWARDS *Perfect. Script.* 482 He was a very morose interpreter.

†**3.** Of a thing: Hard to manage. *Obs.*

1652 L. S. *People's Liberty* xxii. 53 This knot is somewhat morose, and will not easily be untied.

4. *Comb.*, as ***morose-looking, -natured.***

1845 JAMES *Arrah Neil* ii, The elder of the two was a hard-featured somewhat morose-looking personage. **1884** J. PAYN *Lit. Recollect.* 62 A morose-natured man.

morose (mɒˈrəʊs), *a.*[2] *rare.* Cf. MOROUS *a.* [ad. late L. *morōs-us*, f. *mora* delay: see -OSE.]

1. *Casuistry.* Chiefly in the phrase ***morose delectation***, the habit of dwelling with enjoyment upon evil thoughts. So ***morose thoughts.***

Aquinas uses *morosa delectatio* as a term already established, and discusses its meaning, connecting it with *mora* delay and its derivative *immorārī* to linger upon. Cf. St. Augustine *De Civ. Dei* XXII. xxiii, Ne in eo quod male delectat vel visio vel cogitatio remoretur.

1644 HAMMOND *Pract. Catech.* II. §6 (1646) 77 All morose thoughts, i.e. dwelling or insisting on that image, or phansying of such unclean matter with delectation. **1651** JER. TAYLOR *Holy Dying* iii. §9 We may suspect Drunkenness, when it may be also a morose delectation in Unclean thoughts. **1661** BP. NICHOLSON *Exp. Catech.* (1663) 123 In this Commandment are forbidden..All that feeds this sin [adultery], or are incentives to it: as..3. Morose thoughts, that dwell in the phancy with delight.

2. *Civil Law.* (See quot.)

1875 POSTE *Gaius* III. 449 If he is Morose (a debtor chargeable with mora).

morosely (mɒˈrəʊslɪ), *adv.* [f. MOROSE *a.*[1] + -LY[2].] In a morose or sullen manner.

1654 WHITLOCK *Zootomia* 253 Such whole Heads are filled with those Principles of Prejudice..which are either falsly receptive, or morosely exclusive. **1750** JOHNSON *Rambler* No. 74 ¶6 Their singularities therefore are only blameable, when they have imprudently or morosely withdrawn themselves from the world. **1838** GLADSTONE in Morley *Life* (1903) I. 150 Morosely withdrawing himself from the range of human sympathies. **1873** BLACK *Pr. Thule* x. 164 Morosely objecting to pretty nearly everything Lavender said.

moroseness (mɒˈrəʊsnɪs). [f. MOROSE *a.*[1] + -NESS.] The state or quality of being morose.

a **1661** FULLER *Worthies, Northampt.* (1662) II. 291 Always cheerful without the least levity, and grave without any moroseness. **1746** DR. PARSONS in *Phil. Trans.* XLIV. 44, I ..know some, on whose Faces a settled Moroseness always strikes the Beholder. **1875** JOWETT *Plato* (ed. 2) V. 4 The grace and cheerfulness..have disappeared; and a spirit of moroseness..has taken their place.

morosity (mɒˈrɒsɪtɪ). [ad. F. *morosité*, ad. L. *mōrōsitas*, f. *mōrōsus* MOROSE *a.*: see -ITY.] = MOROSENESS. In 17th c. often in particularized sense, †an instance of moroseness.

1534 WHITINTON *Tullyes Offices* I. (1540) 39 Leste..we shulde slyp in to morosyte yuell to please, vnprofytable and odyous to other men. **1563–87** FOXE *A. & M.* (1596) 710/1 The world is come now to such a morossity and peeuish insensibilitie in these contentious and cauilling daies of ours, that [etc.]. **1625** DONNE *Serm.* 3 Apr. 40 There may bee a Jealousie in the Husband, a Morositie in the Father, an Imperiousnesse in the Master. **1649** JER. TAYLOR *Gt. Exemp.* II. Pr. i. 102 Blot out all peevish dispositions and morosities. *a* **1677** BARROW *Serm.* (1810) II. 157 No affected singularities, no supercilious morosities, no frivolous ostentations. **1711** *Vind. Sacheverell* 81 The Stoical Morosities, and mis-tim'd Preachments of these Lay Baptists. **1849** F. W. NEWMAN *Soul* (ed. 2) 176 At least this appears the best way of showing that no morosity mingles with distaste for such things. **1873** MISS BROUGHTON *Nancy* III. 146 By the utter morosity of Algy's face..I conjecture that it is a joke. **1884** C. ROGERS *Soc. Life Scot.* II. xi. 160 James VI sought to repress the prevailing morosity. **1923** E. BOWEN *Encounters* 13 Aunt Willoughby's baffled, bearded morosity. **1965** C. H. SISSON *Christopher Homm* xxi. 162 Even to Dad Christopher's courtship was of some use, as an exercise for morosity.

‖**moˈroso.** *Obs.* Pl. morosi. [It. *moroso* adj., ad. L. *mōrōsus* MOROSE *a.*[1]] A morose person.

1592 *Greene's Vision* G.'s Wks. (Grosart) XII. 215 Feare not then what those Morosi [*printed* Morosie] wil murmure. *a* **1661** FULLER *Worthies, Denbighsh.* (1662) IV. 33 Such as accuse them [*sc.* organs] for superstitious in Churches must allow them lawful in private places. Otherwise such Moroso's deserve not to be owners of an articulate voice.

morosoph (ˈməʊrəsɒf). [a. F. *morosophe* (Rabelais), ad. Gr. μωρόσοφ-ος foolishly wise, f. μωρό-ς foolish + σοφός wise.] †**a.** In Rabelais: A 'wise fool', jester. (Cf. FOOL-SAGE.) *Obs.* **b.** One who is 'foolishly wise'; a foolish pedant or would-be philosopher.

a **1693** *Urquhart's Rabelais* III. xlvii. 377 Our unique Morosoph,..the Lunatick *Triboulet*. **1751** CAMBRIDGE *Scribl.* I. 367, I mark'd where'er the Morosoph appear'd.. How Young and Old, Virgins and Matrons kiss'd The footsteps of the blest Gymnosophist. **1818** T. MOORE *Fudge Fam. Paris* ii. 41 The praises and the trophies Thou gain'st from Morosophs and Sophis. **1835** *Fraser's Mag.* XI. 369 Those who follow the sect of that illustrious morosoph.

So **moˈrosophist** *rare.*, in the same sense; †**moˈrosophy**, foolish pretence of wisdom.

1594 *Mirr. Policy* (1599) 139 As I haue more largely shewed in my Morosophie in these verses. **1610** *Histriomastix* II. 56 That..I may..leave this Idle contemplation To rugged Stoicall Morosophists. **1617** COLLINS *Def. Bp. Ely* II. Contents 6 The Bishops exposition ..is defended against the Adioynders intricate Morosophies. **1794** MATHIAS *Purs. Lit.* (1798) 336 Some Morosophists of the Society. **1870** K. H. DIGBY *Halcyon Hours* 255 Morosophists who love to boast Are those of course who scorn the most This holy maid.

†**moˈrosous,** *a. Obs. rare*$^{-1}$. [f. late L. *morōsus* MOROSE *a.*[2] + -OUS.] = MOROSE *a.*[2] I.

1616 SHELDON *Miracles Ch. Rome* 201 Who..findeth by daily experience either of often lapses, or else of morosous desires..let such a one marrie.

moross, morost, obs. ff. MOROSE, MORASS.

morou, moroun, obs. ff. MORROW, MORN.

†**ˈmorous,** *a. Obs. rare.* [ad. late L. *morōsus* MOROSE *a.*[2]] = MOROSE *a.*[2]

1447 BOKENHAM *Seyntys* (Roxb.) 257 Lyht..ryht furth procedyth wyth owte crokydnesse And a long lyne wyth owte morous dilacyoun. **1594** SOUTHWELL *Magd. Funeral Teares* 128 Guilty consciences are ever morous.

morow(e, obs. forms of MORROW.

morow(e)nyng(e, -ing(e, obs. ff. MORNING.

morowing gift, var. MORWYNGIFT *Sc. Obs.*

moroxite (mɒˈrɒksaɪt). *Min.* [G. *Moroxit* (1798), f. Gr. μόροξ-ος (also μόροχθος) a kind of pipeclay: see -ITE.] A crystallized form of apatite, found in Norway and Finland.

1814 T. ALLAN *Min. Nomencl.* §94. **1879** RUTLEY *Study Rocks* x. 147 Asparagus-stone and moroxite are names given to yellowish-green and blueish-green varieties of apatite.

†**moroˈxylic,** *a. Chem. Obs.* [f. Gr. μόρο-ν, μῶρο-ν mulberry + ξύλ-ον wood + -IC.] ***moroxylic acid***: a supposed acid obtained from a salt of the white mulberry tree. (Cf. MORIC.) So †**moˈroxylate**, a salt of moroxylic acid.

1807 T. THOMSON *Chem.* (ed. 3) II. 274 A peculiar acid, which he [Klaproth] called moroxylic. **1839** *Penny Cycl.* XV. 410/2 Moroxylic acid..is obtained by decomposing the natural moroxylate of lime by acetate of lead.

†**morph**[1]. *Obs. rare*$^{-1}$. [Anglicized form of med.L. *morphea*: see MORPHEW.] = MORPHEW.

1681 GREW *Musæum* I. §vi. i. 131 A Wilk..being burnt.. and mixed with old Oil..is an admirable Remedy against Baldness and Morph of long standing.

morph[2] (mɔːf). *U.S. colloq.* and *slang* shortening of MORPHINE *sb.* (see also quot. 1912).

1912 *Collier's* 21 Sept. 20/2 White 'dope fiends', known in the vernacular of the police as 'hops', 'cokes', or 'morphs'. **1914** JACKSON & HELLYER *Vocab. Criminal Slang* 60 *M*, or *Morph*,..used by morphine fiends. Sulphate of morphia. **1926** J. BLACK *You can't Win* xii. 160 About a spoonful of water and some of their meager store of 'morph' were put in the tin box. **1956** H. GOLD *Man who was not with It* (1965) viii. 65 No morph, no! I had really kicked that one, and would do my own traveling from now on.

morph[3] (mɔːf). *Linguistics.* [f. MORPH(EME.] **a.** = ALLOMORPH[2]. **b.** A phoneme or series of phonemes forming a variant or a number of variants of a morpheme.

1947 C. F. HOCKETT in *Language* XXIII. 322 Recurrent partials not composed of smaller ones (*-way*) are *alternants* or *morphs*... By definition, a morph has the same phonemic shape in all its occurrences... Morphs are not always composed of continuous uninterrupted stretches of phonemes, but they are always composed of phonemes. Every utterance is composed entirely of morphs. **1948** P. K. BENEDICT in *Jrnl. Amer. Oriental Soc.* LXVIII. 185 This nomenclature has obvious advantages from a systematic point of view, and might well be extended to morphology, with the 'morph' as the descriptive unit, and the 'allomorph' as the member of a morpheme. **1952** C. E. BAZELL in E. P. Hamp et al. *Readings in Linguistics II* (1966) 274 The term

morpheme..was used both for the narrower modern concept and for that of the morpheme-alternant or (in American usage) the morph. **1955** *Trans. Philol. Soc. 1954* 69 *Morphemes.* Analytic classification here would obviously refer to morpheme-alternants ('morphs')... Synthetic classification of morphs is implied in the very procedure of defining their morphemic values. For it is on account of their membership in different substitution-classes (selections), that morphs are assigned their different morphemic values, or, as we say, considered to 'represent different morphemes'. **1960** *Amer. Speech* XXXV. 218 He [*sc.* Hoenigswald] believes sound change to be due to nothing but complete borrowing of morphs between only sub-phonemically differing dialects. **1962** H. M. HOENIGSWALD in Householder & Saporta *Problems in Lexicography* 105 There can be no objection to an arrangement by morphs, that is by the phonemic shape of the allomorph or allomorphs making up the morpheme. **1964** E. BACH *Introd. Transformational Gram.* vii. 147 Phonemes have been considered by some to be classes of sounds, morphemes as classes of morphs, and so on. **1965** *Language* XLI. 420 The markers of case are almost always portmanteau morphs that are also involved in expressing other categories..of the noun phrase. **1968** J. LYONS *Introd. Theoretical Linguistics* v. 184 The word *bigger* is analysable into two morphs... Each morph *represents* (or is the exponent of) a particular morpheme... Morphemes may be represented directly by phonological (or orthographical) segments with a particular 'shape' (that is, by morphs). **1972** *Hiberno-English Dialect Questionnaire* 1 Some of the principal morphs found in polysyllables are..included in the questionnaire.

c. *attrib.* and *Comb.*

1947 *Language* XXIII. 337 Intonational morphs..are found spread through such morphs or morph-sequences as *yes, I know, no, maybe,* [etc.]. **1953** C. E. BAZELL *Linguistic Form* ii. 22 The term [*sc.* morphophonemics] has also more recently been used for the study of morph-structure proper. *Ibid.* iv. 47 In many systems no morph-boundaries are found within syllables. **1962** H. M. HOENIGSWALD in Householder & Saporta *Problems in Lexicography* 107 Is it reasonable..to consider the sentence intonations of English on a par with the segmental morph-morphemes? **1964** E. BACH *Introd. Transformational Gram.* vi. 130 The P rules will operate to select the proper morph shapes and allophones. **1965** *Amer. Speech* XL. 297 Orrm's use of double consonants, which is found only in morph-final position or in morph-final clusters, indicates plus juncture rather than shortness of the preceding vowel. **1972** *Archivum Linguisticum* III. 49 There is a regular phonological rule in Nzema and Ahanta which voices certain morph-initial obstruents if they are preceded by a vowel or nasal consonant.

morph[4] (mɔːf). [f. Gr. μορφή form.] A variant form of an animal produced by genetic differences, or (in later use) one of several forms exhibited by an animal in the course of its life cycle. Hence **'morphic** *a.*; **'morphism** = POLYMORPHISM 2.

1955 J. S. HUXLEY in *Heredity* IX. 2, I propose to introduce the term morphism and its derivatives, morphic and morph. *Ibid.* 3, I restrict the term morphism to genetic polymorphism..in which (usually sharply distinct) genetic variants or morphs coexist in temporary or permanent balance within a single interbreeding population in a single spatial region, and in such frequencies that the rarer cannot be due solely to mutation, or to the spread of selectively neutral mutants. *Ibid.* 8 The cuckoo shows a general tendency to morphism..for it shows a plumage dimorphism, barred red and unbarred grey. Among adults, the red morph is confined to a minority, all females. **1955** —— in *Proc. R. Soc.* B. CXLIV. 215 A morphic balance-mechanism must be strong enough to prevent the break-up of the morphism through the disappearance of any morph under adverse selection in periods exceptionally unfavourable to it. **1963** E. MAYR *Animal Species & Evolution* vii. 157 Natural selection may modify the dominance of such morphs. **1968** R. D. MARTIN tr. *Wickler's Mimicry in Plants & Animals* i. 14 A leaf-beetle occurring as two separate morphs is shown. *Ibid.* vi. 61 Both sexes [of *Ityraea nigrocincta*] have two morphs, a green form and a yellow form. **1970** *Nature* 26 Sept. 1368/1 In the autumn the parthenogenetic viviparous morphs of the aphid give birth to nymphs which develop into males and oviparous females. **1974** *Ibid.* 22 Feb. 572/2 The frequencies of colour and banding morphs of the dead animals were compared with those prevailing in the population. **1975** *Jrnl. Zool.* CLXXVII. 336 From considerations of morphism, modality and sex-limitation, a descriptive classification of nine categories is advanced to encompass all situations involving pattern polymorphism and sexual dimorphism in butterflies.

-morph (mɔːf), terminal element (repr. Gr. μορφή form) of sbs. with the sense 'thing having a (certain) form or character', as ISOMORPH, POLYMORPH, ALLELOMORPH, ENDOMORPH.

morphallaxis (mɔːfə'læksɪs). *Zool.* [f. Gr. μορφ-ή form + ἄλλαξις exchange.] Regeneration by the transformation of existing bodily material.

1901 T. H. MORGAN *Regeneration* i. 23 At present there are known two general ways in which regeneration may take place... In order to distinguish broadly these two modes I propose to call those cases of regeneration in which a proliferation of material precedes the development of the new part, 'epimorphosis'. The other mode, in which a part is transformed directly into a new organism, or part of an organism without proliferation at the cut-surfaces, 'morphallaxis'. **1924** G. R. DE BEER *Growth* viii. 53 In regeneration in some cases (where morphallaxis occurs), it [*sc.* material needed for growth] is derived from the other tissues of the organism which thereby undergo reduction. **1956** C. H. WADDINGTON *Princ. Embryol.* xiv. 304 Animals such as coelenterates, flatworms and oligochaetes in which morphallaxis occurs to a considerable extent. **1965** KIORTSIS & MORAITOU in Kiortsis & Trampusch *Regeneration in Animals* 259 If the anteriorly facing cut end of the nerve cord [in the polychaete worm *Spirographis spallanzanii*] is deflected, there is a morphallaxis on one or both sides.

morphe, -phea, var. ff. MORPHEW, -PHŒA.

Morphean (mɔː'fiːən, 'mɔːfiən), *a.* [f. MORPHEUS + -AN.] Of or pertaining to MORPHEUS; hence, sleepy, drowsy.

1694 MOTTEUX *Rabelais* (1737) V. 234 Morphean Visions. **1773** J. ROSS *Fratricide* VI. 557 (MS.) Wak'd by the magic of Morphean spell. **1803** *Edwin* II. xii. 186 He yielded to the Morphean wand, and..Sleep shed its balmy dews over his weary lids. **1809** J. JEBB *Corr.* (1834) I. 523 To work my mind immediately went, even in its morphean state. **1818** KEATS *Endym.* I. 747. **1820** —— *Eve S. Agnes* xxix, O for some drowsy Morphean amulet!

morpheme ('mɔːfiːm). *Linguistics.* [F. *morphème*, f. Gr. μορφή form, after *phonème* PHONEME.] **a.** An element such as an affix, preposition, conjunction, or stress pattern considered in respect of its functional relations in a linguistic system (now little used by linguists). **b.** The smallest meaningful morphological unit of language, one that cannot be analysed into smaller forms.

1896 R. J. LLOYD in *Neueren Sprachen* III. 615 The phonetic elements of a given word are its *phonemes.* But its significant elements, be they root, suffix, prefix, inflection or aught else, are *morphemes.* **1925** P. RADIN tr. *Vendryès's Lang.* II. i. 74 By *semantemes* we understand the linguistic elements which express the ideas of the concepts..and by *morphemes* we understand those elements which express the connexions between the ideas... The morpheme is generally a phonetic element..indicating the grammatical relations between the ideas in the sentence. **1926** L. BLOOMFIELD in *Language* II. 155 A morpheme is a recurrent (meaningful) form which cannot in turn be analyzed into smaller recurrent (meaningful) forms. Hence any unanalyzable word or formative is a morpheme. **1931** *Amer. Jrnl. Philol.* LII. 78 The morpheme of the dependent element indicates merely an unspecialised dependence (gender, number, person, case). *Ibid.* 79 Nouns are semantemes susceptible of morphemes of case. **1933** L. BLOOMFIELD *Language* x. 161 A linguistic form which bears no partial phonetic-semantic resemblance to any other form, is a *simple* form or *morpheme.* Thus, *bird, play, dance, cran-, -y, -ing* are morphemes. Morphemes may show partial phonetic resemblances. **1935** G. K. ZIPF *Psycho-Biol. of Lang.* (1936) i. 15 One may view the same word [sc. *untruthfulness*] as a sequence of five units which we shall term morphemes..i.e. *un-tru-th-ful-ness.* **1948** *Word* Apr. 20 If it is a bound form, the element must—in order to be a morpheme—be active. **1953** C. E. BAZELL *Linguistic Form* i. 5 As used in Europe, it [*sc.* morpheme] answers very approximately to one of two other American terms: (i) the morphemic component, including the morpheme with only one component, or (ii) the morphemic segment or 'morph'. .. (The earlier distinction of morpheme and semanteme is obsolete except in non-structuralist circles.) **1959** *Archivum Linguisticum* XI. 93 In the *Prolegomena*, morphemes ('inflectional elements', not, however, to be identified with morphemes in either the Prague or American [Bloomfieldian] sense) are regarded as constituting part of the content form of language. **1962** E. F. HADEN et al. *Resonance-Theory for Linguistics* iii. 40 The word is here defined..as a free form comprising one or more morphemes, occurring in a given position relative to other words. **1967** *General Linguistics* VII. 65 Maslov discusses the shifts in meaning and utilization which the term 'morpheme' has undergone since its coinage by Baudouin de Courtenay in the 1880's. **1973** *Sci. Amer.* Feb. 57/2 Every language has a stock of several thousand morphemes: the bearers of the basic semantic and grammatical content. An expression such as 'can openers' comprises four morphemes: 'can', 'open', '-er' and '-s'.

c. *attrib.* and *Comb.*, as ***morpheme-class, -combination, -configuration, -count, -sequence, -structure, -theory, -unit, -word; morpheme-based, -initial, -like, -medial*** adjs.; **morpheme alternant** = ALLOMORPH[2].

1942 *Language* XVIII. 171 We divide each expression in the given language into the smallest sequences of phonemes which have what we consider the same meaning when they occur in other expressions... The resultant minimum parts we call not morphemes, but *morpheme alternants.* **1947** *Ibid.* XXIII. 402 Different phonemic shapes of a given base appearing before different suffixes..are morpheme alternants of the same morpheme. **1952, 1955** [see MORPH[3]]. **1963** J. LYONS *Structural Semantics* ii. 11 A word-based grammar seems to be more satisfactory than a morpheme-based grammar for the description of languages of the 'inflecting' type. **1947** *Language* XXIII. 81 Morphemes are assigned to *morpheme-classes* on the basis of the environments in which they occur. Each environment determines one and only one morpheme-class. **1963** ERVIN & MILLER in J. A. Fishman *Readings Sociol. of Lang.* (1968) 76 Morpheme classes can be divided into two groups, lexical and function classes. **1953** C. E. BAZELL *Linguistic Form* vii. 81 But here it is not simply a matter of sorting out incommutable morphemes, but also a case of including commutable morpheme-combinations. **1935** G. K. ZIPF *Psycho-Biol. of Lang.* (1936) iv. 136 If a morpheme-count reveals..that accent tends to settle on morphemes of the greatest average interval..we shall have reached the very heart of the dynamics of accent. *Ibid.* 154 The crystallization of phonemes in a morpheme-configuration. **1964** *Language* XL. 35 Morpheme-initial *s* is replaced by *x* if it is preceded by a vowel or a velar and is followed by a vowel. **1962** H. M. HOENIGSWALD in Householder & Saporta *Problems in Lexicography* 107 There are, in the view of many linguists, morphemes and morpheme-like entities with so-called grammatical meanings. **1965** *Canad. Jrnl. Linguistics* Fall 36 If paralanguage is a dual system, with phoneme and morpheme-like units,..it would be difficult to imagine the primes of a more rudimentary system exceeding in number the primes of a more complex one, language. **1951** Z. S. HARRIS *Methods in Structural Linguistics* x. 129 English has morpheme-medial clusters like /rtr/ (*partridge*) but never like /trt/. **1953** *Language* XXIX. 86 The morphophonemics of a language is then a set of rules for transducing morpheme-sequences to phoneme-sequences. **1955** *Publ. Amer. Dial. Soc.* XXIV. 20 All argots spoken in America are obviously patterned on English, though their specialized morpheme structure usually renders them partially or totally unintelligible to those who speak only the language of the dominant culture. **1972** *Language* XLVIII. 372 The asymmetrical vowel-harmony rule [in Turkish] is accompanied by an accidental gap in the inventory of suffixes, and a systematic morpheme-structure constraint on polysyllabic roots. **1971** D. CRYSTAL *Linguistics* iv. 197 Proponents of the morpheme theory have been..convinced of its validity..as a general explanation for grammatical phenomena. **1942** *Language* XVIII. 171 *Am*, which occurs only in phrases with *I*, and *are*, which never occurs with *I*, are put into one morpheme unit... A morpheme unit is..a group of one or more alternants which have the same meaning and complementary distribution. **1933** L. BLOOMFIELD *Language* xiii. 209 *Morpheme-words*, consisting of a single (free) morpheme: *man, boy, cut, run, red, big.*

Hence **mor'phemic** *a.*, **mor'phemically** *adv.*; also (*rare*) **morphe'matic** *a.*, **morphe'matically** *adv.*, **mor,phemici'zation.**

1930 J. R. FIRTH *Speech* vi. 56 Dutchmen, Danes, Swedes, and Englishmen share many similar morphemic and phonæsthetic habits. **1933** *English Studies* XV. 87 The alternating pairs..of phonemes..evidently form special units which, being conditioned by morphematic circumstances, are called *morphonemes.* **1935** G. K. ZIPF *Psycho-Biol. of Lang.* (1936) i. 15 One may..devise a morphemic alphabet to label all the different morphemes (e.g. prefixes, roots, suffixes, and endings) of a language. **1947** *Language* XXIII. 322 We must have..a set of principles on the basis of which we identify, or refuse to identify, different stretches of speech as morphemically the same. **1953** C. E. BAZELL *Linguistic Form* vii. 83 Only semantic prejudices could lead one to suppose that there was a close content-relation with the morphemically distinct *behind.* **1957** S. POTTER *Modern Linguistics* i. 26 Plural forms of [some] substantives..which happen to end in a dental (nuts, lords..). Here the inflexion -s or -z is felt by the speaker to be morphemic. **1959** R. QUIRK in Quirk & Smith *Teaching of English* i. 34 Many of the curious and amusing forms in *Finnegans Wake*..require us to make morphemic associations in unfamiliar environments. **1964** D. WARD in D. Abercrombie et al. *Daniel Jones* 390 Such a system of orthography..would strip the graphic representation of morphemes..of morphematically conditioned modifications. **1964** E. A. NIDA *Toward Sci. Transl.* v. 102 Similarly, we must be able to analyse the relationships between expressions which are grammatically and morphemically (or lexically) different, but semantically equivalent. **1966** *Amer. Speech* XLI. 116 The phonemicization of *latter:ladder* for those dialects that *clearly* have a voiced intervocalic stop would not be impossible... It would not be so much a problem..as it would be in morphemicization. **1971** *Archivum Linguisticum* II. 49 The 'ambiguity' of morphemic *-s* equally characterizes *-ing*, to name only one further flection. *Ibid.* 59 A morphemically variable noun form.

morphemics (mɔː'fiːmɪks), *sb. pl. Linguistics.* [f. MORPHEM(E: see -IC 2.] The study and description of language in terms of morphemes.

1947 *Language* XXIII. 321 Morphemics and tactics are both necessarily involved in grammar. **1951** TRAGER & SMITH *Outl. Eng. Structure* II. 53 The analysis we are now going to do, the *morphemics* of the language, deals with the recurring patterned partials in utterances. **1960** T. B. W. REID *Historical Philol. & Ling. Sci.* 9 Others maintain that ..phonemics and morphemics alone constitute linguistics, whereas phonetics and semantics are independent disciplines which do not interest them. **1961** D. L. BOLINGER *Generality, Gradience & All-or-None* iii. 35 There is obligatory lengthening in too many places for us to insist that English morphemics be studied in total disregard of it. **1964** M. CRITCHLEY *Developmental Dyslexia* iv. 14 The characters have to cope not only with the phonetic properties of the sound, but also with the problem of meaning. In other words, both phonemics and morphemics must be satisfied. **1966** *Amer. Speech* XLI. 116 If the first and last words in *Betty is in her beddy* are phonetically identical, then for the morphemics, one would have to..set up an allomorph {bɛt} for the morpheme {bɛd}.

So **mor'phemicist**, one who studies morphemics.

1949 KIRBY & WOOLF *Philologica: Malone Anniv. Stud.* 312 In analyzing Joyce's work, the morphemicist would be obliged to construct diagrams in layers, piled one on top of the other.

mor'phetic, *a.* [irregularly f. MORPHEUS + -IC[2].] Pertaining to sleep.

1788 MME. D'ARBLAY *Diary* 26 July, The moment I cease all employment, my thoughts take such an ascendence over my morphetic faculty, that [etc.]. **1796** —— *Camilla* II. iv, I am invulnerably asleep at this very moment! In the very centre of the morphetic dominions.

'morphetine. *Chem.* [a. F. *morphétine*, formed as prec.: see -INE.] A slightly bitter substance obtained from morphine.

1865 in WATTS *Dict. Chem.* III. 1050.

‖**Morpheus** ('mɔːfjuːs). [L.; Ovid's name for the god of dreams, the son of Sleep, as if a. Gr. *Μορφεύς, f. μορφή form.] The god of dreams (popularly often taken as the god of sleep).

c **1369** CHAUCER *Dethe Blaunche* 167 Morpheus, and Eclympasteyre, That was the god of slepes heyre. *c* **1420** LYDG. *Assembly of Gods* 14 Anone came in Morpheus & toke me by the sleue. **1590** SPENSER *F.Q.* I. i. 36, 40. **1605** CHAPMAN *All Fools* III. Plays 1873 I. 146 Or from the Iuory gate Hath Morpheus sent a vision to delude me? **1748** THOMSON *Cast. Indol.* I. xliv, And hither Morpheus sent his kindest dreams. **1857** KINGSLEY *Two Y. Ago* xxiv, Sunk

though he be upon a garret floor, With fumes of Morpheus' crown about his head.

† **morphew** ('mɔːfjuː). *Obs.* Forms: 4-6 **morphe**, 5 **morphu**, **-fu**, **-fw**, **morffue**, 5-6 **morfew**, 5-7 **morphue**, 6 **morfewe**, 6-7 **morphewe**, 5-9 **morphew**. [ad. med.L. *morphea* (written in mod.L. *Morphœa*), a. It. *morfea*, of obscure origin. Cf. F. *morphée* (16th c.).] A leprous or scurfy eruption. ***black, white morphew.***

a **1400** *Stockh. Med. MS.* ii. 962 in *Anglia* XVIII, It distroith þe morphe And disposing to þe lepre. ? *c* **1400** *Lanfranc's Cirurg.* (Brit. Mus. Add. MS.) 4 Cap. iiij of Morfu, ffrakles, .. & Cicatrices of woundes. *Ibid.* 193 Morphue. *Ibid.* 195 Þe white morphu is curid wiþ purgacioun þat purgiþ roten fleume. *Ibid.*, Þe blac morphe is curid wiþ ofte purging of malancoli. *c* **1440** *Promp. Parv.* 343/1 Morfu, sekenesse, *morphea*. **1545** RAYNOLD *Byrth Mankynde* IV. vi. (1634) 201 This is also very good for the Morphew, and other discoloration or staining of the skin. **1562** TURNER *Baths* 1 The bathes of brimstone .. are good for the whyte morphewe and black. **1586** BRIGHT *Melanch.* xxi. 124 Then altereth the colour, and fairenesse is turned into morphe. **1688** HOLME *Armoury* II. 428/1 Morphew is a disease that dyeth the skin yellow. **1748-9** *Gen. Advertiser* No. 4440 Tetters, Ring-worms, Morphew, Sun-burn. **1794-6** E. DARWIN *Zoon.* (1801) III. 124 Morphew or freckles—Tawny blotches on the skin of the face and arms of elderly people. **1810** *Splendid Follies* II. 106 A few morphews and wrinkles incident to her age. **1835** BROWNING *Paracelsus* IV. 117 My outward crust Of lies, which wrap as tetter, morphew, furfair, Wrap the sound flesh.

fig. **1610** BP. HALL *Apol. Brownists* 29 He cannot but acknowledge .. a true face of a Church (though ouer-spreade with some morphue of corruptions). **1647** WARD *Simp. Cobler* 21 No man ever saw a gray haire on the head .. of any Truth, wrinckle, or morphew on its face.

attrib. **1541** R. COPLAND *Guydon's Quest. Chirurg.* Q iv b, The seconde is a morfewe colour & derke. **1640** H. MILL *Nts. Search* 147 The morphew wals are growne so bleake and thin, They have .. lost the outward skin.

Hence '**morphewed** *ppl. a.*, afflicted with morphew; also *fig.*

1598 BP. HALL *Sat.* IV. v. 26 Whose .. sullen rags bewray his Morphew'd skin. **1610** R. TOFTE *Honours Acad.* IV. 150 Thogh the Sunne sheweth himselfe pale, morphewed and ghastly, yet was he by all creatures .. desired. **1646** G. DANIEL *Poems* Wks. 1878 I. 7 Sometime put A gracefull mole, for a dull morphew'd Spot. **1694** WESTMACOTT *Script. Herb.* 65 Mark that, you women, and morphew'd ladies.

morphia ('mɔːfɪə). *Chem.* [mod.L., f. MORPHEUS: see -IA[1]. Cf. MORPHIUM.]

a. = MORPHINE.

1818 A. T. THOMSON *Lond. Disp.* (ed. 2) 286 Robiquet .. has confirm'd his [Sertuerner's] statement regarding the existence of morphia. **1874** GARROD & BAXTER *Mat. Med.* (1880) 193 Apomorphia... Obtained by heating morphia .. with excess of hydrochloric acid. **1876** HARLEY *Mat. Med.* 753 Morphia is the chief and essential constituent of opium.

b. *attrib.*, as in ***morphia habit, lozenge, salt,*** etc.; **morphia syringe**, a syringe for the hypodermic injection of morphia.

1874 GARROD & BAXTER *Mat. Med.* (1880) 198 Morphia Lozenges. *Ibid.* 204 The opium and morphia salts become absorbed. **1881** *Trans. Obstet. Soc. Lond.* XXII. 132 Dr. Godson tapped it with a morphia syringe. **1891** *Daily News* 23 Mar. 5/1 The morphia habit of the deceased.

Hence '**morphiated** *a.*, impregnated or affected with morphia (*Syd. Soc. Lex.* 1891).

morphic ('mɔːfɪk), *a. Biol.* [f. Gr. μορφή form: see -IC.] Of or pertaining to form; relating to the anatomical shape; morphological.

1868 E. D. COPE *Orig. Fittest* (1887) 111 The majority of specific characters are .. 'morphic' as distinguished from developmental. **1894** BUCKMAN *Inf. Ool. Ammonites* (Palæont. Soc.) 382 Morphic equivalents must always be compared. *Ibid.* 444 Such forms are only morphic equivalents.

morphically ('mɔːfɪkəlɪ), *adv.* [f. MORPHIC *a.* + -AL + -LY[2].] In relation to or as regards shape or form; morphologically.

1893 *Proc. Boston Soc. Nat. Hist.* XXVI. 66 This is morphically a free cell.

'**morphil.** *Obs. rare.* [a. F. *morfil*, †*marfil*, a. Sp. *marfil* (= Pg. *marfim*), of Arabic origin (*fil* elephant; the first element is obscure).]

† **1.** Raw ivory. *Obs.*

1698 T. FROGER *Voy.* 11 Their trade consists in Slaves, Gold, Morphil or Ivory, and Wax.

2. Vegetable ivory (see IVORY 2).

1891 in *Syd. Soc. Lex.*

morphinated ('mɔːfɪneɪtɪd), *ppl. a.* [f. MORPHIN-E + -ATE[2] + -ED[1].] Charged with morphine.

1891 in *Syd. Soc. Lex.* **1898** *Rev. Brit. Pharm.* 53 Morphinated water, for use in opium assaying.

morphine ('mɔːfiːn), *sb. Chem.* Also **-in**. [a. G. *morphin* (Sertürner 1816), f. MORPH-EUS: see -INE.] The most important alkaloid narcotic principle of opium, largely used in medicine to alleviate pain.

1828 *Lancet* 2 Feb. 663/1 Morphine .. is the narcotic principle of opium. **1850** MRS. CARLYLE *Lett.* II. 115 Took morphine last night, and slept some. **1856** MAYNE *Expos. Lex.*, *Morphin.* **1899** *Allbutt's Syst. Med.* VI. 734 Morphine is only a palliative.

b. *attrib.*, as ***morphine habit, salt, taker***; **morphine injection**, a hypodermic injection of morphine; **morphine injector**, a medical man addicted to the practice of morphine injection; **morphine syringe** = *morphia syringe.*

1892 GUNTER *Miss Dividends* (1893) 45 Effects more demoralizing than the *morphine habit. **1878** tr. *von Ziemssen's Cycl. Med.* XVII. 857 *Morphine injection also exercises an influence on those addicted to it. *Ibid.* 117 A considerable number of *morphine-injectors have sprung up—chiefly young doctors—who carry on this pernicious practice. *c* **1865** in *Circ. Sci.* I. 417/1 *Morphine salts are .. chiefly employed. **1897** *Allbutt's Syst. Med.* II. 885 The *morphine syringe was invented during my student days. **1899** *Ibid.* VIII. 317 Sulphate of sparteín is used by some *morphine takers.

Hence '**morphine** *v. trans.*, to drug with morphine. **mor'phinic** *a.*, relating to morphine (*Syd. Soc. Lex.* 1891). '**morphinism**, the effect of morphine on the human system; the practice of injecting morphine into the system. '**morphinist**, one who takes morphine to excess; also *attrib.* **morphini'zation**, the producing of the physiological action of morphine in the system by internal administration or hypodermic use (*Syd. Soc. Lex.*). '**morphinize** *v. trans.*, to treat with morphine.

1856 NEALE *Mediæval Preachers* Introd. 15 Their somnolence morphinized into death. **1874** LONGF. in S. Longfellow *Life* (1891) III. 236 When you were morphined out of your wits, anything might pass. **1882** Morphinism [see MORPHIOMANIA]. **1894** *Blackw. Mag.* Nov. 583 Dipsomaniacs, morphinists and epileptics. **1897** *Allbutt's Syst. Med.* II. 882 The children of three morphinist mothers were fairly healthy. **1899** *Ibid.* VIII. 423 The worst case of morphinism I have seen.

morphinomania (ˌmɔːfɪnəʊ'meɪnɪə). *Nosology.* [f. MORPHINE: see -MANIA.] Uncontrollable craving for morphine or opium. Hence **morphino'maniac**, one affected with morphinomania.

1887 *Brit. Med. Jrnl.* 5 Feb. 300 On the Effects of the Sudden Discontinuance of Morphine in Morphinomaniacs suffering from Pneumonia. *Ibid.* 21 May 1003/1 The diagnosis of morphinomania. **1898** *Scotsman* 30 July 11/8 Transformed the dipsomaniac and morphinomaniac into self-controlled and useful members of society.

morphiomania (ˌmɔːfɪəʊ'meɪnɪə). *Nosology.* [f. MORPHI-A + -MANIA.] = MORPHINOMANIA.

1882 *Nature* XXVI. 470 Dr. Landowsky .. deprecated .. this new method of intoxication; he calls it morphiomania or morphinism. **1897** *Allbutt's Syst. Med.* II. 893 Except on withdrawal of the drug I have not seen the excitement or violence to which the name morphiomania would be properly applied.

Hence **morphio'maniac** = MORPHINOMANIAC.

1888 *Pall Mall G.* 8 Sept. 6/1 A Novel for Morphiomaniacs. **1899** *Allbutt's Syst. Med.* VIII. 274 The so-called dipsomaniac or morphiomaniac.

morphism: see MORPH[4].

-morphism ('mɔːfɪz(ə)m), terminal element [f. Gr. μορφή form + -ISM] of sbs. with the sense 'condition or property of having a (certain) form or character', and in *Math.* 'a transformation or correspondence of a (certain) kind': e.g. HETEROMORPHISM, ISOMORPHISM.

†'**morphium.** *Obs.* [mod.L., f. MORPHEUS + -IUM.] Older name for morphia.

1823 J. BADCOCK *Dom. Amusem.* 90 Although .. resembling opium .., it counteracts the evil effects of that dangerous morphium. **1824** *Q. Jrnl. Sci.*, etc. XVII. 170 The tincture of nutgalls a very sensible test of the presence of morphium in fluids. **1856** MAYNE *Expos. Lex.* s.v. *Morphium*, Name given by Sertuerner to morphin.

morpho ('mɔːfəʊ). [mod.L. (J. C. Fabricius 1807, in *Magazin für Insectenkunde* VI. 280), f. Gr. Μορφώ, an epithet of Aphrodite.] A large South American butterfly of the genus so called, often with shiny blue wings. Also *attrib.*

1853 A. R. WALLACE *Travels on Amazon* 14 Among them [*sc.* the butterflies] were .. three Morphos, those splendid large metallic-blue butterflies which are always first noticed by travellers in South America. **1863** H. W. BATES *Naturalist on River Amazons* I. 103 The splendid metallic blue Morphos .. are generally confined to the shady alleys of the forest. **1925** *Glasgow Herald* 1 Aug. 4/2 In the parapet of a fine staircase in one of the Oxford colleges there is a piece of Labradorite with a bewitching blue colour that recalls the tail of a peacock and the wing of a Morpho butterfly. **1926** *Ibid.* 12 June 4 A morpho may have a million and a half scales on its four great wings. **1969** E. BISHOP *Compl. Poems* 210 Oil .. like bits of mirror—no, more blue than that: Like tatters of the *Morpho* butterfly. **1973** *Sci. Amer.* Dec. 67/2 Only here [*sc.* in the tropical rain forest] are found such insects as the brilliant blue morpho butterfly of tropical America.

morphodite ('mɔːfəʊdaɪt). Also **morphodyke, morphodyte.** Colloq. shortening and mispronunciation of HERMAPHRODITE *sb.*

1896 *Dialect Notes* I. 421 *Morphodite*, .. for *hermaphrodite.* **1951** T. CAPOTE *Grass Harp* (1952) i. 3 One of the stories he spread, that Verena was a morphodyte, has never stopped going around. **1956** H. GOLD *Man who was not with It* (1965) xix. 174 He or she waddled by. But I suppose morphodykes are likely to take it personally when people get married.

‖**morphœa** (mɔː'fiːə). *Med.* [mod.L.: see MORPHEW.] A sclerodermatous disease.

1874 T. R. JONES & SIEV. *Phys. Anat.* 94 The skin disease called Morphœa. **1899** *Allbutt's Syst. Med.* VIII. 680 Morphœa generally appears as yellowish white, waxy or ivory like spots, surrounded by a rosy or purplish areola.

morphogen ('mɔːfəʊdʒən). *Biol.* [f. Gr. μορφ-ή form + -O + -GEN.] Any agent which is or might be capable of bringing about or determining morphogenesis.

1952 A. M. TURING in *Phil. Trans. R. Soc.* B. CCXXXVII. 38 The systems actually to be considered consist therefore of masses of tissues which are not growing, but within which certain substances are reacting chemically, and through which they are diffusing. These substances will be called morphogens, the word being intended to convey the idea of a form producer. It is not intended to have any very exact meaning. **1965** *Math. in Biol. & Med.* (Med. Res. Council) VI. 247 Turing considers the behaviour of two chemical substances, A and B, which he calls 'morphogens'. The significance of the name is simply that it is supposed that a high concentration of one or other of these substances can act as an 'inducer' of further differentiation. **1972** *Nature* 13 Oct. 366/1 Many theories for the mechanism of signalling in embryos have been produced; the oldest, and simplest, is that there is a concentration gradient of a 'morphogen' from the animal to vegetal poles, and that cells can measure their ambient concentration and then behave according to their position in the gradient.

‖**morpho'genesis.** [mod.L., f. Gr. μορφ-ή form + γένεσις origin: see GENESIS.]

a. The origination of morphological characters; morphogeny.

1890 *Century Dict.*, *Morphogenesis.* **1899** *Jrnl. R. Microsc. Soc.* 469 Factors in morphogenesis. **1936** P. D. F. MURRAY *Bones* i. 16 These experiments evidently exclude all functional factors as important agents in primary skeletal morphogenesis. **1951** *Nature* 18 Aug. 301/2 Isolated terminal growing points .. afford excellent material for the investigation of the relation between nutrition and morphogenesis. **1974** *Sci. Amer.* Dec. 44/3 They [*sc.* hydras] have a strong capacity for regenerating lost parts, so that one can study morphogenesis not only in developing animals but also in regenerating ones.

b. *Geomorphol.* The formation of landscapes or land forms.

1958 *Geol. Mag.* XCV. 126 Tricart and Cailleux .. claim that a 'sufficiently dense cover of vegetation' interferes very significantly with morphogenesis. **1966** J. A. MABBUTT in G. H. Dury *Essays in Geomorphol.* 102 The hillfoot zone is .. very sensitive to climatically-induced changes of morphogenesis. **1968** R. W. FAIRBRIDGE *Encycl. Geomorphol.* 130/1 An allied form of morphogenesis rather similarly planes, aggrades and deranges drainage in areas of continental glaciation.

So **morphoge'netic** *a.*, of or pertaining to morphogenesis; **morphoge'netically** *adv.*, as regards morphogenesis.

1884 *Q. Jrnl. Microsc. Sci.* XXX. 98 A direct morphogenetic change in the ganglion cells. **1897** *Westm. Gaz.* 20 July 9/2 The force of gravitation is .. the first morphogenetic factor in the individual development of animals. **1905** *Jrnl. Exper. Zool.* II. 155 It seemed to me scarcely possible that all of these strikingly different kinds of oöplasm, each with its own peculiar developmental history and destiny, were nevertheless morphogenetically alike. **1932** J. S. HUXLEY *Probl. Relative Growth* iv. 117 Each such region would be characterized both by the possession of its own growth-gradient and its own morphogenetic field. **1950** *Ann. Assoc. Amer. Geographers* XL. 214 Recently Büdel (1944, 1948) has suggested the recognition of 'formkreisen' or 'morphogenetic regions'. *Ibid.* 232 Within an area in which the climate is essentially homogeneous, the geomorphic effects of climate may be assumed to be similar. These areas are here called morphogenetic regions. **1954** W. D. THORNBURY *Princ. Geomorphol.* iii. 63 The concept of a morphogenetic region is that under a certain set of climatic conditions particular geomorphic processes will predominate and hence will give to the landscape of the region characteristics that will set it off from those of other areas developed under different climatic conditions. **1957** [see FIELD *sb.* 17 c]. **1965** *Science* 29 Oct. 627/3 (*caption*) Possible relation of collagen distribution to morphogenetically active and inactive areas. **1966** SAUNDERS & FALLON in M. Locke *Major Probl. Developmental Biol.* 289 Death of cells is a normal component of most morphogenetic movements such as foldings, detachments, and the confluence of anlagen. **1969** *Oikos* Suppl. XII. 68 (*heading*) Morphogenetic aspects of the agrarian landscape of Öland.

morphogenic (mɔːfəʊ'dʒɛnɪk), *a.* [f. MORPHOGEN(ESIS + -IC.] = MORPHOGENETIC.

1890 in *Cent. Dict.* **1904** *Science* 2 Dec. 749/2 The specific morphogenic factors are connected in some way with specific forms of protoplasm. **1958** C. P. RAVEN *Morphogenesis: Analysis of Molluscan Development* v. 186 The notion of morphogenic substances should not be taken too strictly, as if there were a rectilinear relation between a single substance and the differentiation of a certain organ. **1972** G. D. WINTER in Maibach & Rovee *Epidermal Wound Healing* iv. 104 It is thought that in the normal epidermis the morphogenic force is the pressure of mitosis.

morphogeny (mɔː'fɒdʒɪnɪ). [mod.L., f. Gr. μορφ-ή form + -GENY. Cf. F. *morphogénie.*] = MORPHOGENESIS.

1879 tr. *Haeckel's Evol. Man* I. i. 24 Germ-history of Forms. (Morphogeny.) **1912** *Ann. Assoc. Amer. Geographers* II. 85 Some British observers have recognized levels of erosion or abrasion at several different altitudes, on which they base a more complicated scheme of morphogeny. **1929** *Jrnl. Ecol.* XVII. 374 Of fundamental importance in morphogeny and by no means to be overlooked in adaptation is the correlation of organs and parts, based upon competition within the plant for food.

1950 *Ann. Assoc. Amer. Geographers* XL. 222 Many of the ideas here expressed are explicitly stated in the lectures of Professor Kirk Bryan, whose emphasis on climatic morphogeny has led to the formulation here set forth.

morphographemic (mɔːfəʊgrəˈfiːmɪk), *a.* *Linguistics.* [f. Gr. μορφ-ή form + GRAPHEMIC *a.*] Of or pertaining to the written form of words; spec. ***morphographemic rule***, a rule of writing in transformational grammar (see quot. 1972).

1965 O. THOMAS *Transformational Gram.* iii. 59 If we were interested in how the final sentence was pronounced, rather than in how it is written, we would have a set of *morphophonetic rules* (i.e., rules of pronunciation) rather than *morphographemic rules* (i.e., rules of writing). **1968** J. LYONS *Introd. Theoretical Linguistics* vi. 265 For the written language, 'morphographemic' rules would convert the strings. **1971** F. W. HOUSEHOLDER *Linguistic Speculations* xiii. 255 The immediate output of the lexicon is correct orthography, subject to minor morphographemic adjustments. **1972** R. A. PALMATIER *Gloss. Eng. Transformational Gram.* 98 *Morphographemic rule*,..a rule, of the final section of the grammar, which converts the morphemes of a terminal string into their graphic representations as written words; a spelling rule.

morphographer (mɔːˈfɒgrəfə(r)). [f. Gr. μορφ-ή form + -GRAPHER.]

†**1.** One skilled in the delineation of form. *Obs.*

1697 EVELYN *Numism.* viii. 291 Vandyke..the most incomparable Morphographer and Painter.

2. *Biol.* One who investigates and records facts of morphology.

1888 E. R. LANKESTER in *Encycl. Brit.* XXIV. 817/2 Those of the morphographer and systematist rather than of the bionomist.

morphography (mɔːˈfɒgrəfɪ). [f. Gr. μορφ-ή form + -GRAPHY.] The scientific description of form; descriptive morphology; also, the phenomena which form the object of this.

1856 MAYNE *Expos. Lex., Morphographia*, term for a description or history of external form: morphography. **1888** E. R. LANKESTER in *Encycl. Brit.* XXIV. 803/2 Anatomical study has associated itself with the more superficial morphography. **1898** GÜNTHER in *Nature* 21 Apr. 583/1 Estimating how far the existing superficial configuration or morphography of a volcanic region is an indication of the past history of its development.

Hence **morphoˈgraphic, -graphical** *adjs.*, of or pertaining to morphography.

1856 MAYNE *Expos. Lex.*, *Morphographicus*,.. morphographic. **1888** E. R. LANKESTER in *Encycl. Brit.* XXIV. 818/2 Experimental researches..are not provided for either in the morphographical or physiological laboratories of our universities.

morpholecithal (mɔːfəʊˈlɛsɪθəl). *Biol.* [f. mod.L. *morpholecith-us*, f. Gr. μορφ-ή form + λέκιθος the yolk of an egg + -AL[1].] Pertaining to the yolk of the animal ovum (*Cent. Dict.* 1890).

morpholexical (mɔːfəʊˈlɛksɪkəl), *a.* [f. Gr. μορφ-ή form + LEXICAL *a.*] Of or pertaining to lexical form (cf. also MORPHOPHONEMIC *a.*).

1939 L. BLOOMFIELD in *Travaux du Cercle Ling. de Prague* VIII. 105 It is necessary to distinguish these morphophonemic alterations from certain others, which we may call *morpholexical* variations... These morpholexical variations are quite distinct from internal sandhi. **1940** *Language* XVI. 256 Besides zero and actual element, pairs of forms as -kamy- and -ākamy-, with the meaning identical for both ('water'), are reserved for consideration as morpholexical variations. **1951** Z. S. HARRIS *Structural Linguistics* xiii. 197 It [*sc.* the procedure]..covers regular and irregular phonological alternation, sandhi, morpholexical variation, suppletion, reduplication, and other types of morpheme variants. **1962** CHAVARRIA-AGUILAR & PENZL in Householder & Saporta *Problems in Lexicography* IV. 243 The Pashto Academy..has attempted ..to establish morphological and sometimes morpholexical standards for writers.

morpholine (ˈmɔːfəliːn). *Chem.* [ad. G. *morpholin* (L. Knorr 1889, in *Ber. d. Deut. Chem. Ges.* XXII. 2083), f. *morphin* MORPHINE *sb.* with insertion of *-ol* -OL.] A cyclic amine,

$$\underbrace{CH_2CH_2NHCH_2CH_2O}$$

which is a hygroscopic oil used as a solvent for resins and dyestuffs and whose fatty-acid salts are emulsifying soaps used in floor polishes.

1889 *Jrnl. Chem. Soc.* LVI. 1218 Morpholine (tetrahydroparoxazine) may be regarded as the 'inner anhydride' of dihydroxyethylamine. **1935** *Industr. & Engin. Chem.* Aug. 871/1 Of the derivatives of morpholine, one of the most extensively investigated in the medical field has been morpholine ethanol. **1955** *Sci. Amer.* Aug. 76/3 Dilute solutions of morpholine neither attracted nor repelled salmon but were detectable by them in extremely low concentrations. **1972** *Materials & Technol.* IV. xv. 516 Diethanolamine has also appreciable value as the source of the cyclic ether, morpholine, an important solvent and intermediate in the manufacture of medicinals.

morphologic (mɔːfəʊˈlɒdʒɪk), *a.* [f. MORPHOLOG-Y + -IC: cf. F. *morphologique.*] = next.

1872 in LATHAM *Dict.* **1877** J. E. CARPENTER tr. *Tiele's Hist. Relig.* 2 It is really history, and not a morphologic arrangement of religions. **1936** *Bull. Amer. Assoc. Petroleum Geologists* XX. 859 The peculiar morphologic phenomenon of deep-sea trenches..is confined to the peri-Pacific-Malayan region. **1936** J. KANTOR *Objective Psychol. of Grammar* xi. 158 This morphologic pattern no doubt is as highly evolved as the English. **1944** *Federation Proc.* III. 231/1 An..account of the morphologic changes in muscle following denervation. **1961** A. JUILLAND *Structural Relations* iii. 52 Morphologic segmentation has been explored especially by American structuralists. **1962** H. E. THALMANN tr. *Goguel's Tectonics* ii. 6 The use of morphologic analysis to distinguish rock types..involves great risks of error. **1967** *Word* XXIII. 380 All morphologic composites are based on the same syntagmatic pattern 'determinatum determined by determinant'. **1975** *Language* LI. 142 This fact speaks for the morphologic antiquity of all Type A infinitives cognate with those of Vedic.

morphological (mɔːfəʊˈlɒdʒɪkəl), *a.* [Formed as prec. + -AL[1].]

1. *Biol.* Of, pertaining to, or derived from morphology; such as is described, investigated, or ascertained by morphology.

1830 LINDLEY *Nat. Syst. Bot.* 84 No order can be more instructively studied with a view to morphological inquiries [than the *Pomaceæ*]. **1876** E. R. LANKESTER *Hist. Creat.* I. ii. 30 All the known morphological phenomena in the animal and vegetable kingdoms. **1896** *Allbutt's Syst. Med.* I. 77 The distinctions drawn were..purely morphological.

2. *Philol.* Pertaining to morphology; based on characteristics of form.

1860 FARRAR *Orig. Lang.* ix. 185 Pott's formula for the morphological classification of language. **1861** MAX MÜLLER *Sci. Lang.* 75 In these languages..we shall have to be satisfied with the criteria of a morphological affinity, instead of those of a genealogical relationship.

3. *gen.* Of or pertaining to the history of form; hence *simply*: as regards form; in or of form.

Cf. the parallel sense-development in MORPHOLOGY (sense 4).

1865 LECKY *Ration.* I. 315 Another branch of scientific progress which I may notice on account of its influence upon speculative opinions is the rapid growth of a morphological conception of the universe. **1885** C. F. KEARY in *Numism. Chron.* V. 165 General Pitt-Rivers, taking up the same kind of morphological study in relation to other objects, has arranged a collection of..human implements, and has communicated..papers upon their morphology. *Ibid.* 168 The morphological aspect of the coin-type. **1895** N. STORY-MASKELYNE *Crystallography* i. 3 By reference to this system of planes, it is possible to establish the morphological relationship of all crystals of the same substance, whatever faces they may exhibit. **1918** *Amer. Jrnl. Med. Sci.* CLV. 70 The cardiac signs and symptoms produced as a result of hypothyroidism are not due to morphological alterations in the heart muscle. **1972** D. HERBERT *Urban Geogr.* iii. 66 A clear indication of past functional patterns can often be obtained from the morphological evidence which is left in the urban landscape. **1974** D. MCKIE *Crystalline Solids* xi. 384 Morphological studies are..applicable only to substances which form well developed crystals.

4. *Min.* ***morphological axis*** (see quots.).

1878 GURNEY *Crystallogr.* 38 The axis of hexagonal symmetry in the Rhombohedral System and the axis of tetragonal symmetry in the Pyramidal System are called morphological axes. **1895** STORY-MASKELYNE *Crystallogr.* 128 Where two or more planes of symmetry lying in a zone are conformable, their zone-axis will be termed a morphological axis or axis of form for the system.

morphologically (mɔːfəʊˈlɒdʒɪkəlɪ), *adv.* [f. prec. + -LY[2].] In a morphological manner; with reference to the facts or principles of morphology (in various senses).

1859 *Todd's Cycl. Anat.* V. 220/2 Saprolegnia, which is morphologically so closely related to Vaucheria,..we obtain [etc.]. **1868** MAX MÜLLER *Sel. Ess.* (1881) I. 83 It had been the custom in classifying languages morphologically to represent some languages..as isolating. **1878** GURNEY *Crystallogr.* 40 Directions which are morphologically symmetrical—that is which make equal angles with similar faces. **1899** tr. *von Jaksch's Clin. Diagn.* vi. (ed. 4) 203 A definite and morphologically distinctive parasite occurs in the discharge of cholera patients.

morphologist (mɔːˈfɒlədʒɪst). [f. MORPHOLOGY + -IST.] One versed in morphology; one who pursues morphological investigations.

1845 WHEWELL *Indic. Creator* 34 The morphologists have declared..that they could not allow themselves to ascribe to the Creator any intention. **1857** GOODSIR in *Edin. New Philos. Jrnl.* V. 119 It is..incumbent on the morphologist to ascertain in what respects they correspond. **1899** *Allbutt's Syst. Med.* VIII. 616 But for the morphologist the eruption still runs from dorsum to venter. **1935** [see CLINOGRAPHIC *a.*]. **1972** D. HERBERT *Urban Geogr.* iii. 66 The necessity to incorporate the physical fabric of towns into more general theories of urban growth has long been advocated by urban morphologists. **1974** *Nature* 13 Sept. 100/2 Although glial cells can be studied by morphologists, physiologists know very little about their function.

morphology (mɔːˈfɒlədʒɪ). [f. Gr. μορφ-ή form + -LOGY.] The science of form.

I. 1. *Biol.* That branch of biology which is concerned with the form of animals and plants, and of the structures, homologies, and metamorphoses which govern or influence that form.

1830 R. KNOX *Cloquet's Anat.* 2 It is to this kind of investigation, which has by some been named Morphology, that anatomy belongs. **1859** J. R. GREENE *Protozoa* Introd. 17 By some the word 'morphology' is employed in a restricted sense, to signify the study of homologous organs. **1880** GRAY *Struct. Bot.* 5 *note*, The term Morphology was introduced into science by Goethe, at least as early as the year 1817.

2. *Philol.* **a.** The branch of grammar which is concerned with the form of words (including word-formation and inflexion).

1869 FARRAR *Fam. Speech* iv. 118 By the morphology of a language we mean the general laws of its grammatical structure. **1871** *Public Sch. Lat. Gram.* 21 Morphology or Wordlore..has three divisions:—I. Flexion. II. Derivation. III. Composition. **1907** *Athenæum* 2 Mar. 256/1 Two volumes—one dealing with phonology, morphology, and inflexions, and the other with syntax.

b. *Appos.*, as ***morphology-syntax***. *Comb.*, as ***morphology-based*** adj.

1965 H. A. GLEASON *Linguistics & Eng. Gram.* vi. 118 'Preposition' is available and not needed in the morphology-based system. **1945–9** *Acta Linguistica* V. 125 A problem in morphology-syntax division. **1964** P. L. GARVIN *On Linguistic Method* 157 Morphemic analysis [is]..primarily syntactic for those languages to which the morphology-syntax division applies.

3. *gen.* The history of variation in form.

1885 C. F. KEARY in *Numism. Chron.* V. 165 By the morphology of coins I mean the history of those changes in their form which have resulted..from influences which.. are always affecting..the evolution of coins.

II. 4. Shape, form, external structure or arrangement, esp. as an object of study or classification.

1890 C. P. MITCHELL *Philos. Tumour-Dis.* ii. 52 Facts so varied as those comprised in the morphology of tumours. **1894** *Jrnl. Physiol.* XVII. 81 (*heading*) The morphology and distribution of the wandering cells of Mammalia. **1895** N. STORY-MASKELYNE (*title*) Crystallography: a treatise on the morphology of crystals. **1921** *Geogr. Rev.* XI. 155 (*heading*) Morphology of the Altai Mountains. **1924** A. E. H. TUTTON *Nat. Hist. Crystals* vii. 60 The 'elements' of a crystal.. together with a list of the 'forms' observed, and a table of the interfacial angles, define the morphology of the crystal. **1937** *Rep. Brit. Assoc. Adv. Sci.* 373 (*heading*) A comparative study of the morphology of the North Downs and the Chiltern Hills. **1950** *Jrnl. Gen. Physiol.* XXXIII. 651 Two separate lines of approach..were required: a study of the functional behavior of the [nerve] fibers, and a study of their morphology. **1954** M. BERESFORD *Lost Villages* 23 In the study of village morphology..an opportunity of seeing a medieval village plan without any of the accretions of later building. **1964** R. C. EVANS *Crystal Chem.* (ed. 2) xi. 184 Before the discovery of X-ray diffraction, crystals could be classified only on the basis of morphology, and in terms of their symmetry were assigned to one or other of the thirty-two classes. **1965** E. GURR *Rational Use of Dyes in Biol.* I. 106 (*heading*) Possible influence of molecular morphology in staining. *Ibid.* 107 We can refer to the shape and/or size of a molecule as its morphology. **1971** W. A. PRYOR in R. E. Carver *Procedures Sedimentary Petrol.* vii. 142 Quantitative analysis of grain morphology requires measurement of particle radii, diameters, and lengths. **1974** *Nature* 29 Nov. 377/2 The morphologies found—spheroids, single or paired, filaments, segmented or nonsegmented, 'colonial' structures..—have all been described from prokaryotic groups such as the blue-green algae.

morphomaniac (mɔːfəʊˈmeɪnɪæk). [Irreg. f. MORPHIA + MANIAC *sb.*] = MORPHINOMANIAC.

1906 G. K. CHESTERTON *Dickens* ii. 41 These great popular leaders..become drunkards; they become demagogues; they become morphomaniacs. **1912** L. J. VANCE *Destroying Angel* xii. 165 He's just short of a raving morphomaniac.

morphometric (mɔːfəʊˈmɛtrɪk), *a.* [f. Gr. μορφ-ή form + -O + -METRIC.] Of or pertaining to morphometry or morphometrics; morphometrical.

1931 T. L. WOO in *Biometrika* XXII. 325 A special advantage of taking measurements on the individual bones of the skull is that we thus get some idea of the size and shape of relatively small regions,..giving us a better appreciation of local asymmetries than the run of anthropometric measurements can. I think it might be useful to distinguish the two types of measurements as ethnometric and morphometric, for both are actually anthropometric. **1934** *Geogr. Jrnl.* LXXXIV. 424 Other questions, such as the morphology of arctic regions, morphometric methods, classification and variation of climate. **1952** *Bull. Geol. Soc. Amer.* LXIII. 1117 Detailed morphometric analysis of basins in five sample areas in the equilibrium stage show distinctive, though small, differences in hypsometric integrals and curve forms. **1968** *Mineral. Abstr.* XIX. 240/1 Cumulative curves for the morphometric parameter of the grains composing a sample of sand are figured. **1970** *Evolution* XXIV. 220/2 Morphometric data from 91 crania and 123 mandibles of 2 and 3 year old male white-tailed deer from Michigan were used in this study. **1972** A. YOUNG *Slopes* i. 3 Morphometric analysis takes the river basin as the fundamental unit; this is a consequence of its origin in hydrological studies, in particular in the attempt to predict flood discharge from the landform characteristics of river catchments. **1974** *Nature* 24 May 371/1 A three-fold enrichment (as judged by morphometric analysis of electron micrographs) of synaptic junctions..was obtained.

Hence **morphoˈmetrically** *adv.*

1937 *Trans. Connecticut Acad. Arts & Sci.* XXXIII. 67 The lake is primarily eutrophic, secondarily or morphometrically oligotrophic. **1957** G. E. HUTCHINSON *Treat. Limnol.* I. ii. 170 The number of lakes of maximum depth of over 400 m. will, however, be greatly increased when the large lakes of southern South America become known morphometrically. **1960** *Jrnl. Animal Ecol.* XXIX. 310 The parents were most probably very similar morphometrically to the fledglings.

morphometrics (mɔːfəʊˈmɛtrɪks), *sb. pl.* [f. as prec.: see -IC 2.] Morphometry (esp. of living forms); also, morphometric features or properties.

1960 *Jrnl. Animal Ecol.* XXIX. 309 The shape of an animal, of which morphometrics are a numerical expression, is dependent upon genetically transmitted characters and the modifying influence of the environment on them. *Ibid.* 310 No completely reliable evidence was obtained for either the morphometrics or the behaviour of the parents of two of

the populations studied. **1971** BLACKITH & REYMENT *Multivariate Morphometrics* ii. 9 An essential problem in morphometrics is to measure the degree of similarity of two forms. **1974** *Nature* 22 Mar. 303/3 The chapters on multivariate morphometrics and optical data analysis are particularly good.

morphometry (mɔːˈfɒmɪtrɪ). [f. Gr. μορφ-ή form + -METRY.] The art or process of measuring the external form of objects, esp. in *Geomorphol.*

1856 in MAYNE *Expos. Lex.* **1898** *Nature* 13 Jan. 256/1 Dr. Wilhelm Halbfass has worked out in detail the morphometry of the Lake of Geneva. **1957** G. E. HUTCHINSON *Treat. Limnol.* I. ii. 168 (*heading*) Morphometry of lakes over 400 m. deep. **1958** *Geogr. Jrnl.* CXXIV. 370 (*heading*) Aspects of the morphometry of a 'poly-cyclic' drainage basin. **1961** *Geomorphological Abstr.* Sept. 33 Earlier work showing the dominance of rock type in pebble morphometry is strongly supported. **1963** E. R. WEIBEL (*title*) Morphometry of the human lung. **1970** R. J. SMALL *Study of Landforms* i. 4 Quantification is applied . . to landscape forms, giving rise to the branch of modern geomorphology known as 'morphometry'.

Hence **morphoˈmetrical** *a.*, pertaining to or connected with morphometry.

1856 in MAYNE *Expos. Lex.* **1935** *Geol. Mag.* LXXII. 183 Its [*sc.* the clinographic curve's] utility in delicate morphometrical determinations seems to me undoubted. **1935** *Biometrika* XXVII. 465 (*heading*) Morphometrical indices. **1953** *Anti-Locust Bull.* XVI. (*heading on title-p.*) Morphometrical studies on phases of the Desert Locust (*Schistocerca gregaria* Forskål).

morphon (ˈmɔːfɒn). Also **morphone**. Pl. (badly formed) **morphontes**. [a. G. *morphon* (pl. *morphonten*), invented by Haeckel, who explains it as f. Gr. μορφ-ή form + ὄν being.] **a.** *Biol.* A morphological individual, element, or factor.

1873 W. S. DALLAS (tr. Haeckel) in *Ann. Mag. Nat. Hist.* Ser. IV. XI. 245 Because the morphontes (morphological elements) of the first order which form the sponge-organism . . exhibit a relatively high degree of physiological individuality, and because the personality of the sponges built up of these (the morphon of the third order) was not recognised, the former have been regarded as the 'true individuals' of the sponge. **1880** PASCOE *Zool. Classif.* (ed. 2) 284 *Morphone*, a morphological element. **1883** *Encycl. Brit.* XVI. 842/1 He distinguishes . . the physiological individual (or *bion*) . . from the morphological individual (or *morphon*).

b. *Linguistics.* A term in stratificational grammar for MORPHOPHONEME. Also *attrib.* Hence **morˈphonic** *a.*

1964 S. M. LAMB in *Rep. 15th Ann. Round Table Meeting Ling. & Lang. Stud.* (Georgetown Univ. Inst. Lang.) 105 Morphons (i.e. morphophonemes) often have alternate phonemic realizations. **1965** *Language* XLI. 200, I shall use Lamb's convenient neologism *morphon*. The syntactic component of a correct generative grammar . . yields sentences as strings of morphons. **1966** S. M. LAMB *Outl. Stratificational Gram.* ii. 29 There are three separate alternation patterns, the lexonic, the morphonic, and the phononic. **1967** C. F. HOCKETT *Language, Mathematics, & Linguistics* iii. 95 Relative to the terminal subalphabet T′(G′), a morphon string is a simple (linear) string. **1968** P. M. POSTAL *Aspects Phonol. Theory* iii. 41 It must be emphasized . . that stratificational grammar insists that the morphophonemes, or 'morphons' in their terms, are unanalyzable symbols. **1968** *Language* XLIV. 595 Rules c & e are necessary because the objects on the higher stratum, called 'morphons', are distinct from the objects on the lower stratum, which are bundles of phonons. **1970** G. SAMPSON *Stratificational Gram.* ii. 33 The large number of neutralisations represented by almost every morphon. *Ibid.* iii. 45 In a complete description of English, there would be two further strata, each with its tactics, below the morphon level. . . I am not in a position . . to give the morphonic realisations of the morphemes.

morphoneme (ˈmɔːfəʊniːm). *Linguistics.* [f. Gr. μορφ-ή form + PHO)NEME.] = MORPHOPHONEME. So **morphoˈnemic** *a.*

1933 *English Studies* XV. 87 The alternating pairs (sometimes groups) of phonemes like *ī/e, f/v* evidently form special units which, being conditioned by morphematic circumstances, are called *morphonemes*. **1934** *Language* X. 335 The five Russian vowel morphonemes are very variable . . . The consonant morphonemes are: [p, pj, b, bj . .]. *Ibid.* 340 The interchange here is morphonemic, and does not properly concern us in a purely phonemic study. **1942** *Ibid.* XVIII. 309 Summarizing briefly Trager's article '[The] Phonemes of Russian' (Language 1934, No. 4) and generally valuing its positive outlook, Reformatsky deplores his terminological unclearness connected with [his] use of [the] word 'morphoneme'. **1966** J. VACHEK *Linguistic School of Prague* iv. 81 The generativists after establishing the morphonemic make up of their strings, proceed to 'rewrite' the morphonemes by concrete sounds found in the phonetic implementations of these strings.

morphonology (mɔːfəˈnɒlədʒɪ). *Linguistics.* [f. Gr. μορφ-ή form + PH)ONOLOGY.] A term used by the Prague school of linguists for the study of the phonology of morphemes. So **morphonoˈlogic, morphonoˈlogical** *adjs.*

[**1929** *Travaux du Cercle Linguistique de Prague* I. 85 La grammaire doit comprendre encore un chapitre particulier, qui étudie l'utilisation morphologique des différences phonologiques, et qui peut être appelée la '*morpho-phonologie*' ou, en abrégeant, la '*morphonologie*'.] **1933** *English Studies* XV. 87 That part of phonology which examines the phonological structure of morphemes, is called *morphonology*. **1935** *Amer. Speech* X. 252/2 Another branch of phonology, established by the Prague linguists, called *morphonology*, . . examines the phonological structure of morphemes. **1936** *Ibid.* XI. 114 Morphological phonology or 'morphonology', . . investigates the morphological use of phonemes or groups of phonemes, or more inclusively, for phonological means. **1949** H. SPANG-HANSSEN in *Travaux du Cercle Ling. de Copenhague* V. 69 Morphonologic or morphemic monographs have no direct bearing on this subject either, since they also presuppose that the phoneme inventory has already been established. **1950** *Lingua* II. 241 This morphonology, according to Trubetzkoy, has a threefold task: 1. the investigation of the phonological (i.e. phonematic) structure of the morphemes, 2. the investigation of the combinatorial sound-changes . ., 3. the investigation of the series of sound-changes . . which have a morphological function. **1966** J. VACHEK *Linguistic School of Prague* iv. 81 The other recent trend in linguistic thinking that has substantially contributed to the revival of interest in morphonology is the stratificational approach by Sydney M. Lamb and his colleagues. *Ibid.*, The first language to be characterized from the morphonological point of view was . . Russian. **1971** tr. *Akhmanova's Phonology, Morphonology, Morphology* ii. 82 Professor Vachek speaks of the present state of morphonological research. . . The 'generativist and transformationist' morphonology is, perhaps, best described as 'codificational morphonology'.

morphonomy (mɔːˈfɒnəmɪ). *Nat. Hist.* [f. Gr. μορφ-ή form + -νομία, f. νόμος law.] The science concerned with the laws of form in animals, plants, and crystals.

1856 in MAYNE *Expos. Lex.*, and in later Dicts.

Hence **morphoˈnomic** *a.*, of or pertaining to morphonomy (*Cent. Dict.* 1890).

morphophoneme (mɔːfəʊˈfəʊniːm). *Linguistics.* [f. Gr. μορφ-ή form + PHONEME.] One of the variant phonemes which belong to the same morpheme.

1934 M. SWADESH in *Language* X. 129 Morphologically distinct phonemes are called morpho-phonemes. A morpho-phoneme is one of a class of like phonemes considered as components of actual morphemes which behave alike morphologically, i.e., have a like place in the same mutation series. **1939** L. BLOOMFIELD in *Travaux du Cercle Linguistique de Prague* VIII. 106 The morphophoneme u seems to occur in only one suffix. **1947** C. F. HOCKETT in *Language* XXIII. 323 Morphophonemic statements may involve morphophonemes—that is, the symbols used for phonemes, plus supplementary ones, with special definitions as to phonemic value under varying circumstances—or they may not. **1957** N. CHOMSKY *Syntactic Structures* iv. 33 The elements that figure in the rules can be classified into a finite set of levels (e.g. phonemes and morphemes; or, perhaps, phonemes, morphophonemes, and morphemes). **1964** E. BACH *Introd. Transformational Gram.* ii. 25 We distinguish the final morphophonemes in *laugh* and *wife* on the basis of their plural formation. **1968** *Language* XLIV. 508 The major thesis of this paper is that the most efficient description of morpheme alternants requires the use of morphophonemes, and, moreover, that these morphophonemes do in fact constitute psychologically real units. **1972** *Ibid.* XLVIII. 372 In Turkish, the target is satisfied at a level preceding the application of the first law of vowel harmony, which maps the morphophonemes *A I U* onto their respective phonetic reflexes.

Hence **morphophoneˈmatic** (*rare*), **morphophoˈnemic** *adjs.*, **morphophoˈnemically** *adv.*

1939 [see MORPHOLEXICAL *a.*]. **1944** *Amer. Speech* XIX. 136 The 'neutrality' of *e* in Hungarian and Finnish is not phonetic but morphophonemic. **1951** Z. S. HARRIS *Methods in Structural Linguistics* xiv. 239 The *al* of *moral* would appear to be morphophonemically /æL/, where /L/ represents phonemic zero before *ly*, but /l/ otherwise. **1957** *Publ. Amer. Dial. Soc.* XXVIII. 58 Morphophonemically *be* behaves like an auxiliary, regardless of its complement. **1960** C. E. BAZELL in *Year's Work in Eng. Studies 1958* 47/2 Evidence for the diphthongal character of Gothic *iu* is largely morphophonemic (e.g. the alternation *triu/triwa*). **1964** D. WARD in D. Abercrombie et al. *Daniel Jones* 390 There are some departures from the morphophonematic principle in Russian, including such sporadic ones as, for example, *nozdri* 'nostrils' (cp. *nos* 'nose'). **1965** *Canad. Jrnl. Linguistics* Spring 169 Most noun stems [in Eyak] are morphophonemically invariable. **1968** P. M. POSTAL *Aspects Phonol. Theory* vi. 117 Even setting up new allomorphs like 'is', etc. does not avoid the consequence that the morphophonemic rules must appeal to categorial properties. **1970** *Bible Translator* XXI. 25 There is reason to believe that most function morphemes should be read at sight rather than 'sounded out', and this also supports the idea of writing such morphemes morphophonemically. **1971** tr. *Akhmanova's Phonology, Morphonology, Morphology* ii. 72 It is quite impossible to formulate any morphophonemic rules to explain the would-be substitution of [-a] for [-i] or [:y].

morphophonemics (ˌmɔːfəʊfəˈniːmɪks), *sb. pl.* [f. prec. + -ICS.] The study and description of the phonemic aspects of the constitution of morphemes.

1939 L. BLOOMFIELD in *Travaux du Cercle Linguistique de Prague* VIII. 105 The present paper describes . . the *internal sandhi* or *morphophonemics* of the language. **1953** [see *morpheme-sequence*]. **1957** S. POTTER *Mod. Linguistics* vii. 146 As we proceed from morphophonemics, and morphology proper, to syntax, so we observe a rise in the scale of semantic values. **1965** B. M. H. STRANG *Metaphors & Models* 15 The study of how a language encodes its different meanings is called *morphophonemics*. **1968** *Amer. Speech* XLIII. 233 The author includes a description of Jamaican Creole . . morphophonemics. **1972** *Language* XLVIII. 805 This negative is realized from the sentence modality without going through the morphophonemics of pre-verbal location. **1973** *Computers & Humanities* VII. 218 How does one handle the unbelievably complex morphophonemics in choosing headwords?

morphophonics (mɔːfəʊˈfɒnɪks), *sb. pl.* [f. Gr. μορφ-ή form + PHONICS *sb. pl.*]

= MORPHOPHONEMICS *sb. pl.* (see also quot. 1962). Also ˈ**morphophone**, a unit representing the class of phonemes occurring in dialectally different pronunciations of morphemes; **morphoˈphonic** *a.*

1962 E. F. HADEN et al. *Resonance-Theory for Linguistics* iii. 30 Such sets of allophones, as expressions of morphological units, are *morphophonic expressions*. *Ibid.* 40 Morphophonics . . is the intermediate area between phonology and morphology. . . Morphophonics is the process of transposing phonemic entities from the context of phonology into the context of morphology. **1967** H. L. SMITH in *Language* XLIII. I. 306 A three-stratum, twenty-seven level model for linguistic analysis indicates structural units—the *morphophones*—between phoneme and morpheme. Morphophones are seen as the basic units of the morphemes, and are themselves composed of dialectally different phonemic variants, which are non-contrasting in the same lexical items. *Ibid.* 311 From one point of view, the morphophone can be seen as a sort of 'holding company' or 'super-family' of different phonemes which are non-contrasting in the same words. But from another point of view, the morphophone is a unit of the language as a whole, and as a unit furnishes the basis of what might be thought of as 'higher order' or 'higher level' contrasts. *Ibid.* 323 Substitutions and interchanges are aspects of the morphophonic system. *Ibid.* 341 The donor language's morphophonics have been subject to a pretty thorough Anglicization. **1972** G. L. TRAGER *Lang. & Languages* iii. 49 The diacritic part of morphology, which examines the items of which morphemes are composed, may be called *morphophonics* (more commonly the term is *morphophonemics*, but there are good theoretical reasons for omitting the *-em-*). *Ibid.* 56 Morphemes with more than one allomorph are made up of or composed of morphophones, and it follows that morphemes with only one allomorph are also composed of morphophones. . . The morphophonic alternations that occur can then be considered as relations between (simple) morphophones.

morphophonology (ˌmɔːfəʊfəˈnɒlədʒɪ). *Linguistics.* [f. Gr. μορφ-ή form + PHONOLOGY.] = MORPHONOLOGY. So **morphophonoˈlogical** *a.*

1934 *Language* X. 128 Morpho-phonology includes, in addition to the study of the phonemic structure of morphemes, the study of interchange between phonemes as a morphologic process. **1938** *Trans. Philol. Soc.* 106 The morpheme in the sense of Skalička and of the Prague Linguistic Circle is a morphophonological unit, and the corresponding phonomorphological unit is the phonemic function. **1953** K. JACKSON *Lang. & Hist. in Early Britain* II. 548 The development of IE. *p* cannot be connected in any way with lenition, since it does not follow the special morphophonological rules for its occurrence. **1970** G. C. LEPSCHY *Survey Structural Linguistics* iii. 56 [One of the] main tasks of synchronic phonology [is] . . to describe the morphological utilization of phonological differences (morphophonology or morphonology). **1973** *Archivum Linguisticum* IV. 47 No account is being taken here of regular, if often quite subtle morphophonological alternations, as between . . viyis and vayas. *Ibid.* 50 The lengthening of the vowel of -ha in the example . . belongs rather to the (morpho)phonology of the language.

morphophyly (mɔːˈfɒfɪlɪ). *Biol.* [f. Gr. μορφ-ή form + φῦλ-ον tribe + -Y.] The tribal history of living forms; that branch of phylogeny which treats only of form.

1879 tr. *Haeckel's Evol. Man* I. i. 24 Tribal history of forms (Morphophyly). **1890** in *Century Dict.*

morphoplasm (ˈmɔːfəʊplæz(ə)m). *Biol.* [f. Gr. μορφ-ή form + πλάσμα PLASMA, PLASM.] The vital substance of an organic cell.

1893 W. N. PARKER tr. *Weismann's Germ-Plasm* 38, I shall . . call the vital substance of the cell the 'formative plasm' or morphoplasm . . in contrast to the idioplasm.

morphoˈscopic, *a.* [f. Gr. μορφ-ή form + σκοπ-εῖν to look: see -IC.] Having regard to form.

1816 BENTHAM *Chrestom.* Wks. 1843 VIII. 85 Morphoscopic Posology. [Proposed as a better name for Geometry.]

morphoscopy (mɔːˈfɒskəpɪ). *Biol.* [f. Gr. μορφ-ή form + σκοπ-εῖν to look (see -SCOPE) + -Y.] = MORPHOLOGY (*Syd. Soc. Lex.* 1891).

morphosis (mɔːˈfəʊsɪs). Pl. **morphoses** (mɔːˈfəʊsiːz). [mod.L., a. Gr. μόρφωσις a shaping, f. μορφοῦν to shape, fashion, f. μορφή form.]

†**1.** Form, figure, configuration. *Obs.*

1675 SIR E. SHERBURNE tr. *Manilius* Pref. 3 As they [the Constellations] are distinguished into prophane and Sacred Figures or Morphoses according to the different Uranography of the Antient Ethnicks. **1676** OWEN *Nat. Apostasy* ii. 115 Instead of that Mystical spiritual Union with himself and among themselves which Christ prayed for, and purchased for his Disciples, they have substituted the *Morphosis* or *Mormo* of an Agreement in professing Subjection to the Pope of Rome.

2. *Bot.* The manner or order of development of an organ or organism.

1857 M. J. BERKELEY *Cryptog. Bot.* §94. 114 The morphosis of the production has not yet been properly observed. **1874** R. BROWN *Man. Bot.* 609 *Morphosis*, order or mode of development of any organ or organs.

b. Used for METAMORPHOSIS. (Cf. sense 3.)

1882 G. MAW in *Jrnl. Linn. Soc., Bot* XIX. 370 The only other point I have to refer to is the tendency to morphosis of nearly every part of a Crocus. **1886** —— *Monogr. Crocus* 19 *Morphosis.* Nearly every organ of a Crocus has a strong tendency to metamorphosis.

3. *Med.* A morbid formation; organic disease.

1856 in MAYNE *Epos. Lex.* **1891** in *Syd. Soc. Lex.*

morphosyntax (mɔːfəʊˈsɪntæks). *Linguistics.* [f. Gr. μορφ-ή form + SYNTAX 2.] A branch of

linguistic study which combines the study of morphology and syntax.

1961 F. W. HOUSEHOLDER in Saporta & Bastian *Psycholinguistics* 23/2 So also in morpho-syntax it should be possible to agree on definitions for terms like 'noun phrase', 'verb phrase', 'sentence', etc. **1967** *Word* XXIII. 472 In morpho-syntax the sequential chain model should perhaps not be completely disregarded. **1968** Y. MALKIEL *Essays on Linguistic Themes* i. 3 A few scholars have gone so far as to consolidate all of morphology and syntax into the single domain of 'morphosyntax', which forms the hard, inalienable kernel of linguistics. **1969** tr. *Akhmanova & Mikael'an's Theory Syntax Mod. Linguistics* ii. 26 He [*sc.* Brøndal] not only remained faithful to his conception of 'morphology' and syntax, but also developed it by introducing the notion of 'morphosyntax' to cover such phenomena as the functioning of words in sentences, the semantic modification of words in context, [etc.]. **1972** *Archivum Linguisticum* III. 89 As a final instance of the general validity of a systematic approach to diachronic morpho-syntax, let us examine a well-documented change within the verbal system of Romance.

Hence **morphosyn'tactic** *a.*, **morpho-syn'tactically** *adv.*

1959 F. W. HOUSEHOLDER in *Word* XV. 232 It does not appear that languages have a semantic structure which is separate and distinct from the morpho-syntactic one. **1962** H. C. CONKLIN in Householder & Saporta *Problems in Lexicography* 119 While an 'appeal' to meaning does not improve grammatical analysis, neither does an intuitive appeal to morphosyntactic form yield the most appropriate analysis of meaning and reference. *Ibid.* 121 The compounds *firewater* and *silverfish*..are endocentric morphosyntactically. **1968** *Word* XXIV. 55 The United States dialect refers to any variety of English set off from other varieties of English, phonetically, morphosyntactically, or lexically. **1969** tr. *Akhmanova & Mikael'an's Theory Syntax Mod. Linguistics* v. 119 The *words*..had to have canonical phonemic shapes, to 'behave' morphophonemically and morphosyntactically. **1970** *Language* XLVI. 332 The proposal does not spell out how one gets from the morphosyntactic surface structure to the phonemics.

morphotactics (mɔːfəʊ'tæktɪks). *sb. pl. Linguistics.* [F. Gr. μορφ-ή form + TACTICS.] The study of the sequence of morphemes in a language (MORPHEME b). Hence **morpho'tactic** *a.*; **morpho'tactically** *adv.*

1958 A. A. HILL *Introd. Linguistic Structures* vi. 68 The term 'phonotactics', now widely used, as well as other terms in -'tactics' to indicate sequences of items such as 'morphotactics' and 'logotactics', I owe to an unpublished lecture by Robert P. Stockwell delivered before the Linguistic Institute held at the Georgetown University Institute of Languages and Linguistics in 1954. *Ibid.* viii. 120 With most prebases, it is a morphotactic characteristic which identifies them. *Ibid.*, These are the 'grammatical endings' of familiar terminology. They can be defined morphotactically as morphemes which stand frequently before terminal junctures. *Ibid.* xxi. 414 Morphotactics gives us the partial predictability of morphemes and allomorphs. **1962** E. F. HADEN et al. *Resonance-Theory for Linguistics* iii. 35 Whereas in morphemics our task is to identify the form and the property of a grammatically functioning unit, in morphotactics we focus our attention on such a unit occurring in a sequence of morphemes... The morphotactic identification will be made with the same criteria for determining Form and Property as in morphemics. *Ibid.* 40 Morphotactics complements morphemics with morphology in a manner exactly parallel to phonotactics and phonemics within phonology. **1966** S. M. LAMB *Outl. Stratif. Gram.* ii. 23 When a lexonic ordering is of elements belonging to different morphotactic classes, e.g. verb stem and verb suffix, it is up to the morphotactics to determine their relative order. **1967** D. G. HAYS *Introd. Computational Linguistics* xi. 184 The morphotactic rules come to light as restrictions on sequence are found... The establishment of the morphotactics can be exceedingly simple or as complex as the development of a full syntax. **1970** G. SAMPSON *Stratificational Gram.* vi. 59 The morphotactics generates sequences of 'words' (M-Word), separated by the downward-determined element 'word-boundary'. *Ibid.* 62 The preference value of this derivation is six, one from the semotactic trace, four from the lexotactic, and one from the morphotactic.

morphotectonics (ˌmɔːfəʊtɛk'tɒnɪks), *sb. pl.* [f. Gr. μορφ-ή form + -O + TECTONICS.] The branch of geomorphology concerned with the form and structure of the larger features of the earth's surface (as continents, mountain ranges, river basins); also, the morphotectonic character or features of a region.

1956 E. S. HILLS in *Jrnl. Geol. Soc. Austral.* III. 1 (*heading*) A contribution to the morphotectonics of Australia. *Ibid.*, A model of this size does in fact afford a unique basis for the study of morphotectonics, since no other medium can present a synoptic view of the topography of an area as large as [a] continent. **1961** —— in *Q. Jrnl. Geol. Soc.* CXVII. 79 What I have called morphotectonics implies, as well as structural geomorphology, something broader and applicable to regional study on a large scale, using topography as the primary criterion, but of course not neglecting all that may be known as to geology and geophysics. **1968** R. W. FAIRBRIDGE *Encycl. Geomorphol.* 734/1 The concept of 'Gondwanaland' in the southern hemisphere..evolved in the late nineteenth century..on the basis of extraordinarily similar morphotectonics, as much as from common features of stratigraphy, paleontology and paleoclimate. *Ibid.* 734/2 Up till now only one attempt has been made at a detailed world survey of morphotectonics.

Hence **morphotec'tonic** *a.*, of or pertaining to or seen from the point of view of morphotectonics.

1961 *Q. Jrnl. Geol. Soc.* CXVII. 84 A purely morphotectonic map for Egypt..shows, firstly, that it is not possible to conceive of the region as an elliptical upwarp. **1967** *Geogr. Abstr.* A. 280 The Provence foldings south-east of the Durance and the Verdon confluent give a good summary of the morphotectonic evolution of the Provence Range. **1973** *Nature* 2 Mar. 43/2 The morphotectonic features shown in Figs. 1 and 3 show a close agreement between structure and topography.

morphotic (mɔː'fɒtɪk), *a. Biol.* [ad. Gr. type *μορφωτικός, f. μορφοῦν to form, f. μορφή form.] Formative; contributory to organic structure.

1876 BARTHOLOW *Mat. Med.* (1879) 544 Cupping and leeching..may diminish..the proportion of the morphotic elements. **1891** in *Syd. Soc. Lex.*

morphotomy (mɒr'fɒtəmɪ). *Biol.* [f. Gr. μορφ-ή form + -τομία cutting, f. τομ-, τέμνειν to cut, after *anatomy*.] The art of dissecting the different parts of any organized body for purposes of morphological investigation (*Syd. Soc. Lex.* 1891).

morphotropism (mɔː'fɒtrəpɪz(ə)m). *Cryst.* [f. as next: see -ISM.] = next.

1905 *Amer. Chem. Jrnl.* XXXIV. 104 The chapter on Morphotropism deals with the dependence of the crystal structure on the chemical constitution of the body. **1959** tr. *W. F. de Jong's Crystallogr.* 184 If a change of structure that occurs by replacement becomes so great that we no longer want to use the term 'isomorphism', we speak of morphotropism. **1966** *McGraw-Hill Encycl. Sci. & Technol.* VIII. 599/1 Organic compounds also show morphotropism.

morphotropy (mɔː'fɒtrəpɪ). *Cryst.* [ad. G. *morphotropie* (P. Groth 1870, in *Ann. d. Physik und Chem.* CXLI. 39), f. Gr. μορφ-ή form + τροπή turning.] (The study of) the progressive change in crystal structure brought about by replacing one of the species of atom or radical in a crystal by other species.

1900 *Rep. Brit. Assoc. Adv. Sci. 1900* 167 Morphotropy and isomorphism have a common cause, and..this is more likely to be discovered by the crystallographic study of substances showing morphotropic relationships than from the examination merely of materials likely to exhibit isomorphism. **1924** W. S. STILES tr. *F. Rinne's Crystals & Fine Struct. Matter* ix. 105 P. v. Groth has founded the science of morphotropy. By comparing crystalline forms, he succeeded in showing how the replacement of H by (OH), NO_2, NH_2, CH_3, Cl, in benzene (C_6H_6) manifests itself in changes of corresponding angles, and ultimately the symmetry. **1939** R. C. EVANS *Introd. Crystal Chem.* iii. 60 The structural importance of the quantitative lattice theory ..lies in the light which it throws on..the problems of polymorphism and morphotropy.

So **morpho'tropic** *a.*, characteristic of or exhibiting morphotropy.

1899 *Mineral. Mag.* XII. 66 The three minerals may be members of a morphotropic series, in which the vertical crystallographic axis increases in length with an increase in the amount of lead. **1937** W. L. BRAGG *Atomic Struct. Minerals* ix. 150 The members of the chondrodite series are interesting because of the morphotropic relationships which exist between them. **1959** tr. *W. F. de Jong's Gen. Crystallogr.* 184 A morphotropic range of compounds is one in which the replacing atoms differ gradually in one property—for example, in size or polarizability. **1973** A. I. KITAIGORODSKY *Molec. Crystals & Molecules* i. 18 Morphotropic changes associated with a loss of symmetry are accompanied by an increase in the packing density.

morphous ('mɔːfəs), *a. rare.* [f. Gr. μορφ-ή form: see -OUS.] Having a determinate shape; opposed to *amorphous*.

1885 ROBERTS *Urin. & Renal Dis.* I. iv. (ed. 4) 166 A large quantity of amorphous, or barely morphous granular debris.

morphrodite: see MOPHRODITE.

morphu(e, variant forms of MORPHEW.

morpion ('mɔːpɪən), [a. F. *morpion.*] †**1.** = CRAB 4. *Obs.*

1597 LOWE *Chirurg.* (1634) 126 The Morpions..are found chiefly about the privy parts. **1678** BUTLER *Hud.* III. i. 437 His Flea, his Morpion, and Punese, H' had gotten for his proper ease. **1826** KIRBY & SP. *Entomol.* III. xxviii. 26 *Phthirus* Leach, or the Morpion.

2. *transf.* Applied scornfully to a person. *rare*$^{-1}$.

1954 S. BECKETT *Waiting for Godot* II. 48 Moron!.. Vermin!..Abortion!..Morpion!

morpunkee, variant of MOORPUNKY.

morra, variant of MORA[2]; obs. form of MURREY.

morraine, obs. form of MURRAIN.

morral, variant of MOREL[1].

morrane: see MARRAM.

morrass(h)e, morre(i)s, obs. ff. MORRIS *sb.*[1]

morre, morreine: see MURR, MURRAIN.

morrell, obs. form of MEREL.

1627 W. HAWKINS *Apollo Shroving* III. iv. 49 That can set his three along in a row, And that is fippeny morrell.

morrell(e, -lo, var. ff. MOREL *sb.*[3], MORELLO.

morrenian (mɒ'riːnɪən), *a. Zool.* [f. the name of C. F. A. *Morren* (1807–58), Belgian naturalist: see -IAN.] Epithet of certain glands in worms, whose function appears to be to adapt the ingesta for nutrition (*Cent. Dict.* 1890).

morres, morrey, obs. ff. MORRIS, MURREY.

morreyn(e, obs. forms of MURRAIN.

‖**morrhua** ('mɒruːə). [mod.L. *Morrhua*, a genus of fishes of which the cod (now *Gadus morrhua*) was typical, a. med.L. *morua, moruca, moruta* cod. Cf. F. *morue*.] Used *attrib.* in ***morrhua-oil***, cod-liver oil (Cassell 1885).

morrhuine ('mɒruːaɪn). *Chem.* Also 9 -in. [f. prec. + -INE.] (See quot. 1897.)

1891 *Syd. Soc. Lex., Morrhuin.* **1897** C. W. LYMAN in *New York Voice* 19 Aug. 7/3 Cod-liver oil..contains minute amounts of a substance secreted in the liver, 'gaduine', or 'morrhuine'.

Hence **morrhu'inic** *a. Chem.*, in ***morrhuinic acid*** = GADINIC *acid* (*Syd. Soc. Lex.* 1891).

morrian, morrice, obs. ff. MORION, MORRIS.

morricer ('mɒrɪsə(r)). [f. *morrice* MORRIS *sb.*[1] + -ER[1].] A morris-dancer.

1810 SCOTT *Lady of L.* v. xxii, There morricers with bell at heel, And blade in hand, their mazes wheel.

morries, obs. form of MORRIS *sb.*[1]

morrillo, var. MORILLO.

morrion, obs. form of MORION.

morris ('mɒrɪs), *sb.*[1] Forms: 5 moreys, mourish, 6 mor(r)es, moreis, -yce, -ys, morrass(h)e, morreis, 6–7 moris, morrisse, 6–8 morice, 6–9 morrice, 7 morise, 6– morris. [subst. use of *morys* obs. var. MOORISH *a.*[2] Cf. OF. *morisque, morixe* sb., in the same sense.]

1. = MORRIS-DANCE. †***to dance the morris***, to take part in a morris-dance.

1512 [see MONSIEUR 1]. **1513** DOUGLAS *Æneis* XIII. ix. 112 Thar morisis and syk riot. **1589** R. HARVEY *Pl. Perc.* 8 All the picked youth,..footing the Morris about a May pole. **1617** MORYSON *Itin.* IV. 477 Setting vp maypooles daunsing the morris with hobby horses, bringing home the lady of the harvest. **1712** *Spect.* No. 425 ¶3 Four Reapers, who danced a Morrice to the Sound of Oaten Pipes. **1817** SOUTHEY *Wat Tyler* I. i, Since we were boys together, And play'd at barley-brake, and danced the morris. **1856** BOKER *Leonor de Guzman* I. ii. Poems (1857) I. 261 I'll dance the morrice, and you'll ride the horse With an alms-pipkin at your saddle-bow.

2. A body of morris-dancers.

1500–20 DUNBAR *Poems* lvii. 8 Sum lait at evin bringis in the moreis. **1554** *Burgh Recs. Edinb.* (1871) II. 193 Vtheris that furneist the grayth to the convoy of the moris to the Abbay. **1603** HARSNET *Pop. Impost.* 49 The Fidler comes in with his Taber and Pipe and a whole Morice after him with Motly Visards. **1616** *Pasquil & Katherine* I. 51 Oh, a Morrice is come, obserue our country sport. **1621** BP. MOUNTAGU *Diatribæ* 448 A certaine Lasse..came with others, in a Morrice vnto the Church of Enyalius. **1636** RANDOLPH in *Ann. Dubrensia* C3b, These teach that Dancing is a Iezabell,..The Morrice, Idolls.

3. *transf.* and *fig.*

1547 COVERDALE *Old Faith* To Rdr., The man wyll not daunce in the deuyls morys with them. **1571** *Satir. Poems Reform.* xxix. 35 Sum for þe hure garris heid þameselff, and is not þat a morreis? **1613** FLETCHER *Captain* v. i, Certainly my body Is of a wild-fire For my head rings backward Or else I have a morise in my braines. **1634** MILTON *Comus* 116 The Sounds and Seas with all their finny drove Now to the Moon in wavering Morrice move. **1698** FRYER *Acc. E. India & P.* 23 A Chorus of Porpoises had taken the Sea in their Dance; which Morris once over, the Seas were quiet. **1892** HENLEY *Song of Sword*, etc. Rhymes xi. 1 Gulls in an aëry morrice Gleam and vanish and gleam. **1894** K. GRAHAME *Pagan Papers* 23 And all the attendant hurry and scurry of the human morrice.

4. *attrib.*, as ***morris feast, garment, mate, train***; **morris bell**, one of many small metal bells attached to the clothing of morris dancers.

1560 *Churchw. Acc. St. Helen's, Abingdon* in *Archæologia* I. 17 For two dossin of *Morres belles 1[s]. **1748** SMOLLETT *Rod. Rand.* xiii. (1804) 70 His fears had magnified..the sound of small morrice bells to the clanking of massy chains. **1750** W. ELLIS *Mod. Husbandm.* IV. xvii. 185 A fourth way Is to tie a Morrice-Bell about the Neck of a catch'd rat. **1621** BP. MOUNTAGU *Diatribæ* 488 The Salij, the habite they vsed in those *Morrice-Feasts. **1507** in Lysons *Envir. Lond.* (1792) I. 226 [Kingston upon Thames] For 4 plyts and ¼ of laun for the *mores garments 0. 2. 11. *c* **1621** ROWLEY, etc. *Witch of Edmont.* III. i. (1658) 26, I pray you, good *Morrice-mates, now leave me. **1802** WORDSW. *To Daisy* 17 In shoals and bands, a *morrice train, Thou greet'st the traveller in the lane.

morris ('mɒrɪs), *sb.*[2] *Obs.* exc. *Hist.* [Corruption of *merels*: see MEREL 2.] = MEREL 2. Chiefly ***nine men's (peg) morris.***

1590 SHAKS. *Mids. N.* II. i. 98 The nine mens Morris is fild vp with mud. **1706** PHILLIPS (ed. Kersey), *Merils*, a Play among Boys, otherwise call'd *Fivepenny Morris.* **1825** J. NEAL *Bro. Jonathan* I. 7 Peters had beaten him..at fox and geese; then at morris; then at checquers, or draughts. **1835**

CLARE *Rural Muse* 119 Oft we may track his haunts..By nine-peg-morris nicked upon the green. **1865** S. EVANS *Bro. Fabian's MS.* 9 He found his abacus expressly scored For nine-men's morris on an indoor scale.

morris ('mɒrɪs), *sb.*[3] *Nat. Hist.* [f. the name of William *Morris* of Holyhead.] An elongated flat eel-like fish formerly named *Leptocephalus morrisii*, but now regarded as the aborted young of the conger-eel. Also ***Anglesea morris***.

1769 PENNANT *Brit. Zool.* III. 125. **1781** —— *Tours Wales* II. 252 The Beaumaris Shark,..the Morris, and the trifurcated Hake..are new species taken in this sea. **1835** JENYNS *Brit. Vertebr. Anim.* 480 *Leptocephalus Morrisii*, Gmel. (Angelsea Morris).

Morris ('mɒrɪs), *sb.*[4] The name of William *Morris* (1834–96), poet and craftsman, used *attrib.* of styles of furniture, wallpaper, etc., designed by him or made in his factory or at the Kelmscott Press, *spec.* as **Morris chair**, a type of easy chair with open padded arms and an adjustable back. Also **Morris-papered** *a.*, papered with Morris wallpaper.

1880 LADY JEBB *Let.* 6 Mar. in A. Adburgham *Shops & Shopping* (1964) xvi. 173, I wish you could see Mrs Sellar's drawing-room..; Morris papers on the walls, Burne-Jones' photographs. **1900** *T. Eaton & Co. Catal.* Spring & Summer 235/3 Morris chair, golden oak or mahogany finish. **1912** T. E. LAWRENCE *Let.* 20 May in *Home Lett.* (1954) 209 The piece of Morris tapestry I have. **1912** E. WORDSWORTH *Glimpses of Past* xii. 140 Those were the days of green serge gowns, and Morris papers, depicting miniature orange trees and pomegranates, daisies, and sunflowers. **1920** J. GALSWORTHY *In Chancery* III. iii. 257 On a wall, not yet Morris-papered, was a print of the Queen. **1925** G. B. SHAW *Let.* 24 Feb. in *To a Young Actress* (1960) 83 Morris made all sorts of chairs: there is no particular Morris chair that I know of. **1935** N. MITCHISON *We have been Warned* I. 107 The Morris curtains would be drawn. **1936** J. DOS PASSOS *Big Money* 248 He let himself drop into the morrischair. **1937** V. WOOLF *Years* 54 There she was among the Morris wall-papers and the cabinets. **1938** J. CARY *Castle Corner* 274 A Bible in Morris binding. *Ibid.* 303 I'm quite sure our Morris sugar sifter is far greater than Milan. **1958** *Listener* 28 Aug. 317/1 The Morris dining-room. **1961** A. MILLER *Misfits* iii. 31 The complete assortment of furniture, from the Morris chair to the studio couch. **1967** O. LANCASTER *Eye to Future* v. 123 A charming cottage, stone-walled and Morris-papered. **1972** D. MARLOWE *Do you remember England?* i. 20 The warm bottle of Malvern water by the bedside, Morris wallpaper, and a train-journey biography.

Hence **'Morrisan, Mo'rrisian** *a.*, of, pertaining to, or characteristic of William Morris or his work; also **'Morrisite**, a follower or adherent of the principles, etc., of William Morris.

1897 A. BEARDSLEY *Let.* 26 Dec. (1971) 413 On the art side I suggest that it [*sc.* a projected new periodical] should attack *untiringly and unflinchingly* the Burne-Jones and Morrisian medieval business. **1918** A. BENNETT *Roll-Call* I. ix. 187 A quiet, inexpensive blue dress, embroidered at the neck in the Morrisian manner. **1936** *Archit. Rev.* LXXX. 179/3 Morris's passionate campaign is famous enough, but there were true Morrisites before Morris, men such as Pugin and Semper. **1936** W. R. TITTERTON *G. K. Chesterton* I. i. 23 The S.D.F.ers had always been Marxian in theory, though revolutionary Morrisites in sentiment. **1949** G. B. SHAW *Sixteen Self Sketches* x. 57 A lady in the esthetic dress momentarily fashionable in Morrisan cliques just then. **1970** *New Society* 31 Dec. 1151/2 It seemed plausibly argued that plastic would demean all our sensations and our contact with nature... This kind of approach had wood in mind—more Morrisite than luddite, perhaps. **1972** *Listener* 6 Apr. 458/2 Ernie's father, killed just before the Armistice, had been a Morrisian socialist and preached an end to deference.

morris, morrice ('mɒrɪs), *v.* [f. MORRIS *sb.*[1]]

1. *intr.* To dance. Also *slang* (see quot. 1725).

1725 *New Cant. Dict.*, *Morris*, to hang dangling in the Air, to be executed. **1861** M. COLLINS in *Temple Bar* I. 268 Where the unseen fairies gaily morriced.

2. *slang.* To move away rapidly; to decamp. Also with *off.* ? *Obs.*

1765 COWPER *Let. to Hill* 8 Nov., Wks. 1837 XV. 6, I think the Welshman must *morris.* **1773** GOLDSM. *Stoops to Conq.* III. ii, Zounds! here they are. Morrice! Prance! **1796** MRS. M. ROBINSON *Angelina* II. 81 You'll be pleased to morrice off while you are in a whole skin. **1838** DICKENS *O. Twist* viii, Up with you on your pins. There! Now then! Morrice!

†**b.** To move at a rapid pace. *Obs.*

1826 *Sporting Mag.* XVII. 333 They [horses] are not large, but they can all 'morris' a little.

3. *trans.* To dance (a particular measure).

a **1845** HOOD *Forge* i. 4 However it's quite As wild a night As ever was known on that sinister height Since the Demon-Dance was morriced.

'morris-dance. Forms: see MORRIS *sb.*[1] [f. MORRIS *sb.*[1] (or *morys* MOORISH *a.*[2]) + DANCE *sb.* Cf. Flemish *mooriske dans* (perh. the immediate source), Du. *Moorsche dans*, early mod.G. *moriskentanz*, F. *danse moresque*.]

A grotesque dance performed by persons in fancy costume, usually representing characters from the Robin Hood legend, esp. Maid Marian and Friar Tuck. Hence, any mumming performance of which fantastic dancing is an important feature. Also, a representation of the dance.

1458 *Will of Wetenhale* (Somerset Ho.), Ciphos argenti sculpt. cum moreys daunce. **1494** in *Excerpta Hist.* (1831) 95 For playing of the Mourice dance. **1510** *Will of Jackson* (Somerset Ho.), My cuppe wt the morres daunce. **1532** *Lett. & Pap. Hen. VIII*, V. 739 A gold salt, called the Moresdaunce, with 5 Moresdauncers and a tabrett. **1552** LATIMER *Serm.* (1562) 148 Such felowes are more meete to daunce the morrice daunce, then to bee admitted to preache. **1633** FORD *Love's Sacrif.* I. ii, Thou wouldst sweare A Morris-dance were but a Tragedy Compar'd to that. **1708** J. CHAMBERLAYNE *St. Gt. Brit.* I. I. v. (1743) 35 In the reign of King James the First, 8 old men danced a morice-dance.. whose ages put together made 800 years. **1801** STRUTT *Sports & Past.* III. v. 201, I make no doubt the morris-dance ..originated from the fool's dance.

b. *transf.* and *fig.*

1662 STILLINGFL. *Orig. Sacræ* II. iv. §17 The Dithyrambus was..a kind of extatick Morice-dance. *a* **1639** WOTTON *Parallel Essex & Buckhm.* (1641) 11 Whilest the Queene stood in some doubt of a Spanish Invasion (though it proved but a Morrice dance upon our Waves). **1781** COWPER *Table-T.* 519, I judged a man of sense could scarce do worse Than caper in the morris-dance of verse.

Hence **'morris-dancer**, (*a*) one who takes part in a morris-dance. †(*b*) *pl.* The aurora borealis. **'morris-dancing** *vbl. sb.* and *ppl. a.*

1507 in Jupp *Acc. Carpenters' Comp.* (1887) 200 Itm payd to ye morys daunsers viijd. **1532** [see MORRIS DANCE]. **1612** ROWLANDS *Knave of Hearts* B 1 b, My Sleeues are like some Morris-dancing fellow. **1612** PEACHAM *Gentl. Exerc.* I. xii. 45 Those peeces that shewed..a countrey village, faire or market,..Morrice dancing, peasants together by the eares, and the like. **1621** B. JONSON *Gypsies Met.* (1640) 65 They should be Morris-dancers by their gingle. *a* **1680** BUTLER *Rem.* (1759) I. 224 A Morrice-dancer drest with Bells. **1755** tr. *Pontoppidan's Nat. Hist. Norway* I. 4 *note*, In England.. the north light..is..called Morrice-dancers, Merry dancers, and streamers. **1825** SCOTT *Talism.* xx, How wouldst like such beverage thyself after such a morrice dancing? **1856** VAUGHAN *Mystics* (1860) I. 248 All the year is May for the morris-dancers.

Morrison ('mɒrɪsən). Name of Herbert S. *Morrison*, Secretary of State for Home Affairs and Home Security (1940–5), used *attrib.* in **Morrison hour** (see quot. 1963); **Morrison shelter**, a transportable indoor steel table-shaped air-raid shelter.

1945 S. SPENDER *Citizens in War* 21 In addition to the Anderson shelters, Morrison shelters and Surface shelters were built at the time of the Blitz. **1948** *Hansard Commons* 18 Mar. 2268 Why should Anderson shelters rust more than Morrison shelters? **1952** *Oxf. Jun. Encycl.* X. 89/1 Morrison shelters, also made of steel and shaped like a rectangular dinner-table, could be set up inside a house to give protection if the house collapsed. **1963** T. & P. MORRIS *Pentonville* iv. 84 Some men complain that though at the time of joining they are told of the so-called 'Morrison Hour' they are not told about compulsory overtime. *Ibid.*, The 'Morrison Hour' is one extra hour worked at the end of the day from Monday to Friday and is compulsory. It dates from 1943... Herbert Morrison was Home Secretary at the time.

morris-pike ('mɒrɪspaɪk). *Obs.* exc. *Hist.* Forms: 5 **mareyspyke, marespike, 6 moryspeke, -peik, -pike, -pyke, morryspike, morespike, -pycke, morrespike, mo(o)rishe pike, pyke, morrisshe pike, morishpike, morest spycke,** 6, 8 **morispike,** 7, 9 **morrice-, morris-pike.** [f. *morys*, obs. var. MOORISH *a.*[2]: cf. MORRIS *sb.*[1]] A form of pike supposed to be of Moorish origin.

1487 *Rolls of Parlt.* VI. 397/2 Marespikes, Bowes, Gonnes,..and many other Wepyns. **1517** TORKINGTON *Pilgr.* (1884) 8 Halbardes, Sperys, Moryspekys. **1545** in *St. Papers Hen. VIII*, III. 543 Item, Morest Spyckes, laden with wylde fyer. **1548** *Rutland MSS.* (1905) IV. 568 [Thirty] morrispykes. **1548** *Acts Privy Council* (1890) II. 197 The municions folowing..morispikes, ml. *Ibid.*, Morryspikes, ijml vijc. **1608** [A. MUNDAY] *Reynard's Deliv. Christians* B, The English Mariners so laid about them with ..browne bills,..and morris pikes, that [etc.]. **1641** BAKER *Chron., Hen. VIII* (1653) 369 They entred the Gallies again with Morris Pikes, and began a new fight. **1709** STRYPE *Ann. Ref.* xv. 190 They marched out of London..with guns, moris pikes, halberds, and flags. **1808** SCOTT *Marm.* I. x, The guards their morrice-pikes advanc'd. **1877** MISS YONGE *Cameos* III. 188 The men who knew how to use harquebuses and morris-pikes were stationed round them.

†**b.** *transf.* A morris-pike-man. *Obs.*

1600 HEYWOOD *1st Pt. Edw. IV*, III. ii. (1613) F 4, With our Gunnes and billes browne O the French were beaten downe, Morrys pikes and bowmen.

morrisse, obs. form of MORRIS *sb.*[1]

Morris tube. [From the name of Richard *Morris* (died 1891), the inventor.] A small-bore rifle barrel capable of being inserted in a large-bore rifle or shot-gun for shooting practice; patented in 1881. Also *attrib.*

1884 *Army Gen. Orders* 2 Instructions with regard to the employment of Morris's Aiming Tubes in Government rifles have been approved. **1887** *Ibid.* 160 Morris Aiming Tubes... The issue of Morris tubes to battalions of Militia is deferred. **1896** GREENER *Gun* (ed. 6) 649 The chief use of a Morris tube is to convert a large bore or powerful rifle into a weapon of the saloon rifle type for gallery practice. **1901** *Scotsman* 28 Feb. 8/2 The question of providing Morris-tube ranges in the public parks.

morrow ('mɒrəʊ), *sb.* Now only *literary* and *dial.* (see E.D.D.). Forms: 3–4 **moru,** 3–5 **mor(e)we,** 4–6 **morow(e,** 5 **morue, morou, mor(e)w,** 6–7 **morrowe,** 6– **morrow.** [ME. *morwe, moru*, shortened variant of *morwen* MORN.]

1. = MORN 1, MORNING 1. Occas. as a salutation = GOOD MORROW. *Obs.* exc. *dial.*

c **1275** LAY. 877 He lette clemben an heþ and swiþe loude clepie þat þane ilke morewe come al his gode folke. *c* **1374** CHAUCER *Compl. Mars* 12 The glad nyght ys worthe an heuy morowe. *c* **1386** —— *Prol.* 336 Wel loved he by the morwe a sop in wyn. *c* **1450** *M. E. Med. Bk.* (Heinrich) 94 Let þe seek drinke þer of..at euen hot an morew colde. **1530** PALSGR. 549/1 The two hostes fought togyder from morowe to nyght. **1597** BP. HALL *Sat.* I. vii, Shee's white as morrows milk, or flakes new blowne. **1632** MASSINGER *Maid of Hon.* I. i, Morrow to my Vncle. **1706–7** FARQUHAR *Beaux' Strat.* II. i, Morrow, my dear Sister; are you for Church this Morning? **1710–11** SWIFT *Jrnl. to Stella* 4 Jan., Morning. Morrow, little dears.

2. The day next after the present; the day subsequent to any specified day. ***the morrow***, frequently used advb. = on the following day.

c **1290** *St. Cross* 37 in *S. Eng. Leg.* 2 Þene Morewe aftur Midewinter day to deþe huy him brouȝte. **1297** R. GLOUC. (Rolls) 7842 Þe morwe after seinte mari day. **1310** in Wright *Lyric P.* 41 In morewe men he sohte, At under mo he brohte. *c* **1449** PECOCK *Repr.* I. v. 24 Whanne heuen is rody in the euentid a cleer dai schal be the morewe. **1535** COVERDALE *Exod.* ix. 6 Tomorow shal the Lorde do this vpon earth. And the Lorde dyd the same on the morow. *Ibid. Matt.* vi. 34 Care not then for the morow, for the morow shall care for it self. *a* **1626** BACON *New Atl.* (1900) 8 The Morrow after our three dayes were past, ther came to us a new Man. **1693** DRYDEN *Persius* v. (1697) 475 Unhappy he who does this Work adjourn, And to morrow wou'd the search delay: His lazy morrow will be like to day. **1712** M. HENRY *Daily Commun.* Wks. 1855 I. 242/1 Taking thought for the morrow is the great hinderance of our peace in the night. **1813** BYRON *Br. Abydos* II. xxvii, There late was laid a marble stone; Eve saw it placed—the Morrow gone! **1817** WOLFE *Burial Sir J. Moore* iv, We bitterly thought of the morrow. **1878** BROWNING *La Saisiaz* 12 With yourself it rests to have a month of morrows like to-day!

†**b.** ***the next morrow***: the day after. ***the third morrow***: the day but one after. *Obs.*

a **1300** *Cursor M.* 24549 He hight to rise þe thrid moru. *a* **1310** in Wright *Lyric P.* 82 Hire blisse sprong the thridde morewe. **1390** GOWER *Conf.* I. 250 Wherof his lord, which was deceived, A seknesse er the thridde morwe Conceived hath of dedly sorwe. *c* **1430** *Syr Gener.* (Roxb.) 175 On the third morow Bellins the king Rose erlie or the day ganne spring. **1565** STAPLETON tr. *Bede's Hist. Ch. Eng.* 104 If Sonday were not the next morow after the fourtenth day of the chaunge of the Moone,..he taryed for the Sonday. **1647** W. BROWNE tr. *Polexander* I. 65 The Assembly..thought it fit to resolve of nothing that day, but that they should meet againe the next morrow to conclude all things.

3. *transf.* and *fig.*, esp. in the sense: The time immediately following a particular event.

a **1586** C'TESS PEMBROKE *Ps.* CXLIII. iv, Let mercies morrow Soone chase my night of sorrow. **1646** CRASHAW *Steps to Temple* 40 Let them sleepe on, Till this stormy night be gone, And th' eternall morrow dawne. **1834** HT. MARTINEAU *Farrers* ii. 22 This morrow of a piece of good fortune. **1886** J. FISKE in *Atlantic Monthly* LVIII. 377 On the morrow of a long and costly war, it was not strange that the whole country was in some measure pauperized. **1887** *New Princeton Rev.* III. 1 The morrow of the death of a public favorite is apt to be severe upon his memory.

4. *attrib.* (now only *poet.*), as ***morrow*** †***dew***, †***letter, light, morn, noon, song***; **morrow day**, (*a*) the next day, the morrow; (*b*) daybreak; †**morrow part** = MORNING GIFT (cf. MORDELL); †**morrow priest**, a priest who says morrow-mass; †**morrow star** = MORNING STAR 1.

a **1300** *Cursor M.* 5993 Moises praid þe *moru dai, All þe fleies ware went awai. **1390** GOWER *Conf.* II. 63 Wherof erli the morwe day..he gan to fare Into the field. *c* **1530** *Crt. of Love* 437 Seven at midnight, seven at morow-day. **1582** N. T. (Rhem.) *Matt.* vi. 34 The morow day shal be careful for it self. **1820** KEATS *St. Agnes* xxvii, Flown, like a thought, until the morrow-day. **1398** TREVISA *Barth. De P. R.* XVI. lxii. (Tollemache MS.), White margarites..þat ben conceyuid of þe *morow dewe ben made dym with þe eyer of þe euentide. **1619** HALES *Gold. Rem.* II. (1673) 82 In my *morrow Letters I will not fail..to send your honour the transcripts. **1582** BENTLEY *Mon. Matrones* 107 O Lord, I beseech thee, that..thy grace may spring in my heart with the *morrowe light of thy comfort. **1830** TENNYSON *Poems* 96 The ocean with the morrow light Will be both blue and calm. **1798** COLERIDGE *Anc. Mar.* VII. ad fin., A sadder and a wiser man He rose the *morrow morn. *c* **1489** CAXTON *Blanchardyn* v. 22 A grete forest, in whiche he entred and rode styl tyl the *morowe none, wythout ony adueunture. **1557–8** *Will of W. Rayner* (Somerset Ho.), Unto maude my wif for her full Dowery and *morrowe parte. **1563** BECON *Acts of Christ*, etc. Wks. III. 414 This *morowe priest and that morowe priest. *c* **1386** CHAUCER *Prol.* 832 If even-song and *morwe-song acorde, Lat se now who shal telle the firste tale. *c* **1440** *Promp. Parv.* 344/2 *Morow sterre..,*Lucifer.* **1526** *Pilgr. Perf.* (W. de W. 1531) 67 b, The morowe sterre that commeth before the daye.

morrow ('mɒrəʊ), *v. rare.* [f. MORROW *sb.*] *intr.* To dawn. Also (*nonce-use*) in *passive*, to be endowed with mornings.

1839–52 BAILEY *Festus* 157 When earth was dayed—was morrowed—the first ray Perched on his pen, and diamonded its way. *Ibid.* 228, I have turned to thee, moon, from my heart,..And have hoped it might mix, as I watched thee depart, Like thyself, with the morn which had morrowed. **1884** J. PAYNE *Tales fr. Arabic* I. 70 When the morning morrowed..he summoned the chief of his viziers.

morrow-ȝyfe, var. MORYEVE, 'morning-gift'.

† **'morrowing**, *vbl. sb. Obs. rare.* [f. MORROW *sb.* + -ING[1]: cf. *morning*; in sense 2 implying a vb. **morrow* to procrastinate.]

1. Morning; dawning.

c **1374** CHAUCER *Compl. Mars* (Tanner MS.) 26 Yit will I ..synge The sentence of the compleynt.. That wofull mars made at the departynge Fro fressh venus in a morowynge [*Trin. MS.* morownyng]. *c* **1385** —— *L.G.W.* 1483 The morwynge [*Trin. MS.* morowyng; *Selden MS.* morowenyng] attempre was & fayr. **1508** DUNBAR *Gold. Targe* 247 Suete war the vapouris, soft the morowing.

2. A postponing till 'the morrow'.

1602 BRETON *Mother's Blessing* lxvi. D 3 b, If he importune thee with borrowing,.. Or daily put thee off with morrowing, Till want do make thee wearie of thy lending.

morrowing gift, var. MORWYNGIFT *Obs. Sc.*

morrowless ('mɒrəʊlɪs), *a. rare.* [f. MORROW *sb.* + -LESS.] Not subject to time; without end.

1871 W. D. HOWELLS *Suburban Sk.* 163 Sometimes this choice company sits on the curbing that goes around the terrace..and then I envy every soul in it, so tranquil it seems, so cool, so careless, so morrowless. **1954** J. R. R. TOLKIEN *Fellowship of Ring* xi. 205 Through halls of iron and darkling door, And woods of nightshade morrowless.

† **'morrow-mass.** *Obs.* The first mass of the day.

c **1440** *Jacob's Well* 116 ȝe, þat heryn noȝt full dyvyn seruyse in ȝoure parysch-cherche, but a morwemasse. **1484** *Rec. St. Mary at Hill* (1905) 116 Payd to syr Iohn plommer for hys labur to syng the morowmas. **1584** R. SCOT *Discov. Witchcr.* v. iii. (1886) 76 He heard a little saccaring bell ring to the elevation of a morrowe masse. **1601** F. GODWIN *Bps. of Eng.* 304 He built..a little Chappell for morrow masse. **1849** ROCK *Ch. of Fathers* IV. 8 After Terce, the first mass of the day, or the 'morrow mass' was sung.

b. *attrib.*, as ***morrow-mass altar, monger, priest.***

1494 FABYAN *Chron.* VII. 617 The morowe masse preest of Bowe Churche in Chepe was moste commendyd. **1512** in *Jacob's Hist. Faversham* (1774) 164 At the Morrow Masse Awter. **1556** *Rec. St. Mary at Hill* (1905) 401 Payed to sir William Rychard, morrowmas prest, for halfe a yeare ended at midsomer 1556. *a* **1603** T. CARTWRIGHT *Confut. Rhem. N. T.* (1618) 703 A Popish Sheppard, or Morrow-Masse-Priest. **1624** BP. MOUNTAGU *Gagg* 57 Let you morrow Massmungers when they masse it alone, use Iaponian, or Mexico Language. **1635** PAGITT *Christianogr.* 216 Monks, Nuns, and morrow Masse Priests.

morrow-speech: see MORN-SPEECH.

† **'morrow-tide.** *Obs.* Also 5 mortyde. [Cf. MORN-TIDE.] = MORNINGTIDE.

c **1290** *Beket* 49 in *S. Eng. Leg.* 108 In þe morewe-tide heo weren i-souȝt. *c* **1380** *Sir Ferumb.* 2895 Erly on þe morwe-tyde after þat þay were there, þe Amyral wolde no leng abyde bot þe Galwys let arere. *c* **1386** CHAUCER *Merch. T.* 981 And so bifel, that brighte morwe-tyde, That [etc.]. *c* **1420** *Chron. Vilod.* 1441 In þe mortyde þo, whenne hit was day. **1481** CAXTON *Reynard* (Arb.) 37 It happed so that on a morowtyde erly that grymbert my neuew was of wyne almost dronke. **1504** ATKYNSON tr. *De Imitatione* I. xx. 169 A mery euentyde foloweth a sory morow tyde. **1520** *Myrr. our Ladye* 13 In some chirches they say mattyns in the morow tyde.

morryeve, var. MORYEVE, 'morning-gift'.

Morryoune, obs. form of MORIAN.

† **mors**, *v. Obs.* [aphetic a. F. *amorcer* to prime (a gun), to prepare for an operation.]

1. *trans.* To grease (firearms).

1533 *Acc. Ld. Treas. Scotl.* (1905) VI. 160 For walx and talloune to mors the hagbutis.

2. To prime (a gun). Implied in MORSING *vbl. sb.*

mors, morsall, obs. ff. MORSE *sb.*[2], MORSEL.

† **'morsare.** *Obs.* [aphetic a. F. *amorçoir*, f. *amorcer*: see MORS *v.*] A priming-flask for a cannon.

1540 *Ld. Treas. Acc.* in Pitcairn *Crim. Trials* I. 304* Ane morsare to þe Kingis grace Culvering, quhilk wes of siluer.

morsbunker: see MOSSBUNKER.

morscel, obs. form of MORSEL.

morse (mɔːs), *sb.*[1] Also 5 mors. [a. OF. *mors* (Godef. 1380), ad. L. *mors-us* bite, catch (of a buckle), f. *mordēre* to bite.] The clasp or fastening of a cope, frequently made of gold or silver, and set with precious stones.

1404 *Durh. Acc. Rolls* (Surtees) 394 Item j mors cum lapidibus. **1489** *Will of Atwode* (Somerset Ho.), A mortuary cloth of blac velvett the orfraies & mors wᵗ flowres. **1489–90** *Rec. St. Mary at Hill* (1905) 150 Item, for Cere clothe to the orpharas, the hode & the moose [? *read* morse] of the saide coope. **1536** in *Antiq. Sarisb.* (1771) 197 Six copes..having in the Morse red and white Roses of pearls. *c* **1540** *Invent.* in *Trans. Lond. & Mdsx. Archæol. Soc.* IV. 329, iij copes of white bawdekyn with ffewres of gold and dases..and thys letter I in the morses. *Ibid.* 349, xxvij newe morsys for copys. **1826** MRS. BRAY *De Foix* ii. (1884) 15 His tunic was fastened in front by a morse, or brooch, richly enamelled,.. and representing the Virgin Mary.

morse (mɔːs), *sb.*[2] Forms: 5–8 mors, 6 morsse, 7 morss, moss, 8 morsh, 6– morse. [a. Lapp. *morsa*, *morssa*, or the equivalent Finnish *mursu*. Cf. F. *morse* (first in *morce marin* = Caxton's *mors marine*), Russian *morzh*.]

1. The sea-horse or walrus, *Trichechus rosmarus.*

1482 CAXTON *Chron. Eng.* cclvii. 336 This yere were take iiij grete fisshes bytwene Eerethe and london, that one was callyd mors marine [etc.]. *c* **1553** CHANCELOUR in *Hakluyt's Voy.* (1599) I. 237 There are also a fishes teeth, which fish is called a Morsse. *c* **1614** *Voy.* [*to Spitzbergen*] in *Archæologia Amer.* (1860) IV. 313 Theise morses use to goe ashoare vpon some beach or pointe of lowe land. **1710** WHITWORTH *Acc. Russia* (1758) 83 Morses, or sea-horses, from Nova Zembla, used to load thirty boats a year with blubber. **1855** W. S. DALLAS in *Syst. Nat. Hist.* II. 471 The Walrus, Morse, or Sea-Horse,..is an inhabitant of the Arctic portions of both Hemispheres.

† **2.** Erroneously applied to the hippopotamus.

1775 ASH, *Morse*, the hippopotamus, the river horse. **1891** *Syd. Soc. Lex.*, *Morse teeth*, a name given to the teeth of the hippopotamus used for making artificial teeth.

3. *attrib.*, as ***morse-hide, -ivory, -teeth.***

1681 GREW *Musæum* I. § v. i. 89 A piece of a *Morse-Hide. **1877** W. JONES *Finger-ring* 89 A *morse ivory thumb-ring of an Earl of Shrewsbury. **1618** T. BARKER in *St. Papers Col., E. Indies* 1617–21 (1870) 159 Tin, brass, *morse teeth, Muscovy hides.

Morse (mɔːs), *sb.*[3] *Telegraphy.* The name of the American electrician S. F. B. *Morse* (1791–1872), the inventor of the recording telegraph, and of the alphabet (in which the letters are expressed by combinations of dots and dashes) used for sending messages by this instrument. Used *attrib.* in designations of these inventions and things pertaining to them; also *ellipt.* as *sb.* = 'Morse telegraph'.

[**1847** 'PETER PROGRESS' *Electr. Telegr.* 63 Morse's Telegraph. This variety of the Electric Telegraph is employed on all the American lines.] **1858** in G. B. Prescott *Hist. Electr. Telegraph* (1860) xiv. 191 We work with Morse key and detector. **1860** PRESCOTT *Electr. Telegr.* III. v. 73 Electric telegraph apparatus. The Morse system. **1867** SABINE *Electr. Telegr.* 84 Simple Morse Circuit.—In its simplest form the Morse telegraph consists of a transmitting key [etc.]. *Ibid.* 86 Embossing Instrument with movable Magnet. This is a construction of the Morse by Messrs. Siemens and Halske. *Ibid.* 87 The Morse Code. *Ibid.* 90 The Morse alphabet. *Ibid.* 149 The Morse recorder. **1876** PREECE & SIVEWRIGHT *Telegraphy* 105 In England we never do use the Morse on such circuits... It is an exceedingly rare thing to fix more than four stations on one Morse circuit. **1889** PREECE & MAIER *Telephone* 110 Ordinary Morse signals. **1898** R. KERR *Wireless Telegr.* 93 The Morse inker. *Ibid.* 97 A small Morse key. **1916** [see DASH *sb.*[1] 7 f]. **1931** F. L. ALLEN *Only Yesterday* 13 A mechanically inclined boy has a wireless set, with which, if he knows the Morse code, he may listen to messages from ships at sea. **1972** V. PITT *First Look At Signals* 38 The most famous distress signal is S.O.S... It may be tapped out in Morse Code.

Hence **Morse** *v. intr.* and *trans.*, to signal by means of the Morse alphabet.

1906 KIPLING in *Windsor Mag.* Jan. 232/2 Ah! now she's Morsing against the fog. **1920** *Punch* 31 Mar. 245/1 It can be used for Morsing instructions about breakfast to the cook. **1944** *Jrnl. R. Aeronaut. Soc.* XLVIII. 534 Sudden load changes of 18 kw. (29 h.p. at 85 per cent. efficiency) could be thrown on and off the engine by violently 'morsing' the switch on the load panel without upsetting stability.

Morse (mɔːs), *sb.*[4] *Engin.* [prob. f. the name of the *Morse* Twist Drill Co., now Morse Cutting Tools, of New Bedford, Mass., U.S.A.] ***Morse taper***: a taper on a shank or socket that is one of a standard series having specified dimensions and angles; also *ellipt.*

The word *Morse* is a registered proprietary term in the U.S.

1894 *Machinery* (N.Y.) Nov. p. ii (Advt.), The Standard Tool Company, Cleveland, Ohio. Manufacturers of..Taps, Milling Cutters, Morse Taper Reamers. **1896** R. GRIMSHAW *Shop Kinks* 96 'Morse' and 'American' Tapers. There are still shops which have twist-drills and sockets of the old 'American' taper, and sometimes it is bothersome to work them in with the 'Morse' , as the American is 9–16 inch to the foot, and the Morse is ⅝ inch. **1906** *Official Gaz.* (U.S. Patent Office) 28 Aug. 2956/2 Morse Twist Drill & Machine Company, New Bedford, Mass. Filed May 29, 1905. Used ten years. *Morse* [for] Drills, Reamers, Taps,..and Milling Cutters. **1930** *Engineering* 25 Apr. 539/2 The centres, both of the workhead and tailstock..are 2½ in. in diameter. They have shanks with a No. 6 Morse taper. **1964** S. CRAWFORD *Basic Engin. Processes* v. 114 The barrel is hollow, at one end a morse-taper bore locates the dead centre, and also provides the location for drill and reamer shanks. **1971** B. SCHARF *Engin. & its Lang.* x. 87 Morse tapers which are numbered from 0 to 7 make it possible to interchange drills, sockets, etc. as required.

morsebonker: see MOSSBUNKER.

morseed, obs. variant of MAWSEED.

1724 *Weekly Jrnl.* No. 276 Very fine singing Nightingales, with a fine Parcel of Morseed, to be sold.

morsel ('mɔːsəl), *sb.* Forms: 3 mossel, 4–5 mussel(e, mossele, 5 mussell(e, mossell(e; 4 morsele, morcele, 4–6 morselle, 4–7 morsell, 4–8 morcel, 5 morssel, murssell, morsylle, 5–7 morcell, 6 morssell, *Sc.* morsall, 3– morsel. [a. OF. *morsel* (mod.F. *morceau*: see MORCEAU) = It. *morsello*, med.L. *morsellum*, dim. of F. *mors*, It. *morso* a bite:—L. *morsum*, neut. pa. pple. of *mordēre* to bite.]

1. A bite; a mouthful; a small piece of food.

Now apprehended as a contextual use of sense 2.

1297 R. GLOUC. (Rolls) 7028 þe mossel he dude in to is mouþ..Hit bileuede amidde is þ rote. *a* **1300** *Cursor M.* 13485 Qua had o penis thre hundreth Bred for to bi, þai ar sua fele, War til ilkan bot a morsel. *c* **1375** BARBOUR *Bruce* IX. 398 Our lordis of France, that ay With gud morsellis farsis thair panch. **1382** WYCLIF *Ps.* cxlvii. 17 He sendeth his cristal as musselis [*v.r.* morselis]. *c* **1450** *M.E. Med. Bk.* (Heinrich) 219 Ete þat at fyve mosseles, & þenne drynk a gret drawȝt of good wyn. **1486** *Bk. St. Albans* a v, Take .iij. cornes of whete and put hem in a morcell of flesh and yeue thessame morcellis to the hawke. **1565** T. STAPLETON *Fortr. Faith* 30 This apple is all rotten, and yet there are some sound morsells in him. **1663** H. COGAN tr. *Pinto's Trav.* lviii. 230 She eat of the Fruit, and made her Husband likewise to eat of it, whence it ensued that they were both of them by that unhappy Morsel subjected to the pains of Death. **1665** SIR T. HERBERT *Trav.* (1677) 334 They..wrap it in a leaf of Betele..and chew it in morsels. **1758** JOHNSON *Idler* No. 19 §8 The first morsel is in his mouth. **1828** SCOTT *F.M. Perth* vi, He took a cake in his hand, broke it, and was about to eat a morsel, when the effort to swallow seemed almost too much for him. **1860** TYNDALL *Glac.* I. xxvii. 202 At the spring..the men paused to have a morsel of bread.

b. with omission of *of.*

1297 R. GLOUC. (Rolls) 7025, & al so late þis mossel bred þoru mi þrote wende. *c* **1450** *Merlin* i. 6 Yef we hadde but a mossell brede, we haue more ioye..than ye haue with alle the delicatys of the worlde. **1528** PAYNELL *Salerne's Regim.* Q j b, They eate a morsell breadde.

c. A choice dish; a 'tit-bit'.

c **1440** LYDG. *Horse, Goose & Sheep* 207 A fatt goos..a morsel [*v.r.* mussell] agreable. *a* **1450** *Knt. de la Tour* 22, I wolle telle you an ensaumple of a woman that ete the good morsell in the absence of her husbonde. *Ibid.*, No woman shulde ete no lycorous morcelles in the absens..of her husbond. **1848** W. H. BARTLETT *Egypt to Pal.* x. (1879) 225 The Sheikh brought me, as choice morsels, two or three clusters of large sorrel, which tasted very refreshing.

d. A small meal; a 'snack'.

† *to bring (a person) to a morsel*: ? to bring to poverty. **1470–85** MALORY *Arth.* XVI. viii. 675 She prayd hym to take a lytyl morsel to dyne. **1655** TERRY *Voy. E. India* 8 The Shark..will make a morsell of any thing he can catch, master, and devour. *a* **1734** NORTH *Life Ld. Kpr. Guilford* (1742) 291 But his Vices, in the Way of Women and the Bottle, were so ungoverned, as brought him to a Morsel. **1765** BICKERSTAFFE *Maid of Mill* I. iii. 8 Thou'lt come and eat a morsel of dinner with us. **1818** LADY MORGAN *Autobiog.* (1859) 154 We were eating our morsel at home. **1898** W. F. CLARK *N. Gleams* 56 (E.D.D.) Janey was gettin' ready some kind o' morsel.

e. *transf.* and *fig.*

c **1412** HOCCLEVE *De Reg. Princ.* 3434 Rauyssht of þe beaute of þis womman, This tendir yong morsel, þis doghter, I seye. **1471** CAXTON *Recuyell* (Sommer) 413 Whan the hisperyens sawe hym brought to that sorowe as for to taste the bitter morsell of deth, alle lefte their armes. **1500–20** DUNBAR *Poems* xxxii. 23 Scho wes an morsall of delyte. **1538** BALE *Thre Lawes* 713 He shall be at the last a morsell for the deuyll. **1597** SHAKS. *2 Hen. IV*, II. iv. 396 Now comes in the sweetest Morsell of the night, and wee must hence, and leaue it vnpickt. **1625** BURGES *Pers. Tithes* 33 Tithes which is a sweet morsell that they are loath to part with. **1649** MILTON *Eikon.* ix. 81 That revenge was no unpleasing morsel to him. *a* **1676** GUTHRIE *Mem.* (1702) 91 The Rent of the Chapel Royal (esteem'd formerly a Morsel sufficient for a Bishop). **1742** YOUNG *Nt. Th.* IX. 2044 Few years, the sport Of fortune; then, the morsel of despair. **1775** HARRIS *Philos. Arrangem.* Wks. (1841) 382 Many choice morsels, both from Greek and Roman writers. **1848** L. HUNT *Jar of Honey* Pref. 2 With this sauce a man might swallow some of the bitterest morsels of life. **1874** DEUTSCH *Rem.* 74 Scores of other tough morsels in the Koran.

f. *jocularly* applied to a person.

1610 SHAKS. *Temp.* II. i. 286 You doing thus, To the perpetuall winke for aye might put This ancient morsell: this Sir Prudence. **1838** MRS. CARLYLE *New Lett.* (1903) I. 69 Beware..how you encourage that little morsel of yours to follow the trade of being a Genius.

2. A small piece (of anything), esp. a portion cut or broken from a mass; a little piece; a fragment. Also *Comb.* † **morsel-meal** *adv.*, piecemeal.

c **1290** *St. Kath.* 247 in *S. Eng. Leg.* 99 Hire tetes heo to-drowe Fram hire bodi mossel mele. *a* **1400–50** *Alexander* 1268 Maistris & mynistris menere & grettir, þat was in morsels magged. *c* **1430** *Two Cookery-bks.* I. 30 Take Applys, & pare hem, an smal screde hem in mossellys. **1597** HOOKER *Eccl. Pol.* v. lxxix. 5 He simply deliuered vp a large morsell whereby the value of that which remained was betrayed. **1662** EVELYN *Chalcogr.* 92 A morcel of St. Peters by it self. **1693** TATE *Juvenal* XVI. (1697) 374 An Ombite Wretch..is Pris'ner made: Whose Flesh torn off by Lumps, the rav'nous Foe In Morsels cut, to make it farther go. **1800** tr. *Lagrange's Chem.* I. 349 When dry, it appears in white morsels, which may be reduced by the fingers into an exceedingly fine powder. **1839** URE *Dict. Arts* 815 The small morsels of quicksilver ore. **1860** MOTLEY *Netherl.* (1868) I. i. 8 A morsel of territory.

fig. **1860** A. TROLLOPE *Castle Richm.* I. vi. 106 I'm blessed if I've a morsel of feeling in my toes. **1873** BURTON *Hist. Scot.* VI. lxxiv. 391 No morsel of the system could now be counted an open question.

morsel ('mɔːsəl), *v.* [f. MORSEL *sb.* Cf. F. *morceler*.]

1. *trans.* To divide into 'morsels' or small pieces.

1598 FLORIO, *Morsecchiare*, to morsell, to bite. **1621** MOLLE *Camerar. Liv. Libr.* IV. xvii. 301 Chopping into peeces, morselling and deuouring their prisoners.

2. With *out*: To distribute (property, etc.) in small parcels or quantities.

1855 MRS. GORE *Mammon* I. 7 Their estates have been morselled out; while ours remain intact. **1859** MASSON *Brit. Novelists* i. 50 The total mass.. was shaped, adjusted, and again morselled out in parts by subsequent minstrels.

Hence **'morselled** *ppl. a.*; **'morselling** *vbl. sb.*

1799 BEDDOES *Contrib. Phys. & Med. Knowl.* 536 advt., The practice..of tantalizing readers by morselled information. **1844** M. HENNELL *Soc. Syst.* 188 Civilization and all historic periods known, have their narrow foundation on family management, or morselling. **1861** LYTTON & FANE *Tannhäuser* 95 The split and morselled crags.

morselize ('mɔːsəlaɪz), *v. rare.* [f. MORSEL *sb.* + -IZE.] *trans.* To break up into small pieces. Hence **morseli'zation**, the act of dividing into small pieces.

1886 A. G. WARNER tr. Le Play in *Pop. Sci. Monthly* Oct. 793 The chaotic..condition of the foremost nations of Europe resulted..from the 'infinite morselization'..of interests. **1893** *19th Cent.* Feb. 214 The plan..has been called in America the 'morcelization of government'. **1894** G. S. HALL in *Forum* Apr. 158 We have morselized the old curriculum.

morsh, obs. form of MORSE *sb.*[2]

morsicant ('mɔːsɪkənt), *a.* [ad. L. *morsicant-em*, pres. pple. of *morsicāre* to bite continually, f. *mors-, mordēre* to bite.] (See quot.)

1891 *Syd. Soc. Lex.*, *Morsicant*, producing a sensation as of repeated biting or pricking.

'morsing, *vbl. sb. Sc. Obs.* exc. *Hist.* Also *corruptly* 7 **mosine**; (in Comb.) 8–9 **motion-**, 9 **moshin-**. [f. MORS *v.* + -ING[1].] The action of priming (a gun). In quot. *concr.*, priming-powder, priming.

1629 Z. BOYD *Last Battell* I. 374 They..cry, Peace, peace, euen while God is putting the fierie lunt into the mosine of their sudden destruction.

b. *attrib.* as ***morsing-horn, -powder***; **morsing-hole**, touch-hole.

1552 *Reg. Privy Council Scot.* I. 131 Hagbutteris, furnischit with powldir flask, morsing hornis, and all uthair geir. **1568** *Satir. P. Reform.* xlvii. 54 Ȝe want 30[r] morsing powder. **1789** DAVIDSON *Seasons* 26 An', frae the flake..He whips the carabine.—The motion-hole Frae rust unspik'd.. Adown the bank he hastens. **1805** SCOTT *Last Minstr.* IV. xviii, Buff coats, all frounc'd and 'broidered o'er, And morsing-horns and scarfs they wore. **1824** MACTAGGART *Gallovid. Encycl.*, *Moshin-hole*, the touch-hole of a piece of ordnance; '*pike the moshin-hole*'..means, to clean out the touch-hole. **1828** MOIR *Mansie Wauch* xii, The piker for clearing the motion-hole. **1867** SMYTH *Sailor's Word-bk.* 485 *Morsing powder*, an old term for priming powder.

morsi'tation. *rare*[−0]. [n. of action f. late L. *morsitāre* (found only as v.r. for *morsicāre*: see MORSICANT), freq. of *mordēre* to bite.] (See quot.)

1819 SEAGER, *Morsitation*, the act of biting frequently and slightly; gnawing. Whence in later Dicts.

morspeche, obs. form of MORROW-SPEECH.

morss(e, obs. forms of MORSE *sb.*[2]

† **'morsure.** *Obs.* [a. F. *morsure* (Hatz.-Darm. 13th c.), ad. L. *morsūra*, f. *mors-, mordēre* to bite.] The action or an act of biting; a bite.

a **1400–50** *Alexander* 4088 Þan wald his pepill & his princes haue past ouir þe bourne, And miȝt noȝt for þe morsure & mayning of bestis. **1614** D. T. *Dove & Serp.* Ded., Whereby to free those which behold it from the morsures of such vipers. **1730** *Hist. Litt.* I. 31 He opened a Salamander's Mouth, and endeavoured to make it bite..a Chicken... At last he..succeeded in forcing it to make several morsures. **1819** H. BUSK *Tea* 183 Shall I..The morsure of their fang escape alone?

mort (mɔːt), *sb.*[1] Also 5–7 **morte**. [Partly a. F. *mort* (= Pr. *mort-z*, Sp. *muerte*, Pg., It. *morte*):—L. *mort-em*; partly a. F. *mort* (fem. *morte*), adj. (= Pr. *mort-z*, Sp. *muerto*, Pg., It. *morto*):—pop.L. **mort-um* for L. *mortuum* dead.]

† **1.** Death, slaughter. *Obs.*

c **1330** *Arth. & Merl.* 9066 (Kölbing), Þo stode Herui bi Bohort, Boþe in peril of mort. *a* **1400–50** *Alexander* 1279 (Dublin MS.), The morte of all þe masydons & of þe mony grekez. **1536** *Exhort. to North* in Furnivall *Ballads fr. MSS.* I. 306 Noitt dowtyng off them to maike gret morte. **1560** ROLLAND *Crt. Venus* I. 834 Ouirset with slicht sulphurious, And suddant mort.

2. *Hunting.* **a.** The note sounded on a horn at the death of the deer. Chiefly in ***to blow a mort***.

App. an alteration of the earlier MOTE *sb.*[3] perh. by association with Fr. phr. *à mort*.

Various edd. of the ballad of *Chevy Chase* l. 31, read *mort*, but MS. Ashm. 48 has *mot* (= MOTE *sb.*[3]).

? *a* **1500** in Blount *Anc. Tenures* (1679) 170 As soone as the Bukks head is offered uppe all the kepers shall blowe a Morte three tymes. **1589** R. ROBINSON *Gold. Mirr.* (1851) 14 Presently, the Mort the Hunts-man blew. *a* **1592** GREENE *Card of Fancie* (1593) H, He that bloweth the Mort before the fall of the Buck, may verie well misse of his fees. **1611** SHAKS. *Wint. T.* I. ii. 118 And then to sigh, as 'twere The Mort o' th' Deere. **1677** N. COX *Gentl. Recreat.* I. 80 Then, having blown the Mort, and all the company come in [etc.]. **1741** *Compl. Fam.-Piece* II. i. 292 Then sound the Mort or Morts. **1821** SCOTT *Kenilw.* xxxiii, The horns again poured on her ear the melancholy yet wild strain of the mort, or death-note. **1845** BROWNING *Flight of the Duchess* xi, When horns wind a mort and the deer is at siege.

b. A dead stag. ? *nonce-use*.

1827 HOOD *Mids. Fairies* cx, 'Tis these befriend the timid, trembling stag,..And prompt fresh shifts in his alarum'd ears, So piteously they view all bloody morts.

c. The death, the kill. *arch.*

1855 KINGSLEY *Westw. Ho!* iv, You will..be enabled yourselves to see the mort more pleasantly.

3. The skin of a sheep or lamb that has died a natural death. Also ***mort skin***. *dial.*

1592 GREENE *Upst. Courtier* F 3, The Sadler..makes the lether of them of morts, or tand sheeps skinnes. **1611–12** *Rutland MSS.* (1905) IV. 486 Sheepeskinnes slaughtered hath bin sold by great, for xxiiijs. the dozen, good and bad, mortes and all included. **1624** in *Naworth Househ. Bks.* 212 Received of my Lady for mort skins, iij[li] vj[s] viij[d]. **1752** *Rec. Elgin* (New Spald. Club 1903) I. 464 Ilk dozen of mort lamb skins 2*d.* **1798** R. DOUGLAS *Agric. Surv. Roxb. & Selkirk* 259 *note*, Morts are the skins of sheep and lambs who die. **1816** SCOTT *Bl. Dwarf* i, He'll be unco busy amang the morts this season.

4. ? A dead body, corpse. ? *Obs.*

1658 FRANCK *North. Mem.* (1694) 7 Every Generation since Adam, has so diminished that Beauty and Lustre, that from Men we are almost dwindled into Morts. *a* **1839** GALT *Demon Destiny* 14 The gathering myriads of the famous great—All skeletons, like morts, derisive grin. **1888** H. JAMES *Let.* 31 July (1920) I. 138 You have become a beautiful myth—a kind of unnatural uncomfortable unburied *mort*.

5. *Comb.*: †**mort bell** *Sc.*, a funeral bell; †**mort cape** *Sc.*, a funeral cope; **mort head** *dial.*, a death's head; †**mort mumblings** *Sc.*, mumbled prayers for the dead; **mort note** (quasi-*arch.*) = sense 2; **mort safe** *Sc.*, an iron frame placed over a coffin or at the entrance to a grave as a protection against resurrectionists in Scotland; **mort-skin** *Sc.* and *dial.* (see sense 3); **mort stand** *Sc.*, app. a bier or catafalque; †**mort stone**, a stone on which the bearers of a dead body rested the coffin.

1590 *Burgh Rec. Glasgow* (1876) I. 153 Thair twa commoun bellis, viz. the *mort and skellet bellis. **1612** *Ibid.* 326 The provest, bailleis and counsale, haifing continwit Thomas Kilmawris in the office of the mort bell to this day. **1824** GALT *Rothelan* III. VI. i. 13 From the hour that the mort-bell was again heard in the land, men relapsed into their wonted customs. **1554–5** *Burgh Rec. Edin.* (1871) II. 359 To mak twa *mortcaippis. *Ibid.*, Item, for half ane quarter quhit sating to be the *mort heids, iiij[r]. **1691** R. KIRK *Secret Commonwealth* i. §7 'Tis as the constrained grinning of a Mort-head. **1722** NISBET *Syst. Her.* 267 Crest, a Mort-head, with two Leg-Bones, Saltier-ways proper. *c* **1560** A. SCOTT *Poems* (S.T.S.) i. 92 Mantand *mort mvmblingis mixt w[t] monye leis. **1830** MRS. BRAY *Fitz of Fitz-ford* xvi. (1884) 134 The woods rang with the clamour of blowing the stag to bay, or the triumph of the *mort-note. **1821** A. THOMSON *Jrnl.* 1 Mar. in *Life & Ministry* (1869) iii. 285 The *mort-safe was for the first time put into his grave. **1888** *North. N. & Q.* III. 51 The coffin is then lowered, the cage-like mortsafe put over it, and the hinged rods, the tops of which interlace, bent over and padlocked... The grave is then filled up. **1896** J. B. BAILEY *Diary Resurrectionist* 76 Mort-safes, or strong iron guards, were placed over newly-made graves for protection. **1503** *Acc. Ld. Treas. Scotl.* (1900) II. 290 The *mortstand, with tua tunycales with offrez of fine gold, ane gret caip of the mortstand with sternys of gold on it and offrez of gold. **1561** *Extracts Aberd. Reg.* (1844) I. 330 Ane croce of siluer, the forclayth of the hie altar,..ane erress bed, ane siluer spune, the mort stand [etc.]. **1842** SIR H. TAYLOR *Edwin* v. vii. 227 Oh me! the *mortstone!

† **mort**, *sb.*[2] *Obs.* Also 6 **mortes** (?). [Form and origin uncertain; but cf. MORTAR *sb.*[1] 2.] A kind of wax candle (? or a set of wax candles).

1394 in Gough *Sepulchral Mon.* (1786) I. 170* Fynolx, morts, brennynges, croppes, tapres quarrez. *c* **1530** LD. BERNERS *Arth. Lyt. Bryt.* (1814) 56 The foure mortees of waxe [orig. *quatre cierges ardans*] y[t] stode brennynge before her beddes fete. **1546** in Blomefield *Topogr. Hist. Norfolk* (1806) III. 216 An herse with 120 lyghts and dyverse floryshes, hangyngs and a mortes of wax.

mort (mɔːt), *sb.*[3] Also 6 **morte**. [Origin unknown.] A name for the salmon in its third year.

1530 PALSGR. 246/2 Morte a fysshe. **1584** COGAN *Haven Health* clxxxii. 145 The mort is of like nature, for it is the young Salmon. *a* **1672** WILLUGHBY *Hist. Pisc.* IV. iv. 189 Nostratibus in fluvio Ribble agri Eboracensis Salmones primo ætatis anno Smelts dicuntur; secundo Sprods; tertio Morts. **1753** CHAMBERS *Cycl. Supp.* s.v. *Salmon*. **1861** [see PEAL *sb.*[2]]. **1872** *Dairy News* 13 Aug., Nine fish were killed.. namely, one mort, one smelt, three brandlings, and four river trout. **1904** *Peterite* XIX. 147 Sea-trout, or 'mort' as they are locally termed.

mort (mɔːt), *sb.*[4] *Cant.* Also 6 **morte**, 8–9 **mot**, 9 **mott**. [Origin unknown.] **a.** A girl or woman. Often with qualifying word, as *autem, gentry,* KINCHIN-, *strolling, walking mort* (q.v.).

1561–75 AWDELAY *Frat. Vacab.* (1869) 5 A Kitchin Mortes [*sic*] is a Gyrle. **1592** CHETTLE *Kind-harts Dr.* (1841) 57 It happened, within these few yeeres, about Hampshire there wandered a walking mort, that went about the countrey selling of tape. **1611** MIDDLETON & DEKKER *Roaring Girl* K 4 b, Ben mort (good wench) shal you and I heaue a booth? **1621** B. JONSON *Gypsies Met.* (1640) 65 Male Gipsies all, not a Mort among them. *a* **1700** B. E. *Dict. Cant. Crew*, *Morts*, Yeomen's Daughters; also a Wife, Woman, or Wench. **1837** *Gambler's Dream* III. 225 Every cove and every mot Brings in some swag to boil the pot. **1851** MAYHEW *Lond. Labour* I. 217 After some altercation with the 'mot' of the 'ken' (mistress of the lodging-house). **1922** JOYCE *Ulysses* 247 He saw the image of Marie Kendall, charming soubrette... One of them mots that do be in the packets of fags. **1969** J. BLACKBURN *Bury him Darkly* 10 'Look at them two mots, Fergus.' Dan pointed at two mini-skirted girls.

b. A harlot, a loose woman.

1567 HARMAN *Caveat* (1869) 32 Their harlots, which they terme Mortes and Doxes. **1601** A. MUNDAY *Downf. Rbt. Earl Huntington* III. ii. F 2 b, If I can get the girle to goe with mee, Disguis'd in habit, like a Pedlers mort. **1622** FLETCHER *Beggar's Bush* II. i, Each man shall..enjoy His owne deare Dell, Doxy, or Mort, at night. **1708** *Motteux's Rabelais Pantagr. Prognost.* v, Those whom Venus is said to rule, as..Morts, Doxies. **1773** in Partridge *Dict. Underworld* (1949) 451/1 The first time I saw the flaming mot, Was at the sign of the Porter Pot. *a* **1790** H. J. POTTER *New Dict. Cant & Flash* (1795) 42 *Morts*, or *motts*, lewd women, whores, shop-lifters, &c. **1796** F. GROSE *Olio* 228 Our regiment has not so fine a blowen; Nor all the seven battalions such a mot. **1812** J. H. VAUX *Flash Dict.*, *Mott*, a blowen, or woman of the town. **1821** P. EGAN *Real Life in London* I. xii. 223 The Hon. Tom Dashall..was in close conversation with his *mott*. **1846** *Swell's Night Guide* 60, I don't think as how he ever doss'd with a mott or could fake a shiver if he had it for nix. **1866** E. SELLON *Let.* 4 Mar. in 'Pisanus Fraxi' *Index Librorum Prohibitorum* (1877) 394, I! who had expected some swell mot or other, soon found myself seated beside the most beautiful young lady I ever beheld.

mort (mɔːt), *sb.*[5] Also **mord**. [? Celtic Cornish; cf. Welsh *mêr* marrow.] Lard; pig's grease.

1610 MARKHAM *Masterp.* II. cxiii. 408 You shall adde therto of hogges mort, and fresh butter, of each a pound. **1839** MRS. PALMER *Dial. Dev. Dial.* I. 15 Their high-peak'd loady heads, wi' a wallage o' hair, plaster'd with mort and flour. **1864** QUILLER-COUCH *E. Cornw. Wds.* in *Jrnl. R. Inst. Cornw.* Mar., *Mord*, lard, pig's grease. **1865** T. GARLAND *W. Cornw. Wds.* ibid. Apr., *Mort*, unmelted lard. **1886** *West Somerset Gloss.* s.v., Nif any-body-v a got a bad leg or ort, there idn no fineder thing vor-t-n mort-n chalk.

mort (mɔːt), *sb.*[6] *dial.* [Origin obscure.

The suggestion that it is derived from ON. *mart*, neut. of *margr* great, as in *mart manna* a great number of people, is not supported by the form, chronology, or locality of the Eng. word. It is possibly a dial. corruption of *mortal* used as an intensive (e.g. with such a sb. as *deal*). The existence of the north. dial. MURTH (ON. *mergð*) in the same sense may have assisted its development.]

A great quantity or number; a great deal. Usually const. *of*; rarely *absol.* Also *pl.* (cf. *quantities*).

1694 ECHARD *Plautus* 94 They had a mort o' Prisoners. **1708** *Brit. Apollo* No. 44. 3/2 You having zuch a Mort of Wit. **1775** SHERIDAN *Rivals* I. i, Here's a mort o' merry-making, hey? **1821** CLARE *Vill. Minstr.* I. 123 She talk'd of morts of luck. **1850** DICKENS *Dav. Copp.* xxxii, 'We have had a mort of talk, sir', said Mr. Peggotty to me. **1868** HELPS *Realmah* ii, My Betsy..knew a mort more than I do. **1887** H. SMART *Cleverly won* i. 7 There's a mort of money to be made off the farm in a good year.

b. ***a mort*** used advb.

1887 HALL CAINE *A Son of Hagar* I. Prol., I'll not say but other folks look a mort madder nor ever I looked. **1904** WEYMAN *Abb. Vlaye* viii, You've fared better with me, ay, a *mort* better, than you'd have fared if the Captain had been here.

† **mort**, *a. Obs.* Also 5 **morte**. [a. F. *mort* (fem. *morte*): see MORT *sb.*[1]] Dead.

14.. *Sir Beues* 1696 (MS. E), He was so ffeynt in hys hurte, þer ffore he was al most al morte. *c* **1440** *Pol. Rel. & L. Poems* (E.E.T.S.) 189/127 Thy mede is markyd, when thow art mort, in blysse. *c* **1485** *Digby Myst.* (1882) III. 455 My mynd waxit mort. **1658** C. HOOLE *Sentences for Children* A 3, The many difficulties that attend the work (especially in a Mort language).

b. ***battle mort, mort battle***: war to the death. *Sc.*

1501 DOUGLAS *Pal. Hon.* III. xviii, Plesand pastance, and mony lustie sport, Thair saw we als, and sum time battell mort. **1535** STEWART *Cron. Scot.* II. 297 With mort battell agane King Edelfryde. **1560** ROLLAND *Crt. Venus* II. 272 Of Infidelis mony he did downe thring Be battell mort.

† **mort**, *v. Obs. rare*[−1]. [a. OF. *mortir*, f. *mort* (see MORT *sb.*[1]).] *trans.* To put to death.

c **1440** *York Myst.* xxvi. 77 *Pil.* Howe mene ȝe? *Cay.* Sir, to mort hym for mouyng of menne.

Mortaban: see MARTABAN.

mortadella (mɔːtə'dɛlə). Pl. **mortadelle**. Also **mortadel, mortadello**. [It. dim., irreg. f. L. *murtātum* (sausage) seasoned with myrtle berries.] A large spiced pork sausage; Bologna sausage.

1613 [see CERVELAT 1]. **1732** LD. ESSEX *Let.* 26 Aug. in R. B. Peake *Mem. Colman Family* (1841) I. ii. 30 If you would let your steward buy for me a good Parmesan cheese and some Mortadellos. **1846** R. FORD *Gatherings from Spain* xi. 129 The savoury piquant *embuchados*, which are akin to the *mortadelle* of Bologna, only less hard. **1921** D. H. LAWRENCE *Sea & Sardinia* iii. 118 There is mortadella, the enormous Bologna sausage, thick as a church pillar. **1934** F. SCOTT FITZGERALD *Tender is Night* I. xiii. 76 They ate sandwiches of *mortadel* sausage. **1950** E. HEMINGWAY *Across River & into Trees* xxii. 162 People at home think *mortadella* is a sausage. **1962** G. BUTLER *Coffin in Oxford* xi. 151 A plate of mortadella. **1972** M. HOWELLS *Pop. Ital. Cookery* 13 *Mortadella*. There are many varieties of this sausage, in different sizes and shapes. **1973** E. MCGIRR *Bardel's Murder* ii. 54 If you'd seen the knife he was using to cut up the mortadella sausage, guv'nor, you'd have gone peacefully away.

mortagon(e, obs. forms of MARTAGON.

a **1400** *Stockholm Med. MS.* ii. 367 in *Anglia* XVIII. 316 Mortulaca & mortagon Of swiche an erbe name is on. *c* **1440** *Promp. Parv.* 344/1 Mortagone, herbe, *herba Martis*.

mortaill, mortaise, obs. ff. MORTAL, MORTISE.

mortal (ˈmɔːtəl), *sb.* [f. MORTAL *a.*]

1. Mortal thing or substance (see quot.).

1526 TINDALE *1 Cor.* xv. 53 For this corruptible must putt on incorruptibilite, and this mortall [Gr. τὸ θνητὸν τοῦτο, Vulg. *mortale hoc*] must put on immortalite. **1611** *Ibid.*

2. One who is mortal; a human being in contrast with an immortal.

1567 *Gude & Godlie Ball.* (S.T.S.) 133 Lord I am heir ane wratcheit mortall. **1590** SHAKS. *Mids. N.* III. ii. 115 Lord, what fooles these mortals be! **1651** HOBBES *Leviath.* III. xxxiv. 213 Names..are usefull onely to the short memories of Mortalls. **1713** ADDISON *Cato* I. ii, 'Tis not in Mortals to command Success. **1882** W. S. GILBERT *Iolanthe* I. 4 By our laws, the fairy who marries a mortal, dies!

b. Often used playfully for 'person'. In negative contexts an emphatic equivalent for '(any) one', '(no) one'. Cf. MORTAL *a.* 8 b.

1718 PRIOR *'Her Eyebrow-Box'*, I can behold no Mortal now: For what's an Eye without a Brow? **1728** BERKELEY *Let.* Wks. 1871 IV. 149 Speak not, therefore, one syllable of it to any mortal whatsoever. **1846** W. E. FORSTER in Reid *Life* (1888) I. vi. 186 What a strange little mortal he [Lord J. Russell] is, to be ruler of a mighty nation! **1860** READE *Cloister & H.* lxxviii, She dared not trust such a treasure to mortal. **1864** A. McKAY *Hist. Kilmarnock* 164 Sandy and the other jolly mortals.

mortal (ˈmɔːtəl), *a.* Forms: 4–5 **mortail(e, -taill,** 4–7 **mortall,** 5 **mortalle,** 5–6 **mortale,** 4– **mortal;** *β.* 4–5 **mortel(e, -teil, -tiel,** 4–6 **mortell.** See also MORTUAL. [a. OF. *mortel, mortiel, mortal* (mod.F. *mortel*), or ad. L. *mortāl-is*, f. *mort-, mors* death.]

1. a. Subject to death, destined to die.

Often in the tautologically emphatic phrase ***mortal man***.

c **1374** CHAUCER *Troylus* III. 376 Al were my lyf eterne, As I am mortal. *c* **1391** —— *Astrol.* Prol. (1872) 1 Alle the conclusiouns..ben vn-knowe perfitly to any mortal man in this regioun. *c* **1450** *Godstow Reg.* 524 And the forsaid abbesse and Couente and ther successours shold warantiȝe and defende for euer the forsaid tenement,..to the forsaid Rector and scolers and to ther successours ayenst all mortall men. **1594** SHAKS. *Rich. III*, I. ii. 44–5 Are you all affraid? Alas, I blame you not, for you are Mortall, And Mortall eyes cannot endure the Diuell. **1613** PURCHAS *Pilgrimage* (1614) 355 No mortall man might ascend the Seat. **1667** SIR W. TEMPLE *Let. M. Gourville* Wks. 1731 II. 31 I begin to think that King and his Ministers are mortal like other People. **1697** DRYDEN *Virg. Georg.* IV. 643 What Madness cou'd provoke A Mortal Man t'invade a sleeping God? **1728** YOUNG *Love Fame* vi. 174 Old-age will come; disease may come before; Fifteen is full as mortal as three-score. **1820** SHELLEY *Prometh. Unb.* IV. 297 Whose population which the earth grew over Was mortal, but not human. **1836** C. FORSTER *Life Jebb* (1851) 325 His mortal remains were laid in St. Paul's Churchyard, Clapham. **1853** M. ARNOLD *Scholar-Gypsy* xv, For what wears out the life of mortal men?

†**b.** Doomed to immediate death. *Obs.*

1513 DOUGLAS *Æneis* X. xi. 45 Gif thow askis a resput or delay,..Of this evident deyd of Turnus ȝing,..Allthocht he mortale be rycht sone we knaw. *c* **1622** ROWLEY, etc. *Witch Edmonton* III. (1658) 34 Not yet mortal? I would not linger you, Or leave you a tongue to blab. ? **1624** CHAPMAN *Revenge for Honour* III. ii, Not pledg my peerlesse Mistresse health? Souldier, thou'rt mortall, if thou refuse it.

2. a. Causing death, deadly, fatal. Const. *to*. Now only of diseases, wounds, and blows.

† ***mortal nightshade*** = deadly nightshade: see DEADLY 4 c.

c **1385** CHAUCER *L.G.W.* 2252 The furies thre with al here mortal brond. *c* **1407** LYDG. *Reson & Sens.* 3418 This mortal beverage So noyous ys and so doutable. *c* **1489** CAXTON *Blanchardyn* xxxviii. 141 He..made in his body a grete wounde mortall. **1551** ROBINSON tr. *More's Utopia* II. viii. (1895) 262 At hande strokes they vse not swordes but pollaxes, whiche be mortall, aswel in sharpenes as in weyghte. **1578** LYTE *Dodoens* III. xxiii. 448 Mortall Nightshade. **1604** E. G[RIMSTONE] *D'Acosta's Hist. Indies* IV. x. 236 It is a dangerous thing to frequent so perillous and mortall a creature [quicksilver]. **1604** SHAKS. *Oth.* V. ii. 205, I am glad thy Father's dead, Thy Match was mortall to him. **1665–6** *Phil. Trans.* I. 161 It is mortal to eat of the Flesh of creatures killed by Vipers. **1667** MILTON *P.L.* I. 2. **1682** BUNYAN *Holy War* 284 Since the sickness had been so mortal in Mansoul. **1763** *Museum Rust.* I. lxxxiii. 369 To avoid the early frosts, which are mortal to them. **1805** JEFFERSON *Let.* 8 Feb. (1829) IV. 33 Strangers..find this fever as mortal as the genuine yellow fever. **1814** SCOTT *Ld. of Isles* III. xxix, The master'd felon press'd the ground, And gasp'd beneath a mortal wound.

b. *fig.* Destructive or fatal (*to* a thing).

1670 BAXTER *Cure Ch. Div.* Pref. 2, I know that these principles are as mortal to the Churches, as they are to Souls. **1769** BURKE *Late St. Nat.* Wks. 1842 I. 83, I will shew him a fact more that is mortal to his assertions. **1802** PALEY *Nat. Theol.* (1819) 324 Here therefore might seem to be a mortal defect in their constitution. **1832–4** DE QUINCEY *Cæsars* Wks. 1859 X. 100 Even the more innocent exhibitions, in which brutes only were the sufferers, could not but be mortal to all the finer sensibilities.

c. Of a season or region: Characterized by many deaths. (Cf. MORTALITY.) ? *Obs.*

1649 EVELYN *Diary* 30 Oct., This was a very sickly and mortal Autumne. **1741** *Lett. James Murray, Loyalist* (1901) 62 So sickly and mortal a place as So. Carolina. **1775** ABIGAIL ADAMS *Fam. Lett.* lix. (1876) 95 So sickly and so mortal a time the oldest man does not remember. **1803** MALTHUS *Popul.* II. ii. 207 The years 1757 and 1758 [in Sweden] were barren, and comparatively mortal years. *Ibid.* 209 Notwithstanding the mortal year of 1789, it appeared..that the general healthiness of the country had increased.

†**d.** ***mortal place***: the 'vital part'. *Obs. rare*⁻¹.

1670 MILTON *Hist. Gt. Brit.* II. 96 Last of all against himself he turns his Sword; but missing the mortal place, with his poinard finishes the work.

e. ***mortal mind***: according to Christian Scientists, the source in man of all delusion and error, creating the illusion of bodily sensations, pain, and illness.

1875 M. B. EDDY *Science & Health* vii. 341 Faith is all that ever made a drug remedy the ailments of a man. Mortal mind is belief, the immortal is understanding, the latter is Spirit, the former personal sense; we must learn to hold the immortal and mortal mind or belief separate. **1881** —— *Ibid.* (ed. 3) I. ii. 108 Mortal mind, and not muscles, nerves, bones, etc., determines the condition of its own body. *Ibid.* 114 Mortal mind is the remote cause of all suffering and sickness. **1903** 'MARK TWAIN' in *North Amer. Rev.* Apr. 508 In Christian Science terminology, 'claims' are errors of mortal mind, fictions of the imagination. **1910** *Encycl. Relig. & Ethics* III. 577/2 In Christian Science this lying material sense, or sense of evil, is termed 'mortal mind'. **1970** F. S. MEAD *Handbk. of Denominations in U.S.* (ed. 5) 71/1 Certain terms are important in the exposition of Christian Science. .. Mortal mind is 'the flesh opposed to Spirit'.

3. Aiming at the destruction of an adversary.

a. Of war, a battle, etc.: Fought to the death.

c **1386** CHAUCER *Prol.* 61 At mortal [*v.r.* mortel] batailles had he ben fiftene. **1393** LANGL. *P. Pl.* XVIII. 290 Among here enemys in morteils [*v.r.* mortel(e, mortail] bateles To be culled and ouercome. *c* **1420** LYDG. *Assembly of Gods* 732 For he was lyke to endure that day A gret mortall shoure.. With Vyce. *c* **1500** *Melusine* 144 There bygan a mortal medlee. *c* **1600** SHAKS. *Sonn.* xlvi. 1 Mine eye and heart are at a mortall warre How to deuide the conquest of thy sight. **1603** KNOLLES *Hist. Turks* (1621) 512 The undoubted flower..of his army, which were in that mortall battell almost all slaine. **1697** DRYDEN *Virg. Georg.* IV. 115 The shocking Squadrons meet in mortal Fight.

b. Of an enemy: That will be satisfied only with the death of the object of his hostility; relentless, implacable. Also *fig.*

c **1386** CHAUCER *Knt.'s T.* 732 For I am Palamon thy mortal [*v.r.* mortel] foo. **1390** GOWER *Conf.* I. 347 To grieve his mortiel enemy. *c* **1407** LYDG. *Reson & Sens.* 3134 But that they be..Mortal foon to chastite. **1456** SIR G. HAYE *Law Arms* (S.T.S.) 124 He suld..hald him..for his inymy mortall. **1579** G. HARVEY *Letter-bk.* (Camden) 60 The mortallest enemy I have in this world? **1646** SIR T. BROWNE *Pseud. Ep.* I. vi. 20 The mortallest enemy unto knowledge. **1742** YOUNG *Nt. Th.* v. 38 Pleasure and pride, by nature mortal foes. **1849** MACAULAY *Hist. Eng.* iv. I. 445 Halifax was the mortal enemy of despotism and of Popery.

c. Of enmity, hatred, and the like: Pursued to the death, unappeasable; 'deadly'. Hence *fig.* or *hyperbolically*, as ***a mortal aversion***.

14.. in *Tundale's Vis.* (1843) 107 Thou Herode of malice most mortall. **1585** T. WASHINGTON tr. *Nicholay's Voy.* III. i. 69 From childly & fatherly kindnes to mortal enmity. **1586** J. HOOKER *Hist. Irel.* 162/2 in *Holinshed*, Betwixt whome was a mortall hatred. **1665** SIR W. TEMPLE *Let. to Sir J. Temple* Wks. 1731 II. 4 He has a mortal Hatred to the Dutch for their supporting his City of Munster against him. **1714** ADDISON *Spect.* No. 562 ¶ 5 A Tribe of Egotists for whom I have always had a mortal Aversion. **1761** HUME *Hist. Eng.* I. xix. 459 This great and unusual act of authority in the council gave the Roman pontiffs ever after a mortal antipathy to those assemblies. **1849** MACAULAY *Hist. Eng.* vi. II. 117 The Popish Chancellor became an object of mortal hatred. **1885** O. W. HOLMES (*title*) A Mortal Antipathy.

4. Of pain, grief, fear, and the like: Such as might cause death; deadly in its effects. Often used hyperbolically and jocularly.

c **1368** CHAUCER *Compl. Pite* 61 Sheweth unto your rial excellence Your servaunt, if I durste me so calle, His mortal harm, in which he is y-falle. *c* **1402** LYDG. *Compl. Bl. Knt.* 214 To here this man,..His mortal wo, and his grete perturbaunce Compleyning. **1426** —— *De Guil. Pilgr.* 13679 Lyk a bryd..Wych, in hyr gret mortal ffer,..begynneth quake. **1509** HAWES *Past. Pleas.* xxx. (Percy Soc.) 148 He thinketh long after delyveracion Of his great wo and eke mortall paynes. **1603** KNOLLES *Hist. Turks* (1621) 477 By such meanes as he least feared might have procured any such mortall distrust or danger. **1693** DRYDEN *Ovid's Met.* I. *Daphne* 128 The nymph grew pale, and in a mortal fright. **1822** W. IRVING *Braceb. Hall* xviii. 158 Her finery at church on Sundays has given mortal offence to her former intimates in the village. **1849–50** ALISON *Hist. Europe* V. xxix. §51. 221 Reports of the failure of the enterprise were generally spread, and diffused the most mortal disquietude. **1864** MEREDITH *Sandra Belloni* xxv, Poor Braintop..sat in mortal fear lest his admiration of Emilia was perceived. **1879** M. ARNOLD *Mixed Ess., Falkland* 210 The marriage gave mortal offence to his father.

5. Of sin: Entailing spiritual death; = DEADLY 5. Opposed to *venial*.

1426 LYDG. *De Guil. Pilgr.* 12486 Dedly synne..The wych ycallyd ys 'mortal' Be-cause hys hurtys ffynally Ben in effect verray dedly. *c* **1485** *Digby Myst.* (1882) II. 510 Ther be vij mortall synnes. ? **1566** (*title*) Whether it be mortall sinne to transgresse ciuil lawes which be the commaundements of ciuill Magistrates. *a* **1602** W. PERKINS *Cases Consc.* I. ii. (1609) 10 Now though euery sinne of it selfe be mortall, yet all are not equally mortall: but some more, some lesse. **1667** MILTON *P.L.* III. 215 Mans mortal crime. *Ibid.* IX. 1003. **1887** LECKY *Eng. in 18th C.* VI. 266 The Church had pronounced it to be a sin of that 'mortal' kind which excludes from heaven.

fig. **1581** PETTIE tr. *Guazzo's Civ. Conv.* II. (1586) 66 b, If the fault in wordes be veniall, the fault in sentence and matter is mortall.

6. Pertaining to or accompanying death.

1542 UDALL *Erasm. Apoph.* 154 When he [Diogenes] was awaked out of his mortal slepe, that is to saye, the last that euer he had before his death. **1638** BAKER tr. *Balzac's Lett.* (vol. III.) 79 To reade nothing but pitifull stories, and mortall predictions. **1672** SIR. T. BROWNE *Let. Friend* §x, All these, with many more, were so drowned in a mortal visage and last face of Hippocrates, that [etc.]. **1702** STEELE *Funeral* I. (1724) 16 This Fellow has a good mortal Look—place him near the Corps. **1732** POPE *Ess. Man* I. 288 Safe in the hand of one disposing Pow'r, Or in the natal, or the mortal hour. **1807** WORDSW. *White Doe* I. 336 A tale of tears, a mortal story! **1821** SHELLEY *Hellas* 851 Thou seest the mortal throes Of that whose birth was but the same. **1871** MORLEY *Condorcet* in *Crit. Misc.* Ser. I. (1878) 38 The mortal struggles of a society in revolution.

7. *transf.* (from sense 1.) Of or pertaining to man as a creature living on this earth and destined to die; relating to humanity.

1426 LYDG. *De Guil. Pilgr.* 9306 In thys mortal lyff. **1565** T. STAPLETON *Fortr. Faith* 45 This Testament is written in mens hartes,..not in tables of stone or mortall mettall. **1596** SPENSER *Hymn Heav. Beauty* 153 How then can mortall tongue hope to expresse The image of such endlesse perfectnesse? **1602** SHAKS. *Ham.* III. i. 67 When we haue shuffel'd off this mortall coile. **1637** MILTON *Lycidas* 78 Fame is no plant that grows on mortal soil. **1651** *Fuller's Abel Rediv.* 487 About this time Queen Elizabeth exchanged her mortall crown with an immortall. **1700** DRYDEN *Pal. & Arc.* II. 68 In Brakes and Brambles hid, and shunning Mortal Sight. **1839** KEIGHTLEY *Hist. Eng.* II. 31 The axe descending, terminated his mortal existence. **1842** BORROW *Bible in Spain* vi, He..possessed the largest head which I ever beheld upon mortal shoulders. **1842** TENNYSON *Sir Galahad* 70 This mortal armour that I wear.

absol. **1749** FIELDING *Tom Jones* IX. v, Heroes..have certainly more of mortal than divine about them.

8. In colloquial and slang uses.

a. Extremely great, 'awful'; = DEADLY 8.

App. arising from hyperbolical or jocular applications of senses 3 and 4.

1716 C'TESS COWPER *Diary* (1864) 69 Lord Nottingham and the Duchess of Roxburgh take mortal pains to make the Princess think well of the Tories. **1762** BICKERSTAFFE *Love in Village* I. vi. (1765) 12, I never saw such a mortal throng in our village in all my born days again. **1772** FOOTE *Nabob* II. Wks. 1799 II. 307 They do a mortal deal of harm in the country. **1852** DICKENS *Bleak Ho.* v, I was a mortal sight younger then. **1865** —— *Mut. Fr.* I. xv, I'm not in a mortal hurry.

b. As an emphatic expletive (with *any*, *every*, or a negative). Cf. 'earthly', and sense 7 above.

1609 B. JONSON *Silent Woman* IV. v, *Cle.* Shall I goe fetch the Ladies to the Catastrophe?..*Daup.* By no mortall meanes. **1843** FR. A. KEMBLE *Later Life* III. 36, I have every mortal thing to pack with my own single pair of hands. **1892** *Daily News* 19 Nov. 5/4 We have the authority of Sir James Sawyer for saying that 'we may eat any mortal thing we like'.

c. *slang.* Long and tedious. [Cf. F. 'quinze mortels jours', etc.]

1820 SCOTT *Monast.* xxx, The interior one,..occupied them for three mortal hours. **1838** DICKENS *O. Twist* xxxix, You..take no more notice of me, all this mortal time, than if I was that 'ere dog. **1842** LYTTON *Zanoni* Introd. 19 And so on for 940 mortal pages in foolscap! **1878** STEVENSON *Inland Voy.* 232 The marionettes..performed a piece, called *Pyramus and Thisbe*, in five mortal acts.

d. Short for ***mortal drunk*** = dead drunk (see 10). *Sc.* and *north. dial.*

1824 MACTAGGART *Gallovid. Encycl.* 54 He was often carried home to his crue, on a hand-barrow, just mortal. **1825** JAMIESON, *Mortal*, dead drunk. **1867** A. DAWSON *Rambling Recoll.* (1868) 21 They had tasted of the bottles of the whole fifteen by which time they were one and all of them 'mortal'. **1891** BARRIE *Little Minister* xxiv, He doesna strike me except when he's mortal.

9. *Comb.*

1670 DRYDEN *2nd Pt. Conq. Granada* IV. iii, Instruct thy mortal elemented son. **1697** —— *Æneid* XII. 1073 The mortal-temper'd steel deceiv'd his hand. **1814** SCOTT *Ld. of Isles* II. xi, Or, mortal-moulded, comest thou here From England's love, or France's fear?

10. *adv.* = MORTALLY. Now only *dial.* or *vulgar* in the sense: Extremely, excessively, 'deadly' (cf. 8 a).

mortal drunk = dead drunk.

c **1407** LYDG. *Reson & Sens.* 3665 The pereyl ys so mortal strong. *c* **1500** *Melusine* 175 The batayll was there mortall fyers & doubtous for bothe partyes. **1753** WARBURTON in W. & Hurd *Lett.* (1809) 156 St. John's well, after the name of a mortal cold bath in Nottinghamshire. **1778** SUSAN BURNEY *Let.* 16 July in *Mme. D'Arblay's Early Diary* (1889) II. 247 She is mortal fond of the book, and has got it by heart. **1784** R. BAGE *Barham Downs* I. 9 A mortal rich gentleman. **1816** BYRON *Siege of Corinth* xxvi, Though slight was that grasp so mortal cold. **1844** W. CROSS *Disruption* xxvi. (E.D.D.), The mistress o' the house was 'mortal drunk' in bed. **1855** THACKERAY *Newcomes* II. 35 Missis was mortal angry. **1850** R. G. CUMMING *Hunter's Life S. Afr.* (1902) 92/1 All hands were mortal drunk. **1867** A. TROLLOPE *Last Chron. Barset* (1869) I. xxxiii. 352, I wouldn't speak if I warn't well nigh mortal sure.

† **morˈtalian.** *Obs.* = MORTALIST.

1647 WARD *Simp. Cobler* 11 Brownists, Mortalians [etc.].

† **ˈmortalism.** *Obs.* [f. MORTAL *a.* + -ISM.] The belief that the soul is mortal: see MORTALIST 1.

1646 T. EDWARDS *Gangræna* I. 114 From that he fell to Anabaptisme..and to Mortalisme, holding the Soul Mortall.

† **ˈmortalist.** *Obs.* [f. MORTAL *a.* + -IST.] One who holds the soul to be mortal (see quot.).

1646 R. BAILLIE *Anabaptism* (1647) 99 The Familistick Anabaptists..are not onely for the sleeping of the soul at death, but for its annihilation... At first these mortallists did grant a resurrection of the body,..but now..they deny any resurrection after death, all life either of body or soul.

appositively. **1757** MRS. GRIFFITH *Lett. Henry & Frances* (1767) II. 26 A mortalist Deist sinks into an Atheist.

mortality (mɔː'tælɪtɪ). Forms: 4–6 **mortalite, -itee,** 5 **-ytee, -ytie,** 5–6 **-yte,** 5–7 **-itie,** 6 **-itye,** 7 **mortallitie, -ity,** 6– **mortality.** [ad. F. *mortalité* (12th c.), ad. L. *mortālitāt-em*, f. *mortālis*: see MORTAL *a.* and -ITY.]

1. a. The condition of being mortal or subject to death; mortal nature or existence.

a **1340** HAMPOLE *Psalter* xxix. 14 The mortalite of my fleysse..thou distroyd in my resurreccioun. **1446** LYDG. *Nightingale* I. 149 This hygh forfet whych Adam sone had don Was grounde & cause of oure mortalite. **1447** BOKENHAM *Seyntys* 55, & for my mete is inuysible & my drink celestyal It may not be seyn in þis mortalyte. **1509** FISHER *Funeral Serm. C'tess Richmond* Wks. (1876) 302 *In diebus carnis sue*..That is to say in the dayes of his mortalite. **1526** TINDALE *2 Cor.* v. 4 That mortalite [Gr. τὸ θνητόν] myght be swalowed vppe of lyfe. **1641** J. JACKSON *True Evang. T.* II. 137 Elizabeth Folks,..when her soule was ready to take flight out of her body, concluded her mortality with these words. **1644** HEYLIN *Brief Relat. Laud* 23 Never did man put off mortality with a braver courage. **1703** MAUNDRELL *Journ. Jerus.* (1732) 79 The Sepulcher out of which he [Lazarus] was rais'd to a second Mortality. **1742** YOUNG *Nt. Th.* IX. 65 Life's gayest scenes speak man's mortality. **1820** WORDSW. *Vaudracour & Julia* 53 A man too happy for mortality! **1847** R. W. HAMILTON *Rewards & Punishm.* iii. (1853) 122 Mortality is the rule of all mere animal life. **1867** JOLLY *Sunday Serv.* 301 He passed from mortality, to eternal felicity.

b. Mortals collectively. Now *rare* or *Obs.*

?**1601** DANIEL *Epist. Lady Margaret, C'tess Cumberland* vi, The perplexed State Of troublous and distrest mortalitie, That thus make way vnto the ougly birth Of their owne sorrowes. **1654** FULLER *Two Serm.* 56 All Mortalitie shall be tryed by one of these Two Statutes.

c. *pl.* Mortal properties or attributes. *rare.*

1832 L. HUNT *Poems* 227 (tr. Theocr. xxiv), And in Trachinia shall the funeral pyre Purge his mortalities away with fire.

2. a. Loss of life on a large scale; abnormal frequency of death, as by war or pestilence; †*spec.* a visitation of deadly plague.

c **1400** MAUNDEV. (1839) xviii. 189 But alle weys thei maken gret mortalitee of poeple. *c* **1440** *Alphabet of Tales* 321 þe infeccion of þe ayre þat was cauce in Rome of grete dead & mortalitie. *c* **1450** *Merlin* iii. 56 In that bataile was grete mortalite on bothe parties. **1523** LD. BERNERS *Froiss.* I. cccxxxi. 210 Ther fell suche a mortalyte in the hoost, that of fyue ther dyed thre. *a* **1548** HALL *Chron., Hen. VIII* 109 There was slain at the siege .lxiiii. thousande Turkes, and .xl. thousande dedde of mortalitie and mo. **1596** S. FINCH in Ducarel *Hist. Croydon* (1783) App. 154 Some waste place wherin (in the tyme of some mortalitie) they did burie in. **1654** EARL MONM. tr. *Bentivoglio's Wars Flanders* 185 The conflict lasted many hours, and great was the mortality on all sides. **1693** LUTTRELL *Brief Rel.* (1857) III. 5 Our merchants have an account from Jamaica that there has been a mortality there since the late earthquake. **1727–52** CHAMBERS *Cycl.*, *Mortality*, a term frequently used to signify a contagious disease, which destroys great numbers of either men or beasts. **1761–2** HUME *Hist. Eng.* (1806) III. xlii. 501 Many of these adventurers were killed..; a great mortality seized the rest. **1776** ADAM SMITH *W.N.* I. viii, Years of dearth..are generally among the common people years of sickness and mortality. **1842** BORROW *Bible in Spain* xxv, The mortality amongst the horses..being frightful. **1863** FROUDE *Hist. Eng.* VII. 42 The mortality in the Tudor race which had raised her to the throne had left her also with scarcely a relation in the world.

b. The number of deaths which occur in a given area or period, from a particular disease, etc.; average frequency of death, death-rate.

1645–1854 *Bill of mortality* [see BILL *sb.*[3] 10]. **1672** PETTY *Pol. Anat.* (1691) 17 If 250 Ministers would serve all Ireland, then 10 per Ann. will supply their Mortality. **1843** R. J. GRAVES *Syst. Clin. Med.* ix. 99 It is this which constitutes the great difference between the mortality in private and hospital practice. **1845** *Encycl. Metrop.* II. 459 The method of forming tables of mortality. **1887** *Brit. Med. Jrnl.* 10 Dec. 1257 Hysterectomy..its mortality is out of all proportion to the benefits received by the few. **1899** LD. LISTER in *Daily News* 1 Dec. 3/4 The case-mortality in the inoculated is less by 50 per cent. than that in the uninoculated.

†**c.** Death, decease (of individuals). *Obs.*

1582 STANYHURST *Æneis* I. (Arb.) 20 Eeche thing mortalitye threatneth [L. *intentant omnia mortem*]. **1591** SHAKS. *1 Hen. VI*, IV. v. 32 Here on my knee I begge Mortalitie, Rather then Life preseru'd with Infamie. **1655** FULLER *Ch. Hist.* IX. 191 Amongst the mortalities of this year [1587], most remarkable the death of Richard Barnes Bishop of Durham. **1703** J. LOGAN in *Pa. Hist. Soc. Mem.* IX. 267 With power to succeed the governor in case of absence or mortality. **1723** DK. WHARTON *True Briton* No. 59 II. 509 Ever since the Mortality of the Immortal Queen Anne. **1760–72** H. BROOKE *Fool of Qual.* (1809) II. 70 You will prove a father to her in case of my mortality.

d. The mortal part of man; mortal remains.

1827 SOUTHEY *Hist. Penins. War* II. 132 It happened not unfrequently that these piles of mortality were struck by a shell, and the shattered bodies scattered in all directions. **1871** R. ELLIS tr. *Catullus* lxviii. 99 Now on a distant shore, no kind mortality near him,..Tomb'd in Troy the malign.

3. Deadliness, power to kill.

1430–40 LYDG. *Bochas* I. xx. (1494) e viij, O swetnesse ful of mortalite. **1727** SWIFT *God's Rev. agst. Punning* ¶1 That destructive Pestilence, whose mortality was so fatal, as to sweep away..five millions of Christian Souls.

4. Of a sin: The quality of being mortal.

1532 MORE *Confut. Tindale* Wks. 476/2 Such sinnes, as were either veniall in the begynnyng, or from mortall tourned to veniall by the forgeuenesse of the mortalitie. **1681** DRYDEN *Span. Friar* II. iii, Actions of Charity do alleviate, as I may say, and take off from the Mortality of the Sin.

5. *attrib.*, as (sense 2 b) ***mortality bill, rate, returns, statistics, table***; †**mortality walk**, the occupation of collecting obituary notices for a newspaper.

1665 PEPYS *Diary* 29 June, The *Mortality Bill is come to 267. **1909** *Daily Chron.* 27 Jan. 3/3 Dr. Millsom points out that..the want of air, ventilation, and light are dangerous or injurious to the health of the residents, and that the *mortality rate from all diseases (especially consumption) is very high. **1966** *Lancet* 24 Dec. 1371/1 In an attempt to reduce the mortality-rate, clinicians used ever-increasing amounts of antitetanic serum. **1899** *Daily News* 13 Sept. 5/1 The fall in temperature..has been followed by an immediate diminution in the *mortality returns. **1970** PASSMORE & ROBSON *Compan. Med. Stud.* II. xxxiv. 10/1 The death certificate is both a legal and a statistical document. Its form has been agreed internationally to provide for worldwide comparisons of *mortality statistics. **1880** *Encycl. Brit.* XIII. 169/2 These were very limited data upon which to found a *mortality table. **1773** FOOTE *Bankrupt* III. Wks. 1799 II. 129, I shall quit the *mortality walk, so provide yourself as soon as you can.

mortalize ('mɔːtəlaɪz), *v.* [f. MORTAL + -IZE.]

1. *intr.* To become mortal. *rare.*

1598 SYLVESTER *Du Bartas* II. i. I. *Eden* 7 Tell who (immortall) mortalizing, brought us The balm from heav'n wch hoped health hath wrought us.

2. *trans.* To make mortal; also, to consider or represent as mortal. Hence **'mortalized** *ppl. a.*

1633 T. ADAMS *Exp. 2 Peter* iii. 7 If we look inwards, there we find a depraved soul, a mortalized body. **1643** R. O. *Man's Mortality* i. (1644) 1 What of Adam was immortall through Innocency, was to be mortallized by Transgression. **1706** S. CLARKE *Let. to Mr. Dodwell* 10 That the Soul is by Nature Immortal, and must be mortalized by the Omnipotence of God, if ever it perish. **1831** KEIGHTLEY *Mythol. Anc. Greece & Italy* 477 In later times he [*sc.* Faunus] was mortalised like all the other Italian gods.

mortally ('mɔːtəlɪ), *adv.* Also 4–5 **mortelly, mortali, mortaily.** [f. MORTAL *a.* + -LY[2].]

1. In such a manner that death ensues; so as to cause death; †(to fight) to the death.

c **1386** CHAUCER *Man of Law's T.* 308 This scorpioun..Caste vnder this ful mortally to stynge. *c* **1400** *Brut* lxix. 64 þai fouȝten togeder mortaily. **1426** LYDG. *De Guil. Pilgr.* 21374 And thogh they berke nat On A man, fful mortally they byten kan. **1611** SHAKS. *Cymb.* v. iii. 10 The Enemy..strooke downe Some mortally, some slightly touch'd. **1700** DRYDEN *Fables* Ded. C1b, When you were not only dangerously, but in all appearance mortally wounded. **1798** LD. CLARE in *Ld. Auckland's Corr.* (1862) III. 422 None of the parties, however, are hurt mortally. **1839** THIRLWALL *Greece* VI. 243 They left him mortally wounded.

2. In reference to hatred, jealousy, fear, disquietude, offence, etc.: Bitterly, grievously, intensely. (Cf. MORTAL *a.* 3, 4.)

c **1386** CHAUCER *Manciple's T.* 209 He wol yow haten mortally [*v.r.* mortelly], certeyn. **1553** HOOPER in Foxe *A. & M.* (1583) 1513/2 They hate it mortally, & of all things most detest Gods holy worde. **1625** BACON *Ess., Envy* ¶8 Adrian the Emperour, that mortally Enuied Poets, and Painters, and Artificers, in Works, wherein he had a veine to excell. **1692** R. L'ESTRANGE *Fables* xxxviii. 40 Who would have Imagin'd..that the want of a Cap, or a Cringe, should so Mortally Discompose him. **1693** DRYDEN *Juvenal* Ded. (1697) 89 In Holiday and Stapylton, my Ears..are mortally offended. **1711** SWIFT *Jrnl. to Stella* 16 Sept., I hate these suppers mortally. **1847** C. BRONTE *J. Eyre* v, Mortally apprehensive of some one coming in and kidnapping me. **1849** MACAULAY *Hist. Eng.* vi. II. 104 Johnson was one of those persons who are mortally hated by their opponents. **1885** *Manch. Exam.* 13 June 5/3 The sober and well-to-do would be mortally offended.

3. In the way of mortal sin (see MORTAL *a.*).

1526 *Pilgr. Perf.* (W. de W. 1531) 80 b, I graunt my selfe therin to have..offended mortally, commyttynge deedly synne and dampnable. **1662** J. DAVIES tr. *Olearius' Voy. Ambass.* 142 For which they give this reason, that about that age [*viz.* seven] one begins to sin mortally.

†**4.** In the manner of mortals, as a mortal.

1608 SHAKS. *Per.* v. i. 105 Yet I was mortally brought forth, and am No other then I appeare.

5. *colloq.* Extremely, exceedingly, 'terribly'. (Cf. MORTAL *a.* 8.)

1759 *Rec. Town Counc. Newburgh* in A. Laing *Lindores Abbey*, etc. xxi. (1876) 275 Many become mortally drunk. **1771** SMOLLETT *Humph. Cl.* (1815) 33 His pupil, who seemed to be about the age of three-score, stooped mortally. **1789** A. YOUNG *Trav. France* (1890) 278 The people are in general mortally ugly and dwarfish. **1831** MRS. CARLYLE *New Lett.* (1903) I. 35 It was very stormy, and I was mortally sick the whole twenty four hours. **1883** STEVENSON *Merry Men, Treas. Franchard* vi, With swollen eyes and looking mortally sheepish. **1895** CROCKETT *Men of Mosshags* 37 He was indeed mortally fond of her girdle-cakes.

†**'mortalness.** *Obs.* [f. MORTAL *a.* + -NESS.] The quality of being mortal (in various senses).

1530 PALSGR. 246/2 Mortalnesse, *mortalité*. **1591** SAVILE *Tacitus, Hist.* I. [c. 79] 44 In the one place the mortalnesse, in the other the misery of their woundes wasted them all. **1638** BP. REYNOLDS *Medit. Last Supper* xv. Wks. (1658) 623 Though we are not perfectly cleansed from the soil [of sin], yet are we soundly healed from the mortalness and bruises of it. **1659** *Gentl. Calling* v. §16 Those edgeless weapons may vie with the keenest for the mortalness of their effects.

mortancestry (mɔː'tænsɪstrɪ). *Scots Law.* Corrupt Sc. form of MORT D'ANCESTOR. Chiefly in ***brieve of mortancestry***, which corresponds to the Eng. 'writ of assize of mort d'ancestor'.

1609 SKENE *Reg. Maj.* 58 Qvhen ane man deceisses saised in frie tenement, swa that he is vest and saised therein in propertie, and as of fie: his heire may seik saising thereof: and gif he be of perfite age, he sall haue the brieve of mortancestrie. **1678** SIR G. MACKENZIE *Crim. Laws Scot.* II. xv. §ii. (1699) 212 They were Judges to Recognitions, Brieves of Mortancestrie [etc.]. *a* **1768** ERSKINE *Inst. Law Scot.* III. viii. §62 (1773) 576 Though the brief of inquest sometimes gets the name of the brief of mortancestry..these two were originally distinct. **1746–7** *Act 20 Geo. II*, c. 50 §3 Upon the brief of mortancestry of any heir or heirs. **1838** W. BELL *Dict. Law Scot.* 659 The brieve of mortancestry was used for calling into court those in possession of the ancestor's property, for trying the title under which they possessed.

mortar ('mɔːtə(r)), *sb.*[1] Forms: 1, 4–6 **mortere,** 3–8 **morter,** 4–5 **mortyer,** (5 **moorter, morteer, -ier,** 6 **mortre,** 7 **mortore, -ure**), 5–6 **mortare,** 6– **mortar.** [In sense 1 perh. partly repr. OE. *mortere* masc., a. L. *mortārium*, of obscure origin, whence also MLG. *mortêr, mottêr, morten*, OHG. *morsâri, morsali* (perh. affected by popular etymology, as if f. Teut. *mors-* to crush), also without sound-shifting *mortâri* (MHG. *morsære, morsel*, mod.G. *mörser, mörsel*), OSw. *mortare* (mod.Sw., Da. *morter*). It is, however, doubtful whether the word survived beyond OE.; if not, the existing word must be regarded as wholly a. F. *mortier* (whence Du. *mortier*), to which several of the ME. forms are clearly due. Senses 2, 3, 4 were taken from Fr.; the Fr. lexicographers regard them as transferred applications to objects more or less similar in shape to the 'mortar' of pharmacy.

Cf. Pr. *mortier-s* (in sense 1), Rumanian *mozeriu* (sense 1), It. *mortajo* (senses 1, 3), Sp. *mortero* (senses 1, 2, 3, 4), Pg. *morteiro* (senses 1, 3).]

1. a. A vessel of a hard material (e.g. marble, brass, wood, glass), having a cup-shaped cavity, in which ingredients used in pharmacy, cookery, etc., are pounded with a pestle.

c **1000** *Sax. Leechd.* I. 216 ȝepuna þonne eall tosomne on anum mortere. *c* **1050** *Voc.* in Wr.-Wülcker 448/29 *Mortariola*, mortere. **13..** *K. Alis.* 332 Herbes he tok in an herber, And stamped heom in a morter. *c* **1420** *Liber Cocorum* (1862) 7 Take wete,..And do hit in a morter shene; Bray hit a lytelle. **15..** in *Vicary's Anat.* App. IX. i. (1888) 220 Take the rootes of marche mallowes..and brysse them a lytle in a mortre. **1599** *Acc. Bk. W. Wray* in *Antiquary* XXXII. 243 One little brasse morter and ij pesteles. **1653** WALTON *Angler* I. viii. 171 Then beat these together in a Mortar. **1681** BELON *New Myst. Physick* Introd. 26 Take of good red Coral,..make it into a gross Powder, in a Marble Mortar. **1747** MRS. GLASSE *Cookery* ii. (1767) 57 Make a force-meat with half a pound of veal [etc.]..all beat fine together in a marble mortar. **1839** URE *Dict. Arts*, etc. 438 By bruising a piece of enamel in an agate or porcelain mortar to a coarse powder like sand.

fig. **1377** LANGL. *P. Pl.* B. XIII. 44 Ac her sauce was..vnsauourely grounde, In a morter, post-mortem of many bitter peyne. **1382** WYCLIF *Prov.* xxvii. 22 If thou bete togidere a fool in a morter..shal not ben take awei fro hym his folie. **1535, 1610, 1664, 1855** [see BRAY *v.*[2] 1 b]. **1662** M. W. *Marriage Broker* v. i, This Pestle shall ne're pound i' th widows mortar. [Cf. It. *mortaro* (ad fin.) Florio.]

†**b.** As an instrument of punishment (see quots.).

[**1423** *Maldon* (Essex) *Court Rolls* (Bundle 14. no. 1^v^), Uxor Johannis Morys est communis litigatrix et portabit mortarium.] **1468** *Maldon* (Essex) *Liber* B. fol. 12 b, Alle maner of brethelde brauleres..for ther braulyng shull bere the morter accordyng to the olde custum of this toun. **1572** in A. Clark *Shirburn Ball.* (1907) 47 [At Maldon, Essex.] To the sonne of Simon Sawyer for the ringinge of the bason borne before the surgeon wearinge the morter about his necke for baudry. **1637** in Boys *Coll. Hist. Sandwich* (1789) 708 A woman carries a wooden mortar throughout the town, hanging on the handle of an old broom upon her shoulder..for abusing mrs mayoress. **1789** BOYS *ibid.* 789 The..wooden mortar for punishment of scolds.

†**c.** Proverb. ***to fly to Rome with a mortar on one's head***: app. a legendary achievement of some famous wizard. *Obs.*

1600 KEMP *Nine Daies Wonder* Ep. Ded., Me thinkes I could flye to Rome (at least hop to Rome, as the olde Prouerb is) with a morter on my head. *a* **1625** FLETCHER *Fair Maid Inn* v. ii, He did measure the starres with a false yard, and may now travaile to Rome with a morter on's head to see if he can recover his mony that way.

d. *transf.* (*a*) In early use, a literalism of translation; (*b*) later, applied to various mechanical appliances in which materials are pounded or ground.

(*a*) *c* **1420** *Pallad. on Husb.* IV. 113 A morter [orig. *mortarium* = hole] faste is maad aboute the tre. **1601** HOLLAND *Pliny* II. 594 In Greece they have a cast by themselves, to temper and beat in morters, the mortar made of lime and sand..with a great wooden pestill. **1728** T. COOKE tr. *Hesiod, Wks. & Days* II. 60 Provide a Mortar three Feet deep, and strong; And let the Pistil be three Cubits long.

(*b*) **1766** C. LEADBETTER *Roy. Gauger* II. xiv. (ed. 6) 370 The Rags..are put into Troughs called Mortars, each Mortar having to it five Hammers. **1839** URE *Dict. Arts* 1255 For grinding the tobacco leaves into snuff, conical mortars are employed. **1881** RAYMOND *Mining Gloss.*, *Mortar*,..the receptacle beneath the stamps in a stamp mill, in which the dies are placed, and into which the rock is fed to be crushed. **1902** HALL & NEAL *Anc. Ruins Rhodesia* vi. 77 In no ruin, so far discovered, have the ancient mortars, or crushing-stones, or even gold quartz been discovered.

2. A bowl of wax or oil with a floating wick, and later a kind of thick candle, used esp. as a night-light. *Obs.* exc. *Hist.*

13.. *E.E. Allit. P.* B. 1487, & oþer louelych lyȝt þat lemed ful fayre As mony morteres of wax merkked withoute. *c* **1374** CHAUCER *Troylus* IV. 1245 For, by this morter which that I see brenne, Knowe I ful wel that day is not far henne. *c* **1430** *Bk. Curtasye* 503 in *Babees Bk.*, A morter of wax . . þat alle nyȝt brennes in bassyn clere, To saue þo chambur on nyȝt for fyre. **1530** in *Archæologia* III. 156 Returning to the chaundry all the remains of mortars, torches, quarries, prickets and sizes. *a* **1603** in Nichols *Progr. Q. Eliz.* II. 56 Quarriers, Torches, and Mortroses. **1604** *Househ. Ord.* (1790) 305 Mortores, Torchetts, Torches, Quarrioures. **1641** J. MURRELL *Cookery & Carving* 184 When your Soueraigne is in bed, draw the Curtaines, and see there be morter or waxe of perchours ready. **1852** ROCK *Ch. of Fathers* III. viii. 89. *c* **1865** LETHEBY in *Circ. Sci.* I. 93/2 The wicks of wax mortars and nightlights are made of flax.

3. a. orig. †***mortar-piece***: A short piece of ordnance with a large bore and with trunnions on its breech for throwing shells at high angles.

1558 *Voy. Osep Napea* in *A. Jenkinson's Voy. & Trav.* (Hakl. Soc.) II. 360 They haue also a great many of morter pieces or potguns, out of which pieces they shoote wild fire. **1613** SHAKS. *Hen. VIII*, v. iv. 48 Hee stands there like a Morter-piece to blow vs. **1667** PEPYS *Diary* 28 Apr., Stone-shot of thirty-six inches' diameter, which they shot out of mortar-pieces. **1687** EVELYN *Diary* 16 Mar., Those . . Engines called bombs, shot out of the Mortar-piece on Blackheath. **1760** STERNE *Tr. Shandy* III. xxii, They are two mortar-pieces for a siege next summer.

1627 CAPT. SMITH *Seaman's Gram.* xiv. 68 For Morters, or such chambers are only vsed for triumphs, there is no vse for them in this seruice. **1691** *Lond. Gaz.* No. 2699/4, 8 Mortars, two of which are of 18 Inches diameter. **1727–52** CHAMBERS *Cycl.* s.v. *Mortar-piece*, There are two kinds of mortars: the one hung or mounted on a carriage . .; called pendent or hanging mortars: the other fixed on an immoveable base, called standing mortars. **1800** WELLINGTON in Gurw. *Desp.* (1834) I. 112 Howitzers will not answer at Jemalabad; and I have therefore ordered there a thirteen and a ten inch mortar. **1858** GREENER *Gunnery* 65 Mortars are intended for three purposes; firstly, to bombard a town, or injure the defenders' artillery; secondly, to fire or overthrow the works; thirdly, to break through the vaulted roofs of barracks and magazines. **1875** *Encycl. Brit.* II. 664 The number of men required is calculated for three reliefs, . . 15 per large mortar, and 9 per small mortar.

b. *transf.* Applied to contrivances for firing 'shells' in pyrotechnic displays and for throwing a life-line (cf. *life-mortar* s.v. LIFE *sb.* 17).

1669 STURMY *Mariner's Mag.* v. xiii. 83 Of Artificial Fire-Works. To make the Mortar-Piece of Wood and Past-Board. Provide a Wooden-Ruler of such bigness as you desire to make the Diameter of the Morter. **1749** *Descr. Machine for the Fireworks* 9, 12 Mortars with Air Ballons. **1792** *Trans. Soc. Arts* X. 203 Trials were made, by throwing a loaded Shell on shore, from a small mortar... To the Shell was attached a rope. **1829** MRS. OPIE in Brightwell *Life* (1854) 223 To . . watch, lest any vessel should be in distress on the coast, that the mortar might be used. **1873** *Cornhill Mag.* XXVIII. 72 The rocket and mortar apparatus . . has frequently done good service where a lifeboat would have been useless. **1878** T. KENTISH *Pyrotechn. Treas.* 117 Shells are hollow paper globes, fired vertically, from mortars.

†**4.** = MORTIER. Also *mortar cap. Obs.*

The sense can hardly be said to have really existed in Eng. Quot. 1604 is a mere literalism of translation, and the examples cited in recent Dicts. belong to 1 c. Davies *Suppl. Gloss.* erroneously places under this sense a passage from Fuller *Pisgah* (1650) IV. vi. 107, based on an obscure Talmudic text which (as translated by some scholars) describes the hypocritical Pharisee as 'hanging down his head like a pestle in a mortar'.

1604 E. G[RIMSTONE] *D'Acosta's Hist. Indies* VI. xvi. 467 In some parts [they wear] as it were little morters [Sp. *morteretes*] or hattes. **1686** CHARDIN *Coronat. Solyman* 40 A flat Bonnet, somewhat like the Mortar Caps of the Presidents of the French Parliaments.

5. *attrib.* and *Comb.*, as (sense 1) ***mortar-fashioned*** adj., †***pestle***; (sense 1 d) ***mortar-crushing***; (sense 2) ***mortar-light***; (sense 3) ***mortar-battery***, ***-carriage***, ***-man***, ***-platform***, ***-shell***; (sense 3 b) ***mortar station***.

1708 *Lond. Gaz.* No. 4470/2 The *Mortar Battery on the Counterscarp . . began to play. **1810** WELLINGTON in Gurw. *Desp.* (1838) VI. 360 They have not yet broken ground . . excepting to construct what I conceive to be a mortar battery. **1875** *Encycl. Brit.* II. 664/1 *Mortar-carriages. **1877** RAYMOND *Statist. Mines & Mining* 246 About two tons [of ore] treated by hand (*mortar-crushing) yielded $8,000. **1753** CHAMBERS *Cycl. Supp.* s.v. *Lycoperdon*, The *mortar fashioned lycoperdon. **1856** *Orr's Circ. Sci., Pract. Chem.* 460 The best description of candle manufactured from wax is the **mortar-light*, which is used either for night-watching or for heating dishes on the table. **1952** G. E. THORNTON *Hand-bk. Weapon Training* x. 109 The auxiliaries are placed in position by the mortarman's assistant, who works backwards in co-operation with the *mortarman. **1965** M. W. BROWNE *New Face of War* iii. 19 They lack optical sighting devices, but good mortarmen don't need gadgets like that. **1970** *Globe & Mail* (Toronto) 25 Sept. 9/8 U.S. mortarmen mistakenly fired 36 rounds into an element of U.S. infantrymen. **14..** *Metr. Voc.* in Wr.-Wülcker 626 *Mortare pestelle, *mortarium*, *pila*. **1876** VOYLE & STEVENSON *Milit. Dict.* (ed. 3) s.v. *Platform*, **Mortar Platform*, a platform similar to that used with siege guns, but of smaller dimensions. **1879** *Man. Artill. Exerc.* II. 40 *Mortar shells have no wooden bottom attached. **1812** in G. W. Manby *Ess. Preserv. Shipwr. Persons* 32 Ships in danger of being wrecked on parts of the coast intermediate to the *mortar stations.

b. Special comb.: **mortar-bed**, (*a*) see BED *sb.* 12 a; (*b*) the bed on which the ore is crushed in a stamp-mill; **mortar-block**, the foundation-timber of a stamp-mill; **mortar body**, a paste used in the manufacture of porcelain mortars; †**mortar-cap** (see 4); **mortar casemate** (see quot.); **mortar-hole**, a hole in a rock used as a mortar in primitive ore-crushing; **mortar-man** *nonce-wd.*, an apothecary; †**mortar-piece** (see 3); **mortar-press**, the trough in which tobacco leaves are pressed before cutting; **mortar vessel** (see quot.); **mortar ware**, a very hard porcelain biscuit invented by Wedgwood and used by him in the manufacture of mortars.

1769 FALCONER *Dict. Marine* (1776) s.v. *Mortar*, The middle . . is bent . . to embrace the trunnions, and keep them fast in the *mortar-bed. **1802** C. JAMES *Milit. Dict.* s.v. *Mortar*, Land-Mortar-Beds, are made of very solid timber. **1811, 1816** [see BED *sb.* 12 a]. **1874** RAYMOND *6th Rep. Mines* 353 The mortar-beds constitute a series of inclined terraces, . . and the pulp passing through the screens of one battery is discharged immediately into the one next in front. **1889** C. G. W. LOCK *Pract. Gold-mining* 429 Mortars are often fixed directly upon vertical *mortar-blocks. **1839** URE *Dict. Arts* 1020 *Mortar body, is a paste composed of 6 parts of clay [etc.]. **1879** *Cassell's Techn. Educ.* IV. 138/2 *Mortar casemates are vaulted chambers without a front wall employed . . to secure the mortars of the fortresses from vertical fire. **1902** HALL & NEAL *Anc. Ruins Rhodesia* vi. 78 Shallow hollows on the rocks where the quartz powdered in the *mortar-holes was evidently reduced to the fineness required for washing. **1756** TOLDERVY *Hist. 2 Orphans* I. 17 Prithee fellow its one of thy lies, replied the *mortar-man. **1843** *Penny Cycl.* XXV. 17/2 The damp [tobacco] leaves are . . laid in what is called a '*mortar-press'. **1864** *Chamb. Encycl.*, **Mortar-vessel*, a class of gun-boat for mounting sea-service mortars. **1865** JEWITT *Wedgwoods* x. 187 Josiah Wedgwood's inventions and discoveries... Basaltes, . . jasper, bamboo and *mortar wares.

mortar ('mɔːtə(r)), *sb.*[2] Forms: 3–7 **morter**, 5 **-ere**, **-yer**, 6 **-are**, 7– **mortar**. [ME. *morter*, *mortier*, a. F. *mortier* (13th c. in Littré):—L. *mortārium*. Cf. MDu. *morter*, *mortel* (Du. *mortel*), MHG. *mortel*, *morter* (G. *mörtel*), from Latin or Fr.

The L. *mortārium* in the sense 'product of trituration' (applied by Juvenal to drugs, and by Vitruvius to mortar) is commonly regarded as a transferred use of *mortārium* MORTAR *sb.*[1] 1, which was applied by extension to the trough in which mortar was mixed. It is possible, however, that the two senses of the Latin word are equally original, the suffix *-ārium* being employed in two different functions.]

A material consisting of lime and sand mixed with water, which is used to make the joints between stones and bricks in building, and which, when set, binds them together into a solid mass. Also applied to materials of other composition used for the same purpose.

Various kinds are *gauged*, *hydraulic*, *pointing*, *pozzolana*, *trass*, *water mortar*, etc.; see the qualifying words.

The collocations ***stone and mortar***, ***bricks and mortar***, are freq. used to denote the essential materials used in building; the latter phrase is also employed colloq. for 'houses' or 'house property' (sometimes attrib.).

c **1290** *S. Eng. Leg.* I. 37/125 Þo he ne miȝhte non oþur do þe churche for-to a-rere, he . . bar morter þar-to. *a* **1300** *Cursor M.* 2246 Þe wark þai raised . . Wit tile and ter, witvten stan Oþer morter was þer nan. **1340** *Ayenb.* 116 Þet guode mortyer huer-of me makeþ þe guode walles sarzineys. **1426** LYDG. *De Guil. Pilgr.* 23504 The morter Was not . . Stably among the stoones layd. **1534** *Act 26 Hen. VIII* c. 8 If the owner . . doo not . . with walles of morter and stone sufficiently inclose the same vacant grounde. **1592** GREENE *Upst. Courtier* F 4 An so spoiles hee much good morter and bricke. **1611** BIBLE *Exod.* i. 14 They made their liues bitter, with hard bondage, in morter and in bricke. *a* **1745** SWIFT *Char. of Legion Club* 178 We must give them better Quarter, For their Ancestor trod Mortar. **1825** J. NICHOLSON *Operat. Mechanic* 530 In making mortar, particular attention must be paid to the quality of the sand. **1836** N. PATERSON *Manse Garden* (1860) 29 The legal fence is one of stone and mortar. **1848** DICKENS *Dombey* xxiii, Fragments of mortar . . came dropping down. **1863** P. BARRY *Dockyard Econ.* 116 The plant must be sold, the brick and mortar walls demolished. **1895** *Daily News* 28 Oct. 9/3 Business . . will be practically confined to small metropolitan brick and mortar investments.

b. *transf.* (See quots.)

c **1440** *Promp. Parv.* 344/2 Morter, for playsterynge . ., *litura*. **1573** BARET *Alv.* M 435 Morter or clay mixed with straw, wherewith walles are dawbed, *aceratum*. **1605** SHAKS. *Lear* II. ii. 71, I will tread this vnboulted villaine into morter, and daube the wall of a Iakes with him. **1607** TOPSELL *Four-f. Beasts* (1658) 398 To keep mice from corn, make morter of the froth of oyl mingled together with chaff, . . then plaister the walls of your garnery therewith. *c* **1710** CELIA FIENNES *Diary* (1888) 101 The mill . . pounded the raggs to morter for ye paper. **1797** *Statist. Acc. Scotl.* XIX. 339 *note*, That coarse red clay, called mortar, is the basis of all the grounds in this part of Strathmore. **1842–59** GWILT *Archit.* II. iii. §2235 The sorts of it [*sc.* plaster] are various; as for instance, white lime and hair mortar on bare walls. **1892** Pit-mortar [see PIT *sb.* 15].

†**c.** (*a*) Building, masonry; (*b*) *fig.* building operations. *Obs.*

1582 STANYHURST *Aeneis* II. (1880) 59 No man, no morter can his onset forcibil hynder. **1665** GERBIER *Brief Disc.* 3 Those who say, That a wise man never ought to put his finger into Morter. **1798** W. HUTTON *Life* 43, I . . altered the plan . . till, when put in execution, it cost more than 700*l.* Mortar is rather apt to corrode the pocket.

d. *fig.*

1377 LANGL. *P. Pl.* B. XIX. 321 And of his baptesme & blode þat he bledde on Rode He made a maner morter & mercy it hiȝte. **1480** CAXTON *Chron. Eng.* v. (1520) 43/1 The morter of a werke that I have begon behoveth to be tempred with your blood. **1562** WINȜET *Cert. Tractates* Wks. (S.T.S.) I. 14 The prophetis of it, spargeonit thaim with vntemperit morter [cf. Ezek. xxii. 28]. **1649** J. OWEN *Shaking Heaven & Earth* Wks. 1851 VIII. 277 All that antichristian mortar wherewith from their first chaos, they have been cemented. **1827** CARLYLE *Misc.* (1857) I. 2 A trowel or two of biographic mortar. **1903** *Speaker* 21 Mar. 612/1 They regarded faith as the mortar which kept the bricks of society sticking together.

e. *attrib.* and *Comb.*, as ***mortar-built*** adj., ***-engine***, ***-joint***, ***-like*** adj., ***-maker***, ***-making***, ***-mill***, ***-tempering***, †***-treader***, †***-treading***, ***-tub***; **mortar-bed**, the layer of mortar between courses of brickwork or masonry; **mortar-liquid** = GROUT; **mortar-man** *nonce-wd.*, a builder; **mortar-wash**, thin mortar.

1842 GWILT *Archit.* §1900 The propriety of the *mortar beds being as thin as possible. **1900** A. LANG *Hist. Scotl.* I. iv. 68 *Mortar-built stone edifices. **1875** KNIGHT *Dict. Mech.*, **Mortar-engine*, a machine for grinding and combining materials into mortar. **1878** SIR G. SCOTT *Lect. Archit.* (1879) II. 40 A steep skewback being formed for their springings to . . moderate the thickness of the *mortar-joint. **1704** LONDON & WISE *Compl. Gardener* III. xx. (ed. 4) 89 Rainy weather being apt to reduce the Mould to a *Mortar-like consistence. **1888** C. H. FAGGE *Syst. Med.* (ed. 3) I. 105 The calcified growth has a peculiar dull white chalky, or mortar-like appearance. **1776** G. SEMPLE *Building in Water* 78 The Antients filled up their Work with *Mortar-liquid. **1606** HOLYOKE *Rider's Dict.*, A *morter maker or dawber, *cæmentarius*. **1825** [see *mortar tub*]. **1596** S. FINCH in Ducarel *Hist. Croydon* (1783) App. 152 Nowe we take *morter-makinge in hande. **1659** GAUDEN *Tears Ch.* IV. xvi. 513 While Ministers preach . . with divided tongues, . . they are likely to produce no better successes . . than those . . *morter-men did, whose work deserved the nick-name of Babel. **1878** *Dict. Archit.* (Arch. Publ. Soc.), *Mortar mill. **1904** *Athenæum* 31 Dec. 908/2 Poplar and St. Pancras both run fan-engines, clinker-crushers, and mortar-mills. **1878** *Dict. Archit.* (Arch. Publ. Soc.) s.v. *Mortar mill*, The *mortar-tempering machine. **1602** DEKKER *Satirom.* Wks. 1873 I. 234, I smelt the foule-fisted *Morter-treader. **1586** SIDNEY *Arcadia* IV. (1622) 427 Parting with his sword one of his legs from him, left him to make a roring lamentation that his *morter-treading was marred for euer. **1825** J. NICHOLSON *Operat. Mechanic* 806 The Floor of the gallery where the mortar makers and smiths worked; shewing the situation of the *mortar tubs. **1778** *Phil. Trans.* LXVIII. 889 They ought to be washed over with a brush, wet with *mortar-wash.

†'**mortar**, *v.*[1] *Obs. rare.* [f. MORTAR *sb.*[1]] *intr.* To use a mortar (and pestle). Only in **mortaring** *ppl. a.*

1596 NASHE *Saffron Walden* O 4, He may be such another craftie mortoring Druggeir.

mortar ('mɔːtə(r)), *v.*[2] [f. MORTAR *sb.*[2]] **a.** *trans.* To plaster with mortar; to fix or join with mortar or a mortar-like substance.

1382 [see *ppl. a.* below]. **1563** HYLL *Art Garden.* (1593) 6 They made their inclosure . . with earth and stones mortered together. **1623** BINGHAM *Xenophon* 33 The Wall . . was built of Bricke mortered with asphalt. **1641** BEST *Farm. Bks.* (Surtees) 145 When they come to morter the rigge of an howse. **1658** SIR T. BROWNE *Hydriot.* iii. 12 We found the bones and ashes half mortered unto the sand and sides of the Urne. **1859** R. F. BURTON *Centr. Afr.* in *Jrnl. Geog. Soc.* XXIX. 67 *note*, Bowls of broken china and pottery are mortared into the tombs. **1861** SMILES *Engineers* II. 182 *note*, Every stone being fitted, mortared, and laid with studious accuracy.

b. in fig. context.

1610 DONNE *Pseudo-martyr* Pref. C 3, You are euer after his [*sc.* the Pope's] instruments, to build vp his spirituall Monarchy . . and your selues must ciment and morter the wals with your blood. **1619** BP. WILLIAMS *Serm. Apparell* (1620) 8 This rotten house of ours, the which (were it not continually mortered and repaired with meat and drinke) [etc.]. **1633** BP. HALL *Hard Texts, N.T.* 292 Ye are living stones, ye must bee . . firmly mortered upon the foundation of Christ.

Hence '**mortared** *ppl. a.*, plastered, cemented, or daubed with mortar; '**mortaring** *vbl. sb.*

1382 WYCLIF *Amos* vii. 7 A wall teerid, or morterd [1388 plastrid, Vulg. *murum litum*]. **1892** T. B. F. EMINSON *Epidemic Pneumonia at Scotter* 11 A catch-pit of mortared or unmortared brick. **1897** *Harper's Mag.* Apr. 730 Workers . . are thus spared the mortification of intruding . . mortared or sooty shoes . . among the well-dressed passengers. **1905** HOLMAN HUNT *Pre-Raphlm.* II. 276 The unlovely stone and mortared wall. **1954** M. BERESFORD *Lost Villages* ii. 73 Packing and mortaring had been carefully executed, and both faces of the wall were regular and straight.

mortar, *v.*[3] [f. MORTAR *sb.*[1] 3.] *trans.* To direct mortar fire upon; to hit with mortar shells.

1951 in *Conc. Oxf. Dict.* (ed. 4). **1967** C. CONNELL *World's Greatest Sieges* xxix. 239 The Germans followed the rear-guard down to the water's edge . . mortaring men and boats indiscriminately. **1974** *Times* 18 Mar. 6/6 In the towns, he said, the Arab garrisons had mortared and bombed Kurdish quarters.

Hence '**mortaring** *vbl. sb.*

[**1920** G. M. CHURCHER in *R. Artillery War Commem. Bk.* II. 43/2 The infantry were more than friends... Without their help trench-mortaring . . would not have been the fun it was.] **1971** B. W. ALDISS *Soldier Erect* 229 All that shelling, mortaring and machine-gunning hadn't put a single bunker out of action, although it had spread the jungle about the place. **1972** L. LAMB *Picture Frame* ii. 21 Mortaring started just as he reached the Bois Mesnil lane.

'**mortar-board.** [f. MORTAR *sb.*[2] + BOARD *sb.*]

1. A board for holding mortar: (*a*) see quot. 1876; (*b*) the small square board on which a bricklayer carries mortar; = HAWK *sb.*[3]

1876 Papworth in *Encycl. Brit.* IV. 457 (art. *Building*) The mortar is placed on ledged boards about 3 feet square ..; and the bricks are strewn on the scaffold between the mortar boards. **1882** Young *Every Man his own Mech.* §1141 The mortar-board..is held in the left hand by the handle below while pointing.

2. A popular name for the academic or college cap, which consists of a stiffened head-piece surmounted by a square of 'board', the whole being covered with black cloth.

1854 'C. Bede' *Verdant Green* II. iii, 'I don't mind this ere mortar-board',..as he pointed to the academical cap.

† **mor'tarian**, *a. Obs.* [f. mortar *sb.*[1] + -ian.] Of or pertaining to a (druggist's) mortar.

1651 Biggs *New Disp.* ¶34. 12 The Schools in the Remedies of Diseases, both of simples and their mortarian labour of Compositions, have apply'd themselves [etc.].

mortarie, obs. (*erron.*) form of mortuary *sb.*

mortarium (mɔːˈtɑːrɪəm). Pl. **mortaria**. [L.] A Roman mortar (see quots.).

1842 W. Smith *Dict. Gk. & Rom. Antiquities* 622/1 *Mortarium*, also called Pila and Pilum. **1863** W. Chaffers *Marks & Monograms on Pott. & Porc.* 18, Fig. 24 is a mortarium; 10⅜ inches diameter, of light brown ware, unglazed... Mortaria are sometimes found of the red lustrous ware, called Samian. **1937** *Discovery* Apr. 98/1 They have unearthed..bits of a mortarium. **1938** [see *find-spot* s.v. find *sb.* 4].

ˈ**mortarize**, *v.*[1] *rare.* [f. mortar *sb.*[1] + -ize.] *trans.* To pound in a mortar (*fig.*).

1615 *Curry-Combe for a Coxe-Combe* Contents, Lipsian Miracles morterized.

mortarize, *v.*[2] *rare.* [f. mortar *sb.*[2] + -ize.] *trans.* To bring to the consistency of mortar.

1852 Dickinson in *Jrnl. R. Agric. Soc.* XIII. I. 237 The wet clays were mortarized (to use a coined term).

mortarless (ˈmɔːtəlɪs), *a.* [f. mortar *sb.*[2] + -less.] Without mortar.

1667 Waterhous *Fire Lond.* 87 The Stones of Structures Mortarless. **1886** *Athenæum* 31 July 152 The remains of mortarless stone churches. **1891** Atkinson *Moorland Parish* 38 A..mortarless stone wall or dike.

ˈ**mortar-stone**. Chiefly *Sc.* and *north. dial.* (*Sc.* and *north.* **-stane**). [f. mortar *sb.*[1] Cf. MDu. *mortiersteen*.] A block of stone hollowed to form a mortar; *spec.* 'a stone formerly used for preparing barley, by separating it from the husks' (Jam.).

1480–1 *Durham Acc. Rolls* (Surtees) 97, ij morterstanez cum iij pilis lign. **1500–20** Dunbar *Poems* lx. 60 Mell-heidit lyk ane mortar-stane. **1580** *Reg. Privy Council Scot.* Ser. I. III. 320 Item, in the kitchene..ane mortar stane. **1696** *Invent.* in W. Hector *Select. Judic. Rec. Renfrewsh.* (1876) 304 Ane morter-stone and ane mell yrto. **1865** Lubbock *Prehist. Times* 249 The objects of stone found in the bone caves..are flakes,..hammers, and mortar-stones.

mortary (ˈmɔːtərɪ), *a.* [f. mortar *sb.*[2] + -y.] Of the nature of, consisting of, or resembling mortar.

1805 R. W. Dickson *Pract. Agric.* II. 643 The mortary rubbish from old walls. **1845** *Jrnl. R. Agric. Soc.* V. II. 432 A mortary loam, and a strong clay. **1876** Bristowe *Th. & Pract. Med.* (1878) 435 Yellow tubercle not unfrequently undergoes retrogressive changes..first, into a mortary, and lastly, into a calcareous inert mass.

b. Having mortar obtrusively present. *rare.*

1855 *Househ. Words* XII. 194 We are a little mortary and limey at present, but we are getting on capitally. **1858** Dickens *Lett.* (1880) II. 52 The room..is new and mortary.

mortas(e, mortays(e, obs. forms of mortise.

mortaunceter, variant of mort d'ancestor.

†ˈ**mortcharge**. *Sc. Obs.* [a. F. *morte charge* 'dead load'.] = dead-weight 1 b.

1541 *Burgh Rec. Edin.* (1871) II. 105 That is to say fra Scotis men xx s. greit the mortcharge and xxj s. greit the lycht guddis. **1553** *Ibid.* 184.

Mortclake: see Mortlake.

mortcloth (ˈmɔːtklɒθ, -ɔː-). *Sc.* [f. mort *sb.*[1] + cloth *sb.*]

1. A funeral pall.

(Used by Carlyle in the sense of: Funeral hangings.)

1511 *Acc. Ld. Treas. Scot.* (1902) IV. 195, xvj elnis iij quartaris blak weluus to be ane mort claitht, to ly one King James the Secundis tumbe. *a* **1670** Spalding *Troub. Chas. I* (Bannatyne Club) I. 43 Haveing above his chist a rich mortcloath of black velvet. **1678** Calderwood *Hist. Ch. Scot.* 826 It was reported that they were to use a white cloth above the mort-cloth [at a funeral in 1579]... Answer was returned, that the mort-cloth should be covered with black velvet. **1799** J. Robertson *Agric. Perth* 80 Certain dues for the proclamation of banns, the use of the mort-cloth..and other casualties. **18..** Hogg *Tales & Sk.* (1837) II. 189 When I saw the mortclaith drawn off the coffin. **1837** Carlyle *Fr. Rev.* II. II. vi, The vast Champ-de-Mars wholly hung round with black mortcloth.

2. Fees paid for the use of a pall.

1794 *Statist. Acc. Scotl.* XI. 452 The fund for their support arises from..the weekly collections..mortcloths, proclamation money [etc.]. **1876** Grant *Burgh Sch. Scot.* II. xiv. 457 In 1762 the schoolmaster of Banff derived part of his salary from the town's bells and Mort Cloth.

3. *attrib.* and *Comb.*

1768 *Parish Rec. Leslie* in Small *Hist. U.P. Congreg.* (1904) I. 280 Mortcloth dues for Mr James Clunie. **1902** A. Thomson *Lauder & Lauderdale* vii. 83 Alexander Creze was mortcloth keeper.

mort d'ancestor (mɔːˈdænsɪstə(r)). *Old Law.* Also 6 **mortaunceter, mort(d)auncesto(u)r**, 7, 9 **mortdancester**, (8, -or), 7 **mort d'ancester, mordauncester**. [a. AF. *mordancestre, mort d'auncestre* 'ancestor's death'.] The term applied to an assize brought by the right heir against one who wrongfully took possession of his inheritance on the death of his ancestor (see *Britton* III. vi.).

1523 Fitzherb. *Survey.* 13 The kynges writ of assise of nouell disseson or of assise of mortaunceter. **1540** *Act 32 Hen. VIII*, c. 2 §2 That no maner of persone..shall herafter have sue or maintain any issue of Mortauncestor [etc.]. **1543** tr. *Act 9 Hen. III*, c. 12 Assyses of newe dysseisin, and of mortdauncestour. **1642** tr. *Perkins' Prof. Bk.* v. §383. 165 If Tenant in Taile of land hath issue and dyeth and a stranger abateth..and the issue in tayle bring an Assise of Mordauncester. **1833** *Act 3 & 4 Will. IV*, c. 27 §36 No Writ ..of Mort d'ancestor..shall be brought after the Thirty-first Day of December One thousand eight hundred and thirty-four. **1875** Digby *Real Prop.* ii. §9 The writ of assize of Mort d'Ancestor was perhaps instituted by the ordinance called the Assize of Northampton, A.D. 1176.

‖**mort-de-chien**. *Obs.* [Fr.; lit. 'dog's death', but this is an etymologizing perversion of the Pg. *mordexim* (mɔrdeˈʃĩ): see mordisheen.] A name used by Europeans in India for cholera.

1780 Impey in Sir J. F. Stephen *Nuncomar & Impey* (1885) II. 239 *note*, I am once or twice a year subject to violent attacks of cholera morbus, here called the *mort de chien*, and to other disorders. **1813** J. Johnson *Infl. of Tropical Climate* (1815) 405 Mort de chien is nothing more than the highest degree of Cholera Morbus.

‖**mort dieu**, *int. Obs.* In 6 **mortdew, mordu**. [Fr. = 'God's death'.] An oath.

1593 Marlowe *Massacre Paris* C, *Mor du*, wert not the fruit within thy wombe..This wrathfull hand should strike thee to the hart. **1605** *Tryall Chev.* II. ii. in Bullen *O. Pl.* (1884) III. 292 Mortdew! Ile be reveng'd, by heaven I will.

mortdore, obs. form of mordore.

† **morteaulx**. *Obs.* [? Error for *marteaulx*.] = martel *sb.*[1] 2.

1472 in *Archæologia* (1836) XXVI. 277 The quene had there [in her chamber] her ladyes playinge at the morteaulx.

† **mortechien**. *Sc. Obs.* Forms: 7 **mortiechein, morticheyne**, 8 *corruptly* **mord de chien**, 9 **mortersheen**. [Of difficult etymology.

Identical with the alleged F. *mort d'eschine* (lit. death of the spine), for which Fitzherbert 1534 (*Husb.* §119) quotes the proverb 'Mort de langue et de eschine sont maladyes saunce medecine'. It is probable that *mort* here is a mistake for *morve*, running of the nose, glanders (for which, or its dial. variant *mourve*, Cotgr. has erroneously *mourrüe*). The notion that the morbid matter of glanders came from the spine was generally held. The 16th c. Eng. name for the disease, mourning *of the chine* is prob. a corruption of the original form of the Fr. term. Fountainhall's *mord de chien* is pseudo-etymological (as if ' bite of dog').]

= glanders.

1637 *Rec. Elgin* (New Spald. Club) I. 257 Anent horses that ar suspectit to haue the mortiechein. *a* **1670** Spalding *Troub. Chas. I* (Bannatyne Club) II. 299 Seing the uther tuo hors regimentis..wes scatterit heir and thair, and mony deid in the morticheyne [ed. 1792 mortichien]. **1759** Fountainhall *Decisions* I. 406 Anent the horse infected with the mord de chien. ? **1816** Duff *Poems* 86 (Jam.) And now he's [*sc.* a horse] tane the mortersheen.

mortegon, obs. f. martagon.

morteise, obs. f. mortise.

Mortelack, obs. f. Mortlake.

mortemale, var. mormal.

morterews, obs. var. mortress.

mortersheen, var. mortechien.

mortes(ce, -es(s)e, obs. ff. mortise.

† **mortesse**. *Obs.* App. error for mortar.

1614 *Inv.* in *Trans. Cumb. & Westm. Arch. Soc.* III. 114 One mortesse with pestell.

mortesse, ? erron. var. mortress.

morteys(e, obs. forms of mortise.

mortfundit, Sc. pa. pple. of morfound.

mortgage (ˈmɔːgɪdʒ), *sb.* Forms: 4–7 **morgage**, 6 **mortegage**, 6– **mortgage**. [a. OF. *mortgage* (13th c.) lit. 'dead pledge' (see mort *a.* and gage *sb.*): whence med.L. *mortuum vadium* and *mor(t)gagium*.

For the explanation of the etymological meaning of the term current among 17th c. lawyers, see the following quot.

1628 Coke *On Litt.* 205 It seemeth that the cause why it is called mortgage is, for that it is doubtful whether the Feoffor will pay at the day limited such summe or not, & if he doth not pay, then the Land which is put in pledge vpon condition for the payment of the money, is taken from him for euer, and so dead to him vpon condition, &c. And if he doth pay the money, then the pledge is dead as to the Tenant, &c.]

Law. The conveyance of real or personal property by a debtor (called the *mortgagor*) to a creditor (called the *mortgagee*) as security for a money debt, with the proviso that the property shall be reconveyed upon payment to the mortgagee of the sum secured within a certain period. Also applied to the deed by which the transaction is effected, the rights thereby conferred on the mortgagee, and the condition of being mortgaged.

'The general object of mortgage is to secure a money debt by making it a charge on land, so that, if the debt be not paid by a time agreed upon between the parties, the creditor may sell the land and pay himself out of the proceeds' (*Encycl. Brit.* s.v.).

1475 *Rolls of Parlt.* VI. 147/2 That all Maners, Londes [etc.]..of the which any persone..were seased, or had any astate, title,..or possession..in any maner morgage. **1542–3** *Act 34 & 35 Hen. VIII*, c. 26 §37 Mortgages of landes tenementes or hereditamentes made or had after the saide feaste of Sainct John Baptest. *a* **1634** Randolph *Muses Looking Gl.* II. iv, A glibbery heir With all his lands melted into a mortgage. **1642** Chas. I *Sp.* Wks. 1662 I. 412, I will ..expose all My Land to Sale or Morgage. **1663** Cowley *Cutter Coleman St.* v. i, I have some Hold now upon my Estate again; (tho' she, I confess, be a Clog upon it worse than a Mortgage). **1708** *Act 7 Anne* c. 19 In like Manner as Trustees or Mortgagees of full Age are compellable to convey or assign their Trust Estates or Mortgages. **1728** Young *Love Fame* vi. (1757) 149 His lordship's rent-roll is exceeding great—But mortgages will sap the best estate. **1828** R. Peters *Cases Supreme Crt. U.S.* I. 441 In discussions in Courts of Equity, a mortgage is sometimes called a lien for a debt. **1856** W. R. Fisher *Law Mortgage* 3 The Welsh mortgage, by which the estate is conveyed absolutely to the creditor, without condition; the rents and profits being enjoyed by him in lieu of interest. **1865** Trollope *Belton Est.* i. 2 Mortgages were paid off the property with his wife's money. **1872** W. W. Barry *Forms & Prec. Convey.* 31 A mortgage is made by the same form of assurance as a conveyance, and contains somewhat similar recitals. **1878** Jevons *Prim. Pol. Econ.* 84 They can borrow money by the mortgage of the buildings and machinery belonging to the company.

b. Phrases. † ***in mortgage***: mortgaged. † ***to lay in*** or ***to mortgage***, † ***set to mortgage***: to mortgage. ***to lend on mortgage***: to advance (money) on the security of property, esp. houses or land.

[**1390**: see c.] *c* **1430** Lydg. *Min. Poems* (Percy Soc.) 50 My purse and I be callid to the lure, Of indigence oure stuff leyde in morgage. **1448** Marg. Paston in *Paston Lett.* (1897) I. 69 That he wyl sett hys gode to morgage to Heydon. *c* **1460** *Pol. Rel. & L. Poems* (1866) 24 And whethir it [*sc.* the land] be in any morgage. **1530** Tindale *Pract. Prel.* F viij b, Then to do the kinge seruyce the lordes sell or laye their londes to morgage. **1544** tr. *Littleton's Tenures* 77 b, As a man may make a feoffement in fee in Mortgage, so may a man make a gyft of the tayle in Mortgage. *c* **1595** *Office Alien.* in *Bacon's Wks.* (1730) III. 559 Sometime the land is given in mortgage only, with full intention to be redeemed within one year. **1719** *State Trials, Ralegh* (1730) I. 209, I knew her own Subjects..would not lend her Majesty Money, without Lands in Mortgage. **1844** J. Williams *Real Prop.* IV. (1845) 295 The larger proportion of the lands in this kingdom is at present in mortgage. **1849** Lyell *2nd Visit U.S.* II. 62 Those to whom portions of the borrowed money were lent on mortgage. **1870** L'Estrange *Life Miss Mitford* III. vi. 88 The debts [were] paid, and the residue [of the money] placed out on mortgage.

c. *fig.* (Cf. mortgage *v.* b.)

1390 Gower *Conf.* III. 234 In mariage His trouthe plight lith in morgage. *c* **1430** Lydg. *Min. Poems* (Percy Soc.) 166 Of eche thyng [he] medlithe, his thrift lithe to morgage. **1629** Massinger *Picture* v. iii, I know not..how to redeeme This morgage of her manners. **1633** Marmion *Antiquary* IV. i, If I plot not so, to make all hit, Then you shall take the morgage of my wit. **1684** T. Hockin *God's Decrees* 363 Men ..suffer themselves..to be..ensnared into unhappy contracts and morgages of themselves. **1822** Hazlitt *Table-t.* Ser. II. vi. (1869) 128 They will purchase the hollow happiness of the next five minutes, by a mortgage on the independance and comfort of years. **1866** Lowell *Biglow P.* Ser. II. Introd., Poems (1890) II. 199 A man speaking to me once of a very rocky clearing said, 'Stone's got a pretty heavy mortgage on that land'.

† **d.** *transf.* A pledge. *Obs. rare*$^{-1}$.

1598 Manwood *Lawes Forest* xvi. §11. 99 b, If it be found, that the dogge that was so deliuered to be kept, was a pledge, or a morgage for money.

e. *attrib.*, as ***mortgage bond, debt, deed***, † ***man, money, security, term***; **mortgage rate**, the rate of interest charged by the mortgagee on a loan secured by mortgage; freq. used to refer to a common rate of interest on such loans agreed among building societies, etc.

1890 *Century Dict.*, **Mortgage-bond*, a bond secured by a mortgage. **1839** *Penny Cycl.* XVI. 422/2 The mortgagee may..by express declaration, convert the *mortgage debt into land. **1818** Cruise *Digest* (ed. 2) II. 158 That the second *mortgage deed, comprising all the mortgaged premises, put it in the power of the mortgagee..to [etc.]. **1864** *Chamb. Encycl.* VI. 580/1 The ordinary form of a mortgage-deed resembles an absolute conveyance. **1708** *Rhode Island Col. Rec.* (1859) IV. 50 The said committee..there heard the claims and pretended titles of those gentlemen, called the *mortgage men. **1797** *Encycl. Brit.* (ed. 3) XII. 367/1 With condition to be void on repayment of the *mortgage-money. **1858** Ld. St. Leonards *Handy-Bk. Prop. Law* xiv. 92 Unless the mortgagor will pay off the mortgage-money at a short day. **1935** H. Bellman *Thrifty Three Millions* xii. 263

The *mortgage rate is regarded as being chiefly dominated by the long-term rate of interest. **1952** *Statist* 8 Mar. 349/1 A 4 per cent mortgage rate to borrowing members. **1986** *Economist* 10 May 19/2 Not only has the basic mortgage rate been cut, but competition between building societies and banks has forced them to offer better terms. **1864** *Chamb. Encycl.* VI. 580/1 Trustees are entitled to invest their funds there [*sc.* in Scotland] in *mortgage security. **1827** Jarman *Powell's Devises* II. 139 The question was whether a *mortgage term passed with copyholds, under a devise of all that his (testator's) estate in Bassey, to M. B. and her heirs.

mortgage ('mɔːgɪdʒ), *v.* Also 6–7 **morgage**. [a. obs. F. *mor(t)gager*, or f. prec. sb.] *trans.* To make over (property, esp. houses or land) as security for a money debt, on condition that if the debt is discharged the grant shall be void.

In early use, chiefly in pa. pple.

1530 Palsgr. 640/2 He hath nat solde his lande out ryght, but he hath mortgaged it for more than it is worthe. **1536** Layton in *Lett. Suppress. Monasteries* (Camden) 93 The howse is in dett gretly, the landes solde and morgagede, the fermes let owte. **1612** Dekker *If it be not good* E 3, This day ..a Gallants bound To pay 400. Crownes to free his Landes Fast morgag'de to mee. **1663** Cowley *Verses & Ess.* (1669) 90 [He] Does like an unthrift morgage his Estate Before it falls into his Hand. **1769** Robertson *Chas. V*, V. iv. 361 Lannoy, by mortgaging the revenues of Naples, procured some money. **1817** Wheaton *Cases Supreme Crt. U.S.* II. 396 If..the debtor has made a *bona fide* conveyance of his estate to a third person, or has mortgaged it to secure a debt. **1864** *Chamb. Encycl.* VI. 580/1 In Scotland there is no such practice as mortgaging lands with banks by merely depositing the title-deeds. **1875** Miss Braddon *Strange World* I. iv. 64 The Bellingham estate was mortgaged up to the hilt when he inherited it.

absol. **1790** Burke *Fr. Rev.* (1824) 270 If he wishes to mortgage, he falls the value of his land. **1819** *Stat. Realm* VI. 405 *marg.*, Persons having mortgaged and mortgaging again without Notice to the Second..Mortgagee.

b. *fig.* To pledge; to make liable; *esp.* to establish a claim in advance upon (an income or the like); hence *pass.* to be attached or pledged (*to* something) in advance.

1588 J. Udall *Demonstr. Discipl.* (Arb.) 3 Haue you morgaged the saluation of your soules and bodies, for the present fruition of your pompe and plesure? **1590** Spenser *F.Q.* i. v. 46 Mortgaging their lives to Covetise. *c* **1600** Shaks. *Sonn.* cxxxiv, And I my selfe am morgag'd to thy will. **1651** Biggs *New Disp.* ¶ 290 Morgaged, and benighted to eternall dulnesse. **1712** Steele *Spect.* No. 493 ¶ 1 When Suitors of no Consideration will have Confidence enough to press upon their Superiors, those in Power..are mortgaged into Promises out of their Impatience of Importunity. *a* **1732** Gay *Mad-dog* Poems (1737) II. 67 Gaming succeeds; if fortune crosses, Then virtue's mortgag'd for her losses. **1822** Lamb *Elia* Ser. ii. *Conf. Drunkard*, To mortgage miserable morrows for nights of madness. **1838** Lytton *Alice* iii. i, His income was already deeply mortgaged. **1838** Emerson *Lit. Ethics* (1875) II. 207 The new man must feel that he has not come into the world mortgaged to the opinions and usages of Europe. **1873** Miss Braddon *Str. & Pilgr.* ii. ii. 164 Every man's autumn is mortgaged before the spring is over. **1887** Huxley in *Life* (1900) II. x. 163 What little energy I possess is mortgaged to quite other occupations.

Hence '**mortgaging** *vbl. sb.* and *ppl. a.*

1625 Bacon *Ess.*, *Usury* (Arb.) 543 As for Mortgaging, or Pawning, it will little mend the matter. **1768** Hume *Ess.*, *Publ. Credit* 208 The abuses of mortgaging are more certain and inevitable. **1892** *Daily News* 25 Nov. 7/3 Large capitalist houses have continually taken over numbers of farms left by the mortgaging farmers.

mortgageable ('mɔːgɪdʒəb(ə)l), *a.* [f. mortgage + -able.] Capable of being mortgaged.

1862 T. A. Trollope *Marietta* I. ii. 36 Value of a mortgageable property. **1888** *Univ. Rev.* Nov. 424 There were mortgageable debts to dealers in curiosities [etc.].

mortgaged ('mɔːgɪdʒd), *ppl. a.* [f. mortgage *v.* + -ed[1].] Of land, etc.: Having a mortgage on it; made over as a security for a debt. Also said of debts.

1614 Beaum. & Fl. *Wit at Sev. Weap.* i, To redeem morgag'd Land. **1718** *Free-thinker* No. 42. 307 He will redeem his mortgaged Estate at any Price. **1765** Blackstone *Comm.* I. 173 That in mortgaged or trust-estates, the person in possession..shall have the vote. **1868** Rogers *Pol. Econ.* xiii. (1876) 172 Peasant proprietors are often heavily burdened with mortgaged debts. **1890** Kipling *Departm. Ditties*, etc. *Masque of Plenty*, His speech is of mortgaged bedding, On his kine he borrows yet.

fig. **1643** Lightfoot *Glean. Ex.* 32 Moses Law..taught Israel to expect that one..should redeeme for him morgaged heaven. **1667** *Decay Chr. Piety* vi. 136 Let men consider themselves..as ensnar'd in that unhappy contract which has rendered them part of the Devils possession, and contrive how they may..disentangle their Mortgag'd Souls.

mortgagee (mɔːgɪ'dʒiː). [f. mortgage *v.* + -ee[1].] The person to whom property is mortgaged; one who lends money on mortgage.

1584 in *10th Rep. Hist. MSS. Comm.* App. v. 439 Yt.. shalbe lawfull to and for the morgagee to challenge the morgagor for the resydue. **1628** Coke *On Litt.* 207 The Morgagee or his heire agreeing thereunto may re-enter into the land. **1648** *Art. Peace* xxvi. in *Milton's Wks.* 1851 II. 529 Where Entry hath been made by the Mortgagers against Law..and detained wrongfully by them without giving any satisfaction to the Mortgagees. **1708** [see mortgage *sb.*]. **1827** Jarman *Powell's Devises* II. 147 A testator, who was a mortgagee in fee. **1831** Macaulay *Ess.*, *Civil Disab. Jews*, If we were to say that a Jew mortgagee would not foreclose because [etc.]. **1878** Jevons *Prim. Pol. Econ.* 90 The mortgagee or lender of the money then becomes part-owner of the land and capital.

mortgager ('mɔːgɪdʒə(r)). [f. mortgage *v.* + -er[1].] = mortgagor.

1638 Sanderson *Serm.* (1681) II. 94 So as the mortgager is upon the point the proprietary still. **1648** [see prec.]. **1692** *Act 4 Will. & Mar.* c. 16 The Mortgager or Mortgagers of the said Lands and Tenements. **1790** Burke *Fr. Rev.* 169 Those are to answer the debt who neither were lenders or borrowers, mortgagers or mortgagees. **1839** *Penny Cycl.* XV. 421/2 After the mortgage is made, the mortgager cannot make a lease of the lands without the mortgagee's consent. **1883** *Encycl. Brit.* XVI. 848/1 In equity the mortgager remains the real owner, and the mortgagee is merely an encumbrancer.

mortgagor (mɔːgɪ'dʒɔː(r)). *Law.* Also 6–7 **morgagor**, 9 **mortgageor**. [f. mortgage + -or.

An attempt has been made in some Dicts. to rectify the anomalous spelling *mortgagor*, in which *g* before *o* is pronounced (dʒ), by the insertion of *e*; but the form *mortgageor* is not recorded in actual use. (Cf., however, *obligeor*, s.v. obligor.)]

A person who mortgages or makes over property as a security for debt.

1584 [see mortgagee]. **1628** Coke *On Litt.* 206 The Executors or Administrators of the Mortgagor. **1708** *Act 7 Anne* c. 19 By the Direction of the Cestuy que Trust or Mortgagor. **1766** Blackstone *Comm.* II. 157 That the mortgagee shall re-convey the estate to the mortgagor. **1861** *Law Jrnl. Repts.* XXX. (Com. Pl.) 180 Sold..to pay the debts of the mortgagor. **1875** Digby *Real Prop.* v. (1876) 251 A mortgagor, after default in payment of the mortgage debt, cannot make a valid lease of the lands without the concurrence of the mortgagee. **1890** Hall Caine *Bondman* ii. x, Jacob..bargained to be made Mortgagor.

morth: see murth.

morther: see mauther, murder.

mortice: see mortise.

mortician (mɔː'tɪʃən). *U.S.* [f. L. *mors*, *mort-* death (cf. mort *sb.*[1]) + -ician.] An undertaker; one who arranges funerals.

1895 *Columbus* (Ohio) *Dispatch* 14 Aug. (Advt.), We, Mank & Webb, are the only Morticians in the city who do not belong to the Funeral Director's Protective Association. **1915** *Literary Digest* 16 Jan. 130/3 The word 'mortician' is a recent innovation due to a need felt by undertakers for a word more in keeping with, and descriptive of, their calling. **1927** *Glasgow Herald* 1 Oct. 10/7 As the jury troop out of their boxes every tread of their heels will mean another call for the mortician. **1930** *Punch* 18 June 696 He passed me on to a mortician... His prices..were huge, but then he was mortician to all the best movie-stars' husbands. **1948** *Christian Cent.* 4 Feb. 146/1 Give the morticians credit—their cosmetic arts are highly skilled. **1951** M. McLuhan *Mech. Bride* (1967) 14/2 This sentiment also fits glovelike over the mortician chapel. *Ibid.* 43/2 It is therefore ironic that the present *Life* feature..should have so mortician-like an air. *Ibid.* 62/1 Our refusal to face death at all in the mortician parlor. **1953** 'M. Innes' *Christmas at Candleshoe* i. 10 He is a bald pale person from Buffalo, where he carries on the profession of mortician. **1958** *Oxf. Mag.* 30 Oct. 49/2 Well—hush!—there it is, a thing of beauty in a mortician's parlour; embalmed but—see there!—quite conscious. **1972** *Lebende Sprachen* XVII. 34/1 US *mortician*..undertaker.

mortiechein, variant of mortechien.

mortiel, obs. form of mortal.

‖**mortier** (mɔrtje). [Fr. (Cf. mortar *sb.*[1] 4.)] A cap formerly worn by high officials of France.

1727–52 Chambers *Cycl.*, *Mortier*, a badge or ensign of dignity, borne by the chancellors, and great presidents, of the parliaments of Paris. **1820** Ranken *Hist. France* VIII. i. ii. 28 The first president... His cap, or mortier,..was ornamented with a double round of gold lace. **1830** James *Darnley* xxxix, The star and collar of St. Michael, with the velvet mortier and short white plume.

† '**mortifer**. *Obs. nonce-wd.* [f. L. *morti-*, *mors* death + *-fer* bearing.] A bringer of death.

1667 [see noctifer].

mortiferous (mɔː'tɪfərəs), *a.* Now *rare.* [f. L. *mortifer*, *-fer-us*: see mort *sb.*[1] and -ferous. Cf. F. *mortifère.*] Bringing or producing death; death-dealing, deadly.

1535 Stewart *Cron. Scot.* I. 20 The perelus poysoun, mortiferus melancolie,..In that distres hes done him for to de. **1660** H. More *Myst. Godl.* vi. x. 240 Burnt up by this mortiferous Fever. **1699** Evelyn *Acetaria* 74 The Cicuta.. whatever it is in any other Country 'tis certainly Mortiferous in ours. **1702** C. Mather *Magn. Chr.* vii. vi. (1852) 555 Many of them..were a fair mark for the mortiferous bullets. **1859** R. F. Burton *Centr. Afr.* in *Jrnl. Geog. Soc.* XXIX. 40 That fevers are in these regions the natural expression of mortiferous influences generally. **1902** *Fortn. Rev.* June 1019 If such a 'mortiferous' action really exists, perhaps it could be checked chemically.

b. *transf.* Bringing spiritual death.

1542 Becon *Christmas Banq.* iii. F iij, In the body of him, which without ony carnall entysemente & mortiferous delectacion was conceyued. **1654** Hammond *Fundam.* viii. 73 While we make no distinction of sins, and deem every invincible infirmity..to be as dangerous and mortiferous as the most wilful act. **1844** S. R. Maitland *Dark Ages* 117 [tr. Eligius] Whenever you sin, do not wait in mortiferous security until your wounds putrefy. **1851** Sir F. Palgrave *Norm. & Eng.* I. 198 Every erroneous doctrine..is only the repetition of an earlier error,..the venom enfeebled or more mortiferous.

Hence **mor'tiferously** *adv.*, in a mortiferous or deadly manner; **mor'tiferousness**, deadliness.

1685 H. More *Paralip. Prophet.* xlii. 364 That was not the healing of the Beast, but the mortiferously wounding the Dragon. **1856** Ruskin *Mod. Paint.* IV. v. xix. §21 The pure mortiferousness of this mind, capable neither of patience, fidelity, grace, or wit.

mortific (mɔː'tɪfɪk), *a. rare.* [ad. eccl.L. *mortific-us*: see mort *sb.*[1] and -fic.] Death-producing; deadly. So **mor'tifical** *a.*

1651 Biggs *New Disp.* ¶ 100 Mortifick distempers and maladies. **1657** Tomlinson *Renou's Disp.* iii. i. 97 That Medicament must be given..which..will free from such a mortificall cause. **1657** *Physical Dict.*, *Mortifical.* **1808** *Sporting Mag.* XXXII. 195 With such rapidity did the mortific matter attack his system, that he became a corpse.

† **mor'tificate**, *ppl. a.* and *sb. Obs. rare.* [ad. L. *mortificāt-us*, pa. pple. of *mortificāre* to mortify: see -ate[3].] **a.** *adj.* Killed. **b.** *sb.* ? One who is mortified or dead to the world.

1471 Ripley *Comp. Alch.* i. xx. in Ashm. (1652) 134 Our Tode of the Erth whych etyth hys fyll: Sum name hyt by whych it ys mortyfycat The spyryt of the Erth with venome intoxycate. **1600** W. Watson *Decacordon* (1602) 67 No Prince or prelate liuing can escape their [the Jesuits'] tongs, ..vntill these mortificats haue their wils.

mortification (mɔːtɪfɪ'keɪʃən). [a. F. *mortification* (14th c.), or ad. eccl.L. *mortificātiōn-em*, n. of action f. *mortificāre* to mortify.]

1. In religious use: The action of mortifying the flesh or its lusts: the subjection of one's appetites and passions by the practice of austere living, esp. by the self-infliction of bodily pain or discomfort. **a.** in phr. ***mortification of the body***, ***of sin***, etc.

c **1386** Chaucer *Pars. T.* ¶ 1006 This blisfull regne mow men purchace by pouertee espirituell..the lyf by deth and mortificacion of synne. **1426** Lydg. *De Guil. Pilgr.* 12010 Mortyfycacioun off the body. **1526** *Pilgr. Perf.* (W. de W. 1531) 1 b, Goostly exercyse, or mortifycacyon of the senses. **1532** More *Confut. Tindale* Wks. 700/2 The mortificacion of the fleshly woorkes. *c* **1535** Nisbet *Prol. Romans* (S.T.S.) III. 342 Thann exhorttis he to gude werkis, and vnto contynewall mortificatiounn of fleische. **1671** Tillotson *Serm.* 219 Mortification of our lusts and passions, though.. it have something in it that is troublesome, yet [etc.]. **1674** Owen *Holy Spirit* iv. viii. 483 The Foundation of all Mortification of Sin, is from the Inhabitation of the Spirit in us. **1780** Bentham *Introd. Princ. Morals* ii. §8 (1789) 10 Saints who, for the good of their souls, and the mortification of their bodies, have voluntarily yielded themselves a prey to vermin. **1836** J. H. Newman *Par. Serm.* II. xvii. 221 Self-denial, mortification of life, bearing our cross, are especially insisted on by Christ.

b. simply, without qualification.

1577 tr. *Bullinger's Decades* iv. ii. 562 But we in this disputation of ours, will vse Repentaunce for a conuerting or turning to the Lord..for mortification, and the beginning to leade a newe life. *a* **1633** Austin *Medit.* (1635) 101 It is Lent: a time of Mortification. **1657** Trapp *Comm. Ps.* lxii. 8 Give not over the practice of Mortification untill you feel your hearts part asunder in your bosoms. **1709** Lady M. W. Montagu *Let. to Mrs. Wortley* lx. 99, I must content myself with reckoning it of the mortifications proper to this devout time [Ash Wednesday]. **1775** Sheridan *Duenna* iii. v, Ye eat and swill and sleep..while we are wasting in mortification. **1841** Elphinstone *Hist. Ind.* I. 109 A Bramin..after having passed through a period of solitude and mortification as an anchoret. **1848** Mrs. Jameson *Sacr. & Leg. Art* (1850) 201 He destroyed his health by his austerity and mortifications.

2. *Path.* The death of a part of the body while the rest is living; gangrene, necrosis.

1555 Bonner *Homilies* 69 Mortification, putrifaction, and other suche lyke thinges. **1597** A. M. tr. *Guillemeau's Fr. Chirurg.* 2/3 There ensuethe a Gangræna or mortificatione. **1677** Gale *Crt. Gentiles* iii. 122 A gangrene properly signifies the mortification of some carnose part by reason of an inflammation. **1725** De Foe *Voy. round World* (1840) 90 Pickling, that is to say, throwing salt and vinegar on the back after the whipping..is certainly the way to prevent mortification. **1779–81** Johnson *L.P.*, *Dryden* Wks. II. 358 He died..of a mortification in his leg. **1826** S. Cooper *First Lines Surg.* (ed. 5) 3 In parts of inferior vascularity, like tendons, fasciæ, &c. inflammation readily occasions mortification. **1878** T. Bryant *Pract. Surg.* I. 35 Mortification of any part of the body signifies its death.

transf. **1601** Holland *Pliny* I. 540 A seuerall kind of blasting or mortification there is besides in vines..which is called Roratio.

† **3.** Deadening or destruction of vital or active qualities; devitalization. In 17–18th c. often applied to the state of torpor and insensibility preceding death. *Obs.*

1542 Borde *Dyetary* ii. (1870) 235 Mortyfycation of the vytall, and anymall, and spyrytuall powers. **1596** Norden *Prepar. Spec. Brit.* 11 There seemeth a mortification of the nedles vertue, which staggereth vncertainly. **1654** Whitlock *Zootomia* 25 Inchoate mortifications lessening the horrour of (that must-be-done) Dying. **1706** Stanhope *Paraphr.* III. 259 The Mortification of some old, and quickening of some contrary Principle, in a spiritual Sense. **1732** Arbuthnot *Rules of Diet* (1736) 367 A sudden Remission of the Pain, with cold Sweats [etc.]..are Signs of a Mortification and approaching Death. **1770** Gray *Let. to Nicholls* 25 Nov. (1843) 115 If a mortification does not come to release her, [she] may lie in this agony for months.

† **4.** *Old Chem.* Alteration of the form of metals, etc.; destruction or neutralization of the active qualities of chemical substances. Cf. mortify 6.

1605 TIMME *Quersit.* I. ii. 44 The sole elements, separated from those three beginnings, doe bring nothing but impurities, corruption, and mortification. 1610 B. JONSON *Alch.* II. v, *Sub.* And when comes Viuification? *Fac.* After Mortification. 1678 PHILLIPS, *Mortification*..that by which Mixts are as it were destroyed, and lose the vertues of their first nature, to acquire others more efficacious by the help of revivification. 1706 —— (ed. Kersey).

5. *Scots Law.* The act of disposing of property for religious, or, since the Reformation, for charitable or public purposes. Also, property given for such purposes. (Cf. MORTMAIN.)

1498 *Exch. Rolls Scot.* XI. 81 *note,* We haue gevin and perpetualy mortifyt to the cathedrale kirk of Orkna..the..ile of Burra..as our charter of gift and mortification..mar fullily purportis. 1652 Z. BOYD in *Zion's Flowers* (1855) App. 25/1 Reservand furth of this mortificatioune..the sowme of ane thowsand punds. 1685 in *Buccleuch MSS.* (*15th Rep. Hist. MSS. Comm.* App. VIII.) 119 Thomas Moodie's mortification for building a kirk in Edinburgh. 1700 LAW *Council of Trade* (1751) 11 All gifts, charities, and mortifications already given, or to be given, and appropriated to the poor. 1775 L. SHAW *Moray* (1827) 362 Mortifications for the poor are £650 Scots. 1858 RAMSAY *Remin.* (ed. 2) 58 One of the bailies died and left it [*sc.* a hospital] 10,000 pounds, which was really a great mortification. 1863 A. H. CHARTERIS *Life J. Robertson* ii. 22 A deed of mortification.

6. The feeling of humiliation caused by a disappointment, a rebuff or slight, or an untoward accident; the sense of disappointment or vexation. Also, an instance of this; a cause or source of such humiliation.

1645 EVELYN *Diary* June, Which..frustrated my designe, to my very greate mortification. 1692 R. L'ESTRANGE *Fables* cccxxvii. 285 It is one of the most vexatious Mortifications perhaps, of..a Studious Mans Life to have his Thoughts disorder'd..by the Importunity of a Tedious..Visit. 1748 *Anson's Voy.* I. ii. 21 We had the mortification to be forty days in our passage. 1769 *Junius Lett.* xvi. 73 Let them spare us..the mortification of being amused and deluded like children. 1849 MACAULAY *Hist. Eng.* vi. II. 75 He continued to offer his advice daily, and had the mortification to find it daily rejected. 1872 BLACK *Adv. Phaeton* iii. 31 A blush of shame and exceeding mortification.

7. *attrib.*: **mortification root**, marsh mallow, *Malva officinalis.*

1897-8 BRITTON & BROWN *Flora North. U.S. & Canada.*

† **'mortificative**, *a.* *Obs. rare*⁻¹. [a. OF. *mortificatif*, ad. med.L. **mortificātivus* (see MORTIFY and -ATIVE).] ? That deadens pain.

a 1400 *Stockholm Med. MS.* 12 Anoþer clister þat is clepyd mortificatyf.

mortified ('mɔːtɪfaɪd), *ppl. a.* [f. MORTIFY *v.* + -ED[1].]

1. In religious use, of persons, their actions or occupations: Dead to sin or the world; having the appetites and passions in subjection; ascetic. Now *rare.*

1526 *Pilgr. Perf.* (W. de W. 1531) 143 How euery mortifyed soule..sholde resorte to yᵉ arke of clere conscyence & there counseyle with god. 1579 TOMSON *Calvin's Serm. Tim.* 488/2 Ho, thou art of the companie of hypocrites, thou art mortified. 1588 SHAKS. *L.L.L.* I. i. 28. 1646 BUCK *Rich. III*, I. 4 Such a mortified and perilous Pilgrimage to Jerusalem. 1651 WOOD *Life* (O.H.S.) I. 166 He became a mortified and pious minister in Shropshire. 1656 EARL MONM. tr. *Boccalini's Advts. fr. Parnass.* I. lxiii. (1674) 79 That laudable zeal of Reputation, which is most intense in even the most mortified Vertuosi. *a* 1668 LASSELS *Voy. Italy* II. (1670) 19 They content themselves to go bare foot, and teach only the lower Schools, and first rudiments; ..A strange mortified trade. 1704 NELSON *Fest. & Fasts* II. *Prel. Instr.* (1707) 436 St. James the Great and St. John were very eminent for a mortified Life. 1720 STRYPE *Stow's Surv.* 17/1 A long Beard, Eyes sunk, and an old mortified Face. 1829 SOUTHEY *All for Love* IV. iv. Poet. Wks. VII. 170 To carnal wishes would it turn The mortified intent? 1844 LINGARD *Anglo-Sax. Ch.* (1858) I. iii. 120 An abstemious and mortified life.

† **b.** *mortified to* (rarely *of*): dead to (the world or its pleasures); hence occas. = insensible to. *Obs.*

1659 *Gentl. Calling* ix. §8, I fear there are few so mortified to wealth, as to do it upon the score of self-denial. 1660 INGELO *Bentiv. & Ur.* II. (1682) 89 He is mortified to all sense of Ingenuous Principles. 1670 EACHARD *Cont. Clergy* 90 An hardy and labouring clergy, that is mortified to an horse, and all such pampering vanities. 1676 RAY *Corr.* (1848) 123 Reputation (to the vanity of any affectation whereof I desire to be wholly mortified). 1748 MRS. HARRISON *House-keeper's Pocket-Bk.* Pref., There are but few Philosophers..who are so..mortified to the world as to prefer a dish of Roots. 1809 MALKIN *Gil Blas* x. i, You are mortified to all the pomps and vanities of the world.

† **c.** In jocular use: Abstemious. *Obs.*

1665 PEPYS *Diary* 16 Oct., I observing Mr. Povy's being mightily mortifyed in his eating.

† **2.** Dead, slain. *Obs.*

1593 R. HARVEY *Philad.* 17 If any man will raise them from the graue, who will beleeue their mortified Ghosts? 1603 KNOLLES *Hist. Turks* (1638) 270 Having ended his speech, he shewed vnto them the grisely mortified heads. 1625 FLETCHER & SHIRLEY *Night Walker* II, My young Mistriss, that is mortified.

† **3.** Deadened; numbed; insensible. *Obs.*

1601 SHAKS. *Jul. C.* II. i. 324 Thou like an Exorcist, hast coniur'd vp My mortified Spirit. 1605 —— *Lear* II. iii. 15 Bedlam beggers, who with roaring voices, Strike in their num'd and mortified Armes, Pins, Wodden-prickes, Nayles.

4. Affected by gangrene or necrosis.

1597 A. M. tr. *Guillemeau's Fr. Chirurg.* 33 b, It is necessarye that the vivificent parte expelle from it the mortified. *a* 1676 HALE *Prim. Orig. Man.* I. i. (1677) 23 A mortified Limb or Member. 1695 *New Light Chirurg. put out* 52 His Arm was but little swell'd and not at all mortified. 1720 DE FOE *Capt. Singleton* xi. (1840) 196 He cut off a great deal of mortified flesh. 1801 *Med. Jrnl.* V. 534, I found the fingers and thumb exhibiting a mortified appearance. 1822-34 *Good's Study Med.* (ed. 4) II. 656 The mortified parts..are cast off.

† **b.** *transf.* Of plants: Decayed. *Obs.*

1672-3 GREW *Anat. Plants, Anat. Roots* II. (1682) 83 Divers of the Succiferous Vessels..lying next the Soil, usually more or less mortified.

† **5.** Of meat: see MORTIFY *v.* 6. *Obs.*

1617 MORYSON *Itin.* III. 134 The French alone delight in mortified meates. 1733 TULL *Horse-hoeing Husb.* 38 Palates, accustom'd to the Goût of..mortify'd Venison.

6. *Scots Law.* (See MORTIFY *v.* 5.)

1655 in Z. Boyd *Zion's Flowers* (1855) App. 38/2 The aforsaid mortified sowmes. 1813 CARLISLE *Topogr. Dict. Scot.* II. s.v. *Hoddom*, £400..arising from two mortified sums.

7. Humiliated deeply; vexed, chagrined.

1717 LADY M. W. MONTAGU *Lett.* II. xlv. 29 As I prefer English to all the rest, I am extremely mortified at the daily decay of it in my head. 1725 DE FOE *Voy. round World* (1840) 341 They came home to the rest mortified, wet, and almost famished. 1833 HT. MARTINEAU *Loom & Lugger* II. iii. 54 They were mortified at finding the house shut. 1838 LYTTON *Alice* I. iii, The mortified pride of affection. 1885 S. COX *Expos.* xxv. 343 Base greed and mortified ambition moved him to betray his master.

Hence **'mortifiedly** *adv.*, **'mortifiedness.**

1593 NASHE *Christ's T.* (1613) 127 If..a young Student sets not a grave face on it, or seemes not mortifiedly religious. 1643 T. GOODWIN *Trial Chr. Growth* 122 So much mortifiednesse, so much constancie. 1832 T. SCOTT *Comm. 2 Kings* i. 8 In this manner he showed his mortifiedness to the world. 1846 LANDOR *Exam. Shaks.* Wks. II. 298 Whereunto Sir Thomas replied mortifiedly.

mortifier ('mɔːtɪfaɪə(r)). [f. MORTIFY *v.* + -ER[1].] One who or that which mortifies. † **a.** One who practises mortification; an ascetic (*obs.*). **b.** One who or a thing which causes mortification (in various senses). **c.** *Scots Law* (see MORTIFY *v.* 5).

a. 1649 JER. TAYLOR *Gt. Exemp.* I. Disc. ii. 76 The Sarabaites..were stricter mortifiers than the religious in families and Colledges. 1756 W. DODD *Fasting* (ed. 2) 9 The daily fast of great mortifiers.

b. 1658 PITMAN & BATT *Truth Vind.* 5 None can know him a Justifier, but they who know him a Sanctifier and a Mortifier. 1712 STEELE *Spect.* No. 450 ¶6 The Love of Business and Money is the greatest Mortifier of inordinate Desires imaginable. 1801 LAMB *John Woodvil* III, I want.. Some strokes of the old mortifier Calamity, To take these swellings down. 1841 HOR. SMITH *Moneyed Man* III. iv. 104 How sweet it is when a fallen man can thus mortify his intended mortifiers!

c. 1655 in Z. Boyd *Zion's Flowers* (1855) App. 38/2 Quhich by the will of the mortifiers comes not to be payable untill [etc.]. 1820 J. CLELAND *Rise & Progr. Glasgow* 222 A preference is to be given to the mortifier's relatives.

mortify ('mɔːtɪfaɪ), *v.* Also 5-7 **mortefy**, 6-7 **mortyfy**. [a. F. *mortifier*, ad. L. *mortificāre*, f. *morti-*, *mors* MORT *sb.*[1]: see -FY.]

† **1.** *trans.* To deprive of life; to kill, put to death. (In first quot. *absol.*) Also, to make as if dead; to render insensible. *Obs.*

1382 WYCLIF *1 Kings* ii. 6 The Lord mortifieth, and quykeneth. *c* 1412 HOCCLEVE *De Reg. Princ.* 608 Thogh men sowen seed Of vertu in a yong man, it is deed As blyue, his rebel goost it mortifieþ. 1483 CAXTON *Gold. Leg.* 67 b/1, His herte was mortefyed wythin hym, and he was deed lyke a stone. *a* 1533 LD. BERNERS *Gold. Bk. M. Aurel.* (1546) Q ii b, It is..a swounyng, that incontinently mortifieth al the membres. 1565 COOPER *Thesaurus, Caprimulgi*, Birdes.. that in the night sucke goates and mortifie their vdders. 1600 SURFLET *Country Farm* I. xxviii. 176 It were better to writh about and mortifie their cods altogither with pincers, then to geld them all at once. 1615 BRATHWAIT *Strappado* (1878) 153 Thou.. hast well neere my senses mortefied. 1664 EVELYN *Sylva* ix. (1679) 53 If of the principal Stem so left, the frost mortifie any part. 1688 *Persec. Piedmont* 33 These Ruffians mortified her little Daughter about seven months old before her face. 1692 RAY *Disc.* III. ii. (1732) 415 Their seeds..will..be mortified and destroyed.

† **b.** To bruise. [Cf. OF.] *Obs.*

1609 ROWLANDS *Crew of Kind Gossips* 11, I set a little stoole, And ouer that, downe comes my reeling foole:..I am sure it mortified his shins.

† **c.** *intr.* for *pass.* To lose vitality. *Obs.*

1701 STEELE *Funeral* III. (1702) 42 To see one that was a Beauty unfortunately move with the same languor,..that once was Charming in her—To see, I say, her Mortify that us'd to Kill—ha ha ha! 1707 MORTIMER *Husb.* (1721) II. 9 Their Roots are very apt to mortifie or harden and wither by the wind.

† **2.** *trans.* To kill (in transf. and fig. senses); to destroy the vitality, vigour, or activity of; to neutralize the effect or value of; to deaden (pain); to dull (colour), etc. *Obs.*

c 1386 CHAUCER *Pars. T.* ¶159 The gode werkes, that he dide..been al mortified..by the ofte sinning. *c* 1400 *Lanfranc's Cirurg.* (1894) 96 If þat þou dredist wheþer þat it be symple vlcus or a cankre..bigynne to mortifie it wiþ sum maner of poudre. 1489 CAXTON *Faytes of A.* III. viii. 183 Yf cas be that he goo hys waye so he mortyfyeth his hyre..for seruyce ought not to haue noo hyre tyl that hit be complisshed. 1553 BRENDE *Q. Curtius* D iij, His face waxed pale, and the livelye heate was mortified in all partes of his body. 1555 EDEN *Decades* (Arb.) 113 An herbe which quencheth and mortifieth the violent poyson of the herbe. 1590 MARLOWE *2nd Pt. Tamburl.* III. ii. H 3 My mothers death hath mortified my mind, And sorrow stops the passage of my speech. 1599 SHAKS. *Hen. V*, I. i. 26 His wildnesse, mortify'd in him, Seem'd to dye too. 1651 HOBBES *Leviath.* I. xii. 60 With other signes of private interest, enough to mortifie the most lively Faith. 1682 SIR T. BROWNE *Chr. Mor.* (1756) 112 The knowledge of future evils mortifies present felicities. 1711 SHAFTESB. *Charac.* III. VI. v. 373 He must take care at least so to mortify his Colours, that these plain poor Men may not appear,.. adorn'd like so many Lords.

b. *Irish Gram.* (See quot.)

1843 NEILSON *Introd. Irish Lang.* 5 *B, c, d, f, g, m, p, s, t,* are called mutable, because they can be aspirated, or mortified, i.e. change or lose their sound, by the addition of *h.*

† **3.** *Old Chem.* (See quot. 1704.) *Obs.*

c 1386 CHAUCER *Can. Yeom. T.* 573 This quik-silver wol I mortifye. 1460-70 *Bk. Quintessence* 19 Take also a litil quantite of Mer[curie?] & mortifie it wiþ fastynge spotil. 1558 WARDE tr. *Alexis' Secr.* (1568) 101 b, It will be good.. for to mortifie other Quick Sylver. 1601 HOLLAND *Pliny* I. 257 Clodius..to know what tast pearles had, mortified them in vinegre, and drunke them up. 1657 STARKEY *Helmont's Vind.* 315 The sharpnesse of the salt is totally mortified. 1694 SALMON *Bate's Dispens.* 681/2 This Salt is..used in opening and purging Medicines to mortifie the Acids, which excite Fermentations in our Bodies. 1704 J. HARRIS *Lex. Techn.* I. s.v. *Mortifie*, The Chymists say a thing is Mortify'd when its outward Form is altered or destroyed, as particularly when Mercury, or any other Metal is dissolved in an Acid Menstruum. Sometimes they say also, that Spirits are Mortified, when they are mix'd with such things as destroy their strength, and hinder their Operation.

4. To bring into subjection (the body, its appetites and passions) by the practice of self-denial, abstinence, or bodily discipline.

c 1412 HOCCLEVE *De Reg. Princ.* 3665 Than oghte vs cristen men þat vice fleeme, And swiche lustes in vs mortifie. *c* 1450 tr. *De Imitatione* I. xi. 11 þei studied to mortefie hemself in all wises fro erþely desires. 1477 EARL RIVERS (Caxton) *Dictes* 33 He that wol the lif of his saule lete hym mortifie hit & yeue it payne in this world. 1526 TINDALE *Rom.* viii. 13 But if ye mortifie the dedes off the body by the helpe off the sprete ye shall live. —— *Col.* iii. 5 Mortifie therfore youre members which are on the erth, fornicacion [etc.]. *c* 1535 NISBET *Prol. Romans* (S.T.S.) III. 340 Quhilk spret..subdewis, and mortifyis the fleiss. 1660 JER. TAYLOR *Worthy Commun.* i. §6. 110 Give me strength to subdue my passions, to mortifie my inordinations. 1842 TENNYSON *St. Simeon Stylites* 176 Mortify Your flesh.. with scourges and with thorns. 1853 KINGSLEY *Hypatia* xxiv, Can she not mortify these base affections? 1864 W. W. STORY *Roba di R.* (ed. 3) III. 39 They really mortify the flesh by penance, fasting, and wretched fare.

† **b.** To render 'dead' to the world and the flesh. Cf. MORTIFIED 1. *Obs.*

1556 J. HEYWOOD *Spider & F.* B b, I am not mortified to beare distres. 1567 DK. NORFOLK in Strype *Ann. Ref.* (1709) I. 501, I am too well mortified to care for slanderous reports. 1581 PETTIE tr. *Guazzo's Civ. Conv.* II. (1586) 111 b, Your philosophie perchaunce hath so mortified you, that you can promise your selfe the constancie of that Philosopher whome a woman tooke for an image.

† **c.** *absol.* or *intr.* To practise mortification; to be an ascetic. *Obs.*

1568 H. B. tr. *Peter Mart. On Rom.* 203 To mortefy is nothing els, but for a man to be violent against himselfe, and to withstand and resist wicked lustes. 1709 COLLIER *Ess. Mor. Subj.* II. (1722) 147 What can be a more wretched Sight, than to see a Man mortify without Religion? 1742 YOUNG *Nt. Th.* IX. 2389 They mortify, they starve, on wealth, fame, power. 1753 RICHARDSON *Grandison* VI. xxxii. 223 She is retired to Shirley-manor to mortify, after so rich a regale. 1784 R. BAGE *Barham Downs* I. 164 If you will mortify with me to-night upon toasted cheese and ale. 1804 JANE AUSTEN *Watsons* (1879) 327 Imagine him mortifying with his barrel of oysters in dreary solitude. 1842 BARHAM *Ingol. Leg.* Ser. II. *Nell Cook*, And a Warden-pie's a dainty dish to mortify withal.

5. *trans.* *Scots Law.* To dispose of (property) by mortification.

1498 [see MORTIFICATION 5]. 1652 Z. BOYD *Zion's Flowers* (1855) App. 23/2 Mr. Zacharias Boyd..mortifies and dispones to the..colledge.., the..bands contracts debtis. 1742 RICHARDSON *Pamela* (1785) IV. 49 She has.. mortify'd, as the Scots call it, 150*l.* as a Fund for Loans, without Interest. 1842 J. AITON *Domest. Econ.* (1857) 157 When a minister and heritors disagree as to the propriety of cutting trees on a glebe, the matter must be determined by the Judge Ordinary, and their value, when cut, mortified for behoof of the benefice. 1885 A. MACKAY in *Dict. Nat. Biog.* III. 154 In 1380..Barbour mortified his pension of twenty shillings in favour of the cathedral.

6. *Cookery.* To make (raw meat, game, etc.) tender by hanging, keeping, etc. Also *intr.* for *pass.* *Obs.*

1594 R. ASHLEY tr. *Loys Le Roy* 15 b, Raw flesh..which they do presse betweene two stones..or els do mortifie it on the backe of a horse when a man is on him. 1611 COTGR., *Faisander*, to mortifie fowle. 1626 BACON *Sylva* §891 Try it also with Capon..laid abroad, to see whether it will mortifie and become tender sooner. 1632 MASSINGER *Maid of Hon.* III. i, With a worthy loyne of veale, and valiant Capon, Mortifi'd to grow tender. 1718 OZELL tr. *Tournefort's Voy.* I. 192 They presented us..a goat which proved very good, because we let it mortify some hours. [1733: see MORTIFIED 5.] 1790 GOUV. MORRIS *Diary* 22 Jan. (1889) I. 276 As that day does not suit the company, poor Monsieur Trout must e'en mortify two days longer.

transf. 1572 MASCALL *Plant. & Graff.* (1592) Exhort., Ye must digge your holes a yeere before ye plant that the earth may be the better seasoned, mortified and wax tender. 1658 EVELYN *Fr. Gard.* (1675) 284 Let them lie..in the sun to mortifie them a little, that they may the better receive in the salt.

7. *intr.* *Path.* To become mortified or gangrenous. Also (rarely) *trans.*, to render mortified.

1603 KNOLLES *Hist. Turks* (1638) 120 The wound..began to mortifie and grow blacke. 1708 SWIFT *Predictions for*

1708, Wks. 1751 IV. 195 The Swellings in his Legs breaking, and the Flesh mortifying, [he] will die on the 11th instant. **1748** *Anson's Voy.* I. viii. 78 Snow and sleet.. disabling many of them, by mortifying their toes and fingers. **1847** GROTE *Greece* xxxvi. IV. 494 His injured limb mortified.

8. *trans.* To cause to feel humiliated; to cause (a person) mortification (freq. in *pass.*).

1691 LUTTRELL *Brief Rel.* (1857) II. 193 The bull of the last pope had extreamly mortifyed that court. **1699** BENTLEY *Phal.* Pref. 35, I had no design in't, but to mortifie him a little for his pertness. **1726** SWIFT *Gulliver* II. iii, Nothing angered and mortified me so much as the Queen's Dwarf. **1769** ROBERTSON *Chas. V*, IV. Wks. 1851 III. 611 He was fond of mortifying a man whom he had many reasons to hate. **1796–7** JANE AUSTEN *Pride & Prej.* v, I could easily forgive his pride, if he had not mortified mine. **1837** DISRAELI *Venetia* I. vii, No one was more mortified by her rages.

ˈmortifying, *vbl. sb.* [-ING[1].] The action of the vb. MORTIFY.

1382 WYCLIF *2 Cor.* iv. 10 Euermore beringe aboute the mortifyinge [*gloss* that is, the dyuerse tourmentynge] of Jhesu Crist in oure body. *c* **1450** tr. *De Imitatione* II. xii. 56 þere is non oþer way to lyfe.. but þe way of þe holy crosse, and of quotidian mortifieng. **1530** TINDALE *Prol. Lev.* Wks. (1573) 14/2 Baptisme signifieth vnto vs repentaunce, and the mortifying of our vnruly members, and bodyes of sinne, to walke in a new life. **1674** OWEN *Serm.* Wks. 1851 IX. 469 If our hearts are not engaged to the mortifying of all sin.

ˈmortifying, *ppl. a.* [-ING[2].] That mortifies.

1. Involving mortification or repression of natural appetites and desires. Formerly also, that practises self-denial; austere, self-denying, abstemious.

1596 SHAKS. *Merch. V.* I. i. 82 And let my Liuer rather heate with wine, Then my heart coole with mortifying grones. **1638** RAWLEY tr. *Bacon's Life & Death* (1650) 18 His Life was Austere and Mortifying. **1654** A. GRAY *Spirit. Warfare* iii. (1736) 49 A mortifying Christian is a most Experienced Christian. *a* **1697** AUBREY *Lives* (1898) I. 132 Here he had several mortifying and divine motto's. **1706** STANHOPE *Paraphr.* III. 517 It will not decline the most mortifying Severities, when used as Expedients to secure his good Graces. **1835** I. TAYLOR *Spir. Despot.* III. 86 The mortifying purity of the ministers of heaven.

2. Causing death; mortal, fatal; deadly.

1683 TRYON *Country-Mans Comp.* title-p., To preserve Sheep from that Monsterous, Mortifying Distemper, The Rot. *a* **1691** BOYLE *Hist. Air* (1692) 167 The cold in the woods.. was yet not so mortifying as the other. **1706** E. WARD *Wooden World Diss.* (1708) 103 Mortifying, gripe-gut Beer. **1707** MORTIMER *Husb.* (1721) I. 117 Urine.. is reckoned to be of a destructive, mortifying Nature to Vegetables. **1896** ROSEBERY in *Times* 12 Feb. 6/2 The noble duke's icy cold spray has been turned on, and no political plant with which I am acquainted has survived that mortifying process.

†**b.** Dying (hours). *Obs.*

1649 MILTON *Eikon.* xxviii. 226 Those few mortifying howers that should have been most at peace from all disquiet.

3. Marked by mortification or necrosis.

1797 DOWNING *Disord. Horned Cattle* 18 A swelling attended with lameness and a mortifying blackness. **1901** *Daily Chron.* 25 July 3/2 The explorer held the mortifying finger upright during many a weary march.

4. Causing humiliation of feeling, vexation, or depression; vexatious, annoying; depressing.

1726 SWIFT *Gulliver* III. x, They were the most mortifying Sight I ever beheld; and the Women more horrible than the Men. **1756** COWPER *Wks.* (1837) XV. 270, I live in hourly apprehensions of more mortifying adventures. **1823** LAMB *Elia* II. *Stage Illusion*, The most mortifying infirmity in human nature.. is, perhaps, cowardice. **1879** PEROWNE in *Expositor* X. 166 The disappointment was naturally the more acute and mortifying.

Hence **ˈmortifyingly** *adv.*

1748 RICHARDSON *Clarissa* (1811) III. 284 How tender, how mortifyingly tender now in him! **1832** *Examiner* 293/1 A time mortifyingly short. **1853** C. BRONTE *Villette* xxvii, What she said.. was of a purpose somewhat mortifyingly below the standard of the occasion.

mortilage, -oge, etc., altered ff. MARTILOGE.

1500 *Will of Treffry* (Somerset Ho.), In the mortlage boke & in the commune bederoll. **1523** *Test. Ebor.* (Surtees) V. 172 To have my name writtyn on ther Mortilage booke. **1527** *Trevisa's Higden* v. iv, The mortylogye [*Rolls ed.* martiloge]. *c* **1640** J. SMYTH *Lives Berkeleys* (1883) I. 215 The day of theire deaths shall be written in their mortiloge.

†**mortisate,** *pa. pple. Obs. rare*$^{-1}$. [For **amortizate*, ad. med.L. *amortizātus*: see AMORTIZE *v.*] Given in mortmain.

c **1535** *Art. Inquis. Monast.* in T. West *Antiq. Furness* (1805) 146 What evedence haue ye to shewe for all.. yowre possessions, mortisate and giuen unto you, and this your monasterie?

mortise, mortice (ˈmɔːtɪs), *sb.* Forms: 5–6 **mortas(e, mortays(e, -eys(e, -es(e, -esse, mortyse,** 5–7 **morteis,** 5–8 **mortaise,** (6 **mortress(e, morteise),** 6–7 **mortess,** 7 **mortis(s(e,** (**mortesce, mortize, mortuis),** 7–9 **mortoise, mortes,** 6– **mortise,** 8– **mortice.** [a. F. *mortaise* (13th c. *mortoise* in Hatz.-Darm.), of unknown origin. Cf. Sp. *mortaja*.]

1. A cavity or hole into which the end of some other part of a framework or structure is fitted so as to form a joint; also, a groove or slot for the reception or passage of a rope, an adjustable pin, etc.

Frequently used in 15–16 c. Legends and Mystery Plays for the socket into which the foot of the Cross was set.

c **1400** MAUNDEV. (Roxb.) ii. 5 And þe stock [of the cross] þat stude in þe erthe, in þe whilk was made a mortas [orig. F. *vne morteise*], was of cedre. *Ibid.* x. 38–9 And þe crosse was sette in a mortays in the roche... And þat es now called Golgatha. **1483** CAXTON *Gold. Leg.* 167 b/1, And another piece wherin the sokette or morteys was maad that the body of the crosse stood in. **1541** R. COPLAND *Guydon's Quest. Chirurg.* K iv b, In the ioynynge with the bygger bone doth they [*sc.* the tibia and fibula] make one holowe pyt or morteys wherin the fyrste bone of the fote is receyued. **1611** COTGR. s.v. *Orbite, L'orbite d'une poulie*, the mortaise wherein the shiuer of a Pullie runnes. **1676** *Phil. Trans.* XI. 680 Each Lever is pierced in the middle by a Mortaise,.. in which an iron-nail.. turns round. **1733** TULL *Horse-hoeing Husb.* xxi. 304 The Socket is a Mortise of about a Foot long, at the upper part; two Inches deep. **1825** J. NICHOLSON *Operat. Mechanic* 406 The screw passes through a groove or mortise at the end of the wheel frame. **1844** H. STEPHENS *Bk. Farm* I. 413 The coulter-box is formed by piercing an oblong mortice through the bar. **1844** *Civil Eng. & Arch. Jrnl.* VII. 107/2 The mortoise, in the cap, should be made exactly to suit the mortoise in the piston-rod. **1857** R. TOMES *Amer. in Japan* ix. 198 The cylinders.. are arranged in a row, with a mortise between them to regulate their approach.

2. *spec.* in *Carpentry* and *Joinery*: The counterpart of a TENON[1]; a cavity or hole, usually rectangular in shape, cut in the surface of a piece of timber, etc., to receive the shaped end (called a 'tenon') of another piece.

chase, chased, or ***pulley mortise***, a long mortise in which a tenon may be inserted transversely and driven home. ***double mortise***, (*a*) = prec.; (*b*) one consisting of two holes cut side by side to receive a double tenon. ***stub mortise***, one that is cut only partially through the timber.

c **1440** *Promp. Parv.* 344/1 Morteys of a tenowne, *gumphus.* **1546** GARDINER *Declar. Art. Joye* 35 b, That were euen as wysely done of vs, as if a man wolde frame a tenaunte without a mortesse. **1570** LEVINS *Manip.* 85/19 A mortresse, *cumphus.* **1590** GREENE *Upst. Courtier* F 3, The ioyner though an honest man, yet he maketh his ioynts weake, and putteth in sappe in the morteses. **1663** GERBIER *Counsel* 42 That the Carpenters be good husbands.. in.. sparing to make double Mortises, which doe but weaken the Summers. **1678** MOXON *Mech. Exerc.* v. 80 If you were to make a Tennant upon a piece of Fur, and a Mortess to receive it in a piece of Oak. **1697** BP. PATRICK *Comm. Exodus* xxvi. 19 There were two silver Sockets for each Plank, whose Tenons, sinking into these Mortaises [etc.]. **1753** F. PRICE *Brit. Carpenter* (ed. 3) 8 Double, or pully mortices, (as they are call'd). **1823** P. NICHOLSON *Pract. Build.* 119 Girders.. are made with mortises, in order to receive the tenons at the end of the binding-joists. *Ibid.*, These long mortises are called pulley-mortises, or chase-mortises. **1842** GWILT *Archit.* §2019 The bridging joists are notched;.. though sometimes they are framed between with chased mortices. **1860** WORCESTER (citing Loudon), Stub mortise. **1875** KNIGHT *Dict. Mech.* s.v. *Mortise-chisel*, The chisel.. is a double one, each limb having two lips, adapting the tool to cut a double mortise.

transf. *c* **1710** CELIA FIENNES *Diary* (1888) 10 Two stones stands up and one laid on their tops with morteses into each other. **1852** T. WRIGHT *Celt, Rom., Sax.* ii. 59 Each of the upright stones had two tenons.. which fitted into mortices or hollows.

b. ***mortise and tenon, tenon and mortise***, as the component parts of a particular kind of joint; hence, a joint composed of a mortise and a tenon. Also *collect.* as a method of joining material.

1610 HOLLAND *Camden's Brit.* 251 [Stonehenge].. certaine mighty and unwrought stones.. upon the heads of which, others like ouerthwart peeces do beare and rest crossewise, with a small tenents and mortescis. **1623** GOUGE *Serm. Extent God's Provid.* §15 Two girders were by tenents and mortaises let into the midst of it. **1624** A. WOTTON *Runne from Rome* i. 4, I am instructed to take the frame in sunder..; to trie how every tenant and mortuis is fitted each to other. **1631** WEEVER *Anc. Funeral Mon.* 317 With Mortis and tenents. **1757** *Phil. Trans.* L. 200 They were joined together at the ends with mortoise and tenon. **1801** *Encycl. Brit.* (ed. 3) Suppl. I. 171/1 Where the beams stand square with each other.. the common mortise and tenon is the most perfect junction. **1859** JEPHSON *Brittany* xii. 200 Horizontal stones are laid across the tops of the menhirs, and fastened with mortise and tenon.

attrib. **1791** SMEATON *Edystone L.* §158 The stones.. were all curiously joined together at the ends, mortoise and tenon fashion. **1802** PALEY *Nat. Theol.* ix. 118 There is the hinge joint, and the mortice and tenon joint. **1904** WINDLE *Rem. Preh. Age Eng.* viii. 185 An ellipse of hewn sarsen trilithons, with mortise and tenon connections.

c. *Her.* (See quot.)

1725 COATS *Dict. Her.*, *Mortaise*, or *Mortise*, as our Carpenters and Joyners call it, is.. a square Piece of Wood, with a square Hole through it. **1828–40** BERRY *Encycl. Her.*

3. *nonce-use.* [From the vb.] State of being mortised.

1875 TENNYSON *Q. Mary* III. i, And oversea they say this state of yours Hath no more mortice than a tower of cards.

4. *attrib.* and *Comb.*: †**mortise-articulation** = GOMPHOSIS; **mortise-bolt** (see quot.); †**mortise bones**, the tibia and fibula, the ends of which together form a cavity into which the ball of the ankle-joint is placed; **mortise chisel**, a chisel with a stout blade used in cutting mortises; **mortise clamp**, a clamp mortised at the ends; so **mortise-clamped** *a.*, furnished with such a clamp; **mortise gauge** (see GAUGE *sb.* 11); **mortise-hole** = sense 1 above; hence *fig.*, an obscure place; **mortise-joint**, a mortise and tenon joint; **mortise lock**, one made for insertion in a mortise cut in the edge of the lock-rail of a door; also *attrib.*, as **mortise lock bit, chisel**, tools for cutting a mortise for this lock; †**mortise-piece**, a joining piece; **mortise wheel**, a cast iron wheel having cogs of wood set into mortises; †**mortise wimble**, a tool for boring a mortise.

1658 SIR T. BROWNE *Gard. Cyrus* iii. 57 The seeds.. lockt up in sockets after a gomphosis or *mortis-articulation, diffuse themselves circularly into branches. *Ibid.* 59. **1875** KNIGHT *Dict. Mech.*, **Mortise-bolt*, one let into a mortise in a door. **1541** R. COPLAND *Guydon's Quest. Chirurg.* K iv b, There be two [bones in the knee] that be called yᵉ *morteys bones. *Ibid.* L j, In the vpper roundnes therof is affyrmed the holownesse of the pyt or morteys bones, and there the fote is moued. **1678** MOXON *Mech. Exerc.* iv. 74 The *Mortess Chissel.. is a narrow Chissel but hath its Blade much thicker, and.. stronger... Its Office is to cut.. Mortesses in.. wood. **1852–61** *Archit. Publ. Soc. Dict.* s.v. *Clamp*, *Mortise clamp. **1825** J. NICHOLSON *Operat. Mechanic* 602 Boards.. *mortise-clamped. **1812** P. NICHOLSON *Mech. Exerc.* 140 The *Mortice Gauge.. has two teeth instead of one... The use of this gauge is.. for gauging mortices and tenons. **1585** J. HIGINS *Junius' Nomenclator* 205/2 *Columbaria*... The *mortesse holes: the holes wherein the endes of rafters and quarters are fastened. *a* **1654** SELDEN *Table T.* (Arb.) 43 They do it in a Corner, in a Mortice-hole, not in the Market-place. **1882** OGILVIE s.v. *Mortise*, *Mortise-joint. **1780** *Birmingham*, etc. *Directory* 79 Foxall, William, *mortice lock maker. **1852–61** *Archit. Publ. Soc. Dict.* s.v. *Bit*, Those excellent tools the mortise lock bits. **1875** KNIGHT *Dict. Mech.*, *Mortise-lock Chisel*... It has a peculiar shape, in order to pull out the wood. **1577** B. GOOGE *Heresbach's Husb.* II. 108 For Rafters, and *Mortisse peeces [orig. L. *coagmentationes*] the Elme and the Ashe, by reason of theyr length serues best. **1843** HOLTZAPFFEL *Turning*, etc. I. 351 A *mortise wheel.. with spaces around its edge.. to be filled with wooden cogs. **1407–8** in *Fabric Rolls York Minster* (Surtees) 207 *note*, j *mortas wymbyll, j bandwymbyll.

mortise, mortice (ˈmɔːtɪs), *v.*[1] Forms: see the sb.: also 6–9 **mortize.** [f. MORTISE *sb.*; cf. F. *mortaiser* (OF. *mortissier*, 1302 in Hatz.-Darm.).]

1. *trans.* To fasten or join securely; to fix in or join together closely and firmly; *spec.* in *Carpentry* and *Joinery*, to join with a mortise; to fasten *into* or *to* by means of mortise and tenon; to secure (a tenon) with a mortise. Also *fig.*

c **1440** *York Myst.* xxvi. 163, I fele by a figure in youre fals face, It is but foly to feste affeccioun in ȝou. For Mars he hath morteysed his mark, Eftir all lynes of my lore. **1530** PALSGR. 640/2, I mortayse a thynge in byldyng, as a carpenter dothe... Mortayse this study in to this princypall. **1547** J. HARRISON *Exhort. Scottes* H v, I wote not whether firme concorde be otherwise more sureli mortized in mens hartes, then when [etc.]. **1568** GRAFTON *Chron.* II. 409 When King Henry had thus mortised himselfe and his issue so sure and fast, as he thought, that the same was not possible to be remooued, then [etc.]. **1570** FOXE *A. & M.* (ed. 2) 1387/1 Which Image was mortrest in a wall behynd the hye altare. **1602** SHAKS. *Ham.* III. iii. 20 Maiestie.. is a massie wheele.. To whose huge Spoakes, ten thousand lesser things Are mortiz'd and adioyn'd. **1620–55** I. JONES *Stone-Heng* (1725) 40 Each Stone having two Tenons mortaised into the Architrave. *Ibid.* 41 The Architrave.. being mortaised into them. **1637** GILLESPIE *Eng. Pop. Cerem.* Ep. B 2, We must therefore be mortaised togither.. by the bands of Trueth. **1727** ARBUTHNOT *Coins*, etc. 236 The Ship was built by halves, and the one half being finished.. the other half was join'd to it by great Brass Nails.. mortiz'd with Lead. **1777** ROBERTSON *Hist. Amer.* (1783) III. 392 The Peruvians could not mortize two beams together, or give.. stability to any work composed of timber. **1794** W. FELTON *Carriages* (1801) I. 13 The door-case rails are.. morticed on the standing pillars. **1800** COLERIDGE *Piccolom.* III. iii, So will he, falling, draw down.. All us, who're fixed and mortised to his fortune. **1863** *Q. Rev.* CXIV. 310 The.. ingenuity with which that great engineer mortised his tall tower to the wave-worn rock. **1899** R. MUNRO *Prehist. Scotl.* x. 335 A rectangularly shaped framework of oak beams, mortised at the corners.

absol. **1876** W. PAPWORTH in *Encycl. Brit.* IV. 479/1 But as this exposes the tenon.. to the risk of being torn off, we are obliged to mortise further down.

b. *intr.* for *passive.* To be fixed firmly *into.*

1861 BERESF. HOPE *Eng. Cathedr. 19th C.* vi. 229 The aisles.. require a horizontal wall-space in the nave, between the arcade and the clerestory, for the roofing to mortice into.

2. To cut a mortise in; also with *through.*

1703 T. N. *City & C. Purchaser* 23 These Posts are.. made by the Piece.. and ½*d.* per Hole for Morticing them. **1753** F. PRICE *Brit. Carpenter* (ed. 3) 6 You may mortice through both flitches. **1782** SMEATON in *Phil. Trans.* LXXII. 347 The cross-piece.. is mortoised through, to let the rods pass. **1846** HOLTZAPFFEL *Turning*, etc. II. 716 The several styles to be mortised.. are placed side by side.

†**mortise,** *v.*[2] *Obs.* Also 4–5 **mortese,** 5 **mort(e)yse, -eise,** 5–6 **mortayse,** 6 **mortis(s)ie.** [Aphetic form of AMORTIZE, -ISE.] *trans.* To alienate in mortmain; = AMORTIZE *v.* 3.

c **1380** WYCLIF *Wks.* (1880) 123 Here temporaltees ben mortesid, þat is confermyd in þis deþ. *c* **1450** in *9th Rep. Hist. MSS. Comm.* App. I. 285/2 James of Pecham yaff and morteysed to the sayed brygg the manor of Nerschenden. **1496–7** *Act 12 Hen. VII*, c. 13 §17 Londis.. mortised appropried or belonging to any College in any of the Universitees. **1530** PALSGR. 640/2 He hath mortaysed twenty pounde a yere to founde a chaunterye. **1533** MORE *Debell. Salem* Wks. 943/2 Some one hath thought that it wolde be.. profytable to the realme, that the lordes had the landes whose auncestours had mortisied them. **1546** *Galway Arch.* in *10th Rep. Hist. MSS. Comm.* App. v. 411 Shall not

in leasse set nor mortissie any manner landes,..nor.. mortissie any of the said teithes or revnus.

mortised, morticed ('mɔːtɪst), *ppl. a.* [f. MORTISE *v.*[1] + -ED[1].]

1. In the senses of the verb.

1800 *Vitruvius' Archit., Lexicon* 13/2 *Cardinatus*.. Mortised. **1823** P. NICHOLSON *Pract. Build.* 129 The joint is sometimes made partly parallel, and partly perpendicular, to the mortised piece. **1833** LOUDON *Encycl. Archit.* §239 Doors..having good mortised locks. **1867** SMYTH *Sailor's Word-bk.*, A morticed block is one made out of a single block of wood, chiselled for one or more sheaves; in distinction from a made block. **1875** *Carpentry & Join.* 56 When the pieces of wood to be framed are too thin to allow tenoned and morticed joints to be made.

2. *Her.* = ENCLAVE *a.*

1828–40 in BERRY *Encycl. Her.* **1899** in ELVIN *Dict. Her.*

† **mortisement.** *Obs.* [Aphetic form of AMORTIZEMENT: cf. MORTISE *v.*[2]] An investment in mortmain.

c **1465** *Eng. Chron.* (Camden 1856) 113 The relygious of Esex and of Northfolke..scholde schewe to hem ther wrytynge of ther mortysementes.

mortising, morticing ('mɔːtɪsɪŋ), *vbl. sb.* [f. MORTISE *v.*[1] + -ING[1].] The action of the verb MORTISE in its various senses.

1606 HOLYOKE *Rider's Dict.*, A kind of building, where there is a mortising of timber and stones one within another, *orthostata*. *a* **1676** HALE *Prim. Orig. Man.* IV. iv. 327 The admirable accommodation of the several Parts of the Human Body..the mortising of the Bones one into another [etc.]. **1678** MOXON *Mech. Exerc.* v. 80 You must take care in Mortessing and Tennanting, that [etc.]. **1873** J. RICHARDS *Wood-working Factories* 150 All the mortising in France..is performed by rotary machines.

b. *attrib.*

1819 *Rees' Cycl.* XXII. s.v. *Machinery*, The Mortising Machine which cuts out the mortises for the reception of the sheaves. **1844** H. STEPHENS *Bk. Farm* III. 1156 The enlargement of the hole is then performed either with the mortising-chisel..or by the mortising-machine. **1846** HOLTZAPFFEL *Turning*, etc. II. 505 One rectilinear planing machine that is exclusively intended for cutting across the grain, namely, the morticing engine.

Mortivan, mortize, obs. ff. MARTABAN, MORTISE.

mortkin, var. MORKIN.

mortlage: see MORTILAGE.

Mortlake ('mɔːtleɪk). Also 7 **Mortclake, Mortelack,** 7–8 **Moreclack.** **1.** The name of the Surrey town *Mortlake* used *attrib.* in ***Mortlake hangings, tapestry***, a kind of tapestry woven there in the reigns of James I and Charles I. *Obs.* exc. *Hist.*

[**1639** MAYNE *City Match* II. iii, Why Lady doe you think me Wrought in a Loome, some Dutch peece weavd at Mooreclack?] **1682** OLDHAM *Imit. 3rd Sat. Juvenal* Wks. III. (1686) 198 A rich Suit of Moreclack-Tapestry. **1690** EVELYN *Mundus Muliebris* 8 With Moreclack Tapistry, Damask Bed. **1691** *Lond. Gaz.* No. 2655/4 Two pieces of Mortelack Hangings of Boys and Landskips. **1888** *Encycl. Brit.* XXIII. 213/1 Most of the Mortlake tapestry has distinct marks, such as the shield of St. George with F. C. (F. Crane).

2. (Written **mortlake, mort-lake.**) = *ox-bow lake.*

1902 LD. AVEBURY *Scenery Eng.* ix. 303 The loop often remains as a dead river-channel or 'Mortlake'. Such loop-lakes are known in America by the special name of 'Ox-bows'. **1937** [see CUT-OFF *sb.* 2]. **1957** G. E. HUTCHINSON *Treat. Limnol.* I. i. 123 The term *mortlake*, presumably derived from the place name, has been used in some English works as the equivalent of *bras mort* or *Altwasser*. **1962** READ & WATSON *Introd. Geol.* iv. 172 When the loop of the meander becomes large it is liable to be cut-off across its neck, leaving an abandoned separated portion which may remain as an oxbow-lake or mort-lake. **1968** *Geogr. Abstr.* B. 112 The fish fauna of various rivers, peat hags and mortlakes was examined.

† **'mortle.** *Obs.* [var. of MORTAR *sb.*[1], perh. through association with *pestle*; but cf. Icel. *morteel* (1396 in *Dipl. Isl.* III. 614; in Vigf. erron. given as *mortil*).] A mortar.

1570 in *Wills & Inv. N. C.* (Surtees) I. 327, I gyue to my m[rs] brandlinge my marble mortle wth ye pestell.

mortling, variant of MORLING.

mortmain ('mɔːtmeɪn), *sb. Law.* Forms: 5–6 **mortmayn(e, mortemayn(e,** 6 **mortemeyn, morttmayne,** 6–8 **mortmaine,** 6– **mortmain.** [a. OF. *mortemain*, AF. *morte mayn* (Britton *c* 1290), ad. med.L. *mortua manus*, *manus mortua* (cf. F. *mainmorte*, Sp. *manos muertas*, Pg. *mão morta*, It. *mano morta*) 'dead hand' (L. *mortua*, fem. of *mortuus* dead, *manus* hand).

It seems probable that 'dead hand' in English legal use is a metaphorical expression for impersonal ownership, and is unconnected with the older feudal use of *manus mortua* to denote the custom by which serfs (and other classes included under the term *homines manus mortuæ*) had no power of testamentary disposition, their possessions, if they died without legitimate offspring, reverting to the lord.]

The condition of lands or tenements held inalienably by an ecclesiastical or other corporation. Also *attrib.*

Alienations in mortmain, as being injurious to the rights of the crown and the mesne lords, were forbidden by 7 Edw. I, st. 2 (see quot. 1279) and many subsequent Acts, known as the 'Statutes of Mortmain'. The intention of these statutes was to a great extent evaded by judicial interpretations. *The Mortmain Act*: the statute 9 Geo. II, cap. 36, passed in 1736, imposing restrictions on the devising of property to charitable uses; also, the title of various later statutes having a similar object. *licence of mortmain*: an instrument conveying the permission of the king to alienate property in mortmain.

[**1279** *Act 7 Edw. I* (*Statutum de Viris Religiosis*), Providimus..quod nullus Religiosus aut alius quicumque terras..emere vel vendere..præ sumat..per quod ad manum mortuam terre..hujusmodi deveniant quoquo modo.] *c* **1450** *Godstow Reg.* 446 That hit shold not be lawfull to Religious peple to entre the fee of ony or of other, so that hit shold come into morte-mayne, without his licence. **1494** FABYAN *Chron.* VII. 385 This yere was the statute of Mortmayn enacted firste. *c* **1550** BALE *K. Johan* (Camden) 8 This cumpany hath provyded for me morttmayne. **1590** SWINBURNE *Testaments* 71 Citizens, burgesses and freemen, maie bequeath their burgage landes to Mortmain, which others can not doe. **1623** SIR T. CREW *Sp. Ho. Com.* in Rushw. *Hist. Coll.* (1659) I. 117 The Subjects thereby were enabled to found Hospitals without Licence of Mortmain. **1642** D. ROGERS *Naaman* 165 There was a Statute we know of Mortmaine,..to cut of the validity of such gifts as were given to the Clergy for Popish ends. **1736** LD. BRUCE in *Buccleuch MSS.* (Hist. MSS. Comm.) I. 389, I intend being at London..to attend the Mortmain Bill. **1827** JARMAN *Powell's Devises* (ed. 3) II. 13 The statute 7 and 8 Wm. III. c. 37..provides that the Crown..may grant licenses to aliene, or take in mortmain, of whomsoever the tenements shall be holden. **1844** WILLIAMS *Real Prop.* (1877) 69 The stringency of the provisions in the Mortmain Act. **1846** MCCULLOCH *Acc. Brit. Empire* (1854) II. 373 In some parishes..money has been placed in mortmain..for the better endowment of parish schools. **1903** A. ROBERTSON *Rom. Cath. Ch. in It.* v. (1905) 114 The Mortmain Statutes were framed to prevent the Church Corporations from getting hold of real property.

b. A licence of mortmain.

1567 in W. H. Turner *Select. Rec. Oxford* (1880) 320 In purchasinge a mortmayne. **1596** SPENSER *State Irel.* Wks. (Globe) 680/2 For mayntenaunce of..which [school-houses] it were meete that some severall portion of lande were allotted, sith no more mortmains are to be looked for. **1655** FULLER *Hist. Cambr.* 153 They humbly requested of Her Highnesse a Mortmaine to found a Colledge. *a* **1661** —— *Worthies, Northumbld.* (1662) II. 308 He bought three tenements..and (by a Mortmain procured from King Edward the fourth) erected of them a small Colledge.

c. *transf.* and *fig.*

The figurative use is often based on the notion that the 'dead hand' means the posthumous control exercised by the testator over the uses to which the property is to be applied.

1625 JACKSON *Creed* v. xxi. §3 Alexander..seeks afterward to solace his griefs by procuring mortmain from the oracle for his dead friend to hold greater honours than this great conqueror..could have bestowed upon him. **1852** LONGF. *Haunted Houses* v, Owners and occupants of earlier dates From graves forgotten stretch their dusty hands, And hold in mortmain still their old estates. **1876** LOWELL *Among my Bks.* Ser. II. 228 Sir George Beaumont, dying in 1827,..contrived to hold his affection in mortmain by the legacy of an annuity of £100. **1876** J. B. MAYOR in *Contemp. Rev.* XXVII. 892 There was a time when the thought of Christendom was in mortmain no less than its land.

Hence †**'mortmain** *v. trans.*, to grant in mortmain. †**mort'mainer** (*nonce-wd.*), one who lays a 'dead hand' *upon*.

1530 PALSGR. 641/1, I mortmayne landes, I gyve landes to the churche to be payed for... He hath mortmayned his chiefe maner..to the next abbaye to hym. **1534** CRANMER *Let. to Crumwell* in *Misc. Writ.* (Parker Soc.) II. 287 The said lands, which the said prebendaries shall have of him, to be mortmained by a certain day. **1808** J. W. CROKER *Sk. St. Irel.* (ed. 2) 39 One-third of them [*sc.* clergy] are not resident-absentees from their duties-mortmainers upon the land!

mortmal(l, -mayn(e: see MORMAL, MORTMAIN.

mortne, erroneous form of MORNÉ.

mortoise, obs. form of MORTISE.

Morton's Fork ('mɔːtənz fɔːk). [f. the name of John *Morton* (*c* 1420–1500), Archbishop of Canterbury and minister of Henry VII + FORK *sb.* 1.] John Morton's method of levying forced loans by arguing that those who were obviously rich could afford to pay, and those who lived frugally must have savings. Cf. quot. 1622 *s.v.* CROTCH 7. Also *transf.*

1889 J. GAIRDNER *Henry Seventh* x. 151 One article suggested an argument familiarly known as 'Morton's fork'. **1930** SELLAR & YEATMAN *1066 and all That* xxix. 49 Henry VII was a miser and very good at statecraft; he invented some extremely clever policies such as the one called Morton's Fork. **1964** *New Statesman* 28 Feb. 318/1 The political consequence of this is that he is now—publicly at least—caught on Morton's Fork. **1965** *Listener* 16 Sept. 429/2, I don't think Mr. Smith can altogether pass unscratched between the twin prongs of that Morton's fork. **1973** *Times Lit. Suppl.* 17 Aug. 957/5 A fine Morton's fork technique this—those who went were conspirators and those who stayed away were cowards. **1974** *Cosmopolitan* May 132/1 'Morton's Fork,' she laughed wryly. 'Young and torpid or old and energetic.'

† **mort-pay.** *Obs.* [a. F. *morte-paye*, lit. 'dead pay'.] = DEAD PAY 2.

1622 BACON *Hen. VII* 101 The Seuere punishing of Mort-payes, and keeping backe of Souldiours wages in Captaines.

mortre, obs. form of MORTAR.

† **mortrel.** *Obs.* Also 4 **morterel,** 5 **moteryl,** 7 **mortrell.** [a. OF. *morterel*, *morteruel* (pl. *mortreux*), a kind of milk soup.] = MORTRESS.

1377 LANGL. *P. Pl.* B. XIII. 62 He eet many sondry metes mortrewes [*Camb. MS.* mortreux, *Bodl. MS.* mortrels] and puddynges. **1381** *Form of Cury* (1780) 92 Morterelys. Nym hennyn and porke and seth hem togedere [etc.]. **14..** *Nom.* in Wr.-Wülcker 725/6 *Hoc pepe*, moteryls. **15..** in Cullum *Hist. Hawsted* (1813) 11 To a baker of Bury S[t]. Edmund's for wastle bread to make morterels. **1758** LOWTH *Wm. of Wykeham* 75 Each of the Thirteen secular Brethren [of the Hospital of St. Cross, Winchester] had daily..three messes at Dinner, namely, one mess called Mortrell, made of milk and Wastelbred [etc.].

† **'mortress.** *Obs.* Forms: 4 **mortreux,** 4–5 **mortrewes, -treuus,** 4–5 (9) **mortrews,** 5 **mortrewys, -trow(e)s, -trw(y)s, -terews, -treus, -trowis, -trowse,** 5–6 **mortrus,** 6 **mortesse** (? erron.), 6–7 **mortresse,** 7 **mortress.** [OF. *mortreux*, *-tereoux*, *mourtereoux* (ONF. *moitrou*, *matrou*), pl. of *morterel*, *morteruel*: see MORTREL.] A kind of soup or pottage, made either of bread and milk or of various kinds of meat.

1377 LANGL. *P. Pl.* B. XIII. 41 Ac þei ete mete of more coste mortrewes and potages. *c* **1386** CHAUCER *Prol.* 384 He koude..Maken Mortreux. *c* **1430** *Two Cookery-bks.* 14 Mortrewes of Fysshe... Caste þer-to Sugre and Salt, an serue it forth as other Mortrewys. *c* **1450** *Ibid.* 70 Mortreus de Chare. *Ibid.* 71 Put hit in disshes in maner of Mortrewes. **1513** *Bk. Keruynge* in *Babees Bk.* (1868) 164 In the second course, potage, mortrus, or conyes. **1530** PALSGR. 246/2 Mortesse meate. **1626** BACON *Sylva* §48 A Mortresse made with the Brawne of Capons.

mortress(e, rare obs. forms of MORTISE.

mortrus, variant of MORTRESS *Obs.*

† **'mortual,** *a. Obs. rare.* [var. MORTAL. Cf. OF. *mortuel* (*rare*).]

1. = MORTAL *a.*

c **1440** *Generydes* 6399 The corde is made, the mortuall werre is sese. *c* **1500** MEDWALL *Nature* I. 84 (Brandl) As chyef possessyoner of thyngys mortuall.

2. = MORTUARY *a.* 1.

1514 *MS. Acc. St. John's Hosp., Canterb.*, Rec. for wast of iiij mortualle taperys for Ser Wellyam.

mortuary ('mɔːtjuːərɪ), *a.* and *sb.* Also 6 *erron.* **mortarie.** [ad. L. *mortuāri-us* adj. (med.L. *mortuārium* neut., used as sb.), f. *mortu-us* dead: see -ARY. Cf. F. *mortuaire* (AF. *mortuarie* sb., 1302–3), Pg. *mortuario*.]

A. *adj.*

1. Of or belonging to the burial of the dead.

1514 *MS. Acc. St. John's Hosp., Canterb.*, Rec..for þe wast off iiij mortuary taperys. **1705** GREENHILL *Art Embalm.* 323 Near the Pyramids and mortuary Caves. **1791** COWPER *Wks.* (1837) XV. 227, I enclose a copy of my last mortuary verses. **1826** SCOTT *Diary* 8 Apr. in Lockhart *Life*, He carried me with him as often as he could to these mortuary ceremonies. **1878** BOSW. SMITH *Carthage* 415 The ancient mortuary chambers were filled, after the lapse of centuries, by new occupants. **1904** *Westm. Gaz.* 13 Feb. 5/1 The mortuary chapel which now rises over his grave was only erected some thirty years ago.

2. Of, concerned with, or depending upon death; relating to or reminiscent of death.

1540 TAVERNER *Postils, Passion Sondaye*, Pourge oure consciences from dead or mortuarie workes. **1651** MARIUS *Adv. Conc. Bills Exch.* 65 You must..demand the mony of his Executors..at his Mortuary House or last dwelling House. **1796** BURKE *Let. Noble Ld.* Wks. VIII. 6 His attack upon me and my mortuary pension. [Cf. *supra*, p. 5, where Burke speaks of himself as 'hardly to be classed with the living'.] **1855** *Jrnl. Archæol. Assoc.* XI. 234 These mortuary badges are generally in the form of a heart. *Ibid.* 236 A mortuary ring..is described in the *Gentleman's Magazine* of July 1823.

B. *sb.*

1. A customary gift formerly claimed by the incumbent of a parish from the estate of a deceased parishioner.

c **1380** WYCLIF *Sel. Wks.* III. 285 Or ellis þei schullen not be cristened, ne oyntid, ne biried wiþouten mortuarie. **1469** in *Somerset Med. Wills* (1901) 216, I will that the parson of Brympton have for me to his mortuarie a donne hors of mine. **1560** DAUS tr. *Sleidane's Comm.* 119b, The parson and vicar wyll have for a mortuary..the best thynge that is about the house. **1647** *Husbandman's Plea agst. Tithes* 40 They must have a mortuary, of every dead mans goods, and that was to be the second best of the dead mans moveable goods or cattell. **1775** J. WATSON *Hist. Halifax* 399 These two chapelries have also contended for the mortuaries within their respective divisions. **1852** ROCK *Ch. of Fathers* III. viii. 25 Soul shot, under another though not so fit a name-mortuary-continued to be paid. **1897** *Athenæum* 7 Aug. 184 Mortuaries have been claimed by rectors and vicars within the memory of the present generation.

attrib. **17..** POPE *Happy Life of Country Parson* 6 Tithe-Pig, and mortuary Guinea. **1875** STUBBS *Const. Hist.* I. viii. 229 The clergy received..soul-scot or mortuary-dues.

†**b.** A fine payable to certain ecclesiastical dignitaries on the death of a priest within their respective jurisdictions. *Obs.*

1590 SWINBURNE *Testaments* 232 It shall be lawfull to the Bishops of Bangors, Landaffe, Saint Dauids and Saint Asse, and likewise to the Archdeacon of Chester, to take such Mortuaries of the Priests..as heretofore hath beene accustomed. **1778** PENNANT *Tour Wales* (1883) I. 110 Northop is a sinecure, annexed to the bishopric of St. Asaph,..to compensate for the mortuaries due to the bishop on the death of every beneficed clergyman in the diocese.

†**2.** A funeral; obsequies. *Obs.*

c **1440** *Jacob's Well* 56 þ ey schulde noȝt offeryn at weddynges, at puryficacyouns, at mortuaryes, but o messepeny. **1594** *Selimus* H 3, When thus they see me with religious pompe, To celebrate his tomb-blacke mortarie. **1598** GRENEWEY *Tacitus' Ann.* I. xiii. (1622) 25 A Generall honored with the Augurall dignitie..ought not to meddle in mortuaries. **1600** HOLLAND *Livy* xxx. xliv. 772 Yee keepe a weeping and wailing, as in some publicke funerall and mortuarie carried forth. **1613** PURCHAS *Pilgrimage* VIII. xii. (1614) 804 At these mortuaries they did eate and drinke.

†**3.** A burial place, sepulchre. *Obs.*

1654 WHITLOCK *Zootomia* 36 Look on thy full Table as a Mortuary of the dispeopled Elements. **1658** PHILLIPS, A *Mortuarie*, a Funeral, a burying place.

†**4.** An obituary record. *Obs. rare*$^{-1}$.

1715 M. DAVIES *Athen. Brit.* I. 180 Bale fixes his Death at the Year 1359, but..Waræus places it to the Mortuary of 1360.

5. A building or room in which dead bodies are kept for a time; a dead-house. Also, a place specially prepared for the temporary reception of a corpse.

1865 *Morning Star* 1 June, This mortuary is open every day. **1894** *Times* 19 Dec. 9/6 A mortuary will be erected in the cabin, which will be draped.

attrib. **1898** *Westm. Gaz.* 18 Mar. 5/1 Mortuary keeper. **1905** *Brit. Med. Jrnl.* 16 Sept. 688 Mortuary attendant.

mortylogye: see MORTILAGE.

†ˈ**mortyn.** *Sc. Obs. rare.* Also 5 **mortoun, martoune.** Some kind of wild-fowl.

c **1450** HOLLAND *Howlat* 213 The Martoune [*Bannat. MS.* mortoun], the Murcoke, the Myresnype in ane, Lichtit, as lerit men, law by that laike. **1599** *Sc. Acts Jas. VI* (1816) IV. 180/2 Teillis atteillis Goldyndis mortynis [etc.]. **1600** *Ibid.* 236/2.

moru(e, obs. forms of MORROW.

‖**morucho** (moˈrutʃo). [Sp.] A half-breed bull reared in Spain; originally the name of a thoroughbred race of cattle in the Salamanca area.

1932 E. HEMINGWAY *Death in Afternoon* xii. 128 Half-bred bulls or bulls in which there is a little fighting blood, called moruchos in Spanish, are often very brave while calves. **1957** A. MACNAB *Bulls of Iberia* i. 8 There do exist animals of mixed race, called *moruchos*, half fighting blood and half tame blood of the Salamanca area. **1959** V. J. KEHOE *Aficionado!* iv. 67/2 Another variety of Spanish toro is the half-breed *morucho*. This type, which extends from the Salamanca area down to the Guadarrama range section, does not have animals of the fine form, perseverance of charge and nobility as do the pure breeds.

moruȝiue, var. MORYEVE, 'morning-gift'.

‖**morula** (ˈmɔər(j)ʊlə). [mod.L., dim. of L. *mōrum* mulberry: see MORO^{1}.]

1. *Path.* In various uses (see quots.).

1856 MAYNE *Expos. Lex.*, *Morula*, term for a mulberry-formed, fungous excrescence: a morule. **1891** *Syd. Soc. Lex.*, *Morula*... Also, a synonym of *Frambœsia.* **1897** *Allbutt's Syst. Med.* II. 506 Frambœsia is..essentially a disease of the tropics, though possibly the 'morula', or button-scurvy of Ireland..was closely allied to..it.

2. *Embryol.* Haeckel's term for that stage of development of an ovum in which it has become completely segmented; an ovum at this stage of development.

1874 E. R. LANKESTER in *Phil. Trans.* CLXV. 33 The name *Gastrula* is given by Professor Haeckel to the embryonic form which I had proposed to designate by the old name *Planula*; and the multicellular blastosphere, from which the *Gastrula* is developed, which I had proposed to speak of as a *polyplast*, he well christens the *Morula.* **1875** HUXLEY in *Encycl. Brit.* II. 51/1 All the *Metazoa*, in fact, commence their existence in the form of an ovum... The ovum, after impregnation, divides into cleavage masses, or *blastomeres*, giving rise to a *Morula.*

Hence ˈ**morular** *a.*, 'relating to a morula' (*Syd. Soc. Lex.* 1891); **moruˈlation,** the conversion of the vitellus or yolk of an ovum into a morula (*Cent. Dict.* 1890); ˈ**moruloid** *a.*, having the character of, or resembling a morula (*Ibid.*).

morula, var. MARULA.

morule (ˈmɔə(j)rəl). *Path.* Anglicized form of MORULA.

1856 [see MORULA 1].

‖ˈ**morum.** *Path. rare*$^{-0}$. [mod.L., f. L. *mōrum* a mulberry: see MORULA.] = MORO^{1}.

1693 tr. *Blancard's Phys. Dict.* (ed. 2), *Morum*, the same that *Pladarosis.* **1706** PHILLIPS (ed. Kersey), *Morum*, a Mulberry; Also a little soft Swelling under the Eye-lids.

morun, obs. form of MORN, MOURN *v.*

morunga, variant of MORINGA.

morvenite (ˈmɔːvənaɪt). *Min.* [Named by T. Thomson from *Morven* in Scotland, its locality: see -ITE.] A variety or synonym of HARMOTOME.

1836 T. THOMSON *Min., Geol.*, etc. I. 351 The third species [of harmotome], to which I have given the name of morvenite. **1883** M. F. HEDDLE in *Encycl. Brit.* XVI. 423/1.

morw(e, obs. forms of MORROW.

morw(e-)ȝyve, variant forms of MORYEVE.

morwen, obs. form of MORN.

morwening(e, -yng(e, obs. forms of MORNING.

morwhen, obs. form of MORN.

morwnyng(e, obs. forms of MORNING.

‖**morwong** (ˈmɔːwɒŋ). *Austral.* [The native name.] A fish of the genus *Chilodactylus.*

1880 INGLIS *Austral. Cousins* 298 From Broken Bay to Terrigal,..there are splendid fishing grounds, and the capture of..morwong, travallay, salmon, and hundreds of other varieties, would give exciting sport. **1883** E. P. RAMSAY *Food Fishes N.S. Wales* 13 (Fish. Exhib. Publ.) The Morwongs—*Chilodactylus macropterus*, *C. morwong* (sp. nov.), and *C. fuscus*—are more plentiful, and find a ready sale.

morwoun, morwyng(e, obs. forms of MORN.

†ˈ**morwyngift.** *Sc. Obs.* Also **mor(r)owing gift.** [f. *morwyn* MORN *sb.* + GIFT.] = MORYEVE: cf. MORNING-GIFT.

1503 *Sc. Acts Jas. IV* (1814) II. 240/1 þe qwenis drowry & morwyngift. **1592** *Sc. Acts Jas. VI* (1814) III. 565/1 The Morowing gift gevin be his hienes to his darrest spous. **1593** *Ibid.* (1816) IV. 24/2 His hienes for þe singular luif and affectioune borne toward hir [*sc.* his queen], Gaif, grantit and confirmit to hir in forme of morrowing gift [(ed. 1597) 143 morning gift], All and haill the lordschip of dumfermling w^{t} all baronies, landis [etc.].

morxi, variant of MORDISHEEN.

mory, obs. form of MOORY *a.*

mor-yah, var. MOYA *int.*

moryce, obs. form of MORRIS *sb.*^{1}

Moryen, var. of MORIAN; obs. f. MURRAIN.

†**moryeve.** *Obs.* Forms: *α.* 1 **morᵹenᵹifu, -ᵹyfu, morᵹanᵹifu,** 3 **marhenȝiue, morȝen-ȝiue;** *β.* 3 **mærȝeue, morȝeue, mor(h)ȝiue,** 5 **mor(r)yve;** *γ.* 3 **mareȝeue, marechȝeue, marheȝeue, mahre-ȝiue, moru-ȝiue,** 4 **morw(e-)ȝyve, morow-ȝyfe, more ȝif.** [OE. *morᵹenᵹifu*, f. *morᵹen* MORN, MORROW + *ᵹifu* gift, YEVE; corresponding to OHG. **morgangeba* (*morganegiba* in Gregory of Tours, 6th c.); cf. the synonymous MHG. *morgengâbe*, mod.G. *morgengabe, morgengift.*] The gift made by the husband to the wife on the morning after the consummation of the marriage. Also sometimes misused for *dowry.* Also *fig.* Cf. MORNING-GIFT.

c **974** *Will* in Birch *Cartul. Sax.* III. 630 Ic cyþe hwæt ic minum wiue to morᵹenᵹyue sealde; þæt is Beadewan [etc.]. *c* **1000** ÆLFRIC *Gloss.* in Wr.-Wülcker 115/13 *Dos*, morᵹanᵹifu. *c* **1205** LAY. 14394 Maiden he heo hæfde, & mærȝeue hire bi-tahte. *Ibid.* 31090 He wulle hire to morȝeue þene Mans bitæchen. *a* **1225** *Ancr. R.* 94 Ancren þeos two morhȝiuen [*MS. C.* marechȝeuen, *MS. T.* marhenȝiues] habben biuoren oðre. *c* **1230** *Hali Meid.* 54 (Bodl. MS.) Eadi is his spuse..hwas marheȝeue [*MS. Tit.* mahre-ȝiue] is þe kinedom of heouene. *c* **1250** *Gen. & Ex.* 1428 Siðen men hauen holden skil, first to freinen ðe wimmanes wil, Or or men hire to louerd ȝiue, for wedding or for morȝen-ȝiwe. *c* **1290** *S. Eng. Leg.* I. 257/24 A lauedi of a gret contreie, and of grete moruȝiue al-so. *c* **1380** WYCLIF *Serm.* Sel. Wks. I. 142 And þis morwȝyve [*v.r.* morwe-ȝyve, morowȝyfe, more ȝif] is clepid of clerkes, dower of bodily sutiltc. *c* **1440** *Promp. Parv.* 343/2 Moryve (morryve, *S.*), *dos.*

moryhen, obs. form of MORN.

moryn, obs. form of MORION, MORN.

moryn(e, obs. forms of MURRAIN.

Moryon, variant of MORIAN and MORION.

Morys, obs. form of MOORISH *a.*^{2}, MORRIS *sb.*^{1}

morysh, obs. form of MOORISH *a.*^{1}

moryspeik, -peke, obs. ff. MORRIS PIKE.

moryssh(e, mos, obs. ff. MOORISH *a.*^{1}, MOSS.

mosaic (məʊˈzeɪɪk), *a.*^{1} and *sb.* Forms: *α.* 5 **musycke,** 6 **mousaique,** 6–7 **musaique,** 7 **musaic(k, musai(c)ke;** *β.* 6–8 **mosaique,** 7 **mosaiq, mosaike,** 7–8 (9) **mosaick,** 7– **mosaic.** [a. F. *mosaïque* adj., used subst. in masc. (OF. *mosaicq, musaicq, musec, music* adj., used subst. in masc. and fem.) = Pr. *muzec* adj., Sp. *mosáico* (used subst. in fem.), Pr. *mosaico* (used subst. in fem.), It. *mosaico, musaico* (used subst. in masc.), ad. med.L. *mosaicus, mūsaicus*, as if a. Gr. *μουσαϊκός f. *μουσαῖος by-form of μούσειος pertaining to the muses (cf. late Gr. μουσεῖον mosaic work, whence late L. *opus mūsīvum* in the same sense), f. μοῦσα MUSE *sb.*]

A. *adj.*

1. a. Pertaining to that form of art in which pictures and decorative patterns are produced by the joining together of minute pieces of glass, stone, or other hard substances of different colours; produced by this method.

1585 T. WASHINGTON tr. *Nicholay's Voy.* I. xvi. 17 b, The court is pauid with Mosaique stone. *Ibid.* II. xx. 57 S. Sophia ..within is most artificially made with Mosaique figures. **1615** G. SANDYS *Trav.* 31 Mosaike painting: an antique kind of worke, composed of little square peeces of marble. **1665** SIR T. HERBERT *Trav.* (1677) 63 A stately monument, graced with three fair Courts, each of which is paved with stone, the outside Fabrick (after the Persian mode) being pargettred or plaistered, and polished in Mosaick order. *a* **1680** BUTLER *Rem.* (1759) I. 173 And join it by Mosaic Art, In graceful Order, Part to Part. **1703** MAUNDRELL *Journ. Jerus.* 18 Mar. (1721) 43 We saw many Granite Pillars and remnants of Mosaick Floors. **1816** BYRON *Siege Cor.* xxxi, The vaults beneath the mosaic stone Contain'd the dead of ages gone. **1845** STOCQUELER *Handbk. Brit. India* (1854) 330 The inlaid or Mosaic work-boxes, card-cases, writing-desks, &c. **1893** *Archæologia* LIII. 566 The mosaic panel is not worn at all.

b. *fig.*

1644 BULWER *Chiron.* 141 And from it Eloquence receives her beauteous colours, her Musive or Mosaique Excellency. **1710** HEARNE *Collect.* (O.H.S.) III. 41 After a farrago of English, Greek, and Latin—'You'l pardon this way of writing—I never use it but in an Epistolary Way. I rem. a Gent. lately found fault wth it: and call'd it Mosaic'. **1824** CARLYLE *Misc., Richter* (1869) 16 Let the mosaic brain of old Burton give forth the workings of this strange union. **1882** W. T. DOBSON *Poet. Ingenuities* 225 The next..is a mosaic compilation from poems written to the memory of Robert Burns.

c. Resembling the colours or patterns of mosaic work.

c **1890** tr. *T. de Dillmont's Encycl. Needlework* 133 *Mosaic stitch*.., the first row consists of one short and one long stitch, alternately; the second, of short stitches only, set between the long stitches of the first row; the third row is a repetition of the first, and so on. **1900** E. JACKSON *Hist. Hand-Made Lace* 127 The Lace resembling Duchesse made in Venice in the present day is called Mosaic lace, on account of small sprigs being used to build up the pattern as the pieces of stone and glass are used in Mosaic work. **1934** M. THOMAS *Dict. Embroidery Stitches* 151 *Mosaic filling*, a drawn fabric stitch. **1960** H. HAYWARD *Antique Coll.* 191/1 *Mosaic binding*, book-binding with polychrome decoration. **1961** J. CARTER *ABC for Bk.-Collectors* (ed. 3) 136 *Mosaic bindings*, leather bindings decorated with contrasting colours, whether inlaid, onlaid or painted.

2. ***mosaic wool-work***: a kind of work used in rugs, carpets, and the like, in which coloured threads are arranged side by side so that the cross-section shows a pattern resembling that of mosaic. So ***mosaic carpet***, etc. ***mosaic canvas***: see quot.

1864 WEBSTER, *Mosaic wool-work.* **1879** *Cassell's Techn. Educ.* IV. 390/2 This is..the plan on which the so-called 'mosaic carpet' is made. **1882** CAULFEILD & SAWARD *Dict. Needlework*, *Mosaic Canvas*, the finest descriptions of canvas employed for Embroidery, whether of silk, thread, or cotton, have acquired the popular appellation of Mosaic.

3. Applied to a variety of tile (see quot.).

1875 KNIGHT *Dict. Mech.*, *Mosaic Tile*, a tile molded with different colored clays, arranged in patterns in imitation of the associated pieces of colored stones in true mosaic. **1903** *Edin. Even. News* 12 Oct. 4 A mosaic tile layer.

4. ***mosaic vision***: the manner of vision of the compound eye of an arthropod. ***mosaic theory***: any theory in explanation of the vision of arthropods with compound eyes.

1880 HUXLEY *Crayfish* iii. 12 The theory of mosaic vision propounded by Johannes Müller. **1888** LUBBOCK *Senses Anim.* vii. (1889) 166 Plateau regards the mosaic theory of Müller as definitely abandoned, but seems rather to have had in his mind that of Gottsche.

5. *Embryol.* Of, pertaining to, or characterized by that mode of development in which regions in an embryo are predetermined by the corresponding regions in that embryo at an earlier stage of development.

1893 *Jrnl. Morphol.* VIII. 579 (*heading*) Amphioxus, and the mosaic theory of development. **1904** *Jrnl. Exper. Zoöl.* I. 2 Similar views were more or less clearly expressed by Van Beneden, Flemming, Platner and others prior to the definite formulation of the mosaic-theory of development by Roux in 1888. *Ibid.* Such 'mosaic eggs' as those of mollusks or ctenophores. **1933** J. H. WOODGER tr. *L. von Bertalanffy's Mod. Theories Development* x. 143 After injury we obtain partial embryos from mosaic eggs and whole embryos from the regulative ones. **1963** J. COHEN *Living Embryos* 11 In the Annelid worms and the Molluscs, almost all of the interactions between parts of the egg occur before cleavage commences, and in consequence, if the cells are separated at the 4-cell or 8-cell stage they have already been determined in their fates and can only produce parts of animals. This kind of development is called determinate or mosaic, and is also shown by many primitive Chordates. **1970** AMBROSE & EASTY *Cell Biol.* xiii. 422 Eggs of this kind, in which the cytoplasm is clearly divided into different regions required for the development of specific regions of the embryo, are known as mosaic eggs.

6. ***mosaic disease*** [tr. G. *mosaikkrankheit* (A. Mayer 1886, in *Die Landwirtschaftlichen Versuchsstationen* XXXII. 453)], a virus disease affecting plants, characterized by a mottled

pattern of discoloration on the leaves; also *absol.*; cf. *tobacco mosaic* (TOBACCO 3).

1894 *Jrnl. Mycol.* VII. 382 The first symptom [of tobacco mosaic] is a geographic or mosaic coloring of the leaf surface, light and dark green... The name 'mosaic disease' was given by Dr. Mayer. **1925** *Contemp. Rev.* Dec. 753 Cuba..is finding soil depletion and mosaic disease increasingly serious matters. **1930** *Discovery* June 196/1 The first virus disease to be discovered was the 'mosaic' of tobacco, which manifests itself in a bright mottling and spotting of the foliage. **1940** *Sun* (Baltimore) 29 Jan. 5/6 First reports of a new disease spreading into Pennsylvania peach orchards have located the dread 'mosaic' in the Spring Grove section of York county. **1970** LIEBSCHER & KOEHLER tr. *Fröhlich & Rodenwald's Pests & Diseases of Tropical Crops* 39 A number of virus diseases, such as mosaic disease, infectious chlorosis, and 'heart rot', manifest themselves by retarded growth, discoloration, and leaf curl.

7. *Biol.* Having or composed of cells of two genetically different types.

1902 W. BATESON et al. *Rep. Evolution Comm. R. Soc.* I. 23 Among the large number of capsules examined, there were some of the mosaic type, in which part of the capsule was prickly and the remainder smooth. *Ibid.* 127 'Mosaic' fruits in *Datura*, where..the otherwise pure extracted recessives (thornless) showed exceptionally a thorny patch... Such a phenomenon may be taken as indicating that the germ-cells may also have been mosaic. **1926**, etc. [see CHIMERA, CHIMÆRA 3 d]. **1968** [see *gynandromorph* s.v. GYNANDRO-]. **1969** *New Scientist* 16 Jan. 133/1 Cytogeneticists have found human mosaic individuals. **1974** S. L. ROBBINS *Pathologic Basis Dis.* vi. 178/1 Nondisjunction after zygote formation yields a mosaic individual who has more than one chromosome count in his body cells.

8. Photogr. ***mosaic screen***, a screen containing a pattern of small filters of each of the primary colours which was placed in front of the emulsion for both exposure and viewing in some methods of colour photography; so ***mosaic process***.

1908 *Brit. Jrnl. Photogr.* Suppl. 3 Jan. 13 To make the Krayn mosaic screen..line-screens are again cemented together and form a block. **1935** *Discovery* July 188/2 The well-known 'screen' or 'mosaic' processes, in which the photograph is recorded through a regular or irregular pattern of coloured rulings or grains. **1942** C. B. NEBLETTE *Photography* (ed. 4) xxxii. 786 The irregular mosaic screens are made from a mixture of small colored particles. **1957** R. W. G. HUNT *Reprod. Colour* iii. 30 In photography, the mosaic processes have had a long and distinguished career.

9. Chiefly *Aerial Photogr.* Applied to a composite photograph made up of a number of separate photographs of overlapping areas.

1920 H. E. IVES *Airplane Photography* xxvi. 316 (*heading*) Arranging prints for a mosaic map. **1930** *Air Ann. British Empire* 207 A photographic survey was made for a railway company, the mosaic strip..being produced on a scale of 130 inches to the mile. **1934** *Discovery* June 15/1 The chief photographic contribution..is an aerial mosaic map of an area of about 200 square miles. **1972** *Sci. Amer.* Mar. 10/2 In the past six months the first complete aerial-mosaic map of Manhattan Island has been assembled, and photographic prints are being made on a scale that brings out a wealth of interesting detail.

10. *Ecol.* Applied to an area in which plant associations occur in an alternating pattern.

1930 G. E. DU RIETZ in *Svensk Bot. Tidskr.* XXIV. 496 Phytocoenose-complexes are vegetational units consisting of phytocoenoses with little or no relationship to each other but more or less regularly alternating. They are of several kinds. Good examples for [*sic*] mosaic complexes are furnished by the..Scandinavian bogs, maritime rocks, etc. **1970** P. OLIVER *Savannah Syncopators* 41 As one moves north from the rain forest and into the tropical woodlands and savannah mosaic regions, the trees become fewer and smaller.

11. *Cryst.* Applied to (the structure of) crystals made up of small blocks of perfect lattices set at very slight angles to one another.

1934 W. P. DAVEY *Study Cryst. Struct. & Applic.* xii. 363 It will be of interest..to examine the various ways in which crystals may be grown in the hope of finding mechanisms of crystal growth which will lead easily to the mosaic type rather than the perfect type of structure. **1938** W. A. WOOSTER *Text-bk. Crystal Physics* ii. 62 The mosaic crystal was imagined to be built up of a number of small blocks of perfect crystal, of not more than some 500 A.U. side, arranged nearly parallel to each other. **1964** R. C. EVANS *Introd. Crystal. Chem.* (ed. 2) ix. 206 As normally prepared, a crystal has a pronounced mosaic structure. **1970** R. A. LAUDISE *Growth Single Crystals* i. 17 There is a continuous series of states of order between mosaic structures and structures showing conventional low-angle grain boundaries.

12. Biol. ***mosaic evolution*** (see quots.).

1963 E. MAYR *Animal Species & Evolution* xix. 598 There is not a steady and harmonious change of all parts of the 'type', as envisioned by the school of idealistic morphology, but rather a 'mosaic evolution'. Every evolutionary type is a mosaic of primitive and advanced characters, of general and specialized features. **1971** J. Z. YOUNG *Introd. Study Man* xxxiii. 457 The human character appears in some features (the gait) before others (size of brain); this is the phenomenon called mosaic evolution.

B. *sb.* (= MOSAIC WORK.)

1. a. The process of producing pictures or decorative patterns by cementing together small pieces of stone, glass, or other hard material of various colours; pictures or patterns produced in this manner; the constructive or decorative material composed of small pieces of coloured material cemented together.

c **1400** *Destr. Troy* 1662 Within this palis of prise was a proude halle,..With a flore þat was fret all of fyne stones, Pauyt prudly all with proude colours, Made after musycke, men on to loke. **1585** T. WASHINGTON tr. *Nicholay's Voy.* II. vii. 37 b, A church..which esteemed to be the fayrest..in al those Ilands.., being artificially made of Mosaique. *Ibid.* II. xx. 57 The Images of Mosaique and other flat pictures. **1596** DANETT tr. *Comines* (1614) 279 It is built throughout of the curious worke called Musaique [*marg.* Mousaique], or Marqueterie. **1687** A. LOVELL tr. *Thevenot's Trav.* I. 141 The seeling..is in many places gilt and painted in Mosaick. **1756** NUGENT *Gr. Tour, Italy* III. 53 The name of Mosaic is given to all works composed of little inlaid pieces, whether they be of stone, wood, ivory, enamel, or any other natural or artificial matter. **1832** G. DOWNES *Lett. Cont. Countries* I. 282 Some of the apartments are painted in fresco, with floors in mosaic. **1845** STOCQUELER *Handbk. Brit. India* (1854) 330 The Mosaic is sometimes used as a sort of veneer over the whole surface of an article, and at others, simply as an inlaid bordering on cedar or ivory. **1883** *Encycl. Brit.* XVI. 854/2 The modern so-called 'Roman mosaic' is formed of short and slender sticks of coloured glass fixed in cement, the ends, which form the pattern, being finally rubbed down and polished.

b. *transf.* and *fig.*

1667 MILTON *P.L.* IV. 700 Each beauteous flour, Iris all hues, Roses, and Gessamin Rear'd high thir flourisht heads between, and wrought Mosaic. *a* **1711** KEN *Sion* Poet. Wks. 1721 IV. 332 From various Flowers which she together brought, In sweet Mosaick she a story wrought. **1753** HOGARTH *Anal. Beauty* iv. 23 The pine-apple, which nature has particularly distinguished by bestowing ornaments of rich mosaic upon it. **1899** *Allbutt's Syst. Med.* VII. 489 The disc of bone removed was cut into pieces and packed in mosaic in the wound [*sc.* a trephine-hole in the skull].

c. Applied to work in various other materials analogous to mosaic in method of production, or resembling it in appearance; usually with defining word, as ***paper, straw, wood, wool mosaic***.

1727–52 CHAMBERS *Cycl.* s.v., Mosaic work of wood, more properly called *marquetry*, or inlaid work. **1875** W. BEMROSE (*title*) Mosaicon: or paper mosaic, and how to make it. **1875** KNIGHT *Dict. Mech.* s.v., The Tunbridge wood-mosaic is made of colored parallelopipeds of wood glued together so as to show a pattern at their ends or sections.

2. a. A piece of mosaic work; a design in mosaic.

1699 M. LISTER *Journ. Paris* 124 By the application of a good Eye-glass, I could readily distinguish the squares of all colours, as in other Mosaiques. **1756** BURKE *Subl. & B.* II. xvi, Much of guilding, mosaicks, painting, or statues, contribute but little to the sublime. **1762–71** H. WALPOLE *Vertue's Anecd. Paint.* (1786) II. 30 *note*, [He] fitted up entire windows with them, and with mosaics of plain glass of different colours. **1841** W. SPALDING *Italy & It. Isl.* I. 155 A Mosaic lately found, representing one of Alexander's battles. **1874** MICKLETHWAITE *Mod. Par. Churches* 318 Modern mosaics have nearly always a great deal of gold.

b. *transf.* and *fig.*

a **1678** MARVELL *Appleton House* 582 What Rome, Greece, Palestine, ere said I in this light Mosaick read. **1774** BURKE *Sp. Amer. Taxation* 40 He [Pitt in 1766] made an administration, so checkered..; a cabinet so variously inlaid; such a piece of diversified Mosaic;..that it was indeed a very curious show. **1853** RUSKIN *Stones Ven.* II. vi. §8. 156 We do not enough conceive for ourselves that variegated mosaic of the world's surface which a bird sees in its migration. **1882** W. T. DOBSON *Poet. Ingenuities* 224 Centones or Mosaics. **1882** FARRAR *Early Chr.* I. 352 He does so in a mosaic of magnificent quotations from the.. Psalms. **1896** tr. *Boas' Zool.* 384 The buccal teeth are low knobs (sometimes pointed) or plates, which are arranged in several rows and form a mosaic over the edges of the jaws.

3. a. In various scientific uses.

1877 FOSTER *Phys.* III. ii. (1878) 420 The mosaic of rods and cones is the basis of distinct vision. **1888** LUBBOCK *Senses Anim.* vii. (1889) 166 Plateau..states that, according to Müller, the mosaic [*sc.* the image presented by the compound eye of an arthropod] is formed by a number of partial images, each occupying the base of one of the elements composing the compound eye. **1891** *Syd. Soc. Lex.*, *Mosaic of muscle compartments*, the polygonal areas surrounded by dark lines seen on fresh section of a muscular fibre, without addition of reagents or with acetic acid alone. *Ibid.*, *Mosaic of pigment cells of eye*, the appearance presented by the inner surface of the choroid tunic.

b. *Biol.* An individual (commonly an animal) composed of cells of two genetically different types. Cf. CHIMERA, CHIMÆRA 3 d.

1902 W. BATESON et al. *Rep. Evolution Comm. R. Soc.* I. 23 These mosaics occurred as rarities both on prickly individuals and on smooth ones still more rarely. **1946** R. R. GATES *Human Genetics* I. ix. 281 Case I. 1 was an albino and it is said that two of her children were albino mosaics, the girl having half her hair white and half black, with one blue eye and one black. **1949** DARLINGTON & MATHER *Elem. Genetics* v. 112 In animals the effects of somatic mutation are slightly different [from those in plants]... The changed cells give flakes and sectors instead of layers and the product is known as a mosaic instead of a chimaera. **1968** *New Scientist* 14 Nov. 383/2 Chimaeras, or mosaics—animals containing cells from two sets of parents—have been made experimentally before. **1974** S. L. ROBBINS *Pathologic Basis Dis.* vi. 187/2 Approximately 2 per cent of 'mongoloids' are mosaics (trisomy 21/normal).

c. *Photogr.* = *mosaic screen* (in A. 8 above).

1911 A. WATKINS *Photography* (ed. 5) xii. 227 The Thames colour plate. This is a regular mosaic, formed by three printings (each being dyed) on bichromated colloid; the pattern originating with a 200-line half-tone screen. **1957** R. W. G. HUNT *Reprod. Colour* iii. 30 The Autochrome plate, which consisted of a random mosaic of red, green and blue starch grains with the interstices filled with carbon black, came on the market in 1907. **1973** D. A. SPENCER *Focal Dict. Photogr. Technol.* 395 After exposure through this mosaic the emulsion is reversal processed to a positive transparency.

d. Chiefly *Aerial Photogr.* A mosaic map or photograph (see A. 9 above).

1920 H. E. IVES *Airplane Photography* xxvi. 316 For a mosaic of any size an accurate outline map must be drawn on the surface of which the prints are to be attached. **1920** *Flight* XII. 187/2 He then showed the similarities and differences between a photographic mosaic and a map, and outlined the various difficulties that had to be contended with. **1940** *War Illustr.* 2 Feb. 45 The map-like pictures are afterwards assembled in a big mosaic..which forms a complete plan of the area photographed. **1971** R. DENTRY *Encounter at Kharmel* vii. 113 The Yanks updated their U2 mosaic of the area. **1972** *Nature* 18 Feb. 391/2 Electron micrographs of the inner plexiform layer at a magnification of 25,000 times were used to construct mosaics covering the area from the ganglion cell layer to the vitreal margin.

e. An array of many small photo-emissive metal plates, each of which temporarily stores a charge dependent on the amount of light falling on it, that forms the target plate in some television camera tubes (e.g. the iconoscope); also, an array of piezo-electric transducers in a detector of ultrasound.

1928 *Discovery* Nov. 337/1 Carey's idea was to replace the mosaic of the retina by a mosaic of a large number of minute selenium cells..and, further, to replace the nerve fibres by separately insulated electric wires carrying an electric current from a battery, and to use this device to vary the light given by a number of very minute electric lamps..so placed that each lamp would correspond in position to each of the selenium cells. **1933** *Proc. Wireless Section Inst. Electr. Engin.* VIII. 220/2 The charge acquired by each element of the mosaic is released by the cathode-ray beam once in each repetition of the picture. **1953** AMOS & BIRKINSHAW *Television Engineering* I. iv. 54 The mosaic must be of very fine construction with a number of individual cells to each element otherwise the cells show up in the reproduced image as a grain. **1961** G. N. PATCHETT *Television Servicing* III. vii. 197 The mosaic is composed of antimony islands which are made photo-sensitive with caesium. **1966** *McGraw-Hill Encycl. Sci. & Technol.* XIII. 464/2 The mosaic is electrically coupled to the signal plate by electrostatic capacitance between the two. **1969** J. S. WOOD tr. *L. D. Rozenberg's Sources of High-Intensity Ultrasound* II. II. iv. 215 The construction of ultrasonic receivers in which a kind of 'mosaic' was used, consisting of several piezoelectric cylinders mounted on a large-diameter diaphragm.

4. *Comb.*, as ***mosaic-drawn, -floored, -like, -paved***.

1726 POPE *Odyss.* XIX. 265 In the rich woof a hound, *Mosaic-drawn Bore on full stretch, and seized a dappled fawn. **1888** *Pall Mall G.* 1 Feb. 5/2 A glass-covered, *mosaic-floored, plant-furnished promenade. **1901** *Scribner's Mag.* XXIX. 512/2 A delicate *mosaic-like effect was obtained. **1803** MARY CHARLTON *Wife & Mistress* IV. 157 Ponderous gates, that led into a *Mosaic-paved court.

Mosaic (məʊˈzeɪɪk), *a.*² [a. mod.L. *Mōsāicus*, f. L. *Mōsēs*. Cf. F. *mosaïque* (Calvin, 16th c), G. *mosaisch.*] Of, pertaining, or relating to Moses the lawgiver of the Hebrews, or the writings and institutions attributed to him.

Mosaic law, the ancient law of the Hebrews, contained in the Pentateuch.

1662 STILLINGFL. *Orig. Sacr.* III. iii. §6 The Mosaick history of the Creation. **1701** GREW *Cosm. Sacra* IV. i. §8 A Greek copy of the Mosaick Law. **1895** SALMOND *Chr. Doctr. Immort.* II. iii. 226 The silence of the Mosaic books on the subject of future awards was a stock argument with the Deistical School.

moˈsaic, *v. rare.* [f. MOSAIC *a.*¹ and *sb.*]

1. *trans.* To adorn with mosaics. Also *transf.*

1839 *Tait's Mag.* VI. 255 A cottage..embosomed, or rather matted and mosaicked, by roses and honeysuckles. *c* **1850** *Arab. Nts.* (Rtldg.) 239 Its walks were mosaicked with small stones of various colours. **1890** FREEMAN in W. R. W. Stephens *Life & Lett.* (1895) II. 418 It also wants William the Bad to mosaic the walls. **1895** MRS. A. C. WILSON *5 Years India* 294 A boy with a face mosaiced out in different squares of colour like a clown.

2. To combine as if into a mosaic; also, to produce by such combination.

1841 MOTLEY *Corr.* 18 Nov., Prussia..is new, and an artifical patchwork, without natural coherence, mosaiced out of bought, stolen, and plundered provinces. **1867** *Even. Stand.* 13 July 3 After all the rest of the world had been created the best bits were neatly cut out and mosaicked, so as to form Arcachon. **1889** W. S. GILBERT *Foggerty's Fairy*, etc. (1892) 331 They have mosaiced a hundred of his pithy apophthegms into our daily conversation.

†**moˈsaical**, *a.*¹ *Obs.* Also 6 **museacall**, 7 **musaicall**. [Formed as MOSAIC *a.*¹ + -ICAL.] = MOSAIC *a.*¹ Also ***mosaical work*** = MOSAIC WORK.

a **1586** SIDNEY *Arcadia* I. (1622) 7 New beds of flowers, which being vnder the trees, the trees were to them a Pauillion, and they to the trees a Mosaicall floore. **1592** R. D. *Hypnerotomachia* 49 b, Little flying Byrdes, excellently imphrygiated of museacall paynting. **1604** PARSONS *3rd Pt. Three Convers. Eng.* 346 One Ricimerus..had adorned that Church with diuers sacred pictures of Christ and his Apostles in Musaicall worke. **1613** PURCHAS *Pilgrimage* (1614) 457 The Mosaicall floore pouldred with pearles. **1632** LITHGOW *Trav.* IX. 401 A delicate Roome, and Artificially decored with Mosaical Worke. **1687** A. LOVELL tr. *Thevenot's Trav.* I. 203 We went into the Church, which is ..full of the pictures of the Saints, after the Mosaical way, and paved also in that manner.

Mosaical (məʊˈzeɪɪkəl), *a.*² (and *sb.*) Also 7 **Moysaicall**. [Formed as MOSAIC *a.*²: see -ICAL.]

A. *adj.*

1. Pertaining to or resembling what is Mosaic. †Formerly also often = MOSAIC *a.*²

1563 WINȜET *Four Scoir Thre Quest.* To Rdr., Wks. (S.T.S.) I. 53 Blindit be feruent zele towart the Mosaical law. **1586** HOOKER *Disc. Justif.* (1617) 56 They..saw not how repugnant their beleeuing the necessitie of Mosaicall Ceremonies was to their faith in Iesus Christ. **1615** G. SANDYS *Trav.* 8 As in some cases commanded by the Moysaicall Law. **1753** BP. CLAYTON *Jrnl. Cairo to Sinai* 18 Sept. an. 1722 *note*, The truth of the Mosaical history. **1869** ALFORD in *Gd. Words* 1 Apr. 277 Too frequently, while the practice of a family on the Lord's Day is thoroughly Christian, the theory is as thoroughly Mosaical.

†**2.** ***Mosaical rod*** (see quot. 1778). *Obs.*

a **1681** LILLY *Life & Times* (1715) 33 One John Scott, who pretended the Use of the Mosaical Rods. **1778** PENNANT *Tour Wales* I. 54 [The divining rod] from the rod of Moses, was also profanely called the Mosaical rod.

†**B.** *sb. pl.* Things belonging to the Mosaic Law.

1643 W. GREENHILL *Axe at Root* 13 Shall wee reject truth and light? it's feared we stick too much to Mosaicalls, Prelaticalls, and Traditionalls.

mosaically (məʊˈzeɪɪkəlɪ), *adv. rare.* [f. MOSAICAL *a.*[1] + -LY[2].] In a mosaic manner.

1614 EARL STIRLING *Domes-day, Twelfth Houre* viii, They (mix'd in workes) mosaically grow, And yet each part doth every kinde bestow. *a* **1849** POE *Longfellow*, etc. Wks. 1864 III. 325 What is here not taken from Tennyson, is made up mosaically from the death scene of Cordelia. **1856** DORAN *Knts. & their Days* iii. 45 Illustrative materials, such as anecdotes..he worked mosaically together.

mosaiced: see MOSAICKED *a.*

mosaic gold. [MOSAIC *a.*[1] and *sb.*]

†**1.** [= F. *or de mosaïque* (*Dict. de Trévoux*).] (See quot. 1727–41.) *Obs.*

1727–41 CHAMBERS *Cycl.* s.v. *Gold*, Mosaic Gold, is gold applied in panels on a proper ground, distributed into squares, lozenges, and other compartments; part whereof is shadowed to raise or heighten the rest.

2. [tr. late L. *aurum mūsivum.*] A disulphide of tin.

1746 H. PEMBERTON *Dispens.* 220 *Aurum Musivum.* Mosaic Gold. Take of tin one pound; of flowers of sulphur seven ounces; sal-ammoniac [etc.]. **1890** BRANNT *Metal Worker's Handy-Bk.* 149 Red Bronze is produced by the application of red bronze lacquer or red bronze powder or red mosaic gold.

3. An alloy of copper and zinc, used for cheap jewellery and ornamental metal work; = ORMOLU.

1839 in URE *Dict. Arts* 869. **1852** MRS. SMYTHIES *Bride Elect* xiv, The metal was mosaic gold..and the emeralds..were bits of green glass.

mosaicism (məʊˈzeɪɪsɪz(ə)m). *Biol.* [f. MOSAIC *a.*[1] and *sb.* + -ISM.] The quality or state of being mosaic (MOSAIC *a.*[1] 7).

1926 *Jrnl. Genetics* XVI. 230 No attempt to represent analytically the genetical behaviour of irregular mosaicism in plants has been altogether satisfactory. **1932** *Genetics* XVII. 39 The facts secured from the different breeding tests demonstrate that the mosaicism is due to an unstable translocation. **1947** *Nature* 11 Jan. 66/2 Chemical treatment of female embryos [of *Drosophila melanogaster*] leads to high frequency of mosaicism. **1961** [see MONGOLOID *a.* and *sb.* A. 2]. **1963** *Lancet* 13 May 1028/2 The term mosaicism, in cytogenetic usage, describes a condition in which a substantial minority of cells differ from the majority in their chromosomal content. **1971** *Nature* 11 June 388/2 We have recently had the opportunity to study the rare association of mixed gonadal dysgenesis in a female child and X/XY/XYY mosaicism in karyotypes from blood and fibroblast cultures.

mosaicist (məʊˈzeɪɪsɪst). [f. MOSAIC *sb.* + -IST.] One who makes, or deals in, mosaic work; a worker in mosaic.

1847 LD. LINDSAY *Chr. Art* I. 140 Through the influence of the Byzantine revival, a school of native mosaicists arose in Italy. **1853** RUSKIN *Stones Ven.* II. iv. §57. 103 The art of the mosaicist. **1877** MRS. OLIPHANT *Makers Flor.* iv. 120 Tafi..was more a mosaicist than a painter.

Mosaicity (məʊzeɪˈɪsɪtɪ). *rare.* [f. MOSAIC *a.*[2] + -ITY.] The fact of being of Mosaic origin.

1885 tr. *Wellhausen's Prolegom. to Hist. Israel* 160 It is possible with Bleek to explain the transcendence of history as Mosaicity. **1892** A. B. BRUCE *Apologetics* II. iv. 211 The Mosaicity of the first table of the Decalogue thus appears to be intrinsically credible.

mosaicked (məʊˈzeɪɪkt), *a.* Also **mosaiced.** [f. MOSAIC *sb.* + -ED[2].] Ornamented with, or composed of, mosaic work.

1849 ROCK *Ch. of Fathers* II. 138 *note*, The mosaiced apse belonging to one of those large halls built in the Lateran palace, at Rome, by Leo III..still remains. **1902** *Longm. Mag.* Mar. 426 The finely mosaicked floor.

moˈsaiculture. *Gardening.* [f. MOSAI(C *sb.* + CULTURE.] = *carpet-bedding* (see CARPET *sb.* 5).

1881 *Encycl. Brit.* XII. 261/2 *Carpet Bedding* or *Mosaiculture.*

mosaic work. Now *rare.*

1. = MOSAIC *sb.* 1. Also *transf.* and *fig.*

1606 SYLVESTER *Du Bartas* II. iv. II. *Tropheis* (1633) 202 For, in the bottom of this liquid Ice, Made of Musaick worke, with quaint device The cunning work-man had contrived trim Carpes, Pikes, and Dolphins seeming even to swim. **1643** EVELYN *Diary* 11 Mar., They also shew'd us the picture of Secretary Cecil in mosaiq worke, very well don by some Italian hand. *a* **1680** BUTLER *Rem.* (1759) II. 110 His Writings are like a Taylor's Cushion, of mosaic Work, made up of several Scraps sewed together. **1779** J. MOORE *View Soc. Fr.* (1789) II. lv. 53 This art of copying paintings in Mosaic work. **1842** H. ROGERS *Ess.* (1874) I. 28 That curious mosaic work of different tongues, which is so common in the pages of Burton and Taylor. **1878** SIR G. G. SCOTT *Lect. Archit.* I. 312 Of mosaic-work, whether of porphyry or enamel, you will find abundant examples.

2. = MOSAIC *sb.* 2. ? *Obs.* Also *fig.*

1687 A. LOVELL tr. *Thevenot's Trav.* II. 76 The different colours of these Flints make a pretty pleasant Mosaick work. **1749** CHESTERF. *Let. to Son* 15 May, The several pieces of a Mosaic work, though separately of little value or beauty, when properly joined, form those beautiful figures which please every body. **1756–7** tr. *Keysler's Trav.* (1760) II. 22 At the entrance..hangs a Mosaic work, representing an owl. **1839** HALLAM *Hist. Lit.* II. II. i. 18 *note*, Language is always a mosaic work, made up of associated fragments, not of separate molecules.

So **mosaic-worker**, one who works in mosaic; **mosaic-working** *vbl. sb.*

1878 SIR G. G. SCOTT *Lect. Archit.* I. 178 The bringing to England of two master mosaic-workers. **1883** J. H. MIDDLETON in *Encycl. Brit.* XVI. 853/2 The period when mosaic-working was a real art.

mosaiq(ue obs. forms of MOSAIC *a.*[1] and *sb.*

Mosaism (ˈməʊzeɪɪz(ə)m). *Theol.* [ad. mod.L. *Mōsāismus*, f. *Mōsēs*: see -ISM.] The religious system, laws and ceremonies prescribed by Moses; adherence to the Mosaic system or doctrines.

1845 KITTO *Cycl. Bibl. Lit.* s.v. *Theology*, The period of Mosaism extends from the commencement of the exile..to about the year B.C. 400. **1882** FARRAR *Early Chr.* I. 64 It [Christianity] even tended to render those who were born Jews indifferent to the institutions of Mosaism.

mosaist[1] (ˈməʊzeɪɪst). *rare.* [ad. It. *mosaïsta*, irreg. f. *mosaico*: see -IST. Cf. F. *mosaïste.*] = MOSAICIST.

1864 CROWE & CAVALCASELLE *Hist. Painting Italy* II. 192 Della Valle mentions Angioletto of Gubbio as a mosaist at Orvieto in 1321–1329. **1887** *Athenæum* 20 Aug. 242/1 The two master mosaists, or workers in mosaic, of which it treats are Francesco and Valerio Zuccato.

Mosaist[2] (ˈməʊzeɪɪst). *rare.* [Formed as MOSAISM: see -IST.] One who believes in the Mosaic history of the creation. Also (*nonce-use*) the writer of that history.

1887 HUXLEY *Life & Lett. Darwin* II. 196 Inclined to say to both Mosaists and Evolutionists, 'a plague on both your houses!' **1890** GLADSTONE in *Gd. Words* May 303/1 The recorder of the Creation Story in Genesis I may designate by the name of the Mosaist or the Mosaic writer.

†**mosal.** *Obs. rare.* [repr. the proper name *Mosul*: see MUSLIN.] Muslin.

1657 S. CLARKE *Geog. Descr.* 56 [Grand Cairo] They sell ..cloth called Mosal, of a marvellous bredth and finenesse, whereof the greatest persons make shirts.

Mosan (ˈməʊzən), *a.* [Fr., of or pertaining to the Meuse river, f. L. *Mosa* Meuse.] Pertaining to the style of decorative art developed in the Meuse valley in the 11th to 13th centuries.

[**1882** C. DE LINAS *L'Art et l'Industrie d'autrefois dans les Régions de la Meuse Belge* i. 12 Le temps a pu faire surgir un art..ni rhénan, ni flamand, ni français, bien qu'il se rattache à tous les trois... Cet art,..il faudrait aujourd'hui lui donner un nom: pourquoi pas *art mosan*?] **1910** *Archaeologia* LXII. 22 The appearance of these medallions is of unusual brilliancy and richness, even for the productions of the Mosan school of enamelling. **1933** *Burlington Mag.* Apr. 198/1 The term Mosan art was introduced forty years ago by Charles de Linas, who maintained that the art of the middle, that is Belgian, section of the Meuse country was original. **1957** G. ZARNECKI *Eng. Romanesque Lead Sculpture* 12 It has been generally accepted that this manuscript was influenced by Mosan art. The blending of Winchester and Mosan features found in it was probably not confined to this manuscript alone. **1972** *Times* 6 Dec. 1/6 (*caption*) The exquisitely delicate little statue..is characteristic of the Mosan style of the eleventh and twelfth centuries.

Mosan (ˈməʊsən), *sb.* [f. *mōs*, lit. 'four' in various N. Amer. Indian languages + -AN.] The name of a North American language group comprising Chemakuan, Salish, and Wakashan.

1929 *Encycl. Brit.* V. 139/1 The following reductions of linguistic stocks which have been proposed may be looked upon as either probable or very possible:..5, *Mosan*, consisting of Salish, Chimakuan and Wakashan. **1955** H. A. GLEASON *Introd. Descriptive Linguistics* xxiv. 368 The Pacific Northwest from the Columbia River Valley to southern Alaska is occupied by a number of languages... Most of the languages fall into three families which are related in one phylum known as *Mosan.* **1965** *Canad. Jrnl. Linguistics* Spring 78 It was suggested by Sapir, in..1929, that Kutenai may be distinctly related to both Algonkian and Mosan. *Ibid.* 98 Algonkian-Wakashan has perhaps been more commonly known as Mosan-Algonkian. **1968** *Encycl. Brit.* I. 728/2 Tsimshian and Maidu have probably been considerably influenced by contact with Mosan.

mosandrite (məʊˈzændraɪt). *Min.* Also **mosanderite.** [Named after K. G. *Mosander*, a Swedish chemist (1797–1858) + -ITE.] 'A silicate of the cerium metals, calcium and sodium, with titanium and fluorine' (Chester *Dict. Min.* 1896).

1846 *Penny Cycl.* Suppl. II. 308/2 *Mosanderite* occurs massive and fibrous, and crystallized in flat prisms. **1855** *Orr's Circ. Sci., Min.* 530 *Mosandrite.*

Mosarabic, variant of MOZARABIC *a.*

mosard, -ry, variant ff. MUSARD, MUSARDRY.

‖**Mosasaurus** (məʊsəˈsɔːrəs). *Palæont.* Also Moso-, Mosæ-. Pl. -i. [mod.L. (W. D. Conybeare), f. L. *Mosa* the river Meuse or Maas + Gr. σαῦρος lizard.] A genus of large extinct marine reptiles, combining the characters of a saurian reptile with those of a snake. It was first discovered near Maestricht (on the Meuse) in 1780.

1830 MORTON in *Amer. Jrnl. Sci.* XVII. 289 Mosasaurus. **1833** MANTELL *Geog. S. E. Eng.* 146 The Mososaurus, or Fossil Monitor of Maestricht. **1836** BUCKLAND *Geol. & Min.* xiv. §7 (1837) I. 215 The Mosasaurus. **1875** C. MACLAREN in *Encycl. Brit.* I. 679/2.

Hence **ˈmosasaur**, a reptile of the genus *Mosasaurus*. **mosaˈsaurian** *a.*, of or pertaining to the mosasaurus; belonging to the sub-order *Mosasauria*; *sb.*, a reptile of this sub-order. **mosaˈsaurid**, a reptile of the family *Mosasauridæ*. **mosaˈsauroid** *a.*, having the form or characters of a mosasaurus; *sb.*, a mosasauroid reptile.

1841 OWEN in *Brit. Assoc. Rep.* (1842) 60 The shape of the tooth thus approximates very closely to that of the Mosasaur. **1850** —— in F. Dixon *Geol. & Fossils Sussex* 384 They demonstrate another Mosasaurian character. *Ibid.* 385 That genus of Mosasauroid Lizards. **1877** —— in *Q. Jrnl. Geol. Soc.* XXXIII. 690 The type of the genus and family of Mosasauroids. **1878** *Ann. & Mag. Nat. Hist.* July 92 In the single occipital condyle and the composite structure of the mandible the Mosasaurians are Reptilian. *Ibid.* Oct. 341 Since then [1851] Prof. O. C. Marsh has published a reconstruction of the fore limb of the Mosasaurid *Lestosaurus simus.* **1895** *Funk's Stand. Dict.*, *Mosasaurid.* **1966** *McGraw-Hill Encycl. Sci. & Technol.* VII. 474/1 Suborder Lacertilia... The group..includes modern lizards..and extinct marine mosasaurs (Cretaceous). **1968** A. S. ROMER *Procession of Life* xi. 195 The mosasaurs..had a long, flexible trunk and a highly developed tail, and hence were able to use body and tail undulation for forward progression in somewhat fish-like fashion. **1971** *Nature* 15 Jan. 172/1 In a great many aquatic and marine reptiles, past and present, ichthyosaurs..mosasaurs..the external nares are just in front of the eyes.

mosaul, obs. form of MUSSAL.

‖**moscarˈdino.** *Obs.* Pl. -ini. [It., 'a kinde of Muske-comfets' (Florio 1611), f. med.L. *moschus* MUSK *sb.*] A sweetmeat flavoured with musk.

1599 B. JONSON *Cynthia's Rev.* v. iv, Give mee my confects, my moscardini.

moscatel, variant of MOSCHATEL.

moscato (məˈskɑːtəʊ). Also **moscatto.** [It.: see MUSCAT.] A range of sweet Italian dessert wines; also, the grape from which the wine is produced.

1903 *Consular Reports* (U.S. Bur. Foreign Commerce) July 336 For each liter of sparkling wine, as Margarita, moscatto, moselle, etc., 1 peso (36.1 cents). **1925** A. HUXLEY *Those Barren Leaves* IV. vi. 314 We'll have a bottle of the sweet *moscato.* **1961** *Guardian* 21 Nov. 14/2 (Advt.), *Moscato.* Semi-sweet, fragrant, sparkling..9/0. **1972** *Times* 25 Mar. 10/6 The moscato grape from which Asti Spumante is made.

mosch, obs. form of MOSQUE, MUSK.

†**moschat.** *Obs.* Also **moschatte.** [ad. mod.L. *moschātus*, f. *moschus* MUSK.] = MUSK-CAT.

1607 TOPSELL *Four-f. Beasts* 551 Of the Moschatte, or Mus-kat. **1629** SYMMER *Spir. Posie* Epist. A ij b, The Moschat, Sivet, &c.

†**moschata.** *Obs. rare.* Also **muscata.** [a. mod.L. *moschāta*, *muscāta*, fem. of *moschātus*, *muscātus*: see next.]

1. *Erodium moschatum*, stork's-bill.

1578 LYTE *Dodoens* I. xxxii. 47 The first kinde [of Geranium] is called..in English..of some Moschata. **1611** COTGR. s.v. *Aiguille*, Musked Pinkneedle..; Muscata.

2. *Nux moschata*: the nutmeg.

1587 MASCALL *Govt. Cattle, Horses* (1627) 176 Take..of *baccarum lauri*..of *nux muscata*, of each two ounces. **1706** PHILLIPS (ed. Kersey), *Moschata Nux*, or *Moschocaryon*, Nutmeg, an Indian Spice. **1823** CRABB *Technol. Dict.*

moschate (ˈmɒskeɪt), *a.* [ad. mod.L. *moschātus*, f. med.L. *moschus* MUSK.] Exhaling or having the odour of musk.

1826 KIRBY & SP. *Entomol.* IV. xlvi. 301 Moschate (*Moschatus*). A scent of musk. **1880** A. GRAY *Struct. Bot.* 420.

moschatel (mɒskəˈtɛl). *Bot.* Also 8 moscatell, 8–9 moschatell, 9 muskatel, moscatel. [a. F. *moscatelle*, ad. It. *moscatella*, f. *moscato* musk.] An inconspicuous plant (*Adoxa Moschatellina*, N.O. *Caprifoliaceæ*) 4 or 5 inches high, having

pale-green flowers with a musky smell, found in shady places; freq. ***tuberous moschatel.***

1732 J. MARTYN *Tournefort's Hist. Plants* II. 124 *Moschatellina*... Tuberous Moscatell. **1756** WATSON in *Phil. Trans.* XLIX. 831 Tuberous Moschatell, or Musk-wood Crowfoot. **1854** DOBELL *Balder* xi, Inglorious moschatel..Sickening below the nightshade. **1866** R. BUCHANAN *Lond. Poems* 185 The musk and the muskatel That grow on the window sill. **1874** T. HARDY *Far fr. Mad. Crowd* xxii, The square-headed moschatel, the odd cuckoo-pint.

moschatous ('mɒskətəs), *a.* [Formed as MOSCHATE + -OUS.] = MOSCHATE *a.*

1866 *Treas. Bot., Moschatous,* having the smell of musk.

mosche(a, moschee, obs. forms of MOSQUE.

moschet, obs. form of MUSKET *sb.*[1]

moschet(t)o, obs. forms of MOSQUITO.

moschey, obs. form of MOSQUE.

†**Moschical,** *a. Obs. rare*⁻¹. [f. *Mosche,* an occasional transliteration of Heb. *Mōsheʰ* Moses + -ICAL.] = MOSAICAL *a.*[2]

1687 H. MORE *Answ. Psychop.* (1689) 136 Seems..to have been the old Moschical or Mosaical Philosophy.

moschie, obs. form of MOSQUE.

moschiferous (mɒ'skɪfərəs), *a. Zool.* [f. med.L. *mosch-us* MUSK + -(I)FEROUS.] Bearing or producing musk.

1856 in MAYNE *Expos. Lex.* **1890** *Century Dict.* s.v., Moschiferous organs; a moschiferous animal. **1902** *Webster's Suppl.* s.v., The moschiferous glands of the musk deer.

moschine ('mɒskɪn), *a.* (and *sb.*) *Zool.* [f. mod.L. *Moschin-æ* (f. *Moschus* the typical genus): see -INE[1].] **a.** *adj.* Of, pertaining to, or having the characters of the *Moschinæ,* an Asiatic family of *Cervidæ,* containing the two genera *Moschus* and *Hydropotes.* **b.** *sb.* An animal of the family *Moschinæ,* a musk-deer.

In recent Dicts.

moschite, obs. form of MESQUITA, mosque.

1593 DONNE *Sat.* iv. 199 Would not Heraclitus laugh to see Macrine, From hat, to shooe, himselfe at doore refine, As if the Presence were a Moschite.

moschito, obs. form of MOSQUITO.

mosc(h)o, moschy, obs. ff. MOSQUE.

Moschovite, obs. form of MUSCOVITE.

mosc(h)yon, obs. form of MOTION.

Moscov-: see MUSCOV-.

Moscow ('mɒskəʊ, *U.S.* 'mɒskaʊ). **1.** The name of the capital of the U.S.S.R. used allusively to describe the government, political influence, ideology, etc., of the U.S.S.R.

1957 C. HUNT *Guide to Communist Jargon* xxiii. 82 Moscow-appointed officials of a non-Russian Soviet republic. **1967** H. ARENDT *Origins of Totalit.* (new ed.) xi. 371 The European Communist parties became branches of a Moscow-directed Bolshevik movement. **1971** P. O'DONNELL *Impossible Virgin* ii. 46 He wants a list of our local agents in Prague. Moscow will pay him the earth for that. **1972** T. LILLEY *K Section* viii. 57 A Moscow-trained and dedicated Communist. **1974** *Times* 27 Aug. 4/8 Mr Florakis leads the Moscow-orientated rump of the [Greek Communist] party.

2. ***Moscow mule,*** a cocktail containing vodka.

1963 *House & Garden* Mar. 114/2 A Moscow Mule (vodka, ginger beer, ice and half a lime). **1965** O. A. MENDELSOHN *Dict. Drink* 229 *Moscow mule,* cocktail of vodka, ginger beer and lime. The concoction is reported to be unknown in Russia. **1969** [see MARGARITA 2].

So '**Moscowism.**

1938 *Times Lit. Suppl.* 19 Mar. 182/1 'What Are We To Do?' is less a work of new thinking than of the application and adaptation of Moscowism. **1940** *Manch. Guardian Weekly* 17 May 388 'This book on Poland,' says Cardinal Hinsley in his foreword, 'shows that Nazism and Moscowism agree in two broad lines—Godlessness and ruthlessness.'

†**mose,** *sb. Obs. rare.* [OE. *máse* wk. fem. = MDu. *mêze* (Du. *mees*: see MEESE), OHG. *meisa* (MHG., mod.G. *meise*); ON. has only the derivative *meising-r,* whence F. *mésange.* Cf. COALMOUSE, TITMOUSE, where *-mose* has been corrupted into *-mouse.*] The titmouse.

a **700** *Epinal Gloss.* 806 *Parrula,* masae. *c* **1050** *Voc.* in Wr.-Wülcker 286/14-15 *Parra,* colmase. *Parrula,* spicmase. *a* **1250** *Owl & Night.* 503 þu..pipest al so doþ a mose.

†**mose,** *v. Obs. rare*⁻¹. [Etymology obscure; possibly a corruption.] = MOURN *v.*[2]

1596 SHAKS. *Tam. Shrew* III. ii. 51 His horse..possest with the glanders, and like to mose in the chine.

mose, obs. f. MOOSE, MOSS, MUSA[1] (banana).

moseache, moseak, obs. forms of MOSQUE.

mosel(l, obs. forms of MUZZLE.

Moselle (məʊ'zɛl). Also 8 mossel. [The Fr. name (= G. *Mosel,* L. *Mosella*) of a river which joins the Rhine at Coblentz.] In full ***Moselle wine***: a dry white wine, produced near the Moselle.

1687 CARTE in *Magd. Coll. & Jas. II* (O.H.S.) 158 A glass of Moselle wine. **1693** [R. AMES] *Bacch. Sessions* Rhenish, Hock, Old and Young, Moselle, and Backrag. **1703** *Art & Myst. Vintners* 60 Put into the Vessel 20 ounces of mossel. **1839** BAILEY *Festus* xvi. (1852) 180 Thy wit..Is like cool moselle. **1869** BLACK *In Silk Attire* II. 240 He..contemplatively stirred his Moselle with a bit of biscuit. **1879** VIZETELLY *Facts about Champagne* xvi. 176 The sparkling moselles..are largely dosed with the preparation of elder-flowers, which imparts to them their well-known muscatel flavour and perfume.

moseque, obs. form of MOSQUE.

Moses ('məʊzɪz). Forms: 6-7 Moyses, 7 (*pl.* Mosesses), 7- Moses. [a. L. *Mōses, Mōÿses,* Gr. *Μωσῆς, Μωυσῆς,* ad. Heb. *Mōsheʰ.*]

1. a. Applied allusively to some one resembling Moses, esp. in his character as lawgiver or leader.

1528 TINDALE *Obed. Chr. Man* 13 How cometh it that our Moyseses..commaunde vs the contrary. **1624** T. TAYLOR *2 Serm.* ii. 23 As Israel had not only Ioshua fighting..but also Moses praying..; so wee have many Mosesses lifting up hands, and praiers. **1652** OWEN *Advantage Kingd. of Christ* Wks. 1851 VIII. 320 They will not understand that such Moseses will be deliverers. **1660** *Iter Australe* 12 A second, Moses styled him [*sc.* Cromwell] (for why His Shining Nose made the Synecdoche). **1888** *Times* (weekly ed.) 22 June 14/3 He prayed for another Moses to limit the wanderings of the..party to four years instead of 40.

b. *slang.* (See quots.); also ***to stand Moses.***

[**1611** COTGR., *Moyse,* Holie Moyses; whose ordinarie counterfeit hauing on either side of the head an eminence, or luster arising somewhat in the forme of a horne, hath imbouldened a prophane Author to stile Cuckolds, *Parents de Moyse.*] **1796** *Grose's Dict. Vulg. T.* s.v., A man is said to stand *Moses* when he has another man's bastard child fathered upon him, and he is obliged by the parish to maintain it. **1859** MATSELL *Voc.* s.v. (Farmer), *Moses,* a man that fathers another man's child for a consideration.

c. Used as an oath or expletive.

1840 in *Amer. Speech* (1965) XL. 130 Oh! Moses how they opened dare eyes. **1842** S. LOVER *Handy Andy* xiv. 123 O'Grady, casting a look of mingled rage and contempt on the fisherman, merely uttered the ejaculation, 'Oh Moses!' and threw himself back in his chair. **1855** STRANG *Glasgow & Its Clubs* (1856) 295 Very well the front rank; but holy Moses! what a rear! **1858** O. W. HOLMES *Aut. Breakf.-t.* (1883) 222 The parson..stopped perplexed At what the—Moses—was coming next. **1872** SCHELE DE VERE *Americanisms* 595 By the Ever-Living Jumping Moses. **1890** H. NISBET *Bail Up!* xxx. 212 'And, by the piper that played before Moses, so they did.'

d. A derogatory appellation for a Jew.

1844 *Punch* 6 July 19/1 (*heading*) A hint for Moses... Passing by the eminent establishment of E. Aaron and Co., ..I was naturally attracted..to examine the beauteous objects of gent.'s attire, which are exhibited in their unrivalled plate-glass windows. **1858** *Ibid.* 10 July 12/2 The Jews are no more a disqualified caste, And *moses* will henceforth in Parliament sit.

2. †**a.** A kind of boat used in the West Indies (see quot.). *Obs.* **b.** ***Moses boat***: a kind of boat used in Massachusetts.

Whether these two applications have a common origin is doubtful. The Massachusetts use has been said to be derived from the name of *Moses* Lowell, a famous boat-builder at Salisbury, Mass.

a. 1768 *Boston Chron.* 2-9 May 195/3 An advertisement appeared in the Antigua Gazette, offering forty pistoles, for apprehending one —Scott who was mate of a sloop,..and two sailors, for robbing said sloop, then lying at Antigua, of a moses boat, two barrels of beef [etc.]. **1769** FALCONER *Dict. Marine* (1780) F iv b, A moses is a very flat broad boat, used by merchant-ships amongst the Carribbee-islands, to bring hogsheads of sugar off..to the shipping. **1775** ROMANS *Florida* App. 87 In almost every gut among the many islands in this bay, I have found it as much as four stout men could do, to stem the current in a Moses.

b. 1765 *Mass. Gaz.* 25 Apr. **1766** *Ibid.* 16 Oct., A Moses Boat, about fourteen Foot long. **1770** *Boston Gaz.* 23 Apr. 3/2 Taken from Long Side a Schooner at the North-End, the 13th Inst. a Moses Boat, 16 Feet. **1775** *New. Eng. Chron.* 18-25 May 4/3 A Moses Boat, 13 Feet long, went adrift about a Month ago from Beverly. **1812** *Boston Gaz.* 26 Oct. Suppl. (Advt.) (Th.), On Saturday was picked up, on Dorchester Flats, a small Moses boat. **1970** *Brewer's Dict. Phr. & Fable* 731/2 *Moses boat,* a type of boat made..by a famous boat-builder, Moses Lowell, in the 18th century.

3. *Comb.*: **Moses basket**, a basket used for carrying babies; **Moses' law** (see quot., and cf. Deut. xxv. 3); **Moses' rod**, a divining-rod (cf. MOSAICAL *a.*[2] 2); **Moses-seam** (see quot.); **Moses' tables**, see quot. 1803 [in allusion to Exodus xx].

1945 N. MITFORD *Pursuit of Love* x. 84 She..returned carrying a *Moses basket full of wails. **1948** M. DICKENS *Joy & Josephine* I. i. 13 She was trying to make out whether the young officer were the father of the baby in the Moses basket. **1949** E. TAYLOR *Wreath of Roses* vii. 100 Carrying the baby between them in a Moses basket. **1959** 'A. STAFFORD' *Custody of Anne* I. 45 She shook the moses basket so that the child stirred and whimpered. **1974** 'J. MELVILLE' *Nun's Castle* i. 22 A display of nursery furniture, including an elegant Moses basket of natural straw lined with soft cotton. **1867** SMYTH *Sailor's Word-bk.,* *Moses' law, the term among pirates for inflicting thirty-nine lashes on the bare back—forty save one. **1646** SIR T. BROWNE *Pseud. Ep.* v. xxi. 271 A forked hazell, commonly called *Moses his rod, which freely held forth, will stirre and play if any mine be under it. **1875** KNIGHT *Dict. Mech.,* *Moses-seam, a sail-maker's seam, as the selvages of the canvas lap past each other. **1803** *Gazetteer Scot.* Introd. 12 At Portsoy is found that singular kind of granite called *Moses' Tables, which, when polished, resembles the Hebrew characters on a white ground.

mosesite ('məʊzɪzaɪt). *Min.* [f. the name of Alfred J. *Moses* (1859–1920), U.S. mineralogist + -ITE[1].] A hydrated nitrogen compound of mercury which is found as yellow isometric crystals and has the formula $Hg_2NX.H_2O$, where X represents chiefly chloride and sulphate.

1910 F. A. CANFIELD et al. in *Amer. Jrnl. Sci.* XXX. 202 We propose the name *mosesite,* which name, besides perpetuating the high attainments of Professor Moses in the science of mineralogy, is particularly appropriate as it links his name with a group of minerals which he first definitely put on record. **1953** *Amer. Mineralogist* XXXVIII. 1225 Mosesite from El Doctor, Mexico, contains AsO_4 and very little MoO_4, but that from Terlingua, Texas, has only Cl and SO_4 as anions. *Ibid.* 1234 Mosesite may be easily synthesized by treating HgCl with dilute ammonium hydroxide. **1959** *Prof. Papers U.S. Geol. Surv.* No. 312. 70/1 The kleinite and mosesite..furnish direct evidence that they were formed at temperatures well above those to be expected during weathering.

mosetale, obs. form of MOUSETAIL.

mosette (məʊ'zɛt). [a. F. *mosette,* ad. It. *mozzetta*: see AMICE[2].] = MOZZETTA.

1862 F. C. HUSENBETH *Bp. Milner* 339 Representing the Bishop seated in rocket, mosette, and stole.

mosey ('məʊzɪ), *v. slang* (orig. *U.S.*).

intr. To go away quickly; to decamp. Also, to make haste, 'be lively'; to jog *along* (*lit.* and *fig.*).

18.. *New York Tribune* (Bartlett 1877), I'll get a room nicely furnished, and my wife and I will jes mosey along till the election trouble is over, an' den dere'll be a powerful sight of whitewashin' to be done. **1829** *Virginia Lit. Museum* 30 Dec. 459 *Mosey,* to move off. **1836** *Public Ledger* (Philadelphia) 2 Dec. (Th.), You'r not going to smoke me. So mosey off. **1838** J. C. NEAL *Charcoal Sk.* i. (1850) 17 If your tongue wasn't so thick I'd say you must mosey; but moseying is only to be done when a gemman's half shot. *a* **1859** *N. Y. Family Companion* (Bartlett), After you left me, when them fellows told you to mosey off before the boat went to sea. **1871** J. HAY *Banty Tim* 7 The nigger has got to mosey From the limits o' Spunky P'int! **1885** MISS M. N. MURFREE *Prophet Gt. Smoky Mts.* xiii. 233 Hurry 'long, D'rindy,..you-uns ain't goin' ter reel a hank ef ye don't mosey. **1870** 'MARK TWAIN' *Curious Republic Gondour* (1919) 57, I hain't got time to be palavering along here—got to..mosey along. **1874** —— in *Atlantic Monthly* Nov. 592/2 De way dey made dem sojers mosey roun'! **1891** KIPLING *Naulahka* vi, I'll mosey along somehow. **1901** 'H. MCHUGH' *John Henry* 42 Abie had moseyed away. **1902** W. N. HARBEN *Abner Daniel* 59 Now I must mosey on down-stairs. **1903** A. ADAMS *Log Cowboy* ix. 124 You fellows just mosey along up the trail. **1918** *Punch* 27 Mar. 206/1 Her funnel's caked with Cape Horn ice and blistered in the sun, She's moseyed round above a bit, and, poor old ship, she's done. **1961** C. MCCULLERS *Clock without Hands* v. 111 While Mr Malone made up the Coca-Cola, Jester moseyed over to the scales and stood on them. **1966** T. PYNCHON *Crying of Lot 49* v. 110 She was moseying along a street..when she collided with a gang of guided tourists. **1973** *Daily Tel.* (Colour Suppl.) 16 Mar. 22/3 Map in hand he moseys round the alleys and yards of Southwark. **1974** *Black World* June 70/2, I had moseyed over to see what they were yakking about. **1974** D. RAMSAY *No Cause to Kill* II. 134, I thought I'd mosey on over to the liquor store.

mosey, var. MOSY *a. dial.*

mosged, obs. form of MASJID, mosque.

1594 R. ASHLEY tr. *Loys le Roy* 101 Not suffering in his Mosgedes, or Temples, any corruptible thing whatsoeuer.

mosh, dial. var. MUSH *sb.*[1] and *v.*[2]

‖**moshav** ('məʊʃɑːv). Also **moshaev, moshavah.** Pl. **moshavim.** [ad. mod. Heb. *mōshābh* dwelling, colony.] In Israel: a group of agricultural smallholdings worked co-operatively. So **moshav-ovdim, moshav-shitufi** (see quot. 1950).

1931 [see KIBBUTZ]. **1934** *Cook's Traveller's Handbk. to Palestine, Syria & Iraq* (ed. 6) 48 The *Moshav,* in which small holdings of land are allotted to families on hereditary lease by the Jewish National Fund... The co-operative principle is applied in the purchase and sale of produce and agricultural requirements. **1944** H. F. INFIELD *Co-operative Living in Palestine* (1946) iii. 46 The Moshav is intermediate between individualism and the Kvutza. Here the settler lives in his own house, owns a piece of land and some cattle. *Ibid.* xi. 122 From 1936 to 1939, new Kvutzot were 26, new Moshve-Ovdim only 9. The ration of Kvutzot to Moshve established has doubled. **1950** G. MIKES *Milk & Honey* 136 Some halfway solutions have been attempted. First the *Moshav Ovdim,* in which each family has its own unit of land. The purchase of supplies and the marketing of agricultural products is on a cooperative basis. These..are smallholders' settlements in which every farmer shoulders his own risks... Then there is the *Moshav Shitufi,* in which the women have to work four or five hours a day for the community, but otherwise the family is a separate unit. No personal risk, no private enterprise but more private life. **1959** *Economist* 16 May 640/1 The *moshavim* (the farming settlements where the families rent their own land but co-operate over marketing, tractor stations, seed buying, etc.). **1969** P. WORSLEY in Ionescu & Gellner *Populism* 231 Since

family-farming units and communitarian village life are perfectly compatible, forms resembling the *moshav*, or the Saskatchewan Group Farm, have been the favoured models. **1972** C. RAPHAEL *Feast of History* i. 13/1 A *moshav* (smallholders' settlement) in Galilee. **1973** *Times Lit. Suppl.* 18 May 544/4 A moshav is a village devoted to agricultural pursuits and run on cooperative lines. It is not as austere as some of the kibbutzim. **1973** *Jewish Chron.* 6 July 3/2 The first families moved into the second moshav . . occupying 30 of the 40 houses built.

Moshi, Mosi, varr. MOSSI.

moshin, mosine, corrupt ff. MORSING *vbl. sb.*, *Sc.*

moshrump, obs. form of MUSHROOM.

mosie, var. MOSY *a. dial.*

mosing: see MOZING, MOZE *v.*

mosk (mɒsk), *v. slang.* [Shortened from MOSKENEER.] = MOSKENEER *v.*

1902 *Standard* 5 June 10/2 The practice of obtaining a living by professional pawning—known as 'mosking'.

mosk, variant of MOSQUE; obs. form of MUSK.

moskalonge: see MUSKELLUNGE.

moskee, mos'keh, obs. forms of MOSQUE.

moskeneer (mɒskə'nɪə(r)), *v. slang.* Also **moschkener, moshkeneer, moskuiner, moskeener.** [Of Yiddish origin, f. mod.Heb. *mashkōn* a pledge, whence *mishkēn* to pawn (Dalman *Aram.-neuhebr. Wb.*).] *trans.* To pawn (an article) for more than it is worth.

1874 in *Slang Dict.* **1887** HENLEY *Villon's Straight Tip* 10 Fiddle, or fence, or mace, or mack; Or moskeneer, or flash the drag. **1890** BARRÈRE & LELAND *Dict. Slang*, etc., *Moshkeneer.* **1893** P. H. EMERSON *Signor Lippo* xxii. 100 He moschkeners from twenty to thirty supers a week.

mosker ('mɒskə(r)), *sb. slang.* [f. MOSK *v.* + -ER[1].] One who 'moskeneers'.

1883 *Daily Tel.* 9 July 3/1 The 'mosker' . . is, in slang vernacular, one who makes a living by taking advantage of the business incapacity of persons engaged in the pawnbroking trade. **1905** *Daily News* 1 Mar. 6 There is an average loss to the pawnbroker on these unredeemed pledges, which are often bought cheaply and in bulk by the 'mosker'. Then they are artfully retailed, one by one, and in the character of personal belongings, to unwary pawnbrokers.

mosker ('mɒskə(r)), *v. Obs.* exc. *dial.* (Yorks., Linc.: see E.D.D.) [Of obscure origin.] *intr.* To decay, rot; to crumble or moulder *away*. Hence **'moskered, 'moskering** *ppl. adjs.*

1612 CAPT. SMITH *Map Virginia* 15 Some moskered shining stones and spangles which the waters brought down. **1621** T. GRANGER *Comm. Eccles.* xii. 320 The teeth stand thin, or loose, or moskerd at the root. **1641** BEST *Farm. Bks.* (Surtees) 122 The first decay of wilfes is allwayes att the hearte, for they will rotte, mosker, and bee hollowe within, soe that [etc.]. **1691** RAY *N.C. Words* 50 To *Mosker*; to Rot, or contract Corruption, perhaps from gathering Mosse; as a Moskerd Tree, a Moskerd Tooth.

moskie, moskuee, obs. forms of MOSQUE.

moskito, obs. form of MOSQUITO.

‖**moskonfyt** ('mɒskɒnˌfeɪt). *S. Afr.* [Afrikaans, f. *mos* must + *konfyt* jam.] A thick syrup prepared from grapes.

1891 *Pall Mall Gaz.* Extra No. 58, Oct. 13/2 It was *moskomfyt*, I found, made with grape-juice. **1905** *Agric. Jrnl. Cape of Good Hope* 483 (Pettman), The first idea in planting vines is to provide *mos confyt*, a kind of grape sugar syrup, which is given as part of their rations to the coloured labourers. **1931** T. J. HAARHOFF *Vergil in Experience S. Afr.* i. 3 '*Moskonfyt*' is used, as it was by the Romans, partly as a syrup and partly to break down the acidity of wines. **1953** *Cape Times* 10 Mar. 2/4 A consignment of 600 110-gallon drums of *moskonfyt*, which will be processed into wine in Britain. **1975** *Daily Dispatch* (East London, Cape Province) 20 Sept. 5 A grape for raisins and also for the production of sweet wines, moskonfyt and even jam.

moskyta, var. MESQUITA, MESQUIT, a mosque.

Moslem: see MUSLIM.

Moslemah, used erron. as a pl. of MUSLIM, MUSLEM.

1825 SCOTT *Talism.* ii, Dried hogs-flesh, the abomination of the Moslemah.

Mosleyite ('məʊzlɪaɪt). [f. the name of Sir Oswald Ernald *Mosley* (born 1896) + -ITE[1].] A follower or supporter of Sir Oswald Mosley or his views; a British fascist. Also *attrib.* or as *adj.*

1932 AUDEN *Orators* III. 104 The Simonites, the Mosleyites and the I.L.P. **1944** H. G. WELLS *'42 to '44* 33 The Mosleyites running like the wind down Regent Street from the Jewish prizefighters. **1960** *Economist* 8 Oct. 141/2 The lunatic Mosleyite fringe. **1961** *Ibid.* 17 June 1266/1 The alliance of politicians, civil servants and 'sound' outside minds which generally rules England did not go Mosleyite. **1973** *Guardian* 10 Apr. 1/2 Mr Jonathan Guiness said: 'I am supposed to say that . . it is a question between the Powellites and the Mosleyites . . because I am Sir Oswald Mosley's son-in-law.'

moslings ('mɒzlɪŋz), *sb. pl.* [? = **mosselings*, f. *mossel*, vulgar form of MORSEL *v.*] (See quots.)

1850 HOLTZAPFFEL *Turning*, etc. III. 1080 *Moslings*, the thin shreds or shavings of leather shaved off by the currier in dressing cow, or calf skins. **1875** KNIGHT *Dict. Mech.*, *Moslings*, the thin shreds or scrapings of leather shaved off by the currier in dressing skins. They are used in wiping off metals while grinding and polishing.

mosole, variant of MAUSOLE, MAUSOLEE.

1663 GERBIER *Counsel* c iij b, A glorious Mosole.

mosolem, var. MUSELLIM (a Turkish officer).

mosolyd, obs. form of MUZZLED.

mosque (mɒsk). Forms: 4 **moseak, moseache;** 6 **muskey, muskaye,** 6–7 **mosquee,** 7 **moschy, -ee, -ie, -ey, muskie, mos'keh, moskuee, moski(e, -ee, mosquy, mozki,** 7 **mosquey;** 6–7 **moschea,** 7 **muskia;** 7 **mosquo, mosco, moscho;** 7 **moseque,** 7–8 **mosch(e,** 8–9 **mosk,** 6– **mosque.** [In 16th c. *mosquee* (later shortened to *mosque*), a. F. *mosquée*, a. It. *moschea* (whence G. *moschee*), a. Arab. *masgid* (so pronounced in N. Africa; elsewhere *masjid*), f. *sagada* (*sajada*) to worship.

Cf. early mod.F. *mosquete*, Sp. *mezquita*, Pg. *mesquita*, It. *meschita* (see MESQUITA[1]). Eng. writers have occas. used forms directly taken from Arabic, as MASJID, MOSGED, MUSCHID. Some of the forms above are from Italian; the precise history of the forms in Mandeville is obscure.]

1. A Muslim temple or place of worship.

c **1400** MAUNDEV. (Roxb.) xxv. 114 þaire tempill, þe whilk es called Moseak [ed. 1839 xxii. 232 Moseache]. **1511** *Guylforde's Pilgr.* (Camden) 50 The Sarrasyns wyll suffre no man to come into this place . . bycause it is theyr muskey. **1544** in *Lett. & Pap. Hen. VIII*, XIX. II. 452 [The Turk made offers in his] muskaye. **1551** THOMAS tr. *Barbaro's Trav. Persia* (1873) 10 He . . was lodged in an auncient Moschea. **1585** T. WASHINGTON tr. *Nicholay's Voy.* I. xii. 13 b, A very faire and sumptuous Mosquee. *Ibid.* Table 164 b, S. Sophia and other Mosques of Constantinople. **1603** KNOLLES *Hist. Turks* (1638) 341 The Temple of S. Sophia . . (now reduced vnto the form of a Mahometan Moschy, . .)is most beautifull. **1609** W. BIDDULPH in T. Lavender *Trav.* (1612) 105 There is built in the place thereof [Temple at Jerusalem] a Muskia or Turkish Church. **1613** PURCHAS *Pilgrimage* II. xxii. §4 (1617) 249 Demolishing their Moschees. *Ibid.* III. ix. 325 Mahomet . . therefore appointed publike Prayers in all the Mosques of his dominion. **1624** SIR T. ROE *Negotiations* (1740) 343 The building of so many Mahometan moschyes. **1628** ROBSON *News fr. Aleppo* 16 The Courts of their Mos'kehs or Churches. **1632** LITHGOW *Trav.* VI. 279 The Viccario shewed vs a little Moskee, kept by Turkes. **1648** W. BROWNE *Polex.* IV. II. 191 The daily denying my ransomer in the Mosquo of his adversary. *a* **1659** OSBORN *Observ. Turks* Wks. (1673) 297 By which means such Baths and Moscos are erected. *a* **1668** LASSELLS *Voy. Italy* II. (1670) 31 The great Moski at Fez. **1673** *Lady's Call.* I. v. §49 The present Mahometans . . permit none to sit in their moschos. **1696** tr. *Du Mont's Voy. Levant* 157 Sancta Sophia, which was formerly a Christian Church, and is now a Turkish Mosquee. **1717** LADY M. W. MONTAGU *Let. to Abbé Conti* 1 Apr., They . . go to the mosques on Fridays and the church on Sundays. **1788** GIBBON *Decl. & F.* lxviii. VI. 509 The same model was imitated in the *jami* or royal moschs. **1828** LANDOR *Imag. Conv.*, *Soliman & Mufti* Wks. (1853) I. 355/1 My commands are, . . that praises be offered up in every mosk. **1877** A. B. EDWARDS *Up Nile* ii. 30 A Mahommedan mosque is as much a place of refuge and rest as of prayer. **1896** H. C. TRUMBULL *Threshold Covenant* I. iv. 37 A Muhammadan is always careful to put his right foot first in crossing over the threshold of a mosk.

b. *the mosque*: Those who worship in mosques; the body of Muslims.

1779 BURKE *Corr.* (1844) II. 270, I could not justify to myself to give to the synagogue, the mosque, or the pagoda, the language which your pulpits so liberally bestow upon a great part of the Christian world. **1856** R. A. VAUGHAN *Mystics* I. 326 Those Sufis who proclaimed the difference between the Church and the Mosque of little moment.

2. *attrib.* (or *adj.*) and *Comb.*, as ***mosque-lamp, -tower, worship***; ***mosque-like*** adj. Also **mosque Gothic,** ? a variety of Gothic influenced by Saracenic architecture.

1753 H. WALPOLE *Let. to Chute* 4 Aug., The style has a propensity to the Venetian or *mosque Gothic. **1900** *Daily News* 7 Apr. 5/5 A *mosque lamp that is 14th century Arab work. **1857** S. OSBORN *Quedah* xx. 274 In the centre of the town a *mosquelike building rose amongst the trees. **1892** E. REEVES *Homeward Bound* 224 At 9 p.m. a Moor ascends to the top of the *mosque tower and calls the hour of prayer. **1711** SHAFTESB. *Charac.* (1737) I. 26 There is hardly now in the world so good a Christian . . who, if he happen'd to live at Constantinople, or elsewhere under the protection of the Turks, wou'd think it fitting or decent to give any disturbance to their *mosque-worship.

Hence **mosqued** *a.*, abounding in mosques; **'mosquelet,** a little mosque; **'mosquish** *a.*, resembling, pertaining to, characteristic of, a mosque.

1902 F. THOMPSON in *Academy* 12 Apr. 378/1 The mosquèd Cairene. **1888** *Cornh. Mag.* June 374 A tiny domed mosquelet in a close-set hedge of prickly pear. **1813** FORSYTH *Rem. Excurs. Italy* 362 A roof hooded all over with mosquish cupolas.

mosquet, obs. form of MUSKET.

mosqueto(e, obs. forms of MOSQUITO.

mosquettier, obs. form of MUSKETEER.

mosquetto, mosquit(e, mosquita, variant forms of MESQUITA, MESQUIT, a mosque.

mosquital (mɒ'skiːtəl), *a.* [f. MOSQUIT(O + -AL[1].] Of or pertaining to a mosquito.

1890 *Century Dict.* s.v., Mosquital saliva. **1901** *Brit. Med. Jrnl.* 6 Apr. 842/1 In support of the 'mosquital origin of malarial fever' Dr. King [in 1883] cited numerous medical authorities.

mosquito (mə'skiːtəʊ, mɒ-). Forms: 6 **muskyto, mosqueta,** 6–8 **musketa,** 7 **muskeito, musceto, muscheto, muskitto, musqueeto, muskeeto,** 7–8 **musketoe, muscato, musket(t)o,** 8 **moskito, muskeitoe, mosqueto,** 8–9 **moschet(t)o, moschito, musqueto, musquitto,** 9 **musquitoe, mosquetoe,** 6– **muskito,** 7–9 **musquito,** 7– **mosquito.** [a. Sp. and Pg. *mosquito*, dim. of *mosca* (:—L. *musca*) fly.

Cf. F. *moustique* (whence MOUSTICK *Obs.*), a metathetic alteration of the Sp. word.]

1. A 'gnat' of several different species of the genus *Culex* (esp. *C. mosquito*) and other allied genera, the female of which has a long proboscis, by means of which it punctures the skins of animals (including man) and sucks their blood.

Certain kinds of mosquito are the agents by which the germs of malaria are introduced into the human body.

c **1583** M. PHILLIPS in *Hakluyt's Voy.* (1589) 568 We were also oftentimes greatly annoyed with a kinde of flie, . . the Spanyards called them Musketas. **1600** O. E. *Repl. Libel* III. vii. 35 He is like a flye, or rather, because he speaketh so much for Spaniards, a Spanish mosqueta. **1623** WHITBOURNE *Newfoundland* 99 A very little nimble fly . . which is called a Muskeito. **1625** G. PERCY in Purchas *Pilgrims* IV. 1685 Their bodies are all painted red to keepe away the biting of Muscetos. **1634** W. WOOD *New Eng. Prosp.* (1865) 51 The fourth is a Musketoe which is not unlike to our Gnats in England. **1655** E. TERRY *Voy. E. India* 123 In the night we were . . very much disquieted with another sort [of fly] called Musqueetoes. **1665** SIR T. HERBERT *Trav.* (1677) 121 Howbeit the Muskitto or Gnats pestered us extreamly. **1672** W. HUGHES *Amer. Phys.* 9 That very small black and poysonous Fly, called a Muscato. **1674** JOSSELYN *Voy. New Eng.* (1675) 95 The countrie is strangely incommodated with flies, which the English call Musketaes. **1702** C. MATHER *Magn. Chr.* VI. i. (1852) 351 They were . . grievously infested with moschetos. **1745** *Lond. Mag.* 396 Peach Trees . . which are Nurseries of Muskettos and other Vermin. **1747** FRANKLIN *Lett.* Wks. 1887 II. 98 If a musqueto . . were to light on one of them. **1796** STEDMAN *Surinam* II. xx. 90 We were almost devoured by the clouds of gnats or musquitoes, which arose from a neigbouring marsh. **1825** J. NEAL *Bro. Jonathan* I. 217 Kept awake all the night before by the wolves or moschettoes. **1837** LANDOR *Pentameron* i. Wks. 1853 II. 310/2 The peopled region is peopled chiefly with monsters and moschitoes. **1858** LYTTON *Alice* IV. ix, At Venice I was bit to death by musquitoes. **1902** *19th Cent.* Nov. 679 The great drawback to the far north of Sweden is the Mosquitoes.

fig. **1739** CIBBER *Apol.* xvi (1740) 340 While these buzzing Muscatos have been fluttering round their Eyes and Ears. **1863** READE *Hard Cash* I. vii. 210 When a man has a deep anxiety, some human midge or mosquito buzzes at him.

2. *attrib.* and *Comb.*, as ***mosquito-bite, -season, -sting***; ***mosquito-borne, -bred, -breeding, -carried, -free, -thin*** adjs.

1805 *Med. Jrnl.* XIV. 113 Small lumps resembling *mosquito bites. **1961** M. HYNES *Med. Bacteriol.* (ed. 7) xxv. 392 The Venezuelan virus is also *mosquito-borne, but the reservoir is uncertain. **1898** P. MANSON *Trop. Diseases* i. 17 The *mosquito-bred plasmodial spore. **1926** M. LEINSTER *Dew on Leaf* 208 *Mosquito-breeding ponds. **1909** *Westm. Gaz.* 11 Feb. 2/3 The City of Rio de Janeiro, as regards *mosquito-carried diseases, has . . undergone a complete transformation. **1904** *Brit. Med. Jrnl.* 17 Sept. 642 The measures taken at Ismailia, which have made it a *mosquito-free and malaria-free sanatorium. **1900** *Ibid.* 10 Feb. 301 In Italy the *mosquito season . . extends from the first warm days of spring to the first cold days of autumn or winter. **1899** *Allbutt's Syst. Med.* VIII. 798 The scar of a *mosquito sting. **1933** R. CAMPBELL *Flowering Reeds* 26 When to their roost the sacred ibis file, *Mosquito-thin against the fading West.

b. Special comb.: **mosquito-bar** *U.S.*, a kind of mosquito net; **mosquito-bee** (see quot.); †**mosquito-bier** (? mistake for *mosquito-bar*); **mosquito-blight**, a plant-bug of the East Indian genus *Helopeltis*; **mosquito-boot**, a boot worn to protect the foot from mosquitos; **mosquito brigade**, a body of persons engaged in destroying mosquitoes, with a view to the prevention of malaria; **mosquito-bush**, a West Indian shrub (see quot.); **mosquito-canopy, -curtain**, a canopy or curtain of gauze to keep off mosquitoes; **mosquito coil**, a spiral made from a dried paste of pyrethrum powder with a combustion-supporting substance, which when ignited burns slowly and produces a smoke that inhibits mosquitoes from biting; **mosquito door**, a door designed to exclude mosquitoes from a house; **mosquito-dope** *N. Amer.*, insect repellent; **mosquito-fire**, a fire to keep away mosquitoes; **mosquito-fly, -gnat** (= sense 1); **mosquito hawk** *N. Amer.*, (*a*) the night-hawk, *Chordeiles minor*; (*b*) any dragon-fly which preys upon mosquitoes; **mosquito-net**, a net (of lace, gauze, etc.) to keep off mosquitoes; so

mosquito-netting, a coarse fabric with open meshes, used for mosquito-nets; **mosquito room**, a room from which mosquitoes are excluded; **Mosquito State** *U.S.*, a nickname for New Jersey; **mosquito trousers**, trousers designed to protect the legs from mosquitoes; **mosquito wire**, wire mesh used to exclude mosquitoes.

1828 J. HALE *Lett. fr. West* 227 The *musquitoe bar..is a curtain, of the thinnest gauze, or leno, or some such slight fabric, which admits the air, and excludes the mosquitoe. **1889** MARY E. BAMFORD *Up & Down Brooks* 65 A section of mosquito-bar was tied over the whole. **1899** D. SHARP *Insects* II. 61 Some of these Insects [*Melipona*] are amongst the smallest of bees, so that one, or more, species go by the name of 'Mosquito-bees'. **1814** LEWIS & CLARKE *Exped. Missouri* (1893) III. 1082 The mosquitoes have been so troublesome that it was impossible even to write without the assistance of a *mosquito-bier. **1899** D. SHARP *Insects* II. 562 They are known as *Mosquito blight. The egg is of comparatively large size, and is placed by the bug in the stems of the tea plant. **1774** E. LONG *Hist. Jamaica* III. 884 In those places where they [*sc.* mosquitoes] are very numerous..the usual guard for the legs is the *muskeeto-boot, or a kind of half-trouzer, made of linen, tied above the knee, and reaching to the shoes. **1945** *Tee Emm* (Air Ministry) V. 36 Mosquito-boots, which are issued to airmen ..are meant to be worn in the evenings. This is a malaria precaution. **1956** E. AMBLER *Night-Comers* i. 1 The mosquito boots and the sweat-stained hats. **1904** *Brit. Med. Jrnl.* 17 Sept. 631 The operations of the *mosquito brigade were very largely devoted to treating cesspits which were the breeding grounds of *Stegomyia*. **1750** G. HUGHES *Barbadoes* 169 *Musketo-Bush. This derives its name from its either real or pretended service in driving away by its smell Musketoes from bed-chambers. **1885** *Cassell's Encycl. Dict.*, *Mosquito-canopy. **1963** *Pyrethrum Post* VII. 22/2 *Mosquito coils, as their name implies, are used to prevent adult mosquitoes from biting, particularly during the hours of sleep and are therefore designed to burn for about 8 hours. **1971** *Inside Kenya Today* Mar. 46/2 The prospects for a mosquito coils market [*printed* marker] in the Far East are very promising, and if this market is fully exploited, pyrethrum powder will be a more important product of the pyrethrum industry than it is now. **1972** D. SALE *Love Bite* ii. 31 There are some mosquito coils there, too. Light them at dusk..and you won't be troubled. **1819** BOWDICH *Mission to Ashantee* II. xiii. 439 They sleep on bedsteads encircled with *musquito curtains of bamboo cloth. **1967** P. M. HUBBARD *Custom of Country* (1969) vi. 68 A servant who had been sitting in the veranda got up and held open the *mosquito door. **1903** S. E. WHITE *Forest* 383 Pack one, or absolute necessities for hard trip... Knife; *mosquito-dope; compass; match box. **1948** *Chicago Tribune* 11 July 7/1 New mosquito dopes are being tested by fishermen now that the insects are buzzing. **1826** J. F. COOPER *Mohicans* xiv, The smoke which settles above a *mosquetoe fire. **1802** BINGLEY *Anim. Biog.* (1813) III. 329 The *Musqueto-fly is..a large variety of the Common Gnat. **1828** G. W. BRIDGES *Ann. Jamaica* II. xiii. 130 *Culex pipiens*, the *mosquito gnat. **1709** J. LAWSON *New Voyage to Carolina* 144 East-India Bats or *Musqueto Hawks, are the Bigness of a Cuckoo, and much of the same colour. **1737** J. BRICKELL *Nat. Hist. N. Carolina* 163 The Muskeetoe-Hawks, are Insects, so called, from their continually hunting after Muskeetoes, and killing and eating them. **1782** P. H. BRUCE *Mem.* 424 Musketo hawks. **1832** J. PICKERING *Inquiries of Emigrant* 59 Thousands of long large flies, similar to the English dragon fly, but a little smaller, are flying about the fields; they are called musquito hawks, on account of their killing and living on those insects. **1851** *Southern Planter* (Richmond, Va.) July 195/2 Unlike the..mosquito hawk of the South [the joint worm] does not make its appearance suddenly. **1866** W. R. KING *Sportsman & Naturalist in Canada* 108 The somewhat rare swallow-tail or musquito-hawk,..soaring in pursuit of insects. **1894** NEWTON *Dict. Birds* 593 *Mosquito-hawk*, a name in America for the species of *Chordiles* (Nightjar). **1938** G. CASH *I like Brit. Columbia* 187 A mosquito hawk zoomed belatedly overhead. **1967** E. B. NICKERSON *Kayaks to Arctic* ix. 77 We learned..that in my father's childhood they [*sc.* dragon-flies] had been called 'mosquito hawks'. **1745** *London Mag.* Nov. 551/2 To scorn Umbrellas and *Musketto-Nets, as Jamaican and Carolinean Effeminacies. **1764** SMOLLETT *Trav.* xxiii. (1766) I. 354 Instead of curtains, there is a.. mosquito net, made of a kind of gauze. **1867** M. E. HERBERT *Cradle Lands* i. 3 One comfort only was wanting in this hotel, and that was mosquito-nets. **1969** I. KEMP *Brit. G.I. in Vietnam* viii. 160 The unexpected comforts of a camp bed, an air mattress, and a mosquito net. **1974** P. DICKINSON *Poison Oracle* iv. 111 He had packed the medicines, clothes, mosquito net, compass. **1840** J. B. FRASER *Trav. Koordistan*, etc. I. viii. 221 The bed being without curtains or *mosquito netting. **1885** *Encycl. Brit.* XVIII. 829/2 A piece of.. mosquito-netting made into a bag. **1949** M. MEAD *Male & Female* viii. 171 We asked Tomi..to.. stop up the crevices between the mosquito wire and the..floor of our *mosquito-room. **1923** *World Almanac* (N.Y.) 422 Nicknames of the States... N.J. 'Jersey Blues', 'Garden', 'New Spain', '*Mosquito'. **1930** in G. E. Shankle *Amer. Nicknames* (1937) 376 We get the scornful title, the *Mosquito State*, because we seem to have our share of these industrious and bloodthirsty insects. **1792** SCOTT *Let.* 10 Sept. (1932) I. 22 Wading through the mosses upon this errand, accoutred with the long gun, a jacket, *mosquito trowsers, and a rough cap. **1828** MRS. B. HALL *Let.* 27 Apr. in *Aristocratic Journey* (1931) 261 We got her a pair of mosquito trowsers. **1949** *Mosquito wire [see *mosquito room*].

c. mosquito boat, (*a*) (see quot. 1914); (*b*) a motor-torpedo boat; **mosquito craft**, small light vessels adapted for rapid manœuvring. So **mosquito fleet**, a fleet of such vessels; **mosquito-built** *a.*, said of a light vessel adapted for being rapidly manœuvred.

1804 LARWOOD *No Gun Boats* 18 Man and victual the Musquitoe Fleet (as Wit in its wantonness has described it). **1824** W. IRVING *T. Trav.* II. 242 A little rakish, musquito-built vessell, that could run into all kinds of waters. **1850** H. MELVILLE *White Jacket* II. iii. 12 All the musquito craft of Abba Thule, king of the Pelews. **1884** *Pall Mall G.* 15 Sept. 1/2 Have we a sufficiently numerous mosquito fleet of torpedo boats, steam launches, and picket boats? **1914** *Dialect Notes* IV. 150 *Mosquito boat*, small river craft carrying light guns. **1940** *Topeka* (Kan.) *State Jrnl.* 29 Apr. 2 (*headline*) Trial run for 'mosquito boat'. **1944** in R. W. Zandvoort et al. *Wartime Eng.* (1957) 158 You always drive a boat; but do not refer to any of them as mosquito craft.

Hence **mo'squitoey**, **mo'squitoish** *adjs.*, infested with mosquitoes.

1857 THOREAU *Maine W.* (1894) 259 The bank would often be too steep, or else too low and grassy, and therefore mosquitoey. **1880** SENIOR *Trav. & Trout in Antipodes* 185, I was assured it was unbearably hot, muggy, mosquitoish, rainy, and stormy at Auckland. **1888** LEES & CLUTTERBUCK *B.C.* 1887: *Brit. Columbia* xxxv. (1892) 382 Golden..looked ..not nearly so mosquitoey as when we last saw it.

mosquito, variant of MESQUITA, a mosque.

Mosquito, var. MISKITO *a.* and *sb.*

mosquo, -quy, obs. forms of MOSQUE.

moss (mɒs), *sb.*[1] Forms: 1, 3, 6 **mos**, 2, 6 **mose**, 4–6 **mosse**, 5 **moos**, **mosh**, 4– **moss**. [OE. *mos* neut., bog (also 12th c. *mose* moss), corresponding to MDu., MLG. *mos* bog, also moss, lichen, mildew (Du. *mos* moss), OHG., MHG. *mos* (mod.G. *moos*) bog, moss, MSw., Da. *mos*:—OTeut. **muso*^{m}; declensional variants are represented by Flemish *moze* mud, ON. *mose* wk. masc., bog, moss, Sw. *mosse* masc., bog, *mossa* fem., moss. From a different ablaut-grade of the same root (OTeut. **meus-*, *meuz-*) are OE. *méos* (? masc.) moss (see MESE *sb.*[1]), OHG. *mios* masc., moss (mod.G. *mies* masc., neut., moss, lichen; in some dialects bog), ON. *mýr-r* MIRE *sb.*[1] Cognates outside Teut. (f. Indogermanic **mus-*) are L. *muscus* moss, OSl. *mŭchŭ* moss, ? Lith. *musai* scum on sour milk. The Fr. *mousse* fem. (Pr. *mossa*), moss, is prob. of Teut. origin.

All branches of Teut. exc. Gothic have the word or its cognates in both the senses 'bog' and 'moss' (the plant). As moss is the characteristic plant of bogs, there is no reason for doubting the identity of the word in the two senses. Which is the prior sense is doubtful; the fact that the cognates outside Teut. have the sense 'moss' only is not decisive. The sense 'bog' is the only one known in OE.; but the use as the name of the plant (called in OE. *méos*) presumably existed in OE., as a late adoption from continental Teut. would be very improbable. The 12th c. northern form *mose* (sense 3, quot. *c* 1150) is perh. adopted from ON.; it cannot be the ancestor of the mod. form with unvoiced (s).]

I. 1. a. A bog, swamp, or morass; a peat-bog. (Chiefly *Sc.* and *north. dial.*)

975 *Grant* in Birch *Cartul. Sax.* III. 646 Of þære dic in þæt micle mos; of þæm mose in þæt sic. *c* **1260** [cf. PEAT-MOSS 1]. **1375** BARBOUR *Bruce* VIII. 167 Apon athir syde Wes a gret moss, mekill & braid. ? *a* **1400** *Morte Arth.* 2014 The mosse and the marrasse. **1485** *Rolls of Parlt.* VI. 382/1 Oure Mosse of Penwortham, otherwise called there the Kings Mosse, in oure Countie of Lancastre. **1486** *Bk. St. Albans* E iv b, In moore or in moos he hidyth hem fast. **1535** COVERDALE *Jer.* xiv. 6 The wilde Asses shall stonde in the Mosse. **1535** STEWART *Cron. Scot.* (Rolls) I. 19 The mos, the mure, the craigis, and the clewis. **1573** *Satir. Poems Reform.* xxxix. 347 He raid throw montanes many, mose, and myre. *a* **1706** EVELYN *Sylva* I. xviii (1776) 228 In many of the mosses of the West-Riding of Yorkshire are often dug up Birch-trees that burn and flame like Fir. **1790** BURNS *Tam o' Shanter* 7 We think na on the lang Scots miles, The mosses, waters, slaps, and styles. **1810** SCOTT *Lady of L.* I. v, With anxious eye he wandered o'er Mountain and meadow, moss and moor. **1813** BAKEWELL *Introd. Geol.* (1815) 259 The great moss of Cree in Galloway lies close upon the sea, on a bed of clay. **1880** HAUGHTON *Phys. Geog.* v. 221 The White Nile takes its origin in a gigantic boggy plain or moss.

b. Wet spongy soil; bog.

1596 DALRYMPLE tr. *Leslie's Hist. Scot.* I. 9 Scharpe and hard hillis full of mosse, more and marrase. **1769** *De Foe's Tour Gt. Brit.* (ed. 7) III. 332 A Tract of Ground full of Holes, filled with a boggy Substance, which in this Country is called Moss. **1773** *Gentl. Mag.* XLIII. 265 The Solway-flow contains 1300 acres of very deep and tender moss. **1887** STEVENSON *Merry Men* i, The road..went over rough boulders, so that a man had to leap from one to another, and through soft bottoms where the moss came nearly to the knee.

2. *Border dial.* [Short for *moss-crop*: see 6 b.] Cotton-grass, *Eriophorum vaginatum*.

1798 R. DOUGLAS *Agric. Surv. Roxb.* 108 Early in spring, sheep, in marshy districts, feed much upon the *Eriophorum vaginatum*, called by the farmers and their shepherds *moss*. **1893** *Northumbld. Gloss.*, *Moss*, the first shoots and the flower stalks of the cotton grass, *Eriophorum vaginatum*.

II. The plant.

3. Any of the small herbaceous cryptogamous plants constituting the class *Musci*, some of which form the characteristic vegetation of bogs, while others grow in crowded masses covering the surface of the ground, or of stones, trees, etc. In popular language, the term is often extended to small cryptogams of other orders, esp. lichens and lycopods, and occas. to small phanerogams resembling mosses in appearance and habit.

a. *collect.* Plants of this kind massed together.

Formerly often referred to as a material for filling the chinks between roofing slabs or slates, or for stopping crevices in mill-dams; also as bedding for cattle.

? *c* **1150** *Durham Gloss.*, *Muscus*, mose. **1324–5** *Durham Acc. Rolls* (Surtees) 15 Mulieribus colligentibus mosse pro eodem [stagno]. **1355–6** *Ibid.* 557 Cum colleccione Bruerae et Mos pro eodem [molendino]. ? **1370** *Robt. Cicyle* 59 Fyftene yere he levyd thare, Wyth rotys, and grasse, and evylle fare, And alle of mosse hys clothyng was. **1377** LANGL. *P. Pl.* B. xv. 282 Poule *primus heremita* had parroked hym-selue, þat no man miȝte hym se for mosse and for leues. *c* **1400** MAUNDEV. (1839) xxx. 304 The Walles ben covered alle over with Mosse. **1447** BOKENHAM *Seyntys* (Roxb.) 51 A sparow fedyng hyr bryddes she seye In a nest made of mosh & cleye. **1485** CAXTON *St. Wenefr.* 5 The mosse that groweth vpon the sayde stones smellyth lyke encense. **1502** *Mem. Ripon* (Surtees) III. 267 Rogero Sclayter, 6*d.*, tegenti super cameram..Sclaytston, 4*d.*, ad idem opus, ac del mose, 1*d.*, pro dicto opere. **1523** FITZHERB. *Husb.* §132 Croppe them [*sc.* the trees] in wynter that thy beestes maye eate..the mosse of the bowes. **1573–4** *Rewley Accts.* (Feuillerat) 193 Torchebearers vj attyred in Mosse & Ivye. **1588** SHAKS. *Tit. A.* II. iii. 95 The Trees..Ore-come with Mosse, and balefull Misselto. **1626** BACON *Sylva* §340 Mosse is a Kinde of Mould, of the Earth, and Trees. But it may be better sorted as a Rudiment of Germination. **1657** W. COLES *Adam in Eden* xv. 31 The last [sort] which is the Mosse of a dead Mans Skull is oftner brought out of Ireland, then found with Us. **1712** STEELE *Spect.* No. 514 ⁋2, I saw three figures seated on a bank of moss. **1727–41** CHAMBERS *Cycl.* s.v., There is also a kind of greenish moss growing on human skulls that have been long exposed to the air, called *usnea humana*, or *muscus calvarius*. The antients made a deal of use of it as an astringent, &c. **1765** A. DICKSON *Treat. Agric.* IV. vi. (ed. 2) 483 Moss is commonly ranked in the class of vegetables. **1784** COWPER *Task* i. 270 Hence, ancle-deep in moss and flow'ry thyme, We mount again. **1809** *Med. Jrnl.* XXI. 398, I packed it carefully in fresh moss. *c* **1830** MRS. SHERWOOD in *Houlston Tracts* III. lxi. 8 Is it not a deal, a great deal to me, to see the one whom I love best in all the world wearing away like moss under a dripping rock, from trouble and from weariness. **1864** SKEAT *Uhland's Poems* 312 On couch of moss sat Merlin.

fig. **1559** *Mirr. Mag.*, *Dk. Suffolk* xx, Affirming me to have brought the realme to mosse. **1679** C. NESSE *Antichrist* Ded., Nobility..is but the moss of time. **1680** H. MORE *Apocal. Apoc.* 353 The rest being no part of that.. Christianity, but at best mere moss and filth added to it.

b. Proverb. ***a rolling stone gathers no moss***: used to imply that a man who restlessly roams from place to place, or constantly changes his employment will never grow rich. Hence, in *slang* or allusive use, *moss* occas. = money.

[Cf. Cotgrave s.v. *Mousse*, *Jamais tu ne cueilleras mousse*, Thou wilt neuer grow rich; from the Prouerbe; *Pierre qui se remue n'accueille point de mousse*; Pro. The rolling stone gathers no Mosse.]

[**1362**, *c* **1460**: cf. MOSS *v.* 1 a.] *a* **1541** WYATT *How to use the Court* 4 On the stone that styll doth turne about, There groweth no mosse. These prouerbes yet do last. **1546** J. HEYWOOD *Prov.* (1867) 26 The rollyng stone neuer gatherth mosse. **1548** BRADFORD *Let.* in Foxe *A. & M.* (1583) 1662/2 A tumblyng stone gathereth no mosse. **1621** SANDERSON *Serm.* I. 212 Some men are ever restless,..every new crotchet putteth them into a new course. But thes rowling stones carry their curse with them; they seldom gather moss. *a* **1635** NAUNTON *Fragm. Reg.* (Arb.) 48 He [Rawleigh] foresaw his own destiny; that he was first to roul..before he could come to a repose, and as the stone doth by long lying gather moss. **1853**, **1866** [see ROLLING STONE 1]. **1914** G. B. SHAW *Misalliance* p. lxxxiv, We keep repeating the silly proverb that a rolling stone gathers no moss, as if moss were a desirable parasite. **1936** A. CHRISTIE *ABC Murders* xxxiv. 241 You have been the rolling stone—and you have gathered very little moss. You were bitterly jealous of your brother's wealth.

c. With *a* and *pl.*: A species or kind of moss.

1562 TURNER *Herbal* II. 36 Lichen..cleueth vnto watery stones, or such as at the leste are somtyme sprynkled wyth water as a mosse. **1691** RAY *Creation* I (1692) 100 Such Mosses as grow upon Walls, the Roofs of Houses [etc.]. **1785** MARTYN *Rousseau's Bot.* xxxii. (1794) 491 The Mosses, have leaves like the more perfect vegetables, distinct from the stalk. **1814** SCOTT *Ld. of Isles* III. xiv, On high Benmore green mosses grow. **1849** LYELL *2nd Visit U.S.* (1850) II. xxxii. 215, I saw, on the damp ground beneath the trees, abundance of mosses, with scarcely a blade of grass. **1866** *Treas. Bot.* s.v. *Mosses*, Small species of *Sedum*..are sometimes termed Mosses—of course merely on account of their habit. **1882** VINES tr. *Sachs' Bot.* 903 Such as the Ferns, Equisetaceæ, the Mosses, and others.

d. Applied to sea-weed. *rare.*

1543 TRAHERON *Vigo's Chirurg.* (1586) 436 Coraline, corolina, is thought to be Brion, which is mosse growing to stones in the sea. **1601** CHESTER *Love's Mart.* (1878) 82 Mosse of the Sea, and yellow Succorie. **1830** TENNYSON *Mermaid* 49 In the hueless mosses under the sea. **1895** MAR. L. POOL *Boss* in *Chapbook* III. 478 Granny often wheeled her to the breakwater where she could see the moss gathered. *Ibid.*, The water had gone far out so that one could get to one of the ledges where the moss grew.

4. With defining word.

American moss, the dried stems of Florida moss, which are used in upholstery; **animal moss** = *moss-animal*; **black moss** = *Florida moss*; **Canary moss**, *Parmelia perlata*, a lichen used for dyeing (*Treas. Bot.* 1866); **Ceylon moss**, the common name for *Plocaria candida*, which is imported from Sri Lanka (Ceylon) with some other species (*Treas. Bot.*); see also quot. 1889; †**chin-cough moss**, ? = *chalice-moss* (CHALICE 4); **club-foot moss** = CLUB-MOSS (*Cent. Dict.* 1890); **Corsican moss** (see quot. 1866); **film moss**, *Hymenostomum* (Treas. Bot.); **Florida moss**, *Tillandsia usneoides*; **flowering moss** *U.S.*, (*a*) the creeping evergreen plant, *Pyxidanthera barbulata*; (*b*) = *moss-pink* (see 7 d); (*c*) *Sedum pulchellum* (Britton & Brown *Flora* 1896–8); †**hairy moss**, ? = *hair moss* (HAIR *sb.* 10); †**head moss** (see quot. 1688); **heath-moss** (see quot. 1753); **idle-moss** (see quot. 1866); **Jaffna moss**, *Alectoria sarmentosa*, a dye lichen collected in Sri Lanka (Ceylon) (*Treas. Bot.* 1866); see also quot. 1889; **snake moss**, *Lycopodium clavatum* (Treas. Bot.,

Suppl. 1874); **velvet moss**, *Gyrophora murina* (Ibid.); **white moss**, a name for various lichens. Also BEARD-*moss*, BOG-*moss*, CARRAGEEN *moss*, CHALICE *moss*, CLUB-MOSS, HORNED *moss*, ICELAND MOSS, LONG-*moss*, etc., q.v. as main words or under their first element.

1597 Hairy moss [see GOLDEN *a.* 10b]. **1610** Chin-cough moss [see *chalice-moss*, CHALICE 4]. **1653** WALTON *Angler* iv. 96 White Moss, which grows on some heaths, and is hard to be found. **1753** CHAMBERS *Cycl. Supp.*, *Heath-moss, Coralloides*, in botany, the name of a genus of the mosses. *Ibid.* s.v. *Heath-moss*, Of the Cup-mosses, with less perfect cups, the following are the known species: 1. The skewer *Coralloides*... It is commonly called *horned Moss.* **1796** W. MARSHALL *W. England* I. 222 During the winter months, a West Devonshire Orchard.., appears as if hung with hoar frost; owing to the *white moss* which hangs in ribbons from its boughs. **1857** GRAY *First Lessons Bot.* (1866) 34 We have two or three flowering air-plants in the Southern States,.. one of them is..the Long-Moss, or Black Moss, so called. **1866** *Treas. Bot.*, *Moss, Corsican*, a supposed vermifuge, once in some repute, but now almost exploded. If genuine, it should consist of *Gracilaria Helminthochorton*, one of the rose-spored *Algæ*, but for this the common *Laurencia obtusa* is frequently substituted. *Ibid.*, *Moss, idle*, an old name for various tree lichens, especially those which are pendulous. **1882** J. SMITH *Dict. Econ. Plants* 277 American or New Orleans Moss. **1884** *Cassell's Fam. Mag.* Apr. 316/2 A new material for paper..is the white moss which grows so largely in Norway and Sweden. **1888** Florida moss [see *moss-head* in 7d below]. **1889** G. S. BOULGER *Uses of Plants* 50 Ceylon Moss, Jaffna Moss..(*Sphærococcus lichenioides*, Agardh) another of the Florideæ from..Ceylon, Burma, etc...now used as a demulcent food jelly for invalids. **1890** *Century Dict.*, Animal moss.

5. *transf.* **a.** An excrescence or incrustation resembling moss; esp. the mossy covering of the stalk and calyx of the moss rose.

1607 TOPSELL *Four-f. Beasts* 278 The Hedg-hog..is..beset..with sharpe thorney haires,..and those sharpe prickles are couered with a kind of soft mosse. **1837** T. RIVERS *Rose Amateur's Guide* 6 The Double Moss Rose..covered with that glandular excrescence which we term moss. **1864** LOWELL *Fireside Trav.* 10 Coals, over which a gray, soft moss of ashes grew.

b. *Confectionery.* (See quots.) ? *Obs.*

1706 PHILLIPS (ed. Kersey), *Moss*,..Also a kind of fine Sugar-Work, made by Confectioners, in Imitation of Moss. **1727** BRADLEY *Fam. Dict.* s.v. *Confectioner*, Pastils and Mosses which are sugar works that may be made in the season. **1841** *Guide to Trade, Baker* 64 [Cakes] *Moss.*—Rub a little rout cake paste through a fine sieve, and it will look like moss. Gently squeeze a little together, about the size of half-a-crown, and bake them.

c. *slang.* (See quot.)

1796 *Grose's Dict. Vulgar T.* (ed. 3), *Moss*, a cant term for lead, because both are found on the tops of buildings.

d. Ellipt. for *moss green.*

1897 *Sears Roebuck Catal.* 333/1 Crepe Tissue Paper..in the following colors..Apple, Moss, Grass, Nile and Sea Green. **1923** *Daily Mail* 26 May 1 (Advt.), Superb colours, including: Rose Pink,..Moss, Tomato. **1971** *Vogue* Dec. 148/2 Jersey.. colours..rosewood, oak, moss.

e. Hair. *slang.*

1942 in BERREY & VAN DEN BARK *Amer. Thes. Slang* §121/43. **1966** J. S. COX *Illustr. Dict. Hairdressing* 99/2 *Moss.* (1) Head hair. Slang. (2) Pubic hair. Vulgarism.

III. Combinations.

6. In sense 1.

a. General comb., as ***moss-bank***, ***-bound*** adj., ***-cart***, ***-field***, ***-fog*** (FOG *sb.*[1] 2), ***-ground***, ***-hole***, ***-land***, ***-pit***, ***-pot*** (= hole), ***-sod***, ***-traversing*** adj., ***-work***.

1799 J. ROBERTSON *Agric. Perth* 494 He then digs a new drain at the foot of the *moss-bank. **1840** J. BUEL *Farmer's Comp.* 206 If the land is poor, or *moss-bound. **1834** *Brit. Husb.* I. 165 A peculiar sort of cart..called a *moss-cart, which appears to be admirably adapted to the application of marl..to the surface of peaty soils. **1527** in *Lanc. Wills* (Chetham Soc.) I. 25, I will that the seid John have..the *mosse fylds..in the severall holldings of the seid John Dutton [and others]. **1831** W. PATRICK *Pop. Descr. Plants Lanarksh.* Pref. 20 Tracts of land,..yielding chiefly Heather ..and *Moss-fogs, such as Sphagnums, Bryums, Polytrichums. **1584** COGAN *Haven Health* (1636) 258 In Lankashire, in their *mosse grounds where they dig their turves, there is great store of it. **1746** *Compl. Farmer* s.v. *Watering Flax*, *Moss-holes..frequently answer well for watering the flax. **1887** T. DARLINGTON *Folk-Speech S. Cheshire* 264 **Moss-land*, boggy land. **1934** *Geogr. Jrnl.* LXXXIII. 425 The surviving mosslands of the Lancashire plain. **1971** *Daily Tel.* 3 July 9/2 Greater provision for visitors is planned for the Wildfowl Trust's projected reserve at Martin Mere, on the mosslands east of Southport. *c* **1510** *Reg. Burrough* lf. v. b (P.R.O.), Hey hille lyes betwix the scharthe Hylle and *Mosse pyttes. **1845** JANE ROBINSON *Whitehall* xl. II. 191 What hath any of us done, that grace should come and lug us out of the *moss-pot into which we have strayed of our own folly? **1844** STEPHENS *Bk. Farm* III. 1038, I cover with *moss-sods (from the turf-banks) laid perfectly close, the shear of each fitted to the other. **1785** BURNS *Address to Deil* 73 And aft your *moss-traversin Spunkies Decoy the wight that late an' drunk is. **1799** J. ROBERTSON *Agric. Perth* 509 Though *moss-work be laborious.

b. In names of plants growing in bogs: as **moss-berry**, the cranberry, *Vaccinium Oxycoccos*; **moss-corn**, the silverweed, *Potentilla anserina*; **moss-crop**, (*a*) applied to various species of cotton-grass, esp. *Eriophorum vaginatum* and *E. polystachion*; (*b*) see *moss-corn* above; (*c*) the tufted club-rush, *Scirpus cæspitosus*; **moss-rush**, goose-corn, *Juncus squarrosus*; **moss-whin**, *Genista anglica*; **moss-willow**, ? *Salix fusca.*

1732 J. MARTYN *Tournefort's Hist. Plants* II. 153 Oxycoccus... Cran-berries,..*Moss-berries, or Moor-berries. **1868** *Rep. U.S. Commissioner Agric.* (1869) 178 Among them [*sc.* small fruits] may be noted..mossberries [etc.]. **1818** HOGG *Brownie of B.* etc. II. 269 He [*sc.* a boar] found nothing to eat, save one or two *moss-corns [etc.]. *c* **1475** *Cath. Angl.* 244/2 (Addit. MS.) A *Mosse croppe. **1696** PLUKENET *Opera Bot.* (1769) II. 201 Juncus Alpinus cum caudâ Leporina... *Moss-Crops* Vestmorlandicis dicitur. **1808–18** JAMIESON, *Moss-corns*, Silver-weed,..also called *Moss-crops*, and *Moor-grass.* **1815** *Pennecuik's Descr. Tweed.* 53 *note*, Their [*sc.* sheep's] earliest spring food is a plant bearing a white cotton head, vulgarly designed *Moss-crop.* **1879** J. LUCAS in *Zoologist* Sept. 356 Sheep feed greedily on the flowers of the moor-silk (cotton-grass), or, as it is termed in the dale [Nidderdale] 'Mosscrops and cutthroats'. **1762** W. HUDSON *Flora Angl.* 130 *Juncus culmo nudo*,..*Moss-rush or Goose-corn. **1863** PRIOR *Plant-n.* 154 *Moor-whin*, or **Moss-whin*, a whin that grows on bleak heaths and mosses. *Genista anglica*, L. *a* **1869** C. SPENCE *Fr. Braes of Carse* (1898) 60 Lichen, and liver grass, And the *moss willow Curtain the narrow pass.

c. Special comb.: **moss-cheeper**, (*a*) the meadow pipit, *Anthus pratensis*; (*b*) ***white winged moss-cheeper***, the reed-bunting, *Emberiza schœniclus*; **moss-earth**, earth composed of, or largely mixed with, peat; **moss-flow**, a semi-fluid part of a bog or morass; **moss-oak**, oak-wood preserved in a black state in peat-bogs, etc., bog-oak; also, a seat made out of bog-oak; **moss-reeve**, 'a bailiff or reeve appointed to regulate claims for land on the mosses' (*Cheshire Gloss.* 1886); **moss-tenant**, the tenant of a moorland farm; **moss-wood**, the wood of trees found buried in peat-bogs. Also MOSS-HAG, MOSS-TROOPER.

1684 SIBBALD *Scotia Illustrata* II. II. 22 *Titlinga*, Titling, or *Moss-cheeper. **1901** *Shooting Times* 22 June 21/2 The reed bunting is almost entirely known in the North of Ireland as the 'white winged moss-cheeper'. **1805** W. AITON (*title*) A Treatise on the origin, qualities, and cultivation of *Moss-earth. **1816** SCOTT *Old Mort.* viii, The hundreds forced from their ain habitations to the deserts, mountains, muirs, mosses, *moss-flows, and peat-hags. **1785** BURNS *Halloween* xxiii, He taks a swirlie, auld *moss-oak, For some black, grousome Carlin. **1824** MACTAGGART *Gallovid. Encycl.* (1876) 23 He claps his auld bum down on the mossaik by the cheek o' the chaumer door. **1552** in Picton *L'pool Munic. Rec.* (1883) I. 59 *Moss Reeves Thos Eyre Jno Sudley. **1799** J. ROBERTSON *Agric. Perth* 496 The obloquy of becoming a *moss-tenant gradually became less regarded. **1686** PLOT *Staffordsh.* 217 This *moss-wood (as some call it) grew not far from where found.

7. In sense 3.

a. simple attrib., as ***moss-bank***, ***-bed***, ***-root***.

1742 COLLINS *Oriental Ecl.* III. 18 The violet-blue, that on the moss-bank grows. **1830** TENNYSON *Merman* 39 Soft are the moss-beds under the sea. **1883** G. MEREDITH *Poems & Lyrics* 131 Rich with life as moss-roots breathe of earth In the first plucking of them.

b. instrumental, as ***moss-bearded***, †***-begrown***, ***-bordered***, ***-cankered***, ***-clad***, ***-covered***, ***crowned***, ***-dappled***, ***-hung***, ***-inwoven***, ***-lain***, ***-lined***, ***mantled***, ***shadowed***, †***-thrummed***, ***woven***.

1851 H. MELVILLE *Moby Dick* III. ii. 26 Venerable *moss-bearded Daniel Boone. **1959** D. DAVIE *Forests of Lithuania* iv. 37 A moss-bearded oak that bears The weight of full five hundred years. *c* **1400** MAUNDEV. (Roxb.) xxxiii. 150 It es all *mosse begrowen and couerd so with mosse and with bruschez. **1668** H. MORE *Div. Dial.* v. xxxiii. (1713) 507 *Philoth.*.. It was not still to have ly'n unpolished or Moss-begrown. **1849** M. ARNOLD *New Sirens* xxx, By *moss-border'd statues sitting. **1904** KIPLING *Traffics & Discoveries* 304 The *moss-cankered oak and beech. **1747** LD. LYTTELTON *Mem. Lady* 90 Or under Campden's *moss-clad mountains hoar. **1792** MARY WOLLSTONECR. *Rights Wom.* v. 253 *Moss-covered opinions..indolently adopted only because age has given them a venerable aspect. **1742** COLLINS *Oriental Ecl.* ii. 24 Here, where no springs in murmurs break away, Or *moss-crown'd fountains mitigate the day. **1945** J. BETJEMAN *New Bats in Old Belfries* 6 The view from my bedroom of *moss-dappled path. **1869** 'MARK TWAIN' *Innoc. Abr.* 421 Look down upon these *moss-hung ruins. **1818** SHELLEY *Marenghi* xiv, And hillocks heaped of *moss-inwoven turf. **1819** KEATS *Ode to Psyche* 57 There by zephyrs, streams, and birds, and bees, The *moss-lain Dryads shall be lulled to sleep. **1727–46** THOMSON *Summer* 625 An ample chair, *moss-lined and overhead, By flowering umbrage shaded. **1923** R. GRAVES *Feather Bed* 11 By falls of scree, *moss-mantled slippery rock. **1931** C. DAY LEWIS *From Feathers to Iron* 19 The virgin spring moss-shadowed near the shore. **1613–16** W. BROWNE *Brit. Past.* II. i, Each *mosse-thrumb'd mountaine bends. **1779** MASON *Eng. Gard.* III. 205 Their *moss-woven nest.

c. similative, as ***moss-like***.

1648 HERRICK *Hesper.*, *Oberon's Palace* 42 *Mosse-like silk. **1881** TYNDALL *Floating Matter of Air* 161 Patches of moss-like matter would appear here and there in the field of the microscope.

d. Special comb.: **moss-agate**, a popular name for a variety of agate containing brown or black moss-like dendritic forms; **moss-animal**, **-animalcule**, a bryozoon or polyzoon (see BRYOZOA and POLYZOA); **moss-bag** *Canad.* (see quot. 1865); **moss-basket** (see quot.); **moss-bass**, 'the large-mouthed black-bass, *Micropterus salmoides*' (*Cent. Dict.* 1890); **moss-bee** = *moss-carder bee* (see below); **moss-box** *Coal-mining*, a stuffing-box filled with moss, used in Kind and Chaudron's method of sinking shafts through water-bearing strata; **moss campion**, a dwarf, perennial, tufted moss-like plant (*Silene acaulis*) with purple flowers, growing in northern latitudes; **moss-carder**, also **moss-carder bee**, *Bombus muscorum*, a variety of humble-bee; **moss-copper** (see quot.); **moss-coral** = *moss-animalcule* (see above); **moss crêpe** (see quots.); **moss-fibre** *Anat.* (see quot. 1906); **moss-gold**, a fungus, *Clavaria muscoides*; **moss green**, a green colour resembling that of moss; †**moss hair**, hair resembling moss, 'woolly' hair; **moss-head**, a name given by the Negroes of Charleston, South Carolina, to the hooded merganser, *Mergus cucullatus*; **moss horn** = *mossy horn*; **moss-house**, a garden shelter lined or covered with moss; **moss-locust**, an American name for the rose acacia, *Robinia hispida*; **moss opal**, a variety of opal containing dendritic markings like those of moss-agate; **moss-peat**, peat formed from mosses, esp. those of the genus *Sphagnum*; **moss pink**, a species of phlox (*Phlox subulata*), with dark purple flowers, growing on rocky hills and sandy soils in the central United States; **moss-polyp** = *moss-animalcule* (see above); **moss-rake**, a kind of rake used in gathering Irish moss; **moss-seat**, a mossy seat; also, a seat artificially mossed; **moss-starch** = LICHENIN; †**moss-work**, (*a*) decoration resembling moss; (*b*) moss arranged so as to form a covering. See also MOSS-BACK, MOSS-ROSE.

1798 G. MITCHELL tr. *D. L. G. Karsten's Description Minerals in Leskean Mus.* I. 98 Milk white *Moss Agate, traversed by brownish particles; from Ceylon. **1837** J. D. DANA *Syst. Min.* VI. 343 *Dendrachates*..was our moss agate. **1845** J. C. ATKINSON in *Proc. Berw. Nat. Club* II. No. 13. 132 Chert, hornstone, and moss agate, may be found. **1904** L. J. SPENCER tr. *M. Bauer's Precious Stones* II. 507 Moss-agate is characterised by the presence of green enclosures, such as are found in many specimens of rock crystal. These enclosures..have the general effect of a piece of moss; hence the term moss-agate. **1943** R. D. GEORGE *Minerals & Rocks* xix. 414 Moss agate is similar to agate, but the coloring is in arborescent or moss-like forms. **1947** J. C. RICH *Materials & Methods of Sculpture* viii. 236 Moss agate is a variety of agate whose decorative appearance militates against its use as a sculptural medium. **1962** R. WEBSTER *Gems* I. x. 178 In England and America the term mocha stone is used synonymously with moss agate, but in European countries the green moss agate alone is known as moss agate while the black and red coloured dendritic agate is termed mocha stone. **1881** *Cassell's Nat. Hist.* V. 269 The Bryozoa, or *Moss-animals. **1890** *Century Dict.*, **Moss-animalcule.* **1865** MILTON & CHEADLE *N.W. Passage by Land* vi. 85 The '*moss-bag' or Indian cradle. This is a board with two side flaps of cloth, which lace together up the centre. The child is laid on its back on the board, packed with soft moss, and laced firmly down, with its arms to its side, and only its head at liberty. **1960** J. J. ROWLANDS *Spindrift* 120 A baby whimpered in its moss bag laced to a back-board. **1963** *Beaver* Summer 37/2 The 15-day-old baby sleeping in a moss bag. **1858** SIMMONDS *Dict. Trade*, **Moss-basket*, a fancy basket for a room, conservatory, &c., covered with moss. **1863** *Chamb. Encycl.* V. 454/1 One of the most abundant [species of the humble-bee] is the yellow and orange **Moss-bee* (*Bombus muscorum*), the *Foggie* of the Scotch. **1877** H. BAUERMAN in *Encycl. Brit.* VI. 63/1 *Moss-box. **1791** CHARLOTTE SMITH *Celestina* IV. 191 Lichen and *moss campion. **1853** *Zoologist* XI. 4097 A *moss-carders' nest. **1861** PERCY *Metallurgy, Fuel*, etc. 359 **Moss-copper.* In copper-works this term is commonly used to designate those accumulations of filamentous, or moss-like copper, which are formed in cavities in pigs of certain kinds of regulus. **1955** E. OSTICK *Draper's Encycl.* iii. 84 *Moss crêpe is a dress fabric which relies for its characteristic effect on a special yarn called a moss crêpe yarn. **1966** E. PALMER *Plains of Camdeboo* ii. 20 The people of Pearston district in dark suits and moss crêpe demurely assembling for church on a Sunday. **1906** CUNNINGHAM *Text-bk. Anat.* (ed. 2) 514 The fibres which end in the granular layer are called **moss-fibres* ..because..they present at certain points moss-like thickenings. **1887** HAY *Brit. Fungi* 117 *Clavaria muscoides*, the *Moss-gold. **1884** *West. Daily Press* 29 May 3/7 The rest of the trimmings are in *moss green. **1938** R. FIELD *All this & Heaven Too* (1939) xxiii. 302 She..selected her best dress, the moss-green moire with bands of russet. **1972** H. C. RAE *Shooting Gallery* iii. 210 Tight broadcloth pants in moss green. **1689** *Lond. Gaz.* No. 2433/4 Run away.., a Negro Man of a Tawny Complexion, with *Mosse Hair. **1888** G. TRUMBULL *Bird Names* 75 The colored women often use a large bunch of 'Florida moss', *Tillandsia usneoides*, as a cushion for the heavy loads they carry on their heads, and I am inclined to believe that '*Moss-head' was suggested by this practice, rather than by any resemblance to moss in the bird's crest. **1944** H. WENTWORTH *Amer. Dial. Dict.* 398/1 **Mosshorn, n.*, old cattle; an old cowboy. **1948** H. L. MENCKEN *Amer. Lang.* Suppl. II. xi. 742 *Mosshorn*, an old steer; also, an old cowboy. **1968** R. F. ADAMS *Western Words* (rev. ed.) 201/1 *Mossy horn*,..also called *moss horn.* ? **1793** COWPER (*title*) Inscription for a *Moss-house in the Shrubbery at Weston. **1824** LOUDON *Encycl. Gard.* (ed. 2) §1816 Roofed seats, boat-houses, moss houses [etc.], are different modes of forming resting-places containing seats. **1890** *Century Dict.*, **Moss-locust.* **1904** L. J. SPENCER tr. *M. Bauer's Precious Stones* II. 386 Milk-opal sometimes exhibits black arborescent markings, or dendrites so-called, similar to those in certain varieties of chalcedony. Opal of this kind is known as *moss-opal. It is cut so as to bring the markings..near the surface. **1966** J. SINKANKAS *Mineralogy* II. 447 If containing dendritic or mossy inclusions, it is called moss opal. **1875** S. F. PECKHAM in *Amer. Cycl.* XIII. 217/2 *Moss-peat is oftenest fibrous, and when dried forms elastic masses. **1955** *Times* 21 May 10/6 Bracken..is admirable as a mulch, having all the good qualities of moss-peat, plus a high nutrition value. **1974** *Country Life* 2 May 1076/1 Moss peat can be bought from all suppliers of horticultural sundries, in bags or bales. **1856**

GRAY *Man. Bot.* (1860) 332 *Phlox subulata* (Ground or *Moss Pink). **1879** tr. *Haeckel's Evol. Man.* II. 369 The *moss-polyps (*Bryozoa*). **1883** *Fisheries Exhib. Catal.* 195 Sponge-hook, *moss-rakes. **1806** J. BLACK *Falls of Clyde* III. i. 139 Upon a *moss-seat Jamie sits alone, In pensive guise. **1821** SCOTT *Kenilw.* xxxiii, A grotto, ornamented with rustic work and moss-seats. **1615** G. SANDYS *Trav.* 181 The compassed roofe adorned with *mos-worke and Mosaique guilding. **1648** HERRICK *Hesper.*, *To Robin Red-brest*, Laid out for dead, let thy last kindnesse be With leaves and mosse-work for to cover me.

†**moss**, *sb.*² *Obs.* [? A use of prec.; ? or repr. some eastern word.] A 'head' of raw silk.

1753 HANWAY *Trav.* I. I. v. 18 The moss, or head of silk, often appears fair to the eye, when much coarseness is concealed under it. *Ibid.*, A moss, which is about 60 inches in the round, can be most conveniently reeled off. *Ibid.*, They generally comb the heads of the mosses to deceive the buyer.

moss, *sb.*³ Short for MOSS ROSE.

1837 T. RIVERS *Rose Amateur's Guide* 8 The Perpetual White Moss is a Damask Rose. *Ibid.* 9 The New Striped Moss has not yet bloomed here. **1869** S. R. HOLE *Bk. about Roses* 103 He admires the.. Mosses, Chinas and Bourbons.

moss (mɒs), *v.* Forms: 4-5 **mose**, 6-8 **mos**, 7- **moss.** [f. MOSS *sb.*¹]

1. *intr.* To become mossy (in various senses).

1362 LANGL. *P. Pl.* A. x. 101 Selden Moseþ þe Marbelston þat men ofte treden. *c* **1460** in *Q. Eliz. Acad.* (1869) 39 Syldon mossyth the stone þat oftyn ys tornynd & wende. **1654** GAYTON *Pleas. Notes* II. iii. 42 Sancho's face moss'd, and his chinne had a down sprung out. **1939** G. GREENE *Lawless Roads* iv. 119 Would the Cupid's bow just moss a little more as the flowers dropped?

2. To gather or collect moss.

1700, etc. [implied in MOSSING *vbl. sb.*]. **1895** MAR. L. POOL *Boss* in *Chapbk.* III. 480 I've moss'd twenty year, 'n' I never slipped to speak of before.

3. *trans.* †**a.** To cover with moss. *Obs.*

c **1420** *Pallad. on Husb.* III. 365 Do cley vppon and mose hit al aboute. *Ibid.* 419 Bende as a bowe or vynes that men pleche, And cleme hit, mose it, bynd hit soft abowte.

b. To cover with a growth of moss.

1600 SHAKS. *A.Y.L.* IV. iii. 105 Vnder an old Oake, whose bows were moss'd with age. **1797** W. NICOL *Sc. Forcing Gardener* 175 Washing the branches and stem of trees, which are anywise mossed, with soapsuds and sulphur. **1836** MRS. BROWNING *Poet's Vow* v. x, When years had mossed the stone. **1862** *Macm. Mag.* Sept. 426 How was it [the island] lichened and mossed, ferned and heathered.

fig. **1660** WATERHOUSE *Arms & Arm.* 3 But when they are sober, learned, and usefull, to let them be Mossed over with the scurfe of neglect. **1839** BAILEY *Festus* xxix. (1852) 477 The world shall rest, and moss itself with peace.

†**c.** To roof with moss (*i.e.* to put moss between or under the slates or tiles). *Obs.*

1591 *Churchw. Acc. Minchinhampton* in *Archæologia* (1853) XXXV. 436 To William Webbe, the tyler, upon a bargin for mosing and tiling and pynting of the church house and pentises, vij s. **1657** *Churchw. Acc. Prestwich* in *Ch. Times* 24 Mar. (1905) 395 Pd. to George Milln's son ffor mossinge the church 01. 06. 08. **1722** *Churchw. Acc. Finghall* (MS.), Pd. for liming & mossing yᵉ Ch'ch, 10s 6d.

d. To cover the trunks of (cinchona trees) with moss to increase the yield of alkaloid.

1863-4 W. G. MᶜIVOR *Extract fr. Rep. Govt. Chinchona Plantations* §35 With the permission of Government I will at once moss from 7,000 to 10,000 of our largest plants. **1876** *Encycl. Brit.* V. 781/2.

†**4.** To remove moss from (trees, etc.). *Obs.*

1677 *Dade's Prognostication* A vij, May...Weed your Hop-Gardens, and take away superfluous Branches, and Moss your Gardens. **1707** MORTIMER *Husb.* (1721) II. 78 If the Moss is much and long..it may..do well to prune off the greatest part of the Branches, and to Moss the rest.

5. *intr.* To work in a peat-bog; to cut and prepare peats.

1866 W. GREGOR *Dial. Banffsh.* 115.

mossalagee, obs. f. MUSSALCHEE.

ˈ**moss-back.** Also **mossy-.** [f. MOSS *sb.*¹ + BACK *sb.*; ? orig. a perversion of *mossbunker.*]

1. *U.S.* **a.** A name for the menhaden or mossbunker. **b.** 'A large and old fish, as a bass: so called by anglers, in allusion to the growth of seaweed, etc., which may be found on its back' (*Cent. Dict.* 1890).

1872 SCHELE DE VERE *Americanisms* 87 In the State of New York the same fish [Menhaden] appear under the name of Mossy Back or Mossbunkers.

2. *slang.* **a.** During the civil war in the United States, one who hid himself to avoid the conscription for the Southern army. *U.S.*

1872 SCHELE DE VERE *Americanisms* 283 The Mossyback ...was the man of the South, who secreted himself in a remote forest, or an inaccessible swamp, in order to escape conscription. His name was derived from the quaint fancy that he was determined to keep in hiding till 'the moss should grow on his back'. **1890** *Century Dict.*, *Moss-back.*

b. One 'behind the times'; one attached to antiquated notions; an extreme conservative. Often applied to the farmers of the Western States. Chiefly *N. Amer.*

1878 C. HALLOCK *Amer. Club List & Sportsman's Gloss.* p. viii, *Mossback*, a settler; a homesteader; a pioneer farmer. (Western.) **1884** *Nor'Wester* (Calgary) 3 June 4/1 The local mossback refers to the recent picking up of stones on Stephen Avenue. **1885** *Boston* (Mass.) *Jrnl.* 5 Mar. 2/3 Everybody rejoices over the passage of the bill... We say everybody—we except a few intense mossbacks, who were known during the war as copperheads. **1891** C. ROBERTS *Adrift Amer.* App. 249 He was followed to the very verge of the wood, and then the exhausted 'mossback' left him to return to the house. **1924** J. BUCHAN *Three Hostages* i. 10, I was becoming such a mossback that I had almost stopped reading the papers. **1935** E. POUND *Let.* 28 Jan. (1971) 266 With De Vechii at Ministry of Education there wd. be more chance of *action* than with some aesthetic mossback, sentimentalizing over Dela Crusca. **1937** J. D. CARR *To wake the Dead* xi. 162 Oh, Chris, you are an old mossback! **1941** J. SMILEY *Hash House Lingo* 38 *Moss back*, conservative eater. **1959** W. A. LEISING *Arctic Wings* 97, I listened to old mossbacks, prospectors, and trappers. **1973** 'TREVANIAN' *Loo Sanction* (1974) 212 The moss-backs of the National Gallery had pulled off quite a coup in securing the Marini Horse for a one-day exhibition.

attrib. **1886** *N.Y. Sch. Jrnl.* XXXI. 245 You visit a poor drunkard's wife, and in comes the husband, peremptorily ordering you out of door, quoting the moss-back maxim as his authority.

So **moss-backed, mossy-backed** *adjs.*

1876 *Congress Rec.* 13 Jan. 411/1 [In the cotton states] those too cowardly to fight..were known as 'mossy-backed rangers' during the war. **1881** *Harper's Mag.* Sept. 640/2 A thorough-bred, mossy-backed mountaineer. **1889** 'MARK TWAIN' *Let.* (1917) II. 520 Still mouthing empty reverence for those moss-backed frauds. **1893** *Outing* (U.S.) XXII. 121/2 Earth-worms, fresh from the garden, will lure many a mossy-backed hermit from his lair. **1900** *Speaker* 17 Mar. 644/1 A few malcontents and mossbacked mugwumps. **1963** *Economist* 7 Sept. 826/1 Bankers..found themselves looking hopelessly moss-backed. **1975** G. V. HIGGINS *City on Hill* vi. 148 He's mossbacked and close to a fascist, but he's perfectly sincere.

Mössbauer (ˈmœsbauə(r)). *Physics.* The name of Rudolf L. *Mössbauer* (b. 1929), W. German physicist, used *attrib.* with reference to an effect he reported in 1958, in which gamma rays emitted by an atomic nucleus bound in a crystal exhibit very little Doppler line-broadening (owing to the absence of translational motion of the nucleus) and have almost all the energy released in the transition between nuclear states (owing to the entire mass of the crystal being involved in the recoil of the emitting nucleus, which is consequently very small), so that it is possible to obtain resonance absorption in another similar nucleus with a high degree of precision and hence derive information about the energies and widths of nuclear energy levels; so ***Mössbauer effect, spectroscopy***, etc.

1960 *Physical Rev. Lett.* IV. 28 (*heading*) Observations on the Mössbauer effect in Fe^{57}. **1960** *Ibid.* V. 364/2 The Mössbauer spectrum was observed with an Fe absorber, enriched to 75% Fe^{57} and of equivalent thickness 2·2 mg/cm². **1962** *Listener* 6 Dec. 964/2 Physicists all over the world scramble to examine the 'Mössbauer effect' to find out by how much gravity makes a clock run slow. **1965** PHILLIPS & WILLIAMS *Inorg. Chem.* I. v. 146 The Mössbauer shift can then be correlated with the degree of ionic bonding. Thus the shift of the γ-ray energy from the value found in metallic Sn increases from SnI_4 through $SnBr_4$, $SnCl_4$, and SnO_2 to SnF_4. **1966** *Jrnl. Physics & Chem. Solids* XXVII. 85 The Mössbauer effect was used to measure the line shifts and electric quadrupole splittings of the 14·4 keV level of Fe^{57} in absorbers at 81°K and 300°K of the marcasite structure compounds FeS_2, $FeSe_2$, $FeTe_2$, and $FeSb_2$. **1970** *Physics Bull.* June 247/1 The Mössbauer nuclear resonance is the narrowest spectral line so far available. **1971** GREENWOOD & GIBB *Mössbauer Spectrosc.* i. 1 The Mössbauer effect has been detected in a total of 88 γ-ray transitions in 72 isotopes of 42 different elements. **1971** *Sci. Amer.* Oct. 86/2 Mössbauer-effect spectroscopy is now used extensively for studying chemical bonds, the architecture of molecules and the distribution of electronic charge around atoms. **1973** G. M. BANCROFT *Mössbauer Spectrosc.* iii. 47 In comparison to many spectroscopic experiments, the basic Mössbauer equipment is rather simple and inexpensive. *Ibid.*, A Mössbauer spectrum consists of a plot of the number of gamma ray photons transmitted through an absorber as a function of the instantaneous relative velocity of the source with respect to an absorber.

mossbunker (ˈmɒsbʌŋkə(r)). Forms: 8 **mosbanker**, 8-9 **mossbonker**, 9 **mossbanker**; 9 (in Du. form) **marshbanker**; (in mod. Dicts. **massbanker, marshbunker, morsebonker, morsbunker, mousebunker**); 9- **mossbunker.** [a. Du. *marsbanker* (formerly also *masbank*), of obscure etymology.] The menhaden.

1792 [see MENHADEN]. **1796** MORSE *Amer. Geog.* I. 222 Mossbonker. **1809** W. IRVING *Knickerb.* (1861) 264 A huge moss-bonker. **1868** W. WHITMAN *Poems, Salut au monde* 145, I see ten fishermen waiting—they discover now a thick school of mossbonkers—they drop the joined sein-ends in the water. **1880** GÜNTHER *Fishes* 659 The 'Mossbanker', common on the Atlantic coasts of the United States. **1884** GOODE, etc. *Nat. Hist. Aquatic Anim.* I. 569 This name [Mossbunker]..[has] evidently been transferred from the 'Scad', or 'Horse Mackerel'..known to the Hollanders as the 'Marshbanker' [**1888** —— *Amer. Fishes* 386 'Marsbanker']. New Jersey uses the New York name with its local variations, such as 'Bunker' and 'Marshbanker'.

attrib. **1881** *N.Y. Times* in Goode *Amer. Fishes* (1888) 112 These smacks are engaged in the menhaden or 'mossbunker' fishery.

mosschette, obs. variant of MACHETE.

1827 ROBERTS *Voy. Centr. Amer.* 36 We gave them Mosschettes (or G. R. Cutlass-blades) and a variety of toys.

‖**mosse.** *Obs.* [G. *mass* measure.] (See quot.)

1617 MORYSON *Itin.* III. 235 Two small fennings for each Mosse or measure of wine.

mosse, obs. form of MORSE *sb.*²

mossed (mɒst), *ppl. a.* [f. MOSS *sb.*¹ + -ED².] Covered over, or overgrown, with moss.

1744 HANMER *Shaks. Timon* IV. iii. 223 Those moss'd [1623 moyst] trees. **1830** TENNYSON *Claribel* ii, At noon the wild bee hummeth About the moss'd headstone. **1876** MRS. OLIPHANT *Curate in Charge* (ed. 5) I. x. 240 Wild old gardens and mossed apple-trees.

mossel(e, -ll(e, obs. ff. MORSEL, MUZZLE.

mosser (ˈmɒsə(r)). [f. MOSS *sb.*¹ or *v.* + -ER¹.]

†**1.** One who 'mosses' or roofs with moss.

1708 *Baslow Parish Reg.* 21 July in *Sheffield Gloss.* 322 [Buried,] Edmundus Litlewood de Totley, Moser.

2. A moss-trooper.

1854 DENHAM *Tracts* (1892) 176 These gentry were also called prickers, riders,..bogtrotters, mossers, snatchers.

3. One who works in a 'moss' or bog; one who is engaged in cutting and preparing peats.

1866 W. GREGOR *Dial. Banffsh.* 115. **1880** in JAMIESON.

4. A collector or gatherer of moss.

1880 P. FURNIVALL *Let.* (*MS.*) 5 Sept. **1895** MAR. L. POOL *Boss* in *Chapbk.* III. 478 Granny had no boat as most of the mossers had.

ˈ**mossery.** A place where mosses are grown.

1895 *Scotsman* 25 Oct. 6/6 Visiting the Botanic Gardens in Glasgow the other day, I observed in the 'mossery'..a peculiar-looking selaginella.

mossful (ˈmɒsfʊl), *a.* [f. MOSS *sb.*¹ + -FUL.] Full of, or covered with, moss.

1862 CHR. G. ROSSETTI *Goblin Market*, etc. (1884) 185 Primrose and veined violet In the mossful earth are set.

ˈ**moss-grown**, *a.* [f. MOSS *sb.*¹ + GROWN.] Overgrown with moss.

13.. *Metr. Hom.* (Vernon MS.) in *Archiv Stud. neu. Spr.* LVII. 277 A Mos growen wal he gan fynde þer þe 3ate was wont to be. **1596** SHAKS. *1 Hen. IV*, III. i. 33 Which.. tombles downe Steeples, and mosse-growne Towers. **1820** W. IRVING *Sketch Bk.* (1859) 46 Every antique farm-house and moss-grown cottage is a picture.

b. *fig.* Antiquated.

1893 L. F. TOWNSEND in J. H. Barrows *Parl. Relig.* II. 1221 Dr. Channing..saw, as he thought, the speedy.. burial of the moss-grown doctrines of Bible orthodoxy. **1902** A. B. DAVIDSON *Called of God* viii. 215 Even the holiest things had become mouldy, moss-grown and eaten away.

ˈ**moss-hag.** *Sc.* [f. MOSS *sb.*¹ + HAG *sb.*⁴] Broken ground from which peat has been taken; a pit or hole from which peat has been dug.

1816 SCOTT *Old Mort.* viii, A sour fit o' the batts wi' sitting amang the wat moss-hags for four hours at a yoking. **1818** —— *Hrt. Midl.* xii, When I was in the moss-haggs and moors, wi' precious Donald Cameron, and worthy Mr. Blackadder. **1884** SPEEDY *Sport* xx. 398 Concealing themselves among the moss-hags before daybreak.

Hence ˈ**moss-hagger**, a dweller among moss-hags.

1902 W. S. CROCKETT *Scott. Country* xvi. 412 A coveted sheltering place for many a poor oppressed moss-hager.

Mossi (ˈmɒsɪ). Also **Moshi, Mosi.** Pl. **Mossi, Mossis.** The name of a Negroid people living in Burkina Faso in West Africa. Also *attrib.*

1858 H. BARTH *Trav. N. & Cent. Afr.* IV. 551 The strongest among these pagan kingdoms..is that of the Mósi, although the country is split into a number of small principalities..paying only some slight homage to the ruler of the principality of Wóghodogó. **1911** F. W. H. MIGEOD *Lang. W. Afr.* I. i. 38 The powerful nation of the Moshis and other kindred tribes evidently prevented the extension of the Nta in a northerly direction. **1930** C. G. SELIGMAN *Races of Afr.* iii. 63 The Mossi are agriculturalists, with millet as the staple crop. **1959** *Chambers's Encycl.* XIV. 197/2 Upper Volta..was originally created..in order to stimulate the economic development of the densely peopled Mossi country lying north..of the British Gold Coast. **1964** E. A. NIDA *Toward Sci. Transl.* iii. 54 The Mossis of Haute Volta in West Africa speak of most emotional states in terms of the heart.

mossie¹ (ˈmɒsɪ). *S. Afr.* [Afrikaans, f. Du. *mosje* dim. of *mos* sparrow.] The Cape sparrow, *Passer melanurus.*

1884 R. B. SHARPE *Layard's Birds S. Afr.* (rev. ed.) 479 The 'Mossie', like its cousin the English bird, is essentially a 'cit'. **1936** E. L. GILL *First Guide S. Afr. Birds* 21 The cock Mossie, with his black head, white eye-stripe and cinnamon back, is a handsome and unmistakable bird. **1959** *Cape Argus* 22 Aug. 5/6 The mossies in her neighbourhood never seem to stray more than a few blocks away. **1974** *Stand. Encycl. S. Afr.* X. 209/2 The Cape Sparrow (*Passer melanurus*) has the same size, and much the same habits as the European sparrow, but the male has a different and more handsome plumage, with a black head and throat and a white curved spot on the side. Mossies, as they are called locally, are common birds in South Africa, especially on farms, occurring in flocks during the non-breeding season.

mossie² (ˈmɒsɪ, ˈmɒzɪ). Also **mozzie, mozzy.** Slang abbrev. of MOSQUITO.

1941 BAKER *Dict. Austral. Slang* 47 *Mossie, mozzie*, a mosquito. **1954** R. S. PORTEOUS in *Coast to Coast 1953-4* 117 Blast these mossies. There's more inside this net than out of it. **1964** M. DICKSON *World Elsewhere* v. 182 Sleeping bags, 'mossie' nets and other equipment. **1971** B. W. ALDISS *Soldier Erect* 167 When we were off guard, we kipped on one of the station platforms outside the RTO office, under our mozzy-nets. **1973** *Shooting Times & Country Mag.* 7 July 14/2 If it *has* chosen unwisely, then the newly-hatched

mossies rise triumphantly from the surface only to hit their heads on the caterpillars' safety net and fall back into the liquid.

'mossify, *v. nonce-wd.* [f. MOSS *sb.*[1] + -FY.] *trans.* To make mossy. (In quot. *absol.*)

1822 MRS. E. NATHAN *Langreath* I. 25 You may mossify and poetize if you choose.

mossiness ('mɒsɪnɪs). [f. MOSSY *a.* + -NESS.] The condition of being mossy (in senses of the adj.); *concr.* a mossy substance or growth.

[**1538**: see MOSINESS under MOSY *a.*] **1558** WARDE tr. *Alexis' Secr.* I. iv. (1580) 75 b, The firste softe haire, or mossinesse of the face. **1625** BACON *Ess., Gardens* (Arb.) 561 That the Water be neuer by Rest Discoloured, Greene, or Red, or the like; Or gather any Mossinesse or Putrefaction. **1725** BRADLEY *Fam. Dict.* s.v. *Oak*, The frequent Mossiness of most Trees on the North Side. **1817** KEATS *Spec. Induct. to Poem* 22 Th' half seen mossiness of linnets' nests. **1893** BURRELL & CUTHELL *Indian Mem.* 175 A Himalayan forest is a wealth of leafiness and mossiness.

mossing ('mɒsɪŋ), *vbl. sb.* [-ING[1].] The action of the vb. MOSS in various senses.

1700 O. HEYWOOD *Diaries*, etc. (1885) IV. 231 Sam. Stocks came a mossing. **1856** KANE *Arct. Expl.* I. xxvii. 355 All hands..are out 'mossing'. This mossing..is a frightfully wintry operation.

attrib. **1880** C. R. MARKHAM *Peruv. Bark* 329 This mossing process for renewing the bark

mossite ('mɒsaɪt). *Min.* [ad. G. *mossit* (W. C. Brögger 1897, in *Skrifter udgivne af Videnskabsselskabet i Christiania*: *Mat.-nat. Kl.* VII. 4), f. *Moss*, the name of the city in Norway near which it was found: see -ITE[1].] **a.** A mineral, $(Fe,Mn)(Ta,Nb)_2O_6$, similar to tapiolite but containing a high proportion of niobium. **b.** The end member of the series obtained by substituting niobium for tantalum in tapiolite.

1898 *Jrnl. Chem. Soc.* LXXIV. II. 387 The new mineral, mossite, occurs with yttrotantalite and columbite in a pegmatite vein at Berg in the parish of Råde, near Moss, in Norway. **1917** *Mineral. Mag.* XVIII. 120 The relationship which strüverite and ilmenorutile bear to rutile, on the one hand, and to tapiolite and mossite, on the other hand, may be graphically illustrated. **1955** *Amer. Mineralogist* XL. 445 These features lead one to question the existence of mossite and of a complete tetragonal mossite-tapiolite series. **1968** I. KOSTOV *Mineralogy* II. iv. 247 Tapiolite and mossite have a rutile type of structure in which two $[(Ta, Nb)O_6]$ octahedra alternate with one $[FeO_6]$ octahedron along the tetragonal axis.

mossless ('mɒslɪs), *a.* [f. MOSS *sb.*[1] + -LESS.] Without moss; having no moss.

1880 'MARK TWAIN' *Tramp Abroad* I. 201 The mossless spots were places where repairs had been made by the insertion of bright new masses of yellow straw.

mosso ('mosso), *a.* [It., pa. pple. of *muovere* to move.] Of musical movement: rapid; animated.

1876 STAINER & BARRETT *Dict. Mus. Terms* 297/1 *Mosso* (It.), moved, as *più mosso*, more moved or faster; *meno mosso*, less fast. **1952** H. HUNTER *Gram. Mus.* 87 *Italian terms relating to speed*... Più mosso, Più tosto, Stretto, [etc.]. **1962** *Listener* 26 Apr. 749/3 The intense urgency of the 'Libera me', especially of the *più mosso* middle section with the threatening syncopations of the brass.

mossoljee, obs. form of MUSSALCHEE.

mossoo (mə'su:). A vulgar mispronunciation of MONSIEUR, used in representations of illiterate speech or in derisive allusion to English patriotic prejudices. Cf. MOUNSEER.

1870 MISS BRIDGMAN *R. Lynne* II. vi. 129 You pick out any Mossoo you like. **1886** ASHBY-STERRY *Lazy Minstrel* 68 A stout fur-capped Mossoo.

moss rose. [MOSS *sb.*[1]] A garden variety of the cabbage rose, *Rosa centifolia*; so called from the moss-like growth on its calyx and stalk.

[**1731** MILLER *Gard. Dict., Rosa Provincialis, spinosissima, pedunculo muscoso.* The Moss Province Rose.] **1776** *Ann. Reg.* 118 Half a guinea for some moss roses. **1800** COLERIDGE *Keepsake* 30 There..she sate and stretched The silk upon the frame, and worked her name Between the Moss-Rose and Forget-me-not. **1888** S. HIBBERD in *Times* 20 Aug. 10/3 To the question..Is the white moss rose becoming extinct? the proper answer is, No.

mosstick, obs. form of MAULSTICK.

1658 PHILLIPS, A *Mosstick*,..a round stick about a yard long, which the artist doth rest upon when he paints.

'moss-trooper. [MOSS *sb.*[1] 1.] One of a class of marauders who infested the 'mosses' of the Scottish Border, in the middle of the seventeenth century; a border freebooter.

1651 WHITELOCKE *Mem.* 14 Feb. (1853) III. 289 The Scots, in a village called Geddard..set upon captain Dawson as he returned from pursuing some moss-troopers. *a* **1661** FULLER *Worthies, Northumb.* (1662) II. 303 A sprigg of these Borderers hath lately been revived (disguised under the new name of Moss-Troopers). **1805** SCOTT *Last Minstr.* I. xix. **1849** MACAULAY *Hist. Eng.* iii. I. 294 A single troop of dragoons..was stationed near Berwick, for the purpose of keeping the peace among the mosstroopers of the border.

b. *transf.* A bandit or raider.

1701 COLLIER tr. *M. Anton.* 187 A fourth sort value themselves extremely upon their Hunting the Sarmatian Moss Troopers. **1809** W. IRVING *Knickerb.* (1861) 121 These moss-troopers of the east. **1900** L. S. AMERY *Times' Hist. War S. Afr.* I. viii. 188 Dr. Jameson and his band of moss-troopers.

So **'mosstroopery**, the practices of the moss-troopers; **'moss-trooping** *vbl. sb.* and *ppl. a.*

1805 SCOTT *Last Minstr.* I. xxi, A stark moss-trooping Scott was he. **1845** CARLYLE *Cromwell* vi. II. 150 Rebellion ..with much mosstroopery and horsestealing. **1881** J. RUSSELL *Haigs* v. 89 A moss-trooping and reiving race. **1884** GARDINER *Hist. Eng.* I. 338 Still, the old mosstrooping spirit was not to be changed in a day.

mossy ('mɒsɪ), *a.* [f. MOSS *sb.*[1] + -Y[1].]

I. [Cf. MOSS *sb.*[1] I.]

1. *Sc.* and *dial.* Marshy, boggy, peaty.

1596 DALRYMPLE tr. *Leslie's Hist. Scot.* I. 35 This land.. will be sax, sevin, or viii cubites hich of fat mossie ground as glew, bot maist barren. **1661** J. CHILDREY *Brit. Baconica* 167 Chatmos in this shire is a low mossey ground. **1792** BURNS '*Yon wild, mossy mountains*' ii, Not Gowrie's rich valley, nor Forth's sunny shores, To me hae the charms o' yon wild, mossy moors. **1796** MORSE *Amer. Geog.* II. 175 The rains of so many ages subsiding on the lower grounds, have converted most of the extensive plains into mossy morasses. **1845** *New Statist. Acct. Scotl.* XIV. 120 Many of the natives drink mossy and surface water.

II. [Cf. MOSS *sb.*[1] II.]

2. Overgrown or covered with moss, abounding in moss. Also of a fountain, spring, pool, etc.: Encircled with moss; issuing from, or existing in, a moss-grown rock, etc.

1565 COOPER *Thesaurus* s.v. *Muscosus, Solum muscosum*, a mossie grounde. **1579** LANGHAM *Gard. Health* (1633) 41 The Mossie barke of an Ash. **1628** W. L[ISLE] tr. *Virg. Bucol.* VII. 61 Ye mossy Fountaines [L. *muscosi fontes*] and yee Hearbs which bee Softer then sleepe. **1665** BOYLE *Occas. Refl.* II. ii. (1848) 18 To..conjure up wormeaten Carkases out of their Mossy Graves. **1712** POPE *Messiah* 3 The mossy fountains, and the sylvan shades,..Delight no more. **1818** SHELLEY *Woodman & Nightingale* 23 And every bird lulled on its mossy bough. **1875** MRS. RANDOLPH *W. Hyacinth* I. 3 The soft mossy turf. **1885-94** R. BRIDGES *Eros & Psyche* Oct. iv, Echo, sweet Echo, watching up on high, Say hast thou seen to-day my love go by, Or where thou sittest by thy mossy spring?

3. Covered with something resembling moss; appearing as if covered with moss; downy, velvety.

15.. *An Other Balade* in *Chaucer's Wks.* (1561) 344 b, O Mossie Quince hangyng by your stalke. **1573** in Cunningham *Revels at Crt.* (1842) 58, vj paier of Mossy buskins. **1602** DOLMAN *La Primaud. Fr. Acad.* (1618) III. 796 The myrrh which heere wee haue..is blacke, and as if it were scorched, mouldy and mossie on the outside. **1668** WILKINS *Real Char.* 112 Bearing mossy flowers. **1837** T. RIVERS *Rose Amateur's Guide* 5 The Moss Rose, or Mossy Provence Rose.

4. Resembling moss; formerly applied to down or young growth of hair. Cf. MOSY *a.*

1579 E. K. *Gloss to Spenser's Sheph. Cal.* May 187 Young and mossie heares. **1585** HIGINS tr. *Junius' Nomencl.* 18 *Ephebus*..a stripling, that hauing passed 14 yeares, beginneth to haue a mossie beard. **1698** FRYER *Acc. E. India & P.* 390 His Beard is Cut neatly, and the Whiskers kept in Cases,..not so mossy or slovenly, as either Turkish or Indian Mahometans. **1796** KIRWAN *Elem. Min.* (ed. 2) II. 132 It [*sc.* malachite] is found either massive, or..mossy. **1861** J. R. GREENE *Man. Anim. Kingd., Cœlent.* 83 The slender mossy threads which compose the connecting stem of smaller species. **1887** D. MAGUIRE *Art Massage* ii. (ed. 4) 19 The strigil is a bent instrument in the form of a sickle mossy on its edge, and terminating with a handle at one of its extremities, the other rounded off and mossy.

5. †**a.** *slang* or *jocular*. Stupid, dull. *Obs.*

1597 *Pilgr. Parnass.* II. 168 Woulde anie leaden Mydas, anie mossie patron, have his asses ears deified, let him [etc.]. **1597** *1st Pt. Return fr. Parnass.* I. i. 110 Mossy idiotts. **1602** *2nd Pt. Return fr. Parnass.* II. i. 574 Mossy barbarians the spectators be, That sit and laugh at our calamity.

b. Extremely conservative or reactionary; old-fashioned, out of date; old. *U.S. slang.*

1904 *Collier's* 20 Feb. 1 Arthur Lynch's release has the approval of all England except a few peculiarly mossy old Tories. **1932** *Amer. Speech* VII. 402 That's a mossy hat he wears. **1942** BERREY & VAN DEN BARK *Amer. Thes. Slang* §116/6 Old; aged,..*mossy*. *Ibid.* §233/12 Old-fashioned,.. *mossy*.

6. *Comb.*, as ***mossy-chinned, -footed, -tinctured*** adjs.; **mossy-back, -backed** *a.* (see MOSS-BACK), **mossy crêpe** = *moss crêpe*; **mossy-cup oak**, the bur-oak, *Quercus macrocarpa*; **mossy horn** *U.S.*, an old steer; also, an old cowboy; **mossy stonecrop**, *Sedum acre* (Syd. Soc. Lex. 1891).

1694 MOTTEUX *Rabelais* IV. xxix. (1737) 119 A *Mossy-chin'd Demy-giant. **1832** *Planting* 115 (Libr. Usef. Knowl.) The American *mossy-cup oak. **1883** MEREDITH *Woods of Westermain* 16 *Mossy-footed squirrels leap, Soft as winnowing plumes of Sleep. **1885** C. A. SIRINGO *Texas Cow Boy* viii. 75 They were all old *mossy horn fellows from seven to twenty-seven years old. **1944** R. F. ADAMS *Western Words* 101/2 *Mossy-horn*, a Texas longhorn steer, six or more years old, whose horns have become wrinkled and scaly... The term sometimes is slangily applied to an old cowman. **1955** FOSTER-HARRIS *Old West* viii. 227 Little wrinkles would begin to grow up from the bases of the horns, and the older the steer got, the more the wrinkles would show, giving rise to the term 'mossy horns', meaning old-timers. **1973** R. D. SYMONS *Where Wagon Led* I. vi. 93 It only takes one ole' mossy-horn to take fright at his own shadder to start the whole lot off. **1728-46** THOMSON *Spring* 381 When..whitening down their *mossy-tinctured stream Descends the billowy foam. **1945** M. D. POTTER *Fiber to Fabric* xii. 239 *Mossy crepe*,..fabric with texture giving fine moss effect.

most (məʊst), *a.* (*sb.*) and *adv.* Forms: α. 1 **mǽst**, (**mǽsð**), *Merc.* and *Kent.* **mést**, 3 **mæst**, 2-5 **mest**, 3 **meast**, 4 **meste**, 5 *Norfolk* **myst**. β. 1 *north.* **mást**, (**maast, másð**), 3-5 **mast**, (3 *Orm.* **masst**), 4-6 **moste**, **moost(e**, (5-6 *Sc. poet.* **moiste**), 3- **most**; also *Sc.* and *north. dial.* 4-7 **mast(e**, 4-6 **mayst**, 6 **maiste**, 4-9 **maist**, (9 **meast**). [Com. Teut.: OE. *mǽst* (Northumb. *mást*) = OFris. *mâst, maest*, OS. *mêst* (Du. *meest*), OHG. (MHG., mod.G.) *meist*, ON. *mest-r* (Sw., Da. *mest*), Goth. *maist-s*:—OTeut. **maisto-*, formed with superlative suffix *-isto-* (see -EST) from the root of **maiz*, MO *adv.*, quasi-*sb.*[1] and *a.*

The OE. *mást*, the normal representative of the Com. Teut. type, has been found only in Northumbrian, but it is not certain that it existed only in that dialect. The ordinary OE. form (WS. *mǽst*, Kentish *mést*) has abnormal umlaut, and seems to descend from a prehistoric **má-ist*, a re-formation due to a consciousness of the grammatical relation of the word to *má* MO. The umlaut form survived, in the south, down to the 15th c., but seems to have now entirely disappeared even in dialects. (The 19th c. northern form *meast* represents OE. *mást*; the coincidence with the early ME. *meast*:—OE. *mǽst* is accidental.) The establishment of *most* as the only form in the midlands and south was probably due to the influence of the related *mo, more*.

The southern form *most*, occasionally spelt *moist*, was often used, esp. in rimes, by the Sc. poets of the 15-16th c.]

A. *adj.* **I.** (The senses 1, 2, 3 express respectively the superlative of the three adjectival notions now denoted by *great, much*, and *many*.)

1. = GREATEST *a.*, in various applications.

†**a.** with reference to size, bulk, or stature. *Obs.*

c **1000** *Ags. Gosp.* Matt. xiii. 32 Soðlice þanne hyt wexað hyt ys alre wyrte mæst. *c* **1220** *Bestiary* 500 Cethegrande is a fis ðe moste ðat in water is. **13..** *E. E. Allit. P.* B. 385 Þe moste mountaynez on mor þenne was no more dryȝe. *c* **1450** *Merlin* xiv. 210 Kynge Clarion, that was the moste man of the hoste of alle the Geauntes. **1548-77** VICARY *Anat.* iv. (1888) 30 The braine is diuided into three partes..of which the foremost part is the moste.

†**b.** with reference to amount or degree. (*a*) As superlative of comparison: Greatest in degree or extent, often passing into 'utmost', 'chief', occas. used predicatively. (*b*) As intensive superlative: Very great. *Obs.*

(*a*) *c* **893** K. ÆLFRED *Oros.* IV. xi. §6 Þonne þæt ȝefeoht mæst wære. *c* **1200** ORMIN 5328 Þe maste lufe he shæweþþ þær þatt aniȝ mann maȝȝ shæwenn. *c* **1386** CHAUCER *Sqr.'s T.* 191 But eueremoore hir mooste wonder was How þat it [the hors] koude go and was of bras. **1470-85** MALORY *Arthur* XVII. v. 695 The swerd fayled hym at his moost nede. *c* **1586** SANDERS in *Hakluyt's Voy.* (1599) II. I. 190, I had the Italian & Spanish tongues, by which their most trafique in that countrey is. **1603** SHAKS. *Meas. for M.* III. i. 78 The sence of death is most in apprehension. **1702** ECHARD *Eccl. Hist.* (1710) 609 The most imaginable fatigue and industry.

(*b*) *c* **1380** WYCLIF *Wks.* (1880) 174 Þes prestis þat wole not helpe here maistris out of þis moste peril. **1479** J. PASTON in *P. Lett.* III. 266, I wryght not so largely to yow as I wold do, for I have not most leyser. **1555** in Strype *Eccl. Mem.* (1721) III. App. xliii. 118 So likewise is freewil a most untruth undoubtedly.

c. said of a numerical aggregate, proportion, etc. *Obs.* except in the phr. (*the*) ***most part***.

most part (without article) may be used advb. In quot. *c* 1205 the adverbial accus. *mesten dæl* is used subst. as a nominative.

c **1205** LAY. 7864 And heom sælliche i-lomp þæt mesten dæl com a lond. *a* **1225** *Ancr. R.* 330 Scheome is þe meste del ..of ure penitence. *c* **1330** R. BRUNNE *Chron. Wace* (Rolls) 12839 In to þe most pres Ider þen sprong. **1483** CAXTON *Gold. Leg.* 394/2 The moste parte of the peple of the cyte. *c* **1511** [see DEAL *sb.*[1] 1 d]. **1532** in *Thanes Cawdor* (Spalding Club) 155 The landis and barony of Schancar or the mast part thereof. **1579** in *10th Rep. Hist. MSS. Comm.* App. v. 429 The most noumber shall have the choice and election. **1632** LITHGOW *Trav.* I. 20 Blood-sucking Inquisitors, of which the most part were mine owne Country-men. **1700** S. L. tr. *Fryke's Voy. E. Ind.* 2, I went and took a view of most part of Hungary.

d. ***for the most part*** (also †***party***, †***deal***): usually; in the main. †Also rarely without *the*.

1387 [see DEAL *sb.*[1] 1 d]. *c* **1400** MAUNDEV. (1839) xxix. 294 Thei holden for the moste partye, the..gode manneres, as men of the Contree aboue seyd. **1523** LD. BERNERS *Froiss.* (1812) I. ccccxxvi. 746 Yᵉ lorde of Coucy went to Mortayn ..and there refresshed hym and his company; but for the most partye he hymselfe was with the kyng at Turney. **1545** RAYNOLD *Byrth Mankynde* 90 For the moste parte when there be two at once, the one is masculyne, and the other femenyne. **1561** T. HOBY tr. *Castiglione's Courtyer* III. G g ij, For moste part these kinde of iniurious persons..are menne wel stricken in yeeres. **1647** TRAPP *Comm.* 2 *Cor.* vii. 3 Such faithful friends are in this age all for the most part gone in pilgrimage. **1715** ADDISON *Freeholder* No. 20 ¶8 A House of Commons, which..must consist for the most part of Landed Men. **1871** SMILES *Charac.* viii. (1876) 220 Men of the greatest genius have been for the most part cheerful, contented men.

†**e.** with reference to (*a*) power, authority; (*b*) importance, consequence. ***most master***: ruler, commander; also, one who is 'master' in a contest, etc. *Obs.*

c **950** *Lindisf. Gosp.* Matt. xviii. 1 Hia cueðende huelc wenes ðu maast is in ric heofna. *a* **1225** *Leg. Kath.* 816 Þe meast kempe is icud & kenest of ow alle of þe creft. *c* **1350** *Will. Palerne* 2735 Þe segges were a-slepe..al but þe mest maister. **1382** WYCLIF *Matt.* xxii. 38 This is the firste and the most maundement. **1470-85** MALORY *Arthur* XXI. i. 840 He that was the moost kyng and knyght of the world. **1571**

CAMPION *Hist. Irel.* iii. (1633) 9 Turffe and Sea-coales is their most fuell. **1591** SHAKS. *1 Hen. VI*, I. iii. 149 Shee'le.. dandle thee like a Baby: Though in this place most Master weare no Breeches.

†**f.** Const. *in*, *of*. *Obs.*

a **1300** *Cursor M.* 205 How he þat o myght es mast Send in till erth his haly gast. *c* **1380** WYCLIF *Serm.* Sel. Wks. I. 316 þis Cesare was moost in generalte and larges, and pees of his lordship. *c* **1440** *Sir Gowther* 755 (end) Gyff us myȝt with hym to won, þat lord, þat is most of meyn! Amen. **1533** in Furnivall *Ballads fr. MSS.* I. 380 Wheron to rest, And build hir nest, God graunte hir, moste of might!

†**g.** Oldest. *Obs.*

c **1205** LAY. 11567 Mauric, þe mæst of his childeren. *c* **1250** *Gen. & Ex.* 900 For he [Melchisedech] was boðen king and prest, of elde most, of wit heȝest.

h. qualifying the designation of a person: Entitled to the designation in the highest degree. *Obs.*

c **1300** *Havelok* 323 Godard was.. þe moste swike, þat eure in erþe shaped was. **13..** *Sir Beues* (A.) 1611 The meste wreche of alle Wiþ a strok me doþ adoun falle. **1483** CAXTON *Gold. Leg.* 207 b/2 Fle hens thou moste wretche. *a* **1553** UDALL *Royster D.* IV. iv. (Arb.) 66 The moste loute and dastarde that euer on grounde trode. **1605** CHAPMAN *All Fooles* Wks. 1873 I. 149 These politicians.. are our most fooles. **1624** MIDDLETON *Game at Chess* III. ii. (end), She's caught, and, which is strange, by her most wronger. **1690** W. WALKER *Idiomat. Anglo-Lat.* 439 He had been a most Mad-man had he stood against them.

i. ***the most thing that***, the chief thing that; what... most. *Obs.* exc. *dial.*

a **1450** *Knt. de la Tour* 65 The most thinge that greuid her was her good and gay clothing. *c* **1460** *How Wise Man taught Son* 182 in Hazl. *E.P.P.* I. 177 For deth ys, sone, as I trowe, The most thyng that certyn ys. **1474** CAXTON *Chesse* I. iii, Ryght dere lord and kynge, the grettest and most thinge that I desire is that [etc.]. **1835** D. WEBSTER *Sc. Rhymes* 4 (E.D.D.) The maist thing that troubled the bodies, I think was their hungry wames.

j. †**most end** (*obs.*), **most an end** *dial.* [? OE. **mǽstan ende*, advb. accus.]: see END *sb.* 5 c.

2. a. With *sb.* in *pl.* (†occas. with *the*): The greatest number of; the majority of. †***most times***, usually, in the majority of cases.

a **900** *O. E. Chron.* an. 894, & him mon eac mid oþrum floccum sohte mæstra daȝa ælce, oþþe on dæȝ oþþe on niht. **1377** LANGL. *P. Pl.* B. XIX. 150 And who þat moste maistries can, be myldest of berynge. **1473** WARKW. *Chron.* (Camden) 5 Whereof the most peple were sory. **1579** LYLY *Euphues* (Arb.) 53 Vertue is harboured in the heart of him that most men esteeme mishapen. **1628** BP. HALL *Old Relig.* Ded., I have passed my most and best hours in quiet meditation. **1643** TRAPP *Comm. Gen.* xxiii. 7 Abrahams behaviour to these Hittites may shame the most Christians. **1701** TUTTELL *Descr. & Expl. Math. Instrum.* 1 Most Questions in Arithmetick. **1888** BRYCE *Amer. Commw.* II. lx. 427 Party loyalty is strong enough, with most people.

†**b.** With *sb.* in *sing.*: Numerically strongest.

1638 in *10th Rep. Hist. MSS. Comm.* App. v. 487 It was .. agreed upon, by comon consent and most voice in oppen court.

3. Existing in the greatest quantity, amount, or degree; the greatest amount or quantity of.

This use, like the corresponding uses of *much* and *more*, prob. arose mainly from the absolute use 5, with virtual ellipsis of *of*. When used with abstract sbs. this sense is hard to distinguish from the obsolete sense 'greatest' (1 b).

c **1380** WYCLIF *Sel. Wks.* III. 406 Bot moste harm in þis mater stondes in þis; þat þei perverte þo feythe of þo gospel. *c* **1460** *Towneley Myst.* iii. 16 Of all angels in brightnes God gaf lucifer most lightnes. **1502** ARNOLDE *Chron.* (1811) 16 Our trewe men doo vs to vnderstonde that moost prayeng and leste profyt myght falle to the same cite and to me. **1720** OZELL *Vertot's Rom. Rep.* I. IV. 20 At those tumultuous Assemblies.. such had most Authority as could make most Noise. **1727** SWIFT *Gulliver's Let. to Sympson* Wks. 1751 IX. 143 Have not I the most Reason to complain? **1856** RUSKIN *Mod. Paint.* IV. v. xvi. §42 The work will.. have most power which was begun with most patience.

II. *absol.* (quasi-*sb.*)

4. a. Absolute uses of sense 1. The greatest persons (or, rarely, things); chiefly, with reference to rank or importance. Usually in association with *least*. Now only *poet.* in ***most and least*** = 'all without exception' (in ME. verse often as a metrical tag).

c **1250** *Gen. & Ex.* 198 And for his sinne oc he to munen, ðat moste and leiste him ben binumen. *a* **1300** *Cursor M.* 1659 Fra þe mast dun to þe lest Sal neþer liue ne fouul ne best. *c* **1386** CHAUCER *Clerk's T.* 75 We wol.. Chese yow a wyf.. Born of the gentilleste and of the meeste Of al this land. **1483** CAXTON *Gold. Leg.* 59 b/1, Moyses.. gadred all the most of byrthe. **1526** TINDALE *Heb.* viii. 11 They shall a knowe me, from the lest to the moste off them. **1600** FAIRFAX *Tasso* VIII. lxxii, Enuenoming the hearts of most and least. **1879** BROWNING *Pheidippides* 78 Then praise Pan who fought in the ranks with you most and least.

b. *slang.* The best, (something that is) extremely good, most exciting; also as quasi-*adv.*

1953 *Time* 17 Aug. 3/1 It's the most! **1954** *Time* 1 Feb. 14/1 Last week the general and even the Pentagon conceded that the bop campaign was the most, to say the least. **1958** *Sunday News* (N.Y.) 11 May 2 Of her husband, she said, 'Adam and I dig each other the most. We have a perfect understanding. It couldn't be better.' **1958** *News Chron.* 22 May 4/5 When a man is found to be attractive—he's the most. **1959** *Punch* 16 Sept. 167/2 It has in fact been voted 'The Sleeve With the Most'.. by the editors of the *Beat Disc Review and Pop Chronicle.* **1960** *Guardian* 17 Mar. 4/1 American women get the *most*! **1968** *Listener* 7 Mar. 314/3, I would infinitely prefer to listen to the Kenny Everett programme—'the show that's the most with your tea and toast', as that masterly DJ himself puts it. **1969** H. WAUGH *Young Prey* (1970) 6 'So—you like the ride?'.. 'No kidding, it was the most!'

5. a. The greatest amount or quantity.

c **1122** *O. E. Chron.* an. 1011, þonne hi mæst to yfele ȝedon hæfdon. *a* **1200** *Moral Ode* 112 þe ðe lest wat biseið ofte mest. *c* **1200** ORMIN 15278 þiss follc iss laȝhesst, & tiss lott Addleþþ þe læste mede, Forr þatt teȝȝ hafenn allre masst Off þeȝȝre flæshess wille. *c* **1290** *S. Eng. Leg.* I. 318/671 Ho-so hath of þe eorþe mest, he is slouȝ as þe Asse. **1419** in *Thanes Cawdor* (Spalding Club) 6 To sel thaim to hym or to ony uthir that wil gif mast for thaim. **1500-20** DUNBAR *Poems* lviii. 29 Quha maist hes than sall maist repent. **1648** GAGE *West Ind.* 162 Four hundred Crowns had been the most that my old Predecessor had given yearly. *a* **1908** *Mod.* This is really the most that I can concede.

†**b.** Const. *genitive*. Only OE. and early ME.

c **888** K. ÆLFRED *Boeth.* xxiv. §3 Forðæm þæt he þurh ðæt mæȝe mæst bearna beȝitan. *c* **1200** *Trin. Coll. Hom.* 169 Mest manne him gremede mid scorne *a* **1225** *St. Marher.* 6 Ant tu schalt wummon meast wunne ant weole welden.

†**c.** ***all*** (***one's***) ***most***: (one's) utmost. *Obs.* In quot. used *advb.*

1375 BARBOUR *Bruce* XVII. 818 Quhen all thair mast assalȝeit thai, And the schot thikkest [wes] with-all [etc.].

d. ***to make the most of*** (†***to make most of***): (*a*) To employ to the best advantage; (*b*) To treat with the greatest consideration; (*c*) To represent or exhibit at the best or worst.

1526 *Pilgr. Perf.* (W. de W. 1531) 13 He maketh moost of vs & cheryssheth vs. **1588** *Marprel. Epist.* (Arb.) 22 Thackwell is.. permitted to make the most he could of his presse and letters. *a* **1627** HAYWARD *Edw. VI* (1630) 73 The most [was] made of that which was true, and many falsities added. **1660** FULLER *Mixt Contempl.* (1841) 237, I always made the most of the youngest. **1727** GAY *Begg. Op.* I. iv, How to make the most of her beauty. **1859** FITZGERALD tr. *Omar* xxiii, Ah, make the most of what we yet may spend. **1891** *Temple Bar* June 167 He.. made the most of his opportunity.

e. ***the most of***: the greatest part of, the majority of.

1790 in *Eng. Dial. Dict.* (1903) IV. 170/2. **1843** T. WILSON *Pitman's Pay* 27 The myest of which was left below. **1862** M. D. COLT *Went to Kansas* 192, I.. have taken leave of the most of my friends. **1879** STEVENSON *Travels with Donkey* iii. 96 Without doubt, the most of mankind grossly overeat themselves. **1931** H. BELLOC *Hist. Eng.* IV. i. 127 Much of the most of English wealth in 1536 came from tillage. **1963** C. D. SIMAK *They walked like Men* ix. 49 'You say all my neighbors have lost their leases or sold out?' 'The most of them.'

6. Governed by a prep. forming an advb. phrase.

a. at most, at the most (ME. *atte meste*). A qualifying phrase, attached to a quantitative designation to indicate that the amount, number, or quantity is the largest admissible. Also in wider sense, appended to a statement to denote that it expresses not less, but probably more, than the truth.

c **1300** *St. Brandan* (Percy Soc.) 31 Ther thu schalt fourti dayes bileve atte meste. *c* **1374** CHAUCER *Troylus* v. 947 He spak y-now for o day at þe meste. **1453** in *Trevelyan Papers* (Camden) 25 If the chaplen dy, elec another honest man.. within foure monethis at the most. **1535** COVERDALE *Isa.* xxx. 17 A thousand of you shal fle for one, or at the most for fyue. **1662** J. DAVIES tr. *Olearius' Voy. Ambass.* 196 One degree of Longitude under the thirty seventh degree of Latitude,.. consists but of fifty minutes at the most. **1756** MRS. F. BROOKE *Old Maid* No. 30. 177 After these entered a tall child, at most but in her thirteenth year. **1885** *Law Times* LXXIX. 38/1 The duty of the magistrate should be at most ancillary to that of the doctor.

†**b. for the most.** For the most part. *Obs.*

c **1531** LATIMER in Strype *Eccl. Mem.* (1822) I. II. 177 Those other, for the most, teach nothing, but that whych ys manifest in the Scripture. **1603** SHAKS. *Meas. for M.* v. i. 445 They say best men are moulded out of faults, And for the most, become much more the better For being a little bad.

†**c. with the most.** In the utmost degree; in the greatest quantity; to the full. *Obs.*

c **1205** LAY. 2547 Ah Menbriz dude vnwreste he wes swike mid þan meste. **13..** *Guy Warw.* (A.) 274 Now is Gij in gret tempest Sorwe he makeþ wiþ þe mest [*MS. C.* Sorowe he maketh with the moste] Of Felice þat feir may. *a* **1440** *Sir Degrev.* 1404 Ther ware metus with the maste, I do ȝow to wytte. *a* **1586** SIR H. SIDNEY *Godly Let. to his son Philip*, Feed them well, and pay them with the most. **1628** GAULE *Pract. Theorists Panegyr.* 10 Our gratefull acknowledgement of his Goodnesse, when it is with the most; is but a slender requitall for his Benefits.

7. (Construed as *pl.*) The greatest number. Now usually without article; in early use *most* and *the most* were both common.

a. The most numerous part of an aggregate specified or implied; the majority. Const. *of*.

1470-85 MALORY *Arthur* II. i. 77 Moost of all the barons .. assayed alle by rewe but ther myght none spede. **1535** COVERDALE *Matt.* xi. 20 The cities, in the which most of his miracles were done. **1588** J. UDALL *Diotrephes* (Arb.) 12 The most of them woulde neuer deale in that lawe at home. **1611** SHAKS. *Wint. T.* IV. iv. 594 For she seemes a Mistresse To most that teach. **1635** J. HAYWARD tr. *Biondi's Banish'd Virg.* 173 Moste of the Fleete came lagging on by ones and two's. **1687** A. LOVELL tr. *Thevenot's Trav.* II. 32 Most of these Divans have large Windows. **1767** *Jrnl. Byron's Voy. round World* 10 The most of the priests are negroes. **1796** BURKE *Let. Noble Ld.* Wks. VIII. 63, I looked over a number of fine portraits, most of them of persons now dead. **1852** G. W. CURTIS *Wand. in Syria* 161 We found a spot less dreary than the most. **1875** JOWETT *Plato* (ed. 2) I. 9, I found a number of persons, most of whom I knew. **1882** STEVENSON *New Arab. Nts.* (1884) 30 The most of my patrons are boys.

b. = *most persons*: the majority of people.

1608 WILLET *Hexapla Exod.* 38 The most here doe vnderstand this signe. **1670** LADY MARY BERTIE in *12th Rep. Hist. MSS. Comm.* App. v. 21 Upon the Queene's Birthday most wore embraudered bodys. **1791** *Gentl. Mag.* 22/2 A gentleman.. who felt the infirmities of age at an earlier period than most do. **1833** HT. MARTINEAU *Charmed Sea* i, Her indifference was towards.. most who crossed her daily path. **1852** M. ARNOLD *Youth of Nature* 71 Sunk.. Too deep for the most to discern.

B. *adv.*

1. As a superlative of comparison: In the greatest degree; to the greatest extent.

a. qualifying a verb, a ppl. adj., or an adjectival or advb. phrase.

c **893** K. ÆLFRED *Oros.* I. iv. §1 þara nytena meolc þe hy mæst bi libbað. *a* **1200** *Moral Ode* 217 þe þe deþ is wille mest, he haueð wurst mede. *c* **1200** ORMIN 2595, & ȝho þatt cwemmde himm allre mæst Off all mannkinn onn eorþe. **1390** GOWER *Conf.* I. 238 Most of alle his herte is set.. upon these grete Offices. *a* **1450** MYRC *Festial* 24 For þat a man loueth most yn þys world, þat ys callet his god and his mawmet. **1537** WRIOTHESLEY *Chron.* (Camden) I. 104 The Bishopp of Rochester.. had occupied preachinge most at Pawles Crosse of any bishopp. *a* **1548** HALL *Chron.*, *Hen. VIII* 107 b, He.. thought it most for his honor & profite. **1624** CAPT. SMITH *Virginia* 3 The soyle is most plentifull, sweete,.. and fruitfull of all other. **1723** DK. WHARTON *True Briton* No. 26. I. 228 Their most obliged Creatures have shunn'd them most. **1790** BURNS *To Gentl. who sent a Newspaper* 3 How guess'd ye, sir, what maist I wanted? **1853** M. ARNOLD *Scholar-Gipsy* viii, For most, I know, thou lov'st retired ground!

b. Prefixed to an adj. or adv. to form the superl.

For the conditions under which the comparison with *more* and *most* is used, see MORE *adv.* 1 b, c.

c **1230** *Hali Meid.* (MS. Bodl.) I. 585 For þah he beo richest,.. þ e alre measte poure þe him to were cheoseð, is him wel icweme. **1390** GOWER *Conf.* I. 52 The moste principal of alle. *c* **1400** MAUNDEV. (1839) v. 56 This Weye is most schort. **1610** SHAKS. *Temp.* II. i. 227 Ebbing men, indeed (Most often) do so neere the bottome run By their owne feare, or sloth. **1613** PURCHAS *Pilgrimage* (1614) 283 Hee had some warres.. against the Christians, more vnnaturall against his brother, but most most vnnaturall and monstrous against his sonne Selym. **1617** MORYSON *Itin.* I. 146 The most sweete walke that ever I beheld. **1725** T. THOMAS in *Portland Papers* VI. (Hist. MSS. Comm.) 122 One of the Kirks most Commodious for its largeness. **1818** COLERIDGE *Lett.* (1895) 698 These lectures will be found by far the most interesting.. of any that I have yet delivered. **1892** *Bookman* Oct. 27/2 The most dogged of fighters, the most dangerous of enemies.

c. prefixed pleonastically to the superl. of the *adj.* or *adv.* Now only *poet.* exc. in illiterate use.

c **1400** MAUNDEV. (1839) xxvii. 279 The most fairest Damyselles that myghte be. **1535** [see HIGHEST B. 1]. **1586** A. DAY *Eng. Secretary* I. (1625) 40 The three battels.. by him in his most yongest yeares so miraculously foughten. **1683** PENN *Let. conc. Pennsylvania* 6 One of the most wretchedst Spectacles in the World. **1878** T. HARDY *Ret. Native* IV. vii, I was always first in the most gallantest scrapes in my younger days! **1881** E. H. HICKEY in *Macm. Mag.* XLIII. 236 My most extremest time of misery.

2. As an intensive superlative qualifying adjs. and advs.: In the greatest possible degree.

For the ceremonial titles, *Most Christian*, *Most Honourable*, *Most Noble*, *Most Reverend*, etc., see those adjs.

1508 DUNBAR *Poems* vii. 3 Most wyse, most valyeand, most laureat hie wictour. **1536** *Act 27 Hen. VIII*, c. 42 §1 The Kynges mooste Riall Magestie. **1559** ABP. PARKER *Corr.* (Parker Soc.) 70, I ought and do, acknowledge my most bound duty, to be a faithful orator for your grace during my life. **1602** SHAKS. *Ham.* I. v. 80 Oh horrible, Oh horrible, most horrible. **1631** in Ellis *Orig. Lett.* Ser. III. III. 205 To the King's most excellent Majesty. **1634** SIR T. HERBERT *Trav.* 183 The rinde or skin peeles off most easily. **1688** in Ellis *Orig. Lett.* Ser. III. III. 316, I am, S^r, your most affectionate friend and servant, Sunderland P. **1710** HEARNE *Collect.* (O.H.S.) II. 351 A most vile, stinking Whigg. **1775** JOHNSON *Let. to Earl Chesterfield* in *Boswell*, I am.. your lordship's most humble, most obedient servant. **1853** DICKENS *Let.* 21 Sept., Ever.. Most affectionately yours. **1879** BAIN *Higher Engl. Gram.* 150 His argument was most convincing.

†**3. a.** Mostly; for the most part. *Obs.*

a **1300** *Cursor M.* 2118 þis land lies mast vnto þe south þer þe blamen mast er cuth. **1451** CAPGRAVE *Life St. Aug.* (E.E.T.S.) 1/27 We rede of hym þat whan he cam to lerne dyuers sciens which were þan most in Greke tonge þat he hated þe Greke letteris and loued weel þe Latyn. **1523** FITZHERB. *Husb.* §21 They vse most to pul them [*i.e.* certain weeds] vppe with theyr handes. **1530** PALSGR. 598/1 Where kepeth he his resydence moste? **1605** BACON *Adv. Learn.* II. ii. §9 Although .. States are most collected into Monarchies. **1635** PAGITT *Christianogr.* I. ii. (1636) 72 Those that now inhabite Egypt, are most Moores. **1726** *Adv. Capt. R. Boyle* (1768) 107 As to the Nature of the Inhabitants, they are most of a tawny Complexion. *a* **1734** NORTH *Lives* (1826) III. 388 He took most to silence,.. yet, when he did speak, it was much to the purpose.

b. Qualifying *all*. (In this use the sense 'for the most part' passes into that of 'nearly': see ALMOST.) Similarly ***everich mest***, nearly every one. *Obs.*

a **1000-1130** [see ALMOST 1]. *a* **1200** *Moral Ode* 7 Mest al þet ich habbe idon bi-fealt to child-hade. *c* **1200** *Trin. Coll. Hom.* 181 Mast alle þe hund limen hersumieð þe onre wombe. *a* **1225** *Ancr. R.* 88 Euerich mest, haueð on olde cwene to ueden hire earen. *c* **1230** *Hali Meid.* 103 As gentille wimmen mest alle nu o worlde. **1627** SCLATER *Exp. 2 Thess.* iii. 12 (1629) 275 Wee are most all of Issachars Tribe: therefore vsually choose callings of greatest ease.

4. a. Almost, nearly. Now *dial.* and *U.S.*

It is doubtful whether this is not merely an aphetic form of *almost* (Sc. *amaist*); it is often written *'maist*, *'most*.

*a*1584 MONTGOMERIE *Cherrie & Slae* 243 Sum tyme I musit and maist gane mad. 1613–39 I. JONES in Leoni *Palladio's Archit.* (1742) II. 49 This Architrave returns the Cornice most to the solid of the Pilasters. 1621 LADY M. WROTH *Urania* 541 Her forehead was most couered with her Hat. 1775 in *Essex Inst. Hist. Coll.* (1877) XIII. 198 It is so long since I saw, or heard direct from you that I most forgit you. 1785 BURNS *Addr. Deil* xvi, Ye..gied the infant warld a shog, 'Maist ruin'd a'. 1800 *Farmers' Register* (Greensburgh, Pa.) 8 Nov. (Th.), And though he squeez'd me most to death, I could not help it, no, not I. 1803 *Port Folio* (Philad.) III. 97 (Th.), You know how it most makes you blind, in winter, to look on the snow. 1808 FORSYTH *Beauties Scotl.* V. 344 The distance of most three leagues. 1825 J. NEAL *Bro. Jonathan* I. 107 Most off the handle, some o' the tribe I guess. 1874 J. W. LONG *Amer. Wild-fowl Shooting* 151 You..wade out, most to the edge of the open water. 1883 'MARK TWAIN' *Life Miss.* iii. 26 Then they both got at it.., swelling round and round each other, and punching their fists most into each other's faces. 1901 MERWIN & WEBSTER *Calumet 'K'* i. 6, I 'most met my death climbing up just now. *a*1911 D. G. PHILLIPS *Susan Lenox* (1917) II. iv. 87 The street girls..they 'most starve. 1935 in Z. N. Hurston *Mules & Men* (1970) I. i. 26 He moved by jerks, and he had most no tail.

b. With *all*, *any*, *every*, etc.

1770 WASHINGTON *Diary* 25 Aug. (1925) I. 395 As the Tassels of most all the Corn..was entirely dry. 1775 J. ANDREWS *Let.* 11 Apr. in *Mass. Hist. Soc. Proc.* (1866) VIII. 403, I think it exceeds most every thing of the kind. 1834 C. A. DAVIS *Lett. J. Downing* 35 Most all these southern folks are good fellows. 1854 J. E. COOKE *Virginia Comedians* I. viii. 50 'Never argues with women!' adds Kate, 'as if he was not arguing with me all the time 'most!' 1855 THACKERAY *Newcomes* xxv, Most everybody's here. 1865 'MARK TWAIN' *Celebr. Jumping Frog* (1867) 10 He was lucky,..he most always come out winner. 1894 [see HELLGRAMITE]. 1897 KIPLING *Captains Courageous* i. 5 She's 'most always sick on the ocean. 1904 *Sun* (N.Y.) 16 Aug. 5 Most everybody in the Twelfth Ward was there. 1926 *Publishers' Weekly* 10 July 117 Most any bookbinder will be glad to tell you all about du Pont Fabrikoid. 1956 *Rev. Sci. Instrum.* XXVII. 961/2 If *K* > 1, which is most always the case, then [etc.]. 1964 W. B. HUIE *Hiroshima Pilot* ii. 15 By 1923 most every surviving Confederate veteran had 'been with Pickett'. 1968 *Wall Street Jrnl.* 28 Feb. 16/1 In most any organization, the man who succeeds a reformer faces the task of consolidating the reforms while smoothing feathers the reformer has ruffled. 1968 *Amer. N. & Q.* Mar. 108/1 A book which touches most all of the high spots for the jet set.

†**C.** *Comb.*: **mostwhat** *adv.*, for the most part (common in 17th c.); also quasi-*adj.*, the greater part of; **mostwhen** *adv.*, most frequently, on most occasions; **mostwhere** *adv.*, in most places.

*c*1175 *Lamb. Hom.* 137 þesne lehter habbeð mest hwat alle men. *a*1300 *Cursor M.* 14571 þe freindes þou has aurquar, We wat mast quat er þai þar. *a*1400 in Halliwell *Rara Math.* (1841) 56 A Tretis of Geometrie wherby you may knowe the heghte, depnes, and the brede of mostwhat erthely thynges. 1494 FABYAN *Chron.* v. cxxxvii. 123 The kynge kepte mooste what his paleys. 1562 J. HEYWOOD *Prov. & Epigr.* (1867) 164 Here and there sum: But most when and most where no sum doth cum. 1581 MULCASTER *Positions* i. (1887) 3 The parentes and freindes with whom I haue to deale, be most-what no latinistes. 1602 CAREW *Cornwall* 13 b, The Lord of the soyle is most where allowed libertie to place one workman in euerie fifteene for himself. 1681 H. MORE *Exp. Dan.* i. 5 That State..being most-what supported by the Supreme Power of their Two Consuls. 1737 in *N. & Q.* 8th Ser. (1895) VII. 405/1 This Month was mostwhat inclin'd to wet and very changable wether.

Hence †'**masthede** [-HEAD], supreme greatness, majesty; †'**mostness**, maximal size.

*a*1300 *E. E. Psalter* xxviii. 3 God of masthede þonnered he. 1674 N. FAIRFAX *Bulk & Selv.* 99 From the leastness and mostness, not from the things themselves, it is, that [etc.].

most, obs. form of MUST *sb.* and *v.*

-most (məʊst, məst), *suffix*, forming adjs. in the superlative degree (many of which are also used as advs.), is an altered form of OE. *-mest* (= Goth. *-umist*), a combination of two distinct OTeut. (and Indogermanic) superlative suffixes, *-mo-* (which occurs, e.g., in OE. *forma* first, *hindema* last, and in L. *prīmus* first), and *-isto-* -EST. Those OE. superlatives in *-mest* which either descend from OTeut., or are extensions of OTeut. superlatives in *-mo-*, are formed not on adjs. but on prepositional or demonstrative stems; examples are *æftemest* (see AFTERMOST), *formest* or *fyrmest* FOREMOST, *inmest* INMOST, *niðemest* lowest, *ufemest* or *yfemest* (see OVEMEST), *útmest* or *ýtmest* UTMOST, *ýmest* (= Goth. *auhumists*) highest; the only instance (among the words belonging to this primary group) of formation on an adj.-stem is *midmest* MIDMOST. On the analogy of these older words, the suffix *-mest* was in OE. used to form superlatives of several adjs. of local and temporal signification, as *lætmest*, *síðemest* latest, *éastmest*, *westmest* (also *westema*), *norðmest*, *súðmest*.

In late OE. the adjs. in *-mest* came to be regarded as compounds of *mǽst* MOST, as the frequent spelling *-mæst* shows. The subsequent history of the written form of the suffix coincides with that of the adj., exc. that the absence of stress led to the occasional retention of the spelling *-mest* (beside the quasi-etymological *-most*) down to the 16th c. In mod. English the formal pronunciation of the suffix is assimilated to that of the adj., though colloq. the normal pronunciation (məst) is usual.

As the superlatives in *-mest*, *-most* corresponded to comparatives in *-er*, analogy led to the insertion of *r* or *er* before the suffix: thus *aftemest* was in early ME. altered to *aftermest*, and *ovemest* was replaced by *overmost*. In the 15th and 16th c. the suffix *-most* (interpreted as identical with MOST *a.*) was added to many comparatives in *-er*, on the analogy of earlier adverbial formations in -MORE, as in *furthermost*, *hindermost*, *innermost*, *lowermost*, *outermost*, *uppermost*, *uttermost*.

In ME. and modern English, the suffix has been appended to certain positive adjs.; to sbs. used adjectively, as in *backmost*, *bottommost*, *topmost*; and to advs., as in *downmost*, *upmost*, *hithermost*.

The restriction of the application of the suffix to words denoting position in place, time, or serial order, which existed in OE., has almost universally been adhered to in the subsequent formations; the only exception, in a word that has obtained any degree of currency, is *bettermost*. The only other violations of the rule occur in mere nonce-words, as in the following quot.

*a*1618 SYLVESTER *Ded. Sonn.* i, *To Maidens Blush*, Accept a Heart which to Your Highnesse owes whole Hecatombs of Happy-most Desires.

mostache, -chium, -choe, obs. ff. MOUSTACHE.

mostar-de-velis, variant of MUSTERDEVILLERS.

moste, obs. form of MUST *sb.* and *v.*, MOIST *a.*

moster, var. MOISTURE *v.*

1567 MAPLET *Gr. Forest* 87 The cricket..He useth..to dig and bore in the harde Earth and mostered places.

moster, obs. form of MUSTER.

mostesa, -tese, obs. forms of MESTIZO.

mostest ('məʊstɪst), dial. and joc. var. MOST *a.* (*sb.*) and *adv.* Esp. ***the mostest***, the greatest amount or degree (of something).

Regarded by many users as a double or strengthened superlative.

1885 *Indianapolis Jrnl.* 15 Nov. 10/4 We set around the kitchen fire an' has the mostest fun. 1887 PARISH & SHAW *Dict. Kentish Dial.* 104 *Mostest*, farthest; greatest distance. 'The mostest that he's bin from home is 'bout eighteen miles.' 1892 E. TERRY *Let.* 4 July in *Ellen Terry & Bernard Shaw* (1931) 9 It's mostest kind to write to me so about my young friend. 1905 *Memphis* (Tenn.) *Commercial Appeal* 14 May II. 4/6 It is one of the favorite arguments of his detractors that General Nathan Bedford Forrest, the noted Confederate cavalry leader, was an illiterate man... One [story]..gives Gen. Forrest's answer to the question, 'How do you manage to win your battles?' 'Git thar fust with the mostest men,' is the reputed reply. 1909 M. DIVER *Candles in Wind* xxv. 360 'I'm her friend, Paul—just as much as you are...' 'No, I'm the mostest. She said so.' 1935 *Word Study* Oct. 2/2 One of their favorite games was called 'The Ten Mostest'. Each player would choose 30 words: 10 that he or she considered the most beautiful words, 10 funniest words, and 10 most descriptive words. 1940 C. BOOTHE *Europe in Spring* vii. 172 Norway of all countries was the kind of country which, if you 'got there fust with mostest men', you couldn't be got out of in a day or a year, perhaps ever. 1949 O. NASH *Versus* 68 K is for Keeler.. The fustest and mostest To hit where they ain't. 1958 *Daily Herald* 25 Mar. 5/7 Here's the hostess with the mostest... Her guests all agreed Sophia was pretty good..well, pretty, anyway. 1959 *Times* 14 Sept. 3/5 A great ambition to be there firstest with the mostest. 1960 *Time & Tide* 24 Dec. 1599/1 Eddie Byrnes..he's the mostest act on scope. 1971 *Engineering* Apr. 57 But we make the mostest. 1973 A. HUNTER *Gently French* vii. 64, I reckon you admire the mostest in anything.

most-favoured-nation: see FAVOURED *ppl. a.*[1]

mostic(k, obs. variant forms of MAULSTICK.

mostlings ('məʊstlɪŋz). *dial.* [f. MOST *a.* + -LING[2], -LINGS.] Mostly, for the most part; usually.

1855 ROBINSON *Whitby Gloss.* s.v., It's mostlings rainy now-a-days, I think. 1870 E. PEACOCK *Ralf Skirl.* I. 35 That greasy green coat ye mostlins wears. 1889 TENNYSON *Owd Roä* 38 But Dicky, the Ghoäst moästlins was nobbut a rat or a mouse.

mostly ('məʊstlɪ), *adv.* [f. MOST *a.* + -LY[2].]

1. For the most part; in the main.

1594 CAREW *Huarte's Exam. Wits* 42 Mostly he made complements of verses very well composed. 1627 W. SCLATER *Exp. 2 Thess.* (1629) 42 Our Religion is mostly talke and discourse. 1719 W. WOOD *Surv. Trade* 82 The Goods after they are manufactured are mostly sent Abroad. 1850 CARLYLE *Latter-d. Pamph.* vi. *Parliaments*, Twenty-seven millions mostly fools. 1904 H. BLACK *Pract. Self-Culture* iii. 77 A man whose mind has been mostly fallow ground will not easily take to the mental plough and hoe.

†**2.** In the greatest degree; to the greatest extent; most. *Obs.*

1691 *Emilianne's Observ. Journ. Naples* 311 Those Women who mostly frequent the Confessionals..become [etc.]. 1754 SHEBBEARE *Matrimony* (1766) I. 90 It [the epithet] was applied to those Things which were mostly esteemed. 1768 *Woman of Honor* I. 14 Children..being susceptible of any impressions,..mostly so of good ones.

mostour, obs. form of MOISTURE.

‖**mostra** ('mɒstrə). *Mus.* [It., a mark, indicator, vbl. sb. f. *mostrare* to show.] A 'direct'; a small mark at the end of a line indicating the note with which the next line begins.

1724 *Short Explic. For. Words Mus.*, *Mostra*, is a little Mark or Character in Musick. 1752 AVISON *Ess. Mus. Express.* 131, I have ventured to introduce a new musical character, namely, this Mostra (√) or Index. In mod. Dicts.

mostre, mostur, obs. ff. MUSTER *sb.* and *v.*

mostwhat, -when, -where: see MOST C.

mostyrdewyk: see MUSTERDEVILLERS.

†**mosy,** *sb. Obs.* A dish in cookery.

14.. in *Househ. Ord.* (1790) 460 Mosy for Soper in Somer. Take smale chekyns and chop hom [etc.].

mosy ('məʊzɪ), *a. Obs.* exc. *dial.* Also 5 **moosy,** 6 **moocie,** 7, 9 **mozy,** 9 **mosey, mosie, moosie, moozy, mouzy.** [ME. *mosy* (? OE. **mosiȝ*), f. *mos* MOSS *sb.*[1] + -Y. Cf. MOSSY *a.*, which is a later formation with the same elements.] Downy, hairy; = MOSSY *a.* 3 and 4.

1426 LYDG. *De Guil. Pilgr.* 13704 Pyled and seynt as any kaat, And moosy [*v.r.* mosy] heryd as a raat. 1559 ELYOT *Dict.* s.v. *Barba*, *Incipiens barba*..a younge moocie bearde. 1570 LEVINS *Manip.* 108/34 Mosy, *puber*. 1578 LYTE *Dodoens* II. lxxxviii. 267 Dictam, is..a hoate and sharp herbe..his leaues be..somewhat hoare or mosy with a certaine fine downe. 1615 CROOKE *Body of Man* 159 It is of a fungous or Mozy substance. *a*1825 FORBY *Voc. E. Anglia*, *Mozy*, shaggy; covered with hair. The clown, who shaves but once a week, is of course very mozy when he comes under the barber's hands.

Hence '**mosiness.**

1538 ELYOT *Dict.*, *Iulus*,..the mosynesse of the outwarde parte of fruites.. *Iuli*, be also the mosynesse or softe heares, whiche do growe on the beardes & visages of yong men, before that they be shauen.

†**mot**[1]. *Obs.* Also 6 **mote,** 6–7 **mott(e.** [a. F. *mot* word, saying, motto = Pr. *mot-z*, It. *motto* (see MOTTO):—popular L. **mottum*, altered form of earlier *muttum* (Lucilius) uttered sound, cogn. w. *muttīre*, *mūtīre* to murmur.]

1. A motto.

1586 FERNE *Blaz. Gentrie* II. 7 To what purpose the cote of a Gentleman is manteled and doubled, why some haue assumed motes or wordes, &c. 1593 SHAKS. *Lucr.* 830 Reproch is stampt in Colatinvs face, And Tarqvins eye maie read the mot a farre, 'How he in peace is wounded not in warre'. 1600 AGARD in *Hearne's Collect.* (1771) I. 261 As for motts, I am of that opynyon that they took theyre first beginninge from men's conceits of there being some speciall vertues in them; or from the etymologye of theyre own names. 1602 MARSTON *Ant. & Mel.* v. Wks. 1856 I. 55, I did send for you to drawe me a devise, an Imprezza, by Sinecdoche a Mott. 1659 HOWELL *Lexicon*, *Let. French Prov.*, When you have cast an eye upon this Letter which goeth stuff'd with all Proverbs, old Motts, and Adages.

2. A word.

*c*1645 HOWELL *Lett.* I. II. xv, I haue been long in the Survay of these [the United] Provinces..[and] will conclude with a mot or two of the people.

‖**mot**[2] (mo). [Fr.: see prec.] A witty saying.

[1631 BRATHWAIT *Eng. Gentlew.* 198 That Mot of the Athenians to Pompey the Great, Thou art so much a God, as thou acknowledgest thy selfe to be a man, was no ill saying.] 1813 JEFFREY *Contrib. Edin. Rev.* (1844) I. 345 Another *mot* of hers became an established canon at all the tables of Paris. 1861 DUTTON COOK *P. Foster's Dau.* vii, At length the day came when the Chevalier had uttered his last mot.

mot[3] (mɒt). *dial.* Also **motte;** and see MOTTY. [? a. F. *motte* hillock; also, 'a butt to shoot at' (Cotgr.).] A mark for players at quoits.

1847 in HALLIWELL. 1851 MAYHEW *Lond. Labour* Answ. to Corr. 2 Dec., In the Country the mark in Quoit playing is termed a 'motte'.

mot, var. MORT *sb.*[4], MOTTE.

mota, var. MOOTAH, MOOTER.

†'**motable,** *a. Obs.*[−0] [ad. late L. *mōtābilis* (Vulg. *Gen.* i. 21), f. L. *mōtāre*, freq. of *movēre* (ppl. stem *mōt-*) to MOVE.] (See quot.)

1656 BLOUNT *Glossogr.*, *Motable*..alwayes moving, still in motion.

motacil ('məʊtəsɪl). *rare.* [Anglicized form of next: cf. F. *motacille*.] A bird of the genus *Motacilla*, a wagtail.

1828–32 in WEBSTER.

‖**motacilla** (məʊtə'sɪlə). [L. *mōtacilla* wagtail, perh. f. *mōtāre* to keep moving; according to Varro so called 'quod semper movet caudam';

cf. the Eng. name.] A genus of birds, now restricted to the wagtails, but formerly of wider extent; a bird of this genus.

1752 J. HILL *Hist. Anim.* 505 The Motacilla, with a black breast. The common Wagtail. **1808** A. WILSON *Amer. Ornithol.* (1831) I. 256, I saw him..pursuing what I took to be a species of motacilla.

Hence **mota'cillid, -ine, -oid** *adjs.*, belonging to or resembling the family *Motacillidæ* or the sub-family *Motacillinæ*, of which the genus *Motacilla* is the type. (In recent Dicts.)

‖**motard** (mɔtar). [Fr.] A French motorcycle policeman.

1963 'B. ABRO' *July 14 Assassination* vi. 43 Two motards were by the door... They..kicked their machines into life. **1966** 'D. RUTHERFORD' *Black Leather Murders* xi. 223 They were stopped by a motor-cycle patrolman... The *motard* raised a white gloved hand to his equally white helmet in salute. **1972** D. LEES *Zodiac* 136 Two blue-shirted, crash-helmeted *motards* sitting on their bikes.

†**mo'tation.** [a. L. *mōtātiōn-em*, f. *mōtāre*: see MOTABLE *a.*] Frequent movement.

1721 BAILEY, *Motation*, an often moving to and fro.

motatorious (məʊtə'tɔərɪəs), *a.* [Formed as next + -OUS.] Vibratory, in constant motion; applied to the legs of some insects.

1826 KIRBY & SP. *Entomol.* xlvi. IV. 345 Motatorious (*Motatorii*). Legs, which when the insect is at rest, are in a perpetual vibratory motion.

motatory ('məʊtətərɪ), *a. Ent.* [ad. mod.L. *mōtātōrius*, f. L. *mōtātor*, agent-n. f. *mōtāre*: see MOTABLE.] = prec.

[**1818** KIRBY & SP. *Entomol.* xxiii. (ed. 2) II. 306 Long anterior legs..denominated *pedes motatorii* by Linné.] **1856** MAYNE *Expos. Lex.*, *Motatorius* [Kirby],..motatory.

motazilite (məʊ'tæzɪlaɪt), *sb.* and *a.* Also 8 **moatazalite,** 9 **motazelite, mutazalite.** [f. Arab. *muʿtazil* seceder (active pple. of *iʿtazala* to secede, 8th conj. of *ʿazala* to go) + -ITE.]

a. *sb.* A member of a heretical Muslim sect, which denied predestination and the possibility of assigning definite attributes to the Deity. **b.** *adj.* Of or pertaining to this sect.

1727–41 CHAMBERS *Cycl.*, *Moatazalites.* **1734** G. SALE tr. *Koran, Prel. Disc.* viii. 158 Wasel..and his followers being thenceforth called Motazalites or Separatists.

‖**mot d'ordre** (mo dɔrdr). [Fr. (MOT²), lit. 'word of command'.] A political slogan or watchword; an expression of policy; an oral directive or plan.

1855 *Newsp. & Gen. Reader's Compan.* I. §159 'A *mot d'ordre* was given by the Legitimist leaders of the fusion'; that is to say, A watchword, &c. **1878** L. W. M. LOCKHART *Mine is Thine* I. vii. 144 Another kind of success was to be procured by occasional fits of recalcitrancy against the *mots d'ordre* of the party. **1884** E. W. HAMILTON *Diary* 18 Nov. (1972) II. 735 The Tory Party held their meeting at the Carlton this morning; and *Pax* was the *mot d'ordre*, much to the discomfiture of the hot-headed ones. **1905** B'NESS ORCZY *Scarlet Pimpernel* xii. 119 Evidently expecting to meet their chief—and perhaps to get a fresh *mot d'ordre* from him. **1930** *Observer* 13 Apr. 17/5 The official *mot d'ordre* is that Mr. Gandhi's salt campaign must be treated with a sense of humour. **1947** *Ann. Reg. 1946* 217 The sustained Soviet offensive..against Great Britain and the United States had the appearance of conformity with a *mot d'ordre*.

mote (məʊt), *sb.*¹ Forms: 1–5 **mot,** 4 **moot,** 4–6 **moote,** 6 **moet, moit, motte,** 6–7 **moate,** (? **moth**), 6–8 **moat,** 7 **mothe, mott,** 9 (sense 3 b) **moit, moiet,** 4– **mote.** [OE. *mot* neut. (dat. *mote*), perh. cogn. w. Du. *mot* dust from turf, sawdust, grit (MDu. found only in combs. *steenmot, turfmot*), also fine rain, LG. (EFris.) *mut* dust, grit; connexion with SMUT is possible. With sense 3 b cf. Sp. *mota*, knot in cloth, which however is of uncertain origin.]

1. a. A particle of dust; esp. one of the innumerable minute specks seen floating in the sunbeam; an irritating particle in the eye or throat.

a mote in the eye: often *fig.* (*a*) with allusion to Matt. vii. 3, a relatively trifling fault observed in another person by one who ignores a greater fault of his own (cf. BEAM *sb.*¹ 3 c); †(*b*) a cause of irritation or annoyance.

c **1000** *Ags. Gosp.* Matt. vii. 3 To hwi ȝesihst þu þæt mot on þines broþer eȝan. *c* **1050** *Voc.* in Wr.-Wülcker 355/24 *Atomo*, mote. **1340** *Ayenb.* 175 Þet y-zyeþ þet mot ine þe oþres eȝe. *c* **1375** *Sc. Leg. Saints* xx. (*Blasius*) 345 Quhasa-euire in þare throt seknes has, awne ore mot [etc.]. *Ibid.* xxviii. (*Margaret*) 494 As motis ar in Sown-beme fare. **1481** CAXTON *Reynard* (Arb.) 84 What man loked in the glasse had he ony dissease of prickyng or motes smarte or perles in his eyen he shold be anon heled of it. **1513** DOUGLAS *Æneis, Direction* 66 Quhilk in myne E fast staris a moit to spy. **1546** BALE *1st Exam. Anne Askew* 21 b, Johan Frith is a great moate in their eyes. **1563** T. GALE *Antidot.* II. 8 Pouders.. made subtile and fyne lyke mootes of the sonne, as they call them. **1627** ABP. ABBOT in Rushw. *Hist. Coll.* (1659) I. 454 The first of these is Sir Dudley Diggs, a very great Mote in the Dukes Eye, as I am informed. **1632** MILTON *Penseroso* 8 As the gay motes that people the Sun Beams. **1789** W. BUCHAN *Dom. Med.* (1790) 259 Sometimes he imagines his eyes are full of motes. **1800** HELENA WELLS *Constantia Neville* (ed. 2) II. 243 He pretended to shew to his brethren the moat that he had discovered in their's. **1821** SHELLEY *Hellas* 781 All that it inherits Are motes of a sick eye, bubbles and dreams. **1880** W. WALLACE *Epicureanism* viii. 192 Moving freely about like the motes we see in the sunbeam.

b. A minute solid particle of foreign matter in food or drink. ? Now chiefly *dial.* †***to make no motes of***: not to scruple at.

c **1290** *S. Eng. Leg.* I. 284/204 And Ine blessede nouȝt mi drinke: and a swuch mot þare was Inne, And with þat drinke þat ich dronk: it schet me sone with-Inne. *c* **1460** J. RUSSELL *Bk. Nurture* 272 Ne put youre fyngurs in the cuppe mootes for to seche. **1816** SCOTT *Antiq.* xxiii, I ne'er noticed it afore, and it's nae sic mote neither but what ane might see it in their parritch. **1842** J. AITON *Domest. Econ.* (1857) 221 A corn sickle is then drawn through the butter several cross ways, in order to take out any hairs that may remain in it; and if any other motes appear, they are also taken out.

fig. **1637** RUTHERFORD *Lett.* (1664) 114, I speak it for your encouragement, that ye may make the best out of your joyes ye can, albeit ye finde them mixed with motes. **1637–50** Row *Hist. Kirk* (Wodrow Soc.) 422 Some made no motts of it to subscryve simplie and absolutelie. **1822** GALT *Sir A. Wylie* I. vii. 51 The ragged coat o' the callant was ne'er a mot in the man's marriage.

†**c.** A minute particle of anything, an atom; something very minute or trivial, a trifle. (***not***) ***a mote***: (not) a jot. *Obs.*

a **1300** *Body & Soul* 266 in *Map's Poems* (Camden) 343 That no mon cou nou fynden a mote Of hem, ne of mooder that hem bar. *c* **1374** CHAUCER *Troylus* III. 1554 (1603) It myghte nought a mot in þat suffise. *c* **1412** HOCCLEVE *De Reg. Princ.* 943 Nat wold I rekke as mochel as a mote. *c* **1550** BALE *K. Johan* 1826 Whie wert thu cast in preson?.. For conjurynge, calkynge, and coynynge of newe grotes, For clippynge of nobles, with such lyke pratye motes. **1611** BEAUM. & FL. *Maid's Trag.* II. i, Let me know the man that wrongs me so, That I may cut his body into motes. **1632** MASSINGER *City Madam* v. iii, I presume the sight Would move you to compassion. *Luke.* Not a mote. **1725** BRADLEY *Fam. Dict.* s.v. *Milk*, Where not the least Mote of any Filth may by any means appear.

†**d.** = ATOM *sb.* 2. *Obs.*

1580 SIR E. DYER *Prayse of Nothing* Poems (Grosart) 75 For whilst they traueyled (Curiositie being their guide) to find out in the numbers of Pythagorus the moets of Epicure [etc.]. **1601** HOLLAND *Pliny* II. 136 He saith that this diuersitie proceedeth from those little motes or bodies that go to the making of all things.

†**2.** A spot, a blemish. *Obs.*

13.. *E.E. Allit. P.* A. 763 For mote ne spot is non in þe. *c* **1485** *Digby Myst.* (1882) IV. 1329 In your conscience..is noȝt so great mot. **1530** PALSGR. 246/2 Mote on a gowne or garment, *povtie*. *c* **1586** C'TESS PEMBROKE *Ps.* LXIX. iii, Mote, nor spott, nor least disgrace, But for thee, could taint my face. **1599** SHAKS. *Hen. V*, IV. i. 189 Therefore should euery Souldier..wash euery Moth out of his Conscience. *a* **1711** KEN *Hymns Evang.* Poet. Wks. 1721 I. 71 In your bright souls endure no wilful Mote.

3. †**a.** A tuft of wool forming the nap on cloth. *Obs.*

1583 *Leg. Bp. St. Androis* 779 in *Satir. Poems Reform.*, To sponge his cloak durst not be done. It hurte the woole, and wrought it bair, Puld off the mottes, and did no mair.

b. An imperfection in wool or cotton.

1842 in J. S. BASSETT *Southern Plantation Overseer* (1925) 166 The gin dos not doo good work it draws too many motes through. **1851** *Catal. Gt. Exhib.* II. 490 Burry and motey wool, with the same cleaned from the burs and motes. **1879** *Cassell's Techn. Educ.* IV. 340/1 Many wools contain peculiar seeds called 'burrs' and 'moiets' very difficult to remove, as they are covered with prickles. **1902** W. HANNAN *Textile Fibres* 102 The fragmental portions of cotton seeds carry a tuft of attached fibres on the outer membrane; this is termed a bearded *mote*, and is regarded as an imperfection or impurity. **1903** F. M. LUPTON in *Eng. Dial. Dict.*, *Moit*, the seed of an Australasian plant, which clings to wool, and is unravelled by the scribbler, without being separated from the wool.

4. a. 'A single straw or a single stalk of hay; a part of a single straw; a slender twig' (E.D.D.). Now only *dial.*

1578 LYTE *Dodoens* IV. xiii. 467 Otes..in grassic leaues, and knottie strawe or motes, are somwhat like to wheate. **1747** GOULD *Eng. Ants* 69 The Hill Ants collect a vast Quantity of Pieces of dry Sticks, Chips, Straw-Motes, and other Rubbish. **1930** H. WILLIAMSON *Village Bk.* 328 It had looked like a sheaf of reed motts—the unbruised wheaten stalks used for thatching. **1959** *Times* 19 Aug. 9/7 The 'motts' (or stems) are carefully bumped together, butts down, before being tied in bundles for thatching.

b. *Mining.* (See quot. 1883.)

1881 in RAYMOND *Mining Gloss.* **1883** GRESLEY *Gloss. Coal Mining* 171 *Mote* or *Moat*, a straw filled with gun-powder for igniting a shot.

5. *Comb.* ***mote-laden, -like*** adjs.; **mote-knife,** a knife in a carding machine for removing motes from textile fibres.

1592 NASHE *Four Lett. Confut.* H 2, Thou impotent moate-catching carper. **1896** W. S. TAGGART *Cotton Spinning* I. 132 The cotton is no sooner taken from the feed than it is carried past one or two bars C and D with sharp edges, known as mote knives. **1951** S. SPENDER *World within World* iii. 123 The characters of his novels radiate round him under a glowing cloud of dirty varnish, not unlike the mote-laden lighting of Fräulein Thurau's apartment. **1956** H. GOLD *Man who was not with It* (1965) xii. 102 The mote-laden rays striking guide-rope and stand. *a* **1889** G. M. HOPKINS *Poems* (1967) 194 Swayed about Mote-like in thy mighty glow. **1929** W. FAULKNER *Sartoris* III. 168 It oozed chaff and a sifting dust, motelike in the sun.

mote (məʊt), *sb.*² *Obs.* exc. *Hist.* Forms: 3–7, 9 **mote,** 5, 8 **mot,** 9 *arch.* **moat(e.** [ME. *mote*, a. OF. *mote, motte* clod, hillock, mound, castle-hill, castle (mod.F. *motte* clod, mound), whence med.L. *mota, motta*, MDu. *mote* mound, castle-hill, castle; cf. Pr. *mota* (Levy) hill, castle, Sp. *mota* embankment, dam, Pg. *mota* terrace, rampart, dam; the It. *motta* (obs.) landslip, and *mota* mud, are commonly cited as cognate, but this is doubtful. See MOAT *sb.*¹, which seems to be orig. the same word.

The Rom. word is commonly supposed to be of Teut. origin; cf. Mid.Ger. *mot* moor, bog, HG. dial. *mott* peaty soil, peat, stack of peats (? cogn. w. Eng. MUD).]

1. a. A mound, eminence, hill, esp. as the seat of a camp, city, castle, fort, or other building; also, an embankment. Cf. MOTTE *sb.*²

a **1272** *Luue Ron* 121 in *O.E. Misc.* 97 Hit stont vppon a treowe mote þar hit neuer truke ne schal. *c* **1330** R. BRUNNE *Chron.* (1810) 165 Doun of the kastelle mote Isaac douhter cam, & felle R. to fote gretand. **1419** in *Surtees Misc.* (1888) 14 That nane entir..to defoule the walles na the motes, bot thay that has taken tham to ferme, the whilke sall kytte the herbage that grewys apon the mote. **1533** BELLENDEN *Livy* v. xvii. (S.T.S.) II. 206 Ane litill mote [L. *editus locus*] in quhilk was laid ane buschement full of armit men. *c* **1630** RISDON *Surv. Devon* §225 (1810) 241 Above the clifts appear the banks and motes rudely cast up, called *Clovelly Dikes*. **1768** ROSS *Helenore* III. 116 Frae aff a rising mot, He cry'd to stop, an' crying stampt the ground, Until the hillock gae a trembling sound. **1884** G. T. CLARK *Mediæval Military Archit. in England* I. ii. 27 Many of these mounds under the name of motes (motæ) retained their timber defences to the twelfth and thirteenth centuries. **1898** D. CHRISTISON *Early Fortifications Scotl.* I. i. 3 The motes of which I have to speak are..fortresses..and consist essentially of conical flat-topped mounds, which were defended by palisades. **1919** *Proc. Soc. Antiquaries Scotl.* LIII. 43 Alexander Elphinstone in 1507 took up his residence upon the old deserted Norman mote.

†**b.** *poet.* A castle, fortress; a city. *Obs.*

13.. *E.E. Allit. P.* A. 936 Þat mote þou menez in Iudy londe, Þat is þe cite þat [etc.]. **13..** *Gaw. & Gr. Knt.* 635 Voyded of vche vylany, wyth vertuez ennourned in mote. *a* **1400** *Min. Poems fr. Vernon MS.* 489/173 Boþe þe Mot and þe molde Schon al on red golde.

2. A barrow, tumulus.

1513 DOUGLAS *Æneis* VII. i. 13 Enee..Apon the sepulture, as custum was and gise, An hepe of erd and litle mote gart wpraise. **1724** *Macfarlane's Geog. Collect.* (S.H.S. 1906) I. 8 Hard by this Church..stands a remarkable artificial Mote or little hill rising up like a Piramide. **1886** G. T. STOKES *Irel. & Celtic Ch.* (1888) 72 The interior chamber of the New Grange Moat.

3. *Comb.*, as **mote-castle** = *motte-castle* (MOTTE *sb.*² 2).

1919 *Proc. Soc. Antiquaries Scotl.* LIII. 42 Such a fortress is well represented in the mote-castles of Dinan, Hastings and Rennes, in the Bayeux tapestry.

mote, *sb.*³ *Hunting. Obs.* exc. *arch.* Forms: 4 **moot,** 4–6 **mote,** 4, 7 **mot,** 5 ? **motye,** 6 **mott,** 8–9 *arch.* **moot,** 9 *arch.* **mot.** [a. F. *mot* (see MOT¹), similarly used in French hunting.] A note of a horn or bugle.

13.. *Gaw. & Gr. Knt.* 1364 Baldely þay blw prys.. Strakande ful stoutly mony stif motez. *c* **1369** CHAUCER *Dethe Blaunche* 376 The mayster hunte..With his horne blewe thre mote At the vncouplynge of his houndes. **1470–85** MALORY *Arthur* VII. viii. 223 There he blewe thre dedely motys. **15..** *Chevy Chace* 16 in Wright *Songs & Ballads* (1860) 24 The blwe a mot uppone the bent. **1575** TURBERV. *Venerie* 86 Blowyng two motts with his horne to call in his fellowes and to cause the reste of the kenell to approche. **1819** SCOTT *Ivanhoe* xli, Three mots on this bugle will..bring round..a jolly band of yonder honest yeomen.

†**mote,** *sb.*⁴ *Astr. Obs.* [ad. L. *mōtus* (*u* stem), f. *mō-, movēre* to MOVE.] Motion (of a heavenly body).

c **1391** CHAUCER *Astrol.* II. §44 That thou findest in directe wryte in thy slate under thy rote, and adde hit to-geder, and that is thy mene mote. **1535** STEWART *Cron. Scot.* (Rolls) I. 89 [The sun's] proper muyn and his mot raptyue. **1839** BAILEY *Festus* xix. (1852) 299 As motion in an atom leads at last To a world's orbit—mote and motion given.

†**mote,** *sb.*⁵ *Gardening. Obs.* [a. F. *motte* (†*mote*) clod.] The soil clinging to the roots of a plant.

1693 EVELYN *De La Quint. Compl. Gard.* II. 61 Not that the Water of Rains often penetrates the Body of the Mote.

mote (məʊt), *sb.*⁶ (See quots.)

1858 SIMMONDS *Dict. Trade*, *Mote*,..a name for the nut of the *Carapa guineensis*, used for extracting oil in Sierra-Leone. **1887** BENTLEY *Man. Bot.* (ed. 5) 508 An oil of a similar nature is also obtained from *Carapa Touloucouna*; it has been imported under the name of mote-grease.

mote (məʊt), *v.*¹ *arch.* Forms: α. 1 **mót** (*pl.* **móton,** *subj.* **móte,** *pl.* **móten**), 2–9 **mot** (2–5 *pl.* **mote(n,** 2–4 *subj. sing.* **mote**), 4–5 **moot(e, mut,** 5 **mowte, mutt,** 5–6 **mott(e,** 6 **moit,** (**mothe**), 6–7 **mought,** 6, 8 *Sc.* **mat,** 4– **mote;** β. *2nd sing.* 1 **móst,** 2–5 **most,** 4–5 **moste,** 4 **must.** [A WGer. and Gothic preterite-present verb (wanting in Scandinavian): OE. *mót* corresp. to OFris. *môt*, OS. *môt, muot* may, must (Du. *moet* must), OHG., MHG. *muoz* may, must (mod.G. *muss* must), Goth. *ga-mōt* (it) has room, related to OHG. *muoza* (mod.G. *musse*) leisure:—OTeut. type **mōtā*.

The primary sense seems to be that preserved in Gothic, from which the sense 'is permitted, may' can easily have been developed. The transition from this to the sense 'is obliged, must' is more difficult to explain; it may have arisen

from the use in negative contexts, where the two senses ('may not', 'must not') are nearly coincident. Normally, OTeut. **mōt* should be the perfect of a verb **mat-*, but there is no trace of a vb. of this form with a suitable sense; the word may be related to **met-* to measure (see METE *v.*).

If the verb had come down to mod. English, its form would have been *moot*. Exc. in northern dialects, it seems not to have survived in colloquial use beyond the 15th c., or at latest the middle of the 16th c. In the 16th c. it was often confused with *mought* (see MAY *v.*), with which it was prob. identical in sound. In the early part of the 16th c., the verb was still used correctly as a present tense, though commonly misspelt *mought*. In the archaistic use of Spenser and later writers, on the other hand, it is, even when written *mote*, almost always a preterite except in traditional phrases.

The pa. t. (OE. *móste*) is treated under MUST. The survival of the inflected 2nd person (OE. *móst*) is doubtful after the early part of the 15th c., on account of its formal coincidence with the pa. t., which by that time had already assumed the function of a present.]

1. Expressing permission or possibility; = MAY.

†In early use sometimes with ellipsis of a verb of motion.

Beowulf 347 ȝif he us ȝeunnan wile, þæt we hine swa godne gretan moton. *a* **1000** *Cædmon's Gen.* 2473 (Gr.) Onfoð þæm fæmnum, lætað frið agon ȝistas mine, þa ic for gode wille ȝemundbyrdan, ȝif ic mot, for eow! *c* **1200** ORMIN 1266 ȝif þu..ȝeornesst tatt tu mote skët Uppcumenn inntill heoffne. *a* **1300** *X Commandm.* 2 in *E.E.P.* (1862) 15 ȝif vs grace to wirch workis gode to heuen þat we mot enter inn. *c* **1385** CHAUCER *L.G.W.* 903 (*Thisbe*) We preyen ȝow.. That in on graue that we motyn lye. **1390** GOWER *Conf.* I. 6 God grante I mot it wel achieve. **1437** *Libel Eng. Policy* in *Pol. Poems* (Rolls) II. 188, I beseche God that some prayers devoute Mutt lett the seyde apparaunce probable Thys disposed wythought feyned fable. **1562** WINȜET *Cert. Tractatis* i. Wks. (S.T.S.) I. 10 To the intent that all errour and abuse being cuttit away, we al on baith sydis mot knaw the veritie. **1596** SPENSER *F.Q.* VI. viii. 46 Now mote ye understand that [etc.]. **1812** BYRON *Ch. Har.* I. i, Nor mote my shell awake the weary Nine To grace so plain a tale.

β. *Beowulf* 1671 Ic hit þe þonne ȝehate þæt þu on Heorote most sorhleas swefan.

¶**b.** Used as pa. t. (ind. or subj.) = *might, could.*

c **1440** *Alphabet of Tales* 93 He was so strang in his selfe, þat he mott withstond any temptacion of þe devull. **1596** SPENSER *F.Q.* IV. ii. 8 Therefore he her did court, did serve, did wooe, With humblest suit that he imagine mot. **1600** FAIRFAX *Tasso* III. xiii, Within the postern stood Argantes stout To rescue her, if ill mote her betide. **1763–5** CHURCHILL *Prophecy of Fam.* Poems 1769 I. 116 And from that day Mote never Sawny tune the merry lay.

c. In wishes, forming a periphrastic subjunctive; = MAY. Often in asseverative phrases, ***so mote I thee, so mote I go***, etc.

c **1275** *Passion Our Lord* 71 in *O.E. Misc.* 39 Iblessed hi seyde mote he beo þe cumeþ on godes nome. *a* **1300** *Cursor M.* 5150 'Sais þou soth?' 'yaa, sa mot i the'. *c* **1386** CHAUCER *Frankl. T.* 49 Lerneth to suffre or elles so moot I goon Ye shul it lerne. **1471** MARG. PASTON in *P. Lett.* III. 25 Goddes blissyng and myn mut ye have both. *a* **1518** SKELTON *Magnyf.* 2072 Ye, mary, is it, ye, so mote I goo. **1533** MORE *Apol.* 158 The kynge our souerayne lorde that now is and longe mote be, hath [etc.]. **1546** *Primer Hen. VIII* 72 Our sin forgive, Lord gratious, And our darknes mought lightened be. **1573** *Satir. Poems Reform.* xxxix. 271 Long moit thir countreis leue in pace togidder. **1586** FERNE *Blaz. Gentrie* 22 All is too litile for himzelfe and our yong maisters his zon full ill mought they both thee. **1590** SPENSER *F.Q.* II. i. 33 Well mote yee thee, as well can wish your thought. **1595** DUNCAN *App. Etymol.* (E.D.S.) 71 *Meherclе, hercle*; so Hercules mot be my helpe. **1598** R. BERNARD tr. *Terence, Heauton.* v. iv. 261 So mought thou liue after me and my husband Chremes, as thou art his and mine. **1775** W. PRESTON *Illustr. Masonry* (1781) 37 *Amen.* So mote it be. *a* **1800** *Sang Outlaw Murray* xix. in Scott *Minstr. Scott. Bord.* (1869) 62 God mot thee save, brave Outlaw Murray.

β. *c* **1374** CHAUCER *To Scriv.* 3 Adam scryveyne if euer it þee byfalle Boece or Troylus to wryten nuwe Vnder þy long lokkes þowe most haue þe scalle But affter my makyng þowe wryte more truwe.

2. Expressing necessity or obligation: = MUST.

In early use sometimes with ellipsis of verb, esp. of a verb of motion.

Beowulf 2886 Londrihtes mot þære mægburȝe monna æghwylc idel hweorfan. *c* **1200** *Trin. Coll. Hom.* 19 And þarto moten fif þing to bileuen in god. *c* **1205** LAY. 1051 Ah heo mot nede beien þe mon þe ibunden bið. *a* **1225** *Ancr. R.* 64, & hwon ȝe alles moten uorð, creoiseð ful ȝeorne our muð, earen, & eien. **1377** LANGL. *P. Pl.* B. XIII. 261 For ar I haue bred of mele ofte mote I swete. *c* **1386** CHAUCER *Man of Law's T.* 196 Bot forth she moot wher so she wepe or synge. *a* **1450** *Ibid.* 11587 (Laud MS.) Ye mote nedis [*MS. Cotton* For yow behoues] alle thre Into Egipt lond fle. **1470–85** MALORY *Arthur* I. xxi. 67, I merueylle moche of thy wordes that I mote dye in bataille. **1579** SPENSER *Sheph. Cal.* vii. 154 But shepheard mought be meeke and mylde, Well-eyed, as Argus was.

β. *a* **1225** *Ancr. R.* 102 Cheos nu þu on of þeos two; vor þet oðer þu most leten. *c* **1386** CHAUCER *Man of Law's Prol.* 6 Maugree thyn heed thou most for Indigence Or stele, or begge, or borwe thy despence. *a* **1450** MYRC 14 ȝef thou plese thy sauyoure, ȝef thow be not grete clerk, Loke thow moste on thys werk.

¶**b.** Incorrectly used as pa. t.

1596 SPENSER *F.Q.* v. viii. 5 However loth he were his way to slake, Yet mote he algates now abide, and answere make. **1685** H. MORE *Paralip. Prophet.* xiv. 115 Sith he mought needs sail by Judaea.

mote (məʊt), *v.*[2] Also (sense 2) 7 moat, 9 moit. [f. MOTE *sb.*[1]]

†**1.** *intr.* ? To pick motes, to find fault. *Obs. rare*[−1].

1513 DOUGLAS *Æneis, Exclam. aganis Detractouris* 28 Far eithar is, quha list syt doun to mote, Ane othir sayaris faltis to spy and note.

2. *trans.* To remove motes from wool.

1681, 1876 [see vbl. sb. below].

3. *intr.* Of wool: To show or form motes.

1880 *MS. Cotton Rep. U.S. Census*, The lint rating about the same from old or fresh land, the former motes worse in ginning.

Hence **'moting** *vbl. sb.* (also *attrib.*). Also **'moter**, a workman who removes motes from wool.

1681 in *New Mills Cloth Manuf.* (S.H.S.) Introd. 86 The refuse and losse upon moating and scouring of the Spanish wooll. **1843** *Penny Cycl.* XXVII. 551/2 Such are afterwards picked out by boys or women, called 'wool-moaters', or 'wool-pickers'. **1876** W. CUDWORTH *Round about Bradford* 373 Extensive premises..containing willeying, moiting,.. and condensing machinery. **1881** *Instr. Census Clerks* (1885) 64 Woollen cloth manufacture... Moater.

mote (məʊt), *v.*[3] *colloq.* [Back-formation from MOTOR.] *intr.* To drive, or ride in, a motor car. Hence **'moting** *vbl. sb.*

1890 *Prospectus of 'Gen. Electric Power & Traction' Co.* June, This practical demonstration of 'Moting' is likely to prove very attractive. **1898** *Westm. Gaz.* 18 Jan. 4/1 Leaving London about midday we shall mote to Ascot.

mote obs. f. MOAT, MOOT, MOT, MOTH.

'moted, *a.* [f. MOTE *sb.*[1] + -ED[2].] Full of motes.

1821 BYRON *Foscari* III. i. 101 Those moted rays of light Peopled with dusty atoms.

'mote-hill. *Antiq.* Also 7 mott hill, 9 moat hill. = MOTE *sb.*[2] 1. (Cf. MOOT-HILL.)

c **1682** J. OCHTERLONY *Acc. Forfar* in *Spottisw. Misc.* (1844) I. 328 Dundie Law is at the back thereof, ane exceeding high mott hill. **1805** SCOTT *Last Minstr.* I. xxv, Dimly he view'd the Moat-hills mound, Where Druid shades still flitted round. **1851** D. WILSON *Preh. Ann.* (1863) II. III. iii. 87 Of the aboriginal strongholds we have the Mote-hill or earthen mound, steeply escarped.

motel (məʊ'tɛl). [f. MOT(OR *sb.* and *a.* + HOT)EL *sb.*] A hotel catering primarily for motorists, *spec.* one comprising self-contained accommodation with adjacent parking space. Also *attrib.* and *Comb.*

1925 *Hotel Monthly* Mar. 37/2 The Milestone Interstate Corporation..proposes to build and operate a chain of motor hotels between San Diego and Seattle, the hotels to have the name 'Motel'. **1931** *Sociology & Social Research* XV. 372 The new kind of cottage hotel (e.g., 'Motel'), luxuriously furnished and served like any other hotel, but placed directly on the highway. **1947** A. HUXLEY *Let.* 14 Nov. (1969) 575 From the Blue Bird Motel in Little Rock, Ark, where we have been held up by torrential rains, I take this opportunity of telling you how grateful we all are. **1950** *Archit. Rev.* CVIII. 394 The motel is a new kind of hotel; like an hotel it has an attached restaurant and various services that earlier and more primitive sorts of roadside hostelries omit. **1955** *Times* 28 June 5/7 Although the 'motel' is still regarded as a novelty in the United Kingdom, an establishment of that kind was opened (and is still operating) at Boroughbridge..some time before the war. **1958** *Times* 24 Nov. (Canada Suppl.) p. viii/6 He has almost no contact with..the motel employees. *Ibid.* p. viii/7 The motel business is a field for individual..enterprise. **1962** *Listener* 25 Oct. 692/3 The vast motel-resort..now in the process of erection outside Seoul. **1970** *Homes & Gardens* June 150/1 In a motel the car is meant to be beside your room, but is not invariably. **1970** *New Yorker* 10 Oct. 141/1 A motelkeeper..was serving our breakfast. **1974** *Washington Post* 11 May E23/1 The oldest motel in America is alive and well..in San Luis Obispo, Calif. *Ibid.*, The establishment..opened Dec. 12, 1925, as the Motel Inn.

Hence **mo'tel** *v. intr.*, to stay at a motel; **mo'telland** (*nonce-wd.*), the realm of motels; **mo'telier**, the owner of a motel; **mo'telled** *a.*, provided with motels.

1959 *Guardian* 6 Nov. 8/3 He, the over-fastidious European, is dragged by her through the appalling delights of motelland. **1959** S. H. COURTIER *Death in Dream Time* i. 5 A *motelier's* aspirations. **1963** *Economist* 17 Aug. 595/1 The conventional hotel trade from whose custom, as American moteliers..have found out, the growth must be drawn. **1965** *Punch* 1 Dec. 798/1, I drove through twenty-seven states with a freedom and foot-loose mobility unknown in a nation so thinly motelled as Britain. **1968** G. DE FRAGA *Murder at Cookout* xii. 56 They're motelling in Canberra for a night or two. **1972** *Sydney Morning Herald* 26 Aug. 37/3 Tasmanian motelier Four Seasons Motels Ltd increased profit by 14 per cent.

motele, moteley, obs. forms of MOTLEY.

moteless ('məʊtlɪs), *a.* [f. MOTE *sb.*[1] + -LESS.]

†**1.** Without blemish, spotless. *Obs.*

13.. *E. E. Allit. P.* A. 898 þat moteles meyny. **1648** EARL OF WESTMORLAND *Otia Sacra* 46 (*My Looking-glass*) For if thou shouldst like to thy self, rubb'd ore, Give All for Moteless that comes Thee before.

2. Free from motes or minute dust-particles.

1876 *City-Road Mag.* 141/1 When the air was rendered moteless. **1880** W. S. KENT *Infusoria* I. 127 Those pure and moteless optic conditions of the atmosphere. **1882** *American* 19 Aug. 298/2 In this moteless air were placed test-tubes containing various organic infusions. **1890** TYNDALL in *Fortn. Rev.* 1 Jan. 7 Into one of these rooms, which was stocked with my moteless chambers, I took Mr. Carlyle. **1932** [see *beam-blindness*].

'moteling. *rare.* [f. MOTE *sb.*[1] + -LING.] A little mote; something very small.

1605 SYLVESTER *Du Bartas* II. iii. I. *Vocation* 335 A cloud of Moatlings hums Above our heads. *a* **1618** —— tr. *Pibrac* Wks. (Grosart) II. 24/1 It is a moatling hatcht of th' Unity. **1824** LAMB. *Lett. to Hood* in E. V. Lucas *Life* II. 130, I wash my hands in fishets that come through the pump every morning thick as motelings.

motely, obs. form of MOTLEY.

moten, obs. pa. pple. of METE *v.*[1]

moten(e, obs. forms of MUTTON.

moter: see MOTE *v.*[2]; obs. form of MOTOR *sb.*

moteryl, variant of MORTREL *Obs.*

motet (məʊ'tɛt). *Mus.* Forms: 4–5 **motete**, 5 **motide**, 7 **mottet(t**, 7–9 **motette**, 4– **motet**. See also MOTTETTO. [a. F. *motet* (13th c. in Hatz.-Darm.), dim. of *mot* word (see MOT). Cf. med.L. *motetum*, Sp. *motete*, It. *mottetto.*] †**a.** A melody. *Obs.* **b.** A vocal composition in harmony, set usually to words from Scripture, intended for church use.

c **1380** WYCLIF *Wks.* (1880) 91 þei don not here sacrifices bi mekenesse of herte..but wiþ knackynge of newe song, as orgen or deschant & motetis of holouris. *c* **1430** LYDG. *Min. Poems* (Percy Soc.) 242 The amerous fowlys with motetys and carollys, Salwe that sesoun every morwenyng. **1483** *Cath. Angl.* 244/1 Motide of musyk, *modulus.* **1597** MORLEY *Introd. Mus.* 179 A Motet is properlie a song made for the church, either vpon some hymne or Antheme, or such like. **1664** PEPYS *Diary* 4 Sept., The boy and I again to the singing of Mr. Porter's mottets. **1763** J. BROWN *Poetry & Mus.* xii. 208 The Admission of Hymns or Motets as a Part of divine Service. **1875** OUSELEY *Mus. Form* xii. 57 Many of the Motetts of Haydn and Mozart are written strictly in the modern binary form.

motetto, obs. form of MOTTETTO.

†**motewoke,** *a. Obs.*[−0] Forms: see quot. [f. **mōt* (? Scandinavian: cf. MSw. *māt, māta*, mod.Sw. *mått* measure, Icel. *mát* moderation) + *wōk*:—OE. *wác* soft: see WEAK *a.*] Moderately soft.

c **1440** *Promp. Parv.* 345/1 Mothe woke, neyder to nesche, ne to harde (*H.* moothewyc, or mothwoc, neþer to neysch, ne to hard, *S.* motewoke, *P.* mothwyc, or mothwoc), *dimollis. Ibid.* 430/2 Rere, or motewoke (*S.* mothewoke).

†**'motey,** *sb. Obs.* ? Some pigment.

1426–7 *Rec. St. Mary at Hill* (1905) 66 Also for vj dischis cole & xij lb moty..x d. **1446–7** in Willis & Clark *Cambridge* (1886) I. 395 Et in empcione .x. dd motey pro superornacione caminorum..iijs. **1510** *Ibid.* II. 199 Mastyke vernysch yelowe moty orpment vermylyon.

motey ('məʊtɪ), *a.* Also 8 motie, 9 moatie, moity. [f. MOTE *sb.*[1] + -Y. Cf. MOTTY.]

1. Full of tiny particles; full of specks, spotty.

a **1758** RAMSAY *Highland Lassie* ii, [Lasses] wha mak their cheeks with patches motie. **1893** R. BRIDGES *Shorter Poems* v. *Winnowers* 21 The sunbeams on the motey air Streamed through the open door.

2. Of wool: Full of small hard pieces.

1851 [see MOTE *sb.*[1]]. **1878** *Yorkshireman* Aug. 93 (E.D.D.) A splendid lot [of wool].., not moity, and free from burr.

moth (mɒθ), *sb.*[1] Forms: 1 **moþþe**, *Northumb.* **mohðe, mohða**, 2 **moȝðe**, 2–3 **mohþe**, 4 **moghe, moȝhe, moȝte, moththe, mouȝthe, mouthe, mowȝhe**, 4–5 **motthe, moþþe, moughte, mouȝte**, 5 **moghte, mote, mougthe, mowght(e**, 5–6 **mought**, 5–7 **mothe**, 6 **moght, mowthe**, 6–7 **moath**, 6– **moth**. Also *Sc.* MOCH *sb.* [OE. *moþþe, mohðe* wk. fem., corresponds to MDu. *motte* (mod.Du. *mot* fem.), late MHG. and mod.G. *motte* fem. (? from LG.), ON. *motte* wk. masc. (Sw., Norw. *mott* maggot, weevil).

The phonology is obscure. The word has usually been supposed to be cogn. w. OE. *maða* maggot (see MATHE), which is plausible as regards the sense; but the OE. form *mohð e* points rather to the Teut. root **mug-* as in MIDGE.]

1. a. A small nocturnal lepidopterous insect of the genus *Tinea*, which breeds in cloth, furs, etc., on which its larva feeds; a clothes-moth. In early use, the name seems to have been applied rather to the larva than to the insect itself. From the 16th c. it has been taken to denote primarily the insect in its winged state, and applied to any nocturnal lepidopterous insect of similar appearance.

†*false moth* (tr. mod.L. *pseudo-tinea*, Réaumur): an insect closely resembling the clothes-moth, but feeding on leaves.

c **950** *Lindisf. Gosp.* Matt. vi. 20 Ðer ne hrust ne ec mohðe ȝespilles. *c* **1000** *Ags. Gosp.* Luke xii. 33 þyder ðeof ne ȝenealæcð ne ne (*sic*) moððe [*c* **1160** *Hatton* moȝðe] ne ȝewemð. *c* **1230** *Hali Meid.* 29 Mohðe fret te claðes & cwalm slað þat ahte. **1340** HAMPOLE *Pr. Consc.* 5572 And wormes and moghes on þe same manere, þat in þair clathes has bred here. **1398** TREVISA *Barth. De P.R.* XVIII. cv. (1495) 849 A moughte hyght Tinea and is a worme of clothes. *c* **1412** HOCCLEVE *De Reg. Princ.* 225 As motthes to a cloþe annoyen, And of his wolle maken it al bare. *c* **1440** *Promp. Parv.* 346/1 Mowȝte, clothe wyrme (*K.* mowhe, *S.* mow, *P.* mowghe), *tinea. c* **1520** ANDREW *Noble Lyfe* III. xvi, The Asshes of hym is gode to make white tethe & to kepe the motes out of the clothes. **1534** *Inv. Wardr. Kath. Arragon* in *Camden Misc.* (1855) 30 Oone counterpoynte..sore perisshid withe mowthis. *a* **1586** SIDNEY *Ps.* VI. vi, Woe, lyke a moth, my face's beauty eates. **1626** BACON *Sylva* §696 The Moath breedeth upon Cloth;..It delighteth to be about the Flame of a Candle. **1683** SOAME & DRYDEN tr. *Boileau's Art Poetry*

III. 48 Neglected heaps we in by-corners lay, Where they become to Worms and Moths a prey. **1755** Johnson, *Moth*, a small winged insect that eats cloths and hangings. **1763** Mills *Syst. Pract. Husb.* III. 53 False Moth. **1857** Mrs. Carlyle *Lett.* (1883) II. 313 She let the moths get into my fur last year.

b. *fig.* Something that eats away, gnaws or wastes gradually and silently. Now *rare*.

1577 Whetstone *Life Gascoigne* xxvi, The valiant man, so playes a pleasant parte: When mothes of mone, doo gnaw vppon his hart. **1605** Bacon *Adv. Learn.* II. ii. §4 The Corruptions and Mothes of Historie, which are Epitomes. *c* **1680** Beveridge *Serm.* (1729) I. 535 That which ye have unlawfully gotten..will be a moth in your estates, which will..eat them up. **1861** Dora Greenwell *Poems* 208 This garment old And fretted by the moth Thy love hath borne Upon Thee.

c. in allusion to the insignificance or fragility of the moth, or to its liability to be attracted by the flame of a candle to its own destruction.

1596 Shaks. *Merch. V.* II. ix. 79 Thus hath the candle sing'd the moath. **1613** Chamberlain in *Court & Times Jas. I* (1848) I. 264 But you had not need meet with many such poor moths as Master Pory, who must have both meat and money. **1784** Cowper *Task* VI. 211 So man, the moth, is not afraid, it seems, To span Omnipotence. **1866** Ruskin in Collingwood *Life* (1893) II. 63 We don't deserve either such blessing or cursing, it seems to poor moth me.

†**d.** Applied vaguely to various kinds of animal parasites or 'vermin', as lice, bugs, cockroaches.

c **1460** J. Russell *Bk. Nurture* 280 Ne youre heere ye stryke, ne pyke to pralle for a flesche mought. **1578** Lyte *Dodoens* II. xxxvii. 196 This herbe dryueth away and killeth the stinking wormes or Mothes called Cimici. **1658** Rowland tr. *Moufet's Theat. Ins.* 998 There are three sorts of Blattæ; the soft Moth, the mill Moth, and the unsavoury or stinking Moth. **1748** tr. *Vegetius' Distemp. Horses* 83 Small Maggots or Moths, which others call Lice cause an intolerable Pain in the Intestines.

†**e.** transl. of L. *tinea*: A disease of the scalp.

1600 Surflet *Country Farm* I. xii. 84 For the falling of the haire called the moth, wash the head [etc.].

f. A prostitute. *slang*.

1896 in Farmer & Henley *Slang* IV. 360/1. **1935** A. J. Pollock *Underworld Speaks* 78/1 *Moth*, a female of easy virtue.

2. *Ent.* **a.** Any insect of that one of the two great divisions of the *Lepidoptera* which includes the 'moths' in the older sense.

According to the ordinary modern use, the 'moths' are the same as the *Heterocera*, which are distinguished from the *Rhopalocera* ('butterflies') in that their antennæ are not clubbed. Most of them are of nocturnal habit.

1753 Chambers *Cycl. Supp.*, *Phalenæ*..the name by which authors distinguish those butterflies which fly by night, and which the French thence call *papilions nocturnes*, and we vulgarly *moths*. *Ibid.*, Those moths which have large and heavy bodies..always make a great noise in flying. **1759** Johnson *Idler* No. 64 ¶5, I happened to catch a moth of peculiar variegation. **1847** Tennyson *Princess* II. 5 When these were on, And we as rich as moths from dusk cocoons. **1902** Cornish *Naturalist Thames* 43 The first butterfly, to use an Irishism, was a moth, a sphinx moth.

b. With defining word, in popular names of particular species or genera, as burnet-*moth*, codling-*moth*, gipsy-*moth*, hawk-moth, etc.

3. *attrib.* and *Comb.*, as ***moth-face***, ***-flit***, ***-grub***, ***-hour***, ***-light***, ***-repellent***, ***-trap***, ***-wing***; ***moth-coloured***, ***-hung***, ***-resistant***, ***-soft***, ***-white*** adjs.; ***moth-like*** adj. and adv.; ***moth-hunting*** vbl. sb.; **moth-blight**, various species of homopterous insects of the genus *Aleurodes*, which are destructive to plants; **moth-borer**, the larval forms of various moths which damage plants by boring into stems, etc., esp. the sugar-cane borer, *Diatræa saccharalis*; **moth-fly** = *moth-gnat*; **moth freckle**, 'a term for *Chloasma*' (*Syd. Soc. Lex.* 1891); †**moth-fretten** *a.*, moth-eaten; **moth-gnat**, a dipterous insect of the family *Psychodidæ*; **moth-hunter**, (*a*) one who hunts for moths; (*b*) a name for the Nightjar; **moth-miller**, one of several moths with white-flecked, powdery-looking wings; **moth orchid**, an orchid of the genus *Phalænopsis*, the flower of which resembles a moth; **moth patch**, 'a synonym of *Chloasma*' (*Syd. Soc. Lex.*); **moth sphinx**, 'a moth of the family *Castniidæ*' (Cassell's *Suppl.* 1902); **moth spot** = *moth patch*; **moth-time**, the time of evening when moths abound; †**moth-weed** = *mothwort*; **moth-worm**, the larva of a moth; †**mothwort**, the plant *Helichrysum Stœchas*.

1855 Ogilvie Suppl., **Moth-blight*. **1900** *Nature* 21 June 182/2 A considerable number of the eggs of the *moth borer (which are laid in patches on the leaves of the sugar-cane) are attacked by parasites. **1931** *Discovery* Sept. 300/1 The attacks of the giant moth-borer..and many other pests began in comparatively recent times [in the West Indies]. **1957** *Encycl. Brit.* XXI. 525/2 The giant moth borer (*Castnia licoides*) is particularly destructive in Trinidad and the Guianas. **1974** *Encycl. Brit. Macropædia* XVII. 771/1 The moth borer, *Diatraea saccharalis*, which is widely distributed throughout cane-growing areas, is capable of causing extensive damage when out of control. **1931** V. Woolf *Waves* 254 Jinny's yellow scarf is *moth-coloured in this light. *a* **1963** S. Plath *Crossing Water* (1971) 38 The *moth-face of her husband, moonwhite and ill, Circles her. **1921** W. de la Mare *Veil* 68 Soundless the *moth-flit, crisp the death-watch tick. **1668** Charleton *Ornomast.* 47 *Blatta*..the *Moth-fly, produced out of the Meal-Worm. **1791** *Trans. Soc. Arts* IX. 114 The moth-fly..gets in and lays her eggs in the comb. **1899** D. Sharp *Insects* II. 470 Fam. 7—*Psychodidae* (Moth Flies).—Extremely small, helpless flies [etc.]. **13..** *St. Erkenwolde* 85 in Horstm. *Altengl. Leg.* (1881) 268 Oþer of moulynge oþer of motes opir *moght fretene. **1855** Ogilvie Suppl., **Moth-gnats*. **1890** W. B. Yeats *Countess Kathleen* (1892) 108 At the *moth-hour of eve. **1909** E. Pound *Personae* 23 The moth-hour of our day is upon us Holding the dawn. **1933** W. de la Mare *Fleeting* 161 The secret scent of the *moth-hung flower. **1840** *Cuvier's Anim. Kingd.* 196 The *Moth-hunters bear the same relationship to the Swifts (not to the Swallows) that the Owls do to the Hawks. **1910** W. de la Mare *Three Mulla-Mulgars* 166 Andy's eyes was never made for *moth-hunting. **1930** E. Blunden *Poems* 326 The fete grows late and dark, The King in *moth-light traverses the park. **1934** T. S. Eliot *Rock* II. 84 Moon light and star light, owl and moth light. **1797** Mary Wollstonecr. in C. K. Paul *W. Godwin* (1876) I. 242, I spare the *moth-like appearance. **1804–8** Blake *Milton* I. xi, in *Compl. Writings* (1972) 492 Her moth-like elegance shone over the Assembly. **1839** Bailey *Festus* ix. (1852) 121 From him who hovereth, mothlike, round the sun To six-mooned Ouranus. **1885** W. B. Yeats in *Dublin Univ. Rev.* July 136/1 Gently shook their moth-like wings. **1904** W. H. Hudson *Green Mansions* xiii. 174 She, too, moth-like, had vanished from my side. **1934** S. Spender *Poems* (ed. 2) 36 The mothlike lips at dusk. **1865** *Harper's Weekly* 25 Nov. 747/3 If there is *one* little hole in your linen or paper, some industrious *moth-miller is pretty sure to discover it. **1885** S. O. Jewett *Marsh Isl.* xiii, Come and sit down, and don't flit about so, mother; you make me think of a singed moth-miller. **1880** F. W. Burbidge *Gardens of Sun* ii. 18 In Singaporean gardens the rarest of *moth orchids are planted in cocoanut-shells. **1942** G. G. Denny *Fabrics* (ed. 5) II. 119 Dry cleaners and laundries may apply *moth-repellent treatment. **1958** S. Hyland *Who goes Hang?* xli. 200 Paradichlorbenzene was sold for the first time in the shops as moth repellant in 1932. **1964** N. G. Clark *Mod. Organic Chem.* xix. 390 It [*sc.* naphthalene] has been employed in the manufacture of fire-lighters, and as a moth-repellent and insecticide. **1970** *Which?* Sept. 265/2 The carpet is moth-resistant. **1876** G. M. Hopkins *Wreck of Deutschland* xxvi, in *Poems* (1967) 60 Or night, still higher, With belled fire and the *moth-soft Milky Way. **1958** L. Durrell *Balthazar* i. 17 Brightly lit up in the moth-soft darkness of the Aegean night. **1922** F. Courtenay *Physical Beauty* 26 The so-called '*moth spots', brown spots or patches which appear after middle life, are due to this tan pigment. **1819** Keats *Lamia* I. 222 Now on the *moth-time of that evening dim He would return that way. **1890** *Cent. Dict.*, *Moth-trap. **1928** Metcalf & Flint *Destructive & Useful Insects* ix. 263 Mechanical devices, such as..fly traps, moth traps, maggot traps,..have been used successfully for catching and killing a variety of insects. **1970** *Daily Tel.* 19 Oct. 11/8 A moth new to Britain, Plusia accentifera, has been caught in Mr Terry Dillon's moth-trap at Halsted. **1597** Gerarde *Herbal* II. cxcvi. 520 The branches and leaues laid among clothes keepeth them from moths, whereupon it [*Eliochryson*] hath bene called of some *Mothweede or Mothwoort. **1920** D. H. Lawrence *Lost Girl* xi. 275 Irises rearing purple and *moth-white. **1612** Ainsworth *Annot. Ps.* VI. 8 Ghnash is a *moth-worme, Psalm 39. 12. that fretteth garments. **1885** H. C. McCook *Tenants of Old Farm* 91 The moth-worms pass the summer within these silk-lined rolls. **1578** Lyte *Dodoens* I. lxi. 89 Called..in English Golde floure, *Mothewort, or Golden Stechados. **1597** Gerarde *Herbal* II. cxcvi. 519 Of Golden Mothwoort, or Cudweede.

moth, *sb.*[2] [f. Hind. *moth* moth bean.] In full, ***moth bean***. An Indian bean, *Phaseolus aconitifolius*, of the family Leguminosæ, cultivated in tropical and sub-tropical countries as food for both man and livestock.

[**1832** W. Roxburgh et al. *Flora Indica* III. 299 *P[haseolus] aconitifolius*... *Hind.* Moot. This plant I have reared from seed sent me by Dr. Hunter from the province of Oude where it is much cultivated..and used for feeding cattle.] **1840** *Penny Cycl.* XVIII. 58/1 *P[haseolus] aconitifolius*, Moth of the natives, is cultivated in the north-western provinces, and used for feeding cattle. **1884** tr. *A. de Candolle's Origin of Cultivated Plants* v. 345 Moth, or Aconite-leaved Kidney Bean... An annual species grown in India as fodder, and of which the seeds are eatable, though but little valued. The Hindustani name is *mout*, among the Sikhs *moth*. **1886** A. H. Church *Food-Grains of India* 152 The moth-bean..is found from the Himálaya to Ceylon... It is not esteemed as a food for man, for although it is rich in nutrients, it is generally thought to possess heating properties. **1923** H. C. Thompson *Veg. Crops* xxiv. 334 The term 'bean' as used in the United States includes..several species of oriental beans, including adsuki,..moth and rice beans belonging to the genus Phaseolus. **1972** G. A. C. Herklots *Vegetables in South-east Asia* 244 (*heading*) Moth bean... A slender annual with decumbent branches growing to 18 inches or a foot in length.

moth (mɒθ), *v.* [f. Moth *sb.*[1]] *intr.* To hunt for moths. Chiefly in **'mothing** *vbl. sb.*

1826 Kirby & Sp. *Entomol.* IV. l. 518 The former colour ..is most proper for mothing in the night. **1894** *Naturalist* 14 Geometræ have been on the whole very scarce, and mothing at and after dusk uniformly unproductive.

moth, obs. form of Mote *sb.*[1], Mouth *sb.*

'mothball, *sb.* Also moth ball, moth-ball. [Ball *sb.*[1]] **1.** A ball of naphthalene (sometimes mixed with other substances) used among stored fabrics to repel moths. Also *fig.*

1906 'O. Henry' in *Munsey's Mag.* Dec. 288/1 Me and Solly..prepared to shake off our moth-balls and wing our way against the arc-lights of the joyous and tuneful East. **1911** G. S. Porter *Harvester* xiii. 282 Wouldn't she like me to wear her things better than to have them lying in moth balls? **1916** M. Lees-Dods *Ideal Home* x. 161 When furs are kept by a lady in her own house, a plentiful supply of pieces of camphor, or moth-ball, should be wrapped in tissue paper and distributed amongst the folds. **1932** *Conc. Househ. Encycl.* 808 The round balls sold as moth balls consist of naphthalene, a product of the distillation of coal tar. **1958** S. Hyland *Who goes Hang?* xli. 199 Synthetic camphor wasn't used for moth-balls until 1914! **1964** *Horlicks Home Bk.* 178 In the past naphthalene (usually in the shape of moth balls) was used. **1974** 'J. Melville' *Nun's Castle* I. 10 She had conceived the idea of staging afresh the forgotten Victorian tournament..wearing the original clothes, most of which were still packed away in mothballs.

2. orig. *U.S.* Used *attrib.* to designate armaments or installations stored away, held in reserve, or disused. Similarly ***in mothballs***, laid up, put out of use or action for a long time.

1946 *Amer. N. & Q.* Apr. 7/2 '*Mothball fleet*': inactive U.S. Navy ships to be preserved for long periods by newly-developed techniques. **1946** *Newsweek* 13 May 22/2 The Navy plans to reduce yard personnel to peace-time proportions by early fall. The moth-ball laying-up program will be complete by that time. **1947** *N.Y. Times* 26 Jan. E. 6/5 The moth ball fleet consists of United States warships now undergoing preservative treatment which will enable them to be put back in use rapidly if needed. **1948** *Sun* (Baltimore) 16 Jan. 1/1 The 45,000-ton New Jersey and Wisconsin had been put in 'moth-balls' January 1. **1950** *Hansard Commons* 22 Mar. 2079 We have a 'moth-ball fleet', as it is somewhat vulgarly termed in some countries, reasonably widely dispersed..round the United Kingdom. **1958** *Oxford Mail* 12 Aug. 1/2 The United States is to sell for cash 47 liberty ships kept in 'moth balls' since the last war. **1967** *Boston Sunday Herald* 30 Apr. I. 7/1 A..port improvement paid for by the MPA has remained in mothballs.., because no container ships have been scheduled to or from Boston. **1970** *Globe & Mail* (Toronto) 26 Sept. 6/3 Seventy-four of these fighter-bombers are going directly into mothballs as they roll off the production line at Canadair Ltd. **1972** *Guardian* 14 Jan. 1/5 Orange dust found in crater Shorty could mean..that Apollo hardware put in mothballs..could be brought out for another final journey. **1974** *Evening Standard* 15 July 11/2 (*heading*) Air fleets may be put in moth-balls.

3. *transf.* and *fig.*

1943 Baker *Dict. Austral. Slang* (ed. 3) 51 *Moth balls*, tracer bullets. **1945** L. Shelly *Jive Talk Dict.* 29 *Moth ball*, an aggravating person. **1951** *Football Record* (Melbourne) 8 Sept. 5 And now for eight teams it's mothballs until 1952. **1966** *Listener* 28 Apr. 629/1 The work..was certainly interesting to hear even if it now has to be put back in moth balls. **1971** M. Tak *Truck Talk* 109 *Moth-balls*, balls of ether used by truckers to start cold diesel engines. **1974** *Guardian* 31 Jan. 1/5 The distinguished BBC cheerfully took the most improbable creations [*sc.* films] out of mothballs.

'mothball, *v.* [f. prec.] *trans.* To place in mothballs, in the senses of the sb. Hence **'mothballed** *ppl. a.*

1943 R. Malkin *Marriage, Morals & War* xi. 159 His civvies, all dusted off, were mothballed, and shipped back home. **1949** *Jane's Fighting Ships 1949–50* 357 *Princeton*, *Tarawa* and *Antietam* are also being 'mothballed'. **1957** P. Frank *Seven Days to Never* ii. 80 We've got two thousand Fifty-Twos and Forty-Sevens mothballed, lined up on every desert in Arizona. **1959** *Times* 18 May 5/3 The best service a retired general could perform 'is to turn in his tongue along with his suit and mothball his opinions'. **1959** *Time* (Atlantic ed.) 24 Aug. 52/3 Both plants..will have to be mothballed unless they can be adapted to produce other chemicals. **1965** *New Scientist* 2 Dec. 642/1 The capability now coming on stream cannot be mothballed. We must use it or see its value erode. **1966** *Aviation Week & Space Technology* 5 Dec. 22/3 Essential consideration to the proposal is that the separately orbited satellite modules could be mothballed in space—fully equipped with all experiments, however—until ready for use. **1973** *Wall St. Jrnl.* 28 Nov. 1/2 Mobil Oil plans to 'mothball' its aging East Chicago, Ind., petroleum refinery. **1974** *Evening Standard* 15 July 11/2 There is no doubt that the Trident One may be mothballed.

†**mothe**, *a.* *Obs.* [? a. ON. *móð-r* weary (OSw. *móþ-er* annoyed, disquieted.] ? Disquieted, annoyed.

c **1450** *St. Cuthbert* (Surtees) 859 Þe childre wer confused and mothe. *Ibid.* 6186 He wald noȝt trowe, bot made him mothe, And said he wald it se.

mothe, obs. f. Mote *sb.*[1] and *v.*[1], Mouth *sb.*

†**moth-eat**, *v.* *Obs.* [Back-formation from next.] *trans.* To eat away by or as by moths.

1598 Florio, *Carolare*..to worme or moth-eate. **1638** Sir T. Herbert *Trav.* (ed. 2) 61 From whence ruine and neglect have moatheaten her. **1721** Wodrow *Hist. Suff. Ch. Scot.* (1829) II. II. xiii. 498 The younger ministers did either motheat or too much suffer to be motheaten by the Vulgar the reputation of such who did not follow their way.

'moth-eaten, *a.* Eaten away or destroyed by moths. Often *fig.*

1377 Langl. *P. Pl.* B. x. 362 Owre bakkes þat moth-eten be. **1551** Robinson tr. *More's Utopia* Ep. (1895) 25 Whatsoeuer is not stuffed full of olde moughteaten termes. *a* **1660** *Contemp. Hist. Irel.* (Ir. Archæol. Soc.) III. 85 Sufficient motiue to moue the moat-eaten conferences of these poysonall anti-Catholicks. **1796** Mrs. M. Robinson *Angelina* I. 241 Like a bale of cotton..grown yellow by keeping, and moth-eaten by ill-nature. **1809** E. S. Barrett *Setting Sun* I. 28 The old system is moth-eaten, and kings have had a severe lesson. **1882** J. Hawthorne *Fort. Fool* I. x, The mortality symbolised by the poor moth-eaten clothes.

mothed (mɒθt), *ppl. a.* [f. Moth *v.* + -ed[1].] Full of moths, moth-eaten.

1835 Browning *Paracelsus* IV. 212 From closet long to quiet vowed, With mothed and dropping arras hung. **1930** W. de la Mare *Desert Islands* 39 Stuffed, glass-eyed, a little mothed and dusty.

†'**mothen**, *a. Obs.* [f. MOTH + -EN[4] (if not a misprint for *moth-eaten*).] Full of moths.

1580 FULKE *Confut. Allen* 125 We rake not vp olde, mouldie, and mothen parchementes to seeke our progenitours names. [Hence 1818 in TODD; and in later Dicts.]

mother ('mʌðə(r)), *sb.*[1] Forms: 1 móder, -or, -ur, (módder), *dat.* méd(d)er, mœ́der, 3 moderr, (? moðer), *pl.* modren, 4–5 modire, modre, modur, modyr(e, mooder, 5 modure, 6 moeder, mothir, *Sc.* muddir, muder, 8–9 *Sc.* mither, 5– mother. [Com. Teut. (but wanting in Gothic) and Indo-Germanic: OE. *módor* = OFris. *môdar*, OS. *môdar*, *muodar* (Du. *moeder*, LG. *moder*), OHG. *muotar*, *-er* (MHG. *muoter*, mod.G. *mutter*), ON. *móðer* (Sw., Da. *moder*):—OTeut. **mōdar-* (cons.-stem):—pre-Teut. **mā́ter-*, cogn. w. Skr. **mātr*, *mātar-*, Gr. μᾱ́τηρ-, μᾱτέρ- (Doric), μήτηρ, μητέρ- (Attic and Ionic), L. *māter*, OSl. *mati*, OIrish *māthir*.

As in the case of FATHER, the substitution of *th* for the earlier *d* dates from the beginning of the 16th c., though the pronunciation with (ð) probably existed earlier. The occasional occurrence of the spelling *moþer* in the 14th c. (e.g. in the Göttingen MS. of the Cursor Mundi) has prob. no phonetic significance, being due to association with words like *broþer*, *oþer*, which in fact occur in the immediate context of several of the examples. The development of OE. *ó* to mod.E. (ʌ) (through uː, u, ʊ) is normal in the case of words in *-ther*, *-der*: cf. *brother*, *other*, *rudder*. In OE. the genitive sing. normally coincided in form with the nom., and many instances of the uninflected genitive occur in ME. and early mod.E. (see also 15b). The genitive *móderes* is common in the Northumbrian gospels (10th c.).]

I. 1. a. A female parent; a woman who has given birth to a child. Correlative with *son* or *daughter*.

As with other terms of relationship, *my* is (exc. in poetic language) commonly omitted before *mother* used vocatively. On the other hand, in the 3rd person the use of *mother* for *my mother* is colloquial and familiar; in the middle of the 19th c. it was regarded as vulgar, or at least as unfashionable, but has now regained currency.

Mother is also used colloquially by a husband addressing or referring to his wife.

c **1050** *Voc.* in Wr.-Wülcker 450/25 *Mater*, anes cildes modor. *Materfamilias*, maniȝra cilda modur. *c* **1200** ORMIN 168 He beþ full off Haliȝ Gast ȝet in his moderr wambe. *a* **1225** *Leg. Kath.* 931 Of his feader soð godd, & of his moder soð mon. *c* **1250** *Gen. & Ex.* 1434 Ysaac..wunede ðor in ðoȝt and care, for moderes dead and sondes care. **1340** HAMPOLE *Pr. Consc.* 447 He was consayved synfully Within his awen moder body. **1340** *Ayenb.* 67 Þis zenne is ine uele maneres ase..ine children aye hare uaderes and hare modren. *c* **1386** CHAUCER *Doctor's T.* 93 Ye fadres and ye moodres. *c* **1425** WYNTOUN *Cron.* II. vi. 488 And thare modyre banys ta. *c* **1511** *1st Eng. Bk. Amer.* (Arb.) Introd. 33/1 The[y] ete theym all rawe, both there one fader or moeder. **1526** *Pilgr. Perf.* (W. de W. 1531) 13 As infantes or tender babes newe borne of theyr mother. **1556** *Chron. Gr. Friars* (Camden) 25 The qwenys moder dicessyd. **1588** SHAKS. *L.L.L.* II. i. 255 Then was Venus like her mother, for her father is but grim. **1607** — *Cor.* IV. i. 15 Nay Mother. *Ibid.* 27 My Mother, you wot well [etc.]. *c* **1633** MILTON *Arcades* 22 Cybele, Mother of a hundred gods. *c* **1702** C. MATHER *Magn. Chr.* VI. ii. (1852) 356 She lived to be a mother of several children. **1790** COWPER *Receipt Mother's Picture* 21 My mother! when I learn'd that thou wast dead. *c* **1830** T. H. BAYLY *Song, 'We met—'twas in a crowd'*, Oh, thou hast been the cause of this anguish, My mother!

1855 DICKENS *Dorrit* (1857) I. ii. 13 Mother (my usual name for Mrs. Meagles) began to cry so, that it was necessary to take her out. 'What's the matter, Mother?' said I..'you are frightening Pet.'.. 'Yes, I know that, Father,' says Mother. **1898** J. D. BRAYSHAW *Slum Silhouettes* 156 'Sit yer down, mother,' said Joe, taking his seat at the head of the table. **1932** A. CHRISTIE *Peril at End House* v. 68 Mother and I..feel it's only neighbourly to do what we can. **1970** P. CARLON *Souvenir* ii. 35 Don't you *loathe* the way old folks call each other Mother and Dad?

b. Said of animals.

Rare in ME. and early mod.E., being superseded by DAM *sb.*[2] 2, which afterwards became restricted to quadrupeds, and is now rarely used exc. of mares.

a **900** *Laws Alfred* xvi, ȝif mon cu oððe stodmyran forstele & folan oððe cealf ofadrife, forȝelde mid scill. & þa moder be hiora weorðe. **1382** WYCLIF *Exod.* xxiii. 19 Thow shalt not seethe a kydde in the mylk of his moder. [So all later versions.] **1632** LITHGOW *Trav.* IX. 380 Young Chickens, which are not hatched by their mothers, but in the Fernace. **1692** R. L'ESTRANGE *Fables* ccxxi. 193 Pray Mother (says the Young Crab) do but set the Example your self, and I'll follow ye. **1868** TENNYSON *Lucretius* 100 And lambs are glad Nosing the mother's udder.

c. ***Mother of God, God's Mother*** (= Gr. Θεοτόκος): a frequent designation of the Virgin Mary in Catholic use.

c **1122** *O.E. Chron.* an. 994 (Laud MS.) Se haliȝe Godes modor. *c* **1410** HOCCLEVE *Mother of God* 1 Modir of god, and virgyn undeffouled. *c* **1440** *Gesta Rom.* lxxxv. 405 (Add. MS.) That blessyd ladie, goddis modre. **1483** *Cath. Angl.* 161/1 Goddes modyr; *mater dei, theoticus.* **1591** SHAKS. *1 Hen. VI*, I. ii. 78. **1898** W. K. JOHNSON *Terra Tenebr.* 105 Mother of God, we here enthrone Thee, thy slain Son, within thy house.

d. *abstr.* (*a*) Womanish qualities inherited from the mother. (*b*) That which is characteristic of motherhood; maternal affection.

1599 SHAKS. *Hen. V*, IV. vi. 31 But I had not so much of man in mee, And all my mother came into my eyes, And gaue me vp to teares. **1725** POPE *Odyss.* XI. 188 Strait all the mother in her soul awakes. **1747** RICHARDSON *Clarissa* I. 121, I thought, by the glass before me, I saw the mother in her soften'd eye cast towards me. **1807** J. BARLOW *Columb.* III. 186 Thrice have those lovely lips the victim prest, And all the mother torn that tender breast. **1847** MARY HOWITT *Ballads* 33 The mother in my soul was strong. **1884** TENNYSON *Becket* V. ii, Look! how this love, this mother, runs thro' all The world God made.

e. In extended sense: A female ancestress. Now *rare* exc. in ***our first mother***.

c **1050** *Suppl. Ælfric's Gloss.* in Wr.-Wülcker 173/11 *Proauuia*, þridde moder. *a* **1300** *Cursor M.* 934 Eue sco hight eue fra þat dai, þat moder of mani es for to sai. **14..** *Nom.* in Wr.-Wülcker 689/41 *Hec proava*, the forne modyre. **1611** BIBLE *Gen.* xvii. 16 Yea I wil blesse her, and she shalbe a mother of nations. **1667** MILTON *P.L.* XI. 159 Whence Haile to thee Eve rightly call'd, Mother of all Mankind.

f. Applied to a stepmother or a mother-in-law.

c **1546** EDW. VI *Let. to Q. Cath. Parr* in Ellis *Orig. Lett.* Ser. I. II. 131 Most honorable and entirely beloued mother. **1589** *Reg. Privy Council Scot.* IV. 444 His Hienes, invited be his darrest moder the Quene of Denmarkis..letters. **1859** TENNYSON *Geraint* 779 O my new mother, be not wroth or grieved At thy new son, for my petition to her.

g. Proverbs and proverbial phrases. †***to take one's*** (own) ***mother for a maid***: app. orig. intended to exemplify extreme simplicity. ***to have too much of his mother's blessing***: said of a youth who is unreasonably prudish or scrupulous. ***does your mother know you're out?*** (slang): a jeering question addressed to one who shows excessive simplicity or juvenile presumption. ***(just) like mother makes*** (or ***used to make***) ***(it)***: having the qualities of home cooking; exactly to one's taste; also *fig.*

[**1598** SHAKS. *Merry W.* II. ii. 40 *Fal.* Good-morrow, good-wife. *Qui.* Not so and't please your worship. *Fal.* Good maid, then. *Qui.* Ile be sworne, As my mother was the first houre I was borne.] **1606** BRYSKETT *Civ. Life* 102 Too much, is harmeful euen in iustice it self: whereupon is growne..our English prouerbe, that too much of a mans mothers blessing is not good. **1664** COTTON *Scarron.* I. 48 So smug she [Venus] was, and so array'd He took his Mother for a Maid. **16..** *MS. Ashm.* 36 lf. 112 If euor Ice doe come heare againe, Ice zaid, Chil give thee my Mother vor a maid. **1838** ? T. MARTIN in *Bentley's Miscell.* III. 416 And she asked me 'How's your mother? Does she know that you are out?' **1842** BARHAM *Ingol. Leg., Misadv. Margate*, 'Sir, does your mother know that you are out?' **1919** WODEHOUSE *Damsel in Distress* i. 18 There's a new musical comedy at the Regal. Opened last night, and seems to be just like mother makes. **1927** W. E. COLLINSON *Contemp. Eng.* 52 The notice outside some eating-houses, beef-steak pie like mother makes it! **1963** WODEHOUSE *Stiff Upper Lip, Jeeves* v. 39 Its facade, its spreading grounds..and what not were all just like Mother makes. **1975** D. CLARK *Premedicated Murder* iv. 68 Just like my old mother used to make. A bit of candied peel in a bun can't be beat.

h. Used as an exclamation of surprise, dismay, etc.; freq. ***my mother!***

1869 'MARK TWAIN' *Innoc. Abr.* 52 Twenty-five cigars, at 100 reis, 2500 reis! Oh, my sainted mother! **1909** *Sat. Even. Post* 22 May 6/3 'Gee, what a peach of an idea!' 'Oh, mother!' **1959** N. MAILER *Advts. for Myself* (1961) 93 He roared with laughter now. 'Oh, my mother.' **1972** C. ACHEBE *Girls at War* 107 'Plane!' screamed his boy from the kitchen. 'My mother!' screamed Gladys.

i. ***mothers and fathers***: a game in which children act out the roles of mother and father.

1903 G. R. SIMS *Living London* XXXIII. 271/1 Sometimes ..they [*sc.* the boys] will join the girls in a mimic domestic drama of 'Mothers and Fathers'. **1969** [see INFANT-SCHOOL]. **1972** J. WILSON *Hide & Seek* vii. 130 Shall we play mothers and fathers with our dolls?

j. Ellipt. for *mother-fucker. U.S. slang.*

[**1948** MANONE & VANDERVOORT *Trumpet on Wing* 70 'I'll be a motheree if I'll wear any damn bedpan intern's suit,' I screamed.] **1955** S. WHITMORE *Solo* iii. 42 Jaeger said, ..'He's..so weak now, he can't blow note one.' 'Hell, this mother never could,' Alfred laughed. **1959** N. MAILER *Advts. for Myself* (1961) 358 Old K, he's nothing but a mother. **1967** *Melody Maker* 14 Jan. 8 *Mother*, term of abuse. As in 'You're a mother, baby!' **1972** *Sunday Times* 7 May 10/6 'Man we must just get out of here before those mothers get us all..,' he shouted at me. **1973** *New Yorker* 17 Feb. 62/2 Out the parachute, out the radio, change the c.g., and the mother will go. **1975** *N.Y. Times* 8 Sept. 33/2 'You mothers! I ain't been out five minutes and I just got *outta* the pen this morning!' Her name is Judy, and although she is white, she talks black jive.

2. *fig.* Applied to things more or less personified, with reference either to a metaphorical giving birth, to the protecting care exercised by a mother, or to the affectionate reverence due to a mother.

a. Said of a quality, condition, event, etc., that gives rise to some other.

c **1386** CHAUCER *Pard. T.* 263 Hasard is verray mooder of lesynges, And of deceite and cursed forswerynges. *c* **1449** PECOCK *Repr.* V. xiv. 555 Loue to money..is moder of passing myche yuel. **1463–4** *Rolls of Parlt.* V. 507/1 Ydelnes, moder of all vyces. **1573** *New Custom* I. i, That I Ignorance am the mother of true deuotion. **1597** HOOKER *Eccl. Pol.* V. xv. §1 The mother of such magnificence (they thinke) is but only a proude ambitious desire to be spoken of farre and wide. **1611** B. JONSON *Catiline* III. ii, For 'tis despaire that is the mother of madnesse. **1766** FRANKLIN *Let.* Wks. 1887 III. 463, I congratulate you on the repeal of that mother of mischiefs, the Stamp Act. **1799** *Hull Advertiser* 21 Dec. 4/2 The..maxim that 'freight is the mother of wages'. **1824** LAMB *Elia* Ser. II. *Blakesmoor in H—shire*, The solitude of childhood is not so much the mother of thought.

b. Said of the earth. See also MOTHER EARTH.

a **1000** *Charms* i. 69 Hal wes þu, folde, fira modor. *c* **1250** *Gen. & Ex.* 122 Of euerilc ouȝt, of euerilc sed, Was erðe mad moder of sped. **1600** SURFLET *Country Farm* I. iv. 13 As for the earth..it beareth all manner of corne, fruits,..and other things,..and heereupon old writers haue iustly giuen vnto it the due name of mother. **1625** BACON *Ess., Riches* (Arb.) 235 Our Great Mothers Blessing, the Earths. **1667** MILTON *P.L.* V. 338 Whatever Earth all-bearing Mother yeilds In India East or West. **1822** SHELLEY tr. *Calderon's Mag. Prodig.* ii. 79 O Beloved earth, dear mother. **1821** LAMB *Elia* Ser. I. *Old Benchers*, But the common mother of us all in no long time after received him gently into her lap. **1876** [see MOTHERLY 3].

c. Said of the church: see CHURCH *sb.* 8.

Mother Church is either treated as a quasi-proper name (though initial capitals are not always used) or preceded by a possessive pronoun.

1377 LANGL. *P. Pl.* B. XVI. 197 Children of charite & holicherche þe moder. *c* **1460** *Wisdom* 992 in *Macro Plays* 68 Now haue ye for-yeffnes þat were fylyde, To prey yowur modyr chyrche of her proteccion. **1539** PERY in Ellis *Orig. Lett.* Ser. II. II. 145 According to the lawdebwll usse and costom of owr holly mother Chwrche. **1630** YAXLEE *Morbus & Antid.* To Rdr., The obedient sonne of my deare Mother the true Church of England. **1695** J. EDWARDS *Perfect. Script.* 589 A learned and pious son of our mother. **1726** AYLIFFE *Parergon* 22 The Good of Mother Church, as well as that of Civil Society, renders a Judicial Practice in criminal Cases entirely necessary. **1784** COWPER *Task* II. 576 So we, no longer taught By monitors that mother church supplies [etc.]. **1833** *Tracts for Times* No. 13. 6 The mysterious time of Christmas approaching, our Mother, with true parental anxiety, takes up..the thread of her instructions anew.

d. Said of a country, city, etc., in relation to its natives; *spec.* in ***Mother Russia***.

[**1382** WYCLIF *Gal.* iv. 26: literally from Vulg.] *c* **1550** BALE *K. Johan* (Camden) 66 O Englande, Englande! showe now thyselfe a mother, Thy people wyll els be slayne here without nomber. **1593** SHAKS. *Rich. II*, I. iii. 307 Then Englands ground farewell: sweet soil adieu, My Mother, and my Nurse. **1699** *Rhode Isl. Col. Rec.* (1858) III. 374 We being wholly ruled and governed by the good and wholesome [laws] of our Mother, the kingdom of England. **1726** SWIFT *Gulliver* II. vii, I have always borne that laudable Partiality to my own Country, which [etc.]..: I would hide the Frailties and Deformities of my political Mother. **1786** BURNS *Ernest Cry & Pr.* Postscr. vii, Scotland, my auld, respected Mither! **1851** BORROW *Lavengro* xvi, 'What horse is that?'..'The best in mother England', said the very old man. **1901** HENLEY *Hawthorn & Lavender*, etc. 102 Blow, you bugles of England, blow Over the camps of the fallen foe—Blow glory and pity to the victor Mother, Sad, O, sad in her sacrificial dead! **1966** J. BINGHAM *Double Agent* v. 71, I love Russia... Great Mother Russia. **1972** P. RUELL *Red Christmas* xv. 153 Came as quite a shock to them when they realised we weren't doing it all for Mother Russia. **1973** D. BAGLEY *Tightrope Men* xxiv. 164 'See that tower over there?'..'A Russian observation tower. That's Mother Russia.'

e. Said of one's university. Cf. ALMA MATER.

1647–8 Wood *Life* 15 Feb. (O.H.S.) I. 140 Who fed with the papp of Aristotle at twenty or thirtie yeares of age, and suck at the duggs of their mother the University. **1721** AMHERST *Terræ Fil.* Ded. (1754) 5, I had much rather have your approbation than your censure, and enjoy the favour of my dear mother.

f. Applied to Nature, and occasionally to other personified abstractions represented as protecting or controlling powers.

1601 R. JOHNSON *Kingd. & Commw.* (1603) 35 Whereas mother Nature hath interlaced so riotously her golden and siluer veins in the bosom and wombe of Peru. **1617** MORYSON *Itin.* I. 181 Experience, the mother of fooles. **1764** GOLDSM. *Trav.* 81 Nature, a mother kind alike to all. **1813** SHELLEY *Q. Mab.* VI. 198 Necessity! thou mother of the world! **1866** M. ARNOLD *Thyrsis* xviii, And now in happier air Wandering with the great Mother's train divine.

g. Said of a city, country, institution from which another originates as an offshoot.

1560 DAUS tr. *Sleidane's Comm.* 280b, The churche of Rome, mother and maistres of al others. **1838** THIRLWALL *Greece* II. xii. 106 It [Sinope] became in its turn the mother of several flourishing cities.

h. In physical sense: The material source of a substance; also, the parent stock on which anything grows, or the main stem or channel from which others branch off.

c **1384** CHAUCER *H. Fame* 1983 Auenture, That is the moder of tydynges, As the see of welles and sprynges. **1604** E. G[RIMSTONE] *D'Acosta's Hist. Indies* V. xviii. 378 Saying, that these shells were daughters of the sea, the mother of all waters. **1611** COTGR., *Artere aorte*, the great Arterie, mother Arterie, or mother of arteries. **1668** CULPEPPER & COLE *Barthol. Anat.* Man. I. iii. 306 All the Veins of the whole Body are referred unto two as their Mothers. **1675** EVELYN *Terra* (1676) 44 Water..was by some thought to be the Mother of Earth. **1681** GREW *Musæum* III. I. iv. 283 Another clear Crystal, growing on a Semiperspicuous Mother. **1721** BRADLEY *Philos. Acc. Wks. Nat.* 41 The fruit of the Indian Fig..will strike Root and become a Plant as perfect as the mother it was taken from. **1868** LOCKYER *Elem. Astron.* iii. §15 (1879) 85 Aqueous vapour is the great mother of clouds.

3. A woman who exercises control like that of a mother, or who is looked up to as a mother.

a. One who has religious authority or dignity. Often applied to the Virgin Mary (cf. 1 c).

c **1366** CHAUCER *A.B.C.* 133 Mooder, of whom oure merci gan to springe Beth ye my juge & eek my soules leche. *c* **1375** *Sc. Leg. Saints* xviii. (*Egipciane*) 307 Spirituale modyr, quhat-sa þu be, for godis sak schau þe to me! **1563** WINȜET *Four Scoir Thre Quest.* Wks. (S.T.S.) I. 73 The glorius Virgine, the Mothir. *a* **1711** KEN *Psyche* Poet. Wks. 1721 IV. 165 Sophronia..Who of her sex the guidance nicely skill'd, ..Heav'n for their Ghostly Mother had design'd. **1868** SIR H. W. BAKER in *Hymns A. & M.* App. No. 376 Shall we not love thee, Mother dear, Whom Jesus loves so well?

b. A title given to the head or superior of a female religious community.

1603 SHAKS. *Meas. for M.* I. iv. 86, I will about it strait, No longer staying, but to giue the Mother Notice of my affaire. **1611** BEAUM. & FL. *Philaster* II. ii, The reuerend mother sent

me word, They would all be for the garden. **1798** JOANNA BAILLIE *De Monfort* v. vi, *Freberg* [to Abbess] And you have wisely done, my rev'rend mother. **1820** SCOTT *Abbot* xii, They call me Lady Abbess, or Mother at the least, who address me. **1883** MRS. CRAIK in *Longm. Mag.* Jan. 306, I could understand how the Mother was just the woman to be head of a community like this. **1907** *Athenæum* 2 Nov. 545/3 The astute yet saintly mother-superior.

†**c.** ***mother of the maids***: the head of the maids of honour in a Royal household. *Obs.*

1577–8 *New Yr.'s Gifts* in Nichols *Progr. Eliz.* (1823) II. 88 To Mrs. Hyde, Mother of the Mades. **1633** BROME *North. Lass* I. iv, She might ha' been Mother o' the Maids. **1682** LUTTRELL *Brief Rel.* (1857) I. 159 The lady Sanderson, mother of the maids of honour to her majestie, was interred in the abby. **1711** HEARNE *Collect.* (O.H.S.) III. 132 Mrs. *** Mother of the Maids to K. James II^{ds} Queen.

d. In occasional uses.

1897 *Daily News* 13 July 8/7 Separate cottage buildings, each under the charge of a person called a 'mother', had been established [as homes for girls].

e. Colloq. phr. ***to be mother***: to serve out portions of food or drink; *spec.* to pour out tea.

[**1926** G. B. SHAW *Glimpse of Reality* in *Translations & Tomfooleries* 184 Let us get to work at the supper. You shall be the mother of the family and give us our portions, Giulietta.] **1958** 'J. BROGAN' *Cummings Report* ii. 17 We'll go and have tea, and you be Mother. **1967** J. PORTER *Dover & Unkindest Cut* iv. 41 MacGregor, hearing the tea cups rattling outside..opened the door again. 'Shall I be mother, sir?' **1974** J. MITCHELL *Death & Bright Water* xx. 243 'Shall I be mother?' Callan nodded, and Blythe's strong fingers popped the cork, the champagne foamed into the glasses.

f. The female owner of a pet, esp. of a dog. *colloq.*

1924 GALSWORTHY *White Monkey* I. vi. 39 Ting was.. trying to climb a railing whereon was..a black cat... 'Give him to me, Ellen. Come with Mother, darling!' **1940** N. MITFORD *Pigeon Pie* ix. 139 Many mothers of dogs had fetched their little ones home.

4. a. A term of address for an elderly woman of the lower class. Also used (instead of *Mrs.*) as a prefix to the surname of such a person.

c **1386** CHAUCER *Wife's T.* 149 My leeue mooder, quod this knyght [etc.]. **1476** *Paston Lett.* III. 148 That owther Syme or Mother Brown maye deliver it me to morow. **1496–7** *Rec. St. Mary at Hill* (1905) 34 Item, a Towell of the gyfte of Mother Ienet. **1533** J. HEYWOOD *Play of Love* C iij b, Mother quoth I how doth my dere darlyng. **1588** *Nottingham Rec.* IV. 221 At one wyddoez house named Mother Jane. **1593** *Tell-troth's N.Y. Gift* (1876) 13 While mother trot and her fellowes were descanting on others honesty. **1847** C. BRONTE *Jane Eyre* xix, 'Well, and you want your fortune told', she said... 'I don't care about it, mother; you may please yourself'.

b. ***Mother Bunch*** [f. the name of a noted ale-wife of late Elizabethan times]: (*a*) *Obs. slang*, water; (*b*) a stout or untidy old woman. ***Mother Carey's Chicken, Goose***: see CHICKEN *sb.*^{1} 4, GOOSE 2. ***Mother Hubbard***: a kind of cloak (named after a person celebrated in a well-known nursery rime); also, a kind of loose-fitting garment (chiefly *U.S.*). ***Mother Shipton***: the name of a legendary 'prophetess' of the 16th c.; adopted as the name of a moth, *Euclidea mi* (also called the *Shipton moth*).

1591 SPENSER (*title*) Prosopopoia, or Mother Hubberds Tale. **1600** DEKKER *Shoemaker's Holiday* sig. H2^v Am I sure that Paules steeple is a handful higher than London stone? or that the pissing conduit leakes nothing but pure mother Bunch? **1847** C. BRONTË *Jane Eyre* II. iii. 81 You talked of going..to visit the gipsy camp;..one of the old Mother Bunches is in the servants' hall at this moment. **1861** G. J. WHYTE-MELVILLE *Market Harborough* viii. 94, I *have* seen mammas whom the fairest of Eve's daughters might be proud to resemble; but it is sometimes hard upon the young Phœbe to have..at her side the shapeless Mother Bunch, into the *fac-simile* of which she must eventually grow. **1878** F. M. A. ROE *Army Lett. from Officer's Wife* (1909) 186, I made a Mother Hubbard apron of white paper-cambric. **1882** *Wide Awake* (Boston, Mass.) Jan. 18/2 A little girl in a sort of Mother Hubbard cap..is starting off on a journey. **1882** W. F. KIRBY *Europ. Butterflies & M.* (1903) Plate xlii, Euclidia Mi—Mother Shipton. **1883** *Fort. Rev.* 1 Sept. 351 The ugly and unbecoming covering so long popular as the Mother Hubbard cloak. **1884** *Nat. Police Gaz.* (U.S.) 30 Aug. 12/3 Mattoon's Chief of Police issued an order that any woman appearing on the streets wearing a Mother Hubbard dress would be arrested and lodged in jail. **1894** *Outing* XXIV. 271/1 Six years ago the finest dress to be seen was a calico Mother Hubbard. **1911** *Daily Colonist* (Victoria, B.C.) 19 Apr. 24/4 Overall Aprons, of navy print with white dots, made in Mother Hubbard style. **1919** W. S. MAUGHAM *Moon & Sixpence* xlix. 212 Tiaré Johnson..was dressed usually in a pink Mother Hubbard. **1939** J. STEINBECK *Grapes of Wrath* viii. 99 Ma..wore a loose Mother Hubbard of grey cloth... The dress came down to her ankles. **1943** H. W. KRIEGER *Island Peoples of Western Pacific* 40 The native dress of the women [of the Gilbert Islands], a grass skirt extending from the waist to the knee, has been for the most part replaced by the 'Mother Hubbard', which is made of imported cotton print cloth. **1964** *Guardian* 28 Dec. 6/4 She no more looks like a Mother Bunch than sounds like one.. a fairly plump but elegant, well-dressed woman. **1966** 'R. STANDISH' *Widow Hack* viii. 87, I can persuade you to swim wearing a Mother Hubbard over your swimsuit. Then I'll be able to concentrate.

II. Technical applications.

5. In obsolete scientific uses: after L. *mater*.

†**a.** *Anat.* In the names of certain structures in the brain. ***hard mother*** = DURA MATER; ***godly, meek, mild, soft mother*** = PIA MATER. *Obs.*

1398 TREVISA *Barth. De P.R.* v. i. (Tollem. MS.), þe harde moder and þe milde moder. *Ibid.* v. iii. (1495) 105. *Ibid.* 106 The seconde webbe and skynne of the brayne hyghte pia mater the meke moder. **1541** R. COPLAND *Guydon's Quest. Chirurg.* Ej, The soft moder by vaynes. **1594** [see GODLY *a.* 3]. **1615** CROOKE *Body of Man* 444 The one of these..is thicke and called *dura mater* the hard Mother, the other..thinne called *pia mater*, the deere or neere Mother.

b. *Astrol.* = MATER 1. *Obs.*

c **1391** CHAUCER *Astrol.* I. §3 The Moder of thyn Astrolabie is the thikkeste plate.

c. *Geomancy.* (See quot. 1591.) *Obs.*

1591 SPARRY tr. *Cattan's Geomancie* 8 These four figures be called the mothers, whereof the first is attributed to the Fire, the second to the Aire, the third to the Water, the fourth to the Earthe. **1653** R. SANDERS *Physiogn.* 32, I erected my Figure, drawing from my points and lines, a Mother. **1889** *Sat. Rev.* 16 Feb. 175/1 You then have in all four geomantic figures, which are called the mothers. The top spot (or pair of spots) of each mother is called the head, the second the neck, &c.

6. = ***mother-liquor, -water***: see 17 a.

1611 FLORIO, *Acqua Maestra*, the master-water. Salt-peeter men call it mother of Salt peeter. **1674** RAY *Collection* 136 (Manner of making Vitriol) The liquor that remains after the vitriol is crystallized, they call the mother. **1678** *Phil. Trans.* XII. 1055 When the Work is begun, and Alum once made, then they save the Liquour which comes from the Alum, or wherein the Alum shoots, which they call Mothers. **1681** GREW *Musæum* III. §iii. i. 343 The Lee after the first shooting of the Alum; is called Mothers. **1758** REID tr. *Macquer's Chym.* I. 240 Evaporate and crystallize... Repeat the same operation till the liquor will yield no more crystals: it will then be very thick, and goes by the name of *Mother of Nitre*. **1839** *Penny Cycl.* XV. 448/1 *Mother-water.* When any saline solution has been evaporated so as to deposit crystals on cooling, the remaining solution is termed the mother-water, or sometimes merely the mothers.

7. (More fully, ***artificial mother***.) An apparatus for rearing chickens artificially.

1807 *Trans. Soc. Arts* XXV. 25 Artificial mothers for the chickens to run under. **1830** 'B. MOUBRAY' *Dom. Poultry* (ed. 6) 48 An artificial mother cannot be dispensed with, under which the chickens may brood and shelter. **1884** KNIGHT *Dict. Mech.* Suppl., *Mother*, the hen-mother at Baker's Cresshill poultry farm is of hollow zinc, filled with hot water [etc.]. **1906** *Westm. Gaz.* 14 Nov. 8/3 Incubators, and poultry 'mothers'.

8. A cask or vat used in vinegar-making.

1830 M. DONOVAN *Dom. Econ.* I. 329 Into each vat or mother are poured twenty-two gallons of good vinegar boiling. **1839** URE *Dict. Arts* 3 The vessels employed for carrying on the fermentation are casks, called mothers.

9. The inner bark of a cork-tree.

1862 *Illustr. Lond. News* 25 Jan. 101/1 The first act of the cultivator is to separate it [the 'male'] from the trunk, which thus leaves exposed the liber, termed 'mother'.

10. *Naut.* = ***mother-ship***: see 17 a, below.

1907 *Daily Chron.* 5 Aug. 4/4 Four 'mothers' and the 'Sapphire', flagship of Admiral Montgomerie.

11. A disc with grooves that is made from the plating of an electrotyped master matrix and is used to make a stamper for gramophone records.

1918 H. SEYMOUR *Reproduction of Sound* 182 The obverse impressions of the original matrix are called 'mothers' in the trade, in view of their office in reproducing matrices from the 'master'. **1935** H. C. BRYSON *Gramophone Record* vi. 134 The mother, usually about ·03 inch thick, is then stripped from the master by inserting a blunt knife carefully between them and prising them apart. **1952** GODFREY & AMOS *Sound Recording & Reproduction* v. 139 A second negative copy known as the 'stamper' or 'working matrix' is obtained from the mother. **1968** *Jazz Monthly* Feb. 4/1 John Steiner.. owns the rights to what remains of the Paramount company, including numerous masters and mothers, so it is likely that the actual recording quality will be a great deal better than that on most past Paramount-derived reissues.

III. 12. a. The womb. *Obs.*

1398 TREVISA *Barth. De P.R.* v. xlix. (1495) 166 The moder in wymen is synguler membre disposyd as a bladder. **14..** *Parts of Hum. Body* in Wr.-Wülcker 632/7 Modure, *matrix.* **1545** RAYNOLD *Byrth Mankynde* 9 These thre woordes, the matrix, the mother, and the wombe do sygnyfie but one thyng. **1609** HOLLAND *Amm. Marcell.* 55 The daintie meat made of the mother..of a young sow. **1657** W. COLES *Adam in Eden* ix. 20 The lesser Lavander is much commended in all Diseases of the Mother. **1681** W. ROBERTSON *Phraseol. Gen.* (1693) 897 The mother or womb; *matrix.* **1706** PHILLIPS (ed. Kersey), *Hystera*, the Mother or Womb.

fig. **1398** TREVISA *Barth. De P.R.* XI. xiv. (Tollem. MS.), As Gregory sayeþ, he [lightning] comeþ oute of his moder [L. *de matrice sua*] as a twynkelynge of an ye. **1610** WILLET *Hexapla Dan.* 291 That first law was the mother and wombe as it were of all Gods precepts.

†**b.** ***rising*** (***suffocation, swelling upward,*** etc.) ***of the mother***: Hysteria.

1527 ANDREW *Brunswyke's Distyll. Waters* M iv, Dronke of the same water..is very good for women whose moder dooth ronne upwarde to the harte. **1601** HOLLAND *Pliny* II. 40 The rising or suffocation of the mother in women,..it cureth. **1626** BACON *Sylva* §935 They doe use for the Accident of the Mother, to burn Feathers [etc.]: and by those Ill Smels the Rising of the Mother is put down.

13. Hysteria: equivalent to the phrases in 12 b. Also ***fits of the mother***. *Obs.* or *arch.*

14.. *Stockh. Med. MS.* II. 314 in *Anglia* XVIII. 315 It is good to playster & many oþer thyng For þe moder & to drynkyng. **1545** RAYNOLD *Byrth Mankynde* 116 [Diseases of infants.] Fearefulnesse in the dreames: the mother: yssuynge out of the fundament gut. **1605** SHAKS. *Lear* II. iv. 56 Oh how this Mother swels vp toward my heart! *Historica passio*, downe thou climing sorrow. **1607** TOPSELL *Hist. Fourf. Beasts* (1658) 104 It pacifieth the milt,..expelleth away mothers. **1615** CROOKE *Body of Man* 231 Many passions called *Hystericæ*, which we call fits of the Mother. **1620** VENNER *Via Recta* (1650) 63 It is not fit for women to use that are subject to hystericall fits, which they call the Mother. **1672** JOSSELYN *New Eng. Rarities* 86 Mayweed, excellent for the mother. **1706–7** FARQUHAR *Beaux Strat.* I. i, She cures..fits of the mother, in women. **1792** SIBLY *Occult Sciences* I. 103 The particular diseases of this sign are ..hardness of the spleen, mother, hypocondriac melancholy. **1820** MAIR *Tyro's Dict.* (ed. 10) 373 *Strangulatus*, a disease in women called the mother.

IV. Quasi-adj. and in Combination.

14. Used *appositively*: = 'that is a mother'.

a. *lit.*, of animals.

a **1300** *Cursor M.* 14969 A moder ass yee sal þar find, And yee hir sal vn-do vte of hir band. **1465** *Paston Lett.* II. 211 There lefte behynde of Heylesdonfolde of my mastre schepe xlj modreschep. **1630** in R. Griffiths *Ess. Conservancy Thames* (1746) 74 No Trinck shall stand to fish before any Breach Mouth at the rising or sinking of any Mother-Fishes, or in the Time of Spawn or Brood of Fishes. **1697** DRYDEN *Virg. Georg.* III. 87 The Mother Cow must wear a low'ring Look. **1793** COWPER *A Tale* 45 The mother-bird is gone to sea. **1817** COLERIDGE *Zapolya* II. ii, The mother-falcon hath her nest above it. **1882** FLOYER *Unexpl. Baluchistan* 202 Then there were four old mother goats.

b. of a woman or a goddess.

1625 K. LONG tr. *Barclay's Argenis* I. xx. 58 Pallas, whose young and tender yeeres No Mother-goddesse dandeled. **1675** HAN. WOOLLEY *Gentlew. Companion* 3 Be ye Mother-patterns of Virtue to your Daughters. **1759** GRAINGER *Tibullus* I. 41 Thee, Orpheus, what avail'd..Thy Mother-muse and beast-enchanting song. **1904** W. M. RAMSAY *Lett. to Seven Ch.* xix. 258 The tutelary deity of Smyrna was the Mother-goddess Cybele.

c. *transf.* and *fig.* of things (see sense 2); *spec.* **mother-house**, the founding house of a religious order.

a **1225** *Ancr. R.* 216 ȝe habbeð iherd..of þeo þet me cleopeð ȝe seoue moder sunnen. **1479** *Priory of Hexham* (Surtees) II. 24 Molendinum..cum stagno et le modir-dame. **1594** HOOKER *Eccl. Pol.* I. iii. §2 Those principall & mother elements of the world, wherof all things in this lower world are made. **1604** HIERON *Wks.* I. 484 Because ignorance is a mother sin, therefore [etc.]. **1611** COTGR., *Veine saphene*, the mother veine. *c* **1611** CHAPMAN *Iliad* XXII. 129 Till they reacht, where those two mother springs, Of deepe Scamander, pour'd abroad, their siluer murmurings. **1645** RUTHERFORD *Tryal & Tri. Faith* (1845) 85 Christ hath covenant-right to the promises by this mother-right, that God is his God by covenant. **1661** *Manifest publisht to their Brethren by General Chapter of Catholick English Clergy* 3 Dr. Leyburn does calumniate us, as being Enemies to our Mother-house, the Colledge of Doway. **1691** NORRIS *Pract. Disc.* 118 Love..is a general Mother-Vertue, the principle of a more particular and special Obedience. **1763** MILLS *Syst. Pract. Husb.* IV. 403 The layers..must be allowed two years to take root, before they are cut off from the mother-tree. *a* **1773** A. BUTLER *Lives Saints* (1779) III. 243 When in 1504 the abbey of Mount Cassino joined this Congregation, it took the name of this mother-house. **1784** M. WEIGHTON *Drainage Award* 9 The mother drain, or navigable canal, now made. **1791** E. DARWIN *Bot. Gard.* I. 32 Lifts proud Anteus from his mother-plains. **1798** COLERIDGE *Fears in Solit.* 176 O dear Britain! O my Mother Isle! **1840** [see *branch house* s.v. BRANCH *sb.* 13]. **1854** STANLEY *Mem. Canterb.* i. (1857) 26 The Cathedral of Canterbury [is] the mother cathedral of England. **1874** RAYMOND *Statist. Mines & Mining* 342 On the supposition that it is the mother-vein of the country from which the ores of the Silver Flat..are derived. **1932** C. P. CURRAN in F. J. Sheed *Irish Way* 269 In this spirit she worked for ten years in the Mother-house and novitiate. **1956** K. HUME *Nun's Story* i. 12 The Order was established at the end of the eighteenth century. How many postulants had passed through this mother house could never be guessed.

d. In modern Biology and Pathology, of structures or growths from which others proceed, as ***mother-abscess, -meristem, nucleus, -vesicle***.

1898 P. MANSON *Trop. Diseases* xxiii. 361 Generally the pulmonary abscess communicates with the *mother-abscess in the liver. **1874** *Q. Jrnl. Microsc. Sci.* XIV. 304 The *mother-meristem of the fibro-vascular system. **1891** *Syd. Soc. Lex.*, **Mother nucleus.* **1885–8** FAGGE & PYE-SMITH *Princ. Med.* (ed. 2) I. 28 In such cases [of infection by inoculation] however, there is developed a 'primary' or '*mother-vesicle'.

15. a. Simple attrib. (more or less *rhetorical*): as ***mother arms, bosom, heart, -instinct, love, mind, pain, pang, pity, -sentiment, smile, want***; objective, as ***mother †queller, -slayer***; ***mother murdering*** adj.; instrumental, as ***mother-centred, -dominated, murdered*** adj.; parasynthetic, as ***mother hearted*** adj. Also ***motherwards, motherwise*** advs.

1843 CARLYLE *Past & Pr.* III. viii. 235 In how many ways ..does she, as with blessed *mother-arms, enfold us all! **1837** —— *Fr. Rev.* I. III. ii. 135 How she will reabsorb the former into her *Mother-bosom. **1956** FIRTH & DJAMOUR in R. Firth *Two Studies of Kinship in London* ii. 41 Some United States sociologists..have suggested the term '*mother-centred families' for households in which the mother has the dominant role. **1965** *Observer* 4 Apr. 26/4 Pirandello..was a mother-centred man. **1963** *Times* 23 Apr. 16/4 The *mother-dominated hero. **1881** 'MARK TWAIN' *Prince & Pauper* 114 Her sharp *mother-instinct seemed to detect it. **1920** T. P. NUNN *Education* xi. 131 A thorough-going misogynist could make out a case for applying the adjectives 'mechanical', 'blind', 'unintelligent', even to human mother-instinct. **1854** [DE POWYS] *Uriel*, etc. (1857) 106 All things rest,..Lulled in Mary's *mother-love. **1647** COWLEY *Mistr., My Hrt. Discovered* 16 Thoughts..Fair and chast, as *Mother-Mind. *a* **1592** MARLOWE *Ovid's Eleg.* II. xiv. 30 *Mother-murder'd Itys. **1590** C'TESS PEMBROKE *Antonie* 58 Orestes torche, Which sometimes burnt his *mother-murdering soule. **1709** MRS. MANLEY *Secret Mem.* (1736) II. 44 When the *Mother-Pains came upon her. *Ibid.* III. 15 Like..Abortives under the *Mother Pangs. **1819** J. H. PAYNE *Brutus* v. iii, To strike their country in the mother-pangs Of struggling child-birth. **1878** PATER *Wks.* (1901) V. 110 His [C. Lamb's] simple *mother-pity for

those who suffer. *c* **1440** *Promp. Parv.* 341/2 *Modyr qwellare,.. *matricida.* **1920** *Mother-sentiment [see FATHER *sb.* 11 b]. *c* **1375** *Sc. Leg. Saints* xvi. (*Magdalena*) 462 Allace! nov is þe barne sa borne *modyr-slaar. **1483** *Cath. Angl.* 242/1 A Modyr slaer, *matricida.* **1838** MRS. BROWNING *Rom. Ganges* xix, Press deeper down thy *mother-smile His glossy curls among. **1856** —— *Aur. Leigh* I. 40, I felt a *mother-want about the world. **1893** *Tablet* 15 July 110 It does not forbid the dying son to cast his eyes *motherwards. **1890** LE GALLIENNE *Meredith* 52 She smiles on them *motherwise.

b. with the sense 'inherited or learned from one's mother', 'native', as in MOTHER TONGUE and combinations imitated from this; also in MOTHER-WIT, ***mother-sense***.

1603 OWEN *Pembrokeshire* iii. (1892) 36 For otherwise the Englishe tongue had not ben theire comon and mother speache as it was. **1611** BEAUM. & FL. *Philaster* v. iv, Let.. your nimble tongs forget your mother Gibberish. **1644** MILTON *Educ.* 2 He were nothing so much to be esteem'd a learned man, as any..tradesman competently wise in his mother dialect only. **1732** LAW *Serious C.* xix. (1761) 324 As we call our first language our mother-tongue, so we may as justly call our first tempers our mother-tempers. **1851** BORROW *Lavengro* xvii, You want two things, brother: mother sense, and gentle Rommany. **1904** J. WELLS *J. H. Wilson* vi. 64 A racy and powerful evangelist in his mother-Scotch.

16. a. Genitive combinations, as **mother's bairn** Sc. (said of a spoiled child); **mother's blessing** (see quot. 1861); **mother's boy**, a boy or man who resembles or is dominated by, or excessively attached to, his mother; a sissy; **mother's darling** = *mother's boy*; **Mother's** (or **Mothers'**) **Day** orig. *U.S.*, a day on which mothers are particularly honoured: in the U.S., the second Sunday in May; in Britain = *Mothering Sunday*; also *attrib.*; **mother's help**, a person who helps a mother, mainly by looking after children; **mothers' meeting**, a meeting (usually weekly) of mothers (of the working classes) connected with a parish or congregation, for the purpose of receiving instruction and counsel; also *fig.*; **mother's milk** (see MILK *sb.* 1 c); **mother's pet** = PET *sb.*[1] 2 a; also, the youngest child of a family; **mother's ruin** *slang*, gin (cf. RUIN *sb.* 10); **Mothers' Union**, an organization for mothers to meet together regularly. Also, (*every*) MOTHER'S SON, MOTHER'S CHILD (†in ME. *moder bern*), **daughter** = (every) person.

a **1225** *St. Marher.* 2 Ha..walde ȝeorne ȝef godes wille were þæt ha moste beon an of þe moder bern þæt so muche drohen for drihtin. **1896** A. LANG *Monk of Fife* i. 3 Of me, in our country speech, it used to be said that I was 'a mother's bairn'. **1861** MAYHEW *London Labour* (1862) Extra vol. 245/2 My husband..can't do nothink but give the babies a dose of 'Mother's Blessing' (that's laudanum, sir, or some sich stuff) to sleep 'em when they's squally. **1880** F. STEVENSON *Let.* July in J. Pope-Hennessy *R. L. Stevenson* (1974) vii. 142 Louis is, as I know, a mother's boy..and I am sure he looks like you. **1924** D. H. LAWRENCE *Phoenix II* (1968) 619 Oh, women, beware the mother's boy! **1945** 'L. LEWIS' *Birthday Murder* (1951) ii. 26 Stan's happy as he is being supported by his mother. He's a mother's boy. **1973** W. J. BURLEY *Death in Salubrious Place* ii. 42 Mother's boy —that's his trouble, but it takes all sorts. **1857** LYTTON *What will he do with It?* (1859) I. I. i. 7 He looked like a mother's darling—perhaps he was one. **1922** JOYCE *Ulysses* 33 That knockkneed mother's darling. **1936** 'J. TEY' *Shilling for Candles* iv. 41 Mother's darlings had those eyes; so, sometimes, had womanizers. **1675** COTTON *Burlesque upon B.* 147 Ladies! thou (Paris) moov'st my laughter, They'r Deities ev'ry Mothers Daughter. **1908** *Congr. Rec.* 9 May 5971/1 *Resolved*, That Sunday, May 10, 1908, be recognized as Mothers' Day. **1926** A. HUXLEY *Jesting Pilate* IV. 264 In the First Methodist Church..they were going to distribute 'Mother's Day Flowers to all Worshippers'. (On Mother's Day you must wear a red carnation if your mother is alive, a white one if she is dead.) **1958** *Listener* 27 Nov. 874/1 As uniquely and inimitably American as John Foster Dulles or Mothers' Day. **1959** I. & P. OPIE *Lore & Lang. Schoolch.* xii. 242 In 1956 the majority of High Street shops [in Britain] were displaying 'Mother's Day' gifts in their windows. **1962** *Listener* 12 Apr. 628/1 Last Mother's Day—a retail selling device imported from the United States—the flower-shops were as busy as ice-cream vans during a heat wave. **1881** *Instr. Census Clerks* (1885) 30 Mother's Help. **1908** A. S. M. HUTCHINSON *Once aboard Lugger* I. vii. 41 She is not exactly my friend; she is my—my employer. I'm a mother's-help. **1961** *Evening Standard* 14 July 25/5 (Advt.), A Mother's Help..for happy family. **1865** C. M. YONGE *Clever Woman of the Family* II. xxx. 312 The mothers' meetings for the soldiers' wives. **1887** 'EDNA LYALL' *Knt. Errant* (1889) 282, I was trying to get the Mothers'-Meeting accounts right. **1925** FRASER & GIBBONS *Soldier & Sailor Words* 159 *Mother's meeting*, an occasional name among bluejackets for the captain's address to a ship's company. **1946** D. HAMSON *We fell among Greeks* xviii. 195, I noticed one particular squad which was openly idling... 'Why do you stop work and hold a mother's meeting when I go away?' **1824** J. MACTAGGART *Scottish Gallovidian Encycl.* 348 *Mithers-pet*, the youngest child of a family; the mother's greatest favourite; the *Tony Lumpkin* of the house. **1830** A. PICKEN *Dominie's Legacy* I. 104 He was..as raw looking, overgrown, gawky a youth, as any mother's pet of a student. **1937** PARTRIDGE *Dict. Slang* 535/1 Mother's ruin. **1955** P. JONES *Birthday Honours* I. 10, I have been to a party, darling. .. What would you like? 'Mother's Ruin'? **1970** *New Scientist* 23 Apr. 165/2 Gin, as shown by the old temperance demonstration of dropping earthworms into adjacent glasses of water and mother's ruin, can certainly eliminate unwanted planarians. **1888** MRS. G. SUMNER *To Mothers of Higher Classes* vi. 55 The 'Mothers' Union', now started in the Winchester Diocese, and in other Dioceses, is a very simple plan. **1972** L. LAMB *Picture Frame* xiv. 123, I shall have to run a mothers' union or something.

†**b.** The uninflected genitive survived late in Sc. in certain combinations, as ***mother-brother***, ***sister***, a maternal uncle or aunt; ***mother half***, ***motherside*** = mother's side (with reference to descent). *Obs.*

1483 CAXTON *Gold. Leg.* 70/2 This thamar was Absalons suster by the moder syde. *a* **1500** *Burgh Lawis* xcviii. (1868) 48 That ayre..sal be in yemsell of his frendis on the mudyr-half. **1513** in *Fam. Rose of Kilravock* (Spalding Club) 183 Valter Ross of Kinstary moder broder to the said vmquhile Archibalde. *a* **1578** LINDESAY (Pitscottie) *Chron. Scot.* (S.T.S.) II. 175 Thair captane Monsr de Gwise our quens mother brother. **1596** DALRYMPLE tr. *Leslie's Hist. Scot.* IX. 181 He was the kingis mother brother. **1622** MABBE tr. *Aleman's Guzman d'Alf.* II. 184 His kinswoman by the mother-side. **1678** *Wedderburn's Vocab.* 11 (Jam.) *Avunculus*, the mother-brother. *Ibid.*, *Matertera*, the mother-sister. **1768** BOSWELL *Corsica* ii. (ed. 2) 58 Being uncle by the mother-side to Eurysthenes.

17. Special comb.: **a.** attrib. (and genitive), **mother-alkali**, alkali obtained from the mother-liquor left after crystallization; **mother-and-baby home**, an establishment serving as a maternity home for unmarried mothers, usu. with pre- and post-natal services; **mother-bomb** (see quot. 1971); †**mother-borough** = *mother-city* (*a*); **mother-cell** *Biol.*, a cell which later undergoes cell division and gives rise to daughter-cells; *spec.* a cell which later undergoes meiotic division; **mother-child** *a.*, of or pertaining to a mother and her child; **mother-city**, (*a*) = METROPOLIS in various senses; (*b*) a city regarded as serving as a mother to someone; **mother-clove** (see quot. 1866); **mother coal**, mineral charcoal; **mother complex**, a complex (see COMPLEX 3) about one's mother; **mother-cult**, the worship of a mother-goddess; **mother-daughter** *a.*, of or pertaining to a mother and her daughter; †**mother descent**, descent by the mother's side; **mother-feryer** *U.S. slang* = *mother-fucker*; **mother figure**, a person or thing endowed with some of the attributes of a mother; **mother fit** = 'fit of the mother', a hysteric attack; **mother fixation**, a fixation (see FIXATION 3 b) on one's mother; **mother-fucker** *coarse slang* (orig. and chiefly *U.S.*), a base, despicable person; someone or something that is very unpleasant; hence **mother-fucking** *ppl. a.*, despicable, base; unpleasant; = BLOODY *a.* 10; **mother gate** *Coal-mining* [GATE *sb.*[2]] (see quot. 1860); **mother-grabbing** *ppl. a.* (*U.S. slang*) = *mother-fucking* ppl. adj.; **mother idea** [= F. *idée mère*], the fundamental idea (of something, e.g. of an institution, a literary work); **mother image, imago**, the mental or realized image of an idealized or archetypal mother; **mother-in** (or **and**)**-babe**, used *attrib.* to designate a wooden bobbin, the hollow shank of which contains another smaller bobbin; **mother liquid, liquor** = the liquid left after crystallization, e.g. of sea-salt; **mother-lode** *Min.*, the principal vein of ore; also *fig.*; **mother-loving** *ppl. a.*, (*a*) that loves one's mother; (*b*) = *mother-fucking* ppl. adj.; freq. used as a vague intensive; **mother-lye**, the mother-liquor of an alkali; **mother maid, -maiden**, the Virgin Mary; **mother mark** (? *obs.*), **mother's mark**, a nævus; **mother mould** *Sculpture*, a rigid mould which holds casting material; **mother pian** = *mamma pian*; **mother plane** orig. *U.S.*, an aircraft which launches or controls another aircraft; **mother plant**, (*a*) a parent plant from which other plants have been derived; (*b*) the female or seed-bearing parent of a hybrid (B. D. Jackson *Gloss. Bot. Terms* 1900); **mother queen** = QUEEN-MOTHER; also applied to a queen-bee; **mother-raper** *U.S. slang* = *mother-fucker*; **mother-raping** *ppl. a.* (*U.S. slang*) = *mother-fucking* ppl. adj.; **mother right**, (*a*) = MATRIARCHY; (*b*) the custom by which dynastic succession passes only in the female line; **mother ship**, (*a*) a ship or airship escorting or having charge of a number of other, usu. smaller, craft; also *transf.*; (*b*) an aircraft or rocket from which another aircraft or rocket is launched or controlled; = *mother plane*; **mother sick** *a.*, pining for one's mother (cf. *mammy-sick*); **mother skein**, 'a continuous ribbon-like figure of chromatin in the early stages of nuclear division' (B. D. Jackson); **mother-son** *a.*, of or pertaining to a mother and her son; †**mother spar**, the matrix of an ore; **mother spot** = *mother's mark*; **mother star** = MONASTER; **mother stone**, (*a*) the matrix of a mineral; also, a stone from which other minerals are derived by structural or chemical change; (*b*) see quot. 1770–4; **mother substitute, surrogate**, a person or thing that takes the place of the mother; †**mother suppository**, a suppository for the womb, a pessary; **mother-symbol**, that which is symbolic of the mother or of motherhood; **mother thought** = *mother idea*; **mother tincture**, in Homœopathy, a pure undiluted tincture of a drug; **mother-to-be**, an expectant mother; †**mother wasp** (see quot.); **mother-water** = *mother-liquor*; **mother wool** (see quot.); **mother yaw** = *mamma pian*.

1880 LOMAS *Alkali Trade* 244 'Weak' or '*mother' alkali is a fine powdery substance. **1965** HALL & HOWES *Church in Social Work* v. 90 The county council was running its own *mother and baby home. **1972** *Guardian* 14 July 11/2 Miss McM will not consider going into a mother and baby home and is against adoption. **1971** *New Scientist* 21 Jan. 135/2 Shrapnel grenades..are dropped individually, or in clusters from canisters ('*mother-bombs'). *a* **1225** *Leg. Kath.* 46 Þe *moder burh of Alexandres riche. **1845** *Encycl. Metrop.* VII. 239/1 This may depend either upon the walls of the *mother-cell having been originally thicker, or [etc.]. **1875** BENNETT & DYER *Sachs' Bot.* 440 The pollen-grains, when free from their mother-cells, are unicellular and spherical. **1875** Mother-cell [see ASCOMYCETES]. **1920** W. E. AGAR *Cytology* vii. 212 The diagrams start with the pollen mother-cell in the male and the embryo-sac mother-cell in the female—in each case the last cell generation of the diploid phase. **1932** C. D. DARLINGTON *Rec. Adv. Cytol.* i. 5 In a 'mother-cell' two nuclear divisions follow one another rapidly while the chromosomes only divide once. **1959** W. ANDREW *Textbk. Compar. Histol.* xii. 486 Earlier workers believed this cell to be a mother cell for the successive groups of spermatogonia. **1937** H. READ *Art & Society* v. 191 At first these instincts are concentrated on the mother, and any being that threatens to interfere with the *mother-child bond incurs the child's enmity. **1963** AUDEN *Dyer's Hand* 440 The mother-child relationship..stands for the kind of love that is unaffected by time. **1563–87** FOXE *A. & M.* (1596) 10/2 Bishops of the *mother citie and archbishops were all one. **1575–85** ABP. SANDYS *Serm.* viii. 132 The mother Citie of the Realme is reasonably furnished with faithfull preachers. **1908** *Westm. Gaz.* 4 Aug. 5/1 Capetown ..is in the truest sense the μητρόπολις of South Africa, the 'mother-city' from which the rest have sprung. **1935** L. MACNEICE *Poems* 20 See Belfast... This was my mother-city, these my paps... I cannot be Anyone else than what this land engendered me. **1690** BLANCARD *Lex. Med.* 41 *Anthophylli*...Angl. *Mother cloves. **1693** A. VAN LEEUWENHOEK in *Phil. Trans.* XVII. 952, I chose some of the largest Cloves I could find, called Mother-Cloves. **1866** *Treas. Bot.*, *Mother cloves*, a name in the East for the fully expanded flower-buds of *Caryophyllus aromaticus*. **1873** DAWSON *Earth & Man* vi. 118 A dusty fibrous substance, like charcoal, called '*mother-coal' by miners. **1919** M. K. BRADBY *Psycho-Analysis* v. 59 If sexual fixation takes place at the third stage, the '*mother-complex' will create an obstacle to a man's happiness in married life. **1924** *Spectator* 16 Aug. 229/1, I got a mother-complex. **1936** C. DAY LEWIS *Friendly Tree* I. vi. 87 He sucks a pipe constantly. The mother-complex. Infantilism. **1948** *Yearbk. Psychoanal.* IV. 172 (*title*) The mother complex in literature. **1960** R. F. C. HULL tr. *Jung's Structure & Dynamics of Psyche* in *Coll. Wks.* (1966) VIII. v. 369 Analysis shows an infantile longing for the mother, a so-called mother complex. **1909** *Westm. Gaz.* 2 Feb. 5/1 From the trend of recent writings in Hindu literature it is suggested that the *Mother cult has been revived. **1969** C. FREMLIN *Possession* ii. 17 The closeness of the *mother-daughter relationship. **1974** —— *By Horror Haunted* 138 An ordinary, typical mother-daughter misunderstanding. **1642** FULLER *Holy & Prof. St.* IV. xv. 313 Her royall birth by her Fathers side doth comparatively make her *Mother-descent seem low. **1946** MEZZROW & WOLFE *Really Blues* 4 A *motherferyer that would cut your throat for looking. **1953** *New Biol.* XIV. 29 In birds, for instance, we have the astonishing phenomenon called imprinting, by which the sign stimulus of the IRM to follow a *mother-figure differentiates. **1957** *Economist* 7 Sept. 821/2 The commonest illusion..is that the United Nations is a miraculous mother-figure which will give suck and shelter to all comers. **1970** *Daily Tel.* 22 Sept. 14 Mrs Meir is both a superb politician and a Jewish mother-figure which the young State [of Israel] may well need. **1971** *Ibid.* 18 Jan. 10/7 The association also says there should be a 'mother figure' in each nursing school to whom students can turn for advice. **1657** P. HENRY *Diary & Lett.* (1882) 65 *Mother-fits. **1681** GREW *Musæum* I. i. 4 A Thong hereof ty'd about the middle, is of good use..especially against Mother-Fits. **1921** *Internat. Jrnl. Psychoanal.* II. 55 Jesus is no longer satisfied to make Joseph his ideal (a hard task for a boy with a strong *Mother-fixation of love). **1954** *Scott. Jrnl. Theol.* VII. 393 Rationalism has handed the problem [of worship] over to the psychologist to explain in terms of repressions, mother-fixations, infantile-regressions and the like. **1969** C. ALLEN *Textbk. Psychosexual Disorders* (ed. 2) xvii. 375 Sailors usually carry..the mother's photograph... There is strong mother-fixation in their choice of prostitutes. **1956** *Amer. Speech* XXXI. 111 This linguistic vacuum is being filled by a new obscenity symbol, **mother-fucker*. **1960** J. BALDWIN in *Partisan Rev.* Spring 292 You've got to fight with the elevator boy because the motherf*****'s *white*! **1970** R. D. ABRAHAMS *Positively Black* ii. 45 I'm one motherfucker that don't mind dying. **1971** B. W. ALDISS *Soldier Erect* 142 Jock..looked up into my face. 'The bastards, the fucking mean scab-devouring mankey-minded shower of mother-fuckers!' **1971** J. MANDELKAU *Buttons* xiii. 149 These mother-fuckers had been whining they had no food to sell the people—and this place was stacked! **1973** *Black Panther* 21 July 16/1 We will kill any motherfucker that stands in the way of our freedom. **1959** N. MAILER *Advts. for Myself* (1961) 351 They could smash some *mother-f——ing Reds. **1968** *Rat* 13–16 May 10/2 The police were interminably long in getting into Math. Good mother-fucking barricades. **1969** P. ROTH *Portnoy's Complaint* 106 You muff-diving, mother-fucking son of a bitch! **1974** S. ELLIN *Stronghold* 23 'You motherfucking black clown,' Harvey says without heat, 'nothing is changed.' **1839** *Penny Cycl.* XV. 247 When the bord or '*mother-gate' has proceeded some distance on both sides of

the pit [etc.]. **1860** *Eng. & For. Min. Gloss* (Newc. Terms), *Mothergate*, the bord along which the coals are trammed from a district of workings. **1959** M. RUSS *Half Moon Haven* (1961) I. 60 There isn't one item on this *mother-grabbing planet that I 'like'. **1858** O. W. HOLMES *Aut. Breakf.-t* x, There is a *mother-idea in each particular kind of tree, which, if well marked, is probably embodied in the poetry of every language. **1941** L. MACNEICE *Poetry of W. B. Yeats* vii. 138 It would be tempting to regard Cathleen ni Houlihan, the Poor Old Woman, as a *mother image and so to refer much of Irish nationalism to a mother-fixation. **1968** C. RYCROFT *Crit. Dict. Psychoanal.* 93 Conceptions of the mother existing in the infant's mind formed by splitting of the mother image. **1973** J. SINGER *Boundaries of Soul* iv. 91 The Mother image appeared under strange circumstances to my analysand Margaret. **1916** B. M. HINKLE tr. *Jung's Psychol. of Unconscious* v. 250 That amount of libido which unconsciously is fastened to the *mother-imago. **1956** R. F. C. HULL tr. *Jung's Symbols of Transformation* in *Coll. Wks.* V. II. v. 222 The water and tree symbolism..likewise refer to the libido that is unconsciously attached to the mother-imago. **1919** T. WRIGHT *Romance Lace Pillow* xiii. 126 **Mother-in-Babe Bobbins*, in the hollowed shank of which a tiny wooden bobbin rattles. **1928** G. WHITING *Tools & Toys of Stitching* 220 The Cow-and-Calf and Mother-and-Babe bobbins—they are a perfect, never-ending joy and a masterpiece of the Midlands! **1969** E. H. PINTO *Treen* xxi. 311 Collectively, they are known as church window bobbins, but those with smaller bobbins inside the windows are described as mother-in-babe types. **1839** URE *Dict. Arts* 1133 The more of the crystalline particles are drained from the metallic bath, the richer does the *mother liquid become in silver. **1796** KIRWAN *Elem. Min.* (ed. 2) II. 362 The *mother liquor poured off. **1890** ABNEY *Photogr.* (ed. 6) 73 The mother liquor may be employed for intensifying. *c* **1882** J. H. BEADLE *Western Wilds* xxxiv. 561 What miners call a '*mother lode' is often like a tree in its upward development: below is the main trunk, above the branches diverge. **1927** B. A. MCKELVIE *Black Canyon* p. vi, They started up-stream in search of the mother-lode. **1960** *Encounter* XIV. III. 74 The pages of the T.L.S. were the very mother-lode of academic inanity. **1965** G. J. WILLIAMS *Econ. Geol. N.Z.* v. 58/1 The mother-lode that had been envisaged as the source of the gold in the Blue-spur 'cement'. **1972** *Times Lit. Suppl.* 25 Feb. 219/1 It is mother lode, with rich ore; but it lacks the refining that the author intended to give it. **1964** O. E. MIDDLETON in C. K. Stead *N.Z. Short Stories* (1966) 198 We'd all be drawing the dole like every other *mother-loving beach-comber. **1969** 'J. MORRIS' *Fever Grass* i. 6 Get her out of that mother-lovin' joint an' into the cab. **1800** *Med. Jrnl.* III. 82 These *mother-leys still contain a certain quantity of caustic soda. *c* **1865** *Circ. Sci.* I. 331/2 The fluid from which crystals are precipitated is called mother-lye. **1612** DONNE *Progr. Soul, 2nd Anniv.* 341 Where thou shalt see the blessed *Mother-maid. *c* **1425** *St. Mary of Oignies* II. viii. in *Anglia* VIII. 173 Lyke a childe soukynge þe pappes of þe *moder-mayden. **1797** *Encycl. Brit.* (ed. 3) XII. 615/2 *Nævus*, a mole on the skin, generally called a **mother's mark*. **1822–34** *Good's Study Med.* (ed. 4) IV. 536 These [moles] differ essentially from nævi or genuine mother marks. **1884** *Encycl. Brit.* XVII. 163/1 It is often congenital, hence the term 'mother's mark', or it may appear in early childhood. **1898** C. R. ASHBEE tr. *Cellini's Treat. Goldsmithing & Sculpture* 116 Put them into the cavities..in the mould... Or '*mother mould' as the sculptors would call it. **1947** J. C. RICH *Materials & Methods of Sculpture* v. 100 A heavily bodied plaster mix can be applied over the agar impression to form a mother mold or casing. **1969** R. MAYER *Dict. Art Terms & Techniques* 254/1 *Mother mold*, an outer case or container for a negative mold made of gelatin, rubber, or another weak, flexible substance. The mother mold is made of a rigid material. **1898** *Mother-pian [see MAMMA[1] e]. **1936** *Sun* (Baltimore) 6 July 9/1 Progress on the pick-a-back airplane, a combination in which a '*mother' plane will carry on its back a smaller long range seaplane for 'launching' at high altitude is more secret. **1945** *Time* 19 Nov. 52/2 Everything it sees is projected by radio on a screen in the mother plane. **1962** *Daily Tel.* 10 Sept. 18/4 The 'mother' plane would carry pick-a-back a plane which would be launched at the fringe of space. **1655–87** H. MORE *App. Antid.* (1712) 211 Now this regular conformation of the Seed came from the uniform motion of particles in the *Mother-plant. **1707** MORTIMER *Husb.* (1721) II. 48, I think those raised by Layers from a Mother-plant make the best Trees. **1868** DARWIN *Anim. & Pl.* xxvii. II. 365 Foreign pollen occasionally affects the mother-plant in a direct manner. **1591** *Troub. Reigne K. John* ii. 55 The *Mother Queene she taketh on amisse Gainst Ladie Constance. **1595** SHAKS. *John* II. i. 62 With him along is come the Mother Queene. **1816** KIRBY & SP. *Entomol.* xviii. (1818) II. 117 When the mother-queen was removed, several of the small females contended for the cell with indescribable rage. **1966** C. HIMES *Heat's On* iii. 30 Some *mother-raper is shooting at me with water-melon seeds. *Ibid.* ii. 22 The dirty mother-raping white nigger! **1969** Mother-raping [see *cock-sucking* ppl. adj. s.v. COCK *sb.*[1] 23]. **1885** *Mother right [see MATRIARCHY]. **1907** *Q. Rev.* July 195 Matriarchy, or rule of the mother, is not to be confused with mother-right, or rule through the mother. **1890** *Pall Mall G.* 2 June 2/1 In the case of the picket-boats, they should be entirely independent of a *mother-ship. **1902** H. C. FYFE *Submarine Warfare* v. 108 A wire-less message.. has been sent to the commander of the 'mother ship'. **1903** *Daily Chron.* 10 Jan. 5/1 The torpedo gunboat Hazard, which was stationed at Barrow to act as 'mother-ship' to the five tiny diving torpedo-boats. **1909** *Q. Rev.* Oct. 575 Depôt ships for destroyers, mother-ships for submarines, and oil-supply vessels. **1922** *Encycl. Brit.* XXX. 17/2 Scouts were flown off lighters at sea against airships, and off the decks of battleships and 'mother' ships. **1926** H. T. WILKINS *Marvels Mod. Mech.* 215 An engineer, aboard the airship, opened the telescopic apparatus which left the aeroplane swaying in space some 60 feet below the mother ship. **1938** *Flight* 8 Sept. 197/1 They [*sc.* engineers] designed for catapult launch from a mother ship;..they used diesel engines. **1946** in *Amer. Speech* (1947) XXII. 230/2 The Navy's drones will be sent into the cloud by one mother ship. **1962** J. TUNSTALL *Fishermen* ii. 46 The fleet of catching vessels transfers its fish..to a mother ship, which processes and freezes the fish at sea. **1967** *Times Rev. Industry* Apr. 48/3 Trailers, operating from the central plant and acting as 'mother ships' to the delivery vans, can replace the depots. **1969** *Observer* 20 July 7/3 After it has docked with the mother ship the astronauts will spend four hours going over every inch of the LEM. **1973** *Sci. Amer.* Nov. 23/1 The small 'killer' satellites in a 'mother ship' equipped with central guidance and detection devices. On command the mother ship would have oriented itself and determined when, at what rate and in what direction to launch its subsatellites. **1759** SARAH FIELDING *C'tess of Dellwyn* I. 112 In fact, she was Husband-sick in a Manner the very reverse of what is generally termed *Mother-sick; for Girls are so called when they pine on being separated from their Mothers. **1927** B. MALINOWSKI *Sex & Repression in Savage Society* II. iii. 100 Not one single case of *mother-son incest could be found. **1949** M. MEAD *Male & Female* xvi. 326 A mother-son combination is classified as bad for the son. **1681** GREW *Musæum* III. I. v. 306 The *Mother-Spar of the Tin-Ore. **1690** BLANCARD *Lex. Med.* 388 *Macula Matricalis* ..Angl. The *mother spot. **1849** CRAIG, *Mother-spots.* **1889** *Mother star [see MONASTER]. **1442** in Willis & Clark *Cambridge* (1886) I. 386 Cariage of xviij lodis of *modrestone. **1770–4** A. HUNTER *Georg. Ess.* (1803) I. 506 It's abounding with the stone, called in Hertfordshire, mother-stone (a concretion of many small blue pebbles). **1796** KIRWAN *Elem. Min.* (ed. 2) I. 433 Granite..is the mother-stone, by whose fusion basalt is produced. **1799** J. ROBERTSON *Agric. Perth* 17 Which some farmers call motherstone soil. **1855** J. R. LEIFCHILD *Cornwall Mines* 91 Quartz generally prevails in the matrix (mother stone). **1943** J. S. HUXLEY *Evolutionary Ethics* ii. 16 The absence in the infant's life of a mother or effective *mother-substitute during the crucial period from about one to three years old. **1965** F. SARGESON *Memoirs of Peon* vi. 173 Two young sparrow-legged ruffians..engaged in selling my mother-substitute a large trolley-load of empty bottles. **1578** LYTE *Dodoens* I. lxxxviii. 130 Pessarie (whiche is a *mother suppositorie). **1959** *Science* 21 Aug. 422/3 We took the calculated risk of constructing and using inanimate *mother surrogates rather than real mothers. **1969** E. STOTLAND *Psychol. of Hope* viii. 126 Cloth-covered objects..appear to satisfy a need for contact and closeness; the babies cling to these mother surrogates while they do not cling to those made of uncovered wire. **1956** R. F. C. HULL tr. *Jung's Symbols of Transformation* in *Coll. Wks.* V. 301 At this stage the *mother-symbol..points towards the unconscious as the creative matrix of the future. **1861** MOTLEY in *Corr.* (1889) I. 368 As to the *mother-thought of the book, it is to me original. **1902** *Encycl. Brit.* XXIX. 312/2 The pure tinctures are denominated '*mother tinctures'. **1906** W. DE MORGAN *Joseph Vance* xvi. 149 She makes some concession to my feelings on the subject of High Dilutions, and (at great risk to myself, she says) allows me to have Mother-Tinctures. **1960** C. DALE *Spring of Love* i. 26 She would take a magazine..and reread..Sister Jane's advice to *mothers-to-be. **1973** A. MORICE *Death & Dutiful Daughter* vii. 68 Has our little mother-to-be surfaced yet? **1679** M. RUSDEN *Further Discov. Bees* 4 The Male among Wasps, which some call the *Mother-Wasp, stings more venemously than the common Wasp doth. **1758** REID tr. *Macquer's Chym.* I. 245 All saline solutions in general, after having yielded a certain quantity of crystals, grow thick, and refuse to part with any more, though they still contain much Salt. They are called **Mother-waters.* **1854** J. SCOFFERN in *Orr's Circ. Sci., Chem.* 14 To clear away from any crystalline product the *mother-water.* **1727–41** CHAMBERS *Cycl.* s.v. *Wool*, The French and English usually separate each fleece into three sorts; viz. 1. **Mother-wool*, which is that of the back and neck. **1822–34** *Good's Study Med.* (ed. 4) II. 433 The master fungus being named [in St. Domingo] the mama-pian or *mother yaw.

b. Phrasal combinations with *of*: **† mother of amethyst**, ? = BLUE JOHN 2; **mother of anchovies**, the scad or horse-mackerel, *Trachurus saurus*; **mother of cloves** = *mother clove* (see 17 a); **mother of coal** = *mother coal* (see 17 a); **Mother of Commonwealths** *U.S.*, Virginia; **† mother of emeralds** (see quot.); **† mother of gold**, a mineral supposed to indicate the presence of gold (quot. 1596 identifies the word with MOTHER *sb.*[2]); **mother of the herrings** (see HERRING 1 c); **mother of millions**, the ivy-leaved toad-flax, *Cymbalaria muralis*; **† mother of the mine** (see quot.); **mother of (the) months**, the moon; **Mother of Parliaments**, (*a*) England; (*b*) the British Parliament; **Mother of Presidents** *U.S.*, (*a*) Virginia; (*b*) Ohio; **Mother of States** *U.S.*, (*a*) Connecticut; (*b*) Virginia; **mother of thousands**, (*a*) = mother of millions; (*b*) the common daisy, *Bellis perennis*; (*c*) *Saxifraga sarmentosa*; (*d*) the double blue creeping campanula (Britten & Holl.); (*e*) = HELXINE; **mother of wheat** (see quot.); **mother of the wood**, 'the *Asperula odorata*' (*Syd. Soc. Lex.* 1891); **mother of yaws** = *mother yaw* (*Ibid.*).

1797 *Encycl. Brit.* (ed. 3) XII. 79/1 What we call *amethyst root*, or **mother of amethyst*, is but a sparry fluor, of which we have plenty in Derbyshire. **1668** CHARLETON *Onomasticon* 143 *Trachurus*..the *Mother of Anchovies. **1727–52** CHAMBERS *Cycl.* s.v. *Clove*, *Mother of cloves. **1867** W. W. SMYTH *Coal & Coal-mining* 34 Soft mineral charcoal or 'mother-of-coal'. **1879** *Congress. Rec.* 10 Jan. 413/2 To pour out the vials of his impotent wrath upon the '*Mother of Commonwealths'. **1797** *Encycl. Brit.* (ed. 3) VI. 567/2 Hence the green cochle spar brought from Egypt may have obtained the name of **mother of emeralds.* **1596** RALEIGH *Discov. Guiana* To Rdr., In Guiana..the rocks..are in effect thorow-shining..which being tried to be no Marcasite..but are no other then *El* [*sic*] *madre del oro*..the *mother of golde, or as it is saide by others the scum of golde. **1712** E. COOKE *Voy. S. Sea* 26, I am of Opinion there is also Gold in the Island because we took up the Mother of Gold in several places by the Water-side. **1836** MRS. BRAY *Tamar & Tavy* I. xviii. 318 *Mother of millions, with its numerous small drooping flowers. **1794** W. HUTCHINSON *Hist. Cumbld.* I. *Catal. Anim.* etc. 52 Heterogeneous Iron Ores, Calx of Iron, mixed with calcareous earth. Sparry Iron Ore... Miners call it *mother of the mine. **1613** PURCHAS *Pilgrimage* (1614) 13 The silent Moone; which..is Queene of the Night,..*Mother of moneths. **1820** SHELLEY *Witch of Atlas* 73 Ten times the Mother of the Months had bent Her bow beside the folding-star. **1865** J. BRIGHT in *Birmingham Daily Post* 19 Jan. 5/1 We may be proud of this, that England is the ancient country of Parliaments... England is the *mother of Parliaments. **1910** *Encycl. Brit.* VII. 15/1 The early date at which the principle of self-government was established in England, the steady growth of the principle, the absence of civil dissension, and the preservation in the midst of change of so much of the old organization, have given its constitution a great influence over the ideas of politicians in other countries. This fact is expressed in the proverbial phrase—'England is the mother of parliaments'. **1918** *Daily Mirror* 12 Nov. 6/2 Never has the Mother of Parliaments seen such a scene of enthusiasm as when Mr. Lloyd George read out the armistice terms yesterday. **1926** FOWLER *Mod. Eng. Usage* 548/1 Mother of Parliaments (British Parliament). **1974** *Times* 24 Aug. 2/4 *France Soir*..went on to explain why in the country of the 'Mother of Parliaments' social tension has grown. **1827** A. SHERWOOD *Gaz. Georgia* 98 James Monroe..was born in Va., the *mother of Presidents. **1897** *Chicago Record* 8 Mar. 4/1 Ohio may claim to take rank with Virginia as a 'mother of presidents'. **1904** *N.Y. Tribune* 12 June 8 Virginia concluded not to indorse any candidate. The 'Mother of Presidents' is a trifle particular. **1948** *Chicago Daily News* 21 Apr. 1/5 Ohio is the mother of Presidents, and Taft is one of her sons. **1834** W. A. CARUTHERS *Kentuckian in N.Y.* ii. 195 Virginia has been the *mother of states. **1838** *Yale Lit. Mag.* III. 86 To thee, Mother of States! to thee, good old Connecticut, do our praises most belong. **1855** *Southern Lit. Messenger* XXI. 675/1 Virginia..[was] hailed as 'the Mother of States'. [**1731** P. MILLER *Gardeners Dict.* s.v. *Linaria*, The first of these Plants [*sc.* common yellow toad-flax] grows in great Plenty upon the Sides of dry Banks in most Parts of England and is seldom cultivated in Gardens, for it is a very troublesome Plant to keep within Bounds, the roots being very apt to spread under-ground, and rise at a great Distance from the Mother Plant, whereby it greatly injures whatever Plants stand near it.] **1855** A. PRATT *Flowering Plants & Ferns Gt. Brit.* IV. 126 This plant [sc. *Linaria cymbalaria*] is familiarly known to many persons by the name of *Mother of Thousands. **1866** *Treas. Bot.* 684/1 *Linaria Cymbalaria*, Ivy-leaved Toadflax or *Mother-of-thousands, is frequent on..old garden walls. **1910** T. W. SANDERS *Window & Indoor Gardening* xi. 111 Ivy-leaved Pelargoniums..make delightful basket plants... So, too, [do] Saxifraga sarmentosa (Mother-o'-Thousands or Wandering Jew). **1952** A. R. CLAPHAM et al. *Flora Brit. Is.* 713 *H*[*elxine*] *soleirolii* Req. Mind-your-own-business, Mother of thousands... Naturalized on walls and damp banks. **1958** *N. & Q.* Sept. 411/2 Have your readers ever heard of a plant called 'Mother of Thousands' or 'Wandering Sailor'? *Ibid.* Oct. 452/1 Mother of thousands. .. I believe this plant is *Saxifraga sarmentosa*. *Ibid.* Nov. 488/2 'Mother of thousands'... The name is given to the Ivy-leaved Toad-flax which is also known as 'Mother of Millions'. **1961** *Countryman* LVIII. III. 547 Mother-of-thousands (ivy-leaved toadflax). **1971** K. G. MESSENGER *Flora of Rutland* 69/1 *S*[*oleirolia*] *soleirolii*... Mother-of-Thousands... Pavements, Uppingham, 1961... Intrusive alien. **1975** *Times* 22 Nov. 10/5 The elegant climber..the mother of thousands..produces small plantlets on thread-like runners. **1876** *Hardwicke's Science Gossip* 39 *Veronica hederifolia* is named by farmers [near Kelso] the '*mother-of-wheat'.

mother ('mʌðə(r)), *sb.*[2] [Corresponds in meaning to MDu. *moeder*, *moer* (in mod.Du. *moer*), G. *mutter*, identical in form and gender with the equivalent of MOTHER *sb.*[1]

Comparison with the synonymous It., Sp. *madre* scum of liquids, F. *mère* (*de vinaigre*), OF. *mere* 'vendange pressée' (= sense 3 below), seems to show that this word, in Eng., Du., and Ger., is really an application of MOTHER *sb.*[1] The transition of sense is difficult to explain; but most probably the scum or dregs of distilled waters and the like was regarded as being a portion of the 'mother' or original crude substance which had remained mixed with the refined product, from which in course of time it separated itself. (The term may possibly have belonged originally to the vocabulary of alchemy.) An explanation sometimes given, that 'mother of vinegar' was so called on account of its effect in promoting acetous fermentation, does not agree with the history of the use. It has been pointed out that Gr. γραῦς, old woman, is used in the sense 'scum, as of boiled milk', but the coincidence is prob. accidental.

Most etymologists have regarded the word (with its Du. and Ger. equivalents) as altered by popular etymology from Du. *modder* masc., mud, mire (for which Middle Du. has a rare variant *moeder*, occurring chiefly in derivatives) = LG. *modder*, *moder* (whence mod.G. *moder*), HG. dial. *motter* masc. (for which a variant *mutter* occurs). This notion goes back to Kilian's (Du. or Flemish) dictionary of 1598, which contains the two following entries: (1) '*Modder, moder, moyer, more, moer*, limus, cœnum mollius, lutum, volutabrum; Ang. *mire, mudde*'; and (2) '*Modder, moeyer, moeder, grondsoppe*, fæx, fæces, crassamen, crassamentum; Ang. *mother*'. But there appears to be no evidence that the form *modder* was ever used for 'mother' or 'scum', nor is that sense recorded for Ger. dial. *motter*.]

† 1. Dregs, scum. In the 16th c. examples always the dregs or scum of oil (chiefly rendering L. *amurca*); later applied chiefly to the scum rising to the surface of fermenting liquors. *Obs.*

1538 ELYOT *Dict.*, *Amurca*, the mother or foam of all oyles. **1563** HYLL *Art Garden.* (1593) 31 The new mother or fome of oyle. **1577** B. GOOGE *Heresbach's Husb.* II. (1586) 69 Powre into a Platter the thickest mother of oile. **1600** SURFLET *Country Farm* III. xlix. 529 Else your cyder will.. growe couered with much white mother swimming aloft. **1601** HOLLAND *Pliny* II. 159 The mother or lees of oile oliue. **1609** C. BUTLER *Fem. Mon.* x. L5 The Meth in time wilbe covered with a mother. **1611** COTGR., *Fleur du vin*, the mother of wine; the white, or mouldie spots that float on the top of old wine. **1626** BACON *Sylva* §339 If the Body be liquid and not apt to putrefie totally, it will cast up a Mother in the Top; As the Mothers of Distilled Waters. **1676** GREW

Anat. Leaves I. vi. §4 The Cuticular and other Concretions, commonly called Mothers, in Distill'd Waters, Vinegar, and other Liquors. **1814** CARY *Dante, Paradise* XII. 106 That, mouldy mother is, where late were lees. **1870** *Henfrey's Bot.* (ed. 2) §558 Distribution [of filamentous Fungi or 'Moulds']. Universal, .. occurring constantly in infusions of organic matter .. as 'mother', producing various fermentations.

2. *spec.* (In full ***mother of vinegar***.) A ropy mucilaginous substance produced in vinegar during the process of acetous fermentation (which it hastens) by a mould-fungus called *Mycoderma aceti*.

1601 HOLLAND *Pliny* II. 334 A pultesse made of beasts dung & the mother of vineger tempered together. **1676** [see 1]. **1839** URE *Dict. Arts* 460 The slimy sediment of vinegar casks called mother. **1870** LOWELL *Study Wind.* (1871) 95 Unhappily the bit of mother from Swift's vinegar-barrel has had strength enough to sour all the rest [of Carlyle]. **1879** *Encycl. Brit.* IX. 98/2 Mother of vinegar .. is the 'non-aerobiotic' form of the mycoderma.

†**3.** ***mother of grapes***: the solid mass of skins, etc., left after the expression of the juice by the winepress; = MARC. *Obs.*

1611 COTGR., *Espeé* .. a certaine round staffe, that lies betweene the vpper boords of a Vinepresse, and the mother, or substance of the grapes. **1694** MOTTEUX *Rabelais* V. vii, For fear there should still lurk some Juice among the Husks, and Hullings, in the Mother of the Grape. **1725** BRADLEY *Fam. Dict.* s.v. *Vinegar*, To make strong Vinegar, dry the Mother of Grapes for the space of two Days.

mother ('mʌðə(r)), *v.*[1] [f. MOTHER *sb.*[1]]

1. *trans.* To be the mother of, give birth to; in quots. *fig.*, to be the source of, give rise to, produce.

1548 GEST *Pr. Masse* A vj, This pryuate masse whych mothereth so manyfolde and haynouse vyces. **1850** BLACKIE *Æschylus* II. 189 But tears are vain, And weeping might but mother worser woe. **1900** *Nation* (N.Y.) 15 Nov. 389/1 The historic college at Querétaro, which mothered the evangelization of so enormous a share of the North American wilderness.

2. a. To take care of or protect as a mother.

1863 C. E. B. *Work for All* 68 You would like to take Lizzie Reed into our house, for a time, and mother her till something can be found for her. **1878** *Scribner's Mag.* XV. 555/1 Some mothers 'mother' their children too much. **1894** MRS. H. WARD *Marcella* I. 127 Someone .. will take up Marcella and mother her.

fig. **1889** *Chicago Advance* 21 Feb., The weak churches do feel deeply the need of brotherhood. They want to be mothered. **1899** BARING-GOULD *Bk. of West* I. xii. 208 Okehampton .. is not fathered by the castle, nor mothered by the church.

b. *Naut.* in *passive*. Of a torpedo-boat: To be protected by a 'mother'.

1901 *Blackw. Mag.* Oct. 449 Torpedo craft could also be 'mothered'.

3. To profess to be the mother of; to acknowledge (truly or falsely) the maternity of (a child).

1622 FLETCHER & MASS. *Span. Curate* V. iii, You Sir, that Would have me mother Bastards, being unable To honour me with one Child of mine owne. **1679** W. HOWELL *Medulla Hist. Angl.* (1687) 284 That the Queen, to have put lady Elizabeth besides the Crown, would have mothered another bodies Child; but King Philip scorn'd to father it.

fig. **1788** ANNA SEWARD *Lett.* (1811) II. 41 The congenial rants which pretend to reply to them, are from the same pen, whoever Mr. Merry may persuade to mother them. **1840** T. A. TROLLOPE *Summ. Brittany* II. 370 It is evident throughout the country that 'Our Lady' was called on to mother every Pagan worship that could not be otherwise disposed of. **1884** *Pall Mall G.* 12 June 4/2 Such books are translated by some humble hand, and fathered or mothered by another of some literary standing.

4. Const. *on, upon*. **a.** *lit.* To attribute the maternity of (a child) to (a woman).

1542 UDALL *Erasm. Apoph.* 139 A childe mothered on a woman that neuer beare it, or a chaungelyng. **1888** 'R. BOLDREWOOD' *Robbery under Arms* (1890) 234 They must have changed her, and mothered the wrong child on the old woman.

b. *fig.* To attribute the authorship of (something) to (a woman); also, to ascribe the origin of (something) to something else.

1644 J. GOODWIN *Innoc. Triumph.* (1645) 35 That conception .. is indifferently fathered, or mothered rather, upon them all. **1675** TRAHERNE *Chr. Ethics* 300 Which accident is wholly to be fathered on Adams fondness to please his wife, and to be mothered upon her lightness and credulity. **1831** *Fraser's Mag.* IV. 11 [She] wrote the greater portion of a novel which was mothered on Miss Spence. **1907** *Blackw. Mag.* May 668/2 Many venerable repartees were mothered on her.

5. To find a mother for (a lamb or calf). Also, to pick out from a flock the mother of (a particular lamb). Also *intr.*, *transf.*, and const. *up, upon*.

1844 STEPHENS *Bk. Farm* II. 609 It is necessary when a lamb is left an orphan, or is supernumerary, to *mother it*, as it is termed, upon another ewe. **1888** 'R. BOLDREWOOD' *Robbery under Arms* xlviii, Mothering the calves, bailing up, leg-roping, and all the rest of it. **1889** *Zealandia* I. 30 He pretended to give me every opportunity at 'mothering' (as it is called) my missing lambs, but for fifteen ewes I could find but four. **1890** *Cornh. Mag.* Oct. 386, I was shepherding for Gasgarth, and his missus said to me, 'Jem, mother that 'un,' and I went reight intill middle o' t' flock and browt out t' mother on it. **1898** —— *Rom. Canvass Town* 92 It is vitally necessary to turn-out all the lambs and get them 'mothered' as soon as they are 'tailed'. **1950** *N. Z. Jrnl. Agric.* Sept. 197/3 All lambs can be properly mothered up before nightfall. *Ibid.* 202/1 Do not move the ewes until all the lambs have mothered. **1957** *New Biol.* XXII. 101 Some lambs failed to 'mother' after treatment. **1961** R. M. PATTERSON *Buffalo Head* iv. 134 At Bull Creek we stopped for a little while to give the calves a chance to 'mother-up'; very soon every cow had her calf. **1962** [see *hay-bale* (HAY *sb.*[1] 4)]. **1972** *Country Life* 30 Mar. 812/3 Both lambs and ewes are marked with identical letters to facilitate shepherding, particularly the mothering up, at night, which is very important with winter lambing.

mother ('mʌðə(r)), *v.*[2] [f. MOTHER *sb.*[2]] *intr.* To become mothery. Hence '**mothering** *vbl. sb.*

1718 QUINCY *Compl. Disp.* 228 It's an insipid Phlegm .. and will not keep long without mothering and stinking. **1728** E. SMITH *Compl. Homew.* (1750) 109 If your pickle mothers, boil it again. **1750** JOHNSON *Rambler* No. 51 ¶15 Her conserves mould, her wines sour, and pickles mother. **1863** *Fownes' Elem. Chem.* (ed. 9) 481 Frequently a little sulphuric acid is afterwards added, with a view of checking further decomposition, or mothering.

mother, obs. var. MAUTHER *dial.*, young girl.

'**motherage.** *nonce-wd.* [f. MOTHER *sb.*[1] + -AGE.] The condition or state of being a mother.

a **1591** H. SMITH *Serm.* (1614) 13 Mariage is called Matrimonie, which signifieth motherage [*earlier edd.* Mothers], because it makes them mothers which were virgins before.

mother-church. (See also MOTHER *sb.*[1] 2 c.)

1. † **a.** A parish church, as distinguished from a chapel of ease. *Obs.*

c **1325** *Chron. Eng.* (Ritson) 923 Fifti moder chirchen ant mo He lette falle, ant chapeles bo. *c* **1450** *Godstow Reg.* 649 Except the tethys of wolle & lambys of the modur-churche of Bloxham. **1546** *Yorks. Chantry Surv.* (Surtees) II. 228 The same chauntery is distaunt from the parysshe church .. whych they calle the mother church, ij myles. **1712** ADDISON *Spect.* No. 452 ¶7 We are informed from Pankridge, that a dozen Weddings were lately celebrated in the Mother Church of that Place. **1778** *Eng. Gazetteer* (ed. 2) s.v. *Weymouth*, Some of the inhabitants go to Radipole church, .. others to Wyke-Regis the mother-church.

attrib. **1688** R. HOLME *Armoury* III. xiii. 473 A Square Steeple, or Parochiall, or Mother Church Steeple.

b. The principal church of a country, region, or city; sometimes a cathedral or a metropolitan church. Now *rare*.

1387 TREVISA *Higden* (Rolls) II. 77 Þe þridde chirche was þe chief moderchirche of al Wales. **1513** BRADSHAW *St. Werburge* II. 464 Whiche churche was principall to all the citie, And the mouther-church called withouten doubt. **1738** J. CHAMBERLAYNE *St. Gt. Brit.* I. ix. (ed. 8) 106 St. Paul's, the Mother Church of London Diocese. **1871** FREEMAN *Norm. Conq.* (1876) IV. xviii. 125 The mother church of the whole land, the church of Christ at Canterbury.

2. The church (i.e. organized body of Christians) of which another church is a 'daughter' or offshoot; also, the oldest or original church from which all others have sprung.

1574 G. SCOT *Treat. agst. Err. Rom. Ch.* A iii b, Herein that wicked mother-churche We may to witnes call. **1667** POOLE *Dial. betw. Protest. & Papist* (1735) 31 Not Rome, but Jerusalem should be the Mother-Church. **1882** FARRAR *Early Chr.* I. 94 In reading St. James we can realise the sentiments of the Mother-Church of Jerusalem.

mother country.

1. A country in relation to its colonies.

1587 GOLDING *De Mornay* xxxiii. (1592) 530 After the custome of their Mother country Persia from whence they descend. **1732** BERKELEY *Serm. to S.P.G.* Wks. 1871 III. 245 No fashions are so much followed by our Colonies as those of the mother-country. **1861** LD. BROUGHAM *Brit. Const.* App. I. 405 If Canada were separated from the mother country.

2. One's native country.

So F. *terre mère*. In Caxton's *Eneydos* (1490) the words *la doulce terre mere* of the Fr. original are rendered simply *the swete countrey* (ed. E.E.T.S. p. 29).

1595 DANIEL *Civ. Wars* I. lxxxviii, Thy Mother-countrey, whence thyself didst spring. **1639** MASSINGER *Unnat. Combat* I. i, To joyne with them to lift a wicked arme against my mother Countrey, this Marsellis. **1723** SHAFTESB. *Charac.* III. 143 *note*, Absolute Power annuls the Publick: And where there is no Publick, or Constitution, there is in reality no Mother-Country or Nation. **1824** LADY GRANVILLE *Lett.* 13 Dec., She seems a very charming person .. with *l'air noble* and not a shade of her mother-country.

mothercraft ('mʌðəkrɑːft, -æ-). [f. MOTHER *sb.*[1] + CRAFT *sb.*] The 'craft' or business of a mother; knowledge of, and skill in, the care of children. Also *attrib.*

1911 *Progress* VI. 52 St. Pancras School .. aims .. to become 'a school for mothercraft'. **1914** *Times* 25 Apr. 10/3 The School of Mothercraft. **1917** B. VAUGHAN *Menace Empty Cradle* 44 How much better it would be to teach them mothercraft. **1922** *Daily Mail* 28 Oct. 7 A Mothercraft question set by the Association of Infant Welfare. **1945** [see KARITANE]. **1969** *Sydney Morning Herald* 7 June 4/2 A man wearing a white stocking mask with eye-slits stuck a pistol into the ribs of a mothercraft nurse in a $14,200 payroll robbery at the Royal Hospital for Women, Paddington, yesterday. **1970** *Globe & Mail* (Toronto) 28 Sept. 7/6 As the mother of a child in the Mothercraft nursery may I be permitted to clear the distorted view some of your .. readers have.

†'**motherdom.** *Obs. rare*[−1]. [f. MOTHER *sb.*[1] + -DOM.] Maternal status or authority.

a **1638** MEDE *Wks.* V. (1672) 921 All joyntly as one Body anew acknowledging the Motherdom of the Roman City.

mother earth.

1. The earth considered as the mother of its inhabitants and productions; also (in somewhat jocular use, with allusion to this), the ground.

Cf. L. *Terra mater* (as a goddess). In Eng. the personification remains so far that the article is commonly omitted as before a proper name, although initial capitals are rarely used. Often with possessive, *my, your*, etc.

c **1586** C'TESS PEMBROKE *Ps.* CXLVI. ii, His strength is none, if any in his breath; Which vapor'd foorth to mother earth he goes. **1590** SPENSER *F.Q.* I. ii. 19 He .. With bloody mouth his mother earth did kis. **1600** SHAKS. *A.Y.L.* I. ii. 213. **1667** MILTON *P.L.* I. 687 Men also .. Rifl'd the bowels of their mother Earth For Treasures better hid. **1696** TATE & BRADY *Ps.* civ. 29 Forthwith to mother Earth return. **1766** *Compl. Farmer* s.v. *Vegetation*, The sun, .. cannot either help the mother earth in her pregnancy, nor [etc.]. **1851** D. JERROLD *St. Giles* xiv. 137 It is .. made a misdemeanour against mother earth to sleep .. with only the heavens above the sleeper. **1890** 'R. BOLDREWOOD' *Col. Reformer* (1891) 292 The unbounded treasures of mother earth.

2. (See quots.)

1731 MILLER *Gard. Dict.* s.v. *Earth*, Some by Loam mean that Sort of Earth that equally partakes of Sand and Clay, being a Medium between Sand and Clay, which they call Mother-Earth. **1766** *Compl. Farmer* s.v. *Mould, Mould*, a loose kind of earth, every where obvious on the surface of the ground, called by some mother earth, and by others loam.

mothered ('mʌðəd), *a.*[1] [f. MOTHER *sb.*[1] + -ED[2].] In parasynthetic formations and with advs.: Having a mother.

1669 GALE *Crt. Gentiles* I. II. iii. 29 The Poets fable Bacchus to be .. double mothered. **1791** CUMBERLAND *Observer* No. 151 V. 275 Three such high-blooded bards as Linus, Orpheus, and Musæus, so fathered and so mothered, were enough to people all Greece with poets and musicians.

†'**mothered,** *a.*[2] *Obs.* [f. MOTHER *sb.*[2] or *v.*[2] + -ED.] Containing mother.

1697 DRYDEN *Virg. Georg.* III. 683 They oint their naked Limbs with mother'd Oyl. **1728** T. SHERIDAN *Persius* IV. 61 *note*, Mothered wine.

motherer ('mʌðərə(r)). *Austral.* [f. MOTHER *v.*[1] + -ER[1].] A person employed to 'mother' lambs (cf. MOTHER *v.*[1] 5).

1890 'R. BOLDREWOOD' *Squatter's Dream* vii. 65 No more shepherds and 'motherers' to pay in that humbugging way next year.

†'**motherful,** *a. Obs.* [f. MOTHER *sb.*[1] + -FUL.] Of or pertaining to a mother; motherly.

c **1450** *Mirour Saluacioun* 212 Oure ladie tholed in sawle be moderfull compassionne.

motherhead ('mʌðəhɛd). *Obs.* exc. *arch.* [f. MOTHER *sb.*[1] + -HEAD.] **a.** The state or condition of being a mother. **b.** Motherly care. **c.** *concr.* An embodiment of maternal qualities.

c **1315** SHOREHAM V. 24 Wanne he þat al pys worlde schel welde To hyre worschipe hys yhelde For here moder-hede. **1357** *Lay Folks Catech.* 124 Withouten ony merryng of hir modirhede. **1390** GOWER *Conf.* I. 195 So mot I nedes be that weie For Moderhed and for tendresse. *c* **1440** *York Myst.* xliii. 201 My modirhed, John, schall þou haue, And for my sone I wolle þe take. **1879** E. ARNOLD *Lt. Asia* I. (1881) 9 Countless Devas worship her and wait Attendant on that radiant Motherhead.

motherhood ('mʌðəhʊd). [+ -HOOD.]

1. a. The condition or fact of being a mother.

1603 FLORIO *Montaigne* (1634) 463 For my part, I no more acknowledge Venus without Cupid, then a mother-hood without an off-spring. **1681** W. ROBERTSON *Phraseol. Gen.* (1693) 897 Mother-hood, *Maternitas*. **1837** C. LOFFT *Self-formation* II. 103 Rejoicing in thy motherhood. **1869** MRS. HEATON *A. Dürer* I. iii. (1881) 62 Some women need the warm sun of motherhood to ripen their true nature.

transf. and *fig.* **1623** LISLE *Ælfric on O. & N. Test.* Pref. 8 That were against his owne Apostleship, and the motherhood Rome by him got here. **1672** STILLINGFL. *Idol. Ch. Rome* (ed. 2) 225 Three properties in the Holy Trinity, of the Fatherhood, of the Motherhood, and of the Lordship. **1873** B. GREGORY *Holy Cath. Ch.* xv. 156 The motherhood of the Church was manifested .. in her respect for the individuality of her children.

b. The spirit of a mother; the feeling or love of a mother.

1593 NASHE *Christ's T.* 33 b, Not hate but hunger, taught Miriam to forget mother-hood. **1875** MISS MULOCK *Serm. out of Ch.* iii. (1881) 99 The mere fact of bringing eight or ten children into the world does not in the least imply true motherhood.

c. *transf.* Used *attrib.* of an issue, report, etc.: protective, withholding the worst aspects. *N. Amer.*

1973 *Ottawa Jrnl.* 4 Apr. 6/2 They think public participation is such a motherhood issue in politics these days that it must be paid homage to at all cost. **1974** *Evening Herald* (Rock Hill, S. Carolina) 18 Apr. 4/4 At the meeting, officials from Kaiser, Reynolds, Southwire, Alcoa and others agreed that a 'motherhood' package concealing the dangers of aluminium wiring was the best way to deal with the hearings of the Consumer Product Safety Commission in Los Angeles. **1974** *Ottawa Citizen* 14 Nov. 37/2 Opposition spokesmen attacked him for presenting a 'motherhood' report which told nothing of the real situation of the peacekeeping forces, only that Canadian troops are loved overseas.

2. Used collectively for mothers.

1835 *Tait's Mag.* II. 101 The motherhood of Great Britain was in a conspiracy to entrap him.

3. *Anthropology*. A clan constituted by kinship through the mother.

1884 A. LANG *Custom & Myth* 108 A man of the Mouse 'motherhood', as the totem kindred is locally styled, may not eat mice.

mothering ('mʌðərɪŋ), *vbl. sb.*¹ [f. MOTHER *v.*¹ and *sb.*¹ + -ING¹.]

1. The action of the vb. MOTHER; motherly care or supervision.

1868 STEVENSON *Let.* in *Scribner's Mag.* (1899) XXV. 30/1 Her mothering and thought for others displays itself in advice against hard-boiled eggs, well-done meat, and late dinners. **1892** 'G. TRAVERS' *Mona Maclean* (1893) I. 86 Mothering is woman's work without a doubt.

2. The custom of visiting parents and giving or receiving presents on Mid-lent Sunday, hence called *Mothering Sunday*.

1648 HERRICK *Hesper.*, *To Dianeme, A Ceremonie in Glocester*, Ile to thee a Simnell bring, 'Gainst thou go'st a mothering. **1720** [see MIDLENTING]. **1825** HONE *Everyday Bk.* I. 359 It is still a custom on Mid-Lent Sunday in many parts of England, for servants.. to carry cakes.. as presents to their parents; and in other parts, to visit their mother for a meal of furmity, or to receive cakes.. with her blessing. This is called going a mothering. **1845** *Encycl. Metrop.* XXI. 379 Midlent Sunday.. has also a vulgar name of *Mothering* Sunday. **1883** C. S. BURNE *Shropsh. Folk Lore* 325 'Shrewsbury Simnels'.. are eaten by many who do not heed the pious habit of 'mothering' which they were intended to celebrate.

mothering, *vbl. sb.*²: see MOTHER *v.*²

mothering ('mʌðərɪŋ), *ppl. a.* [f. MOTHER *v.*¹ + -ING².] **1.** That acts as a mother.

1855 BAILEY *Spiritual Leg.* in *Mystic*, etc. 68 Earth's all mothering bosom. **1894** H. DRUMMOND *Ascent Man* 344 The Botanist.. places the mothering plants at the top of his department of Nature. **1901** HENLEY *Hawthorn & Lavender* 30 The clement rain, the mothering dew.

2. *U.S. slang.* = *mother-fucking* ppl. adj.

1968 L. W. ROBINSON *Assassin* (1969) ii. 8 We are lost in the motherin' fog. **1970** 'J. MORRIS' *Candywine Development* xxiii. 253 What I don't see is how those motherin' hijackers expect to get away with it. **1975** *New Yorker* 23 June 40/2 I'm out there cutting that mothering grass all day!

'mother-in-law. Also 6 moder of law, motherelawe, 7 mother law. [See -IN-LAW.]

1. The mother of one's husband or wife.

α. *c* **1440** *Promp. Parv.* 341/1 Moodur in lawe, *socrus.* **1477** *Paston Lett.* III. 175, I trow ther is not a kynder woman leveing then I shall have to my modyr in lawe. **1540** HYRDE tr. *Vives' Instr. Chr. Wom.* (1592) A a v, It is said, that mothers in lawes beare a stepmothers hate unto their daughters in lawes. **1688** PENTON *Guard. Instr.* (1897) 26 The everlasting Din of Mothers-in-law. **1781** GIBBON *Decl. & F.* xix. II. 130 *note*, His only crime was a refusal to gratify the desires of his mother-in-law. **1880** FISON & HOWITT *Kamilaroi* 203 Among the Kamilaroi, if a man be compelled to speak with his mother-in-law, the pair will turn their backs upon one another.

β. **1538** *Extracts Aberdeen Reg.* (1844) I. 154 Jonat Barbour, hir moder of law.

γ. **1526** TINDALE *Luke* xii. 53 The motherelawe agaynst the doughterelawe. **1637** in *Bury Wills* (Camden) 169 My mother lawes children.

2. = STEPMOTHER. Now regarded as incorrect.

1516 *St. Bridget* in *Myrr. our Ladye* p. xlviii, Hir moder in lawe. **1642** FULLER *Holy & Prof. St.* I. x. 26 If she becomes a mother in law, there is no difference betwixt her carriage to her own and her second husbands children. **1732** FIELDING *Miser* IV. xiv, I know the word mother-in-law has a terrible sound; but perhaps I may make a better than you imagine. **1848** THACKERAY *Van. Fair* xiv, Miss Sharp will be your mother-in-law.. that's what will happen.

3. *slang.* (See quot. 1886.)

1884 *Daily Tel.* 3 July 5/4 (Farmer). **1886** 'J. BICKERDYKE' *Curios. Ale & Beer* 392 Mother-in-law... The drink of this name is composed of equal proportions of 'old and bitter'.

4. mother-in-law's tongue, a tropical African herbaceous plant, *Sansevieria trifasciata* or its variety *laurentii*, of the family Liliaceæ, distinguished by a rosette of long, pointed leaves with white or yellow markings, and often cultivated as a house plant.

1958 *Times* 29 Nov. 9/5 Probably the most long-suffering house plant is the 'Mother-in-law's Tongue'. **1961** *Amateur Gardening* 11 Nov. 7/1 The sansevieria, because of its sword-like shape has received the unsympathetic name of Mother-in-Law's Tongue. **1970** 'D. HALLIDAY' *Dolly & Cookie Bird* ii. 15 The place was modern and airy and full of.. mother-in-law's tongue in long boxes. **1974** *Times* 5 Oct. 12/1 The real tough ones include aspidistras,.. mother in law's tongue *Sansevieria laurentii* and the rubber plant *Ficus elastica*.

Hence **mother-in-law** *v. nonce-wd.*, to rule as a mother-in-law.

1855 DICKENS *Dorrit* II. xiv, I will not.. submit to be mother-in-lawed by Mrs. General.

motherkin ('mʌðəkɪn), **-kins.** [f. MOTHER *sb.*¹ + -KIN.] An affectionate diminutive for 'mother'.

1879 BROWNING *Ivan Ivanovitch* 55 See, motherkin, your friends! **1896** MRS. CAFFYN *Quaker Grandmother* viii. 89 'Oh, frivolous motherkin', he said. **1905** MRS. BARNES-GRUNDY *Vacill. Hazel* 259 'What is the matter?' 'Nothing'. .. 'Really?'.. 'Really, motherkins', I replied.

motherland ('mʌðəlænd, -lənd). [f. MOTHER *sb.*¹ + LAND *sb.*¹] **a.** A country as the mother or producer of anything. **b.** The country of one's origin; one's native country.

1711 SHAFTESB. *Charac.* III. 42 It happen'd of old in [Egypt] this Mother-Land of Superstition. *c* **1823** SOUTHEY *Inscr. at Clachnacharry*, Egypt, mother-land of all the arts. **1828** CARLYLE *Misc.* (1857) I. 218 Our own stern Motherland. **1846** PROWETT *Prometh. Bound* 53 Scythia was to the Greeks the mother-land of iron. **1881** MRS. C. PRAED *Policy & Passion* II. 246 The longing for one's motherland. **1890** 'R. BOLDREWOOD' *Col. Reformer* (1891) 40 The way-farer from the misty mother-lands.

mother language. Also (in sense 1) 5 modiris, modris langage.

1. One's native language.

c **1380** WYCLIF *Sel. Wks.* II. 393 Sum men wolde seie it in her modir langage as þei cunnen. *c* **1449** PECOCK *Repr.* I. xiii. 66 Thei of the lay parti which han vsid the hool Bible or oonli the Newe Testament in her modris langage. *a* **1568** ASCHAM *Scholem.* II. (Arb.) 117 In the rudest contrie, and most barbarous mother language, may be found yat can speake verie wiselie. **1659** H. THORNDIKE *Wks.* (1846) II. 599 Whether translations in mother languages are to be had. **1805** SOUTHEY *Madoc in Azt.* v, The very mother-language which I learnt, A lisping baby on my mother's knees.

2. A language from which others have sprung.

1680 *High Dutch Minerva a-la-mode* (title-p.) Whereby the English may both easily and exactly learne the Neatest Dialect of the German Mother-Language. **1846** GROTE *Greece* II. ii. II. 315 They seem capable of being traced back to a certain ideal mother-language. **1902** GREENOUGH & KITTREDGE *Words* 161 Similar processes enable us to postulate a number of similar mother-languages, as Celtic, Slavic, Greek, and so on.

†**3.** The language in which something was written.

1651 C. CARTWRIGHT *Cert. Relig.* I. 364 Which also the antient Fathers have subscribed, which (I suppose) the Marquesse doth mean by the Scriptures Mother-language.

motherless ('mʌðəlɪs), *a.*¹ [f. MOTHER *sb.*¹ + -LESS.] Having no mother.

a **1023** WULFSTAN *Hom.* xlv. (Napier) 228 Fylstan widewum and fæderleasum and moderleasum cildum. *a* **1225** *Leg. Kath.* 78 Ðis meiden was baðe faderles & moderles. **1382** WYCLIF *Jas.* i. 27 To visite pupilles, that is fadirles or modirles. **1477** EARL RIVERS (Caxton) *Dictes* 79 Many poure children that wer fadir and modir lees. **1548** CRANMER *Catech.* 100 b, Oppressers of fatherles and motherles children. **1631** GOUGE *God's Arrows* II. Ep. Ded., To become a mother to the motherlesse. **1712** ARBUTHNOT *John Bull* II. iv, The three poor Motherless Children. **1829** SOUTHEY *All for Love* III. iii, An only child and motherless. **1901** G. S. LAYARD *Mrs. Lynn Linton* i. 3 Eliza's was practically a motherless childhood.

b. As an intensive quasi-*adv.*, esp. in phr. *stone motherless broke. Austral. colloq.*

1898 *Bulletin* (Sydney) 17 Dec. Red Page, To these are prefixed the adjectives *motherless* and *dead*, thus *dead motherless broke.* **1916** A. WRIGHT *Under Cloud* 35 I'm stone motherless meself an' I could do with that hundred Booth is offerin'. **1925** E. S. SORENSON *Murty Brown* 135 That leaves me stony, motherless broke again. **1945** G. CASEY *Downhill is Easier* I. 20 I'd only known Reg when we were both stone motherless broke. **1972** A. MACDONALD *Ukulele Player under Red Lamp* 147 Happy, full as a boot, and stone motherless broke.

Hence **'motherlessness**.

1889 ADEL. SERGEANT *E. Denison* v. xxxvii, An indefinitely lonely and neglected look hung about the two—the look of motherlessness.

†**'motherless**, *a.*² *Obs.* [f. MOTHER *sb.*² + -LESS.] Free from 'mother'.

1607 *Lingua* IV. iii, Steeped seven days in change of motherless rose-water.

motherlike ('mʌðəlaɪk), *a.* and *adv.* [f. MOTHER *sb.*¹ + -LIKE.]

A. *adj.* Resembling a mother; having the qualities of a mother; proper to a mother.

1530 PALSGR. 319/1 Motherlyke belongyng to a mother, *maternal.* **1605** BP. HALL *Medit. & Vows* III. §98 Wks. (1625) 68 It is a mother-like fauour of the Earth, that she beares and nourishes me. **1647** TRAPP *Comm. 1 Thess.* ii. 11 Here he tempers his mother-like meekness with the gravity and authority of a father. **1856** MRS. CARLYLE *Lett.* II. 282 She was so glad over me, so motherlike.

B. *adv.* After the manner of a mother.

1589 WARNER *Alb. Eng.* v. xxviii. 124 Mother-like I moane their death. **1878** SMILES *Robt. Dick* ii. 13 Mother-like.. she could not but regard these young things as intruders.

motherliness ('mʌðəlɪnɪs). [f. MOTHERLY *a.* + -NESS.] The quality of being motherly.

a **1637** B. JONSON *Eng. Gram.* I. vii. (1640) 54 [The word is accented] mótherlinesse. **1727** in BAILEY vol. II. **1856** MISS MULOCK *J. Halifax* xxxix, The sweet motherliness of character which had come to her so early. **1882** *Spectator* 18 Mar. 345 The people will be deeply touched both by its piety and motherliness.

motherling ('mʌðəlɪŋ). [f. MOTHER + -LING.] A term of endearment for a mother. = MOTHERKIN.

1865 MISS YONGE *Dove in Eagle's Nest* xix, 'Nay, motherling', he added [etc.]. **1886** CORBETT *Fall of Asgard* I. 145 'Motherling', she heard him say softly, 'it is very beautiful'.

motherly ('mʌðəlɪ), *a.* [OE. *módorlic*: see MOTHER *sb.*¹ and -LY¹. Cf. MDu., Du. *moederlijk*, OHG. *muoterlîh* (MHG. *mueterlich*, mod.G. *mütterlich*).]

1. Of or pertaining to a mother. *rare.*

† *motherly language*: = 'mother tongue'.

c **1000** ÆLFRIC *Gram.* v. (Z.) 15 *Maternus*, modorlic. **1597** HOOKER *Eccl. Pol.* v. viii. §5 In them who can owe no lesse then childlike obedience to her that hath more then motherly power. **1597** A. M. tr. *Guillemeau's Fr. Chirurg.* *v, The secretes of Physicke in their maternall and motherlye language. **1871** R. ELLIS *Catullus* lxi. 56 You from motherly lap the bright Girl can sever.

2. Befitting or characteristic of a mother.

a **1240** *Wohunge* in *Cott. Hom.* 285 þu.. seh al þis sorhe vpo þi deore wurðe sune was wiðinne martird iþi moderliche herte. *c* **1422** LYDG. *Thebes* I. in *Chaucer's Wks.* (1561) 358/1 Bidding the quene, whan the childe wer borne, Without mercie, or moderly pitee That he be dedde. *c* **1440** *Gesta Rom.* lii. 232 (Harl. MS.) Certeinly Crist is oure fader, For he hathe to vs a fadirlye affeccion, and not a modirly. *c* **1530** LD. BERNERS *Arth. Lyt. Brit.* (1814) 437 Syr, syth ye are lefte me in the stede of my moder, for Goddes sake man leue your faderly herte and take a moderly herte vnto you. **1611** BIBLE *Transl. Pref.* ¶9 Now the Church of Rome would seeme at the length to beare a motherly affection towards her children. **1671** MILTON *P.R.* II. 64 Within her brest.. Motherly cares and fears got head. **1712** ADDISON *Spect.* No. 500 ¶3 When I see the Motherly Airs of my little Daughters when playing with their Puppets. **1848** DICKENS *Dombey* v, Mrs. Chick interposed with some motherly words about going to sleep like a dear. **1874** BURNAND *My time* xiii. 112 She pressed her lips on my forehead with another loving motherly kiss. **1885–94** R. BRIDGES *Eros & Psyche* Oct. xxii, Motherly pity, bend thy face and grant One beam of ruth to thy poor suppliant.

3. Resembling a mother; having the character, manner, or appearance befitting a mother.

1530 PALSGR. 246/2 Motherly woman, *matrone.* **1576** BAKER *Jewell of Health* 162 b, Mydwives and other motherlye women. **1752** J. LOUTHIAN *Form of Process* (ed. 2) 215 To cause to come twelve good and motherly Women, by whom the Prisoner's Plea of Pregnancy may be tried. **1787** BURNS *Border Tour* Wed. 10 May, *Pr. Wks.* 127 Mrs. Somerville an excellent, motherly, agreeable woman, and a fine family. **1815** JANE AUSTEN *Emma* iii, Mrs. Goddard was a plain, motherly kind of woman. **1825** CARLYLE *Schiller* III. (1845) 197 The sky is so blue, and all is so calm, and motherly, and safe. **1876** SWINBURNE *Erechtheus* 20 O holy and general mother of all men born, But mother most and motherliest of mine, Earth. **1882** L. STEPHEN *Swift* i. 10 A brisk, wholesome, motherly body.

motherly ('mʌðəlɪ), *adv.* [f. MOTHER *sb.*¹ + -LY².] In a motherly manner.

1433 LYDG. *St. Edmund* I. 726 in Horstm. *Altengl. Leg.* (1881) 389 Whan she hir sone gan kyssen and enbrace And in hir armys moderly hym streyne. **1554** BRADFORD in Coverdale *Lett. Martyrs* (1564) 288 The mother.. casteth the rodde into the fier, and colleth the childe, geueth it an apple, and dandleth it moste motherly. **1663** COWLEY *Verses & Ess.* x. *Danger Procrast.* (1669) 140 Those studies to which Nature had so Motherly inclined me. **1887** G. MACDONALD *Home Again* vii, The forehead his mother had been so motherly proud of.

'mother 'naked, *a.* [Cf. MDu. *moeder naect* (Du. *-naakt*), MHG. *muoternacket* (G. *mutternackt*).] As naked as at birth; stark-naked.

c **1400** *Sege Jerus.* 346 Sayþ, y bidde hem be boun, bishopes & oþer, To morow or mydday modur nakyd alle. *c* **1440** CAPGRAVE *Life St. Kath.* v. 608 Take this mayden and strype hir modir-naked. **1526** *Pilgr. Perf.* (W. de W. 1531) 260 He all mother naked, spredyng hym selfe on the crosse for vs moost pacyently. **1622** in Pitcairn *Crim. Trials* III. 539 Mother-naikit as he was borne. **1760–72** H. BROOKE *Fool of Qual.* (1809) I. 2 Harry.. would run about, mother-naked.. in a frosty morning. **1872** RUSKIN *Fors Clav.* xxiii. 4 Mother-naked sits Theseus.

mother of pearl. Also 6 moder perl, mother perle, 7–8 mother pearl(e. [Cf. F. †*mère perle* pearl oyster (16th c. in Godef.), It., Sp. *madreperla*, G. *perlenmutter* (late MHG. *perelmuoter*), Du. *parel-*, *paarlmoeder*, *-moer.*]

1. a. A smooth shining iridescent substance forming the inner layer of some shells. = NACRE 2.

a **1510** *Inv. York Minster* in Raine *Abps. of York* (Rolls) III. 388 Unum pece de moder perl. **1552** *Invent. Ch. Goods* (Surtees No. 97) 86 An ymage of the birth of Our Lord, of mother of perle, sylver and gylt. **1590** SPENSER *F.Q.* I. vii. 30 Handle strong Of mother perle. **1698** *Lond. Gaz.* No. 3358/4 A large Cabinet Frame inlaid with Mother Pearle. **1748** *Anson's Voy.* II. viii. 218 They saw.. great heaps of shells of fine mother of pearl scattered up and down. **1827** *Gentl. Mag.* XCVII. II. 70 A screen, curiously wrought with mother-o'-pearl. *c* **1850** *Arab. Nts.* (Rtldg.) 724 Inlaid with mother-of-pearl and ebony. **1889** 'J. S. WINTER' *Mrs. Bob* (1891) 4 The useful and highly-ornamental mother-o'-pearl.

b. Used as an exclamation.

1632 ROWLEY *New Wonder* I. i, Mother a pearle woman, shew your husband the cause.

2. A shell fish yielding mother of pearl. = NACRE I.

1601 HOLLAND *Pliny* I. 255 The shell that is the mother of Pearle. *Ibid.* II. 451 Sundry sorts of other shell fish, and among them, those that.. beare pearles, and therof be called Mother-pearls. **1658** tr. *Porta's Nat. Magic* IX. xii. 241 There are.. shells, we call the Mothers of pearl. **1703** PETIVER *Musei Petiver.* 81 The Sea-Ear, Mother of Pearl, and by some Normans or Norman Shell. **1864** *Chamb. Encycl.* VI. 588/2 *Mother of pearl*, the shells of the large bivalve mollusc *Meleagrina margaritifera*.

fig. **1593** G. HARVEY *Pierce's Super.* 16 It is superexcellent wit, that is the mother pearle of precious Inuention.

†**3.** ? = NACRITE. *Obs.*

1796 MORSE *Amer. Geog.* II. 40 The bowels of the earth abound with.. mother-of-pearl, and some other productions of the mineral kingdom.

4. a. *attrib.*, as in ***mother-of-pearl oyster, shell***; with the sense 'made of mother-of-pearl', as in ***mother-of-pearl button***, etc.; also similative, as in ***mother-of-pearl gloss, -tint***.

1797 *Encycl. Brit.* (ed. 3) XII. 610/1 The margaritiferus, or pearl-bearing mussel... This is the *mater perlarum* of Rumphius, or mother of pearl shell. **1799** Kirwan *Geol. Ess.* 229 The shells found in limestone strata are commonly entire; some preserve their internal mother of pearl gloss. **1802** *Brookes' Gazetteer* (ed. 12) s.v. *Pelew Isl.*, The best knives are made of a piece of the large mother-of-pearl oyster. **1802** Wollaston in *Phil. Trans.* XCIII. 8 The.. angles were taken with a mother-of-pearl micrometer. **1810** *Sporting Mag.* XXXV. 293 A blue jacket with mother-of-pearl buttons on it. **1849** Mrs. Carlyle *Lett.* (1883) II. 64 Button-hook with the mother-of-pearl handle. **1899** *Allbutt's Syst. Med.* VIII. 871 A peculiar white 'mother-of-pearl' tint.

b. *Comb.*: **mother-of-pearl cloud** *Meteorol.* [tr. Norw. *perlemorsky* (H. Mohn 1893, in *Forh. i Vidensk.-Selsk. i Christiania* 1)], a kind of iridescent cloud occurring above the tropopause which is sometimes seen in high latitudes after sunset; cf. *noctilucent cloud* s.v. noctI-; **mother-of-pearl moth** (see quots. 1829, 1850); **mother-of-pearl work**, a kind of embroidery in which pieces of mother-of-pearl are sewn on velvet or silk.

1932 *Q. Jrnl. R. Meteorol. Soc.* LVIII. 307 The remarkable stratosphere clouds which the late Professor Mohn called mother-of-pearl clouds again appeared over Scandinavia several times during the months of January and February this year. **1957** Ludlam & Scorer *Cloud Study* 69 Mother of pearl clouds are rare. They have been seen most often in Norway (but occasionally also in Scotland, Iceland and Alaska), and then only in the months between November and March. **1972** R. Scorer *Clouds of World* v. 74 Mother of pearl clouds are at altitudes between 19 and 30 km. where they may be brightly illuminated by the sun after sunset at the ground, and after the sun has ceased to illuminate the troposphere where most of the blue colour of the sky originates. **1829** J. F. Stephens *Catal. Insects* II. 165 *Margaritia verticalis*.. Mother of Pearl M. **1850** —— *Catal. Lepidoptera* 240 *Botys verticalis*. The Mother-of-Pearl. *Ibid.* 241 *Botys perpendicularis*. The Scarce Mother-of-Pearl. **1882** Caulfeild & Saward *Dict. Needlework* 351 Mother-of-Pearl Work.

mother of thyme. Also 8 **mother thyme**. **a.** The wild thyme, *Thymus Serpyllum*. **b.** *Calamintha Acinos* (Britten & Holland).

1597 Gerarde *Herbal* II. clxiv. 457 Wild Time is called.. in English.. Mother of Time, and our Ladies Bedstrawe. **1693** Dale *Pharmacol.* 234 *Serpullum vulgare*... Mother of Thyme. **1741** *Compl. Fam.-Piece* I. iv. 254 Take.. Agrimony, Mother-thyme,.. Roman Wormwood, Carduus Benedictus. **1845** *Encycl. Metrop.* XXV. 627/2 *Thymus Serpyllum* is the Wild Thyme or Mother of Thyme.

attrib. **1747** Wesley *Prim. Physic* (1762) 86 Let his breakfast be Mother of Thyme tea.

mother's brother. *Anthropol.* The maternal uncle, usu. with reference to his importance in kinship affairs and social customs. Also *attrib.*

1871 L. H. Morgan in *Smithsonian Contrib. Knowl.* No. 218 12 My father's brothers and my mother's brothers, in English, are generalized into one class, and the term *uncle* is employed... The relationships to *Ego* of the two classes of persons are equal in their degree of nearness, but not of the same kind; wherefore, the Roman method is preferable, which employed *patruus* to express the former, and *avunculus* to indicate the latter. *Ibid.* 13 In Seneca-Iroquois, for example, my father's brother is my father... My mother's brother, on the contrary, is my uncle. **1934** R. H. Lowie *Cultural Anthropol.* xiii. 251 A preponderant position of the mother's brother may occur even without matrilocal residence and is termed 'avunculate'. **1949** E. E. Evans-Pritchard in M. Fortes *Social Structure* 95 It is worse with a mother's brother's daughter than with a father's brother's daughter. **1951** R. Firth *Elem. Social Organization* ii. 48 Reference has been made.. to the importance of the mother's brother relationship in Oceanic communities. **1972** J. S. La Fontaine *Interpretation of Ritual* 166 While all non-agnatic kin ceremonially recognize a girl's maturity, the primary ritual figure, to the exclusion of her father or senior agnates, is her mother's brother.

†**mother's child.** *Obs.* A person, chiefly in phrase ***every mother's child.*** (Cf. mother's son.)

a **1300** *K. Horn* 664 (Camb. MS.) At hom lefte ffikenhild, Þat was þe wurste moder child. *c* **1305** *St. Lucy* 93 in *E.E.P.* (1862) 104 Beo ilad oþer ibore And þer schal menie a moder child. **1608** Dod & Cleaver *Expos. Prov.* xi-xii. 167 It was a fault in Dauid to swear so peremptorily that he would kill Nabal, his familie, and euery mothers child of them. **1692** R. L'Estrange *Fables* ccxvii. 190 We have our Failings, Every Mothers Child of us.

mothership ('mʌðəʃɪp). Also 5 **moderchypp, -ship, modyrchep.** [f. mother *sb.*[1] + -ship.] The office of a mother; motherly care.

c **1440** *Partonope* 3589 For on your modership shall I neuer trust. **1453** *Paston Lett.* I. 258 He hathe seyde as myche ther ageyns as he dar do to have hyr gode modyrchep. **1478** *Ibid.* III. 225, I recomaund me on to yowr good moderchypp. **1905** *Blackw. Mag.* Feb. 239/1 Even had self-defence impelled Clarie to abandon her mothership.

†**b.** (See mother *sb.*[1] 3 c.)

1624 Middleton *Game at Chess* iv. ii, I haue promis'd The Mother-ship 'oth Maids.

'**mothersome,** *a. dial.* [f. mother (? *v.*[1]) + -some.] Anxious like a mother.

1840 Mrs. Trollope *M. Armstrong* xv. II. 96, I hope excuse, miss, if I seem over mothersome and foolish about him,.. but he's a precious boy to me.

mother's son.

1. A man. Chiefly in phr., ***every mother's son.***

a **1240** *Wohunge* in *Cott. Hom.* 269 Luue iwile þe mi leue lif, moder sune feirest. *a* **1300** *Cursor M.* 7061 Mani modir son was feld, Als it es in þe stori teld. **13..** *Sir Beues* (A.) 4102 Þat þai ner ded vpon þe grene, Eueri moder sone, i wene. *a* **1400–50** *Alexander* 1429 Þe first modire son he mett .. Was Balaan þe bald berne. **1470–85** Malory *Arthur* x. xxix. 460 He casteth that we shalle neuer escape moder sone of vs. **1542** Udall *Erasm. Apoph.* 330 Tydeus slewe theim euery mothers soonne excepte one. **1590** Shaks. *Mids. N.* I. ii. 80. **1665** J. Webb *Stone-Heng* (1725) 223 The English.. massacred them all, every Mother's Son of them. **1694** Motteux *Rabelais* IV. i. (1737) 5 Each Mother's Son retired on board his own Ship. **1865** Tennyson *Captain* 50 Every mother's son—Down they dropt. **1896** A. E. Housman *Shropshire Lad* xliii, 'Tis that every mother's son Travails with a skeleton.

2. A spoilt child.

1882 'Edna Lyall' *Donovan* xxiv, He's never been allowed to shift for himself, he's a mother's son.

mother tongue. Also (in sense 1) 6–7 **mothers tongue.** [In sense 1, *mother* was originally the uninflected genitive; cf. the form *mothers tongue* in 16–17th c.]

1. One's native language.

c **1380** Wyclif *Sel. Wks.* III. 114 Secler lordys schuld, in defawte of prelatys, lerne and preche þe law of God in here modyr tonge. *c* **1400** *Brut* (E.E.T.S.) 315 Hit was ordeyned ..þat men of lawe.. fro þat tyme forth shold plede in her moder tunge. *c* **1470** Henryson *Mor. Fab.* Prol. v, In mother toung of lating I wald preif To mak ane maner of translatioun. **1519** *Interl. 4 Elements* (Percy Soc.) 3 The Grekes, the Romayns, with many other mo, In their moder tonge wrot warkes excellent. **1540** Cranmer *Pref. to Gt. Bible* 1 The Saxones tonge whiche at that tyme was oure mothers tonge. **1617** Moryson *Itin.* III. 2 Children.. soone learne forraigne languages, and sooner forget the same, yea and their mothers tongue also. **1766** Fordyce *Serm. Yng. Wom.* (1767) I. vii. 294 The.. just pronunciation of their mother-tongue. **1874** Blackie *Self-Cult.* 34 Without the intervention of the mother tongue.

attrib. **1615** J. Stephens *Ess. & Char.* (1857) 256 The learning which lyes in mother-tongue translations.

b. *transf.*

1781 Gibbon *Decl. & F.* III. 15 *note*, His [Shakespeare's] mother-tongue, the language of nature, is the same in Cappadocia and in Britain. **1865** Tylor *Early Hist. Man.* ii. 17 The mother-tongue of the deaf and dumb, is the language of signs.

2. An original language from which others spring.

c **1645** Howell *Lett.* (1892) II. 475 The Mother-Tongues of Europe are thirteen. **1727–41** Chambers *Cycl.* s.v., Of *mother tongues*, Scaliger reckons ten in Europe. **1848** Latham *Eng. Lang.* II. iv. (ed. 2) 83 It [American English] was earliest separated from the mother-tongue.

mother wit. Also 5 **moderis wytte.** Native or natural wit; common sense.

Often in *Proverb*: see clergy 5.

c **1440** Capgrave *Life St. Kath.* v. 1710 Thei cowde neuere resorte on-to her moderis wytte. **1529** More *Dyaloge* I. Wks. 153/2 One speciall thynge, without which all lernynge is halfe lame. What is that quod he. Mary quod I, a good mother wyt. **1596** Spenser *F.Q.* IV. x. 21 For all that nature by her mother-wit Could frame in earth,.. Was there. **1697** J. Sergeant *Solid Philos.* 428 Such Forms of Reasoning were, certainly, never intended.. for Men of good Mother-Wits. **1760** C. Johnston *Chrysal* (1822) I. 263 Well supplied with what is called mother-wit. **1860** Emerson *Cond. Life* vi. (1861) 125 The cure for false theology is motherwit. **1885** J. Martineau *Types Eth. Theory* I. 49 The domain of accidental judgment and mother-wit.

†**b.** ? One who possesses mother wit. *Obs.*

1586 Marlowe *1st Pt. Tamburl.* Prol. 1 From iygging vaines of riming mother wits.

Hence **mother witted** *a.*, having mother-wit.

1593 Nashe *Christ's T.* 67 Discontent,.. if [it light] on a man of puissance, (be he not more then mother-witted circumspect,) to him and his family it is no lesse fatall.

'**motherwort.** Also 4–6 **moderwort(e**, 5 **moderuurt, modir-wort, modyr worte**, 6 **motherwoorte**, 6–7 **motherworte**, 8 **motherworth.** [f. mother *sb.*[1] (in sense 11) + wort.]

1. A name for various plants formerly supposed to be valuable in diseases of the womb; now chiefly applied to *Leonurus Cardiaca*; formerly often to the mugwort, *Artemisia vulgaris*.

a **1387** *Sinon. Barthol.* (Anecd. Oxon.) 36/2 *Regina prati*, moderwort. **14..** *Stockholm Med. MS.* II. 247 in *Anglia* XVIII. 313 Off modir-wort I wyl þe tellyn.. Off þat erbe arn spycys iij. *c* **1440** *Promp. Parv.* 341/2 Modyr worte, herbe (or mugworte, *infra*), *artemesia*. *c* **1450** *Alphita* (Anecd. Oxon.) 106/2 *Matricaria aquatica*.. modeuurt. **1533** Elyot *Cast. Helthe* (1541) A ij, Arthemisia queene of Caria, founde the vertues of motherworte, which in latyne bearith her name. **1548** Turner *Names of Herbes* 50 Lycopus is called of the commune Herbaries Cardiaca, in englishe Motherwurt. **1607** Topsell *Four-f. Beasts* 350 Take of Camomile and Motherwort, of each two or three handfuls. **1747** Wesley *Prim. Physic* (1762) 88 A Decoction of Mother Wort. **1760** J. Lee *Introd. Bot.* App. 319 Mother-wort, *Leonurus*. **1807** T. Thomson *Chem.* (ed. 3) II. 431 Some are brown... Others blue, as camomile, mother-wort. **1856** Miss Pratt *Flower. Pl.* (1861) IV. 179.

2. man's motherwort (see man *sb.* 21). **stinking motherwort**, *Chenopodium vulvaria*.

1578 Lyte *Dodoens* v. iv. 549, I haue named it in Englishe, The ranke stinking Goate, or stinking Motherwort.

mothery ('mʌðərɪ), *a.* [f. mother *sb.*[2] + -y.] Mouldy, feculent.

1709 *Brit. Apollo* No. 65. 2/1 The Wine.. turns Mothery. **1759** Sterne *Tr. Shandy* II. xix, If there is such a juice.., is it not enough to make the clearest liquid in the world both feculent and mothery? **1861** H. Macmillan *Footn. fr. Page Nat.* 239 Wine.. vinegar, catsup, not unfrequently become mothery.

Hence '**motheriness.**

1742 H. Baker *Microsc.* II. iii. 76 A sort of whitish Scum or Motheriness will appear upon the Surface.

'**mothless,** *a. nonce-word.* [f. moth *sb.*[1] + -less.] Void of moths.

a **1763** Shenstone *To the Virtuosi* vii, Tis you protect their pregnant hour; And when the birth's at hand, Exerting your obstetric pow'r Prevent a mothless land.

mothley, obs. form of motley.

moth mullein. [See quot. 1597.] The plant *Verbascum Blattaria*.

1578 Lyte *Dodoens* I. lxxxii. 122 It may be called in English Purple, or Mothe Mulleyn. **1597** Gerarde *Herbal* II. cclviii. 634 Concerning the plants comprehended vnder the titles of *Blattaria*, or Moth Mulleins, I finde nothing written of them, sauing that mothes, butterflies, and all manner of smaller flies and bats, do resort vnto the place wheresoeuer these herbes be laide or strowed. **1607** Topsell *Four-f. Beasts* 538 The Hearbe called Purple, or Moth-mullein. **1778** R. Weston *Gard. Calendar* (ed. 2) 303 Moth Mullein. Yellow Moth Mullein. White. **1838** Mary Howitt *Woodpecker* ii, The moth-mullein.. with its pale yellow flowers.

attrib. **1731** Miller *Gard. Dict.* s.v. *Verbascum*, Mullein with a dark Moth-Mullein Leaf.

motho, obs. form of motto.

moth-proof ('mɒθpruːf), *a.* Also **moth proof, mothproof.** [f. moth *sb.* + proof *a.*] Resistant to damage by moths.

1893 *Ladies' Home Jrnl.* May 13/4 Moth proof bag. **1907** *Yesterday's Shopping* (1969) 275/2 Moth proof Cotton underlay to go between wire bottom of bed and mattress. **1916** *Independent* (N.Y.) 15 May 248/2 Colorfast, reversible moth-proof rugs. **1922** *Sci. Amer.* 22 Oct. 260/1 Making wool moth-proof. **1924** *Ibid.* July 39/4 (*heading*) Making the closet moth-proof. **1931** *Daily Express* 21 Sept. 7/5 Hygienic, dustproof, mothproof and washable. **1959** *Times* 12 Jan. 11/3 Courlene.. is.. rot and moth-proof, washable and quick drying. **1960** *Which?* Jan. 18/2 Wool can be made mothproof by the application of certain chemicals, and mothproof wool is available from some manufacturers and is particularly desirable for carpets.

Hence as *v. trans.*, to render moth-proof; so **moth-proofing** *vbl. sb.*; **moth-proofer**, a substance for moth-proofing clothes or textile fibres.

1925 *Chem. Abstr.* XIX. 184 (*title*) Mothproofing fibrous materials. *Ibid.* 993 (*title*) Moth-proofing fabrics. **1932** *Discovery* Oct. 321/2 Science has provided sufficient moth-proofing substances and means for combating this pest [*sc.* the moth]. **1938** *Chatelaine* May 79/1 Her lovely clothes at Columbia Studios are mothproofed with *Larvex*. **1958** *Spectator* 4 July 15/3 Expert mending, dying to pattern, mothproofing. **1960** *Which?* June 130/1 For woollens that have not been mothproofed in manufacture, the consumer can use *household mothproofers*—liquids which impregnate the material and kill the larvae —or *moth repellents*. **1961** *Times* 13 Dec. 21/7 Air fresheners.. mothproofers.

moththe, mothwoc: see moth, motewoke.

mothy ('mɒθɪ), *a.* [f. moth *sb.*[1] + -y.] Infested by moths; characterized by the presence of moths; suggestive of a moth, resembling the movements of the wings of a moth.

1596 Shaks. *Tam. Shr.* III. ii. 49 His horse hip'd with an olde mothy saddle, and stirrops of no kindred. **1598** Florio, *Tarmoso*, mothie, full of mothes or wormes. **1613** *Uncasing of Machivils Instr.* 16 Raile on a Broker whose clothes are mothie. **1890** *Illustr. Lond. News* 27 Dec. 810/1 Their mothy leathern covers. **1898** Hardy *Wessex Poems* 155 At mothy curfew-tide. **1917** —— *Moments of Vision* 255 Some nocturnal blackness, mothy and warm. **1949** E. Bowen *Heat of Day* vi. 113 Your mothy way of blinking and laziness about keeping your eyelids open.

motif (məʊ'tiːf, ‖motif). [Fr.: see motive *sb.*]

1. a. In painting, sculpture, architecture, decoration, etc.: A constituent feature of a composition; an object or group of objects forming a distinct element of a design; a particular type of subject for artistic treatment. Also used for: The structural principle or the dominant idea of a work.

1848 Mrs. Jameson *Sacr. & Leg. Art* (1850) 87 The *motif* is simple and not easily mistaken. **1850** *Ecclesiologist* XI. 121 Regular stalls would not have suited the *motif* of the arrangement. **1881** *Cornh. Mag.* Mar. 309 The main motif of this landscape was the indescribable Carrara range. **1883** A. H. Church *Prec. Stones* 29 Arrangements of precious stones in which the leading *motif* is either identity, or seriation, or contrast.

b. In literary composition: A type of incident, a particular situation, an ethical problem, or the like, which may be treated in a work of imagination. Also in *Folklore*, a recurrent character, event, situation, or theme.

1857 Kingsley *Two Years Ago* I. vi. 161, I owe you a debt, sir, for having furnished me with one of the most striking 'motifs' I ever had. **1877** *International Rev.* (N.Y.) Jan. 73 Having endeavored to discover the *motif* and

purpose of George Eliot's work. **1884** A. LANG in R.M. Dorson *Peasant Customs* (1968) I. 312 Turning from the Samoyeds and the Epirotes to Africa, we find the *motif* (escape of brother and sister) in a Kaffir tale. **1897** 'EDNA LYALL' *Mrs. Gaskell* in *Women Novelists* 125 The difficult subject which forms the *motif* of 'Ruth'. **1902** W. W. LAWRENCE in *Jrnl. Eng. & Gmc. Philol.* IV. 476 Repetition of motifs and consequent disturbance of logical arrangement is characteristic of Anglo-Saxon poetry. **1935** A. C. BARTLETT *Larger Rhet. Patterns Anglo-Saxon Poetry* 80 The conception of the hereafter clothed in definite form is, in Germanic poetry, found only in Anglo-Saxon, and.. it is a favorite motif in poems not bound by Bible text. **1941** G. G. SCHOLEM *Major Trends in Jewish Mysticism* ii. 67 Some of the oldest mythical motifs are to be found.. in an extremely interesting.. text. **1968** P. OLIVER *Screening Blues* ii. 63 The parody sermons, as Stith Thompson shows, are one of the more popular of folk-tale motifs and they abound in Negro folk-lore. **1971** *English Studies* LII. 501 In addition to the motif of longing, the themes of former happiness and of present estrangement from friends also unify the poem.

c. *Music.* Used in various senses, respectively = FIGURE *sb.* 24, LEITMOTIV, and SUBJECT *sb.*

1882 MRS. A. EDWARDES *Ballroom Repent.* I. 189, I feel original. I have got hold of a *motif*! Oh, if we had.. a sheet of scored paper! **1907** in *Grove's Dict. Mus.* II. 377/1.

2. *Dress-making.* An ornament of lace, braid, or the like, sewn separately on a dress.

1882 CAULFEILD & SAWARD *Dict. Needlework, Motifs*, a French term, used to distinguish the pattern of a piece of embroidery from the groundwork or material. **1897** *Westm. Gaz.* 26 Aug. 3/2 Motifs, braces, epaulettes,.. may be created from bold patterned guipure lace. **1906** *Times* 4 May 10/2 The skirt was bordered.. with large jetted lace motifs.

¶ **3.** Often used instead of MOTIVE in senses not specially Fr., in order to avoid the customary associations of the Eng. word as denoting an influence determining volition.

1874 DYKES *Relat. Kingd.* 163 The very *motif* to such false teaching is a desire to broaden somewhat the excessive straitness of the gospel path to life. **1887** G. T. LADD *Physiol. Psychol.* 463 The *motifs* or data which the mind would have for constructing such a surface must be found in the series of sensations of light and color.

4. *attrib.* and *Comb.*, as ***motif classification, framework, research, -work; motif-less, -like*** adjs.; **motif-index**, an index of standard folklore motifs.

1966 K. LUOMALA in M. Jacobs *Anthropologist looks at Myth* 164 Kirtley's *Motif-Index*.. follows Stith Thompson's system for motif-classification. **1971** R. L. WELSCH tr. *Krohn's Folklore Methodology* iii. 31 The fact that it occurs more or less incidentally in other complexes is due to the influence of the motif framework. **1932** S. THOMPSON in *Indiana Univ. Stud.* No. 96 (*heading*) Motif-index of folk literature. **1958** T. P. COFFIN *Analytical Index to Jrnl. Amer. Folklore* 239 It was deemed advisable not to attempt a complete Thompson-style motif-index of the Journal. **1972** *Jrnl. Amer. Folklore* LXXXV. 278 One would hope this *Index* would be shelved in every library beside the Thompson Type and Motif indexes. **1973** A. DUNDES *Mother Wit* 114 These tools include various tale type indices and motif indices... By using tale type and motif indices, Dorson is able to demonstrate the European provenience of the greater portion of the tales. **1970** *Daily Tel.* 27 June 7 This work, while not.. unmotivated, is entirely motif-less —introductory clinking of pebbles, toneless blowing into instruments built for lusher uses. **1964** *English Studies* XLV. 446 Two terms which characterize Christina's.. reputation through their motif-like occurrence, *caprice* and *banality*, are a source of insight and confusion. **1938** P. S. WATSON tr. *Nygren's Agape & Eros: Part 2* I. 23 The answer can only be supplied by motif-research, that is, by an enquiry which detects the motif behind the formed expression. **1948** L. SPITZER *Linguistics & Lit. Hist.* v. 193 This.. movement is incarnated in.. the rhythm—as in the verbal motif-work.

motif, obs. form of MOTIVE.

motiferous (məʊ'tɪfərəs), *a. Phys.* [f. L. *mōt-us* motion + -FEROUS.] Conveying motion or motor impulses.

1836–9 *Todd's Cycl. Anat.* II. 375/1 There are fibrils which extend between the motiferous part of the cerebrospinal axis and the sympathetic. **1839–47** *Ibid.* III. 893/1 Motiferous filaments.

motific (məʊ'tɪfɪk), *a. Phys.* [f. L. *mōt-us* motion + -FIC.] Producing motion.

1822 GOOD *Study Med.* III. 30 *margin*, Motific, or irritative power of a lower description than sensific. **1835–6** *Todd's Cycl. Anat.* I. 800/2 Convulsion.. is an affection of the motific not of the sensific part of the nervous system.

† **'motild.** *Obs.* [f. *mote*, MOOT *v.*[1] + *-ild* fem. suffix (see GRUCCHILD).] A female disputant.

a **1225** *Leg. Kath.* 418 Ʒef ha þeos modi motild [L. *hanc contionatricem temerariam*] ouercumen mahten. *a* **1240** *Lofsong* in *Cott. Hom.* 205 Ich.. bidde þin ore ðet tu beo mi motild aȝeines mine soule fon.

motile ('məʊtaɪl, -ɪl), *a.* (and *sb.*) [ad. L. type **mōtilis*, f. *mōt-*, ppl. stem of *movēre* to move: see -ILE.] **1.** In *Zool.*, *Bot.*, etc.: Capable of motion; characterized by motion.

1864 *Q. Jrnl. Microsc. Sci.* IV. 189 The motile phenomena hitherto observed in sponges. **1867** J. HOGG *Microsc.* II. i. 261 Still or motile cells of Protococcus. **1890** COOKE *Introd. Fresh-w. Algæ* 143 Active motile cells are so common amongst algæ that they scarce need description.

2. *Psychol.* Of or relating to responses that involve motor imagery. Cf. MOTOR *a.* 3. Also as *sb.*, one who responds to perceptions more readily in terms of motor or kinæsthetic imagery than in terms of auditory or visual.

1886 *Mind* XI. 415 This division of men into visuals, audiles, motiles and indifferents.. is of great interest and importance. **1889** *Proc. Soc. Psychical Res.* V. 536 A 'motile' reading the above question will dimly imagine the movements of his own larynx in uttering the word elephant. **1890** W. JAMES *Princ. Psychol.* II. xviii. 61 Persons who belong to this type (*les moteurs*, in French, *motiles*, as Mr. Galton proposes to call them in English) make use, in memory, reasoning, and all their intellectual operations, of images derived from movement. *Ibid.* 62 Professor Stricker of Vienna.. seems to have the motile form of imagination developed in unusual strength. **1892** —— *Text-bk. Psychol.* xix. 308 All blind persons must belong to the 'tactile' and 'motile' types of the French authors. **1909** [see AUDILE *a.*].

motility (məʊ'tɪlɪtɪ). *Phys.* [Formed as prec. + -ITY.] Capability or power of moving (as a quality of organisms).

1835–6 *Todd's Cycl. Anat.* I. 40/2 Motility and Sensation. **1836–9** *Ibid.* II. 675/1 Cold.. tends to diminish sensibility and motility. **1860** *Encycl. Brit.* (ed. 8) XXI. 1000/2 The changes and motility of their cilia. **1875** BENNETT & DYER *Sachs' Bot.* 645 Motile leaves.. lose their motility when oxygen is withheld from them. **1878** A. M. HAMILTON *Nerv. Dis.* 90 A very small lesion may produce very decided impairment of motility.

Motilon (məʊtɪ'ləʊn). Also **Motilone.** Pl. **Motilon, Motilones.** [Sp., of Amer. Ind. origin.] A Cariban Indian people of Colombia; a member of this people; also, their language. Also *attrib.*

1913 P. J. EDER *Colombia* xii. 186 The white settlers have at times been driven away by the onslaughts of the Motilones Indians, who dwell in the forests of the Eastern Cordillera to the east. **1937** T. ROURKE *Tyrant of Andes* 26 The Motilones are no myth. They.. have been sending the six-foot arrows flying from the bush into the American.. geologists working for the oil companies. **1949** L. S. & E. JUDSON *Let's go to Colombia* v. 213 The Motilone Indians. Of fierce Carib origin the Motilones were never subdued by the Spaniards. **1950** J. A. MASON in J. H. Steward *Handbk. S. Amer. Indians* VI. 232 The *Cariban* affinities of *Motilón* .. have always been accepted. **1957** *Encycl. Brit.* XXI. 80/1 They [*sc.* the Carib] reached the Andes on the west and small groups entered Colombia (Motilon, Opon and Carare Indians). **1964** E. A. NIDA *Toward Sci. Transl.* iii. 37 The Motilones in Colombia have borrowed the Spanish word *purisima* 'most pure' from the phrase *María purísima* 'Mary, most pure', but have given it the meaning of 'the devil'. **1965** MOSER & TAYLOR *Cocaine Eaters* IV. ii. 151 The arrow is the most treasured object a Motilon possesses. *Ibid.* iii. 157 We had been intrigued by the question of death amongst the Motilon. *Ibid.* 179 The Motilon chiefs. **1968** G. ANTHONY *Colombia: Land of Tomorrow* xiii. 160 It was left as a souvenir of a raid by the Motilone Indians... The Motilones, who live along the mountainous border between Colombia and Venezuela, are still amongst the fiercest and least-known of all Colombia's Indians.

motion ('məʊʃən), *sb.* Forms: 4–6 **mocioun**, 5 **mocyoun, moscyoun**, 5–6 **mocyon**, 5–7 **mocion**, 6 **mocyone, motione, motioun, motyon**, 5– **motion.** [a. F. *motion* (13th c.), ad. L. *mōtiōn-em*, n. of action f. *movēre* to MOVE.

The Eng. uses correspond not only to those of L. *mōtio*, but also, and perhaps more commonly, to those of *mōtus* (It., Sp. *moto*).]

1. a. The process of moving, i.e. of undergoing change of place; the condition of a body (in mathematical theory also of a point, line, surface, etc.) when at each successive instant it occupies a different position in space. Also, in particularized uses: An instance, or a particular kind or variety (discriminated according to direction, velocity, etc.) of this process or condition. (In early use chiefly of the movements of the heavenly bodies.)

motion of ROTATION, *of* TRANSLATION: see those words. *laws of motion*: see LAW *sb.* 17 b.

1412–20 LYDG. *Chron. Troy* I. 1706 Þe grete Tholome.. telleþ þe cause why.. Bothe of Eclips and coniunccioun, And whi þei falle by natural mocioun. *c* **1430** —— *Min. Poems* (Percy Soc.) 85 The cheildren of Seth.. Founde first the crafte of hevenly mocyouns. **1570** BILLINGSLEY *Euclid* I. def. xvi. 3 A point, by his motion or draught, describeth a line. **1590** SHAKS. *Com. Err.* III. ii. 24 We in your motion turne, and you may moue vs. **1629** MASSINGER *Roman Actor* II. i, The motion of the Spheares are out of time, Her musicall notes but heard. **1642** FULLER *Holy & Prof. St.* IV. ix. 277 Diogenes confuted him who denyed there was any motion, by saying nothing but walking before his eyes. **1670** H. STUBBE *Plus Ultra* 163 The superiour part of the Air or Atmosphere.. hath another motion or lation then that which is more low. **1690** LOCKE *Hum. Und.* II. xiv. §7 This .. is the Reason, why Motions very slow, though they are constant, are not perceived by us. **1701** GREW *Cosmol. Sacra* I. i. 4 The two Visible Parts of the Universe are Matter and Motion. **1710** J. CLARKE *Rohault's Nat. Phil.* (1729) I. 165 The Particles of the Water having less Motion, than our Bodies have in all those Parts which are near the Heart, they receive some Motion from us. **1812–16** PLAYFAIR *Nat. Phil.* (1819) I. Introd. 9 No body loses motion in any direction, without communicating an equal quantity to other bodies in that same direction. **1829** *Nat. Philos.* I. *Mechanics* II. xiii. 53 (Usef. Knowl. Soc.) Generally speaking,.. the motions which we meet with in the use of machinery may be resolved into rectilinear and circular. **1860** TYNDALL *Glac.* I. xi. 82 The clouds at a distance lay.. with scarcely visible motion. **1875** JOWETT *Plato* (ed. 2) V. 150 The motion.. was circular, as in the motion of a top. **1883** *Encycl. Brit.* XV. 687/1 We must now consider the composition of simple harmonic motions in directions at right angles to each other.

b. *fig.* (e.g. of the progress of time.)

1681 DRYDEN *Abs. & Achit.* 254 Heaven has to all allotted, soon or late, Some lucky Revolution of their Fate: Whose Motions, if we watch and guide with Skill [etc.]. **1822** BYRON *Heav. & Earth* I. iii. 83 Nor years, nor heart-break, nor time's sapping motion.

c. *Philos.* (now only *Hist.*) By many writers *motion* (Gr. κίνησις) was applied in a wider sense to all kinds of change, the term ***local motion*** being employed to distinguish change of place from the other kinds of 'motion'.

1678 CUDWORTH *Intell. Syst.* I. i. §41. 50 To assert that Life and Sense, Reason and Understanding, were really nothing else but Local Motion. **1727–41** CHAMBERS *Cycl.* s.v., The antient philosophers considered *motion* in a more general and extensive manner. They defined it, a passage out of one state into another: and thus made six kinds of motion, viz. Creation, generation, corruption, augmentation, diminution, and lation, or local motion.

† **d.** Change of abode; a flitting from one place to another. *Obs.*

1634 SIR T. HERBERT *Trav.* 130 Hee seldome resides in Cities, or any one place long, but affects perpetuall motion. **1643** EVELYN *Diary* 23 July, Which had been a greate cause of my perpetual motions hitherto between Wotton and London. **1645** [see 6 a]. *a* **1661** FULLER *Worthies, Staffs.* (1662) III. 46 William Gifford.. was a man of much Motion.

† **e.** The action of moving or setting in movement, the fact of being moved. *Obs. rare.*

1667 MILTON *P.L.* XII. 592 And see the Guards, By mee encampt on yonder Hill, expect Thir motion, at whose Front a flaming Sword, In signal of remove, waves fiercely round.

† **f.** *fig.* Advancement, promotion. *Obs. rare.*

1641 W. MOUNTAGU in *Buccleuch MSS.* (Hist. MSS. Comm.) I. 288 The lawyers also must have their motions: Banks must be Baron and Lord Treasurer, the Attorney Chief Justice.

2. a. Change of place, whether voluntary or automatic, in an animate body or its parts; an instance of this, a movement.

1588 SHAKS. *L.L.L.* IV. ii. 403 O! neuer will I trust to speeches pen'd, Nor to the motion of a Schoole-boies tongue. **1615** CROOKE *Body of Man* 740 Men.. in their sleepe haue not so strong Tonnical motions as when they are awake. **1644** [see LOCAL A. 1 c]. **1645** EVELYN *Diary* 7 Jan., A Sermon was preach'd to the Jewes.., who are constrained to sit till the houre is don; but it is with so much.. spitting, hum'ing, coughing, and motion, that [etc.]. **1727–41** CHAMBERS *Cycl.* s.v., *Animal Motion*, is that whereby the situation, figure, magnitude, &c. of the parts, members, &c. of animals are changed. **1742** YOUNG *Nt. Th.* VIII. 541 The love of pleasure: that, thro' ev'ry vein, Throws motion, warmth. **1799** *Med. Jrnl.* II. 423 To retard the motion of the heart and circulating fluids. **1803** *Ibid.* X. 433 This translation of sensation and motion to parts remote from the place where impressions are made. **1813** BYRON *Br. Abydos* II. xxvi, That hand, whose motion is not life, Yet feebly seems to menace strife.

† **b.** In artistic use.

1598 HAYDOCKE tr. *Lomazzo* I. 23 By Motion, the Painters meane that comelines, and grace in the proportion and disposition of a picture, which is also called the spirite and life of a picture.

c. Power of movement, capability of moving (as the property of an animate body).

1603 SHAKS. *Meas. for M.* III. i. 120 This sensible warme motion, to become A kneaded clod. **1667** MILTON *P.L.* II. 151 Devoid of sense and motion. **1698** ROKEBY in *Misc.* (Surtees No. 37) 62, I was taken with a very great indisposition.. my motion in a manner wholly lost.. I was necessitated to be carryed up staires.

d. The action of moving the body in walking, running, etc. Also, manner of walking or stepping; gait, carriage.

1598 SHAKS. *Merry W.* III. iii. 68 The firme fixture of thy foote would giue an excellent motion to thy gate, in a semi-circled Farthingale. **1607–12** BACON *Ess., Beauty* (Arb.) 212 Yf it be true that the principall part of Beautie is in decent mocion. **1647** CLARENDON *Hist. Reb.* I. §119 He had in his person, in his aspect and countenance, the appearance of a great man, which he preserved in his gait and motion. **1674** *Ibid.* XII. §89 The men.. must be good horsemen, otherwise they could not obey the quick motion and turns of their horses. **1711** STEELE *Spect.* No. 4 ¶6 Her Air has the Beauty of Motion, and her Look the Force of Language.

† **e.** Bodily exertion (tending to fatigue); *pl.* = bodily exercises. *Obs.*

1602 SHAKS. *Ham.* IV. vii. 158 When in your motion you are hot and dry. **1605** BACON *Adv. Learn.* II. viii. §3 By Ambages of diets, bathings, annointings, Medicines, motions, and the like, prolong life. **1689** WOOD *Life* 20 Dec. (O.H.S.) III. 318 His violent motion going up Shotover Hill on foot. **1695** DRYDEN *Du Fresnoy's Art Paint.* Pref. 50 But that Poet was always in a Foam at his setting out, even before the Motion of the Race had warm'd him.

3. a. An act of moving the body (or its members); a change of posture; an external or visible movement, a gesture; in bad sense, †a grimace, antic.

1608 MACHIN *Dumb Knt.* I. i, In her lookes Each motion hath a speaking maiesty. **1621** FLETCHER *Wildgoose Chase* III. i. (init.), These Gim-cracks, made of Mops, and Motions. **1667** MILTON *P.L.* VIII. 223 Speaking or mute all comliness and grace Attends thee, and each word, each motion formes. **1798** JOANNA BAILLIE *Tryal* II. ii. *Plays on Passions* (1821) I. 230 [stage-direction] Agnes, making a slight motion of her hand to fasten some pin in her dress. **1804** WORDSW. '*She was a Phantom of Delight*', Her household motions light and free, And steps of virgin-liberty. **1807–26** S. COOPER *First Lines Surg.* (ed. 5) 346 By a slight motion of the hand backward. **1842** TENNYSON *Locksley Hall* 22 And her eyes on all my motions with a mute observance hung.

b. Phrases. ***to make a motion*** or ***motions***: to beckon, invite by gestures (*to do* something). ***to go through the motions of***: to perform by way of simulation gestures or movements such as are used in (some specified action); also *fig.*, to do something only perfunctorily; to pretend; also with ellipsis of 'of' and following phr; so ***going-through-the-motions***.

1719 De Foe *Crusoe* I. (Globe) 207 Upon this my Savage ..made a Motion to me to lend him my Sword. 1743 Bulkeley & Cummins *Voy. S. Seas* 130 As soon as we discover'd them, we made Motions to them to come down. 1816 Scott *Old Mortality* in *Tales my Landlord* 1st Ser. II. x. 255 She pressed her handkerchief to her face, sobbed with great vehemence, and either wept, or managed, as Halliday might have said, to go through the motions wonderfully well. 1850 'M. Tensas' *Odd Leaves Life Louisiana Swamp Doctor* 88 Cuss you! I was only going through the motions; the rifle ain't loaded! 1856 Dickens *Dorrit* (1857) I. xxxvi. 316 Mr. Dorrit urbanely went through the motions of playing a game at skittles with the Collegian who was the next oldest inhabitant to himself. 1900 'Mark Twain' *Man that corrupted Hadleyburg* 298 A Government cannot satisfy all these public opinions; it can only go through the motions of trying. This Government does that. It goes through the motions, and they do not succeed. 1933 Auden *Poems* (ed. 2) 58 Go through the motions of exploring the familiar. 1944 H. Croome *You've gone Astray* xvi. 166 It was pleasant, undoubtedly pleasant. But both of them felt..that in some fundamental sense they were merely going through the motions. 1958 *Spectator* 22 Aug. 247/1 Her gaoler is called her secretary and in public goes through the motions of secretaryhood. 1963 *Times Lit. Suppl.* 11 Jan. 27/4 A mere exasperated going-through-the-motions. 1973 W. J. Burley *Death in Salubrious Place* i. 24 It's really a diplomatic mission... It would be better if we at least go through the motions of an investigation.

c. A practised and regulated movement of the body; a step, gesture, or other movement acquired by drill and training (e.g. in *Fencing* and in the *Manège*). Also *fig.*

1601 Shaks. *Twel. N.* III. iv. 304 He giues me the stucke in with such a mortall motion that it is ineuitable. 1602 —— *Ham.* IV. vii. 102 (1604 Qo.) The Scrimures of their nation, He swore had neither motion, guard, nor eye, If you opposd them. 1650 Milton *Tenure of Kings* (ed. 2) 57 For Divines, if we observe them, have thir postures and thir motions no less expertly, and with no less variety then they that practice feats in the Artillery-ground. *a*1763 Shenstone *Ess.* Wks. 1765 II. 141 As a race-horse hurts his motions by condescending to draw in a team. 1809 Roland *Fencing* 98, I do not..recommend this motion to be adopted by young beginners, as it is apt to give rise to bad habits.

d. *Mil.* Each of the several successive actions of which a prescribed exercise of arms consists.

1635 Barriffe (*title*) Military Discipline..together with the exercise of the foot in their motions. 1718 *Act New Hampshire* in *Outing* (U.S.) (1895) XXVII. 78/2 To exercise them in motions, the use of arms, and shooting at marks. 1760 *New Manual Exerc.* (ed. 3) 7 The Officers face to the Left-about in 3 Motions. 1802 C. James *Milit. Dict.*, *Manual Exercise*..consists in seven motions of the firelock. .. The motions in the manual exercise will, in future, be performed slower than heretofore, leaving three seconds between each motion. 1859 [see extension 10].

4. Commotion, agitated condition (e.g. of water); irregular movement, shaking, oscillation (of a ship, a vehicle). †Also, in immaterial applications, a political agitation or commotion; excitement, agitation (of the mind or feelings). See also 6b.

1387 Trevisa *Higden* (Rolls) VI. 277 In token of þe mocioun of Ierusalem þat fel þre hondred ȝere afterward. 1423 *Coventry Leet Bk.* (E.E.T.S.) 45 For-asmoche as dyssencions, stirrynges and mocions haue byn had a-fore tyme..for certen comen. 1535 Coverdale *2 Esdras* vi. 14 There shal come a greate mocion [Vulg. *commotio*], but yͤ place where thou stondest shal not be moued. 1582 *Reg. Privy Council Scot.* III. 516 To contene thamselffis peciable ..unattempting ony further motioun or trouble. 1644 S. Kem *Messengers Prepar.* 22 It's good stepping into the poole upon the motion of the waters. 1697 Potter *Antiq. Greece* I. iv. (1715) 15 The State continu'd all that time unsettl'd, and in continual motions. 1700 Dryden *Cymon & Iphig.* 30 Love..brushing o'er, adds motion to the pool. 1715 Gay *What D'ye Call It* II. viii. *Ballad*, Cease, cease, thou cruel Ocean, And let my Lover rest; Ah! what's thy troubled Motion To that within my Breast? 1719 De Foe *Crusoe* II. (Globe) 592 He spoke this with so much Warmth in his Temper, so much Earnestness and Motion of his Spirits. 1771 T. Percival *Ess.* (1777) I. 127 The mixtures..seemed to have some little fermentative motion in them. 1798 Coleridge *Anc. Mar.* v. xxi, But in a minute she 'gan stir, With a short uneasy motion—Backwards and forwards half her length. 1807 Crabbe *Par. Reg.* III. 572 His groans now told the motions of the cart. 1864 Dickens *Mrs. Lirriper's Leg.* i, in *All Year Round* Extra Christmas No., 1 Dec. 7/1 Not much motion on the whole, though me with a swimming in the head. 1971 E. R. Seary *Place Names Avalon Penin. Newfoundland* v. 90 Petty Harbour Point, now Motion Head..derived its latest name..from The Motion, the heavy cross sea caused by the irregular and broken ground.

5. a. *pl.* Activities or 'movements' on the part of a person or body of persons, when pursuing an affair; esp. the movements of an army in the field. (Now *rare.*) †Formerly also *sing.*

1674 Clarendon *Hist. Reb.* XIV. §137 That his coming into Zealand, and his continuance there, was known to Cromwell, with all the particulars of his motion. 1693 *Humours Town* 24 Whose motions she has always as certain advice of as a Commander has of those of an Enemy. 1705 Stanhope *Paraphr.* I. 298 Joseph taking the Advantage of the Night to conceal his Motions, went away with Jesus and the Virgin, and dwelt in Egypt. 1769 Robertson *Chas. V*, IV. Wks. 1813 V. 406 All the emperor's motions, depending on himself alone, were more brisk and better concerted. 1775 Sheridan *St. Patr. Day* I. ii, My chief business with you is to watch the motions of a rake-helly fellow here. 1828 Scott *F.M. Perth* viii, He had associated himself to the Smith, whose motions he had watched for the purpose of joining him.

b. Phr. ***to make a motion***: to begin to move in a particular direction or with some specified purpose.

1633 G. Herbert *Temple, Holy Script.* II. i, This verse marks that, and both do make a motion unto a third, that ten leaves off doth lie. 1709 *Tatler* No. 43 ⁋11 The French Army had laid Bridges over the Sharp, and made a Motion as if they intended to pass that River. 1719 De Foe *Crusoe* II. (Globe) 604 About an Hour after they made a Motion to attack us again. 1800 Mrs. Hervey *Mourtray Fam.* III. 204 She made a motion towards the door.

6. in motion. a. *lit.* In a state of moving or of being moved; in a state of activity or moving about. Opposed to *at rest*. (Also †***upon motion.***) Phr. ***to put in*** (†***into***, †***to***) ***motion***, ***to set in motion***.

1601 Shaks. *Twel. N.* III. i. 87 Taste your legges sir, put them to motion. *c*1645 Howell *Lett.* I. xiv. 27 My last unto you was from the Low-Countreys, wher I was in motion to and fro above four months. 1647 Cowley *Mistr.*, *Called Inconst.* iii, As Men in Motion think the Trees move too. 1659 H. More *Immort. Soul* (1662) 233 The whole matter of the Universe, and all the parts thereof, are ever upon motion. 1662 Stillingfl. *Orig. Sacr.* III. ii. §18 There must be an infinitely powerful..God, who must..put matter into motion. 1774 Goldsm. *Nat. Hist.* (1776) I. 116 Not a breeze, not a cloud which might be supposed to put all Nature thus into motion. 1836–41 Brande *Chem.* (ed. 5) 337 All the effects we are about to describe depend..upon electricity in motion, or upon electric currents. 1841 R. Willis *Princ. Mechanism* 18 Each of which is so connected with the frame-work of the machine, that when in motion every point of it is constrained to move in a certain path.

b. *fig.* In a state of activity, excitement, commotion, or the like; occas. †***in great motion.*** ***to put*** or ***set in motion***, to set going or working.

1596 Shaks. *1 Hen. IV*, I. iii. 226 To keepe his anger still in motion. 1599 —— *Hen. V*, I. ii. 185 Setting endeuour in continual motion. 1611 —— *Cymb.* IV. iii. 31 The want is, but to put those Powres in motion, That long to moue. 1673 Temple *Ess.*, *Ireland* Wks. 1731 I. 110 When Things are once in Motion, Trade begets Trade. 1748 *Anson's Voy.* II. vi. 192 Our people..observed..lights hurrying backwards and forwards in the fort, and other marks of the inhabitants being in great motion. 1772 *Ann. Reg.* XV. 94/2 We have now in our gaol sixteen rioters from Sudbury, and it is an alarming circumstance that the whole country seems in motion. 1804 G. Rose *Diaries* (1860) II. 139 My writ was moved for this day,..but my patent was not put in motion. 1855 Prescott *Philip II*, II. v. I. 197 They..who set a revolution in motion have not always the power to stop it.

†7. a. The action of moving, prompting, or urging (a person to do something, or that something be done); a proposal, suggestion (esp. in phr. ***to make a motion***); an instigation, prompting, or bidding. *Obs.* in general sense (see 8).

*c*1374 Chaucer *Troylus* IV. 1263 (1291) þoo wordes.. Nys but to shewe yow my mocion To fynde vn-to oure helpe þe beste weye. 1412 Hoccleve *De Reg. Princ.* 4989 To god þi sone make a mocioun, How he þi seruaunt was, mayden marie. 1432–50 tr. *Higden* (Rolls) VI. 15 Heraclius themperour..errede from the feithe thro the mocioun of Cirus..and of Sergius [L. *suadentibus ad hoc Cyro..et Sergio*]. 1530 Palsgr. 647/1, I opyn a mater, I make first mocyon of it, or breke a mater to one, *je entame*. 1539 in Ellis *Orig. Lett.* Ser. II. II. 131 Ye marvelle that I and my brotherne do nott frelye..surrendure upe owre Howse at the mocyone off the Kyngs Commissinars. 1611 Bible *Transl. Pref.* ⁋5 To whom..a sealed booke was deliuered, with this motion, Reade this, I pray thee. 1632 Lithgow *Trav.* III. 126 A Traueller..must alwayes at the first motion content these Rascals. 1682 Bunyan *Holy War* 19 Then they all with one consent said to this Bramble, do thou Reign over us. So he accepted the motion and became the King of the Town of Mansoul. 1720 De Foe *Capt. Singleton* x. (1840) 174 My friend made a motion to me, that we should desire Captain Wilmot to put us into the sloop. 1773 *Life N. Frowde* 26 The Mate applauded this Motion, and accordingly we went on shore. 1796 *Hist. Ned Evans* I. 21 Does she know..that I have been sent for, or was it only a mere motion of your own?

b. ? Persuasive force. *Obs. rare*$^{-1}$.

*a*1591 H. Smith *Serm.* (1614) 265 If I had the wordes of motion to speake that which might be spoken of this matter, it would fright Iudas himselfe.

8. *spec.* **a.** A proposition or proposal formally made in a deliberative assembly.

1579–80 North *Plutarch, Aristides* (1595) 364 A generall counsell..in the which Aristides made a motion, that all the cities of Greece should [etc.]. 1605 *Nottingham Rec.* IV. 278 The mocion of 20 to be added to the Councell shalbe assented vnto. 1692 R. L'Estrange *Fables* cccix. 271 And upon this Ground, there was a Motion put up, for Changing the Monarchy into a Republique. 1710 Hearne *Collect.* (O.H.S.) III. 84, I mov'd that it might be bought for the Publick Library. My Motion not listen'd to. 1712 Steele *Spect.* No. 298 ⁋5 The Motion being made, and the Question being put. 1838 Thirlwall *Greece* IV. xxxiv. 334 This motion was carried. 1880 McCarthy *Own Times* III. xliv. 327 The motion was never pressed to a division.

b. *Law.* An application made to a court or judge by a party to an action or his counsel, to obtain some rule or order of court necessary to the progress of the action.

*a*1726 Gilbert *Tenures* (1757) 290 Upon motion to the court, it was agreed by the four justices, that [etc.]. 1729 Jacob *Law Dict.* s.v., In the Courts of Chancery, King's Bench, &c. Motions are made by Barristers and Counsellors at Law, for what concerns their Clients Causes... One ought not to move for several Things in one Motion; and where a Motion hath been denied, the same Matter may not be moved again by another Counsel, without acquainting the Court thereof. 1818 Cruise *Digest* (ed. 2) I. 289 The motion was refused. 1838 Dickens *O. Twist* xli, He.. quitted the Bar in disgust because he had only one brief and a motion of course in twenty years.

9. †a. An inward prompting or impulse; an instigation or incitement from within; a desire or inclination (*to* or *towards*). Also, a stirring of the soul, an emotion. *Obs.*

1430–40 Lydg. *Bochas* II. iii. (1494) f viij, This body must haue a soule of life To queke the membres with goostly mocions. 1504 Lady Margaret tr. *De Imitatione* IV. vii. 269 So full of mocyons and concupyscences [L. *tam plenus concupiscentiarum motibus*]. 1597 Hooker *Eccl. Pol.* v. ii. §3 Whereas vnto mens inward cogitations, vnto the priuie intents and motions of their harts, religion serueth for a bridle. 1604 Shaks. *Oth.* I. iii. 335 We haue Reason to coole our raging Motions. 1607–12 Bacon *Ess.*, *Nobility* (Arb.) 190 He that standeth at a stay when others rise, can hardlye avoyd mocions of envye. 1625 *Ibid.*, *Love* 449 There is in Mans Nature, a secret Inclination, and Motion, towards loue of others. *a*1680 Charnock *Sinfuln. & Cure of Evil Th.* Wks. (1849) 123 Good motions cherished will spring up in good actions. 1692 Dryden *St. Euremont's Ess.* 9 Whether he killed his Sons by a motion of Heroick Vertue. 1718 Hickes & Nelson *J. Kettlewell* III. cx. 464 He got the Mastery of his Passions, and brought the Motions of his Mind into Subjection to the Law of Christ. 1726 Swift *Gulliver* III. i, The natural Love of Life gave me some inward Motions of Joy.

†b. *spec.* A working of God in the soul. *Obs.*

1526 *Pilgr. Perf.* (W. de W. 1531) 19 That all our actes and dedes be ordred and wrought after the inclynacyon or mocyon of grace. 1548–9 (Mar.) *Bk. Com. Prayer, Coll. 1st Sund. in Lent*, That..wee maye euer obeye thy Godlye mocions. 1670 Walton *Lives* I. 37 God..mark'd him with ..a blessing of obedience to the motions of his blessed Spirit. 1760–72 H. Brooke *Fool of Qual.* (1809) II. 158 Abandoned by God, and unvisited by his gracious motions in the heart.

c. Phr. ***of*** (†***upon***) ***one's own*** (or †***proper***) ***motion*** = of one's own accord. Now *arch.* Similarly †***of a*** (specified) ***motion***.

1426 Lydg. *De Guil. Pilgr.* 19495 And my burdoun I heelde ryghte ffaste..And seyde (off sodeyne moscyoun) 'Bordoun' [etc.]. 1462 *Paston Lett.* II. 112 The parson comyth not of hyse owyn mocyon. 1489 Caxton *Faytes of A.* I. v. 11 The ladies them self of theyr propre mocion brought theyr jewellis. 1533 Cromwell in Merriman *Life & Lett.* (1902) I. 370 Ye shall not moche nede to travayle.. to procure answer other then of their owne mocyons they shall declare unto you. 1577–87 Holinshed *Chron.* III. 1211 He also of a godlie motion builded a conuenient roome in Pauls churchyard. 1597 Hooker *Eccl. Pol.* v. lxxvii. §13 Ye choose not me, but I of mine own voluntarie motion made choice of you. 1652 Needham tr. *Selden's Mare Cl.* 21 Not at the instance of any one, but of their own proper motions. 1730 Wesley *Wks.* (1830) I. 12, I do not say you would be too officious should you of your own motions seek out the persons that want your instructions. 1903 *Expositor* Apr. 268 Christ of his own motion went further afield.

†10. A motive, reason; a ground or cause of action. *Obs.*

1533 Bellenden tr. *Livy* II. vii. (S.T.S.) I. 155 þai war all resolute of ane mynde..; And for þir mociouns [L. *proinde*] desirit porsena [etc.]. 1549 *Compl. Scot.* iii. 27 Thai [the English] ar, ande alse hes beene, the special motione of the iniust veyris that hes trublit cristianite thir sex hundretht ȝeir by past. 1657–8 in *Burton's Diary* (1828) II. 354 They have openly and avowedly trod God's people under foot, on that very motion and account; that they were Protestants.

11. The involuntary action of the intestines, leading to discharge of their contents; an evacuation of the bowels. Also, chiefly in *plural*, that which is evacuated; the fæces.

1598 Shaks. *Merry W.* III. i. 105 Shall I loose my Doctor? No, hee giues me the Potions and the Motions. 1766 [Anstey] *Bath Guide* ii. 50 We must swallow a Potion For driving out Wind after every Motion. 1786 R. Willan in *Med. Commun.* II. 118 He had..two or three loose motions. 1843 R. J. Graves *Syst. Clin. Med.* x. 111 Those who are dissatisfied with less than two or three motions in the day. 1871 Napheys *Prev. & Cure Dis.* III. ix. 995 The motions of the bowels present a pale drab or clay color. 1897 *Allbutt's Syst. Med.* III. 737 In sprue the motions are generally very frothy.

12. *Mus.* **†a.** Movement (quick or slow); tempo.

1674 Playford *Skill Mus.* I. x. 33 This Mood..is of two Motions, the one slow, the other more swift. 1727–52 Chambers *Cycl.* s.v., The *motion*, in songs composed in double time, differs from that in those in triple time. It is the *motion* that distinguishes courants and sarabands, from gavots, borees, chacones, &c.

b. (*a*) The melodic progression of a single part with reference to the intervals taken by it. See conjunct *a.* 6, disjunct *a.* 3. (*b*) The progression of two or more parts with relation to each other. For ***parallel***, ***direct***, ***similar***, ***oblique***, ***contrary motion***, see those adjs.

1731, 1811, etc. [see contrary *a.* 5b, oblique *a.* 6, etc.].

†13. a. A puppet-show. *Obs.*

1589 Nashe *Pasquill & Marforius* 12 Pompes, Pagents, Motions, Maskes. 1599 B. Jonson *Ev. Man out of Hum.* II. iii, They say, there's a new Motion of the city of Niniueh, with Ionas, and the whale, to be seene at Fleet-bridge. 1611 Shaks. *Wint. T.* IV. iii. 103 Then hee compast a Motion of the Prodigall sonne. 1677 *Lond. Gaz.* No. 1170/4 All Persons exposing publickly any Shows, Motions, Stage-Playes, or strange Sights. 1678 *Norwich Court-Bks.* 21 Dec. (1905) 152 Oliver Batt licensed to show a motion called 'Arte and Vartue'.

b. A puppet. Also applied contemptuously to a person. *Obs.*

1591 SHAKS. *Two Gent.* II. i. 100 Oh excellent motion; oh exceeding Puppet. **1601** B. JONSON *Poetaster* III. iv, What's he, with the halfe-armes there, that salutes vs out of his cloke, like a motion? **1609** —— *Sil. Wom.* III. iv, Did you thinke you had married a statue? or a motion, onely? **1623** FLETCHER *Rule a Wife* II. i, Goe, find me out this man, and let me see him, If he be that motion that you tell me of, And make no more noise, I shall entertain him. **1633** MARMION *Antiquary* I. i, This travelling motion has been abroad in quest of strange fashions. **1663** KILLIGREW *Parson's Wedd.* IV. i, One that never..sleepes in a whole skin, but is taken to pieces like a Motion, as if she were too long. **1689** SWIFT *Ode to Sir W. Temple* vii, As in a theatre the ignorant fry, Because the cords escape their eye, Wonder to see the motions fly.

14. A piece of mechanism which itself moves, or which sets other pieces moving or modifies their motion; †the MOVEMENT *sb.* of a watch. Also *fig.*

perpetual motion: see PERPETUAL *a.* 1 b. ***parallel motion***: see PARALLEL *a.*

1605 DANIEL *Philotas* III. ii. D 2 b, This great motion of a state we see Doth turne on many wheeles. *a* **1626** BACON *New Atl.* (1900) 36 Engines for Multiplying and Enforcing of Windes, to set also on going diverse Motions. *Ibid.* 43 Wee have divers curious Clocks; And other like Motions of Returne: And some Perpetuall Motions. **1678** *Lond. Gaz.* No. 1315/4 A silver Watch with several motions. **1682** *True Protest. Mercury* No. 151. 2/2 Two silver Watches, the one a large one with a rising motion. **1727–41** CHAMBERS *Cycl.*, *Motion* is also used among mechanics, for the inside of a watch, &c. more commonly called *movement*. **1793** W. & S. JONES *Catal. Optical*, etc. *Instr.* 2 Reflecting telescopes.. with rack-work motions. **1894** *Times* 23 Mar. 4/6 The engine-driver..might know whether the line was clear even ..while he was oiling the motion.

15. *attrib.* and *Comb.*, as (sense 8 b) ***motion-day***; (sense 14) ***motion-maker***, ***wheel***; **motion-bar**, a guide-bar in a steam-engine; **motion-block** (see quot.); †**motion-man**, the worker or exhibitor of a puppet-show; **motion photography**, the photographing of moving subjects, later known as *cinematography*; **motion picture**, a 'moving picture'; a cinema film; also *attrib.*; **motion sickness**, nausea induced by motion; travel sickness; **motion study**, the study of the movements necessary for the most effective and least tiring method of performing a task; also *attrib.*; **motion-work**, the mechanism for moving the hands of a watch or clock.

1871 *Routledge's Ev. Boy's Ann.* Sept. 534 Flat guides, called *motion-bars, or guide-bars. **1879** *Cassell's Techn. Educ.* II. 74 The *motion-block which forms a connection between the piston-rod and connecting-rod. **1887** G. C. V. HOLMES *Steam Engine* 214 The guides or motion blocks.. which prevent the end of the piston rod from being deflected as the connecting rod assumes an angular position. **1904** E. MANSON *Builders of our Law* (ed. 2) 229 *Motion-day at the Rolls was a scene to be remembered. **1818** BENTHAM *Ch. Eng.* 118 Of these same *motion-makers, the third..is Earl Nelson. **1614** B. JONSON *Barth. Fair* I. v, A Puppet-play.. that I writ for the *motion man. *a* **1680** BUTLER *Rem.* (1759) I. 102 When truly all their Feats have been As well perform'd by Motion-men. **1912** F. A. TALBOT *Moving Pictures* xxviii. 312 *Motion photography as an educational force. **1913** *Chambers's Jrnl.* Sept. 688/1 In the early days the long exposure necessary rendered motion-photography well-nigh impossible. [**1891** *Leisure Hour* Aug. 711/1 A highly composite mechanism which is to be known as the 'kinetograph', or *motion-picture.] **1896** *Boston Even. Transcript* 7 Nov. 16/4 The cinematographe motion picture programme will be augmented daily. **1913** F. A. TALBOT *Pract. Cinematogr.* 129 Plate, The first motion-pictures of an opening flower, taken at the Marey Institute. The complete opening of a convolvulus is shown in fifteen pictures. **1915** WODEHOUSE *Something Fresh* v. 117 The maiden in distress..was merely earning the salary paid her by some motion-picture firm. **1917** H. GARLAND in Ade *Lett.* (1973) 69 What a change is indicated in a few words. The motor car, the telephone,..and the Motion Picture Theater! **1923** R. D. PAINE *Comr. Rolling Ocean* vii. 112 There were a few stores, a church,..but not a solitary motion-picture theater. **1929** M. R. WERNER *Bryan* 264 Between 1916 and 1919 Bryan was engaged in negotiations for a motion picture on the curse of drink, of which he was to be the star. **1934** *Discovery* June 171/1 Fifty thousand feet of standard motion-picture film will be exposed. **1952** *Manch. Guardian Weekly* 5 June 7/2 The nine judges of the United States Supreme Court handed down a unanimous decision this week that exerts an historic restraint on the censorship of motion pictures. **1972** D. SHIPMAN *Great Movie Stars: Internat. Yrs.* p. v, The coming of Sound to the motion-picture medium killed it as a means of almost effortless international communication. **1973** L. SNELLING *Heresy* I. i. 8 This was a visual generation and the motion-picture its natural medium. **1942** *Sci. News Let.* 12 Dec. 378/1 Air sickness can be prevented or cured if you know how. So can sea-sickness and the other kinds of *motion sickness that attack men lurching over battlefields in tanks and jeeps. **1953** A. SMITH *Blind White Fish in Persia* x. 189 We had been asked to investigate the effectiveness of Kwells pills against the motion sickness occasionally experienced in riding camels. **1971** *Jrnl. Gen. Psychol.* LXXXV. 87 (*heading*) A psychophysiological test for motion-sickness susceptibility. **1973** *Times* 1 Aug. 6/1 Still suffering from the motion sickness which has put their mission behind schedule, the three Skylab astronauts today started to tidy up the orbiting laboratory. **1911** F. B. GILBRETH (*title*) *Motion study. *Ibid.* p. v, The phrase 'Motion Study' explains itself. The aim of motion study is to find and perpetuate the scheme of perfection... Standardizing the trades is the world's most important work to-day, and motion study is the first factor in that work. **1918** C. S. MYERS *Present-Day Applications of Psychol.* 17 Yet in regard to industry, the need for good method and the need for systematic training are only just beginning to be realised, as is instanced in the following illustrations of what is now technically known as 'motion-study'. **1933** M. S. VITELES *Industrial Psychol.* xx. 436 In the practical application of motion study techniques the emphasis is upon the ease of work, upon *human* and not primarily upon *economic* efficiency. **1960** M. SPARK *Ballad of Peckham Rye* ii. 15 Motion study did marvels in the factory. **1764** *Ann. Reg.* I. 79/1 Two *motion wheels [in a watch]. **1795** J. AIKIN *Manchester* 311 They..excel in what is called *motion-work, such as dial wheels, locking springs [etc.]. **1884** F. J. BRITTEN *Watch & Clockm.* 179 In turret clocks, where the striking is not discharged by the motion work.

motion ('məʊʃən), *v.* Also 5 mocyon, 6 moshion, -yon, mocion. [f. MOTION *sb.*]

†**1. a.** *trans.* To propose, move, bring forward. Const. *to*, *unto*. *Obs.*

1505 in *10th Rep. Hist. MSS. Comm.* App. v. 391 Anye discord..or ingerous wordes or langauge spokin, movid or moshioned betwixte anny brother or neighboure. **1535** in *Lett. Suppress. Monasteries* (Camden) 77 Your humble oratour, disquietly vexede without cause or any pretenced occasion motioned of your said oratours partie. **1577** *F. de L'isle's Legendarie* D iij, Which was by motioning a double alliance. **1581** SAVILE *Tacitus' Hist.* III. lxx. (1591) 157 Till Vitellius began first to motion a parle. **1586** HOOKER *Suppl. Irish Chron.* 136/2 in *Holinshed*, Tirlough..making the like sutes as his wife before his comming had motioned vnto his lordship. **1611** BIBLE *Transl. Pref.* ¶ 2 It was made a capitall crime, once to motion the making of a new Law for the abrogating of an old. **1635** J. HAYWARD tr. *Biondi's Banish'd Virg.* 169, I..never entertained a thought of motioning love unto you, otherwise than in a lawfull and honourable way. **1648** GAGE *West Ind.* xviii. (1655) 136 This Fryer hath writ of this Countrey, and hath gone to Spain to the Court to motion the conquering of it. **1666** PEPYS *Diary* 8 June, Creed and I down the river as low as Sir W. Warren's, with whom I did motion a business that may be of profit to me. **1714** *New Hampshire Prov. Papers* (1868) II. 662 His Honour..often motioned it to the Council to be gratified. **1721** J. WINDHAM *Let.* 5 Jan. in *Pall Mall G.* (1891) 25 June 3/2 A bill is ordered to be brought in to make it felony for [etc.]... Motioned by Sir Joseph Jekyll, seconded by H. Walpole and others. **1802** C. JAMES *Milit. Dict.*, *To motion a thing*, to propose it in a military or civil meeting.

b. with *infinitive* or *clause* as object. *Obs.*

1524 DK. SUFFOLK in Ellis *Orig. Lett.* Ser. III. I. 331 So it is as I am enformed, vpon malice it is mocioned vnto your Grace to take into the Kingis handes..the Pryory of Conyssed [etc.]. **1536** STAFFORD in *Lett. Suppress. Monasteries* (Camden) 122 Where I desyred Mr. Bryan to be so good master unto me as to moshion unto your mastership to helpe me to the gift of the priorie of Fynshed. *a* **1648** LD. HERBERT *Hen. VIII* (1683) 363 One Tempse..who motion'd that they all should Petition the King to take his Queen again. **1676** NEWTON in Rigaud *Corr. Sci. Men* (1841) II. 395, I am now to return you thanks..for motioning to get the experiment in controversy tried before the Royal Society. **1676** W. ROW *Contn. Blair's Autobiog.* x. (1848) 271 They motioned in the Committee that John Hamilton should be general-major of the army. **1688** *Col. Rec. Pennsylv.* I. 233 Samll Richardson..motion'd that The order of This board..was Contrary to Law. **1823** W. FAUX *Mem. Days Amer.* 323 Another rising to say, 'I motion, that as some cannot command money they should bring vegetables'.

c. To propose or recommend (a person) for employment, or as a partner in marriage. *Obs.*

1577 HOLINSHED *Chron.* II. 553 Hugh le Brun..(vnto whom Queene Isabell..had beene promised in mariage before that King Iohn was motioned vnto hir..). *a* **1641** BP. MOUNTAGU *Acts & Mon.* (1642) 282 He refused the Kings daughter in marriage, being motioned to him, and married that slave. **1641** HINDE *J. Bruen* vii. 24 A daughter of one M. Hardware,..was commended to the Father, and so by him motioned unto his Sonne. *a* **1694** M. ROBINSON *Autobiog.* (1856) 9 Our young student..being motioned to the lord general Fairfax as a page.

d. To approach with a request; to petition or suggest to (a person). *Obs.*

1476 J. PASTON in *P. Lett.* III. 158 John Redwe mocyond hym onys myche aftyr thys intent. **1528** ABBESS OF WILTON *Let. to Wolsey* (P.R.O.), I have oft tymes mocioned my systers to be reclused within oure monastery. **1538** in Ellis *Orig. Lett.* Ser. III. III. 218 And forasmoche as I found your Lordeschipp gudd Lorde unto me in my [former] suyte..I am now the bolder to motyon yowr Lordeschippe for my neybors of Oxford. **1544** BALE *Chron. Sir J. Oldcastle* Pref. 7 b, This noble lorde Cobham with certen other more, mocyoned the kynge at Westmynstre..that it were verye commodyouse to Englande yf the Romyshe Bysshoppes auctorite extended no forther than the Occeane see.

e. In *passive*: To have an inward motion, be tempted. *Obs.*

a **1591** H. SMITH *Serm.* (1637) 790 Marke whensoever thou art motioned to evill, if it doe not promise thee some goodesse to come of it.

†**2.** *intr.* or *absol.* To make a proposal, bring forward a motion, offer a plan. *Obs. rare.*

1509 in *Mem. Hen. VII* (Rolls) 437 And that they that had so moschyonyd unto the kynge hys lord had no good ground nor reson so for to do. **1539** LATIMER *Let. to Cromwell* 17 Jan. *Remains* (Parker Soc.) 413, I doubt not, but the king's highness..will remember his poor subjects now in Lent as touching white meat, of the which I now motion unto your lordship, to the intent it may come betime among them. **1560** DAUS tr. *Sleidane's Comm.* 461 The Quene motioned for the restoring of abbey landes. **1599** A. M. tr. *Gabelhouer's Bk. Physicke* 352/1 [A prescription] When anye Membre is so extreamlye inflamed that it wexeth blacke, and the Chirurgiane beginneth to motion of the extirpation therof. **1667** MILTON *P.L.* IX. 229 Well hast thou motion'd, wel thy thoughts imployed How we might [etc.]. **1694** *New Hampshire Prov. Papers* (1868) II. 115 The Lieut. Governor motioned to this Board of a citadel to be built in this fourt. **1839** CARLYLE *Chartism* i. 112 For what end at all are men.. sent to St. Stephen's,..kept talking, struggling, motioning and counter-motioning?

3. *trans.* To direct or guide by a sign, or significant gesture or movement. Const. *to* with *inf.*; also with *adv.* or *advb. phrase.*

1787 MME. D'ARBLAY *Diary* 1 Nov., When I produced it [a present], she motioned it away with her hand. **1820** L. HUNT *Indicator* No. 43 (1822) I. 340 She motioned him..to be silent. **1838** DICKENS *Nich. Nick.* i, Nickleby..motioning them all out of the room, embraced his wife and children. **1869** A. W. WARD tr. *Curtius' Hist. Greece* II. II. iv. 5 It was their duty..to motion off any one who approached the gods of the state without the right of so doing. **1895** SCULLY *Kafir Stories* 158 Whitson sat down on a stone, and motioned his companion to do the same.

4. *intr.* **a.** To make a motion or movement as if intending *to do* something. ? *Obs.*

1747 RICHARDSON *Clarissa* (1811) II. xxxiv. 248 Snatching my hand from my brother who was insolently motioning to give it to Mr. Solmes. **1754** —— *Grandison* VI. xlii. 262, I..motioned to quit the hall for the parlour. **1800** HELENA WELLS *Constantia Neville* (ed. 2) II. 79, I.. requested he would be seated. This he declined, motioning at the same time to go away. **1803** MARY CHARLTON *Wife & Mistress* IV. 187 She..motioned to depart.

b. To make a significant movement or gesture for the purpose of directing or guiding.

1788 CHARLOTTE SMITH *Emmeline* (1816) IV. 216 Lady Adelina.., still motioning with her hand for Fitz Edward to leave her, moved on. **1802** MRS. RADCLIFFE *Gaston de Blondeville* Posth. Wks. 1826 II. 377 The King motioned with his arm; the Archbishop made a sign in the air. **1856** MRS. BROWNING *Aur. Leigh* VIII. 81 'Will you sit?' I asked, and motioned to a chair. **1897** HALL CAINE *Christian* x, She ..motioned to him to stand by her side. **1899** T. M. ELLIS *Three Cats-eye Rings* 130 Clayside motioned to the men to cover in the dead.

5. *trans.* To impart motion to.

1929 BRIDGES *Test. Beauty* I. 24 Wisdom..choosing to be call'd Athena daughter of Zeus Motion'd the marble to her living grace.

motionable ('məʊʃənəb(ə)l), *a. rare.* [f. MOTION *sb.* + -ABLE.] Capable of motion.

1840 *P. Parley's Ann.* I. 149 She gave it a gentle pat with her paw, to see if it were motionable. **1893** R. BRIDGES *Shorter P.* v. xv. 11 The frost-bound country held Nought motionable or alive.

motional ('məʊʃənəl), *a.* [f. MOTION *sb.* + -AL[1].] Of or pertaining to motion; characterized by (certain) motions. In *Electr.* applied *spec.* to an impedance that arises out of the motion of a conductor in a magnetic field.

1679 tr. *Willis's Pharmac. Rationalis* I. I. ii. 7 This Coat contains manifold orders of motional Fibres. *a* **1831** BENTHAM *Language* Wks. 1843 VIII. 300/2 The existence of any expressible state of things, or of persons,..whether it be quiescent, or motional,..is what is called *a fact*. **1879** THOMSON & TAIT *Nat. Phil.* I. I. §343 A system so constituted that the positional forces are proportional to displacements and the motional to velocities. **1892** O. HEAVISIDE *Electr. Papers* I. 446 In general **h** = VD**v** × 4π, where **D** is the displacement of the field, **v** the velocity, **h** the induced magnetic force, and V is as in equation (3). [*Note*] The force [so defined]..I now term the motional magnetic force, and its companion (21*a*) below, the motional electric force. **1912** KENNELLY & PIERCE in *Proc. Amer. Acad. Sci.* XLVIII. 113 The difference obtained by subtracting the damped values from the corresponding free values may be called the motional values of resistance, inductance, etc.; since such differences are due to the motion of the diaphragm. *Ibid.* 144 This means that the impedance of the receiver has become increased, through the vibration of the diaphragm, by a motional impedance. **1957** W. FRASER *Telecommun.* xvi. 510 The movement of the speech coil in the air gap induces a back e.m.f. in the coil so that the loudspeaker has a motional impedance under dynamic conditions. **1969** F. A. BOVEY *Nuclear Magn. Resonance Spectrosc.* i. 14 In liquids of ordinary viscosity..the local variations in magnetic field strength have become so short-lived that motional averaging is complete.

motionally ('məʊʃənəlɪ), *adv.* [f. MOTIONAL *a.* + -LY[2].] As regards motion.

1974 *Nature* 7 June 593/3 As the average pore radius approaches 100 Å, the amount of motionally restricted water in the Vycor glass is reduced to below 10% (v/v).

†'**motionary**, *a. Obs. rare*[−1]. [f. MOTION *sb.* + -ARY[1]; cf. STATIONARY.] Having a motion; moving, or causing motion.

1612 R. DABORNE *Christian turn'd Turke* 230 We are sway'd As are the motionary ingines of a clocke.

†'**motionated**, *a. Obs. rare*[−1]. [f. MOTION *sb.* + -ATE + -ED[1].] That is moved or set in motion.

1666 G. ALSOP *Maryland* (1869) 48 He might..then with a Spade, like his Grandsire Adam, turn up the face of the Creation, purchasing his bread by the sweat of his brows, that before was got by the motionated Water-works of his jaws.

†'**motioner.** *Obs.* [f. MOTION *sb.* or *v.* + -ER[1].] One who 'motions'; a proposer, instigator.

? **1536** LATIMER in *Lett. Suppress. Monasteries* (Camden) 149 Butt now, syr, another thynge, that by your favour I myght be a motionare unto you, at the request [etc.]. *c* **1560** R. MORICE in *Lett. Lit. Men* (Camden) 26 Dr. Butts was the firste motioner of his preferment. **1577** *F. de L'isle's Legendarie* H v b, They..had bene the chiefe motioners of the estates to call for accomptes. **1665** MARQ. WORCESTER in Dircks *Life* (1865) 278 You are no motioner of this; you do but lay before him my reasonable petition therein.

b. *transf.* of a thing. (Frequent in Hales.)

1616 HIERON *Wks.* II. 37 Where religion was not the first motioner, the issue of the marriage without great repentance can neuer bee comfortable. **1617** HALES *Gold. Rem.* I. (1673)

2 We will consider, First, the sin it self..: where we will briefly consider what it is, and what causes and motioners it finds in our corrupt understandings.

motion-hole: see MORSING b.

motioning ('məʊʃənɪŋ), *vbl. sb.* [f. MOTION *v.* + -ING[1].] The action of the verb MOTION; †the proposing or suggesting (of something).

1620 in Gutch *Coll. Cur.* I. 170 The motioning of that Match maketh a general fear. **1652** COTTERELL *Cassandra* II. (1676) 22 A visit of his own motioning. **1786** MME. D'ARBLAY *Diary* Oct., After this, the Smelts, at royal motioning, returned the visit of Mrs. Delany.

†'**motionist.** *Obs.* [f. MOTION *sb.* + -IST.] One skilled in motions.

1650 MILTON *Tenure Kings* (ed. 2) 58 If there come a truth to be defended which..seemes not so profitable, strait these nimble motionists can finde no eev'n leggs to stand upon.

motionless ('məʊʃənlɪs), *a.* [f. MOTION *sb.* + -LESS.] Having no motion or movement, not moving. Also, incapable of motion.

1599 SHAKS. *Hen. V*, IV. ii. 50 And in their pale dull mouthes the Iymold Bitt Lyes foule with chaw'd grasse, still and motionlesse. **1634** MILTON *Comus* 819 The Lady that sits here In stony fetters fixt, and motionless. **1742** YOUNG *Nt. Th.* v. 189 All the live-long night, Rigid in thought, and motionless, he stands. **1802** BINGLEY *Anim. Biog.* (1813) I. 38 The tongue [of fish] is in general motionless, obtuse, and fleshy. **1883** J. GILMOUR *Mongols* 362 Etiquette requiring them to remain motionless at the board.

Hence '**motionlessness**.

1817 J. GILCHRIST *Intell. Patrimony* 23 The agreeableness that the sentient frame finds in motionlessness. **1840** THACKERAY *Paris Sk.-bk.* Wks. 1900 V. 207 The silence and motionlessness of the whole added to its awfulness.

'**motionlessly**, *adv.* [f. MOTIONLESS *a.* + -LY[2].] Without motion, stilly; in a motionless manner.

1887 W. JAMES in *Pop. Sci. Monthly* June 170 It is the very same instinct which leads a boy playing 'I spy' to hold his very breath when the seeker is near, and which makes the beast of prey..motionlessly lie in wait for his victim.

†'**motist.** *Obs. rare.* [ad. It. *motista*, f. *moto*:—L. *mōtus* movement.] One skilled in depicting or describing movement.

1598 R. HAYDOCKE tr. *Lomazzo* II. 13 Here then the diligent Motist [orig. *il diligente motista*] ought to obserue, how much any one humor aboundeth in the body, so that he may learne to expresse the motions accordingly. *Ibid.* 15 Whence I holde it most convenient for that Painter, which would prooue a cunning Motist, to be..precise in diligent observing of the aboue named rules. *Ibid.* 21 Those excellent Motistes Al. Magnus, Abbas Tritemius, and Rai. **1644** BULWER *Chirol.* A j b, Thy Hand hath, like a cunning Motist, found In all the Senses, wherein they abound.

motitation (məʊtɪ'teɪʃən). *rare.* [n. of action f. L. *mōtitāre*, freq. of *mōt-*, *movēre* to MOVE: see -ATION.] A quivering movement.

1641 BP. HALL *Serm. Lent* Wks. 1837 V. 434 What shall we say to those men..that love to dance upon a quaking earth? yea, that affect to be actors in these unkindly motitations? **1649** BULWER *Pathomyot.* II. i. 67 If you rest a trembling Head upon a cushion, you shall soon stay the trembling, and free it from that motitation. **1884** J. PAYNE *1001 Nights* VIII. 105 With Cairene motitations and Yemani wrigglings..and Hindi torsions.

motivate ('məʊtɪveɪt), *v.* [f. MOTIVE *sb.* + -ATE[3], after F. *motiver*, G. *motiviren*.] **1.** *trans.* = MOTIVE *v.*; to provide with a stimulus to some kind of action; to direct (a person's energy or behaviour) towards certain goals.

1885 *Athenæum* 14 Feb. 213/1 The chief defect [of the novel] is that the principal events are not sufficiently 'motivated'. **1901** MEADER *Lat. Pronouns is, hic*, etc. 80 Various reasons might have motivated the change. **1924** W. B. SELBIE *Psychol. Relig.* iv. 89 Freud has shown very clearly that forgetting is not the unconscious process that we think, but that it is generally motivated. **1949** *Here & Now* (N.Z.) Oct. 29/2 The vast majority of pictures are sexually motivated. **1953** 'M. INNES' *Christmas at Candleshoe* v. 53 When at fifteen he was eventually packed off to apprenticeship in the city, the action was motivated only by the plain fact that there was nothing else to do with him. **1964** M. ARGYLE *Psychol. & Social Probl.* xii. 152 A special feature of the teacher's job is the need for him to motivate the pupils—there is no wage incentive for school work, and the competitive marks system is only a partial solution. **1966** J. PARTRIDGE *Middle School* vii. 139 A Secondary Modern in which boys are poorly motivated towards their school work at the best of times. **1971** E. DICHTER (*title*) Motivating human behavior. **1974** *Daily Tel.* 2 May 22 (Advt.), Can you motivate salesmen? Not an easy task, because these people are supposed to be self-starters.

absol. **1863** LYTTON *Caxtoniana* II. 259 But Goethe's art was not dramatic; he himself tells us so,..he adds..that, from the philosophical turn of his mind, he 'motivates' too much for the stage.

2. To serve as or provide a motive for; to justify.

1970 *Nature* 4 Apr. 44/1 The publisher motivates the slim size of these volumes by claiming it makes them more likely to be read. **1973** *Physics Bull.* Apr. 234/3 The demand for a relativistically acceptable version of momentum conservation is used to motivate the introduction of relativistic concepts of dynamics.

Hence '**motivated**, '**motivating** *ppl. adjs.*

1909 *Proc. Mod. Lang. Assoc.* XXIV. 175 The motivating reason is of another sort. **1928** C. J. WARDEN *Outl. Compar. Psychol.* v. 126 Punishment was introduced as a motivating stimulus. **1959** B. WOOTTON *Social Sci. & Social Path.* viii. 245 Their actions appear motiveless or strangely motivated. **1963** *Economist* 23 Nov. 767/2 Some form of sales promotion (the motivated-sell). **1968** R. WEST *Sketches from Vietnam* iii. 75 The Americans concede with regret that the Vietcong tend to be more highly motivated than the government supporters. **1973** *Jrnl. Genetic Psychol.* CXXII. 198 The majority of subjects..could be regarded as highly motivated to enter university.

motivation (məʊtɪ'veɪʃən). [f. MOTIVE *v.*: see -ATION.] **1. a.** The action of the verb MOTIVE.

1873 *Contemp. Rev.* XXI. 446 He [Schopenhauer] distinguishes the sufficient reason of Becoming, of Knowledge, of Being, and of Action... The fourth is the law of motivation. **1902** *Edin. Rev.* July 203 Still less are we referring to the structure of the Robertsonian drama, the 'motivation' of its plot.

b. *Psychol.* and *Sociol.* The conscious or unconscious stimulus for action towards a desired goal provided by psychological or social factors; that which gives purpose or direction to behaviour.

1904 *Psychol. Rev. Monogr. Suppl.* V. II. 11 (*heading*) The egoistic and the social in motivation. **1922** R. S. WOODWORTH *Psychol.* viii. 137 The instincts are extraordinarily important in the study of motivation. **1932** W. MCDOUGALL *Energies of Men* xvi. 245 It is in relation to the problems of motivation that the postulation of subconscious activities is most urgently required. **1937** T. PARSONS *Struct. of Social Action* III. xvi. 637 Weber's work necessitated the ideal-typical formulation of systems of ideas which are relevant to concrete motivation. **1950** LUCAS & BRITT *Advertising Psychol. & Res.* II. v. 107 Lists of human wants and related advertising appeals are included in this chapter mainly for the purpose of illustrating the theory of motivation. **1954** R. F. C. HULL tr. *Jung's Coll. Works* XVII. vii. 193 The real motivations are sought and real discoveries are made. **1966** *Rep. Comm. Inquiry Univ. Oxf.* I. 69 Weight can properly be given to evidence about their motivation,..the nature of their schooling, or their non-academic interests and activities. **1972** *Sci. Amer.* Feb. 48/1 There are other important motivations for attempting to synthesize speech. One is learning how speech is produced in the human vocal tract. **1973** B. O'CONNELL *Aspects of Learning* vi. 103 Motivation may be considered as either intrinsic or extrinsic; intrinsic motives include those of exploration and curiosity, and extrinsic those of status and social approval.

2. Manner or means of movement.

1946 M. PEAKE *Titus Groan* 407 There could be no mistaking that nimble, yet shuffling and edgeways-on—that horribly deliberate motivation that was neither walking nor running. **1948** M. H. NICOLSON *Voyages to Moon* v. 195 Swift's flying chariot remains unique in the history of literature..both for its vast size..and for the plausibility of its principle of motivation.

3. *attrib.* and *Comb.*, esp. in connection with market research and advertising, as ***motivation analyst, department, psychology, study***; **motivation research**, research, usu. with the object of increasing a product's sales, undertaken to discover the underlying psychological and social motives that influence people; so **motivation researcher**; cf. MOTIVATIONAL *a.* b.

1958 A. HUXLEY *Let.* 15 Feb. (1969) 846 American advertising techniques as perfected by the Motivation Analysts. **1957** V. PACKARD *Hidden Persuaders* iii. 29 The McCann-Erickson advertising agency in New York had five psychologists manning a special motivation department. **1961** *Daily Tel.* 14 Mar. 17/2 The 'motivation psychology' that allows a driver to be placid and content at one moment and at the next makes him rush forward 'like a raging lunatic'. *Ibid.*, He described 'motivation psychology' as the study of what makes the individual road user tick. **1953** *Business Week* 5 Sept. 40/2 The publication of a..book called 'An Introductory Bibliography of Motivation Research'. **1960** *Times Rev. Industry* July p. ii/2 Motivation research and ergonomics are but two examples of new terms... The one seeks the reasons for decisions and actions; the other is devoted to the study of man and his working environment. **1967** M. ARGYLE *Psychol. Interpersonal Behaviour* ix. 153 A number of special methods are used in motivation research interviews to get at genuine feelings. **1968** M. RICHLER *Cocksure* xxii. 139 The Motivation Research boys, the pollsters, covered America for us, and came back with 20,000 completed forms. **1954** G. H. SMITH *Motivation Res.* I. ii. 23 In order to do profitable work at this level, the motivation researcher should be familiar with the major concepts of psychiatry and abnormal psychology. **1967** G. STEINER *Lang. & Silence* 45 'Motivation researchers', those grave-diggers of literate speech, tell us that the perfect advertisement should neither contain words of more than two syllables nor sentences with dependent clauses. **1954** G. H. SMITH *Motivation Res.* v. xvii. 206 Perhaps the best single person to guide a motivation study is a social psychologist.

motivational (məʊtɪ'veɪʃənəl), *a.* [f. prec. + -AL.] Of or pertaining to motivation.

1931 L. T. TROLAND in *Psychologies of 1930* 460 Narrowly and popularly conceived, motivational psychology would be concerned primarily with 'motives', but broadly and scientifically considered, it deals with all of the determinative functions and dynamics of mind. **1940** *Q. Rev. Biol.* Dec. 403 These conventional categories proved satisfactory only so long as each individual was looked upon as a discrete action-centre without intimate motivational connections with others of his species. **1943** *Mind* LII. 137 As to its motivational aspects, one can at least imagine that the cross connections just mentioned make it relatively easy to tap at least one of the just active hungers. **1951** G. HUMPHREY *Thinking* vi. 183 The mechanism of thinking was at least in the earlier work still associational though this was supplemented by motivational factors. **1958** M. ARGYLE *Relig. Behaviour* xii. 144 This is because the [social learning] theory shows how religion is passed on but does not show the motivational forces maintaining it. **1967** L. B. ARCHER in Wills & Yearsley *Handbk. Managem. Technol.* 131 Even in the most technical situations, motivational and aesthetic considerations have a material bearing upon performance. **1970** *Nature* 26 Sept. 1369/2 Investigations of animal learning usually include motivational components which activate and direct behaviour to relevant goals. **1974** *Ibid.* 15 Mar. 195/2 Problems of such motivational 'conflicts' are of great interest in finding out how behaviour in general is organised.

b. Special collocations: ***motivational analyst, consultant, selling***; **motivational research** = *motivation research*; **motivational researcher** = *motivation researcher*.

1957 V. PACKARD *Hidden Persuaders* i. 8 These motivational analysts..are adding depth to the selling of ideas and products. **1959** *Times Rev. Industry* Nov. 4/2 The copywriter has been joined by the art director, and round them have formed phalanxes of executives and research departments and motivational consultants. **1953** *Reporter* (N.Y.) 13 Oct. 27/3 Motivational research means just what it seems to—exploration into..the real reasons why a consumer buys..a product or service. **1957** *Observer* 22 Sept. 11/6 Last week he [*sc.* Dr. Ernest Dichter] described to an audience of advertising people what motivational research—M.R. to its friends—is, and what it does. 'It takes the social sciences out of the seminar,' he says, 'and into the supermarket.' **1960** *Sunday Express* 12 June 14/5 'You are not *typical*,' say the Motivational Research boys. **1960** E. DICHTER *Strategy of Desire* (1961) 15 Often the assignment given our organization for conducting motivational research was a very sober and concrete one. **1971** —— *Motivating Human Behavior* 3 Some people begin to question the manipulative nature of motivational research. **1964** M. MCLUHAN *Understanding Media* xxii. 223 These tales from the Vienna Woods, dreamed up by motivational researchers. **1963** *Horizon* (U.S.) July 36/2 The *beau idéal* of all motivational selling is the use of language to conceal the *absence* of thought.

Hence **moti'vationally** *adv.*, as regards or in terms of motivation.

1952 T. PARSONS *Social System* i. 4 Only in so far as his relation to the situation is in this sense motivationally relevant will it be treated in this work as action. **1967** M. ARGYLE *Psychol. Interpersonal Behaviour* iii. 52 Synchronization is necessary along a number of different dimensions for smooth and motivationally satisfying interaction to take place.

motivative ('məʊtɪveɪtɪv), *a.* [f. MOTIVAT(E *v.* + -IVE.] Serving to motivate; providing a reason for, or a stimulus to, action or thought.

1949 *Mind* LVIII. 37 It might be said that..commands..are unreliable from the logical point of view, because their real function is motivative. **1963** R. CARNAP in P. A. Schilpp *Philos. R. Carnap* 45 Metaphysical theses..often have other meaning components, e.g. emotive or motivative ones.

motivator ('məʊtɪveɪtə(r)). [f. MOTIVAT(E *v.* + -OR 2 c.] Something or someone that initiates, or is a stimulus to, action or behaviour.

1943 *Mind* LII. 124 The hypothesis that the prime motivators, such as hunger, thirst, pain-avoidance, and sex, are the driving power, the source of energy behind the whole infinitely complex pattern of socio-psychological behaviour. **1956** A. HUXLEY *Adonis & Alphabet* 41 Meaningless pseudo-knowledge has at all times been one of the principal motivators of individual and collective action. **1958** *Listener* 18 Sept. 414/2 Sex is clearly vitally associated with survival and is a primary motivator. **1959** HALAS & MANVELL *Technique Film Animation* 17 Television is now the main motivator of the increased output of animation. **1972** M. ARGYLE *Social Psychol. of Work* ix. 241 Herzberg and his colleagues concluded that 'motivators' (achievement, etc.) mainly affect satisfaction.

motive ('məʊtɪv), *sb.* Forms: 4 **motif(f**, 4–5 **motyf**, 4–6 **motyve**, 6 **motife, -yfe, moitive**, 6– **motive.** [a. F. *motif* masc. (in Oresme, 14th c.), subst. use of OF. *motif* MOTIVE *a.* Cf. Sp., Pg., It. *motivo*; also G. *motiv* (from Fr.).]

†**1.** Something moved or brought forward; a motion, proposition; esp. in ***to move*** (or ***make***) ***a motive*** (cf. MOTION). *Obs.*

1362 LANGL. *P. Pl.* A. XI. 70 Suche Motyues þei meuen þis Maistres in heor glorie. **1451** CAPGRAVE *Life St. Aug.* 12/25 Tho seid þei whan þei were concluded with argumentis on all sides þat Faustus schuld come and he schuld make answere on-to all þese motyues. **1523** SKELTON *Garl. Laurel* 114 Madame..Vnto your grace then make I this motyue, Whereto made ye [etc.]? **1586** FERNE *Blaz. Gentrie* I. 261 Questions of the lawes of armes with their solucions which he hath deuided into fourteene motiues. **1602** *North's Plutarch, Philip* (1612) 1135 So he [Philip] made a motiue, that he desired to speake with the townes openly. **1652** EARL MONM. tr. *Bentivoglio's Hist. Relat.* 8 If..the great Assembly of the States Generall be to be called for any new extraordinary business..this Councell drawes up the motives and sends them to the particular States of every Province.

†**2. a.** ? A moving impression on the mind. *Obs.*

c **1386** CHAUCER *Man of Law's T.* 530 This gentil kyng hath caught a greet motyf Of this witnesse.

b. An inward prompting or impulse; chiefly in ***of, from one's own*** (or ***proper***) ***motive***. Chiefly *Sc.* Cf. MOTION *sb.* 9. *Obs.*

1456 SIR G. HAYE *Law Arms* (S.T.S.) 60 Thre worthi princis come till him of thair awin curage and propre motyf. **1546** *Reg. Privy Council Scot.* I. 55 Of his awin fre will and motive, uncompellit or coactit. **1600** HOLLAND *Livy* XXI. xviii. 403 An enterprise proceeding from his owne motife.

c. ? A (supernatural) prompting or inciting. *Obs.*

1611 Tourneur *Ath. Trag.* v. ii, Heau'n..Whose gracious motiues made me still forbeare To be mine owne Reuenger. **1637** Earl Monm. tr. *Malvezzi's Rom. & Tarquin* 235 Many have beleeved, that in man also there are certaine seeds of Divination of future things..: I should beleeve them to bee the motives of our tutelary Angels [etc.].

†**3.** An argument, means of producing conviction. *Obs.*

c **1449** Pecock *Repr.* v. ii. (Rolls) 489 Forto proue that these religiouns ben sectis of perdicioun, he muste take his euydencis and hise motyues in othir place out and fro the seid text of Peter.

4. a. That which 'moves' or induces a person to act in a certain way; a desire, fear, or other emotion, or a consideration of reason, which influences or tends to influence a person's volition; also often applied to a contemplated result or object the desire of which tends to influence volition.

Writers of the 17–18th c. commonly speak of acting *on* a motive; the usual prep. now is *from*, though occasionally *with* or *for* is employed.

c **1412** Hoccleve *De Reg. Princ.* 1559 What was þi cause why þou toke a wyf? Was it..for luste, or muk? what was þi motyf? **1586** *Reg. Privy Council Scot.* IV. 78 Lying undir dangear of horning, or proces of forfaltour, or uthirwayes upoun sum uthir motive, thay durst not compeir. **1594** Hooker *Eccl. Pol.* II. viii. §4 Hereof wee haue no commandement either in nature or scripture..yet those motiues there are in both which drawe most effectually our mindes vnto them. **1602** Shaks. *Ham.* I. i. 105 And this (I take it) Is the maine Motiue of our Preparations. **1647** Clarendon *Hist. Reb.* I. §60 [Felton answered] that the motives thereunto would appear if his hat were found, in which he had..fixed them. **1694** Locke *Hum. Und.* II. xxi. §29 (ed. 2) 133 The motive to change, is always some uneasiness... This is the great motive that works on the Mind to put it upon Action. **1710** Steele *Tatler* No. 211 ¶4 There is no other motive of action that can carry us. **1754** Edwards *Freed. Will* I. ii. (1762) 5 By Motive, I mean the whole of that which moves, excites, or invites the Mind to Volition. **1796** Charlotte Smith *Marchmont* III. 147 He married her on the most laudable motives. **1813** Byron *Br. Abydos* I. xii, Now I have motive to be brave. **1824** Chr. Wordsworth *Who wrote Εἰκὼν Βασιλική* 164, I am compelled to declare, that, from the motives upon which he writes.. his testimony adds very little. **1868** Bain *Ment. & Mor. Sci.* 346 The Motives, or Ends of action, are our Pleasures and Pains. **1884** F. Temple *Relat. Relig. & Sci.* iii. (1885) 80 The freedom of the will is not shown in acting without motive, but in choosing between motives.

†**b.** A moving or inciting cause. *Obs.*

1591 Sylvester *Du Bartas* I. ii. 249 Now the chiefe Motive of these Accidents Is the dire discord of our Elements. **1634** Sir T. Herbert *Trav.* 65 You shall finde no motiues to beget Alexanders Riot, except barren Mountaines..can procure Epicurisme. **1727** *Philip Quarll* (1816) 75 He discovered a sail.., which quite altered the motive of his former fears: no monster, said he, has devoured him.

†**5.** A mover, instigator, promoter. *Obs.*

1600 Holland *Livy* XXIII. xxxvii. 500 Vercellius and Sicilius the motifes and chieftains of that rebellion. **1611** Bible *Transl. Pref.* ¶11 They were the principall motiues of it, and therefore ought least to quarrell it. **1681** Nevile *Plato Rediv.* 19 He cannot be denied to be a great motive of the Peoples unquietness.

†**6.** A moving limb or organ. (Only in Shaks.)

1593 Shaks. *Rich. II*, I. i. 193 My teeth shall teare The slauish motiue of recanting feare. **1606** —— *Tr. & Cr.* IV. v. 57 Her wanton spirites looke out At euery ioynt, and motiue of her body.

7. a. In Art and Literature: = motif 1, 2. Also in extended use.

1851 tr. *Kugler's Hand-bk. Paint.* 18 The positions and *motives* in both [are] too conventional. **1851** Eastlake *ibid., note*, This word..as generally used by the author,..means the principle of action, attitude and composition in a single figure or group; thus it has been observed, that in some antique gems which are defective in execution, the motives are frequently fine. **1853** Kingsley *Hypatia* xxii, A dance.. in which every attitude was a fresh motive for a sculptor of the purest school. **1860** Ruskin *Mod. Paint.* V. VIII. ii. §1 A great composition always has a leading emotional purpose, technically called its motive, to which all its lines and forms have some relation. Undulating lines, for instance, are expressive of action; and would be false in effect if the motive of the picture was one of repose. **1865** F. B. Palliser *Hist. Lace* xxxv. 425 The French, by adopting what is technically termed eight 'motives', produce their lace of a finer make and more complex pattern. **1868** C. L. Eastlake *Hints Household Taste* ix. 201 Some of the table-china is also very good in what may be called the *motive* of its design. **1889** *Academy* 25 May 365/2 The motive [of the picture] is of the simplest. **1893** *Jrnl. Amer. Folklore* VI. 255 The motive that Brer Wolf seeks protection from his pursuers with Brer Rabbit..is akin to the episode in the Roman de Renart. **1928** *Daily Express* 21 Apr. 6/2 These motives are mounted in various designs on a background of satin. **1930** S. W. Cheney *New World Archit.* i. 20 The primary 'motive' [of New York] is the repeated pier-line, the chief relieving factor the occasional terrace. **1931** A. U. Dilley *Oriental Rugs & Carpets* plate 16 (*caption*) Vestibule of the Madrassa (college) Mader-i-Shah (Mother of Shah) Sultan Hussein (1700), Ispahan. Compare ceiling motive with rug medallion.

b. *Mus.* = motivo, motif 1 c. *leading motive*: see leading *ppl. a.* 1 b.

1866 Engel *Nat. Mus.* ii. 82 Motive is the term which may most properly be applied to the shortest musical idea. **1883** F. Hueffer *Wagner* (ed. 2) 88 As if to remind him of this limit of his power, the orchestra intones a solemn theme which might be called the 'law or bond motive'.

8. *attrib.* and *Comb.*, as ***motive-hunter***, ***-hunting***, ***-pattern***; **motive-grinder**, **-mill-wright**, *nonce-wds.*, a laborious searcher after motives; **motive-monger**, one who 'traffics' in motives; so **motive-mongering**; †**motive-wise** *adv.*, as a motive of conduct or action.

1831 Carlyle *Sart. Res.* II. vii, Foolish Wordmonger and *Motive-grinder, who in thy Logic-mill hast an earthly mechanism for the Godlike itself. **1905** *Spectator* 28 Jan. 141/1 He is..a *motive-hunter, seeking on every side for little justifications for his pride. **1907** Raleigh *Shakespeare* 180 Regan and Goneril do not go *motive-hunting like Iago. **1831** Carlyle *Sart. Res.* III. iii, *Motive-Mill-wrights. **1762** Sterne *Tr. Shandy* VI. xxxi, My father, who was a great *motive-monger. *a* **1834** Coleridge *Notes & Lect.* (1849) I. 233 O what a lesson concerning..the folly of all *motive-mongering, while the individual self remains! **1941** Koestler *Scum of Earth* 232 No attempt to discriminate, to discover political *motive-patterns. **1674** Allen *Danger Enthus.* 134 Because Faith is thus *Motive-wise such an Operative Principle of a good and Holy Life.

motive ('məʊtɪv), *a.* Also 6 moitive, motyfe. [ad. OF. *motif* or med.L. *mōtīv-us* (Erigena, *c* 860), f. L. *mōt-*, *movēre* to move: see -ive.

Erigena renders τὸ τῆς φύσεως κινητικόν (Pseudo-Dionysius) by *naturæ motiva capacitas*.]

1. a. That moves or tends to move a person to a particular course of action; that constitutes a motive for action. Now somewhat *rare*.

1502 *Ord. Crysten Men* (W. de W. 1506) v. vii. 426 The cause motyue of the composycyon of this present boke. **1594** Hooker *Eccl. Pol.* I. ix. §1 What we doe against our wills.. we are not properly said to do it; because the motiue cause of doing it is not in our selues. *Ibid.* IV. xi. §12 Shall euery motiue argument vsed in such kinde of conferences be made a rule for others still to conclude the like by? **1654** Z. Coke *Logick* 9 The Causes motive of men to invent this Art, were first, The defect of mans nature. **1858** Sears *Athan.* III. x. 333 Those..whose motive principles are selfish. **1870** J. H. Newman *Gram. Assent* II. x. 469 The Emperor Marcus seems to consider obstinacy as the ultimate motive-cause to which their unnatural conduct was traceable. **1879** R. T. Smith *Basil the Great* x. 116 He held sacramental doctrine, yet we do not find the sacraments used as motive arguments.

†**b.** Powerful to move or incite. *Obs.*

1577–87 Holinshed *Chron.* I. 43/1 The oration of queene Voadicia..wherein she rippeth up the..shamefull wrongs which their enemies inflicted upon them, with other matters verie motive. **1649** Jer. Taylor *Gt. Exemp.* Disc. iii. §8 Generals, even in spiritual things are less perceived and less motive than particulars.

2. a. Having the quality of initiating movement; productive of or used in the production of physical or mechanical motion; spec. in *Physics*, etc. ***motive energy***: see energy 6. ***motive power***, the power acting upon matter to move it, moving or impelling power (so also ***motive force***); also, the mechanical energy (as steam, electricity, air, etc.) used to drive machinery.

1578 Banister *Hist. Man* IV. 44 A Muscle..is construct.. wᵗ Nerues, that it might cary with it the moitiue vertue that springeth from the brayne. **1625** N. Carpenter *Geog. Del.* I. iii. (1635) 48 In the Reasonable soule of man, we haue two faculties.., a motiue, and a directiue power. **1641** Wilkins *Math. Magick* I. v. (1648) 29 The Nerves serve for the conveyance of the motive faculty from the brain. **1708** *Brit. Apollo* No. 62. 2/1 The absolute motive force of the Muscles. **1835** Whewell in *Trans. Cambr. Philos. Soc.* V. 160 That property of a force..which we may call the motive quantity of the force. **1849** Noad *Electricity* (ed. 3) 360 A machine with a motive wheel of about 2½ feet in diameter.. to propel a Napier's printing press. **1862** H. Spencer *First Princ.* II. xiv. §114 (1875) 325 When horse-power and man-power were alone employed, the motive agent was not bound up with the tool moved. **1889** G. Findlay *Eng. Railway* 6 The question of the motive power to be employed was left an open one. **1936** *Discovery* Nov. 380/1 Motive-power accessories—like electric batteries—are not required.

b. *transf.* and *fig.*

1865 M. Arnold *Ess. Crit.* i. (1875) 11 The French Revolution..found..its motive power in the intelligence of men. **1889** *Spectator* 14 Dec. 845 The usual motive-power of industrial enterprises,—the desire of human beings to grow rich.

c. Of nerves = motor *a.* 2.

1668 Culpepper & Cole *Barthol. Anat.* Man. III. ii. 325 These two motive-nerves are so united as to touch one another. **1843** R. J. Graves *Syst. Clin. Med.* Introd. Lect. 14 In cases of tic douloureux we divide the sentient and not the motive nerves.

3. Concerned with or having the function or quality of initiating action.

1569 *Reg. Privy Council Scot.* I. 684 Bayth the partiis comperand personalie, of thair awin motive willis. **1575** *Ibid.* II. 451. **1650** Hobbes *Hum. Nat.* 4 Of the powers of the Mind there be two sorts, Cognitive and Imaginative, or Conceptive and Motive. **1844** Disraeli *Coningsby* v. ii, Public reputation is a motive power. **1892** N. Smyth *Chr. Ethics* I. iii. 189 Historical Christianity, on the ethical side of it, is increased divine motive power for man.

4. Of the limbs: Concerned with the faculty of motion or locomotion. ? *Obs.*

1541 Copland *Guydon's Quest. Chirurg.* C iv b, The seconde [purpose of the sinews is] to gyue moeuynge to the motyfe or styrynge membres. **1658** Sir T. Browne *Gard. Cyrus* iii. 58 In the motive parts of animals may be discovered mutuall proportions. **1835** Kirby *Hab. & Inst. Anim.* II. xvii. 93 The motive organs may be divided into two classes, those that are employed by an animal in locomotion, and those that are used for prehension.

†**5. a.** Having the faculty of motion; capable of movement; mobile. *Obs.*

1579–80 North *Plutarch, Camillus* (1595) 152 Fire.. is the most motiue & quickest substance that is of all naturall things. **1603** Holland *Plutarch's Mor.* 993 Cold is stationarie and heat motive. **1628** Feltham *Resolves* II. [I.] xxvi. 84 Nature is motiue in the quest of ill.

b. ? Moving readily, mobile. *Obs.*

1615 Brathwait *Strappado* 88 So pure her skin, so motiue to the eie, As it did seeme compos'd of Iuorie. **1621** —— *Nat. Embassie* 97 Faire in proportion, motiue in her pace.

motive ('məʊtɪv), *v.* [f. motive *sb.*; cf. F. *motiver*, G. *motiviren*.]

1. *trans.* To furnish with a motive or inciting cause; to give or supply a motive to; to be the motive of; also *pass.*, to be prompted by (something) as a motive.

a **1650** May *Satir. Puppy* (1657) 86 He carried himself as altogether unsensible of any beating, and demands what motiv'd that mirth. **1815** J. C. Hobhouse *Substance Lett.* (1816) I. 431 Lord Castlereagh, lest anything..absurd should be wanting to motive the war, reads a forged letter. **1830** W. Taylor *Hist. Surv. Germ. Poetry* I. 197 The salary was augmented so liberally as to motive his migration. **1874** W. G. Ward *Ess. Philos. Theism* (1884) I. 258 An act need not be motived by pleasure at all; and yet a very large amount of pleasure may be annexed to its performance.

2. In *passive*, of incidents in a drama or work of fiction: To be provided with a motive; to be rendered credible by what is revealed of the character, circumstances, or antecedent history of the persons.

1858 Hawthorne *Ancestral Footstep* (1883) 486 His malice must be motived in some satisfactory way. **1884** Symonds *Shaks. Predecess.* xi. 478 Where the witch's malice might have been motived and brought into play.

motived ('məʊtɪvd), *a.* [f. motive *v.* + -ed[1].] In senses of the vb.

1862 T. A. Trollope *Marietta* II. vii. 118 A collective and motived judgement. **1900** *Daily News* 28 Nov. 9/2 His work is always delicate, suggestive, motived, and..sincere.

motiveless ('məʊtɪvlɪs), *a.* [f. motive *sb.* + -less.] Having no motive.

1817 Godwin *Mandeville* II. 75 Had not that accident given us rather a motiveless contempt and abhorrence for others? **1879** Miss Braddon *Clov. Foot* i, Ah!..he wants something of me. This liberality is not motiveless.

Hence '**motivelessly** *adv.*, '**motivelessness**.

1876 Geo. Eliot *Dan. Der.* III. xxiv, That calm which Gwendolen had promised herself to maintain had changed into sick motivelessness. **1892** *Illustr. Lond. News* 22 Oct. 515/1 Feelings..unreasonably, motivelessly strong. **1933** L. Strachey *Characters & Commentaries* IV. ix. 315 This triumphant invention of the motivelessness of Iago has been dwelt upon by innumerable commentators. **1970** G. Greer *Female Eunuch* 37 When men began to grow their hair in our generation they were not acting motivelessly.

motiveness ('məʊtɪvnɪs). [f. motive *a.* + -ness.] Capability of locomotion.

1828 J. Ballantyne *Exam. Hum. Mind* 427 As to motiveness, they [*sc.* the lower animals] frequently discover a degree of agility to which man can make no pretensions.

motivic ('məʊtɪvɪk), *a.* *Mus.* [f. motiv(e *sb.* + -ic.] Of or pertaining to a musical motive or motives. Also *Comb.* So **mo'tivically** *adv.*

1947 A. Einstein *Mus. Romantic Era* vii. 67 The thematic connection of the introductory *Andante* with the *Allegro ma non troppo*, a motivic 'safeguard' that one will not as yet find so clearly stressed in the Classics. *Ibid.* xi. 144 He [*sc.* Liszt] also feels doubly strongly the need for grappling the parts of the whole together motivically. **1957** E. T. Cone in N. Frye *Sound & Poetry* I. 4 The motivic shapes..of the music. **1959** *Listener* 16 July 114/1 These processes are not entirely explained by either motivic-contrapuntal or expansive-polyphonic methods. **1961** *Times* 13 Oct. 18/6 Webern's instrumentation of the Ricercare is not..so cannibalistic as a single hearing might lead one to suppose. A letter which he wrote..shows that his principal aim..was with its motivic coherence. **1964** *Listener* 13 Aug. 250/2 *Erwartung* is composed without proper themes, without continuity of motivic work, [etc.]. **1970** *Daily Tel.* 19 Nov. 14/5 A wealth of further motivic events in these two slowish movements.

‖**motiviert** (moti'virt), *a.* Also **motivirt**. [G., pa. pple. of *motivieren* to motivate.] Motivated. Also **Moti'vierung**, motivation.

1812 H. C. Robinson *Diary* 20 Aug. in *On Bks. & their Writers* (1938) I. 108 He [*sc.* Coleridge] thinks the character of Faust himself not *motiviert*. **1866** Geo. Eliot *Let.* 10 Apr. (1956) IV. 237, I feel sure that there are deficiencies..in what the Germans call the *Motivirung* seen from a legal point of view. **1890** G. B. Shaw *Let.* 17 Aug. (1965) 255, I also opined that the fatalistic apathy of Christ..was inadequately motivirt.

motivity (məʊ'tɪvɪtɪ). [f. motive *a.* + -ity.] The quality or capacity of initiating motion; *spec.* in *Dynamics*, kinetic energy.

1690 Locke *Hum. Und.* II. xxiii. 145 The active power of Moving, or, as I may call it, Motivity. **1822** Good *Study Med.* III. 6 The first a nerve of hearing, the second of feeling, and the third of motivity. **1865** Bushnell *Vicar. Sacr.* i. (1868) 49 All God's quickening motivity and power are taken away from the feeling.

‖**motivo** (mo'tivo). *Mus.* [It.: see motive *sb.* Cf. motif.] The leading subject of an air, etc.; a subject or theme out of which a movement is developed. Also (see quot. 1876).

1789 Burney *Hist. Mus.* IV. 145 It is a graceful and pleasing air, the *motivo* of which has been often used in the present century. **1811** Busby *Dict. Mus.* (ed. 3). **1875** Ouseley *Mus. Form* ix. 48 Variations may be constructed.. upon an original theme or motivo. **1876** Stainer & Barrett *Dict. Mus. Terms, Motivo* (It.)..(1) The sort of movement

indicated by the opening notes of a sentence. (2) A subject proposed for development.

‖**mot juste** (mo ʒyst). [Fr., lit. 'exact word'.] The precisely appropriate expression.

1912 *Nation* (N.Y.) 14 Mar. 264 Here and throughout we have conspicuously the *mot juste*, not one too many and each where it will tell. **1915** E. POUND in Joyce *Lett.* (1966) II. 364 My head is a squeezed rag, so don't expect le mot juste in this letter. **1916** [see DIM *a.* 4 b]. **1932** WODEHOUSE *Louder & Funnier* 8 Most of these essays were written..at a time when the wolf at the door left little leisure for careful thought and the patient search for the *mot juste*. **1955** E. POUND *Section: Rock-Drill* lxxxv. 17 Get the mot juste before action. **1966** J. DOS PASSOS *Best Times* (1968) ii. 44 For years I'd been reading Flaubert: letters, short stories... I caught his obsession for the *mot juste*.

motled, obs. form of MOTTLED.

motley ('mɒtlɪ), *a.* (*adv.*), *sb.* Forms: 4 motteley, 4–5 mottelay, 4,6–8 motly, 5 motle(e, motele, motleye, 6–7 moatl(e)y, (7 mothly), 7–8 motely, 5– motley. [Of obscure origin.

The early forms (with which cf. those of MEDLEY) suggest adoption of an AF. *motelé, which may possibly have been formed on the native Eng. MOTE *sb.*[1], speck, spot; cf. *speckled*, with which in some early examples *motley* seems nearly synonymous. Formally the word might be derived from OF. *motel*, early mod.F. *motteau* little clod, also 'clot of congealed moisture' (Cotgr.), dim. of *mote*, *motte* clod, but this does not seem quite satisfactory with regard to sense. Connexion with early mod.F. *mattelé* 'clotted, knottie, curdled, or curd-like' (Cotgr.) is improbable on grounds both of form and meaning.]

A. *adj.*

1. Diversified in colour; variegated; particoloured; chequered.

[**1388** *Calverley Chart.* (1904) 204 Pur j gowne de bloy mottelay et j chaperon de scharlete.] **1390–1** *Earl Derby's Exp.* (Camden) 8 Pro xxiiij virgis de rubano motteley. **1415** in Rymer *Fœdera* IX. 274/2 Duas Copas de Motley Velwet nigro, rubeo, & viridi cum Orfreis de Velvet rubeo. *c* **1430** *Two Cookery-bks.* I. 36 And ȝif þow wolt haue it Motley, take þre pottys, and make letlardys in eche, & coloure [them].. so þat þey ben dyuerse; an..caste al togederys in-to on, an stere hem..and he wol be Motley whan he ys lechyd. **1483** CAXTON *Gold. Leg.* 49/1 Israhel lovyd Joseph..and made for hym a motley cote. **1504–5** *Norwich Sacr. Roll* (MS.), In factura unius panni de Motley velveto. **1587** TURBERV. *Trag. T.* 16 b, When May, with motly robes began his raigne. **1606** SYLVESTER *Du Bartas* II. iv. II. *Magnif.* 313 He, whose count-less Heards for pasture Dis-robe (alone) mount Carmel's moatly Vesture. **1620** SHELTON *Quix.* IV. xxiii. (1652) 131 An artificiall Fountain wrought of motly Jasper and smooth Marble. **1686** PLOT *Staffordsh.* 123 All the colours being..given by the variety of Slips, except the Motley-colour which is procured by blending the Lead with Manganese. **1687** A. LOVELL tr. *Thevenot's Trav.* III. 36 They make the..motely colours [orig. *bigarures*] that are upon the Stuffs with Moulds. **1755** SMOLLETT *Quix.* (1803) IV. 31 Two of thom..are green, two carnation, two blue, and one motley. **1757** DYER *Fleece* II. 111 Where pitch.. must stain your motley flock, To mark your property. *a* **1839** PRAED *Poems* (1864) II. 159 A motley page Of black and white. **1851** LAYARD *Pop. Acc. Discov. Nineveh* viii. 185 About thirty Cawals in their motley dresses of black and white.

b. *esp.* of a fool's dress. Hence ***motley fool***.

1600 SHAKS. *A.Y.L.* II. vii. 13, I met a foole i'th Forrest, A motley Foole. *Ibid.* 43 O that I were a foole, I am ambitious for a motley coat. **1603** DEKKER & CHETTLE *Grissil* I. (Hübsch 1893) 14 Its hard sir for this motley Ierkin to find friendship with this fine doublet. **1812** BYRON *Ch. Har.* II. lxxviii, In motley robe to dance at masking ball. **1820** HAZLITT *Lect. Dram. Lit.* 49 Shakspear has contrived to clothe..the same sort of character with a motley garb.

c. *Path.* in ***motley dandruff***, a dandruff which produces a variegated appearance of the skin. Also (by association with 'mottle'), of the skin in disease: Mottled in appearance.

1822 GOOD *Study Med.* IV. 573 The variegated or Motley Dandriff, pityriasis versicolor. **1843** R. G. GRAVES *Syst. Clin. Med.* iv. 51 In some instances the eruption was papular, or a motley appearance of the skin.

2. *transf.* and *fig.* Composed of elements of diverse or varied character: **a.** of things.

1824 WOTTON *Archit.* II. 98, I could wish such medlie and motlie Designes confined onely to the Ornament of Freezes. **1641** MILTON *Animadv.* Wks. 1851 III. 208 The motley incoherence of a patch'd missall. **1693** DRYDEN *Persius' Sat.* I. 158 One would enquire from whence this motley Style Did first our Roman Purity defile. **1728** POPE *Dunc.* I. 63 There motley images her fancy strike, Figures ill-paired, and Similics unlike. **1796** ELIZA HAMILTON *Lett. Hindoo Rajah* (1811) I. 138 Motely tales of love and murder. **1864** BURTON *Scot Abr.* I. i. 14 The language of France..has left to our day some motley relics. **1871** B. TAYLOR *Faust* (1875) II. I. iii. 25 Motley fancies blossom may For the fashion of the day.

b. of an assembly of persons.

1687 T. BROWN *Saints in Uproar* Wks. 1730 I. 77 What a motly checquer'd assembly of red-coats and wastecoateers! **1748** *Anson's Voy.* I. iii. 28 With this motly crew..Pizarro set sail. **1846** ARNOLD *Later Hist. Rome* I. viii. 477 The infantry were..a motley force of Greeks, Cretans, Syrians, and natives of Pontus. **1879** LUBBOCK *Addr. Pol. & Educ.* i. 2 In..Singapore, we see a motley population attracted from China, the Malay Peninsula and India.

†**3.** Varying in character or mood; changeable in form. *Obs.*

1593 DONNE *Sat.* i. 1 Away thou changeling motley humorist. **1755** YOUNG *Centaur* v. (1757) IV. 221 So motley a creature is man; as mutable, as God is fixed.

†**4.** Made of the cloth called motley. *Obs.*

1589 *Marprel. Epit.* G j, He deserueth to be cased in a good moatley cloakbagg for his labor. **1615** BRATHWAIT *Strappado* (1878) 130, I had Smaw gere (at tat tide) but a lether-bagge, A Motley iacket, an a slop of blew, It was my Fadders, I mun tell thee true.

5. *Comb.*, chiefly parasynthetic, as ***motley coloured***, ***-minded***, ***-peopled***, ***-speckled*** adjs.; also † **motley-scorn** (see quot.).

1799 STRUTT *Dress & Habits* II. 279 The Merchand [in the *Cant. T.*]..is clothed in a *motley-coloured garment. **1600** SHAKS. *A.Y.L.* v. iv. 41 This is the *Motley-minded Gentleman. **1845** STOCQUELER *Handbk. Brit. India* (1854) 135 This..*motley-peopled capital. **1600** DEKKER *Fortunatus* C 4, Poore Vertue Why is this *Motley-scorne [*sc.* a cockscomb] set on thy head? **1676** *Lond. Gaz.* No. 1114/4 Lost.. a *Motly-speckled Greyhound.

B. *sb.*

†**1.** A cloth of a mixed colour; a mixture. *Obs.*

c **1386** CHAUCER *Prol.* 271 (Lansd. MS.) A marchant was þere with a forked berde In motteley [*Ellesm.*, *Heng.* motlee; *Camb.*, *Petw.* motle; *Corp.* mottle; *Harl.* motteleye] and hye on hors he satte. **1394–5** *Durham Acc. Rolls* (Surtees) 598 In uno panno viridi cum xx uln. de motly pro garniamentis estivalibus. **14..** *Voc.* in Wr.-Wülcker 603/46 *Polimitus*, Ray or motle or medler. **1467–8** *Rolls of Parlt.* V. 620/1 Double Motleys, VII yerdes longe..and sengle Motleys, VI yerdes longe. **1487–8** *Rec. St. Mary at Hill* (1905) 135 Paide for mendyng of a vestmente of worstede Motleye, xij d. **1556** WITHALS *Dict.* (1568) 34 a/1 He that maketh motley, *polymitarius*. **1617** MORYSON *Itin.* III. 170 His [*sc.* the king of Denmark's] chiefe Courtiers..were all attired in an English cloth, which they call Kentish cloth, we call Motley, but much finer then that whereof we make cloakebags.

†**b.** *transf.* (Common in Lydgate.) In *pl.* as the material of the flowery 'mantle' of the earth. Similarly, ***white motley***, as the clothing of the hawthorn. *Obs.*

c **1402** LYDG. *Compl. Bl. Knt.* xi, Ther saw I eek the fresshe hawethorn In whyte motle, that so swote doth smelle. *c* **1407** —— *Reson & Sens.* 117 Hys [*sc.* the earth's] mantel ys so lusty hewed..wyth motles fressh and fyne. *c* **1450** —— *Secrees* 1378 This sesoun fflora that is of fflours quene, hire fressh motlees she tournyth now Citryne. *c* **1515** *Cocke Lorell's B.* (Percy Soc.) 7 The walles shallbe of hauthorne..And hanged wᵗ whyte motly yᵗ swete doth smell.

2. A variegated, chequered, or mixed colour; also *transf.* and *fig.* an incongruous mixture.

c **1440** *Promp. Parv.* 345/2 Motle, colowre, *stromaticus*. **1530** PALSGR. 246/2 Motley[,] colour, *biguarrure*. **1552** *Act 5 & 6 Edw. VI*, c. 6 §23 Clothes..of anye other color or colors then..watchett shepes color lyon color motteley or tren [*v.r.* Iren] grey. **1698** FRYER *Acc. E. India & P.* 366 By their joint perverting the Holy Bible sprang up this motly of Blasphemous Dotages. **1864** D. G. MITCHELL *Wet Days at Edgewood* (1884) 72 Interlacing the pages into a motley of patchwork. **1889** *Amer. Nat.* May 494 A motley of white and gray on the head, neck, shoulders, and back.

Comb. **1611** COTGR., *Bigarrément*, diuersly, of sundrie colours, motley-like.

3. A parti-coloured dress which was the recognized attire of a professional fool or jester, freq. in phr. *to wear motley*; hence, allusively, foolery, nonsense. ***a piece of motley***, a fool. *Obs.* exc. *Hist.*

1600 SHAKS. *A.Y.L.* II. vii. 34 A worthy foole: Motley's the onely weare. *a* **1619** FLETCHER *Wit without M.* III. iv, Never hope after I cast you off, you men of Motley. **1623–34** FLETCHER & MASS. *Lover's Progr.* I. i, How have you work'd This piece of motley to your ends? *a* **1680** BUTLER *Rem.* (1759) I. 225 Their poring upon black and white too subt'ly Has turn'd the Insides of their Brains to motly. **1842** H. ROGERS *Ess.* (1874) I. i. 21 So exuberant is Fuller's wit, that ..his very wisdom wears motley.

b. A fool, jester.

c **1600** SHAKS. *Sonn.* cx, I haue gone here and there And made my selfe a motley to the view. **1616** HAUGHTON *Englishm. for my Money* F 3 b, Will not this monsieur Motley take his answer? **1873–4** DIXON *Two Queens* III. XIV. viii. 113 Wolsey, in his gown and band, beat all the motleys with their caps and bells.

motley ('mɒtlɪ), *v.* [f. MOTLEY *sb.*] *trans.* To make motley or parti-coloured in hue; to diversify in character; to mix incongruously. Hence '**motleyed** *ppl. a.*

1447 BOKENHAM *Seyntys* (Roxb.) Introd. 3 Poetrye Enbelshyd wyth colours of rethoryk So plenteuously that fully it lyk In may was neuere no medews sene Motleyed wᵗ flours on hys verdure grene. **1598** SYLVESTER *Du Bartas* II. i. I. *Eden* 89 With thousand Dies he motleys all the Meades. *c* **1610** F. DAVISON *Ps.* xxiii, Motlied [*so MS. Rawl. Poet.* 61 (1626); *edd.* mottled] with Springs flowry painting. **1630** DRAYTON *Muses' Elys.* vi. 57 The motlied Meadowes then, ..Shot vp their spicy sweets. **1742** COLLINS *Oriental Ecl.* iii. 17 Gay-motley'd pinks and sweet jonquils she chose. **1798** A. P. *Tour in Wales* 35 (MS.) They were a motleyed throng of quadrupeds and the human species. **1830** MOIR in *Blackw. Mag.* XXVII. 341 Some ruins motleyed with the weeds That love the salt-breeze.

motleyness ('mɒtlɪnɪs). [f. MOTLEY *a.* + -NESS.] The condition or quality of being motley.

1819 *Edin. Rev.* XXXII. 358 All other dogs are prized.. for the motleyness of their coats. **1846** LD. COCKBURN *Jrnl.* (1874) II. 161 The folly was the only bond that united Sir Culling's supporters. Hence their motleyness.

motmot ('mɒtmɒt). [mod.L. (in 17th c. also *momot*, whence *Momotus* name of the typical genus); app. echoic of the bird's note.] A bird of the family *Momotidæ* or *Prionitidæ*, native of Mexico and South America.

[**1635** NIEREMBERG *Hist. Nat.* 209 De momot. **1651** HERNANDEZ *Nov. Plant. Anim. et Min. Mexicanorum Hist.*, *Hist. Anim.*, etc. 52 De Motmot.] **1837** SWAINSON *Nat. Hist. Birds* II. 141 Every writer, since the days of Linnæus..has placed the motmots (*Prionites*) and the toucans (*Ramphastos*) close together. **1884** NEWTON in *Encycl. Brit.* XVII. 3/2 The Motmots are a purely Neotropical form.. the majority of the species inhabit Central America.

‖**moto** ('moto). *Mus.* [It.] In regard to musical tempo: motion, pace; *spec.* in **moto perpetuo**, a rapid instrumental composition consisting mainly of notes of equal value.

1740 J. GRASSINEAU *Mus. Dict.* 145 *Moto*,..is a term that has many significations in music; sometimes it means only a motion or passage from one note to another... Sometimes it regards the quickness and slowness of such motion, as a brisk, slow, lively or languid motion. **1801** BUSBY *Dict. Mus.*, *Moto contrario* (Ital.), an expression applied to that progression of the different harmonic parts of a composition by which they move in opposite directions. **1884** F. NIECKS *Conc. Dict. Mus. Terms* 177 *Moto* (It.), (1) Motion... (2) Movement... *Moto contrario* (It.), contrary motion. *Moto misto* (It.), mixed motion. *Moto obliquo* (It.), oblique motion. *Moto perpetuo* (It.), perpetual motion. **1901** G. B. SHAW *London Music in 1888–89* (1937) 389 A light-fingered and humorous *moto perpetuo* which might have come straight out of a Mendelssohn concerto. **1969** *Times* 30 Oct. 13/4 A brief moto perpetuo (with splendidly clean, disciplined figuration) by way of conclusion.

moto, obs. form of MOTTO.

moto-, irreg. repr. L. *mōt-* (as in MOTION, MOTIVE, MOTOR), used in various combinations.

a. *Anat.* as in **moto-sensitive** *a.*, composed of motor and sensitive nerve-fibres; *Biol.* as in **moto-plastic** *a.*, ? suffering change in the process of motion.

1835–6 R. OWEN in *Todd's Cycl. Anat.* I. 551/1 The great moto-sensitive chords. *Ibid.*, Those two large moto-sensitive columns, which evidently represent..the spinal cord of the *Vertebrata*. **1862** H. J. CARTER in *Ann. & Mag. Nat. Hist.* Ser. III. IX. 446 A mass of minute polymorphic cells (*Amœbæ*) which..soon separated from their globular aggregation, and crept away from each other under moto-plastic forms.

b. in various combinations for explanation of which see MOTOR *sb.* 5. **moto-cross**, cross-country motor-cycle racing.

1895 *Review of Rev.* Nov. 395/2 The motocycle, as the horseless carriage is to be named in future, has come to stay. **1900** *Pall Mall G.* 17 Apr. 9/2 The only lady moto-cyclist who has met with any success in road races with men. **1901** *Pall Mall Mag.* Sept. 64/2 The moto-cyclette. **1951** *Motor Cycle Sport in Pictures* 9 (*caption*) 1950 Moto-Cross victors. Left to right, B. W. Hall (B.S.A.), G. J. Draper (B.S.A.) and H. H. Lines (Ariel), three of the British team of 12 which won the Moto-Cross des Nations in Sweden. **1960** *Motor Cycling Sports Yearbk.* 81 (*heading*) Scrambles and Moto-cross. *Ibid.*, A dark cloud which has passed over the moto-cross world. **1968** K. BIRD *Smash Glass Image* vii. 85 His machine kicked over the ground as if he were taking part in moto-cross.

motograph ('məʊtəgrɑːf, -æ-). [f. MOTO- + -GRAPH.] (In full ***electro-motograph***.) A receiver for an electric telegraph or telephone, invented by Edison.

1877 *Eng. Mechanic* 1 June 276/1 Edison's Motograph. **1883** J. MAIER *Hospitalier's Mod. Appl. Electr.* II. 96 A principle which was first applied by the inventor [Edison] to a telegraphic relay, under the name of electro-motograph. **1894** DICKSON *Edison* 83 Motograph receiving and transmitting telephone.

Hence '**motographic** *a.*

1884 KNIGHT *Dict. Mech.* Suppl., *Motographic Receiver*, an invention of Edison, by which the volume of sound is increased in a telephonic receiver. Called also Electro-motograph.

motometer (məʊ'tɒmɪtə(r)). [Formed as prec. + -METER.] (See quot.)

1876 *Catal. Sci. App. S. Kens.* 7 'The Motometer', a machine to indicate the number of revolutions made..by a steam engine or revolving shaft.

moton. *Antiq.* [Origin obscure.] Some portion of the armour of the 15th century.

Its place in the list suggests that it may be the plate often figured as attached to the rerebrace to protect the armpit. See Visct. Dillon *The Besague or Moton* in *Archæol. Jrnl.* LXIV. 15 ff.

c **1470** *Abilmentis for Justus* [i.e. *Jousts*] of Pees (Lansd. MS. 285, fol. 9 b; also in Hastings MS., *Archæologia* LVII), A rerebrace. A Moton. A vambrace and a gaynepayne [etc.]. **1824** MEYRICK *Anc. Armour* III. Gloss., *Moton*, a piece of armour used in the time of Henry VI, Edward IV and Richard III, and appears to have been for the protection of the right armpit. **1846** in FAIRHOLT *Costume* Gloss.

moton(e, obs. forms of MOUTON, MUTTON.

motoneurone (məʊtəʊ'njʊərəʊn). *Biol.* Also **motoneuron.** [f. MOTO-: see NEURON, NEURONE.] = *motor neurone* s.v. MOTOR *sb.* and *a.* B. 2.

1908 *Nature* 6 Feb. 333/2 The inhibition of the motoneurones is..followed by a superactivity in them. **1943** *Jrnl. Neurophysiol.* VI. 311 Few if any extensor motoneurones could have discharged in the earlier reflex. **1964** J. Z. YOUNG *Model of Brain* iv. 50 In a mammal the largest motoneurons of the spinal cord may have a dendrite spread of 1 m. **1973** *Nature* 3 Aug. 254/1 The authors rule out the possibility that this occurs *via* the neural feedback loop involving the sensory fibres from the muscle to the motoneurone.

motonne, obs. form of MUTTON.

Motopia (mə'təʊpɪə). [f. MO(TOR *sb.* + U)TOPIA.] A name for an urban environment designed to meet the needs of a pedestrian society by strict limitation of the use of the motor car. So **Mo'topian** *a.*

1959 *Engineering* 18 Sept. 206 (*heading*) Motopia: where traffic and pedestrians never meet. **1961** G. A. Jellicoe *Motopia* 7 Motopia..arises..from the realization that our present physical conditions are being thrown into chaos by the advent of one car per family and even one per person. *Ibid.* 15 The English preference..fixed the shape and alignment of the Motopian rectangle. **1968** C. A. Doxiadis *Between Dystopia & Utopia* 20 Such efforts as the *Motopia* of 1961, all of whose cars were to circulate on the tops of the roofs of the buildings.

motor ('məʊtə(r)), *sb.* and *a.* Also 7 moter. [a. L. *mōtor* (whence F. *moteur*, Sp., Pg. *motor*, It. *motore*), agent-n. from L. *movēre* to MOVE.]

A. *sb.*

1. One who or something which imparts motion.

a. *first* or *prime motor* [= med.L. *primus motor*]: †(*a*) in mediæval astronomy, = PRIMUM MOBILE 1; (*b*) applied (allusively) to God, as the cause of the motion of the heavens; †(*c*) the first instigator, or the chief director, e.g. of a plot, a political organization, etc.; †(*d*) the part that initiates motion in a piece of mechanism. (Cf. *prime mover*.)

(*a*) **1586** B. Young *Guazzo's Civ. Conv.* IV. 197b, How the Heauens and Planets make their neuer ceasing course, Vnder their Motor first and great, from whence they had their source. **1604** E. G[rimstone] *D'Acosta's Hist. Indies* III. vi. 136 The earth is not mooved, by reason of her heavinesse,..being far from this first motor.

(*b*) **1620** Melton *Astrolog.* 26 From God, that is the true Prime Moter. **1678** Gale *Crt. Gentiles* IV. III. iii. 51 Al our movements or motions are from God as the prime Motor... Is he not then the first Cause and Motor of al our motions? Doth not Aristotle..strongly demonstrate, That al our natural motions must arise from one first immobile Motor? **1952** G. Sarton *Hist. Sci.* I. xix. 498 God exists, for it is the necessary principle and end of everything, the first motor.

(*c*) **1600** E. Blount tr. *Conestaggio* 187 One of the first moters of this popular humour which made him king. *a* **1660** *Contemp. Hist. Irel.* (Ir. Archæol. Soc.) I. 93 Bagnall that was prime motor in the counties of Katarlagh and Kilkeny. **1685** Cotton tr. *Montaigne* (1711) I. xxii. 149 The Fruits of publick Commotion are seldom enjoyed by him who was the first Motor.

(*d*) **1656** *Artif. Handsom.* 41 Whose prime moter or spring ..being set true,..the outward wheeles, motions and indications cannot go amisse.

b. An agent or force that produces mechanical motion.

1644 Digby *Nat. Soul* x. §4. 426 In heauy thinges, their easy following..an other way then downewardes, testifyeth that their motion downewardes hath an extrinsecall motor. **1674** Grew *Anat. Trunks* I. vi. §6 Convolvula's do not wind by any peculiar Nature..but because their Parts are disposed so, as to render them more sequaceous to the external Motor. **1685** Boyle *Effects of Mot.* Suppl. 147 The heavier part of the Stople broke off from the other..and was carry'd from it by invisible motors to a great distance. **1839** *Civil Eng. & Arch. Jrnl.* II. 405/1 The true motor of the system would..be the weight of the atmosphere.

c. *fig.* in various applications.

1594 Lodge & Greene *Looking Glass* (1598) G, Thine eyes the motors to command my world. **1641** Gauden *Love of Truth* 22 Love is the weight and motor of the soul. **1847** Lewes *Hist. Philos.* (1867) I. 182 Happiness was the aim.. of all men—the motor of all action.

2. *Anat.* a. A muscle designed to move a particular part of the animal frame. b. A nerve whose function it is to excite muscular activity in a particular part of the animal body.

1808 Barclay *Muscular Motions* 300 In every motion.. there must always be a number of muscles employed, some as motors, some as directors, some as moderators. **1824** C. Bell *Nerves* 33 We cannot forget that this nerve is entirely devoted to the muscles of the tongue; that it is the motor of the tongue. **1840** Elliotson *Hum. Physiol.* 323 Three [nerves] conveying volition to the muscles of the eyes, the common motors [etc.]. **1846** Worcester, *Motor*..(Anat.) a moving muscle.

c. A person in whom motor representations of perceptions predominate over auditory or visual ones.

1890 W. James *Princ. Psychol.* II. xviii. 62 The young savage was a *motor*. **1902** —— *Var. Relig. Exper.* xiv. 347 The shrew-type is defined as possessing an 'active unimpassioned temperament'. In other words, shrews are the 'motors', rather than the 'sensories'. **1929** J. Adams *Everyman's Psychol.* vii. 155 Men fall into two classes of sensories and motors... Motors have to receive sense impressions, and sensories have to send out messages leading to actions. *Ibid.* 156 The motor is often on the edge of action, eager to go.

3. a. An apparatus for employing the energy of some natural agent or force for the impulsion of machinery; a machine that supplies the motive power for the propulsion of a vehicle or vessel. In recent use also in a narrower sense excluding steam engines.

1856 Emerson *Eng. Traits* v. 91 They adopt every improvement in rig, in motor, in weapons; but they fundamentally believe that the best strategem in naval war is to lay your ship close alongside of the enemy's ship. **1881** *Eng. Mechanic* 27 May 286/1 A water-motor sufficient to drive a sewing-machine would not be reliable to drive a lathe. **1884** Cotterill *Appl. Mechanics* 482 Hydraulic motors are classed according to the mode in which the water operates upon them. **1892** *Electrical Engineer* 16 Sept. 284/2 There is little difficulty in designing a cart to be driven by a motor, the motor also being able to be used for other purposes, such as winding a drum.

b. Short for MOTOR CAR and *motor carriage*.

1900 *Chamb. Jrnl.* 28 Apr. 344 The purchase by the Prince of Wales of a six horse-power Daimler motor should still further..popularise automobilism. **1902** Harmsworth *Motors & Motor-driving* 64 Many doctors who use motors have joined the Automobile Club. **1912** E. M. Forster *Let.* 25 Dec. in *Hill of Devi* (1953) 17 The Luards..got the Maharajah of Indore's motor. **1929** M. de la Roche *Whiteoaks* xxviii. 381 They were going by motor to the lakes.

4. *Math.* An operator of quantity which represents the displacement of a rigid body.

1873 Clifford *Math. Papers* (1882) 183, I propose to call this quantity a *motor*; the simplest type of it being the general motion of a rigid body. And we shall say that in general the sum of rotors is a motor, but that in particular cases it may degenerate into a rotor or vector. **1878** —— *Elem. Dynamic* I. 125 A quantity like a twist-velocity, which has magnitude, direction, position, and pitch, is called a *motor*, from the twist-velocity which is the simplest example of it.

5. *attrib.*, designating a vehicle driven by a motor, as ***motor-ambulance, bicycle, cab, carriage, -hearse, -landau, -lorry, -plough, -sledge, toboggan, -tractor, tricycle, -truck, vehicle, -wagon*** etc.; also designating sea vessels, aircraft, and other devices driven or powered by a motor, as ***motor-cannon, -craft, -cruiser, -launch, -liner, meter, -mower, -ship, -sloop, torpedo-boat, -vessel, yacht.***

1915 Motor-ambulance [see JOY-RIDE *sb.*]. **1917** W. Owen *Let.* 25 Mar. (1967) 447, I went a joy ride on a Motor Ambulance, a Daimler. **1931** *Times Lit. Suppl.* 18 June 478/4 The occasional British practice of sending on billeting-parties in motor-ambulances. **1894** *Westm. Gaz.* 14 June 7/2 A newly-invented motor-bicycle. **1904** *Daily Chron.* 8 Jan. 9/5 A motor-cab costs twice as much to build as an ordinary hansom. **1889** F. R. Stockton *Great War Syndicate* 79 She carried one motor-cannon of large size. **1939** *War Illustr.* 9 Dec. 390 It was to a similar type of French engine that the first successful 'motor-cannon', or shell gun, firing between the arms of the 'V', was fitted. **1896** *Daily News* 5 Feb. 5/3 The first International Motor-Carriage Exhibition will be held at the Imperial Institute in May. **1905** *Daily Chron.* 17 June 9/1 The latest regulation that no small boat should 'lock' with a motor-craft appears to have caused considerable surprise. **1921** *Daily Colonist* (Victoria, B.C.) 9 Oct. 23/2 The motor cruiser Speejacks was reported safe last night. **1936** *Discovery* Sept. 272/2 Charting the coast from a small motor-cruiser. **1975** *Times* 19 Sept. 4 (Advt.), A boat test on the fast 33' motor cruiser Cleopatra. **1904** *Daily Chron.* 8 Jan. 9/5 The County Council insists that the motor hansom shall also be registered. **1924** P. Creswick *Beaten Path* xxxiii. 180, I see there are motor-hearses now. **1973** 'R. MacLeod' *Burial in Portugal* i. 23 An elderly motor hearse with black paintwork and tarnished chrome..carried a polished oak coffin. **1916** 'R. Dehan' *Earth to Earth* 73 The motor-landau in waiting for him at Covertsham Station, Deershire, was destined to receive a second passenger. **1912** W. Owen *Let.* 31 Aug. (1967) 158, I was asked to accompany them & Vicar on a motor-launch-trip. **1935** *Discovery* Dec. 372/2 A little undecked motor-launch for inshore work. **1975** 'D. Rutherford' *Mystery Tour* iii. 40 The trip by motor launch through the canals. **1913** *Chambers's Jrnl.* Jan. 31/1 The motor-liner above mentioned and her two sister-ships were built. **1931** *Evening Standard* 16 Jan. 9/1 (*caption*) The new motor-liner Warwick Castle leaving Belfast for her final trials. **1902** Kipling *Traffics & Discoveries* (1904) 391 There's a heavy load of grist just in from Lamber's Wood. Eleven miles it came in an hour and a half in our new motor-lorry. **1926** *Daily Chron.* 13 May 2/6 Three men were each sentenced to three months hard labour for inciting a crowd of people to set fire to a railway motor lorry in the city. **1934** *Discovery* Apr. 94/1 In most portions of the globe explorers under the new order have the valuable aids of aeroplane and motor-lorry. **1903** L. C. Reed *Amer. Meter Practice* iii. 37 These ten watts are the input into the motor meter, and the efficiency of this motor meter will give the ratio of the torque exerted on the armature. **1971** *Gloss. Electrotechnical, Power Terms (B.S.I.)* I. iv. 12 *Motor meter*, meter incorporating a motor. **1923** *Punch* 15 Aug. 165 (*caption*) The motor-mower takes charge. **1959** *Oxf. Univ. Gaz.* 1 Dec. 345/2 One new motor-mower was acquired in replacement of an old one now worn out and for which spare parts are no longer available. **1972** 'H. Carmichael' *Naked to Grave* vi. 74 Through the window he saw a motor mower, cans of paint, fertilizer in paper sacks. **1896** Beaumont in *Jrnl. Soc. Arts* 10 Jan. 161 The motor omnibus shown by Fig. 48. **1901** *Chambers's Jrnl.* Nov. 764/2 Great things are anticipated of a new method of land culture by means of a motor-plough. **1916** *Daily Colonist* (Victoria, B.C.) 25 July 11/3 The motor-ship City of Portland..has been given her trial trip. **1929** *Times* 2 Nov. 10/2 The Tuscan Star..is the first motor-ship ordered by the Blue Star Line. **1955** *Times* 3 May 15/6 The construction of two motor ships of about 1,300 tons deadweight, designed to operate in our short sea services. **1910** *Chambers's Jrnl.* Aug. 546/2 The 'final dash' [to the Pole]..will be made with the help of motor-sledges. **1936** *Discovery* July 215/1 Captain Scott took motor-sledges to the Antarctic in 1910. **1931** *Times Lit. Suppl.* 15 Jan. 33/3 M. Knut Stubbendorff..chartered the motor-sloop Isbjörn. **1948** *New Deal for Saskatchewan Fisheries* 20 Motor toboggans..manoeuver in almost any kind of terrain. **1940** Motor torpedo-boat [see E-BOAT]. **1928** *Punch* 29 Feb. 248/3 The world is still a stage; the ruling factors Are petrol and pink legs and motor-tractors. **1934** *Discovery* June 143/2 Although aircraft and motor tractor have been used they are in no sense in competition with the dog-sledge. **1896** Beaumont in *Jrnl. Soc. Arts* 10 Jan. 152 The motor tricycle shown by Fig. 34 is an oil motor cycle made in 1883. **1916** *Daily Colonist* (Victoria, B.C.) 2 July 15/5 The iron-shod war horse of former days has evolved into the padded wheel motor car, motor truck, and motor cycle of 1916. **1937** *Discovery* Nov. 359/1 The sandy wastes of the Gobi are being cut to ribbons by motor-truck tyres. **1898** *Daily News* 2 Apr. 2/6 The Post Office and Motor Vans.—A motor van service for the conveyance of the mails. **1890** J. W. Quinn *U.S. Pat. 431,993*, I..have invented certain new and useful Improvements in Motor-Vehicles. **1937** *Discovery* July 194/2 The noise from motor vehicles. **1959** P. Bull *I know Face* ix. 148 He was referring to his motor-vehicle. **1931** *Daily Tel.* 21 May 7/5 Pioneers of motor-vessels to the East. **1969** *Jane's Freight Containers 1968–69* 394/1 This service is carried out by motor-vessels of 600–1,500 tons. **1909** *Chambers's Jrnl.* June 343/2 Large warehouses have their veritable fleets of motor-wagons. **1929** J. Buchan *Courts of Morning* III. i. 320 The raiders..helped themselves.. loading the loot into light motor-wagons. **1905** *Outing* May 218/2 A 90 foot motor yacht was launched late last season. **1973** 'I. Drummond' *Jaws of Watchdog* i. 31 A fast, low-profile motor yacht five miles out to sea.

b. Of, pertaining to, or designed for use in motors, motor vehicles, or motoring, as ***motor accident, age, bonnet, cap, -chassis, club, -coat, -dealer, -driver, fitter, garage, -goggles, -hooter, horn, -house, insurance, lantern, licence, -mania, -mask, mechanic, oil, race, -racing, -ride, -road, run, salesman, scarf, show, -smash, -spectacles, -tour, track, traffic, transport, -travel, -travelling, trip, trouble, tyre, -veil.***

1910 'Saki' *Reginald in Russia* 17 What I had mistaken for a motor accident was evidently a case of savage assault and murder. **1972** M. Yorke *Silent Witness* vi. 123 Roy's father had been killed in a motor accident. **1937** *Amer. Speech* XII. 317/1 The influence of..the motor age. **1963** *Daily Tel.* 28 Nov. 16/2 The root of the trouble is that our cities were never built for the motor age. **1910** *Blackw. Mag.* Nov. 604/2 My wife..had been patiently sitting in the hall wearing a new motor-bonnet. **1937** J. Laver *Taste & Fashion* x. 151 The latest trimming for these motor bonnets. **1906** *Daily Colonist* (Victoria, B.C.) 5 Jan. 3/4 (Advt.), Motor Caps. 50c, 75c, $1.00 reduced to 40c. **1907** Motor cap [see *ear-flap*]. **1915** *Pearson's Mag.* Jan. 25 Great lines of these old motor-chassis, mounted with a serviceable lorry body, are to be met with on all the roads of France. **1934** *Amer. Speech* IX. 111/1 Such motor clubs as the *A.A.A.*, the *A.M.A.*, and the *Automobile Club of Southern California*. **1909** W. J. Locke *Septimus* iv. 57 Shrugging himself into his motor-coat, which the chauffeur brought him. **1910** *Blackw. Mag.* Apr. 480/1 A long leather motor-coat. **1937** *Discovery* May 164/1 Motor dealers in South America..order what they need by air mail. **1902** *Pall Mall Mag.* XXVIII. 410/1 Should motor drivers be subject to an examination as to proficiency? **1968** J. H. Burn *Lect. Notes Pharmacol.* (ed. 9) 7 It is good for a motor-driver driving through the night. **1961** *Evening Standard* 26 July 22/6 Skilled..motor fitter required. **1973** *Times* 16 Oct. 6/8 Christopher Smart, aged 25, a motor fitter. **1974** P. Wright *Lang. Brit. Industry* ix. 77 He's a mechanic, but he'd rather be called a motor fitter. **1902** Motor garage [see GARAGE *sb.* 1]. **1922** W. J. Locke *Tale of Triona* xxiv. 273 An ex-officer..who has just set up a motor garage. **1914** Beerbohm *Seven Men* (1919) 127 He did not wear motor-goggles. **1922** Joyce *Ulysses* 483 In motor jerkin, green motorgoggles on his brow. **1911** Beerbohm *Zuleika D.* xix. 291 All along the soaked towing-path lay strewn the horns, the rattles, the motor-hooters, that the youths had flung aside. **1909** *Chambers's Jrnl.* June 401/1 The predominant sounds..were not those of wheels or whistles or motor-horns. **1931** M. Allingham *Look to Lady* x. 105 The squawk of a motor-horn. **1970** V. Canning *Great Affair* xii. 211 A chorus of motor horns began to blow in anger at some road block. **1902** D. Salomons in A. C. Harmsworth et al. *Motors* vi. 84 A well-built motor-house should cost nothing in the up-keep. **1971** *Daily Tel.* (Colour Suppl.) 18 June 33/4 There is the medium-sized house with its own tennis court and 'motor house', as garages were first called. **1955** *Times* 3 May 16/1 Motor insurance, which constitutes a substantial portion of our Accident business. **1975** *Times* 24 Sept. 3/2 The estimated cost of motor insurance premiums in 1975 was £580m. **1914** Chesterton *Flying Inn* xxi. 248 Humphrey had hung one of the motor lanterns on to a branch. **1907** *Yesterday's Shopping* (1969) 413/2 The motor licence case. **1957** *Railway Mag.* June 392/1 The beginnings of a reaction from the worst of motor-mania are bringing the uninitiated back on to the narrow gauge. **1966** *Punch* 16 Feb. 232 The ingenuity, energy and wealth that mechanised intellectual Peter Pans devote to indulgence of their motor-mania. **1916** *War Illustr.* V. 451/3 Our goggles..are shaped like a motor-mask. **1930** *Daily Express* 6 Oct. 7/4 James Horn, aged thirty-one, a motor mechanic. **1961** *Evening Standard* 25 July 15/1 (Advt.), Motor Mechanics required. **1939** G. B. Shaw *Geneva* II. 45 Motor oil is a sanction when you withhold it. Castor oil is a sanction when you administer it. **1900** *Racing Rules & Regulations* (Motor Car Club) 11 In all Motor Races held under the Rules of the Motor Car Club it must be stated on all Entry Forms..that they are so held. **1936** J. B. Priestley *They walk in City* iii. 41 An aeroplane parade, a motor race, a parade of cadets. **1905** *Official Programme Internat. Tourist Trophy* 4 A new departure in the history of motor racing. **1956** *Nature* 11 Feb. 246/2 The establishment of a motor-racing circuit on public roads in the Peak District National Park. **1974** J. Gardner *Corner Men.* ii. 19 Most of the books were..concerned with motor cars or motor-racing. **1914** Chesterton *Flying Inn* xx. 241 You owe me a motor-ride, you know. **1919** G. B. Shaw *Inca of Perusalem* Prologue in *Heartbreak House* 234 Dresses, hats, furs, gloves, motor rides: one bill after another. **1909** *Westm. Gaz.* 27 Aug. 2/2 Of more dramatic interest is the second part of the Bill, with its proposal for the creation of motor-roads. **1926** T. E. Lawrence *Seven Pillars* (1935) VII. lxxxii. 457 Gilman and Dowsett..had spent months in Wadi Itm, building, like engineers, a motor road through the gorge. **1949** *Archit. Rev.* CV. 118/1 The average speed of 30 m.p.h. here allowed for the surface plan is high, but, even allowing this figure, the advantage of elevated motor-roads is obvious. **1975** *Listener* 14 Aug. 199/1 A new motor road roaring past their windows. **1936** Joyce *Let.* 18 Nov. (1966) III. 393 Perhaps you could make your suggested motor run to the school at Zug? **1936** J. B. Priestley *They walk in City* i. 17 Mysterious and vaguely amorous gentlemen friends, usually commercial travellers or motor salesman, loom and soar and suddenly vanish. **1973** A. Behrend *Samarai Affair* vi. 65

That Bromborough motor salesman chap separated from his wife. **1899** in A. Adburgham *Shops & Shopping* (1964) xxii. 261 Motor scarves. **1911** *Daily Colonist* (Victoria, B.C.) 28 Apr. 20/6 Waterproof Motor Scarf of good size..each 75¢. **1905** S. A. Barnett *Let.* 2 Dec. in H. Barnett *Canon Barnett* (1918) II. 194 We have been to the Motor Show, when vast Olympia was crammed by a fashionable crowd. **1965** A. Christie *At Bertram's Hotel* i. 13 He could talk racing shop, cricket..give Motor Show information. **1972** *Nature* 31 Mar. 193/1 It is difficult to believe that international motor shows are instrumental in selling cars. **1916** W. Owen *Let.* 3 July (1967) 398, I was so happy to learn that your motor-smash came to no harm. **1931** R. Lehmann *Letter to Sister* 22 Things happen to you... You have been in a motor smash. **1911** D. H. Lawrence *White Peacock* II. iii. 262 She disengaged her arms to take off his disfiguring motor-spectacles. **1909** *London Mag.* Sept. 18/2 Excursions through the sky..are to become as common as motor-tours. **1915** J. Buchan *39 Steps* iv. 90 That's the end of my Scotch motor tour. **1928** *Manch. Guardian Weekly* 19 Oct. 301/2 Motor traffic and the urbanisation of large rural stretches are producing a hideous outbreak of advertisement hoardings, petrol pumps..and gaunt new motor-tracks. **1933** G. Robey *Looking Back on Life* xxviii. 306 Lord Dewar ..made the famous epigram about there being only two classes of pedestrians in these days of reckless motor traffic—the quick, and the dead. **1926** *Brit. Gaz.* 12 May 2/4 At Liverpool there have been a few cases of interference with motor transport, for which heavy sentences have been inflicted. **1936** *Discovery* June 189/1 An ever-extending network of good macadamised roads is increasingly introducing the use of motor transport. **1923** A. E. Housman *Let.* 18 Aug. (1971) 215 Blazing hot all the time while motor-travel could temper it [*sc.* the weather]. **1909** *Chambers's Jrnl.* June 342/2 Putting the accidents on railways and on the roads together, motor-travelling included. **1934** Joyce *Let.* 25 Apr. (1966) III. 304, I was swept off..to make my first motor trip. **1950** M. Laski in *Contact* May–June 26/1 It is, of course, possible to take an extended motor-trip abroad without ever coming into contact with the Art of Navigation. **1911** *Chambers's Jrnl.* Jan. 55/1 Cleaver and Latham dropped into the Mediterranean..because of motor trouble. **1907** *Nature* 14 Feb. 383/1 Chemical composition of some motor-tyre rubbers. **1937** *Discovery* June 186/1 The wayside was strewn with motor tyres and broken down cars. **1970** Y. Carter *Mr. Campion's Falcon* vii. 59 Packing-cases, old motor tyres, drums of paint. **1907** *Yesterday's Shopping* (1969) 320 D/3 Motor veil. In Crêpe de Chine. **1926** W. de la Mare *Connoisseur* 70 She was a rare one for the fashions: scarves and motor-veils, and that kind of thing.

c. Instrumental, as ***motor-assisted***, ***-driven***, ***-dusted***, ***-infested***, ***-mad***, ***-paced*** adjs.

1954 *Highway Code* 32 To motor cyclists and riders of motor-assisted pedal cycles..*you must not* carry more than one passenger on a two-wheeled machine. **1904** *Motor Cycle* 6 June 551 A motor-driven roundabout. **1937** *Discovery* Dec. 387/1 The motor-driven fan. **1967** Karch & Buber *Offset Processes* v. 168 Motor-driven lenses, or hit-or-miss methods involving tricky out-of-focus photographic and lighting techniques are used. **1974** H. R. F. Keating *Bats fly up for Inspector Ghote* iii. 31 A powerful motor-driven dhow. **1909** M. B. Saunders *Litany Lane* III. xviii. 236 His eyes were fixed on the white, motor-dusted hedges. **1909** *Q. Rev.* Jan. 143 This singularly congested and motor-infested country. **1931** T. H. Pear *Voice & Personality* 43 Today's world of motor-infested 'beauty-spots'. **1922** W. J. Locke *Tale of Triona* xxvi. 292 England ran motor-mad that summer. **1938** *Encycl. Brit. Bk. of Year* 100/1 Mills also set up a new record of 2 mins. 1½ secs. for the mile, standing start, unpaced; while Albert Marquet did the distance in 41⅗ secs. from a flying start and motor paced. **1973** *Observer* 16 Sept. 26/6 Instead of winning a motor-paced race by 10 laps, he would come from behind in the final lap to take it on the line.

6. motor-bandit *Obs.*, a thief who uses a motor car; **motor-bicycle** *v. intr.*, to travel on a motor bicycle (*rare*); so ***motor-bicycling*** vbl. sb., ***motor-bicyclist***; **motor-bike** = motor-cycle *sb.*; hence as *v. intr.*, to travel on a motor-bike; so ***motor-biking*** vbl. sb.; **motor-bus**, a motor-driven omnibus; hence as *v. intr.*, to travel by motor-bus; **motor camp** orig. *U.S.*, a place where a motorist may park his car and set up camp; **motor caravan**, (*a*) a caravan designed to be towed by a motor car; (*b*) (see quot. 1964); **motor-coach**, (*a*) a single-decker motor-bus; (*b*) (see quot. 1940); **motor-coaster**, (*a*) a motorized vessel employed in sailing along the coast; (*b*) a type of big dipper at a fun-fair; **motor cop** *U.S. colloq.* = *motor-cycle cop*; **motor court** *U.S.*, (*a*) (see quot. 1936); (*b*) a motel; **motor-drive**, (*a*) a drive or journey in a motor-car; (*b*) driving power provided by a motor or engine; **motordrome** *Obs.*, a course for motor-racing; **motor generator** *Electr.*, an apparatus consisting of an electric motor and a generator with their armature shafts mechanically coupled which may be used to change the voltage, frequency, or number of phases of a supply; **motor glider**, an aircraft constructed like a glider but having an engine (now used in training glider pilots); **motor-home** *N. Amer.*, a very large vehicle equipped as a self-contained home; **motor hotel**, a hotel designed particularly for use by motorists; a motel; **motor inn** = *motor hotel*; **motor lodge**, a motel; **motor mate** *Obs.*, one who attends to the motor of an airship; **motor mouth** *U.S. slang*, a person who talks incessantly, and often to little purpose; **motor park**, (*a*) *U.S.* = *motor court* (*a*); (*b*) a car-park; **motor-sailer**, a boat equipped with both sails and a motor; **motor-school**, a school where the driving of motor vehicles is taught; **motor-scooter**, a two- or three-wheeled vehicle resembling a child's scooter, propelled by a small engine; hence **motor-scooterist**, one who rides a motor-scooter.

1913 *Punch* 19 Feb. 133/3 On top of all this Motor Bandit business comes the news that two men have been charged.. with breaking into a bakery and stealing a sponge-cake, value one penny. **1935** *Ibid.* 6 Mar. 253/3 Returning from a jumble sale a man was held up by a motor-bandit. **1960** J. Betjeman *Summoned by Bells* v. 49 He motor-bicycled his life away, Looking for orchids in the Wytham Woods. **1912** W. Owen *Let.* 16 Aug. (1967) 155 Captain Wigan has had a motor-bicycling accident! **1908** R. Brooke *Let.* 4 Aug. (1968) 136 Abercrombie..is a Metrical Motor Bicyclist, a mumbly Wump, but often splendid. **1903** *Work* 18 Apr. 176/3 (Advt.), Motor Bike, 1½-h-p. **1911** W. Elmhirst *Freshman's Diary* (1969) 20 He went over to Malvern yesterday on his motor bike. **1927** H. G. Wells *Short Stories* 627, I remember my wild rush on my motor-bike to London. **1944** F. Clune *Red Heart* 33 He motor-biked to Alice Springs. **1958** J. Betjeman *Coll. Poems* 224 Along the village street the sunset strikes On young men tuning up their motor-bikes. **1972** M. Gee *In my Father's Den* 27 That motor-bike gang. **1913** G. B. Shaw *Let.* 21 Mar. in *B. Shaw & Mrs. Campbell* (1952) 100 It looked like a superb stroke of motorbiking. **1901** H. G. Wells in *Strand Mag.* Dec. 623/2 'You really think such a thing *is* possible?'.. 'As possible,' said Gibberne, and glanced at something that went throbbing by the window, 'as a motor-bus.' **1914** A. D. Godley *Let.* 10 Jan. in *Reliquiae* (1926) I. 292 What is this that roareth thus? Can it be a Motor Bus? **1915** D. O. Barnett *Lett.* 39 We came on from our last stopping place, whither we motor-bused, in a car. **1972** *Daily Tel.* 24 Mar. 15/1 Trolleys were a merger of motorbus and tram. **1925** *Sat. Even. Post* 10 Oct. 98/1 The average motor camp is too well known to need any description. **1926** *Daily Colonist* (Victoria, B.C.) 4 July 1/4 Motor Camp is Winning Favor. **1970** *N.Z. Listener* 21 Dec. 8/3 Don't join a joker in a motor camp cabin for the night... Try yelling for help in a motor camp in the holiday season, mate. **1930** *Daily Express* 1 Aug. 9/2 The most modern form of holiday transport—the motor-caravan, or trailer caravan. **1959** *Motor* 7 Oct. 246 Motor Caravans as practical vehicles. **1964** *Which?* Apr. 35/1 A motor caravan is basically an ordinary van that has been fitted with windows, beds and cupboards, a table, cooker and sink. **1923** Motor coach [see coach *sb.* 1 e]. **1926** *Times* 6 May 3/5 Intimidation of owners and drivers of motor-cars and motor-coaches plying for public hire is reported to-day in several localities. **1940** *Chambers's Techn. Dict.* 559/2 *Motor-coach*, a passenger coach, equipped with its own motors, for use on electrified railways; it is commonly used in conjunction with trailer coaches to make up a multiple-unit train. **1958** J. Betjeman *Coll. Poems* 153 Then the mystery tour By motor-coach inland this afternoon. **1972** *Modern Railways* Sept. 334 Bob [*sc.* Berner Oberland Bahn] trains are motorcoach-hauled and not fitted for push-pull operation. **1973** J. Porter *It's Murder with Dover* v. 42 All the cars and motor coaches..streaming through the village. **1928** *Daily Express* 5 Dec. 11/4 It is feared that the London motor-coaster, Wander (82 tons), has been lost, with a crew of five. **1974** *Amer. Speech* 1971 XLVI. 84 Fast moving amusement rides on elevated rails: toboggan, high rides,..shoot the chutes, motor coasters. **1915** *Policeman's Monthly* Oct. 14/1 The motor cops were brought in on the 'carpet'. **1918** R. Wagner *Film Folk* 23 If one goes home some afternoon and finds an ambulance or a motor cop outside the door, he instinctively looks for the camera. **1936** *Pop. Mechanics* LXVI. 674/1 The motor court is a recent development of the motor age. It's not a tourist park, it's not an auto camp... It's a collection of miniature homes clustered around a central service and administration building. **1962** I. Fleming *Spy who loved Me* i. 15 'Motel' isn't a good word any longer. It has become smart to use 'Motor Court' or 'Ranch Cabins'. **1906** Beerbohm *Around Theatres* (1924) II. 221 The details of the motor-drive are quite plausible. **1936** *Discovery* Apr. 113/2 The compressor, or vacuum pump, has an independent motor drive. **1971** *Amateur Photographer* 13 Jan. 51/1 The exposure system is powered by the motor drive batteries but a bridge circuit makes it independent of their precise voltage as they run down. **1908** *Westm. Gaz.* 4 Aug. 4/3 Mr. Locke-King has spent a large fortune in building this wonderful motordrome. **1887** *Electrician* 2 Dec. 74/1 We are enabled to reproduce photographs and sectional drawings of the Paris and Scott motor generator which recently underwent some tests at the Newcastle Exhibition. **1907** Parshall & Hobart *Electr. Railway Engin.* ix. 351 The locomotive is equipped with a motor-generator set comprising a single-phase motor directly connected to a continuous-current generator. **1930** *Engineering* 28 Feb. 278/2 The electrical load is consequently divided between the steam-driven sets and motor-generator sets in accordance with the demand for heating steam. **1966** *McGraw-Hill Encycl. Sci. & Technol.* VIII. 617/1 Motor-generator sets are used for a variety of purposes, such as providing a precisely regulated dc current for a welding application, a high frequency ac power for an induction-heating application, or a continuously and rapidly adjustable dc voltage to the armature of a dc motor employed in a position control system. **1923** *Jrnl. R. Aeronaut. Soc.* XXVII. 531 One of the things that instantly occurred to most people..was that the motor glider heralded the dawn of a new era in commercial aeronautics. **1969** *Sailplane & Gliding* XX. 491/2 The flying training will be based on glider and motor glider experience. **1971** D. Piggott *Gliding* (ed. 3) i. 8 The two-seater motor glider has proved an unqualified success for all stages of training. **1966** *Economist* 15 Jan. 181/1 There is the 'motor home', especially built on a lorry or bus chassis, an elaborate 'land yacht'. **1970** *Globe & Mail* (Toronto) 25 Sept. 38/9 (Advt.), Wanted Motor home, used, good condition. **1973** *Sci. Amer.* Apr. 1/1 (Advt.), These air springs are the only ones of their kind on motorhomes. **1974** *Trailer Life* Nov. 92 Writers, editors and publishers, who formerly had only the word trailer to contend with when referring to recreational vehicles now had to wrestle with trailers, pickup campers, chassis-mounts and the few then-existing motorhomes. **1965** *Punch* 1 Dec. 798 They call themselves motor lodges, motor courts, motor hotels, even tourtels and autotels, but motel is the word that blisters the night sky of the American suburbs. **1967** *Autocar* 5 Oct. 44/1 (*caption*) New motor hotels—not motels—specially designed for motorists, are being opened by the Trust House group. **1967** *Time* 21 Apr. 25, 46 restaurants and six motor inns. **1974** *Country Life* 21 Mar. 693/2 This privately owned Motor Inn situated on the water's edge. **1965** Motor lodge [see *motor hotel*]. **1975** *Globe & Mail* (Toronto) 24 May 10/2 Judge Dunlap dismissed two charges of procuring, one of attempting to procure and a charge of keeping a common bawdy house in a motor lodge here. **1928** C. F. S. Gamble *Story N. Sea Air Station* xxii. 411 One of the motor-mates of the amidships gondola raised the black curtain. **1971** *Soaring* July 6 (*caption*) The motormouth..can be heard broadcasting across three states any weekend. **1977** *National Observer* (U.S.) 22 Jan. 12/1 The increasing number of 'motor mouths' posing as sports broadcasters,..statisticians and whatever. **1986** *Washington Post* 22 May D11/1 [They] have been cut from the same inspirational motormouth mold... They'll invite you into their office..and break every bone in your inner ear. **1939** *New Yorker* 14 Oct. 72 The usual phrase for cabin colonies in California is 'auto court'; 'motor park', perhaps copied from 'trail park'. **1965** W. Soyinka *Road* I. 1 The motor-park lay-abouts are sprawled on the floor and on benches. **1972** C. Achebe *Girls at War* 60 Everybody, even a motor-park tout, knows what school fees are for. **1934** *Yachting* (N.Y.) Jan. 39 A consideration of the motor-sailer. **1937** [see fifty-fifty *adv.* and *a.*]. **1971** J. R. L. Anderson *Reckoning in Ice* vi. 111 His boat was what is called a motor-sailer, which generally means..more engine than sail. **1974** *Country Life* 24 Jan. 153/1 We have pure sailing craft, motor sailers and motor yachts, excellently crewed..from £15 to £100 per person per day. **1909** *Chambers's Jrnl.* June 342/1 The..gentleman..is now getting his country grooms trained at a motor-school. **1919** Motor-scooter [see buller *sb.*[4]]. **1938** *Times* 28 Feb. 12/2 He then tears down the course on a motor-scooter. **1956** *Railway Mag.* Nov. 722/2 Goods agents..have been provided with motor scooters, to enable them to cover ground more quickly. **1957** J. I. M. Stewart *Use of Riches* 58 The age of the motor-scooter had brought little of modernity to Castelarbia as yet. **1960** *News Chron.* 22 Mar. 7/8, I saw White running behind one of the motor-scooterists. **1965** J. Creasey *Toff & Spider* ii. 22 The motor-scooterist had turned into the Square and was slowing down.

B. *adj.* [After F. *moteur*, *motrice*, which like other agent-nouns in Fr. is often used as adj.]

1. Giving, imparting or producing motion.

1872 Lyell *Princ. Geol.* (1875) I. II. xx. 506 The accelerating force produced..would be inefficient as a motor power. **1880** Kinglake *Crimea* VI. iv. 75 The second of the three motor forces had its origin in the same puissant will. **1899** *Daily News* 15 June 6/5 The motor power of the future was not to be steam..but electricity.

2. *Phys.* Of nerves (opposed to *sensory*), muscles, etc.: Conveying or imparting an impulse which results or tends to result in motion. So ***motor area*** (***region***, ***zone***): that part of the cortex of the brain from which motor impulses are directed to the various parts of the animal body; ***motor cortex***, the part of the cerebral cortex which has a motor function; ***motor neurone***, a neurone having a motor function; ***motor root***, the anterior or ventral root of spinal or certain cranial nerves, containing axons of motor neurones; ***motor unit***, a neuroanatomical unit which comprises a single motor neurone and the muscle fibres on which it acts.

1824 C. Bell *Nerves* 30 The motor nerves. **1836–9** *Todd's Cycl. Anat.* II. 372/1 Those [*sc.* ganglia] which have connected with them both motor and sentient nerves. **1839–47** *Ibid.* III. 720/2 A nerve may contain sentient and motor fibres. **1840** W. J. E. Wilson *Anatomist's Vade Mecum* viii. 387 There are thirty-one pairs of spinal nerves, each arising by two roots, an anterior or motor root, and a posterior or sensitive root. **1848** E. Forbes *Naked-eyed Medusæ* 3 The muscular system usually consists of a marginal motor ring. **1878** *Jrnl. Nerv. & Mental Dis.* V. 766 The largest nerves of the human body (sciatics) arise precisely from that point of the lumbar cord where we find the largest, so-called motor, cells. **1881** *Nature* XXIII. 236 Reactions of the motor-zone of the brain. **1885** McKendrick in *Encycl. Brit.* XIX. 41/1 The evidence, therefore, is strongly in favour of the view that there are definite motor areas of grey matter on the cortex. **1890** W. James *Princ. Psychol.* I. ii. 61 The motor cortex might be sensitive as well as motor. **1893** W. R. Gowers *Man. Dis. Nerv. Syst.* (ed. 2) II. 4 This [parietal lobule] also forms part of the motor region. **1898** *Jrnl. Compar. Neurol.* VII. 185 The neuraxis of the motor neuron loses its medullary sheath before piercing the sarcolemma. **1925** Liddell & Sherrington in *Proc. R. Soc.* B. XCVII. 516 The experimental results suggest that a reflex maintains maximal response of the individual 'motor-unit' by a degree of central excitation which is commonly 'supramaximal'. **1926** J. S. Huxley *Essays Pop. Sci.* 286 The rest of the [spinal] cord, however, and in particular the motor areas and motor roots, show no increase in size, showing that the number of muscle-fibres to be supplied does not stimulate the growth of the supplying cells. **1942** O. Larsell *Anat. Nervous Syst.* xxiv. 326 The upper motor neuron fibers of the pyramidal tract terminate in synaptic relation to large motor cells in the anterior column of the gray matter of the spinal cord. **1970** M. Hollander tr. *Monnier's Functions Nervous Syst.* II. xxvi. 572 (*heading*) Functions of the motor cortex and pyramidal system. **1970** J. G. Chusid *Correlative Neuroanat. & Functional Neurol.* (ed. 14) ii. 76/2 The motor unit is made up of the anterior horn cell of the spinal cord and the muscle group it innervates. **1973** *Gray's Anat.* (ed. 35) 1002/2 The motor nucleus of the trigeminal nerve gives rise to the fibres of the motor root. **1974** Passmore & Robson *Compan. Med. Studies* III. xxxiv. 53/2 Motor neurone disease may present with any combination of upper and lower motor neurone signs.

3. Of, pertaining to, or involving muscular movement; based upon or received through the movement of parts of the body.

1878 tr. *Ziemssen's Cycl. Pract. Med.* XIII. 474 Motor pareses and paralyses. **1880** W. JAMES *Coll. Ess. & Rev.* (1920) 163 Wundt says that were our motor feelings of an afferent nature, 'it ought to be expected that they would increase and diminish with the amount of inner or outer work actually effected in contraction.' **1884** J. SULLY *Outl. Psychol.* vii. 247 In general the motor representations are weak as compared with the sensory. **1890** W. JAMES *Princ. Psychol.* II. xix. 131 The facts shade off into the phenomena of motor automatism, trance, etc. **1899** *Allbutt's Syst. Med.* VI. 790 Unilateral motor trigeminal palsy. **1899** A. G. WHYTE tr. *Binet's Psychol. of Reasoning* 24 When we think of the ball, this idea must comprise the images of these muscular sensations, as it comprises the images of the sensations of sight and touch. Such is the motor image. **1925** C. FOX *Educational Psychol.* 228 Walking is not bringing into use unconscious motor-images. **1936** *Amer. Speech* XI. 88/2 Speech responses are so complex that they can hardly be considered identical with motor reflexes. **1942** A. T. POFFENBERGER *Princ. Appl. Psychol.* vi. 105 The fineness of motor control or coördination is..an essential factor in many forms of adjustment. **1951** A. D. WOODRUFF *Psychol. of Teaching* (ed. 3) xvi. 270 Motor behavior that is guided by perceptual cues, such as playing the piano. **1951** C. I. HOVLAND in S. S. Stevens *Handbk. Exper. Psychol.* xvii. 627/2 An important change with practice in motor learning is change in muscular tension. **1958** M. ARGYLE *Relig. Behaviour* v. 56 Evidence drawn from actual studies of conversion shows that people converted at public meetings are more easily hypnotized, display more motor automatisms and can therefore be classified to some extent as hysterics. **1962** *Canadian Jrnl. Linguistics* VII. 65 The assumption that the ability to speak is simply a motor-skill which can be measured by tests of imitation and reading aloud. **1969** MILLER & MCNEILL in Lindzey & Aronson *Handbk. Social Psychol.* (ed. 2) III. xxvi. 687 At the other [extreme] would be the so-called 'motor theory' of speech, which holds that a listener can recognize speech only by imitating (at least covertly) the motor movements that would produce it. **1971** *Jrnl. Gen. Psychol.* LXXXV. 208 In the events intervening between stimulus input and motor output, there is ordinarily first the operation of cognition.

motor (ˈməʊtə(r)), *v.* [f. the sb.] **a.** *trans.* To convey in a motor car; to traverse (a distance) in a motor vehicle; also *intr.*, to travel or drive in a motor car.

1896 *Westm. Gaz.* 10 Sept. 7/2 The cost of 'motoring' cotton to Manchester. **1898** *Autocar* 11 June 379 On May 12th my wife and I motored. *Ibid.* 18 June 392 We motored back. **1919** WODEHOUSE *Damsel in Distress* viii. 103, I motored down with a boy I know. **1928** 'S. S. VAN DINE' *Greene Murder Case* xii. 141 Vance and Ada and I motored the few blocks to 18, Broad Street. **1932** J. BUCHAN *Gap in Curtain* i. 31 Mayot had motored to Cirencester to meet a friend. **1972** *Daily Tel.* (Colour Suppl.) 27 Oct. 86/3 From Sidmouth I walked (though most people motor) to Salcombe Regis. **1972** *Listener* 21 Dec. 849/1 If we were opening a show with a Boxing Day matinee, we should have finished rehearsing on Friday night and then have motored to our respective homes.

b. *intr.* To travel in a motor-boat; to use the engine in a sailing-boat.

1968 'D. HALLIDAY' *Dolly & Singing Bird* xiii. 147 'You don't deny you were motoring?' Johnson kept his voice reasonable. 'We used the engine..to South Rona and back. At Portree, we changed over to sail.' **1971** P. M. HUBBARD *High Tide* xiii. 134 There was no wind to sail with. I could motor down river and hope to pick up something of a sailing breeze outside.

motorable (ˈməʊtərəb(ə)l), *a.* [f. MOTOR *v.* + -ABLE.] Of a road or district: suitable for motor vehicles; capable of being travelled over in a motor vehicle.

1920 A. L. BAGLEY *Holiday Rambles N. Wales* 178 This is certainly not a motorable road. **1953** X. FIELDING *Stronghold* 93 The only motorable highway in the whole of Sphakia province. **1972** P. M. HUBBARD *Whisper in Glen* iii. 25 Roads which were a little alarming but just about motorable. **1974** *Country Life* 24 Jan. 144/2 We..thought of a certain lake. Ten hours by pony from the nearest motorable road.

Motorail (ˈməʊtəʊreɪl). [Blend of MOTOR *sb.* and RAIL *sb.*[2]] A service whereby cars, with their drivers and passengers, are transported by railway. Also *attrib.*

1968 *Daily Tel.* 6 Jan. 10/6 This year British Rail will have nearly 100 more Motorail trains, giving a total carrying space for 90,000 cars. **1971** *Country Life* 25 Nov. 1463/3 British Rail unveiled their plans for 1972 Motorail... The 27 routes to be operated will have a combined capacity for 120,000 cars and over half a million passengers. **1974** *Ibid.* 18 Apr. 965/4 Excellent train service to Penzance..and Motorail links throughout Britain.

Motorama (məʊtəˈrɑːmə). [Blend of MOTOR *sb.* 3 b and *-or)ama* after PANORAMA.] An exhibition of motor vehicles.

1950 *Richmond* (Va.) *News Leader* 18 Jan. 38/1 General Motors opens its auto show here. The display which General Motors calls 'Mid-century Motorama' brings..38 of GM's 1950 model cars. **1954** *Amer. Speech* XXIX. 157 *Motorama*, an automobile exhibit. **1974** *John O'Groat Jrnl.* (Wick) 6 Sept. 2/2 *Motorama*, Wick & District Round Table present Motorama Spectacular at Ackergill on Sunday, 15th September at 2 p.m.

ˈmotor-boat, *sb.* A motor-driven boat or launch.

1902 *New Liberal Rev.* Apr. 440 The paraffin motor..is.. impossible in anything but an open motor-boat. **1913** E. F. BENSON *Thorley Weir* i. 11 If I must go on the river, give me a motor-boat. **1973** A. BEHREND *Samarai Affair* ii. 24 He would..step overside into the boarding punt, a small-sized motor-boat. **1973** *Fisheries Fact Sheet* (Environment Canada Fisheries & Marine Service) No. 1. 2/2 Individual fishermen fishing near their homes from small row-boats or motor-boats.

ˈmotor-boating, *vbl. sb.* Also without hyphen and as two words. [f. prec. + -ING[1].] **1.** Travel in a motor-boat.

1918 *Chambers's Jrnl.* Aug. 541/1 The water is never dangerously rough, and provides the finest possible field for motor-boating. **1961** *Guardian* 8 Feb. 10/2 The sports of motor-boating and water-skiing.

2. *Electronics.* Oscillation in an amplifier that is of such a low frequency that individual cycles may be heard, giving a characteristic sound, and caused by feedback from the output to the input of earlier stages, often through a common voltage supply.

1930 J. H. REYNER *Testing Radio Sets* vi. 84 Back-coupling with a mains unit usually takes the form known as motor-boating. The oscillation set up is of a low frequency and gives a continuous 'pop, pop, pop'. **1943** F. E. TERMAN *Radio Engineers' Handbk.* v. 409 A power supply having low internal impedance at low frequencies is also helpful in eliminating motorboating. **1945** *Electronic Engin.* XVII. 429 Regeneration may lead to low-frequency oscillation (about 5 to 10 c/s) known as 'motor boating'. **1965** G. J. KING *Radio & Audio Servicing Handbk.* iii. 78 Decoupling prevents signals which could occur in an element common to two or more stages from getting back into the input circuits and causing oscillation or motorboating.

So **ˈmotor-boat** *v. intr.*, (*a*) to travel in a motor-boat; (*b*) (of an amplifier) to exhibit motor-boating.

1922 *Contemp. Rev.* Mar. 409 The scenery through which he tramped or motor-boated. **1932** F. E. TERMAN *Radio Engin.* vii. 277 Amplifiers receiving their plate voltage from a common dry battery have a tendency to motor-boat when the batteries are near the end of their useful life, particularly when the amplification is high. **1970** *Nature* 28 Nov. 797/2 Two men motor-boating on the loch collided with a large object.

motorcade (ˈməʊtəkeɪd). orig. *U.S.* [f. MOTOR *sb.* + -CADE.] A procession of motor vehicles.

1913 *Arizona Republican* (Phoenix) 5 June 2/4 The motorcade can make its music self supporting and donate large and salubrious gobs of melody to the natives at all points along the line. *Ibid.* 4 July 4/2 This 'motorcade' came from a suggestion thrown out by the sporting editor of the Republican. It was immediately accepted by several local automobile owners, whereupon, the sporting editor [*sc.* Lyle Abbott] became the busiest man in Phoenix and hammered away at the 'motorcade' a term which, by the way, he had invented sometime before in order that newspapers might keep pace with the developments of vehicular transportation. **1924** *N. & Q.* 19 Apr. 288/1 A parade of motor cars..was termed in the local [Florida] papers a 'motorcade'. **1928** in *Amer. Speech* (1930) VI. 155 The North Dakota farmers' motorcade started to-day on its long drive to the Republican Convention at Kansas City. **1933** *Sun* (Baltimore) 19 Aug. 3/1 The action was taken after a telegram from the Governor was read to workers who came into Mahanoy City in a motorcade. **1936** [see -CADE]. **1942** S. L. A. MARSHALL *Armies on Wheels* vi. 99 A motor-cade in which the cars become bogged down. **1953** *Times* 13 July 3/5 The word 'motorcade'..is..no novelty. Some years before the war it was employed—and perhaps coined—by the Salvation Army in advertisements of a procession of cars which bore the Army's principal officers on a tour of the main towns of the country. **1969** *Wall St. Jrnl.* 28 Jan. 1/6 He rides in Presidential motorcades. **1972** *Guardian* 25 Oct. 2 The old-style motorcade..is hard to beat as a campaigning technique. **1974** *Northern Times* (Golspie, Sutherland) 23 Aug. 7/6 Mr. George Reid, M.P. for Clackmannan and East Stirling, accompanied by Mr. Sutherland, will be in a motorcade covering Helmsdale, Brora, Golspie, Dornoch and Bonar-Bridge.

ˈmotor car. [MOTOR *sb.* 5.] A wheeled vehicle or 'horseless carriage', propelled by a motor engine and used esp. as a private conveyance on the road; an automobile. Also *attrib.*

1895 *Westm. Gaz.* 10 Sept. 3/2 The chief reason why motor-cars have not been more generally adopted in America lies in the roughness..of the roads. **1895** *Daily Chron.* 29 Oct. 5/1 A name has not yet been found for horseless carriages... The latest suggestion we have had is 'motor car'. Mr. F. R. Sims, who is responsible for it, urges [etc.]. **1896** *Daily News* 5 Feb. 5/3 The Motor Car Club. **1909** *Daily Graphic* 26 July 7/4 Numbers came from all the neighbouring towns, while motor-car parties came from considerable distances. **1931** H. G. WELLS *Work, Wealth & Happiness of Mankind* (1932) 21 The motor-car 'bandit'. **1970** 'D. HALLIDAY' *Dolly & Cookie Bird* i. 4 George is a motor-car salesman. **1972** *Daily Tel.* (Colour Suppl.) 20 Oct. 52/1 The Rolls-Royce approach to making motor cars (they are never just 'cars' at Crewe). **1974** *Times* 4 Dec. 17/2 The motor-car industry..has been the most important single engine of economic development in industrial countries for the past fifty years.

Hence **ˈmotor-carist**, a motorist; **ˈmotor-carring**, travel in a motor car.

1899 *Motor-Car World* I. 37/2 Many of the disabilities under which motorcarists suffer in England will be removed. **1901** 'SAKI' *Let.* 17 Aug. in *Square Egg* (1924) 61 Travelling with Aunt Tom is more exciting than motorcarring. **1903** *Westm. Gaz.* 12 Jan. 10/1 The champion motor-carist of the House of Commons.

ˈmotor-cycle, *sb.* [MOTOR *sb.* 5.] A form of bicycle, usually larger and heavier than an ordinary bicycle, having a small (usu. petrol) motor by which it is propelled. Also *attrib.*, as **motor-cycle cop** (*U.S. colloq.*), **policeman**, a policeman who rides a motor-cycle.

1896 *Daily News* 5 Feb. 5/3 This Exhibition..will comprise motor-cycles and carriages. **1902** *Motor Cycling* 12 Feb. 24/1 In a year or two motor cycles will be as plentiful as the ordinary cycle is to-day. **1919**, **1928** [see COMBINATION 10 b]. **1927** K. EUBANK *Horse & Buggy Days* 33 There's always some fool motor-cycle cop coming along to interfere. **1928** 'S. S. VAN DINE' *Greene Murder Case* xxv. 288 On North Broadway we were forced to the kerb by a motor-cycle policeman. **1934** T. S. ELIOT *Rock* i. 21 Every son would have his motor cycle. **1958** *New Statesman* 22 Feb. 220/1 A motor-cycle policeman seized his shoulder and flung him along the pavement. **1972** C. WESTON *Poor, Poor Ophelia* (1973) vii. 39 All those sex-mad motorcycle toughies. **1972** R. ADAMS *Watership Down* xix. 111 Few places are far from human noise—cars, buses, motorcycles, tractors, lorries. **1974** *Times* 18 Mar. 7/1 Five people were killed here in a running battle between motorcycle gangs.

Hence **ˈmotor-cycle** *v. intr.*, to ride a motor-cycle; **ˈmotor-cycling** *vbl. sb.*; **ˈmotor-cyclist**, one who uses a motor-cycle.

1902 *Motor Cycling* 12 Feb. 24/1 Now that motor cycling has come to stay..it may not be out of place to say where improvements may be made that will be beneficial to..all those who motor-cycle. *Ibid.* 19 Feb. 32 Motor cyclists will not require palatial club premises. **1912** G. W. E. RUSSELL *Afterthoughts* xx. 184 Motorists and cyclists, and those strange hybrids the motor-cyclists, seem to disregard weather. **1925** E. F. NORTON *Fight for Everest, 1924* v. 103, I wore a fur-lined leather motor-cycling helmet. **1956** G. N. PATTERSON *God's Fool* ii. 17 Pulling on his motor-cycling gloves savagely, he stalked out. **1972** 'J. & E. BONETT' *No Time to Kill* i. 5 The chef's elder daughter..motor-cycled out for a free lunch in the hotel kitchen. **1973** J. WAINWRIGHT *Pride of Pigs* 92 The motor-cyclist was pinned under his machine.

motordom (ˈməʊtədəm). [f. MOTOR *sb.* + -DOM.] The realm or world of motors; motor vehicles, the people who use them, or those who deal in them, considered collectively.

1900 *Captain* III. 225/1 In the world of motordom. **1909** *Westm. Gaz.* 2 Nov. 2/3 There is scarcely a woman in London who has not had to sacrifice the cadences of talk to the Moloch of Motordom. **1910** [see CRACKER 4 b]. **1916** W. J. LOCKE *Wonderful Year* vi. 84 Fashionable motordom halted at the Hôtel des Grottes. **1961** L. MUMFORD *City in Hist.* xv. 474 The 'progressive' metropolises of motordom, like Los Angeles, exhibit..all the urban evils of the palaeotechnic period.

ˈmotored, *a.* [f. MOTOR *sb.* + -ED[2].] Provided with a motor.

1928 *Daily Express* 17 Nov. 9/3 The Wright brothers completed their motored glider—the first real airplane—in their bicycle shop at Dayton on Nov. 17th 1903.

motorial (məʊˈtɔːrɪəl), *a.* [f. L. *mōtōri-us* (see MOTORY) + -AL[1].] Of or pertaining to motion; *spec.* of or pertaining to a motor nerve; motor.

1843 J. G. WILKINSON *Swedenborg's Anim. Kingd.* I. i. 39 Itself [*i.e.* the tongue] and its organic parts, motorial and sensorial. **1860** FORBES WINSLOW *Obscure Dis. Brain & Mind* ii. 25 Apparently in full possession of their intellectual, sensorial, and motorial [*ed.* 4 (1868) motor] powers. **1883** T. LAUDER BRUNTON in *Nature* XXVII. 421 The motorial..fibres..being stimulated by a slight touch. **1899** *Allbutt's Syst. Med.* VI. 507 Such nervous affections as are marked by nervous and motorial excitement.

motoric (məˈtɔːrɪk), *a.* [f. MOTOR *sb.* and *a.* + -IC.] **a.** Of, pertaining to, or characterized by muscular movement.

1930 *Program 47th Meeting Mod. Lang. Assoc. Amer.* 12 An attempt to illustrate the present status of *Schallanalyse* in its visual, acoustic, and motoric approach. **1958** *New Scientist* 14 Aug. 610/2 A simple motoric rhythm in which the animal repeatedly pulled the brush towards himself. **1971** *Nature* 18 June 470/2 The reasons for favouring this method are not quite clear. Motoric convenience, for example, seems an inadequate explanation, in view of normal writing practice.

b. Of a piece of music or its performance: marked by much movement or energy.

1937 *Sat. Rev. Lit.* (U.S.) 23 Jan. 6 Stravinsky's crisp sentences, often naked in their brevity, recall the 'motoric' rhythms of his *Noces*. **1942** *Ann. Reg. 1941* 338 The Symphony..was an interesting..example of what the continental critics used to call 'motoric music'. **1972** *Daily Tel.* 4 May 14/3 Its determined progress was crisply outlined without excessively motoric playing.

motoring (ˈməʊtərɪŋ), *vbl. sb.* [f. MOTOR *v.* + -ING[1].] **1.** The action of driving or travelling in a motor car.

1897 *Truth* 28 Jan. 219 The delights of motoring on a Gladys.

2. *attrib.*, as ***motoring-cap***, ***chocolate***, ***coat***, ***glove***, ***goggles***, ***map***, ***offence***, ***veil***.

1909 *Chambers's Jrnl.* Sept. 588/2 She raised a little gloved hand and patted the hair under a dainty motoring-cap. **1966** D. HOLBROOK *Flesh Wounds* 130 In handy places here and there the tank men kept their round tins of cigarettes and their bars of motoring chocolate. **1907** G. B. SHAW *John Bull's Other Island* IV. 83 Broadbent enters, soiled and disordered as to his motoring coat. **1931** M. ALLINGHAM *Look to Lady* xx. 204 Mr. Campion in a motoring coat and hatless. **1920** W. J. LOCKE *House of Baltazar* viii. 101 Drawing on his motoring gloves. **1942** *R.A.F. Jrnl.* 3 Oct. 30 There were those first flights..in all the glory of an old flying helmet and motoring gloves. **1903** G. B. SHAW *Man & Superman* III. 78 Tanner and Straker, in their motoring goggles, leather coats, and caps, are led in from the road by the brigands. **1975** 'M. DUKE' *Death of Holy Murderer* ii. 37 She removed a pair of antique motoring goggles. **1926–7**

Army & Navy Stores Catal. 915/1 Contour Motoring Map of British Isles. **1931** R. H. HEATON *Perfect Hostess* 133 A set of motoring maps of England and Scotland. **1974** *Camping & Caravanning* Sept. 12/1 The R.A.C. have introduced two new series of motoring maps. **1933** M. ALLINGHAM *Sweet Danger* xvii. 213 The young gents who were wanted for a motoring offence. **1972** *Police Rev.* 17 Nov. 1484/1 Although penalties for motoring offences may be low, it is a truism that purely in financial terms it works out cheaper being a petty criminal than being a forgetful motorist. **1973** P. MOYES *Curious Affair of Third Dog* i. 20 He's not a *criminal*... It was only a motoring offence—but unfortunately he killed somebody. **1955** N. MARSH *Scales of Justice* vii. 160 Illustrations of young women in dustcoats and motoring veils. **1971** *Country Life* 14 Oct. 966/3 Intrepid ladies in large hats, goggles, motoring veils and dust-coats. **1974** I. MURDOCH *Sacred & Profane Love Machine* 229 She now donned a floppy green hat and tied it over her head with a sort of motoring veil.

motorism ('məʊtərɪz(ə)m). [f. MOTOR *sb.* + -ISM.] The use or prevalence of motor vehicles; the world of motoring.

1913 *Chambers's Jrnl.* Feb. 132/2 It is but ten or twelve years since the time when the tide of motorism began to flow. **1930** *Time & Tide* 24 Jan. 101 The death-dealing motorism of the highway. **1952** *Birmingham* (Alabama) *News* 20 Sept. 4 If you want to be in the forefront of motorism these days, it seems you have to have headlamps outside the fenders, mudguards that only partially protect, and if possible wire wheels.

motorist ('məʊtərɪst). [f. MOTOR *sb.* + -IST.] An amateur of motoring; one who rides in a motor car.

1896 *Daily News* 14 Nov. 3/1 The glorious company of motorists will include such well-known men as Lord Cardross [etc.]. **1902** in Cassell's *Encycl. Dict., Suppl.* **1912** *Collier's* 5 Oct. 30/1 In the new Model C-Six the motorist is constantly in a position of rest and free from care or strain. **1960** *Spectator* 30 Sept. 479 Gibberd gave a motorist's-eye view of the town. **1975** *Times* 10 Sept. 3/2 Motorists.. would be.. invited to discuss their driving with road safety officials.

motorium (məʊ'tɔərɪəm). [mod.L., f. *mōtōrius* moving, f. L. *mōt-*, stem of *movēre* to move: cf. -ORY^1.] **1.** *Psychol.* Collectively, the centres in the brain concerned in the function of voluntary muscle; that system of the body capable of initiating and putting into effect muscular movement.

1885 J. ROSS *Handbk. Dis. Nervous Syst.* 73 The central ends of the individual sensory mechanisms are unified by a collective centre—the *sensorium commune*—which is the general centre of nervous connections on the afferent side. It may also be supposed that the individual motor centres are unified by a general centre of nervous connections which may be regarded as a *motorium commune*. **1900** DORLAND *Med. Dict.* 398/1 *Motorium*, (1) a motor center; especially the common center of motor influences; (2) the motor apparatus of the body. **1924** R. M. OGDEN tr. *Koffka's Growth of Mind* 80 The optical sensorium and motorium can not be regarded as two independent pieces of apparatus, since for many types of performance they constitute a unitary organ. **1959** S. KOCH *Psychology* II. 76 For certain purposes, in dealing with transactions with the physical world (walking, performing a motor task, driving a car, etc.), the motorium may be considered to be the muscular apparatus of the organism. Even in such cases, however, it may prove to be useful to consider tools as a part of the motorium.

2. *Zool.* A cytoplasmic structure in some ciliate protozoa forming the centre of the neuromotor apparatus.

1914 R. G. SHARP in *Univ. Calif. Publ. Zool.* XIII. 83 We now come to the description of what is believed to be the most interesting structure in the anatomy of this organism [*sc.* the protozoan *Diplodinium ecaudatum*]... The possibility of this structure functioning.. as a neuromotor apparatus is suggested and.. the designation neuromotor apparatus will be used, and its constituent parts will be described as a motorium or motor mass. **1926** G. N. CALKINS *Biol. Protozoa* ii. 104 Certain special types of cytoplasmic kinetic elements such as myonemes, motorium, and conductile fibers, are characteristic of the ciliates. **1940** L. H. HYMAN *Invertebrates* I. iii. 65 All these fibrils may center in a small body, the motorium. **1966** *New Scientist* 3 Nov. 242/1 Another interesting feature of *Euplotes* is that, as Taylor first noticed in 1920, some of the cirri are connected by a system of minute fibrils to a structure near the front of the animal. This he called the motorium.

motorization (ˌməʊtəraɪ'zeɪʃən). [f. next + -ATION.] **1.** *Psychol.* The process of making a presentation motorial in character. *rare.*

1901 *Amer. Jrnl. Psychol.* XII. 304 The motorization of an exposed word would suggest another similar in sound. *Ibid.* 309 The single-word motorization does not make so much noise in consciousness.

2. The introduction, use, or possession of motor vehicles; equipment with motor vehicles.

1913 in WEBSTER Add. **1919** *N.Y. Times Mag.* 6 Apr. 11 During the war the motorization of artillery proceeded at an unprecedented rate. **1929** H. ROWAN-ROBINSON *Further Aspects of Mechanization* ii. 9 The motorization of infantry and cavalry divisions furnishes.. additional strategic mobility. **1930** *Time & Tide* 13 Sept. 1134 The world moves largely on rubber, which alone makes motorization possible. **1960** H. HONDERMARD in E. Davies *Roads & their Traffic* vi. 130 The extent of motorization, expressed by the number of vehicles per 1000 inhabitants, has had to be periodically reviewed. *Ibid.* 132 Fig. 6.1.. shows a significant correlation between the degree of motorization and national income in different countries. **1960** G. MIKES *How to be Inimitable* 57 This motorisation has developed into a war between the motorists and the authorities. **1969** *Daily Tel.* 26 Aug. 14/3 Full motorisation of Britain's cities.. might go as high as £12,000 million.

motorize ('məʊtəraɪz), *v.* [f. MOTOR *sb.* and *a.* + -IZE.] *trans.* **1.** *Psychol.* To convert (visual or auditory sensations or images) into motorial presentations; to apprehend in a motorial manner. Also *intr.* or *absol. rare.*

1901 *Amer. Jrnl. Psychol.* XII. 308 The word.. seems to be motorized as soon as singly presented. *Ibid.* 309 This.. has reference to readers who motorize.

2. To provide or furnish with a motor or with motor vehicles. Hence **'motorized** *ppl. a.*; **'motorizing** *vbl. sb.*

1913 WEBSTER Add., *Motorize*, to substitute motor-driven vehicles or automobiles, for the horses and horse-drawn vehicles of (a fire department, city, etc.). **1922** *Daily Mail* 24 Nov. 6 These machines have gone beyond the stage of motorised pedal cycles and are in all respects real motor-cycles. **1924** *Public Opinion* 8 Aug. 130/3 If one should dream of motorising the entire world on the scale of the United States. **1927** *Glasgow Herald* 5 Apr. 8 Serried ranks of tanks advancing against each other.. with motorised artillery bringing up the rear. **1933** ADE *Let.* 13 Nov. (1973) Now there ain't no income from the darn stuff [*sc.* farm lands]. I think it is entirely because of the fact that the world has become motorized but I am not proposing any remedies. **1938** *Times* 16 May 9/1 The extension of the air arm and the motorizing of units. **1938** *Sun* (Baltimore) 31 Aug. 20/3 The regiment is motorized and will come over the Governor Nice Highway to the city. **1958** *Edmonton* (Alberta) *Jrnl.* 24 June IV. 16/6 Motorized toboggans have made their appearance in the Mackenzie River delta. **1972** *Physics Bull.* July 402/2 The construction of a motorized drill table for physically handicapped operators. **1972** 'G. BLACK' *Bitter Tea* (1973) ii. 26 Angels mightn't be watching over them, but a good third of the motorized police in the State were.

motorless ('məʊtəlɪs), *a.* [f. MOTOR *sb.* + -LESS.] **1.** Not provided with a motor; performed without the use of a motor; esp. of gliders or flying in gliders.

1897 [see *air-sailer (-or)* s.v. AIR *sb.*^{1} B. III. 5]. **1908** [see *aerodone* s.v. AERO- b]. **1930** V. W. PAGÉ *Henley's ABC of Gliding & Sailflying* (1931) i. 11 They had proved their aëronautical theories with motorless ships which actually stayed aloft a short-time, supported only by air currents. *Ibid.* iii. 49 (*caption*) Outline Drawings.. Showing How Bird Form is Approximated in Creations Intended for Motorless Flight.

2. Of a road, etc.: having little or no traffic.

1970 *Daily Tel.* 19 Sept. 12 Experiments with motorless zones in wild and remote country. **1972** *Listener* 21 Dec. 849 We should drive on motorless roads, praying that conditions would be good.

'motor-man. [f. MOTOR *sb.* (sense 3).] The driver of a motor car or carriage; *spec.* the hired driver of a public motor-driven conveyance.

1890 *Boston* (Mass.) *Jrnl.* 12 Apr. 4/4 Has it, then, become the established policy of the West End road, from the late vice president to the motor-men, that the public must learn that the electric cars cannot be fooled with? **1901** *Daily Record & Mail* 11 July 3 Hours and Wages of Motormen and Conductors. **1904** F. LYNDE *Grafters* xxiv. 298 The conductor and motorman of an early morning electric car. **1908** [see *dead man's handle* s.v. DEAD MAN]. **1935** 'J. GUTHRIE' *Little Country* xxv. 367 Ernest.. climbed on board a tram... The motorman, instead of moving off immediately, waited a moment. **1956** *Railway Mag.* Nov. 744/1 The back of the motorman's compartment is formed by a glass panel so that passengers can enjoy a good view of the track. **1971** *Railway World* Mar. 127 Someone in High Office.. gave orders that motormen should count ten between releasing the air brakes and re-applying power.

motor-minded (stress variable), *a.* [f. MOTOR *sb.* and *a.* + MINDED *ppl. a.*] **1.** *Psychol.* Having a mind in which motor images predominate over visual and auditory ones; thinking largely in terms of movements.

1897 *Psychol. Rev. Monogr. Suppl.* II. I. 40 This, in itself, does not prove that motor-minded persons are less intelligent readers than auditory- or visual-minded. **1900** *Amer. Jrnl. Psychol.* XI. 297 Consonants were not thought to be generally more important than vowels for word perception. The relative importance of these elements might depend upon the reader's tendency to be motor or auditory minded. **1904** W. JAMES in *Atlantic Monthly* Jan. 98/1 Every one knows that in some of us the material of thought is mainly optical, in others auditory, etc., and the classification of human beings into the eye-minded, the ear-minded, and the motor-minded, is familiar.

2. Interested in motor vehicles.

1927 *Glasgow Herald* 14 Oct. 8 With motor trade exhibitions running.. in London (at Olympia) and in Paris .., the motor-minded have got quite a lot to talk about.

So **ˌmotor-'mindedness**, the state of being motor-minded (sense 1).

1897 *Psychol. Rev. Monogr. Suppl.* II. I. 41 It is evident that motor-mindedness is far from being an advantage to a reader. **1902** [see EAR-MINDEDNESS].

mo'torpathy. *U.S.* $rare^{-0}$. [f. MOTOR *sb.* + -PATHY.] The movement cure. Hence **motor'pathic** *a.*

1864 in WEBSTER.

† motorphobe ('məʊtəfəʊb). *Obs.* [f. MOTOR *sb.* + -PHOBE.] One who has a morbid dread or hatred of motor vehicles.

1905 *Automobile Topics* 27 May 448 The time will come when.. the motorphobes will wonder what ever possessed them to act so foolishly. **1911** *Chambers's Jrnl.* Aug. 533/1 A motorphobe was quoted as declaring solemnly in 1906, 'In another ten years there will not be half the autocars on the roads that there are now.'

motorway ('məʊtəweɪ). [f. MOTOR *sb.* + WAY^1.] A specially designated class of highway with two or more lanes in each direction, designed and regulated for use by fast motor traffic. Also *attrib.*, as **motorway box**, a rectangular system of motorways; **motorway madness** *colloq.*, reckless driving on a motorway, esp. in fog.

1903 *Car* 4 Nov. 327 (*title*) Concerning motor-ways. *Ibid.* 327/1 The Motor-way is *bound* to come! **1930** TROUBRIDGE & MARSHALL *John Ld. Montagu of Beaulieu* xx. 254 Where the economic conditions guarantee an adequate volume of traffic, as between large cities, direct roads solely for fast traffic, *i.e.* motorways, must be constructed. **1937** [see AUTOBAHN]. **1955** *Times* 6 July 10/1 Motorways, 345 miles in total length, for motor traffic only, are to be built by the Government. **1959** *Radio Times* 23 Oct. 3/1 A motorway differs from all other types of roads in that it has no crossroads, no traffic lights, no pedestrian crossings. Certain categories of road-users are barred from it altogether; these include pedal cyclists, invalid carriages and 'L' drivers. **1964** *Daily Tel.* 22 Jan. 14 The British are relative newcomers to the motorway age. **1967** *Economist* 4 Nov. 495/1 The more central, shorter, but more expensive 'motorway box' favoured by the GLC. **1971** *Daily Tel.* 14 Sept. 2/6 This supports the 'motorway madness' theory of a false sense of security which makes drivers behave quite differently on motor-ways than on ordinary roads. **1972** J. MANN *Mrs Knox's Profession* v. 31 She had pulled into the motorway café, hating the look of it. **1973** R. BUSBY *Pattern of Violence* i. 15 He.. gave them a name and the time of arrival of a motorway coach. **1973** *Guardian* 15 Oct. 14/1 Fog is the number one motorway menace with irresponsible .. driving coming second. Mix the two, and the headlines next morning scream 'Motorway madness' yet again.

motory ('məʊtərɪ), *a.* [ad. late L. *mōtōri-us*, f. *mōtor*: see MOTOR.]

1. *Phys.* = MOTOR *a.* 2, 3.

1691 RAY *Creation* II. (1692) 58 The motory Muscles. **1763** JOHNSTONE in *Phil. Trans.* LIV. 184 These nerves are equally motory and sensory. **1865** *Q. Jrnl. Sci.* II. 137 Some peculiar motory phenomena not heretofore observed in the Sponges. **1885** J. MARTINEAU *Types Eth. Th.* I. 138 The sensory and motory nerves.

2. *gen.* That causes motion. Cf. MOTOR *a.* 1.

1799 SIR H. DAVY in Beddoes *Contrib. Phys. & Med. Knowl.* 23 The effect of a peculiar motory or vibratory impulse. **1817** COLERIDGE *Biog. Lit.* I. xiii. 288 A motory force of a body in one direction and an equal force of the same body in an opposite direction is not incompatible.

‖**motoscafo** (mɔtɔs'kafo). Pl. motoscafi. [It.] In Italy: a motor-boat; esp. such a boat used as a public conveyance on the Venetian canals.

1942 *Britannica Bk. of Year* (U.S.) 468 Another type developed considerably in scope and design was the motor torpedo boat... Before the war the Italians were proud of their vessels of this category, officially classed as M.A.S. (*motoscafi anti-sommergibili*) but these had accomplished singularly little. **1950** E. HEMINGWAY *Across River* xxxiv. 210, I will get into the *motoscafo*.. and.. we will not ever see one another again. **1971** P. LORAINE *Photographs have been Sent* v. i. 143 The father gave up his gondola and bought himself a nice new *motoscafo*. **1975** 'D. RUTHERFORD' *Mystery Tour* iii. 40 There are no motor vehicles in Venice, so.. you will be conveyed to the hotel by *motoscafo*.

motoun, obs. f. MUTTON.

Motown ('məʊtaʊn). [Shortening of *Motor Town*, nickname for Detroit, Michigan, U.S.A., an important car-manufacturing city.] Music of a type made popular by Black musicians and singers from Detroit. Also *attrib.* Cf. TAMLA MOTOWN.

1970 *Melody Maker* 11 July 19/7 Some of their songs are extremely unusual, for example 'Jesus Buddha Moses Gauranga' which starts with a bit of 2001 string sound and contains one line which is pure Motown. **1971** *New Yorker* 25 Sept. 127 The set included several songs from each of the Band's three albums.. and two Motown oldies.

motre, obs. f. MUTTER *v.*

motricity (məʊ'trɪsɪtɪ). $rare^{-1}$. [ad. F. *motricité*, f. (*force*) *motrice*: see MOTOR *a.*] The motor function.

1903 F. W. H. MYERS *Human Personality* I. 55 So soon as the cause of each accident of this kind was traced.., the perversion of sensibility or of motricity disappeared.

†'motrix. *Obs.* $rare^{-1}$. Feminine, in Latin form, of MOTOR.

1650 CHARLETON *Paradoxes* 82 The phansy, which is the motrix of those qualities.

motso, var. MATZAH.

mott, obs. pa. t. of METE *v.*^{1}

mott, var. MOAT *sb.*^{1}, MORT *sb.*^{4}, MOTE *sb.*^{1}

motte (mɒt), *sb.*^{1} *U.S.* Also mot, mott. [ad. Amer. Sp. *mata* grove, plant, f. Sp. *mata* bush, clump.] A clump of trees in a prairie (*Funk's Stand. Dict.* 1895).

1844 KENDALL *Santa Fé Exped.* I. 41 All that was necessary was to keep a bright look-out.. while passing the different *mots* and ravines scattered along our trail. **1848** C. W. WEBBER *Old Hicks* v. 52 Our course bearing west of north, over broken prairie, diversified by clumps or motts of

scrubby growth. **1857** Olmsted *Journ. thro' Texas* 137 Before us [were] very beautiful prairies,..and little belts, mottes and groups of live-oak. **1880** R. H. Loughridge *U.S. Census Rep. on Cotton for Texas*, Motts of Timber. Motts of live oak. **1962** E. B. Atwood *Regional Vocab. Texas* iii. 42 A small group of trees together, surrounded by open country... *Mott* is rather heavily concentrated in South Central and West Texas.

motte (mɒt), *sb.*² [after F. *motte* mound: see mote *sb.*²] = mote *sb.*² 1 a, esp. in phr. ***motte and bailey***, denoting the principal type or design of castle built in Britain by the Normans, consisting of a fort surmounting a mound (*motte*) at the foot of which was an enclosed bailey or court.

1884 G. T. Clark *Mediæval Mil. Archit. Eng.* I. ii. 16 This 'mound', 'motte', or 'burh'..was formed from the contents of a broad and deep circumscribing ditch. **1892** J. H. Round *Geoffrey de Mandeville* 336 The *motte*, though its name was occasionally extended to the whole fortress, was essentially the actual keep, the crowned mound. **1900** *Proc. Soc. Antiquaries Scotl.* XXXIV. 269 As these are the proper Norman names, and there are no others, I shall henceforth speak of this type of castle as the motte-and-bailey type. **1912** E. S. Armitage *Early Norman Castles Brit. Isles* vi. 80 The motte-and-bailey type of castle is to be found throughout feudal Europe. **1934** *Proc. Soc. Antiquaries Scotl.* LXVIII. 59 The Peel of Kirkintilloch had been a medieval fortress of the motte-and-bailey type. **1947** T. H. White *Elephant & Kangaroo* (1948) xxi. 169 A Norman castle on a motte. **1962** C. W. Hollister *Anglo-Saxon Mil. Inst.* vii. 142 The motte-and-bailey style was unknown to them, just as it was unknown to their contemporaries on the Continent. **1967** J. B. Nellist *Brit. Archit.* vi. 145/1 Although the bailey might be captured, the motte as a self-contained unit could still offer resistance. **1971** *Country Life* 27 May 1297/1 At Dunsany the present castle was apparently built in succession to an earlier motte and bailey castle, the mound of which exists to the north-east of the present house. *Ibid.* 11 Nov. 1280/4 The building stands on a raised motte; it had a moat on the south-west side.

2. *Comb.*, as **motte-castle**, a (Norman) fort standing on a motte.

1912 E. S. Armitage *Early Norman Castles Brit. Isles* vi. 83 It is rare indeed to find a motte-castle in a wild, mountainous situation in England. **1926** *Archæologia Cambrensis* LXXXI. 223 The earthen mounds of two of the earlier 'motte' castles—moated mounts which once had wooden towers upon their summits.

motte, obs. form of moat, mot, mote.

motted (ˈmɒtɪd), *ppl. a. rare.* [f. mott(e *sb.*² + -ed¹.] Situated upon a motte or mound.

1947 Auden *Nones* (1952) 64 Do they sponsor In us the mornes and motted mammelons?

motteleye, -tet(t, obs. ff. motley, motet.

‖**mottetto** (motˈteto, mɒˈtɛtəʊ), *pl.* **-ti** (-ti). Also 8–9 motetto. [It.: see motet.] = motet b.

1644 Evelyn *Diary* 8 Nov., This being finish'd began their Motettos, which..were sung by eunuchs. **1724** *Short Explic. For. Words Mus., Motetto*, or *Motetti*, are what we call Motets. **1855** Motley *Dutch Rep.* (1861) I. 276 Full orchestra performed several fine Motettos. **1878** E. H. Pember in Grove *Dict. Mus.* I. 108 The rest..consist principally of masses, madrigals, mottetti, and psalms.

motthe, mott hill, obs. ff. moth, mote-hill.

mottie, variant of motey *a.*

mottle (ˈmɒt(ə)l), *sb.* Also 7 **mottel**. [Prob. a back-formation from motley *a.*]

1. One of a number of adjacent and confluent spots or blotches, by which a surface is diversified or variegated. Also *fig.*

1676 [see mottled *ppl. a.*]. **1683** *Lond. Gaz.* No. 1847/8 Her marks are black Mottels upon all her Legs and Nose. **1829** Landor *Imag. Conv.* Wks. 1853 I. 517/1 Is the rouge off my face? It is rather in streaks and mottles. **1855** Browning *Epist. Karshish* 47 There's a spider here.. Sprinkled with mottles on an ash-grey back.

2. The arrangement of spots or confluent blotches of colour forming a mottled surface.

1858 Greener *Gunnery* 173 The effect..is to give a beautiful mottle to the [gun] barrel. **1873** E. Spon *Workshop Receipts* Ser. i. 424/1 The mottle of these woods has very little variety. **1896** A. Morrison *Child of the Jago* 136 His chest and flanks were a mottle of bruises.

b. A kind of woollen yarn of variegated colour.

1887 *Daily News* 20 June 2/5 There is also rather more inquiry in single-hank yarns, in lustres, in mottles and in genappes. **1888** *Ibid.* 10 Sept. 2/6 A variety of yarns, including lustres, mottles, and mélanges.

mottle (ˈmɒt(ə)l), *a.* [Formed as prec.] = mottled *a.* Also Comb. ***mottle-faced***, ***-legged*** adjs.

1676 *Lond. Gaz.* No. 1153/4 A light gray Gelding,..motle Nosed. **1678** *Ibid.* No. 1308/4 Lost..a..Spaniel Dog, belonging to His Majesty, his legs and nose mottel. **1837** Dickens *Pickw.* xliii, The mottle-faced gentleman spoke with great energy. **1872** *Routledge's Ev. Boy's Ann.* 2 One mottle-legged, chubby-cheeked boy.

mottle (ˈmɒt(ə)l), *v.* [Formed as mottle *sb.*] *trans.* To mark or cover with spots or blotches; to variegate or cloud with irregular spots or streaks; *spec.* in *Soap making*, to impart a mottled appearance to white soap by the addition of chemicals.

1676 [see mottled *ppl. a.*]. **1775** M. Harris *Eng. Lepidoptera* 12 Light brown, beautifully mottled with dark brown. **1814** Southey *Roderick* xv. 4 Her beams Mottle with mazy shades the orchard slope. **1820** W. Irving *Sketch Bk.* II. 44 He has..a broad full face, curiously mottled with red. **1862** Miller *Elem. Chem.* (ed. 2) III. 271 Marseilles and Castile soaps..are mottled by the addition of green vitriol and sulphuretted lye.

fig. **1841** D'Israeli *Amen. Lit.* (1867) 128 Our national idiom has been mottled by foreign neologisms.

mottled (ˈmɒt(ə)ld), *ppl. a.* [f. prec. + -ed¹.]

1. Dappled with spots or blotches; marked with spots, streaks, or patches of different colour.

1676 *Lond. Gaz.* No. 1143/4 A little motled Bitch, with yellow motles from head to toe. *c* **1765** Flloyd *Tartarian T.* (1785) 114/2, I put a pair of..baskets on a mottled goat. **1794** Herschel in *Phil. Trans.* LXXXV. 71 The mottled appearance of the sun is owing to an inequality in the level of the surface. **1808** *Times* 29 Feb. 1/2 Followed a Person, a Mottled Pointer Dog. **1813** *Gentl. Mag.* LXXXIII. i. 95 Soap..Mottled 114*s*..per Doz. **1848** Thackeray *Bk. Snobs* xxvii, Scrubbing.. Polly's dumpy nose with mottled soap. **1868** Princess Alice *Mem.* 29 Dec. (1884) 207 My babies.. look so mottled and healthy. **1874** Garrod & Baxter *Mat. Med.* (1880) 330 The leaves are..pale green when fresh, mottled-brown when dry.

b. *transf.* and *fig.*

1857 Buckle *Civiliz.* I. xiii. 744 The real lack of ideas which their barbarous and mottled dialect strives to hide. **1891** J. Strong *New Era* 201 A mottled population, containing the worst elements of society.

2. Special collocations: **mottled baboon**, the common baboon, *Cynocephalus papio*; **mottled calf**, a variegated leather used for book-binding; **mottled iron**, a soft kind of cast iron; **mottled grampus** (see quot.); **mottled owl**, a North American owl, *Scops asio*; **mottled pig**, a kind of pig-iron (see quot.). Also in collectors' names for many British moths, as **mottled beauty, bran, carpet, grey**, etc. (see Rennie *Butterflies & Moths*. 1832, *passim*).

1802 Bingley *Anim. Biog.* (1813) I. 73 The Common or *Mottled Baboon. **1895** J. Zaehnsdorf *Hist. Bookbinding* 27 *Mottled Calf.—Pale-coloured calf, decorated by the sprinkling of acids in drops. **1884** G. B. Goode, etc. *Nat. Hist. Aquatic Anim.* 14 On the California coast occurs the Whiteheaded or *Mottled Grampus, *Grampus Stearnsii* Dall. **1836–41** Brande *Chem.* (ed. 5) 763 Gray or *mottled-iron is softer and less brittle. **1884** W. H. Greenwood *Steel & Iron* iv. 48 The characteristic dappled appearance peculiar to mottled iron. **1781** Latham *Gen. Synopsis Birds* I. i. 126 *Mottled Owl. **1880** *Encycl. Brit.* XIII. 284/2 Sometimes a pig will solidify partly as white iron partly as grey..; such iron is known as '*mottled pig'. **1749** B. Wilkes *Eng. Moths & Butterflies* 36 The *mottled Umber-moth.

Hence **ˈmottledness**, mottled condition.

1830 J. Wilson in *Blackw. Mag.* XXVIII. 386 The red and brown mottledness o' its striped and starry beauty.

mottledy (ˈmɒt(ə)ldɪ), *a. rare.* [f. mottled *ppl. a.* + -y¹.] Having a mottled appearance.

1929 E. Bowen *Last September* i. vii. 78 Her grey-and-blue 'mottledy' foulard.

mottlement (ˈmɒt(ə)lmənt). [f. mottle *v.* + -ment.] The condition of being mottled.

1853 G. J. Cayley *Las Alforjas* II. 2 A confused mottlement of every shade of red.

mottler (ˈmɒt(ə)lə(r)). [f. mottle *v.* + -er¹.]

a. A workman who mottles soap. **b.** A house-painter's brush for mottling.

1839 Ure *Dict. Arts* 1143 As soon as the mottler has broken the paste,..he ceases to push his rake from right to left. **1875** Davidson *House-painting*, etc. 106 Lay the colour over the whole panel, and work it level with a hog-hair mottler—a flat tool mounted in tin.

mottling (ˈmɒt(ə)lɪŋ), *vbl. sb.* [f. mottle *v.* + -ing¹.] The production of a mottled appearance. Also, the appearance itself.

1839 Ure *Dict. Arts* 1143 Mottling is usually given..by introducing into the nearly finished soap..a certain quantity of the strong lye of crude soda. **1851** Nichol *Archit. Heav.* 49 The stippling is no illusion, as its dark mottling moves with the stars. **1874** Wood *Nat. Hist.* 281 Longitudinal mottlings of variously tinted brown. **1875** Davidson *House-painting*, etc. 107 The over-graining of maple should be done on the same day as the mottling. **1897** *St. George's Hosp. Rep.* IX. 127 The cheeks and extremities showed conspicuous dusky mottling.

motto (ˈmɒtəʊ). Pl. **-os, -oes**. Also 7 **mot(h)o**; pl. **motti**. [a. It. *motto* = F. *mot*: see mot¹.]

1. a. Originally, a word, sentence, or phrase attached as a legend to an 'impresa' or emblematical design, and serving to explain or emphasize its symbolic import. Hence, in wider sense, a short sentence or phrase inscribed on some object, and expressing a reflection or sentiment considered to be appropriate to its purpose or destination; also, a proverbial or pithy maxim adopted by a person as his rule of conduct.

1589 Greene *Span. Masquerado* A 3 b, The Spanish Masquerado with the Mottos. 1 The Pope, hauing put off his triple Crowne,..saith thus. *Neque Petrus, neque Paulus, quid igitur restat?* 2 Phillip king of Spaine..saith thus. *Iubet Ecclesia, dissentire non audeo* [etc.]. **1608** Shaks. *Per.* ii. ii. 44 The fift, an Hand enuironed with Clouds, Holding out Gold, that's by the Touch-stone tride: The motto thus *Sic spectanda fides*. **1643** *Plain English* 2 We have found it not impossible to be miserable under the Motto of *Beati pacifici*. **1720** Swift *Let. Advice Yng. Poet* Misc. (1722) 91 Posies of Rings, Motto's of Snuff-Boxes, the Humours of Sign-Posts [etc.]. **1796** Burke *Let. Noble Ld.* Wks. VIII. 27 'Nitor in adversum' is the motto for a man like me. **1860** Trollope *Castle Richm.* I. vi. 106 Strike when the iron's hot; that's my motto.

b. *spec.* in *Her.* A significant word or sentence usually placed upon a scroll, either below an achievement of arms or above the crest, occas. having some reference to the name or exploits of the bearer, to the charges upon the shield or to the crest, but more often expressing merely a pious aspiration or exalted sentiment.

1600 Camden in Hearne *Collect.* (1771) I. 267 Mr. Richard Carew..used under his armes this Italian motto, *Chiveracc durera*, which also conteyneth his name anagramatically. **1605** *Relat. Journ. Earl of Nottingham* 14 His *Moto* or word being *Desir N'a Repos*. **1610** Guillim *Heraldry* vi. vi. 271 An other ornament there is externally annexed to Coat-armour, and that is the Motto, or Word. **1644** Bp. Hall *Serm.* 9 June, Wks. 1837 V. 498 The motto that was wont to be written upon the Scottish coin, as the emblem of their Thistle, *Nemo me impunè lacesset*. **1784** H. Clark *Hist. Knighthd.* I. 101 All between three Imperial crowns, placed within the motto of the Order; viz. *Tria Juncta in Uno*. **1882** Cussans *Her.* (1893) 196 *Festina Lente*—'Hasten slowly', or 'On slow', is the Motto of the Onslow family; and *Doe no yll, quoth D'Oyle*, that of Doyley.

c. The poetical lines contained in a motto-kiss or paper-cracker.

1848 A. H. Clough *Bothie* ii. 12 You ask me to join you in snapping—What but a pink-paper comfit, with motto romantic inside it? **1850** Dickens *Dav. Copp.* xxxiii. 340 There were crackers..with the tenderest mottos. **1869** W. S. Gilbert *Ferd. & Elvira* 30 Tell me, Henry Wadsworth ..or Mister Tupper Do you write the bonbon mottoes my Elvira pulls at supper?

†**2.** A pithy expression, a saying. Cf. mot².

1614 Tomkis *Albumazar* iv. xiii, You tip your speeches with Italian Motti, Spanish Refranes, and English Quoth Hee's. *a* **1660** *Contemp. Hist. Irel.* (Ir. Archæol. Soc.) I. 183 That evangelicall motho arundinem vento agitatam.

3. A short quotation (or sometimes an original passage simulating a quotation) prefixed to a literary work or to one of its parts, and expressing some idea appropriate to the contents.

1711 Addison *Spect.* No. 221 ¶4 But as for my unlearned Friends, if they cannot relish the Motto, I take care to make Provision for them in the Body of my Paper. **1894** J. L. Robertson in *Scott's Poet. Wks.* Pref. 3 The mottoes and lyrical fragments of the Novels are of all Scott's work the most difficult part to edit.

4. *Mus.* A recurrent phrase. Freq. *attrib.*, as ***motto theme***.

1891 *Times* 10 Oct. 11/1 In the final number the 'motto' or recurrent phrase of four notes is subjected to double diminution. **1934** C. Lambert *Music Ho!* v. 316 The ascription of actual individuality to a recurrent or 'motto theme' and the attaching of symbolic significance to its later transformations, devices wholly at variance with the classic principles of symphonic form, are here perfectly justified. **1935** *Downside Rev.* LIII. 30 Against the noble motto-theme of the introduction is set a restless surging subject in the distant tonality of D minor. **1962** *Times* 13 June 13/1 The symphony's motto-theme. **1964** *Listener* 2 Apr. 570/3 The sixth quartet is more difficult to analyse, though the crucial factor is probably the motto-theme which appears in increasingly contrapuntal guise before each movement. **1966** *Ibid.* 17 Nov. 746/3 The first (*Largo*) begins with imitative entries of the 'motto' and quotes the opening of the first symphony, twice.

5. *U.S.* = *motto-kiss*.

1835 *Southern Lit. Messenger* I. 358, I only ate..a few macaronies and mottoes. **1860** *North-West* (Port Townsend, Washington) 5 July 3/3 Candies, Gum drops, Mottoes. **1890** in *Century Dict.*

6. *attrib.*, as ***motto-band*** (Her.), ***-monger***, ***-pamphlet***, ***-scroll***; **motto-kiss**, a sweetmeat wrapped in fancy paper, having a motto or scrap of poetry inclosed with it.

1716 M. Davies *Athen. Brit.* II. 53 His Motto-Pamphlet still remaineth in each Window, *Misericordias Domini in æternum Cantabo*. **1748** Richardson *Clarissa* Wks. 1883 VIII. 480, I..ever was a censurer of the motto-mongers among our weekly and daily scribblers. **1858** Simmonds *Dict. Trade, Motto-kisses*. **1864** Boutell *Her. Hist. & Pop.* xvii. (ed. 3) 282 The Motto-Scroll forms both a convenient and sufficiently secure standing-place for Supporters. *Ibid.* xviii. 289 Standards were also generally divided bend-wise into compartments by Motto-Bands.

Hence **ˈmotto** *v. trans.*, to inscribe with a motto. **ˈmottoed** *ppl. a.*, inscribed with a motto †or legend. **ˈmottoless**, without a motto.

1738 *Gentl. Mag.* VIII. 212/2 A motto'd silk garter. **1765** E. Thompson *Meretriciad* (ed. 6) 45 My Lord makes his approach, But at the corner leaves the motto'd Coach. **1827** Hone *Every-day Bk.* 16 Nov. II. 1546 The engraving that pictures [this incident] is mottoed, 'The Spoiled Child!' **1835** Beckford *Recoll.* 87 Every armorial device, every mottoed lambel. *a* **1845** Hood *To Moon* v, Thou art a sadder dial..Than ever I have found..Motto'd with stern and melancholy rhyme. **1891** *Standard* 14 May 5/2 The London Municipality is at this moment armless, and crestless, and mottoless.

motton, obs. form of mouton, mutton.

mottramite ('mɒtrəmaɪt). *Min.* [f. *Mottram* (see quot. 1876) + -ITE.] Vanadate of lead and copper occurring rarely in black incrustations.
1876 ROSCOE in *Proc. Roy. Soc.* XXV. 111 The second vanadium mineral, to which I propose to give the name of Mottramite, occurs as a crystalline incrustation on Keuper sandstone found at Alderley Edge and at Mottram St. Andrew's, in Cheshire. **1896** in CHESTER *Dict. Min.* 181.

mottun, obs. pa. pple. of METE *v.*[1]

motty ('mɒtɪ), *sb. dial.* [Cf. MOT[3].] = MOT[3].
a **1800** PEGGE *Suppl. to Grose* (1814) 389 *Motty*, the mark at which the quoits (or coits) are thrown. Derb.

motty ('mɒtɪ), *a. Sc.* Also **mottie**. [f. *mot*, Sc. pronunciation of MOTE *sb.*[1] + -Y. Cf. MOTEY.] Containing motes.
1599 A. HUME *Day Estivall* 53 The subtile mottie rayons light. **1725** RAMSAY *Gentle Sheph.* v. ii. Prol., The rising sun shines motty through the reek. **1785** BURNS *Vision* I. iv, All in this mottie, misty clime. **1865** ALEX. SMITH *Summer in Skye* (1880) 331 Where the motty sunbeam from the pane.. struck him.

Motu ('məʊtuː), *sb.* and *a.* [Native word.]
A. *sb.* A Melanesian people of New Guinea inhabiting the area of Port Moresby. Also, their language. **B.** *adj.* Of or pertaining to this people. Also, **Motuan**.
1880 O. C. STONE *Few Months New Guinea* iv. 46 The inhabitants of Anuapata and the neighbourhood consist principally of the Motu tribe. **1885** W. B. LAWES *Motu Gram. & Vocab.* p. v, In the grammar of the Motu dialect of New Guinea one peculiarity is in the use of letters so much alike as to be scarcely distinguishable..b and p,..d and t [etc.]... The Motuan language seems to be a strange mixture of Papuan and Eastern Polynesian. **1894** A. C. HADDON *Decorative Art Brit. New Guinea* 236 Port Moresby ..is the centre of the Motu tribe... The Motu make great trading voyages to the Gulf of Papua. **1910** C. G. SELIGMANN *Melanesians Brit. New Guinea* 16 The Koita.. have for generations intermarried with the Motu... Although the Koita still speak a Papuan language the majority of the males speak Motu, a Melanesian language, and have adopted..certain Motu customs. **1965** *Language* XLI. 169 Motu...is spoken fluently..by a few thousand Koitabuans intermingled among the Motuans themselves. **1967** 'E. LINDALL' *Time Too Soon* xviii. 197 He spoke in Motuan for the valley folk..and then in English for the white man. **1971** *Guardian* 4 Aug. 5/4 Motu, the language of the Port Moresby district.

‖**motuca** (məʊ'tuːkə). Also **motuka**. [Native name.] A Brazilian horse-fly, *Hadrus lepidotus*, of the family Tabanidæ.
1836 H. W. BATES *Naturalist on River Amazons* I. vii. 306 In the daytime the Motúca, a much larger and more formidable fly than the mosquito, insisted upon levying his tax of blood. *Ibid.*, The Motúca is of a bronzed-black colour; its proboscis is formed of a bundle of horny lancets... Its puncture does not produce much pain, but it makes such a large gash in the flesh that the blood trickles forth in little streams. **1914** *Chambers's Jrnl.* Oct. 630/1 Hornets dispute with motucas and other biting flies over the luckless intruder. **1927** W. M. MCGOVERN *Jungle Paths & Inca Ruins* 224 Unlike the vampire bat, the motuka inflicted a very painful sting. **1933** P. FLEMING *Brazilian Adventure* I. xvii. 145 There were also *motuca* flies, which looked like a lethal and slightly futuristic form of blue-bottle, and whose bites drew blood and oaths but had no worse effects.

‖**motu proprio** ('məʊtuː 'prɒprɪəʊ). [L., 'on his, its, etc., own impulse'.] Of one's own volition, on one's own initiative, spontaneously. Also as *sb.*, an edict issued by the Pope personally to the Roman Catholic Church, or to a part of it. Also *attrib.*
1603 C. HEYDON *Defence Judicial Astrol.* xxi. 447 But the Moone and other Planets moove also motu proprio. **1613** J. CHAMBERLAIN *Let.* 14 Oct. in T. Birch *Court & Times James I* (1848) I. 278 Signor Gabellione, the Duke of Savoy's ambassador, came *motu proprio* about three weeks since to Ware Park. **1620** N. BRENT tr. *Soave's Hist. Council of Trent* IV. 354 Dispatching the dispensations under the name of Motu proprio, or with other clauses, with which the Chancery doth abound. **1848** GODDE DE LIANCOURT & MANNING *Pius IX* II. xv. 404 The Pope published, on the 2nd of October at Rome, a new *motu proprio* for the organisation of a Senate. **1911** *Catholic Encycl.* X. 602/2 *Motu proprio*, the name given to certain papal rescripts... The words signify that the provisions of the rescript were decided on by the pope personally, that is, not on the advice of the cardinals or others. *Ibid.*, A favour granted *motu proprio* is valid even when counter to ecclesiastical law. **1938** *Oxf. Compan. Mus.* 596/2 *Motu proprio*... The word is often heard in connexion with church music on account of the Motu Proprio of Pius X, issued in the year of his becoming Pope (1903)... Instruments other than the organ were not to be employed without the bishop's special permission. **1964** P. F. ANSON *Bishops at Large* x. 455 The Patriarch of the West (in the person of Pope Pius XI) might have been forced to issue a *motu proprio* denouncing the Patriarch of Glastonbury. **1972** *Daily Tel.* 15 Sept. 8/7 Restatement of celibacy rules for deacons and priests came in a separate *motu proprio* decree.

moty, -tye: see MOTEY *sb.*, MOTE *sb.*[3]

motyfe, obs. variant of MOTIVE.

motza, var. MATZAH.

‖**mou**[1] (muː). Also **mow, mu**. [Chinese.] A Chinese unit of area, varying according to locality but usu. equivalent to about 670 square metres (800 square yards).
1876 *Encycl. Brit.* V. 39/1 A ground-rent of 15,000 cash (about £3) per *mow* (a third of an acre). **1924** *Other Lands* Jan. 56/2 Having acquired a tract of land on the north bank of thirty to forty thousand mow it has been very successful. **1937** E. SNOW *Red Star over China* ii. 71 Here in Shensi a peasant may own as much as 100 *mou* of land and yet be a poor man. **1955** *Ann. Reg. 1954* 305 'Of the over 80 million mou of the still flooded farmlands, 30 million mou have not yet been drained.'.. A mou was almost exactly one-sixth of an acre. **1957** *Encycl. Brit.* XV. 140/2 Mou... Commonly 806.65 sq. yd. Varies locally. Shanghai = 6,600 sq. ft. (Municipal Council). By Customs Treaty = 920.417 sq. yd., based on ch'ih of 14.1 inches. **1973** *Times* 21 Mar. (China Trade Suppl.) p. xiv/3 Since a *mu* is one sixth of an acre, and a catty is 1.1 lb. these figures come out at 18 cwt and 24 cwt of unhusked rice an acre.

mou', mou[2] (muː), *Sc.* Also 6, 8 **mow**. [var. of MOUTH *sb.*; the dropping of the *th* is abnormal.] = MOUTH in various senses.
a **1510** DOUGLAS *K. Hart* II. 531 For he hes gottin morsellis on the mow. **1719** D'URFEY *Pills* V. 89 He..kist her bonny Mow. **1794** BURNS *Sic a Wife as Willie had*, She has..A whiskin' beard about her mou'. **1858** PORTEOUS *Real 'Souter Johnny'* 13 He..took care..to..fill the jinglin' stoup wi mair To gust their mou.

mou, obs. form of MAY *v.*[1]

mou, obs. form of MOW *sb.*

mouch (muːtʃ), *v. Obs.* exc. *dial.* [? cogn. w. MUNCH *v.*] *trans.* To eat up, to eat greedily.
1570 LEVINS *Manip.* 216/42 To Mouche [*rimed with* couche, touche, auouche], eate, *mandere*. **1658** in PHILLIPS. **1866** BROGDEN *Prov. Words Linc.* 130.
Hence †'**moucher**, a great eater; †'**mouching**, ? eating greedily.
1570 LEVINS *Manip.* 71/19 A Moucher, *manduco*. **1607** DEKKER & WEBSTER *Sir T. Wyat* Wks. 1873 III. 103 *Clowne*. O poore shrimpe, how art thou falne away for want of mouching?

mouch, mouchache: see MOOCH, MUSTACHIO.

‖**moucharaby** (muː'ʃærəbɪ). Also 9 **moucharabey, musharab(a)yeh, -biyeh**. [Fr.; corruptly a. mod.Arab. *mashrabiyyah* (Dozy).] In northern Africa: An external balcony inclosed with latticework. Also *attrib.*
1884 *Health Exhib. Catal.* p. lvii/2 Panels of Musharabyeh Woodwork. **1888** ALICE MEYNELL in *Art Jrnl.* II. 138/1 The actress in her mousharabiyeh chair. **1891** *Pall Mall G.* 23 May 2/1 White-curtained moucharabies. **1894** *Daily News* 22 Sept. 6/5 The Cairo musharabayeh, and the fluted silk of to-day, would have been regarded as eccentric in the extreme.
¶ In 1843 MM. Mérimée and Lenoir (*Archit. Mil. au Moyen-Age*) fancifully applied the name *moucharaby* to a kind of balcony projecting from the walls of certain European mediæval castles. It does not appear that this application of the word ever had any actual currency either in Fr. or Eng.; but *moucharaby* was inserted with this explanation (its proper sense being ignored) in Ogilvie's *Imperial Dictionary* (1850), and the entry has been copied with verbal alterations and expansions into various later Eng. Dicts.

‖**mouchard** (muʃar). [F. *mouchard*, f. *mouche* fly (used fig. for 'spy').] A police spy. Hence '**mouchardism**.
1802 in C. JAMES *Milit. Dict.* **1834** *Tait's Mag.* I. 663/1 Would you and your *mouchards* have me believe [etc.]? **1891** R. BUCHANAN *Coming Terror* 9 The increased corruption and *mouchardism* of an irresponsible Press. **1901** *Daily Express* 18 Mar. 7/1 At Marseilles, he had made friends with a man who turned out to be a mouchard.

mouchato(e: see MUSTACHIO.

mouche. *rare.* Also **mouch**. [a. F. *mouche*, a fly, hence a spot, ad. L. *musca*, a fly.] †**a.** A patch of black plaster worn on the face. *Obs.*
1676 WISEMAN *Surg.* I. xxii. 119 From which time it hath continued well, she not having worn any Mouch upon it of late years. **1690** EVELYN *Mundus Muliebris* 6 Mouches for pushes, to be sure, From Paris the tré-fine procure.
b. A natural mark on the face similar in appearance to a patch of plaster.
1859 G. A. SALA *Twice round Clock* 143 In a hoop petticoat, a point lace apron, red-heeled *mules*, a *toupet* and a *mouche* on the left cheek. **1959** M. STEEN *Woman in Back Seat* I. i. 8 At the angle of the jaw,..there should be a dark brown *mouche*, about the size of a small pea.
So †**mou'chet** in the same sense. *Obs.*
a **1700** B. E. *Dict. Cant. Crew*, Mouchets, Patches for Ladies Faces. **1725** in *New Cant. Dict.*

mouche, variant of MOOCH *v.*, MUCH *adv.*

moucheacheo: see MUSTACHIO.

moucher, variant of MOOCHER.

mouchette (muː'ʃɛt). *Archit.* [a. Fr.] A motif in curvilinear tracery having the shape of a curved dagger.
1927 *Proc. Soc. Antiquaries Scotl.* LX. 388 The space under the arch bears an heraldic shield supported by a composition of *soufflets* and *mouchettes*. **1949** *Archit. Rev.* CV. 4/1 The mouchettes of the Court School are equally distinctive... They change only within certain fixed limits, ..and yet in a very subtle manner the mouchettes create changes of style. **1955** M. HASTINGS *St Stephen's Chapel* 179 The fan tracery of Henry VII's chapel is no more than an extremely elaborate combination of mouchettes. **1967** J. B. NELLIST *Brit. Archit.* ii. 43/1 The elaborate tracery is almost entirely composed of mouchette shapes.

mouching: see MOOCHING *vbl. sb.* and *ppl. a.*

‖**mouchoir** (muʃwar). [Fr.] A handkerchief.
1690 EVELYN *Mundus Muliebris* 3 Of Pocket Mouchoirs, Nose to drain, A dozen lac'd, a dozen plain. **1753** *Lond. Mag.* Oct. 481 A mouchoir with musk his spirits to chear. **1833** M. SCOTT *Tom Cringle* xi. (1842) 248 First wiping my shoes with his *mouchoir*. **1848** THACKERAY *Van. Fair* xlviii, Her mouchoirs, aprons, scarfs..and other female gimcracks.

moucht(e, mouct(h)e, obs. pa. t. of MAY *v.*[1]

moud, obs. form of MOOD *sb.*[1]

moude, obs. form of MUD.

mouden, obs. form of MUEZZIN.

moudewarp, -wart, -iewark, -iwarp, obs. ff. MOULDWARP.

moudie, moudy ('maʊdɪ). *Sc. dial.* Also 8 moody, mowdy, 9 mowdie. [Short for *moudiwarp* MOULDWARP.] A mole; freq. *attrib.* Also, a mole-catcher.
c **1720** *Bewick & Graham* xlviii. in Child *Ballads* IV. 148/1 Then he stuck his sword in a moody-hill. **1789** DAVIDSON *Seasons* 62 List'ning to the chirp O' wand'ring mouse, or moudy's carkin hoke. **1828** *Craven Gloss.*, *Moudy*, a mole catcher. *a* **1869** C. SPENCE *Fr. Braes of Carse* (1898) 186 There field mice and moudies litter.

moudon, moudre, obs. ff. MUEZZIN, MOULDER.

moudy, obs. form of MUDDY.

moue (muː), *sb.* [Fr.: see MOW *sb.*[2]] A pout.
1850 THACKERAY *Pendennis* lx[i]v, With a charming *moue*. **1883** J. HAWTHORNE *Dust* viii. 58 'You don't seem glad to see me, Uncle Francis?' she exclaimed, making a *moue* of lovely irony. **1908** A. BENNETT *Old Wives' Tale* IV. i. 429 She gave a *moue* and a flounce in reply, and swished out. **1955** *Times* 18 July 3/1 The hero..seeks the male companionship of sea life only to collapse powerless before the frail charm, the irresistible *moue*, and the wide eyed Frenchness of a passenger on the boat. **1974** 'J. LE CARRÉ' *Tinker, Tailor* xii. 103 'Why, George..it was you who arranged the deal!' With a quaint moue of professional vanity, Smiley conceded ..it.

moue (muː), *v.* [f. the sb.] **1.** *trans.* **a.** To ogle; stare at. **b.** To utter (words) with a moue.
1909 HARDY in *Daily Chron.* 1 Apr. 4/6 Whither have danced those damsels now; Is Death the partner who doth moue Their wormy chaps and bare? **1938** G. GREENE *Brighton Rock* V. v. 213 'Work, work, work,' she moued at them.
2. *intr.* To make a moue.
1938 G. GREENE *Brighton Rock* VII. ix. 346 They looked up and moued to each other, as much as to say—'Oh well, she wasn't really worth the trouble.' **1968** *Punch* 7 Aug. 202/3 The girls look the same young flappers to me, moueing and mincing and doing the long-lashed come-hither look.

moue, obs. form of MOW.

mouedhin, variant of MUEZZIN.

mouf (maʊf), repr. a pronunc. of MOUTH *sb.*
The examples are taken from Black English sources in the U.S. but the pronunciation is also characteristic of Cockney speech in London.
1909 *Dialect Notes* III. 350 *Mouf*, mouth: a negroism rapidly gaining ground among the whites, especially in the derivatives, as *mouffle* (mouthful). **1935** Z. N. HURSTON *Mules & Men* (1970) I. ii. 49 She got plenty hips, plenty mouf and no brains. **1969** R. FAIR in A. Chapman *New Black Voices* (1972) 114 Oh, shut yo mouf up man. **1971** *Black World* Oct. 63/2 Like I got hoof and mouf disease and there ain't no hope at all.

†**mouffette**. *Nat. Hist. Obs.* Also 8 **moufette, moufete**. [a. F. *moufette* (Buffon), *mofette*, *mouffette*: see MOFETTE.] Any one of the fetid American skunks of the genus *Mephitis*.
1774 GOLDSM. *Nat. Hist.* II. 304 The Weasel kind.. comprehends..all the varieties of the American Moufettes. **1797** *Encycl. Brit.* (ed. 3) XI. 673/1 The animals which he allows to be common to both countries are, the Mexican hog, the moufete, the opossum [etc.]. **1833** *Penny Cycl.* I. 443/1 The mouffettes..are likewise a genus peculiar to the New World. **1868** *Nat. Encycl.* I. 615.

mouflon ('muːflɒn). *Nat. Hist.* Also 8– **moufflon**, 8–9 **mufflon**. [a. F. *mouflon*, ad. early Sard. **mofrone* (whence the mod. forms *murvoni*, *murone*):—late L. *mufron* (Polemius Silvius, 5th c.). Cf. MUFFLE *sb.*] **1.** A wild sheep, esp. *Ovis musimon*, native of the mountainous regions of southern Europe, as Sardinia, Corsica, and the Isles of Greece. ***maned, ruffled mouflon***, the wild sheep of Barbary, *Ammotragus tragelaphus*.
1774 GOLDSM. *Nat. Hist.* III. 39 The moufflon, which is the sheep in a savage state, is a bold, fleet creature. **1792** BELKNAP *Hist. New Hampsh.* III. 144 The breed might be renewed and improved by importing from Barbary the

mufflon. **1843** J. SAUNDERS in C. Knight *London* V. cxvii. 261 In the centre..is a curious little open hut, with projecting eaves... A horned sheep, the mouflon, is confined in it. **1864** J. ORMSBY *Autumn Rambles in N. Afr.* 70 The Feshtall is the maned moufflon of the Atlas. **1888** *Encycl. Brit.* XXIII. 635/1 Of ruminants..we find one mufflon (*Musimon vignei*). **1905** *Blackw. Mag.* Mar. 321/2 A large number of gazelle and muflon—Barbary wild sheep —were allowed to roam at will. **1970** *Ashmolean Mus. Rep. Visitors 1969* 14 Omphalos bronze bowl decorated on the inside with mouflon among the trees. **1974** *Environmental Conservation* I. 9/1 Antelope, mouflon, and ostriches, have been exterminated over large areas.

attrib. **1893** LYDEKKER *Horns & Hoofs* 85 An..account of mouflon shooting is given. **1932** J. S. HUXLEY *Probl. Relative Growth* iii. 88 The adult wild Mouflon ewe is in its proportions but little in advance of the improved Suffolk lamb.

2. The fur of the mouflon; woollen fabric made from the mouflon's coat. Occas. used erron. of the fur of the Mongolian goat. Also *attrib.*

1905 *Westm. Gaz.* 29 Sept. 13/2 With moufflon fur. **1910** *Encycl. Brit.* XI. 351/2 Many Mongolian goats with the long hairs pulled out are sold as mouflon. **1949** *Amer. Speech* XXIV. 98 There is a species of goat from the mountains of northern China characterized by pelts of downy underhair. .. These furs are widely used and are called *moufflons* or *pulled goat.* **1952** C. W. CUNNINGTON *Eng. Women's Clothing* 295 *Moufflon serge* ('18), 'a kind of brushed woollen textile'. **1962** *Guardian* 21 July 4/7 A mist of softest peltry —chinchilla, sables, mink, and millinery moufflon. **1973** *Ibid.* 27 Feb. 11/2 Coat in white mouflon wool.

moufti, mough, obs. forms of MUFTI, MOW.

mought, obs. forms of MOTE, MOTH, MOUTH.

mought(e, obs. and dial. pa. t. of MAY *v.*[1]

mougnon, variant of MONION.

mougth, mougthe, obs. ff. MOUTH, MOTH.

mouht, obs. pa. t. of MAY *v.*[1]

mouie, variant of MOWE *Obs.*, kinswoman.

‖**mouillé** (muje). *French Gram.* [pa. pple. of F. *mouiller* to wet, moisten.] Of a consonant, chiefly *l*, also *n*, *r*: Palatalized or 'fronted', changed into (ʎ, ɲ, rj).

1833 *Penny Cycl.* I. 385/1 The *mouillé* sound of the French *ll*.

‖**moujik, muzhik** ('muːʒɪk, ‖muˈʒik). Now *Hist.* Forms: 6 musick, mousike, 6–7 mousick, 8 mugike, 9 mougik, -jik, muzhik, mooshik, -zheek; mouzhik, 9– mujik. [Russ. *muzhik* peasant.]

1. A Russian peasant.

1568 TURBERV. *Trag. T.*, etc. (1587) 184 One [licour] called Kuas, whereby the Musick liues. **1591** G. FLETCHER *Russe Commw.* (Hakl. Soc.) 12 The marchants and mousicks ..are very much discouraged by..exactions. **1799** *Monthly Rev.* XXX. 548 The mugikes, or serfs. **1833** R. PINKERTON *Russia* 352 Set a mujik at your table, he will soon lay up his legs on it. **1877** MAR. M. GRANT *Sun-Maid* xxxii, His mougik still wore his sheep-skin wrapped close round his chin. **1877** D. M. WALLACE *Russia* xxvi. (ed. 2) II. 151 There stood the patient bearded *muzhik* (peasant) in his well-worn sheep-skins. **1892** *Daily News* 26 Jan. 6/2 All the mooshiks without exception are workmen. **1934** *Discovery* Dec. 364/2 The mujiks know that Lenin hath given, but Stalin hath taken away. **1949** I. DEUTSCHER *Stalin* iii. 67 Eight or nine soldiers out of ten were mouzhiks. **1961** *Observer* 10 Dec. 7/2 The most fascinating Khrushchev of all is the high-powered *mouzhik*, the super *kulak.* **1963** V. NABOKOV *Gift* iv. 216 He began dabbling in propaganda by conversing with mujiks.

2. (In full *moujik blouse, coat*). A loose fur cape for ladies' wear.

1897 *Westm. Gaz.* 30 Sept. 3/2 This moujik coat..is.. now too popular. **1901** *Ibid.* 4 July 3/1 The moujik, that little blouse coat, cut low in the neck and with open fronts [etc.].

mouk(e, obs. forms of MUCK *sb.*